The Universal Dictionary of the English Language

THE UNIVERSAL DICTIONARY
— *of the* —
ENGLISH LANGUAGE

Edited by
HENRY CECIL WYLD
With an Appendix by
ERIC PARTRIDGE

Wordsworth Editions

28906.

First published in Great Britain by Routledge & Kegan Paul.

This edition published 1989 by Wordsworth Editions Ltd, 8b East Street, Ware, Hertfordshire, under licence from the proprietor.

ISBN 1-85326-940-9

Printed and bound in Great Britain by Mackays of Chatham PLC.

Preface

IT is not without some misgivings and searchings of heart that a man at the present time can put his name on the title-page of a new Dictionary as its Editor. There are so many good English dictionaries, varying in size and scope, from the great Oxford Dictionary—that wonder of the age—down to those cheap and humble volumes whose chief object seems to be to aid in the solution of cross-word puzzles. It is therefore reasonable to ask whether there is room for yet another English dictionary, whether there is still some void among works of this class which remains to be filled. The present writer confesses that had he been asked these questions seven or eight years ago, he would probably have said No to both. When one reflects that, apart from the unapproachable Oxford Dictionary, there are such medium-sized works as the new Webster, Funk and Wagnall, the Imperial Dictionary, and the smaller but most admirable Concise Oxford, besides Chambers, Annandale, and others, while in etymology pure and simple there are Skeat and Weekley, it may well seem that the field is handsomely covered for many years to come.

When, however, the Publishers determined to embark upon the publication of an English Dictionary, and did the present writer the honour of inviting him to compile and edit it, it became necessary to review the situation and inquire how far it might still be possible to produce a work that should be of service to the public in such a way as to justify the undertaking. The essential features of a dictionary are its size, its scope, and the manner in which the material it contains is presented. The approximate size of this work was determined by the Publisher. It was to be a book of moderate and medium size. It was to be distinctly smaller than Webster, but considerably larger than the Concise Oxford. From the latter work, it was agreed that the present dictionary should be distinguished, not so much by the inclusion of a larger number of words, as by a fuller and less condensed mode of treatment. More space was allowed for actual definitions, illustrative examples, etymologies, discussions of changes in meaning, and so on.

It fell to the Editor to devise in detail the plan of the book, its scope, and the method of arrangement. It was decided, with the consent and approval of the Publishers, that the book should be above all things a book of words, their derivations and their meanings, and not an encyclopaedia. We deal primarily with words and their uses, and not with things. But since a dictionary necessarily includes the names of thousands of material objects of all kinds, it is impossible to avoid descriptions of these. Similarly, in dealing with the name of a scientific, philosophical, or religious doctrine, it is necessary to give a certain amount of information of a kind which is normally to be sought in an encyclopaedia or a special treatise. In these and many other instances the distinction between a dictionary of words and an encyclopaedia becomes rather faint, and the 'word-book' encroaches upon the functions of works of quite a different kind. This encyclopaedic element is here reduced to the lowest minimum.

Passing to the positive features of this dictionary, the pronunciation of each word is recorded both in a simple and exact phonetic notation, and in a less exact and popular mode of spelling which the Publishers believe to be more generally intelligible. The pronunciations indicated are those current in good society, and where more than one pronunciation of the same word are current, both are given, that preferred by the Editor being put first.

The etymologies are given with greater fullness than is usual in dictionaries of this size and scope. It will be noticed that when a word is a loan from another language, the usual practice in the smaller dictionaries of merely indicating that the word is derived from Latin, French, and so on, is extended, and the etymology of the Latin or French word in question is given as far as possible. In all cases the attempt has been made to indicate the relation or original identity of the word under immediate discussion with others in English, and full cross-references are given to related or cognate words. An attempt is also made as far as possible to trace the development of meaning from the most primitive starting-point down to the present-day usage in English.

It is hoped that those readers who, although unfamiliar with the methods of philological science, are sufficiently interested in etymology to take a little trouble will be able to follow the line of argument adopted in the discussions of the forms and meanings of words by reference to the introductory sections of the book. Unfortunately no means have yet been discovered whereby the results of a highly developed science such as that of etymology, with its own body of facts, and special modes of reasoning upon them, can be made available to readers previously ignorant of both facts and methods without the expenditure of some mental effort on the readers' part.

In selecting the words for inclusion in the dictionary, the net has been cast fairly widely. The greatest importance is naturally attached to words current in literary and colloquial use at the present day. At the same time, a large number of purely technical and scientific words and terms have been included, since many of these necessarily play a considerable part in the lives of important sections of the community. Many of these words have been deliberately concocted by men of science to meet the needs, and embody the theories and views, of the moment, and many will probably pass out of use with a change of scientific outlook.

The definitions have been thought out with a view to clearness and completeness. The various meanings and shades of meaning are carefully distinguished, and each is illustrated, when necessary, by a brief sentence, usually of a colloquial character. Special meanings or shades of meaning, especially when poetical, are occasionally exhibited in short quotations from the poets. It must be borne in mind that this dictionary is primarily designed to set forth contemporary usage; when necessary, words, or particular uses of words, are designated as *Archaic*, *Obsolescent*, *Obsolete*. When a word or usage is no longer current in colloquial speech, it is marked as *Poetical* or *Literary*. Similarly when a particular usage is purely Colloquial or Familiar, this is indicated. Special care has been directed to giving idiomatic usages and phrases. These are included under that particular meaning of a word from which the idiom sprang. The Editor has not hesitated to include words and idioms which belong to current slang. Such words must be regarded as very real elements of colloquial speech.

The main aim of the book is to give, in dictionary form, a picture of English usage at the present time, both literary and colloquial. The Editor is conscious of many shortcomings, and this is said neither from false modesty, nor as an attempt to disarm criticism, but as the expression of what is perhaps a natural feeling in one who has just completed a long and laborious piece of work. In spite of its defects, the book contains much that will probably interest, amuse, and instruct the general reader.

No claim is made to original research in the etymologies. The Editor's task has been mainly that of collecting, and selecting from, the materials supplied by such masters as Bradley, Skeat, Kluge, Meyer-Lübke, Walde, Boisacq, and others, and presenting their results so as to throw light upon particular problems. Here and there an original suggestion has been thrown out.

The work of defining and mapping out the meanings of each word was carried out, in the first instance, independently of other dictionaries, as will usually appear from the actual terms of the definitions, and from the general arrangement of divisions and subdivisions of meaning. Other dictionaries, notably the new large Webster, Funk and Wagnall, the Concise Oxford, and the great Oxford Dictionary were consulted after the treatment of a word had been roughed out, to ensure a reasonable completeness in the enumeration of the various meanings. The compiler of a dictionary, if he reads a definition given in another book *before* he has determined the form of his own, is apt to be so hypnotized by the former that he finds it difficult to get away from it, and tends to reproduce its phraseology. The Editor has tried, when revising this work, to eliminate the results of such suggestion so far as he could detect them. For purely technical and scientific terms recourse was had to encyclopaedias, or, when possible, to the advice of experts. The Editor then attempted to give in his own words a clear and intelligible account of the term's implication and submitted this to the expert for criticism.

The Editor has, in conclusion, the duty and pleasure of making certain acknowledgements.

First to Sir John Hammerton, who is in a real sense the 'only begetter' of the book, and has acted throughout as its Managing Editor. He has afforded the Editor every help in his power by providing skilled assistance, expert and clerical. His unfailing personal kindness and courtesy have been a great support.

To those who have assisted him in the actual compilation the Editor tenders his sincere gratitude. In especial he wishes to thank Miss Mary Serjeantson, M.A. (Liverpool), D.Phil. (Oxford), Reader in English in the University of London, who has taken part in the work from an early stage, and Mr. Cecil Weatherly, B.A. (Oxford), Barrister-at-Law, who was engaged on the dictionary from about the middle, and who, together with Miss Serjeantson, has taken an active part in the revision and correction of the proofs of practically the entire work. It is impossible to exaggerate the debt which the Editor owes to the untiring devotion and loyalty of Dr. Serjeantson and Mr. Weatherly, as well as to their expert knowledge in various fields.

Dr. A. B. Gough has rendered invaluable help, partly in compilation, but more especially by his keen-eyed reading of the final proofs. Much is owed to his judicious suggestions.

The Editor wishes to pay a special tribute to the most helpful collaboration of Miss G. M. Holland and her colleagues, whose unflagging interest and labours in the tedious task of incorporating corrections in the proofs and securing typographical exactitude have been of the greatest service. But whatever the various parts played by these ladies and gentlemen, the Editor must take responsibility for the work in its final form and for its shortcomings.

HENRY CECIL WYLD

OXFORD.

Introduction

I

General Remarks on English Etymology

By the Editor

We all of us use words, in the ordinary affairs of life, in our business and in our everyday pleasures, as well as in our more solemn moments of exalted emotion, whether of joy or of sorrow, or, it may be, in the expression of still loftier aspirations associated with religion. For the normal man or woman life without that means of communication with our fellow-creatures which we call *language*, that is *words*, is unthinkable.

If we reflect upon the subject at all, we shall soon realize that even our own English language which we know so well, and use so readily, though familiar is yet mysterious. Many persons who have but little time for special studies, though they may read and think about many things outside their daily routine of cares and duties, so far as their leisure may permit, have been unable to devote much attention to the study of the words of their native tongue. They can speak it and read it and write it; they can say all, or nearly all, they want to say in it—and this is no mean accomplishment—and yet there are whole aspects of English of which, from the circumstances of their lives, they are totally unaware. English speech plays an enormous part in the lives of all of us, and yet when we come to think, we find that we know next to nothing about it.

What then, it may be asked, is there to know about this most familiar thing the English Language, beyond that it is (or ought to be) pronounced in a certain way, that its words have this or that meaning, and that certain grammatical constructions are said to be 'correct' while others are not?

First of all we might suggest a few rather large questions such as: Where did English come from? Why do we sometimes notice that English words resemble words with the same or similar meaning in other languages? Was English always as it is now; was it always pronounced as at present; did the words always bear the same meanings as they now do? How did English words come to mean just what they do? How is it that the same English word may have many different meanings and shades of meaning?

Now, concerning these, and many other questions of a similar kind, considerable curiosity exists fairly widely, even among those who are sometimes referred to as 'general readers'.

It may be possible, to some extent, to gratify such natural and praiseworthy curiosity where it exists, and perhaps even to stimulate it among some of those who have never felt it.

It may be asserted that to understand something of the ancient relationships of words, of the gradual changes of form that befall them through the centuries, and of the well-nigh incredible developments of meaning—now in the way of expansion, now by a process of restriction and specialization—to understand something of all this, I say, adds enormously to the interest with which we speak, hear, or read our native language. It is not extravagant to say that such knowledge opens up new worlds of thought and speculation.

An Etymological Dictionary, rightly used, may guide on to the right path. In this Dictionary no little pains have been devoted to etymologies. In fact these are discussed here more fully than is usual in works of its size. A large number of words are cited from many languages, and changes of meaning are often discussed at some length. The justification for giving so large a collection of words from languages more or less remote from, but ultimately related to, English is that often only in this way is it possible to understand how a meaning has developed from another which at the first glance appears to have no connexion with it.

It is no doubt to be lamented, but it is a fact, that there is no royal road to Etymology, any more than to any other branch of knowledge. Etymology is not an easy science—'the wayfaring man', even though he be not 'a fool', is very liable 'to err therein', unless he is willing to take a certain amount of trouble to understand what it is desired to do, and the means by which we attempt to accomplish this.

The Meaning of Etymology

The 'etymology' of a word means, briefly, an *account of the history of its form*, as far back as we can get it, and an account of the *chief developments of meaning* which it has undergone.

To those unacquainted with the science of philology and its methods, and with the historical relationships of languages, the treatment of the etymologies of words displayed in this, or any other Dictionary which deals with the subject, is apt to be puzzling and confusing. The difficulty can unfortunately only be removed by a more or less thorough training in methods and studies which the 'general reader' cannot be assumed to possess. Nor is it possible in a short introduction such as this to supply an equivalent to such a training.

On the other hand it is necessary to make an attempt, by stating, as clearly as may be, certain elementary facts about English and its relation to other languages, to get rid of some of the worst misunderstandings to which our treatment of etymologies might give rise, and prevent this from completely misleading the uninitiated.

Ancestry of English

The oldest form of English which we find recorded in written documents is about 1200 years old. This is known as *Anglo-Saxon*, or more generally, among students of the subject, as *Old English*. But Old English does not suddenly appear as an isolated phenomenon in these islands. We know that this language was brought here in the 5th century by various tribes from Northern Germany, known as Angles, Saxons, and Jutes. It turns out that there are several languages on the Continent, also preserved in ancient documents, which so closely resemble Old English (O.E.) in vocabulary, grammatical forms, and in the structure of the sentence, that we cannot escape the conviction that these tongues must have had a close affinity to O.E., in fact that all of them had a common ancestor. This group of related languages, O.E., Old Frisian, Old Saxon, Old High German, represented at the present time by Frisian, Dutch, and various other Low German dialects, and Modern German, is known as the West Germanic (W. Gmc.) group, and their immediate common ancestor, which survives only in its offspring, as West Germanic.

But this is not all. There are two other groups of languages the individuals of which are as closely related to each other as those of the W. Gmc. group, and which further have a remoter, though unmistakable resemblance to this.

One of these groups consists of the Scandinavian languages (Icelandic, Danish, Norwegian, Swedish), old forms of which are also preserved in written documents, going back, in some cases, well over 1000 years. This is called the North Germanic (N. Gmc.) group. Yet a third pair of old languages bearing marked resemblance to both W. and N. Gmc. existed. The more important is that of the Goths, preserved in fairly copious documents (a translation of the New Testament, and parts of the Old, and a commentary). This translation was made by the Gothic Bishop Wulfila in the 4th century. Another language of this type, that of the Vandals, is represented only in a number of personal names occurring in Latin and other manuscripts. We call the group to which Gothic and Vandalic belong the East Germanic (E. Gmc.) group. These three groups, the N. Gmc., the E. Gmc., and the W. Gmc., are all derived from a common ancestor which we call Primitive Germanic (Pr. Gmc.).

Now the first thing to decide about an English word is whether it is a pure *native word*, or whether it came into our language by borrowing from some other language, and is what is called a loan-word. If a word is not native, we endeavour to find out whence it came, when it passed into English, and all that is discoverable about it in the language from which we, or our ancestors, took it.

If, for instance, we look up the word *tooth*, we find that in O.E. it was written *tōþ* (*þ* = *th*), and that words closely resembling it are recorded in all the W. Gmc. languages, which shows that it was not only a native English word but also a common W. Gmc. word. But we shall find that other words with the same meaning and very similar forms are mentioned, from Old Norse and from Gothic. This shows that *tooth* goes back not merely to W. Gmc., but that it was part of the common stock of Pr. Gmc. words, since otherwise cognate forms could not occur in both E. and N. Gmc. groups which were differentiated from each other and from W. Gmc. centuries before the oldest records.

Even this is not the end of the story. In our account of the word *tooth*, a number of forms are included from several other languages, which all bear even to the layman's eye some faint resemblance to the English word in form, and which all have the same meaning. The words are Sanscrit *danta*, Greek *odont-*, Latin *dent-*, Welsh *dant*. One important difference between these and the oldest English form *tōþ* is that the latter lacks *n*, which the others all have. Yes, but it appears that Gothic, the most primitive type of Gmc. known to us, has *tunþus*, and O.H.G., like English a W. Gmc. tongue, had *zand*. Now from what we know of the sound changes peculiar to O.E. and O.H.G. we are able to say with certainty that both these old forms are derived from a W. Gmc. **tanþ-*, which has had a different development in O.E. and O.H.G. respectively.

The Ancient Mother Tongue and its Descendants

What about the other words, in Greek, Latin, and so on? What have they to do with English and Gmc.? The answer is that Gmc. is derived from a still older language which we call Primitive Aryan, or simply Aryan, a fruitful mother of languages and families of languages. Just as N., E., and W. Gmc. were all descended from, or differentiated out of, Pr. Gmc., so was Pr. Gmc. itself sprung, together with other great families of speech, from Pr. Aryan.

This ancient Mother Tongue, spoken it may be in Northern or Eastern Europe, it may be in Asia, was, at some very remote period, split up into a number of dialects each of which in its turn (if it survived) became the ancestor of another family of speech, the speakers of which wandered farther and farther afield from the original 'home' or 'cradle', and carried Aryan speech in its various forms over the greater part of Europe into Persia, and into large parts of India. Of these forms Pr. Gmc. was one. The chief others were: (1) the Indian branch, i.e. Sanscrit, the ancient sacred language of India, and later Indian languages; (2) old and later Persian; (3) Balto-Slavic, which split into Baltic, represented by Lithuanian, Lettish, and Old Prussian on the one hand, and the Slavonic tongues on the other, represented by Old Slavonic, and the present Russian, Polish, Czech, and Serbian &c.; (4) the Hellenic branch, which includes the various Greek dialects; (5) Italic: Latin, and the other old dialects of Italy; (6) Celtic, including ancient Gaulish, and the ancient languages of Ireland, Wales, the Highlands of Scotland, the Isle of Man, and the modern descendants of these. Breton is an offshoot of Welsh. Cornish, of which some literary remains are preserved, died out, as a spoken language, about 200 years ago.

The gist of this statement may be put in the form of a rough genealogical tree which makes it easy to see at a glance the relation between English and the other chief languages of the Aryan family. This is attempted in the table on p. ix.

It has been noted that great differences often exist in the various families between forms of what we allege to be originally the same word, that is, one fully cognate, and derived from the same ancestral form in Pr. Aryan. These differences are due to tendencies which existed in each family to develop along different lines. This means that the speakers of the various primitive communities, who all started with the same language, as they drew further and further away from each other in their migrations, gradually came to pronounce the same original sounds, vowels and consonants, and otherwise alter their language, in different ways. These differences were accentuated with time and distance, until it is often very difficult at first to discern the original identity of a word under the very different forms it has assumed in widely separated families. It is the business of philologists to discover and formulate the laws of change as they affect every sound among the various groups of languages, so as to be able to recognize identity in spite of difference.

Regularity of Change in Speech Sounds

We soon learn to appreciate the truth of the great principle which guides all philological study, that a given sound is always changed, in one and the same dialect, in the same way, under the same conditions. Thus, for instance, in Gk. initial *s* becomes the aspirate *h*, and between vowels is lost altogether; in Celtic initial *p* is lost; in Sanscrit, Pers., and the Balto-Slav. families a sound which appears as *k* in Gk. and Lat. and as *h* in Gmc., develops into the sound of *sh* or *s*; Gmc. has changed old *p*, *t*, *k* into *f*, *þ*, *h* respectively, and so on. These changes take place everywhere, in all words containing these sounds, not in only isolated words here and there.

It often happens that in seeking for cognates of an English word outside Gmc. we are unable to find a word completely identical with it, but only a base, or as it used to be called, a 'root'. Thus *food*, O.E. *fōda*, a Gmc. word, has no complete cognate elsewhere, but part of the word (that corresponding to *fō-* from Aryan *pā-*) is found, with various different formative elements, in Lat. *pā-bulum*, 'food', *pā-nis*, 'bread', *pā-scere*, 'to feed', drive to pasture, *pā-stor*, 'shepherd'—originally 'the feeder' (of sheep &c.)—

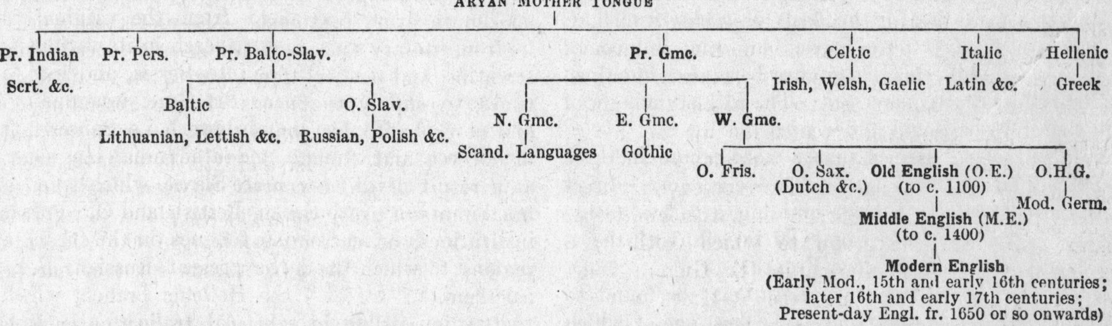

pāstura, 'pasture', which words are further discussed in the Dictionary under their English forms *pabulum*, *pastor*, *pasture*, which have all been borrowed straight from Latin. Again, the word *stream*, O.E. *strēam*, a Gmc. word, is cognate with Gk. *hréein*, 'to flow' (or, as it is sometimes spelt, *rhéein*), which in Aryan must have been **srew-ein*. We know that *sr-* becomes *hr-* in Gk. and also that in Gmc. it becomes *str-*. We know further that between vowels *w* disappears altogether in Gk., but becomes *u*, a vowel, when followed by another consonant. Hence we are able to assert that the Gk. word *hreûma*, 'a flow, flux', is cognate with *hréein*, and that its earlier form must have been **srew-ma*. Now this would become **streum* in Gmc. This is very much like the Pr. Gmc. form from which O.E. *strēam* is descended, but it is not quite the same, for the Gmc. ancestor of this was **straum*, and it is preserved unaltered in O.H.G. *straum*. Now this would be **sroum-* in Aryan, and we therefore have to assume two original Aryan types, this, and **sreum-* the ancestor of Gk. *hreûma*. But it is known that in Aryan the diphthongs *eu* and *ou* interchanged in the same base, by virtue of a principle known as Gradation which we cannot discuss here. Further, a third possible form was *u* with loss of the first element of the diphthong, so that we might predict a third form of our base, **sru-* or, with the *-m-* suffix, **sru-m-*. The former is actually found in the Sanscrit *sru*, 'to flow'. This form also establishes the primitive *sr-* which became *str-* in Gmc., *hr-* in Gk., but remained unchanged in the Indian branch of the Aryan language. The Gk. word *hreûma* was later borrowed in Latin as *rheuma*, whence it passed into French, and thence into English, and will be found under *rheum* in the Dictionary.

English Borrowings from Other Tongues

The beginner in etymology must be warned against the error of supposing that when a number of words are given from other Gmc. languages, to illustrate the history of a native English word, it is suggested that the English word is derived from any of these. They are quoted as sister forms, sprung from a common parent, and they enable us to reconstruct the parent in the light of the known laws of sound change, and further, sometimes to observe different shades of meaning developed in the several languages. Similarly, when remoter cognates are cited from Scrt., Gk., Lat., or Slav., none of these is the ancestor of Gmc., but a sister form descended from a common mother. This should have become clear from the foregoing remarks and illustrations.

But it is time to turn to borrowings, or loan-words in English. Throughout her history our language has borrowed from many sources. The chief of these are Latin, the great culture language of the Mediaeval Western world, Norse through the Scandinavian invaders of England, and French, partly in a special form through the Normans, partly by many later borrowings from Central French. Some Latin words came into English through popular speech in the Continental period, and are found in O.E. and the other old Gmc. languages (see *street* and *(tur-)nip* in the Dictionary). Others came in later from Celtic speakers of Latin in Britain (see *provost*), and yet more through the influence of the Roman Church in Anglo-Saxon England (see *Pope*, *Mass*, *rule*, *disciple* &c.).

Throughout the Middle Ages Latin continued to influence English, many words coming from the Latin Vulgate as well as from profane sources; Latin authors were read, and Latin was used as a living language among the learned in speaking and writing. How readily words direct from Latin become naturalized in English is shown by the hundreds, some commonly current, some purely the possession of the learned, with such endings as *-ate*, *-ation*, *-ion*, *-tude*, *-ance*, *-ence*, and so on, and by others, equally numerous, with the prefixes *ab-*, *ad-*, *al-* &c., *de-*, *con-* &c., *ex-*, *in-*, *pre-*, *pro-*. It is the words with these and other Latin prefixes and suffixes which contribute to make any English Dictionary that is at all complete so extremely bulky.

Latin and Romance Words in English

Latin words borrowed since the Anglo-Saxon period are almost entirely derived from literary sources. In this they differ from a large part of the French words in English, a considerable portion of which, especially those borrowed from Norman French during the three centuries that followed the Conquest, were derived from direct contact with French speakers — Normans — in England. The Normans were originally Norsemen who had settled in Neustria, later Normandy, early in the 10th century, and had acquired French. It is perhaps desirable to say something of the origin of French and its nearest linguistic connexions. French belongs to what are known as the Romance or Neo-Latin languages. These are all derived from popular forms of Latin as it was spoken in the various provinces of the far-flung Empire of ancient Rome. The principal other members of this family are Italian — in many respects nearest to Latin — Spanish, Portuguese, Provençal. Most of these tongues have given words to English at one time or another, though none in such numbers as French.

In giving the etymology of a word from French or any other Romance language, we indicate the Latin word whence it comes, and discuss the etymology of the latter. It naturally often happens that the same Latin base appears both as the ancestor of a word of French origin occurring in English, and again in a word borrowed direct from Latin. Thus *faith* comes from a Norman-French form of Lat. *fides*, 'faith', and this word is also the basis of *fidelity* from Lat. *fidelitāt-*. Again *royal* is pure French in form, and comes from Lat. *regālis*, but this latter word is also found in English, almost unaltered, as *regal*. The full etymology of *royal* will therefore be found under *regal*.

Again it will often happen that a word occurs in three or even four different forms in English—e.g. *hospital* direct from Low Latin *hospitale*, 'a large building, a palace' (a by-form of this is *spital*); *hostel* from Old French, with the *-s-* still preserved; *hotel* from Modern French.

A French word when traced to Latin may be found to have remoter cognates in the Gmc. languages, one of which cognates may occur in English. Thus *flower* in Middle English (Chaucer &c.) and O. French is *flour*, which is derived from Lat. *flōrem*, accusative form of *flōs*, 'a flower', and this is found again in *floral* derived straight from Lat. *flōrālis*. But the Lat. *flōs* is cognate with O.E. *blōstma*, which survives in English as *blossom*, and also with O.E. *blōwan*, 'to bloom, flourish', Mod. Engl. *to blow*. A further Gmc. cognate is O.N. *blōm*, 'a flower', not found in O.E., but borrowed later from Norse, and surviving as the common word *bloom*. As a rule, before we can establish the remote relations of a French word with a native English word, we must inquire into the ancestral Latin form of the former, and then discuss the Gmc. and English cognates with this Latin word.

Scandinavian Influence on English Vocabulary

Lastly, among the most copious sources of our borrowings, the Scandinavian languages must be mentioned. English speakers were brought into direct contact with Danes and Norsemen (who, as we saw, spoke a North Gmc. language) as a result of repeated raids carried out by these pirates, and the ultimate settlement by them of large tracts of England under King Alfred. Old Danish and Norse were in many ways very close to Old English, and a considerable part of the vocabulary was common to both peoples, although the pronunciation was different. The interpenetration of English with Norse words was tolerably thorough, and many words thus derived appear from the 12th century onwards to be firmly established, and to be in process of gradually ousting the old native words. Only a very few out of several hundred can be mentioned here. How vital these words have become to us is shown by the following, all of which are indispensable in ordinary life: *dairy, egg, husband, skin, sky, ill, weak, die* (verb), *thrive, give, get, take, raise, split, though, they, them.* A curious case of Scandinavian influence is seen in *dream*, a pure English word so far as its form goes, derived from O.E. *drēam*, but its present meaning, 'vision', is pure Scandinavian. The Old Norse word is *draumr*, which had the same sense as the Modern English word. But the English word, in O.E. and early Middle English, meant 'noise, cheerful noise, revelry; happiness', and never by any chance had the sense of 'vision'. The word was gradually influenced in meaning by the Old Norse word—its exact cognate—and entirely lost its old senses. (See discussion of the development of meaning under *dream* in the Dictionary.)

Other Sources of the English Vocabulary

In addition to those, the most important elements in the English vocabulary, already referred to, there are large numbers of words, borrowed at different periods, and used with varying degrees of frequency, adopted from languages spoken in every continent. Many of these words come to us from literary sources, many others, especially philosophic, scientific, and medical terms, are taken straight, in modern times, to supply the needs of ever-extending knowledge and new philosophic conceptions, from the ancient tongues of Greece and Rome. Many others have been adopted as a result of direct contact between Englishmen and the inhabitants of every corner of the globe, to express objects, institutions, or customs familiar in the life of those far regions to which the adventurous spirit of our people has led them.

It is impossible, in a brief Introduction such as this, to go in detail into these varied elements of our vocabulary. It must suffice to specify as sources such historical facts as the long British occupation of India, and the existence of large classes of military and civil officers of British blood who, after service in India, return to their own country; the colonization of North America by the English in the 17th century, and the later contact between ourselves and the citizens of the American Republic; the colonization of Canada, of South Africa, of Australia.

Nothing is more remarkable in the history of language than the changes undergone in the meanings of words. One reason, in discussing etymologies, for collecting together a large number of cognates from various languages is that often by this means alone is it possible to discover the fundamental meaning which underlies them all, from which all the varied senses have sprung, and to trace the manner in which the meanings have branched out in innumerable directions. One has only to look through the various cognate words and their meanings brought together in this dictionary under the words *pax, pay, pacify, pale* (I.), *page* (II.), and *fair* (II.), and consider the well-established relationships between all these words, both in form and meaning, together with the various shades of meaning of *pay* and *fair* developed in English itself, in order to realize what is possible in the way of variation in sense. Here we start apparently with the material sense of 'joining, fitting together', and upon this theme the human mind has played, using the old words to express now a material, now a non-material conception; now extending, now narrowing the connotation, twisting and turning in every imaginable and unimaginable direction.

And yet, at the end of it all, we are able to recognize a unifying principle pervading the whole, so that the links in the chain of meaning are never entirely lost, or are at least recoverable.

One of the charms of etymology is that it reveals the human mind at work, for ever striving to express new ideas and shades of meaning, adapting and readapting material which is as old as man himself, so that it shall reflect the modes of thought, the needs and hopes, the occupations and habits, of every age and of every manner of life.

II

By M. S. Serjeantson

A—The Sounds of Primitive Aryan, and the Characteristic Treatment of these in the Several Chief Families of Aryan Languages

FROM the Primitive Aryan Mother Tongue there sprang, as was stated above, p. viii, several daughter languages, each of which became, by a natural process of differentiation, a fruitful mother of languages and dialects. Among the members of each of the communities into which the original Aryan community was broken up, there gradually arose different habits of pronunciation, and tendencies to change the primitive sounds in different ways. The table of the Aryan languages and their relationships is repeated here for convenience of reference.

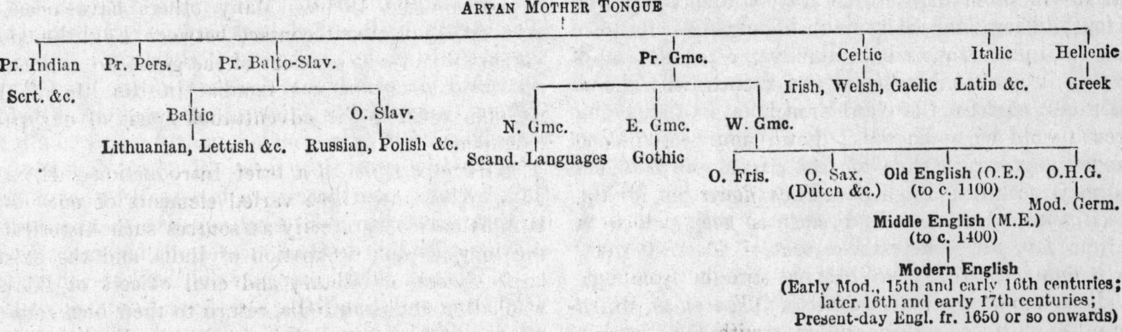

We then proceed to summarize the differences in the treatment of the original sounds which are most characteristic of the several families of languages.

The Sounds of Primitive Aryan

According to modern philologists, who have made a hypothetical reconstruction, the Aryan Mother Tongue had the following sounds :—consonants : stops, *b*, *d*, *g*, *g⁀*, g^w ; *p*, *t*, *k*, *k⁀*, k^w ; these with aspiration : *bh*, *gh*, *ph*, *kh* &c. ; the trill *r* ; the divided consonant *l* ; the nasals *m*, *n*, ŋ ; the open consonants *j*, *w*, *s*, and perhaps þ. The distinction between *g⁀* and *g*, *k⁀* and *k*, lies in the fact that the latter of each pair (*g*, *k*) is pronounced with the tongue farther back in the mouth than the former (cp. the consonants of *go*, *cow* (*g*, *k*), with those of *give*, *key* (*g⁀*, *k⁀*)) ; g^w, k^w are pronounced like *g*, *k*, but with the lips protruded. The vowels were : *ī*, *i*, *ē*, *e*, *ā*, *a*, *ō*, *o*, *ū*, *u*, ə ; diphthongs : *ei*, *ai*, *oi* ; *eu*, *au*, *ou* ; the same with the first element long : *ēi*, *āi* &c. ; əi, əu. There were also syllabic *l*, *n*, *m*, *r*, usually written by philologists *l̥*, *n̥*, *m̥*, *r̥* (cp. the final syllables of *bottle*, *mutton* = [bɔ́tl, mátn]). These occurred only in unstressed syllables, and arose from the reduction or elimination of the full vowel which preceded *l*, *m* &c.

Sound Changes which occur in the Derived Families of Languages

1. Indian Group. This includes (*a*) the Sanscrit of the ancient sacred writings (including the Vedas, the oldest part of which dates from the 10th or 11th century B.C.), and (*b*) Classical and Epic Sanscrit, of the later literature. Sanscrit developed into the two dialects of Prākrit and Pāli ; from the latter came many of the modern Indian dialects, including Hindustani and Bengali.

Sanscrit levelled Aryan *ă̄*, *ŏ̄*, *ĕ̄* under *ă̄* ; *ĭ̄* and *ŭ̄* remained ; ə became *i* or *a*. Cp. Scrt. *bhárati*, 'he bears' (fr. **bher-*, see **bear (I.)**) ; Scrt. *á-dhām*, 'I put' (fr. **dhēm-*, see **fact**) ; Scrt. *aštáu*, 'eight', fr. **ok⁀t-*, see **eight** ; Scrt. *sthitáš*, 'standing', fr. **stə-*, see **state (I.)**. The diphthongs are monophthongized, *ei*, *ai*, *oi* becoming *ē*, and *eu*, *au*, *ou* becoming *ō*. Cp. Scrt. *édhaš*, 'firewood', fr. **aidh-*, see **aedile** ; *éti*, 'he goes', fr. **ei-*, see **itinerate** ; Scrt. *ṓjaš*, 'strength', fr. **aug-*, see **auction** ; *yōš*, 'safety', fr. **jou-*, see **jus**.

Scrt. retains the Aryan lip and point stops, both aspirated and unaspirated. But if two aspirated consonants occur in the same word, the first loses its aspiration. This is known as Grassman's Law ; a similar process occurs in Greek. Cp. Scrt. *bandhati*, 'he binds', fr. **bhendh-*, see **bind (I.)**. The lip-modified back stops, k^w, g^w, g^wh, are levelled under the full back stops *k*, *g*, *gh*, becoming respectively *k* (*c*), *g* or *j*, *gh* or *h* ; cp. Scrt. *stighnati*, 'he climbs', fr. **stigh-*, see **sty (I.)** ; Scrt. *gharmáš*, 'glow', fr. g^wh-, see **warm**. But Aryan k^w, g^w become respectively *č*, *j* in Scrt. before front vowels ; e.g. Aryan *k^w*etwər*, 'four', becomes in Scrt. *čatur-* (cp. Lat. *quatuor*, where the initial consonant has undergone little change) ; see **four**. The Aryan back-advanced stops, *k⁀*, *g⁀*, *g⁀h*, undergo a characteristic change in Primitive Indian (similar to that in Iranian and Balto-Slavonic), by which *k⌒* becomes *š* = [ʃ], *g⌒* becomes *j* = [dž], *g⌒h* becomes *h*; cp. Scrt. *šatám*, Lat. *centum*, see **hundred**; Scrt. *jānāmi*, 'I know', fr. **g⌒nō-*, see **know**. Aryan *j* and *w* remain in Scrt. (transcribed as *y*, *v*), as in Scrt. *yunákti*, 'harnesses', cp. Lat. *jungere*, see **join (I.)**; *vēdaš*, 'I know', see **Veda**. Nasal consonants and *r* usually remain in Scrt. Aryan *l* often appears as *r*. Thus Scrt. *rōkáš*, 'bright', is cognate with Gk. *leukós*, 'white', and Lat. *lux*, 'light', see **leuco-**. Scrt. *bhrāj-*, 'to shine', and Gk. *phlégein*, 'to burn', are both fr. an Aryan base **bhlē̆-* &c., 'to burn'; see **flagrant**.

2. Iranian developed into Old Bactrian (East Iranian) and Old Persian (West Iranian, extant in cuneiform inscriptions). The former is the language of the Zoroastrian sacred writings known as the Zend-Avesta; the latter is the ancestor of the modern Persian dialects, of Afghan &c.

The vowel-system of Iranian resembles that of Sanscrit, except that the Idg. diphthongs are not monophthongized. Iranian has *ai* for the *i*-diphthongs (Idg. *ai*, *oi*, *ei*), *au* for the *u*-diphthongs (Idg. *au*, *ou*, *eu*); these two, *ai* and *au*, remain in Persian, but become respectively *aē* or *ōi*, *au* or *əu*, in Old Bactrian (thus Zend has *dvaētha*, 'menace', fr. Iranian **dwai-*, fr. Aryan **dwei-*; cp. Gk. *dei-nós*, 'terrible', and see **dire**). Iranian eventually loses the Idg. aspirated stops, *bh*, *dh* becoming *b*, *d*. It has, however, *š*, *s* for Idg. *k⌒* (back-advanced) as in Scrt., *z* for Idg. *g⌒*, *g⌒h* (see **quiet (II.)**).

3. The Balto-Slavonic group includes (A) the Baltic dialects of Old Prussian (since the 17th century no longer spoken), Lithuanian, and Lettish; (B) the Slavonic dialects: (*a*) Russian and its varieties; (*b*) Polish and Czech; (*c*) Bulgarian, Serbian, and Slovenian. The oldest form of Bulgarian is that extant in a 9th-century translation of the Gospels; this form is sometimes called Old Church Slavonic. As regards the vowels of the Balto-Slavonic dialects, it should be noted that Idg. *ā* is rounded to *ō*, but *o* unrounded to *a* (cp. Lith. *dalìs*, 'part', fr. Aryan **dol-*, see under **daedal**); *ō* is diphthongized to *uo* (written *ů*; e.g. Lith. *jũkas*, 'jest', fr. Aryan **jŏk-*, cognate with Lat. *jocus*, 'joke', fr. **jòk-*, see **joke**); the symbol ˜ over a vowel denotes length. The Idg. diphthongs are not monophthongized, *ei*, *ai*, *oi* appearing respectively as *ei*, *ai*, *ai*, or being levelled under *ė* (= [ie]); *eu*, *au*, *ou* become *au* (as in Lith. *auszra*, 'red of dawn', cognate with **aurora**, q.v.). In Slavonic, Idg. *a* and *o* both appear as *o*; *ō* is unrounded to *ā*; *y* (= [ÿ]) represents Idg. *ū*; the symbol *ĭ* is used for a Slavonic raised *i*, *ŭ* for a raised *o*; the diphthongs are monophthongized, *ei*, *ai*, *oi* to *ě* (apparently [ē]), *eu*, *au*, *ou* to *u* (cp. O. Slav. *uši*, 'ears', fr. Aryan base **ōus-*, 'ear', see **ear**). Both the Baltic and Slavonic groups keep the Aryan lip and point stops, but these when aspirated lose their aspiration. Both branches develop *s* or *z* for the back-advanced stops (*k⌒*, *g⌒* &c.), resembling in this respect Sanscrit and Iranian (see **hound**, fr. Aryan **k⌒wn-*, and cognate with Lith. *szun-*, Russ. *su-ka*, 'bitch'). Baltic usually levels the full back stops (*k*, *g*, *gh*) and the lip-modified back stops (k^w, g^w, g^wh) under *k*, *g*, *g*, but Slavonic has in certain forms *č*, *ž* (*z*), *ž* (*z*) instead of *k*, *g*, *g*, for Idg. *k*, *g*, *gh*, and k^w, g^w, g^wh. (Thus O. Slav. *četyre*, 'four', represents Aryan *k^w*etwər*, see **four**; and O. Slav. *žlŭtŭ*, 'yellow', is fr. the Aryan base **g⌒hel-*, **g⌒hl-* &c., see **gold**.)

4. Hellenic comprises three chief groups: (*a*) Ionic (including also Euboean and Attic); (*b*) Achaean (with Aeolian, Thessalian, and Boeotian; Arcadian, Cyprian, and Pamphylian); (*c*) Doric (including Laconian, Corinthian, and others, and the North-Western dialects of Epirus, Locris, Phocis, Achaia &c.). The history of Greek can be traced from the 8th century B.C. By the end of the 4th century B.C., Attic had become in some degree a 'standard' language in all parts of Greece, and also in Asia Minor; it is the ancestor of the modern Greek dialects.

One of the chief features of Attic phonology, and one which is shared also by the rest of the Ionic group, is its change of Idg. *ā* to *ē* (as for instance in Gk. *mḗtēr*, 'mother', fr. Aryan **mā-*, see **mother**). Otherwise, most of the Aryan vowels remain in Greek; *ū*, however, becomes [ÿ] (written *u*) in the Ionic-Attic group. The diphthongs were preserved for a time, but later *ei* became [ē] and, perhaps by the 3rd century B.C., [ī]; while *ou* by about the 5th century B.C. became *ū*.

Idg. *w*, written Ϝ (digamma) in early Gk., disappears before vowels (cp. Gk. *épos*, 'a word', earlier **wep-*, for **wek*^{w}*-*, 'to speak', see **epos**; Gk. *aúra*, earlier **awer-*, 'air', see **aura**), or becomes an aspirate (see **Hesperian**); before consonants it becomes the vowel *u*. Idg. *j* becomes an aspirate ('rough breathing') or *z* (see Gk. *hṓra* for **jōra*, 'hour', under **hour**; see also **zeugma**); Idg. *s* becomes an aspirate which remains initially, but otherwise usually disappears before vowels, and before *j*, *w*, *l*, *m*, *n*, *r*. Idg. lip and point stops remain in Greek, the voiced aspirated stops are unvoiced, e.g. *bh* > *ph*, *dh* > *th*; for instance, Gk. *thūmós*, 'breath', is fr. Aryan **dhū-*; see **fume**. As in Sanscrit, an initial aspirated stop loses its aspiration if the next syllable begins with an aspirated stop (see **bind**). Back-advanced and full back stops are levelled in Greek: *k*, *k⌒* both become *k*; *g*, *g⌒* > *g*; *gh*, *g⌒h* > *kh* (χ) with unvoicing as in the case of *bh*, *dh*. Cp. Gk. *khandánein*, 'to hold', fr. Aryan **ghe(n)d-* &c., see **get**. The Aryan lip-modified back stops, k^w, g^w, g^wh, (*a*) become respectively *p*, *b*, *ph*, before back vowels (other than *u*), *i* + vowel, or consonants (other than *j*); cp. Gk. *poinḗ*, fr. *k^w*oin-*, see **penal**; (*b*) k^w > *t*, g^w > *d*, g^wh > *th* before front vowels (see Gk. *téttares* under **quadri-**); (*c*) k^w > *k* before *j*, *u*; g^w > *z* before *j*, *g* before *u*; cp. Gk. *zōós*, fr. *g^w*jō-*, see **zoo-**. Idg. syllabic *m̥*, *n̥* become *a* in Greek before a consonant, so that the Aryan unstressed negative prefix *n̥* becomes Gk. *a-*, corresponding to Gmc. *un-* (see under **un-**).

5. Italic. This comprises two main branches: (*a*) Oscan, Umbrian, and Sabellian, the last including such dialects as Sabine, Volscian, and Faliscan; all these are known chiefly from inscriptions, and from forms quoted by Latin grammarians; (*b*) Latin, which developed on the one hand into the literary language of the classical period, and on the other into the popular, spoken dialect known as Low or Vulgar Latin, which was eventually carried by soldier and merchant over the whole of the Roman Empire. By the end of the 6th century A.D. Low Latin had split up into the so-called Romance dialects which now include French, Provençal, Spanish, Portuguese, Italian, Roumanian, Walachian, and Rhaeto-Romanic.

The Aryan simple vowels are for the most part preserved in Latin, but *e* tends to become *i* before a nasal (see **imbricate**, fr. earlier **embh-*), and *e* becomes *o* before *w* (written *v*; see **novel**); the group **swe* becomes *swo-*, *so-* (see Lat. *soror* under **sister**), and **we* becomes *wo* (*vo*) before *l* or *m* followed by a back vowel (see *volo* under **volition**). The Idg. diphthongs remained at first in Italic, and later developed as follows: *ei* > *ī* (see Lat. *dīcere*, 'to tell', under **diction**), *ai* > *ae* (see **laevo-**, earlier **laiwo-*), *oi* > *oe* > *ū* (see **mural**), *əi* > *ai* > *ae* (see secular, fr. **səik-*), *eu* > *ou* > *ū* (see *dūcere*, 'to lead', under **duke**); *au* remained in classical Latin, but became *ō* in Low Latin (see under **cloisonné**), *ou* > *ū* (see **lucus**, Lat. *lūc-*, 'light', fr. earlier **louk-*). Idg. syllabic *m̥*, *n̥*, > *em*, *en* in Latin (as in *densus*, 'thick', fr. Aryan **dn̥-t-*, whence also Gk.

dasús, 'thick', see **dasy-**). The non-aspirated stops, *p*, *t*, *k*, *b*, *d*, *g*, remain in Latin, and *k⁀*, *g⁀* become *k*, *g*. The aspirated voiced stops change considerably: *bh* > *ph* > *f* initially, *b* medially (see **future**, **nebula**); *dh* > *th* > þ, which develops further to (*a*) *f* initially (as for instance in the Aryan base **dhək-* &c., 'to place', Lat. *fac-ere*, 'to do', see **fact**), (*b*) *b* medially before and after *r*, and before *w* or *l* (see **verb**, earlier **werdh-*), (*c*) *d* under other conditions (see **media**). Oscan &c. had *f* for Idg. *dh* in all these positions. Idg. *g⁀h* usually became *h* initially (as in Lat. *hortus*, 'garden', Aryan **g⁀hort-*, see **hortus siccus**), but *f* before *u* (see **futile**); medially, *g⁀h* usually became *h* (see **vehicle**). Idg. *gh* became *h* (see **host (I.)**); *gʷh* > *f* initially, *gu* after a nasal; otherwise, *v* medially (cp. Lat. *ninguit*, 'it snows', *niv-em*, 'snow', and see **snow**). It should also be noted that Idg. *s* became Italic *z* between vowels, and this became Latin *r* (see Lat. *soror*, under **sister**, and cp. also Lat. *altāria*, 'altar', fr. **alt-āra* for **alt-āsa*, see **altar**).

6. Celtic has three main divisions: (A) Gaulish, which was supplanted in ancient Gaul by Low Latin at the beginning of the present era, surviving only in inscriptions, and in personal names and loan-words in Latin writings (see, for instance, **palfrey**); (B) Brythonic, including Welsh, Cornish, and Breton; (C) Gaelic, including Scotch and Irish Gaelic, and Manx.

The Celtic phonological developments are too complicated to summarize briefly. Some of the changes of Primitive Celtic will be seen in the Tables. It may be mentioned, however, (*a*) that Idg. *ē* becomes *ī* (see Celtic *rīg-*, 'king', under **rich**); (*b*) that Idg. initial *w* appears as *f* in Old Irish (see O. Ir. *fot*, 'length', under **vast**), *v* in Gaulish, *gw* in Brythonic; (*c*) that Idg. *kʷ* becomes *k* (*c*) in Gaelic (as in O. Ir. *cethir*, 'four', Aryan **kʷetwər*, q.v. under **four**) but *p* in Brythonic and Gaulish; (*d*) that Idg. *gʷ* becomes *b* (see O. Ir. *biad*, 'means of life', fr. **gʷī-*, under **vital**); (*e*) that Idg. *p* disappears initially and between vowels (cp. O. Ir. *iasc*, 'fish', with Lat. *piscis*, q.v. under **fish**).

7. Germanic. The Primitive Germanic language became differentiated into three branches, called, from the relative positions of the areas in which they were spoken, East, North, and West Germanic.

East Germanic included the dialects of the Goths, Vandals, Heruli, and Gepidae, all now dead languages, and mostly surviving only in Place and Personal Names in Greek and Latin writings. Gothic, however, is represented by a translation of parts of the Bible, made in the 4th century by the West Gothic bishop Wulfila, and by part of a commentary on the Gospel of St. John. These are now extant only in 6th-century manuscripts, but they constitute (except for some Scandinavian runic inscriptions) the earliest recorded form of any of the Germanic dialects. An East Gothic dialect, Crimean Gothic, survived for some centuries, but all we know of it is a list of some sixty or seventy words taken down in the 16th century by a certain Flemish envoy of the Emperor, O. G. von Busbecq.

North Germanic in its oldest recorded form is known as Old Norse, represented by runic inscriptions of which the oldest are of the 3rd and 4th centuries (from Denmark and Schleswig). By the end of the Viking period (c. 700–1050), the language had begun to be differentiated into East Scandinavian, including Swedish and Danish, and West Scandinavian, comprising Norwegian and Icelandic.

West Germanic includes: (*a*) Old English, the earliest records of which are of the late 7th century; (*b*) Old Frisian, from the 14th century; (*c*) Old Saxon, formerly spoken in the area from the Harz Mountains to the North Sea between the Elbe and Zuider Zee, known from the 9th century; (*d*) Old Low Franconian, from which Modern Dutch and Flemish are mainly derived; (*e*) Old High German, the speech of Central and Southern Germany and parts of Switzerland and Austria, and the ancestor of the Modern German dialects; (*f*) the language of the Lombards, which is known chiefly from proper names, and which has long been extinct.

Primitive Germanic was distinguished from the Aryan mother-tongue, and from its sister languages, Celtic, Italic, Hellenic &c., partly by vowel changes and partly by a series of striking consonantal changes, affecting first the aspirated and non-aspirated stops, and known as *the First Sound-shifting*. The developments involved must have been spread over several centuries, and were for the most part complete probably a century or more before the beginning of this era. The Primitive Germanic vowel changes were somewhat later. Gothic resembles Primitive Germanic more closely than any other dialect, and forms quoted from Gothic illustrate the first developments from Indo-Germanic more clearly than do forms from Old English, Old High German, Old Norse &c., obscured as these are by many subsequent changes. (It will be seen, however, from the Tables that Gothic does in certain respects differ strikingly from Primitive Germanic.) The most characteristic Pr. Gmc. vowel changes are: (*a*) Idg. *o* > *a* (e.g. Goth. *dags*, fr. Aryan **dhogʷh-*, see **day**; see also the Gmc. words under **host (I.)**, **eight**); (*b*) Idg. *ā* > *ō* (see O.E. *mōdor*, Aryan **māt-*, under **mother**); (*c*) Idg. *ei* > *ī* (see O.E. *drīfan*, 'to drive', Aryan **dhreibh-*, under **drive**); (*d*) Idg. *oi* > *ai* (e.g. Goth. *ains*, Aryan **oin-*, see **one**); (*e*) Idg. *ou* > *au* (see **red**). Further, Idg. *l̥*, *m̥*, *n̥*, *r̥* become Gmc. *ul*, *um*, *un*, *ur* (see **corn (I.)**, **hundred**, **tush (II.)**, **wolf**). The consonant changes are more far-reaching. The chief are: (1) Idg. *p*, *t*, *k*, and *ph*, *th*, *kh*, become respectively *f*, þ, χ (*k⁀* and *k⁀h* are levelled under *k* and *kh*); see **father**, **thumb**, **horn**. (2) Idg. *bh*, *dh*, *gh* (*g⁀h*) become *ƀ*, *đ*, ʒ, later *b*, *d*, *g*; see **bear**, **do**, **goose (I.)**. (3) Gmc. *s*, *f*, þ, χ (see (1) above) are voiced to *z*, *ƀ*, *đ*, ʒ medially when the chief accent of the word did not precede them; for instance, O.E. *fæder*, 'father', represents Gmc. **fađer*, fr. earlier Gmc. **faþér*; see **father**. This change is referred to as *Verner's Law*. (4) Idg. *b*, *d*, *g* became *p*, *t*, *k*; see **pool (I.)**, **tree**, **crane**. These changes are sometimes referred to as *the First* (*Germanic*) *Sound-shift*.

In the Germanic dialects *ƀ*, *đ*, ʒ appear as *b*, *d*, *g* initially and after nasals. A special feature of North and West Germanic is the development of medial *z* (see (3) above) to *r*; see **hoard**, O.E. *hord*, 'treasure', which is cognate with Goth. (E. Gmc.) *huzd*; final *z* is, however, lost in West Germanic. The Old High German dialects are distinguished from the other West Germanic dialects by a further series of consonantal changes (*the Second Sound-shift*). This took place during the 6th and 7th centuries, and included, among other changes, the development of *t* to *z* [*ts*] or *ss* (see O.H.G. *zīt*, 'time', under **tide**, and Germ. *hass*, 'hatred', Gmc. **hat-*, under **hate**); of *k* to *ch* [χ] (see **acre**, O.H.G. *acchar*); of *p* to *pf* or *f* (see O.H.G. *helfan*, Gmc. **help-*, under **help**).

B—The History of English in England

During the 5th century, Britain was invaded and settled by Germanic-speaking tribes from Western Europe, Angles, Saxons, and Jutes. At the time of the settlement there was probably little differentiation between their common tongue and the other dialects which eventually developed from West Germanic. Probably most of the changes which characterize English took place actually in this country, though a few may have begun on the Continent. Since the 5th century, the story of English is one of continual change and of the rise of innumerable dialects. Before the Conquest, one dialect had risen to the importance of a *written* standard language—that of Wessex, the kingdom of the West Saxons—and a very large proportion of the Old English literature is extant in this dialect. At the beginning of the Middle English period the supremacy of West Saxon as a literary language had diminished, and dialects from all parts of the country contributed to the literature of the period. It was not until the late 14th century that a South-East Midland dialect came into prominence—again as a *written*, not a *spoken*, standard. This was the dialect of London, influenced to some degree by that of neighbouring areas, and its gradual rise in importance was due to the city's authority as a centre of trade and of government. During the Elizabethan period a certain standard of *speech* became recognized, at first among men of the Court and of the Universities, and afterwards over a wider area; this, like the written standard, was based on London English—or rather on the speech of a certain class of speakers in London and its environs. (There were already variants arising among the other classes of speakers in London, from which the modern London dialects are derived.) This spoken standard developed into what is now known as Received Standard English, which is definitely not a local dialect but a class dialect, and may be heard in any part of the country without a tinge of regional peculiarities. The written language has followed the spoken standard in such matters as style and vocabulary, though always slightly more archaic; it is the *pronunciation* of Received Standard English which is its chief characteristic.

Modern English spelling, conventionalized by the 15th-century printers on a basis of late 14th-century spelling, fails to reflect any of the important changes in pronunciation which took place during the late 14th and early 15th century and afterwards, when almost every vowel in the English language changed in quality.

In the following notes on the characteristic development of Old and Middle English, only such changes are dealt with as left a permanent impression on the language (or are necessary to explain the form of O. and M.E. words), and owing to the exigencies of space only the most important of these are included.

1. Changes distinguishing Old English from West Germanic

(*a*) Isolative:

(i.) W. Gmc. *a* > *æ* (except before a nasal), see O.E. *cræft*, W. Gmc. **kraft*, under **craft**; O.E. *æcer*, **acre**, W. Gmc. **akr-*. (ii.) W. Gmc. *ā* > *ǣ* (except before a nasal), see **deed** which is fr. O.E. *dǣd*, W. Gmc. **dād*. (iii.) W. Gmc. *ai* > *ā*; thus W. Gmc. **hair-*, **hail-*, become O.E. *hār*, *hāl*, see **hoar**, **holy**. (iv.) W. Gmc. *au* > *ēa*, as in O.E. *drēam*, W. Gmc. **draum*, see **dream**. (v.) W. Gmc. *eu* > *ēo*, e.g. W. Gmc. **deur*, O.E. *dēor*, see **deer**.

(*b*) Combinative:

(i.) W. Gmc. *a*, *i*, *u* + nasal + *f*, *s*, or *þ*, became nasalized and lengthened, the nasal being lost; then the vowel was denasalized, *ā̆* becoming *ō̆*, *ī̆* > *ī*, *ū̆* > *ū*; e.g. W. Gmc. **munþ* becomes O.E. *mūþ*, see **mouth**; W. Gmc. **gans* becomes O.E. *gōs*, see **goose**.

(ii.) W. Gmc. *ā* became *ō* before a nasal; see O.E. *spōn*, W. Gmc. **spān*, under **spoon**.

(iii.) Early O.E. *i*, *e*, *æ* (W. Gmc. *i*, *e*, *a*) tended to become diphthongized (to *io*, *eo*, *ea*) before *h*, *r* or *l* + another consonant; e.g. O.E. *heard*, fr. **hærd*, W. Gmc. **hard*, see **hard**; O.E. *heall*, W. Gmc. **hall*, see **hall**; O.E. *feoh*, W. Gmc. **feχ*. see **fee**. This change is commonly known as Fracture. (*æ* was diphthongized before *l* + cons. in the South, but not in the Midlands or North.)

(iv.) Prim. O.E. back vowels were fronted when followed in the next syllable by *i* or *j* (both these usually disappeared subsequently); thus *ū̆* > *ȳ̆*; *ā* > *ǣ*; *ō* > [*ϕ*], later *ē*. Similarly, *æ* (fr. W. Gmc. *a*) > *e*; *ēa* > *ē* (*īe* in West Saxon). This process is called *i*-mutation. For instance, W. Gmc. **tākjan*, 'to show', appears in O.E. as *tǣċan*, 'to point out, teach', cp. the unmutated *tācn*, 'a sign', see **token** and **teach**; W. Gmc. **mūsi-*, pl. of **mūs*, 'mouse', see **mouse**, is in O.E. *mȳs*, whence Mod. Engl. *mice*; W. Gmc. **fōdjan*, 'to feed', > in O.E. *fēdan*, see **feed**, cp. the unmutated noun *fōda*, **food**.

(v.) Of the consonant changes in O.E., the most striking are the developments of W. Gmc. *k*, *ʒ*. The former is fronted to [ṫ] (voiceless front stop), later [tʃ], initially before a front vowel, and also medially and finally after *ī̆*; see **chin**, **chaff**, **pitch**, where the O.E. fronted cons. is printed *ċ* = *ċin*, *ċeaf* &c., W. Gmc. **kinn*, **kaf*. W. Gmc. *sk* always becomes [ʃ], written *sc*; see **shall**, W. Gmc. **skal*, O.E. *sċeal*.

W. Gmc. *ʒ* is fronted to [j] (voiced front open cons.) initially before front vowels (as in O.E. *ġeldan*, 'to pay' (where the dotted *g* indicates its front quality), see **yield**), and also medially and finally after front vowels (see **day**); but *ʒ* becomes [g] before back vowels (see **good**, **go**), and remains [ʒ] (voiced back open) between back vowels (see **saw (I.)**). O.E. spelling does not distinguish between [k] and [tʃ], or between [j], [ʒ], and [g], but the changes can still be traced in the modern pronunciation.

W. Gmc. *gg* > O.E. [dd], later [dž], written *cg*, before *j* (as in O.E. *bryċġ* [brydž], fr. W. Gmc. **bruggj-*, see **bridge**).

2. Changes distinguishing M.E. from Old English

During the 11th and 12th centuries there were a considerable number of changes in English pronunciation, which were gradually reflected in the spelling of the written language. Diphthongs were monophthongized, and subsequently new diphthongs arose from various sources. There were several important isolative changes in the quality of single vowels, while the chief combinative changes are changes in quantity. Further, the vowels of unstressed syllables began to lose their distinct character and to become levelled under one sound.

(*a*) Isolative changes:

(i.) O.E. *æ* > *a*; see O.E. *fæder*, M.E. *fader*, under **father.** (ii.) O.E. *ā* > *ō* [*ǭ*], slack: O.E. *hām* > M.E. *hōm*; see **home.** (iii.) O.E. *ǣ* > *ē*: O.E. *hǣlan*, 'to heal', > M.E. *hēlen*, see **heal.** (iv.) O.E. *ȳ* > *ī*, *ĕ* or *ŭ*, *ü* [*y*]; see **hill, bride; knell, left** (I.); **thrush.** (v.) O.E. *ēa* > [*ē*], written *e*, *ee*: O.E. *drēam* > M.E. *drēm*, see **dream.** (vi.) O.E. *ēo* > [*ē*]: O.E. *dēop* > M.E. *dēp*, see **deep.** (vii.) O.E. ʒ (between back vowels) > *w*; see **saw** (I.), **law,** M.E. *sawe*, *lawe*, O.E. *sagu*, *lagu*.

(*b*) Combinative:

The chief are quantitative changes: (i.) The short vowels *a*, *e*, *o* are lengthened in open syllables to *ā*, *ē* [*ē*], *ō*; cp. L.O.E. *tacan*, M.E. *tāken*, **take**; O.E. *mete*, M.E. *mēte*, **meat.** (ii.) Long vowels are shortened before groups of two or more consonants; cp. L.O.E. *dēpþe*, M.E. *dĕpþe*, **depth**; and cp. M.E. *kēpen*, 'to keep' (see **keep**), Pret. *kĕpte*, 'kept', O.E. *cēpan*, *cēpte*.

(*c*) Orthographical:

It must not be forgotten that there was considerable French influence on the spelling in the Post-Conquest period. Among the important innovations of French scribes were the following: (i.) The use of *ch* for the sound [tʃ], cp. **child**; (ii.) *sh* for O.E. *sc* [ʃ], see **shall**; (iii.) *th* for O.E. þ, ð, cp. **thorn, this**; (iv.) *v* for O.E. *f* when the latter stood for [v], cp. **love**; (v.) *ou* for [ū], see **mouth**; (vi.) *o* for [u] in the neighbourhood of *n*, *m*, see **son, monk**; (*u* and *n*, *m* were easily confused in writing); (vii.) *y* is now used for the sound [ī]; (viii.) the sound [ȳ], expressed in O.E. by *y*, is now written *u*.

3. Changes distinguishing Modern English from Middle English

Modern English changes in pronunciation are not reflected in the modern spelling, which remains, as has been already said, based on the conventional spelling of Late Middle English. Many, if not all, of the changes characteristic of Early Modern English had, however, begun before 1400, and from the beginning of the 15th century, and in some cases earlier, we find spellings indicating clearly the writer's realization that the old spelling does not fit the sound. For instance, when a 15th century letter-writer has *dipe* for 'deep', or *ceme* for 'came', we must believe that he no longer pronounced [dēp, kām] as in Middle English, but something nearly approaching the modern sounds. Such 'phonetic' spellings, which are numerous enough to supply satisfactory evidence for the date of most of the modern changes, occur for the most part in letters, diaries &c. which did not get into the hands of the early printers, and so did not have their spelling conventionalized. Similar 'occasional spellings', as they are called, are found in letters &c. right down to the 18th century. When Queen Elizabeth, for example, writes *offen* for 'often', and *stauke* for 'stalk', we can hardly be in doubt as to how she pronounced them. These unconventional forms are one of our best sources of information in the modern period.

We may give a few of the most striking developments of the vowels in Early Modern English.

(i.) M.E. *ā* > [ei], cp. **take,** M.E. *tāken*; (ii.) M.E. *ai*, *ei* > [ei], cp. **day,** M.E. [d*ai*]; (iii.) M.E. *ī* > [*ai*], cp. **life,** M.E. *līf*; (iv.) M.E. [*ǭ*] > [*ou*], cp. **home**; (v.) M.E. [ō] > [ū, *u*, a], cp. **food, foot, flood,** M.E. *fōde*, *fōt*, *flōd*; (vi.) M.E. *ē*, *ē* have both as a rule become [ī], cp. **deep,** M.E. [dēp]; **meat,** M.E. [mēt]; (vii.) M.E. *u* > [a, *u*], cp. **but, love, full**; (viii.) M.E. *er* > *ar*, which remains in many words, cp. **far,** M.E. *fer*; (ix.) M.E. *ū* > [*au*], cp. **house,** M.E. *hūs*; (x.) M.E. *au*, *ou* > [ǭ], cp. **pause,** M.E. *pause*, fr. Fr. Among combinative changes we may note the change of *al* to *aul* (later [ǭl]), cp. **all**; the rounding of *wa* to *wo*, except before a back consonant, cp. **what, wash,** contrasted with **wag**; the raising of *e* to *i* before *ng*, cp. **England, linger** (M.E. *lengen*).

Changes in quantity are also important. One of the commonest is the lengthening of short vowels before *r*, the latter being lost subsequently; cp. **hard, are, earth** &c. The vowel *a*, and often *o*, is lengthened also before *f*, *s*, þ; cp. **pass, after, path**; **soft, cross.** On the other hand, shortening has often taken place, especially before point consonants; cp. **dead, hot, flood, breath.**

Consonant changes which occur regularly are: (i.) the loss of *r* finally and before another consonant; (ii.) the loss of M.E. [χ], written *h* or *gh*, finally or before *t*, or the development of the same consonant to *f*, cp. **bough, night, enough, laughter**; (iii.) the loss of *l* before certain consonants, cp. **talk, half**; (iv.) the change of [sj] to [ʃ], cp. **assure, tissue**; (v.) the change of [tj] to [tʃ], cp. **nature, fortune.** There were, however, many other consonantal changes which took place during the Early Modern period, some of which have been swept away by a regrettable tendency among some speakers, especially noticeable during the past century, to attempt to fit the sound to the spelling; this tendency, for instance, has 'restored' the *w* in such a word as *forward* (*w* having been lost in this position in the 13th century or earlier), for which [fǭwəd] is now the usual pronunciation even in Received Standard English, in place of the normally developed Early Modern Standard [fǭrəd].

The vowels of unstressed syllables began a process of reduction and shortening in Middle English and even earlier, and these 'obscured' forms usually remain as the normal types. The general tendency is to reduce all unstressed vowels to [ə] or to [*i*], long vowels being shortened, diphthongs monophthongized, and round vowels unrounded. The modern spelling often indicates the original quality of the vowel. Cp. **private** [pr*ái*v*i*t]; **nature** [néitʃə]; **pigeon** [p*í*dž*i*n]; **biscuit** [b*í*sk*i*t]; **tortoise** [tǭtəs].

Present-day English

By the side of the widespread central type which is recognized as a standard, English speech at the present time exhibits many varieties or dialects. Some of these have grown up, and are spoken in particular parts of the country, and we speak of the dialect of Norfolk, of Kent, of Oxfordshire, and so on. These are called *Regional Dialects.* Other types of English, again, are not primarily of local or regional origin, but are current among certain sections or classes of the population, and owe such peculiarities as distinguish them from other dialects to differences of social status and occupation. These factors tend, on the one hand, to separate groups of speakers from others belonging to a different social grade, and, on the other, to bring those of the same social grade into closer association with each other than they enjoy with speakers of other grades who follow callings of a different kind. We call those varieties or dialects which have grown up within particular sections or social divisions *Class Dialects.*

Regional Dialect has generally an ancient independent development of its own. The features of pronunciation, grammar, and vocabulary which distinguish severally the speech of the different geographical areas are established by continuous tradition, and however much they may depart from the usage of literature or of the upper reaches of society, these dialects are nevertheless perfectly 'correct' within the particular regions where they are spoken. The ultimate test of 'correctness' is usage. A pronunciation or a grammatical form which is current throughout a region is *ipso facto* 'correct' in that dialect. When purely regional peculiarities are used by speakers who are attempting to use standard English, they are out of place, and we call them *provincialisms.* The various Class Dialects are on rather a different footing. These are usually not independently developed as are the pure Regional Dialects, but are mere modifications of standard English, whose divergences from this are due partly to class isolation, partly to the influence of the nearest Regional Dialect. We generally regard these results of class and Regional Dialect as *vulgarisms.*

Of the two general types of English just considered, pure Regional Dialects are limited to particular parts of the country, while the Class Dialects vary from class to class, and also from district to district. None of these types is, or ever could be, regarded as a suitable vehicle for the highest expression of the national mind and culture. Like most peoples who have an ancient civilization, and an elaborate social and political system, the English have developed a common dialect or *koinê* which is used in writing by all Englishmen, no matter what Regional or Class Dialect they may speak; it has long been the form in which literature is embodied, and it is used in the ordinary affairs of life by large sections of the community, as well as in the transaction of public business.

This dialect is that which is now often called *Received Standard English.* It was regional in origin, and is now quite definitely, a Class Dialect. It developed during the 14th century from one of the contemporary variants of London English—that spoken primarily in court circles and among men of rank generally, and it has remained, during the whole period of its evolution, as the dialect of the upper classes. It has been influenced in some measure at various stages by other Class Dialects, and, to a less extent, by Regional Dialects. It has been variously called *Good English, Upper Class English,* or *Public School English,* but *Received Standard,* the name now often applied to it, is perhaps the least ambiguous. Perhaps it should be pointed out again that, as Received Standard is not a Regional Dialect, it is not confined to any one area, but may be heard with but slight variations in any part of the country. This dialect has throughout the Modern English period been the chief vehicle of our literature. Those whose normal dialect it is speak it entirely without hesitation, affectation, or self-consciousness; in fact, most of them think about it very little, but simply accept it as a purely natural thing, which indeed it is. The variations occasionally heard in Received Standard are comparatively few, and the majority of them are such differences as naturally occur between older and younger generations of speakers.

Received Standard English is, however, rather elusive, and not always easily acquired by those who do not speak it from childhood, and there have grown up recently a number of dialects approximating to Received Standard, but not perfectly uniform with it in all points of pronunciation, idiom, and vocabulary. These dialects may be called Modified Standard English. Some people do not realize, or refuse to recognize, that there is a distinction between this and Received Standard, and many are content to label *any* form of Modified Standard 'correct English', 'the King's English', 'the standard language', and so on. Various forms of Modified Standard are spoken by thousands or even millions of educated people all over the country. These 'modified' forms of English, however, are not identical with Received Standard. In point of fact, many highly educated people speak very distinct forms of English, variously 'modified' by regional or by different class dialects. Little difference between Received and Modified Standard English can be traced in the written language, for the two are more or less uniform in grammar and syntax; it is in pronunciation and colloquial idiom that the distinction emerges.

Among the classes of words the pronunciation of which is most difficult to establish are those recently concocted or introduced from foreign sources. These include many 'learned' words, most of which are scientific terms with a Greek or Latin basis. As these have no 'history' in English, they have no traditional pronunciation, except such as are based on earlier established models. Words of this kind come to be habitually pronounced in a certain way among those who commonly use them, and this convention is eventually recognized as 'correct'.

A completely uniform dialect will probably never be spoken all over England, let alone in other English-speaking countries. It is quite possible that Received Standard English will remain the speech of a comparatively small proportion of the population. Whether this is to be regretted or not need not be discussed here. But so long as people turn to Received Standard English as a model, it must be remembered that the best, often unconscious, authorities on this dialect are those who speak it naturally; that the traditional pronunciation of a word for the last several centuries determines its present-day pronunciation, and is therefore of great importance in deciding between variants; that over-carefulness is not 'correctness', and that slovenliness is to be avoided, no less than the fantastic 'rules' of purists and the introduction of new pronunciations merely in order to approximate to the spelling.

I. The Consonants of the Aryan Languages

Primitive Aryan.	Sanscrit.	Iranian.	Baltic.	Slavonic.	Hellenic.	Italic.	Celtic.	Germanic.
p	p	p	p	p	p	p	—	f (ƀ)
ph	ph	p, f	p	p	ph	f		f
b	b	b	b	b	b	b	b	p
bh	bh	b	b	b	ph	f, b	b	ƀ
t	t	t, þ	t	t	t	t	t	þ
th	th	þ	t	t	th	t	t	þ (đ)
d	d	d	d	d	d	d	d	t
dh	dh	d	d	d	th	f, b, d	d	đ

I. The Consonants of the Aryan Languages—*continued*

Primitive Aryan.	Sanscrit.	Iranian.	Baltic.	Slavonic.	Hellenic.	Italic.	Celtic.	Germanic.
k	k, c	k, χ	k	k, č	k	c	c	χ (ʒ)
kh	kh	k, χ			kh	h		χ (ʒ)
k̂	š	s	sz	s	k	c	c	χ (ʒ)
k^w	č, k	k, χ	k	k, č	p, t, k	qu, c	c, p	χ^w, χ, f
g	g, j	g	g	g, ž, z	g	g	g	k
gh	gh, h	g	g	g, ž, z	kh	h, g	g	ʒ
ĝ	j	z, d	z	z	g	g	g	k
ĝh	h	z, d	z	z	kh	h, g	g	ʒ
g^w	g, j	g	g	g, ž, z	b, d, g, z	gu, v, g	b	kw, k, p
g^wh	gh, h	g	g	g, ž, z	ph, th. kh	f, gu, v, g	g	ʒw, ʒ, ƀ
n	n	n	n	n	n	n	n	n
m	m	m	m	m	m	m	m	m
ŋ	ŋ	ŋ	ŋ	ŋ	ŋ	ŋ	ŋ	ŋ
l	r, l	l	l	l	l	l	l	l
r	r	r	r	r	r	r	r	r
s	s	s	s	s	h, s	s, r	s	s (z)
j	y	y	j	j	h, z	j	j, —	j
w	v	v	v	v	ϝ, h	v	f, v, gw	w

II. The Vowels of the Aryan Languages

Primitive Aryan.	Sanscrit.	Iranian.	Baltic.	Slavonic.	Hellenic.	Italic.	Celtic.	Germanic.
a	a	a	a	o, e	a	a	a	a
ā	ā	ā	ō	a	ē, ā	ā	ā	ō
e	a	a	e	e, ĭ	e	e	e, i	e, i
ē	ā	ā	ė	ě, a	ē	ē	ī	ǣ
i	i	i	i	ĭ	i	i	i, e	i
ī	ī	ī	ȳ	i	ī	ī	ī	ī
o	a	a	a	o, e	o	o	o	a
ō	ā	ā	ō, ů	a	ō	ō	ā	ō
u	u	u	u	ŭ	u	u	u, o	u
ū	ū	ū	ū	y	ū	ū	ū	ū
ə	i, a	i, a	a	o, e	a	a	a	a
ei	ē	aē, ōi	ei, ë	ě	ei	ei, ī	ē, ia	ī
ai	ē	aē, ōi	ai, ë	ě	ai	ai, ae	ae	ai
oi	ē	aē, ōi	ai, ë	ě	oi	oi, ū	oe	ai
eu	ō	ao, əu	au	u	eu	ou, ū	ō, ua	eu, iu
au	ō	ao, əu	au	u	au	au	ō, ua	au
ou	ō	ao, əu	au	u	ou	ou, ū	ō, ua	au

III. The Vowels of West, East, and North Germanic

Primitive Germanic.	West Germanic.	East Germanic.	North Germanic.
a	a	a	a
ǣ	ā	ē	ā
e	e	i, e (aí)	e
i	i	i	i
ī	ī	ī (ei)	ī
ō	ō	ō	ō
u	u, o	u, o (aú)	u, o
ū	ū	ū	ū
ai	ai	ái	ei
au	au	áu	au
eu	eu	iu	jō
iu	iu	iu	jū

Rules for Pronunciation

(1) Key to the Popular Phonetic Spelling for the use of the General Reader
(2) The System of Phonetic Notation summarized for Advanced Students

THE accepted spelling of English is by no means always a reliable guide to pronunciation. Owing to various historical circumstances English spelling has come to be considerably divorced from the pronunciation. It is *inconsistent*—the same letter does not always stand for the same sound; it is *redundant*—the spelling of many words contains letters which represent no sound at all; it is *incomplete*—some words contain sounds of which the spelling takes no account and for which no letter is written. The important element of accentuation is entirely disregarded.

Under these circumstances, if we wish to indicate the actual pronunciation of English words, we must employ what is called a *phonetic notation*. This is a means of remedying the defects of ordinary spelling. The general characteristics of a phonetic system of spelling are (1) that it is consistent—the same letter, or combination of letters, always stands for the same sound; (2) letters are not written where no sound is pronounced (e.g. *gh* are not wanted in *right*); (3) differences of quantity, or length, are distinguished; (4) accented syllables are marked; the acute accent ʹ implies the chief or strongest stress, or accent, the grave accent ` implies secondary or weaker accent; unstressed syllables are unmarked.

Throughout this Dictionary two systems of phonetic notation are employed, numbered respectively 1. and 2., these phonetic spellings being enclosed in square brackets [ ]. The following are examples of their use:

advocacy, n. [1. ádvokasi; 2. ǽdvəkəsi].
afford, vb. trans. [1. afórd; 2. əfɔ̄́d].
affranchise, vb. trans. [1. afránchīz; 2. əfrǽntʃaiz].
agitation, n. [1. àjitáshun; 2. æ̀džitéiʃən].

System No. 1 may be preferred by the general reader because it contains no unfamiliar letters or symbols. By this system a very fairly accurate idea of the pronunciation can be conveyed.

System No. 2 is more precise, and distinguishes more minutely the various sounds and shades of sound which occur in English speech. It contains, however, a number of letters or symbols which are unfamiliar to the general reader, and on this account he may prefer to disregard it, and to trust to system No. 1. This more elaborate system (No. 2) is, however, in accordance with the principles demanded by exact notation, and such systems are commonly employed by philologists today in scientific descriptions of pronunciation, and in the discussion of linguistic facts.

The keys provided below should make clear the phonetic values of the symbols of both systems.

It must be borne in mind that no system of this kind, whether popular in character or of a more exact kind, can be self-explanatory, but demands that the reader should make himself familiar, by constant reference to the key, with the sound values attached to the various symbols.

Key to System No. 1

a as in h*a*t
ah as in f*a*ther
ā as in h*a*te
ār as in h*are*
e as in b*e*ll
ē as in b*e*
ēr as in d*eer*
ë as in h*er*d, b*ir*d
i as in b*i*t
ī as in b*i*te
īr as in f*ire*
o as in n*o*t
ō as in n*o*te
ōr as in m*ore*
u as in b*u*t
ū as in t*u*ne
ūr as in l*ure*
oo as in p*u*t
ōō as in b*oo*n
ou as in n*ow*, *ou*t
th as in *th*ink
dh as in *th*ere
gh as in lo*ch*
zh as in plea*s*ure

Key to System No. 2

Simple Vowels

(Symbols)	(Phonetic Values)
ā	as in h*a*! f*a*ther, h*ar*d.
æ	as in Standard Southern English h*a*t, str*a*p.
a	as in b*u*t, r*u*st, bl*oo*d, M*o*nday.
ɛ	as in h*e*n g*e*t.
i	as in p*i*n, h*i*d, priv*a*te.
ī	as in s*ea*t, h*ee*d, mach*i*ne.
ɔ	as in h*o*t, w*a*nt.
ɔ̄	as in *awe*, c*augh*t, t*o*rn, h*a*ll.
ʌ̄	as in b*ir*d, t*ur*n, l*ear*n, w*or*d.
ə	only in unstressed or unaccented syllables, as butt*er*, tog*e*th*er*, th*e* dog, p*er*haps.
ū	as in h*oo*t, br*oo*d, r*u*de, r*ue*.
u	as in p*u*t, p*u*ll, f*oo*t, c*ou*ld.

In French words, &c.

(Symbols)	(Phonetic Values)
a	as in Fr. p*a*tte.
y	as in Fr. p*u*re.
e	as in Fr. d*é*.
ē	as in Ital. cr*e*dere.
i	as in Fr. s*i*.
ø	as in Fr. p*eu*.
o	as in Fr. b*eau*.
ã	as in Fr. *an*, *an*ge, p*en*ser.
ɔ̃	as in Fr. s*on*.
æ̃	as in Fr. v*in*, s*in*ge.
ø̃	as in Fr. *un*.

Diphthongs

(i.e. combinations of two vowel sounds of which only the first is accented and syllabic)

(Symbols)	(Phonetic Values)
au	as in h*ou*se, c*ow*, pl*ou*gh.
o*u*	as in st*o*ne, gr*ow*.
a*i*	as in wh*i*te, n*i*ght, *I*, fl*y*.
ɔ*i*	as in t*oy*, b*oi*l.
ɛə	as in *air*, b*are*, th*eir*.
e*i*	as in m*a*de, t*a*ke, ag*ai*n, v*ei*n.
*i*ə	as in h*ear*, qu*eer*, b*ier*, imper*i*al.
īə	as in f*ie*ld, kn*ee*l, s*ea*led.
*u*ə	as in one pronunciation of s*ure*, p*oor*.

Consonants

(Symbols)	(Phonetic Values)
b	as in *b*at.
p	as in *p*ot.
v	as in *v*ain, o*f*.
f	as in *f*at, enou*gh*.
d	as in *d*ark.
t	as in *t*ake, dance*d*, min*t*.
ð	as in *th*is, bo*th*er.
þ	as in *th*ink, brea*th*.
l	as in *l*ook.
l̥	as in Fr. souff*le*.
j	as in *y*acht, *y*ear, few [fjū].
ž	as in Fr. *j*our; Engl. plea*s*ure [plɛžə], bridge [br*i*dž].
ʃ	as in *sh*ip, wi*sh*, cheap [tʃīp], na*t*ion [ne*i*ʃən].
z	as in la*z*y, cau*s*e, dog*s*, i*s*.
s	as in *s*ip, cat*s*, piece.
g	as in *g*ood, be*g*.
k	as in *k*ite, cat, lo*ck*.
n	as in *n*o, *kn*ow, *gn*aw.
m	as in *m*ill, li*mb*, hy*mn*.
ŋ	as in si*ng*, lo*ng*, thi*n*k [þ*i*ŋk].
r	as in *r*ing, *wr*ite, ve*r*y.
r̥	as in Fr. renconť*re*.
h	as in *h*ome.
w	as in *w*ill, d*w*ell, q*u*een.
ʒ	as in Germ. ta*g*.
χ	as in Scots lo*ch*.
j̥	as in Germ. Rei*ch*.

Principles of Strict Phonetic Notation Explained

By using a phonetic notation we attempt to convey, as accurately as this can be done by graphic symbols, some of the actual facts concerning pronunciation. In order to accomplish this, it is necessary (*a*) that there should be a separate symbol for every sound which occurs in the language, and (*b*) that every time a given sound occurs it should be represented by the same symbol. The first two essentials, then, are completeness in the set of symbols employed, and consistency in using them.

A third condition which must be observed is that no symbol be written uselessly, that is, a letter is not written where no sound is pronounced. Thus there is no sound corresponding to *l* in *talk*; it has long since disappeared from English pronunciation. Therefore when this or similar words are expressed by phonetic notation, no symbol is written between the vowel and the final consonant. We think of the word simply as it appeals to the ear, as a combination of sounds, every one of which must be expressed by a symbol. Where no sound is heard, no symbol is written.

Quantity. Long vowels are marked by placing the ordinary mark of length over them, as [ā, ī] &c. Short vowels are left unmarked [æ, *i*] &c.

Some vowels popularly called ' long ' are in reality diphthongs, that is, they consist of two distinct vowel sounds; they are therefore written with two symbols. Thus ' long *i* ' as in *white* consists of the two short vowels [*a*] as in German *mann*, and [*i*] as in Engl. *bit*. This diphthong is therefore written [*ai*]. The vowels in *take* and *stone* are often referred to respectively as ' long *a* ' and ' long *o* '. In reality, in educated English speech, they also are diphthongs, and are therefore written [ei, ou].

Stress or Accent. The stressed or accented syllable of a word is indicated by placing an acute accent over the vowel, thus [fā́ðə]. If a word, such as certain compounds, has a strong stress on two syllables, both are marked, as [*hái*hǽnd*id*] ' high-handed '.

Where a word of several syllables has, in addition to the chief stress and the unstressed or weak syllables, also one which has a secondary or weaker stress than that of the syllable which has the chief or strongest stress, this secondary stress is marked by placing the grave accent over it, as [ìndɪfǽtɪgəbl] ' indefatigable .'

It must be remembered that what a phonetic notation as used in a dictionary can accomplish is to show in which words and syllables certain sounds are used. It cannot, without entering into long discussions which would be almost useless to those who had not received a special training in Phonetics, inform the reader what is the precise nature and character of *the sounds themselves.* Thus the vowel sound in *hand* may be pronounced in a dozen different ways in different English dialects; that is to say, that all over England perhaps a dozen different vowel sounds may be heard in this word. When therefore, in this Dictionary, the pronunciation of *hand* is indicated as [hænd] the reader is not informed which of the exact varieties is intended. All he can discover is that the writer of the Dictionary states that the same vowel is pronounced here as in all other words in which the symbol [æ] is written.

When it is said, then, that a Dictionary tells us how to pronounce, the claim as a rule is, in reality, too wide. All it does is to show the *distribution of sounds*, to indicate in which words the same sounds occur. It also tells us where the accent is placed, and whether the vowels are short or long. But it does not give what a phonetician would call an exact analysis of the sounds themselves. Key words are given as a guide to what is called ' the values ' of the symbols, but since different people may have different pronunciations of the words given, none can be certain that his sound in a given word is exactly that intended by the person who drew up the tables. All that can be said is that the sounds which the writer of this Dictionary had in mind are those in use among the majority of persons who speak Southern *Standard*, or better, *Received Standard English.* If this description is considered too vague, it must suffice here to say that *Received Standard* is that type of English which is spoken by those who have been educated at one of the older Public Schools. It is by no means the exclusive property of these, but from them at any rate we may be pretty sure of hearing it.

Note on Method of Arrangement

As the plan of this Dictionary differs in some details from that of others of its size, a short exposition of this is given here.

Each entry appears in black type, followed immediately by the part of speech, noun, verb, preposition etc. Homonyms, i.e. words having the same form but different sense (e.g. *bear*, the verb, and *bear*, the animal), are given separate entries, followed by Roman figures enclosed in brackets : **bear (I.)**, vb.; **bear (II.)**, n. This plan is also usually followed for words used as two or more different parts of speech : **account (I.)**, n.; **account (II.)**, vb.

Next comes the pronunciation in the two forms of phonetic notation, enclosed in square brackets.

Following the pronunciation, and preceding the definition of the word, its origin is indicated. This may consist merely in a reference to another entry (e.g. See prec.; See next word &c.) or in a reference in black type to one or more other entries (e.g. under *aeroplane*, See **aero-** & **plane**) where the various parts of the word are fully dealt with. Under the main etymology is given the history of the word as far as it can be traced, working back, for example, from the modern form to Old English, Germanic, and finally to the most primitive Aryan form, or through Middle English to French, Latin, and possibly Greek. The relation of the word to words in other languages is indicated, and references are given in black type to other entries in the Dictionary which should be looked up in order to trace the interesting connexion which often exists between words apparently unrelated. See under **abstruse, affray, agglomerate, air (I.)**.

It may happen occasionally that the etymology of a simple word is so long and interesting as completely to overshadow the short definition which appears at the end of the entry. An instance of this occurs under **albatross.**

After the history of the word comes its use in present-day English. For greater clarity this is usually subdivided. In the case of a verb which is used transitively and intransitively, the main divisions are headed, e.g. **A.** trans., **B.** intrans. (see **act (II.)**). Each of these divisions is divided into minor divisions, numbered **1, 2, 3,** and so on, and each of these subdivisions may be further divided into **a, b, c** &c. Occasionally one of these small subdivisions is again divided into (i.), (ii.), (iii.).

In addition to defining the meaning of a word in all its developments and applications, short sentences illustrating its various uses are given in *italics*. Special idiomatic uses, including colloquialisms and slang expressions, are given, preceded by Phr., e.g. Phr. *that cock won't fight,* q.v. under **cock (I.)**.

Abbreviations used in this Dictionary

abbr. abbreviated, abbreviation
abl. ablative
absol. absolute(ly)
acc. accusative
A.D. Anno Domini
ad. adapted
adj. adjective
adv. adverb
advbl. adverbial
aeron. aeronautics
A.-Fr. Anglo-French
Afr. African
agric. agriculture
alchem. alchemy
alg. algebra
Am. American
anal. analogy
anat. anatomy
anct. ancient
anthropol. anthropology
antiq. antiquities
Arab. Arabic
archaeol. archaeology
archit. architecture
arith. arithmetic
art. article
astrol. astrology
astron. astronomy
attrib. attributive(ly)
auxil. auxiliary
A.V. Authorized Version
bacter. bacteriology
Balto-Slav. Balto-Slavic
B.C. Before Christ
Bib. Biblical
bibliog. bibliography
biog. biography
biol. biology
bot. botany
Brazil. Brazilian
Bret. Breton
B.V.M. Blessed Virgin Mary
c. circa (about)
cap. capital
Carib. Caribbean
cd. could
Celt. Celtic
cent. century
Ch. church
chem. chemistry
Chin. Chinese
class. classical
cogn. cognate
coll. collective(ly)
colloq. colloquial
commerc. commercial
compar. comparative
conj. conjunction
conn. connected
Copt. Coptic
Corn. Cornish
correl. correlative
corrupt. corruption
cp. compare
crystal. crystallography
Dan. Danish
dat. dative
def. definite
demons. demonstrative
dial. dialect
dimin. diminutive
dist. distinguished
Du. Dutch
E. East
eccles. ecclesiastical
econ. economics
educ. education
e.g. exempli gratia (for example)
Egyptol. Egyptology
elect. electricity
engin. engineering
Engl. English
entom. entomology
equiv. equivalent
esp. especially
ethnol. ethnology
etymol. etymology
facet. facetious
fem. feminine
feud. feudal(ism)
fig. figurative
Finn. Finnish
Flem. Flemish
foll. following
fort. fortification
Fr. French
fr. from
freq. frequentative
Fris. Frisian
fut. future
Gael. Gaelic
Gaul. Gaulish
gen. generally
geneal. genealogy
genit. genitive
geog. geography
geol. geology
geom. geometry
Germ. German (modern)
Gk. Greek
Gmc. Germanic
Goth. Gothic
gram. grammar
Heb. Hebrew
her. heraldry
Hind. Hindustani, Hindi
hist. history
horol. horology
hort. horticulture
ibid. ibidem (the same)
Icel. Icelandic
i.e. id est (that is)
illit. illiterate
imit. imitative
imperat. imperative
imperf. imperfect
impers. impersonal
indef. indefinite
indic. indicative
infin. infinitive
intens. intensive
interj. interjection
internat. international
interrog. interrogative
intrans. intransitive
Ir. Irish
iron. ironical(ly)
irreg. irregular
Ital. Italian
Jap. Japanese
Jav. Javanese
L. Late
Lat. Latin
Lett. Lettish
L.G. Low German
lit. literal(ly)
liter. literature, literary
Lith. Lithuanian
log. logic
mach. machinery
Malay. Malayan
manuf. manufacturing
masc. masculine
math. mathematics
M. Du. Middle Dutch
M.E. Middle English
mechan. mechanics
Med. Mediaeval
med. medical, medicine
metal. metallurgy
metaph. metaphysics
meteor. meteorology
M. Fr. Middle French
M.H.G. Middle High German
mil. military
min. mining
mineral. mineralogy
M.L.G. Middle Low German
Mod. Modern
mus. music
mythol. mythology
N. North
n. noun
nat. hist. natural history
nat. sc. natural science
naut. nautical
nav. naval
neg. negative
neut. neuter
nom. nominative
Norm. Norman
Norw. Norwegian
N.T. New Testament
Nthn. northern
numis. numismatics
O. Old
obs. obsolete
obsolesc. obsolescent
O.D. Old Dutch
O.E. Old English
O. Fr. Old French
O. Fris. Old Frisian
O.H.G. Old High German
O.L.G. Old Low German
O.N. Old Norse
opt. optics
orig. original(ly)
ornith. ornithology
O.S. Old Saxon
O.T. Old Testament
paint. painting
palaeont. palaeontology
parl. parliamentary
pass. passive
pathol. pathology
perf. perfect
perh. perhaps
Pers. Persian
pers. person
Peruv. Peruvian
pharm. pharmacology
philol. philology
philos. philosophy
phon. phonetic(s)
photog. photography
Phr. phrase
phren. phrenology
phys. physics
physiol. physiology
pl. plural
Pl.-N. Place-Name
poet. poetry, poetical
Pol. Polish
polit. political
Port. Portuguese
possess. possessive
P.P. past participle
Pr. Primitive
prec. preceding
pred. predicate, predicatively
pref. prefix
prep. preposition
Pres. Part. present participle
pret. preterite
print. printing
priv. privative
prob. probably
pron. pronoun
Prot. Protestant
Provenç. Provençal
provinc. provincial
psychol. psychology
punct. punctuation
q.v. quod vide (which see)
R.C. Roman Catholic
redupl. reduplicated
ref. reference
reflex. reflexive
reg. regular
rel. relative
relig. religion
rhet. rhetorical
Rom. Roman
Russ. Russian
R.V. Revised Version
S. South
sc. scilicet (namely)
Scand. Scandinavian
Scrt. Sanscrit
sculp. sculpture
shd. should
sing. singular
Slav. Slavonic
Span. Spanish
specif. specific(ally)
spirit. spiritualism
Sthn. southern
subj. subjunctive
suff. suffix
superl. superlative
surg. surgery
surv. surveying
Swed. Swedish
syll. syllable
techn. technical, technology
teleg. telegraphy
teleph. telephony
theatr. theatrical
theol. theology
theos. theosophy
trans. transitive
transf. transference, transferred
transl. translated, translation
trig. trigonometry
Turk. Turkish
typog. typography
univ. university
U.S.A. United States of America
usu. usually
vb. verb
vbl. n. verbal noun
veter. veterinary
vulg. vulgar
W. Welsh
w. with
wd. would
W. Gmc. West Germanic
wh. which
wk. weak
W.S. West Saxon
zool. zoology

An asterisk (*) preceding a word indicates a form of which there is no actual record, but which is reconstructed in accordance with known rules of development.

Bibliographical Note

In the etymologies reference is frequently made to authorities on philology, whose opinions are quoted, e.g. 'According to Skeat . . .', 'Walde says that . . .' &c. We give below the titles of the works from which such quotations are made and others that have been consulted.

Berneker, E. Slavisches etymologisches Wörterbuch, vol. I. Heidelberg, 1908–13.

Boisacq, Émile. Dictionnaire étymologique de la langue grecque. 2nd ed. Heidelberg and Paris, 1923.

Bosworth-Toller. Anglo-Saxon Dictionary. Oxford. Supplement (Toller). Oxford, 1921.

(Stratmann-)Bradley. Middle English Dictionary. Oxford, 1891.

Concise Oxford Dictionary of Current English. (H. W. and F. G. Fowler.) Oxford, 1929.

Hellquist, E. Svensk Etymologisk Ordbok. Lund, 1921.

Kluge, F. Etymologisches Wörterbuch der deutschen Sprache. 9th ed. Berlin and Leipzig, 1921.

Lewis and Short. A Latin Dictionary. Oxford, 1927.

Liddell and Scott. A Greek-English Lexicon. Oxford, 1929.

Meyer-Lübke, W. Romanisches etymologisches Wörterbuch. 2nd ed. Heidelberg, 1924.

New Standard Dictionary of the English Language. Funk & Wagnalls Company, New York, 1930.

Oxford English Dictionary. A New English Dictionary on Historical Principles. Edited by Sir James Murray, Henry Bradley, W. A. Craigie, and C. T. Onions. Oxford, 1884–1928. (Abbr. O.E.D.)

Roget, Peter. Thesaurus of English Words. New ed. 1920.

Skeat, W. W. An Etymological Dictionary of the English Language. New ed. Oxford, Clarendon Press, 1910.

Uhlenbeck, C. Kurz gefasstes etymologisches Wörterbuch der gotischen Sprache. 1896.

Walde, Alois. Lateinisches etymologisches Wörterbuch. 2nd ed. Heidelberg, 1910.

Webster's New International Dictionary of the English Language. G. Bell & Sons, London, 1924.

Weekley, E. An Etymological Dictionary of the English Language. London, 1921.

Yule, Henry, and Burnell, A. C. Hobson-Jobson, A Glossary of Colloquial Anglo-Indian Words and Phrases. New ed. by W. Crooke. London, Murray, 1903.

The Universal Dictionary of the English Language

A, a [1. ā; 2. ei]. **1.** The first letter of the English and other cognate alphabets; for the various sounds see *Rules for Pronunciation*, and for abbreviations see end of Dictionary. **2.** As symbol, denoting the first in order or quality of a series, esp. **a** in classification of shipping according to rate of seaworthiness, in Lloyd's Register, with addition of numeral: **A 1**, first class, in general, first rate, superior; **b** (alg.) denoting the first of a series of known quantities; **c** (mus.) the sixth note in the diatonic scale of C major; the scale in which the keynote is A.

a (I.), indef. art. (before consonant sounds) [1. ā, a; 2. ei, ə]; **an** (before vowel sounds) [1. an; 2. ən]. O.E. *ān*, 'one, a', in M.E. differentiated in form, into *a, an*, 'a' when unstressed, and *ōn, ō*, 'one', when stressed; see **one. a** Used primarily before nouns in sing.; **b** before collectives which imply a number of persons or things: *a dozen, a few* &c.; **c** before a proper name used as type of character &c.: *a Napoleon, a Milton*, one like, such a man as &c.; **d** with distributive force: *a mile a minute, a hundred a year* &c., where the second *a* is now felt as indef. art. but is historically a prep. See next word.

a (II.), prep. Weakened form of O.E. *on*, 'in, into, on'. See **on. 1.** Used as prefix in such adverbial compounds as *abed, afloat, ashore* &c., q.v. See also **a-**. **2.** Written with hyphen or separate, as in *now-a-days, once a month* (in latter phrase *a* has same origin and function as in former). **3.** With verbal nouns, in sense of in process of, in act of: *a-building, a ringing, a hunting*.

a-, pref. **a** fr. O.E. *on*, prep., used to form adv. See prec.: *ashore* &c. **b** O.E. *ā-*, intens.: *arise*; used also to form trans. fr. intrans. vbs.: *await*. **c**=Lat. *ab*, 'from'. See **ab-**. **d**=Lat. *ad*, 'to'. See **ad-**. **e**=Gk. *a-, an-*, neg., or priv. part. See **an-** & **in-**. **f**=Fr. *a-*, fr. Lat. *ex-*, 'out of'. See **ex-**.

aardvark, n. [1. árdvark; 2. ādvāk]. Dutch, lit. 'earth pig'. See Engl. cognates **earth** & **farrow**. A South African burrowing quadruped which feeds entirely on ants.

aardwolf, n. [1. árdwoolf; 2. ādwulf]. Du. See **earth** & **wolf**. A South African carnivorous animal, somewhat resembling the hyena and civet.

Aaron's beard, n. [1. árunz bérd; 2. éərənz bíəd]. See Ps. cxxxiii. Popular name of plants some part of which resembles a beard, esp. the Great St. John's wort, *Hypericum calycinum*, and the mother of thousands, *Saxifraga sarmentosa*.

Aaron's rod, n. [1. árunz ród; 2. éərənz rɔ́d]. See Exod. vii. 9 and Num. xvii. **a** (archit.) A straight, long, upright moulding with leafage and scroll work; **b** (bot.) popular name of the common mullein, *Verbascum thapsus*, and the golden-rod, *Solidago*.

ab-, pref. Lat. prep., used also as pref., implying motion away from, departure, separation, consumption, absence, difference. Cogn. w. Gk. *apó*, 'away, from'; Scrt. *ápa*, 'away, back'; O.H.G. *aba, ab*, 'from, off', O.E. *æf, of*. See **of**.

aback, adv. [1. abák; 2. əbǽk], fr. **a-** & **back**. Backwards, towards or to the back. **1.** (naut.) Backward against the mast; said of sails of a ship, or of ship itself, when sails are pressed against the mast by a head wind. **2.** (fig.) Surprised: *taken aback*.

abacus, n. [1. ábakus; 2. ǽbəkəs], fr. Lat. *abacus, abax*; Gk. *ábax*, genit. *ábakos*, 'square board strewn with sand for tracing figures; tablet', fr. Heb. *ābāq*, 'dust'. **1.** A calculating frame with balls sliding on wires, the Pythagorean multiplication table. **2.** (archit.) A slab forming the uppermost member of the capital of a column. **3.** A sideboard or cupboard divided into compartments for holding cups, bottles &c.

Abaddon, n. [1. abádun; 2. əbǽdən]. Heb., 'abyss, destruction'. **1.** Sheol, hell, place of the lost souls; the bottomless pit. **2.** The destroying angel, Apollyon.

abaft, adv. & prep. [1. abáhft; 2. əbáft], fr. O.E. elements *on-be-æftan*, 'behind'. **1.** adv. (naut.) On or towards the stern or hinder part of a ship. **2.** prep. (naut.) Behind, towards the stern.

abalone, n. [1. abalónā; æbəlóunei]. Span.; origin unknown. A shell-fish, haliotis or ear-shell, with perforated dark blue and green shell, lined with mother-of-pearl.

abandon (I.), vb. trans. [1. abándun; 2. əbǽndən]. In M.E., fr. O. Fr. *a bandon*, 'in the power of, at one's disposal, at liberty, according to one's desire', see **ban** (II.). **1. a** To give up, relinquish entirely: *to abandon a career, a mode of life, a purpose, plan &c.*; **b** to leave, depart from (a place or dwelling): *to abandon one's house, country* &c.; **c** to give up (one state of mind for another): *to abandon hope*; **d** to forsake, generally in a heartless and illegal manner: *to abandon one's wife, children, friends*. **2.** (reflex., oneself &c.) To cease to control one's passions and feelings, give oneself up entirely to these: *to abandon oneself to vice, despair* &c.

abandon (II.), n. [1. abándun; 2. abā́dɔ̃], also [əbǽndən]. Fr., fr. prec. A giving-up to natural impulses, generally with the idea of passionate fervour; letting oneself go: *singing, acting, speaking &c. with abandon*.

abandoned, adj. [1. abándund; 2. əbǽndənd]; fr. **abandon** (I.). Lacking moral principle, vicious, immoral, profligate: *an abandoned woman*.

abandonment, n. [1. abándunment; 2. əbǽndənmənt]. **abandon** (I.) & **-ment. 1.** The act of giving up, relinquishing, or forsaking. **2.** The state of being forsaken.

abase, vb. trans. [1. abā́s; 2. əbéis], fr. O. Fr. *abaissier*, 'to bring low'. **a-** & **base**. To lower, cast down, reduce in rank, humble, degrade (only in fig. sense).

abasement, n. [1. abā́sment; 2. əbéismənt]. Prec. & **-ment**. State of being abased; humiliation.

abash, vb. trans. [1. abásh; 2. əbǽʃ]. In M.E., fr. O. Fr. *esbahir, esbahiss-*, 'astonish', lit. 'shout bah! at'; Lat. **ex-** & word of imitative origin; see **-ish**, vbl. suff. To put to shame, destroy (a person's self-possession); confound, disconcert, discomfit.

abashed, adj. [1. abásht; 2. əbǽʃt]. Confounded, disconcerted: *to stand abashed*.

abate, vb. trans. & intrans. [1. abā́t; 2. əbéit], fr. O. Fr. *abattre*, 'to beat down'. See **a-** & **batter** (I.). **A.** trans. **1.** To bring down, diminish, reduce, lessen; **a** (in material senses) *to abate a tax, price* &c.; **b** (in non-material senses) *to abate one's pride* &c. **2.** (law) To bring to an end, to do away with: *to abate a nuisance*. **B.** intrans. **1.** To decrease, grow less, grow smaller, of storm, flood, disease &c. **2.** (law) To become less proportionately in amount, of claims, legacies &c., when all assets are insufficient to pay in full.

abatement, n. [1. abā́tment; 2. əbéitmənt]. Prec. & **-ment. 1.** Decrease, reduction. **2.** (law) **a** Removal, destruction of cause: *abatement of nuisance*; **b** entrance by a stranger on freehold before the entry of an heir or devisee: *abatement of freehold*; **c** deduction proportionately when assets are insufficient for payment in full: *abatement of debts, legacies*.

abat(t)is, n. [1. ábatis, -tē; 2. ǽbətis, -tī]. Fr. *abatis*, 'mass of things felled, or thrown down', fr. *abattre*. See **abate** & **batter** (II.). (mil.) Defence, or obstacle, e.g. on a road, or round a fort, consisting of felled trees fastened together with butts inwards.

abattoir, n. [1. ábatwar; 2. ǽbətwā]. Fr., meaning place where animals are felled, i.e. slaughtered. See **abate** & **batter** (I.) & **-ory**. Slaughter-house.

abb, n. [1. ab; 2. æb]. O.E. *āb, āweb*. See **a-** & **web**. Yarn for the woof.

abbacy, n. [1. ábasi; 2. ǽbəsi], fr. eccles. Lat. *abbātia*, fr. *abbās*, 'an abbot'. See **abbot**. The dignity, jurisdiction, or tenure of an abbot.

abbé, n. [1. ábā; 2. ǽbei]. Fr., fr. Lat. *abbāt(em), abbās*. See **abbot**. Title of respect used in France to a priest; also applied to ecclesiastics in minor orders, e.g. *the Abbé Liszt*.

abbess, n. [1. ábes; 2. ǽbes]. O. Fr. *abaesse*, L. Lat. *abbatissa*. Lady at the head of a nunnery.

abbey, n. [1. ábi; 2. ǽbi]. M.E., fr. O. Fr. *abaie*, popular form fr. eccles. Lat. *abbātia*. See **abbacy**. **1.** A monastery or society of celibate persons of either sex secluded from the world and devoted to religion. **2.** The collection of buildings in which such a society resides. **3. a** A church formerly belonging to an abbey; **b** a building, once an abbey, converted into a private dwelling house.

abbot, n. [1. ábut; 2. ǽbət]. Borrowed already fr. Lat. *abbāt-(is)* in O.E. in form *abbod*, M.E. also *abbot*. The word came through Gk. fr. Syriac *abbā*, 'father'. The male head or superior of an abbey or monastery.

abbreviate, vb. trans. [1. abrḗviāt; 2. əbrívieit], fr. Lat. *abbreviāt-(um)*, P.P. type of *abbreviāre*, 'shorten fr. *ab* & *breviāre*, 'to shorten', fr. *brevis*, 'short'. See **ab-**, **brief**, **-ate**. **a** To make brief, to shorten (esp. a speech or narrative); **b** to shorten (a word) by writing part for the whole.

abbreviation, n. [1. abrèviáshun; 2. əbrīviéiʃən]. Prec. & **-ion**. Curtailment, shortening; act of shortening; esp. of a word in writing, e.g. *Bart.* for *Baronet*.

abbreviator, n. [1. abrḗviātur; 2. əbrívieitə]. See prec. & **-or**. One who abbreviates, esp. one who cuts a book down to smaller compass.

abdicate, vb. trans. [1. ábdikāt; 2. ǽbdikeit], fr. Lat. *abdicāt-(um)*, P.P. type of *abdicāre*, 'disown, reject'. See **ab-** & **dictate**. **a** To give up, withdraw from exercise of (office or power); **b** (often absol., of reigning monarchs) to relinquish the crown.

abdication, n. [1. àbdikáshun; 2. æ̀bdikéiʃən]. Prec. & **-ion**. The act of laying down an office; specif., formal withdrawal from office by reigning monarch.

abdomen, n. [1. ábdomen; 2. ǽbdəmən]. Lat. *abdōmen, abdūmen*, the etymol. of which is very doubtful. Perh. related to Gk. *-dus* in *nēdǘs*, 'belly, womb', & *dúō*, 'clothe, enter', see **ecdysis**. (anat.) The belly; that part of the human or animal body between the thorax and the pelvis, including stomach, bowels &c.; part of insect behind legs.

abdominal, adj. [1. abdóminal; 2. æbdɔ́minəl]. Lat. *abdōmen* & adj. suff. *-ālis*; see **-al**. Pertaining to the abdomen or belly, and the lower part of the body: *abdominal region*; *abdominal section*, cutting into abdomen.

abducent, adj. [1. abdúsent; 2. æbdjúsənt]. Pres. Part. type fr. Lat. *abdūcere*, 'lead away from'. See **abduct**. (anat.) Drawing back or away, esp. *abducent muscles*, those which pull back parts they are attached to. See **abductor**.

abduct, vb. trans. [1. abdúkt; 2. æbdʌ́kt]. Lat. *abduct-(um)*, P.P. type of *abdūcere*, 'to lead away', fr. *ab* & *dūcere*, 'to lead'. See **duct**. **1.** (rare) To draw, or lead, away. **2.** To take away illegally, to kidnap; specif., to carry off a woman unlawfully.

abduction, n. [1. abdúkshun; 2. æbdʌ́kʃən], fr. Lat. *abductiōn-(em)*. See prec. & **-ion**. The act of abducting. Specif. **1.** (law) the unlawful carrying off of a person (esp. a young woman or ward). **2.** (anat.) **a** Muscular action of moving a limb &c. away from the body, or from another limb or part; **b** (surg.) gaping through shrinkage, of edges of a wound. **3.** (log.) A syllogism of which the minor premise, and therefore the conclusion, is merely probable.

abductor, n. [1. abdúkter; 2. æbdʌ́ktə]. See **abduct** & **-or**. (anat.) Muscle which moves parts of the body away from each other.

abeam, adv. [1. abḗm; 2. əbím]. See **a-** & **beam**. (naut.) **a** At right angles to the ship's length or keel; **b** opposite the middle of the ship's side.

abecedarian, adj. [1. àbēsēdárian; 2. èibīsīdéəriən], fr. first four letters of the alphabet, & **-arian**. **a** Arranged alphabetically; **b** belonging to ABC of a subject, hence elementary.

abed, adv. [1. abéd; 2. əbéd], fr. O.E. *on bedde*, 'in bed'. See **a-** & **bed**. (archaic) In bed or on the bed. Phr. *to lie abed*.

abele, n. [1. abḗl; 2. əbíəl]. Du. *abeel*, fr. O. Fr. *abel, aubel*. Low Lat. *albellus*, 'little white thing (tree)', dimin. of *albus*, 'white'. See **alb**. White poplar.

Aberdeen terrier, n. [1. áberdḗn térier; 2. ǽbədín tériə], fr. Aberdeen, in Scotland. The Scotch terrier, q.v.

aberdevine, n. [1. àberdevín; 2. æ̀bədəváin]. Origin unknown. Bird-fancier's name for the siskin.

aberrance, **aberrancy**, n. [1. abérans(i); 2. æbérəns(i)], fr. Lat. *aberrantia*, formed fr. Pres. Part. of *aberrāre*, 'wander away, go astray'. See **ab-** & **err**. **1.** A moral wandering or lapse, straying from the path of rectitude. **2.** (geom.) *Aberrancy of curvature*, the deviation of a curve from its circle of curvature at any point.

aberrant, adj. [1. abérant; 2. æbérənt]. See prec. **a** (fig.) Straying from the right way; **b** specif. (biol.) deviating from the natural type, abnormal.

aberration, n. [1. aberáshun; 2. æbəréiʃən]. Lat. *aberrātiōn-(em)*, 'a wandering', fr. *aberrāt-(um)*, P.P. type of *aberrāre*. See **aberrance**. (gen. sense) Departure from normal or expected course. **1.** Moral or intellectual wandering, deviation from right course of thought or conduct; error, moral or mental lapse. **2.** (astron.) Displacement of a heavenly body's true position to the observer; difference between true and observed positions of a heavenly body. **3.** (biol.) Departure, deviation from type. **4.** (opt.) The non-convergence of rays to one focus.

abet, vb. trans. [1. abét; 2. əbét]. M.E. *abetten*, 'instigate', fr. O. Fr. *abeter*, lit. 'to cause to bite, lure', fr. O.N. *beita*, q.v. under **bait (I.)**. To assist, encourage, or incite in or to an action; instigate, countenance, chiefly in bad sense, esp. *aid and abet*.

abetment, n. [1. abétment; 2. əbétmənt]. Prec. & **-ment**. The act of abetting; inciting or egging-on a person, esp. to do something wrong.

abettal, n. [1. abétl; 2. əbétl]. **abet** & **-al**. Abetment.

abetter, **abettor**, n. [1. abéter; 2. əbétə]. See prec. & **-er**, **-or**. One who incites; a supporter, confederate.

abeyance, n. [1. abáans; 2. əbéiəns]. A.-Fr. *abeiance*, 'suspension', fr. O. Fr. vb. *béer*, 'gape', as in expectation of something, fr. Low Lat. *badāre*, 'gape'. Orig. 'gaping expectancy'. (law) State of temporary suspension or inhibition; a dormant or latent condition capable of revival, esp. in Phrs. *in abeyance*; *to fall into abeyance*; esp. of hereditary title; also of a law, rule, or custom temporarily suspended.

abhor, vb. trans. [1. abhór; 2. əbhɔ́], fr. Lat. *abhorrēre*, 'to shrink away from'. See **ab-** & **horrid**. To feel extreme hatred or loathing for, to shrink from with horror; to regard with disgust, to detest.

abhorrence, n. [1. abhórens; 2. əbhɔ́rəns]. See prec. & **-ence**. **a** Extreme hatred, detestation; **b** something that is detested: *hypocrisy is my abhorrence*.

abhorrent, adj. [1. abhórent; 2. əbhɔ́rənt]. See **abhor** & **-ent**. Inspiring disgust, hateful: *to be abhorrent to*.

abide, vb. intrans. & trans. [1. abíd; 2. əbáid]. In M.E., O.E. *onbidan*, 'wait for, expect'. See **a-** & **bide**. **A.** intrans. **1.** To dwell, stay, take up one's abode (archaic). **2.** To remain fixed in a certain state, to continue: *abide by*, to remain faithful to, adhere to, stick to a bargain, decision, undertaking, promise &c. **B.** trans. **1.** To wait for, be prepared for, watch for: '*Who may abide the day of His Coming?*' **2.** (colloq., vulg., or facetious) To endure, put up with, tolerate (gen. with neg.): *I can't abide that.*

abiding, adj. [1. abíding; 2. əbáidiŋ]. As fr. Pres. Part. of prec. Permanent, continual, which does not fade or pass away.

abidingly, adv. Prec. & **-ly**. Continually.

abies, n. [1. ábiēz; 2. ǽbiīz]. Lat., 'the silver fir'; etymol. uncertain. (bot.) A genus of coniferous trees, including the true firs, with straight, erect cones and separate needles not joined at the base.

abigail, n. [1. ábigāl; 2. ǽbigeil]. Biblical woman's name. A waiting-woman or lady's maid. See 1 Sam. xxv. 41.

ability, n. [1. abíliti; 2. əbíliti]. O. Fr. *ableté*, fr. Lat. *habilitāt-(em)*, 'aptitude, ability', fr. *habilis*, 'handy, easy to manage', fr. *habēre*, 'have, hold, control'. See **habit**. **a** Power to perform, whether physical or intellectual; skill or competence, cleverness in doing something. Phr. *to the best of one's ability*, as well as one can; **b** (in pl.) limited to sense of cleverness, intellectual capacity.

ab initio. See **initio**.

abiogenesis, n. [1. àbīōjénesis; 2. éibaioudžénisis], fr. Gk. **a-**, 'without', & *bios*, 'life', see **biology**, & **genesis**. Spontaneous generation; the doctrine that living organism can be produced from lifeless matter.

abiogenetic, adj. [1. àbīōjenétik; 2. èibaioudženétik]. See prec. & **-genetic**. Relating to theory of spontaneous generation.

abiogenetically, adv. [1. àbīōjenétikali; 2. èibaioudženétikəli]. Prec. & **-al-** & **-ly**. (of forms of life) Produced without previously existing life.

abiogenist, n. [1. àbīójenist; 2. èibaióudžənist]. See **abiogenesis** & **-ist**. One who holds the doctrine of spontaneous generation.

abject (I.), adj. [1. ábjekt; 2. ǽbdžekt], fr. Lat. *abject-(um)*, P.P. type of *abjicere*, 'to throw away', fr. **ab-** and *jacere*, 'to throw'. See **jactitation**. **1.** (of condition, state) Degraded, wretched: *in abject poverty*. **2.** (of persons) Contemptible, miserable, servile, spiritless, cowardly: *the most abject of flatterers*; *an abject time-server*. **3.** (of actions) Grovelling, despicable: *to make an abject apology*.

abject (II.), n. fr. prec. (archaic and Bib.) A person in a low condition, a despicable wretch, an outcast: '*the very abjects came together against me*' (Ps. xxxv. 15).

abjection, n. [1. abjékshun; 2. æbdžékʃən], fr. Lat. *abjectiōn-(em)*. See **abject (I.)** & **-ion**. (rare) A low state; degradation, abasement.

abjectly, adv. [1. ábjektli; 2. ǽbdžektli]. **abject (I.)** & **-ly**. In an abject manner; contemptibly, servilely.

abjectness, n. [1. ábjektnes; 2. ǽbdžektnis]. See prec. & **-ness**. Misery; cringing timidity, servility.

abjuration, n. [1. àbjooráshun; 2. æ̀bdžuréiʃən], fr. Lat. *abjūrātiōn-(em)*. See **abjure**. Renunciation on oath.

abjure, vb. trans. [1. abjóor; 2. əbdžɔ́, əbdžúə], fr. Lat. *abjurāre*, 'to deny on oath'. See **ab-** & **juror**. **1.** To renounce upon oath, swear off from, e.g. allegiance to a person or cause. **2.** To give up, surrender (a claim &c.). **3.** To relinquish formally (an opinion, religious doctrine, heresy &c.).

ablactation, n. [1. àblaktáshun; 2. æ̀blæktéiʃən], fr. Lat. *ablactātiōn-(em)*, lit. 'putting away of milk, weaning'. See **ab-** & **lactation**. Weaning of a child from the breast.

ablation, n. [1. abláshun; 2. æbléiʃən], fr. Lat. *ablātiōn-(em)*, fr. *ablāt-(um)*, used as P.P. of *auferre*, 'to carry, take away'; the base *lāt-* is for **tlāt-*, & occurs in Lat. also in another form as *toll-*. See **tolerate** & **thole (I.)**. Lit. 'a taking away'; specif. **a** removal of any part of the body by surgical operation; **b** wearing away of a glacier or rock by melting or action of water.

ablative, adj. & n. [1. áblativ; 2. ǽblətiv]. Lat. *ablātīvus*, fr. *ablātus*, see prec., & adj. suff. *-īvus*, see **-ive**. Lit. 'that which takes away'. Name invented by Julius Caesar for a Lat. case in nouns, expressing origin, agent, instrument &c.; a case with similar functions is found in all the older Aryan languages.

ablaut, n. [1. áblout; 2. áblaut]. German word. Term invented by Grimm for the vowel changes which occur in Aryan languages within the same base, due primarily to conditions and nature of original stress and intonation: *ride—rode—ridden*; Lat. *sed-eo*, *sēd-i*, *nidus*, 'nest', fr. **ni-sd-o* &c. Those who prefer English words generally call the process Gradation, q.v. The German word is literally 'sound deviation', or 'variation'.

O.H.G. and Germ. *ab*, 'from', & *laut*, 'sound', see **loud**.

ablaze, adv. & adj. [1. abláz; 2. əbléiz]. See **a- & blaze**. **1.** adv. On fire, in a blaze (of buildings &c.). **2.** adj. (fig.) **a** (of material objects) Aglow, gleaming, flashing *ablaze with light, jewels* &c.; **b** (of mental condition) excited, wrought up: *ablaze with anger, indignation* &c.

able, adj. [1. ábl; 2. éibl]. O. Fr., Mod. Fr. *hable*, fr. Lat. *habilis*, 'handy, manageable, fit' &c., fr. *habēre*, 'to have, hold'. See **ability**. **1. a** Having the means, skill, strength, opportunity, being in a position to accomplish something; specif. **b** (law) legally qualified for an office, inheritance &c. **2. a** (of persons) Competent, clever, possessing abilities: *an able writer* &c.; **b** (of human performance) competently done, showing knowledge, skill, cleverness: *an able speech* &c.

-able, suff. [1. abl; 2. əbl], fr. Lat. vbl. stems in *-ā*, & *-bilis*. See **-ble**. Used in Fr. with vbs. of all conjugations. Living suffix in English; compounded with words of native and other origin as well as with those of Lat. origin. **a** Able to be, suitable for: *sizable, eatable*; liable to or for: *taxable*; **b** possessing qualities of, resembling, pertaining to, likely to: *comfortable, knowledgeable, peaceable, suitable, likable*. Often associated and confused with independent *able*, as prob. in *understandable, un-get-at-able* &c.

able-bodied, adj. [1. ábl bódid; 2. éibl bɔ́did]. Sound, strong of body, physically fit and active. *Able-bodied seaman* (abbrev. A.B.), one who is able to perform all the duties of seamanship, and who has a special rating.

ablet, n. [1. áblet; 2. ǽblit], fr. Fr. *ablette*, fr. Low Lat. *abula* for *albula*, dimin. of *alba*, 'white'. See **alb**. A small fresh-water fish, the bleak.

abloom, adv. & adj. [1. ablóōm; 2. əblúm]. **a- & bloom**. In bloom; blooming.

ablution, n. [1. ablóōshun; 2. əblúʃən]. Lat. *ablūtiōn-(em)*, 'a washing, cleansing', fr. *abluere*, 'to wash off, wash away'; fr. **ab-** & *luere*, 'to wash', cogn. w. Lat. *lavāre*, 'wash'. See **lave**. **1. a** Act of washing, esp. of person; **b** (gen. pl.) the act of washing or cleansing: *to perform one's ablutions*; specif., a ceremonial washing of person, hands, or sacred vessels before or after solemn religious rites, e.g. at celebration of Eucharist. **2.** (sing.) Water used in ceremonial ablution.

ablutionary, adj. [1. ablóōshunari; 2. əblúʃənəri]. Prec. & **-ary**. Pertaining to washing and cleansing.

ably, adv. [1. ábli; 2. éibli]. See **able & -y**. In an able manner; skilfully, competently.

abnegate, vb. trans. [1. ábnegāt; 2. ǽbnigeit], fr. Lat. *abnegāt-(um)*, P.P. type of *abnegāre*, 'to refuse, deny'. See **ab- & negate**. To renounce, deny oneself, give up, relinquish.

abnegation, n. [1. àbnegáshun; 2. ǽbnigéiʃən], fr. Lat. *abnegātiōn-(em)*. See prec. & **-ion**. Renunciation, denial, self-denial.

abnormal, adj. [1. abnórmal; 2. æbnɔ́məl], fr. Lat. adj. *abnormis*, 'deviating from rule', & *-ālis*. See **ab- & norm & -al**. Not conforming to rule, deviating from a type or standard, irregular, exceptional: *an abnormal condition of affairs*.

abnormality, n. [1. àbnormáliti; 2. ǽbnɔmǽliti]. Prec. & **-ity**. Deviation from regular type or form; eccentricity of mind, deformity of person; an abnormal thing or person.

abnormally, adv. [1. abnórmali; 2. æbnɔ́məli]. **abnormal & -ly**. In an irregular, eccentric manner; exceptionally.

abnormity, n. [1. abnórmiti; 2. æbnɔ́miti]. Lat. *abnormitāt-(em)*, 'irregularity'. See **abnormal & -ity**. Irregularity, anything which deviates from type, or departs from custom; irregularity of form, monstrosity.

aboard, adv. & prep. [1. abórd; 2. əbɔ́d]. See **a- & board**. **1.** adv. (naut.) On board, into, within a ship or boat. Phr. *all aboard!*, warning of departure. **2.** adv. Alongside: *to keep the land aboard*; *close aboard, hard aboard*. **3.** prep. On board of: *to go aboard a ship*.

abode (I.), n. [1. abód; 2. əbóud]. Recent word (17th cent.) formed fr. Pret. type of **abide**. Dwelling-place, house, dwelling. Phr. *take up, make one's abode*.

abode (II.), vb. Pret. of **abide**. O.E. *abād*, M.E. *abood*.

abolish, vb. trans. [1. abólish; 2. əbɔ́liʃ], fr. Fr. *aboliss-*, *abolir*, fr. Lat. *abolescere*, 'to decay, die away', inceptive form of *abolēre*, 'to destroy', prob. cogn. w. Gk. *ólethros*, 'ruin', *óllumi*, 'destroy'; see **Apollyon**. To destroy, wipe out, extirpate, to do away with altogether.

abolition, n. [1. abolíshun; 2. æbəlíʃən], fr. Lat. *abolitiōn-(em)*, fr. *abolit-(um)*, P.P. type of *abolēre*. See **abolish & -ion**. The act or fact of doing away with, wiping out, as laws, customs, taxes, debts &c.; complete destruction; specif. destruction of some recognized abuse, such as negro slavery.

abolitionism, n. [1. abolíshunizm; 2. æbəlíʃənizəm]. Prec. & **-ism**. Principles, theory, policy, which demand abolition of something.

abolitionist, n. [1. abolíshunist; 2. æbəlíʃənist]. See prec. & **-ist**. One who favours abolition, esp. of negro slavery.

abomasum, n. [1. àbomásum; 2. æboumeísəm]. Neo-Lat. See **ab- & omasum**. The fourth, digesting stomach of a ruminant animal.

abominable, adj. [1. abóminabl; 2. əbɔ́minəbl], fr. Lat. *abōmĭnābilis*. See **abominate & -able**. **a** Causing intense horror and disgust, detestable, atrocious, esp. morally odious; **b** (colloq.) expressing more or less mild dislike: *an abominable dinner* &c.

abominably, adv. Prec. & **-ly**. In an abominable manner.

abominate, vb. trans. [1. abóminăt; 2. əbɔ́mineit], fr. Lat. *abōmināt-(um)*, P.P. type of *abōminārī*, 'to deprecate as an ill omen', hence 'detest'. See **ab- & omen**. To loathe and detest, hold in horror; also merely, to dislike: *I abominate cold mutton*.

abomination, n. [1. abòmináshun; 2. əbɔ̀minéiʃən], fr. Lat. *abōminātiōn-(em)*. See **abominate & -ion**. **1.** Act of abominating; loathing, detestation: *to hold a thing in abomination*. **2.** Something abominable or detestable; disgusting, degrading practice; an object of loathing and disgust. Phr. *the abomination of desolation*, the desecration of the Temple at Jerusalem, see Dan. ix. 27 &c., and Matt. xxiv. 15.

aboriginal, adj. & n. [1. aboríjinal; 2. æbərídžinəl]. See **ab- & original** & cp. **aborigines**. **1.** adj. Existing from the beginning, before earliest records; indigenous, esp. in reference to indigenous races, flora, fauna &c. of a region as distinct from later immigrants and imported plants and animals. **2.** n. An aboriginal person, plant, animal &c.; in pl. usually **aborigines**.

aboriginally, adv. Prec. & **-ly**. From the earliest time.

aborigines, n. pl. [1. aboríjinēz; 2. æbərídžiniz]. Lat. *aborīginēs*, 'first inhabitants' (esp. of Latium), fr. *ab origine*, 'from the beginning'. See **ab- & origin**. The primitive inhabitants of a country, supposed to have sprung from the soil; applied also, more rarely, to flora and fauna.

abort, vb. intrans. [1. abórt; 2. əbɔ́t], fr. Lat. *abort-(um)*, P.P. type of *aborīri*, 'to miscarry', fr. *ab-* & *orīri*, 'to be born'. See **origin, orient**. **1.** To miscarry, give birth to offspring prematurely. **2.** (fig.) (of schemes, plans &c.) To come to nothing, go awry, fail.

abortifacient, n. & adj. [1. abórtifásient; 2. əbɔ̄tifǽsiənt]. See prec. & **-facient**. **a** n. Drug or other means for producing abortion; **b** adj., causing, producing, abortion.

abortion, n. [1. abórshun; 2. əbɔ́ʃən], fr. Lat. *abortiōn-(em)*, 'miscarriage'. See **abort & -ion**. **1. a** Miscarriage of birth; **b** (criminal law) miscarriage deliberately and illegally procured. **2.** One born out of due season, hence a monstrous, misshapen, or stunted creature.

abortionist, n. [1. abórshunist; 2. əbɔ́ʃənist]. Prec. & **-ist**. One who procures illegal abortion.

abortive, adj. & n. [1. abórtiv; 2. əbɔ́tiv], fr. Lat. *abortīvus*, 'born prematurely'. See **abort & -ive**. **1.** adj. **a** (fig., of plans, actions &c.) Badly devised and matured, therefore unsuccessful, coming to nought; **b** (biol.) imperfectly developed. **2.** n. (med.) A medicine for producing abortion.

abortively, adv. Prec. & **-ly**. (fig.) In an immature manner, without success, awry.

abound, vb. intrans. [1. abóund; 2. əbáund], fr. O. Fr. *abonder*, fr. Lat. *abundāre*, 'to overflow'; fig., 'to abound', fr. **ab-** & *unda*, 'a wave'. See **undulate**. **1.** To be plentiful, exist in large quantities: *wild birds abound in Oxfordshire*. **2. a** (with *in*) *To abound in*, to be well stocked with, to possess in great quantity; expressing possession of things which are characteristic in a given place, as *the streams abound in trout*; moral qualities which are inherent, as *he abounds in courage* &c.; **b** (followed by *with*) *to abound with*, to be plentifully stocked with: *the British Museum abounds with old statues*.

abounding, adj. [1. abóunding; 2. əbáundiŋ], fr. Pres. Part. of prec. **a** Being plentiful, abundant. Phr. *grace abounding*; **b** *abounding in, abounding with*. See prec.

about (I.), adv. [1. abóut; 2. əbáut]. O.E. *ābūtan, onbūtan*, 'around', of time, 'about'. M.E. *aboute(n)*. See **a- & but**, conj. **1.** On all sides, around; here and there, in various directions: *to look, walk, move about*. **2.** In circuit, around the outside (archaic): *a mile about*; *to come about*, to take place, happen; *to bring about*, to cause to take place. **3.** Nearly, approximately; closely corresponding to in quality, manner, degree &c.: *about as high as, about a mile* &c.; (colloq.) *just about enough*, quite enough. **4.** To a reversed position, in the opposite direction: *to face about*; (mil.) *about turn!*, face the opposite direction; (naut.) *about ship!*, order to place a ship on the other tack; Phrs. *to go, set, about something*, prepare to do, start doing; *going about* (of news, report &c.), current; *out and about*, able to pursue one's ordinary occupations (after illness &c.); *to be about, up and about*, to be astir, not in bed; *to put about*, see **put (I.)**; *to send about one's business*, dismiss; *turn and turn about*, alternately.

about (II.), prep. See prec. **1.** Around, all around: *bind the chains about him*; on every side of: *look about you*; here and there in, to and fro in: *to walk about the streets* &c. Phr. *to beat about the bush*, approach a subject indirectly, not to come straight to the point. **2.** Near to, in close proximity to; by one's person: *everything handsome about him*; *about the Court*. **3.** Engaged in, concerned with (archaic): '*I must be about My Father's business*'. **4. a** Concerning, with regard to, on the subject of: *to talk about business*; *a book about gardening*; **b** in connexion with, appertaining to: *her dress is the best thing about her*. **5.** (before an infin.) On the point of, in the act of (forming Fut. Part.): *about to shoot, about to speak* &c.

above, adv., prep., & adj. [1. abúv; 2. əbáv]. M.E. *aboven*, O.E. *ābūfan*, fr. **a-**, *be*, '**by**', q.v., & *ufan*, 'upwards', cogn. w. Germ. *auf*. See **over**. **1.** adv. **a** In a higher place, overhead, expressing (i.) motion to: *to soar above*, (ii.) rest at: *the sky above*; **b** higher in power, superior in rank: *it was referred to the court above*; **c** earlier in order, higher in the same page (of books &c.), earlier in same book: *as is stated above*; **d** in Heaven: *there is a God above*. **2.** prep. **a** Higher than, over (of physical relation), expressing (i.) motion to: *to fly above the clouds*, (ii.) rest at: *the balloon was floating* *above our heads*; Phr. *to keep one's head above water*, to keep safe; **b** superior to in any respect, beyond: *above others in ability*; Phrs. *above comprehension, above reproach, above suspicion, praise* &c.; *above meanness*, superior to; (mod. colloq. slang) *to be above oneself*, give oneself airs, be too conceited; **c** surpassing in number or quantity, more than: *above 200 members*. **3.** adj. Placed, written, mentioned above or before: *the above facts, statements* &c.

above-board, adv. & adj. Above the board or table (perh. orig. card-table), in open sight, without concealment or trick, honourable: *open and above-board*.

above-mentioned, adj. [1. abúv ménshund; 2. əbáv ménʃənd]. Referred to, mentioned before, in same book, page &c.

ab ovo, adv. [1. ab ōvō; 2. æb óuvou]. Lat., 'from the egg', see **ab-** & **ovum**. From the very beginning.

abracadabra, n. [1. ábrakadábra; 2. ǽbrəkədǽbrə]. Origin unknown. A spell, magic formula, a catchword.

abrade, vb. trans. [1. abrād; 2. əbréid], fr. Lat. *abrādere*, 'to scrape off', fr. **ab-** & *rādere*, 'to scrape off, shave'. See **raze**. To rub or wear off, wear away by friction, graze, esp. of skin.

Abraham man, n. [1. ábraham màn; 2. éibrəhæm mæ̀n], fr. the parable of Lazarus (Luke xvi.). (hist.) A lunatic beggar of the 16th and 17th cents., licensed to beg by Bethlehem Hospital; also one of a set of vagrant beggars pretending to be lunatics under licence.

abranchiate, adj. & n. [1. abrángkiāt; 2. əbrǽŋkieit]. **a-**, 'without', & **branchiate**. **a** adj. Not provided with gills; **b** n., animal that is not provided with gills at any stage of development.

abrasion, n. [1. abrázhun; 2. əbréižən], fr. Lat. *abrāsiōn-(em)*, fr. *abrās-(um)*, P.P. type of *abrādere*. See **abrade**. **1. a** Grazing, rubbing, or scraping off, as of the skin; **b** place where skin is scraped off. **2. a** A wearing down, rubbing away, as of rocks, machinery &c.; **b** place showing this.

abrasive, adj. & n. [1. abrāziv; 2. əbréiziv]. Prec. w. Lat. suff. *-īvus*. See **-ive**. **1.** adj. **a** Tending to graze, scrape the skin; **b** tending to wear down, rub away rocks &c. **2.** n. Substance, such as emery &c., used for grinding, polishing &c.

abraxas, n. [1. abráksas; 2. əbrǽksəs]. Formed of the Gk. letters, as numerals, equiv. to 365. **1. a** A mystic name, used by the Egyptian Gnostics, of the Supreme Being as ruling 365 heavens; **b** a gem engraved with this name, used as a talisman. **2.** (entom.) A genus of buff-coloured moths spotted with black, the magpie moth.

abreast, adv. [1. abrést; 2. əbrést]. See **a-** & **breast**. **a** On a level with, when facing or moving in same direction; **b** (fig.) *abreast of*, or, more rarely, *with*, keeping up with, not behind the advance of science, thought &c.: *abreast of the times, of what is going on* &c.

abridge, vb. trans. [1. abríj; 2. əbrídž]. M.E. *abregge*, fr. O. Fr. *abregier*, 'shorten', Mod. Fr. *abréger*, fr. Lat. *abbreviāre*, 'to shorten'. See **abbreviate**. To make shorter, lessen, diminish, curtail; esp. to shorten by using fewer words, to condense (books &c.).

abridg(e)ment, n. [1. abríjment; 2. əbrídžmənt]. Prec. & **-ment**. Shortening, reduction, diminution, condensation; curtailment (of rights); specif., reduced or condensed form of a book.

abroad, adv. [1. abráwd; 2. əbrɔ́d]. M.E. *abrood*. See **a-** & **broad**. **1. a** Broadly, widely, at large, over a wide space: *publish, spread abroad* (of rumour, news &c.); **b** current, going about (of rumours &c.): *there is a rumour abroad*. **2.** Outside one's abode, out of doors: *to be abroad early*. **3.** Beyond the bounds of a country; in foreign lands: *to go, travel, abroad*; (colloq., fig.) *to be all abroad*, to be puzzled, confused in mind. Treated as a noun in Phr. *from abroad* &c.

abrogate, vb. trans. [1. ábrogāt; 2. ǽbrəgeit], fr. Lat. *abrogāt-(um)*, P.P. type of *abrogāre*, 'to repeal' (law &c.), fr. **ab-** & *rogāre*, 'to ask, propose' (as a law). See **rogation**. To repeal, annul, abolish (laws or customs).

abrogation, n. [1. abrogáshun; 2. æbrəgéiʃən], fr. Lat. *abrogātiōn-(em)*. See prec. & **-ion**. Act of repealing by authority.

abrupt, adj. [1. abrúpt; 2. əbrʌ́pt], fr. Lat. *abrupt-(um)*. P.P. type of *abrumpere*, 'to break off'. See **ab-** & **rupture**. **1.** Broken off, steep, craggy (of rocks, banks, precipices). **2.** Sudden, hasty, unexpected; **a** (of actions) *abrupt entrance, departure* &c.; **b** (of manners) short, uncivil, gruff. **3.** (of style) Breaking off suddenly, disconnected, passing from one thought to another without proper transition. **4.** (geol., of strata) Suddenly cropping out.

abruptly, adv. Prec. & **-ly**. In an abrupt manner; suddenly, without warning.

abruptness, n. See prec. & **-ness**. Quality of being abrupt; suddenness, unceremonious haste in speech, manners &c.

abscess, n. [1. ábses, -sis; 2. ǽbsεs, -sis]. Lat. *abscessus*, 'going away', fr. *abscēdere*, 'go away', fr. *abs-* (for **ab-**) & *cēdere*, see **cede**; sense being 'flowing of humours into one channel'. Inflamed swelling on the body containing pus; sac or cavity filled with pus in an organ of the body.

abscind, vb. trans. [1. absínd; 2. əbsínd], fr. Lat. *abscindere*, 'to cut off', fr. **ab-** & *scindere*, 'to cut, split', Pret. *scidi*, P.P. *scissum* (fr. **scid-tom*), cogn. w. Gk. *skhizō*, 'split', *skhisma*, 'cleft, division'. See **schism**. From variant of same base, Aryan **skhit-*, we get Goth. *skaidan*, 'divide', O.E. *sc(e)ādan*, 'divide, distinguish'. See **shed (I.)**. To cut off (obs.).

abscissa, n. [1. absísa; 2. əbsísə]. Lat. *abscissa (līnea)*, see prec. word. A line cut off, as point of reference in geometry.

abscission, n. [1. absíshun; 2. əbsíʃən], fr. Lat. *absciss-(um)*, P.P. type of *abscindere*, see **abscind**, & **-ion**. Cutting off; state of separation.

abscond, vb. intrans. [1. abskónd; 2. əbskɔ́nd], fr. Lat. *abscondere*, 'to put out of sight, conceal', fr. *abs-* (for **ab-**) & *condere*. The history of this vb. is remarkable. It comes fr. Lat. *cum*, 'together', & base **dhē-*, 'make, place', cogn. w. Lat. *facio*, 'make', Pret. *fē-ci*. Orig. sense is 'put together, build', then 'put away together, store up', then 'to hide'. For other words fr. base **dhē-* see **do, deed, thesis, fact**. To depart secretly and suddenly; steal off and hide oneself; esp. to run away to escape the law.

absconder, n. [1. abskónder; 2. əbskɔ́ndə]. Prec. & **-er**. One who absconds.

absence, n. [1. ábsens; 2. ǽbsəns]. Fr., fr. Lat. *absentia*, fr. *absens*, Pres. Part. of *abesse*, 'to be absent', fr. **ab-** & *esse*, 'to be'. See **essence**. **1.** The state of being away from a place or from company; opposed to *presence*. **2.** The time of being away: *long absence* &c. **3.** Non-existence, lack, want of: *absence of evidence* &c. **4.** Mental abstraction, inattention, esp. in Phr. *absence of mind*. **5.** (at Eton College) Roll-call.

absent (I.), adj. [1. ábsent; 2. ǽbsənt], fr. Lat. *absens, absentis*, Pres. Part. of *abesse*. See **absence**. **1.** Not present, being away in another place: *absent friends*. **2.** Mentally abstracted, inattentive to what is going on around one, preoccupied, having the mind withdrawn from what is passing; absent-minded: *an absent air*.

absent (II.), vb. trans. [1. absént; 2. əbsént], fr. Fr. *absenter*, fr. Lat. *absentāre*. See prec. (used reflex.) To remain away, withdraw (oneself) intentionally: *to absent oneself from a meeting* &c.

absentee, n. [1. àbsenté; 2. æ̀bsəntí], fr. **absent** & **-ee**. A person not present, esp. one who absents himself on an occasion when he ought to be present; one habitually living away from home; specif., a landlord not living on his estate.

absenteeism, n. [1. àbsentéizm; 2. æ̀bsəntíizəm]. Prec. & **-ism**. The practice of absenting oneself from one's duty, dwelling &c., esp. of a landlord living away from his estates.

absently, adv. [1. ábsentli; 2. ǽbsəntli]. See **absent (I.)** & **-ly**. (of mental state) In an absent, inattentive, or preoccupied manner.

absent-minded, adj. See **absent (I.)** & **minded**. Preoccupied, inattentive; unconscious of what is passing around one.

absent-mindedly, adv. Prec. & **-ly**. In a preoccupied manner.

absent-mindedness, n. See prec. & **-ness**. Condition or habit of being preoccupied.

absinth(e), n. [1. ábsinth; 2. ǽbsinþ]. Fr. *absinthe*, fr. Lat. *absinthium*, 'wormwood', fr. Gk. *apsinthion*, pre-Hellenic word. A green, aromatic liqueur flavoured with wormwood and anise.

absolute, adj. [1. ábsolūt; 2. ǽbsəljūt], fr. Lat. *absolūtus*, 'loosened or freed from', P.P. of *absolvere*. See **absolve**. **1.** Free from imperfection; complete, perfect: *absolute beauty*; unmixed, pure: *absolute alcohol*. **2. a** Freed from limitation or condition; unconditional: *an absolute promise*; unqualified, complete, thorough: *absolute trust*; *an absolute fool!*; **b** free from external restraint or limitations; authoritative: *an absolute monarch*; *absolute ownership*. **3. a** Considered without reference to other things, complete in itself: *absolute knowledge*; **b** positive, actual, real, certain, definite: *an absolute fact*; *absolute proof*; **c** (gram.) standing apart from its usual construction with another word or words: *ablative absolute*; **d** (log.) not involving reference to anything else; taken in its essential nature; categorical: *an absolute proposition*. **4.** As n., *the absolute*, cp. **3.**

absolutely, adv. Prec. & **-ly**. In an absolute manner; unconditionally, unrestrictedly, completely.

absolution, n. [1. absolúshun; 2. æbsəljúʃən]. Lat. *absolūtiōn-(em)*, 'an acquittal', fr. *absolvere*. See **absolute** & **-ion**, & **absolve**. **1.** (eccles.) **a** A formal remission of guilt or sin by a duly ordained priest, after confession and penitence on the part of the sinner: *to give absolution*; **b** the act of pronouncing such remission; **c** regular form of words in which remission is given: *to pronounce the Absolution*. **2.** (law) Formal declaration of acquittal by the judge.

absolutism, n. [1. ábsolūtizm; 2. ǽbsəljūtizəm]. See **absolute** & **-ism**. Political theory which favours government by an absolute ruler.

absolve, vb. trans. [1. abzólv; 2. əbzɔ́lv], fr. Lat. *absolvere*, 'to loosen, set free', fr. **ab-** & *solvere*. See **solve**. **a** To grant absolution to (in eccles. sense); **b** to acquit, declare, acknowledge free from blame, guilt, responsibility, a vow, oath &c.

absorb, vb. trans. [1. absórb; 2. əbsɔ́b], fr. Lat. *absorbēre*, 'to swallow up', fr. **ab-** & *sorbēre*, 'to suck in, swallow up'; cp. also Lat. *sorbitio*, 'potion, broth'; cogn. w. Gk. *hrophéō* (fr. **sroph-*), 'gulp down, sup up greedily', & *hróphos*, 'a gulping down, that which is gulped down, broth &c.'; Lith. *srebiù*, 'I swallow', *surbiù*, 'I suck'. **1. a** (lit., of porous substances taking up moisture). To take up, suck in, drink up; also of animals taking drink, or nourishment generally; **b** (fig., of mental process) to take in, assimilate (learning, ideas, knowledge &c.). **2.** (fig.) To engross, take up, occupy (the attention, energies, time &c.).

absorbefacient, adj. & n. [1. absòrbefásient; 2. əbsɔ̀biféiʃənt]. See **absorb** & **-facient**. (med.) **1.** adj. Tending to promote or induce absorption, as of fluids, pus &c. **2.** n. Substance, drug &c. which promotes such absorption.

absorbent, adj. & n. [1. absórbent; 2. əbsɔ́bənt], fr. Pres. Part. of Lat. *absorbēre*, 'drink up' &c. See **absorb**. **1.** adj. Inclined, liable, ready to absorb fluids. **2.** n. A substance which absorbs moisture readily.

absorbing, adj. [1. absórbing; 2. əbsɔ́biŋ], fr. Pres. Part. of **absorb**. (fig.) Engrossing, taking up completely, the attention, thoughts, interest &c.: *absorbing studies, interests.*

absorption, n. [1. absórpshun; 2. əbsɔ́pʃən]. Lat. *absorptiōn-(em)*, lit. 'a sucking down; a drink, beverage'. fr. *absorpt-(um)*, P.P. type of *absorbēre*. See **absorb**. **1. a** Process of sucking up, drinking in of fluids or moisture by porous substances, or by the air (active and passive); **b** (vulg. and colloq.) drinking, taking of food generally. **2. a** Incorporation and assimilation by animal tissues of nutriment by phýsiological process, through the blood or otherwise; **b** taking up and dispersal of fluid or pus, by surrounding tissues of animal body, e.g. from a blister &c. **3.** (fig.) Preoccupation, engrossing of the mind, attention &c. by thought, objects of interest &c.

abstain, vb. intrans. [1. abstā́n; 2. əbstéin]. Fr. *abstenir*, 'refrain from', Lat. *abstinēre*, 'to keep away from', fr. *abs-* (for **ab-**) & *tenēre*, 'to hold'. See **tenable**. *Abstain from*, to hold oneself back voluntarily from, refrain from, avoid.

abstainer, n. [1. abstā́ner; 2. əbstéinə]. See prec. & **-er**. Specif., one who does not take alcoholic drink: *total abstainer.*

abstemious, adj. [1. abstémius; 2. əbstímjəs]. Lat. *abstēmius*, 'sober, temperate', fr. *abs-* (for **ab-**) and *tēmētum*, 'intoxicating drink'; cp. also *tēmulentus*, 'drunken'; perh. related to Scrt. *tam-*, 'be breathless, choke'; *tāmyati*, 'is exhausted'. Sparing in food, drink, or enjoyment; given to self-denial; temperate, not self-indulgent.

abstemiously, adv. Prec. & **-ly**. Sparingly (esp. of eating and drinking).

abstemiousness, n. See prec. & **-ness**. Practice, habit, of being abstemious.

abstergent, adj. & n. [1. abstérjent; 2. əbstə́dʒənt], fr. Lat. *abstergent-(em)*, Pres. Part. type of *abstergēre*, 'to wipe away', fr. *abs-* (for **ab-**) & *tergēre*, 'to rub or wipe off'. Etymol. doubtful. **a** adj. Serving to cleanse; **b** n., a cleansing substance, e.g. soap.

abstersion, n. [1. abstérshun; 2. əbstə́ʃən], fr. Lat. *absters-(um)*, P.P. type of *abstergēre*. See prec. & **-ion**. Act or process of cleansing.

abstersive, adj. [1. abstérsiv; 2. əbstə́siv]. See prec. & **-ive**. Cleansing.

abstinence, n. [1. ábstinens; 2. ǽbstinəns]. Fr., fr. Lat. *abstinentia*, fr. *abstinent-(em)*, Pres. Part. type of *abstinēre*. See **abstain** & **-ence**. Deliberate self-deprivation; refraining from (food, drink, pleasure); temperance. Specif., *total abstinence*, complete abstention from alcoholic liquors.

abstinent, adj. [1. ábstinent; 2. ǽbstinənt]. See prec. Given to abstinence; temperate.

abstract (I.), adj. [1. ábstrakt; 2. ǽbstrækt]. Lat. *abstract-(um)*, 'separated from', P.P. type of *abstrahere*, 'to draw away', *abs-* (for **ab-**) & *trahere*, 'to draw'. See **tract** (I.). Existing, or thought of as existing, apart from material objects, opposed to *concrete*; hence, ideal, not practical. As n., esp. Phr. *in the abstract*, the ideal or theoretical way of regarding things.

abstract (II.), n. See next word. Something taken out, summary, epitome (of statement, narrative, speech &c.).

abstract (III.), vb. trans. [1. abstrákt; 2. əbstrǽkt], fr. P.P. type of Lat. *abstrahere*. See **abstract** (I.) **1.** To remove, take away, whether by a mental or physical operation. **2.** (euphemistic) To remove someone else's property illegally; to steal.

abstracted, adj. [1. abstrákted; 2. əbstrǽktid]. (lit.) Withdrawn, removed; (fig.) absent-minded, preoccupied in mind.

abstractedly, adv. Prec. & **-ly**. Absent-mindedly.

abstractedness, n. See prec. & **-ness**. State, habit, of absent-mindedness.

abstruse, adj. [1. abstrṓōs; 2. əbstrū́s]. Lat. *abstrūs-(um)*, P.P. type of *abstrūdere*, to thrust away, conceal', fr. *abs-* (for **ab-**) & *trūdere*, 'to thrust, push', cogn. w. O. Slav. *truditi*, 'oppress', *trudŭ*, 'misery', Goth. *us-þriutan*, 'threaten, afflict', O.E. *þrūtian*, 'swell with anger, threaten', also *þrēat*, 'punishment, threat'. See **intrude**, **thrust**, **threat**. (lit.) Thrust away, hidden; hence, difficult to understand, obscure, unintelligible, deep (of subjects, thought, statement).

abstrusely, adv. Prec. & **-ly**. Obscurely, vaguely; profoundly.

abstruseness, n. See prec. & **-ness**. Difficulty, profundity (of thought, study &c.).

absurd, adj. [1. absérd; 2. əbsə́d]. Fr., fr. Lat. *absurdus*, 'out of tune, harsh, senseless, unsuitable', fr. base **swer-*, 'to sound', whence Lat. *susurrus*, 'whisper'; cp. Scrt. *sváriti*, 'resounds', *sváraš*, 'sound, tone'; also Gk. *sûrinx*, 'flute'. See **susurration**. **a** Inconsistent with known fact, or with normal order of things; eccentric, odd; **b** foolish, ridiculous; **c** comical, laughable.

absurdity, n. [1. absérditi; 2. əbsə́diti]. Fr. *absurdité*, Lat. *absurditāt-(em)*. See prec. & **-ity**. **1.** The state or quality of being absurd; folly, nonsense. **2.** Specific thing which is absurd, e.g. a statement, action, appearance &c.; something silly yet comical.

absurdly, adv. [1. absérdli; 2. əbsə́dli]. **absurd** & **-ly**. In an absurd manner.

absurdness, n. [1. absérdnes; 2. əbsə́dnis]. See prec. & **-ness**. Same as **absurdity**, **1**.

abundance, n. [1. abúndans; 2. əbʌ́ndəns]. Fr. *abondance*, fr. Lat. *abundantia*, 'an overflowing', fr. *abundant-(em)*, Pres. Part. type of *abundāre*, 'to overflow'. See **abound** & **-ance**. **1.** An overflow, overflowing fullness, great plenty, copiousness: *an abundance of good things.* **2.** (of quantity) More than sufficiency: *abundance of food.* **3.** Specif., plentiful supply of the good things of life, wealth, affluence: *to live in abundance.* **4.** (solo whist) Call of player who undertakes to take nine tricks from his own hand.

abundant, adj. [1. abúndant; 2. əbʌ́ndənt]. Fr. *abondant*, fr. Lat. *abundant-(em)*, Pres. Part. type. of *abundāre*. See **abound** & **-ant**. (of things) Plentiful, ample, more than sufficient, rich in.

abundantly, adv. Prec. & **-ly**. Plentifully, amply, sufficiently.

abuse (I.), vb. trans. [1. abū́z; 2. əbjū́z], fr. Fr. *abuser*, fr. Lat. *abūti*, *abūsus*, 'to misuse, abuse'. See **ab-** & **use**. **1.** To put to a wrong use, misuse: *to abuse one's authority, position, power, wealth* &c. **2. a** To treat badly, handle roughly or cruelly, injure by so doing (of animals, machines); **b** to presume upon, take advantage of (kindness, generosity, hospitality); **c** to betray (confidence, secret &c.). **3. a** To subject to verbal insult; scold loudly and coarsely, revile; **b** (in mild sense) blame, express disapproval of, find fault with. **4.** To mislead, deceive (archaic & obs. except in passive).

abuse (II.), n. [1. abū́s; 2. əbjū́s], fr. Fr. *abus*, fr. Lat. *abūsus*. See **abuse** (I.) **1.** Misuse, perverted use, application to a bad or wrong purpose: *abuse of power* &c.; *abuse of language, terms* &c., in perverted, inexact sense. **2.** A corrupt, oppressive, or unjust practice or custom (often in pl.). **3.** Vituperation; loud, coarse, insulting speech (often accompanied by oaths): *torrent of abuse*; *term, word of abuse*, oath, foul name.

abusive, adj. [1. abū́siv; 2. əbjū́siv]. See **abuse** & **-ive**. **1. a** Containing abuse; vituperative, scurrilous: *an abusive speech, expression*; **b** (of persons) insulting in language: *he became abusive.* **2.** (archaic) Wrongly used, irregular: *an abusive grammatical construction, as 'mutual' for 'reciprocal'.*

abusively, adv. Prec. & **-ly**. In an insulting manner.

abusiveness, n. See prec. & **-ness**. Habit of employing abuse.

abut, vb. intrans. [1. abút; 2. əbʌ́t]. O. Fr. *abouter*, 'place end to end'. See **butt** (II.). **1.** *Abut (up)on*, to end at, border on, touch at some point: *his garden abuts on the road.* **2.** (of parts of a building) To end *on* or *against*, to touch by projecting, to lean on.

abutilon, n. [1. abū́tilon; 2. əbjū́tilən], fr. Arab. *aubūtīlōn*. (bot.) Genus of shrubby plants, of the mallow family, with brightly coloured bell-shaped flowers.

abutment, n. [1. abútment; 2. əbʌ́tmənt]. See **abut** & **-ment**. (archit.) Support on which an arch rests; point where support and thing supported meet.

abysm, n. [1. abízm; 2. əbízəm], fr. O. Fr. *abisme*, fr. Low Lat. **abyssimus*, superl. of Lat. *abyssus*. See **abyss**. (poet.) Abyss.

abysmal, adj. [1. abízmal; 2. əbízməl]. Prec. & **-al**. Bottomless; (esp. fig.) profound, unfathomable, as *abysmal ignorance.*

abyss, n. [1. abís; 2. əbís], fr. Lat. *abyssus*, fr. Gk. *ábussos*, 'bottomless', fr. **a-** (priv.) & *bússos*, 'bottom', origin of which is unknown. **1.** A bottomless gulf or chasm; hence, primeval chaos; the bowels of the earth; the infernal pit, hell. **2.** Any unfathomable cavity; hence, (fig.) anything profound and unfathomable: *abyss of despair, of time.* **3.** (her.) The centre of an escutcheon.

abyssal, adj. [1. abísal; 2. əbísəl]. Prec. & **-al**. Belonging to the lowest depths of the sea.

-ac, suff. [1. ak; 2. æk], fr. Gk. *-akos*, Lat. *-acus*, or Fr. *-aque*, used to form adjs., e.g. *elegiac, iliac* &c., or ns., e.g. *aphrodisiac.*

acacia, n. [1. akā́sha; 2. əkéiʃə]. Lat. *acācia*; Gk. *akakia, akakalís*, 'Egyptian tamarisk', prob. Egyptian word. **a** Genus of trees, of mimosa tribe; **b** (in England) the locust-tree, q.v., or false acacia, *Robinia*, a graceful ornamental tree planted on lawns, having sharp thorns on the smaller branches.

academe, n. [1. ákadēm; 2. ǽkədīm]. See **academy**.

academic, adj. [1. àkadémik; 2. ækədémik]. See **academy** & **-ic**. **1.** Pertaining to an academy, esp. relating to a university: *academic degree, curriculum* &c.; *academic interests.* **2.** (derived from above) Pedantic, too much occupied with the rules of an academy or university; hence, unpractical: *academic manner*; *academic discussion*, purely theoretical, having no practical result. **3.** Frigid, inhuman (of men and manners). **4.** n. pl. *Academics*, discussions which are purely theoretical.

academical, adj. & n. [1. àkadémikl; 2. ækədémikl]. Prec. & **-al**. **a** adj. Belonging to an academy or university; **b** n. pl., *academicals*, university robes &c. Phr. *in full academicals*, gown, hood, bands, and cap.

academically, adv. Prec. & **-ly**. In an academic manner; precisely, pedantically; in theory only, not practically.

academician, n. [1. akàdemísyan, -íshan; 2. əkædəmísjən, -íʃən]. Fr. *académicien*. See **academic** & **-ian**. Member of an Academy of Art, or of a learned society; specif. (cap.) a member of the English Royal Academy, or of the French Academy.

academy, n. [1. akádemi; 2. əkǽdəmi]. Fr. *académie*, Lat. *acadēmia*, fr. Gk. *akadḗmeia*, 'the Academy', from the hero *Akadēmos* (after whom Plato's garden was named). **1.** (class. hist., and philos.) **a** The garden near Athens in which Plato taught; **b** the followers of Plato; the school or system of philosophy founded by Plato. **2.** A chartered corporation of scholars, artists, men of letters, men of science, as *The Royal Academy, French Academy* &c. **3.** An educational institution or school, usually not of university standing, as *The Edinburgh Academy*; often a pretentious term for a private school: *a young ladies' academy.*

acajou, n. [1. ákazhōō; 2. ǽkəʒū]. Fr. See **cashew**. **a** The cashew tree or its fruit; **b** (French use) mahogany.

acalephe, n. [1. ákalēf; 2. ǽkəlīf]. Gk. *akalḗphē*, 'a nettle', fr. Heb. *halīfōt*, 'prickly leaves of the spinach', fr. base meaning 'pierce, cut'. (zool.) Jelly-fish.

acanthus, n. [1. akánthus; 2. əkǽnþəs]. Lat., fr. Gk. *ákanthos*, fr. *ákis*, 'spine, thorn'. See **acute**. **1.** (bot.) Genus of prickly plants found in South Europe and Asia Minor. **2.** (archit.) *Acanthus leaf*, conventional representation of leaves of plant, esp. in capital of Corinthian column.

acarid, n. [1. ákarid; 2. ǽkərid], fr. Gk. *ákari*, 'mite', fr. *akárēs*, 'too short to be cut; minute, tiny', fr. **a-** (priv.) & *keírein*, 'to cut', see **shear (I.)**. (entom.) Any member of an order of arachnids which includes the mites and ticks; a mite, tick.

acarpous, adj. [1. akárpus; 2. əkā́pəs], fr. Gk. *ákarpos*, 'unfruitful', fr. **a-** (priv.) & *karpós*, 'fruit'; cogn. w. Lat. *carpere*, 'to pluck, gather'; O.E. *hærfest*, 'harvest', O.H.G. *herbist*, Mod. Germ. *herbst*, 'autumn, season of fruits'. From the idea of 'plucking' in different sense comes **harp**. See **harvest & -ous**. (bot.) Not producing fruit.

acatalectic, adj. [1. akàtaléktik; 2. əkæ̀təléktik], fr. Gk. *akatalēktós*, fr. **a-** (priv.) & *katalḗgein*, 'to leave off, stop'. See **catalectic**. (of verse) Complete, having the full number of feet or syllables.

acatalepsy, n. [1. akátalepsi; 2. əkǽtəlepsi], fr. Gk. *akatálēpsis*, 'not understanding', fr. **a-** (priv.), *katá*, 'down', & *lēpsis*, 'a taking'. See **catalepsy**. (philos.) Incomprehensibility, term of ancient scepticism, of knowledge as probable only and not certain.

acataleptic, adj. [1. akàtaléptik; 2. əkæ̀təléptik], fr. Gk. *akatalēptikós*. See prec. & **-ic**. (philos.) Incomprehensible.

acaulous, adj. [1. akáwlus; 2. əkṓləs]. Gk. *ákaulos*, fr. **a-** (priv.) & *kaulós*, 'a stalk, stem, shaft'; cp. Gk. *koîlos*, 'hollow', Lat. *caulis*, 'stem of plant'. See **cauliflower, colewort, kail, hollow**. (bot.) Having no stem, or a very short stem.

Accadian, Akkadian, adj. & n. [1. akā́dian; 2. əkéidiən], fr. Heb. *Akkad*, Gen. x. 10. **1.** adj. Of, pertaining to, a primitive race and language of ancient Babylonia. **2.** n. **a** Member of this race; **b** its language, earliest form of cuneiform.

accede, vb. intrans. [1. aksḗd; 2. æksíd], fr. Lat. *accēdere*, 'to approach, come over (to); to give assent', fr. *ad*, 'to', & *cēdere*, 'to go, yield'. See **ad- & cede** & cp. **access** &c. (followed by *to* or absol.) **1.** To enter on, attain to, succeed to: *to accede to the throne, power, an estate, office* &c. **2.** To come over to, to join: *to accede to a party, government* &c. **3.** To become a party to; to agree, assent to: *to accede to a treaty, request, proposal* &c.

accelerando, adv. [1. aksèlerándō; 2. æksèlərǽndou]. Ital., fr. Lat. gerund. See **accelerate**. (mus. direction) With gradually increased speed.

accelerant, n. [1. aksélerant; 2. æksélərənt], fr. Lat. *accelerant-(em)*, Pres. Part. type of *accelerāre*. See **accelerate & -ant**. Substance which accelerates or increases the speed of any process, esp. of the chemical process of catalysis; a catalyser.

accelerate, vb. trans. & intrans. [1. aksélerāt; 2. æksélereit], fr. Lat. *accelerāt-(um)*, P.P. type of *accelerāre*, 'to hasten', fr. *ad* & *celer*, 'swift'. See **ad- & celerity**. **1.** trans. To increase the speed of (any motion or action), cause to go quickly, hasten. **2.** intrans. (of motion or process) To become swifter.

accelerated, adj. [1. aksélerāted; 2. æksélereitid]. P.P. of prec. Increased in speed of motion, made to go quicker.

accelerating, adj. [1. akséleràting; 2. æksélereitiŋ]. Pres. Part. of **accelerate**. Causing quicker motion: *an accelerating force*.

acceleration, n. [1. aksèleráshun; 2. æksèləréiʃən], fr. Lat. *accelerātiōn-(em)*, 'a hastening'. See **accelerate & -ion**. **1. a** The act of increasing speed; **b** increase of speed. **2.** (mechan.) The rate of change of velocity of a body in motion per unit of time.

accelerative, adj. [1. akséleràtiv; 2. æksélərətiv]. See **accelerate & -ive**. Tending to increase speed.

accelerator, n. [1. aksélerāter; 2. æksélereitə]. See **accelerate & -or**. Anything which increases speed of motion. Specif. **a** Contrivance for producing greater speed in a machine (e.g. motor-car); **b** (anat.) a nerve or muscle which hastens a motion.

accent (I.), n. [1. áksent; 2. ǽksənt], fr. Lat. *accentus*, 'accentuation, tone', fr. *ad* & *cantus*, 'tone, melody', fr. *cantum*, P.P. of *canere*, 'to sing'. See **ad- & cant**. **1.** (phon.) Includes both **a** emphasis, stress, and **b** tone, pitch; (fig.) emphasis, intensity, sharp distinction. **2.** Mode of utterance, style of pronunciation: *a good French accent*; *a strong Scots accent*. **3.** A mark placed over a letter in writing and printing to indicate emphasis, pitch, vowel quality. **4.** (gen. pl., poet.) **a** Verse, poetical composition, poetry; **b** speech, voice, utterance: *he spoke in accents mild*. **5.** (mus.) Stress or beat, recurring at intervals.

accent (II.), vb. trans. [1. aksént; 2. æksént]. See prec. **a** To put marks of accent upon (letter) in writing and printing; **b** to emphasize, more correctly, *accentuate*.

accentor, n. [1. aksénter; 2. ækséntə]. Lat., 'one who sings with another', fr. *ad-* & *cantor*, 'singer'. See **accent (I.) & cant**. (ornith., cap.) Name of a group of small singing birds, esp. the hedge-sparrow or hedge-warbler.

accentual, adj. [1. akséntūal; 2. ækséntjuəl], fr. Lat. *accentus*, 'accent', & **-al**. Pertaining to accent: *accentual verse*, that in which stress and not quantity is the basis of rhythm.

accentuate, vb. trans. [1. akséntūāt; 2. ækséntjueit]. Med. Lat. *accentuāt-(um)*, P.P. type of *accentuāre*. See **accent (I.)**. To place emphasis upon (a word or syllable) in speech; (fig.) to give prominence, importance to, to emphasize, increase force or value of (expression of an idea, command &c.; a colour, musical note, physical feature).

accentuation, n. [1. aksèntūáshun; 2. æksèntjuéiʃən], fr. Med. Lat. *accentuātiōn-(em)*. See prec. & **-ion**. The act of putting on accent (in any sense).

accept, vb. trans. [1. aksépt; 2. əksépt], fr. Lat. *acceptāre*, freq. of *accipere*, *acceptum*, 'to take, receive', fr. **ad-** & *capere*, 'to take', see **captive**. **1. a** To consent to take, receive (what is offered or given): *to accept a gift, invitation, kindness, an honour* &c.; **b** to undertake duties of: *to accept an office, appointment* &c. **2. a** To consent to, agree to, admit, permit: *the accepted truth*; *to accept the correctness of a statement, a correction, an amendment* &c.; **b** (law) to receive personally: *to accept service of writ*; **c** (commerc., of bills) to take responsibility for, promise to pay, agree to meet. *Accept of* can be used in all above senses, except **2. b**, but is now old-fashioned and formal.

acceptability, n. [1. aksèptabíliti; 2. əksèptəbíliti]. See **acceptable & -ity**. Suitability, worthiness for acceptance.

acceptable, adj. [1. akséptabl; 2. əkséptəbl], fr. prec. & **-able**. Worth accepting, pleasant to receive; gratifying, agreeable, welcome (of something given or conferred).

acceptableness, n. Prec. & **-ness**. Acceptability.

acceptably, adv. See prec. & **-ly**. In a way, or on an occasion, that gratifies receiver.

acceptance, n. [1. akséptans; 2. əkséptəns], fr. **accept & -ance**. **1.** Taking of what is offered; act of consenting to receive: *acceptance of an invitation, gift, benefit, honour* &c. **2.** Intellectual assent to, belief in: *acceptance of a statement, theory, doctrine* &c. **3.** (commerc.) **a** The acknowledgement of a liability; an undertaking to pay a bill when presented; **b** document proving such acceptance of liability &c.

acceptation, n. [1. àkseptáshun; 2. æ̀ksepté iʃən], fr. Low Lat. *acceptātiōn-(em)*, 'taking'. See **accept & -ation**. The received meaning of a word or expression; the sense in which it is usually taken and understood.

acceptilation, n. [1. aksèptiláshun; 2. æksèptiléiʃən], fr. Lat. *acceptilātiōn-(em)*, fr. *accept-(um)*, P.P. type of *accipere*. See **accept**. **a** (Roman and Scots law) Formal, verbal release from a verbal contract, whether payment has been made or not; **b** (theol.) the free remission of sins.

acceptor, n. [1. aksépter; 2. ækséptə], fr. **accept & -or**. Specif., one who accepts or undertakes the payment of a bill of exchange.

access, n. [1. ákses; 2. ǽkses], fr. Lat. *accessus*, 'an approach', fr. *accēdere*, *accessum*, 'to come near, approach'. See **accede**. **1.** The act of coming to, approach to a place or person: *prayer of humble access* (in Communion Service: '*We do not presume to come*' &c.). **2.** Means, or way of approach (to places): *the only access to the house was through a farmyard*. **3.** Opportunity, or right of approach, entry, or use: *access to books, to means of education* &c.; *Peers have access to the Sovereign at all times*; *access to the house and property was granted on completion of purchase*. **4.** (law) Opportunity for exercising marital rights: '*Access of the husband shall be presumed, unless the contrary be shown*' (Blackstone). **5. a** (med.) A fit or attack of disease; **b** an outburst, paroxysm (of anger or passion).

accessary, accessory (I.), n. [1. àksésari; 2. æ̀ksésəri]. Lat. *accessōrius*, fr. *access-(um)*, P.P. type of *accēdere*; spelling confused w. that of Lat. suff. *-ārius*. See **accede**. **1.** Something subordinate but contributing to the principal cause producing a general result; adjunct. Specif. (derived usage, gen. pl. and spelt *accessories*) extra and additional details of equipment to anything, furnishings, garnishings &c., as *the accessories of a motor-car*, which, though indispensable, are not part of the original structure (e.g. lamps, horn, tool-chest, oil-cans, air-pump &c.). **2.** (law, gen. spelt *accessary*) One privy to, and aiding in, a crime: *accessary before, after, the fact*.

accessary (II.), adj. See prec. Additional, subordinate, adventitious.

accessibility, n. [1. aksèsibíliti; 2. æksèsibíliti], fr. Lat. *accessibilitāt-(em)*. See **accessible & -ity**. The condition (of things) or quality (of persons) of being accessible.

accessible, adj. [1. aksésibl; 2. æksésibl], fr. Lat. *accessibilis*. See **access & -ible**. **1. a** (of places &c.) Capable of being entered or reached; get-at-able; **b** (of persons) easy of access or approach. **2.** Attainable, to be got at: *accessible information*. **3.** (fig., with *to*) Easily moved by, open to the influence of, amenable to certain motives: *accessible to reason, pity, bribery* &c.

accessibly, adv. Prec. & **-ly**. (Situated) in such a manner as to be easily reached.

accession, n. [1. akséshun; 2. ækséʃən], fr. Lat. *accessiōn-(em)*, 'a coming to, approach; addition'. See **access & -ion**. **1.** The act of coming; approach; esp. coming to or reaching a condition, state, office, dignity, power, esp. the throne: *the king's accession*. **2.** A coming to as an addition; **a** joining, addition: *accession to a party, corporate body, society* &c.; **b** thing added, acquisition: *list of accessions* (to a library, &c.); **c** valuable, agreeable addition: *a great accession to the neighbourhood*. **3.** (law) Increment, addition to value of property (by improvements or natural growth).

accessory. See **accessary**.

accidence, n. [1. áksidens; 2. ǽksidəns], fr. O. Fr. *accidens*, fr. Lat. *accidentia*, neut. pl. See **accident**. That part of grammar, or of a treatise on grammar, which deals with inflexions.

accident, n. [1. áksident; 2. ǽksidənt], fr. Lat. *accident-(em)*, *accidens*, 'an accident'; also Pres. Part. of *accidere*, 'to fall at, to, to happen, fall out'; fr. **ad-** & *cadere*, 'to fall', see **cadence**. That which befalls or happens. **1.** Unexpected event, one that occurs without design or apparent cause: *a mere accident of birth.* Hence Phr. *by accident*, by chance. **2.** An unexpected event, or undesigned act, of an unfortunate character; misfortune, injury, disaster. Phr. *to meet with an accident.* **3.** (philos.) A property of a thing which is a mere contingent attribute, not part of its essential nature. **4.** (geol. and geog.) Irregularity, diversity in surface of a stretch of country. **5.** (her.) An additional, but unessential, mark in an escutcheon which may be retained or omitted.

accidental, adj. & n. [1. àksidéntal; 2. ǽksidéntəl]. Prec. & **-al**. **1.** adj. **a** Happening by chance or unexpectedly; **b** incidental, contingent, attributive, not essential to nature of a thing. **2.** n. (mus.) **a** A sharp, flat, or natural occurring incidentally in a piece of music though not naturally belonging to the key in which the piece is written; **b** the symbol of such in musical notation.

accidentally, adv. Prec. & **-ly**. In an accidental manner, by chance; without intention or design.

accidie, n. [1. ákside; 2. ǽksidī]. Variant of **acedia**.

accipiter, n. [1. aksípiter; 2. æksípitə]. Lat., lit. 'the seizer', fr. **ad-** & base *cap-*, 'seize, hold', q.v. under **captive**, hence 'hawk' or other bird of this kind, 'bird of prey'; see **accept**. **1.** (zool.) A bird of prey of the order *Accipitres* or *Raptores*, including eagles, falcons, hawks &c. **2.** (surg.) A bandage over the nose, resembling a hawk's claw.

accipitral, adj. [1. aksípitral; 2. æksípitrəl], fr. prec. & **-al**. Of, pertaining to, the *Accipitres* or hawks; hawklike.

acclaim (I.), vb. trans. [1. aklám; 2. əkléim], fr. Lat. *acclāmāre*, 'to cry out at', fr. **ad-** & *clāmāre*, 'to cry out, shout', see **claim, clamant, clamour. 1.** To greet with loud applause; to acknowledge, recognize as, announce, indicate such recognition by applause: *acclaim the victor*; *acclaim him (as) king.* **2.** To shout, call out.

acclaim (II.), n., fr. prec. Shout of applause, or approbation (poet. and rare).

acclamation, n. [1. aklamáshun; 2. ækləméiʃən], fr. Lat. *acclāmātiōn-(em)*, 'a shout of favour or approbation', fr. *acclāmāre.* See **acclaim** & **-ation**. Loud public applause; a shout or other demonstration of approval, joy, welcome &c. made by a multitude. Phr. (in public meetings, of a motion) *carried by acclamation*, by loudly expressed approval, without counting votes.

acclamatory, adj. [1. aklámateri; 2. əklǽmətəri]. See prec. & **-ory**. Expressing joy, approval &c. by acclamation.

acclimatization, n. [1. aklīmatīzáshun; 2. əklàimətaizéiʃən]. See **acclimatize** & **-ation**. **a** Act or process of inuring, accustoming, to new conditions of climate &c.; **b** state of being so inured.

acclimatize, vb. trans. [1. aklímatīz; 2. əkláimətaiz], fr. Fr. *acclimater*, fr. *à*, 'to', & *climat.* See **climate** & **-ize**. **a** To inure, accustom, habituate (men, animals, plants) to a new climate, different from the native one; **b** (fig., reflex.) to get accustomed to new surroundings and conditions of life.

acclimatized, adj. [1. aklímatīzd; 2. əkláimətaizd]. P.P. of prec. Accustomed to new climate, to new conditions of life.

acclivity, n. [1. aklíviti; 2. əklíviti], fr. Lat. *acclivitas*, 'a rise, ascent', fr. **ad-** & *clīvus*, 'a slope'; the latter word is cogn. w. Goth. *hlaiw*, O.E. *hlǣw*, *hlāw*, 'burial mound', cp. *-low*, *-law* in Mod. Engl. Place-Names. The same orig. base, w. different formative elements, appears also in Lat. *clīno*, 'bend, turn'. See **decline, incline** &c. A slope of the earth, as the side of a hill, considered as ascending and opposed to *declivity.*

accolade, n. [1. akolád; 2. ækəléid]. Fr., fr. Ital. *accollata*, fr. *accollare*, 'embrace round the neck', fr. Lat. *ad*, 'to', & *collum*, 'neck'. See **collar (I.)**. The act or ceremony of conferring knighthood, formerly often consisting of an embrace, now of the laying of a sword on the shoulder of the person to receive the honour, by virtue of which act, together with the words pronounced by the Sovereign or his deputy, a man becomes a knight: *to receive the accolade*, to be knighted.

accollé, adj. [1. akólā; 2. ækɔ́lei]. Fr., fr. Lat. *ad* & *collum*, 'neck.' See **collar (I.)**. **a** (her.) Having the neck encircled (of animals &c.); **b** (numis.) joined at the neck, as profile portraits on a medallion or coin.

accommodate, vb. trans. [1. akómodāt; 2. əkɔ́mədeit]. Lat., fr. *accommodāt-(um)*, P.P. type of *accommodāre*, 'to fit, adapt', fr. *ad* & *commodāre*, 'to fit, adapt', fr. *con*, 'with', & *modus*, 'measure'. See **ad-, con-,** & **mode. 1.** To adapt, adjust (esp. one-, him-, her- self &c.) *to* anything: *accommodate oneself to circumstances.* **2.** To adapt or reconcile (what appears to be incongruous or inconsistent): *to accommodate facts, statistics &c. to theory.* **3.** (followed by *with*) To furnish, fit out, supply with something that is required, as **a** money, to lend; **b** lodgings &c.: *to accommodate for the night*; **c** (used by tradesmen) to oblige (a customer).

accommodating, adj. [1. akómodāting; 2. əkɔ́mədeitiŋ]. See **accommodate** & **-ing**. (of persons) Obliging, easy-going; free from scruple, willing for slight inducement to adapt principles to suit circumstances.

accommodatingly, adv. Prec. & **-ly**. In an accommodating manner; obligingly.

accommodation, n. [1. akòmodáshun; 2. əkɔ̀mədéiʃən], fr. Lat. *accommodātiōn-(em)*, 'an adapting or adjusting of one thing to another'. See **accommodate** & **-ion**. Various uses corresponding to verb: **1.** Adjustment, adaptation (to given purpose); reconcilement (of differences, opinions &c.). **2.** Lodging, quarters: *good, poor, accommodation.* **3.** Loan of money at an agreed rate of interest.

accompaniment, n. [1. akúmpaniment; 2. əkámpənimənt], fr. Fr. *accompagnement.* See **accompany** & **-ment**. **1.** A thing which naturally co-exists with another: *disease is a frequent accompaniment of famine.* **2.** (mus.) Part played on musical instrument in conjunction with, and supporting, voice or another instrument.

accompanist, -yist, n. [1. akúmpanist, -iist; 2. əkámpənist, -iist]. See **accompany** & **-ist**. (mus.) One who plays an accompaniment.

accompany, vb. trans. [1. akúmpani; 2. əkámpəni], fr. Fr. *accompagner*, fr. *à*, 'to', & *compagne*, 'companion'. See **company, companion. 1.** To perform two or more actions simultaneously or in immediate succession: *accompany one's speech with gesture*; *he accompanied his orders with blows.* **2.** To attend, go with; to perform a journey &c. in association with (some other person or thing), bear company: *to accompany a person to the door*; *the cruiser accompanied the merchant-ships down the channel.* **3.** (mus.) To support, by playing on a musical instrument in co-operation with him, a person who is singing, dancing, or playing on some other instrument; also, to play in conjunction with the voice, a song, another instrument &c.: *to accompany a singer* &c.; *to accompany a song, the violin &c., on the piano.*

accomplice, n. [1. akómplis; 2. əkɔ́mplis]. Fr. *complice.* First syll. perh. orig. indef. art.; otherwise fr. **ad-**; & L. Lat. *complex*, *complicis*, 'a confederate', fr. Lat. *complicāre*, 'to fold together', fr. **com-** & *plicāre*, 'to fold'. See **complex, complicate.** One, generally a subordinate, who participates, shares, is associated with another, in the perpetration of a crime, or who is privy to the committing of an offence; one who shares a guilty secret; a confederate.

accomplish, vb. trans. [1. akómplish; 2. əkɔ́mpliʃ], fr. O. Fr. *ac(c)omplir*, fr. Lat. *ad* & *complēre*, 'to fill up, complete'. See **ad-** & **complete** & vbl. suff. **-ish**. To carry out, bring to a conclusion, succeed in finishing or completing (used of work, task, designs &c.).

accomplished, adj. [1. akómplisht; 2. əkɔ́mpliʃt]; old-fashioned [1. akúmplisht; 2. əkámpliʃt]. P.P. of prec. (of persons) Perfected by education and training, possessed of certain acquired knowledge, social arts, and graces; cultivated.

accomplishment, n. [1. akómplishment; 2. əkɔ́mpliʃmənt]. See **accomplish** & **-ment**. **1.** The act or process of accomplishing; completion, fulfilment. **2. a** Quality possessed by an accomplished person; **b** (pl.) acquired knowledge, arts, and graces.

accord (I.), vb. intrans. & trans. [1. akórd; 2. əkɔ́d]. In M.E. *accorden*, 'agree, admit', fr. O. Fr. *acorder*, fr. Low Lat. *accordāre*, 'to be of one mind, agree, harmonize' &c., fr. Lat. *ad* & *cor, cordis*, 'heart, soul'. See **cordate. 1.** intrans. To be in harmony, to be consistent (usually followed by *with*): *to accord with one's hopes, wishes, desires* &c.; *that does not accord with what has gone before.* **2.** trans. To grant, bestow on (a person): *to accord him praise* &c.; to grant to: *to accord praise to him.*

accord (II.), n. O. Fr. *acord*, 'agreement'. See prec. Consent, mutual agreement, harmony, consonance, consistency: *with one accord*; *in accord with one's hopes, principles.* In Phr. *of one's own accord*, i.e. spontaneously, *accord* has sense of assent, impulse.

accordance, n. [1. akórdans; 2. əkɔ́dəns]. O. Fr. See **accord (II.)** & **-ance**. Agreement, conformity: *in accordance with* (a person or thing), in agreement with, in conformity to: *I am in accordance with him in this matter*; *in accordance with custom.*

accordant, adj. [1. akórdant; 2. əkɔ́dənt]. In M.E., fr. O. Fr. Pres. Part. of *accorder.* See **accord (I.)** & **-ant**. In tune with; in agreement with (followed by *to* or *with*): *accordant to reason, with truth.*

according, adv. [1. akórding; 2. əkɔ́diŋ], fr. Pres. Part. of **accord (I.)**. Chiefly used now in the phrases *according as* and *according to.* *According as*, in proportion as, to the extent that: *according as you behave yourself so you will be well treated.* *According to*: **a** in a manner consistent with, in conformity with: *according to one's lights*, to the best of one's abilities, following the knowledge one has; **b** on the authority of, following the statement of: *according to Macaulay, King Charles was weak and treacherous.*

accordingly, adv. Prec. & **-ly**. In a conformable, corresponding manner; therefore.

accordion, n. [1. akórdiun; 2. əkɔ́djən]. Invented word, fr. *accord* in sense of 'harmony', & suff. *-ion*, on anal. of **clarion**. (mus.) A small, portable musical wind instrument with stops, held with both hands, one of which does the fingering; the bellows lie between either end of the instrument, which is alternately pulled out and squeezed together by action of the hands.

accordion-pleat, n. One of a series of pleats of equal size resembling the folds in bellows of an accordion, used in women's skirts.

accost, vb. trans. [1. akóst; 2. əkɔ́st], fr. Fr. *accoster*, fr. L. Lat. *accostāre*, fr. Lat. *ad* & *costa*, 'a rib'. See **costal**. Literal meaning 'to come up to a person's side'. To come up to, and speak to a person; to speak first, before one is addressed; begin conversation. Now often in bad sense, of prostitutes &c., to speak to a stranger for immoral purpose.

accouchement, n. [1. akóoshmon; 2. akūʃmɑ̃]. Fr. See **couch** & **-ment**. Confinement, childbirth, delivery.

accoucheur, n. [1. àkooshér; 2. ækūʃʌ́]. Fr. Medical man who specializes in midwifery.

accoucheuse, n. [1. àkōōshĕz; 2. ǽkūʃáz]. Fr. A midwife.

account (I.), n. [1. akóunt; 2. əkáunt], fr. O. Fr. *aconte*, Mod. Fr. *compte*, Low Lat. *comptum*, fr. *computum*, 'reckoning'. See **compute**. **1.** Reckoning, calculation, record, of money transactions; statement of money owing; bill: *keep one's accounts in order*; *tradesman's account* &c. **2.** Statement of manner in which pecuniary matters and responsibilities have been dealt with: *to give, render, an account of one's stewardship.* Phr. *to pay money on account*, pay part of a larger sum which is owing. **3.** Grounds, reason, cause, motive, conditions: esp. in Phrs. *on no account*, under no circumstances; *on account of*, because of; *on my account*, for my sake; *on one's own account*, on one's own responsibility; for one's own advantage, independently. **4.** Description, descriptive statement, narrative. Phr. *give a good, bad, account of*, speak favourably, unfavourably. **5.** Judgement, estimate, opinion. In Phr. *to take account of, into account*, consider; *take no account of*, neglect, overlook; *not to hold of much account*, to have poor opinion of; *of no account*, unimportant, negligible. **6.** Advantage, profit: in Phr. *to turn to (good) account*, make (good) use of.

account (II.), vb. trans. & intrans., fr. prec. **A.** trans. **1. a** To hold, esteem, estimate, judge: *to account it a fortunate circumstance that* &c.; **b** (reflex.) *to account oneself happy* &c. **B.** intrans. *Account for*: **a** To provide a satisfactory explanation for, render intelligible, explain: *only illness could account for his behaviour*; *not to be able to account for*, to be unable to explain, understand; **b** give a statement showing how money or other property entrusted to one's care has been spent or dealt with: *you will have to account for every penny you have had* (always with *for* of things, and *to* of persons).

accountability, n. [1. akòuntabíliti; 2. əkàuntəbíliti]. See **accountable** & **-ity**. Condition of being accountable; liability, responsibility.

accountable, adj. [1. akóuntabl; 2. əkáuntəbl]. See **account (II.)** & **-able**. **1.** Liable to be called on to explain; answerable, responsible, for (*to* persons, *for* things): *he is accountable to me for what he does.* Phr. *not accountable for one's actions* &c., not right in the head, irresponsible. **2.** Able to be accounted for, explicable (rare).

accountably, adv. Prec. & **-ly**. In a manner that can be accounted for.

accountancy, n. [1. akóuntansi; 2. əkáuntənsi]. See **accountant** & **-ancy**. The profession, occupation, of an accountant.

accountant, n. [1. akóuntant; 2. əkáuntənt]. Cp. O. Fr. *acontant, accomptant.* See **account** & **-ant**. One whose profession it is to inspect and audit accounts.

account-book, n., fr. **account (I.)** & **book**. A book in which accounts (usually private) are kept.

accoutre, vb. trans. [1. akōōter; 2. əkūtə]. Fr. *accoutrer*, orig. simply 'clothe, deck out', now 'dress in grotesque, fantastic fashion'. Etymol. doubtful. Meyer-Lübke ventures on none at all. Others have guessed: **a** O. Fr. *coustre*, fr. Low Lat. *custor*, 'guardian, sacristan, one having charge of vestments' &c., Lat. *custos*, see **custody**; **b** O. Fr. *cousture*, Mod. Fr. *couture*, 'sewing', fr. Lat. *consutūra*, connected with *con* & *suere*, 'sew', see **suture**. Both are improbable. To dress, fit out with costume; equip, esp. for military service. Chiefly in P.P. *accoutred.*

accoutrement, n. [1. akōōtrement; 2. əkūtrəmənt]. See prec. & **-ment**. **a** Dress, and personal outfit generally; **b** (esp. in pl.) military outfit, including everything except actual clothes, and weapons.

accredit, vb. trans. [1. akrédit; 2. əkrédit], fr. Fr. *accréditer*, fr. Lat. *ad* & *crēdere, crēditum*, 'to trust'. See **ad-** & **credit**. To invest with credit, sanction; specif. (gen. in P.P.) to send an official envoy or ambassador to foreign court, duly provided with credentials from his own government; also of any intermediary or representative: *an accredited minister, agent.*

accretion, n. [1. akréshun; 2. əkríʃən]. Lat. *accrētiōn-(em)*, 'an increasing', fr. *accrēt-(um)*, P.P. type of *accrescere*, 'to increase'. See **crescent**. **1.** Increase in size, esp. by external addition as distinct from organic growth: '*A mineral augments not by growth, but by accretion*' (Owen). **2.** The matter added in such growth or accumulation. **3.** (law) **a** Accession, q.v.; **b** increase of legacy &c. by addition of share of co-legatee who dies before legacy falls due.

accrue, vb. intrans. [1. akrōō; 2. əkrú], fr. Fr. *accrue*, n., 'increase', fr. *accrû*, P.P. of *accroître*, 'to increase', fr. Lat. *accrescere*. See **accretion**. To come, fall due (to a person), as a gain or advantage, as result of natural increase, esp. of interest on money; of any advantage arising from a process or action which falls to a person. '*And unto meeting, when we meet, Delight a hundredfold accrue*' (Tennyson).

accumbent, adj. [1. akúmbent; 2. əkámbənt], fr. Lat. *accumbent-(em)*, Pres. Part. of *accumbere*, 'to lean, recline towards or against', fr. *ad*, 'to', & *cumbere*, 'to lie, recline'. See **cubicle**. (bot.) Folded on their faces, of the cotyledons of such plants as the wallflower.

accumulate, vb. trans. & intrans. [1. akúmūlāt; 2. əkjūmjuleit], fr. Lat. *accumulāt-(um)*, P.P. type of *accumulāre*, 'to heap up', fr. **ad-** & *cumulus*, 'a heap', see **cumulus**. **1.** trans. To heap up, pile up, bring together by degrees, amass (money, possessions &c.). **2.** intrans. To increase in number or mass; to gather together, become thick (lit. and fig.): *dust soon accumulates in houses which are not cleaned; disasters accumulated round his path.*

accumulated, adj. [1. akúmūlāted; 2. əkjūmjuleitid]. P.P. of prec. Heaped, stored up, amassed, brought together: *accumulated wealth, crimes, wisdom of ages* &c.

accumulation, n. [1. akūmūláshun; 2. əkjūmjuléiʃən]. See **accumulate** & **-ion**. **1.** The act or process of accumulating, heaping up, amassing. **2. a** That which has been accumulated; collection, pile, often in rather unfavourable sense: *accumulation of rubbish*; *a troublesome accumulation of papers* &c.; specif. **b** growth of capital by addition of interest.

accumulative, adj. [1. akúmūlātiv; 2. əkjūmjuleitiv]. See **accumulate** & **-ive**. **1.** Resulting from accumulation; more usually *cumulative*, q.v. **2.** (of persons) Acquisitive, given to heaping up (wealth &c.).

accumulatively, adv. Prec. & **-ly**. By accumulation.

accumulator, n. [1. akúmūlāter; 2. əkjūmjuleitə]. See **accumulate** & **-or**. **a** (rare) One who accumulates or amasses (wealth &c.); a money-maker; specif. **b** an apparatus for storing energy, electricity &c.

accuracy, n. [1. ákūrasi; 2. ǽkjurəsi]. See **accurate** & **-acy**. Exactness, precision, correctness.

accurate, adj. [1. ákūrat; 2. ǽkjurət], fr. Lat. *accūrātus*, 'prepared with care', fr. *accūrāre*, fr. **ad-** & *cūra*, 'care'. See **cure (I.)**. **1.** (of persons) Careful, painstaking, exact. **2.** (of statements, descriptions &c.) Free from mis-statement; strictly true, precise. **3.** (of apparatus, machines &c.) Giving precise results; working according to design.

accurately, adv. Prec. & **-ly**. In an accurate manner; with accuracy.

accursed, accurst, adj. [1. akérsed, akérst; 2. əkə́sid, əkə́st]. P.P. of obs. *accurse.* See **curse (II.)**. The *-ed* pronounced as separate syllable when the word is followed by a noun; two-syllabled form only used absolutely. Under a curse, ill-fated; hence, abominable, detestable. Often in colloquial speech used to express mere annoyance; troublesome; equivalent to, but much stronger than, *confounded.*

accusation, n. [1. akūzáshun; 2. ækjuzéiʃən], fr. Lat. *accūsātiōn-(em)*, fr. *accūsāt-(um)*, P.P. type of *accūsāre*. See **accuse** & **-ion**. **a** Act of accusing; charge or imputation of an offence or crime; **b** (law) an indictment. Phrs. *to be under an accusation*; *bring an accusation against.*

accusative, adj. & n. [1. akúzativ; 2. əkjúzətiv]. Lat. *accūsātīvus*, fr. *accūsāre*, 'blame' &c. See prec. & **-ive**. **a** adj. Accusing; **b** n., name of case of direct object of transitive verb. In inflected languages the accusative has specific and characteristic suffix; in uninflected languages like French or English there is properly no accusative case, but the object of a transitive verb stands in this case-relation though it has no suffix.

accuse, vb. trans. [1. akúz; 2. əkjúz]. Fr. *accuser*, Lat. *accūsāre*, 'accuse, blame', fr. *cūdere*, 'strike, beat, pound', fr. Aryan base **kʷou-*, whence also Lith. *kauti*, 'hew, strike, forge', O.H.G. *houwan*, Germ. *hauen*, O.E. *hēawan*, 'hew, strike'. See **cause (I.)** & **hew**. To impute guilt to; to bring a charge against, indict (a person *of* an offence); to blame, lay the fault on.

accused, n. [1. akúzd; 2. əkjúzd], fr. P.P. of prec. Person against whom a criminal charge is brought in a court of law.

accuser, n. [1. akúzer; 2. əkjúzə]. See **accuse** & **-er**. One who brings an accusation, charge, indictment, or imputation.

accusing, adj. [1. akúzing; 2. əkjúziŋ]. Pres. Part. of **accuse**. Imputing guilt: *to point an accusing finger at (a person).*

accusingly, adv. Prec. & **-ly**. In an accusing manner.

accustom, vb. trans. [1. akústum; 2. əkástəm], fr. O. Fr. *acostumer* (Fr. *accoutumer*), fr. *à*, 'to', & **custom**. To make familiar by use or habit, to habituate, inure, familiarize, train (a person or animal *to* something, or *to do* something): *to accustom a dog to the gun*; (often used in pass.) to be in the habit of, be used to: *to be accustomed to hard work, bad food* &c.; (also reflex.) *to accustom oneself to.*

accustomed, adj. [1. akústumd; 2. əkástəmd]. P.P. of prec. Usual, habitual, customary, characteristic: *to fight with accustomed bravery.*

ace, n. [1. ās; 2. eis], fr. Fr. *as*, 'ace at dice or cards', Lat. *as*, 'unity, unit', see **as (II.)**. **1.** A unit; esp. a single point or spot on playing-cards or dice; the card so marked: *ace of spades* &c.; Phr. *within an ace of*, failing, or escaping by a hair's-breadth. **2.** (fig.) The highest, best (from *ace* at cards); specif. (flying) *an ace*, any particularly brilliant airman who brought down a large number of enemy planes.

-acea, suff. [1. ásia; 2. éisiə]. Lat. neut. pl., sc. *animalia*, of *-āceus*, used in zoological terminology for names of orders and classes, as *Crustacea* &c.

-aceae, suff. [1. ásiē; 2. éisiī]. Lat. fem. pl., sc. *plantae*, of *-āceus*, used in botanical terminology for names of orders and families, as *Malvaceae* &c.

-acean, suff. [1. áshan; 2. éiʃən], fr. Lat. *-āceānus*. See prec. & **-an**; forming **a** adjs. = **-aceous**; **b** n., of members of orders in *-acea*: *a crustacean.*

acedia, n. [1. asédia; 2. əsídiə]. Med. Lat., fr. Gk. *akēdia*, 'torpor, indifference', fr. *akēdēs*, 'uncared for, unheeded; careless', fr. **a-** (priv.) & *kēdos*, 'care'. Sloth, torpor, lethargy, one of the seven deadly sins.

Aceldama, n. [1. aséldama; 2. əséldəmə]. Gk. *Akeldamá*, Acts i. 19. A field of bloodshed or slaughter.

-aceous, suff. [1. áshus; 2. éiʃəs], fr. Lat. *-āceus*, see **-acea** & **-ous**, used to form adjs. fr. zool. & bot. ns. in *-acea* & *-aceae.*

acephalous, adj. [1. aséfalus; 2. əséfələs], fr. Gk. *aképhalos*, 'headless', fr. **a-** (priv.) & *kephalḗ*, 'head'. See **cephalic**. Headless; specif. (zool.) having no part of the body specially differentiated as a head.

acerbity, n. [1. asérbiti; 2. əsǽbiti], fr. Fr. *acerbité*, Lat. *acerbitāt-(em)*, 'sourness, harshness', fr. *acerbus*, 'sour, harsh, unripe'. See **acrid**. **1.** Sourness, astringency of taste. **2.** (fig.) Sharpness, harshness, bitterness of temper, speech, actions, manner &c.

acerose, adj. [1. áserōs; 2. ǽsərous], fr. Lat. *acerōsus*, 'full of chaff, chaffy', fr. *acer-(is)*, *acus*, 'chaff'. See **awn**, & cp. **acrid**. Second sense as if fr. Lat. *acus*, 'needle'. (bot.) **a** Mixed with chaff; chaffy; **b** needle-shaped, as the leaves of pines.

acervate, adj. [1. asérvāt; 2. əsǽveit], fr. Lat. *acervāt-(um)*, P.P. type of *acervāre*, 'to heap up', fr. *acervus*, 'heap, pile'; etymol. doubtful. (bot.) Heaped up, growing in heaps or clusters, as certain fungi &c.

acetabulum, n. [1. àsetábūlum; 2. æ̀sətǽbjuləm]. Lat., 'a little cup for vinegar', fr. *acētum*, 'vinegar'. See **acetic**. (anat.) **1.** The cup-shaped socket of the hip into which the thigh bone fits. **2.** A sucker of an octopus, leech &c.

acetarious, adj. [1. àsetárius; 2. æ̀sitéəriəs]. Lat. *acētāria* (pl.), 'vegetables prepared with vinegar', fr. *acētum*, 'vinegar'. See **acetic** & **-ary** & **-ous**. (of plants) Used in salads, as lettuce, mustard and cress &c.

acetate, n. [1. ásetāt; 2. ǽsiteit]. See **acetic** & **-ate**. (chem.) A salt of acetic acid: *copper acetate*, verdigris.

acetic, adj. [1. asétik; 2. əsítik], fr. Lat. *acētum*, 'that which has grown sour', hence 'vinegar', & **-ic**; *acētum*, P.P. of vb. *acēre*, 'be sour', cogn. w. *ăcer*, 'sharp', see **acrid**. Pertaining to vinegar; specif. (chem.) *acetic acid*, organic acid compound found in juices of plants, giving its sour taste to vinegar.

acetify, vb. trans. & intrans. [1. asétifī; 2. əsítifai]. See prec. & **-fy**. **a** trans. To turn into vinegar; **b** intrans., to become sour.

acetone, n. [1. ásetōn; 2. ǽsitoun]. See **acetic** & **-one**. (chem.) The representative type of a group of organic compounds, *ketones*, q.v., derived from the distillation of wood alcohol or acetates.

acetous, adj. [1. asétus; 2. əsítəs]. See **acetic** & **-ous**. Pertaining to, producing, vinegar; sour: *acetous acid* (obs.), vinegar.

acetyl, n. [1. ásetil; 2. ǽsitil]. See **acetic** & **-yl**. (chem.) The radical or base of acetic acid.

acetylene, n. [1. asétilēn; 2. əsétilīn], fr. prec. & **-ene**. A colourless gas, compound of carbon and hydrogen, obtained by the action of water on calcium carbide, burning with a very bright white flame and having an unpleasant and powerful smell.

ache (I.), n. [1. āk; 2. eik]. O.E. **æce*, M.E. *āche*. In early Mod. Engl. the n. was normally pronounced [1. āch; 2. ētʃ]. The present pronunciation is due to anal. w. vb.; the infin. & 1st sing. pres. were in O.E. *acan*, *ace*, M.E. *āken*, *āke*. Cogn. w. Lat. *ag-ere*, 'set in motion', & numerous derived meanings. See **agent**. A pain, esp. a dull, continuous pain as opposed to a sudden sharp one; used both of physical pain (toothache, earache &c.) and mental or emotional sensations (heartache &c.).

ache (II.), vb. intrans. See prec. Present spelling due to that of noun. **1. a** (of a part of the body) To be continuously and dully painful: *my head, ear, arm &c. aches*; **b** (with pers. pron.) to suffer continuous, dull pain: *I am aching all over*. **2.** (fig.) Expressing strong longing for something: *I was aching to join in the fight*.

achene, n. [1. akḗn; 2. əkín], fr. Gk. **a-** (priv.) & *khainein*, 'to gape'. See **chaos**. (bot.) A small dry carpel containing a single seed, which does not burst when ripe.

Acheron, n. [1. ákeron; 2. ǽkərən]. Lat., fr. Gk. *Akhérōn*, fr. *ákhos*, 'grief, woe', fr. the base seen in **anguish**. (class. mythol.) The river of woe, one of the rivers of Hades, hence the infernal regions, the underworld.

Acheulian, adj. [1. ashúlian; 2. æʃjúliən], fr. Fr. *Acheulien*, fr. St. Acheul, France, where remains were first discovered. (archaeol.) Of, denoting, a stage of palaeolithic culture, succeeding the *Chellean* and preceding the *Mousterian*.

achieve, vb. trans. [1. achḗv; 2. ətʃív], fr. Fr. *achever*, 'to accomplish, complete', fr. *à chef venir*, fr. Low Lat. *ad caput venīre*, 'to come to a head (with)'. To gain, effect something, reach, esp. *to achieve one's purpose, object* &c.

achievement, n. [1. achḗvment; 2. ətʃívmənt]. Fr. *achèvement*. See **achieve** & **-ment**. **1.** Something completed, brought to successful conclusion, esp. by skill, valour, exertion, industry; an exploit. **2.** (her.) Hatchment.

Achilles tendon, n. [1. akílēz téndon; 2. əkílīz téndən]. Lat. *tendo Achillis*, from the legend of the infant Achilles being held by the heel when Thetis dipped him in Styx to render him invulnerable. (anat.) The tendon at the back of the heel, attached to the thick muscle of the calf.

achromatic, adj. [1. àkromátik; 2. æ̀kroumǽtik]. Gk. **a-**, 'lacking', & *khrôma*, *khrṓmatos*, 'colour', cp. Gk. *khroiá*, 'skin, colour, surface'. See **chrome**. Colourless; specif. (optics) *achromatic lens*, one which transmits white light without decomposing it into the component colours.

achromatism, n. [1. akrṓmatizm; 2. əkróumətizəm]. Prec. & **-ism**. Want of colour.

achromatize, vb. trans. [1. akrṓmatīz; 2. əkróumətaiz]. Prec. & **-ize**. To deprive of colour.

achromatopsy, n. [1. akrṓmatopsi; 2. əkróumətɔpsi]. See **achromatic** & **optic**. (lit.) Colour-lacking sight, i.e. colour-blindness.

acicular, aciculate, adjs. [1. asíkūlar, -lāt; 2. əsíkjulə, -leit], fr. Lat. *acicula*, dimin. of *acus*, 'needle', see **acrid** & **-ar** & **-ate**. (bot. and zool.) **a** Shaped like a needle, sharp-pointed; **b** having sharp, finely-pointed bristles or needles.

acid (I.), adj. [1. ásid; 2. ǽsid], fr. Lat. *acidus*, 'sour', cogn. w. *acētum*. See **acetic** & **acrid**. **1.** Sour, sharp, to the taste (of fruits, liquors &c.). **2.** (fig., of the temper, countenance, manner of speaking &c.) Ill-natured, testy, gloomy. **3.** (chem.) Having the essential properties of an acid. See **acid** (II.).

acid (II.), n., fr. prec. A sour substance, such as vinegar; specif. (chem.) a substance containing hydrogen from which salts are formed by substitution of the hydrogen by a metal, distinguished by turning blue vegetable colours, as litmus paper, red. Phr. *acid test*, a final, crucial test of anything, proving the true value, genuineness &c.; from the use of acid in proving gold.

acidify, vb. trans. & intrans. [1. asídifī; 2. əsídifai]. See **acid** (I.) & **-fy**. **1.** trans. **a** To make sour; specif. **b** (chem.) to convert into an acid. **2.** intrans. To become sour.

acidimeter, n. [1. àsidímeter; 2. æ̀sidímitə]. See **acid** (I.) & **-meter**. Instrument for measuring the strength of acids.

acidity, n. [1. asíditi; 2. æsíditi], fr. Lat. *aciditāt-(em)*. See **acid** (I.) & **-ity**. The quality of being acid or sour.

acidosis, n. [1. àsidṓsis; 2. æ̀sidóusis]. Hybrid form. See **acid** (I.) & **-osis**. (pathol.) A morbid bodily condition, found with diabetes &c., due to an accumulation of fatty acids in the blood and tissues.

acidulate, vb. trans. [1. asídūlāt; 2. æsídjuleit], fr. Lat. *acidulus*, 'slightly sour', dimin. of *acidus*. See **acid** (I.) & **-ate**. To make somewhat acid, to make acid in a moderate degree. (Rare.)

acidulated, adj. [1. asídūlāted; 2. æsídjuleitid]. P.P. of prec. Made somewhat acid or sour; **a** of things: *acidulated drops*; **b** of persons, temper &c.: *an acidulated old maid*.

aciform, adj. [1. ásiform; 2. ǽsifɔ̄m], fr. Lat. *acus*, 'needle'. See **acrid** & **-form**. (bot. and zool.) Sharp, fine, like a needle or bristle.

aciniform, adj. [1. asíniform; 2. æsínifɔ̄m]. See **acinus** & **-form**. (bot.) Having the form of an acinus; clustered, as the drupels of a berry.

acinus, n. [1. ásinus; 2. ǽsinəs]. Lat., 'cluster of grapes; berry'; etymol. doubtful. (bot.) **a** A fruit, as the blackberry, raspberry &c., composed of clustered drupels; **b** one of such drupels.

-acious, suff. [1. āshus; 2. éiʃəs], fr. Lat. *-ax*, *-acis*, & **-ous**, forming adjs. w. meaning 'given, tending to, abounding in, full of': *mendacious, tenacious* &c.

-acity, suff. [1. ásiti; 2. ǽsiti], fr. Lat. *-acitāt-(em)*, or Fr. *-acité*, forming ns. corresponding to adjs. in *-acious*: *mendacity, tenacity* &c.

acknowledge, vb. trans. [1. aknólej; 2. əknɔ́lidž], fr. **a-** & **knowledge**. **1.** To admit, own: *to acknowledge the necessity of a proceeding*. **2.** To recognize the authority, claims of: *acknowledge a man as one's superior*. **3. a** To own with gratitude and reward: *acknowledge kindness*; **b** state as a fact: *acknowledge receipt of a letter*. **4.** (law) To own as genuine, avow in legal form.

acknowledg(e)ment, n. [1. aknólejment; 2. əknɔ́lidžmənt]. See prec. & **-ment**. **1.** The act of acknowledging; an admission, confession, avowal (of a fault; of the existence, authority, or truth of a person or thing). **2.** The owning or recognition of a benefit, obligation, by expressing gratitude or giving something in return: *a small acknowledgement of kindness received*; *to bow one's acknowledgements* (*of applause* &c.).

aclinic, adj. [1. aklínik; 2. əklínik], fr. **a-** (priv.), Gk. *klinein*, 'to bend', & **-ic**. See **clinic**. (of magnetic needle) **a** Not dipping; **b** situated where the needle does not dip: *aclinic line*, the magnetic equator.

acme, n. [1. ákmi; 2. ǽkmi]. Gk. *akmḗ*, 'a point, edge', fig., 'flower of age, prime of life', cp. Gk. *akḗ*, 'point', Lat. *aciēs*, 'point, edge'; cogn. also w. Engl. **edge**. See also **acrid**. The top or highest culminating point, esp. (fig.) point of perfection &c.: *the acme of perfection, of one's hopes*.

acne, n. [1. ákni; 2. ǽkni]. Etymol. unknown; possibly corruption of prec. word. A common skin disease; a small hard pimple, chiefly affecting the forehead and nose or chest, caused by the blocking and inflammation of the sebaceous glands.

acolyte, n. [1. ákolīt; 2. ǽkəlait], fr. Low Lat. *acolythus*, Gk. *akólouthos*, 'a follower', cp. *akolutheō*, 'follow, go with', cogn. w. *kéleuthos*, 'road, track, journey', cp. Lith. *keliáuju*, 'I journey', & Lat. *callis*, 'footpath'. Cp. **anacoluthon**. (eccles.) **a** Person in minor orders in R.C. Church whose business it is to serve at Mass; layman who performs similar offices in Church of England; **b** (fig.) an assistant, devoted follower and attendant.

aconite, n. [1. ákonīt; 2. ǽkənait], fr. Fr. *aconit*, fr. Lat. *aconītum*, fr. Gk. *akónīton*, 'monk's-hood'; origin unknown. **1. a** The plant monk's-hood; **b** poisonous drug extracted from this. **2.** *Yellow Aconite*, Eranthis hiemalis.

acorn, n. [1. ákorn; 2. éikɔ̄n]. O.E. *æcern*, 'acorn', O.N. *akarn*, Goth. *akran*, 'fruit'. Some Engl. dialects pronounce the word [ætʃərn], wh. wd. appear to be the normal Mod. form fr. O.E. The exact ancestor of our form is, however, found in M.E. *ācorne*. It has been suggested that *æcern* was related to *æcer*, 'field', see **acre**, and meant simply 'fruits of the field'. This is doubtful. In any case the present form has been influenced by supposed connexion with *corn*. The fruit of the oak tree.

acotyledon, n. [1. akòtilḗdon; 2. əkɔ̀tilídən]. **a-** (priv.) & **cotyledon**. (bot.) Any plant which has no cotyledons, including all flowerless plants, such as mosses, lichens, ferns &c., now usually styled cryptogams.

acotyledonous, adj. [1. akòtilédonus; 2. əkɔ̀tilídənəs]. Prec. & **-ous**. (bot.) Having no cotyledons; cryptogamous.

acoustic, adj. & n. [1. akóustik; 2. əkáustik]. Fr. *acoustique*, Gk. *akoustikós*, fr. *akoúō*, 'I hear', earlier *kous-, cogn. w. Lat. *cus-tos*, 'guardian', see **custody** (idea of watching, listening), Goth. *hausjan*, 'hear', O.E. *hieran*, see **hear**. *a-* is fr. Aryan *sm̥, 'one', and is here copulative. See **simplex**. **1.** adj. Connected with sense of hearing, or with the physical theory of sounds. **2.** n. (gen. in pl.) *Acoustics*, the theory of sound; properties of audibility and resonance, dependent on the structural features and proportions of a building (theatre, lecture-hall &c.).

acquaint, vb. trans. [1. akwánt; 2. əkwéint], fr. O. Fr. *acointer*, fr. L. Lat. *accognitāre*, fr. Lat. *ad* & *cognit-(um)*, P.P. type of *cognoscere*, 'to get to know'. See **cognoscible**. **1. a** To inform, make aware of, let know: *to acquaint* (a person) *with* (a fact); also *acquaint* (person) *that*; **b** (reflex.) *acquaint oneself*, to acquire information concerning, to make oneself familiar *with*. **2.** (in pass.) *To be acquainted with* (a person or thing), to have personal knowledge of. Phrs. *to make one acquainted with* (things), to inform; (with persons) to introduce; also, archaic and liter.: *to bring (a person) acquainted with*.

acquaintance, n. [1. akwántans; 2. əkwéintəns], fr. O. Fr. *acointance*. See **acquaint** & **-ance**. **1.** Knowledge of (a person) gained by direct or epistolary intercourse, but not amounting to intimate friendship; (of facts) knowledge, without qualifications as to degree: *a slight, an intimate, acquaintance with astronomy*. **2.** A person with whom one is acquainted, whom one knows slightly, but not intimately, as distinct from a *friend*.

acquiesce, vb. intrans. [1. àkwiés; 2. æ̀kwiés]. Fr. *acquiescer*, Lat. *acquiescere*, 'to rest', fig., 'to rest, be satisfied, assent to', fr. *ad* & *quiescere*, 'to keep quiet'. See **ad-** & **quiescent**. To agree tacitly to, accept; consent unwillingly to a suggestion, plan, proposal &c.: *he will never acquiesce; they have acquiesced in his resignation.*

acquiescence, n. [1. àkwiésens; 2. æ̀kwiésəns]. Fr. See prec. & **-ence**. Passive compliance, assent, unenthusiastic consent.

acquiescent, adj. [1. àkwiésent; 2. æ̀kwiésənt]. Fr., fr. Lat. *acquiescent-(em)*, Pres. Part. of *acquiescere*. See **acquiesce**. Tacitly agreeing, consenting without protest, permitting.

acquiescently, adv. Prec. & **-ly**. In an acquiescent manner.

acquire, vb. trans. [1. akwír; 2. əkwáiə], fr. Lat. *acquīrere*, 'seek in addition, add to, acquire', fr. *ad* & *quaerere*, 'to seek, search', for **quais-ere*, perh. =*quā*, or some form of interrog. pron., & base **ais-*, 'ask', found in Scrt. *ēšati*, 'seeks, inquires', & **ask**. See **query, question**. **1.** To gain by and for oneself, through one's own efforts or actions: *to acquire the art of public speaking; to acquire a bad reputation*. **2.** To get as one's own, come into possession of, by whatever means: *acquire a title, wealth* &c.

acquired, adj. [1. akwírd; 2. əkwáiəd]. P.P. of prec. Of a quality or trait attained by practice or experience as distinct from what is inherited, innate, or natural, as *an acquired taste* &c.; specif. (biol.) *acquired characters*, mental or physical characteristics gained through influence of environment, and not inherited from parents.

acquirement, n. [1. akwírment; 2. əkwáiəmənt]. See **acquire** & **-ment**. **1.** The act of acquiring. **2.** That which is acquired; specif., an acquired mental faculty, accomplishment.

acquisition, n. [1. àkwizíshun; 2. æ̀kwizíʃən]. Lat. *acquisitiōn-(em)*, fr. *acquisīt-(um)*, P.P. type of *acquīrere*. See **acquire** & **-ion**. **1.** Act or process of acquiring: *the acquisition of money, land* &c. **2.** That which is acquired or gained, esp. something added to what already existed (of persons or things), in favourable sense: *the new member is a distinct acquisition to the party*.

acquisitive, adj. [1. akwízitiv; 2. əkwízitiv]. See prec. & **-ive**. Desirous, capable, of acquiring and retaining, tending to acquire and retain (knowledge, wealth, power &c.): *an acquisitive mind; the acquisitive instinct*.

acquisitiveness, n. Prec. & **-ness**. **1.** The desire, tendency, to acquire. **2.** (phren.) The supposed mental faculty to which is attributed this tendency.

acquit, vb. trans. [1. akwít; 2. əkwít], fr. O. Fr. *aquiter*, Lat. *ad* & *quiētāre*, 'to settle', fr. *quiēs*, *-ētis*, 'rest'. See **ad-** & **quiet**. **1.** To declare, after considering evidence, (a person) not guilty (*of* an offence); consider and declare (a person) not responsible for something done amiss, or as not possessing some bad quality of which he was suspected. **2.** (reflex.) To bear or conduct oneself, to perform one's part, to behave: *to acquit oneself well, ill*.

acquittal, n. [1. akwítal; 2. əkwítəl]. Prec. & **-al**. Specif. (law) the act of acquitting; a setting free from the charge of an offence by legal verdict.

acquittance, n. [1. akwítans; 2. əkwítəns]. O. Fr. *aquitance*. See **acquit** & **-ance**. Discharge from debt or other liability; the documentary evidence of such discharge; a receipt in full.

acre, n. [1. áker; 2. éikə]. O.E. *æcer*, 'field; land-measure', M.E. *āker*, O.H.G. *acchar*, Goth. *akrs*, 'field', cp. Lat. *ager*, under **agrarian**. **1.** A measure of land, 4840 sq. yds. **2.** A field, now only in special phrases, as *broad acres*, large property; *God's Acre*, churchyard.

acreage, n. [1. ákerij; 2. éikəridž]. **acre** & **-age**. The number of acres in a piece of land; acres collectively: *acreage of a farm* &c.; *reduce one's acreage*.

acrid, adj. [1. ákrid; 2. ǽkrid]. Formed on anal. of *acid* (Lat. *acidus*), fr. Lat. *ācer*, *ācris*, 'sharp, bitter', cp. Lat. *acus*, 'needle'; Gk. *ákris*, 'peak, hill-top', also *ákis*, 'point, barb', Scrt. *áçriš*, 'edge, slope', Lith. *asztrùs*, 'sharp', O. Slav. *osŭtŭ*, 'prickle', O.E. *egl*, 'awn, beard of barley', O.N. *eggja*, 'sharpen, incite'. See **egg** (on), vb., **edge, acid**. **1.** (of things) Bitter, stinging, irritating, esp. to the taste or smell. **2.** (fig., of persons, temper, disposition &c.) Bitter, cross-grained, irritating, caustic.

acridity, n. [1. akríditi; 2. ækríditi]. Prec. & **-ity**. Acridness.

acridness, n. [1. ákridnes; 2. ǽkridnis]. **acrid** & **-ness**. The quality of being acrid.

acrimonious, adj. [1. àkrimṓnius; 2. æ̀krimóuniəs]. See **acrimony** & **-ous**. (of non-material things) Bitter, rankling, embittered (of quarrel, strife &c.).

acrimoniously, adv. Prec. & **-ly**. In an acrimonious manner.

acrimony, n. [1. ákrimuni; 2. ǽkriməni], fr. Lat. *ācrimōnia*, 'sharpness, pungency', fr. *ācer*, *ācr-(is)*, 'sharp'. See **acrid** & **-mony**. Severity, harshness, bitterness, asperity of temper, manner, speech &c.

acrisia, n. [1. akrísia; 2. əkrísiə]. Gk. *akrisia*, fr. **a-**, neg. particle, & *krísis*, 'judgement'. See **critic**. (med.) A condition of disease which presents no decided symptoms from which diagnosis can be made.

acritical, adj. [1. akrítikl; 2. əkrítikəl], fr. prec. & **-al**. See **critical**. (med.) Giving no indications of a crisis.

acro-, pref., fr. Gk. *ákros*, 'at the end, topmost, outermost', fr. *aké*, 'edge'. See **acid, acrid**. At highest point; at the tip; extreme.

acrobat, n. [1. ákrobat; 2. ǽkrəbæt]. Fr. *acrobate*, fr. Gk. *akrobátein*, 'to walk on tiptoe', *akróbatos*, 'one who so walks', fr. *ákros*, 'tip' &c., & *bat-*, 'going', cp. *batós*, 'passable', fr. *bainō*, 'I go'. See **acro-** & **basis**. Highly skilled gymnast, tightrope walker, tumbler &c.

acrobatic, adj. [1. àkrobátik; 2. æ̀krəbǽtik]. Prec. & **-ic**. Pertaining to an acrobat or his performance.

acrobatics, n. pl., fr. prec. Acrobatic performances.

acrocarpous, adj. [1. àkrokárpus; 2. æ̀krəkā́pəs], fr. **acro-** & Gk. *karpós*, 'fruit', see **carpel**, & **-ous**. (bot.) Producing fruit at end of stalk.

acrocephalic, acrocephalous, adj. [1. àkrōsefálik, -séfalus,; 2. æ̀krousəfǽlik, -séfələs]. See **acro-** & **cephalic** & **cephalous**. Having a pointed skull.

acrogen, n. [1. ákrojen; 2. ǽkrədžən]. **acro-** & **-gen**. Lit. 'growing at the top'. Specif. (bot.) plant of cryptogam class, having a perennial stem whence fresh growths take place, as in ferns, mosses &c.

acrogenous, adj. [1. akrójenus; 2. əkrɔ́džənəs]. Prec. & **-ous**. (bot.) Belonging to the class of acrogens.

acrolith, n. [1. ákrolith; 2. ǽkrəliþ], fr. **acro-** & Gk. *líthos*, 'a stone'. See **litho-**. Ancient form of statue having the trunk of wood and the head and other extremities of stone.

acromegaly, n. [1. àkrōmégali; 2. æ̀kroumégəli]. Modern concoction fr. Gk. *ákros*, 'at the end, outermost, on the top', cp. *ákros*, 'peak, summit' &c., see **acro-**, & Gk. base *megal-* as in gen. &c. of *mégas*, 'great, tall, long' &c., q.v. under **mega-** & **megalo-**. (med.) Abnormal, permanent, and excessive enlargement of the extremities, involving esp. the head, hands, and feet.

acronycal, adj. [1. akrónikal; 2. əkrɔ́nikəl]. Gk. *akrónukhos*, 'at nightfall', fr. *akro-* (in sense of 'edge'), see **acro-**, & *núkh-(os)*, *núx*, see **night**. (astron.) Happening at nightfall or sunset; applied to the rising and setting of stars.

acronycally, adv. Prec. & **-ly**. At nightfall or sunset.

acropolis, n. [1. akrópolis; 2. əkrɔ́pəlis]. Gk. *akrópolis*, 'higher city', fr. **acro-** & *pólis*, 'city'. See **policy** (I.), **politic**. The fortified upper part or citadel of a Greek city, esp. that of Athens.

across, adv. & prep. [1. akráws; 2. əkrɔ́s], fr. **a-** & **cross** (III.). **1.** adv. **a** Crosswise; in a position or direction crossing the line of length transversely from side to side; athwart: *write across* (e.g. back of a letter); **b** in a position resulting from crossing: *to get across (river, road)*. **2.** prep. **a** (expressing direction) Forming a cross with; at an angle with; from side to side of; completely over: *a bridge across the river*; **b** (expressing motion, position) over in any direction except lengthwise; from one side to the other: *to run across the road; lie across the bed*. Phrs. *across country*, direct from point to point; not following the roads; *to run, come, across* (person or thing), to come into contact with, meet unexpectedly, by accident; *to get across a person*, quarrel with him; *to be across a horse's back*, ride.

acrostic, n. [1. akróstik; 2. əkrɔ́stik], fr. Gk. *akrostikhion*, fr. **acro-** & *stíkhos*, 'order, row, line', fr. *steikhein*, 'go, come, go in order, march'. Cogn. w. O.E. *stīgan*, 'go, rise'. See second element in **distich, stile** &c. **a** Poem, the initial letters of the lines of which form words: **b** problem, puzzle, the solution of which consists in discovering a series of words which, written one below another, spell other words when the initial, sometimes also the final and middle letters, are read from top to bottom.

acroterium, n., pl. **acroteria** [1. àkrōtḗrium, -ia; 2. æ̀kroutíəriəm, -iə]. Lat., fr. Gk. *akrōtḗrion*, 'summit, apex, top', fr. *ákros*, 'topmost'. See **acro-**. (class. archit.) **a** The plinth or pedestal for a statue or other ornamental figure, placed on the apex and lower corners of a pediment; **b** figure placed on such pedestal.

act (I.), n. [1. akt; 2. ækt]. Fr. *acte*, 'action', fr. Lat. *actus*, 'a moving, impulse', fr. *actum*, 'something done', P.P. of *agere*, 'set in motion, drive; do &c.; cogn. w. Gk. *ágein*, 'lead, guide, carry off', cp. Scrt. *ájati*, 'goes, drives', *ájiraš*, 'active, moving'. See further under **agent, agonistic**. **1.** A thing done; an action, deed, (good or bad) performance, exploit: *we are all responsible for our acts*; *act of kindness*; specif., *The Acts* (*of the Apostles*), New Testament book describing the history of the Early Church immediately after Our Lord's death; *act of God*, operation of natural forces, lightning, tempest, earthquake &c., esp. in causing disaster; something beyond human control; *act of grace*, something done voluntarily, not under compulsion or as part of a duty. **2.** Process of doing; action: *in the* (*very*) *act*; while doing something: *caught in the act*. **3.** Transaction of a legislative body; a legislative measure; the same embodied in a document: *Act of Parliament* (this fr. Lat. *acta*, neut. pl. of P.P. 'what has been done', a record of this). **4.** One of the main divisions of a play, in which the development of the action reaches a definite stage.

act (**II.**), vb. trans. & intrans., fr. prec. **A.** trans. (only of dramatic performance and fig. uses derived from this) **1.** (of a whole company) To perform (a play), represent (a story, incident &c.). **2.** (of a single person) **a** To personate, assume the character of, on the stage: *to act a, the, part* (*of*); *to act the Ghost in* '*Hamlet*'; **b** to simulate (a feeling), behave as: *to act outraged dignity, act the knave.* (fig.) *To act a part* (in bad sense), to play the hypocrite: *he is merely acting a part. To act the part of* (in good or bad sense), to fulfil the character or duties of: *to act the part of benefactor. To act one's part*, to do one's duty; *to act one's part well*, to fulfil the duties imposed on one. **B.** intrans. **1.** To perform actions, do things (in the widest sense); to take steps; to carry into effect by action ideas, decisions of the mind &c.: *the time for thinking is past; we must act immediately. To act as*, to do the work of, serve as: *to act as interpreter, guide* &c. *To act on, upon*, to behave in a certain way on account of something: *to act on an assumption*; *to act on someone's advice*; *to act on one's own responsibility* &c. *To act up to* (*one's reputation, ideals* &c.), to realize by one's actions a certain standard. **2.** To behave, comport, or bear oneself under given circumstances: *to act wisely, foolishly* &c. **3.** Specif., to perform on the stage; to follow profession of an actor. **4.** To take a specific part in a legal or other transaction: *to act on one's behalf*; *to act for one*; *to act in the matter.* **5.** (of things) To produce effects; fulfil proper functions; succeed: *the brake won't act*; special use (of the bowels), produce evacuation. *To act on*, to influence, affect: *acid acts on stone*; (of a drug) *to act on the stomach, heart* &c.

acting, n. & adj. [1. ákting; 2. ǽktiŋ]. Vbl. n. & Pres. Part. fr. **act** (**II.**). **1.** n. **a** Performance of a play on the stage: *a play unsuitable for acting*; **b** manner in which the actors play their parts: *bad, good, acting*; **c** exercise of the dramatic art: *fond of acting*. **2.** adj. Performing temporary services, holding temporary rank or position in another's absence, deputizing for, as *Acting Captain, Acting Manager*.

actinic, adj. [1. aktínik; 2. æktínik], fr. Gk. *aktīn-(os), áktīs*, 'ray, radiance, brightness', & **-ic**. Cogn. w. Scrt. *aktúš*, 'light'; Goth. *ūhtwō*, 'dawn', fr. **uŋχtwō*; in gradational relation to **night**. (phys.) Of, pertaining to, the ultra-violet, invisible rays of the spectrum which produce chemical change.

actinism, n. [1. áktinizm; 2. ǽktinizəm]. See prec. & **-ism**. **a** Property, possessed by ultra-violet rays, of producing chemical change; **b** chemical change effected by such rays.

actinium, n. [1. aktínium; 2. æktíniəm]. See prec. & **-ium**. A radio-active substance found in pitchblende, with actinic or chemical properties.

actino-, pref. Form, fr. **actinic**, used in compounds, signifying **a** (phys.) of, pertaining to, actinic rays or actinism; **b** (zool.) having a radial or radiated structure.

actinometer, n. [1. àktinómeter; 2. æ̀ktinɔ́mitə]. **actino-** & **-meter**. Instrument for measuring the actinic or chemical effect of ultra-violet rays.

actinomyces, n. [1. àktinōmísēz; 2. æ̀ktinoumáisīz]. See **actino-** & Gk. *múkēs*, 'fungus'. Cp. Gk. *múxa*, 'mucus', see **mucus**. (bacter.) A genus of minute parasitic rayed fungi.

actinomycosis, n. [1. àktinōmīkósis; 2. æ̀ktinoumaikóusis]. Prec. & **-osis**. (pathol.) An inflammatory disease, affecting cattle and, more rarely, man, marked by suppurating tumours in the jaw &c., and caused by infection by the actinomyces and other bacteria.

actinotherapy, n. [1. àktinothérapi; 2. æ̀ktinouþérəpi]. **actino-** & **therapy**. The use of actinic rays of light for healing diseases of the skin, tuberculosis of the joints &c.

actinozoa, n. [1. àktinōzóa; 2. æ̀ktinouzóuə]. **actino-** & **-zoa**. (zool.) A group of rayed polyps, including the corals and sea-anemones.

action, n. [1. ákshun; 2. ǽkʃən]. Fr. *action*, fr. Lat. *actiōn-(em)*, 'action', formed fr. base *act-*, cp. Lat. *actus* under **act** (**I.**), & **-ion**. **1.** Exertion of force or energy, process of doing or operating, departure from state of inertia and quiescence; used (without art.) of physical and mental process: *action of any kind is better than doing nothing*; *the Government promised to suspend all action for the moment*; *his mind seemed incapable of action.* Special uses: *conscious, unconscious, action*, performed as result of volition, without act of will. *Action* is often used with definite sense of contrast to inactivity, inertia: *a man of action* &c. Phrs. *to take action* (*in* a matter), begin to do something; *line, mode, of action*, form which action has; *action of the mind, mental action.* **2.** Specific act, or form of activity, deed, operation: *I resent his action in this matter*; *a pious, generous, spirited, mean, action.* **3.** Function, special series of movements peculiar and proper to an organ: *action of the heart, lungs, liver* &c. (med.) *Action of the bowels*, evacuation of excreta. **4.** Mode or style of bodily and physical movement: *fine, graceful, clumsy, action* (of a horse or human being in performing any natural movements). **5.** Characteristic direction or mode of movement of a machine: *reversible action*; hence, *to be put out of action*, (gen.) be deprived of power of action, be incapacitated. **6.** (chem. and phys.) Effects exerted by matter, heat, light: *action of acids* &c. **7.** (mil.) A battle, hostile encounter between opposing forces. Phrs. *to break off an action*, stop the battle; *to accept action*, engage in a battle. **8.** (law) A legal suit, or process. Phr. *to take, bring an, action* (*against*). **9.** The series of events and actions, or the representation of these (as distinct from portrayal of character and passion) in a play or narrative which make up the plot. **10.** (phys.) See **quantum theory**.

actionable, adj. [1. ákshunabl; 2. ǽkʃənəbl]. See **action** & **-able**. (law) Liable to, or giving cause for, an action at law.

active, adj. [1. áktiv; 2. ǽktiv]. Fr. *actif*, Lat. *actīvus*, fr. base *act-* as in P.P. of *agere*. See **act**. **1.** Inclined, disposed, to action or movement; nimble, agile, alert; used of mind and body: *active in one's movements*; *an active pair of legs*; *an active mind, brain, intelligence* &c.; *a man of active sympathies*, easily evoked. Phr. *as active as a kitten*, extremely active. **2.** Energetic, busy, bustling, used of persons, life, character &c.: *an active manager*; *to lead an active life*; *to be active in one's habits*; special use: *on active service*, in Army or Navy, engaged in fighting. **3.** Possessed of full or adequate powers of mind and body: *to be still active*; *not to be as active as one was.* **4.** Practical, actual, real, effective: *to take, play, an active part in affairs*; *to take an active interest in what is going on*; *to give active help.* **5.** Occupied in, with, involved in, having responsible part in: *to be an active party to a transaction*; *active list* in the Army or Navy, the list of those who have not retired from the Service. Phr. *on the active list*, still engaged in one's duties; (gen.) able to take part in affairs. **6.** Lively, subject to movement in various directions: *an active market, barometer.* **7.** (gram.) An *active verb* is one which has as a subject the name of the person or thing that performs the action which it expresses. Opposed to *passive*.

actively, adv. Prec. & **-ly**. In an active manner (with all senses of adj.).

activeness, n. See prec. & **-ness**. State of being active; activity.

activity, n. [1. aktíviti; 2. æktíviti], fr. Fr. *activité*, fr. Low Lat. *actīvitāt-(em)*. See **active** & **-ity**. State and quality of being *active* in mind and body. **1.** Agility, nimbleness, alertness; power of movement of mind and body. **2.** Normal bodily and mental power: *his time of full activity is past.* **3.** (in pl.) Specific doings in spheres of action: *the various activities of enemy spies in our midst are well known*; *his manifold activities were paralysed by the indifference of others*; *human activities*, any actions or enterprises carried out by men. **4.** Movement, liveliness: *activity of trade, of the market, of the legislature* &c.

acton, n. [1. áktun; 2. ǽktən]. O.F. *auqueton*, 'padded jacket', Span. *alcoton*, fr. Arab. *al-qutun*, 'the cotton'. See **cotton**. A stuffed jacket worn under the mail as additional protection in mediaeval times.

actor, n. [1. ákter; 2. ǽktə]. Lat., 'doer'. See **act** (**II.**) & **-or**. **a** One who plays a part in a drama on the stage; professional performer of plays; **b** (fig.) one who takes part in any notable action.

actress, n. [1. áktres; 2. ǽktris]. See prec. & **-ess**. A female performer of stage plays.

actual, adj. [1. áktūal, ákchooal; 2. ǽktjuəl, ǽktʃuəl], fr. Fr. *actuel*, fr. L. Lat. *actuālis*, fr. *act-us*, see **act** (**I.**) & **-al**. **1.** Really existing as a fact, as distinguished from potential or possible. **2.** In existence at the present moment: *the actual position.*

actuality, n. [1. àktūáliti, àkchooáliti; 2. æ̀ktjuǽliti, æ̀ktʃuǽliti], fr. Med. Lat. *actuālitāt-(em)*. See prec. & **-ity**. State of being actual; reality, realism.

actualization, n. [1. àktūalīzáshun; 2. æ̀ktjuəlaizéiʃən]. **actualize** & **-ation**. A making actual or real.

actualize, vb. trans. [1. áktūalīz, ákchooalīz; 2. ǽktjuəlaiz, ǽktʃuəlaiz]. **actual** & **-ize**. To make (a project, idea) actual, to realize in action; render real by description.

actually, adv. [1. áktūali, ákchooali; 2. ǽktjuəli, ǽktʃuəli]. **actual** & **-ly**. **a** At the present moment, now; **b** really, in truth; often used with statements which appear improbable: *he not only ran in the race, but actually won it.*

actuarial, adj. [1. àktūárial; 2. æ̀ktjuéəriəl]. **actuary** & **-al**. Pertaining to the theory by which insurance risks are estimated, and the premiums adjusted.

actuary, n. [1. áktūari; 2. ǽktjuəri]. Lat. *actuārius*, 'a clerk, registrar', fr. *acta*, 'events, records'. See *actum* under **act** (**I.**). An official in an insurance office who calculates insurance risks and fixes premiums according to tables of mortality &c.

actuate, vb. trans. [1. ǽktūeit, ákchooāt; 2. ǽktjueit, ǽktʃueit], fr. *actuāt-(um)*, P.P. type of Med. Lat. *actuāre*. See **act** (**I.**). To act upon, influence; to provide, serve as, motive for (action).

acuity, n. [1. akūiti; 2. əkjúiti], fr. Fr. *acuité*, fr. Low Lat. *acuitāt-(em)*, fr. *acus, -ūs*, 'a needle', cp. *acuere*, 'to sharpen'. See **acute** & also **acid, acrid**. **a** Sharpness (of a point); **b** intensity (of disease); **c** keenness (of wit, intelligence).

aculeate, adj. [1. akūliāt; 2. əkjúlieit], fr. Lat. *acūleāt-(um)*, fr. *acūleus*, dimin. of *acus*, 'needle'. See **acuity** & **-ate**. **a** (bot.) Having sharp prickles or points; **b** (zool.) having stings (of insects).

acumen, n. [1. akúmen; 2. əkjúmen]. Lat. *acūmen*, 'sharpened point', also 'mental sharpness, keenness of intelligence', fr. *acuere*, 'to sharpen'. See **acute**. Acuteness of mind; penetration.

acuminate, adj. [1. akúminat; 2. əkjúmineit], fr. Lat. *acūmināt-(um)*, P.P. of *acūmināre*, 'to sharpen', see **acumen** & **-ate**. (bot.) Pointed, tapering to a sharp point.

acupressure, n. [1. àkūprésher; 2. ækjuprésə], fr. Lat. *acus*, 'needle', see **acuity** & **pressure**. (med.) Method of checking bleeding by the pressure of a needle on the blood-vessel near the point of escape.

acupuncture, n. [1. àkūpúngkchur; 2. ækju-pŋktʃə], fr. Lat. *acus*, 'needle', see **acuity**, & **puncture**. (med.) A method of relieving pain, as in lumbago &c. by puncture of the inflamed part with a needle.

acute, adj. [1. akút; 2. əkjút], fr. Lat. *acūtus*, 'sharp-pointed', fr. *acuere*, 'to sharpen'. See **acid** & **acrid**. **1.** Sharp, pointed, coming to a sharp point; specif. (geom.) *an acute angle*, one less than a right angle, opposite to *obtuse*. **2. a** (of intellectual qualities) Keen, sharp, penetrating, shrewd; **b** (of the senses) keen, sharp. **3.** (of any emotional or physical condition) Intense, severe, poignant: *acute pain, pleasure, jealousy* &c. **4.** (of sounds) Sharp, shrill, high. **5.** (of writing and print.) *Acute accent*, line sloping from right to left, placed over letter, as Fr. *é*. **6.** (med., of a disease &c.) Severe; in the stage of violent symptoms, when the suffering is most intense; as distinct from *chronic*.

acutely, adv. Prec. & **-ly**. Sharply, keenly (of the senses, feelings, and mental faculties).

acuteness, n. See prec. & **-ness**. **a** The quality of being acute (of mental faculties, senses, emotions); **b** (med., of disease) condition of being severe, intense.

-acy, suff. [1. asi; 2. əsi]. Fr. *-atie*, Lat. *-acia*. Used in forming abstract nouns, which arose **a** fr. adjectives w. stem *-aci-* (nom. *-ax*: *fallax, fallaci-*); or **b** fr. adj. of *-ātus* type, Engl. *-ate*, when corresponding noun in Lat. is formed in *-ātio*, Med. Lat. *-ātia*, whence Fr. *-atie* [asī]. The suffix has been widely extended by analogy in Fr. and Engl., and forms abstract nouns also fr. concrete nouns in *-ate*: *magistrate, magistracy*.

ad-, pref., fr. Lat. prep. *ad*, 'to' &c., cogn. w. Gmc. *at*, as in Goth., O.S.; O.H.G. *az*, O.E. *æt*, 'at, near, from'. The word has various meanings in Lat.: direction towards, with or without motion; proximity, near to, by, at; up to, about, a certain time or number. In composition *ad-* expresses: (1) motion to; (2) addition; (3) completion; (4) nearness; (5) award to; (6) beginning of an action. The form remains unchanged before vowels & *b, d, h, m, v*; before *c, f, g, l, n, p, r, s, t*, the *d* in *ad* is assimilated, & it becomes *ac-, af-, ag-, al-* &c. The above applies to words direct fr. Lat. In O. Fr. *ad-* normally becomes *a-*, but in many words it was later Latinized, either in Fr. or Engl. The process is often carried further in Engl., wh. may have *ad-* in words where M.E. & Fr. retain the older *a-* form.

-ad, suff. **1.** From Gk. *-ad* as in *triad*, the number three, fr. Gk. *triás*, genit. *triád-os*, used **a** to form collective numerals; **b** in fem. patronymics, *dryad* &c.; **c** names of poems, '*Iliad*'; **d** names of plants, *liliad*. **2.** From Fr. *-ade*, as in *ballad*. See **-ade**.

adage, n. [1. ádij; 2. ædidž]. Fr. *adage*, fr. Lat. *adagium*, 'adage, proverb', fr. **ad-** & *agi-*, fr. base of *aiō*, fr. **agjō*, 'I say, relate'; cp. Gk. *ēmí* for **ēgmi*, 'speak'. Cp. **prodigy**. An old saying, a proverbial maxim, a proverb.

adagio, adv. & n. [1. adáhjō; 2. ədádžou]. Ital., 'leisurely'. (mus.) **a** adv. Slowly, leisurely; **b** n., a slow movement.

Adam, n. [1. ádam; 2. ædəm]. Heb. Name of the first man; hence, human frailty, sin: *the old Adam*, unregenerate human nature. Phrs. *Adam's ale, Adam's wine*, water; *Adam's apple*, the prominence in a man's throat, the thyroid cartilage of the larynx; (colloq.) *not to know (a person) from Adam*, not to know at all.

adamant, n. [1. ádamant; 2. ædəmənt]. O. Fr., fr. Lat. *adamas, adamantis*, 'hardest iron or steel', & fig. of character, 'unyielding, inexorable'; fr. Gk. *adámas, adámantos*, same meaning as in Lat.; fr. **a-** (priv.) & *damáō*, 'I tame', cogn. w. Lat. *domāre*, 'tame, subdue', & *domitāre*, 'break in', &c. See **daunt**. **a** A hard, unyielding stone such as the diamond; **b** any hard, unyielding substance, esp. in Phr. *as hard as adamant*, and fig. (of the character, resolution, will &c.): *adamant to entreaties, temptations* &c.

adamantine, adj. [1. adamántīn; 2. ædəmæntain), fr. prec. & **-ine**. **1.** Made of, having the qualities of, adamant; unbreakable: '*adamantine chains*' (Milton). **2.** (fig., of non-material qualities) Firm, unyielding: *adamantine courage* &c.

Adamite, n. [1. ádamīt; 2. ædəmait], fr. **Adam** & **-ite**. **1.** Descendant of Adam; human being. **2.** Member of a sect which abandoned clothes in imitation of Adam.

adapt, vb. trans. [1. adápt; 2. ədæpt], fr. Fr. *adapter*, fr. Lat. *adaptāre*, 'to fit to'. See **ad-** & **apt**. **1. a** (of material things) To make to fit in a new place or to alter in such a way as to make more suitable for a particular place or purpose; special uses: (i.) *to adapt a play*, or *to adapt a novel* so as to make it suitable for dramatic representation; (ii.) to give a new application to: *Pope adapted Horace*; **b** (of non-material things) to make fit for, make suitable to, accommodate, chiefly to the mental and intellectual capacities and to the habits and customs of others: *to adapt one's remarks to one's audience*; *to adapt one's behaviour, manners &c. to one's company*; *to adapt plans to suit new circumstances* &c. **2.** (reflex.) *Adapt oneself to*, to shape, modify, one's conduct, habits &c., so as to make them more suitable or agreeable to others: *to adapt oneself to one's company, social surroundings* &c.

adaptability, n. [1. adáptabíliti; 2. ədæptəbíliti]. See next word & **-ity**. The quality of being adaptable; capacity of being made suitable, fit, for new purpose or place; power of fitting oneself for situation, of modifying one's habits, desires, manners, to suit one's surroundings &c.

adaptable, adj. [1. adáptabl; 2. ədæptəbl], fr. **adapt** & **-able**. (See various senses of this vb.) **a** (of things) Capable of being adapted; **b** (of persons) able to adapt oneself to circumstances &c., pliable; also in bad sense.

adaptation, n. [1. àdaptáshun; 2. ædæptéiʃən]. See **adapt** & **-ation**. **a** The act or process of making a thing fit, of altering it to make it more suitable for a place or purpose; **b** that which is so adapted.

adapted, adj. [1. adápted; 2. ədæptid], fr. P.P. of **adapt**. Suitable, convenient, proper, fit, for a particular purpose (with *for*): *clothes adapted for winter wear*. (The sense of alteration to make suitable, seen in vb., is lost in the adj.)

ad captandum, adj. [1. ád kaptándum; 2. æd kæptændəm], fr. Lat. phr. *ad captandum vulgus*, for 'capturing the mob'. See **captive**. Calculated, intended, to attract the notice, fancy, of the public (esp. in bad sense), superficially attractive: *ad captandum arguments*.

add, vb. trans. & intrans. [1. ad; 2. æd], fr. Lat. *addere*, 'put to, lay on, give in addition'. See **ad-**; second element is fr. Lat. *dare*, 'place, put, give', of wh. see base under **date (I.)**, **donation**. **A.** trans. **1. a** To join one thing to another; increase the amount of something: *to add milk to one's tea*; *to add more water*; Phr. *to add insult to injury*; **b** to combine two or more numbers into a single sum; compute sum total resulting from such a combination of numbers. **2.** To make further statement, say further. **B.** intrans. *Add to*, to increase the sum of, make addition to: *it adds to my pleasure to see you here today*.

addax, n. [1. ádaks; 2. ædæks]. Lat., orig. a native African word. A North African and Arabian antelope with spiral horns.

added, adj. [1. áded; 2. ædid], fr. P.P. of **add**. Increased, additional: *an added sorrow, pleasure* &c.

addendum, n. [1. adéndum; 2. ædéndəm]. Lat., 'that which must be added', gerundive of *addere*. See **add**. Something added; an appendix or addition, esp. to a literary work or document; (in pl.) *addenda*, of a series of additions.

adder, n. [1. áder; 2. ædə]. O.E. *nǣddre*, M.E. *naddere, addere* &c., O.S. *nādra*, O.H.G. *nātara*; Goth., w. different gradation vowel, *nadrs*; cogn. w. Lat. *natrix*, 'water snake', & ultimately connected w. base in Lat. *nēre*, 'spin, interlace, entwine', q.v. under **needle**, fr. the serpent's habit of writhing & coiling. The Mod. Engl. form is fr. *an adder* for *a nadder*. See similar loss of initial *n-* in **umpire**. Name given to various poisonous snakes of the viper family; the common adder, or viper, is the only poisonous British snake.

addict (I.), vb. trans. [1. adíkt; 2. ədíkt]. Lat. *addictus*, P.P. of *addīcere*, 'to award, assign, devote to', fr. *ad*, 'to', & cp. *dicāre*, 'to dedicate', *dīcere*, 'tell, declare, show', q.v. under **diction**, **indicate** &c. **a** To devote, give up (*to*), habituate, accustom (one's mind, obs.); **b** (now only reflex.) to give oneself up to (a practice, habit): *to addict oneself to vice, to scientific studies* &c.

addict (II.), n. [1. ádikt; 2. ædikt], fr. prec. Person addicted to some habit, esp. to bad habits, such as drug-taking &c.

addicted, adj. [1. adíkted; 2. ədíktid], fr. P.P. of **addict (I.)**. Devoted or given up *to* a practice; attached, prone *to*; (chiefly in bad sense) given up to bad habits: *addicted to drink*; *addicted to stealing* &c.

addiction, n. [1. adíkshun; 2. ədíkʃən]. Act of addicting; state of being addicted or devoted *to* a habit &c.; propensity.

Addison's disease, n. [1. ádisunz dizéz; 2. ædisənz dizíz], fr. its discoverer, Dr. Addison, 1855. A disease marked by progressive anaemia, asthenia, and discoloration of the skin &c., caused by loss of function in the suprarenal glands.

addition, n. [1. adíshun; 2. ədíʃən]. Fr., fr. Lat. *additiōn-(em)*, fr. *addit-(um)*, P.P. type of *addere*, see **add** & **-ion**. **a** The act and process of adding; specif., in arithmetic, the uniting of two or more numbers into one sum; extended in mathematics to express the process of simplifying, by grouping into one expression, a series of terms connected by positive and negative signs; Phr. *in addition (to)*, also, as well as, over and above; additionally; **b** that which is added: *addition to one's income, family*; **c** (her.) something added to a coat of arms as a mark of honour.

additional, adj. [1. adíshunal; 2. ədíʃənəl]. See **addition** & **-al**. Coming as an addition, added, supplementary.

additionally, adv. Prec. & **-ly**. In addition.

addle, adj. (only in compounds), vb. trans. & intrans. [1. ádl; 2. ædl]. O.E. *adel*, 'putrid mud, filth'; cp. M.L.G. *adele*, 'mud'. **1.** adj. In such phrases as *addle-head, addle-pate*, empty, muddle-headed. **2.** vb. **a** trans. To cause to become addled, (chiefly fig.) to muddle, confuse: *to addle one's head* or *brain*; **b** intrans., to grow addled (of eggs).

addled, adj. [1. ádld; 2. ædld], fr. M.E. *adele*, 'mud', see prec., & **-ed**. **a** (only of eggs) Rotten, incapable of producing a chicken; **b** (fig., of the brain) confused, muddled.

address (I.), vb. trans. [1. adrés; 2. ədrés]. Fr. *adresser*, fr. Low Lat. *addrictiāre* for *-direct-*. See **direct** & **dress (I.)**. **1.** To make straight, direct the course of, aim. (obs. except in golf) *To address the ball*, to take aim at the ball, adjusting the position of the body and the grip on the club so that the ball, when hit, shall take the desired course. **2.** To indicate by an inscription the person to whom and the place at which a thing is to be delivered: *to address a letter, parcel* &c. (*to* a person). Special use: (of ships) to consign to an agent. **3. a** To direct speech, words, prayers &c. *to* a person: *to address one's remarks to*; (reflex.) *to address oneself to a person*; **b** to speak directly to; deliver a speech, sermon &c. to: *to address a person, an audience, a meeting, one's constituents* &c. **4.** (reflex.) To apply oneself *to*, direct one's energies *to*, an object: *to address oneself to a task.*

address (II.), n., fr. prec. **1. a** The indication inscribed on or attached to anything sent by messenger, post, or any mode of transit (e.g. letter, parcel, package &c.) stating name of recipient and place at which it is to be delivered; **b** the place where a person resides and to which his or her letters are to be addressed: *to change one's address.* **2. a** A formal speech of congratulation, thanks, petition &c.; specif., *the Address*, the reply to the King's Speech in the Houses of Parliament at beginning of a Parliament or Session; **b** a speech, lecture, sermon &c. to an audience; **c** manner of speaking, conversational bearing: *a man of pleasing address.* **3.** Graceful skill and tact, esp. in the conduct of affairs: *he had all the address of an accomplished diplomat.* **4.** (pl.) Courtship of a lady: *to pay one's addresses to a lady.*

addressee, n. [1. àdresé; 2. ædresí], fr. **address (I.)** & **-ee.** Person to whom letter &c. is addressed.

adduce, vb. trans. [1. adús; 2. ədjús], fr. Lat. *addūcere*, 'to lead or bring to', fr. **ad-** & *dūcere*, 'to lead', see **duct.** To bring forward in a statement (written or spoken) as evidence or illustration; to cite, allege (arguments, reasons &c.) in support of or as proof of a statement or case.

adducent, adj. [1. adúsent; 2. ədjúsənt]. Prec. & **-ent.** (anat., of muscles) Having the function of drawing together certain parts of the body; adductor; opposed to *abducent.*

adducible, adj. [1. adúsibl; 2. ədjúsibl], fr. **adduce** & **-ible.** Capable of being adduced.

adduct, vb. trans. [1. adúkt; 2. ædákt]. See **adduce.** (anat., of muscles) To draw (parts of the body) together.

adduction, n. [1. adúkshun; 2. ədákʃən]. Fr., fr. Lat. *adductiōn-(em).* See prec. & **-ion.** (anat.) The act of adducting; the action by which parts of the body are drawn together or a limb drawn towards the axis of the body.

adductor, adj. & n. [1. adúkter; 2. ədáktə], fr. **adduct** & **-or.** (anat.) **a** adj. Adducent; **b** n., adducent muscle.

-ade, suff. [1. ād; 2. eid]. **1.** Fr., in words borrowed fr. Span. or Port. *-ada*, Lat. *-āta*, fem. sing. of P.P. of 1st conj. The regular Fr. development is *-ée*, wh. has often been replaced by above, though *-ée* is found in O. Fr. A living suff. used in formation of various words: *lemonade, masquerade, ambuscade.* **2.** Fr. *-ade*, as in *decade*, fr. Gk. *-ad.* See **-ad.** **3.** From Span. or Ital. *-ado*: *renegade.*

ademption, n. [1. adémpshun; 2. ədémpʃən]. Lat. *ademptiōn-(em)*, fr. *adempt-(um)*, P.P. type of *adimere*, 'to take away', fr. *ad* & *emere*, 'to buy', orig. 'to take'. See **exempt**, & cp. **redemption.** (law) Revocation of grant or bequest.

adenoid, adj. [1. ádenoid; 2. ǽdənɔid], fr. Gk. *adḗn*, genit. *adénos*, 'acorn, gland', & **-oid.** *Adḗn* is fr. Aryan **ŋgʷēn*, & is cogn. w. Lat. *inguen*, 'groin, generative organs', & w. O.N. *økkuen*, & O.H.G. *ancweiz*, 'pustule, swelling'. Orig. sense of base seems to have been 'swelling', then 'gland', & as the Lat. & Gk. cognates show, it was variously applied to glands generally. Gland-like, glandular: *adenoid growth.*

adenoids, n. pl., fr. prec. (med.) Growths in back of the nose, near the throat, which cause defects in speaking and breathing. So named from shape, 'like an acorn'.

adept, adj. & n. [1. adépt ádept; 2. ədépt, ǽdept], fr. Lat. *adeptus*, 'reached, attained', P.P. of *adipisci*, 'to arrive at, reach, attain to, obtain', fr. **ad-** & *apiscor*, 'reach, come up with', ultimately a freq. of **apio*, 'bind', see **copula** for *co-apula*; cogn. w. Lat. *aptus*, 'attached to', see **apt**, & *apud*, 'near, by, with'. Cp. further Scrt. *āpnóti*, 'reaches, gains', *āpta*, 'clever, skilful'. **1.** adj. Well-skilled, thoroughly proficient, expert. **2.** n. One who is proficient or well-skilled, expert, *in* anything (esp. an art, science, profession &c.); (colloq.) *an adept at* (prob. on the anal. of *very good at*). Specif. (formerly) an alchemist who had discovered, or was supposed to have discovered, the Philosopher's Stone; now applied to a person (esp. in Buddhism) who as a mystic thinker and ascetic has attained to knowledge of the mysteries of nature and science.

adequacy, n. [1. ádekwasi; 2. ǽdikwəsi]. See **adequate** & **-acy.** The state or quality of being adequate; sufficiency in amount, quality, or mental equipment for a given purpose.

adequate, adj. [1. ádekwit, -kwat; 2. ǽdikwit, -kwət], fr. Lat. *adaequātum*, P.P. of *adaequāre*, 'to make equal to'. See **ad-** & **equal.** Equal to, commensurate with, a requirement or occasion, fully sufficient for a purpose; proportional to a specific need; **a** (of material things) *adequate amount, quantity* &c.; **b** (of non-material things) *adequate intelligence, mental qualities*; **c** (of causes) reasonably sufficient to justify an action: *adequate reasons* &c.; **d** (gen. of persons) competent: *to be quite adequate to one's post.*

adequately, adv. Prec. & **-ly.** In an adequate manner; to an adequate extent, amount.

ad eundem, adj. & adv. [1. ad eúndem; 2. æd iándem]. Lat., sc. *gradum*, 'to the same degree'. **ad-** & acc. sing. of **idem**, 'same'. Of admission of a graduate of one university to the same degree at another without further examination.

adhere, vb. intrans. [1. ad-hḗr; 2. ədhíə], fr. Lat. *adhaerēre*, 'to stick to, cling to', fr. **ad-** & *haerēre*, 'to stick, cling'; P.P. *haesum.* Prob. cogn. w. Goth. *(us)gaisnan*, 'to be frightened', & w. Lith. *gaisztú*, 'hesitate', *gaiszínti*, 'hinder'; further w. O.H.G. *gīsal*, O.E. *ġīsl*, 'hostage', i.e. 'one who is held fast as a pledge'. Cp. **cohere** & **hesitate.** (with *to* when followed by n.) **1.** (of things) To stick fast, be firmly attached *to*, as mud to clothes, a stamp to an envelope. **2.** (of persons) **a** To hold to, cleave to, be faithful to, give allegiance *to* a person, party, cause, institution, school of thought &c.; **b** to persevere in, stick *to*, an opinion, habit, project, duty &c. (often with implication of opposition, hindrance &c.).

adherence, n. [1. ad-hḗrens; 2. ədhíərəns], fr. **adhere** & **-ence.** (only fig.) Spiritual or mental act or condition of adhering to or being attached to a cause or set of opinions.

adherent, adj. & n. [1. ad-hḗrent; 2. ədhíərənt]. Fr. *adhérent*, fr. Lat. *adhaerent-(em)*, Pres. Part. of *adhaerēre.* See **adhere. 1.** adj. (only of things) Sticky, clinging, attached. **2.** n. (only of persons) One who adheres to or supports a person, party, or system; a follower, supporter *of.*

adhesion, n. [1. ad-hḗzhun; 2. ədhíʒən], fr. Fr. *adhésion*, fr. Lat. *adhaesiōn-(em)*, fr. *adhaes-(um)*, P.P. type of *adhaerēre.* See **adhere** & **-ion. 1.** The physical or material action or condition of adhering or sticking to a thing; the cleaving together of two substances in contact, united by glue, cement &c. (Sometimes confused with, and used figuratively for, *adherence.*) **2. a** (surg.) The reuniting of parts that have been severed; **b** (path.) the union of adjacent parts as a result of inflammation.

adhesive, adj. [1. ad-hḗsiv; 2. ədhísiv]. Fr. *adhésif*, fr. Lat. *-īvus.* See prec. & **-ive.** Sticky, clinging, made so as to stick, as *adhesive plaster*; (also fig.) of persons in habit of thrusting their company upon one, difficult to shake off.

adhesively, adv. Prec. & **-ly.** In an adhesive manner.

adhesiveness, n. See prec. & **-ness.** The quality of being adhesive; stickiness.

adhibit, vb. trans. [1. ad-híbit; 2. ədhíbit], fr. Lat. *adhibit-(um)*, P.P. type of *adhibēre*, 'to hold to, apply to', fr. **ad-** & *habēre*, 'to hold', see **habit.** (rare) **a** To attach, affix; **b** to administer (remedies &c.).

ad hoc, adj. [1. ád hók; 2. ǽd hɔ́k]. Lat., 'for this purpose'. Designed for a particular purpose, specially made, prepared &c.

adiabatic, adj. [1. àdiabátik; 2. æ̀diəbǽtik], fr. Gk. *adiábatos*, 'impassable', fr. **a-** (priv.), *día*, 'through', & *batós*, 'passable', fr. stem of *baínein*, 'to go, pass'. See **basis.** (phys.) Impervious to heat, denoting a change of volume, by compression or expansion, without gain or loss of heat.

adiantum, n. [1. àdiántum; 2. æ̀diǽntəm]. Lat., fr. Gk. *adianton*, 'maidenhair', neut. sing. of *adíantos*, 'unwetted', fr. **a-** (priv.) & *diaínein*, 'to wet, moisten'; etymol. doubtful. (bot.) A genus of ferns, the maidenhair ferns.

adiaphora, n. pl. [1. àdīáfora; 2. æ̀daiǽfərə]. Gk., neut. pl. of *adiáphoros*, 'indifferent', fr. **a-** (priv.) & *diáphoros, diaphérein*, 'to differ', cp. next word. See **dia-** & **-phore.** (Prot. theol.) Things that are indifferent or not essential, as certain matters of ritual or ceremonial observance.

adiaphoresis, n. [1. adīaforḗsis; 2. ædàiəfəríːsis], fr. **a-** (priv.) & **diaphoresis**, 'carrying through', q.v. (med.) Absence of adequate perspiration.

adieu, interj. & n. [1. adú; 2. ədjú] or as Fr. [adjø]. Fr. *à*, 'to', & *Dieu*, 'God', fr. Lat. *deum.* See **deity, divine (I.). 1.** interj. Greeting on taking farewell; good-bye. **2.** n. (pl. *adieux*) [1. adúz; 2. ədjúz]. A farewell, a leave-taking: *to make one's adieux.*

ad infinitum, adv. [1. ad infinítum; 2. æd infináitəm]. Lat., 'for ever, without ceasing'. See **infinite.**

ad interim, adv. [1. ad ínterim; 2. æd íntərim]. Lat. See **interim.** Meanwhile, temporarily.

adipocere, n. [1. àdiposḗr; 2. æ̀dipousíə], fr. Lat. *adeps, adipis*, 'soft animal fat', & *cēra*, 'wax'. See **adipose** & **cere.** A waxy or oily substance into which the soft tissues of dead animal bodies are converted when exposed to moisture.

adipose, adj. & n. [1. ádipōs; 2. ǽdipous], fr. Lat. *adeps, adipis*, 'fat of animals', & **-ose.** *Adeps*, Low Lat. *alipes*, is borrowed fr. Gk. *áleipha*, 'unguent, oil used in funeral sacrifices'; the class. Lat. form perh. influenced by *adep-tus*, fr. *adipiscor*, see **adept**; the Gk. word has a derived vb. *aleíphō*, 'anoint', & there is also *alinein*, 'anoint', cogn. w. Lat. *linīre*, 'to smear'. See **liniment. 1.** adj. Fat, fatty: *adipose tissue.* **2.** n. Animal fat.

adiposity, n. [1. àdipósiti; 2. æ̀dipɔ́siti]. Prec. & **-ity.** State of being fat; obesity.

adit, n. [1. ádit; 2. ǽdit], fr. Lat. *aditus*, 'an approach', fr. P.P. type of *adīre*, 'to approach', fr. *ad* & *īre*, 'to go'. The Aryan base **ei-, *ej-, *i-* &c., 'go', is found in various forms in most of the derived languages. See further under **itinerate.** An approach, entrance; specif., a horizontal opening into a mine.

adjacency, n. [1. ajásensi; 2. ədžéisənsi]. See next word & **-cy.** The state of being adjacent.

adjacent, adj. [1. ajásent; 2. ədžéisənt], fr. Lat. *adjacent-(em)*, Pres. Part. type of *adjacēre*, 'to lie at or near', fr. **ad-** & *jacēre*, 'to lie', lit. 'cast oneself down'. This vb. is related to the other Lat. vb. *jacio*, infin. *jacere*, 'cast, hurl'. See **jactitation** & **jet (III.).** Lying near to, neighbouring, but not necessarily in contact with: *adjacent villages, houses* &c.

adjacently, adv. Prec. & **-ly**. In an adjacent place, close to.

adjectival, adj. [1. àjektíval; 2. ǽdžiktáivəl]. **adjective** & **-al**. Having character or function of an adjective; related to the adjective.

adjectivally, adv. Prec. & **-ly**. By means of an adjective.

adjective, n. [1. ájektiv; 2. ǽdžiktiv], fr. Lat. *adject-īvus*, 'added', fr. P.P. type of *adjicere*, 'throw to, add', fr. **ad-** & *jacere*, 'to throw', see *jacere*, under **adjacent**, & **-ive**. (gram.) Part of speech expressing a quality or attribute, further limiting, defining, and describing the thing expressed by a noun.

adjoin, vb. trans. & intrans. [1. ajóin; 2. ədžóin]. See **ad-** & **join**. **1.** trans. To join on to, lie next to, be in contact with, be united to; (loosely) to be very near to (of houses, land &c.): *the field adjoins the house.* **2.** intrans. To be in contact or in close proximity: *the two houses adjoin.*

adjoining, adj. [1. ajóining; 2. ədžóiniŋ]. Pres. Part. of prec. Being in contact, neighbouring, adjacent (of houses, land &c.).

adjourn, vb. trans. & intrans. [1. ajérn; 2. ədžə́n), fr. O. Fr. *ajorner*, fr. Low Lat. *adjurnāre*, fr. *ad* & *jurnus*, 'day', Lat. *diurnus*, 'daily', fr. *dies*, 'day'. See **journal**, **diurnal**. **A.** trans. To put off till another day, or from day to day, to postpone; esp. of deliberative and legislative bodies, *to adjourn a meeting*, to put off or postpone its further proceedings, to put an end to its activities for the day in order to resume and continue them at another time. **B.** intrans. **1.** (of an assembly of persons) To suspend business, joint proceedings &c., and disperse either for an agreed or an indefinite period of time (*sine die*). **2.** (colloq.) To go to another place (lit., put off further conversation in actual place): *to adjourn to the drawing-room.*

adjournment, n. [1. ajérnment; 2. ədžə́nmənt]. Prec. & **-ment**. **1.** The act of adjourning or putting off. **2.** The state of being adjourned; the time for which a legislative or deliberative body adjourns: *a week's adjournment* &c.

adjudge, vb. trans. [1. ajúj; 2. ədžádž], fr. O. Fr. *ajuger*. See **ad-** & **judge**. **1.** To arrive at and pronounce a judicial decision in regard to a person or matter: *to adjudge a man guilty.* **2.** To award something (as costs in legal action, prize in a competition &c.) to a person as a result of judicial consideration.

adjudgement, n. [1. ajújment; 2. ədžádžmənt]. Prec. & **-ment**. A judicial decree or award.

adjudicate, vb. trans. & intrans. [1. ajóōdikāt; 2. ədžū́dikeit], fr. Lat. *adjūdicāt-(um)*, P.P. type of *adjūdicāre*, 'to adjudge, decide, impute, ascribe', fr. **ad-** & *jūdicāre*, 'to judge'. See **judge**, **judicial**. **1.** trans. (of a judge or court) To come to and pronounce a judicial decision concerning a person or matter: *to adjudicate a claim* &c. **2.** intrans. (adjudicate *on* a matter, *in* a case) To sit as a judge and give judicial decision.

adjudication, n. [1. ajóōdikáshun; 2. ədžū̀dikéiʃən]. Prec. & **-ion**. Legal finding of a judge or court; sentence or award; specif., decree in bankruptcy.

adjudicator, n. [1. ajóōdikāter; 2. ədžū́dikeitə]. See prec. & **-or**. One who settles a controversy, or awards a prize.

adjunct, n. [1. ájungkt; 2. ǽdžaŋkt], fr. Lat. *adjunctum*, neut. sing. of P.P. of *adjungere*, 'to join'. See **ad-** & **junction**. **1.** Something joined or added to another thing, but subordinate to and not an essential part of it: *a mere adjunct*; *a cushion is a useful adjunct to a sofa*; (also of persons) a person joined to, or associated with, another or others in some office, service &c. **2.** (gram.) Words added to amplify other words; an adjective, adjectival phrase, adverb or adverbial phrase. **3.** (logic) A non-essential property or attribute.

adjunctive, adj. [1. ajúngktiv; 2. ədžáŋktiv]. Prec. & **-ive**. Having the character of an adjunct.

adjunctively, adv. Prec. & **-ly**. As, by way of, an adjunct.

adjuration, n. [1. àjoorāshun; 2. ǽdžuréiʃən], fr. Lat. *adjūrātiōn-(em)*, formed fr. P.P. type *adjūrāt-(um)* of *adjūrāre*, 'swear to, confirm by oath'. See **ad-** & base of *jūs, jūris*, 'law', &c. under **jus**. The act of adjuring; an earnest or solemn charge or appeal; specif. (in exorcism) *adjuration of the devil*, a solemn command, in the name of God, to depart from the body of the person possessed.

adjuratory, adj. [1. àjoorāturi; 2. ǽdžuréitəri]. Containing an adjuration.

adjure, vb. trans. [1. ajóōr; 2. ədžɔ́, ədžúə], fr. Lat. *adjūrāre*, 'to swear', fr. **ad-** & *jūrāre*, 'to swear'. See **adjuration**. To charge under solemn oath; entreat earnestly, solemnly.

adjust, vb. trans. [1. ajúst; 2. ədžást], fr. 16th-cent. Fr. *adjuster*, Mod. Fr. *ajuster*; Med. Lat. *adjustāre*, fr. Low Lat. *adjuxtāre*, 'to bring together', fr. **ad-** & *juxta*, 'near', fr. base **jug-*, 'join', cp. *jugum*, 'yoke', *jungere*, 'join'. See **join**, **junction**, **yoke**. **1. a** To arrange, settle, put in order, bring to a satisfactory state, harmonize (differences, quarrels); **b** to arrange properly, put in right position (one's clothes &c.). **2.** To fit, suit, adapt, make (a thing) suitable for its function, regulate for use: *to adjust piece of machinery, telescope, sights of a gun* &c.

adjustable, adj. [1. ajústabl; 2. ədžástəbl]. Prec. & **-able**. Capable of being adjusted, regulated, for particular purpose.

adjustment, n. [1. ajústment; 2. ədžástmənt]. **adjust** & **-ment**. The act of adjusting; specif. (marine insurance) settlement of amount payable to insured person for goods lost at sea.

adjutancy, n. [1. ájutansi; 2. ǽdžətənsi]. See next word & **-cy**. The office or position of an adjutant.

adjutant, n. [1. ájutant; 2. ǽdžətənt], fr. Lat. *adjūtant-(em)*, Pres. Part. type of *adjūtāre*, 'to help', freq. of *adjuvāre*, 'to help', fr. **ad-** & *juvāre*, 'to help, support'. See **coadjutor**. **1.** A regimental officer, not above the rank of major, whose duty is to assist the commanding officer of a battalion, depôt &c. in administrative and other duties. *Adjutant-general*, the second executive officer of the Imperial General Staff of the army, whose duties are concerned with recruiting, training, and discipline. **2.** Also *adjutant-bird*, a large species of stork, found in India, feeding on snakes and carrion, and acting as a scavenger.

ad libitum, adv. [1. àd líbitum; 2. ǽd líbitəm]. Lat., 'at pleasure'. To any extent, without restriction, as much as is desired; often abbr. *ad lib.*

admeasure, vb. trans. [1. admézhur; 2. ædméžə]. See **ad-** & **measure**. To measure; ascertain proper proportionate share.

admeasurement, n. [1. admézhurment; 2. ædméžəmənt]. Prec. & **-ment**. Process, act, of admeasuring; adjustment of proportional shares &c.

administer, vb. trans. [1. admínister; 2. ædmínistə]. Fr. *administrer*, fr. Lat. *administrāre*, 'to manage, carry out, accomplish; to attend, wait, serve'. See **ad-** & **minister** (II.). **1.** To manage, govern, arrange financial transactions, as a steward or executor: *to administer an estate* &c. **2. a** To apply or direct the application of laws or discipline; to dispense: *to administer justice, punishment* &c.; **b** to conduct or execute religious offices, dispense rites: *to administer the Blessed Sacrament* (*to*). **3. a** To furnish with, give, bring (help, food, medicine &c.) *to* (a person); **b** to offer, tender: *to administer an oath.*

administrant, n. [1. admínistrant; 2. ædmínistrənt], fr. Lat. *administrans, -antis*, Pres. Part. of *administrāre*. See **administer**. One who administers.

administration, n. [1. admìnistrāshun; 2. ædmìnistréiʃən], fr. Lat. *administrātiōn-(em)*, fr. *administrāt-(um)*, P.P. type of *administrāre*, see **administer** & **-ion**. **1. a** Management of business, of an estate &c.; specif. (law) the management of a deceased person's estate; **b** management of public affairs, government; also, the power or party that administers the government of the country; the Ministry, the Government. **2.** The effective application of laws by a person in authority: *the administration of justice.* **3.** The dispensation of the Sacrament. **4.** Application of remedies &c.

administrative, adj. [1. admínistrativ; 2. ædmínistrətiv], fr. Lat. *administrātīvus*. See prec. & **-ive**. Connected with administration, with practical details of management of affairs; executive.

administratively, adv. Prec. & **-ly**. In an administrative manner.

administrator, n. [1. admínistrāter; 2. ædmínistreitə]. Lat., 'manager, agent'. See **administration** & **-or**. One who manages or directs practical details of organization; specif. (law) person authorized to manage, or distribute rent &c. from, estate of deceased person, or of a minor.

administratorship, n. [1. admínistrātership; 2. ədmínistreitəʃip]. See prec. & **-ship**. The office of an administrator.

administratrix, n. [1. admínistrātriks; 2. ædmínistreitriks]. See **administrator** & **-ix**. Woman administrator.

admirable, adj. [1. ádmirabl; 2. ǽdmirəbl], fr. Fr., fr. Lat. *admīrābilis*. See **admire** & **-able**. Worthy of admiration; of a character to excite wonder, pleasure, esteem; hence, excellent, wonderfully good.

admirably, adv. Prec. & **-ly**. In an admirable manner.

admiral, n. [1. ádmeral; 2. ǽdmərəl]. O. Fr. *amiral*, fr. Arab. *amir al*, 'commander of the', in various titles, as *amir al mumenin*, 'Commander of the faithful', *al bahr*, 'of the sea', &c., remodelled on anal. of *admir-able*; see **emir**. **1. a** Naval officer commanding fleet or squadron; one above rank of captain; in British Navy of four grades, *Admiral of the Fleet, Admiral, Vice-Admiral, and Rear-Admiral*; **b** title given to the chief captain of a fishing fleet. **2.** (entom.) Popular name of two species of butterfly, *Red Admiral*, Vanessa Atalanta, and *White Admiral*, Limenitis Sibylla.

Admiralty, n. [1. ádmeralti; 2. ǽdmərəlti]. Prec. & **-ity**. **1. a** The board of commissioners, *Lords of the Admiralty*, appointed for the administration of naval affairs; **b** building where this board transacts business. **2.** (rhet. or poet.) Naval power, sea power: '*the price of Admiralty*'. **3.** (law) *Admiralty Court*, a division of the Supreme Court with jurisdiction in maritime affairs.

admiration, n. [1. àdmirāshun; 2. ǽdmiréiʃən], fr. Lat. *admīrātiōn-(em)*, 'wondering at, admiration'. See **admire** & **-ation**. **a** Sentiment of wonder, approval, pleasure, excited by contemplation of beauty, skill, merit, or excellence of any kind; **b** object which inspires the sentiment: *she was the admiration of all beholders.*

admire, vb. trans. [1. admír; 2. ədmáiə], fr. Fr. *admirer*, fr. Lat. *admīrāri*, 'to wonder at', fr. **ad-** & *mīrāri*, 'to wonder'. Cp. Lat. *mīrus*, 'marvellous'. Orig. meaning of base seems to be 'smile, laugh'; in other languages it appears w. initial *s-*: Scrt. *smēraš*, 'smiling', *smáyatē*, 'he smiles'; O.E. *bismer* = *bi-smer*, 'insult, mockery, joke', lit. 'something to laugh at', further *smær(e)*, 'lip'. **1.** To regard a person or thing with wonder of pleasurable kind, with approval; hence, to have a great esteem for. **2.** (formerly) Merely, to wonder at, feel surprise at (not always in favourable sense). Now obsolete in this sense.

admirer, n. [1. admírer; 2. ədmáiərə]. See **admire** & **-er**. One who admires; specif., one who admires a woman; a suitor for woman's hand.

admiring, adj. [1. admíring; 2. ədmáiəriŋ]. Pres. Part. of **admire**. Filled with admiration: *admiring glances*.

admiringly, adv. Prec. & **-ly**. With admiration.

admissible, adj. [1. admísibl; 2. ədmísibl]. Fr., fr. Low Lat. *admissibilis*, fr. *admissum*, P.P. of *admittere*, 'to let in', see **admit** & **-ible**. **1.** (of an idea, plan &c.) Deserving, possible, to be held, entertained, or allowed. **2.** (law, esp. of evidence) Entitled to be brought forward and accepted as proof. **3.** Entitled to admission to an office &c.

admission, n. [1. admíshun; 2. ədmíʃən], fr. Lat. *admissiōn-(em)*, 'letting in to an interview', fr. *admiss-(um)*, P.P. type of *admittere*, see **admit** & **-ion**. **1.** Letting in to, allowing to enter; right of entry to (a building, corporation of any kind, society &c.): *admission by ticket* (see **admit, 1**). **2. a** Something admitted or conceded as being true; confession: *a serious admission*; **b** acknowledgement, expressed or implied statement that something is true.

admit, vb. trans. [1. admít; 2. ədmít], fr. Lat. *admittere*, 'to allow to enter or approach', fr. **ad-** & *mittere*, 'to send'; for second element see **mission**. **1.** To permit or allow (a person &c.) to enter, to let in, give access *to* (a place, society, corporation, privileges &c.). **2.** (of rooms, buildings &c.) To have space for: *the theatre only admits 1000 persons*. **3.** To receive as true, to allow, acknowledge, confess: *to admit the force of arguments, that one was wrong* &c.; *if that were true, though I don't admit it*... **4.** *To admit of*, to allow, be capable, patient, of: *to admit of doubt, improvement, delay* &c.

admittance, n. [1. admítans; 2. ədmítəns], fr. **admit** & **-ance**. Permission, right, to enter: *to grant, refuse* (a person) *admittance to* (a building, entertainment &c.).

admitted, adj. [1. admíted; 2. ədmítid], fr. P.P. of **admit**. (prec. n.) Acknowledged, recognized as true, valid: *an admitted fact* &c.

admittedly, adv. Prec. & **-ly**. By general acknowledgement, consent, or agreement.

admix, vb. trans. [1. admíks; 2. ədmíks]. See **ad-** & **mix**. To mix *with* something else.

admixture, n. [1. admíkschur; 2. ədmíkstʃə]. See **ad-** & **mixture**. Addition made by mixing another ingredient; compound so formed.

admonish, vb. trans. [1. admónish; 2. ədmóniʃ], fr. Lat. *admonēre*, fr. **ad-** & *monēre*, 'to warn', with suff. **-ish**. See base under **monition, mental, mind**. **1.** To exhort, advise (a person) *to do, to be, that* he should do or be &c.; to reprove mildly and warn against an offence: *to admonish a person to be more careful*. **2.** To warn (a person) *of* (something); to inform, remind *of*.

admonishment, n. [1. admónishment; 2. ədmóniʃmənt], fr. prec. & **-ment**. Act of admonishing; warning or reproof conveyed.

admonition, n. [1. admonishun; 2. ædmoníʃən], fr. Lat. *admonitiōn-(em)*, 'a warning'. See **admonish** & **-ion**. A warning, mild reproof.

admonitory, adj. [1. admóniteri; 2. ədmónitəri]. See prec. & **-ory**. Conveying warning or reproof; advising caution.

ad nauseam, adv. [1. ád náwsiam; 2. ǽd nɔ́siæm]. Lat., lit. 'to the point of sickness'. See **nausea**. To the point of being disgusting; esp. by continued repetition, or prolonged duration.

ado, n. [1. adóō; 2. ədú]. M.E. *at dō*, 'to do', *at* being Scand. Phr. orig. North. Engl. See **do**. Cp. Engl. *a sad to-do* in same sense. Fuss, bustle, stir, difficulty, trouble: *to make too much ado*; *without more ado* &c.

adobe, n. & adj. [1. adób(i); 2. ædóub(i)]. Span.-Amer., fr. Span. *adobar*, 'to plaster'. **1.** n. **a** A sun-baked brick; **b** house, wall &c. built of such bricks. **2.** adj. Made, built of sun-baked bricks.

adolescence, n. [1. àdolésens; 2. æ̀dəlésəns]. Fr., fr. Lat. *adolescentia*, fr. *adolescere*, 'to grow up', fr. **ad-** & **olescere*, inceptive form of **olēre*, 'to grow', cogn. w. *alere*, 'to nourish'. See **alimentary, adult**. The state of growing up; time of life from childhood to manhood or womanhood, between puberty and full maturity; youth.

adolescent, adj. & n. [1. adolésent; 2. ædəlésənt], fr. Lat. Pres. Part. *adolescent-(em.)* See prec. **1.** adj. In process of growing up; growing from childhood to maturity. **2.** n. Boy, girl, growing up.

Adonis, n. [1. adṓnis; 2. ədóunis]. Greek mythol.; name of a youth beloved by Aphrodite (Venus) for his beauty. A handsome man.

adopt, vb. trans. [1. adópt; 2. ədɔ́pt], fr. Fr. *adopter*, fr. Lat. *adoptāre*, 'to choose, select, adopt as a child', fr. **ad-** & *optāre*, 'to wish for, desire; choose', see **option**. **1.** To take a child of other parents voluntarily into one's family and consider and treat him in all ways as one's own; (by extension) to take into close relationship, in one's household, some person from outside. **2.** (of non-material things) To appropriate, accept deliberately, make one's own (a set of opinions, theories, religious beliefs, ideas, methods &c. which one did not formerly hold or act on).

adoptability, n. [1. adòptabíliti; 2. ədɔ̀ptəbíliti]. See **adoptable** & **-ity**. The state or quality of being adoptable.

adoptable, adj. [1. adóptabl; 2. ədɔ́ptəbl], fr. **adopt** & **-able**. Capable of being, or suitable to be, adopted.

adopted, adj. [1. adópted; 2. ədɔ́ptid]. P.P. of **adopt**. Taken by adoption: *an adopted son*.

adoption, n. [1. adópshun; 2. ədɔ́pʃən], fr. Lat. *adoptiōn-(em)*. See **ad-** & **option**. **1.** The act of taking voluntarily as one's own a child of other parents. **2.** Taking over, acceptance (of a plan, view, policy, resolution, opinion &c); special use: *adoption of a candidate* by a political party to represent it in a Parliamentary election. **3.** (philol.) The taking of a foreign word into regular use in a language without changing its form to any appreciable extent.

adoptive, adj. [1. adóptiv; 2. ədɔ́ptiv], fr. Lat. *adoptīvus*, 'pertaining to adoption, made or acquired by adoption'. See **adopt** & **-ive**. Acquired by adoption: *an adoptive son*; constituted by adoption: *an adoptive father*.

adorable, adj. [1. adórabl; 2. ədɔ́rəbl], fr. **adore** & **-able**. Worthy of being adored or loved devotedly; capable of inspiring devoted attachment.

adorableness, n. Prec. & **-ness**. The quality of being adorable.

adorably, adv. See prec. & **-ly**. In an adorable manner.

adoration, n. [1. adoráshun; 2. ædəréiʃən]. Fr., fr. Lat. *adōrātiōn-(em)*. See next word & **-ation**. **1.** The act of worshipping or paying devotion to God or to some sacred person or object; prayer. **2.** Intense affection, regard, devoted love.

adore, vb. trans. [1. adór; 2. ədɔ́]. Fr. *adorer*, fr. Lat. *adōrāre*, 'speak to, entreat, ask for, in prayer, worship', fr. **ad-** & *ōrāre*, 'speak, pray, beseech'. See **oration, orison**. **1.** To worship, honour as divine, venerate. **2.** (of earthly things) To love devotedly, love to distraction, idolize; (colloq., in weakened sense) to like very much: *I simply adore plum-pudding*.

adorer, n. [1. adórer; 2. ədɔ́rə]. See **adore** & **-er**. **a** One who adores; one who worships, venerates; **b** one who loves devotedly, an ardent admirer, a lover.

adoring, adj. [1. adóring; 2. ədɔ́riŋ]. Pres. Part. of **adore**. Showing or expressing worship, reverence, ardent devotion, love &c.: *adoring glances*.

adoringly, adv. Prec. & **-ly**. In an adoring manner, with adoration.

adorn, vb. trans. [1. adórn; 2. ədɔ́n], fr. Fr. *adorner*, fr. Lat. *adornāre*, fr. **ad-** & *ornāre*, 'to deck, embellish, beautify'. See **ad-** & **ornament**. To deck, decorate, dress with ornaments &c.; embellish, set off to advantage, enhance the beauty or attractiveness of (**lit.** and fig.); **a** (lit.) *to adorn oneself with jewels, fine clothes* &c.; *to adorn a room with flowers* &c.; **b** (fig.) to add distinction, importance, beauty, to something: *to adorn the stage, the pulpit, episcopal bench* &c.

adornment, n. [1. adórnment; 2. ədɔ́nmənt], fr. **adorn** & **-ment**. **a** The act of adorning: *adornment of one's person* &c.; **b** an ornament or decoration; (also in pl.) *adornment(s) of a church*.

adown, adv. [1. adóun; 2. ədáun]. O.E. *of dūne*, lit. 'from the hill', down. See **down (II.)** & **(III.)**. (archaic and poet.) Down.

ad rem, adv. & adj. [1. ád rém; 2. ǽd rém]. Lat. **ad-** & acc. sing. of *rēs*, 'thing, matter' &c. See **real (I.)**. To the point, to the purpose.

adrenalin, n. [1. adrénalin; 2. ædrénəlin], fr. **ad-**, **renal** & **-in(e)**. A chemical substance secreted by the suprarenal glands, forming the active principle of an extract used for various diseases, as Addison's disease &c., and for checking bleeding on account of its constricting effect on the blood-vessels.

adrift, adv. & adj. [1. adríft; 2. ədríft]. **a-** fr. O.E. *on-*, & **drift**. **a** (of ships and boats) Loose from moorings, driven hither and thither by wind and tide: *to cut a ship, boat, adrift, go adrift*; **b** (fig., of human beings) without guidance or moral direction; at the mercy of gusts of passion and impulse. Phr. *to turn (a person) adrift*, turn him out of house and home, loose upon the world; dismiss from service.

adroit, adj. [1. adróit; 2. ədróit]. **Fr.**, 'dexterous', orig. 'rightly', fr. *à*, 'to', & *droit*, 'right'. See **direct**. (of persons and human actions) Dexterous, skilful, active, clever; possessing readiness of skill or resource, either physical or mental: *an adroit workman*; *adroit debater*.

adroitly, adv. Prec. & **-ly**. In an adroit manner; skilfully, dexterously, cleverly.

adroitness, n. See prec. & **-ness**. The quality of being adroit; dexterity, cleverness.

adscript, n. [1. ádskript; 2. ǽdskript]. Lat. *ascrīptus*, P.P. of *ascrībere*, 'to enrol', fr. **ad-** & *scrībere*, 'to write'. See **scribe**. (of serfs &c.) Attached to particular region or manor.

adsum, n. [1. ádsum; 2. ǽdsam]. Lat., 'I am present', as answer in a roll-call &c.

adulate, vb. trans. [1. ádūlāt; 2. ǽdjuleit], fr. Lat. *adūlāt-(um)*, P.P. type of *adūlāri*, 'to fawn like a dog, wag the tail'; base *ūl-* cogn. w. Scrt. *vālaś*, 'tail'. To praise excessively, flatter in servile manner.

adulation, n. [1. àdūláshun; 2. æ̀djuléiʃən], fr. Lat. *adūlātiōn-(em)*, 'fawning'. See prec. & **-ion**. Servile flattery.

adulatory, adj. [1. ádūlātori; 2. ǽdjuleitəri], fr. **adulate** & **-ory**. Full of praise, flattering.

Adullamite, n. [1. adúlamīt; 2. ədáləmait], fr. the cave of *Adullam*, 1 Sam. xxii. 1. (polit. slang) Name given to seceders from a political party, who form a 'cave' or isolated group.

adult, adj. & n. [1. adúlt; 2. ədált]. Lat. *adultus*, 'grown up', P.P. of *adolescere*, see **adolescence**. **a** adj. Grown up, having reached maturity: *adult voters*; **b n.**, **a** person who has reached maturity.

adulterant, adj. & n. [1. adúlterant; 2. ədáltərənt]. Lat. *adulterant-(em)*, Pres. Part. of *adulterāre*, 'defile'. See **adulterate (II.)**. Substance used in adulterating, e.g. water in milk.

adulterate (I.), adj. [1. adúlterat; 2. ədáltərət]. See next word. **a** (of persons) Guilty of adultery; made illegitimate by adultery of parents: *adulterate offspring*; **b** (of substances) not perfectly genuine, having foreign substance added.

adulterate (II.), vb. trans. [1. adúlterāt; 2. ədáltəreit], fr. Lat. *adulterāt-(um)*, P.P. type of *adulterāre*. See **adulterer**. To falsify substances by adding inferior materials.

adulteration, n. [1. adùlteráshun; 2. ədàltəréiʃən]. Prec. & **-ion**. The act of adulterating; state of being adulterated or debased.

adulterer, n. [1. adúlterer; 2. ədáltərə], fr. Lat. *adulter*, 'adulterer', & **-er**, derived fr. vb. *adulterāre*, wh. stands for *ad alterāre*, fr. *alter*, 'other' (see **alter, alternative**), 'change to something different', hence, 'falsify, corrupt'; w. specialization of meaning to above sense. A man guilty of adultery.

adulteress, n. [1. adúltres; 2. ədáltris]. Prec. & **-ess**. Woman guilty of adultery.

adulterine, adj. [1. adúlterin; 2. ədáltərin], fr. Lat. *adulterīnus*, 'bastard, not genuine, counterfeit'. See **adulterer** & **-ine**. **1.** Resulting from adultery; born of adultery, esp. *adulterine bastardy*. **2.** Counterfeit, spurious.

adulterous, adj. [1. adúlterus; 2. ədáltərəs]. See **adulterer** & **-ous**. (of persons) Guilty of adultery; (of conduct) having character of adultery.

adulterously, adv. Prec. & **-ly**. In an adulterous manner.

adultery, n. [1. adúlteri; 2. ədáltəri], fr. Lat. *adulterium*, n. See **adulterer**. Breach, by either sex, of marriage vows of fidelity to the spouse.

adumbrate, vb. trans. [1. ádumbrāt; 2. ǽdambreit], fr. P.P. in *-ātum* of Lat. vb. *adumbrāre*, 'to cast a shadow, delineate in outline', fr. **ad-** & *umbrāre*, fr. *umbra*, 'shade, shadow'. See **umbra**. To sketch in outline, forecast, indicate character of something still to come.

adumbration, n. [1. àdumbrā́shun; 2. æ̀dambréiʃən], fr. Lat. *adumbrātiōn-(em)*, 'a sketching in outline'. See prec. & **-ion**. Sketch, shadowing forth, forecast of intentions for future action, nature of statement yet to be made &c.

adumbrative, adj. [1. adúmbrativ; 2. ædámbrətiv]. **adumbrate** & **-ive**. Having, being in, the nature of an adumbration.

adust, adj. [1. adúst; 2. ədást], fr. Lat. *adustus*, 'burned', P.P. of *adūrere*, 'to burn up', fr. *ad* & *ūrere*, P.P. *ustum*, 'to burn', for earlier **ūsere*, cp. Gk. *eúō*, 'singe', for **eusō*; Scrt. *ōšati*, 'burns', *ušnáš*, 'hot', *uštaš*, 'burnt', exactly corresponding to Lat. P.P.; further O.E. *ysla*, 'glowing cinders' &c., fr. **us-il-*. See **combustion**. Scorched, dried up with heat, parched; sunburnt.

ad valorem, adj. & adv. [1. àd valṓrem; 2. æ̀d vælɔ́rem]. Lat., 'according to value'. See **valour**. Generally of taxes, levied according to value of taxable property.

advance (I.), vb. trans. & intrans. [1. adváhns; 2. ədvā́ns]. O. Fr. & Fr. *avancer*; M.E. *avancen*; *d* inserted in 16th cent. spelling, as though pref. were Lat. *ad*. It really comes fr. Lat. *ab*, 'through', Fr. *av*. The second element is Lat. *ante*, 'before, in front' (see **ante-**). From the combination *abante*, wh. produced Fr. *avant* & Ital. *avanti*, 'before', a Low Lat. vb. **avanteāre* was formed, whence Fr. *avancer*, Ital. *avanzare*, Span. *avanzar* &c. **A.** trans. **1. a** (of material objects) To move, bring, push forward; **b** (fig.) to bring forward, put forward, propose, as a plan, suggestion, claim &c. **2.** To promote (a person or his interests); to raise to a higher rank or position, help forward: *advanced to the rank of General*; *to advance one's fortunes*. **3.** To move forward, fix earlier date for; hasten (events); cause progress to be made. **4.** To raise (prices). **5. a** To pay (money) before date when it legally falls due; to pay on security; **b** to lend (money &c.), esp. on security. **B.** intrans. **1.** To come, move, forward; specif. (mil.) to attack the enemy, occupy territory which he holds. Also *advance against*, to attack. **2.** (fig., of persons) To make progress; to rise in rank, position &c.: *to advance in one's profession*. **3.** (fig., commerc., of prices) To rise, go up, become dearer, higher.

advance (II.), n., fr. prec. **1. a** A moving forward from one place to another; forward movement: *our troops could not check the enemy's advance*; **b** of passage of time: *advance of evening, old age* &c.; advbl. phr.: *in advance*, before, beforehand (of place or time); prepositional phr.: *in advance of*, in front of, before. Fig. uses: **2.** Progress, improvement in a task, social position, rank, office, health, knowledge &c.: *advance in one's career*; *in science* &c. **3.** (chiefly pl.) Approaches made to gain favour, to form an acquaintance, to make up a difference &c.; overtures of friendship, love &c.: *to encourage, repel (a person's) advances*. **4.** Rise in price, value, wages &c.: *advance in the cost of living*. **5.** Payment beforehand; a loan (of money &c.): *temporary advance*.

advanced, adj. [1. adváhnst; 2. ədvā́nst]. P.P. of **advance** (I.). **1.** Far on in progress: *advanced ideas, opinions, studies, thinkers*; also derived from this, too far advanced, therefore supposed to have abandoned the old habits and principles; lax in conduct &c.: *rather an advanced young woman*. **2.** Far on in life, old: *advanced in years*. **3.** *Advance(d) guard*, detachment of troops sent forward in advance of main body.

advancement, n. [1. adváhnsment; 2. ədvā́nsmənt], fr. **advance** (I.) & **-ment**. **a** The act of advancing: *advancement of learning, of one's hopes*; **b** state of being advanced (lit. and fig.); progress, improvement, promotion, upward progress, success: *advancement in life, career, fortunes* &c.

advantage (I.), n. [1. adváhntij; 2. ədvā́ntidž], fr. Fr. *avantage*, fr. *avant*, 'before', & **-age**. See **advance**. **1. a** Any condition, circumstance, event, of favourable character, likely to promote success, happiness; means of gaining desired end; source of benefit or profit: *the advantages of the proposal outweigh the disadvantages*; Phr. *to take advantage of* (a favourable circumstance, opportunity &c.), to avail oneself of, profit by; **b** benefit, gain, profit: *the advantage of a good education*. **2.** Superiority, better position, with *of* or *over* (a person): *to have the advantage of, gain an advantage over (a person)*. Phr., specif. (ironical) *you have the advantage of me*, said to stranger who knows one's name, and claims acquaintance. Phr. *to take advantage of a person*, to deceive, outwit, overreach; also, to seduce (a woman). **3.** Specif., first point scored in lawn tennis when both sides have made 40 (gen. *vantage*).

advantage (II.), vb. trans., fr. Fr. *avantager*. See prec. To cause, give rise to advantage; be beneficial to; promote, benefit, profit.

advantageous, adj. [1. àdvantā́jus; 2. æ̀dvəntéidžəs]. Fr. *avantageux*. See **advantage** (I.) & **-ous**. Fraught with, yielding, advantage; beneficial, profitable, useful.

advantageously, adv. Prec. & **-ly**. With advantage; profitably.

advent, n. [1. ádvent; 2. ǽdvent], fr. Lat. *adventus*, 'an arrival', P.P. of *advenīre*, 'to come to, arrive at', fr. **ad-** & *venīre*, 'to come', q.v. under **venue**, & see **come**. **1.** A coming or arrival; specif. (with cap.) the Incarnation of Christ; also, the expected second coming of Christ to earth. **2.** (eccles., with cap.) The season (including four Sundays) immediately before Christmas.

Adventism, n. [1. ádventizm; 2. ǽdventizəm]. Prec. & **-ism**. Doctrine that the second coming or Advent of Christ, to rule the earth, is at hand.

Adventist, n. [1. ádventist; 2. ǽdventist]. See prec. & **-ist**. One who accepts the doctrine of Adventism.

adventitious, adj. [1. àdventíshus; 2. æ̀dventiʃəs]. Lat. *adventīcius*, 'coming from abroad, foreign, extraneous'. See **advent** & **-itious**. Added extraneously, not inherent; casual, accidental; specif. (law, of property) coming from a stranger or by collateral succession.

adventitiously, adv. Prec. & **-ly**. In an adventitious manner; casually, accidentally.

adventure (I.), n. [1. advénchur; 2. ədvéntʃə], fr. Fr. *aventure*, fr. Low Lat. *adventūra*, fr. Lat. *adventūrus*, Fut. Part. of *advenīre*, 'to arrive'. See **advent, venture**. **1.** Daring, hazardous, enterprise; encountering of risks, participation in strange and exciting events: *love of adventure*. **2.** An unexpected, exciting incident, a remarkable experience; a strange and striking event, attended by risk and danger: *a strange adventure*. **3.** A speculative venture in commerce.

adventure (II.), vb. trans. & intrans., fr. prec. Now more usually **venture**. **1.** trans. To risk, take risk of, endanger, take chance of success or failure of. **2.** intrans. To be put to the test, try chance, take risks.

adventurer, n. [1. advénchurer; 2. ədvéntʃərə], fr. **adventure** & **-er**. Now chiefly restricted to bad sense, one, often of dubious antecedents, who lives by his wits; one bent on obtaining, by equivocal means, wealth and position, without deserving them by honest service; unscrupulous, plausible rogue.

adventuresome, adj. [1. advénchersum; 2. ədvéntʃəsəm]. **adventure** & **-some**. (rarely used) Given to, fond of adventure(s). See **venturesome**.

adventuress, n. [1. advénchures; 2. ədvéntʃəris]. Fem. of **adventurer**.

adventurous, adj. [1. advénchurus; 2. ədvéntʃərəs], fr. O. Fr. *aventuros*. See **adventure** & **-ous**. **1.** (of persons) Fond of adventure; enterprising, venturesome. **2.** (of actions &c.) Hazardous, risky, attended by danger.

adventurously, adv. Prec. & **-ly**. In an adventurous manner, boldly; rashly.

adverb, n. [1. ádvërb; 2. ǽdvʌ̄b], fr. Fr. *adverbe*, fr. Lat. *adverbium*, fr. **ad-** & *verbum*, 'a word'. See **verb** & **word**. (gram.) A word that qualifies verb, adjective, or other adverb, expressing place, time, manner &c., answering questions How? When? Where?

adverbial, adj. [1. advërbial; 2. ædvʌ́biəl], fr. Lat. *adverbiālis*. Prec. & **-al**. Of, pertaining to, an adverb.

adverbially, adv. Prec. & **-ly**. With function of an adverb.

adversaria, n. pl. [1. adversā́ria; 2. ædvəséəriə]. Lat., sc. *scripta*, 'writings', lit. 'things turned towards one'. See **adversary**. Miscellaneous notes or jottings; memoranda; hence, a commonplace book.

adversary, n. [1. ádversari; 2. ǽdvəsəri], fr. Lat. *adversārius*, lit. 'one turned towards'. See **adverse, advert**. Person or party opposed, hostile to, contending with, one; enemy, opponent.

adversative, adj. [1. advërsativ; 2. ædvʌ́sətiv], fr. Lat. *adversātīvus*. See next word & **-ive**. (of terms, words &c.) Denoting, expressing, opposition or antithesis.

adverse, adj. [1. ádvërs, advërs; 2. ǽdvʌ̄s, ədvʌ́s], fr. Lat. *adversus*, 'turned towards, opposite to, against', adj. & P.P. of *advertere*, 'to turn to', fr. *ad* & *vertere*, 'to turn'. See **advert**. Opposed, hostile, unfavourable to, contrary: *adverse fate, winds, criticism, judgement* (in law).

adversely, adv. Prec. & **-ly**. In a hostile, prejudicial manner: *acting adversely to one's interests*.

adversity, n. [1. advërsiti; 2. ədvʌ́siti], fr. O. Fr. *aversité*, fr. Lat. *adversitāt-(em)*. See **adverse** & **-ity**. State of ill fortune; misfortune, distress, misery, affliction.

advert, vb. intrans. [1. advërt; 2. ədvʌ́t], fr. Lat. *advertere*, 'to turn to, direct towards', fr. **ad-** & *vertere*, 'to turn, change'. The Aryan base **wert-, *wort-* &c., 'turn, change', is widespread in the derived languages; cp. Scrt. *vártati*, 'he turns', *vartulaš*, 'round'; O. Slav. *vrŭtěti*, 'turn, twist', Lith. *versti*, 'turn'; Goth. *wairþan*, 'become, come to pass', O.S. *werthan*, O.E. *weorþan*, 'become, be, turn out to be, happen', O.H.G. *werdan*. See also **vertex, version, & worth (III.)** (in phr. *woe worth*). *Advert to*, to turn to, in thought; refer, allude *to*, in speech or writing.

advertise, vb. trans. & intrans. [1. ádvertīz; 2. ǽdvətaiz]. Fr. *avertir*, formerly *advertir*, 'to warn, give notice to', fr. Lat. *advertere*, 'to turn to', see **advert**, & **-ise**. **A.** trans. **1.** To give public notice of; to announce publicly, esp. *by* a printed notice *in* a newspaper or elsewhere: *to advertise one's wares*. **2.** (archaic)

To inform, notify, warn (a person) *of* (a thing). **B.** intrans. **a** (absol. or followed by *for*) To put a notice, warning, demand &c. in a newspaper or public place: *if you can't find a house, you had better advertise*; also **b** in bad sense, to put oneself forward, urge one's merits and claims to recognition, call attention to oneself: *it's a pity he advertises so much.*

advertisement, n. [1. advértisment; 2. ədvÁtismənt], fr. Fr. *avertissement.* See prec. & **-ment.** A public notice or announcement of news, goods for sale, and needs, esp. in newspapers, on placards &c.

advertiser, n. [1. ádvertīzer; 2. ǽdvətaizə]. **advertise** & **-er.** One who advertises.

advice, n. [1. advís; 2. ədváis]. M.E. *avis*, 'opinion', fr. O. Fr. This word wd. correspond to Lat. *ad visum*, 'according to my view, as I see it'; fr. Lat. vb. *vidēre*, 'see, look at, consider, reflect upon'. See **vision, wit. 1. a** Considered opinion regarding a matter, set of circumstances &c., and recommendation as to how to deal with it successfully; counsel; Phr. *to give, tender, ask, take, advice*; *act on advice*; **b** specif., skilled professional opinion of doctor or lawyer, consulted in a medical or legal case. **2.** Information, notification, report, intelligence; (gen. pl.) **a** diplomatic and political official report; **b** (commerc.) statement regarding business transactions, bills of exchange &c.: *letter of advice.*

advisability, n. [1. advīzabíliti; 2. ədvaizəbíliti]. See next word & **-ity.** The quality of being advisable (of line of action).

advisable, adj. [1. advízabl; 2. ədváizəbl], fr. **advise** & **-able.** Proper to be advised, or recommended; therefore, in accordance with prudence, expedient.

advisableness, n. Prec. & **-ness.** Advisability.

advisably, adv. See prec. & **-ly.** With advice; wisely, prudently.

advise, vb. trans. & intrans. [1. advíz; 2. ədváiz], fr. Fr. *aviser*, 'inform (trans. & reflex.), reflect upon', fr. Low Lat. *advisāre*, **ad-** & *visāre*, fr. Lat. *vidēre, visum*, 'to see'. See **advice. A.** trans. **1.** To give advice to, express view as to best thing to do, counsel. **2.** To give notice to, to inform (a person) *of* a thing (tradesman's English): *we will advise you when we hear* &c. = let you know. **B.** intrans. *Advise with* (a person) *on*, or *about* (something), to take counsel, consult *with*: (rare and archaic) *I must advise with you on the situation.*

advised, adj. [1. advízd; 2. ədváizd]. Only in **ill-advised, well-advised.**

advisedly, adv. [1. advízedli; 2. ədváizidli]. Prec. & **-ly.** Deliberately, of set purpose.

advisedness, n. [1. advízednes; 2. ədváizidnis]. See prec. & **-ness.** Careful deliberation, caution.

adviser, -or, n. [1. advízer; 2. ədváizə]. See **advise,** & **-er** & **-or.** One who gives advice.

advisory, adj. [1. advízeri; 2. ədváizəri], fr. **advise** & **-ory. a** Empowered to give advice, existing for purpose of consultation: *an advisory body*; **b** containing advice: *advisory letter.*

advocacy, n. [1. ádvokasi; 2. ǽdvəkəsi], fr. Fr. *advocacie*, fr. Med. Lat. *advocātia.* See **advocate** & **-acy.** The act of pleading in support *of*; intercession.

advocate (I.), n. [1. ádvokit; 2. ǽdvəkit], fr. O. Fr. *avocat*, fr. Lat. *advocātus*, 'one called in to aid another, in legal cause, an advocate', fr. *advocāre*, 'to call to one's aid', fr. **ad-** & *vocāre*, 'to call'. See **vocal, vocation. 1.** One who pleads the cause of another; specif., in Scotland, a barrister. *Faculty of Advocates*, the Scottish Bar; *Lord Advocate*, principal law officer of the Crown, and public prosecutor, in Scotland; *Devil's advocate*, Med. Lat. *advocatus diaboli*, legal representative of the case for opposing canonization; hence, a deprecator. **2.** One who supports, defends, and recommends verbally a cause, proposal, line of action &c.: *an advocate of tariff reform, of a milk diet, of early rising* &c.

advocate (II.), vb. trans. [1. ádvokāt; 2. ǽdvəkeit], fr. prec. To plead in favour of, defend by argument; to support, recommend: *to advocate reform.*

advowson, n. [1. advóusn; 2. ədváusn], fr. M.E. *avoweisoun*, O. Fr. *avoëson*, fr. Lat. *advocātiōn-(em)*; Med. Lat., 'right of a patron'. See **advocate (I.).** (Engl. law) The right of patronage of, presentation to, a church benefice.

adynamia, n. [1. àdinámia; 2. æ̀dinéimiə], fr. Gk. *adunamía*, 'want of strength', fr. **a-**, 'not', & *dúnamis*, 'power, strength'. See **dynamic.** (med.) Lack of vital force or strength.

adynamic, adj. [1. àdīnámik; 2. æ̀dainǽmik]. Prec. & **-ic.** (med.) Weak, lacking strength.

adytum, n. [1. áditum; 2. ǽditəm]. Lat. *adytum*, fr. Gk. *áduton*, lit. 'a place not to be entered', fr. **a-** (priv.) & *dúein*, 'to enter, penetrate into', see **ecdysis.** The innermost part, shrine, of a temple; hence, private room, sanctum.

adz(e), n. [1. adz; 2. ædz]. O.E. *adesa.* Etymol. unknown. A tool something like an axe, but with curved blade set with the cutting edge at right angles to the handle, used for cutting away the surface of wood. It resembles in shape and mode of use what is known as a grubbing axe.

aedile, n. [1. ēdīl; 2. ídail]. Lat. *aedīlis*, fr. *aedēs*, 'a building, temple, dwelling-house' &c. Orig. a place with a hearth or fire. Cp. *aestus*, 'fire', *aestas*, 'hot season, summer'; cp. Gk. *aíthō*, 'burn', *aîthos*, 'burning heat, fire'; Scrt. *ēdhaś*, 'wood for burning'; O.H.G. *eit*, O.E. *ād*, 'funeral pile, fire'. See **aestivate, edifice, edify.** A magistrate who, in Ancient Rome, had charge of public and private buildings, roads &c., together with other duties of supervision.

aegis, n. [1. ējis; 2. ídžis]. Lat. *aegis*, fr. Gk. *aigís*, the shield of Zeus, lit. 'one covered with goat-skin', fr. *aig-*, stem of *aix*, 'goat'. Cogns. in other languages, apart fr. Armenian *aic*, 'goat', are not identified w. certainty. The word appears to have no connexion w. Gk. *aíssō*, 'move with quick, darting motion'. **1.** (class. mythol.) The shield given by Zeus to Athene. **2.** (fig.) Protection, support: *to appear under the aegis of (a person).*

aegrotat, n. [1. ēgrōtat; 2. igróutæt]. Lat., 'he is sick', 3rd sing. of *aegrōtāre*, 'to be sick', fr. *aeger*, 'sick'; cogn. w. O. Slav. *jęza*, 'illness'; Lett. *īgstu*, 'to be annoyed'. (in English universities) A certificate that an examination candidate is unable through illness to take certain of the papers; the word after candidate's name on a class list, issued by examiners, indicates that he has reached a standard entitling to a degree, though not to a class, in that part of the examination which he was able to undertake.

Aeolian, adj. [1. ēólian; 2. ióuliən], fr. Lat. *Aeolius*, of *Aeolus*, Gk. *Aiolos*, 'the god of the winds', & **-an.** Of, pertaining to, moved by, the wind; esp. *Aeolian harp*, a musical instrument consisting of a rectangular box on or in which are stretched strings or wires, producing musical sounds as the wind passes across them.

aeon, n. [1. éon; 2. íən, íɔn]. Gk. *aiṓn*, 'age, eternity', for **aiwōm*, cogn. w. Lat. *aevum*, 'space of time, eternity'; Goth. *aiws*, 'an age, eternity', *aiw*, adv., 'ever', O.E. *ā*, 'always, ever', further, w. specialization of meaning, O.E. *ǣ(w)*, fr. **aiwi-*, O.H.G. *ēwa*, 'custom, law, marriage', lit. 'something established from time immemorial'. See **ever, never.** An indefinite, but vast and immeasurable period of time.

Aepyornis, n. [1. èpiórnis; 2. ìpiɔ́nis]. Gk. *aipús*, 'tall', & *ornis*, 'bird'. The etymol. of the first element is doubtful; for the second, see **ornithology.** Large, extinct bird of Madagascar.

aerate, vb. trans. [1. árāt; 2. éəreit], fr. Lat. *āēr*, Gk. *āḗr*, 'air'. See **air** & **-ate. a** To expose to the action of the air; **b** to fill with, charge (liquid) with, gas so that it sparkles: *aerated waters* &c.

aeration, n. [1. ārāshun; 2. ɛəréiʃən]. See prec. & **-ion. a** Exposure to the action of the air; **b** process of filling, charging liquids with air.

aerial (I.), adj. [1. árial; 2. éəriəl], fr. Lat. *āerius*, Gk. *āérios*, & **-al.** See **air. a** Of air, gaseous; **b** connected with the air; **c** like air, thin, unsubstantial (lit. and fig.).

aerial (II.), n., fr. prec. Aerial wire or antenna as used in wireless telegraphy.

aerially, adv. [1. áriali; 2. éəriəli]. **aerial (I.)** & **-ly.** In an aerial manner; in the air.

aerie, aery, n. [1. ári; 2. éəri], fr. Med. Lat. *aeria, āria*, fr. O. Fr. *aire*, of doubtful origin; either fr. Lat. *ārea*, 'level piece of ground' (see **area**), or fr. Lat. *ātrium*, 'court, hall' (see **atrium**); the later Engl. variant spelling **eyrie** is due to a confusion w. M.E. *ey*, 'egg'. **1. a** The lofty nest of an eagle or other bird of prey; **b** the brood of an eagle or other bird of prey. **2.** (by transf.) A house, castle, stronghold, situated on a high rock or hill.

aeriform, adj. [1. áriform; 2. éərifɔ̄m], fr. Lat. *āēr*, 'air', & **-form.** Having the form or nature of air; (fig.) unreal.

aero-, pref. Form used to make compound words, fr. Gk. *aér-(os)*, *āḗr*, **air.**

aerobic, adj. [1. ārṓbik; 2. ɛəróubik], fr. **aero-** & Gk. *bíos*, 'life'. See **bio-.** (biol.) **a** (of bacteria) Living and growing only in the presence of oxygen; **b** produced by such bacteria: *aerobic fermentation* &c.

aerodrome, n. [1. árodrōm; 2. éərədroum]. Formed on analogy of **hippodrome,** fr. **aero-** & Gk. *drómos*, 'course'. See **dromedary.** A large, open, level tract of ground, used for the starting and landing of aeroplanes, equipped with hangars, workshops &c.; a flying ground.

aerodynamics, n. [1. árōdīnámiks; 2. éəroudainǽmiks]. **aero-** & **dynamics.** (physics) That branch of dynamics which deals with the forces of air or gases in motion, of resistance to bodies moving in air, and of pressure exerted by air &c.

aerolite, n. [1. árolīt; 2. éərəlait]. **aero-** & **-lite.** Meteorite.

aerometer, n. [1. ārómeter; 2. ɛərɔ́mitə]. **aero-** & **-meter.** Instrument for measuring and comparing the weight and density of gases.

aeronaut, n. [1. áronawt; 2. éərənɔ̄t]. **aero-** & Gk. *naút-(ēs)*, 'sailor'. See **nautical.** One who navigates or sails the air; a balloonist; the navigator or pilot of an airship or other flying machine lighter than air.

aeronautic(al), adj. [1. āronáwtik(l); 2. ɛərənɔ̄́tik(l)]. Prec. & **-ic** & **-al.** Of, pertaining to, aeronautics.

aeronautics, n. [1. āronáwtiks; 2. ɛərənɔ̄́tiks]. Science, practice, of navigating the air in balloons or flying machines of any kind.

aerophone, n. [1. árofōn; 2. éərəfoun]. **aero-** & **-phone.** Instrument for increasing the intensity of sound in the air, used in aeronautics for detecting the sound and position of flying machines.

aerophore, n. [1. árofōr; 2. éərəfɔ̄]. **aero-** & **-phore.** Apparatus carrying a supply of compressed air, oxygen &c. for breathing, as used in mining accidents, by workers under water, firemen &c.

aerophyte, n. [1. árofīt; 2. éərəfait]. **aero-** & **-phyte.** (bot.) An air plant or epiphyte, as orchids, lichens &c. which grow on other plants though they are not parasitic, but derive nourishment, as moisture &c., directly from the air.

aeroplane, n. [1. ároplān; 2. éərəplein]. See **aero-** & **plane.** Any one of the different kinds of flying machines which are heavier than air, and which are supported in the air by planes or wings, and propelled forward and upward by a revolving propeller.

aerostat, n. [1. árostat; 2. éərəstæt]. **aero-** & Gk. *statós*, 'placed'. See **statics.** Any flying machine lighter than air, as balloon or airship.

aerostatics, n. [1. ārostátiks; 2. εərəstǽtiks]. **aero-** & **statics. 1.** Science which deals with the equilibrium of elastic fluids, such as air or gases, or of bodies suspended or moving in them. **2.** Aeronautics.

aerostation, n. [1. ārostáshun; 2. εərəstéiʃən]. **aerostat** & **-ion.** Science, practice, of navigating flying machines lighter than air, as airships or balloons; contrasted with *aviation.*

aeruginous, adj. [1. ēro͞ojinus; 2. iərúdžinəs], fr. Lat. *aerūginōsus*, fr. *aerūgin-(em)*, *aerūgo*, 'copper-rust', fr. *aer-*, 'copper', see **iron** & **-ous.** Pertaining to, of the colour of, like, copper-rust or verdigris.

aery (I.). See **aerie.**

aery (II.), adj. [1. ári; 2. éəri]. See **aerial** & **-y.** (poet.) Aerial.

Aesculapian, adj. [1. èskūlápian; 2. ìskjūléipiən], fr. Lat. *Aesculāpi-(us)*, fr. Gk. *Asklēpiós*, son of Apollo & Coronis, deified for his skill in medicine. Of, pertaining to, the art of healing.

aesthete, n. [1. ésthēt; 2. ísþīt], fr. Gk. *aisthētḗs*, 'one who perceives'. The first syll. in this word is fr. earlier *awis- & is connected w. Gk. *aiō*, 'hear', fr. *awisō, & w. Lat. *audio*, 'hear', fr. *awiz-dio; see **audible.** The origin of the second element in the last is uncertain, but it apparently reappears in Gk., in form of *-th-*, both in above Gk. n. & in related vb. *aisthánomai*, 'I perceive'. One who affects an extravagant appreciation of the beautiful in nature and art.

aesthetic, adj. [1. ēsthétik; 2. ìsþétik], fr. Gk. *aisthētikós*, 'capable of perception', connected w. *aisthánomai*, 'I perceive, feel'. Cp. prec. **a** Relating to perception of the beautiful, esp. in art; hence, artistic, connected with canons and principles of beauty underlying any of the arts: *aesthetic point of view, criticism* (contrasted with *scientific* or *historical*); *aesthetic tastes* &c.; **b** (of persons) having appreciation of beauty.

aesthetically, adv. [1. ēsthétikali; 2. ìsþétikəli]. Prec. & **-al** & **-ly. a** In an aesthetic manner; **b** from the point of view of aesthetics.

aestheticism, n. [1. ēsthétisizm; 2. ìsþétisizəm], fr. **aesthetic** & **-ism.** Exaggerated cult of the beautiful, and of artistic taste.

aesthetics, n. [1. ēsthétiks; 2. ìsþétiks]. The science which seeks to determine the canons of taste upon which criticism of the arts is based.

aestho-physiology, n. [1. ésthō fiziólojі; 2. ísþou fizióledži]. See **aesthetic** & **physiology.** Physiology of the organs of sense.

aestival, adj. [1. ēstíval; 2. ìstáivəl]. Lat. *aestīvālis, aestīvus*, fr. *aestas*, 'hot season, summer'. See **aedile** & **aestivate.** Of, belonging to, the hot season, summer.

aestivate, vb. intrans. [1. éstivāt; 2. ístiveit], fr. Lat. *aestīvāt-(um)*, P.P. type of *aestīvāre*, 'to spend or pass the summer'; fr. Aryan base *aidh-, 'heat, fire' &c., q.v. under **aedile.** To spend the summer; specif. (of certain animals) to spend the summer in a state of suspended animation; cp. *hibernate.*

aestivation, n. [1. ēstiváshun; 2. ìstivéiʃən], fr. prec. & **-ion. a** (zool.) Habit of aestivating; **b** (bot.) arrangement of petals in flower bud before opening; cp. *vernation.*

aether, n. See **ether.**

aetiological, adj. [1. ētiolójikal; 2. ìtiəlódžikəl]. See next word & **-ic** & **-al.** Dealing with, explaining, causes; esp. *aetiological myth*, one that has arisen in order to explain the origin of a name, custom &c.

aetiology, n. [1. ētióloji; 2. ìtiólədži], fr. Gk. *aitia*, 'cause, origin' (etymol. obscure), & **-logy. a** The science or philosophy of causes and origins; **b** specif., study of the origin of diseases.

afar, adv. [1. afár; 2. əfá]. See **a-** (fr. **on**) & **far.** (poet.) At a distance: *the drums were heard afar*; (in prose) from a distance; often preceded by *from*, as *to see something from afar, to come from afar*; or followed by *off*: *to stand afar off.* (Archaic and literary.)

affability, n. [1. àfabíliti; 2. æ̀fəbíliti], fr. Fr. *affabilité*, fr. Lat. *affābilitāt-(em)*. See **affable** & **-ity.** Ease, pleasantness, courtesy, of address.

affable, adj. [1. áfabl; 2. ǽfəbl]. Fr. *affable*, fr. Lat. *affābilis*, lit. 'able to be spoken to', fr. *affāri*, 'to speak to', fr. **ad-** & *fāri*, 'to speak', fr. base *bhā-, 'speak', q.v. under **ban** & **fable.** Easy of access for conversation, hence pleasant-spoken, courteous, polite, in conversation and address.

affableness, n. Prec. & **-ness.** Affability.

affably, adv. See prec. & **-ly.** In an affable manner, courteously.

affair, n. [1. afár; 2. əféə], fr. O. Fr. *afaire*, Fr. *affaire*, fr. *à faire*, 'to do', cp. **ado**; fr. Lat. *facere*, see **fact. 1.** Something done or to be done; business: *one's own affair*; (pl.) business of any kind, transactions, proceedings: *occupied with affairs*; *public affairs*; *one's private affairs*; *affairs of the State* &c. **2.** A matter, event, or action, referred to in vague terms: *the whole episode was a strange affair*; *affair of honour, of the heart* &c. **3.** (colloq.) Used in vague reference to material objects in general, equivalent to 'thing': e.g. (of a woman's dress &c.) *a wonderful affair*; *the coach was a strange, old-fashioned affair.*

affect (I.), vb. trans. [1. afékt; 2. əfékt], fr. Lat. *affect-(um)*, P.P. type of *afficere*, 'to do something to, touch, work upon', fr. **ad-** & *facere*, 'to do, make', see **fact, facile. 1.** To act upon, produce a result on something, cause change (for better or worse) in: *to affect the health, conduct, opinions* &c.; *be affected by heat, cold, hunger* &c. **2.** (fig.) To move, touch, stir, influence, work on the feelings, emotions, passions: *to be deeply affected*, have one's emotions stirred.

affect (II.), vb. trans. Fr. *affecter*, fr. Lat. *affectāre*, 'to strive after, aim at; to assume falsely, feign'; freq. of *afficere.* See **affect (I.). 1.** To show a partiality, preference, for; make use of: *to affect my company, bright colours, a foreign style of dress* &c. **2.** To feign, assume, make a pretence of: *to affect ignorance, indifference, an air of benevolence, a military appearance* &c.

affectation, n. [1. àfektáshun; 2. æ̀fiktéiʃən]. Lat. *affectātiōn-(em)*, 'eager desire for, careful study prompted by fondness', fr. Lat. *affectāt-*, as in P.P. of *affectāre*, 'make efforts to do' &c., fr. *affect-*, as in P.P. of *afficere.* See **affect (II.).** Display of sentiments which are not genuine, or assumption of mannerism in behaviour or speech which is not natural; deliberate artificiality in any artistic work; applied both to the false feelings and emotions themselves, and their outward expression in act or word: *an affectation of kindness, good breeding*; *affectation of speech, literary style* &c.

affected (I.), adj. [1. afékted; 2. əféktid], fr. P.P. of **affect (I.). 1. a** Influenced, showing results of a process or action: *affected by disease*; **b** influenced morally or emotionally; touched, moved. **2.** (gen. preceded by *well-* or *ill-*) Disposed, inclined, conditioned.

affected (II.), adj. As fr. P.P. of **affect (II.).** (of persons, habits, manners &c.) Artificial, filled with affectation, false; put on, not natural.

affectedly, adv. Prec. & **-ly.** In an affected or artificial manner.

affecting, adj. [1. afékting; 2. əféktiŋ], fr. Pres. Part. of **affect (I.).** Apt to move, stir, the emotions; touching, pathetic: *an affecting sight* &c.

affectingly, adv. Prec. & **-ly.** In an affecting manner.

affection (I.), n. [1. afékshun; 2. əfékʃen]. Lat. *affectiōn-(em)*, 'the being affected, feeling; frame of mind; right feelings; favourable disposition, love, goodwill'. See **affect (I.)** & **-ion. 1. a** Mental state or disposition; feeling, emotion, impulse, desire, passion; **b** kind feeling, goodwill, fondness, love, attachment (*for* or *towards*). **2.** (med.) Disease, complaint: *an affection of the lungs* &c.

affection (II.), vb. trans., fr. prec. To have an affection, liking, for. (Obsolesc. and rare.)

affectionate, adj. [1. afékshunat; 2. əfékʃənit], fr. **affection** & **-ate. a** (of persons) Possessing and exhibiting affection; having a loving disposition, tender; **b** (of things) expressive of affection: *an affectionate greeting, letter, embrace* &c.

affectionately, adv. Prec. & **-ly.** In an affectionate manner.

affectionateness, n. See prec. & **-ness.** The quality of being affectionate.

affective, adj. [1. afékti v; 2. əféktiv]. See **affect (II.)** & **-ive.** Pertaining to the emotional element in a mental condition.

afferent, adj. [1. áferent; 2. ǽfərənt], fr. Lat. *afferent-(em)*, Pres. Part. of *afferre*, 'to bring or carry to', fr. **ad-** & *ferre*, 'to bear, carry', cogn. w. **bear (I.).** See also **fertile, -ferous.** (physiol., of nerves and blood-vessels) Conducting inwards; converse of *efferent.*

affettuoso, adv. [1. afetōōósō; 2. əfetuóusou]. Ital. (mus. direction) With feeling.

affiance (I.), n. [1. afíans; 2. əfáiəns], fr. O. Fr. *afiance*, 'trust, confidence', fr. *afier*, 'to trust', fr. Low Lat. *affidantia*, fr. *affidāre*, 'to trust', fr. **ad-** & *fidāre*, 'to trust, to pledge one's faith', fr. Lat. *fides*, 'faith', see **fidelity. a** Firmly rooted faith, trust; reliance, confidence: '*That he may evermore have affiance in Thee*' &c. (Prayer for King's Majesty); **b** pledging of faith, esp. exchange of vows in marriage.

affiance (II.), vb. trans., fr. O. Fr. *afiancer*, fr. *afiance.* See prec. To promise (oneself or another) solemnly in marriage; become engaged (gen. P.P.). Also as adj.: *the affianced bride.*

affidavit, n. [1. àfidávit; 2. æ̀fidéivit], fr. Low Lat. 3rd sing. perf. indic. of *affidāre*, 'to pledge one's faith', fr. Lat. **ad-** & *fides*, 'faith'. See **affiance** & **fidelity.** (law) A statement or declaration in writing made on oath before a commissioner of oaths or other person authorized to administer an oath.

affiliate, vb. trans. [1. afíliāt; 2. əfílieit], fr. Low Lat. *adfiliāre, affiliāre*, 'to adopt as a son', fr. Lat. **ad-** & *filius*, 'a son', see **filial. 1.** (of an institution) To receive, accept, incorporate (persons) as members; to attach (other bodies) as branches; also *affiliate to* (of persons or institutions) in above senses. **2.** (law) To determine the paternity of (an illegitimate child). **3.** (fig.) *Affiliate with*, to trace the origin and relations, e.g. of a language: *English must be affiliated with Dutch and other West Germanic tongues.*

affiliation, n. [1. afiliáshun; 2. əfiliéiʃən]. Fr. *affiliation*, fr. Low Lat. *affiliātiōn-(em)*. See **affiliate** & **-ion. 1. a** The reception of a person or body into a society or corporation (as a member, branch &c.); incorporation; **b** act or condition of being affiliated. **2.** (law) Determination of paternity of an illegitimate child. **3.** (fig.) The tracing of anything to its origin, and showing its relations with other things.

affinity, n. [1. afíniti; 2. əfíniti], fr. Fr. *affinité*, fr. Lat. *affīnitāt-(em)*, 'neighbourhood; relationship by marriage', fr. *affīnis*, lit. 'at the border, adjacent, related', fr. **ad-** & *fīnis*, 'border, boundary'. See **finis. 1.** Relationship by marriage; as opposed to *consanguinity.* **2.** Close relationship between, implying common origin of, several varieties of animals, plants, languages, types of civilization &c.; the aggregate of resemblances upon which the assumption of a common origin is based. **3.** (chem.) Tendency of certain bodies to unite with others.

affirm, vb. trans. & intrans. [1. aférm; 2. əfə́m], fr. Lat. *affirmāre*, fr. *ad* & *firmāre*, 'to make firm'. See **ad-** & **firm. A.** trans. **1.** To declare, state positively, assert to be true; opposed to *deny*: *to affirm one's loyalty*; *affirm that it was so.* 2. (law) To confirm, ratify: *affirm a judgement, decision* &c. B. intrans. (law) To declare solemnly by affirmation instead of by oath.

affirmation, n. [1. afermáshun; 2. æfəméiʃən], fr. Fr. *affirmation*, fr. Lat. *affirmātiōn-(em)*. See **affirm** & **-ation**. **a** The act of affirming; **b** that which is affirmed; strong, positive statement that something is true; specif. (law) a solemn declaration made instead of an oath by a person of delicate conscience, held to be legally equivalent to an oath; statements of this kind made in Court of Law are punishable as perjury if untrue.

affirmative, adj. & n. [1. afërmativ; 2. əfǽmətiv]. Fr. *affirmatif, -ive*, fr. Lat. *affirmātīvus*. See **affirm**. 1. adj. Asserting that such a thing exists, is a fact, that such a statement is true; saying 'yes'; opposed to *negative*. 2. n. That which affirms, esp. in *to answer in the affirmative*, to say 'yes'.

affirmatively, adv. Prec. & **-ly**. In the affirmative; yes.

affix (I.), vb. trans. [1. afíks; 2. əfíks], fr. Lat. *affix-(um)*, P.P. type of *affīgere*, 'to fasten to', fr. *ad* & *fīgere*, 'to fasten'. See **ad-** & **fix**. 1. To fix, fasten, stick (a thing *to* another), to attach: *to affix a label to a parcel, a stamp to a letter* &c. 2. To apportion, attach (esp. blame) to a person. 3. To put down in writing, add, at the end of a document; attach, append *to*: *to affix one's signature.*

affix (II.), n. [1. áfiks; 2. ǽfiks), fr. Fr. *affixe*, fr. Lat. *affixum*. See **affix (I.)**. That which is affixed, added, stuck on; specif. (gram.), formative element, prefix or suffix, added to a stem or base, which has the function of modifying and further defining original meaning, or of expressing a syntactic relation.

afflatus, n. [1. aflátus; 2. əfléitəs], fr. Lat. *afflātus*, lit. 'a blowing on, breathing; breeze, blast; inspiration, enthusiasm', fr. P.P. of *afflāre*, 'to blow, breathe, inspire'. See **ad-** & **flatus**. Lat. *flāre*, 'blow', is cogn. w. **blow (I.)**. **a** A breath, blast; **b** inspiration, strong impulse, esp. of poets, prophets.

afflict, vb. trans. [1. aflíkt; 2. əflíkt], fr. Lat. *afflict-(um)*, P.P. type of *affligere*, 'to dash down, damage' (also *afflictāre*, intens. of *affligere*, 'to dash against; to distress'); **ad-** & *flictus*, 'a striking, dashing together', fr. *fligere*, 'to strike'; cogn. w. Goth. *bliggwan*, 'strike', *blaggw*, 'a blow' &c. Cp. **inflict** & **thlipsis**. To cause pain or suffering to body or mind; to distress, torment, grieve, make sad.

afflicting, adj. [1. aflíkting; 2. əflíktiŋ], fr. Pres. Part. of prec. Distressing, grievous, productive of sorrow.

affliction, n. [1. aflíkshun; 2. əflíkʃən], fr. Fr. *affliction*, fr. Lat. *afflictiōn-(em)*. See **afflict** & **-ion**. **a** A state of mental suffering, grief, misery, distress, adversity; **b** *an affliction*, anything which gives rise to such suffering; calamity, misfortune, blow.

afflictive, adj. [1. aflíktiv; 2. əflíktiv], fr. **afflict** & **-ive**. Cp. Fr. *afflictif*. Giving or causing grief.

affluence, n. [1. áflooens; 2. ǽfluəns], fr. Fr. *affluence*, fr. Lat. *affluentia*, fr. *affluent-(em)*, Pres. Part. of *affluere*, 'to flow to', fr. **ad-** & *fluere*, 'to flow', see **fluent**. Abundance, profusion, copiousness; specif., riches, wealth.

affluent (I.), adj. [1. áflooent; 2. ǽfluənt], fr. Lat. *affluentem*. See prec. **a** (lit.) Flowing freely, abundant; **b** (of persons) abounding in goods or riches, wealthy.

affluent (II.), n. Same as prec. Used in literal sense of 'flowing to'. Stream which flows into another; tributary.

afflux, n. [1. áfluks; 2. ǽflaks], fr. Lat. *afflux-(um)*, P.P. of *affluere*, 'to flow to'. See **ad-** & **flux**, & cp. **affluence**. A flowing towards, of water, a crowd of people, moving objects generally; (med.) flow of blood to some part.

afford, vb. trans. [1. afórd; 2. əfɔ́d]. The pref. is historically O.E. *ġe-*, later weakened to *a-* & confused w. O. Fr. or Lat. *af-*, fr. **ad-** & *f-*; O.E. *forþian*, 'help forward, promote well-being of'; *ġe-forþian*, 'put forth, contribute, prosper, promote well-being of, carry out' &c., is formed fr. O.E. adv. *forþ*, 'forwards' &c. See **forth, further**, adv. & vb. 1. **a** (of material things) To give forth, yield, supply, provide with, furnish from natural resources: *the trees afford a pleasant shade*; *the coco-nut affords a sweet and refreshing milk*; also **b** (of non-material things) *it affords me great satisfaction to be able to help you.* 2. (preceded by *can, can't, be able*) To be able to pay for, be rich enough to buy; have enough to spare: *he can* (or *is able to*) *afford to keep a motor-car, but not to hunt as well*; *I can't afford the time for so-and-so.*

afforest, vb. trans. [1. afórest; 2. æfɔ́rist]. See **ad-** & **forest**. To plant trees systematically on, cover (land) with forest, convert into forest.

afforestation, n. [1. àforestáshun; 2. æ̀fɔristéiʃən], fr. prec. & **-ation**. Act or process, natural or artificial, of planting a forest.

affranchise, vb. trans. [1. afránchīz; 2. əfrǽntʃaiz]. See **ad-** & **franchise**. To make free; to release from obligation.

affray, n. [1. afrá; 2. əfréi]. See also **fray (I.)**. Orig. a vb., 'to frighten' (still so used by Shakespeare), cp. **afraid**, fr. O. Fr. *effraier*, Mod. Fr. *effrayer*, cp. also n. *effroi*, 'fear, terror'. The word is a hybrid, fr. Lat. **ex-**, 'out of', & Gmc. **friþ-*, 'peace', cp. O.H.G. *fridu* (whence Fr. form), O.S. *frithu*, O.E. *friðu*, all ultimately fr. Aryan base **pri-*, 'love, protect'. Cp. **free, friend**. Breach of the peace, fighting, esp. a public riot; brush, contest, between small parties of opposing sides in a war.

affright (I.), vb. trans. [1. afrít; 2. əfráit]. Late formation, so far as spelling is concerned, fr. *af-*=**ad-** & **fright (I.)**; the O.E. compound *āfyrhtan*, 'frighten', M.E. *afrihte*, is the true ancestor of the uttered form, though the spelling has been altered fr. erroneous view as to origin of pref. To frighten, terrify, scare (archaic and poet.).

affright (II.), n., fr. prec. Fear, terror, panic (archaic and poet.).

affront (I.), vb. trans. [1. afrúnt; 2. əfrʌ́nt], fr. O. Fr. *afronter*, fr. Low Lat. *affrontāre*, 'to strike against', fr. Lat. **ad-** & *front-em*, 'forehead, front'. See **front**. 1. **a** To insult, offend, put a slight upon (a person); **b** to offend pride or modesty of. 2. To confront, dare, face: *to affront death a hundred times.*

affront (II.), n., fr. prec. An impudent, offensive speech or act; insult. Phr. *to offer, put an affront upon.*

affronté, adj. [1. afróntā; 2. æfrɔ̃tei]. Fr., P.P. of *affronter*. See **affront (I.)**. (her.) **a** (of two animals &c. on shield) Face to face, facing each other; **b** facing full to the front.

affronted, adj. [1. afrúnted; 2. əfrʌ́ntid], fr. P.P. of **affront (I.)**. Deeply offended, wounded in feelings, having sense of being insulted.

affusion, n. [1. afúzhun; 2. əfjúʒən]. Lat. *affūsiōn-(em)*, fr. *affūs-(um)*, P.P. type of *affundere*, 'to pour upon', fr. *ad* & *fundere*, 'to pour'. See **ad-** & **fusion**. Specif., the act of pouring of water upon the body in baptism.

afield, adv. [1. aféld; 2. əfíəld]. O.E. *on felda*, 'in the field'. See **a-** & **field**. **a** In the field, out (of troops and agricultural labourers); **b** far away (from home), at, to, a distance; esp. *far afield*, remote, out of the way; *go too far afield*, out of one's way.

afire, adv. & p. adj. [1. afír; 2. əfáiə]. See **a-** & **fire**. On fire (lit. and fig., of passion &c.): *with heart afire.*

aflame, adv. & adj. [1. aflám; 2. əfléim]. See **a-** & **flame**. In a flame, ablaze; in a glow, glowing; esp. *aflame with colour, with enthusiasm*; (of human face) *aflame with blushes.*

afloat, adv. [1. aflót; 2. əflóut]. O.E. *on flote*, 'on the sea', fr. *flot*, 'sea'. See **float**. 1. **a** At sea, on board ship as distinct from being on land; **b** floating about (of objects in water); **c** flooded with water (of the floor &c.). Phr. *to keep afloat*, stay at surface of water, prevent (oneself or another) from sinking; (fig.) keep out of debt. 2. (fig.) Current, widely known and circulated (of report, rumour &c.).

afoot, adv. & adj. [1. afóot; 2. əfút]. See **a-** & **foot**. **a** On foot (archaic); **b** on the move, stirring, astir, going about: *to be early afoot*; (fig.) *mischief afoot.*

afore, adv. & prep. [1. afór; 2. əfɔ́]. O.E. *on foran*, 'before'. See **a-** & **fore**. (naut.) In front of: esp. *to serve afore the mast*, as one of the crew.

afore-, in compounds such as *afore-said, aforementioned*, said, mentioned, earlier or previously.

a fortiori, adv. [1. á fòrtiórī; 2. éi fɔ̀tiɔ́rai]. Lat., 'by, with the stronger reason'; compar. of *fortis*, 'strong'. See **fort**. All the stronger, with all the more force.

afraid, adj. [1. afrád; 2. əfréid]. Orig. P.P. of *affray*, 'to frighten', see **affray**. Filled with fear, frightened: *afraid of* (before nouns), *that* (before verbs).

afreet, afrit, afrite, n. [1. áfrēt; 2. ǽfrīt]. Arab. An evil demon, monstrous malevolent giant.

afresh, adv. [1. afrésh; 2. əfréʃ]. **a-** & **fresh**, formed on model of orig. Engl. advs. Anew, again, once more.

Afrikander, n. [1. àfrikánder; 2. æ̀frikǽndə]. S. Afr. Du. A settler in South Africa, of European, esp. of Dutch, blood.

aft, adv. [1. ahft; 2. āft]. O.E. *æftan*, 'from behind', Goth. *aft*, 'behind', adv. *aftana*, 'from behind', fr. *af*, 'from, out of, by', O.E. *æf, af, of*, O.H.G. *aba, abe* &c., & *-ta*, superl. suff.; *af* &c. is cogn. w. Scrt. *ápa*, 'away from', Gk. *ápo, apó*, 'from, away from, down from', Lat. *ab*, 'from' &c. (naut.) Towards the stern of a vessel. Phr. *fore and aft*, lengthwise, from stem to stern.

after, prep. & adv. & adj. [1. áhfter; 2. ā́ftə]. O.E. *æfter*, 'behind, in place, time, order; through, during, in consequence of'. Orig. compar. of **æft*. See **aft**. **A**. prep. 1. **a** (of place) Later, behind: *shut the door after you*; *come into the room after me*; **b** (of order) next to, following: *my name comes after yours.* Phrs. *day after day, year after year*, continuously; *one after another*, consecutively. 2. (of time) Later than, subsequent to: *King John reigned after King Richard.* 3. (expressing relation of cause and effect) **a** In consequence, as result of: *I shall not go after what has happened*; **b** in spite of: *after all my trouble he has learnt nothing.* 4. (with certain verbs) Expressing object, purpose: *to look after, see after, ask after, run after.* 5. In accordance with manner of, in imitation of: *a portrait after Romney.* Phr. *after a manner*, up to a point, rather badly. 6. In accordance with, in conformity with: *he behaved after his nature.* **B**. adv. of time. Later, subsequently: *a year after*; *after he had gone away.* **C**. adj. Later, succeeding, chiefly in *after days, years.*

afterbirth, n. [1. áhfterbërth; 2. ā́ftəbāþ]. See **after** & **birth**. (med.) Membrane which envelops foetus in pre-natal state and which is expelled together with the placenta after birth of child.

after-crop, n. A second crop on same land in the same year.

after-damp, n. Poisonous gas which remains after an explosion in mines.

after-glow, n. The light which remains in the west some time after the sun has gone down.

after-grass, n. The grass that grows after the hay has been mown; aftermath.

aftermath, n. [1. áhftermath; 2. ā́ftəmæþ], fr. **after** & obs. *math*, 'mowing', O.E. *mǣþ*. See **mow (III.)**. After-grass; (also fig.) results of some catastrophe, esp. *aftermath of war.*

afternoon, n. [1. áhfternōōn; 2. áftənūn]. Period between noon and evening.

after-pains, n. pl. (med.) The pains which succeed childbirth, esp. resulting from the expulsion of afterbirth, or the natural shrinking of the womb.

afterthought, n. [1. áhfterthawt; 2. áftəþōt]. **a** Reflection upon an act or event which is past; **b** idea, thought, answer, repartee &c. which occurs after, and generally too late for the occasion or circumstances in which it might have served.

afterwards, adv. [1. áhfterwardz; 2. áftəwədz]. Later, subsequently.

aga, agha, n. [1. áhga; 2. ágə]. Turk. An oriental title of rank, esp. in the Turkish army; *Aga Khan*, hereditary title held by the head of a family tracing descent from Ali, having spiritual authority over certain Moslem sects in India &c.

again, adv. [1. agán; 2. əgéin], in M.E., fr. O.E. *ongēan*, 'in front of, opposite, again', O.H.G. & O.S. *gegin*, Mod. Germ. *gegen*, 'opposite, against', O.N. *gagn*. Origin obscure, but sense is primarily 'opposition' in position, whence various differentiations of meaning; cp. Germ. *gegner*, 'opponent', *begegnen*, 'to meet', of one coming in contrary direction, *gegend*, 'countryside' &c. The following all have underlying sense of 'over against, coming to meet one, back' &c. **1.** Back to the original place, position, condition &c.: *to come back, home, again*; *be all right again*; *to be oneself again*, recover from illness. **2.** (of sound) In return, in response, giving echo back: *he shouted till the valleys rang again*. **3.** (expressing repetition) Once more, a second time: *do it again*; *again and again*, more than once, repeatedly; *time and again*, repeatedly; *now and again*, occasionally. **4.** (expressing increased quantity) *As much again*, twice as much; *half as large again*. **5.** Moreover, besides, further: *again, we must remember* &c. **6.** On the other hand: *this is better, but then again it costs more.*

against, prep. [1. agánst; 2. əgéinst]. O.E. *ongēanes, tōgēanes*, adv., fr. prec. w. advbl. genit. suff. & 'excrescent' *t*, cp. **betwixt, amongst**. M.E. has *ayeynst* &c. See remarks on **again**, the orig. senses of wh. are fully preserved in present word. **1. a** Facing, opposite to, usually preceded by *over*: *over against the church*; **b** expressing contrast: *against a pale sky*. **2.** Coming into collision, contact with: *to push against*; *waves beating against the shore*; (colloq.) *to run (up) against (a person)*, meet by chance. **3.** In anticipation of, in preparation for: *against a rainy day*; *against his coming* (obsolesc.) **4.** (expressing hostility) In opposition, hostile, counter, to; contrary to (lit. and fig.): *to struggle, fight, against*; *to be against a proposal*; *it's against reason*; *against one's will, wishes, expectations* &c.; *for and against*; *a race against time*; *against the stream*; *(to go) against the grain*; (also fig.) contrary to inclination. NOTE: meanings **3** and **4** are mingled in the expression *to be warned against (a person or thing)*.

agama, n. [1. ágama; 2. ǽgəmə], fr. a native Carib word for a lizard. A species of lizard, related to the iguanas, brightly coloured and changing colour like the chameleon.

agamous, adj. [1. ágamus; 2. ǽgəməs], fr. Gk. **a-**, 'without', & *gámos*, 'marriage', fr. base **gem-*, 'unite', whence also Lat. *gener*, 'son-in-law', *geminus*, 'twin', Scrt. *jāmiš*, 'brother or sister'; see **gamo-**. Non-sexual.

agape, adv. & adj. [1. agáp; 2. əgéip]. See **a-** & **gape**. Gaping, open-mouthed (with surprise, expectation &c.).

agape, n. [1. ágapē; 2. ǽgəpī]. Gk. *agápē*, 'love', pl. *agápai*, 'love-feast'. The vb. *agapáō*, 'love', whence the n. comes, is so far unexplained. Meal of which early Christians partook in connexion with Holy Communion.

agar-agar, n. [1. ágar ágar; 2. éigār éigā]. Malay. A gelatinous substance obtained from various East Indian seaweeds, used as a culture for bacteria, and in the East for making soups.

agaric, n. & adj. [1. ágarik; 2. ǽgərik], fr. Gk. *agarikón*, 'a kind of tree-fungus'. Prob. fr. a Pl.-N. (bot.) Kind of mushroom or fungus.

agate, n. [1. ágat; 2. ǽgit], fr. Fr. *agat(h)e*, fr. Ital. *agata*, fr. Lat. *achātes*, fr. Gk. *akhā́tēs*. **a** Semi-precious, variegated, very hard stone; variety of chalcedony; **b** burnishing instrument tipped with agate.

agave, n. [1. agávi; 2. əgéivi]. Lat., fr. Gk. *Agauḗ*, name of the mother of Pentheus, in Gk. mythol., fem. sing. of *agauós*, 'noble'. Etymol. doubtful. (bot.) A genus of plants, which includes the S. American aloe or century plant, from which sisal-hemp is made.

agaze, adv. [1. agáz; 2. əgéiz]. See **a-** & **gaze**. Gazing, on the gaze (esp. with surprise).

age (I.), n. [1. āj; 2. eidž]. Fr. *âge*, fr. Low Lat. *aetāticum* for *aevitāticum*, Lat. *aetāt-(em)*. See **aeon, eternal**. **1.** Whole period of existence of a person or thing, from his or its birth or beginning down to a given time, esp. the number of years a person has lived: *the age of Westminster Abbey*, *of human life upon the earth* &c.; *the ordinary age for entering a university is between 18 and 19*; *of tender, advanced, age*; *10 years of age*. **2.** The time of a man's life at and after which maturity is reached, when full legal rights are enjoyed and personal responsibility can be accepted; period of maturity in animals and plants: *to come, be, of age*, to reach, pass, 21 years. **3.** The latter part of life, the state of being old, opposed to *youth*: *the infirmities of age.* **4. a** Historical period; stage of development of civilization, art &c.: *the Stone, Bronze, Iron, Age*; *the Dark, Middle, Ages* &c.; **b** generation of men living at given period: '*The age to come would say this poet lies*' (Shakespeare). **5.** A great stretch of time: **a** great geological epoch in the earth's history: *Ice Age, Silurian Age* &c.; **b** very long, indefinite period of time: '*A thousand ages in thy sight Are like an evening gone*,' (Dr. Watts); (also colloq.) *what an age you have been!* **6.** (poker) The player on the left hand of dealer who draws cards and bets last.

age (II.), vb. intrans. & trans., fr. prec. **1.** intrans. To grow old, show signs of, have appearance of, old age: *to age rapidly.* **2.** trans. To cause to grow old, produce signs of old age: *worry and illness age a man.*

-age, [1. ij; 2. idž]. O. Fr., fr. Lat. *-aticum*. Suff. used to form ns.; expressing **1.** act, process, function, collectives of these: *breakage, leakage, marriage, driftage, wreckage, passage* &c.; **2.** rank, status, condition, and collectives relating to these: *baronage, peerage, pupilage* &c.

aged, adj. **1.** [1. ájed; 2. éidžid], well stricken in years, old (fr. P.P. of **age (II.)**). **2.** [1. ājd; 2. eidžd] **a** having attained age of maturity, esp. of horses (fr. **age (I.), 2**); **b** being of, having, a certain age: *aged 15* &c.

ageless, adj. [1. ájles; 2. éidžlis]. **age (I.)** & **-less**. Not old, having no old age, not subject to changes and infirmities of (old) age.

agency, n. [1. ájensi; 2. éidžənsi], fr. L. Lat. *agentia*, fr. Lat. *agens, agentis*. Cp. Fr. *agence*. See **agent** & **-cy**. **1. a** Motive power, force, mode of action: *electricity is a mysterious agency*; **b** effort, exertion, influence, instrumentality (of persons): *through the agency of powerful friends, he obtained the post.* **2.** (commerc.) **a** The occupation, function, of an agent; **b** place or office where an agent does his business.

agenda, n. [1. ajénda; 2. ədžéndə]. Lat. *agenda*, 'things that must be done', neut. pl. gerundive of *agere*, 'to do', q.v. under **agent**. Things to be done; list of details of business to be brought up at a meeting.

agent, n. [1. ájent; 2. éidžənt], fr. Lat. *agent-(em)*, Pres. Part. of *agere*, one of the most widely differentiated vbs. as to meaning in Lat. Among the chief meanings are: set in motion, physically and morally; drive, conduct, go; incite, rouse, urge; to do, act, deal with; spend time; manage, transact business; play a part as an actor &c. Cp. Gk. *ágō*, 'drive, lead'; Scrt. *ajati*, 'goes, drives'. The orig. & simplest sense of the base is 'movement, move'. See **act, agile, agony, agrarian, examine** &c. **1.** (of persons) An active being; one who does things, exerts power to bring something about: *a free agent*; (*passive agent* is really a contradiction in terms). **2.** (of persons) One who acts for another; one who is entrusted with the business of another; a substitute, deputy, generally one who manages and organizes, develops a business: specif., a land-agent, house-agent. **3.** A force in nature producing definite results upon various forms of matter, esp. *physical, medical, chemical agent.*

agglomerate (I.), vb. trans. & intrans. [1. aglómerāt; 2. əglɔ́mərèit], fr. Lat. *agglomerāt-(um)*, P.P. type of *agglomerāre*, 'to wind (as into a ball), to join, attach', fr. **ad-** & *glomerāre*, 'to gather into ball or heap, gather together', fr. *glomus, glomeris*, 'a ball of yarn'. The latter is fr. base **gel-*, **gl-*, 'gather, stick together', wh. appears also in Scrt. *gúlmaš*, 'swelling in the belly'; M.H.G. *klamm*, 'clamp, fetter'; O.E. *clamm*, 'grasp, bond'; & w. other formative elements, in a large number of words. See **agglutinate, clay, clot, clump** &c. To collect various objects or fragments, haphazard, into a mass, pile, heap.

agglomerate (II.), adj. & n. **1.** adj. Gathered together into a ball or mass. **2.** n. A confused pile or mass of unrelated objects, or irregular fragments; specif. (geol.) a collection of volcanic fragments fused by action of heat into single mass.

agglomeration, n. [1. aglòmeráshun; 2. əglɔ̀məréiʃən]. See **agglomerate (I.)** & **-ion.** **a** The process of collecting, or being collected, into a mass; **b** confused mass of disparate elements.

agglomerative, adj. [1. aglómerativ; 2. əglɔ́mərətiv]. See prec. & **-ive.** Having a tendency to heap together. (Rare.)

agglutinate (I.), vb. trans. & intrans. [1. aglṓōtināt; 2. əglū́tineit], fr. Lat. *agglūtināt-(um)*; P.P. type of *agglūtināre*, 'to glue, stick on', fr. **ad-** & *glūtināre*, 'to glue', fr. *glūten, glūtin-(is)*, 'glue'. See **glue** & **glutinous. 1.** trans. **a** To stick (things) together, as with glue; **b** to break down into glue-like substance. **2.** intrans. **a** To unite, cleave together; **b** to become broken down into glue-like substance.

agglutinate (II.), agglutinated, adj. [1. aglṓōtināt(ed); 2. əglū́tineit(id)]. See prec. Stuck together.

agglutination, n. [1. aglōōtináshun; 2. əglū̀tinéiʃən]. See **agglutinate (I.)** & **-ion. 1.** Act or process of sticking things together by means of glue &c.; the state of being thus stuck together. **2.** (philol.) Mode of combining together originally distinct elements in language, in which the fusion appears to be less intimate than in so-called inflexion, but which serves the same purpose as the latter. Sometimes applied to ordinary compounds in which neither word undergoes any change of form or meaning, e.g. *pig-sty.*

agglutinative, adj. [1. aglṓōtinativ; 2. əglū́tinətiv]. See **agglutinate** & **-ive. 1.** Tending to agglutinate, adhesive. **2.** (philol.) **a** Formed by agglutination: *agglutinative form, compound*; **b** characterized by agglutination: *agglutinative language.*

aggrandize, vb. trans. [1. ágrandīz; 2. ǽgrəndaiz]. Fr. *agrandir*; *a* for Lat. **ad-**, & *grandis*, 'large', see **grand** & **-ize.** To make larger; specif., to increase the standing and importance of person, institution, or state, esp. by addition of wealth, rank, or power.

aggrandizement, n. [1. agrándizment; 2. əgrǽndizmənt], fr. prec. & **-ment.** Increase of wealth or power, importance; elevation to higher rank.

ravate, vb. trans. [1. ágravāt; 2. ǽgrəveit], . Lat. *aggravāt-(um)*, P.P. type of *aggravāre*, t. 'to make heavy', fr. *ad* & *gravis*, 'heavy'. ee **ad-** & **grave (IV.)**. **1. a** To make worse, intensify the gravity of, make more burdensome (affliction, illness &c.); **b** to add to (an offence), make it worse. **2.** (incorrect and colloq.) To exasperate, incense, annoy (a person).

aggravated, adj. [1. ágravāted; 2. ǽgrəveitid]. P.P. of prec. **1.** Increased in gravity, made worse by some additional circumstance: *aggravated assault*. **2.** (colloq. and incorrect) Exasperated, incensed: *to feel aggravated*.

aggravating, adj. [1. ágravāting; 2. ǽgrəveitiŋ], fr. Pres. Part. of **aggravate**. **a** Making worse, more heinous, adding gravity to: *aggravating circumstances*; **b** (colloq. and incorrect) exasperating, annoying, provoking: *how aggravating to be interrupted*.

aggravatingly, adv. Prec. & **-ly**. In an aggravating manner.

aggravation, n. [1. àgraváshun; 2. æ̀grəvéiʃən], fr. L. Lat. *aggravātiōn-(em)*. See **aggravate** & **-ion**. Act or circumstance which adds to, and makes more grievous, heinous: *aggravation of sorrow, guilt* &c.

aggregate (I.), vb. trans. [1. ágregāt; 2. ǽgrigeit], fr. Lat. *aggregāt-(um)*, P.P. type of *aggregāre*, lit. 'to bring to the flock', fr. **ad-** & *grex, gregis*, 'flock, herd'. See **gregarious**. **a** (obs.) To collect, join together into a party or mass; **b** to amount to, work out at (of a given number of persons or things being estimated).

aggregate (II.), adj. & n. [1. ágregat; 2. ǽgrigit]. **a** adj. (of many individuals) Collected into a single body and viewed as a whole, total; **b** n., sum total, group as a whole; esp. in Phr. *in the aggregate*, on the whole, taken as a whole.

aggregation, n. [1. àgregáshun; 2. æ̀grigéiʃen], fr. L. Lat. *aggregātiōn-(em)*. See **aggregate (I.)** & **-ion**. Association, massing together into mass, crowd &c. of a number of separate individuals, persons, or things.

aggress, vb. intrans. [1. agrés; 2. əgrés], fr. Fr. *aggresser*, fr. Low Lat. *aggressāre*, freq. of *aggredi*, formed fr. *aggress-(um)*, P.P. type of latter, 'to approach, attack', fr. **ad-** & *gradi*, 'to step, go', fr. *gradus*, 'a step'. See **gradus**. (a dictionary word) To become an aggressor.

aggression, n. [1. agréshun; 2. əgréʃən], fr. Lat. *aggressiōn-(em)*. See prec. & **-ion**. An unprovoked attack upon; invasion of rights &c.

aggressive, adj. [1. agrésiv; 2. əgrésiv]. See **aggression** & **-ive**. (chiefly of persons) Having quarrelsome manner and disposition, fond of, and prone to start, controversy, and to attack in words, cantankerous: *aggressive person, manner, tone of voice, utterances* &c. Phr. *to assume, take, the aggressive*, to attack, take the offensive; be offensive.

aggressively, adv. Prec. & **-ly**. In an aggressive manner.

aggressiveness, n. See prec. & **-ness**. The habit and act of being aggressive.

aggressor, n. [1. agréser; 2. əgrésə], fr. Lat. *aggressor*. See **aggress** & **-or**. The person who begins a quarrel, or who first makes an attack.

aggrieved, adj. [1. agrḗvd; 2. əgrívd]. P.P. of *aggrieve* (the other parts of the vb. are hardly ever used), fr. O. Fr. *agrever*, 'to weigh down', fr. Lat. *gravāre*, 'to weigh down, oppress', fr. *gravis*, 'heavy'. See **grieve**. Injured in one's feelings, slighted; having one's just rights and claims disregarded: *to be, feel, aggrieved*.

aghast, adj. [1. agáhst; 2. əgást]. Old P.P. of obs. vb., O.E. *gǣstan*. See **ghastly, ghost**. Frightened, terrified; struck with sudden dismay, horror, amazement.

agile, adj. [1. ájil; 2. ǽdžail], fr. Fr. *agile*, fr. Lat. *agilis*, 'that moves easily, nimble', fr. *agere*, 'to move'. See **agent**. Nimble, active; swift of movement; also of the mind or intelligence.

agilely, adv. Prec. & **-ly**. Nimbly.

agility, n. [1. ajíliti; 2. ədžíliti], fr. Fr. *agilité*, fr. Lat. *agilitāt-(em)*. See **agile** & **-ity**. Nimbleness, quickness in movement (also of the intelligence).

agio, n. [1. ájō, ā́jō; 2. ǽdžou, éidžou]. Ital., 'discount', lit. 'ease', cp. **adagio**. **a** The discount or premium payable in exchanging the metallic currency of one country for that of another, or of depreciated for undepreciated currencies &c.; **b** agiotage.

agiotage, n. [1. ájotij; 2. ǽdžətidž], fr. prec. Exchange business.

agist, vb. trans. [1. ajíst; 2. ədžíst], fr. O. Fr. *agister*, cp. *giste*, 'lodging', Mod. Fr. *gîte*, fr. Lat. *jacitāre*, formed fr. *jacēre*, 'to lie'. See **adjacent**. (law) To feed one's cattle on another's land on payment of rent; to take in another's cattle to pasture on one's land for a rent.

agistment, n. [1. ajístment; 2. ədžístmənt]. Prec. & **-ment**. (law) **a** Agreement to take and feed cattle on one's land for a rent; **b** profit derived from this.

agitate, vb. trans. & intrans. [1. ájitāt; 2. ǽdžiteit], fr. Lat. *agitāt-(um)*, P.P. type of *agitāre*, 'to put in constant motion', freq. of *agere*, 'to move'. See **agent**. **1.** trans. **a** (of material things) To move, shake, cause to tremble; **b** (of the mind and emotions) to disturb, cause painful excitement, fluster. **2.** intrans. To stir up political, industrial, or civil unrest; *to agitate for*, excite, influence, public opinion in favour of.

agitated, adj. [1. ájitātid; 2. ǽdžiteitid]. P.P. of prec. Disturbed, disquieted, excited, moved (of the mind, and of material things).

agitatedly, adv. Prec. & **-ly**. In an excited, perturbed manner.

agitation, n. [1. àjitáshun; 2. æ̀džitéiʃən], fr. Lat. *agitātiōn-(em)*. See **agitate** & **-ion**. **1.** Mental or bodily disturbance, painful, tremulous, or fussy excitement. **2. a** Act of exciting mind of the public so as to cause unrest, esp. for political ends; **b** public disturbance or excitement so aroused.

agitato, adv. [1. àjitáhtō; 2. æ̀džitátou]. Ital. (musical direction) As with extreme, excited emotion, with rapid, tremulous movement.

agitator, n. [1. ájitāter; 2. ǽdžiteitə], fr. Lat. *agitator*. See **agitate** & **-or**. One who agitates, esp. one who stirs up political and civil excitement.

aglet, n. [1. áglet; 2. ǽglit], fr. Fr. *aiguillette*, 'a point', fr. *aiguille*, 'a needle', fr. Lat. *acucula* = *acicula*, dimin. of *acus*, 'a needle', cogn. w. *ăcer*, 'sharp'. See **acid, acrid, acute**. Metal tag of a lace.

agley, adv. [1. aglḗ; 2. əglí], fr. **a-** & Scots *gley*, 'to squint'. (Scots) Askew, awry.

aglow, adv. (used pred. as adj.) [1. agló; 2. əglóu]. **a-** & **glow**. (lit.) In a glow, glowing; (fig.) excited.

agnail, n. [1. ágnāl; 2. ǽgneil]. O.E. *angnægl*, 'corn on foot'. The first element is cogn. w. Goth. *aggwus*, 'narrow, oppressive, painful', O.H.G. *angi*, O.E. *eng*; cp. further Lat. *angor*, 'suffocation, torment', *angere*, 'press tight, throttle', *angustus*, 'narrow'. See **anguish, anxious**. The second element is O.E. *nægl*, 'nail'. An obs. word, preserved in English dictionaries & in dialect glossaries; but current in form *hangnail*. Meanings various, according to the dictionaries: a whitlow; torn skin at base of a nail.

agnate, adj. & n. [1. ágnāt; 2. ǽgneit], fr. Lat. *agnātus*, 'a relation (on the father's side)', fr. *agnasci*, **ad-** & *nasci*, 'to be born'. See **natal**. **a** adj. Sprung from same male ancestor on father's side; (fig.) allied, akin; **b** n., one so descended and related to another.

agnatic, adj. [1. agnátik; 2. ægnǽtik]. Prec. & **-ic**. Pertaining to agnation, q.v.; related through males.

agnation, n. [1. agnáshun; 2. ægnéiʃən], fr. Lat. *agnātiōn-(em)*. See **agnate** & **-ion**. Relationship by descent from common male ancestor on father's side.

agnomen, n. [1. agnṓmen; 2. ægnóumen]. Lat. fr. **ad-** & *gnōmen*, 'name'; old form of *nomen*, q.v. under **nominal**. Name added to surname; nickname.

agnostic, n. & adj. [1. agnóstik; 2. ægnóstik], fr. Gk. *ágnōstos*, 'not knowing', fr. **a-**, 'not', & stem of *gignṓskō*, 'I know'. See **gnostic**. **a** n. One who believes that nothing is, or can be, known concerning God or a future life, and that knowledge is limited to material phenomena; **b** adj., pertaining to, holding, this doctrine.

agnosticism, n. [1. agnóstisizm; 2. ægnóstisizəm], fr. **agnostic** & **-ism**. The negative doctrine held by agnostics.

agnus castus, n. [1. ágnus kástus; 2. ǽgnəs kǽstəs]. Lat. *agnus*, fr. Gk. *ágnos*, 'a willow-like tree used at religious festivals', confused w. *hagnós*, 'chaste', & Lat. *castus*, 'chaste'. Etymol. of first element doubtful, perh. Heb. For *castus* see **chaste**. Ornamental tree with white or blue flowers.

Agnus Dei, n. [1. ágnus dḗī; 2. ǽgnəs díai]. Lat., 'lamb of God'. See **yean**. **1. a** Part of the Mass beginning 'Agnus Dei'; or in English Eucharist, 'O Lamb of God that takest away the sins of the world' &c.; **b** music to which this is sung. **2. a** The figure of a lamb representing Christ, bearing a flag and cross; **b** a cake of wax stamped with this figure, blessed by the Pope.

ago, adv. [1. agṓ; 2. əgóu]. O.E. *āgān*, P.P. 'gone away, past'; M.E. *agoon*, used as adv. Pref. *ā-* had no very definite meaning; its function was chiefly intens. See **go**. Gone by, past, in the past: *ten years, a long, short, time ago* &c.; *long ago*, in the distant past.

agog, adv. & pred. adj. [1. agóg; 2. əgóg], fr. Fr. *en gogues*, 'mirthful'; the origin of *gogue* is unknown. Cp. Fr. *en goguettes*, 'joyous, merry', *goguenard*, 'facetious'. Astir, in a state of excitement, expecting something to happen; esp. *all agog (to hear the news)*.

agonic, adj. [1. agónik; 2. əgónik]. Gk. **a-**, 'not', & *gōnia*, 'an angle, corner', wh. is cogn. w. Gk. *gónu*, 'knee'. The latter word has cognates in most Aryan languages w. sense of 'knee' (see **knee**), wh. is prob. the root meaning unless the still more general one of 'joint' be the starting-point. An angle fr. the Pr. Gk. point of view, was a thing in the shape of the bent knee. Not forming an angle: specif., *agonic line*, imaginary line on earth's surface on which the magnetic and true north are the same.

agonistic, adj. [1. àgonístik; 2. æ̀gənístik], fr. Gk. *agōnistikós*, 'pertaining to a combatant', fr. *agōnistḗs*, 'one who contends in the games', fr. *agṓn*, 'assembly, place of contest, struggle, contest'; fr. base **ag-* as in Gk. *ágō*, 'lead, bring up' &c.; cp. Lat. *agere*, q.v. under **agent**. Pertaining to contest, esp. in athletic games; also of intellectual strife.

agonize, vb. intrans. & trans. [1. ágonīz; 2. ǽgənaiz], fr. Fr. *agoniser*, 'to be in death agony, at the last gasp', fr. Low Lat. *agonizāre*, fr. Gk. *agōnízomai*, 'contend for a prize, struggle', esp. in the public games, but also in gen. sense. See **agonistic**. **1.** intrans. To suffer intense pain. **2.** trans. To torture, cause to suffer great pain.

agonizing, adj. [1. ágonīzing; 2. ǽgənaiziŋ], fr. Pres. Part. of **agonize**. Causing intense pain and suffering, physical or mental.

agonizingly, adv. Prec. & **-ly**. In an agonizing manner.

agony, n. [1. ágoni; 2. ǽgəni], fr. Vulgate Lat. *agonia*, cp. Fr. *agonie*, 'death struggle', fr. Gk. *agōnia*, 'a struggle for victory in the games; anguish of mind'. See **agonistic**. **1.** Extreme bodily or physical pain or suffering: *in agonies of pain*. **2.** The last death struggle, the pangs of death: *the death agony*. **3.** Specif., the last sufferings, physical and spiritual, of the Saviour before the Crucifixion: *the Agony in the garden*; *by thine Agony and Bloody Sweat* (Litany). **4.** Extreme mental suffering: *agony of mind*; *in all the* *agony of doubt, despair.* Phr. *agony column* (in newspapers), one in which appear personal advertisements for missing friends, private messages (often in cipher), appeals for charity &c.

agoraphobia, n. [1. àgorafóbia; 2. ǽgərəfóubiə], fr. Gk. *agorá*, 'market-place, place of assembly', see second element in **panegyric**, & **-phobia.** (pathol.) A morbid fear of being in open spaces or a public place.

agouti, n. [1. agōōtē; 2. əgūti]. Fr., fr. Span. *aguti*, fr. native name. (zool.) A Central American and West Indian rodent, genus *Dasyprocta*, about the size of a rabbit, nocturnal in habit and very destructive to sugar plantations &c.

agrarian, adj. [1. agrárian; 2. əgréəriən], fr. Lat. *agrārius*, 'pertaining to land', fr. *ager*, 'land, a field', & adj. suff. **-an.** The Lat. *ager* is cogn. w. Gk. *agrós*, 'field', & Engl. **acre.** These are all derived fr. Aryan base **ag-*, 'go', &c., see **agent**, so that *acre* &c. is orig. that wh. is traversed. **1.** Relating to land or landed interest of any kind; specif., relating to cultivated land, and landed property. *Agrarian laws*, those relating to tenure and distribution of land. **2.** (bot., of plants) Growing in a field.

agree, vb. intrans. [1. agrḗ; 2. əgrī], fr. Fr. *agréer*, 'to accept or receive with favour', fr. *à* (Lat. *ad*) & *gré*, 'favour, good will', fr. Lat. *grātus*, 'acceptable, pleasing, agreeable'. See **grateful. 1.** *Agree to*: to consent, assent, to a proposal, offer; concur in, accept, statement, view &c.; also *agree to do . . .*; & absol.: *I agree*, I accept your view, proposal &c. **2.** *Agree with*: **a** (of persons) (i.) To be of same mind, share opinions of; (ii.) (used absolutely) to be in harmony, get on together: *he and I don't agree at all*; **b** (of things) to be conformable, to correspond: *your account hardly agrees with the facts*; **c** (gram.) to correspond in gender, number, case, person. **3.** To suit the health of; esp. in neg., *smoking doesn't agree with him.*

agreeable, adj. [1. agrḗabl; 2. əgrīəbl]. Cp. Fr. *agréable*, fr. **agree** & **-able. 1.** Pleasing, pleasant, delightful; (of persons) well-mannered, charming. **2.** (of persons) Willing, ready to consent: *agreeable to a plan, suggestion* &c.; also (colloq. and vulg.), *I'm quite agreeable*, I am ready to do what you want.

agreeableness, n. Prec. & **-ness.** The quality of being agreeable.

agreeably, adv. See prec. & **-ly. 1.** In an agreeable manner; delightfully, pleasingly: *to sing agreeably*; *agreeably surprised*, i.e. that something is better than one expected. **2.** In accordance with; conformably to: *agreeably to my instructions.*

agreement, n. [1. agrḗment; 2. əgrīmənt], fr. **agree** & **-ment.** Cp. Fr. *agrément.* **1.** Harmony, unanimity, of opinion; correspondence of feelings, sympathies, tastes &c.; conformity of statement. **2.** A mutual understanding, bargain, arrangement &c.; specif. (law), a legal instrument in nature of an undertaking or contract which is binding on the signatories. **3.** (gram.) Concord of words with others in gender, number, case, person.

agrestic, adj. [1. agréstik; 2. əgréstik], fr. Lat. *agrestis*, fr. *ager*, 'field'. See **agrarian** & **-ic.** Rustic, rural, unpolished, uncouth.

agricultural, adj. [1. àgrikúlchural; 2. ǽgrikáltʃərəl]. See **agriculture** & **-al.** Connected with, pertaining to, agriculture. *Agricultural show*, exhibition of farming produce and live-stock, also of implements used in the various branches of agriculture.

agriculturalist, n. [1. àgrikúlchuralist; 2. ǽgrikáltʃərəlist]. See **agriculture** & **-ist.** A farmer; person concerned with, or having a special knowledge of, agriculture.

agriculture, n. [1. ágrikùlchur; 2. ǽgrikàltʃə], fr. Lat. *agricultūra*, fr. *ager*, 'a field', & *cultūra*, 'cultivation'. See **agrarian, culture.** Art and theory of farming, including cultivation of the ground, sowing and harvesting of crops, and the raising of live-stock.

agriculturist, n. [1. àgrikúlchurist; 2. ǽgrikáltʃərist]. Prec. & **-ist.** One engaged or skilled in agriculture. (Rare.) See **agriculturalist.**

agrimony, n. [1. ágrimuni; 2. ǽgriməni]. Lat. *agrimōnia*, fr. Gk. *argemṓnē*, etymol. unknown. (bot.) A common hedgerow perennial plant, with spike of small yellow flowers & hooked, clinging fruit; also name of other plants not belonging to the genus *Agrimonia.*

agrimotor, n. [1. ágrimòter; 2. ǽgrimòutə], fr. Lat. *ager, agri-*, 'field', see **agrarian**, & **motor.** A mechanically driven machine, used in agriculture, to draw ploughs &c.

agronomic(al), adj. [1. àgronómik(l); 2. ǽgrənómik(l)]. Cp. Fr. *agronomique.* See **agronomy.** Pertaining to management and cultivation of land and production of crops.

agronomics, n. [1. àgronómiks; 2. ǽgrənómiks]. See **agronomy.** The science of the management of land and production of crops.

agronomist, n. [1. agrónomist; 2. ægrónəmist]. See **agronomy** & **-ist.** One versed in agronomy.

agronomy, n. [1. agrónomi; 2. ægrónəmi], fr. Fr. *agronomie*, fr. Gk. *agronómos*, 'rural, wild', also as n., 'steward, overseer of land'; *agrós*, 'field, land', q.v. under **agrarian**, & *nomós*, 'pasture, place for cattle', which word is cogn. w. Gk. *némō*, 'apportion, assign, manage; also drive (cattle) to pasture, feed'. See further under **nomad.** Theory and practice of production of crops; management of land.

aground, adv. [1. agróund; 2. əgráund]. See **a-** & **ground.** (naut.) On, or touching, the bottom in shallow water, and therefore unable to float; stranded: *to go, run, aground* (of ships).

ague, n. [1. ágū; 2. éigjū]. O. Fr., fr. Lat. (*febris*) *acūta*, 'acute fever'. See **acute.** A fever recurring periodically, accompanied by shivering fits, esp. malarial fever.

aguish, adj. [1. águish; 2. éigjūiʃ]. Prec. & **-ish. a** (of fever) Resembling an ague; **b** (of persons) subject to ague and shivering.

ah, interj. [1. ah; 2. ā]. Prob. fr. Fr. An exclamation expressing surprise, delight, pity, threats, regret &c.

aha, interj. [1. ah-háh; 2. āhā]. Exclamation expressing esp. triumph, mockery, irony &c.

ahead, adv. [1. ahéd; 2. əhéd]. See **a-** & **head. 1.** (expressing movement) **a** In advance, in front of, leading: *to walk ahead of*; **b** forward, onward: *to go, drive, run &c., ahead*; (colloq.) *go ahead*, go on, continue (story, work &c.); also *straight ahead.* **2.** (expressing position) Before, in front of (lit. and fig.). Phr. *breakers ahead!* **3.** *Ahead of*, in front of, in advance of (lit. and fig.): *to be, get, ahead of*, further forward than, in advance of; (fig.) succeed better than, surpass: *to be, get, ahead of all others in a race, business, knowledge* &c.

aheap, adv. [1. ahḗp; 2. əhīp]. **a-** & **heap.** In a heap, in a pile, piled up.

ahem, interj. [1. ahém; 2. əhém]. Conventionalized, literary form to express a deliberate cough of warning, surreptitious calling of attention &c. Pronunciation from spelling.

ahoy, interj. [1. ahói; 2. əhói]. Probably literary mode of expressing a shout; perh. influenced by **hoy.** Call used in hailing ships: *ship ahoy!*

ahull, adv. [1. ahúl; 2. əhál]. See **a-** & **hull.** (naut., applied to ship prepared to meet a storm) With sails furled &c., suggesting that vessel is reduced to a mere hull.

aï, n. [1. áh-ē; 2. ái]. Imitative, fr. the cry of the animal. The three-toed sloth of S. America.

aid (I.), vb. trans. [1. ād; 2. eid], fr. Fr. *aider*, O. Fr. *aidier*, fr. Lat. *adjūtāre*, 'to help', freq. of *adjuvāre*, 'cherish, sustain, help', fr. **ad-** & *juvāre*, 'to help'. See second element in **coadjutor.** To help, assist, in any way, bring succour to: *to aid a person to do something; aid a person in an enterprise.*

aid (II.), n., fr. Fr. *aide.* See **aid** (I.). **1.** Help, assistance of any kind. **2.** Person who, or thing which, supports, helps, assists: *he was my chief aid in the business*; *books are a great aid to reflection.* **3.** (constitutional hist.) Grant of money to the King for particular purpose, hence, tax levied for this purpose.

aide-de-camp, pl. **aides-**, n. Anglicized Fr. pronunciation [1. ād de kòm; 2. éid də kā]. Fr., 'assistant in the field'. (mil.) An officer personally appointed by a general to assist him in various ways in carrying out his duties.

aigrette, n. [1. āgrét; 2. èigrét]. Fr. *aigrette.* See **egret. a** The egret; **b** a plume or tuft of feathers, used as an ornament for the hair.

aiguille, n. Anglicized pronunciation [1. āgwḗl; 2. eigwīl]. Fr., 'needle'. See **aglet.** A sharply pointed peak of a mountain.

aiguillette, n. [1. àgwēlét; 2. èigwīlét]. Fr. dimin. of prec. Aglet, q.v.

ail, vb. trans. & intrans. [1. āl; 2. eil]. O.E. *eglan*, 'to molest, trouble', cp. adj. *egle*, 'horrible, repulsive; sad'; Goth. *aglō*, 'tribulation', *aglus*, 'hard, difficult', (*us-*)*agljan*, 'to trouble, afflict, weary'. The word is prob. cogn. w. O.E. *ege*, 'terror', Goth. *agis*; O.H.G. *egi*, 'fear'; Goth. (*af-*)*agjan*, 'frighten'. Cp. further Gk. *ákhos*, 'distress, mental pain', *ákhomai*, 'suffer' &c. **a** trans., usually impers. To cause pain, trouble, afflict: *it ails me greatly that* &c.; *what ails you?*, what's the matter?; **b** intrans., to be, grow, weak and ill: *he ailed sadly during the winter.*

aileron, n. [1. áleron; 2. éilərō]. Fr., 'little wing, fin', dimin. of *aile*, 'wing', Lat. *āla*, 'wing', orig. 'shoulder', fr. **aksla*; cp. Lat. dimin. *axilla*, 'armpit', cogn. w. O.E. *eaxl*, 'shoulder'. See further under **aisle, axil, axillary.** (aeronautics) Hinged flap attached to each end of main plane of a flying machine, which serves to preserve balance, and is used in turning sharply.

ailette, n. [1. àlét; 2. èilét]. Fr., fr. *aile*, 'wing', see prec., & *-ette*, dimin. suff. Projecting plate of steel, somewhat resembling miniature wing, fixed so as to afford protection to shoulder when chain armour was worn.

ailing, adj. [1. áling; 2. éiliŋ], fr. Pres. Part. of **ail.** Sickly, ill, suffering, esp. in body.

ailment, n. [1. álment; 2. éilmənt], fr. **ail** & **-ment.** Illness, indisposition, infirmity, chiefly applied to one of a trifling character: *little, slight, ailment*; occasionally: *serious ailment.*

aim (I.), vb. intrans. & trans. [1. ām; 2. eim]. M.E. *aimen* &c., 'estimate, intend', fr. O. Fr. *esmer, aesmer*, fr. Lat. *ad* & *aestimāre*, 'to estimate'. See **esteem** & cp. **estimate.** The Mod. Engl. meaning implies calculated direction of effort to a given end. **A.** intrans. *Aim at*: **1. a** To point, direct, level, a weapon or blow at a person or object with the intention of hitting him or it; **b** (fig.) to direct an action, or remark at a person, with intention of affecting him in some way: *in doing* (*or saying*) *this I am not aiming at you.* **2.** To direct the will or desires towards the attainment of an object, strive for particular purpose: *to aim at gaining the prize.* Phr. *to aim high*, desire, strive for success, fine results &c. **B.** trans. **a** To point, direct, level (a weapon, missile, blow) *at* a mark: *to aim a gun, a stone, a shot &c., at*; **b** (fig.) to direct, level, an action or utterance, *at*: *to aim one's efforts at*; *aim innuendoes, satire &c., at.*

aim (II.), n., fr. prec. **1.** The act of directing a weapon, blow, or missile towards the object intended to be hit; direction of a missile: *to take aim* (*at*). **2.** Purpose, design, intention, object to attainment of which one's efforts are directed.

aimless, adj. [1. ámles; 2. éimlis], fr. prec. & **-less.** (only fig.) Without any particular aim, purpose, design; hence, trivial, futile.

aimlessly, adv. Prec. & **-ly.** In an aimless manner.

aimlessness, n. See prec. & **-ness.** Lack of fixed purpose.

-ain, suff. Fr. form of Lat. adj. suff. *-āneus*; see **-an.**

air (I.), n. [1. ār; 2. ɛə], in M.E., fr. O. Fr., fr. Lat. *āĕr*, 'air', fr. Gk. *āér*, 'lower air surrounding earth', for **awēr*, cp. Gk. *aémi*, fr. **awémi*, 'I blow'. The Aryan base is **wē-*, the *a-* in Gk. being a pref. The cognates are Scrt. *vātaš*, 'wind'; O. Slav. *vejati*, 'blow', Lith. *véjas*, 'wind'; Goth. *waian*, O.H.G. *wājan*, O.E. *wāwan*, 'blow'. See further under **vent, wind. 1. a** The invisible, elastic, gaseous substance which surrounds the earth; atmosphere; **b** (gen.) space above the earth; the sky: *birds of the air*; *to leap into the air*. Fig. Phrs. *in the air* (i.) (of rumours) current, (ii.) (of projects &c.) having no foundation in reality, or not fully matured, shadowy; *to take the air*, to go out of doors; *hot air*, boastful, blustering, talk; *to tread upon air*, to be in an exalted condition of mind; *to beat the air*, to engage in futile pursuits or attempts; (*to build*) *castles in the air*, form fanciful schemes, unrealizable projects. **2.** A particular state or quality of the atmosphere: *fresh, bracing, air*; *Brighton is noted for its good air.* **3.** A breeze; movement of the atmosphere: *a nice air*; *a slight air stirring* &c. **4.** (mus.) A tune, melody, esp. the predominant motif, soprano part in harmonized compositions. **5.** Outward appearance, mien, bearing, deportment, style, manner: *an air of importance*; *a lofty air*; *a triumphant air.* **6.** (pl.) An affected or haughty manner; assumption of superiority in bearing: *to put on airs*; *to give oneself airs.* Phr. *too many airs and graces*, affectations of manner, finnicking mannerisms.

air (II.), vb. trans. & intrans., fr. prec. **A.** trans. **1. a** To expose to, put out in, the air for the purpose of drying, purifying &c.: *to air clothes* &c.; **b** to let air into, ventilate: *to air rooms*; **c** to expose to heat in order to remove dampness: *to air a bed, damp clothes* &c. **2.** (fig.) To publish abroad, parade: *to air one's opinions, theories, grievances* &c. **B.** intrans. To become aired, dried, purified: *to hang out clothes to air.*

air-base, n. The base of operations for aircraft, including repair-shops &c.

air-bed, n. A mattress inflated with air.

air-bladder, n. A sac containing air, found in most fishes, the swim-bladder or sound.

air-brake, n. A railway brake worked by air pressure.

air-cell, n. (anat.) Cavity or receptacle for air in the body.

air-chamber, n. Cavity filled with air.

air chief marshal, n. Title, rank, of an officer of the Royal Air Force, ranking next below the marshal and above an air marshal, equivalent to a general in the army.

air-cock, n. Small tap or vent to allow escape of air from engine or pipe.

air commodore, n. Title, rank, of an officer in the Royal Air Force, corresponding to colonel-commandant in the army or rear-admiral in the navy.

air-cooled, adj. [1. ār kōōld; 2. ɛ́ə kúld]. (esp. of engines in motors) Cooled by means of radiators exposed to the air.

aircraft, n. [1. ārkrahft; 2. ɛ́əkrāft]. Any kind of flying machine.

aircraft-carrier, n. A ship designed to carry naval aeroplanes, with special decks for starting and landing.

air-cushion, n. Cushion inflated with air.

Airedale, n. [1. ārdāl; 2. ɛ́ədeil]. Place name in Yorkshire. A large variety of terrier.

air-engine, n. Engine worked by heated or compressed air.

airer, n. [1. ārer; 2. ɛ́ərə]. **air** (II.) & **-er.** A frame on which clothes are aired or dried.

air force, n. That branch of the armed forces of the realm which fights in the air, in aeroplanes or airships, the full title being Royal Air Force.

air-gas, n. A gas used for lighting or heating obtained by saturating dry atmospheric air with vapour from various hydrocarbons, as petrol &c.

air-gun, n. A gun from which the ball is discharged by compressed air.

air-hole, n. One made to allow air to pass in or out; specif., hole in ice where a spring or current has prevented freezing, or one artificially made.

airily, adv. [1. ārili; 2. ɛ́ərili]. See **airy** & **-ly.** (of behaving, speaking) In an airy manner; lightly, jauntily, flippantly.

airiness, n. [1. ārines; 2. ɛ́ərinis]. See **airy** & **-ness. 1.** The condition or quality of being airy, exposed to, permeated by, fresh air. **2.** Lightness of spirits, gaiety; levity.

airing, n. [1. āring; 2. ɛ́əriŋ], fr. Pres. Part. of **air** (II.). **1.** Exposure to air or heat for warming or drying: *to give clothes, room, an airing.* **2.** Exercise in the open air for the sake of health: *to take an airing.*

airless, adj. [1. ārles; 2. ɛ́əlis]. **air** (I.) & **-less.** Deprived of, void of, air; unventilated, not communicating with the open air; stuffy.

airlessness, n. Prec. & **-ness.** State, quality, of being airless.

air-lock, n. Block caused in water-pipe by bubble of air which prevents flow of water.

airman, n. [1. ārman; 2. ɛ́əmən]. An aviator.

air marshal, n. Title, rank, of an officer in the Royal Air Force, equivalent to lieutenant-general in the army.

air-pillow, n. Pillow inflated with air.

airplane, n. [1. ārplān; 2. ɛ́əplein]. (American usage) Aeroplane.

air-plant, n. An epiphyte.

air-pocket, n. (aeronaut.) Current or aerial disturbance which causes aircraft to drop suddenly a considerable distance.

air-port, n. An aerodrome for the transport of passengers and goods by air, esp. one with a customs-house attached, for the collection of duties, examination of passports &c.

air-route, n. Established route which aircraft take from place to place, for passenger and commercial traffic.

air-shaft, n. Passage for admitting fresh air into a mine or tunnel.

airship, n. [1. ārship; 2. ɛ́əʃip]. A machine for navigating the air, capable of being steered, supported by gas-bags, and propelled by an engine or engines.

air-sickness, n. An illness experienced in flying at great altitudes, akin to mountain sickness.

air-space, n. Space containing air; extent of respirable air in a hall, room, or building.

air-tight, adj. Impermeable to air.

air vice-marshal, n. Title, rank, of an officer in the Royal Air Force, equivalent to major-general in the army.

airway, n. [1. ārwā; 2. ɛ́əwei]. **a** The passage in a coal or other mine in which the current of air, for ventilation, is carried; **b** an air-route for aeroplanes.

airy, adj. [1. āri; 2. ɛ́əri], fr. **air** (I.) & **-y. 1.** Exposed to the air; breezy: *an airy situation.* **2. a** Resembling air, thin, unsubstantial: '*an airy spirit*' (Shakespeare); **b** empty, visionary: *airy notions.* **3. a** Light, sprightly, graceful, delicate: *airy tread*; **b** light-hearted, vivacious, gay: *airy mood, manner* &c.; **c** from **air** (I.), **6** (in unfavourable sense), showing levity, flippant, off-hand.

aisle, n. [1. īl; 2. ail]. O. Fr. *ele*, fr. Lat. *āla*, 'wing', q.v. under **aileron.** The *s* is due to association w. Med. Lat. *ascella* fr. *axilla*, 'armpit', wh. is dimin. of *āla.* A side division of a church parallel to the nave, and separated from it by a row of pillars; passage between two rows of pews in a church.

ait, n. [1. āt; 2. eit]. See **eyot.**

aitch-bone, n. [1. āchbōn; 2. éitʃbòun], fr. *a nache bone* (15th cent.); O. Fr. *nache*, pl. *naches*, 'rump, buttocks', is fr. Low Lat. *naticas* (acc. pl.), Lat. *natis*, 'rump' &c. This is cogn. w. Gk. *nôton, nôtos*, 'back', further relations are unknown. The rump bone; cut of beef over this bone.

ajar (I.), adv. [1. ajár; 2. ədžā́]. M.E. *on char* (of window), fr. **a-** = O.E. *on* & *ċerre, ċierre*, 'turn'. Cp. Germ. *kehren.* See **char** (I.), **charwoman.** (of a door or casement window) Not quite closed and latched, so that it will move in either direction.

ajar (II.), adv. **a-** & **jar** (II.). (fig.) In a state of discord, in a jarring state, out of harmony.

akimbo, adv. [1. akímbō; 2. əkímbou]. M.E. *in kene bowe*, 'in a sharp curve'. See **keen** & **bow.** On the other hand, *-kim* may be connected w. **kink**, and the word may represent the Icel. *kengbojinn*, 'bent in a crook'. Only in Phr. *with arms akimbo*, with hands on hips and elbows bent.

akin, pred. adj. [1. akín; 2. əkín], fr. **a-** & **kin. a** (of persons) Of one blood or kin, related; often *akin to*; **b** (of things) having similar properties, resembling, connected with: '*pity is akin to love*'

Akkadian. See **Accadian.**

-al, adj. suff. **a** From Lat. *-ālis*, direct or through Fr. A living suff. used in forming adjs. fr. ns. of Lat. or Gk. origin; **b** fr. Lat. *-al* as in *animal*, or *-ālia*, neut. pl. of *-ālis*, used as n., direct or fr. M.E. *-aile*, fr. Fr. Living suff. used in forming ns. fr. vbs., as *avowal* &c.

alabaster, n. & adj. [1. álabahster; 2. ǽləbāstə]. Lat. *alabaster*, Gk. *alábastros* & *alábastron*, prob. derived fr. *Alabastron*, name of a town in Egypt. **1.** n. A soft white semi-transparent stone capable of receiving a high polish. **2.** adj. **a** Made of alabaster; **b** like alabaster, as being smooth and white.

à la carte, adv. & adj., Engl. pronunciation [1. àh lah kárt; 2. *à la kā́t*]. Fr. (of a meal at a hotel or restaurant) Ordered course by course, as desired, from the bill of fare; contrasted with *table d'hôte*; **a** adv., *to dine à la carte*; **b** adj., *an à la carte dinner.*

alack, interj. [1. alák; 2. əlǽk]. Perh. fr. **a-** & **lack.** Exclamation expressing sorrow or dismay, regret; also *alack-a-day, alas and alack* (obs. or lit.).

alacrity, n. [1. alákriti; 2. əlǽkriti], fr. Lat. *alacritāt-(em), alacritas*, 'cheerfulness, ardour, eagerness', fr. *alacer*, 'cheerful, brisk'; connected w. Gk. *elaúnō*, 'set in motion'; Goth. *aljan*, 'zeal', O.E. *ellen*, 'courage'. Eager and willing readiness.

alalia, n. [1. alália; 2. əléiljə]. Gk. *alaliā*, fr. *álalos*, 'speechless', **a-**, 'not', & *lálos*, 'talkative', cp. *laléō*, 'chatter, babble, make an inarticulate noise'. Base belongs to a group of imitative words; cp. Scrt. *lalalla*, imitation of stammering; Lat. *lallāre*, 'to sing a child to sleep'. Cp. further Mod. Germ. *lallen*, 'stammer'; Lith. *lalúti*, 'stammer'. (med.) Speechlessness, loss of speech.

alar, adj. [1. āler; 2. éilə], fr. Lat. *ālāris*, fr. *āla*, 'a wing'. Cp. **aileron. a** Connected with, having, wings; wing-shaped; **b** (anat.) axillary.

alarm (I.), n. [1. alárm; 2. əlā́m], fr. Fr. *alarme*, fr. Ital. *allarme*= *all'arme*, '**to arms!**' See **arm** (II.). **1.** A sudden call to arms; a warning of danger: *to sound, give, the alarm.* **2.** The emotion caused by anticipation of danger, fear, anxiety.

alarm (II.), vb. trans. fr. prec. **1.** (mil.) To call to arms; to give warning of danger, rouse to action. **2.** To cause dread or anxiety to, frighten, make anxious.

alarm clock, n. A clock which can be set to rouse sleepers at a given time by a noisy beating of a small gong.

alarmed, adj. [1. alármd; 2. əlā́md], fr. **P.P.** of **alarm** (II.). **a** Roused to action and vigilance; **b** frightened, dismayed.

alarming, adj. [1. alárming; 2. əlā́miŋ], fr. Pres. Part. of **alarm** (II.). Causing anxiety, fear, anticipation of danger or disaster.

alarmist, n. [1. alármist; 2. əlā́mist], fr. **alarm** (I.) & **-ist.** A nervous, timid person, given to anticipating the worst; one who starts rumours of disaster on a slight basis.

alarum, n. [1. alárum; 2. əlǽrəm]. Same as **alarm** (I.). **1.** Poetical for **alarm. 2.** Sound made by alarm clock; mechanical device for making this sound.

alary, adj. [1. ālari; 2. éiləri], fr. Lat. *ālārius*, fr. *āla*, 'a wing'. See **alar, aileron.** Alar.

alas, interj. [1. aláhs; 2. əlā́s]. Fr. *hélas*, fr. *ha*, exclamatory, & *las*, 'wretched'. See **lassitude**. Exclamation expressing regret, sorrow, pity, or apprehension.

alastrim, n. [1. álastrim; 2. ǽləstrim]. Invented word. (med.) An infectious disease, accompanied by fever and a rash, apparently a mild form of smallpox.

alate(d), adj. [1. ālāt(ed); 2. éileit(id)], fr. Lat. *ālātus*, 'furnished with wings, winged', fr. *āla*, 'a wing'. See **aileron**. Winged.

alb, n. [1. alb; 2. ælb], fr. Lat. *alba* (*vestis*), 'white (garment)'. *Albus*, 'white', has but few cognates outside Lat., but cp. Gk. *alphós*, *alōphós* (rare), 'white', & the old Gmc. word for 'swan', O.H.G. *albiz*, *elbiz*, O.E. *elfet*, lit. 'the white bird'. *Albion* (England) & *Alba*, Ir. for Scotland, are prob. Celt. representatives of the base, meaning the 'white land', the former named fr. the cliffs, the latter possibly fr. its snow-covered mountains. 'The white vestment', a long white vestment with a girdle and tight sleeves, worn by the celebrant at Mass over the cassock and under the chasuble.

albacore, n. [1. álbakōr; 2. ǽlbəkō], fr. Span. *albacora*, & Port. *albacor*, fr. Arab. *al*, 'the', & *bukr*, 'young camel, heifer, pig'. A large species of tunny, allied to the bonito.

albatross, n. [1. álbatros; 2. ǽlbətrəs]. Thus in Todd's 'Johnson', 1773. Perh. influenced by Lat. *albus*, 'white'. The name is apparently 'corrupted' by Dampier (d. 1712), who writes *algatrosses*, fr. Port. *alcatraz*, 'cormorant, or other large sea-bird', wh. is a variant of Port. *alcatruz*, 'bucket on a water-wheel'; this is an Arab. word, *al-qādūs*, 'the water-carrier, pelican', because it carries water in its pouch; the Arab. word is itself borrowed fr. Gk. *kádos*, 'cask, jar'; the Gk. word is said by Boisacq to be borrowed fr. Phoenician. Large web-footed sea-bird related to the petrels, genus *Diomedea*, found chiefly in the Southern hemisphere.

albeit, conj. [1. awlbḗit; 2. ōlbī́it] = al(though) it (so) be (that). Even though, although; nevertheless.

albert, n. [1. álbert; 2. ǽlbət]. Kind of watch chain named after Prince Albert; also *Albert chain*.

albescent, adj. [1. albésent; 2. ælbésənt], fr. Lat. *albescent-(em)*, Pres. Part. type of *albescere*, 'to become white', fr. *albus*, 'white'. See **alb**. Becoming white, passing into a whitish shade.

albinism, n. [1. álbinizm; 2. ǽlbinizəm]. See **albino** & **-ism**. Physical condition in men and animals, in which the proper amount of pigment or colouring matter is lacking.

albinistic, adj. [1. àlbinístik; 2. æ̀lbinístik]. See next word & **-ist** & **-ic**. Affected with albinism.

albino, n. [1. albḗnō; 2. ælbínou]. Span. or Port. *albīno*, 'whitish', fr. Lat. *albus* 'white', see **alb**; the term was originally applied by the Portuguese to negroes on the coast of Africa who were mottled with white spots. Man or animal suffering congenitally from a lack of pigment; true albinos have white hair and either pink or very pale blue eyes, which are unable to bear strong light.

albite, n. [1. álbīt; 2. ǽlbait]. Fr., fr. Lat. *albus*, 'white'. See **alb** & **-ite**. (mineral.) A white felspar, a silicate of aluminium and sodium.

album, n. [1. álbum; 2. ǽlbəm], fr. Lat. *album*, 'a white tablet on which anything is inscribed', neut. sing. as n. of *albus*, 'white'. See **alb**. A book, with blank pages, in which photographs, literary extracts, autographs, newspaper-cuttings, or stamps &c. are inserted or fixed.

albumen, n. [1. álbūmen; 2. ǽlbjumen], fr. Lat. *albūmen* (found once, in Pliny), fr. *albus*, 'white'. See **alb**. **a** White of egg; **b** a complicated chemical constituent of most organic matter; in scientific terminology, usually *albumin*.

albumenize, vb. trans. [1. albū́menīz; 2. ælbjū́minaiz], fr. **albumen** & **-ize**. To cover, coat, with albumen; to treat with an albuminous solution.

albumin, n. [1. álbūmin; 2. ǽlbjumin]. (chem.) Albumen, one of a class of proteids.

albuminoid, adj. & n. [1. albū́minoid; 2. ælbjū́minɔid], fr. **albumen** & **-oid**. **a** adj. Like albumen; **b** n., (usually in pl.) a chemical constituent of organic matter; proteids.

albuminous, adj. [1. albū́minus; 2. ælbjū́minəs]. **albumen** & **-ous**. Belonging to, containing, albumen.

albuminuria, n. [1. albùminū́ria; 2. ælbjùminjṓriə], fr. **albumen** & Gk. *-ouria*, fr. *oûron*, 'urine', q.v. The presence of albumen in the urine, usually, but not necessarily, a symptom of kidney disease.

alburnum, n. [1. albérnum; 2. ælbʌ́nəm]. Lat., fr. *albus*, 'white'; see **alb**. Soft white wood growing between the bark of trees and the heartwood or duramen; sap-wood.

alcahest. See **alkahest**.

alcaic, adj. & n. [1. alkā́ik; 2. ælkéi-ik], fr. Lat. *Alcaicus*, Gk. *Alkaikós*, fr. *Alkaîos* (*Alcaeus*), a lyric poet of Mitylene, contemporary w. Sappho (610 B.C.). **a** adj. Pertaining to Alcaeus, or to the metre invented by him; esp. *alcaic metre*; **b** n., *alcaics*, lines written in this metre: cp. Tennyson's '*Milton, a name to resound for ages*'.

alchemic(al), adj. [1. alkémik(l); 2. ælkémik(l)]. See **alchemy** & **-ic** & **-al**. Relating to alchemy.

alchemically, adv. Prec. & **-ly**. By alchemy or its processes.

alchemist, n. [1. álkemist; 2. ǽlkəmist]. See **alchemy** & **-ist**. Student or professor of alchemy.

alchemy, n. [1. álkemi; 2. ǽlkəmi]. In M.E. *alkenamye*, *alconomye* &c., on anal. of *astronomye*. O. Fr. *alchemie*, *arquemie*, fr. Arab. *al-kimia*, fr. *al-*, def. art., & Gk. *khēmeía*, 'transmutation' of metals; later 'alchemy, chemistry'; of doubtful origin, possibly fr. *Khēmía*, 'the black land', fr. *Khemi*, the Egyptian name for Egypt, & so meant orig. 'the art practised by the Egyptians'; in later Gk. the word was confused w. *khūmós*, 'juice', fr. *khéein*, 'to pour'; cogn. w. Lat. *fundere*; see **found** (**II.**), cp. **chemist** & **chemistry**. Chemistry as practised down to middle of 17th cent., the main objects of which were the discovery of the philosopher's stone (for transmuting all metals to gold), and the elixir of eternal youth.

alcohol, n. [1. álkohòl; 2. ǽlkəhɔ̀l], fr. Arab. *al kohl*, orig. a fine powder of antimony; the change of meaning to rectified spirit is European in origin. **1. a** Pure, rectified spirit, a volatile, intoxicating fermentation product contained in wine, beer, spirits, or other distilled or fermented liquors; specif., *ethyl alcohol*, obtained by fermentation of saccharine solutions; **b** (by extension) intoxicating liquor containing this: *not to touch alcohol*, drink no intoxicating drink. **2.** (chem.) A large group, the *alcohols*, of compounds analogous to ordinary 'ethyl' alcohol, which are hydroxides derived from hydrocarbons; common examples are *methyl-alcohol*, wood spirit, and *amyl-alcohol*, the main constituent of fusel oil.

alcoholate, n. [1. álkoholāt; 2. ǽlkəhɔleit], fr. **alcohol** & **-ate**. (chem.) A compound of an alcohol and a metal.

alcoholic, adj. & n. [1. àlkohólik; 2. æ̀lkəhɔ́lik]. Prec. & **-ic**. **1.** adj. **a** Of, pertaining to, alcohol; containing alcohol: *alcoholic drinks*; **b** caused by alcohol: *alcoholic gastritis*. **2.** n. A person who makes a habit of drinking alcoholic liquors in excess, and whose health is thereby impaired.

alcoholism, n. [1. álkoholizm; 2. ǽlkəhɔlizəm]. **alcohol** & **-ism**. The condition of an habitual drunkard; diseased state of the system caused by excessive use of alcoholic liquors: *chronic alcoholism*.

alcoholize, vb. trans. [1. álkoholīz; 2. ǽlkəhɔlaiz]. **alcohol** & **-ize**. To steep in, bring under influence of, alcohol.

alcoholometer, n. [1. àlkoholómeter; 2. æ̀lkəhɔlɔ́mitə]. **alcohol** & **-o-** & **-meter**. Instrument for measuring the alcoholic strength of spirits by weight or volume; hydrometer.

Alcoran, n. [1. àlkoráhn; 2. æ̀lkərā́n]. *Al*, Arab. = 'the'. See **Koran**.

alcove, n. [1. álkōv; 2. ǽlkouv]. Fr., fr. Span. *alcoba*, fr. Arab. *al-qobbah*, 'vault'. A recess, esp. in the wall of a room; summer-house in a garden; private apartment.

aldehyde, n. [1. áldihīd; 2. ǽldihaid]. Shortened fr. *alcohol dehydrogenatum*, i.e. deprived of hydrogen. (chem.) A volatile colourless liquid, with offensive pungent smell, obtained by the oxidation of alcohol.

alder, n. [1. áwlder; 2. ṓldə]. O.E. *alor*, O.H.G. *elira*, Mod. Germ. *erle*; cp. also Lat. *alnus*, 'alder', fr. **alisnos*; Lith. *alksnis*. Same orig. base as Lat. *ulmus*, 'elm'. See **elm**. Small European tree related to birch.

alderman, n. [1. áwlderman; 2. ṓldəmən]. O.E. (*e*)*aldormann*, 'prince, chief, governor'; fr. *ealdor*, 'chief' &c., fr. *eald*, 'old, senior'. See **old**. One of the senior members of a city or county council, distinguished from ordinary councillors by being elected for a long period or for life, so that they are not obliged to contest their seats.

aldermanic, adj. [1. awldermánik; 2. ōldəmǽnik]. Prec. & **-ic**. Pertaining to an alderman; characteristic of an alderman.

aldermanry, n. [1. áwldermanri; 2. ṓldəmənri]. **alderman** & **-ry**. **a** The office or dignity of an alderman; **b** a district or ward of a borough represented on the city council by an alderman.

aldermanship, n. [1. áwldermanship; 2. ṓldəmənʃip]. **alderman** & **-ship**. The office of an alderman.

Aldine, adj. [1. áwldīn; 2. ṓldain]. See below & **-ine**. (bibliog., of editions of books) *Aldine edition*, printed by Aldus Manutius and his family in Venice between 1490 and 1597, bearing the sign of an anchor entwined by a dolphin.

ale, n. [1. āl; 2. eil]. O.E. *ealu*, *alu*, 'ale, beer', genit. (*e*)*aloþ*; O.N., Swed., Dan. *öl*. The word occurs in no W. Gmc. language except Engl., where it is very old. It exists also in O. Slav. *olu*, & Lith. *alus*, 'kind of beer', & perhaps in **alum**. In some compounds *-al*(*e*) formerly meant a feast at which the liquor was consumed. See **bridal**. In general popular usage this word and beer, q.v., are applied indifferently to a thinnish, fermented malt liquor.

aleatory, adj. [1. ā́leatri; 2. éiliətri], fr. Lat. *āleātōrius*, fr. *āleātor*, 'dice-player, gambler', fr. *ālea*, 'die'. Etymol. contested; perh. fr. **acslea*, cogn. w. Scrt. *akšáš*, 'die'; possibly fr. same base as *oculus*, 'eye' (see **ocular**), meaning 'studded with eyes' or spots; another suggested connexion is w. Gk. *ēleós*, *ēlós*, 'crazed, distracted', w. wh. cp. also Gk. *alḗ*, 'wandering of the mind, madness', & *alā́omai*, 'wander about'. Depending on chance, on cast of a die; hence (law) depending on some uncertain event such as bets, lotteries: *aleatory contract*.

ale-conner, n. [1. ā́l kóner; 2. éil kɔ́nə]. See **ale** & **con** (**I.**) & **-er**. (hist.) An old manorial official who tested quality of ale and measures used in sale &c.

alee, adv. [1. alḗ; 2. əlī́]. See **a-**, 'on', & **lee**. (naut.) On the lee side of a ship; to leeward.

alegar, n. [1. ā́legar; 2. éiligā], fr. **ale**, & Fr. *aigre*, 'sour'. Cp. **vinegar**. (provinc.) Sour ale; vinegar made of this.

ale-house, n. Humble public-house; shop where ale is sold.

alembic, n. [1. alémbik; 2. əlémbik]. In M.E. *alembykes*, Fr. *alambic*, fr. Arab. *al-ambīq*, 'the still', borrowed fr. Gk. *ámbik-(os)*, *ámbix*, 'cup'. An apparatus, of glass or metal, formerly used in distilling; (also fig.) *alembic of the mind* &c.

alert, adj. [1. alért; 2. ələ́t], fr. Fr. *alerte*, formerly *allerte* & *à l'airte*; Ital. *all'erta*, 'on the alert', lit. 'on the look-out', fr. *erta*, 'a look-out, a watch-tower', fem. of *erto*, P.P. of *ergere*, Lat. *ērigere*, 'to raise or set up'. See **erect**. Watchful, vigilant, wide-awake, ready, in mind and body; esp. in Phr. *on the alert*.

alertly, adv. Prec. & **-ly**. In an alert manner.

alertness, n. See prec. & **-ness**. The state or quality of being alert; briskness, activity.

aleuron(e), n. [1. alūron; 2. əljúərən], fr. Gk. *áleuron*, 'wheat-flour or meal', fr. *aléō*, 'grind', cogn. w. Scrt. *áṇuš*, 'thin, fine'. (bot.) A proteid substance found, as minute granules, in the ripening seeds of wheat and other cereals.

alevin, n. [1. álevin; 2. ǽlivin], fr. Fr. *alevine*, fr. O. Fr. *alever*, 'to raise, rear', fr. Lat. *ēlevāre*, see **elevate**. The young newly-hatched fry of trout or other fish of the salmon family while the yolk-sac is still attached.

ale-wife, n. **ale** & **wife**. **a** Female proprietor of ale-house; **b** (in U.S.A.) popular name of a species of herring.

Alexandrine, n. [1. àlekzáhndrīn; 2. ǽlik-zǽndrain], fr. Fr. *alexandrin*. Perh. because this style of verse was used in O. Fr. in poems on Alexander the Great. (pros.) In English poetry a line with six stresses, e.g.: '*A needless Alexandrine ends the song, That, like a wounded snake, drags its slow length along*' (Pope).

alexandrite, n. [1. àlekzáhndrīt; 2. ǽlik-zǽndrait], fr. Alexander II. of Russia & **-ite**. A dark-green gem stone, with red reflections, a variety of chrysoberyl.

alexipharmic, adj. & n. [1. alèksifármik; 2. ælèksifámik], fr. Gk. *alexiphármakos*, 'warding off poison', fr. *aléxein*, 'to ward, drive, keep off', & *phármakon*, 'drug, poison'. See **pharmacology**. The first element is cogn. w. Scrt. *rákṣati*, 'to protect'; O.E. *ealgian*, 'to defend', *ealh*, 'temple'; Lett. *elks*, 'idol'. **a** adj. Able to drive away, counteract, poison; having the quality of an antidote; **b** n., an antidote.

alfa, n. [1. álfa; 2. ǽlfə], fr. Arab. *halfa*. Esparto grass.

alfalfa, n. [1. alfálfa; 2. ælfǽlfə]. Span., fr. Arab. *alfaçfaçah*, 'good fodder'. Lucerne.

alfresco, adv. & adj. [1. álfréskō; 2. ǽlfrés-kou], fr. Ital. *al fresco*, lit. 'in the fresh (air)'. **a** adv. In the open air; **b** adj., open air: *an alfresco luncheon*.

alga, n., pl. **algae** [1. álga, áljē; 2. ǽlgə, ǽldžī]. Lat. *alga* (pl. *algae*), 'seaweed'. Cp. Norw. *ulka*, 'sticky slime'. (bot.) The name of a large group of lowly organized plants, not differentiated into root, stem, or leaf, but possessing chlorophyll, including the seaweeds and similar weeds found in stagnant or slow-flowing fresh water.

algebra, n. [1. áljebra; 2. ǽldžibrə]. Arab. *al jēbr*, 'putting together of fragments'. Branch of mathematics dealing with relations and properties of numbers by means of symbols.

algebraic(al), adj. [1. àljebráik(l); 2. ǽldži-bréi-ik(l)]. Prec. & **-ic** & **-al**. Concerned with, relating to, algebra.

algebraically, adv. Prec. & **-ly**. By means of algebra.

algebraist, n. [1. àljebráist; 2. ǽldžibréi-ist]. **algebra** & **-ist**. Student of, expert in, algebra.

-algia [1. áldzhia; 2. ǽldžiə]. Suff. representing Gk. *álgos*, 'pain', see **neglect**, & **-ia**. Pain; e.g. *neuralgia*.

algoid, adj. [1. álgoid; 2. ǽlgɔid], fr. **alga** & **-oid**. (bot.) Resembling algae.

algological, adj. [1. algolójikal; 2. ælgə-lɔ́džikəl]. **algology** & **-ical**. Of, pertaining to, algology.

algologist, n. [1. algólojist; 2. ælgɔ́lədžist]. See prec. & **-ist**. Student of algology.

algology, n. [1. algóloji; 2. ælgɔ́lədži], fr. **alga** & **-logy**. Study of algae; that branch of botany which deals with algae.

algorism, n. [1. álgorizm; 2. ǽlgərizəm], fr. Med. Lat. *algorismus*, fr. Arab. *al-Khwarizmi*, 'the man of Khiva', Abu Ja'far ben Musa, Arab mathematician of 9th cent., the transl. of whose work introduced the Arabic numerals to Europe. **a** Arabic system of notation of 1-9 and 0; **b** the Arabic numerals.

algum, n. [1. álgum; 2. ǽlgəm]. Heb. A tree and its wood, mentioned in A.V. 2 Chron. ii. 8 &c. Also transliterated **almug**.

Alhambra, n. [1. alhámbra; 2. ælhǽmbrə]. Arab. *al hamra*, 'the red house'. The ancient royal Moorish palace at Granada in Spain.

alhambresque, adj. [1. álhambrésk; 2. ǽl-hæmbrésk]. Prec. & **-esque**. Made or decorated like the Alhambra.

alias, adv. & n. [1. ālias; 2. éiliæs]. Lat. *alias*, 'at another place, at another time', fr. *alius*, 'another'; Gk. *állos*, 'other'; cp. Goth. *aljis*, 'other', *aljar*, 'elsewhere', O.E. *elles*, 'otherwise' (cp. **else**). See **alien**, **alibi**, **altruist**. **a** adv. Otherwise, otherwise called: *Israel Cohen alias Ian Colquhoun*; **b** n., assumed name.

alibi, n. [álibī; 2. ǽlibai]. Lat. *alibi*, 'elsewhere, at another place', *alius*, 'other', & *ibi*, 'there'; cp. prec. word. (law) Plea in criminal charge that accused was somewhere else when the crime was committed, and therefore cannot be guilty of it. Phrs. *to set up an alibi*; *prove an alibi*.

alidade, n. [1. álidād; 2. ǽlideid]. Fr., fr. Arab. *al-hidāda*, 'a rule'. **a** The moving indicator of an astrolabe; **b** the vernier or indicator of optical or surveying instruments.

alien, adj. & n. [1. ályen; 2. éiljən], fr. Lat. *aliēnus*, 'belonging to another', fr. *alius*, 'another'. See **alias**, **else** &c. **1.** adj. **a** Belonging to another country, race; strange, foreign: *alien subjects*, *alien shores* &c.; **b** *alien to*, strange, remote from, repugnant to, out of harmony with: *quite alien to my thoughts*. **2.** n. A foreigner, stranger; specif., a non-naturalized, foreign-born resident in a country.

alienability, n. [1. ālyenabíliti; 2. èiljən-əbíliti]. See next word & **-ity**. Liability to be alienated.

alienable, adj. [1. ályenabl; 2. éiljənəbl]. **alien** & **-able**. Capable of being separated from one ownership and transferred to another (of property).

alienage, n. [1. ályenij; 2. éiljənidž]. **alien** & **-age**. Condition of being an alien.

alienate, vb. trans. [1. ályenāt; 2. éiljəneit], fr. Lat. *aliēnāt-(um)*, P.P. type of *aliēnāre*, 'to make different; to surrender, give up, lose; to estrange', fr. *aliēnus*, 'belonging to another'. See **alien**. **1.** To estrange, render unfriendly, lose friendship of (a person), to turn away affection, regard &c. *from*. **2.** (of property) To transfer to another's ownership.

alienation, n. [1. àlyenāshun; 2. èiljənéiʃən], fr. Lat. *aliēnātiōn-(em)*, 'a transferring or surrendering of a thing to a person; aversion, hatred; insanity, madness'. See **alien** & **-ation**. The act of alienating or state of being alienated; specif. **a** estrangement (of a person); turning away elsewhere (his affection &c.); **b** (law) legal conveyance of property to another; **c** derangement of the mind, insanity (not strictly an English usage).

alienator, n. [1. ályenāter; 2. éiljəneitə]. **alienate** & **-or**. One who alienates, esp. in legal sense.

alienee, n. [1. ālyené; 2. eiljənī]. (law) One to whom property is transferred.

alienist, n. [1. ályenist; 2. éiljənist]. **alienation** & **-ist**. Specialist in mental diseases.

aliform, adj. [1. āliform; 2. éilifɔ̄m], fr. Lat. *āla*, 'wing', & **-form**. See **aileron** & related words. Wing-shaped.

alight (I.), vb. intrans. [1. alít; 2. əláit]. O.E. *ālihtan*. See **light (V.)**. **1.** To get down, dismount (from a horse, a vehicle &c.); hence, to conclude one's journey: *to alight at Oxford*. **2. a** To descend and settle, come to rest, as from air to earth (of birds, aeroplanes); **b** *alight on*, strike with in falling or jumping: *to alight on one's feet*.

alight (II.), adj. See **a-** & **light (I.)**, n. Lighted (up), in a flame, on fire (lit. and fig.).

align, vb. trans. & intrans. [1. alín; 2. əláin], fr. Fr. *aligner*, fr. *à* (Lat. *ad*) & *ligne* (Lat. *līnea*), 'line'. See **line**. **1.** trans. To range, draw up, in line, bring into line. **2.** intrans. To form in line, fall into line (of troops).

alignment, n. [1. alínment; 2. əláinmənt], fr. Fr. *alignement*. See **align** & **-ment**. **1.** Arrangement in a line; formation in a straight line, esp. of soldiers on parade; also of sights of gun and target. **2.** (engin.) The ground plan of a railway or road as distinct from gradient or profile.

alike, adj. & adv. [1. alík; 2. əláik]. O.E. *ġe-līć*, 'like'. See **a-** & **like (I.)**. **1.** adj. (only used pred.) Similar, having strong resemblance, without difference. **2.** adv. In the same manner or degree; similarly, equally. Phr. *share and share alike*, to share equally.

aliment, n. [1. áliment; 2. ǽlimənt], fr. Lat. *alimentum*, 'nourishment', fr. *alere*, 'to rear, nourish, support'; cp. Goth. *alan*, 'grow up' (cp. Lat. *adolesco* under **adolescent**); O.N. *ala*, 'nourish'. The same base is found also in O.E. *ēald*, *āld*, 'old', Goth. *alþeis*, O.H.G. *alt*, the sense of wh. was 'grown, matured, old'. See **old**. Food, nutriment, means of support.

alimental, adj. [1. àliméntal; 2. ǽliméntəl]. See prec. & **-al**. Supplying food; nourishing.

alimentary, adj. [1. àliméntari; 2. ǽliméntəri], fr. Lat. *alimentārius*, 'of or relating to nourishment'. See **aliment** & **-ary**. **1.** Nutritive. **2.** Belonging to nutrition or functions of organs of nutrition; *alimentary canal*, channel in animal body through which food passes, including whole length from the mouth, through intestines to natural exit.

alimentation, n. [1. àlimentáshun; 2. ǽli-mentéiʃən], fr. Low Lat. *alimentātiōn-(em)*. See **aliment** & **-ation**. Nutrition; the act of providing nourishment, condition of being nourished.

alimony, n. [1. álimuni; 2. ǽliməni], fr. Lat. *alimōnia*, 'nourishment, sustenance', fr. *alere*, 'to nourish'. See **aliment**. Maintenance, means of living; specif. (law) provision made for support of a woman out of her husband's income after a legal separation.

aliphatic, adj. [1. àlifátik; 2. ǽlifǽtik], fr. Gk. *aleíphat-(os)*, *áleiphar*, 'oil, fat'. Cp. **adipose** & see **-ic**. Derived from fat, fatty, specif. (organic chem.) of a series of hydrocarbons.

aliquant, adj. & n. [1. álikwant; 2. ǽlikwənt], fr. Lat. *aliquantum*, 'somewhat', fr. *ali-(us)*, 'other', & *quantus*, 'how great'. **1.** adj. Not dividing without remainder: *6 is an aliquant part of 16.* **2.** n. An aliquant number.

aliquot, adj. & n. [1. álikwot; 2. ǽlikwɔt]. Lat., 'some, several', fr. *ali-(us)*, 'other', & *quot*, 'how many'. **1.** adj. Dividing exactly without remainder: *6 is an aliquot part of 18.* **2.** n. An aliquot number.

alive, adj. [1. alív; 2. əláiv]. O.E. *on līfe*, 'in life, living'. See **on** & **life**. (gen. used pred.) **1.** Living, possessing life, in a living state, not dead (of bodily and spiritual life). **2.** In force, being, operation; existent, unextinguished: *to keep a right, claim, alive.* **3.** Active, brisk, lively, alert, vigorous: *very much alive*; *a man who is thoroughly alive*; advbl., *look alive*, be brisk, be quick; (colloq. expletive) *man alive!*; *sakes alive!* **4.** *Alive with*, swarming, thronged with: *a pool alive with fish*; *alive with vermin.* **5.** *Alive to*, susceptible to, aware of, able to perceive: *alive to a fact, to possibilities, dangers.*

alizarin, n. [1. alízarēn; 2. əlízərīn]. Fr., fr. *alizari*, 'madder', prob. fr. Arab. *al-açārah*, 'juice of a plant', fr. *açara*, 'to press'. A red or reddish-yellow dye, originally obtained from madder, now produced synthetically from anthracene.

alkahest, n. [1. álkahest; 2. ǽlkəhest]. A pseudo-Arab. word, prob. coined by Paracelsus. A supposed liquid which would dissolve gold and all other substances; one of the objects of search of the alchemists.

alkali, n. [1. álkali; 2. ǽlkəli]. Fr., fr. Arab. *al-qāli*, 'charred ashes'. **1.** The soluble product obtained from the charred ashes of certain plants, soda ash or potash. Specif. **2.** (chem.) a base or compound which neutralizes an acid and forms a salt; particularly, one of the hydrates of sodium and potassium or of the alkali metals, cæsium, lithium, and rubidium, also ammonia solution, distinguished from an acid by turning red vegetable colours, as litmus paper, blue.

alkalimeter, n. [1. alkalímeter; 2. ælkəlímitə]. **alkali** & **-meter.** Instrument for ascertaining the strength of alkalis or alkaline mixtures.

alkaline, adj. [1. álkalīn; 2. ǽlkəlain]. Prec. & **-ine.** Belonging to, having the character of, an alkali.

alkalinity, n. [1. alkalíniti; 2. ælkəlíniti]. Prec. & **-ity.** Quality, property, of an alkali; alkaline property.

alkaloid, n. [1. álkaloid; 2. ǽlkəlɔid]. **alkali** & **-oid.** (chem.) Any of various nitrogenous organic substances having basic or alkaline properties, esp. such as are derived from plants, as contrasted with the ptomaines, usually highly poisonous and of acrid taste; many, as morphine, strychnine &c., are used as drugs.

alkanet, n. [1. álkanet; 2. ǽlkənɛt], fr. Span. *alcana*, fr. Arab. *al-ḥenna*, 'the henna plant', & **-et.** **a** A kind of anchusa or bugloss, the root of which yields a red dye; **b** dye obtained from this plant.

all, adj., n., & adv. [1. awl; 2. ɔl]. O.E. & M.E. *all*; in all Gmc. languages. Apparently no cognates outside Gmc. **1.** adj. **a** The entire amount, quantity, extent of; the whole of: *all day*; *all night*; *all the time*; *all his life*; *all England*; Phrs. *for good and all*, for ever, finally; *once for all*, implying never again; **b** the greatest possible: *with all speed*; *in all haste*; *with all respect*; **c** every, every one of, every kind of: *all men*; *in all directions*; *on all sides*; *all manner of*; *at all points*; *in all respects*; *at all times*; *at all events*, in any case; *maid-of-all-work*. **2.** n. The whole number, quantity, amount; everything or everybody: *all is lost*; *that's all*; *all in good time*; *all are agreed*, i.e. all men; *to lose one's all*, everything one has; with *of*=the whole: *all of it*; every one: *all of you*. Phrs. *after all*, when everything has been taken into account; nevertheless: *after all, it might have been worse*; *all-in-all (to me)*, my best-loved object; *all's one (for that)*, it's just the same; *and all*, and everything else, and the rest; *in all*, altogether, in total number: *a dozen in all*; *all told*, all counted; *at all* (esp. in neg. or interrog. sentences), in the least degree, to the least extent: *not at all stupid*; *is he at all suitable for the post?* **3.** adv. Wholly, completely, altogether, entirely, quite: *he's all agog with excitement*; *all covered with mud*; *all over*; *all too soon*; *all the better*; (colloq.) *you're all wrong!* Phrs. *all at once*, suddenly; *all but*, almost, nearly: *he all but collapsed*; *all right!*, (colloq.) expressing assent or approbation; *all one*, just the same thing, immaterial, indifferent; *all the same*, nevertheless; *all over*, (colloq.) resembling in all respects: *that's John all over*, what one would expect from John; *it's all over with*, *all up with (him* &c.), (colloq.) he is ruined, finished, done for.

Allah, n. [1. ála; 2. ǽlə]. Arab., 'God'.

allantois, n. [1. alántōis; 2. əlǽntouis], fr. Gk. *allānt-(os)*, *allās*, 'sausage'. (anat.) A membranous sac in the fœtus or embryo of mammals, birds, and reptiles.

allay, vb. trans. [1. alā́; 2. əléi]. O.E. *ālecgan*, 'put down, diminish' &c., M.E. *aleyen*. See **a-** & **lay (III.)**. **1.** To quiet, put to rest, appease, calm (a disturbance, excitement &c.). **2.** To alleviate, assuage, relieve (of pain, anxiety, trouble &c.).

allegation, n. [àligā́shun; 2. æ̀ligéiʃən], fr. Lat. *allēgātiōn-(em)*, 'despatching a mission', fr. *allēgāre*, 'despatch on business'; by metonymy, 'allege, adduce'. See **legate.** **1.** An assertion, affirmation, statement, esp. one not supported by evidence, cp. *a mere allegation*. **2.** (law) Statement made before a court of law &c. of something which it is proposed to prove by evidence.

allege, vb. trans. [1. aléj; 2. əlédž]. M.E. *alleggen*, 'bring forward as evidence', fr. A.-Fr. *alegier*, Central O. Fr. *esligier*, 'to clear at law', as fr. Lat. *exlītigāre*. Cp. **litigate.** **1.** To affirm, assert positively: *to allege as a fact*. **2.** To bring forward as an argument, plea, excuse, extenuating circumstance &c.: *to allege illness, error of judgement* &c.

allegiance, n. [1. aléjens; 2. əlídžəns]. M.E., fr. O. Fr. *ligeaunce*. See **liege.** (in feudalism) Duty, loyalty which a man owes to his sovereign or overlord; hence generally, loyalty, devotion.

allegoric(al), adj. [1. àligórik(l); 2. æ̀ligɔ́rik(l)], fr. Fr. *allégorique*, fr. Lat. *allēgoricus* & *-ālis*, fr. Gk. *allēgorikós*. See **allegory.** Pertaining to allegory, figurative, symbolical.

allegorically, adv. Prec. & **-ly.** By means of allegory.

allegorist, n. [1. áligorist; 2. ǽligərist]. Cp. Fr. *allégoriste*. See **allegory** & **-ist.** One who uses allegory; a writer of allegory.

allegorize, vb. trans. [1. áligorīz; 2. ǽligəraiz], fr. Fr. *allégoriser*, fr. Lat. *allēgorīzāre*. See **allegory** & **-ize.** To turn into, treat as, allegory.

allegory, n. [1. áligori; 2. ǽligəri], fr. Lat. *allēgoria*, fr. Gk. *allēgoría*, 'speech made in public assembly', fr. *állos*, 'other', see **alias**, & *agoreúō*, 'I speak (in the assembly)', fr. *agorá*, 'place of assembly'. See base **ag-* under **agent.** Description, or narrative conveyed by means of another differing from it, but resembling it sufficiently to suggest it; a figurative story in the nature of a parable, the purpose of which is often to enforce a series of moral teachings.

allegretto, n., adj., & adv. [1. àlegrétō; 2. æ̀ligrétou]. Ital., dimin. of **allegro.** (mus.) **1.** n. A movement in music not quite as brisk as *allegro*. **2.** adj. Rather brisk, somewhat brisk. **3.** adv. Rather briskly.

allegro, n., adj., & adv. [1. alā́grō; 2. æléigrou]. Ital., lit. 'cheerful, gay', fr. Lat. *alacer*, 'lively'. See **alacrity.** (mus.) **1.** n. A quick movement in music intermediate between *andante* and *presto*. **2.** adj. Quick, brisk. **3.** adv. Quickly, briskly.

alleluia, n. & interj. [1. àlilóōya; 2. æ̀lilújə]. Lat. form, fr. Gk. *allēloúia*, of Heb. *hallēlūyāh*. See **hallelujah. a** n. Song of praise; **b** interj., exclamation of joy, praise, and exultation.

allergy, n. [1. álerji; 2. ǽlədži]. A coined term, fr. Gk. *állos*, 'other, different'; see **alias** & **else**, & **energy.** (physiol.) Condition in which the reaction to a second infection by a toxin, serum &c. differs from that following a first infection, cp. *anaphylaxis*.

allerion, n. [1. alḗriun; 2. əlíəriən]. Fr., also *alerion*; etymol. doubtful. (her.) An eagle, displayed with expanded wings but with feet cut off and no beak.

alleviate, vb. trans. [1. alḗviāt; 2. əlívieit], fr. L. Lat. *alleviāt-(um)*, P.P. type of *alleviāre*, fr. Lat. *allevāre*, fr. **ad-** & *levāre*, 'to lighten, ease', fr. *levis*, adj., 'light'. See **levity.** To lighten, lessen, mitigate, relieve (pain and suffering of body or mind).

alleviation, n. [1. alèviā́shun; 2. əlìviéiʃən], fr. prec. & **-ion.** The act or process of lightening, relieving pain, sorrow &c; relief, mitigation.

alleviative, adj. & n. [1. alḗviativ; 2. əlíviətiv]. See prec. & **-ive. a** adj. Tending to alleviate; **b** n., that which alleviates.

alley (I.), n. [1. áli; 2. ǽli]. O. Fr. *alee*, 'a going, passage'. Cp. Fr. *aller*, 'go, walk' &c. Etymol. of this common word is doubtful, but Meyer-Lübke suggests Lat. *ambulāre*, 'go, walk', w. assimilation of *mb* to *l*, through intermediate *amblar*. The Lat. word itself is not satisfactorily explained; connexion w. Gk. *aláomai*, 'wander', is suggested, the first element being *amb-* (cp. *ambi*, 'around'), the second *ul-*, cogn. w. Gk. *al-*, 'wander'. Cp. **amble (I.)**. See **aleatory. 1.** Path, shady walk bordered by trees &c. in pleasure grounds. **2.** Narrow passage between buildings; a narrow squalid street in a slum; *blind alley*, (lit. and fig.) path, way, that leads nowhere. **3.** Narrow, enclosed space for bowls or skittles.

alley (II.), n. See **ally (III.)**.

All Fools' Day, n. The 1st of April, when people are made April fools.

all fours, n. [1. áwl fórz; 2. ɔ́l fɔ́z]. **1. a** All four legs of an animal; **b** the two arms and legs of a human being. Phr. *on all fours with*, exactly corresponding, alike. **2.** A card game, also called 'seven up'.

All-Hallows, n. [1. áwl hálōz; 2. ɔ́l hǽlouz]. See **all** & **hallow.** All Saints' Day, the 1st of November.

All-Hallow's Eve. See **Hallowe'en.**

alliacious, adj. [1. àliā́shus; 2. æ̀liéiʃəs], fr. Lat. *allium*, *ālium*, 'garlic', & **-aceous**; *ālium*, orig. 'the strong-smelling plant', is fr. earlier **an-slom*, fr. base **an-* 'breathe, smell', see **animus.** (bot.) Of, belonging to, the genus of plants, *Allium*, which includes the onion and leek as well as garlic.

alliance, n. [1. alī́ans; 2. əláiəns]. M.E. *aliaunce*, O. Fr. *aliance*, Fr. *alliance*, fr. O. Fr. *alier*, Fr. *allier*. See **ally (I.)**. **a** A union between families by marriage: *matrimonial alliance*; **b** a friendly union between states, nations, parties &c., esp. by treaty or pact, for achievement of a common interest in peace, war, politics &c.

allied, adj. [1. alī́d; 2. əláid], fr. P.P. of **ally (I.)**. **a** United together, connected by marriage (of families), or by treaties (of states); **b** akin, related, connected by similarity of character: *history and allied subjects*.

alligator, n. [1. áligāter; 2. ǽligèitə], fr. Span. *el lagarto*, 'the lizard', fr. Lat. *lacertus*, also *lacerta*, 'a lizard'. See **lizard.** (zool.) Large carnivorous aquatic reptile of the crocodile family, found only in America and China, having rather shorter blunter snout than the crocodile, and teeth in lower jaw which shut into indentations in upper.

alligator apple, n. A tree of the West Indies and tropical America with wood used as cork and a pulpy fruit or berry, an inferior kind of custard-apple.

alligator pear, n. A tree of the West Indies and tropical America; the avocado.

alligator tortoise, n. The snapping turtle.

alliterate, vb. intrans. [1. alíterāt; 2. əlítərèit], fr. Lat. *al* for **ad-** & *littera*, 'a letter of the alphabet', see **letter, literal**, w. vb. suff. **-ate**, on anal. w. **obliterate. a** (of words in sentence or group) To begin with the same consonantal sound or with the same or a different vowel sound; **b** (of writers and speakers) to construct phrases, sentences, verses, of words which begin with same sound.

alliteration, n. [1. aliterā́shun; 2. əlitəréiʃən], fr. prec. & **-ion.** Recurrence of the same consonantal sound in stressed syllables of several words in a series, in prose or verse.

alliterative, adj. [1. alíterativ; 2. əlítərətiv]. **alliterate** & **-ive.** Connected with, characterized by, alliteration: *alliterative poetry*, that in which alliteration is a structural feature, as in O.E. and in some M.E. poems.

alliteratively, adv. Prec. & **-ly.** According to the principles of alliteration.

allocate, vb. trans. [1. álokāt; 2. ǽləkeit], fr. Low Lat. *allocāt-(um)*, P.P. type of *allocāre*, fr. Lat. *ad* & *locāre*, 'to place'. See **ad-** & **locate.** To assign, allot.

allocation, n. [1. alokáshun; 2. æləkéiʃən]. See prec. & **-ion.** Apportionment.

allocution, n. [1. àlokúshun; 2. æ̀ləkjúʃən], fr. Lat. *allocūtiōn-(em)*, 'an address', fr. *alloqui*, 'to speak to', fr. **ad-** & *loqui*, 'to speak'. See **locution.** An address, esp. of an authoritative, admonitory character.

al(l)odial, adj. [1. alódial; 2. ælóudiəl], fr. Med. Lat. *allōdiālis*. See **al(l)odium.** Referring to system of land-tenure which existed to some extent among the Anglo-Saxons, and more widely, and down to a later age, in Norway, in which land was held without obligation to an overlord, practically equivalent to freehold; contrasted with *feudal*.

al(l)odialism, n. [1. alódializm; 2. ælóudiəlizəm], fr. prec. & **-ism.** The allodial system.

al(l)odialist, n. [1. ælódialist; 2. ælóudiəlist]. **al(l)odial** & **-ist.** One who holds allodial land.

al(l)odially, adv. [1. alódiali; 2. ælóudiəli]. **al(l)odial** & **-ly.** By allodial tenure.

al(l)odium, n. [1. alódium; 2. ælóudiəm], fr. Med. Lat. *allōdium*. The word is pure Gmc., being derived fr. Frankish *alōd*, 'entire property', fr. *all* (see **all**) & *ōd*, 'property', O.H.G. *ōt*, O.E. *ēad*, 'prosperity, wealth'; cp. O.E. *ēadig*, 'prosperous, rich, blessed'; also O.E. *ēaden*, 'granted'; extra-Gmc. cognates appear to be lacking. (law) Land held as the absolute property of the owner without being subject to any rent, or service, due to an overlord. See **al(l)odial.**

allo-, pref. used in forming many scientific compounds, fr. Gk. *állos*, 'other'. See **alias** & **else.**

allogamy, n. [1. alógami; 2. əlɔ́gəmi]. See **allo-** & **-gamy.** (bot.) Fertilization of one plant by pollen from another, cross-pollination, contrasted with *autogamy*.

allomerism, n. [1. alómerizm; 2. əlɔ́mərizəm]. See next word & **-ism.** (mineral. and chem.) Quality, state, of being allomerous.

allomerous, adj. [1. alómerus; 2. əlɔ́mərəs]. See **allo-** & **-merous.** (mineral. and chem.) Varying in chemical composition without change of form.

allopath, n. [1. álōpath; 2. æ̀loupæþ]. See **allopathy.** Allopathist.

allopathic, adj. [1. àlopáthik; 2. æ̀ləpǽþik]. Cp. Fr. *allopathique*. See **allopathy.** Belonging to allopathy.

allopathist, n. [1. alópathist; 2. ælɔ́pəþist]. **allopathy** & **-ist.** One who practises allopathy.

allopathy, n. [1. alópathi; 2. ælɔ́pəþi]. See **allo-** & **-pathy.** (med.) The ordinary system of medical treatment which aims at curing disease by remedies having an opposite effect upon the body to that caused by the disease. Name given in contrast to *homeopathy*.

allophylian, adj. & n. [1. àlofílian; 2. æ̀ləfíliən], fr. Gk. *allóphūlos*, 'foreign, of another tribe', fr. *állos*, 'other', see **allo-**, & *phūlḗ*, 'tribe', *phūlon*, 'stock, race', see **phylo-.** Of another race, foreign. Specif., applied to the non-Aryan peoples and languages of Europe and Asia.

allot, vb. trans. [1. alót; 2. əlɔ́t]. O. Fr. *aloter*; of Gmc. origin. See **lot.** To distribute; apportion, assign, as a share or lot, *to*.

allotment, n. [1. alótment; 2. əlɔ́tmənt]. Fr. *allotement*. See **allot** & **-ment.** **1.** The act of allotting or apportioning. **2.** That which is allotted; a share or portion granted to a person; specif. **a** a small portion of land let out at a low rent for cultivation under various enactments such as the Allotments and Small Holdings Acts; **b** appropriation of shares in a company to applicant, on issue.

allotropic(al), adj. [1. àlotrópik(al); 2. æ̀lətrɔ́pik(əl)]. See **allotropy** & **-ic.** Of or pertaining to allotropy.

allotropically, adv. Prec. & **-ly.** By allotropy.

allotropism, n. [1. alótropizm; 2. əlɔ́trəpizəm]. See **allotropy** & **-ism.** Allotropy.

allotropy, n. [1. alótropi; 2. ælɔ́trəpi], fr. Gk. *állos*, 'other', see **allo-**, & *trópos*, 'turn, direction, way'. See **trope.** (chem.) Property possessed by certain chemical elements, such as carbon, of existing in two or more distinct forms.

all-overish, adj. [1. àwlóverish; 2. ɔ̀lóuvəriʃ]. See **all, over, -ish.** (colloq.) Having general sensation of discomfort and indisposition: *to feel rather all-overish*.

all-overishness, n. Prec. & **-ness.** (colloq.) Condition of health in which general discomfort and uneasiness are felt.

allow, vb. trans. & intrans. [1. alóu; 2. əláu]. M.E. *alouen*. Two orig. distinct vbs. have been confused; O. Fr. *alouer*, 'place, use, assign', fr. Low Lat. *allocāre* (see **allocate**), & O. Fr. *aloer*, 'approve', Lat. *adlaudāre*, 'extol'. See **laud.** **A.** trans. **1.** To permit, give consent, assent to, **a** an action being done: *smoking is not allowed here*; **b** permission to (a person) doing something: *I can't allow you to behave like that.* **2.** To give, yield, provide, accord, make possible: *this gate allows access to the garden.* **3.** To make a fixed, periodical grant or payment: *to allow a person so much a year.* **4.** To acknowledge, admit, concede, accept as true or valid: *allow a claim*; *argument* &c.; *I allow that I was a bit hasty.* **5.** To make a deduction from payment due: *to allow a shilling in the pound*; *allow discount* &c. **B.** intrans. *Allow of* (*an excuse* &c.), admit; *allow for*, take into consideration, provide for.

allowable, adj. [1. alóuabl; 2. əláuəbl]. **allow** & **-able.** Of such a character that it can be allowed; permissible, lawful.

allowably, adv. Prec. & **-ly.** In a manner that may be allowed; permissibly.

allowance (I.), n. [1. alóuans; 2. əláuəns], fr. O. Fr. *alouance*. See **allow** & **-ance.** **1.** The act of allowing; permission; (rare in this sense). **2.** Something which is allowed; a fixed quantity or ration of anything which is periodically served out, e.g. of food, money &c.; specif., periodical payment of money to a person. **3. a** Deduction, discount: *an allowance for cash on a bill*; **b** the taking into account of extenuating circumstances: *to make allowance for his youth.*

allowance (II.), vb. trans., fr. prec. To put (persons) on an allowance of money, food &c., to assign definite amounts of food or money &c., at fixed and regularly recurring periods.

alloy (I.), n. [1. alói; 2. əlɔ́i]. O. Fr. *alei, aloi*, fr. *aleier*, 'combine', fr. Lat. *alligāre*, 'bind'. See **ligature.** **1.** Combination, mixture, fusion, of two or more metals. **2.** The standard of purity of gold or silver. **3. a** Base metal mixed with precious one; **b** (fig.) something bad combined, mingled, with something superior: *pleasure without alloy.*

alloy (II.), vb. trans., fr. prec. **1.** To reduce the purity of a metal by mixing it with a baser metal. **2.** To mix (metals). **3.** (fig.) To debase, impair, detract from the value of.

All Saints' Day, n. Festival in honour of all the Saints, Nov. 1st; All-Hallows.

All Souls, n. The faithful departed; often used as a title of dedication of a church &c.

All Souls' Day, n. Nov. 2nd, a day on which prayer is offered, esp. in R.C. Ch., for the souls of the faithful departed.

allspice, n. [1. áwlspīs; 2. ɔ́lspais], fr. **all** & **spice.** A highly pungent West Indian spice, *Pimenta pimenta*, supposed to combine the flavour of several different condiments.

allude, vb. intrans. [1. alúd; 2. əljúd], fr. Lat. *allūdere*, 'to play with, joke; to refer to', fr. **ad-** & *lūdere*, 'to play a game, frisk'. See further under **ludicrous.** Followed by *to*: **a** to refer to in speech or writing; **b** (often with idea of furtiveness) to refer to indirectly, covertly, to hint at; **c** to mean, intend to say: *when I say a hero, I allude to my friend opposite.*

allure, vb. trans. [1. alyór, alúr; 2. əljɔ́, əljúə], fr. O. Fr. *alleurer*. See **ad-** & **lure.** To draw on, tempt, by a lure; to entice, win over; to attract, charm (often in a bad sense).

allurement, n. [1. alyórment; 2. əljɔ́mənt]. Prec. & **-ment.** That which allures; enticement, attraction, fascination; often in bad sense: *the allurements of the wicked world.*

alluring, adj. [1. alyóring; 2. əljɔ́riŋ], fr. Pres. Part. of **allure.** Attractive, enticing, tempting.

alluringly, adv. Prec. & **-ly.** In an alluring, enticing, manner.

allusion, n. [1. alúzhun; 2. əljúžən], fr. Lat. *allūsiōn-(em)*, fr. *allūs-(um)*, P.P. type of *allūdere*, see **allude**, & **-ion.** A reference *to*, in speech or writing, whether direct or indirect and covert.

allusive, adj. [1. alúsiv; 2. əljúsiv], fr. base seen in prec. & **-ive.** **1.** Containing an allusion (*to*); full of allusions. **2.** (her.) *Allusive arms*, canting arms, q.v.

allusively, adv. Prec. & **-ly.** By way of allusion; by implication or suggestion.

allusiveness, n. See prec. & **-ness.** The quality of being allusive.

alluvial, adj. [1. alóóvial; 2. əlúviəl]. See next word & **-al.** Relating to, composed of, alluvium; of soil washed from one place and deposited in another by flowing water.

alluvion, n. [1. alóóviun; 2. əlúviən]. Fr. *alluvion*, fr. Lat. *alluviōn-(em)*, lit. 'an overflow, inundation'; also 'alluvial land'; fr. *alluere*, 'to wash against', fr. **ad-** & *luere*, 'to wash', cogn. also w. Lat. *lavāre* & *lavere*, Gk. *loúō*, 'wash'. See **lave.** Addition to land bordering on sea or river caused by gradual silting up of soil; new land formed in this way.

alluvium, n. [1. alóóvium; 2. əlúviəm]. Lat., neut. of adj. *alluvius*. See **alluvion.** (geol.) Matter derived from natural waste of rocks, carried away by running water, and gradually deposited in some other place, there forming new soil.

ally (I.), vb. trans. [1. alí; 2. əlái], fr. O. Fr. *alier*, Fr. *allier*, 'to join, unite', fr. Lat. *alligāre*, fr. **ad-** & *ligāre*, 'to bind'. See **alliance** & **ligature.** **1.** To combine, unite, bind together, esp. of individuals and families by marriage, of states by treaty, and of political parties; (gen. used in the pass. or reflex., followed by *with*) *to ally oneself with (a family or party)*; *England and France were allied in the Great War.* **2.** (in pass.) *To be allied to*, closely connected, by common descent or strong resemblance; having similar character or constituents: *English is nearly allied to Dutch*; *physical disease and insanity are often allied*; *coal is chemically allied to the diamond.*

ally (II.), n., fr. prec. **a** A state united with another by agreement or treaty, for political or warlike objects; **b** an individual who cooperates with, supports, helps, another, in a particular work, for common object; supporter, friend.

ally (III.), **alley**, n. [1. áli; 2. æli]. Prob. an abbr. form of **alabaster.** A large, choice marble or taw, used in playing marbles.

almagest, n. [1. álmajest; 2. ǽlmədžest]. Fr., fr. Arab. *al-majistī*, 'the greatest work', fr. Arab. *al-*, 'the', & Gk. *megístē*, fem. sing. of *mégistos*, 'greatest', superl. of *mégas*, 'great'. See **mega-.** The name given by the Arabs to their translation of the great astronomical work of Ptolemy of Alexandria, hence later applied to other astronomical and astrological treatises.

Alma Mater, n. [1. álma máter; 2. ǽlmə méitə]. Lat., 'fostering mother'. *Almus, -a, -um* is connected w. vb. *alo*, 'rear, nourish, support'. See further **adult, adolescent, aliment, old.** Applied to the university, college, or school at which a person has been educated.

almanac, n. [1. áwlmanak; 2. ɔ́lmənæk]. Low Lat., also in Fr., Span., & Ital. Origin unknown. List or table of days, months of the year, together with astronomical data, and indications of feasts, holidays &c. See **calendar.**

almandine, n. [1. álmandīn; 2. ǽlməndain]. For earlier *alabandine*, fr. Lat. *alabandina*, name of gem stone found at Alaband, in Asia

Minor. A deep red variety of garnet, the noble or precious garnet, known as *carbuncle* when cut *en cabochon.*

almighty, adj. & n. [1. àwlmíti; 2. ɔ̄lmáiti]. O.E. *ealmihtiġ, ælmihtiġ.* See **all**, adv., & **mighty. 1.** adj. All-powerful, omnipotent. **2.** n. *The Almighty*, God.

almond, n. [1. áhmund; 2. ámənd], fr. O. Fr. *almande*, Fr. *amande*, Ital. *amandola*, fr. Lat. *amygdala*, Gk. *amugdálē*, 'an almond'; etymols. proposed are not satisfactory; the word is prob. a foreign loan into Gk. Agreeably flavoured kernel of the stone-fruit of the almond tree, allied to the peach and plum, eaten as a nut; the fruit itself is not edible.

almond-eyed, adj. Having long, almond-shaped eyes, esp. of Mongolian type.

almoner, n. [1. áhmuner; 2. ámənə]. O. Fr. *aumoner*, fr. Low Lat. *almosinārius, eleēmosynārius.* See **alms.** Official distributor of alms, esp. in Royal Household. *Lord High, Hereditary Grand, Almoner.*

almonry, n. [1. áhmunri; 2. ámənri]. Fr. *aumônerie.* See prec. word. Official residence of almoner; place where alms are distributed.

almost, adv. [1. áwlmōst; 2. ɔ́lmoust]. O.E. *eallmǣst.* See **all & most**, adv. Nearly, all but.

alms, n. [1. ahmz; 2. āmz]. O.E. *ælmysse*, fr. Lat. *eleēmosyna*, fr. Gk. *eleēmosúnē*, 'mercy, alms'. Cp. *éleos*, 'pity, mercy, compassion', *eleéō*, 'pity, show mercy upon'. The etymol. of these Gk. words is unknown. Money given in charity for relief of the poor; specif., money given in church for charitable and religious purposes.

almsfolk, n. [1. áhmzfōk; 2. ámzfouk]. Persons living on alms (archaic).

almsgiver, n. [1. áhmzgiver; 2. ámzgivə]. One who gives money &c. for charitable purposes.

almsgiving, n. [1. áhmzgiving; 2. ámzgiviŋ]. Act and practice of giving money for charity.

almshouse, n. [1. áhmz-hòus; 2. ámzhàus]. A house endowed by private charity for the housing and maintenance of a certain number of aged or disabled poor.

almsman, n. [1. áhmzman; 2. ámzmən]. A person supported by charity.

almug, n. [1. álmug; 2. ǽlmag]. Name of a tree and its wood, probably sandal-wood, referred to in 1 Kings x. 11, 12. Also **algum.**

alnage, n. [1. álnij; 2. ǽlnidž], fr. O. Fr. *aulnage*, fr. *aulne*, **ell**, & see **-age.** (hist.) Measurement and inspection of woollen cloth by the ell.

alnager, n. [1. álnijer; 2. ǽlnidžə]. Prec. & **-er.** (hist.) Official charged with the inspection and measurement of woollen cloth.

aloe, n. [1. álō; 2. ǽlou], fr. Lat. *aloē*, Gk. *alóē*. **1.** (bot.) **a** A genus of liliaceous plants, with spikes of red or yellow flowers and fleshy leaves yielding a bitter juice; *the American aloe*, the agave, q.v., or century plant. **2.** (med., pl.). A purgative drug obtained from the bitter resinous juice of aloe leaves.

aloetic, adj. & n. [1. àlōétik; 2. æ̀louétik]. Cp. Fr. *aloétique.* See prec. & **-ic. a** adj. Containing aloes; of the nature of aloes; **b** n., a medicine containing aloes.

aloft, adv. [1. aláwft; 2. əlɔ́ft], fr. Scand., for *on lofte*, 'in the air', cogn. w. O.E. *lyft*, 'air'. See **loft & lift.** On high, high up; specif. (naut.) at the mast-head, up among the rigging; overhead; hence (fig. and colloq.) in Heaven, to Heaven: *to go aloft*, to die.

alone, adj. (following the n.) [1. alṓn; 2. əlóun], fr. **all & one**, the latter in O.E. sense of 'alone, sole'. **a** By oneself; apart from others; exclusive of others; solitary: *to be, live, alone*; *all, quite, alone*; **b** only, exclusively, solely: *I alone know the story.* Phrs. *to let, leave, alone*, refrain from interfering with; *let alone that . . .*, not to mention.

along, adv. & prep. [1. alóng; 2. əlɔ́ŋ]. O.E. *andlang*, 'continuous', M.E. *anlong.* See **long (I.).** *And-*, 'facing, against', is found in O.H.G., Goth., & other Gmc. languages. It is further cogn. w. Lat. *ante*, 'before', Gk. *antí*, 'over against, opposite'. See **ante-, anti-. 1.** adv. **a** On, onward, forward, away from present position: *to go along*; *to get along*, go, get, away from here (colloq.); **b** *along with*, in company with; together with: *come along (with me)*; **c** (of time) throughout whole duration, all the time; in Phr. *all along*: *I knew it all along.* **2.** prep. (expressing movement and position) By or through the length; from one end of anything towards the other end (or any part of the length) of, opposed to *across*: *along the road, the river.*

alongshore, adv. [1. alòngshṓr; 2. əlɔ̀ŋʃɔ́]. In the water near or by the shore.

alongside, adv. & prep. [1. alóngsíd; 2. əlɔ́ŋsáid]. **1.** adv. By the side; esp. (naut.) **a** (of small boat) close to the side of larger ship; **b** (of ship) close to side of dock or landing-place. **2.** prep. *Alongside of*, by the side of; side by side with: *to sit, walk, alongside of.*

aloof, adv. & pred. adj. [1. alóof; 2. əlúf]. Lit. 'on the luff'. Formed fr. Du. *loef*, a naut. word, q.v. under **luff**, with *a-*, on anal. of *afoot, aground* &c. At a distance; apart; away (lit. and fig.): *to stand aloof, hold aloof from* &c. (Sometimes used as pred. adj., esp. in moral sense.)

aloofness, n. Prec. & **-ness.** The state of being aloof (lit. and fig.).

alopecia, n. [1. àlōpésia; 2. æ̀loupíʃiə], fr. Gk. *alōpekía*, 'mange of foxes, bald patch on head', fr. *alṓpēx*, apparently cogn. w. Scrt. *lōpāčaš*, 'fox'. The medical term for baldness.

aloud, adv. [1. alóud; 2. əláud], formed fr. *a-* (as though fr. *on*) on anal. of *abed, ahead* & other advs., & **loud.** (lit.) In a loud manner. Loudly, with some resonance of voice, so as to be generally audible; not whispered or smothered: *to speak, read, laugh, aloud.*

alow, adv. [1. alṓ; 2. əlóu]. See **a-** for *on*, & **low (III.).** (naut.) In a lower part of a vessel; below.

alp, n. [1. alp; 2. ælp]. Fr., fr. Lat. *alpēs*, pl. 'alps'; Celt. word, prob. cogn. w. Lat. *albus*, 'white'. See **alb.** A high mountain; specif. pl. *the Alps*, the lofty mountain ranges of Switzerland, France, and N. Italy; note that in the Swiss valleys *alp* (in Tirol, *alm*) is used of a summer mountain pasture below snow level.

alpaca, n. [1. alpáka; 2. ælpǽkə]. Span., fr. Arab. *al-*, 'the', & Peruv. *paco*, name of animal. **1. a** Kind of llama found in Peru having long woolly hair; **b** the wool of this animal. **2.** Very thin, light cloth made from the wool of this animal, often mixed with silk or cotton; much cloth sold as alpaca is made from mohair with silk or cotton admixtures.

alpenstock, n. [1. álpenstok; 2. ǽlpinstɔk]. Germ. Lit. 'Alp stick'. A long staff with an iron point used in climbing mountains, esp. in Switzerland.

alpha, n. [1. álfa; 2. ǽlfə]. Gk. *álpha*, Heb. *aleph.* **1.** The first letter in the Greek alphabet; hence, the first or the beginning: *the Alpha and Omega*, the beginning and end. **2.** In astronomic and other scientific terminology, the first of a series, as *Alpha Centauri*, the first, brightest star in that constellation; *Alpha rays* &c.

alphabet, n. [1. álfabet; 2. ǽlfəbɛt], fr. Gk. *álpha* & *bêta*, the first two letters of the Greek alphabet. **a** Whole series of letters used in writing a language, generally arranged and learnt in a particular order; **b** (fig.) the elements of any study.

alphabetic(al), adj. [1. àlfabétik(l); 2. æ̀lfəbétik(l)], fr. prec. & adj. suffs. **-ic & -al.** Connected with the alphabet; esp. *alphabetical order*, arranged according to usual order of the letters.

alphabetically, adv. Prec. & **-ly.** In the order in which the letters of the alphabet are arranged.

Alpine, adj. [1. álpīn; 2. ǽlpain], fr. Lat. *Alpīnus*, 'of or belonging to the Alps', fr. *Alpēs*, 'the Alps'. See **alp. 1.** Of or pertaining to the Alps or any high mountains; belonging to lofty regions: *Alpine flora*; *Alpine snows* &c. **2.** Like the Alps; lofty: *Alpine heights.*

Alpinist, n. [1. álpinist; 2. ǽlpinist]. Prec. & **-ist.** One who climbs the Alps or other high mountains; one skilled in mountain climbing.

already, adv. [1. awlrédi; 2. ɔ̄lrédi]. See **all**, adv., & **ready.** Prior to a specified time (past, present, or future); beforehand, previously; by this time.

alright. Wrong form of *all right.* See all, adv.

Alsatia, n. [1. alsáshya; 2. ælséiʃjə]. Low Lat. name of Fr. Alsace, Germ. Elsass. **1.** Name of an old French province lying between France and Germany, on the border of Switzerland, long a 'debatable ground' or 'no man's land'. **2. a** (hist.) A district, in Whitefriars, between Fleet Street and the Thames, in London, which during the 16th and 17th cents. was a recognized 'sanctuary' for debtors and criminals till 1697: '*With his bravoes of Alsatia and his pages of Whitehall*' (Macaulay); **b** any asylum or refuge.

Alsatian, adj. & n. [1. alsáshun; 2. ælséiʃən]. Prec. & **-an. 1.** adj. Of, pertaining to, Alsace or its inhabitants. **2.** n. **a** An inhabitant of Alsace; **b** an Alsatian dog.

Alsatian dog, n. A large breed of sheep dog, bred originally in Alsace, having a distinct strain f wolf.

also, adv. & conj. [1. áwlsō; 2. ɔ́lsou]. O.E. *al(l)-swā*, 'likewise, just as, as'. See **all & so.** In like manner, in addition; besides; as well.

alt, n. [1. alt; 2. ælt], fr. Lat. *altus*, 'high, lofty, tall; shrill' (of the voice). The word orig. meant 'well-nourished', hence 'fully grown, tall', & is connected w. vb. *alo*, 'nourish', q.v. under **adult, adolescent, & old.** (mus.) First octave of musical notes above treble stave: *C in alt.*

altar, n. [1. áwlter; 2. ɔ́ltə]. Already in O.E., fr. L. Lat. *altar, altāre, altārium*; Lat. *altāria* (only in pl.), (1) 'things pertaining to the altar, that which was placed upon the altar for burning of victim', (2) 'a high altar' (poet.), fr. *alta āra*, 'a high altar'. For *altus, -a*, cp. **alt.** *Āra* (earlier *āsa*) is an altar, perh. orig. one for burning sacrifices. Some connect the word w. Lat. *āreo*, 'become dry, parched', & *āridus*, 'dry', *ardeo*, 'burn', fr. base ***ās-**, 'burn', as in Scrt. *ásaš*, 'ash' (cp. **ash (I.)**). Others consider the fundamental meaning of *āra*, to be 'mound, shelf of rock', & cp. Gk. *ēiṓn*, fr. **āsiōn*, 'sea-bank, river-bank, beach'. **1.** A raised structure or block, of stone or wood, with a flat top, upon which sacrifices were offered to a deity. **2.** (in Christian Church) Stone structure upon which the sacrifice of the Mass is offered; Communion Table. Phr. *to lead (a bride) to the altar*, to marry.

altar-cloth, n. Cloth of silk, linen &c., often richly embroidered and embossed, which hangs down from top and covers front of altar in Christian churches.

altar-piece, n. Ornamental carving behind and above altar; reredos.

altar-rail, n. Railing fencing off altar and steps leading to it from the rest of the chancel; flat top to this, upon which communicants may lean in kneeling or rising.

altar-tomb, n. Tomb built in form of an altar.

altazimuth, n. [1. altázimuth; 2. æltǽzimaþ]. Combination of **altitude & azimuth.** An astronomical instrument attached to a telescope for observing simultaneously the altitude and azimuth of a star and thus fixing its exact apparent position.

alter, vb. trans. & intrans. [1. áwlter; 2. ɔ́ltə], fr. Fr. *altérer*, fr. Low Lat. *alterāre*, 'to change', fr. Lat. *alter*, 'the other (of two)'. The last word is prob. fr. same base as *alius*, 'another' (see **alias, alibi**), & suff. **-tero-*, identical w. that of compar., & here (in *al-ter*) limiting the choice to one of two. Cp. **-ther**. **1.** trans. **a** To change in some respect; to make different; to vary: *to alter one's course, one's mode of life* &c.; **b** to modify (a decree &c.); *alter a house*, change style of architecture, disposition and size of rooms &c.; *alter clothes*, make them fit better, adapt for different purpose &c. **2.** intrans. To become different; to change, vary; specif. (of persons) to change for the worse in appearance, show signs of age or illness.

alterability, n. [1. àwlterabíliti; 2. ɔ̀ltərəbíliti]. See next word & **-ity**. Capacity for being altered or of altering.

alterable, adj. [1. áwlterabl; 2. ɔ́ltərəbl], fr. **alter** & **-able**. Capable of being altered.

alteration, n. [1. àwlteráshun; 2. ɔ̀ltəréiʃən]. See **alter** & **-ation**. **a** Act of altering anything; **b** condition of being altered; change.

alterative, adj. & n. [1. áwlterativ; 2. ɔ́ltərətiv]. See **alter** & **-ative**. **1.** adj. Liable to, causing, change. **2.** n. (med.) Medicine or treatment which produces certain changes in the system.

altercate, vb. intrans. [1. áwlterkāt; 2. ɔ́ltəkeit], fr. Lat. *altercāri, altercātus*, 'to wrangle, quarrel, with another', fr. *alter*, 'another'. See **alter**. (rarely used) To contend in words, to dispute, wrangle (with).

altercation, n. [1. àwlterkáshun; 2. ɔ̀ltəkéiʃən], fr. Lat. *altercātiōn-(em)*, 'a wrangling, dispute', see prec. & **-ion**. A wordy contest; a hot dispute, noisy wrangle.

alter ego, n. [1. álter égō; 2. ǽltər égou]. Lat., lit. 'other I'. One's other self; an intimate friend who is constantly with one and who shares one's tastes and thoughts.

alternant, adj. [1. awltérnant; 2. ɔltə́nənt], fr. Lat. *alternant-(em)*, Pres. Part. type of *alternāre*. See **alternate**. (of geol. structure) Composed of alternating layers.

alternate (**I.**), vb. trans. & intrans. [1. áwlternāt; 2. ɔ́ltəneit], fr. Lat. *alternāt-(um)*, P.P. type of *alternāre*, 'to do first one thing then another', fr. *alternus*, 'every other, alternate', fr. *alter*, 'the other (of two)'. See **alter**. **1.** trans. To carry out, or cause to happen, two actions severally, by turns: *to alternate weakness with severity*. **2.** intrans. **a** (of two events) To happen successively, first one, then another: *good harvests alternate with bad*; *hope and fear alternate in my breast*; **b** (of electrical current) to change direction and reverse periodically.

alternate (**II.**), adj. [1. àwltérnat; 2. ɔ̀ltə́nit]. Lat. *alternātus*. See prec. Occurring by turns, in time or position: *each alternate day*; *Shakespeare's sonnets have twelve lines with rhymes in alternate lines, and a rhyming couplet at the end.*

alternately, adv. Prec. & **-ly**. In alternate order or succession.

alternating, adj. [1. áwlternāting; 2. ɔ́ltəneitiŋ], fr. Pres. Part. of **alternate** (**I.**). Changing in turns or in succession; specif., *alternating current*, electric current which passes through a repeated cycle of changes of magnitude and direction at regular intervals.

alternation, n. [1. awlternáshun; 2. ɔltənéiʃən]. Act of alternating; state of being alternate.

alternative, adj. & n. [1. awltérnativ; 2. ɔltə́nətiv], fr. Med. Lat. *alternātīvus*. See **alternate** (**I.**) & **-ive**. **1.** adj. Offering choice of two things; (less correctly) of several. **2.** n. **a** Choice (limited to one) between two possible things, or lines of action; **b** (less correctly) choice of one among more than two things, or lines of action.

alternatively, adv. Prec. & **-ly**. In an alternative manner; with the choice of two things.

alt-horn, n., fr. **alt** & **horn**. (mus.) A brass wind-instrument used in military bands. See **saxhorn**.

although, conj. [1. awldhṓ; 2. ɔlðóu], fr. **all**, adv., & **though**. Though, notwithstanding, in spite of the fact that.

altigraph, n. [1. áltigrahf; 2. ǽltigrāf], fr. **altitude** & **-graph**. A form of aneroid barometer which automatically records on a chart altitudes reached, as in flying.

altimeter, n. [1. altímeter; 2. æltímitə]. **altitude** & **-meter**. An aneroid barometer with dial marked in meters or feet, recording the altitude reached, as in flying.

altitude, n. [1. áltitūd; 2. ǽltitjūd], fr. Lat. *altitūdo*, fr. *altus*, 'high'. See **alt**. **1. a** Height of objects from bottom to top (not applicable to that of human beings); **b** height above sea-level; **c** high place, region (esp. in pl.). **2.** Specif. (astron.) angular height in degrees of a star above the astronomical horizon.

alto, n. [1. áltō; 2. ǽltou]. Ital., fr. Lat. *altus*, 'high'. See **alt**. (mus.) **1. a** Highest male voice, counter-tenor; now, the lowest female, or boy's, voice, contralto; **b** the part in a score taken by this voice. **2.** An alto singer.

altogether, adv. [1. àwltogédher; 2. ɔ̀ltəgéðə]. See **all, together**. **a** Wholly, completely, totally, entirely: *altogether bad*; **b** all things considered, on the whole: *altogether, I'm not sorry I stayed after all.*

alto-relievo or **alto-rilievo**, n. [1. áltō relḗvo, áltō riliévō; 2. ǽltou rilívou, ǽlto riliévo]. Ital. (*ri-*), 'in high relief'. See **alt** & **relief** (**II.**), n. (sculp.) High relief, a term designating that kind of sculpture in which the figures project from their background by more than half their thickness, and in which the limbs and head are often entirely detached from background; contrasted with *bas-relief*.

altruism, n. [1. áltrooizm; 2. ǽltruizəm], fr. Fr. *altruisme*, O. Fr. *altrui*, Mod. Fr. *autrui*, & **-ism**, fr. Lat. *alteri huic*, 'to this other'. See **alter**. The principle of putting the interests of others before one's own interests, unselfishness. Converse of *egoism*.

altruist, n. [1. áltrooist; 2. ǽltruist]. See prec. & **-ist**. One whose conduct is governed by what he conceives to be in the interest of others rather than of himself.

altruistic, adj. [1. àltrooístik; 2. æ̀ltruístik]. Prec. & **-ic**. Regardful of others, unselfish.

altruistically, adv. [1. àltrooístikali; 2. æ̀ltruístikəli]. Prec. & **-al** & **-ly**. In an altruistic manner; unselfishly.

alum, n. [1. álum; 2. ǽləm], fr. O. Fr. *alum*, Mod. Fr. *alun*, fr. Lat. *alūmen*; prob. cogn. w. Gmc. **aluþ*, 'beer', whence O.E. *ealu*, see **ale**. **a** A chemical crystalline substance, the double sulphate of aluminium and potassium, used as a styptic and astringent; **b** (chem.) any of a series of sulphates, including above, in which sodium, ammonium &c. takes the place of potassium, and chromium or other metal that of aluminium.

alumina, n. [1. alúmina; 2. æljúminə], fr. Lat. *alūmen*, **alum**. (chem.) A mineral earth, the oxide of aluminium.

aluminium, n. [1. àlūmínium; 2. æ̀ljumíniəm]. See **alum**. A white metal of remarkable lightness and malleability.

alumnus, n., pl. **alumni** [1. alúmnus, -ī; 2. əlámnəs, -ai]. Lat. *alumnus*, 'a nursling, foster-son, disciple', fr. *alere*, 'to nourish'. See **adult** & words there referred to. One who has received his education at a given school, college, university, or other institution; a member of such institutions.

alveolar, adj. [1. alvḗoler; 2. ælvíələ]. See **alveolus** & **-ar**. (anat.) Of, pertaining to, or resembling, alveoli. See **alveolus**. (phon.) *Point alveolar consonants*, those formed by point of tongue against the alveoli, or honeycomb structure just behind upper teeth.

alveolate, adj. [1. alvḗolat; 2. ælvíəlit], fr. Lat. *alveolātus*, fr. *alveolus*. (bot.) Pitted with small cavities like a honeycomb.

alveolus, n., pl. **alveoli** [1. alvḗolus, -ī; 2. ælvíələs, -ai]. Lat. *alveolus*, dimin. of *alveus*, 'a hollow, cavity'. **a** (anat.) A small hollow, esp. the socket of a tooth; structure in roof of mouth just behind upper teeth; **b** (zool.) a small cavity as in a shell, fossil, or coral; **c** a cell in a honeycomb.

alway, adv. [1. áwlwā; 2. ɔ́lwei]. See **always**. (archaic or poet.) Always.

always, adv. [1. áwlwaz; 2. ɔ́lwiz]. O.E. *ealne weġ*, 'the whole way, always'. The final *s* in present-day form is that of an adv. genit. **a** At all times, ever, continually; **b** on all occasions; invariably, uniformly; opposed to *sometimes* or *occasionally*.

alyssum, n. [1. álisum; 2. ǽlisəm], fr. Gk. *álusson*, name of a plant used to cure hiccup, fr. **a-** (priv.) & *lúzein*, 'to hiccup'; cogn. w. M.H.G. *slucken*, 'to swallow'. (bot.) Genus of rock plants with hairy leaves and clusters of yellow or white flowers.

am, vb. [1. am, m; 2. æm, əm, m]. O.E. *eom, eam*. In Gmc. this form is found only in O.E., and in O.N. *em*, & Goth. *im*; but cp. further Scrt. *ásmi*; Gk. *eimi* (for **esmi*); O. Lat. *esum*, Lat. *sum*; O. Slav. *jesmĭ*, Lith. *esmi*; Ir. *am*. The final *m* is a survival of the ending *-mi*, orig. 1st pers. pron. 1st pers. sing. of vb. **be**.

amadou, n. [1. ámadōō; 2. ǽmədū]. Fr., fr. Provenç., Port. *amador*, fr. Lat. *amātor*, 'lover'; so called from the substance easily catching fire. See **amatory**. Spongy substance made from a species of fungus; used as tinder.

amain, adv. [1. amā́n; 2. əméin]. As though fr. O.E. *on mæġne*, 'with force', on anal. of *asleep, ashore* &c., 16th cent. See **a-** & **main**. (archaic and poet.) Vigorously, violently; at full speed.

amalgam, n. [1. amálgam; 2. əmǽlgəm], fr. Fr. *amalgame*, Med. Lat. *amalgama*, prob. fr. Lat. *malagma*, fr. Gk. *málagma*, 'a soft mass', fr. *malássō*, 'I make soft', fr. *malakós*, 'soft'. The base **mal-* is found in other forms in Lat. *mollis*, 'soft', *molĕre*, 'grind in a mill', *mulcāre*, 'beat', *mulcēre*, 'stroke, touch gently'. See **emulsion, mill, molar, meal** (**I.**). **a** Mixture of a metal or metals with mercury; **b** any loose combination or mixture of different substances; also fig.

amalgamate, vb. trans. & intrans. [1. amálgamāt; 2. əmǽlgəmeit]. Prec. & **-ate**. **A.** trans. **1.** To form an amalgam of (metals). **2.** (by transf. and fig.) To combine, consolidate: *to amalgamate companies, businesses, interests* &c. **B.** intrans. **1.** (of metals) To combine in an amalgam. **2.** (by transf. and fig., of persons, classes, ideas &c.) To mix, unite; to blend satisfactorily, agree.

amalgamation, n. [1. amàlgamáshun; 2. əmæ̀lgəméiʃən]. See prec. & **-ion**. **1.** The mixing or blending of different groups of human beings, races, societies &c.; the union of two or more bodies into one: *amalgamation of railway companies, businesses* &c. **2.** The act of mixing or compounding mercury with another metal.

amalgamative, adj. [1. amálgamativ; 2. əmǽlgəmətiv]. See **amalgamate** & **-ive**. Inclined, tending, to amalgamate.

amanuensis, n. [1. amànūénsis; 2. əmæ̀njuénsis]. Lat., 'clerk, secretary', *a(b) manu*, 'from, by, the hand', & adj. suff. *-ensis*. See **manual**. Person employed to write what another dictates or copy what he has written; a literary assistant; secretary.

amaranth, n. [1. ámaranth; 2. ǽmərænþ]. Gk. *amárantos*, 'unfading', fr. **a-**, 'not', & *marainō*, 'put out, quench, waste away' (*-th* is due to confusion w. Gk. *ánthos*, 'flower'); cp. Lat. *marcēre*, 'wither, droop, fade'; Goth. *ga-maurgjan*, 'shorten', fr. wh. base comes also O.E. *myrġe, myriġ*, 'pleasant, delightful', orig. 'transitory, lasting but a short time'. See **merry**. **1.** Poetical name of an imaginary flower supposed never to fade. **2.** (bot.) A genus of annual plants with richly coloured flowers (esp. purple or crimson), including 'Love-lies-bleeding'.

amaranthine, adj. [1. àmaránthīn; 2. æ̀mərǽnþain], fr. prec. & **-ine**. Of or pertaining to amaranth. **a** Unfading, undying: *''Tis hers to pluck the amaranthine flower of Faith'* (Wordsworth); **b** of a purple colour.

amaryllis, n. [1. amarílis; 2. æmərílis]. Lat., fr. Gk. *Amarullis*, the name of a country girl in Theocritus and Virgil. **1.** (poet.) Conventional name for a maiden in pastoral poetry. Cp. '*To sport with Amaryllis in the shade*' (Milton, 'Lycidas'). **2.** (hort.) A family of bulbous plants.

amass, vb. trans. [1. amás; 2. əmǽs], fr. Fr. *amasser*, fr. Low Lat. *amassāre*, fr. Lat. **ad-** & *massa*, 'a lump, mass'. See **mass.** To pile up, heap together, accumulate (esp. riches, treasure(s) &c.).

amateur, n. [1. àmatḗr, ámatūr; 2. æ̀mətə́, ǽmətjō]. Fr., 'one who is fond of something', fr. Lat. *amātōr-(em)*, 'a lover', fr. *amāre*, 'to love'. See **amative, amatory. a** One who pursues any form of study, art, sport &c. from a natural love of it, not to make money; **b** (in disparaging sense) one who lacks complete knowledge of a subject, or skill in a pursuit, through insufficient training and practice: *a mere amateur.* Opposed to *professional.*

amateurish, adj. [1. àmatḗrish; 2. æ̀mətə́riʃ]. Prec. & **-ish.** Like, after the manner of, an amateur; like the works of one; hence, betraying lack of skill and practice (of persons); not well done, clumsy &c. (of work).

amateurishly, adv. Prec. & **-ly.** In an amateurish manner.

amateurishness, n. See prec. & **-ness.** Lack of skill and practice.

amateurism, n. [1. àmatḗrizm; 2. æ̀mətə́rizəm]. **amateur** & **-ism.** Amateurishness.

Amati, n. [1. amáhti; 2. əmáti]. Violin made at Cremona in 16th or 17th cent. by member of the Amati family of violin-makers.

amative, adj. [1. ámativ; 2. ǽmətiv]. Fr. *amatif*, fr. Lat. *amātus*, P.P. of *amāre*, 'to love', & *-īvus*, see **-ive.** The origin of this base is very uncertain; Walde compares *amita*, 'father's sister' (see **aunt**), & thinks the starting-point was a childish word of endearment. **a** Pertaining to love; **b** inclined, disposed, to love; amatory.

amativeness, n. Prec. & **-ness.** Propensity to be affected by feeling for the opposite sex.

amatol, n. [1. ámatol; 2. ǽmətəl]. Combination of **ammonium** & **toluene.** A high explosive, a mixture of ammonium, nitrate, and trinitrotoluene.

amatory, adj. [1. ámateri; 2. ǽmətəri], fr. Lat. *amātōrius*, fr. *amātor*, 'lover', fr. *amāre*, 'to love'. See **amative.** Pertaining to, inducing, love for opposite sex.

amaurosis, n. [1. amorṓsis; 2. æmərόusis]. Gk., fr. *amaurós*, 'dark, dim, faint', prob. fr. **a-**, 'without', & stem **mar-*, seen in *marmaírein*, 'to shine, glimmer', see **marble,** & **-osis.** (pathol.) Partial or total decay or loss of sight, due to disease of the optic nerve, without change in the external eye.

amaze (**I.**), vb. trans. [1. amáz; 2. əméiz]. O.E. *āmasian.* See **maze.** To fill with astonishment, to surprise, astound.

amaze (**II.**), n. (poet.) Amazement, bewilderment.

amazed, adj. [1. amázd; 2. əméizd], fr. P.P. of **amaze** (**I.**). Filled with astonishment, astounded.

amazedly, adv. [1. amázedli; 2. əméizidli]. Prec. & **-ly.** In an amazed, astounded manner; with astonishment.

amazedness, n. [1. amázednes; 2. əméizidnis]. See prec. & **-ness.** Astonishment, surprise.

amazement, n. [1. amázment; 2. əméizmənt]. **amaze** & **-ment.** The condition of mind produced by something unexpected; wonder, astonishment.

amazing, adj. [1. amázing; 2. əméiziŋ], fr. Pres. Part. of **amaze** (**I.**). Causing amazement; wonderful, surprising.

amazingly, adv. Prec. & **-ly.** To an extent, in a manner, which causes amazement.

Amazon, n. [1. ámazun; 2. ǽməzən]. Gk. *amazṓn.* A foreign word, but derived by Greeks by popular etymol. fr. **a-**, 'without', & *mazós*, 'breast', the Amazons being supposed to cut off a breast to facilitate use of the bow; *mastós*, another dialect form of the word, means 'hillock' as well as 'breast'. The ultimate connexions are doubtful; some authorities connect the base w. words meaning 'flowing', others w. those meaning 'fat, plump', others again w. supposed cognates meaning 'nourishment'; see Boisacq, under *madân.* **1.** Female warrior belonging to fabulous race in Scythia. **2.** A tall, strong woman of masculine habits and mind.

Amazonian, adj. [1. amazṓnian; 2. æməzóuniən]. Prec. & **-ian.** Of, pertaining to, or like an Amazon, war-like; of masculine manners.

amazonite, n. [1. ámazunīt; 2. ǽməzənait], fr. river Amazon & **-ite.** A semi-precious stone of a bright green colour; also called *Amazon stone.*

ambages, n. [1. ambájēz; 2. æmbéidžiz]. Lat., 'roundabout way'; also 'shuffling, quibbling, ambiguity'; fr. *ambi-*, 'about', & base **ag-*, 'go, drive'. See **ambi-** & **agent.** (now chiefly in fig. sense) Roundabout way of speaking or acting.

ambagious, adj. [1. ambájus; 2. æmbéidžəs], fr. prec. & **-ous.** Roundabout, circuitous (fig., more rarely lit.).

ambassador, n. [1. ambásader; 2. æmbǽsədə], fr. Fr. *ambassadeur*, fr. Ital. *ambasciatore*; cp. Low Lat. *ambaxiāre*, 'relate, announce', also *ambactus*, 'vassal depending upon a lord'. This is believed to be a Celt. word, containing base **ag-*, common to Lat. & Celt., meaning 'drive' &c. (cp. **agent**), the pref. being *ambi-*, 'about'. The word is also borrowed in Goth. *andbahts*, 'servant'; *andbahti*, 'service'. **1.** A messenger, herald, bringer of news: *an ambassador of peace.* **2.** An agent or intermediary: *to act as another's ambassador in a negotiation.* **3.** Specif., an official of highest rank, employed by the supreme power in a state to represent it abroad, esp. at a foreign court, and to transact diplomatic business between the two countries.

ambassadorial, adj. [1. àmbasadṓrial; 2. æ̀mbæsədɔ́riəl], fr. prec. & adj. suff. **-al.** Of, connected with, an ambassador.

ambassadress, n. [1. ambásadres; 2. æmbǽsədrɛs, -is]. **ambassador** & **-ess. a** The wife of an ambassador; **b** female employed as intermediary in a negotiation.

amber, n. & adj. [1. ámber; 2. ǽmbə], fr. Fr. *ambre*, Ital. *ambra*, Span. *ámbar*, fr. Arab. *alambar*, 'ambergris'. **1.** n. Hard, palish yellow, transparent fossil resin found upon certain seashores. **2.** adj. Having colour of amber. The word originally referred to *ambergris*, q.v.

ambergris, n. [1. ámbergrēs; 2. ǽmbəgrīs], fr. Fr. *ambre gris*, 'grey amber'. Substance of wax-like consistency found floating in tropical seas, used in perfumery; a secretion of sperm whale.

ambi-, pref. representing a Lat. *ambi*, 'about, around', cogn. w. Gk. *amphí*; O.S. & O.H.G. *ambi*, O.E. *ymb*, (*emb*), 'around'; **b** Lat. *ambō*, 'both', cogn. w. Gk. *ámphō.* The forms are cogn.

ambidexter, n. [1. àmbidékster; 2. æ̀mbidékstə], fr. Lat. *ambo*, 'both', see **ambi-, b,** & *dexter*, 'right hand'. See **ambidextrous.** A person who can use both hands with equal facility.

ambidexterity, n. [1. àmbidekstériti; 2. æ̀mbidekstériti]. Prec. & **-ity.** See **ambidextrous.** The faculty of using both hands equally well.

ambidextrous, adj. [1. àmbidékstrus; 2. æ̀mbidékstrəs]. See **ambi-** & **dextrous.** Capable of using both hands with equal facility and skill; esp. able to perform with left hand acts usually performed only with right.

ambidextrously, adv. Prec. & **-ly.** With both hands equally well.

ambidextrousness, n. See prec. & **-ness.** Ambidexterity.

ambient, adj. [1. ámbient; 2. ǽmbiənt]. Lat. *ambient-(em)*, 'going round', Pres. Part. of *ambīre*, 'to surround', fr. *ambi*, 'around', & *īre*, 'to go'. See **ambi-** & **itinerant.** Surrounding, encompassing.

ambiguity, n. [1. àmbigū́iti; 2. æ̀mbigjúiti], fr. Lat. *ambiguitāt-(em)*, 'double meaning', fr. *ambiguus.* See **ambiguous.** The quality or state of being ambiguous; double meaning; hence obscurity, lack of clearness.

ambiguous, adj. [1. ambíguus; 2. æmbígjuəs], fr. Lat. *ambiguus*, 'shifting, changeable, doubtful', fr. **ambi-**, 'about', & *agere*, 'to go', see **agent,** & **-ous.** The first element may be used in sense of 'in two directions'. Cp., however, Lat. *ambigere*, 'wander about, go around'. Doubtful, obscure, liable to be understood in more than one way; equivocal (of a statement, style &c.)

ambiguously, adv. Prec. & **-ly.** In an ambiguous manner.

ambiguousness, n. See prec. & **-ness.** Ambiguity.

ambit, n. [1. ámbit; 2. ǽmbit]. Lat. *ambitus*, 'a going round, circuit'. See **ambient.** Circuit, compass, sphere, scope, extent.

ambition, n. [1. àmbíshun; 2. æ̀mbíʃən]. Lat. *ambitiōn-(em)*, 'a going round of candidates canvassing for office', hence 'a seeking after fame', fr. *ambīre.* See **ambient. 1.** Strong desire for success **a** in worldly matters, e.g. personal distinction, prosperity, advancement; **b** in accomplishment of aspirations and ideals. **2.** The object of such desires and aspirations.

ambitious, adj. [1. ambíshus; 2. æmbíʃəs], fr. Lat. *ambitiōsus*, 'going about in order to solicit', hence 'obsequious, anxious to please; fond of display, ostentatious'. See **ambition** & **-ous. 1.** (of persons) **a** Possessing ambition; anxious to attain success, fame, distinction, power &c.; filled with inordinate desire for these; **b** desiring strongly, eager for; (followed by *of* before n.) *ambitious of wealth, power* &c. **2.** (of human action, works, ideas) Characterized by, showing, arising out of, ambition; hence aspiring: *an ambitious attempt, conception, scheme* &c.

ambitiously, adv. Prec. & **-ly.** In an ambitious manner.

ambitiousness, n. See prec. & **-ness.** Ambition.

amble (**I.**), vb. intrans. [1. ámbl; 2. ǽmbl], fr. O. Fr. *ambler*, Lat. *ambulāre*, 'to go about, walk', fr. *amb-*, 'about' (cp. **ambi-**), & a base found also in Gk. *al-ē̃*, 'ceaseless roaming', *al-áomai*, 'wander about', *al-ḗtēs*, 'vagabond'. See **alley** (**I.**). **a** To move at an easy, unhurried pace (of horse); **b** (of persons) to move in a way resembling this pace, esp. *to amble along, about.*

amble (**II.**), n. fr. prec. **a** Pace of horse when it ambles; **b** of persons who walk in manner resembling such pace.

ambling, adj. [1. ámbling; 2. ǽmbliŋ], fr. Pres. Part. of **amble** (**I.**). Moving at an easy, unhurried pace: *ambling trot.*

amblyopia, n. [1. àmbliṓpia; 2. æ̀mblióupiə]. Gk., fr. *amblús*, 'dull, blunt, dim', cogn. w. *malakós*, 'soft', see **malaco-,** & *ṓps*, 'eye', see **optic.** (pathol.) A weakening, gradual impairment of eyesight, the incipient stage of amaurosis, q.v.

ambo, n. [1. ámbō; 2. ǽmbou]. Low Lat., fr. Gk. *ámbōn*, 'a ridge, raised place', later 'pulpit'; usually derived fr. *anabaínein*, 'to go up, ascend', but more prob. cog. w. Lat. *umbo*, 'boss', see **omphalo-, umbilicus,** & **navel.** (eccles. archit.) A large, ornamental reading desk, in Romanesque and Byzantine churches, from which the Epistle and Gospel are read and sermons preached.

amboyna, amboina (**wood**), n. [1. ambóina (wood); 2. æmbóinə (wud)], fr. Amboyna, one of the Molucca Islands. Finely grained wood from tree growing in Amboyna.

ambrosia, n. [1. ambrṓzia; 2. æmbróuziə]. Gk. *ambrosía*, fr. *ámbrotos*, 'immortal', fr. **a-**, 'not', & *brotós*, 'mortal', fr. **mbrotós*, wh. stands for **mrotos* & is cogn. w. Lat. *mort-em* &c., 'death'. Cp. Scrt. *amṛtaś*, 'immortal'.

See **mortal** (III.), & **murder**. **1.** (Gk. mythol.) The food of the gods. **2.** (fig.) Anything having a delicious taste.

ambrosial, adj. [1. ambrṓzial; 2. æmbróuziəl], fr. prec. & **-al**. Pertaining to, resembling, ambrosia in taste, therefore delicious; also (poet.) fragrant: *ambrosial locks.*

ambry, aumbry, n. [1. ámbri, áwmbri; 2. ǽmbri, ɔ́mbri], earlier form *almary*; hence often taken to be a contraction of **almonry**; more prob. fr. O. Fr. **almarie*, fr. *armarie*, Mod. Fr. *armoire*, 'cupboard', fr. Med. Lat. *armăria*, 'bookcase, cupboard', *armărium*, 'armoury', fr. Lat. *arma*, 'arms, tools, implements'. See **arm** (II.). **1.** (archaic) A cupboard, repository. **2.** (specif. eccles.) A closed recess or small alcove, usually on the north side of the chancel in a church, in which were kept the Eucharistic vessels or the reserved Sacrament.

ambs-ace, n. [1. ámz ās; 2. éimz eis]. O. Fr. *ambes as*, Lat. *ambas*, 'both', & *as*. See **ace**. Double aces, the lowest throw at dice.

ambulance, n. [1. ámbūlans; 2. ǽmbjuləns]. Fr., fr. Lat. *ambulāre*, 'to walk', & **-ance**. See **amble**. **1.** A moving hospital attached to an army in the field; organization for giving first aid, and for conveying sick or injured people to hospital. **2.** A vehicle for conveying wounded from battle; one for carrying sick or injured people to hospital.

ambulatory (I.), adj. [1. ámbūlatri; 2. ǽmbjulətri]. Lat. *ambulātōrius*, 'movable', fr. *ambulāt-(um)*, P.P. of *ambulāre*, 'to walk', see **amble** (I.), & **-ory**. **a** Connected with walking; **b** movable.

ambulatory (II.), n. (archit.) A covered way in which to walk, as a cloister, or arcade, esp. a processional way round the eastern end of a cathedral behind the high altar.

ambuscade (I.), n. [1. àmbooskā́d; 2. æ̀mbuskéid]. Fr. *embuscade*, Span. *emboscada*. See **ambush**. (mil.) **a** Concealment of troops in a secret place for the purpose of a surprise attack; **b** place where such troops lie concealed; **c** trap laid for enemy, an ambush.

ambuscade (II.), vb. trans. & intrans. **1.** To conceal troops in ambush; **2.** To attack from a hidden place or ambush.

ambush (I.), vb. trans. [1. ámboosh; 2. ǽmbuʃ]. Earlier *embush*, O. Fr. *embuscher*, fr. Low Lat. *imboscāre*, lit. 'to set in a bush'. See **boscage, bush**. **a** To place troops in hiding, or in ambush for surprise attack; **b** to surprise, and attack from an ambush.

ambush (II.), n., fr. prec. **a** Arrangement of troops in concealed position for surprise attack; **b** body of troops so concealed; **c** place in which troops are concealed.

ameer, amir, n. [1. amḗr; 2. əmíə]. Arab., 'commander, nobleman, prince'. See **emir**. Title adopted by various Mohammedan rulers, esp. those of Afghanistan and Bokhara.

ameliorate, vb. trans. & intrans. [1. amḗlyurāt; 2. əmíljəreit]. Fr. *améliorer*, Lat. **ad-** & *melior*, 'better', & *āt-*, on anal. of many vbs. in 1st conjug. The base **mel-* has sense of 'strong, great, good'; cp. Gk. *mála*, adv., 'very, very much, quite', *malerós*, 'very strong'; also *amalós*, 'soft, feeble, lit. 'not strong' (*a-* = 'not'). Another form of same base is seen in Lat. *multus*, 'many'. See **multi-**. **a** trans. To make better, improve; **b** intrans., to become better.

amelioration, n. [1. amèlyurā́shun; 2. əmìljəréiʃən]. See prec. & **-ion**. **a** Act of making better; **b** state of being improved; **c** improvement, betterment.

ameliorative, adj. [1. amḗlyurātiv; 2. əmíljəreitiv]. See **ameliorate** & **-ive**. Tending, conducing, to improvement.

amen, interj. & n. [1. ā́mén, áhmén; 2. éimén, ɑ́mén]. Gk. *amḗn*, 'verily', fr. Heb., the root meaning being 'strength, stability'. **a** interj. So be it! Phr. *to say amen to*, be in agreement with; **b** as n., the word itself uttered at end of a prayer &c.: *to sing the amen.*

amenability, n. [1. amènabíliti; 2. əmìnəbíliti]. See next word & **-ity**. Condition of being amenable (in various senses).

amenable, adj. [1. amḗnabl; 2. əmínəbl], fr. Fr. *amener*, 'lead, bring up to', & **-able**. The Fr. vb. is fr. Low Lat. *amināre*, fr. *a-* 'to', & *mināre*, 'lead, conduct', also 'drive out, chase'; Lat. *minārī*, 'to threaten'. See **menace, minatory**. **1.** Liable to be called to account; answerable, responsible; (followed by *to*, or absol.) *amenable to justice.* **2. a** Tractable, submissive, willing to yield; (followed by *to*, or absol.) *amenable to discipline*; **b** capable of being won over by, responsive to: *amenable to flattery.*

amenableness, n. Prec. & **-ness**. Quality or condition of being amenable.

amenably, adv. See prec. & **-ly**. In an amenable manner; agreeably to, in accordance with: *amenably to the rules.*

amend, vb. trans. & intrans. [1. améndː; 2. əménd]. Fr. *amender*, fr. Lat. *ēmendāre*, 'to free from faults', fr. *ē-*, 'out, out of', & *mendum*, 'error, blunder'; cp. also *menda*, 'defect, blemish'; these words are cogn. w. Scrt. *mindā́*, 'bodily defect'. Cp. **emend**. **A.** trans. **1.** To correct, free from faults or error, improve: *to amend one's life, conduct* &c. **2.** To alter wording of a bill before Parliament, or of a motion before a legislative or administrative body, so as to render it more generally acceptable. **B.** intrans. To reform oneself, improve in conduct, behave better.

amendment, n. [1. améndment; 2. əméndmənt]. Prec. & **-ment**. **1.** Improvement, reform, of life and conduct. **2.** Alteration of text of legislative measure; specif., alternative form of words proposed at meeting of legislative body, instead of those standing in text as first presented; counter proposal brought forward at a public discussion of measures: *to move, propose, second, an amendment.*

amends, n. pl. [1. améndz; 2. əméndz]. Fr. *amende*, 'a fine'. See **amend**. Reparation, compensation, made in consideration of a loss, injury, insult, inflicted: *to make amends.*

amenity, n. [1. amḗniti; 2. əmíniti]. Fr. *aménité*, Lat. *amoenitāt-(em)*, 'delightfulness, a pleasure', fr. *amoenus*, 'pleasant, charming'. Connected w. *amāre*, 'love'. See **amative**. Quality of delightfulness, agreeableness, **a** (in places, buildings) arising from beauty of site, pleasantness of climate, suitability of design &c.; **b** (in persons) attractiveness due to urbane and courteous manners, gentleness of disposition &c.

ament, n. [1. áment; 2. ǽmənt], fr. Lat. *āmentum, ammentum*, 'thong, strap', prob. fr. **apmentum*, fr. base seen in **apere*, 'to bind', see **apt**. (bot.) The drooping, downy flower-spike or inflorescence of the willow, hazel &c.; catkin.

amentaceous, adj. [1. amentā́shus; 2. æmənteíʃəs]. Prec. & **-aceous**. (bot.) **a** Like, formed of, aments or catkins; **b** amentiferous.

amentiferous, adj. [1. amentíferus; 2. æməntífərəs]. See prec. & **-ferous**. (bot.) Bearing aments or catkins.

amerce, vb. trans. [1. amḗrs; 2. əmə́s]. M.E. *amercen*, 'to fine', A.-Fr. *amercier*, fr. Low Lat. *amerciāre*, 'to fine', formed fr. *a-*, 'to, at', & *mercēs*, 'pay, salary; reward; cost, retribution, punishment'. Cp. further Lat. *merx*, 'goods, wares', *mercārī*, 'to trade'; the base is possibly connected w. O.H.G. *marah*, O.E. *mearh*, 'mare'. For transference of meaning cp. **fee**. See **mercy**. To fine; more generally, to punish.

amercement, n. [1. amḗrsment; 2. əmə́smənt], fr. prec. & **-ment**. **a** Infliction of a fine by a court; **b** the fine or penalty imposed.

amerciable, adj. [1. amḗrsiabl; 2. əmə́siəbl]. See **amerce** & **-able**. Liable to infliction of amercement.

American, adj. & n. [1. amérikan; 2. əmérikən], fr. America, fr. Amerigo (Americus) Vespucci, & **-an**. **1.** adj. **a** Of, pertaining to, the continent of America, North, Central, and South: *American Indian* &c.; **b** of, pertaining to, the United States of America: *American politics, the American navy* &c. **2.** n. **a** An aboriginal inhabitant of America; Amerindian; **b** citizen of the United States of America; **c** inhabitant of South or Central America, of European descent: *Latin or Spanish American.*

American cloth, n. A textile fabric, of cotton or linen, with a surface imitating leather.

Americanism, n. [1. amérikanizm; 2. əmérikənizəm]. **American** & **-ism**. Peculiarity, esp. of pronunciation, idiom, vocabulary, manners &c., common to Americans, i.e. of the United States, or derived through American influence.

Americanize, vb. trans. [1. amérikanīz; 2. əmérikənaiz]. See prec. & **-ize**. (of speech, manners, ideas &c.) To mould or modify according to American (U.S.A.) models and practice.

Amerindian, n. [1. ameríndian; 2. æmərı́ndiən]. **American** & **Indian**. (ethnol.) A member of the native, aboriginal races of North, Central, or South America.

amethyst, n. [1. ámithist; 2. ǽmiþist], fr. Gk. *améthustos*, 'a remedy against drunkenness', fr. **a-**, neg., & *methúein*, 'to be drunken', *méthusis*, 'drunkenness' &c.; the stone *amethyst* was supposed to have the power of preventing intoxication; the above Gk. words are fr. Gk. *méthu*, 'wine', see **methyl** & **mead** (I.). A precious stone, usually of a purple colour.

amethystine, adj. [1. àmithístīn; 2. æ̀miþístain]. Prec. & **-ine**. Made of, resembling, amethyst, esp. in colour.

amiability, n. [1. àmiabíliti; 2. èimiəbíliti]. See **amiable** & **-ity**. The quality of being amiable.

amiable, adj. [1. ā́miabl; 2. éimiəbl]. O. Fr. *amiable*, fr. Lat. *amīcābilis*, 'friendly', see **amicable**. Exhibiting, and evoking, affection; lovable, pleasant, affable (of persons and manners); good-natured, of such a character as facilitates easy and agreeable social intercourse; ingratiating, friendly.

amiably, adv. Prec. & **-ly**. In an amiable or pleasant manner (of behaviour, mode of address &c.): *to speak, behave, amiably.*

amianthus, n. [1. àmiánthus; 2. æ̀miǽnþəs]. Corrupt. of Gk. *amiantos*, 'undefiled, pure', fr. *a-* (priv.) & *miainein*, 'to stain' (see **miasma**); the word was applied specif. to a greenish stone. A fine variety of asbestos, with long, silky fibres.

amicability, n. [1. àmikabíliti; 2. æ̀mikəbíliti]. See next word & **-ity**. Quality of being amicable.

amicable, adj. [1. ámikabl; 2. ǽmikəbl]. Lat. *amīcābilis*, 'friendly', fr. *amīcus*, 'friend', fr. *amāre*, 'to love'. See **amative**. Friendly, peaceful; carried out in friendly spirit: *an amicable meeting, settlement.*

amicableness, n. Prec. & **-ness**. Friendliness, goodwill.

amicably, adv. See prec. & **-ly**. In an amicable manner.

amice (I.), n. [1. ámis; 2. ǽmis]. M.E. *amyse*, O. Fr. *amis, amit*, fr. Lat. *amictus*, 'mantle, cloak', fr. P.P. of *amicīre*, 'wrap, throw around', fr. *amb-*, 'around', & *jacere*, 'throw, fling'. See **ambi-** & **jactitation**. (eccles.) Vestment worn by the celebrant at the Mass, consisting of a square piece of white linen placed round the neck and shoulders.

amice (II.), n. Often confused with above, fr. O. Fr. *aumuce*, Low Lat. *almucia*. Origin unknown. Fur-lined hood worn formerly by the clergy and by pilgrims.

amid, amidst, prep. [1. amíd(st); 2. əmíd(st)]. O.E. form *on middan*, 'in the middle', M.E. *on midden, amidde(n)*, whence *amid*, or w. common advbl. (genit.) *-s*, *amiddes* &c. The final *-t* is due to a common tendency of pronunciation (cp. *agains-t*) and has no functional significance. See **a-** & **mid**. In, or into, the middle of; surrounded by.

amide, n. [1. ámīd; 2. ǽmaid]. See **ammonia** & **-ide**. (chem.) A compound derived from ammonia by replacing one hydrogen atom by an element.

amidin, n. [1. ámidin; 2. ǽmidin]. Fr. *amidon*, Lat. *amylum*, 'starch', fr. Gk. *ámulon*, 'fine meal', see **amyl**. Hard, transparent substance produced by subjecting starch to heat.

amidships, adv. [1. amídships; 2. əmídʃips]. See **amid** & **ship**. In the middle of the ship.

amidst. See **amid**.

amine, n. [1. ámīn; 2. ǽmain]. See **ammonia** & **-ine**. (chem.) Name of a class of basic substances obtained by replacing the hydrogen atoms of ammonia by alcohol radicals.

amir. See **ameer**.

amiss, adv. & adj. [1. amís; 2. əmís]. See **a-** & **miss (III.)**. (Chiefly in Phrs.) **1.** adv. **a** Wrongly, ill, badly; in a wrong way: *to do something amiss*, do it badly, wrong; *that which we have done amiss*, the sins committed; *there's something amiss with him*, he is ill, or in trouble; *to take something amiss*, to be offended; **b** inopportunely, distastefully; in negative constructions only: *nothing came amiss to him*, he was prepared for, would welcome, could do, anything. **2.** adj. (as pred. in neg. constructions) *This house, dinner, arrangement &c. is not amiss.*

amity, n. [1. ámiti; 2. ǽmiti]. Fr. *amitié*, Lat. *amīcitia*, 'friendship', fr. *amīcus*, 'friend', fr. base of *amāre*, 'to love'. See **amative**. Friendship, friendly relations, harmony, mutual goodwill.

ammeter, n. [1. ámiter; 2. ǽmitə], fr. contraction of Ampère, name of electrician, used as designation for unit of electric force, & **-meter**. Instrument for measuring the force of electric current in terms of ampères.

ammonal, n. [1. ámonal; 2. ǽmənəl], fr. **ammonia** & **aluminium**. Name of a class of high explosives, formed by a combination of aluminium and ammonium nitrate, used for grenades, bombs &c.

ammonia, n. [1. amṓnia; 2. əmóunjə]. Mod. contraction for (*sal*) *ammoniac*. See next word. (chem.) Volatile, pungent, alkaline gas, composed of hydrogen and nitrogen, formerly obtained from hartshorn, hence also known as *spirits of hartshorn*; it is used in medicine and industry, and combines with acids to form ammonium salts.

ammoniac, adj. & n. [1. amṓniak; 2. əmóuniæk]. Lat. *ammōniacum*, fr. Gk. *ammōniakón*, pertaining to Ammōn, an Ethiopian god, identified w. Zeus (Jupiter); ammonia was said to be obtained near the temple of Jupiter Ammōn. **a** adj. Having nature of ammonia; *sal ammoniac*, a hard salt used medicinally; **b** n., usually *gum ammoniac*, a bitter resin used in medicine, obtained from tree of same name.

ammoniacal, adj. [1. àmonī́akl; 2. æ̀moundiəkl]. Prec. & **-al**. Containing, or having the properties of, ammonia.

ammoniated, adj. [1. amṓniāted; 2. əmóunieitid], fr. **ammonia** & Lat. suff. **-ate** & Engl. **-ed**. Combined, impregnated, with ammonia.

ammonite, n. [1. ámonīt; 2. ǽmənait], fr. (Jupiter) Ammōn (see **ammoniac**), who was represented with ram's horns. An extinct cephalopod mollusc allied to the nautilus; its flat, spiral fossil shell, resembling ram's horn.

ammonium, n. [1. amṓnium; 2. əmóuniəm]. Neo-Lat. fr. **ammonia**. (chem.) A compound radical acting as an alkaline base, which has not been separated; it is ammonia with extra atom of hydrogen; compounds such as ammonium chloride (sal ammoniac) are produced by the reaction of ammonia to acids.

ammunition, n. [1. àmūníshun; 2. æ̀mjuniʃən]. Fr. (prob. = *la munition*) *amunition*, Lat. *mūnītio*, 'defence'. See **munition**. **1.** Formerly applied to all kinds of military stores and still as adj. See below. **2.** Collective name for articles used to charge firearms of all kinds, as shells, cartridges, explosives, primers &c.

ammunition boots, n. (In this word *ammunition* keeps its old general sense.) Boots supplied to soldiers from military stores as part of their equipment.

ammunition-wag(g)on, n. A waggon used to carry ammunition.

amnesia, n. [1. àmnḗzia; 2. æ̀mníziə], fr. Gk. **a-**, 'not', & *mnḗsi-(os)*, 'of memory'. Cp. Gk. *mnáomai*, 'I remember', fr. base **men-* &c., 'mind, memory' &c., wh. occurs in its several gradational forms in many Aryan languages. See under **memory, mental, mind**. (med.) Loss of memory.

amnesty, n. [1. ámnisti; 2. ǽmnisti]. Fr. *amnestie*, fr. Gk. *amnēstía*, 'forgetfulness', fr. **a-**, 'not', & *mnēstis*, 'remembrance', fr. base **men-* &c. See prec. Pardon granted by a sovereign, or a state, for an offence, esp. for one of a political character.

amnion, n. [1. ámnion; 2. ǽmniən]. Gk., 'bowl in which the blood of victims was caught; membrane round foetus'. Perh. fr. **sambnion*, Aryan **sangwen-*, 'blood', & cogn. w. Lat. *sanguin-em* &c., 'blood', q.v. under **sanguine**. The secondary meaning of *amnion* may be derived from the presence of blood in the fluid of the prenatal sac, or may be due to supposed resemblance in shape between the latter and a bowl. (anat.) The membrane in which the foetus or embryo of mammals, birds, and reptiles is enclosed before birth.

amoeba, n. [1. amḗba; 2. əmíbə]. Gk. *amoibḗ*, 'change', cp. *ameíbō*, 'I change'. The *b* in these words is for Aryan g^w, & they may thus be connected w. Lat. *migrāre*, 'to change one's abode'. See **migrate**. (zool.) Elementary microscopic organism which constantly changes its shape.

amoebaean, adj. [1. àmēbḗan; 2. æ̀mībíən], fr. Gk. *amoibaîos*, 'interchanging, alternate', fr. *amoibḗ*, 'change'. See prec. & **-an**. Interchanging, alternating, answering back, specif. of verses: *amoebaean strains.*

among, amongst, prep. [1. amúng(st); 2. əmáŋ(st)]. O.E. *on ġemang*, 'into midst of', lit. 'into a crowd', or 'mixture', fr. same base the vb. *menġan*, 'mingle, associate with', is derived, see **mingle**. M.E. *amonges* has genit. suff. used adverbially; to this *-t* has been added, as in *against, amidst* &c. **1.** (expressing position) **a** (without movement) Surrounded by, in the midst of: *to live among(st) one's people*; *among the mountains*; **b** entrance into a group, movement into new surroundings: *to go among people*. **2.** (expressing currency or distribution throughout a group of persons) *A practice frequent among the Esquimaux.* **3.** (expressing association, connexion, with a group or class) *Numbered among the dead*; *blessed among women*; *one among many.* **4. a** (expressing distribution throughout all the members of a group) *Not five pounds among them*; *divided among the heirs*; **b** (expressing reciprocity in action by members of a group) *to discuss, quarrel, agree, among themselves.*

amontillado, n. [1. amòntilyáhdo; 2. əmɔ̀ntiljádo]. Span., fr. Montilla, town in Spain. A variety of sherry, usually sweet and full-bodied.

amorist, n. [1. ámorist; 2. ǽmərist], fr. Lat. *amor*, 'love'. See next word & **-ist**. One who cultivates and practises love and gallantry.

amorous, adj. [1. ámorus; 2. ǽmərəs], fr. Fr. *amoureux*, fr. Low Lat. *amōrōsus*, fr. Lat. *amor*, 'love', & *-ōsus*. See base **ama-* &c. in **amative**, & **-ous**. **1.** (of persons) **a** Constitutionally prone to love of opposite sex; **b** in a state of sexual excitement. **2.** Expressing, inciting to, arising from, sexual love: *amorous songs, glances, sighs* &c.

amorously, adj. Prec. & **-ly**. In an amorous manner.

amorousness, n. See prec. & **-ness**. Propensity to sexual love; condition of sexual excitement.

amorphism, n. [1. amórfizm; 2. əmɔ́fizəm]. See next word & **-ism**. Shapelessness; (specif. mineral.) absence of crystalline structure.

amorphous, adj. [1. amórfus; 2. əmɔ́fəs]. Gk. *ámorphos*, 'shapeless', **a-**, 'not', *morphḗ*, 'shape, form', see **morphology**, & **-ous**. **a** Shapeless, formless; badly constructed, ill-designed; **b** (mineral.) uncrystallized.

amortizable, adj. [1. amórtizabl; 2. əmɔ́tizəbl]. See **amortize** & **-able**. (of debts) Capable of being paid off.

amortization, n. [1. amòrtizáshun; 2. əmɔ̀tizéiʃən]. See **amortize** & **-ation**. **a** Act of liquidating, paying off a debt; **b** sum devoted to this purpose.

amortize, vb. trans. [1. amórtīz; 2. əmɔ́taiz]. Low Lat. *admortizāre*, **ad-** & *mort-*, 'dead, death'; cp. Fr. *amortir*, 'deaden, reduce in violence'. See **mortal** & **-ize**. (lit.) To make as if dead, destroy; hence (legal) **a** to convey property to a corporation or 'alienate in mortmain'; **b** to pay off, liquidate, extinguish (a debt).

amount (I.), vb. intrans. [1. amóunt; 2. əmáunt], fr. O. Fr. *amonter*, 'amount to', fr. *amont*, 'upwards', *a*, 'to', & *mont*, 'hill, mountain', fr. Lat. *mons, montis*. See **mount (I.)**. *Amount to*, **1.** to reach, come up to (of number of things, figures, sums of money &c.); **2.** result in, come to, be equivalent to; Phrs. *to amount to very little, not to amount to much*, to be unimportant, insignificant.

amount (II.), n., fr. prec. **a** Sum total of several sums or quantities; **b** quantity: *a large, small, trifling, amount.*

amour, n. [1. amóor; 2. əmúə]. Fr., fr. Lat. *amōr-(em), amor*, 'love'. See **amative**. A love affair; now usually as euphemism to describe one of a discreditable, or illicit, character.

ampelopsis, n. [1. àmpilópsis; 2. æ̀mpilɔ́psis]. Gk., 'looking like a vine', fr. *ámpelos*, 'vine', & *ópsis*, 'appearance'. *Ámpelos* prob. stands for earlier **ankʷelos*, & may be connected w. Gk. *agkúlos*, 'curved', *ógkos*, 'hook' &c. See **anchor** & **angle (III.)**. The second element is fr. the Gk. base *op-*, fr. **okʷ-*, 'to see', concerning wh. see **optic**. Virginia creeper.

amperage, n. [1. ampáraj; 2. æmpéəridž]. See foll. & **-age**. Number of ampères in an electric current.

ampère, n. [1. ampár; 2. æmpéə]. Fr. [ãpēr]. Name of French electrician (1755–1836). Unit of force in an electric current.

ampersand, n. [1. ámpersand; 2. ǽmpəsænd]. Chiefly a dictionary word; the symbol & = *and*. Said to stand for *and per se* (Lat., 'by itself'), *and*.

amphi-, pref. Gk. *amphí*, 'on both sides, of both kinds', cogn. w. Lat. **ambi-**.

Amphibia, n. pl. [1. amfíbia; 2. æmfíbiə]. See **amphibious**. Animals capable of living both in the water and on land.

amphibian, adj. & n. [1. amfíbian; 2. æmfíbjən]. See **amphibious** & **-an**. **a** adj. Having character and habits of an amphibious animal; **b** n., an amphibious animal.

amphibious, adj. [1. amfíbius; 2. æmfíbjəs]. Gk. *amphíbios*, 'living a double life' (i.e. on land and in water), applied to frogs; fr. **amphi-** & *bíos*, life. See **biology**. **a** (of plants and animals) Able to live both on land and in water; **b** (fig.) having double character.

amphibole, n. [1. ámfibōl; 2. ǽmfiboul], fr. Gk. *amphíbolos*, 'doubtful'. See next word. Name given to a group of rock-forming minerals of various forms and colours, including hornblende.

amphibology, n. [1. àmfibóloji; 2. æ̀mfibɔ́lədži]. Gk. *amphíbolos*, 'attacked on both sides; doubtful, ambiguous'. See **amphi-**, & cp. *bólos*, 'a throw', *bolís*, 'missile', *bállein*, 'to throw, strike' &c., q.v. under **ballistics**, & **-logy**. Phrase or statement capable of being interpreted in more than one way; ambiguous expression; quibble.

amphibolous, adj. [1. amfíbolus; 2. æmfíbələs]. See prec. & **-ous**. Ambiguous, capable of two meanings.

amphibrach, n. [1. ámfibrak; 2. ǽmfibræk]. Gk. *amphíbrakhus*, 'short at both ends', fr. **amphi-**, & *brakhús*, 'short', q.v. under **brachy-**. (pros.) **a** Metrical foot; in quantitative languages, one of three syllables, the first and third being short and the middle one long (◡ – ◡); **b** in languages in which metre depends mainly on stress, a stressed syllable flanked on either side by one devoid of stress, e.g. *appearing* [əpíəriŋ].

amphictyonic, adj. [1. amfiktiónik; 2. æmfìktiɔ́nik]. **amphictyony** & **-ic**. (Gk. hist.) Of, belonging to, an amphictyony; *amphictyonic council*, the council of a league of Greek states, centred first at Delos, then at Delphi.

amphictyony, n. [1. amfíktioni; 2. æmfíktiəni]. Gk. *amphiktuonia*, fr. *amphiktíones*, 'neighbours, those that dwell round about a place', fr. **amphi-** & base of *ktízein*, 'to people, colonize, found a city', cogn. w. Lat. *situs*, 'position', see **site**. (Gk. hist.) A form of federation or league of different Greek states, centring round a shrine, as at Delos or Delphi.

amphimixis, n. [1. àmfimíksis; 2. æ̀mfimíksis]. Biological term coined fr. Gk. **amphi-**, 'both sides', & *mîxis*, 'mingling, sexual intercourse'. See **mix**. (biol.) Union of germ cells of two individuals.

amphipod, n. [1. ámfipod; 2. ǽmfipɔd], fr. **amphi-** & **-pod**. (zool.) Member of a large suborder of Crustaceans, of small size, with two sets of limbs, one for swimming, the other for jumping, including the freshwater shrimps, sand-fleas, and sand-hoppers &c.

amphisbaena, n. [1. àmfisbḗna; 2. æ̀mfisbínə]. Gk. *amphísbaina*, 'fabulous monster with a head at either end, capable of going in either direction'; *amphis*, 'at both sides', (see **amphi-**) & *bainein*, 'go', see **basis**. '*Amphisbaena dire*' (Milton).

amphitheatre, n. [1. ámfithèater; 2. ǽmfiþìətə]. Gk. *amphithéātron*. See **amphi-** & **theatre**. Oval or circular space, or arena, surrounded by seats rising tier upon tier, and commanding view of the whole space.

Amphitryon, n. [1. amfítrion; 2. æmphítriən]. Gk. *Amphitrúōn*, in whose person Zeus gave a feast. Cp. also Molière's play of the name, and the saying 'le véritable Amphitryon, est l'Amphitryon où l'on dîne'. Host, hospitable entertainer.

amphora, n. [1. ámfora; 2. ǽmfɔrə]. Lat. *amphora*, Gk. *amphoreús*, 'cinerary urn', fr. **amphi-** & *phoréus*, 'bearer', fr. *phoréō*, 'I carry' (fr. its two handles). See this base under **bear (I.)** (class. archaeol.) A vessel, usually made of clay, with two handles and a narrow neck, used for holding and storing wine, oil, corn &c.

ample, adj. [1. ámpl; 2. ǽmpl]. Fr., fr. Lat. *amplus*, 'large, spacious', perh. fr. **ambplo-*, 'large on all sides', fr. *ambo*, 'both', see under **ambi-**, & **plo-*, 'full', connected w. *plēnus*, 'full', q.v. under **plenum**; but this is doubtful. **a** Large, of great size, spacious; abundant, copious; **b** large enough: *ample room for everyone*.

amplification, n. [1. àmplifikā́shun; 2. æ̀mplifikéiʃən]. See **amplify** & **-fication**. Act of amplifying; enlargement, extension.

amplifier, n. [1. ámplifier; 2. ǽmplifaiə]. **a** (micros.) Device for enlarging field of vision; **b** (in wireless teleg.) device by which radio waves, before and (or) after rectification, are increased in power without change in wave form, thus magnifying signals received and increasing the loudness of the sounds into which they are converted.

amplify, vb. trans. [1. ámplifī; 2. ǽmplifai]. Fr. *amplifier*, 'to enlarge', fr. Lat. *ampli-* (see **ample**) & **-fy**. To increase, make larger; (of narrative, statement &c.) to make fuller, state in greater detail.

amplitude, n. [1. ámplitūd; 2. ǽmplitjūd]. Fr., fr. Lat. *amplitūdo*, fr. *amplus*, 'large', see **ample**. Spaciousness, (great) width or size; sufficiency.

ampulla, n. [1. ampóola; 2. æmpúlə]. Lat., 'globular vessel for holding liquids, ointments &c.'; dimin. fr. Gk. word *amphoreús*. See **amphora**. Specif. **a** cruet for wine and water at Mass; **b** mediaeval pilgrims' bottle; **c** vessel for holding the chrism or oil used in ceremonial anointing, as at the coronation &c.

amputate, vb. trans. [1. ámpūtāt; 2. ǽmpjuteit], fr. Lat. *amputāt-(um)*, P.P. type of *amputāre*, 'to cut off', esp. of plants, 'to prune', fr. **ambi-** & *putāre*, 'to prune' (trees &c.). The base, according to Walde, occurs also in Lat. *pavīre*, 'strike, ram, tread down', whence *pavimentum* (see **pavement**), *puteus*, 'well, pit, dungeon' (primarily a hole cut or hewn in the ground); cp. further Gk. *paíō* for **pawjō*, 'strike'; Lith. *piáuti*, 'strike'. **a** (surg.) To cut off whole or part of a limb or projecting part of body; **b** cut off larger boughs of trees.

amputation, n. [1. àmpūtā́shun; 2. æ̀mpjutéiʃən]. Lat. *amputātiōn-(em)*, 'a pruning, lopping off'. See **amputate** & **-ion**. (surg.) Operation involving removal of whole or part of a limb.

amuck, amok, adv. [1. amúk; 2. əmák]. Malay. *āmuq*, 'rushing in a state of frenzy to the commission of indiscriminate murder'. Cit. Skeat, fr. Marsden's Malay Dictionary. See elaborate and informing article on the word in Yule and Burnell's 'Hobson Jobson'. Only in *to run amuck*, to rush about in furious manner intent on shedding blood; (fig. in less specif. sense) to get out of control and perpetrate acts of violence (of body of rioters &c.).

amulet, n. [1. ámūlet; 2. ǽmjulɛt]. Fr. *amulette*, 'charm, esp. one carried on the person', Lat. *amulētum*, 'sympathetic preservative against sickness, amulet hung round the neck'; prob. connected with Lat. *āmōlīrī*, 'carry away, remove', fr. *a(b)*, 'from', *mōlīrī*, 'exert oneself, cast, hurl, remove', fr. *mōlēs*, 'mass, burden'. See **molecule**. Talisman, charm (esp. one hung round the neck).

amuse, vb. trans. [1. amū́z; 2. əmjúz], fr. Fr. *amuser*. See **a-**, fr. *ad*, 'to', & **muse (II.)**. **1.** To occupy the attention, cause to muse; bewilder (obs.). **2.** To occupy attention in a pleasant manner, esp. so as to give recreation, keep mind agreeably employed, excite interest, provoke mirth, divert: *to amuse the children*; *amuse oneself with gardening*; *to amuse one's leisure*; *to be much amused by a joke, play* &c.

amused, adj. [1. amū́zd; 2. əmjúzd], fr. P.P. of **amuse**. (of persons) Filled with interest in, pleasurably occupied, having the mind affected by interesting or mirthful ideas or preoccupations: *to keep a person amused*.

amusement, n. [1. amū́zment; 2. əmjúzmənt]. See **amuse** & **-ment**. **1.** The emotion or state of mind of being amused: *to cause, provoke, great amusement*; *his amusement was great*. **2.** That which causes amusement, which occupies the attention in a pleasurable manner; pastime, diversion, entertainment: *his chief amusement is reading novels*; (also in pl.) entertainments, diversions: *the amusements of the London season*.

amusing, adj. [1. amū́zing; 2. əmjúziŋ], fr. Pres. Part. of **amuse**. Tending to cause amusement, provoking pleasurable interest or mirth, diverting.

amusive, adj. [1. amū́ziv; 2. əmjúziv]. See **amuse** & **-ive**. **a** (rare) Amusing; **b** (obs.) tending to occupy the mind so as to delude.

amygdala, n. [1. amígdala; 2. əmígdələ]. Lat. *amygdalum*, *-a*, 'an almond', Gk. *amugdálē*, q.v. under **almond**. **a** (obs.) An almond; **b** one of the tonsils (from shape).

amygdalic, adj. [1. àmigdálik; 2. æ̀migdǽlik], fr. prec. & **-ic**. Made from, relating to, almonds.

amygdaloid, adj. & n. [1. amígdaloid; 2. əmígdəlɔid]. **amygdala** & **-oid**. **a** adj. Almond-shaped; **b** n., (geol.) a kind of rock with almond-shaped kernels embedded in it.

amyl, n. [1. ámil; 2. ǽmil], fr. Lat. *amylum*, Gk. *ámulon*, 'fine meal, starch', fr. **a-**, 'not', & *múlē*, or *múlos*, 'mill'. See base under **mill**. **1.** (obs.) Starch. **2.** (chem.) A hydrocarbon radical, found as compounds, as *amyl alcohol*, in fusel oil, *amyl nitrite*, used in medicine as a specific for angina pectoris &c.

amyloid, adj. & n. [1. ámiloid; 2. ǽmilɔid], fr. prec. & **-oid**. **a** adj. Starchy, starch-like; **b** n., starchy substance.

an (I.), form of indef. art. (before words beginning with a vowel) w. stress on foll. n. [1. an; 2. ən]. O.E. *ān*, 'an, one', M.E. *an*, unstressed, shortened form of *ān*; the nasal lost already in M.E. before a foll. cons. See **a**, indef. art., & **one**.

an (II.), conj., also **and**, of wh. the former is a variant; special use of *and* found in M.E. & common in 16th cent. See **and**. (obs.) If, and if.

an-, a-, neg. pref., fr. Gk. *an-*, *a-*, cogn. w. Lat. *in-* & Gmc. *un-*. See **in-** & **un-**.

-an, suff. representing Lat. *-ānus*, in adjs. (or ns. fr. these) directly fr. Lat., or through Fr. **-ain**; denoting 'connected with, of the nature of, coming from', e.g. *human, Anglican, American, saurian*. Cp. **-ane**, **-ian**.

ana-, pref. Gk. *ána*, *aná*, 'up', &c.; in composition 'up to, up, again, anew', = Lat. *re-*, 'towards', also 'backwards'. Cp. Lat. *an-* in *antēlāre*, 'to breathe hard', Goth. *ana*, 'on, upon, towards', O.E. *an*, *on*, O.H.G. *ana*. See **on**.

-ana, suff. [1. ā́na, áhna; 2. éinə, ánə], neut. pl. of Lat. adjs. in *-ānus*, see **-an**, suff.; added to names to form ns., meaning 'sayings of, personal anecdotes, information' &c., as *Johnsoniana*. See **ana**.

ana, n., fr. prec. Collection of personal or literary anecdotes, pieces of information, reminiscences &c.

anabaptism, n. [1. ànabáptizm; 2. æ̀nəbǽptizəm]. See **ana-** & **baptism**. Religious tenets of Anabaptists.

Anabaptist, n. [1. ànabáptist; 2. æ̀nəbǽptist]. See **ana-** & **baptist**. Name given to body of Protestant fanatics in 16th cent. who, among other practices, insisted upon re-baptism of adults and upon total immersion.

anabas, n. [1. ánabas; 2. ǽnəbæs], fr. Gk. *anabás*, *anabánt-(os)*, P.P. of *anabainein*, 'to go up, climb', fr. **ana-**, 'up', & *bainein*, 'to go'. See next word. (zool.) Name of a genus of East Indian and African freshwater fishes, the so-called 'climbing perch', with modified gills and stiff fins, which enable it to travel some distance on land from stream to stream.

anabasis, n. [1. anábasis; 2. ənǽbəsis]. Gk. *anábasis*, 'a going up', fr. **ana-** & *básis*, 'a going'. See **basis**. Military expedition, specif. that of Cyrus the younger against the Persian Artaxerxes, described by Xenophon in book of above name.

anableps, n. [1. ánableps; 2. ǽnəblɛps], fr. Gk. *anáblepsis*, 'a looking up', fr. **ana-** & *blépein*, 'to look, see', etymol. doubtful. (zool.) A fish of S. and Central America, with projecting eyes divided into two parts, for vision in water and air.

anabolic, adj. [1. ànabólik; 2. æ̀nəbɔ́lik]. Gk. *anabolḗ*, 'that which is thrown up', fr. **ana-** & *bállō*, 'I throw'. See **ballistics**. (biol.) Belonging to, characterized by, anabolism.

anabolism, n. [1. anábolizm; 2. ənǽbəlizəm]. See prec. & **-ism**. (biol.) Physiological processes involved in building up nutritive substances into living protoplasm, the constructive form of metabolism, q.v.; contrasted with *catabolism*.

anacatharsis, n. [1. ànakathársis; 2. æ̀nəkæþásis]. Gk., 'clearing away', fr. **ana-** & *kátharsis*, 'cleansing'. See **catharsis**. (med.) Vomiting, expectoration.

anacathartic, adj. & n. [1. ànakathártik; 2. æ̀nəkæþátik]. See prec. & **-ic**. **a** adj. Causing vomiting &c.; **b** n., an emetic, expectorant.

anachronism, n. [1. anákronizm; 2. ənǽkrənizəm]. Fr. *anachronisme*, fr. Gk. *anakhronismós*, **ana-** & *khrónos*, 'time', & **-ism**. See **chronic**. **a** Error in assigning date to historical event; **b** event or thing which is, or would be, incompatible or out of keeping with, incongruous in, the period at which it happens or exists, or is alleged to have happened or existed.

anachronistic, adj. [1. anàkronístik; 2. ænæ̀krənístik]. Characterized by, involving, anachronism.

anaclastic, adj. [1. anaklástik; 2. ænəklǽstik], fr. Gk. *anáklastos*, 'bent back, refracted', fr. **ana-** & *klásis*, 'breaking', connected w. *kláein*, 'to break'; cp. further Gk. *kladarós*, 'fragile', & Lat. *clādes*, 'disaster, calamity'. See also variants & cognates of same base under **halt (I.)**, 'lame', &c. (opt.) Produced by the refraction of light.

anacoluthon, n., pl. **anacolutha** [1. ànakolúthon, -tha; 2. æ̀nəkɔljúþɔn, -þə]. Gk., 'inconsequent', fr. *an-*, 'not', & *akólouthos*, 'following, agreeing with'; the adj. is fr. **sm*, 'one' (wh. base see under **simple**), & Gk. *kéleuthos*, 'road, path, track', w. wh. cp. Lat. *callis*, 'mountain track', Lith. *keliáuju*, 'I travel'; remoter connection w. Goth. *hlaupan*, O.E. *hlēapan*, 'leap', is possible. See **leap** & cp. **acolyte**. Defect of style, consisting in ill-constructed sentence in which the syntax of second part is not in agreement with that of first part; lack of grammatical sequence.

anaconda, n. [1. ànakónda; 2. æ̀nəkɔ́ndə]. Perh. Ceylonese. **1. a** Name originally given to a python of Ceylon; **b** hence, in popular language, any large snake which crushes its victim. **2.** (zool.) A large water-snake, of the Boa family, of tropical S. America.

anacreontic, adj. & n. [1. ànakriόntik; 2. æ̀nækriɔ́ntik], fr. Anacreon, Gk. lyrical poet, c. 560 B.C. **a** adj. (of poetry) Having lyrical character and manner of Anacreon's poems; **b** n. (pl.) lyrical poetry written in this style, celebrating love and wine.

anacrusis, n. [1. ànakrōōsis; 2. æ̀nəkrúsis]. Gk. *anákrousis*, 'a pushing back, checking', fr. *anakroúein*, 'to thrust back, check', fr. **ana-** & *kroúein*, 'to knock'. Cp. O. Slav. *krušiti*, 'snap off', Lith. *krùszti*, 'smash'. (pros.) Unstressed syllable(s) preceding stressed syllable in a verse which normally begins with a stress.

anadem, n. [1. ánadem; 2. ǽnədem]. Gk. *anádēma*, 'a head-band', fr. *ana-déō*, 'bind, up, bind round'; cp. Lat. *re-dimīre*, 'bind, wreathe round'; Scrt. *dāma*, 'bond'. See **diadem**. Garland, chaplet, wreath.

anadromous, adj. [1. anádrōmus; 2. ænǽdroumәs], fr. Gk. *anádromos*, 'running upward'. See **ana-** & first element of **dromedary**. (of fish) Going up rivers from sea to spawn, e.g. the salmon.

anaemia, n. [1. anḗmia; 2. ænímiə]. Gk. *anhaimía*, 'bloodlessness', fr. *an-*, 'without', see **an-**, & *haîma*, 'blood', fr. **saima*. Cp. O.N. *hunangs-seimr*, O.H.G. *seim*, 'virgin honey'. See also **haemal**. (med.) Deficiency of blood, or unhealthy condition of this, generally indicated by pallor of complexion.

anaemic, adj. [1. anḗmik; 2. ænímik], fr. prec. & **-ic**. Pertaining to, associated with, disease of anaemia; bloodless. *Anaemic-looking*, pallid.

anaerobic, adj. [1. ànārṓbik; 2. æ̀nεəróubik], fr. Gk. **an-**, 'not', & *āḗr*, 'air', see **air**, & *bíos*, 'life', see **biology**. Capable of living without air, esp. of bacteria which do not require oxygen for their existence.

anaesthesia, n. [1. ànesthḗzia; 2. æ̀nisþíziə]. Gk., 'insensibility', *an-* (priv.), see **an-**, & *aísthēsis*, 'perception by the senses, feeling', fr. *aisthánomai*, 'I feel'. See **aesthete**. General or local insensibility, usually caused by disease, drugs, or specif. by anaesthetics.

anaesthetic, n. & adj. [1. ànesthétik; 2. æ̀nisþétik], fr. Gk. *anaisthētos*, 'without feeling, unfelt'. See prec. & **-ic**. (med.) **1.** n. Substance which induces local or general insensibility, such as chloroform or ether; commonly used during surgical operations. **2.** adj. Having property of producing insensibility.

anaesthetist, n. [1. anḗsthetist; 2. ænísþətist]. See prec. & **-ist**. Medical attendant whose duty it is to administer anaesthetics during surgical operations.

anaesthetize, vb. trans. [1. anḗsthetīz; 2. ænísþətaiz]. See **anaesthetic** & **-ize**. To administer anaesthetics to, render insensible by administering anaesthetics.

anaglyph, n. [1. ánaglif; 2. ǽnəglif]. Gk. *anágluphon*, 'sculptured in relief', fr. **ana-** & *glúphein*, 'hollow out, engrave', cogn. w. Lat. *glūbere*, 'deprive of bark, peel', O.S. *klioban*, O.E. *clēofan*, O.H.G. *klioban*, 'split, cleave'. Cp. also Germ. *kluft*, Engl. *cleft*. See **cleave**. Embossed ornament, sculptured in low relief, such as a cameo.

anagogic(al), adj. [1. anagójik(l); 2. ænəgɔ́džik(l)]. See **anagogy** & **-ic** & **-al**. Of, pertaining to, using anagogy; mystical, spiritual, allegorical.

anagogy, n. [1. ánagōji; 2. ǽnəgoudži], fr. Gk. *anagōgḗ*, 'a leading up', fr. **ana-**, 'up', & *ágein*, 'to lead'. See **agent**. A mystical, spiritual, or allegorical interpretation of the Scriptures, esp. of the Old Testament.

anagram, n. [1. ánagram; 2. ǽnəgræm], fr. Gk. *ánā*, 'back', see **ana-**, & *grámma*, 'a written character, a letter'. See **grammar**. New phrase or word made out of a phrase or word by transposing the letters.

anagrammatical, adj. [1. ànagramátikl; 2. æ̀nəgrəmǽtikl]. See **ana-** & **grammatical**. Arranged as, containing an anagram.

anagrammatically, adv. Prec. & **-ly**. By means of, as an anagram.

anal, adj. [1. ánal; 2. éinəl]. See **anus** & **-al**. (anat.) Connected with the anus.

analects, analecta, n. pl. [1. ánalekts, ànalékta; 2. ǽnəlekts, æ̀nəléktə]. Gk. *análekta*, 'things gathered up, chosen', fr. **ana-**, & base **leg-*, 'choose, pick out', cp. Gk. *légein*, 'speak', earlier, 'choose words'. See **lecture**. Collection of literary fragments.

analeptic, adj. & n. [1. analéptik; 2. ænəléptik], fr. Gk. *analēptikós*, 'restorative', fr. *analambánein*, 'to take up, restore'. See **ana-** & **catalepsy**. (med.) **1.** adj. Restorative, invigorating, tonic, of medicines &c. **2.** n. A restorative medicine, a tonic.

analgesia, n. [1. ànaljḗsia; 2. æ̀nældžísiə]. Gk., 'want of feeling', fr. **an-** & *álgos*, 'pain', see **-algia**. **a** Absence of pain; **b** (med.) diminution or loss of the sense of pain; local insensibility to pain.

analgesic, adj. & n. [1. ànaljésik; 2. æ̀nældžésik]. Prec. & **-ic**. **1.** adj. Producing analgesia; diminishing, stopping pain. **2.** n. Drug &c. which effects this; an anodyne.

analogical, adj. [1. ànalójikl; 2. æ̀nəlɔ́džikl]. See **analogy** & **-ic** & **-al**. Resulting from, based upon, analogy.

analogist, n. [1. análojist; 2. ənǽlədžist]. See **analogy** & **-ist**. One who uses or reasons by analogy.

analogize, vb. trans. & intrans. [1. análojīz; 2. ənǽlədžaiz]. See prec. & **-ize**. **1.** trans. To explain, represent, by analogy. **2.** intrans. **a** To use analogies; **b** to reason, argue, by analogy.

analogous, adj. [1. análogus; 2. ənǽləgəs]. See **analogy** & **-ous**. Comparable, corresponding, similar, to.

analogously, adv. Prec. & **-ly**. By analogy.

analogue, n. [1. ánalōg; 2. ǽnəloug]. Fr., fr. Gk. *análogon*, neut. adj., 'according to due ratio or proportion'. See next word. That which corresponds to, or is compared with, something else.

analogy, n. [1. análoji; 2. ənǽlədži]. Fr. *analogie*, Gk. *analogia*, 'proportion'. See **ana-**, & **logic, lecture** for base, **log-*, **leg-*. **1.** (gen. sense) Partial resemblance or agreement between two things; esp. those points of agreement upon which a comparison between two things is based: *there is a certain analogy between the functions of a chairman and those of the Speaker of the House of Commons.* **2.** Specif. (philol.) process whereby words and grammatical forms are built up on the model of others with which they have points of resemblance in meaning, grammatical function, or sound: *new forms are often constructed on the analogy of* (*by analogy with*) *words originally unrelated.* **3.** (log.) Form of reasoning whereby it is concluded that if two or more things agree in certain respects, they will probably do so in others also.

analphabetic, adj. [1. ànalfabétik; 2. æ̀nælfəbétik], fr. **an-** & **alphabetic**. Expressing the sounds of speech by some other graphic means than by letters.

analyse, vb. trans. [1. ánalīz; 2. ǽnəlaiz], fr. Fr. *analyser*, fr. **analysis**; ending confused w. vbs. in **-ize**. **1.** To resolve, divide, any compound substance into the elements of which it is composed; specif. **a** to discover constituent parts of (a compound) by chemical process; **b** (gram.) to examine minutely the structure of (a sentence) and distinguish precise function of each word. **2.** (fig.) To examine critically (a statement, argument &c.); separate out, distinguish the true from the false, test the soundness of.

analysis, n. [1. análisis; 2. ənǽlisis], fr. Gk. *análusis*, 'a loosing, releasing', fr. **ana-** & *lúsis*, 'a loosing', fr. *lúein*, 'to loose'; cogn. w. **loose**. **1.** Separation, decomposition of any compound substance into its component parts (specif. in chem.). **2.** (fig.) **a** Critical examination, testing, of an argument, statement &c.; **b** parsing of a sentence.

analyst, n. [1. ánalist; 2. ǽnəlist]. See prec. & **-ist**. One who analyses, esp. one who applies chemical tests to discover constituent parts of substances, or to test their purity; an analytical chemist.

analytic(al), adj. [1. ànalítik(l); 2. æ̀nəlítik(l)], fr. Gk. *analutikós*. See **analysis** & **-ic** (& **-al**). **a** Relating to, apt at, accustomed to carry out, analysis: *an analytic mind*; *analytical chemist*; **b** (of languages), contrasted with *inflexional*, expressing grammatical relations by separate words instead of by inflexions.

analytically, adv. Prec. & **-ly**. By analysis or analytical methods.

anamnesis, n. [1. ànamnḗsis; 2. æ̀næmnísis]. Gk., 'recollection', fr. **ana-** & root **mna-*, of *mimnḗskein*, 'to remember'. See **mnemonics**. Recollection, remembrance, esp. of events &c. of a supposed previous existence.

anamorphosis, n. [1. anamórfosis; 2. ænəmɔ́fəsis]. Gk., fr. *anamorphóein*, 'to change the form of, to transform', fr. **ana-** & *morphḗ*, 'form, shape', see **morphology**. **1.** A distorted drawing or projection of an object, as seen in a reflection in a convex mirror &c., which assumes its proper shape when looked at from a certain angle or when reflected in such mirror. **2.** (biol.) A gradual change in form, in the evolution of a type, not amounting to metamorphosis. **3.** (bot.) An abnormal change or degeneration in form, giving the appearance of a different species, as in certain fungi &c.

ananas, n. [1. anáhnas; 2. ənɑ́nəs]. Span., fr. Peruv. *nānās*. (rarely used) Pineapple.

anandrous, adj. [1. anándrus; 2. ænǽndrəs], fr. Gk. *anandrós*, 'husbandless; unmanly', fr. **an-**, & *ándr-(os)*, *anḗr*, 'man'. See **androgynous**. (bot.) Having no stamens.

Ananias, n. [1. ananías; 2. æ̀nənáiəs], fr. name of Biblical character, Acts v. A liar (colloq. and vulg.).

anapaest, n. [1. ánapēst; 2. ǽnəpist]. Lat. *anapaestus*, fr. Gk. *anápaistos*, 'struck back, rebounding', fr. **ana-** & *paíein*, 'to strike'. See base **paw-* &c., 'strike', under **amputate**. (pros.) A reversed dactyl, i.e. a foot consisting of two short syllables followed by a long, or two unstressed syllables followed by a stressed, e.g. Engl. *overcóme, to the gráve*.

anapaestic, adj. [1. ànapḗstik; 2. æ̀nəpístik]. Prec. & **-ic**. Pertaining to, consisting of, anapaests.

anaphora, n. [1. anáfora; 2. ənǽfərə]. Gk., fr. **ana-** & *phérein*, 'to bear'. See **-ferous** & **bear (I.)**. **a** The Eucharistic service in the Greek Orthodox Church; **b** (rhet.) **a**

repetition of words or phrases at the beginning of a succession of clauses.

anaphrodisiac, adj. & n. [1. ànafrodíziak; 2. ǽnæfrədíziæk]. Gk. **an-**, & *aphrodīsiakós*, 'venereal', see **aphrodisiac.** (med.) **1.** adj. Tending to subdue or reduce sexual appetite. **2.** n. A drug having this property.

anaphylaxis, n. [1. ànafilάksis; 2. ǽnəfiləæksis]. An invented word. See **ana-** & **prophylaxis.** (med.) A term applied to an exaggerated susceptibility to a second injection of a protein substance, such as a serum, following a first injection, after a certain interval of time; also applied to the susceptibility of some people to illness after eating shell-fish, raisins &c.

anarch, n. [1. ánark; 2. ǽnāk]. Gk. *ánarkhos*, 'without a head or chief', fr. **an-** & *arkhós*, 'leader, chief', cogn. w. Gk. *arkhḗ*, 'beginning, origin'. See **arch-**. Leader in anarchy, one who excites lawlessness.

anarchic (al), adj. [1. anárkik(l); 2. ænάkik(l)], fr. prec. & **-ic** & **-al.** Having character of anarchy.

anarchically, adv. Prec. & **-ly.** In an anarchical manner.

anarchism, n. [1. ánarkizm; 2. ǽnəkizəm], fr. **anarchy** & **-ism.** Political theory on which anarchy is based, that organized government is an evil.

anarchist, n. [1. ánarkist; 2. ǽnəkist]. **anarchy** & **-ist.** One who supports anarchy; one who practises or supports active political agitation to the point of terrorism.

anarchy, n. [1. ánarki; 2. ǽnəki]. Gk. *anarkhía*, 'state of being without government', fr. *ánarkhos*. See **anarch. 1.** Political condition in which there is no government, no supreme power in the state; hence, absence of order, political and social confusion. **2.** (by extension) Absence of order and discipline generally, in any sphere; chaos.

anarthrous, adj. [1. anárthrus; 2. ənάþrəs], fr. Gk. *ánarthros*, 'without joints', fr. **an-** & *árthron*, 'joint', see **arthritis,** & **-ous. 1.** (Gk. gram.) Used without the article. **2.** (zool.) Having no joints, unarticulated.

anasarca, n. [1. anasárka; ænəsάkə], fr. **ana-**, & Gk. *sark-(ós)*, *sárx*, 'flesh'. See **sarco-.** A diffused form of subcutaneous dropsy.

anastomose, vb. intrans. [1. anástomōs; 2. ænǽstəmous]. See next word. To communicate, join by anastomosis.

anastomosis, n. [1. ànastomósis; 2. ǽnæstəmóusis]. Gk., fr. *anastomóein*, 'to furnish with a mouth or opening', fr. **ana-** & *stóma*, 'mouth'. See **stomach.** Intercommunication of branched vessels, as arteries, veins; of the veins or sap-vessels of leaves of plants &c., or of channels of a river system, and the like.

anastomotic, adj. [1. ànastomótik; 2. ǽnæstəmɔ́tik]. See prec. & **-otic.** Pertaining to, exhibiting, joined by, anastomosis.

anathema, n. [1. anáthema; 2. ənǽþimə]. Lat. *anathema*, 'an excommunicated person, or the curse of excommunication', fr. Gk. *anáthema*, orig. 'a thing devoted', later, 'a thing devoted to evil, a thing accursed', variant of *anáthēma*, 'a thing set up', fr. *anatithēmi*, 'I set up', fr. **ana-** & *títhēmi*, 'I place'; for base of this vb. see **thesis** (Gk.), **fact** (Lat.), **do** (Engl. & Gmc.). **1.** A curse or ban pronounced with and by ecclesiastical authority, accompanied by excommunication. **2.** Strong imprecation, malediction, uttered by anyone. **3. a** Person or thing against whom *anathema*, **1**, is pronounced; **b** person who or thing which is heartily disliked, condemned, reprobated; for the combination *Anathema Maranatha*, 1 Cor. xvi. 22, see **maranatha.**

anathematization, n. [1. anáthematīzáshun; 2. ənǽþimətaizéiʃən]. See next word & **-ation.** Pronouncement of anathema against a person or thing; denunciation.

anathematize, vb. trans. [1. anáthematīz; 2. ənǽþimətaiz], fr. Gk. *anathematizein.* See **anathema** & **-ize.** To pronounce an anathema against, put under a ban, denounce.

anatomic(al), adj. [1. anatómik(l); 2. ænətɔ́mik(l)]. Fr. *anatomique*, Lat. *anatomicus*, fr. Gk. *anatomikós*, 'skilled in anatomy'. See **anatomy** & **-ic** (& **-al**). Relating to, connected with, anatomy or dissection, or to the details of structure of the animal body.

anatomically, adv. Prec. & **-ly.** From the point of view of anatomical science.

anatomist, n. [1. anátomist; 2. ənǽtəmist]. **anatomy** & **-ist.** One skilled in, a student of, anatomical science; a dissector.

anatomize, vb. trans. [1. anátomīz; 2. ənǽtəmaiz]. See prec. & **-ize.** To dissect animal bodies in order to study their structure.

anatomy, n. [1. anátomi; 2. ənǽtəmi], fr. Fr. *anatomie*, Lat. *anatomia*, cp. Gk. *anatomḗ*, 'dissection', connected w. *anatémnein*, 'I cut up', fr. **ana-** & *témnein*, 'cut'. Cp. also Gk. *tomḗ*, 'place from which something has been cut', *tómos*, 'a cut slice', *tomós*, adj., 'cutting, sharp'; O. Slav. *tēti*, 'to split', Ir. *tamnaim*, 'I mutilate'. **1.** Meaning originally dissection of bodies for the purpose of studying their structure, the word has come to mean **a** the art of dissection; **b** the science of animal (including human) structure, learnt from dissection; **c** the details of animal structure of which the science treats; **d** a treatise on anatomic science, or on the structure of particular animals. (The word is also applied to the structure of plants, though less commonly.) **2.** A skeleton (popular and archaic); sometimes shortened to **atomy,** as though = 'an atomy'.

anatto, annatto, n. [1. anátō; 2. ənǽtou], prob. a native name. An orange-red colouring matter, obtained from the seeds of a South American tree, *Bixa orellana*, used for colouring cheeses.

anbury, ambury, n. [1. ánberi; 2. ǽnbəri]. Etymol. doubtful, prob. fr. O.E. *ang-*, 'painful', see **agnail,** & **berry. a** A soft tumour or wart on a horse's or ox's neck; **b** a disease of cabbages, turnips, and other plants, affecting the roots, due to a slime fungus; also called club-root, or finger-and-toe.

-ance, suff. [1. ans; 2. əns], fr. O. Fr. *-ance*, direct fr. Lat. *-antia*, forming abstract ns. of quality, action &c., fr. Pres. Part. stems in *-ant.* Cp. **-ence.**

ancestor, n. [1. ánsester; 2. ǽnsistə]. O. Fr. *ancestre*, *ancessor*, Mod. Fr. *ancêtre*, fr. Lat. *antecessor*, 'predecessor', fr. *ante*, before, & *cess-*, P.P. type of *cēdere*, 'go'. See **cede. 1.** One from whom a person is directly descended, whether on father's or mother's side; forebear, forefather. **2.** (biol. &c.) Individual animal or plant from which later animals or plants are derived; progenitor. **3.** (law) Person from whom an estate is derived by legal succession, independent of whether he be the progenitor of the heir.

ancestral, adj. [1. anséstral; 2. ænséstrəl], fr. O. Fr. *ancestrel.* See prec. & **-al.** Connected with, derived from, having character of, ancestors: *ancestral possessions*; *ancestral forms* (*of life* &c.).

ancestry, n. [1. ánsestri; 2. ǽnsistri]. Cp. O. Fr. *ancesserie.* See **ancestor** & **-y.** Series of ancestors, lineage, descent.

anchar. See **antiar.**

anchor (I.), n. [1. ángker; 2. ǽŋkə]. O.E. *ancor*, fr. Lat. *ancora*, Gk. *ágkūra*, 'an anchor', fr. *agkṓn*, 'a bend'; cp. *agkúlos*, 'crooked, curved', cogn. w. Lat. *uncus*, 'hook'. See **uncinal. 1.** Instrument for mooring ships and boats when floating in the water, consisting usually of a strong iron or steel bar having at one end curved arms with a fluke or hook at each extremity, which becomes embedded in sea or river bottom, and at the other end a ring to which a cable is attached that is fastened to the ship. Phrs. *to cast anchor*, let anchor down into sea from ship; *weigh anchor*, to haul anchor out of the sea, therefore (of ships) to start upon a voyage; *to come to anchor*, let anchor down into the sea, cease sailing; *ride at anchor*, be made fast to, and held safe by anchor. **2.** (fig.) Anything which gives feeling of security from being fixed and steady. *Sheet anchor*, formerly name of largest type of anchor, now chiefly (fig.) that upon which one mainly relies for support.

anchor (II.), vb. trans. & intrans. **a** trans. To make a ship fast by letting down anchor: *anchor a ship in the bay*; **b** intrans., to come to anchor.

anchorage, n. [1. ángkerij; 2. ǽŋkəridž]. See **anchor** & **-age.** Place suitable, specially prepared, for ships to anchor.

anchoress, n. [1. ángkeres; 2. ǽŋkərɛs]. See **anchoret** & **-ess.** Female recluse.

anchoret, anchorite, n. [1. ángkeret, ángkerīt; 2. ǽŋkərɛt, ǽŋkərait]. The former is the more historical form, the latter that more commonly used now; fr. Lat *anachōrēta*, Gk. *anakhōrētḗs*, fr. *anakhōréō*, 'I retire', fr. **ana-** & *khōréō*, 'give place, withdraw', cp. *khôros*, 'room, free space', see **chori-.** With this, Gk. *khêros*, 'empty, deprived of', *khḗrā*, 'widow', *khēróō*, 'make desolate, widow' &c., are prob. cogn., & further, Lat. *hēres*, 'heir'. See further under **heir.** Person who renounces the world, esp. for religious reasons; hermit, recluse.

anchovy, n. [1. ánchuvi, ànchóvi; 2. ǽntʃəvi, ǽntʃóuvi]. Span. *anchova.* Origin doubtful. Small fish resembling herring in appearance, possessing very rich pungent flavour, much used in savouries and sauces.

anchusa, n. [1. ànkúza; 2. ǽnkjúzə]; popularly, [1. ànchóoza; 2. ǽntʃúzə]. Lat. *anchūsa*, fr. Gk. *ágkhousa*, 'plant whose root yields a red dye'. (hort.) Various species of plants of borage family, with prickly leaves and stems, cultivated for their graceful clusters of purple or bright blue blossom.

anchylosed, adj. [1. ángkilōzd; 2. ǽŋkilouzd]. As though P.P. of vb. to *anchylose*, wh. hardly exists. See **anchylosis.** Afflicted with anchylosis or stiffening of the joints.

anchylosis, n. [1. àngkilósis; 2. ǽŋkilóusis]. Gk., fr. *agkúlos*, 'crooked'. See **anchor, angle (I.).** Stiffening of the joints through formation of adhesions.

ancient (I.), adj. & n. [1. ánshent; 2. éinʃənt], fr. Fr. *ancien*; cp. Span. *anciano*, Ital. *anziano*, fr. Low Lat. *antiānus*, 'old, former', fr. Lat. *ante*, 'before'; the final *t* is inorganic. See **ante-. 1.** adj. Old, of long standing, having existed from times past (of persons and things, now chiefly of latter, application to persons being archaic or literary); specif. (law) enjoyed without interruption for twenty years or more: *ancient lights*, right to uninterrupted light to windows of house &c. **2.** n. **a** An old man (archaic); **b** *Ancient of Days*, God; **c** in pl. *the ancients*, those who lived in antiquity; specif., one of the classical writers.

ancient (II.), n. corrupt. of **ensign.** (archaic) **a** A standard, ensign; **b** bearer of a standard; ensign.

anciently, adv. **ancient (I.)** & **-ly.** In times gone by, in ancient days, formerly.

ancientness, n. See prec. & **-ness.** Antiquity.

ancillary, adj. [1. ansílari; 2. ænsíləri]. Lat. *ancillāris*, 'relating to female servants', fr. *ancilla*, 'maid-servant'. Cp. also Lat. *anculus*, 'servant'; both are dimin. of a Sabine word *ancus*, 'servant', the earlier history of wh. is obscure. Subordinate, auxiliary.

ancipital, ancipitous, adj. [1. ansípital, -us; 2. ænsípitəl, -əs], fr. Lat. *anceps*, *ancipit-is*, 'having two heads, double', fr. *an*, for *amb-*, see **ambi-,** & base of *caput*, 'head'. See **capital** & **-al, -ous.** (bot.) Of stems of certain grasses &c., having two edges, flattened, not rounded.

ancle. See **ankle.**

ancon, n. [1. ángkon; 2. ǽŋkən]. Lat., fr. Gk. *agkṓn*, 'a bend, elbow'. See **anchor (I.). a** (anat.) The elbow; **b** (archit.) a console bracket for supporting the cornice of a doorway.

-ancy, suff. [1. ansi; 2. ənsi]. Variant of **-ance**; cp. **-ency** & see **-y.** Forming ns., denoting quality or state, as *ascendancy* &c.

and, conj. [1. an(d); 2. ænd, ən(d)]. O.E. *and*, O.H.G. *anti*, *enti*, *unti* &c., Mod. Germ. *und*; the same element occurs in Gk. *antí*, *ánta*, 'opposite, over against', Lat. *ante*, 'before, in front of, facing' (see **ante-**, **anti-**); the idea of 'opposite, over against' is still expressed in Germ. particle *ent-* in *entgegen*, 'against, over against', in *antworten*, 'answer, give word for word', & in O.E. *and-swerian*, see **answer**. From the sense of opposing something else to what has been said comes finally the sense of addition, whence the copulative function arises; note that the final *-d* of Engl. *and* shows that the form arose in an unstressed position. The word serves as link joining parts of a sentence, and expresses an addition to what has already been expressed. **a** It is equivalent to 'also', 'in addition', 'moreover' &c.; **b** in order to, (colloq.) after *try*, *come*, *go*: *try and do it*, *come and see*; *go and look at it*.

andante, adv. & n. [1. àhndáhnte; 2. àndǽnte]. Ital., Pres. Part. of *andare*, 'to go', the etymol. of wh. is unknown. (musical term) **a** adv. (play) Slowly; **b** n., a slow movement.

andiron, n. [1. ándīern; 2. ǽndaiən]. M.E. *anderne*, *aundirne*, *aundyre(n)* &c., O. Fr. *andier*, Mod. Fr. *landier*, fr. *l'andier*; remoter history obscure; the latter part of Engl. word has certainly been influenced by *iron*. Iron utensil consisting of an upright bar supported by two feet in front, and another bar at right angles to it supported by one foot, used for supporting burning logs on a flat, open hearth.

androecium, n. [1. andrḗsium; 2. ændrísiəm]. Neo-Lat., fr. Gk. *andro-*, 'male', see next word, & *oîkos*, 'house'. See **economy**. (bot.) The stamens of a flower, taken collectively.

androgynous, adj. [1. àndróginus, -jinus; 2. ændrɔ́ginəs, -džinəs]. Gk. *andrógunos*, 'a man-woman, hermaphrodite', fr. *anḗr*, *andrós*, 'man', & *gunḗ*, 'woman'. See latter under **gynaeco-**, **quean** & **queen**. Gk. *anḗr* is cogn. w. Lat. (Sabine) *nēria*, 'bravery', & *nero*, 'strong'; cp. further Scrt. *náryaš*, 'virile', & O. Ir. *nertaim*, 'I strengthen'. Uniting the characters of male and female, hermaphrodite, esp. (bot.) having stamens and pistils in the same flower.

androphobia, n. [1. àndrofóbia; 2. ændrəfóubiə]. Gk. *andro-*, fr. *anḗr*, 'man' (see prec.), & *phóbos*, 'fear, flight'. See **-phobia**. Unhealthy dread of the male sex.

-androus, suff. [1. ándrus; 2. ǽndrəs], fr. Gk. *andro-*, 'male', see **androgynous**, & **-ous**, used esp. in botanical terminology to form compounds indicating presence of stamens.

-ane, suff. [1. ān; 2. ein]. Variant form of **-an**, fr. Lat. *-ānus*. **a** As parallel form of *-an*, often with differentiation of meaning, as *human*, *humane*; *urban*, *urbane* &c.; **b** (chem.) of paraffin series of hydrocarbons: *methane* &c.

anear, prep. & adv. [1. anḗr; 2. əníə]. **a-** & **near**. (rare) Near.

anecdotage, n. [1. ánekdōtij; 2. ǽnɛkdoutidž]. See **anecdote** & **-age**. **a** Collection of anecdotes (rare); **b** (facet.) time of life at which trivial anecdotes form staple of a person's conversation. (Formed jocosely, fr. **dotage**).

anecdotal, adj. [1. ánekdòtal; 2. ǽnɛkdòutəl]. See next word & **-al**. Concerned with, teeming with, anecdotes.

anecdote, n. [1. ánekdōt; 2. ǽnikdout]. Fr., fr. Gk. *anékdota*, 'unpublished things', fr. **an-** & *ékdota*, fr. *ekdidōmi*, 'I give out', *ek*, 'out', & *didōmi*, 'I give', redupl. form of base **dō-*, 'give'. See **donation** for other Aryan cognates. Account of an isolated event; a biographical detail; trivial story.

anele, vb. trans. [1. anḗl; 2. ənı́l]. M.E. *anelien*, 'anoint with oil', fr. O.E. *an* & *ele*, 'oil', loan-word fr. Lat. *oleum*. See **oil**. (archaic or obs.) Lit. to put oil upon, that is, specif., to administer Extreme Unction to. Cp. 'Hamlet': *unhouseled, unaneled*.

anemometer, n. [1. ànemómeter; 2. ænɛmɔ́mitə]. Gk. *ánemos*, 'wind', see **anemone**, & **meter**. Gauge for measuring speed of wind.

anemone, n. [1. anémuni; 2. ənémәni]. Gk. *anemṓnē*, 'the wind-flower', lit. 'daughter of the wind', fr. *ánemos*, 'wind', & *-ṓnē*, fem. patronymic suff.; Lat. *animus*, 'soul' &c., & Goth. *us-anan*, 'breathe out', are cognates. See **animus**. **1.** (bot.) White, star-shaped, woodland flower, the windflower, *Anemone nemorosa*; also in other many-coloured wild and cultivated species. **2.** (zool.) Sea-anemone.

anent, prep. [1. anént; 2. ənént]. O.E. *on efen*, *onemn*, 'near to, close by', M.E. *anen*, *onefent*, *anentis* &c., 'near to, against'; the final *t* is excrescent; fr. *an-*, *on-*, & *efen*, *emn*, 'even, equal'. The compound is an old one, &, first of all, expressed physical propinquity, cp. O.H.G. *ineben*, *neben*, Mod. Germ. *neben*, 'near, by the side of'; O.S. *on eƀan*. The first sense was 'on a level with'. See **on** & **even (II.)** (rare and obsolesc.) **a** With regard to, about, concerning; **b** over against, near.

-aneous, suff. [1. āneus; 2. éiniəs], fr. Lat. adj. in *-āneus*. See **-an** & **-ous**.

aneroid, adj. & n. [1. áneroid; 2. ǽnərɔid]. Fr. *anéroïde*, Gk. *a*, 'not', see **an-**, & *nērós*, *nārós*, 'flowing, liquid', & **-oid**; *nārós* is connected w. vb. *náein*, 'flow, water'. See further under **nereid**. **a** adj. Dry, containing no liquid mercury (of a kind of barometer); **b** n., barometer of this kind, in which the air-pressure acts on the elastic lid of a container from which most of the air has been exhausted.

aneurism, n. [1. ánūrizm; 2. ǽnjurizəm], fr. Gk. *aneurusmós*, 'dilatation', fr. *aná* & *eurús*, 'wide', cogn. w. Scrt. *urúš*, 'wide'. (med.) Pathological distension of the walls of an artery.

anew, adv. [1. anū́; 2. ənjū́], fr. **a-**, unstressed form of **of**, & **new**. Afresh, again, once more.

anfractuosity, n. [1. ánfraktūósiti; 2. ǽnfræktjuɔ́siti]. Fr. *anfractuosité*, Lat. *anfractus*, 'curving, circuitous route'; (fig.) 'prolixity in speech', fr. *an-*, for **ambi-**, and see **fracture**. Circuitousness (lit. and fig.).

angary, n. [1. ánggari; 2. ǽŋgəri], fr. Fr. *angarie*, fr. Med. Lat. *angaria*, 'compulsory service, especially for the Imperial post', fr. Gk. *aggareía*, 'office of a courier', fr. *ággaros*, 'courier'. See **angel**. (internat. law) In French, *droit d'angarie*, the right of a state at war to seize and use the property of an enemy or neutral on belligerent territory for its own military purposes, or to prevent its use by the enemy.

angel, n. [1. ānjl; 2. éindžl], fr. Lat. *angelus*, fr. Gk. *ággelos*, 'a messenger', cp. *aggéllō*, 'I announce'. The word, in the form *engel*, was borrowed fr. Lat. in the O.E. period, but the Mod. Engl. form is not derived direct fr. this, as the vowel of the first syll. shows, wh. presupposes a M.E. *āngel*, a form underivable fr. the O.E. form; it is possible that Fr. *ange* may have influenced the first vowel in the M.E. form, & that the rest of the word is fr. the O.E. type. The Gk. word is cogn. w. Gk. *ággaros*, 'Persian messenger', see prec. word, & w. Scrt. *áŋgiraš*, 'divine being'. See **evangel**. **1. a** Supernatural, celestial being, endued with immortality, and greater than human powers and intelligence; messenger from God to man; **b** guardian spirit, spiritual protector. Phrs.: *to rush in where angels fear to tread*, interfere foolishly and presumptuously in what does not concern one; *to entertain angels unawares*, not to appreciate fully the merits or importance of one's company. **2.** (fig.) Human being of either sex of great beauty or goodness (esp. of beautiful children, and of women who are both good and lovely). **3.** Formerly the name of an English gold coin worth about ten shillings, from its bearing figure of St. Michael.

angel-fish, n. A fish, *Angelus squatina*, a kind of ray or skate, allied to the sharks, with wing-like pectoral fins.

angelic, adj. [1. anjélik; 2. ændželik]. **angel** & **-ic**. **a** Like an angel in appearance or character; appearing at once beautiful and benign: *an angelic expression of countenance*; **b** coming from, belonging to, angel or angels: *angelic voices*.

angelica, n. [1. ànjélika; 2. ændželikə], fr. Med. Lat. *angelica herba*, 'the angelic herb', fr. its medicinal properties. **a** Pungent herb used for flavouring, also formerly in medicine; **b** sweetmeat made from root of this plant candied.

angelical, adj. [1. anjélikl; 2. ændželikl]. **angelic** & **-al**. Chiefly in *Angelical doctor*, St. Thomas Aquinas.

angelically, adv. Prec. & **-ly**. After the manner of an angel: *to behave angelically*.

angel lights, n. Prob. corrupt. of 'angle lights'. (archit.) The small lights on the outside at the top of a perpendicular window.

angelolatry, n. [1. ānjelólatri; 2. éindžəlɔ́lətri]. See **angel** & **-latry**. Worship of angels.

angelus, n. [1. ánjelus; 2. ǽndžiləs]. Devotion of the Roman Catholic Church which commemorates the Incarnation; so called from opening words, *Angelus Domini nuntiavit Mariae*, recited three times a day, at 6 A.M., noon, and 6 P.M. *Angelus bell*, one rung to announce the hour of the service.

anger (I.), n. [1. ángger; 2. ǽŋgə]. M.E. *anger*, fr. O.N. *angr*, 'affliction, sorrow'; Goth. *aggwus*, 'narrow', O.H.G. *angi*, *engi*, O.E. *eng*, 'narrow, painful', are cogn., & outside Gmc., Lat. *angere*, 'to throttle, to cause pain, to torment', Gk. *ágkhein*, 'choke, throttle'. Rousing of wrathful passion, stirring of resentful displeasure and strong antagonism, by sense of injury or insult; wrath, indignation, rage, ire.

anger (II.), vb. trans., fr. prec. To rouse antagonistic, resentful emotion in a person, provoke anger; to incense: *he was greatly angered by his friend's ingratitude*.

angina, n. [1. ánjina, ànjína; 2. ǽndžinə, ændžáinə]. Lat. *angina*, 'quinsy', cp. *angere*, 'press tight, throttle' &c., Gk. *ágkhein*, 'throttle' &c., fr. same base as **anger**. (med.) Constriction and spasmodic affection of throat and chest; esp. *angina pectoris*, spasmodic contraction of the great blood-vessels of the heart.

anginal, adj. [ánjinal; 2. ǽndžinəl]. Prec. & **-al**. Relating to, caused by, indicative of, angina.

angio-, pref., fr. Gk. *aggeîon*, 'vessel, receptacle', dimin. of *ággos*, 'chest, box'; cogn. w. O. Ir. *aigen*, 'dish'. Form used in making compound words, meaning contained in, covered by, a vessel, as seed- or blood-vessels.

angiosperm, n. [1. ánjiospêrm; 2. ǽndžiəspȧm]. **angio-** & **sperm**. (bot.) Any of a very large class or primary division of plants, including all flowering plants whose seeds are enclosed in an ovary, contrasted with *gymnosperm*.

angle (I.), n. [1. ánggl; 2. ǽŋgl]. Fr. *angle*, fr. Lat. *angulus*, 'an angle, corner', cp. Gk. *agkṓn*, 'bend, angle'. See **anchor** & **uncinal**. **1.** (geom.) Space near meeting-place of, and between two lines converging to a point. **2.** The sharp corner of anything resembling or forming an angle in shape.

angle (II.), n. O.E. *angel*, also in other W. Gmc. languages, fr. same base as above. Fish-hook; fishing tackle generally (archaic).

angle (III.), vb. intrans., fr. prec. **a** To use an angle for fishing, to fish: *to angle for trout* &c.; **b** (fig.) To use some device, trick, intrigue, to obtain one's ends; hold out cunning inducements to a person to do something: *to angle for promotion*.

Angle (IV.), n. Lat. *Anglus*, fr. Gmc. **angl-*, see **English**. Member of a Germanic tribe which settled in Northern, Eastern, & Central England.

angler, n. [1. ánggler; 2. ǽŋglə], fr. **angle (III.)** & **-er**. **a** One who angles, a fisherman; **b** species of fish which attracts smaller fish near its jaws by means of filaments attached to its head, which somewhat resemble the line and bait of a fisherman.

Anglican, adj. & n. [1. ánggl̇ikan; 2. ǽŋglikən]. Med. Lat. *Anglicānus*, 'English', fr. *Anglicus*,

'English', fr. *Anglus,* see **Angle (IV.)**. **a** adj. Belonging to, connected with, the Church of England; **b** n., a member of the Church of England.

Anglicanism, n. [1. ánglikanizm; 2. ǽŋglikənizəm]. Prec. & **-ism.** The theological principles and practice of the Church of England.

anglice, adv. [1. ánglisi; 2. ǽŋglisi]. Lat. In English.

anglicism, n. [1. ánglisizm; 2. ǽŋglisizəm]. See **Anglican** & **-ism.** English principles, practice, custom; specif., English idiom wrongly introduced into another language.

anglicize, vb. trans. [1. ánglisīz; 2. ǽŋglisaiz]. See prec. & **-ize. a** To render (a person) English in character, habits, feelings, appearance &c.; **b** to turn into English speech, or idiom.

angling, vbl. n. [1. ángling; 2. ǽŋgliŋ] fr. **angle (III.)**. Fishing, the art of the fisherman.

Anglo-, pref. [1. ánglō; 2. ǽŋglou], fr. **Angle (IV.)**. Pertaining to the English, originating in England; e.g. *Anglo-Catholic; Anglo-Indian,* **a** British by birth, but living in India; **b** Eurasian.

anglomania, n. [1. ànglōmánia; 2. æ̀ŋgloumèiniə]. **Anglo-** & **mania.** Exaggerated admiration for, and imitation of, English customs, institutions &c., esp. on the part of foreigners.

anglophobia, n. [1. ànglōfóbia; 2. æ̀ŋgloufóubiə]. **Anglo-** & Gk. *phóbos,* 'fear'. See **-phobia** & **-phobe.** (reverse of prec.) Hatred or fear of all things English, of England, and the English.

Anglo-Saxon, adj. & n. [1. ánglō sáksun; 2. ǽŋglou sǽksən]. **1.** adj. **a** Pertaining to the Germanic tribes which settled in England in the fifth century: *Anglo-Saxon institutions;* **b** pertaining to the English race; of English birth or descent. **2.** n. **a** Member of Anglo-Saxon tribes; **b** language spoken in England before the Conquest; now usually called *Old English.*

angola, angora, n. [1. anggóla, anggóra; 2. æŋgóulə, æŋgórə]. Latter fr. name of town in Asia Minor; former a substitution for the name. A cloth made from hair of Angora goat or from some other soft fine wool resembling this.

angora cat, n. One with long, silky fur.

angostura, adj. [1. ànggostúra; 2. æ̀ŋgəstjúrə], fr. place in Venezuela. **a** *Angostura bark,* bark of South American tree having pungent taste, and used as tonic; **b** *Angostura bitters,* liquor used as appetizer made from above.

angrily, adv. [1. ánggrili; 2. ǽŋgrili], fr. next word & **-ly.** In an angry manner.

angry, adj. [1. ánggri; 2. ǽŋgri], fr. **anger** & adj. suff. **-y.** (The word expresses rather a passing mood than a permanent trait of character). **a** Filled with anger, stirred by wrathful passion; enraged: *angry (with a person) about, at (a thing);* **b** (fig., of a wound or sore) inflamed.

anguine, adj. [1. ánggwin; 2. ǽŋgwin]. Lat. *anguīnus,* fr. *anguis,* 'a snake', cogn. w. Gk. *ékhis,* 'viper'. See **echidna.** (rare) Snake-like, serpentine.

anguish, n. [1. ánggwish; 2. ǽŋgwiʃ]. M.E. *anguys* &c., O. Fr. *anguisse,* Mod. Fr. *angoisse,* fr. Lat. *angustia,* 'narrowness, deficiency, perplexity', fr. *angustus,* 'narrow, critical, difficult' &c.; fr. same base as in **angina. a** Intense physical pain, bodily suffering, torment, agony; **b** (fig.) acute mental and moral suffering, grief, anxiety: *anguish of body and mind.*

angular, adj. [1. ánggūlar; 2. ǽŋgjulə], fr. Lat. *angulāris,* fr. *angulus.* See **angle (I.)**. Having angles, sharp-cornered. (of persons) **a** Gaunt, lacking in natural degree of plumpness; **b** cantankerous, inclined to quarrel, hard to get on with.

angularity, n. [1. ànggūláriti; 2. æ̀ŋgjulǽriti], fr. prec. & **-ity.** Quality of being angular (lit. and fig.).

angularly, adv. [1. ánggūlarli; 2. ǽŋgjuləli], fr. **angular** & **-ly.** With angles, in an angular manner.

angulate, adj. [1. ánggūlāt; 2. ǽŋgjuleit]. See **angle (I.)** & **-ate.** Having angles in literal sense.

anhydrite, n. [1. anhídrīt; 2. ænháidrait]. See next word & **-ite.** Anhydrous calcium sulphate.

anhydrous, adj. [1. anhídrus; 2. ænháidrəs], fr. Gk. *ánudros,* 'waterless', fr. **an-** & *húdōr,* 'water', see **hydro-**, & **-ous.** (chem. and mineral.) Of substances which have no water in their composition, esp. of crystals which have lost the water of crystallization; as *anhydrous calcium sulphate.*

anigh, adv. [1. aní; 2. ənái]. Modern formation on anal. of **afar** &c. See **a-** & **nigh.** Near, nigh.

anights, usually **o'nights**, adv. [1. anīts; 2. ənáits]. Adv. fr. **night**, w. double formation, O.E. *on niht(e),* 'at night', with addition of advbl. genit. suff. (archaic) At night, by night, nightly.

anil, n. [1. ánil; 2. ǽnil]. Fr., fr. Span., fr. Arab., fr. Scrt. *nīla,* 'dark blue'. Shrub from which West Indian indigo is made.

anile, adj. [1. ánīl; 2. éinail]. Lat. *anīlis,* fr. *anus,* 'an old woman', cp. O.H.G. *ana,* 'great grandmother', *ano,* 'great grandfather', Mod. Germ. *ahnen,* 'ancestors', also Mod. Germ. *amme,* 'nurse'. Like an old woman; verging on imbecility.

aniline, n. & adj. [1. ánilīn; 2. ǽnilain]. See **anil** & **-ine. 1.** n. Chemical product used in manufacture of dyes, originally obtained from indigo, now chiefly from coal-tar. **2.** adj. Of, pertaining to, aniline: *aniline dyes* &c.

anility, n. [1. aníliti; 2. əníliti]. See **anile** & **-ity.** Condition of being anile; senility, dotage.

animadversion, n. [1. ànimadvérshun; 2. æ̀nimædvə́ʃən]. Lat. *animadversiōn-(em),* 'attention, inquiry, censure', fr. *animadvers-(um),* P.P. type of *animadvertere,* 'to notice, punish'. See **animadvert.** Depreciatory reference to, or remarks upon; blame (followed by *on*).

animadversive, adj. [1. ànimadvérsiv; 2. æ̀nimædvə́siv]. See prec. & **-ive.** Imputing blame, disparaging. (Rare.)

animadvert, vb. intrans. [1. æ̀nimadvért; 2. æ̀nimædvə́t], fr. Lat. *animadvertere,* 'to notice', contracted fr. *animum advertere,* fr. *animus,* 'mind', & *ad,* 'to', & *vertere,* 'to turn'. See **animus** & **version.** To refer, allude to, comment upon (usually with implied disapproval); hence, to blame, censure: *to animadvert upon a person's conduct* &c.

animal (I.), n. [1. ánimal; 2. ǽniməl]. Lat. *animal,* 'a living being', fr. *animālis,* 'of air, living', fr. *anima,* 'air, breath, life', & adj. suff. *-ālis.* See **animus** & **-al. 1.** Living creature possessing power of voluntary motion, as distinguished from, and contrasted with, *plant,* on one hand, and from *man,* human being, on the other. Often also *lower animals.* **2.** A man of low type and character, a brutish, sensual human being.

animal (II.), adj. fr. prec. **1.** Pertaining to living beings: *animal life, habits* &c. **2.** Pertaining to lower nature and physical appetites of human beings; sensual, carnal: *man's animal nature, passions, desires* &c.

animalcular, adj. [1. ànimálkūlar; 2. æ̀nimǽlkjulə], fr. **animalcule** & **-ar.** Pertaining to, of the nature of, an animalcule.

animalcule, n. [1. ànimálkūl; 2. æ̀nimǽlkjūl]. Low Lat. *animalculum,* dimin. of Lat. *animal.* See **animal (I.)**. Minute living creature, perceptible only by means of a microscope.

animalism, n. [1. ánimalizm; 2. ǽniməlizəm]. **animal** & **-ism.** Animal character, lower nature; sensuality.

animalize, vb. trans. [1. ánimalīz; 2. ǽniməlaiz]. **animal** & **-ize.** To render like an animal, develop, emphasize, lower nature.

animate (I.), vb. trans. [1. ánimāt; 2. ǽnimeit]. Lat. *animātus,* P.P. of *animāre,* 'to fill with breath or air,' fr. *anima,* 'air'. See **animus** & **-ate.** To give life to, fill with life, enliven; inspire.

animate (II.), adj., fr. prec. Living, organic, as distinct from lifeless and inorganic: *animate nature.*

animated, adj. [1. ánimāted; 2. ǽnimeitid], fr. P.P. of **animate (I.)**. **a** Full of life, lively, active, mobile, spirited, brisk, vivacious: *an animated gesture, conversation, expression, face* &c.; **b** inspired with or by, actuated, influenced: *animated by* (or *with*) *the highest motives* &c.

animatedly, adv. Prec. & **-ly.** In a lively, spirited manner.

animating, adj. [1. ánimāting; 2. ǽnimeitiŋ], fr. Pres. Part. of **animate (I.)**. Life-giving, inspiring: *an animating impulse, motive* &c.

animation, n. [1. ànimáshun; 2. æ̀niméiʃən]. **animate (I.)** & **-ion.** Life, liveliness, spirit; condition of being brisk, vivacious: *a face devoid of animation; a speech delivered with animation.*

animism, n. [1. ánimizm; 2. ǽnimizəm], fr. Lat. *animus,* 'soul'. See **animus** & **-ism.** Name given to various doctrines or theories concerning the soul, of which the chief are: **a** Doctrine that the soul is the vital principle which produces all forms of organic life; **b** primitive religious belief found among many savage tribes, that all objects, even inanimate things, possess life and are endowed with souls; this belief has various developments and forms.

animist, n. [1. ánimist; 2. ǽnimist]. See prec. & **-ist.** One who holds any of the various forms of animism.

animosity, n. [1. ànimósiti; 2. æ̀nimɔ́siti]. Lat. *animōsitāt-(em),* 'boldness, vehemence, enmity', fr. *animōsus,* 'bold, spirited' fr. *animus,* 'courage, spirit, passion'. See **animus** & **-ity.** Violent hatred, dislike, prejudice, often leading to outward expressions of hostility.

animus, n. [1. ánimus; 2. ǽniməs]. Lat., meaning 'spiritual principle of human life, rational soul; disposition, courage, pride; vehemence, wrath'. The primitive sense, wh. underlies the large group of words in Lat. related to this, is found in *anima,* wh. means 'air, breeze; the breath; principle of animal life' (as distinct fr. *animus,* 'living being'); outside Lat. we have Gk. *ánemos,* 'wind' (see **anemone**); Goth. *us-anan,* 'breathe out', O.E. *anda,* 'malice, anger' &c.; O.N. *andi, ond,* 'soul, spirit'; O. Slav. *vonja,* 'vapour, breath'. **1.** In English chiefly used in bad sense of animosity, prejudice, grudge: *to have, feel, show, (an) animus against a person.* **2.** (specif., law) Intention, as in Lat. Phrs. *animus furandi,* of stealing; *testandi,* of making a will &c.

anise, n. [1. ánis; 2. ǽnis]. Fr. *anise,* fr. Lat. *anīsum,* fr. Gk. *ánīson,* 'anise, dill'; origin unknown. Plant with pungent, aromatic seeds, used for flavouring and in manufacture of the liqueur anisette.

aniseed, n. [1. ánisēd; 2. ǽnisīd]. Seed of anise, used for flavouring cakes &c.; also yielding an aromatic, carminative oil.

anisette, n. [1. ànisét; 2. æ̀nisét]. Fr., dimin. of **anise.** Sweet, strong-flavoured liqueur made from aniseed.

aniso-, pref., fr. Gk. *ánisos,* 'unequal', fr. *an-,* neg. pref., & *ísos,* 'equal'. See **an-** & **iso-.** Form used in making scientific terms, meaning 'unequal, dissimilar, unsymmetrical', as converse of those in **iso-.**

anker, n. [1. ángker; 2. ǽŋkə]. Du. & Germ., etymol. doubtful; Low Lat. has *anceria,* 'keg, vat'. **a** An old liquid measure for spirits, about 8½ imperial gallons; **b** keg containing such quantity.

ankh, n. [1. angk; 2. æŋk]. Egyptian. The ancient Egyptian symbol of life, a tau-cross or T, surmounted by an oval.

ankle, ancle, n. [1. ángkl; 2. ǽŋkl]. M.E. *ancle,* prob. Scand.; cp. Du. & Swed. *ankel,* cogn. w. Lat. *angulus,* 'angle, corner', Scrt. *áŋam,* 'limb'. See further cognates under anchor, angle (I.), uncinal. a The joint in human beings which connects the foot with the leg; b slender part of the leg between this joint and the calf.

anklet, n. [1. ángklet; 2. ǽŋklit], fr. prec. & dimin. suff. **-let**. Ring for the ankle, whether worn as ornament or as a fetter.

ankus, n. [1. ángkus; ǽŋkəs]. Hind. An elephant goad, consisting of a pointed spike with hook attached, applied to the head by the mahout.

ankylosed. See **anchylosed**.

ankylostomiasis, n. [1. àngkilōstōmíasis; 2. æ̀ŋkiloustoumáiəsis], fr. Gk. *agkúlos*, 'crooked', see **anchor**, & *stóma*, 'mouth', see **stomach**, & **-iasis**. (pathol.) Disease caused by the parasitic 'hookworm', characterized by great anæmia, esp. affecting miners.

anlace, n. [1. ánles; 2. ǽnlɛs]. Etymol. unknown. A short dagger with broad, tapering blade, formerly worn in the girdle.

anna, n. [1. ána; 2. ǽnə]. Hind. *āna*. a An Indian monetary term (no coin of one anna exists); the sixteenth part of a rupee; b applied colloquially in India to persons of mixed blood: *to have so many annas of dark blood.*

annalist, n. [1. ánalist; 2. ǽnəlist]. See next word & **-ist**. Writer of annals.

annals, n. pl. [1. ánalz; 2. ǽnəlz]. Fr. *annales*, fr. Lat. *annāles* (*sc. libri*), 'chronicles, yearly records', pl. of *annālis*, 'pertaining to a year', fr. *annus*, 'year'. See **annual**. a Yearly record of events, yearly chronicle; historical records, history; b periodic publication containing record of progress of knowledge in science &c.

annates, n. pl. [1. ánāts; 2. ǽneits]. L. Lat. *annāta*, fr. *annus*, 'year'. See **annual**. First-fruits of an ecclesiastical benefice, paid to the Pope in Roman Church.

anneal, vb. trans. [1. anḗl; 2. əníəl]. O.E. *on-ǣlan*, 'burn, kindle, inflame', M.E. *anēlen*, 'burn, melt', O.E. *ǣlan*, fr. **ailjan*, earlier **aiþl-jan*, cogn. w. Lat. *aedes*, 'hearth' &c.; it belongs to group of words discussed under **aedile, aestivate** &c. The M.E. & Mod. Engl. forms may have been influenced to some extent by O. Fr. *neeler*, 'coat with black enamel', fr. Low Lat. *nigellāre*, fr. *nigellus*, dimin. of *niger*, 'black'. See under **negro**. To temper glass or metals by subjecting them to heat, for purpose of reducing brittleness.

Annelida, n. [1. anélida; 2. ənélidə]. Lat. *annellus, ānellus*, 'a little ring', dimin. of *ānulus*, & Gk. *eîdos*, 'form, shape'. See **annular & idol**. (zool.) Division of segmented worms, so-called from their being formed, as it were, from a number of small rings.

annex (I.), vb. trans. [1. anéks; 2. ənéks]. Lat. *annexus*, P.P. of *annectere*, 'to bind to', fr. **ad-** & *nexum*, 'bound', cp. **nexus**. 1. To add, join, attach, append *to*. 2. Specif. (of a state) to add territory or another smaller state to itself by bringing the former under its control and governance.

annex(e) (II.), n. [1. áneks; 2. ǽnɛks], fr. prec. or Fr. *annexe*. Something joined on; specif., a smaller building added to larger one, either in actual communication with it or situated sufficiently near to provide extra accommodation for the inhabitants of main building, esp. an *annex(e) to a hotel.*

annexation, n. [1. ànekzā́shun; 2. æ̀nɛkzéiʃən]. See **annex** (I.) & **-ation**. Act or process of taking over of extra territory, or another smaller state, by one which is more powerful, and placing it under the control of the latter.

annihilate, vb. trans. [1. aníilāt; 2. ənáiəleit], fr. Lat. *annihilāt-(um)*, P.P. type of *annihilāre*, fr. **ad-** & *nihil*, 'nothing'. See **nil, nihilist**. To bring to nothing, demolish, destroy utterly.

annihilation, n. [1. aniilā́shun; 2. ənàiəléiʃən]. See prec. & **-ion**. Destruction, complete demolition.

anniversary, n. & adj. [1. àniversari; 2. æ̀nivə́səri]. Lat. *anniversārius*, 'yearly', fr. *annus*, 'year', & *vertere, versum*, 'to turn'. See **annual & version**. 1. n. a The day of the year on which an event happened or is celebrated; b the yearly celebration of an event. 2. adj. Belonging to an anniversary.

Anno Domini, adv. [1. ánō dóminī; 2. ǽnou dɔ́minai]. Lat. In the year of our Lord, i.e. of Christian era, usually in abbreviation A.D.

annotate, vb. trans. [1. ánōtāt; 2. ǽnouteit], fr. Lat. *annotāt-(um), annotāre*, 'to note down', fr. **ad-** & *notāre*, 'to mark, note', see **note** (I.). To supply explanatory notes or commentary to a document, esp. to literary text or treatise.

annotated, adj. [1. ánōtāted; 2. ǽnouteitid], fr. P.P. of prec. Containing, supplied with, explanatory notes: *an annotated edition.*

annotation, n. [1. ànōtā́shun; 2. æ̀noutéiʃən]. See **annotate & -ion**. Act of annotating; note(s) supplied to a text by way of explanation or commentary.

annotator, n. [1. ánōtātur; 2. ǽnouteitə]. See **annotate & -or**. One who writes notes upon a text.

announce, vb. trans. [1. anóuns; 2. ənáuns], fr. Fr. *annoncer*, fr. Lat. *annunciāre*, fr. **ad-** & *nunciāre, nuntiāre*, 'to relate, report', fr. *nuntius*, 'messenger'. See **nuncio**. 1. a To declare, publish (news &c.); b give notice of (a visitor's) arrival by calling out his name: *the servant announced Mr. and Mrs. Jones.* 2. To convey information through the senses, otherwise than by word or written message: *an occasional shot announced the presence of the enemy.*

announcement, n. [1. anóunsment; 2. ənáunsmənt]. See prec. & **-ment**. Public statement, made verbally, or in writing or print, giving notice that an event has happened, or is to take place in the future.

announcer, n. [1. anóunser; 2. ənáunsə]. See prec. & **-er**. One who announces, esp. official who introduces each item of a broadcast programme, reads the news &c.

annoy (I.), vb. trans. [1. anói; 2. ənɔ́i]. O. Fr. *anoier*, fr. *anoi*, 'vexation', Mod. Fr. *ennui*, fr. Lat. *in odio*, as *mihi est in odio*, 'it is hateful to me'. See **noisome & odium**. To trouble, vex, worry, harass.

annoy (II.), n. See prec. (rare and obsolesc.) Injury, worry, something distasteful; painful emotion caused by what is distasteful.

annoyance, n. [1. anóians; 2. ənɔ́iəns]. See **annoy** (I.) & **-ance**. a Act of annoying; b that which annoys; c feeling of irritation caused by action or event which is unpleasant.

annoying, adj. [1. anói-ing; 2. ənɔ́i-iŋ], fr. Pres. Part. of **annoy** (I.). Causing, productive of, annoyance, irritating, vexatious.

annoyingly, adv. Prec. & **-ly**. In a manner which annoys.

annual (I.), adj. [1. ánūal; 2. ǽnjuəl]. L. Lat. *annuālis*, fr. *annus*, 'year', wh. stands for **atnos*, & is thus exactly cogn. w. Goth. *aþn*, 'year'. The base of both occurs also in Scrt. *át-ati*, 'he goes, moves on'. Yearly, coming every year.

annual (II.), n. a Something which appears each year, e.g. a periodical volume published once a year: *The Boy's Own Annual*; or b a plant which springs up, flowers, seeds, and dies within a year, and which does not come up again, contrasted with *perennial*. Phr. *hardy annual*, (facetious) an event which recurs each year with wearisome iteration.

annually, adv. See **annual** (I.) & **-ly**. Each, every, year.

annuitant, n. [1. anū́itant; 2. ənjúitənt]. See **annuity & -ant**. One receiving an annuity.

annuity, n. [1. anū́iti; 2. ənjúiti]. Fr. *annuité*, fr. Lat. *annuus*, 'yearly', fr. *annus*, 'year'. See **annual & -ity**. Fixed sum paid every year as income, at one or more regular intervals, during lifetime of recipient.

annul, vb. trans. [1. anúl; 2. ənál]. Fr. *annuler*, fr. Lat. *ad nullum*, 'to nothing'. See **null**. To render null and void, to make of no effect, nullify, do away with (esp. of laws, legal decisions, customs &c.).

annular, adj. [1. ánūlar; 2. ǽnjulə], fr. Lat. *ān(n)ulāris*, fr. *ān(n)ulus*, dimin. of *ānus*, 'a ring'; the latter is perh. fr. **ancno-*, & in this case may be compared w. Scrt. *aknáš*, 'curved', & further w. Lat. *uncus*, 'crooked', see under **uncial**. Ring-like; *annular eclipse*, one in which a ring of light is left on sun's disk.

annulate(d), adj. [1. ánūlāt(ed); 2. ǽnjuleit(id)]. See **annular** & **-ate(d)**. Furnished with rings; formed of rings.

annulation, n. [1. ànūlā́shun; 2. æ̀njuléiʃən]. See prec. & **-ion**. A ring-like formation.

annulet, n. [1. ánūlet; 2. ǽnjulɛt]. Dimin. formed fr. Lat. *ān(n)ulus*, 'a ring'. See **annular**. A small ring; specif. (her.) small ring borne as a charge.

annulment, n. [1. anúlment; 2. ənálmənt]. See **annul** & **-ment**. a The act of annulling; b declaration that a law &c. is null and void.

annuloid, annulose, adj. [1. ánūloid, ánūlōs; 2. ǽnjulɔid, ǽnjulous], fr. Lat. *ān(n)ulus*, 'ring'. See **annular & -oid & -ose**. Ring-like; formed of ring-like segments.

annunciate, vb. trans. [1. anúnsiāt; 2. ənánsieit], fr. Lat. *annunciāt-(um)*, P.P. type of *annunciāre*. See **announce & -ate**. (rare) To announce.

annunciation, n. [1. anùnsiā́shun; 2. ənànsiéiʃən]. Lat. *annunciātiōn-(em)*. See prec. & **-ion**. 1. The act of announcing. 2. Specif. (cap.) announcement by the angel Gabriel to the B.V.M. of the Incarnation. 3. Festival of Christian Church commemorating this, falling on March 25th.

anode, n. [1. ánōd; 2. ǽnoud], fr. Gk. *ánodos*, 'way up', fr. **ana-** & *hodós*, 'way' (see **hodometer**), wh. is cogn. w. O. Slav. *choditi*, 'to walk'. Ultimately fr. same base as **sed-*, 'sit' (see **sit**), of wh. orig. sense was 'to place' either part of the person upon a seat, or the foot upon the road in order to go. Positive electric pole; specif. (wireless) element of thermionic valve which attracts electrons emitted by its filament, also styled *plate*.

anodyne, adj. & n. [1. ánōdīn; 2. ǽnoudain], fr. Lat. *anōdynus*, fr. Gk. *anṓdunos*, 'painless', fr. **an-** & *odúnē*, 'pain'. The most plausible etymol. is that connecting the latter word w. Gk. *dúē*, 'distress', & *daíō*, 'light up' (fr. **dawjō*); further w. Scrt. *dunṓti*, 'afflict, ill-treat, burn', & the Scrt. n. *davaš*, 'conflagration', *dōman*, 'torment' (the pref. *o-* in *odúnē* is unexplained). With the above words may be equated O.E. *tēon*, 'suffering, injury, wrong', see **teen**. a adj. Allaying pain, soothing; b n., anything which soothes pain; something which calms the mind; specif., drug which soothes and relieves pain.

anoint, vb. trans. [1. anóint; 2. ənɔ́int]. O. Fr. *enoint*, P.P. of *enoindre*, fr. Lat. *inunct-(um)*, P.P. type of *inungere*, fr. *in*, 'on', & *ungere*, 'to smear'. See **ointment & unction**. 1. To apply ointment to, pour oil upon, smear or rub with oil or ointment. 2. Specif., to induct (priest or king) to an office by the use of consecrated oil as a religious ceremony.

anointed, adj. [1. anóinted; 2. ənɔ́intid]. P.P. of **anoint**. 1. Smeared or rubbed with oil or ointment. 2. (absol.) *The Lord's Anointed*, a Christ, the Messiah; b a king by divine right.

anointing, n. [1. anóinting; 2. ənɔ́intiŋ], fr. Pres. Part. of **anoint**. a Act of applying ointment; b consecration of a king &c. by such an act.

anomalism, n. [1. anómalizm; 2. ənɔ́məlizəm]. See **anomaly & -ism**. State of being anomalous or irregular; an anomaly.

anomalistic, adj. [1. anòmalístik; 2. ənɔ̀məlístik]. See **anomaly & -ist & -ic**. Tending to be anomalous; esp. (astron.) *anomalistic month*, time taken by moon to pass from perigee to perigee; *anomalistic year*, time taken by earth or other planet to pass from perihelion to perihelion.

anomalous, adj. [1. anómalus; 2. ənɔ́mələs], fr. Lat. *anōmalus*, fr. Gk. *anṓmalos*, 'uneven, irregular'. See next word & **-ous.** Deviating from the ordinary rule or procedure; irregular, abnormal, unusual.

anomaly, n. [1. anómali; 2. ənɔ́məli], fr. Lat. *anōmalia*, fr. Gk. *anōmalía*, 'inequality', fr. **an-** (priv.) & *homalós*, 'even, level, of like degree', fr. *homós*, 'one and the same, belonging to two or more jointly'. This word stands for **somós*, & is cogn. w. Scrt. *sám*, 'together with', O. Slav. *sa*, 'with', Goth. *sama*, 'same' (cp. **same**). With the longer form *homalós*, cp. Lat. *similis*, 'like' (see **similar**), & further under **homo-**. **1. a** Irregularity, departure from a common rule (applied to natural phenomena and to apparent irregularities in grammar &c.); **b** inconsistency, paradox (in human affairs and conduct). **2.** Specif. (astron.) **a** angular distance of a planet from its perihelion or satellite from its perigee; **b** angle measuring apparent irregularities in planet's motion.

anomo-, pref. In composition, 'irregular'; chiefly in scientific terminology, fr. Gk. *ánomos*, 'without law', fr. **a-**, 'not, lacking', & *nómos*, 'anything assigned, usage, custom, enactment, law', cogn. w. Gk. *némō*, 'distribute, assign, allot, hold, possess, control'; cp. Goth., O.E. &c. *niman*, 'take'. See **nomad, numb.**

anon (**I.**), adv. [1. anón; 2. ənɔ́n]. O.E. *on ān*, *on ānum*, adv., 'continually, continuously, immediately', M.E. *anoon*. See **on & one.** Soon, in a little while, directly. *Ever and anon*, from time to time, every now and then.

anon (**II.**), adj. Abbr. of **anonymous.**

anonaceous, adj. [1. ànonáshus; 2. æ̀nənéiʃəs], fr. Mod. Lat. *anona*, 'pine-apple', see **ananas & -aceous.** (bot.) Relating, belonging, to the pine-apple.

anonym, n. [1. ánonim; 2. ǽnənim]. Fr. *anonyme*, Lat. *anōnymus*, fr. Gk. *anṓnumos*, **an-**, 'without', *ónoma*, 'name', cogn. w. Lat. *nōmen*, 'name', Goth. *namō*, O.E. *nama*. See **name, nominal. a** A person whose name is not revealed; **b** a pseudonym, an assumed or false name.

anonymity, n. [1. ànonímiti; 2. æ̀nənímiti]. See prec. & **-ity.** Condition of being anonymous.

anonymous, adj. [1. anónimus; 2. ənɔ́niməs]. See **anonym & -ous. a** (of persons) Not named; having one's name concealed: *to remain anonymous; an anonymous donor* &c.; **b** (of liter. and other works) not bearing author's name: *an anonymous book, letter* &c.

anonymously, adv. Prec. & **-ly.** Without revealing, publishing, bearing, a name: (of a book) *published anonymously.*

anopheles, n. [1. anófelēz; 2. ənɔ́fəlīz]. Gk. *anōphelḗs*, 'useless, harmful', fr. **an-**, 'without', & *óphelos*, 'use, help', cogn. w. Scrt. *phála-*, 'gain, success'. A genus of blood-sucking mosquitoes, which act as carriers of the malaria parasite.

anosmia, n. [1. anósmia; 2. ənɔ́smiə]. Gk. **an-**, 'without', & *osmḗ*, 'scent, odour', the Attic form fr. **odsmā́*, cp. Doric *odmā́*, Hom. *odmḗ*, 'stench', cogn. w. Lat. *odor*, 'scent'. See **odour.** (med.) Loss of the sense of smell.

another, pron., n., & adj. [1. anúdher; 2. ənáðə]. See **an** (**I.**) & **other. 1.** (of things and persons) Something different: **a** as n., *I don't like this one, show me another*; **b** as adj., *I must put on another coat before going to the party; I saw one play yesterday, and another, much better one, today.* **2. a** as n. Something in addition; a further, additional thing: *I've had one cup of tea, but I should like another*; **b** as adj., followed by a n., *have another try.* **3.** (reciprocally, preceded by one) *Love one another*, let each one love the other, or others. **4.** adj. or n. One (person or thing) of the same character, class, degree, kind as, one closely resembling, one that has preceded: *for all we know this young man may turn out another Keats; I have had one house that exactly suited me, and I can hardly expect to find another.*

anourous, adj. [1. anóorus; 2. ənúərəs], fr. Gk. **an-**, 'without', & *ourá*, 'tail', wh. is cogn. w. Gk. *ouríakhos*, 'butt end of a spear'; Lat. *urruncum*, 'lower part of an ear of corn', cp. **uro-.** (zool.) Tailless.

anserine, adj. [1. ánserin; 2. ǽnsərain]. Lat. *anserīnus*, fr. *anser*, 'goose', for **g̑hans-*, cp. Gk. *khḗn*, Scrt. *hasa-*, O.H.G. *gans*, O.E. *gōs*, whence **goose.** Like, pertaining to, a goose.

answer (**I.**), n. [1. áhnser; 2. ā́nsə]. O.E. *andswaru*, M.E. *andsware, answere*, 'a reply', orig. a statement made on oath, affirmation. *And-* here has the sense of 'in reply, in return'. See **and & swear. 1.** Statement, spoken or written, made in reply to a question; reply, response. **2.** Solution of a problem, esp. in mathematics. **3. a** Statement made, or **b** action taken, in reply to an attack or accusation; **c** (law) defence (in criminal case), pleading of defendant (in civil action).

answer (**II.**), vb. trans. & intrans. O.E. *andswerian, andswarian*, 'answer, reply', M.E. *answere* &c., fr. prec. **A.** trans. **1. a** To reply in speech or writing, or by signal, to (a question, remark &c., stated or written): *to answer a question*; **b** to write in return for (a letter received) not necessarily involving reply to questions): *to answer a letter.* Phr. *answer (a person) back*: to make an impertinent reply. **2.** To do something in return for, or by way of retaliation: *answer blows with blows.* **3.** To respond to (a summons): *answer a call, the bell* &c. **4.** To suit, be adequate to, be adapted to, fulfil (a purpose &c.): *that will answer my turn; to answer its purpose.* **B.** intrans. **1. a** To make a reply: *I asked him several questions, but he never answered*; **b** to write in return for letter received: *I wrote to him last week, but he hasn't answered yet*; **c** to indicate by word or sign that one has heard a call: *when I call you, you should answer at once.* Phr. *answer to a name*, acknowledge it as one's own by replying when one is addressed by it. **2.** To succeed, achieve the desired end: *our plan, experiment, hasn't answered at all.* **C.** Followed by prepositions. *Answer for*, **a** to be responsible for: *I can't answer for his honesty, for the truth of the statement*; **b** to suffer the consequences of: *we must all answer for our sins some day. Answer to*, **a** to correspond with, agree with: *answer to a description*; **b** to act in response to action on the part of another, react to external stimulus: (of a horse) *to answer to the whip; to answer to medical treatment.*

answerable, adj. [1. áhnserabl; 2. ā́nsərəbl]. Prec. & **-able.** (Followed by *to* before names of persons, and *for* before names of actions.) **1.** Responsible, liable to be called to account: *you are answerable to me for your conduct*; (also absol.) *irregularities have occurred, and some-one must be answerable.* **2.** Corresponding, in proportion to, commensurate with: *the results were not answerable to the hopes that had been formed.* **3.** Capable of being answered (rare); cp. *unanswerable.*

answering, adj. [1. áhnsering; 2. ā́nsəriŋ], fr. Pres. Part. of **answer** (**II.**). **a** Replying: *an answering voice*; **b** corresponding, agreeing with: *a person answering to this description.*

ant, n. [1. ahnt; 2. ānt]; more rarely [1. ant; 2. ænt], to distinguish fr. **aunt.** O.E. *ǣmete*, whose variant *ēmete* produced **emmet**; M.E. *amte* &c. This must be a common W. Gmc. word, cp. O.H.G. *ameizza*, Mod. Germ. *ameise*. Perh. connected w. Goth. *maitan*, 'to cut', O.H.G. *meizan*, cp. Mod. Germ. *meissel*, 'chisel'. The W. Gmc. form fr. wh. the O.E. & O.H.G. words for *ant* come wd. be **āmaitjō-*, & might mean orig. 'the insect that cuts (bites) off', in reference to its habit of biting through the stems & roots of plants &c.; the origin of the word, however, is by no means certain. Small gregarious insect of the family *Formicidae*, varying in colour according to species, sometimes provided with wings, having highly-developed social organization; very active, and strong for its size, and constructing 'hills' or piles of pine-needles &c. in which chambers and passages are formed.

-ant, suff. [1. ant; 2. ənt]. Through Fr. or direct fr. Lat. *-ant(em), -ent(em)*, Pres. Part. Expresses agent or instrument in nouns: *applicant, irritant.*

antacid, adj. & n. [1. antásid; 2. æntǽsid]. See **anti- & acid.** (chem. and med.) **a** adj., Counteracting, neutralizing, an acid; preventing acidity; **b** n., substance, as an alkali, which counteracts or neutralizes an acid; a preventive of acidity.

antae, n. pl. [1. ántē; 2. ǽntī]. Lat., perhaps fr. **ante**, 'in front, before', or cogn. w. Scrt. *ā́tā*, 'door-frame'; O.N. *ǫnd*, 'ante-room'. (class. archit.) Projecting flat pilasters or piers at each corner of the portico of a temple &c. Phr. *in antis*, of columns between these pilasters.

antagonism, n. [1. àntágonizm; 2. æ̀ntǽgənizəm], fr. Gk. *antagṓnisma*, fr. *antagōnizomai*, 'struggle against'. See **antagonize. 1.** State or condition of being opposed to something; active opposition (*to* or *against*): *to be or act in antagonism to; to be, come into, be brought into antagonism with.* **2.** Mutual hostility of forces, principles, persons: *antagonism between Capital and Labour.*

antagonist, n. [1. àntágonist; 2. æ̀ntǽgənist], fr. L. Lat. *antagōnista*, fr. Gk. *antagōnistḗs*, 'rival'. See **antagonize & -ist.** One pitted against, and striving with, another in any kind of contest; enemy, opponent; **a** rival in a competition for the same object.

antagonistic(al), adj. [1. antàgonístik(l); 2. æntæ̀gənístik(l)]. Prec. & **-ic & -al.** Opposed to, hostile to, incompatible with.

antagonistically, adv. Prec. & **-ly.** In an antagonistic manner.

antagonize, vb. trans. [1. antágonīz; 2. æntǽgənaiz], fr. Gk. *antagōnízomai*, 'struggle against', fr. **anti-** & *agōnízomai*, 'I struggle', fr. *agṓn*, 'a contest', see **agonistic. 1.** To oppose, contend with, dispute the mastery with (of like forces). **2.** To bring into opposition, render hostile, make an enemy of.

antalkali, n. [1. antálkali; 2. æntǽlkəlai]. **anti- & alkali.** (chem.) Substance which counteracts or neutralizes an alkali.

antalkaline, adj. [1. antálkalīn; 2. æntǽlkəlain]. Prec. & **-ine.** Counteracting, neutralizing, an alkali.

antaphrodisiac, adj. & n. [1. àntafrodíziak; 2. æ̀ntæfrədíziæk]. See **anti- & aphrodisiac. a** adj. Counteracting sexual desire; **b** n., medicine, drug &c. used for this purpose.

antarctic, adj. & n. [1. antárktik; 2. æntā́ktik]. See **anti- & arctic. a** adj. Opposite to the north, or arctic, pole; pertaining to the south pole or the regions near the south pole; **b** n., (caps. & with def. art.) *the Antarctic*, south pole or south polar regions.

ant-bear, n. The great ant-eater.

ante-, pref. [1. ánti; 2. ǽnti]. Lat., 'before, in front of', of space & position; 'earlier than, before', in time, cogn. w. Gk. *antí* (see **anti-**) & **and.** Cp. also first element in **answer.**

ant-eater, n. Name given to various edentate mammals, chiefly of tropical America, which live on ants licked up by their long sticky tongue; the great ant-eater or **ant-bear**, the pangolin, tamandua &c.

antecedence, n. [1. àntisḗdens; 2. æ̀ntisídəns], fr. Lat. *antecēdentia*. See **antecedent. 1.** Action of going before, state of being before, in point of time; precedence, priority. **2.** (astron.) Retrograde motion of a planet.

antecedent (**I.**), adj. [1. àntisḗdent; 2. æ̀ntisídənt], fr. Fr. *antécédent*, fr. Lat. *antecēdent-(em)*, Pres. Part. of *antecēdere*, fr. *ante*, 'before', & *cēdere*, 'to go'. See **ante- & cede.** Being or going before in time, prior, preceding, previous (*to*).

antecedent (**II.**), n., fr. prec. **1. a** Something which precedes, goes before, happens before; a thing or circumstance which goes before in time or order; hence, **b** word or clause referred to by pronoun, esp. by a relative pronoun. **2.** (pl.) Facts or circumstances that have happened before in the history of a person's life, such as ancestry, education, past actions and employment &c.

antechamber, n. [1. ántichāmber; 2. ǽntitʃeimbə]. Fr. *antichambre*. See **ante-** & **chamber**. Room leading into another, larger, apartment.

antechapel, n. [1. ántichapl; 2. ǽntitʃæpl]. See **ante-** & **chapel**. That part of the west end of a church or collegiate chapel which is separated from the nave by the rood-screen; in cruciform buildings it forms a transept.

antedate (I.), n. [1. àntidā́t; 2. æ̀ntidéit]. See **ante-** & **date**. (rare) A prior date; a date earlier than the true one.

antedate (II.), vb. trans., fr. prec. **1.** To date back, assign a date earlier than the true one to (a letter, document, event &c.). **2.** To precede in point of time. **3.** (rare) To bring about before due time, to accelerate. **4.** To imagine (something) as occurring or existing before it actually happens or comes into existence, to anticipate.

antediluvian, adj. & n. [1. àntidilōōvian; 2. æ̀ntidilúviən], fr. **ante-** & Lat. *dīluvium*, 'flood, deluge', fr. *dīluere*, 'to wash away'. See **dilute, diluvial**. **1.** adj. Pertaining to the time before the Flood; existing before the Flood; hence, antiquated, primitive. **2.** n. **a** Anybody or anything living before the Flood; **b** (fig.) a very old or old-fashioned person.

antefixa, n. pl. [1. àntifíksa; 2. æ̀ntifíksə]. Lat., fr. *antefixus*, 'fixed in front'. See **ante-** & **fix**. (class. archit.) Small decorative fixtures placed at the eaves of roofs to conceal the ends of the tiles.

antelope, n. [1. ántilōp; 2. ǽntiloup]. Fr. *antilope*, fr. Gk. *anthólops*. Origin unknown. General term of a group containing several varieties of ruminant, horned animals, which generally resemble deer in their lightness and agility, but are classed as bovines, and are allied to goats.

ante meridiem, adv. [1. ànti merídiem; 2. æ̀nti mərídiəm], abbr. as a.m. [éi ém]. Lat. acc. of *merīdies*, 'mid-day'; for *medi-*, 'mid', cp. *medius*, q.v. under **medial**, & *dies*, 'day', see **dies non**. Cp. **meridian**. Before noon.

antemundane, adj. [1. àntimúndān; 2. æ̀ntimándein]. See **ante-** & **mundane**. Existing or happening before the creation of the world.

antenatal, adj. [1. àntinā́tl; 2. æ̀ntinéitl]. See **ante-** & **natal**. Existing or happening before birth.

antenna, usually in pl. **antennae**, n. [1. anténa, anténē; 2. æntḗnə, æntḗnī]. Lat., 'a sail-yard', fr. Gk. *anateinō*, 'stretch, spread out'; *teinō*, 'stretch', is fr. **tenjō*, & is cogn. w. Lat. *tenuis*, 'thin' &c., q.v. under **attenuate**, & further w. **thin**. **1.** Feeler or horn of an insect or crustacean which projects from the head. **2.** The wires or aerials used for transmitting and receiving the electric waves in wireless telegraphy or telephony.

antenuptial, adj. [1. àntinúpshal; 2. æ̀ntinápʃl]. See **ante-** & **nuptial**. Prior to marriage, esp. (law) of marriage settlements.

antepenult, adj. [1. àntipenùlt; 2. ǽntipinàlt]. See next word. Antepenultimate.

antepenultima, n. [1. àntipenúltima; 2. æ̀ntipináltimə]. Lat. **ante-**, & *paenultima*, 'last but one', fr. *paene*, 'almost', & *ultima*, 'last'. See **penultimate**. The last but two; usually of the syllables in a word.

antepenultimate, adj. [1. àntipenúltimat; 2. æ̀ntipináltimit], fr. prec. & **-ate**. Last but two, of syllables in a word.

anteprandial, adj. [1. àntiprándial; 2. æ̀ntiprǽndiəl], fr. **ante-** & Lat. *prandium*, 'dinner'. See **post-prandial**. Before dinner.

anterior, adj. [1. antḗrier; 2. æntíəriə], fr. Lat. *anterior*, 'fore, former', compar. fr. *ante*, 'before', see **ante-**. Cp. Fr. *antérieur*. Followed by *to*: **a** (of place) before, more in front; **b** (of time, events &c.) before, earlier, preceding.

anteriorly, adv. Prec. & **-ly**. Before.

ante-room, n. [1. ánti room; 2. ǽnti rum]. See **ante-** & **room**. Room through which another, generally a larger room, is entered; waiting-room.

antetype, n. [1. ántitīp; 2. ǽntitaip]. See **ante-** & **type**. Prototype.

anth-, pref. **anti-** before aspirates.

anthelion, pl. **anthelia**, n. [1. anthḗliun, -a; 2. ænþíliən, -iə]. L. Gk., neut. sing. of *anthḗlios*, 'opposite the sun', fr. **anti-** & *hḗlios*, 'sun', see **heliacal**. A halo, or luminous ring, seen surrounding the shadow of an object cast by the sun on a cloud or fog bank, as in polar or alpine regions.

anthelmintic, adj. & n. [1. ànthelmíntik; 2. æ̀nþelmíntik]. **anth-, anti-**, & Gk. *hél-minth-(os)*, *hélmis*, 'worm', see **helminthic**. (med.) **a** adj. Destroying, expelling intestinal parasitic worms; **b** n., an anthelmintic remedy; vermifuge.

anthem, n. [1. ánthem; 2. ǽnþem]. Already in O.E., *antefn*, whence M.E. *antem*, fr. Lat. *antiphōna*, fr. Gk. *antiphōna*, neut. pl. of *antiphōnos*, 'sounding in response to'. See **antiphone**. **1.** Prose passage, usually from Scripture, set to music and sung in churches, after the third collect at matins or evensong in the English liturgy; equivalent of the Roman Catholic and Lutheran *motet*. **2.** Any triumphant, joyous song.

anther, n. [1. ánther; 2. ǽnþə], fr. Gk. *anthērós*, 'flowery', fr. *ánthos*, 'a flower'; cp. Scrt. *ándhaś*, 'grass'. (bot.) That part of the stamen of a flower which contains the pollen.

ant-hill, n. **ant** & **hill**. An ant's nest; esp. used of the high conical mounds made by the termites or so-called white ants; (also fig.) a densely populated district or town.

anthologist, n. [1. anthólojist; 2. æ̀nþólədžist]. See **anthology** & **-ist**. One who compiles an anthology or collection of poems.

anthology, n. [1. anthóloji; 2. æ̀nþólədži], fr. Lat. *anthologia*, fr. Gk. *anthologia*, 'garland, collection of small poems', fr. *ánthos*, 'flower' (cp. **anther**), & *logia*, 'collection', fr. *légō*, 'I gather'. See **-logy**. Collection of carefully chosen poems; specif., *Greek anthology*, collection of Greek epigrams.

Anthony pig, n. [1. ántoni pig; 2. ǽntəni píg], fr. St. Anthony, the patron saint of swine-herds, to whom a pig from each litter was usually vowed. (provinc.) Smallest pig of a litter.

Anthozoa, n. pl. [1. ànthōzṓa; 2. æ̀nþouzóuə], fr. Gk. *ánthos*, 'flower', see **anther**, & **-zoa**. (zool.) A class or order of marine polyps, the corals.

anthracene, n. [1. ánthrasēn; 2. ǽnþrəsīn]. See next word & **-ene**. (chem.) A hydrocarbon obtained by the distillation of coal-tar, used esp. for the production of alizarin dyes.

anthracite, n. [1. ánthrasīt; 2. ǽnþrəsait]. Lat. *anthracītēs*, fr. Gk. *anthrakítēs*, 'coal-like', fr. *ánthrax*, *ánthrakos*, 'coal'; the base perh. represents Aryan **sn̥dhro-*, in wh. case the word wd. be cogn. w. O.E. *sindar*, O.H.G. *sintar*, 'refuse of coal, dross'; **cinder** is fr. O.E. *sindar*, but has been influenced by Fr. Kind of hard, slow-burning coal.

anthrax, n. [1. ánthraks; 2. ǽnþræks], fr. Lat. *anthrax*, '(1) coal, (2) an ulcer, carbuncle', fr. Gk. *ánthrax*. See **anthracite**. Infectious pustular disease in animals, caused by bacteria; it may also be caught by human beings.

anthropo-, pref., fr. Gk. *ánthrōpos*, 'man'. The etymol. relation, if any, between the two Gk. words for 'man', the above & *anḗr* (see **androgynous**), is doubtful. The latter is fr. base *andr-*, cp. genit. *andrós*, & it is a tempting suggestion that the longer word is fr. **andr-ōps*, 'having the face, or appearance, of a man'. For Gk. *ṓps*, 'eye, face, countenance', see **optic**. Pertaining to man, or the study of man.

anthropocentric, adj. [1. ánthrōposéntrik; 2. ǽnþroupəséntrik]. **anthropo-** & **centric**. Centring in man, regarding man as the centre or pivot of the universe.

anthropogeography, n. [1. anthrṓpōjēógrafi; 2. ænþróupoudžiógrəfi]. See **anthropo-** & **geography**. Called also *human geography*; study of the geographical distribution of the human race, and the relation of man to his physical environment.

anthropography, n. [1. ànthrōpógrafi; 2. ǽnþroupógrəfi]. See **anthropo-** & **-graphy**. Branch of anthropology dealing primarily with the physical characteristics of the different races of mankind.

anthropoid, adj. & n. [1. ánthropoid; 2. ǽnþrəpoid], fr. Gk. *anthrōpoeidḗs*, 'of human form'. See **anthropo-** & **-oid**. Cp. Fr. *anthropoïde*. **a** adj. Resembling man in form: *anthropoid ape*, one of a group of apes most closely related to man, as the chimpanzee, gibbon, gorilla &c.; **b** n., one of the group of animals who are nearest to man in anatomical structure, and, as it is supposed, nearest to him also in the scale of nature; one of the larger apes.

anthropological, adj. [1. ánthrōpolójikl; 2. ǽnþroupəlódžikl]. See **anthropo-** & **-logical**. Connected with the study of anthropology, and the group of phenomena with which it deals.

anthropologist, n. [1. ánthropólojist; 2. ǽn-þrəpólədžist]. See next word & **-ist**. A student of anthropology.

anthropology, n. [1. ánthropóloji; 2. ǽn-þrəpólədži]. See **anthropo-** & **-logy**. In its widest sense, the science of man in his physical and psychological aspects (often used specif. to denote the study of primitive customs, myths, and religion).

anthropometric(al), adj. [1. ànthropométrik(l); 2. æ̀nþroupəmétrik(l)]. See **anthropo-** & **metric**. Connected with anthropometry.

anthropometrist, n. [1. ànthropómetrist; 2. æ̀nþrəpómetrist]. Prec. & **-ist**. One skilled in or practising anthropometry.

anthropometry, n. [1. ànthropómetri; 2. æ̀nþrəpómetri]. **anthropo-** & **-metry** on anal. of **geometry** &c. Art of minute measurement of parts of human body and determination of the relative proportions, **as a** means of identification of individuals.

anthropomorphic(al), adj. [1. ánthrōpomórfik(l); 2. ǽnþroupəmṓfik(l)]. See **anthropomorphous** & **-ic** (& **-al**). Having nature of, resembling, tending to, anthropomorphism.

anthropomorphism, n. [1. ánthrōpomórfizm; 2. ǽnþroupəmṓfizəm]. See **anthropomorphous** & **-ism**. Conception, representation, of God under the form of a man; attribution of human thoughts, passions &c. to the Deity.

anthropomorphist, n. [1. ánthrōpomórfist; 2. ǽnþroupəmṓfist]. See prec. & **-ist**. One who holds anthropomorphic views of the Deity.

anthropomorphize, vb. trans. & intrans. [1. ánthrōpomórfiz; 2. ǽnþroupəmṓfaiz]. See next word & **-ize**. To conceive, represent, the Deity with human form and attributes.

anthropomorphous, adj. [1. ánthrōpomórfus; 2. ǽnþroupəmṓfəs], fr. Gk. *anthrōpómorphos*, 'of human form', fr. **anthropo-** & *morphḗ*, 'form', see **morphology**, & **-ous**. Resembling, having form and appearance of, a man.

anthropophagi, n. pl. [1. ánthrōpófajī; 2. ǽnþroupófədžai]. Gk. *anthrōpo-phágos*, 'cannibal', fr. **anthropo-** & Gk. *phageîn*, 'to eat', q.v. under **-phagous**. Man-eaters, cannibals.

anthropophagic, adj. [1. ánthrōpofájik; 2. ǽnþroupəfǽdžik]. See prec. & **-ic**. Connected with cannibalism.

anthropophagous, adj. [1. ánthrōpófagus; 2. ǽnþroupófəgəs]. See **anthropophagi** & **-ous**. Addicted to cannibalism.

anthropophagy, n. [1. ánthrōpófaji; 2. ǽn-þroupófədži]. Fr. *anthropophagie*, fr. Gk. *anthrōpophagía*. See **anthropophagi**. Practice of eating human flesh; cannibalism.

anti-, pref. [1. ánti; 2. ǽnti]. Gk. *anti*, 'against'; cogn. w. Lat. **ante-** & Engl. **and**; used in various senses in Gk. compounds, of wh.

opposition is one; in Engl. this pref. is freely used to form new compounds (ns. & adjs.), & its general force is 'opposition, hostility, rivalry': *antipope, anti-slavery, anti-social* &c. In names of drugs & curative agents the pref. expresses opposition to, abolition, cure, of the disease: *anti-scorbutic, anti-bilious* &c. Note that in some words, fr. old Lat. compounds, *anti-* represents compounded form of Lat. **ante.**

anti-aircraft, adj. [1. ánti árkrahft; 2. ǽnti ɛ́əkrāft]. **anti- & aircraft.** Used in defence against attack by an enemy's air forces, as guns, searchlights &c.

antiar, anchar, n. [1. ántiar, ánchar; 2. ǽntiā, ǽntʃā], fr. Jav. *antjar.* **a** The upas tree, *Antiaris toxicaria*; **b** cardiac, virulent poison derived from the resin of this tree.

antibody, n. [1. àntibódi; 2. æ̀ntibɔ́di]. **anti- & body.** (physiol.) A substance produced in the blood as a natural antidote to infection.

antic, adj. & n. [1. ántik; 2. ǽntik]. Ital. *antico,* Lat. *antīquus,* 'old'. See **antique. a** (archaic, as adj.) Formerly used in sense of grotesque, fantastic; **b** n. (often in pl.), grotesque gestures, whimsical, frolicsome capers; **c** a jester, merry-andrew (archaic).

antichrist, n. [1. ántikrist; 2. ǽntikraist]. See **anti- & Christ.** One hostile to Christ and His teaching; a false prophet; specif., the great personal enemy and opponent of Christ who is expected to appear before the second coming of Christ, at which antichrist will be finally destroyed.

antichristian, adj. [1. ántikríschan; 2. ǽntikrístʃən]. See **anti- & Christian.** Opposed to Christianity and Christians; tending to destroy Christian influence.

anticipant, adj. & n. [1. antísipant; 2. æntísipənt], fr. Lat. *anticipant-(em),* Pres. Part. type of *anticipāre.* See **anticipate & -ant. a** adj. Expecting, anticipating; **b** n., one who anticipates.

anticipate, vb. trans. [1. àntísipāt; 2. æntísipeit], fr. Lat. *anticipāre,* 'take beforehand', fr. *ante,* 'before', & **-cipāre,* fr. *capere,* 'to take, seize, grasp', in physical and intellectual senses. See **ante- & captive. 1. a** To enjoy, make use of, in advance, prematurely and before proper time: *to anticipate one's next quarter's salary* &c.; **b** to realize and suffer from in advance: *do not let us anticipate miseries which may never arise.* **2. a** To be beforehand with a person in taking action; thus, to forestall, prevent: *the British general had anticipated the enemy's move, which was therefore ineffective*; **b** to foresee, and take steps to meet (of non-material things): *to anticipate an argument.* **3.** To foresee (another's order, wish &c.), and carry it out in advance. **4.** To expect, look forward to, **a** hopefully: *I anticipate deriving much instruction from your book*; **b** with gloomy foreboding: *I anticipate very little pleasure from my visit.*

anticipation, n. [1. àntisipáshun; 2. æntisipéiʃən]. Prec. & **-ion.** Act of anticipating in any of various senses of vb. Phr. *in anticipation of,* anticipating. Also specific meanings: **1.** (law) Assignment of income of trust estate before it is due. **2.** (mus.) Beginning of one or more tones of a chord before preceding chord has ceased. **3.** Hope of good things; foreboding of bad.

anticipative, adj. [1. antísipātiv; 2. æntísipeitiv]. **anticipate & -ive.** Belonging to, filled with, anticipation: *anticipative action.*

anticipatory, adj. [1. antísipāteri; 2. æntísipèitəri]. **anticipate & -ory.** Happening, being, made, in advance: *an anticipatory account of a book about to be published.*

anticlerical, adj. [1. àntiklérikl; 2. æ̀ntiklérikl]. See **anti- & clerical.** Opposed to undue influence of the clergy, esp. in politics; or to existence of organized clerical hierarchy.

anticlericalism, n. [1. àntiklérikalizm; 2. æ̀ntiklérikəlizəm], fr. prec. & **-ism.** Hostility to clerical power and influence.

anticlimax, n. [1. àntiklímaks; 2. æ̀ntiklάimæks]. See **anti- & climax.** (rhet.) Sudden drop in dignity in style caused by addition of a trivial expression, esp. a commonplace idea which contrasts too sharply with what has gone before.

anticlinal, adj. [1. àntiklínal; 2. æ̀ntiklάinəl], fr. **anti- & Gk.** *klínein,* 'to bend, lean', see **clinic, & -al.** Leaning, inclined in opposite directions; specif. (geol.) of, pertaining to, an anticline.

anticline, n. [1. ántiklīn; 2. ǽntiklain], fr. prec. (geol.) A convex fold in which the upheaved strata slope down from the axis in opposite directions; opposed to *syncline.*

anticyclone, n. [1. àntisíklōn; 2. æ̀ntisáikloun]. See **anti- & cyclone.** State of the atmosphere the reverse of a *cyclone,* tending to produce a change of weather for better and more settled conditions.

anticyclonic, adj. [1. àntisīklónik; 2. æ̀ntisaiklɔ́nik]. Prec. & **-ic.** Of, pertaining to, an anticyclone.

antidiphtheritic, adj. & n. [1. ántidiftherítik; 2. ǽntidifþərítik]. See **anti- & diphtheritic. a** adj. Having property of curing or preventing diphtheria; **b** n., a medicine or serum with such property.

antidotal, adj. [1. àntidótal; 2. æ̀ntidóutəl]. See next word & **-al.** Having qualities of an antidote.

antidote, n. [1. ántidōt; 2. ǽntidout], fr. Lat. *antidotum,* fr. Gk. *antídoton,* 'a remedy', lit. 'given against', fr. *antí,* 'against', & *dotós,* 'given', fr. *didōmi,* 'I give'. See **anti-** & base under **donation.** A specific against a poison; (fig.) a remedy for spiritual evil. Phr. *bane and antidote,* poison and cure.

antigen, n. [1. ántijen; 2. ǽntidʒen]. **anti- & -gen.** (physiol.) Substance, such as an antitoxin, which on being introduced into the blood causes the production of an antibody.

antigropelos, n. pl. [1. àntigrópelōz; 2. æ̀ntigrɔ́pilouz]. Gk., **anti-,** & *hugrós,* 'moist, liquid', see **hygro-,** & *pēlós,* 'clay, mud', etymol. unknown. Facet.; used by Calverley in parody of Browning, in sense of gaiters, or goloshes.

antihelix, n. [1. àntihéliks; 2. æ̀ntihíliks], fr. Gk. *anthélix.* See **anth-, anti-, & helix.** Rounded portion of cartilage of outer ear, inside, and in front of the outer rim or helix.

anti-Jacobin, n. [1. ànti jákobin; 2. æ̀nti dʒǽkəbin]. **anti- & Jacobin. 1.** One opposed to Jacobins and Jacobinism, i.e. to revolutionary ideas &c., esp. of a political party and club in the French Revolution. **2.** Name of a weekly periodical, founded 1797, by George Canning.

antilogous, adj. [1. antílogus; 2. æntíləgəs]. See **antilogy & -ous.** Contradictory; of contrary name, reverse of *analogous.*

antilogy, n. [1. antíloji; 2. æntílədʒi]. Gk. *antilogía.* See **anti- & -logy.** A contradiction in terms or ideas.

antimacassar, n. [1. àntimakáser; 2. æ̀ntiməkǽsə]. See **anti- & macassar.** Cloth, or piece of muslin &c., often embroidered and ornamented, used originally for protecting backs of chairs from hair-grease; later applied to small piece of fabric used as ornament on tables &c. during part of the Victorian epoch.

antimonarchical, adj. [1. àntimonárkikl; 2. æ̀ntimənάkikl]. See **anti- & monarchical.** Opposed to system of government by a king as head of the State; likely to prejudice continuance of such a system: *antimonarchical views, propaganda* &c.

antimonarchist, n. [1. àntimónarkist; 2. æ̀ntimɔ́nəkist]. See **anti- & monarchist.** One who is opposed to government by a king.

antimony, n. [1. ántimuni; 2. ǽntiməni]. Fr., fr. Lat. *antimonium,* prob. fr. Arab. *i(n)thmad,* cp. Gk. *stímmi,* & Lat. **stibium.** Metallic element, symbol *Sb* = *stibium,* of crystalline, brittle texture and silvery white, shining colour; used in the arts as an alloy, and medicinally; an irritant poison; *antimony tartrate,* tartar emetic.

Antinomian, n. & adj. [1. àntinómian; 2. æ̀ntinóumiən]. **antinomy** & adj. suff. **-an. a** n. Member of a sect which maintained that under the Gospel dispensation the moral law was not binding, since faith alone was sufficient to salvation; **b** adj., pertaining to the doctrines of the Antinomians.

antinomy, n. [1. antínumi; 2. æntínəmi], fr. Gk. *antinomía,* 'an ambiguity in the law', fr. **anti-** & *nómos,* 'law', q.v. under **anomo- & nomad.** Contradiction or inconsistency between two laws or principles; opposition of one law or principle to another.

antipathetic, adj. [1. àntipathétik; 2. æ̀ntipəþétik]. See **anti- & pathetic & antipathy.** Incompatible in character and sentiments; inspiring antipathy.

antipathetically, adv. [1. àntipathétikali; 2. æ̀ntipəþétikəli]. Prec. & **-al & -ly.** In an antipathetic manner.

antipathy, n. [1. antípathi; 2. æntípəþi]. Fr. *antipathie,* fr. Lat. *antipathīa,* fr. Gk. *antipátheia,* fr. *antipathés,* 'opposed in feeling', fr. **anti-** & *páthos,* 'feeling'. See **pathos. 1.** Deep-rooted aversion, repugnance to, or dislike for, a person, springing from radical irreconcilability of character and feeling. **2.** Object of such dislike and repugnance. **3.** Essential difference between substances (e.g. oil and water) which precludes intermingling.

antiperiodic, n. [1. àntipēriódik; 2. æ̀ntipiəriɔ́dik]. See **anti- & periodic.** (med.) Preventive of periodic return of attacks of disease.

antiphlogistic, adj. & n. [1. àntiflōjístik; 2. æ̀ntifloudʒístik]. **anti- & phlogistic.** (med.) **a** adj. Tending to counteract, reduce, inflammation; **b** n., antiphlogistic substance.

antiphon, n. [1. ántifon; 2. ǽntifən], fr. Fr. *antiphone,* fr. Low Lat. *antiphōna,* fr. Gk. *tà antíphōna,* neut. pl., 'musical accords', lit. 'things sounding in response', fr. *antí,* 'in return', see **anti-,** & *phōnḗ,* 'sound, tone, voice'. See **phone (I.),** & cp. **anthem. a** Versicle sung by one side of a church choir in response to one sung by the other side; **b** anything composed, or arranged, to be sung in such a manner.

antiphonal, adj. & n. [1. antífonal; 2. æntífənəl]. See prec. & **-al. a** adj. Pertaining to the alternate singing by the two sides of a choir; suitable, adapted, for singing as an antiphon; **b** n., collection of antiphons.

antiphonally, adv. Prec. & **-ly.** After the manner of an antiphon.

antiphony, n. [1. antífoni; 2. æntífəni]. **antiphon & -y.** Anthem, chant, or other musical composition, sung alternately by two sides of a choir, or by choir and congregation.

antipodal, adj. [1. antípodal; 2. æntípədəl]. See **antipodes & -al. a** Pertaining to the antipodes; on the opposite side of the globe; **b** (fig.) opposite, forming strong contrast to.

antipodes, n. pl. [1. antípodēz; 2. æntípədiz], fr. Lat. *antipodes,* fr. Gk. *antípodes,* pl. of *antípous,* lit. 'having the feet opposite', fr. **anti-,** & *poús, podós,* 'foot'. See **-pod, pedal, & foot. 1.** Those regions lying on the opposite side of the globe from any given point. **2.** (fig.) Anything diametrically opposed to, or utterly different from, something else: *at the exact antipodes of opinion* &c.

antipope, n. [1. ántipōp; 2. ǽntipoup]. See **anti- & pope.** Rival to properly elected Pope; one elected illegally in opposition to the Pope who has been canonically elected, as in a period of schism.

antipyretic, adj. & n. [1. àntipīrétik; 2. æ̀ntipaiərétik]. See **anti- & pyretic.** (med.) **a** adj. Tending to reduce fever; **b** n., remedy which does this.

antipyrin(e), n. [1. àntipírin; 2. æ̀ntipάiərin]. See prec. & **-ine.** Trade name of a drug, derived from coal-tar, used as an antipyretic.

antiquarian, adj. & n. [1. àntikwárian; 2. æ̀ntikwɛ́əriən], fr. Lat. *antīquārius.* See **antiquary & -an. 1. a** adj. Connected with study of antiquities; **b** n., an antiquary (recent use). **2.** Large size of drawing-paper.

antiquarianism, n. [1. àntikwấrianizm; 2. æntikwéəriənizəm]. Prec. & **-ism.** Study and love of antiquities.

antiquary, n. [1. ántikweri; 2. ǽntikwəri], fr. Lat. *antīquārius*, fr. *antīquus*, 'old', & adj. suff. *-ārius*, see **-ary.** See **antique. a** One who makes a study of, who collects, antiquities; **b** dealer in antiquities.

antiquated, adj. [1. ántikwāted; 2. ǽntikweitid], fr. Lat. *antīquātum*, P.P. type of *antīquāre*, fr. *antīquus*, & **-ed**; the Engl. vb. *antiquate*, 'to make obsolete', can hardly be said to exist now, though formerly in occasional use; the Lat. vb. fr. wh. it was formed had an entirely different meaning, 'to reject a bill', derived fr. sense of restoring something to its orig. condition. There is therefore no continuity of meaning w. the Mod. Engl. word, wh. was rather formed afresh fr. **antique.** (of things) Rendered, or become old, and therefore unfit for use; out of date; (of persons) wedded to old-fashioned, obsolete ways and ideas.

antique (I.), adj. [1. antḗk; 2. æntík]. A variant of **antic.** Mod. pronunciation influenced by that of Fr. or Ital., Lat. *antīquus*, *antīcus*, 'former, what was formerly, earlier, old'. The first element of the word is **ante-**, 'before', & the second, *-īq-*, may be compared w. that in Lat. *post-īcus*, 'hinder', & further w. Scrt. *prátīk-aś*, 'reversed', *pratīk-am*, 'countenance', *an-īk-am*, 'presence'. It is suggested that *-īk-* is a form of base **okʷ-*, 'eye, face' (cp. Lat. *oculus*, 'eye', q.v. under **ocular, oculist**). In this case *antīquus, antīcus*, wd. mean 'with the face turned to what went before'. **1. a** Belonging to the past, dating from antiquity, old: *the antique world*; *an antique gem*; **b** old, not belonging, or adapted to present time, archaic, old-fashioned, out of date. **2.** (typog.) Style of bold type.

antique (II.), n., fr. prec. **1.** Something dating from the past; an object of ancient art or craftsmanship. **2.** (coll.) *The antique*, ancient art and culture: *a lover of the antique.*

antiquity, n. [1. antíkwiti; 2. æntíkwiti], fr. Fr. *antiquité*, fr. Lat. *antīquitāt-(em)*, 'ancient times', formed fr. *antīquus*, see **antique,** & **-ity. 1. a** The remote past, very ancient times (esp. before the Middle Ages): *the nations of antiquity*; **b** the ancient world, the people who lived in it and their civilization &c.: *a history of antiquity*; **c** great age, persistence through a long period of time: *a family of great antiquity.* **2.** (coll. in pl.) *Antiquities*, the products and remains of all kinds of the ancient world, including relics of ancient culture generally, buildings, documents, objects of art: *Greek and Roman antiquities.*

antirrhinum, n. [1. àntirínum; 2. æntiráinəm], fr. Gk. *antírrhīnon*, fr. *anti*, 'equal to, like', see **anti-**, & *rhís, rhīnós*, 'nose'. See **rhino-.** (bot.) Large genus of flowering plants popularly called snapdragon.

antisabbatarian, n. [1. ántisàbatấrian; 2. ǽntisæbətéəriən]. See **anti-** & **sabbatarian.** One who is opposed to very strict observance of Sunday as a day in which no pleasures and amusements may be enjoyed.

anti-Semite, n. [1. ánti sḗmīt; 2. ǽnti símait]. See **anti-** & **Semite.** One who holds that the moral and social influence of Jews in European civilization is pernicious, and who therefore aims at counteracting and destroying it; one who hates Jews.

anti-Semitic, adj. [1. ánti semítik; 2. ǽnti simítik]. See prec. & **-ic.** Connected with anti-Semites and anti-Semitism.

anti-Semitism, n. [1. ánti sémitizm; 2. ǽnti sémitizəm]. Prec. & **-ism.** The principles and aims of anti-Semites; organized political movement which seeks to realize these.

antiseptic, adj. & n. [1. àntiséptik; 2. æntiséptik]. See **anti-** & **septic. 1.** adj. Tending to destroy, to destruction of, the bacteria which cause putrefaction in the dead, and the formation of pus in the living organism. **2.** n. Chemical or other agent which produces this result.

antiseptically, adv. [1. àntiséptikali; 2. æntiséptikəli], fr. prec. & **-al** & **-ly.** By means of antiseptics.

anti-social, adj. [1. ànti sṓshal; 2. ǽnti sóuʃl]. See **anti-** & **social.** Opposed to, incompatible with, the principles and conditions which underlie organized society.

antistrophe, n. [1. antístrofē, àntistrṓfē; 2. æntístrəfi, æntistróufi]. Gk., lit. 'a turning back'. See **anti-** & **strophe.** The return of the chorus in Greek drama to answer to a previous strophe; hence, the lines recited on their return.

antistrophic, adj. [1. àntistrófik; 2. æntistrɔ́fik], fr. prec. & **-ic.** Belonging to the antistrophe.

antithesis, n. [1. antíthesis; 2. æntíþisis], fr. Gk. *antíthesis*, 'opposition', fr. *antitithēmi*, 'set one thing against another, compare, oppose'. See **anti-** & **thesis. 1.** (rhet.) Emphatic contrast, or opposition made between two words (as expressing contrast of two ideas), often effected by placing the words respectively at the beginning and at the end of the sentence. **2.** Marked contrast; direct opposite.

antithetic(al), adj. [1. àntithétik(l); 2. æntiþétik(l)], fr. prec. Having the character of an antithesis; contrasted.

antithetically, adv. Prec. & **-ly.** By antithesis or contrast.

antitoxic, adj. [1. àntitóksik; 2. æntitɔ́ksik]. See **anti-** & **toxic.** Of, pertaining to, having the power of, an antitoxin.

antitoxin, n. [1. àntitóksin; 2. æntitɔ́ksin], fr. Lat. *toxicum*, 'poison', orig. one for smearing on arrow-heads. See prec. & **-in.** Chemical compound occurring in the blood, under certain conditions, which has the power of neutralizing poisonous substances, esp. of a bacteriological character.

anti-trades, n. pl. [1. ánti tràdz; 2. ǽnti trèidz]. **anti-** & **trade.** Certain tropical winds of the upper air which blow in a contrary direction to the trade winds.

antitype, n. [1. ántitīp; 2. ǽntitaip], fr. Gk. *antítupos*, 'struck back, echoed, answering to, correspondent'. See **anti-** & **type.** That which is represented by a type or symbol.

antler, n. [1. ántler; 2. ǽntlə]. M.E. *auntelere*, O. Fr. *antoillier*, fr. Low Lat. *antoculārem (rāmum)*, 'branch before the eye', that is, orig., the lowest branch of a stag's horn. See **ante-** & **ocular.** The whole, or any part, of a stag's horn.

antlered, adj. [1. ántlerd; 2. ǽntləd], fr. prec. & **-ed.** Having, bearing, antlers.

ant-lion, n., fr. **ant** & **lion.** Popular name of the larva of a large, winged insect, *Myrmeleon*, resembling a dragon-fly, which digs a pit in loose sand into which its prey, such as ants and other small insects, falls.

antonomasia, n. [1. àntonomấzia; 2. æntənəméiziə]. Lat., fr. Gk., fr. *antonomázein*, 'to name instead, call by a new name', fr. **anti-** & *ónoma*, 'name', cogn. w. Lat. *nōmen*. See **name.** Use, substitution, of an epithet or descriptive phrase for a proper name, or of a proper name for a class of persons or things, as *the little Corporal* for Napoleon, *a Nero* for a cruel person &c.

antonym, n. [1. ántonim; 2. ǽntənim]. As if fr. Gk. **antṓnumos*, fr. **anti-** & *ónoma*, 'name'. See prec. A word which expresses the exact opposite of another word, as *white, black* &c.; contrasted with *synonym.*

antrum, n. [1. ántrum; 2. ǽntrəm]. Lat., fr. Gk. *ántron*, 'cave'; etymol. doubtful. (anat.) A cavity, esp. one or other of the two cavities in the upper jaw communicating with the nose.

anus, n. [1. ánus; 2. éinəs]. Lat., 'ring', cp. **annular.** (anat.) External lower opening of alimentary canal.

anvil, n. [1. ánvil; 2. ǽnvil]. O.E. *anfilte*, 'anvil', M.E. *anfelt, -velt, -vilt*, cp. O.H.G. *anafalz*, Du. *aanbeld*. Kluge connects these w. Mod. Germ. *falz*, 'a groove, furrow', & *falzen*, vb., & identifies the Gmc. base w. that in Lat. *pello*, 'strike', *pulsus*, 'blow'. See **compel, pulse (I.), felt (I.).** The *v* in second syllable of *anvil* shows the Western type, as in **vixen.** Heavy block of iron upon which the smith works and hammers metals.

anxiety, n. [1. angzíeti; 2. æŋzáiəti], fr. Lat. *anxietāt-(em)*, *anxietas*, fr. *anxius*, 'solicitous, uneasy, painfully uncertain'. See **anxious. 1.** Distress, uneasiness, of mind caused by dread of impending evil, or uncertainty, arising from imperfect information, as to how an event will turn out, esp. if the knowledge possessed points to probability of ill-fortune; concern, misgiving, foreboding. **2.** Eager desire to do, or to possess, something: *my chief anxiety is to help in every way.*

anxious, adj. [1. ángshus; 2. ǽŋʃəs], fr. Lat. *anxius*, 'solicitous, uneasy', fr. *angere*, 'to press tight, throttle, cause pain, vex'. See **anger. 1.** Distressed, disturbed in mind, filled with misgivings, by uncertainty as to issue of an event, esp. when there is foreboding or anticipation of evil; the word may refer to a permanent, habitual state of mind: *an anxious person*; or, more commonly, to one produced by specific causes: *I'm very anxious about your health*; *I shall be anxious till I hear they have got safe home.* **2.** Eager, strongly desirous to do, or obtain, something: *anxious to do one's best, for success, wealth* &c.

anxiously, adv. Prec. & **-ly.** In a state of painful anxiety: *to wait anxiously for news.*

any, adj. & pron. [1. éni; 2. éni]. O.E. *ǣniġ*, M.E. *ány, ę̄ny*; cp. O.H.G. *einig*, Du. *eenig*, fr. Gmc. **ain-ig-*, fr. **ain*, 'one', see **one,** & suff. *-ig*, the precise force of wh. is doubtful. Used chiefly in interrogative, negative, and conditional phrases; also, affirmatively, with reference **a** to quality, no matter what quality, good or bad: *any sort would be better than none at all*; *any port in a storm*; *any one of the plans will do*; **b** to quantity and number, one, some, whatsoever quantity or number, large or small: *haven't you any money at all?*; *I wish I had any*; *if he had any intelligence at all he would keep silent*; *have we any chance of success?*; *any help you can give will be valuable*; **c** whichever, which . . . soever; *any surgeon can set a broken leg.* Phrs. *at any rate*, at least; *in any case*, under all circumstances, whatever happens.

anybody, n. & pron. [1. énibodi; 2. énibɔdi]. See **any** & **body. a** Any person, someone: *I haven't seen anybody*; **b** somebody, a person of importance: *I don't think she was anybody before her marriage.*

anyhow, adv. [1. énihou; 2. énihau]. See **any** & **how. a** By any means, in any possible way: *I could not get in anyhow*; **b** whatever happens, in any case, at least: *you won't be late anyhow*; **c** carelessly, in a happy-go-lucky way: *the work was done anyhow.* Phr. *to feel anyhow*, upset, ill.

anyone, n. [1. éniwun; 2. éniwan]. See **any** & **one. a** Anybody, any person at all: *I don't think anyone was at home*; **b** any person at all, taken at random, the first person you meet: *anyone could have told you that*; *I will take anyone I can get.*

anything, n. & pron. [1. énithing; 2. éniþiŋ]. See **any** & **thing.** A single thing; whatever thing you like, no matter which: *I have not found anything*; *take anything you fancy.*

anyway, adv. [1. éniwā; 2. éniwei]. See **any** & **way.** In any case, at all events; anyhow.

anywhere, adv. [1. éniwār; 2. éniwɛə]. See **any** & **where.** In, to, any place: *I don't want to go anywhere, I'll stay where I am.* Phr. *not, never, to go anywhere*, to live a retired life.

anywhither, adv. [1. éniwidher; 2. éniwiðə]. See **any** & **whither.** (archaic and obsolesc.) To any (particular) place, in any direction (implying motion towards).

anywise, adv. [1. éniwīz; 2. éniwaiz]. See **any** & **wise (II.).** In any manner, in any wise.

Anzac, adj. & n. [1. ánzak; 2. ǽnzæk], fr. initials of Australian & New Zealand Army

Corps. **a** adj. Of, belonging to this corps; **b** n., a member of this corps.

aorist, n. [1. ā́orist; 2. éərist], fr. Gk. *aóristos*, 'indefinite', fr. **a-**, 'without, not', & *horistós*, fr. *horízō*, 'I limit, define', fr. *hóros*, 'boundary'. See **an-** & **horizon**. (Gk. gram.) Name of the tense expressing that an action took place in the past, with no definition as to completion, repetition, or continuance.

aorta, n. [1. āórta; 2. eiɔ́tə]. Low Lat. fr. Gk. *aortḗ*, 'that which is slung', hence, 'a knapsack', later, the great artery, fr. *aeírō*, lift', fr. **-werjō*; see **arsis**. (anat.) The great blood-vessel which, through its branches, carries blood from the heart to every part of the body.

à outrance, adv. [1. ah ōōtráhns; 2. ā ūtrā̃s]. Fr. (see **outrance**). To an excessive degree, without truce; (of a duel) to the death.

apace, adv. [1. apā́s; əpéis]. **a-**, 'on', & **pace (I.)**. Quickly, with speed: *old age comes on apace.*

apache, n. [1. ahpáhsh; 2. apā́ʃ]. Fr. **a** Name of warlike tribe of American Indians; **b** Parisian rough, robber, and assassin.

apanage. See **appanage**.

apart, adv. [1. apárt; 2. əpā́t], fr. Fr. *à part*, Lat. *ad partem*, 'to the one side or part'. See **ad-** & **part**. **a** (referring to space) On one side, separately, remote from: *the house stood apart from others*; **b** (expressing separation in character, purpose, distinctiveness) *the two friends had grown much apart latterly*; *the various shades of meaning of a word must be kept clearly apart in a dictionary.* Phrs. *to set something apart*, devote it to particular purpose; *joking apart*, joking being remote from my intention.

apartment, n. [1. apártment; 2. əpā́tmənt]. Fr. *appartement*, 'set of rooms reserved for exclusive use of an individual or family'. See **apart** & **-ment**. The French sense of a suite or set of rooms is now obsolete in English; the word is applied to a single room, but its use is now felt as rather pretentious; more usually *apartments* (coll.), n. pl., specif., set of rooms, part of a house, usually furnished, hired from occupier of the house, generally by the week or other limited period, for the private use of an individual or family.

apathetic, adj. [1. àpathétik; 2. æ̀pəþétik], fr. **apathy**, on anal. of **pathetic**. Devoid of feeling, insensible to emotion; indifferent.

apathy, n. [1. ápathi; 2. ǽpəþi], fr. Fr. *apathie*, fr. Lat. *apathīa*, fr. Gk. *apátheia*, 'insensibility to suffering', fr. *apathḗs*, 'without feeling', **a-**, 'without', & **pathos**. Listlessness, indifference, sluggishness of mind.

ape (I.), n. [1. āp; 2. eip]. O.E. *apa*, M.E. *āpe*, O.H.G. *affo*; possibly an old loan-word fr. some unknown foreign source. **a** A monkey, esp. one of the tailless species, most nearly related to man; **b** an imitator, mimic.

ape (II.), vb. trans., fr. prec. **1.** To imitate, attempt to emulate, a person, his manners, bearing, etc.; to profess another's opinions, etc.: *a vulgar fellow may ape the manners of a gentleman.* **2.** To assume, pretend to have, qualities one does not possess: *pride which apes humility.*

apeak, adv. [1. apḗk; 2. əpík]. Fr. *à pic*, 'perpendicularly'. (naut.) In a vertical line.

apepsia, apepsy, n. [1. apépsia, apépsi; 2. əpépsiə, əpépsi], fr. Fr. *apepsie*, Gk. *apepsía*, 'indigestion', fr. **a-** (priv.) & *péptein*, 'to digest'. See **pepsin**. Indigestion.

aperçu, n. (Anglicized Fr. pronunciation) [1. apársū; 2. āpéəsy]. Fr. *aperçu*, P.P. of *apercevoir*, 'to perceive', used as n. in sense of 'brief summary'. See **perceive**. Summary, outline (of a book, argument &c.).

aperient, adj. & n. [1. apḗrient; 2. əpíəriənt], fr. Lat. *aperient-(em)*, Pres. Part. type of *aperīre*, 'uncover, lay bare, open', fr. **ap-weri-*, fr. **ab-** & **wero-*, 'door'; cogn. w. Lith. *veriu*, 'I open'; O. Slav. *vora*, 'partition'; cp. **vestibule** & **cover**. (med.) **a** adj. Tending to produce laxity of the bowels; **b** n., medicinal substance or drug which produces this effect.

aperitive, adj. & n. [1. apéritiv; 2. əpéritiv]. Fr. *apéritif*, 'opening drug or liquid, an appetiser', Lat. *aperitīvus*, fr. *aperīre*, 'open'. See prec. **a** Aperient; **b** more usually in French sense, appetizer.

aperture, n. [1. áperchur; 2. ǽpətʃə], fr. L. Lat. *apertūra*, 'an opening', fr. *aperīre*, 'to open'. See **aperient**. Hole, gap, opening.

apetalous, adj. [1. apétalus; 2. əpétələs], fr. Gk. *apétalos*, 'leafless', fr. **a-**, 'without', & *pétalon*, 'leaf', see **petal**, & **-ous**. (bot.) Having no petals.

apex, n. [1. ā́peks; 2. éipɛks]. Lat. *apex*, 'point, summit; conical cap of a priest', (fig.) 'the highest honour'; origin doubtful. Highest point, top, summit of anything; (fig.) *the apex of one's fortunes.*

aphæresis, n. [1. afḗresis; 2. əfíərisis]. Gk. *aphaíresis*, 'a taking away', fr. *aphairéō*, 'I take away', fr. *apó*, 'off, away', & *hairéō*, 'I take, seize'. Of uncertain etymol. (gram.) Loss of a syllable at the beginning of a word.

aphasia, n. [1. afā́zia; 2. əféiziə]. Gk. *aphasía*, 'speechlessness', fr. **a-** (priv.) & *phásis*, 'speech', fr. *phēmí*, 'I say, speak', cogn. w. Lat. *fāma*, 'talk, rumour'. See **fame**. (med.) Loss of power of speech, usually owing to an injury to the brain.

aphasiac, n. [1. afā́ziak; 2. əféiziæk]. Prec. & **-ac**. One suffering from aphasia.

aphasic, adj. [1. afā́zik; 2. əféizik]. See prec. & **-ic**. Connected with, tending to, aphasia.

aphelion, n. [1. afḗlion; 2. æfíliən], fr. Gk. **apo-**, 'off, from', & *hḗlios*, 'sun'. See **heliacal**. (astron.) That point in the course of a planet or comet which is farthest from the sun.

apheliotropic, adj. [1. àfēliōtrópik; 2. æ̀filiou-trɔ́pik], fr. **apo-** & *hḗlios*, 'sun', & *tropikós*, 'relating to a turn'. See **heliotropic**. Property possessed by certain plants, or parts of plants, of turning away from the sun.

aphesis, n. [1. áfisis; 2. ǽfisis]. Gk. *áphesis*, 'a letting go', fr. *aphíēmi*, 'I let go', fr. **apo-** & *híēmi*, 'I send', see **jet (III.)** & cp. **jactitation**. Elimination of a short unstressed syllable at beginning of a word.

aphetic, adj. [1. afétik; 2. əfétik], fr. prec. & **-ic**. Belonging to, resulting from, aphesis.

aphis, n. [1. áfis, ā́fis; 2. ǽfis, éifis], pl. **aphides** [1. áfidēz; 2. ǽfidiz]. Origin unknown. Green-fly; species of lice which infest leaves and flower stems of plants.

aphonia, n. [1. afṓnia; 2. əfóuniə]. Gk. *aphōnía*, fr. *áphōnos*, 'voiceless', fr. **a-**, 'without', & *phōnḗ*, 'sound, tone, voice'. See **phone (I.)**. (med.) Total loss of voice.

aphonic, adj. [1. afónik; 2. æfɔ́nik]. See prec. & **-ic**. Having no sound, not pronounced; voiceless.

aphorism, n. [1. áforizm; 2. ǽfərizəm], fr. Gk. *aphorismós*, 'a definition', fr. *aphorízein*, 'to determine, define', fr. **apo-**, & *horízein*, 'to set bounds', fr. *hóros*, boundary. See **horizon**. Concise definition of a general principle; brief, pithy saying, maxim.

aphorist, n. [1. áforist; 2. ǽfərist]. See prec. & **-ist**. One who makes aphorisms.

aphoristic(al), adj. [1. àforístik(l); 2. æfəríst-ik(l)]. See prec. & **-ic** (& **-al**). Having the character of, abounding in, aphorisms.

aphrodisia, n. [1. àfrodízia; 2. æ̀frədíziə]. See next word. Strong sexual passion.

aphrodisiac, adj. & n. [1. àfrodíziak; 2. æ̀frə-díziæk], fr. Gk. *aphrodīsiakós*, 'venereal', fr. *Aphrodítē*, the Greek goddess of love, Venus. **a** adj. Tending to produce sexual desire; **b** n., drug or other agent which does this.

aphtha, n., pl. **aphthae** [1. áftha, áfthē; 2. ǽfþə, ǽfþī]. Lat., fr. Gk., 'inflammation, eruption', in pl. 'thrush', fr. *háptein*, 'to set on fire'; no cognates known outside Gk. **1. a** The disease of children usually called 'thrush'; **b** aphthous fever or foot-and-mouth disease. **2.** (pl.) The white, inflamed pustules in mouth or throat, characteristic of thrush and of aphthous fever.

aphthous, adj. [1. áfthus; 2. ǽfþəs]. Prec. & **-ous**. Marked, caused, by aphthae; *aphthous fever*, foot-and-mouth disease; *apthous stomatitis*, thrush.

aphyllous, adj. [1. afílus; 2. əfíləs], fr. Gk. *áphullos*, 'leafless', fr. **a-**, 'without', & *phúllon*, 'leaf'. See **phyllo-**. (bot.) Having no leaves.

apiarian, adj. & n. [1. āpiā́rian; 2. eipiéəriən]. Lat. *apiārius*, 'belonging to bees; a bee-keeper'; *apiārium*, 'a bee-house', fr. **apis**. **a** adj. Pertaining to bee-hives or bee-keeping; **b** n., apiarist.

apiarist, n. [1. ā́piarist; 2. éipiərist]. See prec. & **-ist**. One who keeps bees.

apiary, n. [1. ā́piari; 2. éipiəri]. Lat. *apiārium*, 'a bee-house', fr. *apis*, 'bee', the etymol. of wh. is unknown. A place where bees are kept; collection of bee-hives.

apical, adj. [1. ápikal; 2. ǽpikəl], fr. Lat. *apic-is*, *apex*, see **apex** & **-al**. Of, pertaining to, an apex or tip.

apiculture, n. [1. ā́pikulchur; 2. éipikaltʃə], fr. Lat. *apis*, 'bee', see **apis**, & *cultūra*, 'care, tending'. See **culture**. Rearing and care of bees.

apiece, adv. [1. apḗs; 2. əpís]. **a-** & **piece**. (of persons and things) Severally, to or for each: *to cost a penny apiece*; *to be fined ten pounds apiece.*

apiology, n. [1. āpiólogi; 2. èipiɔ́lədʒi], fr. Lat. *apis*, 'bee', see next word, & **-logy**. Scientific study of bees.

apis, n. [1. ā́pis; 2. éipis]. Lat., 'bee'; etymol. unknown. The bee of any species.

apish, adj. [1. ā́pish; 2. éipiʃ]. **ape (I.)** & **-ish**. Like an ape; given to slavish imitation; foolish, mischievous.

apivorous, adj. [1. āpíverus; 2. eipívərəs]. Lat., **apis**, 'bee', & **-vorous**. Bee-eating.

aplomb, n. [1. ahplóm; 2. aplɔ̃]. Fr., lit. 'perpendicularity', hence, 'balance, assurance', fr. *à*, 'to', & *plomb*, 'lead'. See **plumb**. Self-possession, assurance in manner and conduct.

apnoea, n. [1. apnḗa; 2. æpníə], fr. Gk. *ápnoia*, fr. *ápnoos*, *ápnous*, 'without breath', fr. **a-** (priv.) & *pnéō*, 'I breathe', q.v. under **pneuma**. (med.) Suspension of breathing.

apo-, pref. Gk., as pref. & prep., 'from, derived from; asunder, away; back again'; general sense, 'separation, cutting off, sending away'. In mod. chem., *apo-* expresses origin, derivation from: *apo-caffeine*, a compound derived from caffeine. The word is cogn. w. Lat. *ab*, Goth. *af*, O.E. *æf*, O.H.G. *ab*, &c. in approximately same sense as the Gk.

apocalypse, n. [1. apókalips; 2. əpɔ́kəlips], fr. Lat. *apocalypsis*, fr. Gk. *apokálupsis*, 'revelation', fr. *apokalúptein*, 'uncover, disclose', fr. **apo-** & *kalúptein*, 'to cover', wh. is cogn. w. Gk. *kalúbē*, 'cabin', *kálumma*, 'woman's veil'; fr. Aryan base **kel-* &c., 'hide, cover', cp. Lat. *cēlāre*, 'hide', *occulo*, 'hide'. See **conceal, occult**. A revelation of the last things; specif., that made to St. John and recorded by him in the last book of the New Testament, called also the *Book of the Revelation of St. John the Divine.*

apocalyptic, adj. [1. apòkalíptik; 2. əpɔ̀kəlíp-tik], fr. Gk. *apokaluptikós*. See **apocalypse** & **-ic**. Pertaining to revelation, or to the Apocalypse.

apocalyptist, n. [1. apòkalíptist; 2. əpɔ̀kəlípt-ist]. See **apocalypse** & **-ist**. The writer of the Apocalypse (rare).

apocopate, vb. trans. [1. apókopāt; 2. əpɔ́kə-peit], fr. Gk. *apokóptein*, 'to cut off', fr. **apo-**, 'off', *kóptein*, 'to strike, cut'; cp. Gk. *kopís*, 'knife', *kopḗ*, 'incision', & further Gk. *kápōn*, Lat. *cāpo*, 'capon, emasculated cock'. See **capon**. (inelegant word rarely used) To cut off, esp. to cut off or drop the last sound or syllable of a word.

apocope, n. [1. apókopi; 2. əpɔ́kəpi]. Gk. *apokopḗ*, 'a cutting off'. See prec. The cutting off or omission of the last sound or syllable of a word.

Apocrypha, n. [1. apókrifa; 2. əpókrifə], fr. Gk. *apókruphos*, 'hidden', fr. **apo-** & *krúptein*, 'to hide'. See **crypt**. Certain books of the Old Testament contained in Septuagint and Vulgate, but not regarded as part of the Canon either by the Jews or by the Protestant Reformers.

apocryphal, adj. [1. apókrifal; 2. əpókrifəl]. See prec. & **-al**. **a** Belonging to, connected with, the Apocrypha; **b** of doubtful authority, not genuine; fictitious, false.

apodal, adj. [1. ápodal; 2. ǽpədəl], fr. Gk. *ápous, ápod-(os)*, 'footless', fr. **a-** (priv.) & *pod-(ós), poús*, 'foot', &c. See **pedal** & **-pod**. (zool.) Lacking feet or pelvic fins.

apodeictic, adj. [1. àpodíktik; 2. æ̀pədáiktik], fr. Gk. *apodeiktikós*, fr. *apodeiknūmi*, 'to point out, show, prove by argument'. See **apo-** & **deictic**. (log.) Capable of being clearly proved or demonstrated; absolutely certain; clearly proved and established.

apodeictically, adv. [1. àpodíktikali; 2. æ̀pədáiktikəli]. Prec. & **-al** & **-ly**. In an apodeictic manner; by clear proof or demonstration.

apodosis, n. [1. apódosis; 2. əpódəsis]. Gk., 'a giving back, return', fr. *apodidómai*, 'to give back', fr. **apo-** & *didōmi*, 'I give'. See base under **donation**. The consequent clause, expressing the result, in a conditional sentence; correlative of *protasis*.

apogee, n. [1. àpojḗ; 2. æ̀pədží]. Fr. *apogée*, fr. Gk. *apógaios*, 'away from land', more directly fr. **apo-** & *gê*, 'earth'; see **geo-**. The point at which a heavenly body in its course is farthest away from the earth; contrasted with *perigee*.

apolaustic, adj. [1. àpoláwstik; 2. æ̀pəlɔ́stik], fr. Gk. *apolaustikós*, fr. *apolaúein*, 'to enjoy'; the base **lau-*, wh. does not occur uncompounded in Gk., is cogn. w. Lat. *lucrum*, 'profit, gain'; Scrt. *lṓtam*, 'booty', Goth. *launs*, O.E. *lēan*, 'reward, wages', see **lucre** & **loot**. Given over to pleasure.

Apollo, n. [1. apólō; 2. əpólou]. Gk. *Apóllōn*, earlier *Apéllōn*. Etymol. doubtful. Boisacq tentatively suggests an Aryan base **apel-*, 'to promote, provoke, excite, cause to grow', etc., whence perhaps also Gk. *ápella*, 'assembly'. The Greek god of the sun and of poetry.

Apollyon, n. [1. apólion; 2. əpólion], fr. Gk. *apollúōn*, Pres. Part. of *apollúein*, 'to destroy utterly', fr. **apo-** & *ollúein*, 'to destroy', cogn. w. Gk. *ólethros*, 'loss, ruin, death'; Lat. *(ab)olēre*, 'to destroy'. See **abolish**. The destroying angel of the bottomless pit, Rev. ix. 11; hence, the Devil.

apologetic (I.), also **apologetical**, adj. [1. apòlojétik(l); 2. əpɔ̀lədžétik(l)], fr. Fr. *apologétique*, fr. Lat. *apologēticus*, fr. Gk. *apologētikós*, 'fit for defence', fr. *apologéomai*, 'speak in defence, defend oneself against a charge'. See **apology**. (The primary sense has now become secondary.) **1. a** Excusing with regret, and with desire to conciliate, a wrong done, or slight offered, whether deliberately or inadvertently, by word or deed: *he was very apologetic*; *make an apologetic speech* &c.; **b** (of manner &c.) conciliatory, deferential: *an apologetic tone*. **2.** Defending (statements, opinions &c.) against attack; explanatory, though not admitting wrong (of an essay, treatise &c.).

apologetic (II.), n., fr. prec. **a** Formal apology or defence written or spoken; **b** (in pl.) *apologetics*, specif., that branch of theology concerned with reasoned defence of revealed religion.

apologetically, adv. [1. apòlojétikali; 2. əpɔ̀lədžétikəli], fr. **apologetic (I.)** & **-ly**. So as to convey regret and excuse: *to speak apologetically*.

apologist, n. [1. apólojist; 2. əpólədžist], fr. Fr. *apologiste*. See **apology** & **-ist**. **a** One who defends a person, cause, or institution; **b** specif., one who defends religious and theological doctrines against attack.

apologize, vb. intrans. [1. apólojīz; 2. əpólədžaiz], fr. Gk. *apologízomai*, 'give a full account of', fr. *apología*, [see prec., & **-ize**. Engl. meaning more closely associated w. those of **apology**. To acknowledge slight or injury inflicted, whether intentionally or inadvertently, and express regret: *if I have offended you, I apologize*; *to apologize to a person, for rudeness* &c.

apologue, n. [1. ápolōg; 2. ǽpəloug]. Gk. *apólogos*, 'story, tale'. See **apo-** & **logos**. Story invented to enforce a moral truth; moral fable.

apology, n. [1. apóloji; 2. əpólədži], fr. Gk. *apología*, 'a speech in defence'. See **apo-** & **-logy**. **1.** Expression of regret for slight or injury that one has inflicted on a person, or for discourtesy, rudeness &c. towards him, in deed or speech; explanation that no offence was intended: *to offer, accept, an apology*. **2.** Vindication, defence. See **apologetic (II.)**. **3.** A poor substitute for something else; makeshift: *a mere apology for a dinner*.

apophthegm, apothegm, n. [1. ápo(f)them; 2. ǽpə(f)þem]. Gk. *apóphthegma*, 'thing uttered, sententious answer, terse saying', fr. *apophthéggomai*, 'speak one's opinion plainly', fr. **apo-** & vb. *phthéggomai*, cp. *phthégma*, 'voice, saying, cry, roar'. This is in gradational relation to Gk. *phthóggos*, 'voice, speech, sound'. No cognates known. Cp. second element in **diphthong**. Terse, pithy, instructive saying, moral maxim.

apophysis, n. [1. apófisis; 2. əpófisis]. Gk. *apóphusis*, 'off-shoot'; fr. **apo-** & *phúsis*, 'nature, natural growth', see **physio-**. **a** (anat.) A protuberance or process on a bone; **b** (bot.) swelling on the spore-cases of mosses.

apoplectic, adj. [1. àpopléktik; 2. æ̀pəpléktik], fr. Gk. *apoplēktikós*, 'disabled by a stroke, crippled; astounded'. See **apoplexy** & **-ic**. **a** Having character of, tending to cause, apoplexy; **b** (of persons) liable to be attacked by apoplexy.

apoplectically, adv. [1. àpopléktikali; 2. æ̀pəpléktikəli]. Prec. & **-al** & **-ly**. In an apoplectic manner.

apoplexy, n. [1. ápopleksi; 2. ǽpəpleksi], fr. Fr. *apoplexie*, fr. Lat. *apoplēxia*, fr. Gk. *apoplēxía*, fr. *apoplḗssein*, 'strike down, disable', fr. **apo-** & *plḗssein*, 'strike, smite, wound'; cp. further, Gk. *plēgḗ*, 'blow', Doric *plāgā́*, borrowed into Lat. as *plāga*, whence **plague**. Sudden loss of sensation and consciousness, usually caused by rupture of a blood-vessel in the brain.

aposiopesis, n. [1. apòsiopḗsis; 2. əpɔ̀siəpísis]. Lat., fr. Gk. *aposiṓpēsis*, fr. *aposiōpáō*, 'I am silent', fr. *siōpḗ*, 'silence'. The origin of this word is very obscure, & its relations outside Gk. very dubious; connexion suggested w. Goth. *sweiban*, 'to cease', or w. O.H.G. *swīgēn*, Mod. Germ. *schweigen*, 'be silent', is hardly possible. Rhetorical device, which consists in suddenly breaking off speaking in the middle of a sentence, e.g.: *when I looked into the room, the first thing I saw—— but I dare not describe that dreadful sight.*

apostasy, n. [1. apóstasi; 2. əpóstəsi], fr. Lat. *apostasia*, fr. Gk. *apostasía*, lit. 'standing away from', i.e. 'defection, revolt', later form fr. *apóstasis*. See **apo-** & **stasis**. **a** Voluntary and deliberate desertion or renunciation of, defection from, one's faith, principles, as formerly professed; **b** desertion of a cause which one has championed.

apostate, n. & adj. [1. apóstat, apóstāt; 2. əpóstit, -eit], fr. Fr. *apostat*, fr. Lat. *apostata*, fr. Gk. *apostátēs*. See **apostasy**. **a** n. One guilty of apostasy; **b** adj., guilty of apostasy.

apostatize, vb. intrans. [1. apóstatīz; 2. əpóstətaiz]. See prec. & **-ize**. To become an apostate; desert, betray one cause &c. for another: *to apostatize from Monarchism to Bolshevism*.

a posteriori, adv. & adj. [1. á posteriṓrī; 2. éi pɔsteriɔ́rai]. Lat., 'from what comes after'. See **posterior**. (log.) Applied to mode of reasoning which arrives at general principles from the observation of facts, which infers causes from effects: adv., *to reason a posteriori*; adj., *a posteriori argument*; contrast *a priori*.

apostle, n. [1. apósl; 2. əpósl], fr. Gk. *apóstolos*, lit. 'one sent forth, a messenger', fr. **apo-** & *stéllein*, 'set in order, equip, dispatch, send'. See **stele** & cp. **epistle** & **stole (I.)**. **1.** One who is sent forth to preach, to advocate a cause; a messenger; specif. **a** (cap.) one of the twelve sent forth by Christ to preach the Gospel; **b** (cap.) the first Christian missionary to a country: *St. Augustine was the Apostle of the English*; **c** a zealous advocate of a moral, social, or political measure or reform: *an apostle of Free Trade, of Protection* &c. **2.** One of the twelve officials of the Mormon sect.

Apostles' Creed, n. Creed of the Christian Church, said at morning and evening prayer; it is the earliest of the creeds, at least in origin, if not in the present form.

apostleship, n. [1. apóslship; 2. əpóslʃip]. Prec. & **-ship**. Condition, state, of being an apostle.

apostle spoon, n. Silver or silver-gilt spoon with figure of one of the Apostles on the handle.

apostolate, n. [1. apóstolāt; 2. əpóstəleit]. See **apostle** & **-ate**. Office, authority, functions, of an apostle.

apostolic(al), adj. [1. àpostólik(l); 2. æ̀pəstólik(l)]. Gk. *apostolikós*. See prec. & **-ic** & **-al**. **1.** Belonging to, connected with, the Apostles and their times. **2.** Derived from, according with the spirit of, the Apostles: *Apostolic Church*; *Apostolic doctrine, teaching* &c.; *Apostolic(al) Succession*, continuity of Orders from the Apostles. **3.** Connected with St. Peter, chief of the Apostles, hence, with the Pope: *the Apostolic See*, i.e. Rome.

apostolically, adv. Prec. & **-ly**. **a** After the manner of the Apostles; **b** by, through, the Apostles.

apostrophe, n. [1. apóstrofi; 2. əpóstrəfi]. Gk. *apostrophḗ*, 'a turning away'. A figure in rhetoric in which the orator turned away from rest of audience to address one person. See **apo-** & **strophe**. **1.** An exclamatory, hortatory address to a person or thing, present or absent; occurring either in a speech or a literary work. **2.** The mark (') in punctuation; used when a letter is omitted, and before or after the possessive suffix *-s* in the singular or plural respectively of nouns.

apostrophize, vb. trans. [1. apóstrofīz; 2. əpóstrəfaiz]. Prec. & **-ize**. To address an apostrophe (**1**) to.

apothecary, n. [1. apóthekari; 2. əpóþikəri], fr. Lat. *apothēcārius*, 'a warehouseman', fr. *apothēca*, 'storehouse (esp. of wine)', fr. Gk. *apothḗkē*, fr. *apotithēmi*, 'I put away', fr. **apo-** & *tithēmi*, 'I place', q.v. under **thesis**. Obs. in ordinary use, except as title of the *Society of Apothecaries*. One who prepares medicines and sells drugs, pharmaceutical chemist; formerly, the apothecary was a subordinate and inferior kind of medical practitioner who prescribed, as well as dispensed, medicines.

apothegm. See **apophthegm**.

apothem, n. [1. ápothem; 2. ǽpəþem], fr. **apo-** & Gk. *théma*, 'that which is placed', fr. *tithénai*, 'to place, set down'. See **thesis**. (math.) Perpendicular drawn from the centre to any one of the sides of a polygon.

apotheosis, n. [1. apòtheṓsis; 2. əpɔ̀þióusis]. Lat., fr. Gk. *apothéōsis*, fr. *apotheóō*, 'deify, make a god of', fr. **apo-** & *theós*, 'god'. See **theo-**. **1.** Raising of a mortal to the rank of a divinity; act of putting a mortal among the gods and counting him as divine. **2.** Supreme exaltation, glorification, of a person or thing.

apotheosize, vb. trans. [1. apótheōsīz; 2. əpóþiousaiz]. See prec. & **-ize**. To exalt to rank of a divinity, make a god of.

appal, vb. trans. [1. apáwl; 2. əpɔ́l]. M.E. *apallen*, 'make, become, pale'; fr. O. Fr. *apallir*, 'grow pale'. See **pale, pallid**. To terrify, horrify, dismay.

appalling, adj. [1. apáwling ; 2. əpɔ́liŋ], fr. Pres. Part. of prec. Terrible, horrifying.

appallingly, adv. Prec. & **-ly**. To a shocking extent ; in a deplorable manner.

appanage, apanage, n. [1. ápanij ; 2. ǽpənidž], fr. Fr. *apanage*, fr. O. Fr. *apaner*, lit. 'to provide with bread, to endow, provide with means of subsistence ', fr. Lat. **ad-** & *pānis*, 'bread '. See **panification** & other words referred to under that heading. **1.** Provision made from Crown property for younger members of a royal house. **2.** Dependency ; property or emolument attached as a perquisite to an office. **3.** (fig.) A personal quality, attribute, or endowment which accrues by nature, right, or custom : *admiration is a natural appanage of beauty.*

apparatus, n. [1. àparā́tus ; 2. æ̀pəréitəs]. Lat., 'preparation, making ready ', fr. *apparāre*, 'to make ready for ', fr. **ad-** & *parāre*, 'to make ready '. See **pare**, & cp. **parade** & **prepare**. **1.** Instruments devised, arranged, and got ready for accomplishing a desired end ; **a** collection of utensils, or mechanical contrivances, for carrying out a given work : *an apparatus for pumping water, driving piles, heating a building* &c. ; **b** delicate and complex instruments for experiments in physics, chemistry &c. : *scientific apparatus* ; **c** group of bodily organs which co-operate in a given set of functions : *digestive, respiratory, apparatus* &c. **2.** Collection of literary, historical, and other materials necessary for critical study of a document : *apparatus criticus* or *critical apparatus.*

apparel (I.), n. [1. apárel ; 2. əpǽrəl]. M.E. *appareil*, fr. O. Fr., fr. vb. *apareiller*, 'clothe', fr. *à* & *pareiller*, lit. 'to put together things of the same kind '; cp. Fr. *pareil*, 'like, similar ', fr. Low Lat. *pariculus*, 'like ' ; all fr. Lat. base *pār*, 'equal, similar '. See **par, peer (I.)**. Clothing, dress, attire.

apparel (II.), vb. trans. M.E. *aparailen*, fr. O. Fr. *apareiller*. See prec. To clothe, dress.

apparent, adj. [1. apā́rent ; 2. əpéərənt], fr. Lat. *appārent-(em)*, Pres. Part. type of *appārēre*, 'to become visible, appear ', fr. **ad-** & *pārēre*, 'to appear '. See **appear**. **1. a** Visible, capable of being seen : *apparent to the naked eye* ; **b** easily seen, obvious, plain : *apparent to the most casual observer. Heir apparent*, the next direct heir by birth to the sovereign, or holder of hereditary title or estate (contrasted with *heir presumptive*). **2.** According to appearances ; seeming : *the apparent cause of his illness was excessive drinking.*

apparently, adv. Prec. & **-ly**. So far as can be judged by appearances, actually as it appears to the eye or the mind, but not necessarily really and truly so : *he was apparently a loyal and devoted friend.*

apparition, n. [1. àparíshun ; 2. æ̀pəríʃən]. Fr., fr. Lat. *appāritiōn-(em)*, 'service, attendants', fr. *appārit-(um)*, P.P. type of *appārēre*. See **apparent** & **appear**. Something which appears, esp. suddenly and inexplicably ; hence, supernatural visual impression ; ghost.

apparitor, n. [1. apáritor ; 2. æpǽritɔ]. Lat. *appāritor*, 'an attendant, public servant, lictor ', see prec. & **-or**. **a** An officer in attendance on judges and magistrates in a civil court ; **b** one who executes the orders, esp. in serving summonses, in an ecclesiastical court.

appeal (I.), vb. intrans. & trans. [1. apḗl ; 2. əpíl], fr. Fr. *appeler*, 'to call ', fr. Lat. *appellāre*, 'to call upon, address, entreat ', fr. **ad-** & *pell-*, wh. occurs in various other compounds & is prob. cogn. w. Goth. *spillōn*, 'inform, recount ', O.H.G. *spellōn*, 'recount ', *spill*, 'narrative ', O.E. *spell*, 'narrative, message ', see **spell (I.)**. **A.** intrans. **1. a** To call upon another to decide a question, confirm one's statement or opinion : *I appeal to you to say whether I'm not right, speaking the truth* &c. ; *to appeal to the umpire* ; **b** to call to witness in corroboration of one's statement : *I appeal to history, and to the common experience of mankind.* **2.** To make an urgent demand, request, for help : *we must appeal to the public on behalf of the hospitals.* **3.** (of politicians, esp. the party in power) *To appeal to the country*, take the feeling of the constituencies at a general election as to whether they approve the policy proposed by the government. **4.** (law) To demand the judgement of a higher tribunal to quash or reverse that of a lower : *to appeal against a decision* ; (also absol.) *to appeal*, carry a case to a higher court. **5.** (fig.) To make a successful demand, hence, to move the feelings, attract : *these pictures do not appeal to me* ; *the prospect of happiness thus presented appealed to him strongly.* **B.** trans. (legal hist. and archaic) To challenge, call before a court to meet a charge of treason or other heinous crime.

appeal (II.), n. Fr. *apel*. See prec. **1. a** Urgent demand for aid ; entreaty, challenge : *to make an appeal to one's feelings, charity* &c. ; **b** request for a decision : *an appeal to the umpire.* **2.** (law) Action by which a cause is brought by an unsuccessful party from a lower to a higher court, in hope of obtaining a favourable decision ; *court of appeal*, any court of law to which cases from a lower court may be brought for revision &c.

appealable, adj. [1. apḗlabl ; 2. əpíləbl]. See **appeal (I.)** & **-able**. (rare) That can be appealed, **a** against ; **b** to.

appealing, adj. [1. apḗling ; 2. əpíliŋ], fr. Pres. Part. of **appeal (I.)**. Full of entreaty ; of a nature to move the feelings : *an appealing gesture, tone, glance.*

appealingly, adv. Prec. & **-ly**. In an appealing manner.

appear, vb. intrans. [1. apḗr ; 2. əpíə], fr. O. Fr. *apparoir*, fr. Lat. *appārēre*, fr. **ad-**, 'to ', & *pārēre*, 'to come forth, show oneself '. See **pare**. **1.** To come before the eyes, become perceptible to sense of sight, become visible : *to appear on the horizon* ; *the swallow has appeared in the south of England.* **2. a** To be brought before a judge, magistrate, tribunal &c. : *appear before* (as prisoner to be tried) ; **b** to present oneself before a court of justice as an advocate or as a person to be tried for an offence, or as plaintiff or defendant in a suit : *to appear for the prosecution.* **3. a** To come before the public as writer, actor, lecturer, entertainer &c. : *to appear in public, at Covent Garden* ; **b** to go into society : *to appear in society, at social gatherings* ; **c** (of a book) to be published, come out. **4.** To be obvious, manifest to the mind : **a** (impers.) *it appears from what you say, that* &c. ; *it appears to me that you are all wrong* ; **b** to seem, to convey the impression : *to appear to be suffering.*

appearance, n. [1. apḗrans ; 2. əpíərəns], fr. **appear** & **-ance**. **1. a** The act or process of appearing : *the comet duly made its appearance as predicted.* Phr. *to put in an appearance*, to appear ; **b** specif., act of appearing in a court &c. : *to enter an appearance.* **2. a** The act of coming before the public, esp. on the stage ; **b** the publication of a book &c. **3. a** The condition or form in which a person or thing appears ; outward semblance, look, aspect : *to have a very poor appearance* ; *the sky had a threatening appearance.* Phr. *to all appearance*, as far as can be seen ; **b** something conveying particular impression : *to have the appearance of being half-starved* ; **c** outward look, show, as distinguished from reality : *to keep up appearances.* **4.** Something appearing mysteriously and inexplicably ; esp. **a** a strange phenomenon : *a queer appearance in the sky* ; **b** a phantom, ghost.

appeasable, adj. [1. apḗzabl ; 2. əpízəbl]. See next word & **-able**. Capable of being appeased, in all senses.

appease, vb. trans. [1. apḗz ; 2. əpíz], fr. Fr. *apaiser*, 'to bring to peace, pacify ', fr. *à* & O. Fr. *pais*, fr. Lat. *pāx, pācis*, 'peace '. See **pax** & **pacify**. **1. a** To pacify, soothe, propitiate, conciliate (an angry person) ; **b** to calm, assuage &c. (passions and emotions of the mind, anger, indignation, greed &c.). **2.** To satisfy, content, physical needs : *appease hunger, thirst, one's appetite* &c.

appeasement, n. [1. apḗzment ; 2. əpízmənt]. Prec. & **-ment**. Cp. Fr. *apaisement.* Process of appeasing, assuaging, satisfying.

appellant, adj. & n. [1. apélant ; 2. əpélənt], fr. Fr. *appellant*, Pres. Part. of *appeller*, fr. Lat. *appellant-(em)*, Pres. Part. of *appellāre.* See **appeal (I.)**. (law) **1.** adj. Appealing, pertaining to an appeal. **2.** n. Person who appeals to higher court.

appellate, adj. [1. apélāt ; 2. əpéleit], fr. Lat. *appellāt-(um)*, P.P. of *appellāre.* See **appeal.** (law) Having power to hear and determine appeals : *appellate jurisdiction* &c.

appellation, n. [1. àpelā́shun ; 2. æ̀peléiʃən], fr. Lat. *appellātiōn-(em)*, fr. *appellāre*, 'to call upon '. See **appeal (I.)** & **-ation**. Name, title, designation, by which particular person or thing is known.

appellative, n. & adj. [1. apélativ ; 2. əpélətiv]. See prec. & **-ive**. **a** n. Appellation ; **b** adj., pertaining to a common noun ; naming.

appellatively, adv. Prec. & **-ly**. By name.

appellee, n. [1. àpelḗ ; 2. æ̀pelí], fr. Fr. *appelé*, P.P. of *appeler.* See **appeal (I.)**. (law) The defendant in an appeal ; one tried for an offence at the instance of another, as distinct from *appellant.*

append, vb. trans. [1. apénd ; 2. əpénd], fr. Lat. *appendere*, 'to hang something on ', fr. **ad-** & *pendere*, 'to hang '. See **pendant.** **1.** To hang something on, attach it (esp. by a string &c.) to, something else : *to append a label to a trunk* ; *append a seal to legal document.* **2.** To add something in writing ; send, enclose, an additional message, or another document, together with a letter &c. ; furnish further matter by way of supplement to a book : *I append X's letter herewith* ; *to append a list of names (to a document)*, or *notes, a bibliography* &c. *(to a book).*

appendage, n. [1. apéndij ; 2. əpéndidž]. Prec. & **-age**. Something hung on, attached to, hanging from, in literal sense.

appendant, adj. & n. [1. apéndant ; 2. əpéndənt]. Fr., Pres. Part. of *appendre.* See **append** & **-ant**. **1.** adj. **a** (rare) Attached to, dependent from : *a notice appendant to a door* ; **b** specif. (law, of rights &c.) attached by prescription to an estate in land, contrasted with *appurtenant.* **2.** n. Something attached, hung on, an adjunct.

appendicitis, n. [1. apèndisítis ; 2. əpèndisáitis]. See **appendix** & **-itis**. (med.) Inflammation of the vermiform appendix.

appendix, n. [1. apéndiks ; 2. əpéndiks], pl. **appendices** [1. apéndisēz ; 2. əpéndisiz]. Lat., 'something hung on, appendage ', fr. *appendere*, 'to hang to '. See **append.** **1.** Something appended or added afterwards ; supplement, addition to a book, document &c. **2.** (anat.) *Vermiform appendix* (first word often omitted where no ambiguity can exist), small narrow tube with blind end leading out of the caecum, q.v.

apperception, n. [1. apersépshun ; 2. æpəsépʃən]. Fr. *aperception*, fr. Lat. See **ad-** & **perception**. Consciousness of act of perceiving ; self-consciousness.

appertain, vb. intrans. [1. àpertā́n ; 2. æ̀pətéin], fr. Fr. *appartenir*, fr. Lat. *ad* & *pertinēre.* See **ad-** & **pertain**. To belong to, as a right conferred by nature, custom, or office, or by possession : *the power of ordaining priests appertains only to the Episcopate.*

appetence, n. [1. ápetens ; 2. ǽpitəns]. Fr., 'instinctive desire ', fr. Lat. *appetentia*, 'longing after something, desire ', fr. *appetent-(em)*, Pres. Part. of *appetere*, 'seek after, try to get ', fr. **ad-** & *petere*, 'demand, require '. See **petition.** Strong natural desire ; specif., sexual appetite.

appetency, n. [1. ápetensi ; 2. ǽpitənsi]. See prec. & **-cy**. **a** Natural desire, appetite, appetence ; **b** natural propensity, inclination (of animals) towards certain habits and behaviour ; **c** (of inanimate objects) affinity, attraction.

appetent, adj. [1. ápetent; 2. ǽpitənt]. Fr., fr. Lat. *appetent-(em)*, Pres. Part. See **appetence**. Possessing, filled with, appetence.

appetite, n. [1. ápetīt; 2. ǽpitait]. O. Fr. *apetit*, fr. Lat. *appetītus*, 'onset', & (fig.) 'passion, desire', fr. P.P. of *appetere*, q.v. under **appetence**. **1.** Natural desire, inclination, craving **a** for gratification of a physical need: *human, animal, appetites*; **b** specif., desire for food; hence, the gusto with which a hungry person eats: *to have a good, poor, appetite*; *lose, spoil, one's appetite*, through illness, eating too much at wrong time &c. **2.** (fig.) Desire for mental or emotional stimulus, satisfaction, and enjoyment: *an appetite for work, reading, music* &c.

appetizer, n. [1. ápetīzer; 2. ǽpitaizə]. On model of Fr. *appétissant*, 'appetizing', as though fr. 'to appetize', & **-er**. Anything taken to give an appetite or relish for a meal.

appetizing, adj. [1. ápetīzing; 2. ǽpitaiziŋ], as though fr. Pres. Part. of vb. *appetize*. See prec. & **appetite**. Provoking the appetite, savoury (of food); attractive, pleasing.

appetizingly, adv. Prec. & **-ly**. In such a way as to provoke the appetite.

applaud, vb. intrans. & trans. [1. apláwd; 2. əplɔ́d], fr. Lat. *applaudere*, fr. **ad-** & *plaudere*, 'to clap the hands in approbation'. See **plaudit**. **1.** intrans. To express approbation and agreement by clapping the hands, cheering &c. **2.** trans. **a** To express approval of by clapping hands &c.; **b** to approve, commend: *I applaud your decision.*

applause, n. [1. apláwz; 2. əplɔ́z], fr. Lat. *applaus-(um)*, P.P. type of *applaudere*. See **applaud**. **a** Expression of approbation, agreement, concurrence, by clapping of hands, shouting &c.; **b** approval, concurrence, commendation: *he won general applause by his scientific discoveries.*

applausive, adj. [1. apláwsiv; 2. əplɔ́siv], fr. prec. & **-ive**. Expressing applause.

apple, n. [1. ápl; 2. ǽpl]. O.E. *æppel*, O.H.G. *aphul*, Mod. Germ. *apfel*; cp. W. *afal*, Russ. *jábloko*. Origin of word unknown. Well-known round or oval red and yellow fruit, with firm, juicy flesh and smooth skin, of the genus *Malus*. Special uses: *apple of one's eye*, (i.) the pupil of the eye, (ii.) much cherished object; *apple of discord*, one contended for by Juno, Minerva, and Venus, hence, cause, subject, of dispute; *apples of Sodom*, fruit which turned into ashes when one bit it. Phr. *to upset the, a person's, apple-cart*, to spoil his plans, put spoke in a wheel.

apple-cheese, n. Cake of pomace from cider press.

apple-jack, n. Spirit distilled from apple-juice or cider.

apple pie, n. Tart made of apples. Phrs. *apple-pie bed*, one in which upper or lower sheet has been so folded as to prevent a person from getting into it; *apple-pie order*, thoroughly good order.

apple pomace, n. Pulp of apples from which the juice has been pressed in making cider.

appliance, n. [1. aplíans; 2. əpláiəns]. See **apply** & **-ance**. **1.** Mechanical device or contrivance, used as a means to a particular end; apparatus. **2.** Act of applying; application (rare and obs.).

applicability, n. [1. àplikabíliti; 2. æ̀plikəbíliti]. See **applicable** & **-ity**. **a** Capacity for being used for, or applied to, a particular end or purpose; **b** appropriateness in reference to particular person or object.

applicable, adj. [1. áplikabl; 2. ǽplikəbl], fr. Lat. *applic-(āre)*, 'to apply', & **-able**. See **apply**. **a** Capable of being applied *to* particular purpose; **b** having reference *to* particular person or object; appropriate.

applicableness, n. See prec. & **-ness**. Appropriateness.

applicant, n. [1. áplikant; 2. ǽplikənt], fr. Lat. *applicant-(em)*, Pres. Part. of *applicāre*. See **apply**. One who applies for anything; specif., candidate applying for a situation or appointment.

application, n. [1. àplikáshun; 2. æ̀plikéiʃən], fr. Lat. *applicātiōn-(em)*, fr. *applicāt-(um)*, P.P. type of *applicāre*. See **apply**. **1.** Putting of one thing upon, or over against, another (in various senses, lit. and fig.): **a** (lit.) act of applying, placing, directly upon: *application of a dressing, plaster, to a wound*; **b** (fig.) act of using for particular purpose: *application of drastic remedies, punishment* &c.; *application of a theory in actual practice* &c.; **c** (fig.) (i.) use or mention of a term as referring to a person or thing: *the application of the title 'Good' to Henry VIII. would hardly be appropriate*; (ii.) appropriateness, relevancy of such use: *such terms as 'cruel' or 'kind' have no application in connexion with Justice*; **d** act of directing the mind intently upon intellectual objects; diligence: *to show application in one's studies.* **2. a** Act of demanding, soliciting, requesting: *I was unsuccessful in my application to the Minister*; **b** the demand, request, itself: *I have seen your application and must refuse it.* **3.** Specif., act of presenting oneself as candidate for a post; the document announcing the candidature.

appliqué, adj. & n. (Anglicized pronunciation) [1. aplékā; 2. æplíkei]. Fr., P.P. of *appliquer*. See **apply**. **a** adj. Applied, attached, of ornament, pattern of one material laid or put on the surface of another, as in metal work, embroidery &c.: *appliqué work*; **b** n., appliqué work.

apply, vb. trans. & intrans. [1. aplí; 2. əplái], fr. O. Fr. *aplier*, Lat. *applicāre*, 'to fasten, attach to; (fig.) connect with; to direct intently upon, devote to', fr. **ad-**, 'to', & *plicāre*, 'fold, lay together, fasten', see **plicate**. **A.** trans. **1.** To place upon, or close to, bring into contact with: *to apply a cautery to a wound*; *apply a match to a candle*; *apply one's eye to a telescope* &c. **2.** To turn to use, employ for particular purpose, devote to: *to apply a sum of money to the relief of taxation, for the benefit of the mentally afflicted* &c.; *apply skill and care to.* **3.** To use (epithet or term) in reference to, and as appropriate to, a person or thing: *I should hardly apply the term scholarship to such learning as his.* **4.** (of the mind, attention &c.) To direct intently upon: *to apply one's mind to study.* **5.** (reflex.) *Apply oneself to*, betake, set oneself to, direct one's attention upon. **B.** intrans. **1.** To fit, suit, be relevant, have relation to: *that argument does not apply in this case.* **2. a** To make an application, turn, go to a person in order to obtain something: *apply to me for instructions* &c.; **b** offer oneself as candidate for a post, appointment: *very few have applied for the vacant office.*

appoggiatura, n. [1. apòjatóōra; 2. apòdžatúra]. Ital., 'a support', fr. Lat. **ad-**, 'to', & *podium*, 'elevated place', fr. Gk. *pódion*, 'footstool, gallery to lean on', cp. Ital. *poggio*, 'support', fr. base **ped-*, **pod-*, 'foot'. See **pedal** & **foot**. (mus.) A grace-note.

appoint, vb. trans. [1. apóint; 2. əpɔ́int]. M.E. *appointen*, fr. O. Fr. *apointer*, 'arrange, settle', Low Lat. *appunctāre*, fr. **ad-** & *punct-(um)*, P.P. type of *pungere*, 'to prick, sting'. The idea seems to be to bring to a point or head. See **point, puncture**. **1. a** To decree, ordain, prescribe, set down as lawful and binding: *each man performed his appointed task*; *prayers appointed to be read in churches*; **b** to arrange, organize, set in good order, govern: *to appoint one's house, estates* &c. *on sound lines.* **2.** To fix, determine (time, place) *for*: *to come at the time appointed.* **3.** To nominate (a person) to, and place (him) in, an office, employment; designate by authority: *to appoint a man ambassador*; *appoint to a professorship* &c. **4.** (law) To determine disposition of (an estate).

appointment, n. [1. apóintment; 2. əpɔ́intmənt]. See prec. & **-ment**. **1.** A fixed arrangement for a meeting, an assignation; engagement: *to keep, break, an appointment*; *an appointment for 6 o'clock.* **2. a** The act of authoritatively placing a person in an office or position; **b** the office assigned: *to receive a good appointment.* **3.** (law) Disposition of an estate by deed or will, esp. by means of a *power of appointment.* **4.** (pl.) Outfit, equipment, esp. the furniture &c. of a house: *all the appointments were good.*

apport, n. [1. apórt; 2. əpɔ́t]. Fr., fr. *apporter*, 'to bring', fr. Lat. *apportāre*, see **ad-** & **port (IV.)**. (in spiritualistic parlance) A material object appearing at a séance without visible agency.

apportion, vb. trans. [1. apórshun; 2. əpɔ́ʃən]. Fr. *apportionner*, fr. Low Lat. *apportionāre*, 'divide into portions'. See **portion**. To divide out, distribute justly and suitably, assign in due proportion: *to apportion one's time between various occupations*; *to apportion blame, praise, credit* (among several persons).

apportioned, adj. [1. apórshund; 2. əpɔ́ʃənd], fr. P.P. of prec. Allotted, assigned: *an apportioned task.*

apportionment, n. [1. apórshunment; 2. əpɔ́ʃənmənt]. See **apportion** & **-ment**. **a** Act of apportioning; **b** results of this act, the distribution, mode of sharing arrived at.

apposite, adj. [1. ápozit; 2. ǽpəzit], fr. Lat. *apposit-(um)*, P.P. type of *appōnere*, 'put near, by side of, apply to', fr. **ad-**, 'to', & *pōnere*, 'to place, put'. See **depose** & **position**. Apt, to the point; relevant (to): *an apposite remark.*

appositely, adv. Prec. & **-ly**. To the point, suitably, appropriately.

appositeness, n. See prec. & **-ness**. Suitability, relevance.

apposition, n. [1. àpozíshun; 2. æ̀pəzíʃən]. Lat. *appositiōn-(em)*. See **apposite** & **-ion**. **1.** a Placing in conjunction; **b** (specif.) appending (of seal). **2.** (gram.) Placing of a word, esp. a noun, in same syntactic relation as another in the same sentence.

appraisal, n. [1. aprázal; 2. æpréizəl]. See next word & **-al**. Act of appraising, valuation, estimate.

appraise, vb. trans. [1. apráz; 2. æpréiz], fr. O. Fr. *apreiser*, Lat. *appretiāre*, fr. *pretium*, 'price'. See **appreciate** & **price**. To set a price on, fix, estimate the value of anything, specif., of an article of commerce (by a professional valuer); also of non-material things and qualities, to estimate moral or aesthetic worth and merit of.

appraisement, n. [1. aprázment; 2. æpréizmənt]. See prec. & **-ment**. **a** Action of estimating monetary value; **b** estimated value; **c** in both senses, of non-material things.

appraiser, n. [1. aprázer; 2. æpréizə]. See **appraise** & **-er**. Professional valuer.

appreciable, adj. [1. apréshiabl, aprésiabl; 2. əpríʃiəbl, əprísiəbl]. Fr. See **appreciate** & **-able**. Capable of being estimated; large enough to be perceived.

appreciably, adv. Prec. & **-ly**. To an appreciable extent.

appreciate, vb. trans. & intrans. [1. apréshiāt, aprésiāt; 2. əpríʃieit, əprísieit], fr. Lat. *appretiāt-(um)*, P.P. type of *appretiāre*, 'to set a price to', fr. **ad-** & *pretium*, 'price'; cp. Fr. *apprécier*. See **appraise** & **price**. **A.** trans. **1.** (archaic) To set a price to, estimate the value of, judge to be worth so much. **2.** To judge correctly, estimate at true value, feel the force of: *to appreciate the full meaning of what is said*; *appreciate the difficulties of a situation* &c. **3.** (of non-material qualities) **a** To estimate correctly, set high value on, feel grateful for: *I greatly appreciate your kindness*; **b** to distinguish fully the merits of, be sensible of, alive to qualities of, judge with discriminating enjoyment: *to appreciate poetry keenly*; *to appreciate a rest after hard work.* **B.** intrans. To increase in value (of material and non-material things); opposite of *depreciate.*

appreciation, n. [1. aprèsiáshun; 2. əprìsiéiʃən], fr. Fr. *appréciation*. See prec. & **-ion**. **1. a** Act of appreciating in all senses; **b** correct estimate, exact perception: *ap-*

preciation of the beauties of Shakespeare; c grateful recognition of merit, goodness &c.: *appreciation of kindness received.* 2. Increase in value.

appreciative, adj. [1. apréshiativ; 2. əpríʃiətiv]. See **appreciate** & **-ive**. Feeling, showing, appreciation (in various senses).

appreciatively, adv. Prec. & **-ly**. In such a way as to manifest appreciation.

appreciatory, adj. [1. apréshiateri; 2. əpríʃiətəri]. See **appreciate** & **-ory**. Appreciative.

apprehend, vb. trans. [1. àprehénd; 2. æprihénd], fr. Lat. *apprehendere*, fr. **ad-** & *prehendere*, 'to seize'. See **prehensile**. 1. To arrest, take into custody. 2. (fig.) To grasp with the mind, understand, perceive meaning of. 3. To foresee, look forward to, anticipate, esp. with anxiety; hence, to dread.

apprehensibility, n. [1. àprehènsibíliti; 2. æprihènsibíliti]. See next word & **-ity**. Capacity for being apprehended.

apprehensible, adj. [1. àprehénsibl; 2. æprihénsibl], fr. Lat. *apprehensibilis*, fr. *apprehens-(um)*, P.P. type of *apprehendere*, see **apprehend**, & **-ible**. Capable of being apprehended.

apprehension, n. [1. àprihénshun; 2. æprihénʃən], fr. L. Lat. *apprehensiōn-(em)*, fr. *apprehens-(um)*, P.P. type of *apprehendere*, see **apprehend**, & **-ion**. 1. Act of apprehending; a (lit., rare) seizing, grasping: *the hand is for apprehension*; b grasping with the mind, faculty of understanding: *a person of feeble apprehension*; c mental perception. 2. Arrest, seizure (of criminals). 3. Gloomy foreboding, dread anticipation (often in pl.).

apprehensive, adj. [1. àprehénsiv; 2. æprihénsiv]. See prec. & **-ive**. 1. Capable of apprehending, apt at understanding (of persons). 2. Relating to, connected with, sensuous perception, or intellectual understanding. 3. Full of fears, uneasy in mind, prone to anticipate evil things.

apprehensively, adv. Prec. & **-ly**. In an apprehensive manner (in various senses).

apprehensiveness, n. See prec. & **-ness**. a Power, faculty, of intellectual apprehension; b condition of habitual anticipation of evil.

apprentice (I.), n. [1. apréntis; 2. əpréntis]. Fr. *aprentis*, through Low Lat. **apprenditus*, 'one laid hold of', fr. Lat. *apprehendere*, 'seize'. See **apprehend**. 1. One who is learning a craft or trade, and who is bound by agreement to serve his employer for a specified time in return for instruction. Phr. *To bind apprentice to (a tradesman)*. 2. A novice, tiro (rather rare).

apprentice (II.), vb. trans., fr. prec. To make or bind a person apprentice: *his father apprenticed him to a butcher.*

apprenticeship, n. [1. apréntisship; 2. əpréntisʃip]. See **apprentice (I.)** & **-ship**. a State of being an apprentice; b service rendered as an apprentice; c period or term during which the service lasts. Phr. *to serve one's apprenticeship.*

apprise, vb. trans. [1. apríz; 2. əpráiz], fr. Fr. *appris*, 'instructed', P.P. of *apprendre*, 'to learn, teach', fr. Lat. *apprehendere*. See **apprehend**. To inform: *to apprise a person of something.*

approach (I.), vb. trans. & intrans. [1. apróch; 2. əpróutʃ], fr. Fr. *approcher*, fr. Low Lat. *appropiāre*, fr. *ad-*, 'to', & *propiāre*, 'to draw near', fr. *prope*, 'near', the origin of wh. is doubtful. See **propinquity**. A. trans. 1. To move towards, come near to, arrive close to: *to approach the city, one's home.* 2. (in transferred or fig. senses) a To get within close proximity to, to draw near to: *to approach manhood*; *to approach completion*; b to attain similarity, almost equality to, in quality, amount, character: *something approaching perfection, the required sum, success* &c.; c to make advances, overtures, to (a person), open negotiations with: *will you approach the General on the matter?* B. intrans. 1. To lessen the distance between some person or thing by moving towards him or it, to come near, nearer: *to be unable to approach any nearer.* 2. (in transferred or fig. senses) To draw near, come on (of time, events &c.): *winter, death, the end, approaches.*

approach (II.), n., fr. prec. Act or process of coming near or nearer (in various senses, lit. and fig.). 1. a (in space) *The enemy fled at our approach*; b (in time) *the approach of night*; c (in amount, extent, character &c.) resemblance, approximation to: *some approach to truth.* 2. a District, country surrounding a place, which must be crossed before place can be reached: *the approach to the village was wild and desolate*; b specif., made road leading to a house; drive, avenue; c (fig.) preliminaries, mode of access to a subject of study or discussion: *practical study of living languages is an excellent approach to philology*; d specif. (golf) stroke to land ball on green. 3. (pl.) Attempts to open personal relations, enter into negotiations: *the other's approaches were not encouraged by the great man.*

approachability, n. [1. apròchabíliti; 2. əpròutʃəbíliti]. See next word & **-ity**. a (of things, places) Quality of being easily reached; accessibility; b (of persons) disposition which receives personal advances from others with patience and courtesy.

approachable, adj. [1. apróchabl; 2. əpróutʃəbl]. See **approach (I.)** & **-able**. a Easy of access; b welcoming, friendly to, advances.

approaching, adj. & n. [1. apróching; 2. əpróutʃiŋ], fr. **approach (I.)** & **-ing**. 1. adj. Advancing towards one, coming nearer: *approaching footsteps, death* &c. 2. n. (golf) That part of the game which consists in playing the ball on to the putting-green.

approbation, n. [1. àprobáshun; 2. æprəbéiʃən], fr. Lat. *approbātiōn-(em)*, fr. *approbāt-(um)*, P.P. type of *approbāre*, 'to approve, assent to', fr. **ad-**, 'to', & *probāre*, 'try the goodness of', fr. *probus*, 'good'. See **probate** & cp. **approve**. Act of assenting to, sanctioning, something done, with a certain pleasure; hence also commendation, approval.

approbatory, adj. [1. aprốbatori; 2. əpróubətri]. See prec. & **-ory**. Marked by approbation.

appropriate (I.), adj. [1. aprópriat; 2. əpróupriət], fr. Lat. *appropriāt-(um)*, P.P. type of *appropriāre*, 'to make one's own', fr. **ad-**, 'to', & *proprius*, 'one's own'. See **proper**. Originally, set apart for a particular purpose or person; hence, suited, adapted to particular purpose; fit, suitable, for particular person, thing, occasion.

appropriate (II.), vb. trans. [1. aprópriāt; 2. əpróuprieit]. See prec. 1. a To take, and convert to one's own exclusive use; b to do this illegally, by force or fraud; to steal. 2. To devote, set apart, assign to particular use or person.

appropriately, adv. [1. aprópriatli; 2. əpróupriətli], fr. **appropriate (I.)** & **-ly**. In an appropriate manner; suitably.

appropriateness, n. See prec. & **-ness**. State, quality, of being appropriate.

appropriation, n. [1. apròpriáshun; 2. əpròupriéiʃən]. See **appropriate (II.)** & **-ion**. 1. a Act of appropriating, setting aside something and assigning it to a particular person or use; b conversion of something to one's own use. 2. Ecclesiastical benefice which is in the hands of a bishop or a spiritual corporation; as distinct from *impropriation*.

appropriative, adj. [1. aprópriativ; 2. əpróupriətiv]. See prec. & **-ive**. Having nature of, tending to, appropriation.

appropriator, n. [1. aprópriāter; 2. əpróuprièitə]. See prec. & **-or**. Holder of an ecclesiastical benefice, as a bishop or spiritual corporation, as distinct from *impropriator*.

approval, n. [1. aprōōval; 2. əprúvəl]. See **approve** & **-al**. 1. Approbation, consent to, sanction of an act: *the scheme had the approval of the committee.* 2. Critical examination, judgement, verdict (implying expectation that this will be favourable, though the reverse is possible): *I should like to submit what I have written for your approval.* Phr. *to send goods on approval*, for customer's decision whether he will buy or not.

approve, vb. trans. & intrans. [1. aprōōv; 2. əprúv], fr. Fr. *approuver*, O. Fr. *aprover*, fr. Lat. *approbāre*. See **approbation** & **probate**. 1. a trans. To hold, and express, favourable opinion concerning; consider and pronounce good; also, and more usually, *approve of*: *I quite approve (of) your choice*; *I don't approve (of) his conduct*; b intrans., *I have heard all the proposals, and I don't approve at all.* 2. trans. (of a legislative or administrative body) To sanction formally, confirm by resolution: *to approve a report.* 3. (reflex.) To demonstrate, prove, give evidence of, one's quality: *to approve oneself a good teacher.*

approver, n. [1. aprōōver; 2. əprúvə]. Prec. & **-er**. An informer, one who turns King's evidence.

approximate (I.), adj. [1. apróksimat; 2. əpróksimit], fr. L. Lat. *approximāt-(um)*, P.P. type of *approximāre*, 'to come near to', fr. **ad-**, 'to', & *proximus*, 'nearest, very near'. See **proximal**. Approaching correctness, fairly exact; esp. coming very near to in amount, extent, quality &c.; nearly resembling: *an approximate account of what happened*; *approximate value, cost, distance* &c.

approximate (II.), vb. trans. & intrans. [1. apróksimāt; 2. əpróksimeit], fr. prec. a trans. (rare) To bring close to, cause to come near; b intrans., to come near to, approach, be nearly equal to, or identical with, almost correspond with, esp. in amount, extent, quality &c.: *to approximate to the truth, to what was said, to the description.*

approximately, adv. [1. apróksimatli; 2. əpróksimitli]. See **approximate (I.)** & **-ly**. In a manner, to an extent, which is nearly exact; almost, very nearly, to all intents and purposes: *approximately what I want*; *approximately correct.*

approximation, n. [1. apròksimáshun; 2. əpròksiméiʃən]. See **approximate (II.)** & **-ion**. Act of coming near, of becoming almost identical; something which comes near to exact identity, equality, resemblance &c.: *a very close approximation to the truth*; *a mere approximation*, that is, not accurate in every particular.

appui, n. [1. apwḗ; 2. əpwí]. Fr., fr. *appuyer*, 'to prop, support', fr. Low Lat. *appodiāre*, fr. **ad-** & *podium*, 'pedestal, support'. See **pedal**. (mil.) Support, base, esp. in Phr. *point d'appui* [1. pwán dapwḗ; 2. pwǣ dəpwí], a fixed point on which troops pivot in manœuvres.

appurtenance, n. [1. apértinans; 2. əpə́tinəns]. A.-Fr. *apurtenance*. See **appertain**, **pertain**, & **-ance**. 1. That which appertains to something else larger or more important; an adjunct, accessory to something which is regarded as the principal object of the group. 2. (law) Right, property, subsidiary or accessory to property, acquired otherwise than by prescription, contrasted with *appendant*

appurtenant, adj. & n. [1. apértinant; 2. əpə́tinənt]. a adj. Annexed to some other more important thing; accessory, incident, to; b n., an appurtenance.

apricot, n. [1. áprikot; 2. éiprikɔt]. Formerly *apricock*, *abricot*; the word has been chased through a number of languages, first to Fr. *abricot*, thence to Port. *albricoque*, & Span. *albaricoque*, & further still to Arab. *al barqūq* (*al*, 'the'); but it does not stop here. The word was borrowed by the Arabs fr. Med. Gk. *praikókion*, wh. is itself fr. Lat. *praecoqua*, 'apricots', neut. pl. of *praecoquus*, another form of *praecox*, 'early ripe'. See **precocious** & **cook**. 1. Round, soft, stone fruit, deep orange red in colour, allied to plum and peach. 2. Orange-red colour, also attributive, *apricot colour.*

April, n. [1. ápril; 2. éiprəl, éipril]. M.E. *aprille*, fr. Lat. *aprīlis*; orig. the second month of a year wh. began in March, cp. Lat. *quintīlis*, 'July', *sextīlis*, 'August'; *April* means prob. 'second month', & is connected w. Scrt. *áparaś*, 'later, second', cp. Goth. *afar*, 'afterwards'; the Latins took it as contraction of **aperīlis*, 'opening', sc. *mensis*, 'month', fr. *aperīre*, 'to open'. The fourth month of the year; *April fool*, one who has tricks played upon him on April 1st.

a priori, adv. & adj. [1. á prīórī; 2. éi praiórai]. Lat. *ā*, 'from', & *priōri*, 'something going before', fr. *prior, prius*, 'former, previous'. See **prior**. **a** adv. In Phr. *to reason a priori*, that is, from cause to effect, deductively; **b** adj., *a priori reasoning, argument*, deductive reasoning; contrast *a posteriori*.

apron, n. [1. áprun; 2. éiprən], fr. M.E. *a napron*, fr. O. Fr. *naperon*, 'napkin, cloth', fr. *nappe*, 'cloth', fr. Lat. *mappa*, 'cloth'. See **map**. **1.** A piece of cloth, leather, or other material, of varying length, worn suspended in front to keep the clothes clean. **2. a** Part of the official dress of bishops, deans, and archdeacons, properly a short form of cassock; **b** square, coloured cloth, with symbolic ornamentation, worn, hanging from the waist, as part of the ceremonial dress of freemasons. **3.** In various special uses, generally applied to objects which resemble an apron in shape or function, e.g. the *apron of a carriage*, one made of thick waterproof material, serving to protect persons on the box from cold and wet; the projecting flooring at the sill of dock- and lock-gates and weirs; the piece of wood which holds the blade of a carpenter's plane &c.

aproned, adj. [1. áprund; 2. éiprənd]. Prec. & **-ed**. Clad in, covered or protected by, an apron.

apron-stage, n. Stage of a theatre with projection into the auditorium, used in imitation of the Elizabethan stage, in which the audience were on three sides of the actors.

apron-string, n. String by which an apron is suspended from the neck or tied round the waist; esp. in Phr. *tied to one's mother's apron-strings*, too much or too long dependent on or controlled by one's mother.

apropos, adj. & adv. [1. àpropó; 2. æprəpóu]. Fr. *à*, 'to', & *propos*, 'purpose, plan', fr. Lat. *prōpositum*, P.P. of *prōpōnere*, 'to put forth, set forth, propose'. See **purpose**. **1.** adj. To the point or purpose; opportune, opportunely: *the remark was very apropos*. **2.** adv. *Apropos of . . .*, with regard to (in reference to something already mentioned, to which it is desired to return in conversation).

apse, n. [1. aps; 2. æps], fr. Lat. *apsis*. See **apsis**. (archit.) Semicircular projection, or recess at end of a church, with vaulted roof.

apsidal, adj. [1. ápsidal; 2. ǽpsidəl], fr. Lat. *apsīdis*, genit. sing. of *apsis*. See next word & **-al**. (archit.) Relating to, having character of, an apse: *apsidal recess*.

apsis, n., pl. **apsides** [1. ápsis, ápsidēz; 2. ǽpsis, ǽpsidiz]. Lat. *apsis, absis* (genit. sing. *apsīdis, absīdis*), 'an arch or vault', fr. Gk. *(h)ápsis*, 'a fastening, felloe of a wheel', also 'an arch or vault', connected w. *háptein*, 'to fasten, adjust, touch'. Further connexions unknown. (astron.) Apogee and perigee of moon; aphelion and perihelion of a planet.

apt, adj. [1. apt; 2. æpt], fr. Lat. *aptus*, 'fitted, suited', P.P. of obs. vb. **apere* 'fasten', used as P.P. of *apiscor*, 'reach after, attain to, get', &c.; prob. cogn. w. Scrt. *āptáś*, 'fitting, skilful'. **1.** Fit, suited, suitable, appropriate to the occasion: *an apt quotation*. **2.** Skilled, promising: *an apt pupil*. **3.** Likely *to*, having a tendency *to*, inclined *to* (do), in danger of (doing): *an idle person is apt to get into mischief*.

apterous, adj. [1. ápterus; 2. ǽptərəs], fr. Gk. *ápteros*, 'wingless', fr. **a-**, 'without', & *pterón*, 'wing'; the latter word shows the 'vanishing' grade of the base, **pet-*, 'go, fly', as in Lat. *petere*, 'go, travel to', & Gk. *pétomai*, 'I fly, dart, rush' &c. The Gmc. form, almost exactly corresponding to *pterón*, but w. different grade in first syllable, is seen in O.E. *feþer*, 'feather, pen'; cp. also Lat. *penna*, 'feather, pen', fr. **petna*. See **ptero-, feather, & pen** (III.). (zool.) Lacking wings (of certain insects).

apteryx, n. [1. ápteriks; 2. ǽptəriks], fr. Gk. **a-**, 'without', & *ptérux*, 'wing'. The latter is closely cogn. w. Gk. *pterón*, 'wing' (see prec. word), but has different formative suff. (zool.) Species of bird peculiar to New Zealand, with rudimentary wings and no tail, the kiwi.

aptitude, n. [1. áptitūd; 2. ǽptitjūd], fr. Low Lat. *aptitūdin-(em) aptitūdo*, fr. *aptus*. See **apt**; cp. **attitude**. Natural capacity, propensity, special disposition for some particular action or pursuit.

aptly, adv. [1. áptli; 2. ǽptli]. **apt & -ly**. Suitably, fittingly.

aptness, n. See prec. & **-ness**. Fitness, suitability, appropriateness.

apyretic, adj. [1. àpīrétik; 2. èipaiərétik], fr. Gk. *apúretos*, 'without fever', fr. **a-**, 'without', & *puretós*, 'feverish heat, fever', fr. *pûr*, 'fire'. See **pyre, pyretic**. (med.) Free from fever.

aqua fortis, n. [1. ákwa fórtis; 2. ǽkwə fɔ́tis]. Lat. = 'strong water'. See **aquatic & fort**. Nitric acid.

aquamarine, n. [1. àkwamarḗn; 2. æ̀kwəmərín], fr. Lat. *aqua marīna*, 'sea-water', fr. *aqua*, 'water' & *marīnus, -a, -um*, 'of the sea', fr. *mare*, 'sea'. See **aquatic & marine**. (mineral.) Bluish-green, transparent stone, variety of beryl.

aqua regia, n. [1. ákwa rḗjia; 2. ǽkwə rídžiə]. Lat., 'royal water'. See **aquatic & regal**. A mixture of nitric and hydrochloric acid, so called from its power to dissolve the 'royal metal', gold, also platinum.

aquarelle, n. [1. akwarél; 2. ækwərél], Fr., fr. Ital. *acquerella*, 'water-colour', dimin. of *acqua*, Lat. *aqua*, 'water'. See **aquatic**. A water-colour drawing.

aquarellist, n. [1. akwarélist; 2. ækwərélist]. Prec. & **-ist**. One who paints in water-colour.

aquarium, n. [1. akwā́rium; 2. əkwɛ́əriəm]. Lat., neut. sing. of *aquārius*. See **aquatic & -ary**. **a** Artificial pond, or tank with glass sides, in which living water plants, fish, and animals are kept; **b** place where such tanks are exhibited.

Aquarius, n. [1. akwā́rius; 2. əkwɛ́əriəs]. Lat., 'water carrier'. See prec. (astron.) A constellation and eleventh sign of the Zodiac.

aquatic, adj. [1. akwátik; 2. əkwǽtik]. Fr. *aquatique*, fr. Lat. *aquāticus*, 'found in the water, watery', Lat. *aqua*, 'water', cogn. w. Goth. *ahwa*, O.H.G. *aha*, O.E. *ēa*, 'water'; the suff. of above is fr. Lat. *-āticus*, see **-atic**. **1.** Belonging to water; growing, living, in water: *aquatic plants* &c. **2.** (of sports &c.) Taking place on or in the water.

aquatint(a), n. [1. ákwatint(a); 2. ǽkwətint(ə)], fr. Fr. *aquatinte*, Ital. *acqua tinta*, fr. Lat. *aqua tincta, aqua*, 'water', & *tinctus*, P.P. of *tingere*, 'to dye'. See prec. & **tint**. Form of engraving and etching, produced by aqua fortis on copper.

aqua tofana, n. [1. ákwa tofáhna; 2. ǽkwə təfánə]. Lat., 'water of Tōfana', name of a supposed Sicilian poisoner of 17th cent. A colourless, tasteless, poisonous liquid, of secret preparation, probably of arsenic.

aqua vitae, n. [1. ákwa vītē; 2. ǽkwə váitī]. Lat., 'water of life'. See **aquatic & vital**. **a** Brandy or other spirituous liquor; **b** (old chem.) rectified spirit of wine.

aqueduct, n. [1. ákwedukt; 2. ǽkwidakt], fr. Lat. *aquaeductus*, lit. 'a conveyance of water, conduit', fr. *aqua*, 'water', & *ductus*, P.P. of *dūcere*, 'to lead'. See **aquatic, duct, & duke**. **1.** An artificial channel or conduit for water; esp. one constructed upon raised piers of masonry, for carrying large quantities of water for a long distance, often crossing valleys and rivers. **2.** (anat.) Small passage connecting different organs, or parts of same organ, e.g. *aqueduct of Sylvius* (in the brain).

aqueous, adj. [1. ákwius; 2. éikwiəs]. Coined fr. Lat. *aqua*, 'water', & **-ous**, the Lat. word being *aquōsus*, 'abounding in water'. See **aquatic**. Watery; made with water; thin, and resembling water in consistency: *aqueous solution*; *aqueous humour*.

Aquilegia, n. [1. àkwiléjia; 2. æ̀kwilídžiə]. Earlier also *aquileia*; origin unknown. Botanical name of the columbines.

aquiline, adj. [1. ákwilīn; 2. ǽkwilain], fr. Lat. *aquilīnus*, 'pertaining to the eagle', fr. *aquila*, 'eagle', now supposed to be fr. *aquilus*, 'dark-coloured'. See **eagle & -ine**. Hooked, curved, like an eagle's beak: *aquiline nose, features*.

-ar, suff. representing Lat. *-ārius* or *-āris*, taken direct or imitated fr. Lat. Often for Engl. **-er**, as in *beggar* on model of *scholar* &c.

Arab, n. [1. árab; 2. ǽrəb]. Fr. *arabe*, fr. Lat. *arabs, arabis*, fr. Gk. *áraps, árabos*. **1. a** Inhabitant of Arabia; **b** Arab horse. **2.** *Street arab*, homeless urchin of either sex; probably from his or her nomad habits.

arabesque, adj. & n. [1. àrabésk; 2. æ̀rəbésk], fr. Fr. *arabesque*, 'Arabian'. Prec. & **-esque**. **a** adj. (of style of decoration) Derived from the Moors and Arabs, exhibiting fantastic patterns, painted or in low relief, of intertwined scroll-work, leaves &c.; **b** n., ornament of this type.

Arabian, adj. & n. [1. arā́bian; 2. əréibiən]. Arabia & **-an**. **1.** adj. Of, belonging to, Arabia. **2.** n. **a** An Arab; **b** Arabic.

Arabic, adj. & n. [1. árabik; 2. ǽrəbik], fr. Lat. *arabicus*. See **Arab & -ic**. **1.** adj. Arabian; *gum arabic*, resin of species of acacia; *Arabic numerals*, those in use today, as opposed to Roman numerals &c. **2.** n. Language of the Arabs and Arabia, one of the family of Semitic languages.

arabis, n. [1. árabis; 2. ǽrəbis]. Med. Lat. *arabis*, fr. Gk., 'Arabian'. See **Arab**. Genus of low-growing, clustering plants with smooth leaves and white or purple flowers.

Arabist, n. [1. árabist; 2. ǽrəbist]. **Arab & -ist**. Arabic scholar, student of Arabic.

arable, adj. & n. [1. árabl; 2. ǽrəbl]. Fr., fr. Lat. *arābilis*, fr. *ar-*, as in *arāre*, 'to plough', & **-able**; this is a very primitive base, & is common to nearly all Aryan languages: Gk. *aróō*, 'I plough', *árotron*, Lat. *aratrum*, 'a plough'; O. Slav. *orati*, 'to plough'; Goth. *arjan*, 'to plough'; O.E. *erian*; O.H.G. *erran*; M. Ir. *airim*, 'I plough', *arathar*, 'a plough'; remoter relation exists between this group of words & the bases of Lat. *rādere*, 'scratch, scrape', & *rōdere*, 'gnaw'. See further **rat, rodent**. **a** adj. Fit for ploughing; usually ploughed: *arable land*, land which is ploughed, as distinct from *meadow land*; **b** n., arable land, plough land.

arachnid, n. [1. aráknid; 2. ərǽknid]. Gk. *arákhnē*, 'spider's web', *arákhnēs*, 'spider, cobweb', wh. is perh. for **araksnā* &c., & connected w. Gk. *árkus*, 'net'. (zool.) Member of the class *Arachnida*, which includes spiders, scorpions, mites &c.

arachnitis, n. [1. àrakni̇́tis; 2. æ̀rækn áitis]. Gk. See *arákhnēs*, 'cobweb', under prec., & **-itis**. (med.) Disease of arachnoid membrane.

arachnoid, adj. [1. aráknoid; 2. ərǽknɔid]. Cp. Gk. *arachno-eidés*, 'cobweb-like'. See **arachnid & -oid**. **1.** (anat.) Applied to thin membrane which covers the brain and the spinal cord: *arachnoid membrane*. **2.** (bot.) Covered with fine hairs like a cobweb.

araneid, n. [1. arā́nēid; 2. əréini-id], fr. Lat. *arānea*, 'spider', prob. fr. **araksnā*. Cp. **arachnid**. (zool.) Member of the order *Araneida*, which include the spiders, belonging to the class *Arachnida*.

araucaria, n. [1. àrawkā́ria; 2. æ̀rɔ̄kɛ́əriə], fr. the territory of Araucania & the province of

Arauco, south of Chile. (bot.) Genus of trees of which the *monkey-puzzle* is the best known.

arbalest, arblast, n. [1. árbalest, árblahst; 2. ábəlɛst, áblāst]. In M.E., fr. O. Fr. *arbaleste*, Lat. *arcuballista*, 'a catapult fitted with a contrivance like a powerful bow', fr. *arcus*, 'bow'. See **arc** & **ballistics**. Kind of powerful cross-bow, with mechanical device for bending the bow, and a trigger which released the string and fired the dart.

arbalester, n. [1. árbalester; 2. ábəlɛstə]. M.E. *arblastere*, O. Fr. *arbalestier*. Prec. & **-er**. Man who fights with an arbalest; cross-bow man.

arbiter, n. [1. árbiter; 2. ábitə]. Lat., 'spectator, hearer, umpire, judge'; the first element is simply **ad-**, 'to', the second is derived fr. base in *baeto, bēto, bīto*, 'I go'. This is possibly a dialectal form of *gʷe- &c., 'go, come', & thus related to Lat. *venio*, Gk. *baino* &c.; but this is doubtful. In any case, *arbiter* is orig. merely one who goes to a place. **a** One having power and authority to decide in a dispute; judge; **b** one who has absolute control: *arbiter of our fate*; in first sense, *arbitrator*, q.v., is now more usual.

arbitrable, adj. [1. árbitrabl; 2. ábitrəbl], fr. Lat. *arbitrāri*, 'to decide'. See prec. & **-able**. Capable of, subject to, settlement by arbitration.

arbitrage, n. [1. árbitrij; 2. ábitridž]. Fr. See **arbiter** & **-age**. **a** Calculation of the difference between the prices of stocks and shares, bills of exchange, currency &c. in the home and a foreign market; **b** business of buying and selling shares on the basis of this calculation in order to make a profit.

arbitral, adj. [1. árbitral; 2. ábitrəl], fr. L. Lat. *arbitrālis*. See **arbiter** & **-al**. Pertaining to arbitration.

arbitrament, n. [1. arbítrament; 2. ābítrəmənt]. Fr. *arbitrement*, Lat. *arbītrium*, 'judgement, decision'. See **arbiter** & **-ment**. **a** Decision of a dispute by an arbitrator; **b** authoritative and final decision and judgement: *the arbitrament of war*.

arbitrarily, adv. [1. árbitrarili; 2. ábitrərili]. **arbitrary** & **-ly**. In an arbitrary manner.

arbitrariness, n. See prec. & **-ness**. State, quality, of being arbitrary.

arbitrary, adj. [1. árbitrari; 2. ábitrəri], fr. Lat. *arbītrārius*, 'at the discretion of an arbiter or umpire; not fixed, uncertain'. See **arbiter** & **-ary**. In accordance with impulse and whim, rather than of reasoned judgement; despotic, high-handed.

arbitrate, vb. intrans. [1. árbitrāt; 2. ábitreit], fr. Lat. *arbītrāt-(um)*, P.P. type of *arbītrāri*, 'to decide, judge'. See **arbiter**. **1.** To give a decision as between two parties in a dispute. **2.** Of international disputes, to refer them to, and decide them by, arbitration.

arbitration, n. [1. àrbitráshun; 2. àbitréiʃən], fr. Lat. *arbitrātiōn-(em)*, 'judgement, will', fr. *arbitrātus*, 'will, decision'. See **arbitrate** & **-ion**. Act of arbitrating; settlement of a dispute by decision of an arbitrator: *to submit a difference of opinion to arbitration*.

arbitrator, n. [1. árbitrātur; 2. ábitreitə]. Lat. *arbītrātor*. See **arbitrate** & **-or**. One who arbitrates, esp. a person agreed upon by both sides in a dispute to decide the question at issue.

arbor, n. [1. árbur; 2. ábə]. Lat., 'tree, stock'. See **arboreal**. Meaning is taken fr. Fr. *arbre*. The spindle, axis of a wheel, esp. of clocks and watches.

arboraceous, adj. [1. arburáshus; 2. ābəréiʃəs]. See Lat. *arbor*, 'tree', under **arboreal**, & **-aceous**. **a** Tree-like in growth and structure; **b** wooded.

arboreal, adj. [1. arbóreal; 2. ābóriəl], formed w. **-al**, fr. Lat. *arboreus*, fr. *arbor*, 'tree'. This word is perh. derived fr. Aryan suff. *ardhos, 'pertaining to trees', meaning 'lofty, well-grown', w. wh. etymologists connect also Lat. *arduus*, 'lofty, steep', some explaining the *-d-* in the latter as due to Celt. *ard*, 'high' (cp. *Arduenna silva, Ardennes*), & others by assuming double forms, *ardh- & *ard-, in Aryan itself; Gk. *orthós*, 'straight, standing erect, upright', see **ortho-**, is fr. same base, & further Gk. *ptórthos*, 'young branch, shoot, sapling', wh. is assumed to come fr. *pj-orthos*, the pref. being reduced form of *epi*, 'at' &c., see **epi-**. **a** Belonging to, having character of, a tree: *arboreal vegetation*; **b** living in, given to frequenting, trees: *arboreal life, arboreal monkeys*.

arboreous, adj. [1. arbóreus; 2. ābóriəs]. Lat. *arboreus*. See prec. & **-ous**. **a** (of country) Thickly set with trees, wooded; **b** having the growth and structure of a tree, as distinct from those of herbs and shrubs.

arborescent, adj. [1. arburésent; 2. ābərésənt]. Lat. *arborescent-(em)*, Pres. Part. of *arborescere*, 'to grow into a tree', fr. *arbor*, 'tree'. See **arboreal**. Becoming tree-like, becoming woody in the stalk.

arboretum, n. [1. arburétum; 2. ābərítəm]. Lat., 'place grown with trees, plantation', said to be an ignoble word, the dignified one being *arbustum*, fr. *arbor*, 'tree', & *-ētum*, a suff. used in the coll. sense of 'group of trees' in **pinetum**, *pomētum*, 'apple orchard' &c. See Gmc. form of this suff. in **frith**. Place where specimen trees are planted and carefully tended; collection of trees.

arboricultural, adj. [1. arbórikùlchural; 2. ābórikàltʃərəl]. **arboriculture** & **-al**. Pertaining to arboriculture.

arboriculture, n. [1. arbórikùlchur; 2. ābórikàltʃə], fr. Lat. *arbor*, 'tree', & *cultūra*, 'tending, cultivation'. See **arboreal** & **culture**. Scientific cultivation of trees and shrubs; branch of study which deals with methods of tree culture.

arboriculturist, n. [1. arbòrikúlchurist; 2. ābòrikáltʃərist]. See prec. & **-ist**. One who studies and practises scientific tree culture.

arborization, n. [1. àrburīzáshun; 2. àbəraizéiʃən], fr. Lat. *arbor*, 'tree', see **arboreal**, & **-ize** & **-ation**. Tree-like appearance, figure with ramifications like branches of a tree; **a** in certain fossils; **b** caused by distension of blood-vessels in certain inflammatory conditions.

arbor vitae, n. [1. árbur vítē; 2. ábə váitī]. Lat., 'tree of life'. See **arboreal** & **vital**. Name of several evergreen trees of the genus *Thuja*.

arbour, n. [1. árbur; 2. ábə]. M.E. *herbere*, *erbere*, 'a herb garden', fr. O. Fr. *herbier*, Lat. *herbārium*, 'collection of dried plants', fr. *herba*, 'grass, green crops, herb' &c; the present form of the Engl. word, & to some extent perh. the meaning, has been influenced by association w. Lat. *arbor*, 'tree'. See **herb, herbarium**. Shady retreat in a garden, in the nature of a summer-house, largely formed by shrubs and climbing plants trained over a wooden or iron framework.

arbutus, n. [1. arbútus; 2. ābjútəs]. Lat. *arbutus*, 'the wild strawberry-tree'. The origin of the word is obscure, but it is not, apparently, related to *arbor*, 'tree'; cp. the undoubted derivative of the latter word, *arbustus*. Name applied to several evergreens, of which the strawberry-tree is one.

arc, n. [1. ark; 2. āk], fr. Lat. *arcus*, 'bow, arch, curve'. It seems certain that Goth. *arhwazna*, 'arrow', & O.E. *earh*, 'arrow', are cogn.; beyond this, relationships are obscure. See **arch** & **arrow**. **1.** (geom.) Portion of a curved line: *arc of a circle*. **2.** Applied to various objects having similar shape, e.g. forms and colourations of light of curved, arc-like shape: **a** the rainbow; **b** luminous glow produced in certain kinds of electric lamps: *an arc light, electric arc*; **c** the curve apparently traversed by the sun between rising and setting.

arcade, n. [1. arkád; 2. ākéid]. Fr., fr. Med. Lat. *arcāta*, 'arch', lit. 'arched things', fr. Lat. *arcus*, a bow, see **arc**, & **-ade**. **a** A series of arches supported by a row of columns; **b** arched passage, whether open or closed at sides; **c** specif., passage with arched roof and shops leading out of it on both sides.

arcaded, adj. [1. arkáded; 2. ākéidid]. Prec. & **-ed**. Having, furnished, decorated with arcades.

Arcadia, n. [1. arkádia; 2. ākéidiə]. Gk. *Arkadía*, mountainous district in Peloponnesus, whose inhabitants were supposed to be simple and contented; hence, **a** simple, quiet, rural district; **b** condition of simplicity, content, and innocence supposed to exist in such a spot.

Arcadian, adj. [1. arkádian; 2. ākéidiən]. Prec. & **-an**. Characteristic of Arcadia; therefore, simple, innocent, rural.

Arcady, n. [1. árkadi; 2. ákədi]. Poetical form of **Arcadia**; cp. Keats: '*in Tempe or the vales of Arcady*'.

arcanum, n. [1. arkánum; 2. ākéinəm]. Lat. *arcānum*, 'shut up, closed, secret', fr. *arca*, 'chest, strong-box, coffin' &c.; cp. *arcēre*, 'enclose, keep away, ward off', & Gk. *arkéō*, 'resist, keep off', *árkios*, 'safe, sure'. (gen. in pl., *arcana*) A secret, a mystery.

arch (I.), n. [1. arch; 2. ātʃ]. O. Fr. *arche*, fr. Lat. *arcus*, 'a bow'. See **arc**. **1.** Curved structure of masonry supporting a superstructure; used esp. for spanning an opening in building, door, window; for connecting pillars, supporting bridge &c. by converting the vertical pressure of the weight of masonry above into horizontal or diagonal thrust. **2.** Entrance or passage covered by arched structure; archway. **3.** Anything shaped like an arch, even although it bear no superstructure, esp. an arch-shaped construction, of any material, through which a road or path passes: *triumphal arch*, one erected across a roadway, through which procession passes; *rose arch*, light structure of lattice or wire over a garden path &c.

arch (II.), vb. trans., fr. prec. **1.** To build an arch over, supply with, span by means of, an arch. **2.** (fig.) To curve, form something into shape of an arch: *to arch the eye-brows; a horse arches its neck; a cat arches its back*.

arch (III.), adj. See **arch-**. **1.** Chief, principal (now rarely used without hyphen). See following. **2.** Hence, from frequent association with such words as *wag, rogue* &c., slily mischievous, possessing and expressing innocent roguishness: *arch smiles*; *to look arch*.

arch-, pref. [1. arch; 2. ātʃ], also in some words [1. ark; 2. āk]. Already in O.E. we find *ærće-, erće*, in the words *erćebisćop, erćediacon*, in wh. the pref. is an early borrowing fr. Lat. *archi-*; this normally gives the pronunciation [ātʃ] in Mod. Engl., and this is doubtless the origin of one ordinary type, wh. has been extended to many compounds wh. did not exist in O.E. In those words where [āk] is pronounced, this is due to a recent borrowing direct fr. the Gk. The ultimate origin of the pref. is Gk. *arkhi-*, 'chief', the form in composition of *arkhós*, 'leader, chief', connected w. *arkhḗ*, 'beginning, origin', & *árkhō*, 'begin'. It has been suggested that this Gk. base is fr. Aryan *m̥rghō-, 'to be first'. See further under **brain**. The force of the pref. in Engl. words is to some extent differentiated, but all the senses spring from the idea of 'chief, leader': **a** *arch-priest* &c.; **b** *arch-buffoon*; **c** (with inversion of sense before words having sense of reproach &c.) *arch-liar*.

archaean, adj. [1. arkéan; 2. ākíən]. Gk. *arkhaîos*, 'ancient', fr. *arkhḗ*, 'beginning'. See **arch-**. Belonging to the most ancient geological period.

archaeological, adj. [1. àrkeolójikl; 2. àkiəlódžikl]. **archaeology** & **-ic** & **-al**. Connected with archaeology.

archaeologist, n. [1. àrkiólojist; 2. àkiólədžist]. Next word & **-ist**. Student of archaeology.

archaeology, n. [1. àrkióloji; 2. àkiólədži]. See **archaean** & **-logy**. Study of human antiquities, of the art, customs, and beliefs of the most ancient peoples.

archaeopteryx, n. [1. àrkēóptериks; 2. ākiɔ́ptəriks], fr. Gk. *arkhaîos*, 'ancient', see **archaean**, & *ptérux*, 'wing', see **ptero-**. Name of a fossilized bird with marked reptilian characteristics, type of a link between birds and reptiles.

archaic, adj. [1. arkāik; 2. ākéi-ik], fr. Gk. *arkhāikós*, 'antiquated', fr. *arkhaios*, 'ancient'. See **arch-** & **archaean** & **-ic**. Old-fashioned, primitive, antiquated; (esp. of language) belonging to an early period, no longer in ordinary current use.

archaically, adv. [1. arkāikali; 2. ākéiikəli]. Prec. & **-al** & **-ly**. In an archaic manner, as an archaism.

archaism, n. [1. árkāizm; 2. ákei-izəm], fr. Gk. *arkhaios*, 'ancient'. See **archaean** & **-ism**. **a** Use of an old or obsolete word, idiom or form in speech, or literary style; **b** an obsolete word or expression.

archaist, n. [1. árkāist; 2. ákei-ist]. See prec. & **-ist**. One given to the use of, partial to, archaism.

archaistic, adj. [1. àrkāístik; 2. ākei-ístik]. Prec. & **-ic**. Characterized by archaism.

archaize, vb. trans. & intrans. [1. árkāīz; 2. ákeiaiz], fr. Gk. *arkhaizein*. See **archaic** & **-ize**. **1.** trans. To make archaic or archaistic. **2.** intrans. To use archaisms.

archangel, n. [1. àrkánjel; 2. ākéindžəl]. See **arch-** & **angel**. Principal, chief, angel.

archbishop, n. [1. àrchbíshup; 2. ātʃbíʃəp]. O.E. *ærcebiscop*. See **arch-** & **bishop**. Bishop at the head of an ecclesiastical province; metropolitan.

archbishopric, n. [1. àrchbíshuprik; 2. ātʃbíʃəprik]. See prec. & suff. in **bishopric**. **a** Ecclesiastical province over which an archbishop's jurisdiction extends; **b** office of an archbishop.

archdeacon, n. [1. àrchdékun; 2. ātʃdíkən]. O.E. *ærcediacon*. See **arch-** & **deacon**. Ecclesiastical dignitary, having special charge, under the bishop, of a part of a diocese, in respect of discipline and other matters. The archdeacon, as such, is a priest, though it may happen that he is in episcopal orders.

archdeaconry, n. [1. àrchdékunri; 2. ātʃdíkənri]. Prec. & **-ry**. A division of a diocese, made for ecclesiastical purposes, governed under the bishop, by an archdeacon.

archdiocese, n. [1. àrchdíosis; 2. ātʃdáiəsis]. See **arch-** & **diocese**. The diocese (as distinct from the province) ruled over by an archbishop.

archducal, adj. [1. àrchdúkal; 2. ātʃdjúkəl]. See **arch-** & **ducal**. Connected with an archduke.

archduchess, n. [1. àrchdúches; 2. ātʃdátʃis]. See **arch-** & **duchess**. Wife of an archduke; princess of the Imperial house of Austria.

archduchy, n. [1. àrchdúchi; 2. ātʃdátʃi]. See **arch-** & **duchy**. Territory ruled by an archduke.

archduke, n. [1. àrchdúk; 2. ātʃdjúk]. See **arch-** & **duke**. Prince of the Imperial house of Austria.

arch-enemy, n. [1. árch énemi; 2. átʃ énimi]. See **arch-** & **enemy**. Chief enemy; *the arch-enemy (of mankind)*, Satan.

archer, n. [1. árcher; 2. átʃə]. A.-Fr., O. Fr. *archier*, Lat. *arcārius*, fr. Lat. *arcus*, 'bow'. See **arc** & **-ary**. One who shoots with a bow and arrows; bowman.

archer fish, n. A small East Indian fish, *Toxotes jaculator*, which squirts drops of water at the insects on which it feeds.

archery, n. [1. árcheri; 2. átʃəri], fr. **archer** & **-y**. **a** Use of bow and arrow in war or in hunting; **b** the art of shooting with bow and arrows; **c** organized force of archers.

Arches, Court of, n. [1. árchez, kórt ov; 2. átʃiz, kɔ́t əv]. See **arch (I.)**. An ecclesiastical court of appeal for the province of Canterbury, originally sitting in St. Mary-le-Bow Church, *Beata Maria de Arcubus*; *Dean of Arches*, judge of this Court.

archetype, n. [1. árkitīp; 2. ákitaip], fr. Gk. *archétupon*, 'pattern, model'. See **arch-** & **-type**. Original pattern, prototype.

archfiend, n. [1. árchfénd; 2. átʃfínd]. See **arch-** & **fiend**. The chief, or worst, of fiends; Satan.

Archibald, n. [1. árchibawld; 2. átʃibōld]. (in Great War) Soldier's term for an anti-aircraft gun; usually abbreviated, Archie.

archidiaconal, adj. [1. àrchidīákunal, àrki-; 2. àtʃidaiækənəl, āki-]. See **arch-** & **diaconal**. Belonging to, connected with, an archdeacon or archdeacons.

archidiocese, n. See **archdiocese**.

archiepiscopacy, n. [1. àrchiepískopasi, àrki-; 2. ātʃi-ipískəpəsi, āki-]. See **arch-** & **episcopacy**. System of ecclesiastical government in which archbishops have chief power.

archiepiscopal, adj. [1. àrchiepískopal, àrki-; 2. ātʃi-ipískəpəl, āki-]. See **arch-** & **episcopal**. Belonging to, connected with, an archbishop or his office.

archiepiscopate, n. [1. àrchiepískopāt, àrki-; 2. ātʃi-ipískəpeit, āki-]. See **archi-** & **episcopate**. Office, reign, state, of an archbishop.

archil, n. [1. árchil; 2. átʃil]. O. Fr. *orchel*, Ital. *orcello*. Etymol. unknown. A violet dye obtained from lichen.

archimandrite, n. [1. àrkimándrīt; 2. ākimǽndrait]. L. Lat. *archimandrīta*, fr. L. Gk. *arkhimandrítēs*, 'principal of a monastery'. See **arch-**. *Mándra* meant orig. 'a stable, fold'. Cp. Scrt. *mandurā*, 'stable', *mandirám*, 'room, house, palace, temple'. (eccles.) In Greek Church the superior of a large monastery, or group of monasteries, corresponding to *abbot* in Western Church.

Archimedean, adj. [1. àrkimédian; 2. ākimídiən], fr. Archimedes, a Gk. mathematician c. 230 B.C. **a** Pertaining to Archimedes; **b** esp. *Archimedean principle*, (i.) the lever; (ii.) the doctrine of the relation of the weight of a body immersed in water, to the amount of water it displaces &c; *Archimedean screw*, one formerly used for raising water, rotating in a hollow cylinder, which is in a slanting position and partly immersed.

archipelago, n. [1. àrkipélagō; 2. ākipéləgou]. Ital. *arcipelago*, fr. Gk. *arkhi-*, 'chief', see **arch-**, & *pélagos*, 'sea', see **pelagic**. Lit. 'chief sea'. **1. a** The Aegean Sea between Greece and Asia Minor; hence, **b** any sea or sheet of water in which there are numerous islands. **2.** A group of islands.

architect, n. [1. árkitekt; 2. ákitekt]. Fr. *architecte*, fr. Lat. *architectus*, fr. Gk. *arkhitéktōn*, 'master-builder, director of works'. Gk. *téktōn*, 'carpenter, builder', is related to Gk. *tékhnē*, 'art, skill, craft' &c., & w. Scrt. *táksan*, 'carpenter'. See **arch-** & **technical**. **1.** A professional student of building as an art and a science, who designs buildings, draws plans, and directs process of construction; the term is extended also to a designer of ships, a *naval architect*. **2.** (fig.) One who creates, shapes, and moulds non-material things: *the architect of his fortunes*. Phr. *the Great Architect of the Universe*, God as Creator.

architectonic, adj. [1. àrkitektónik; 2. ākitektɔ́nik]. Gk. *arkhi-*, 'chief', & *tektonikós*, 'skilled in building'. See prec. **a** Related to architects and architecture; **b** constructive; **c** connected with the systematization of knowledge.

architectonics, n. pl., fr. prec. The architectural art and technique.

architectural, adj. [1. àrkitékchural; 2. ākitéktʃərəl]. **architecture** & **-al**. Connected with, having the qualities of, architecture.

architecturally, adv. Prec. & **-ly**. From point of view of, after the manner of, architecture.

architecture, n. [1. árkitekchur; 2. ákitektʃə]. Fr., fr. Lat. *architectūra*. See **architect** & **-ure**. **1.** The science and art of building and construction in masonry, esp. of houses, churches, bridges. **2.** Style, mode, design of building, as having certain distinguishing features according to the period and nationality of the work. **3.** Construction generally, creative workmanship: *the architecture of a parliamentary bill, of a speech* &c.

architrave, n. [1. árkitrāv; 2. ákitreiv], fr. Ital. *architrave*, fr. Gk. *archi-*, see **arch-**, & Lat. *trabs, trabis*, 'a beam'. See **trabeation**. (archit.) **a** Lowest part of the entablature which rests directly upon the column; **b** moulding above and on either side of the top of the opening of a door or window.

archival, adj. [1. àrkíval; 2. ākáivəl]. See **archive** & **-al**. Belonging to, contained in, archives.

archive(s), n. [1. árkīv(z); 2. ákaiv(z)]. Fr., fr. L. Lat. *archī(v)um*, fr. Gk. *arkheîon*, 'public building, residence of chief magistrate'. Cp. **archon** & see **arch-**. **a** Place where public records and documents are kept; **b** records and historical documents stored in such a place.

archivist, n. [1. árkivist; 2. ákivist]. Prec. & **-ist**. Keeper of public records.

archivolt, n. [1. árkivolt; 2. ákivəlt], fr. Ital. *archivolto*, fr. Lat. *arcus*, 'bow, arch', see **arch (I.)**, & *volto*, q.v. under **vault**. Inner part of curve of an arch; moulding surrounding the curve of an arch.

archon, n. [1. árkon; 2. ákən]. Gk. *árkhōn*, 'ruler, magistrate', fr. *árkhō*, 'I rule'. See this base under **arch-**. One of the nine chief magistrates of ancient Athens.

archpriest, n. [1. árchprést; 2. átʃpríst]. See **arch-** & **priest**. Formerly a priest who acted as chief assistant under a bishop.

archway, n. [1. árchwā; 2. átʃwei]. See **arch (I.)** & **way**. Passage going through an arch.

arciform, adj. [1. árkifōrm; 2. ákifōm], fr. Lat. *arcus*, 'bow'. See **arch (I.)** & **-form**. Curved, shaped, like a bow or arch.

arctic, adj. & n. [1. árktik; 2. áktik], fr. Lat. *arcticus*, fr. Gk. *arktikós*, 'of the Bear, northern', fr. *árktos*, 'bear; the constellation of the Great Bear, the North'; w. *árktos* cp. the cognates Lat. *ursus*, fr. **urcsos*, see **Ursa**, Scrt. *ṛkšaš*, W. *arth*. **1.** adj. **a** Belonging to the extreme Northern latitudes; polar; **b** very cold, as in arctic regions: *the weather has become absolutely arctic*. **2.** n. (usually cap.) The arctic circle or regions.

arcuate(d), adj. [1. árkuat(ed); 2. ákjueit(id)], fr. Lat. *arcuātus*, P.P. of *arcuāre*, 'to curve like a bow', fr. *arcus*, 'bow'. See **arc**. Curved, bent, like a bow.

arcuation, n. [1. àrkūáshun; 2. ākjuéiʃən]. Prec. & **-ion**. **a** Act of curving or arching; **b** (archit.) use of arches in building; **c** series of arches.

-ard, suff. [1. ard; 2. əd], forming ns., fr. O. Fr., fr. Gmc., cogn. w. **hard**; also spelled **-art**; as in *drunkard, sluggard, braggart* &c.

ardency, n. [1. árdensi; 2. ádənsi]. See next word & **-cy**. Condition of being ardent; heat of emotion; vehemence.

ardent, adj. [1. árdent; 2. ádənt], fr. Lat. *ardent-(em)*, Pres. Part. of *ardēre* for **āridēre*, 'to burn, glow', lit. & fig., fr. *āridus*, 'parched', w. wh. cp. also *ārēre*, 'become dry' &c. The *r* in these Lat. words is for *z*, earlier *s*; the base was therefore orig. **as-*, & is found in Scrt. *ása-*, 'ash, dust', *ásita-*, 'black, ash-coloured'; the same base appears in Gmc. w. an additional formative suff., Goth. *azgō*, 'ash', O.H.G. *asca*, O.E. *æsc(e)*. See further under **ash (I.)** & **arid**. **1.** Burning, fiery, hot, glowing, shining. The figurative use is now more common than the literal. The latter survives, however, in *ardent heat* (esp. of sun); *ardent spirits*, referring to parching, hot effect on the throat. **2.** Otherwise, the word is applied, **a** to emotional states, to express vehemence: *ardent love, hate, hopes, desires* &c.; **b** to persons, in sense of eager, zealous: *an ardent admirer, supporter* &c.

ardently, adv. Prec. & **-ly**. In an ardent, eager manner; with ardour, eagerly.

ardour, n. [1. árdur; 2. ádə]. Lat. *ardor*, 'heat, flame'; also 'eagerness'. See **ardent** & **-or**. **a** Warmth, violence, of passion, emotion, feelings; **b** zeal, earnestness: *patriotic, religious ardour.*

arduous, adj. [1. árdūus; 2. ádjuəs], fr. Lat. *arduus*, 'high, steep, difficult', cogn. w. Gk. *orthós*, 'straight, erect'. See **ortho-**, also **arboreal**. **1.** High, steep, difficult to climb (obs.): '*arduous paths*' (Pope). **2.** Difficult to accomplish, laborious, severe: *an arduous task.* **3.** (of persons, transferred sense) Capable of accomplishing difficult tasks, therefore energetic, strenuous.

arduously, adv. Prec. & **-ly**. With hard work and toil; laboriously.

arduousness, n. See prec. & **-ness**. State, quality, of being arduous.

are (I.), vb. [1. ar; 2. ā] &c., pres. pl. indic. of **be**, fr. O.E. Northumbrian type *aron*, M.E. *āre(n)*. *Ar-* here is fr. earlier **az-*, Aryan **os-*, w. wh. cp. forms w. different gradation in *es-*, q.v. under **am**.

are (II.), n. [1. ar; 2. ā]. Fr., fr. Lat. *ārea*. See next word. In metric system, a unit of surface = 100 sq. metres, 119·6 sq. yards.

area, n. [1. ária; 2. éəriə]. Lat. *ārea*, 'vacant piece of ground (esp. in a town), building plot'. Origin doubtful; perh. related to Lith. *óras*, 'the open air'. **1.** Space, extent of ground, whether enclosed or not; it may be applied to **a** the surface expanse of floor of a building, such as a church or hall; **b** enclosed space upon which a building stands; **c** specif., sunk, paved court or yard, before a town house, railed off from street, approached from ground level by steps, and giving access and light to basement. **2.** Particular tract of the earth's surface, region: *wheat-growing area; areas of population.* **3.** (fig.) Range, scope: *area of thought, investigation* &c.

areca, n. [1. áreka, aréka; 2. ǽrikə, ərīkə]. Port., fr. Canarese. Species of palm found in parts of Asia, and in Malay Archipelago, bearing pungent, astringent fruit.

areca nut, n. Fruit of areca, used for chewing; betel.

arena, n. [1. aréna; 2. ərīnə]. Lat. *arēna*, *harēna*, 'sand, sandy place; seashore; place of combat (fr. being strewn with sand) in Roman amphitheatre'; hence 'the combats in the amphitheatre'; prob. fr. **ghasesnā*, & cogn. w. M. Ir. *ganem*, 'sand', fr. **ghasnimā*; further relationships doubtful. **1.** Used in above Latin senses, except that the notion of sand has been entirely lost. **2.** (fig.) The scene of any conflict or vigorous action: *the arena of the World War; to enter the arena of politics.*

arenaceous, adj. [1. àrenáshus; 2. æ̀rənéiʃəs], formed fr. Lat. *arēnāce-(us)*, 'sandy', & *-ōsus*, fr. *arēna*, 'sand'. See prec. & **-aceous**. Sandy, resembling sand.

areola, n. [1. aréola; 2. ərīələ]. Lat., 'small open space', dimin. of **area**. **a** Very small area, e.g. between veins of a leaf, or between the stiffening ribs of an insect's wing; **b** (anat., med.) rosy circle surrounding nipple; red inflamed ring round a pustule.

areometer, n. [1. àreómeter; 2. æ̀riɔ́mitə], fr. Gk. *araiós*, 'thin, not dense, rare'; cogn. w. Scrt. *ṛté*, 'without'; O. Slav. *oriti*, 'to dissolve'; & perh. w. Gk. *érēmos*, 'solitary', see **hermit**; & **-meter**. Hydrometer.

Areopagite, n. [1. àreópagīt; 2. æ̀riɔ́pəgait], fr. Gk. *Areiopagītēs*. See next word. (Gk. hist.) Member of the Areopagus.

Areopagus, n. [1. àreópagus; 2. æ̀riɔ́pəgəs]. Lat., fr. Gk. *Areiópagos*, also *Areios págos*, 'hill of Ares or Mars'. For the second element see under **pax**. (Gk. hist.) **a** Hill west of the Acropolis, Athens, seat of an ancient judicial tribunal. **b** this tribunal.

arête, n. [1. arát; 2. æréit]. Fr., 'a fish-bone', also 'sharp ridge of roofing', fr. Lat. *arista*, 'awn or beard of an ear of grain'; origin uncertain. Sharp ridge or crest of mountain.

argala, n. [1. árgala; 2. ágələ]. Hind. *hargila*. Large Indian stork, adjutant-bird.

argali, n. [1. árgali; 2. ágəli]. Tatar name. Large, wild Asiatic sheep, *Ovis ammon*, with large, curved horns.

argand burner, n. [1. árgand bérner; 2. ágænd bə́nə]. Burner (for gas) for the argand lamp.

argand lamp, n. [1. árgand làmp; 2. ágənd læ̀mp], fr. name of Swiss physicist, Aimé Argand (1755–1803). Lamp with cylindrical wick, allowing current of air inside as well as out.

argent, n. & adj. [1. árjent; 2. ádžənt]. Fr., fr. Lat. *argentum*, lit. 'the white metal, silver'; cp. Gk. *argós*, 'bright, white'. See **argil**. **1.** n. **a** The metal silver (archaic or poet.); **b** (poet.) whiteness, something white: '*The polished argent of her breast*' (Tennyson); **c** (her.) silver tincture on shield. **2.** adj. Resembling silver, silvery-white, white.

argentiferous, adj. [1. àrjentíferus; 2. àdžəntífərəs]. See **argent** & **-ferous**. (of ore) Containing silver.

argentine, adj. [1. árjentīn; 2. ádžəntain]. Lat. *argentīnus*, 'of silver'. **argent** & **-ine**. Resembling silver in colour; made of silver; giving out a clear silvery sound when struck.

argil, n. [1. árjil; 2. ádžil], fr. Fr. *argile*, 'clay', fr. Lat. *argilla*, fr. Gk. *árgillos*, 'white clay, potter's earth'. Cp. Gk. *argḗs*, 'white', *argós*, 'shining, bright, glistening'; the last word, & not 'white', is apparently the primitive sense. Cp. the cogn. Scrt. *ṛjráś*, 'red, glowing'. See **argent**. Potter's clay.

argillaceous, adj. [1. àrjiláshus; 2. àdžiléiʃəs], fr. prec. & **-aceous**. Resembling, having nature of, containing, clay; clayey.

argilliferous, adj. [1. àrjilíferus; 2. àdžilífərəs]. See **argil** & **-ferous**. Bearing, rich in, clay.

Argive, n. [1. árjīv; 2. ádžaiv]. Lat. *Argīvus*, 'a Greek of Argos; a Greek', fr. *Argos* & **-ive**. **a** An inhabitant of Argos in Peloponnesus; **b** (by extension) any (ancient) Greek (poet.).

argon, n. [1. árgon; 2. ágɔn], fr. Gk. *argós*, 'idle, inert', fr. *aergós*, fr. **a-**, 'not, without', & *érgon*, 'work'. See **ergon**, & cp. also **work**. (chem.) Inert gas existing in the atmosphere.

Argonaut, n. [1. árgonawt; 2. ágənɔ̄t], fr. Lat. *Argonauta*, fr. Gk. *Argonaútēs*, 'a sailor in the ship Argo', fr. *Argṓ* & *naútēs*, 'sailor'. See **nautical**. **1.** (Gk. mythol.) One of the heroes who sailed with Jason in the ship Argo in quest of the Golden Fleece. **2.** (zool.) Genus of mollusc, allied to the cuttle-fish, found in the Mediterranean; the paper nautilus.

argosy, n. [1. árgosi; 2. ágəsi]. Formerly *Ragusyes* (in pl.), 'richly laden merchantships', from the Dalmatian port Ragusa. Large ship, esp. a merchantman.

argot, n. [1. árgō; 2. ágou]. Fr. Etymol. unknown. Low, popular slang, esp. of Paris. Specif., thieves' slang.

arguable, adj. [1. árgūabl; 2. ágjuəbl]. See **argue** & **-able**. (of a proposition) Having sufficient probability, basis of possible truth, to be capable of support by argument.

argue, vb. trans. & intrans. [1. árgū; 2. ágju], fr. O. Fr. *arguer*, fr. Lat. *argūtāre*, freq. of *arguere*, 'make clear, prove'; fr. same base as Lat. *argentum*, 'silver', see **argent**, the primitive meaning of wh. is 'shining, clear'. Cp. **argute**. **A.** trans. **1. a** To debate, discuss, bring reasons for and against: *to argue a case, question* &c.; **b** to persuade by discussion and reasoning: *to argue a man out of an opinion* &c. **2.** To prove, indicate: *his action argues him a man of weak intelligence.* **B.** intrans. To maintain an opinion by giving reasons; to reason, dispute keenly: *to argue in favour of a theory* &c.; *to argue that black is white. Argue against* (a person), oppose in argument; (a proposition) try to prove by argument that it is false; *argue about* (a thing), dispute concerning; *argue with* (a person), exchange arguments with.

argument, n. [1. árgūment; 2. ágjumənt]. Fr., fr. Lat. *argūmentum*, 'argument, proof, evidence', fr. *arguere*. See prec. & **-ment**. **1.** Reasons, line of reasoning, adopted for purpose of convincing others of truth of a proposition; reason, or series of reasons adduced to influence, and persuade to acceptance of conclusions: *strong, weak, unconvincing, argument(s).* **2.** Process of reasoning, controversy, discussion, debate: *to rely on, trust to, argument for persuasion.* **3.** Summary of the subject-matter of a book, plot of a story &c.

argumentation, n. [1. àrgūmentáshun; 2. àgjumentéiʃən]. Fr. *argumentacion*, fr. Lat. *argūmentātiōn-(em)*, 'adducing of proof', fr. *argūmentāri*, 'to argue', see **argument**, & **-ation**. Act, process, of adducing reasons and drawing conclusions; debate.

argumentative, adj. [1. àrgūméntativ; 2. àgjuméntətiv]. Fr. *argumentatif*, see prec. & **-ive**. **a** (of persons) Fond of, given to dispute and argument; disputatious; **b** (of utterances &c.) abounding in, characterized by, argument; controversial.

argumentatively, adv. Prec. & **-ly**. In an argumentative manner.

argumentativeness, n. See prec. & **-ness**. Argumentative, disputatious habit of mind.

Argus, n. [1. árgus; 2. ágəs]. Lat. *Argus*, fr. Gk. *Argós*, a mythological person with a hundred eyes. Chiefly in *argus-eyed*, keen-sighted, observant, vigilant; *argus-pheasant*, n., a bird of the East Indies, resembling a pheasant, but allied to the peacock, the male having large, ocellated wing-feathers and tail.

argute, adj. [1. árgūt; 2. ágjūt]. Lat. *argūtus*, lit. 'made clear, clear, sharp; acute, witty, cunning', &c., fr. *arguere*, 'make clear'. See **argue**. Quick, sharp (in physical or mental activities).

argyrodite, n. [1. árjirōdīt; 2. ádžiroudait], fr. Gk. *argurṓdes*, 'rich in silver', fr. *árguros*, 'silver', fr. *argós*, 'shining, bright', see **argil**, & *eîdos*, 'shape, form', see **idol** & **idea**. A rare, steel-grey mineral, containing silver and germanium.

aria, n. [1. áhria; 2. ária]. Ital., fr. Lat. *āēr*, 'air'. See **air**. (mus.) An air, tune, melody; esp. elaborate air sung by a single voice in an oratorio.

Arian, adj. & n. [1. árian; 2. éəriən], fr. Lat. *Ariānus*, fr. *Arius*, *Arīus*, Gk. *Arīos*, *Areîos*, name of a heretic of Alexandria in 4th cent. A.D., who taught that Christ is merely the first and noblest of all created things; that the Son is not of the same substance as the Father. **a** adj. Pertaining to the doctrine of Arius; **b** n., one who holds this doctrine.

-arian, suff. [1. árian; 2. éəriən], fr. Lat. *-āri(us)* & *-ān(us)*. See **-ary** & **-an**. Used in forming adjs. & ns.; generally a sect, class, school of thought &c., e.g. *proletarian, humanitarian, Unitarian.*

Arianism, n. [1. árianizm; 2. éəriənizəm]. **Arian** & **-ism**. The heretical doctrines of Arius and the Arians.

arid, adj. [1. árid; 2. ǽrid], fr. Lat. *āridus*, 'dry, parched', fr. *ārēre*, 'to be dry'. See **ardent**. **a** (of soil &c.) Dry, parched; barren; **b** (fig., of the mind and the products of mental activity) barren, jejune, uninteresting.

aridity, n. [1. aríditi; 2. æríditi]. Fr. *aridité*, Lat. *āriditāt-(em)*, 'dryness', fr. *āridus*, see **arid**, & **-ity**. State of being arid (lit. and fig.).

ariel, n. [1. áriel; 2. éəriəl]. Arab. *aryil*, 'stag'. Arabian gazelle.

Aries, n. [1. áriēz; 2. éəriīz]. Lat., 'ram', genit. *arietis*. Cp. Gk. *ériphos*, 'kid', Lith. *erýtis*, 'lamb', Ir. *earb*, 'kid'. (astron.) Constellation, the first of signs of the zodiac.

aright, adv. [1. arīt; 2. ərait]. **a-**, for *on*, & **right**. Rightly.

aril, n. [1. áril; 2. ǽril], fr. Low Lat. *arillus*, 'dried grape'. (bot.) An accessory seed-covering, developing after fertilization, as in the passion flower.

arioso, adv. [1. ahriṓsō; 2. ariósо]. Ital., fr. **aria**, & *-oso* = Lat. *-ōsus*, adj. suff. See **-ous**. (mus.) In a flowing, melodious manner.

arise, vb. intrans. [1. aríz; 2. əráiz]. **a- & rise.** **1.** (archaic and poet.) To get up, rise from bed, from recumbent position, from lower to higher position; (of persons, and esp. of heavenly bodies). **2.** To spring up; to come into existence, action, notice; be born: *great confusion arose*; *many false prophets shall arise*; *many great men have arisen from very humble beginnings*; (fig., of sound) *a shout arose from the crowd*, became audible. **3.** To spring from, proceed, issue, result from: *great consequences may arise from trifling causes*; *nothing arises out of that statement.*

arista, n. [1. arísta; 2. əristə]. Lat. See **arête.** (bot.) The awn or beard of grain, grasses &c.

aristate, adj. [1. arístāt; 2. əristeit], fr. prec. & **-ate.** Bearded (of grains).

aristocracy, n. [1. àristókrasi; 2. æ̀ristókrəsi]. Fr. *aristocratie*, fr. Lat. *aristocratia*, fr. Gk. *aristokratia*, 'rule of the best', fr. *áristos*, 'best'; cp. Gk. *areiōn*, 'better', *aretē*, 'virtue', *aréskein*, 'to make good, conciliate, please' &c., & see **-cracy.** **1.** Government by the best citizens (i.e. those most distinguished by birth, fortune &c.); therefore, government by a small class; oligarchy. **2.** Body from whom ruling class comes; the nobility of birth. **3.** Best and most distinguished representatives of a body, class: *aristocracy of talent, intellect* &c.

aristocrat, n. [1. áristokrat; 2. ǽristəkræt], fr. Fr. *aristocrate*, fr. *aristocratie*, *aristocratique*. See prec. & **-crat.** Person of ancient and distinguished birth; a member of the hereditary nobility, whether titled or not.

aristocratic, adj. [1. àristokrátik; 2. æ̀ristəkrǽtik], fr. Fr. *aristocratique*, fr. Gk. *aristokratikós*. See prec. & **-ic.** **1.** Pertaining to, favouring, an aristocracy: *to have aristocratic leanings, sympathies* &c. **2.** Belonging to the aristocracy by birth, well-born; resembling an aristocrat; having distinguished bearing and manners.

aristocratical, adj. [1. àristokrátikl; 2. æ̀ristəkrǽtikl]. Prec. & **-al.** (rare) Aristocratic.

aristocratically, adv. Prec. & **-ly.** In the manner of, like, an aristocracy or aristocrats.

arithmetic, n. [1. aríthmetik; 2. əríþmətik], fr. Lat. *arithmētica*, fr. Gk. *hē arithmētikḗ* (sc. *tékhnē*), 'art of counting', fr. *arithmētikós*, adj., fr. *arithméō*, 'I number, count, reckon up', fr. *arithmós*, 'number; a numbering or counting', perh. connected w. Lat. *reor*, P.P. *ratus*, 'to think, imagine', & Lat. *ratio*, 'process of thinking, reckoning', see **rate (I.)**, also w. Goth. *raþjō*, 'number, account'. **a** The science of numbers; art of computing; **b** treatise on this subject.

arithmetical, adj. [1. àrithmétikl; 2. æ̀riþmétikl]. Prec. & **-al.** Pertaining to, connected with, based on, arithmetic.

arithmetically, adv. Prec. & **-ly.** By means of arithmetic.

arithmetician, n. [1. arìthmetíshun; 2. əriþmətíʃən]. See **arithmetic & -ician.** One proficient in arithmetic.

arithmometer, n. [1. àrithmómeter; 2. æ̀riþmɔ́mitə], fr. Fr. *arithmomètre*, fr. Gk. *arithmós*, 'number', see **arithmetic, & -meter.** A calculating machine.

ark, n. [1. ark; 2. āk]. O.E. *arc*, *earc*, 'Noah's Ark, a box, coffin', fr. Lat. *arca*, 'chest'. See **arcanum.** **1.** A chest, receptacle (rare and poet.); specif., *Ark of the Covenant*, Jewish receptacle of sacred things. **2.** Specif. **a** the vessel in which Noah was saved from the Flood; **b** *Noah's ark*, child's toy in imitation of the ark, containing wooden figures supposed to resemble men and animals.

arles, n. [1. arlz; 2. ālz]. Scots & Nthn. variant of obs. *erles*. See **earnest (III.).** Earnest-money.

arm (I.), n. [1. arm; 2. ām]. O.E. *earm*, *arm*, Common Gmc. *arm-, cogn. w. Lat. *armus*, 'shoulder where it joins the shoulder-blade', Gk. *harmós*, 'joint', fr. same orig. base as **arm (II.).** **1.** Upper limb of the human body between the shoulder and the hand. Phrs. *to walk arm-in-arm (with)*; *to give, offer, one's arm (to)*; *to take one's arm*; *to receive a person with open arms*, very cordially; *a child in arms*, very young child who must be carried; *to keep (a person) at arm's length*, treat coldly; *make a long arm*, stretch arm out to its fullest length. **2. a** Part of clothing covering an arm; a sleeve: *the arm of a coat*; **b** that part of a chair or other seat which supports the arm of sitter. **3.** (fig.) Grip, power, authority: *the arm of the law.* **4.** Anything remotely resembling the arm in shape: *arm of a tree*, big branch; *of a river*, river fork; *of the sea*, estuary.

arm (II.), n., commonly in pl., **arms**, fr. Fr. *arme*, fr. Lat. *arma* (only in pl.), 'implements of war, weapons'; also 'implements of agriculture, the tackle of a ship' &c.; ultimately fr. same base *ar-, 'join, fix' &c., as seen in **arm (I.)**; cp. further, Gk. *hárma*, 'chariot, chariot and horses', *ármena*, 'tackle, rigging of a ship, any tools or implements'; *armózein*, 'to fit together, join, prepare, make ready'. See also **art, arthritis.** **1.** Weapon, instrument of attack or defence: *fire-arm*; *small arms*, pistol, rifle. Phrs. *to take up arms (against)*, enter into hostilities; *to arms*., call to take up arms; *to bear arms*, to be a soldier; *to lay down arms*, cease hostilities, either **a** to surrender, or **b** to grant peace; *in arms*, armed, ready to fight; *up in arms*, roused to indignant protest; *under arms*, armed and organized as fighting force; *deeds of arms*, military exploits. **2.** A branch of the fighting services of a state; the cavalry, infantry, or artillery; also of navy or air-force. **3.** pl. (her.) Devices borne by members of a family on a shield, banner &c. as hereditary marks of distinction; similar heraldic devices used by countries, cities, institutions &c.; *coat of arms*, shield bearing proper heraldic devices; *King at, of, Arms*, one of the chief officials at Herald's Office or College of Arms; *sergeant at arms*, the mace-bearer of the Lord Chancellor and Speaker, responsible for discipline.

arm (III.), vb. trans. & intrans., fr. Fr. *armer*, fr. Lat. *armāre*, 'to furnish with weapons, implements &c.; to equip'. See prec. **A.** trans. **1.** To furnish, equip, with weapons. **2. a** To furnish with tools, or appliances, suitable for particular work, or to meet circumstances (extended to any form of equipment): *to be armed with umbrella and goloshes*; **b** (of mental and moral preparation) *to be armed at all points, with information, arguments* &c. **3.** (reflex.) *to arm oneself* (lit. and fig.). **B.** intrans. To take up, provide oneself with, arms: *war is certain, we should arm without delay.*

armada, n. [1. armáda; 2. āméidə]. Span., fr. Lat. *armātus, -a, -um*, 'equipped, armed', P.P. of *armāre*. See **arm (III.).** A fleet of warships, specif. that fleet sent by Philip II. of Spain against England in 1588: *the Spanish*, also *Invincible, Armada.*

armadillo, n. [1. armadílō; 2. āmədílou]. Span. dimin. of *armado*, 'armed creature', fr. Lat. *armātus*, P.P. of *armāre*. See **arm (III.).** (zool.) S. American toothless, burrowing mammal, which is protected by small hard bony plates resembling armour.

Armageddon, n. [1. àrmagédon; 2. ȧməgédən], fr. Gk. *Harmagedon*, in Rev. xvi. 16; etymol. doubtful, usually taken as equiv. to Heb. *har megiddon*, district of Megiddo, in Palestine, scene of many great battles; possibly the word represents the name of an old Babylonian deity. **a** Place where the last great battle before the Day of Judgement is to be fought; **b** (by transf.) a great final or decisive battle between the nations.

armament, n. [1. ármament; 2. ámәmәnt], fr. Lat. *armāmenta* (pl.), 'implements, fittings for any purpose', fr. *armāre*, 'to arm, equip'. See **arm (III.) & -ment.** **a** Forces, esp. naval, equipped and armed for war; **b** great guns of men-of-war, together with torpedoes and ammunition of all kinds; **c** act or process of fitting out army and navy for war.

armature, n. [1. ármachur; 2. ámətʃə]. Lat. *armātūra*, 'armour', fr. *armāre*, 'to arm'. See **arm (III.).** **1. a** Armour, anything worn to protect the body; hence, **b** any covering of a protective character, e.g. means of protection of animals or plants, wire covering round a cable &c. Specif. **2. a** (elect.) core of laminated iron wound round by coils of insulated copper-wire, the part of a dynamo which rotates in the magnetic field; **b** a short bar of iron across the poles of a horse-shoe magnet.

armchair, n. [1. ármchâr; 2. ámtʃέə]. See **arm (I.) & chair.** Chair with supports for the arms.

arme blanche, n. [1. arm blahnsh; 2. ārm blɑ̃ʃ]. Fr., 'white arm'. **a** The cavalry sabre; **b** cavalry.

armed (I.), adj. [1. armd; 2. āmd]. **arm (I.) & -ed.** Relating to the human arm; usually in compounds, *long-armed*, *white-armed* &c.

armed (II.), adj., fr. P.P. of **arm (III.).** Furnished with weapons.

armet, n. [1. ármet; 2. ámεt], fr. O. Fr. *armetta*, dimin. of *arme*. See **arm (II.) & -et.** A steel helmet, of the 15th cent., with closely fitting round head-piece, a movable visor, and a jointed neck-piece.

armful, n. [1. ármfool; 2. ámful]. See **arm (I.) & -ful.** As much as can be held in the arms; hence, a large quantity: *an armful of hay.*

armiger, n. [1. ármijer; 2. ámidžə]. Lat., 'weapon-bearer', fr. *arma*, 'weapons', & *gerere*, 'to bear, carry'. See **gerent.** An esquire; person possessing, and entitled to bear, heraldic arms.

armigerous, adj. [1. armíjerus; 2. āmídžərəs], fr. prec. & **-ous.** Possessing, entitled to bear, arms: *an armigerous family.*

armillary, adj. [1. armílari; 2. āmíləri], fr. Lat. *armilla*, 'armlet, bracelet', fr. *armus*, 'shoulder', see **arm (I.), & -ary.** **a** Pertaining to a bracelet or ring; **b** consisting of rings, or spheres. *Armillary sphere*, ancient astronomical instrument consisting of a hollow sphere made up of series of circles, and turning upon its polar axis.

arming, n. [1. árming; 2. ámiŋ]. See **arm (III.) & -ing.** **a** Act or process of supplying arms; **b** heraldic arms.

Arminian, n. & adj. [1. armínian; 2. āmíniən], fr. Arminius, Dutch theologian, d. 1609. **a** n. Adherent of Arminianism; **b** adj., pertaining to Arminianism.

Arminianism, n. [1. armínianizm; 2. āmíniənizəm]. Prec. & **-ism.** The anti-Calvinistic theological doctrines of Arminius.

armistice, n. [1. ármistis; 2. ámistis]. Fr., fr. Low Lat. *armistitium, fr. Lat. *arma*, 'weapons' (see **arm (II.)**), & *-sistere*, *-stitum* (in compounds), fr. *sistere*, 'to cause to stand (still), stop', fr. *stāre*, 'to stand', see **state**, on anal. of *solstitium*, 'standing still of the sun'. (mil.) A suspension of hostilities by mutual agreement between belligerents; a truce.

armlet, n. [1. ármlet; 2. ámlit]. **arm (I.) & -let.** **1.** Band, or circlet, of cloth or other material worn round the arm. **2.** A small inlet of the sea; branch of a river.

armorial, adj. & n. [1. armórial; 2. āmɔ́riəl]. See **armory & -al.** (her.) **a** adj. Pertaining to heraldic arms: *armorial bearings*; **b** n., a book of coats of arms.

armory, n. [1. ármori; 2. áməri], fr. O. Fr. *armoierie*, *armoirie*, fr. *armoier*, *armoyer*, 'to blazon heraldic arms', fr. Lat. *arma* 'arms', see **arm (II.).** Science and art of heraldry.

armour (I.), n. [1. ármur; 2. ámə], fr. O. Fr. *armeüre*, fr. Lat. *armātūra*. See **armature.** **1.** Protective covering for the body in war, made either of chain mail, or of metal plates fitted to the trunk, arms, legs, and head (that for the latter being the *helmet*), and riveted together. **2.** Steel plates used to protect ships, forts, motor-cars, tanks &c. from artillery or rifle fire.

armour (II.), vb. trans., fr. prec. To furnish

with steel plates as a protective covering; usually in P.P., **armoured.**

armour-bearer, n. See **armour (I.)** & **bearer.** Man who carried the armour of a superior.

armour-clad, adj. See **armour (I.)** & **clad.** Covered, protected, by armour: *armour-clad warriors; armour-clad ships.*

armoured, adj. [1. ármurd; 2. ámәd], fr. P.P. of **armour (II.).** Furnished with, protected by, armour: *armoured cruiser.*

armourer, n. [1. ármurer; 2. ámәrә], fr. O. Fr. *armurier, armeurier,* fr. *armeüre,* 'armour'. See **armour (I.)** & **-er. 1. a** Formerly, one who made, repaired, cleaned, and fitted armour; **b** one who makes and repairs arms. **2.** One in charge of the small arms of a ship or a regiment.

armour-plate, n. See **armour (I.)** & **plate.** Steel plate used as armour of ships.

armour-plated, adj. Provided with armour-plate.

armoury, n. [1. ármuri; 2. ámәri]. **armour (I.)** & **-y.** Place where arms of war are kept.

army, n. [1. ármi; 2. ámi], fr. Fr. *armée,* lit. 'armed force', cogn. w. Span. **armada,** Ital. *armata,* fr. Lat. *armātus,* P.P. of *armāre,* 'to arm'. See **arm (II. & III.). 1. a** Organized body of men, trained, armed, and equipped for fighting against the enemies of their country; specif. **b** the whole of such men belonging to a state: *Great Britain's army is very small in relation to her responsibilities;* Phr. *to enter, go into, join, the army; standing army,* one consisting of professional soldiers, permanently under arms; **c** military unit consisting of two army corps, commanded by a general. **2.** An organized body of persons engaged in special work: *Salvation Army.* **3.** A very large number, great multitude: *a whole army of workmen were engaged upon the new road.*

army corps, n. See **army** & **corps.** Military unit consisting (in the Great War, according to English organization) of three infantry divisions, with various corps troops of artillery, engineers, cavalry, and auxiliary services, commanded by a lieutenant-general.

army list, n. See **army** & **list.** Official list published at regular intervals, giving name, rank, regiment, or actual post, of every officer holding His Majesty's commission.

arnica, n. [1. árnika; 2. ánikә]. Etymol. unknown. **a** Genus of plants; **b** drug or tincture made from the root of the plant, used for sprains, bruises &c.

aroint, interj. [1. aróint; 2. әróint]. Etymol. doubtful. Skeat suggests derivation fr. O.E. (*ġe*)*rȳm* (*þū*), 'make room', fr. O.E. *rūm,* 'spacious, wide'. See **room.** Usually in Phr. *aroint thee!,* Be off! Begone! (obs.)

aroma, n. [1. aróma; 2. әróumә]. Lat., fr. Gk. *árōma,* 'seasoning, spice'. Etymol. obscure. Fragrance; delicate, clinging perfume, flavour; (also fig.) characteristic quality or atmosphere in work of art.

aromatic, adj. [1. àromátik; 2. ærәmǽtik], fr. Fr. *aromatique,* fr. Lat. *arōmaticus,* fr. Gk. *arōmatikós.* See **aroma** & **-atic.** Giving off a fragrant, spicy odour.

arose, vb. [1. arṓz; 2. әróuz]. Pret. of **arise.** O.E. *ārās,* M.E. *aroos.*

around, adv. & prep. [1. aróund; 2. әráund]. **a-,** fr. *on,* & **round. 1.** adv. See **round (I.)** Round about, in circles, to and fro in the neighbourhood: *to prowl around;* (colloq.) *to hang, fool, around.* **2.** prep. See **round (II.).** On all sides of, about, encompassing.

arousal, n. [1. aróuzal; 2. әráuzәl]. See next word & **-al.** (rare or archaic) The act of arousing; the fact of being aroused.

arouse, vb. trans. [1. aróuz; 2. әráuz]. See **a-** & **rouse. a** (of persons) To awaken from sleep, stir up from inactivity; **b** (of passions, emotions) to excite, cause to become active.

arpeggio, n. [1. arpéjō; 2. ā(r)pédžo]. Ital., fr. *arpeggiare,* 'play the harp', fr. *arpa,* 'harp', see **harp.** (mus.) Playing of notes of a chord in rapid succession, resembling harp-playing, instead of simultaneously.

arquebus, also **harquebus,** n. [1. árkwibus; 2. ákwibәs], fr. Fr. (*h*)*arquebuse,* fr. Ital. *archibuso;* of Gmc. origin, cp. M.H.G. *hakenbüchse* & L.G. *hakkebuse,* lit. 'hook gun', so called because orig. slung fr. a hook; the first element is cogn. w. **hook,** but has been influenced by Ital. *arco,* bow for shooting'; the second element is Germ. *büchse,* 'box', then 'a gun'. See **box,** & cp. *-bus* in **blunderbus.** The earliest form of hand-gun, precursor of the musket; it was of large bore, and had a hook near the muzzle by which it could be attached to a rest stuck in the ground from which it was fired.

arquebusier, harquebusier, n. [1. àrkwibûzier; 2. ākwibjūziә]. Prec. & **-ier.** Soldier armed with an arquebus.

arrack, n. [1. árak; 2. ǽræk]. O. Fr., fr. Arab. *'arak,* wh. meant first 'sweat', then 'the exudation of sap drawn from date palm'; finally, 'strong drink, distilled spirit' (Yule and Burnell). In the East the name is also applied to spirit made from rice or molasses.

arraign (I.), vb. trans. [1. arán; 2. әréin]. M.E. *areinen* &c., fr. A.-Fr. *aresner, arreiner,* fr. Lat. **ad-,** 'to', *ratiōn-*(*em*), 'reason, account'. See **ratio** & **rate (I.). 1.** (law) To indict on a criminal charge. Hence, **2,** to call to account, call in question, examine publicly and critically: *to arraign before the bar of public opinion.*

arraign (II.), n., fr. prec. (law) Arraignment, indictment, only in *Clerk of Arraigns,* deputy of the Clerk of Assize, who reads the indictment.

arraignment, n. [1. aránment; 2. әréinmәnt]. See **arraign (I.)** & **-ment.** Process or act of arraigning or indicting, or of being arraigned.

arrange, vb. trans. & intrans. [1. aránj; 2. әréindž]. Late M.E., fr. O. Fr. *arangier,* fr. *a,* 'to', & *ranger* &c., 'put into line'. See **range (I.).,** & **rank. A.** trans. **1. a** To put into order; to group, place, in systematic manner; classify, sort (of persons and things): *to arrange an audience (in their proper seats); arrange one's house, affairs; arrange one's books, papers, collections* &c.; **b** (fig., of non-material things) *to arrange one's arguments, ideas* &c. **2. a** To settle a dispute, esp. by agreement between the parties: *let us arrange our differences;* **b** to settle controversial questions in advance by a mutual understanding: *the discussion was a sham, everything had been arranged before the meeting.* **3.** To adapt a piece of music, or a literary work, to a new purpose, or give it a new form: *to arrange a piece for four voices, for the violin; arrange a novel for the stage.* **B.** intrans. **a** To come to an agreement: *arrange with a person about a matter;* **b** to manage, smoothe out difficulties, get something done: *I will arrange somehow; I will arrange to do as you wish* &c.

arrangement, n. [1. aránjment; 2. әréin(d)žmәnt]. See **arrange** & **-ment. 1.** The act or process of arranging, putting in order, classifying &c.: *the arrangement of a library takes a long time.* **2.** Result of above process, manner of grouping, classifying: *the arrangement adopted in this library makes it difficult to find the book required.* **3.** (pl.) Preparation, measures for the carrying out of a purpose: *to make one's own arrangements.* **4.** Settlement, adjustment of a dispute, agreement: *to come to an arrangement.* **5.** Adaptation of a musical or literary composition.

arrant, adj. [1. árant; 2. ǽrәnt]. Variant of **errant. 1.** Wandering, vagrant (obs.). Hence, **2,** notorious, outstandingly bad, unmitigated, thorough: *an arrant thief, rogue, hypocrite* &c.; *arrant nonsense* &c.

arrantly, adv. Prec. & **-ly.** Notoriously, infamously.

arras, n. [1. áras; 2. ǽrәs], fr. town in Artois, France, where this fabric was manufactured. **a** Rich figured tapestry; **b** hangings, wall-coverings, of such material.

array (I.), vb. trans. [1. arā́; 2. әréi]. M.E. *arraien,* O. Fr. *araier,* 'array, prepare, arrange'; all fr. Romanic type **arredāre,* as in Ital., formed w. Lat. pref. *ar-* (i.e. **ad-** before *-r-*), & W. Gmc. **reidi,* 'ready, equipped', cp. O. Fris. *rēde,* 'ready', O.E. *rǣde,* ready, mounted', & O.E. *ġerǣdu,* 'trappings, armour'; cp. also Goth. cogn. *garaiþs,* 'fixed, ordained'. See **ready. 1.** To place, set, in order, line; esp. **a** to marshal, dispose (of troops, for battle); **b** to impanel a jury; (fig., of parties in a debate, counsel in law case): *a formidable list of counsel was arrayed against us.* **2.** To dress up, deck out, adorn (lit. and fig.). **3.** (reflex.) *To array oneself in all one's finery.*

array (II.), n. See prec. **1.** Order, line, of battle, disposition of troops: *battle array.* **2.** A military assemblage; troops. **3.** A panel of jurors. **4.** An imposing assemblage or display of persons or things, massed, aligned, grouped together: *a formidable array of eminent men, of authorities* &c. **4.** Dress, apparel, equipment: *in fine array.*

arrear, n. [1. arḗr; 2. әríә]. O. Fr. *arere,* cp. Mod. Fr. *arrière,* 'behind', fr. L. Lat. *ad retrō,* 'backwards'. See **retro-.** (in pl.) **a** That in which one has fallen behind: *arrears of work, correspondence* &c.; **b** specif., debt unpaid and overdue: *arrears of rent, wages* &c. Phr. *in arrear(s),* behindhand, esp. in paying a debt.

arrearage, n. [1. arḗrij; 2. әríәridž]. Prec. & **-age.** (archaic, rare) That which remains behindhand; that remaining unpaid.

arrect, adj. [1. arékt; 2. әrékt], fr. Lat. *arrect-*(*um*), P.P. type of *arrigere,* 'to set upright, to raise, erect', fr. *ad,* 'to', & *regere,* 'to stretch, to keep or lead in a straight line', then 'to guide, lead, direct, rule'. See base in **right.** Pricked, cocked (of the ears); on the alert (rare).

arrest (I.), vb. trans. [1. arést; 2. әrést], fr. O. Fr. *arester,* 'stop', Mod. Fr. *arrêter,* cp. Ital. *arrestare,* fr. Low Lat. *adrestāre,* fr. **ad-,** 'to', & *restāre,* 'to stop', fr. **re-,** 'back', & *stāre,* 'to stand'. See **state** & cp. **rest (III.) 1. a** To stop, check the course of, retard, slow down: *to arrest progress, development;* **b** (law) to delay proceedings on ground of error: *to arrest judgement.* **2.** (law) To take into legal custody, seize (a person) by legal authority, for a crime &c. **3.** (of mental activities) To attract and fix, catch and hold: *to arrest one's attention.*

arrest (II.), n., fr. O. Fr. *areste,* 'stoppage, delay', & *arest,* 'act of arresting'. See prec. **1.** Stoppage, check, retarding (of movement). **2.** (law) **a** The seizure or detainment of a person in custody by legal authority; Phr. *under arrest,* in custody; **b** *arrest of judgement,* staying (of judgement) for legal cause.

arresting, adj. [1. arésting; 2. әréstiŋ], fr. Pres. Part of **arrest (I.).** Having the property of attracting or exciting the attention and interest; interesting, striking: *an arresting speech, work of art* &c.

arrestive, adj. [1. aréstiv; 2. әréstiv]. See **arrest (I.)** & **-ive.** Having tendency to fix and hold the attention.

arrestment, n. [1. aréstment; 2. әréstmәnt]. O. Fr. **arrest (I.)** & **-ment.** (rare) Act or fact of arresting; detention.

arriere ban, n. [1. áriār bán; 2. ǽriεә bǽn]. Fr., fr. O. Fr. *arier-ban,* fr. O.H.G. *hari-ban;* for second element see **ban (II.);** first element is O.H.G. *hari,* Mod. Germ. *heer,* 'host, army', see **harry (I.);** in secondary sense this was confused w. *arrière,* 'behind', fr. L. Lat. *ad retrō,* 'backwards'. See **retro-.** (hist.) **1. a** Summons to war issued by the French kings to their vassals; **b** body of vassals so summoned. **2.** (incorrectly) The summons of the vassals to their tenants, as inferior vassals; hence, Phr. *ban et arrière-ban.*

arriere pensee, n. [1. áriār páhnsā; 2. ǽriεә pãsei]. Fr. Thought which one hides, while revealing another; reluctance.

arris, n. [1. áris; 2. ǽris], fr. O. Fr. *areste,* Mod. Fr. *arête,* Lat. *arista,* 'ear of grain'. See **arête.** Sharp ridge formed by junction of two surfaces at different angles; esp. edge of mouldings.

arrival, n. [1. arrîval; 2. ərάivəl]. M.E. *arrivaille*. See **arrive** & **-al**. **1. a** The act of coming to the end of one's journey, of reaching destination; advent; **b** coming to port, or station, of a ship or train. **2.** Person or thing which arrives or has arrived: *new arrivals at a hotel* &c.

arrive, vb. intrans. [1. arív; 2. ərάiv], fr. O. Fr. *ariver*, cogn. w. Ital. *arrivare*, Span. *arribar*, fr. Low Lat. *arrībāre*, *arrīpāre*, 'come to shore', fr. *adrīpāre*, fr. **ad-**, 'to', & *rīpa*, 'shore, bank'. See **riparian**. **1.** To come to, reach, destination, come to end of a journey; to appear on the scene; be brought: *to arrive at last, early, in London, upon the scene* &c. **2.** (fig.) **a** To come to, reach, a state of mind: *to arrive at a conclusion, conviction* &c.; **b** to reach a state, time, of life: *to arrive at the age of discretion*. **3.** (of time) To come: *the time, day, has arrived*. **4.** Used trans. by Milton: '*ere he arrive The happy isle*' (P.L. ii. 409, 10).

arrogance, n. [1. árogans; 2. ǽrəgəns]. O. Fr., fr. Lat. *arrogantia*. See **arrogant** & **-ance**. The assertion of one's own importance, together with contempt of others; disdainful assumption of dignity or authority; haughtiness.

arrogant, adj. [1. árogant; 2. ǽrəgənt], fr. O. Fr. *arrogant*, fr. Lat. *arrogant-em*, Pres. Part. type of *arrogāre*, 'to claim what is not one's own'. See **arrogate**. Self-asserting, given to insisting on one's own fancied rights and importance; haughty, overbearing.

arrogantly, adv. Prec. & **-ly**. In an arrogant manner; with arrogance; haughtily, disdainfully.

arrogate, vb. trans. [1. árogāt; 2. ǽrəgeit], fr. Lat. *arrogāt-(um)*, P.P. type of *arrogāre*, 'to ask for oneself, to claim what is not one's own', fr. **ad-**, 'to', & *rogāre*, 'to ask'. See **rogation**. **1.** To lay claim to something, claim for oneself, without just cause, advance undue pretension to: *to arrogate the rights of a superior*; also *to arrogate to oneself* (more usual). **2.** To ascribe, attribute, to another.

arrogation, n. [1. àrogáshun; 2. æ̀rəgéiʃən]. Prec. & **-ion**. Act of taking, or claiming, more than one is entitled to; a presumptuous claim.

arrondissement, n. [1. arondésmon; 2. arɔ̃dismɑ̃]. Fr., fr. *arrondir*, 'to round, fill out', fr. *à* & *rond*, **round**. Subordinate administrative district of a department or city.

arrow, n. [1. árō; 2. ǽrou]. O.E. *earh*, *arh*, M.E. *arewe*, cogn. w. Goth. *arhwazna*, 'arrow'; the words are cogn. w. Lat. *arcus*, 'bow', & meant orig. 'missile for a bow'. See **arc** & **arch**. A straight, slender rod with a sharp point, and a feathered end, shot from a bow.

arrow-head, n. See **arrow** & **head**. **a** The head of an arrow; **b** mark on British Government stores: *the broad arrow*, q.v.

arrowroot, n. [1. árōrōōt; 2. ǽrourūt]. See **arrow** & **root**. So called from its juice used by natives as an antidote for poisoned arrows. West Indian plant, from which a nutritive, starchy powder is derived, used as food for invalids.

arse, n. [1. ars; 2. ās]. O.E. *ears*, *ærs*, M.E. *ers*, *ars*, cogn. w. Gk. *órros*, fr. **orsos*, 'tail, rump', & *ourá*, fr. **orswa*, 'tail', see **uro- (II.)**. The buttocks (familiar and vulgar).

arsenal, n. [1. ársenal; 2. ásənəl]. Fr., fr. Ital. *arsenale*, fr. Arab. *dar accinā'ah*, 'house where things are made', fr. *dar*, 'house', *al*, 'the', *cinā'ah*, 'art'. The final *-al* in Fr. & Engl. is fr. Ital. *-ale*. State establishment where ammunition and guns are manufactured and stored.

arsenic (I.), n. [1. ársenik; 2. ásənik], fr. O. Fr., fr. Lat. *arsenicum*, fr. Gk. *arsenikón*, *arrenikón*, 'yellow orpiment', fr. Heb. *zarnīq*, fr. Pers. **zarnīka*; the word was associated in Gk., by popular etymol., w. *arren-*, *arsenikós*, 'male', fr. *ársēn*, 'male', cogn. w. O. Pers. *aršan*, 'man'. The alchemists divided the elements into male and female. **a** A metallic poison, white arsenic, trioxide of arsenic; **b** (chem.) a semi-metallic element of a steely-grey colour, usually found in the arsenic ores, orpiment, and realgar &c.

arsenic(al) (II.), adj. [1. arsénik(l); 2. āsénik(l)]. Prec. & **-al**. Of, containing, arsenic; caused by arsenic: *arsenical poisoning*.

arsenious, adj. [1. arsḗnius; 2. āsíniəs]. See **arsenic** & **-ous**. Connected with, containing, arsenic; (chem.) of trivalent compounds of arsenic: *arsenious oxide*, white arsenic.

arsis, n. [1. ársis; 2. ásis]. Lat. *arsis*, fr. Gk. *ársis*, 'raising, lifting', fr. *aeírō*, fr. **awerjō*, & *aírō*, fr. **warjō*, 'I raise, lift'; Scrt. *várṣma*, 'height, point', Lat. *verrūca*, fr. **versūca*, 'wart, swelling', see **verruca**, O.E. *wearr*, 'swelling', fr. **wars-*, are apparently cognates. (pros.) The unaccented part of a foot in Greek and Latin prosody; in English prosody by reversal of usage, the stressed part.

arson, n. [1. ársun; 2. ásən]. O. Fr., fr. L. Lat. *arsiōn-(em)*, 'a burning', fr. Lat. *ardēre*, *arsum*, 'to burn'. See **ardent**. The act of deliberately and intentionally setting fire to property, whether one's own to obtain insurance money, or another's as a piece of malice or revenge.

art, n. [1. art; 2. āt], fr. O. Fr. *art*, fr. Lat. *artem*, acc. of *ars*, fr. **art-s*; Scrt. *ṛtám*, 'use, usage', *ṛtí*, 'manner, mode'; connected w. Lat. *artus*, 'joint, limb', & Gk. *artizein*, 'to prepare'. See also **arm (I. & II.)**; all these are fr. base **ar-*, 'join, put together'; *art* orig. is 'a fitting, adjusting, joining'. **1. a** Human skill and industry as applied to adapting and modifying natural objects to man's requirements; human intervention for this purpose, as opposed to the action of natural forces: *a cavern hollowed out partly by nature, partly by art*; **b** human effort, skill, practice, applied to non-material things: *a fine voice comes by nature, but is assisted by art*. **2.** Certain branches of human thought and learning considered as instruments of intellectual development, such as grammar, logic, and mathematics: *the liberal arts*; *a Master of Arts*; *Faculty of Arts* (in a university). **3.** Set of principles, rules, precepts, gained by experience, which teach a systematic method for carrying out operations requiring skill and training, such as the exercise of a craft, or performance of any series of complex activities: *the art of building*; *the industrial arts*; *the art of war*; *the healing art* &c.; *the Black Art*, magic, necromancy. **4.** Application of skill, dexterity, knowledge, taste, to the æsthetic expression of feeling and emotion, or production of beauty, through the medium of colour, form, words, musical sound &c.: *the art of the painter, sculptor, poet, musician*; *the Fine Arts*; *the art of Shakespeare or of Beethoven* &c. **5.** Cunning, artifice, skilful contrivance to persuade or deceive, craftiness: *she put forth all her arts of attraction*.

artefact, variant of **artifact**.

Artemisia, n. [1. àrtemízia; 2. àtimíziə]. Gk., 'wormwood'. (bot.) A genus of plants which includes southernwood, or lad's love, and wormwood.

arterial, adj. [1. artḗrial; 2. ātíəriəl]. Fr. (16th cent.); Mod. Fr. *artériel*. See **artery** & **-al**. Connected with, having character of, an artery or arteries: *arterial blood*, as opposed to *venous*, see **arterialize**; *arterial road*, a main road; *arterial traffic* &c.

arterialization, n. [1. artḗrializáshun; 2. ātìəriəlaizéiʃən], fr. next word & **-ation**. The conversion of venous into arterial blood.

arterialize, vb. trans. [1. artḗrialīz; 2. ātíəriəlaiz]. Fr. *artérialiser*. **arterial** & **-ize**. (of blood) To transform venous blood into arterial blood by impregnating it with oxygen, a process carried out in or through the lungs.

arteriotomy, n. [1. ártēriótomi; 2. ātìəriɔ́təmi], tr. Lat. *artēriotomia*, fr. Gk. *artēriotomía*, see **artery** & **-tomy**. (med.) The cutting open of an artery.

artery, n. [1. árteri; 2. átəri], fr. Lat. *artēria*, fr. Gk. *artēría*, 'the windpipe, artery'; origin doubtful; prob. related to Gk. *aeirein*, 'to raise', see **arsis**, fr. wh. base also **aorta**. **a** One of the larger blood-vessels, which carry blood from the heart to all parts of the body; **b** (fig.) something which serves as a channel of supplies, e.g. a river or main road.

artesian, adj. [1. artḗzian, -ḗzhan; 2. ātíziən, -íʒən], fr. Fr. *artésien*, fr. O. Fr. *Arteis*, Mod. Artois, an old province of France. *Artesian well*, one which is bored into a water-bearing stratum, from which a constant supply of water rises through a narrow pipe.

artful, adj. [1. ártfool; 2. átfəl]. See **art**, **5**, & **-ful**. (of persons and actions) Deceitful, cunning, crafty.

artfully, adv. Prec. & **-ly**. In an artful manner; cunningly, craftily.

artfulness, n. See prec. & **-ness**. Cunning, skill in deceiving, craftiness.

arthritic, adj. [1. arthrítik; 2. āþrítik], fr. Lat. *arthrīticus*, fr. Gk. *arthrītikós*. See **arthritis** & **-ic**. Liable to, suffering from, affected by, having nature of, arthritis.

arthritis, n. [1. arthrîtis; 2. āþráitis]. Lat. *arthrītis*, fr. Gk. *arthrîtis*, fr. *árthron*, 'a joint', & **-itis**. *Arthron* is fr. base **ar-*, 'join' &c., seen in **arm**, **art**. (med.) Chronic inflammation of the joints, often leading to stiffening and deformity.

arthropod, n. [1. árthropod; 2. áþrəpɔd], fr. Gk. *árthron*, 'joint', see prec., & **-pod**. (zool.) Any member of the great phylum *Arthropoda*, which includes the crustaceans, arachnids, and true insects.

artichoke, n. [1. ártichōk; 2. átitʃouk], fr. Ital. *articiocco*, a corrupt. of Arab. *alkharshuf*. **a** A plant somewhat resembling a large thistle, whose flower-heads have scales or bracts at the bottom, with fleshy edible bases, called also *globe artichoke*; **b** *Jerusalem artichoke*, an entirely different plant, in reality a kind of sunflower, the edible portion of which is the root; *Jerusalem* is a popular adaptation of Ital. *girasole*, 'sunflower', see **girasole**.

article (I.), n. [1. ártikl; 2. átikl]. Fr., fr. Lat. *articulus*, dimin. of *artus*, 'joint', fr. **ar-*, 'fit, join'. See **arm**, **art**. **1.** An item; particular material object, considered as separate and distinct from others of same class, or a substance representing a class, as distinct from other classes: *to buy several articles at a shop*; *coal and iron are important articles of trade*. **2.** Separate portion or clause of a document, setting forth a distinct principle, precept, condition, point, in a statute, treaty, contract, agreement, profession of faith &c.; each charge or count in an indictment: *The Thirty-nine Articles* (in Book of Common Prayer); *articles of apprenticeship* (also specif. called *Articles*); *Articles of Association*, of a joint stock company &c. **3.** A literary composition dealing with a particular topic, and included in, and forming part of, a newspaper, magazine, encyclopaedia &c., but self-contained and independent. **4.** (gram.) Small word (*a*, *the*) standing before nouns, or adjectives followed by nouns, with a slight defining function.

article (II.), vb. trans. See prec. **a** To bind by articles of apprenticeship (see prec., **2.**); **b** to detail charges against accused in an indictment.

articled, adj. [1. ártikld; 2. átikld], fr. prec. & **-ed**. Bound by articles: *articled clerk, apprentice*.

articular, adj. [1. artíkūlar; 2. ātíkjulə], fr. Lat. *articulāris*, fr. *articulus*. See **article** & **-ar**. Connected with the joints.

articulate (I.), vb. trans. & intrans. [1. artíkūlāt; 2. ātíkjuleit], fr. Lat. *articulāt-(um)*, P.P. of *articulāre*, 'to separate into natural divisions'; of speech, 'to utter distinctly', fr. *articulus*, 'joint'. See **article**. **A.** trans. **1.** (anat.) To connect the joints of a skeleton by wires, so that it forms a unity with each separate bone in its right place. **2.** To put speech sounds and words together into properly connected utterance; pronounce, utter distinctly; give utterance to ideas. **B.** intrans. **1.** (anat.) To form a joint *with* (of the extremities of two bones united by, and moving by means of joint). **2.** To utter speech sounds, pronounce words, speak, distinctly.

articulate (II.), adj. [1. artíkūlat; 2. ātíkjulit]. See prec. **1.** (zool., bot., and anat.) Provided with joints. **2. a** (of human speech) Consisting of distinct sounds and words, clearly distinguishable from each other, as contrasted with the cries of animals; **b** (of human beings) clear in utterance, speaking, able to express their thoughts and ideas, expressive; **c** (of products of the mind, treatises &c.), clear, systematically arranged.

articulation, n. [1. artìkūláshun; 2. ātikjuléiʃən], fr. Lat. *articulātiōn-(em)*, 'jointing', of vines, 'putting forth new joints', fr. *articulāt-(um)*, P.P. type of *articulāre*. See **articulate** & **-ion**. **1. a** (anat.) Junction, joint, between two bones; **b** (bot.) junction between two parts in plants, capable of spontaneous separation. **2.** Act of putting together, jointing. **3.** Act, mode, of articulating, or uttering speech sounds; enunciation; speech.

articulatory, adj. [1. artíkūlāturi; 2. ātíkjuleitəri]. See **articulate** & **-ory**. Of, or pertaining to, articulation in any sense.

artifact, n. [1. ártifakt; 2. ātifækt], fr. Lat. *ars, art-(em)*, 'art', & *fact-us*, 'made'. See **artifice** & **fact**. (archaeol.) Object, such as early palaeolithic flint, made and shaped by human art and skill, as opposed to natural object, shaped by weather, water &c.

artifice, n. [1. ártifis; 2. ātifis]. Fr., fr. Lat. *artificium*, 'skilled handicraft, skill, ingenuity', also in bad sense 'cunning device', cp. *artifex, -fic-(em)*, 'craftsman', *art-(em)*, 'art', see **art**, & *-fic-*, 'make', form of *facere*, 'to make'. See **fact**. **a** A device, contrivance, ingenious expedient; **b** (in bad sense) trick, cunning device.

artificer, n. [1. artífiser; 2. ātífisə]. Prec. & **-er**. **a** A skilled worker, craftsman, mechanic; **b** a petty officer in the engineering branch of the navy.

artificial, adj. [1. àrtifíshal; 2. ātifíʃəl], fr. Lat. *artificiālis*. See **artifice** & **-al**. **1.** (of things) Made by art, as contrasted with what is produced by nature; produced or contrived by human skill as a substitute for, or in imitation of, what is real, natural: *artificial flowers, artificial limbs, artificial teeth.* **2.** (of persons, emotions &c.) Feigned, fictitious, not genuine; affected: *artificial smile, manner* &c.

artificiality, n. [1. àrtifishiáliti; 2. ātifiʃiǽliti]. See prec. & **-ity**. The state or quality of being artificial.

artificialize, vb. trans. [1. àrtifíshalīz; 2. ātifíʃəlaiz], fr. **artificial** & **-ize**. Render, make, artificial.

artificially, adv. [1. àrtifíshali; 2. ātifíʃəli]. **artificial** & **-ly**. **a** By means of art, not naturally: *chicks artificially hatched*; **b** in an affected manner.

artificialness, n. [1. àrtifíshalnes; 2. ātifíʃəlnis]. See prec. & **-ness**. Artificiality.

artillerist, n. [1. artílerist; 2. ātílərist]. See next word & **-ist**. Artilleryman, gunner.

artillery, n. [1. artíleri; 2. ātíləri], fr. O. Fr. *artillerie*, fr. *artiller*, 'to fortify, provide with engines of war'; fr. Low Lat. *articulārius*, fr. *articula*, neut. pl., dimin. of *art-(em)*, 'art, skill, device' &c. See **article** & **art**. **1.** Big guns (not including machine-guns), cannon, for discharging shells, as opposed to *small-arms*. **2.** That branch or arm of the army which has the management of the big guns.

artilleryman, n. [1. artíleriman; 2. ātílərimən]. See **artillery** & **man**. One who serves a gun; one belonging to the artillery; gunner.

artisan, n. [1. àrtizán; 2. ātizǽn]. Fr., fr. Ital. *artigiano* (fr. Low Lat. **artitiānus*), fr. Lat. *artītus*, P.P. of *artīre*, 'to instruct in arts', fr. *art-(em)*. See **art**. One employed in an industrial art; mechanic, handicraftsman.

artist, n. [1. ártist; 2. ātist]. Fr. *artiste*, fr. Ital., fr. Low Lat. *artista*, fr. *art-(em)*, see **art**, & **-ist**. **1.** A skilled performer, one who is proficient, one possessing address, competence, neatness in execution, combined with aesthetic feeling and taste: *a true, thorough, artist.* **2.** Person who practises one of the fine arts as a profession; (in popular usage) a painter of pictures.

artiste, n. [1. artést; 2. ātíst]. Fr. See prec. Term applied (generally by themselves) to public professional performers on the music-hall stage, in the circus &c., quite independently of merit.

artistic, adj. [1. artístik; 2. ātístik]. Fr. *artistique*. See **artist** & **-ic**. **a** Possessed of aesthetic knowledge and sensibility, combined with skill in execution of one of the fine arts; **b** fond of, appreciative of, the arts.

artistically, adv. [1. artístikali; 2. ātístikəli]. Prec. & **-al** & **-ly**. After the manner of an artist, so as to show artistic skill.

artistry, n. [1. ártistri; 2. ātistri]. See **artist** & **-ry**. The qualities of aesthetic sensibility and taste combined with skill, possessed by an artist.

artless, adj. [1. ártles; 2. ātlis]. See **art** & **-less**. Free from art in bad sense, not cunning, crafty, insinuating, or artificial; natural, simple, unaffected, innocent, unsophisticated, naïve.

artlessly, adv. Prec. & **-ly**. In an artless manner; naturally, innocently.

artlessness, n. See prec. & **-ness**. Quality of being artless; simplicity, innocence.

arum, n. [1. árum; 2. ɛ́ərəm]. Lat., fr. Gk. *áron*, cogn. w. Lat. *(h)arundo*, 'reed'. **a** (bot.) The wild lily, *Arum maculatum*, also called 'cuckoo-pint', 'lords and ladies', 'wake-robin'; **b** popular name of cultivated white lily, usually *arum lily, Richardia.*

-ary, suff. [1. ari; 2. əri], forming adjs. & ns., fr. Lat. *-ārius, -a, -um*. Occurring in words borrowed direct fr. Lat., or if fr. Fr. w. corresponding suff. *-aire*, re-formed on Lat. model.

Aryan (I.), adj. [1. árian; 2. ɛ́əriən], fr. Scrt. *ārya*, 'noble', & **-an**; cp. also the cogn. Pers. *Irān*, 'Persia', cp. *Iranian*. Perh. cogn. also w. Gk. *áristos*, 'best', see **aristocrat**. The Gk. name *Areía* for Eastern Persia is borrowed fr. the Scrt. **1.** adj. **a** Belonging to, forming part of, the large family of languages, called also *Indo-European*, and *Indo-Germanic*, which includes those Indian dialects and languages related to Sanscrit; Persian; and most of the European families of speech, Albanian, Armenian, Hellenic, Italic, Slavonic, Germanic, Celtic; the term was first used by Max Müller; **b** specif., connected with the hypothetical ancestor of all Aryan languages; **c** connected with the Sanscrit and Persian branches of Indo-Germanic. **2. a** Belonging to the race which spoke the original Aryan language; **b** belonging to a race using Aryan speech. It was formerly held that identity of language implied identity of race, a view now abandoned. Since it is uncertain which of the races using Aryan speech were the original transmitters of it, the term is now, if applied to race, generally used in sense **b**.

Aryan (II.), n., fr. prec. **1. a** Aryan speech in general; **b** specif., primitive Aryan, the hypothetical mother tongue from which all the Aryan families of speech are derived. The term is used in this sense in the etymological discussions in this book. **2. a** A speaker of an Aryan language; **b** (i.) a member of the supposed primitive Aryan race or a descendant of this race; (ii.) a European or Asiatic speaking an Aryan language (see remarks under **Aryan** (I.), **2. b**); contrasted esp. with *Semite.*

as (I.), adv., conj., & rel. pron. [1. az; 2. æz, əz]. O.E. *ealswā, alswā*, whence in M.E. *alsō*, in stressed positions, & *alse, als, as* in unstressed, the loss of *l* occurring orig. in the latter. See **also**. In various senses and functions. **1. a** Expressing identity of or equivalence in amount, degree, manner: *history will regard this man as the saviour of his country* (cp. different force of *as* in **2. b**); *ye shall be as gods*; *do as you are told*; *I promise to do this as I hope for salvation*; '*I see men as trees walking*'; **b** followed by infin. *to*: *be so good as to obey*; **c** in comparisons asserting equality: *as good as I am.* **2.** Expressing a substitution of a person or thing for another; symbolization, characterization, representation by a person or thing of another; in the character of, in the capacity of, in the light of: *to act as commander-in-chief*; *to appear as Macbeth*; **b** limitation to one special aspect: *from one point of view he may be regarded as the saviour of his country* (cp. different force of *as* in **1. a**): *as prose style this is bad.* **3.** Denoting time during or at which: *he was shot as he was escaping*; often preceded by *just*, at the very moment that: *just as he was speaking there was a loud explosion.* **4.** Introducing a fact or condition from which certain results follow; since, seeing that: *as he had been properly taught he had no difficulty in dealing with the matter*; *as you are sorry I'll forgive you.* **5.** Implying, a mitigation of, attenuation of, allowance for insufficiency or incompleteness: *bad as this horse is, it's the only one I have*; *I was glad of his help, slight as it was*; **b** depreciation, detraction, from a certain stated degree of adequacy: *good as it is, it's not enough.* **6.** Introducing words standing for particular instances or illustrations of a general statement; for example, for instance: *some animals, as the fox and the squirrel, have bushy tails.* **7.** Expressing equality in comparison: *as old as the hills*; cp. (with neg.) *not so young as he looks.* **8.** Adverbial phrases of various kinds, expressing a degree or extent: *as far as*: *as far as the eye could reach*; (fig.) *all right as far as it goes*; **b** time: *as soon as*, simultaneously with; *as yet*, so far, up to now; *as long as*, to such time as, for a certain duration of time: *keep it as long as you like*; *as often as*, whenever, every time that; **c** conditional: *as long as*, provided that: *as long as you apologize I'm satisfied*; **d** resemblance, probability, *as if*: *he looks as if he hadn't long to live*; *as though*: *he spoke as though he were thoroughly frightened*; **e** relationship: *as to, as for, as regards*, with reference to, speaking of, with regard to; **f** purpose: *so as to*, in order that. **9.** Idiomatic phrases: *as good as*; *as good as dead*, very nearly; *as good as one's word*, equivalent to, performing what one promised; *(just) as well*: *it is (just) as well you did come to-day*, fortunate that; *as well as*: *hit in the leg as well as in the head*, in addition to; *as much*: *I thought as much*, I expected this; *as such*: *a poor teacher as such, but a learned man*; *as it were, as who should say*, so to speak. **10.** Pronominal uses: *such as*, those **who**; *as many as*, all who.

as (II.), n. [1. as; 2. æs]. Lat. Perh. orig. 'thin piece of metal'. Cp. Lat. *assis*, 'plank, disk, slice'. See also **ace**. Roman copper coin.

asafoetida, n. [1. ásafétida; 2. ǽsəfítidə]. Span. *azafedida*, fr. Pers. *āzā*, 'resin', & Lat. *foetida*, 'stinking'. See **fetid**. A gum derived from a Persian umbelliferous plant, with a very nauseous taste and smell.

asbestine, adj. [1. azbéstin; 2. æzbéstain], fr. Lat. *asbestinus*, fr. Gk. *asbéstinos*. See next word & **-ine**. Pertaining to, or having the properties of, asbestos; non-combustible.

asbestos, n. [1. àzbéstos; 2. æzbéstəs]. Lat., fr. Gk. *ásbestos*, lit. 'unquenchable', fr. **a-**, 'not', & *sbestós*, fr. *sbénnūmi*, 'I quench'. The base fr. wh. these forms spring is believed to be **zgwēs-*, & to occur also in Lith. *gèsti*, O. Slav. *gasiti*, 'to go out', & in Goth. *qistjan*, 'destroy', O.H.G. *quistan*. White or greyish mineral substance, found in form of long fibres which can be compressed and moulded into any shape required, or woven into a kind of fabric; asbestos is completely non-combustible, and is much used for fireproof curtains, roofing &c., and mixed with clay and other substances for use in gas-fires &c.

ascend, vb. trans. & intrans. [1. asénd; 2. əsénd], fr. Lat. *ascendere*, 'climb up, mount', fr. **ad-**, 'to', & *scandere*, 'to climb'. See **scan**. **A**. intrans. **1**. **a** (of persons, animals &c.) To go up, come up to a higher position: '*I ascend unto My Father*'. **b** (of inanimate things, cries, smoke &c.) to be raised, be borne, to rise, to a higher level; **c** (of musical notes) rise in pitch: *an ascending scale*; **d** to slope, lead upwards: *the path ascends here*. **2**. (fig.) To improve in quality, rise in rank (rare). **B**. trans. To climb, mount, go to top of: *ascend the stairs, a ladder, a mountain* &c. Phr. (fig.) *ascend the throne*, become king.

ascendancy, -ency, n. [1. aséndansi; 2. əsénd-ənsi]. See **ascendant** & **-ancy, -ency**. Control, dominating influence, domination: *to obtain ascendancy over*.

ascendant, -ent, n. & adj. [1. aséndant; 2. əséndənt], fr. O. Fr. *ascendant*, fr. Lat. *ascendent-(em)*, Pres. Part. type of *ascendere*. See **ascend**. **1**. n. **a** (astrol.) That sign of the zodiac which is above the horizon, at a given time, esp. that of a person's birth, which is supposed to influence his fortunes; hence: (fig.) *in the ascendant*, increasing in importance and influence; **b** (rare) superiority, supremacy *over*; **c** (rare) an ancestor (opp. to *descendant*), one who precedes in the genealogical line. **2**. adj. **a** Ascending, rising; (specif. astron.) rising towards the zenith; **b** superior, dominating.

ascension, n. [1. asénshun; 2. əsénʃən]. Lat. *ascensiōn-(em)*, 'ascent', fr. *ascens-(um)*, P.P. type of *ascendere*. See **ascend**. **a** Act of ascending; process of climbing up, mounting; **b** specif., the visible rising to heaven of the Saviour after the Resurrection (with caps. *the Ascension*).

ascensional, adj. [1. asénshunal; 2. əsénʃənəl]. **ascension** & **-al**. Connected with ascension or ascent; ascensive.

Ascension Day, n. Day of feast of the Church commemorating the Ascension of Christ.

Ascension tide, n. The period between Ascension Day and Whitsunday.

ascensive, adj. [1. asénsiv; 2. əsénsiv]. See prec. & **-ive**. Tending, causing, to rise.

ascent, n. [1. asént; 2. əsént], fr. **ascend**, on the anal. of **descent**, fr. **descend**. **1**. The act of ascending, climbing: *the ascent of a mountain*. **2**. Act of rising, upward movement: *the ascent of a balloon*. **3**. Slope, gradient, of a hill &c.: *a rapid ascent*. **4**. Way, path, road, leading upwards.

ascertain, vb. trans. [1. àsertân; 2. æsətéin], fr. O. Fr. *acertener*, fr. *à*, 'to', & *certain*. See **certain**. To find out, discover, become informed about. The 18th cent. meanings, cause to be certain, apprise; render certain, definite; (of facts &c.) are now obsolete.

ascertainable, adj. [1. asertânabl; 2. æsətéinəbl]. **ascertain** & **-able**. Capable of being discovered, found out.

ascertainment, n. [1. ascertânment; 2. æsətéinmənt]. **ascertain** & **-ment**. Process, act of making certain, discovery.

ascetic, n. & adj. [1. asétik; 2. əsétik], fr. Gk. *askētikós*, 'practised, industrious, athletic', fr. *askētés*, 'one who practises any art, an athlete'; used by ecclesiastic writers in sense of 'exercise in, or devotion to, divine things', hence 'separated from intercourse with the world, a monk, hermit'; this is the starting-point of our usage; the origin of the above Gk. words and of the allied *askéō*, 'fashion curiously; honour a divinity; practice, exercise', is obscure. **1**. n. One who practises great self-denial in respect of, and abstinence from, material pleasures and enjoyments; one who represses and mortifies the appetites of the flesh, and leads a life of severe self-discipline and often of hardship. **2**. adj. Also *ascetical*, given to self-denial, and strict austerity of life.

ascetically, adv. [1. asétikali; 2. əsétikəli]. Prec. & **-al** & **-ly**. In an ascetic manner; with self-denial and austerity.

asceticism, n. [1. asétisizm; 2. əsétisizəm]. See **ascetic** & **-ism**. The practice, habits, and general mode of life of an ascetic; system of self-denial, abstinence from material satisfactions.

ascidian, -ium, n. [1. asídian, -um; 2. əsídiən, -əm], fr. Gk. *askídion*, dimin. of *askós*, 'leather bag, wineskin', origin uncertain. Member of a genus of molluscs with tough outer sac; sea-squirt.

ascites, n. [1. asítēz; 2. əsáitīz]. Gk. *askítēs*, 'dropsy', fr. *askós*, 'leather bag', cp. prec. (med.) Accumulation of fluid in the cavity of the peritoneum, a symptom of various diseases of the liver, of Bright's disease &c.

ascribable, adj. [1. askríbabl; 2. əskráibəbl]. **ascribe** & **-able**. Capable of being attributed to; due to.

ascribe, vb. trans. [1. askríb; 2. əskráib], fr. Lat. *ascrībere*, 'to add to in a writing, attribute', fr. **ad-**, 'to', & *scrībere*, 'to write'. See **scribe**. To attribute, impute, put down *to*: *to ascribe all honour to a person*; *to ascribe one's failure to fate* &c.

ascription, n. [1. askrípshun; 2. əskrípʃən]. Lat. *ascriptiōn-(em)*, 'addition in writing', fr. *ascript-(um)*, P.P. type of *ascrībere*. See **ascribe**. **a** Act of ascribing; **b** that which is ascribed or imputed.

asepsis, n. [1. ásépsis, asépsis; 2. éisépsis, əsépsis], fr. Gk. **a-**, 'not', & *sépsis*, 'putrefaction'. See next word. Condition of wounds, sores, or parts of animal body, in which there is no formation of pus.

aseptic, adj. [1. āséptik; 2. éiséptik]. Gk. **a-**, 'not', & *sēptikós*, 'putrefactive', cp. *sépō*, 'putrefy'. See **septic**. Not forming, free from, pus, free from pus-forming bacteria; surgically clean (of wounds, sores, surgical instruments, dressings &c.)

asexual, adj. [1. ásékshooal; 2. éisékʃuəl]. **a-**, 'without', & **sexual**. Lacking characteristics of specific sex; lacking sexual instinct; (of mode of reproduction) without union of sexes, or of germ cells from different sexes.

asexuality, n. [1. āsekshooáliti; 2. éisekʃuǽliti]. Prec. & **-ity**. Condition of being asexual.

ash (I.), n. [1. ash; 2. æʃ]. O.E. *asce*, *æsce*, M.E. *asch*, *esch*, O.H.G. *asca*; Goth. has variant formation *asgō*; this Gmc. base is represented in several other Aryan languages; Scrt. *āsaš*, 'ashes, dust'; w. *-d-* formative element in Gk. *ázō*, 'dry up, parch', *áza*, 'dryness, heat', fr. **azd-*; Lat. *āreo*, 'to be dry, parched' &c., *āridus*, 'dry, parched', *ardēre*, 'burn', all fr. base **āz-*. See **ardent, arid**. **1**. **a** Dry, powdery, white or greyish substance which remains after burning anything: *this coal leaves a great deal of ash*; *a cigar ash* &c.; **b** specif., of chemical products, *soda ash, potash* &c. **2**. (more often in pl.) *Ashes*, a collection of ash left after burning: *the whole village was burnt to ashes*; **b** specif., remains of human body after cremation: *his ashes were scattered to the winds*; **c** (fig. and poet.) the dead human body, human remains when life has gone out, esp. considered as in disintegration: '*e'en in our ashes live our wonted fires*' (Gray); *his ashes repose in Westminster Abbey*. Cp. use of *dust* in this sense. Phrs. *to turn to dust and ashes*, (fig.) of shattered hopes; *to repent in sackcloth and ashes*, in token of humiliation.

ash (II.), n. O.E. *æsc*, M.E. *asch* &c.; O.H.G. *asc*, Mod. Germ. *esche*, O.N. *askr*, Bulg. *jasika*, 'poplar'. **a** Tree of the genus *Fraxinus*, with hard, tough, elastic wood; **b** wood of this tree; **c** *mountain ash*, the rowan tree.

ashamed, adj. [1. ashâmd; 2. əʃéimd], fr. P.P. *āscámod*, of O.E. vb. *ā-scamian*, 'to be ashamed'. See **a-** & **shame**. (only pred.) Stricken with shame, disconcerted, covered with confusion by consciousness of guilt, or of having committed discreditable action: *to be thoroughly ashamed*. Followed by *of* before noun expressing cause of shame: *ashamed of one's folly*; by infinitive: *ashamed to tell*; reflexive: *ashamed of oneself for having done so and so*; followed by *that*: *I'm ashamed that you should see me like this*.

ashen, adj. [1. áshen; 2. ǽʃən]. **1**. From **ash (I.)** & adj. suff. **-en**. Livid, pale, white, applied chiefly to human complexion: *ashen face*; *to turn ashen*. **2**. From **ash (II.)** & **-en**. Connected with ash-tree; made of ash-wood (archaic).

ashlar, n. [1. áshlar; 2. ǽʃlə]. M.E. *ascheler*, fr. O. Fr. *aisselier*, Lat. *axillāris*, fr. *axilla*, dimin. of *axis*, 'board, plank'. *Axis* in this sense is referred by Walde to Lat. *asser*, 'pole, stake', & said to be unexplained; cp. also **as (II.)**; most dictionaries do not distinguish this word fr. Lat. *axis*, 'axle', q.v. under **aileron, alar, axle**. Dressed, hewn block of stone used on outer surface of wall.

ashlaring, n. [1. áshlaring; 2. ǽʃləriŋ], fr. prec. & **-ing**. Masonry composed of ashlars.

ashore, adv. [1. ashŏr; 2. əʃɔ́]. See **a-** & **shore**. (naut.) On, or to, the shore, land, as distinct from being on a ship on the water: *to come, go, ashore*, i.e. (from a ship on the water) on to the land, or (of a swimmer) out of the water.

Ash Wednesday, n. See **ash (I.)** & **Wednesday**. The first day of Lent, following Shrove Tuesday; so called from the penitential use of ashes in the Roman Catholic Church.

ashy, adj. [1. áshi; 2. ǽʃi]. **ash (I.)** & **-y**. **a** Consisting of, covered with, ashes; **b** ash-coloured, pale. Same as **ashen**.

Asiatic, adj. & n. [1. âshiátik; 2. èiʃiǽtik], fr. Lat., fr. Gk. *Asiatikós*, 'of Asia', fr. *Asía*, 'a district in Lydia; Asia Minor; Asia'. **1**. adj. Connected with, coming from, Asia. **2**. n. A native of Asia.

aside (I.), adv. [1. asíd; 2. əsáid]. See **a-** & **side**. (always with sense of movement or motion) On one side, to one side, out of the direct path. Special uses: **1**. Banished, dismissed from further use: *to lay aside bad habits*; (law) *to set aside a verdict*, dismiss, make of none effect, quash. **2**. Put on one side for use on another occasion: *to put aside money for an emergency*; *to put a book aside for reference*; *to lay* or *put aside one's winter clothes*. **3**. (of persons) Excluded from office or rank in favour of another: *in filling up places in the Cabinet, Mr. X was set aside*. **4**. Away from the direct course (on a journey &c.); or from the main stream of an argument &c.: *to turn aside for a moment*. Phrs. **a** *to speak aside* (of actors &c.), to utter something which is not part of the dialogue addressed to other persons on the stage, but which is intended to be heard by the audience; **b** *to take (a person) aside*, to lead away from a company for private conversation.

aside (II.), n., fr. prec. *An aside*, speech uttered by actor according to Phr. **a** above.

asinine, adj. [1. ásinīn; 2. ǽsinain], fr. Lat. *asininus*, fr. *asinus*, 'ass, dolt, blockhead'. The Lat. word for 'ass' is supposed to be derived fr. Asia Minor, & fr. Lat. it has passed into most European languages; fr. the same Asiatic source comes Gk. *ónos* (q.v. under **onager**), & for the Gmc. type see **ass**. (chiefly fig.) Like an ass, silly, stupid, unintelligent (of persons, actions, remarks &c.).

-asis, suff. [1. asis; 2. əsis], fr. Lat., fr. Gk., of ns. denoting 'state, condition', fr. vbs. ending in *-aein*; in Engl. usages in medical terminology of diseases, e.g. *psoriasis* &c.

ask, vb. trans. & intrans. [1. ahsk; 2. āsk]. O.E. *āscian*, *ācsian*, *āxian*, O.S. *ēscōn*, O.H.G. *eiscōn*, Mod. Germ. *heischen* (w. *h-* fr. association w. *heissen*, see **hight**), O. Slav. *iskati*, 'to seek', Scrt. *icchā́ti*, 'wishes'. **A**. trans. **1**. **a** (of things) To inquire, solicit information, express desire to be told: *to ask the way*; *ask a question*; *ask the name of somebody or something*; **b** (of persons) interrogate, put a question to: *ask him the way*. **2**. **a** (of persons) To request, beg, urge upon:

to ask one to do something; ask the doctor to come; **b** (of things) to solicit, beg for, request to be given: *to ask a favour, advice; to ask too much.* **3.** To demand as a price for, as remuneration for services: *to ask 200 guineas for a horse; to ask 10s. a day wages.* **4.** To publish (banns of marriage): *to ask the banns, have one's banns asked*; (also of persons) *to be asked*, to have one's banns called (archaic). **5.** **a** To invite (a person) to go somewhere, or to do something: *to ask a person to dinner; to ask one down to the country (on a visit)*; **b** (colloq., specif.) to invite to marry, propose to. **B.** intrans. **1.** (followed by *for*) To make a demand or request: *to ask for help, money* &c. **2.** (followed by *after, about, for*) To make inquiry for or concerning: *to ask after a person's health; ask about the latest news someone has been asking for you.*

askance, adv. [1. askáhns; 2. əskǽns]. Origin dubious. Sideways, to one side; chiefly fig., in Phr. *to look askance at*, regard with suspicion or disapproval.

askari, n. [1. askáhri; 2. æskǽri]. Arab., fr. *askar*, 'army'. Native soldier of East Africa trained and commanded by European officers.

askew, adv. [1. askū́; 2. əskjū́]. See **a-** & **skew.** Out of the straight line, in a crooked position; awry: *to hang a picture askew.*

aslant, adv. & prep. [1. asláhnt; 2. əslǽnt]. **a-** & **slant.** (archaic) **a** adv. In a slanting direction; across; **b** prep., slantingly across: '*There is a willow grows aslant a brook*' (Shakespeare).

asleep, adv. & pred. adj. [1. aslḗp; 2. əslī́p]. O.E. *on slǣpe*, see **a-** & **sleep.** Cp. *David fell on sleep*, as late as Authorized Version. **1.** **a** Into a condition of sleep; sleeping: *to fall asleep; to be asleep*; **b** (of parts of the body), in a numbed condition, temporarily numb; insensitive owing to compression of blood-vessels. **2.** (fig., of mental condition) Reverse of alert or lively; obtuse, dulled, in a condition of mental torpor.

aslope, adv. [1. aslṓp; 2. əslóup]. 'On the slope'. **a-** & **slope.** In a sloping position, slanting.

asp (I.), n. [1. asp; 2. æsp], fr. O. Fr. *aspe*, fr. Lat. *aspis*, fr. Gk. *aspís*, wh. is perh. of Semitic origin. **1.** A small snake of the viper family of N. Africa, esp. the horned adder, *Cerastes cornutus.* **2.** Any small venomous serpent.

asp (II.). See **aspen.**

asparagus, n. [1. aspáragus; 2. əspǽrəgəs]. O.E. *sparagi*, 16th-cent. *sparage, sperage*; O. Fr. *esperage*, O. Ital. *sparagi*, Lat. *asparagus*, fr. Gk. *aspáragos, aspháragos*, 'asparagus', also 'tender shoots of other plants'. The ultimate origin of the word is doubtful, the form w. *-ph-* being the true one, but there can be little doubt that it was in Gk. itself associated w. *spargáein*, 'to be full to bursting, swell, be ripe' &c.; a cogn. of this is Lith. *sprógti*, 'to bud', & *spragḗti*, 'germinate, sprout, bud'; further, Lat. *spargere*, 'throw here and there, scatter, strew', see **spark** & **sparse.** A vegetable with tender succulent shoots, coming straight from the root and sticking through the ground.

asparagus bed. n. Specially prepared portion of ground in kitchen garden in which the asparagus roots ('crowns') are planted.

aspect, n. [1. áspekt; 2. ǽspekt]. Fr., fr. Lat. *aspectus*, 'glance; view of', fr. *aspect-(um)*, P.P. type of *aspicere*, 'to look at', fr. **ad-**, 'to', & *specere*, 'to look', see **spectacle, spy.** **1.** Characteristic outward appearance; expression, mien (of human beings): *of mild and gentle aspect.* **2.** Way, direction, towards which anything presents itself or faces; view; **a** (of physical position) *the house has a north aspect*; **b** mode of presentment to the mind, particular way in which a problem, question, may be considered: *the aspect of affairs; to consider a question in all its aspects.*

aspen, n. [1. áspen; 2. ǽspen]. O.E. *æspe, æps*, 'white poplar'; O.H.G. *aspa*, Mod. Germ. *espe*, Lett. *apse*, O. Slav. *osina.* Origin unknown. The suff. is adjectival, cp. **ashen, oaken** &c. The form **asp** is now never used. Species of peculiarly tremulous poplar, the leaves of which are paler at the back than on the outward surface. Phr. *to tremble like an aspen leaf.*

asperges, n. [1. aspḗrjēz; 2. æspə́dʒiz]. Lat., 2nd pers. sing. fut. indic. of *aspergere*, 'to sprinkle upon', fr. **ad-** & *spargere*, 'to sprinkle', cogn. w. Gk. *spargáein*, 'to swell'. See **asparagus** & **sparse.** (R.C. Ch.) Short service before High Mass at which altar, clergy, and people are sprinkled with holy water; from the opening words '*Asperges me hyssopo*'.

aspergill(um), n. [1. àspērjil, asperjílum; 2. ǽspədʒil, æspədʒíləm]. Lat., fr. *asperg-(ere)* & *-illum*, dimin. suff. See **asperges.** Small brush used in ceremony of asperges.

asperifoliate, adj. [1. àsperifṓliāt; 2. ǽsperifóulieit], fr. Lat. *asper*, 'rough', & *folium*, 'leaf'. See **asperity** & **foliate.** (bot.) Having rough leaves.

asperity, n. [1. aspériti; 2. æspériti], fr. Lat. *asperitāt-(em), asperitas*, 'roughness', fr. *asper*, 'rough'. This word means lit. 'thrusting away, rejecting', & is fr. Lat. *a-spernere*, 'thrust aside, reject'. See further under **spurn.** (chiefly fig.) Roughness, harshness, sharpness, acerbity, severity (of temper, manner, voice &c.); (also of external conditions) severity, discomfort: *the asperities of a winter campaign.*

asperse, vb. trans. [1. aspḗrs; 2. æspə́s]. Fr., fr. Lat. *aspers-(um)*, P.P. type of *aspergere*, 'sprinkle'. See **asperges. 1.** (eccles.) To sprinkle with water as in baptism &c. **2.** (fig.) To besmirch, detract from, attribute wrong-doing, spread evil rumours concerning, calumniate a person: *to asperse a person's character, good name, honour* &c.

aspersed, adj. [1. aspḗrst; 2. æspə́st]. Prec. & **-ed.** **a** Calumniated; **b** specif. (her.) having small charges scattered over surface of shield.

aspersion, n. [1. aspḗrshun; 2. æspə́ʃən], fr. Lat. *aspersiōn-(em)*, 'sprinkling', fr. *aspers-(um)*, P.P. type of *aspergere*, 'sprinkle'. See **asperse** & **-ion. 1.** (eccles.) The act of aspersing (1). **2.** Act of aspersing (2); slander, backbiting, disparagement, detraction, innuendo: *to cast aspersions on a person, his character* &c.

asphalt, n. & vb. trans. [1. ásfalt; 2. ǽsfælt]. Lat. *asphaltum*, fr. Gk. *ásphaltos*, 'bitumen'. Of Semitic origin. **1.** n. **a** Kind of inflammable pitch; **b** a mixture of this pitch with sand, gravel &c. used for the surface of roads &c. **2.** vb. To cover with asphalt.

asphaltic, adj. [1. asfáltik; 2. æsfǽltik]. Prec. & **-ic.** Composed of, containing, asphalt.

asphodel, n. [1. ásfodel, àsfodél; 2. ǽsfədel, æsfədél]. Gk. *asphódelos.* Origin obscure. See **daffodil. a** (bot.) Flowering plant of the lily tribe; **b** (class. mythol.) the flower which blooms eternally in the fields of the dead.

asphyxia, n. [1. asfíksia; 2. əsfíksiə], fr. Gk. *asphuxia*, fr. **a-**, 'without', & *sphúxis*, 'pulsation'; cp. *sphugmós*, 'throbbing pulse', & *sphúazein*, 'to beat, throb'. See **sphygmus.** Suspended animation; suffocation, insensibility, caused by shortage of oxygen in the system.

asphyxiate, vb. trans. [1. asfíksiāt; 2. əsfíksieit]. See prec. & **-ate.** To suffocate.

asphyxiation, n. [1. asfiksiā́shun; 2. əsfiksiéiʃən]. Prec. & **-ion.** Suffocation.

aspic (I.), n. [1. áspik; 2. ǽspik]. Fr., fr. earlier *espic.* Etymol. dubious. A savoury meat jelly, used for enclosing chicken &c.

aspic (II.), n. 16th cent. Provenç. *aspic*, 'asp', Lat. *aspid-(em)*, acc. of *aspis.* See **asp** (I.). (archaic) An asp or small venomous serpent.

aspidistra, n. [1. àspidistra; 2. æspidístrə]. Recent coinage fr. Gk. *aspis*, 'shield', & *ástron*, 'star'. Some authorities connect *aspis* w. Gk. *áspris*, 'kind of oak'. This word is fr. **askʷ-*, & is perh. connected w. Gmc. *ask-.* See **ash** (II.). *Aspis* wd. appear orig. to have been a wooden shield. For *ástron* see **astral.** Flowering plant with variegated leaves, originally from China and Japan.

aspirant, n. & adj. [1. aspírant; 2. əspáiərənt]. Fr. *aspirant*, Pres. Part. of *aspirer*, fr. Lat. *aspīrant-(em)*, Pres. Part. of *aspīrāre*, 'to breathe, endeavour to attain to'. See **aspire. 1.** n. One who aspires to, seeks, hopes to reach, a high position, or to gain an object: *an aspirant to honours.* **2.** adj. (rare) **a** Breathing, aspiring; **b** rising: '*There with flames all around him aspirant*' (Swinburne).

aspirate (I.), n. [1. áspirat; 2. ǽspərit], fr. Lat. *aspīrāt-(um)*, P.P. type of *aspīrāre.* See **aspire.** (phon.) The sound usually expressed by the letter *h*, which consists merely of emphasis or stress falling upon the unmodified breath-stream; in ordinary speech this only occurs initially, before a vowel, or after a voiceless consonant before a vowel, popularly called 'rough breathing': *to be rather shaky in one's aspirates; to put the aspirate in the wrong place*; popularly called 'dropping the *h*' or 'putting it in'.

aspirate (II.), vb. trans. [1. áspirāt; 2. ǽspəreit]. **1.** To pronounce with an aspirate; to utter the sound of an aspirate: *to aspirate a vowel* (popularly, to pronounce *h* before it); *to aspirate a consonant*, pronounce a stressed, 'rough' breathing after it. **2.** (med.) To draw off (fluid, gas &c.) from a cavity by means of an aspirator.

aspirated, adj. [1. áspirāted; 2. ǽspəreitid]. Pronounced with an aspirate: *aspirated consonant* (in Ir.-Engl. pronunciation of boy &c. = bhoy [bhɔi].

aspiration, n. [1. àspirā́shun; 2. æspiréiʃən], fr. Lat. *aspīrātiōn-(em)*, 'breathing to or upon', fr. *aspīrāre.* See **aspire. 1.** Act of breathing (rare). **2.** Pronunciation of an aspirate or aspirated sound. **3.** (fig.) Strong desire, hope, to attain an ideal; specific desire of this kind, wish to attain particular ideal. **4.** (med.) Withdrawal of fluid &c. from a cavity by an aspirator.

aspirator, n. [1. áspirāter; 2. ǽspireitə]. **aspirate (II.)** & **-or.** (med.) Instrument composed of a tubular needle attached to a syringe by which fluid, as pus or gases, can be withdrawn from a cavity, as in cases of empyaema from the pleural cavity or from a deep-seated abscess &c.

aspire, vb. intrans. [1. aspír; 2. əspáiə], fr. Lat. *aspīrāre*, fr. *ad*, 'to, at', & *spīrāre*, 'breathe'. See **spirant, spirit.** (followed by *to* or *after*, or by infin.) **1.** To desire eagerly, set one's hopes upon, seek to attain, some high aim or object of a material or non-material kind; *to aspire to the highest excellence, to honours* &c.; *to aspire to rule, lead* &c. **2.** To rise, tower up (poet. & archaic): '*Beholds a sudden Thebes aspire*' (Pope, 'Temp. of Fame', 86).

aspirin, n. [1. áspirin; 2. ǽspərin]. Invented word. Trade name for a special preparation of salicylic acid, used in rheumatism, and relief of neuralgic and other pains.

asquint, adv. & adj. [1. askwínt; 2. əskwínt]. See **a-** & **squint.** (very rare) Squintingly, crookedly.

ass, n. [1. ahs, as; 2. ās, æs]. O.E. *assa*, an exceptional form cpd. w. other Gmc. languages. O.E. has also *eosol*, fr. **asil*, alternating w. **asal*; cp. also Goth. *asilus*, O.H.G. & Mod. Germ. *esel*, all fr. Lat. *asinus*, w. change fr. *n* to *l* (as in Gmc. **katil-*, 'kettle', Goth. *katilus*, O.E. *ċietel* &c., fr. Lat. *catinus*, 'bowl, pot'). See further under **asinine** & **onager. 1.** Quadruped, related to, but smaller than, the horse, having coat of longish, coarse hair, long ears, and a dark mark in form of a cross passing along the back and over each shoulder. **2.** (fig.) A stupid person, a fool.

assagai, assegai, n. [1. ásagī; 2. ǽsəgai]. Port. *azagaia*, O. Fr. *azagaye*, fr. a Berber word. Spear or lance of hard wood tipped with iron, used as a missile or for stabbing by tribes in South Africa.

assail, vb. trans. [1. asā́l; 2. əséil]. M.E. *assailen*, O. Fr. *asaillir*, *asalir*, fr. Low Lat. *adsalīre*, fr. *ad* & *salīre*, 'to leap, spring', cp. Lat. *assilīre*, 'to leap, spring upon'. See **salient**. **1.** To make a violent physical attack upon, assault (a person, fortress, or military position). **2.** To attack with arguments, hostile criticism, ridicule &c.; to overwhelm with questions, entreaties &c.; also *assailed by doubts, fears, temptation*. **3.** To tackle a difficulty, obstacle &c. in the determination to overcome it.

assailable, adj. [1. asā́labl; 2. əséiləbl], fr. prec. & **-able**. Capable of being attacked, liable to attack (lit. and fig.).

assailant, n. [1. asā́lant; 2. əséilənt], fr. Fr. *assaillant*, Pres. Part. of *assaillir*. See **assail**. One who assails, attacks; an enemy.

assart, n. & vb. [1. asárt; 2. æsát]. O. Fr. *essart*, 'grubbing up of trees', Low Lat. *exartum*, fr. Lat. **ex-**, 'out', *sarrīre*, 'to grub, hoe', cp. *sarculum*, fr. **sart-lom*, 'hoe'; w. these cp. Gk. *sáron*, 'besom', *saróō*, 'I sweep, cleanse', also *sairō*, fr. **sarjō*, 'I sweep away', & further Scrt. *sṛnis*, 'elephant goad', *sṛni*, 'sickle'. **1.** n. **a** Act (formerly an illegal act) of grubbing up trees, bushes &c., in converting forest into arable land; **b** land so cleared of trees. **2.** vb. To clear land of wood, make a clearance or assart.

assassin, n. [1. asásin; 2. əsǽsin]. Fr., fr. Ital. *assassino*, fr. Arab. *hashīshī*, 'drinkers of haschish', q.v., sect of fanatics in Palestine in 13th cent., whose chief object was to stab Crusaders; fr. 15th cent. *assassin* became equiv. to murderer. A secret, treacherous murderer.

assassinate, vb. trans. [1. asásināt; 2. əsǽsineit], fr. prec. & **-ate**. To strike down treacherously, murder by violence.

assassination, n. [1. asàsināshun; 2. əsæ̀sinéiʃən]. Prec. & **-ion**. Treacherous, violent murder; a single, specific act of this.

assault (I.), n. [1. asáwlt; 2. əsɔ́lt], fr. O. Fr. *asaut*, Fr. *assaut*, fr. Lat. **ad-** & *saltus*, 'a leap', fr. *salīre*, 'to leap, spring'. See **assail** & **salient**. **1. a** A military attack, by sudden rush upon a fortified post: *to take a town, fortress &c. by assault*; **b** a violent physical attack upon a person; **c** (law) either performance, or threat, of physical violence, if latter be accompanied by menacing gesture, such as raising stick or clenched fist. **2.** An attack upon a person by words, arguments &c.; an attack upon institutions, customs, opinions, made in the hope of destroying them.

assault (II.), vb. trans. See prec. **1. a** To attack (fortress &c.) by a sudden rush; **b** to attack (person) with physical violence. **2.** (archaic) To attack with hostile words, abuse, severe criticism &c.

assay (I.), n. [1. asā́; 2. æséi], fr. O. Fr. *assai*, *assay*, cogn. w. Ital. *assaggio*, fr. Lat. *exagium*, 'a weighing', fr. *exigere*, 'to weigh, measure, examine', fr. **ex-** & *agere*, see **agent**. See also **essay**. Trial, test, esp. of the weight, quality, value &c. of gold, silver, and other metals.

assay (II.), vb. trans., fr. prec. **a** To make trial of, to test; specif., to test the purity of valuable metals (gold, silver &c.), or to discover the constituents of a metal or ore; **b** to attempt, endeavour.

assayable, adj. [1. asā́abl; 2. æséiəbl]. Prec. & **-able**. Capable of being assayed.

assayer, n. [1. asā́er; 2. æséiə]. See prec. & **-er**. One who assays metals, esp. one who practises assaying as a profession.

assaying, n. [1. asā́ing; 2. æséiiŋ]. **assay** (II.) & **-ing**. The trial, testing, of metals.

assemblage, n. [1. asémblij; 2. əsémblidž], fr. Fr. *assemblage*, fr. *assembler*, see **assemble**, & **-age**. **1. a** The act of assembling, of coming, of bringing, together; **b** act or process of putting, fitting, together, parts of an engine or other machine. **2.** A collection of persons, a gathering, company, concourse; (less formal than *assembly*). **3.** A collection of things, a group, cluster.

assemble, vb. trans. & intrans. [1. asémbl; 2. əsémbl], fr. Fr. *assembler*, cogn. w. Span. *asemblar*, Ital. *assemblare*, fr. Lat. *assimulāre*, in late sense of 'to collect at the same time', fr. **ad-** & *simul*, 'at the same time, together'. See **simulate**. **A.** trans. **1.** To collect, cause to come together, into one place, to bring together, convene: *to assemble an audience* &c. **2.** To put together the parts of some mechanism: *to assemble a watch, an engine* &c. **B.** intrans. To come, meet, together, to congregate (of a number of individuals).

assembly, n. [1. asémbli; 2. əsémbli], fr. O. Fr. *asemblee*, n., fr. fem. P.P. of *assembler*. See prec. **1.** The act of assembling, or the state of being assembled, a meeting, gathering: *the assembly of Parliament*. **2.** (only of persons) A company of persons collected together for a common purpose (e.g. legislation, deliberation, entertainment); *assembly room*, a room in which persons gather together for social entertainment. **3.** (mil.) Signal by drum or bugle for troops to assemble.

assent (I.), vb. intrans. [1. asént; 2. əsént], fr. O. Fr. *assenter*, Lat. *assentīre*, fr. **ad-** & *sentīre*, 'feel, perceive' &c. See **sense**, **sentient**. To agree to, acquiesce in: *to assent to a proposal*; (also absol.) *some demurred, but most assented*.

assent (II.), n. O. Fr. *assente*. See prec. The mental act of agreeing to a thing, agreement, acquiescence, consent: *to give one's assent*. *Royal assent*, formal approval given by the British sovereign in Parliament to a bill which has passed both Houses.

assentation, n. [1. àsentā́shun; 2. æ̀sentéiʃən], fr. Lat. *assentātiōn-(em)*, fr. *assentāri*, 'to assent habitually, to flatter'. See **assent** & **-ation**. (rare) Ready assent; pretended agreement.

assentient, adj. & n. [1. asénshient; 2. əsénʃiənt], fr. Lat. *assentient-(em)*, Pres. Part. of *assentīre*. See **assent** (I.). **a** adj. Assenting; **b** n., one who assents.

assentive, adj. [1. aséntiv; 2. əséntiv]. See prec. & **-ive**. Assenting, complying.

assert, vb. trans. [1. asért; 2. əsə́t], fr. Lat. *assert-(um)*, P.P. type of *asserere*, 'to join to, lay claim to, vindicate, protect, defend', fr. **ad-** & *serere*, 'to join, connect, range in a row'. See **series**. **1.** To maintain, defend, support (a cause or claim), vindicate a claim to: *to assert one's rights, liberties*. **2.** To declare, affirm, state positively, aver: *to assert that such a thing happened*. **3.** (reflex.) *Assert oneself*: **a** to vindicate one's rights, claim to be heard; **b** (in bad sense) to claim too much, thrust oneself forward unduly.

assertion, n. [1. asérshun; 2. əsə́ʃən], fr. Lat. *assertiōn-(em)*, 'a formal declaration respecting the freedom or servitude of a person', fr. *asserere*. See **assert** & **-ion**. **1.** The act of insisting on, urging, claims, rights &c.; *self-assertion*, undue insistence on one's rights, claims, importance &c. **2. a** Declaration, positive statement; **b** a statement unsupported by evidence: *a mere assertion*.

assertive, adj. [1. asértiv; 2. əsə́tiv]. **assert** & **-ive**. Positive, given to asserting, claiming, esp. with undue insistence and confidence.

assertively, adv. Prec. & **-ly**. Dogmatically, peremptorily.

assertiveness, n. See prec. & **-ness**. Action, esp. when habitual, of asserting with confidence and insistence.

assess, vb. trans. [1. asés; 2. əsés], fr. O. Fr. *assesser*, fr. Low Lat. *assessāre*, fr. Lat. *assess-(um)*, P.P. type of *assidēre*, 'to sit beside, to assist in office' (e.g. as an assessor), in Low Lat. specif. 'to apportion a tax', fr. **ad-** & *sedēre*, 'to sit'. See **sedentary**, **sit**. **a** To estimate value of property, esp. with view to imposition of a tax or fine, payable by owner to the state; **b** to estimate amount of damage done to property and the fine payable to owner in respect of this; **c** judge (person) liable for fine of so much: *to assess (a person) in damages of such an amount*.

assessable, adj. [1. asésabl; 2. əsésəbl], fr. prec. & **-able**. Capable of being assessed; liable to be assessed.

assessment, n. [1. asésment; 2. əsésmənt], fr. **assess** & **-ment**. **1. a** Act of assessing, determining, the amount of taxation, fine &c. to be paid by a person or persons; **b** the amount so determined. **2.** Valuation of income, property &c. for purpose of taxation; the value assigned.

assessor, n. [1. aséser; 2. əsésə], fr. **assess** & **-or**. **1.** (law) **a** A person sitting with judge or magistrate to assist and advise in technical questions; **b** one who acts as expert consultant to, without being an actual member of, a commission, committee &c. **2.** One who assesses taxes or estimates the value of property for purpose of taxation.

assets, n. [1. ásets; 2. ǽsets]. O. Fr. *asez* (*z = ts*), Mod. Fr. *assez*, 'enough', fr. Lat. *ad satis*, 'sufficiently'. See **satis**. *Assets* was orig. an adv., then used as an adj., & finally as a n. In this function it was a sing., but is now felt & used as pl., fr. wh. a new sing., *asset*, has been formed. **1.** (law) Property of a deceased person which is liable to be applied to discharging his debts and paying legacies. **2.** Whole property, of every kind, of an insolvent individual or corporation, liable to be administered for benefit of the creditors. **3.** (by extension) **a** Possessions, property generally (often as singular referring to a single object); **b** a valuable object, favourable circumstance, which adds strength, support, or which benefits in any way: *good health is a great asset*; *you will be a valuable asset to our society*.

asseverate, vb. trans. [1. asévərāt; 2. əsévəreit], fr. Lat. *asseverāt-(um)*, P.P. type of *asseverāre*, lit. 'to act with earnestness'; of speech, 'to assert strongly', fr. **ad-** & *sevērus*, adj., 'serious, stern, hard, firm'. See **severe**. To affirm solemnly, aver, assert positively.

asseveration, n. [1. asèverā́shun; 2. əsèvəréiʃən], fr. Lat. *asseverātiōn-(em)*. See **asseverate** & **-ion**. Solemn, positive, declaration.

assibilate, vb. trans. [1. asíbilāt; 2. əsíbileit], fr. Lat. *assibilāt-(um)*, P.P. type of *assibilāre*, fr. **ad-** & *sībilāre*, 'to hiss'. See **sibilant**. To make sibilant, give a hissing sound to. (Vague, unscientific term not applicable in exact phonetic terminology.)

assibilation, n. [1. asìbilā́shun; 2. əsìbiléiʃən]. Prec. & **-ion**. Action or process of assibilating.

assiduity, n. [1. àsidū́iti; 2. æ̀sidjúiti], fr. Lat. *assiduitāt-(em)*, 'attendance', fr. *assiduus*, lit. 'sitting by', hence 'in constant attendance, indefatigable, industrious', fr. *assidēre*, fr. **ad-**, 'by, near', & *sedēre*, 'to sit'. See **sedentary**. Constant and unremitting attention, persistent application, directed to a particular end; diligence, industry.

assiduous, adj. [1. asídūus; 2. əsídjuəs], fr. Lat. *assiduus*. See prec. & **-ous**. **a** Having capacity of sticking to a task; **b** solicitously attentive.

assiduously, adv. Prec. & **-ly**. In an assiduous manner; perseveringly, diligently.

assiduousness, n. See prec. & **-ness**. The quality of constant, careful, conscientious attention to duty, to a specific task &c. (applied to permanent feature of character or to specific manifestation of it).

assign (I.), vb. trans. [1. asī́n; 2. əsáin], fr. Fr. *assigner*, fr. Lat. *assignāre*, 'to mark out for, allot', fr. **ad-** & *signāre*, 'to mark, mark out', fr. *signum*, 'mark, token, sign'. See **sign**. (Always followed by *to* before names of persons.) **1.** (law) To make over, transfer (property &c.), to another. **2. a** To allot (things to persons); **b** appoint, designate (persons for particular duties). **3.** To fix, determine, appoint, a time (*for*); or a limit (*to*) something. **4.** To ascribe, attribute an event, custom &c. to a particular date; credit a person with particular words, actions. **5. a** To ascribe, a motive &c. *to* a person; **b** to fix upon, discover, reason *for* an action.

assign (II.), n. (law) One to whom property, right, or interest is legally transferred, esp. in Phr. *heirs and assigns*. See **assignee.**

assignable, adj. [1. asínabl; 2. əsáinəbl]. **assign** (I.), & **-able.** Capable of being assigned (in any sense): *assignable property*; *assignable reason* &c.

assignat, n. [1. ásignat; 2. ǽsignæt]. Fr. See **assign** (I.). Paper money issued by the French revolutionary government, 1790, on security of lands confiscated by the State.

assignation, n. [1. àsignáshun; 2. æ̀signéiʃən]. **assign** (I.) & **-ation. 1. a** An appointment to meet at particular place and time; **b** often used of meeting arranged between lovers; **c** sometimes in unfavourable sense of secret, illicit meeting. **2.** Assignment, **1.**

assignee, n. [1. àsiné; 2. æ̀siní]. O. Fr. *assigné*, fr. P.P. of *assigner*, see **assign** (I.) & **-ee.** (law) **a** Person empowered to act for another; **b** an assign.

assignment, n. [1. asínment; 2. əsáinmənt]. **assign** (I.) & **-ment. 1. a** Legal transference of a right or property; **b** document authorizing such transference. **2.** Act of assigning, attributing, referring to.

assimilate, vb. trans. & intrans. [1. asímilāt; 2. əsímileit], fr. Lat. *assimilāt-(um)*, P.P. type of *assimilāre*, 'to liken', fr. **ad-**, 'to', & *similis*, 'like', see **similar. A.** trans. **1.** To make alike, cause to resemble: *to assimilate one's mode of speech to that of one's companions.* **2.** (of living organisms) To convert, by physiological process, matter which is different from, into matter identical with, that of which the organism is composed; to incorporate into the system, digest. **3.** (fig.) **a** (of mental process) To absorb into the mind, grasp, thoroughly understand, appropriate as part of one's thought, knowledge, or principles &c.: *to assimilate the idiom of French*; **b** (of an institution, political or other organization) to incorporate with itself, absorb: *the old Russian Empire assimilated innumerable smaller peoples and states.* **B.** intrans. To become absorbed, blend, amalgamate: *Europeans and Jews do not readily assimilate.*

assimilation, n. [1. asìmiláshun; 2. əsìmiléiʃən], fr. Lat. *assimilātiōn-(em)*. See prec. & **-ion. a** The act or process of assimilating; **b** state or condition of being assimilated (in any sense).

assimilative, adj. [1. asímilātiv; 2. əsímileitiv]. **assimilate** & **-ive.** Tending to, inclined to, assimilate.

assist, vb. trans. & intrans. [1. asíst; 2. əsíst], fr. Fr. *assister*, 'to stand by, help', fr. Lat. *assistere*, 'to stand by', fr. **ad-** & *sistere*, 'to place, to stand', redupl. form of *stāre*, 'to stand' &c., see **state** & **stand. A.** trans. **1. a** To help (a person); **b** to further, advance (an undertaking, process &c.). **2.** Specif., to give financial help to. **B.** intrans. To be present, as a spectator, at a ceremony, public meeting &c.: *assist at* (a French idiom).

assistance, n. [1. asístans; 2. əsístəns]. Prec. & **-ance. a** Help, succour, support; **b** persons present, as spectators &c. (Gallicism).

assistant, n. [1. asístant; 2. əsístənt]. See **assist** & **-ant.** One who assists another, esp. as permanent helper or co-worker in a specific occupation.

assize, n. [1. asíz; 2. əsáiz]. M.E., fr. O. Fr. *assise*, fem. P.P. of *asseoir*, 'to be seated', fr. Lat. *assidēre*, 'sit at, or near'. See **assess. 1. a** Trial, inquiry, inquest, before a jury; **b** (also in pl.) *Assizes*, periodical sessions of judges in every English county to try criminal and civil cases; Phr. *the Great Assize*, the Day of Judgement. **2.** (hist.) Rules of a court fixing the price and weight and regulating the sale of bread, ale &c.

associate, (I.) vb. trans. & intrans. [1. asóshiāt; 2. əsóuʃieit], fr. Lat. *associāt-(um)*, P.P. type of *associāre*, 'to join to, unite with', fr. **ad-** & *socius*, 'companion, ally'. See **sociable. A.** trans. **1.** (of persons) To join, unite with, as partner, colleague, participator, in an office, business, or enterprise &c.: *the Government was only too glad to associate Mr. X with their other supporters in the House.* **2.** To connect (ideas) together in the mind, consider as related: *we naturally associate the name of Darwin with the doctrine of evolution.* **3.** To connect, join together verbally (esp. of names): *a toast associated with the name of the chairman*; *the names of these two persons were freely associated by public rumour.* **4.** (reflex.) *Associate oneself with*, adhere to, express agreement with (a proposal, opinion, views, hopes &c.): *to associate oneself with the remarks of So-and-so*, that is with sentiments expressed thereby. **B.** intrans. *Associate with*, frequent society of, keep company with, as a habit: *he associates with very undesirable characters.*

associate (II.), n. [1. asóshiat; 2. əsóuʃiət], fr. Lat. *associātus*, 'joined with, in company'. See prec. **1. a** One united with others by common ties of occupation, enterprise, interest; colleague, partner, confederate; **b** one united with another by ties of social intimacy, one often in another's company; companion, familiar friend. **2.** Implying membership of a subordinate or inferior character, of certain institutions: e.g. **a** of certain universities, in which *Associate* is a title conferred on persons who have pursued a truncated course of study, and passed examinations of a less thorough character than those required for a degree; or, **b** of academies of art in which the term is applied to juniors who have not yet attained to full membership as Fellows or Academicians: *Associate of the Royal Academy*, A.R.A. **3.** (law) A member of a body of officials of the High Court of Justice, arranging the business of the court to which they are attached.

associate (III.), adj. **a** Closely connected, affiliated: *a group of associate societies*; **b** sometimes prefixed to names of titles or offices, implying usually co-operation, and intimate relation, without full status and responsibility: *associate professor, judge* &c.

association, n. [1. asòshiáshun, -siáshun; 2. əsòuʃiéiʃen, -siéiʃən]. Prec. & **-ion. 1. a** Act of associating; **b** state of being associated, companionship, intimacy. **2.** Connexion, bond, between ideas, relation, existing in the mind: *association of ideas.* **3.** Group of persons, united and organized, generally under conditions set forth in a legal bond, and acting together for some specific purpose, in furtherance of common aims, of a political, commercial, philanthropic character: *Conservative Association*; *Trading, Temperance, Association* &c.; *articles, deed, of association*, legal document determining conditions under which an association, such as a partnership, company &c., exists and acts. **4.** Association football.

associational, adj. [1. asòshiáshunal; 2. əsòuʃiéiʃənəl]. Prec. & **-al.** Pertaining to, based on, the association of ideas.

associationalism, n. [1. asòshiáshunalizm; 2. əsòuʃiéiʃənəlizəm]. See prec. & **-ism.** Philosophic doctrines of the associationalists.

associationalist, n. [1. asòshiáshunalist; 2. əsòuʃiéiʃənəlist]. See prec. & **-ist.** Believer in system of philosophy which finds a basis in the association of ideas.

association football, n. One of the two main forms of the game of football, in which there are eleven players a side; the ball is round, and has to be kicked through the goal posts under the cross-bar; no handling of the ball is allowed except by goal-keeper. Cp. *rugby.*

assoil, vb. trans. [1. asóil; 2. əsóil]. M.E. *assoilen*, O. Fr. & A.-Fr. *assoiler*, Lat. *absolvere*, 'loosen, free from, acquit'. See **absolve.** (archaic) To absolve (from sin); pardon, acquit of guilt.

assoilzie, vb. trans. [1. asóilyi; 2. əsóilji]. Scots form of prec. (Scots law) To acquit.

assonance, n. [1. ásonans; 2. ǽsənəns]. Fr., as though fr. Lat. **assonantia*, fr. Lat. *assonant-em*, Pres. Part. of *assonāre*, 'to sound, respond to', fr. **ad-**, 'to', & *sonāre*, 'to sound'. See **sonant** & **sound** (I.). **a** Agreement in sound between two words as regards the stressed vowels, although the following consonant sounds are different, thus forming an imperfect rhyme, e.g. *take—fate*, or *sharper—garter*; **b** practice of using assonances as rhymes in verse.

assonant, adj. [1. ásonant; 2. ǽsənənt], fr. Lat. *assonant-(em)*, cp. prec. See **sonant.** Agreeing, corresponding to, in vowel sound.

assonate, vb. intrans. [1. ásonāt; 2. ǽsəneit], fr. Lat. *assonāt-(um)*, P.P. type of *assonāre*, see **assonance.** (followed by *with*) To agree with in vowel sound (of two words).

assort, vb. trans. & intrans. [1. asórt; 2. əsɔ́t], fr. Fr. *assortir*, 'sort, match', O. Fr. *assorter*, fr. *à*, 'to', & *sorte.* See **sort. A.** trans. **1.** (chiefly in P.P.) To separate and group into sorts or classes, classify according to similarity, or identity of character, appearance &c.: *a well-assorted, ill-assorted pair, company* &c. **2.** To furnish (goods) in an assortment or variety (chiefly in P.P.): *assorted chocolates.* **B.** intrans. *Assort with*, to belong to same class, to match, suit (with), agree: *to assort well, ill, with.*

assortment, n. [1. asórtment; 2. əsɔ́tmənt], Prec. & **-ment. 1.** Act of assorting, classifying &c. **2.** Collection of objects classified and grouped according to their kind; set of several such groups.

assuage, vb. trans. [1. aswáj; 2. əswéidž], fr. O. Fr. *assouager, assouagier*, fr. Lat. **ad-**, 'to', & *suāvis*, 'sweet, pleasant', see **suave. a** To allay, mitigate, reduce, soothe (physical suffering, pain, unrest &c.); **b** (fig.) to soften, still, render less acute (mental suffering, grief, anxiety, fear &c.); **c** to calm, soothe, relieve (passion, desire, anger &c.). Generally applied rather to sensations and emotions than to the persons who experience them. Intransitive use, to grow, become calm &c., now obsolete.

assuagement, n. [1. aswájment; 2. əswéidžmənt]. Prec. & **-ment.** Act or process of assuaging.

assumable, adj. [1. asúmabl; 2. əsjúməbl]. **assume** & **-able.** Capable of being, open to being, assumed.

assumably, adv. Prec. & **-ly.** By way of an assumption.

assume, vb. trans. & intrans. [1. asúm; 2. əsjúm], fr. Lat. *assūmere*, 'to take to, adopt, usurp', fr. **ad-** & *sūmere*, 'to take'; this vb. is fr. **sub-**, 'under', & *emere*, 'take, buy'. See **exempt. A.** trans. **1.** To take to oneself, appropriate, seize, adopt: *to assume the reins of government*; *assume control of.* Phr. (fig.) *to assume the offensive.* **2.** (of inanimate things) To take the form of, become like, present appearance of: *his illness assumed a very grave character.* **3.** To pretend to possess, put on, counterfeit: *to assume an air of innocence, importance* &c.; *assume voice, manner, of someone else.* **4.** To take for granted, suppose without definite proof: *to assume something for the sake of argument.* **B.** intrans. To be presumptuous, pretentious, to claim undue importance, display too great familiarity of manner.

assumed, adj. [1. asúmd; 2. əsjúmd], fr. P.P. of prec. **1.** Pretended, adopted in order to deceive; feigned, not real: *an assumed name, assumed air of benevolence.* **2.** Taken for granted, supposed.

assuming, adj. [1. asúming; 2. əsjúmiŋ], fr. Pres. Part. of **assume.** Presumptuous.

assumption, n. [1. asúmpshun; 2. əsámpʃən], fr. Lat. *assumptiōn-(em)*, 'a taking, receiving', fr. P.P. type *assumpt-(um).* See **assume** & **-ion. 1.** The act **a** of assuming, seizing, adopting, by exercise of force or right: *assumption of power, authority*; **b** of pretending to possess, adopting air or semblance of a quality or manner: *assumption of dignity, honesty* &c. **2. a** The act of taking for granted, without proof, that something exists, or that an event has happened; **b** that which is so taken as being true, or as having happened: *a mere, an unwarrantable, assumption.* **3.** (cap.) Miraculous removal from earth, without death, and reception into heaven, of the natural bodies of certain saints, esp. of the B.V.M.; the feast of the Church commemorating the latter on Aug. 15th.

assumptive, adj. [1. asúmptiv; 2. əsámptiv]. See prec. & **-ive**. **1.** Having nature of an assumption; capable of being assumed; presumptuous. **2.** (her.) *Assumptive arms*, arms granted, or assumed, as a distinction to commemorate a particular achievement.

assurance, n. [1. ashórans; 2. əʃɔ́rəns], fr. O. Fr. *aseurance*. See **assure** & **-ance**. **1. a** A declaration or assertion, positive statement based on certitude and tending to inspire confidence; **b** statement of the nature of a promise or guarantee: *to give an assurance that a debt will be paid.* **2.** The state of being sure; certainty, confidence: *we may have full assurance that everything possible was done.* **3. a** (in good sense) Confidence in oneself; self-possession, self-reliance, firmness: *an easy assurance of manner which bespeaks familiarity with the polite world*; **b** (in an unfavourable sense) overweening self-confidence, self-conceit, presumption: *a young man of unbounded assurance; he actually had the assurance to take all the credit for himself.* **4.** A variant of insurance, q.v.; only of life insurance. **5.** (law) Evidence of the conveyance of property.

assure, vb. trans. [1. ashór; 2. əʃɔ́]. O. Fr. *aseurer*, formed fr. Lat. *secūrus*, 'safe'. See **secure, sure**. **1.** To make safe and certain; secure, ensure: *this will assure your comfort.* **2. a** *To assure a person*, to assert with confidence, state positively (to a person) that a thing is so: *I assured him of our affection; we assured him that we were glad he was present*; **b** to convince a person, inspire certainty in him, by such statement that a thing is true: *I wish I could be assured that what you hope will come to pass; in spite of all I said I was unable to assure him of the fact*; **c** (reflex.) to persuade, convince, oneself by investigation that something is true: *before deciding I must assure myself of all the circumstances.* **3.** To undertake, state, confidently that certain things will be; to promise: *I can assure you (of) a hearty welcome.* **4.** To insure.

assured, adj. [1. ashórd; 2. əʃɔ́d], fr. P.P. of prec. **a** Made sure, safe: *success is assured; an assured position*; **b** insured.

assuredly, adv. [1. ashóredli; 2. əʃɔ́ridli]. Prec. & **-ly**. Certainly, without doubt.

assuredness, n. [1. ashórednes; 2. əʃɔ́ridnis]. See prec. & **-ness**. Certainty, self-confidence (esp. in bad sense).

assurgent, adj. [1. asérjent; 2. əsə́dʒənt], fr. Lat. *assurgent-(em)*, Pres. Part. of *assurgere*, 'to rise up', fr. **ad-** & *surgere*, 'to rise'. See **surge**. Rising, specif. **a** (her.) blazoned as rising from the sea; **b** (bot., of stems) curving upward.

Assyriology, n. [1. asìriólojì; 2. æsìriɔ́lədʒi] *Assyria* & **-logy**. The study of the antiquities, ancient civilization, language &c., of Assyria.

astatic, adj. [1. ástátik; 2. éistǽtik], fr. Gk. *ástatos*, 'not steadfast, unstable', fr. **a-**, 'not', & *statós*, 'standing', vbl. adj. of *hístēmi*, 'I make to stand'. See **static**. **a** (of magnetic needle) Without tendency to keep in one position, unaffected by magnetism of the earth; **b** (in electricity) of coils so wound that currents passed through them produce no external magnetic field.

aster, n. [1. áster; 2. ǽstə], fr. Lat. *aster*, fr. Gk. *astḗr*, 'star'. See **astral**. (bot.) Genus of herbaceous plants, with showy flowers of various colours; in England blooming in autumn. *China aster*, variety of this flower.

aster, Lat. suff., also in O. Fr. *-astre*; expresses similarity as in Lat. *oleaster*, 'wild olive tree', or diminutiveness, & inferiority, as in *poetaster*, a second-rate, would-be, poet.

asterisk, n. [1. ásterisk; 2. ǽstərisk], fr. Lat. *asteriscus*, fr. Gk. *asterískos*, dimin. of *astḗr*, 'star', q.v. under **astral**. The figure of a star (*) used in writing and printing to mark words for reference &c., or to indicate a hypothetical form, or to fill up spaces in a line where something is omitted.

asterism, n. [1. ásterizm; 2. ǽstərizəm], fr. Gk. *asterismós*, 'constellation', fr. *astḗr*, 'star'. See **astral**. **a** (astron.) A cluster of stars, constellation; **b** three asterisks (⁎*⁎) together, in writing and printing, calling special attention to a word or passage.

astern, adv. [1. astérn, astárn; 2. əstə́n, əstɑ́n]. **a-**, 'on', & **stern** (II.). (naut.) Towards, at, in back part of ship; backwards, as in *full speed astern.*

asteroid, adj. & n. [1. ásteroid; 2. ǽstərɔid], fr. Gk. *asteroeidḗs*, 'star-like', fr. *astḗr*, 'star'; see **astral** & **-oid**. **1.** adj. Star-shaped, star-like. **2.** n. **a** (astron.) One of the small planets whose orbits are between Mars and Jupiter; **b** (zool.) one of the *Asteroidea*, a starfish.

asthenia, n. [1. asthenía, asthḗnia; 2. æsþənáiə, æspíniə], fr. Gk. *asthéneia*, 'weakness', fr. **a-** (priv.) & *sthénos*, 'strength', of wh. the origin is obscure. (med.) Weakness, debility.

asthenic, adj. [1. asthénik; 2. æspénik]. Prec. & **-ic**. Weak, debilitated.

asthma, n. [1. ásma; 2. ǽsmə], fr. Gk. *âsthma*, 'hard-drawn breath, panting, gasping'; connected w. Gk. *áēmi*, 'breathe hard, blow', fr. **a-wē-mi*; the base **wā-*, 'blow', occurs in Scrt. *vā́ti*, 'blows', O. Slav. *vějati*, Lat. *ventus*, 'wind', Goth. *waian*, 'blow' &c. See **air, wind**. (med.) Chronic, or recurrent, affection of organs of respiration, attended by difficulty in breathing and constant wheezing and coughing.

asthmatic, adj. & n. [1. àsmátik; 2. æ̀smǽtik], fr. Lat. *asthmaticus*, fr. Gk. *asthmatikós*. See prec. **a** adj. Connected with asthma; suffering from asthma; **b** n., person afflicted with asthma.

asthmatically, adv. [1. àsmátikali; 2. æ̀smǽtikəli]. Prec. & **-al** & **-ly**. As if suffering from asthma.

astigmatic, adj. [1. àstigmátik; 2. æ̀stigmǽtik], fr. Gk. **a-**, 'not', & *stigma, stigmatos*, 'a puncture, mark, spot'. See **stigma, stigmatic**. (med. and opt.) **a** Pertaining to, suffering from, astigmatism; **b** suitable for, correcting, astigmatism: *astigmatic lenses* &c.

astigmatism, n. [1. astígmatizm; 2. əstígmətizəm]. See prec. & **-ism**. (med. and opt.) Structural defect of the eye which prevents the rays of light from being focussed to a single point on the retina, causing indistinctness of vision.

astir, adv. & adj. [1. astér; 2. əstə́]. **a-** & **stir** (II.). Agog, in motion; up from bed; in state of excitement: *to be early astir; the whole town was astir with the news.*

astonish, vb. trans. [1. astónish; 2. əstɔ́niʃ]. M.E. *astonen*, 'astound', fr. O. Fr. *estuner*, Mod. Fr. *étonner*, L. Lat. *ex-tonāre*, 'strike, shock', cp. *tonāre*, 'to thunder'. To this old vb. the suff. **-ish** (II.) has been added, on anal. of *extinguish* &c. See **astound**. To excite the emotion caused by the unexpected, strike with wonder, to surprise, amaze.

astonished, adj. [1. astónisht; 2. əstɔ́niʃt], fr. P.P. of prec. Filled with surprise, amazed.

astonishing, adj. [1. astónishing; 2. əstɔ́niʃiŋ], fr. Pres. Part. of **astonish**. Causing surprise, wonderful.

astonishingly, adv. Prec. & **-ly**. In an unexpected manner, to an unexpected extent.

astonishment, n. [1. astónishment; 2. əstɔ́niʃmənt]. **astonish** & **-ment**. The mental state produced by something unexpected; wonder, surprise, amazement.

astound, vb. trans. [1. astóund; 2. əstáund], fr. M.E. *aston(i)en*, wh. see under **astonish**, w. 'inorganic' final *-d* as in **sound** (I.) & (II.). The earlier ancestral type must have been *astoun* [ū]. The Low Lat. form is *ex-tonāre*, the second element of wh. is *tonāre*, 'to thunder', fr. a base found very widely, Scrt. *tányati*, 'roars, thunders', Gk. *stónos*, 'sigh, groan', *sténein*, 'to wail, groan', further O.E. *þunian*, 'resound', & *þunor*, 'thunder'. The development of meaning of *astound* is paralleled by our expression '*thunderstruck*'. See **thunder**. To fill with amazement, strike with stupefaction by presenting something unexpected to the attention (more forcible than *astonish*).

astounding, adj. [1. astóunding; 2. əstáundiŋ], fr. Pres. Part. of prec. Of a nature to astound; amazing, marvellous.

astraddle, adv. [1. astrádl; 2. əstrǽdl]. See **straddle**. In a straddling position, with a leg on either side of something.

astragal, n. [1. ástragal; 2. ǽstrəgəl], fr. Lat. *astragalus*, fr. Gk. *astrágalos*, 'one of the vertebrae of the neck; ball of ankle-joint; moulding in the capital of Ionic column'; prob. connected w. *ostéon*, 'bone', *óstrakon*, 'hard shell, as of snails' &c. **a** (archit.) Convex, rounded moulding; **b** moulding, or ring, round cannon near the mouth.

astragalus, n. [1. astrágalus; 2. əstrǽgələs]. See prec. (anat.) Ball of ankle-joint.

astrakhan, n. [1. àstrakán; 2. æ̀strəkǽn], fr. Astrakhan in Russia. The pelt of still-born or young lambs from Astrakhan, which is black, with small tight curls; used for trimming coats &c.

astral, adj. [1. ástral; 2. ǽstrəl]. Fr., fr. Lat. *astrālis*, adj., fr. *astrum*, 'star', fr. Gk. *ástron*, same base as Gk. *astḗr* (see **aster**); cogn. w. Lat. *stella*, fr. **ster-la*, Goth. *stair-nō*, O.H.G. *sterro*, O.E. *steorra*. See **star** & **stellar**. **1.** Pertaining to the stars: *astral influence.* **2.** (theos.) *Astral body*, one alleged to exist and to consist of highly rarefied form of matter.

astray, adv. [1. astrá; 2. əstréi]. **a-**, 'on', & **stray**, on anal. of *abroad* &c.; the second element is only found as a verb. Esp. in Phr. *to go, to lead, to be led, astray*, **a** (lit.) in, on, wrong path, in wrong direction, off the right track; **b** fig., of intellectual error, or **c** of moral lapse.

astrict, vb. trans. [1. astríkt; 2. əstríkt], fr. Lat. *astrict-(um)*, P.P. type of *astringere*, 'to draw close, bind, tighten'. See **astringe**. (rare or obs.) To bind, confine; constrict, restrict.

astriction, n. [1. astríkshun; 2. əstríkʃən]. Prec. & **-ion**. (med.) Contraction of parts; action of an astringent.

astrictive, adj. & n. [1. astríktiv; 2. əstríktiv]. **astrict** & **-ive**. **a** adj. Having action of an astringent; **b** n., an astringent.

astride, adv. & prep. [1. astríd; 2. əstráid]. **a-**, 'on', & **stride**. With one leg on either side of: **a** adv., *to ride astride*; **b** prep., *to sit astride* (or *astride of*) *a horse.*

astringe, vb. trans. [1. astrínj; 2. əstríndʒ], fr. Lat. *adstringere*, fr. **ad-**, 'to', & *stringere*, 'draw or tie tight, to bind'; w. this word may be cpd. Gk. *strággō*, 'draw tight, bind, squeeze'; & the Gmc. group of words connected w. O.E. *strang* &c., 'strong'. See **strain, strong**. (rare or obs.) To constrict, compress.

astringency, n. [1. astrínjensi; 2. əstríndʒənsi]. See prec. & foll. words & **stringency**. The property of being astringent.

astringent, adj. & n. [1. astrínjent; 2. əstríndʒənt], fr. Pres. Part. *astringent-(em)*. See **astringe**. **a** adj. Having the property of drawing together soft tissues, contracting severed vessels, thus checking flow of blood &c.; **b** n., a drug or other agent which effects this.

astro-, pref. Form used in composition, in sense of 'star-', 'connected with the heavenly bodies' &c., fr. Gk. *ástron*, 'star'. See **aster, astral**.

astrolabe, n. [1. ástrōlàb; 2. ǽstroulèib]. In M.E., & O. Fr. *astrelabe*, fr. **astro-** & Gk. base *lab-*, seen in *la(m)bánein*, 'to take, seize'. See **catalepsy**. Instrument used formerly by astrologers for ascertaining the positions of the heavenly bodies; a kind of primitive sextant.

astrologer, n. [1. astrólojer; 2. əstrɔ́lədžə]. See **astrology** & **-er**. Student of astrology, esp. one who professed to foretell events from an observation of the heavenly bodies.

astrological, adj. [1. astrolójikl; 2. æstrəlɔ́džikl]. Gk. **astro-** & **-logy** & **-ic** & **-al**. Connected with astrology.

astrology, n. [1. astróloji; 2. əstrɔ́lədži], fr. Fr. *astrologie*, fr. Lat. *astrologia*, fr. Gk. *astrologia*. See **astro-** & **-logy**. Study of the stars; primitive astronomy; now a pseudo-science mainly concerned with prediction of events by means of deductions from relative position of the heavenly bodies at a given moment.

astrometer, n. [1. astrómeter; 2. æstrɔ́mitə]. See **astro-** & **meter**. Instrument for determining the brightness of stars.

astronomer, n. [1. astrónomer; 2. əstrɔ́nəmə]. See **astronomy** & **-er**. One skilled in, a student of, the science of astronomy.

astronomic(al), adj. [1. astronómik(l); 2. æstrənɔ́mik(l). See **astronomy** & **-ic** & **-al**. Relating to, concerned with, depending on, astronomy.

astronomically, adv. Prec. & **-ly**. In accordance with, from the point of view of, astronomy.

astronomy, n. [1. astrónomi; 2. əstrɔ́nəmi]. M.E., fr. O. Fr. *astronomie*, fr. Gk. *astronomía*, fr. *astro-nómos*, 'classing the stars; an astronomer', see **astro-**, **astral**, & Gk. *nómos*, 'anything assigned or apportioned, custom, law', see **nomad**. The science of stars or the other heavenly bodies.

astrophysics, n. [1. àstrōfíziks; 2. æ̀strou-fíziks]. **astro-** & **physics**. That branch of astronomy which deals with the physical and chemical properties of the planets and stars.

astute, adj. [1. astút; 2. əstjút]. Lat. *astūtus*, 'artful, clever, crafty, cunning', fr. *astus*, 'cleverness, craft, cunning'. Origin doubtful. Shrewd, sagacious; wily, cunning, crafty.

astutely, adv. Prec. & **-ly**. Cleverly, knowingly, craftily.

astuteness, n. See prec. & **-ness**. Sagacity, cunning.

asunder, adv. [1. asúnder; 2. əsándə]. O.E. *on sundran*. See **a-** & **sunder**. **1.** (of a single object) Right through, in two halves, in pieces: *the cup fell, broke, was broken asunder*. **2.** (of two or more things) Implying separation; **a** by moving, or being moved, away from each other, apart, in different directions: *to fly, rush, be driven asunder*; **b** by position in space, remote from each other: *the two places lay far asunder*. **3.** (fig., of persons) Separated; different in character.

asylum, n. [1. asílum; 2. əsáiləm]. Lat., fr. Gk. *ásūlon*, 'refuge, sanctuary', neut. of adj. *ásūlos*, 'free from plunder, unharmed, inviolable', fr. **a-**, 'not', & *sū́lē, sûlon*, 'right of seizure', cp. *sūlā́ō*, 'I strip, plunder, carry off'. Etymol. obscure. **1.** Place of refuge and protection; sanctuary. **2.** (now chiefly specif.) Institution for the care and skilled treatment of the blind, deaf, or insane.

asymmetrical, adj. [1. ásimétrikl; 2. éisimétrikl]. Next word & **-ic** & **-al**. Not symmetrical, unequal in size or shape of its two sides, irregular.

asymmetry, n. [1. ásímetri; 2. éisímitri], fr. Gk. *asummetría*, fr. *asúmmetros*, fr. **a-**, 'not', & *súmmetros*. See **symmetry**. Absence of symmetry, esp. between two sides of same thing; irregularity.

asymptote, n. [1. ásimtōt; 2. ǽsimtout], fr. Gk. *asúmptōtos*, 'not falling together', fr. **a-**, 'not', *sún*, 'with', & *ptōtós*, vbl. adj. fr. *píptein*, 'to fall'. See **symptom**. (math.) A line continually approaching a curve but never meeting it; a tangent at infinity.

asyndeton, n. [1. asíndeton; 2. æsínditən], fr. Gk. *asúndetos, -on*, 'unconnected', fr. **a-**, 'not', & *sún*, 'together', & *déō*, 'I bind', cp. for last element, **diadem**. (rhet.) A figure of speech in which conjunctions are omitted.

at, prep. [1. at; 2. æt, ət]. O.E. *æt*, 'in, at' of place; time when; expresses also motion towards; source, origin; deprivation, equivalence, price; M.E. *at*, Goth. *at*, 'at, by, from', O. Sax. *at*, O.H.G. *az*, cogn. w. Lat. *ad*, 'towards', with or without motion; 'near to, by, at'; of time, 'towards, about, in, at'. See **ad-**. Other relations are doubtful. **1.** **a** Expresses place in which, or where, anything is; used before names of places, except that of London: *at Brighton, Oxford, Edinburgh* &c.; **b** position in which anything remains, stands: *at the top of the house*; *at the head of the line*; Phr. *at close quarters*, very near; **c** expresses point reached, after motion, attainment of object of a journey: *to arrive at the bank of the river, at the end of the journey, at one's destination*. **2.** (of time, before names of hours and of certain seasons; not before names of days, months, the four seasons) When an event takes place, or action is performed: *at Christmas, Easter*; *at noon*; *at 5 o'clock*; *at dinner-time*; *at the beginning*. **3.** Expresses mode of occupation; concerned with, engaged in: *to be at work, play*; *at breakfast, at prayer*. Phr. *to be at, what are you at now?*, what are you doing? **4.** Expresses state or condition: *at peace, at war, at one's disposal*. Phrs. *at peace*, specif., dead; *at loggerheads (with)*, in hostility, having a quarrel (with); *at daggers drawn*, in a state of violent hostility. **5.** Expresses manner in which something is done: *at a bound, at a (the) run*; *at a gallop*. Phrs. *at one fell swoop*, with a single act; *at a sitting*, after one continuous effort; *at a pinch*, as a matter of absolute necessity. **6.** Expresses motion towards: **a** *to run, rush, jump at*; *let me get at him*; **b** direction towards: *to point at, aim at, shoot at, look at*. **7.** Expresses origin, source; from: *to drink at the brook*; *to get (information) at the fountain-head*; *to receive something at a person's hands*. **8.** Expresses amount, number, price; equivalent to so much, so many: *to reckon one's expenses at so much a week*; *to estimate a crowd at ten thousand*; *to engage labour at 5s. a day per man*; *to sell, buy, at such and such a price*. **9.** In a large number of adverbial phrases denoting **a** relations in space, e.g. *at a distance, at hand, at sea*; **b** time: *at once, at last*; **c** manner or condition: *at all, not at all, at least, at bay*; **d** position: *at attention* (of soldiers); *at home*.

atavism, n. [1. átavizm; 2. ǽtəvizəm], fr. Fr. *atavisme*, fr. Lat. *atavus*, 'father of a great-grandfather, ancestor', fr. *at-*, 'beyond', & *avus*, 'grandfather'. *At-* is prob. the same word as Lat. *at*, 'but', cogn. w. Scrt. *áti*, 'over and above, beyond', & O. Slav. *otŭ*, 'away from'. *Avus* & *ava*, 'grandmother', belong to a primitive Aryan group of relationship words; Goth. has *awō*, 'grandmother'; O. Prussian *awis*, 'uncle', Lith. *avýnas*, 'uncle', O. Ir. *aue*, 'nephew, grandson'. See further under **avuncular**, **eme**. (biol.) Recurrence in a descendant of some physical character or mental trait, derived from a remote ancestor, rather than from the immediate progenitors.

atavistic, adj. [1. àtavístik; 2. æ̀təvístik]. See prec. & **-istic**. Due to, produced by, atavism (of the character); having tendency to atavism (of the individual organism).

ataxia, -xy, n. [1. atáksia, atáksi; 2. ətǽksiə, ətǽksi]. Gk., 'want of order, discipline', fr. **a-**, 'not', & *táxis*, 'arrangement, disposition, battle-order, order'; cp. *tássō*, 'I arrange, put in order'. See **tactic**. (med.) Disease affecting the motor nerves and muscles, characterized by loss of control of these and lack of co-ordinated movement, esp. in the disease known as *locomotor ataxy* or tabes.

ataxic, adj. [1. atáksik; 2. ətǽksik], fr. prec. & **-ic**. Connected with, due to, ataxia.

ate, vb. [1. āt; 2. eit]. Pret. of **eat**. This form is now obsolesc. & rarely used, the normal past tense being *eat* [1. et; 2. ɛt]. *Ate* presupposes M.E. *āte*, formed on the **anal.** of *brake, spake*.

-ate, suff. [1. āt, at; 2. eit, ət]. **1.** From Lat. P.P. *-ātum*, in vbs. of first (*-āre*) conjugation; **a** used to form adjectives like *disconsolate, inviolate, sedate, ornate*; **b** to form English verbs on model of Latin verbs of first conjugation, *separate, venerate*; or verbs which Latin did not form from nouns with stems in *-āt-*, such as *felicitate, facilitate*, from Latin (acc.) *felicitāt-(em), facilitāt-(em)* &c.; **c** to form adjectival, participial nouns as *delegate*, one delegated; **d** (chem.) forming names of salts of acids, usually ending in **-ic**, as *nitrate*, from nitric acid &c. **2.** From Latin forms in *-ātus*, genit. *-ātūs*, not from P.P.; the words express office, dignity, rank &c., and form nouns such as *episcopate, vice-cancellariate, professoriate* &c.

atelier, n., Engl.-Fr. [1. áteliā; 2. ǽtəliei]. Fr., fr. O. Fr. *astelier*, fr. Low Lat. **hastellarium*, place where **hastellae* or small planks were made; the latter is for Lat. *hastula*, dimin. of *hasta*, 'spear, shaft', wh. is cogn. w. Goth. *gazds*, 'goad', see **hastate**. Workshop; artist's studio.

Athanasian Creed, n. [1. àthanā́shan; 2. æ̀þənéiʃən]. Creed attributed to Athanasius, bishop of Alexandria, d. 373 A.D., the defender of orthodox Christianity against Arianism; beginning with the words *Quicunque vult*, 'Whosoever will be saved'.

atheism, n. [1. áthēizm; 2. éiþi-izəm], fr. Gk. *átheos*, fr. **a-**, 'without', & *théos*, 'God', & **-ism**. See **theo-**. Disbelief in the existence of a God or supreme Being (this is sometimes called *moral atheism*).

atheist, n. [1. áthēist; 2. éiþi-ist]. See prec. & **-ist**. One who does not believe in the existence of God; one who believes that God does not exist, and who proclaims this negative dogma.

atheistic(al), n. [1. àthēístik(l); 2. èiþiístik(l)]. Prec. & **-ic** & **-al**. Pertaining to atheists and atheism; tending to the latter.

atheistically, adv. Prec. & **-ly**. After the manner of atheists.

Athenaeum, n. [1. àthenḗum; 2. æ̀þəníəm]. Lat. form of Gk. *Athḗnaion*, the temple of *Athḗnē*, goddess of wisdom. **a** A literary or scientific club; **b** building in which such a club and its library are housed.

athirst, pred. adj. [1. athérst; 2. əþə́st]. **a-**, 'on', & **thirst**. The form might possibly be derived fr. O.E. *of-þyrst*, P.P.; if not it is a new formation on a common pattern. **a** Thirsty (archaic and poet.); **b** (followed by *for* before a noun) eager, longing for, esp. *athirst for information* &c.

athlete, n. [1. áthlēt; 2. ǽþlīt], fr. Lat. *athlēta*, fr. Gk. *athlētḗs*, 'a combatant', fr. *athléō*, 'I contend for a prize', fr. *âthlos*, 'contest', *âthlon*, 'the prize of contest'. This is contracted fr. earlier *áethlon*, wh. is for **awethlon*; the first part of this, **awe-*, may be cogn. w. Scrt. *vā́-yati*, 'fatigue, exhaust oneself'. The old suggestion that the Aryan base was **wedh-*, connected w. Goth. *wadi*, 'pledge', Lat. *vas* for **vad-s*, 'surety', is now commonly rejected. See these words under **wed**. One devoted to, and skilled in, physical exercises, esp. in running, jumping &c.; the term is also applied to persons addicted to such games as cricket and football.

athletic, adj. [1. athlétik; 2. æþlétik], fr. Lat. *āthlēticus*, Gk. *athlētikós*, fr. *athlētḗs*, see **athlete**, & **-ic**. **a** Pertaining to athletes or their pursuits &c.: *athletic sports*; **b** like an athlete, physically strong, active, skilled in exercises and outdoor games.

athletically, adv. [1. athlétikali; 2. æþlétikəli]. Prec. & **-al** & **-ly**. In an athletic manner, like an athlete.

athleticism, n. [1. athlétisizm; 2. æþlétisizəm]. See **athletic** & **-ism**. The practice of athletics; devotion to athletics.

athletics, n. pl. [1. athlétiks; 2. æþlétiks]. Collective name for physical exercises and games requiring skill and activity.

at-home, n. [1. at (h)ṓm; 2. ət (h)óum]. Social function at which guests are received at an appointed hour.

athwart, adv. & prep. [1. athwórt; 2. əþwɔ́t]. See **a-**, 'on', & **thwart (II.)**. **1.** adv. **a** Across, from side to side; **b** (lit. and fig.) across the course, implying opposition. **2.** prep. **a** Across, extending from side to side of; **b** (lit. and fig.) across the course, path of; implying hindrance or opposition.

-atic, suff. [1. átik; 2. ǽtik], used to form adjs., *dramatic* &c., & these used as ns., *fanatic*, fr. Fr. *-atique*, Lat. *-aticus*.

atilt, adv. & adj. [1. atílt; 2. ətílt]. See **a-** & **tilt**. Only in Phr. *to ride, run, atilt*, run at as though tilting with a lance.

-ation, suff. [1. áshun; 2. éiʃən]. Used for forming abstract ns. fr. vbs., fr. Lat. *-ātiōn-(em)*, formed fr. P.P. type, *-āt-*, of vbs. of 1st conjugation in *-āre*; it occurs in Fr. & Engl. in words derived straight fr. Lat. words of this type, but also by extension of the type in many others formed on model of these; the frequency of this suff. in Fr. & Engl. is due to the former using the type of 1st Lat. conjugation as the commonest verbal type.

-ative, adj. suff. [1. ātiv, ativ; 2. éitiv, ətiv]. Fr. *-atif*, Lat. *-ātīvus*. Chiefly in formations fr. vbs. in *-ate*, *demonstrative* &c., but sometimes extended to adjs. formed fr. Engl. vbs., *talkative*.

atlantes, n. pl. [1. atlántēz; 2. ətlǽntīz]. Gk., pl. of *Atlas*. See **atlas**. (archit.) Pillars supporting an entablature, sculptured to represent men with arms upraised as if carrying a heavy burden.

Atlantic, n. & adj. [1. atlántik; 2. ətlǽntik]. Lat. *Atlanticus*, fr. Gk. *Atlantikós*, fr. stem of *Atlās*, the Atlas Mountains in N.W. Africa, fr. the name of the god *Atlas*, see next word. **1.** n. The ocean dividing the American continent from Europe and Africa. **2.** adj. Connected with, found or situated in, this ocean: *an Atlantic liner, voyage*; *the Atlantic islands*.

atlas, n. [1. átlas; 2. ǽtləs], fr. name of a Gk. god who was supposed to bear the world upon his shoulders. The *-tl-* is prob. a reduced form of Aryan base **tol-*, **tel-*, 'to bear'. See this under **thole (I.)**, & **tolerate**. The figure of Atlas supporting the globe was frequently put on front page of an atlas. **1.** A collection of maps bound into a volume. **2.** (anat.) The top vertebra of spinal column which bears the skull.

atmolysis, n. [1. atmólisis; 2. ætmɔ́lisis]. See first element in **atmosphere**, & **-lysis**. (physics) Separation of mixed gases by making use of the different rates at which they are diffused through porous substances.

atmometer, n. [1. atmómeter; 2. ætmɔ́mitə]. See first element in **atmosphere**, & **-meter**. Instrument for measuring the rate of evaporation.

atmosphere, n. [1. átmosfēr; 2. ǽtməsfiə], fr. Gk. *atmós*, 'smoke, vapour', *sphaîra*, 'ball, sphere'. The first element is either for **awe-tmos*, & cogn. w. Gk. *áēmi*, 'blow', see **air, vent, wind (I.)**; or it is cogn. w. Scrt. *ātmā* & O.E. *ǣþm*, 'breath'. For second element see **sphere**. **1.** Gaseous envelope surrounding the earth or other heavenly body. **2.** The condition of the air in any particular locality, esp. as affected by heat, cold &c.: *cold, stuffy, atmosphere of a room* &c. **3.** (fig.) Any surrounding mental or moral influence or environment: *a tense, electric atmosphere prevailed at the meeting*.

atmospheric(al), adj. [1. àtmosférik(l); 2. ætməsférik(l)]. See **atmosphere** & **-ic** & **-al**. Belonging to, connected with, the atmosphere.

atmospherics, n. pl. [1. àtmosfériks; 2. ætməsfériks], fr. prec. Strong ether waves, due to natural causes, as lightning, which interfere with the reception of signals in wireless.

atoll, n. [1. atól; 2. ətɔ́l]. Malay. A coral island; belt of coral reef surrounding a lagoon.

atom, n. [1. átum; 2. ǽtəm], fr. Fr. *atome*, fr. Lat. *atomus*, fr. Gk. *átomos*, 'atom', lit. 'uncut, indivisible', fr. **a-**, 'not', & *tomós*, vbl. adj. of *témnō*, 'I cut, split'. This base occurs also in M. Ir. *tamnaim*, 'I mutilate'; O. Slav. *tĕti*, fr. **tenti*, 'to split'. See **tome**. **1. a** Originally, the smallest ultimate and indivisible theoretical portion of matter, now, however, divisible into electrons; see next word; **b** (in chem.) the smallest portion of an element which exists alone or combined with other similar portions of an element; see next word. **2.** A minute portion of anything; some very small thing. Phr. *to smash, break, to atoms*.

atomic, adj. [1. atómik; 2. ətɔ́mik]. See prec. & **-ic**. Of, connected with, atoms. *Atomic theory*, a theory of the constitution of matter propounded by Democritus and other Greek philosophers; as first formulated in scientific shape by John Dalton, it declares that matter consists of uniform indivisible particles, atoms, alone or in combination, of a definite number of elements; modern research into the electrical theories of matter by J. J. Thomson and others has shown that atoms consist of complex systems of electrical charges (electrons) in rapid orbital motion. *Atomic weight*, relative weight of an atom of an element, taken usually from hydrogen as unity or from oxygen as 16; elements are arranged in order of their atomic weights, and from these tables the existence of previously unknown elements has been deduced.

atomicity, n. [1. àtomísiti; 2. ætəmísiti]. See prec. & **-ity**. Number of atoms in a molecule.

atomism, n. [1. átomizm; 2. ǽtəmizəm]. See **atom** & **-ism**. Doctrine that physical universe is composed of indivisible atoms.

atomist, n. [1. átomist; 2. ǽtəmist]. See prec. & **-ist**. One who holds doctrine of atomism.

atomization, n. [1. àtomīzáshun; 2. ætəmaizéiʃən]. See next word & **-ation**. Process or act of atomizing.

atomize, vb. trans. [1. átomīz; 2. ǽtəmaiz], fr. **atom** & **-ize**. To reduce to atoms; convert liquids into fine spray.

atomizer, n. [1. átomīzer; 2. ǽtəmaizə]. Prec. & **-er**. Instrument for converting liquids to fine spray, esp. for purposes of disinfection.

atomy (I.), n. [1. átomi; 2. ǽtəmi], fr. **anatomy**, the first syll. being taken for indef. art. Skeleton; (by extension) thin, emaciated person.

atomy (II.), n. See **atom** & **-y**. Atom; minute creature.

at one, adv. See separate words. In agreement, of one mind, in harmony.

atone, vb. intrans. [1. atṓn; 2. ətóun], fr. **at, one**, & preserving old type of latter word. In earlier Mod. Engl. *atone* is used in physical sense of unite; this and the trans. use, *to atone a crime* &c., are now entirely obs. Now always *atone for*: to expiate, make reparation, amends, give satisfaction, for an offence, crime &c. (often implying further suffering on part of person who atones).

atonement, n. [1. atṓnment; 2. ətóunmənt], fr. **atone** & **-ment**. **a** Act of atoning, expiation; **b** specif., *the Atonement*, the expiatory work of the Saviour, in redeeming man and reuniting him to God.

atonic, adj. [1. atónik; 2. ətɔ́nik], fr. Gk. *átonos*, 'without tone', fr. **a-**, 'without', & *tónos*. See **tonic**. **a** In vague terminology of popular phonetics used in sense both of unaccented (of syllables), and voiceless (of sounds) (best avoided in either of these senses); **b** (med.) lacking vital energy; characterized by, arising from, such a lack: *atonic disease*.

atrabilious, adj. [1. átrabílius; 2. ǽtrəbíljəs], fr. Lat. *āter*, *ātra*, 'dark, black', & *bīliōsus*, 'bilious', fr. *bīlis*, 'bile, gall'. See this under **bilious**; Lat. *āter* is prob. connected w. O. Pers. *ātarš*, 'fire', & perh. w. Serb. & Little Russ. *vátra*, 'fire, hearth'; the Lat. word apparently meant orig. 'burnt, burnt black'. Melancholy, hypochondriacal, cantankerous, lit. 'suffering from black bile'.

atrabiliousness, n. Prec. & **-ness**. State of being atrabilious.

atrip, adv. [1. atríp; 2. ətríp]. **a-**, 'on', & **trip**. (naut.) Of an anchor, just clear of the ground when being drawn up.

atrium, n. [1. ātrium; 2. éitriəm]. Lat.; etymol. is obscure, but connexion w. Etruscan *ātar*, 'stone', is suggested; the Lat. word meant perh. orig. 'stone court, or chamber'. **1.** Central court or chief apartment of a Roman house. **2.** (anat.) A chamber, cavity, esp. of an auricle of the heart, or the tympanum of the ear.

atrocious, adj. [1. atrṓshus; 2. ətróuʃəs], fr. Lat. *ātrōx*, *ātrōcis*, 'cruel', & **-ous**; none of the proposed etymols. is very convincing, but the suggestion that the word is *āter*, 'black' (see **atrabilious**), & **ōx*, fr. **ōkʷ-*, 'eye' (cp. Gk. *ṓps* & compound *glaukṓpis*), is interesting. See **ferocious**. **a** Extremely cruel or wicked, heinous; **b** horrible, horrifying, abominable.

atrociously, adv. Prec. & **-ly**. In an atrocious manner; colloquially used to express mere disapproval or dislike: *atrociously bad sermon, dinner, manners* &c.; thus used, the word has no sense of moral depravity.

atrociousness, n. See prec. & **-ness**. Condition of being atrocious; action of atrocious character.

atrocity, n. [1. atrósiti; 2. ətrɔ́siti], fr. Lat. *ātrōcitāt-(em)*, fr. *ātrōx*, 'fierce, cruel'. See **atrocious**. **a** Condition of being atrocious; **b** an act of extreme brutality, cruelty, or outrageous wickedness; (in pl.) a series of shocking, cruel, and abominable deeds.

atrophic, adj. [1. atrófik; 2. ætrɔ́fik], fr. **atrophy** & **-ic**. Connected with, arising from, atrophy.

atrophied, adj. [1. átrofid; 2. ǽtrəfid], fr. P.P. of **atrophy (II.)**. Shrunk, reduced in bulk or amount through lack of nourishment, or through disuse.

atrophy (I.), n. [1. átrofi; 2. ǽtrəfi]. Fr. *atrophie*, fr. Lat. *atrophia*, fr. Gk. *atrophía*, fr. *átrophos*, 'not nourished', fr. **a-**, 'not', & *trophḗ*, 'nourishment'; cp. Gk. *tréphō*, 'fatten, nourish', also 'thicken, coagulate'; cp. also *trophalís*, 'curdled milk'. The base is Aryan **dhrebh-*, **dhrobh-*, whence O.E. *drōf*, 'turbid, muddy', *drēfan* (fr. **drōfjan*), 'make turbid (of water &c.); ruffle, trouble (the mind)'; Goth. *drōbjan*, 'excite, cause trouble'; O.H.G. *truobi*, 'dark, turbid' &c., Mod. Germ. *trübe*, & O.H.G. *truoben*, 'make cloudy, disturb' &c.; cp. further Lith. *drebti*, 'splash with thick liquid, mud' &c. See **draff**. **a** Shrinkage, wasting, diminution in bulk through lack of nourishment, esp. of an organ of the body: *atrophy of the lungs, liver* &c.; **b** (biol.) cessation of development of a part or organ in animals or plants, supposed to be due to disuse during many generations of the species; **c** (fig.) diminution, withering of moral qualities: *atrophy of conscience, virtue* &c.

atrophy (II.), vb. intrans. & trans., fr. prec. **a** intrans. To waste away, shrink, become weak and useless through atrophy (lit. and fig.); **b** trans., to cause to waste away, produce atrophy in.

atropine, n. [1. átropēn; 2. ǽtrəpīn], fr. Gk. *átropa*, 'deadly nightshade', cp. also *átropos*, 'inflexible, what cannot be turned aside', name of one of the Fates, fr. **a-**, 'not', & *tropḗ*, 'turn, change', see **trope**, & **-ine**. Alkaloid poison extracted from the belladonna or deadly nightshade.

attach, vb. trans. & intrans. [1. atách; 2. ətǽtʃ]. M.E. *attachen*, 'arrest a prisoner', fr. O. Fr. *attachier*; *a*, 'to', & *tach-*, prob. of Gmc. origin. Cp. **tack (I.)**, 'small nail'. **A.** trans. **1.** (law) To arrest (a person), or seize (property) by legal authority. **2.** To fasten (one thing to another), by sticking, tying, binding &c.: *to attach a stamp, a label, weight* &c. **3.** (fig., of persons) **a** To cause to adhere, gain over to one's side, party, interests; **b** to connect with, allot to, by authority: *to attach an officer to a regiment, the staff* &c.; **c** to win affection, admiration, and, by these, the help and co-operation, of a person; attract; **d** (reflex.) *attach oneself*, to join, unite with, another person, party, society &c. **4.** (of non-material things) **a** To affix, assign: *attach a name, blame, to*; **b** to attribute, ascribe to: *to attach importance, significance &c. to.* **B.** intrans. To inhere in, be incident to: *great responsibilities attach to power and position.*

attachable, adj. [1. atáchabl; 2. ətǽtʃəbl], fr. prec. & **-able**. Capable of being attached.

attaché, n. [1. atáshā; 2. ətǽʃei]. Fr., P.P. of *attacher*, 'to attach'. See prec. **a** Junior official, usually without salary, attached to staff of an ambassador, or minister plenipotentiary at a foreign court; **b** military or naval officer connected with the embassy of his own sovereign at a foreign court in order to report on military and naval affairs: *military, naval, attaché.*

attaché case, n. Small, flat leather bag for carrying papers and documents.

attached, adj. [1. atácht; 2. ətǽtʃt], fr. P.P. of **attach**. **a** (of things) Fastened, fixed, appended to; **b** (of persons) officially connected with, assigned, allotted, to a particular post, office, set of duties &c.; **c** (of persons) joined by taste, inclination, or affection; devoted to: *attached to one's friends*; *the brothers were deeply attached.*

attachment, n. [1. atáchment; 2. ətǽtʃmənt], fr. **attach** & **-ment**. **1.** Means whereby one thing is attached to another. **2.** Moral bond between persons, springing from affection and respect; affection: *to form an attachment for.* **3.** (law) Arrest or seizure by legal authority.

attack (I.), vb. trans. [1. aták; 2. ətǽk]. Variant of **attach**, fr. Fr. *attaquer*, 'attack', Ital. *attaccare*, 'fasten, attack'. **1. a** To make a violent physical assault upon with intent to cause injury; **b** specif. (mil.) to initiate hostile action with armed forces against enemy in the field; take the offensive; assail with military forces and appliances. **2.** (fig.) To assail with hostile speech or writing; blame violently, direct strong unfavourable criticism against: *to attack a person, or a policy, on the platform, in the press* &c. **3.** To set to work upon, begin operations upon (a task or problem). **4.** (of disease, the elements &c.) **a** To act injuriously upon, affect prejudicially: *to be attacked by gout, malaria &c.*; *the damp is attacking the walls*; **b** (of chemical action) to act upon, cause wasting: *acid attacks metals.*

attack (II.), n., fr. prec. **1.** Violent hostile physical assault, **a** generally, of any such violence; **b** (mil.) specif., offensive operation by organized armed force upon another; opposite of *defence*; **c** strong adverse criticism, invective, directed against persons or measures, by speech or writing: *an attack in the House, in the press, against a minister, against the policy of government* &c. **2.** Onslaught of disease; bout, access, fit: *an attack of measles, gout* &c. **3.** Mode of beginning an action, esp. **a** in speaking or singing, process of beginning utterance of a sound, way of uttering note at beginning of a passage; **b** in games such as cricket, tennis &c., way of playing a stroke.

attacker, n. [1. atáker; 2. ətǽkə]. Prec. & **-er**. One who attacks.

attain, vb. trans. & intrans. [1. atā́n; 2. ətéin], fr. O. Fr. *ataign-*, *ateign-*, stem of *ataindre, ateindre*, fr. Lat. *attingere*, 'to come in contact with, touch, reach', fr. **ad-**, 'to', & *tangere*, 'to touch'. See **tangent**. **1.** trans. To gain, reach, achieve, accomplish, as result of effort (aims, ideals, aspirations &c.). **2.** intrans. *Attain to*, to reach, arrive at, come up to; (esp. of non-material things) **a** by natural development: *attain to man's estate*; **b** by deliberate effort: *to attain to power, prosperity &c.*; **c** by moral or intellectual effort: *to attain to wisdom, knowledge* &c.

attainability, n. [1. atā̀nabíliti; 2. ətèinəbíliti], fr. next word & **-ity**. Quality of being attainable.

attainable, adj. [1. atā́nabl; 2. ətéinəbl], fr. **attain** & **-able**. Capable of being attained.

attainableness, n. Prec. & **-ness**. Attainability.

attainder, n. [1. atā́nder; 2. ətéində], fr. O. Fr. *ataindre, ateindre*, 'accuse, condemn', fr. Lat. *attingere*. See **attain, attaint**. (law) Act of attainting; condition, result, of being attainted, that is, loss of civil rights through judicial or legislative sentence; the extinction of civil and legal rights as the result of a sentence of death or of outlawry; *bill of attainder*, legislative act inflicting results of attainder without judicial trial.

attainment, n. [1. atā́nment; 2. ətéinmənt], fr. **attain** & **-ment**. **1.** Act or process of attaining. **2.** Something attained, esp. a personal mental accomplishment or acquisition; proficiency in any branch of knowledge &c. (often in pl.): *a man of varied attainments.*

attaint (I.) vb. trans. [1. atā́nt; 2. ətéint]. O. Fr. *ataindre*, 'accuse, convict'. See **attainder**. Confused with **taint**. **1. a** To convict of crime (obs.); **b** to convict of crime punishable by attainder; to subject to attainder. **2.** To sully, dishonour (partly through confusion with *taint*).

attaint (II.), n., fr. prec. **1.** a Touch, hit (in a tournament, obs.); **b** specif., wound on horse's leg caused by an overreach. **2.** Stain, disgrace (confusion with *taint*).

attar, n. [1. áter; 2. ǽtə], also [1. ótō; 2. ɔ́tou]. Pers. *'ater*, 'perfume', fr. Arab. *'atara*, 'to smell sweet'. Cp. **otto**. Pungent, volatile oil distilled from flowers, used in perfumery; esp. *attar of roses.*

attemper, vb. trans. [1. atémper; 2. ətémpə], fr. Lat. *attemperāre*, fr. **ad-** & *temperāre*, 'to divide or proportion duly, to qualify, temper; to control, manage; to moderate or restrain oneself'. See **temper** (I.), wh. in all senses is now more usual. **1.** To mix in due proportion; to qualify by mixing; (of metals) to temper. **2.** To modify, moderate, soothe. **3.** To accommodate to, adapt.

attempered, adj. [1. atémperd; 2. ətémpəd], fr. P.P. of prec. Tempered, regulated, adapted.

attemperment, n. [1. atémperment; 2. ətémpəmənt]. See **attemper** & **-ment**. Act or process of attempering.

attempt (I.), vb. trans. [1. atémpt; 2. ətémpt]. O. Fr. *attempter*, fr. Lat. *attemptāre, attentāre*, 'strive after, attempt', fr. **ad-**, 'to', & *temptāre*, 'try, test'. See **tempt**. **1.** To try, endeavour, to do, or secure, something; **a** (followed by vbl. n. or infin.) *to attempt flying, to fly*; **b** (followed by n., vb. 'to do' &c. being understood) *to attempt a difficult task*; *attempt the mountain* (*to climb* understood); *attempt too much*; *attempt a settlement of the dispute.* **2.** To endeavour to master, or prevail over by force: *to attempt a person's life*; *to attempt a capture.*

attempt (II.), n., fr. prec. **1.** An endeavour to do something, effort, esp. to overcome a difficulty: *an attempt to save life, to stamp out disease, to do one's duty* &c. **2.** An endeavour to overcome someone, or obtain something by force; hence, an attack, assault (on life, virtue &c. of a person).

attend, vb. intrans & trans. [1. aténd; 2. əténd], fr. Fr. *attendre*, 'expect, wait for', Lat. *attendere*, orig. 'to stretch, bend mind to'. See **ad-**, 'to', & **tend**. **A.** intrans. **1.** (followed by *to*) **a** To direct the mind upon, fix one's thoughts on, give heed to, pay attention to: *to attend to what is said, to what is going on, to what one is doing*; **b** to take care of, look after, give care in promoting or directing: *to attend to one's own business*; *to attend to the education of one's children*; *attend to another's comfort*; *to have a great deal to attend to.* **2.** (followed by *upon*) **a** Wait upon (persons) with solicitude, in order to perform services, and carry out orders or wishes; (of servants, officials): *the duchess was attended upon by her own maid*; *the first secretary attended upon the ambassador*; **b** to listen, wait for, orders, instructions &c.: *to attend upon a person's wishes, orders* &c. **3.** (absol). To listen with care, direct thought in certain direction: *if you don't attend, you won't understand.* **B.** trans. **1.** To be present at, take part in: *to attend a course of lectures, a church service, public meeting.* **2.** To wait upon, be with, for purpose of rendering services, esp. professionally, as a medical man: *the patient was attended by the best doctors*; *the army surgeon attended him daily.* **3. a** To accompany, wait upon: *the equerry attended the prince on his journey*; **b** to be present with, accompany as a consequence, or inseparable incident: *his plan was attended with great difficulties*; *may good luck attend you.*

attendance, n. [1. aténdans; 2. əténdəns]. **attend** & **-ance**. **1. a** The act of attending: *to be in attendance on a person*; *attendance at a meeting* &c. Phr. *to dance attendance upon* (*a person*), to attend his (her) convenience; **b** specif., *medical attendance*, skilled care bestowed by doctor on patient. **2.** Those present at, or attending, a meeting, lecture &c.: *a large, small, attendance.*

attendant (I.), adj. [1. aténdant; 2. əténdənt]. Fr., fr. Pres. Part. See **attend**. **a** Being present in attendance, in waiting: *the queen and her attendant train of ladies*; **b** accompanying, consequential, connected: *war and its attendant horrors.*

attendant (II.), n. Same as prec. One who attends upon, accompanies, in any capacity, as friend, companion, keeper, servant.

attention, n. [1. aténshun; 2. aténʃən]. Fr., fr. Lat. *attentiōn-(em)*, 'bending of the mind', fr. *attent-(um)*, P.P. type of *attendere*, see **attend**, & **-ion**. **1.** Act of directing, applying, the mind or senses (in various shades of meaning); **a** careful observation, consideration, and thought: *to give one's best attention to*; **b** careful, watchful notice, or observation by the senses: *to pay attention to a sound, sight &c.*; *to attract attention*; **c** care, solicitude, serviceable kindness: *to receive immediate attention* (e.g. from a doctor or nurse). **2. a** Act of courtesy and kindness: *I regard this as a delicate attention on your part*; (or in pl.) *they showed me a hundred little attentions*; **b** specif., ceremonious politeness, or assiduous court, paid to a lady by a suitor: *to pay a lady marked attentions.* **3.** (mil.) **a** Interjectional word of command: *Attention!*, cautionary word, given before one ordering a movement or manœuvre; **b** as noun in Phrs. *to stand at, come to, attention*, be in, assume, attitude of readiness preparatory to executing the next command.

attentive, adj. [1. aténtiv; 2. əténtiv], fr. Fr. *attentif*. See prec. & **-ive**. Given to attending, or to paying attention; heedful, observant: **a** *attentive to what is said*; **b** careful, assiduous: *attentive to duty*; **c** specif., solicitous for well-being of others; or **d** solicitous in paying court to ladies.

attentively, adv. Prec. & **-ly**. In an attentive manner; carefully.

attentiveness, n. See prec. & **-ness**. Quality of being attentive.

attenuant, adj. & n. [1. aténūant; 2. əténjuənt]. Fr., fr. Lat. *attenuant-(em)*, Pres. Part. of *attenuāre*. See **attenuate**. **a** adj. Tending to make (fluids) thin, to dilute; **b** n., medicine which does this.

attenuate (I.), vb. trans. & intrans. [1. aténūāt; 2. əténjueit], fr. Lat. *attenuāt-(um)*, P.P. type of *attenuāre*, fr. **ad-**, 'to', & *tenuāre*, 'to make thin', fr. *tenuis*, 'thin'; the latter has cognates in many Aryan languages; Scrt. *tanuš*, 'long, stretched out, tender', Gk. *tanu-* (in composition), 'long, slender', also *tanúō*, 'I stretch', O.H.G. *dunni*, O.E. *þynne*, 'thin', O. Slav. *tĭnŭkŭ*, 'thin', W. *teneu*, 'thin'; orig. sense of base is 'stretched'. See **tense, tender (IV.), thin.** **A.** trans. **1.** To make thin or slender; reduce in density; weaken consistency or potency of. **2.** (fig., rare) To minimize, reduce force, severity, or gravity of. **B.** intrans. (rare) To become thin; to grow less.

attenuate (II.), **attenuated**, adj. [1. aténūat, aténūāted; 2. ətén*juə*t, ətén*jueit*id], fr. Lat. *attenuātus.* See prec. Made thin or slender; (of liquids, gases) diluted, rarefied.

attenuation, n. [1. atènūā́shun; 2. ətenjuéiʃən]. See prec. & **-ion.** Act or process of attenuating in literal and figurative senses.

attest, vb. trans. & intrans. [1. atést; 2. ətést], fr. Fr. *attester*, fr. Lat. *attestāri*, fr. **ad-**, 'to', & *testāri*, 'to bear witness'. See **testament. A.** trans. **1. a** To testify, certify, vouch, bear witness to; specif., *to attest a signature*, witness officially; **b** to give proof of, manifest the truth of: *the antiquity of the building is attested by the style of its architecture.* **2.** To put (a person) on oath. **B.** intrans. (followed by *to*) To bear witness to.

attestation, n. [1. àtestā́shun; 2. ætestéiʃən]. Fr., fr. Lat. *attestātiōn-(em)*, fr. *attestāri.* See prec. & **-ation. a** The act of attesting; **b** evidence by which anything is attested.

attestor, n. [1. atéster; 2. ætéstə], fr. **attest** & **-or.** One who attests or vouches for.

Attic (I.), adj. [1. átik; 2. ǽtik], fr. Lat. *Atticus*, Gk. *Attikós*, of Attica. **1.** (of liter. and artistic taste or productions) Resembling the style and taste of Attica or Athens; simple, elegant, restrained: *Attic wit, taste* &c. **2.** (archit.) *Attic base*, that characteristic of Ionic and Corinthian columns.

attic (II.), n., fr. Fr. *attique*, 'upper part of a house', so called as belonging to the Attic order of architecture. See prec. **a** Apartment or room on top storey of a house, generally immediately under the roof and having not a flat ceiling, but one following the angle of the roof; **b** hence, a mean room (on top floor), a garret; **c** (in pl.) *the attics*, the whole top storey of a house, and rooms in this.

atticism, n. [1. átisizm; 2. ǽtisizəm], fr. Gk. *attikismós.* See **Attic** (I.) & **-ism.** Feature of style typical of Attic Greek language and literature; hence, a refined, elegant expression.

atticize, vb. trans. & intrans. [1. átisīz; 2. ǽtisaiz], fr. Gk. *attikizein.* See **Attic** (I.) & **-ize. a** trans. To make conformable to the speech or idiom, style, manners &c. of Attica or Athens; **b** intrans., to affect Attic or Greek style, speech, manners &c.

attire (I.), vb. trans. [1. atīr; 2. ətáiə]. Used in M.E. (one *t*); the n. *atyr* occurs in A.-Fr., but not in Old Continental Fr.; vb. *atirier*, 'set in order, adorn', occurs in O. Fr., fr. Fr. *tiere, tire*, 'row, rank, order'. The origin of this word is obscure, but see **tier.** A connexion has been suggested with a Gmc. word, O.E. *tīr*, 'glory', wh. it is hard to connect w. O.H.G. *ziari*, 'beauty, adornment', Mod. Germ. *zier*; the further etymol. of both of these words is unknown. To dress up, array; esp. of dressing in official or splendid garments for ceremonial occasions; the word is often used reflexively, *to attire oneself.*

attire (II.), n., fr. prec. **a** Dress, clothing, covering of the body; **b** (fig., of covering and adornment of Nature) *the attire of spring* &c.

attitude, n. [1. átitūd; 2. ǽtitjūd]. Fr., fr. Ital. *attitudine*, 'aptness, promptitude, posture', fr. dat. of Low Lat. *aptitūdo.* See **aptitude. 1. a** Disposition of head and limbs, posture, position of body and limbs, bearing, mien, esp. when deliberately adopted to express some emotional state, as on the stage, for a picture &c.; Phr. *to strike an attitude*, adopt affected, mock heroic, or grotesque, gestures and bearing; **b** specif., disposition of human figure in painting and sculpture. **2.** (fig.) Mental or moral condition, disposition; way of regarding, and of relating mind to, life and events; course of action adopted in relation to these: *attitude of mind*; *an unfavourable attitude towards a person* &c.

attitudinize, vb. intrans. [1. àtitū́diniz; 2. ætitjū́dinaiz]. See prec. & **-ize.** To posture, assume deliberately an attitude, physical or mental, to produce an effect; adopt an affected deportment and gestures.

attorn, vb. trans. [1. atérn; 2. ətə́n]. O. Fr. *atorner*, lit. 'turn to'. See **turn.** (law) **a** To transfer homage from one over-lord to another; **b** to agree to become tenant of property under a new landlord, on transfer of estate from one owner to another, esp. in Phr. *to attorn tenant, of* estate, *to* owner.

attorney (I.), n. [1. atérni; 2. ətə́ni]. O. Fr. *atorné*, P.P. of *atorner.* See **attorn. a** One authorized to act for another; specif., a legal practitioner who so acts in legal business; Phr. *by attorney* opposed to *in person*; **b** in popular usage, a solicitor, or law agent. *Attorney-general*, the chief legal officer of the Crown, a member of the ministry in power.

attorney (II.), n. O. Fr. *atornée*, P.P. fem. See prec. *Letter, warrant, of attorney*, document by which authority is given by a person to another to act for him; *power of attorney*, authority thus conferred.

attract, vb. trans. [1. atrákt; 2. ətrǽkt], fr. Lat. *attract-(um)*, P.P. type of *attrahere*, 'to draw to', fr. **ad-** & *trahere*, 'to draw'. See **tract** (I.). To draw anything towards one. **a** (of physical forces) To draw towards, cause to approach, or combine: *a magnet attracts iron*; *trees attract lightning*; *particles of matter attract each other*; **b** (fig., of influence exerted on sentient beings) to draw towards, to cause desire to approach by exciting feelings of interest, pleasure, admiration &c.; to allure, entice, charm: *youth is attracted by pleasure*; *crowds of people were attracted by the music*; *flowers attract bees*; **c** to provoke, draw, observation towards, upon, oneself: *to attract notice, attention* &c.

attraction, n. [1. atrákshun; 2. ətrǽkʃən], fr. Lat. *attractiōn-(em)*, n., fr. *attract-(um).* See **attract** & **-ion. a** The process or property of attracting by action of natural forces as *magnetic attraction*; **b** (fig.) influence exerted on sentient beings by anything which delights, interests, allures (see **attract, b**): *as life advances the pleasures of the senses have less attraction than those of the mind and affections*; **c** that which delights, allures, attracts: *the shops and theatres offer many and various attractions.*

attractive, adj. [1. atráktiv; 2. ətrǽktiv]. See **attract** & **-ive.** Having the property of attracting, alluring, charming; seductive, engaging.

attractively, adv. Prec. & **-ly.** In an attractive manner.

attractiveness, n. See prec. & **-ness.** The quality of being attractive; charm.

attrahent, adj. & n. [1. atrā́ent; 2. ətréiənt], fr. Lat. *attrahent-(em)*, Pres. Part. of *attrahere*, 'to draw to'. See **attract. a** adj. Attracting, drawing; **b** n., (med.) that which by producing external irritation (such as a blister) causes action in the part.

attribute (I.), vb. trans. [1. atríbūt; 2. ətríbjūt], fr. Lat. *attribūt-(um)*, P.P. type of *attribuere*, 'add, assign, bestow, give, impute to', fr. **ad-**, 'to', & *tribuere*, 'distribute, assign, grant', see **tribute.** Followed by *to*: **1.** To ascribe, assign, to a person, give person credit for possessing a quality; to consider as belonging or appropriate to: *to attribute all the virtues to one's parents.* **2.** To suppose, assume (something) to be the result of a given cause, to ascribe, put down to: *to attribute one's success to hard work*; *attribute one's good health to total abstinence.* **3.** (rare) To assign an event to specific time or place.

attribute (II.), n. [1. átribūt; 2. ǽtribjūt], fr. Lat. *attribūtum*, neut. n., fr. *attribūtus*, P.P. of *attribuere.* See prec. **1.** A quality ascribed to, and considered as inherent in and essential to, any person or thing; characteristic quality: *mercy is an attribute of God.* **2.** Material object especially depicted in pictorial and plastic art, as a symbol of a person or his office: *a crown and sceptre are attributes of kings, a sword of warriors, a trident of Neptune* &c. **3.** (gram.) Word denoting an attribute or quality, i.e. an adjective.

attribution, n. [1. àtribū́shun; 2. ætribjū́ʃən]. Fr., fr. Lat. *attribūtiōn-(em)*, n., fr. P.P. type *attribūt-(um)* & **-ion.** See **attribute** (II.). **a** Act of attributing; **b** that which is attributed.

attributive, adj. & n. [1. atríbūtiv; 2. ətríbjutiv]. See **attribute** (II.) & **-ive. 1.** adj. **a** Of the nature of an attribute; **b** (gram.) of adjectives expressing quality that is taken for granted, e.g. *red hair*; contrasted with *predicative.* **2.** n. Adjectival word used attributively, i.e. not as a predicate.

attributively, adv. Prec. & **-ly.** As an attribute.

attrite(d), adj. [1. atrít(ed); 2. ətráit(id)], fr. Lat. *attrītum*, 'worn away', P.P. of *atterere*, 'rub against', fr. **ad-** & *terere*, 'to rub, crush', see **trite** & cp. **triturate.** (rare) Worn away by friction.

attrition, n. [1. atríshun; 2. ətríʃən], fr. Lat. *attrītiōn-(em).* See prec. & **-ion. 1. a** The act or process of wearing away by friction; **b** state of being so worn. **2.** (theol.) The least measure of sorrow for sin, arising from fear of punishment; contrasted with *contrition*, the highest degree of repentance.

attune, vb. trans. [1. atū́n; 2. ətjū́n], fr. *at* (for **ad-**) & **tune. a** (poet.) To put in tune, make musical instrument, or voice, accord with others; **b** (fig.) bring into spiritual or moral harmony or agreement with; make fit, adapt: *hearts attuned to worship.*

aubade, n. [1. ōbáhd; 2. oubā́d]. Fr., 'morning serenade', lit. 'song to be sung at dawn'; fr. Fr. *aube*, 'dawn', w. suff. **-ade** as in *serenade* &c. See **alb. a** Morning serenade; **b** the morning song of birds.

aubergine, n. [1. ṓbārzhēn; 2. óubeəžīn]. Fr. dimin. of *auberge, alberge*, 'a kind of peach'. The egg-plant, q.v.

auburn, adj. [1. áwbun, áwbērn; 2. ɔ́bən, ɔ́bə̄n]. M.E. *auburne*, 'whitish', O. Fr. *alborne, auborne*, Low Lat. *alburnus*, 'whitish', fr. *albus*, 'white'. See **alb.** (of human hair) Reddish-brown, of a chestnut or golden-brown colour; (like most colour words, this has travelled far in meaning and has probably been influenced by a confusion with *brown*).

auction (I.), n. [1. áwkshun; 2. ɔ́kʃən], fr. Lat. *auctiōn-(em)*, acc., 'an increase, a public sale (by increasing bids)', fr. *augēre, auctum*, 'to increase'. The base **aug-* is found in Goth. *aukan*, 'grow, increase', O.H.G. *ouhhōn*, O.E. *ēacian*, 'to increase', *ēac*, 'moreover, also' (see **eke**); Scrt. *ójaś*, 'strength', Lith. *áugu*, 'I grow', Gk. *aúxō*, 'I increase'. See **augment**, & a different gradational form of same base under **wax** (III.). A public sale, in which purchase is made by the highest of a series of bidders, each of whom increases price offered by the last. *Dutch auction*, a sale at which the auctioneer starts by offering articles to be sold at a high price and keeps reducing it till a purchaser is found. *Auction bridge*, card game (see **bridge**).

auction (II.), vb. trans., fr. prec. To sell by auction.

auctioneer, n. [1. àwkshunḗr; 2. ɔ̀kʃəníə]. Prec. & **-eer.** Person licensed to sell property by auction.

auctioneering, n. [1. àwkshunḗring; 2. ɔ̀kʃəníəriŋ]. See prec. & **-ing.** Profession of an auctioneer.

audacious, adj. [1. awdā́shus; 2. ɔdéiʃəs]. Fr. *audacieux*, 'bold', fr. Lat. *audāci-*, stem of *audax*, 'bold', & **-ous.** This word, & *audēre*, 'venture, dare', are prob. for **avidax*, **avidēre*, & related to Lat. *avēre*, 'to be eager for', *avidus*, 'desirous, greedy', & *avārus*, 'greedy' &c., cp. **avid, avarice. a** Daring, bold, foolhardy (of persons and actions); **b** (of persons) overstepping limits of decorum, impudent; despising law and custom; presumptuous, shameless, insolent; **c** (of actions and conduct) based on, arising from, contempt for decorum and decency; shameless, brazen.

audaciously, adv. Prec. & **-ly.** In an audacious manner (in various meanings).

audaciousness, n. See prec. & **-ness.** Audacity, chiefly in bad sense.

audacity, n. [1. awdásiti; 2. ōdǽsiti], as fr. Lat. *audācitāt-(em)*. See **audacious** & **-ity**. **a** (in good sense) Daring, careless bravery, high-spirited courage; **b** (in bad sense) overweening presumption, impudence, insolent boldness.
audibility, n. [1. àwdibíliti; 2. ōdibíliti]. See next word & **-ity**. Capacity, capability, of being heard; power of making oneself heard when speaking.
audible, adj. [1. áwdibl; 2. ōdibl], fr. Low Lat. *audībilis*, fr. *audīre*, 'to hear', wh. stands for **auzdiō, *awizdiō*, cp. Scrt. *āvíš*, 'open, public', & Lat. *auris*, 'ear', fr. **auzis*; Gk. *oûs*, fr. **ousos*; Lith. *ausis*; Goth. *ausō*, O.E. *ēare*, 'ear'. See **ear**. **a** (of sound) Capable of being heard; perceptible to the ear; actually heard; **b** (of persons) capable of making oneself heard when speaking.
audibly, adv. Prec. & **-ly**. So as to be heard.
audience, n. [1. áwdiens; 2. ōdiəns]. Fr., fr. Lat. *audientia*, 'a hearing, audience, attention', fr. *audient-(em)*, Pres. Part. of *audīre*, 'to hear'. See **audible**. **a** A hearing, esp. formal interview granted by a ruler or other important person; **b** a session of a judge to hear cases; **c** assemblage of persons present at a lecture, concert, theatrical performance, speech-making &c.
audiometer, n. [1. àwdiómeter; 2. ōdiómitə], fr. Lat. base, *audi-*, 'hearing' (see **audible**), & **-meter**. Instrument for testing hearing-power, or for measuring intensity of sounds.
audiphone, n. [1. áwdifōn; 2. ōdifoun]. Hybrid concoction fr. Lat. *audi-*, 'hearing', & Gk. *phōnḗ*, 'sound', see **phone**. An instrument for improving imperfect sense of hearing, consisting of a plate which vibrates to sound waves, and transmits them to auditory nerve on being pressed against the upper teeth.
audit (**I.**), n. [1. áwdit; 2. ōdit], fr. Lat. *audītus*, 'a hearing', fr. *audīre*, 'to hear', see **audible**. **a** Official scrutiny of accounts, esp. of trading concern, or of an institution; **b** settlement of accounts between landlord and tenant.
audit (**II.**), vb. trans., fr. prec. To make an official scrutiny and testing of accounts, esp. with help of skilled professional accountants.
audit ale, n. Extra strong ale, originally brewed at the universities for days of audit.
audition, n. [1. awdíshun; 2. ōdíʃən], fr. Lat. *audītiōn-(em)*, 'a hearing', fr. *audīre*, 'to hear'. See **audible**. **a** Act of experiencing auditory sensations; act of hearing or listening; **b** the sense of hearing; **c** a hearing given to a singer, actor &c. to test qualities for an engagement (U.S.A.).
auditive, adj. [1. áwditiv; 2. ōditiv]. See **auditory** & **-ive**. (rare) Pertaining to sense of hearing.
auditor, n. [1. áwditer; 2. ōditə]. Lat., 'hearer'. See **audit** & **-or**. **1.** (archaic) A hearer, listener. **2.** Specif., one who audits accounts.
auditorial, adj. [1. àwditórial; 2. ōditóriəl]. Prec. & Lat. adj. suff. *-iāl(is)*. See **-al**. Connected with an auditor or auditing.
auditorium, n. [1. àwditórium; 2. ōditóriəm]. Lat. See **auditory** (**II.**) Building or part of building in which the audience sit to hear lectures, speeches &c.; same part in a theatre or concert hall.
auditory (**I.**), adj. [1. áwditeri; 2. ōditəri]. Lat. *audītōrius*, cp. *audītor*, *audiō*, 'hear'. See **audible** & **-ory**. **1.** **a** Connected with sense of hearing: *auditory nerve*; **b** connected with sound in relation to its perception by organs of hearing: *auditory sensation*.
auditory (**II.**), n. Lat. *audītōrium*, 'place for listening, hall of justice' &c. See prec. (rare) **a** Part of building in which an audience sit; **b** those who sit there; audience.
Augean, adj. [1. awjḗan; 2. ōdžíən], fr. Lat. *Augēas*, Gk. *Augeias*, in Gk. mythology a king of Elis, whose stable remained uncleansed for 30 years until Hercules cleansed it in a day. Filthy, esp. in Phr. *Augean stable*; used literally, and metaphorically of moral impurity or dishonesty.
auger, n. [1. áwger; 2. ōgə], for *a nauger*; M.E. *auger*, earlier *nauger*, O.E. *nafugār*, lit. 'nave-piercer', fr. *nafu*, '**nave**', of a wheel', & *gār*, 'spear, javelin', see **gore** (**II.**). Carpenter's tool, larger than a gimlet, for boring holes.
aught, n. & adv. [1. awt; 2. ōt]. M.E. *auht*, O.E. *āwiht*, 'anything, at all', fr. *ā*, 'ever', & *wiht*, 'thing, creature'. See **whit** & **wight**. **a** n. Anything; **b** adv., at all, in any way, to any extent.
augite, n. [1. áwjīt; 2. ōdžait], fr. Gk. *augītēs*, fr. *augḗ*, 'brightness'. Cp. O. Slav. *jugŭ*, 'south', *jutro*, 'morning'. (mineral.) A rock-forming mineral, usually black or dark green, a variety of pyroxene.
augment (**I.**), vb. trans. & intrans. [1. awgmént; 2. ōgmént], fr. Fr. *augmenter*, fr. Lat. *augmentāre*, 'to increase', fr. *augmentum*, n., 'increase', fr. base of Lat. *augēre*, 'to increase', see **auction** & **eke**. **1.** trans. **a** To make larger in size or extent, cause to increase; **b** to prefix augment to (see next word). **2.** intrans. To grow larger, increase.
augment (**II.**), n. [1. áwgment; 2. ōgmənt]. See prec. Vowel prefixed to the past tenses of the verb in Sanscrit and Greek.
augmentation, n. [1. àwgmentáshun; 2. ōgmentéiʃən]. Fr., fr. Low Lat. *augmentātiōn-(em)*, fr. *augmentāre*, see **augment** (**I.**), & **-ation**. **a** Act or process of increasing, adding to; **b** condition of being increased; **c** that which constitutes the increase; addition, enlargement; **d** (specif., her.) addition to a coat of arms, granted as an honour; **e** (mus.) repetition of a motif in notes of greater value.
augmentative, adj. & n. [1. awgméntativ; 2. ōgméntətiv], fr. Fr. *augmentatif*. See prec. & **-ive**. **1.** adj. **a** Tending to increase, having function of increasing; **b** (gram., of words or inflexional elements) having function of intensifying idea expressed. **2.** n. (gram.) Word, or inflexional element, prefix, suffix, which intensifies or extends the meaning.
augur (**I.**), n. [1. áwger; 2. ōgə]. Lat., member of the college of priests in ancient Rome who foretold the future, esp. by observing flight or notes of birds; the word is for **avi-ger*, the first element of wh. is *avis*, 'bird', see **aviary**, & the second prob. fr. Lat. *gerere*, wh. has many & various meanings, e.g. 'bear, conduct, direct, manage' (see **gerent**); the view that *-gur* is fr. an old vb. meaning 'look at, consider', & cogn. w. O. Slav. *zĭrěti*, 'see, glance at' &c., is now thought less probable. One who predicts events; fortune-teller, soothsayer.
augur (**II.**), vb. trans. & intrans., fr. prec. **1.** trans. To portend, betoken, presage: *this closeness augurs a thunderstorm*; also of persons, predict, infer: *to augur misfortune from what has happened*. **2.** intrans. **a** To make a prediction, draw an inference from what has happened as to probable future happenings: *from what you tell me I cannot augur well for the future*; **b** to imply future developments: *this augurs well for your success*.
augural, adj. [1. áwgūral; 2. ōgjurəl], fr. Lat. *augurālis*, fr. *augur*. See prec. & **-al**. Pertaining to augurs; ominous.
augury, n. [1. áwgūri; 2. ōgjuri]. O. Fr. *augurie*, Lat. *augurium*, 'profession of an augur; divination, soothsaying'; see **augur** (**I.**). **a** Art and practice of divination and prophecy; **b** omen; **c** specific inference drawn from omens, prediction.
August (**I.**), n. [1. áwgust; 2. ōgəst]. Named after Augustus Caesar, the first Roman Emperor; see **august** (**II.**). The name of the eighth month of the calendar year.
august (**II.**), adj. [1. awgúst; 2. ōgást], fr. Lat. *augustus*, 'consecrated, venerable, majestic', fr. base in *augēre*, 'increase', wh. has also fig. sense of 'to exalt, praise, extol'; see **augment** & **auction**. Majestic, imposing, awe-inspiring, dread: *an august personage*; *august assemblage*; *august decree* &c.
Augustan, adj. [1. awgústan; 2. ōgástən], fr. Lat. *augustānus*, fr. Augustus, name of Roman Emperor, see **August** (**I.**). Esp. in Phr. *Augustan Age*, which is applied to that period of any nation when its literature and art reach the highest point of elegance, purity, and refinement. In connexion with Rome the name refers to the age of Augustus Caesar; in England to that of Queen Anne.
augustly, adv. [1. awgústli; 2. ōgástli], fr. **august** (**II.**) & **-ly**. Majestically, imposingly.
augustness, n. [1. awgústnes; 2. ōgástnis]. See prec. & **-ness**. Quality of being august.
auk, n. [1. awk; 2. ōk]. Scand. Cp. Dan. *alke*, Swed. *alka*. A web-footed sea-bird resembling a puffin or penguin, with short wings which it uses only as paddles; the great auk or garefowl is extinct.
aula, n. [1. áwla; 2. ōlə]. Lat., fr. Gk. *aulḗ*, 'court'. Cp. Gk. *iaúō*, 'I rest', fr. base **au-*, 'rest'. Large hall, room for public meetings.
aulic, adj. [1. áwlik; 2. ōlik], fr. Fr. *aulique*, fr. Lat. *aulicus*, fr. Gk. *aulikós*, fr. *aulḗ*, 'court', see prec. Pertaining to an aula. Specif. *Aulic Council*, court of justice of the Holy Roman Empire established by Maximilian I. in 1499 and abolished in 1806.
aumbry. See **ambry**.
aunt, n. [1. ahnt; 2. ānt], fr. O. Fr. *aunte*, *ante*, fr. Lat. *amita*, 'father's sister'. Cp. various relationship words fr. same base, Gk. *ammás*, *ámmia*, 'mother'; O.N. *amma*, 'grandmother'; all these prob. connected w. *amāre*, 'love' &c. See **amative**. Father's or mother's sister; uncle's wife.
Aunt Sally, n. [1. áhnt sáli; 2. ánt sǽli]. **a** Popular diversion which consists in trying to knock a pipe out of the mouth of a wooden dummy, by shying sticks at it; the figure at which sticks are thrown; **b** (fig.) any person or institution which becomes a mark for popular attack and abuse.
aura, n. [1. áwra; 2. ōrə]. Lat., fr. Gk. *aúra*, 'air in motion, breeze', fr. **awer-*, cogn. w. Gk. *āḗr*, 'air', fr. **āwēr-*. See **air**. **1.** **a** Emanation, effluvium, aroma, as from flowers, blood &c.; **b** also fig., of associations of words &c. **2.** Name given by believers in mesmerism to an invisible fluid which is alleged to convey the mesmeric influence between operator and patient. **3.** (med.) A sensation, as of oppression, palpitation &c., a premonitory symptom of an attack of epilepsy.
aural (**I.**), adj. [1. áwral; 2. ōrəl], fr. prec. & **-al**. Connected with an aura.
aural (**II.**), adj., fr. Lat. *auris*, 'ear' & adj. suff. *-ālis*, see **-al**. *Auris* stands for **auzis*; cp. **audible** & **ear**. Pertaining to, derived through, concerned with, the ear: *aural impressions*, *aural surgeon*.
aurally, adv. Prec. & **-ly**. By means of the ear or sense of hearing.
aureate, adj. [1. áwriāt; 2. ōrieit]. Lat. *aureus*, 'golden', & **-ate**; Lat. *aurum*, 'gold', lit. 'the shining metal', is connected w. *aurōra*, 'dawn', see **aurora**. (rare or poet.) Golden, gilded, splendid.
aurelia, n. [1. awrḗlia; 2. ōríliə], fr. Ital. *aurelia*, fem. of *aurelio*, 'shining like gold, golden', fr. Lat. *aurum*, 'gold'. See prec. **a** (obs.) Butterfly chrysalis; **b** (cap.) genus of large disk-shaped jelly-fish.
aurelian, adj. [1. awrḗlian; 2. ōríliən], fr. prec. & **-an**. Belonging to an aurelia or the Aurelia.
aureola, aureole, n. [1. awrḗola, áwreōl; 2. ōríələ, ōrioul]. Lat. *aureola* (*corōna*), 'golden crown', fem. of *aureolus*, 'golden', dimin. of *aureus*, 'golden', fr. *aurum*, 'gold', see **aureate**. **a** Celestial crown, supposed to be granted, in addition to the joys of heaven, to the saints, virgins, martyrs, and doctors; **b** pictorial representation of this, in form either of a golden ring, or a golden disk, painted behind and around head of the wearer, cp. *halo* & *nimbus*.

auric, adj. [1. áwrik; 2. ṓrik], fr. Lat. *aurum*, 'gold', & **-ic**. See **aureate** & **aurora**. Pertaining to, derived from, gold.

auricle, n. [1. áwrikl; 2. ṓrikl], fr. Lat. *auricula*, 'external ear', dimin. of *auris*, 'ear'. See **aural (II.)**. **a** The external ear of animals; **b** (anat.) one of the two chambers of the heart which receives blood from the veins and forces it into the ventricles. So called from supposed resemblance to an ear in shape.

auricled, adj. [1. áwrikld; 2. ṓrikld], fr. prec. Auriculate.

auricula, n. [1. awríkūla; 2. ɔ̄ríkjulə]. Lat. See **auricle**. (bot.) Alpine primula, a species of primrose, of which there are many cultivated varieties, so-called from shape of leaf.

auricular, adj. [1. awríkūlar; 2. ɔ̄ríkjulə]. Prec. & adj. suff. *-āris*, see **-ar**. **1.** Connected with the ear or with hearing: *auricular confession*, one heard by a priest. **2.** Connected with the auricles of the heart.

auriculate, adj. [1. awríkūlāt; 2. ɔ̄ríkjuleit]. See prec. & **-ate**. Having lobes or appendages shaped like ears.

auriferous, adj. [1. awríferus; 2. ɔ̄ríf ərəs], fr. Lat. *aurifer*, 'gold-bearing', fr. *aurum*, 'gold', see **aureate**, & **-ferous**. Containing, yielding, gold (of ores, mines &c.).

auriform, adj. [1. áwriform; 2. ṓrifɔ̄m], fr. Lat. *auri(s)*, 'ear'. See **audible** & **form**. Ear-shaped.

Aurignacian, adj. [1. ȯrignáshun, ȯrinyáshun; 2. ɔ̀rignéiʃən, òurinjéiʃən], fr. Aurignac, France, where remains were first discovered. Belonging to the latest period of palaeolithic culture, succeeding the Mousterian period; the peoples belonging to it, a race of hunter-artists, were probably the first of modern European man.

aurilave, n. [1. áwrilāv; 2. ṓrileiv], fr. Lat. *auri-(s)*, 'ear', see **audible** & **ear**, & **lave**. Ear-cleaner.

aurist, n. [1. áwrist; 2. ṓrist], fr. Lat. *auri-*, stem of *auris*, 'ear', see **audible**, & **-ist**. Surgeon specially skilled in diseases of the ear.

aurochs, n. [1. áwroks; 2. ṓrɔks]. The Engl. form is eccentric and is apparently due, as regards the spelling, to Mod. Germ. *auerochs*. The O.E. *ūr* is 'bison', O.H.G. *ūr* & *ūrochso*. The base *ūr-* is cogn. w. Scrt. *-usrá*, 'ox', orig. 'reddish-coloured animal', see **ox**. Primitive European bison, now nearly extinct.

aurora, n. [1. awrṓra; 2. ɔ̄rṓrə]. Lat., 'dawn', stands for **ausōza*, cp. also Gk. (Attic) *héōs*, Aeolic *aúōs*, 'dawn', & Scrt. *uṣā́s*, 'early light'; Lith. *auszrà*, 'red of dawn'; orig. meaning of the base is 'shining'; Lat. *aurum*, 'gold', is prob. also a cogn. & so certainly is Engl. **east**. See **combustion**. (poet.) **a** The dawn; **b** goddess of dawn; **c** the colour of the sky at sunrise. *Aurora Borealis*, luminous, quivering glow, seen at night in the sky in northern latitudes; *Aurora Australis*, similar phenomenon seen in southern latitudes. See further **boreal**.

aurum, n. [1. áwrum; 2. ṓrəm]. Lat., see **aurora**. The chemical name for gold.

auscultate, vb. trans. & intrans. [1. áwskultāt; 2. ṓskalteit], fr. P.P. type *auscultāt-(um)*, of Lat. *auscultāre*, 'listen'. See next word. To practise auscultation.

auscultation, n. [1. àwskultáshun; ɔ̀skaltéiʃən]. Lat. *auscultātiōn-(em)*, fr. *auscultāre*, 'to listen to'; *aus-* preserves the *-s-*, wh. has been lost in Lat. *audio*, 'hear' (see **audible**), & changed to *z*, & then to *r*, in *auris*, 'ear' (see **auricle** &c.). (med.) Art of sounding or listening to noises made by heart, lungs, and other internal organs, and thence diagnosing their condition by applying ear to a stethoscope placed against chest, back &c.

auscultator, n. [1. áwskultāter; 2. ṓskalteitə]. Lat., 'hearer, listener'. See prec. & **-or**. One who practises auscultation.

auscultatory, adj. [1. awskúltateri; 2. ɔ̄skáltətəri]. See prec. & **-ory**. Pertaining to auscultation.

auspice, n. [1. áwspis; 2. ṓspis]. Fr., fr. Lat. *auspicium*, lit. 'a bird-watching', fr. *avi-*, 'bird', & *spec-*, 'look at, watch'. For first element see **augur** & **aviary**; for second see **species** & **spy**. Cp. Lat. *auspex*, 'bird-watcher', one who told the future fr. flight of birds; *auspicāre*, 'to take the omens' by this means. **a** Omen, generally in favourable sense; **b** (usually in pl.) patronage, protection: esp. *under the auspices of*.

auspicious, adj. [1. awspíshus; 2. ɔ̄spíʃəs]. Lat. *auspici-* & *-ōsus*. See prec. & **-ous**. Having favourable tokens or omens; accompanied by circumstances which promise well for the future; favourable, fortunate: *an auspicious event, circumstance, beginning* &c.

auspiciously, adv. Prec. & **-ly**. Favourably, under happy conditions, promising well for the future.

auspiciousness, n. See prec. & **-ness**. Good omen, something portending good fortune.

austere, adj. [1. awstḗr; 2. ɔ̄stíə]. Fr., fr. Lat. *austērus*, 'dry, harsh, stern', fr. Gk. *austērós*, 'making the tongue dry and rough', hence 'harsh, stern', fr. *aúō*, 'I dry', cp. *aûos*, 'dry', fr. **sausos*, cp. Lith. *saũsas*, 'dry'. See further under **sear (I.)**. **a** (of moral conditions, manners &c.) Harsh, stern, forbidding; **b** (of mode of life) severely simple, ascetic; **c** (of style in literature or other art) severe, sparing in ornament, chaste.

austerely. adv. Prec. & **-ly**. In an austere manner.

austereness, n. See prec. & **-ness**. Austerity.

austerity, n. [1. awstériti; 2. ɔ̄stériti]. Fr. *austérité*. See **austere** & **-ity**. The quality of being austere (in various senses).

austral, adj. [1. áwstral; 2. ṓstrəl], fr. Lat. *austrālis*, 'southern', cp. *auster*, 'south wind'; this word is fr. **ausra-*, & cogn. w. Scrt. *usrā́ś*, adj., 'of the morning, rosy'; Lith. *auszrà*, 'red of the morning, dawn'; further O.H.G. *ōstra*, 'east'. See **aurora** & **east**. Southern, southerly.

authentic, adj. [1. awthéntik; 2. ɔ̄þéntik]. M.E. *autentik*, O. Fr. *autentique*, fr. Lat. *authenticus*, fr. Gk. *authentikós*, 'original, genuine', fr. *authéntēs*, 'one who does a thing himself, absolute master; murderer'; also *auto-éntēs*, see **auto-**, 'self' &c., & *ent-* for **sent-*, w. wh. cp. Lat. *sons* for *sont-s*, 'guilty, criminal'. Walde, however, disputes connexion of *sons* w. above Gk. word. See **sooth**. **a** Of known origin, being what it purports to be, genuine: *an authentic signature*; **b** having approved authority, reliable: *authentic news*; **c** (law) properly and formally attested.

authentically, adv. [1. awthéntikali; 2. ɔ̄þéntikəli], fr. prec. & **-al** & **-ly**. In an authentic manner.

authenticate, vb. trans. [1. awthéntikāt; 2. ɔ̄þéntikeit], fr. Low Lat. *authenticāt-(um)*, P.P. type of *authenticāre*, 'to make authentic'. See **authentic**. **a** To make authentic by formal attestation; **b** to prove genuine, establish beyond doubt the origin of.

authentication, n. [1. awthèntikáshun; 2. ɔ̄þèntikéiʃən]. Prec. & **-ion**. The act of authenticating.

authenticity, n. [1. àwthentísiti; 2. ɔ̀þentísiti], fr. **authentic** & **-ity**. **a** State or quality of being authentic, of established authority: *the authenticity of the Gospels*; **b** genuineness.

author, n. [1. áwther; 2. ṓþə]. M.E. *au(c)tor*, fr. O. Fr. *autor*, *auteur*, fr. Lat. *auctor*, 'one who enlarges, originates; master, one entitled to decide on a matter, author of a literary work', fr. *auct-(um)*, P.P. of *augēre*, 'to make to grow, to increase'. The *-th-* was at first merely scribal, but became fixed, & has influenced the pronunciation. See **auction**. **1.** One who brings something into being; originator, creator of anything: *God the Author of our being*; *the author of mischief*. **2.** Specif., one who produces literary work, writer: *author of a novel* &c. **3.** (by extension) The works of an author: *to have many authors on one's shelves*, i.e. their works.

authoress, n. [1. áwthures; 2. ṓþərəs]. Prec. & **-ess**. A female author.

authoritarian, n. & adj. [1. àwthoritárian; 2. ɔ̄þɔritéəriən]. See **authority** & **-arian**. **a** n. Believer in rigid exercise of authority; **b** adj., pertaining to (exercise of) authority.

authoritative, adj. [1. awthóritativ; 2. ɔ̄þɔ́ritətiv]. See **authority**, **-ate**, & **-ive**. **1.** (of persons) Accustomed to exercise authority, to give orders and be obeyed; fond of command, inclined to assert authority; dictatorial, peremptory. **2.** (of statements, commands, documentary evidence &c.) Having the sanction, weight, of authority; entitled to credit as proceeding from established authority, recognized knowledge &c.: *an authoritative statement, opinion*.

authoritatively, adv. Prec. & **-ly**. In an authoritative manner.

authoritativeness, n. See prec. & **-ness**. Quality of being authoritative.

authority, n. [1. awthóriti; 2. ɔ̄þɔ́riti]. Fr. *autorité*, fr. Lat. *auctōritāt-(em)* &c., 'personal influence, importance; leading, command, responsibility' &c. See **author** & **-ity**. **1. a** Power, legal right to command and to enforce obedience: *the authority of Parliament, of commanding officer* &c.; '*a man set in authority*'; **b** permission, right, to exercise, justification, sanction, for using, such power when delegated by legally constituted government: *to act, speak, with the authority of the Law, of the Church* &c.; *by what authority was this order given?* **2.** (often in pl.) Person or body of persons possessing authority, having right to govern, direct, control affairs, make laws &c.: *the Municipal, County, Authority (-ies)*; *the Authorities of the Army and Navy*. **3.** Moral, intellectual weight, influence, power, derived from a person's character, knowledge, rank, position &c., and the esteem and prestige which these carry: '*Authority forgets a dying king*' (Tennyson); *to have authority with the people*. **4. a** Person who is relied upon, by reason of his special knowledge, experience, study, to give trustworthy testimony or a weighty and credible opinion on particular facts and events: *to be an authority on Roman law, philology* &c.; **b** books or documents in which such knowledge, experience, and opinions are embodied: *Walpole's Memoirs are an important authority for the social and political life of his time*; **c** weight of opinion, bulk of testimony: *the authority is overwhelming for the view I take* &c.

authorizable, adj. [1. áwthorīzabl; 2. ṓþəraizəbl], fr. **authorize** & **-able**. Capable of being, suitable to be, authorized.

authorization, n. [1. àwthorīzáshun; 2. ɔ̄þəraizéiʃən]. Fr., fr. Lat. See next word & **-ation**. Act of authorizing; warrant, sanction.

authorize, vb. trans. [1. áwthorīz; 2. ṓþəraiz], fr. *autoriser*, O. Fr. *auctoriser*, *authoriser*, fr. Low Lat. *auctōrizāre*, fr. *auctor*, see **author**, & **-ize**. **1.** To give authority to, empower, commission, (a person) to do something: *to authorize a person to act for one*. **2. a** To sanction, permit (an action): *conduct authorized by the law*; **b** to justify, furnish adequate reasons for: *his action was authorized by the situation*.

authorized, adj. [1. áwthorīzd; 2. ṓþəraizd]. P.P. of prec. **a** Sanctioned, by law, custom, authority, or general approval; **b** (of persons) approved, commissioned by responsible authority to act: *an authorized agent* &c.

Authorized Version, n. The translation of the Bible issued by authority in 1611.

authorship, n. [1. áwthorship; 2. ṓþəʃip]. **author** & **-ship**. **a** Profession, business, of writer of books &c.; **b** origin, question who was the author of a literary work: *a book of doubtful authorship*.

auto-, pref. Gk. *auto-*, in composition, fr. *autós*, 'same, self', the origin of wh. is doubtful, but wh. is perh. for **asu-to*, & related to Scrt. *ásuṣ*, 'life, life of the soul', in wh. case the orig. meaning wd. be 'essence, essential principle' &c.; this pref. occurs in Engl. words borrowed directly, or indirectly, fr. Gk. & already thus compounded, e.g. *autocracy*, also in a host of recent scientific or popular concoctions, in wh. the second element may be fr. almost any source, e.g. *auto-suggestion, auto-closing* &c. The force of *auto-* in compounds is 'done by and for oneself, independent, without the action and interference of others, spontaneous, absolute', e.g. *automaton*, 'acting by and through itself', *autocrat*, 'absolute ruler', and so on.

auto, n. [1. áwtō; 2. ɔ́tou]. Abbreviation for *automobile*, q.v. (colloq.; not much used).

autobiographer, n. [1. àwtōbīógrafer; 2. ɔ̀toubaiɔ́grəfə]. See **auto-** & **biographer**. One who writes an account of his own life.

autobiographic(al), adj. [1. àwtōbīōgráfik(l); 2. ɔ̀toubaiougrǽfik(l). Prec. & **-ic** (& **-al**). Connected with details of one's own life or with autobiography.

autobiographically, adv. Prec. & **-ly**. In a manner relating to one's own life; by way of autobiography.

autobiography, n. [1. àwtōbīógrafi; 2. ɔ̀toubaiɔ́grəfi]. Gk. *autobiographía*. See **auto-** & **biography**. **a** Art and practice of writing a narrative of one's own life; **b** particular work dealing with a person's life, written by himself.

autocar, n. [1. áwtokar; 2. ɔ́toukā]. See **auto-** & **car**. Another name for automobile or motor-car; a road car propelled by its own engine.

autocephalous, adj. [1. àwtōséfalus; 2. ɔ̀touséfələs], fr. **auto-** & Gk. *kephalḗ*, 'head', see **cephalic**, & **-ous**. (of a Church or community) Having its own governing head; independent.

autochthon, n. [1. awtókthon; 2. ɔtɔ́kþən]. Gk. *autokhthōn*, 'from the land itself', fr. **auto-** & Gk. *khthṓn, khthonós*, 'earth, soil', fr. **g̑hzōm-*; cogn. w. Scrt. *kṣā́ma-*, 'earth', & w. Lat. *humus*, 'earth', see **humus**. (Usually in pl., *autochthones*.) One of the primitive original inhabitants of a country, who have dwelt there since before earliest history; an aboriginal.

autochthonal, -ous, -ic, adj. [1. awtókthonal, -us, àwtokthónik; 2. ɔtɔ́kþənəl, -əs, ɔ̀təkþɔ́nik]. See prec. & various suffs. Aboriginal, belonging to earliest known inhabitants of a country.

autochthonism, n. [1. awtókthonizm; 2. ɔtɔ́kþənizəm]. See prec. & **-ism**. State of being an aboriginal of a country.

autocracy, n. [1. awtókrasi; 2. ɔtɔ́krəsi]. Fr. *autocratie*, fr. Gk. *autokráteia*, fr. *autokratḗs*. See next word & **-cracy**. **a** System of government by a single, absolute ruler; **b** a government carried on according to this system; **c** a supreme and independent controlling influence in government: *this statesman was said to have turned his office into an autocracy.*

autocrat, n. [1. áwtokrat; 2. ɔ́təkræt]. Fr. *autocrate*, fr. Gk. *autokratḗs*, 'ruling by oneself', fr. **auto-** & *krátos*, 'might, power', see **-cracy**. **1.** An absolute monarch, or other ruler, who has supreme and independent control of the government; the reverse of a constitutional ruler. **2.** One who conducts affairs of any kind on his own initiative and authority, without consulting the views of others; a dictatorial, overbearing person.

autocratic, adj. [1. àwtōkrátik; 2. ɔ̀toukrǽtik], fr. **autocrat** & **-ic**. Pertaining to, resembling, characteristic of, an autocrat, or an autocracy; high-handed, dictatorial.

autocratically, adv. [1. àwtōkrátikali; 2. ɔ̀toukrǽtikəli]. Prec. & **-al** & **-ly**. After the manner of an autocrat, or an autocracy.

auto-da-fé, n., pl. **autos-da-fé** [1. áwtō dah fā́; 2. ɔ̀tou dā féi]. Port. & Span., 'act of faith'. **a** The ceremony of the trial and sentence of a heretic by the Inquisition; **b** the carrying out of the sentence by burning.

autogamous, adj. [1. awtógamus; 2. ɔtɔ́gəməs]. See **auto-** & **-gamous**. (bot.) Self-fertilizing, of flower which is fertilized by its own pollen.

autogenesis, n. [1. àwtōjénesis; 2. ɔ̀toudženisis]. Gk. See **auto-** & **genesis**. Spontaneous generation.

autogenetic, adj. [1. àwtōjenétik; 2. ɔ̀toudženétik]. See **auto-** & **genetic**. Pertaining to autogenesis.

autogenous, adj. [1. awtójenus; 2. ɔtɔ́džinəs], fr. Gk. *autogenḗs, -és*, 'self-produced', fr. **auto-** & **-genous**. Self-generating or self-generated.

autogeny, n. [1. awtójeni; 2. ɔtɔ́džini]. See prec. & **-geny**. Spontaneous generation.

autograph (I.), n. [1. áwtograhf; 2. ɔ́təgrāf], fr. Lat. *autographum*, fr. Gk. *autógraphos*. See **auto-** & **graph**. **a** A person's own handwriting; esp. in common usage, a person's signature: *autograph album*, one containing specimens of the handwriting of different persons; **b** author's own manuscript of a literary work; **c** copy of writing reproduced by lithography.

autograph (II.), vb. trans., fr. prec. **a** To write with one's own hand, esp. to write one's name on a document. (Popular and common for *write one's name on, put one's name to*); **b** to copy by lithography.

autographic(al), adj. [1. àwtōgráfik(l); 2. ɔ̀tougrǽfik(l)]. See prec. & **-ic** & **-al**. **a** In one's, a person's, own handwriting; **b** in lithographic reproduction.

autography, n. [1. awtógrafi; 2. ɔtɔ́grəfi]. See **autograph**. Direct reproduction of writing or drawing by lithographic process.

autogravure, n. [1. àwtōgravū́r, -vyṓr; 2. ɔ̀tougrævjúə, -vjɔ̄]. See **auto-** & **grave** (I.), & **-ure**. Process for reproducing photographs, a form of photogravure.

autogyro, n. [1. àwtōjírō; 2. ɔ̀toudžáiərou]. Span. *autogiro*. See **auto-** & **gyro-**. Type of aeroplane, designed for vertical ascent and descent, the main feature being an extra horizontal screw rotating under wind-pressure.

auto-intoxication, n. [1. áwtō intoksikā́shun; 2. ɔ́tou intɔksikéiʃən]. See **auto-** & **intoxication**. (med.) Self-poisoning; poisoning by toxic substances produced within the body.

automatic(al), adj. [1. àwtomátik(l); 2. ɔ̀təmǽtik(l)], fr. Gk. *autómat-(os)*, see **automaton** & **-ic** & **-al**. **1.** Having power of spontaneous motion (esp. of machinery and mechanical contrivances), working of itself: *automatic telephone, pistol* (in latter sense, also absolutely, as noun). **2.** (of movements or actions of human and other organic beings) Not resulting from volition; unconscious, merely mechanical.

automatically, adv. Prec. & **-ly**. By automatic action.

automatism, n. [1. awtómatizm; 2. ɔtɔ́mətizəm], fr. **automaton**. **a** State of being automatic; **b** power of movement without either volitional effort or external control, such as beating of the heart; **c** doctrine that the actions and movements of animals are not directed by consciousness but by purely physiological causes.

automaton, n. [1. awtómaton; 2. ɔtɔ́mətən], fr. Gk. *autómaton*, neut. of adj. *autómatos*, 'self-moving'. See **auto-**. The second element is fr. Aryan **mn̥t-ós*, 'thinking', fr. wh. base comes also Lat. *mens*, 'mind', fr. **ment-s*, see **mental**, & Goth. *ga-munds*, 'memory', O.E. *ġe-mynd*, 'memory', see **mind**. Something which moves and acts of itself; specif. **a** mechanical device which does this; and **b** human being who acts unintelligently and mechanically, merely following a prescribed and customary routine.

automobile (I.), adj. [1. àwtōmṓbīl; 2. ɔ̀toumóubail]. Hybrid Gk. & Lat. See **auto-** & **mobile**. Self-moving or self-movable.

automobile (II.), n. [1. àwtōmōbḗl; 2. ɔ̀toumoubíl], fr. Fr., as prec. Specifically used to denote a vehicle propelled by an engine worked by petrol, less commonly by steam; more commonly *motor-car* or *motor*.

autonomic, adj. [1. àwtōnómik; 2. ɔ̀tounɔ́mik]. See **autonomous** & **-ic**. (rare) Autonomous.

autonomist, n. [1. awtónomist; 2. ɔtɔ́nəmist]. See next word & **-ist**. One in favour of independent self-government.

autonomous, adj. [1. awtónomus; 2. ɔtɔ́nəməs], fr. Gk. *autónomos*, 'making or having one's own laws', fr. **auto-** & *nómos*, 'law', q.v. under **nomad**, & **-ous**. (of states, political units, institutions) Possessing political independence or self-government.

autonomy, n. [1. awtónomi; 2. ɔtɔ́nəmi], fr. Gk. *autonomía*, 'independence', see **autonomous**. (of states and institutions) a Condition of possessing and enjoying political independence, self-government; **b** political independence, self-government; **c** community, political unit, possessing self-government.

autoplasty, n. [1. áwtōplasti; 2. ɔ́touplæsti], fr. Gk. *autóplastos*, 'self-formed', see **auto-** & **plasma, plastic**. (surg.) Restoration of destroyed skin and tissue by grafting healthy portions taken from other parts of the body of same person.

autopsy, n. [1. áwtopsi; 2. ɔ́təpsi], fr. Gk. *autopsía*, 'a seeing with one's own eyes', fr. **auto-** & *ópsis*, 'a sight; the power of sight', see **optic**. Personal inspection; specif., post-mortem examination of a body. This is the common sense of the word in English.

auto-suggestion, n. [1. áwtō sujéschun; 2. ɔ́tou sədžéstʃən]. Hybrid Gk. & Lat. See **auto-** & **suggestion**. Suggestion coming from within, from one's own consciousness, and not received from outside.

autotoxin, n. [1. àwtōtóksin; 2. ɔ̀toutɔ́ksin]. See **auto-** & **toxin**. (pathol.) A toxic poisonous substance produced by changes within the body, as contrasted with external bacterial infection &c.

autotype, n. & vb. [1. áwtōtīp; 2. ɔ́toutaip]. See **auto-** & **type**. **1.** n. **a** Facsimile of writing or of a picture; **b** process of reproducing permanent copy of a photograph; copy made by this process. **2.** vb. To reproduce by this process.

autotypography, n. [1. áwtōtīpógrafi; 2. ɔ̀toutaipɔ́grəfi]. See **auto-** & **typography**. The process of making autotypes.

autumn, n. [1. áwtum; 2. ɔ́təm]. O. Fr. *autompne*, Fr. *automne*, fr. Lat. *autumnus*. The etymol. is uncertain, but it has been plausibly suggested that *aut-* may be cogn. w. the group of Gmc. words, Goth. *aud-ags*, 'rich, happy'; O.S. *ōd-ag*, O.H.G. *ōt-ag*, O.E. *ēad-iġ*, 'prosperous, happy, rich'. *Autumn* wd. thus mean the 'season of plenty'. **a** The third season of the year, between summer and winter; **b** (fig.) period of full maturity of life and development, when youth is past and decline has not yet set in.

autumnal, adj. [1. awtúmnal; 2. ɔtʌ́mnəl], fr. prec. & **-al**. Of or pertaining to, happening in, autumn; **a** (of plants) blooming or fruiting in autumn; **b** (fig.) connected with the middle period of life.

auxanometer, n. [1. awkzanómeter; 2. ɔkzənɔ́mitə], fr. Gk. *auxánein*, 'to increase'. See **auction** & **-meter**. An instrument for measuring the growth of plants.

auxiliary, adj. & n. [1. awgzíliari; 2. ɔgzíliəri], fr. Lat. *auxiliāris*, 'helpful', fr. *auxilium*, 'addition, help', fr. base **aug-*, 'increase', q.v. under **auction**, & **-ary**. **1.** adj. Helping, assisting, subsidiary: *auxiliary troops. Auxiliary verb*, one like *be, shall, will* and often *have*, which has no function apart from the full verb whose mood or tense it helps to express. **2.** n. A helper, assistant; specif. (in pl.) foreign troops serving with another nation in war.

avail (I.), vb. intrans. & trans. [1. avā́l; 2. əvéil], fr. *a-* (for Lat. **ad-**, 'to') & Fr. *vaille*, fr. *valoir*, 'to be worth', fr. Lat. *valēre*, 'to be strong, to be effective'. See **valiant**. **1.** intrans. To be of use, worth, value, profit; to serve a purpose: '*Ah! what avails the sceptred race*' (Landor). **2.** (reflex.) *To avail oneself of*, to profit by, take advantage, make use of: *to avail oneself of an offer, opportunity* &c. **3.** trans. To profit, benefit &c.: *our wealth avails us nothing, all must die.*

avail (II.), n., fr. prec. Use, profit, benefit, advantage; only in a few phrases such as: *of no avail*, useless; *of little avail*, very little good; *of what avail is it* &c.

availability, n. [1. avàlabíliti; 2. əvèiləbíliti]. See next word & **-ity**. Quality of, capacity for, being available.

available, adj. [1. avấlabl; 2. əvéiləbl], fr. **avail** & **-able**. **a** Capable of being used, handy, near at hand and easy to be obtained; **b** (special use confined to trading companies &c.) *tickets* (for railway or theatre) *available on day of issue only*, i.e. lawfully usable.

avalanche, n. [1. ávalahnsh; 2. ǽvəlānʃ]. Fr. dial. form of *avalance*, 'descent', fr. *avaler*, 'to descend', cp. *à val*, 'down hill', lit. 'to the valley'. **a** A mass of snow and ice loosened by thaw which rushes down a mountain-side collecting more and more snow, together with earth &c., in its descent; **b** (fig.) a thick shower of blows, missiles &c.; a huge influx of papers, letters, circulars &c. by post.

avant-courier, n. (compromise Engl.-Fr. pronunciation) [1. ávahn kòorier; 2. ǽvā kùriə], fr. Fr. *avant*, 'before'. See **advance** & **courier**. One who goes on ahead, before main body or principal person, in order to reconnoitre or to give notice of approach; pl., scouts, advance-guard.

avanturine. See **aventurine**.

avarice, n. [1. ávaris; 2. ǽvəris], fr. O. Fr., fr. Lat. *avāritia*, 'greed', fr. *avārus*, 'greedy', fr. *avēre*, 'to long for, covet'. See **audacious** & **ave** & cp. **avid**. Greed for riches; eager desire to obtain and to hoard wealth; covetousness, cupidity.

avaricious, adj. [1. àvaríshus; 2. ǽvəríʃəs]. Fr. *avaricieux*, see prec. Afflicted with avarice; afraid of losing or spending money; greedy, miserly, stingy.

avariciously, adv. Prec. & **-ly**. In an avaricious manner.

avast, interj. [1. aváhst; 2. əvā́st]. Prob. fr. Du. *houd vast*, 'hold fast'. (naut.) Stop! leave off!

avatar, n. [1. ávatar; 2. ǽvətā], fr. Scrt. *avatāra*, 'descent', fr. *áva*, 'down' (cogn. w. Lat. *au*, 'away', as in *aufero*, 'carry away'), & *tar-*, 'go, cross over', as in *tarati*, 'crosses'. (Hind. mythol.) Descent to earth of a Hindu deity and his incarnation as man or animal.

avaunt, interj. [1. aváwnt; 2. əvɔ́nt], fr. Fr. *avant*, 'to the front, forward!' fr. Lat. *ab ante*, 'from before'. See **advance**. Begone! (archaic, now only in mock heroics).

ave, interj. & n. [1. áhvi; 2. ā́vi]. Lat., 'hail, farewell', imperat. of *avēre*, 'to be happy, fare well', w. wh. the following are cognates: Scrt. *ávati*, 'he rejoices, helps, protects', *avitár*, 'helper, protector', *āviš*, 'favourable'; Gk. *enēés* for **en-ēwēs*, 'affable', *aítās* for **avi-tās*, 'benevolent, gentle', &, finally, Goth. *awi-liuþ*, 'thanksgiving, song of praise'. **1.** Interjectional greeting (esp. of farewell). **2.** n. **a** A devotional address or prayer to the B.V.M., from *Ave Maria*, first words of the prayer: *to say so many Aves*; **b** a farewell.

avenge, vb. trans. [1. avénj; 2. əvéndž], fr. O. Fr. *avengier*, fr. *à*, 'to', & *vengier*, fr. Lat. *vindicāre*, 'to claim as one's own; to avenge, punish'. See **vengeance**, **vindicate**. **a** To take satisfaction for an injury &c. by inflicting punishment upon the wrongdoer; inflict retribution: *to avenge a wrong*; *to avenge a wronged person upon the oppressor*; **b** *to avenge oneself, to be avenged*, to exact retribution for a wrong.

avenger, n. [1. avénjer; 2. əvéndžə]. Prec. & **-er**. He who avenges.

avenging, adj. [1. avénjing; 2. əvéndžiŋ]. Pres. Part. of **avenge**. Of, pertaining to, the person who or that which inflicts vengeance; exacting vengeance.

avens, n. [1. ávenz; 2. ǽvenz], fr. O. Fr. *avence*; etymol. doubtful. Rosaceous plant, herb bennet, wild species of the genus *Geum*.

aventurine, n. [1. avéntūrin; 2. ævéntjurin]. Fr., fr. Ital. *avventurino*, fr. *avventura*, 'chance', cp. **adventure**, so called because discovered by accident. **1.** Kind of Venetian glass of brownish colour with gold spangles enclosed in it. **2.** A variety of silica, or crystalline quartz, traversed by fissures which reflect the light, and give a spangled appearance.

avenue, n. [1. ávenū; 2. ǽvinjū]. Fr., fr. fem. P.P. of *avenir*, fr. Lat. *advenīre*, fr. **ad-**, 'to', & *venīre*, 'to come', see **venue**. A way of approach. **1. a** Principal road, or one of several, passing through private grounds to a house, usually bordered by trees on either side; drive; **b** roadway bordered by trees; a double row of trees without a road. **2.** A wide street with houses on either side, with or without rows of trees. **3.** (fig.) Means of access or approach to non-material things: *an avenue to success, prosperity* &c.

aver, vb. trans. [1. avě́r; 2. əvə̄́], fr. Fr. *avérer*, 'assert', fr. Lat. **ad**, 'to', & *vērum*, 'true thing, truth'. See **very**, **verity** &c. **a** To declare to be true, assert, affirm, declare positively: usually, *to aver that an event happened*, or absolutely, *as he avers*; **b** (law) to prove or justify (a plea).

average (I.), n. [1. áverij; 2. ǽvəridž]. O. Fr., fr. Med. Lat. *averāgium*, 'property, cattle', fr. Lat. *habēre*, 'have', see **habit**; cp. O. Fr. *aveir*, vb. & n., 'goods'; there is also another word, Fr. *avarie*, 'damage to goods in transit', at one time used of payment due to a port for each ship moored there. The relationship, if any, between the two words is not clear, nor is the precise development of meaning. There seems to have been confusion in English between the two words. There is also a word *arriage* in Scots law, associated with *carriage* in leases, implying some kind of service to be rendered by a tenant to his feudal lord. **1. a** Mean proportion; the mean value or quantity of any number of sums, values, or quantities, obtained by dividing the totals by the number of the former; medial estimate: *on an* (*the*) *average*; *a cricketer's batting or bowling average*; hence, **b** generally prevailing rate, common standard: *well up to the average*. **2.** Estimate of probability or proportion, derived by generalization from number of specific cases: *to strike an average*; esp. in insurance (the original sense), **a** estimated proportion of actual compensation for loss to be paid, having regard to total amount of loss, and relation of this to the value actually insured; **b** (in marine insurance) *general average*, proportion of loss to be borne by all parties or insurers for damage through intentional acts done to save ship or cargo; *particular average*, that to be borne by owners or insurers for accidental damage.

average (II.), adj. See prec. **a** Arrived at by process of average, containing a mean value: *average monthly rainfall* &c.; **b** of a usual standard; ordinary, normal: *average height, intelligence*.

average (III.), vb. trans., fr. **average** (I.). **a** To estimate, arrive at, the average of; **b** to distribute in a proportion arrived at by average: *to average a loss* &c.; **c** to amount to, work out at, on an average: *to average a certain monthly expenditure*.

averment, n. [1. avěrment; 2. əvə̄́mənt], fr. **aver** & **-ment**. **1.** Act of averring; something averred; positive asseveration, declaration. **2.** (law) Offer to prove a plea; proof of a plea.

averruncator, n. [1. àverungkấter; 2. ævəraŋkéitə], fr. obs. vb. *averruncate* & **-or**, fr. Lat. *averruncāt-*(*um*), P.P. of *averruncāre*, 'to ward off, remove', fr. *ā*, *ab*, 'off', & *verruncāre*, 'to turn'; also 'to turn out well'; an old religious word; erroneously confused in meaning w. Lat. *ēruncāre*, 'to root out'; the word should be avoided. Device consisting of two curved pincer-like blades at the end of a long pole, worked by a wire, used for pruning and lopping small boughs and shoots growing high above one's head. (The instrument is far commoner than the name.)

averse, adj. [1. avěrs; 2. əvə̄́s], fr. Lat. *āvers-*(*um*), 'turned away', P.P. of *āvertere*, see **avert**. Set against, opposed to, reluctant, disinclined for. Normally and usually followed by *to* (before Pres. Parts. and vbl. and other ns.): *averse to coming*; *not averse to a good dinner*; or less frequently by infin.: *averse to do*. (Very rarely, and now chiefly in affected style, followed by *from*.)

averseness, n. Prec. & **-ness**. State of being averse.

aversion, n. [1. avěrshun; 2. əvə̄́ʃən], fr. Lat. *āversiōn-*(*em*), 'a turning away', fr. *āvers-*(*um*), *āvertere*, see **avert**. **1.** Strong feeling of dislike, antipathy, repugnance (followed by *to*). **2.** Person or thing which inspires antipathy: *my chief aversion*.

avert, vb. trans. [1. avěrt; 2. əvə̄́t], fr. O. Fr. *avertir*, fr. Lat. *āvertere*, 'turn aside from', fr. *ā*, 'from', & *vertere*, 'to turn'. See **version**. **1. a** To turn away from, turn aside in another direction: *to avert one's eyes, glance &c. from*; **b** to ward off, prevent from producing effect: *to avert a blow*. **2.** (fig.) To ward off, prevent, a disaster, illness &c.

averted, adj. [1. avěrted; 2. əvə̄́tid], fr. P.P. of prec. Turned away (esp. of the eyes), as though ashamed or horrified.

avertible, adj. [1. avěrtibl; 2. əvə̄́tibl]. **avert** & **-ible**. (of non-material things) Capable of being averted or prevented.

aviarist, n. [1. ấviarist; 2. éiviərist]. See **aviary** & **-ist**. One who keeps an aviary.

aviary, n. [1. ấviari; 2. éiviəri], fr. Lat. *aviārium*, fr. *avis*, 'a bird'. The undoubted cognates of this common Lat. word are not numerous, but include prob. Scrt. *viš*, 'bird', & Gk. *aietós*, *aetós*, 'eagle' (for **awjetos*). See **augur**, **auspice**. Large cage or enclosed space for keeping birds.

aviation, n. [1. àviấshun; 2. èiviéiʃən], concocted fr. Lat. *avi-*(*s*), 'bird', see prec. & **-ation**. Art of flight through the air by mechanical means, including everything connected with management of flying-machines in the air.

aviator, n. [1. ấviàter; 2. éivièitə], fr. Lat. *avi-*(*s*), 'bird', & *-ātor*, on anal. of *viator* &c. See prec. & **aviary**. One who flies by mechanical means; flying-man; one skilled in aviation.

aviculture, n. [1. ấvikulchur; 2. éivikaltʃə], fr. Lat. *avi*(*s*), 'bird', see **aviary**, & **culture**. Breeding and care of birds.

avid, adj. [1. ávid; 2. ǽvid], fr. Lat. *avidus*, fr. *avēre*, 'to be eager for, to desire', see **audacious** & **ave** & cp. **avarice**. Eager for, desirous of, greedy, followed by *of* or *for*.

avidity, n. [1. avíditi; 2. əvíditi], fr. Fr. *avidité*, fr. Lat. *aviditas*, 'longing, vehement desire', fr. *avidus*. See prec. & **-ity**. Ardent desire, eagerness, greed, hunger (lit. and fig.): *to accept, to eat, with avidity*.

avidly, adv. [1. ávidli; 2. ǽvidli]. **avid** & **-ly**. Eagerly, hungrily.

avifauna, n. [1. ấvifàwna; 2. éivifɔ̀nə], fr. Lat. *avis*, 'bird', see **aviary**, & **fauna**. All the species of birds collectively distributed in a given region.

avizandum, n. [1. àvizándum; 2. ævizǽndəm]. Med. Lat., gerund of *advizāre*, 'to consider', see **advise**. (Scots law) Withdrawal or suspending of a case by a judge for further consideration.

avocado, n. [1. àvōkáhdō; 2. ævoukā́dou]. Span., 'advocate'. Corrupt. of Mexican name *ahuācall*. The fruit of a tropical American and W. Indian tree, shaped like a pear; the alligator-pear.

avocation, n. [1. àvōkấshun; 2. ævoukéiʃən], fr. Lat. *āvocātiōn-*(*em*), 'a calling off, diversion', fr. *āvocāre*, *-ātum*, fr. *ā*, 'from, off', & *vocāre*, 'to call', see **vocation**. (Original meanings, diversion, distraction of attention, now obsolete.) **a** One's regular, habitual business, customary occupation, calling (also in pl.); **b** minor, subsidiary, employments, occupations other than regular habitual business (in pl.).

avocet, avoset, n. [1. ávōset; 2. ǽvouset], fr. Fr. *avocette*, fr. Ital. *avosetta*. Genus of bird with webbed feet; allied to the stilt.

avoid, vb. trans. [1. avóid; 2. əvɔ́id], fr. O. Fr. *esvuidier*, 'to empty', fr. Lat. **ex-** & **void**, w. change of pref. to a-, 'from'. (Old meanings, to void; to depart; extricate oneself from &c., are now obsolete.) To keep away from; eschew. Specif. **1. a** to shun, give the slip to, escape meeting, refrain from society of (a person); **b** keep away from, abstain from going to (a place); **c** escape, prevent oneself, from (suffering, calamity &c.); **d** evade, refrain from doing (an action, one's duty &c.). **2.** (law) To annul (a plea); to make void, invalidate, quash (a sentence).

avoidable, adj. [1. avóidabl; 2. əvɔ́idəbl]. Prec. & **-able**. Capable of being avoided.

avoidably, adv. Prec. & **-ly**. In an avoidable manner.

avoidance, n. [1. avóidans; 2. əvɔ́idəns]. See **avoid** & **-ance**. **1.** The act of avoiding: *avoidance of difficulties.* **2.** The vacation of an office or benefice. **3.** (law) In *Plea of Confession and Avoidance*, where in a defence to an action, certain facts are admitted but with new facts sufficient to 'avoid' or annul the legal effect of what is admitted.

avoirdupois, adj. & n. [1. àverdepóiz; 2. æ̀vədəpɔ́iz]. Incorrect form of *avoir de pois*, in O. Fr. *aveir de pois*, 'goods of weight', fr. *aveir*, later *avoir*, 'goods', fr. Lat. *habēre*, 'to have', cp. first element in **average**, & O. Fr. *pois*, 'weight', see **poise**. **1.** *Avoirdupois* or as adj. *avoirdupois weight*, system of weights used in all English-speaking countries for all articles except precious metals and medicines. **2.** (colloq. and vulg.) Excessive weight and stoutness of a person.

avouch, vb. trans. & intrans. [1. avóuch; 2. əváutʃ], fr. O. Fr. *avochier*, fr. Lat. *advocāre*, 'to call, summon, as (legal) defender', fr. **ad-** & *vocāre*, 'to call'. See **vouch**. **1.** trans. **a** To avow, assert, affirm, that something is true; **b** to confess, acknowledge openly. **2.** intrans. To give assurance; to assert.

avow, vb. trans. [1. avóu; 2. əváu], fr. O. Fr. *avouer*, *avoer*, fr. Lat. *advōtāre*. See **vow** & **vote**. The meanings show confusion between *advōtāre*, 'vow', & *advocāre*, 'call upon'. See prec. **1. a** To declare openly, admit, confess: *to avow one's errors*; **b** (reflex.) to declare, admit, oneself to be: *avow oneself a believer in spiritualism.* **2.** (law) To justify an act done, make avowry of.

avowable, adj. [1. avóuabl; 2. əváuəbl], fr. **avow** & **-able**. Capable of being avowed or acknowledged without discredit.

avowal, n. [1. avóual; 2. əváuəl]. See **avow** & **-al**. Free and open admission, confession.

avowed, adj. [1. avóud; 2. əváud], fr. P.P. of **avow**. Self-acknowledged, freely admitted, recognized: *an avowed Jew*; *the avowed author of the plot.*

avowedly, adv. [1. avóuedli; 2. əváuidli]. Prec. & **-ly**. By admission and acknowledgement.

avowry, n. [1. avóuri; 2. əváuəri]. O. Fr. *avouerie*. See **avow** & **-ry**. (law) Action of avowing; specif., justification of action by one distraining goods.

avulsion, n. [1. avúlshun; 2. əvʌ́lʃən]. Lat. *āvulsiōn-(em)*, 'a tearing off', fr. *āvuls-(um)*, P.P. type of *avellere*, 'pull off, tear away', fr. *ā*, 'away', & *vellere*, 'pull, pluck, twitch', see **vellicate**; the base is prob. the same as that in Lat. *vellum*, 'shorn fleece' (see **wool**), & possibly Lat. *vulnus*, 'wound'; cp. also Goth. *wilwan*, 'to rob, take by force', also W. *gwellaif*, 'tongs'. **1.** A tearing away, forcible separation. **2.** Specif. (law) sudden removal, or cutting off, of land by flood, or alteration in course of a river, from estate of one person, so that it is joined to that of another.

avuncular, adj. [1. avúngkūlar; 2. əvʌ́ŋkjulə], fr. Lat. *avunculus*, 'maternal uncle', dimin. of *avus*, 'grandfather', & **-ar**; see **atavism** & **eme**, & cp. **uncle**. Pertaining to, in relationship of, an uncle.

await, vb. trans. [1. awā́t; 2. əwéit]. Norman Fr. *awaitier*, fr. *a*, 'to', & **wait**. **1.** (of persons) To wait for, be on look-out for, expect: *to await a person*; *await arrival of*, *await a decision.* **2.** (of things) To be prepared for, in store for; to overtake, follow of necessity: *a hearty welcome awaits you*; *death awaits us all.*

awake (I.), vb. trans. & intrans. [1. awā́k; 2. əwéik]. Formally fr. O.E. *āwacan* & *āwacian*, see **wake (I.)**, wh. were intrans.; the O.E. trans. vb. was *aweċċan*, M.E. *awecchen*. See also **watch (II.)**. **A.** trans. **a** To rouse from sleep; **b** (fig.) to rouse, stir up (a person), from mental lethargy, or indifference, inaction; excite into action or activity of any kind: *to awake a person from ignorance and sloth*; **c** make a person conscious, aware of (followed by *to*): *awake a person to a sense of sin*; **d** excite lively feelings of interest, sorrow, delight &c.: *to awake old memories, awake a desire for knowledge.* **B.** intrans. **a** To come out of sleep, cease to sleep; **b** (fig.) to enter upon bodily or mental activity, rouse oneself from indifference or inactivity; **c** *to awake to*, to become conscious, aware, of, to realize: *to awake to one's danger, responsibilities* &c.

awake (II.), pred. adj. M.E. *awāke(n)*, str. P.P. of prec. Roused from sleep, no longer sleeping; (lit. and fig.) vigilant, mentally alert. *Awake to*, conscious of, aware of, alive to: *to be fully awake to difficulties* &c.

awaken, vb. trans. & intrans. [1. awā́ken; 2. əwéikən]. O.E. *āwæcnian*, intrans., 'come to life, come into being'. To awake, in various senses, lit. & fig., esp. to arouse to a sense of.

award (I.), vb. trans. [1. awórd; 2. əwɔ́d]. O. Fr. *awarder*. See **ward (I.)**. **a** To give, allow (something claimed), by judicial pronouncement; **b** to assign, allot, something, esp. a prize, palm, to a person after careful weighing of merits of various candidates; **c** to grant, allow to.

award (II.), n. See prec. **a** Judicial decision, judgement, esp. of arbitrators; **b** payment awarded by such decision.

aware, adj. [1. awā́r; 2. əwέə]. O.E. *ġewær*. See **ware, wary**. Knowing, conscious, informed: *aware of the facts*; *aware that there is danger.*

awash, adv. & pred. adj. [1. awósh; 2. əwɔ́ʃ], fr. **a-**, 'on', & **wash**. (of a rock, sunken ship &c.) On a level with the surface of the water so as to be washed by it.

away, adv. [1. awā́; 2. əwéi]. O.E. *onweġ*, M.E. *awei* &c., 'away'. See **a-**, 'on', & **way**. (Orig. 'on the way' then w. sense of removal to another place, & many differentiations of meaning.) **1.** (denoting rest or position) At a distance from given place or person: *far away*; *away from home*; *away at the wars* &c. **2. a** (expressing motion, removal) To a distance, to another place, or in a different direction: *to go away*; *throw away*; *run away*; *to lean away from.* Phrs. *away with you*; *away with it*, take it away; *to fire away one's ammunition*; *explain away*, minimize, lessen force of; *whither away?*, where are you going? **b** expressing loss, diminution, destruction: *to drain away*; *ebb away*; *waste, pine, wither, away*; *take away (from).* Phrs. *to pass away*, die; *to fall away (from)*, desert, withdraw support or adherence. **3.** Expressing the idea of immediate action; forthwith, without delay: *straight away, right away.* **4.** Denoting continuous movement, or action; without intermission: *work away, peg away (at).* **5.** (used as mere intens.) *Far and away the best.*

awe (I.), n. [1. aw; 2. ɔ]. Scand.; M.E. *āȝe*, *āwe*, fr. O.N. *agi*, cogn. w. Goth. *agis*, 'fear, anguish', O.H.G. *agi*, *egiso* (cp. O.E. *eġesa*, 'fear', & that wh. inspires it). The corresponding O.E. word is *eġe*, 'fear', wh. has been lost. Outside Gmc. there is the cogn. Gk. *ákhos*, 'grief', & *ákhomai*, 'I am afflicted'. Respect mingled with fear; dread, startled wonder; feeling inspired by something at once terrifying and majestic or sublime: *to stand, be, in awe of*; *a feeling of awe.*

awe (II.), vb. trans., fr. prec. To inspire with awe, to strike with respectful dread.

aweary, adj. [1. a-wḗri; 2. əwíəri], fr. **a-** & **weary**. (poet.) Weary.

aweless, adj. [1. áwles; 2. ɔ́lis], fr. **awe (I.)** & **-less**. **a** Not inspiring awe; **b** not feeling awe.

awesome, adj. [1. áwsum; 2. ɔ́səm], fr. **awe (I.)** & **-some**. Inspiring awe, dreadful.

awestruck, adj. [1. áwstruk; 2. ɔ́strʌk], fr. **awe (I.)** & **struck**. Deeply affected with awe.

awful, adj. [1. áwfool; 2. ɔ́fəl], fr. **awe (I.)** & **-ful**. **1. a** Apt to fill others with awe, inspiring awe; dreadful, appalling; **b** deserving and inspiring respect and reverence, solemnly impressive: *awful dignity.* **2.** (colloq.) Used as a mere intensive: *an awful nuisance*; *awful nonsense.*

awfully, adv. Prec. & **-ly**. **a** In an awful manner; **b** (colloq., mere intens.) very, extremely: *awfully good* &c.

awfulness, n. See prec. & **-ness**. **a** Quality or fact of being awful; **b** (colloq.) unpleasantness, disagreeableness, specif., bad behaviour &c.

awhile, adv. [1. awī́l; 2. əwáil]. *a*, indef. art., as in O.E. *āne hwīle*, or 'on', on anal. of other old advbs. thus formed, & **while**; in any case the pref. is gen. felt as the art., cp. *wait awhile*, or *wait a little while.* For a short time.

awkward, adj. [1. áwkward; 2. ɔ́kwəd]. Orig. an adv. meaning 'wrong way round, contrary', fr. *auk*, 'wrong, contrary', & *-ward*, adv. suff., as in *forward* (see **-ward**). *Auk* is fr. O.N. *ǒfug*, 'turning the wrong way, back foremost', of wh. *ǒf* is for *af* (see **off, of**); & *-ug*, Goth. *-uh*, O.S. & O.H.G. *-uh*, as in O.S. *abuh*, 'perverse, evil', O.H.G. *apuh*, 'turned away' (corresponding to O.N. *ǒfug*), is a suff., the precise force of wh. is difficult to determine: it is supposed to be cogn. w. Lat. *que*, 'and'. The history of *awkward* is thoroughly elucidated by Skeat. **1. a** (of material things) Difficult or dangerous to use or handle, inconvenient for particular purpose: *an awkward door to open*; *an awkward handle to hold*; **b** (of non-material things) embarrassing, inopportune, disconcerting: *an awkward situation*; *an awkward remark, pause*; *an awkward time for it to occur.* **2.** (of persons or their actions) **a** Clumsy, ungraceful, embarrassed: *an awkward boy*; *awkward in his movements*; *awkward in society*; Phr. *the awkward age*, adolescence; **b** lacking dexterity, bungling: *an awkward workman*; **c** (colloq.) dangerous, formidable: *an awkward customer.*

awkwardly, adv. Prec. & **-ly**. In an awkward manner.

awkwardness, n. See prec. & **-ness**. Quality of being awkward, in all senses; inconvenience; clumsiness; inopportuneness; lack of grace or dexterity.

awl, n. [1. awl; 2. ɔl]. O.E. *æl*, M.E. *al*, *all*; cognate w. O.N. *ala*, O.H.G. *ala*. A small pointed tool for boring holes in wood, leather &c., distinct from a gimlet in having a pear-shaped handle, and no thread or arm.

awn, n. [1. awn; 2. ɔn]. Same in M.E.; O.E. has *eġenu* (pl., fr. **æġin-*), 'chaff', but our present form must go back to an O.E. **agan-*, without mutation, or may be a Scand. loan-word, cp. Swed. *agn*, 'husk'; the word is well represented in Gmc. languages, cp. O.H.G. *agana*, Goth. *ahana*, 'chaff'; these are cogn. w. Lat. *agna* (fr. **acna*), 'straw', & Gk. *ákhnē*, 'husk of wheat' &c., pl. *ákhnai*, 'chaff'. All these words are derived fr. Aryan base **ak(h)*, 'sharp, pricking', whence come also a large number of words meaning 'cutting edge, point, prickle', also (fig.) 'pain, grief' &c. See **acid, acerbity, acrid, acuity, acute, ail, edge.** Spiky growth from end of the ears of oats, barley, some kinds of wheat, and from many kinds of grasses; called also *beard.*

awned, adj. [1. awnd; 2. ōnd], fr. prec. & **-ed**. Furnished with spikes or beard, like oats &c.

awning, n. [1. áwning; 2. ṓniŋ]. Etymol. doubtful, but cp. Fr. *auvent*, 'shed, penthouse'. Canvas sheet stretched on framework used as a protection from the sun, esp. on deck of a ship.

awnless, adj. [1. áwnles; 2. ṓnlis], fr. **awn** & **-less**. Devoid of awn.

awoke, vb. [1. awṓk; 2. əwóuk]. Pret. of **awake**; see **woke**.

awry, adv. & pred. adj. [1. arī́; 2.ərái], fr. **a-**, & **wry**. **1.** adv. **a** Crookedly, askew, unevenly; **b** (fig., of human actions, events &c.) wrong, erroneously, in a wrong manner or direction: *everything has gone awry*, gone wrong, failed. **2.** pred. adj. Twisted, crooked, distorted (lit. and fig.): *the picture is all awry*; *his life was awry*.

axe, n. [1. aks; 2. æks]. O.E. *acus*, *æx* &c., O.H.G. *acchus*, Goth. *akwizi*, cp. Lat. *ascia* for **acsia*, 'axe', also 'mason's trowel', Gk. *axī́nē*, 'axe'. Tool for cutting and splitting timber, with a heavy head, having one sharp edge and a long handle by which it is swung; Phrs. *the axe*, (i.) execution by beheading; (ii.) drastic reduction of public expenditure; *to have an axe to grind*, to have personal, usually financial, advantages to gain by a certain course of action.

axial, adj. [1. ákzial; 2. ǽkziəl], fr. **axis** & **-al**. Of, belonging to, connected with, an axis.

axil, n. [1. ákzil; 2. ǽkzil], fr. Lat. *axilla*, 'armpit'; see **aisle** & **axle**. Point at which a bough springs from the tree or a leaf from its stem.

axile, adj. [1. áksīl; 2. ǽksail], fr. **axis** & **-ile**. Belonging to, situated in, the axis.

axilla, n. [1. akzíla; 2. ækzílə]. Lat., 'armpit', dimin. of *āla* (fr. **acsla*), 'wing'; see **aileron, aisle, axle**. **a** (anat.) The armpit; **b** (bot.) axil, q.v.

axillary, adj. [1. akzílari; 2. ækzíləri], fr. **axilla** & **-ary**. **1.** (anat.) Connected with the armpit. **2.** (bot.) Connected with, arising from, the axil: *axillary bud*.

axiom, n. [1. áksium; 2. ǽksiəm], fr. Fr. *axiome*, fr. Lat. *axiōma*, fr. Gk. *axíōma*, 'that which is thought fit or worthy', (philos.) 'self-evident proposition', fr. *axió-ō*, 'I deem worthy, estimate', fr. *áxios*, 'worthy'; cp. also *ágō*, 'weigh, estimate'; cp. Lat. *agīna*, 'frame of a balance', *exagium*, 'weight'; all ultimately fr. base **ag-*, 'go, move' &c.; see **act, action, agent** &c. **1.** An accepted principle or assumption such as those upon which sciences are based. **2.** (math. and log.) A self-evident proposition, one which is so evident that it needs no proof or demonstration.

axiomatic(al), adj. [1. àksiōmátik(l); 2. æ̀ksioumǽtik(l)], fr. Gk. *axiōmatikós*, fr. *axíōma*. See **axiom**. Of the nature of an axiom; belonging to, based on, undisputed principles.

axiomatically, adv. Prec. & **-ly**. By the use of axioms, as based on axioms.

axis, n., pl. **axes** [1. áksis, -ēz; 2. ǽksis, -īz]. Lat., 'axle of a waggon, axis of the world, north pole, the whole sky', cogn. w. Gk. *áxōn*, 'axle of a wheel', Scrt. *ákšaš*, same base as **axilla**; see also **axle, aisle, aileron.** Hypothetical central line of a body; in various special uses: **1.** (geom. and drawing) Real or imaginary line which divides a figure into two symmetrical parts. **2.** (astron.) An imaginary line about which a body rotates or may rotate. *Axis of the equator*, imaginary straight line on which the earth rotates and which passes through the imaginary points called poles. **3.** (bot.) Stem or central line along which the growths and organs of a plant are arranged.

axle, n. [1. áksl; 2. ǽksl]. M.E. *axel* &c., *axeltree*; the uncompounded *eaxl*, *axl*, means 'shoulder' in O.E.; the Gmc. cognates are O.H.G. *ahsala*, Mod. Germ. *achsel*, O.S. *ahsla*, O.N. *öxul(l)* &c. For this base in other families of language, see **axilla, axis, aileron, aisle. a** (rather loosely in common usage) The rod or bar which connects two opposite wheels, and on, or with, which the wheel revolves; **b** more exactly, the *axles* are the two ends of the bar which connects the wheels, the bar itself being strictly the *axle-tree*. *Axle-box*, box closed by detachable cap, in nave of wheel, through which the ends of the axle-tree pass.

Axminster, adj. & n. [1. áksminster; 2. ǽksminstə], fr. name of town in Devon, where carpets were formerly woven by hand. Name of a type of carpet now made at Wilton near Salisbury.

axolotl, n. [1. àksolótl; 2. æ̀ksəlɔ́tl]. Mexican word. Kind of amphibian water lizard or salamander found in Mexico, which retains the gills of its tadpole form and breeds as such in the lakes where it lives, but has power of developing lungs and attaining its true salamander form on land.

ay, aye, interj. & n. [1. ī; 2. ai]. Perh. same as **aye**. **1.** interj. Yes. **2.** n. An answer in the affirmative; (pl.) *ayes*, those who vote in the affirmative or in favour of a motion. Parliamentary Phr. *the ayes have it*, those in favour of the motion are in a majority.

ayah, n. [1. ī́ya; 2. áijə]. Anglo-Indian word, said to be from Span. *āya*, Port. *aia*, 'governess'. Native Hindu nurse or lady's maid, esp. one waiting on Europeans in India.

aye, adv. [1. ā; 2. ei]. M.E. *ei*, *ai* &c., fr. O.N. *ei*, 'ever, always'; the native Engl. word cogn. w. this is *ā*, 'always'; O.H.G. *eo*, Goth. *aiw*, 'always'. These are fr. the ns., O.E. *ǣ(w)*, 'time, eternity', O.H.G. *ēwa*, Goth. *aiws*; see further on this base under **aeon, age, eternal, ever.** Ever, always, forever; also *for aye*, eternally: *for ever and aye*.

aye-aye, n. [1. ī́yī; 2. áijai]. Madagascar word, perh. fr. cry of animal. Small rodent about the size of a cat, with a bushy tail like a squirrel, a nocturnal lemur, *Chiromys*, found in Madagascar.

azalea, n. [1. azália; 2. əzéiliə], fr. Gk. *azaléa*, fem. of *azaléos*, adj., 'burnt, dry'; so named because the plant flourishes in a dry soil. Cp. Gk. *áza*, 'soot', *ázō*, 'to dry, burn'. The Gk. base is fr. **azd-*, cp. Czech *ozditi*, 'to dry up'; fr. same base, without *-d*, Goth. *azgō*, 'cinder' (see **ash**), and Lat. *aridus*, 'dry', *ardēre*, 'burn', fr. **azidus*, **azidiō*. See **ardent, arid.** Genus of shrubs with richly scented white, pink, yellow, or red blooms, allied to the rhododendron, chiefly natives of North America and China.

azarole, n. [1. ázarōl; 2. ǽzəroul], fr. Fr. *azerole*, fr. Ital. *azzeruolo*, fr. an Arab. word. Fruit of Neapolitan medlar; tree which bears this.

Azilian, adj. [1. azílian; 2. əzíliən], fr. name of cavern, Mas d'Azil, French Pyrenees, where remains were found. Pertaining to a stage of prehistoric culture linking the palaeolithic and neolithic periods.

azimuth, n. [1. ázimuth; 2. ǽzimaþ]. M.E. *azimute* (in Chaucer's 'Astrolabe'), fr. Arab. *as-samūt*, 'the paths'. See **zenith.** Distance of a star in angular degrees from N. or S. point of the meridian.

azimuthal, adj. [1. àzimū́dhal; 2. æ̀zimjū́ðəl]. Prec. & **-al.** Pertaining to the azimuth.

azimuth compass, n. Special form of compass with vertical sights used for taking the azimuth of a star.

azo-, pref., fr. **azote**, old name for nitrogen; used in chemistry to form words denoting compounds containing nitrogen in various combinations.

azoic, adj. [1. azṓik; 2. əzóuik], fr. Gk. *ázō-(os,)* fr. **a-**, 'without', & *zōḗ*, 'life'. See **zoic, zoology.** (geol.) Belonging to that period of geological time before the appearance of organic life on the earth: *azoic age*.

azonic, adj. [1. azónik; 2. əzɔ́nik], fr. Gk. *azōnikós*, *ázōnos*, fr. **a-**, 'not', & *zṓnē*, 'belt, zone, region'. See **zone.** Not limited to a particular region or zone.

azote, n. [1. azṓt; 2. əzóut]. Fr., fr. Gk. **a-**, 'not', & *zōḗ*, 'life'. See **zoic.** Old name for nitrogen, so called because it is incapable of supporting organic life.

azotic, adj. [1. azótik; 2. əzɔ́tik]. Fr. *azotique*. See prec. & **-ic.** Pertaining to azote or nitrogen.

azotite, n. [1. ázotīt; 2. ǽzətait], fr. **azote** & **-ite.** (obs.) A salt of nitrous acid.

azotize, vb. trans. [1. ázotīz; 2. ǽzətaiz], fr. **azote** & **-ize.** To nitrogenize; to deprive of oxygen.

azure, adj. & n. [1. ázhur, ā́zhur; 2. ǽžə, éižə]. M.E., fr. O. Fr. *azur*, fr. Med. Lat. *azura* (cp. Span. & Port. *azul*), fr. Arab. *al-lazward*. See **lapis lazuli. 1.** adj. Of a sky-blue colour, of the sky, sea, and human eyes. **2.** n. **a** The colour sky-blue; **b** (poet.) the sky itself when blue and cloudless; **c** heraldic name for blue.

azurite, n. [1. ázhūrīt; 2. ǽžjurait]. Prec. & **-ite.** Basic carbonate of copper, from its colour.

azygous, adj. [1. ázigus; 2. ǽzigəs], fr. Gk. *ázugos*, 'unyoked', fr. **a-**, 'not', & *zugón*, 'yoke'. See **zygo-.** (anat., of an organic part, a muscle &c.). Not one of a pair.

B

B, b [1. bē; 2. bī]. **1.** The second letter of the English and other cognate alphabets; for its use in abbreviations see end of Dictionary. **2.** As symbol, denoting the second in order or quality of a series; specif. **a** (alg.) the second of a series of known numbers; **b** (mus.) the seventh note in the diatonic scale of C major; the scale in which the keynote is B.

baa, vb. & n. [1. bah; 2. bā]. Imitative. **a** vb. To bleat, of sheep and lambs; **b** n., the cry made by these animals.

Baal, n. [1. bāl; 2. beil]. Semitic, 'lord'. God of the Phoenicians; (fig.) a false god or idol.

baa-lamb, n. Childish name for a lamb or sheep.

babacoote, n. [1. bábakōōt; 2. bǽbəkūt], fr. Malagasy *babakoto*. (zool.) Species of lemur found in Madagascar.

babble (I.), vb. intrans. & trans. [1. bábl; 2. bǽbl]. Imit., cp. Swed. *babbla*; also Lat. *babulāre*, Fr. *babiller*. **1.** To speak inarticulately or incoherently; to utter a stream of trivialities. **2.** To tell what had best been kept secret, reveal secrets inadvisedly. **3.** (of streams) To murmur, make gentle sound in flowing.

babble (II.), n., fr. prec. Childish chatter; foolish talk; confused sound of conversation, as of crowds; badly articulated speech; the sound of streams.

babbler, n. [1. bábler; 2. bǽblə]. **babble** (I.) & **-er. 1.** One who babbles (in various senses). **2.** Species of thrush.

babe, n. [1. bāb; 2. beib]. Prob. connected w. **babble. a** Baby, very young child; **b** an innocent, inexperienced person: *a mere babe in the ways of the world*.

babel, n. [1. bábl; 2. béibl]. Heb. *Bābel*, name of capital of Babylonia; place where, in the O.T. narrative, human speech was confounded. **1. a** Confused sound produced by a number of persons speaking together at the same time; a chattering; **b** sound produced by a number of persons speaking different languages. **2. a** Place where there is a babel of sound; **b** place where several different languages are spoken.

babiroussa, n. [1. bàbiro͞osa; 2. bæ̀birúsə]. Malay., 'hog deer'. Species of Indian hog, native of Celebes and Buru.

baboo, n. [1. báhbo͞o; 2. bắbū]. Hind. *babu*. Hindu title = Mr. Generally used contemptuously of an Indian who has had a European education and adopts English speech and manners.

baboon, n. [1. babo͞on; 2. bəbún]. M.E. *baboin* &c., Fr. *babouin*. Origin uncertain. A kind of large ape with short tail, dog-like muzzle, and bare, coloured patches on cheeks and buttocks, typical genus *Papio*.

babouche, n. [1. babo͞osh; 2. bəbúʃ]. Fr. *babouche*, fr. Arab. *babush*, Pers. *pa-posh*, 'foot-covering'. An Oriental heelless slipper.

baby, n. [1. bắbi; 2. béibi]. Dimin. of **babe**. **1.** Very young child; applied also familiarly to young animals, esp. monkeys. **2.** One having the behaviour or character of a baby; a frivolous, foolish, or cowardly person. Phrs. *a regular baby*; *cry-baby*, a child who cries for nothing. **3.** A thing of small size of its kind: *baby grand piano.*

baby-farmer, n. A woman who makes money by taking in unwanted babies to board; esp. one who neglects and ill-treats her charges.

babyhood, n. [1. bắbihood; 2. béibihud]. **baby** & **-hood**. Condition of being a baby.

babyish, adj. [1. bắbi-ish; 2. béibi-iʃ]. **baby** & **-ish**. Like a baby, esp. in sense **2**.

baccalaureate, n. [1. bàkaláwriat; 2. bækəlɔ́riət]. Med. Lat. *baccalaureātus*, fr. Lat. *baccalāris*, see **bachelor**, influenced by Lat. *laurus*, 'laurel'. Lowest academic degree, that of Bachelor.

baccarat, n. [1. bákarah; 2. bǽkərā]. Fr., perh. fr. name of town. Gambling card game.

baccate, adj. [1. bákāt; 2. bǽkeit]. Lat. *bacca*, 'berry', see **bacci-**, & **-ate**. Bearing berries.

bacchanal, n. & adj. [1. bákanal; 2. bǽkənəl], fr. Lat. *Bacchānālis*, belonging to Bacchus (god of wine) & his rites; fr. Gk. *Bákkhos*, see **bacci-**. **a** n. A roysterer, noisy, drunken reveller; **b** adj., belonging to, characteristic of, such a reveller.

Bacchanalia, n. [1. bàkanália; 2. bækənéiliə]. Lat., neut. pl.; see prec. The feasts and orgies of Bacchus. Applied to noisy, drunken revelry.

Bacchanalian, adj. [1. bàkanálian; 2. bækənéiliən]. Prec. & **-an**. Belonging to noisy, drunken feasts.

Bacchant(e), n. [1. bákant, bakánti; 2. bǽkənt, bəkǽnti], fr. Lat. *bacchant-*, Pres. Part. of *bacchāri*, 'to celebrate the festival of Bacchus'. A male or (esp.) female devotee of Bacchus; a woman given to wine and noisy mirth.

Bacchic, adj. [1. bákik; 2. bǽkik]. Gk. *Bakkhik-(ós)*, fr. *Bákkhos*, see next word, & **-ic**. Relating to Bacchus.

bacci-, pref. Form of Lat. *bacca*, *băca*, 'berry', used in compounds; the word prob. meant orig. 'grape', & is connected w. Gk. *Bákkhos*, the god of wine. Cp. **Bacchante**.

bacciferous, adj. [1. baksíferus; 2. bæksífərəs]. Prec. & **-ferous**. Berry-bearing.

bacciform, adj. [1. báksiform; 2. bǽksifɔ̄m]. **bacci-** & **-form**. Shaped like a berry.

baccivorous, adj. [1. baksíverus; 2. bæksívərəs]. **bacci-** & **-vorous**. Berry-eating; feeding, living, on berries.

baccy, n. [1. báki; 2. bǽki]. Colloq. abbr. for tobacco.

bacdore, n. [1. bàkdṓr; 2. bækdɔ̄]. Hind. *bāg-dor*, 'bridle-cord'. Anglo-Indian, a halter or leading rein.

bachelor, n. [1. bácheler; 2. bǽtʃilə]. M.E. *bachelere*, fr. O. Fr., fr. Lat. *baccalāris*, 'tenant of a *baccalāria* or small farm'; connected w. *bacca*, 'berry'. See **bacci-**. Perh. confused w. *bacca-laureus*, 'laurel-berry'. Precise derivation of Fr. word uncertain. Old sense in Fr., 'a young man aspiring to knighthood', then, 'a junior member of guild or university; a *young* unmarried man'. These senses all survive in Engl. usage, together w. others derived & extended fr. them. **1.** An unmarried man of any age; very commonly *old bachelor*. Phr. *bachelor girl*, young unmarried woman living a free, unconventional life. **2.** One who holds a junior degree at a university: *Bachelor of Arts, Medicine* &c. **3.** The lowest rank of knighthood: *Knight Bachelor.*

bachelordom, n. [1. báchelerdum; 2. bǽtʃilədəm]. **bachelor** & **-dom**. State of being an unmarried man.

bachelorhood, n. [1. báchelerhood; 2. bǽtʃiləhud]. **bachelor** & **-hood**. Bachelordom.

bachelor's button, n. Popular name of several species of flowers belonging to the *Centaurea*, from their resemblance to buttons in shape.

bacillary, adj. [1. basílari; 2. bəsíləri]. See **bacillus** & **-ary**. Rod-shaped; consisting of or resembling small rods; pertaining to bacilli.

bacilliform, adj. [1. basíliform; 2. bəsílifɔ̄m]. **bacillus** & **-form**. Shaped like a rod or bacillus.

bacillus, pl. **bacilli**, n. [1. basílus, -ī; 2. bəsíləs, -ai]. Coined fr. Lat. dimin. *bacillum*, 'rod, staff'; cp. same base w. different formative element, in Gk. *báktron*, 'staff'; see **bacteria**; cp. O. Ir. *bacc*, 'crutch'; **peg** is prob. fr. same base. See further **imbecile**. Name given from their shape to a large genus of minute plant organisms, schizomycetes or bacteria, both harmful and harmless, which exist under a variety of conditions in many substances.

back (I.), n. [1. bak; 2. bæk]. O.E. *bæc*, M.E. *bak*, O.N. *bak*, O.H.G. *bahho*, 'ham'. See **bacon**. **1.** The hinder part of the human body which extends from the base of the neck to the end of the spine; the corresponding part in other animals; (by extension) *the back of a wave*, upper surface, from resemblance to back of large animal. Phrs. *behind one's back*, without one's knowledge; *to put one's back into anything*, work hard at, to use great efforts, to accomplish; *to put a person's back up* (as of a cat), to make him angry. **2.** That portion of a chair or couch which supports the back of a sitter. **3.** The hinder part of anything, farthest from the front; the part of anything remotest from that which normally faces outwards towards the person using it: *back of a drawer, box, cupboard*; *back of a grate*; *back of the mouth, throat*, the part farthest from the lips, in which the uvula is situated; *back of the tongue*, that part of upper surface farthest from tip, nearest root. Phr. *at the back of one's mind*, existing in the memory, but not prominent in one's consciousness. **4.** That part of anything which is at the opposite side from that brought into play when it is in use: *back of the hand*, that portion of the hand which is uppermost when the palm is turned downwards; *back of a brush*, that uppermost when bristles are turned downwards; *back of a knife*, the non-cutting side of blade, opposite edge; *back of a picture*, the unpainted side of canvas; *back of a house*, rear part, that face which has not principal entrance. *The Backs* at Cambridge, part of a park, into which the rear sides of several colleges look. **5.** In games such as football, hockey &c., position nearest the goal, behind front line of players; a player who occupies this position.

back (II.), vb. trans. & intrans., fr. prec. **A.** trans. **1.** To form or provide a back for. **2.** To give support, help, countenance: *the Government's declaration of war was backed by the whole nation*; *his friends backed him strongly in his candidature.* **3.** To put one's name on the back of a legal or financial document, bill &c., thus making oneself responsible: *to back a bill for a friend* &c. **4.** To bet a sum of money on a competitor in a contest of chance or skill: *to back horses for the Derby.* **5.** To cause to go or move backwards: *to back a car, a horse*; *to back oars, to back water*, row backwards. **B.** intrans. **1.** To move backwards: *the horses of the mounted police backed into the crowd.* **2.** To adjoin, be near to, look out on, at the back: *my garden backs on to a mews.* **C.** Followed by adverbs. *Back down*, to give up, abandon claim, charge &c. *Back out of*, to withdraw from a promise, undertaking &c. *Back up*, to follow up in support, esp. at games.

back (III.), adj. **back** (I.) used attributively. **1.** Being behind, situated in the rear: *back door, garden, entrance*; *back brake*, one on hind wheel of a bicycle. **2.** (phon.) *Back vowel, consonant*, made with the *back* of the tongue, that part farthest from the tip; in more archaic and less accurate terminology, *guttural vowel* &c. **3.** No longer current, having appeared at an earlier date: *back number* of a magazine or serial publication; also fig., of a person of reactionary tendencies and obsolete opinions.

back (IV.), adv., fr. **back** (I.). **1.** To the rear, to the opposite direction from the front; expresses movement towards, position at, in place and time: *to go, move, stand, back*; *go back several years*; *some time back*; *look back*, (lit. and fig.) survey, consider events of a former period; (colloq.) *never to look back*, to have no reversal of health or prosperity. Phrs. *to go back on* (*one's friends*), to betray them; (*on one's word, principles*) repudiate, be false to; *to keep back*, conceal fact, sum of money &c. (usually in bad sense). **2.** Expressing return to original place, position, state &c.: *to give, pay, back*; *hand, send, back*; *go back to one's home*; *go back for something*, return to one's starting-point; *take back* (an offensive remark &c.), withdraw, cancel. Phrs. *to pay a man back* (*in his own coin*), treat him as he has treated oneself; *to answer back*, reply to what has been said, esp. in an impertinent way.

back (V.), n., fr. Du. *bak*, 'tub', cp. Fr. *bac*, 'punt, ferry-boat'. A shallow vat or tray used by brewers, dyers &c.

backache, n. [1. bákāk; 2. bǽkeik]. Pain in the back; lumbago.

backband, n. [1. bákband; 2. bǽkbænd]. Strap passing over horse's saddle and supporting shafts of cart or carriage.

backbite, vb. trans. & intrans. [1. bákbīt; 2. bǽkbait]. **a** trans. To speak maliciously of (persons) when absent; **b** intrans., to speak maliciously of absent persons.

backbiter, n. [1. bákbīter; 2. bǽkbaitə]. Prec. & **-er**. Person given to backbiting.

backbiting, n. [1. bákbīting; 2. bǽkbaitiŋ]. **backbite** & **-ing**. Action of one who backbites; malicious remarks about, censure of, the absent.

back-blocks, n. (Australia, colloq.) District difficult of access, esp. pastoral areas, far away from a railway, river, or sea-coast.

backboard, n. [1. bákbord; 2. bǽkbɔ̄d]. **1.** Board placed at the back of anything; e.g. *backboard of a cart*, movable board closing it at the back; *backboard of a picture*, one fastened behind it for support. **2.** Board strapped for a certain time each day to the back of a young person with a weak or curved spine to give support to or straighten it &c.

backbone, n. [1. bákbōn; 2. bǽkboun]. **1. a** The spine; **b** (fig.) strength of character, firmness, courage, resolution, moral fibre. **2.** (fig.) Principal support, vital, sustaining element or principle: *the squirearchy was formerly the backbone of the country*; *the backbone of a defence, a religion* &c.

backboned, adj. [1. bákbōnd; 2. bǽkbound]. Prec. & **-ed**. Having a backbone; vertebrate.

back-chat, n. (colloq.) Interchange of facetious or insolent remarks between two persons; insolence.

backdoor, adj. [1. bákdṓr; 2. bǽkdɔ̄]. (fig.) Secret, covert, underhand: *backdoor methods, influence* &c.

backdown, n. [1. bákdoun; 2. bǽkdaun]. Retreat, withdrawal, from one's position; surrender.
backed, adj. [1. bakt; 2. bækt]. **back (I.)** & **-ed**. **1.** Covered, lined, at the back: *a curtain backed with satin.* **2.** Chiefly in compounds, having a back of a specified kind: *straight-backed* &c.
back end, n. (provinc.) The late autumn.
backer, n. [1. báker; 2. bǽkə]. **back (II.)** & **-er**. One who backs (in varying senses); **a** one who bets on a horse, or on a sporting event; **b** one who assists, supports, believes in merits of, advocates cause of, another; a supporter, protector: *a young man is fortunate to secure powerful backers early in his career.*
backfall, n. [1. bákfawl; 2. bǽkfɔ̄l]. Fall on the back sustained in wrestling.
back fire, n. [1. bák fír; 2. bǽk fáiə]. Premature explosion of gas in an internal-combustion engine, which causes the piston to travel in reverse of the desired direction.
back-fire, vb. intrans. [1. bàk fír; 2. bæ̀k fáiə]. (of internal-combustion engine) To undergo, produce, a back fire.
back-formation, n. Grammatical form derived from another by a secondary and later process of analogy, the later form having the appearance of being the basal form from which the other is derived; e.g. *to grovel*, formed from *grovelling*, as though the latter were a Pres. Part. of a verb, instead of being an old adverb.
backgammon, n. [1. ba(k)gámun; 2. bæ(k)-gǽmən], fr. **back** & **gammon**; see also **game**. Game played on a special board, with draughtsmen and dice.
background, n. [1. bákgrọund; 2. bǽk-graund]. The hinder area in a landscape; representation of this in a picture; the darker, less important part of a picture which is, or is represented as being, farthest from the eye, and against which the chief figures and images are grouped; the hinder part of a scene in a theatre. Phr. *to keep in the background*, to remain in comparative obscurity during an action or event.
backhand (I.), n. [1. bákhand; 2. bǽkhænd]. **1.** Type of hand-writing in which the strokes are sloped backwards, that is, from left to right. **2.** Stroke, in a game &c., delivered with the back of the hand turned outwards, the movement of the arm being from the player's left side towards his right.
backhand (II.), adj., fr. prec. Made with the back of the hand turned outwards and held in the same direction as that in which the stroke is delivered.
backhanded, adj. [1. bàkhánded; 2. bæ̀k-hǽndid]. **backhand (I.)** & **-ed**. **1.** Backhand: *a backhanded stroke, blow* &c. **2.** (of written letters) Sloped backwards. **3.** (fig.) Ambiguous, equivocal, uttered in, expressing, sarcasm: *a backhanded compliment.*
backhandedly, adv. Prec. & **-ly**. In a backhanded manner.
backhandedness, n. See prec. & **-ness**. Quality of being backhanded.
backhander, n. [1. bàkhánder; 2. bæ̀khǽndə]. **backhand** & **-er**. **1.** Backhanded blow, or stroke. **2.** Glass of wine poured out by person at a table for his right-hand neighbour before passing the bottle on in the proper direction from right to left.
backing, n. [1. báking; 2. bǽkiŋ]. **back (II.)** & **-ing**. **1.** Substance used to cover the back of an object: *mirrors have a backing of quicksilver.* **2. a** Act of one who backs (horses &c.); **b** wagers, bets, laid on a sporting event; **c** (fig.) assistance, moral support afforded by one person to another; efforts used in behalf of another with a view to furthering his interests: *he had strong academic backing in his candidature.*
back page, n. Left-hand page of a book.
backsaw, n. [1. báksaw; 2. bǽksɔ̄]. Saw with a bar of stiff metal welded to the upper edge to give strength and rigidity.
backshish. See **baksheesh**.
backside, n. [1. bàksíd; 2. bæ̀ksáid]. **1.** (archaic) The back, rear, remoter side of anything: *the backside of the desert* (Bib.); now written *back side.* **2.** The hinder parts, the buttocks, rump.
back slang, n. Form of jargon or argot in which words are disguised by being spelt backwards and given the pronunciation thus suggested; e.g. *gip* for *pig*, *ecrip* for *price*, *slop* for *police.*
backslide, vb. intrans. [1. bàkslíd; 2. bæ̀k-sláid]. To fall away from a condition of grace, honesty, uprightness &c.; to relapse.
backslider, n. [1. bàkslíder; 2. bæ̀ksláidə]. Prec. & **-er**. Person who backslides; one who falls back into sin, or relapses into bad habits.
backsliding, n. [1. bàkslíding; 2. bæ̀ksláidiŋ]. See prec. & **-ing**. Act of one who backslides; relapse into sin, error &c.; fall from grace.
backstairs, n. [1. bákstárz; 2. bǽkstéəz]. A staircase in a house leading from the servants' quarters, having a special entrance to each landing usually shut off by a door; contrasted with *front stairs, principal staircase.* Phr. *backstairs influence*, secret, underhand, covert influence.
backstay, n. [1. bákstā; 2. bǽkstei]. Rope, set of ropes, extending from the mast-head to the side of a ship, sloping towards the stern, used to keep the mast in position and give it support.
backstop, n. [1. bákstop; 2. bǽkstɔp]. **1.** Fence behind the home base in baseball to stop the balls that pass the catcher. **2.** (cricket) Player who fields in a straight line behind the wicket-keeper; longstop.
backstrap, n. [1. bákstrap; 2. bǽkstræp]. Strap passing along horse's backbone, from the saddle to the crupper.
backstroke, n. [1. bákstrōk; 2. bǽkstrouk]. Backhanded stroke.
backsword, n. [1. báksord; 2. bǽksɔ̄d]. Sword with only one cutting edge; a broadsword.
backward, adj. [1. bákward; 2. bǽkwəd]. **back (I.)** & **-ward**. **1.** Not advanced; standing, being, moving, towards the back: *a backward position; a backward movement.* **2.** Lagging behind, retarded, not having made progress, in mental development, knowledge, studies, civilization &c.: *a backward child; a backward people; a backward state of society.* **3.** Slow, reluctant, disinclined to take action: *backward in asserting oneself, taking one's proper position* &c. **4.** Behind time, late: *backward in one's preparations.*
backwardation, n. [1. bàkwardáshun; 2. bæ̀k-wədéiʃən]. **backward** & **-ation**. (Stock Exchange) Postponement of delivery of stocks and shares by mutual consent of buyer and seller, on payment of a premium to the former.
backward(s), adv. [1. bákward(z); 2. bǽk-wəd(z)]. **back (I.)** & **-ward**. In a rearward direction, away from front, opposite of *forward*; in reverse direction to the normal: *the enemy's line was pressed backwards a few yards; to glance backwards over one's shoulder; to say something backwards*, begin at the end; *sitting backwards on a horse*, i.e. looking towards its tail; *to walk backwards*, in contrary direction to that in which one is looking; *to make an engine &c. go backwards*, revolve the contrary way from usual, from right to left; *ring bells backwards.*
backwash, n. [1. bákwosh; 2. bǽkwɔʃ]. Waves, motion of water, caused by the passage of a vessel.
backwater, n. [1. bákwàwter; 2. bǽkwɔ̀tə]. **1.** Small creek containing stagnant water, leading into a stream or river. **2.** (fig.) **a** Condition of intellectual stagnation, and inaccessibility to new ideas &c.; **b** group of persons among whom such a condition exists, place where such a group lives: *I live in a backwater in this small village.*
backwoods, n. pl. [1. bákwọ̀odz; 2. bǽk-wùdz]. Wild, only partially cleared forest region, remote from civilization; esp. in Canada or U.S.A.
backwoodsman, n. [1. bákwọ̀odzman; 2. bǽk-wùdzmən]. **1.** A settler, dweller, in the backwoods. **2.** (colloq., facet.) A person who habitually lives in the depths of the country and rarely visits towns; specif., a peer who rarely visits the House of Lords, except when whipped up to vote on some special occasion.
bacon, n. [1. bắkun; 2. béikən]. M.E. *bācoun*, O. Fr. & Med. Lat. *baco(n)*, fr. O.H.G. *bahho*, 'buttock', cogn. w. O.E. *bæc*, 'back'. See **back (I.)**. Salted, pickled, flesh of the pig. Phr. *to save one's bacon*, escape loss or injury.
Baconian, adj. & n. [1. bākṓnian; 2. beikóun-iən], fr. name of Francis Bacon, Lord Verulam (1561–1626), & **-ian**. **1.** adj. Pertaining to Francis Bacon and his philosophy. **2.** n. **a** A student of Bacon's works; **b** supporter of the theory that Bacon was the real author of Shakespeare's plays.
bacteria, n. pl. [1. baktḗria; 2. bæktíəriə]. More rarely used in sing. **bacterium** [1. baktḗrium; 2. bæktíəriəm]. Latinized form of Gk. *baktḗrion*, dimin. of *báktron*, 'staff'. See also **bacillus** & **baculus**. A group of minute parasitic plant organisms, schizomycetes, which exist in the air, water, soil, and the bodies of animals and plants. Some are the cause of diseases, others convert dead organic matter into food for plants.
bacterial, adj. [1. baktḗrial; 2. bæktíəriəl]. Prec. & **-al**. Belonging to, consisting of, caused by, bacteria.
bactericide, n. [1. baktḗrisīd; 2. bæktíərisaid]. **bacteria** & **-cide**. Substance which destroys bacteria; a disinfectant, antiseptic.
bacterio-, pref. Form of **bacteria**, used in compounds.
bacteriological, adj. [1. bàktēriolójikl; 2. bæktìəriəlɔ́dʒikl]. **bacteriology** & **-ic** & **-al**. Belonging to, concerned with, bacteriology.
bacteriologist, n. [1. bàktēriólojist; 2. bæk-tìəriɔ́lədʒist]. See next word & **-ist**. One devoted to the study of bacteriology.
bacteriology, n. [1. bàktērióloji; 2. bæktìəri-ɔ́lədʒi]. **bacterio-** & **-logy**. Science or study of bacteria.
bacterioscopy, n. [1. bàktērióskopi; 2. bæk-tìəriɔ́skəpi]. **bacterio-** & **-scopy**. Microscopic investigation of bacteria.
bacteroid, n. [1. báktēroid; 2. bǽktíərɔid]. **bacterio-** & **-oid**. Minute organism occurring in roots of leguminous plants.
bacteroid(al), adj. [1. bàktēróid(al); 2. bæk-tiərɔ́id(əl)]. Prec. & **-al**. Having form of, resembling, bacteria.
baculus, n. [1. bákūlus; 2. bǽkjuləs]. Lat., 'a rod', also *baculum*, see **bacillus**. Official staff or rod, emblem of authority.
bad, adj. [1. bad; 2. bæd]. Not found in O.E., but M.E. *badde* in present sense **1.** Perh. related to O.E. *bæddel*, 'hermaphrodite', *bædling*, 'effeminate person', wh. may contain base **bǣd-*, as in O.E. *bǣdan*, 'oppress' (see **bide**), orig. 'restrain, cause to remain'. The sense may have been 'hindered in growth, undeveloped, imperfect', whence sense of 'perverse' might easily arise. Opposite of *good*; morally evil, vicious, imperfect, wrong. Various shades of meaning and applications: **1.** Wicked, vicious, immoral, unrighteous: *bad men, habits, laws* &c. Phrs. *bad woman*, one who is unchaste; *bad language*, verbal obscenity or profanity; *a bad word*, one which is profane or obscene; *to go to the bad*, be morally ruined; *the bad disease*, venereal; *go from bad to worse* (of persons and institutions &c.), become steadily demoralized or ruined; *bad debt*, one which will never be paid; *act in bad faith*, dishonestly, insincerely; *bad name (for)*, evil reputation; *bad fairy*, evil genius; *bad hat* (fig., colloq.), good-for-nothing fellow, also *bad lot* (of men and women); *put a bad construction on something*, interpret unfavourably; *be in a bad temper*, be angry or cross; *in a bad way* (of health or fortunes). **2.** (fol-

lowed by *for*) Injurious, dangerous, hurtful, unsuited to; *bad for the health, the eyes, morals, children* &c. **3**. Offensive to the senses; nasty, disagreeable: *a bad smell, taste* &c. Phr. *to be in bad odour*, in disfavour. **4**. Imperfect, inadequate, unsuitable; below standard, not reaching desired degree of excellence: *a bad light, dinner, clothes, manner, joke, voice*. Phrs. *not bad* (colloq.), good, fairly satisfactory; *not bad fun*, amusing; *not a bad idea*, a good suggestion; *with a bad grace*, unwillingly, awkwardly; *to see something in a bad light*, regard it unfavourably; *to have bad luck*, be unfortunate; *to be* (*taken*) *bad*, be, fall, ill; *a bad leg, eye*, sore, painful; *a bad half-crown*, counterfeit; *bad law*, unsound. **5**. Decayed, rotten: *a bad egg*; *this meat, fish, is bad*; *a bad tooth*. Phrs. *to go bad*, become rotten, putrefy, esp. of food, fruit &c.; *a bad egg*, an untrustworthy, disreputable person. **6**. Severe, intense (said of something which in itself is 'bad'): *a bad cold*; *bad pain*; *is the pain very bad?*; *bad attack of the gout*; *bad headache*; heinous: *a bad crime* &c.

baddish, adj. [1. bádish; 2. bǽdiʃ]. Prec. & **-ish**. Rather bad; either not very bad, or having considerable bad qualities.

bade, vb. [1. bad, bād; 2. bæd, beid]. Pret. of **bid**. The first type of pronunciation represents O.E. *bæd*, M.E. *bad*; the second, M.E. *bāde*, apparently fr. M.E. *bad* w. the vowel lengthened through the influence of the long vowel of the Pret. pl. & P.P. Cp. **spake**.

badge, n. [1. baj; 2. bædž]. 15th cent. *bage, bagge*. Etymol. unknown. Distinctive mark, or sign, worn to indicate particular office or rank: *badge of rank*, in army, worn on cuff or epaulettes; *policeman's badge*.

badgeer, badgir, n. [1. báhdgēr; 2. bádgiə], fr. Pers. *bād-gīr*, 'wind-catch'. Arrangement common in Persia and in Sind for bringing air down into a house, for purposes of ventilation.

badger (I.), n. [1. bájer; 2. bǽdžə]. Etymol. unknown; not found before modern period. The old name, *brock*, still survives in northern dialects and in Place-Names. Large wild mammal, *Meles taxus*, of a grey colour, with long claws for burrowing, which lives in earths or burrows, and is still fairly plentiful in some parts of England.

badger (II.), vb. trans., fr. prec. To treat like a badger; hence (fig.) to worry, tease, pester; to heckle with troublesome questions and contentious discussion.

badger-baiting, n. [1. bájer bāting; 2. bǽdžə bèitiŋ]. The baiting or worrying of the badger by dogs, formerly a favourite sport.

badinage, n. [1. bádinàhzh; 2. bǽdinàž]. Fr., fr. *badin*, 'jester', *badiner*, vb., 'jest, chaff', cp. O. Fr. (Provenç.) *badar*, & **-age**. Light, good-natured pleasantry; chaff.

badly, adv. [1. bádli; 2. bǽdli]. **bad** & **-ly**. In a bad, unsatisfactory, inadequate manner; ill, reverse of *well*.

badminton, n. [1. bádmintun; 2. bǽdmintən], fr. Duke of Beaufort's seat of that name. **1**. A game played with shuttlecocks and racquets over a net. **2**. A compound summer drink.

badness, n. [1. bádnes; 2. bǽdnis]. **bad** & **-ness**. Quality of being bad.

baffle, vb. trans. [1. bafl; 2. bǽfl]. Perh. connected w. archaic Fr. *beffler*, 'ridicule', & *bafouer*, 'set at naught, hold up to contempt'. Provinc. Engl. *baff*, 'useless, worthless', & Germ. *baff machen*, 'to astound', are prob. related. Origin of base perh. imitative of sudden, unexpected blow which produces bewilderment. **a** To puzzle, disconcert, bring to bewilderment; check, delude (persons); **b** to hinder, thwart, impede progress, prevent accomplishment of (plans, efforts &c.).

baffling, adj. [1. báfling; 2. bǽfliŋ]. Pres. Part. of prec. Puzzling, producing hindrance, making obstacles; (of persons) inscrutable, difficult to understand.

baffy, n. [1. báfi; 2. bǽfi]. Perh. related to first syll. of **baffle**; cp. provinc. Engl. *baff*, 'a blow'. Wooden golf club used for 'lofting' a ball.

bag (I.), n. [1. bag; 2. bæg]. M.E. *bagge*, fr. O.N. *baggi*. Origin doubtful. **1. a** Receptacle, made in various shapes and sizes, of leather, cloth, carpet &c., for holding and transporting movable articles of property: *travelling-bag*, one for carrying clothes &c. on a journey; *lawyer's bag*, in which he carries briefs &c.; *mail-bag*, for holding letters &c. consigned to the post; *game-bag*, for carrying game which has been shot; *blue-bag*, containing blue powder used in laundry work; *string bag*, one made of net for carrying very light articles; *money-bags* (fig.), wealth. Phrs. *bag-of-bones*, very thin person or animal; *whole bag of tricks*, every possible device, all the accessories of anything; *to let the cat out of the bag*, divulge a secret inadvertently; *to clear out, bag and baggage*, with all one's belongings, completely; **b** pl. (*pair of*) *bags* (colloq.), trousers. **2**. All the game shot by a sportsman on a single expedition, (lit.) contents of his *game-bag*; applied to everything that he kills, including big game, elephant &c. **3**. In various fig., colloq., and jocose uses, e.g. **a** number of the evil-doers whose names are taken down by a university proctor; **b** of material, esp. if new and illuminative, collected by a scholar during his researches &c.

bag (II.), vb. trans., fr. prec. To put into a bag. Used in various senses: **1**. (of sportsmen) To kill, secure as result of day's sport: *to bag a hare, to bag so many partridges* &c.; (fig.) to collect, obtain possession of, cp. **bag** (I.) **2**: *to bag subscriptions, anecdotes, butterflies* (of a collector) &c. **2**. To obtain possession of without permission, help oneself to, other people's property (esp. when of small value); mild term not implying dishonesty as a rule; (colloq.) *I have bagged some of your cigarettes, matches* &c.

bag (III.), vb. intrans., fr. **bag** (I.). **a** To swell, as a sail in the wind, or garments in water; **b** to become baggy.

bag (IV.), vb. trans. Provinc. Engl. Etymol. doubtful. To cut, esp. of hedges, rough grass, weeds &c., with a stout hook; hence, *bagging-hook*.

bagasse, n. [1. bagás; 2. bəgǽs]. Fr. Etymol. doubtful. Sugar-cane after it has been crushed in the mill, sometimes used as fuel.

bagatelle, n. [1. bàgatél; 2. bægətél]. Fr., fr. Ital. *bagatella*, 'trifle, worthless thing'. Perh. fr. *bacca*, 'berry', fr. Lat. *bacca*, see **bacci-**, w. dimin. suff., 'something small and valueless'. **1**. A trifle, something unimportant (often with *mere*). **2**. A game played on a board, with holes instead of pockets, with ivory balls and small cues; a kind of inferior billiards.

baggage, n. [1. bágij; 2. bǽgidž]. **bag** (I.) & **-age**. **1**. Collection of bags and packets, esp. of travellers, of an army on active service &c.; luggage. **2**. (by extension from sense of collection of worthless articles, now obs.) An impudent, immoral woman; a jade, a hussy; esp. *an impudent baggage*. Also in playful sense, with no evil suggestion, a merry, thoughtless young girl. *Baggage animals, mules*, used to carry baggage of army or exploring party; *baggage train*, waggons carrying army's baggage.

bagginess, n. [1. bágines; 2. bǽginis]. Next word & **-ness**. Condition of being baggy.

baggy, adj. [1. bági; 2. bǽgi]. **bag** (I.) & **-y**. Puffy; suggesting a bag; hanging in an irregular fold: *trousers baggy at the knees*; *baggy skin below the eyes*.

bagman, n. [1. bágman; 2. bǽgmən]. (colloq.) A commercial traveller, from the habit of carrying his samples about with him in a bag.

bagnio, n. [1. báhnyō; 2. bánjou]. Ital. *bagno*, 'bath', fr. Lat. *balneum*, see **balneal**, whence also Fr. *bain*, 'bath,' *se baigner*, 'take a bath'; cp. Fr. *baigne*, fr. Ital. word used in sense of convict prison. **1**. A bath, as applied to Italian and Oriental *bagno*, otherwise obsolete. **2**. A prison. **3**. A brothel.

bagpipe, n. [1. bágpīp; 2. bǽgpaip]. Wind instrument in vogue among the Scottish Highlanders, with a mouthpiece and fingering stops, the air being supplied from a leather bag which acts as the bellows, and is kept filled with air by the player, who holds it under his left arm and regulates the pressure by squeezing.

bahadur, n. [1. baháhdur; 2. bəhádə]. **Hind.**, 'hero, champion'. Title used in India, and affixed to names of European officers in documents, or in speaking ceremoniously, by natives—as *Brown Sahib Bahadur*, equivalent to 'the gallant officer'. Among Europeans in India the term is applied to a haughty, pompous personage.

baignoire, n. [1. bānwar; 2. béinwā]. **Fr.**, fr. Lat. *balneum*, 'bath', see under **balneal**, & *-orium*, see **-ory**; the word means 'bath, bathroom; box at the theatre'; meaning extended apparently through intermediate sense of small private apartment. **Stage box at a theatre.**

bail (I.), n. [1. bāl; 2. beil]. O. Fr. *bail*, 'custody', Low Lat. *ballium*, connected w. Lat. *bajulus*, 'porter', *bajulāre*, 'bear a burden'. The transition of meaning is not clear. Mod. sense of Fr. *bail* is 'lease'. The etymol. of *bajulus* is unknown. Sum paid as security for an accused person's appearance at his trial, pending which he is released. Phrs. *to surrender to one's bail*, appear duly at trial; *out on bail*, released from prison pending trial, bail having been paid; *to forfeit one's bail*, i.e. by non-appearance; (colloq.) *take leg bail*, to run away; (fig.) *I'll go bail*, I feel sure of something and therefore will bet on it, I'll be bound.

bail (II.), vb., fr. prec. Generally, *bail out*, to pay the sum demanded as security or bail for a person's appearance at his trial, thus securing his release on bail.

bail (III.), n., fr. O. Fr. *bail*, fr. Lat. *baculum*, 'little stick', q.v. under **bacillus**. (cricket) One of two small pieces of wood laid across the top of the wicket, resting on all three stumps; the batsman is 'out' when either of these is knocked off by the ball when bowled, or when player is stumped, or run out.

bail (IV.), also **bale**, vb. intrans. & trans., fr. Fr. *baille*, 'bucket', fr. L. Lat. *bācula*, dimin. of Lat. *bāca*, *bacca*, 'berry, grape'; also 'wine jar'; see **bacci-**. **1**. intrans. To throw water out of a boat by dipping into it some small vessel or bucket held in the hand. **2**. trans. *Bail out*, to bail the water out of a boat.

bailable, adj. [1. bālabl; 2. béiləbl]. **bail** (II.) & **-able**. Allowing of bail; of lighter offences.

bailee, n. [1. bālḗ; 2. beilí]. **bail** (I.) & **-ee**. Person to whom goods are committed in trust, and who has temporary property in them, under a contract of bailment, q.v.

bailer, n. [1. bāler; 2. béilə], fr. **bail** (IV.) & **-er**. **a** Person who bails; **b** vessel used in bailing.

bailey, n. [1. bāli; 2. béili]. O. Fr. *baille*, 'palisade, enclosure', Med. Lat. *ballium*. Courts or wards of a castle formed by spaces between the circuits of defences which surrounded the keep. Name often retained after castle and its defences have disappeared, e.g. *Old Bailey*, the central criminal court of London which stands in what was the bailey of the City Wall; *St. Peter's le Bailey*, Oxford.

bailie, n. [1. bāli; 2. béili]. Form of **bailiff**. City magistrate in Scotland.

bailiff, n. [1. bālif; 2. béilif], fr. O. Fr. *baillif*, 'custodian, magistrate', fr. Low Lat. *bajulivus*, fr. *bajulus*, 'porter', see **bail** (I.). **1**. Originally a king's officer; now a sheriff's officer. **2**. A land agent, or one who manages the practical working of a farm for a landowner.

bailiwick, n. [1. bāliwik; 2. béiliwik]. See **bailie** & **-wick**. The district, jurisdiction, of a bailie.

bailment, n. [1. bālment; 2. béilmənt]. See **bail (I.)** & **-ment.** (law) The delivery of goods by a bailor to a bailee, on trust, under an express or implied contract to hand them back after the purpose for which they were delivered has been accomplished.

bailor, n. [1. bālur; 2. béilə]. See **bail (I.)** & **-or.** Person who commits goods to another, the *bailee*, in trust, under a contract of bailment.

bain-marie, n. [1. bán márē; 2. bǽ marī]. Fr. Vessel or pan for cooking or heating food; it does not come into direct contact with the fire, but stands in another vessel which is filled with water and placed on fire.

Bairam, n. [1. bíram; 2. báiəræm]. Turk. One of two Moslem festivals, one of which (*Lesser Bairam*) is held immediately after the fast called Ramadan, and the other (*Greater Bairam*) seventy days after this.

bairn, n. [1. bārn; 2. beən]. Scots, partially adopted into English. O.E. *bearn, barn*, cogn. w. **bear (I.)**. A young child; a child of any age, offspring.

bait (I.), vb. trans. [1. bāt; 2. beit]. O.N. *beita*, 'make to bite', cogn. w. O.E. *bītan*, q.v. under **bite. 1.** To worry (bears, badgers, bulls) with dogs, as an ancient form of sport. **2.** (fig.) To tease (persons) excessively, to exasperate by continuous series of insults.

bait (II.), vb. trans. Prob. same as prec. w. differentiated meaning, fr. O.N. *beita*, M.E. *bayte*. **1.** To give food to (esp. of horses). **2.** To stop for food on a journey (men and horses). **3.** To put *bait* (see below) in a trap for animals, or on a fish-hook. Phr. (fig.) *to bait the hook*, to offer some inducement to a person to act in a particular way, allure (gen. in unfavourable sense).

bait (III.), n. See prec. **1.** Fodder for horses. **2.** Food, or imitation of it, put in traps or on hooks to attract animals or fish.

baize, n. [1. bāz; 2. beiz]. Orig. pl. *baies*, O. Fr. *baie*, 'bay-coloured', see **bay (V.)**. Coarse woollen cloth, usually green.

bake, vb. trans. & intrans. [1. bāk; 2. beik]. O.E. *bacan*, M.E. *bāke*, O.H.G. *bahhan*; cogn. w. Gk. *phṓgein*, 'roast'; connexion w. Lat. *focus*, 'fireplace, hearth', is improbable. See **focus**; cp. also **batch. 1.** trans. **a** To cook by dry heat, usually in a closed chamber or oven; **b** used also of the sun's action when excessively strong, when it is said to *bake the ground*, harden and cake it; (fig.) *half-baked*, imperfect, undeveloped, immature (of persons and things). **2.** intrans. To undergo process of baking; to become baked: *bread bakes in the oven.*

bakehouse, n. [1. bākhous; 2. béikhaus]. Part of a baker's premises containing ovens, where baking is carried on.

baker, n. [1. bāker; 2. béikə]. O.E. *bæcere*. **bake** & **-er.** One who bakes; specif., a tradesman whose employment is to bake bread. Phr. *pull devil, pull baker*, said of a contest in which both sides struggle hard without decisive victory to either.

baker's dozen, n. **a** Thirteen buns, small cakes &c., sold for the price of twelve; **b** thirteen objects of any kind.

bakery, n. [1. bākeri; 2. béikəri]. **bake** & **-ery. a** Place where bread is baked; **a** bakehouse; **b** shop where bread is sold.

baking, adj. & adv. [1. bāking; 2. béikiŋ]. Pres. Part. of **bake.** (colloq.) **1.** adj. Very hot: *the weather was simply baking.* **2.** adv. In Phr. *baking hot*, so hot as to bake.

baking powder, n. Powder containing cream of tartar, used in baking instead of yeast.

baksheesh, backshish, bucksheesh, n. [1. bákshēsh; 2. bǽkʃīʃ]. Pers.-Hind. *bakhshish.* Gratuity, tip; a bribe; used in Turkish, Persian, and Hindustani.

balalaika, n. [1. bàlalíka; 2. bæ̀ləláikə]. Russ. **1.** Kind of guitar used, esp. among the gypsies, in Eastern Europe. **2.** Concert of Russian folk-songs and popular music.

balance (I.), n. [1. bálans; 2. bǽləns]. Fr., fr. Lat. *bi-*, 'two', see **bi-**, & *lanx*, 'plate, dish', esp. 'scale of weighing-machine'. *Lanx* is cogn. w. Gk. *lékos, lekis, lekánē*, 'dish'. Etymol. doubtful. **1.** Machine for weighing, the essential feature of which is a lever suspended by the middle, from either end of which a 'scale' or plate depends. When the weights placed respectively in either scale are exactly equal, the lever is straight; when they are unequal, the heavier causes that end of the lever to sink, while the lighter end rises. All the derived senses spring from the fundamental idea of *weighing*, and of comparing one thing with another as regards weight, and the behaviour of the lever or beam by means of which this is accomplished. There are many types of *balance*, for measuring the weight of different things, and possessing greater or less degrees of accuracy according to the nature of the substances to be weighed. Phr. (mostly fig.) (*trembling*) *in the balance*, undecided, depending on some slight cause to determine one way or another (of human actions, judgements, fate). **2. a** State of equipoise maintained between two weights; opposing forces, as in walking, riding &c., or tendencies, as good and evil (lit. and fig.); hence, equilibrium generally, state of order and stability; Phrs. *keep, preserve, lose, one's balance*; *to be* (*thrown*) *off one's balance*; *balance of power* (between states); *balance of probabilities*; **b** special use, gymnastics, exercise on horizontal or parallel bars: *long arm balance*; **c** mental equipoise, orderly, normal, reasonable state of mind. **3. a** Equality, exact correspondence between debit and credit side of an account; specif. **b** that sum existing on credit side (esp. *balance at the bank*); (popular) remnant, remainder, that left over: *he gave the balance of his dinner to his dog.*

balance (II.), vb. trans., fr. prec. **A.** trans. **1.** To maintain anything in a state of balance, equipoise, equilibrium: *to balance a pole*, as a juggler, i.e. keep it upright over one's head &c. without propping or grasping it, merely by distributing the weight so that the pressure falls straight down, from the centre of highest point to that end which rests on the head &c.; *to balance* (*oneself*) *on the edge of a chair*, to sit on extreme edge in a position requiring careful distribution of weight to avoid a fall. **2.** To weigh one possibility &c. against another in one's mind, estimate relative value of two or more proposals, suggestions, plans. **3.** To show relation of expenditure and income, profit and loss in accounts: *balance one's accounts, books.* **B.** intrans. To become, be, balanced: *account would not balance.*

balance-sheet, n. Statement of receipts and expenditure, assets and liabilities, esp. in a commercial enterprise, or business house.

balaniferous, adj. [1. bàlaníferus; 2. bæ̀ləníſərəs]. Lat. *balanus*, fr. Gk. *bálanos*, 'acorn', & **-ferous**; Gk. *bálanos* is fr. base **gʷəl-*, **gʷel-* &c., 'gland'; cp. O. Slav. *želadĭ*, Lat. *glans*, & see **gland.** (bot.) Acorn-bearing.

balanoid, adj. & n. [1. bálanoid; 2. bǽlənoid]. First element of prec. & **-oid.** Acorn-shaped.

balas, n. [1. bálas; 2. bǽləs]. Fr. *balais*, Med. Lat. *balascus*, fr. Arab. *balakhshī.* A kind of ruby or red spinel.

balaustine, n. [1. baláwstin; 2. bælɔ́stin]. Gk. *balaústion*, flower of pomegranate tree, cp. **baluster**, & **-ine.** The pomegranate tree.

Balbriggan, n. [1. balbrígan; 2. bælbrígən]. From place of that name in Ireland. Knitted cotton fabric used for hosiery &c.

balcony, n. [1. bálkuni; 2. bǽlkəni], earlier [bælkóuni], fr. Ital. *balcóne*, cp. Ital. *balco*, 'scaffold'; loan-word fr. O.H.G. *balcho*, 'beam', Germ. *balken.* See **balk** (of timber). **a** Structure in the nature of a platform, supported by stone or wooden brackets, or on pillars, on outside of a building; it is protected by a railing or parapet, and windows open upon it; **b** in theatre, the tier of seats below the gallery and above the dress-circle.

bald, adj. [1. bawld; 2. bɔld]. M.E. *balled*, 'bald', orig. 'white', prob. fr. W. *bali*, 'whiteness'; cogn. w. O. Slav. *bjělĭ*, 'white'; see further under **phalarope**, & cp. **fuller (I.)**. **1. a** Devoid of natural covering, esp. of hair: *bald man, bald head.* Phrs. *bald as an egg, as a coot, as a billiard ball*; **b** (of mountain-tops) bare, having no vegetation. **2.** (fig.) **a** Destitute of ornament, free from superfluous adornment; therefore, simple, plain: *a bald statement of fact*; **b** lacking all the graces; therefore, poor, ugly, uninteresting: *a bald style*; *verse which is rather bald* &c. **3.** (zool.) Of certain birds and animals whose heads are devoid of feathers or hair, or have a white spot. In the latter case the original sense is preserved: *bald-headed coot, bald-faced stag.* Cp. for sense *piebald, skewbald.*

baldachin, n. [1. báwldakin; 2. bɔ́ldəkin], fr. Fr. *baldequin*, also in Ital. form *baldacchino* [1. bàldakḗnō; 2. bàldakínou], fr. *Baldacco*, Ital. name for Bagdad. Originally the word was applied to a richly woven cloth coming from Bagdad, then a covering or canopy made of such material, used esp. for ecclesiastical purposes. The present uses are: **a** covering or canopy of silk borne on four poles, carried over the Pope, and over the Blessed Sacrament; **b** the canopy over a Bishop's throne; **c** a structure of stone or marble supported by four pillars built over the altar.

balderdash, n. [1. báwlderdàsh; 2. bɔ́ldədæ̀ʃ]. Origin uncertain. **1.** (obs.) A poor kind of mixed drink. **2.** Now only used in sense of foolish talk, or argument, devoid of sense.

bald-headed, adj. & adv. **1.** adj. Having a bald head, one partially or entirely devoid of hair. **2.** adv. In Phr. *to go for a thing, or person, bald-headed*, to pursue an object, attack a person, with the utmost vigour, and with disregard of everything else, esp. of the consequences of one's action.

baldish, adj. [1. báwldish; 2. bɔ́ldiʃ]. **bald** & **-ish.** Rather bald, just becoming bald.

baldly, adv. [1. báwldli; 2. bɔ́ldli]. **bald** & **-ly.** In a bald manner. Only fig., cp. **bald, 2**: *to write rather baldly.* Phr. *to put it* (*quite*) *baldly*, without any toning-down, brutally and plainly.

baldness, n. [1. báwldnes; 2. bɔ́ldnis]. See prec. & **-ness.** State, quality, of being bald.

bald-pate, n. See **bald** & **pate.** A bald-headed person.

baldrib, n. [1. báwldrib; 2. bɔ́ldrib]. A special cut of pork from near the rump and lacking fat.

baldric, n. [1. báwldrik; 2. bɔ́ldrik]. M.E. *baldric, baudric* &c., fr. O. Fr. *bau(l)deric*, perh. through Med. Lat. *balderingus*, borrowed fr. O.H.G. *balderich*; cogn. w. **belt.** A belt, usually of leather or silk, worn over one shoulder and under opposite arm, from which a sword or bugle was hung.

bale (I.), n. [1. bāl; 2. beil]. M.E., fr. O. Fr. *bāle*; perh. connected w., & borrowed fr., O.H.G. *balla*, 'round package' &c.; cp. **ball.** Large bundle or package (esp. of merchandise packed for shipment); (pl.) *bales*, often used almost in mere sense of goods, merchandise, wares, with but slight underlying sense of 'wares made into bundles'.

bale (II.), n. O.E. *bealu, -o, balu*, 'calamity, injury, wickedness', M.E. *bāle*; O.S. *balu*, O.H.G. *balu*; cp. Goth. *balw-jan* 'to torment', *balwa-weisei*, 'wickedness'. Outside Gmc., Gk. *phēlós*, 'deceitful', & other derived words; Lat. *fallere*, 'cause to fall, to deceive, trick', see **false, fail**; O. Slav. *boli*, 'disease', *bolěti*, 'suffer pain', are prob. cogn. (poet. or archaic) Misfortune, injury, grief.

bale (III.). Variant of **bail (IV.)**.

baleen, n. [1. balḗn; 2. bælín], fr. O. Fr. *baleine*, fr. Lat. *bālaena, ballaena*, apparently borrowed fr. Gk. *phállaina*, 'whale', but initial *b* instead of *p* or *ph* has not been explained. The Gk. word is possibly cogn. w. **whale**, but this is doubtful. Whalebone.

balefire, n. [1. bālfīr; 2. béilfaiə]. M.E. *bāle*, O.E. *bǣl*, 'blazing fire', cogn. w. O.N. *bāl*, 'large fire', cp. Gk. *phalós*, 'bright', Scrt. *bhāla-m*, 'brightness'; see further under phalarope & fuller (I.); the second element is a late addition & tautological. A beacon fire; funeral pyre.

baleful, adj. [1. bálfool; 2. béilful]. **bale (II.)** & **-ful**. Harmful, injurious, pernicious; malicious, sinister. (Much commoner than the noun.)

balefully, adv. Prec. & **-ly**. In a baleful, harmful, manner.

balefulness, n. See prec. & **-ness**. The quality of being baleful; harmfulness.

balinger, n. [1. bálinjer; 2. bǽlindžə]. O. Fr. *balengier*, 'whale ship', cp. Lat. *ballaena*, *bālaena*, 'whale'. See **baleen**. (obs.) Small ship, originally a whaler.

balk, **baulk** (I.), n. [1. bawk; 2. bɔ̄k]. O.E. *balca*, 'ridge between furrows'; M.E. *balke* is found in same sense, & later, meaning 'beam'; O.S. *balcō*, O.H.G. *balcho*, Mod. Germ. *balken*, & O.N. *bjalki*, all mean 'a beam of wood'. Something like this, the original, meaning is preserved in O.E. cogn. *bolca*, '(wooden) gangway of a ship'. The Gk. *phálagx*, 'trunk or log of wood', see **phalanx**, is possibly a remoter cogn. fr. same base. It seems that the original meaning was a piece of timber, & the O.E. form may have been used in that sense, although it is not recorded. The sense 'boundary, partition' is found in O.N. *bālkr*. The development of the various meanings expressed by different forms of this base was apparently 'a log or piece of timber', whence **a** 'a wooden plank used as a gangway', & **b** 'a wooden partition'; whence 'a dividing line generally', finally, 'the dividing ridge between furrows'. **1.** Piece of land left unploughed between furrows; formerly, a strip of unploughed land dividing acres or fields in common land. **2.** Large timber or a principal beam in a house. **3.** A division of a billiard table at bottom end, from which play begins. A ball is said to be *in balk* after it has been in a pocket, when it can only be played, in first instance, at balls which are *outside balk*. **4.** A hindrance, obstacle, cause of delay.

balk (II.), vb. trans. & intrans., fr. prec. **1.** trans. To hinder, prevent, frustrate: *to be balked in a jump*, put off at last moment; *to be balked of one's purpose, desires* &c. **2.** intrans. To hesitate, refuse, jib (esp. of a horse in jumping).

Balkanize, vb. trans. [1. báwlkanīz; 2. bɔ́lkənaiz]. Recent, fr. Balkan & **-ize**. To introduce a political condition such as exists in the Balkans; set up or create a group of mutually hostile national and political units.

ball (I.), n. [1. bawl; 2. bɔ̄l]. M.E. *balle*, 'ball', fr. Fr. *balle*; Gmc. loan-word, cp. O.H.G. *ballo*. The orig. meaning appears to be 'something swelled or blown out into a rounded form'. Cp. **bowl**, w. wh. *ball* is connected; also **belly, bellows**. A round or roundish body or mass, solid or hollow, composed of any substance and of any size. In great variety of uses, e.g. *ball of earth, ball of string, ball of the eye* &c. *Three balls*, pawnbroker's sign. **1.** (poet.) Referring to the earth: *this terrestrial ball*. **2.** A missile fired by any kind of firearm, from a pistol to a cannon. (Latter now more often *shell*.) **3. a** Object used in various games: large, inflated, and either round or egg-shaped, in *football*; round, medium-sized, and hard in *cricket, hockey, fives, polo*; small, round, inflated, in *lawn-tennis*; **b** the mode in which the ball is delivered in one of these games: *a good ball, slow ball, difficult ball* &c. Phrs. *to have the ball at one's feet*, to have a favourable opportunity of making one's career; *keep the ball rolling*, keep anything going, esp. conversation. **4.** Large pill given to a sick animal, esp. to a horse or cow.

ball (II.), vb. intrans., fr. prec. To collect or harden into a ball, as of snow in a horse's hoof.

ball (III.), n. Fr. *bal*, O. Fr. *baller*, 'dance', fr. Lat. *ballāre*, 'to dance'. The Lat. word is borrowed fr. Gk. *bállein*, 'throw', & fr. the same base comes Gk. *ballizein*, 'to throw the legs about', hence 'jump, dance'. The basal meaning is 'to throw one's legs, or oneself, about'. Cp. **ballad, ballet,** & see **ballistic**. Social gathering, party for dancing. Phr. *to open the ball*, to start, make a beginning of, an action; begin operations.

ballad, n. [1. bálad; 2. bǽləd]. O. Fr. *ballade*, fr. Provenç. *ballada*. Cp. **ball (III.)**. Originally a song accompanied by a dance; **a** a traditional popular story in a simple metre, supposed by some to have grown up among the people and to have been produced by combined effort of a company, each one adding something: *ballad poetry*; **b** any simple song, generally of a pathetic character: *drawing-room ballad*.

ballade, n. [baláhd; 2. bælā́d]. Late borrowing from Fr., see prec., with specific sense of a poem with three verses of eight lines each and an *envoy* of four; each verse and the envoy end with the same line or *refrain*.

ballade royal, n. Special form of *ballade*, each verse of which has eight or ten lines.

balladmonger, n. [1. báladmùngger; 2. bǽlədmàŋgə]. One who makes or sells popular ballads; derisively of an inferior poet.

balladry, n. [1. báladri; 2. bǽlədri]. **ballad** & **-ry**. (archaic) Ballad poetry in general.

ballast (I.), n. [1. bálast; 2. bǽləst], fr. Swed. *ballast*, O. Swed. *bar-last*. The origin of first element is doubtful. The second is a common Gmc. word meaning 'burden'; cp. O.E. *hlæst*, 'burden, freight', O.H.G. *hlast*, which is from same base as O.E. *hladan*, 'to lade, load', see **lade**. **1. a** Any heavy material, iron, stone, water, placed in hold of ship, or sand in balloon, to keep it straight and steady; **b** gravel, broken stone &c. laid between railway lines to give steadiness. **2.** (fig.) *Mental ballast*, elements of character which give steadiness and stability and poise.

ballast (II.), vb., fr. above. To provide with ballast; to place this in position.

ballasting, n. [1. bálasting; 2. bǽləstiŋ]. Material used as *ballast*.

ball-bearing, n. Bearing in which revolving parts of a machine turn upon steel balls, which diminish the friction.

ball-cartridge, n. Cartridge loaded with ball or bullet, as contrasted with *blank-cartridge*.

ball-cock, n. Device for regulating inflow of water, esp. into cisterns, consisting of a floating ball which rises or falls with the height of the water, thereby shutting or opening valve of pipe through which the water comes in.

ballerina, n. [1. baleréna; 2. bælərínə]. Ital. See **ballet**. A female ballet-dancer.

ballet, n. [1. bálā; 2. bǽlei]. Fr., fr. Ital. *balletto*, dimin. of *ballo*, 'dance'. See **ball (III.)**. An elaborate series of dances forming a theatrical display, in which a number of persons take part.

ballet-dancer, n. Person, usually a woman, who takes part in a ballet.

ball-flower, n. (archit.) Form of moulding, esp. characteristic of 14th-century Decorated, consisting of a ball placed within a globular flower whose petals form a cup to hold it.

ballistic, adj. [1. balístik; 2. bəlístik], fr. Lat. *ballista*, 'a large catapult for hurling stones', formed fr. Gk. base *ball-*, as in *bállein*, 'throw'. The Aryan base was **gʷel-*, whence Scrt. *gálati*, 'drip, fall', O.H.G. *quellen*, 'spurt out', O.N. *kelda*, 'spring of water'; cp. *-keld* in Engl. Pl.-Ns. Pertaining to projectiles, or to the science and art of controlling the flight of these.

ballistics, n. pl. [1. balístiks; 2. bəlístiks], fr. prec. The theory, science, and art of projectiles and the means of propelling these, and of controlling the flight, direction, and distance of projectiles propelled by explosion.

ballon d'essai, n. [1. balon desā; 2. balɔ̃ desɛ]. Fr., lit. 'trial balloon', see **balloon** & **essay (II)**. A proposal, suggestion, put forward to test public opinion; experimental feeler.

ballonet, n. [1. bàlonét; 2. bæ̀lənét]. Fr., dimin. of *ballon*. See **balloon**. One of set of small subsidiary gas- or air-bags, placed within the envelope of observation balloons or airships to maintain buoyancy or rigidity.

balloon (I.), n. [1. baloōn; 2. bəlū́n]. Fr. *ballon*, fr. Ital. *ballone*, orig. applied to a football. First applied in present sense in reference to invention of the Montgolfier brothers (1783). Cp. **ball** (I.) & **-oon**. Large bag of silk or other light material filled with gas and used for lifting weights, persons &c. into the air and travelling considerable distances; used also of the inflated bag which supports a modern airship in the air. Varieties of *balloon*: *observation balloon*, one allowed to rise to considerable height and anchored to the ground, in which an observer sits during a battle to report on movements and positions of the enemy's troops, guns &c.; *dirigible balloon*, one capable of being guided or directed in the air, an airship.

balloon (II.), vb., fr. prec. To puff or swell out like a balloon; said of sails &c.

balloonist, n. [1. baloōnist; 2. bəlū́nist]. **balloon** (I.) & **-ist**. Person who practises ascents in a balloon.

balloon-tire, n. A motor tire of large section for use under low pressure.

ballot (I.), n. [1. bálot; 2. bǽlət], fr. Fr. *ballotte*, fr. Ital. *ballotta*, 'little ball', dimin. of *ballo*. Cp. **ball (I.)**. **1.** Originally a small ball used in secret voting; hence any object used for this purpose, whether a ball or paper or ticket. **2.** Act of voting secretly, by whatever method, for a candidate, esp. for election to Parliament, or to any post filled by votes of electors. Hence, **3,** any voting by a paper or ticket, whether secret or not, for a person, or a motion at a legislative body. Phrs. *to take a ballot*; *elect, vote, by ballot*.

ballot (II.), vb. intrans., fr. prec. **1.** To vote for, or elect, by means of a paper or ticket signifying one's choice of a candidate. **2.** To vote (esp. secretly) for or against a resolution.

ballot box, n. Box into which the voting papers are put at an election.

ballroom, n. [1. báwlroom; 2. bɔ́lrum]. See **ball (III.) & room**. **a** Apartment in which a ball takes place; **b** room specially built for dancing.

ballyrag, vb. trans. & intrans. [1. bálirag; 2. bǽliræg]. Origin uncertain, but cp. *to rag*, in similar sense. **1.** trans. **a** To treat (person) with rough, boisterous horse-play; **b** to scold, censure, severely, take to task. **2.** intrans. **a** To indulge in rough, noisy play; **b** to scold.

balm, n. [1. bahm; 2. bām]. M.E. *basme*, *baume*, fr. O. Fr. *ba(u)sme*, Mod. Fr. *baume*. The O. Fr. form comes regularly fr. Lat. *balsamum*, 'gum of balsam tree', itself borrowed fr. Gk. *bálsamon*, 'balsam tree, resin of this tree'; cp. **balsam**. The *l* in the spelling of Mod. Engl. word is introduced fr. Lat. form. The word is perh. Semitic in origin. **1.** (bot.) Perennial garden herb, *Melissa officinalis*, with fragrant, aromatic leaves and flowers. **2.** Aromatic, medicinal gum resin, obtained from various trees and plants; balsam; *Balm of Gilead*, fragrant ointment made from the resin of a tree which grows in Asia and Africa. **3.** Any fragrant, healing ointment. **4.** (fig.) Anything which heals mental pain: *balm for a sad heart* &c. Phr. *to pour balm into a person's wounds* (fig.).

balmily, adv. [1. báhmili, 2. bā́mili]. **balmy** & **-ly**. In a balmy manner.

balminess, n. See prec. & **-ness**. Quality, state, of being balmy.

Balmoral, n. [1. balmóral; 2. bælmɔ́rəl], fr. the Royal residence, Balmoral Castle, in Scotland. **a** A kind of striped woollen petticoat; **b** a laced walking shoe or boot.

balmy, adj. [1. báhmi; 2. bā́mi]. **1. a** Possessing balm, or the qualities of this; **b** fragrant, aromatic, soothing: *balmy breeze* &c. **2.** (colloq. and vulg., more correctly **barmy**) Weak in the intellect.

balneal, adj. [1. bálneal; 2. bǽlniəl], fr. Lat. *balneum*, 'bath', & **-al**. *Balneum* is contracted fr. *balineum*, a form of Gk. *balaneion*.

This is cogn. w. Gk. *blúein*, 'gush out, bubble', & w. *bállein*, 'hurl, throw', & it is possible that Scrt. *gālayati*, 'pours forth', & *jálam*, 'water, that which is poured or which gushes out', also come fr. the same base; Aryan **gʷel-*, 'gush, pour'; if so, then Germ. *quelle*, 'source, well-spring', may also be connected; the fundamental meaning of *balaneîon* wd. thus appear to be a place into wh. water gushes. Pertaining to baths.

balneology, n. [1. bàlneóloji; 2. bælniɔ́lədži]. Lat. *balneum*, 'bath', see prec., & **-logy**. The science of the therapeutic use of natural and medicinal baths and waters.

balsam, n. [1. báwlsam; 2. bɔ́lsəm], fr. Lat. *balsamum*, q.v. under **balm**. An aromatic resin; anything healing, soothing, restorative (lit. and fig.).

balsam fir, n. American coniferous tree, *Abies balsamea*.

balsamic, adj. [1. bawlsámik; 2. bɔlsǽmik]. Prec. & **-ic**. Resembling balsam; soothing, fragrant.

balsam poplar, n. American poplar, whose buds are covered with an aromatic resin.

baltheus, n. [1. báltius; 2. bǽltiəs]. Low Lat., fr. Lat. *balteus*, 'belt'; of Gmc. origin; see **belt**. Girdle or belt worn by the Pope, bishops, and other clergy of the Roman Catholic Church.

baluster, n. [1. báluster; 2. bǽləstə]. Earlier form of **banister**. Fr. *balustre*, 'small pillar', fr. Ital. *balaustro*, Lat. *balaustium*, fr. Gk. *balaústion*, 'flower of wild pomegranate'. Applied to pillar in allusion to its shape. (archit.) Small pillar, usually swelling out in the middle and more slender at the top and base, supporting a coping or handrail.

balustrade, n. [1. bálustràd; 2. bǽləstrèid]. Prec. & **-ade**. Set or series of *balusters*, together with rail or coping which they support, used as ornamental parapet to a terrace &c.

bam, vb. trans. & intrans. [1. bam; 2. bæm]. Abbr. of **bamboozle** in 18th-cent. slang. The phrase, '*Her Ladyship was plaguily bamb'd*', occurs in Swift's 'Polite Conversations'. He refers to *bam* in the Introduction as a truncated form of *bamboozle*, as *pozz* is of *positive*. The meaning seems to be 'to annoy, worry, tease, puzzle, take in'. Also occasionally used as noun in 18th cent.: *a bam*, hoax, fraud &c.

bambino, n. [1. bambḗnō; 2. bæmbínou]. Ital., 'baby'. Specif., the Infant Jesus displayed with the B.V.M. in a picture &c.

bamboo, n. [1. bàmbóō; 2. bæmbū́]. Orig. in Engl. *bambus*, fr. Du. form *bamboes*, borrowed fr. Malay. or Jav. *bambu*. Origin doubtful; found also in forms *mambu*, *banbu*. Name given to variety of giant grasses with hard, jointed stems growing in Africa, Asia, and America.

bamboo cane, n. A walking cane of bamboo.

bamboozle, vb. trans. [1. bambóōzl; 2. bæmbū́zl]. 18th-cent. coinage, according to Swift. Perh. fr. *bambino*, 'child, baby', w. an ending formed fr. association w. **foozle**. Cp., however, Fr. *bamboche*, 'marionette', *bambocher*, 'play the fool'. (colloq. and fam.) To make a fool of, puzzle, take in, deceive; to confuse (a person) as to an issue.

ban (I.), vb. trans. [1. ban; 2. bæn]. Common Gmc. base **ban*, w. slightly differentiated meanings; O.E. *bannan*, 'to summon, call out, proclaim, command; O.N. *banna*, 'forbid, prohibit, curse'. This base is cogn. w. that in Lat. *fā-ma*, 'common talk, report' &c., & *fa-tur*, 'he speaks' &c.; Gk. *phé-*, *phā́-mi*, 'I speak, tell' &c.; see **fame**. To prohibit, forbid, interdict; to curse.

ban (II.), n. Same base as above. O.E. (*ge*)-*bann*, 'summons, interdict', O.N. *bann*, 'prohibition', O.H.G. *ban*, Mod. Germ. *bann*, 'prohibition'. Cp. also **banns**. **a** Curse, anathema and excommunication proclaimed by ecclesiastical authority; **b** outlawry from Holy Roman Empire; **c** milder form of public disapproval tacitly expressed though not formally pronounced: **d** any kind of interdict or prohibition; Phrs. *to put under a ban*; *under the ban*, excommunicated, in a condition of ostracism; **e** (med. hist.) proclamation calling out the king's vassals for military service; troops so called out, often *ban et arrière ban*, see **arrière ban**.

ban (III.), n. Pers. *bān*, 'lord, master'. Governor of a province, banat, in Hungary.

banal, adj. [1. bánal, banáhl; 2. bǽnæl, bænā́l]. Fr. *banal*, fr. Gmc. **bann*, see **ban** (II.), w. adj. suff. **-al**. Originally a feudal word referring to something which all vassals had to do by order of their lord. Since these duties were incumbent upon everyone, *banal*, from 'compulsory (for all)', came to mean 'common to all', whence it is but a step to its present meaning. Trite, commonplace, matter-of-fact.

banality, n. [1. banáliti; 2. bænǽliti]. See prec. & **-ity**. Triteness; commonplace, trivial idea or expression.

banana, n. [1. banáhna; 2. bənā́nə]. Span., fr. S. Am. native name. Tropical fruit tree; the long, narrow, curved fruit of this tree, which is covered by a thickish, tough skin, yellow when ripe, pulpy in texture, without much juice, and faintly sweet in taste.

banat, n. [1. bánat; 2. bǽnæt]. See **ban** (III.). Jurisdiction of a ban.

Banbury cake, n. [1. bánburi kák; 2. bǽnbəri kéik], fr. name of Oxfordshire town. A cake of light, sweet paste filled with mincemeat.

banc, banco, n. [1. bángk(ō); 2. bǽŋk(ou)]. O. Fr. *banc*, fr. Low Lat. *bancus*, 'bench'; Gmc. loan-word, see **bank** (I.) & **bench**. **1.** Bench on which judges sit. Phr. *in banc*, *in banco* (Lat. abl.), on the bench, in session; used of the Supreme Court of Common Law. **2.** *Banco* (school slang, Charterhouse), evening preparation of work for following day, carried out in each 'house'.

band (I.), n. [1. band; 2. bænd]. O.E. *band*, common to all Gmc. languages; see **bind**. The original and fundamental meaning is that of something which *binds*, attaches, fastens one thing to another, or which acts as a fetter or shackle. Various shades of meaning: **1.** A ligament or tie of any material with which a loose bundle (as hay &c.) or a number of objects (as a faggot) may be fastened and kept together, so as to form a single more or less compact mass: *hay band*, often of twisted strands of hay, to fasten a truss; *withy band*, one of twisted withies to tie up a faggot, also called *faggot band*; *iron band*, e.g. which surrounds a cask and holds the staves of which it is composed in position; *india-rubber band*, flat ring for holding papers &c. **2.** (archit.) 'Flat face or fascia, square moulding, or continuous tablet; series of ornaments encircling a building or continued along a wall' (Parker). **3.** Flat strip of cloth making part of certain garments, and encircling a part of the body: *neckband*, *waistband*, *wristband*. **4. a** Anything in the form of a flat strip, distinctive in material, texture, or colour from the rest of the object upon which it is applied: a *band of iron* across a door or box; a *band of colour*, e.g. upon a garment, shawl &c., differing from the colour of the rest; specif. **b** (pl.) *bands*, short strips of white material hanging down in front from the neck, worn as part of academic dress at universities by the Vice-Chancellor, Doctors of Divinity, Proctors &c.; also in legal dress, as by barristers &c. **5.** (probably associated with and influenced by sense of **ban**, i.e. persons outlawed. Cp. **bandit**). **a** Body of persons united for a common purpose, association: *band of robbers*, *brigands*; *band of brothers*, said of Nelson and his captains; **b** special use: company of musicians: *German band*; *regimental band*.

band (II.), vb. trans. & intrans., fr. prec. Often *band together*, to bring together, collect, unite, (of persons): *to band people together for a certain purpose*; *to band together to resist oppression* &c.

bandage (I.), n. [1. bándij; 2. bǽndidž]. Fr., fr. *bande*, of Gmc. origin, see **band** (I.), & **-age**. Strip of soft pliable material, used esp. for binding wounds and injuries.

bandage (II.), vb. trans., fr. prec. To apply a bandage to; to surround with, secure, or protect with a bandage: *to bandage a broken head, a cut finger*.

bandan(n)a, n. [1. bandána; 2. bændǽnə]. Hind. *bandhnu*, 'a mode of dyeing in which the material to be dyed is tied in various places so that these do not receive the dye'. The word is doubtless connected w. Scrt. *bandh-*, 'tie, bind'. See **bind**. Bright-coloured and spotted red or yellow handkerchief, generally of silk, also attrib.: *bandanna silk handkerchief*.

bandbox, n. [1. bán(d)boks; 2. bǽn(d)bɔks]. Originally a case in which a clergyman kept his linen bands; now a light case of cardboard for holding light articles, esp. hats. Phr. *to look as if one had just come out of a bandbox*, look very smart, spick and span.

band brake, n. Brake attached to a bicycle, motor-car &c., consisting of a steel band which acts by being tightened so as to grip the axle of the wheel.

bandeau, n. [1. bándō; 2. bǽndou]. Fr., fr. earlier *bandel*, fr. *bande*, Gmc. loan-word, see **band** (I.), & dimin. suff. **-el**. Fillet for a woman's head.

banded, adj. [1. bánded; 2. bǽndid], fr. P.P. of **band** (II.). United, federated: *banded hosts*.

banderilla, n. [1. bànderílya; 2. bændərílјə]. Span. dimin. of *bandera*, **banner**. A barbed dart with a small streamer stuck into the bull by the *bandilleros* in a bullfight.

banderol(e), n. [1. bánderòl; 2. bǽndəròul]. Fr., fr. Ital. *banderuola*, 'a long narrow flag or streamer attached to mast-head, or to the end of a knight's lance, with armorial or other devices upon it'. Dimin. of **banner**. **1.** Used in above sense. **2.** (archit.) A flat band with inscription, used on buildings of Renaissance period.

bandicoot, n. [1. bándikōōt; 2. bǽndikūt], fr. Telegu, meaning 'pig-rat'. Large species of rat found in India and Ceylon.

bandit, n. [1. bándit; 2. bǽndit]. Fr., fr. Ital. *banditto*, 'outlawed', fr. *bandire*, 'banish'. See **ban** (I.) & **banish**. Robber, brigand; dishonest, rascally person.

banditti, n. [1. banditi; 2. bændíti]. Ital., pl. of *banditto*. See prec. Members of organized bands of robbers; such bands generally.

bandmaster, n. [1. bán(d)màhster; 2. bǽn(d)-mā̀stə). Conductor of a musical band or orchestra.

bandog, n. [1. bándog; 2. bǽndɔg]. **band** (I.) & **dog**. A dog kept chained up as a watch-dog, or on account of his ferocity; hence specif., a mastiff or bloodhound.

bandolier, bandoleer, n. [1. bàndolḗr; 2. bændəlíə], fr. Fr. *bandoulière*, Ital. *bandoliera*, fr. *bandola*, dimin. of *banda*, of Gmc. origin; see **band** (I.). Shoulder-belt with small pockets for holding cartridges.

bandstand, n. [1. bándstand; 2. bǽndstænd]. Raised and covered place, open on all or most sides, in which a musical band plays in the open air.

bandy (I.), vb. trans. [1. bándi; 2. bǽndi]. Prob. fr. the game **bandy** (II.). To throw about, toss backwards and forwards, esp. *to bandy words* (*with a person*), to exchange rapid remarks, to engage in altercation; *to bandy a rumour, story, about*, to pass it on from one person to another; *to have one's name bandied about*, to have it talked of, generally unfavourably, in connexion with something.

bandy (II.), n. Perh. fr. **bend**, in reference to the stick used. **a** Once a form of the game of tennis, now a form of hockey; **b** the stick, with a curved end, used in the game.

bandy (III.), adj. Perh. connected w. *bend*, cp. prec. Of the legs, having bowed or curved shin bones which bend outwards from the knees.

bandy (**IV.**), n. Telegu *baṇḍi*, 'cart, vehicle'. A carriage, bullock-cart, or buggy, used in many parts of India.

bandy-legged, adj. Having bandy legs.

bane, n. [1. bān; 2. bein]. O.E. *bana*, 'murder; murderer, slayer', M.E. *bāne*, 'destroyer, destruction', O.H.G. *bano*, 'death, destruction', O.S. *bano*, 'slayer', cogn. w. Goth. *banja*, 'wound', O.E. *benn*. The Aryan base **bhon-* does not seem to survive outside Gmc. Gk. *phónos*, 'murder' &c., formerly often connected in the dictionaries w. *bane*, has nothing to do w. it, but goes back to Aryan **gʷhon-* &c., wh. see under **gonfalon**. The older meanings are now obsolete. In the compound *rat's-bane*, the second element means poison; apart from this the independent word only occurs in such phrases as *the bane of my life* &c., with sense of cause of ruin, source of evil, worry, curse &c.; or, occasionally, *idleness has always been his bane* &c., ruin, cause of injury.

baneful, adj. [1. bánfool; 2. béinfəl]. Prec. & **-ful**. More used than n. Harmful, pernicious, destructive, injurious, deadly, causing injury; esp. *baneful influence, effect(s)*. Also used of disease.

banefully, adv. Prec. & **-ly**. In a baneful or injurious manner.

banefulness, n. See prec. & **-ness**. (rather rare) Property or character of being baneful.

bang (**I.**), vb. trans. & intrans. [1. bang; 2. bæŋ]. Of imitative origin; cp. also O.N. *banga*, 'hammer', & L.G. *bangen*, 'to strike'. **A.** trans. **1. a** To strike violently and noisily; to thump: *to bang a drum, a gong*; **b** to bring into violent collision with something; to strike violently; to butt forcibly against: *to bang one's head*; *to bang oneself against a tree*; *to bang one's fist on the table*, to bring the fist down noisily and violently on the table. **2.** To close violently and noisily; to slam: *to bang a door*; *to bang the lid of a box down*; *to bang a window down*; *to bang a door to*, cause it to shut noisily by a violent movement. **3.** (colloq. and vulg.) To beat, thrash; knock (person) about roughly and brutally. **4.** *Bang off (ammunition)*, to fire it off, esp. uselessly. **B.** intrans. **1.** To explode, be fired, with a loud noise: *the gun banged*. **2. a** (of door, window, lid of a box &c.) To shut violently with a loud noise; to slam: *the door banged after him*; *I heard a window bang in the basement*; **b** *bang to*, to close, be closed, with a loud noise.

bang (**II.**), n. See prec. **1.** A violent blow, a hard knock: *to get a bang on the head*. **2.** Loud, sudden noise accompanying a violent action or movement: *to shut the door with a bang*. **3.** Loud, sudden explosion, or report of fire-arms: *the gun went off with a bang*.

bang (**III.**), interj. & adv. See **bang** (**I.**). **1.** interj. Exclamation imitative of loud, sudden sound or explosion, often called forth by hearing this: *bang!*; *bang went the gun, and the bird fell*. **2.** adv. **a** Applied to an unexpected action or event, or to one beyond recall: *bang goes sixpence!*; **b** describing effect of a sudden blow, movement &c.; precisely, exactly, just: *hit him bang in the eye*; *the picture fell bang on his head*; **c** completely, straight, right, clean &c.: *he jumped bang out of the window*.

bang (**IV.**), n. & vb. trans. Origin doubtful. (archaic, colloq.) **1.** n. Hair cut straight across the forehead; a fringe. **2.** vb. To cut (hair) in this fashion.

bang (**V.**) or **bhang**, n. Hind. *bhāng*. Dried leaves and small stalks of Indian hemp which have an intoxicating effect when either smoked or consumed in a sweetmeat.

banged, adj. [1. bángd; 2. bæŋd], fr. prec. Under the influence of **bang** (**V.**), intoxicated. Phr. *banged up to the eyes*.

bangle, n. [1. bánggl; 2. bǽŋgl]. Hind. *bangrī*, 'a ring of coloured glass worn on the wrist by women'; *bangle* is applied to any native ring-bracelet or anklet. **1.** Originally a circlet of glass or metal worn round the wrist or ankle by Indian women. **2.** A bracelet of gold or silver, consisting usually of a slender circlet, or small chain, worn by women, and sometimes by men, in Europe.

banian, banyan, n. [1. bányàn; 2. bǽnjæ̀n]. Port., fr. Arab. *banyan*. Said to come fr. Gujerati *vāṇiya*, 'a man of the trading caste', fr. Scrt. *vaṇij*, 'merchant'. **1.** A Hindu trader, esp. from province of Gujerat; sometimes used by early travellers of persons of the Hindu religion generally. **2.** Extended to mean a broker, secretary, or steward. **3.** An undershirt such as that worn by Hindus, of muslin, wool, or silk; a loose garment resembling a dressing-gown, similar to that worn by Hindu tradesmen, and adopted formerly by Englishmen in India as a form of undress.

banian-, banyan-day, n. See prec. Day on which no meat is eaten; so called from the fact that the banian, or merchant caste, profess so great a respect for animal life as to abstain from all animal flesh.

banian-, banyan-tree, n. A species of Indian fig. The name is said to have been given to a famous tree of the kind growing near Gombroon (old name for place on Persian Gulf now called Bandar Abbas), under which the *Banians* or Indian traders who settled there had built a little pagoda. The branches of this tree are said, on touching the ground, to take root and send up new shoots, which in turn grow into trees.

banish, vb. trans. [1. bánish; 2. bǽniʃ]. O. Fr. *banir*, 'put under a *ban*, to outlaw', see **ban** (**I.**) & **-ish**. **1.** To condemn a person to leave his country, drive into exile. **2.** Generally, to send away, drive away, dismiss: *to banish a person from one's presence*. **3.** (of mental action) To put away, remove: *to banish fear, shyness, anxiety, care* &c.

banishment, n. [1. bánishment; 2. bǽniʃmənt]. Prec. & **-ment**. **1.** Act of banishing; sentence of exile. **2.** State of being banished; exile.

banister, n. [1. bánister; 2. bǽnistə]. Popular, & now universal, form of **baluster**. Usually pl. *banisters*. The hand-rail and supporting pillars or bars which protect the open side or sides of a staircase in a house.

banjo, n. [1. bánjō; 2. bǽndžou]. Corrupted, in American Negro pronunciation, fr. *banjore*, earlier *bandore*, Lat. *pandura*, fr. Gk. *pandoûra*, 'a three-stringed musical instrument'; see **pandora**. Musical instrument having long neck and strings like a guitar, and a body with a front made of parchment like a tambourine, over which the strings pass, and which imparts a peculiar resonance to their note when they are plucked. Phr. *to play the cat and banjo with*, reduce to confusion; upset.

banjoist, n. [1. bánjōist; 2. bǽndžouist]. Prec. & **-ist**. Player of, performer on, the banjo.

bank (**I.**), n. [1. bangk; 2. bæŋk]. Not in O.E.; M.E. *banke*, perh. Scand., O.N. *bakki*, cogn. w. **bench**. **1.** A heap or mound of earth raised above level of immediate surroundings, often dividing fields, with a ditch on one side from which the earth forming the *bank* has been dug; hence, any mound resembling this, piled up by wind or water, as *bank of snow, snow bank*; *bank of clouds*; further, shelving ground at bottom of sea, higher than surrounding floor and causing a shoal: *sand bank*; *the banks of Newfoundland*; the same in an estuary. **2.** The land along the edge of a river or other watercourse: *the banks of the Thames*; *river-bank*; *to bring a boat to the bank*; *reach the bank* (when swimming in a river &c.); *a river flows between its banks*. **3.** (naut.) **a** The bench or seat on which the rowers sit in a galley; **b** (by extension) those seated upon it: *a bank of rowers*. **4.** (min.) Face of coal which is in process of working.

bank (**II.**), vb. trans. & intrans., fr. prec. **1.** trans. **a** To pile up earth &c. in form of a bank; to put a bank so as to narrow, impede, or stop the flow of a watercourse—often *to bank up (a stream* &c.). **2.** intrans. **a** (aeron.) To put machine at an angle in turning, so as to avoid a side-slip; **b** (of sand &c. in an estuary) to become piled up and form a bank or shallow.

bank (**III.**), n. See **banc** & **bench**. **1. a** Originally the table or counter of a money-changer; hence, **b** an institution or establishment where money is dealt with; **c** the building in which the business of such an institution is conducted. Phrs. *the Bank*, the Bank of England; *safe as the Bank*, very safe; *to have money in the bank*, (fig.) to have savings. **2. a** Sum of money held by keeper of, or stakeholder at, gaming-table from which he pays his losses; **b** a gambling game of cards, also *banker*.

bank (**IV.**), vb. intrans. & trans., fr. prec. **A.** intrans. **1. a** To keep a bank; **b** to keep the bank in certain gambling games. **2.** To keep money in a bank: *he banks with Barclay's*. **B.** trans. To pay (money) into a bank: *to bank one's earnings each week*.

bank-bill, n. Bill of exchange drawn by or on a bank.

bank book, n. One in which the accounts of each customer of a bank are kept.

banker (**I.**), n. [1. bángker; 2. bǽŋkə]. **bank** (**I.**) & **-er**. A horse which has been trained to jump banks.

banker (**II.**), n. **bank** (**IV.**) & **-er**. **1.** One who keeps, or conducts the business of, a bank; (pl.) a group of persons, or company, which does this: *merchants and bankers*. **2.** (gaming) **a** Person who acts as stakeholder and pays losses from common fund called *the bank*; **b** a game of cards.

banket, n. [1. bángket; 2. bǽŋkit]. S. Afr. Du., orig. name of a hard kind of almond toffee, Du. form of **banquet**. (min.) A conglomerate gold-mining reef in the Witwatersrand gold district of the Transvaal.

bank holiday, n. One of several days in the year, other than Sundays, on which the banks are closed; day kept as a general holiday; specif. (cap.) one of the four statutory annual holidays.

banking, n. [1. bángking; 2. bǽŋkiŋ]. **1.** See **bank** (**IV.**). The act of carrying on trade of a banker; the art and method of this business; the business itself: *he was engaged in the lucrative trade of banking*; *he had mastered all the mysteries of banking*. **2.** See **bank** (**II.**). A manœuvre, an operation, executed when turning an aeroplane, to avoid a side-slip.

bank-note, n. Paper money, in form of a promissory note, payable on demand, whose face value is guaranteed by the bank which issues it.

bank paper, n. Bank-notes collectively; bills and drafts accepted by a bank.

bank rate, n. Amount of discount fixed by Bank of England for doing business.

bankrupt (**I.**), n. [1. bángkrupt; 2. bǽŋkrapt]. Cp. Fr. *banqueroute*, fr. Ital. *bancarotta*, fr. **bank** (**III.**) & Lat. *rupt-(um)*, P.P. type of *rumpere*, 'to break, burst'. See **rupture**. **1.** Technically, a person who has been declared on his own or others' petition to be liable to bankruptcy laws, and who is therefore subject to have his property administered for the benefit of his creditors. **2.** Popularly, an insolvent person.

bankrupt (**II.**), adj., fr. prec. **1.** In the condition of being a bankrupt, in technical or popular sense. Phr. *to go bankrupt*, (i.) to be made a technical bankrupt; (ii.) to become insolvent, be ruined. **2.** Devoid of, destitute in, wholly lacking, something one ought to possess: *bankrupt in reputation, policy, ability, intelligence* &c.; *to be morally bankrupt*.

bankrupt (**III.**), vb. trans. See prec. To cause to become bankrupt, to make bankrupt.

bankruptcy, n. [1. bángkrupsi; 2. bǽŋkrəpsi]. **bankrupt** & **-cy**. **a** Condition of being or becoming bankrupt; **b** moral or intellectual poverty.

banksia, n. [1. bángksia; 2. bǽŋksiə], fr. the botanist Sir Joseph Banks, d. 1820. A genus of Australian evergreen shrubs, with clusters of small yellow flowers.

banner, n. [1. báner; 2. bǽnə]. M.E. *banére*, fr. Fr. *baniere*, earlier **bandiere*, cp. Ital. *bandiera*, fr. Low Lat. *bandum*, 'flag', itself a Gmc. loan-word, cp. Goth. *bandwō*, 'sign'. The connexion of this base w. **ban** or **bind**, or w. Gk. *phainein*, 'show', see **fantasy**, is doubtful. The development of meaning is 'sign, symbol', particular kind of symbol, hence 'a flag'. A flag of any kind supported on a pole; esp. (fig.) as symbol of a nation, a cause, or a person: *the banner of freedom, revolt* &c.; *the banner of England was unfurled*; *to fight under the banner of a leader, under Christ's banner*; *to unfurl one's banner*, to proclaim one's cause, opinions, enthusiasms.

banner-bearer, n. **a** One who carries a banner; **b** (fig.) one who proclaims a cause.

banneret, n. [1. báneret; 2. bǽnərɛt]. M.E. *baneret*, fr. Fr.; see **banner** & **-et**. An order of knighthood superior to that of knights bachelor; originally a knight who could lead his vassals under his own banner; hence *knight banneret*.

bannerole, n. [1. bánerōl; 2. bænəroul]. Variant of **banderole**. Banner displayed at a funeral and placed over tomb.

banner screen, n. Small fire-screen in form of a banner, and hung from a rod.

bannock, n. [1. bánok; 2. bǽnək]. O.E. *bannuc*, 'cake' (*-uc* dimin. ending); Gael. *bonnach* is prob. borrowed fr. this. A flat kind of cake made of oatmeal, barley, and sometimes of shortbread. (Word used only in Scotland or among Scots.)

banns, n. pl. [1. banz; 2. bænz]. For etymol. see **ban (II.)**. Specialized use of *ban*; the public announcement that two persons are to be married, which must be made in the parish church of both parties on three successive Sundays before the marriage can take place in a church. Phrs. *to call the banns*; *have one's banns called*.

banquet (I.), n. [1. bángkwet; 2. bǽŋkwit]. Fr., fr. Ital. *banchetto*, dimin. of *banco*, 'bench'. See **banc** & **bench**. **a** A feast, esp. of an official character: *Lord Mayor's banquet*; *Royal banquet* &c.; **b** any sumptuous, elaborate feast or repast: *a regular banquet*, a very good dinner.

banquet (II.), vb. trans. & intrans., fr. prec. **1.** trans. To treat to, regale with, a banquet. **2.** intrans. To regale, treat oneself, with (to) a banquet; to feast, as at a banquet.

banqueter, n. [1. bángkweter; 2. bǽŋkwitə]. Prec. & **-er**. Partaker of a banquet.

banquette, n. [1. bangkét; 2. bæŋkét]. Fr. dimin. of *banc*, of Gmc. origin; see **bank (I.)**. (mil.) The fire step of a trench.

banshee, n. [1. bánshē; 2. bǽnʃī]. Ir. *bean*, 'woman', & *sidh*, 'fairy'. The first element is cogn. w. Engl. **quean, queen**. A supernatural creature who in Ireland is believed to be connected with certain families, whom she warns, and terrifies, on the death of a member, by a dreadful wailing; the banshee is said to *cry*.

bantam, n. [1. bántam; 2. bǽntəm], fr. name of province of Bāntan at the western extremity of Java. **1.** Name given to various kinds of dwarf poultry brought by travellers from the above-mentioned part of Java. They are said originally to have come from Japan. **2.** (pl.) Name given in the Great War to small but strong and healthy recruits, who were for a time formed into special battalions.

bantam weight, n. Boxer not exceeding 116 pounds in weight.

banter (I.), vb. trans. & intrans. [1. bánter; 2. bǽntə]. Origin unknown. **1.** trans. To chaff, tease playfully and good-naturedly, subject to humorous and kindly raillery. **2.** intrans. To indulge in good-humoured raillery or persiflage; to be jocular.

banter (II.), n., fr. prec. Light, good-natured chaff, persiflage, raillery, jesting.

banting, n. [1. bánting; 2. bǽntiŋ]. System for reducing weight by avoiding sugar, fats, and farinaceous foods, proposed by William Banting (1797–1878), and named after him. While the word was still in use there was a tendency to regard it as a Pres. Part. or vbl. n. in such phrases as, *you'd better try banting*, and an infin. *to bant* was formed quite naturally.

bantling, n. [1. bántling; 2. bǽntliŋ]. Possibly fr. older Germ. *bänkling*, see **bank (I.)** & **-ling**, & cp. origin of **bastard**. A young child, young creature; often contemptuously.

Bantu, n. & adj. [1. bántōō; 2. bǽntū], fr. native *ba-ntu*, 'men, mankind'. **1.** n. **a** An African group or family of languages, embracing most of those spoken in Africa south of the Equator; **b** a member of any of the various African races which speak Bantu. **2.** adj. Pertaining to Bantu, as language or speaker.

banyan, banyan-tree. See **banian, banian-tree**.

banzai, interj. [1. bánzī; 2. bǽnzái]. Jap. '(may you live) ten thousand (years)'. Form of greeting used to the Emperor of Japan.

baobab, n. [1. bāobab; 2. béiəbæb]. Native name of an African tree, the trunk of which sometimes attains 30 ft. in diameter.

bap, n. [1. bap; 2. bæp]. Scots. Origin unknown. A small loaf or roll of bread with thin, soft crust.

baptism, n. [1. báptizm; 2. bǽptizəm]. M.E. *baptesme, baptim, baptism* &c., fr. O. Fr. *baptesme*, fr. Gk. *baptismós*, 'dipping in water', cp. *báptein*, 'dip', *baphḗ*, 'dyeing'. The Aryan base is **gabh-*, wh. seems to have the meaning 'to plunge', cp. Scrt. *gabhirāś*, 'deep', *gámbha*, 'abyss'. A sacrament of the Christian Church by means of which persons are admitted to membership. The essentials of the rite are sprinkling with, or immersion in, water, and the utterance of the words stating that it is performed in the Name of all three Persons of the Holy Trinity, who are severally mentioned; christening. The ceremony is generally accompanied by name-giving. Fig. uses: *baptism of fire*, a soldier's first battle or a severe ordeal; *baptism of blood*, martyrdom.

baptismal, adj. [1. baptízmal; 2. bæptízməl]. Prec. & **-al**. Relating to, made, conferred, in, baptism: *baptismal vows*; *baptismal name*.

baptist, n. [1. báptist; 2. bǽptist]. O.F. *baptiste*, Lat. *baptista*, fr. Gk. *baptistḗs*, 'one who dips, a dyer', later 'baptist' in Christian sense; cp. **baptism**. **1.** One who baptizes, esp. used of *St. John (the) Baptist*, the forerunner of Christ. **2.** Member of a sect (Baptists) who insist on total immersion at baptism, and believe that this sacrament should only be administered to believers in Christianity. They deny validity of infant baptism.

baptist(e)ry, n. [1. báptistri; 2. bǽptistri]. O.F. *baptisterie*, fr. Gk. *baptistḗrion*, 'bathing-place, swimming-bath', later adopted in Christian sense. See **baptist** & **-ery**. **a** Originally a separate building for the administration of baptism; **b** in Baptist chapels, a large tank used for complete immersion at the ceremony of baptism; **c** in the English and Roman Catholic Churches, that part of the church, sometimes separate from the rest, where the font stands, and where baptism is administered.

baptize, vb. trans. & intrans. [1. baptíz; 2. bæptáiz]. M.E. *baptīsen*, Fr. *baptiser*, fr. Gk. *baptizein*, 'to dip under, baptize'; see **baptism**. **1.** trans. To administer the sacrament of baptism to; to admit (person) as member of Christian Church by the rite of baptism; to christen. **2.** intrans. To perform, practise, the rite of baptism: *Quakers do not baptize*.

bar (I.), n. [1. bar; 2. bā]. M.E. *barre*, 'bar' (in various senses), O. Fr. *barre*, Low Lat. *barra*, etymol. unknown. A strip or rod of metal or wood long in proportion to its breadth. Numerous derived meanings and special uses, generally with fundamental idea of obstruction, hindrance, or separation. **1. a** Strip or rod of iron or wood used for purposes of obstruction, esp. *bar of a door, shutter, window*; extended use: *prison bars*, prison; *behind bolt and bar*, in secure confinement; **b** (fig.) moral and intellectual obstruction or hindrance: *a bar to progress, to happiness*. **2.** Any long, narrow piece or rod of metal, e.g. *crow-bar*, called also *bar*, or *iron bar*; the rounded piece of iron which goes into a horse's mouth, part of a *bar bit*; *handle-bar*, of bicycle. **3.** Piece or mass of any material which is long in proportion to its breadth and thickness: *bar of soap, lead, gold*; (fig.) a ridge of any kind: '*And over those ethereal eyes The bar of Michael Angelo*' (Tennyson, 'In Memoriam'). **4. a** Obstruction, gatehouse, or gate closing a road, which could not be passed without payment of a *toll*; also *toll bar*; **b** gatehouse in fortified town or castle: *Temple Bar*. **5.** A non-material obstacle, hindrance, impediment: *poverty is not necessarily a bar to happiness, though it often is to worldly success*. **6.** Bank of sand or gravel silted up at mouth of a harbour &c. **7. a** Narrow strip of metal, crossing and sometimes clasping the riband of a military medal, with name of battle at which holder was present; in some campaigns a *bar* is added for every battle fought; **b** in some Crosses and Orders—Victoria Cross, Distinguished Service Order, Military Cross &c.—the addition of a *bar* indicates that the distinction has been gained more than once by the wearer. **8.** (her.) Stripe or band crossing the shield horizontally, not exceeding in breadth one-fifth of total length of shield; popularly and improperly used instead of *bend*, in *bar sinister*, mark of illegitimacy. **9.** (mus.) **a** A vertical line drawn across the stave in the score; **b** the musical unit or division of notes indicated by this. **10.** Strip or shaft of colour or light. **11.** Final destruction of a claim, or action in law. **12.** Railing in a court of law which separates from rest of the hall the part where the judges sit, where prisoners are put for trial, and where the business of the court is carried on: *to be tried at Bar*. **13.** Barrier in Inns of Court separating benchers and readers from the students. The latter took their seats at the bar on becoming entitled to take part in the debates and to become barristers. Hence, *to be called to the Bar*, enter the legal profession as a barrister; *to be at the Bar*, be a barrister; *to go to the Bar*, become a barrister. **14.** *The Bar*, the whole body of qualified and admitted barristers. **15. a** Railing in House of Commons to which persons are brought to be censured or examined by the House: *the bar of the House*; hence **b** a tribunal, esp. an intellectual or moral tribunal. Phr. *the bar of public opinion*. **16. a** A counter in a hotel or public-house where drinks are sold; **b** the room in which the bar is.

bar (II.), vb. trans., fr. O. Fr. *barrer*; see prec. **1.** To place a bar in position so as to make obstruction more complete; secure by means of a bar: *to bar a door, window-shutter* &c.; *to bar out (the masters)*, form of schoolboy insubordination. **2.** To hinder, obstruct, in any way (lit. and fig.): *that way is barred*; *all exits are barred*; *my prospects of success are barred*. **3. a** To exclude, rule out, prohibit: *bar one*, in betting; *spot barred* (billiards), game in which a player is not allowed to hole the red from spot more than twice in succession; *to bar discussion of a point*, rule out, forbid; **b** (as prep.) except, all but: *the list is complete bar (barring) a few names*. Phr. *bar none*, with no exceptions. **4.** (colloq.) To object to, dislike: *what I bar is a man who talks of what he doesn't understand*. **5.** To mark with streaks or bars of different colour or material: *the sky was barred with black clouds*; *crimson barred*.

bar (III.), n. Fr. Large sea fish.

barb (**I.**), n. [1. barb; 2. bāb]. Fr. *barbe*, 'beard', Lat. *barba*, 'beard'; cogn. w. O.E. *beard*; see **beard**. **1.** Appendage suggestive of a beard, e.g. the wattles of a *barbel* (fish), q.v. **2.** That part of a piercing implement or weapon (fish-hook, arrow, spear &c.) which projects downwards a little below the point, having itself a sharp penetrating point, which prevents the hook or weapon from being withdrawn. **3.** That part, filament, of a feather which springs directly from the shaft. **4.** Linen cloth worn by nuns, which covers the throat and sometimes the chin.

barb (**II.**), vb. trans., fr. prec. To supply, furnish, with a barb.

barb (**III.**), n., fr. Fr. *barbe*. A breed of horse from Barbary.

barbara, n. [1. bárbara; 2. bábərə]. (log.) The name of the first mood of the syllogism, from the scholastic Latin doggerel mnemonic beginning *barbara celarent* &c.

barbarian (**I.**), n. [1. barbárian; 2. bābéərjən]. Lat., fr. Gk. *barbar-*, see **barbaric**, & **-ian**. In M.E. the form *barbar*, direct fr. Fr., was used as a n. **1.** A person belonging to a savage, uncivilized race. **2.** A person who behaves like a savage, esp. in having rough, coarse manners, and no refinement or cultivation of mind. **3.** Matthew Arnold defined his use of the word, and gave some currency to such usage, as expressing the aristocrat whose mind was diverted from culture by sports and pleasures, rather than by any active dislike to art and literature in themselves. In this respect Arnold distinguished the '*Barbarian*' from the '*Philistine*', q.v. Gray had used the word in somewhat the same way; cp. '*young barbarians at play*', referring to boys at Eton, in 'Ode on Distant Prospect of Eton College.'

barbarian (**II.**), adj., fr. prec. Pertaining to barbarians; strange, foreign.

barbaric, adj. [1. barbárik; 2. bābǽrik]. Older Fr. *barbarique*, Lat. *barbaricus*, 'outlandish, foreign', fr. Gk. *barbarikós*. These words, and Gk. *bárbaros*, Lat. *barbarus*, were applied to anything foreign, as distinct from what was respectively Gk. and Roman. The Gk. pl. *hoi barbaroi*, 'the barbarians', was applied to foreigners generally, or to those who did not speak Greek, very much as the Jews called all who were not Jews Gentiles. The base, which is found in various forms in several Aryan languages, is ultimately of imitative origin, and refers to the speech, meaning stammering, stuttering, jabbering, uttering gibberish &c.; cp. Scrt. *barbaraś*, 'stammering, foreign', i.e. not speaking Scrt.; Lat. *balbus*, 'stammering, stammerer', Lith. *blebénti*, 'babble', Bulg. *blábolja*, 'jabber', Russ. *bolobólit*, 'chatter, jabber'. Outlandish, rude, uncultivated; esp. in reference to taste, ideals of splendour &c. Cp. Milton's—'*Or where the gorgeous East with richest hand Showers on her kings barbaric pearl and gold*'.

barbarism, n. [1. bárbarizm; 2. bábərizəm]. Fr. *barbarisme*, Lat. *barbarismus*, fr. Gk. *barbarismós*, 'impropriety of speech', such as a foreigner would commit; see **barbaric** & **-ism**. **1.** In English the word retains the Greek and Latin meaning as a special sense, *barbarism* in speech or writing, esp. introduction of foreign words and phrases. **2.** The general sense is the condition of being uncivilized and savage, ignorant: *to relapse into a state of barbarism*, esp. of savages, when civilizing influence is withdrawn. **3.** Special sense derived from **2**, cruelty; more often *barbarity*, q.v.

barbarity, n. [1. barbáriti; 2. bābǽriti]. *Barbar-*, as in **barbarian** &c., & **-ity**. Behaviour and conduct characteristic of barbarians; specif., cruelty, ferocity, mercilessness: *to be treated with the greatest barbarity*.

barbarize, vb. trans. [1. bárbarīz; 2. bábəraiz], fr. Fr. *barbariser*, fr. Gk. *barbarízō*, 'speak or behave like the barbarians'. See **barbaric** & **-ize**. **a** To make barbarous, introduce savage customs among (a people); **b** to corrupt (a style) by introduction of foreign expressions &c.

barbarous, adj. [1. bárbarus; 2. bábərəs]. Lat. *barbarus*, fr. Gk. *bárbaros*. See **barbaric** & **-ous**. **a** Savage, uncivilized, like a barbarian; **b** cruel, merciless; **c** unrefined, coarse &c.; applied to persons, conduct, habits, tastes &c.

barbarously, adv. Prec. & **-ly**. In a barbarous manner; rudely, cruelly.

barbarousness, n. See prec. & **-ness**. Barbarity, barbarism.

barbary, n. [1. bárbari; 2. bábəri]. Fr. *barbarie*; *barbar-* as in **barbaric** & **-y**. (archaic) Barbarous, pagan, lands and peoples; paganism; formerly, specif. used of the Saracens.

Barbary ape, n., fr. *Barbary*, old name of N. Africa. Large tailless N. African ape, found also on the rock of Gibraltar.

Barbary sheep, n. Wild sheep with large horns of N. Africa.

barbate(d), adj. [1. bárbāt(ed); 2. bábeit(id)]. Lat. *barbātus*, 'bearded', cp. **barb** (**I.**), & **-ate**. (bot. and zool.) Bearded, provided with hairy tufts or awns, as barley, oats &c.

barbecue (**I.**), n. [1. bárbekū; 2. bábikjū]. Span. *barbacoa*, fr. native Haiti term. **a** Originally a wooden framework to sleep on; or on which meat was smoked or roasted; **b** animal roasted whole for a feast.

barbecue (**II.**), vb. trans., fr. prec. To roast (an animal) whole: '*Send me, ye Gods, a whole hog barbecued*' (Pope).

barbed, adj. [1. barbd; 2. bābd]. **barb** (**I.**) & **-ed**. **a** Furnished with barbs; esp. *barbed wire*, strands of galvanized wire with sharp spikes or barbs interspersed, used for fencing, wire entanglements &c.; **b** (fig.) *barbed words, wit* &c., stinging, sharp, wounding.

barbel, n. [1. bárbel; 2. bábəl]. Fr. See **barb** (**I.**) & **-el**. Large fresh-water fish with filaments growing from mouth.

bar-bell, n. [1. bár bĕl; 2. bá bĕl]. Object resembling a dumb-bell for developing the muscles, consisting of an iron bar with a round lump of iron at either end.

barber, n. [1. bárber; 2. bábə]. M.E. *barbour* &c., O. Fr. *barbeor*, Fr. *barbe*, Lat. *barba*; see **barb** (**I.**) & **beard**. (lit.) One who trims and shaves beards; now generally a hairdresser; *barber surgeon*, formerly one who both shaved and bled his clients when necessary; *barber's pole*, a pole used as a trade sign, hung out over a barber's shop. It was painted in two colours to resemble strips of cloth or bandages twined round it, and symbolized the barber's function of bandaging his clients' arms after bleeding.

barberry, n. [1. bárberi; 2. bábəri]. Form of **berberis**, with influence of **berry** in second element.

barbet, n. [1. bárbet; 2. bábit], fr. Lat. *barbātus*; see **barbate**. (lit.) The bearded creature. Specif. **1.** several kinds of tropical birds with short stumpy bill, from the base of which there grow, as it were, bristles. **2.** A kind of hairy French poodle.

barbette, n. [1. barbét; 2. bābét]. Fr. The name prob. given fr. the supposed resemblance of the row of guns mounted on the mound to a fringe of beard. See **barb** (**I.**) & **-ette**. **a** Platform, or mound of earth for mounting guns within a fortress, high enough to allow of the guns being fired over the parapet; **b** circular armoured platform with hood protecting heavy guns in warships.

barbican, n. [1. bárbikan; 2. bábikən]. M.E. *barbecan*, O. Fr. *barbican* &c., 'outwork of a fortress'. Prob. fr. Arab. *bābkhāna*, 'gatehouse', or Pers. *barbar-khānah*, 'house on the wall'. The O. Fr. always has *r* (*bar-*), wh. perhaps makes the latter more probable; origin is, however, uncertain. Outer defences of a city or fortress, such as strongly defended gateway or bridge.

barbicel, n. [1. bárbisĕl; 2. bábisĕl]. Lat. *barbicella*, dimin. of *barba*, 'beard'; see **barbate**. Minute process on the barbule of a bird's feather.

barbiton, n. [1. bárbiton; 2. bábitən]. Gk., prob. a foreign loan-word. An ancient instrument of music like a lyre, having many strings.

barbule, n. [1. bárbūl; 2. bábjūl]. Lat. *barbula*, dimin. of *barba*, 'beard'. See **barbate**. A process along the edge of the barb of a feather, serving to unite the barbs into an unbroken surface.

barcarol(le), n. [1. bárkarōl; 2. bákəroul]. Fr. *barcarolle*, Ital. *barcaruola*, 'boatman's song', fr. *barca*, 'boat', see **bark** (**V.**). Song of Venetian boatmen; any piece in similar rhythm.

bard, n. [1. bard; 2. bād]. Gael. & Ir. *bardh*, *bard*. **1.** A Celtic tribal singer, minstrel, poet, and chronicler; still used for recognized singer at the Welsh musical festival, Eisteddfod. **2.** (archaic and liter.) A poet; *the Bard of Avon*, Shakespeare.

bardic, adj. [1. bárdik; 2. bádik]. Prec. & **-ic**. Belonging to, characteristic of, composed by, a bard; esp. of old lays, *bardic poetry*.

bardolater, n. [1. bardólater; 2. bādólətə]. See **bard** & **idolater**. Worshipper, idolater, enthusiastic, uncritical admirer of the Bard, i.e. Shakespeare.

bardolatry, n. [1. bardólatri; 2. bādólətri]. See prec. & **-latry**. Worship, idolatry, of Shakespeare.

Bardolph, n. [1. bárdolf; 2. bádəlf], fr. name of Shakespeare's character in 'Henry IV.' &c. A red-faced, tippling old rascal.

bare (**I.**), adj. [1. bār; 2. bɛə]. O.E. *bær*, M.E. *bāre*, O.H.G. *bar*. The Gmc. base was perh. *_baz-_, in wh. case the word must be cogn. w. O. Slav. *bosŭ*, & Lith. *basas*, 'barefooted'; these, together w. Armen. *bok*, 'naked' (fr. *_bhos-ko_), go back to Aryan *_bhos-_, *_bhes_, fr. wh. latter form Germ. *ent-behren*, O.H.G. *inberan*, 'to dispense with, go without, lack', are perh. derived. **1.** Naked; devoid of customary or usual covering: *bare feet*, without shoes and stockings; *to have one's head bare*, without a hat; *a bare floor*, without a carpet. Phrs. *the bare boards*, same as *bare floor*; *in one's bare skin*, naked; *to pick a bone, joint, bare*, strip it of all the meat; *to lay bare*, uncover, display; *to lay bare one's inner feelings*, reveal, make known. **2. a** Empty, destitute (of), stripped, bereft (of): *the house was quite bare*; *the larder was bare*, had no food in it; *the room looked very bare*, empty of furniture; **b** in a moral sense: *to be bare of credit*, have a bad or no reputation. **3. a** Just enough; mere, so much and no more, hardly as much as: *a bare majority*; *the bare supposition, idea* &c.; *a bare hundred pounds*; **b** very slightest, lowest possible: *bare(st) possibility, chance*. **4.** Nothing beyond what is mentioned: *to believe a thing on one's bare word*, without further evidence.

bare (**II.**), vb. trans., fr. prec. **a** To make, lay, bare; to uncover: '*This sea that bares her bosom to the moon*' (Wordsworth); specif., *to bare one's head*, take off one's hat; **b** in non-material sense, *to bare one's heart, soul, thoughts* &c., to reveal, confess.

bareback, adj. & adv. [1. bárbak; 2. béəbæk]. **a** adj. (of a horse) Without a saddle; **b** adv. (of manner of riding) without using a saddle: *to ride bareback*.

barebacked, adj. [1. bárbakt; 2. béəbækt]. Prec. & **-ed**. Without a saddle.

barefaced, adj. [1. bárfāst; 2. béəfeist]. Insolent, without shame or concealment, unblushing: *barefaced impudence*.

barefacedly, adv. [1. bárfásedli; 2. béəféisidli]. In a barefaced manner; impudently, shamelessly.

barefacedness, n. [1. bárfásednes; 2. béəféisidnis]. Impudence, shamelessness.

barefoot, adj. & adv. [1. bárfoot; 2. béəfut]. With bare feet, without shoes and stockings: *to be, go, walk, barefoot*.

barefooted, adj. [1. bárfóoted; 2. bɛəfútid]. Prec. & **-ed**. Having bare feet.

bareheaded, adj. & adv. [1. bårhéded; 2. bèəhédid]. Having no covering, hat &c. on the head; without a hat: *a bareheaded mendicant*; *to stand bareheaded.*

barelegged, adj. [1. bårlégd; 2. bèəlégd]. Having the legs bare; generally referring to bareness of knees and part of the calf of the leg, as of children with short skirts or breeches, and low socks, or persons wearing Highland kilt.

barely, adv. [1. bårli; 2. béəli]. **bare** (I.) & **-ly. 1.** In a bare manner; without cover, adornment &c., nakedly. **2.** (rare) Openly, without reserve, explicitly. **3.** Scarcely, only just, merely.

barenecked, adj. [1. bårnékt; 2. bèənékt]. Having the neck bare, or uncovered, of ladies in low dresses.

bareness, n. [1. bårnes; 2. béənis]. **bare** (I.) & **-ness.** State, quality, of being bare.

baresark, adj. & adv. [1. bårsàrk; 2. béəsàk]. See **bare** (I.) & **sark.** Without shirt or coat of mail. Modern form, based on wrong interpretation of **berserker.** Said of ancient Norse warriors, who were supposed, when excited in battle, to strip off part of their armour so as to fight with greater fury and vigour.

bargain (I.), n. [1. bárgin; 2. bágin], M.E. *bargaine, bargein* &c., fr. O. Fr. *bargaigne.* Origin doubtful, but see next word. **1.** Pact or agreement reached, after discussion, between two or more parties, in regard to commercial transaction, buying and selling; agreement so reached concerning affairs generally. Phrs. *to drive a bargain,* carry on negotiations with energy; *make a bargain with,* come to an agreement; *strike a bargain,* conclude an agreement; *a good, bad, bargain,* favourable, unfavourable terms; *a hard bargain,* one in which one party gets rather severe terms; *make the best of a bad bargain,* face misfortune cheerfully; *into the bargain,* (i.) in addition to agreed terms; also by extension, (ii.) besides, also, as *he saved the lady from drowning, and married her into the bargain*; *that's a bargain,* that is settled; *a bargain's a bargain,* we must stick to our agreement. **2.** Something obtained for a small price, esp. below its real value: *to pick up bargains* (at a sale); *the house and grounds would be a bargain at such a price.*

bargain (II.), vb. intrans. O. Fr. *bargainer,* fr. Low Lat. *barcaniāre*; origin doubtful, but perh. fr. *barca,* ('trading) vessel', wh. brings goods to a port, & takes others away. See **bark** (V.) **1.** (*with* a person, *about* a transaction) To haggle, discuss conditions of commercial or other transaction, with a view to buying something at a lower price than that asked, selling at as high a price as possible, or, generally, of getting the most favourable and profitable terms for oneself. **2.** *To bargain for* (gen. with neg.), to expect, be prepared for, be willing to accept or agree to: *I didn't bargain for that, for all this trouble* &c., this was not in the agreement, I didn't expect, cannot consent to undertake it; *more than one bargained for,* an unpleasant surprise.

bargainer, n. [1. bárginer; 2. báginə]. **bargain** (II.) & **-er.** One who bargains.

bargain hunter, n. One on the look out for *bargains* (2), esp. in pictures, old books, old furniture &c.

barge (I.), n. [1. barj; 2. bādž]. Prob. a variant of **bark** (V.), **barque. a** A broad, flat boat, now used for transporting heavy goods on canals and broad rivers, and drawn or towed by horses; formerly a fashionable means of locomotion for passengers, up and down the Thames, when the barge was propelled by rowers; **b** large, ornamented rowing boat, for ceremonial use, usually *state-barge*; **c** college boat-house, or house-boat, at Oxford.

barge (II.), vb. intrans., fr. prec. (colloq.) **a** *Barge about,* of a clumsy, rough person, or a bad rider on a horse, to plunge, or leap about without care or proper control of one's movements and direction; **b** *barge into,* run into, collide with (person or things) in a clumsy, awkward, rough fashion, whether from accident or design.

barge-board, n. Gen. derived fr. *verge-board,* but w. no explanation of change, unknown in Engl. since O.E. period, of *v* to *b.* Possibly the initial of *verge* has been influenced by *b-* in O.E. *beorgan,* M.E. *berȝen* &c., 'to protect'. Thick boarding, generally more or less decorated, which hangs down at right angles from outer edge of a gable, fastened so as to protect the projecting ends of the roof-timbers.

bargee, n. [1. bàrjḗ; 2. bàdžī]. **barge** (I.) & **-ee.** A man who conducts a barge; (by extension) a rough, insolent fellow: *a regular bargee*; Phr. *to swear like a bargee,* with copiousness, force, and variety.

baritone. See **barytone.**

barium, n. [1. bárium; 2. béəriəm], fr. Gk. *barús,* 'heavy', see **baro-.** (chem.) Silver-white or pale yellow metallic element of alkaline group, found in barytes.

bark (I.), n. [1. bark; 2. bāk]. Scand. Cp. Dan. & Swed. *bark*; perh. cogn. w. O.E. *beorc,* 'birch tree', q.v. under **birch. 1.** Outer covering or rind of trees, which envelops trunk, boughs &c. down to smallest branches and twigs. **2.** Special kind of bark, used medicinally, esp. that of a Peruvian tree, cinchona, called also *Peruvian,* and *Jesuits' bark.*

bark (II.), vb. trans., fr. prec. **1.** To remove or strip bark from (a tree). **2.** (colloq.) To take the skin off: *to bark one's shins, elbows* &c.

bark (III.), vb. intrans. O.E. *beorcan,* O.N. *berkja,* 'bark', as a dog. The base is not found in the other Gmc. languages. The O.E. vb. is strong, & has forms *beorc-, bearc, burc-,* (*borc-*). These would represent Aryan **bherg-,* **bhorg-,* **bhr̥g-* respectively. If we might assume an orig. base **bhereg-,* it might be possible to connect *beorcan* w. Lat. *fragor,* 'crash, noise, din'. This word is, however, gen. derived fr. **sphrag-,* & compared w. Gk. *spharágos,* 'noise'. See under **speak. 1.** Of certain animals, esp. dog, fox &c., to utter the cry natural and peculiar to them. **2. a** To make a noise resembling dog's bark, esp. to cough loudly; also of a revolver, to explode noisily.

bark (IV.), n., fr. prec. The noise, or cry, made by dog or fox. Phr. *his bark is worse than his bite,* of an ill-tempered, scolding person who is not actively harmful.

bark (V.), also **barque**, n. Fr. *barque,* Ital. *barca.* **1.** A particular kind of three- or four-masted sailing-ship, with the fore-mast and main-mast square-rigged, and mizzen with fore-and-aft rig. **2.** (poet.) Any kind of boat.

bark-bound, adj. Of a tree, stunted in its growth by reason of the bark not expanding properly, and kept small and thin within a hard tight bark.

barkentine, barquentine, n. [1. bárkentēn; 2. bákəntīn]. See **bark** (V.). Three-masted sailing-vessel with square-rigged fore-mast, and two after-masts fore-and-aft rigged.

barker, n. [1. bárker; 2. bákə]. **bark** (III.) & **-er.** One who, that which, barks, esp. (colloq.) a revolver.

barking (I.), n. [1. bárking; 2. bákiŋ]. **bark** (III.) & **-ing.** Sound made by a dog when it barks.

barking (II.), adj., fr. Pres. Part. of **bark** (III.). Given to uttering noisy barks: *a barking dog is a great nuisance.*

barley, n. [1. bárli; 2. báli]. O.E. *bere,* also *bærlīc,* prob. 'barley-like'. This base is found in O.N. *barr,* 'grain', & Goth. *bariz-eins,* adj., 'made of barley'. Outside Gmc., we have O. Slav. *braš-ĭno,* 'food', Russ. *borošno,* 'rye-meal'; Lat. *far,* genit. *farris,* fr. **fars-,* 'grain, spelt', also *farīna,* 'meal', fr. earlier **farrīna* fr. **farsīna,* see **farina.** The Aryan base was **bhors-,* & must have referred orig. to some kind of wild cereal, whose name was transferred among the various Aryan tribes to different species wh. they severally first cultivated. A cereal plant, *Hordeum vulgare,* and the grain derived from it, esp. used for malt in brewing and distilling; *pot barley,* grain of barley with the hard outer husk peeled off; *pearl barley,* the white inner kernel.

barley-brake, -break, n. Rural game in which one person chases a number of others, who 'break', or disperse, when pursued.

barleycorn, n. [1. bárlikorn; 2. bálikōn]. **1. a** A grain of barley; **b** an old measure, the third of an inch, based on approximate length of a grain of barley. **2.** *John Barleycorn,* name given to whisky, or other malt liquor; from personification of the grain.

barley-sugar, n. Transparent sweetmeat made from pure sugar, generally flavoured with lemon.

barley-water, n. A drink for invalids made from pearl barley, which is boiled in water and strained off, leaving a clear or translucent liquid.

barm, n. [1. barm; 2. bām]. O.E. *beorma,* M.E. *berme,* L.G. *barme,* Germ. *bärme,* 'yeast', cogn. w. Lat. *fermentum,* 'leaven, yeast' (cp. **ferment**), wh. perh. comes fr. **fervimentum,* & is related to Lat. *fervēre,* 'boil, glow', & older *fervere* w. same meaning, also to *fretum,* 'heat, violence'. The above Lat. words are not connected w. Lat. *formus,* 'hot', q.v. under **warm.** The orig. meaning of the Aryan base **bherew-* is 'boil, bubble (with heat)', & other cognates are Ir. *brennim,* 'bubble, spout forth'; remoter relations are Goth. *brinnan,* 'burn', & the various words in Gmc. languages connected therewith. See these under **burn** (I.). Yeast, leaven, which are now the more usual words, except provincially.

barmaid, n. [1. bármād; 2. bámeid]. See **bar** (I.) & **maid.** Woman or girl who serves customers in a bar where liquors are sold, chiefly in hotel or public-house.

barm brack, n. [1. bárm brák; 2. bām bræk]. A kind of cake or scone made with yeast, chiefly used in Ireland.

Barmecide, adj. [1. bármesīd; 2. bámisaid], fr. name of giver of such a feast in the *Arabian Nights.* Only in Phr. *Barmecide feast,* an apparently luxurious but in reality disappointing, miserable feast or entertainment.

barmy, adj. [1. bármi; 2. bámi]. **barm** & **-y.** Frothy, like barm; (fig.) light-headed, silly. (In this sense often confused with, and written, *balmy.*) (colloq. and vulg.) *Barmy on the crumpet,* light-headed, touched in the head, mad; *to go barmy,* become foolish or mad.

barn, n. [1. barn; 2. bān]. O.E. *bærn, bern,* fr. *bere,* 'barley' (see **barley**), & *ærn,* 'house, receptacle'. The older form of the latter is *ræn-, ren-,* wh. survives in a few compounds in O.E. It is possible that the word is cogn. w. Goth. *razn,* 'house', O.N. *rann,* wh., it is suggested, are cogn. w. Goth. *rasta,* O.E. *ræsta,* 'place of rest'; see **rest.** Building for storage of grain or hay, and other produce of a farm.

barnacle (I.), n. [1. bárnakl; 2. bánəkl]. M.E. *bernakile, bernacle* &c., 'a kind of bit for a horse', O. Fr. *bernac, bernicle(s)*; etymol. unknown. **1. a** Formerly a species of pincers used as an instrument of torture; **b** an instrument (also called *twitch*) put on a horse's nose to hold him by, and keep him quiet when being shod or clipped. **2.** (her.) Representation of the pincers, displayed upon a shield. **3.** Since 16th cent. (in pl.) spectacles, in allusion to the instrument put on a horse's nose (**1. b** above).

barnacle (II.), n. M.E. *bernak, barnakille* &c., a kind of wild goose, popularly supposed to come fr. the shellfish of this name. It is suggested that the origin of the name of the crustacean may be Gael. *bairneach,* 'limpet'. The name was then transferred to the bird. Cp. Fr. *barnache* & *bernacle,* wh. are applied both to the goose & to the shellfish. **1.** The word in English is now used more particularly of those shellfish which remain permanently attached to rocks, the bottoms of ships, also to piers and masonry which are regularly covered by the sea at each tide. **2.** (fig.) Person who adheres closely and refuses to be moved, esp. from a post or office &c.

barnacle goose, also **bernicle**, n. See prec. Goose found in Northern Europe, allied to the brant-goose.

barn dance, n. A kind of dance resembling a schottische, of rustic origin, of the kind which was in vogue among country folk using a barn as a ball-room.

barn-door, n. Large double doors, big enough to admit loaded waggon and horse, which give entrance to a barn. Phrs. *as big as a barn-door*, very big and broad; *not to be able to hit a barn-door* (in shooting), to be a very bad shot.

barn-door fowl, n. Common domestic, farm-yard fowl.

barn-owl, n. Large brown and grey owl which frequents uninhabited buildings, such as barns, church towers &c.

barn-stormer, n. See **storm (II.)**. Strolling actor who plays in buildings such as barns where a theatre is not available; the implication of the name is that such an actor delights and takes by storm the simple, rustic audience in a barn, but would not impress more experienced hearers; hence, an inferior actor.

barn-storming, n. The practice or profession of performing as a strolling player.

baro-, pref., fr. Gk. *báros*, 'weight', cp. *barús*, 'heavy', fr. Aryan *$*g^{w}$ǝro-* &c., fr. wh. base comes also Lat. *gravis*, 'heavy'; see **grave (IV.)** & **gravid**. Used in words of scientific origin, expressing idea of atmospheric pressure.

barograph, n. [1. bárograhf; 2. bǽrǝgrāf]. Prec. & **-graph**. A recording barometer which traces, on a revolving cylinder, by means of a style attached to a lever connected with the quicksilver which forms the barometer, a line showing the effects upon the latter, of the varying pressure of the atmosphere during a given period of time.

barology, n. [1. baróloji; 2. bærɔ́lǝdži]. See **baro- & -logy**. Science of weight or gravity.

barometer, n. [1. barómeter; 2. bǝrɔ́mitǝ]. See **baro- & -meter**. Instrument for measuring the degree of pressure of the atmosphere by means of quicksilver enclosed in a glass tube.

barometric(al), adj. [1. bàrométrik(l); 2. bærǝmétrik(l)]. See prec. & **-metric**, & **-al**. Pertaining to, measured by, a barometer: *barometric pressure* &c.

barometrically, adv. Prec. & **-ly**. By means of a barometer.

baron, n. [1. bárun; 2. bǽrǝn]. O. Fr. *barun*, orig. acc. of *ber(s)*, 'man, hero, warrior', also 'baron' in feudal sense. The etymol. of the word is much disputed. Med. Lat. *baro, barōnis* &c. is certainly the starting-point of the O. Fr. form. The problem is whether this is derived fr. Lat. *bāro*, 'fool, blockhead', or borrowed fr. a Gmc. word seen in O.H.G. *baro*, 'man, free man', therefore one competent to render military service to the king. In this case we may cp. O.N. *berja*, 'strike', & esp. (reflex.) *berja-sk*, 'fight' (cp. Germ. *sich schlagen* & Fr. *se battre*). With this base there is a large number of cognates outside Gmc.; Lat. *ferīre*, 'strike, smite, thrust', O. Slav. *borja*, 'I strive, fight', Czech. *boriti*, 'destroy', Lith. *bariù*, 'I strive in words, quarrel', Ir. *berraim*, 'I cleave, cut'. With all these Gk. *phárō*, 'cleave, divide' &c. is also cogn. The etymol. fr. older Lat. *bāro*, 'fool', may be dismissed as improbable on many grounds, & that fr. O.H.G. *baro*, 'fighting man' may be accepted. The cognates given above show that the fundamental idea connected w. *baron* is 'a warrior', one who strikes, fights, cleaves his way through his enemies. The original meaning of *baron* in feudal times was one of a class of tenants holding his lands by military service from the king, or other superior lord. The term was soon restricted to king's barons who were summoned by writ to the council. The practice grew up that those once summoned had a right to attend, and the honour and privilege became hereditary. Present-day usage: 1. Lowest rank in hereditary peerage; used only in stating a man's rank: *he is a baron*, i.e. not of higher rank; also in enumerating a man's titles, and in legal descriptions: *Baron X of Y*. A baron is addressed and spoken of as *Lord X*, never as *Baron X*, except only in the case of foreign titles. See however **baroness**. 2. A judge of the Court of the Exchequer was called a *Baron of the Exchequer*; he was spoken of and addressed as *Baron X*. The office and title are now abolished. 3. A foreign nobleman: *a German, Dutch, baron* &c. 4. (law) Man, husband; contrasted with *feme*, woman, wife. 5. *Baron of beef*, a double sirloin of beef.

baronage, n. [1. bárunij; 2. bǽrǝnidž]. Prec. & **-age**. a The body of peers (strictly only *the barons*) of the realm; b a book which gives a list of these.

baroness, n. [1. bárunes; 2. bǽrǝnis]. **baron & -ess**. 1. a Wife of a baron; b lady who has inherited a barony, or who has had this honour conferred upon her personally. The word is never used as a title for English women, apart from official or legal descriptions, and in enumerations of peeresses, except in cases which come under b. 2. Foreign lady who is the wife or daughter of a baron; in these cases the word is used as a mode of address, and as title prefixed to the name.

baronet (I.), n. [1. bárunet; 2. bǽrǝnit]. **baron** & dimin. suff. **-et**. A person holding lowest hereditary English title. This title and status were created by James I. in 1611, as a means of raising money. Landholders and others of sufficient wealth and antiquity could obtain the rank on payment of £1000. Baronets are addressed, like knights, as *Sir John* &c., according to their Christian name, and their style is *Sir X. Y., Bart.*; their wives are officially styled *Dame Margaret G.* &c. or simply *Lady G.*

baronet (II.), vb. trans. To raise to rank of baronet, esp. in P.P. *baronetted*, made a baronet.

baronetage, n. [1. bárunetij; 2. bǽrǝnǝtidž]. **baronet & -age**. a Whole body of baronets; b book containing list of these.

baronetcy, n. [1. bárunetsi; 2. bǽrǝnǝtsi]. **baronet & -cy**. Rank and status of baronet: *to confer a baronetcy upon.*

baronial, adj. [1. barṓnial; 2. bærόuniǝl]. **baron & -ial**. 1. Belonging to the condition of *baron*: *baronial rank* &c. 2. Splendid, stately, spacious, ample, as befitting a baron or important person: *baronial splendour, magnificence* &c. 3. (archit.) Often slightly derisive, of a style of building found in some large, modern houses which exhibits a wealth of turrets and castellated parapets &c.: *the Scots baronial style of architecture.*

barony, n. [1. báruni; 2. bǽrǝni]. M.E. *baronie*, fr. O. Fr.; **baron & -y**. 1. The domain of a baron: *bishops sat in the House of Lords originally as representing their baronies.* 2. Status, rank, of baron: *he gained his barony for his service in the Great War.* 3. An old division of an Irish county, corresponding to the English *hundred.*

baroque, adj. [1. barók; 2. bǝrɔ́k]. Fr., as adj., *une perle baroque*, Ital. *barocco*, Port. *barrocco*, orig. 'irregularly shaped pearl'; etymol. doubtful. 1. Grotesque, queer, fantastical; applied to architecture, often equivalent to *rococo*, q.v.; (of taste) corrupt, bizarre &c. 2. As noun, *the baroque*, baroque style, taste &c.

baroscope, n. [1. bároskōp; 2. bǽrǝskòup]. **baro- & -scope**. Instrument which shows the changes of pressure in the atmosphere.

barouche, n. [1. barṓōsh; 2. bærúʃ], fr. Germ. *barutsche*, fr. Ital. *baroccio*, earlier *biroccio*, L. Lat. *birrotium*, 'two-wheeled chariot', Lat. *birotus* for **bis-rotus*, adj., 'two-wheeled'. See **bi- & rota**. A style of carriage now obsolete, having four wheels, a seat or box for driver, two double seats inside, and a flexible folding hood behind; it was drawn usually by two horses.

barque, barquentine, n. See **bark (V.)**, **barkentine**.

barrack (I.), n. [1. bárak; 2. bǽrǝk], fr. Fr. *baraque*, 'wooden hut or shed', Ital. *baracca* &c.; perh. related to **bar**, in sense of a temporary shelter put together fr. boards & strengthened by stronger pieces of wood. 1. (usually pl.) *Barracks*, a set of buildings, or a single large building, for housing a military garrison. These buildings are usually rather plain and devoid of architectural beauty. Hence, 2. a large rambling, ugly house: *a regular barrack of a place.*

barrack (II.), vb. trans., fr. prec. 1. To quarter (troops) in barracks. 2. (Australian cricket slang, of crowd of spectators) To utter cries of derision at, cheer derisively at, in order to upset, opposing players.

barracuda, barracouta, n. [1. bàrakṓōda, -kṓōta; 2. bærǝkúdǝ, -kútǝ]. Span., prob. fr. native name. A large, voracious, edible sea-fish, of the Caribbean Sea.

barrage, n. [1. bárahzh; 2. bǽrāž]. Fr., orig. a series or system of bars; see **bar**. 1. (engin.) Artificial obstruction placed in a river or watercourse to direct the stream, or cause increase of depth. 2. (mil.) During the Great War *barrage* was used for a curtain of artillery fire concentrated upon a part of the enemy's line, or upon an area between this and the Allies' lines for the purpose of preventing the enemy leaving his trenches to attack; a *barrage* was also concentrated just ahead of our troops when they went forward to attack, and so adjusted that it more or less conformed to their movements, *creeping barrage*. Phr. *to lift the barrage*, lengthen the range of a barrage.

barrator, n. [1. báratur; 2. bǽrǝtǝ]. M.E. *baratour*, 'rioter, quarrelsome person', O. Fr. *barateor*, 'swindler'. See **barter**. One guilty of the crime of barratry.

barratrous, adj. [1. báratrus; 2. bǽrǝtrǝs]. See next word & **-ous**. (law) a Of persons, inclined to; b of conduct, savouring of, tending to, barratry.

barratry, n. [1. báratri; 2. bǽrǝtri]. O. Fr. *barrater*, 'to deceive'. See **barter & -ry**. (law) 1. (marine) Fraudulent or negligent breach of duty on part of master and crew of a ship whereby the interests of the owners are endangered. 2. (gen.) Incitement to, or encouragement of, litigation and quarrels.

barrel (I.), n. [1. bárel; 2. bǽrǝl]. M.E. *barel*, fr. O. Fr. *bareil* &c.; origin doubtful, but perh. connected w. **bar**. 1. Cylindrical vessel or cask made of shaped wooden boards or staves, bound round each end and the middle by iron hoops, with flat boards shaped so as to close either end. Barrels are so made as to bulge in the middle and become smaller top and bottom. 2. a The contents of a barrel, esp. of beer or cider; also *barrel of pork, herrings, oysters*; b liquors are often measured by the barrel, which may be of varying sizes, usually to contain 36, 18, or 9 gallons. 3. a Metal tube of gun, rifle, revolver &c. through which projectile passes; b revolving cylinder in a watch &c. 4. The body (excluding head and legs) of a horse or cow: *not enough barrel*, too slight in the body.

barrel (II.), vb. trans., fr. prec. To put (liquor) &c. in barrels.

barrelled, adj. [1. báreld; 2. bǽrǝld]. P.P. of prec. 1. Provided with a *barrel*; a of guns &c., chiefly in compounds: *double-, single-barrelled*; b of horses &c., *well barrelled*, with big girth of body. 2. Put in barrels, as liquor &c.

barrel-organ, n. Instrument for producing music by means of a revolving cylinder turned by a handle, studded with pegs, which act upon vibrating tongues of metal; chiefly used as a means of obtaining money in the street.

barrel-vault, n. A vault, which presents a uniform concave surface throughout its whole length.

barren, adj. [1. báren; 2. bǽrǝn]. M.E. *barain*, fr. O. Fr. *brehaigne, baraigne*; origin obscure. 1. (of women) Sterile, incapable of bearing children. 2. (of plants and trees) Unproductive of seed or fruit; unprolific. 3. (of land, soil) Poor, unproductive, not yielding crops; as n. pl., *barrens*, tract of barren country. 4. a (of persons and their mental faculties) Unproductive, arid, jejune; lacking creative power and initiative; b (of intellectual or literary output) devoid of spirit, interest, fire, or life; arid, dreary. 5. Devoid of, lacking: *barren of ideas, of interest, charm* &c.

barrenness, n. [1. bárennes; 2. bǽrənnis]. Prec. & **-ness**. Condition of being barren.

barricade, n. & vb. trans. [1. bàrikád; 2. bæ̀ri-kéid]. Fr., fr. Ital. *barricata*, or Span. *barricada*, 'a barring up'. Perh. fr. Span. *barrica*, 'cask', or fr. Low Lat. *barra*, 'bar', & **-ade**. 1. n. A defence, or obstruction, esp. across a street, hastily built of trees, earth, rough timber &c. 2. vb. To close, surround, protect, with a barricade.

barrier, n. [1. bárier; 2. bǽriə]. M.E. *barrere*, Fr. *barrière*, 'obstacle', derived fr. *barre* &c. See **bar (I.)** & **-ier**. 1. a An obstacle of any kind; anything which separates from, or prevents access to, anything; b a structure erected to keep the public away from certain parts of a building, e.g. a railway station; or from the roadway when a public procession is passing &c. 2. Non-material obstacle, hindrance, bar, impediment: *barrier to progress, education* &c.; *barrier to one's affection* &c.; *the barriers of class or caste.*

barrister, n. [1. bárister; 2. bǽristə], fr. O. Fr. *barre*, see **bar (I.)**, & **-ster**. Qualified member of that branch of the legal profession whose province is to plead in court as an advocate, or counsel; a member of the Bar; full form is *barrister-at-law.*

barrow (I.), n. [1. bárō; 2. bǽrou]. O.E. *bearwe*, M.E. *barewe*, 'barrow'; prob. derived fr. *bær-*, a form of base 'to bear'. See **bear (I.)**, **bier** &c. A small hand-cart, generally with one or not more than two wheels, provided with handles to push it by, for conveying articles too bulky or heavy to be carried; also *hand-, wheel-barrow.*

barrow (II.), n. O.E. *beorg*, 'hill, (burial) mound', M.E. *berewe, barewe*; cp. O.H.G. *berg*, 'hill', Goth. *bairg-ahei*, 'mountain', O.N. *bjarg*, 'rock'. Outside Gmc. the cognates are Scrt. *bṛhant-*, 'high', & O. Slav. *brěgŭ*, 'shore, bank'. The fundamental meaning is 'something piled up, a heap'. See further under **borough** & **bury**. Mound, tumulus, esp. of ancient burial mounds: *long barrows*, of Neolithic age; *round barrows*, of Bronze age.

barrulet, n. [1. bárūlet; 2. bǽrjulit]. Low Lat. *barrula*, dimin. of *barra*, see **bar**, & **-et**. (her.) Small bar, one-fourth the width of a bar.

barruly, adj. [1. bárūli; 2. bǽrjuli]. (her., of the field) Traversed by barrulets.

barry, adj. [1. bári; 2. bǽri]. Fr. *barré*, 'barred'. See **bar (I.)**. (her.) Traversed horizontally by an even number of *bars.*

barry-bendy, adj. See prec. & **bendy**. (her., of the field) Divided by *bars* and *bends* with colours alternate.

barry-nebuly, adj. **barry** & **nebuly**. (her.) Barry with wavy lines.

barry-pily, adj. **barry** & **pily**. (her.) Traversed by piles arranged barry.

barse, n. [1. bars; 2. bās]. O.E. *bærs*, 'perch', prob. fr. the same base as **bristle**. Cp. also **bass (III.)**. Common perch.

bars-gemels, n. [1. bárz jémelz; 2. bā́z džéməlz]. See **bar** & **gemel**. (her.) Barrulets arranged in pairs; double bars.

bar-shot, n. Double shot, or two shots linked by a bar; formerly used in naval warfare to cut enemy's masts and rigging.

barter (I.), vb. intrans. & trans. [1. bárter; 2. bā́tə]. M.E. *bartren* &c., O. Fr. *barater*, 'to cheat'. Origin doubtful; cp. O. Ir. *brath*, 'treachery'. 1. intrans. The original sense of cheating over a bargain has passed away, though a certain unfavourable shade of meaning still lingers; to haggle over a transaction, to traffic. 2. trans. To exchange: *to barter one thing for, against, another*; *barter away*, sell at too low a price; (chiefly fig.) of *freedom, position, honour* &c., to part with these for an illusory advantage.

barter (II.), n., fr. prec. Exchange, traffic in, goods, usually without intervention of money; often *exchange and barter.*

Bartholomew Fair, n. [1. barthólomū fár; 2. bāþóləmjū féə]. Great annual fair beginning on St. Bartholomew's Day, Aug. 24th.

bartisan, n. [1. bàrtizán; 2. bā̀tizǽn]. Introduced by Sir Walter Scott, apparently from a popular 17th-cent. Scottish spelling *bertisene*, for **bratticing**. Small tower or turret projecting from a larger tower or from battlements.

barton, n. [1. bártun; 2. bā́t(ə)n]. O.E. *beretūn*, 'threshing floor, barn', lit. 'barley enclosure', M.E. *bertun* &c. See **barley** & **town**, & cp. **barn**. A *barton* was a barn, or group of barns, in which the grain from the farms of a manor was collected. The word is common in place names all over England, and still used provincially for 'barn'.

bar tracery, n. **bar** & **tracery**. (archit.) Ornamental window tracery, the patterns of which are formed by the intersections and curves of the mullions.

baruria, n. [1. baróōria; 2. bærúriə]. Gk. *barús*, 'heavy', see **bary-**, & *oûron*, 'urine', see **urine**. Pathological condition in which the urine shows an abnormal specific gravity, as in diabetes.

bary-, pref., 'heavy', Gk. *barús*, 'heavy'. See **baro-**.

barycentre, n. [1. bárisenter; 2. bǽrisɛntə]. See prec. & **central**. Centre of gravity.

barycentric, adj. [1. bàriséntrik; 2. bæ̀ri-séntrik]. Prec. & **-ic**. Belonging to the centre of gravity.

baryta, n. [1. baríta; 2. bærái tə]. Modern formation. See **bary-** & **barium**. (chem.) Barium monoxide.

barytic, adj. [1. barítik; 2. bæráitik]. Prec. & **-ic**. Connected with baryta.

barytone, baritone, adj. & n. [1. báritōn; 2. bǽritoun]. The Ital. spelling w. *-i-* is usually now commoner in the musical sense. Gk. *barútonos*, 'heavy, low-toned'. See **bary-** & **tone**. 1. adj. (of the human voice) Between bass and tenor, and partaking of some of the quality of each. 2. n. a A baritone voice; b singer possessing such a voice. 3. (Gk. gram.) A word not having an accent marked on final syllable, the grave accent being understood.

basal, adj. [1. básal; 2. béisl], fr. **base** & **-al**. Relating to, situated at, the base. Esp. common in fig. uses, fundamental, at the bottom of, therefore that on which the whole (argument &c.) is built, or from which it proceeds; hence, fundamentally important: *a basal argument, principle, condition* &c.

basally, adv. Prec. & **-ly**. In a basal, fundamental, manner; from the bottom; altogether: *basally wrong, unsound* &c.

basalt, n. [1. básawlt, basáwlt; 2. bǽsɔlt, bəsɔ́lt]. Lat. *basaltes*, African word, 'a hard, dark marble found in parts of Africa'. 1. (geol.) Any dark-coloured rock of volcanic origin; the columns of rock in the Giant's Causeway (Ireland) are of this character. 2. A black kind of porcelain, made by Wedgwood.

basaltic, adj. [1. basáwltik; 2. bəsɔ́ltik]. Prec. & **-ic**. Of the nature of basalt.

bascule, n. [1. báskūl; 2. bǽskjūl]. Fr., 'seesaw'. Origin doubtful. Apparatus in which one end rises when weight or pressure is put upon the other, on the principle of the seesaw; esp. *bascule bridge*, a kind of drawbridge, raised and lowered by a system of weights and balances, e.g. the Tower Bridge, London.

base (I.), n. [1. bās; 2. beis]. Fr. *base*, fr. Lat. *basis*, 'a stepping; pedestal, foot, base, foundation', fr. Gk. *básis*, 'step, walk, that on which one steps, ground, a pedestal'. The word is related to Gk. *bainō*, 'come, go, walk, step', wh. goes back to earlier **ban-jō*, Aryan **gʷ(ə)m̥jō*, as *básis* to earlier **bátis*, fr. Aryan **gʷm̥tis*; cp. Scrt. *gáti-*, 'going', wh. is the exact cogn., as is also Goth. *ga-qumþs*, 'coming together'. See further under **come**, & cp. **basis**. 1. Bottom; fundamental, lowest, part of anything, that upon which it rests; pediment, foot, support, foundation: *base of a mountain, pillar, building*. 2. (archit.) Lowest part, pediment of a column considered as a separate feature, or design, complete in itself, and having an independent design. 3. (chem.) A substance which combines with and neutralizes an acid, forming a salt; in general, an oxide. 4. Substance used as a mordant in dyeing. 5. (her.) The lower part of the field. 6. (mil.) The place or area from which the units of an army advance, from which it derives its reinforcements and supplies of all kinds, and from which the communications lead to the various sections of the force as they proceed towards their objectives. 7. Starting-point or goal in several ball games, e.g. *baseball*. 8. (philol.) A theoretical result of the last analysis of a word; that which is left when the various suffixes and prefixes have been stripped off; that common element which is recognizable in a group of cognate words; formerly called the root.

base (II.), vb. trans., fr. prec. To build, place, found, rest, anything upon something else as a foundation or support; use as point of departure; chiefly in fig. use: *to base one's hopes upon*; *base one's inferences, arguments, conclusions, upon facts.*

base (III.), adj. M.E. *bās*, O. Fr. *bas*, 'low', Lat. *bassus*, only as cognomen, Low Lat. w. sense of 'thick, stumpy', perh. borrowed fr. Gk. *pássōn*, compar. of *pakhús*, 'thick, stout, coarse'. The connexion of the latter w. Lat. *pinguis*, 'fat, plump', see **pinguid**, is now disputed. 1. (of persons) a Low, low-born, mean; b having low motives and a vicious character. 2. (of action, conduct, thoughts, motives) Unworthy, mean, sordid, reverse of lofty; dishonourable, wicked. 3. (metal.) *Base metal*, metal of inferior value, i.e. not gold or silver. 4. (of language) Not classical; impure, debased: *base Latin* &c.

baseball, n. [1. básbawl; 2 béisbɔl]. Chief national game of U.S.A., somewhat resembling rounders highly elaborated and developed; played with a hard ball, four bases, and nine players on each side.

base-born, adj. 1. Of low, mean, humble, birth. 2. Of illegitimate birth.

basely, adv. [1. básli; 2. béisli]. **base (III.)** & **-ly**. In a base manner, esp. in moral senses.

basement, n. [1. básment; 2. béismənt]. **base (I.)** & **-ment**. That part of a house which is below the ground; rooms, cellars &c. constructed in the foundations, often having windows looking into a sunk, open area or yard, lighted from above.

baseness, n. [1. básnes; 2. béisnis]. **base (III.)** & **-ness**. The quality or condition of being base, chiefly of moral qualities; meanness, unworthiness, wickedness of character and conduct.

bash, vb. trans. [1. bash; 2. bæʃ]. Origin doubtful, but cp. Dan. *baske*, 'beat'. The form of the word has perh. been influenced by *smash*. (colloq.) To strike violently; to hit or beat (a person) brutally and roughly, to thrash: *to bash one's head against a tree*; *to bash a person on the head.*

bashaw, n. [1. basháw; 2. bæʃɔ́]. Variant of **pasha**. (archaic) Sometimes applied disrespectfully to an official who takes himself and his functions too seriously, and attempts to hector.

bashful, adj. [1. báshfool; 2. bǽʃful], fr. M.E. *bash*, 'to strike with confusion', see **abash**, & **-ful**. Timid, shy, retiring, modest, coy; inclined to shun social prominence; backward in asserting or claiming one's rights.

bashfully, adv. Prec. & **-ly**. In a bashful manner, shyly, timidly.

bashfulness, n. See prec. & **-ness**. Timidity, shyness, coyness; reluctance to assert oneself.

bashi-bazouk, n. [1. báshi bazóok; 2. bǽʃi bəzúk]. Turk. A Turkish irregular soldier.

basic, adj. [1. básik; 2. béisik], fr. **base** (I.) & **-ic**. **1.** Pertaining to, at, the base of; fundamental; esp. of non-material things: *basic principles.* **2.** (chem. &c.) Having the properties of a base or an excess of base or fundamental constituents, esp. of a process of steel manufacture in which the furnace is lined with lime and magnesia which combine with and remove the phosphorus from the iron, forming phosphates, 'basic slag'.

basic slag, n. Agricultural fertilizer made from a by-product of steel manufacture. See prec. under **2**.

basil (I.), n. [1. bázil; 2. bǽzil]. O. Fr. *basile*, Lat. *basilisca*, 'plant, supposed antidote to basilisk's bite', Gk. *basilískos*, 'kind of serpent, basilisk'. Cp. **basilisk**. One of a group of aromatic plants of the mint family.

basil (II.), n. Corrupt form of earlier & obs. *basan*, fr. O. Fr. *basane*, fr. Arab. *bizanah*, 'lining'. Sheepskin tanned with oak or other bark.

basilic, adj. [1. basílik; 2. bəsílik]. Fr. *basilique*. See **basilica**. **a** Belonging to a basilica q.v.; **b** (anat.) *basilic vein*, an important vein of the upper arm running from elbow to armpit.

basilica, n. [1. basílika; 2. bəsílikə]. Lat., 'public hall with aisles and colonnades', for administration of justice, or other business, fr. Gk. *basiliké* (*stoá*), lit. 'royal cloister, or roofed colonnade', fr. *basileús*, 'king'. See next word. **1.** The Roman basilicas were later often converted into churches, and the ground plan of these buildings was generally followed in the early churches which were built as such. The *basilica* was a long oblong hall, with rows of columns down the aisles, and divided into the *atrium* or entrance chamber, the *nave*, and the *apse* or semicircular projecting chamber at the end farthest from the entrance. **2.** Name given by the Pope to several churches in Rome as a title of honour. **3.** A church built on the plan of the old *basilica*.

basilisk, n. [1. bázilisk; 2. bǽzilisk], fr. Lat. *basiliscus*, 'a kind of lizard', fr. Gk. *basilískos*, 'little king', dimin. of *basileús*, 'king'; name given to a kind of serpent & to the golden-crested wren. The Gk. word for king, orig. 'leader in battle', is derived fr. *basi-*, 'one who goes before, leads', cp. **base** (I.), & *lāós*, 'people, host, army', etymol. unknown. For the development of meaning, cp. **duke**, & the O.E. *heretoga*, 'army leader', Mod. Germ. *herzog*, 'duke', usually a reigning duke. **1.** A fabulous creature of the African desert whose glance and breath were supposed fatal. **2.** A species of lizard with an erectile crest down the middle of the back. **3.** Antiquated form of cannon ornamented with devices of serpents.

basin, n. [1. básn, básin; 2. béisn, béisin]. O. Fr. *bacin*, Low Lat. *bachinon*, referred to by Gregory of Tours as a rustic word. The origin of this is obscure. **1.** A hollow vessel or receptacle, of porcelain, earthenware, metal &c., usually shallow for its girth, with curving or sloping sides, for containing water for washing or any other purpose, or milk in dairies from which cream is to be skimmed. **2.** Contents of a basin: *basin of water.* **3.** Hollow space, natural or artificial, containing water, e.g. a bathing-pool, deep part of a harbour &c. **4.** Tract of country drained by a river: *a river basin*; *the Thames basin.* **5.** (anat.) Cavity of the pelvis.

basinet, basnet, n. [1. básinet, básnet; 2. bǽsinɛt, bǽsnɛt]. M.E. & O. Fr. *bacinet* &c. Dimin. of **basin**. See **-et**. Light steel helmet, originally open in front and worn under heavier battle-helmet; later made with visor.

basis, n. [1. básis; 2. béisis]. Direct fr. Gk. *básis*, 'going', whence 'that upon which one walks', &c. See **base** (I.). That upon which anything rests; ground-work, foundation; **a** (in material sense) *the physical basis of life*; **b** (in non-material sense) *the basis of religion, morals, of an argument.*

bask, vb. intrans. & reflex. [1. bahsk; 2. bāsk]. M.E. *baske* (rare), fr. O.N. *baða-sk*, reflex., lit. 'to bathe oneself'; *baða* is cogn. w. **bathe**; *-sk* is for O.N. *sik*, reflex. pron.; cp. Mod. Germ. *sich*. **1.** To steep, immerse, oneself in with enjoyment, to luxuriate in, expose oneself with delight to : *to bask in the sun, in the heat, in the sunlight* &c.; (also absolutely) *I want merely to bask on a day like this.* **2.** (of moral enjoyment) To be favoured with, to experience and take delight in: *to bask in a lady's smiles, in the patronage, favour, of the great, in the smiles of Fortune.*

basket, n. [1. báhsket; 2. báskit]. M.E. *bascate, baskete*. Prob. dimin. of O. Fr. *basche*, 'basket'. This is apparently fr. a Lat. word *bascauda*, found in Juvenal, & said to mean a brazen vessel. This word is supposed to be of Gaulish or British (Celt.) origin. The transference of meaning of the word in Fr. fr. a brazen receptacle to one of a totally different material is by no means improbable. The Celt. *bascauda* may well be cogn. w. Lat. *fascia*, 'band, girth, fillet' &c., & *fascis*, 'bundle', as suggested by Walde. *Bascauda* may have been primarily a vessel bound w. hoops, wh. might apply equally either to one made of metal or of wicker. *Fascis* &c., are cogn. w. Ir. *basc*, 'neckband', & prob. w. O.E. *bast*, 'inner bark of a tree', present-day **bast**. A basket wd. seem to be orig. a receptacle bound or twisted together, or simply one w. hoops. The W. *basged* is borrowed fr. Engl. **1.** A receptacle made of withies, cane, rushes, grass, or other flexible material, plaited and twisted into a frame of stiffer rods, and often strengthened by being bound round the top, middle, and bottom by twisted bands through which the uprights of the frame and the flexible materials of the main fabric pass. **2.** By extension, a receptacle of metal or other material, somewhat resembling a basket in general structure, e.g. a receptacle of iron bars for holding coal or logs in a fireplace: *fire-basket.* **3.** The contents or amount of stuff contained in a basket; a basketful: *a basket of eggs, apples, vegetables* &c.

basket-ball, n. Ball game played with inflated ball which is tossed into goals resembling baskets.

basketful, n. [1. báhsketfool; 2. báskitful]. Contents of a basket; as much as a basket will hold.

basket-hilt, n. Sword-hilt made in form of basket-work, to protect the hand.

basketry, n. [1. báhsketri; 2. báskitri]. **basket** & **-ry**. Art of making baskets; basket-work.

basket-stitch, n. Kind of stitch in embroidery, worked over a cord which gives it somewhat the appearance of basket-work.

basket-wood, n. Kind of West Indian climbing shrub, the stems of which are used in basket-making.

basket-work, n. Interlaced work such as that used in making baskets.

basking shark, n. [1. báhsking shark; 2. báskiŋ ʃák]. A large, small-toothed shark of the N. Atlantic, also called sailfish and sunfish.

bason. See **basin**.

Basque (I.), n. [1. bahsk; 2. bāsk]. **1. a** One of a distinct race inhabiting the Western Pyrenees; **b** the language of this people. **2. a** Formerly a man's doublet with a skirt-like continuation; **b** now, woman's bodice with short skirt.

Basque (II.), adj., fr. prec. Pertaining to the Basques or their language.

bas-relief, bass-relief, n. [1. bàs reléf; 2. bǽs rilíf]. Fr., *bas*, 'low', *relief*, 'raised work'; Ital. *basso-rilievo*. See next word & **relief**. Sculpture in which the design projects but slightly from a flat surface, but is more raised than the design on a coin or medal.

bass (I.), adj. [1. bās; 2. beis]. Fr. *bas*, 'low', Ital. *basso*, fr. Low Lat. *bassus*, 'fat, thick, stumpy'. See **base** (III.). (mus.) Low in tone, having a deep compass: *bass voice*; *bass notes.*

bass (II.), n., fr. prec. **1. a** Clef that marks the bass or low range of notes; **b** the lower part of the musical register. **2. a** The deep notes of a man's voice; **b** a voice of deep quality; **c** a man possessing such a voice.

bass (III.), n. [1. bas; 2. bæs]. Form of **barse**. Species of fish of N. America, resembling a perch; also, *sea bass*, a European and American fish resembling a salmon.

Bassarid, n. [1. básarid; 2. bǽsərid]. Gk. (Thracian) *bassaris*, 'fox', genit. *-idos*. A Mænad, Bacchante.

bass-bar, n. [1. básbar; 2. béisbā]. Strip of wood put lengthwise within the body of violins or other instruments of that class to give additional strength to withstand the string pressure upon the bridge.

bass drum, n. [1. bās drúm; 2. béis drám]. The largest-sized drum, with very deep note.

basset, n. [1. báset; 2. bǽsit], also **basset hound**. Fr., fr. *bas*, 'low', see **base** (III.), & **-et**. Variety of small hound, of French origin, with short legs.

basset griffon, n. Wire-haired variety of basset hound.

basset-horn, n. Ital. *corno di bassetto*, fr. dimin. of *basso*, 'bass', see **bass** (I.). Musical wood wind instrument with alto or tenor quality of tone. The end at which is the reed mouthpiece is bent, and the other end is bell-shaped and bent outwards.

bassinet, n. [1. bàsinét; 2. bæ̀sinét]. Fr., dimin. of *bassin*. See **basin**. Child's cradle made of wicker-work with a hood or canopy at one end; also type of perambulator.

basso, n. [1. básō; 2. bǽsou]. Ital. See **bass** (I.). **a** Deep bass voice; **b** man with deep bass voice.

basso buffo, n. [1. básō bóofō; 2. bǽsou búfou]. Ital. See **bass** & **buffoon**. Comic bass singer.

bassoon, n. [1. basóon; 2. bəsún]. Fr. *basson*. See **bass** (I.) & **-oon**. Musical wood wind instrument with bass quality of tone, having a long curved reed mouthpiece; the bass hautboy or oboe; the tube is furnished with holes, some of which are stopped by the fingers, some by keys.

bassoonist, n. [1. basóonist; 2. bəsúnist]. Prec. & **-ist**. Player of a bassoon.

basso profundo, n. [1. básō profúndō; 2. bǽsou prəfándou]. Ital. See **bass** (I.) & **profound**. **a** Bass voice of exceptional depth; **b** man possessing such a voice.

basso-rilievo, n. [1. básō riliévō; 2. bǽsou riliévou]. Ital. Bas-relief.

bass viol, n. [1. bás víol; 2. béis váiəl]. A violoncello.

basswood, n. [1. báswood; 2. bǽswud]. Corrupt. of **bast**. Tree of genus *Tilia* or lime, or its wood; applied also to tulip tree.

bast, n. [1. bast, bas; 2. bæst, bæs]. O.E. *bæst, bast*, cogn. w. Lat. *fascia*, 'band, bandage, fillet' &c., & *fascis*, 'bundle', lit. 'that which is tied or bound up'; see **fasces**. The essential meaning of the Engl. & Gmc. word is 'stuff, or strips for tying'. Wooden fibre from certain trees, which forms long, tough strips, which are used for making cordage, mats &c., and by gardeners for tying up plants to stakes, pergolas &c.

bastard, n. & adj. [1. bástard; 2. bǽstəd]. M.E., fr. O. Fr. *bastard*, Mod. Fr. *bâtard*; called also in O. Fr. *fils de bast*, 'son of a pack-saddle', *bast*, 'saddle', & Gmc. suff. *-art*. Cp. **bantling**. *Bât, bast* is fr. Low Lat. *bastum*, 'pack-saddle', wh. is prob. related to Lat. *bastaga*, 'carriage of baggage', *bastayārius*, 'baggage-master', *basterna*, 'litter, sedan chair', carried between mules. These words are all formed fr. a Gk. loan-word, *bastázō*, 'I carry', wh. may ultimately be cogn. w. Lat. *gerere*, 'to bear, carry about', P.P. *gestum*; see **gerent, gest, gesture,**

& w. Goth. *kas*, 'vessel, jug', O.N. *kasta*, 'to throw', see **cast**. **1.** n. A child begotten outside lawful wedlock; an illegitimate, baseborn child. **2.** adj. **a** Not genuine, spurious, esp. of an imitation of genuine thing; sham: *bastard good nature, charity, patriotism* &c.; **b** (by extension) applied to all sorts of things which are more or less abnormal in shape, size &c., or which differ in some way from standard type: *bastard apple, acacia, cherry, pine* &c.; *bastard wheat*; *bastard type*, having face larger or smaller than size proper to the body &c.

bastardization, n. [1. bàstardīzā́shun; 2. bǽstədaizéiʃən]. See next word & **-ation**. The act or process of making illegitimate.

bastardize, vb. trans. [1. bástardīz; 2. bǽstədaiz]. See **bastard** & **-ize**. To render illegitimate, make a bastard of; as when a marriage is annulled, the offspring of it thereby become illegitimate.

bastardy, n. [1. bástardi; 2. bǽstədi]. O. Fr. *bastardie*. See **bastard** & **-y**. State or condition of being illegitimate.

baste (I.), vb. trans. [1. bāst; 2. beist]. O. Fr. *basser*, 'soak'. Origin unknown. **1.** To soak, moisten (roasting meat) with melted fat or gravy, the fat or gravy being poured over the joint with a ladle from time to time while the process of roasting is going on. **2. a** To thrash, or beat soundly; **b** (fig.) to heckle, make verbal attack on, abuse.

baste (II.), vb. trans. O. Fr. *bastir*, fr. O.H.G. *bestan*, 'sew with bast'. Cp. **bast**. To sew loosely, and temporarily, with big stitches.

bastille, n. [1. bàstḗl; 2. bæstíəl]. Fr., 'a fortress', fr. O. Fr. *bastir*, 'to build'. See **bastion**. Originally, a tower or shelter used in defence of a fortress, separate from the main structure of the fortifications: *The Bastille*, ancient state prison in Paris, taken and destroyed by the mob in the Revolution, July 14, 1789.

bastinado, n. & vb. trans. [1. bàstinā́dō; 2. bæstinéidou]. Span. *bastonada*, Fr. *bastonnade*, 'a cudgelling'. Cp. **baton**. **1.** n. Form of punishment formerly practised by some Orientals, such as the Turks and the Chinese, consisting of a severe beating with a stick administered to the soles of the feet. **2.** vb. To administer the bastinado to.

basting (I.), n. [1. bā́sting; 2. béistiŋ]. **baste (I.)** & **-ing**. Action of one who bastes; process of being basted.

basting (II.), n. **baste (II.)** & **-ing**. Action or process of sewing loosely.

bastion, n. [1. bástiun, bástyun; 2. bǽstiən, bǽstjən]. Fr., fr. Ital. *bastione*; cp. O. Fr. *bastir*, Ital *bastire*, 'to build', same as Low Lat. vb. This is perh. borrowed fr. Gk. *bastázein*, 'lift, carry', w. idea of bearing a weight; cp. **bastard**. A projecting part of a fortification, either in the form of a round half-tower built into the surface of the main wall, or constructed so as to form a salient angle with two faces.

bastioned, adj. [1. bástiund; 2. bǽstiənd]. Prec. & **-ed**. Provided with bastions.

bat (I.), n. [1. bat; 2. bæt]. O.E. *batt*, 'club, stick', M.E. *batte*, 'cudgel'. The Fr. *batte* is a mallet with a long handle, something like a bittle or beetle, & is presumably connected w. *battre*, 'beat'. The resemblance between the Engl. & Fr. words is in this case accidental. The origin of *bat* is unknown. **1.** Now applied almost entirely to the wooden implement with a flat blade and a cane handle used in the game of cricket, and, much more rarely, to a tennis-racquet. Phr. *to carry one's bat*, to stay in till the end of an innings without being put out. **2.** A person who uses the bat in cricket; batsman; *a good, a useful bat* &c. **3.** (slang) A sharp blow. **4.** (colloq.) Pace, rate of speed: *to go full bat*.

bat (II.), vb. intrans., fr. prec. To use a bat, that is to 'go in' in cricket, and endeavour to make runs.

bat (III.), n. Apparently a dial. development of M.E. *backe*, wh. is possibly of Scand. origin, cp. Dan. *-bakke*, Swed. *-backa*, 'bat', but may be a genuine Engl. word, though not recorded in O.E. A small nocturnal mammal, like a mouse, with long forelegs joined to its hindlegs by a tough membranous structure which projects beneath the lower part of the body and enables it to fly or flit about with great swiftness. Phr. *as blind as a bat*, very blind.

batata, n. [1. batáhta; 2. bætā́tə]. Span. form of a native Am. word. The sweet potato.

batch, n. [1. bach; 2. bætʃ]. M.E. *bacche*, 'batch'. The O.E. equiv. is not recorded, but wd. be either *bæċ* or *bæċċe*, derived fr. *bacan*, 'to bake', q.v. under **bake**. **1.** The whole product of a single baking, esp. of loaves, cakes &c.; also of china and pottery. **2.** A number, collection of things, or quantity of material produced by one effort, action or operation, or coming from same place of origin, or received as result of a single order; (of very wide application): *a batch of cigars, batch of luggage, books, parcels, correspondence* &c.; said also of collections of persons closely associated by belonging to same family, occupation, institution or organization: *a batch of relatives, batch of recruits, batch of workmen, batch of undergraduates* &c.

bate (I.), n. & vb. trans. [1. bāt; 2. beit]. Prob. connected w. Swed. *beta*, 'to tan', & thus cogn. w. **bait (I.)** & **bite**. **1.** n. An alkaline solution used in tanning. **2.** vb. To steep (leather) in bate.

bate (II.), n. Etymol. uncertain; possibly variant of **bait (I.)**. (colloq.) Rage, temper: *to get in a bate about anything*.

bate (III.), vb. trans., fr. **abate**. To diminish, reduce, mitigate, take something off from: *to bate one's demands, charges, claims* &c.

bated, adj. [1. bā́ted; 2. béitid]. Prec. & **-ed**. Reduced, suspended; chiefly in Phr. *with bated breath*, in a state of suspense, anxiety, expectation, or awe.

bat-eyed, adj. Mentally blind, obtuse, unobservant, liable to miss the finer shades of thought and feeling.

batfowl, vb. intrans. [1. bátfoul; 2. bǽtfaul]. **bat (I.)**. To catch birds at night by dazzling them with a light, and knocking them down when they fly towards it.

batfowling, n. [1. bátfouling; 2. bǽtfauliŋ]. Prec. & **-ing**. Sport, action, of catching birds in manner described above.

bath (I.), n. [1. bahth; 2. bāþ]; pl. [1. bahdhz; 2. bāðz]. O.E. *bæð*; M.E. *bath*; O.H.G. *bad*, O.N. *baþ*. The word is found in every branch of Gmc. speech except Goth. The final *-þ* is derivative & the base may be associated w. that in Germ. *bähen*, 'to warm by covering with hot bandages, foment'. Cognates outside Gmc. are very doubtful. Connexion with Lat. *fomentum* (fr. **fowementum*) & *fovēre*, 'to warm' &c., see **foment**, has been proposed by some and rejected by others. Possibly we have here the same base as in **bake**. The fundamental meaning wd. in that case be 'hot immersion, or washing'. **1.** A vessel or receptacle in wood, metal, or porcelain made to contain water, in which the person may be immersed and washed. **2.** A washing or cleansing of the person in a bath: *to have, take, a bath*; *a hot bath*, a wash or immersion in (a bath of) hot water; *mud bath*, immersion in mud or earth containing medicinal qualities; *Order of the Bath*, a British order of knighthood with civil and military division and three classes. **3.** (in pl.) *Baths*, an institution where baths of various kinds may be taken: *Turkish baths, swimming baths, sea-water baths*, &c. **4.** Liquid, or vessel containing it, in which objects are immersed to undergo a chemical process, e.g. *hypo bath*, for developing photographs. **5.** Vessel or chamber in which certain parts of machinery work in a water, air, or oil medium: *oil bath* &c.

bath (II.), vb. trans. New formation direct fr. prec. To give a bath to; esp. to give a child its bath: *to bath the baby*.

Bath (III.), n. Town in Somerset, named from its hot, mineral springs. Various attributive uses: **a** *Bath-brick*, a compound of various earths, used for cleaning metal and stone; **b** *Bath-bun*, spiced fruit bun with knobbly, sugared surface; **c** *Bath-chair*, three-wheeled invalid chair for a single person; **d** *Bath-stone*, kind of limestone.

bathe (I.), vb. intrans. & trans. [1. bādh; 2. beið]. O.E. *baðian*, M.E. *bāð(i)e(n)*, fr. O.E. *bæþ*, q.v. under **bath (I.)**. Note the difference in vowel sound & final consonant wh. show derivation fr. the O.E. vb., as distinct fr. vb. *bath*, derived direct fr. the n. in Mod. period. **A.** intrans. **1.** To take a bath; **a** to immerse oneself in water for purpose of washing; **b** to immerse oneself in the sea, in a river or lake for enjoyment, swimming &c. The word implies this as a rule, unless the context shows that it refers to washing in a bath. **B.** trans. **1.** To soak, immerse, steep, in water; apply water to: *to bathe one's face, eyes, feet* &c.; *to bathe an injured part or limb*. **2.** (fig.) To embrue: *to bathe one's hands in blood*, be guilty of a person's death by violence. **3. a** To lave, wash, wet, flow past, reach to, touch, of the waters of river or lake which are said to *bathe the shores, the foot of a cliff* &c.; **b** (of light, warmth &c.) to surround, play upon, encompass.

bathe (II.), n., fr. prec. The act or process of bathing in the sea, a swimming bath, river &c.: *to have a pleasant, long, rapid bathe*, &c.

bather, n. [1. bā́dher; 2. béiðə]. **bathe (I.)** & **-er**. **a** One who bathes, in the sea, river &c.; **b** one who takes medicinal baths at a watering-place.

bathetic, adj. [1. bathétik; 2. bæþétik], fr. **bathos**, on anal. of *pathetic*. Trite, characterized by bathos.

bathing, n. [1. bā́dhing; 2. béiðiŋ]. See **bathe (I.)** & **-ing**. The act or habit of entering the sea &c.: *to be fond of bathing*; *good bathing may be had from the beach*; *the bathing here is rather dangerous*.

bathing machine, n. Small hut on wheels, which can be drawn down to the water's edge at low tide, used by sea-bathers for undressing and dressing.

bathometer, n. [1. bathómeter; 2. bæþɔ́mitə]. See **bathos** & **meter**. Lit. 'depth measurer'; an instrument for taking soundings and gauging depth, also called bathymeter.

bathorse, n. [1. bát-hòrs; 2. bǽthɔ̄s]. First element is fr. Fr. *bât*, 'pack-saddle', for etymol. of wh. see **bastard**. A horse which carries baggage, esp. in a military campaign.

bathos, n. [1. bā́thos; 2. béiþɔs], fr. Gk. *báthos*, 'depth, height', fr. *bathús*, 'deep', etymol. unknown. A descent from the sublime to the ridiculous in style; triteness, triviality, matter-of-factness in style.

bathybius, n. [1. bathíbius; 2. bæþíbiəs]. Name invented by Huxley, fr. Gk. *bathús*, 'deep', see prec., & *bíos*, 'life', see **bio-**. A slimy, gelatinous substance dredged up from the ocean bed at great depths and supposed, wrongly, to consist of protoplasm; it is now proved to be an inorganic substance.

bathymeter, n. [1. bathímeter; 2. bæþímitə], fr. Gk. *bathús*, 'deep', see **bathos**, & **-meter**. Instrument for measuring the depth of water as in the sea, lakes &c., also *bathometer*.

bathymetric, adj. [1. bàthimétrik; 2. bæþimétrik], fr. Gk. *bathús*, 'deep', see **bathos**, & **-metric**. Pertaining to bathymetry or the measurement of the depth of water, as in the sea, a lake &c.

bathymetry, n. [1. bathímetri; 2. bæþímitri]. See prec. & **-metry**. Science of measuring the depths of seas, lakes &c.

batik, n. [1. bátik; 2. bǽtik]. Malay *batik*. Method of colouring fabrics in marbled designs, originating in Java, in which the parts not to be dyed are protected by a coat of wax.

batiste, n. [1. batḗst; 2. bətíst]. Fr., fr. name of first maker, *Baptiste of Cambrai*. **a** A fine lawn or cambric of linen; **b** a fine cotton muslin.

batman, n. [1. bátman; 2. bǽtmən]. See first element of **bathorse**. (mil.) **a** Originally one who looked after the baggage animals; **b** now an officer's servant generally.

batmoney, n. [1. bátmuni; 2. bǽtmani]. The first element is prob. quite distinct fr. that in prec. word, & comes fr. Hind. *bhāt*, 'advances made to ploughmen without interest', & by extension, 'extra allowances made to officers on special grounds'. The Anglo-Indian form is *batta*. Field allowance to an officer on active service.

baton, n. [1. bátn; 2. bǽtn], fr. Fr. *bâton*, 'stick, staff', O. Fr. *baston*; etymol. unknown. **1.** A staff of office, symbol of rank, e.g. *Field-Marshal's baton*. **2.** Short, thick staff, also called *truncheon*, used by the police for defence and attack. **3.** A slender staff used by the conductor of an orchestra for beating time. **4.** (her.) An ordinary, in form of a bend (q.v.) with its ends cut off, and one fourth the breadth.

Batrachia, n. pl. [1. batrákia; 2. bætréikiə]. Latinized coinage fr. Gk. *batrákheios*, 'pertaining to a frog', fr. *bátrakhos*, 'frog'; etymol. doubtful. **a** Amphibians generally; **b** specif., family of frogs and toads.

batrachian, adj. [1. batrákian; 2. bætréikiən]. Prec. & **-an**. Pertaining to, resembling, the batrachia.

batta, n. See **batmoney**.

battalion, n. [1. batályun; 2. bətǽljən], fr. Fr. *bataillon*, fr. Ital. *battaglione*. See **battle** & **-oon**. **1.** (mil.) A unit of an infantry regiment, consisting of four companies. As a rule the full strength of a battalion in the English Army is about 1000 men. **2.** Extended general use, a large company, number, a band of people (rather rare): *whole battalions of spies*.

battel(s), n. pl. [1. bátlz; 2. bǽtlz] & vb. intrans. [1. bátl; 2. bǽtl]. Origin uncertain. **1.** n. In the University of Oxford, college accounts for provision and stores of all kinds are so called. **2.** vb. *To battel*, to live from the college kitchen and stores.

batten (I.), vb. intrans. & trans. [1. bátn; 2. bǽtn]. O.N. *batna*, 'to improve, grow better'. The base *bat-* is cogn. w. O.E. *bet*, 'better', wh. comes fr. **bati-*. See etymol. under **better**, cp. also **boot (I.)**. **a** intrans. To thrive, grow fat, to luxuriate in comfort and plenty; **b** trans., to nourish, refresh, fatten: '*Battening our flocks on the rich dews of night*' (Milton, 'Lycidas').

batten (II.), n. & vb. trans. Variant of **baton**. **1.** n. Board or spar of timber from 2 to 6 inches wide, and from ⅝ to 2 inches thick, used in flooring, and also to make firm the laths upon which plaster is laid. **2.** vb. **a** To make firm with battens; **b** *batten down*, to fasten down securely, esp. of the hatches in a ship, by nailing battens across.

battening, n. [1. bát(e)ning; 2. bǽt(ə)niŋ]. Prec. & **-ing**. Woodwork consisting of battens nailed upon a frame.

batter (I.), vb. trans. & intrans. [1. báter; 2. bǽtə]. M.E. *batteren*, O. Fr. *batre*, Fr. *battre*, Lat. *battuere*, *bātuere*, 'strike, beat', borrowed fr. Celt. *bathu*, 'strike'. The genuine Lat. forms of the base are seen in *con-fūtāre*, lit. 'strike down, check, repress', *re-fūtāre*, 'restrain, repress', also in *fatuus*, 'stupid, foolish', lit. 'struck silly'; see **fatuous**. The Aryan base was **bhāw*, 'strike', wh. occurs also in **beat (I.)**. **1.** trans. To beat, strike violently with repeated blows, with intent to injure, demolish, or make a loud noise: *to batter someone about the head*; *batter down, to batter a door, wall, down*. **2.** intrans. *To batter at the door*, make loud noise by striking.

batter (II.), n., fr. prec. A mixture of flour, eggs, and milk beaten up together and boiled, baked, or fried.

batter (III.), n., perh. fr. **batter (I.)**. (archit.) **a** A slight slope inwards given to the walls of a tower, so that the circumference is smaller at the top than at the base; **b** a similar slope given to both sides of a wall in its construction, so that it is less thick at the top than at the base.

batter (IV.), n. **bat (II.)** & **-er**. Batsman at cricket.

battered, adj. [1. báterd; 2. bǽtəd], fr. P.P. of **batter (I.)**. **1.** (of persons) Rugged, weather-beaten, in appearance; showing effects of the stress of life. **2.** (of things) dilapidated, shabby, showing marks of wear and tear: *a battered top-hat*.

battering-ram, n. [1. bátering ràm; 2. bǽtəriŋ rǽm]. **1.** Military engine formerly used for knocking down walls, consisting of a large, heavily weighted beam, often with a head of iron moulded in the form of a ram's head, and swung between two supports or wheels. **2.** Any heavy object, such as a log or long pole, wielded and swung by several persons, for beating down a wall, a door &c.

battering-train, n. [1. bátering tràn; 2. bǽtəriŋ trèin]. (mil.) Train of heavy artillery for a siege; now more often called siege train.

battery, n. [1. báteri; 2. bǽtəri]. Fr. *batterie*, fr. *battre*, 'beat', see **batter (I.)**, & **-ry**. **1.** (law) Unlawful beating and assaulting of a person, esp. in Phr. *assault and battery*. **2.** (mil.) **a** An artillery unit, consisting of a certain number of guns under a single command, including the officers, men, and ammunition necessary for working the guns; **b** any group of guns on a warship. **3.** (elect.) Group of cells in apparatus for generating an electric current.

batting, n. [1. báting; 2. bǽtiŋ], fr. **bat (II.)** & **-ing**. **1.** Action of one who bats, as at cricket. **2.** Cotton, or cotton wool, in sheets for use in quilts &c.

battle (I.), n. [1. bátl; 2. bǽtl]. M.E. *batáile*, O. Fr. *bataille*, Lat. *battālia*, *battuālia*, 'fighting and fencing exercises of soldiers and gladiators'. See **batter (I.)**. **1.** A conflict, encounter, contest of arms, fighting, between opposing armies on land, between ships of war at sea, or between airships and aeroplanes in the air: *to win, lose, the battle* (lit. and fig.). Phr. *half the battle*, the advantage or better part in a discussion, cause &c. **2.** Extended from particular combats to war generally: *the light of battle*; *the love of battle is natural to all men*. **3.** (fig.) Struggle against moral forces, or against hardship, misfortune, fate &c.: *the battle of life*; *the battle against sin*.

battle (II.), vb. intrans., fr. prec. Cp. Fr. *batallier*; see prec. To fight, struggle, contend: *to battle with, against, the wind, opponents, misfortunes* &c.; *to battle for the right, one's friends* &c.

battle-array, n. Order, line, of battle; equipment, armour &c.

battle-axe, n. Heavy, long-handled axe, formerly an important weapon of offence.

battle-cruiser, n. A large, fast, and heavily armed cruiser.

battle-cry, n. **1.** Word or cry used to rally troops round a leader, collect men of the same side in a fight, or to encourage soldiers to special efforts for a common cause. **2.** (fig.) Phrase or word embodying or expressing a principle or ideal, and used by those who are combatting for a cause; slogan.

battledore, n. [1. bátldòr; 2. bǽtldɔ̀]. M.E. *batyldor*, 'instrument for beating'; prob. fr. Span. *batallador*, 'a great warrior, champion'. See **battle** & **-tor**. **1.** Wooden implement with a long handle and a flat round blade, shaped like a tennis racquet, used for beating clothes that are being washed. **2.** Similarly shaped instrument, having the blade strung with cat-gut, or covered with stout parchment, used in the game of *battledore and shuttlecock*.

battle-field, n. Locality, scene, of a battle; the place where a battle is being or has just been fought.

battle-ground, n. Same as **battle-field**; also (fig.) the cause for which men dispute; the subject of controversy.

battlement, n. [1. bátlment; 2. bǽtlmənt]. M.E. *batelment*, O. Fr. *bataillement*; cp. also O. Fr. *bastiller*, 'to fortify', see **bastille**. See **battle (I.)** & **-ment**; the first element was prob. associated w. the idea of 'building, or fortifying', as well as the closely connected one of 'combat', though the words, similar also in form, are quite distinct in origin. A parapet on tower or wall, built with alternate open spaces and blocks of solid wall; originally for purposes of defence, later constructed as an ornamental feature.

battle-piece, n. Painting of a battle.

battle royal, n. A severely contested fight; (lit. and fig.) used of fight between game-cocks, prize-fighters, and of a general scrimmage; also of a heated argument between two disputants.

battle-ship, n. Naval vessel, armed with guns and protected with armour-plates. The name is now given specifically to a particular class of vessels, namely the largest and most powerfully armed, corresponding to the old ship of the line.

battue, n. [1. bátū; 2. bǽtjū]. Fr., lit. 'beating'. Cp. **batter (I.)**. **a** Beating of woods and covers for game, which are shot as they pass the guns; also **b** the game shot as a result of the process.

batz, n. [1. bats; 2. bæts], fr. M.H.G. *petz*, *betz*, 'a bear', the etymol. of wh. is obscure. Small coin of low value bearing image of a bear, formerly struck in Berne, and current in Switzerland, now no longer in use.

bauble, n. [1. báwbl; 2. bɔ́bl]. M.E. *bābel*, fr. O. Fr. *baubel*, 'toy'; perh. connected w. **babe**. **1.** (archaic) Professional jester's stick or plaything, emblematic of his calling. **2. a** A trifling, glittering object of small intrinsic value, a gewgaw; **b** (contemptuous) earthly pomp; an emblem of human greatness, symbol of rank, wealth &c., regarded as transitory and worthless by the side of the infinite and eternal.

baudechin, n. [1. báwdekin; 2. bɔ́dikin]. In M.E. 'precious silk stuff', fr. O. Fr. *baudequin*. See **baldachin**, wh. is fr. the Ital. form of same word.

baulk. See **balk**.

bauxite, n. [1. báwksīt; 2. bɔ́ksait], fr. Les Baux, France, & **-ite**. A clayey mineral, a hydrate of alumina, one of the chief sources of aluminium.

bawbee, n. [1. bawbḗ; 2. bɔbí]. Etymol. uncertain. (Scots, colloq.) A halfpenny.

bawd, n. [1. bawd; 2. bɔd], M.E. *baude*, 'pander, procurer', O. Fr. *baude*. The M.E. adj. has the less reprehensible meaning of 'joyous, boastful', & *bauderie* means 'gaiety, mirth', but also 'the act of a pander'. The Fr. word is borrowed fr. Gmc. **bald*, **bold**. The word is now rare in English, and survives only in literary use, or as a deliberate archaism. Still used in 17th and 18th cent. Its meaning is procuress, sometimes prostitute.

bawdry, n. [1. báwdri; 2. bɔ́dri]. See prec. & **-ry**. Obscenity, unchastity of conduct, lewdness. Still used more widely than *bawd*.

bawdy, adj. [1. báwdi; 2. bɔ́di], fr. **bawd** & **-y**. In M.E. *baudi* means simply 'dirty'. Obscene, lewd, unchaste, esp. of conversation: *bawdy talk, bawdy stories*. Hardly in popular use, but current among educated persons who deliberately adopt archaic and literary words.

bawdy-house, n. A brothel.

bawl (I.), vb. intrans. & trans. [1. bawl; 2. bɔl]. Mod. Icel. *baula*, 'to low', O.N. *baula*, 'cow'. It is almost inconceivable that this word shd. be borrowed fr. Mod. Icel., & we must suppose that it was an old Scand. word. It is not recorded apparently in M.E. The relation of Med. Lat. *baulāre*, 'bark as a dog', is obscure. The latter may be a purely imitative word. The word is now only used of human action. **1.** intrans. **a** To utter loud, discordant cries, whether inarticulate as in weeping and lamentation, or articulate as in loud speech; the word always has a disparaging sense. It is not generally used of shrill, high sounds, but is applied to the loud shouts of unruly children, the harsh, ugly sounds made by uncultivated persons in conversation shouted across some distance, in scolding, or in calling each other: *to bawl across the street, to bawl about the house*; Phr. *to bawl and squall*, to utter a series of loud, ugly noises and shouts in speaking or singing; **b** to speak or sing unnecessarily loud; to speak or sing with effort and strain: *you needn't bawl, I can hear quite well*; *his delivery is very bad, he simply bawls*. **2.** trans. To utter loudly: *to bawl the news*. **3.** Followed by adverbs and prepositions. *To bawl at (a person)*, address him rudely with the voice raised; *to bawl out*, **a** intrans., to shout suddenly, call out; also **b** trans., *to bawl out abuse*.

bawl (II.), n., fr. prec. A loud shout or cry.

bay (I.), n. [1. bā; 2. bei]. Fr. *baie*, Low Lat. *baia*. Etymol. uncertain, but perh. connected w. Gmc. base, **baug-*, **bug-*, 'bend', wh. occurs in O.E. *būgan*, 'bend, bow', also in O.E. *boga*, 'bow' (for shooting arrows), *bēag*, 'ring' &c.; cp. this base under **bow (I.)** & **(II.)**; see also **bight**, 'bay'. Deep indentation of the land bordering on the sea or a lake, and forming an inlet for the water. The land forms a curve round, and partly encloses, this portion of the water.

bay (II.), n. Fr. *baie*, O. Fr. *baee*, 'an opening'. Connected w. *bayer*, 'gape', wh. now survives only in Pres. Part. as adj. *béant*, & P.P. *(bouche) bée*, 'gaping, yawning'; cp. Ital. *badare*, 'to open'. **1.** A principal division, or compartment, of a building, marked by some important feature, such as columns, pillars, pilasters, which divide up the building into regular portions. **2.** Recess in wall of a room. See **bay window**. **3.** A part of a railway station consisting of a side line which forms a terminus, and a platform, separate from the main lines and platforms. **4.** Part of deck of ship where sick or wounded are placed: *sick-bay*.

bay (III.), vb. intrans. & trans, fr. earlier *abaie*, O. Fr. *abayer*, 'to bark', Lat. **ad-** & *baubāri*, 'to bark, howl' (of dogs). The Gk. cognate is *baúzein*, 'bark, wail', lit. 'to utter *baú, baú*', wh. corresponds to our *bow-wow*. The same imitative base occurs in Lith. *baũbti*, 'to low'. **a** intrans. To bark, esp. continuously and with a deep note, as of hounds in full chase; **b** trans., as in Shakespeare's '*to bay the moon*', is hardly current now.

bay (IV.), n., fr. prec. Deep bark, esp. as of a pack of hounds. Phr. *at bay*, adv., **a** said of hunted animal on which the hounds or hunters have gained, and which is obliged to face its foes and defend itself to the last; also (fig., of persons, nations) *to be at bay*, to be in desperate straits and compelled to carry on a fierce defence as a last chance; **b** *to keep someone or something at bay*, to keep at arm's length, prevent from coming beyond a safe distance, to ward off: *to keep an enemy, a danger, a disease &c., at bay*; *to bring (an enemy &c.) to bay*, to reduce him to his last efforts of resistance, bring to account.

bay (V.), adj. & n. Fr. *bai*, 'brown', of a horse, Lat. *badius*, 'chestnut brown', only of horses; cp. Ir. *buide*, 'yellow'. **1.** adj. Of a reddish-brown colour; used only of horses. **2.** n. *The bay, a fine bay* &c., bay horse.

bay (VI.), also **bay tree**, n. [1. bá (trē); 2. béi (trī)]. Fr. *baie*, fr. Lat. *bac(c)a*, 'berry'; see **baccate**. **1.** Species of laurel with leaves which are very aromatic when crushed. **2.** (pl.) *Bays*, (fig.) honours, rewards, fame, bestowed or gained in recognition of meritorious exploits and achievements; from the garland of bay formerly bestowed upon a victor &c.

bayadère, n. [1. bậyadǻr; 2. bèijədéə]. Fr., fr. Port. *bailadeira*, 'ballet-dancer', fr. *bailar*, 'to dance', see **ballet**. A female dancer, esp. one attached to a temple in Southern India.

Bayard, n. [1. bǻard; 2. béiād], fr. the name of a celebrated French warrior, the Chevalier Bayard (1476–1524). A very highly bred, chivalrous gentleman, of high courage and exquisite manners.

bayberry, n. [1. bábèri; 2. béibèri]. See **bay (VI.)**. **a** Fruit of the bay tree; **b** West Indian myrtaceous tree.

bayonet, n. & vb. trans. [1. báonet; 2. béənit], fr. Fr. *baionnette*, prob. fr. Bayonne, where these weapons are said to have first been made. The dialect forms *bagonet, bagnet* can hardly be normal variants of Fr. word, but are perh. due to association w. *bag*, 'to cut or hack a hedge', & *bagging hook*, the hook used for this purpose. **1.** n. A long dagger affixed to the muzzle of a rifle, and used in hand-to-hand fighting: *to charge with the bayonet*; *bayonet charge*, charge of infantry with fixed bayonets; *bayonet drill*, military training and exercises in the effective use of the bayonet in attack and defence. Bayonets are sometimes made with a handle, so that they resemble a short sword, and can be used independently of the rifle, both for fighting and for cutting brushwood &c. **2.** vb. To thrust with the bayonet at (an enemy); to kill with the bayonet.

bayou, n. [1. bíōō; 2. báiū], fr. Amer.-Ind., *bayuk*. A sluggish, marshy, tideless inlet or creek, on the sea coast, or of a lake or river, in the southern states of the U.S.A.

bay rum, n. Aromatic liquid used in the toilet, distilled from West Indian bayberry.

bay-salt, n. Perh. fr. **bay (I.)**. Coarse salt obtained by evaporation of sea-water.

bay window, n. Window built in a recess, or bay, in a room, projecting from outer wall, and usually having lights on three sides.

bazaar, n. [1. bazár; 2. bəzā́], fr. Pers. *bāzār*, 'permanent market, or street of shops'. The word is Arab. & Turk., & has spread into most European languages. **1.** In the Oriental meaning when referring to the East. **2.** A large shop where a variety of fancy articles are on sale; a special department of a shop, e.g. *a Christmas bazaar* &c. **3.** A sale of articles of all kinds, presented to the organizers of the undertaking, but generally sold at prices rather exceeding their value, for some philanthropic object, e.g. to raise money for a church, a mission, a hospital &c. The term is applied both to the sale itself and the building where it is held.

bdellium, n. [1. délium; 2. déliəm]. Through Lat., fr. Gk. *bdéllion*, 'a fragrant gum', prob. of Semitic origin. **1.** A substance mentioned in the Bible, Gen. ii. 12 and Num. xi. 7, and there variously understood to mean a resin or a precious stone. **2.** A gum resin obtained from various species of balsam trees.

be, vb. intrans., copula, auxil. [1. bē; 2. bī]. In the conjugation of this vb. three quite distinct bases are used, those seen respectively in *be—been, am—is, was—were*. The etymol. of these is dealt w. under the heading of each; that of the base *be* is dealt w. here. In O.E., in the pres. indic., the sing. forms *bēo(m), bist, biþ* are used, & in the pl. *bēoþ*. These survive in M.E., esp. in the S. & S. Midl., as *ich bē(o)* &c., *bist, biþ, būþ* &c., & in pl. *bēn, bēþ, būþ* &c. At the present time *be* is only used in the pres. in some provinc. (Sthn. & S.-W. Midl.) dialects. The O.E. infin. is *bēon*, M.E. *bēn, been, bē*. The P.P. in O.E. has a form fr. a different vb., *ġe-worden*, as a rule, but in M.E. *ibē(n)*, *bē(n)*, whence our *been*. The base is used in the pres. sing. of vb. 'to be', in O.H.G. & Mod. Germ. *bin*, O.S. *bium*, & in Lat. in various tenses: *fui*, 'I have been', *fueram, futūrus* &c. The Balto-Slav. languages also employ the same base: Lith. *búti*, 'to be', *bùwo*, 'he was'; O. Slav. *byti*, 'to be', *bylu*, 'was'; further Ir. *buith*, 'to be', *boi*, 'was', *bud*, 'will be' &c. This base is seen also in Lat. in the fut. & imperf. in *-bo, -bam*. The base **bheu-*, **bhū-*, fr. wh. these are derived is widely spread throughout the Gmc. & other Aryan languages, w. the sense of 'remaining, dwelling', & so on. Cp. O.E., O.H.G. *būan*, O.N. *būa*, 'dwell', Gk. *phúomai*, 'I become, grow', *phúsis*, 'nature', see **physio-**; Scrt. *bhávati*, 'exists, happens', *bhūmis*, 'earth'; Lith. *bùtas*, 'house', *bŭklà*, 'home, dwelling-place'; Ir. *both*, 'hut'; cp. Scot. *bothie*. **1.** To exist, have existence; come to pass, happen: '*whatever is, is right*'; *I think, therefore I am*; *how can such things be?*; *the memory of what has been, and never more shall be*; *it was not to be*. **2.** As auxiliary: **a** (with P.P. of other vbs. to form pass.) *the enemy were well beaten*; *the city was destroyed by the mob*; *I was deceived* &c.; (expressing futurity) '*Man never is, but always to be, blest*' (Pope); **b** (with Pres. Part.) to express (i.) action, or process still going on, not yet complete, or continuous: *he was knocked down as he was crossing the street*; *I was talking to my son at the time*; *life is passing away, and we are doing nothing*; *as I write this the train is passing through the mountains*; (ii.) (with *come* and *go*, the latter followed by another vb., expressing intention of future action) *I am coming home tomorrow*; *he is leaving next week*; *I am coming to see you today*; *I am going to write to him at once* &c. (see **go**). **3.** As mere copula joining subject and predicate: **a** (expressing mere relation, or indicating some quality and character) *this man is the king*; *he is my father*; *trees are green*; *iron is hard*; *Alfred was king of all England*; **b** (expressing identity) *true contentment is real happiness*; *gold is the most precious metal*; *a straight line is one which lies evenly between its extreme points*; '*Thou wert my guide, philosopher, and friend*' (Pope). **4.** To possess a certain value or price, to cost: *how much is this?*, i.e. what does it cost?, *this one is half-a-crown*. **5.** To be equivalent to, to amount to; to be the cause of &c.; to stand for, as a symbol: *to be the envy of all beholders*; *that will be the death of me*; '*all the world's a stage*'.

be-, pref. O.E. *be-*, weak form of *bī* (see **by**). As an independent prep. O.E. *be* has the senses 'by, along, near (of place)'; concerning; according to'; as a pref. it makes intrans. vbs. trans., & acts as intensifier. In O.H.G. both *bi* & *bī* exist, the latter used as a pref., as in Engl.; in O.S. *be, bi*; in Goth. *bi* only is found, & is used there also in composition. The base prob. occurs in O.E. *ymbe*, 'around', O.H.G. *umbi*, w. wh. compare Lat. *amb-ō*, Gk. *amphi*, Scrt. *abhi*, 'about'. See **both**. Prefix, used to modify sense of verbs, or to make other words into verbs. It has various functions, more than one of which sometimes are combined in the same verb. Almost any verb might conceivably receive this prefix, and the same is true of almost any noun, but in practice, most of the verbs so made, which occur in the dictionaries, do not exist, except as fleeting literary, or jocular colloquial creations. The main functions of *be-* are: **1.** To make an intransitive verb transitive: *bemoan, bestride*. **2.** To act as an intensive, express thoroughness, completeness of action or process: *bespatter, besmirch, bedeck* (with flowers &c.), *belabour*. **3.** To form verbs from nouns. The most commonly used forms of verbs so made are the past participles used as adjectives: *bewigged, bejewelled, beringed, bewhiskered* &c.

beach (I.), n. [1. bēch; 2. bītʃ]. Origin very doubtful. Not found in O. or M.E. It may be connected w. O.E. *beċe*, 'brook', wh. is cogn. w. Germ. *bach*, 'brook, stream', O.H.G. *bah*. The Engl. *beċe* appears in Pl. Ns., as *-beach* & *-batch*. It appears improbable that *beach*, if it be connected w. this, is derived fr. this identical form; it may go back to a cogn. w. a different grade, O.E. **bǣċ*, meaning 'the bed, or margin by the side of a brook'; thence, since this is often pebbly, coming to mean 'margin of pebbles or shingle by the side of water, of a lake, of the sea'. This is purely conjectural, but not impossible. To this hypothetical O.E. **bǣċ*, the Gk. *pēgé*, 'spring, source', wd. be an exact equiv.; cp. **Pegasus.** The shore by the margin of a lake, estuary, or of the sea, esp. when composed of pebbles or sand. The word is most often used of the fringe of shingle between the edge of the sea and the land. Phr. *to be on the beach*, to be hard up, ruined. For original meaning see **beachcomber.**

beach (**II.**), vb. trans., fr. prec. **a** To run (ship, boat &c.) on a beach; **b** to haul (boat &c.) on to a beach.

beachcomber, n. [1. béchkómer; 2. bítʃ-kóumə]. **beach & comber**, in sense of wave. (an Australian and Pacific Islands usage) **a** A large, long wave rolling in from the ocean on to the beach; **b** (slang) a vagrant, loafer, who picks up a living somehow by haunting the shore and seaports of Pacific Islands, Australia &c.

beachy, adj. [1. béchi; 2. bítʃi]. **beach** (**I.**) **& -y.** Covered with beach, like a beach; pebbly and sandy.

beacon (**I.**), n. [1. békun; 2. bíkən]. O.E. *bēac(e)n*, 'sign, token', also 'banner', M.E. *beekne*. The certain cognates in other Gmc. languages are O. Fris. *bēken*, O.S. *bōkan*, O.H.G. *pouhhan*. Beyond this the etymol. seems not to have been carried, so far. We have here a Gmc. base **bauk-*, for wh. we may confidently reconstruct an Aryan predecessor **bhoug-*, wh. wd. have also the grades **bheug-*, **bhŭg-*. Such a base appears in Gk. *pheúgō*, 'flee', *phúza* (fr. **phug-ja*), 'headlong flight, rout'; Lat. *fugĭre*, 'flee', *fuga*, 'flight'. With these the etymologists connect Lith. *búgti*, 'terrify', *baugùs*, 'frightful' &c. (See the prob. related Gmc. base **biug-*, **bŭg-* &c. under **bight, bow** (**I. & II.**), where the development of meaning has gone on quite different lines.) The base **bheug-* then seems to have the sense of running away fr. something wh. frightens one. It is now suggested that the base in Gmc. came to mean 'fear of something dangerous, danger, sign of danger, warning', then, 'a sign or token' generally. Cp. also **beckon. 1.** A prominent object or landmark, such as a tower, or clump of trees on a hill: e.g. *Crowborough Beacon*, in Sussex. **2.** Specif., a lighthouse or beacon fire. **3.** (fig.) A warning, summons, call to action in support of a cause &c.

beacon (**II.**), vb. intrans., fr. prec. To act as a beacon, to warn, give notice, summon, encourage: '*The soul of Adonaïs like a star, Beacons from the abode where the eternal are*' (Shelley, 'Adonais', lv.).

beacon fire, light, n. One lighted as a warning, or to notify that some hoped-for event has happened.

bead (**I.**), n. [1. bēd; 2. bīd]. O.E. *ġe-bed*, 'prayer', M.E. *bēde(s)*, 'prayer(s)', also 'beads', O. Fris. *bede*, O.S. *beda*, O.H.G. *beta*, Goth. *bida*. The O.E. vb. is *biddan* (reflex.), 'pray', fr. **bed-jan*. It has been proposed to equate w. this base Scrt. *bādhatē*, 'compels, presses, urges'. The base apparently means 'urge with entreaties, importune with demands, beg and pray'. See also **bid** (**I.**). The Mod. Engl. meaning of *bead* is an interesting case of transference fr. the prayer itself to the small round objects on a string (rosary), used to help illiterate persons to remember how many prayers they had uttered, & wh. particular prayer had been reached. **1.** Small globular object of glass, wood &c., pierced so that it can be threaded on a wire or string: *glass beads, pearl beads* &c. *To tell one's beads*, make use of rosary, therefore to say one's prayers, though this is secondary, and the old meaning is lost in a direct application; *draw a bead on something*, to take aim. **2.** Small round drop of moisture: *beads of sweat, blood, pus* &c. **3.** (archit.) Small semicircular moulding; same as *astragal*; moulding in Norman work resembling a row of beads. **4.** (in pl.) Prayers (obs.). Still used in certain public schools, apparently without any reference to 'beads' in modern sense. Often spelt *bede*. The old sense survives vaguely in *bead-roll*, list of persons whose memory is kept in mind, originally list of those whose souls were prayed for; *beadsman*, person receiving charity, originally one who was bound to pray for his benefactors.

bead (**II.**), vb., fr. prec. **1.** To cover, bedeck, with beads, as embroidery &c. **2.** To say one's prayers; still, or until recently, used in special school slang at Charterhouse.

beaded, adj. [1. béded; 2. bídid]. Having, provided with, beset with, beads; beadlike in shape: '*With beaded bubbles winking at the brim*' (Keats).

beading, n. [1. béding; 2. bídiŋ]. **bead** (**I.**) **& -ing.** (archit.) Moulding; wooden strip applied as a finish to a frieze on the walls of buildings.

beadle, n. [1. bédl; 2. bídl]. O.E. *bydel*, S. Eastern *bedel*, 'messenger, herald', M.E. *budel, bēdel*, O.H.G. *butil*. The word is formed fr. the grade *bud-* of base seen in O.E. *bēodan*, 'announce', O.H.G. *biotan*, Goth. *-biudan*. (This vb. has been confused w. *biddan*, the meaning of wh. it has influenced. Cp. **bid**). Cogn. w. Gmc. **beud-*, **bud-*, fr. Aryan **bheudh-*, **bhudh-*, are Gk. *peúthomai*, 'ask, inquire, learn by asking', aor. *e-puthómēn*, cp. *peuthṓ*, 'tidings, news', O. Slav. *budéti*, 'wake, watch', Scrt. *bódhati*, 'he watches, pays attention, considers', *buddhiš*, 'perception' &c. A subordinate parish officer, now obsolete, who acted as official for the vestry in relief of the poor, also kept order in churches &c. Cp. **bumble**, & see also **bedell.**

beadledom, n. [1. bédldum; 2. bídldəm]. Prec. **& -dom.** Fussy, stupid interference of subordinate officials; bumbledom.

bead-roll, beadsman. See note at end of **bead** (**I.**).

beady, adj. [1. bédi; 2. bídi]. **bead** (**I.**) **& -y.** Bead-like, esp. *beady eyes*, small, bright, round, and slightly prominent.

beagle, n. [1. bégl; 2. bígl]. M.E. *begle*, of O. Fr. origin; etymol. obscure. A small, short-legged, smooth-coated hound, used chiefly for hunting hares when those who take part follow the hunt on foot and not on horseback: *a pack of beagles.*

beagling, n. [1. bégling; 2. bígliŋ]. Prec. **& -ing.** The sport of hunting hares with beagles.

beak, n. [1. bēk; 2. bīk], fr. Fr. *bec*, fr. Lat. *beccus*; said by Suetonius to be of Celt. origin. **1.** The horny projections from the mouths of birds, corresponding to the lips in mammals; the bill or nib of a bird. **2.** A human nose which is hooked and prominent. **3.** (by extension) Applied occasionally to the projecting portion of various objects, e.g. the rostrum of an ancient galley, ram of a warship, the mouthpiece of a flute &c. **4.** (colloq.) **a** A magistrate: *to be brought before the beak*; **b** (schoolboy slang), a schoolmaster, esp. the headmaster.

beaked, adj. [1. bēkt; 2. bīkt]. Prec. **& -ed.** Having, provided with, a beak (of birds); (also of land, rock &c.) jutting out: *beaked promontory.*

beaker, n. [1. béker; 2. bíkə]. The late 15th cent. *biker*, 'drinking-cup' &c., cannot be the ancestor of present-day form wh. must go back to M.E. (Nthn. ?) **bēker*, wh., however, is not recorded, or, as seems more probable, to Du. *beeker*. The word is found in most Gmc. languages, O.H.G. *behhar*, Germ. *becher*, O.N. *bikarr*, wh. is the starting-point of the only recorded early Mod. Engl. form. The word is clearly a loan-word in Gmc. & must be related to L. Lat. *bacar*, 'wine-vessel, wine-glass', & *bacris*, 'vessel with a long handle, ladle'. The Ital. *bicchiere* is certainly related to this, but more closely resembles Gk. *bîkos*, 'wine-jar'. The origin of this is obscure. **a** Goblet, cup, drinking-vessel; *beaker-folk*, round-headed race which introduced round barrows and a knowledge of metal into Great Britain at the end of the Neolithic period, their culture being typified by a specific kind of beaker; **b** contents of such a vessel: (gen. poet.) '*O for a beaker full of the warm South, Full of the true, the blushful Hippocrene*' (Keats, 'Nightingale').

beaky, adj. [1. béki; 2. bíki]. **beak & -y.** Like a beak, said esp. in reference to a human nose which is hooked or prominent.

beam (**I.**), n. [1. bēm; 2. bīm]. O.E. *bēam*, M.E. *bēme*, 'tree, beam (of wood), column of light', M.E. *bēmes*, 'beams of light', O. Fris. *bām*, O.H.G. *baum*, O.S. *bōm*, Du. *boom*, 'tree'. It is certain that the W. Gmc. base was **baum-*; whether Goth. *bagms* & O.N. *baðm*, 'tree', are fr. the same orig., & if so, how their forms are to be accounted for, does not concern us here. The Aryan base, whence the W. Gmc. type was derived, must have been **bheum-*, **bhoum-*, **bhum-* &c., corresponding to Gk. *phúma*, 'swelling, tumour, growth upon the body', lit. 'that which grows, is put forth', fr. the base **phu-* (Aryan **bhu-*), 'to become, produce' &c., seen in Gk. *phúein*, 'to bring forth, engender', *phúsis*, 'nature' &c.; this is believed to be identical w. **bheu-* &c. discussed under **be.** The common orig. meaning of the W. Gmc. base is undoubtedly 'tree', whence in Engl. considerable differentiation of meaning has taken place. The specific meaning 'tree' appears to be a specialized limitation of the earlier meaning 'growth'. The development of meaning in Engl. is interesting: tree; then, roughly hewn trunk, a large piece of timber used in building &c. From this meaning has branched off, at an early date, that of 'a pillar, column of fire, or light'. It seems strange at first sight that the name of so solid an object as a *beam* shd. be transferred to light, but cp. **ray**, fr. Fr. *raie*, Lat. *radius*, 'staff', & **shaft**, orig. a 'pole, handle' &c., for smaller streams of light. Already in O.E. we get *sunnebēam*, 'sunbeam', & the compound *lēohtbēamede*, adj., 'having beams of light'. The O.E. *bīeme*, 'trumpet', is usually connected w. *bēam*, & the meaning of this may possibly be, as seems to be gen. assumed, 'a wooden thing', but this is not very convincing. *Bīeme* may mean orig. 'the instrument which sends forth "beams" of sound', *peals* as we shd. say. In O.E. the same word is often applied both to sight & sound, cp. *swutol*, 'clear', both 'bright' of light & other visible things, & 'ringing, echoing', of voices, sounds &c.; cp. further *hādor*, wh. means both 'bright, shining', & 'clear, resonant' of voices &c. **1.** A thick piece of timber, esp. one of the principal horizontal timbers in a building or a ship. Hence, **2**, the extreme breadth of a vessel at widest part. Also (fig.) of animals, and (colloq.) of persons: *broad in the beam.* Phr. *to be on one's beam-ends*, helpless. **3.** Various special uses: **a** bar of a balance, from ends of which the scales depend; **b** wooden cylinder forming part of weaving loom; **c** pole of a two-horse carriage or waggon, on and to either side of which the horses are harnessed (archaic); **d** part of a plough to which the share and coulter are attached, and by which it is drawn; **e** long quill in wing of a hawk, *beam feather*; **f** main stem of stag's horn. **4. a** A shaft, ray or stream of light, generally also of the sun, moon, stars; **b** (in wireless telegraphy and telephony) system which uses low power and short wave, using reflectors to direct and increase the strength of the signals: *the beam system*; **c** (fig.) a cheerful, kindly glance; goodness and kindness exhibited in looks and expression of countenance, or felt as an influence exerted: *the beams of a smile*; *to enjoy the beams of a person's kindness, charity* &c.

beam (**II.**), vb. intrans., fr. prec. **1.** To shine, shed light, esp. poetical and literary. **2.** (fig.) To smile happily and benevolently; to wear an expression of cheerful content and benevolence: *he said nothing, but merely sat and beamed*; *to beam upon a person.*

beaming, adj. [1. bḗming; 2. bímiŋ]. Pres. Part. of prec. Radiant, cheerful, happy, benign; esp. *beaming face, smile, expression of countenance, glance* &c.

beamish, adj. [1. bḗmish; 2. bímiʃ], fr. **beam** (I.), 4, & **-ish.** Word invented by Lewis Carroll in 'Through the Looking Glass,' Jabberwocky: *Come to my arms, my beamish boy,* apparently with some such sense as fine, flourishing, fortunate, successful &c.

bean, n. [1. bēn; 2. bīn]. O.E. *bēan*, M.E. *bēne* (note phrase *not worth a bene* (Chaucer), 'worthless'), O.H.G. *bōna*, Germ. *bohne*, O.N. *baun*. The connexion of this Gmc. word w. Gk. *phakós*, 'lentil', Lat. *faba*, 'bean' &c., has never been explained & is very dubious; see **fabaceous.** A kind of leguminous plant of order known as *Fabaceae*; seed of these plants, some of which are used as human food, while others of coarser kind are fed to horses: *French beans, runner beans, kidney beans, broad beans* &c. Phrs. (usually colloq.) *full of beans, to have too much beans,* said of horses who show spirit and liveliness, and by extension, of human beings, in sense of spirited, full of activity, vigour, and go; *to give (a person) beans,* to give him a thrashing, treat him severely, hurt him; also said of a wound or injury: *it gave me beans,* it hurt, caused much pain; *old bean,* (slang) form of familiar address; cp. Fr. *mon vieux haricot.*

bean-feast, n. Originally referring to favourite popular dish of *beans and bacon*; a village banquet, then (colloq.) any kind of festive, hilarious celebration, generally, but not necessarily, including some sort of banquet or other meal.

beano, n. [1. bḗnō; 2. bínou], fr. prec. (colloq. and vulg.) Bean-feast.

bean-pod, n. Legume, or seed-vessel of the bean plant.

bear (I.), vb. trans. & intrans. [1. bār; 2. bɛə]. O.E. *beran*, M.E. *bēre(n)*, O.H.G., O.S. *beran*; Goth. *bairan*; O.N. *bera*; all the Gmc. languages use the word in double sense of 'carry' & 'bear children'; Gk. *phérein*, 'carry, bring forth', Lat. *fero*, 'I bear', see **-ferous**; Scrt. *bhárati*, 'he bears'; O. Slav. *berą*, 'I collect, bring together'. The Aryan base in its various forms is **bher-*, **bhēr-*, **bhor-*, **bhōr-*, **bhr̥-*, corresponding respectively to Gmc. **ber-*, **bǣr-*, **bar-*, **bōr-*, **bur-*. Cp. **bairn, bier, born.** N.B.—The P.P. in present-day Engl. is always written *borne*, except in sense 2 below. In the primary senses *bear*, **1**, is now largely displaced by *carry* and **2** by *have*, at any rate in colloq. speech. On the other hand, the word is much used in the various derived meanings, & in many idiomatic phrases. **1.** To carry, transport: *his shoulders can bear a heavy load* (lit. and fig.); *the mules bearing the baggage remained behind*; *the ship bore him to a distant country.* Various idiomatic uses derived from primary sense 'carry': *bear arms,* to be provided with weapons; also (her.) to possess armorial bearings; *bear the marks, signs, traces of* (ill-treatment, wounds, punishment &c.), to exhibit traces of; *bear a grudge, malice* &c., to have a grievance *against* (a person) *for* (an injury); *bear a hand,* to help, give assistance; *bear a part in,* to take part, or share in; *bear away the bell, bear the palm,* excel in a competition or in comparison with several others; *bear a person company,* to remain in society of, accompany; *bear false witness against,* testify wrongly, give wrong evidence; *bear off,* deviate from course, go away in different direction; *bear out* (evidence, conclusion &c.), confirm, correspond to, agree with; *bear down on,* come rapidly towards, esp. of a ship; also (fig.) to walk quickly in a person's direction. **2.** To bring forth, produce: **a** of women, *to bear children,* now generally, *to have children*; P.P.: *she has borne many children*; *he was born in 1815*; **b** of plants, trees, *to bear fruit.* **3.** To support, sustain, a weight, strain &c.; **a** trans., *this beam bears the whole weight of the upper floor*; **b** intrans., to be equal to a strain, be strong enough, be capable of sustaining a weight: *will the ice bear to-day?*, is it strong enough? **4. a** To endure, undergo, suffer with fortitude: *he bears pain well*; *he bore the operation satisfactorily.* Phrs. *bear the brunt,* play chief part in any action, suffer first or severest attack, have most of the trouble in an affair; *bear up* (*against*) misfortune &c., resist, show courage in face of; *to be unable to bear* (pain &c.), not to be strong, courageous enough; **b** to tolerate, put up with, like; esp. with *can't*: *I can't bear that fellow*; *he couldn't bear living alone* (in this sense *bear* is strongly stressed); *bear with* (a person or circumstance), endure with patience; *there is no bearing* (*with*) (persons and circumstances), he, it, they cannot be endured, tolerated. **5.** To lean heavily upon, for support: *to bear heavily on a stick* &c. **6.** To have relation to, have influence or bearing upon: *this fact bears upon the subject of our conversation.* **7.** (reflex.) **a** (lit.) Carry oneself, walk &c.: *he bears himself like a man who has been well drilled*; **b** (fig.) comport, conduct oneself, behave: *he bore himself with great dignity under difficult circumstances.*

bear (II.), n. O.E. *bera*, O.H.G. *bero*. The Gmc. languages have abandoned the Aryan name for this animal seen in Gk. *árktos*, Lat. *ursus* (fr. **urcsos*), W. *arth*, Scrt. *r̥kšas*. The attempts to connect *bera* w. Lat. *furvus*, 'dusky, black', or w. Lat. *ferus*, 'wild', must be rejected. The former is most prob. connected w. O.E. *deorc*, 'dark', see **dark**, & the latter is certainly cogn. w. Gk. *thḗr*, 'wild beast', q.v. under **fierce.** There seems no objection to connecting *bera* w. the base seen in **brown** & in **beaver.** We must assume for this word an Aryan **bhere*, cp. Lith. *béras*, O. Slav. *brŭ-logŭ*, 'lair of the bear'. The *bear* according to this is merely 'the brown animal', a designation wh. he shares w. the beaver. **1. a** Heavy, clumsy mammal, belonging to the genus *Ursus*, with rough, thick coat and long claws, of which there are many species, found in many parts of Europe, Africa, and America, whose diet consists partly of flesh, partly of fruit and honey. Phr. *to sell the skin before one has killed the bear*; **b** (astron.) name of two Northern constellations, Great and Little Bear, Ursa Major and Minor. **2.** (fig.) A clumsy, loutish, rough-mannered man. **3.** (Stock Exchange) One who is waiting for a fall in the price of securities, so that he may buy them before settling day at a lower price than that at which he had previously sold them. Cp. *bull.*

bear (III.), vb. trans., fr. prec., sense **3.** To act as a bear in selling and buying shares.

bearable, adj. [1. bārabl; 2. bɛ́ərəbl]. See **bear** (I.) & **-able.** Tolerable, capable of being endured: *the pain though unpleasant was quite bearable.*

bear-baiting, n. [1. bār bā̆ting; 2. bɛ́ə bèitiŋ]. Old sport of baiting a bear with dogs.

beard (I.), n. [1. bērd; 2. bíəd]. O.E. *beard*, O.H.G. *bart*, O.N. *barðr*; Lat. *barba* (fr. **farba*, fr. **bhardha*), Lith. *barzdà*, O. Slav. *brada*, all meaning 'beard'. **1.** The hair on a man's cheeks and chin, formerly used also of hair on upper lip; hair on chin of a he-goat, lion, and other animals. Phr. *to speak in one's beard,* mumble, mutter indistinctly. **2.** Fringed gills of oyster. **3.** Spike or awn on oats, barley, or other cereals.

beard (II.), vb. trans., fr. prec. To approach a person, esp. one who inspires awe, boldly with a request, open a subject of dispute with him (from idea of seizing by the beard, and thus having a formidable foe at one's mercy); esp. *to beard a man in his den.*

bearded, adj. [1. bērded; 2. bíədid], fr. P.P. of prec. Furnished with a beard.

beardless, adj. [1. bērdles; 2. bíədlis]. **beard** (I.) & **-less.** Without a beard; not yet growing hair on the face; hence, youthful.

beardlessness, n. Prec. & **-ness.** State of being beardless.

bearer, n. [1. bārer; 2. bɛ́ərə]. **bear** (I.) & **-er.** **1.** One who bears or carries: *a bearer of burdens*; specif. **a** one of those who carry the coffin of the dead to the grave; also *pall-bearer*, one of those who walk beside the coffin draped with a pall, in honour of the dead; **b** a Hindu domestic servant, who originally helped to carry a litter or palanquin; **c** presenter of a cheque not made payable to order; *bearer securities,* stocks and bonds the scrip or certificate of which has no owner's name on it and can change hands without formal transfer. **2.** That which produces (of crops, plants &c.): *a good, poor, bearer.*

bear-garden, n. Place where bears used to be kept for the sport of bear-baiting, hence (fig.) noisy, rowdy place or assembly.

bearing, n. [1. bāring; 2. bɛ́əriŋ]. See **bear** (I.) & **-ing.** **1. a** Personal carriage, deportment: *a man of noble, lofty bearing*; **b** manner, behaviour: *his kindly bearing endeared him to all.* **2.** Relation to something else; meaning, drift, purport: *what you say has no bearing upon the question*; *I fail to see the bearing of that remark*; *what is the precise bearing of the word in this passage?* **3.** (naut., surveying, map reading &c.) Direction, position, of any object in relation to a ship or other fixed point from which direction is to be ascertained: *to take the bearings,* find out direction of ship's course &c.; (extended and fig. meaning) sense of physical direction generally, and sense of relation in intellectual matters: *I have lost my bearings, am out of my bearings,* have lost my way, or, am puzzled. **4.** Endurance, possibility of being endured: *his conduct is beyond, past, all bearing.* **5.** (mechan.) *Bearings,* part of a machine in which the moving parts turn, or revolve, as *ball bearings.* **6.** (her.) All the charges, or emblems on a coat of arms, in Phr. *armorial bearings.* **7.** The capacity for, process of, producing a crop in trees and plants; the season of such production: *by judicious pruning fruit trees can be kept in bearing for many years.*

bearing rein, n. A short strap fastened from the top of the bridle to the saddle or other part of the harness to keep a horse's head up.

bearish, adj. [1. bārish; 2. bɛ́əriʃ], fr. **bear** (II.) & **-ish.** Like a bear, rough, rude in manners.

bearishness, n. Prec. & **-ness.** A rough, surly manner.

bear-leader, n. **bear** (II.) & **leader.** One who acts as tutor or travelling companion to a rich young man.

bear's grease, n. Fat, grease, of the bear, perfumed and used as a hair pomade.

bearskin, n. [1. bārskin; 2. bɛ́əskin], fr. **bear** (II.) & **skin.** Tall furry hat worn by Guards' regiments.

beast, n. [1. bēst; 2. bīst]. M.E. *bēste*, fr. O. Fr. *bēste*, fr. Lat. *bēstia*, 'beast', as distinct fr. man, esp. a wild animal. Walde derives the word fr. Aryan **dhwēsdhia*, wh. becomes first **dwēsdia* then *bēstia* (*b* fr. *dw-* being normal Lat. change). The base, different forms of wh. are **dhewēs-*, **dhwēs*, -**dhūs-* &c., means orig. 'to breathe', & fr. it are also derived Lith. *dvēs-ti*, 'pant', *dvãse*, 'breath, spirit', *daũsos*, 'higher air', Lett. *dwēs-ele*, 'breath, soul, life'; O. Slav. *dychati*, 'breathe', *duchŭ*, 'breath', *duša*, 'breath, soul'; w. these may also be compared Gk. *theós*, 'god', fr. earlier **thwesos*, Aryan **dhwesos*, lit. 'spirit, breath', see **theo-**; cp. further Scrt. *dhū-má*, 'smoke, steam' &c. This base, the fundamental meaning of wh. is 'vapour, breath' (as a visible mist), appears, variously modified by different formative elements, in many words in all Aryan languages, & is used to express the more complex ideas of 'life, spirit' &c. *Bēstia* is orig. 'the living, breathing creature'. The base appears again w. exactly the same meaning in Gmc. **deus-*, O.E. *dēor*, 'wild animal'. See further under **deer, dust, fume.** **1. a** In widest sense, applied to animals in general in distinction to birds and fishes; esp. to wild, fierce animals: *wild beasts*; *beasts of the forest, jungle* &c.; apart from special combinations such as those above, *animal* is now more usual; **b** specif. (of cows, bullocks &c.) cattle: *farmers are getting good prices for their beasts*. Special uses: *beast of burden*, horses, mules, donkeys; *beast of prey*, lion, tiger &c; *the beast in man*, lower nature. **2. a** A filthy, degraded person of disgusting and brutal habits; **b** in schoolboy slang merely a strict, severe, rather exacting person, esp. of schoolmasters; **c** used jocularly in colloquial speech, without any bad sense, of one who on occasion will not fall in with one's wishes, a disobliging, or obstinate person, e.g. *don't be a beast, do as I ask you*. **3.** *The Beast*, Antichrist, the Beast of the Apocalypse.

beastliness, n. [1. béstlines; 2. bístlinis]. **beastly & -ness.** Condition, quality, of being beastly. **1.** Esp. of moral conditions, nastiness, filthiness: *a mind full of beastliness*. **2.** Obscenity, immorality of speech, thought, and conduct: *to talk beastliness*; *live in a state of beastliness*; *this book is sheer beastliness*.

beastly (I.), adj. [1. béstli; 2. bístli]. See **beast & -ly.** **1.** Like a beast; disgusting, filthy, obscene: *beastly habits, mind, conversation*. **2.** (colloq.) Unpleasant, provoking dislike, often in quite a mild sense, rather bad, not very good: *beastly weather, headache, temper, noise, food*; *this bed is simply beastly*.

beastly (II.), adv. Used colloquially as intensive with adjective expressing anything disagreeable, unpleasant &c.: *beastly bad luck*; *this meat is beastly tough*; *Russian is beastly difficult to learn* &c.

beat (I.), vb. trans. & intrans. [1. bēt; 2. bīt]. O.E. *bēatan*, 'strike, beat, trample, dash', O.H.G. *bōzzen*, cp. also O.H.G. *ana-bōz*, 'anvil', O.N. *bauta*. The Gmc. stem must have been orig. **bau-t-*, the *-t-* being a formative, cp. Lat. *con-fū-tāre*, 'strike down' (Lat. & Eng. *t* cannot be equated). The Lat. word means also 'thrust, strike', & w. it Lat. *fustis*, 'cudgel, staff', is cogn. This may be derived fr. Aryan **bhud-sti*, this form of the base being equiv. to Gmc. **bu-t-*, another gradation of **bau-t-*. The Engl. word seems to have retained the orig. general meaning. **1.** To strike, rain blows upon, with the hand, hammer, stick &c.; *to beat iron, a walnut tree*; *to beat one's breast*; *beat a drum*; *to beat a carpet* (to knock the dust out). Phr. *to beat time*, indicate rhythm of music with a conductor's baton; *a beaten path, track* (lit. and fig.), road which others have travelled before; *beat a retreat*, retire, run away (from idea of drums beating); *beat it!*, (colloq., U.S.A.) go away! clear off! get out!; *beat the bounds* (of a parish), indicate by striking with rods. **2.** Specif., to strike with the hand, a stick, or whip &c., as a punishment, to thrash, flog, castigate: *this boy deserves to be well beaten*; *the man was fined for cruelly beating his horse, dog*. **3. a** To prevail over an opponent in any contest, to win victory over, inflict a defeat on (with *at, in*): *Oxford beat Cambridge at athletics*; *I can easily beat him at golf*; *the English beat the enemy at the Battle of the Somme*. Phrs. *that beats everything I ever heard*, is very surprising; *you won't easily beat that*, improve on; *that beats me*, puzzles, brings me to a standstill; *to beat the band* (of anything astonishing or surprising); *dead beat*, tired out; **b** (by extension) to surpass, be superior to, have particular qualities in excess of some other person or thing: *as a story-teller Chaucer beats all his contemporaries*; *many people think port beats claret as an after-dinner wine*; *England beats most other countries in its green fields*. **4.** To throb, pulsate with regular stroke (of the heart or pulse). Phr. *his heart had ceased to beat*, the man was dead. **5.** To rouse, or 'put up' game. **6.** Various uses and phrases: *to beat about the bush*, talk round a subject before coming to the point; *beat the air*, (fig.) pursue a useless or fruitless task; *beat against*, dash (of waves on rocks &c.); *beat down*, lower, reduce (of a price); suppress, destroy: *beat down opposition*; *beat into* (one's head), teach with difficulty; *beat off*, thrust aside, repel (of attacks); *beat up*, to whisk, cause to froth (of eggs &c.); *beat up recruits*, collect; *beat up quarters of*, visit; *beat out* (metal), hammer it thin; (fig.) to elucidate, bring to light: *beat out the meaning* of something.

beat (II.), n., fr. prec. **1.** A regular, recurrent stroke, as of the heart, drums, of a clock, or bells; recurrent emphasis in rhythm or music: *heart beats*; *beat of drum*, implies the sound made by beating. **2.** A particular round or course regularly traversed: *a policeman's* (&c.) *beat*, the precise path on which he comes and goes when on duty. Phr. *to be on the* (*his*) *beat*, in the act of going his rounds; (fig.) *to be off, out of, one's beat*, to be on unfamiliar ground, in subject or pursuit different from one's usual studies and habits. **3.** Act of beating for game, in hunting and shooting.

beaten, adj. [1. bétn; 2. bítn], fr. P.P. of **beat** (I.). O.E. *bēaten*, M.E. *bēten*. **1.** Having received a beating: *a beaten hound*. **2.** Conquered, defeated: *a beaten enemy*; *the enemy were thoroughly beaten*. **3.** Wrought, smoothed, by beating or treading: *beaten gold*; *beaten track*, familiar, well-worn path; also fig.

beater, n. [1. béter; 2. bítə]. **beat** (I.) & **-er.** **1. a** One who beats; in most senses of **beat** (I.), specif. **b** man employed to beat up game; used also technically in various senses in different industries &c., e.g. *gold beater*. **2.** Instrument which beats: *a mechanical carpet-beater, egg-beater* &c.

beatific(al), adj. [1. bèatífik(l); 2. bìətífik(l)], fr. L. Lat. *beātificus*, fr. *beātus*, 'blessed'. See **beatitude** & **beauty** & **-fic.** **a** Having the power of making blessed. *Beatific vision*, immediate sight of God granted to the saints; **b** (in gen. sense) radiating happiness; charming, delightful: *a beatific smile*.

beatification, n. [1. biàtifikáshun; 2. biæ̀tifikéiʃən]. Prec. & **-ation.** Process of making blessed. In the Christian Church (esp. now in Roman Catholic and Orthodox Churches) the word means a public, authoritative recognition that one who is dead has attained to the second degree of sanctity, is one of *the Blessed*, and is entitled to public religious veneration; this state is next in order to full canonization.

beatify, vb. trans. [1. biátifī; 2. biǽtifai], fr. L. Lat. *beātificāre*. See **beatitude** & **-fy.** **a** To declare officially that a departed person is one of *the Blessed*, and has reached the state of *beatification*; **b** (in gen. sense) to make happy.

beating, vbl. n. [1. béting; 2. bítiŋ], fr. **beat** (I.) & **-ing.** **1.** The action of one who beats (in various senses); the process involved in that action. Specif., a thrashing, whipping; infliction of defeat &c.: *to give a boy, the enemy &c. a good beating*. **2.** Pulsation, recurrent stroke: *beating of the heart*; fluttering, flapping: *beating of wings*. Also in various uses related to meanings of the verb.

beatitude, n. [1. biátitūd; 2. biǽtitjūd], fr. Lat. *beātitūdo*, 'happiness, blessedness'. Formed fr. *beātus*, 'blessed', P.P. of *beāre*, 'make happy', fr. base **dwe-*, 'to honour' &c. See **beauty.** **1.** Blessedness, happiness: *a state of beatitude*. **2.** One of the precepts laid down in the *Sermon on the Mount* (gen. pl., *The Beatitudes*).

beau, n. [1. bō; 2. bou]. Fr. *beau*, O. Fr. *bel*, Lat. *bellus*. See **beauty.** **1.** A dandy, a buck; man who sets up as a model of fashion and elegance in dress and manners. Formerly used as a half-contemptuous title before the surname of such persons, as *Beau Nash*, *Beau Brummel*. **2.** A cavalier, squire of dames, lady's escort; one paying polite attentions and rendering small services to a lady. **3.** (as vb.) To act as a *beau* (2), dance attendance on ladies.

beau ideal, n. As though Engl. [1. bō īdéal; 2. bóu aidíəl]. Fr., 'ideal beauty'. See prec. Generally felt in English to be the opposite, 'beautiful ideal'. The highest standard of excellence one can conceive: *he is my beau ideal of a gentleman, soldier* &c.

Beaune, n. [1. bōn; 2. boun], fr. name of town & wine-growing district in France. A brand of Burgundy wine.

beauteous, adj. [1. bútius, búchus; 2. bjútiəs, bjútʃəs]. Formed fr. O. Fr. *bealte*, q.v. under **beauty, & -ous.** Beautiful, with hardly any difference in meaning compared with this, but used far less frequently.

beautiful (I.), adj. [1. bútifool; 2. bjútif(ə)l]. See **beauty & -ful.** Possessing beauty; comely, lovely.

beautiful (II.), n., fr. prec. **a** Abstract n. That which has beauty; the quality or principle of beauty (always preceded by *the*): *a love of the beautiful*; *Burke on the Sublime and Beautiful*; **b** those who possess beauty; beautiful persons: '*The young, the beautiful, the brave*' (Byron).

beautifully, adv. **beautiful** (I.) & **-ly.** In a beautiful manner (with various senses); pleasantly, satisfactorily, successfully; *you have done it beautifully*; *the car ran beautifully*; *to get on beautifully*; *to paint, write, play, beautifully*.

beautify, vb. trans. [1. bútifī; 2. bjútifai]. See next word & **-fy.** To make beautiful, adorn, give additional beauty to.

beauty, n. [1. búti; 2. bjúti]. M.E. *bealtē*, *beautē*, *beutē*, O. Fr. *beltét*, *belté*, fr. Lat. *bellitāt-(em)*, fr. adj. *bellus*, 'charming, lovely, agreeable'; *bellus* is fr. earlier **benlos*, connected w. *bene*, 'well', *bonus*, 'good', wh. come fr. **dwen-*. The most probable relationships of this base, outside Italic, are Scrt. *dúvaś*, 'honour, respect, homage', & other derived Scrt. words w. same sense. The Lat. *beāre*, 'bless, gladden', P.P. *beātus*, 'blessed, happy', are fr. same base. Cp. **beatitude.** **1.** The abstract quality. **a** *Beauty of sight and sound*: that visual impression of fitness, suitability, satisfaction and pleasure produced, upon the eye or sight, by a sense of just proportion in the relative size of the various parts of a design, by grace of line and perfection of form, by certain absolute qualities of colour, or by the effect of one colour in relation to others. The pleasure and satisfaction to the ear which results from the absolute quality of sounds, or is produced by the harmony of sounds in combination, and by regularity of rhythm. The main elements in beauty of sight and sound are suitability, proportion, harmony. The word *beauty* refers both to the sensations of the kind described and to the combination of qualities and circumstances which produce them. We speak of the *beauty* of a face, feature, of woman, of a building, scene, picture; *beauty* of voice, of a melody, verse, style; **b** *moral and spiritual beauty*: the sense of moral elation, exaltation, rightness which results from the perception and contemplation of such qualities of mind, thought, feeling as are felt to be in accordance with truth, sincerity, justice, benevolence, and so forth. By *beauty* in this sense is meant both the combination of moral qualities and the effect which the perception of them produces upon the mind. We speak of the *beauty of holiness*; *beauty of mind, thought, feeling, character*; *beauty of kindness, unselfishness* &c. Since works of art, painting, sculpture, poetry, literature generally are the expression of moral states by means which appeal to the eye or the ear, the word *beauty* in reference to any of them nearly always implies a combination of what is defined under both **a** and **b**. **2.** Particular example, exhibition of grace, charm, virtue, or excellence as defined under **1. a** and **b**: (often in pl.) *her smile was one of her chief* *beauties; she has many beauties of mind and person; the landscape had a beauty all its own; 'Paradise Lost' contains a thousand beauties.* **3. a** A beautiful person, esp. of a woman: *she was very attractive, but hardly a beauty; the pages of Grammont mention many once famous but now long-forgotten beauties;* **b** used colloquially, in irony, in reference to a person who is the reverse of beautiful, or with whom the speaker is annoyed: *she's a regular beauty, isn't she; well, you are a beauty, you've lost me the game;* **c** used jocularly, and affectionately in addressing persons and animals (esp. dogs and horses): *come along, my beauties.*

beauty sleep, n. Sleep before midnight, popularly supposed to be specially beneficial.

beauty spot, n. Small patch of black plaster stuck on face to enhance, by contrast, the freshness of the complexion.

beaver (I.), n. [1. bévər; 2. bívə]. O.E. *beofor* (fr. **bifur*), O.H.G. *bibar*, O.N. *björr*, Du. *bever*, cogn. w. Lat. *fiber*, O. Slav. *bebrŭ*, Lith. *bébrus*, Scrt. *babhrúš*, 'brown', then 'larger ichneumon'. The Aryan base **bhru-* meant 'brown'; the word **bhe-bhru*, 'beaver', is simply a reduplication of this; *beaver*, therefore, is 'the brown animal'. Cp. **bear (II.)** & **brown. 1.** A large rodent, genus *Castor*, with a flat scaly tail, living in kind of huts, or 'lodges', which it constructs in streams; found in Europe and America. **2. a** The fur of the beaver: *trimmed with beaver;* **b** originally this was used for making what are now called *top-hats*, and the word was transferred to designate a hat of this kind, also *beaver-hat* (already in Chaucer).

beaver (II.), n. Late 15th cent. *baviere*, fr. identical O. Fr. form; lit. 'a bib', something to catch saliva, O. Fr. & Mod. Fr. *bave*, 'saliva, foam from an animal's mouth', etymol. unknown. (obs.) Lower, movable part of a helmet, protecting the chin and lips, worn with a vizor. '*O yes, my lord, he wore his beaver up*' (Shakespeare, 'Hamlet').

becalm, vb. trans. [1. bekáhm; 2. bikám]. See **be-** & **calm.** Now chiefly in pass., w. P.P. *becalmed*, of a ship, deprived of wind and unable to make progress by sailing.

became, vb. [1. bekám; 2. bikéim]. Pret. of **become**; see **came.**

because, adv. [1. bekóz; 2. bikóz], fr. **be-**, wk. form of **by**, & **cause.** For the reason that: *he does it because he thinks it right, not because he likes doing it; because of*, on account of, owing to.

beccafico, n. [1. bekaféko; 2. bekəfíkou]. Ital., lit. 'fig-pecker', fr. *beccare*, 'to peck', fr. *becca*, 'beak', fr. Lat. *beccus*, see **beak,** & *fico*, see **fig.** The name given to various small autumnal migrant birds, haunting fig trees and vineyards, netted for food and esteemed a great delicacy; specif., a kind of garden warbler; cp. *ortolan.*

bechamel, n. [1. béshamel; 2. béʃəmel]. Fr., name of its inventor. A rich white sauce.

bechance, vb. [1. becháhns; 2. bitʃáns]. See **be-** & **chance.** To happen, come about.

bêche-de-mer, n. [1. báshdemār; 2. beʃdəméər]. Fr. corrupt. of Port. *bicho do mar*, 'sea-slug'. The sea-slug, trepang; a favourite Chinese dish.

beck (I.), n. [1. bek; 2. bek], fr. obs. vb., shortened form of **beckon.** A nod, sign made with the hand in greeting &c.: '*Nods and becks and wreathed smiles*' (Milton, 'L'Allegro'). Phr. *to be at a person's beck and call*, to be constantly liable to come and go at his bidding.

beck (II.), n., fr. O.N. *bekkr.* Prob. cogn. w. **beach.** Small stream; chiefly Nthn.

becket, n. [1. béket; 2. békit]. Etymol. doubtful; prob. fr. Du. *bek*, 'beak', w. dimin. suff. **-et.** (naut.) Name of various devices, such as a ring or loop of rope, for securing loose ends of rope, tackle &c.

beckon, vb. trans. & intrans. [1. békun; 2. békən]. O.E. *bēacnian*, 'make signs, point out'. Cp. **beacon.** To make a sign with hand or finger to (a person), consisting of a rapid sweeping motion inwards, usually indicating a summons to approach.

becloud, vb. trans. [1. beklóud; 2. bikláud]. **be-** & **cloud.** To dim, make dark, obscure, overshadow. Often fig. of the eyes, the mind, or intelligence.

become, vb. intrans. & trans. [1. bikúm; 2. bikám]. **be-** & **come. A.** intrans. **1.** To pass from one state, condition, or set of circumstances, into another: *he became stupid as he grew old; he became king on his father's death; what was formerly a secondary matter, now becomes one of the highest importance.* **2.** To happen to, befall (followed by *of*): *what will become of the children left unprovided for?* Special use (colloq.): '*What's become of Waring?*' (Browning), where is he? **B.** intrans. To beseem, befit, suit, sit well upon: *it does not become me to speak on such a subject; his modesty became well so great a man; this style of dress becomes you very well.*

becoming (I.), adj. [1. bikúming; 2. bikámiŋ], fr. Pres. Part. of prec. Suitable, appropriate, befitting; **a** (of conduct and action) *it is not at all becoming in a man to speak with disrespect of his friend;* **b** (of personal dress) specially suitable for a particular person, as setting off his or her personal advantages: *she wore a most becoming hat.*

becoming (II.), n. **become** & **-ing.** A coming into existence, or life, the beginning of the process of any kind of development; chiefly used in philosophy, perhaps as a translation of the German phrase *Werden und Vergehen*, lit. *becoming and passing away.*

becomingly, adv. **becoming** (I.) & **-ly.** In a becoming manner.

bed (I.), n. [1. bed; 2. bed]. O.E. *bedd*, O.H.G. *beti, betti*, Goth. *badi*, 'bed'. The O.E. word is used not only in sense of 'couch', but also, in compounds, in that of 'garden bed, place where plants grow'; cp. *wyrt-bedd*, 'bed of plants or vegetables', *hrēod-bedd*, 'reed-bed'; in Germ. also, *beet*, variant of *bett*, means 'garden bed'. This sense is apparently rather nearer than that of 'couch' to the primitive meaning, wh. seems to be 'place dug, or hollowed out'. Lat. *fodio* has senses 'dig' & 'pierce, prick, stab', the first meaning being derived apparently fr. the idea of thrusting a spade into the ground. Other Aryan languages employ the base sometimes in sense of 'prick, pierce', sometimes in that of 'dig, a place dug out, grave' &c.; Lith. *bed-eti*, 'dig, hollow out'; Lett. *best*, 'bury', *bedre*, 'pit, hollow', *bed-ît*, 'hollow out, bury'; further Lith. *badýti*, 'pierce, prick', O. Slav. *bosti*, 'prick', *bodlĭ*, 'thorn'; Welsh *bedd* means 'grave'; cp. Place-Names such as *Beddgellert*; Gk. *bóthros*, 'hollow', may be fr. same base but this is not certain. The development of meaning of the n. in Gmc. may have been 'place dug, scratched or hollowed out', whence the specialized meanings: **a** place hollowed out by an animal to lie down in, a lair — this is extended to mean 'human resting-place'; **b** 'place where ground is dug up, or naturally broken up, in wh. plants grow'. Thus a *bed* was originally a very primitive form of resting-place. **1.** A piece of furniture upon which human beings sleep or rest; applied generally to the article with all its parts, both the mattress and the wooden or iron frame which supports it. Phrs. *to be brought to bed (of)*, give birth to (a child); *go to bed*, retire for the night, enter one's bed; *take to one's bed*, remain in bed, from illness &c.; *to be too fond of one's bed*, lazy; *stay, lie in bed; bed of roses*, easy, pleasant position; *bed of sickness; die in one's bed*, natural death. **2.** More specif., mattress: *feather bed, flock bed.* **3.** Anything used as a resting-place for men or animals: *bed of straw, hay, leaves* &c. Fig. Phr. *as you make your bed, so you must lie upon it*, you are responsible for your own misfortunes. **4.** (fig.) The grave: '*The cock's shrill clarion nor the echoing horn No more shall rouse them from their lowly bed*' (Gray). **5.** (fig.) The marriage state; condition of intimate relations between man and woman (gen. preceded by poss. pron.): '*I . . . Divorced old barren Reason from my bed, And took the daughter of the vine to spouse*' (FitzGerald, 'Omar Khayyám'); *the king banished his wife from his bed*, separated from her, broke off cohabitation. **6.** Large mass of matter, collection of objects (stones &c.) closely packed together: *bed of clay; the river, ocean bed*, ground underneath the water; *bed of rock, gravel* &c. **7.** Piece of ground dug and prepared for planting, or naturally forming suitable spot in which trees and plants grow: *flower bed; onion bed; bed of peas; bed of rushes, nettles* &c.; *withy bed.* **8.** Foundation of solid substance upon which buildings, machines &c. are fixed; layer or course: *bed of masonry, mortar* &c.

bed (II.), vb. trans., fr. prec. To place in a bed. **1.** Virtually obsolete in sense of *putting to bed.* **2. a** To plant out flowers or plants of any kind in a bed (often with *out*): *to bed out geraniums;* **b** to lay anything on a bed: *to bed stones, bricks &c. in mortar* &c.

bedaub, vb. trans. [1. bedáwb; 2. bidɔ́b], fr. **be-** & **daub.** To daub or splash with moisture or filth.

bed-chamber, n. **bed** & **chamber.** Bedroom; archaic or obs., except in title of certain officials of the Royal Household, as *Groom, Lady, of the Bed-chamber.*

bed-clothes, n. **bed** & **clothes.** Sheets, pillows, blankets &c. for a bed.

bedding, n. [1. béding; 2. bédiŋ]. **bed** (I.) & **-ing.** Bed and bed-clothes; materials, straw or litter, from which a domestic animal's bed is made.

bedeck, vb. trans. [1. bedék; 2. bidék]. **be-** & **deck** (I.). To cover with, ornament, trick out, bedizen: *bedeck with flowers, jewels* &c. (of persons); *bedeck with flags* (of buildings).

bedeguar, -gar, n. [1. bédegar; 2. bédigā]. Fr. *bédeguar*, fr. Pers. *bādāwar*, 'brought by the wind'. A mossy growth on the stems of rose-bushes, caused by a gall-insect.

bedel(l), n. [1. bedél; 2. bedél], fr. Lat. *bedellus.* See **beadle.** A university officer, whose duties are to attend the chancellor or vice-chancellor and carry the mace in procession: *Esquire Bedell.*

bedesman. See **beadsman.**

bedevil, vb. trans. [1. bedévl; 2. bidévl]. **be-** & **devil.** To play havoc with, throw into confusion (of mind or circumstances); to bewitch, play the devil with.

bedew, vb. trans. [1. bedū́; 2. bidjū́]. **be-** & **dew.** To sprinkle with dew; (by extension and fig.) to sprinkle with, or cause drops of moisture of any kind to appear on: *eyes bedewed with tears.*

bedfellow, n. [1. bédfelō; 2. bédfelou]. **bed** (I.) & **fellow. a** One who shares a bed with another; a wife; **b** (fig.) one who is associated with another by circumstances; Phr. *an awkward bedfellow*, a person difficult to live with, or to have to deal with in association; *a strange bedfellow*, an associate whom one would not expect to have owing to difference of tastes, habits, character &c.

bedight, adj. [1. bedít; 2. bidáit], fr. P.P. of obs. vb. 'to adorn, deck'. See **be-** & **dight.** (rare and archaic) Adorned (with).

bedim, vb. trans. [1. bedím; 2. bidím]. **be-** & **dim.** To make dim, esp. of eyes, sight &c.; to cloud, make obscure the vision: *eyes bedimmed with tears* &c.

bedizen, vb. trans. [1. bedízn; 2. bidáizn]. **be-** & **dizen.** To trick out, generally with tawdry, flashy ornaments; to cover to excess with ornaments, jewels &c.; (said of persons, usually reflex.): *bedizen oneself with;* (or in P.P.) *bedizened with* &c.

bedlam, n. [1. bédlam; 2. bédləm]. Old form of *Bethlehem*, found in late M.E. **1. a** (cap.) Originally a hospital, that of *St. Mary of Bethlehem*, London, in which, later, mad people were confined; **b** a madhouse. **2.** Now only used figuratively in sense of a state of affairs, confusion, noise &c. resembling the supposed condition of a madhouse: *a regular bedlam*; *fit for bedlam* (more literal here).

bedlamite, n. [1. bédlamīt; 2. bédləmait]. Prec. & **-ite.** Madman, lunatic.

Bedlington terrier, n. [1. bédlingtun térier; 2. bédliŋtən tériə], fr. Bedlington, village in Northumberland, where first bred. A breed of rough-haired sporting terrier.

bedouin, n. & adj. [1. bédooin; 2. béduin]. Fr., fr. Arab. *badawin*, 'dwellers in the desert', fr. *badw*, 'desert'. **1.** n. (sing. & pl.) A nomad Arab of the desert. **2.** adj. Of, belonging to, the nomad Arabs.

bedraggle, vb. trans. [1. bedrágl; 2. bidrǽgl]. **be-** & **draggle.** To drag through the mire, make filthy; to make untidy (of one's dress, as though with much hard wear): *she looked rather bedraggled.*

bedridden, adj. [1. bédridn; 2. bédridn]. O.E. *bedrida*, *-reda*, 'one bedridden'; lit. a 'bed-rider'; now felt as P.P. Cp. *hag-ridden.* Compelled by illness and infirmity to remain permanently in bed.

bedrock, n. [1. bédrók; 2. bédrɔ́k]. **bed** (**I.**) & **rock.** **a** The bottom layer of rock, lying below superficial formations; **b** (fig.) fundamental principles. Phr. *to get down to bedrock.*

bedroom, n. [1. bédroom; 2. bédrum]. **bed** & **room.** Room containing a bed; sleeping apartment.

bedside, n. [1. bédsīd; 2. bédsaid]. **bed** (**I.**) & **side.** **1.** Side or neighbourhood of a bed: *to keep books at one's bedside.* **2.** (fig.) Of attendance on a sick person: *to watch, be, sit &c. at or by a person's bedside*, to be near, attentive to his wants &c.; *bedside manner*, one combining gentleness, sympathy, and cheerfulness suitable to a person in attendance on invalids: *to have a good bedside manner*, said of doctors, also (sarcastically) of those whose manners are exaggeratedly ingratiating.

bed-sore, n. **bed** (**I.**) & **sore.** A sore on the back or other parts of the body subject to pressure, caused by long lying in bed.

bedstead, n. [1. bédsted; 2. bédsted]. **bed** (**I.**) & **stead.** Frame of wood or iron which supports bed and its appurtenances.

bedstraw, n. [1. bédstraw; 2. bédstrɔ̄]. **bed** (**I.**) & **straw.** Popular name of several plants of the genus *Galium*, esp. *Lady's bedstraw*, with yellow flowers, and *hedge-bedstraw*, with white flowers; the stalks when dry were formerly used for bedding, whence the name.

bedtime, n. [1. bédtīm; 2. bédtaim]. **bed** (**I.**) & **time.** Hour for retiring to bed: *it is past bedtime*; usual, habitual, hour for going to bed: *my bedtime is 11 o'clock.*

bee, n. [1. bē; 2. bī]. O.E. *bēo*, M.E. *bee*, O.H.G. *bīa*, *bi-ni*, Germ. *bie-ne*, O. Swed. *bī*. Outside Gmc., cognates are Lat. *fūcus*, 'drone, male of honey bee', for **bhoi-kos*; Lith. *bi-tė*; Ir. *bech* (w. *-ko-* suff. like *fūcus*). Beyond this the relationships are uncertain. It has been suggested, on the one hand, that *bee* is connected w. the base **bhi-*, 'tremble, fear', wh. appears in O.E. *beofian*, 'quake', O.H.G. *biben*, O. Slav. *boją*, 'I am afraid', Scrt. *bibhéti*, 'he is afraid', wh. wd. imply that the *bee* was orig. thought of as the trembling, flitting creature; &, on the other, that it is named, fr. its habit of constructing nests, fr. the base **bheu-*, 'remain, dwell, make a dwelling', in sense of 'build' as in Germ. *bauen*; in this case the bee is 'the builder'. Cp. under **be** for more information about **bheu*, & under **wasp**, 'the weaver', for example of an insect named after its constructive habits. **1.** Small, flying, humming insect with four wings, six legs, and a formidable sting, which gathers honey from flowers and stores it in wax combs; genus *Apis.* Phrs. *busy as a bee*; *to swarm like bees*, to be very numerous; *to have a bee in one's bonnet*, to be obsessed with an idea, esp. a **fad**, to be slightly mad; *like a bee in a bottle*, of a buzzing noise. **2.** Collection of persons who meet together for pursuit of common purpose, such as a competition, or work of charity. Never much used in England except in term *spelling bee*, a word now as obsolete as the institution.

bee bread, n. Substance made of pollen of flowers, collected by bees for feeding the young brood.

beech, n. [1. bēch; 2. bītʃ]. O.E. *bēce*, 'beech tree', also *bōc*, *bōc-treō* (unmutated) (cp. *buck-* in **buckmast, buckwheat**); O.H.G. *buohha*, Germ. *buche* (fem.); O.N. *bōk*. With this, Lat. *fāgus*, 'beech', & Gk. *phēgos*, *phāgos*, 'oak with edible acorns' are cogn. The name of the tree goes back to Aryan times, but it was applied by different peoples to different trees. It is tempting, in view of the Gk. use, to connect the name of the tree w. Gk. *phágein*, 'to eat' (cogn. w. Scrt. *bhágati*, 'he divides out', *bháktam*, 'portion of food', *bhágaš*, 'lord and master', lit. 'one who gives out food', cp. **lord** & **lady**, & see **-phagous**), in wh. case the *beech* wd. be the 'tree with edible fruit'. This, however, is now considered uncertain. After all, there are several other trees wh. have a more generally edible fruit than either the oak or the beech. Tree of genus *Fagus.*

beechen, adj. [1. bēchen; 2. bītʃən]. O.E. *bēcen-(holt)*, 'beech wood', cp. Lat. *fāginus*, adj. fr. *fāgus*, Gk. *phēgineós.* These show adj. suff. *-ino*, cogn. w. O.E. *-in-*. Pertaining to the beech tree: *beechen wood* (now more or less obs.); made of wood of beech tree.

beechmast, buckmast, n. [1. bēchmahst, búkmahst; 2. bītʃmāst, bákmāst]. **beech** & **mast.** Fruit, nuts, of the beech tree.

bee-eater, n. Name of a family, *Meropidae*, of small, brightly plumaged birds of Southern Europe, which feed on bees, wasps, and other flying insects.

beef, n. [1. bēf; 2. bīf]. M.E. *beef*, *boef* &c., O. Fr. *boef*, *buef*, fr. Lat. *bovem*, acc. of *bōs*, 'ox'. For etymol. of this, see **cow**, w. wh. it is cogn., & **bovine.** **1.** Formerly used of a living ox (pl. *beeves*), now only used for carcase and flesh of an ox or cow considered as food; by extension also *horse beef*, horse-flesh as food. **2.** (fig. and colloq.) **a** Flesh generally, esp. when redundant. Phr. *beef to the heels*, plump to excess; **b** hence, with transference of meaning, strength, vigour, muscle: *to put too much beef into a stroke*, at tennis, billiards &c.

beefeater, n. [1. bēfēter; 2. bīfītə], fr. **beef** & **eater.** One of the Yeomen of the Guard. The former ingenious derivation, fr. *beaufetier*, 'one who waited at the king's sideboard', is now given up; there never was the slightest historical or linguistic evidence in its favour. The word means what it seems to mean. Why it was applied to the Yeomen of the Guard is not known, unless Dr. Johnson was right in saying 'because the commons is beef when on waiting'. The name may be a rather derisive nickname suggesting that the yeomen were well fed, and with the implication, perhaps, that eating was the chief part of their duties. The function of this body was formerly to protect the king's person; they are now purely ceremonial.

beefiness, n. [1. bēfines; 2. bīfinis]. See **beefy** & **-ness.** The quality of being beefy.

beefing, n. [1. bēfing; 2. bīfiŋ], fr. **beef** & **-ing.** Name comes from deep-red colour. A kind of apple, also in variant form *biffin*: *Herefordshire, Yorkshire, beefing.*

beefsteak, n. [1. bēfsták; 2. bīfstéik]. Thick slice of beef.

beef-tea, n. [1. bēf tē; 2. bīf tī]. Strong broth made from beef.

beefwood, n. [1. bēfwood; 2. bīfwud]. **beef** & **wood.** Species of tree found in tropical countries, having slender, drooping, jointed branches and no leaves; it produces a very hard, red-coloured timber, whence its name.

beefy, adj. [1. bēfi; 2. bīfi]. **beef** & **-y.** Well covered with flesh, stout; also strong, vigorous.

bee hive, n. **bee** & **hive.** Straw or wooden structure in which domesticated bees live and store their honey.

bee-line, n. **bee** & **line.** A straight, direct line, shortest line between two points, as bee flies.

Beelzebub, n. [1. bēélzēbub; 2. biélzibab]. Lat., fr. Gk. *Beelzeboúb*, fr. Heb. *Báal-zebūb*, 'the lord or Baal of the flies', a Philistine deity. (in New Testament) The Devil, Satan.

been, vb. [1. bēn; 2. bīn]. P.P. of **be.** O.E. *bēon*, M.E. *bēn.*

bee orchis, n. **bee** & **orchis.** Species of orchis, whose flower bears a resemblance to a bee.

beer, n. [1. bēr; 2. biə]. O.E. *bēor*, O.H.G. *bior*, Germ. *bier*, O.N. *bjōrr*; Fr. *bière* is borrowed fr. M.H.G. *bier*. There is a Gmc. word for 'barley' wh. appears in O.E. as *bēow*, wh. is prob. connected, in wh. case *beer* was orig. 'barley drink'. Well-known fermented drink of malted barley, hops, and water, of variable character, strength, quality, and colour; also of other fermented drinks, as *ginger-beer* &c. *Small beer*, very thin beer; (fig.) anything trifling and unimportant. Phr. *to think no small beer of oneself*, have a very good conceit of oneself.

beer-engine, n. Apparatus for drawing beer from the barrel in the cellar to tap in the bar of a public-house, worked by a lever or *beer-pull.*

beerhouse, n. [1. bērhous; 2. bíəhaus]. Public-house licensed for sale of beer, but not of spirits or wines.

beer money, n. Allowance paid to servants in lieu of supplying them with beer.

beery, adj. [1. bēri; 2. bíəri]. **beer** & **-y.** Like beer in taste or smell; suggesting influence of beer; (of persons) slightly drunk or bemused.

beestings, biestings, n. pl. [1. bēstingz; 2. bīstiŋz]. O.E. *bīesting*, fr. *bēost*, 'first milk of cow after calving', O.H.G. *biost*, Germ. *biest*, *biestmilch*; cp. Goth. *beist*, 'leaven, yeast'. The last-mentioned is certainly connected w. Goth. *beitan*, **bite** &c., & **bitter**, but it is difficult, on account of the vowels, to connect it w. the O.E. & O.H.G. words. The etymol. is uncertain. First milk of a cow after she has calved.

beesty, n. See **bheesty.**

bee's wax, n. [1. bēzwaks; 2. bīzwæks]. Wax secreted by bees for making the honeycombs; used for various purposes, such as making candles, polishing and preserving wood &c.

beeswing, n. [1. bēzwing; 2. bīzwiŋ]. **bee** & **wing.** Thin crust formed on wine, esp. port, after being long in bottle.

beet, n. [1. bēt; 2. bīt]. O.E. *bēte*, borrowed fr. Lat. *bēta*, 'beet', whence Fr. *bette-rave*; the O.H.G. *bieza*, 'beetroot', is also an early loan-word fr. Lat.; etymol. of the latter is unexplained; the word *botva*, 'mangold wurzel', exists in Little Russ. Name of a plant of two kinds, one with a red, sweetish root, used as a vegetable, in salads &c., the other with white root, used for making sugar, *beet sugar*, belonging to family known as *Chenopodiaceae.*

beetle (**I.**), n. [1. bētl; 2. bītl]. O.E. *bitel*, 'beetle', M.E. *bētel*; it seems certain that the word is fr. the base *bit-*, one of the forms of O.E. base *bītan*, 'bite', w. the derivative suff. *-il*, q.v. under **-el**; the beetle is therefore 'the biting insect'. See **bite** (**I.**). Member of the order Coleoptera, of insects, some with wings, others wingless, with a hard scaly covering, of which there are a large number of varieties. Applied also to insects which resemble, but are not properly beetles, as the *black-beetle* or cockroach. Phr. *blind as a beetle*, *beetle blind*, very blind.

beetle (**II.**), adj. & vb. intrans. Suggested relation to **beetle** (**I.**) seems very improbable. *Bitel-browed* already in M.E. **1.** adj. Projecting, overhanging, esp. of eyebrows: *beetle-browed.* **2.** vb. To project, overhang (of eyebrows and cliffs; used esp. in Pres. Part.): *beetling cliffs, brows.*

beetle (**III.**), n. [1. bḗtl, bítl; 2. bítl, bítl]. O.E. *bīetel*, 'mallet'. This word is derived fr. an earlier **bēatil*, lit. 'a beater', the base being that of O.E. *bēat-an*, 'beat'. See **beat** (**I.**). A heavy wooden mallet with a long handle, used for driving wedges into thick pieces of timber in splitting it.

beetroot, n. [1. bḗtrōōt; 2. bítrūt]. **beet** & **root**. Root of the *beet*; a more general name than the uncompounded word, esp. as used in salads.

beet sugar, n. **beet** & **sugar**. Sugar made from the white beet.

befall, vb. intrans. & trans. [1. befáwl; 2. bifɔ́l]. O.E. *befeallan*, 'fall into' (a habit); the mod. word perh. is not a direct descendant of O.E. word, but a later formation, fr. **be-** & **fall** (**I.**), with different sense, associated w. 'fall out' in sense of 'happen'. To happen, happen to, turn out, come to pass: *I fear some evil will befall*; *a strange fate befell him.*

befit, vb. trans. [1. befít; 2. bifít]. See **be-** & **fit** (**III.**). To suit, be fitting for, be seemly.

befitting, adj. [1. befíting; 2. bifítiŋ]. Pres. Part. of prec. Suitable, seemly, well adapted to the circumstances.

befittingly, adv. Prec. & **-ly**. In a suitable, fitting manner.

befog, vb. trans. [1. befóg; 2. bifɔ́g]. See **be-** & **fog**. To surround with fog; (gen. fig.) **a** to obscure, make confused (a subject, explanation &c.); **b** to puzzle, render muddle-headed (persons).

befool, vb. trans. [1. befōōl; 2. bifúl]. **be-** & **fool** (**I.**). To make a fool of, deceive, dupe, cheat.

before, prep. & adv. [1. befór; 2. bifɔ́]. O.E. *beforan*, 'in front of (order and place); in presence of; anterior to (in time)'; M.E. *bi-*, *before(n)*, fr. **be-** & common Gmc. *for*, q.v. under **fore** & **former**. **1.** Expresses **a** precedence in order among a number of persons or objects; **b** position and place; **c** time. **a** *Order*, coming earlier than someone or something else, preceding in order: *King Richard reigned immediately before King John*; *Colonel X was given seniority in the service just before Colonel Y*; *to be before others in class* (at school); (fig.) referring to assumed order of merit: *as a poet Chaucer was before all his English contemporaries*, i.e. excelled, was superior to; **b** *place, position*, in front of, opposite to: *a tree stands before the door of the house*; '*The singers go before, the minstrels follow after*'; *he sat just before me in church*; '*a dainty dish to set before a king*'; (fig.) of events, life &c., still to come, not yet reached: '*The world was all before them where to choose Their place of rest*' (Milton); *his whole life is before him*; Phr. *before the mast*, as a common sailor; *to sail before the wind*, with wind behind; **c** *time*, anterior, antecedent, to, preceding, earlier: *he died before I was born*; *before Christ.* Phrs. and special uses: *before long*, soon, immediately; *before now*, earlier than the present moment; *to be before one's time*, or *age*, to have larger, clearer ideas than, superiority of insight compared with, one's contemporaries. **2.** In the presence of, face to face with: *to stand before kings*; *to walk humbly before God*; *to speak out before everyone*, publicly; *to be brought before a magistrate.* Phrs. (of a question, subject &c.), *to be before the meeting, the House* (of Lords or Commons), to be under discussion, or capable of discussion; *before one's* (*very*) *eyes*, under one's observation; *before one's face*, openly, without secrecy.

beforehand, adv. [1. befórhand; 2. bifɔ́hænd]. Prec. & **hand**. Prior to, previously; in anticipation of; too early, prematurely; in good time: *he was to have spoken at the meeting, but fell ill beforehand*; *I knew what to expect, so was prepared beforehand*; *you are rather beforehand in your suspicions*; *I must be beforehand with my packing.*

before-mentioned, adj. [1. befór ménshund; 2. bifɔ́ ménʃənd]. Mentioned before, in an earlier part of speech or document.

befoul, vb. trans. [1. befóul; 2. bifául]. **be-** & **foul**. To make filthy; (fig.) to cast aspersions on. Phr. *to befoul one's own nest*, injure, make discreditable insinuations against one's family, or those persons and institutions with which one is associated.

befriend, vb. trans. [1. befrénd; 2. bifrénd]. **be-** & **friend**. To act as a friend to; come to assistance of, help, benefit in any way.

befurred. adj. [1. befḗrd; 2. bifʌ́d] **be-** & **fur**. Trimmed with fur: *a befurred gown.*

beg, vb. trans. & intrans. [1. beg; 2. beg]. M.E. *beggen*; possibly contracted fr. O.E. *bed-ecian*, 'beg'; connected w. O.E. *ġebed*, 'prayer' (q.v. under **bead**), but this is very doubtful. Another suggestion is that the word is a contraction of **beguine**, member of mendicant order; the certain solution has, however, not yet been reached. **A.** trans. To ask, supplicate for, demand urgently, esp. an act of charity: *to beg a few pence*; *to beg a meal*; *to beg one's life* (from a judge, or from a murderer). Also, followed by *of*, governing names of persons: *to beg money of charitable people.* Phrs. *to beg one's bread*, live on charity, ask for support without making any return; *to beg leave*, ask permission; *to beg pardon*, ask to be excused; *I beg your pardon*, polite, often meaningless formula of excuse for a real or fancied injury however slight; *to beg the question*, evade the real issue. **B.** intrans. (used absolutely) To ask for charity (for oneself), money, food, clothes &c.: *to beg from door to door*; also to solicit alms &c. disinterestedly, for some charitable object. Phr. *to go begging*, of goods &c., to fail to find a purchaser. **C.** Constructions with prepositions. **a** To ask for, make urgent plea for; followed by *for* governing name of thing demanded: *to beg for money, help* &c.; **b** address urgent petition to, entreat; followed by *of* governing name of person to whom demand is addressed: *I beg of you not to run any risk.*

began, vb. [1. begán; 2. bigǽn]. Pret. of **begin**. O.E. *-gann*; M.E. *-gan.*

beget, vb. trans. [1. begét; 2. bigét]. O.E. *beġietan*, non-W.S. *begetan*, 'acquire, obtain, get; beget offspring'; M.E. *beyēten*, *-gēten*, w. same meanings as in O.E. The vb. *ġetan* only occurs compounded in O.E. (see **be-** & **get**). The compound *bigitan* is found in Goth. in sense of 'come upon, find, reach'. O.N. uncompounded *geta* has these meanings & also that of 'beget'. The mod. sense is secondary. **1.** To engender offspring (of male parent). **2.** (fig.) To produce, result in: *extravagance begets all kinds of misery*; (with *of* in pass. to express cause) *fear is often begotten of guilt.*

begetter, n. [1. begéter; 2. bigétə]. Prec. & **-er**. One who begets.

beggar (**I.**), n. [1. bégar; 2. bégə]. Also in M.E. *beggere*, either fr. **beg**, w. agent suff. **-er**; or fr. O. Fr. *beg(h)ard*, 'a member of a male begging confraternity', corresponding to **beguine**. **1.** One who begs, a mendicant; one in abject poverty; a person in the habit of collecting money for charitable purposes. **2.** Used in a vague and perfectly general sense, equivalent to person, chap, fellow &c.; often with playful, friendly intent: *poor beggar*; *an unfortunate beggar*; *nice little beggars* (of children, young animals &c.).

beggar (**II.**), vb. trans., fr. prec. To reduce to poverty: *to beggar oneself by speculation*; *the war has beggared whole families.*

beggarliness, n. [1. bégarlines; 2. bégəlinis]. See next word & **-ness**. State of poverty, inadequacy.

beggarly, adj. [1. bégarli; 2. bégəli], fr. **beggar** & **-ly**. Poor, mean, inadequate: *a few beggarly pounds*; poor intellectually: *a beggarly amount of learning.*

beggar-my-neighbour, n. [1. bégar mi nā́bur; 2. bégə mi néibə]. A simple card game for two players.

beggary, n. [1. bégari; 2. bégəri]. **beggar** & **-y**. State of poverty and want, esp. *reduce to beggary.*

begging, n. & adj. [1. béging; 2. bégiŋ]. **1.** n. Act of asking alms &c.: *live by begging.* **2.** adj. Concerned with asking alms: *a begging letter*, one in which charity is demanded.

begin, vb. trans. & intrans. [1. begín; 2. bigín]. O.E. *be-ginnan*, *ā-ginnan*, but *on-ginnan*, 'begin', is commoner. In nearly all the Gmc. languages the word is found, & always compounded; O.S. & O.H.G. *biginnan*, O.H.G. also *inginnan*, O. Du. *beginnan*, Goth. *du-ginnan*, 'begin'. The compound is evidently an old one. The etymol. is doubtful. There is an O. Slav. *po-činą*, 'I begin', wh. must be cogn. The Gmc. form must have been orig. **bí-hinnan*, whence, w. voicing of *h* owing to prec. stress, **bi-ʒinnan*, written w. *g* in O.E. It has been suggested that the base **gin-* is connected w. that found in various forms in O.E. *-gīnan*, 'yawn', *ġeonian*, 'yawn, be wide open', & *gānian*, 'yawn'. This cannot be regarded as quite certain, but as far as the meaning goes we may cp. our phrase *to open proceedings* where *open* has sense of 'start, begin'. To commence action of any kind, start, make a start, set about for first time set things going. **1.** trans. *To begin operations*; *begin one's breakfast*, start eating it; *begin French*, start learning it; *begin a new book*, start reading it. **2.** intrans. **a** To start, open, pass from quiescence to activity, come into existence: *the play begins at 1 o'clock*; *who can tell when life on this earth began?*; *the royal house of Wessex begins a few generations before King Alfred.* Phrs. and constructions (in most of the following *begin* can be used both trans. and intrans.): *to begin at*, start from; *begin by* (doing something), start one's activities with a particular action; *begin with* (this or that person or thing), deal with, consider, in first place; *begin on* (a piece of work), set about, start: **b** followed by *to* and verb: *begin to laugh, eat, think* &c.; *I begin to understand you.*

beginner, n. [1. begíner; 2. bigínə]. Prec. & **-er**. One who begins, esp. one who is making a start, doing something for the first time, or is at commencement of his work, training, studies &c., and is therefore inexpert; a **tiro**, untried, inexperienced person: *not bad for a beginner*; *a mere beginner*; *don't trust yourself in an aeroplane with a beginner in the art of flying.*

beginning, n. [1. begíning; 2. bigíniŋ]. **begin** & **-ing**. Start, commencement, opening of operations, inception; source, starting-point, origin: *to make a beginning*; *a good, bad, beginning*; *that was the beginning of all our troubles.* Phr. *the beginning of the end*, first signs of final, hoped for, or inevitable result.

begird, vb. trans., [1. begérd; 2. bigʌ́d]. **be-** & **gird**. Chiefly in P.P. *begirt* (*with*), encircled, girded round, surrounded with.

begone, interj. & vb. intrans. [1. begón; 2. bigɔ́n]. Lit. imperat. *be* & *gone*, P.P. of **go**. Forcible command, meaning 'go away, clear out'. Not very common as imperat.; chiefly used in such phrases as: *tell him to begone at once*; *I wish he'd begone* &c., when the speaker prob. feels the expression sometimes as a single vb. used in infin., sometimes as two words, of wh. first is infin. & the second a P.P.

begonia, n. [1. begṓnia; 2. bigóuniə]. Fr., named in honour of Michel Begon, 1638–1710, a patron of botany. A genus of fleshy-leaved plants or shrubs, native in tropical countries, and much cultivated for their bright-coloured flowers, which have no petals but only sepals.

begot, vb. [1. begót; 2. bigɔ́t]. Pret. of **beget**. For the vowel, see **got**.

begotten, vb. [1. begótn; 2. bigɔ́tn]. P.P. of **beget**. For vowel cp. prec. Cp. O.E. P.P. *beġeten.*

begrime, vb. trans. [1. begrī́m; 2. bigráim]. **be** & **grime**. To cover with grime, make dirty. Chiefly as pass. in P.P. *begrimed.* The word refers esp. to dirt from soot, coal, smoke, but *begrimed with dust* is used.

begrudge, vb. trans. [1. begrúj; 2. bigrʌ́dž]. **be-** & **grudge**. To envy (a person something);

to part with something unwillingly, to be stingy in giving: *to begrudge a man his good fortune*; *I begrudge good wine for such a purpose*; *he begrudges his wife money to buy clothes.*

beguile, vb. trans. [1. begíl; 2. bigáil]. **be-** & **guile**. **1.** To deceive, cheat, mislead, persuade by false statements: *he was beguiled into parting with most of his money.* **2.** To make time, a journey &c., pass quickly and pleasantly, by occupying oneself with something interesting: *he beguiled the weary hours with music*; *our journey was beguiled with pleasant talk.*

beguilement, n. [1. begílment; 2. bigáilmənt]. Prec. & **-ment**. Deception, snare; an amusement or occupation which makes time pass rapidly.

beguiler, n. [1. begíler; 2. bigáilə]. See prec. & **-er**. Deceiver, seducer; one who coaxes and wheedles, either harmlessly, or with sinister motives.

beguilingly, adv. [1. begílingli; 2. bigáiliŋli], fr Pres. Part. of **beguile** as adj., & **-ly**. In an artful, persuasive, charming manner.

beguinage, n. [1. bégēnahzh; 2. bégīnāž]. Name given to cluster of cottages in which the communities of *Beguines* live.

Beguine, n. [1. bégēn; 2. bégīn]. Member of religious community of women founded at Liége in 1170 by Lambert le Bègue, and named after him.

begum, n. [1. bégum; 2. bígam]. Turk. *bīgam*, fem. of *beg*, 'chief, lord'. Applied in India to Moslem princesses and ladies of high rank. Spelt variously *beagam, begun, begom*, by early travellers.

begun, vb. [1. begún; 2. bigán]. P.P. of **begin**. O.E. *-gunnen*, M.E. *-gunne(n)*.

behalf, n. [1. beháhf; 2. biháf]. O.E. *healf, half*, 'half', is also used in sense of 'side, part' in a battle or lawsuit. Hence such phrases in M.E. as *on his halve*, 'on his part', *bi halve him*, 'concerning his part, for his part' &c. From the combination *bi halve* a new n. *behalf* has been formed. The word is only used in such phrases as *on my behalf, on behalf of my friend* &c., meaning, in the interest of, for the sake of &c.

behave, vb. intrans. & reflex. [1. behāv; 2. bihéiv]. See **be** & **have**. O.E. *behabban*, 'detain, restrain'. Fundamental idea is 'control oneself, have oneself in hand'. The pronunciation of *-have* here comes normally fr. M.E. *hāve*, & was used continuously, as rhymes show, in the independent word, right up to the first quarter of 17th cent. When *have* was used as an auxil. vb. it was usually unstressed, & was pronounced w. a short vowel *-hăv* (cp. **have**). The old stressed form w. long vowel, now survives only in *behave* & *behaviour*. **1.** intrans. (gen. with adv.): To conduct, comport oneself, evince a certain manner, *to behave well, beautifully, judiciously* &c., or *to behave ill, badly, shamefully* &c. Said not only of human beings, but also of animals, such as horses and dogs, and (by extension) of machines, in the sense that they go, act, work, well or ill. Applied to human beings, *behave* may refer to manners, breeding &c., as *he behaves admirably in company, he doesn't know how to behave*; or to conduct generally, as *he behaved very badly over the whole business, he behaved very meanly to his children* &c. **2.** reflex. Generally, if unqualified, to conduct oneself well; *to behave oneself, himself* &c., in nearly same senses as **a**, but referring more specifically to manner and bearing: *behave yourself*, conduct yourself properly; *he must learn to behave himself.*

behaviour, n. [1. behāvyur; 2. bihéivjə]. An abnormal formation fr. prec., prob. influenced by obs. *havour*, 'possessions, goods', also *aver*, q.v. under **average**. Way of behaving; conduct; manners, whether good or bad: *a prize for good behaviour*; *he showed excellent behaviour under trying circumstances.* Phrs. *to be on one's good, best, behaviour*, to take special pains to behave well; *to put someone on his good behaviour*, caution him to behave well.

behaviourism, n. [1. behāvyurizm; 2. bihéivjərizm]. Prec. & **-ism**. Term applied to a psychological method in which the conduct or action of a person is observed purely objectively according to his reactions to various physical or mental stimuli.

behead, vb. trans. [1. behéd; 2. bihéd]. O.E. *behēafdian*. **be-** & **head**. To cut the head off.

beheld, vb. [1. behéld; 2. bihéld]. Pret. of **behold**. See **held**.

behemoth, n. [1. bĕhēmōth; 2. bíhimouþ]. Heb., pl. of *behamah*, 'beast', an augmentative use of pl. in sense of 'great'. (Bib.) A huge beast, apparently the hippopotamus, referred to in Job xl. 15.

behest, n. [1. behést; 2. bihést]. O.E. *behǣs*, 'vow', M.E. *beheste*. Uncompounded *hǣs* means a 'command'. It is derived fr. Gmc. **hait-ti* (cp. Goth. *haiti*, 'order'), whence **haissi*, **hāsi*, *hǣs*, the O.E. base being *hāt*, as in *hāt-an*, vb., 'command, be called', further in O.H.G. *heizan*, O.S. *hētan*, Goth. *haitan*, the origin of wh. is doubtful. The final *-t* in *behest*, wh. is found already in M.E., was prob. added on some anal., possibly that of *request*, but such final consonants sometimes develop naturally in English, as in *graft*, q.v., earlier *graffe*. (poet.) Command, order.

behind (I.), prep. & adv. [1. behínd; 2. biháind]. O.E. *behindan*, prep. & adv. 'behind'. See **be-** & **hind (III.)** & **hinder**. **1.** To, or at, the rear, in the direction away from which one is facing, at the back of: *behind the house*; *a cow's ears are behind its horns*; *his tail hung down behind.* Phrs. *behind one's back*, secretly, without one's knowledge; *to have strong support behind one*, backing one up, helping. **2.** On the other (back) side of, hidden by: *get behind a tree*; *behind the mountains*; *behind the curtain* (at a theatre). Phrs. *behind the scenes*, (fig.) in secret; *to be behind the scenes*, to know private affairs, secrets; *there is more behind*, something not suspected or disclosed. **3.** Of time, in the past: *the follies of his youth are now far behind him.* Phr. *to be behind time*, unpunctual, late. **4.** Remaining after one has gone from a place; *to leave one's stick behind* (one); *the enemy in retreating left destruction and ruin behind him.* **5.** Inferior to in merits, attainments &c.: *our success is much behind what I had hoped*; *Swift is a long way behind Pope as a writer of the heroic couplet*; *he is behind other boys of his age.* **6.** In a less advanced position, farther from the goal than others, in a course, journey, race: '*And leave reluctant folly far behind*'; *the leading horse was so fast that he soon left all the rest behind*; *the youngest of the party was still a long way behind when we reached home.* Phrs. *to fall behind*, not keep up (with); (fig.) *behind the times*, old-fashioned.

behind (II.), n., fr. prec. (colloq.) Buttocks, rump.

behindhand, adj. [1. behínd-hand; 2. biháind-hænd]. See **behind** & **hand**. Only used predicatively. Late, behind time; in arrears (with payment, work); out of date: *we must hurry, we are already rather behindhand*; *to be behindhand with one's rent*; *people who live in the country all the year round are apt to get a bit behindhand in their ideas.*

behold, vb. trans. [1. behóld; 2. bihóuld]. **be-** & **hold**. O.E. *behāldan*, 'keep, possess; behave (reflex.); consider, observe (laws); look at'. The compound is an old one, & the last meaning given in O.E. in its simplest sense was 'keep in view, keep one's eye on'. **1.** To perceive by sight, look at, see, contemplate, regard. **2.** Used in imperative in sense of take notice! look!: '*Behold, I bring you good tidings of great joy*' (Bib. and archaic). Phr. *lo and behold*, followed by a statement, in announcing something striking or unexpected.

beholden, adj. [1. behóldn; 2. bihóuldn], fr. old P.P. of above, *behōlden*, in sense of 'held, bound', &c. (with *to*) Under an obligation; bound to someone by a service he has rendered: *I am greatly beholden to you for your kindness.*

beholder, n. [1. behólder; 2. bihóuldə]. **behold** & **-er**. One who sees, esp. some specific object: *her beauty charmed all beholders* (all who saw it).

behoof, n. [1. behóof; 2. bihúf]. Cp. O.E. *behōfian*, vb., 'need, require', *behōf-lić*, 'necessary', O. Fris. *bihōf*, Du. *behoef*, 'advantage', Swed. *behof*, 'need', Germ. *behuf*, M.H.G. *behuof*, 'purpose, advantage'. The base *hōf* is related to **have**, showing gradation *a-ō*, as in O.E. *far-an*, 'go', Pret. *fōr*, or Late O.E. (fr. Scand.) *takan*, 'take', *tōk*, 'took'. Used only in such phrases as *in my, your, his behoof*, for my sake, advantage &c.

behove, vb. impers. [1. behóv; 2. bihóuv]. O.E. *behōfian*. See prec. The present-day form wd. normally be *bihoove* [1. behóov; 2. bihúv]. To be incumbent upon one: *it behoves you to work as hard as you can.*

beige, n. [1. bāzh; 2. beiž]. Fr., in O. Fr. *bise*, L. Lat. *bisus*, 'grey', cp. Ital. *bigio*. **a** A textile fabric, made of unbleached or undyed wool; **b** a greyish-brown colour.

being, n. [1. bēing; 2. bíiŋ]. **be** & **-ing**. **1.** Existence, state of existing: *to come into being*; *the fleet in being.* **2.** A human creature, living person; Deity: *the Supreme Being*; *human beings*; *those unfortunate beings who live by crime.* **3.** Human life: '*This pleasing anxious being*' (Gray's 'Elegy'). **4.** Essence, nature: *thrilled to the very roots of his being.*

belabour, vb. trans. [1. belábur; 2. biléibə]. **be-** & **labour**. To thrash, beat heartily: (lit.) to spend labour upon.

belated, adj. [1. belāted; 2. biléitid]. **be-** & **late** & suff. **-ed**. **a** Overtaken by the night and darkness; **b** too late, unduly deferred: *belated efforts.*

belaud, vb. trans. [1. beláwd; 2. bilɔ́d]. **be-** & **laud**. To praise greatly, overwhelm with praises. Phr. *belauded to the skies.*

belay, vb. [1. belá; 2. biléi]. **be-** & **lay (III.)**. O.E. *belećgan*, 'lay round, cover' &c. (naut. term) To hitch a rope round a (belaying) pin. (naut. slang, in imperat.) *Belay! belay there!*, stop, enough!

belaying pin, n. [1. beláing pìn; 2. biléi-iŋ pìn]. A fixed spike or pin of wood or iron in a ship, for hitching a rope round and making it fast.

belch (I.) vb. intrans. & trans. [1. belsh; 2. belʃ]. O.E. *bealc(i)an*, *belćettan*, neither of wh. is direct ancestor of Mod. Engl. word prob. related to first syll. of **bellow**, w. *-k-* suff., as in **talk**. **1.** intrans. To eructate. **2.** trans. (fig.) **a** To utter violent, obscene language; *belch forth curses, insults* &c.; **b** (also of a volcano, gun, engine) *belch forth, out, flame, smoke* &c.

belch (II.) n., fr. prec. **a** Eructation; **b** spurt of flame, smoke &c.

belcher, n. [1. bélcher; 2. béltʃə]. Generally *belcher handkerchief*; a spotted handkerchief worn round the neck. Named after Jim Belcher, pugilist (1783–1854).

beldam(e), n. [1. béldam; 2. béldəm]. O. Fr. *beldame*, 'grandmother'; orig. term of honour, then used ironically. A hideous, filthy, or violent, old woman.

beleaguer, vb. trans. [1. belēger; 2. bilígə], fr. Du. *belegeren*, 'camp round'. Connected w. **laager**, 'camp'. See also **leaguer** & **lair**. To besiege (lit. and fig.).

belemnite, n. [1. bélemnīt; 2. béləmnait], fr. Gk. *bélemnon*, 'dart', fr. *bélos*, 'dart, anything thrown', & suff. **-ite**; *bélos* is related to Gk. *bállein*, 'throw, hurl', q.v. under **ballistic** & **quell**. A cylindrical, tapering, pointed fossil of a kind of extinct cuttlefish, which derives its name from a fancied resemblance in shape to the end of a dart.

bel esprit, n. [1. bél esprē; 2. bél esprí]. Fr. A wit, an intellectual person of superior parts.

belfry, n. [1. bélfri; 2. bélfri]. The word had orig. no connexion w. **bell**; M.E. *berfray* is fr. O. Fr. *berfroi* (Mod. Fr. *beffroi*, 'watch-tower'); the Fr. word is fr. Low Lat. *berfridus*, a Gmc. loan-word; cp. M.H.G. *bercfrid*, 'watch-tower', *berc*, 'protection' (cp. Germ. *bergen*, cogn. w. O.E. *beorgan*, 'to protect', see **borough**) & *frit*, 'place of security', cogn. w. O.E. *friðu*, 'peace'. Since bells were often hung in these towers for giving the alarm, and since church towers also contained bells, the association was so strong that the meaningless *ber-* was naturally converted, in England, into the intelligible *bel-*, and *belfry* came to be considered primarily as a place in which bells were hung; hence, **a** a bell-tower; **b** place in such a tower where the bells hang.

Belial, n. [1. bélyal; 2. bíljəl]. Heb. *bli-yaal*, 'worthlessness'. **1.** In O.T., esp. in Phr. *sons of Belial*, the wicked, the worthless, cp. 1 Sam. ii. &c. **2.** In N.T., Satan, The Devil, cp. 2 Cor. vi.

belie, vb. trans. [1. belī; 2. biláj]. O.E. *belēogan*, 'deceive', fr. **be-** & *lēogan*, 'tell lies'. See **lie**. **1.** To give a false impression of, show to be false: *his acts belie his words.* **2.** To fall short of a promise, or hope: *the expectations based on his early successes were completely belied later on.*

belief, n. [1. belḗf; 2. bilíf]. O.E. *ġe-lēafa*, 'belief, faith', O.H.G. *geloube, gloube*, Germ. *glaube*, 'faith', O.S. *gilōbo*, Du. *geloof*; the present form arises first in M.E. See **believe**. **1.** Something, a fact or statement, accepted as having an existence, and held to be true. Specif., of a body of religious doctrine, faith: *the belief(s) of the Christian Church*; *The Belief*, the Apostles' Creed. **2.** The conviction existing in the mind that certain things exist, that certain statements or doctrines are true: *his belief in Christianity was strengthened by his experience of life.* **3.** Trust, confidence: (always with *in*) *I have no great belief in doctors*; *I have great belief in early rising.*

believable, adj. [1. belḗvabl; 2. bilívəbl]. **believe** & **-able**. Capable of being believed; credible, probable.

believe, vb. trans. & intrans. [1. belḗv; 2. bilív]. O.E. *ġe-lēfan*, M.E. *be-lēve(n)*, fr. *ġe-léafa*; O.S. *gilóbian*, O.H.G. *gilóuben*. The O.E. base *lēaf-*, Gmc. **lauf*, is cogn. w. O.E. *lēof*, Gmc. **leuf*, 'dear'. Belief, therefore, is originally something one holds dear, & to *believe* is to value something greatly, hold it dear. See further under **lief**. **1.** To hold something to be true, have faith, esp. of religious doctrine: **a** intrans. (used absolutely) *I believe*, that is, I am a Christian, hold the doctrines of Christianity; **b** trans. *to believe a doctrine, statement* &c., to hold, be convinced, that it is true; *to believe a person* means to be convinced that he is speaking the truth. **2.** intrans. **a** *To believe in* (of persons and things), have confidence in, place reliance upon, trust to: *I believe in you*, (i.) hold you to be a man of honour, (ii.) I expect great things of you; *I believe in plenty of exercise*, hold it to be healthy and generally advantageous; **b** *believe in*, applied to the Deity implies faith (cp. uses in **1. a** and **b**); *I believe in God*, means I have the conviction that He exists; **c** the phrase is used in this sense also in relation to the prophets of other religions, to mythical personages, to philosophical or religious systems concerning which different opinions exist: *many millions of men believe in Buddha*; *no one believes nowadays in Jupiter and Neptune*; *many clever men have lately come to believe in spiritualism.*

believer, n. [1. belḗver; 2. bilívə]. Prec. & **-er**. One who believes; specif., one holding a particular form of faith: *he is no longer a believer*, not a Christian; also, followed by *in*, a person having confidence in something: *he is a great believer in small meals.*

believing, adj. [1. belḗving; 2. bilíviŋ], fr. Pres. Part. of **believe**. Having faith in a particular doctrine: *a believing Christian, Jew* &c.

belike, adv. [1. belík; 2. biláik]. **be-** & **like (I.)**, (archaic and provinc.) Probably, perhaps.

belittle, vb. trans. [1. belítl; 2. bilítl]. **be-** & **little**. To make little of, depreciate, minimize, represent as of small account.

bell (I.), n. [1. bel; 2. bɛl]. O.E. *belle*, 'bell', also compounds *bellehring*, 'bell-ringing', *bellehūs*, 'bell-tower'. The vb. *bellan* in O.E. means 'bellow, grunt' (cp. **bell (III.)**), the same word in O.H.G. means 'bark', as a dog. The orig. meaning of the base must have been 'loud noise, cry, shout'. It is possible that Lat. *fleo*, 'I weep' may be fr. same base, as also Lett. *bil-ât*, 'weep', & Lith. *bil-óti*, 'speak'. This association, however, is doubtful. In any case the base appears to be of imitative origin, & used to express noise, sound, of various kinds in different languages. Cp. also **bellow**. **1.** Hollow, usually cup-shaped, vessel of metal, closed at smaller, upper end, open at lower, larger end, which gives out a musical note when struck. The striker, in bells, is suspended inside from the top, except in modern *electric bells* where the striker operates from outside. These are hardly bells at all in the original sense. Phrs. *to bear away the bell*, take the prize, win; *clear as a bell*, very clear, of sound; *with bell, book, and candle*, referring to form of ecclesiastical cursing; *cap and bells*, part of costume worn by a court jester; *passing-bell*, one tolled at moment of death; *sound of marriage-bells*, (fig.) for wedding; *all went merrily as a marriage-bell*, in the most satisfactory manner, successfully. **2.** (naut. pl.), *Bells*, the half-hours of the watch as struck on the ship's bell, *eight bells* being struck at the end of each watch of four hours, at four, eight, and twelve o'clock. **3.** Anything shaped like a bell, esp. the cup of certain flowers. **4.** Metal structure in which persons can go under water without being drowned or wetted: a *diving-bell.*

bell (II.), vb. trans. fr. prec. To furnish with bells. Used only in Phr. *bell the cat*, undertake a dangerous enterprise, with reference to fable of the cat and the mice.

bell (III.), vb. intrans. O.E. *bellan*, 'bellow', &c. Cp. under **bell (I.)**. To make the cry of the stag in the rutting season.

belladonna, n. [1. bèladóna; 2. bèlədɔ́nə]. Ital. *bella donna*, Lat. *bella domina*, 'beautiful woman'. Cp. **beauty** & **dame**. So called from the supposed beautifying effect of the drug as a cosmetic. **1.** (bot.) A poisonous plant, *Atropa belladonna*, with red flowers and lustrous, black berries, popularly called the deadly nightshade. **2.** (med.) A poisonous, medicinal drug extracted from the leaves and root, which also yields the powerful alkaloid *atropine*.

bell-buoy, n. Buoy carrying a bell, which is rung by the movement of the waves; used as a signal of danger from rocks, shoals &c.

belle, n. [1. bel; 2. bɛl]. Fr. fem. adj. used as n. For etymol. see **beauty**. A beautiful woman: *quite a belle*; *the belle of the ball*, the best-looking woman there.

belles-lettres, n. pl. [1. bel létr; 2. bɛl létr]. Fr. See **beauty** & **letter**. Writings which are purely literary, as distinct from technical and scientific works.

belletrist, n. [1. bèlétrist; 2. bèlétrist]. Prec. & **-ist**. One given to the study of belles-lettres.

belletristic, adj. [1. bèletrístik; 2. bèlɛtrístik]. Prec. & **-ic**. Belonging to fine literature.

bell-flower, n. (bot.) Campanula; from shape of the flower.

bell-founder, n. One who founds or casts bells, a maker of bells.

bell-foundry, n. Foundry, place where bells are cast and made.

bell-hanger, n. One whose trade it was to fix bells of the old-fashioned sort, worked by wires and levers, in houses.

bell-hop, n. (colloq. U.S.A.) Page boy at an hotel.

bellicose, adj. [1. bélikōs; 2. bélikous], fr. Lat. *bellicōsus*, 'warlike'; Lat. *bellum*, 'war', is for earlier **dwellum*, lit. 'a struggle between *two* opposing sides', cp. *duo*, 'two'. See **dual** & cp. **duel**. *Bellicōsus* is a formation w. adj. suff. *-ōsus* (cp. **-ous**) added to adj. *bellicus*, 'warlike', wh. itself is formed fr. stem *belli-* by addition of suff. *-ic, -us*. Warlike, given to war and fighting, pugnacious.

bellicosity, n. [1. bèlikósiti; 2. bèlikɔ́siti]. Lat. **bellicōsitāt-(em)*, 'pugnacity'. See prec. & **-ity**. Quality of being bellicose; pugnacity.

belligerency, n. [1. belíjerensi; 2. bɛlídžərənsi]. See next word & **-ency**. The state of being a belligerent.

belligerent, n. & adj. [1. belíjerent; 2. bɛlídžərənt]. Fr. *belligérant*, fr. Lat. *belligerant-(em)*, Pres. Part. type of *belligerāre*, 'wage war', fr. *bellum*, q.v. under **bellicose**, & *gerere*, 'bear, carry on' &c., wh. belongs to different conjugation fr. form used in compound; the Pres. Part. of latter wd. give *-ant*, that of former *-ent*; for *gerere* see **gerent** & **gesture**. **a** n. Nation or party waging regular war; **b** adj., in *belligerent powers*, i.e. those taking part in a war.

bell-metal, n. **bell** & **metal**. Metal used in casting bells, an alloy of copper and tin.

Bellona, n. [1. belṓna; 2. bɛlóunə]. **Lat.** name of goddess of war, sister of Mars. Connected with *bellum*, q.v. under **bellicose**. Personification of war; by extension, a tall fine-looking woman.

bellow, vb. intrans. & n. [1. bélō; 2. bélou]. This vb. is connected w. O.E. *bellan*, q.v. under **bell (I.)**, but not directly derived fr. it. The suff. *-ow*, O.E. *-gian*, M.E. *-ewen, -owen*, may have been added on anal. of other vbs., e.g. *hollow*, or through the influence of O.E. cogn. *bylġean*, fr. **bul-igōjan*; on the other hand *bellow* may be merely the S.E. ('Kentish') form of the latter. **1.** vb. To make a loud outcry; esp. of sound made by oxen; extended also to loud human cries or shouts. A man is said to *bellow* when he speaks unnecessarily loud, or sings loudly without art or expression; also used of the roaring of cannon, thunder, wind. **2.** n. The sound made in bellowing: *a loud bellow.*

bellows, n. pl. [1. bélōz; 2. bélouz]. Variant of **belly (I.)**. Implement for blowing a fire or supplying a wind-instrument, as an organ, with air, consisting essentially of a collapsible leather bag which is alternately squeezed and opened by means of handles, so that it sucks in air and expels it again with some force; usually referred to as *a pair of bellows* when portable, and as *(the) bellows* when fixed, as in a blacksmith's forge or organ.

bell punch, n. A metal case containing a bell and punch, used by ticket-collectors on tramway cars, omnibuses &c.

bell-ringer, n. One who rings church bells; campanologist.

bell-ringing, n. Act of ringing (church) bells; esp. the art and practice of ringing changes on (church) bells; campanology.

bell-tent, n. A conical, bell-shaped tent.

bell wether, n. The leading wether of a flock of sheep, wearing a bell.

belly (I.), n. [1. béli; 2. béli]. O.E. *-belġ*, 'bag, pod', in *bēanbelġ*, fr. earlier **bælgi-*; M.E. *beli*, in mod. sense; Goth. *balg-s* is 'a bag for wine, wine-skin'; O.H.G. *balg* & O.N. *belgr* have same meaning. All these forms are related to the O.E. vb. *belgan*, 'to swell, puff out, be angry', & to the n. *ġe-belġ*, 'anger'. The orig. & basal meaning seems to be 'swell', wh. still survives in **belly (II.)**; the word is a variant of **bellows**. Cp. also O. Ir. *bolg*, 'bag', & *bolgaim*, 'I swell'. **1.** The lower part of the trunk below the diaphragm in man and other mammals, also in fish, thought of from outside, the abdomen. (The polite and usual word now is *stomach*.) Phr. *pot belly*, prominent abdomen. **2.** The stomach itself, receptacle into which food passes: *an empty belly*; *belly-ache*, pain in the stomach, colic.

3. (fig.) **a** Greed, '*Such as for their bellies' sake Creep and intrude and climb into the fold*' (Milton, 'Lycidas'); **b** as the seat of vitality, feeling, and thought: *to have fire in one's belly*, inspiration, genius. **4.** Protuberant, bulging surface of an object, as of a violin.

belly (**II.**), vb., fr. prec. To swell out, as a sail in the wind, esp. *bellying sails.*

belly-band, n. **belly** (**I.**) & **band.** Girth of a horse's harness.

bellyful, n. [1. bélifool; 2. bélifʊl]. **belly** (**I.**) & **-ful.** **a** As much as one wants to eat; **b** (fig.) satisfying amount of anything (esp. of fighting).

belong, vb. intrans. [1. belóng; 2. bilɔ́ŋ]. Not found as vb. w. pref. *be-* in O.E.; *langian* in O.E. means 'grow long; feel tedium; long for; befit, belong'; *ġelang*, adv., means 'at hand, attainable'. Prob. this meaning arose fr. that of 'alongside of', gen. *entlang* in O.E.; thence what was near at hand was thought of as something pertaining, belonging to, in a moral sense. See **along, long** (**I.**), adj., & (**II.**) vb. **1.** To pertain to, be suitable to; to be in place, constitute a duty &c.: *it does not belong to a minister to dictate to his colleagues; this word belongs to this sentence; where do these things belong?* **2.** *Belong to,* to be a possession of: *that belonged to me, but I have given it away.*

belongings, n. pl. [1. belóngingz; 2. bilɔ́ŋiŋz]. See **belong** & **-ing.** Possessions, goods and chattels, luggage.

beloved, adj. & n. [1. belúvd, belúved; 2. bilávd, bilávid]. P.P. used as adj. See **be-** & **love.** **1.** adj. Much loved: *X, the beloved wife of So-and-so; greatly beloved by all who knew him* [belúvd, bilávd]; *he lost his beloved pipe* [belúved, bilávid]. **2.** n. Beloved person; fiancé(e), husband, wife: *he brought his beloved to see us* [belúved, bilávid].

below, adv. & prep. [1. beló; 2. bilóu]. First in M.E.; the second element is Scand., O.N. *lāg-r.* See **be-** & **low** (**III.**). **1.** adv. Beneath, lower, in relation to a given position, at a greater depth: *from the hill-top we could see the plains below; the place below,* hell; *although I was on the third storey, I could hear the noise below,* on a lower storey, or in the street. Phrs. *here below,* the earth, in distinction to heaven; *down below,* in hell; the tomb; the bottom of the sea &c. **2.** prep. **a** Lower, in place, in relation to a given position or level: '*below the seats divine*' (Pope); *below the surface,* under water, under the soil, buried; Phrs. *below ground,* buried; *below the mark,* of inferior quality, in ill-health; *below par* (Stock Exchange, of shares &c.), below nominal value, hence (fig.), in bad health; *below stairs,* the servants' quarters; *to hit below the belt,* of a foul blow in boxing; also fig., to deliver a mean, unfair, attack; **b** inferior intellectually, morally, in rank &c.: *to be below a person in intelligence, character, social standing, in the ranks of a hierarchy* &c.; *below a schoolfellow in class* &c.

belt (**I.**), n. [1. belt; 2. bɛlt]. O.E. *belt,* O.H.G. *balz*; loan-word fr. Lat. *balteus,* wh. perh. stands for older **dwalt-,* possibly cogn. w. Scrt. *dvárati,* 'confines, covers'; this is, however, doubtful. See also **baldric.** **1.** Strap of leather, or any material, which encircles the waist, girdle; band round a woman's waist: *sword belt; Sam Browne belt,* one supported by two straps crossing shoulders to take off weight of sword; specif., as symbol of investiture of an earl or knight, hence, *belted earl* &c. **2.** (mechan.) Strap, or broad leather band used in driving machinery: *driving belt.* **3.** Narrow plantation of trees round a park or field. **4.** **a** Stripe or strip of different colour, or material, superimposed upon another; cp. *band;* **b** the course of armour-plate along the water-line of a warship.

belt (**II.**), vb. trans., fr. prec. **1.** To encircle with a belt; fasten by means of a belt: *to belt on a sword.* **2.** **a** To thrash violently, from use of a leathern belt for this purpose; **b** of violent movement such as running, perhaps suggested by *pelt*: *to belt along the road.*

beltane, n. [1. béltān; 2. béltein]. Ir. *bealteine,* Gael. *bealltuinn,* lit. 'blaze-fire'; for first element see **bale-fire**; second element, O. Ir. *ten,* 'fire', is fr. Celt. type, **tepnos,* cogn. w. Lat. *tepēre,* 'to be warm' (see **tepid**); old connexions w. *Baal, Bel,* have no foundation. An old Celtic festival on May Day.

beluga, n. [1. belōōga; 2. bɛlúgə], fr. Russ. *byeluga,* fr. *byely,* 'white'; cp. Lith. *báltas,* 'white', cogn. w. Gk. *phalós,* 'shining'; see further under **bald, phalarope,** & **fuller.** The 'white whale', a large kind of dolphin, of the Arctic seas, hunted for its blubber, oil, and hide, sold as 'porpoise hide'.

belvedere, n. [1. bélvedēr; 2. bélvidiə]. Ital., 'fine outlook, view'. **a** Turret in a building from which a wide view of surrounding country may be obtained; **b** garden summer-house so placed as to command a view. The word is the Italian equivalent of the English place-name *Belvoir* [1. bḗver; 2. bívə], which is from a French source.

bemoan, vb. trans. [1. bemṓn; 2. bimóun]. **be-** & **moan.** O.E. *be-mǣnan,* 'lament', shows mutation; the unmutated *mān,* 'crime', has entirely different sense. To lament, sorrow for, express grief concerning something.

bemuse, vb. trans. [1. bemū́z; 2. bimjúz]. **be-** & **muse** (**II.**). To render stupid; originally, apparently, to preoccupy, plunge in thought. See, however, etymology of *muse,* vb.

bemused, adj. [1. bemū́zd; 2. bimjúzd], fr. P.P. of prec. Stupefied, esp. with drink or drugs.

ben, n. [1. ben; 2. bɛn]. O.E. *binnan,* 'within', **be-** & *innan,* 'in', see **in,** cp. *būtan,* 'outside'. (Scots) The inner room of a two-roomed cottage, usually *but and ben,* the outer and inner room.

bench, n. [1. bensh; 2. bɛnʃ]. O.E. *benċ*; variant of **bank.** Orig. a long shelf, or seat of wood; fr. this the various senses are developed. **1.** **a** Long seat of wood, generally without a back, esp. in old dining-halls, as in ancient schools and colleges; by extension applied to seats of other material, e.g. *stone bench* in a formal garden, fixed slab of stone without a back; **b** seats in the Houses of Parliament: *ministerial benches, back benches* &c.; **c** thwart of an ancient galley. **2.** **a** Official seat of a judge or magistrate in a court of law, and those seats in the same line, on either side of this: *Mr. Justice D. was on the Bench,* heard the case; *the High Sheriff occupied a seat on the Bench beside the Judge*; **b** (coll. of judges and bishops): '*I call on this Right Reverend, and that most learned Bench*' (Chatham); *the whole Bench of Bishops*; Phr. *to be raised to the Bench,* be made a bishop or judge; **c** *King's Bench,* a division of the High Court of Justice. **3.** Wooden work-table of solid construction at which certain handicrafts are carried on: *carpenter's bench; shoemaker's bench.*

bencher, n. [1. bénsher; 2. bénʃə]. Prec. & **-er.** Member of the governing body of one of the Four Inns of Court.

bench-mark, n. **bench,** in sense of 'bank', & **mark** (**I.**). A surveyor's mark, usually a broad arrow with line drawn through it to mark the line of a level.

bend (**I.**), vb. trans. & intrans. [1. bend; 2. bɛnd]. O.E. *bendan,* 'bind, stretch, bend a bow'. This meant orig. to put a string or *bend* into a bow, the idea of curving it being secondary, although this is now the primary association w. the word. See **band, bind,** & **bundle.** This base in its various forms expresses the idea of 'fastening, tying'. **A.** trans. **1.** To curve, cause to curve or to depart from straight line, or into a different direction; applied chiefly to materials which possess a certain rigidity and offer some resistance, not to unresisting materials which can be folded or coiled, such as cloth or rope: *bend a stick, piece of wire, bar of iron* &c. Phrs. *bend the knee,* bow, pray; *bend the neck,* submit. **2.** (fig.) To apply one's mind, attention, thoughts (*to*): *I can't readily bend my mind to this new work.* **3.** (naut.) To fasten, bind (a rope; only survival of orig. meaning). **4.** To curve (a bow) in order to string it; this, formally, the original use, has, in reality, lost its old force, the uppermost idea now being the curving, not the stringing. **B.** intrans. To depart from straightness; curve, droop, sag; give way: *willow rods bend but do not easily break; if you put much weight on that stick it will bend.*

bend (**II.**), n. O.E. *bend,* 'band, chaplet, bond', & O. Fr. *bende*; variant of **band.** **1.** A curve, departure from straightness: (slang) *get a bend on you,* look sharp, be quick, from the idea of bending the legs in running. **2.** (naut.) A knot in a rope (very near orig. sense). **3.** (her.) Charge on shield consisting of a broad diagonal band drawn from dexter chief to sinister base, or if reversed, from sinister chief to dexter base. The latter is called *bend sinister* and implies bastardy.

bended, adj. [1. bénded; 2. béndid]. Either fr. **bend** (**I.**), w. P.P. suff. **-ed,** used as adj., or formed fr. **bend** (**II.**), w. suff. **-ed.** Having a bend or curve, esp. in Phr. *on bended knees,* in attitude of prayer, and (fig.) very earnestly, urgently, and imploringly; (also poet.) *with bended bow,* strung, and curved by pulling string, ready for discharge of arrow. See also **bent,** adj.

bendy, adj. [1. béndi; 2. béndi], fr. O. Fr. *bendé,* Fr. *bandé.* **bend** (**II.**) **3** & **-y.** (**her.**) Divided by bends (of an escutcheon).

bene-, pref. In compounds of Lat. origin. Lat. *bene,* adv., 'well, happily, prosperously' &c., fr. earlier **dwene,* cogn. w. *bonus,* 'good', fr. **dwenos,* **dwonos*; connected w. Lat. *beāre,* 'bless, make happy'. See further under **beatitude.**

beneath, prep. & adv. [1. benḗth; 2. biníþ]. O.E. *beneoþan,* 'beneath, below', fr. **be-** & *niþ-,* 'low, down', & *-an,* 'from'; cp. **nether**; M.E. *benéthe,* O.H.G. *nidana.* Used in much the same way as **below.** **1.** prep. (of physical position) Below, under, at the foot of, on the ground, at the base of anything higher than the soil: *a pillow beneath his head; sitting beneath a tree; playing beneath my windows.* **2.** prep. (of moral and social position &c.) Inferior in moral worth, esteem, reputation, rank: *to be far beneath someone in intelligence, character, attainments* &c. Phrs. *beneath contempt, beneath notice,* not worth notice; *to marry beneath one,* take a wife or husband of inferior rank to one's own. **3.** adv. Below, at a lower level: *the valley lay beneath.*

Benedicite, n. [1. bènedísiti; 2. bènidáisiti]. Lat. imperat. pl., 'bless ye', of *benedīcere.* See **benediction.** Name of canticle beginning *O all ye works of the Lord, bless ye the Lord* &c., from opening words in Lat. *Benedicite omnia opera.*

Benedick, n. [1. bénedik; 2. bénidik], fr. character in Shakespeare's 'Much Ado'. A newly married man, esp. one supposed to be a confirmed bachelor who marries.

Benedictine, n., fr. name of St. Benedict who founded (c. 520) the order of monks bearing this name. **1.** [1. bènedíktin; 2. bènidíktin]. A monk of this order; the chief duty is the prosecution of study, combined with manual work. **2.** [1. bènedíktēn; 2. bènidíktīn]. A sweet, powerful liqueur made by the Benedictine monks.

benediction, n. [1. bènedíkshun; 2. bènidíkʃən]. Lat. *benedictiōn-(em),* 'blessing', fr. **bene-** & *dictio,* 'speaking, saying, uttering', fr. *dīc-ere,* 'say, tell, declare'. See under **dictate, diction** &c.; also cp. **teach.** Full form of **benison.** **1.** Blessing; utterance of a blessing, esp. that given by the priest at the end of a church service. **2.** (cap.) Special service in Roman Catholic Church in which the priest blesses the people with the Blessed Sacrament.

benedictory, adj. [1. bènedíktori; 2. bènidíktəri], fr. Med. Lat. *benedictōrius.* See prec. & **-ory.** Of, pertaining to, expressing, a blessing.

benefaction, n. [1. bènefákshun; 2. bènifǽkʃən], fr. Lat. *benefactiōn-(em).* **bene-** & *factio,* 'doing, making'; see **faction,** also **deed. 1.** A good deed, act which confers a benefit. **2.** A charitable donation.

benefactor, n. [1. bénefaktur; 2. bénifæktə]. Lat., fr. **bene-** & **factor,** 'doer, maker', fr. *facio,* 'make, do', q.v. under **fact.** One who confers a benefit; esp. one who founds or endows an institution, such as a college or school. Phr. *pious benefactors.*

benefactress, n. fem. [1. bénefaktres; 2. bénifæktris], fr. prec. & **-ess.** Female benefactor.

benefice, n. [1. bénefis; 2. bénifis]. Fr. *bénéfice,* fr. Lat. *beneficium,* wh. in Low Lat. meant 'grant of an estate', & in Class. Lat. 'well-doing, kindness, good turn'. See prec. words & Lat. words there referred to; *-ficium* is form of stem *fac-,* 'do, make' &c. See **fact.** Church living, property held by an ecclesiastical officer for life, or during performance of certain duties. It is applied more especially to livings held by rectors and vicars.

beneficed, adj. [1. bénefist; 2. bénifist], fr. prec. & **-ed.** Provided with a benefice: *a beneficed clergyman.*

beneficence, adj. [1. benéfisens; 2. benéfisəns]. Lat. *beneficentia,* 'active kindness', Fr. *bienfaisance.* See next word & **-ce.** Habit or practice of doing active good; kindness, charity.

beneficent, adj. [1. benéfisent; 2. benéfisənt]. Lat. *beneficent-(em).* Acc. of Pres. Part. of *beneficere,* 'to do good'. See **benefice.** Charitable, kindly, conferring good, merciful (of persons and laws &c.).

beneficently, adv. Prec. & **-ly.** In a beneficent manner.

beneficial, adj. [1. bènefíshal; 2. bènifíʃəl], fr. Lat. *benefici-(ālis).* See **benefice** & **-al.** Not applied to persons. Conferring benefits or advantages; **a** having the quality of doing good to, or improving: *a system of strict discipline has a beneficial effect on conduct; the waters of Bath are very beneficial to the health of rheumatic persons;* **b** (law) giving, having the benefit or usufruct of property, as under a trust: *beneficial ownership.*

beneficially, adv. Prec. & **-ly.** In a beneficial manner.

beneficiary, n. [1. bènefíshiari; 2. bènifíʃiəri]. Lat. *beneficiārius.* See **benefice** & **-ary. 1.** (law) One who holds under feudal tenure; holder of a living. **2.** Now chiefly used for one who benefits, or obtains property or other advantages, under a will or trust.

benefit (**I.**), n. [1. bénefit; 2. bénifit]. M.E. fr. O. Fr. *benfet,* prob. influenced in first element by Lat. form *bene.* Lat. *benefactum,* 'well done'. See prec. compounds & **bene-** & **fact. 1.** Act of kindness; favour: *to confer (a) benefit(s) upon.* **2.** Advantage, profit; improvement in condition: *I get no personal benefit from the business; he derived great benefit from the medicine.* Special use: a performance at a theatre in which the actors give their services free, and the profits of which go to some particular person or charity: *a benefit night.* Phr. *for your special benefit,* for your sake, to please you. **3.** *Benefit of Clergy:* privilege claimed by ecclesiastical courts to deal with clerical offenders, and by persons charged with offences to be tried by these courts; extended so as to apply to all who could read like a clerk, or clergyman, a certain verse of the 51st Psalm. The right was abolished in 1827.

benefit (**II.**), vb. trans. & intrans., fr. prec. **1.** trans. To confer a benefit upon, do something for one's advantage; to cause improvement in health &c. **2.** intrans. (usually with *by*) To derive benefit from some action, treatment &c.

benevolence, n. [1. benévolens; 2. binévələns], fr. O. Fr. *benivolence,* Lat. *benevolentia,* 'goodwill, kindness', fr. **bene-** & n. formed fr. *volent-,* 'willing'. Cp. **volition** & **will** (**II.**). **1.** State of mind which consists in a disposition to do good; kindliness of heart, love of humanity: *a man of great benevolence of character.* **2.** Activity in doing good, and, specif., in showing liberality in giving; munificence: *his widespread benevolence enabled many struggling authors to live.* **3.** (hist.) A form of forced loan, resorted to by several English kings.

benevolent, adj. [1. benévolent; 2. binévələnt]. See prec. Lit. 'well-wishing'; given to *benevolence* in both senses above. *Benevolent society,* one which exists for the purpose of helping distressed persons belonging to certain categories: *Actors', Jews', Benevolent Society.*

benevolently, adv. Prec. & **-ly.** In a benevolent manner.

Bengali, adj. & n. [1. bengáwli; 2. bengɔ́li], fr. name of Indian Province. **1.** adj. Pertaining to, of, Bengal. **2.** n. **a** Native of Bengal; **b** language of the natives.

Bengal light, n. [1. bèngawl lít; 2. bèngɔl láit]. A kind of firework, giving a very bright coloured light of some duration, esp. used as signals of distress &c. at night.

benighted, adj. [1. beníted; 2. bináitid]. **be-** & **night** & **-ed. 1.** Overtaken by the night and darkness. **2.** (fig.) In a condition of moral or intellectual darkness; unenlightened, in a backward state of culture: *the poor benighted heathen.*

benign, adj. [1. benín; 2. bináin]. Fr. *bénigne,* fr. Lat. *benignus,* 'kindly, friendly, kindhearted, affable, fertile, copious' &c.; fr. **bene-,** 'well', & suff. *-*gno-,* 'producing', q.v. under **gender, nature;** cp. also **kin** & **malignant. 1. a** Gracious, kindly, pleasing (of persons); **b** favourable, mild, fruitful (of climate and soil). **2.** (med.) Of a disease, growth &c., not cancerous; as opposed to *malignant.*

benignant, adj. [1. benígnant; 2. binígnənt], new formation direct fr. Lat. on anal. of **malignant,** as if fr. **benignant-em.* Cp. prec. **a** Well-disposed, kindly; **b** (of disease), mild, not cancerous.

benignantly, adv. Prec. & **-ly.** In a benignant manner.

benignity, n. [1. benígniti; 2. binígniti]. M.E. & O. Fr. *benigntee,* Lat. *benignitāt-(em),* fr. *benignus,* q.v. under **benign.** Kindness of heart and character.

benignly, adv. [1. benínli; 2. bináinli]. **benign** & **-ly.** In a benign manner.

benison, n. [1. bénizn; 2. bénizn]. M.E. *benison,* O. Fr. *beneison,* popular form of Lat. *benedictiōn-(em),* q.v. under **benediction,** wh. is straight fr. the Lat. Blessing, benediction.

bennet. See **bent-grass.**

bent (**I.**), adj. [1. bent; 2. bent], fr. old P.P. of *bendan,* q.v. under **bend** (**I.**). Curved, crooked; of a bow &c., same as **bended.**

bent (**II.**), n., fr. prec. or direct fr. P.P. of **bend** (**I.**). Inclination of the mind or taste; aptitude, bias: *to have a natural bent for study* &c. Phr. *to follow one's bent,* pursue one's own inclinations and tastes. For sense cp. *bend one's mind.* See **bend** (**I.**) **2.**

bent-grass or **bent,** n. O.E. *beonet,* O.H.G. *pinuz, binuz,* Mod. Germ. *binse,* 'rush'. No satisfactory etymol. has yet been suggested. **a** Stiff, coarse, reedy grass; **b** land on which such grass grows. The word occurs in the common English Place-Name, *Bent-ley.*

Benthamism, n. [1. bénthamizm; 2. bénþəmizəm]. System of philosophy and ethics propounded by Jeremy Bentham (1748–1832), the leading principle of which was 'the greatest happiness of the greatest number'.

Benthamite, n. [1. bénthamít; 2. bénþəmait]. See prec. & **-ite.** Follower of Jeremy Bentham.

benthos, n. [1. bénthos; 2. bénþɔs], fr. Gk. *bénthos,* 'depth of the sea'; poet. variant of *báthos,* 'depth', see **bathos.** An oceanographical term for various forms of life found at the bottom of the sea; cp. *nekton* & *plankton.*

benumb, vb. trans. [1. benúm; 2. binám]. Really an old P.P. O.E. *benumen,* fr. *beniman,* 'deprive of, take away from'; see **numb;** the final *-b* is unhistorical, but may have been pronounced at one time. To deprive of sensation, esp. by cold; also of the mind (usually in P.P.), *benumbed:* paralysed, deadened, by some strong, sudden emotion, such as terror.

benzene, n. [1. bénzēn; 2. bénzīn], fr. **benzoin.** (chem.) An important hydrocarbon chemically known as phenyl-hydride, a colourless liquid obtained by distillation of coal-tar oil; an immense number of chemical substances called aromatic compounds are derived from it, and it produces aniline, the source of modern dye-stuffs; it is also known as *benzol.*

benzine, n. [1. bénzēn; 2. bénzīn]. See prec. & **-ine.** A mixture of volatile hydrocarbons obtained from crude petroleum, often confused with 'benzene' and sometimes therefore called 'benzoline'; it is a colourless liquid which easily vaporizes and forms with air a dangerously explosive mixture; it dissolves fats, and is used for household cleaning, preparation of varnishes &c.

benzoin, n. [1. bénzōin; 2. bénzouin]. (Also formerly called *gum-benjamin* or *benjamin.*) Resin of the tree called *Styrax benzoin* wh. grows in Sumatra, used medicinally as a disinfectant. The stuff & the name passed fr. Arab traders among European peoples, & was named by the Arabs *lubān-jawī,* 'Java frankincense', whence Span. *benjui,* Port. *beijoim, beijuim,* Ital. *belzoino;* corrupted in Engl. to *benjamin.*

benzol, n. [1. bénzol; 2. bénzəl]. See prec. & **-ol.** Another name for **benzene,** particularly in France and Germany.

benzoline, n. [1. bénzolēn; 2. bénzəlīn]. See prec. & **-ine.** Benzine, q.v.

beplaster, vb. trans. [1. bepláhster; 2. biplástə]. **be-** & **plaster.** To cover thickly with plaster, to plaster over.

bepowder, vb. trans. [1. bepóuder; 2. bipáudə]. **be-** & **powder.** To powder over, cover thickly with powder.

bequeath, vb. trans. [1. bekwédh; 2. bikwíð]. O.E. *becweþan,* 'say, reproach; bequeath', fr. **be-** & *cweðan,* q.v. under **quoth. 1.** To leave property (to a person) by will. Strictly, *bequeath* is used only of *personalty* (i.e. money), not *real estate* (land). **2.** To hand on, transmit (name, works, example &c.) to posterity.

bequest, n. [1. bekwést; 2. bikwést]. M.E. *bequeste,* rare; usual form *bequide,* cp. O.E. *cwide,* 'saying, declaration', fr. earlier **kweði-,* fr. base of *cweþan,* 'say', see **quoth.** The new M.E. form is doubtless influenced by, & made on the anal. of, **quest, request. a** The act of bequeathing; **b** that which is bequeathed.

Berber, n. & adj. [1. bérber; 2. bʌ́bə], fr. Arab. *barbar,* 'people of Barbary'. Origin is doubtful; a similar name is found early in Egypt for a Libyan tribe; possibly connected w. **barbaric. 1.** n. **a** Member of an indigenous race inhabiting the hilly districts of N. Africa; **b** language spoken by this race. **2.** adj. Of, pertaining to, the Berbers or their language.

berberis, n., also **berberry** & **barberry** [1. bérberis; 2. bʌ́bəris], fr. Med. Lat. *berberis, barbaris,* origin unknown. (bot.) A shrub with yellow flowers and long, thin scarlet berries.

bereave, vb. trans. [1. berḗv; 2. birív]. O.E. *berēafian,* 'despoil, deprive one of something', fr. **be-** & *rēafian,* 'to plunder, ravage'. See **reave.** To deprive one of anything, remove, take away from, esp. non-material things, hope, joy, expectations &c.: *nothing can bereave me of my memories of the past.* Most common in P.P., either **bereaved** or **bereft,** which are often used as adjectives.

bereaved, adj. [1. berḗvd; 2. birívd]. See prec. & **-ed.** Usually means, specif., deprived of by death: *to be bereaved of one's parents, wife, friends* &c. Special uses: *the bereaved husband*, one who has just lost his wife; *the bereaved* (sing. or pl.), of those who have just lost some near relation.

bereavement, n. [1. berévment; 2. birívmənt]. **bereave & -ment.** State of being bereaved; esp. loss of a near relative by death.

bereft, adj. [1. beréft; 2. biréft]. P.P. of **bereave.** Has more general meaning than **bereaved**, deprived of: *bereft of home and riches*; special use: *to be utterly bereft*, deprived of something essential to one's happiness or existence; very much afflicted, crippled in power of doing anything, and so on; *bereft of reason*, mad.

beret, n. [1. bérā; 2. bérei]. Fr. *béret*, fr. Ital. *berretta*. See **biretta.** A flat, round woollen cap, fitting close to the skull, as worn by the Basque peasants.

berg, n. [1. bërg; 2. bāg]. Swed., Du., & Germ., 'hill', q.v. under **barrow (II.).** A large mass of ice; an iceberg.

bergamot (I.), n. [1. bërgamot; 2. bāgəmət], fr. Bergamo, Italian city. Aromatic oil, much used in perfumery, extracted from the rind of *Citrus limetta*, or sweet lime.

bergamot (II.), n. Through Ital. fr. Turk. *beg-armudi*, 'pear of a bey or prince'. See **bey.** Name of a highly flavoured pear.

beri-beri, n. [1. béri béri; 2. béri béri]. A Cingalese word, redupl. intens. form, of *beri*, 'weakness'. A tropical, often epidemic, disease, a form of peripheral neuritis, accompanied by wasting, dropsy &c., due probably to the absence of certain vitamins in the food, notably in polished rice when the husk has been removed.

Berkeleian, n. & adj. [1. barklḗan; 2. bāklíən], fr. Bp. Berkeley (1685–1753) & **-ian.** **a** n. Follower of Berkeley, in whose philosophy the objective existence of the external world is questioned; **b** adj., pertaining to, in accordance with, this system of thought.

Berlin, n. [1. bërlín; 2. bʌlín]. A four-wheeled carriage invented in Berlin in the 17th cent., and widely popular in France and England during the 18th. *Berlin black*, a special form of heat-resisting black enamel, used for painting stoves &c.; *Berlin wool*, a fine wool for knitting &c.

berm, n. [1. bërm; 2. bʌm]. Fr. *berme*, fr. Gmc. source; cp. O.N. *barmr*, 'brim', cogn. w. Russ. *boroná*, 'edge'. (mil.) Term in fortification for level ground between parapet and ditch.

berry, n. & vb. intrans. [1. béri; 2. béri]. O.E. *berig(e)*, 'berry', O.H.G. *peri, beri*, Mod. Germ. *beere*, Du. *bes, bezie*, Goth. *-basi*; etymol. doubtful; perh. connected w. Scrt. *ba-, bhas-ti*, 'eats, chews', in wh. case a *berry* wd. be 'the edible fruit'. **1.** n. **a** Small, round, juicy fruit of certain trees and shrubs; **b** egg in roe of lobsters &c. **2.** vb. To fruit up, come into, form berries.

bersaglieri, n. pl. [1. bàrsahliári; 2. bɛəsāliéri]. Ital., lit. 'sharp-shooters', fr. *bersaglio*, 'mark'; etymol. doubtful. A corps d'élite of quick-marching riflemen in the Italian army.

berserker, n. [1. bérsêrker; 2. bā́sʌ̂kə]. O.N. *berserkr*, 'bear-shirt', name given to an ancient Norse warrior who fought with peculiar fierceness and fury. See **bear (II.)** & **sark.** A hard-fighting champion; one given to furious contests. Phr. *berserker rage, fury*, uncontrolled rage.

berth (I.), n. [1. bërth; 2. bāþ]. Etymol. very doubtful; not found in O.E. Possibly same as **birth**, in sense of 'position in the world', or fr. **bear (I.)** in sense of 'make room for by bearing off'; both are quite uncertain. **1.** (naut.) Place, room, for a ship to swing at anchor; ship's place at wharf. Phr. (fig.) *to give one a wide berth*, avoid. **2.** Sleeping quarters in a ship. **3. a** A lodging, quarters, anywhere: *a comfortable berth*, good quarters; **b** a situation, employment, billet, post: *to get a berth in some good business*; *a good berth*, well-paid, suitable situation.

berth (II.), vb. trans. fr. prec. *To berth a ship*, to put a ship into position in harbour, or by the wharfside.

bertha, n. [1. bërtha; 2. bā́þə], fr. woman's name. A broad, round collar, extending over the shoulders, worn by women.

Bertillon system, n. [1. bártiyon sistem; 2. béətījɔ̃ sistim], fr. name of inventor. A system of registering measurements of such parts of the body as the skull, hand, foot, forearm; or as a means of identification, esp. of criminals, a special form of anthropometry.

beryl, n. [1. béril; 2. béril]. Fr. *béryl*, Lat. *bēryllus*, Gk. *bḗrullos*. **a** Gem stone of a sea-green colour; **b** (mineral.) term given to a group of precious stones, crystallized silicates of beryllium and aluminium, which also includes the **emerald, aquamarine,** and chrysoberyl.

beryllium, n. [1. berílium; 2. berílɪəm]. See prec. & **-ium.** A metal chemically related to the *beryl*, very hard and silvery white in colour.

beseech, vb. trans. [1. beséch; 2. bisítʃ]. **be-** & O.E. *sēcan*, M.E. *beseechen*. See **seek.** *Beseech* a person *to do* something, or *for*, something, or *that* one *may*; entreat earnestly, demand urgently, beg, supplicate: *I beseech you to listen*; *he besought his master for permission to go home*; *to beseech that one may be allowed* &c.

beseeching, adj. [1. beséching; 2. bisítʃiŋ], fr. Pres. Part. of prec. Entreating, suppliant, appealing: *beseeching look, voice* &c.

beseechingly, adv. Prec. & **-ly.** In a beseeching, appealing manner.

beseem, vb. impers. [1. besém; 2. bisím]. **be-** & **seem**; M.E. *besēmen*; O.E. (*ġe*)*sēman*, 'satisfy, settle dispute', but sense fr. O.N. *sœma*, 'to honour, appear, befit'. Cp. **seem & seemly.** To befit, be suitable, be appropriate; esp. with *well* and *ill*: *it ill beseems you to be ungrateful*; *her modesty beseemed her well*.

beset, vb. trans. [1. besét; 2. bisét]. O.E. *besettan*, 'set on, appoint, set about, adorn'. See **be-** & **set.** **a** To surround, close in (of persons): *beset withq uestions, difficulties* &c.; **b** to encompass, assail (of temptations, difficulties &c.): '*the sins which do most easily beset us*'; *besetting sin*.

beshrew, vb. trans. [1. beshrōō; 2. biʃrū́]. M.E. *beschrewen*, 'deprave, pervert'. **be-** & **shrew.** Now only in deliberate archaism '*beshrew me*', mock heroic imprecation, 'devil take, confound me'.

beside, prep. [1. besíd; 2. bisáid]. O.E. *be sīdan*, 'by the side of'. See **be-** & **side.** Of position, near by, close to, alongside of: *the house beside the river*; *to lie, walk, beside (one)*. Phrs. *beside the mark, the question*, irrelevant; *beside oneself*, mad.

besides, adv. & prep. 1. besídz; [2. bisáidz]. Same as above, w. advbl. (old genit.) suff. *-(e)s*. In addition, over and above; moreover, in addition to what has been said.

besiege, vb. trans. [1. besḗj; 2. bisídʒ]. **be-** & **siege.** Hybrid compound, w. Gmc. pref. instead of that in O. Fr. *assegier*, fr. L. Lat. *assediāre*. **1.** (mil.) To lay siege to, beset (a city) with armed forces. **2.** (fig.) To crowd round, press in upon, surround: *the War Office was besieged by anxious inquirers*; *as soon as he appeared he was besieged by his delighted constituents*. **3.** To ply with, press upon, demand eagerly or urge acceptance of: *to besiege with attentions, invitations, requests*.

besieger, n. [1. besḗjer; 2. bisídʒə]. Prec. & **-er.** **a** One who besieges (fort, town &c.); **b** (pl.) besieging forces.

besique. See **bezique.**

beslaver, vb. trans. [1. besláver; 2. bislǽvə]. **be-** & **slaver.** To slaver over, cover with slaver, (esp. fig.) to flatter fulsomely: *beslavered with compliments and praises*.

besmear, vb. trans. [1. besmḗr; 2. bismíə]. **be-** & **smear.** To cover with, daub, smear over.

besmirch, vb. trans. [1. besmérch; 2. bismʌ́tʃ]. **be-** & **smirch.** To darken, stain, cast stain upon, soil (esp. in fig. sense); **said** of *character, life* &c.

besom, n. [1. bézum, bḗzum; 2. bézəm, bízəm]. O.E. *bes(e)ma*, 'broom, rod for beating'. M.E. *besum*; O.D. *bessem*, O.H.G. *besamo*; Mod. Germ. *besen*. Etymol. doubtful, but perh. connected w. Gmc. base *basi-, seen in **berry,** as if made fr. berry-bearing shrub. **1.** Broom for sweeping lawns, paths, yards &c., made of a bundle of pliable twigs fastened to a long handle. **2.** (colloq., provinc.) Name of reproach for a woman; a jade.

besotted, adj. [1. besóted; 2. bisɔ́tid]. **be-** & **sot** & **-ed.** Stupefied (with drink); foolish, infatuated.

besought, vb. [1. besáwt; 2. bisɔ́t]. Pret. & P.P. of **beseech.** M.E. *besōht(e)*; see **sought.**

bespangle(d), vb. & adj. [1. bespángl(d); 2. bispǽŋgl(d)]. **be-** & **spangle.** Cover(ed) with spangles.

bespatter, vb. trans. [1. bespáter; 2. bispǽtə]. **be-** & **spatter.** To splash, cover with, mud, slime, liquid dirt.

bespeak, vb. trans. [1. bespḗk; 2. bispík]. O.E. *besprecan*, 'speak about, complain', M.E. *bespēken*, 'speak about'. Cp. Germ. *besprechen*, 'to engage (rooms, seats &c.), in advance'. See **be-** & **speak.** To claim, order in advance: *may I bespeak your interest for X?*; *every room is already bespoken*. The trade phrase *bespoke* is applied to goods that are made to order, as distinct from *ready-made*: *bespoke boots* &c.

besprent, adj. [1. besprént; 2. bisprént]. M.E. *bespreynt*, P.P. of *besprengen*, 'to besprinkle', see **be-** & cp. **sprinkle.** (poet.) Sprinkled, strewn with.

besprinkle, vb. trans. [1. bespríngkl; 2. bispríŋkl]. **be-** & **sprinkle.** To sprinkle something *with* something else.

Bessemer process, n. [1. bésemer prṑses; 2. bésimə pròusɛs], fr. the inventor Sir Henry Bessemer, d. 1898. Process of steel-making in which the iron is decarbonized by a forced draught of air through the molten metal.

Bessemer steel, n. Steel made by the above process.

best (I.), adj. [1. best; 2. bɛst]. O.E. *betst*, 'best', superl. of *gōd*, O.S. *best*, Goth. *batist-s*. The base *bat-, used for compar. & superl. of *good* in all Gmc. languages, appears in another grade in O.E. *bōt*, 'remedy, compensation', cp. **boot (III.)**, & in O.E. *bētan*, 'provide remedy for, compensate', fr. *bōt-jan. Cp. also Goth. *ga-bat-nan*, 'profit, benefit'. O.E. *betst* is exactly equiv. to Goth. *bat-ist-s*, & goes back to an identical form *bat-i-st-, *-st-* being the superl. suff. Connexions outside Gmc. are doubtful. See **better.** **1.** Used as superlative of both *good* and *well*; expresses both comparative and absolute excellence; possessing essential qualities in the greatest possible degree. **a** Having the highest degree of moral or intellectual excellence: *the best heart, character, intentions*; *the best abilities, brains, talents* &c.; **b** having highest degree of suitability and adequacy for a particular purpose: *the best horse, road, cloth, boat*; *best book on the subject, best voice, the best father*. Phr. *the best thing to do*, that most likely to be successful; *what will be the best to do now?*; **c** having greatest amount of completeness and perfection: *the best art, pictures, poetry, architecture*; **d** possessing greatest amount of competency, efficiency, or skill in particular kind of work or activity: *the best painter, scholar, teacher, cook, rider, general* &c.; Phr. *the best man for the job*; **e** having highest degree of equivalence between value and price paid; most profitable in view of effort expended: *the best value, bargain*; *best results*; **f** affording greatest degree of satisfaction to the senses: *the best dinner I have eaten*; *the best cigar, best apple, best view, best scent* &c. **2.** *Best* is also used as mere intensive, expressing thoroughness &c., in such phrases as *the best-hated man*. **3.** Various idiomatic phrases (in several of the following *bcst*, preceded by *the*, is used as a noun). *All for the best*, not so bad as it seems after all; *to do, try, one's best*, take greatest pains; *have the best of it*, win, be successful; *make the best of it*, or *of a bad business*, be cheerful in face of misfortune &c.; *to the best of my ability*, as well as I can; *to the best of my belief*, so far as I know; *the best part of anything*, largest share, nearly all; *make the best of one's time*, be very busy, do as much as possible; *best man*, supporter of bridegroom at wedding; *put one's best foot forward*, go as quickly as possible; *with the best*, as well as anyone; *to be at one's best*, be brilliant; in a good temper; show the utmost one can do; *Sunday best*, or *best clothes*; *make the best of one's way*, go as fast as possible; *at best*, under the most favourable circumstances; *the best of wives*, distinguished among wives for goodness.

best (II.), adv. See prec. **1.** To the highest degree of excellence, competence, suitability: *to work, do anything, best.* **2.** To the greatest extent, most thoroughly: *to love one best*; *I work best early in the morning.* Phr. *we, you &c. had best do something*, it would be suitable, to our advantage &c.

best (III.), vb. trans. fr. **best** (I.). (colloq.) *To best someone*, beat him, have advantage over; sometimes in bad sense to get an advantage over by unfair, dishonest, means.

bestead, adj. [1. bestéd; 2. bistéd], fr. old P.P., M.E. *bestad*, fr. *besteden*, 'place'; O.N. *stad*, 'placed, situated', fr. *steðja*, 'fix, appoint'. See **be-** & **stead.** (archaic) Circumstanced, situated; in *ill-*, *well-bestead.*

bestial, adj. & n. [1. béstial; 2. béstiəl]. Fr. *bestial*, Lat. *bestiālis*. Cp. **beast** & **-al.** **1.** adj. Like a beast; brutal, barbarous, unrestrained, disgusting, obscene. **2.** n. (a Scots usage) Cattle collectively, as on a farm.

bestiality, n. [1. bèstiáliti; 2. bèstiǽliti]. Prec. & **-ity.** **a** Brutishness, beastliness; **b** specif. (law) unnatural sexual crime with an animal.

bestialize, vb. trans. [1. béstialīz; 2. béstiəlaiz]. **bestial** & **-ize.** To make bestial or brutish.

bestially, adv. [1. béstiali; 2. béstiəli]. **bestial** & **-ly.** In a bestial manner.

bestiary, n. [1. béstiari; 2. béstiəri], fr. L. Lat. *bestiārius*. See **beast** & **-ary.** One of the mediaeval collections of fables, allegories, semi-mythical accounts of animals, esp. of wild animals.

bestir, vb. refl. [1. bestér; 2. bistə́]. O.E. *bestyrian* (rare), 'heap up', fr. **be-** & **stir.** To rouse oneself to action, exert oneself.

bestow, vb. trans. [1. bestó; 2. bistóu]. M.E. *bestōwen*, 'place'. **be-** & **stow.** **1.** To place, deposit, put: *I don't know where to bestow all my luggage.* **2.** (with *upon*) To grant, give, confer (a benefit): *he bestowed a fortune upon his nephews*; *Providence had bestowed many advantages upon him.* **3.** (colloq.) To give quarters to, find room for: *can you bestow us somewhere for the night?*

bestowal, n. [1. bestóal; 2. bistóuəl]. Prec. & **-al.** Act of bestowing in any of above senses.

bestrew, vb. trans. [1. bestrṓō; 2. bistrū́]. O.E. *bestrēowian*, 'bestrew, cover'. See **be-** & **strew.** **1.** To scatter over surface (not used of liquids); to cover thickly (*with*): *to bestrew the floor with papers.* **2.** To lie thickly scattered about, over: *the leaves bestrew the lawn in autumn.*

bestrewn, adj. [1. bestrṓōn; 2. bistrū́n], fr. P.P. of prec. Recent formation, the vb. being orig. weak. More usual now than *bestrewed.* Covered with: *the whole place was bestrewn with rubbish.*

bestride, vb. trans. [1. bestríd; 2. bistráid]. O.E. *bestrīdan*, 'mount a horse'. See **be-** & **stride.** **1.** To put one's legs one on either side of anything (a horse, seat, narrow ditch, brook &c.); to sit upon (a horse), ride. **2.** (fig. and poet.) To pass, reach, across, as of a rainbow, beams of sun, sound &c., across a valley, field &c.: '*Winds that the thunder bestrides*' (Swinburne).

bestrode, vb. [1. bestrṓd; 2. bistróud]. Pret. of prec.; see **strode.**

bet (I.), n. [1. bet; 2. bet]. Etymol. quite uncertain; the usual explanation given is that it is a shortened form of **abet.** **1.** A wager, offer to pay a certain sum of money, or give some article in the event of some event happening or not happening. **2.** The amount or thing wagered.

bet (II.), vb. trans. & intrans. fr. prec. **1.** trans. To lay as a wager (with person): *he bet me a pound I would not do it*; *to bet five pounds on or against a horse* &c. Phr. *to bet one's bottom dollar on, that* &c., to be absolutely certain that &c. **2.** intrans. **a** To make practice of making wagers: *he never betted*; **b** to wager with, *on, against*: *to bet on the favourite*; *I'll bet against your winning.* Phr. *you bet*, you may be sure.

beta, n. [1. béta; 2. bítə]. Gk. The second letter of the Greek alphabet (see **B**); fr. Heb. *bēt*; used for the second of a series of objects of which the first is *alpha*, A, as in stars of second brightness in a constellation; *beta-rays* &c.

betake, vb. reflex. [1. beták; 2. bitéik]. M.E. *betāken*, 'entrust, commit to one's keeping'. See **be-** & **take.** To take, convey oneself, go.

betel, n. [1. bétl; 2. bítl]. Portuguese *betre, betle*, fr. Malay. *veṭṭila*, fr. *veru ila*, 'simple, or mere leaf' (Yule and Burnell). 'The leaf of the *Piper betle*, chewed with the dried *areca nut* (which is thence improperly called *betel-nut*)' (Yule and Burnell).

bête noire, n. [1. bát nwár; 2. béit nwā́(r)]. Fr., 'black beast'. A person or thing that one detests specially.

bethel, n. [1. béthel; 2. béþl]. Heb. *beth-el*, 'house of God'. Derisive name for a Nonconformist chapel; esp. *little bethel.*

bethink, vb. reflex. [1. bethíngk; 2. biþíŋk]. O.E. *beþencan*, 'consider; (reflex.) reflect'. See **be-** & **think.** To consider well, remember: *I suddenly bethought me how* &c.

betide, vb. intrans. & trans. [1. betíd; 2. bitáid]. Defective. Used only in 3rd sing. pres. subj. O.E. *tīdan*, 'to happen'. See **be-** & **tide.** **a** intrans. To happen, come to pass: *whate'er betide*; **b** trans., to happen to: *woe betide you.*

betimes, adv. [1. betímz; 2. bitáimz]. **be-** & later formed advbl. genit. of O.E. *tīma*. See **time.** In good time, early: *to rise betimes*, get up early.

betoken, vb. trans. [1. betóken; 2. bitóukən]. **be-** & O.E. *tācnian*, 'signify'; see **token.** To signify, augur, have as a meaning, indicate: *that betokens no good to me.*

betony, n. [1. bétuni; 2. bétəni], fr. Fr. *bétoine*, fr. L. Lat. *betonica*, said to be of Gaulish origin. (bot.) Plant with a purple flower.

betray, vb. trans. & reflex. [1. betrá; 2. bitréi]. Hybrid compound; **be-** & M.E. *traien*; O. Fr. *traïr*, 'betray', Mod. Fr. *trahir*, Lat. *trādere*. Cp. **traitor, treason.** **1.** To play part of traitor towards, give up (a person, object) treacherously to enemies; to act falsely, deceitfully towards. **2.** To reveal (a secret) improperly, or inadvertently. **3.** (reflex.) *Betray oneself*, to reveal one's true character; let out one's secret unconsciously or by momentary inadvertence. **4.** To deceive, seduce (a woman).

betrayal, n. [1. betráal; 2. bitréiəl]. Prec. & **-al.** Act of treachery, treacherous delivery of a person &c. to enemies.

betrayer, n. [1. betráer; 2. bitréiə]. **betray** & **-er.** Traitor; seducer.

betroth, vb. trans. & reflex. [1. betrṓdh; 2. bitróuð]. M.E. *betrewðien*. See **be-** & **troth** & **truth.** To affiance, promise to marry, bind oneself or another, by a promise, to marry someone. Esp. in P.P. *to be betrothed to*, become engaged to; *betroth oneself to.* P.P. as adj., *the betrothed pair.*

betrothal, n. [1. betrṓdhal; 2. bitróuðəl]. Prec. & **-al.** Ceremony or act of becoming affianced.

betrothed, n. [1. betrṓdhd; 2. bitróuðd], fr. P.P. of **betroth.** Engaged person: *the betrothed*, the pair; *my betrothed*, fiancé(e).

better (I.), adj. [1. béter; 2. bétə]. O.E. *bet* (adv.), *betera* (adj.), O.H.G. *beziro*, Mod. Germ. *besser*, Goth. *batiza*. See further under **best.** Compar. of *good* & *well.* Always used in relation to, & expressing comparison w., some other person, thing, or state, & differing in this fr. **best**; generally followed by *than.* **1.** Expressing, generally, superiority to someone or something else. See various categories under **best.** Phrs. *the better the day, the better the deed*; *better than nothing*, might be worse; *no better than he, she should be*, a doubtful character; *one's better feelings*, higher part of one's nature; *better half*, husband, or wife; *be better than one's word*, do more than one promised; *one's betters*, elders, persons of higher rank &c.; *I know better*, I am not such a fool as to believe what you say; *to know better*, be able to judge that one has behaved ill; *think better of something*, change one's mind; *think the better of someone*, have a higher opinion; *to have seen better days*, have been richer, in a better position than at present; *better sort*, superior people; *for better for worse*, in good and bad fortune; *to feel better*, be less ill, recovering; *I am, he &c. is, better*, improved in health; *better late than never*, not too late. Special use: **a** having greater degree of moral excellence, more virtuous &c.: *he is a better man than I am*; **b** *better* is sometimes used positively, and *well* as implying superiority: *he is better, but not well yet*, the word being here contrasted with *ill*, not with *well.*

better (II.), adv. See prec. **1.** In a superior manner: *he does it better than I do.* **2.** More thoroughly, completely: *he is better loved than ever*; *better feared, better served, obeyed* &c. Phr. *we, you &c. had better (do something)*, it would be suitable, to our advantage &c.

better (III.), vb. trans. & reflex., fr. **better** (I.). To improve; improve on; do better than: *John Howard endeavoured to better the condition of prisoners in jails*; *he never bettered his earlier work*; *you can't better that.* *Better oneself*, raise oneself to a position, obtain situation of greater emolument, importance, and responsibility than one has held before: *in a few years he had bettered himself considerably by his talents and industry.*

better, -or, n. See **bet** (II.) & **-er, -or.** One who bets.

betterment, n. [1. béterment; 2. bétəmənt]. **better** (I.) & **-ment.** Improvement; specif. increase in value of a landed estate, otherwise than by mere repairs &c.

betting, n. [1. béting; 2. bétiŋ]. **bet** (II.) & **-ing.** Practice, habit, of laying wagers; the making of bets, esp. on horse-races &c.

betting-book, n. Book in which bets are recorded.

betting-man, n. One who makes a habit of betting.

between, prep. & adv. [1. betwén; 2. bitwín]. O.E. *betwēonan, betwēonum*, 'between', fr. **be-** & *twēonum*, adv. formed fr. base of *twā*, **two**, w. dat. pl. suff. An old construction separated the compound, as *be sǣm twēonum*, 'by seas two, between the seas'. **1.** Original use expresses relation of one to two other units whether individuals or groups, the sense being that one is in the middle with one of the two others on either side. This relation may be: **a** in respect of place, the relation being maintained either (i.) in a state of rest: *the house stands between a river and a wood*; *I sat between John and Henry*; or (ii.) during motion: *to walk between two hedgerows*; *the river flows between wooded banks*; **b** in respect of two places in order, precedence in a series: *between the top and the bottom of the hill*; *majors in the army rank between colonels and captains*; **c** in respect of two periods of time: *between youth and middle age*; *between 1914 and 1918.* Phrs. *between two fires*, attacked on both sides; *between the* *devil and the deep sea*, no escape possible; *between the cup and the lip*, of disappointed hopes; *hit, got, between wind and water*, in a tender spot; *between whiles*, during intervals; *in between*, spaced out among; *betwixt and between*, half and half. **2.** (expressing reciprocity) Confined to (two or more persons) and shared by each: *let us keep this strictly between ourselves*; *the money was divided equally between the crew*. Phrs. *between you and me, ourselves*, speaking confidentially; *settle it between you*. **3.** Expressing separation: *let us have no quarrels between gentlemen*; *let nothing come between us*; *the shadow of the past came between him and happiness*. **4.** Expressing union, bond of connexion, common to: *there was great love between them*; *I cannot quarrel with him after all there is between us*. Phr. *a go-between*, agent between two persons or parties.

betwixt, prep. & adv. [1. betwíkst; 2. bitwíkst]. O.E. *betweox, betwix*, 'between', earlier **twisk-*, M.E. *betwixe*; O.S. *twisk*, O.H.G. *zwisk, zwiski*, 'twofold'; O.H.G. *zwiskēn*, Du. *tusschen*, 'in the middle between two'. Archaic and poet. for **between**; chiefly in Phr. *betwixt and between*, neither one thing nor the other; of indeterminate character.

beurré, n. [1. bērā; 2. bǽrei], fr. Fr. *beurre*, 'butter'. French name, used in England for several kinds of pear: *beurré rance, beurré d'Amanlis* &c.

bevel, n. [1. bévl; 2. bévl]. O. Fr. *bevel*, Mod. Fr. *beveau*; etymol. unknown. A sloping edge; a joiner's tool for adjusting angle of bevel. Also as adj., having a sloping edge; and vb., to impart a bevel to, usually in P.P. *bevelled*.

beverage, n. [1. béverij; 2. bévəridž]. 16th cent. Engl., O. Fr. *bovraige*, Ital. *beveraggio*, 'drink'; cp. also *beverie*, 'action of drinking', *beivre*, 'to drink'; fr. Lat. *bibere*, 'to drink', q.v. under **bibulous**. Liquid used for drinking; that which can be drunk; a drink.

bevy, n. [1. bévi; 2. bévi]. Not found before 16th cent.; fr. Fr. *bevée*, 'flock of larks, or quails', fr. Ital. *beva*. Etymol. doubtful, but perhaps orig. a flock of birds gathered to drink, & hence w. transference of meaning, a company of people come together for social purposes; cp. O. Fr. *bevre*, Ital. *bevere*, 'to drink'. See prec. word. A gathering, troop, company, esp. of *ladies, maidens, beauty*.

bewail, vb. trans. [1. bewā́l; 2. biwéil]. See **be- & wail.** To lament, mourn over; regret deeply, complain of.

beware, vb. [1. bewā́r; 2. biwéə]. Apparently a descendant of O.E. *bewarian*, 'watch over, guard', but now as though fr. vb. *be* & O.E. *wær*, 'cautious, aware of'. See **wary.** To be cautious, careful of, on guard against. Always preceded by another verb unless in imperative, or when *be* would be naturally used, as: *you must beware of bad companions*; *I will beware of lobster at night*; *tell him to beware of strangers*; *beware of the dog!*

bewilder, vb. trans. [1. bewílder; 2. biwíldə]. A late word, though Engl. in origin. O.E. *wildern*, M.E. *wilderen* means 'wilderness'; *bewildern* is lit. 'to lead into the wilderness, or lead astray'; *wildern* survived later in provinc. Engl.; cp. **wilderness.** To puzzle, perplex, throw into confusion of mind.

bewildering, adj. [1. bewíldring; 2. biwíldriŋ], fr. Pres. Part. of prec. Puzzling, confusing, causing confusion of mind.

bewilderment, n. [1. bewílderment; 2. biwíldəmənt]. **bewilder & -ment.** State of being bewildered.

bewitch, vb. trans. [1. bewích; 2. biwítʃ]. See **be- & witch. 1.** To cast a witch's spells over, operate on by magic. **2.** To charm, enchant, fascinate, delight extremely.

bewitched, adj. [1. bewícht; 2. biwítʃt], fr. P.P. of prec. Affected by magic; enchanted, delighted, charmed.

bewitching, adj. [1. bewíching; 2. biwítʃiŋ], fr. Pres. Part. of **bewitch.** Enchanting, delightful, fascinating, captivating.

bewitchingly, adv. Prec. & **-ly.** In an enchanting, captivating manner.

bewray, vb. trans. [1. berā́; 2. biréi]. **be- &** O.E. *wrēgan*, 'accuse', M.E. *be-, biwreyen*, 'reveal, disclose'; w. *wrēgan*, we connect O.E. *wrōh-t*, 'accusation'; also O.H.G. *ruogen*, 'accuse', Mod. Germ. *rügen*, O.S. *wrōgian*, Goth. *wrōh-s*, 'accusation', *wrohjan*, 'accuse'. The base has not been traced outside Gmc. To proclaim, betray, reveal: '*thy speech bewrayeth thee*'.

bey, n. [1. bā; 2. bei]. Turk. *bēg* [bē], 'lord, prince'. **a** A governor of a town or district in the Turkish dominions; placed after the name of the person: *Ismet Bey*; **b** title often borne formerly by English and other European officials, and by English officers of the rank of major in the army serving in Egypt.

beyond, adv. & prep. (& n.) [1. bēyónd; 2. bijɔ́nd]. O.E. *beġeondan*, M.E. *beyonde*, 'beyond'; **be-** compounded w. Gmc. base **jaind-*, 'there'. Cp. **yon, yonder.** *Beyond* means originally 'over there'. **1.** On the other, further, side (of), past, further on: *beyond the river, tree* &c.; *beyond the last house*; (fig.) *beyond the tomb*. Phrs. *beyond one's depth*, into deep water; *beyond seas*, the other side of the ocean. **2.** (of time) Later than, more advanced than: *beyond the hour when he was expected*. **3.** (of non-material things) Out of reach, out of one's range, outside one's understanding, further than one's powers take one; surpassing: *beyond my intelligence*; *beyond my humble powers*; *he has gone far beyond me in learning*. Phrs. *beyond compare*, incomparable, very excellent; *beyond control*, uncontrollable; *beyond one's depth* (fig.), too difficult; *beyond one's expectations*, better than one hoped; *beyond expression*, greater than I can say; *beyond one's grasp*, out of reach; *beyond hope*, hopeless; *beyond the mark*, too far; irrelevant; *beyond possibility*, impossible; *beyond measure*, greater than can be measured, very great(ly); *beyond all praise*; *beyond price*, priceless; *beyond reason*, unreasonable. **4.** (as n.) *The beyond*, the other life. Phr. *the back of beyond*, a very remote place.

bezant, n. [1. bézant; 2. bézənt]. O. Fr. *besan*, Lat. *Bysant(ius nummus)*, 'coin of Byzantium'. **1.** A gold coin current in Eastern Roman Empire and Europe generally from 4th to 15th cents. and current in England in 13th and 14th cents. **2.** (her.) Representation of above, a gold circular figure covered with dots.

bezel, n. [1. bézl; 2. bézl]. O. Fr. *bezel*, Mod. Fr. *bizeau*. Etymol. very doubtful, but possibly Low Lat. *bis-alus*, 'stone which has two angles', or faces. This may be, as Skeat suggests, Lat. *bis ala*, 'double wing'. **a** Sloping faces of a cut gem; sloping edge of a chisel; **b** that part of a ring which holds the stone.

bezique, n. [1. bezḗk; 2. bizík]. Fr. *bésique*. Etymol. unknown. **a** A card game for two or four players; **b** scoring point made by combination of queen of spades and knave of diamonds.

bezoar, n. [1. bḗzōr; 2. bízōə]. Corrupt. of Pers. *pādzahr*, Arab. *bāzahr*, orig. a term in old Oriental *materia medica* for an antidote. Later used for hard concretions found in bodies of certain animals, and supposed to have antidotal properties; sometimes called *snake stone*; the term is also applied to *hair-balls*, q.v.

Bezonian, n. [1. bezṓnian; 2. bizóuniən]. Also *bisonian*, fr. Fr. *bisogne*, 'knave, rogue', fr. Ital. *bisogni*, pl., 'new recruits for an army in need of money', fr. *bisogno*, 'need'. Etymol. doubtful. (archaic) Knave, beggarly fellow, familiar from Pistol's '*under which king, Bezonian* &c.' ('2 Henry IV.').

bhang, n. [1. bang; 2. bæŋ]. See **bang (V.).**

bheesty, n. [1. bḗsti; 2. bísti]. Anglo-Indian word for the domestic who supplies a household with water; a water-carrier generally. Etymol. is dubious; possibly fr. Pers. *bihishti*, 'person', or fr. *bihisht*, 'paradise'.

bi- [1. bī; 2. bai]. Lat. pref. much used in Engl., esp. w. words of Lat. origin, but also w. others. Lat. *bi-*, 'twice', fr. *bis*, w. loss of *-s* in compounds; cp. Lat. *bicornis*, 'two-horned', *bis* & *cornu*, 'horn'. *Bis* is for earlier **dwis*, connected w. *duo*, 'two', q.v. under **dual & two.** Cp. *b* for *dw-* in Lat. *bellum*, q.v. under **bellicose.** The force of the pref. *bi-* is 'double, twice, having two'. The chief uses of *bi-* in Engl. are: **1.** Having two: *bicuspid*, having two cusps or points; doubly, in two ways. **2.** Lasting for two; occurring every two: *biennial, bimonthly*. **3.** (chem.) Having double the amount of acid or base indicated by the uncompounded form: *bicarbonate*.

bias, n. & vb. trans. [1. bías; 2. báiəs]. Fr. *biais*, 'oblique, obliquity'; etymol. doubtful; perh. fr. Lat. *bifax*, acc. *bifacem*, 'two faced', Low Lat., 'crooked'. **1.** n. **a** (i.) Deflection from straight line or course, or in a particular direction; (ii.) that which produces such deflection, whether lopsidedness in shape, or a weight on one side; esp. in bowls, which are so made that they swerve from a straight course when rolled; **b** (fig.) influence brought to bear on the mind or opinions; prejudice, predisposition, for good or ill: *to have a bias against, in favour of, a person, idea* &c.; **c** an oblique line across the texture in a fabric or cloth. **2.** vb. (esp. fig.) To influence, prejudice; usually in unfavourable sense: *to be bias(s)ed against a person* &c.

biaxial, adj. [1. biáksial; 2. baiǽksiəl]. **bi- & axial.** Of crystals, having two axes.

bib (I.) n. [1. bib; 2. bib]. Prob. connected w. following word. Piece of linen worn by young children over the breast at meals, to protect clothes. Phr. *best bib and tucker*, best clothes.

bib (II.), vb., gen. intrans. Prob. fr. Lat. *bibere*, 'drink'. See **bibulous.** To drink, esp. in sense of to partake too frequently or copiously of strong liquor.

bibber, n. [1. bíber; 2. bíbə]. Prec. & **-er.** One given to excessive or too frequent drinking of strong liquor.

bibbing, n. [1. bíbing; 2. bíbiŋ]. **bib (II.) & -ing.** The habit, or act, of excessive drinking.

Bible, n. [1. bíbl; 2. báibl]. M.E. & O. Fr. *bible*, fr. Lat. *biblia*, fr. Gk. *biblia*, 'collection of writings', pl. of *biblion*, 'little book, scroll'. This is a derivative of *biblos*, 'inner bark of papyrus', and is an Egyptian loan-word. **1. a** The collection of sacred writings, or canonical books, which constitute the Holy Scriptures (*The Bible*); **b** a copy of these (*a Bible*). Phr. *Bible oath*, a solemn and binding one, as if taken on a Bible. **2.** (by extension) Any authoritative book: *The Oxford English Dictionary is the Bible of all students of the English vocabulary*.

Bible Christian(s), n. Religious sect, offshoot of Methodists, professing that their tenets are derived solely from what they conceive to be the true interpretation of the Scriptures.

Bible clerk, n. Name applied to a person in position of an exhibitioner at All Souls' College, Oxford, who receives free board and lodging, and has the duty of reading the Lessons in the College Chapel.

biblical, adj. [1. bíblikl; 2. bíblikl]. Lat. *biblicus*, adj. See **Bible & -ic & -al. 1.** Contained in, in accordance with, the Bible; of doctrine, custom, phrase &c.: *biblical teaching, practice, name* &c. **2.** Pertaining to, concerning, text and history of the Bible: *biblical studies*; *biblical scholar*.

biblio-, pref. Form of Gk. *biblion* (cp. **Bible**) used in composition. It refers in some words specifically to the Bible, in others to books in general.

bibliographer, n. [1. bibliógrafer; 2. bibliɔ́grəfə]. See **bibliography & -er.** One concerned with, or occupied by bibliography.

bibliographical, adj. [1. bibliōgráfikl; 2. bibliougrǽfikl]. See **bibliography & -ic & -al.** Belonging to bibliography.

bibliographically, adv. Prec. & **-ly.** By means of, as in, a bibliography; by a bibliographer.

bibliography, n. [1. bìbliógrafi; 2. bìbliɔ́grəfi]. Gk. *bibliographia.* See **biblio-** & **-graphy.** **1.** The study or account of the history of books from the external side as distinct from their subject matter; description of the making up of books, the various editions and impressions and the differences which distinguish these. **2.** List of books and writings dealing with a particular subject, or written by a particular author: *a bibliography of philology, of philological books; a Tennyson bibliography,* list of all editions &c. of Tennyson's works, and of books about him and them.

bibliolater, n. [1. bìbliólater; 2. bìbliɔ́lətə], fr. **biblio-** & Gk. *latréia,* '(hired) service, especially service of the gods, worship'. Cp. Gk. *latreúō,* 'work for hire; serve the gods', *látris,* 'servant, slave', *látron,* 'pay, hire'; Lat. *lātro,* 'hired servant'. These & many other words in the Aryan languages are fr. a base **lē(i)-,* 'possession, safe keeping; earn, gain'. Cp. Gk. *a-léios,* 'poor', lit. 'without corn land'; O. Slav. *leti,* 'permitted'; Goth. *un-lēds,* 'poor', lit. 'without property'; O.E. *lǣþ,* 'division of land, property', & *un-lǣd,* 'poor', lit. 'un-propertied'. See also **idolatry, idolater** & **-latry.** Lit. 'book-worshipper, book-slave'. One who has a great enthusiasm for the Bible, which takes the form of an exaggerated attachment to the literal word of Holy Writ.

bibliolatrous, adj. [1. bìbliólatrus; 2. bìbliɔ́lətrəs]. Prec. & **-ous.** Given to exaggerated reverence for the literal interpretation of the words of the Bible.

bibliolatry, n. [1. bìbliólatri; 2. bìbliɔ́lətri]. See prec. & **-y.** Respect, enthusiasm, for literal meaning of the words of Scripture.

bibliomancy, n. [1. bíbliōmànsi; 2. bíblioumæ̀nsi]. See **biblio-** & **-mancy.** Divination by opening a Bible at random and taking the first verse to meet the eye as a prophecy of future events, guide to conduct &c.

bibliomania, n. [1. bìbliōmánia; 2. bìblioumèiniə]. **biblio-** & **mania.** Book madness; excessive enthusiasm for collecting books.

bibliomaniac, n. [1. bìbliōmániak; 2. bìblioumèiniæk]. See **biblio-** & **maniac.** One afflicted with bibliomania.

bibliophil(e), n. [1. bíbliōfìl, -fil; 2. bíblioufàil, -fìl]. **biblio-** & **-phil(e).** A book-lover, one who is fond of books, rather perhaps as a collector than as a reader.

bibliopole, n. [1. bíbliōpōl; 2. bíbliəupòul]. **biblio-** & Gk. *pōlēs,* 'merchant, seller'; cogn. w. Lith. *pelnas,* 'pay, reward', Russ. *pelonŭ,* 'booty'; O.H.G. *fāli,* Mod. Germ. *feil,* 'to be sold, venal'. Bookseller, esp. seller of rare books.

bibulous, adj. [1. bíbūlus; 2. bíbjuləs]. Lat. *bibulus,* 'given to drinking freely'; Lat. *bibō,* 'I drink', a redupl. form, is fr. earlier **pibō,* w. assimilation of *p* to *b.* The base is found in many forms in Aryan languages & the orig. forms & variants **pōi-, *pō(i)-, *pi-,* are assumed; cp. Gk. *pínō,* 'drink', Scrt. *pibati,* 'he drinks', O. Slav. *piti,* 'to drink', O.W. *iben* for **piben* = Lat. *bibimus,* 'we drank'. Further cognates are: Scrt. *pānam,* 'a drink', *pītáś,* 'having drunk'; Gk. *pótos,* 'drinking bout', *pô-ma,* 'draught, potion'; Lat. *pōtātio,* 'drinking bout', *pōtio,* 'draught', *pōtor,* 'drinker', *pōculum,* 'drinking cup', fr. **pōtlom,* w. wh. cp. Ir. *ol,* 'draught', fr. **potlo;* O. Slav. *pojq,* 'I would have drunk', *pivo,* 'a drink', Russ. *pivo,* 'beer', Lith. *pŷvas,* 'beer'. See **imbibe, poison, potion.** Given to drinking strong liquor; slightly overcome with drink (of persons).

bi-cameral, adj. [1. bīkámeral; 2. baikǽmərəl], fr. **bi-** & Lat. *camera,* 'chamber', & **-al;** see **camera** & **chamber.** Of legislative bodies, having two chambers or houses.

bicarbonate, n. 1. bīkárbonat; 2. bàikáːbənit]. **bi-** & **carbonate.** (chem.) A carbonate with two equivalents of carbonic acid to one of a base, e.g. *bicarbonate of soda.*

bice, n. [1. bīs; 2. bais]. Fr. *bis.* Origin unknown. Blue or green pigment.

bicentenary, n. [1. bìsentḗnari; 2. bàisentínəri]. Lat. **bi-** & *centēnārius,* adj. 'relating to a hundred years'. See **centenary.** Celebration of existence of a building or institution for two hundred years, or of the two-hundredth anniversary of a person's birth or death or of an historical event &c.

bicentennial, adj. [1. bìsenténial; 2. bàisenténiəl]. Lat. **bi-** & *centum,* 'hundred', q.v. under **cent,** & *annus,* 'year', wh. appears as *-enn-* in composition, as in *biennium,* 'period of two years'. See **annual** & **biennial.** Having lasted for two hundred years; occurring every two hundred years.

bicephalous, adj. [1. biséfalus; 2. baiséfələs]. A hybrid word fr. **bi-** & Gk. *kephalḗ,* 'head', see **cephalic,** & **-ous.** Two-headed.

biceps, n. [1. bíseps; 2. báiseps]. Lat. *biceps,* adj., 'two headed', fr. **bi-** & *caput,* 'head'. See **capital, chief.** Name given to flexor muscle with double attachment, esp. that of the upper arm, but also applied to that in leg which bends the knee.

bichloride, n. [1. bīklṓrīd; 2. bàiklɔ́raid]. **bi-** & **chloride.** Chemical compound with double amount of chlorine combining with metals, as *bichloride of mercury,* corrosive sublimate.

bicker, vb. intrans. [1. bíker; 2. bíkə]. M.E. *bikeren;* freq. active vb. formed w. suff. *-er* fr. base *bik-, pik-* &c. See **pick.** To squabble, engage in repeated petty disputes.

bicuspid, n. [1. bīkúspid; 2. báikáspid]. Lat. **bi-** & *cuspis,* 'point'. See **cusp.** Tooth, such as molar, having two points or prominences.

bicycle, n. & vb. intrans. [1. bísikl; 2. báisikl]. Lit., 'two-wheel'. Lat. **bi-** & **cycle,** fr. Gk. *kúklos.* **1.** n. Well-known machine used as mode of progression, with two wheels in same line, a seat for one person, handle-bars by means of which the front wheel is directed as required, and pedals whereby the back wheel is driven; now usually styled a *push-bicycle,* as contrasted with *motor-bicycle.* **2.** vb. To ride upon a bicycle.

bicycling, n. [1. bísikling; 2. báisikliŋ], fr. prec. & **-ing.** Riding of a bicycle.

bicyclist, n. [1. bísiklist; 2. báisiklist]. See **bicycle** & **-ist.** One who rides a bicycle.

bid (I.), vb. trans. [1. bid; 2. bid]. In O.E. there were two strong vbs. wh. had certain meanings in common: *biddan,* Pret. sing. *bæd,* (Pret. pl. *bǣdon*), P.P. *beden,* wh. means 'entreat, request, demand', & the same vb. compounded, *ge-biddan,* (reflex.) meaning 'pray', & *bēodan,* Pret. sing. *bēad* (Pret. pl. *budon*), P.P. *boden,* meaning 'invite, or challenge to fight; announce, proclaim; threaten; command'. It is obvious that the pres. & infin. types of *bid* are fr. *biddan,* that the Pret. *bade* [bæd] is fr. *bæd,* while the P.P. *bidden* cannot be derived fr. those of either of the O.E. vbs., but is after the model of *ridden* &c. of the 'ride' class. During the 15th & 16th cents., *bad* & *bāde* were used in the Pret., while the P.P. had both *bēde(n),* *boden* forms. A form *bidde* was also used in Pret. as early as the 15th cent., & 'Euphues' (1586) has *for-bidden. Bid* corresponds to O.S. *biddian,* Goth. *bidjan,* 'pray, beg', & goes back to a Gmc. **bed-.* Cp. **bead.** With this it is difficult to connect Goth. *beidan,* 'expect', O.E. *bīdan,* 'wait, bide' (cp. **bide**), Lat. *fīdō,* 'trust', or Gk. *peithō,* 'persuade' &c., as is sometimes attempted. O.E. *bēodan,* O.S. *biodan,* 'offer', Goth. *ana-biudan,* 'order, command', go back to Gmc. **beud-,* wh. is cogn. w. Gk. *peúth-omai,* 'ask, inquire, learn', Scrt. *bódhāmi,* 'I observe'. The two bases appear to have overlapped in meaning very early, & the meanings of both are certainly blended in *bid.* **1.** To command, order: '*Bid me discourse, I will enchant thine ear*'; *do as you are bid.* **2.** To invite; (archaic) '*the worthy, bidden guest*' (Milton); chiefly in P.P. *bidden to a feast* &c. Survives in *bidding prayer,* in which congregation are invited to pray for certain things. **3.** To announce, proclaim: only in archaic Phr. *to be bidden,* have one's banns called, *bid defiance,* make known &c., and perhaps in *to bid fair,* promise, show promise. Phr. *to bid farewell, welcome, good-night* &c. This use of the word might belong either to **2** or **3.** **4.** (with *for*) **a** To offer, make an offer at a sale or auction: *to bid twenty pounds for a horse;* **b** also (obsolesc.) to make an offer: *will no one bid (for this horse)?*

bid (II.), n., fr. prec. An offer of a price. Cp. **bid** (I.), **4.**

biddable, adj. [1. bídabl; 2. bídəbl]. **bid** & **-able.** Obedient, easily persuaded, docile (not common).

bidden, vb. [1. bídn; 2. bídn]. P.P. of **bid** (I.).

bidder, n. [1. bíder; 2. bídə]. **bid** (I.) & **-er.** One who bids, esp. at an auction.

bidding, vbl. n. [1. bíding; 2. bídiŋ]. See **bid** (I.) & **-ing.** **1.** Command, order: *to do your bidding,* obey you. **2.** Bids, offers at auction: *bidding was brisk.*

bide, vb. trans. & intrans. [1. bīd; 2. baid]. O.E., O.S. *bīdan,* O.H.G. *bītan,* 'await' &c., Goth. *beidan,* 'await'. It is not quite certain that Lat. *fīdo* 'trust', see **fidelity,** Gk. *peithō,* 'I learn by asking', *Peithṓ,* 'Persuasion' personified as a goddess, *pistis,* 'trust, faith, belief', are cognates of the Gmc. base **bid, *beid-, *baid,* though this & the above Lat. & Gk. words wd. all go back to Aryan **bheidh-, *bhoidh-, *bhidh-.* For **abide** (archaic, poet. and provinc.) to wait, stay, delay. Regularly used in Phr. *to bide one's time,* await a favourable opportunity. Note dialectal use: *you bide where you be,* stay where you are.

bidree, n., also **biddery** [1. bídrē; 2. bídri], fr. Hind. *bidri,* fr. Bidar, town in India. Alloy of zinc, tin, lead, or copper, used for making an Indian ware, *bidree ware,* inlaid with gold and silver decoration.

biennial, adj. & n. [1. biénial; 2. baiéniəl], fr. Lat. *biennis,* adj., *biennium,* n., 'period of two years', fr. **bi-** & *annus,* 'year', q.v. under **annual,** & **-al.** **a** adj. Lasting for two years; recurring every two years; **b** n., a plant which lives for two seasons and then dies off, contrasted with *perennial.*

bienseance, n. [1. byansāahns; 2. bjǣsɑ̃s]. Fr., 'well-beseemingness', fr. *bien,* 'well', Lat. **bene-,** *séance,* n., fr. *séant,* Pres. Part. of *seoir,* 'sit', Lat. *sedēre,* see **sedentary.** That which is fitting and suitable in conduct and morals; decorum, decency.

bier, n. [1. bēr; 2. biə]. O.E. *bǣr,* 'bier, litter', O.H.G. *bāra,* fr. common Gmc. base **ber-,* 'bear'. The same type of gradation occurs in O.E. Pret. pl. *bǣr-on,* Goth. *bērun,* O.H.G. *bār-um.* Lat. *fer-etrum,* 'bier', is fr. same base, but shows a different form of gradation. See further under **bear** (I.). Fr. *bière* is borrowed fr. Gmc. **1.** A frame of wood, sometimes on wheels, on which coffins are borne. **2.** (fig.) Death: *friends who but a short while ago were delighting in his society are now weeping round his bier,* regretting his death.

biff, n. & vb. trans. [1. bif; 2. bif], prob. imitative. (slang, colloq.) **1.** n. Blow, smack: *a biff in the eye;* also fig. **2.** vb. To strike, hit: *biffed on the nose.*

biffin, n. [1. bífin; 2. bífin]. Variant of **beefing.**

bifid, adj. [1. bífid; 2. báifid], fr. Lat. *bifidus,* 'split in two parts', fr. **bi-** & *fid-,* stem of *findere, fiss-um,* 'to split'. See **fissile.** (bot.) Split, divided into two equal parts or lobes.

bifocal, adj. [1. bīfṓkal; 2. bàifóukəl]. **bi-** & **focal.** Of lenses &c., having two foci. See **focus.**

bifoliate, adj. [1. bīfṓliāt; 2. bàifóulieit]. Lat. **bi-** & *foliātus,* 'leaved', see **folio** & **-ate.** Having two leaves.

bifurcate, vb. intrans. & trans. [1. bífĕrkāt; 2. báifākeit]. Lat. **bi-** & *-furca*, 'fork with two prongs', q.v. under **fork**, & **-ate**. To divide into two branches, streams &c., said of a bough, river, road &c.

bifurcate(d), adj. [1. bífĕrkat, -kāted; 2. báifākit, -keitid], fr. P.P. of prec. Forked, divided into two.

bifurcation, n. [1. bìfĕrkáshun; 2. bàifākéiʃən]. See **bifurcate** & **-ion**. Forking, division into two.

big, adj. [1. big; 2. big]. M.E. *big*; origin unknown. **1.** Possessing great size, ampleness, bulk, or magnitude generally. Of things as they extend in space in every dimension; the usual word to describe anything having largeness of any kind; **a** (of bulk, mass) *big lump, clod, loaf, pudding, trunk of tree, body, book* &c.; **b** (of height) *a big man, tree, chimney, spire* &c.; **c** (of width) having great lateral extension, covering wide surface: *big margin, field, shoulders, chest* &c.; **d** having great containing capacity: *big room, cask, box, hole*; **e** (of sound) having great volume, range, compass: *a big voice, big roar, noise* &c. Phrs. *big-bellied*, (obs.) pregnant; *to look big*, assume important air; *talk big*, boast; *big with child, young* (obsolesc. and liter.), pregnant; hence, *big with fate*. **2.** (fig. uses) **a** (of mind, character, affections) Liberal, magnanimous, generous, noble: *big intelligence, nature, heart*; **b** (of persons, offices, news) important, distinguished; also (of persons) having qualities mentioned under **a**. Phr. *a big wig*, important person. **3.** (specif. designation) *The big toe*; *the big house*, chief house in a village.

bigamist, n. [1. bígamist; 2. bígəmist]. See **bigamy** & **-ist**. Man with two wives; woman with two husbands.

bigamous, adj. [1. bígamus; 2. bígəməs]. See **bigamy** & **-ous**. **a** (of person) Guilty of bigamy; **b** (of marriage) involving bigamy.

bigamously, adv. Prec. & **-ly**. In a bigamous manner.

bigamy, n. [1. bígami; 2. bígəmi]. O. Fr. *bigame*, 'twice-married', compounded of Lat. **bi-** & Gk. *gámos*, 'wedding'. This word, together w. Gk. *gaméō*, 'I marry', *gambrós*, 'son-in-law', i.e. one related by marriage, seems to be connected w. a number of words implying relationship, relationship by marriage &c., all sprung, & variously formed, fr. a base **ĝem-*, 'to pair, bind together' & so on. Thus Scrt. *jāmiš*, 'related, in sisterly relation to', *jâmātar*, 'daughter's husband'; Lat. *gener*, 'son-in-law', *geminus*, 'twin, paired, double', are a few words fr. among many other cognates. See others, more remote, under **gender, nature, kin**; cp. **-gamy**. The crime of having two wives or two husbands at the same time.

bigaroon, n. [1. bigaro͞on; 2. bigərúːn]. O. Fr. **bigaron, bigarreau*, fr. *bigarré*, 'variegated'. The latter is perh. **bi-**, & some word connected w. Engl. *garish*, 'bright-coloured'. The etymol. of this, however, is also doubtful. Skeat suggests connexion w. **gaze**, a Scand. word. If *bigarré* belongs to this group, the second element must be a Gmc. loan-word. Large whiteheart cherry; from its striped colouring.

big-horn, n. A mountain sheep of western North America, with curved horns, of a greyish-brown colour, *Ovis canadensis*, also called Rocky Mountain sheep.

bight, n. [1. bīt; 2. bait]. O.E. *byht*, 'a bend', fr. **buhti*. Connected w. O.E. *būgan*, 'bend, bow', q.v. under **bow (I.)**. **a** A twist or hitch in a rope; **b** a bend or curve in a coast-line; a bay.

bigot, n. [1. bígut; 2. bígət]. Fr.; etymol. dubious, perh. fr. form of *Visigoth*; very doubtful. One who holds a creed or opinion in an obstinate, narrow-minded way, and is inaccessible to all reason in respect to it.

bigoted, adj. [1. bíguted; 2. bígətid]. Prec. & **-ed**. Narrow-minded, prejudiced, obstinately imbued with a belief.

bigotry, n. [1. bígutri; 2. bígətri]. **bigot** & **-ry**, cp. Fr. *bigoterie*. The condition of being a bigot.

bijou, n. [1. bézho͞o; 2. bíʒūː]. Fr., 'a jewel, treasure'. Etymol. unknown. Chiefly attrib., as a house-agent's word, implying something small, but perfect and elegant of its kind: *bijou villa, residence, flat* &c.

bijouterie, n. [1. bēzho͞oteri; 2. bìʒúːtəri]. Fr. See prec. Articles of jewelry, trinkets &c.

bike, n. & vb. [1. bīk; 2. baik]. Colloq. abbr. of **bicycle**.

bilateral, adj. [1. bīláteral; 2. bailǽtərəl]. See **bi-** & **lateral**. Having two sides.

bilberry, n. [1. bílberi; 2. bílbəri]. *bil-* is Scand. Cp. Dan. *bölle-bær*, prob. meaning 'ball', a term wh. might be applied to any berry. See **berry**. Small, low-growing, wild shrub with small, blue, sweetish berries; also called *blaeberry* and *whortleberry*.

bilbo, n. [1. bílbō; 2. bílbou], fr. Bilbao in Spain, noted for iron-smelting works and foundries. **1.** (archaic) Kind of sword or rapier. **2.** (pl.) *Bilboes*, fetters with chain and bar, used for confining prisoners on board ship; probably same as **1**; the word occurs earliest in this sense.

bile, n. [1. bīl; 2. bail]. Fr. *bile*, Lat. *bīlis*, 'gall, bile', origin doubtful. **1.** (med.) Secretion of the liver, stored in gall-bladder, which aids digestion. **2.** (fig.) Bitterness of feeling, ill humour.

bilge, n. [1. bilj; 2. bildž]. Said to be a form of O. Fr. *boulge*, Lat. *bulga*, 'leather sack', though the vowel change is difficult to account for; Mod. Fr. is *bouge*, wh. means a low, squalid chamber or hovel. See also **bulge**. **1.** That part of the bottom of a ship which is broadest, and nearest the horizontal. **2. a** Filth and moisture which soak into, and collect in this part of the ship; foul dirt collected in any vessel or sink; **b** (fig. and colloq.) nonsensical, stupid, incompetent writing or talk.

bilge-keel, n. Projecting ridge of timber or steel plating fastened along the side of a ship, at the line of the bilge, to check or prevent rolling.

bilge-water, n. Foul-smelling water collected in ship's bottom.

bilharzia, n. [1. bilhárzia; 2. bilhǽziə], fr. T. Bilharz, discoverer of the worm as cause of the disease. A parasitic trematode worm, which from water, drunk or bathed in, gets into the blood and bladder and causes the chronic disease *Bilharziosis*, common in Egypt, tropical Africa &c., the chief symptom of which is the passing of bloody urine.

biliary, adj. [1. bílyari; 2. bíljəri]. Fr. *biliaire*, Lat. *bīlis*, see **bile**, & *-ārius*, q.v. under **-ary**. Pertaining to bile.

bilingual, adj. [1. bīlínggwal; 2. bailíŋgwəl]. Lat. *bilinguis*, adj., 'speaking two languages', fr. **bi-** & Lat. *lingua*, 'tongue, language', & **-al**. See **lingual**. Speaking two languages, esp. from childhood, as a Welshman speaks Welsh and English without remembering how he learnt either.

bilious, adj. [1. bílyus; 2. bíljəs]. Fr. *bilieux*, Lat. *bīliōsus*. See **bile** & **-ous**. **1.** Connected with, caused by, derangement of bile: *bilious complaint*; *a bilious headache*. **2.** Liable to suffer from such derangement: *bilious subject, patient*. **3.** (fig.) Given to taking a gloomy view of life.

biliousness, n. Prec. & **-ness**. The state of suffering from derangement of bile.

-bility, suff. [1. bíliti; 2. bíliti]. Used to form ns. fr. adjs. ending in **-ble**, fr. Lat. adjs. in *-bilis*, & ns. in *-bilitāt-(em)*, *-bilitas*. See **-able** & **-ity**.

bilk, vb. & n. [1. bilk; 2. bilk]. Origin unknown. **1.** vb. (colloq.) To swindle a person out of money due to him, as by avoiding meeting him or by slipping away without paying: *to bilk a cabman*. **2.** n. One who practises mean, petty evasions of payment; a bilker.

bilker, n. [1. bílker; 2. bílkə]. Prec. & **-er**. One who bilks; petty swindler.

bilking, n. [1. bílking; 2. bílkiŋ]. See **prec.** & **-ing**. The habit and practice of mean swindles.

bill (I.), n. [1. bil; 2. bil]. O.E. *bill*, 'sword', M.E. *bylle* &c., Germ. *bille*, 'pickaxe'; cp. Du. *bijl*, 'axe', Germ. *beil*, Dan. *biil*, O.N. *bildr*, *bilda*. It is hardly possible to separate the two types; perh. *bill* is for **bit-lo*, in wh. case connected w. **bite**, & meaning 'the splitting weapon'. **1.** A type of curved, short, and broad axe or halberd, now obsolete. **2.** A kind of curved chopping-tool for cutting and lopping brushwood, hedges &c. *Billhook* is the more current name for this. It may be that this tool is a survival in a slightly modified form of the O.E. *bill*, put to different uses; cp. use made by soldiers of the bayonet for cutting wood &c.

bill (II.), n. & vb. intrans. O.E. *bile*; etymol. not determined; perh. related to **bill (I.)**. In this case the orig. meaning is 'the splitter'. **1.** n. **a** A bird's beak, that is, the horny, projecting extremity of a bird's mouth; **b** the point of the fluke of an anchor; **c** a small promontory, in Place-Names, e.g. *Portland Bill*. **2.** vb. **a** (of pair of doves or other birds) To touch bills, stroke bill against bill; **b** (fig.) to caress. Phr. *to bill and coo*.

bill (III.), n., fr. Low Lat. *billa*, Lat. *bulla*, orig. a 'bubble, knob, blob', then applied to the blobs of lead or wax affixed to documents which received the impress of the seal; then the seal itself (that is, the impression of it attached to a document); then a sealed document; finally a document in general. See also **bull (III.)**. Term applied to documents of many different kinds: **1.** *Parliamentary Bill*, draft of proposed legislation, as presented to the Houses of Parliament; Phr. *to pass, throw out, the Bill*. **2.** (law) Statement of a case submitted to Grand Jury; Phr. *find a true bill*. **3.** (commerc.) *Bill of exchange*, name given to document or negotiable instrument used in commerce as a means of payment; *bill of lading*, statement or description of freight of a ship; *bill of sale*, document transferring personal property, and authorizing its seizure by money-lender. **4.** List, statement, of various sorts: **a** *bill of fare*, list of food at a hotel or restaurant; **b** *theatre bill*, programme, statement posted up of the forthcoming performances of plays, and other entertainments. **5.** Statement by a tradesman, doctor &c. of money due for goods supplied, or services rendered. Phr. (fig.) *to foot the bill*, bear expenses, accept responsibility for payment.

bill (IV.), vb. trans., fr. prec. To announce, proclaim by means of bills or placards; an actor is *billed to appear* in such and such a part &c.

bill-broker, n. See **bill (III.)** & **broker**. Person who deals in bills of exchange.

bill-discounter, n. [1. bíl diskòunter; 2. bíl diskàuntə]. See **bill (III.)** & **discount (II.)** One who discounts or advances the value of bills of exchange.

billet (I.), n. [1. bílet; 2. bílit]. Dimin. of Fr. *bille*, or modification of Fr. dimin. *billot*, 'block of wood, trunk of a tree'. Origin of word unknown. A block of wood, esp. part of a big log which has to be split up for fuel.

billet (II.), n. Fr. *billet*, fr. O. Fr. *bille*, 'document'. See **bill (III.)**. **1.** A document, and, specif., an order requiring householder to give board and lodging to a soldier. Hence, **2, a** the accommodation so provided; any accommodation or quarters, esp. for soldiers; (often in pl. *billets*) *to be in billets* (of soldiers housed elsewhere than in barracks or in a camp or bivouac); **b** since the Great War especially the word is widely used for lodging quarters by civilians. **3.** (by extension, fig.) An appointment, paid situation, place, occupation: *a good, bad, billet*, well-, ill-paid, situation.

billet (III.), vb. trans., fr. prec. To put a person into a billet (**2, a**): *to billet a man upon a householder*.

billet-doux, n. [1. bìlā dō͞o; 2. bìlei dú]. Fr., 'sweet note', i.e. love-letter. Used in same sense in English; also, ironically, of a letter one would rather not receive, containing a bill or a complaint.

billhook, n. [1. bílhook; 2. bílhuk]. See under **bill (I.)**.

billiards, n. [1. bílyardz; 2. bíljədz]. Fr. *billard*, 'billiard table'. Cotgrave gives Fr. *billard* as meaning a cudgel, & also what we call a *cue* or *queue* at billiards. But Fr. *bille* also means a ball. See **ball, billet (I.)**. Both ideas seem to exist in the name of the game. Game played with ivory balls which are struck with leather-tipped rods, (cues, or queues), upon a large, oblong, fixed table with a slate top covered with tough, smooth, green cloth, and provided with pockets at the corners and in the middle of the long sides. *Billiard ball, cue, table* &c.; *billiard room*, one set apart for the game; *billiard marker*, attendant who keeps the score at the game.

Billingsgate, n. [1. bílingzgāt; 2. bíliŋzgit], fr. Billingsgate, fish market in London. Foul, abusive, obscene, blasphemous language, such as is supposed to be natural and habitual to fishwives.

billion, n. [1. bílyun; 2. bíljən]. Portmanteau word coined fr. **bi-**, or Fr. *bi(s)*, 'again', & *-illion*, fr. **million**. In England a million millions; in France and U.S.A. a thousand millions.

billon, n. [1. bílun; 2. bílən]. Fr., orig. 'lump'. Cp. **billet (I.)**. An alloy of silver with a preponderating amount of copper, used for a debased currency.

billow, n. [1. bílō; 2. bílou], fr. O.N. *bylgja*, 'wave', Swed. *bölja*, Dan. *bölge*. These are all derived fr. Gmc. base **belg-*, **bulg-*, 'to swell', q.v. under **belly, bellows, & bulge**. A wave, esp. a large swelling wave; (poet.) wave, generally, e.g. *the gentle billows*.

billowy, adj. [1. bílōi; 2. bíloui]. Prec. & **-y**. Undulating, broken by waves or swellings (of the surface of the sea, and of land).

bill-poster, -sticker, n. One who posts or sticks placards and advertisements of all kinds on walls or hoardings.

billy, n. [1. bíli; 2. bíli]. Prob. same as the abbr. form of *William*. (Australian colloq.) Tin can used as a camp kettle &c.

billycock, n. [1. bílikok; 2. bílikɔk]. Orig. *bully-cocked*, i.e. 'cocked as bullies wore their hats'. An obsolete name for a hard, round felt hat; a bowler hat.

billy-goat, n. The first element is the man's name; cp. *nanny* for a female goat. A male or he-goat.

bilobate, adj. [1. bìlṓbāt; 2. bàilóubeit]. See **bi- & lobe & -ate**. (bot.) Having two lobes.

biltong, n. [1. bíltong; 2. bíltɔŋ], Du., fr. *bil*, 'rump', & *tong*, 'tongue', wh. the strips resemble in shape. Sun-dried meat, of antelope, oxen &c., cut in long strips; used by hunters &c. in South Africa.

bimanal, bimanous, adj. [1. bìmā́nal, -us; 2. bàiméinəl, -əs]. **bi-** & Lat. *manus*, 'hand', see **manual (I.)**, & suff. **-al, -ous**. (zool.) Having two hands; belonging to two-handed order of mammals, now an obsolete term of scientific classification.

bimane, n. [1. bímān; 2. báimein]. Fr. *bimane*, fr. Lat. Cp. prec. (zool.) Individual belonging to bimanal mammals.

bimetallism, n. [1. bīmétalizm; 2. baimétəlizəm]. See **bi- & metal & -ism**. System of coinage in which two metals, gold and silver, are employed as currency standards and legal tender.

bimetallist, n. [1. bīmétalist; 2. baimétəlist]. See prec. & **-ist**. One who advocates bimetallism.

bi-monthly, adj. [1. bìmúnthli; 2. bàimánþli]. See **bi- & monthly**. Happening, appearing, twice every month.

bin (I.), n. [1. bin; 2. bin]. O.E. *binn*, manger', loan-word fr. L. Lat. *benna*, 'two-wheeled cart with a body of basket-work' itself borrowed fr. Gaul.; the word still exists in W. *benn*, 'cart, vehicle'. **1.** A covered receptacle or box of wood or iron, used in stables to hold corn or other grain. **2.** Receptacle, fixed (of bricks) or movable (of iron), esp. for household rubbish, dust, ashes &c.; whence *dustbin* &c. **3.** Division, in a wine-cellar, usually separated from others by partition of brick, in which wine of a particular vintage is stored.

bin (II.), vb. trans., fr. prec. To place, store, in a bin, esp. used of wine.

bin-, pref. = **bi-**, before vowels.

binary, adj. [1. bínari; 2. báinəri]. Lat. *bīnārius*, 'consisting of two', fr. *bīni*, 'two together', fr. base of **bi-**, & *-ārius*, q.v. under **-ary**. Dual, involving two: (mus.) *binary measure*, having two beats to the bar; (astron.) *binary system*, that of two stars revolving round common centre &c.

binate, adj. [1. bínāt; 2. báineit]. Lat. *bīni*. See **binary & -ate**. (bot.) Double, growing in pairs (of leaves &c.).

bind (I.), vb. trans. & intrans. [1. bīnd; 2. baind]. O.E. *bindan*, 'bind'; in all Gmc. languages; fr. Aryan **bhendh-*, Scrt. *bandhati*, 'he ties up, binds', Gk. *peîsma*, 'cable', fr. **phenth-*, fr. **bhendh-*, *pentherós*, 'father-in-law, connexion (by marriage)'; Lat. *of-fend-ix*, 'knot, band', *of-fend-i-mentum*, 'strap for tying up the chin', Lith. *beñd-ras*, 'companion'. The primitive & fundamental idea expressed by the base is 'tie up, fasten, connect'. Cp. **band, bend, bond, bundle**. **A.** trans. **1.** To tie, make fast, fasten together, or one thing to another, surround, confine one, or a collection of things with a cord or band: *to bind sheaves; bind two spars together; bind one's legs together; bind one to a stake; have one's hands bound* &c. Phr. (fig.) *bound hand and foot*, hindered by circumstances. **2.** (with *up*) To tie up, bandage, esp. of wounds, broken limbs &c. Phr. (fig.) *bound up in*, of one's interests, affections &c., engaged in, identified with, absorbed by. **3.** (reflex.) *Bind oneself to . . .*, to pledge oneself, enter into an undertaking to do something. **4.** To fasten the sheets of a book, manuscript, or other loose sheets together, and fix them in a cover of leather or cloth: *to bind books*. **5.** To fasten some other material (as braid) to the edge of carpet or cloth. **6.** To render costive (of the action on the bowels of certain kinds of food or drugs). **7.** (with *over*, law) To cause one to appear in Court of Justice by means of a bond. **8.** Place under a legal obligation to serve for certain period: *bind an apprentice; to be bound apprentice*. **B.** intrans. To coalesce under pressure into a hard, firm mass (of snow, mud, clay &c.).

bind (II.), n., fr. prec. Hardened clay between coal strata.

binder, n. [1. bínder; 2. báində]. **bind (I.)** & **-er**. A person who, or machine which binds (in various uses).

binding (I.), n. [1. bínding; 2. báindiŋ]. **bind (I.)** & **-ing**. That which binds or covers; esp. (of a book) the material, also the manner and style in which a book is bound.

binding (II.), adj., fr. Pres. Part. of **bind (I.)**. Having force or authority to hold one to a pledge, oath, agreement &c.: *a promise given under compulsion is not binding*.

bindweed, n. [1. bíndwēd; 2. báindwīd]. A weed with long runners which encircle stems of other plants growing near; applied esp. to the wild convolvulus.

bine, n. [1. bīn; 2. bain], for **bind**, w. loss of final *-d*; cp. *lawn* for *laund*. Name applied to plants with runners or climbing stems, esp. to hops; also in names of climbing plants, e.g. *woodbine*.

binnacle, n. [1. bínakl; 2. bínəkl]. Modern form; earlier *bittacle*, fr. Port. *bitacola*, Fr. *habitacle*, all fr. Lat. *habitāculum*, 'little dwelling'. This was formerly applied to a small shelter for the steersman of a ship. See **habitation**. The first syll. may have been influenced by **bin**. Box for a compass on a ship.

binocular, adj. & n. [1. bīnókūlar; 2. bainɔ́kjulə]. Lat. *bīni*, 'two together', see **bi-**, & *oculus*, 'eye', see **ocular**. **1.** adj. **a** Using both eyes at once: *binocular vision*; **b** adapted for such vision: *binocular microscope* &c. **2.** n. (usually pl.) *Binoculars*, field or opera glass through which both eyes look at the same time.

binomial, adj. & n. [1. bìnṓmial; 2. bàinóumiəl], cp. Lat. *binōminis*, adj., 'having two names'. See **bi- & nominal**. The above word is formed as though fr. **binōmius* & *-ālis*. See **-al**. **1.** adj. **a** (alg.) Having, consisting of, two terms: *binomial equation*; *binomial theorem*, of Sir Isaac Newton, formula for expressing the result of raising a binomial equation to any power without multiplication at length; **b** (bot. and zool.) composed of two names or words; more usually binominal, q.v. **2.** n. (alg.) Expression, equation, consisting of two terms, joined by the plus or minus sign.

binominal, adj. [1. bìnóminal; 2. bàinɔ́minəl]. Lat. See prec. Having two names; esp. *binominal system*, that adopted in zoology and botany of describing animals and plants by genus and species.

binturong, n. [1. bínt̄urong; 2. bíntjurɔŋ]. Native Malay name. (zool.) A small animal, allied to the civet-cat, with tufted ears, prehensile tail, and coarse black hair.

bio-, pref. Form of Gk. *bíos*, 'way of life', used in mod. compounds; *bios* is fr. Aryan **gʷiwos*, wh. appears also in Lat. *vīvere*, 'to live', fr. **gʷiwere*, *vīvus*, 'living', fr. **gʷiwos*, see **vital**; Scrt. *jīvati*, 'he lives'; O. Slav. *živą*, 'I live'. Goth. *qius*, 'living', is fr. Gmc. **kwiwas*, the exact representative of Aryan **gʷiwos*. From the same base, though w. an unexplained medial or final *-k-* sound, come further O.E. *cwicu*, O.S. *quik*, O.H.G. *quec*, 'living'; see **quick**. From differing forms of the same orig. base come further Gk. *zā̃ō*, 'I live', infin. *zên*, fr. **gʷjē-* & *zṓos*, 'living', q.v. under **zoo-**.

bio-chemistry, n. [1. bíō kémistri; 2. báiou kémistri]. See **bio- & chemistry**. Branch of physiology which deals with the chemical constitution of the bodies of living animals and plants.

biogenesis, n. [1. bìōgénesis; 2. bàioudžénisis]. See **bio- & genesis**. Lit. 'origin of life'; specif., the name of one particular doctrine concerning the origin of life, that living cells or organisms can only arise from parent organisms like to themselves in character and structure; contrasted with *abiogenesis*.

biograph, n. [1. bíōgrahf; 2. báiougrāf]. See **bio- & -graph**. Lit. 'living picture'; contrivance, also called *cinematograph*, for depicting action and movements by means of a series of photographs, passed rapidly before the eyes, each representing a stage in the movement, so that the effect is natural and continuous.

biographer, n. [1. bìógrafer; 2. bàiɔ́grəfə], fr. **bio-** & Gk. *gráphō*, 'I write', see **graph**, & **-er**. One who writes an account of a person's life.

biographic(al), adj. [1. bìōgráfik(l); 2. bàiougrǽfik(l)]. See prec. & **-ic** & **-al**. Pertaining to biography, consisting of facts about a person's life.

biographically, adv. Prec. & **-ly**. After the manner of biography.

biography, n. [1. bíógrafi; 2. baiɔ́grəfi]. Gk., fr. **bio-** & *graphía*, 'account', q.v. under **-graphy**. History, account, description, of a person's life.

biological, adj. [1. bīōlójikl; 2. bàioulɔ́džikl]. See **biology** & **-ic** & **-al**. Belonging to the science of life; belonging to the life of animals and plants.

biologically, adv. Prec. & **-ly**. From the point of view of biology.

biologist, n. [1. bíólojist; 2. baiɔ́lədžist]. See **biology** & **-ist**. One who is engaged in the study of biology.

biology, n. [1. bíóloji; 2. bàiɔ́lədži]. **bio-** & Gk. *lógos*, 'discourse'. See **-logy**. (lit.)

Science of life. The study of animals and plants; of their physical and other characteristics, their habits and mode of life generally; their genealogical relations one to the other; the distribution of the various genera and species over the earth; the facts concerning their birth, and, as far as is ascertainable, of the origin and nature of life itself.

biometrics, n. pl. [1. bīōmétriks; 2. bàiouméṭriks]. See **bio-** & **metric**. That branch of biology which deals with the statistical, quantitative analysis of the facts of biology.

bionomics, n. pl. [1. bīōnómiks; 2. bàiounómiks]. Formed fr. **bio-** and second element of **economics**. That branch of biology which deals with the adaptation of organisms to their surroundings &c., cp. *ecology*.

bioplasm, n. [1. bíōplàzm; 2. báiouplæ̀zəm]. **bio-** & Gk. *plásma*, 'mould, anything moulded'. See **plasm, plastic**. Germinal matter which lies at the basis of physical life; the germ plasm.

bioplast, n. [1. bíōplast; 2. báiouplæst]. Cp. prec. & Gk. *plastós*, 'moulded'. Bioplasm, germ plasm.

bioscope, n. [1. bíōskōp; 2. báiouskoup], fr. **bio-** & Gk. *skopós*, 'watcher', fr. *skopéo*, 'I look at', see **-scope**. New coinage on anal. of **telescope** &c. Biograph.

bipartite, adj. [1. bīpártīt; 2. baipáṭait]. See **bi-** & **partite**. **1.** (bot.) Divided into two parts: *bipartite leaf* &c. **2.** Having, drawn up in, two corresponding documents, as shared by two parties: *bipartite contract, treaty* &c.

biped, n. & adj. [1. bíped; 2. báiped]. Lat. *bipēs*, adj., 'two-footed', fr. **bi-** & *pēs, ped-is*, 'foot'. See **pedal**. An animal with two feet, such as a man, a monkey, or a bird. Used, though rarely, as an adj.: '*naked, biped beast*' (Byron.)

biplane, n. [1. bíplān; 2. báiplein]. Recent word, coined fr. **bi-** & Lat. *plānum*, 'flat surface'. See **plane**. Aeroplane with two planes.

birch (I.), n. [1. bërch; 2. bʌ̄tʃ]. O.E. *bierće*, O.H.G. *biricha*, 'birch tree'; prob. related to **bark** (I.). **1.** Name of tree with smooth, thin bark, the outer layer of which is white, peels off, and is renewed each year, genus *Betula*. **2.** The timber of this tree; also attrib.: *birch tree, birch bark, birch wood, birch broom*. **3.** A weapon for inflicting corporal punishment, esp. upon schoolboys, consisting of a bundle of twigs like a broom, fastened together; not necessarily of birch twigs; also called *birch rod*.

birch (II.), vb. trans., fr. prec. To inflict corporal punishment upon, to flog, beat, by means of a *birch rod*.

birchen, adj. [1. bërchen; 2. bʌ̄tʃən], fr. **birch** (I.) (archaic) Made of birch wood; consisting of birch trees: *birchen forests*.

bird, n. [1. bërd; 2. bʌ̄d]. O.E. & M.E. *bridd*, later, w.metath., *bird*, 'young bird'. Ordinary word for bird in general in O.E. is *fugol*, q.v. under **fowl**. *Bridd* has given some trouble, since it does not occur in any other Gmc. language. It seems reasonable, so far as the meaning goes, to connect it w. **brood** & **breed**. The difficulty felt in identifying a base w. *-i-* w. one w. *-ō-*, wh. has been a stumbling-block, is, however, not insuperable. *Brood* represents O.E. *brōd*, whose vowel, as O.H.G. *bruot* shows, goes back to Gmc. *ō*. This may well be fr. Aryan *ōi*, wh. wd. have the so-called weak grade *-i-*. If this identification be justified, then O.E. *bridd* means orig. a creature 'hatched out by warmth'. Cp. **bread** & **brew** for further etymol. details. **1.** A feathered biped which lays eggs: *bird of prey*, e.g. hawk, eagle, owl &c.; *game bird*, e.g. partridge, pheasant &c. **2.** Applied to human beings: **a** with affectionate admiration: *my bird* (to a young child), *a bonny bird* (to a pretty young girl); **b** vaguely meaning no more than 'fellow, person' &c.: *a gay bird, a lively bird, a queer bird*; *old bird*, equivalent to *old buffer*. **3.** Phrs. and idioms: (fig.) *a little bird told me*, some unnamed revealer of secrets; *birds of a feather*, persons of the same profession, or character; *a bird in the bush*, unknown possibilities; *a bird in the hand*, something certain, since already gained or known; *the bird is* (or *has*) *flown*, prisoner escaped, person one expected to find, gone away; *fine feathers make* (*do not make*) *fine birds*, well-dressed people may appear superior to what they really are; *kill two birds with one stone*, attain two objects at once; *bird of passage*, migratory bird, or (fig.) a person who stays but a short time in a place; *to sing like a bird*, easily, freely, and clearly; *to do something like a bird*, willingly.

bird-cage, n. Receptacle of wicker, or of wires, with wooden or metal frame, for housing birds in captivity.

bird-fancier, n. One who knows about, is interested in, breeds, and sells, birds.

bird-lime, n. Sticky material, spread on twigs to catch small birds.

bird of paradise, n. Family of birds from New Guinea, with splendid plumage.

bird-seed, n. Small seed, used esp. for feeding birds in cages.

bird's eye, n. See **bird** & **eye**. **a** (bot.) The speedwell; **b** kind of fine-cut tobacco, in which the sections of the stems somewhat resemble the eye of a bird; **c** in Phr. *bird's-eye view*, extensive view of a town or country seen from above; general survey of a subject or argument.

bird's nest, n. Nest of a bird: *bird's-nesting*, search for nests in order to collect eggs.

bireme, n. [1. bírēm; 2. bái(ə)rīm], fr. **bi-** & Lat. *rēmus*, 'oar', wh. may stand for **ret-mo*, cp. Gk. *eretmón*, 'oar', *eréssō*, 'row'; Scrt. *aritraš*, 'propellant, oar', *aritár*, 'rower'. These are all fr. forms of base **eret-*, 'drive forward, row'. See **row** (II.). Galley with two banks of oars.

biretta, n. [1. biréta; 2. birétə]. Ital. *berretta*, Low Lat. *birretum*, fr. *birrus*, 'cape of silk or wool'; perh. fr. Gk. *purrós*, 'yellow, flame-coloured', fr. *pûr*, 'fire', q.v. under **pyre**. Cap of peculiar shape worn by Roman Catholic clergy, cardinals having red, bishops purple, and priests black birettas. This head-gear has recently been adopted also by some clergy of the Church of England.

birth, n. [1. bërth; 2. bʌ̄þ]. The genuine O.E. form is (*ġe-*)*byrd*, 'birth, parentage'; in M.E. this gives place to the form *birthe*, borrowed fr. O.N. *byrþ*(*r*); this is cogn. w. the O.E. form, the *-d* in the latter being due to a type w. the accent on a different syll. in pre-Gmc.—**bhr̥tí* giving the Engl. type, *bhr̥ti* the O.N. type. The orig. base is **bher-*, cp. **bear** (I.), **burden**. Primitive meaning is *bearing*. **1.** The act of bringing forth offspring: *three at a birth*; *childbirth*. **2.** **a** The physical process of being born: *the day of one's birth*; '*Our birth is but a sleep and a forgetting*' (Wordsworth); **b** (fig.) spiritual regeneration: *a birth unto righteousness*. **3.** That produced in child-bearing: *a monstrous birth*. **4.** Descent, lineage, family, pedigree: **a** (gen.) *a man of good, humble, mean, birth*; *he behaved as became his birth*; **b** specif., good, distinguished lineage: *a person of birth, of no birth*. Phr. *a man of birth and breeding*.

birthday, n. [1. bërthdā; 2. bʌ̄þdei]. The day on which anyone's birth takes place; the anniversary of the day. *Birthday-book*, one in which people enter their names under the date of their birth. *Birthday-cake*, specially large, good, decorated cake made for a birthday. *Birthday-honours*, honours and titles bestowed, as is believed, upon deserving persons, in connexion with the birthday of the Sovereign.

birth-mark, n. See **birth** & **mark** (I.). Discoloration, or patch upon some part of the skin of the body, dating from birth, and usually ineradicable; a naevus.

birth-place, n. See **birth** & **place**. House, or town, at which a person is born.

birth-rate, n. See **birth** & **rate** (I.). Proportion of births to population of a country.

birthright, n. [1. bërthrīt; 2. bʌ̄þrait]. That which belongs to one by virtue of his birth; inheritance; that which falls to one because of his nationality or race: *freedom of speech and action is an Englishman's birthright*.

bis, adv. [1. bis; 2. bis]. Fr. & Ital., fr. Lat., 'twice, again'. See under **bi-**. (mus.) Used to denote that a passage is to be played over again; English equivalent, *repeat*.

biscuit, n. [1. bískit; 2. bískit]. Fr. *biscuit*, fr. Lat. *bis coctus*, 'twice cooked'. The spelling *byskit* is found in 15th cent. Engl., implying a pronunciation like our own. See **decoct** & **cook** (III.). A thin, crisp cake, made of flour and eggs, sometimes spiced and mixed with currants, sweetened or unsweetened, made in many varieties and sizes and very popular in England. *Ship's biscuit*, an old-established, coarse kind of biscuit, used at sea as a substitute for bread.

biscuit ware, n. Baked, unglazed **pottery**; a fine pottery imitating china.

bise, n. [1. bēz; 2. bīz]. Fr. Origin unknown. Cold (north-east) wind which blows from snow-covered mountains in Switzerland.

bisect, vb. trans. [1. bīsékt; 2. baisékt], fr. **bi-** & Lat. *sect-*(*um*), P.P. type of *secāre*, 'to cut', see under **sect, section**. (lit.) To cut in two; (usually, esp. in math.) to divide into two equal parts.

bisection, n. [1. bīsékshun; 2. baisékʃən]. Prec. & **-ion**. Act of bisecting.

bisector, bisectrix, n. [1. bīsékter, -triks; 2. baiséktə, -triks]. **bisect** & **-or**. (geom.) Line which bisects a line or an angle.

bisexual, adj. [1. bīsékshooal; 2. baisékʃuəl]. **bi-** & **sexual**. Having both sexes in one individual, as certain plants and hermaphrodite animals.

bishop, n. [1. bíshup; 2. bíʃəp]. O.E. *bisċop*, O.H.G. *biscof*, borrowed in W. Gmc. period at latest, fr. Lat. *episcopus*, fr. Gk. *epískopos*, 'overseer, guardian', fr. *epí*, 'upon, over', & *skopós*, 'watcher'. See **epi-** & **scope**. **1.** An officer of the Christian Church specially consecrated by another bishop and given authority to perform certain duties; he has **a** certain spiritual functions, the conferring of ecclesiastical orders, i.e. the ordaining of deacons and priests, and consecration of other bishops, and confirmation, which he alone can perform; and **b** responsibility for the superintendence, guidance, and organization of the spiritual, educational, and social work of the Church within his sphere of jurisdiction or bishopric; a bishop also performs all the functions of a priest. **2.** Name of a piece in chess which has a top carved into the shape of a bishop's mitre. **3.** Name of a drink made of spiced wine.

bishopric, n. [1. bíshuprik; 2. bíʃəprik]. O.E. *bisċopriċe*, fr. *bisċop*, see prec., & *riċe*, 'realm, dominion', a word found in most Gmc. languages, & prob. borrowed very early fr. Celt. *rīk-s, rī* (cp. personal names such as *Vercingeto-rix* &c., the base of wh. is cogn. w. Lat. *rēx*, 'king', *rego*, 'I rule' &c.; see **rex**. From same stem are Scrt. *rāj-, rājan-*, 'king, rajah', *rājati*, 'he rules, is powerful'; the fundamental meaning is 'powerful'), wh. survives in the O.E. adj. *riċe*, 'powerful, mighty', see **rich**. The forms in other Gmc. languages are: O.S. *rīki*, O.H.G. *rīhhi*; Mod. Germ. *reich*, 'empire, dominion, rule', Goth. *reiki*, 'rule' &c., *reiks*, 'mighty'. The office of bishop; the area or diocese over which the jurisdiction of a bishop extends.

bismillah, interj. [1. bismíla; 2. bismílə]. Arab. *bi-'mi 'llāhi*, 'in the name of God'! Pious ejaculation uttered by Mohammedans before entering upon an enterprise.

bismuth, n. [1. bízmuth; 2. bízməþ]. Origin unknown; first called *wismut* by Basil Valentine who recognized it in 15th cent. One of the metallic elements; used in metallurgy as an alloy, and as a medical drug.

bison, n. [1. bísn; 2. báisn]. Lat. *bisōn, -ontis*, also in Gk., but apparently Gmc. in origin; cp. O.E. *wesend*, O.H.G. *wisunt*, O.N. *vīsundr*. Wild ox of which two species only exist, the European aurochs and North American buffalo, with very powerful humped shoulders, a mane, and short horns.

bisque, n. [1. bisk; 2. bisk]. Fr.; in first sense connected w. **biscuit**; origin of other senses unknown. **1.** Unglazed porcelain used for statuettes. **2.** A rich thick soup, made with crayfish &c. **3.** A point given to another in certain games, which he may take at any stage, as in a sett or at a hole in golf &c.

bissextile, adj. & n. [1. bisékstīl; 2. baisékstail]. Fr. (*année bissextile*), fr. L. Lat. *bissextilis annus*, a year having an extra day intercalated, formerly Feb. 24, wh. was the sixth day before the calends of March (March 1); there were therefore two days of same name, lit. 'twice the 6th'. See **bi-** & **sext** & **-ile**. Name for leap year, still used in French.

bistort, n. [1. bístort; 2. bístōt], fr. Fr. *bistorte*, fr. Low Lat. *bis torta* (*herba*), 'twice twisted plant', fr. *bis*, 'twice', see **bi-**, & *tort-(um)*, P.P. type of *torquēre*, 'to twist'. See **torque**. A perennial plant, allied to buckwheat, with twisted root-stock; the plant yields an astringent medicinal drug.

bistoury, n. [1. bísturi; 2. bístəri], fr. Fr. *bistouri*, of unknown origin. A thin, straight, or slightly curved surgical knife or scalpel.

bistre, n. [1. bíster; 2. bístə]. Fr., origin unknown. A dark-brown pigment or colour.

bit (I.), n. [1. bit; 2. bit]. O.E. *bita*, 'morsel, bit', lit. 'portion bitten off'; connected w. vb. *bītan*, cp. under **bite**. The orig. connexion in sense w. biting has entirely disappeared fr. present-day usage. **1.** A portion, piece, part, detached from some larger thing; a small quantity (in various uses). Phrs. *to give a person a bit of one's mind*, speak plainly in pointing out faults, scold; *a nice bit of money*, a good deal; *to have a bit of dinner*, some dinner; *bit by bit*, gradually; *not a bit better* &c., not at all; *to do one's bit*, one's share of duty &c. **2.** Specif., a small coin: *sixpenny, threepenny, bit* (obsolesc.). **3.** Part of an instrument for boring, a drill, worked by a brace; also *centrebit*.

bit (II.), n. Closely connected w. prec. There is no precise ancestor recorded in O.E.; *bitol*, 'bit for a horse', has dimin. suff.; *ġe-bǣtu*, 'bit and bridle', is fr. earlier **bāti*, a different grade of same stem. The primary meaning is 'something on which (a horse) bites'. A bar of steel, or two short, rounded bars linked together placed in a horse's mouth, from which he is ridden or driven, kept in place by straps, and to which the reins are attached. Phr. *to take the bit between (the, one's) teeth*, (of a horse) to run away; (fig.) to be out of control.

bit (III.), vb. trans., fr. prec. To put a bit in mouth of (horse &c.).

bit (IV.), vb. Pret. of **bite**. M.E. *bit*, fr. the O.E. P.P. type, see **bitten**. The regular M.E. Pret. *bōt*, fr. O.E. *bāt*, survived until the 16th cent.

bitch, n. [1. bich; 2. bitʃ]. O.E. *biċċe*, cogn. w. O.N. *bikkja*. Origin unknown. **1.** Female of dog, wolf, or fox. **2.** (in low speech) Woman of bad character.

bite (I.), vb. trans. & intrans. [1. bīt; 2. bait]. O.E. & O.S. *bītan*, O.H.G. *bīzan*, Goth. *beitan*, O.N. *bīta*, 'bite'. Cogn. w. Lat. *findere*, 'cleave, split', of wh. forms without the nasal are seen in perf. *fid-i*, & P.P. *fissum*, fr. **fid-tom*, see **fissile**; cp. also Scrt. *bhittáś*, 'split' &c., exactly cogn. w. Lat. *fissus* fr. *bhēdāmi*, 'I split, cut, smash'; further Gk. *pheidomai*, 'I am sparing', *pheidṓ*, 'sparing, thrift'. The idea is that of cutting oneself off, from, depriving oneself. The Gmc. languages have specialized the use of the stem for the meaning 'to split, divide, with the teeth'. **1. a** To use the teeth upon, cut into with the teeth; also, cut into, penetrate, of a knife or sword. Phrs. *to bite the dust*, fall to, roll on, the ground; *bite one's thumb at*, (fig.) show contempt for a person; *bite one's lips*, show annoyance; *much bitten with*, taken with, filled with enthusiasm for; **b** (used also with prep.) *bite at*, snap at; *bite into*, make deep incision in; *bite off*, separate, detach, a portion of something with teeth; (fig.) *to bite off more than one can chew*, to undertake something beyond one's powers. **2.** To have a habit of attacking with teeth (of animals) or sting (of insects); use teeth on without provocation: *does your dog bite?; he never bites; I've been dreadfully bitten by a flea, gnat, mosquito; do dragon-flies bite?* **3.** (extended use) **a** To act on by friction, catch, grip (of machinery, wheels): *the rails were so slippery that the wheels of the engine would not bite; the brake will not bite*; **b** to act on chemically, as an acid. **4.** To cause pain to, make to smart; to nip: *this mustard doesn't bite much; the frost will bite the fruit-blossom*; (fig.) to hurt the feelings, wound susceptibilities: *Pope knew how to make his satires bite.* **5.** To take a bait (of fish): *the fish were biting well*; also (fig., of persons), to accept an offer, or suggestion; allow oneself to be cajoled or deceived: *I hinted that I would lend him my house, but he wouldn't bite; he offered great advantages to those who joined the society at once, hoping many would bite.*

bite (II.), n., fr. prec. **1.** A nip, snap, with the teeth. Phr. *his bark is worse than his bite*, not so dangerous as he appears. **2.** Wound inflicted with teeth or sting: *dog's bite, gnat's bite.* **3.** A small quantity of food: *a bite of dinner* &c. **4.** Sharp physical or mental pain, smart, sting: *the bite of a wound; the bite of a lampoon.* **5.** Pungency, sting: *whisky with a bite in it*; (fig.) point, cogency, of style, of an epigram, joke &c. **6. a** Attempt by a fish to take angler's bait; **b** (fig.) tentative offer or advance by a person towards accepting a proposed bargain, suggestion, hint &c.

biter, n. [1. bíter; 2. báitə], fr. **bite (I.)** & **-er**. One who bites, in various senses (lit. and fig.).

biting, adj. [1. bíting; 2. báitiŋ], fr. Pres. Part. of **bite (I.)**. In varying senses: piercing, cold, of wind, hail; stinging, pungent, painful (esp. fig.): *biting sarcasm, irony* &c.

bitingly, adv. Prec. & **-ly**. In a biting manner.

bitten, vb. [1. bítn; 2. bítn]. P.P. of **bite**; O.E. *biten*; M.E. *bitten.*

bitter (I.), adj., adv., & n. [1. bíter; 2. bítə]. O.E. *bitter*, O.S., O.H.G. *bittar*, Goth. *baitrs*, 'bitter', in lit. & fig. senses; connected w. **bite (I.)**. **1.** adj. **a** Tasting acid or sour; the reverse of sweet, as wormwood or quinine; *bitter beer*, light clear beer, with slight astringent taste, due to hops &c.; **b** (fig.) painful, grievous, distressing, hard to be borne; malignant, acrimonious, rankling, envious, relentless: *bitter pain, hardship, grief, disappointment, poverty; bitter quarrel, strife; bitter enemy, bitter rival.* Phr. *to the bitter end*; this may be nautical in origin, cp. next word. **2.** adv. Bitterly: *'tis bitter cold.* **3.** n. **a** Bitterness; **b** (glass of) bitter beer.

bitter (II.), n. See **bitts**. (naut.) Also *bitter end*, the inboard end of a cable fastened to the bitts.

bitter apple, n. Colocynth.

bitterling, n. [1. bíterling; 2. bítəliŋ]. **bitter (I.)** & **-ling**. A small freshwater fish of the carp family, with a bitter flavour.

bitterly, adv. [1. bíterli; 2. bítəli]. **bitter (I.)** & **-ly**. In a bitter manner (esp. fig.): *to regret bitterly; speak bitterly*, resentfully.

bittern (I.), n. [1. bítern; 2. bítʌ̄n]. M.E. *bitour*, fr. Fr. *butor*, fr. Low Lat. *būtōrius*, 'bittern', Lat. *būteo*, 'buzzard', *būtio*, 'bittern'; cp. also Lat. *būbo*, 'owl', *būbīre*, 'to utter the cry of an owl'; cp. further Gk. *búzō*, 'I cry like an owl', *būza*, 'owl'. The stem is imitative in origin & refers to the booming cry of the bird. The final *-n* in the Engl. word may be due to anal. w. *heron, hern*, another marsh bird closely related to the *bittern*. European marsh bird allied to the heron, with speckled and streaked dark plumage and deep booming call.

bittern (II.), n., fr. **bitter (I.)**. The very bitter liquor remaining after crystallization in salt works.

bitterness, n. [1. bíternes; 2. bítənis], fr. **bitter (I.)** & **ness**. **1.** The taste of anything bitter. **2.** (fig., esp. of feelings) Severity, virulence, animosity, grudging, envy, relentlessness, ill-feeling.

bitters, n. pl. [1. bíterz; 2. bítəz]. See **bitter (I.)**. Liquors made from various herbs, alcohol, sugar &c., used mixed with stronger drinks, such as gin, sherry &c. as appetizers.

bitter sweet, n., fr. **bitter (I.)** & **sweet**. A trailing plant, *Solanum dulcamara*, the woody nightshade.

bitts, n. pl. [1. bits; 2. bits]. Earlier (16th cent.) *beetes*. Prob. Scand.; cp. Dan. *beding*, 'bitts'; Swed. *beting*, 'a bitt', & perh. O.N. *bite*, 'beam'. Etymol. doubtful. Pair of heavy vertical timbers or iron posts on ship's deck to which hawsers, cables &c. are secured.

bitumen, n. [1. bitūmen; 2. bítjumən]. Lat. *bitūmen*, 'mineral pitch', an Oscan-Umbrian dialect form, instead of true Lat. **vitumen*. This points to an earlier form of the stem, **gʷitu-*, wh. appears in Scrt. *játu*, 'lac, gum', & in Gmc., in O.E. *cwidu, cudu*, 'gum, resin', & O.H.G. *quiti*, Mod. Germ. *kitt*, 'cement, gum, mastic'. Natural mineral pitch, asphalt.

bituminize, vb. trans. [1. bitū́minīz; 2. bitjū́minaiz]. See **bitumen** & **-ize**. To impregnate, cover, with, convert into, bitumen.

bituminous, adj. [1. bitū́minus; 2. bitjū́minəs]. **bitumen** & **-ous**. Belonging to, impregnated with, having the consistency or smell of bitumen.

bivalence, -cy, n. [1. bīvā́lens(i); 2. baivéiləns(i)], fr. **bi-** & **valency**. (chem.) State, condition, of being bivalent.

bivalent, adj. [1. bīvā́lent; 2. baivéilənt]. (chem.) Having a valency of two, having power of replacing two atoms of hydrogen.

bivalve, n. [1. bívalv; 2. báivælv], fr. **bi-** & **valve**, Lat. *valva*, 'leaf of a door'. Mollusc, such as the oyster or mussel, which has a double, hinged shell.

bivouac (I.), vb. intrans. [1. bívooak; 2. bívuæk]. Fr., earlier *bivac*, introduced during Thirty Years' War, fr. Germ. *beiwache*, lit. 'a guard, a keeping watch', fr. *bei*, prep., q.v. under **by**, & *wache*, q.v. under **wake (I.)**, **watch (I.)**. Originally, to be on guard against surprises. Now, simply to camp temporarily, in improvised shelters, and usually without tents.

bivouac (II.), n. See prec. A temporary night encampment for an army or military detachment.

bizarre, adj. [1. bizár; 2. bizā́]. Fr., fr. Span. *bizarro*, 'valiant', said to be a Basque word. It seems to have originally signified 'furious, enraged', then in 16th cent. Fr. 'brave, intrepid', later 'capricious', & finally 'strange, fantastic'. (of persons) Eccentric, peculiar, queer, having a strange appearance, dress &c.; (of taste, style, art &c.) fantastic, extravagant, grotesque.

blab, vb. intrans. [1. blab; 2. blæb], fr. O.N. *blabbra*, Dan. *blabbre*, 'babble, gabble'. To reveal confidences or secrets.

blabber, n. [1. bláber; 2. blǽbə]. Prec. & **-er**. One who blabs; tale-teller, sneak.

black (I.), adj. [1. blak; 2. blæk]. O.E. *blæc*, 'black', O.H.G. *blah*. It is possible that this word belongs to same group as Lat. *flamma*, 'blazing fire, flame', fr. **flag-ma*, related to *flāgrāre*, 'to blaze, glow, burn'; Gk. *phlég-ein*, 'burn, scorch', *phlég-ma*, 'heat, inflammation', *phlóx* for **phlóg-s*, 'flame, blaze', *phlog-mós* (same suff. as *flamma*), 'blaze' &c., & many other Gk. words of kindred meaning; further Scrt. *bhárg-aś*, 'gleam, radiancy' &c. In this case *black* means primarily, 'burnt, scorched, darkened by fire'. The differentiation in meaning fr. 'glowing, blazing' to 'black' represents different ways of considering the same thing, or different effects of the same cause. See also **flagrant, flame, phlegm.** **1.** Having the property of absorbing the light rays, therefore colourless, dark, sombre, swarthy; colour of soot; the opposite of white: *black clouds, black darkness.* Phrs. *black in the face*, dark red, from passion or effort; *black art*, necromancy, witchcraft, magic; *to be in one's black books*, in disgrace; *black and blue*, very much bruised; *black cap*, worn by judge in pronouncing death sentence; *a black eye*, bruise round orbit; *black flag*, pirates' emblem; signal of execution; *black sheep*, person of bad character; *to prove that black is white*, try to establish a paradox, argue against evidence; *black as soot, as night, as your hat*, very dark. **2.** (fig., in variety of senses) **a** (of thoughts) Gloomy, despondent, sad, dismal; **b** (of the character) wicked, perverse, infamous: *a black soul, heart* &c.; **c** (of appearance, expression of face &c.) sullen, angry, ill-tempered: *black looks*; **d** (of one's fortunes, position in the world, prospect, fate &c.) hopeless, desperate, giving rise to despondency. Phrs. *to look black at one*, disapprovingly; *not so black as he is painted*, better than his reputation.

black (II.), n., fr. prec. **1.** The pigment or colour of *black*; the darkest colour, that of coal or soot. **2.** Applied to a variety of things which are black in colour: **a** clothes: *to wear black*; *clad in decent black*; **b** small particle of soot, such as falls from the atmosphere in towns; **c** a negro; **d** dirt, a smear of any kind: *to have some black on one's hands*; *black and white*, pen-and-ink drawing; *have something (down) in black and white*, keep a written record.

black (III.), vb. trans., fr. **black** (I.). To put black stuff on to certain things, esp. *to black boots* (polish with blacking); *to black a grate*, polish with blacklead; *black out*, obliterate (printed matter) with printer's ink.

blackamoor, n. [1. blákamōr; 2. blǽkəmō]. **black** & **Moor** (I.). Negro.

black-and-tan, n. See **black & tan.** Black with spots or markings of tan or brown colour; esp. *black-and-tan terrier*, a small smooth-haired terrier with such markings; the *Black-and-Tans*, popular name of a special British force employed in Ireland at the end of the War, dressed in khaki uniform with black caps, belts &c., like those of the Royal Irish Constabulary.

black-a-vised, adj. [1. blák a vīzd; 2. blǽk ə vaizd]. Hybrid word. **black** & Fr. *à vis*, 'to sight', & **-ed.** See **visage.** Dark, swarthy, in complexion.

blackball, vb. trans. [1. blákbawl; 2. blǽkbōl]. To vote against in a secret ballot, esp. for membership of a club, by putting a black ball in ballot-box.

blackbeetle, n. [1. blákbētl; 2. blǽkbītl]. Popular name of the cockroach, q.v., which is neither black nor a beetle.

blackberry, n. [1. blákberi; 2. blǽkbəri]. Small black juicy fruit, full of seeds, which grows wild on brambles.

blackbird, n. [1. blákbërd; 2. blǽkbād]. **1.** Common wild bird, *Turdus merula*, allied to the thrushes, with dark plumage, sometimes piebald, with a very sweet note. **2.** In Australia and Pacific Islands, name given to natives, Kanakas, who used to be kidnapped and shipped to work under forced indentures; whence the term *blackbirding* for this practice.

blackboard, n. [1. blákbòrd; 2. blǽkbɔ̄d]. Sheet of wood painted black, used in lecture-rooms and schoolrooms by the teacher, who writes upon it with chalk.

black buck, n. The Indian antelope.

blackcap, n. [1. blákkap; 2. blǽkkæp]. Name of a species of warbler, *Sylvia atracapilla*, the cock having a black-capped head.

blackcock, n. [1. blákkok; 2. blǽkkɔk]. Another name for the black grouse, black game, or heath-cock, the female of which is the 'grey hen'; found in the Highlands of Scotland, north of England, in Ireland, and many parts of Europe and Asia.

black-currant, n. Small black juicy fruit, with peculiar pungent odour and taste, *Ribes nigra.*

Black Death, n. Epidemic, resembling what is now called *bubonic plague*, which spread over the greater part of Europe in 14th century. So called from the symptom of internal haemorrhages which darkened the skin of sufferers.

black-draught, n. Aperient medicine composed of senna and Epsom salts.

Black Eagle, n. Title of the first order of knighthood of the former kingdom of Prussia.

blacken, vb. intrans. & trans. [1. bláken; 2. blǽkən]. **black** (I.) & **-en.** **1.** intrans. To grow black. **2.** trans. **a** To make black: *blacken one's face*; **b** (fig.) to speak ill of, attribute bad conduct &c. to, cast aspersions on reputation: *blacken a person's character.*

blackfellow, n. [1. blákfelō; 2. blǽkfelou]. Popular name of an Australian aboriginal.

Black Friar, n. Friar of Dominican order.

blackguard (I.), n. [1. blágard; 2. blǽgād]. **1.** Name originally given to the lowest class of menials employed in a kitchen, from the dirty nature of their occupation. **2.** A low, disreputable ruffian; a scoundrel, a man of low moral character and devoid of honour.

blackguard (II.), vb. trans., fr. prec. To abuse violently; to call (person) a blackguard.

blackguardism, n. [1. blágardizm; 2. blǽgədizəm]. See prec. & **-ism.** Ruffianly, rowdy behaviour; dishonourable, immoral conduct.

blackguardly, adj. [1. blágardli; 2. blǽgədli]. See prec. & **-ly.** **1.** Having character or appearance of a blackguard: *a blackguardly fellow.* **2.** Disreputable, unprincipled, dishonourable, ruffianly: *blackguardly conduct* &c.

blackhead, n. [1. blákhed; 2. blǽkhed]. Small pimple on the face &c. caused by the blocking of a sebaceous duct, the head of which is blackened by dirt.

black-hearted, adj. Having an evil, malignant nature.

blacking, n. [1. bláking; 2. blǽkiŋ]. **black** (I.) & **-ing.** Black substance used for blackening and polishing boots.

blackish, adj. [1. blákish; 2. blǽkiʃ]. **black** (I.) & **-ish.** Rather black, tending towards black or dark shade of colour, not quite black.

black-jack, n. See **black** (I.) & **jack** (III.). Large leathern cup, or can, for drink (obs.).

black-lead, n. A mineral, graphite, or plumbago, dark grey in colour, quite different from lead, composed of carbon with small proportion of iron; used in making pencils, and for polishing grates.

blackleg, n. [1. bláklèg; 2. blǽklèg]. Origin unknown. **1.** A swindler and cheat, esp. at cards and in racing. **2.** A workman, member of a Trade Union, who, when a strike is threatened or declared, offers to work at lower rate of wages than that for which his Union is contending.

black-letter, n. & adj. **1.** n. Type, also called Gothic, in which earliest books were printed. It still survives in common use in Germany. **2.** adj. Of documents and books written or printed in black-letter type: *black-letter book*, early printed book.

black-list, n. & vb. trans. **1.** n. List of persons against whom charges are made, convictions are recorded &c. **2.** vb. To enter the name of (person) on a black-list.

blackmail, n. & vb. trans. [1. blákmāl; 2. blǽkmeil]. **black** (I.) & obs. *mail*, 'rent', fr. O.N. *māl*, 'agreement'. **1.** n. Extortion of money by threats to expose a discreditable secret. **2.** vb. To threaten a person with exposure unless he pays a price for silence; to extort money from by such threats.

blackmailer, n. [1. blákmāler; 2. blǽkmeilə]. Prec. & **-er.** One who practises blackmail.

black Maria, n. [1. blák maría; 2. blǽk məráiə]. Van, painted black, in which prisoners are conveyed between the gaol and the court of law where they are tried.

black mass, n. **1.** A mass, or eucharistic service, in which the vestments &c. are black, as at a Requiem Mass. **2.** An obscene travesty of the mass, as celebrated by worshippers of Satan.

blackness, n. [1. bláknes; 2. blǽknis]. See **black** (I.) & **-ness.** **1.** The quality of being black: *blackness of the night.* **2.** (fig.) Wickedness: *blackness of men's hearts.*

black-pudding, n. A kind of sausage made from pig's blood, suet &c.

Black Rod, n. A high official of the Order of the Garter acting as usher in the House of Lords, so called from his ebony rod of office.

black-rot, n. A fungus attacking various cultivated vegetables.

black rubric, n. See **rubric.** An ordinance or declaration as to kneeling, printed, in black, not red, and therefore not strictly a 'rubric', at the end of the Communion Service in the Prayer Book of 1661.

black-rust, n. Disease in cereal plants. See **rust.**

blacksmith, n. [1. bláksmith; 2. blǽksmiþ]. See **black** (I.) & **smith.** A smith who works in iron; commonly applied to the smith who shoes horses, properly *farrier.*

black-strap, n. Name given colloquially to a strong, immature, or inferior kind of port wine, also to a mixture of rum and molasses.

blackthorn, n. [1. blákthorn; 2. blǽkþɔ̄n]. See **thorn.** **1.** The species of thorn tree, *Prunus spinosa*, which bears the sloe. **2.** (esp. in Ireland) A stout cudgel cut from this tree.

blackwater fever, n. [1. blákwawter fēver; 2. blǽkwōtə fīvə]. An acute disease, esp. of tropical Africa, characterized by intermittent fever, vomiting, and presence in the urine of haemoglobin, which turns it deep red or black in colour.

bladder, n. [1. bláder; 2. blǽdə]. O.E. *blǣddre*, 'blister, bladder', connected w. Gmc. stem **blǣ(w)-*, 'blow, inflate', q.v. under **blade, blow** (I.), **blast, blossom.** **1.** (anat.) Bag or sac consisting of tough elastic membrane, in the bodies of animals, which holds secreted liquids: *gall-bladder, urinary bladder* &c.; the latter usually called *the bladder.* **2. a** Any tough, inflated membraneous bag, e.g. *football bladder* (of india-rubber, inflated, which keeps the ball tight and in right shape, and resilient), *bladder of lard* &c.; **b** an air-sac, as the *swimming-bladder*, sound of fish; or as in seaweeds &c. **3.** (fig.) A superficial, loquacious person; cp. *windbag.*

bladderwort, n. [1. bláderwërt; 2. blǽdəwʌt]. See prec. & **wort.** An aquatic plant which has small vesicles or sacs which catch floating insects &c.

bladdery, adj. [1. bláderi; 2. blǽdəri]. See prec. & **-y.** Puffed out, inflated, like a bladder.

blade, n. [1. blād; 2. bleid]. O.E. *blæd*, 'leaf', is very rare, the common word being, as now, *lēaf.* In O.H.G. *blat* is the normal word, Mod. Germ. *blatt.* These words belong to the stem seen in O.E. *blōwan*, 'to bloom', *blōstma*, 'blossom', Goth. *blōma*, O.S. *blōmo*, O.H.G. *bluomo*, 'flower', & O.S. *blōian*, O.H.G. *bluojen, bluowen*, 'to flower, bloom' (see **blow** (IV.)). O.E. *blǣd*, a different form of gradation, means 'growth (of trees, plants &c.), fruit, flower'. All these are cogn. w. Lat. *flōs*, 'flower', *flōrēre*, 'to flower', & various other words connected w. 'flower', see **flower.** Ir. has *blāth*, 'a flower'. The Aryan stem was **bhlō-, *bhlē-, *bhlə-*, corresponding respectively to Gmc. **blō-, *blǣ-, *bla-*, as seen in the above Gmc. words. The meaning, 'swell out into bud, to bloom', was early specialized fr. the orig., wh. was 'puff up, swell', in a more general sense. The stem in **blow** (I.), of the wind, is prob. ultimately the same, & further that in **belly** & **bellows.** **1.** *Blade* is now used chiefly of the young narrow leaves of corn, and of grass; otherwise rather vaguely, in poetry of foliage. **2.** (by extension) Applied to various long, narrow, flat objects: **a** *blade of a sword, knife*, the cutting part; **b** *blade* *of an oar, of a paddle* (for steamers); **c** *shoulder-blade*, flat bone; **d** (fig. sense, from **a**) a merry, rollicking, swaggering, boisterous young fellow: *a gay, lively &c. blade*; cp. the use of *muskets, sabres, bayonets*, meaning those who carry them, men, soldiers.

blaeberry, n. [1. bláberi; 2. bléiberi], fr. *blae*, 'blue', see **blue** & **berry**. A name for the bilberry, q.v., or whortleberry.

blah, n. [1. blah; 2. blā]. (slang, U.S.A.) Rubbish, blether.

blain, n. [1. blān; 2. blein]. O.E. *blegen*, M.E. *bleine*, fr. Pr. O.E. **blægin*, fr. stem **blag-*, Aryan **bhlәgh-*, 'swell', the full form of wh. is **bhelegh-*. See remarks under **belly, bulge**, & other words there referred to. *Blain* means ultimately 'swelling'. Small swelling, pimple or pustule.

blame (**I.**), vb. trans. [1. blām; 2. bleim]. Fr. *blâmer*, O. Fr. *blasmer*, fr. Lat. *blasphēmāre*, 'abuse, vituperate', a Gk. loan-word fr. *blasphēméō*, 'I speak profanely, speak ill of'. See **blaspheme**. **1.** To find fault with (a person); gen. with *for*: *he is greatly to be blamed for his negligence.* **2.** To attack, fix responsibility for an offence, failure &c. upon a person, hold culpably responsible: *we know not whom to blame for the disaster; who is to blame for setting the house on fire?* (colloq.) Phr. *To blame something upon a person*, hold him responsible.

blame (**II.**), n., fr. prec. **1.** Censure, fault-finding, expression of disapproval: *he justly incurred great blame for his incompetence.* **2.** Responsibility for an offence or failure: *where does the blame lie for the failure of our diplomacy?; it is small blame to you that you have been unsuccessful.* Phrs. *to lay the blame upon (a person) for; to bear the blame*, take the responsibility, incur reproach.

blameless, adj. [1. blámles; 2. bléimlis]. Prec. & **-less**. Free from blame, innocent, immaculate; virtuous.

blamelessly, adv. Prec. & **-ly**. In a blameless manner.

blamelessness, n. See prec. & **-ness**. Innocence, piety, virtue.

blameworthy, adj. [1. blámwĕrdhi; 2. bléimwāði]. See **blame** (**II.**) & **worthy**. Deserving of blame, of censure.

blanch, vb. trans. & intrans. [1. blahnsh; 2. blānʃ], fr. Fr. *blanchir*, 'make white', fr. *blanc*, 'white'. See **blank** (**I.**). **a** trans. To make white: *to blanch almonds*, take the skin off them; *to blanch sea kale*, and other plants, by keeping them in the dark; **b** intrans., to grow, turn pale, esp. with shame or fear.

blancmange, n., pseudo-Fr. pron. [1. blamónzh; 2. blәmɑ̃ʒ]. Fr. *blancmanger*, 'white food'. See **blank** & **manger**. Sweet dish with insipid, mawkish taste, made in a mould, of milk stiffened with cornflour, isinglass, or gelatine.

bland, adj. [1. bland; 2. blænd], fr. Lat. *blandus*, 'smooth-tongued, having a winning address'. Various explanations have been offered in explanation of this word, several of wh. present phonological difficulties. That wh. connects the word w. Lith. *balañdis*, 'dove', Lett. *blādu, blāst*, 'to chatter', is on the whole the most probable. With it, the Lat. words *blaterāre*, 'to babble, chatter', *balatro*, 'babbler', may also be connected. The ultimate meaning wd. thus be 'talkative, flattering, well-spoken'. **1.** (of manner and address) Ingratiating, courteous, gentle, caressing, pleasant. **2.** (of climate) Mild, balmy, genial, temperate.

blandish, vb. trans. [1. blándish; 2. blǽndiʃ], fr. Lat. *blandīri*, 'flatter', fr. *blandus*, & **-ish**. See **bland**. To flatter, coax, persuade with soft words.

blandishment, n. [1. blándishment; 2. blǽndiʃmәnt]. Prec. & **-ment**. Flattery, persuasion; (often pl.) arts of persuasion; (gen. in slightly unfavourable sense) artful flattery with ulterior motive.

blandly, adv. [1. blándli; 2. blǽndli]. **bland** & **-ly**. In a bland, gentle manner.

blandness, n. See prec. & **-ness**. The quality of being bland; mildness, gentleness.

blank (**I.**), adj. [1. blangk; 2. blæŋk], fr. Fr. *blanc*, cp. Ital. *bianco*. The word is Gmc. in origin, cp. O.H.G. *blanch*, 'white, shining', O.E. *blanca, blonca*, 'white horse', O.N. *blakkr* (for **blank-r*, 'white horse'). Prob. related to **blink**, & ultimately to Gmc. **blīk-*, 'shine', O.E. &c. *blīcan*, 'shine'. See further under **bleach** & **bleak**. Orig. meaning, 'bright, dazzling'. **1.** Empty, vacant, void (chiefly in extended sense, not written on or marked, of paper); original sense of white has practically disappeared: *a blank page* (in a book); *a blank sheet of paper; a blank space* (on a page). Phr. *a blank cheque*, one not filled up; hence (fig.) *to give a blank cheque*, unlimited amount of money; *blank cartridge*, one without shot or bullet. **2.** Empty, unoccupied (of ground): *many blank spaces are still left in the suburbs.* **3.** (fig.) **a** Lacking ideas, having forgotten: *my mind, memory, is perfectly blank on the subject*; **b** lacking expression in the face, as through a shock, disappointment: *a blank look, expression.* **4.** Unrhymed (of verse): *blank verse*, usually of ten syllables, or five feet. **5.** A vulgar expletive, used instead of a genuine oath; this modern vulgarism in speech is due to the habit of printing oaths with the initial followed by ——, as d——.

blank (**II.**), n., fr. prec. **1.** Empty, unoccupied space, gap, esp. on a page (see prec. **1**); a piece of paper with nothing printed or written on it, as a ticket in a lottery which does not win a prize. Phr. *to draw a blank*, (lit.) receive a useless ticket, hence, to fail in any enterprise or quest. **2.** (fig.) Vacancy, emptiness of mind, esp. from shock or strong emotion: *my mind became a complete blank*, I forgot everything. **3.** Space, emptiness, left when something has been lost or removed: (lit.) *now that the picture has been taken down it leaves a great blank on the wall*; (fig.) *her son's death has made a great blank in her life.*

blanket (**I.**), n. [1. blángket; 2. blǽŋkit], fr. Fr. *blanc*, see **blank** (**I.**), & **-et**, dimin. suff., 'the white thing'. **a** Thick, soft woollen cloth, often bleached nearly white, but also sometimes grey, yellow, or striped; **b** covering for a bed made of this material; **c** rug strapped on to a horse in the stable. Phrs. *toss in a blanket*, schoolboy practice of tossing a person from a blanket, into which he falls; *wet blanket*, (fig.) any depressing influence which damps hopes or enthusiasm.

blanket (**II.**), vb. trans., fr. prec. **1.** To cover with a blanket. **2.** (naut.) To take the wind out of the sails of (another vessel) by steering between her and the wind.

blankly, adv. [1. blángkli; 2. blǽŋkli]. **blank** (**I.**) & **-ly**. In a blank manner; esp. **a** (of look, manner &c.) vacantly: *to stare blankly at* &c.; **b** (of statements) flatly; cp. *point blank.*

blankness, n. [1. blángknes; 2. blǽŋknis]. See prec. & **-ness**. State, quality, of being blank.

blare, vb. & n. [1. blār; 2. bleә]. Prob. loan-word, fr. Du. *blaren*; ultimately imitative; cogn. w. **blaze** (**I.**) & **blow** (**I.**). **1.** vb. To peal out, esp. of a trumpet; to utter noisily. **2.** n. Noise made by something which blares: *blare of a trumpet* &c.

blarney, n. & vb. [1. blárni; 2. blɑ́ni], fr. Blarney Castle, in Ireland, where is the *Blarney stone*, wh. if anyone kisses, he is said to receive the gift of being persuasive and agreeable of address. **1.** n. Flattery; pleasant, persuasive, cajoling humbug; insincere compliments. **2.** vb. To flatter, cajole, speak coaxingly and persuasively.

blasé, adj. [1. bláhzā; 2. blɑ́zei]. Fr., P.P. of *blaser*, 'to take the edge off, to pall'. Sated, surfeited; bored through having enjoyed too much of anything.

blaspheme, vb. intrans. & trans. [1. blasfḗm; 2. blæsfím], fr. Gk. *blasphēmein*, 'speak profanely; speak ill of someone', a compound of *blas-* & *phēmi*, 'speak'. The origin of **blas-* is doubtful. It is perh. fr. **mlaps-*, Aryan **mlakʷ-*, or **mlagʷ-*; cp. Gk. *blábē*, 'hurt, damage', & **bláp-tein*, 'to harm' &c.; these are cogn. w. Lat. *mulcāre*, 'to beat', for *mulc-tāre*, & *multa*, 'punishment, fine', for **mulcta* (see **mulct**), perh. w. Scrt. *marčáyati*, 'he insults', & O. Slav. *u-mlŭčiti*, 'to curb, restrain'. Gk. *phēmi*, 'I speak', *phēmis*, 'speech', is cogn. w. Lat. *fā-ri*, 'to speak', *fā-ma*, 'rumour, common talk' &c. See further under **fame**. **a** intrans. To utter impieties, profanities, curse and swear; **b** trans., to rail against with profanity, revile.

blasphemer, n. [1. blasfḗmer; 2. blæsfímә]. Prec. & **-er**. One who utters blasphemies, speaks profanely; one who reviles.

blasphemous, adj. [1. blásfemus; 2. blǽsfimәs]. See prec. & **-ous**. **a** (of persons) Given to blasphemy; **b** (of language &c.) of a blasphemous, profane, character.

blasphemously, adv. Prec. & **-ly**. In a blasphemous, profane, manner.

blasphemy, n. [1. blásfemi; 2. blǽsfimi]. Gk. *blasphēmia*. See **blaspheme** & **-y**. Foul, impious talk, profanity; profane abuse.

blast (**I.**), n. [1. blahst; 2. blāst]. O.E. *blǣst*, 'blast, a blowing', connected w. O.E. *blāwan*, 'blow', & *-st-* formative suff. Cp. **blow** (**I.**). **1.** Sudden, violent movement of the wind, a squall, a boisterous gust of wind. **2.** The draught in a smelting furnace. Phr. *to be in, out of, blast*, of a furnace, working or not; hence (fig.) of any kind of activity, *in full blast.* **3.** Sound of a wind-instrument: *blast of a trumpet* &c. **4.** (fig.) Scorching, withering effect of malicious rumour, lying reports &c.: '*The rage of power, the blast of public breath*' (Pope). **5.** Detonation caused in breaking up rocks by explosives; the charge of explosive used in a single operation of the kind.

blast (**II.**), vb. trans., fr. prec. O.E. *blǣstan*, 'blow'. **1.** To shatter by explosion, blow up, esp. of rocks in quarrying operations. **2.** To wither, shrivel up, scorch as with fire, or excessive cold: *a single night's frost in May often blasts the fruit-buds, and ruins the crop for that year; a blasted woodland, heath* &c. **3.** (fig.) To destroy, ruin, bring to nothing (of reputation, honour, good name, hopes &c.). **4.** An oath (not particularly forcible, but chiefly used in low society): *blast it!*; (adj. fr. P.P.) *a blasted nuisance* &c.

blast-furnace, n. Type of smelting furnace in which hot air is blown in under pressure at the bottom, producing an intense heat.

blastoderm, n. [1. bláhstodĕrm; 2. blɑ́stodām], fr. Gk. *blástos*, 'bud, sprout, growth', & *dérma*, 'skin'. Etymol. of first element doubtful; *dérma*, the usual word for skin, 'hide', means lit. 'that which peels off', & is cogn. w. the base of *dérō*, 'flay'; Goth. *-tairan*, 'to tear', O.H.G. *-zeran*, O.E. *teran*, Mod. Engl. *tear*, derive fr. same base. See **derm** & **tear** (**I.**). (biol.) The layer of cells arising from the germinal disk in the early stages of segmentation in the life of an embryo.

blatancy, n. [1. blátansi; 2. bléitәnsi]. See next word & **-cy**. State, quality, of being blatant.

blatant, adj. [1. blátant; 2. bléitәnt]. Word apparently invented by Spenser in 'Faery Queen'; used of the *Blatant Beast.* The word has no history; the suggestion that it is connected with *bleat* seems highly unlikely. Noisy; vulgarly and ineffectively loud in speech. Applied also to a self-assertive, boisterous manner.

blatantly, adv. Prec. & **-ly**. In a blatant manner.

blather. See **blether**.

blaze (**I.**), n. [1. blāz; 2. bleiz]. O.E. *blæse*, 'torch, fire', M.E. *blāse*, M.H.G. *blass*, 'bald', orig. 'shining' (cp. use of **bald**, 'marked with white', & **blaze** (**III.**)), O.H.G. *biass*, 'white', Mod. Germ. *blass*, 'pale'. The base is that fr. wh. **blast** & **blow** are derived. **1.** Burst or spurt of flame; flame, fire: *the fire sprang into a blaze.* Phr. *in a* *blaze*, on fire. **2.** A patch, or mass, of brilliant, striking colour; strong glow of light: *a blaze of colour, of light.* **3.** (in pl.) *Blazes,* mild expletive, chiefly in phrases: *go to blazes; work, run &c. like blazes,* i.e. excessively, vigorously; *what the blazes am I to do?* &c.

blaze (II.), vb. intrans., fr. prec. **1.** (of fire) To burn brightly, burst into flame; (of eyes, countenance &c.) to gleam, be lit up with strong emotion. Also *blaze up,* burn up. Phrs. (fig.) *blaze up,* to get into a sudden rage; *blaze out (at),* direct violent anger against. **2.** *Blaze off, away,* fire off ammunition rapidly; also merely to fire ammunition: *to blaze away at a rabbit* &c. Phrs. (fig.) *blaze away at one's work* &c., keep vigorously at it; (in imperat.) *blaze away then,* equivalent to 'start, go on, get to work'; *blazing indiscretion,* patent, notorious, rashness; *blazing scent* (in fox-hunting), strong; reverse of a cold scent. **3.** (of light) To shine brilliantly: *lights were blazing in every window.*

blaze (III.), n. & vb. trans., fr. **blaze** (I.). **1.** n. **a** White mark on forehead of a horse or ox; **b** mark on a tree made by hacking off a piece of bark. **2.** vb. To mark a tree for felling by chopping out a piece of bark, thus making a 'blaze' or white spot on it. Phr. *to blaze the trail,* make a path through a wood &c. in above manner.

blaze (IV.), vb. trans. O.N. *blāsa,* 'to blow'; cp. O.H.G. *blāsan,* Goth. *(uf)blēsan,* 'to blow'; cogn. w. **blast, blow** (I.). To publish news loudly and widely. From idea of proclamations made with a trumpet; esp. *blaze about, abroad.*

blazer, n. [1. blā́zer; 2. bléizə]. Lit. 'that which blazes', fr. the bright colours in wh. blazers are often made. See **blaze** (II.). Light flannel coat, often dyed with colours of some particular club or institution, worn instead of ordinary coat, with garments suitable for boating, tennis, cricket, or other games.

blazon (I.), n. [1. blā́zun; 2. bléizən]. O. Fr. *blason,* 'shield', later 'coat of arms'; M.E. *blazon, blazoun,* 'shield' &c. Etymol. somewhat obscure, but the Fr. word wh. we borrowed is prob. due to Germ. *blasen,* 'blow, proclaim'; later this M.E. word was associated w. the M.E. *blāse* 'blow, proclaim' (**blaze** IV.), & the meaning extended fr. 'shield which proclaims a man's lineage &c.', to that of 'proclamation'. **1.** (her.) **a** Shield bearing heraldic devices, coat of arms; **b** scientific heraldic description of arms and bearings. **2.** (fig.) Account, record of virtues, titles to fame.

blazon (II.), vb. trans., fr. prec. **1.** To paint or inscribe a shield with proper arms of bearer. **2.** Esp. *blazon abroad,* proclaim widely. (In this sense partly influenced by *blaze abroad.*)

blazonry, n. [1. blā́znri; 2. bléiznri], fr. prec. & **-ry**. **1.** Display of armorial bearings. **2.** Heraldic art and method of inscribing, arranging on a shield and describing these.

-ble, suff. [1. bl; 2. bl]. Derived through O. Fr., fr. Lat. adj. suff. *-bilis.* See **-able**.

bleach, vb. [1. blēch; 2. blītʃ]. O.E. *blǣcan,* 'make pale, whiten', fr. *blāc,* 'pale, shining' (not to be confused w. O.E. *blæc,* 'black'). *Blāc* is cogn. w. the O.E. vb. *blīcan,* 'shine'; cp. also O.H.G. *bleih,* 'pale', Mod. Germ. *bleich,* O.N. *bleikr,* q.v. under **bleak**. The fundamental meaning of the base appears to be 'shine, glitter' &c., cp. O. Slav. *bliskati,* 'to shine', *blěsku,* 'gleam', n., Mod. Russ. *blestet,* 'flash', & so on. More remote in form are Lat. *flag-rāre,* 'to flame, burn', *flamma,* 'flame', fr. **flagma,* Gk. *phlog-mós* 'a blaze' &c. See **flame** & **black**. Note how the same orig. base may develop meanings wh. are the exact opposite of each other: e.g. O.E. *blāc,* 'shining (like fire), pale', & O.E. *blæc,* 'dark', as though burnt black, scorched, by fire. To whiten, esp. of cloth &c. by exposure to light, or by chemical process.

bleacher, n. [1. blḗcher; 2. blītʃə]. Prec. & **-er**. One who bleaches, esp. one engaged in the business of bleaching linen, cotton, or other textiles.

bleaching powder, n. [1. blḗching pòuder; 2. blītʃiŋ pàudə]. Chemical, such as chlorine, or chloride of lime, used for bleaching.

bleak (I.), adj. [1. blēk; 2. blīk]. Cogn. w. **bleach**, but borrowed in M.E. (in form *blēke*) fr. O.N. *bleikr,* 'pale' &c. The native Engl. adj., O.E. *blāc,* 'pale', precisely cogn. w. *bleikr,* has been lost in Mod. Engl., but survives in M.E. *blōk(e)*; see, however, **bleach**. Original meaning was, lacking in colour; now **a** (of a landscape), dreary, dismal; **b** (of a situation, tract of country) wind-swept, exposed, cold; **c** (fig., of a person's face, expression) harsh, dismal, forbidding; gloomy, sad.

bleak (II.), n., fr. O.N. *bleikja,* cogn. w. prec. Small silvery, cyprinid fish, found in rivers, *Alburnus lucidus*; also allied sea-fish.

bleakly, adv. **bleak** (I.) & **-ly**. In a bleak manner.

bleakness, n. See prec. & **-ness**. State, quality, of being bleak.

blear, adj. & vb. [1. blēr; 2. bliə]. M.E. *blēre*; etymol. doubtful. (rare) Dim-sighted, lustreless. **1.** adj. Esp. in compound, *blear-eyed,* dim-sighted. **2.** vb. **a** To dim the sight; **b** to cast a cloud or vapour over glass or shining surface; **c** to make the outline vague and indistinct, equivalent to *blur.*

bleat, vb. & n. [1. blēt; 2. blīt]. O.E. *blǣtan,* 'bleat'. Of imitative origin, cp. Du. *blaten,* & see **feeble**. **1.** vb. **a** To make the characteristic cry of the sheep; **b** (fig.) to speak in a feeble, quavering voice resembling that of a sheep; **c** to talk nonsense. **2.** n. The cry made by a sheep or lamb; feeble, foolish talk.

bleater, n. [1. blḗter; 2. blītə]. Prec. & **-er**. A foolish, timid person who expresses groundless apprehensions, esp. in a whining voice.

bleating, n. [1. blḗting; 2. blītiŋ]. See **bleat** & **-ing**. Cry of sheep; foolish, trivial talk.

bleb, n. [1. bleb; 2. bleb]. Origin unknown; perh. connected w. *blob,* whose origin is equally obscure. (rare) Small blister.

bled, vb. [1. bled; 2. bled]. Pret. & P.P. of **bleed**. M.E. *bledde, (y)bled,* fr. O.E. *blēdde, ġeblēd(d).*

bleed, vb. intrans. & trans. [1. blēd; 2. blīd]. O.E. *blēdan,* vb., fr. *blōd,* '**blood**'. **1.** intrans. **a** To give out, flow with, blood, lose blood, from any cause: (fig.) *my heart bleeds for you,* I feel grief on your account; **b** (of trees) to lose sap from a cut through the bark, or from place where bough has been lopped or broken off. **2.** trans. **a** To draw or let blood from a patient, for medical reasons; **b** to extort money from.

bleeder, n. [1. blḗder; 2. blīdə]. Prec. & **-er**. Person suffering from a pathological state known as haemophilia, in which bleeding takes place from a very slight blow or injury to any part of the body.

bleeding, n. [1. blḗding; 2. blīdiŋ]. See prec. & **-ing**. **a** Flow of blood, haemorrhage: *bleeding of the nose* &c.; **b** blood-letting.

blemish (I.), vb. trans. [1. blémish; 2. blémiʃ]. Fr. *blêmir,* O. Fr. *blesmir,* 'to grow pale, livid'. Etymol. very doubtful; said to come fr. Gmc. source, but none at all convincing has yet been suggested. The Engl. word is fr. *blemiss-,* as in Fr. Pres. Part. To injure, mar, deface, esp. of beauty, and in a moral sense, reputation &c.

blemish (II.), n., fr. prec. A physical or moral defect or imperfection; anything that detracts from beauty or perfection.

blench, vb. intrans. [1. blench; 2. blentʃ]. O.E. *blenċan,* 'to deceive', M.E. *blenchen,* 'turn aside'. Prob. connected w. **blank**, w. meaning influenced by **blink**. Origin of form & development of meaning both obscure. To flinch, quail.

blend (I.), vb. trans. & intrans. [1. blend; 2. blend]. The O.E. vb. is *blandan,* 'to mix', wh. cannot be the precise ancestor of *blend* nor of M.E. *blendan,* 'to mix', whence the present-day form comes. It is possible that an unrecorded O.E. **blendan* existed, formed fr. **bland-jan,* cp. O.E. *ġe-blond,* 'mixture, mixing, tumult'. The vb. *blandan,* 'mix' is found in O.S., O.H.G., & O.N. The word is undoubtedly connected w. **blind**. **1.** trans. **a** To mix together, mingle things of one sort with others, or varieties of same thing together; used especially in various trades: *to blend tea, coffee, spirits* &c.; **b** used in literary style, chiefly in passive: *good and evil are blended (together) in life; the diverse elements in his character were strangely blended.* (The archaic P.P. *blent* is much used in poetry.) **2.** intrans. To mingle easily and suitably; be adaptable to something different; unite so as to form harmonious whole: *oil and water will not blend; these shades of colour blend beautifully; Orientals and Europeans never really blend.*

blend (II.), n., fr. prec. Mixture of different things or varieties, esp. of tea, spirits, tobacco &c.

blende, n. [1. blend; 2. blend]. (metal.) One of the principal ores of zinc. Name said to be derived fr. Germ. *blendendes erz,* 'deceiving ore', so called because it resembles lead ore although it contains no lead.

blending, n. [1. blénding; 2. bléndiŋ]. **blend** (I.) & **-ing**. Process of mixing different types of the same article (esp. tea, spirits &c.) so as to produce a marketable, and if possible an agreeable, combination.

Blenheim orange, n. [1. blénim órinj; 2. blénim ɔ́rindž]. From Duke of Marlborough's seat. Name of large reddish apple.

Blenheim spaniel, n. A breed of toy spaniels, so called because originally bred at Blenheim.

blenno-, pref., fr. Gk. *blénna,* 'slime, mucus'; see **blenny**, used in medical terminology, e.g. *blennorrhoea,* [1. blènoréa; 2. blènəríə], a morbid discharge of mucus, esp. from the urethra.

blenny, n. [1. bléni; 2. bléni]. Lat. *blennius,* fr. Gk. *blénnos,* name of a fish, fr. *blénna,* 'slime', fr. **gʷlenna,* base **gʷlen-,* 'to stick', cp. M.H.G. *klenen,* 'stick', O. Slav. *glenŭ,* 'slime'. See also **glue**. A small spiny sea-fish, so called from the mucus which covers the skin.

bless, vb. trans. [1. bles; 2. bles], P.P. **blest** & **blessed** [1. blest, blésid; 2. blest, blésid]. O.E. *blēdsian, blētsian,* 'bless, consecrate'. Only found in Engl., but derived fr. Common Gmc. *blōd,* 'blood', w. suff. *-isōjan.* The vb. meant orig. 'to sprinkle with blood', as a priest at a sacrifice. See **blood**. **1.** To pronounce words and perform acts which produce, or are attended by, a supernatural effect; consecrate, dedicate: *the priest blesses the elements at Holy Communion; 'Bless, O Lord, these Thy gifts to our use'.* **2.** To invoke Divine favour upon; pronounce a benediction. (This use has been influenced by translation of Lat. *benedicere* as 'bless'.) *'They brought little children to Him and He blessed them'; at the close of the service the priest blesses the people*; common in colloq. use in Phrs. (*God* being understood, but rarely expressed, before each) *bless me; bless my soul; bless the child; well, I'm blest,* indicating surprise. Special use: *bless oneself,* make sign of cross on one's forehead and breast. Phr. *not a penny to bless oneself with,* very poor. **3.** To praise, venerate, worship: *'We praise Thee, we bless Thee, we glorify Thee'; 'We bless Thy Holy Name'.* **4.** To wish happiness and prosperity for a person; wish well to; feel gratitude towards: *I bless the day I met him; those who enjoy the advantages offered by the ancient colleges of Oxford may well bless the founders.* Phr. *to bless one's stars.* **5.** To render happy, fortunate; cause to prosper (followed by *with*): *their union was blest with numerous offspring; he was blest with an ample fortune*; (followed by *in*) *I am greatly blest in my children.* (This meaning has been influenced by that of *bliss* which has been confused with *bless,* although quite independent in origin.) See **bliss**.

blessed, blest, adj. fr. P.P. of prec. [1. blésed, blest; 2. blésid, blest]. *Blessed* is usual when adj.; *blest* used chiefly in poetry. It is not always easy to distinguish the adj. fr. the P.P. **1.** Deserving of veneration; consecrated, holy: *the Blessed Sacrament*; '*Behold from henceforth, all generations shall call me blessed*'. **2.** Happy, fortunate, favoured: *those were blessed days* (this usage needs to be employed with caution on account of the now more familiar colloquialism; see **5** below). (poet.) '*Araby the blest*' (Milton). **3.** Endowed with, fortunate in possessing (chiefly poetical; but see **bless, 5**): '*Blest with each talent and each art to please*' (Pope). **4. a** In a state of eternal happiness (of those in Paradise): *the blessed ones*; (as a n.) *the islands of the blest*; **b** specif., a title applied to those whom the R.C. Church has recognized as on the way to beatification: *blessed John Postgate* (a holy man who lived in Yorks. in 17th cent.). **5.** Euphemistic expletive (in polite colloq. usage); esp. in *the whole blessed lot*; *every blessed one.*

blessedly, adv. [1. blésedli; 2. blésidli]. Prec. & **-ly.** (rare) In a blessed manner; fortunately, happily.

blessedness, n. [1. blésednes; 2. blésidnis]. See prec. & **-ness.** The state or condition of being blessed; joy, felicity: *we believe that the saints enjoy perpetual blessedness.* Phr. *a state of single blessedness*, the unmarried state (jocular).

blessing, n. [1. blésing; 2. blésiŋ]. O.E. *blētsung*. See **bless** & **-ing. 1. a** Invocation of Divine favour; the benediction pronounced by the priest: *to give the blessing*; **b** (special use) grace, thanksgiving before or after food: usually *to ask a blessing*; **c** solemn wish expressed by human being for another's welfare, often accompanied by a laying of the hands on his head: '*Give me a blessing O my father*'. **2.** Bestowal of Divine favour, mercy, grace: *by the blessing of God his life was saved*; '*May the blessing of God Almighty . . . be amongst you and remain with you always*'. **3.** A gift of God, Nature; a benefit, advantage: *a long, healthy and happy life was a blessing which Providence granted him.* **4.** A thing or circumstance which gives one satisfaction; something which promotes one's happiness or comfort, or which prevents a misfortune: *a good fire is a great blessing in cold weather*; *what a blessing it is the two men did not meet.* Phrs. *a blessing in disguise*, something which turns out well unexpectedly; (jocular) *an unappropriated blessing*, an unmarried woman.

blether, blather, vb. intrans. & n. [1. blédher, bládher; 2. bléðə, blǽðə]. M.E. *blather*, Scots *blether*, fr. O.N. *blaðra*, 'to talk nonsense, gabble'; imitative; cp. M.H.G. *bladeren*; O.H.G. *blabbizōn*. **1.** vb. To talk nonsense, chatter foolishly. **2.** n. Foolish talk.

blew, vb. [1. bloo͞; 2. blū]. Pret. of **blow (I.)**; O.E. *blēow*, M.E. *blew.*

blight (I.), n. [1. blīt; 2. blait]. Not found in O.E. & not used apparently before 17th cent. Thus the history is very obscure. It has been suggested that the word is derived fr. the base found in **bleach.** There is a vb. *bliċettan* in O.E., 'to glitter', & a n. *bliċettung*, 'coruscation', & further, in late M.E., a n. *blickening*, 'pallor', used to translate *rubigo*, 'mildew'. These words seem to be all related to each other, & further to the base ***bhleg-**, 'shine', & it is difficult to separate them fr. the word *blight.* The suggestion of Skeat is that the latter is so called fr. the pale or white appearance it gives to leaves &c. On the other hand, it is possible that the base in this word may have had the other force of 'burn, wither up'. In either case the Engl. word may be fr. an unrecorded O.E. ***bliht**, fr. earlier **blæhti* whence **bleahti*, ***blieht** &c. The word *blecþa*, 'blight', is recorded in O.E. & must be fr. the base referred to, & represent an earlier **blækiþu.* The genuine descendant of this wd. be **bleckth* at the present time. **1.** The word loosely applied to various diseases which affect, and insect pests which attack, the leaves, stems or flowers of plants, such as black rust, mildew, greenfly &c. **2.** Dull cloud or mist which sometimes comes up with an east wind in the summer, and which some believe is composed largely of the insects or spores of the fungi which attack plants: *a blight in the air.* **3.** (fig.) Anything which depresses the spirits, damps enthusiasm, causes the failure of plans &c.; a feeling of depression and hopelessness, disappointment: *the absence, through illness, of the head of the family cast a blight over the party*; *sudden loss of fortune came as a blight to his hopes of a career in diplomacy.*

blight (II.), vb. trans., fr. prec. **1.** To injure, check growth of, or destroy, a plant by mildew, or other disease; also to wither up, blacken leaves, buds &c. through frost. **2.** (fig.) To cut off, shatter, check (hopes, career, prospects, enjoyment &c.).

blighted, adj. [1. blīted; 2. bláitid], fr. P.P. of prec. **1.** (of plants) Withered, destroyed through disease. **2.** (fig., of hopes, affections &c.) Dashed, disappointed, marred.

blighter, n. [1. blīter; 2. bláitə], fr. **blight (II.)** & **-er. a** (lit.) One who blights, whose presence has a devastating influence; **b** (slang) a mildly opprobrious epithet applied to a person who is generally disagreeable, a troublesome, cantankerous fellow. Often used in vague sense equivalent to *fellow, chap.*

Blighty, n. [1. blīti; 2. bláiti], fr. *Billaït*, 'Europe', a word used in India. It is said to come fr. Arab. *wilāyat*, 'kingdom, province'. The adj. *bilāyatī* is applied to various articles of foreign importation, e.g. *bilāyatī pānī*, 'foreign, European, water', i.e. soda water. During the Great War *Blighty* was used by soldiers of the British Army for England. Phr. *a blighty one*, a wound severe enough to necessitate removal of the patient to England.

blimp, n. [1. blimp; 2. blimp]. Invented word. A small non-rigid type of airship, used for scouting at sea near the coast.

blind (I.), adj. [1. blīnd; 2. blaind]. O.E. & Common Gmc. *blind*; connected w. O.E. & Common Gmc. *blandan*, q.v. under **blend (I.).** O.N. has also *blunda*, 'to close the eyes', & *blundr*, 'slumber'. The base is found also in Lith. *blandýti*, 'to shut the eyes', *blįsta*, 'it grows dark', & in O. Slav. *blanditi*, *blęsti*, 'to make a mistake'. The orig. meaning of the base seems to be 'confused, puzzled, dark', thence 'confused in sight'. **1. a** Sightless, unable to see, lacking the power of vision; **b** having imperfect sight, dim-sighted. Phrs. *as blind as a bat*, very blind; *the blind leading the blind*, one incompetent person helping another; *blind alley*, road that leads nowhere, one closed at one end (also fig.); *blind window*, one that has been walled up. **2.** (of moral and intellectual state) Unobservant, obtuse, dull, unenlightened; lacking foresight, understanding, appreciation: *to be blind to a person's faults, to one's own interests, to the beauties of nature, to charms.* **3.** (slang) Drunk, esp. in Phr. *blind to the world.*

blind (II.), vb. trans., fr. prec. **1. a** To deprive of sight, make blind, temporarily or permanently; **b** to bind something round the eyes of, to blindfold. **2.** To obscure mental or moral perception; deceive: *his vanity blinded him to the weakness of his position.*

blind (III.), n., fr. prec. **1.** A screen made of thin strips of wood fastened one above another, and overlapping, on a cord, which is lowered over a window; or one of cloth, which is either lowered from a roller above, or hung on a rod and drawn across, a window to keep out the light: *to draw, pull down, the blind(s)*, (lit. and fig.) as sign of mourning, end of anything. **2.** (fig.) A deception, artifice, misleading action designed to draw off attention from, and hide real intentions: *his genial manner was a mere blind for his swindles.* **3.** (coll.) *The blind*, blind people: *asylum for the blind*, also *Blind Asylum.*

blindfold (I.), vb. trans. [1. blīndfōld; 2. bláindfould]. M.E. *blindfellen*, 'strike blind' (cp. **fell (IV.)**); confused w. *fold* through being principally used in P.P. *-felled.* To deprive of sight by putting a bandage over the eyes.

blindfold (II.), adj. & adv., fr. prec. **a** Having the eyes bandaged; **b** (fig.) deluded, uninstructed: *to be blindfold*; *to act, do something, blindfold.* Phr. *to know one's way blindfold*, be very familiar with the road &c.

blindly, adv. [1. blīndli; 2. bláindli]. **blind (I.)** & **-ly. a** As though unable to see, as one who is blind; esp. **b** (fig.) rashly, without proper foresight or deliberation; ignorantly.

blindman's-buff, n. [1. blīndmanz búf; 2. bláindmænz báf]. See **buffet**, n. Game in which a person with bandaged eyes tries to lay hold of one of the other players, who confuse him by jostling and pushing him.

blindness, n. [1. blīndnes; 2. bláindnis]. **blind (I.)** & **-ness. a** Lack of sight; state of being blind; **b** (fig.) rashness; ignorant folly; state of moral or intellectual unenlightment.

blink (I.), vb. intrans. & trans. [1. blingk; 2. bliŋk]. Borrowed fr. L.G. or Scand. source; cp. Du. *blinken*, 'shine', Dan. *blinke*, 'twinkle'. Prob. connected w. base discussed under **bleach** & **bleak. 1.** intrans. **a** To open and close the eyelids rapidly; often in Phr. to *wink and blink*; **b** (of lights, esp. when seen from a distance) to shine fitfully, twinkle. **2.** trans. (fig. use) To refuse to accept a fact or situation, attempt to evade or conceal it: *it is no good blinking the fact that we have been beaten.*

blink (II.), n., fr. prec. **a** Transitory flash or gleam of light; **b** specif., a white reflection on the horizon from ice-fields; also *ice-blink.*

blinkers, n. pl. [1. blingkerz; 2. bliŋkəz]. See **blink (I.)** & **-er.** Part of harness of carriage or cart horse, consisting of square flaps of leather attached to headpiece which prevent the horse from seeing to the side. Phr. (fig.) *to be, run, in blinkers*, in a state of partial ignorance concerning what is going on around one.

blinking, adj. [1. blingking; 2. bliŋkiŋ], fr. Pres. Part. of **blink (I.).** (colloq. and vulg. slang) A mildish expletive used instead of a stronger expression in low talk; often has no meaning at all, but when it has one this is always derogatory; used in certain classes in any context before any noun.

bliss, n. [1. blis; 2. blis]. O.E. *bliþs, bliss*, 'joy, merriment, happiness', derived fr. *bliþ(e)*, 'gay, happy', q.v. under **blithe.** Perfect enjoyment; specif., the joy of the saints in heaven; content, happiness; physical or spiritual delight and well-being. This word and its O.E. derivative *blissian*, 'rejoice', have been confused with **bless.**

blissful, adj. [1. blísfool; 2. blísful]. Prec. & **-ful.** Happy, pleasant, enjoyable; esp. of places, and states of mind or body: *a blissful state of prosperity* &c.

blissfully, adv. Prec. & **-ly.** In a perfectly happy manner; esp. in Phrs. *blissfully happy*; *blissfully ignorant of*, happy because ignorant.

blissfulness, n. See prec. & **-ness.** State of perfect happiness.

blister, n. & vb. trans. & intrans. [1. blíster; 2. blístə]. M.E. *blester*, fr. O. Fr. *blestre*, of Gmc. origin, cp. O.N. *blāstr*, 'swelling'. Connected w. stem in **blow (I.). 1.** n. **a** Bladder-like swelling on the skin, containing watery fluid, caused by heat or other irritant; **b** similar swelling on painted surface; **c** any irritant used medically to produce a blister. **2.** vb. **a** To cause a blister; produce one by medical means; **b** (fig.) to wither, scarify, with scornful reproaches, bitter sarcasm &c.

blithe, adj. [1. blīdh; 2. blaið]. O.E. *blīþe*, 'joyful, merry, gentle, mild, gracious', O.H.G. *blīdi*, 'gay, friendly', O.S. *blīði*, O.N. *blīðr*, 'mild, gentle', Goth. *bleiþs*, 'friendly, merciful'. It is suggested w. considerable plausibility that this word is for *mlīþ, & that it is connected w. Goth. miliþ, 'honey', O.E. milisć for *miliþ-sk, 'honeyed'. Gk. has méli, 'honey', genit. mélit-os, mélissa, 'bee', & the vb. blíttō (w. bl- for ml-), 'to take honey from the hive'. Cp. also Lat. mel, 'honey', Ir. mil. Further connexion is suggested w. Common Gmc. mild, 'gentle' &c. The Aryan base on this showing wd. be *melit-, or, in other grades, *mleit-, *mlit-, wh. last appears as blit- in Gk. & blīþ- in Gmc. 'Honey' in Gk. melit- & Gmc. miliþ- is 'the mild, the pleasant substance'. See **mild & mellifluous**, & cp. **mildew.** Gay, happy, cheerful (rarely used of persons except pred.): *she seems very blithe*; often *blithe and gay*; esp. used of character, disposition, mood, spirit, heart &c.

blithely, adv. Prec. & **-ly.** Cheerfully, gaily, willingly.

blithesome, adj. [1. blídhsum; 2. bláiðsəm]. See prec. & **-some.** Almost same meaning as **blithe**, but more freely applied to persons.

blithesomeness, n. Prec. & **-ness.** Gaiety of disposition or mood.

blizzard, n. [1. blízard; 2. blízəd]. Mod. invented word; first used in U.S. in 1880; of imitative origin, w. suff. **-ard** added to stem of *blow, blast, blaze* &c. A driving, blinding storm of snow accompanied by violent wind.

bloat, vb. trans. & intrans. [1. blōt; 2. blout], fr. M.E. adj. *blōte.* Precise history doubtful, but connected w., if not borrowed fr., O.N. *blautr*, 'soaked, soft'. The Scand. word is cogn. w. Lat. *fluere*, 'to flow', *fluidus*, 'flowing, liquid', & Gk. *phlúein*, 'boil up'. See **fluent.** **1.** trans. **a** To cure fish by soaking in brine and smoking; **b** to swell, puff out, usually in P.P. *bloated.* **2.** intrans. & trans. To swell, puff out; esp. *bloat out.*

bloated, adj. [1. blṓted; 2. blóutid], fr. P.P. of prec. Swelled, puffed out, puffy, unhealthily fat and large: *a bloated body, face* &c.; *bloated with over-eating, gluttony*; also fig.: *a bloated profiteer.*

bloater, n. [1. blṓter; 2. blóutə], fr. **bloat** in sense **1** & **-er.** A fish, esp. herring, salted and smoked; cp. Swed. *blötfisk*, 'soaked fish'.

blob, n. [1. blob; 2. blɔb]. Origin unknown. **1.** Globular mass of any moist substance, mud, clay &c. **2.** (colloq., in cricket) Nought, a duck's egg.

blobber-lipped, adj. [1. blóber lipt; 2. blɔ́bə lipt]. Cp. **blubber.** With thick, protruding lips.

block (I.), n. [1. blok; 2. blɔk]. Prob. fr. Fr. *bloc*, a Gmc. loan-word, O.H.G. *blok, bloh*, fr. *bi-loh*; the second element is cogn. w. Germ. *loch*, 'hole, opening', O.E. *loc*, 'lock, prison'; cp. Goth. *lūks*, 'opening', & see **lock (II.).** The use of the same word for 'hole' & 'something which closes a hole', is seen in Ir. use of *stone gap*, i.e. the bit of wall which fills a gap. **1.** Lump, unshaped mass of wood, or, more rarely, of stone; *barber's block*, roughly shaped wooden head on which wigs are fitted. Phrs. *to cut blocks with a razor*, use delicate means for a rough task; (fig.) *a chip of the old block*, of a child who resembles his father in person or character. **2.** (special usage of above) The piece of wood on which those condemned to death laid their necks when being beheaded: *to go to the block.* **3.** (derived from **1**) A lumpish, dull, stupid, clumsy person. **4.** Large pulley and its wooden case, as used in rigging of ships. **5.** A mass of buildings; group of connected houses. **6.** An obstruction in passage, pipe, road &c., esp. of congestion of traffic on road or railway line. **7.** That part of cricket pitch close to wicket where batsman stands and rests his bat before playing a ball.

block (II.), vb. trans., fr. prec. **1.** To obstruct (passage, pipe, road &c.). **2.** (fig.) To hinder, esp. advance, progress of measure in Parliament &c. **3.** *Block out*, to plan out in broad lines the general design of a piece of writing, or scheme of any kind; *block in*, to sketch out roughly the arrangement of a picture, as to grouping of figures and masses of colour &c. **4.** (cricket) To stop a ball by keeping bat upright, straight in front of wicket, with the end resting on the ground.

blockade, n. & vb. trans. [1. blokā́d; 2. blɔkéid], fr. **block** & **-ade**, on anal. of **barricade, cannonade** &c. **1.** n. Complete closure of a port from the sea by means of warships, so that ingress and egress are stopped; isolation of a place, town &c. by surrounding it with troops. Phrs. *to raise the blockade*, cease above action; *to run the blockade*, pass in or out of a blockaded place. **2.** vb. To impose a blockade, esp. by sea, of a port or harbour.

blockade-runner, n. A ship which, or person who, slips through the guard of a blockaded port and communicates with the force inside.

block-book, n. Book printed from engraved wooden blocks.

blockhead, n. [1. blókhed; 2. blɔ́k(h)ɛd]. A person with a head like a block; a stupid fool.

block-house, n. Small fortified building, roughly made of logs.

blockish, adj. [1. blókish; 2. blɔ́kiʃ]. **block** (I.) & **-ish.** Like a lump of wood, dull of wit, stupid, obstinate.

bloke, n. [1. blōk; 2. blouk]. Origin unknown. (colloq. slang) General term for one of the male sex; equivalent to fellow, chap &c.; esp. in slightly contemptuous phrase: *old bloke.*

blond(e), adj. & n. [1. blond; 2. blɔnd]. Fr. *blond(e)*, 'fair of complexion', (of hair) 'yellow, pale'; of Gmc. origin, cp. O.E. *blandan*, 'mix', under **blend**; O.E. *blanden-feax* means 'grey-haired', prob. orig. 'mixed, white and original colour, grizzled'. **1.** adj. **a** (of hair) Light in colour, pale auburn or yellow; **b** (of complexion) fair, pink and white; opposite of *brunette.* **2.** n. A person having fair hair and complexion.

blood (I.), n. [1. blud; 2. blad]. O.E. *blōd*, Common Gmc., prob. fr. same base, Aryan **bhlō-*, as in **blossom** & **bloom.** The idea at the bottom of the particular Gmc. specialization of the base, in *blood*, is possibly 'the spirting fluid'. **1. a** The red fluid circulating through the arteries, veins, and capillaries of man and the vertebrate animals; similar fluid in lower animals; (med.) *to let blood*, to bleed surgically; *blood heat*, temperature of human blood, about 98° F.; *to taste blood*, (of dogs or wild animals) to kill and devour an animal they have hunted, thus acquiring a taste for such food; (fig.) to gain a first experience of something which one has desired; **b** (fig.) human nature: *more than flesh and blood can stand.* **2.** The essence, seat of physical life; life itself: *to give one's blood for one's country*; *pour out one's blood like water*; *to spill blood*, take life; *hands stained with blood*, guilty of cruelty, murder; *dip one's hands in blood*, provoke slaughter, kill; *to have a person's blood on one's head*, be responsible for his death, or misfortune; *man of blood*, cruel, guilty of loss of human life; *'s blood*, obsolete oath, for *God's blood.* **3.** Vehicle, seat, of passions; character; essence of being: *my blood ran cold*, I was terrified; *to freeze one's blood*, frighten, horrify; *my blood is up*, in a great passion; *in cold blood*, calmly, deliberately, without provocation; *to make bad blood between persons*, cause ill-feeling; *to make one's blood boil*, arouse one's indignation. **4.** That which constitutes, and through which is transmitted, the character, typical qualities of an individual, family, race; therefore lineage, descent, pedigree; consanguinity: *to be of the same blood*, of common descent; *to have fighting &c. in one's blood*, derive it by descent; *high, blue, blood*, aristocratic birth; *blood royal*, royal family; *prince of the blood*, closely related, through common ancestor, to the sovereign; *noble blood, ennobled in blood*, of recipient of peerage, and his heirs; *base blood*, illegitimacy; *related in blood, in half blood*, relationship through one parent; *blood is thicker than water*, ties of relationship are real. **5.** (derived from **4**) A smart young man of fashion, a dandy; also, more generally, *a young blood*, equivalent to young blade, fellow &c.

blood (II.), vb. trans. **1.** (med., now obs.) To draw blood surgically = *bleed.* **2. a** To give a hound his first taste of blood; **b** (fig.) to initiate to new experience.

blood-guiltiness, n. See next word & **-ness.** Guilt of, responsibility for, murder and bloodshed.

blood-guilty, adj. **blood** & **guilty.** Guilty of, responsible for, murder or bloodshed.

blood-horse, n. Horse whose pedigree is in the Stud Book; thoroughbred.

bloodhound, n. [1. blúd-hound; 2. bládhaund]. Breed of British dog, formerly known as sleuth hound; present name from the keenness with which it follows scent of blood.

bloodily, adv. [1. blúdili; 2. bládili]. See **bloody** & **-ly.** In a bloody manner, in sense **1, a** and **b**, of **blood.**

bloodless, adj. [1. blúdles; 2. bládlis]. **blood** (I.) & **-less.** **1.** Devoid of blood, pale (of lips, cheeks &c.). **2.** Without shedding of blood: *bloodless victory*; *bloodless operation.* **3.** (fig.) Spiritless; lacking in animation, vigour, passion &c.: *a bloodless character, temperament.*

bloodlessly, adv. Prec. & **-ly.** In a bloodless manner; without bloodshed.

blood-letting, n. [1. blúd léting; 2. blád létiŋ]. See **blood** & **let. a** Process of bleeding surgically; **b** (fig.) bloodshed, as in military attack, in a prize-fight &c.

blood-money, n. Reward earned for delivering over to justice one charged with capital offence.

blood orange, n. Variety of orange grafted on pomegranate; its flesh is streaked with red, and the juice is reddish.

blood-poisoning, n. A general term for various acute diseases caused by the entry of poisonous germs into the blood-stream, as pyæmia, septicæmia &c.

blood-pudding, n. Dish composed of pigs' blood, suet &c.; same as *black pudding.*

blood-red, adj. Of the colour of blood.

bloodshed, n. [1. blúdshed; 2. bládʃɛd]. **blood** (I.) & **shed** (I.) **a** Effusion of blood, slaughter of any kind; **b** war.

bloodshot, adj. [1. blúdshot; 2. bládʃɔt]. **blood** (I.) & **shot** (I.). (of the eyes) Suffused with blood, through breaking of small blood-vessels.

blood-stained, adj. [1. blúd stānd; 2. blád steind]. **a** Soiled with, soaked in, blood; **b** (fig.) guilty of murder.

bloodstone, n. [1. blúdstōn; 2. bládstoun]. **blood** (I.) & **stone.** Haematite, variety of chalcedony; a green stone with red streaks.

blood-sucker, n. **a** Leech; **b** (fig.) one guilty of extortion.

bloodthirstiness, n. See next word & **-ness.** Ferocity, cruelty.

bloodthirsty, adj. [1. blúdthërsti; 2. bládþāsti]. **blood** (I.) & **thirsty.** Ferocious, inclined to violence, eager to take life.

blood-vessel, n. Vein or artery; muscular tube through which the blood circulates.

bloodworm, n. [1. blúdwërm; 2. bládwām]. Bright-red worm, used as bait in fishing.

blood-wort, n. Species of plants so called from red juice of the roots.

bloody, adj. [1. blúdi; 2. bládi]. O.E. *blōdiġ.* **blood** (I.) & **-y.** **1. a** Covered or stained with blood: *bloody nose*; **b** (fig.) cruel, murderous, guilty of bloodshed: *bloody tyrant*; *bloody deed* &c.; **c** (her.) *bloody hand*, armorial bearing of Ulster; also borne by baronets. **2.** Low, vulgar, blasphemous epithet; also meaningless adjective much used among very low persons. (The origin of this expression has been much discussed; some believe it to be derived from a blasphemous reference to the Blood of the Redeemer, cp. *God's Blood*, now obsolete; others that it referred to the *bloods*, or fashionable rakes and rufflers, of 17th and early 18th cent. This seems improbable.)

bloody-minded, adj. Cruel, bloodthirsty.

bloom (I.), n. [1. blo͞om; 2. blūm], fr. O.N. *blōm(i)*, found as *blōme* in M.E. The O.E. type is *blōstma*, q.v. under **blossom**. One of the numerous words of variously differentiated meaning, fr. the prolific Aryan base **bhlē-*, **bhlō-* &c., meaning 'swell, blow; sprout, bud, spirt' &c.; among the nearest cognates are Lat. *flō-s*, 'flower', Gk. *blastéo*, 'bud, sprout, burst forth', *blástēma*, *blástē*, *blástos*, 'a bud, sprout, leaf, growth' &c. See further under **blade, blow (IV.), folio. 1.** Flower of a plant. Hence, **2.** The season, or time of life, at which plants and human beings reach greatest degree of perfection, vigour, and beauty; prime: esp. *bloom of youth*; *in full bloom*, (of plants) covered with blossom. **3. a** The dusty, powdery covering on the skin of such fruits as grapes and plums; **b** (fig.) glow, flush of health on the cheeks.

bloom (II.), vb. intrans., fr. prec. **a** To put forth flowers; **b** (fig.) to be in full beauty and perfection, to flourish.

bloom (III.), n. O.E. *blōma*, 'mass of molten metal'. Origin unknown, unless related to *blāwan*, 'blow', see **blow (I.)**. Metallurgical term for rough mass of iron after smelting.

bloomer, n. [1. blo͞omer; 2. blū́mə]. Origin doubtful, prob. connected w. **blooming.** (slang) A mistake, blunder.

bloomer(s), n. [1. blo͞omer(z); 2. blū́mə(z)]. Costume for women, invented by Mrs. Amelia Jenks Bloomer of New York, in 1851. It consisted of a coat with a belt, a short skirt, and baggy trousers fastened in round the ankles. The word is now as obsolete as the garments.

blooming, adj. [1. blo͞oming; 2. blū́miŋ], fr. Pres. Part. of **bloom (II.)**. **a** In a state of flower; **b** (of human beings) presenting an appearance of health or beauty: *she looks blooming*; **c** slightly vulgar, mild expletive or intensive, equivalent to *confounded*; also used with hardly any meaning as useless epithet: *the whole blooming lot*; *every blooming thing* &c. (Owing to this vulgar use of the word, that under **b** is becoming obsolete, except predicatively, since *blooming health*, *blooming cheek* &c. are liable to a ludicrous ambiguity.)

blossom (I.), n. [1. blósum; 2. blɔ́səm]. O.E. *blōstma*, M.E. *blosme*, *blossem*. See cognates & etymol. under **bloom (I.)**. Cp. Gk. *blástēma*, for cogn. w. closely related formation. **a** Flower, esp. on fruit trees; **b** total mass of flower on a tree, esp. a fruit tree.

blossom (II.), vb. intrans., fr. prec. To put forth flowers, to come into flower.

blot (I.), n. [1. blot; 2. blɔt]. Origin doubtful. Found in 14th cent. **1.** A spot or stain, esp. of ink on paper. **2.** (fig.) Disgrace, cause of reproach: *blot on one's character, reputation.* **3.** An ugly, unsightly object, esp. when unsuitable to its surroundings: *a blot on the landscape.*

blot (II.), vb. trans., fr. prec. **a** To make spots or blots of ink on (paper); **b** to blur, smudge (words newly written) before the ink is dry; **c** (poet.) to erase (what is written). *Blot out*, **a** to destroy, obliterate; **b** to obscure from view: *the landscape was blotted out by the fog.*

blotch, n. [1. bloch; 2. blɔtʃ]. Only since 17th cent.; perh. a mixture of *blot* & *patch.* **a** Eruption, spot or pimple on the skin; **b** spot, stain, discolouration on any surface.

blotchy, adj. [1. blóchi; 2. blɔ́tʃi]. Prec. & **-y.** Covered with spots or blotches.

blotting-paper, n. [1. blóting pāper; 2. blɔ́tiŋ pèipə]. Pres. Part. of **blot (II.)** & **paper.** Absorbent paper, used to dry up quickly what has been written in ink.

blouse, n. [1. blouz; 2. blauz]. Fr. word. Etymol. unknown. **a** French workman's cotton or linen overall, belted at waist; **b** loose outer garment, kind of shirt, worn by women on upper part of the body.

blow (I.), vb. intrans. & trans. [1. blō; 2. blou]. O.E. *blāwan*, M.E. *blōwen*, Gmc. **blǣwan*, fr. Aryan base **bhlē-*, 'blow, swell, puff up' &c.; cp. Lat. *flā-re*; no doubt ultimately connected w. base discussed under **bloom, blossom,** & w. that in **blow (IV.)** **A.** intrans. **1.** (of wind, air &c.) To move, stir, produce current or gust: (impers.) *it is blowing very hard*; otherwise with *wind* or *air* as subject: *the wind blows from the east* &c. Phr. *to blow great guns*, of a violent gale. **2.** To expel air forcibly from mouth or nose. Phrs. *to puff and blow*, to pant, labour in breathing; *to blow hot and cold*, keep changing one's opinions or intentions, alternately praise and blame. **B.** trans. **1.** To drive air from one's lungs into a wind instrument, sound it: *to blow a trumpet.* Phr. *to blow one's own trumpet*, boast, praise oneself. **2.** To drive air mechanically into a fire, or organ-pipes: *blow the bellows*, *blow (up) the fire*; *blow an organ* (by means of bellows). **3.** To clear by driving air through: esp. **a** *to blow one's nose*; **b** *to blow an egg*, expel contents by blowing through small hole made in shell. **4.** Mild oath (only in imperat.): *blow it* &c. = confound it &c.; or in P.P. *I'm blowed if I will* &c. (P.P. always *blown* except in this expression). **C.** With various adverbs and prepositions. *Blow over*, (intrans., fig., of misfortune, rumours &c.) to pass away, be forgotten. *Blow out*, extinguish with puff of air (of candles &c.); (trans. and intrans.) to puff up, inflate, distend (of effects of food); special usage: *blow out one's brains* or *blow one's brains out*, kill oneself by shooting in the head. *Blow up*, (trans. and intrans.) (i.) to explode; cause to explode, destroy by means of explosives; (ii.) to pump air into, inflate, pneumatic tire of motor-car or bicycle; (iii.) (slang) to scold, take to task. *Blow upon*, to discredit; take away charm or interest of anything.

blow (II.), n., fr. prec. Airing; whiff, taste, of fresh air: *to go for a blow on the cliffs.*

blow (III.), n. Origin doubtful, not recorded before 15th cent.; possibly fr. **blow (I.)**, starting w. idea of a violent gust of wind; cp. Fr. use of *coup*, 'stroke, blow', in *coup de vent*, *coup de poing*, *coup de destin* &c., though here the meaning 'blow' in general sense is the starting-point. **1. a** A violent stroke, knock, from fist, weapon, or tool, deliberately given; or **b** violent collision, sudden impact, between two objects, one or both of which are in motion: *a blow from a sword*; *blows of a hammer on an anvil*; *blow from a falling stone.* Phrs. *at one blow*, with single stroke, by single action; *come to blows*, begin fighting; *exchange blows*, fight; *without striking a blow*, without effort; *strike a blow for*, help; *strike a blow against*, oppose, try to prevent. **2.** (fig.) Misfortune, sudden disagreeable shock, disaster, disappointment: *a blow to one's hopes, plans* &c.

blow (IV.), vb. intrans. O.E. *blōwan*, 'to flower, bloom, flourish', O.H.G. *bluojan*, Mod. Germ. *blühen*, 'bloom', connected w. **bloom & blossom,** fr. Gmc. base **blō-(w-)*, Aryan **bhlō-*, 'sprout' &c. Cp. also **blood.** O.E. *blāwan*, 'blow', of wind, is ultimately connected, though fr. a different grade, Gmc. **blǣ-(w-)*, Aryan **bhlē-*, of same stem. The differentiation of meaning, as of form, is exceedingly early. To bloom, blossom, put forth flowers.

blow-ball, n. Head of dandelion in seed.

blower, n. [1. blṓer; 2. blóuə]. **blow (I.)** & **-er.** Plate of metal which can be drawn down in front of a grate to create draught.

blow-fly, n. Species of fly to which the meat-fly or bluebottle belongs.

blow-hole, n. Aperture in whale's head, through which it spouts water.

blown, adj. [1. blōn; 2. bloun], fr. P.P. of **blow (I.)**. O.E. *blāwen*, M.E. *blōwen.* Breathless, out of breath from violent exertion.

blow-pipe, n. **a** Pipe through which stream of air is kept playing on a flame so as to increase its intensity; used by plumbers in soldering; **b** long pipe used by some savage tribes, through which a dart is driven by air from the lips.

blowy, adj. [1. blṓi; 2. blóui]. **blow (I.)** & **-y.** Gusty, windy.

blowzy, adj. [1. blóuzi; 2. bláuzi]. Origin unknown. Slatternly, untidy, frumpish (of a sluttish woman).

blub, vb. [1. blub; 2. blab]. Shortened form of **blubber (I.)**.

blubber (I.), vb. intrans. [1. blúber; 2. blábə]. Origin unknown; found as *blober* in M.E., perh. imitative. Schoolboy word meaning to weep, cry, esp. loudly.

blubber (II.), n. M.E. *blober*, 'bubble, foam', perh. imitative. Fat of the whale.

blubber (III.), adj. See prec. (of lips only) Thick, swelled, protruding, as a negro's.

bluchers, n. pl. [1. blo͞ocherz; 2. blū́tʃəz]. Old-fashioned boots which came half-way up the calf. Called after the Prussian Field-Marshal Blücher.

bludgeon, n. & vb. trans. [1. blújun; 2. bládžən]. Origin unknown. **a** n. Stout, heavy stick or cudgel; **b** vb., to use this upon someone, to belabour with heavy weapon so as to injure severely.

blue (I.), adj. [1. blo͞o; 2. blū]. M.E. *blew*, fr. Fr. *bleu*, itself a Gmc. loan-word, cp. O.H.G. *blao.* The word *blǣ-* occurs in O.E. in the compound *blǣ-hǣwen*, 'blue'. The Gmc. base, in spite of the difference of meaning, is cogn. w. Lat. *flāvus*, 'yellow, gold-coloured'; further relations of this base are very doubtful. Ancient colour-words are very variable in meaning when distributed among the different tribes of Aryan speakers. Nothing as a rule is more difficult than to ascertain the precise shade of colour intended even in modern descriptions, unless there be comparison w. some natural object whose colour is more or less fixed, but even that may vary in different lights. Another Gmc. cogn. of *blue* is O.N. *blār*, wh. means 'livid, leaden-hued'. **1.** Any of the various shades of that colour seen in the sky on a clear, sunny day, and, in consequence, in the sea also under certain atmospheric conditions; applied to the pale, greyish, misty shade of distant hills: *the blue hills of Sussex*; also to wreaths of smoke from a wood-fire &c. Various shades designated as *pale blue*, *bright blue*, *cornflower blue*, *dark blue*, *blue-black* &c. Phrs. *to look blue*, disconcerted, dismayed, ill; *in a blue funk*, very much frightened; *till all is blue*, continuously, for very long time; *blue blood*, aristocratic birth; *once in a blue moon*, very rarely; *blue water school*, those who insist on the necessity of a strong navy; *true blue*, loyal to a good cause; *blue ruin*, bad, deleterious gin. **2.** Indecent, obscene (of stories, conversation).

blue (II.), n., fr. prec. The colour of blue; specif. **1.** The sky, esp. in *a bolt from the blue*, (lit.) thunderbolt from the sky; (fig.) anything unforeseen, unexpected, startling. **2. a** Person who plays cricket, football &c. for Oxford or Cambridge University, or who rows in the inter-university boat-race or represents university in athletics: *to be a blue*; **b** the fact of being a member of the principal cricket or football team of one of the universities, or of being one of the crew who row in the boat-race: *to get one's blue.* **3.** *The blues*, esp. *a fit of*, melancholia, extreme depression of spirits (colloq.) **4.** *The Blues*, n., Royal Horse Guards (Blue), from colour of their uniform. **5.** Kind of blue powder used by laundresses in their work.

blue (III.), vb. trans. **1.** (fr. prec.) To treat (laundry) with blue. **2.** Prob. corrupt. of **blew,** Pret. of **blow (I.)**, in sense of 'to scatter'. (slang and colloq.) To squander, waste, spend foolishly (money or other property).

Bluebeard, n. [1. blo͞obērd; 2. blū́biəd]. Person who makes away with several wives; from personage in Perrault's story of the name.

bluebell, n. [1. blo͞obel; 2. blū́bel]. A flower; name applied (esp. in Scotland) to the harebell, a variety of wild campanula; and, in England, to the wild blue hyacinth.

blue-book, n. Official report, or document of any kind, published by authority of Parliament, from colour of paper cover.

blue-bonnet, n. Highlander, esp. Highland warrior, from head-dress.

bluebottle, n. [1. bloōbotl; 2. blúbətl]. Large, buzzing fly with a blue body; the blow-fly.

blue-coat boy, n. Pupil of the *Blue-coat School*, or *Christ's Hospital*, from colour of long-skirted coat worn by them.

blue gum, n. Eucalyptus tree.

bluejacket, n. [1. bloōjaket; 2. blúdžækit]. Seaman belonging to Royal Navy.

blue john, n. (metal.) Purple fluorspar.

blue light(s), n. Firework used in signalling.

Blue Mantle, n. Heraldic title; one of the Pursuivants of Arms, instituted by Edward III. as additional officer of the Order of the Garter.

blue mould, n. Kind of mildew or fungus, esp. on cheese.

blueness, n. [1. bloōnes; 2. blúnis]. **blue** (I.) & **-ness**. Quality of being blue.

Blue Peter, n. (orig. *repeater*) Blue flag with white square in centre, hoisted when a ship is about to sail.

blue pill, n. Pill the medicinal ingredient of which is mercury.

blue ribbon, n. Order of the Garter; hence, any recognized and coveted distinction.

bluestocking, n. [1. bloōstoking; 2. blústəkiŋ]. Learned, pedantic lady. Name given in 18th cent. to clubs of learned and literary ladies and a few men, which met to enjoy improving conversation. Some of the male members wore blue stockings instead of customary black silk, to show contempt for convention.

blue stone, n. Vitriol.

bluethroat, n. [1. bloōthrōt; 2. blúþrout]. Small bird akin to *redstart*, so called from colour of its breast.

blue whale, n. The rorqual.

bluff (I.), adj. [1. bluf; 2. blaf]. Etymol. unknown. **a** (of cliffs, or ships' bows &c.) Having broad, steep, perpendicular front; **b** (of manners or persons) rough, **gruff**, rather rude, but honest, hearty, frank.

bluff (II.), n., fr. prec. Steep headland.

bluff (III.), vb. trans. Origin unknown. Originally used in certain card games, esp. poker; now, generally, to deceive, give false impression, hoodwink, humbug, bamboozle.

bluff (IV.), n., fr. prec. Deception, deliberate giving of false impression.

bluffer, n. [1. blúfer; 2. bláfə]. **bluff (III.)** & **-er**. One who bluffs in order to deceive others.

bluffness, n. [1. blúfnes; 2. bláfnis]. **bluff** (I.) & **-ness**. **a** Steepness (of a cliff); **b** rough honesty (of manner).

bluish, adj. [1. bloōish; 2. blúiʃ]. **blue** (I.) & **-ish**. Somewhat blue in colour; verging on, tinged with, this colour.

blunder (I.), vb. intrans. & trans. [1. blúnder; 2. blándə]. Etymol. doubtful; M.E. *blondren* (in different sense); perh. connected w. O.E. *blandan*, 'mix'. See **blend (I.)** & **blind** (I.). **1.** intrans. **a** To move hesitatingly, clumsily; to stumble over or against objects in one's path; esp. *to blunder about, along, against, into*; **b** to err in judgement, speech, or action, say or do the wrong thing: *he blundered badly in answering the questions put to him.* **2.** trans. To spoil, upset, mismanage (plans, negotiations); do work in clumsy, inefficient manner: *the delicate negotiation was hopelessly blundered by the minister.*

blunder (II.), n., fr. prec. A mistake, error; ill-judged, clumsy speech or action: *there are many blunders in this translation*; *he committed a blunder in refusing to receive the deputation*; *the general's manœuvre was a tactical blunder.*

blunderbuss, n. [1. blúnderbus; 2. blándəbas]. Altered fr. Du. *donderbus*, lit. 'thunder box', *bus* is cogn. w. Germ. *büchse*. See **thunder** & **box**. Short heavy flintlock gun with very wide bore, and sometimes a bell-shaped muzzle, used in 17th and 18th cents.

blunderer, n. [1. blúnderer; 2. blándərə]. **blunder** (I.) & **-er**. One who blunders; a clumsy, tactless, unskilful person.

blundering, adj. [1. blúndering; 2. blándəriŋ], fr. Pres. Part. of **blunder** (I.). Clumsy, tactless, lacking in taste, judgement, or skill.

blunderingly, adv. Prec. & **-ly**. In a blundering manner; clumsily, tactlessly.

blunt (I.), adj. [1. blunt; 2. blant]. Origin unknown. **a** Dull, lacking in point or edge (of piercing and cutting weapons and tools); **b** (fig.) obtuse, lacking in finesse and delicacy (of the understanding, intelligence, feelings); **c** (fig.) lacking in refinement and polish; abrupt, downright; outspoken (of men, manners, mode of address &c.).

blunt (II.), n. (vulg. slang). Coin, money.

blunt (III.), vb. trans., fr. **blunt** (I.). **a** To take the edge or point off (tool or weapon); **b** (fig.) to render insensitive, less acute (of the feelings and intelligence).

bluntly, adv. [1. blúntli; 2. blántli]. **blunt** (I.) & **-ly**. In a blunt manner; (usually fig.) in an abrupt, rough, outspoken manner.

bluntness, n. See prec. & **-ness**. The quality of being blunt in any of senses given under **blunt** (I.).

blur (I.), n. [1. blėr; 2. blā]. Origin unknown. Suggested connexion w. **blear** & **blot** unhelpful, as their origin is equally obscure. A smear, a blot, spot, or blemish which renders outlines of writing or of a picture indistinct; a misty, indistinct view.

blur (II.), vb. trans., fr. prec. **a** To smear or blot writing, or a picture; **b** to render indistinct or dim, any prospect or view: *thick wreaths of smoke blurred the landscape*; **c** to efface from, or weaken image of anything in the memory.

blurb, n. [1. blėrb; 2. blāb]. Invented word. A publisher's laudatory announcement of a book, often printed on the jacket with which it is issued.

blurred, adj. [1. blėrd; 2. blād]. P.P. of **blur** (II.). Dimmed, indistinct, smeary.

blurt, vb. trans. [1. blėrt; 2. blāt]. Origin doubtful; possibly imitative. To utter something suddenly and without deliberation; reveal a secret involuntarily and indiscreetly; usually *to blurt out.*

blush (I.), vb. intrans. [1. blush; 2. blaʃ]. O.E. *blyscan*, 'to blush, grow red'. Etymol. very doubtful; possibly related to **blaze**; cp. O.E. *blysa*, 'torch, blaze', wh. may be connected w. O.E. *blæse*, 'torch, fire', though it is difficult to account for the vowels. **1.** To grow red; (esp. of the face) to be suffused with a reddish glow, under stress of strong emotion. **2.** (fig., extended sense from above) To be ashamed: *to blush for very shame*; *I blush for you*; *I blush to think of such conduct* &c.; '*Do good by stealth and blush to find it fame*' (Pope); '*When statesmen, heroes, kings in dust repose, Whose sons shall blush their fathers were thy foes*' (Pope).

blush (II.), n., fr. prec. Rosy glow which mantles in the cheeks of sensitive and modest persons under stress of strong emotions, such as shame or shocked modesty, indignation &c. Phrs. *to put to the blush*, cause to blush, from modesty &c.; *at the first blush*, at first sight; *spare my blushes*, don't flatter.

blushing, adj. [1. blúshing; 2. bláʃiŋ], fr. Pres. Part. of **blush** (I.). Rosy, covered with blushes, hence modest: *blushing bride.*

blushingly, adv. Prec. & **-ly**. In a shamefaced manner; modestly.

bluster (I.), vb. intrans. [1. blúster; 2. blástə]. Origin unknown. **1.** (of winds and waves) To rage, storm violently and boisterously. **2.** (fig., of persons) To hector, scold, threaten, in a bullying manner; complain in a noisy excited manner; often *to bluster at.*

bluster (II.), n., fr. prec. **a** Noise of stormy wind or waves; **b** (fig.) noisy, fussy, excited complaints, or scolding &c.; empty threats.

blusterer, n. [1. blústerer; 2. blástərə]. Noisy, fussy, excitable, scolding person.

blustering, adj. [1. blústering; 2. blástəriŋ]. Noisy, stormy, violent (of wind &c.); given to loud complaints, threats &c. (of persons).

blusteringly, adv. Prec. & **-ly**. In a blustering manner.

bo!, interj. [1. bō; 2. bou]. Imitative. Exclamation used to startle or frighten someone. Phr. *can't say bo! to a goose*, of person very timid or inarticulately shy.

boa, n. [1. báw-a, bóa; 2. bɔ́ə, bóuə]. S. Am. word. **1. a** Genus of large snakes found in tropical America and Madagascar, sometimes 12 ft. in length; also *boa constrictor*, from its habit of winding itself round its prey and crushing it to death in its folds; **b** python. **2.** Wrap of fur or other material which ladies wind round their throats; presumably so called from fancied resemblance to a snake.

Boanerges, n. [1. bōanérjēz; 2. bouənə́dʒiz]. Heb., 'sons of thunder' (Mk. iii. 17). Applied to a fiery orator with a powerful voice.

boar, n. [1. bōr; 2. bɔ̄]. O.E. *bār*, M.E. *boor* &c.; O.H.G. *pēr*, *bēr*, fr. Gmc. base **bair-*. Origin unknown. The plausible identification w. Lat. *ferus*, 'wild', wh. wd. make the boar 'the wild, savage beast', suggested by many of the dictionaries, breaks down, since not only do the vowels present difficulties, but *ferus* is shown by the Gk. cogn. *thḗr*, see **theriac**, & Lith. *žweris*, 'wild beast', to be fr. Aryan **gʷheros*, wh. at once rules out any identification of these words w. the Gmc. form. No more happy is the proposed identification w. **bear** (the animal). The vowels here again offer serious difficulty. **1. a** The male, ungelded, domestic pig; **b** the wild swine, esp. the male. **2.** Its flesh, esp. of the *boar's head.*

board (I.), n. [1. bord; 2. bɔ̄d]. O.E. *bord*, 'plank, table, shield' &c., also in O.S., O.H.G. *bort*, Goth. *-baurd*, O.N. *borð*. Cp. further the cognates O.E. *bred*, 'board, tablet', O.H.G. *bret*, 'board, shield', Mod. Germ. *brett*, 'board'. Beyond this we cannot at present carry the etymol. See also **border**. **1.** Plank, strip of wood, considerably longer than its width, and rather thin in proportion to length. (Technically, in builders' and joiners' terminology, a *board* is at least 4½ in. broad, and not more than 2½ in. thick. If these dimensions are changed, the piece of wood receives another name.) Phr. *to tread the boards*, be on the stage, be an actor. Many derived senses: **2.** Tablet of wood on legs; table, at which various kinds of work are carried out, and food is eaten. The sense *table* preserved in certain contexts and combinations: *hospitable board*; *groaning board*, plentifully spread table; *above board*, (lit.) on the table, openly (orig. of cards); *sweep the board*, (lit.) take all cards or stakes on the table; (fig.), be very successful, win. Hence, **3.** food received at a board, meals, esp. in sense of meals regularly taken at same house, for stipulated payment: *board and lodging*, food and house-room; cp. *board-wages* below. **4.** Thin slabs of wood covered with leather or cloth, on which certain games, such as chess, draughts, dice &c. are played. **5.** Official, legally constituted body with certain administrative functions, so called from meeting round a table or board: *Board of Admiralty, Trade*; *School Board*; *Board of Directors, Guardians* &c. **6.** (naut.) **a** The side of a ship: *to go by the board*, (of masts &c.) to fall over; (also fig. of plans &c.) to be abandoned, to fail completely; *on board*, aboard, also of train &c.; **b** line of a ship's course between tack and tack.

board (II.), vb. trans. & intrans., fr. prec. **1.** To cover with boards; *to board up*, close by nailing boards across, a window, door &c. **2.** To supply with daily meals; (intrans.) *to board out*, take one's meals in different house from that in which one resides; trans., place (children) in a house or institution other than their homes, where t y are lodged and fed. Phr. *to board wit* receive board and lodging at a person's house in return for agreed payment. **3.** (derived from **board** (I.), **4**; colloq., and gen. pass.) To examine an officer of army or navy before a medical board: *he was boarded yesterday and passed for general service.* **4.** To go into, go on board, a ship, whether for peaceful purposes, or, in a naval action, to enter an enemy ship in order to take possession.

boarder, n. [1. bórder; 2. bɔ́də]. Prec. & **-er.** One who boards at another person's house; a schoolboy who lives at school, contrasted with *day boy.*

boarding, n. [1. bórding; 2. bɔ́diŋ], fr. **board** (I.) & **-ing.** Collection, construction, arrangement, of boards for any purpose.

boarding-house, n. **a** One at which visitors may reside and obtain daily meals in return for payment; **b** house in connexion with a public school where a certain number of boys live in charge of a master.

boarding-school, n. One where boys or girls live entirely, and are housed and fed, during term time, in distinction to a *day school.*

board meeting, n. Meeting of a board of directors &c.

board school, n. Elementary school, administered by a school board; now obsolete.

board-wages, n. See **board** (I.), 3, & **wages.** Wages paid to servants while their masters are away from home, which include cost of food &c.

boar-hound, n. **boar** & **hound.** A large type of hound, of various types, originally specially bred for hunting the wild boar.

boast (I.), n. [1. bōst; 2. boust]. Found in M.E., but etymol. very doubtful. **1.** Vain, arrogant, self-glorifying assertion; self-glorification: *at the beginning of the war, the enemy's boast was that he was invincible.* **2.** Cause for satisfaction, something of which one is justly proud: *Nelson's proud boast, when dying, was that he had done his duty.* Phr. *to make a boast of*, to claim proudly or boastfully. **3.** A stroke off the side wall in tennis.

boast (II.), vb. intrans. & trans., fr. prec. **1.** intrans. **a** To praise oneself; tell stories to one's own credit; extol in vain and arrogant manner, and rather in excess of their deserts, one's own abilities, possessions, position, or anything connected with oneself: *he boasts too much*; *he is always boasting of his house and pictures*; *he boasted of having a fine voice*; Phr. *not much to boast of*, inferior, second-rate; **b** (special usage) to have the advantage of possessing: *the town boasts of a fine church*; *many Oxford colleges can boast of beautiful gardens.* **2.** trans. To assert arrogantly one's superiority to other people; proclaim in a vain manner that one can do certain things, possesses certain aptitudes, abilities &c. (usually *boast that*): *he boasts that he is one of the best shots in the country*; *to boast that one can sing, ride, dance well* &c.; (also in P.P.) *his boasted wealth.*

boaster, n. [1. bōster; 2. bóustə]. Prec. & **-er.** One who boasts, a vain bragging fellow, a braggart.

boastful, adj. [1. bōstfool; 2. bóustful]. **boast** (I.) & **-ful.** **a** (of persons) Inclined to boast, fond of boasting, vainglorious; **b** (of language &c.) expressed in vainglorious words.

boastfully, adv. Prec. & **-ly.** In a boastful manner.

boastfulness, n. See prec. & **-ness.** Quality of being boastful.

boat (I.), n. [1. bōt; 2. bout]. O.E. *bāt*, 'ship, boat', O.N. *beitr*; not found in other languages except as a loan fr. Engl.; etymol. unknown. **1.** Hollow receptacle, whose essential property is that it floats in water and sustains a considerable weight; formerly constructed of wooden planks fastened to a wooden frame, recently also of steel or iron plates on an iron frame. The word is a generic term for water-craft of every description, large or small, whether used on the sea, on rivers or l kes, and no matter how propelled, whether by oars, a single paddle, a pole, steam or in ernal combustion engine, or electricity. Phrs. *to be (all) in the same boat*, in the same circumstances, sharing same risks &c.; *to burn one's boats*, commit oneself irrevocably to a line of action; *the university, college, boat*, the crew who represent the college, university, in boat-races. **2.** Various boat-shaped articles, e.g. **a** a small silver or porcelain receptacle for holding sauce, gravy &c. at table: *sauce-boat*; **b** a boat-shaped swing for two persons at fairs, *swing-boat* or *boat-swing.*

boat (II.), vb. intrans., fr. prec. To go on the water in a boat, esp. for pleasure; travel in a boat: *to boat down the river*; *to go boating.*

boat-bill, n. Name of a large S. American wading bird, allied to the herons, whose bill resembles an upturned boat.

boater, n. [1. bōter; 2. bóutə]. Trade name for hard, flat-brimmed straw hat.

boatful, n. [1. bōtfool; 2. bóutful]. **boat** (I.) & **-ful.** The crew and passengers of a boat or ship.

boat-hook, n. Hook at end of a pole, used to draw a small boat in to shore, or steady it while entering or leaving &c.

boat-house, n. Shed in which small boats are kept; usually either opening on to a wharf or platform sloping towards the water, or constructed over a small creek, or cutting in a river-bank, so that the boats rest in the water under cover.

boating, n. [1. bōting; 2. bóutiŋ]. **boat** (II.) & **-ing.** The sport or amusement of rowing; *boating man*, one who rows in boat-races.

boatman, n. [1. bōtman; 2. bóutmən]. **a** One who lets out boats for hire; **b** person who forms one of the crew of a small boat; one who manages, is in chief charge of, a small boat; **c** a freshwater insect, *water-boatman*, which uses its legs as paddles in swimming on surface of water.

boat-race, n. Competition, trial of speed between crews of two or more specially built rowing-boats; specif., *The Boat-race*, annual race between the rowing crews of the universities of Oxford and Cambridge.

boatswain, n. [1. bōsn; 2. bóusn]. O.E. *bātswegen*, 'boatman', of wh. *swegen* is Late O.E. form of O.N. *sveinn*, 'boy, servant'. See **swain.** Ship's officer who superintends crew on deck, boats, rigging &c., and calls the men to duty by sounding a whistle.

boat train, n. One timed to reach a port in such time that persons travelling by it may catch an out-going steamer; one which brings passengers arriving by steamer at a port to London or other important centre.

bob (I.), vb. intrans. & trans. [1. bob; 2. bɔb]. Etymol. unknown. **1.** intrans. To move rapidly up and down: *to bob up and down, about* (used of any such movement, but esp. of any floating object which appears and disappears on surface of the water). Special uses: *bob up*, of speaker rising hastily and frequently to address meeting; to appear suddenly and unexpectedly after prolonged absence; *bob at someone*, to curtsey, esp. in a rustic ungainly manner. **2.** To go in a bob-sleigh, q.v. **3.** trans. **a** To dock (the tail of horse or dog); **b** to cut (the hair of women) short in form of a mop. Cp. **bob** (III.) **4.** To catch with lips at (cherries held suspended from teeth by the stalk).

bob (II.), n., fr. prec. A jerky, springing movement; a clumsy curtsey.

bob (III.), n., fr. **bob** (I.). Various uses: **a** a short wig, also *bob wig*, contrasted with *full-bottomed* one; **b** any small round mass at the end of something, e.g. weight on pendulum of a clock, on tail of a kite; **c** docked tail of a horse or dog; bobbed hair of a woman.

bob (IV.), n. Etymol. doubtful. Term in bell-ringing, applied to changes in long peals; *bob major, minor, royal* &c.

bob (V.), n. Etymol. doubtful. (slang) A shilling; (does not take *-s* in pl.) *five bob* &c.

bob (VI.), n. Perh. fr. personal name *Robert.* **a** *Dry bob*, boy who plays cricket; *wet bob*, one who rows (school expressions at Eton); **b** *light bob*, old name for soldier in light infantry companies or regiments.

bobbed, adj. [1. bobd; 2. bɔbd]. P.P. of **bob** (I.), **2.** **a** Docked, of tail of horse &c.; **b** cut short like a mop, of woman's hair or of woman with hair so cut.

bobbery, n. [1. bóberi; 2. bɔ́bəri]. Anglo-Indian. Said to be fr. Hindu exclamation of surprise or grief, *bāp-rē*, 'O father' (cp. Engl. colloq. *my aunt!*); hence, that which provokes the exclamation, a disturbance, row.

bobbery-pack, n. Pack of hounds of different breeds, or no breed, used by the British in India and other parts of the East to hunt jackals; hence, a scratch pack.

bobbin, n. [1. bóbin; 2. bɔ́bin]. Fr. *bobine*, 'reel' (for thread). Origin unknown. **a** Cylinder for holding, and paying out, thread, wire, string &c.; reel, spool; **b** small ball of wood hung from a string, which lifts an old-fashioned door-latch.

bobbish, adj. [1. bóbish; 2. bɔ́biʃ]. Connected w. **bob** (I.), vb., & **-ish.** (slang) Lively, cheerful, in good condition.

bobby, n. [1. bóbi; 2. bɔ́bi], fr. Sir Robert Peel. (slang) A policeman.

bobolink, n. [1. bóbolingk; 2. bɔ́bəliŋk]. Said to be fr. *Bob Lincoln*, wh. note of bird is supposed to resemble. Migratory bird of N. America, otherwise called *rice bunting.*

bobsleigh, n. [1. bóbslā; 2. bɔ́bslei]. See **sleigh** (I.), & cp. **bob** (I.). Sledge carrying three or four persons, which runs down snow- or ice-covered incline by its own weight, steered by a movable portion in front, worked by small wheel; used for winter sports in Switzerland.

bobstays, n. [1. bóbstāz; 2. bɔ́bsteiz]. See **bob** (I.) & **stay** (III.). (naut.) The ropes or stays fastened to the cutwater, which hold the bowsprit of a sailing-vessel downwards.

bobtail, adj. & n. [1. bóbtāl; 2. bɔ́bteil]. **bob** (I.) & **tail.** **a** adj. Having the tail cut short, or docked; **b** n., an animal so treated. Vulgarly, of garments, esp. coats cut very short, or outgrown. Phr. *tag, rag, and bobtail*, disreputable rabble; crowd of undistinguished persons.

bob-tailed, adj. Bobtail, adj.

Boche, n. [1. bosh; 2. bɔʃ]. Origin doubtful. (French army slang) A German.

bode, vb. trans. [1. bōd; 2. boud]. O.E. *bodian*, 'announce, foretell', fr. **bud-ōjan*; formed fr. that grade of the stem wh. occurs in O.E. *bod-en*, fr. **bud-an*, P.P. of *bēodan*, 'to announce'. See **bid** & **bead.** To portend, signify, be an omen of (good or ill): *this bodes you no good*; *that bodes a happy ending.*

bodeful, adj. [1. bōdfool; 2. bóudful], fr. prec. or obs. n. & **-ful.** Ominous, threatening.

bodega, n. [1. bodéga; 2. bɔdígə]. Span., fr. Gk. *apothḗkē*, 'place where things are stored, or laid up; a granary, magazine'. See **apothecary.** A wine-shop, where wine is sold on draught and consumed on the premises.

bodice, n. [1. bódis; 2. bɔ́dis]. Orig. pl. (pair of) *bodies*, cp. *stays.* See **body.** Woman's garment covering upper part of person above waist; usually rather close-fitting, with or without sleeves; applied both to a garment worn outside and one worn underneath the outer body-coverings.

-bodied, adj. [1. bódid; 2. bɔ́did]. P.P. of **body** (I.) & **-ed.** Only in compounds: *able-bodied, full-bodied* &c.

bodikin, n. [1. bódikin; 2. bɔ́dikin]. Dimin. of **body.** Entirely obsolete oath; 17th cent. In full, *'Od's bodikin*, '*God's*' &c.

bodiless, adj. [1. bódiles; 2. bɔ́dilis]. **body** & **-less.** Disembodied, divided from the body.

bodily (I.), adj. [1. bódili; 2. bɔ́dili], fr. **body** & **-ly.** Belonging to, concerned with, the body; physical as contrasted with spiritual: *bodily fear*, fear for, of, injury to, the body; *bodily suffering.*

bodily (II.), adv., see prec. **a** In the flesh: *Christ is said to be bodily present in the Blessed Sacrament*; **b** in person, actually: *he came bodily and defended himself against all imputations*; **c** as a whole: *the building was transported bodily to another place.*

boding, adj. [1. bṓding; 2. bóudiŋ], fr. Pres. Part. of **bode**. Ominous; filled with promise of evil: *boding care.*

bodingly, adv. Prec. & **-ly**. In an ominous manner.

bodkin, n. [1. bódkin; 2. bɔ́dkin]. M.E. *boydekin*, 'dagger'. Origin unknown. An instrument, like a very large needle, with blunted or rounded point, for running tape &c. through a loop or hem. Phr. *to sit, travel, bodkin*, of person wedged tightly between two others in a carriage &c.

body (**I.**), n. [1. bódi; 2. bɔ́di]. Exclusively Engl. as regards usage, prob. also as regards the word itself. The etymol. is very uncertain. O.E. *bodiġ*, M.E. *bodi*, have the same sense as their present-day descendant in its primary meaning; beyond that all is obscure. The suggestion has been made that the word is ultimately the Gk. *apothḗkē*, 'storehouse' (see **bodega & apothecary**), through Med. Lat. *butica*, whence also Mod. Germ. *bottich*, 'cask', O.H.G. *botahha*, see **boot** (**I.**). This is a pure speculation, and so far, quite unsupported by any evidence. It is not impossible. More cannot be said in its favour. **1.** The physical organism, corporeal frame, as a whole, of man and animals: '*Your bodies are the temples of the Holy Ghost*'; *if we wish to have healthy bodies we must live healthily and regularly*; *heirs of one's body*, descendants. **2.** The flesh, the physical as distinct from, and contrasted with, the spiritual and intellectual part of human beings: *the Inquisition burnt and destroyed the bodies of heretics in the hope of saving their souls.* Phrs. *to keep body and soul together*, just keep alive; *absent in body, present in spirit.* **3.** The trunk, upper part of the human frame which contains the lungs, heart, and the digestive organs, but exclusive of the head and the limbs: *to be wounded in the body*; *to run a man through the body.* **4.** Dead body, corpse: *several bodies were washed ashore from the wreck*; *Nelson's body was brought to England and buried with great pomp.* **5.** Short, tight-fitting garment, covering the body in sense **3.** Same as *bodice.* **6. a** The main portion of a structure, as distinct from appendages: *the body of a church, hall, ship, aeroplane* &c.; **b** main portion of a literary work, distinct from preface, introduction, notes, appendix &c. **7. a** Group, collection, assembly of human beings: *large bodies of the unemployed were gathered in different parts of the city*; **b** specif., organized assembly of persons with legal status and legislative or administrative or other functions: *body politic*; *legislative body*; *body of electors*; *learned bodies.* **8.** Human being: (colloq.) *a decent honest body*; *poor body.* **9.** Mass, piece of matter, a substance distinct from others: *the heavenly bodies*, sun, moon, stars; *a metallic body.* **10.** Consistency, substance, comparative density (of wine, colour &c.): *a wine of full body.*

body (**II.**), vb. trans., fr. prec. To exhibit in outward form, typify; generally *body forth.*

bodyguard, n. [1. bódigard; 2. bɔ́digād]. **body** (**I.**) & **guard**. **1.** A military corps, attached to and guarding the person of the sovereign, his representative, or other high authority: *His Majesty's Body Guard of the Yeomen of the Guard* &c. **2. a** Escort, force of police &c. watching and protecting a person's life; **b** body of faithful followers, supporters &c.: *his old pupils acted as a bodyguard.*

body-snatcher, n. **body** (**I.**) & **snatch**, 'to seize & **-er**. Name given to one of the 'resurrection men', who stole corpses from graves to sell to anatomists for dissection.

Boer, n. [1. bōor, bōr; 2. buə, bɔ̄ə]. Du. word for 'peasant, farmer', cp. Germ. *bauer*; cogn. w. O.E. *ġebūr*, 'peasant' (see **boor** & also **neighbour**), & cp. O.E. *būr*, 'dwelling' (see **bower & byre**); the Gmc. base **bu-*, whence all these words come, means 'to dwell; to till the land, to plant', cp. O.H.G. *buan* w. these meanings. The ultimate source is Aryan **bhū-*, 'to be, become, spring, produce', whence also Gk. *phûma*, 'growth', *phúsis*, 'nature' (see **physic**); Lat. *fui*, 'I was', *futūrus*, 'about to be' (see **future**); also Scrt. *bhūmi*, 'earth', *bhūti*, 'existence'. See **be**. S. African colonist of Dutch origin.

bog, n. & vb. [1. bog; 2. bɔg], fr. Gael. or Ir. *bog*, 'soft'. **a** n. Soft, wet, marshy, miry ground; a swamp, quicksand; **b** vb. (usually pass.), *to be bogged*, to become stuck in a bog, or in miry ground.

bog butter, n. Greasy mineral substance found in Irish bogs.

bogey (**I.**), n. [1. bṓgi; 2. bóugi]. Origin doubtful. See **boggle**. Ghost, evil spirit, bugbear; something of which one has special dislike or horror; imaginary terror.

bogey (**II.**), n. Said to be fr. *Colonel Bogey*, an imaginary person; fr. prec. (golf) Number of strokes in which a good player should play a hole or get round a course.

boggle (**I.**), n. [1. bógl; 2. bɔ́gl]. A Scotch word, not much used in Engl.; perh. connected w. base in W. *bwg*, 'ghost'. Goblin, spectre, supernatural visitant.

boggle (**II.**), vb. intrans., fr. prec. (always *boggle at*) To shrink from, have a horror of, make difficulties about, feel scruples concerning something: *he boggled at undertaking fresh responsibility*; *he is not the man to boggle at trifles of that kind.*

bogie, n. [1. bṓgi; 2. bóugi]. Etymol. unknown; occurs first as a Northumbrian word. A wheeled, pivoted framework placed beneath the front of a locomotive or long railway coach, enabling the train to take curves more safely and easily.

bog-myrtle, n. **bog & myrtle**. Popular name of **gale**.

bog-oak, n. **bog & oak**. Oak of ancient date, found buried in peat bogs, of deep black ebony colour, often used for carved ornaments &c.

bog-spavin, n. See **bog & spavin**. Soft swelling or tumour on the inner side of the hock of a horse.

bog-trotter, n. **bog & trotter**. Contemptuous name for an Irishman, as living among bogs.

bogus, adj. [1. bṓgus; 2. bóugəs]. Origin unknown; introduced fr. U.S.A. Sham, not genuine.

bogy. See **bogey** (**I.**).

bohea, n. [1. bōhḗ; 2. bouhī́]. Chinese *Wu-i* [1. booē; 2. buī], name of district. Inferior variety of black China tea.

Bohemian, n. & adj. [1. bōhḗmyan; 2. bouhī́mjən], fr. Fr. *Bohémien*, 'gipsy', orig. meaning inhabitant of Bohemia, where the gipsies were supposed to come from. Unconventional (person), given to free-and-easy mode of life, untrammelled by ordinary rules of social life.

boil (**I.**), n. [1. boil; 2. bɔil]. O.E. *bȳl(e)*, M.E. *bīle*, cogn. w. O.H.G. *būlla*, 'swelling', M.H.G. *biule*, Du. *buil*; Goth. *uf-baul-jan*, 'to puff up', might be connected, but this wd. prohibit the more probable relationship w. Lat. *flēmina*, 'swelling on a joint', wh. is supposed to contain base **bhelēi-* (here **bhlē-*), q.v. under **blow** (**I.**), **blast, bloom** &c., & w. Gk. *phli-mélia*, 'bleeding wounds on horses' feet'. The present form of *boil* no doubt influenced by that of **boil** (**II.**); we shd. expect *bile*. Small inflamed swelling, filled with pus, on neck or other part of the body.

boil (**II.**), vb. intrans. & trans. M.E. *boile*, O. Fr. *boillir*, 'to boil', fr. Lat. *bullīre*, 'boil', connected w. *bulla*, 'bubble', fr. an Aryan base **bwel-*, 'swell', parallel to **bhel-*, w. same meaning, see **bold & ball**. Cp. **bulb**. **A.** intrans. **1. a** To bubble, be agitated, as water is when a certain degree of heat is reached: *water boils at 212 degrees Fahrenheit*; **b** to be in the process of boiling (of liquid or food being cooked): *the potatoes are boiling.* Phrs. *boiling hot*, very hot (of food or anything heated by fire; also of weather &c.); *to keep the pot boiling*, to make a living somehow; cp. *potboiler.* **2.** To be violently agitated, churned up, made to bubble, as the sea through action of wind, or swiftly flowing river among rocks, or in a narrow channel &c.: *boiling waves, waters* &c. **3.** (fig.) To be violently excited by some powerful emotion such as anger, indignation: *to boil with rage*; Phr. *to make one's blood boil. Boil away*, (of water) to evaporate in steam; *boil over*, **a** (of liquids) to reach boiling-point and overflow vessel in which they are being boiled; **b** (fig.) to be unable to restrain one's indignation &c. **B.** trans. **1.** To submit liquids to great heat; cause liquids to bubble by raising temperature. **2.** To cook food in a vessel containing water which is kept boiling: *to boil eggs, vegetables* &c. **3.** To submit anything to great heat by immersing in water which is kept boiling: *to boil clothes* (in laundry work); *boil down*, to reduce by boiling.

boil (**III.**), n., fr. prec. Boiling-point; in such Phrs. as *bring to, keep on, at, the boil.*

boiler, n. [1. bóiler; 2. bɔ́ilə]. **boil** (**II.**) & **-er**. **1.** A person who boils something. Chiefly in compounds: *soap-boiler* &c. **2.** Metal vessel in connexion with a furnace in which water is either boiled so as to generate steam (for engines), or in which it is kept hot (for baths, or heating apparatus).

boiling (**I.**), n. [1. bóiling; 2. bɔ́iliŋ]. **boil** (**II.**) & **-ing**. **1.** Act or process of making liquids &c. boil, or of cooking by boiling: *food is often cooked by boiling*; *the skilful boiling of food is a fine art.* **2. a** The whole of a number of things boiled in the same vessel, or by a single act or process: *a boiling of potatoes*; **b** (fig., colloq.) things produced by single process, hence group, party of associated persons or things, esp. *the whole boiling.*

boiling (**II.**), adj., fr. Pres. Part. of **boil** (**II.**). **a** (of liquids) In a state of bubbling from exposure to heat; **b** (lit. and fig. of anything) very hot.

boisterous, adj. [1. bóisterus; 2. bɔ́istərəs]. M.E. *boistous, buistous*, 'rough, clumsy, boisterous'; origin unknown. **a** (of persons) Rude, rough, noisy, exuberant in manner; **b** (of wind, sea, weather &c.) violent, strongly agitated, tempestuous.

boisterously, adv. Prec. & **-ly**. In a rough, boisterous manner.

bolas, n. [1. bṓlas; 2. bóuləs]. Pl. of Span. *bola*, 'ball'. Implement consisting of several heavy balls attached to a thong, used in S. America by the Gauchos for hurling at the legs of horses and cattle to trip them up.

bold, adj. [1. bōld; 2. bould]. O.E. *bāld* (W.S. *beald*), O.H.G. *bald*, O.N. *ballr*, fr. **bald-r*, Goth. *balþei*, 'boldness', *balþs, balþaba*, 'boldly'; possibly fr. Aryan base **bhel-*, 'to swell', q.v. under **ball, billow, belly** &c. **1.** Daring, brave, courageous, stout-hearted. **2.** (in bad sense) Impudent, shameless, immodest, esp. of women: *bold hussy* &c. **3.** Confident, well-assured: *I'll be bold*, or *I make bold, to say* &c., I am sure. **4. a** Prominent, precipitous (of cliffs, promontories &c.); hence, **b** striking, vigorous, emphatic (of drawing, architecture &c.): *bold lines, curves, a bold design.*

bold-faced, adj. **1.** Impudent, lacking in proper modesty. **2.** (typog.) Having conspicuous, heavy face, or style of cutting.

boldly, adv. [1. bṓldli; 2. bóuldli]. **bold & -ly**. **a** In a bold, courageous manner: *to act boldly* &c.; **b** clearly, conspicuously: to *stand out boldly from a background.*

boldness, n. See prec. & **-ness**. **a** Bravery, daring; **b** (in bad sense) effrontery.

bole (**I.**), n. [1. bōl; 2. boul]. M.E. *bōle*, fr. O.N. *bol-r*, 'trunk of a tree', cp. Mod. Germ. *bohle*, 'tree-trunk', cogn. w. Gk. *phálagx*, 'large round piece of wood, log', fr. Aryan stem **bhel-*, 'swell out'. Cp. also **ball, balk, belly** &c. Stem or trunk of a tree.

bole (**II.**), n., fr. Fr. *bol*, 'round mass', Low Lat. *bōlus*, 'lump, clod', fr. Gk. *bōlos*. The latter is cogn. w. Scrt. *glāuš*, 'lump, ball', wh. shows that the Aryan base was **gʷel-*. Another related word is Gk. *bálanos*, 'acorn', see **balaniferous.** Tough red clay, found between layers of basaltic lava, and formed by decay of underlying surface of this.

bolection, n. [1. bōlékshun; 2. boulékʃən]. Origin unknown. (archit.) Portion of a moulding which projects above general surface.

bolero, n. [1. boláro; 2. bəléərou]. Span. **1.** Kind of Spanish dance accompanied by castanets and lively music. **2.** Short female garment or coat reaching to the waist.

boletus, n. [1. bōlétus; 2. boulítəs]. Lat., fr. Gk. *bōlítēs,* 'mushroom, fungus', fr. *bôlos,* 'lump'. See **bole (II.).** A genus of fleshy fungi, growing in woods, often brightly coloured, some being edible.

bolide, n. [1. bólīd; 2. bóulaid]. Gk. *bolís,* genit. *bolíd-os,* 'anything thrown, missile'; connected w. *bállō,* 'I throw', q.v. under **ballistic.** Meteor followed by train of light, often exploding.

boll, n. & vb. [1. bol; 2. bəl]. O.E. *bolla,* 'bowl', M.E. *bolle,* prob. fr. base **bhel-,* 'swell'. Cp. **bole (I.)** & references there given. **1.** n. Round seed-vessel of flax or cotton plant; *boll weevil,* a very destructive small weevil which infects cotton fields. **a.** vb. To form seed pods.

bollard, n. [1. bólard; 2. bóləd]. Prob. **bole (I.)** & **-ard.** Stout post of wood or iron on deck of a ship, or on a landing-stage, around which ropes holding vessels are hitched.

bolo, n. [1. bólō; 2. bóulou]. Span. Long, single-edged knife.

bolometer, n. [1. bōlómeter; 2. boulómitə], fr. Gk. *bolḗ,* 'stroke, blow', fr. *bállein,* 'to throw', see **ballistic,** & **-meter.** (phys.) Instrument for measuring radiant heat.

Bolshevik, n. & adj. [1. bólshevik; 2. bólʃɛvik]. Russ. (pl. *Bolsheviki*), lit. 'one in, those forming a majority', fr. *bolshe,* 'greater, more', for base see second element in **debile;** opposed to *Menshevik;* orig. name given to the party forming a majority at a Russian Socialist conference at Lausanne, 1903. **1.** n. **a** Member of the advanced Communist party of Russia, which established the 'dictatorship of the proletariat' after the revolution of 1917; **b** general name for a Russian Communist or for a Communist or violent revolutionary in any country. **2.** adj. Of, pertaining to, the Bolsheviks or Bolshevism; Bolshevist.

Bolshevism, n. [1. bólshevizm; 2. bólʃɛvizəm]. Prec. & **-ism.** Principles, policy, of the Bolsheviks.

Bolshevist, adj. & n. [1. bólshevist; 2. bólʃɛvist]. See prec. & **-ist. 1.** adj. Of, pertaining to, the Bolsheviks or their policy; communistic, violently revolutionary. **2.** n. A Bolshevik.

bolster (I.), n. [1. bólster; 2. bóulstə]. O.E. *bolster* prob. = 'the puffy, swelled, thing'. See base **bhel-* under **ball, belly, billow** &c. Long, round cushion upon which the pillows on a bed rest.

bolster (II.), vb. trans., fr. prec. To support, prop; (esp. fig.) *bolster up,* to support, a person or cause which is rather insecure, and would collapse without extraneous help.

bolt (I.), n. [1. bōlt; 2. boult]. O.E. *bolt,* 'arrow', O.H.G. & Mod. Germ. *bolz.* Origin doubtful; Kluge suggests that the word may be a refashioning of Lat. *(cata)pulta.* See **catapult. 1.** Short, stout arrow, or dart, fired from a crossbow. Phrs. (fig.) *to shoot one's bolt,* make one's effort, attempt, or attack; *my bolt is shot; bolt upright,* quite straight, straight as a bolt. Cp. *straight as a dart.* **2.** Lightning, meteorite falling from the sky, thunderbolt; esp. in Phr.: *a bolt from the blue,* unexpected occurrence. **3. a** A thick metal bar on a door, which is shot into clasps or hasps fastened to framework, and prevents the door being opened; **b** a catch on a spring fastened to upper sash of a window which locks under a piece of metal placed to receive it on lower sash, and prevents window being opened from outside; **c** sliding bar which locks the breech of a rifle. **4.** One of a variety of similar devices for holding two things together (e.g. a ring, knocker, bolt-fastenings &c. to a door) consisting of an iron pin in form of a screw, which often has a fixed head at one end, and a small flat piece of pierced iron, or nut, which is tightly screwed on to the other.

bolt (II.), vb. trans. & intrans., fr. prec. **1.** To fasten a door or window by means of a bolt: *bolt the door, window* &c. **2.** To run away quickly; said **a** of a horse which is frightened, and cannot be stopped by rider or driver; also **b** of rabbits &c., which run on being aroused from cover into the open; **c** of persons who run away from something which alarms them; **d** (extension of **c**) to run away from home &c. unexpectedly and disappear; elope &c.: *his wife has bolted with her cousin and all his money.* In the above senses the idea doubtless is 'to run as fast as a bolt from a crossbow'. **3.** To swallow food rapidly and greedily: *to bolt one's dinner.*

bolt (III.), n., fr. prec. A rapid run, escape, dash; uncontrolled flight. Phrs. (colloq.) *make a bolt for it; do a bolt,* run away.

bolt (IV.), boult, vb. trans. M.E. *bolte,* 'sift', O. Fr. *buleter, beluter,* Mod. Fr. *bluter,* Low Lat. *buratare;* orig. to sift anything by passing it through a coarse kind of cloth, called in O. Fr. *bure,* L. Lat. *burra.* Cp. also Ital. *buratto,* 'sieve'. See **bureau.** To sift. Obsolete, except in archaic figurative phrase *to bolt to the bran* (already in Chaucer), to sift the evidence, inquire closely into anything.

bolter (I.), n. [1. bólter; 2. bóultə]. **bolt (II.)** & **-er.** One that bolts, esp. of horse given to bolting or running away.

bolter (II.), vb. trans. Provinc., also *balter,* 'to mat, entangle'. Etymol. doubtful. Archaic, esp. in *blood-boltered,* of hair &c., matted with blood, 'Macbeth'.

bolus, n. [1. bólus; 2. bóuləs]. Late Latinized form of Gk. *bôlos,* 'lump' &c. See **bole (II.).** Big pill, esp. one administered to an animal.

bomb (I.), n. [1. bom; 2. bəm]. Fr. *bombe,* fr. Lat. *bombus,* 'deep, humming, or buzzing sound', as of bees, also of a horn, fr. Gk. *bómbos,* same sense, cogn. w. Scrt. *bambaraś,* 'bee', O. Slav. *babinŭ,* 'drum'; of imitative origin, the name being given to the missile on account of the peculiar noise made by its passage through the air. See also **bound (III.). 1. a** Spherical, explosive shell, fired from a mortar, or dropped from an aeroplane or air-ship; **b** general name for various forms of grenade, q.v., thrown by hand, as *Mills' bomb* &c. **2.** (fig.) A startling, unexpected event; statement of surprising character. Cp. **bombshell.**

bomb (II.), vb. trans., fr. prec. To heave bombs at, attack with bombs. (This verb had become obs., but came again into common use during the Great War.)

bombard, vb. trans. [1. bombárd; 2. bəmbád]. Fr. *bombarder,* vb., *bombarde,* n. See **bomb (I.)** & **-ard.** Orig. a noun, 'that which drones or hums', applied to **a** a musical instrument, **b** a primitive cannon. In first sense the word occurs in Engl. in 14th, & in latter in 15th cent. Cp. Ital. *bombarda,* 'kind of cannon'. The Engl. vb. is derived fr. the n. in the sense, 'to use a bombard', i.e. cannon. Shakespeare uses the noun in sense of 'drinking vessel'. **1.** To attack with artillery; also, in milder sense, to pelt: *to bombard with confetti, bouquets* &c. **2.** (fig.) To assail frequently and vigorously with questions, complaints, applications &c.

bombardier, n. [1. bòmbardḗr, bùmbardḗr; 2. bòmbədíə, bàmbədíə], fr. prec. Fr. *bombardier,* 'soldier who throws bombs, artilleryman'. Originally a soldier in charge of a *bombard,* or cannon, for throwing bombs; now lowest rank of non-commissioned officers in Royal Artillery.

bombardment, n. [1. bombárdment; 2. bəmbádmənt]. See **bombard** & **-ment.** Artillery attack.

bombardon, n. [1. bombárdun; 2. bəmbádən]. Ital. *bombardone.* Cp. **bombard. a** Deep-toned musical instrument of bassoon class; **b** one of the stops on an organ.

bombasine. See **bombazine.**

bombast, n. [1. bombást; 2. bəmbǽst]. O. Fr. *bombace,* 'cotton'. Lat. *bombyx,* 'silk-worm, something made of silk, any fine fibre, cotton', fr. Gk. *bómbux,* 'silk-worm, silk'; origin unknown. The development of meaning of *bombace,* fr. 'cotton' to 'padding', & the fig. use of the word is not difficult to follow. The final *-t* of the Engl. word was developed in accordance w. a habit, still found among vulgar speakers, but common in all classes fr. 15th to 18th cent., of pronouncing a *-t* after a final *-s.* Thus *loste* occurs for *loss* in 15th cent. High-sounding, flowery, rather empty and insincere, verbiage; rodomontade.

bombastic, adj. [1. bombástik; 2. bəmbǽstik]. Prec. & **-ic.** (of speech, manner) Pertaining to *bombast;* characterized by high-flown, inflated, rhetorical expression.

bombastically, adv. [1. bombástikali; 2. bəmbǽstikəli]. Prec. & **-al** & **-ly.** In a bombastic manner.

Bombay duck, n. [1. bómbā dúk; 2. bómbei dák]. Anglo-Indian word for a kind of dried fish (the *bummalo*) which has a very strong and rather rank taste; used to give savour to curry &c., and considered a great delicacy.

bombazine, n. [1. bòmbazḗn; 2. bòmbəzín]. O. Fr. *bombasin,* L. Lat. *bombȳcinum,* 'silk fabric', fr. *bombyx.* See further under **bombast.** Kind of twilled fabric, mixture of silk and wool, used for women's dresses, esp. for mourning garments.

bomber, n. [1. bómer; 2. bómə]. **bomb (II.)** & **-er. a** Aeroplane &c. carrying explosive bombs; **b** soldier who throws hand-grenades or bombs.

bombproof, adj. [1. bómproof; 2. bómprūf]. Secure against effects of explosion of bombs; esp. *bombproof shelter,* a specially constructed chamber reinforced in various ways.

bomb-shell, n. Explosive shell, same as **bomb;** (now gen. fig.) *a regular bombshell,* great surprise, source of agitation &c.

bona fide, adj. & adv. [1. bóna fídi; 2. bóunə fáidi]. Lat. words meaning 'in good faith'. Genuine, reverse of sham, or imitation.

bona fides, n. [1. bóna fídēz; 2. bóunə fáidiz]. Legal. Honest intention; good faith.

bonanza, n. [1. bōnánza; 2. bounǽnzə]. Span. Lit. 'good luck, prosperity'. Rich vein of ore in a mine; anything that shows prosperity; run of luck, fine weather and good, plentiful crops on a farm.

bonbon, n. [1. bónbon; 2. bɔ̃bɔ̃]. Fr., reduplicated form of *bon,* 'good', fr. Lat. *bonus,* 'good'. See under **bonus & bene-.** Sweetmeat.

bonbonnière, n. [1. bonboniár; 2. bɔ̃bɔnjḗr]. Fr., fr. prec. A small ornamented box or case for sweetmeats &c.

bond (I.), n. [1. bond; 2. bənd]. O.E. *band, bond.* Variant of **band,** & related to **bind. 1.** Shackle, something which restrains freedom of movement: (only in pl.) '*Let us break their bonds in sunder and cast away their cords from us*'. **2.** (fig.) Anything which unites, a connecting link: *bond of friendship; common tastes form a bond between us.* **3.** (law) **a** An agreement by which one is bound, a covenant: *to enter into a bond with a person;* **b** the document, signed and sealed, which embodies such an agreement. Phr. *his word is as good as his bond,* of a very honest person; **c** (specif., finance) an instrument issued by a government or corporation which acknowledges that a certain sum has been lent, as evidence of debt which the holder can recover. **4.** (building) System of ties, or unions by which adjacent stones or bricks, or courses of stones or bricks, are held together, by overlapping in various ways. **5.** State of certain goods, wines, tobacco &c., kept under government supervision till Customs duties are paid: *in bond, out of bond.*

bond (II.), vb. trans., fr. prec. **1.** To tie materials in building by means of a bond. **2.** To convert a loan into a debt secured by bonds.

bondage, n. [1. bóndij; 2. bɔ́ndidž]. Med. Lat. *bondagium*, fr. O.E. *bōnda*, q.v. under **bond-man**, & *-agium*, q.v. under **-age**. **1.** Condition of being a *bonda* or person cultivating and holding land by villein service; hence, lack of freedom, restraint on liberty of action, subjugation; still further extended to imply slavery, captivity. **2.** (fig.) Any thing or set of circumstances which impose(s) moral restraint or subjection: *bondage of sin, vice* &c.

bonded, adj. [1. bónded; 2. bɔ́ndid], fr. **bond (I.)**, **3** & **5**, & **-ed**. **1.** (finance) Secured by bonds. **2.** Placed in government warehouse called a 'bonded warehouse', pending payment of duty.

bondmaid, n. [1. bóndmād; 2. bɔ́ndmeid]. See **bondman**. Female slave.

bondman, bondsman, n. [1. bóndman, bóndzman; 2. bɔ́ndmən, bɔ́ndzmən]. O.E. *bōnda*, 'householder', later 'a villein', fr. O.N. *bōndi*, older *būandi*, lit. 'dweller, householder', a man who tilled his own land, a freeman. See **Boer**. After the Conquest a change of tenure reduced the status of these small landholders and they become villeins, holding their land fr. the lord of the manor & w. their liberties curtailed. Although quite unconnected historically w. *bond*, 'shackle' &c., *bōnda* became confused w. it, & the meaning changed fr. 'freemen' to 'serf'. Hence *bondsman* now means a person in bonds, a serf.

bond-servant, n. Bond(s)man, serf.

bone (I.), n. [1. bōn; 2. boun]. O.E. *bān*, 'bone', O.H.G. *bein*, 'bone, leg', Mod. Germ. *bein*, 'leg', O.L.G. *bēn*, 'bone'; O.N. *bein*, 'bone', & 'leg'; cp. also O.N. *beinn*, 'straight'. This may be the orig. meaning of the base, in wh. case the derived sense in *bone* &c. wd. start fr. 'straight bones', wh. makes it at least possible that the word referred first of all, to the bones of the thigh & shins as in Germ. The tempting equation of the word w. Lat. *femur*, 'thigh', must be rejected. So far the base seems confined entirely to Gmc. **1.** A portion, one of the parts, of the hard structure which composes the framework or skeleton supporting the soft tissues and organs of vertebrate animals: *the bones of the head, the thigh bone* &c. Phrs. *a bone of contention*, cause of dispute; *to have a bone to pick with someone*, subject of argument, cause of complaint; *to be frozen, drenched, to the bone*, thoroughly, extremely, cold or wet; *to make no bones about*, have, or show no scruple; *dry as a bone*, very dry. **2.** The hard substance of which the bones are formed. **3.** Various hard structures found in the animal body, e.g. *whale bone*, or the hard inner shell of cuttle-fish, also ivory. **4.** (pl., by extension of **1**) The dead body as a whole: *his bones were laid in Westminster*. **5.** (in pl.) Thin strips of ivory or bone, a pair of which is held between the fingers of each hand and clattered together in time to music or rhythmical movement.

bone (II.), vb. trans., fr. prec. **1.** To remove the bones of: *to bone a turkey, leg of mutton* &c. **2.** (slang) To steal, appropriate what does not belong to one.

bone-bed, n. (geol.) Layer of rock containing fragments of bone.

boned, adj. [1. bōnd; 2. bound]. **bone (I.)** & **-ed**. **a** Having bone of particular kind: *large-boned, raw-boned*; **b** having bones removed: *boned turkey* &c.

bone-dry, adj. Dry as an old bone which has been exposed to the weather; (also fig.) very thirsty.

bonedust, n. [1. bṓndust; 2. bóundast]. Finely ground bones, used as manure.

bone-setter, n. A person, generally an unqualified surgeon, who has special skill in manipulating injured or diseased bones and joints, and in setting fractured limbs; an osteopath.

boneshaker, n. [1. bṓnshāker; 2. bóunʃeikə]. Used derisively of a bad, antiquated, dilapidated bicycle.

bone spavin, n. Growth of bone on horse's hock, which causes lameness.

bonfire, n. [1. bónfīr; 2. bɔ́nfaiə]. Perh. fr. **bone**; said to be so called because bones were formerly chief materials used. Large fire lighted on festive occasions as a sign of rejoicing.

bongo, n. [1. bónggō; 2. bɔ́ŋgou]. Native name. A large striped antelope of E. and W. Africa.

bonhomie, n. [1. bónomē; 2. bɔ́nɔmí]. Fr., 'good nature'; *bon*, 'good', *homme*, 'man'. See **bonus** & **bene-** & **homage**. Geniality, good nature, pleasantness of manner.

Boniface, n. [1. bónifās; 2. bɔ́nifeis], fr. name of character in Farquhar's 'Beaux' Stratagem', 1707. Inn-keeper, esp. one who is jovial and genial.

bonito, n. [1. bōnḗtō; 2. bounítou]. Span.; etymol. unknown. Name of various large kinds of tunny of the mackerel family, of Atlantic Ocean &c., esp. the striped tunny which pursues the flying-fish.

bon mot, n. Fr. Lit. 'good word, saying'. Pronounced w. remote imitation of Fr. as [1. bon mō; 2. bɔ̃ mou]. A jest; humorous, witty, pointed saying.

bonne, n. [1. bon; 2. bɔn]. Fr. word, fem. of *bon*, 'good', see **bonus**, specialized in sense of children's nurse, female domestic. In England sometimes used formerly of a Frenchwoman who acted as nurse to English children. Generally *French bonne*; used to be pronounced [1. bun; 2. ban].

bonne bouche, n. [1. bón bṓōsh; 2. bɔ́n búʃ]. Fr., lit. 'good mouth(ful),' fr. fem. of *bon*, 'good', see **bonus** &c., & *bouche*, 'mouth', fr. Lat. *bucca*, 'cheek', see **buccal**; the Engl. sense is not a Fr. one. Tit-bit.

bonnet (I.), n, [1. bónet; 2. bɔ́nit]. O. Fr. *bonet*, Mod. Fr. *bonnet*, Span. *bonete*. Origin unknown. Perh. refers orig. to material of wh. the thing was made. Meyer-Lübke quotes as oldest mention *chapel de bonet*. **1.** Head-dress of various shapes and material; applied either **a** to kind of cap with strings worn on the head out of doors by women; **b** to soft cap covering head and ears worn by babies; **c** to a peculiar kind of flat cap worn in Scotland, esp. by Highlanders. **2.** Extended to various structures which have nothing in common with a *bonnet* in original sense except that they cover something: e.g. **a** cowl or hood fixed to the top of a chimney to regulate draught or prevent down-draught; **b** contrivance to arrest sparks on funnel of locomotive; **c** covering of metal on motor or other machine, to protect valve-chambers, cylinders &c. **3.** (colloq., slang) Decoy, accomplice in a swindle, doubtful gambling transaction, who acts as a cover to the principal.

bonnet (II.), vb. trans., fr. prec. **1.** To provide with a bonnet (rare). **2.** To cover a man's face with his hat, by striking it down over his eyes. **3.** (extended meaning) To cover, protect, as a fire from draught, damp down, extinguish.

bonnet rouge, n. [1. bonā rṓōzh; 2. bɔne rūž]. Fr., 'red cap', fr. head-dress worn by revolutionary mob in French Revolution. A red republican.

bonny, adj. [1. bóni; 2. bɔ́ni]. M.E. *boni*. Origin uncertain; possibly connected w. Fr. *bon*, 'good', see **bonus**. (Not much used in South of England; common in Scotland and North country.) Handsome, buxom; esp. of good looks combined with, or arising from, the glow of health: *a bonny boy*; *her bonny face* &c.

bonspiel, n. [1. bónspēl; 2. bɔ́nspīl]. A Scots usage; earlier *bonspel*; prob. borrowed fr. Du.; the second element is Du. *spel*, Germ. *spiel*, 'game', prob. cogn. w. *spell*, 'turn of work', see **spell (III.)**; first element may be Du. *bond*, 'league'; early sense was that of a match at archery or other game of skill. A match, esp. an important one, at curling.

bonus, n. [1. bṓnus; 2. bóunəs]. Lat. *bonus*, 'good', earlier *duonos*, fr. **dwenos*. Some identify the base w. that in Scrt. *dúvaš*, 'veneration, worship', *duvásyati*, 'respects, acknowledges, praises'. See further under **bene-** & **beauty**. Early proposals to connect **dwenos* w. Gk. *dúnamis* &c., 'power', are now gen. rejected. See further **dynamic**. **1.** A gratuity, additional payment over and above what recipient is strictly entitled to. **2.** Specif., extra sum added, out of accumulated profits, by Life Insurance Co. to the value of a policy above the sum originally insured for.

bony, adj. [1. bṓni; 2. bóuni], fr. **bone** & **-y**. **1.** Like bone in structure, or hardness: *bony growth, bony swelling* &c. **2.** Full of bones: *the herring is a very bony fish*. **3.** Possessing large, prominent bones: *a tall bony man*; *a bony horse* &c.

bonze, n. [1. bonz; 2. bɔnz]. Jap. *bonzi*, *bonzō*. Term applied by Europeans in China to Buddhist priests; originally derived from Japan. Found in forms *bonzō, bonzi*, in English writings from 16th cent.

boo(h), interj. & vb. trans. & intrans. [1. bōō; 2. bū]. Imitative of sound made by a cow. **1.** interj. Exclamation uttered to express disapproval or contempt; also to chase away an animal. **2.** vb. **a** To utter the exclamation, to say *booh!*; **b** to chase away by uttering the cry: *boo a dog out of the garden*; **c** to utter the cry in order to express disapproval of a person or his opinions.

booby, n. [1. bṓōbi; 2. búbi]. Span. *bobo*, 'fool', fr. Lat. *balbus*, 'stammering, stuttering'; cp. Ital. *balbo*, O. Fr. *baup*, Fr. *ébaubi*, 'astonished, amazed', lit. 'struck dumb'. The Lat. word is of ancient imitative origin, & ultimately connected w. Gk. *bárbaros*, 'not Greek, foreign'. See **barbarous**. **a** A clumsy, stupid dunce, a loutish, heavy fellow; **b** a sailor's name for various sea-birds, esp. the gannet.

boobyish, adj. [1. bṓōbi-ish; 2. búbi-iʃ]. Prec. & **-ish**. Like, pertaining to, a booby.

booby-prize, n. Prize awarded in good-natured derision to the last in a race or other competition.

booby-trap, n. Kind of practical joke which consists in placing some object where a person must pass, so that he will trip over it, or that it will fall upon his head.

boodle, n. [1. bṓōdl; 2. búdl]. Perh. fr. **caboodle**, the origin of wh. is unknown. (vulg. slang) Money, cash.

boohoo, n. & vb. intrans. [1. bōōhṓō; 2. būhú]. Imit., redupl. of **boo**. **a** n. Noisy weeping, hence fuss; **b** vb., to utter loud lamentations &c.

book (I.), n. [1. book; 2. buk]. O.E. *bōc*, 'book, document, charter', Common Gmc. word, fr. same stem as **beech** (tree), fr. ancient custom of inscribing runic letters on thin shavings or boards of beech. **1.** **a** Collection of blank, printed, or written sheets or leaves, of paper, or other material, fastened together, and bound in boards, covered with cloth, leather, or paper &c., so as to form a unity or volume: *a note book, account book, book of MS., printed book* &c.; **b** entries in a record: *book of fate*. Phrs. *to bring to book*, call to account; *to be in one's black books*, in disfavour, from idea of a person's name being in a record of misdeeds. **2.** **a** A literary composition, compilation or treatise of any kind, which, when printed and bound, constitutes a *book* in above sense (**1**); **b** (extended fig. meaning) studies: *at one's books*. Phrs. *to speak without the book*, from memory; *the Book, the Good Book*, Bible. **3.** A considerable portion, division, or section of a literary work: *Milton's 'Paradise Lost' consists of twelve books*. **4.** The words which are sung in opera; same as *libretto*: *the music was fine, but the book was very poor*. **5.** The whole of a person's bets on a single race, or at single race-meeting: *to make a book on the Derby*. Phr. (fig.) *to suit one's book*, to be in accordance with one's plans or wishes. **6.** Six tricks taken by one side at whist; the number after which each additional trick taken counts in the score.

book (**II.**), vb. trans., fr. prec. **1.** To enter in a book, esp. of engagements, appointments, orders &c. **2.** (extended use) **a** To retain in advance, ensure enjoyment of at particular time: *to book seats*, for a theatrical performance; *to book a passage for New York*; **b** to ensure in advance that a person will do something, or go somewhere on particular date: *I want to book you to dine with me tomorrow*; *I am booked to go to London next week.*

bookbinder, n. [1. bóokbīnder; 2. búkbaində]. One whose trade it is to bind books.

bookbinding, n. [1. bóokbīnding; 2. búkbaindiŋ]. **a** Trade of bookbinder; **b** the art of binding books; **c** specimens of the art: *exhibition of book-binding.*

bookcase, n. [1. bóokkās; 2. búkkeis]. Set of shelves connected together, for holding books.

booked, adj. [1. bookt; 2. bukt], fr. P.P. of **book** (**II.**). **a** (of things) Engaged, retained, bespoken; **b** (of persons) engaged, bound, under promise to do certain things: *booked up*, completely engaged: *all the seats are booked up*; having many engagements: *I'm booked up for the whole week* (colloq.).

bookie, n. [1. bóoki; 2. búki]. (colloq.) See **book-maker.**

booking, n. [1. bóoking; 2. búkiŋ]. **book** (**II.**) & **-ing**. Act of entering memoranda, engagements &c. in a book; anything so entered, esp. record of accommodation secured in advance; *booking-clerk*, person who makes and keeps records of *bookings*, esp. one who issues tickets at railway stations &c., or who registers passengers' luggage, or who allots seats for a theatre, or rooms to guests in a hotel &c.; *booking-office*, office in railway station, hotel, or theatre, where tickets are issued, or where rooms, or seats, are allotted.

bookish, adj. [1. bóokish; 2. búkiʃ]. **book** (**I.**) & **-ish**. Pertaining to, connected with, books; **a** pertaining to studies: *bookish interests*; **b** studious, fond of books: *bookish person*; **c** based on, derived from, books rather than from life; pedantic: *a bookish speech, bookish mode of thought* &c.

book-keeping, n. Method or art of recording financial receipts and expenditure, keeping of accounts.

bookland, n. [1. bóokland; 2. búklænd]. O.E. *bōcland*. Land held by a 'book' or charter, as old form of tenure.

book-learning, n. Knowledge derived from books, as distinct from personal experience; popularly, knowledge in general, education.

booklet, n. [1. bóoklet; 2. búklit]. A small book or pamphlet.

book-maker, n. **a** Maker or compiler of books rather than an original writer; specif. **b** person who makes a regular profession of betting at horse-races.

book-making, n. Practice, process, of making books in either of above senses.

bookman, n. [1. bóokman; 2. búkmən]. Learned, studious person; scholar.

bookmark, n. [1. bóokmark; 2. búkmāk]. Thin strip of ivory, metal, wood, or paper placed in a book to facilitate rapid finding of particular page or passage.

book-plate, n. Engraved armorial or other design, generally including name of an individual or institution &c. pasted on the inside of a book-cover to mark ownership; ex-libris.

book-post, n. Postal system and rate by which books &c. can be sent by post.

bookseller, n. [1. bóokseler; 2. búksɛlə]. One who sells books as regular occupation and trade.

bookselling, n. [1. bóokseling; 2. búksɛliŋ]. Trade of a bookseller.

bookshelf, n., pl. **-shelves** [1. bóokshelf, -vz; 2. búkʃɛlf, -vz]. Long board, often part of a *bookcase*, upon which books are placed.

bookstall, n. [1. bóokstawl; 2. búkstōl]. Stall, generally in the open air, in a market-place &c., where books are sold.

bookstand, n. [1. bóokstand; 2. búkstænd]. Generally same as *bookcase*, but term implies an independent self-contained piece of furniture, which need not stand against wall, and is often supported on feet.

bookwork, n. [1. bóokwērk; 2. búkwʌk]. Study; systematic use of, and reference to, books.

bookworm, n. [1. bóokwērm; 2. búkwʌm]. **1.** Small worm, properly the larva of a moth or beetle, which burrows into and destroys pages of old books. **2.** (fig.) A person devoted to, engrossed in, the study of books.

boom (**I.**), n. [1. bōōm; 2. būm], fr. Du. *boom*, 'tree, pole', cogn. w. Engl. **beam.** **1.** (naut.) Long pole or spar used to keep the bottom of a sail extended: *jib-boom* &c. **2.** Obstruction made of heavy pieces of timber fastened together, placed at mouth of navigable river &c. to prevent entry by enemy ships.

boom (**II.**), vb. intrans. & trans. M.E. *bomme(n)*, *bumbin*, 'hum'; of imitative origin; cp. Germ. *bummen*. See **bomb** (**I.**). **1.** intrans. To give out a deep resounding, humming note or noise; said of thunder, a drum, artillery, some kinds of birds, esp. the bittern, q.v., and of a person with deep powerful voice. **2.** (fig. and colloq.) **a** To make a stir, sensation, to 'make a noise in the world'; hence to prosper; (of persons) acquire reputation, prestige &c.; (of commodities &c.) to increase in value, become known and sought after: *he was just booming as a painter when he died*; *every market is booming*; **b** (trans. use) to advertise persons or things, make them favourably known: *to boom one's friends, wares* &c.

boom (**III.**), n., fr. prec. **1.** Deep resonant sound as of thunder, artillery, drums &c. **2. a** Access of fame, reputation, value; contrasted with *slump*; **b** system of advertisement which causes this.

boomerang, n. [1. bōōmerang; 2. būməræŋ]. Native Australian word. **1.** Piece of wood, curved and flat, which, when thrown in particular way, performs a series of curves in the air and, after travelling some distance, returns to approximately the same spot from which it was thrown; used by Australian aborigines as a weapon for killing birds &c. **2.** (fig.) Anything, attack, malicious speech &c., which recoils upon the person who starts it.

boon (**I.**), n. [1. bōōn; 2. būn]. O.N. *bōn*, O.E. *bēn*, 'prayer, petition', fr. **bōni*. Etymol. is doubtful; perh. fr. Gmc. **bǣni*, W. Gmc. **bāni*, Pr. O.E. **bōn-i*, & connected w. O.E. *biddan*, 'pray, beg', wh. has Pret. *bǣd-on*; cp. under **bead** (**I.**). This wd. imply a very early difference in formative suff. to base **bhē-* (**bhē-dh-*, & **bhē-n-*). Possibly connected w. Lat. *fā-bula*, 'tale, story' (see **fable**); cp. also Scrt. *bhánati*, 'speaks'. See **ban** (**II.**). **1.** Request, favour: *to ask a boon of someone* (archaic and lit.). **2.** An advantage, blessing, comfort: *open spaces in the centre of towns are a great boon to the inhabitants.* (This usage probably influenced by next word.)

boon (**II.**), adj. Late M.E. *bōn*, O. Fr. *bōn(e)*, 'good', &c., fr. Lat. *bonus*. See **bonus** & **bene-**. **a** Pleasant, benign, delightful, of weather, air &c. (archaic and poet.); **b** genial, jolly, only in *boon companion.*

boor, n. [1. bōōr, bōr; 2. būə, bōə]. Cp. O.E. *gebūr*, 'peasant', but *boor* is prob. borrowed fr. Du. *boer*, wh. is cogn. w. O.E. word. See **Boer. 1.** (archaic or hist.) Peasant, countryman. **2.** A clumsy, mannerless, ill-bred lout.

boorish, adj. [1. bórish; 2. bɔ́əriʃ]. Prec. & **-ish**. Pertaining to a boor; ill-mannered, rude.

boorishness, n. Prec. & **-ness**. Loutishness, bad manners, lack of breeding.

boost, vb. trans. & n. [1. bōōst; 2. būst]. Etymol. unknown; orig. an American slang term. **1.** vb. **a** To lift, raise, push up from behind or below; specif., **b** to increase the value and sale of anything or reputation of a person, by advertising and other methods, to boom. **2.** n. **a** Anything done to boost or advance the value &c. of anything; **b** advance in value owing to such methods, a boom.

booster, n. [1. bōōster; 2. būstə]. Prec. & **-er.** One who boosts; specif. (elect.) device in an accumulator regulating the current and raising the voltage.

boot (**I.**), n. [1. bōōt; 2. būt]. 14th cent. Engl. *bōte*, O. Fr. *bote*, Mod. Fr. *botte*, 'high boot'. The hist. & origin of the word are obscure. It seems to have been borrowed into L. Lat. fr. a High Germ. source & to have passed into most of the Romance languages. The early meanings were **a** 'barrel, tun; leather bag', hence, 'a leather flask or bottle', **b** 'leather covering for the feet and legs', that is 'boot'. The Gmc. base is apparently that in O.H.G. *botahha*, Mod. Germ. *bottich*, 'tub, barrel', & possibly in O.E. *bodig*, Engl. **body,** & O.E. *byden*, 'tub, barrel', & *bytte*, 'leather bottle, wine-skin'. The Fr. *botte* means both 'boot' & 'barrel'. See further under **bottle. 1.** Leather case or covering for the foot, formerly reaching up to, or beyond, the knee; now, a *boot* as distinct from a *shoe*, reaches at least over the ankle, and is fastened by buttons, or by means of laces which pass through eyelet holes, or over blunt, rounded hooks. Other varieties are distinguished as *high boots*, or *riding boots*, which extend to within a few inches of the knee. Phr. *the boot is on the other leg*, truth is in opposite direction from that alleged, or responsibility lies elsewhere; (fig.) *to get the boot*, be dismissed, kicked out; *to die in one's boots*, not in one's bed; *to have one's heart in one's boots*, to be very nervous or frightened, to lose courage. **2.** A portion of an old-fashioned chaise, behind the main part of the body, which contained an extra seat, and in which luggage was placed. **3. a** A leather covering drawn over hoof of a horse and strapped round the pastern, to prevent injury to soft turf of a lawn from the iron shoe by a horse pulling a roller or mowing machine; **b** a kind of pad of leather worn by a horse round fetlock to prevent him from cutting this inside by striking it with shoe of another foot: generally *brushing boot.* **4.** Instrument of torture used formerly to extract confessions from prisoners; an iron case drawn over the foot and lower part of the leg, into which wedges were driven so as to crush the flesh and bones. *Boot and saddle*, cavalry trumpet call as signal to mount, a corruption of Fr. *boute-selle*, 'put saddle on'.

boot (**II.**), vb. trans., fr. prec. **1.** To provide with boots (rare); but see **booted. 2.** To use the boots upon, i.e. to kick; esp. *to boot round (the place), boot out*, kick out; (fig., colloq. and vulg.) to dismiss from situation or office.

boot (**III.**), n. O.E. *bōt*, 'remedy, compensation, cure', O.H.G. *buosza*, 'reparation', Mod. Germ. *busse*, O.S. *bōta*, 'cure', Goth. *bōta*, 'advantage'. Cp. **better, best.** (rare and obsolesc., poet.) Advantage, profit; cp. legal term *estovers*. In ordinary speech chiefly in adv. Phr. *to boot*, in addition, into the bargain.

boot (**IV.**), vb., fr. prec. (largely obs. and poet.) To profit, advantage, benefit: '*What boots it with incessant care To ply the humble slighted shepherd's trade?*' (Milton).

bootblack, n. [1. bōōtblàk; 2. būtblæk]. One who cleans boots and shoes, usually in street.

booted, adj. [1. bōōted; 2. būtid], fr. P.P. of **boot** (**II.**). Provided with, wearing, boots, ready for riding; esp. in Phr. *booted and spurred.*

booth, n. [1. bōōdh; 2. būð]. Not recorded in O.E. but prob. existing, as **bōþ*, M.E. *bōþe* ('*huccsterress bōþe*' early 13th cent.); the cognates are M.H.G. *buode*, 'hut', Mod. Germ. *bude*, M. Du. *boede*, O.N. *būþ*, 'temporary abode, shop, hut' &c. The vowel of the last offers some difficulty, compared w. the others, unless we assume the orig. Aryan base to have been **bhōut-*. The base may be that found in O.E. & O.N. *būa(n)*, 'dwell, remain', & the *-th* may be a derivative suff. as in *youth*, q.v. See **be, build, bower** (**I.**). Cp. also fr. base **bhū-* &c., Lith. *bùtas*, 'house', *būklà*, 'home, dwelling-place'. A shed, shelter, generally of boards; a covered stall in a market.

bootjack, n. [1. bōōtjăk; 2. bútdžæk]. **boot (I.) & jack.** Contrivance consisting of a kind of lever, part of which grips the heel, for pulling off long boots.

bootlace, n. [1. bōōtlās; 2. bútleis]. Lace used for fastening boots, through eyelet holes or round metal hooks.

bootleg, vb. [1. bōōtleg; 2. bútleg]. **boot (I.) & leg.** (slang, U.S.A.) **a** To carry whisky or other prohibited alcoholic liquor concealed on one's person, for consumption or sale, originally by hiding a bottle &c. in the leg of a high boot; hence **b** to traffic in the smuggling or sale of prohibited liquor in any form.

bootlegger, n. [1. bōōtleger; 2. bútlegə]. Prec. & **-er.** One engaged in traffic in prohibited alcoholic liquor.

bootless, adj. [1. bōōtles; 2. bútlis], fr. **boot (III.) & -less.** Without result or advantage, fruitless, unavailing: *a bootless errand, effort.*

bootlessly, adv. Prec. & **-ly.** Unavailingly.

boots, n. [1. bōōts; 2. būts]. Person whose chief duty it is to clean boots, esp. at a hotel.

boot-tree, n. Wooden tree or last inserted in boots or shoes to stretch and keep them in shape.

booty, n. [1. bōōti; 2. búti]. Supposed to be fr. Fr. *butin*, of same meaning, & this again fr. O.N. *býti*, 'exchange, barter'; Ital. has *bottino*. The Engl. word is spelt *buti* by Caxton, & the later spelling may be due to association w. **boot (III.).** The ending can hardly be fr. Fr. *-in*, but must be due rather to anal. of other ns. in *-y*, such as *bounty*, Fr. *-é*. Cp. suff. **-y. 1.** Spoils of war, loot, goods taken from the enemy, plunder. **2.** (law) Specif., spoils taken on land as distinct from *prize*. Booty in war becomes property of captor by right of seizure. **3.** Any valuable or cherished acquisition, without reference to manner in which it was acquired: *the forests of S. America provided a rich booty of specimens for naturalists.*

booze (I.), vb. intrans. & trans. [1. bōōz; 2. būz]. M.E. *bousen*, loan-word fr. M. Du. *būzen*, 'drink', Mod. Du. *buizen*; cp. Mod. Germ. *bausen*, 'tipple', fr. M.H.G. *būs*, 'inflation'. (low, vulg. word) To drink immoderately, and constantly; tipple.

booze (II.), n., fr. prec. Drink, esp. alcoholic drink.

boozed, adj. [1. bōōzd; 2. būzd], fr. P.P. of **booze (I.)** Drunk, intoxicated.

boozy, adj. [1. bōōzi; 2. búzi]. **booze (II.) & -y.** Fuddled with strong drink, half-drunk; inclined to drink too much.

bo-peep, n. [1. bō pēp; 2. bou píp]. **bo & peep.** Childish game, the point of which is to spring out suddenly from half-suspected hiding-place, so as to startle the child mildly.

bora, n. [1. bóra; 2. bórə]. Ital., fr. Lat. *Boreas*, 'the north wind'. See **boreal.** A cold, dry, north-east wind of the Adriatic, blowing in autumn and winter.

boracic, adj. [1. borásik; 2. bərǽsik]. See **borax & -ic.** Of, pertaining to, containing, borax; boric: *boracic* or *boric acid*, crystalline substance, usually powdered, obtained in volcanic districts of Italy and also chemically from boron; used as a preservative for food and as an antiseptic in medicine.

borage, n. [1. búrij; 2. báridž]. M.E. *borage*, fr. O. Fr. *bourage*, Mod. Fr. *bourrache*, L. Lat. *borrāgo*, *borrāgin-(em)*, whence also Ital. *borragine*; formed fr. L. Lat. *burra*, 'hairy, shaggy coat of animals', cp. Fr. *bourre*, 'hair of animals, pad, stopper' &c., & *bourrer*, 'to stuff, pad, stop' &c., wh. have cognates in most of the other Romance languages. Lat. *reburrus*, 'hair standing on end', gives Fr. *rebours*, 'wrong side', *à rebours*, 'against the grain, backwards'. The *b* in the Lat. word is dial. for *f*, hence *burrus* may be derived fr. Aryan **bhr̥s-os*, whence Gmc. **burs-t-*, q.v. under **bristle & brush.** *Borage* is thus 'the hairy plant', a well-chosen name. A genus of plants with bright blue flowers and hairy stems, belonging to the order which includes the anchusa, bugloss &c.

borate, n. [1. bórāt; 2. bóreit], fr. **boron & -ate.** (chem.) A salt of boric acid.

borax, n. [1. bóraks; 2. bóræks]. M.E. & O. Fr. *boras*, L. Lat. *borax*, fr. Arab. *bauraq*. White powder, combination of boric acid and sodium.

bordage, n. [1. bórdij; 2. bódidž], fr. Med. Lat. *bordāgium*. See next word & **-age.** (legal hist.) Tenure of a bordar.

bordar, n. [1. bórdar; 2. bódə], fr. Low Lat. *bordārius*, fr. *borda*, O. Fr. *borde*, 'cottage'; etymol. doubtful, possibly connected w. **board (I.).** (legal hist.) A tenant or villain who held his cottage and small parcel of land from his lord in return for menial services.

Bordeaux, n. [1. bōrdṓ; 2. bōdóu]. Name of town and seaport in France, centre of wine-growing district. Wine grown in the district of Bordeaux and shipped therefrom, whether white or red, the latter being usually known in England as 'claret'.

border (I.), n. [1. bórder; 2. bódə]. M.E., fr. O. Fr. *bordure*, fr. *bord(a)*, 'edge', & Lat. *-ūra*, see **-ure.** This is a Gmc. word, cp. O.E. *borda*, 'fringe', borrowed into Low Lat., & found in most of the Romance languages, Ital. *bordo*, Span. *borde*, 'edge of a ship'. In some of the derived meanings this & the other Gmc. *bord*, q.v. under **board,** have become confused. **1.** Edge, outer rim, fringe, or margin of anything. **2.** Territory at the extreme limits of a country or state; boundary, frontier; specif., *The Border*, between Scotland and England. **3.** A narrow strip, by way of ornament, generally different in colour or material from the rest, forming edge of a robe or woman's garment. **4.** A flower bed which forms the boundary of a portion of a garden, often running at the foot of a wall, or edge of a lawn: *an herbaceous border.*

border (II.), vb. trans., fr. prec. **1.** To provide with a border or edging; (usually pass.) *the lawn was bordered by trees, a stream* &c. **2.** To march with, be contiguous to, run alongside of: *my land borders yours; part of North Berkshire borders the Thames*; also intrans. (with *on, upon*).

bordered, adj. [1. bórderd; 2. bódəd]. P.P. of prec. **1.** Having an ornamental edging, fringe &c. of different colour or material: *a robe bordered with gold lace.* **2.** (her.) Having an edge of specified tincture (i.e. colour): *bordered or.*

borderer, n. [1. bórderer; 2. bódərə]. **border (II.) & -er. 1.** An inhabitant of a frontier region. **2.** (in pl.) Name of certain British regiments: *Scottish Borderers, South Wales Borderers.*

borderland, n. [1. bórderland; 2. bódəlænd]. **1.** Territory adjoining frontiers of two countries. **2.** (fig.) Intermediate condition between two states of mind: *borderland of dreams, consciousness* &c.; region of thought between two branches of knowledge &c.: *borderland between physiology and psychology.*

bordure, n. [1. bórdūr; 2. bódjə]. Fr. See **border (I.).** (her.) Border surrounding shield; when plain, one-fifth of width of shield; broader when charged.

bore (I.), vb. trans., also used absolutely [1. bōr; 2. bō(ə)]. O.E. *borian*, M.E. *bōren*, 'pierce', O.H.G. *borōn*, Mod. Germ. *bohren*, O.N. *bora*. The base is Aryan **bher-*, **bhr̥-* &c., 'pierce, penetrate', wh. appears also in Lat. *for-āre*, 'bore, pierce', *fer-īre*, 'strike, cut, thrust', *fastīgium*, 'gable, top, point', for **farstigium*; Gk. *phároș*, 'plough', *phársos*, 'portion, something cut off'; Scrt. *bhr̥ṣ-ṭi-*, 'prong, point, summit'. The same base occurs in **borage, bristle, brush. 1.** To pierce, penetrate, drive a hole into, or through, anything, esp. by rotating a pointed instrument, such as a drill, gimlet, bradawl &c. **2.** To burrow, or dig, or cut into the earth, as in sinking a well, the shaft of a mine, or in making a tunnel. **3.** (fig.) To produce feeling of tedium and weariness in a person, as by dull, uninteresting conversation, or by urging him to do something which he dislikes, or in which he has no interest; to fatigue by repeated importunities of any kind. (For this particular application of the word cp. Fr. use of *scier*, 'to saw', and *une scie*, 'a bore'.)

bore (II.), n., fr. prec. **1.** An implement for piercing or boring; a drill. **2.** A perforation, hole made by boring. **3. a** The inside of a gun-barrel; **b** the size of a tube, esp. of a gun-barrel; calibre. **4.** (fig.) **a** A tedious, wearisome, uninteresting person; **b** a tedious occupation, one which does not interest one.

bore (III.), n., fr. O.N. *bāra*, 'wave', cogn. w. **bear (I.).** Tidal wave, piling up of water caused by the sea at high tide rushing up a constricted river channel with high cliffs on each side, esp. that of the Severn.

bore (IV.) vb. [1. bōr; 2. bō]. Pret. of **bear (I.).** M.E. *bōre*, fr. P.P. type, see **born.** Cp. O.E. Pret. *bær*, M.E. *bar*.

boreal, adj. [1. bóreal; 2. bóriəl]. Fr. *boréal*, Lat. *boreālis*, 'pertaining to north wind', *boreas* & adj. suff. *-ālis* (see **-al**); a loan-word fr. Gk. *boréās*, 'north wind'; fr. base **gʷor-*, 'mountain', cp. O. Slav. *gora*, Scrt. *giriš*, 'mountain'. Orig., *boreas* was 'the wind from the mountains'. In Lat. & Gk. the north wind was personified under this name. Pertaining to *Boreas*, therefore northern.

bored, adj. [1. bord; 2. bōd]. P.P. of **bore (I.).** Overcome by boredom, oppressed with sense of tedium (of persons).

boredom, n. [1. bórdum; 2. bódəm]. **bore (I.) & -dom.** Condition of being bored, fatigued, uninterested; tedium; anything which induces this condition of mind.

borer, n. [1. bórer; 2. bórə]. **bore (I.) & -er.** Anything which bores or penetrates; a drill. Also applied to certain insects which bore into wood.

boric, adj. [1. bó-, bórik; 2. bó-, bórik], fr. **boron & -ic.** Of, pertaining to, containing, boron or borax; boracic: *boric acid*, boracic acid.

boring, adj. [1. bóring; 2. bóriŋ], fr. Pres. Part. of **bore (I.).** Having the quality of producing sense of tedium, fatigue, boredom.

born, borne, vb. [1. born; 2. bōn]. **P.P.** of **bear (I.).** O.E. *boren*, M.E. *bōren*.

borné, adj. [1. bórnā; 2. bórnei]. Fr., P.P. of *borner*, 'to limit'. See **bourne,** & cp. **bound (I.).** Having limits, narrow-minded; having limited experience and outlook.

boron, n. [1. bóron; 2. bórɔn], fr. **borax &** suff. *-on*, as in **carbon.** (chem.) Non-metallic element occurring in borax and other substances.

borough, n. [1. búro; 2. bárə]. O.E. *burg*, *burug*, M.E. *burgh*, *boru* &c., 'fortified place, town', O.S., O.H.G. *burg*, Goth. *baurgs*, 'town'; Gmc. **burg-us*; connected w. O.E. *beorgan*, to hide, protect, preserve' &c., O.H.G. *bergan*, Goth. *bairgan*, prob. also w. O.E. *beorg*, O.H.G. *berg*, Goth. *bairg*, 'hill, mound' &c., see **barrow (II.).** Outside Gmc. the base occurs (possibly) in Lat. *fortis*, 'strong, bold' &c., fr. O. Lat. *forc-tus*, though this is also otherwise equated (see **fort**); more certainly w. Scrt. *br̥hánt*, 'thick, strong, big', W. *bry*, 'high', O. Celt. *Brigantes*, 'the high ones'. The base expresses the ideas 'strong and high', possibly 'strong, impregnable', & so on, because high. Orig., then, *burg* is 'a strong place'. The word is common in Gmc. languages as the second element in Pl. Ns. The Pl.-N. element *-bury* is fr. O.E. *byriġ*, the dat. sing. See also **borrow, burrow, bury,** vb. Town or **city; a** *municipal borough*, a town or municipality with a mayor and corporation and privileges conferred by charter; **b** *parliamentary borough*, town constituency in England, which returns one or more members to Parliament; in Wales these are grouped; cp. *burgh* for Scottish usage; also *pocket* and *rotten borough.*

borough-English, n. (law) Custom according to which land and tenements in certain towns descended to the youngest instead of to the eldest son. So called because the custom obtained only in certain English boroughs, that in French boroughs being the ordinary one of primogeniture.

borrow, vb. trans. & intrans. [1. bórō; 2. bɔ́rou]. O.E. *borgian*, 'to give or take a loan, to lend, also borrow', formed fr. *borg*, 'pledge, security', connected w. *beorgan*, 'protect' &c., q.v. under **borough**. **A.** trans. **1.** To receive anything, or the right to use anything, belonging to another, as a temporary loan, on promise to pay back the thing or sum of money lent, the lender often holding security of some kind, and receiving interest until repayment is completed: *his necessities compelled him to borrow money at exorbitant interest.* **2.** Applied also to informal temporary loans of other persons' belongings: *may I borrow your pony for the afternoon?* **3.** (arith.) Term used in subtraction when the figure to be subtracted is greater than that from which it is to be subtracted, and one is taken from the next higher denomination and added to the smaller figure. **B.** intrans. **1.** To borrow money: *he is always trying to borrow of his friends.* **2.** (golf) To allow for the effect of wind or a slope on the ball.

borrower, n. [1. bóroer; 2. bɔ́rouə]. Prec. & **-er.** One who borrows.

borrowing, n. [1. bóroing; 2. bɔ́rouiŋ]. See prec. & **-ing.** Act of one who borrows.

Borstal, adj. [1. bórstal; 2. bɔ̄́stəl], fr. name of site of first prison in Kent. Pertaining to Borstal or the system, *Borstal system*, of separate prisons and treatment of young criminals between the age of 16 and 21.

borzoi, n. [1. bórzoi; 2. bɔ̄́zɔi]. Russ., lit. 'swift'. A Russian wolf-hound, a large high-standing hound of greyhound type, but with thick, soft, and silky coat, usually white with yellow markings.

boscage, n. [1. bóskij; 2. bɔ́skidž], fr. O. Fr. *boscage*, 'grove', fr. L. Lat. *boscus, buscus*, 'thicket', & *-agium*, see **-age.** *Buscus*, whence Fr. *buis*, is prob. a form of *buxus*, 'box-tree', wh. appears in Gk. as *púxos* & is thought to be of foreign origin. See further under **bush** & **box (I.).** A woody region, thicket, grove.

bosh, n. [1. bosh; 2. bɔʃ]. Said to be Turkish word w. much the same sense as it has in Engl. **1.** Foolishness in word or deed; nonsense: *what you say is all bosh*; *to talk bosh.* **2.** Used as rather rude exclamation, equivalent to *Nonsense!*; *Humbug!*

bosky, adj. [1. bóski; 2. bɔ́ski], fr. L. Lat. *boscus.* See **boscage** & **-y.** Wooded, covered with woodland; bushy.

bosom, n. [1. bóozum; 2. búzəm]. O.E. *bōsm, bōsum*, O.H.G. *buosum*, O.S. *bōsm*; etymol. doubtful, but perh. for **bōgsma*, & connected w. O.E. *bōg*, 'shoulder, arm', & meaning orig. 'the part covered by the arms when folded in front of one', &, as it were, 'armful, embrace'. Cp. **elbow** & **bough.** Now chiefly used figuratively. **1. a** The human breast (obsolesc. or poet.); **b** that part of the clothing which covers the breast; fold of a dress or robe (obs.): *he thrust the book into his bosom.* Such phrases as *shirt bosom, bosom of a dress* &c. are no longer current in England. **2.** (fig.) The affections, passions; inmost thoughts: *to take someone to one's bosom*; *his sorrows were locked in his own bosom.* Phrs. *wife of one's bosom* (obsolesc.); *bosom friend*, very intimate friend. **3. a** The surface of the earth or sea; **b** the inner depths of the earth, below the surface: *minerals torn from earth's deepest bosom*; **c** embrace, keeping, guardianship: *bosom of the Church*; *bosom of one's family.*

bosomed, adj. [1. bóozumd; 2. búzəmd]. **a** Having a bosom; esp. in combinations: *big-bosomed, deep-bosomed*; **b** (poet.) placed, situated in the bosom, e.g. of a sheet of water, or a wood: *an islet bosomed in the lake*; *a house bosomed in trees*, surrounded by.

boss (I.), n. [1. bos; 2. bɔs]. Fr. *bosse*, 'protuberance', in various applications. Origin unknown; common in various forms in Romance languages; Ital. *bozza*, 'swelling, lump of stone' &c.; *bozzo*, 'rough plan'; perh. cp. **botch.** **1.** Any protuberant part, a knob &c., e.g. a projecting metal stud on a shield. **2.** (archit.) Projecting carving or moulding, used as an ornament, as in arches and roofs.

boss (II.), vb. trans. Perh. same as prec. Cp. Ital. *(ab-)bozzare* & *bozzare*, 'sketch out roughly', Port. *esboçar*, Fr. *ébaucher* &c. See **botch, (II.).** (slang) To bungle, make a bad job of; esp. to miss something aimed at.

boss (III.), n. Du. *baas*, 'master'. (slang, rather vulg.) A master, the head or chief man in any undertaking or institution. In modern sense imported from U.S.A., where the word meant first of all a person who pulled wires in political intrigue. The word in Marlowe's 'Tamburlaine' (1588), applied to a woman: '*Disdainful Turkess and unreverend boss*' ('Tam.' pt. i. Act iii. sc. 3, l. 168), has probably a different origin.

boss (IV.), vb., fr. prec. To play the master or leader; to be too masterful, to attempt to assert undue authority over.

boss-eyed, adj. **boss (II.)** & **eyed.** (colloq.) Squinting; cock-eyed.

boston, n. [1. bóstun; 2. bɔ́stən], fr. town in Massachusetts, U.S.A. **1.** (obs.) Mode of hair-dressing formerly practised by fops. **2.** Kind of valse.

Boswell, n. [1. bózwel; 2. bɔ́zwəl]. One who plays the part of sedulous admirer to a person; esp. one who collects and records sayings of a great man, as James Boswell (1740–95) did for Dr. Johnson: *to be a, act the, Boswell to* &c.

Boswellian, n. [1. bòzwélian; 2. bɔ̀zwélian]. Prec. & **-ian.** Admirer and student of Boswell's Life of Johnson.

Boswellize, vb. trans. [1. bózwelīz: 2. bɔ́zwəlaiz]. See prec. & **-ize.** To deal with a person's life and sayings as Boswell did with those of Dr. Johnson.

bot, bott, n. [1. bot; 2. bɔt]. Origin unknown. Parasitic maggot (of the *bot-fly*) which infests skin and intestines of horses and other animals. *Bots, botts*, pl., disease, an irritable swelling caused by the bot-fly.

botanic(al), adj. [1. botánik(l); 2. bɔtǽnik(l)]. See **botany** & **-ic** & **-al.** Relating to the science of botany; relating to plant life.

botanically, adv. Prec. & **-ly.** From a botanic point of view; according to botany.

botanist, n. [1. bótanist; 2. bɔ́tənist]. See **botany** & **-ist.** Student of botany.

botanize, vb. intrans. [1. bótanīz; 2. bɔ́tənaiz]. See prec. & **-ize.** To collect plants for study; to study plants.

botanizer, n. [1. bótanīzer; 2. bɔ́tənaizə]. Prec. & **-er.** One who botanizes.

botany, n. [1. bótani; 2. bɔ́təni]. Fr. *botanique* in same sense. Engl. *-y* suff. due to anal. of *astronomy* &c., wh. is as fr. Gk. *-nomia*; Gk. *botánē* means 'pasture, fodder', but the adj. *botanikós*, 'relating to herbs', is later applied to the science of botany. The prime meaning of the base is seen in the Gk. vb. *bóskein*, 'to feed, pasture cattle', & in *boskós*, 'feeder of cattle'. The orig. form is **gʷō-*, 'to feed'; cp. Lith. *gauja*, 'herd'. It is possible that Gk. *boûs*, 'ox', is fr. same base; see **bovine** & **cow** & cp. **proboscis.** The science of the structure, growth, and life of plants.

botch (I.), n. [1. boch; 2. bɔtʃ]. M.E. *boche*, O. Fr. *boche*, 'swelling on the skin'. Cp. **boss (I.).** **1.** A swelling, or spot &c., on the skin. **2.** A clumsy piece of work. Originally a lump, shapeless swelling.

botch (II.), vb. trans., fr. prec. **1.** To bungle anything, carry out work clumsily and unskilfully. **2.** To patch roughly (a boot &c.).

botcher, n. [1. bócher; 2. bɔ́tʃə]. A rough sort of cobbler; a bad, clumsy workman.

both, pron., adj., & adv. [1. bōth; 2. bouþ]. M.E. *bōþe, bōthe*, fr. O.N. *bāþar.* The ending *-th* may perh. be fr. the pl. def. art., O.N. *þeir, þær, þau*, O.E. *þā* for all genders; O.H.G., Goth. in *bajō-þs*, adj., & Mod. Germ. have a corresponding ending in *bei-de*, 'both', wh. is lacking in the other languages; O.E. has *bēgen* masc., *bā* fem. & neut., Goth. *bai* masc., *ba* neut. The base is found also in second element of Lat. *am-bō*, 'both', *am-bi-*, 'around, both sides', inseparable pref., Gk. *ám-phō*, 'both', *ám-phi*, 'around', Scrt. *u-bhāu.* The Aryan base was apparently **bhōi-*, **bhēi-*, **bhi-.* See **ambi-.** The word thus occurs in Gmc., Italic, Hellenic, & Scrt., but no further light can be thrown upon its origin. The two (persons or things) together, not excluding either. **a** Used as a pron., as: *are your parents living? Yes, both are*; **b** as an adj.: *both parents are still living*; **c** adv. = two things at once, at same time: *he is both a fool and a knave*; *both a gentleman and a scholar.*

bother (I.), vb. trans. & intrans. [1. bódher; 2. bɔ́ðə]. Etymol. unknown. **1.** trans. To annoy, worry, cause trouble, anxiety, or difficulty to; pester, perplex: *children often bother their parents in many ways*; *the variety of his responsibilities bothered him greatly*; *don't bother me with these trivial details*; *that doesn't bother me, it's quite simple.* Phrs. *to bother one's head about*, feel anxiety, take trouble concerning; *oh, bother (it)!*, confound it! **2.** intrans. To feel anxiety, worry &c.; allow oneself to be made anxious: *he would be much better if he didn't bother so much*; *do your best and don't bother*; *he lets things slide and doesn't bother.* Also, *bother about* (something), feel anxious, and take steps to improve it; either in sense of fussing unduly, or of taking reasonable care: *he is always bothering about things that don't matter*; *this general was defeated because he had not bothered about taking* (or *to take*) *obvious precautions.*

bother (II.), n. See prec. Source of trouble, worry; difficulty, tedium; disturbance, fuss; dispute: *his sons are a great bother to him*; *I find dictionary work a great bother*; *what is all this bother about?*; *I had some bother with him about keeping his appointments.*

botheration, n. [1. bòdheráshun; 2. bɔ̀ðəréiʃən], fr. prec. & **-ation.** Same as **bother (II.)**; also mild expletive = confound it!: *oh, botheration!* Perhaps suggested by *damnation!*

bothy, n. [1. bóthi; 2. bɔ́þi]. Scots; perh. related to **booth.** A small, humble cottage.

botony, adj. [1. bótuni; 2. bɔ́təni]. Fr. *boutonné*, 'provided with a bud, or button'. See **button.** (her., of a cross on the shield) Having a kind of trefoil at the end of each branch.

bo-tree, n. [1. bō trē; 2. bóu trī], fr. Cingalese *bō*; cp. Scrt. *bōdhi*, 'enlightenment', cp. *Buddha.* The pipul or sacred fig tree of India, being the tree under which Gautama (Buddha) was sitting when 'enlightenment' came to him.

bottle (I.), n. [1. bótl; 2. bɔ́tl]. M.E. *botel*, fr. O. Fr. *boteille*, Low Lat. *butticula*, 'flask', dimin. of *buttis*, 'cask', fr. Gk. The word is found in Ital. *bottiglia*, Span. *botella*, Port. *botelha* &c. The further relations of this group of words w. those discussed under **body** & **boot (I.)** are not clear, but it seems probable that *bottle* was orig. a leather flask or wineskin. **1.** A hollow vessel, esp. a receptacle for liquids, usually of glass, without handles, with narrow top or neck, and the part below either swelling out and then continuing straight down to the bottom, or with swelling, bulging sides sloped in towards the bottom. Specif., a small glass receptacle from which babies suck milk: *to bring a child up on the bottle.* Phrs. *wine in bottle and in barrel*; *(make a noise) like a bee in a bottle.* **2.** The contents of, amount contained in, a bottle, esp. of wine: *to drink a whole bottle*; *this decanter will hold a large bottle of wine.* **3.** (fig.) Wine, strong drink, which is usually stored in, and associated with, bottles: *to be too fond of the bottle, to take to the bottle*; '*Go like an Indian, in another life Expect thy dog, thy bottle and thy wife*' (Pope);

discuss something over a bottle, while drinking, in a sociable, friendly manner; *to crack a bottle together,* take wine together, hold friendly intercourse.

bottle (II.), vb. trans., fr. prec. **a** To put into a bottle: *it would be best to bottle this wine at once*; **b** (fig.) *bottle up,* restrain, keep under control, conceal: *discontent and rebellion, long bottled up, now broke out.*

bottle (III.), n. Perh. same as **bottle** (I.), fr. O. Fr. *botel,* dimin. of *botte,* 'bundle'. See **body, butt** (I.). Bundle, truss, esp. *bottle of hay* (obsolesc. and rare).

bottle-brush, n. Brush for cleaning bottles.

bottled, adj. [1. bótld; 2. bɔ́tld]. Put into bottles (of wine, beer &c.).

bottle glass, n. Coarse, green glass.

bottle green, adj. Dark green.

bottle-headed whale, n. Variety of small whale.

bottle-holder, n. Supporter, backer, esp. at a prize-fight.

bottle-nose, n. Cetacean of dolphin family.

bottle-nosed, adj. Having a swelled, reddish, pimply nose, suggestive of owner's fondness for the bottle.

bottle-tit, n. (ornith.) Long-tailed titmouse; so-called from shape of its nest.

bottle-washer, n. One who washes bottles; any menial or underling; drudge, hack.

bottom (I.), n. [1. bótum; 2. bɔ́təm]. O.E. *botm,* 'lowest part, depth, bottom, ship's keel', M.E. *botome, boþem* &c.; O.S. *bodom,* 'soil', O. Fris. *boden,* O.H.G. *bodam,* Mod. Germ. *boden,* 'ground, soil, earth, land', O.N. *botn,* 'bottom of sea, of a ship'. The *t* in O.E., compared w. *d* in O.S. as well as in O.H.G., presents difficulties wh. have not been cleared up. The O.N. form points to Gmc. **buþm-,* wh. wd. square w. O.S. & O. Fris. In spite of irregularities in O.E. & O.H.G., we may compare Lat. *fundus,* for **fudn-os,* 'bottom of anything', but also 'piece of land, farm, estate'; Gk. *puthmēn* for **phuthmēn,* 'foundation, bottom of anything, of the sea, of a cup'; Scrt. *budhnáś,* 'soil, ground'; O. Ir. *bond,* for **bodn,* 'sole of the foot'. In spite of the somewhat various meanings of the above cognates, the root idea, preserved in Gmc., Lat., & Scrt., seems to be 'earth, land'. It is suggested that the Aryan **bhudhn-* meant 'the place of growth' ultimately, & the base is connected w. that of Lat. *fui,* 'I was', *fieri,* 'to become', Engl. **be.** See also **beam** (I.). **1.** The lowest part of anything, farthest from the top; the base, which supports the rest: *the bottom of a tree*; *bottom of a house,* basement; lowest part of a slope: *bottom of the hill.* **2.** The part of a chair which supports the sitter. **3.** That end of a cask which is downwards, upon which the cask rests; either end may become the bottom. **4. a** The lowest part of any vessel, either inside or out: *to leave something at the bottom of the cup*; *the bottom of a well, a bath, bucket, barrel* &c.; **b** (fig.) the depths of one's character, nature, feelings: *a good man at bottom*; *from the bottom of the heart,* sincerely, deeply. **5.** The bed of any body of water: *bottom of the sea, lake, river.* Phrs. *to go to the bottom,* to sink (of a boat, or swimmer); *to touch bottom,* get into shallow water, run aground; (fig.) to reach the lowest possible degree of demerit. **6.** The basis, foundation (esp. fig.) of belief, argument, subject of study &c.: Phrs. *to be at the bottom of something,* to be the cause; *to get to the bottom of,* to understand thoroughly from inquiry; *to go to the bottom of a question,* study deeply, inquire into; *to knock the bottom out of an argument* &c., destroy, refute (perhaps with reference also to **3**). **7. a** The lowest part or keel of a ship: Phr. *bottom upwards,* upside down; **b** (by extension) the whole ship: *the great bulk of the American Army was brought over in British bottoms.* **8.** That part of the human anatomy used in sitting (colloq. and vulg.). **9.** (provinc.) A small valley, or hollow in the ground.

bottom (II.), adj., fr. prec. Lowest, last: *bottom price.* Phr. *to bet one's bottom dollar,* bet all one has, to be absolutely certain of.

bottom (III.), vb. trans. & intrans., fr. **bottom** (I.). **1.** trans. **a** To put a bottom or seat to: *to bottom a chair* &c.; **b** to reach, get to the bottom of anything, to find out about, understand fully, to fathom: *to bottom a man's motives, plans, arguments* &c.; **c** (usually in pass.) to found, base: *his arguments were bottomed on practical good sense.* **2.** intrans. (rare) To rest, be based or grounded, with *on* or *upon*: *on what do his arguments bottom?*

bottom growth, n. Thick, short grass in meadows, below the longer and comparatively sparse growth.

bottom heat, n. Heat at the roots of plants in frames, produced by thick bed of manure or *hotbed* below the soil.

bottomless, adj. [1. bótumles; 2. bɔ́təmlis]. **bottom** (I.) & **-less. a** (lit.) Without bottom, that is, of great depth, unplumbed: *bottomless abyss*; **b** (of a chair) having no seat or bottom; **c** (fig.) without foundation; so deep as to prevent one getting to the end or bottom; unfathomable: *bottomless stupidity, ignorance, incapacity* &c. (always in unfavourable sense).

bottomry, n. [1. bótumri; 2. bɔ́təmri]. See **bottom** (I.), 7, & **-ry.** Cp. Du. *bodmerij.* System of lending money to shipowner for a voyage on security of his ship.

botulism, n. [1. bótūlizm; 2. bɔ́tjulizəm], fr. Lat. *botulus,* 'gut, sausage', & **-ism.** *Botulus* appears to be an Oscan dial. form fr. Aryan **gʷot-ulos,* normal Lat. **votulus.* The base **gʷot-, *gʷet-,* means 'twist, wind, enfold', & fr. it are also derived Goth. *qiþus,* 'belly, womb', O.H.G. *quiti,* 'vulva', O.E. *cwiþ,* 'womb', & possibly Lat. *uterus,* 'womb', wh. some derive fr. **gʷuteros.* The Lat. word was apparently extended fr. its orig. meaning 'guts' to 'sausage' on account of fancied resemblance in shape. For later developments of *botulus* in the Romance languages see **bowel.** The meaning of the word as appears fr. above is lit. 'sausage disease'. The disease, which is generally fatal, arises from poison which is set up by the action of certain bacteria in potted and other preserved meats.

boudoir, n. Fr. pronunciation [1. bŏŏdwar; 2. būdwār]; Engl. [1. bóodwawr; 2. búdwɔ̄]. 18th cent. Fr. word, fr. *bouder,* 'to sulk' (origin unknown), & *-oir,* as in *parloir.* Cp. **parlour.** Literally a place to sulk in. Generally applied to a private sitting-room devoted to the use of the mistress of the house.

bougainvillaea, -ia, n. [1. bŏŏganvílea; 2. būgənvíliə]. Bougainville, an 18th cent. French naval explorer. A genus of tropical plants, the flowers of which have large bright red or purple bracts.

bough, n. [1. bou; 2. bau]. O.E. *bōg, bōh,* 'arm, shoulder, bough' (cp. **bosom**), O.H.G. *buog,* 'upper part of arm', also 'hip', Mod. Germ. *bug.* Engl. is the only language that has extended this word to mean 'limb, arm of a tree, bough'. Cp. outside Gmc., Gk. *pêkhus* for **phākhus,* 'forearm', Scrt. *bāhúś* for **bhāghus,* 'arm, forearm'. Limb of a tree, esp. one of the larger branches.

bought, vb. [1. bawt; 2. bɔ̄t]. Pret. & P.P. of **buy.** O.E. *bohte, (ġe)boht*; M.E. *boht(e).*

bougie, n. [1. bŏŏzhē; 2. búʒi]. Fr., 'wax candle'; fr. Bugia, in Algeria, whence these candles first came to Europe. (surg.) A flexible instrument of rubber, for exploring or dilating wounds, urethra, and other openings in the body.

bouillabaisse, n. [1. bŏŏlyabās; 2. búljəbeis]. Fr., fr. O. Fr. *bueilles,* 'guts, bowels' (cp. **bowel & botulism**), & *abaisse,* 'abbess'. The word then means lit. 'abbess' guts'. A rich fish stew, a characteristic dish in Marseilles.

bouilli, n. [1. bŏŏyē; 2. búji]. Fr., 'boiled meat'. Cp. **bully beef.**

bouillon, n. [1. bŏŏyon; 2. bújɔ̃]. Fr., 'strong broth'. See **boil** (II.). Strong broth, liquid decocted from meat, such as beef-tea.

boulder, n. [1. bṓlder; 2. bóuldə]. M.E. *bulderstōn*; cp. Swed. *bullersten,* 'large stone in a stream', perh. fr. *bullra,* 'roar, rattle'; Dan. *buldre.* The word apparently means 'roaring stone', on account of noise made by a stream flowing round it; perh. connected w. **bellow,** vb. Large, rounded mass of rock; often one which has been brought by ice or water from a distance, and which therefore differs from the surrounding rocks in character. *Boulder clay,* deposit of ancient glaciers containing far-travelled boulders.

boulevard, n. [1. bóolvard; 2. búlvād]; Fr. [1. bŏŏlvar; 2. būlvār]. Mod. Fr., earlier *boulevert, boulevere,* borrowed in early 15th cent. fr. Germ *bollwerk,* 'fortification.' See **bulwark.** A boulevard was originally a public walk, later on planted with trees, upon the top of old fortifications. The term is now used of a broad road with avenues of trees, often having houses on either side, frequented by the public as a promenade.

boulter, n. [1. bṓlter; 2. bóultə]. Etymol. unknown. Long stout line for fishing, with a number of hooks attached.

bounce (I.), vb. intrans. & trans. [1. bouns; 2. bauns]. M.E. *bounse,* 'strike, beat'. L. Germ. *bunsen,* Du. *bonzen,* 'beat', &c. Origin unknown. **A.** intrans. **1.** To rebound on striking anything, as an indiarubber ball, or other resilient body: *the ball bounced over the net*; *the ball doesn't bounce well.* **2.** To move with bounding action, move roughly, violently, noisily, and ungracefully: *a number of ungainly young women were bouncing about in the playing-field*; *to bounce into a room*; *to bounce out of a chair.* **B.** trans. **1.** (rare in this sense) To cause to rebound: *to bounce a ball.* **2.** To bluff, persuade by untrue statements; esp. to hurry someone by these means into hasty, unconsidered action: *he tried to bounce me by concealing half the facts*; *the committee were bounced by wire-pullers into a rash decision.*

bounce (II.), n., fr. prec. **1. a** Power of, capacity for, bouncing; resilience: *the ball has lost its bounce*; **b** act of bouncing: *hit ball on first bounce.* **2. a** Roughness, clumsiness, of motion; **b** impudence, noisy bluster.

bouncing, adj. [1. bóunsing; 2. báunsiŋ], fr. Pres. Part of **bounce** (I.) **a** Given to bouncing, in general sense; **b** healthy, lusty, vigorous: *his wife presented him with two bouncing boys*; **c** large, clumsy, and rough in appearance and movement: *stout, red-cheeked, bouncing damsels.*

bound (I.), n. [1. bound; 2. baund]. (Usually in pl.) M.E. *bounde,* earlier *bunne,* O. Fr. *bonne,* earlier *bodne,* 'limit, boundary', Med. Lat. *bodina,* the origin of wh. is unknown. The Mod. Fr. is *borne*; cp. **bourn(e)** (II.); the final *-d* in *bound* is natural phon. development. **1. a** The limit, outer edge, boundary, confine, esp. fig.: *the bounds of space and time*; *the farthest bounds of ocean*; **b** specific area defined by law or rule as one which may be lawfully entered: *within bounds*; *out of bounds,* within, or beyond such an area (used esp. in schools). **2.** Limitations, restraints, restrictions, confining borders, esp. fig. of those imposed on conduct and thought by law, custom, moral sense, or intelligence: *he went outside the bounds of decency*; *to overstep the bounds of common sense, of possibility.* Phr. *to put, set bounds to,* limit, restrain.

bound (II.), vb. trans., fr. prec. **1.** To serve as a boundary, or confine to: *a line of mountains bounds the landscape*; *England is bounded on the north by Scotland.* **2.** (fig.) To set a limit to, to impose boundaries; place restrictions upon: *we should bound our desires by reason*; *no nice scruples bounded his conduct.*

bound (III.), vb. intrans. Used since 16th cent. in Engl. O. Fr. *bondir,* 'resound, echo' &c., only used in sense of 'leap, spring', in 15th cent., comes fr. L. Lat. *bombitāre,* earlier *bombicāre,* 'buzz, hum', fr. *bombire.* See this base under **bomb** & **bombard.** **1.** To leap, spring, skip, advance with light, rapid, elastic, springy motion, as by a series of leaps; hence, often, simply to walk or run rapidly and actively: *his dog bounded to meet him*, or *along by his side*; '*Like a roe I bounded o'er the mountains*' (Wordsworth). **2.** To recoil, bounce, as a ball or other elastic body; to rebound.

bound (**IV.**), n., fr. prec. A spring, leap; (by extension) a violent beat of the heart (poet.); (fig.) *a bound forward*, sudden and rapid progress. Phrs. *at a single bound*; *by leaps and bounds*, (fig.) very rapidly; *on the bound*, of a ball, after first bounce from the ground.

bound (**V.**), adj. M.E. *boun, būn*, 'prepared, ready', fr. O.N. *būin*, P.P. of *būa*, 'dwell, prepare'. See **be, beam**; also **boor, bower, busk.** **1.** Prepared, ready for (esp. for a journey): *a ship bound for a voyage*; *outward bound*; *homeward bound*; *bound to start on Tuesday* (in the last, often partly confused with P.P. of *bind*, in sense of *constrained, compelled*). **2.** Ready, and intended to go to a certain place: *bound for the Cape, India* &c.

bound (**VI.**), vb., Pret. & P.P. of **bind.** Both fr. M.E. P.P. type *būnde(n)*, see **bounden**; cp. O.E., M.E., Pret. *band*.

boundary, n. [1. bóundri; 2. báundri], fr. Med. Lat. *bonnārium*, a piece of land having a *bonne* or fixed limit; cp. **bound** (**I.**); equiv. to Mod. Fr. *Bonnier*, family name & a measure of land. The Engl. form developed the *-d-* fr. some such form as **būnri*, but was doubtless influenced by **bound** (**I.**). **1.** That which marks and fixes the limits of a piece of land or field, as a ditch, or water-course &c.; or of a province or country, as a river, range of hills &c., or agreed land-marks. **2. a** The limits, frontier &c. so fixed; **b** specif., the fixed limits of a cricket field, marked by a rope or line: *to hit a boundary*, to drive the ball to these limits, upon which so many runs are counted to the batsman. **3.** (fig.) The extreme edge or limit of a subject of study, thought, or speculation: *boundaries of knowledge, science, thought* &c.

bounden, adj. [1. bóunden; 2. báundən], fr. M.E. *bounden*, P.P., fr. O.E. *bunden*, P.P. of *bindan*, **bind.** Literally *bound*, fastened as though with bonds; hence, made obligatory, imposed upon one; survives only in phrase *bounden duty*.

bounder, n. [1. bóunder; 2. báundə]. **bound** (**III.**) & **-er.** Chiefly used in colloquial and familiar English in sense of a vulgar, ill-bred person of the male sex; a cad, an outsider.

boundless, adj. [1. bóundles; 2. báundlis], fr. **bound** (**I.**) & **-less.** Without bound or limit; very great, excessive.

boundlessly, adv. Prec. & **-ly.** Without limits or bounds.

bounteous, adj. [1. bóunteus, -chus; 2. báuntiəs, -tʃəs]. M.E. *bountevous*, fr. O. Fr. *bontif* & *-ous*; *bontif* formed fr. *bontét* & *-īvus*, see **bounty** & **-ive.** Mod. *bounteous*, formed anew as fr. *bounty* & **-ous.** **a** (of persons) Open-handed, liberal, generous; **b** (of things given) freely given; plentiful, abundant.

bounteously, adv. Prec. & **-ly.** In a liberal, bounteous manner; freely.

bounteousness, n. See prec. & **-ness.** Liberality, plentifulness.

bountiful, adj. [1. bóuntifool; 2. báuntiful]. **bounty** & **-ful.** **a** (of persons) Liberal in giving, open-handed; **b** (of things) plentiful, abundant.

bountifully, adv. Prec. & **-ly.** In a bountiful manner.

bountifulness, n. See prec. & **-ness.** Liberality; abundance.

bounty, n. [1. bóunti; 2. báunti]. M.E. *bounté*, fr. O. Fr. *bontét*, fr. Lat. *bonitāt-(em)*, acc., cp. Ital. *bontà*, Engadine dial. *bundét*, Span. *bondád*; fr. Lat. *bonus*, 'good', O. Lat. *dwonos*, fr. **dwenos*, connected w. Scrt. *dúvaš*, 'worship, adoration' &c. Cp. **bonus, beauty, bene-, boon** (**II.**). **1.** Liberality, freedom in giving, generosity, munificence. **2.** That which is given freely and liberally; generous gift, gratuity. **3.** Reward, premium offered, in addition to the price received for the article produced, in order to encourage production, as a *bounty on corn*, offered to induce farmers to grow it.

bouquet, n. [1. bóokā; 2. búkei]. Fr. *bouquet*, fr. *bousquet*, fr. Lat. *buxus*, 'wood, bush' &c., & dimin. suff. **-et.** Cp. **boscage, box** (**I.**) & **bush.** **1.** A bunch of flowers, nosegay. **2.** Perfume, aroma, of wine.

bourdon, n. [1. bóordun; 2. búədən, -ɔ̃], fr. Fr. *bourdon*, 'drone bee, base stop in an organ', Low Lat. *burdo*, 'drone', prob. imitative of humming, buzzing. See **burden** (**III.**). Bass stop in an organ or harmonium.

bourgeois (**I.**), n. & adj. [1. bo͞orzhwah; 2. búržwā]. Fr., fr. Low Lat. *burgensis*; Gmc. **burgus* (q.v. under **borough**) & adj. suff. *-ensis*. **a** n. Middle-class (person); citizen, shopkeeper; **b** adj., relating to habits, and modes of thought belonging to, characteristic of, the town-dwelling middle class.

bourgeois (**II.**), n. [1. bĕrjóis; 2. bʌdžóis]. Perh. fr. name of a typographer. A size of printer's type between long primer and brevier.

bourgeoisie, n. [1. bóorzhwahzē; 2. búržwāzī]. Fr. See **bourgeois** (**I.**). The middle classes collectively.

bourn (**I.**), n. [1. born; 2. bɔ̄(ə)n]. M.E. *burne*, O.E. *brunna*, 'stream, brook', also w. metath. *burna, burne*, Goth. *brunna*, O. Fris. *burna*, O.S. & O.H.G. *brunno*, Mod. Germ. *brunn, brunnen*, O.N. *brunnr*, cogn. w. O. Ir. *brennim*, 'bubble, spout out'; prob. same base as **burn** (**I.**) The Gmc. words quoted are apparently all connected w. Gk. *phréar* for **phréw-ar*, 'tank, cistern, reservoir', fr. Aryan base **bhreu-*, **bhru-* &c., fr. **bherew-* &c., 'bubble, spurt' &c. Cp. also Scrt. *bhurvan*, 'disturbance, agitation (of water)', Gk. *phru-ássomai*, 'tremble, prance, become agitated, (of horses)'. See further under **bird, bread, brew, brood.** Stream, rivulet. The northern (and Scots) form is *burn*.

bourn(e) (**II.**), n. Fr. *borne*, 'limit' &c., q.v. under **bound** (**I.**). Limit, boundary; goal; realm, domain.

bourrée, n. [1. bóorā; 2. búrei]. Fr. **a** An old lively French or Spanish dance, of the gavotte type; **b** music composed for this.

bourse, n. [1. boors; 2. buəs]. Fr. *bourse*, 'purse, Exchange', Low Lat. *bursa*, fr. Gk. *búrsa*, 'hide (stripped off and tanned), leather', hence 'leather bag'. See **bursar.** Name given to place, in foreign countries, corresponding to our (Stock) Exchange, where merchants and financiers meet to transact business.

boustrophedon, adj., adv., also as n. [1. bòustrofédon; 2. bàustrɔfídən]. Gk., as adv. only, lit. 'as ox turns in ploughing', fr. *boûs*, 'ox', see **bovine**, *stroph-*, *stréphein*, 'to turn', see **strophe**, & adv. suff. *-don*. **a** adj. Of old form of writing in which lines run from left to right and then right to left alternately; **b** adv., in this form of writing; **c** n., this form of writing.

bout, n. [1. bout; 2. baut]. Etymol. doubtful. Possibly early Mod. Engl. spelling of obs. *bought*, 'bend', connected w. **bight.** **1.** A spell of activity of any kind; amount of action performed in a continuous period of time: *bout of fighting, work, of drinking* &c. **2.** A contest, struggle, fight; *bout with the gloves*, boxing match; *bout with the enemy*. **3.** Space of time, occasion; turn, fit: *bout of illness, of coughing*.

bouts rimés, n. pl. [1. bo͞o rḗmā; 2. bū rīme]. Fr., lit. 'rhymed ends'. A form of verse-making, in which rhyming words are given to which lines of verse are to be composed.

bovate, n. [1. bṓvāt; 2. bóuveit]. L. Lat. *bovata*, see **bovine.** (obs.) A measure of land of varying extent in different localities; also styled *oxgang*.

bovine, adj. [1. bṓvīn; 2. bóuvain]. Low Lat. *bovīnus*, fr. *bōs, bov-is*, 'ox', adj. suff. *-īnus*, see **-ine.** Lat. *bōs* is an Umbr. dial. form of wh. the true Lat. wd. be **vōs*, cogn. w. Gk. *boûs*, fr. Aryan **gʷōus*, cp. Scrt. *gāuš*, O. Slav. *gov-ędo*, 'ox'. The Gmc. cogn. is **cow.** **a** Ox-like, pertaining to the ox; **b** (fig.) heavy in body and mind, dull.

bow (**I.**), n. [1. bō; 2. bou]. O.E. *boga*, M.E. *bōwe*, 'bow for shooting', O. Fris. *boga*, O.H.G. *bogo*, O.N. *bogi*; all presuppose Gmc. **buga-*, related to O.E. *būgan*, 'to bend, curve'; cp. (w. different gradation form), O.H.G. *biogan*, Goth. *biugan*, wh. go back to Aryan **bheuk-*, **bhuk-*, or **bheugh-*, **bhugh-* &c. The other languages, however, have forms wh. presuppose Aryan **bheug-* &c.; Gk. *pheúgō*, Lat. *fugio*, Perf. *fūgi*, 'I flee' (w. idea of swerving, bending one's course away from), cp. **fugacious**, Scrt. *bhujáti*, 'bends, thrusts aside', *bhugnaš*, 'bent'. O.E. uses *ġe-būgan* in sense of fleeing away from battle. The *bow* is primarily 'the bent, curved' thing or weapon. Cp. also **buxom.** **1.** A primitive weapon. held in left hand with arm extended, made of flexible wood, bent so that a string which is held tightly stretched between the two ends propels arrows by the force of its recoil when released by the finger and thumb of right hand after it has been pulled back towards the shoulder. Phrs. (fig.) *to have two strings to one's bow*, several resources, plans for doing anything; *to draw the long bow*, talk big, exaggerate. **2.** Anything shaped more or less like a bow, esp. a *rainbow*. **3.** The arched front part of a saddle. **4.** Slender piece of wood strung with horse-hair with which the strings of the violin, 'cello &c. are made to sound; formerly called also a fiddle-stick. **5. a** A kind of running knot with a double loop; **b** a piece of silk or lawn tied in this way and used as a necktie &c.

bow (**II.**), vb. intrans., fr. prec. To use the bow (**I.**), **4**, in playing the fiddle: *he bows admirably*.

bow (**III.**), vb. intrans. & trans. [1. bou; 2. bau]. O.E. *būgan*, 'bend, incline, turn aside' &c. From same base as **bow** (**I.**). **A.** intrans. **1. a** To bend, incline head, or body by way of greeting, or in token of respect; **b** (by extension), to remove one's hat, in greeting or respect, without inclining head or body (used only of men in this sense). Phr. *to have a bowing acquaintance with*, very slight acquaintance. **2.** (fig.) To submit to, acknowledge superior knowledge or judgement, yield to greater strength: *I bow to your decision, to his expert knowledge in certain matters*; *we must bow to superior force, resistance is impossible*; *to bow before the inevitable.* **B.** trans. **1.** To usher, conduct (persons) into or out of a room; indicate that they are to enter or to withdraw: *I was bowed into the great man's room by his butler, and shortly afterwards bowed out again by the master of the house himself.* **2.** To bend, prostrate, oppress, crush (lit. and fig.): *the prevailing wind has bowed all the trees towards the east*; *the Jews bowed their necks beneath the severities of Pharaoh*; *our hearts are bowed with grief*; *to bow the knee to*, worship, show respect for. **3.** To express by, or with, a bow, or inclination of head or body: *to bow one's thanks, one's appreciation* &c. **C.** *Bow down* (*to*) intrans., **a** to submit to, show humility, yield to, acknowledge, truckle to: *I'm not going to bow down to people of this sort*; **b** to worship as divine; show reverence for: '*Thou shalt not make to thyself any graven image . . . thou shalt not bow down to them nor worship them*'.

bow (**IV.**), n., fr. prec. An inclination of head or body made as sign of greeting or respect. Phr. *to make one's bow*, take one's leave, retire; bring any public act, speech &c. to an end.

bow (**V.**), n. [1. bou; 2. bau]. Same word as **bough**, fr. O.E. *bōg, bōh*, 'shoulder, limb, bough'; derived fr. *bōg* type. Naut. sense borrowed prob. fr. Dan. *boug*, latter being used in that sense & having approximately same diphthong. The fore part of a boat or ship, which cuts the water when **vessel**

advances, as distinct from the *stern.* Phrs. *on the bow, bow side, bow oar.*

bow chaser, n. (naut.) Ship's gun so placed as to be able to fire at a vessel in front.

bowdlerize, vb. trans. [1. bóudleriz; 2. báudləraiz], fr. name of Dr. Thomas Bowdler, who published in 1818 an edition of Shakespeare intended for family reading, with everything wh. he considered profane or indelicate cut out. To expurgate a book; generally used to imply expurgation carried out without very sound taste and judgement; to emasculate a text.

bowed, adj. [1. bōd; 2. boud]. **bow (I.)**. & **-ed.** Curved, bent, like a bow.

bowel, n. [1. bóuil; 2. báuil]. M.E. *bouel*, fr. O. Fr. *bueille, boel*, 'bowel', Mod. Fr. *boyau*, Lat. *botellus, botulus*, q.v. under **botulism** & **bouillabaisse.** (Gen. used in pl.) **1.** Gut, intestine, entrail, in men or animals, that part of alimentary canal leading out of stomach from below. **2.** (fig.) The innermost, hidden, covered, part of anything, esp. *the bowels of the earth.* **3.** (fig.) The viscera were formerly regarded as the chief seat of the emotions, passions &c.; hence (by extension) the feelings and emotions themselves: *the bowels of mercy, compassion* &c.; '*his bowels yearned after him*' (archaic).

bower (I.), n. [1. bóuer; 2. báuə]. O.E. *būr*, 'chamber', esp. 'women's quarters', also 'dwelling, cottage', M.E. *bour*, 'room, lady's apartment, bower'. (The mod. spelling came in sporadically in words of this type, during the later 15th & 16th cents., to express the tendency to pronounce a second syll. after a long *ū, ī*, or diphthong, before *-r*; cp. *flower*, fr. *flour*, & the common early spelling *fiar, desiar* &c.) O.H.G. *būr, pūr*, in same sense; fr. base **bū-*, 'to dwell'; discussed under **Boer, be**, & cp. **byre.** (obsolesc.) Used rather vaguely in following poet. senses. **1.** Lady's chamber, private apartment. **2.** Leafy, flowery grove; arbour, rustic summer-house in a garden: '*There's a bower of roses by Bendamere's stream*' (Moore). **3.** Rustic cottage, retreat.

bower (II.), n. fr. **bow (V.).** An anchor (and cable) carried at the bow of a ship; also attrib., *bower-anchor, bower-cable.*

bower (III.), n. fr. Germ. *bauer*, 'peasant'; Germ. name for the *knave* in cards. See **Boer.** Expression in card game of euchre for one of the two highest cards used: *right bower*, knave of trumps; *left bower*, knave of same coloured suit as trumps.

bower bird, n. **bower** (I.) & **bird.** Group of Australian birds, such as *bird-of-paradise*; so called from the peculiar and elaborate character of their nests.

bowery, adj. [1. bóueri; 2. báuəri]. **bower** (I.) & **-y.** Leafy, flowery, like a bower.

bowie knife, n. [1. bōi nīf; 2. bóui naif], fr. name of American inventor, Col. Bowie. Knife with a long single-edged blade, the back of which is straight until near the point, when it curves convexly.

bowing, n. [1. bōing; 2. bóuiŋ], fr. **bow** (I.), **4.** & **-ing.** The management of the bow in fiddle playing; player's style in using the bow.

bowl (I.), n. [1. bōl; 2. boul]. O.E. *bolla*, M.E. *bolle*; O. Fris., O.H.G. *bolla*, O.N. *bolli*, fr. Gmc. **bul-*, 'swell', Aryan **bhḷ-* &c. Cp. Lat. *follis*, 'leather bag'. An enormous number of words in all the Aryan languages have been connected w. the various forms of this base. See some of them under **ball, belly, billow, blade.** The *bowl* was the vessel w. a 'swelling', rounded shape. The Mod. Engl. form is abnormal, & we should expect *boll.* It does not help much to say the form of *bowl* has been influenced by that of **bowl (II.)** since that also is abnormal. **1.** A hollow vessel or basin made of wood, china, metal, or glass, of various sizes and used for various purposes: *washing-bowl, slop-bowl, rose-bowl* &c. **2.** Specif., a drinking vessel. Already in 14th cent. *bollere* means 'drunkard', lit. 'one who used the bowl (in excess)'. Now the usage is chiefly confined to poetry, and even there is more often extended to drinking, that is to the use of the bowl on convivial occasions, rather than the thing itself. (See **3** below.) '*Send round the bowl and be happy awhile*' (Moore). Phr. *the flowing bowl* (Pope). *Punch bowl*, one in which punch is brewed, from which it is ladled into glasses for drinking. **3.** (fig.) Convivial drinking: *to sit too long over the bowl*; *the cheerful bowl*, and so on. **4. a** The rounded part of a tobacco pipe into which the tobacco is placed for smoking; **b** hollowed, serviceable part of a spoon.

bowl (II.), n. Fr. *boule*, fr. Lat. *bulla*, 'bubble'. Cp. **bill (III.).** Ultimately connected w. base **bhel-, *bhḷ-* &c., 'blow out, swell', & therefore allied indirectly to **bowl (I.).** Heavy wooden ball, made with a bias, trundled along a flat lawn, in game of bowls.

bowl (III.), vb. trans. & intrans., fr. prec. **1.** trans. **a** To roll, trundle, (a bowl) **(II.)** along the ground, in bowls, or in ninepins; to roll (a child's hoop); **b** to deliver (a ball) to batsman in cricket, which was formerly done under-hand, with the same action as in rolling a bowl; **c** to get a batsman out by bowling, in cricket: *he was bowled in the second over.* Also *bowl out.* Phrs. *to bowl out* (fig. from cricket), to defeat another in any way, frustrate, disconcert, in argument &c., bring to a nonplus; *to bowl over* (fig. from ninepins), to upset, render helpless, put out of action: *I was completely bowled over by the bad news, by illness* &c. **2.** intrans. To roll, move rapidly, esp. in a wheeled vehicle (gen. with *along*): *we bowled along the country roads in a high dog-cart.*

bow-leg, n., fr. **bow** (I.) & **leg. a** (usually in pl.) A leg, or shin bone, which curves outwards from knee in the shape of a bow: *to have bow-legs*; **b** malformation due to this condition: *to suffer from bow-leg.*

bow-legged, adj. Prec. & **-ed.** Having bow-legs.

bowler (I.), n. [1. bōler; 2. bóulə], fr. **bowl** (III.), **1.**, & **-er.** One who bowls; esp. the player who bowls to the batsman in cricket: *a fast, dangerous bowler.*

bowler (II.), n., fr. **bowl** (I.) on account of its shape. A hard round felt hat.

bowline, n. [1. bōlin; 2. bóulin]. **bow** (V.) & **line**; corresponding forms found in the Mod. Gmc. languages. Pronunciation of first element changed as if fr. O.E. *boga*, see **bow** (I.), rather than fr. *bōg.* Rope in ship's rigging running from a sail to bow of ship.

bowling, n. [1. bōling; 2. bóuliŋ], fr. **bowl** (III.) & **-ing. 1. a** The act of delivering the ball in cricket; **b** style in which this is done. **2. a** Game, sport, or act of playing bowls; **b** specif., game, sport of playing skittles on a bowling alley, as distinct from *bowls.*

bowling-alley, n. Covered floor, long, narrow and provided with raised edges as a boundary, upon which skittles or ninepins is played.

bowling-green, n. Specially levelled and prepared lawn upon which bowls is played.

bowls, n. pl. [1. bōlz; 2. boulz]. See **bowl** (II.). Game played on a bowling-green with balls or bowls made with a bias, the object being to lay the bowl near a smaller one called a 'jack'.

bowman, n. [1. bōman; 2. bóumən]. **bow** (I.) & **man.** Person who uses, or fights with, a bow; an archer.

bowshot, n. [1. bōshot; 2. bóuʃɔt]. See prec. & **shot.** The distance which an arrow will carry when shot from a bow; the range of the old English long-bow was 300-400 yards.

bowsprit, n. [1. bō-, bóu-sprit; 2. bóu-, báu-sprit]. **bow** (V.) & O.E. *sprēot*, 'pole, spar'. This is no doubt related to O.E. *sprēotan*, 'sprout', *sprota*, 'sprout, twig', cp. O.H.G. *sprozzo.* See this base under **sprout** (I.). The spar projecting from bow of a ship, which carries a sail, and supports the masts by means of stays.

Bow Street, n. [1. bō strēt; 2. bóu strīt]. Street in London, near Long Acre and Covent Garden, chiefly as name of principal metropolitan police court; whence *Bow-street runner*, the name of a detective or police officer attached to this court, prior to the formation of a London police and detective force.

bowstring (I.), n. [1. bōstring; 2. bóustriŋ]. **bow** (I.) & **string. a** The stout cord of a bow which propels the arrow; **b** cord used in old Turkish Empire for strangling people.

bowstring (II.), vb. trans., fr. prec. To strangle by twisting a bowstring or other cord round the throat.

bow window, n. **bow** (I.) & **window. a** Window built out so as to project in a semi-circular form from the walls of a house; **b** (vulg.) a prominent abdomen.

bowwow, n. [1. bóuwóu; 2. báuwáu]. Imitative. **a** Popular, or childish name for bark of a dog; **b** transferred, in childish talk, to dog itself. (In the latter case accentuated only on first syllable. [1. bóuwou; 2. báuwau]).

bowyer, n. [1. bōyer; 2. bóujə]. M.E. *bowyere.* **bow** (I.) & **-yer.** Man who makes or sells bows. Nearly obsolete, except as a family name.

box (I.), n. [1. boks; 2. bɔks]. O.E. *box*, fr. Lat. *buxus*, borrowed fr. Gk. *púxos*; prob. of foreign (Phrygian ?) origin; connexion w. *puknós*, 'dense, hard', is disputed; cp. **boscage, bush, pyx.** An evergreen shrub or tree with a very hard, pale yellow wood.

box (II.), n. O.E. *box*, 'box tree', also a receptacle made fr. the wood. Perh. same as prec. Also in O.H.G. *buhsa*, 'box wood', & 'case of box wood', Mod. Germ. *büchse.* Orig. a receptacle made of box wood. **1. a** A case, coffer, chest; a receptacle of wood, metal, or card-board &c., of any size, generally with a lid, either square or round. This word has innumerable and very various applications; the special sense in which it is used is often expressed by a qualifying word prefixed: e.g. *horse-box*, a compartment in a train for carrying a horse; *pill-box*, a small card-board case for pills; **b** contents of a box: *to eat a whole box of chocolates.* All the following meanings spring from the fundamental one of a chest or coffer. **2.** A present, gift; now only *Christmas box*; originally the contents of a box (cp. similar use of *bottle, hamper*), then with specialized sense of gifts enclosed in a box. **3.** Driver's seat on a carriage; so named because it was originally made upon the *box* which contained the tools for repairs, spare food for the horses &c. **4.** A private compartment in a theatre, commanding view of the stage, and containing seats for several persons: *stage box* &c. **5. a** A small house or room: *a little box of a place*; **b** small country house, used as temporary residence for specific purpose: *hunting box, shooting box*; **c** a small wooden shelter: *sentry box.* **6.** In various technical senses: e.g. that enclosed part of window frame in which the weights which hold the window at desired height move up and down; also used in type-founding, machinery &c.

box (III.), vb. trans., fr. prec. **1.** To put into a box (in various senses): *to box a horse*, put him into a horse-box &c. **2.** *Box up*, to confine, shut up in a restricted space, restrain freedom of movement: *we were boxed up all night in a railway carriage, in a small room* &c. **3.** *Box the compass*, **a** to repeat in right order all the points; **b** (fig.) to go through various states of opinion or belief, until one comes back to that from which one started.

box (IV.), n. In Chaucer in sense of 'a blow'; possibly borrowed fr. Gk. *púx*, adv., in phr. *púx agathós*, 'good, handy, with the fists'. Cp. **pugnacious.** A blow with the open hand, a slap; now only in *box on the ear.*

box (V.), vb. trans. & intrans., fr. prec. **1.** trans. To slap a person's face or head; only in *to box the ear(s).* **2.** intrans. To fight with the fists, esp. for sport with padded gloves.

box-cloth, n. A thick, heavy, light-brown cloth, made for driving or box coats.

boxer, n. [1. bókser; 2. bóksə]. **box (V.)** & **-er. 1. a** A person who fights with his fists, esp. one who has been trained in the art of self-defence, and is skilled; **b** a professional pugilist, prize-fighter. **2.** (cap.) A member of a Chinese nationalist secret society; translation of Chinese name, 'fist of harmony'.

boxing, n. [1. bóksing; 2. bóksiŋ], fr. **box** & **-ing.** The art of using the fists to fight; pugilism.

Boxing Day, n., fr. **box (II.), 2.** Name given to Dec. 26th, from the custom of giving *Christmas boxes* on that day.

boy, n. [1. boi; 2. bɔi]. Etymol. very dubious; but note early Fris. *boi*, 'young gentleman'. **1. a** A male child from birth to puberty; often applied by elders to young men in the early twenties: **b** applied to elderly or old men as a term of affection or mild contempt: *an old boy; nice old, funny old boy*, equivalent to *fellow, chap, buffer* &c. **2.** A native servant, esp. one belonging to an inferior and subject race.

boycot(t) (I.), vb. trans. [1. bóikot; 2. bóikət], fr. Capt. Boycott, land-agent in Co. Mayo, for whose benefit the treatment, very similar to the Church's Major Excommunication, was first practised in Ireland in 1880. **1.** To combine against (a landowner, farmer, or tradesman), by refusing to hold any social intercourse with him, to sell to, or buy from, him. **2.** (fig.) **a** (of persons) To ostracize, keep aloof from, send to Coventry; **b** (of goods and merchandise) to refrain from using, refuse to buy, forbid entry into a country.

boycot(t) (II.), n., fr. prec. The system of treating persons and goods in the way defined in above entry: *to apply the boycot(t); a system of boycot(t)* &c.

boyhood, n. [1. bóihood; 2. bóihud]. **boy** & **-hood.** The period of a male child's life up to puberty.

boyish, adj. [1. bói-ish; 2. bói-iʃ]. **boy** & **-ish.** Like a boy; both in favourable and unfavourable sense: **a** fresh, high-spirited, cheerful; **b** inexperienced, unpractised

boyishly, adv. Prec. & **-ly.** In a boyish manner, like a boy.

boyishness, n. See prec. & **-ness.** Quality of being boyish.

Boy Scout. See **scout (I.).**

brace (I.), n. [1. brās; 2. breis]. M.E. *brāce*, 'armour for the arms; clasp, clamp; pair'; O. Fr. *brache, brase, brasse*, fr. Lat. pl. *bra(c)chia*, 'arms', fr. Gk. *brakhīōn*, 'arm', the origin of wh. is unknown. The Fr. *brace* &c. means the measure of both arms extended; the M.E. word also refers to armour for *both* arms, & is derived fr. the Lat. pl. *Brace* came then to mean 'a pair of arms' before it meant 'pair' in general. The other meanings of the word in Engl. go back to the idea of clasping w. the arms, or of steadying, supporting oneself with the arms. Cp. **embrace. 1.** That which gives support, solidity, steadiness, to anything, a prop; e.g. cables, ropes &c. which give resistance to masts and other parts of a ship's rigging; iron or wooden props, stanchions, ties, in a building; metal stays in machinery; cords fastened to the side which maintain tension in a drum &c. **2.** (typog.) Bracket connecting two lines of print, or two words on different lines, as {. **3.** Specif. (always pl.), straps passing over the shoulders and crossed on the back, which button on to the trousers back and front, and keep them up. **4.** A pair, esp. of dogs, or hares, pheasants, partridges, and other forms of game; often used colloq. and popularly for a pair generally. **5.** (also in full) *Brace (and bit)* (see **bit (I.)**), tool for boring in which the *bit* is made to revolve by turning part of the brace with one hand, while it is firmly held in position by the other.

brace (II.), vb. trans., fr. prec. **1. a** To strengthen, give support, rigidity, steadiness to, apply a *brace* to, in any of the instances in **brace (I.)**; **b** (reflex.) *brace oneself up*, make a mental or muscular effort, put oneself in a condition to use one's whole strength, and resist the greatest amount of pressure; *brace oneself for a task*, prepare for it by making one's nerves and muscles tense (lit. and fig.). **2.** (fig.) To freshen, invigorate, stimulate, give health and strength to; (of air, climate &c.; also of moral and intellectual influence). **3.** Specif., to support (trousers) with *braces*; often *brace up.*

bracelet, n. [1. brāslet; 2. bréislit]. Fr. *bracelet*, dimin. of O. Fr. *bracel*, 'armlet', fr. Lat. *bracchiāle*, neut. adj., 'thing for the arm'. See **brace (I.). 1.** Band or circlet of metal or other substance worn on the wrist, esp. by women. **2.** (colloq. slang) A handcuff (gen. in pl.).

bracer, n. [1. brāser; 2. bréisə]. M.E., fr. O. Fr. *brasseure*. Cp. **brace (I.). a** Formerly armour protecting the arm; **b** also kind of shield worn in archery, to protect the wrist from the blow of the bowstring.

brach, n. [1. brach; 2. brætʃ]. M.E. *brache*, O. Fr. *brache(t)*, fr. O.H.G. *braccho*, 'hound hunting by scent', Mod. Germ. *bracke*; prob. cogn. w. Lat. *frāgrāre*, 'to smell strongly'; cp. under **fragrant.** The Gmc. word is found also in Ital. *bracco*, Span. *braco*, Ital. *braccare*, O. Fr. *braquer*, 'to trace out, follow by scent'. A bitch hound.

brachial, adj. [1. brākial; 2. bréikiəl], fr. Lat. *bracchiālis*. See **brace** & **bracelet** & **-al. a** Pertaining to the arm: *brachial artery*; **b** resembling an arm, of structures in fish, birds &c.

brachiate, adj. [1. brākiāt; 2. bréikieit]. Lat. *bracchiātus*, 'having boughs, or branches, like arms'. See **brace** & **-ate.** Having branches arranged in pairs, like the maple.

brachy-, pref., 'short', often implying also broadness in proportion to length; used in many modern scientific words; fr. Gk. *brakhús*, 'short', wh. in Gk. compounds becomes *brakhu-*. This is cogn. w. Lat. *brevis*, 'short'; see **brief (I.)** both fr. Aryan **breg'hu-* (the Lat. more directly fr. form **brehwi-*), & prob. also w. O. Slav. *brŭzŭ*, 'rapid'.

brachycephalic, -ous, adj. [1. bràkisefálik, bràkiséfalus; 2. brækisifǽlik, brækiséfələs]. See **brachy-** & **cephalic.** (ethnol.) Short (and broad) headed; having a skull of which breadth is at least four-fifths of length.

brachylogy, n. [1. brakíloji; 2. brækílədʒi]. **brachy-** & **-logy**, fr. Gk. compound *brachylogia*, 'brevity in speech'. Conciseness in speech; specif., omission of word in a sentence which is essential to grammatical construction.

bracing (I.), adj. [1. brāsing; 2. bréisiŋ], fr. Pres. Part of **brace (II.).** Stimulating, invigorating, refreshing (of wind, air, climate); also of moral and intellectual stimulation.

bracing (II.), n., **brace (II.)** & **-ing.** Process or act of stimulating, refreshing &c.: *he needs bracing.*

bracken, n. [1. bráken; 2. brǽkən]. M.E. *braken*; cp. Mod. Swed. *bräken*. Cp. **brake (II.). a** Species of coarse fern, *Pteris aquilina*, which grows in sandy and peaty soil; **b** collectively, a mass of such fern growing.

bracket (I.), n. [1. bráket; 2. brǽkit]. Earliest recorded form, *bragget or staie in building*, 1580 (O.E.D.). The origin is unknown, since the attempts to identify the word w. various words derived fr. Lat. *braccae*, 'breeches', can hardly be accepted. The word must be fr. some derivative of Lat. *bracchium*; cp. **brail** in sense of support. Influence in meaning & form by this group of words is admitted by the O.E.D. **1.** (archit.) Projecting support in a building, often carved, whether of timber or stone. **2.** A shelf, often hinged, supported against a wall by one or two props from below, which are also often hinged so as to be folded flat against wall, allowing the board which forms the shelf to hang down flat in front of them. **3.** A hinged fixture with burner for gas, fastened to end of gaspipe, and projecting from the wall. **4.** A figure used in printing, either *round* ( ), or *square* [ ], the former used for enclosing parenthesis &c., the latter for separating words from the rest of the text for any purpose. See **brace (I.), 2.** Phr. (*in brackets*), as foregoing words. **5.** (gunnery) Firing of a series of shots beyond and short of a target, in range finding.

bracket (II.), vb. trans., fr. prec. **a** To enclose in brackets (as in prec. **4**); **b** to join, or associate, two names of things or persons together in print by enclosing one below the other in a brace, or bracket; **c** (fig.) to associate the names of two persons together for any reason: *X and Y were bracketed for the prize*, adjudged of equal merit; **d** to fire bracket at (target).

brackish, adj. [1. brákish; 2. brǽkiʃ], fr. obs. adj. *brack*, 'salt', cp. Du. *brak*, adj., 'salt', & **-ish.** Rather salt; (of water) between salt and fresh, as that in an estuary &c., and so undrinkable.

bract, n. [1. brakt; 2. brækt], fr. Lat. *bractea*, 'thin metal plate'. Etymol. unknown. (bot.) Small leaf at base of a flower.

bracteate, adj. & n. [1. bráktēāt; 2. brǽktieit], fr. Lat. *bracteātus*, 'covered with thin plates'; see prec. & **-ate. 1.** adj. (bot.) Having bracts. **2.** n. (archaeol.) A thin small plate of silver or gold, used as an ornament &c. in early times.

brad, n. [1. brad; 2. bræd]. M.E. *brod*, 'spike, headless nail', later *brad*, cp. *Gad* for *God*. Prob. fr. O.N. *broddr*, 'spike', cogn. w. O.E. *brord*, 'point', cp. Lat. *fastīgium*, 'point', fr. **farsti-*, cp. Scrt. *bhṛṣṭiś*, 'point, prong'. See further under **borage, bristle, brush.** Name given to various types of nail; generally one which is long and slender with a small head.

bradawl, n. [1. brádawl; 2. brǽdōl]. See **brad** & **awl.** Tool consisting of straight, slender stem of steel with chisel edge for making holes for reception of nails or screws.

Bradbury, n. [1. brádburi; 2. brǽdbəri]. (colloq.) Name for a Treasury note, for £1 or 10s., from signature of official borne by each.

brady-, pref., 'slow', fr. Gk. *bradús*, 'slow', used in scientific terminology as *bradycardia* [1. bràdikárdia; 2. brædikádiə], slow beating or action of the heart; *Bradypus*, genus of three-toed sloths &c. The Gk. word is fr. **gʷr̥du-*, & is cogn. w. Lat. *gurdus*, 'stupid'.

brae, n. [1. brā; 2. brei]. Northern form fr. O.N. *brā*, 'eyelid', borrowed in M.E. & used in sense of 'river-bank, slope', cogn. w. O.E. *brū, brǣw* &c., q.v. under **brow.** Slope, hill-side, bank. North country and Scots word sometimes used by English writers.

brag (I.), vb. intrans. [1. brag; 2. bræg]. M.E. *brag(g)en*, 'boast, sound loudly (of voice)'. Etymol. doubtful. The dictionaries suggest relations either w. Fr. *brague*, 'ostentation', wh. is late, or w. O.N. *braka*, 'to creak', wh. should give **brack*, or **brake*, in Mod. Engl. To boast, to indulge in self-glorification, express undue pride and satisfaction in what concerns oneself, one's achievements or belongings: (gen.) *to brag of, about.*

brag (II.), n., fr. prec. Occurs in 14th cent. English in present sense. **a** A boast, vaunt &c.: *a foolish brag*; (also abstract) self-laudation, noisy, arrogant claim to admiration; **b** an old game of cards, possibly the original of poker.

braggadocio, n. [1. bragadóshiō; 2. brægədóuʃiou]. Formed & used by Spenser (in sense of 'boaster') fr. **brag**, w. Ital. suff. Vain, arrogant, noisy, boasting.

braggart, n. [1. brágart; 2. brǽgət]. **brag** & **-ard.** One who brags; a vain, noisy, boastful fellow.

Brahmapootra, n. & adj. [1. bráhmapòōtra; 2. brámәpūtrə], fr. name of Indian river. Species of fowl, usually in abbreviated form *Brahma.*

Brahmin, n. [1. bráhmin; 2. brámin], fr. Scrt. *Brāhmaṇa*, fr. *Brahma*, 'prayer; divine cause of the world', now used to designate a member of the priestly caste among the Hindus.

Brahminee, n. [1. bràhminē; 2. brāminī], fr. Scrt. *brahmaṇi*, see prec. Female belonging to Brahmin caste.

brahminical, adj. [1. brahmínikl; 2. brāmínikl]. **Brahmin** & **-ic** & **-al.** Pertaining to the Brahmins.

Brahminism, n. [1. bráhminizm; 2. brāminizəm]. **Brahmin** & **-ism.** System of religion, worship, among Brahmins; Hinduism.

Brahminy, -ee, adj. [1. bráhmini; 2. brāmini], fr. **Brahmin**, on anal. of *Bengalee* &c.

braid (I.), vb. trans. [1. brād; 2. breid]. O.E. *bregdan*, M.E. *breiden* &c., 'twist, wrench, draw (sword), plait'. Cp. O.S. *bregdan*. The O.E. vb. has a variety of meanings, all implying rapid, violent movement: to draw (a sword), pull, drag; move the hands (in swimming), brandish, throw; change (colour); weave, & so on. The last meaning is the nearest to present sense of *braid*. None of the dictionaries has suggested any extra Gmc. cognates for the base *bregd-*, but it seems reasonable to connect Lith. *brēžti*, 'scratch', O. Slav. *brěšti*, 'to hurl, throw', & Lat. *fricāre*, 'rub', as probable connexions. See **friction, friable.** **1.** To entwine, weave together, plait, esp. of a woman's hair. **2.** To adorn, trim, anything with braid.

braid (II.), n., fr. prec. **1.** Narrow band of woven material, linen, silk, ribbon, for binding the edges of cloth and garments; braid in this sense may be applied flat to the surface of cloth for the sake of ornamentation. **2.** Flat strip of material woven from fine gold thread as used on military, naval, and diplomatic uniforms: *gold braid.* **3.** A plait in a woman's hair, or plait of hair intertwined with some other substance.

braided, adj. [1. brāded; 2. bréidid]. P.P. of **braid (I.)**. **1.** Trimmed, ornamented, with braid. **2.** Twisted, plaited, intertwined: esp. *braided locks, hair.*

braiding, n. [1. brāding; 2. bréidiŋ]. **braid** & **-ing.** Trimming, as with braid, on a garment: *gold braiding.*

Braidism, n. [1. brādizm; 2. bréidizəm]. Named after Dr. Braid of Manchester (died 1860). Hypnotism. (obsolesc.)

brail, n. & vb. trans. [1. brāl; 2. breil], fr. O. Fr. *braiel*, 'girdle, belt', fr. Low Lat. *bracāle*, in same sense, fr. *brac(c)ae*, 'breeches'; of Celt. origin. See **breech.** **1.** n. (usually pl.) Small ropes at corner of a sail used for hauling in a sail, before furling. **2.** vb. To haul in, shorten, sail by use of brails.

Braille, n. [1. brāl; 2. breil]. Named after inventor Louis Braille (1809–52). System of reading and writing for the blind, in which the letters are formed by raised points pricked on paper.

brain (I.), n. [1. brān; 2. brein]. O.E. *brægen, bregen*, M.E. *brain*, O. Fris. & Du. *brein*; cp. also O.E. *brego*, 'prince, king'; prob. cogn. w. Gk. *brekhmós, brégma*, 'top of the head', if this, as is suggested, stands for earlier **mreghmó*, Pr. Gmc. **mregn-*, of wh. the full form wd. be **mereghm-*. It is further suggested that from a form of the same base w. different gradation in both syllables, **mr̥gh-*, the Gk. *arkhós*, 'leader, chief', *árkhō*, 'I begin', *arkhḗ*, 'beginning, cause' &c. are derived; cp. **arch-.** The fundamental meaning of the base is supposed to be 'top, summit'. If this be accepted *brain* orig. meant 'top of the head'. **1. a** Soft mass of nervous substance contained within the skull of vertebrate animal; (often used in pl. in idioms). Phr. *to blow one's brains out*, shoot fatally in the head; **b** also applied to the nerve ganglion in head of certain invertebrates. **2.** Centre of thought and sensation, therefore (fig.) mind, intelligence, intellect, ability: *to overtax one's brain*; *use one's brains*; *a powerful, weak, clear, muddled, brain.* Phrs. *to cudgel*, or *rack one's brains*, make a special effort of thought or memory; *to have something on the brain*, be obsessed by it; *to pick a man's brains*, utilize his knowledge without troubling to work something out for oneself.

brain (II.), vb. trans., fr. prec. To knock out the brains of.

-brained, adj. [1. brānd; 2. breind]. Having a brain, usually qualified, as in *rattle-brained.*

brain-fever, n. Inflammation of the membrane surrounding the brain; meningitis.

brainless, adj. [1. brānles; 2. bréinlis]. **brain (I.)** & **-less.** Without brains or intelligence, stupid.

brain-pan, n. Upper part of the head.

brainsick, adj. [1. brānsik; 2. bréinsik]. Having a disordered mind.

brain-storm, n. Sudden mental derangement.

brain-wave, n. (colloq.) A sudden inspiration; a bright idea or suggestion.

brainy, adj. [1. brāni; 2. bréini]. **brain (I.)** & **-y.** Having good brains; clever.

braird (I.), n. [1. brārd; 2. brɛəd]. Perh. fr. O.E. & M.E. *brerd*, 'edge, border', cogn. w. *brord*, q.v. under **brad.** Newly sprouted blade of corn or grass. (Orig. Scots).

braird (II.), vb. intrans., fr. prec. To sprout.

braise, vb. [1. brāz; 2. breiz], fr. Fr. *braiser*, 'to stew', fr. *braise*, 'glowing charcoal', said to come fr. a Gmc. base **brasa*, perh. the same as that in **braze.** To stew meat in a closed pot.

brake (I.), n. [1. brāk; 2. breik]. M.E. *brāke*, 'fern'. Cp. **bracken.** **1.** A kind of fern. **2.** A thicket.

brake (II.), n. & vb. trans. O. Du. *braeke*. Related to **break (I.)**. **a** n. An instrument for beating flax and hemp; **b** vb., to crush or beat (flax).

brake (III.), n. Etymol. uncertain. **1.** Contrivance for retarding or stopping the speed of a revolving wheel, either by gripping the axle, or by applying direct friction to the wheel itself; used in various forms on all wheeled vehicles, except two-wheeled horse carts or carriages; otherwise on railway or other engines, motor cars, carriages, and bicycles. *To put on; apply, the brake*, (lit. and fig.) of anything which acts as a check. **2.** (also **break (III.)**) **a** A large, heavy, four-wheeled carriage used for breaking in young horses; **b** a large, open carriage, of the wagonette class, used for excursions &c.

brakeage, n. [1. brākij; 2. bréikidž]. Action of a **brake (III.)**; act or process of applying it.

brake-van, n. Compartment on railway train from which brakes are worked.

bramble, n. [1. brámbl; 2. brǽmbl]. O.E. *brēmel, brēmbl(es)*, fr. **brōmil*, q.v. under **broom**, M.E. *brembel* &c. Any coarse-growing, thorny, trailing plant, e.g. wild-rose; specif., blackberry bush: *bramble jelly*, blackberry jelly.

brambling, n. [1. brámbling; 2. brǽmbliŋ]. Earlier *brambline*, fr. **bramble.** A brightly coloured finch, *Fringilla montifringilla*, of Northern Europe and Asia, the mountain finch.

brambly, adj. [1. brámbli; 2. brǽmbli]. See **bramble** & **-ly.** Like brambles, thorny.

bran, n. [1. bran; 2. bræn]. M.E., fr. O. Fr. *bran, bren*; etymol. very doubtful, but word is found in Provenç. & O. Span. *bren*; cp. further Bret. *bren*, W. *brann*. It is uncertain whether it is a Celt. word, or borrowed in these languages fr. a Fr. source. The inner skin or husk of wheat, oats &c. separated from the grain, and used as coarse meal. Chaucer has '*to bolte it to the bren*', (fig.) to sift a question thoroughly.

brancard, n. [1. brángkard; 2. brǽŋkəd]. Fr., connected w. *branche*. See next word. A horse-litter.

branch (I.), n. [1. brahnch; 2. brān(t)ʃ]. M.E. *branche, braunch*, fr. Fr.; cp. Ital., Span. *branca*, 'claw', Provenç. *branc*, 'twig', Low Lat. *branca*, 'paw'. Meyer-Lübke suggests a Gmc. origin, & that the word is a transposed form of **crampa* (see **cramp** & **cram**), wh. is not very convincing. **1.** Limb of a tree, springing from trunk direct, or from a bough. **2.** (fig. and extended use) Any extension, subdivision, offshoot (in various senses): *branch of a river, road* &c.; also of a family, of group of languages, of division of a subject of knowledge, thought, study &c.

branch (II.), vb. intrans., fr. prec. **a** (of a tree) To put forth branches; often *branch out*, to spread, extend, boughs; **b** (of a river, road) to fork, bifurcate, divide into two or more (*branch off, away*); **c** (of persons) (*branch out*) to launch out into various new enterprises, incur expenses &c.

branchiate, adj. [1. brángkiāt; 2. brǽŋkieit]. Lat. *branchiae*, 'gills of a fish', fr. Gk. *brágkhia*, 'gills', cogn. w. Gk. *brógkhos*, 'tracheal artery', q.v. under **bronchi.** Provided with gills.

brand (I.), n. [1. brand; 2. brænd]. O.E. *brand*, 'fire', poet. 'sword', fr. its flashing when wielded, M.E. 'sword, fire'; O.N. *brandr*, 'flame; sword-blade', O.H.G. *brant*, Mod. Germ. *brand*, 'fire, conflagration'. The base is derived fr. Gmc. base **bren-*, **bran-*, 'to burn'. See **burn.** **1.** Something burning, portion of a fire, piece of burning wood; (poet.) a torch. Phr. (fig.) *to snatch a brand from the burning*, to save somebody, something, from risk of destruction. **2.** Mark formerly put upon criminals with a hot iron; hence. a mark, sign, or evidence of crime, sin, or infamy; a stigma: *the brand of Cain*; *the brand of villainy.* **3. a** A mark put upon an object with a hot iron, with a stencil, or other means, to indicate, e.g. (i.) ownership, as on casks, or on horses, pigs &c.; (ii.) the quality or character, of manufactured goods, fabrics &c.; (iii.) the date of vintage and shipper, as on wine corks; **b** hence, the quality, class, grade of the article branded: *a well-known brand of margarine* &c. **4.** (poet.) A sword. (Very old poetical usage; swords in old English and Germanic poetry are also called 'flames, gleams, of battle', and are described as flashing, shining, blazing &c.)

brand (II.), vb. trans., fr. prec. To mark with a brand in any sense under **brand (I.)**, **2** and **3**; (fig. from **2**) to single out, designate, indicate, as infamous; to denounce: *to brand a man as a liar, coward, rogue* &c.

brander, n. [1. brànder; 2. brǽndə]. Prec. & **-er.** **a** Person who brands; **b** instrument for branding.

brandied, adj. [1. brándid; 2. brǽndid]. See **brandy** & **-ed.** Soaked, saturated, in, flavoured with, brandy: *brandied cherries* &c.

brandish, vb. trans. [1. brándish; 2. brǽndiʃ]. M.E. *brandischen*, fr. O. Fr. *brandiss-*, Mod. Fr. *brandir*, fr. Gmc. *brand* (see **brand (I.)**) & **-ish.** Orig. 'to wave a sword'. To wave, flourish, with raised arm (a weapon, stick, whip &c.), either in a menacing or in a triumphant manner.

brandling, n. [1. brándling; 2. brǽndliŋ], fr. **brand (I.)** & dimin. suff. **-ling.** Name given from bright-red markings. **a** A red worm with bright rings round the body, used as bait by anglers; **b** a young salmon, parr.

brand-new, adj. [1. brán(d) nū; 2. brǽn(d) njū]. Quite new, fresh; (lit.) with the brand still showing; as though only just branded by the maker.

brandreth, n. [1. brándreth; 2. brǽndriþ]. Prob. fr., or at least influenced by, O.N. *brandreið*, 'fire-grate'; the word exists also in O.E., *brandrād, -rida*, & O.H.G. *brantreita*. See **brand (I.)** & **ride.** O.N. *reið* means 'vehicle' &c. Gridiron, iron trivet.

brandy, n. [1. brándi; 2. brǽndi]. Shortened fr. *brande-, brandy-wine*, both of wh. are found in early 17th cent., but later in the cent. the form *brandy* is found; (O.E.D.) fr. Du. *brandewijn*, 'burnt, distilled, wine'. Strong spirit distilled from wine.

brandy-ball, n. A kind of sweetmeat in the form of small round ball, transparent and somewhat of the colour of brandy.

brandy-pawnee, n. [1. brándi páwnē; 2. brǽndi pɔ̄nī]. Old-fashioned Anglo-Indian word, of wh. second element is Hind. *pānī*, 'water'. Brandy and water.

brandy-snap, n. Thin, hard, sticky biscuit resembling ginger-bread in taste.

branks, n. pl. [1. brangks; 2. bræŋks]. Etymol. doubtful; Celt. *brancas, brangas*, 'bridle', are borrowed fr. Engl.; possibly cogn. w. **prong**. A scold's bridle, a sort of iron bridle with gag for the mouth, formerly used in Scotland and England as a punishment for disorderly, scolding women.

brank-ursine, n. [1. brángk ḗrsin; 2. brǽŋk ə́sin], fr. Fr. *branche-ursine*, 'bear's paw, claw', see **branch (I.)** & **ursine**. Popular name of a species of acanthus, also called 'bear's breech'.

bran-new. Variant of **brand-new**.

bran-pie, -tub, n. Large tub filled with bran among which presents are hidden, and in which children 'dip' for a prize.

bransle, n. [1. brahnl; 2. brāl]. O. Fr.; Mod. Fr. *branle*, cp. *branler*, 'shake, swing, move rapidly' &c.; prob. fr. Gmc. *brand* in sense of 'sword', connected w. *brandir*, 'to wave' &c. Cp. **brand (I.)** & **brandish**. **a** Old French dance; **b** music adapted for such a dance.

brantgoose, brent-, n. [1. brántgōōs, brént-; 2. brǽntgūs, brént-]. Cp. Germ. *brandgans*. Perh. connected w. *brand, brant*, 'burnt', so named on account of dark colour. See **brand (I.)**. Small species of wild goose, dark in colour, of Arctic origin, but visiting Britain during the summer; also called 'barnacle' or 'bernacle goose'.

brash (I.), n. [1. brash; 2. bræʃ]. Prob. fr. Fr. *brèche*. See **breccia**. Loose broken stones or rubble, usually *stone-brash*.

brash (II.), n. Etymol. doubtful; possibly imitative. A sudden eructation of acid fluid from the stomach; usually *water-brash*.

brass (I.), n. [1. brahs; 2. brās]. O.E. *bræs*. Etymol. quite uncertain, but connexion w. Lat. *ferrum*, 'iron', wh. is fr. **ferzom*, borrowed fr. Heb. *barzel*, has been suggested. **1.** A hard, ductile alloy of a yellow colour, generally composed of copper and zinc. Phr. *as bold as brass*, very bold and confident (not necessarily in bad sense). **2.** Specif. **a** (pl. *brasses*) an engraved sheet of brass formerly embedded in the floor of a church, consisting of a portrait of some important person connected with the parish; any engraved brass plate set in floor or wall of a building as a memorial of a person or event; **b** *the brass*, the wind-instruments of an orchestra, as made of brass or other metal, as contrasted with *wood*. **3.** (vulg. and colloq.) Money. **4.** (fig., conveying idea of hardness and flashiness) Impudence, shameless effrontery.

brass (II.), adj., fr. prec. Made of brass: *brass rod, ring, bedstead* &c. Phr. *not to care a brass farthing*, be completely indifferent.

brassard, n. [1. brásard; 2. brǽsād]. Fr., fr. *bras*, 'arm'. Cp. **brace (I.)**. Badge worn on the arm.

brass band, n. Group of players of brass musical instruments.

brass-hat, n. (mil. slang) A general or staff-officer, from the gold braid and metal rim to his cap.

Brassica, n. [1. brásika; 2. brǽsikə]. Lat., 'cabbage', possibly a Gaulish word. (bot.) Genus of plants which includes the cabbage, turnip &c.

brassie, -y, n. [1. bráhsi; 2. brā́si]. **brass** & **-y**. Golf-club having a brass plate screwed on to that part of the head which is downwards in playing.

brass plate, n. Specif., one fixed to door of a doctor's house, engraved with his name; one fixed to a coffin, with name and age of deceased.

brassy, adj. [1. bráhsi; 2. brā́si]. See **brassie**. Like brass; having colour or taste resembling brass. Specif. (of voice or other sound), harsh, metallic, discordant.

brat, n. [1. brat; 2. bræt]. Origin very doubtful; perh. fr. O. & M.E. *bratt*, 'cloak, rough garment', wh. is Celt. (Ir. *brat*, 'cloak'), in reference to a beggar child's tattered, nondescript clothes. (familiar and contemptuous) A child.

brattice, bratticing, n. [1. brátis(ing); 2. brǽtis(iŋ)]. M.E. *brutaske, bretasce*, 'bartizan', O. Fr. *bretesche*. Origin fr. Germ. *brett*, 'board', has been suggested, but is now rejected as impossible by Meyer-Lübke, who derives the O. Fr. word & O. Ital. *bertesca*, 'drawbridge', fr. **brittisca*, 'Breton', adj.; Germ. *brett* may, however, have influenced the meaning. The word seems to have been used for a movable wooden structure or tower in a fortress. A 15th-cent. Engl.-Lat. dictionary, Promptorium, gives *propugnaculum* as the meaning of *bretasce, bretays*. At present time *brattice* is used specifically of an air-tight partition or shaft for ventilating mines. It is not necessarily made of, or even lined with, wood.

bravado, n. [1. braváhdō; 2. brəvā́dou], fr. Span. *bravada*, modified by other words in *-ado*. See **brave (I.)**. Display of boldness and daring.

brave (I.), adj. [1. brāv; 2. breiv]. A late word not found in Engl. before Caxton ('*brave deeds*'); fr. Fr., fr. Ital. *bravo*. In O. Port. *bravo* means 'untamed, wild', esp. of young bulls; O. Span. *bravo* is 'a young bull'. The orig. sense is 'wild, violent', thence 'spirited, courageous'. The etymol. is uncertain, but a derivation fr. Lat. *barbarus* is suggested. See **barbaric**. **1. a** (of persons, character) Courageous, bold, gallant; willing to incur danger, not frightened by danger, misfortune, suffering; Phrs. *as brave as a lion*, very brave; *the brave*, brave men; **b** (of actions) requiring courage in the person performing them. **2.** Having a fine, gay, splendid appearance: *a brave show, display*.

brave (II.), n., fr. prec. A brave man, esp. a Red Indian warrior.

brave (III.), vb. trans., fr. prec. Cp. Fr. *braver*, 'to dare, defy'. **1.** To show courage in face of, notwithstanding (danger &c.); take risk of without flinching: *he had braved death a hundred times*. **2.** To dare, defy. Phr. *to brave it out*, to meet suspicion or blame with defiance.

bravely, adv. **brave (I.)** & **-ly**. In a courageous, spirited manner; gaily, splendidly.

bravery, n. [1. bráveri; 2. bréivəri]. **brave** & **-ery**. Cp. Fr. *braverie*. **a** Courage, daring, boldness, intrepidity; **b** finery, splendour, smart dress, trappings, or equipment.

bravo (I.), n. [1. bráhvō; 2. brā́vou]. Ital. See **brave (I.)**. A brigand, desperado, a hired ruffian or assassin.

bravo (II.), n. & interj. [1. bráhvṓ; 2. brā́vóu]. Ital. *bravo*, 'brave man', used in applauding performers, singers &c.; also *bravi* (pl.) & *brava* (to a woman). **a** Exclamation of approval; **b** the utterance of word to express approval, plaudit; often in pl. *-oes*.

bravura, n. [1. bravōōra; 2. bravūra]. Ital., 'spirit, bravery'. See **brave, bravo**. **1.** Spirit, dash, intrepid bearing or conduct. **2.** (mus.) Brilliant, spirited passage.

brawl (I.), vb. intrans. [1. brawl; 2. brōl]. M.E. *braule* &c., 'scold, quarrel'. Etymol. dubious, but note L.G. *brallen*, 'brag' &c., M.H.G. *prālen*, Mod. Germ. *prahlen*, 'speak loud, boast'. **1.** To quarrel noisily and roughly; specif., to create disturbance in church during divine service. **2.** (of streams and brooks) To flow noisily, as over stones.

brawl (II.), n., fr. prec. A rough, noisy quarrel; a row, with fighting, esp. in the public street.

brawler, n. [1. bráwler; 2. brṓlə]. **brawl (I.)** & **-er**. One who creates a disturbance; a noisy, quarrelsome person.

brawling, n. [1. bráwling; 2. brṓliŋ], fr. **brawl (I.)** & **-ing**. Noisy quarrelling; specif., disturbance in church during divine service.

brawn, n. [1. brawn; 2. brōn], fr. O. Fr. *braon*, 'piece of flesh', Low Lat. *bradōn-(em)*, 'ham', M.E. *braun*, 'pig-meat; muscle'. The O. Fr. word is fr. a Gmc. base **brādo*, as in O.H.G. *brāten*, 'roast', O.E. *brǣdan*. Orig. meaning is apparently 'cooked meat'. **1.** Pickled meat, esp. of the pig, cut into slices or lumps, spiced, and compressed into a mould. **2.** Muscle, force, vigour.

brawny, adj. [1. bráwni; 2. brṓni]. Prec. & **-y**. **a** Having large, well-developed muscles; **b** stout, strong, powerful.

braxy, n. & adj. [1. bráksi; 2. brǽksi]. Scots & N. Engl.; etymol. dubious. **1. n.** A disease of sheep, splenic fever or apoplexy. **2.** adj. Affected, tainted, with braxy.

bray (I.), vb. trans. [1. brā; 2. brei]. M.E. *braie(n)*, O. Fr. *breyer*, Mod. Fr. *broyer*, 'crush', fr. O.H.G. *brehhan*, 'break'. See **break (I.)**. To pound, crush, esp. in a mortar.

bray (II.), vb. intrans. M.E. *braye*, O. Fr. & Mod. Fr. *braire*, 'cry out, bray', fr. L. Lat. *bragīre*, (*-ēre*), 'whinny'; perh. Celt., cp. Bret. *breugi*, 'shriek, cry'. **1.** To utter a loud discordant noise or cry; esp. of the ass, or of trumpets. **2.** To bellow, cry, or shout harshly; utter loud, foolish speech, complain loudly. (Always insulting when applied to human utterance.)

bray (III.), n., fr. prec. **1.** A loud discordant bellow; the sound made by the ass; blare of trumpets. **2.** Noisy, foolish talk; noisy protests: '*Exeter Hall sets up its bray*' (Macaulay).

braze, vb. trans. [1. brāz; 2. breiz]. Fr. *braser*, fr. O.N. *brasa*, 'heat with fire'. To unite (two pieces of metal) by heating, or with hard solder.

brazen (I.), adj. [1. brā́zn; 2. bréizn]. O.E. *bræsen*, M.E. *brāsen*. See **brass** & **-en**. **1. a** Made of brass: *brazen image*; **b** giving out, having, a sound such as is yielded by brass: *brazen tones of voice*. **2.** Audacious, shameless, impudent: *a brazen hussy*.

brazen (II.), vb. trans., fr. prec. To adopt impudent, defiant manner, under a charge or suspicion; to justify oneself in an impudent, defiant manner; esp. *to brazen it out*.

brazen-faced, adj. With a face of brass; shameless, impudent: *a brazen-faced hussy*.

brazier (I.), n. [1. brā́zier, brā́zher; 2. bréiziə, bréižə]. M.E. *brasiere*. See **brass**. One who works in brass.

brazier (II.), n. See **braze**, vb. Cp. Fr. *brasier*. Vessel for holding hot coals.

Brazil, n. [1. brazíl; 2. brəzíl]. Also in early form *brasil*, Span., Port., & Fr. name for a red dye-wood fr. the East Indies; later, when such wood was found in S. Am., the name was given to the country now so called. A red dye-wood, *Brazil-wood*, obtained in Brazil and other South American countries.

Brazil-nut, n. A large three-sided nut with edible seeds, the fruit of a gigantic native tree of Brazil.

breach (I.), n. [1. brēch; 2. britʃ]. O.E. **brǣċ(e)* is not recorded; fr. **brǣċi-* (cp. Pret. pl. *brǣc-on*, Lat. *frēg-i*, 'broke'), whence M.E. *brēche* & Mod. form; O.E *bryċe*, 'breaking, fragment', fr. **bruki*, occurs, but cannot be ancestor of *breach*. The word, however, offers no difficulty, being a perfectly normal derivative fr. base **brek-*. Cp. **break (I.)**. On the other hand, *breach* may have been adopted, instead of the descendants of O.E. *bryċe* (S.E. *breċe*), through influence of Fr. *brèche*, wh. has partly the same meanings, &, together w. Ital. *breccia*, is borrowed fr. the Gmc. base **brek-*. Cp. **breccia**. **1.** Action of breaking (now only in fig. use), in sense of violation, infringement, infraction, as of a law, obligation, duty, promise. Specif., *breach of promise*, (in law) failure in promise to marry. Phrs. *custom more honoured in the breach than in the observance*; *breach of faith*, betrayal. **2.** Result of the action of breaking: **a** a rent, gap, opening in a wall, esp. (mil.) of fortifications &c.; **b** result of seditious conduct and speech: *breach of the peace*, riot, civil disturbance. Phr. *to stand, throw oneself, into the breach*, (fig.) bear chief brunt of attack, take chief labour and responsibility.

breach (II.), vb. trans., fr. prec. To make a breach ((I.) 2, a) in walls or fortifications; break through a line of defence.

bread, n. [1. bred; 2. bred]. O.E. *brēad*, 'morsel, crumb, of bread; bread', M.E. *brēde*

&c., O. Fris. *brād*, O.S. *brōd*, fr. **brauð-*, O.H.G. *brōt*, fr. **braud*, O.N. *brauð*. The base fr. wh. all these are derived is Aryan **bh(e)reu-*, 'bubble, boil, spurt' &c., wh. occurs in many words, & w. widely differentiated meanings; cp. **bourn (I.)**, where the root idea is the bubbling of water. For sense of the present word cp. Lat. *de-frŭtum*, 'new wine, must', wh. is connected w. *fervēre*, 'boil, ferment, glow' (see **fervent, ferment**). *Bread* is named fr. the fermentation & rising caused by the yeast, & means lit. 'fermented substance'. See further **bird, brew, brood.** **1.** Form of food made of flour or meal and water mixed with yeast and baked. Phr. *bread and wine*, the Sacred Elements; the Eucharistic Service. **2.** (by extension, and regarded as symbolical of principal element) Human food generally: *daily bread*; *to beg one's bread* &c. Phrs. *to break bread with*, share a meal with; *bread and salt*, symbol of hospitality; *to quarrel with one's bread and butter*, find fault with one's chief source of livelihood; *to eat the bread of idleness*, live on others without working; *to take the bread out of one's mouth*, deprive of livelihood; *earn one's bread*, make a living; *to know on which side one's bread is buttered*, be alive to one's interests; *bread buttered on both sides*, very comfortable circumstances. **3.** Substance resembling bread: *bee bread*.

bread-basket, n. (colloq.) The stomach.

bread-crumb, n. **a** Soft spongy part of bread inside crust; **b** a minute fragment of bread.

bread-fruit, n. Farinaceous fruit of a tree growing in Pacific Islands which, when baked, resembles bread.

bread sauce, n. Bread-crumb and milk seasoned with pepper and onions, eaten with game and poultry.

bread-stuffs, n. Grain, cereals, from which bread is made; bread, biscuit.

breadth, n. [1. bredth; 2. bredþ]. This is a late formation w. suff. *-th* on anal. of M.E. *lengthe*, *heiȝthe* &c., 'height'. The O.E. form is *brǣdu*, 'breadth', fr. **brādi* (w. change of suff.), fr. adj. *brād*. See **broad (I.)**. **1.** Distance from side to side; measure across, at right angles to length; width. Various derived and figurative uses: **2.** Anything measured according to width: *breadth of carpet, cloth* &c. **3.** (fig.) **a** Largeness, amplitude generally; intelligence, generosity, catholicity: *breadth of mind, sympathy, interests* &c.; **b** (in bad sense) lack of due restraint or limit, undue latitude, licence in speech or conduct: *too much breadth in a man's jokes, behaviour* &c. Cp. *broadness* & *broad* in similar sense. **4.** (in a work of art) *Breadth of treatment* is such a mode of subordinating details to the general essentials that the effect is one of spaciousness, largeness, free from meanness and petty points of distraction.

breadthways, -wise, adv. [1. brédthwāz, -īz; 2. brédþweiz, *-aiz*]. In the direction of breadth.

bread-winner, n. Person who supports a family by his or her labour.

break (I.), vb. trans. & intrans. [1. brāk; 2. breik]. O.E. *brecan*, M.E. *brēken*, O.S. *brekan*, O.H.G. *brehhan*, Mod. Germ. *brechen*, Goth. *brikan*; cp. Lat. *frēg-i*, 'I broke', wh. coincides exactly w. O.E. *brǣc-on*, found in Pret. pl. (cp. **breach (I.)**), *frac-tus* for **frag-tos*, 'broken', corresponding w. O.E. *bræc*, 'broke', Pret. sing., & Scrt. *bhraj*, 'breaking, bursting'; see also **fraction.** Another grade of this base occurs in **brook (I.)**. **A.** trans. The general meaning is to divide, separate anything, into two or more parts by some means other than *cutting*, which is gradual, and esp. by a sudden blow or strain. **1.** To fracture, divide, generally into two parts, suddenly and forcibly, snap, disconnect, by jerk, sudden shock, or blow: *to break a rod, stick*; *break one's leg, one's neck*, i.e. the bone; *break the leg of a chair*; *break a twig* &c. Phrs. (mostly fig. of above sense) *break one's heart*, grieve, suffer pain, die of this; *break a lance with*, engage in intellectual contest; *no bones are broken*, no harm done; *break one's head against*, *break one's teeth on*, encounter insuperable difficulties; *break the back of an undertaking*, get an important, or the most difficult, part completed. **2.** To shatter, smash to pieces, as a brittle substance: *to break a window*, i.e. the glass; *break crockery* &c. Phr. *break the ice*, (fig.) make a beginning, overcome initial repugnance, or difficulty. **3.** **a** To crack, rupture surface, burst open, wound, bruise as with blow of blunt instrument: *to break a man's head*, as with a cudgel; *to break the skin*; *break on a wheel*, by striking with iron bar; **b** special uses: (of a fish) *to break the water*, pierce, by jumping partly out; (of a submarine) *to break surface*, come up from under water; (of game) *break cover*, come out. Phrs. *break Priscian's head*, use bad grammar; '*Break a butterfly upon a wheel*' (Pope), use a powerful means for very slight end; *break bread*, (i.) partake of a meal; (ii.) receive Holy Communion. **4.** To open ground for planting, rupture surface by means of plough, pick, spade: *new-broke land, soil* &c. Phr. *to break the ground*, (fig.) make preliminary preparation for any action. **5.** To injure, spoil, render temporarily useless by destroying some essential part (of machine, mechanical contrivance): *to break a clock, sewing-machine, fountain pen* &c. **6.** **a** To ruin, degrade from an office or employment: *to break a general, minister of state*; **b** to ruin financially, make bankrupt: *he was completely broke(n) by the failure of his business.* Phrs. *a broken man*, ruined in health, spirit, fortune, or reputation; (colloq.) *broke*; *stony broke*, ruined, bankrupt. **7.** (fig.) To crush, keep in subjection, deprive of initiative; (of animals) to train, discipline: *to break a man's spirit*; *to break opposition*; *a well-broken horse* (also *break in*), *break a horse to harness*. Phr. *to break one of a habit*, cause to discontinue. **8.** To exceed, go beyond, surpass, beat (of a record). **9.** (in a moral sense) To infringe, violate, act in opposition to: *to break the law, rules*; *break a promise* &c. Phrs. *to break faith with*, deceive, betray; *break one's word*, fail to keep promise. **10.** **a** To interrupt, destroy continuity, discontinue: *to break one's rest, sleep*; *break the peace*; *break one's journey*; Phrs. *break the thread of an argument* &c.; *to break short*, bring to an end; *break a spell*; *break one's fast*, eat after fasting; *break silence*, begin to speak; **b** destroy unity, completeness, disturb symmetry: *to break the line*; *break a set*; *break a sovereign*; *break the balls* (in billiards), play out of balk. **11.** To weaken, mitigate, render less severe: *the bushes broke his fall or he would have been killed.* **12.** To open, reveal, disclose; obs. except in Phr. *to break the (bad) news* &c., which is also partly suggestive of sense in **10.** **B.** intrans. **1.** **a** To come asunder, divide into two or more parts, burst, split, by a sudden rupture from a strain or blow: *the rope will break if you put your weight on it*; *the glass broke to pieces from the frost*; **b** to be liable to come in half, or in pieces as above, owing to the nature of the substance: *brittle things break easily*; *oak may bend but will not break*; Phr. *my heart will break*, I shall die of grief; **c** to burst outwards owing to pressure of unhealthy matter, of a swelling, boil, abscess &c. **2.** To cleave, part asunder, disperse, pass away, as *clouds, darkness, frost*, and (fig.) *gloom* &c. **3.** To dawn, begin to become light (of the day). **4.** To put forth shoots, to sprout, show signs of expanding (of buds on a bough or stem; of bough itself): *if you prune off the ends, the bough will break lower down.* **5.** To twist aside, depart suddenly from original line, or path (of a ball in billiards, cricket &c.); also *break back*. **6.** To change, become harsh, squeaky, and uncontrollable (of a boy's voice in adolescence). **7.** To change (of weather &c.): *the spell of fine weather has broken.* **C.** Combined with prepositions and adverbs. *Break away*, depart from abruptly, escape; (fig.) deviate from habit, ordinary conduct, mode of thought, belief. *Break down*, trans., **a** overthrow by violence, batter down (a wall, door &c.); **b** crush down, suppress, keep under (of opposition, resistance); **c** to dissolve, dissipate; intrans., **a** to collapse, come to nothing (of plans &c.); **b** (i.) to suffer physical or mental collapse; (ii.) to burst into tears. *Break forth*, intrans., **a** to spurt, or spring out (of a stream &c.); fig., of anger, indignation &c.; **b** to burst into sudden, animated speech. *Break in*, **a** trans., to submit (an animal) to discipline and training (esp. of horses); also by extension, to train, discipline (a person); accustom him to new routine &c.; **b** intrans., to enter a house or building by force: *burglars have broken in.* *Break in on*, burst suddenly into a person's presence, disturb, interrupt him; disturb his peace. *Break into*, **a** force one's way into locked house &c. (esp. of burglars); **b** give sudden utterance to: *break into a loud laugh*; **c** change one's mode of movement suddenly: *break into a run, gallop*; **d** to take up, occupy, infringe upon: *break into one's time, leisure.* *Break off*, **a** trans., snap off, sever with force a part of anything; (fig.) interrupt, discontinue abruptly: *break off social relations, an engagement to be married, a conversation, a battle*; **b** intrans., to cease speaking: *break off in the middle of a sentence* &c. *Break out*, intrans., **a** escape: *prisoners have broken out*; **b** make a sudden impulsive utterance; **c** lose one's temper, show sudden violence in speech or conduct; **d** (of disease, pestilence, any violent disorder or calamity) make a sudden appearance, begin to affect people: *measles has broken out at the school, plague in India* &c.; *riots and disturbances broke out in many places.* *Break through*, intrans., **a** burst, make a way, hole, through (any enclosure, obstacle, defence); **b** (fig., of non-material obstacles) penetrate, overcome: *break through a man's reserve, his taciturnity*, &c.; **c** make an appearance, show: *the sun broke through (the clouds).* *Break up*, trans., **a** reduce to fragments, smash anything; **b** (fig.) destroy, scatter, disperse, put to flight, e.g. band of robbers, conspirators &c.; intrans., **c** disintegrate, dissolve, change &c.; (fig., of persons) to lose strength, show signs of age or ill-health; (of school &c.) disperse at end of term for holidays. *Break with*, intrans., **a** discontinue abruptly, leave off, make an end of: *break with old habits* &c.; **b** cease friendly relations with, quarrel with: *associates, friends* &c.

break (II.), n. fr. prec. **1.** A fracture, rupture: *a break in the gas-pipe.* **2.** (fig.) Interruption, disturbance of continuity: *a break in one's life, habits* &c. **3.** Dawn: *break of day.* **4.** Deviation of a cricket or tennis ball on first striking ground. **5.** Continuous score in billiards: *made a break of 500.*

break (III.), n. Perh. fr. **brake (III.)** influenced by *break in.* **a** Carriage-frame on wheels, with driver's seat, but no body, for training young horses; **b** a large kind of wagonette.

breakable, adj. & n. [1. brākabl; 2. bréikəbl]. **break (I.)** & **-able.** **a** Easily broken, fragile; **b** (pl.) things liable to be broken, crockery &c.

breakage, n. [1. brākij; 2. bréikidž]. See prec. & **-age.** **a** Act of breaking; **b** article(s) broken; **c** that place in, or part of, anything, which has been broken, the actual area of breaking.

break-down, n. [1. brāk doun; 2. bréik daun]. See **break (I.), C.** **1.** An accident to a train, to machinery &c., which causes a stoppage or failure in working: *break-down gang*, men with tools &c. ready to deal with a 'break-down' on a railway. **2.** Collapse of physical or mental health. **3.** **a** A step-dance; **b** a negro dance.

breaker (I.), n. [1. bråker; 2. bréikə]. **break** (I.) & **-er**. **a** A person who breaks (in any sense); **b** a wave which breaks in foam on a reef, or on rocky shore; **c** (poet.) a large wave generally. Phr. *breakers ahead*, (fig.) future difficulties.

breaker (II.), n., fr. Span. *barrica*, 'cask'. A small cask, or keg, for water &c., carried in ship's boats.

breakfast, n. [1. brékfast; 2. brékfəst]. See **break** (I.) & **fast** (I.), n. The first meal of the day; so called because at this meal the fast of the night is broken.

breaking, n. [1. bråking; 2. bréikiŋ]. Vbl. n. of **break** (I.). **1.** Breakage, act or process of fracture. **2.** (gram.) Translation of German *brechung*, a phonetic process first described by German philologists, who invented the term. See English term **fracture** (I.) (phon.).

breakneck, adj. [1. bråknek; 2. bréiknɛk]. **break** (I.) & **neck**. So rapid as to cause risk of breaking one's neck: esp. *breakneck speed*.

break-off, n. See **break** (I.), **C**. Metal work of a shot-gun immediately behind breech.

break-up, n. See **break** (I.), **C**. Disruption, commotion, destruction; dispersal (of school) at end of term.

breakwater, n. [1. bråkwawter; 2. bréikwōtə]. **break** (I.) & **water**. A structure of stone, iron, or wood and shingle for breaking force of waves against a coast.

bream (I.), n. [1. brēm; 2. brīm]. O. Fr. *brēme*, fr. *bresme*, borrowed fr. O.H.G. *brahsino*. **a** A freshwater fish, genus *Abramis*, of the carp family; **b** a sea fish, *sea-bream*, genus *Sparus*.

bream (II.), vb. trans. Origin doubtful. To clean a ship's bottom by burning and scraping.

breast (I.), n. [1. brest; 2. brɛst]. O.E. *brēost*, 'breast', M.E. *brēst*, O.S. *briost*, O.N. *brjōst*, & w. different gradation, Goth. *brusts*, 'bowels, heart, breast(s)', & O.H.G. & Mod. Germ. *brust*. The use of this base for part of the body is confined to the Gmc. languages, & indeed it has not been identified outside them hitherto. A connexion w. the group seen in Lat. *fastigium*, 'point, spike', Scrt. *bhṛṣṭiś*, 'spike' &c., is not impossible. The *breast* wd. thus be the 'projecting, swelling, pointed' part of the body. See further cognates & references under **borage, bore** (I.), **brad, bristle**. **1.** The upper front part of the body below the neck between the shoulders in human beings, and (more rarely) the corresponding part in animals. Specif., this part in women considered as the source of milk for young children. Phrs. *a child at the breast*, very young infant still suckled by its mother; *to give the breast to a child*, suckle it. **2.** (fig.) Seat of the emotions, thence the passions, feelings of all kinds, heart in figurative sense: *a troubled, anxious breast*. Phr. *to make a clean breast of*, make frank and full confession. **3. a** Anything supposed to resemble a human breast in shape: *the mountain's breast*; **b** that part of the clothing which covers the breast: *the breast of a coat*, so *breast-pocket*, pocket in that part of a coat.

breast (II.), vb. trans., fr. prec. To present the breast to, hence face resolutely, oppose, struggle with: *to breast the waves* (of a swimmer, or ship); (fig.) *breast the storm* (*of popular abuse, obloquy* &c.).

breast-band, n. Strap which crosses horse's breast and takes the pull, in harness, when a collar is not used.

breast-bone, n. Flat, perpendicular bone in front of breast in mammals from which the ribs spring; sternum.

breast-high, adj. Reaching to height of the breast.

breast-pin, n. Pin with jewelled or ornamented head, formerly worn by men in the old-fashioned stock or neck-cloth; now sometimes stuck into the necktie.

breastplate, n. [1. bréstplāt; 2. bréstpleit]. **a** Part of defensive armour; metal plate protecting breast; **b** strap running across horse's breast; breast-band; **c** vestment worn by Jewish high priest.

breastsummer, n. [1. brésumer; 2. brésəmə]. **breast** (I.) & **summer** (II.). The latter is fr. Fr. *sommier*, 'beast of burden', also 'stone which receives thrust of an arch; beam supporting wall above a door'. This word (cp. L. Lat. *sagmārius*) is derived fr. Fr. *somme*, 'burden', wh. in its turn is L. Lat. *sagma*, 'pack-saddle', whence Ital. *salma, soma*, 'burden'; *sagma* comes fr. Class. Lat. *sagum*, 'rough piece of cloth', hence 'military cloak', said to be a Gaulish word. Thus the word, both in form & meaning, has travelled far. The starting-point of its strange career seems to be the extension of meaning fr. 'coarse military cloak' to a saddle or valise for carrying military clothing & baggage generally; thence to the burden itself, then to any kind of burden; the derivative *sommier*, fr. meaning the bearer of one particular kind of burden, is extended to that wh. bears the weight of a building. *Summer, somer*, 'baggage animal', are found already in M.E. We may either have borrowed the later meaning 'beam' &c. fr. Fr., or have developed it independently. Other Rom. dialects besides Fr. have developed the latter meaning. Large beam or girder running horizontally above the opening of a window, or door, to support the building above.

breastwood, n. [1. bréstwood; 2. bréstwud]. New shoots from principal branches of fruit trees trained against wall, or as espaliers.

breastwork, n. [1. bréstwërk; 2. bréstwāk]. (mil.) Mound, parapet, breast-high above the ground, used for defence instead of a trench.

breath, n. [1. breth; 2. brɛþ]. O.E. *brǣþ*, M.E. *brēth(e)*. The word is peculiarly Engl. in form & meaning, but is closely connected w. O.H.G. *brādem*, Mod. Germ. *brodem*, 'vapour, steam'. The etymol. is very doubtful. Murray in the O.E.D. (in 1888) connects the O.E. w. the O.H.G. word & suggests that both go back to Aryan **bhrēt-*, wh. base, having lost the pref. **bhr-*, & received a formative suff. *-mo*, he sees in O.E. *ǣþm*, 'breath', O.H.G. *ātum*, 'breath, spirit', Mod. Germ. *atem*, O.S. *āðom*, & further in Scrt. *ātmán-*, 'spirit', Gk. *atmós*, 'vapour, steam', see **atmosphere**. Weekley accepts this without discussion, but recent philologists, Walde, Hirt, Boisacq, do not mention the possible connexion of *breath* w. *atem* &c. Hirt derives O.E. *brǣþ* & O.H.G. *brāto* fr. earlier **mrē-t* & compares (w. quite other formative suffs.) O.H.G. *marawi*, 'tender', O.E. *mearu*, also Mod. Germ. *mürbe*; further Gk. *mar-aínō*, 'extinguish, quench', also 'pine away, grow weak'; Lat. *marcēre*, 'wither, droop' &c., see **marcescent**. The development of meaning between these words & one meaning 'vapour' &c. is hard to see. On the other hand, Murray gave no explanation of the mysterious **bhr-*. **1.** Air drawn into or expelled from the lungs. In many fig. Phrs. *to draw one's breath*, live, be alive; *with bated breath*, anxiously, expectantly; *hold one's breath*, (fig.) be in a state of physical and mental tension; *waste breath*, talk in vain; *breath of one's nostrils*, something very precious; (*with*) *the last breath*, (at) the end of life, as a last action; *in the same breath*, at same moment; *speak under one's breath*, in low tones; *take away one's breath, one's breath away*, startle, surprise one; *out of breath*, having difficulty in breathing; *shortness of breath*, difficulty in breathing. **2. a** Air, breeze, movement in the atmosphere: *to get a breath of air*; **b** (fig.) slight sound, murmur (lightly spoken word): *no breath of scandal*; '*The blast of public breath*' (Pope). **3.** Fragrance, exhalation: *breath of spring*. **4.** (phon.) Expiration of air from lungs without vibration of vocal chords; *breath sounds*, those so uttered, cp. *voiceless*.

breathe, vb. intrans. & trans. [1. brēdh; 2. brīð]. O.E. *brǣþan*, M.E. *brēthen*, fr. *brǣþ*, n. See **breath**. **A.** intrans. **1. a** To take in or expel air from the lungs; hence **b** (by extension) to live. Phrs. *still breathing*, just alive; *to breathe freely, breathe again*, to feel reassured, have no anxiety; (trans.) *to breathe one's last*, to die. **2.** To exhale, blow gently (of air, breeze, fragrance &c.): '*There breathes a living fragrance from the shore*' (Byron). **B.** trans. **1.** To cause to use the lungs in breathing **a** moderately and beneficially: *I took the horse a gentle gallop to breathe him*; **b** to put out of breath: *he was so breathed that he could hardly move*; **c** to allow to recover breath: *now you are sufficiently breathed we will push on*. **2.** To utter gently in speech: *to breathe a prayer, blessing* &c. Phrs. *not to breathe a word*, to keep a secret, confidence &c.; (intrans.) *to breathe upon*, express disfavour, disparage. **3.** To give out, proclaim, express, convey: *his words breathe a spirit of humanity and moderation*.

breathed, adj. [1. brēdhd; 2. brīðd]. Prec. & **-ed**. (phon.) Uttered without vibration of vocal chords (of speech sounds, or air-stream from lungs). Cp. *aspirated & voiceless*.

breather, n. [1. brēdher; 2. brīðə]. See **breathe** & **-er**. **1.** One who breathes. **2. a** Violent exercise which puts one out of breath; **b** space of rest to recover one's breath: *to take, have, a breather*.

breath-group, n. (phon.) Series or group of speech sounds (words or syllables) uttered with a single impulse of breath.

breathing, n. [1. brēdhing; 2. brīðiŋ], fr. **breathe** & **-ing**. **1. a** Act, power, of respiration: *his breathing became weaker and more irregular*; **b** (fig.) gentle movements of the air, exhalation, or fragrance as of flowers; gently uttered sounds in speech. **2. a** (phon.) Aspiration, q.v., also *rough breathing*; an impulse of breath from the lungs with stress put upon it; cp. *glide*, n. (phon.); **b** mark in writing or printing put to indicate aspiration.

breathless, adj. [1. bréthles; 2. bréþlis]. **breath** & **-less**. **a** Lacking breath, short of, out of, breath; panting; (poet.) dead, as *breathless corpse*; **b** of such a nature as to cause shortness of breath: *breathless hurry, speed* &c.; (fig.) causing strong emotion, as surprise, interest: *breathless attention, expectation* &c.; **c** sultry, unstirred, not freshened by any breeze: *breathless day, weather* &c.

breathlessly, adv. Prec. & **-ly**. In a breathless manner.

breathlessness, n. See prec. & **-ness**. Lack, shortness of breath, difficulty in breathing.

breathy, adj. [1. bréthi; 2. bréþi]. **breath** & **-y**. (of sounds, esp. of manner of speaking, singing, and playing wind instruments) Characterized by emission of mere breath, as contrasted with musical and sonorous notes; lacking in volume.

breccia, n. [1. brécha, bréshya; 2. brétʃa, bréʃja]. Ital., 'kind of marble consisting of angular fragments held together by natural cement'; of Gmc. origin, cogn. w. Fr. *brèche*, fr. base **brek-*. See **breach** & **break**. Composite rock consisting of angular pieces larger than grains of sand, held together by a natural cement; (by extension) mass of shingle or rough stones held together by frozen snow or ice.

bred, vb. [1. bred; 2. bred]. Pret. & P.P. of **breed**. O.E. *brēdde*, (*ġe*)*brēd*(*d*), M.E. *bredde*, *bred*(*d*).

breech, n., gen. in pl., **breeches** [1. brēch, bríchez; 2. brītʃ, brítʃiz]. O.E. *brēc*, pl. of *brōc*, 'breeches'; of Celt. origin, cp. Lat. *brac*(*c*)*ae*. **1.** (sing.) **a** Lower and hinder part of body, buttock, thigh; **b** rear part of cannon or of rifle or gun-barrel. **2.** (pl.) Garments which cover the lower part of the body and legs; (colloq.) trousers. Specif., garment extending from hips to a few inches below knees, generally tightened and buttoning in at knee, esp. for riding, or *knee-breeches*, in court or official costume. Phr. *to wear the breeches* (of women), have a masculine character, rule their husbands.

breech block, n. The movable block of steel which closes the breech of a gun.

breeched, adj. [1. brēcht; 2. britʃt], as fr. vb. *to breech*, 'to provide with a breech, or with breeches'. **1.** Provided with a breech (of firearms). **2.** Wearing breeches, having attained age when childish garments are left off: *his son was not yet breeched.*

breeches-buoy, n. Pair of canvas breeches attached to a life-buoy, slung along a rope, used for life-saving at sea.

breeching, britchin(g), n. [1. bríching; 2. brítʃiŋ], fr. **breech** & **-ing**. That part of harness, in form of a strap, which passes round quarters of a horse in a cart or carriage and takes the forward thrust of the vehicle.

breechless, adj. [1. brḗchles; 2. brítʃlis]. **breech** & **-less**. Without a breech, or without breeches; **a** of firearms; **b** of children not yet breeched.

breech-loader, n. Gun or rifle loaded at the breech.

breech-loading, adj. [1. brḗch lōding; 2. brítʃ loudiŋ]. (of firearms) Made to be loaded at the breech.

breed (I.), vb. trans. & intrans. [1. brēd; brīd]. O.E. *brēdan*, 'cherish', fr. *brōd*, 'brood' &c. See **brood** (I.). **A.** trans. **1. a** To produce, give birth to, offspring (of animals, rare as trans. in this sense); **b** (fig., of non-material things) to produce, cause to appear, give rise to: *unemployment breeds misery and civil disturbance.* **2.** To rear, bring up, nurture, educate, train (in this sense there is often something of **1** implied): *our parents have bred us to follow in their footsteps*; *he was bred a soldier*; *England still breeds men to fight for her*; *an Englishman born and bred.* **3.** To propagate, cause animals to reproduce their kind by selective pairing of male and female: *to breed horses, cattle, dogs* &c. **B.** intrans. To bear, produce, nourish, rear, young; to propagate, carry on species by natural reproduction: *birds breed in the spring*; *rabbits breed freely in captivity*; *to breed true to type.* Sometimes used forcibly, but coarsely, of human beings.

breed (II.), n., fr. prec. **1.** Variety, or race of animals or men; strain, stock: *breed of cattle, horses* &c.; *Nelson and his captains were of the true English breed.* **2.** Sort, class, kind (esp. of men, more rarely of things); implying possession of common qualities, as though derived from same source: *Newman and Keble were thinkers of much the same breed.*

breeder, n. [1. brḗder; 2. brídə]. **breed** (I.) & **-er.** **1.** An animal thought of as breeding and producing offspring: *elephants are slow breeders.* **2.** A person who carries on the selective propagation of animals: *horse-breeder, dog-breeder* &c.

breeding, n. [1. brḗding; 2. brídiŋ], fr. **breed** (I.) & **-ing.** **1.** Act or process of natural propagation of species; **a** (as carried on by animals themselves) *spring is the season of breeding for most English birds*; **b** (as a deliberate, selective pairing of animals to produce a stock, carried on by men) *the breeding of horses and cattle is an important industry.* **2.** Nurture, training, education: *British officers for the army receive their breeding at Woolwich and Sandhurst.* Hence, **3.** Bearing, manners, deportment; knowledge of customs and conventions of good society, as produced by training and education: *a man of fine breeding*; *he showed rather doubtful breeding.*

breeze (I.), n. [1. brēz; 2. brīz]. Fr. *brise*, Span. *brisa*, Port. *briza*, 'north-east wind'. Meyer-Lübke is doubtful whether this word in Rom. may not be borrowed fr. Engl. Connexion w. **bise** is doubtful. **1.** Light, gentle wind. **2.** (fig.) Slight quarrel; mild disagreement and interchange of apostrophe and retort, esp. at a public meeting.

breeze (II.), n. Perh. fr. O. Fr. *brese*, 'cinders, live coals', connected w. **braise** (II.), **brazier** (II.). **a** Coal dust, cinders, refuse from coal or coke; **b** such refuse mixed with cement and made into slabs for use in buildings.

breeze (III.), n. O.E. *brēosa*, 'gad-fly', M.E. *brēse*. The word prob. means 'the stinging creature', & may be derived fr. Gmc. base **breus-*, **brus-*, Aryan **bhreus-*, **bhrus-*, seen in O.E. *byrst*, 'bristle', *brord*, 'point', fr. **bruzda-*, Scrt. *bhr̥ṣtiš*, 'spike, prong' &c. See **brad, bore, bristle.** Horse-fly, gad-fly.

breezily, adv. [1. brḗzili; 2. brízili]. **breezy** & **-ly.** In a breezy manner.

breeziness, n. [1. brḗzines; 2. brízinis]. See next word & **-ness.** The condition of being breezy in any of its senses.

breezy, adj. [1. brḗzi; 2. brízi]. **breeze** (I.) & **-y.** **a** (of weather) Fresh, windy; **b** (of locality) exposed to wind, airy; **c** (fig., of manner) brisk, cheerful, genial.

bregma, n. [1. brégma; 2. brégmə]. Gk., 'front part of the head', see under **brain.** (anat.) That part of the skull where the frontal and side bones meet.

Brehon, n. [1. bréhon; 2. bríhən]. O. Ir. *brithem*, 'judge'. Ancient Irish judge; *Brehon Laws*, those customary among the ancient Irish.

brent-goose. See **brant-goose.**

bressumer. See **breastsummer.**

brethren, n. [1. brédhren; 2. bréðrin]. Archaic pl. of **brother.**

Breton, adj. & n. [1. bréton; 2. brétən], fr. O. Fr. *Breton*, see **Briton.** **1.** adj. Pertaining to Brittany, or to its inhabitants, or to its Celtic dialect. **2.** n. **a** A native of Brittany; **b** Celtic dialect of Brittany.

Bretwalda, n. [1. bretwólda; 2. bretwɔ́ldə]. O.E.; see **wield.** The ruler of the Britons; title given to some of the early Anglo-Saxon kings.

breve (I.), n. [1. brēv; 2. brīv]. M.E. *brēv*, 'official document'. A variant of *brēf*, q.v. under **brief** (I.). The *v* is derived fr. the inflected cases, cp. *loaf*, pl. *-ves*, where *f* is 'voiced' between vowels. *Brēv* must therefore be fr. the type developed in inflected forms. (obs.) A mandate from a sovereign &c.

breve (II.), n. Lat. *brevis*, 'short'. Cp. **brief** (I.). **a** (mus.) A note consisting of two semibreves (obsolesc.); **b** (typog.) the mark of shortness (˘) placed over a letter.

brevet, n. [1. brévet; 2. brévit]. M.E. *brevet*, fr. O. Fr.; Mod. Fr. *brevet*, 'patent, or diploma awarded by an authoritative body, esp. government'. Derived fr. O. Fr. *breve* in sense of 'official document', see **breve** (I.), & dimin. suff. **-et.** Document or patent conferring a privilege; specif., document conferring upon an officer in the army an army rank one degree superior to that which he holds in his regiment; e.g. *brevet major* is a regimental captain who is granted title and rank of a major in the army, with the right of performing the functions of a major, and of holding appointments for which only majors are eligible, when employed extra-regimentally.

breviary, n. [1. bréviari; 2. brívjəri]. Lat. *breviārium*, 'summary', fr. *brevis*, 'short'. Cp. **brief** (I.). Book used by priests in Roman Catholic Church, containing Divine Office for each day.

brevier, n. [1. brevḗr; 2. brivíə]. (typog.) Small type between *bourgeois* and *minion*, originally used in printing breviaries.

brevity, n. [1. bréviti; 2. bréviti]. Not recorded in M.E. Perh. fr. A.-Fr. *brevete*, but more prob. derived straight fr. Lat. *brevitāt-(em)*, w. suff. *-y* on anal. of many other words in *-ity*. Used in present sense since early 16th cent. See **brief** (I.). Shortness of duration (of non-material things only), absence of prolixity; conciseness: *brevity of human life*; *brevity of speech.*

brew (I.), vb. trans. & intrans. [1. brōō; 2. brū]. O.E. *brēowan*, M.E. *brēwen*, O.H.G. *briowan*. The base is that wh. occurs in **bird, bourn, bread, brood** &c., cogn. w. Lat. *de-frūtum*, 'must', O. Ir. *bruith*, 'cooking', *bruthe*, 'broth'. The Aryan base is **bherewa*, 'boil, bubble, ferment', &c. Cp. further Lat. *fervēre*, 'to be boiling hot, glow'; see **fervent**; Gk. *phréār*, fr. **bhrewār*, 'well, reservoir', q.v. under **bourn** (I.). **1.** trans. **a** To prepare, produce, by steeping, boiling and fermenting; esp. of ale, beer, and malt and hop liquors generally; **b** (extended use) to prepare by boiling, infusion, and mixing of ingredients, e.g. of tea, punch; also, generally, to prepare a drink by mingling ingredients; e.g. of claret-cup &c.; **c** (fig.) to contrive, prepare, bring about, esp. of disaster, trouble, mischief &c. **2.** intrans. **a** To brew beer &c.; **b** (fig.) to gather, form, prepare: *a storm, mischief, is brewing.*

brew (II.), n. fr. prec. That which is brewed, esp. a single making of ale or beer &c.

brewer, n. [1. brōōer; 2. brúə], see prec. & **-er.** One who brews, prepares for consumption, and sells ale and beer.

brewery, n. [1. brōōeri; 2. brúəri]. **brew** & **-ery.** Works or building in which the trade of brewing is carried out.

brewing, n. [1. brōōing; 2. brúiŋ], fr. **brew** (I.) & **-ing.** Act or process of producing malted liquor, ale, beer &c.

brewis, n. [1. brōōis; 2. brúis]. M.E. *brouet, broues, browis* &c., 'broth', wh. have the meaning, but not direct ancestral form, of modern word; fr. O. Fr. *brouet*, wh. is said to be fr. O.H.G. *brod-*, 'broth', & dimin. suff. The base is that in **brew** & other words there referred to. (provinc.) Applied to various kinds of broth and liquid stews.

brewster, n. [1. brōōster; 2. brústə]. **brew** (I.) & old fem. suff. **-ster.** Originally a woman brewer, now only used in *Brewster Sessions*, of certain periodical sittings of licensing magistrates to renew old and grant new licences for the sale of alcoholic liquors.

briar (I.), adj. & n. [1. bríar; 2. bráiə], fr. Fr. *bruyère*, the plant 'heath or broom'; no connexion w. **brier**; the Fr. word is apparently fr. a Low Lat. **brugaria*, wh. is supposed to be derived fr. Celt. **brucus*, 'heath plant'. Cp. **brusque.** **1.** adj. Made of the root of the white heath, *Erica arborea*, esp. used for making tobacco pipes: *briar pipes.* **2.** n. **a** The wood of the white heath; **b** pipe made of this.

briar (II.), n. Prickly shrub. See **brier.**

bribable, adj. [1. bríbabl; 2. bráibəbl]. **bribe** (II.) & **-able.** Capable of being bribed, open to bribery; corrupt.

bribe (I.), n. [1. brīb; 2. braib]. O. Fr. *bribe*, 'large lump of bread'. Etymol. unknown. In M.E. the n. occurs, apparently in present sense, the vb. in sense of 'to beg', also 'to pilfer'; *bribour* means 'thief, rascal'. A reward, favour, bestowed on, or price paid to, a person to induce him to act against his judgement or conscience, illegally or wickedly, in the interests of some person or cause.

bribe (II.), vb. trans., fr. prec. To offer or give a reward or price to (a person) in order to influence his conduct in a particular way.

bribery, n. [1. bríberi; 2. bráibəri]. **bribe** (I.) & **-ery.** An act, or the practice, of payment to a person to influence his action corruptly.

bric-à-brac, n. [1. brík a brak; 2. brík ə bræk]. Fr. Etymol. unknown. Suggestions in the dictionaries are purely speculative and lead nowhere. Collection of antiques and curiosities, usually of small articles; applied also to small miscellaneous articles, used as ornaments; knick-knacks of no great value.

brick (I.), n. [1. brik; 2. brik]. A late word; first found in Engl. 1447. O. Fr. *brique* in sense of 'piece'. Precise origin & hist. obscure. Prob. borrowed fr. a Gmc. language, & connected w. base **brek-*, 'break', cp. O.E. *brice*, 'piece, fragment'. See **break** (I.). **1. a** Oblong, rectangular block of hard, burnt clay, used, instead of stone, in building; Phrs. *as dry, hard, as a brick*; *to make bricks without straw*, undertake hard and fruitless task; **b** the material of which bricks are composed. **2. a** Any mass shaped like a brick, as a compressed block of dried manure containing mushroom spawn for propagating; **b** (in pl.) esp. *box of bricks*, collection of rectangular blocks, usually of wood, of varying lengths with which children construct small forts &c. **3.** (colloq.) A cheerful, kind-hearted, good-natured person: *a regular brick*; *to behave like a brick* &c.

brick (II.), adj., fr. prec. Made of brick: *a brick house* &c. Phr. (*up against*) *a brick wall*, something unyielding or impenetrable.

brick (III.), vb. trans., fr. **brick** (I.). Usually *brick in, up*. To block up (gap &c.) with bricks.

brickbat, n. [1. bríkbat; 2. bríkbæt]. See **bat** (I.). Rough, broken piece of brick.

brick clay, n. Clay suitable for making bricks.

brickdust, n. [1. bríkdust; 2. bríkdast]. Powdered brick, esp. red brick.

brick-field, n. Field in which bricks are moulded and baked.

brick-kiln, n. Kiln or furnace in which bricks are burnt or baked.

bricklayer, n. [1. bríklāer; 2. bríkleiə]. One whose trade it is to build with bricks.

bricklaying, n. [1. bríklāing; 2. bríkleiiŋ]. Act, trade, of building by laying bricks on bed of mortar.

brick red, adj. Dark red, resembling the colour of the common brick.

brick tea, n. China tea compressed into blocks or bricks for transport, esp. in Asia.

brickwork, n. [1. bríkwērk; 2. bríkwāk]. Building, or part of it, made of brick.

bricole, n. [1. bríkōl; 2. bríkoul]. Fr. Etymol. unknown. **a** (obs.) An old military engine for hurling stones at the walls of a fortress; **b** (in real tennis) a stroke off the side wall; **c** (billiards) indirect stroke off the cushion.

bridal (I.), n. [1. brídal; 2. bráidəl]. O.E. *brȳdealu*, 'wedding feast'. See **bride** & **ale**. The latter word is used in O.E. in sense of 'feast, festivity' & prob. confused later w. suff. in *espousal, nuptial*. Ceremony of marriage; festivity held on occasion of a marriage.

bridal (II.), adj., fr. prec.; also perh. new formation fr. **bride** & adj. suff. **-al**. **a** Pertaining to marriage or marriage feast: *bridal bells, banquet* &c.; **b** belonging to a bride: *bridal wreath, veil*; *bridal party* (in sense of bride and her attendants and friends).

bride, n. [1. brīd; 2. braid]. O.E. *brȳd, brīd*, fr. **brūdi*, M.E. *brīd* &c., O.H.G. *brūt*, Mod. Germ. *braut*, Goth. *brūþs*, 'daughter-in-law, bride', O.N. *brūðr*. This common Gmc. base is perh. derived fr. that wh. has produced **brood**, **bread** &c., meaning 'she who produces, rears, offspring'. Relation w. Lat. *Frūtis*, a name for Venus, has been suggested, & this is connected w. Lat. *frut-ex*, 'bush', *fruti-cāre*, 'to sprout, bud', cp. **frutex**, & expresses the idea of fertility. Various more or less plausible origins have been suggested for the last two Lat. words, but whichever be considered the most probable, the underlying meaning of each is pretty much the same. **a** Woman on her wedding-day, before and after ceremony; **b** newly-married woman, for few months after wedding.

bride-cake, n. Rich, highly-decorated cake eaten at weddings.

bridegroom, n. [1. brídgroom; 2. bráidgrūm]. O.E. *brȳdguma*. See **bride**. The second element is due to a substitution of **groom**, q.v., for the old common Gmc. *guma*, 'man', M.E. *gume, gōme*, cp. O.H.G. *brūti-gomo*, Mod. Germ. *bräuti-gam*; this is cogn. w. Lat. *homo*, Aryan **ghom-* &c., cp. Lith. *žmón-es* (pl.), 'mankind'. The word is connected w. Lat. *humus*, 'earth'. See **humus** & **man**. Newly-married man, or one about to be married.

bridesmaid, n. [1. brídzmād; 2. bráidzmeid]. Cp. **bride** & **maid**. Young unmarried woman, usually one of several, who attends the bride at a wedding.

bridesman, n. [1. brídzman; 2. bráidzmən]. Male attendant on bridegroom at a wedding, now usually called *best man*.

bridewell, n. [1. brídwel; 2. bráidwəl]. Named after a former palace wh. was later used as a prison, built near *St. Bride's* (*Bridget's*) *Well* in London. Lock-up for arrested persons, gaol &c.; house of correction for vagabonds and disorderly persons.

bridge (I.), n. [1. brij; 2. bridž]. O.E. *bryċġ, briċġ*, M.E. *brigge* &c.; O.H.G. *brucka*, Mod. Germ. *brücke*, Du. *brugge*. The exact formal cogn. w. the Engl. word in O.N. is *bryggja*, wh. however means 'landing-place, gangway'; the word for 'bridge' in O.N. is *brū*, fr. same base but without the *-ja* suff. The etymol. is very doubtful. **1.** Structure of wood, stone, or iron built across a chasm, e.g. a river, valley, railway-cutting, or road, so as to form a means of passage for foot-passengers and vehicles. Phr. *a golden bridge*, an easy way of retreat or means of extricating oneself from a difficulty. **2.** (naut.) Kind of raised platform extending over and across part of a ship's deck, for the captain or navigating officer. **3.** (variously applied with sense of support or connexion) **a** *Bridge of the nose*, bone which supports the soft structures of the nose, and gives to this its characteristic shape in profile; **b** (mus.) small wooden strut or support which takes the strain of the strings when tightened, in instruments of the fiddle class, and raises them above the belly of the instrument between tail-piece and finger-board; **c** (dentistry) small metal device for keeping false teeth in place by attaching them to existing teeth; **d** rest for the cue in billiards held by the left hand.

bridge (II.), vb. trans., fr. prec. **1.** To span a chasm, to unite the opposing sides of a river, valley &c., by means of a bridge. **2.** (fig.) To overcome obstacles; fill in a break in time: *to bridge over the difficulties of a situation*.

bridge (III.), n. Etymol. unknown; it was a form of whist played first in Greece & Constantinople & called *biritch*, or Russian whist. A card game, resembling whist, in which one player exposes his cards which are played by his partner; the modern game is now *auction bridge*, each player in which bids for right of playing, or a later variety, *contract bridge*.

bridgehead, n. [1. bríjhed; 2. brídžhed]. (fort.) Defensive work protecting approach to a bridge on side nearest to the enemy.

bridle (I.), n. [1. brídl; 2. bráidl]. O.E. *briġdel, brīdel*, fr. **bregd-il*, cp. *breġdan*, 'twist, pull' &c., under **braid** (I.). **1.** Part of horse's harness consisting of the whole head-gear and its appurtenances, including the bit, the various straps which hold it in position, and the reins which control it. **2.** Specif., the reins by which the horse is controlled by the rider.

bridle (II.), vb. trans. & intrans., fr. prec. **1.** trans. **a** To put a bridle on a horse &c.; **b** (fig.) to restrain, check, keep within bounds: *to bridle one's passions, desires, ambitions* &c. **2.** intrans. **a** (of horses) To carry the head with chin drawn in as though tightly reined; **b** (fig., of persons) to show pride, contempt, or resentment by one's bearing, esp. by a haughty tossing of head, and a stiff carriage: *to bridle with anger, bridle at one's remarks*.

bridle hand, n. That hand in which reins are generally held—the left.

bridle path, n. Path along which horses can be ridden or led, but too narrow for vehicles.

bridle rein, n. Rein attached to bit, esp. in riding horses.

bridoon, n. [1. bridóon; 2. bridún]. Fr. *bridon*, fr. *bride*, 'bridle', wh. is borrowed fr. a L.G. source. Cp. **bridle** (I.). Reins and bit, including both snaffle and curb, of a military bridle.

brief (I.), adj. [1. brēf; 2. brīf]. M.E. *brēfe*, fr. Fr. *bref* &c., Lat. *brevis*, 'short', cogn. w. Gk. *brakhús*, 'short', of linear space, & time, O. Slav. *brŭzěja*, 'shallow', Aryan **bhreghu*, cp. **brachy-**. **1.** Lasting only for a short time, having but a short duration in time, short-lived (*brief* is not applied, as is the word *short*, to linear space): *brief life, experience*; *brief remarks*, i.e. few and soon over; *brief hopes*, soon shattered. **2.** **a** (of style) Concise, condensed; **b** (of manner) abrupt, as though anxious to break off conversation.

brief (II.), n., fr. prec. M.E. *brēf*, 'legal or official document'. Orig. a summary, of facts & arguments; official mandate. Specif. **a** papal letter less formal than a 'bull'; **b** (law) document of instructions, prepared by solicitor, giving the barrister or counsel a compendious statement of facts in a case to be tried in court. Phrs. *to hold a brief for*, support, justify, argue in favour of a person or state of things; *to have plenty of briefs* (of a barrister), to be busy in his profession.

brief (III.), vb. trans., fr. prec. **a** To instruct (a barrister), give a brief to; more generally, employ him, e.g. *many eminent counsel were briefed in this case*; **b** (gen.) to give particular information, or instructions regarding a matter, furnish a person with facts and arguments: *if you want me to put your case forcibly, you must brief me thoroughly beforehand*.

briefless, adj. [1. brēfles; 2. bríflis]. **brief** (II.) & **-less**. Lacking briefs (of a barrister), therefore unemployed, unable to make a livelihood from profession of the Law.

briefly, adv. [1. brēfli; 2. brífli]. **brief** (I.) & **-ly**. In a brief manner; succinctly.

brier (I.), **briar**, n. [1. brīer; 2. bráiə]. O.E. *brēr* &c. Etymol. dubious. Relation of Mod. to O.E. form also obscure. Prickly wild shrub with long trailing shoots, esp. that bearing the wild rose.

brier (II.), n. Tobacco pipe. See **briar**.

brig, n. [1. brig; 2. brig]. Short for **brigantine**. A two-masted, square-rigged vessel.

brigade (I.), n. [1. brigád; 2. brigéid]. Fr. *brigade*, Ital. *brigata*, 'troop', fr. Ital. *briga*, 'strife', also in Port. It is supposed that these & other related words are formed fr. the borrowed Gmc. base *brik-* (Goth.) *brek-*, q.v. under **break** (I.). **1.** A unit of the army, smaller than a division, consisting of three or four battalions of infantry or regiments of cavalry, or of three or four batteries of artillery. **2.** Any organized body of persons acting together, or held together by common beliefs and customs: *fire brigade*; *Boys' Brigade*.

brigade (II.), vb. trans., fr. prec. **a** To put (troops) into the same brigade; **b** occasionally, to group, or classify together.

brigade major, n. The chief staff officer of a brigade. He is generally a captain in army rank and does not become a major by virtue of his office.

brigadier, n. [1. brigadḗr; 2. brigədíə]. Fr. *brigadier*. See **brigade** & **-ier**. A military officer commanding a brigade or holding a staff appointment of similar status. He ranks immediately below a major-general. Such officers have also, at different periods in the history of the British Army, been called 'brigadier-generals' and 'colonels-commandant'; 'brigadier' is the present usage. It is not a permanent rank but the style of an appointment.

brigand, n. [1. brígand; 2. brígənd]. O. Fr. *brigant*, 'light-armed soldier', Fr. *brigand* w. different sense, Ital. *brigante*; fr. Low Lat. *brigare*, 'strive', fr. Gmc. base *brik-* &c. Cp. **brigade** & **break** (I.). Lawless person, esp. one of a band, in Southern Europe, who lives by waylaying travellers, stealing their property, and sometimes kidnapping their persons in hope of obtaining a ransom. The term is not applied to English thieves, whose methods are different.

brigandage, n. [1. brígandij; 2. brígəndidž]. Prec. & **-age**. Act and practice of stealing, and behaving as a brigand.

brigantine, n. [1. bríganten; 2. brígəntīn]. Fr. *brigantin*, Ital. *brigantino*. Originally a fighting, esp. a piratical vessel. See **brigand**. Two-masted ship, with square-rigged fore-mast and fore-and-aft rig on mainmast.

bright (I.), adj. [1. brīt; 2. brait]. O.E. *beorht, bryht* &c., 'bright', O.H.G. *beraht*, Goth. *bairhts*, O.N. *bjartr*. Outside Gmc. cp. Lith. *breszko*, 'it dawns', O. Slav. *brězgŭ*, 'dawn', Scrt. *bhrā́jati*, 'it gleams, sparkles'. The base **bhereĝ-* &c. is apparently Common Aryan. It seems probable that the Aryan base *bheleg-, 'shine, flame', whence Lat. *flagrāre*, 'flame, burn' &c., was closely related. See this under **blank, bleak, flagrant**, & cp. **brock**. For other cognates of *bright* see **birch** (tree), **bark** (of tree). **1.** Radiating, emitting, giving out, light; reflecting light; shining; reverse of *dark* and *dull*. Phr. *to look on the bright side*, take a cheerful view of things. **2.** Vivid, conspicuous in tone (of colours): *bright red, blue* &c. **3.** Free from cloudiness; clear, transparent (of liquids, wine, beer &c.). **4.** (fig., of mental qualities) Alert, animated, intelligent, cheerful. **5.** Illustrious: *his reputation was never brighter than just before his death.*

bright (II.), adv., fr. prec. O.E. *beorhte*, adv., 'brightly'. In a bright manner, brilliantly, with much light: '*How bright those glorious spirits shine*' (Watts). Chiefly with vb. *shine*.

brighten, vb. trans. & intrans. [1. brīten; 2. bráit(ə)n]. **bright** (I.) & **-en**. **A.** trans. **1.** To make bright, cause to shine, by cleaning &c.: *to brighten silver*. **2.** To improve by making more cheerful, happier: *to brighten the lot of the poor*. **B.** intrans. To grow, become light, or bright: *the day is brightening*.

brightly, adv. [1. brítli; 2. bráitli]. **bright** (I.) & **-ly**. Same as **bright** (II.), but more extensively used as adv. of *bright* in all senses.

brightness, n. [1. brítnes; 2. bráitnis]. **bright** (I.) & **-ness**. The quality or property of being *bright* in its various senses.

Bright's disease, n. [1. bríts dizḗz; 2. bráits dizíz]. So called after Dr. Richard Bright, who described the complaint in 1827. A malady of the kidneys; acute or chronic nephritis.

brill, n. [1. bril; 2. bril]. Cornish *brilli* is a mackerel; *brith* means 'streaked'. A flat fish allied to the turbot and resembling it in shape and in the quality of its flesh.

brilliance, brilliancy, n. [1. brílyans(i); 2. bríljəns(i)]. See **brilliant** & **-cy**. Quality of being bright, shining, intelligent; brightness, splendour, radiance; keen intelligence, wit.

brilliant (I.), adj. [1. brílyant; 2. bríljənt]. Fr. *brillant*, Pres. Part. of *briller*, 'shine' &c., fr. Low Lat. **beryllāre*, 'shine like a beryl'. Cp. the vbs. Ital. *brillare*, Span. *brillar*. See **beryl**. **a** Bright, glittering, shining; **b** (of non-material things) splendid, having qualities which attract attention, provoke admiration: *brilliant mind, talents, wit, intelligence*; *a brilliant idea* &c.

brilliant (II.), n., fr. prec. **1.** Diamond or other precious stone cut in particular way, with numerous facets, so as to ensure special brilliancy. The ordinary form of brilliant is roughly that of two cones base to base, the upper having a flat top formed by cutting off a part not far from base, the lower having the point cut off. **2.** (typog.) Smallest size of type used in ordinary printing.

brilliantine, n. [1. brílyantēn; 2. bríljəntīn]. Fr. Cp. **brilliant** (I.). Greasy cosmetic used to make the hair lie flat.

brim (I.), n. [1. brim; 2. brim]. O.E. *brymme*, 'border, sea shore', M.E. *brimme*, cp. Germ. *brame*, 'edge' &c.; O.E. *brim*, 'sea', w. wh. the word is confused in O.E., may be cogn., & the orig. meaning of *brymme* may be 'edge of the sea'. In this case *brim* is related prob. to Lat. *fremere*, 'roar, murmur', Gk. *brémein*, 'murmur, resound', *brómos*, 'roaring', *bronté*, 'thunder'. This is by many derived fr. a base **mrem-* & supposed to be cogn. w. **murmur**. For an alternative etymol. see **form** (I.). **1.** Edge, border, shore of river, lake, or sea. **2.** Outer edge, rim of cup or other hollow vessel: '*A beaker . . . With beaded bubbles winking at the brim*' (Keats). Phr. *full to the brim*, completely full. **3.** Part of a hat which projects below the crown; the rim.

brim (II.), vb. intrans. & trans., fr. prec. **1.** intrans. To be full to the brim; *brim over*, to be full to overflowing; (fig.) *brim (over) with health and spirits*. **2.** trans. To fill to the brim (rare).

brimful, adj. [1. brimfóol; 2. brímfúl]. **brim** (I.) & **full**. Full to the brim, very full; (fig.) *brimful of ideas* &c.

brimmed, adj. [1. brimd; 2. brimd]. **brim** (I.) & **-ed**. **a** Provided with a brim; **b** filled very full (of a cup &c.).

brimmer, n. [1. brímer; 2. brímə]. **brim** (I.) & **-er**. A vessel, esp. for drinking, filled to the brim; a copious draught.

brimstone, n. [1. brímstun; 2. brímstən]. M.E. *brinstōn, brenstōn*; O.N. *brennisteinn*. See **burn & stone**. Sulphur. Phrs. *brimstone bitch*, a violent, vituperating woman (obs. and coarse); *brimstone and treacle*, purgative mixture formerly given to children.

brindled, adj. [1. bríndld; 2. bríndld]. Earlier *brinded*. Connected w. **brand**. Streaked, esp. with brown or tawny colour; having streaks of lighter colour on black.

brine, n. [1. brīn; 2. brain]. O.E. *brȳne*. Etymol. doubtful. Perh. fr. **mrīn-*, cp. Lat. *marīnus*, 'belonging to the sea'. See **marine**. **1.** Water strongly impregnated with salt, used for pickling pork &c. Phr. *salt as brine*. **2.** (fig. and poet.) Sea water.

bring, vb. trans. [1. bring; 2. briŋ]. O.E. *bringan*, O.H.G. *bringen*, Goth. *briggan*, strong vb. related to wk. O.E. *brengan*, fr. **brang-jan*, O.S. *brengian* &c. The base as it stands in Gmc. not found in other branches of Aryan languages. It is suggested that Gmc. **bring-*, **brang-*, is an old compound formed fr. the bases **bhrē-* &c., 'bear', cp. **bear** (I.), vb., & **enek-* found in Gk. *enegkein*, 'carry, reach', also Gk. *ógkos*, 'burden, bulk, mass'; cp. also Lat. *nanc-iscor*, 'obtain, light upon', Lith. *nèszti*, 'carry'. See further on this base under **enough**. **1.** To convey, or cause to come, esp. to place where speaker is, or intends to be, whether by carrying, leading, driving, or attracting; convey from more distant to nearer place (said of things and persons): *bring it to me*; *bring him with you to see me*; *they returned to camp bringing in prisoners*; *what brings you here today?* Phrs. *bring into the world* (of maternal parent), give birth to; *bring* (something) *home to* (a person), convict, prove guilt of; *bring pressure to bear on, upon*, use persuasion or compulsion. **2.** To cause, produce, make to come: *hard work sometimes brings its reward*; *my efforts have brought me good luck*; *riches often bring honours along with them*. Phr. *bring to pass*, cause to happen. **3.** To persuade, induce: *I wish I could bring you to see my point*; (also reflex.) *I can't bring myself to take strong action in the matter*. **4.** To procure as a price, to sell for, fetch: *how much did your fruit crop bring last year?*; *his literary work brings him hundreds a year*. **5.** (law) To prefer, adduce, start, as *an action in law, an accusation, charge* &c. **6.** Used in large number of special and idiomatic phrases, with prepositions: *bring about*, cause to happen; *bring back*, remind one, call to mind; *bring down*, cause to fall (lit. and fig.), to abase, ruin (of persons); *bring down the house*, provoke great applause, esp. in theatre; *bring forth*, cause, produce, give birth to (fruit, offspring &c.); *bring forward*, adduce, urge, as an argument, proposal &c.; also in bookkeeping, carry figures from preceding to following page; *bring in* (*guilty* or *not guilty*), pronounce verdict; also, yield as a profit, produce; *bring off*, rescue, esp. from a wreck; carry out, achieve; *bring on*, cause, induce, e.g. *an illness*; also, cause discussion; *bring out*, exhibit clearly (of meaning &c.); publish (a book); introduce to public (an actor, singer); produce (a play); *bring over*, convert to another religion, way of thinking &c.; *bring round*, restore to consciousness, or health; convert by persuasion, to different opinions; *bring through*, guide, through difficulties &c.; help by instruction to pass an examination; restore health to, by medical care during illness; *bring to*, to restore (person) to consciousness; to check (ship &c.); intrans., to come to a stop; *bring under*, subdue; include within (a category &c.); *bring up*, rear, educate; raise (point or argument) for discussion; vomit; cause to stop, arrest; also intrans. to conclude a journey, esp. of a ship: *to bring up at a port*.

brink, n. [1. bringk; 2. briŋk]. M.E., of Scand. origin, cp. Dan. *brink*, 'edge', Swed. *brink*, 'slope, declivity of a hill'. Perh. derived, w. an infixed nasal, fr. Aryan **mreg-*, a form of **marog-*, whence connected w. Lat. *margo*, 'edge, brink, border'. See **margin**, also **mark** (I.). Edge, verge, esp. of a steep descent, lofty height, or deep fissure, chasm &c., in the ground. Fig. uses and Phrs.: *on the brink of the grave*, near death; *brink of eternity*; *brink of ruin*; *to stand shivering on the brink*, of one reluctant to make up the mind, unable to come to a decision.

briny, adj. [1. bríni; 2. bráini]. Prec. & **-y**. Very salt; (poet.) of tears. (used vulgarly as n.) *The briny*, the sea.

brio, n. [1. brēō; 2. bríou]. Ital. Supposed to be Gaulish, fr. hypothetical **brivos*, 'courage, strength', cp. Ir. *brig*, 'strength', W. *bri*, 'honour'. Dash, spirit, vivacity.

brioche, n. [1. brēósh; 2. brióʃ]. Fr. Origin unknown. Kind of light cake or bun.

briquette, n. [1. brikét; 2. brikét]. Fr. *briquette*. See **brick** & dimin. suff. **-ette**. Small brick-shaped mass; esp. of coal-dust mixed with sawdust, ashes, clay &c., used for burning to economize more expensive fuel, or if made of highly inflammable materials, to facilitate lighting of household fires.

brisk (I.), adj. [1. brisk; 2. brisk]. Etymol. uncertain. **1.** (of persons) Lively, active, vigorous, quick in movement. **2.** (of liquors) Sparkling, effervescent; reverse of *flat*.

brisk (II.), vb., fr. prec. Esp. *brisk up*: **a** trans., to enliven, cheer, render brisk; **b** intrans., to grow lively, become brisk.

brisket, n. [1. brísket; 2. brískit]. M.E. *bruskette*, O. Fr. *bruschet, breschet*, Mod. Fr. *bréchet*. Etymol. obscure. Said to be of Celt. origin. Cp. Bret. *brusk, bruched*, W. *brysced*, 'breast of slain animal'. The word may be of Gmc. origin, cp. O.E. *brēost*, q.v. under **breast**. The W. form may be loan-word fr. Engl. The Fr. may be fr. Bret., wh. is ultimately the same as W. Joint of beef cut from breast of the animal extending to between the front legs.

bristle (I.), n. [1. brísl; 2. brísl]. M.E. *bristel, brustel*, fr. O.E. *byrst* & dimin. suff. *-il, (-el)*. The O.E. word is cogn. w. O.H.G. *burst*, Mod. Germ. *borste*, 'brush, bristle'. Outside Gmc., Lat. *fast-īgium*, fr. **farsti-*, 'top, summit, of a roof, gable'; Scrt. *bhṛṣṭiš*, 'point, spike'. Cp. further **borage, brad, breast, burn** (I.). Orig. meaning is 'spike, prickle'. Short, stiff, hair-like, prickly structure on animals, esp. on the neck and back of swine.

bristle (II.), vb. intrans., fr. prec. **1.** To rise, stand on end, as the bristles of an animal when excited. **2.** (fig.) To evince rage, indignation; from analogy of angry animal; esp. *bristle with anger* &c. **3.** **a** To show a number of projecting points, such as masts, steeples, spears, bayonets &c., as though thickly set with bristles: *the city bristles with church-spires*; *a cavalry regiment with bristling lances*; **b** (fig.) to be full of difficult, hard, debatable, points: *the whole subject bristles with difficulties*.

bristling, brisling, n. [1. brísling; 2. bríslíŋ]. Scand.; etymol. obscure. A small sea-fish, of the herring type, of N. European waters, canned in oil, like sardines.

bristly, adj. [1. brísli; 2. brísli]. See **bristle** (I.) & **-y**. **a** Like bristles; full of bristles, rough, spiky, prickly; **b** (of hair) rough, coarse, standing up.

Bristol, adj. [1. brístol; 2. brístəl], fr. name of town, Gloucestershire. Of Bristol; *Bristol board*, a fine, smooth-faced cardboard; *Bristol cream*, a fine brand of sherry; *Bristol diamond*, a kind of rock crystal or spar.

Britannia metal, n. [1. británya métal; 2. britǽnjə métl]. An alloy of tin with antimony and copper, with some zinc or bismuth added, resembling silver in appearance.

Britannic, adj. [1. británik; 2. britǽnik]. Lat. *Britannicus*; cp. **Briton**. Pertaining to Britain; now only in diplomatic Phr. *His Britannic Majesty* &c.

British, adj. [1. brítish; 2. brítiʃ]. O.E. *Brettisċ*; cp. **Briton** & **-ish**. **a** Pertaining to, coming from, Britain; relating to the inhabitants of Britain; *British warm*, short, thick, military overcoat; **b** pertaining to the Celtic inhabitants of Great Britain before the Anglo-Saxon settlement.

Britisher, n. [1. brítisher; 2. brítiʃə]. Perh. American word; formed on anal. of *foreigner*. Native inhabitant of British Isles.

Briton, n. [1. bríton; 2. brítən], fr. O. Fr. *Breton*, fr. Lat. *Brittōn-*, member of the tribe of the *Brittones*. The relation between this form, & Lat. *Britanni*, *Bretanni*, Gk. *Brettanoi*, *Prettanoi*, is very obscure, & the etymol. is doubtful. **1.** One of the native Celtic inhabitants of Great Britain at the time of the Roman invasion. **2.** Native of Great Britain or the British Empire.

brittle, adj. [1. brítl; 2. britl]. M.E. *brutel*, *britel*; formed fr. form **brut-* of base seen in O.E. *brēotan*, 'break, destroy', & adj. suff. *-il*. Gmc. base **breut-*, **brut-*, prob. related to Lat. *frustum*, 'piece, fragment', cp. **frustum**. The further etymol. is obscure. Apt to break in pieces, or snap; fragile.

brittleness, n., fr. prec. & **-ness**. Condition of being liable to break easily.

britzka, n. [1. brítska; 2. brítskə]. Polish, dimin. of *bryka*, 'wagon'. Kind of open carriage (now obs.)

broach (I.), n. [1. brōch; 2. broutʃ]. M.E., fr. Fr. *broche*, fr. Low Lat. *brocca*, Lat. *broccus*, 'having prominent teeth'; cogn. w. Gk. *brū̆kein*, 'bite', *broū̆kos*, 'grasshopper'; O.H.G. *chrouwil*, 'three-pronged fork'. Aryan type **gʷroukʷ-*. See also **brooch.** Spit for roasting; also *broach spire*, a church spire which rises direct from the tower-wall without parapet.

broach (II.), vb. trans., fr. prec. **1.** To pierce a cask of liquor and insert tap for drawing off. **2.** (fig.) To open, approach (a subject of discussion), to moot.

broad (I.), adj. [1. brawd; 2. brɔ̄d]. O.E. *brād*, M.E. *brood*, *brōde* &c., O.H.G. *breit*, *preit*, O.N. *breiðr*, Goth. *braids*. Etymol. obscure. The proposal to connect the Gmc. words w. Lat. *frio*, 'crumble', see **friable**, is not convincing. **1.** Wide, having large measurement across. Phr. *as broad as it's long*, as much to be said for as against, indifferent. **2.** Extending in all directions, spacious: *broad lands*; *the broad ocean*. **3.** Widely diffused, full: *broad daylight*. **4.** Evident, strongly marked, (of speech) *a broad accent*, *broad Scots* &c.; perhaps from idea that provincial speakers utter their dialect with uncouth widening of the mouth. Phr. *a broad hint*, unmistakable. **5.** (fig., of the mind and ideas) Extended, open, free from prejudice, catholic; far-ranging, liberal, not confined within narrow limits: *a broad mind*; *broad culture*, *outlook* &c.; specif., *Broad Church*, applied to a school of theology which insists but little on hard and fast dogma, and which some consider as inclined to latitudinarianism. **6.** Without proper restrictions and control; hence improper, inclined to indecency: *many consider the humour of Rabelais rather too broad.* **7.** Large and essential, general, bold, as opposed to *minute*, *detailed*: *he stated his views in broad outline*; *in this picture the treatment of the subject is broad and strong.*

broad (II.), n., fr. prec. *The Broads*, wide sheets of water in Norfolk.

broad arrow, n. Mark in form of an arrow-head, painted or branded upon stores, horses &c., belonging to the British Government. The mark is also placed upon the prison clothes of convicts in H.M. prisons.

broadcast (I.) adj. [1. bráwdkahst; 2. brɔ́dkāst]. **broad** & **cast** (I.). **1.** (of seed) Scattered upon soil and not sown in drills. **2.** (fig.) Widespread, diffused far and wide (of rumour, report &c.). **3.** As P.P. of next word, of wireless announcements &c.

broadcast (II.), vb. trans. & intrans. (Recently coined & adopted word.) To disseminate, by means of wireless telephony, the sound of speeches, vocal and instrumental music, and dramatic performances as these are being uttered or performed.

broadcasting, n. [1. bráwdkahsting; 2. brɔ́dkāstiŋ]. Prec. & **-ing**. The process of disseminating speeches, music &c. by wireless telephony.

broadcloth, n. [1. bráwdklawth; 2. brɔ́dklɔ̄þ]. A fine, smooth, densely woven cloth, formerly used in making men's clothes, usually made in very broad width.

broaden, vb. trans. & intrans. [1. bráwdn; 2. brɔ́dn]. **broad** (I.) & **-en**. **1.** trans. To make broad, esp. in fig. sense: *to broaden one's mind*. **2.** intrans. (also with *out*). To become broad or wide: *river broadens* (*out*) *at this point.*

broadly, adv. [1. bráwdli; 2. brɔ́dli]. **broad** (I.) & **-ly**. In a broad manner.

broad-minded, adj. Having a liberal mind.

broadness, n. [1. bráwdnes; 2. brɔ́dnis]. **broad** (I.) & **-ness**. State, quality, of being broad.

broadsheet, n. [1. bráwdshēt; 2. brɔ́dʃīt]. Sheet of paper printed on one side only; esp. a popular ballad or tract so printed, sold in the streets. See **broadside, 4.**

broadside, n. [1. bráwdsīd; 2. brɔ́dsaid]. **1.** Side of a ship above water-line, from stem to stern. **2.** All the guns that can be fired simultaneously on same target from one side of a ship; the combined fire of these guns. **3.** (fig.) Volley of abuse; strong attack of any kind launched at the same moment against a single person or party. **4.** (typog.) Sheet of paper consisting of single page, printed on one side only. See **broadsheet.**

broadsword, n. [1. bráwdsord; 2. brɔ́dsɔ̄d]. A large sword with broad cutting blade.

Brobdingnag, n. [1. bróbdingnag; 2. brɔ́bdiŋnæg]. Invented by Swift, *Gulliver's Travels*. Land of giants, whose inhabitants were 60 feet high.

Brobdingnagian, adj. [1. bròbdingnágian; 2. brɔ̀bdiŋnǽgiən]. Prec. & **-ian.** Pertaining to Brobdingnag; applied to anything which is very large; on a huge scale, gigantic.

brocade (I.), n. [1. brōkā́d; 2. broukéid]. Span. *brocado*. Cp. Fr. *brocard*, 'embroidered stuff'. The word means lit. 'pricked, figured, embossed', L. Lat. *brocāre*, 'prick', & is fr. same base as **broach**, 'a spit'. Rich fabric interwoven and embossed with gold and silver thread, or adorned and embossed with raised ornamentation.

brocade (II.), vb. trans., fr. prec. To adorn (silk or linen cloth) with raised figures &c.

broccoli, n. [1. brókoli; 2. brɔ́kəli]. Ital., pl. of *broccolo*, 'sprout', dimin. of *brocco*, 'splinter'. See base under **broach (I.).** Species of cauliflower which puts out numerous sprouts, each like a miniature cauliflower.

broch, n. [1. brogh; 2. brɔχ]. Cp. O.N. *borg*, see **borough**. A prehistoric, round stone tower, of the Orkneys and Shetlands &c.

brochure, n. [1. brṓshoor; 2. bróuʃuə]. Fr. The vb. *brocher* means to fasten sheets of paper together in a paper cover by piercing and sewing, as opposed to fastening them by regular binding. *Brochure* is a collection of sheets so stitched. Cp. **broach (I.)**, n. In English, usually a small pamphlet or tract, irrespective of how it is bound.

brock, n. [1. brok; 2. brɔk]. O.E. *broc*, 'badger'; prob. of Celt. origin, cp. Gael. *broc*; connected w. Ir. & Gael. *breac*, 'speckled'; cogn. w. Gk. *phorkós*, 'grey', & w. base whence comes **bright**. A badger; the old name, now obsolete except provincially and in Place-Names.

brocket, n. [1. bróket; 2. brɔ́kit]. M.E. *broket*, Fr. *brocard*, 'fallow deer of first year'. The name refers to the small spike of the horn; related to group of words under **broach (I.).** Stag of second year.

brogue (I.), n. [1. brōg; 2. broug]. Etymol. doubtful. Prob. Celt. It has been suggested that the word is fr. some Celt. source fr. wh. comes **breeches.** Rough shoe of untanned leather, originally applied to such as were worn by the Irish; now, a strong, thick shoe worn in the country by both sexes.

brogue (II.), n. Same as prec. 'Speech of the brogue-wearing Irish'. Provincial accent, esp. the Irish manner of speaking English.

broider, vb. Archaic. See **embroider.**

broil (I.), vb. trans. & intrans. [1. broil; 2. brɔil]. Etymol. doubtful. M.E. *broilen*, O. Fr. *broiller*, *bruiller*, 'burn'. Fr. *brûler*, O. Fr. *brusler*, is fr. Low Lat. **per-ustulāre* formed fr. *ustus*, P.P. of *ūrere*, 'burn', q.v. under **combustion.** A form *brule* for *broil* is used in 15th-cent. Engl., wh. may have been influenced by *brûler*. There is a Mod. Germ. & M.H.G. *brodeln*, 'bubble', wh. may be the origin of Fr. *broiller*. **1.** trans. To grill, cook, (meat) on a gridiron by direct contact with fire. **2.** (fig.) **a** intrans. To be very hot: *to sit broiling in the sun*; *a broiling day* &c.; **b** trans., *I shall be broiled alive if I stay in this room any longer.*

broil (II.), n., fr. old vb. Cp. Fr. *brouiller*, 'mix', Ital. *imbrogliare*, 'mix, confuse', whence Fr. *brouille*, Ital. *broglio*. These may be fr. a Gmc. word **brōjan*, 'scald', but the relationship is by no means clear. A mix up, row, quarrel, disorder.

broiler, n. [1. bróiler; 2. brɔ́ilə], fr. prec. & **-er.** One who stirs up strife and broils; a quarrelsome fellow.

broke (I.), vb. [1. brōk; 2. brouk]. Pret. of **break (I.).** M.E. *brōk*, fr. the P.P. type; see **broken**; cp. O.E. Pret. *bræc*, M.E. *brak.*

broke (II.), adj. P.P. of **break (I.)**; cp. next word. Archaic, but still used in special senses. **1.** (of ground) *Broke*, *new broke*, turned up by plough. **2.** Ruined financially, bankrupt (colloq.): *I shall be broke if I play with him too often.*

broken, vb. [1. brṓken; 2. bróukən]. Usual P.P. of **break.** O.E. *brocen*, M.E. *brōke(n)*. As adj. Special senses: **1.** Made weak, infirm, spiritless by disease, grief &c.: *a broken man.* Phr. *a broken reed.* **2.** Rough, uneven (of ground): *a broken surface.* **3.** (philol.) A vowel which in O.E. is diphthongized before certain combinations of consonants is, by some writers, called a 'broken vowel'; cp. *fracture.*

broken-down, adj. **1.** Broken in health, enfeebled by illness. **2.** (of horses) Unfit for work, esp. through over-straining of the muscles and tendons of the hind legs. **3.** (of machines) Worn-out; temporarily out of order and unworkable.

broken-hearted, adj. Deeply affected by grief, very unhappy, inconsolable.

brokenly, adv. [1. brṓkenli; 2. bróukənli]. **broken** & **-ly.** With breaks, or sudden interruptions, esp. of voice &c.

broken-winded, adj. (of horses &c.) Breathing with difficulty and noisily, through defective respiratory organs, through overwork &c.

broker, n. [1. brṓker; 2. bróukə]. M.E., O. Fr. *brocour*, 'retailer of wine', lit. 'broacher of casks.' See **broach (II.).** **1.** An agent, or middleman, who acts, for a commission, between buyer and seller, or in other kinds of bargain. **2.** An official charged with selling distrained goods.

brokerage, n. [1. brṓkerij; 2. bróukəridʒ]. Prec. & **-age.** Commission received by broker for conducting a bargain.

broking, n. [1. brṓking; 2. bróukiŋ]. The practice of broker's trade.

brolly, n. [1. bróli; 2. brɔ́li]. (slang) Umbrella.

bromide, n. [1. brṓmīd; 2. bróumaid], fr. base *brom-*, q.v. under next word, & **-ide.** Compound of bromine and a metal, as *potassium bromide* &c.

bromine, n. [1. brṓmīn; 2. bróumain]. Gk. *brômos*, 'stink', of unknown origin, & **-ine.** (chem.) Non-metallic element with a rank smell, used in medicine, as a sedative &c.

bromism, n. [1. brṓmizm; 2. bróumizəm]. See prec. & **-ism.** (med.) Complaint arising from excessive use of bromine.

bronchi, n. pl. [1. bróngkī; 2. brɔ́ŋkai]. Gk. *brógkhos*, 'windpipe'. Etymol. obscure. Cp. Gk. *brókhthos*, 'throat'. Some authorities connect these words, others keep them apart. Some cp. w. the former, Goth. *ana-praggan*, 'tighten, press'. The two branches or tubes into which the windpipe divides before entering the lungs. Called also *bronchial tubes.*

bronchial, adj. [1. bróngkial; 2. brɔ́ŋkiəl]. Prec. & **-al.** Pertaining to the bronchi.

bronchitis, n. [1. bron(g)kítis; 2. brɔŋkáitis, brɔnkáitis]. See **bronchi** & **-itis.** (med.) Inflammation of mucous membrane of the bronchi.

bronchocele, n. [1. bróngkōsēl; 2. brɔ́ŋkousīəl]. **bronchi-** & *-o-* & **-cele.** Goitre.

broncho-pneumonia, n. [1. bróngkō nūmṓnia; 2. brɔ́ŋkou njūmóuniə]. See prec. & **pneumonia.** Acute inflammation of the bronchi and lungs.

bronco, n. [1. bróngkō; 2. brɔ́ŋkou]. Span. word meaning 'rough'. Etymol. obscure & dubious. Wild, rough horse of Western North America.

bronco-buster, n. [1. bróngkō bùster; 2. brɔ́ŋkou bàstə]. (slang, U.S.A.) Cowboy who breaks in broncos.

Brontosaurus, n. [1. brȯntōsáwrus; 2. brɔ̀ntousɔ́rəs]. Invented word fr. Gk. *brontḗ*, 'thunder', & *saûros*, 'lizard'. See **brim** (I.) & **saurian.** A gigantic prehistoric genus of lizards, cp. *dinosaur.*

bronze (I.), n. & adj. [1. bronz; 2. brɔnz]. Fr., fr. Ital. *bronzo, bronzino*, fr. Lat. *aes Brundisīnum*, 'brass from Brindisi'. **1.** n. **a** Alloy of copper and tin; **b** an ornament, statue &c. made from this; also used of copper coins: *seven pence in bronze*; **c** colour of bronze. **2.** adj. Made of, of the colour of, bronze.

bronze (II.), vb. trans. & intrans., fr. prec. **a** To give a colour or surface resembling that of bronze to anything; **b** specif., to become brown from exposure to sun and weather.

Bronze Age, n. Archaeological period extending in Europe roughly from 1800 to 1000 B.C., during which implements of bronze were used, following the later Stone Age and preceding the Iron Age.

brooch, n. [1. brōch; 2. broutʃ]. Variant of **broach** (I.). Ornamental pin, in form of a clasp, often set with jewels, worn in the garments at neck or breast.

brood (I.), n. [1. brōōd; 2. brūd]. O.E. *brōd*; O.H.G. *bruot*, Mod. Germ. *brut*, 'brood', cp. also Du. *broed*, same meaning. The word is derived fr. the fertile Aryan base **bhrēu-*, 'to warm, boil', & has innumerable cognates. See **bourn, bread, brew,** & perh. **bird.** The *-d* in *brood* is a derivative suff., & not part of the orig. base. See also **breed, vb.,** wh. is regularly developed fr. the form *brōd-*. **1.** Young of animals, esp. of birds. **2.** All the young birds hatched at one time in the same nest. **3.** (extended sense) **a** All the young of the same dam, though born at different times; **b** applied to young family of human beings, progeny generally.

brood (II.), vb. intrans., fr. prec. **1.** (of a bird) **a** To sit on and hatch eggs; **b** also to sit quietly in repose, as though sitting on a nest: '*Birds . . . sit brooding on the charmed wave*' (Milton.) **2.** To dwell upon a subject, ponder with care and anxiety: *to brood over one's misfortunes, wrongs* &c. **3.** To hang low and heavily over (as of clouds over mountain-top; and fig., of care, sorrow &c.).

brood (III.), adj., fr. **brood** (I.). Kept for breeding purposes: *a brood mare.*

broody, adj. [1. brōōdi; 2. brūdi]. Found as *brōdiġ*, w. present sense, in O.E. See **brood** (II.) & **-y.** Inclined to brood, or sit on eggs: *a broody hen.*

brook (I.), n. [1. brook; 2. bruk]. O.E. *brōc*, Mod. Du. *broek*, O.H.G. *pruoh, bruoh*; Mod. Germ. *bruch*, gen. 'fracture, something broken', has also specialized sense of 'broken ground, fen, marsh'. *Brook* still has this sense in some of the Engl. regional dialects. The word is fr. a form of the base seen in **break,** & in the ordinary Engl. sense means that which *breaks*, or bursts out of the ground. A small stream of water, not so large as a river.

brook (II.), vb. trans. O.E. *brūcan*, 'make use of, enjoy', wh. is also the sense of O.H.G. *brūhhan*, Mod. Germ. *brauchen* (the latter also means 'to be obliged, compelled to do something'); Goth. has *brūks*, 'useful'. The base is the same as that in Lat. *fruor*, fr. **frugwor*, 'feed oneself with, enjoy, delight in', & in *frūx*, genit. *frūg-is*, 'fruit, produce of the earth', *fructus* for **frug-tus*, 'enjoyment'. See **fruit, frugal, usufruct.** To tolerate, endure, put up with; **a** generally with negative: *it brooks no delay*; *he cannot brook interference*; **b** in poetry without negative: '*The captive thrush may brook the cage*'.

broom, n. [1. broom; 2. brum]. O.E. *brōm*, M.E., *brōme*, O.H.G. *brāmo*, 'broom' (the plant), Mod. Germ. *brombeere*, 'blackberry'; cp. **bramble. 1.** Yellow-flowering shrub of genus *Genista* or *Cytisus.* **2.** Implement for sweeping, consisting either of a bundle of twigs tightly bound together round a handle, or of bristles inserted in flat piece of wood, to the back of which a handle is attached. The former variety was originally made of the twigs of broom plant. Phr. (fig.) *new broom*, newly appointed official, zealous in his duties.

broomstick, n. [1. bróomstik; 2. brúmstik]. Broom-handle.

brose, broase, n. [1. brōz; 2. brouz]. Same as **brewis.** *Athol brose*, drink composed of whisky, honey, and cream.

broth, n. [1. brawth, broth; 2. brɔ̄þ, brɔþ]. O.E. *broþ*, O.H.G. *brod*, fr. base **bhrēu-* &c., 'to boil, heat' &c. See **bread, brew, brood** &c. Liquid in which meat has been cooked; the same flavoured and thickened with vegetables, served as soup. Phr. (Ir. usage) *broth of a boy*, fine fellow.

brothel, n. [1. bróthl; 2. brɔ́þl]. M.E. *brothel*, 'worthless person, prostitute', formed fr. P.P. type *broth-* of O.E. *brēoþan*, 'destroy'. This has been confused in meaning w. O. Fr. *bordel*, 'a poor hut, hovel'; cp. Ital. *bordello*, Span. *burdel*, all fr. Gmc. *bord*, 'plank'. Cp. **board.** House of ill fame.

brothel keeper, n. One who owns or directs a brothel.

brother, n. [1. brúdher; 2. bráðə]. O.E. *brōþor*, O.S. *brōthar*, O.H.G. *pruodar*, Germ. *brüder*, Gk. *phrā́tēr* & *phrā́tōr*, 'member of a tribe or society of kinsmen', Lat. *frāter*, Scrt. *bhrā́tar-*, O. Slav. *bratrŭ, bratŭ*, Lith. *broter-ėlis* (w. dimin. suff.), O. Ir. *brāthir.* This word is common to every branch of Aryan speech. Its origin is doubtful, but relationship w. base **bher-*, q.v. under **bear** (I.), has been suggested; fundamental meaning perh. 'having common parents'. See also **fraternal** & **friar. 1.** A male person (or animal) having same parents as another; persons having only one parent in common are called *half-brothers.* Such a relation commonly referred to as *my, his, brother John* &c. (Archaic pl. *brethren* only in solemn and liturgical use.) **2.** A person united to another by membership of the same society, profession, or rank: *a brother mason*; *brother clergyman, professor* &c. (pl. often *brethren*). Phrs. *band of brothers*, group of persons closely united by common ties of interest and affection; *brothers in arms*, soldiers who have served together; *brother officers*, members of same regiment. Sovereigns and judges on the Bench address each other officially as *Brother.* Term also applied to a officials of certain companies or guilds: *Elder Brother of Trinity House*; **b** members of a religious brotherhood: *Christian Brothers*; cp. *sister.*

brother german, n. See prec. & **german** (I.). Full brother, through both parents; formerly used of those having a common mother (*uterine brother*); now sometimes restricted to brothers through father alone.

brotherhood, n. [1. brúdherhood; 2. bráðəhud]. **brother** & **-hood. 1.** Condition of being in relation of brother in any sense: *our brotherhood in Christ.* **2.** Society, association, guild, or other organized corporation for religious, benevolent, or professional purposes. **3.** Whole group of persons belonging to same profession and business: *the medical brotherhood.*

brother - in - law, n. [1. brúdher in law; 2. bráðər in lɔ̄]. Wife's brother; sister's or wife's sister's husband.

brotherliness, n. [1. brúdherlines; 2. bráðəlinis]. See next word & **-ness.** Friendliness, helpful kindness.

brotherly, adj. [1. brúdherli; 2. bráðəli]. **brother** & **-ly. 1.** Belonging to, becoming in, a brother: *brotherly affection.* **2.** Fraternal, like a brother, kind and friendly: *he treated me from the first in a most brotherly manner.*

brougham, n. [1. brōōam; 2. brúəm]; old-fashioned & obs. [1. brōōm; 2. brūm]. Light, four-wheeled closed carriage, designed by Lord Brougham (1778–1868).

brought, vb. [1. brawt; 2. brɔ̄t]. Pret. & P.P. of **bring.** O.E. *brōhte*, (*ġe*)*brōht*; M.E. *brought*(*e*).

brow, n. [1. brou; 2. brau]. O.E. *brū*, M.E. *browe*, O.H.G. *brāwe*, Mod. Germ. *braue*, O.N. *brūn*, Gk. *o-phrŭs*, 'eye-brow, brow of a hill, edge of beetling cliff', Scrt. *brūš*, O. Slav. *bruvĭ*, O. Ir. *brudd.* Some writers consider that the primitive sense is 'steep cliff, height' &c., & that the widespread application of word to the front of the head is secondary. The base has both senses in several languages. The suggested connexion w. Lat. *frons*, q.v. under **front,** is improbable. The connexion w. **bridge** is widely accepted. **1.** Part of the forehead just above eye-brow; forehead generally. Phr. *to knit the brows*, wrinkle the forehead, frown. **2.** Steep slope of a hill.

browbeat, vb. trans. [1. broubēt; 2. bráubīt]. Prec. & **beat.** To bully, shout down, treat arrogantly, truculently, and overbearingly.

browbeating, n. [1. broubēting; 2. bráubītiŋ]. Process or act of bullying and attempting to disconcert by arrogant speech.

brown (I.), adj. [1. broun; 2. braun]. O.E. *brūn*, M.E. *broun*, O.H.G. *brūn*, Mod. Germ. *braun*, Du. *bruin*, O.N. *brúnn*, 'brown', also 'brilliant', Gk. *phrū́nē*, 'toad', lit. 'brown creature'; cp. also Mod. Slovene *bruny*, 'brown', O. Slav. *bronŭ*, 'brown-and-white horse', Scrt. *babhrúš*, 'brown', applied to a species of ichneumon lizard. Cp. **beaver.** Having a colour of one of various shades between black and red or yellow. Phr. *to do brown*, (slang) to take in, swindle; *brown study*, a deep reverie.

brown (II.), n., fr. prec. **1.** Brown colour. **2.** A brown butterfly. **3.** (vulg.) A copper coin.

brown (III.), vb. intrans. & trans., fr. **brown** (I.). To become or make brown, e.g. to tan from exposure to sun and weather, or by action of fire.

Brown Bess, n. [1. bróun bés; 2. bráun bés]. Old English flint-lock musket.

brown coal, n. Lignite.

Brown George, n. [1. bróun jórj; 2. bráun džɔ́dž]. Name for a large brown earthenware water-jug or pitcher.

brownie, n. [1. bróuni; 2. bráuni]. **brown** (I.) & dimin. **-ie, -y. a** Diminutive, good-natured fairy or elf; **b** a very young member of the Girl Guides, answering to 'Wolf Cub' of the Boy Scouts.

Browning, n. [1. bróuning; 2. bráuniŋ], fr. name of inventor. A type of automatic pistol.

browse, vb. intrans. [1. brouz; 2. brauz]. O. Fr. *brouster*, 'sprout' (of trees &c.), fr. *broust*, Mod. Fr. *brout*, 'sprout, shoot from tree'. The word is of Gmc. origin, cp. O.S. *brustian*, 'sprout, bud', connected w. O.E. *byrst*, q.v. under **bristle,** & w. the base meaning 'spike' &c. there discussed. Thus *browse* orig. meant to crop young shoots of herbage &c. **1.** To feed as animals do, nibble off grass and young shoots &c., to graze. **2.** (extended, fig. use) To read or study in a desultory way.

brucine, n. [1. broōsēn; 2. brūsīn]. Named, w. suff. **-ine**, after James Bruce, Abyssinian traveller (1730–94). (chem.) Poisonous alkali found in seeds of nux vomica plant.

bruin, n. [1. broōin; 2. brūin], fr. Du. *bruin*, 'brown', see **brown (I.)**. Popular name of the bear in fairy tales.

bruise (I.), vb. trans. & intrans. [1. broōz; 2. brūz]. O.E. *brȳsan*, M.E. *brīsen, brūsen* &c. But the Mod. Engl. word is perh. rather fr. O. Fr. *bruiser*, whence Mod. Fr. *briser*, 'break, shatter', said to be fr. Gaulish *brīs-*, 'break'. To injure the flesh by a blow from blunt instrument, or by a fall, without breaking skin or drawing blood, but so as to leave discolouration of the skin: *to bruise one's arm*; *a child's flesh bruises easily*. (Applied also to injury caused to fruit by a fall, or to bark of a tree by a blow.)

bruise (II.), n., fr. prec. Injury caused by blow or fall; contusion.

bruiser, n. [1. broōzer; 2. brūzə], fr. **bruise (I.)** & **-er**. A pugnacious person who enjoys contest of any kind; a pugilist.

bruit (I.), n. [1. broōt; 2. brūt]. M.E. *bruit*, fr. Fr., fr. Lat. *rugītus*, 'roaring', *rugīre*, 'roar'; cp. Homeric Gk. *erúgmēlos*, 'bellowing, lowing' (of oxen), also Gk. *rhúzein*, 'growl' (as a dog), *ōrūgḗ*, 'howl'; O. Slav. *rŭzati*, 'neigh'. O.H.G. *rohōn*, 'roar', is cogn. The initial *b-* in *bruit* is perh. due to influence of *bramer*, 'howl' &c., Ital. *brammare*, wh. is of Gmc. origin, or of Fr. *braire*, **bray**. Report, rumour (rare).

bruit (II.), vb. trans., fr. prec. To spread a rumour, or report; esp. *bruit about, abroad*.

Brumaire, n. [1. broōmār; 2. brūmɛə], or as Fr.; fr. *brume*, 'fog'. See **brumous**. The second month, Oct. 23rd to Nov. 21st, in the French revolutionary calendar.

Brummagem, adj. & n. [1. brúmajem; 2. brámədʒəm]. Variant pronunciation of Birmingham, formerly current, but now a vulgarism. **a** adj. Of inferior quality, cheap and nasty; esp. of cheap jewellery, plated goods &c.; **b** n., cheap, inferior goods.

brumous, adj. [1. broōmus; 2. brūməs]. Fr. *brumeux*, but w. substitution of Lat. suff. *-ōsus*, see **-ous**, Lat. *brūma*, 'shortest day in the year', fr. *brevima*; cp. **brief**. Foggy, misty.

brunette, n. [1. broōnét; 2. brūnét]. Fr., fem. of *brunet*, fr. *brun*, 'brown', fr. Gmc. See **brown (I.)**. A woman with dark hair, eyes, and complexion; contrasted with *blond(e)*.

brunt, n. [1. brunt; 2. brant]. Etymol. unknown. Chief stress, strain, or attack, esp. in Phr. *to bear the brunt*.

brush (I.), n. [1. brush; 2. braʃ]. M.E. *brusshe* &c., O. Fr. *brosse*, 'scrub, bushes', fr. Gmc. base **burst-*, q.v. under **bristle**. **1. a** Implement consisting of bristles set in a flat piece of wood or ivory, generally furnished with a short handle, used for removing dust, cleaning, polishing &c., or for smoothing and tidying the hair; or of tuft of hair &c. set in a handle, used by painters; **b** (extended meaning) of the art of painting: *the brush of Sir Joshua, of Turner* &c. **2.** (elect.) **a** Electrical discharge with rays grouped like the bristles of a brush; **b** a device such as a bunch of copper wire used to conduct current in and out of the armature of a dynamo. **3.** A fox's tail. **4.** Rough, low-growing bushes, scrub, undergrowth. **5.** Slight contact, brief encounter: *a brush with the enemy*.

brush (II.), vb. trans. & intrans., fr. prec. **A.** trans. **1. a** To use brush upon; clean or polish with a brush: *to brush one's clothes, boots, hat, teeth, hair* &c.; **b** to knock off with a hasty movement of hands, esp. *brush off, away*; *brush away a fly*; *brush off speck of dust*; (fig., of trouble, difficulties &c.) *brush aside*, ignore, or dismiss lightly. **2.** *Brush up*, smarten, furbish up: *the house needs to be brushed up*; (fig.) revive memory of, regain skill in by study or practice: *I must brush up my Latin*; *he had to brush up his drill on rejoining his regiment*. **3.** To graze slightly, touch in passing: *the foliage brushed my cheek as I ran through the wood*. **B.** intrans. **1.** *Brush against*; *brush past*, to push heedlessly by or past so as to touch. **2.** (of a horse). To rub one foot against another in trotting, so as to cut or injure it.

brushwood, n. [1. brúshwood; 2. bráʃwud]. Small twigs growing at the end of boughs; scrub, undergrowth.

brushy, adj. [1. brúshi; 2. bráʃi]. **brush (I.)** & **-y**. **1.** Like a brush, bushy, esp. of animal's tail. **2.** Covered, thick, with brush or brushwood.

brusque, adj. [1. broosk; 2. brusk]. Fr. *brusque*, Ital. *brusco*, perh. fr. Lat. *ruscus* (plant), 'butcher's broom', the etymol. of wh. is doubtful, by confusion w. Med. Lat. *brūcus, bruscus*, 'heather', said to be of Gaulish origin. Rough, abrupt, in manner.

brusquely, adv. Prec. & **-ly**. In a brusque manner; roughly, abruptly.

brusqueness, n. See prec. & **-ness**. State, quality, of being brusque.

Brussels, n. [1. brúselz; 2. brásəlz]. Name of capital of Belgium. Used as pref. to various objects: *Brussels carpet, lace* &c.; *Brussels sprouts*, vegetable resembling miniature cabbage, a number of which sprout from one stem.

brut, adj. [1. brūt; 2. bryt]. Fr.; lit. 'raw, crude' &c. Technically applied to wines, esp. champagne, to which the minimum of sweetening liqueur has been added. Cp. *dry*.

brutal, adj. [1. broōtal; 2. brūt(ə)l]. Fr. See **brute**, **-al**. **1.** (lit.) Like a brute; coarse, rough, uncivilized; cruel, inhuman; obscene. **2.** (slang) Disgusting, disagreeable, unpleasant: *the weather is perfectly brutal*.

brutality, n. [1. broōtáliti; 2. brūtǽliti]. Fr. *brutalité*, fr. **brutal** & Lat. suff. *-tāt-*, q.v. under **-ity**. Action which is brutal; savagery, cruelty, inhumanity.

brutalize, vb. trans. [1. broōtalīz; 2. brūtəlaiz]. **brutal** & **-ize**. To render brutal; degrade to level of the brutes, dehumanize; treat with brutality.

brute (I.), n. [1. broōt; 2. brūt]. Fr. *brut*, M.E. *brut*, fr. Lat. *brūtus*, 'heavy, dull, stupid, irrational'; an Umbrian form w. *b* for Aryan *gʷ*; cp. true Lat. form, w. different grade, *gravis*, 'heavy'; the other cognates are Scrt. *gurúš*, Gk. *barús*, Goth. *kaurus*, Lett. *gru-ts*, all meaning 'heavy'. See **grave (IV.)**, **barytone**, **care**. **1.** Any of the lower animals, as distinct from man; a beast. **2.** A man who is like a brute; a coarse, inhuman, cruel, or gross person.

brute (II.), adj. See prec. Irrational, insensate; inanimate, soulless: *a brute beast*; *brute strength*, sheer animal force, as distinct from intelligent, trained skill.

brutish, adj. [1. broōtish; 2. brūtiʃ]. Prec. & **-ish**. Belonging to, resembling, unreasoning brutes; coarse, rude, irrational, stupid.

brutishness, n. Prec. & **-ness**. The quality or state of being brutish.

brutum fulmen, n. [1. broōtum fúlmen; 2. brūtəm fálmɛn]. Lat., 'senseless, vain thunderbolt'. See **brute** & **fulminate**. A vain, empty, threat.

bryologist, n. [1. briólojist; 2. braiɔ́lədʒist]. Gk. *brúon*, 'moss', cogn. w. *brúein*, 'swell, burst forth'; perh. cogn. w. Lat. *frutex*, 'bush, shrub'; fr. base **mru-*, whence also O. Slav. *brŭstĭ*, 'bud', O.N. *brum*, 'bud' &c. Cp. **embryo**. See also **-logy** & **-ist**. One learned in mosses.

bryology, n. [1. briólojі; 2. braiɔ́lədʒi]. See prec. Science of mosses.

bryony, n. [1. brīoni; 2. bráiəni]. Gk. *bruōnía*, cp. base under **bryologist**. Genus of climbing, trailing plants.

Bryophyta, n. [1. brīofíta; 2. braioufáitə]. See **bryologist** & **-phyta**. (bot.) One of the great divisions of plants which includes the mosses and liverworts.

Brythonic, adj. & n. [1. brithónik; 2. briþɔ́nik], fr. W. *Brython*, connected w. **Briton**, & **-ic**. **1.** adj. Of, pertaining to, the Celts of Cornwall, Wales, Brittany, & ancient Cumbria, or their language. Cp. **Gaelic**. **2.** n. The Brythonic language or dialect.

bubble (I.), n. [1. búbl; 2. bábl]. Etymol. doubtful, cp. Swed. *bubbla*, 'bladder, bubble'. **1.** Thin, filmy envelope of liquid filled with air or gas. **2. a** Small globule of air or gas enclosed in liquid, e.g. in sparkling wines or aerated waters; **b** the same enclosed in some solid substance such as glass or iron, when in a molten condition and remaining when the substance cools and hardens. **3.** (fig.) Any plan, enterprise, ambition &c. which lacks solidity and a sound basis for success and realization: *the South Sea Bubble*; (also attrib.) *a bubble company*.

bubble (II.), vb. intrans., fr. prec. **1. a** To give forth bubbles, effervesce (as sparkling liquids); **b** to rise in bubbles, be agitated (of boiling liquids). **2.** To flow with gurgling sound: *a bubbling brook* &c.; *to bubble out* (as water from the ground). **3.** (archaic) To deceive, dupe, swindle; fr. **bubble (I.)**, **3.**

bubble-and-squeak, n. Popular name for a dish of fried meat and cabbage.

bubbly, adj. [1. búbli; 2. bábli]. See **bubble (I.)** & **-y**. **a** Full of, giving forth, bubbles (of liquids in agitation; also of glass &c. containing bubbles of air); **b** (slang) *a bottle of (the) bubbly*, champagne.

bubo, n. [1. būbō; 2. bjūbou]. Gk. *boubṓn*, 'groin', cogn. w. Scrt. *gavīnī*, 'groin', Lat. *boa*, 'swelling of the legs', base **gʷou-*. Swelling and suppuration of gland in the groin or arm-pit.

bubonic, adj. [1. būbónik; 2. bjūbɔ́nik], fr. prec. & **-ic**. Accompanied, characterized, by swelling in groin &c.; esp. *bubonic plague*.

buccal, adj. [1. búkal; 2. bákəl]. Lat. *bucca*, 'cheek, mouth cavity', & **-al**. The base orig. means 'roar, bellow' &c.; cp. Scrt. *bukkāruš*, 'roaring of lions', *buk-kati*, 'barks', Gk. *búktēs*, 'howling', O. Slav. *bŭčati*, 'to bellow, low' &c. Pertaining to the mouth cavity, esp. *buccal cavity*.

buccaneer, n. [1. bukanḗr; 2. bakənίə]. Fr. *boucanier*, fr. *boucan*, said to be an Indian word, meaning 'frame for smoking and roasting meat'; the word was first applied to French settlers in Haiti who hunted wild cattle. A piratical sea-rover, filibuster; unscrupulous adventurer.

buccinator, n. [1. búksināter; 2. báksineitə]. Lat., 'trumpeter', fr. *buccināre*, 'to blow trumpet', fr. *bucca*, 'cheek'. See **buccal**. (anat.) Name of a thin, flat muscle in the cheek.

Bucentaur, n. [1. byooséntōr; 2. bjuséntɔ̄], fr. Gk. *boûs*, 'ox', cp. **bovine**, & *kéntauros*, cp. **centaur**. **1.** Fabulous monster, half-bull, half-man. **2.** Name of the state barge of the old Venetian Republic, probably a corruption of Italian *buzino d' oro*, 'bark of gold'.

Bucephalus, n. [1. byooséfalus; 2. bjuséfələs]. Gk., fr. *boûs*, 'ox', see prec., & *kephalḗ*, 'head', see **cephalic**. **a** Name of Alexander the Great's favourite charger; **b** a high-spirited horse.

buck (I.), n. [1. buk; 2. bak]. O.E. *bucc*, 'male deer', *bucca*, 'he-goat', Common Gmc., cp. Germ. *bock*, Du. *bok*, O.N. *bukkr*. **1.** Specif., a male fallow-deer, stag; also male of several other animals, esp. of deer generally, of hares, rabbits. **2.** Antelope. **3.** A dandy. Phr. *old buck*, old fellow (familiar mode of address). **4.** (slang, U.S.A.) A dollar.

buck (II.), vb. trans. & intrans., fr. prec. **1.** To jump with all four feet together and back arched (of horses): *buck off*, dismount a rider by bucking. **2.** To strut, swagger, boast. **3.** *Buck up*, pull oneself together for greater effort; work with greater vigour; cheer up. Phr. *greatly, much, bucked*, encouraged, cheered.

buck-basket, n., fr. obs. vb. *buck*, 'to soak, wash clothes', M.E. *bouken*, cogn. w. **bucket**. (archaic) Laundry basket, basket to carry dirty clothes to the wash.

buckboard, n. [1. búkbord; 2. bákbōd]. Light, long-bodied, four-wheeled carriage.

buckeen, n. [1. bukḗn; 2. bakín]. Ir. A pretentious, ill-educated, often impoverished member of the smaller gentry.

bucker, n. [1. búker; 2. bákə]. See **buck** (II.) & **-er**. A bucking horse.

bucket (I.), n. [1. búket; 2. bákit]. Etymol. very doubtful. Hardly fr. O.E. *būc*, 'pitcher'; cp. Fr. *baquet*, dimin. of *bac*, wh. Meyer-Lübke derives fr. Gaulish *baccus*, 'trough'; *boket* occurs in M.E. **1.** Vessel for drawing and carrying water, made of wood, galvanized iron &c. Phr. *kick the bucket* (slang), to die. **2.** Applied to various articles which somewhat resemble a *bucket* in function; as **a** the part of a pump which sucks and holds water in pipe; **b** scoop of dredging machine.

bucket (II.), vb. intrans., fr. prec. **a** To ride fast, roughly, and clumsily; **b** to row badly, so as to scoop water with oar, by hurrying the forward swing.

bucket-shop, n. (American slang term.) An office, or business in share-dealing, run by persons who are not members of the Stock Exchange.

buck-horn, n. Material used for knife-handles made from stag's horn.

buck-hound, n. A small variety of staghound, formerly bred for hunting the deer, esp. the carted deer; *Master of the Buckhounds*, an official of the royal household, now abolished.

buck-jumper, n. A bucking horse or mule.

buckle (I.), n. [1. búkl; 2. bákl]. M.E. *bokel*, Fr. *boucle*, Lat. *buccula* (dimin. of *bucca*, 'cheek', see **buccal**), 'that part of a helmet which covers mouth and cheek, the beaver; also, a boss on a shield'. **1.** Device attached to one end of a strap for fastening the two ends together, consisting of a metal frame with a movable tongue or spike attached to one end, which passes through a hole in the other end of strap. **2.** Ornamented clasp, or buckle, for shoes &c., formerly often jewelled.

buckle (II.), vb. trans. & intrans., fr. prec. **1.** To fasten with a buckle. Phr. *buckle to*, to set to work in earnest, begin work. **2.** To crumple up, bend from weight or strain, or heat; esp. of metal work, machines of iron &c.

buckled, adj. [1. búkld; 2. bákld]. P.P. of prec. Provided with buckles (of shoes).

buckler, n. [1. búkler; 2. báklə]. M.E., fr. O. Fr. *bocler*, Fr. *bouclier*; connected w. **buckle**, meaning provided with a boss. Large shield carried on left arm.

buckmast, n. [1. búkmahst; 2. bákmāst]. Variant of **beechmast**.

buckram, n. [1. búkram; 2. bákrəm]. M.E. *bokeram*, O. Fr. *boqueran*. Origin unknown. Perh. influenced by association w. *bouc* & **buck**. **1.** Stiff, coarse linen cloth, used in linings and for binding books. Phr. *men in buckram*, imaginary, non-existent men (from Falstaff in '1 Henry IV.'). **2.** (fig.) Stiffness of bearing or manner.

buckshot, n. [1. búkshot; 2. bákʃət]. Large-sized shot.

buckskin, n. [1. búkskin; 2. bákskin]. Leather made from skin of buck, used for breeches and gloves &c.

buckthorn, n. [1. búkthorn; 2. bákþɔ̄n]. (bot.) A thorny shrub, genus *Rhamnus*, with black bark and black berries, which are strongly purgative and are used in veterinary medicine.

buckwheat, n. [1. búkwēt; 2. bákwit]. Prob. O.E. *bōc*, 'beech', & **wheat**. Cp. Du. *bockweit*, Germ. *buchweizen*. Plant belonging to dock family, with heart-shaped leaves and pinkish-white flowers. The fruits or seeds resemble small beech-nuts, and are used for making cakes and also esp. for poultry food.

bucolic (I.), adj. [1. būkólik; 2. bjukɔ́lik]. Lat. *būcolicus*, fr. Gk. *boukolikós*, 'of herdsmen, pastoral', fr. *boukólos*, 'herdsman' (see **bovine**); *-kólos* is perh. cogn. w. Goth. &c., *haldan*, 'hold, guard'. See **hold** (I.). Pertaining to life of shepherds; pastoral, rustic.

bucolic (II.), n., fr. prec. **a** Pastoral poem; **b** pastoral poet; **c** rustic person, farmer.

bud (I.), n. [1. bud; 2. bad]. M.E. *budde* &c. Origin unknown. **1.** Rudimentary or embryonic shoot, from a main stem or from branch of plant, consisting of tightly folded leaf or flower, whence a new branch, leaf, or flower will develop. **2.** Partly developed, tightly folded blossom; half-opened blossom; (fig., mod. slang) a young undeveloped girl. Phrs. *in bud* (of trees and plants), in process of putting forth leaf or flower buds; (fig.) *nip in the bud*, put an end to something in its beginnings. **3.** Protuberance on body of organism which divides off from parent and forms new organism by gemmation.

bud (II.), vb. intrans. & trans., fr. prec. **1.** intrans. **a** To put forth buds of any kind; start growing (as of plants in spring); **b** *bud off from*, separate, form new organism from parent (also fig. of organizations, institutions, and other corporate bodies). **2.** trans. To graft (a young bud) on to another plant so as to obtain a new shoot, branch &c.

Buddhism, n. [1. bóodizm; 2. búdizəm]. Asiatic religion founded by Gautama Siddartha, called *Buddha*, or 'enlightened'.

Buddhist, n. [1. bóodist; 2. búdist]. One professing the religion of Buddhism.

Buddhistic, adj. [1. boodístik; 2. budístik]. Belonging to Buddhists and Buddhism.

buddleia, n. [1. búdlēa; 2. bádliə], fr. Adam Buddle, botanist. A genus of flowering shrubs, some of which are evergreen, natives of S. America, Asia, and Africa.

budge (I.), vb. intrans. & trans. [1. buj; 2. badž], fr. Fr. *bouger*, 'move', fr. L. Lat. *bullicāre*, 'boil', freq. of *bullīre*, q.v. under **boil**. Cp. Provenç. *bolegar*, 'move'. **1.** intrans. To make a slight movement; to move from, away from, one position to another: (usually with neg.) *he never budged the whole time*; *it won't budge an inch*. **2.** trans. To cause to move; remove: *I cannot budge him from his place* &c.

budge (II.), n. M.E. *bugee*; etymol. uncertain. A kind of fur, usually of lambskin.

budgereegah, n. [1. bújerēgàh; 2. bádžərigà]. Native word. Small bright-coloured parakeet, the Australian love-bird.

budget (I.), n. [1. bújet; 2. bádžit]. M.E. *bouget* &c., O. Fr., dimin. of *bouge*, 'leather bag', cp. Ital. *bolgetta*, fr. Lat. *bulga*, 'leather bag', orig. simply a skin. The word is prob. of Gaulish origin; see **bulge**. Relation to Goth. *balgs*, 'leather bag', q.v. under **bellows**, **belly**, is obscure. **1.** Originally a wallet, pouch (obs.). Hence, **2.** Contents of such a wallet, whence specif., collection, accumulation, esp. *budget of news*. **3.** **a** Financial statement made annually in House of Commons by Chancellor of the Exchequer; **b** proposals for raising sum estimated to be necessary for national expenses for current year; **c** similar statement and estimate presented to other public bodies, municipalities, county councils, universities &c.

budget (II.), vb., fr. prec. To form an estimate of expenses and take measures to meet them (see prec. (I.), 3); usually *to budget for*.

buff (I.), n. [1. buf; 2. baf], fr. Fr. *buffle*, 'buffalo', see **buffalo**. **1.** Thick, soft leather made from skin of buffalo or ox &c., formerly used for military coats. **2.** (fig. and colloq.) Bare skin: *strip to the buff*. **3.** Colour of buff, a pale brownish yellow. **4.** *The Buffs*, East Kent (old 3rd) Regiment of the Line, from colour of their facings.

buff (II.), n., fr. O. Fr. *bouffe*, *bufe*. See **buffer** (II.), **buffet** (I.), also **rebuff**. Thump, blow (obs.).

buffalo, n. [1. búfalō; 2. báfəlou]. Port. *bufalo*, fr. Lat. *būbalus*, fr. Gk. *boúbalos*, 'African gazelle, antelope', later 'buffalo'; cp. also Lat. *būbulus*, adj., 'pertaining to oxen', also Scrt. *gavalaš*, 'wild buffalo'. The formation of the Gk. & Lat. forms is obscure, but the base is the same as in **bovine**. **1.** Any species of wild ox, including Indian, African, and American varieties. **2.** Member of benevolent society, *Ancient and Antediluvian Buffaloes*.

buffalo robe, n. One made of skin of buffalo, in use among N. American Indians.

buffer (I.), n. [1. búfer; 2. báfə]. Perh. lit. 'striker'. Cp. **buff** (II.) & **buffet** (I.). **1.** Device with springs or cushions for lessening or absorbing shock produced when two heavy bodies come into forcible contact; e.g. projecting iron rods with flat heads, working on powerful springs attached to railway engines, carriages, and terminal platforms. **2.** (fig.) Neutral state situated between two possible belligerents which serves to make hostilities less easy and probable.

buffer (II.), n. In M.E. Prob. same as prec., special sense being perh. one who strikes at random, hence a foolish person. Possibly connected w. **buffoon**. Usually *old buffer*, a good-natured, rather foolish, and incompetent fellow, either elderly or appearing so.

buffet (I.), n. [1. búfet; 2. báfit]. Dimin. of O. Fr. *buffe*, 'blow'. See **buff** (II.). **a** A blow, generally one given with hand; **b** (fig.) misfortune, calamity: *buffet of fate*.

buffet (II.), vb. trans., fr. prec. To inflict, give a buffet. Special usage: *buffet the waves*, swim vigorously in sea.

buffet (III.), n. Bad imitation of Fr. pronunciation [1. bóofā; 2. búfei]. Fr. Origin unknown. Refreshment bar, esp. at railway station; room, or table, where refreshments are served at a party.

buffoon, n. [1. bufóon; 2. bafún]. Fr. *buffon*, *bouffon*, fr. Ital. *buffone*, cp. *buffare*, 'blow, puff'; prob. imit. One who makes rough jests, esp. accompanied by grotesque and comical gestures; a droll, amusing comical fellow; also in derogatory sense, one who constantly interposes with unseemly jests.

buffoonery, n. [1. bufóoneri; 2. bafúnəri]. See prec. & **-ery**, cp. Fr. *b(o)uffonnerie*. Act of a buffoon; rough jokes; foolery.

bug, n. [1. bug; 2. bag]. M.E. *bugge*, 'scarecrow'. Etymol. doubtful, but perh. connected w. base in **boggart**, **boggle**. **1.** Nasty, flat, ill-smelling, verminous, wingless insect, genus *Cimex*, found in dirty houses and furniture. **2.** (colloq., esp. American usage) Any small, flying insect, including moths and butterflies and, recently, *bacilli*. **3.** (archaic) A bogey, spectre, awe-inspiring object: '*bugs to fearen babes withal*' (Spenser, 'F. Q.', ii. 12, 25). **4.** (colloq.) *Big bug*, important person, usually ironical.

bugbear, n. [1. búgbār; 2. bágbɛə], also more rarely **buggaboo** [1. búgaboo; 2. bágəbū], n. Etymol. dubious. Cp. **bug**. Source of aversion or fear; fancied object of terror or dislike.

bugger, n. & vb. [1. búger; 2. bágə], fr. Fr. *bougre* for **boulgre*, fr. Med. Lat. *Bulgarus*, 'a Bulgarian', also a heretic; heresy of various kinds, esp. of Manichaean origin or tendency, was rife in the Balkans in 11th cent., & horrible crimes & vices were attributed to adherents. **1.** n. **a** (law) A male person guilty of unnatural sexual crime with another male person, a sodomite; **b** a low form of abuse, without any particular significance. **2.** vb. To commit an unnatural sexual crime on or with another.

buggery, n. [1. búgeri; 2. bágəri]. Unnatural sexual offences; sodomy.

buggy, n. [1. búgi; 2. bági]. Origin unknown. Light vehicle, somewhat resembling dogcart, usually for one horse, and having two wheels.

bughouse, adj. [1. búg-hous; 2. bághaus]. (slang, U.S.A.) Mad, crazy.

bughunting, n. [1. búg hunting; 2. bághantiŋ]. Butterfly-collecting.

bugle (I.), n. & vb. intrans. [1. búgl; 2. bjúgl]. O. Fr., fr. Lat. *būculus*, *būcula*, 'heifer, young ox'; cp. O. Fr. *bugler*, 'to low, blow the horn', Mod. Fr. *beugler*. The base is that in Lat. *bōs*, 'ox' &c. Cp. **bovine** & **cow**. **1.** n. Kind of small brass trumpet, chiefly in military use. **2.** vb. To sound call on a bugle.

bugle (II.), n. Etymol. uncertain, but cp. Du. *beugel*, 'ring', also O.E. *bēag*, 'ring', fr. base in O.E. *būgan*, 'to bend, bow'. Cp. **bow** (III.) Ornament of glass or jet sewn on to woman's dress.

bugle-call, n. Military signal given by various notes on bugle.

bugler, n. [1. búgler; 2. bjúglə]. **bugle** (I.) & **-er**. One who plays the bugle.

bugloss, n. [1. búglos; 2. bjúglɔs]. Fr. *buglosse*, Lat. *būglossa*, fr. Gk. *boúglōssos*, 'ox-tongued', *boûs*, 'ox', *glōssa*, 'tongue'. Cp. *bu-* in **Bucentaur** & **glossary**. Plant allied to borage, so called from shape of leaves, genus *Echium*.

buhl, n. & adj. [1. bool; 2. būl]. Germanized fr. Fr. *boulle*, fr. A. C. Boulle, a French cabinet-maker, temp. Louis XIV. Cabinet work inlaid with brass and tortoise-shell.

build (I.), vb. trans. & intrans. [1. bild; 2. bild]. O.E. *byldan*, fr. **buld-jan*, cp. *bold*, 'a building, house'; fr. Gmc. base **bu-*, 'dwell', Aryan **bhu-*. Cp. **be, Boer, boor, bower** &c., also **future**. **A.** trans. **1.** To construct (any kind of edifice), by putting together various materials, stone, brick, wood &c., in suitable order and position; to erect, rear: *to build a house, church, stable, dam* &c.; *build into*, use as part of an edifice, place in position in a structure: *to build a tablet into a wall* &c. **2.** To construct any large machine or apparatus, which involves systematic putting together and combining various parts, e.g. an organ, engine, ship, railway &c. **3.** (extended use, colloq.) To construct generally, fashion, contrive, e.g. a coat, suit of clothes. **4.** *Build up*, **a** to fill in with masonry, as a door, window; **b** to surround with houses and buildings: *my house and garden are very much built up now*; **c** (fig., of non-material things) to form, develop gradually by steady progression: *to build up a reputation, character, a practice, a business* &c.; also *an argument, case, work of art* &c.; **d** to strengthen, improve, give stability to: *build up one's constitution, health* &c. **5.** (fig.) *Build upon*, base, rest upon with security, place reliance in (of hopes and expectations): *I should not build too many hopes upon his generosity.* **B.** intrans. To engage in operation of building: *I would rather not build, if I can find a suitable house.*

build (II.), n., fr. prec. **a** Style, shape, design, form: *these two houses agree in general build*; **b** general characteristics of proportion and figure of human body: *he and I are pretty much the same build.*

builder, n. [1. bílder; 2. bíldə]. **build** (I.) & **-er**. One who builds; specif., one engaged in the trade of constructing houses &c.; *master builder*, one who employs workmen to build. Special use: *Empire builder*, one who as a soldier, administrator, colonist, trader &c., helps to found civilized community under the British flag.

building, n. [1. bílding; 2. bíldiŋ]. **build** (I.) & **-ing**. **a** Anything built into an edifice, a house, church, hall &c.; **b** specif., *buildings*, secondary structures, round or near main edifice, stables, barns, sheds &c.; also *outbuildings*. *Building land*, land suitable for, and set aside for, building on, as distinct from parks, cultivated land &c.

bulb (I.), n. [1. bulb; 2. balb]. Fr. *bulbe*, fr. Lat. *bulbus*, fr. Gk. *bolbós*. The base is the same as in Lat. *bulla*, 'bubble, knob'; ultimately fr. Aryan **bul-*, **bel-* &c., 'swell'. Cp. **blade** (of grass &c.), **folio**, & words there discussed. **1.** Enlarged, spherical termination of stem in certain orders of plants, such as the onion, daffodil, hyacinth, crocus &c. The *bulb* is usually below ground, and from it the leaves spring upwards, and the roots grow downwards. **2.** A round or ovoid expansion at end of a tube, esp. of glass, as in a thermometer; or a bulb-shaped glass as that containing the incandescent wire in an electric light. **3.** Rounded enlargement at the end of a nerve, and of a hair.

bulb (II.), vb. intrans., fr. prec. To form bulbs; also (hort.) *bulb up*, form a head, as cabbage plant.

bulbed, adj. [1. bulbd; 2. balbd]. **bulb** (I.) & **-ed**. Having a bulb or bulbs.

bulbous, adj. [1. búlbus; 2. bálbəs], fr. **bulb** (I.) & **-ous**. Like a bulb, rounded, swelled.

bulbul, n. [1. bóolbool; 2. búlbul]. Prob. Arab. word. Persian and Arabic name for genus of Asiatic birds of bright plumage and renowned for their singing; often mentioned by Persian poets.

bulge (I.), n. [1. bulj; 2. baldž]. O. Fr. *boulge*, fr. Lat. *bulga*, prob. a Gaulish word. Cp. O. Ir. *bolg*, 'bag', cogn. w. Goth. *balgs*, 'skin bag'. Aryan base **bhelg-*, 'swell'. Cp. **bilge, billow, follicle.** Irregular outward swelling; tendency to swell from flat surface; specif., the outward swell on a ship's side below the water line, esp. constructed as defence against torpedo attack, usually *bulge keel.*

bulge (II.), vb. intrans., fr. prec. **a** To swell outwards irregularly; **b** to swell, as a bag, from being too full.

bulger, n. [1. búljer; 2. báldžə]. **bulge** (II.) & **-er**. A golf-club with convex face.

bulging, adj. [1. búljing; 2. báldžiŋ], fr. Pres. Part. of prec. Showing tendency to swell, as if filled to overflowing: '*the bulging corn-bins of Russia*'. Special use: *bulging eyes*, prominent, starting from the head.

bulimia, n. [1. boolímia; 2. būláimiə]. Gk. *boulimía*, 'excessive hunger', fr. *boûs*, 'ox', q.v. under **bovine** &c., & *līmós*, 'hunger'; perh. cogn. w. Gk. *loimós*, 'plague, pestilence'; Lat. *lētum*, 'death', see **lethal**. Cp. *starve* for association of hunger and death. (med.) Morbid hunger.

bulk (I.), n. [1. bulk; 2. balk]. M.E. *bulke*, 'heap'. Cp. Dan. *bulk*, 'lump', O. Swed. *bulk*, 'crowd, mass'. **1.** Size, volume, esp. great size; huge dimension; great size of body. Phr. *sell in bulk*, in large quantities. **2.** (naut.) Hull and cargo of ship. Phr. *in bulk*, loose, not in package, as grain in a ship. **3.** Main mass, largest part of anything.

bulk (II.), vb. intrans. & trans., fr. prec. **1.** intrans. To assume size or importance, esp. *bulk large.* **2.** trans. To appraise, ascertain, bulk (of a cargo).

bulkhead, n. [1. búlkhed; 2. bálkhed], fr. obs. *bulk*, 'balk, lump of wood', see **balk** & **head**. One of several upright partitions dividing various compartments of a ship.

bulky, adj. [1. búlki; 2. bálki], fr. **bulk** (I.) & **-y**. Having great bulk or dimensions; massive; clumsy, unwieldy.

bull (I.), n. [1. bool; 2. bul]. The uncompounded word does not occur in O.E., but *bulan wylle*, a local designation, prob. contains it, & *bulluc*, 'bull calf', certainly does. M.E. *bule, bole* &c.; M.H.G. *bulle*; O.N. *boli*. The base is almost certainly Aryan **bhel-*, 'swell', but whether the Engl. word is derived fr. secondary meaning seen in **bellow**, or fr. the same specialized sense found in Gk. *phallós*, 'membrum virile', q.v. under **phallic**, it is hard to determine. **1.** Uncastrated male of ox or any of the bovine group — buffalo, bison &c.; also of the elephant, walrus, whale, elk, and moose &c. Phrs. *take the bull by the horns*, face difficulties and dangers, not shirking or evading; (*like*) *a bull in a china shop*, clumsy, rough, or noisy, blatant person in a position where delicacy of movement or feeling, and tact are required; *bull of Bashan*, stout, well-fed, robust, and florid person. **2.** (stock exchange) A speculator who has bought low in expectation of a rise in price. **3.** Constellation, *Taurus*, one of the signs of the Zodiac.

bull (II.), vb., fr. prec. To act as a bull on stock exchange (see **bull** (I.), **2**).

bull (III.), n. Lat. *bulla*, 'seal', primarily a boss or knob (of wax &c.). Cp. **bill** (III.). Official Papal enactment.

bull (IV.), n. Perh. fr. Fr. *boule*, 'lie, deceit', Lat. *bulla*, 'bubble, knob', &c. Cp. **bill** (III.), **boil** &c. This Lat. word, according to Meyer-Lübke, gives rise to a large number of words w. varying meanings, including above Fr. word; also the vbs. Catalan *borboller*, 'confuse', & Fr. *barbouiller*, 'stammer, stutter, speak unclearly'. A comical contradiction in terms; a blunder in speech or conduct. Esp. *Irish bull.*

bullace, n. [1. bóolas; 2. búlis]. M.E. *bolace*, O. Fr. *beloce*, 'sloe', the origin of wh., & of its apparent cognates, seems to be unknown, and suggestions are purely speculative. Hard, round, dark purple plum.

bull-baiting, n. [1. bóolbāting; 2. búlbeitiŋ]. **bull** (I.) & **bait**. Old sport of baiting bulls with dogs.

bulldog, n. [1. bóoldog; 2. búldɔg]. **bull** (I.) & **dog**. **a** Large, powerful, thickset dog, originally bred for baiting bulls, with very strong jaws; **b** (fig.) tenacious, courageous person; **c** (colloq.) university proctor's servant, whose duty it is to chase and arrest undergraduates suspected of any offence; **d** certain pattern of revolver.

bull-doze, vb. trans. [1. bóoldōz; 2. búldouz]. (American slang) To bully, intimidate, threaten with violence, originally a term used in elections in Southern States of U.S.A. of intimidating voters, esp. negroes.

bullet, n. [1. bóolet; 2. búlit]. Cp. Fr. *boulette*, dimin. of *boule*, 'ball', Lat. *bulla*, 'knob', q.v. under **bill** (III.) & **bull** (III.). Round or conical pellet of lead fired from a rifle or revolver.

bullet-headed, adj. Having a round, small head.

bulletin, n. [1. bòoletén, bóoletin; 2. bùlitín, búlitin]. Fr., fr. Ital. *bulletino*, double dimin. fr. Lat. *bulla*, in sense of 'seal'. Cp. **bill** (III.) & **bull** (III.). **a** Brief official announcement; **b** publicly affixed notice of state of health of (distinguished) invalid.

bull fight, n. Spanish sport in which bulls are exasperated by men, mounted and on foot, with lances and darts, and finally skilfully killed.

bullfinch, n. [1. bóolfinch; 2. búlfintʃ]. **bull** (I.) & **finch**. **a** Small bird, *Pyrrhula vulgaris*, with rounded beak and bright plumage; **b** a tall hedge with ditch (the second element a form of *fence*).

bull-frog, n. Very large species of frog.

bullion, n. [1. bóolyun; 2. búljən]. Fr. *bouillon*, 'something boiled', hence 'soup', Lat. *bulliōn-(em)*, fr. *bullīre*. Cp. **boil**. The word refers orig., in the Engl. sense, to molten metal. **1. a** Gold and silver before being coined; **b** also gold and silver money considered as so much precious metal, apart from face value. **2.** Gold and silver lace.

bull-necked, adj. Having a short, thick neck.

bullock, n. [1. bóoluk; 2. búlək]. O.E. *bulluc*, 'bull-calf'. Cp. **bull** (I.) & dimin. suff. **-ock**. **a** A young bull; **b** any castrated male of the ox kind.

bull-ring, n. **bull** (I.) & **ring**. The arena in which bull-fighting takes place.

bull-roarer, n. **bull** (I.) & **roar**. A flat piece of wood with a string passed through a hole, which when swung round the head gives forth a booming, roaring sound, used in various religious ceremonies by Australian aborigines, and called by them *tundun.*

bull's eye, n. **a** The centre of a target; **b** thick convex piece of glass for letting light through a roof, the deck of a ship &c.; **c** a lantern containing a lens made of such a piece of glass; **d** a sweetmeat, round in shape, with black and white stripes, flavoured with peppermint.

bull terrier, n. Breed of dogs, cross between bulldog and a terrier.

bull trout, n. Large trout resembling a small salmon, found in rivers, and in lochs which communicate by a river with the sea; called also *sea trout.*

bully (I.), n. [1. bóoli; 2. búli]. Origin doubtful. Suggested connexion w. Germ. *buhle*, 'lover, sweetheart', is unconvincing. **1.** Blustering, swaggering, tyrannical, cruel ruffian; specif., a big strong schoolboy who torments weaker boys. **2.** A hectoring scoundrel who lives on women's immoral earnings. **3. a** A scrimmage, in Eton game of football; **b** putting of the ball in play at hockey. **4.** as adj. (American colloq.) Fine, splendid.

bully (II.), vb. trans., fr. prec. **1.** To tyrannize over, treat cruelly; scold and punish harshly one too weak to defend himself. **2.** Specif., to treat weaker boys in a school cruelly.

bully beef, n. Prob. Fr. *bouilli*, see **boil**, **(II.)** influenced by **bull (I.)**. Soldiers' term for tinned corned beef supplied as rations in field and camp.

bulrush, n. [1. bóolrush; 2. búlraʃ], fr. **bull (I.)** in sense of 'large', cp. **bull-frog** & **horse-chestnut**. A large species of rush with thick velvety head.

bulwark, n. [1. bóolwark; 2. búlwək]. Du. *bolverk*. Cp. **bole**, of tree, & **work**. **1. a** Rampart, earthwork; **b** raised parapet running round ship's deck. **2.** (fig.) Any form of defence; that which gives security: *law is the bulwark of civilization*.

bum-bailiff, n. [1. bùm bálif; 2. bàm béilif]. Prob. fr. *bum*, vulgar term for 'buttocks, rump', & **bailiff**, as one who touched debtor on back when serving writ &c. A sheriff's officer, bailiff of the court, serving writs, distraint orders &c.

Bumble, n. [1. búmbl; 2. bámbl], fr. name of beadle in Dickens's *Oliver Twist*. A self-important minor official; one who uses his office in an attempt to give himself an importance which he would otherwise lack; an impertinent jack-in-office.

bumble-bee, n., fr. M.E. vb. *bumlen*, 'hum', connected with **boom (II.)** Large species of wild bee with loud hum.

Bumbledom, n. [1. búmbldum; 2. bámbldəm], fr. **Bumble** & **-dom**. The status of a minor official; the possession & exhibition of the qualities of a Bumble.

bumble-foot, n. Etymol. doubtful. Disease in poultry consisting of a swelling containing pus on ball of foot.

bumble-puppy, n. **a** Unscientific whist; **b** game in which two players take part, the object of which is to wind a cord round a post by striking with a racquet a bag of sand fastened to one end of the cord, the other end of which is attached to top of post, each player striking from an opposite direction.

bumbo, n. [1. búmbō; 2. bámbou]. Ital. *bombo*, childish word for drink. Drink made of spirits, spice, sugar and water.

bumboat, n. [1. búmbōt; 2. bámbout]. Dan. *bun*, 'box for fish in a boat'. (naut.) Boat used for removing refuse from ships, also for bringing stores to the ship.

bummalo, n. [1. búmalō; 2. báməlou]. Corrupt. of native name *bombil*. A small Indian fish, dried and eaten with curry as a relish; Bombay duck.

bump (I.), vb. intrans. & trans. [1. bump; 2. bamp]. Etymol. doubtful; perh. imitative. **1.** intrans. **a** To strike heavily against, *bump into, against*; **b** to rumble and jolt along, as of heavy vehicle over a bad road, *bump along*. **2.** trans. **a** To hurt or injure by striking or knocking against anything: *I have bumped my head, knee* &c.; **b** (in boat-racing) to catch up and touch (boat immediately ahead) and win by so doing; **c** *bump off* (slang), to kill, murder.

bump (II.), n. See prec. **1.** Dull heavy blow, esp. one received by running violently against a hard, heavy mass. **2.** A swelling or lump, caused by a *bump* or heavy blow. **3.** (phrenol.) **a** One of several natural protuberances on skull; **b** faculty or characteristic supposed to be indicated by it. **4.** Process of winning a boat-race by catching up and bumping boat immediately ahead.

bumper, n. [1. búmper; 2. bámpə]. **bump (I.)** & **-er.** A full glass or tankard of wine or other alcoholic drink. *Bumper* is used before another noun to express abundance, copiousness, esp. *bumper crop, harvest.*

bumpkin, n. [1. búmpkin; 2. bámpkin]. Etymol. uncertain; prob. a Du. dimin.; perh. *boomken*, 'little tree', in sense of a lumpish block. A clumsy, loutish, unpolished country fellow.

bump supper, n. Feast given in an Oxford or Cambridge college to celebrate success in *bumping races*. See **bump (II.)**, **4.**

bumptious, adj. [1. búmpshus; 2. bámpʃəs]. **bump (II.)** & suff. on anal. of *facetious, fractious* &c. Cp. jocular word *scrumptious*. Arrogant, self-assertive, inclined to claim too much attention and hearing for one's opinions.

bumptiously, adv. Prec. & **-ly**. In a bumptious, self-assertive manner.

bumptiousness, n. See prec. & **-ness**. Quality of being bumptious.

bumpy, adj. [1. búmpi; 2. bámpi]. See **bump (II.)** & **-y**. **a** (of a surface) Uneven, covered with bumps; **b** (of motion of a vehicle) rough, jolting.

bun, n. [1. bun; 2. ban]. M.E. *bunne*. Suggested etymols. appear improbable & to be mere desperate shots. **1.** Small round sweet spongy cake with convex top and too few currants. Buns are of several kinds, and are classified according to price: *penny bun, halfpenny bun*; according to character: *currant bun* (with few or no currants); *bath-bun*, q.v., an entirely different article; (*hot*) *cross bun*, spiced variety of currant bun, with a cruciform depression on top, eaten on Good Friday. Phr. (colloq., slang) *to take the bun*, to be first in anything, to win. **2.** Small round object of anything, a bunch, as of hair &c.

bunch (I.), n. [1. bunsh; 2. banʃ]. No known etymol. **a** Cluster of things growing together, esp. *bunch of grapes, currants*; **b** collection of things fastened together, *bunch of keys, flowers* &c. Phr. *the best of the bunch*, the pick of anything; **c** (slang) group, association, gang, party, of persons.

bunch (II.), vb., chiefly intrans., fr. prec. To gather up into folds, knots, or into a bunch.

bunchy, adj. [1. búnshi; 2. bánʃi]. **bunch (I.)** & **-y**. In form of a bunch, tufty; inclined to grow in bunches.

bunco, vb. trans. [1. búngkō; 2. báŋkou]. Origin doubtful. (slang, U.S.A.) To swindle, esp. at cards.

buncombe, n. See **bunkum.**

buncosteerer, n. [1. búngkōstērer; 2. báŋkoustiərə], fr. **bunco.** (American slang) Swindler, card-sharper.

bundle (I.), n. [1. búndl; 2. bándl]. M.E. *bundel*, as though fr. O.E. **byndel*, earlier **bund-il*, cogn. w. **bind**. **1.** Collection of things fastened together: *bundle of clothes, rags; bundle of hay, sticks* &c. **2.** Specif., things, esp. clothes, rugs &c., folded and fastened together for convenient transport; a package, packet.

bundle (II.), vb. trans. & intrans., fr. prec. **1.** trans. **a** To put together in confused heap: *bundle clothes into a drawer*; **b** *bundle out*, to dismiss from one's presence, room &c. hastily and unceremoniously; to expel. **2.** intrans. *Bundle out*, to depart hastily, in confusion.

bung (I.), n. [1. bung; 2. baŋ]. Etymol. doubtful; O. Du. has *bongh*, 'hole'; possibly fr. Lat. *punct-(um)*, P.P. of *pungere*, 'to prick, punch'. See **pungent**. **a** Large stopper of wood or cork, esp. in a cask; **b** specif., one stopping hole in cask in which the tap is inserted.

bung (II.), vb. trans., fr. prec. **1.** To insert a bung. **2.** Esp. *bung up*, close partially by swelling of surrounding parts: *to have one's eyes bunged up*; also close (passage, pipe &c.) by accumulation of solid matter: *the drain is completely bunged up*. **3.** (schoolboy slang) **a** To hurl, throw; **b** *bung off*, to run away, bunk.

bungaloid, adj. [1. búnggaloid; 2. báŋgəlɔid]. Coined fr. next word & **-oid**, on anal. of **fungoid**. Consisting of, of the nature of, bungalows: *bungaloid growths on the south coast.*

bungalow, n. [1. búnggalō; 2. báŋgəlou], fr. Hind. *Bānglā*, 'belonging to Bengal'. Temporary, lightly built house or cottage of wood, generally one storey high and having a verandah.

bungle (I.), vb. intrans. & trans. [1. búnggl; 2. báŋgl]. Origin doubtful. Prob. modern creation suggested by **bung**, **bang** &c. & *-le*, as in *jingle, stumble*. To blunder over anything, to do it badly and clumsily; to spoil a piece of work or a negotiation by unskilful handling.

bungle (II.), n., fr. prec. A clumsy, unskilful piece of work; a confusion, mistake.

bungler, n. [1. búnggler; 2. báŋglə]. Prec. & **-er.** One who bungles; clumsy workman, stupid, unskilful negotiator.

bungling, n. & adj. [1. búnggling; 2. báŋgliŋ]. See prec. & **-ing**. **a** Result of a bungle; unskilful, clumsy work or handling; **b** clumsy, unskilful, confused (of persons and actions).

bunion, n. [1. búnyun; 2. bánjən]. O. Fr. *bugne*, 'boil, swelling'. Origin doubtful. See **bun.** Inflamed swelling, esp. on large joint of great toe.

bunk (I.), n. [1. bungk; 2. baŋk]. Origin unknown. Perh. connected w. **bank (I.)** & **bench**. **a** Sleeping berth, esp. in ship, consisting of wooden shelf in recess, upon which bedding is placed; **b** (colloq.) flight, escape. Phr. *to do a bunk*, run away.

bunk (II.), vb. intrans. See prec. **a** To retire to one's bunk; (colloq.) to go to bed; **b** (schoolboy slang) to run away.

bunk (III.), n. Short for **bunkum.** (Am. slang) Nonsense, humbug.

bunker (I.), n. [1. búngker; 2. báŋkə]. Origin doubtful. **1.** Receptacle for coal, esp. on ship. **2.** (golf) Hollow or other obstacle, natural or artificial, on golf links.

bunker (II.), vb. trans., fr. prec. To get one's ball into a bunker at golf; esp. in P.P. pass.: *to be badly bunkered.*

bunkum, buncombe, n. [1. búngkum; 2. báŋkəm], fr. name of county in N. Carolina, whose representative in Congress was said to have spoken frequently & needlessly to impress his constituents. Nonsense, futile, senseless talk, flimsy argument.

bunny, n. [1. búni; 2. báni]. Perh. fr. **bun.** Pet name, esp. among children, for a rabbit.

bunodont, n. [1. búnōdont; 2. bjúnoudənt]. Gk. *bounós*, 'mound, hill' (origin unknown), & *odont-*, 'tooth'. See **odont(o)-** & **dent(i)-**, **tooth.** (lit.) Having (small) mounds on the teeth; applied to group of animals, including the pig and the hippopotamus.

Bunsen burner, n. [1. boonsn bérner; 2. búnsn bánə]. After Prof. Bunsen, celebrated German chemist. Contrivance for burning air mixed with gas, which increases the heat.

bunt (I.), n. [1. bunt; 2. bant]. Origin unknown. Disease in wheat, smut.

bunt (II.), n. Cp. Swed. *bunt*, 'bundle'. **a** The bagging part of a fishing-net; **b** the part of a furled sail which is gathered up on to the yard.

bunting (I.), n. [1. búnting; 2. bántiŋ]. Etymol. unknown. Common name for various small birds, forming the family *Emberizidae*, allied to the finches, as the yellow-hammer, the corn-, reed-, snow-bunting &c., the Italian ortolan, and others.

bunting (II.), n. Cp. M.E. *bonten*, 'sift'. Originally, probably, coarse cloth used for sifting. Now applied especially to bright-coloured cloth and flags used for decorating streets and buildings on occasions of festivity.

bunyip, n. [1. búnyip; 2. bánjip]. Australian native word. Fabulous animal, said to be of enormous size. Hence a humbug, sham.

buoy (I.), n. [1. boi; 2. bɔi]. Fr. *bouée*, Ital. *boia*; borrowed fr. a Gmc. language; cp. O.H.G. *bouhhan*, 'sign, signal', cogn. w. O.E. *bēac(e)n*. See under **beacon**. **1.** Contrivance made of wood or metal, hollow, and usually globe-shaped, which floats easily in water, and is moored to the bottom of sea or river, either to mark a channel or indicate position of something, e.g. an anchor left at the bottom. **2.** Contrivance for keeping person afloat in the water, consisting of kind of belt of cork, or one inflated with air; usually *life-buoy*.

buoy (**II.**), vb. trans., fr. prec. Generally *buoy up*. **1. a** To keep afloat, prevent from sinking in water; **b** (fig.) to sustain morally, as *to buoy up with hope* &c. **2.** To mark, indicate, position of anything in water by fixing buoys: *to buoy an anchor, fairway* &c.

buoyage, n. [1. bói-ij; 2. bɔ́i-idž]. **buoy (I.)** & **-age**. Buoys collectively; system of buoys; provision of buoys.

buoyancy, n. [1. bóiansi; 2. bɔ́iənsi]. See next word & **-ancy**. **a** Capacity for floating, tendency to float in water or air; **b** (fig.) lightness, gaiety of spirits &c.

buoyant, adj. [1. bóiant; 2. bɔ́iənt]. **buoy (II.)** & **-ant**. **1.** Liable to float, capable of floating, capable of rising to surface if immersed; capable of keeping things afloat. **2.** (fig., of hopes, spirits &c., also of prices) Showing tendency to rise.

bur, n. See **burr (I.)**.

burble, vb. intrans. [1. bẽrbl; 2. bʌ́bl]. Prob. concocted fr. *bubble* & *gurgle*. To make a gentle gurgling or bubbling sound.

burbot, n. [1. bẽrbot; 2. bʌ́bət], fr. Fr. *bourbotte*, prob. fr. *bourbe*, 'mud'; L. Lat. *borba*, fr. Gk. *bórboros*, 'mud, slime'. Connexion w. O.E. *horh*, 'filth', has been suggested, w. the assumption that the Aryan base was *g^worg^w-*, wh. is difficult to equate w. *horh*, as this shd. represent Gmc. **hwurha-*. Another suggestion is affinity w. Scrt. *barburá*, 'water', wh. does not take us much further. Flat-headed, eel-shaped, freshwater fish, *Lota vulgaris*, with barbels on head and chin, also known as the eel-pout.

burd, n. [1. bẽrd; 2. bʌd]. M.E. *burde*, 'lady, maiden', chiefly poetical. Either fr. O.E. *byrde*, 'well-born, of high rank', or metathesized form of O.E. *brȳd*, 'bride'; or, as Tolkien suggests, fr. O.E. **byrde*, 'embroideress'; cp. O.E. *byrdistre*, O.N. *byrða*. See **bear (I.)**, **birth**, & **bride**. (obs. and lit.) Occurs chiefly in old ballads: *Burd Helen* &c. Lady, well-born young woman.

burden (**I.**), n. [1. bẽrdn; 2. bʌ́dn]. O.E. *byrðen*, 'load', lit. 'something which is carried or borne'. Cp. base in **bear (I.)**, **birth**. **1.** That which is borne, a load; (lit. and fig.): *a horse's burden*; *a burden of care, responsibility* &c. Phr. *beast of burden*, one specially used for carrying loads. **2.** Something difficult or grievous to bear; esp. fig.: *a burden of sin, sorrow, taxation*. Phr. *burden of proof*, responsibility to prove; cp. Latin phrase *onus probandi*. **3.** Carrying capacity of a ship, tonnage: *of 40 tons burden*.

burden (**II.**), vb. trans., fr. prec. To impose a burden (of any kind) upon, to encumber; to oppress with a burden; in various uses: *to burden a man with a heavy coat*; *to burden with tasks, taxation, expenses* &c.

burden (**III.**), n. Variant of **bourdon**. Refrain of a song; something constantly recurring in a speech or statement; gist: *the burden of his remarks was* &c.

burdensome, adj. [1. bẽrdnsum; 2. bʌ́dnsəm]. Cp. **burden (I.)** & **-some**. Troublesome, oppressive, cumbersome; grievous to bear.

burdensomeness, n. Prec. & **-ness**. That which has property of being burdensome.

burdock, n. [1. bẽrdok; 2. bʌ́dək, bʌ́dɔk]. Cp. **burr (I.)** & **dock (I.)**. Plant with leaves like a dock and prickly flower-heads.

bureau, n. [1. bū́rō; 2. bjúərou]. Fr., 'desk, office', O. Fr. *bure*, 'coarse woollen cloth', *burel*, 'woollen covering, a table covered with this', Ital. *burello* &c. The word is ultimately derived fr. Lat. *burra*, 'rough covering' &c., & meant something rough & hairy, prickly. The Lat. word is discussed under **borage**. Further connexions are w. **brad** & **bristle**. **1.** Piece of furniture in form of a table or desk for writing, usually containing drawers and provided with a movable flap. **2. a** An office; hence, **b** a government department.

bureaucracy, n. [1. būrókrasi; 2. bjuərɔ́krəsi]. Prec. & **-cracy**, 'government'. **a** Government by state officials from a central office; **b** system of officialism; **c** officials as a body.

bureaucrat, n. [1. bū́rōkrat; 2. bjúəroukræt]. See prec. & **-crat**. **a** Official who works from or in a bureau or office; **b** narrow-minded jack-in-office who works blindly according to the rules of his office without exercising intelligent judgement; **c** a person who is a believer in efficacy of such a system.

bureaucratic, adj. [1. bûrōkrátik; 2. bjùəroukrǽtik]. Prec. & **-ic**. **a** (of persons) Having the nature of a bureaucrat; slavishly attached to petty rules; **b** (of a system) carried on according to the rules and habits of a bureaucracy.

bureaucratically, adv. [1. bûroukrátikali; 2. bjùəroukrǽtikəli]. Prec. & **-al** & **-ly**. After the manner of a bureaucrat; in a narrow, servile manner, according to the official letter of the law.

burette, n. [1. būrét; 2. bjuərét]. Fr., dimin. of *buire*, 'bottle, vase'. A glass tube, graduated and with stop-cock at bottom, used by chemists for measuring small quantities of liquids.

burgage, n. [1. bẽrgij; 2. bʌ́gidž]. Fr. *bourgage*, Low Lat. *burgagium*, 'township', fr. Gmc. *burg*, 'fortified place, town', q.v. under **borough**, & **-age**. (law) Privileged tenure of land from an overlord, esp. in ancient boroughs, by payment of yearly rental.

burgee, n. [1. bẽrjē; 2. bʌ́džī]. Origin unknown. Small pennant, shaped into single point or swallow-tailed, used by yachts.

burgeon, n. & vb. intrans. [1. bẽrjun; 2. bʌ́džən]. M.E. *borjoun*, Fr. *bourgeon*, the origin of wh. is obscure. Meyer-Lübke derives it fr. Low Lat. **burrio*, 'bud', & suggests connexion w. *burra*, 'hairy garment, fleece' &c., q.v. under **borage** &c. He rejects etymol. usually given, fr. O.H.G. *burjan*, 'raise'. **1.** n. A bud. **2.** vb. To come into bud; put forth buds (obsolesc. and poet.).

burgess, n. [1. bẽrjes; 2. bʌ́džis]. M.E. & O. Fr. *burgeis* &c., Low Lat. *burgensis*, Gmc. loan-word fr. *burg* (see **borough**), & adj. suff. *-ensis*, q.v. under **-ess**. An inhabitant of a town; strictly one who enjoys the municipal rights of the borough (now rarely used).

burgh, n. [1. búro; 2. bárə]. Scottish variant spelling of **borough**.

burgher, n. [1. bẽrger; 2. bʌ́gə]. Du. *burger*, Germ. *bürger*. See **borough**. Town-dweller, inhabitant of particular town who enjoys privileges of a *burgess*, q.v.; not an English word, and applied chiefly to inhabitants of Dutch or German towns.

burglar, n. [1. bẽrglar; 2. bʌ́glə]. Low Lat. or Anglo-Lat. *burgulator*, *burglator*. The O.E. word was *burg-bryče*, 'breaking into a strong place'. On the anal. of this the new word may have been formed, the second element of the latter being prob. suggested by Lat. *latro*, in its secondary meaning of 'robber'. See **borough**. One who breaks into a house by night, i.e. between the hours of nine and six, in order to commit a felony, esp. to steal.

burglarious, adj. [1. bẽrglárius; 2. bʌ̄gléəriəs]. **burglar** & **-ous**. Pertaining to, constituting the crime of, burglary.

burglariously, adv. Prec. & **-ly**. After the manner of a burglar; in such a manner as to constitute burglary.

burglarize, vb. [1. bẽrglarīz; 2. bʌ́gləraiz]. **burglar** & **-ize**. (rare) Same as **burgle**.

burglary, n. [1. bẽrglari; 2. bʌ́gləri]. See **burglar** & **-y**. The crime of breaking into a house by night; specific act of unlawful entry into a house combined with theft.

burgle, vb. intrans. & trans. [1. bẽrgl; 2. bʌ́gl]. Formed afresh fr. **burglar**. But vb. *burgulāre* found 1354 (O.E.D.). **a** intrans. To commit burglary; to break into a house and steal; **b** trans., to rifle (a house, safe, receptacle of any kind).

burgomaster, n. [1. bẽrgomàhster; 2. bʌ́gəmàstə]. Anglicized form of Du. *burgemeester* or Germ. *bürgermeister*. See **borough** & **master**. Chief magistrate of a Dutch, German, or Flemish town, corresponding to an English mayor.

burgonet, n. [1. bẽrgunet; 2. bʌ́gənet]. Fr. *bourguignotte*, fr. *Bourgogne*, *Bourguignon*, 'man of Burgundy'. Light helmet with visor and protections for the cheeks.

burgundy, n. [1. bẽrgundi; 2. bʌ́gəndi]. Wine of Burgundy, esp. red wine.

burial, n. [1. bérial; 2. bériəl]. O.E. *byrgels*, 'burial-place, tomb'. See **bury**, vb. Act or process of placing dead body in the tomb, whether this be in the ground itself or in a vault or chapel &c.

burial-ground, n. Open space set apart for burials; graveyard, cemetery.

burial service, n. Religious ceremony performed at funerals. Specif., part of the liturgy of the Church of England contained in Prayer Book, which is read over bodies of the dead when these are placed in the grave.

burin, n. [1. bū́rin; 2. bjúərin]. Fr., Ital. *burino*. Prob. of Gmc. origin, fr. O.H.G. *borōn*, 'bore'. See **bore (I.)**. Tool for engraving on copper.

burke, vb. trans. [1. bẽrk; 2. bʌk], fr. name of a ruffian hanged in Edinburgh, 1829, for murdering a number of persons by smothering them in order to sell their bodies for dissection. **1.** To murder by smothering. (Obs.; the word is now generally used figuratively.) **2.** To stop discussion of (question or inquiry in parliament or other deliberative bodies); to evade, smother (any discussion or proposed measure).

burl, n. & vb. [1. bẽrl; 2. bʌl]. M.E. *burle*, 'flock of wool, stuffing'. O. Fr. *borel*, *burel*, Ital. *borello*, 'coarse woollen stuff' &c.; fr. the base meaning 'animals' hair, rough cloth' &c., discussed under **borage** & **bureau**. **a** n. Matted lump, or mass, esp. in animal's coat, wool, or cloth; **b** vb., to dress cloth &c. by removing knots.

burlap, n. [1. bẽrlap; 2. bʌ́læp]. Origin doubtful. Perh. related to prec. Coarse cloth of hemp or jute.

burlesque, adj., n., vb. trans. [1. bẽrlésk; 2. bʌlésk], fr. Fr.; cp. Ital. *burlesco*, fr. *burla*, 'jest, mockery'. Meyer-Lübke assumes Low Lat. **būrula* of obscure origin. The word in Engl. implies imitation or reproduction of speech, action, ideas &c. in such a way as to make what is so imitated ridiculous. **1.** adj. Imitative in grotesque or ludicrous way; pertaining to, resembling, such a manner of imitation: *burlesque acting*. **2.** n. **a** Ludicrous imitation, caricatured reproduction, parody; **b** literary, dramatic work of such a type. **3.** vb. To imitate or mimic a person's voice, manner, gestures &c., or the style of a book or author, or the plot and characters of a play &c., in such a way as to make them laughable, ridiculous, grotesque, and generally absurd; especially by exaggerating peculiarities and giving a ludicrous turn to what was meant seriously; to travesty, parody.

burly, adj. [1. bẽrli; 2. bʌ́li]. M.E. *burlich*, *burli*, 'tall, stately'; prob. fr. O.E. *būrlič*, 'handsome, fit for the bower', cp. *būr*, 'bower'. See **bower (I.)**, n. Stout in figure; robust, large and vigorous (of persons).

burn (**I.**), vb. trans. & intrans. [1. bẽrn; 2. bʌn]. O.E. *beornan*, *biernan*, *brinnan*, str. vb., intrans., 'burn'; *bærnan*, wk. vb., trans.; M.E. *bernen*, *brennen*. The latter is Chaucer's form. The present-day *burn* may be a W. Midl. dial. type, representing O.E. *beorn-*, but the influence of M.E. *burne*, 'burnish', may have had something to do w. it. The orig. Aryan base is prob. that so widely differentiated in form & meaning, seen in **bourn** (of water), **burn (III.)** (spring of water), **bread**, **brood** &c., the meaning of wh. was 'bubble, spirt; bubble with heat, boil; glow with heat' &c. **A.** trans. **1.** To consume, annihilate, destroy by subjecting to action of fire. In many idiomatic uses, lit. and fig.: *burn down*, destroy completely by fire, reduce to ashes (of house, village &c.). Phrs. *burn one's boats,* destroy means of retreat, or withdrawal from any position; commit oneself irrevocably to particular line of action; *burn candle at both ends,* exhaust one's strength, resources, by prolonged activity, or on several objects. **2. a** To injure by exposure to fire; (i.) of food, to scorch &c.: *this soup is burnt*; (ii.) of other things: *to burn the carpet,* e.g. by dropping glowing coal. Phr. *to burn one's fingers,* (fig.) to suffer rebuff through interference, or rashness; *to burn a hole,* in clothes &c.; (fig.) *to burn one's money*; *money burns a hole in his pocket,* of inability to keep money, extravagance; **b** specif., to put to death by burning: *Cranmer, Ridley, and Latimer were burnt (alive, at the stake) in Oxford.* **3.** To harden by baking, treat with fire (of bricks, lime &c.) **4.** To utilize for purposes of heating, or lighting: *to burn coal, coke, wood, in one's grate*; *to burn candles, oil.* **5.** (of the action of the sun) **a** On the complexion, to tan, cause freckles; **b** on the ground, to parch up, harden, cause to crack &c.; **c** on plants, herbage &c., to cause to shrivel up, grow brown, wither. **6.** (of action of acids or other irritants) To cause injury to tissues &c.; to produce sensation of burning, in taste: *his hands were badly burnt by vitriol*; *mustard burns the tongue.* **B.** intrans. **1. a** To be on fire, in a state of combustion, and as result produce light and heat; to be capable of, or liable to ignition and combustion: *coal burns well in this grate*; *this gas burns very dimly*; *damp wood will not burn*; *if a spark falls among gorse in summer it burns furiously*; **b** to undergo, and exhibit effects of, exposure to heat of fire or sun; to be scorched or tanned: *delicate skins burn very easily in the sun.* **2.** (fig.) **a** To be animated by intense passion of any kind: *to burn with religious zeal, with enthusiasm, with love, hatred* &c.; **b** to suffer from, and show effects of, high fever: *his hand, forehead, was burning.*

burn (II.), n., fr. prec. Injury caused, esp. to human body, by fire: *the child was rescued from the fire, but died soon after of terrible burns.*

burn (III.), n. Cp. **bourn (I.).** Stream of water; brook, rill.

burner, n. [1. bĕrner; 2. bə́nə]. **burn (I.)** & **-er.** **1.** One who burns anything. **2.** That part of a lamp from which the flame or light comes, often specially designed to secure maximum of light or heat.

burnet, n. [1. bĕrnet; 2. bə́nit]. Variant of **brunette.** Brown-leaved plant resembling sainfoin; *burnet-moth,* group of moths with blue or green front wings with red spots and red hinder wings.

burnie, n. [1. bĕrni; 2. bə́ni]. M.E. *brinie, brunie* &c., fr. O.N. *brunja,* 'coat of mail'. Perh. related to **burn** & **brown.** The O.E. word is *byrne,* & is very common in the old heroic poetry such as 'Beowulf'. Coat of mail covering chest, neck, and back.

burning, adj. [1. bĕrning; 2. bə́niŋ]. Pres. Part. of **burn (I.).** Various fig. uses: esp. **a** *burning question,* one much discussed; **b** *burning disgrace, shame,* notorious, scandalous; **c** *burning zeal, enthusiasm,* intense.

burning bush, n. Name of several shrubs, esp. *Fraxinella,* which give off highly volatile and ignitable oil.

burning-glass, n. Convex lens for concentrating sun's rays, thus producing intense heat.

burnish, vb. trans. & intrans. [1. bĕrnish; 2. bə́niʃ]. M.E. *burnischen* &c., O. Fr. *burnir, brunir,* 'make brown'. See **brown, brunette,** & **-ish.** **1.** trans. To polish, make to shine, make smooth; esp. to make (metal) smooth and bright by rubbing with hard substance. **2.** intrans. To be capable of receiving a polish, to take a polish; esp. *to burnish well.*

burnisher, n. [1. bĕrnisher; 2. bə́niʃə]. Prec. & **-er.** Tool for burnishing, made of some hard smooth substance, e.g. ivory, steel &c., with rounded surface.

burnous(e), n. [1. bernōōz; 2. bənúz], fr. Fr. *burnous,* fr. Arab. *burnus.* Kind of cloak with a hood worn by Arabs and Moors.

burnt-offering, n. [1. bĕrnt ófering; 2. bə́nt ófəriŋ]. P.P. of **burn** & **offering.** Also *burnt sacrifice,* something offered to a deity and burnt on an altar.

burr, bur (I.), n. [1. bĕr; 2. bə̄]. M.E. *burre.* Prob. Fr. *bourre,* 'mass of animal's hair', as used for padding &c. Cp. group of words mentioned under **borage. a** Round, prickly, sticky seed-vessels of certain plants which are easily detached, and adhere to clothes, and the coats of animals; **b** (fig.) anything that clings like a burr; a person who persistently forces his presence upon another.

burr (II.), n. & vb. intrans. & trans. Origin doubtful. **1.** n. Peculiar pronunciation of *r*-sound common in some areas of England, and heard in certain individuals anywhere, which consists of a slight trill made with the uvula. **2.** vb. To pronounce *r* in this manner.

burr (III.), n. Etymol. uncertain. **1.** The rough edge or line left by the etcher's or engraver's tool on copper. **2.** A rough flinty stone, used for millstones and whetstones.

burred, adj. [1. bĕrd; 2. bə̄d]. P.P. of **burr (II.).** Esp. *burred-r,* pronounced with a burr.

burrow (I.), n. [1. búrō; 2. bárou]. Variant of **borough.** See also **bury.** Hole scooped in the ground by certain animals, esp. rabbits, as a shelter, or place to breed in. Cp. discussion of meaning under **borough.**

burrow (II.), vb. trans. & intrans., fr. prec. **1.** To make a burrow, that is, to penetrate into the ground by scooping out the earth as rabbits and moles do. **2.** (fig., with *into*) To work laboriously at a task, esp. to read large books diligently, work at a subject.

bursa, n., pl. **bursae** [1. bĕrsa, -sē; 2. bə́sə, -sī]. Lat. 'bag', see next word. (anat.) A small sac or cavity, esp. one containing synovial fluid in a joint.

bursar, n. [1. bĕrsar; 2. bə́sə]. Med. Lat. *bursarius,* Lat. *bursa, byrsa,* 'leather bag', fr. Gk. *búrsa,* 'hide, leather', wh. is perh. orig. not a Gk. word. The word is perh. connected w. Lat. *burra,* 'shaggy garment', & *reburrus,* 'with bristling hair'. See words discussed under **borage, bristle.** **1.** A treasurer, esp. at an Oxford or Cambridge college. The *bursar* at an Oxford college is often the agent for the college estates. **2.** Person holding a scholarship or endowment for study at a Scotch university.

bursarial, adj. [1. bĕrsârial; 2. bəsέəriəl]. Prec. & **-al.** Pertaining to a bursar.

bursary, n. [1. bĕrsari; 2. bə́səri], fr. **bursar (I.).** **1.** Office in which a college bursar conducts his business. **2.** A scholarship, or endowment for poor students, esp. at a Scotch university.

burst (I.), vb. intrans. & trans. [1. bĕrst; 2. bə̄st]. O.E. *berstan,* M.E. *bersten, bresten* (the latter perh. fr. O.N. *bresta*), cp. O.H.G. *brestan,* Mod. Germ. *bersten.* Prob. connected w. O.E. *brēotan,* 'break, destroy', cp. **brittle,** & *bros-nian,* 'crumble, decay', fr. **brut-snōjan* (?), cp. O.H.G. *brōsma,* 'crumb', & O.E. *brȳsan,* 'to bruise'. A more remote relationship may also exist w. Lat. *frustum,* 'morsel, crumb' (see **frustum**), & an even remoter w. **break.** The mod. spelling is perh. fr. the n. See **burst (II.).** **A.** intrans. **1.** To fly in pieces, break open, rupture, give way, esp. suddenly and forcibly; *either* **a** from internal pressure, as a storm, from atmospheric pressure, a shell through explosion, a bubble through expansion of air within, a tumour, river bank, dam &c., from excess of contents, and so on; *or* **b** owing to violent force or strain exerted from without, as any obstacle, wall, door, window &c., which yields suddenly to battering. Also (fig., of effects of violent emotion): *my heart will burst* (obsolesc.), cp. *break* in this sense. Phr. *ready to burst,* greatly moved, or excited; *to burst with laughing.* **2.** (colloq., often spelt and pronounced *bust*) Also *burst up,* to smash, fail entirely (of business or firm &c.). **3.** (fig.) **a** To be filled to overflowing, plentifully provided with; to be well endowed with (generally used in Pres. Part.): *the storehouses and granaries are bursting with corn*; *he was bursting with health, excitement, happiness* &c.; **b** idiomatic use: *the buds are all bursting,* opening in spring. **4.** (followed by preposition) To come into sudden activity; issue forth violently (of something pent up and suddenly released); appear suddenly and unexpectedly: *burst into flame*; *burst into tears*; *burst out of the ground* (of a river); *burst out laughing*; *burst into a room*; *burst into angry speech*; *the view of the sea burst suddenly upon my sight*; *the knowledge burst upon him all at once.* Phr. *burst out,* begin to speak (violently and suddenly) **B.** trans. **1.** To break, shatter, rend, cause to come asunder, suddenly and violently (esp. by strain or pressure exerted from within): *to burst one's bonds, restraints*; *the river has burst its banks*; *to burst a blood-vessel*; *burst a strap*; *one's clothes* &c.; *burst one's way through a crowd* &c. Phr. *burst one's sides with laughing*; *burst oneself,* injure by excessive effort. **2.** (of non-material things) To destroy, render useless: *to burst a conspiracy.*

burst (II.), n. O.E. *byrst,* 'loss, injury', fr. **bursti,* wh. is a grade of *berst-,* as in vb. *berstan*; cp. **burst (I.).** The M.E. *burst,* wh. reproduces exactly the O.E., is the Western dial. type, & this we have retained. The form of the mod. vb. wh. we shd. have expected to be *berst* is prob. due to the n. The latter, at the present time, is closely related in meaning to the vb., & has lost its old significance. General sense: the act of bursting in the various meanings of **burst (I.).** **1.** Sudden rupture or explosion: *burst of a shell.* **2.** Sudden breaking forth into activity: *burst of applause, laughter, weeping.* Phr. (colloq.) *go on the burst* [1. bust; 2. bast], indulge in bout of drinking and dissipation. **3.** Brief violent effort, spurt: *burst of speed*; *work in sudden bursts.* **4.** Sudden opening, expanse, stretch of country: *a burst of mountain and plain.*

burthen, n. See **burden.**

bury, vb. trans. [1. béri; 2. béri]. O.E. *byrġan, berġan,* M.E. *burien, berien.* The spelling of Mod. Engl. vb. is fr. the M.E. S.W. & Western type, the pronunciation fr. the S.E. type. The word is derived fr. the widespread & widely differentiated base found in **burgh** & **borough.** Cp. **burial** & **burrow.** Orig. meaning is 'to put into a strong, secure place'. **1. a** To put (a dead body) into the ground, or into a tomb of any kind; also to sink a dead body below surface of the sea; **b** (of clergy) to perform Burial Service over; **c** to lose by death: *he has buried all his children.* **2. a** To put anything into, hide away in, the earth; to heap earth or soil or other substances over anything: *to bury treasure, ammunition* &c; *to bury something in sand, leaves, snow.* Phr. *to bury the hatchet,* (fig.) forget quarrels; *bury one's differences*; **b** (fig.) to hide away, immerse, isolate, to remove from sight and observation: *to bury oneself in one's studies,* or *books*; *bury one's face in one's hands*; *bury oneself in the country*; *to bury a poem in an obscure periodical.*

bus, n., pl. **buses** [1. bus; 2. bas]. Abbreviation of **omnibus.** Public conveyance, driven by electricity or petrol, *motor-bus,* or drawn by horses, *horse-bus,* which travels on the ordinary road and not upon rails.

busby, n. [1. búzbi; 2. bázbi]. Origin unknown. Tall hat of fur worn in full parade dress by Hussar regiments and Horse Artillery in British Army.

bush (I.), n. [1. boosh; 2. buʃ]. M.E. *busch* &c., Med. Lat. *boscus.* See **boscage, box** (the plant). **1.** Shrub, low-growing plant with dense foliage, and usually several stems springing from the root, thus distinguished from a tree which has a single main stem. **2. a** Group, or thicket of shrubs; **b** (by extension) tract of country covered with shrubs, esp. uncleared, wild country in the colonies (Australia or Africa): *to live in the bush*, in remote unopened country, in the wilds. **3.** Mass or bunch of foliage, formerly hung out as a vintner's sign. Phr. (fig.) *a good wine needs no bush*, no advertisement.

bush (II.), n. Perh. fr. M. Du. *busse*, 'box', wh. is ultimately fr. same source as above. See **box** &c. (mechan.) Metal lining for cavity in which end of axle rotates.

bushel, n. [1. bóoshel; 2. búʃ(ə)l]. M.E. *buschil*, O. Fr. *boissel*, Mod. Fr. *boisseau*, Med. Lat. *buscellus*, 'little box'. Cp. **box, boscage, bosky** &c. Measure of capacity, equal to eight gallons; used of corn, lime, fruit &c. Phr. *to hide one's light under a bushel*, be too modest in showing one's qualities; *he doesn't hide his light under a bushel*, proclaims his merits too loudly.

bushel basket, n. Basket having capacity of a bushel.

bush-fruit, n. Fruit which grows on a bush as distinct from tree-fruit (apples &c.); specif., currants, raspberries, gooseberries.

bush-harrow, n. Harrow consisting of heavy frame, to which bushes are fastened, used for cleaning land and covering seeds.

bushido, n. [1. bŏŏshēdō; 2. búʃidou]. Jap., 'way of a soldier or knight'. The unwritten chivalrous code of conduct, or life, as observed by the samurai or military class.

bushiness, n. [1. bóoshines; 2. búʃinis]. **bushy & -ness.** Quality of being bushy, thick, tufted.

bushman, n. [1. bóoshman; 2. búʃmən]. Du. *boschjesman*. Dweller in the bush or wilds; esp. (cap.) member of certain primitive South African tribes.

bushranger, n. [1. bóoshrānjer; 2. búʃreindžə]. Australian outlaw, formerly applied to an escaped convict, living as a kind of highwayman in the bush.

bushy, adj. [1. bóoshi; 2. búʃi]. **bush (I.) & -y. a** Covered, overgrown with bushes; **b** thick, tufted, dense, as certain plants; also applied to tails of foxes and other animals.

busily, adv. [1. bízili; 2. bízili]. **busy & -ly.** In a busy manner, laboriously; eagerly; (in bad sense) curiously, inquisitively.

business, n. [1. bíznes; 2. bíznis], fr. **busy & -ness.** The various senses in wh. the word is now used all show loss of relation to those of 'busy'. Cp. **busyness. 1.** Regular, habitual, occupation, trade, profession, followed for a livelihood: *his business was that of a horse-dealer, solicitor, stock-broker, merchant, shopkeeper* &c. **2. a** Commercial transactions, trade, finance &c., contrasted with one of the learned or liberal professions, or with the public services: *business is a more lucrative career than the army*; *he preferred business to medicine*; **b** particular commercial enterprise: *he had a very good business*; *he has sold his business and retired.* Phr. *to go into business*, embrace commercial career; *business is business*, we can't afford to be too generous, or to be governed by sentiment; *not strict business*, not in accordance with ordinary commercial procedure; *go to, come away from, business*, enter or leave office where one's affairs are conducted; *a matter of business*; *business before pleasure*; *to stick to one's business*, (fig.) be attentive to duty; *a good stroke of business*, favourable transaction of any kind; *one's man of business*, agent, legal adviser, solicitor. **3.** That which has to be done, a special duty, or service imposed by a person's position, office, or circumstances: *it is part of a professor's business to add to the knowledge of his subject*; *my business in life is to bring up my family properly*; *the business of an opposition is to oppose*; *that is no business of yours.* Phrs. *to mind one's own business*, keep to one's own duties and not interfere with other people's; *to have no business to do so-and-so*, no right to do it; *to get, come, to business*, start dealing seriously with the matter in hand; *to send a man about his business*, dismiss, snub, reprove; *that will do his business*, be enough for him; (in bad sense) kill. **4.** Affair, subject, matter (also of material things): *I don't understand this business about the disputed election*; *I am sick of the whole business*; *it's a queer*, or *bad, business altogether.* **5.** (dram.) Specific gestures, bodily movements, expressions of face, tones of voice &c. of an actor in interpreting his part, as distinct from the words: *this part has a good deal of comic business as played by X.*

business-like, adj. Prec. & **like.** Exhibiting business qualities; practical, systematic, orderly, efficient, punctual.

busk (I.), n. [1. busk; 2. bask]. Fr. *busc*, 'strip of whalebone or steel for stiffening front of a corset'. Origin doubtful, but perh. connected w. Fr. *bûche*, O. Fr. *busche*, 'piece of wood', wh. is fr. Lat. *boscum*, 'wood'. Cp. **box** (I.), **boscage, bush** &c. Same meaning as French *busc* cited above.

busk (II.), vb. M.E. *busken*, (reflex.) 'get oneself ready', O.N. *būa-sk*, 'prepare oneself'; *-sk* stands for *sek*, 'him &c. self', reflex. pron. *Būa* has various meanings in O.N., chief & prime of wh. is 'dwell, inhabit', but it also has active sense of 'prepare'. The O.E. cogn. *būan* in addition to 'inhabit' has sense of 'cultivate' (land). See **be, Boer.** To get ready, prepare oneself (obs. and liter.). Cp. the ballad beginning '*Busk ye, busk ye, my bonnie, bonnie bride*' &c.

buskin, n. [1. búskin; 2. báskin]. O. Fr. *broissequin*, fr. O. Ital. *borzacchino*, prob. Gmc. loan-word, cp. Du. *broseken*, 'short leather boot'. Mod. Fr. *brodequin*, 'laced boot covering foot and lower part of leg', has perh. been influenced in form by *broder*, 'embroider' &c. The earliest example quoted by O.E.D. is fr. 1503, where the word refers to boots for the queen. Weekley's suggestion that the word is a form of *buckskin*, based on Phr. '*payre bucskyis*' (1481–90), is not quite convincing, though the two words may well have been associated in the minds of some speakers. **1.** Leather boot reaching half-way up the calf. **2.** A thick-soled boot, the *cothurnus*, q.v., worn by Greek and Roman tragic actors, hence, symbol of tragedy: '*The buskin in poetrie is vsed for tragical matter*' (Glossary in Spenser's 'Shepherd's Calendar'). Phr. *to put on the buskins*, assume tragical manner, write tragedy.

buss, n. & vb. [1. bus; 2. bas]. Prob. fr. W. or Gael. *bus*, 'kiss'. The word has no direct connexion w. Lat. *bāsium*, 'kiss', whence Fr. *baiser*, though the Lat. word is perh. borrowed fr. a Celt. source, & therefore ultimately cogn. w. *bus*. The starting-point is Aryan **gʷād-s*, fr. another grade of wh., **gud-s*, Gmc. **kus-*, also comes. Cp. **kiss.** (obs. or liter.) **a** n. A kiss, esp. one which is rough and playful; **b** vb., to kiss.

bust (I.), n. [1. bust; 2. bast]. Fr. *buste*, Ital. *busto*. Origin unknown. **1.** Sculptured representation of human head, neck, and upper chest. **2. a** Part of human body between neck and waist; **b** woman's breast.

bust (II.), slang for **burst.**

bustard, n. [1. bústard; 2. bástəd]. O. Fr. *bistarde* & *oustarde*, the latter being ancestor of Mod. Fr. *outarde*, fr. Lat. *avis tarda*, 'slow bird'. See these Lat. words under **aviary & tardy.** The O. Fr. forms w. & without initial *b* represent two old types, the former *avistarda*, the latter *(*a*)*bistarda*, w. loss of the initial *a-*; O. Ital. *bistarda* & *ustarda*, Mod. Ital. *ottarda*, Provenç. *austarda*, O. Span. *abutarda*, Port. (*a*)*betarda*. A large, swift-running bird, genus *Otis*, found in the Old World, related to cranes and plovers; an Australian species is called *turkey*. The name seems ill-chosen.

bustle (I.), vb. intrans. & trans. [1. búsl; 2. básl]. M.E. *bustlen*, 'wander blindly and aimlessly'; perh. variant of **busklen*, formed fr. **busk** (II.). **1.** intrans. (often with *about*) To hurry about, make show of busy activity; also *bustle up*, bestir oneself, hurry. **2.** trans. To stir up, hurry (others); incite to activity and speed.

bustle (II.), n., fr. prec. Hurry, fussy activity; excited, noisy movement.

bustle (III.), n. Origin doubtful. Old-fashioned device for making woman's skirts project behind.

bustling, adj. [1. búsling; 2. báslin̩], fr. Pres. Part. of **bustle** (I.). Active, busy; noisily busy.

busy (I.), adj. [1. bízi; 2. bízi]. O.E. *bysiġ*, M.E. *busy, bisy*. Example of writing one M.E. dial. type and pronouncing another, as in **bury**, vb. Origin unknown. **1.** Habitually occupied, regularly engaged in some occupation, pursuit, or work; diligent: *a doctor is generally a busy man*; *my dictionary keeps me always busy.* **2.** Occupied, engaged, temporarily; at work, or active for the time being: *I shall be busy all tomorrow*; *I won't disturb you if you're busy.* **3.** Filled with activities and occupations **a** (of times and seasons): *a busy day, time, morning* &c.; **b** (of places) filled with active, occupied persons: *a busy town, station, market-place* &c. **4.** Too much interested in or occupied with other people's affairs; officious: *an idle, busy, interfering woman.*

busy (II.), vb. trans. or reflex. O.E. *bysġian.* Cp. prec. To provide occupation for, cause to be, keep, active and diligent: *she busies herself about the house*; (more rarely) *I have busied the gardener for the afternoon.*

busy-body, n. Meddlesome, officious, interfering person, esp. one who chatters about the affairs of others.

busyness, n. [1. bízines; 2. bízinɛs, -nis]. New formation. Differentiated in spelling and pronunciation fr. **business.** Condition or habit of being busy.

but (I.), conj., adv., prep., rel. pron. [1. but; 2. bat]. O.E. *be-ūtan, būtan*, adv. & prep.; also conj.; M.E. *būten, būt*, & *būt*, adv. & conj. The shortened form, wh. is the ancestor of present form, arose in unstressed positions. See **be- & out.** *But* has very varying uses in the sentence and expresses many shades of meaning. It is often difficult to determine its precise grammatical function in a sentence. Its general function is to express contrast, opposition, exclusion, restriction, with varying degrees of intensity. **A.** conj. **1.** Simple adversative, contrasting two co-existing conditions or qualities; yet, nevertheless: *Naaman was a mighty man, but he was a leper*; *his parents were poor but honest*; *he was handsome and rich, but very stupid*; *I should like to come, but I haven't time.* **2.** Contrasting and opposing positive and negative statement; on the contrary, on the other hand: *I bring not peace, but a sword*; *I was not there, but my father was*; *not Angles, but angels.* **B.** adv. **1.** Excluding some condition or contingency: *I am not such a fool but that I understand you*; *I have no doubt but that all will come right.* **2.** Only just, not more than, only so much as: *he left but an hour since*; *I saw her but a moment*; *he called but once*; *he was but a child*; *I spoke but in jest*; *we did but glance at the horrid sight*; *there is but one chance left*; (poet.) *did she but smile, his heart beat high.* **3.** Unless, if . . . not: *she would have fallen but that he caught her*; *I should dismiss him but that his father was an old and faithful servant.* **4.** (with *can*) In any case, at least: *you can but try.* Adverbial phrase: *all but*, very nearly: *he all but died of his wound.* **C.** prep. **1. a** Excluding, except: '*None but the brave deserves the fair*'; *all but one man were drowned*; *nothing but misery can result*; *nothing remains but to die*; **b** treated as conjunction before personal pronoun: '*All but he had fled*'; **c** colloquially governs dative of personal pronoun: *they killed everyone but him.* **D.** rel. pron. = who . . . not: *there are few men but would risk all for such a prize.*

but (**II.**), vb. & n., fr. prec. Only in Phr. *but me no buts*, i.e. do not use expressions full of objections and qualifications.

but (**III.**), n. In Scots Phr. *but and ben*, the outer room of a two-roomed cottage. See **ben**.

butcher (**I.**), n. [1. bóocher; 2. bútʃə]. O. Fr. *bouchier*, lit. 'one who slaughters bucks', Fr. *bouc*. See **buck**. **1.** One who slaughters animals; tradesman who deals in meat: *pork butcher*, one who sells pig meat, sausages &c. **2.** (fig.) A cruel, bloodthirsty man; a general who wastes lives of soldiers unnecessarily; a murderer. Phrs. *butcher's bill*, (fig.) list of those killed in action; *butcher's meat*, everything sold by a butcher, as distinct from fish and poultry.

butcher (**II.**) vb. trans., fr. prec. To kill, slaughter (animals) for food; to slaughter, kill, (human beings) brutally; to massacre.

butcher-bird, n. Popular name of various kinds of shrike which impale their prey on thorns &c.

butcherly, adj. [1. bóocherli; 2. bútʃəli]. **butcher** (**I.**) & **-ly**. Like, suitable for, a butcher; (fig.) cruel, brutal, murderous.

butcher's broom, n. An evergreen shrub, *Ruscus aculeatus*, with yellow, greenish flowers and red berries.

butchery, n. [1. bóocheri; 2. bútʃəri]. Fr. *boucherie*. **butcher** (**I.**) & **-y**. **1.** Place where animals are slaughtered; shambles. **2.** Butcher's trade, esp. *butchery business*. **3.** Massacre, murder; cruel and unnecessary slaughter of men or animals: *this is not legitimate sport, fighting, but mere butchery*.

butler, n. [1. bútler; 2. bátlə]. M.E. *boteler* &c., O. Fr. *bouteillier*. See **bottle** (**I.**) & **-er**. Specif., servant who looks after wine-cellar, plate &c. Generally, head man-servant indoors.

butt (**I.**), n. [1. but; 2. bat]. O. Fr. *bout*, Fr. & Ital. *botte*. See discussion under **bottle** (**I.**). Large cask for wine or beer.

butt (**II.**), n. O. Fr. *bot*, 'end', Fr. *bout*. Cp. **butt** (**IV.**), strike' &c. Of Gmc. origin. Confusion has taken place between various words & senses, wh. is very difficult to unravel. Cp. **butt** (**III.**). **1.** Thick end of weapon or tool: *the butt* (*end*) *of a whip, spear, fishing-rod* &c., that part of a weapon by which it is wielded, as distinct from blade, or, in case of fire-arms, from the barrel: *butt of a rifle*. Phr. (in fly-fishing) *to give a fish the butt*, put extra pressure upon him by using thick end as lever. **2.** Thickest part of tree-trunk, extending from ground to lowest branches; a stump, thick log. (This sense partly due to **butt** (**III.**)). **3.** Kind of flat fish, turbot, sole &c.

butt (**III.**), n. (usually in pl. in senses **1** & **2** below). Fr. *but*, 'aim, object of aim, end', *butte*, 'mound of earth'. Prob. of Gmc. origin. Meyer-Lübke suggests Frankish *būt* & compares O.N. *būtr*, 'tree-trunk'. Meaning 'aim', or 'that which one strikes', fits better w. source suggested for **butt** (**IV.**). The words have been confused. Fr. *pied-bot*, 'club foot', appears to be near in sense to Gmc. word meaning 'lump of wood'. **1.** Mound of earth behind targets at a shooting-range. **2.** **a** The targets themselves; **b** the group of targets and mounds which form the range, hence shooting-range. **3.** A person who is an object of ridicule, attack, or accusation.

butt (**IV.**), vb. trans. M.E. *butten*, O. Fr. *boter*, Fr. *bouter*, *buter*, 'strike, push'; cp. Ital. *botto*, 'blow'. Meyer-Lübke derives the words fr. Frankish *bōtan*, 'strike'. See this Gmc. base under **beat** (**I.**). **1.** To strike, thrust, esp. with the head, or, of an animal (ram, goat &c.), with the horns: *the prisoner butted the policeman in the stomach*. **2.** To run into (with *against*, *into*): *going round the corner I butted into John*. **3.** To join end of timber to that of another piece without overlapping; to place end flat against wall. (This perhaps belongs under **butt** (**II.**).) **4.** (used absol. with *on*, *out*, &c.) To jut out, project (influenced by **abut**).

butte, n. [1. būt; 2. bjūt]. Fr., cp. **butt** (**II.**). An isolated hill rising steeply from a plain in the western parts of the United States.

butter (**I.**), n. [1. búter; 2. bátə]. O.E. *butere*, common to W. Gmc. languages, borrowed fr. Lat. *būtyrum*, itself fr. Gk. *boútūron*, wh. means lit. 'cow cheese', fr. *boû(s)*, 'ox' &c., cp. **bovine**, & *tūrón*, *tūrós*, 'cheese', perh. connected w. Lat. *turgeo*, 'swell', cp. **turgid**. The Gk. word is, however, thought to be a popular etymol. or lit. translation of a barbarian word. **1.** **a** Greasy, fatty product of firm consistency, derived from cream by churning; **b** similar substance derived from other materials, e.g. *cocoa butter*; *melted butter*, butter melted for sauce for asparagus &c., also insipid white sauce, consisting chiefly of flour and milk. Phrs. *to look as if butter would not melt in one's mouth*, have an innocent appearance; *to know which side one's bread is buttered*, know one's own interests. **2.** (fig.) Adulation, flattery, fair speaking.

butter (**II.**), vb. trans., fr. prec. **a** To cover with butter; **b** to flatter, esp. *butter up*. Phr. *kind* (*soft, fine*) *words butter no parsnips*, tangible evidence of goodwill better than promises.

butter-and-eggs, n. Varieties of flowers whose petals have two shades of yellow; e.g. a variety of daffodil &c.

butter-boat, n. Shallow, boat-shaped vessel for holding sauce.

butter-cooler, n. Device for keeping butter cold and hard by evaporation of water surrounding it.

buttercup, n. [1. búterkup; 2. bátəkap]. Varieties of ranunculus with yellow flowers.

butter-dish, n. Small dish in which butter is placed on the table.

butter-fingered, adj. Having weak or tender fingers; unable to grip firmly.

butter-fingers, n. Person who is unable to hold anything firmly; esp. one who cannot hold a catch or stop a ball at cricket.

butterfly, n. [1. búterflī; 2. bátəflai]. Insect, often brightly coloured, with four wings and knobbed antennae, order *Lepidoptera*, which flies by day. Reason for association with *butter* uncertain; perhaps originally applied to bright yellow varieties. See **fly** (**II.**) & cp. **moth**.

butteris, n. [1. búteris; 2. bátəris]. Perhaps variant of *buttress* with differentiated meaning. Instrument for paring horses' hoofs when affixing shoe.

butter-knife, n. One, usually of silver, with unsharpened edge, for cutting butter at table.

butter-milk, n. Liquid remaining when butter has been churned from cream.

butter-nut, n. Oily, edible nut of walnut family, growing in America.

butterscotch, n. [1. búterskoch; 2. bátəskɔtʃ]. Sweetmeat made by boiling sugar and butter together until mass becomes thick and hardens as it cools.

buttery, n. [1. búteri; 2. bátəri]. Nothing to do w. *butter*, but fr. O. Fr. *boterie*, fr. *bouteillerie*, 'place where bottles and casks are kept'. See **bottle** (**I.**) & cp. **butler**. Place, esp. in colleges and public schools, where provisions such as bread, butter, and ale are kept, and whence they are issued.

buttery-hatch, n. Half-door with sliding shutter, through which provisions are handed into dining-hall from the buttery or kitchen.

buttock, n. [1. bútuk; 2. bátək]. See **butt** (**II.**), 'end', & **-ock**. **1.** Fleshy protuberances at back of hip upon which human being sits; rump. **2.** Move in wrestling, in which one competitor gets his opponent across his back and throws him over his head; esp. in *cross-buttock*; also as vb.

button (**I.**), n. [1. bútn; 2. bátn]. Fr. *bouton*, Ital. *bottone*, 'bud'. Said by Meyer-Lübke to be fr. Fr. *bout*, 'point, end'. See **butt** (**II.**). **1.** **a** Small knob or portion of flattened, rounded metal, bone, horn &c., attached to clothes, which passes through slit or loop in corresponding place on opposite side of garment and keeps this closed; **b** similar small object worn merely as a badge of honour or distinction, or for ornament. **2.** (fig.) Anything worthless: *not worth a button*; *not to care a button*. **3.** Various applications; denoting small, round, knob-shaped objects: **a** small unopened mushroom; **b** piece of leather on an oar to prevent it slipping through rowlock; **c** round piece of leather at end of fencing foil, to prevent injury to opponent from thrusting; **d** knob which on being pressed forms contact and rings electric bell. Phr. *press the button*, in reference to electric machinery set in motion by forming contact and producing current, to start important series of events by simple means; **e** small, hardly formed fruit such as apples &c. **4.** *Buttons*, (colloq.) a page-boy, from usual livery with several rows of metal buttons down front of coat.

button (**II.**), vb. trans. & intrans., fr. prec. **a** trans. To fasten together, close, by means of buttons: *to button one's coat* &c., also *button up*; Phrs. (fig.) *to button up one's mouth*, preserve silence; *button up one's purse*, refuse to give money; **b** intrans., (of garments &c.) to be capable of being closed, made so as to close, with buttons: *this dress buttons down the back*; *my collar won't button*.

buttonhole (**I.**), n. [1. bútnhōl; 2. bátnhoul]. **1.** Hole, slit, in a garment into which a button slips and fastens. **2.** Flower, or small bunch of flowers, worn in a buttonhole.

buttonhole (**II.**), vb. trans., for earlier *buttonhold*, by confusion w. prec. word. To hold (a person) by the button of his coat, so that he cannot get away, and must listen to what you say; to detain, hold (person) in conversation against his will.

button-hook, n. Small metal or bone hooked implement used for fastening the buttons of boots &c.

buttress (**I.**), n. [1. bútres; 2. bátris]. O. Fr. *bouterez*, fr. *bouter*, 'thrust'. Cp. **butt** (**IV.**). **1.** Construction of stone or brick built against outside of a wall to give additional strength by receiving part of the thrust; a prop. **2.** (fig.) Support, prop (of non-material things): *the buttress of a throne, constitution, argument*.

buttress (**II.**), vb. trans., fr. prec. **a** To support, strengthen a building by buttresses; **b** (fig.) to lend strength, support to non-material things. Also *buttress up*, esp. *an argument, case*, support rather weak case by slightly irrelevant considerations.

butty, n. [1. búti; 2. báti]. Etymol. uncertain. **1.** **a** Foreman of gang of workmen; **b** man who contracts for certain work in a coal-mine and pays workmen for this. **2.** (colloq.) Mate, comrade, friend; esp. on board ship.

butyraceous, adj. [1. būtiráshus; 2. bjūtiréiʃəs], fr. Lat. *būtyrum*, Gk. *boútūron*. See **butter** & **-aceous**. Like, resembling butter, of the consistency of butter.

butyrate, n. [1. bútirāt; 2. bjútireit]. See prec. & **-ate**. (chem.) A salt of butyric acid.

butyric, adj. [1. būtírik; 2. bjūtírik]. See prec. & **-ic**. (chem.) Of, pertaining to, related to, butter; specif., *butyric acid*, acid found in rancid butter, rotten cheese, juice of animal flesh &c.

buxom, adj. [1. búksum; 2. báksəm]. M.E. *buhsom*, 'pliable, obedient'; formed fr. O.E. base *būg-* &c., as in *būgan*, 'to bend'. See **bow** (**III.**), & **-some**; cp. Mod. Germ. *biegsam*, 'flexible'. Earlier sense of 'flexible, pliant', now entirely lost; at present, word means good-looking, comely, in a plump, full-blooded way; sonsy (used only in reference to women).

buxomness, n. Prec. & **-ness**. Quality of being buxom; comeliness.

buy, vb. trans. [1. bī; 2. bai]. O.E. *byċġan*, O.S. *buggian*, Goth. *bugjan*, 'buy'. The base has not been identified outside Gmc., & the origin is unknown. M.E. has the forms *biggen* &c., lineally derived fr. O.E. infin., also *bīȝen*, *būyen* &c., whence present-day type. This is a new formation in M.E.

fr. the 2nd & 3rd pers. pres. indic., O.E. *byġ(e)st, byġ(e)þ*. **1.** To obtain in exchange for payment, generally of money, or in exchange for services: *to buy a horse for a hundred pounds*; *money cannot buy happiness*; *the best that money can buy*. Phr. *to buy a pig in a poke*, commit oneself to something without thoroughly knowing all the conditions; be deceived over a bargain. **2.** To obtain at expense of a great sacrifice: *to buy fame with one's life, with bitter experience* &c.; *victory, peace, was dearly bought*. **3.** To gain a person's services, support, by bribery: *the electors were said to have been bought*. Phrs. with preps.: *buy in* (esp. at auction sales), to withdraw anything from sale by mentioning higher price than any yet bid; *buy off*, get rid of a claim, or claimant, esp. unjust claim &c., by payment; *buy out*, to pay a person to give up his interest in property or office; *buy up*, to buy largest obtainable amount of anything.

buyable, adj. [1. bíabl; 2. báiəbl]. Prec. & **-able**. Purchasable, capable of being bought.

buyer, n. [1. bíer; 2. báiə]. **buy** & **-er**. One who buys; purchaser.

buzz (I.), vb. intrans. [1. buz; 2. baz]. Of imitative origin. **1.** To make a humming noise such as is made by certain insects, bees &c., or by machinery in rapid motion. **2.** (colloq.) Transferred sense, **a** to move rapidly, esp. *buzz along*; *buzz about*, move busily and actively from place to place; **b** (trans. use) to hurl, chuck, throw: *to buzz a stone*. **3.** In some companies, to take what wine is left in the bottle or decanter when it reaches one, although it does not make a full glass; the person who does this starts the fresh bottle.

buzz (II.), n. See prec. Sound made by bees &c.; by whirling machinery; by conversation of a number of persons together.

buzzard, n. [1. búzard; 2. bázəd]. O. Fr. *busart*, Lat. *būteo*, 'falcon'; perh. related to Fr. *butor*, q.v. under **bittern**. Name of various kinds of kites or harriers, genus *Buteo*.

buzzer, n. [1. búzer; 2. bázə]. **buzz (I.)** & **-er**. (colloq.) **a** A steam whistle, hooter, syren, used for summoning people to work, as in factory &c.; **b** (elect.) an electromagnetic device in which a vibrating armature produces a buzzing sound; used in wireless to generate weak oscillatory waves for tuning radio receivers.

by, prep. & adv. [1. bī; 2. bai]. O.E. & O.S. *bī, be*, O.H.G. *bī, be*, Mod. Germ. *bei*, Goth. *bi*, 'at, near'. Cp. O.E. *ymb*, 'around', fr. **um-bi*, O.H.G. *umbi*, Gk. *am-phi*, 'around, about, at, near', Scrt. *a-bhi*, 'at, around', & Lat. *am-bi-*, 'around'; cp. **ambi-**. **A.** prep. **1.** Expressing relation in space, **a** near, close to, in neighbourhood of, at hand: *to sit by the fire*; *the house stands by the river bank*; *to have something by one*, within reach, handy; **b** expressing general direction and position: *east by north*. Phr. *to stand by a man*, give him support, backing. **2.** Expressing direction of movement, path followed &c., **a** through, across, over: *I came by the road, by the fields, by Oxford Street* &c.; *some fell by the wayside*; **b** avoidance, past, beyond: *he walked by me without speaking*; *we drove by several fine parks*. **3.** Expressing relations in time, **a** at, in, during a specific time: *to travel by day*; *the enemy attacked by night*; **b** for a certain time, for the duration of certain period: *to hire a horse by the day, to engage a clerk by the month* &c.; **c** not later than a certain time, before expiry of stated interval: *he will certainly come by three o'clock*; *he will be dead by the end of the year*; *I was very tired by the evening*; *he ought to be here by now*. **4.** Expressing agency or means, **a** agency, through instrumentality, work, efforts of (of persons): *St. Paul's was built by Wren*; *Winchester College was founded by William of Wykeham*; *'Rob Roy' was written by Sir Walter Scott*; **b** means, instrument: *an arch supported by massive pillars*; *a weight lifted by a powerful lever*; *an engine driven by electricity, water-power* &c.; *to perish by the sword*; *by this means, by means of*. Phrs. *by all means*, certainly (in acquiescence); *by no means*, not at all, certainly not (refusal, disagreement). **5.** Expressing mode, manner, method, of an action or process: *he found his way by the light of the moon*; *to dine by lamplight*; *the work was accomplished only by untiring effort*; *by the help of God we will conquer our enemies*; *to hang on by one's hands*; (fig.) *to hang by a thread*, be in a dangerous or critical condition; *darkness came on by degrees*; *by birth an Englishman*. **6.** (in solemn affirmations, vows, imprecations, invocations) With sanction of, through help or authority of: *he swore by all the saints*; *I swear by Almighty God that I will speak the truth*. **7.** Expressing various relations and conditions, **a** in accordance with, in agreement with, subject to: *by request of friends*; *by your kind permission, by your leave*; *by the conditions of our bond we are bound to do so and so*; **b** according to a measurement, number, or quantity: *'The wine of life keeps oozing drop by drop, The leaves of life keep falling one by one'* (Omar Khayyám); *apples are sold by the bushel, milk by the gallon*; *to eat oysters by the dozen*; **c** in calling, naming, after: *called by the name of his grandfather*; *addressed by the title Sir, My Lord* &c.; **d** as, in the nature of: *by way of*. **B.** adv. **1.** **a** Expressing position in repose, near, at hand: *many were standing by at the time*; *when no one is by*; **b** expressing close neighbourhood in moving past: *'Pride in their port, defiance in their eye, I see the lords of human kind pass by'* (Goldsmith); (often implying avoidance, missing) *to go by on the other side*; *wealth and fame have passed me by*. Phr. *to stand by* (naut.), be in neighbourhood, in readiness. **2.** (with sense of motion) At one side, aside, esp. *to put by, lay by*. Phr. *laid by*, incapacitated by illness. **3.** adv. Phrs. *By and by*, before long, later on; also as n. *the sweet by-and-by*, the future; *by the by(e)*, by the way, in passing: *by the by(e), I forgot to tell you the news*.

by-, bye-, pref. As pref. has sense of secondary, minor, of less importance, subsidiary; also secret, indirect. *By-* is usually hyphened, *bye* written as separate word. *By* is in some cases prefixed without hyphen.

by-blow, n. Illegitimate child.

bye, n. [1. bī; 2. bai]. **a** Something subordinate, incidental, or subsidiary, esp. in Phr. *by the bye* (see **by**, adv., **3**); **b** (in cricket) run scored for ball that passes batsman and wicket-keeper; **c** in games where competitors are drawn in pairs, the one left over, who waits to compete till next round; the odd man, pair, or team.

bye-bye (I.), n. [1. bíbī; 2. báibai]. Childish word for sleep: *go to bye-bye*.

bye-bye (II.), interj. [1. bíbí; 2. báibái]. (colloq.) Good-bye.

by-election, n. Election to Parliament held by itself, and not during a General Election, in cases where a seat is vacant through death, resignation &c.

bygone, adj. & n. [1. bígon; 2. báigən]. **a** adj. Over and past, belonging to the past: *bygone sorrows, joys* &c.; **b** n., something past and done with, an event, esp. a sorrow, injury, of the past: *let us forget bygones*; *let bygones be bygones*, forgive and forget.

by-law, n. Pref. here is O. Dan. *byr*, borrowed in O.E. as *bȳ, bī*, 'town', cp. *Derby* &c. The word is fr. base of *būa*, 'dwell' &c. Cp. **bound (V.)**, **be** &c. Special law or regulation made by a town council, local authority, or other corporation.

by-pass, n. **a** Side passage in pipe &c. used to control and divert circulation of gas, air &c.; **b** by-road; specif., a new road connecting two points of old road to avoid a town &c.

bypath, n. [1. bípahth; 2. báipāþ]. Indirect, retired path.

byplay, n. [1. bíplā; 2. báiplei]. Play, action, or gesture, taking place apart and aside from a main conversation or argument, esp. on the stage.

byplot, n. [1. bíplot; 2. báiplɔt]. Secondary, subordinate plot within the main course of development of a story or drama.

by-product, n. Something produced in the process of manufacture of another article, as coke and tar in making gas.

byre, n. [1. bīr; 2. baiə]. O.E. *bȳre*; etymol. doubtful, possibly cogn. w. *būr*. See **bower (I.)**. (in provinc. usage) Cow-shed.

byroad, n. [1. bírōd; 2. báiroud]. Side road, one apart from highroad.

Byronic, adj. [1. bīrónik; 2. bairɔ́nik], fr. Lord Byron. Applied to a genre of poetry, and to a general attitude of mind, resembling the poetry and temper of Byron, cynical, misanthropic and yet romantic.

Byronism, n. [1. bíronizm; 2. báiərənizəm]. Attitude of mind, habit of thought, resembling that cultivated by Byron and exhibited in his poetry. See prec.

byssus, n. [1. bísus; 2. bísəs]. Lat. *byssus*, fr. Gk. *bússos*, 'fine linen', a Semitic loanword, Heb. *būs*, 'cloth'. Fine fabric of flax, cotton, or silk made by the ancients, such as that used for wrapping Egyptian mummies.

bystander, n. [1. bístànder; 2. báistændə]. One standing near, but not taking part in an event or action.

bystreet, n. [1. bístrēt; 2. báistrīt]. Street leading out of a main thoroughfare, back street; (in derogatory sense) small, unimportant, poor street.

byway, n. [1. bíwā; 2. báiwei]. Secondary, side road, side track; (fig.) *byway of learning, literature* &c., line of study, research &c. which is off the beaten track, and of secondary importance, though often contributory and accessory to the main theme.

byword, n. [1. bíwërd; 2. báiwɜ̄d]. Originally, a proverb (obs.). Now in bad sense, object of contempt, reproach, and censure.

Byzantine, adj. [1. bīzántīn, bízantīn; 2. baizǽntain, bízəntain]. Cp. **bezant**. Pertaining to Byzantium (Constantinople), esp. of architecture; *Byzantine Church*, the Greek Church, whose headquarters were at Byzantium.

C

C, c [1. sē; 2. sī], the third letter of English and other languages; as symbol, **C** = Lat. *centum*, 100. For use in abbreviations see end of Dictionary. In algebra, the third known quantity; in music, first note of the scale of C major or minor; *C-spring*, see **cee-spring**.

caaba. See **kaaba**.

cab (I.), n. [1. kab; 2. kæb]. Abbr. of **cabriolet**. **1.** Vehicle, usually plying for hire, with two or four wheels; as *hansom cab, taxi-cab* &c. Phr. *to take a cab*, hire, or travel in a cab. **2.** Driver's shelter on a locomotive engine.

cab (II.), vb. intrans., fr. prec. (colloq.) To go somewhere by cab; also *to cab it*.

cabal (I.) n. [1. kabál; 2. kəbǽl]. Fr. *cabale*, fr. L. Lat. *cabbala*, fr. Heb. *qabbālāh*, 'mysterious doctrine received', cp. Heb. *qābal*, 'take, receive'. By an accident the English

Cabinet of 1671 consisted of five men whose initials spelt the word—Clifford, Arlington, Buckingham, Ashley, Lauderdale, hence they were called the *Cabal*. The word was, however, used in English, in sense of 'secret', and as a vb., 'to conspire', some time before. **a** Secret intrigue, political manœuvre; **b** also group of persons who carry on such an intrigue.

cabal (**II.**), vb. intrans., fr. prec. To conspire, intrigue, esp. *cabal against*.

cab(b)ala, n. [1. kabáhla; 2. kæbálə]. See **cabal** (**I.**). Traditional mystic interpretation of the Scriptures preserved among Jewish Rabbis.

cab(b)alistic, adj. [1. kàbalístik; 2. kæbəlístik]. Prec. & **-ist** & **-ic**. Pertaining to the *cabbala*; cryptic, mysterious, magic, esp. of written symbols and inscriptions.

cabaret, n. [1. kábarā; 2. kǽbarei]. Fr. word, the origin & formation of wh. are doubtful. There are words in various Romance languages, related to Lat. *cavus*, 'hollow', cp. Fr. *cave* in special sense of 'cellar', w. wh. *cabaret* may be connected. **1.** Small inn or wine-shop. **2.** **a** Small drinking-place or night restaurant in which singing and dancing performances are given; **b** the entertainment itself.

cabbage, n. [1. kábij; 2. kǽbidž]. Earlier Engl. forms, *caboche*, *caboge*, the former of wh. is a Fr. form wh. still survives, meaning 'big head'; cp. also Ital. *capoccia* in same sense. The word is fr. Low Lat. *capum, 'head', cp. Lat. *caput*, q.v. under **capital** (**I.**). The suff. *-oche*, *-occia* is pejorative. Plant of the order *Brassica*, used as a vegetable, the leaves of which are tightly folded so as to form a large hard 'head'.

cabbage butterfly, n. Common butterfly of pale greenish-yellow colour, the caterpillar of which feeds on leaves of cabbage. Also called *cabbage white*.

cabbage rose, n. Large coarse pink rose.

cabby, n. [1. kábi; 2. kǽbi]. (colloq.) Partly jocose term for *cabman*. Nearly obsolete now with disappearance of horse-cabs.

caber, n. [1. kāber; 2. kéibə]. Gael. *cabar*, 'pole, beam'. Rough pole, usually a young fir tree, used in Highland games for tossing as a trial of strength and skill. Phr. *to toss the caber*.

cabin (**I.**), n. [1. kábin; 2. kǽbin]. M.E. *caban(e)*, 'small house', fr. Fr., derived fr. Ital. *capanna*, *-o* (in Low Lat.), 'hut, shelter'. The origin is very doubtful. Fr. *cabine*, Ital. *cabino*, are borrowed fr. Engl. word. **1.** Small house, hut, humble abode. **2.** Apartment on a ship, esp. for sleeping. **3.** Building on a railway line from which signals and points are worked.

cabin (**II.**), vb. trans., fr. prec. To confine, esp. within narrow limits, to enclose: '*cabin'd, cribb'd, confin'd*' (Shakespeare); '*Her cabined, ample spirit, It fluttered and failed for breath*' (Matthew Arnold).

cabin boy, n. Junior servant on a ship.

cabinet, n. [1. kábinet; 2. kǽbinit]. Dimin. of **cabin**. Cp. Fr. *cabinet*, Ital. *gabinetto*. **1.** Small private room or office. **2.** Piece of furniture, often of fine design, inlaid and decorated, of various kinds; **a** case, set of drawers, esp. for preserving, and sometimes for exhibiting, precious objects, specimens, and curiosities; **b** case with glass doors and shelves for showing china, jewels &c. **3.** (extended use) The collection of valuables contained in a cabinet. **4.** (cap.) Body of ministers, heads of the various departments of state, who initiate policy, and are responsible for the government of a country. **5.** A particular size of photograph, about 7 in. by 5 in.; hence, *cabinet photograph, cabinet size*.

Cabinet Council, n. Meeting of ministers of state to deal with state business.

cabinet-maker, n. **1.** Highly skilled worker in wood, who designs and makes cabinets and other pieces of furniture requiring fine finish. **2.** (facetious) Prime Minister.

cabinet-making, n. Trade, art, process, of making highly finished furniture of the cabinet type.

Cabinet minister, n. A member of the Cabinet.

cabinet pudding, n. One consisting of bread, candied peel, and raisins, covered with hot sauce or syrup.

cabinet-work, n. The work of a cabinet-maker, including the finer woodwork, panelling &c. in interior of a house.

cable (**I.**), n. [1. kābl; 2. kéibl]. M.E. *kābel, cābel*, fr. O. Fr. *cable*, Low Lat. *capulum*, 'halter', fr. *capio*, 'take, hold', q.v. under **captive**. Mod. Fr. *câble* may have different origin. **1.** Thick, strong rope, or line, of hemp, fibre, or wire. **2.** Bundle of wires twisted round hard core, insulated, and protected by waterproof cover, laid on sea-bottom, for conveying electric current. **3.** Message transmitted by means of a cable (2); also *cablegram*: *to send a cable*. **4.** (archit. and goldsmith's work) Twisted ornament resembling a cable.

cable (**II.**), vb. trans. & intrans., fr. prec. **1.** To send (message) to countries across the sea by means of an electric submarine cable. **2.** (archit. &c.) To furnish with cable ornament.

cablegram, n. [1. kāblgràm; 2. kéiblgræ̀m]. See **cable** & **-gram**. Message sent by electric cable.

cablet, n. [1. kāblet; 2. kéiblit]. **cable** & **-et**. Rope less than 10 in. in circumference.

cabman, n. [1. kábman; 2. kǽbmən]. Driver of a cab, esp. of a horse-cab.

cabob(s), n. [1. kābob(z); 2. kéibɔb(z)]. Arab. *kabāb*. Anglo-Indian word, used for roast meat generally; specif., a dish made of highly spiced beef or mutton.

cabochon, n. [1. kaboshon; 2. kabɔʃɔ̃]. Fr., fr. *caboche*, 'head', *cabocher*, 'to cut off'. See under **cabbage**. A gem-stone, such as a ruby, cut with a round unfaceted top, then said to be cut *en cabochon*.

caboodle, n. [1. kabōōdl; 2. kəbúdl]. U.S.A. slang; origin unknown. (slang) In Phr. *the whole caboodle*, everything, everyone; the whole lot.

caboose, n. [1. kabōōs; 2. kəbús], fr. Du. *kabuys*, also *kombuis*, earlier *kaban huis*, 'cabin-house'. Borrowed in Fr. in form *cambuse* (w. same meaning), wh. form sometimes appears as *camboose* in Engl. Room on ship's deck in which cooking is carried out.

caboshed, adj. [1. kabósht; 2. kəbɔ́ʃt], fr. Fr. *caboche*, 'head', q.v. under **cabbage**. (her.) Describes animal's head borne full-face (*affronté*) without showing any part of neck.

cabotage, n. [1. kábotahzh; 2. kǽbɔtāž]. Fr. word whose origin is uncertain. *Cabot* is the name of a fish; *caboter* is to sail along coast touching at the ports, and never going far; possibly the fish sticks close to the shore. Coasting trade carried on by ships which go from port to port.

cabriole, n. & adj. [1. kábriōl; 2. kǽbrioul]. See etymol. of **cabriolet**; reason for name not clear. (of furniture) Kind of curved leg characteristic of Queen Anne period, generally having carved shell at the top, and a foot in form of a claw clasping a ball.

cabriolet, n. [1. kàbriōlā; 2. kæ̀brioulei]. Fr. word for a one-horse vehicle now obs.; dimin. of *cabriole*, 'leap of a goat, caper', fr. idea of using the carriage for a jaunt or party of pleasure. The word is derived fr. Lat. *caper*, 'he-goat'. See **caper**. Light one-horse carriage with two wheels and a hood; word and thing no longer current but survives in shortened form **cab**.

ca' canny, Scots, = call canny. See **canny**.

cacao, n. [1. kakáh-ō; 2. kəkáou]. Span., fr. native Mexican *kakauatl*. Mexican plant from seeds of which *cocoa* and *chocolate* are made.

cachalot, n. [1. káshalot; 2. kǽʃəlɔt]. Fr. word; etymol. uncertain, said to be fr. Southern Fr., Gascon dial. word *cachau*, 'tooth'. Species of whale with teeth in lower jaw, the sperm whale.

cache, n. [1. kash; 2. kæʃ]. Fr. word meaning 'hidden place'; cp. Fr. *cacher*, 'to hide', fr. Low Lat. *coacticāre*, freq. fr. *co-actāre*, 'collect'. See **co-** & **act**. Secret storehouse or hiding-place; esp. **a** of stores left by explorers at different stages along their route, for return journey, or for another party; also **b** of collection of illicitly hidden arms; **c** of store of grain or honey collected by certain animals for winter use.

cachectic, adj. [1. kakéktik; 2. kækéktik], fr. Gk. *kakhektikós*, fr. *kakós*, 'bad', q.v. under **cachexy**. Belonging to, suffering from, cachexy.

cachet, n. [1. káshā; 2. kǽʃei]. Fr. word meaning 'seal, stamp'. Connected w. **cache**. Originally a private mark or seal. Distinguishing mark of excellence or authenticity: *rich vulgarians often send their sons to Eton simply to give them a cachet*. For *lettre de cachet*, see **lettre de cachet**.

cachexy, n. [1. kakéksi; 2. kækéksi]. Gk. *kakhexia*, fr. *kakós*, 'bad', q.v. under **caco-**, & *héxis*, 'permanent state, or habit of body', formed fr. base of *ékhō*, 'hold, possess'. This Gk. vb. is for earlier *seghō, & is cogn. w. Scrt. *sáhatē*, 'to master', *sáhaś*, 'triumphant strength'; Goth. *sigis*, O.E. *sige*, 'victory'. See **epoch**. (med.) Bad general state of bodily health.

cachinnate, vb. intrans. [1. kákinät; 2. kǽkineit], fr. Lat. *cachinnāt-(um)*, P.P. type of *cachinnāre*, 'laugh aloud, burst out laughing'; imitative word, but cp. also Gk. *kakházein* w. same meaning. To laugh loudly and roughly.

cachinnation, n. [1. kàkináshun; 2. kæ̀kinéiʃən]. Lat. *cachinnātiōn-(em)*. See prec. & **-ion**. Loud, rough laughter.

cacholong, n. [1. kásholong; 2. kǽʃɔlɔŋ]. Through Fr. fr. a Calmuck word meaning 'beautiful stone'. Opaque variety of opal, bluish or yellowish in colour.

cachou, n. [1. kashōō; 2. kəʃú]. Fr. See **cashew**. Pill or lozenge, usually silvered, composed of cashew-nut and other condiments; used for removing odour of smoke from the breath.

cachucha, n. [1. kachōōcha; 2. katʃútʃa]. Span. Spanish dance resembling the bolero.

cacique, n. [1. kasēk; 2. kæsík]. Span., fr. native W. Indian word. West Indian chief.

cackle (**I.**), vb. intrans. [1. kákl; 2. kǽkl]. M.E. *kakelen*; perh. Scand. loan-word, cp. Swed. *kackla*. Of imitative origin. **1.** To utter the typical cry of a hen or a goose. **2.** (of human beings) To chatter noisily, esp. in a shrill nasal voice; also to laugh in a shrill, noisy manner.

cackle (**II.**), n., see prec. **1.** The noise made by a hen or a goose. **2.** Loud, shrill chatter or laughter.

cackler, n. [1. kákler; 2. kǽklə]. **cackle** (**I.**) & **-er**. **a** Bird that cackles; **b** person who talks noisily and excessively.

cackling, n. [1. kákling; 2. kǽkliŋ]. **cackle** (**I.**) & **-ing**. **a** The sound made when a bird or person cackles; **b** the act of emitting a cackle; **c** same as **cackle** (**II.**), **2**.

caco-, pref., fr. Gk. *kakós*, 'bad, evil'. The etymol. of this common Gk. word is uncertain. Of the various suggested explanations given by Boisacq none appears worthy of credence. It occurs in many compounds in Gk., equiv. to our *ill-*, *mis-*, or *mal-*; e.g. *kakó-potmos*, 'ill-fated', *kako-súnthetos*, 'ill-put-together', *kako-nomía*, 'misgovernment' &c. The word can serve as a pref. in newly formed words composed of Gk. elements.

cacodyl, n. [1. kákodil; 2. kǽkɔdil]. Gk., fr. *kakós*, 'bad', see **caco-**, & **od-**, cp. *ózō*, 'have a smell', see under **odour**, & *húlē*, 'material, substance', q.v. under **-yl**. Lit. 'ill-smelling stuff'. A poisonous, malodorous compound of arsenic and methyl.

cacoepy, n. [1. kakóepi; 2. kækóuεpi]. Gk., fr. **caco-** & *-épeia*, fr. *épos*, 'word, speech', q.v. under **epic**. Bad pronunciation; the reverse of *orthoepy*.

cacoethes, n. [1. kàkōéthēz; 2. kækouíþīz], fr. Gk. *kako-éthēs*, 'an ill habit'. See **caco-** & **ethic**. Bad habit of body or mind; tendency to ill-health; esp. in Latin Phr. *cacoethes scribendi*, bad habit of writing (too much).

cacography, n. [1. kakógrafi; 2. kækógrəfi]. See **caco-** & **-graphy**. Bad handwriting; bad spelling; the reverse of *calligraphy*.

cacology, n. [1. kakóloji; 2. kækólədži]. Gk. See **caco-** & **logy**. **a** Improper selection of words; **b** bad pronunciation.

caconymic, adj. [1. kàkonímik; 2. kækənímik]. Gk., fr. **caco-** & *ónuma*, 'name', q.v. under **name** & **nominal**, & **-ic**. Having an objectionable, ill-sounding name.

cacoon, n. [1. kakōōn; 2. kəkūn], fr. native name. Tropical bean of West Indies and Central America with very large pods.

cacophonous, adj. [1. kakófunus; 2. kækófənəs]. Gk., fr. **caco-** & *phōnē*, 'sound, tone', q.v. under **phone**, & **-ous**. Harsh, ill-sounding.

cacophony, n. [1. kakófuni; 2. kækófəni], fr. Fr. *cacophonie*. See elements of prec. & **-y**. Discord, ugly sound.

cactaceous, adj. [1. kaktáshus; 2. kæktéiʃəs]. See **cactus** & **-aceous**. Relating to the botanical order *Cactaceae*, to which the cactus belongs.

cactiform, adj. [1. káktiform; 2. kǽktifōm]. **cactus** & **-form**. Resembling a cactus in appearance and structure.

cactus, n. [1. káktus; 2. kǽktəs], pl. *cactuses*; learned pl. *cacti* [1. káktī; 2. kǽktai]. Gk. *káktos*; origin unknown; perh. pre-Hellenic. Family of plants of which there are numerous varieties, all having thick, fleshy leaves studded with prickles.

cacuminal, adj. & n. [1. kakúminal; 2. kækjúminəl], fr. Lat. *cacūmen*, 'tip, peak, summit', & Lat. suff. *-ālis*, q.v. under **-al**. *Cacūmen* is fr. **cacud-*, or **cacub-men*; cp. Scrt. *kakúd-* & *kakúbh*, 'peak, point'. Scrt. *kākúd-* means 'mouth-cavity, roof of the mouth'. The orig. meaning is perh. 'vault', 'something arched', then 'highest point of arch'. (phon.) Applied by some writers to sounds articulated with the point, or tip, of the tongue turned backwards and upwards; also to sounds made with the point of tongue articulating far back against the hard palate, as the Swed. *d* preceded by *r*, as in *jord*, 'earth'.

cad, n. [1. kad; 2. kæd]. Abbr. of Fr. *cadet*, 'a junior'. See **cadet**. The word was originally applied to a junior or inferior servant, esp. at a public school or a college; then applied generally to boys of the town as distinct from members of the school or college, whence it developed a bad sense. In present-day usage the word means **a** an ill-bred, vulgar, bad-mannered person; **b** in a moral sense, a person who lacks proper feelings and instincts, such esp. as fair-mindedness, generosity, and consideration for others, in fact one who is deficient in chivalrous feelings and is the reverse of a gentleman in the best and widest sense. (Rarely applied to a female.)

cadastral, adj. [1. kadástral; 2. kədǽstrəl]. Formed w. adj. suff. **-al**, fr. Fr. *cadastre*, 'a detailed public survey of territorial property'. This is derived fr. Lat. *capitastrum*, register of *capita*, 'heads' or units in a territorial survey; see **capital**. Belonging to, exhibiting, ownership, extent and value of land for purposes of taxation, esp. *cadastral survey, map*.

cadaveric, adj. [1. kadáverik; 2. kədǽvərik]. Lat. *cadāver*, 'corpse', & **-ic**. *Cadāver* is prob. fr. base of *cadere*, 'to fall', q.v. under **cadence**. (med.) Possessing characteristics of a corpse.

cadaverous, adj. [1. kadáverus; 2. kədǽvərəs]. Lat. *cadāver-ōsus*, 'corpse-like'. Cp. prec. & **-ous**. Looking like a corpse; hence pale, pinched, melancholy of countenance.

caddie. See **caddy (I.)**.

caddis fly, n. [1. kádis flī; 2. kǽdis flai]. Etymol. of first word unknown. May-fly and other insects whose larvae live in water; *caddis worm*, the larva of above; used as bait for fishing.

caddish, adj. [1. kádish; 2. kǽdiʃ]. See **cad** & **-ish**. Like, after the manner of, a cad; ill-bred, vulgar, rude, ungentlemanlike; used of persons, their manners, speech, and habits.

caddishly, adv. Prec. & **-ly**. In a caddish manner.

caddy (I.), n. [1. kádi; 2. kǽdi], fr. Fr. *cadet*. See **cadet**. Servant in attendance on golf-player, who carries his clubs, looks for lost balls, and so forth.

caddy (II.), n., fr. Malay *kati*, measure of weight. Usually *tea-caddy*, a small box, of wood, silver &c., used for holding tea.

cadence, n. [1. kádens; 2. kéidəns]. Fr., cp. Ital. *cadenza*. Formed fr. Lat. *cadent-(em)*, Pres. Part. type of *cadere*, 'to fall'. See suff. **-ence**. Etymol. of *cadere* not clear, but cp. Scrt. *čadati*, 'he falls down'. **a** Rhythm, metre, in poetry; **b** rise and fall of the voice in speaking; **c** used by Milton of the sound of wind: '*the sound of blustering winds which . . . now with hoarse cadence lull seafaring men*' (P. L. ii. 286-8); **d** technical term in music for a concluding strain.

cadenced, adj. [1. kádenst; 2. kéidənst]. Prec. & **-ed**. Rhythmical; in metre.

cadency, n. [1. kádnsi; 2. kéidnsi]. See **cadence** & **-y**. (her.) **1.** Descent of younger branch of a family from main line. **2.** Figure on the shield, called also *marks of cadency*, which indicates position of a cadet in relation to head of the family.

cadenza, n. [1. kadéntsa; 2. kədéntsə]. Ital. See under **cadence**. (mus.) Ornamental flourish of voice or instrument, introduced usually towards close of a movement.

cadet, n. [1. kadét; 2. kədét]. Fr., earlier *capdet* formed fr. Lat. *capit-(is)*, *caput*, 'head, chief', w. dimin. suff. *-et*. The word means lit. 'little head, or chief', see **capital**. **1.** Younger son, one junior in position in a family: *cadet branch*, descended from younger son. **2.** Student at naval or military college (usually *Gentleman Cadet*) who is being trained to become an officer. During the War private soldiers specially selected as likely to make good officers, and trained in special courses of instruction, were called *cadets* while in course of training. Member of a Cadet Corps. **3.** (fr. initials K.D.) Member of the former Russian Constitutional Democratic Party.

Cadet Corps, n. An organization at many public and secondary schools for training the elder boys on military lines to qualify as members of an Officers' Training Corps, q.v.

cadge, vb. intrans. & trans. [1. kaj; 2. kædž]. Etymol. doubtful, possibly corrupt. of **catch**. To beg; to sponge on others for money, hospitality &c.

cadger, n. [1. kájer; 2. kǽdžə]. See prec. & **-er**. A beggar; worthless fellow, idle loafer, esp. one who lives on others.

cadi, n. [1. kádi; 2. kéidi]. Arab. *qādī*. Minor judge or magistrate, usually of a small town or village, among Arabs and Turks.

cadmium, n. [1. kádmium; 2. kǽdmiəm], fr. Lat. *cadmia*, fr. Gk. *kadmeia gê*, 'Cadmean earth, calamine'. The place-name *Kadmos* may be of Semitic origin, cogn. w. Heb. *qedem*, 'east'. White ductile metallic element resembling tin, and related to zinc; *cadmium yellow*, intense yellow pigment of which cadmium is an ingredient.

cadre, n. [1. kahdr; 2. kādr]. Fr. word meaning 'frame, framework', fr. Ital. *quadro*, Lat. *quadrum*, 'square', q.v. under **quadri-**. (mil.) Skeleton or permanent nucleus of a military unit, or of a staff.

caduceus, n. [1. kadúseus; 2. kædjúsiəs]. Lat., 'herald's staff', ad. fr. Gk. (Doric) *karukion*, fr. *kārux*, 'herald'. The corresponding Attic forms are *kērúkeion*, *kêrux*. These are all related to the Homeric vb. *karkairō*, 'resound', & cogn. w. Scrt. *čarkarti*, 'mention with praise', *čarkṛtiš*, 'praise, glory'. Gmc. cognates occur in O.E. *hrōþ-or*, 'joy, benefit', & *hrēþ*, 'glory, victory', fr. **hrōþi*; O.H.G. *hruod*, 'glory' (cp. personal name, *Rūd-olf*); Goth. *hrōþ-eigs*, 'glorious'. Lat. *car-men*, 'song', cp. **charm (II.)**, is prob. cogn., & undoubtedly O. Slav. *krasa*, 'beauty', *krasĭnŭ*, 'beautiful', & a large number of words in all the Slav. languages meaning 'beauty', 'bright coloured, brilliant' &c. Russ. *krasnyi* means 'beautiful, glorious' & also 'red'. Orig. the Gk. word for 'herald' meant 'one who proclaimed abroad fame and glory'. In classical antiquity a caduceus was the wand of a herald, made of olive wood, with two serpents twined round it; it was a symbol of peace, and was the wand of Hermes (Mercury) as the messenger of the gods.

caducity, n. [1. kadúsiti; 2. kædjúsiti], fr. Fr. *caducité*, fr. Lat. *cadūcitāt-(em)*, 'perishableness, frailness', fr. adj. *cadūcus*, 'inclined to fall, fleeting, perishable', derived fr. *cadere*, 'to fall', q.v. under **cadence**. Perishableness, transitoriness.

caducous, adj. [1. kadúkus; 2. kædjúkəs], fr. Lat. *cadūcus*. See prec. Prone to fall. (bot., of parts of plants) Falling very early.

caecal, adj. [1. sékal; 2. síkəl]. See **caecum** & **-al**. Belonging to the 'blind gut' or caecum.

caecum, n. [1. sékum; 2. síkəm]. Lat. neut. adj., 'the blind thing'; cogn. w. this word are Goth. *haihs*, 'blind, one-eyed', O. Ir. *caech*, Scrt. *kēkara*, 'squinting'. (anat.) The blind gut, a closed part at the beginning of the large intestine, containing the so-called 'vermiform appendix'.

Caesar, n. [1. sézar; 2. sízə]. Lat., the cognomen or family name of Caius Julius Caesar, derived fr. *caes-(um)*, (fr. **kaid-tom*), P.P. type of *caedere*, 'to cut, strike, hew' &c. See **cement**. **1.** a Title adopted by Augustus and succeeding Roman emperors; **b** an emperor, cp. Russ. *czar*, Germ. *kaiser*. **2.** (by transf.) **a** An autocrat; **b** the civil power, from *render unto Caesar* &c. (Matt. xxii. 21).

Caesarian, adj. [1. sēzárian; 2. sīzéəriən], fr. Lat. *Caesariānus*, 'pertaining to Caesar'. See prec. & **-an**. (surg.) *Caesarian operation*, one for delivering a child by cutting the mother, so called from Julius Caesar, who was born through such an operation.

Caesarism, n. [1. sézarizm; 2. sízərizəm]. **Caesar** & **-ism**. System of autocratic rule.

caesious, adj. [1. sézius; 2. síziəs]. Lat. *caesius*, 'bluish grey', esp. of the eyes (very rare), prob. connected w. *caelum*, 'heaven', q.v. under **ceiling**; cp. **cerulean**. (bot.) Bluish grey.

caesium, n. [1. sézium; 2. síziəm]. See prec. A rare alkaline metal, resembling potassium and rubidium, of silvery colour; the spectrum has two blue lines, whence its name.

caesura, n. [1. sēzúra; 2. sizjúərə]. Lat., formed fr. *caes-* as in P.P. of *caedo*, 'cut' &c. Cp. **Caesar** & see **cement**. (pros.) Break or pause in verse or line.

café, n. [1. káfā; 2. kǽfei]. Fr. form of **coffee**. Originally, place of public entertainment where coffee and other non-alcoholic drinks might be had, a coffee-house. In England the word is now chiefly applied to a restaurant where non-alcoholic drinks only are sold, and where light meals are obtainable. On the Continent *café* is used of restaurants generally.

cafeteria, n. [1. kàfetéria; 2. kæfetíəriə]. Span. for **café**. A restaurant in which the customers help themselves to light dishes &c., without waiters.

caffeine, n. [1. káf(e)ēn; 2. kǽf(i)īn]. See **coffee** & **-ine**. Alkaloid obtained from coffee-plant, tea &c.; used as a drug in medicine.

caftan, n. [1. káftan; 2. kǽftæn], fr. Turk. & Pers. *qaftan*, through Fr. *cafetan*. Long gown with girdle and long sleeves worn in the Levant.

cage (I.), n. [1. kāj; 2. keidž]. Fr. *cage*, cp. Ital. *gabbia*, 'basket for fowls, coop', & *gaggia*, 'basket', wh. are all derived fr. Lat.

cavea, 'hollowed place', also 'stall, cage, coop, bee-hive'. See also **cave, cavern.** **1.** A structure for confining animals, usually with iron bars for large animals, and for small animals and birds a receptacle with top and sides entirely made of a kind of trellis of wire or wicker-work, having a flat wooden or iron floor. **2.** Anything resembling a cage in structure, e.g. the enclosed platform of a lift, esp. one used to take miners up and down the shaft of a mine. **3.** (fig.) Prison: '*Stone walls do not a prison make, Nor iron bars a cage*' (Lovelace).

cage (II.), vb. trans., fr. prec. To confine, shut up as in a cage.

caiman. See **cayman.**

cainozoic. See **kainozoic.**

caique, n. [1. kah-ék; 2. kāík]. Turk. word. Light sailing- or rowing-boat, used on the Bosporus.

caird, n. [1. kārd; 2. kɛəd]. Gael., Ir. *ceard.* (Scots) A wandering tinker.

cairn, n. [1. kārn; 2. kɛən]. Gael. *carn*, genit. *cairn*, 'heap'. Pile of rough stones specially built as a landmark or monument; also a cairn-terrier.

cairngorm, n. [1. kárngórm; 2. kɛ́əngɔ́m, -gɔ̄rm], fr. **cairn**, & Gael. *gorm*, 'blue'. A clear yellow or brownish crystal much used for brooches and other ornaments by the Scots. Named after the mountain in Inverness-shire where it is chiefly found.

cairn - terrier, n. A small shaggy - coated variety of Scotch terrier, so named from ability to burrow in or round cairns.

caisson, n. [1. kāsun; 2. kéisən]. Fr. word w. same meanings as in Engl.; fr. *caisse*, 'wooden box', cp. Ital. *cassa*. These are derived fr. Lat. *capsa*, 'chest, box, receptacle', wh. is formed fr. base seen in *capio*, 'take, seize', also 'receive, hold, contain'. See this word under **captive** & **-oon.** **1.** (mil.) Movable covered chest on wheels, often attached to light guns for containing ammunition; an ammunition wagon. **2.** (engin.) **a** Large water-tight chamber, sunk below surface of a river &c., from which the water is excluded by pumping air into it, and in which men work under water; **b** large iron receptacle sunk into bed of a river and filled with cement in which the piers of a bridge are embedded. *Caisson disease*, disease of workers in compressed air, as in caissons, diving-bells &c.

caitiff, n. [1. kātif; 2. kéitif], fr. O. Fr. *caitif*, fr. Lat. *captīvus*, 'prisoner', see **captive.** (archaic and poet.) Mean, base person; contemptible, cowardly knave.

cajole, vb. trans. [1. kajṓl; 2. kədžóul]. Fr. *cajóler*, 'flatter with ulterior motive'. Etymol. very obscure. Meyer-Lübke arrives at no definite result. **1.** To flatter, caress, praise, make oneself pleasant to a person with a view to persuading him to do what we want. Generally in bad sense, implying trickery. **2.** Hence, to deceive, throw dust in a person's eyes by soft and flattering speeches.

cajolement, n. [1. kajṓlment; 2. kədžóulmənt]. See prec. & **-ment.** Act or process of cajoling, implying that the object of this is accomplished; deception.

cajolery, n. [1. kajṓleri; 2. kədžóuləri]. **cajole** & **-ery.** Act of cajoling, the attempt to flatter one into doing something; considered rather as a process which is going on.

cajoling, adj. [1. kajṓling; 2. kədžóuliŋ], fr. Pres. Part. of **cajole.** Flattering, caressing with intent to persuade or deceive: *cajoling ways, smile* &c.

cajolingly, adv. Prec. & **-ly.** In a cajoling manner.

cake (I.), n. [1. kāk; 2. keik], in M.E., prob. Scand. loan-word, cp. Swed. *kaka*; cp. also Germ. *kuchen*, Du. *koek*. This may be cogn. w. base **kōk-*, 'cook', in wh. case it wd. be a Gmc. formation after the pattern of other words wh. have *ā-ō* gradation (cp. O.N. *taka*, 'take', Pret. *tōk*, 'took'), since *cook* is a very early loan-word fr. Lat. *coquere*. See **cook.** **1.** Kind of confectionery consisting of flour, butter, and eggs, sweetened and baked in a tin mould, often enriched with currants, raisins &c.: *plum cake*. The word is applied both to the material itself (*cake*) and to a portion baked in a mould as a single unity (*a cake*). Phrs. *one cannot eat one's cake and have it too*; *to take the cake* (fam.), win a prize, excel; (ironical) *that takes the cake*, beats everything; *cakes and ale*, merry-making. **2.** (from shape or consistency) **a** Thin wafer-like material, unsweetened, made of oatmeal and water: *oatcake*; **b** compressed food, consisting chiefly of linseed, given to cattle for fatting: *oil-cake*. **3.** Applied to certain nonedible materials which are shaped, moulded, or compressed, e.g. *cake of soap, cake of tobacco*. **4.** Dried, hardened clay or mud, esp. on the clothes or on animals' coats.

cake (II.), vb. trans. & intrans., fr. prec. To form hard or sticky mass, as mud, clay &c.; dry hard, coagulate, as blood: *caked with mud, filth* &c.

cakewalk, n. [1. kākwawk; 2. kéikwɔ̄k]. Grotesque step-dance, the prize for which is a cake; practised by negroes in U.S.A.

calabar bean, n. [1. kálabar bḗn; 2. kǽləbā bīn], fr. Calabar, west coast of Africa. Poisonous bean of a leguminous W. African plant, extract from which is used as a drug in tetanus, also by oculists for dilating the eye.

calabash, n. [1. kàlabásh; 2. kæ̀ləbǽʃ]. Fr. *calebasse*, fr. Span. *calabaza*, fr. Arab. *qar*, 'gourd', *aibas*, 'dry'. **1.** Fruit or gourd of a tropical S. American tree; the tree itself. **2.** Any kind of gourd, esp. one dried, cleaned, and used as a bottle or drinking-vessel; also as a tobacco pipe.

calaboose, n. [1. kàlabṓōs; 2. kæ̀ləbúːs], fr. Span. *calabozo*, 'dungeon, cell'. A prison, gaol, esp. in Southern States of U.S.A.

calamanco, n. [1. kàlamángkō; 2. kæ̀ləmǽŋkou]. Etymol. doubtful. A glossy woollen cloth.

calamander wood, n. [1. kalamánder wòod; 2. kæləmǽndə wùd]. The name of the tree in Cingalese is *kalumederiye*, wh., it is suggested, may be ad. fr. *Coromandel*. Hard, finely veined wood, used in cabinet-making, from tree of same name growing in Ceylon and parts of India.

calamary, n. [1. kálamari; 2. kǽləməri]. Lat. *calamārius*, fr. *calamus*, 'reed, pen', wh. is a loan-word fr. Gk. *kálamos*, cogn. w. Scrt. *kalámas*, 'reed-pen'; another cogn. is Lat. *culmus*, 'stalk, stem'. See further under **haulm** & cp. **culm** (I.). Squid or cuttlefish with pen-shaped inner shell.

calamine, n. [1. kálamīn; 2. kǽləmain]. Fr., fr. Med. Lat. *calamina*, fr. Lat. *cadmia*. See **cadmium.** A kind of zinc ore.

calamint, n. [1. kálamint; 2. kǽləmint], fr. Gk. *kalaminthē*, connected w. *kálamos*, see **calamary.** (bot.) An aromatic herb, *Calamintha*, of the mint family.

calamitous, adj. [1. kalámitus; 2. kəlǽmitəs]. Lat. *calamitōsus*. See **calamity** & **-ous.** Fraught with, productive of, calamity; disastrous.

calamitously, adv. Prec. & **-ly.** In a calamitous manner.

calamitousness, n. See prec. & **-ness.** State of calamity, misery.

calamity, n. [1. kalámiti; 2. kəlǽmiti]. Fr. *calamité*, fr. Lat. *calamitāt-(em)*, (acc. of *calamitas*). This word meant primarily 'misfortune in war, defeat', & orig. is said to have been applied to injury caused to crops by hail. The older form of word is *cadamitas*, & it has nothing to do w. Lat. (*in*)-*columis*, 'uninjured', as the older dictionaries state, nor w. Lat. *cadō*, 'fall'. Genuine cognates are Gk. *kḗdō*, 'I destroy, afflict', & Scrt. *kadanam*, 'destruction'. A terrible, disastrous event; misfortune, misery.

calamus, n. [1. kálamus; 2. kǽləməs]. Lat., 'reed'. See **calamary.** **1.** (bot.) **a** Name of various reeds, as sweet-flag &c.; **b** a genus of palms, the stems of which make rattan-canes. **2.** A reed-pen, as used by the ancients and in the East.

calash, n. [1. kalásh; 2. kəlǽʃ]. Fr. *calèche*; borrowed also into Germ. as *kalesche*. A Slav. word orig.; O. Slav. *koleso*, 'wheel' &c.; the word *kolo* &c. is used in various Slav. dialects, in pl. in sense of 'cart, waggon'. The Russ. *kolyáska*, 'calash', is reborrowed fr. a Romance source. The Aryan base, whence the Slav. words come, is **kʷel-*, 'turn, move', whence also the various words for 'wheel' noted under **cycle, pole** (II.), & **wheel.** **a** Obsolete form of carriage with four wheels, seats for four inside, a box for coachman, and a movable hood; **b** a silk hood worn by women in 18th cent.

calcareous, adj. [1. kalkārius; 2. kælkɛ́əriəs]. Lat. *calcārius*, 'pertaining to lime', fr. *calx*, 'stone, lime', cp. **chalk**; perh. fr. base **skʷel-*, in wh. case Lat. *silex*, fr. earlier **scilex*, 'pebble, flint-stone', q.v. under **silica,** is cogn. Pertaining to, containing, lime or limestone.

calceolaria, n. [1. kàlsēōlária; 2. kæ̀lsioulɛ́əriə]. Lat. *calceolārius*, 'shoe-maker', fr. *calceolus*, 'little shoe', dimin. of *calceus*, 'half-boot', fr. *calc-(is)*, *calx*, 'heel'. There are various cognates in the Slav. languages referring to parts of the leg, e.g. O. Slav. *klŭka*, 'knee, ham', Bulg. *klŭkŭ*, 'thigh' &c. (bot.) A genus of S. American plants, the flower of which is supposed to resemble an ancient make of slipper.

calciferous, adj. [1. kalsíferus; 2. kælsífərəs]. Lat. *calci-*, fr. *calx*, 'lime', q.v. under **calcareous,** & **-ferous.** Lit. 'lime-bearing', producing or containing carbonate of lime.

calcification, n. [1. kàlsifikāshun; 2. kæ̀lsifikéiʃən], fr. Lat. *calci-ficatiōn-(em)*. See prec., & **-fy** & **-ation.** Petrifaction through impregnation with lime; (med.) hardening and stiffening of joint or muscle through limy deposit; ossification.

calcify, vb. intrans. & trans. [1. kálsifī; 2. kǽlsifai]. Fr. *calcifier*. See prec. To become hard, or render hard, through deposit of lime.

calcinate, vb. trans. [1. kálsināt; 2. kǽlsineit], fr. Lat. *calcināt-(um)*, P.P. type of *calcināre*, see **calcine.** To calcine.

calcination, n. [1. kàlsinā́shun; 2. kæ̀lsinéiʃən]. Lat. *calcinātiōn-(em)*. See prec. & **-ion.** Process of calcining, or reducing to powder by action of heat.

calcine, vb. trans. & intrans. [1. kálsīn; 2. kǽlsain]. Fr. *calciner*, Lat. *calcināre*, 'reduce to lime' (*calx*). See **calcareous.** Reduce, by burning, to lime, in form of powder, or friable substance; to disintegrate by burning; frequently used of bones, esp. in P.P. *calcined*.

calcite, n. [1. kálsīt; 2. kǽlsait], fr. Lat. *calc-(is)*, *calx*, 'lime', see **calcareous,** & **-ite.** Native calcium carbonate or carbonate of lime.

calcium, n. [1. kálsium; 2. kǽlsiəm]. Formed fr. Lat. *calc-(is)*. See prec. A metallic chemical element, the metallic base of lime, not found free in nature, but in compounds; *calcium carbide*, formed by electrical heating of carbon and lime, used for production of acetylene gas for lighting.

calculable, adj. [1. kálkūlabl; 2. kǽlkjuləbl], fr. Fr. *calculable*, Lat. *calcul-(āre)*, see **calculate,** & **-able.** Capable of being calculated; ascertainable by calculation; hence, deducible from given data; to be reckoned upon as likely to happen.

calculate, vb. trans. [1. kálkūlāt; 2. kǽlkjuleit]. Lat. *calculāt-(um)*, P.P. type of *calculāre*, 'to reckon, compute, by means of a **calculus**'. **1.** To reckon, compute, by mathematical processes, esp. by arithmetic; (also intrans. with *upon, on*), to be sure of, rely upon: *you cannot calculate upon fine weather.* **2.** To ascertain by mathematical process date of recurring movements of heavenly bodies, eclipses, phases of the moon &c. **3.** **a** To plan, fit, adapt for particular purpose: *these laws are not calculated for modern conditions*; hence, **b** to act, speak, design something deliberately and of set purpose, esp. in P.P.: *a calculated lie, insult, crime* &c. 4. (colloq., U.S.A.) To draw an inference, suppose, presume, believe: *I calculate we're going to have thunder.*

calculating, adj. [1. kálkūlāting; 2. kǽlkjuleitiŋ], fr. Pres. Part. of prec. 1. Making a calculation: *a calculating machine*, one that performs arithmetical and other processes automatically. 2. Shrewd, cautious: *a calculating mind*; (often in bad sense) cunning, scheming.

calculation, n. [1. kàlkūlā́shun; 2. kælkjuléiʃən]. See **calculate** & **-ion**. 1. a Act, process, of calculating or reckoning; b that which is calculated, result of an arithmetical or other process. 2. Forethought, plan, scheme: *done without calculation.*

calculus, n. [1. kálkūlus; 2. kǽlkjuləs]. Lat., 'a pebble, small stone', dimin. of *calx*, 'stone' &c., q.v. under **calcareous**. The Lat. word was applied to a counter used in playing draughts, further, to a stone used for reckoning, and hence to a reckoning, computation. 1. (med.) Limy deposit forming a stone in some part of the body; e.g. in the kidneys or bladder. 2. (math.) Mode of calculation; e.g. *integral calculus.*

caldarium, n. [1. kaldárium; 2. kældéəriəm]. Lat., fr. neut. form of *cal(i)dārius*, 'warm', fr. *calidus*, 'hot'; see **cauldron**. (archaeol.) Hot room in Roman bath.

caldron. See **cauldron**.

calefacient, n. & adj. [1. kàlifā́sient; 2. kælifeíʃiənt]. Lat. Pres. Part. *calefacient-(em)*, 'growing, making warm', of *calefacio*, fr. *caleo*, 'be hot, glow with heat', connected w. *calidus*, 'hot', q.v. under **cauldron**, & *facere*, 'make', see **fact**. (med.) Producing heat.

calefactory, n. & adj. [1. kàlefákturi; 2. kælifǽktəri]. Same meaning as prec. & w. same derivation (except that *-fact-* is fr. P.P. type of *facere*), & adj. suff. *-ōrius*, see **-ory**.

calembour, n. [1. kalombōōr; 2. kalābūr]. Fr. word. Pun.

calendar (I.), n. [1. kálendar; 2. kǽlində]. O. Fr. *calendier*, Lat. *calendārium*, 'account book of interest' kept by money-changers; so called because interest was due on the *calendae* or first day of the month. See further under **calends**. 1. System for fixing the beginning, end, and principal days of the year. 2. a Almanac; list of days, months, saints' days, and other church festivals and fasts &c. of a given year; b special list of important days throughout the year, adapted for certain classes, or interests, when certain events, public meetings, examinations &c. are held, as *university calendar*, or when certain operations should be performed (e.g. sowing of certain crops &c.), as in a *gardener's calendar*. 3. List or index of official documents contained in a given collection, e.g. charters, state papers, rolls &c., giving date of each document and brief abstract of its contents.

calendar (II.), vb. trans., fr. prec. To make list or index of official or other documents with dates and abstracts. See prec. 3.

calender (I.), n. & vb. trans. [1. kálender; 2. kǽlində]. Cp. Fr. *calandre*, 'machine for smoothing and polishing paper or cloth', fr. Med. Lat. *celendra*, prob. popular form of *cylindrus*, fr. Gk. *kúlindros*, 'roller', see **cylinder**. a n. Machine with rollers for smoothing and polishing cloth, paper &c.; b vb., to submit cloth to the process of smoothing. In Cowper's 'John Gilpin' the word is used of the tradesman who treats cloth in this way; the normal form would be *calenderer.*

calender (II.), n., fr. Pers. *qalender*. A wandering, mendicant dervish.

calends, n. pl. [1. kálendz; 2. kǽləndz]. Found already in form *cālend*, 'month, allotted span of life', in O.E., fr. Lat. *calendae*, *kalendae*, wh. has been reborrowed in M.E. The Lat. word means the first day of the month, so called because these dates were 'called out' or proclaimed publicly. The base **kal-* is seen in Lat. *calāre*, 'proclaim, convoke', also in *clāmor*, 'a shout' &c. (see **clamour**), *clārus* (see **clear**); Gk. *kaléō*, 'call', & O.E. *hlōwan*, 'to low', are also cognates. See **low** (I.). The base has nothing to do with Engl. **call**. Phr. *Greek calends*, a date or occasion which never comes.

calenture, n. [1. kálentūr; 2. kǽlintjə]. Fr., fr. Span. *calentura*, derived fr. Lat. Pres. Part. type *calent-(em)*, fr. *calēre*, 'to be hot', see **cauldron**. Tropical fever, attended with delirium, due to exposure to excessive heat.

calescence, n. [1. kalésens; 2. kəlésəns], fr. Lat. *calescent-(em)*, Pres. Part. type of *calescere*, 'to grow hot', fr. *calēre*, 'to be hot'. See **cauldron**. Increasing heat or warmth.

calf (I.), n. [1. kahf; 2. kāf]. O.E. (W.S.) *ċealf*, Anglian *calf*; Common Gmc., O.H.G. *chalb*, Mod. Germ. *kalb*, Goth. *kalbō*, 'calf, heifer', O.N. *kalfr*. The Aryan base is **gʷelbh-* &c., the fundamental meaning of wh. was 'to swell out'. The meaning has been differentiated into 'that which is swelled', & 'that which causes the swelling'. The former survives in Gk. *delphús*, 'womb, belly', Goth. *kilþei*, 'womb', Scrt. *gárbhaś*, 'womb', also 'fruit of the womb, foetus', Lat. *galba*, a Gaulish word, 'fat paunch'; the latter in *calf* &c., & Gk. *délphax*, 'young pig'. Cp. also **calf** (II.). The orig. meaning of the Gmc. words, then, is 'a young animal fresh from the womb'. 1. The young of the cow; applied also to the young of hippopotamus, rhinoceros, seal, whale, and moose-deer. 2. Leather made from skin of the calf, used for boots and bookbinding. Phr. *bound in calf*. 3. Undeveloped, foolish, loutish young man. Phr. *calf love*, transitory affection of immature youth for one of opposite sex.

calf (II.), n. Cp. O.N. *kalfi*, 'calf of leg'. This word is fr. same base as **calf** (I.), & shows the primary meaning 'swell'. The fleshy part of the leg of human beings at the back of the shin-bone between the knee and the ankle.

calf's-foot, n. [1. káhvz foot; 2. kā́vz fut]. Dish made from feet of calves boiled and seasoned.

calf's-foot jelly, n. Jelly made from gelatinous substance in calves' feet strained out after boiling.

Caliban, n. [1. káliban; 2. kǽlibæn], fr. character in Shakespeare's 'Tempest'. See **cannibal**. An ugly semi-human monster; an ugly, ill-shapen, brutal man.

calibrate, vb. trans. [1. kálibrāt; 2. kǽlibreit], fr. **calibre** & **-ate**. 1. To ascertain the internal diameter of gun-barrel or other tube. 2. To determine and verify the scale of a measuring instrument with a standard.

calibration, n. [1. kàlibrā́shun; 2. kælibréiʃən]. Prec. & **-ion**. Accurate measurement and testing of the calibre of a gun &c., also of scale of instrument by a standard.

calibre, n. [1. káliber, kalḗber; 2. kǽlibə, kəlíbə]. Fr., but further origin doubtful; perh. fr. Arab. *qālib*, 'mould, model'. 1. a Diameter of bore of a rifle or cannon; b diameter of bullet or shell. 2. (fig.) Extent, capacity, quality, of mind or character: *a man of poor, excellent, calibre.*

calicle, n. [1. kálikl; 2. kǽlikl]. Lat. *caliculus*, 'little cup', dimin. of **calyx**. Small cup-like cavity, as the hollows in structure of coral.

calico, n. [1. káliko; 2. kǽlikou]. Spelt *calicut*, *calecut* in 16th cent., the name being derived fr. Calicut in the E. Indies. The Mod. Engl. form prob. derived through Fr. *calicot*. A fine cotton cloth originally of India, now generally of European make.

calico-ball, n. A fancy-dress ball or dance at which only cotton dresses are worn.

calico-printer, n. One who follows the trade of stamping coloured figures or patterns on calico.

calicular, adj. [1. kalíkūlar; 2. kəlíkjulə]. See **calicle** & **-ar**. Having the form of a calicle.

calipash, calipee, n. [1. kálipash, kálipē; 2. kǽlipæʃ, kǽlipī]. Prob. W. Indian words. See **carapace**. The 'fat', or gelatinous substance, found inside the turtle's shell, regarded as a dainty. *Calipash* is dull green in colour, *calipee*, palish yellow.

caliper. See **cal(l)iper**.

caliph, n. [1. kā́lif, kálif; 2. kéilif, kǽlif]. Found in M.E., derived through Fr. *caliphe*, fr. Arab. *khalīfah*, 'successor', fr. *khalafa*, 'to succeed'. Title given to the descendants and successors of Mahomet as spiritual and temporal rulers; claimed by Sultans of Turkey, who held it simply by right of conquest; the title is now in abeyance.

caliphate, n. [1. kálifāt, kálifāt; 2. kéilifeit, kǽlifeit]. Through Fr. fr. Arab. *khilafat*. The office, dignity, and jurisdiction of a caliph.

calk. See **caulk**.

calkin, n. [1. kál-, káwkin; 2. kǽl-, kṓkin], fr. O. Fr. *calcain*, Lat. *calcāneum*, 'heel', fr. *calx*, 'heel'. See **calceolaria**. Turned-down portions at ends of horse's shoe which project and give the animal a grip on the ground and prevent slipping.

call (I.), vb. intrans. & trans. [1. kawl; 2. kōl]. O.E. *callian* (W.S. *ceallian*), 'shout', O.H.G. *kallōn*, 'talk loudly', O.N. *kalla*, 'name, call'. The most obvious cogn. outside Gmc. is Lat. *gallus*, 'cock', fr. **gal-nos*. The base is widespread in the Slav. languages: O. Slav. *glasŭ*, 'voice', Russ. *gólos*, 'voice', *golosit*, 'speak or sing loudly', Serb.-Croat. *glasa*, 'voice, news, call', *glásiti*, 'announce, tell, call' &c. See further under **gallinaceous** & **glory**. A. intrans. 1. To shout, cry out, utter words in such a tone as to attract attention, and with deliberate purpose of so doing: *I thought I heard someone calling*; *did you call, sir?*; (often specif.) to summon help: *I called and called but no one came to my assistance*. *Call out*, cry or shout loudly, as when in pain, or in summoning help. 2. To pay a brief visit at another's house: *we have only been here a month, and very few neighbours have called yet*; *I was out when he called*. *To call at (a house)*; *call on (a person)*. B. trans. 1. a To summon by means of the voice, esp. by crying out loudly: *he is near enough to hear you if you call him*; b to summon in any way, as by sending note or message, or by a signal of any kind: *I've broken my leg, call the doctor*; *call a cab*; *the airship kept calling us by wireless*. Phrs. *to call the banns*, announce or publish banns of marriage in church; *call a halt*, demand cessation of activities; *call a meeting*, issue notices desiring attendance of members of a deliberative or legislative body; *call a person over the coals*, rebuke, blame for something; *call attention to*, indicate, point out; *call a man to the bar*, summon to bar of court, i.e. to make him a barrister; *call into being, existence*, create, produce; *call to mind*, remember; *call in question*, throw doubt upon; *call to order*, demand orderly conduct at public meeting (action of chairman); *call the time*, determine and direct course of events, have control of actions. 2. a To give a name to, as in baptism: *to call one's child John*; (in pass.) to go by, have the name of; b to designate, indicate, distinguish by a certain name or nickname: *our butler's name is Brown but we always call him Dawkins*; *the woodpecker is called the yaffle in some parts of the country*. Phrs. *to call a person names*, to abuse, insult him; *to call a spade a spade*, or *call things by their names*, to speak plainly and without mincing matters; use strong language; *call cousin with*, claim relationship with (a person). 3. To rouse from sleep, awaken, summon to rise from bed: *don't forget to call me at 8 o'clock*. 4. To consider as being, or as equivalent, or approximate to: *I call this a very good house*; *you may call it twenty miles from here to Oxford*. Phr. *to have nothing to call one's own*, to be penniless, possess nothing. 5. To summon authoritatively to a particular office or duty, as to the ministry of the Christian Church, to a responsible position in the state &c.

C. Special uses with prepositions. *Call away,* summon away, call a person from place where he is to that from which summons comes; *call back,* recall, summon to return; *call down,* invoke from above: *call down a blessing upon one*; cause to descend: *his wickedness called down Divine wrath*; *call for,* demand, require: *the occasion called for instant and drastic measures*; visit a person with a view to accompanying him to another place; *call forth,* bring out, elicit: *the crisis called forth all his energies*; *call in,* a give orders for return of (e.g. of worn coin to Mint); b demand payment of (debts); c summon, request attendance of: *to call in a doctor*; *call on,* pay visit to (a person); apply to a person for particular service: *call on one for a speech* &c.; *call off,* divert, summon away from; give signal to discontinue an attack; *call out,* summon to activity, mobilize (armed forces); challenge to fight; *call over* (*names*), read out names in order to ascertain who is present at a gathering; *call up,* a summon to one's presence; b summon to join a military unit; c summon on telephone by giving registered number to operator; d (fig.) imagine, form, evoke, mental picture of event, or person: *call up visions of the past.*

call (II.), n., fr. prec. 1. A cry, shout; cry uttered for purpose of attracting attention, esp. a summons for help made by the voice. Phr. *within call,* close at hand, within hearing. 2. a Summons made by signal of any kind, e.g. by flags, telephone, wireless &c.; Phr. *a close call,* narrow escape; b reading out of list of names in public so as to discover absentees. 3. a Summons or invitation to undertake particular duty: *a call to a bishopric, professorial chair* &c.; specif., *call to the Bar*; b inward conviction that one should undertake a certain office (esp. that of the Christian ministry); vocation. 4. Short visit paid by a one person at the house of another, or by tradesman &c. on regular round: *the baker's, postman's, call*; b by a ship at a port, or a train at a station. Phrs. *a place of call,* place at which regular calls are made; *house of call,* public house. 5. Necessity, obligation (often with neg.): *there is no call for you to worry over his affairs.* 6. Strong attraction, impulse towards, or in favour of something: *the call of the wild, the sea* &c. 7. Note or cry of birds or animals. 8. a Urgent demand, claim, for money or services: *to have many calls on one's income, on one's time*; b specif., authorized demand by financial concern, on shareholders, for payment of sums due in certain eventualities. 9. Signal made to partner in card games, by playing cards in particular order, that he should lead a certain suit: *a call for trumps.*

calla, n. [1. kála; 2. kǽlə]. Invented Lat. word. (bot.) a Genus of plants which includes the water-arum; b usually *calla-lily,* the arum lily.

callant, n. [1. kálant; 2. kǽlənt]. Provinc. Engl., fr. O. Fr. *calland,* cp. Fr. (different dial.) *chaland,* 'customer'. The etymol. of this is very obscure. A lad, young fellow.

call-boy, n. **call** (I.) & **boy.** Boy employed at a theatre to 'call' the actors when it is time for them to go on the stage.

caller (I.), n. [1. káwler; 2. kɔ̄lə], fr. **call** (I.) & **-er.** Specif., one who pays a visit. Cp. **call** (II.) 4.

caller (II.), adj. [1. káler; 2. kǽlə]. Scots; etymol. doubtful. a Fresh, not stale (of herrings &c.); b cool, fresh, brisk (of wind, weather &c.).

calligraphy, n. [1. kalígrafi; 2. kælígrəfi]. Gk. *kállos,* 'beauty', & **-graphy**; Gk. *kállos,* fr. **kʷalwos,* & *kalós* (*kalli-* in composition), 'beautiful', are cogn. w. Scrt. *kalyaš,* 'healthy', & *kalyā́naš,* 'beautiful, agreeable, wholesome'. Beautiful writing; handwriting generally.

calling, n. [1. káwling; 2. kɔ̄liŋ]. See **call** (I.) & **-ing.** Occupation, profession, trade, vocation.

cal(l)iper, n. [1. káliper; 2. kǽlipə]. Prob. variant of **calibre.** Usually in pl. (*pair of callipers*). Instrument resembling a pair of compasses, with two legs, usually curved, which, fastened together at one end by a hinge, can be adjusted at varying distances apart, for measuring thickness or diameter of objects, or distance between two opposite surfaces, e.g. the walls of a box.

cal(l)isthenic, adj. [1. kàlisthénik; 2. kælisþénik]. See next word. Belonging to callisthenics.

cal(l)isthenics, n. pl. [1. kàlisthéniks; 2. kælisþéniks], fr. Gk. *kalli-,* q.v. under **calligraphy,** & *sthénos,* 'strength'. Concerning the origin of the second element the etymologists can cast very little light. Art and practice of bodily exercises calculated to produce strength and grace.

callosity, n. [1. kalósiti; 2. kælɔ́siti]. Fr. *callosité,* 'hardening of the skin', fr. Lat. *callus,* 'hardened skin', & common suff. *-itāt-,* q.v. under **-ity.** Cp. also *callōsus,* adj., 'thick-skinned'. There is possibly a distant connexion w. Lat. *clādēs,* 'disaster, defeat', wh. is gen. derived fr. Aryan base **kel-* &c., 'strike', see **clado-.** The development of meaning of *callus* &c. in this case wd. be 'blow, wound, scar, hardening of skin as result of blow' &c. Hardening, hard lump on the skin, from friction, esp. on hands, feet, and horses' legs.

callous, adj. [1. kálus; 2. kǽləs]. Lat. *callōsus.* See prec. & **-ous.** 1. Hardened (of skin). 2. (fig.) Morally insensitive, hardhearted, indifferent to suffering of others.

callously, adv. Prec. & **-ly.** In a callous manner (in fig. sense).

callousness, n. See prec. & **-ness.** State, quality, of being callous.

callow, adj. [1. kálō; 2. kǽlou]. O.E. *calu,* 'bald, bare' (of boughs &c.), O.H.G. *kalo,* Mod. Germ. *kahl.* It now seems certain that the Gmc. words are not borrowed fr. Lat. *calvus,* 'bald', as formerly supposed, but are orig. Gmc. words & cogn. w. a large group of words in Slav., e.g. O. Slav. *golŭ,* 'naked', Russ. *gol,* 'naked, bare, bald', Slovene, *gol,* 'naked, bald, immature', & *goləs,* 'beardless boy, unfledged bird'. The above & other related words in the Slav. languages have a meaning very much akin to that of the Mod. Engl. word. 1. Bare, esp. of unfledged birds; chiefly in Phr. *callow brood, young* &c. 2. (fig.) Raw, undeveloped, inexperienced (of boys and very young men); derived from sense of 'beardless': *callow youth* (applied both to a young man, and to his time of life).

callus, n. [1. kálus; 2. kǽləs]. See **callosity.** (med.) Thickened and hardened skin or soft fleshy tissue; bony lump formed round broken bone when healing.

calm (I.), n. [1. kahm; 2. kām]. Fr. *calme,* adj., fr. Ital. or Span. *calma,* 'absence of wind, tranquillity', fr. Gk. *kaûma,* 'burning heat of sun, fever'. In Fr. & Engl. the word seems to have been primarily an adj. & the n. to have been derived fr. this, though in Ital. &c. the n. comes first, as is natural fr. the Gk. word. The *-l-* may be due to association w. the Lat. words *calēre,* 'to be hot', *calidus,* 'hot', *caldor, calor,* 'heat', wh. are fr. base **k̑elē-,* & related to Lith. *szilaũ,* 'become warm', *szìltas,* 'warm', & more remotely to O.E. *hlēowan,* 'become warm'. See **cauldron** & **lukewarm.** The Gk. *kaûma* is related to *kaiō,* 'I become hot', wh. is fr. **kawjō,* fr. base **kʷēw-* &c., 'glow', cogn. w. Goth. *haúri* (fr. **hurja-*), 'coal' &c. a Atmospheric condition of windlessness when ships cannot sail; b (fig.) peacefulness, tranquillity of mind, or in social and political affairs. Phr. *the calm before the storm* (lit. and fig.). The noun is less used than the adjective in English.

calm (II.), adj. See prec. 1. Quiet, peaceful; a (of weather) Devoid of wind; b (of the sea, or waters of a lake) still, not in violent movement, smooth, unruffled; c (of bodily condition, esp. of movements of heart, pulses, breathing) quiet, regular. 2. (fig.) a (of the mind and temper) Not agitated; peaceful, free from excitement, under control, restrained; leisurely; b also of persons possessing such state or qualities of mind; c (of political and social conditions) peaceful, free from disputes, war, riots. 3. (colloq.) Casual, too easy-going; hence, impertinent, presuming: *it was rather calm of him to expect me to take so much trouble for a stranger.*

calm (III.), vb. trans. & intrans., fr. prec. To render calm, to tranquillize (physically or mentally); pacify. *Calm down*: a trans., to soften, assuage (anger, rage, excitement); b intrans., to become calm after violent agitation (of the sea, the human temper, human beings, political conditions &c.).

calmative, n. [1. káhmativ; 2. kā́mətiv]. Prec. & **-ative.** (med.) That which calms, a sedative.

calmly, adv. [1. káhmli; 2. kā́mli]. **calm** (II.) & **-ly.** In a calm manner; a quietly, without showing emotion; b coolly, with casualness.

calmness, n. [1. káhmnes; 2. kā́mnis]. See prec. & **-ness.** The quality of being calm.

calomel, n. [1. kálōmel; 2. kǽloumel]. Fr., fr. Gk. *kalós,* 'fair', see first element of **calligraphy,** & *mélas,* 'black', see first element of **melancholy.** Perhaps so called because it is a white substance, though prepared from a dark one. (med.) Preparation of mercury, used as a purgative.

calorescence, n. [1. kàlorésens; 2. kælərésəns]. Should be *calescence,* Lat. *calescere,* Pres. Part. *calescent-(em),* 'to grow hot', but formed on anal. of type *calor-,* see **calori-.** (phys.) Transference of light rays into heat rays.

calori-, pref. Form used in compounds fr. Lat. *calor,* 'heat', q.v. under **calm** (I.).

calorie, n. [1. kálori; 2. kǽləri]. Fr. See prec. Unit of heat; specif., in relation to the value of food.

calorifacient, adj. & n. [1. kàlorifáshient; 2. kæləriféiʃiənt], fr. **calori-** & Lat. Pres. Part. *facient-,* 'making'. See **fact.** a adj. Heat-producing; b n., substance producing heat.

calorific, adj. [1. kàlorífik; 2. kælərífik]. Fr. *calorifique,* Lat. *-ficus,* fr. *fac-,* 'make'. See prec. & **fact.** Heat-producing; pertaining to heat: *calorific properties of coke.*

calorification, n. [1. kalórifikáshun; 2. kælɔ̀rifikéiʃn]. Prec. & **-ation.** Production of (esp. animal) heat.

calorifics, n. [1. kalorífiks; 2. kælərífiks]. See **calorific.** The doctrine or science of heat.

calorimeter, n. [1. kalorímeter; 2. kælɔrímitə]. **calori-** & **-meter.** Apparatus for measuring amount of heat developed by combustion or friction.

calotte, n. [1. kalót; 2. kælɔ́t]. Fr., fr. Ital. *calotta,* prob. fr. Gk. *kalúptra,* 'woman's veil'. Meyer-Lübke points out that the word is earlier & more widespread than Fr. *cale,* whence our **caul,** fr. wh. *calotte* &c. is derived by some etymologists. The above Gk. n. is fr. vb. *kalúptō,* 'I cover, conceal', wh. is cogn. w. Lat. *oc-culo,* 'cover'. See **occult.** Small skull-cap worn chiefly by ecclesiastics.

caltrop, n. [1. kál-, káwltrup; 2. kǽl-, kɔ̄ltrəp]. The forms *colte-træppe, -trippe, calca-træppe,* a plant-name, kind of thorn, are found in O.E. *Colte* is a 'colt', see **colt,** *calca* is a Lat. loan-word for 'heel', see **calceolaria**; evidently popular etymol. was at work early in producing the doublet. The second element = **trap.** 1. Small instrument used in mediaeval warfare for laming horses, consisting of a small iron ball with three or four spikes so arranged that one always projected outwards. They were scattered over the ground where enemy cavalry had to pass. 2. (bot.) Kind of plant, having spines on head of the flower or fruit.

calumet, n. [1. kálūmet; 2. kǽljumet]. Fr. dimin. of Lat. *calamus,* 'reed'. See **calamary** & **haulm.** Pipe with long stem, smoked on ceremonial occasions by North American Indians; also called *pipe of peace.*

calumniate, vb. trans. [1. kalúmniāt; 2. kəlámnieit]. See **calumny** & **-ate**. To slander, bring false accusation against, malign.

calumniation, n. [1. kalùmniā́shun; 2. kəlàmniéiʃn]. Prec. & **-ion**. Act of slandering.

calumniator, n. [1. kalúmniāter; 2. kəlámnieitə]. One who brings false charge.

calumnious, adj. [1. kalúmnius; 2. kəlámniəs]. See **calumny** & **-ous**. Pertaining to, smacking of, calumny.

calumny, n. [1. kálumni; 2. kǽləmni]. Fr. *calomnie*, Lat. *calumnia*, 'intrigue, trick; false accusation', connected w. *calvor*, 'devise tricks, deceive'; cp. also Gk. *kēlis*, 'stain, disgrace', *kēléō*, 'bewitch, seduce, beguile'; further, in Gmc., Goth. *hōlōn*, 'deceive', O.E. *hōl*, 'slander'. Slander, false accusation, unjust description of a person.

calvary, n. [1. kálvari; 2. kǽlvəri]. Lat. *calvāria*, 'skull', fr. *calva*, 'hairless scalp'; Gk. *kelébē*, 'cup, drinking-vessel', fr. **kalébē*, Aryan **kalᵊgʷā*. Lat. *calvus*, 'bald', gen. associated w. these words, has prob. nothing to do w. them. **1.** Place of the Crucifixion; a translation of Heb. *gulgōleth*, 'skull', Gk. form *golgothá*. **2.** Representation of the Crucifixion, consisting of three crosses or crucifixes representing the Saviour and the two thieves placed together in the open air, generally on a high place.

calve, vb. intrans. & trans. [1. kahv; 2. kāv]. O.E. *calfian*. See **calf (I.)**. **1.** intrans. To bring forth, give birth to, a calf. **2.** trans. (of glaciers and icebergs) To shed, part with, a portion.

Calvinism, n. [1. kálvinizm; 2. kǽlvinizəm], fr. John Calvin, 1509-64, & **-ism**. System of theology and religious doctrine devised by Calvin; adherence to Calvin's views and doctrines.

Calvinist, n. [1. kálvinist; 2. kǽlvinist]. See prec. & **-ist**. Member of Calvin's sect; one whose religious opinions resemble those of Calvin.

Calvinistic, adj. [1. kalvinístik; 2. kælvinístik]. Prec. & **-ic**. Belonging to, agreeing with, Calvinism.

calvities, n. [1. kalvíshiēz; 2. kælvíʃiīz]. Lat. 'baldness', fr. *calvus*, 'bald'; cogn. w. Scrt. *kulvaś*, 'bald'. (med.) Baldness.

calx, n. [1. kalks; 2. kælks]. Lat. word, 'stone, lime'. See first element of **calcareous**. Residual earthy powder left when a metal or mineral has been burnt.

calyc-, calyci-, pref. Forms of **calyx**, used in compounds. Used in botanical names.

calyx, n. [1. kāliks; 2. kéiliks]. Lat., fr. Gk. *kálux*, 'cup, outer envelope, calyx, of a flower, bud'; cogn. w. Gk. *kúlix*, 'cup', Scrt. *kalikā*, 'flower-bud', *kaláśaś*, 'pot, cup'. Outer series of leaves, forming a cup, from which the petals of a flower spring.

cam, n. [1. kam; 2. kæm]. Du. *kam*, 'comb', cogn. w. **comb**. (mechan.) Projecting portion from edge of wheel which gives desired peculiar motion to another wheel or roller which moves against edge of first wheel.

camaraderie, n. [1. kàmaráhderē; 2. kæ̀mərádəri]. Fr. See **comrade**. Lit. 'comradeship'; good will, intimacy, mutual trust and helpfulness, as among comrades.

camarilla, n. [1. kàmarélya; 2. kæ̀mərílja]. Span. dimin. of Lat. *camera*, 'room'. See **camera**. Originally a 'little chamber', esp. a private audience chamber in royal palace; hence, group of persons meeting privately; political clique, caucus, cabal.

camber, n. [1. kámber; 2. kǽmbə]. Fr. *cambrer*, 'to curve, bend', Lat. *camerāre*, 'to arch', fr. *camera*, 'arch, vault', see **camera**. Slight convexity, or curve, on surface of a road, beam, floor, or deck.

cambist, n. [1. kámbist; 2. kǽmbist]. Fr. *cambiste*, 'changer', fr. Lat. *cambium*, 'exchange'. Cp. **cambium** & **change**. **a** One who deals in bills of exchange; **b** an expert in theory of exchanges.

cambium, n. [1. kámbium; 2. kǽmbiəm]. Lat. word meaning 'change'; the related vb. *cambīre*, *cambiāre*, is a Celt. loan-word, cp. O. Ir. *cimb*, 'tribute'. Further light is lacking. See **change**, **excambion**. Soft formative tissue of annual growth between wood and bark in large roots, stems, and boughs of trees, from which both wood and bark originate.

cambrel, n. [1. kámbrel; 2. kǽmbrəl]. Etymol. dubious. Possibly fr. W. *cam-*, 'bent', & *pren*, 'wood'. Piece of bent, shaped wood used by butchers for hanging carcases by the legs.

Cambrian, adj. & n. [1. kámbrian; 2. kǽmbriən], fr. Lat. *Cambria*, 'Wales', fr. Celt. *Cymru*. (geol.) **a** adj. Of system of rocks lying below the Silurian, the earliest of palaeozoic rocks; **b** n., such rocks.

cambric, n. [1. kā́mbrik; 2. kéimbrik], fr. Kamerijk, Flemish form of name of town in Flanders, better known by French name Cambrai. Fine white linen cloth.

came, vb. [1. kām; 2. keim]. Pret. of **come**. M.E. *cām*, fr. earlier *cam*, w. vowel lengthened through the influence of the long vowel of the Pret. pl. *cōmen*. The O.E. Pret. sing. is *c(w)ōm*; the M.E. form *cam* is perh. on the anal. of *nam*, Pret. sing. of *niman*, 'to take'.

camel, n. [1. kámel; 2. kǽməl]. Heb. *gāmāl*, cogn. w. Arab. *jamala*, 'to carry', through Lat. *camēlus*, fr. Gk. *kámēlos*; forms in M.E. are *camel*, *camail*, *chamel* &c. Large Asiatic hornless, ruminant quadruped with a long neck, thick hairy coat, large flat feet with hard soles, and either one (Arabian variety or dromedary) or two humps (Bactrian variety); much used in desert country, both for riding and carrying burdens.

cameleer, n. [1. kameléːr; 2. kæməlíə]. Prec. & **-eer**. Camel driver.

camellia, n. [1. kamélya; 2. kəmílјə]. Named after Jesuit traveller, Joseph Kamel. Evergreen Chinese and Japanese shrub, with large red or white flower resembling a rose in form.

camelopard, n. properly [1. kàmélōpàrd; 2. kæ̀méloupàd]; now usually in jocose form [1. kámel-lépard; 2. kǽməl-lépəd]. Lat. *camelopardus*. See **camel** & **pard**. Hardly ever used in old sense applied to giraffe. With second pronunciation given above sometimes used colloquially for a tall, scraggy, ungraceful woman.

camelry, n. [1. kámelri; 2. kǽməlri]. See **camel** & **-ry**. **a** Train of camels; **b** soldiers mounted on camels.

camel's hair, n. & adj. **a** Hair of camel woven into cloth; also used for painters' brushes (now usually of hair of squirrel's tail); **b** the cloth itself; **c** adj., made of camel's hair: *camel's-hair brush*.

Camembert, n. [1. kámembār; 2. kǽməmbɛə]. Name of village in Normandy. Soft, rich, strong-smelling, but delicately flavoured cheese.

cameo, n. [1. kámeō; 2. kǽmiou]. Ital. *caméo*, fr. Med. Lat. *cammaeus*. Origin unknown. Carved gem, esp. agate, sardonyx, or shell, in which the figure is cut in relief in one layer, the next, usually of different colour, serving as background.

cameo ware, n. Pottery with figures moulded in relief on ground of different colour, such as was designed for Wedgwood by Flaxman.

camera, n. [1. kámera; 2. kǽmərə]. Lat., 'vault, arched roof, arch', fr. Gk. *kamára*, 'anything with an arched or vaulted roof or covering, covered carriage'; w. this, the native Lat. *camur*, 'crooked, bent inwards', is cogn.; further, Scrt. *kmárati*, 'to be bent, curved', &, w. different suff., O.H.G., O.S. *himil*, 'heaven', Mod. Germ. *himmel*. See also **chamber**. **1.** Legal, *in camera*, in judge's private room, privately. **2.** Photographic apparatus containing sensitive plate or film, and lens for directing and concentrating light rays upon it. **3.** *Camera obscura*, 'dark room', a darkened chamber in which by means of lens and reflectors in roof, the image of surrounding landscape and all it contains is reflected upon a white sheet.

camerlengo, n. [1. kàmerléngō; 2. kæ̀məléŋgou]. Ital., cogn. w. **chamberlain**. Papal chamberlain; cardinal in charge of papal treasury.

Cameronian, n. [1. kàmerṓnian; 2. kæ̀məróunjən]. From Richard Cameron, Scottish Covenanter, d. 1680. **1.** Follower of Cameron, believer in doctrines which he taught as founder of Reformed Presbyterian Church; member of sect which adheres to these. Also used as adj., pertaining to the sect or doctrines. **2.** (pl.) The old 26th Scottish Infantry Regiment in British Army, now 1st Battalion Scottish Rifles, as originally recruited from Cameron's followers.

camisole, n. [1. kámisōl; 2. kǽmisoul]. Fr., fr. Span. *camisole*, fr. Lat. *camisia*, q.v. under **chemise**. Woman's loose linen jacket worn under dress.

camisole de force, n. [1. kamisol de fors; 2. kamisol də fors]. Fr. Cp. prec. & **force**. Strait-jacket.

camlet, n. [1. kámlet; 2. kǽmlit]. Fr. *camelot*, orig. camel's-hair cloth, now cheap, shoddy woollen cloth. Prob. fr. **camel**. Originally a fine oriental woven material, now applied to various kinds of light inferior cloth.

camomile, n. [1. kámomīl; 2. kǽməmail]. Fr. *camomille*, fr. Lat. *chamomilla*, fr. Gk. *khamai*, 'on the ground', & *mēlon*, 'apple'; cp. first element of **chameleon** & **melon**. Aromatic plant, from flowers of which an infusion is made for medicinal purposes; *camomile tea*, infusion of camomile flowers.

camorra, n. [1. kamóra; 2. kæmɔ́rə]. Ital. Secret society at Naples, whose aims are partly political and partly criminal.

camouflage (I.), n. [1. kámooflahzh; 2. kǽmuflāž]. Fr., fr. vb. *camoufler*, 'disguise'; cp. *camouflet*, 'puff of smoke'. (Much used during Great War.) **1.** Disguise, or concealment of objects from the enemy, e.g. guns, ships, whereabouts of troops. **2.** Deception of any kind, whereby an object is made to look like something else, or concealed altogether.

camouflage (II.), vb. trans. See prec. To disguise, alter appearance of anything, conceal.

camp (I.), n. [1. kamp; 2. kæmp]. Fr., 'place where an army is located', fr. Ital. *campo*, in special sense, fr. Lat. *campus*, 'flat space, plain'. The real Fr. form of this word is *champ*, q.v. under **champaign**. The orig. meaning of the base whence *campus* is derived was 'curved, bent, crooked', & the Lat. word must first have meant 'undulating country', then 'valley', then 'flat space at the foot of hills'; numerous cognates in Gk. express idea of bending, winding &c.: *kampé*, 'winding of a river', *kámpsis*, 'bending, turning', *kampúlos*, 'bent, curved', *kámptein*, 'to bend, bow' &c.; cp. further, Lith. *kum̃pas*, 'crooked', O.H.G. *hamf*, Goth. *hamfs*, 'crippled', O.E. *hōfer*, 'hump, swelling'. Prob. related ultimately to the base seen in **camera**. **1. a** Open space in which tents or huts are placed as dwelling-places, esp. for military units; the collection of tents and huts erected for soldiers; **b** (fig., by extension) the adventurous, wandering, rough life of a soldier: *his experience lay rather in the camp than in the court*. **2.** Any temporary shelter erected nightly, or for a brief space, in the open air, for gipsies, hunters, travellers &c. to eat and sleep in. **3.** (fig., fr. **1, a**) Group of persons sharing same ideals, religious or political views, or jointly supporting a cause, or body of doctrines of any kind: *Gladstone and Disraeli were always in different camps*. Phr. *in the same camp*, on the same side.

camp (II.), vb. intrans., fr. prec. **1.** To form, build, place a camp of any kind. **2.** To lodge temporarily, as a makeshift, under uncomfortable conditions, pending complete installation, as in partly furnished house; often *camp out*, to sleep in open air with or without tent or hut.

campagna, n. [1. kampáhnya; 2. kæmpánja]. Ital., fr. Lat. *Campānia*, name of district, fr. *campāneus*, 'belonging to a campus, or open country'. See **camp (I.)**. Tract of open country, esp. the undulating plain in neighbourhood of Rome.

campaign, n. & vb. intrans. [1. kàmpân; 2. kæmpéin]. Fr. *campagne*, 'open country'. Same word as **campagna** & **champaign**, fr. Lat. *campus* & adj. suff. *-āneus*. **1.** n. **a** Series of military actions in the field, continuously conducted with definite objective in view: *the Waterloo campaign*; **b** organized, preconcerted action of any kind for attainment of particular purpose: *a political campaign*. **2.** vb. To go, serve on, organize a campaign, military or political. Phr. *to go campaigning*.

campaigner, n. [1. kampâner; 2. kæmpéinə]. Prec. & **-er**. One who has experience in military operations. Phr. *an old campaigner*, an experienced old hand.

campanile, n., Ital. pl. **campanili** [1. kàmpanéle, -ē; 2. kæmpəníle, -ī]. Ital., 'bell-tower', fr. Low Lat. *campana*, 'bell'. Etymol. uncertain. Detached tower of considerable height in which bells are hung.

campanologist, n. [1. kàmpanólojist; 2. kæmpənólədžist]. Next word & **-ist**. One who studies bells, their founding and ringing.

campanology, n. [1. kàmpanóloji; 2. kæmpənólədži]. Cp. **campanile**; fr. Low Lat. *campana* & **-logy**. Study and science of the founding and ringing of bells.

campanula, n. [1. kampánūla; 2. kæmpænjulə]. Mod. Lat. dimin. of *campana*, 'bell', see **campanile**. A genus of plants with bell-shaped flowers, including the harebell and Canterbury bell.

campanulate, adj. [1. kampánūlāt; 2. kæmpænjuleit]. Prec. & **-ate**. Bell-shaped.

camp-bed, n. See **camp (I.)** & **bed**. Narrow, folding, portable bed, occupying little space.

camp-chair, n. See **camp (I.)** & **chair**. Folding, portable chair, usually made of strips of canvas supported by sticks.

campeachy wood, n. [1. kampéchi wòod; 2. kæmpítʃi wùd], fr. Campeche, town in Mexico. Logwood.

camp-follower, n. See **camp (I.)** & **follower**. Non-military male or female hanger-on of army on the march.

camphor, n. [1. kámfer; 2. kǽmfə]. Ultimately fr. Arab. *kāfur*, through Fr., M.E. *camphere*, Mod. Fr. *camfre*. **a** Highly aromatic and volatile white transparent substance, obtained by distillation from various plants, esp. from the camphor-laurel of Formosa &c., used in medicine &c.; **b** (chem.) alcoholic derivative of terpenes.

camphorated, adj. [1. kámforāted; 2. kǽmfəreitid], as though fr. P.P. of *camphorate. Prec., & **-ate** & **-ed**. Impregnated with camphor: *camphorated oil*.

camphoric, adj. [1. kamfórik; 2. kæmfórik]. **camphor** & **-ic**. Of, containing, camphor.

campion, n. [1. kámpiun; 2. kǽmpiən]. Etymol. doubtful. General name for plants of the genus *Lychnis*, esp. that known as 'ragged robin'.

campo santo, n. [1. kámpō sántō; 2. kǽmpou sǽntou]. Ital., 'sacred field'. Cp. **camp** & **saint**. A cemetery.

camp-shot, n. Etymol. of first element doubtful; second element apparently as in **wainscot**. Timber facing to a weir, river-bank &c. made of piles and boarding, also called *camp-shed, camp-sheeting* &c.

camp-stool, n. See **camp (I.)** & **stool**. Folding seat of canvas and wood or metal, without back, easily carried.

campus, n. [1. kámpus; 2. kǽmpəs]. Lat., 'field', see **camp**. Term for the principal grounds of an American school or university.

camwood, n. [1. kámwood; 2. kǽmwud]. Etymol. unknown. Hard red wood from W. Africa yielding stain used in dyeing.

can (I.), auxil. Pret. Pres. vb. [1. kan; 2. kæn]. Exists in all Gmc. languages w. senses of 'know' & 'be able'. The vb. is defective & 'irregular' in the other Gmc. languages as in Engl. O.E. infin. *cunnan*, Pres. *ic cann*, pl. *wē cunnon*. The word is cogn. w. Lat. *gnōscō*, 'know', & Gk. *gi-gnṓskō*. See also **could** & **ken, know**. (Always followed by vb. in infin.) **1.** To be able, in sense **a** to have intellectual capacity to do something: *he can learn anything with the greatest ease*, or **b** to possess physical power of doing something: *he can run a mile in less than five minutes*. **2.** To be, or feel, morally justified in an action: *I can hardly go away and leave you all alone*. **3.** To have permission to do something: *you can go away as soon as you like*. **4.** Construction with following verb suppressed: *God alone can all things = can do* &c. Negative forms: *cannot* [1. kánot; 2. kǽnɔt], (colloq.) *can't* [1. kahnt; 2. kānt].

can (II.), n. O.E. *canne*, gloss to Lat. *crātēr*, 'cup', M.E. *canne*, 'jar, drinking-vessel'; common W. Gmc.; M.H.G. *kanna*, O.H.G. *channa*, Mod. Germ. *kanne*; also O.N. *kanna*. The word appears to be native Gmc., & not borrowed, as formerly suggested, fr. Gk. *kántharos*, 'drinking-cup'. **a** Vessel for holding and carrying liquids, generally of iron, tin, or copper, with a spout for pouring, and two handles, one circular over the top for carrying or lifting, and the other on the side for directing stream from spout; **b** small tin vessel used by workmen for carrying tea &c., also used to drink from.

can (III.), vb. trans., fr. prec. To put into a can or tin; specif., to preserve meat, fruit, and other foods by enclosing them in air-tight tin box.

Canadian canoe. See **canoe**.

canaille, n. [1. kanîe; 2. kænáij]. Fr., fr. Ital. *canaglia*, lit. 'pack of hounds', O. Fr. *chenaille*. See **canine**. Contemptuous expression for lower orders; rabble, vulgar herd.

canal, n. [1. kanál; 2. kənǽl]. Fr., fr. Lat. *canālis*, 'water-pipe', formed fr. *canna*, 'reed', wh. is borrowed fr. Gk. *kánna*, 'reed'. The Gk. word is itself borrowed fr. Assyrian *kanū*, 'reed'. See **cane (I.)** & **channel**. **1.** Artificial water-way cut across land for navigation or irrigation. **2.** A channel, pipe, or course for liquids, esp. a duct or passage in animal body: *alimentary canal* &c.

canalization, n. [1. kànalīzáshun; 2. kǽnəlaizéiʃən]. **canalize** & **-ation**. **a** The making of canals; **b** system of canals.

canalize, vb. trans. [1. kánalīz; 2. kǽnəlaiz], fr. **canal** & **-ize**. To make into a canal, or system of canals; to adapt (river) by embanking, so as to form a canal or part of canal.

canard, n. [1. kanáhr; 2. kænā́(r)]. Fr. word for 'duck'; also 'false report'.

canariensis, n. [1. kanàriénsis; 2. kənèəriénsis], fr. **canary** & Lat. adj. suff. Canary-creeper.

canary, n. [1. kanâri; 2. kənéəri], fr. Canary Islands. **1.** A bright yellow bird with shrill, persistent song. **2.** Wine much drunk in England in 16th and 17th cent. Also as adj.: *canary bird*; *canary wine*.

canary-coloured, adj. Of bright, light yellow colour, resembling that of the bird.

canary-creeper, n. Trailing plant with bright yellow flowers; canariensis.

canaster, n. [1. kanáster; 2. kænǽstə]. Span. *canastro*, through Lat. *canistrum*, or direct fr. Gk. *kánastron*, 'wicker basket'. See **canister**. Kind of coarsely cut tobacco, so called from the rush basket originally used for packing.

can-can, n. [1. kán kan; 2. kǽn kæn]. Fr. A wild, extravagant kind of dance, with much kicking of the legs.

cancel (I.), vb. trans. [1. kánsl; 2. kǽnsl]. Lat. *cancellāre*, 'to make or enclose with a lattice; to cancel with cross-wise strokes', fr. *cancelli*, n. pl., 'place enclosed by railing or lattice', dimin. of *cancer*, 'lattice', late word wh. has nothing to do w. word for crab (see **cancer**), but developed by dissimilation fr. *carcer*, 'enclosure', hence 'prison'. This is cogn. w. O. E. *hearg*, 'hedge, enclosure, temple, or place of sacrifice', O.H.G. *harug*, O.N. *horgr*, w. same meaning, all starting fr. idea of 'space enclosed, set apart'. The starting-point of Lat. *cancelli* &c. is the lattice, or cross woodwork, by which the enclosure was accomplished. See also **chancel**, **chancellor**, **chancery**. To cross out, originally by drawing pen through written word; hence, obliterate, delete, do away with, abolish, make void. Used in various contexts: *to cancel debts*; *cancel permission, leave* &c. Specif. in arith., to strike out the same factor from numerator and denominator; also intrans., *cancel out*, of numbers &c.

cancel (II.), n., fr. prec. **a** Something suppressed or cancelled, e.g. printer's proof; **b** implement used in cancelling, as ticket-punch.

cancellated, adj. [1. kánselāted; 2. kǽnsəleitid]. Formed fr. Lat. *cancellātus*, 'latticed'. See **cancel** & **-ate**. Marked with cross-lines or ridges; reticulated.

cancellation, n. [1. kanseláshun; 2. kænsəléiʃən]. **cancel (I.)** & **-ation**. Act or fact of cancelling; abolition, annulment.

cancer, n. [1. kánser; 2. kǽnsə]. Lat., 'a crab', cogn. w. Gk. *karkínos*, 'crab', & Scrt. *karkaṡ*, 'hard'. **1.** One of the signs of the Zodiac: *Tropic of Cancer*, parallel of latitude N. of equator. See **tropic**. **2.** Malignant disease which attacks and destroys the tissues of the body. **3.** (fig.) Moral or social evil which corrodes and destroys like a cancer.

cancerous, adj. [1. kánserus; 2. kǽnsərəs], fr. prec. & **-ous**. **a** Belonging to, characteristic of, cancer; **b** liable to, suffering from, cancer.

cancroid, adj. [1. kángkroid; 2. kǽŋkrɔid], fr. Lat. *cancer*, see **cancer**, & Gk. suff. **-oid**, 'like'. **a** Like a crab; **b** like a cancer.

candelabrum, n., pl. **-a**; also **candelabra** as sing., pl. **-as** [1. kàndelâbrum, -áhbrum; 2. kændiléibrəm, -ā́brəm]. Lat. for 'candlestick'. Cp. **candle**. Large branched candlestick for holding three or more candles.

candescence, n. [1. kandésens; 2. kændésəns]. See next word & **-ence**. Bright glow, as of white-hot metal.

candescent, adj. [1. kandésent; 2. kændésənt], fr. Lat. Pres. Part. *candescent-(em)*, 'growing white', fr. *candescere*, freq. of *candēre*, 'shine, glow', cp. **candid**. Glowing as if white hot.

candid, adj. [1. kándid; 2. kǽndid]. Fr. *candide*, 'single-minded, honest', fr. Lat. *candidus*, 'white, glowing; beautiful; pure, honest, upright'. The fundamental meaning of the base is 'bright, shining, glowing'; Gk. *kándaros*, 'glowing coal', Scrt. *ćand-*, 'shine'. Cp. also Lat. *-cend-* as in *incendere*, 'set on fire'; see **incendiary**. Frank, honest, outspoken, telling the truth whether agreeable or not. Phr. *candid friend*, one who enjoys telling unpleasant truths; *to be perfectly, quite, candid*, not to mince words.

candidate, n. [1. kándidāt; 2. kǽndideit, -it]. Lat. *candidātus*, one aspiring to office who was clothed in a white toga. See **candid** & **-ate**. **a** One who offers himself for appointment to an office, election to parliament &c.; **b** a person thought likely to be considered for an office, although he does not offer himself for appointment.

candidature, n. [1. kándidàchur; 2. kǽndidèitʃə]. See prec. & **-ure**. Act or fact of standing, becoming candidate, for an appointment, election &c.

candidly, adv. [1. kándidli; 2. kǽndidli]. **candid** & **-ly**. In a candid manner; frankly, outspokenly.

candidness, n. [1. kándidnes; 2. kǽndidnis]. See prec. & **-ness**. Quality of being candid; honest expression of truth.

candied, adj. [1. kándid; 2. kǽndid]. See **candy** & **-ed**. Sugared, preserved by boiling in sugar: *candied peel* &c.

candle, n. [1. kándl; 2. kǽndl]. O.E. *candel*, fr. Lat. *candēla*, 'tallow candle, taper'; connected w. *candēre*, 'glow, burn' &c., q.v. under **candid**. See also **chandelier**. **1.** Slender cylindrical mass of wax, tallow, or spermaceti &c. containing a wick, for giving light. Phrs. *not fit to hold a candle to*, much inferior; *with bell, book, and candle*, in due form (properly of excommunication); *the game is not worth the candle*, more trouble, or expense, than it is worth; *burn the candle at both ends*, see **burn**. 2. Anything shaped like a candle, e.g. **a** *sulphur candle*, lighted for fumigation; **b** cylindrical portions of porous material through which water passes in a filter.

candle-berry, n. **a** A N. American shrub, also *candle-berry myrtle*, or wax-myrtle, the berries of which are covered with a greenish-white wax; **b** the candle-nut.

candle-end, n. Stump of a candle which has burnt down.

candle-light, n. Illumination of a room by candles; *by candle-light*, in the evening, after daylight has gone.

Candlemas, n. [1. kándlmas; 2. kǽndlməs]. O.E. *candelmæsse*. **candle** & **mass**. Feast of the Purification of B.V.M., Feb. 2nd; so called because candles for use on the altar are blessed then.

candle-nut, n. Fruit of a Pacific island shrub which burns with a bright light.

candle-power, n. Mode of measuring illuminating power of any form of light in terms of that of a standard sperm candle burning so much per hour.

candlestick, n. [1. kándlstik; 2. kǽndlstik]. O.E. *candelsticca*. See **candle** & **stick (II.)**. Implement of various shapes for holding a candle, of metal, porcelain, wood &c.

candle-tree, n. **a** The candle-berry; **b** the shrub which bears the candle-nut.

candour, n. [1. kándur; 2. kǽndə]. Lat. *candor*, 'whiteness'. Cp. **candid**. Open-mindedness, impartiality, frankness.

candy, n. & vb. [1. kándi; 2. kǽndi], fr. Fr. (*sucre*) *candi*, 'crystallized sugar', cp. also Ital. *zucchero candito*, in both cases P.P. of vbs. *candir, candire* respectively; fr. Arab. & Pers. *qand*, 'sugar'. **1.** n. Crystallized sugar, prepared by boiling and evaporating; used as sweetmeat and for sweetening coffee. (In U.S.A. applied to sweetmeats generally.) **2.** vb. To crystallize sugar by boiling; to preserve fruit &c. by boiling and saturating in sugar, and coating with sugar crystals, esp. in P.P. *candied*.

candytuft, n. [1. kándituft; 2. kǽnditaft], fr. Candia (Crete) & **tuft**. Species of plant, genus *Iberis*, with pink, white, or purple tufted flowers.

cane (I.), n. [1. kān; 2. kein]. M.E. *cane, canne*, fr. O. Fr., Mod. Fr. *canne*, 'walking-stick', through Lat. fr. Gk. *kánna*, 'reed', q.v. under **canal**. **1.** Hard, slender, hollow, jointed, flexible stem of certain plants such as bamboo, malacca, rattan &c., and the sugar-cane. **2.** (hort.) Stem of bush fruit plants such as the raspberry or loganberry which spring straight from the root each year. **3.** Canes split and treated, ready for various industrial uses, such as making seats of chairs &c.: *a chair seated and backed with cane*. **4.** A slender rod, whether actually a cane or not, used by schoolmasters for whipping boys: *a few strokes of the cane would do him good*. **5.** A slender walking-stick, originally a malacca cane, now applied indifferently to sticks of other kinds.

cane (II.), vb. trans., fr. prec. **1.** To use cane in manufacture, e.g. to place and fasten into frame, strips of cane interwoven to form seat or back of a chair. **2. a** To administer corporal punishment with a cane, as to a boy at school; **b** euphemism for a beating administered with a stick of any kind. Phr. *to have one's lessons thoroughly caned into one*, enforced by means of constant punishment.

cane chair, n. One made entirely of thickish, stiff cane, bent and woven so as to form frame-work, legs, seat, and back.

canephorus, n. [1. kānéforus; 2. keinéfərəs]. Gk. *kanēphóros*, 'basket-bearing', *kánē*, form of *kánna*, 'reed, rush basket', & *-phóros*, fr. *phérō*, 'I carry'. See **canal** & **-phore**. Greek sculpture representing a youth or maiden bearing a basket containing the sacred things in feasts &c.

cane-sugar, n. Sugar obtained from the sugar-cane as contrasted with beet-sugar &c.

cangue, n. [1. kangg; 2. kæŋg]. Fr., fr. Port. *canga*, 'yoke'. Heavy board worn round neck by Chinese criminals, which prevents them from lying down.

canine, adj. [1. kánīn, kánīn; 2. kǽnain, kéinain]. Lat. *caninus*, fr. *canis*, 'dog'. The word has cognates in most Aryan tongues; Gk. *kúōn*, Scrt. *śvan-*, genit. *śúnaś*; Lith. *szû*, genit. *szuñs*; O. Ir. *cú*, genit. *con*; Goth. *hunds*, O.E. *hund*. Cp. **hound** & see **cynic**. Belonging to, related to, the dog: *canine species*; *canine teeth*, the four pointed teeth (in men) between incisors and molars.

caning, n. [1. kāning; 2. kéiniŋ]. **cane (II.)** & **-ing**. A thrashing administered with a cane.

canister, n. [1. kánister; 2. kǽnistə]. Lat. *canistrum*, 'wicker basket', fr. Gk. *kánastron*, fr. *kánna*, 'reed', q.v. under **canal**. Cp. also **canaster**. **1.** Box, usually of metal, for keeping tea, tobacco &c. **2.** Specif., metal box containing wafers before consecration at the Eucharist. **3.** *Canister shot*, old-fashioned form of artillery ammunition, consisting of a number of shot contained in a case which burst so that the shot scattered after the manner of shrapnel.

canker (I.), n. [1. kángker; 2. kǽŋkə], fr. Fr. *cancre*, Lat. *cancr-*, inflected type of **cancer**. **a** Ulcerous sore in men and animals; **b** disease in trees which destroys the wood; **c** (fig.) devastating, corrupting moral influence, or tendency.

canker (II.), vb. trans. & intrans., fr. prec. **a** trans., To destroy or affect by canker in any sense; **b** intrans., to fall a prey to, suffer from, canker.

cankerous, adj. [1. kángkerus; 2. kǽŋkərəs]. **canker (I.)** & **-ous**. Affected by canker; resembling canker.

canker worm, n. Caterpillar which destroys leaves and buds.

canna, n. [1. kána; 2. kǽnə]. Lat. for **cane**. A genus of American tropical plants with large decorative leaves and brightly coloured flowers.

cannabis, n. [1. kánabis; 2. kǽnəbis]. Lat., 'hemp', fr. Gk. See **canvas**. (bot.) The genus of plants which includes hemp, esp. *Cannabis indica*, from which the narcotic drug hashish is obtained.

canned, adj. [1. kand; 2. kænd], fr. P.P. of **can (III.)**. (of foods) Preserved by being enclosed in air-tight tin box.

cannel coal, n. [1. kánel kōl; 2. kǽnəl koul]. First word prob. dialectal variant of **candle**. It has been suggested that the name was applied because this kind of coal burns brightly and without smoke.

cannibal, n. & adj. [1. kánibal; 2. kǽnibəl]. Span. A variant of *Caribal*, inhabitant of Carib Islands; form perh. influenced by Span. *canino*, 'like a dog, voracious'. **Caliban** is prob. also a variant of this. Human being who eats human flesh; also as adj., e.g. *cannibal feast*.

cannibalism, n. [1. kánibalizm; 2. kǽnibəlizəm]. Prec. & **-ism**. Habit of eating human flesh.

cannibalistic, adj. [1. kànibalístik; 2. kæ̀nibəlístik]. See prec., & **-ist** & **-ic**. Pertaining to, having character, after manner, of a cannibal.

cannikin, n. [1. kánikin; 2. kǽnikin]. See **can (II.)** & **-kin**. Small can; drinking-vessel.

canning, n. [1. káning; 2. kǽniŋ]. **can (III.)** & **-ing**. Process of preserving meat, fish, fruit &c. in hermetically sealed cans of tin-plate.

cannon (I.), n. [1. kánun; 2. kǽnən]. Used in mod. sense since 16th cent.; cp. Ital. *cannone*, 'a great tube or pipe'; ultimately fr. Gk. *kánna*, 'reed, pipe' &c. See **canal**, **cane**, **canon**. **1.** Large engine or gun for firing heavy projectiles; large mounted piece of ordnance. Now more and more giving place to *gun*. **2.** The cannon-bone (of a horse &c.).

cannon (II.), n., fr. prec. or adaptation of **carom**. Stroke in billiards in which player causes his own ball to strike both the other balls in succession, either by glancing off one directly on to the other, or by passing from one ball to the cushion, and thence on to the other.

cannon (III.), vb. intrans., fr. prec. **a** To make a cannon in billiards; **b** *cannon into*, run violently against; **c** *cannon off*, to make a cannon in billiards from one ball on to the other: *cannon off the red*, strike first, and rebound from.

cannonade, n. [1. kánunád; 2. kæ̀nənéid]. **cannon (I.)** & **-ade**. **a** A discharge of artillery; **b** noise made by discharge.

cannon-ball, n. Formerly, round heavy iron ball fired from a cannon. Now rarely used, being superseded by *shell*.

cannon-bone, n. Bone between knee or hock and fetlock, in hoofed animals.

cannonry, n. [1. kánunri; 2. kǽnənri]. **cannon (I.)** & **-ry**. (rare) Collection of artillery; discharge of artillery.

canny, adj. & adv. [1. káni; 2. kǽni]. Provinc. Engl. O.N. *kænn*, 'skilled' &c. Cp. **ken**, **know**. Clever, shrewd, cautious: *a canny Scot*. Phr. *call canny*, usually *ca' canny*, Scots 'drive carefully'; used by English workmen for the principle of not being too industrious during working hours, and not doing the full amount of work in a given time, thus restricting output, for various purposes.

canoe (I.), n. [1. kanōō; 2. kənú]. Span. *canoa*, W. Ind. word. Very light boat propelled either by paddles with one blade, *Canadian canoe*, or long paddle with blade at either end, *Rob Roy canoe*.

canoe (II.), vb. intrans., fr. prec. To travel in or by canoe: *to canoe from Oxford to Lechlade*.

canoeist, n. [1. kanōōist; 2. kənúist]. Prec. & **-ist**. Person who uses, one skilled in management of, a canoe.

canon (I.), n. [1. kánun; 2. kǽnən]. M.E. *canūn, canoun* &c., O. Fr. through Lat. fr. Gk. *kanṓn*, 'straight rod or bar, carpenter's rule, rule or standard of excellence'. The class. Gk. authors were called *kanónes*, 'models of excellence'. The word is ultimately derived fr. Gk. *kánna*, 'reed', wh. is discussed under **canal**, & is closely related to **cannon (I.)**. **1.** (eccles.) Rule, law, or body of laws, enacted by Church as the standard of order, doctrine, and discipline. *Canon law*, ancient system of Church law sanctioned by civil authorities, and recognized, before the Reformation, as binding in all Christian countries in Western Europe. **2. a** General rule, principle, standard, of conduct, taste, thought; criterion by which scientific judgements are reached and tested; **b** specif., tests by which the genuine works attributed to an author are distinguished from the spurious. **3. a** Body of sacred writings accepted as inspired, and as guides to faith and morals by the historic Christian Church: *Books of the Canon*; **b** body of writings of an author which are accepted as genuine: *the Chaucer Canon*. **4.** *Canon of the Mass*: the second part of the Eucharistic service, after the Sanctus, which includes the Words of Institution, beginning *Te igitur clementissime Pater*, to the end of service. So called because it includes the fixed unvarying form according to which the Mass is offered. **5.** (mus.) A round or continued fugue. **6.** (typog.) Largest type with special name.

canon (II.), n. M.E. *canun*, O. Fr. *canoine*, Fr. *chanoine*, Lat. *canonicus*, 'one subject to rule, or canon'. See prec. word for etymol. **1. a** Ecclesiastical dignitary, usually a member of a Cathedral Chapter; **b** *minor canon*, or priest-vicar, a priest who conducts the services in a Cathedral, not a member of the Chapter; **c** R.C. Ch., *canon-regular*, member of the order of Augustinian canons. **2.** Title, form of address given to canons: *the Rev. Canon X Y Z.*

canon (**III.**). See **canyon.**

canoness, n. [1. kánunes; 2. kǽnənes]. **canon** (**II.**) & **-ess**. Woman living in religious community, under a vow, and holding an ecclesiastical benefice or canonry.

canonical, adj. & n. [1. kanónikl; 2. kənɔ́nikl]. See next word & **-al**. **a** adj. According to the canon; regular, authorized. *Canonical books* of the Bible, those forming part of the **canon** (**I.**). **b** n. pl. *canonicals*, robes, vestments belonging to particular ecclesiastical or academic status: *in full canonicals.*

canonicity, n. [1. kànonísiti; 2. kæ̀nənísiti]. Lat. *canonic-(us)*, see **canon** (**I.**), & **-ity**. Conformity to, agreement with, the canon; regularity, genuineness.

canonist, n. [1. kánunist; 2. kǽnənist]. **canon** (**I.**) & **-ist**. One skilled in canon law.

canonization, n. [1. kànunīzáshun; 2. kæ̀nənaizéiʃən]. **canon** (**I.**), & **-ize** & **-ation**. *Canon* is here used in extended sense of a roll of persons officially recognized and approved as worthy of saintship. **a** Process whereby a deceased person is officially recognized and proclaimed by the Christian Church as a saint, to whom veneration is due, and whose aid may be invoked; the names of those canonized are added to the calendar or roll of saints; **b** the act and fact of such official recognition.

canonize, vb. trans. [1. kánunīz; 2. kǽnənaiz]. **canon** (**I.**) & **-ize**. To recognize officially the claims of sainthood in a deceased person; to proclaim the fact of his sainthood and add his name to the calendar or canon of saints.

canopic, adj. [1. kanṓpik; 2. kænóupik], fr. Canopus, town of ancient Egypt. *Canopic jar*, one of the four jars or urns which contained the entrails of an embalmed body and were placed in the tomb with the mummy.

canopy (**I.**), n. [1. kánopi; 2. kǽnəpi]. Lat. *canopeum*, fr. Gk. *kōnōpeîon*, 'mosquito net', fr. *kṓnōps*, 'gnat'. Apparently a compound of *kônos*, 'pine cone', & *ōps*, 'eye, face', on account of shape of its head. See **cone** & **optic**. **1.** Roof-like covering, supported on pillars, of a bed; one supported by poles, held or carried over kings and potentates on ceremonial occasions. **2.** (fig.) A lofty, spacious covering, esp. *canopy of heaven.* **3.** (archit.) Structure of wood or stone forming kind of roof to a pulpit, shelter for statue in a niche, or cover for a font &c.

canopy (**II.**), vb. trans., fr. prec. To cover overhead as with a canopy.

canorous, adj. [1. kanṓrus; 2. kənɔ́rəs]. Lat. *canōrus*, 'tuneful, harmonious', fr. base of *cano*, 'sing', q.v. under **cant** (**I.**). Melodious, sonorous.

cant (**I.**), vb. intrans. & n. [1. kant; 2. kænt]. Lat. *cantāre*, 'sing, declaim in a singing tone, drawl', fr. *canere*, 'sing'; cogn. w. Gk. *kanássō*, 'make a gurgling sound', *kanázo*, 'resound', also *kanakhḗ*, 'ringing sound, clash', & *ēi-kanós*, 'singer of the dawn', Hesychius, (*ēi* same as Gk. *ēoîos*, 'early', Att. *heōos*, 'early, at dawn', q.v. under **aurora**); O. Ir. *canim*, 'I sing'; Goth. *hana*, 'cock', O.E. *hana*, 'cock', & *henn*, 'hen', O.H.G. *hano*, Mod. Germ. *hahn*. See **hen.** Term first applied to whining of beggars, then to peculiar secret slang of beggars and thieves: *thieves' cant.* **1.** vb. (ordinary usage now) To utter hypocritical platitudes; to reproduce the stereotyped formulae of a religious or political faction, esp. insincerely and without conviction. **2.** n. **a** Hypocritical, insincere expression of pious or religious sentiments; **b** catchword(s) of a faction or clique; **c** (obs.) secret slang of tramps, beggars, and thieves.

cant (**II.**) n. & vb. trans. & intrans. Swed. & Dan. *kant*, 'corner', O. Fr. *cant*, Ital. *canto*, 'corner', through L. Lat. *cantus*, fr. Gk. *kanthós*, 'corner of the eye', origin unknown. **1.** n. **a** Corner, slope (infrequent); **b** a slope, slant (referring to direction and position). **2.** vb. **a** trans. To give a slope to, cause to slant; **b** intrans., to slope, lean to one side, in slanting direction.

Cantab., n. [1. kántab; 2. kǽntæb], fr. *Cantabrigia*, Cambridge. Member of University of Cambridge.

cantabile, adv. [1. kantáhbile; 2. kæntā́bile]. Ital. Cp. **cant** (**I.**). Of voice &c.; as musical direction, to be sung in an easy, flowing, melodious way.

cantaloup, n. [1. kántalōōp; 2. kǽntəlūp]. Fr., fr. Ital. *Cantalupo*, fr. castle of that name, near Rome. Kind of melon with rough rind.

cantankerous, adj. [1. kantángkerus; 2. kæntǽŋkərəs]. Cp. M.E. *contek*, *contak*, 'strife', & **-or** & **-ous**; prob. influenced by *rancorous*. Ill-natured, cross-grained, quarrelsome.

cantankerously, adv. Prec. & **-ly**. Ill-naturedly.

cantankerousness, n. See prec. & **-ness**. Ill-nature, proneness to quarrel.

cantar. See **kantar.**

cantata, n. [1. kantáhta; 2. kæntā́tə]. Ital., formed fr. Lat. *cantāre*, 'sing', q.v. under **cant** (**I.**). (mus.) Choral composition; setting to a narrative or dramatic poem, with solos, choruses, interludes, sung, but not acted.

cantatrice, n. [1. kántatrēs; 2. kǽntətrīs]. Fr., fr. Ital. Professional female singer.

canteen, n. [1. kàntḗn; 2. kæ̀ntīn]. Fr. *cantine*, Ital. *cantina*, 'wine-cellar'; perh. dimin. fr. L. Lat. *cantus*, 'corner'. See **cant** (**II.**). **a** Place where drinks and provisions are sold, esp. in a camp or barracks; also at bazaars and fêtes; **b** soldier's water-bottle or drinking-vessel.

canter, n. & vb. [1. kánter; 2. kǽntə]. Contracted fr. *Canterbury pace*, in allusion to the slow rate at which the pilgrims rode. **1.** n. An easy hand-gallop. Phrs. *win at a canter*, easily; *preliminary canter*, a short breather for a horse before a race, also (fig.) of a trial trip &c. **2.** vb. To ride at such a pace; **a** trans., *to canter a horse*, make him go at a canter; **b** intrans., *to canter along the road* &c.

canterbury, n. [1. kánterberi; 2. kǽntəbəri], fr. place-name Canterbury. Piece of furniture, consisting of set of divisions for music or papers, standing on short legs.

Canterbury bell, n. (hort.) Large kind of campanula, white, pink, or purple.

cantharides, n. [1. kàntháridēz; 2. kæ̀nþǽridiz]. Lat. *cantharid-*, stem of *cantharis*, fr. Gk. *kantharis*, *-idos*, 'blister fly', *kántharos*, kind of beetle regarded as sacred in Egypt. Etymol. unknown. (med.) Concoction of dried so-called Spanish fly, or beetles, which is used as an irritant to cause blistering.

canticle, n. [1. kántikl; 2. kǽntikl]. Lat. *canticulum*, 'little song', dimin. of *cantus*, 'song', q.v. under **cant** (**I.**). Short hymn or chant; one of the Prayer Book hymns, e.g. the *Nunc dimittis*, *Venite*, *Magnificat* &c.; pl. *Canticles*, the Song of Solomon.

cantilever, n. [1. kàntilḗver; 2. kæ̀ntilívə]. See **cant** (**II.**) & **lever** (**I.**). (engin.) Device for distributing strains and thrusts in bridge-building, which consists of a series of piers each of which has on either side an iron girder sloping outwards from pier or pillar, joining another which slopes inwards from it and thrusts against the same pier below. These girders are interlaced with those springing from next pier, and so on.

canting, adj. [1. kánting; 2. kǽntiŋ], fr. Pres. Part. of **cant** (**I.**). **1.** Given to the use of cant (of persons): *a canting rogue*, a whining, hypocritical knave; smacking of cant, hypocrisy, insincerity (of modes of expression, forms of speech): *a canting appeal* &c. **2.** (her., said of crests) Device on shield, or motto which constitutes a pun on the family name of bearer, as a neat's head borne by family of *Neate.*

cantle, n. [1. kántl; 2. kǽntl]. O. Fr. *cantel*, dimin. of **cant** (**II.**). Hinder part of a saddle which rises slightly.

canto, n. [1. kántō; 2. kǽntou]. Ital., fr. Lat. *cantus*, 'song'. Cp. **cant** (**I.**). A chief division of a long poem: *the 'Faery Queen' has seven Books, each containing several cantos.*

canton (**I.**), n. O. Fr., 'corner', fr. **cant** (**II.**). **1.** [1. kánton; 2. kǽntən]. A state in the Swiss Republic; one of the great territorial divisions of Switzerland. **2.** [1. kántun; 2. kǽntən]. **a** (her.) Small square bearing device in upper corner (usually dexter) of shield; **b** also of a flag or standard.

canton (**II.**), vb. trans. fr. prec. **a** [1. kántun; 2. kǽntən]. To place (device &c.) in the canton of a shield or flag; **b** [1. kantṓōn; 2. kæntūn]. To quarter (troops) in cantonments.

cantonment, n. [1. kantṓōnment; 2. kəntūnmənt], fr. **canton** (**I.**) & **-ment.** (mil., usually in pl.) Place assigned as quarters to troops.

cantoris, n. [1. kantṓris; 2. kæntɔ́ris]. Lat. genit. sing. of *cantor*, 'singer, precentor'. See **cant** (**I.**) & **-or.** (mus.) Direction in music book used by church or cathedral choir, meaning that the passage so marked is to be sung by that portion of the choir who sit on the same side as the precentor, i.e. the north side; contrasted with *decani.*

cantus firmus, n. [1. kántus férmus; 2. kǽntəs fə́məs]. Med. Lat., 'firm', or 'fixed song'. Plain-song.

Canuck, n. [1. kanúk; 2. kənák]. (slang) A Canadian, esp. a French Canadian.

canvas, n. [1. kánvas; 2. kǽnvəs]. Fr. *canevas*, fr. Lat. *cannabis*, fr. Gk. *kánnabis*, 'hemp'. See further under **hemp.** Strong coarse cloth of hemp or flax, used in making sails, tents, sacks &c. Phr. *under canvas*, **a** of troops, in tents; **b** of ships, under sail.

canvas-back duck, n. A N. American duck, esteemed as a delicacy, with grey-and-white mottled back feathers, resembling canvas.

canvass, vb. trans. & intrans. [1. kánvas; 2. kǽnvəs], fr. **canvas** (**I.**), orig. sense being to sift through canvas; perhaps from shaking up papers in a bag. **1.** To discuss, examine, a question thoroughly. **2.** To solicit votes from (persons) for (a cause or a candidate for a post).

canvasser, n. [1. kánvaser; 2. kǽnvəsə]. Prec. & **-er.** One who solicits votes.

canyon, n. [1. kányun; 2. kǽnjən]. Span. *cañon*, 'deep, hollow gorge', fr. Lat. *canna*, 'reed, pipe' &c. See **canal, cane.** Deep gorge between cliffs with river or stream flowing through it.

canzonet, n. [1. kànzonét; 2. kæ̀nzənét]. Ital. *canzonetta*, dimin. of *canzone*, Lat. *cantiōne*, abl. of *cantio*, 'song'. See **cant** (**I.**). Short, light song.

caoutchouc, n. & adj. [1. kóuchōōk; 2. káutʃūk]. Fr., fr. Carib. word. **a** n. Indiarubber; **b** adj., made of this.

cap (**I.**), n. [1. kap; 2. kæp]. O.E. *cæppe*, fr. L. Lat. *cappa*, fr. *caput*, 'head'. See **cape** (**I.**). **1.** Head-dress of various shape, of cloth or soft material, for men and women; distinguished from a hat by having no brim. The word, when applied to women's headgear, formerly referred to a light covering of muslin, lawn, or lace, worn in the house, esp. by elderly ladies; now it may also refer to out-of-doors head-dress. Specif., *cap* (for men) may refer to **a** academic head-dress with flat top and a tassel: *cap and gown*; **b** a cardinal's cap; **c** head-dress belonging to military uniform; **d** head-dress of court jester: *cap and bells*, *fool's cap* (also conical hat of paper worn formerly by children as a punishment); **e** (her.) *cap of maintenance*, figure of sort of cap placed below a crest; also as symbol of authority, borne before the sovereign; **f** (in sports) head-dress with the team's colours, badge &c., as sign of membership of team: *to get one's cap*; **g** special forms or shapes, as *huntsman's*, *jockey's*, *cap.* Phrs. *to come cap in hand*, (fig.) as a humble suppliant, humbly; *if the cap fits, wear it*, if the remark suits your case, apply it; *to set one's cap at* (of a woman), try to gain a man as an admirer; *feather in one's cap*, a distinction, something to be proud of. **2.** Round or cap-like covering of various kinds; **a** as a protection on projecting top or end of beam, stick, over place on bough of tree which has been broken or sawn off; **b** whitish zone visible at either pole of the planet Mars; **c** small metal covering containing slight explosive placed on nipple of gun to detonate charge, *percussion cap*; **d** (anat.) *knee-cap*, bony plate covering front of knee-joint; **e** end of boot or shoe, *toe-cap*.

cap (II.), vb. trans. fr. prec. **1.** To place cap on person's head (esp. when conferring academic degree). **2.** To place cap, in sense under **cap** (I.), 2, upon anything. **3.** To remove one's headgear by way of salute to a person. **4. a** To match or surpass: *to cap an anecdote*, tell one as good as, or better than, that just told; **b** *cap verses*, to supply a quotation, in a game, beginning with the last letter of the passage previously quoted. **5.** (veter. surg.). To injure a projecting joint, as the hock of an animal or the elbow of a person: esp. *a capped hock*. **6.** (fox-hunting). To collect subscriptions from (meet &c.) in cap of master or huntsman.

capability, n. [1. kăpabíliti; 2. kèipəbíliti]. See **capable** & **-ity**. Power of, capacity for, practical action; ability; also in pl.

capable, adj. [1. kā́pabl; 2. kéipəbl]. Fr., fr. Lat. *capābilis*, 'able to grasp', fr. *capere*, 'take, seize, hold', q.v. under **captive**. **1.** (of persons) **a** (gen.) Having power or ability, esp. intellectual, clever, intelligent, shrewd; **b** (for a special purpose or duty) *capable for*, available, competent, qualified. Phr. *capable of* (followed by n. or Pres. Part., usually in bad sense), wicked enough for. **2.** (of things) Susceptible of, liable to, patient of: (of a situation, circumstances) *capable of improvement*; (of verbal formulae) *capable of such and such an interpretation*, the words may bear such a meaning.

capableness, n. Prec. & **-ness**. Quality of being capable; cleverness, ability.

capably, adv. See prec. & **-ly**. In a capable manner.

capacious, adj. [1. kapā́shus; 2. kəpéiʃəs], fr. Lat. *capāc-*, stem of *capax*, 'able to hold much, spacious', base *cap-*, 'hold, grasp', &c., see **captive**, & **-ous**. **a** Able to hold a great deal: *a capacious stomach, mouth* &c.; **b** wide, spacious: *a capacious room*; **c** (of non-material things) *capacious mind*, broad, receptive &c.

capacitate, vb. trans. [1. kapásităt; 2. kəpǽsiteit]. See next word & **-ate**. To render capable for, prepare for; make legally eligible, or competent, for.

capacity, n. [1. kapásiti; 2. kəpǽsiti]. Fr. *capacité*, Lat. *capācitāt-(em)*, 'power of holding'. See **capacious** & **-ity**. **1.** Power of holding, grasping, containing (of material and non-material things); power of holding knowledge and ideas; ability, grasp: *he overestimated the capacity of his bag, stomach*; *a mind of great capacity*, powerful, having grasp. **2.** Relation to circumstances, character: *he came in the capacity of a friend*. **3.** (in elect.) Quantity of electricity required to raise a conductor to unit potential when all neighbouring conductors are at zero potential; the unit is a farad, generally converted to a microfarad.

cap-a-pie, adv. [1. káp a pḗ; 2. kǽp ə pí]. O. Fr., 'from head to foot'. See **cap** & **pedal**. Fully armed, prepared &c.

caparison, n. [1. kapárizun; 2. kəpǽrizən]. O. Fr. *caparasson*, Lat. **co-apparātiōn-(em)*, 'preparation'. See **co-** & **prepare**. Harness, equipment, esp. of horses and armed men.

cape (I.), n. [1. kăp; 2. keip]. In M.E. & M. Fr., 'short, sleeveless cloak', fr. Span. *capa*, orig. 'head covering', & connected w. Lat. *caput*, 'head', q.v. under **capital** (I.). See also **cap**. Kind of short, sleeveless cloak, covering neck and shoulders, now chiefly a woman's garment, or of certain military uniforms, chiefly foreign; it is either part of a long coat or a separate garment.

cape (II.), n. Fr. *cap*, Ital. *capo*, fr. Lat. *caput*, 'head'. See prec. Headland, promontory, part of coast jutting into the sea; also (cap.) as prefix: *Cape Cod* &c.; *the Cape*, Cape of Good Hope; whence as adj. *Cape Colony* &c.

capelin, n. [1. kápelin; 2. kǽpəlin]. Fr., fr. Span. *capelan*. Etymol. doubtful. A small seafish, allied to the smelt, found in great shoals off the Atlantic coast of N. America, used as bait for cod-fishing and also smoked and dried for food.

caper (I.), vb. intrans. & n. [1. kā́per; 2. kéipə]. Prob. shortened form of **capriole**. **a** vb. To skip about, frisk, leap about in a lively manner; (fig.) to act in a jaunty, foolish manner, likely to attract attention; **b** n., a brisk, lively, and skipping motion; (fig., often in pl.) thoughtless, foolish conduct; silly pranks, hare-brained escapades: *I am tired of his capers and his follies*. Phr. *to cut capers*, (i.) to dance about in an active, sprightly way; (ii.) (fig.) to play foolish pranks.

caper (II.), n. M.E. *caperes* (sing.), through L. Lat., fr. Gk. *kápparis*, foreign word of unknown origin. **a** Prickly shrub from Mediterranean area; **b** flower-bud of this or seed vessels of nasturtium pickled in vinegar, and used as a flavouring in sauce: *caper sauce*.

capercailzie, n. [1. kāperkā́l(y)ē; 2. kèipəkéil(j)i], fr. Gael. *capul*, 'horse' (cp. Low Lat. *caballus*, Fr. *cheval*), & *coille*, 'wood'. Largest species of grouse, the wood grouse or cock of the woods, *Tetrao urogallus*, found in Europe, still surviving in Scotland.

capful, n. [1. kápfool; 2. kǽpful]. **cap** (I.) & **-ful**. In Phr. *capful of wind*, a transient gust.

capias, n. [1. kā́pias; 2. kéipiæs]. Lat., 'thou may'st take', fr. form of document. See Lat. *capere*, 'to take', under **captive**. (legal) A writ authorizing officer to arrest the person mentioned.

capillaire, n. [1. kàpilā́r; 2. kæ̀piléə]. Fr. See **capillary**. The wild maiden-hair fern, an extract from which is used in making preserves, syrups &c.

capillarity, n. [1. kàpiláriti; 2. kæ̀pilǽriti]. Fr. *capillarité*. See next word & **-ity**. Property, capacity, of exercising capillary attraction.

capillary, adj. & n. [1. kapílari; 2. kəpíləri]. Lat. *capillāris*, adj., fr. *capillus*, 'hair'. By most etymologists connected w. Lat. *caput*, 'head', & Scrt. *kapālam*, 'skull', O.E. *hafola*, 'head'; but Walde suggests relation w. Lat. *caper(r)āre*, 'to wrinkle', the further relations of wh. are obscure. **1.** adj. Belonging to the hair; hair-like, thin as a hair: *capillary tube*, very fine blood-vessel; *capillary attraction*, physical process of 'attraction' between liquids and solids. **2. n.** One of the thin, hair-like blood-vessels.

capital (I.), adj. [1. kápitl; 2. kǽpitl]. Lat. *capitālis*, 'pertaining to the head, or life', fr. *caput*, gen. *capit-(is)*, & adj. suff. *-ālis*, q.v. under **-al**. The relation of *caput* to words for 'head' in cogn. languages is obscure. The connexion between it & Goth. *haubiþ*, O.E. *hēafod*, 'head', O.H.G. *houbit* &c., wh. was for long a truism of philology, is in reality very doubtful on account of the orig. *au* of the Gmc. group. In spite of different formative suff., Scrt. *kapālam*, 'skull', & O.E. *hafola*, 'head', must be connected w. *caput*. An ultimate origin fr. base **kap-*, 'hold, contain' &c. (see **captive**) has been suggested, in wh. case *caput* wd. mean orig. the 'container'. It may be asked, *container of what?* The answer prob. is either the brains, or the mind, life &c. See also the form *-cep-* in **biceps**. **1.** (as survival of Lat. sense) Belonging to life, affecting life, or forfeiture of life: *capital offence*; *capital punishment*. **2.** Of prime importance, vital; chief (in political sense): *capital city* &c. **3.** At the head, leading; in expression *capital letter*, 'large' letter, used at beginning of a sentence, and as initial letter in proper names. **4.** Excellent, very good: *a capital speech*; *capital fellow*.

capital (II.), n., fr. prec. The fundamental meaning is something which is at the head, which leads, is important; there are numerous differentiations of meaning. **1.** The chief city (of a country or county), the seat of government and administration. **2.** A capital letter. **3.** (econ.) **a** Accumulated wealth owned by individual or corporation at a given moment, as distinct from income received during a certain period; principal: *tax, levy, on capital*; **b** amount of property employed in a given business, for the production of more wealth: *the capital of a company*; **c** (usually *Capital*), private ownership of wealth personified, as contrasted with Labour. **4.** (fig.) Something which adds to one's power and influence; an advantage: *he tried to make political capital out of the misfortunes of a section of the community*.

capital (III.) n. Lat. *capitellum*, 'little head', dimin. of *caput*. See **capital** (I.). (archit.) The head, or uppermost part (member), of a column, of various characteristic styles, e.g. Doric, Corinthian, Gothic &c.

capitalism, n. [1. kápitalizm; 2. kǽpitəlizəm], fr. **capital** (II.), 3, & **-ism**. System of individual ownership of capital or wealth.

capitalist, n. [1. kápitalist; 2. kǽpitəlist]. See prec. & **-ist**. Owner of capital, as distinct from one who lives entirely by what he earns.

capitalistic, adj. [1. kàpitalístik; 2. kæ̀pitəlístik]. **a** Pertaining to, characteristic of, a capitalist; **b** after the manner of the system of capitalism.

capitalization, n. [1. kàpitalīzā́shun; 2. kæ̀pitəlaizéiʃən]. Next word & **-ation**. Act, or process, of converting annual payment into capital sum.

capitalize, vb. trans. [1. kapítalīz, kápitalīz; 2. kəpítəlaiz, kǽpitəlaiz], fr. **capital** (II.), 3, & **-ize**. **a** To convert into, or use as, capital; **b** to compute capital value of, or convert income or annuity into a single payment of a sum equivalent to that which yields the income.

capitally, adv. [1. kápitali; 2. kǽpitəli], fr. **capital** (I.), 4, & **-y**. Very well, in an excellent manner.

capitate(d), adj. [1. kápităt(ed); 2. kǽpiteit(id)]. Lat. *capit-ātus*, 'headed', fr. *caput*. See **capital** (I.). Having a form like a head; (bot.) having a head with clustered flowers.

capitation, n. [1. kàpitā́shun; 2. kæ̀pitéiʃən]. L. Lat. *capitātiōn-(em)*, 'poll tax', fr. *caput*, *capit-(is)*, 'head'. See **capital** (I.) & **-ation**. Tax payable by, or on, each person; *capitation fee*, one payable by each person, as by every member of a school or college; *capitation grant*, one made to an institution, school, hospital &c., in respect of each one of their inmates, members &c.

Capitol, n. [1. kápitol; 2. kǽpitəl]. Lat. *Capitōlium*, Temple of Jupiter on one of the seven hills of Rome; connected w. *caput*, 'head', see **capital** (I.). Name given to important state or public building, usually in classical style; e.g. the seat of the legislature at Washington, U.S.A.

capitoline, adj. [1. kapítolīn; 2. kəpítəlain]. Lat. *mons capitōlīnus*. Of, pertaining to, the hill at Rome upon which the Capitol stood.

capitular, adj. & n. [1. kapítūlar; 2. kəpítjulə]. Med. Lat. *capitulāris*, fr. Lat. *capitulum*, dimin. of *caput*, 'head'. See **capital** (I.), & cp. **chapter**. **a** adj. Pertaining to a *chapter*, q.v. in its various senses. **b** n., a member of a (cathedral) chapter.

capitulary, n. [1. kapítūlari; 2. kəpítjuləri], fr. Med. Lat. *capitulārium*. See prec. & **-ary**. Collection of decrees, ordinances, laws &c., as of chapter of cathedral or, specif., of early Frankish kings.

capitulate, vb. intrans. [1. kapítūlăt; 2. kəpítjuleit]. Med. Lat. *capitulāre*, 'to draw up, agreement &c., under heads' (*caput*). See **capital** (I.) & **chapter**, & **-ate**. **a** (mil.) To surrender subject to stipulated terms; **b** generally, to surrender, give in, cease to contend.

capitulation, n. [1. kapìtūláshun; 2. kəpìtʃuléiʃən]. See prec. & **-ion.** Originally a document in which heads, or terms, of agreement were stated; now: **a** act of surrendering; **b** document in which terms of surrender are laid down (rare); **c** specif., pl. *capitulations*, treaty &c., under which foreign powers are granted ex-territorial rights and jurisdiction in another state, esp. in Asiatic states, as formerly in Turkey &c.

capon, n. [1. kápun; 2. kéipən]. M.E. *capun*, fr. O. Fr.; Lat. *capōn-(em)* &c. The word is connected w. a base meaning 'cut, hack, hew' &c., & often appears w. initial *sk-*; Gk. *skaptō*, 'I dig', also *kápetos* (for **skápetos*), 'grave, trench', O. Slav. *skopiti*, 'to castrate', *skopĭsĭ*, 'castrated person', Lith. *skapoti*, 'scrape', *skopti*, 'dig out with a knife', *kapóti*, 'hack, hew'; the Gmc. form appears in Goth. *skaban*, 'cut, shave (the hair)', O.H.G. *skapan*, O.E. *scafan*, 'shave, scrape'; cp. **shave.** **a** A castrated domestic fowl, esp. when prepared for the table; **b** (fig.) a cowardly, poor-spirited fellow.

caponier, n. [1. kàponḗr; 2. kæpəníə]. Fr., lit. 'cage for capons'. See prec. In fortification a term for a construction placed across a ditch or trench, so as to enfilade it.

caponize, vb. trans. [1. kápunīz; 2. kéipənaiz], fr. **capon** & **-ize.** To make a capon of, castrate.

caporal, n. [1. kaporáhl; 2. kæpərál]. Fr., 'corporal'. A kind of French tobacco.

capot, n. & vb. trans. [1. kapót; 2. kæpót]. Fr. **1.** n. Winning of all the tricks at the game of piquet. **2.** vb. To win all the tricks at piquet against (player).

capric, adj. [1. káprik, káprik; 2. kéiprik, kæprik]. Lat. *caper*, 'he-goat'; cogn. w. Gk. *kápros*, 'wild boar', O.N. *hafr*, O.E. *hæfer*, 'he-goat'. These are prob. all related to Scrt. *kaprt*, 'membrum virile'. *Capric acid, oil*, obtained from butter, or coco-nut; so called from its rank smell.

capriccio, n. [1. kaprḗchō; 2. kæprítʃou]. Ital. for **caprice.** (mus.) A composition of light, irregular form.

caprice, n. [1. kaprḗs; 2. kəprís]. Fr., fr. Ital. *capriccio*, 'sudden start', fr. Lat. *caper*, 'he-goat'. See **capric.** **a** A whim, freakish idea, passing fancy; also **b** in art, a work of sportive, wayward fancy.

capricious, adj. [1. kapríshus; 2. kəpríʃəs]. Fr. *capricieux*, Ital. *capriccioso*; see prec. & **-ous.** Full of caprices, whimsical; unstable, inconstant; unreliable, incalculable.

capriciously, adv. Prec. & **-ly.** In a capricious, inconstant, incalculable manner.

capriciousness, n. See prec. & **-ness.** The quality of being capricious; specific conduct &c., which exhibits this.

Capricorn, n. [1. káprikorn; 2. kæprikɔ̄n]. Lit. 'goat-horn', Lat. *caper*, see **capric**, & *cornu*, 'horn', see **corn (II.)** & **horn.** One of the constellations; sign of the Zodiac representing this; *Tropic of Capricorn*, parallel of latitude S. of Equator, see **tropic.**

caprification, n. [1. kàprifikáshun; 2. kæprifikéiʃən]. Lat. *caprificātiōn-(em)*, fr. *caprificus*, 'wild fig', fr. *caper*, 'goat', see **capric**, & *fīcus*, 'fig', see **fig.** Process of hastening the ripening of figs by means of the stings of gall-insects.

caprine, adj. [1. káprīn; 2. kæprain]. Lat. *caprīnus*, fr. *caper*, q.v. under **capric.** Belonging to, like a (he-)goat.

capriole, vb. intrans. & n. [1. kápriōl; 2. kæprioul]. Ital. *capriola*, dimin. fr. Lat. *capra*, 'she-goat'. See Lat. *caper*, under **capric**; also **cab, cabriolet.** **a** vb. To caper, kick up the heels (from skipping of a goat); **b** n., a leap, caper, esp. of a horse.

Capsicum, n. [1. kápsikum; 2. kæpsikəm]. Lat. *capsa*, 'box' &c. See **case.** Genus of tropical plants, red peppers, the pods and seeds of which are very hot and pungent and are used whole, as *chillies*, or powdered, as *cayenne pepper*; they also yield a medicinal drug.

capsize, vb. trans. & intrans. [1. kapsíz; 2. kæpsáiz]. Skeat has suggested that the word is an Engl. refashioning of Span. *cabezar* or *cabuzar*, 'sink (a ship) by the head', fr. *cabo*, 'head', Lat. *caput.* See **capital (I.).** To upset, overturn, or cause to do so (esp. of boats and ships, but also carriage, cart &c.).

capstan, n. [1. kápstan; 2. kæpstən]. In M.E., fr. Fr. *cabestan*, fr. Lat. *capistrum*, 'halter', derived fr. base *cap-*, 'to hold', q.v. under **captive.** Device for hauling up anchors, or for drawing light boats above high watermark. It consists of an upright cylinder on which the cable is wound, revolving upon a pivot; poles or 'bars' which act as levers for turning, are inserted in holes made at intervals in upper part of cylinder, the cable coiling round below these.

capsular, adj. [1. kápsūlar; 2. kæpsjulə]. Next word & **-ar.** Shaped like, in the nature of, acting as, a capsule.

capsule, n. [1. kápsūl; 2. kæpsjūl], fr. Lat. *capsula*, dimin. of *capsa*, 'chest, receptacle' &c. See **case (I.).** Small case or sheath (in various senses); **a** (anat.) membranous sac or envelope enclosing certain parts or organs, e.g. the kidneys; **b** (bot.) case or vessel enclosing seeds or spores, which opens or bursts when ripe and allows contents to be dispersed; **c** (med.) thin gelatine case in which unpalatable powders &c., are swallowed; **d** thin, tight-fitting covering of metal or india-rubber for the top of a bottle, or end of a tube or pipe.

captain (I.), n. [1. káptin; 2. kæptin] M.E., fr. O. Fr. *capitain*, fr. Lat. *capitāneus*, adj., 'head, chief', fr. *capit-(is)*, *caput*, 'head' (see **capital**), & Fr. suff. *-ain*; cogn. w. **chieftain.** **1. a** Naval or military officer; in navy, between commander and rear-admiral; in army, one commanding a company (infantry) or a troop (cavalry), and ranking above a lieutenant and below a major; also, *group captain*, officer in Air Force, equivalent to colonel in army; **b** title prefixed to name of above: *Captain A* &c. **2. a** Officer commanding a merchant ship; or **b** a fire-brigade &c.; **c** person who acts as leader and chief of crew of racing-boat; **d** chief of a sporting club, or of a polo, cricket, or football team &c. **3.** A great leader in war, whether by sea or land; applied to such commanders as *Julius Caesar, Marlborough, Napoleon.* **4.** (by extension) A leader, pioneer in any enterprise: *a captain of industry.*

captain (II.), vb. trans., fr. prec. To act as captain or leader of (not in naval or military sense) but esp. in sense **2, b, c,** and **d** above.

captaincy, n. [1. káptinsi; 2. kæptinsi]. **captain (I.)** & **-cy.** The rank and status of a captain; term of tenure of this office.

captainship, n. [1. káptinship; 2. kæptinʃip]. See prec. & **-ship.** Function of leader or captain; exercise of this.

captation, n. [1. kàptáshun; 2. kæptéiʃən]. Lat. *captātiōn-(em)* acc., 'reaching after, catching at', fr. P.P. type of *captāre*, 'to reach after', fr. *capt-(um)*, see **captive**, & **-ation.** A reaching out after, appeal for, applause, or favour.

caption, n. [1. kápshun; 2. kæpʃən]. Lat. *captiōn-(em)*, 'a taking, seizing' fr. *capt-(um)*, see **captive. 1.** (law) **a** Act of taking or seizing; **b** legal arrest; **c** certificate attached to legal document which shows by what authority, when, &c., it was taken or executed. **2.** Heading, short title of a division of a book, as chapter, page &c., or of a scene in a cinematograph.

captious, adj. [1. kápshus; 2. kæpʃəs]. Lat. *captiōsus*, 'fallacious, deceptive, sophistical', fr. base *cap-*, 'take', q.v. under **captive**, & **-ous. a** (of persons) Anxious to catch, trip up, others in argument; (chiefly used in derogatory sense) apt to cavil, fond of making objections, and finding fault; **b** (of remarks, criticism, arguments) made for the sake of finding fault and carping, rather than to promote cause of truth.

captiously, adv. Prec. & **-ly.** In a carping, fault-finding manner.

captiousness, n. See prec. & **-ness.** Act, habit, of fault-finding for its own sake, sophistical argument.

captivate, vb. trans. [1. káptivāt; 2. kæptiveit]. L. Lat. *captivāt-(um)*, P.P. type of *captivāre*, 'take captive', fr. *captīvus*, q.v. under **captive.** To capture, delight, the fancy; to enchant, fascinate, charm.

captivating, adj. [1. káptivāting; 2. kæptiveitiŋ], fr. Pres. Part. of prec. Delightful, enchanting, winning, alluring.

captivation, n. [1. kàptiváshun; 2. kæptivéiʃən]. See **captivate** & **-ion. a** That which delights and charms; **b** the act of captivating, ability to enchant and captivate.

captive, adj. & n. [1. káptiv; 2. kæptiv]. Fr. *captif*, fr. Lat. *captīvus*, adj., 'caught, taken prisoner', formed fr. base *cap-*, w. *-t-* as in P.P. type *captus*, 'caught', fr. *capere*, 'take, receive, seize, hold' &c., & adj. suff. *-īvus*, q.v. under **-ive.** The base appears further in Gk. *káptō*, 'swallow greedily, gulp down', *kṓpē*, 'handle of anything, haft of a sword' &c.; Scrt. *kapaṭī*, 'two handfuls'; Lith. *kepju*, 'I seize, grasp', O. Slav. *čepĭ* 'a chain'; Goth. *hafjan*, 'heave, carry' &c., O.H.G. *heffan*, Mod. Germ. *heben*, 'heave', O.E. *hebban*, 'raise, lift up'. Goth. *hafts*, 'joined, bound', O.S., O.H.G. *haft*, 'bound, caught', O.E. *hæft*, (1) 'handle', (2) 'bond, fetter, captivity', have exactly the same formation as Lat. *capt-*. The various shades of meaning seen in above cognates all spring fr. the central idea, 'grasp, seize' &c. Cp. further the various Engl. words derived fr. this base: **cable, capable, capacity** &c.; further **case (I.), catch, chase** &c. **a** adj. Taken, caught, held, kept prisoner; *captive balloon*, one tethered to the ground; **b** n., a person or animal that is caught, and kept prisoner. (The word is more commonly used as a noun than as an adjective.)

captivity, n. [1. kaptíviti; 2. kæptíviti]. Fr. *captivité*, fr. Lat. *captīvitāt-(em)*, acc., fr. prec. & **-ity. 1.** State or condition of being a prisoner, or having liberty of movement and action impeded. **2.** Specif., *the Captivity*, that of the Jews in Babylon.

captor, n. [1. kápter; 2. kæptə], fr. Lat. base *capt-*, see **captive**, & **-or.** One who takes a prisoner; (said also of a ship which takes another prisoner).

capture, n. & vb. trans. [1. kápchur; 2. kæptʃə]. Lat. *captūra*, 'taking; quarry'. See prec. & **-ure. 1.** n. **a** The act or process of taking, of making a prisoner; **b** the person, animal, or thing caught, or seized. **2.** vb. To catch, take prisoner.

Capuchin, n. [1. kápūchin; 2. kæpju(t)ʃin]. Fr. *capucin*, earlier *capuch-*, fr. Ital. *capuccino*, 'little cowl', double dimin., fr. *capuccio*, fr. *capo*, 'head covering', Lat. *caput*, 'head'. See **capital, cape** &c. Order of Franciscans, from peculiar brown habit with pointed cowl. *Capuchin monkey*, South American monkey, *Cebus*, with thick hair forming sort of cowl over the head; *capuchin pigeon*, breed of pigeon with crested head.

capybara, n. [1. kàpibáhra; 2. kæpibárə]. Native name. A large South American tailless rodent, living a semi-aquatic life on banks of rivers and lakes, allied to the guinea pig.

car, n. [1. kar; 2. kā]. M.E., fr. O. Fr. *carre*, Lat. *carrus*, 'kind of four-wheeled wagon', a Celt. loan-word, cp. *carr* in Ir., W., & Bret., 'cart, vehicle'. The word is distinct fr., but cogn. w., Lat. *currus*, 'car, wain', &c., q.v. under **curricle.** A wheeled vehicle, in various uses. **1.** Poetical word for chariot: '*I saw the Master of the sun, he stood High in his luminous car*'. . . . (Aubrey de Vere). In Phr. *triumphal car*, decorated chariot. **2.** Specif. **a** an Irish two-wheeled carriage of peculiar make, drawn by one horse, having seats on each side, parallel to wheels, and projecting beyond these; called also *outside* *car, jaunting car*, and (in England) *Irish car*; **b** certain compartments on a railway train: *luncheon car, sleeping car*; (never used in England of the ordinary railway passenger carriage); **c** large public vehicle running on a rail through streets, plying for hire: *tramway-car; tram-car*. **3.** Recent colloquial expression, now very generally used, for an *automobile*, or *motor-car*: *it is too far to ride, I will come in a car*; also *side-car*, small carriage for one person attached to a motor bicycle.

carabineer, carbineer, n. [1. kàra-, kàrbinḗr; 2. kærə-, kābiniə], fr. Fr. *carbinier*. See **carbine**. **a** A mounted soldier carrying a carbine; **b** specif., *the Carabineers*, 6th Dragoon Guards.

carabinieri, n. pl. [1. kàrabiniári; 2. kàrabiniḗri]. Ital. See prec. The mounted police or gendarmes of Italy.

caracal, n. [1. kárakal; 2. kǽrəkæl]. Fr., fr. Pers., Turkish *qarah-qulaq*, 'black ear'. **a** A kind of lynx, *Lynx caracal*, of Asia and Africa, with reddish fur, black-tipped ears, and white spot over eyes; **b** its fur.

carack, carrack, n. [1. kárak; 2. kǽræk], fr. Fr. *caraque*, fr. Low Lat. *carraca*, Span. & Port. *caraca*, Ital. *caracca*; etymol. doubtful, perh. fr. Arab. *qaraqīr*, pl. of *qorqūr*, 'merchant ship'. (hist.) An armed merchantman of Spain and Portugal.

caracole, n. & vb. intrans. [1. kárakōl; 2. kǽrəkoul]. Fr. *caracoler*, 'prance', fr. Fr. *caracole* 'a spiral, turns to right and left', fr. Ital. *caracollo*, fr. Span. *caracol*, 'snail', also 'winding staircase' and 'wheeling about'. The ultimate etymol. of the large group of Romance words w. very various meanings, wh. Meyer-Lübke cites under *cochlea*, 'snail', is doubtful & obscure so far as the chain of meaning is concerned, nor is the form of above Span. word fully explained. Our word seems, however, to be derived, w. some unexplained refashioning, through the Lat. *coc(h)lea*, fr. Gk. *kokhlías*, 'snail', itself derived fr. *kógkhos* (see **conch**), 'mussel or cockle', or *kógkhē*, 'mussel-shell'. In Romance the word appears to mean a 'snail', then a spiral shell, then, as applied to a horse's movements, 'to prance about in a spiral'. **a** n. A horse's leaps and prancings from side to side; **b** vb., to leap from side to side, prance about.

carafe, n. [1. karáhf; 2. kærā́f]. Fr., also Ital. *caraffa*, Span. *garrafa*. Etymol. doubtful; perh. fr. Arab. *gharafa*, 'draw water'. Glass bottle for water at table or toilet.

caramel, n. [1. káramel; 2. kǽrəmɛl]. Fr., fr. Span. *caramelo*, O. Fr. *calemele*, L. Lat. *calamellus* (perh. influenced by Lat. *calamus*, 'reed'), fr. *canna mellis*, 'sugar cane', fr. **canna** & *mel*, 'honey'. See **cane, canal, & melliferous**. **a** Burnt sugar used for colouring; **b** thin coating of burnt sugar on a pudding; **c** a sticky sweetmeat.

carapace, n. [1. kárapās; 2. kǽrəpeis]. Fr., fr. Span. *carapacho*. Etymol. unknown. **a** Thick upper shell of a turtle; **b** upper shell of a crab or other crustacean.

carat, n. [1. kárat; 2. kǽrət]. Fr., fr. Ital. *carato*, O. Port. *quilate*, Arab. *qīrāt*, perh. fr. Gk. *kerátion*, 'little horn', dimin. of *kéras*, 'horn'. See **keratin**. **a** Unit of weight for diamonds and pearls, about 3¼ grains; **b** measure of proportionate purity of gold: 24 c. is pure gold, 18 c. has 6 parts alloy &c.

caravan, n. [1. kàraván; 2. kærəvǽn]. Fr. *caravane*, earlier *karouan*, fr. Pers. *karwan*. **1.** Party of travellers, their baggage and beasts of burden, journeying together, esp. across desert. **2. a** Covered cart or waggon, used as a travelling house by gipsies or other vagrants who travel slowly from place to place and camp at night; **b** the waggons, whether conveying persons or animals, of travelling circus.

caravanserai, n. [1. kàravánserā, -seri; 2. kærəvǽnsərei, -sərī], fr. prec. & Pers. *sara*, 'mansion'. Eastern inn with large courtyard where caravans rest for the night.

caravel, carvel, n. [1. káravel, kárvel; 2. kǽrəvɛl, kāvɛl]. Fr. *caravelle*, 'Turkish, Italian, or Spanish ship with four masts'; Ital. *caravella*, fr. Gk. *kárabos*, 'kind of beetle; crayfish; a light vessel'. Etymol. doubtful. Applied to light vessels of various kinds; used in 16th cent. (obs.). *Carvel-built*, of boats &c. in which the planks are flush with the side; contrasted with *clinker-built*, where they overlap.

caraway, n. [1. kárawā; 2. kǽrəwei]. Fr. & Span. *carvi*, fr. Arab. *karwiā*, fr. Gk. *káron*, 'cummin seed'. Etymol. unknown. Plant with pungent, aromatic seeds, used for flavouring cakes, and for distilling into a liqueur, and as a carminative drug.

carb(o)-, pref., form used in compounds of **carbon**.

carbide, n. [1. kárbīd; 2. kābaid]. **carb(o)- & -ide**. (chem.) A compound of carbon with another element, usually a metal, as *calcium carbide*, from which acetylene gas is obtained.

carbine, n. [1. kárbīn; 2. kābain]. Fr. *carabine*, Ital. *carabina*, concerning wh. various conjectures have been put forward, notably a derivation fr. Gk. *katabolé*, 'overthrow' &c., wh. is definitely rejected as impossible by the latest authority, Meyer-Lübke. Etymol. unknown. Short rifle carried by mounted troops.

carbo-hydrate, n. [1. kárbō hīdrāt; 2. kābou háidreit]. **carb(o)- & hydrate**. (chem.) A group of organic compounds, such as starch, sugar, cellulose &c., of carbon, oxygen, and hydrogen.

carbolic, adj. & n. [1. karbólik; 2. kābɔ́lik], fr. **carb(o)-, & -ol** (fr. Lat. *oleum*, 'oil', see **oil**), **& -ic**. **a** adj. (chem.) Derived from carbon, as coal or coal tar; specif., *carbolic acid*, phenol, acid obtained by distillation from coal tar, used as a powerful germicide and antiseptic; **b** n., (colloq.) carbolic acid.

carbolize, vb. trans. [1. kárbulīz; 2. kābəlaiz]. Prec. & **-ize**. To sterilize, impregnate with carbolic acid.

carbon, n. [1. kárbun; 2. kābən]. Lat. *carbōn-(em)*, 'piece of burning, or charred, wood, charcoal', fr. **kar-dhō*; cp. O. Slav. *krada*, 'hearth', Lith. *kárztas*, 'hot', Goth. *haurja* (= **hurja*), 'coals' (only in pl.). With different gradation, also O.E. *heorþ*, 'hearth, fire', Germ. *herd*, Mod. Engl. **hearth**. **1.** (chem.) One of the non-metallic elements, occurring in various forms, e.g. the diamond, graphite, or 'black lead' &c., and in all animal and vegetable tissues, as also in charcoal, coal, petroleum &c. **2. a** A stick of carbon, as in electric arc-lamps; **b** duplicate copy of letters &c. obtained by use of *carbon paper*, covered with black substance which is placed between two sheets of writing-paper and produces on the lower a copy of what is written on that above.

carbonaceous, adj. [1. kàrbonáshus; 2. kābənéiʃəs]. **carbon & -aceous**. **a** Like coal; **b** containing coal or carbon.

carbonari, n. pl. [1. kàrbonáhri; 2. kābənā́ri]. Ital. Secret political society in Italy, esp. in kingdom of Naples during early 19th cent.; said to derive its name from early members being charcoal burners.

carbonate (I.), n. [1. kárbunat; 2. kābənit]. **carbon & -ate**. Salt of carbonic acid.

carbonate (II.), vb. trans. [1. kárbunāt; 2. kābəneit]. **carbon & -ate**. To burn to carbon; carbonize.

carbonic, adj. [1. karbónik; 2. kābɔ́nik]. **carbon & -ic**. Belonging to, derived from, carbon; specif., *carbonic acid*, carbon dioxide, produced by combustion of carbon or decomposition of organic matter, by respiration and fermentation; it is a colourless, heavy, odourless gas, non-inflammable and non-breathable, and is the 'choke-damp' of coal-mines.

carboniferous, adj. [1. kàrbuníferus; 2. kābəníførəs]. **carbon & -ferous**. Coal-bearing; (of geol. strata) coal-producing. *Carboniferous period*, that in which these strata were laid down.

carbonize, vb. trans. [1. kárbunīz; 2. kābənaiz]. **carbon & -ize**. **a** To reduce to carbon by burning; **b** impregnate with carbon.

carborundum, n. [1. karborúndum; 2. kābərándəm]. **carb(o)- & corundum**. A crystalline compound of carbon and silicon, used as an abrasive in tool-grinding.

carboy, n. [1. kárboi; 2. kābɔi]. Pers.-Arab. *qarābah*, 'large flagon'. Large glass jar enclosed in basket-work, used for holding corrosive chemicals, as nitric acid, vitriol &c.

carbuncle, n. [1. kárbungkl; 2. kābaŋkl]. In M.E.; O. Fr. type *charboucle*, Lat. *carbunculus*, dimin. of *carbo*, 'small coal; bright-red precious stone'. **1.** Large inflamed boil or tumour. **2.** Bright, deep-red precious stone, esp. a garnet cut with smooth rounded surface.

carburet, vb. trans. [1. kàrbūrét; 2. kābjurét], fr. **carbon**, *-ur*, on anal. of *sulphur*, & **-et**. (chem.) To combine any element with carbon, esp. in P.P., as *carburetted hydrogen*.

carburetter, -or, n. [1. kàrbūréter; 2. kābjurétə]. Prec. & **-er**. Device for combining air or gas with carbon or its compounds; specif., an apparatus attached to internal combustion engines for mixing air with the spray of petrol to form an explosive vapour.

carcanet, n. [1. kárkanet; 2. kākənɛt]. Fr. *carcan*, 'an iron collar used formerly for attaching animals to a post for public exhibition'; fr. Low Lat. *carcannum*, loan-word fr. O.H.G. *kwerka*, 'neck, throat'; cp. O.N. *kverk*, 'crop', & see **gurgitation**. Ornamented chain for the neck, often set with jewels. (Archaic.)

carcass, -case, n. [1. kárkas; 2. kākəs]. M.E. *carcays, carkeys*, O. Fr. *carcois*, Mod. Fr. *carcasse*, fr. Ital. *carcassa*, 'kind of bomb'; all fr. Low Lat. *carcosium*. Etymol. unknown. **1.** Dead body of an animal, esp. when prepared for sale by butcher. **2. a** Dead human body (a contemptuous sense); **b** the human body alive or dead, now only in contemptuous, humorous, or depreciatory reference; the mere mortal body. **3.** Skeleton, framework. of a building or ship.

carcinoma, n., pl. **-ata** [1. kàrsinóma, -mata; 2. kāsinóumə, -mətə]. Lat., fr. Gk. *karkinōma*, 'ulcer, cancer', fr. *karkínos*, 'crab'. Cp. **cancer**. (med.) A form of cancer.

card (I.), vb. trans. & n. [1. kard; 2. kād]. Fr. *carde*, 'machine with interlaced metal points for combing cloth' &c., Lat. *carduus*, 'thistle'. The orig. meaning of the base is 'cut, scrape', cp. Lat. *carēre*, 'to be without, lack', orig. 'to be cut off from something'. Cp. also Lat. *curtus*, 'shortened, truncated', *curto*, 'shorten, diminish', *corium*, 'hide, leather'; Gk. *keírō*, 'clip, cut, hew off', fr. **kerjō*; Scrt. *kr̥ṇāti*, 'injures, kills'; O.E. *hierwan*, 'deride, insult, injure', is perh. also cogn. See further under **carnal**. (chiefly used now as vb.) To cleanse, comb, disentangle hair, wool, hemp &c. with a *card* (see Fr. word above cited).

card (II.), n. Fr. *carte*, Ital. *carta*, fr. Lat. *charta*, later *carta*, 'leaf of paper, or Egyptian papyrus', fr. Gk. *khártēs*, 'leaf of papyrus'. Origin unknown, prob. Egyptian. **1.** One of 52 variously figured pieces of thin, smooth pasteboard, the designs on which are coloured black or red, used in large number of games—whist, bridge &c.: *playing cards*; *pack of cards*. Phrs. *to play one's cards well* (fig)., conduct affairs with judgement and discretion; *on the cards*, likely to happen (from use of playing-cards in telling fortunes); *put one's cards on the table*, disclose one's plans, abandon secrecy; *a house of cards*, visionary project which soon collapses; *one's best card*, strongest argument; best means of getting one's own way; *speak by the card*, with assurance, clearly; *the correct card*, the proper thing. **2.** Piece of thin pasteboard used for variety of purposes: **a** bearing name and address engraved upon it: *visiting card*; Phr. *to leave cards (on)*, call, pay a visit; **b** piece of cardboard with device, and compliments or good wishes for particular occasions: *Christmas, birthday, card* &c.; **c** one of a series arranged alphabetically, bearing written or printed entry of name and author of a book: *card catalogue, index* &c.; **d** piece of pasteboard bearing name and address of person for whom intended on one side, and a message, notice, or communication on the other, sent through the post: *post card*; **e** printed pasteboard, giving names, score, and other details of a race, game &c., as programme: *race-card, score-card* &c. **3.** A droll, original, eccentric fellow: (familiar, colloq., and vulg.) *a queer card.*

cardamom, cardamum, n. [1. kárdamom; 2. kādəməm, -əm]. Gk. *kardámōmon,* 'kind of cress; the seed, eaten as a flavouring'. Etymol. unknown. Aromatic East Indian fruit and its seed, used as a condiment.

cardboard, n. [1. kárdbord; 2. kādbōd]. Thick, stiff paper or pasteboard used for making boxes &c.

card-case, n. See **card (II.)** & **case.** Leather case for carrying visiting-cards in the pocket.

cardiac, adj. [1. kárdiak; 2. kādiæk]. Gk. *kardiakós,* fr. *kardía,* 'heart'. This word is cogn. w. Engl. **heart,** & Lat. *cor,* q.v. under **cordial.** Concerned with the heart, esp. in disease: *cardiac symptoms,* i.e. of heart disease.

cardigan, n. [1. kárdigan; 2. kādigən], fr. Earl of Cardigan, 1855. Woollen waistcoat worn over ordinary waistcoat.

cardinal (I.), adj. [1. kárdinal; 2. kādinəl]. Fr., fr. Lat. *cardinālis,* adj., fr. Lat. *cardō,* genit. *cardin-(is),* 'hinge of a door, pivot; that on which all depends'. Cp. Gk. *kradaínō,* 'brandish, shake', *kórdax,* 'dance', Scrt. *kūrdati,* 'leaps, hops'. Connected with that on which things hinge or depend; of chief importance: **a** *cardinal virtues* (see **virtue**); *cardinal numbers,* simple numbers: one, two, three &c.; *cardinal points* (of compass), north, south &c.; **b** *cardinal church,* one of the 70 principal churches of Rome, to which the rest are subordinate; see **cardinal (II.).**

cardinal (II.), n., fr. prec. Prince of Roman Church, member of Pope's Council or Sacred College, one of whose duties it is to elect the Pope. So called from his important position in the constitution of the Church.

cardinalate, n. [1. kárdinalāt; 2. kādinəleit]. Prec. & **-ate.** **a** Rank or dignity of a cardinal; **b** body of cardinals collectively.

cardinal red, n. A bright scarlet-red colour; from colour of cardinal's robes.

cardio-, pref., form of Gk. *kardía,* 'heart', used in compounds. See **heart.**

cardiology, n. [1. kàrdiólojі; 2. kādiɔ́lədži]. Prec. & **-logy.** Science or study of the heart and its functions.

cardiometer, n. [1. kàrdiómeter; 2. kādiɔ́mitə]. See prec. & **-meter.** Apparatus for measuring the beat of the heart.

carditis, n. [1. kardítis; 2. kādáitis]. Gk. *kardía,* 'heart', see **cardio-** & **-itis.** Inflammation of the heart.

cardoon, n. [1. kardóon; 2. kādū́n]. O. Fr. *cardon,* 'thistle'. See **card (I.).** Vegetable allied to artichoke and thistle, the globe artichoke.

card-sharper, n. One who sharps or cheats at cards.

care (I.), n. [1. kār; 2. keə]. O.E. *caru,* 'anxiety, grief, trouble, care', M.E. *cāre,* O.S. *cara,* 'sorrow, suffering', O.H.G. *chara,* 'complaint, lamentation', Goth. *kara,* 'sorrow'; cp. also Goth. *kaúrus,* 'heavy, burdensome', fr. *kurus, w. different form of gradation (cp. Gmc. *bar-, *bur-, Goth. *bar-, baúr-,* q.v. under **bear (I.), burden** &c.). The orig. sense of the base is 'something heavy, hard to bear', then 'something grievous, troublesome, painful' &c. Outside Gmc. the cognates are Lat. *gravis,* 'heavy, weighty, important' &c. (see **grave (III.),** adj.); Gk. *barús,* fr. **gʷrús,* 'heavy, grievous, troublesome', *báros,* 'weight, burden, misery'; Scrt. *gurúš,* 'heavy'. Lat. *brūtus,* 'heavy', is an Umbrian form, = Lat. **grūtus,* see **brute.** See also **chary.** **1.** Anxiety, grief (poet. and archaic): '. . . *care sat on his faded cheek*' (Milton); *care had aged him before his time.* **2.** Occasion for, cause of, anxiety, grief &c. (esp. in pl.): *he was wealthy and free from cares of every kind.* **3.** Serious attention of mind, solicitude, watchfulness, pains: *to bestow great care upon one's work.* Phrs. *take care*; *have a care,* be prudent. **4.** Object of solicitude and peculiar attention: *everything connected with the farm was his especial care.* **5.** Protection, charge, responsible management, direction: *the orphans were left to the care of their grandfather*; *the sick man was placed under the care of the best physicians.* Phr. *care of* (written c/o), placed on letters before name of owner of house in which addressee of letter is staying.

care (II.), vb. intrans. O.E. *carian,* 'reck, be anxious', M.E. *cāren,* fr. prec. **1.** **a** To feel strongly, esp. interest, sorrow, anxiety: *although he does not show it, he really cares a great deal*; **b** (more frequently with neg.) to be indifferent to, unmoved by, not to be afraid &c., in various idiomatic Phrs. *I don't care,* have no interest, am indifferent; *I don't care what happens now*; (often with expletive) *I don't care a damn, a straw, a button, a brass farthing* &c. **2.** (with *for* followed by n.) **a** To feel a strong liking, or affection, for: *do you think she ever really cared for her husband?*; **b** to look after, take charge of, provide for: *the country must care for those who were crippled in the war*; **c** (more usual with neg.) to dislike, prefer to dispense with: *I don't care for him at all*; *I don't much care for mustard with mutton.* Phr. (colloq. and vulg.) *I don't care if I do,* I am willing, do not object.

careen, vb. trans. & intrans. [1. karḗn; 2. kərín]. Lat. *carīna,* 'keel of a ship'; cp. Gk. *karúa, káruon,* 'nut'; Scrt. *kárakaš,* 'shell of coconut, water vessel made therefrom'. (lit.) To expose a ship's keel. (naut.) **a** To cause a vessel to be over on one side, on beach, or in dock, so as to expose keel, for cleaning and repairs; **b** to (cause a vessel to) heel over on one side when in the water.

careenage, n. [1. karḗnij; 2. kərínidž]. Prec. & **-age.** Act of careening a ship; place adapted for this work; cost of work.

career (I.), n. [1. karḗr; 2. kəríə], fr. Fr. *carrière,* Lat. *carrāria (via),* 'carriage (way)', fr. *carrus.* See **car.** **1.** Rapid course, impetuous motion onwards; esp. *in full career, mad career.* **2.** Mode of living; course, progress through life; way of earning a living; success in profession or business.

career (II.), vb. intrans., fr. prec. To rush wildly, rapidly, as in a frolic or high spirits; often *career about.*

careerist, n. [1. karḗrist; 2. kəríərist]. **career (I.)** & **-ist.** One concerned mainly with his own success in life, to the exclusion of other considerations.

careful, adj. [1. kárfool; 2. kéəfl]. See **care (I.),** & **-ful.** Orig. meaning 'full of care, anxious, troubled', is now archaic & obs. **a** (of persons) Painstaking, given to bestowing attention; prudent in judgement, cautious in action; provident, thrifty; **b** (of mode of performance of a mental or physical act) executed with care; exact, thorough: *a careful study, careful painting* &c.

carefully, adv. Prec. & **-ly.** In a painstaking, exact manner.

carefulness, n. See prec. & **-ness.** Bestowal of care, exactness.

careless, adj. [1. kárles; 2. kéəlis]. See **care (I.)** & **-less.** **1.** Free from anxiety, lighthearted: *happy, careless youth.* **2.** *Careless of,* indifferent to, unheeding, undeterred by: *he performed his task, careless of danger and discomfort.* **3.** Thoughtless, negligent; hence, incompetent (of persons and their acts).

carelessly, adv. Prec. & **-ly.** In a careless manner.

carelessness, n. See prec. & **-ness.** Mental habit of inattention, negligence &c.; result of this in action. Phr. *a piece of carelessness.*

caress (I.), n. [1. karés; 2. kərés]. Fr. *caresse,* fr. Ital. *carezza,* Low Lat. *caritia, 'endearment', fr. *cārus,* 'dear, beloved'; cp. Scrt. *čāruš,* 'pleasant, agreeable', O. Ir. *caraim,* 'I love'. See **charity.** Gesture or act expressing love or affection, such as a kiss, embrace, pat &c.

caress (II.), vb. trans., fr. prec. **a** To fondle, kiss &c., in a loving, affectionate way; **b** to flatter, employ blandishments towards, soothe.

caressing, adj. [1. karésing; 2. kərésiŋ], fr. Pres. Part. of prec. (of manner, voice, tone, look, touch) Endearing, loving, expressive of affection, soothing.

caressingly, adv. Prec. & **-ly.** In a caressing manner.

caret, n. [1. káret; 2. kǽrɛt]. Lat., 'it needs, is lacking', pres. indic. of *carēre,* 'to be without'. See base under **card (I.).** Mark (^) placed after a word in written page or printed proof to indicate where something is to be added.

caretaker, n. [1. kártāker; 2. kéətèikə]. See **care (I.)** & **take.** A subordinate employee whose business it is to take care of, look after, clean, protect from unauthorized intrusion, a building, esp. an unoccupied house, a museum or picture-gallery, a church &c.

careworn, adj. [1. kárworn; 2. kéəwōn]. Oppressed by cares and anxiety; showing traces of this in appearance; tired, haggard, weary looking.

Carex, n. [1. kāreks; 2. kéəreks]. Lat., 'rush, sedge'; etymol. unknown. (bot.) Genus of plants which includes the sedges.

carfax, n. [1. kárfaks; 2. kāfæks]. M.E. *carfoukes,* fr. O. Fr. *carrefourg,* fr. L. Lat. *quadrifurcum,* fr. Lat. *quadri-,* fr. *quatuor,* 'four', & *furcus,* 'fork'. See **four & fork** & Skeat's note on the word. Place where four roads meet, now only surviving as name of such in towns, as at Oxford &c.

cargo, n. [1. kárgō; 2. kāgou]. Span., fr. Low Lat. *carricum,* lit. 'a cart-load', fr. Lat. *carrus,* 'car'. See **car & charge (I.).** Freight of a ship.

caribou, -boo, n. [1. kàribóo; 2. kæribū́]. Am. Ind. word, said to mean, 'pawer, scratcher'. The N. American reindeer.

caricature, n. & vb. trans. [1. kàrikatū́r; 2. kærikətjúə(ə)]. Ital. *caricatura,* fr. *caricare,* 'to load, charge, blame', fr. Low Lat. *carricāre,* 'to load a car' (see **car & charge (I.)**). Orig. something overloaded, overcharged, distorted. **1.** n. **a** Grotesque, laughable representation (i.) of a person, in a drawing, of his manner, voice &c., by mimicry, or (ii.) of the style of a writer, composer, painter &c. The essential feature of caricature is exaggeration of some characteristic feature or mannerism; **b** said also of a person or thing which is very ugly, ill-shaped, badly made: '*A caricature of a face*' (Gilbert). **2.** vb. To make a caricature of, to represent in caricature.

caricaturist, n. [1. kàrikatū́rist; 2. kærikətjúərist]. Prec. & **-ist.** Person who draws or makes caricatures.

caries, n. [1. kāriēz; 2. kéəriiz]. Lat., 'rottenness, decay'; cp. Scrt. *śṛṇāti,* 'smashes, destroys', *śūrtáš,* 'broken to pieces'; Gk. *kḗr,* 'death, destruction, disease'. It is possible that Scrt. *śáru,* 'shot', Goth. *hairus,* O.E. *heoru,* 'sword' = 'instrument of destruction', belong to the same group of words. Decay, esp. of bones and teeth.

carillon, n. [1. kárilyun; 2. kǽriljən], or as Fr. [karijɔ̃]. Fr., 'peal of bells'. Derivation is suggested fr. Med. Lat. *quadrilionem,* 'set of four bells'. **a** A peal or chime of bells, arranged so that tunes &c. can be played by one person, the *carilloneur*; **b** tune, melody played on such set of bells.

carinate, adj. [1. kárinàt; 2. kǽrineit], fr. Lat. *carīnāt-(us),* fr. *carīna,* 'keel'. See **careen.** Shaped like the keel of a ship, with ridge down the centre; **a** (bot.) of leaves &c.; **b** (zool.) of sternum or breast-bone of birds.

carious, adj. [1. kárius; 2. kéərіəs]. Lat. *cariōsus*, 'decayed', fr. **caries** & **-ous**. Decayed.

carking, adj. [1. kárking; 2. kákiŋ]. O. Fr. *carkier*, fr. Low Lat. *carricāre*, 'load'. See **car** & **cargo**. Cp. obs. vb. *to cark*. Oppressive, irritating; chiefly in Phr. *carking care*.

carl(e), n. [1. karl; 2. kāl]. O.N. *karl*, also in O.E. *hūs-carl*, cp. Germ. *kerl*, & see cogn. form under **churl**. (Scots) Fellow; rude, rustic kind of man.

carline (I.), n. [1. kárlin; 2. kálin]. Cp. O.N. *kerling*; fr. prec. w. fem. suff. (Scots) Old woman.

carline (II.), n. Fr., fr. Med. Lat. *carlina*, said to be for *Carolina*, fem. adj. fr. *Carolus*, 'Charles', i.e. Charlemagne. (bot.) Genus of plants, resembling the thistle.

carmagnole, n. [1. kàrmanyṓl; 2. kàmænjóul]. Fr. **a** Originally a kind of short jacket worn during French Revolution; **b** a round dance of a rowdy, licentious character, much in vogue among the lower order of Revolutionaries at that time. This is the only sense now borne by the word in English.

carman, n. [1. kárman; 2. kámən]. See **car** & **man**. Person employed to drive a horse waggon or lorry, esp. one carrying goods and parcels; a carter. (Never applied to driver of vehicle propelled by petrol or steam.)

Carmelite, n. & adj. [1. kármelīt; 2. kámilait], fr. Mount Carmel, place of foundation in 12th cent. **a** n. One of an order of mendicant friars, the White Friars; **b** adj., belonging to this order.

carminative, adj. & n. [1. kárminativ; 2. káminətiv], fr. Lat. *carmināt-(um)*, P.P. type of *carmināre*, 'card wool', hence 'cleanse', fr. same base as **card** (I.). (med.) **a** adj. Expelling, removing, flatulence; **b** n., drug, medicine, which does this, as dill, caraway &c.

carmine, n. & adj. [1. kármīn; 2. kámain]. Fr. & Span. *carmin*; fuller Span. form *carmesin*, Med. Lat. *carmesīnus*. See **crimson**. A crimson-red colour with touch of purple.

carnage, n. [1. kárnij; 2. kánidž]. Fr., fr. Ital. *carnaggio*, L. Lat. *carnāticum*. See **carnal** & **-age**. Severe slaughter, esp. of human beings.

carnal, adj. [1. kárnal; 2. kánl], fr. Lat. *carn-*, stem of *caro*, 'flesh', orig. 'piece of flesh, portion cut from a carcass', & adj. suff. *-ālis* (see **-al**). *Caro* is cogn. w. Gk. *keirō*, 'I cut off' (fr. **ker-jō*); Scrt. *kṛntáti*, 'he cuts', Lith. *kertù*, 'hack'. O.H.G. *sceran*, 'cut', O.E. *sceran*, 'cut, shear', are fr. a variant, **sker-*, of same base. The Lat. word shows therefore a highly specialized use of a base meaning 'to cut', & must orig. have meant merely 'a slice'. See other development of same base under **card** (I.). Not related to Gk. *kréas*, 'flesh', q.v. under **crude** & **raw**. Pertaining to the flesh, esp. in figurative sense of lower nature and its appetites, as opposed to the spirit; sensual, material, worldly: *carnal affections, lusts, desires*; *carnal knowledge* (*of*), sexual intercourse.

carnality, n. [1. karnáliti; 2. kānǽliti]. Prec. & **-ity**. Fleshly appetite, lust; indulgence in this.

carnally, adv. [1. kárnali; 2. kánəli]. **carnal** & **-ly**. In the body; according to the flesh, or the lower nature: '*to be carnally minded is death*'.

carnation, n. [1. karnáshun; 2. kānéiʃən]. Fr., 'flesh tint, complexion', fr. Lat. *carnātiōn-(em)*, fr. *carn-(is)*, *caro*, 'flesh'. See **carnal**. **1.** A bright rosy or pink colour, as of flesh; also as adjective. **2.** A cultivated variety of the clove pink, of different colours; in this sense the word appears first as *coronation*, *cornation* &c., and may have meant shaped like a *corona*, 'crown', from its indented petals.

carnelian, n. [1. karnélian; 2. kānīljən]. Variant of **cornelian**. Influenced by association w. various words of *carn-* type, fr. the colour. See **carnal** & **carnation**. (mineral.) Stone of fine red or reddish-white colour.

carnival, n. [1. kárnival; 2. kánivəl]. Fr., Ital. *carnevale*, older *carnelevale*, 'putting away of flesh' (as food). See **carnal** & **lever**. **1.** Week just before Lent; festivities and frolics held at this season in Roman Catholic countries. **2.** Generally, revelry, verging on riotousness.

Carnivora, n. [1. karnívora; 2. kānívərə]. Lat. neut. pl., 'flesh-eating'. See **carnal** & **voracious**. (zool.) Order of flesh-eating mammals.

carnivore, n. [1. kárnivōr; 2. kánivɔ̄]. Fr., fr. Lat. *carnivorus*. See prec. A flesh-eating mammal.

carnivorous, adj. [1. karnívorus; 2. kānívərəs]. See prec. & **-ous**. Flesh-eating; of animals, and also of certain plants.

carob, n. [1. károb; 2. kǽrəb]. Fr. *carobe*, fr. Arab. *kharrūb*, 'pod, bean'. An evergreen Mediterranean tree, with edible seed-pods.

carol, n. [1. károl; 2. kǽrəl]. O. Fr. *carole*, Ital. *carola*, 'a dance in a ring', fr. Med. Lat. **choraula*, 'a dance to the flute', fr. Gk. *khoraúlēs*, 'player on flute for a dance', fr. *khorós*, 'dance in a ring, festive choral dance', & *aulós*, 'flute'. See **choral**. With the second element cp. Gk. *aulṓn*, 'valley; ditch'; O. Prussian *aulis*, 'pipe'; O. Slav. *ulica*, 'lane'. **a** A merry, joyful song; esp. of Christmas hymns; **b** (poet.) the song of birds.

Caroline, adj. [1. károlīn; 2. kǽrəlain], fr. Lat. form *Carolus*, 'Charles'. Belonging to the time of Charles I. or II.: *Caroline poetry*.

Carolingian, adj. [1. kàrolínjian; 2. kærəlíndžiən]. See prec. Belonging to the time of Charlemagne, or to the dynasty founded by him; also Carlovingian.

carom, n. [1. kárum; 2. kǽrəm], fr. Fr. *carambolage*, 'a cannon in billiards', *caramboler*, 'to make a cannon', fr. *carambole*, 'the red ball'; etymol. doubtful. (billiards) Cannon; now obsolete, except for French and American billiards played on table without pockets.

carotid (I.), adj. & n. [1. karótid; 2. kərɔ́tid]. Fr. *carotide*, fr. Gk. *karōtídes*, 'the great arteries of the neck', fr. *káros*, 'heavy sleep, torpor', fr. belief that drowsiness was caused by the carotids. Etymol. obscure. **a** adj. Pertaining to, situated near, one of the carotids: *carotid gland* &c.; **b** n., also *carotid artery*, one of the two great arteries of the neck.

carousal, n. [1. karóuzl; 2. kəráuzl]. See **carouse** & **-al**. A hilarious, jovial feast; noisy drinking-bout.

carouse, vb. intrans. & n. [1. karóuz; 2. kəráuz]. Fr. *carousse*, fr. Germ. *gar aus*, 'right out, to the bottom', in reference to emptying the cup at one gulp in drinking. **1.** vb. To drink deeply and with joviality, to feast, engage in a carousal. **2.** n. Act of carousing, a jolly, copious feast accompanied by plentiful potations.

carp (I.), n. [1. karp; 2. kāp]. Occurs not only in most Gmc. languages, but in nearly identical form in Lat. *carpa*, Russ. *karp*, Lith. *karpa*, W. *karp*. Perh. a pre-Aryan word in Europe wh. penetrated through Gmc. into other languages; cp. also Gk. *kuprînos*, Scrt. *śapharaś* &c. **a** (zool.) A family of fresh-water fish, *Cyprinidae*, which includes the common carp, also gudgeon, chub, roach &c.; **b** the common carp, often bred in lakes and ponds; the 'gold fish' of China is a special variety.

carp (II.), vb. intrans. M.E. *carpen*, 'say, speak', fr. O.N. *karpa*, 'boast', but later sense influenced by Lat. *carpere*, 'to pluck'. See this base under **carpel**. To find fault unreasonably, in a sharp, biting, unpleasant manner (usually *carp at*; esp. in Pres. Part. form as adj.): *carping criticism* &c.

carpal, adj. & n. [1. kárpl; 2. kápl], fr. **carpus** & **-al**. **a** adj. Pertaining to the carpus, or wrist, or the corresponding part in the fore-limb of vertebrates; **b** n., the carpal bone or carpus.

carpel, n. [1. kárpel; 2. kápel]. Lat. *carpellum*, new formation, dimin. of Gk. *karpós*, 'fruit', the orig. meaning of wh. is 'that which is plucked or gathered'; cp. the cogn. Lat. *carpere*, 'pluck, cull, gather'; further Gk. *krópion*, 'scythe'; Scrt. *kṛpāṇaś*, 'sword'; Lith. *kir̃pti*, 'cut with scissors, shear'. See the same base w. specialized meanings under **harvest**, **harp**. (bot.) Single-celled pistil; one cell of a compound pistil.

carpenter (I.), n. [1. kárpinter; 2. kápintə]. In M.E. fr. O. Fr. *carpentier*, Low Lat. *carpentārius*, 'waggon or carriage builder', earlier 'a waggon driver', fr. *carpentum*, 'two-wheeled covered carriage, coach, chariot; agricultural cart'; cp. *carpentāria*, 'waggon-maker's workshop'. *Carpentum* is prob. a Gaulish word, cp. O. Ir. *carpat*, 'waggon', W. *kerbyd*, 'coach'. **a** One whose trade it is to cut and fix wood used in construction of buildings, e.g. roof timbers, floors, panels, doors, and other timber-work fittings; he also makes movable wooden articles of a rough kind, such as boxes and frames, but not household furniture; a joiner; **b** an amateur who makes wooden articles, does repairs in woodwork &c.: *quite a clever carpenter*.

carpenter (II.), vb., fr. prec. To do carpenter's work.

carpenter-ant, n. A black ant that builds elaborate nests in wood.

carpenter-bee, n. Wild, solitary bee which lays its eggs in holes bored in wood.

carpentry, n. [1. kárpintri; 2. kápintri]. **carpenter** & **-y**. **a** The art of cutting and joining timber, constructing in wood; **b** the work of a carpenter.

carpet (I.), n. [1. kárpit; 2. kápit]. Found in M.E. as early as 1284; O. Fr. *carpite*, L. Lat. *carpita*, 'kind of thick cloth'; prob. fr. Lat. *carpere*, 'pluck' &c. (see **carpel**), either fr. action in weaving, or fr. the cloth being made of shreds, cp. L. Lat. *carpia*, Fr. *charpie*, 'lint'. **1.** A thick, heavy woven fabric of wool, silk, or jute &c. used for covering floors; also compressed compound of cork &c., *cork-carpet*. **2.** A square, or strip of this, forming a unity, used for a room or corridor. Phr. *on the carpet*, **a** (of a topic, question, project) under consideration; **b** (colloq., of employé &c.) reprimanded. **3.** Anything resembling a carpet by covering the ground evenly: *a carpet of moss, leaves, flowers*.

carpet (II.), vb. trans. fr. prec. **a** To cover with (a) carpet: *to carpet the stairs*; **b** to strew, or cover evenly and thickly, as leaves, flowers &c.: *carpeted with flowers*; **c** (colloq., of employer &c.) to summon (servant, employé &c.) into room in order to reprimand him.

carpet-bag, n. Old-fashioned travelling-bag made of carpet.

carpet-bagger, n. [1. kárpit báger; 2. kápit bǽgə]. Prec. & **-er**. Parliamentary candidate or member imported from another district; one who does not reside in constituency, but visits it occasionally for a few nights; originally an American political slang term, of shady candidates from the Northern States in the South, during period after Civil War.

carpet-bedding, n. (hort.) System of planting a garden bed thickly with low-growing herbaceous plants with bright colouring arranged in geometrical patterns.

carpeting, n. [1. kárpiting; 2. kápitiŋ]. **carpet** & **-ing**. Material for carpets; floor-coverings.

carpet-knight, n. (in disparaging sense) A knight or soldier who has never served in the field, but has gained all his experience at home under safe and comfortable conditions.

carpetless, adj. [1. kárpitles; 2. kápitlis], fr. **carpet** & **-less**. Without a carpet; uncarpeted.

carpet-rod, n., fr. **carpet** & **rod**. Metal rod for holding stair-carpet in position, one being fixed at base of each stair. (Also *stair-rod*.)

carpet-sweeper, n. Mechanical device for sweeping carpets, consisting of a revolving brush set in a covered receptacle on wheels; often worked by electricity.

carpo- (I.), pref. Form of **carpus**, used in composition.

carpo- (II.), pref. Form of Gk. *karpós*, 'fruit', used in composition. See **carpel**.

carpology, n. [1. karpóloji; 2. kāpɔ́lədži]. See prec. & **-logy**. Study of the structure of fruits.

carpus, n. [1. kárpus; 2. kápəs]. Lat., fr. Gk. *karpós*, 'wrist', fr. *k^wrp-, lit. 'part which turns, moves'. Cp. Goth. *hwairban*, 'throw (oneself), walk', O.E. *hweorfan*, 'go, move', O.H.G. *hwerfan*, Mod. Germ. *werfen*, 'throw'. Cp. **wharf**. (anat.) In man, the wrist, the joint between hand and forearm; the corresponding part in other vertebrates.

carrack. See **carack**.

carrageen, also **carrageen moss**, n. [1. kára-gēn; 2. kǽrəgīn], fr. place-name Carragheen. Edible sea-weed found on coasts of Ireland.

carriage, n. [1. kárij; 2. kǽridž]. O. Fr. *cariage*, 'that which is carried, luggage'. Mod. Engl. sense of 'vehicle', prob. influenced by the obs. *caroche*, 'coach, carriage', fr. O. Fr. *carroche*, 'stately, luxurious form of coach'. **carry** & **-age**. **1.** Act, or process of carrying, conveying, transporting anything; specif., transport and delivery of goods by rail, ship &c.: *railway companies undertake the carriage of goods*. **2.** Cost of, charge made for, carrying goods &c., expenses of carriage: *the carriage on these parcels will be heavy*. **3. a** Mode of holding, bearing, poising, head, limbs, and person generally; deportment, bearing: *an awkward, a graceful, carriage*; **b** (fig., in moral sense) demeanour, behaviour, manners (archaic and obsolesc.). **4. a** Any of several varieties of wheeled vehicle, esp. a private one with four wheels, drawn by horse, mule, or donkey, for conveying persons: *private carriage*; *carriage and pair*; *pony-carriage*; Phrs. *to start, set up, a carriage*, to own a carriage for first time; *to keep, drive, a carriage*, to have a private carriage; **b** compartment of a coach on a railway, reserved for passengers and light luggage; **c** that part of a motor-car, distinct from wheels, engine &c., in which the passengers sit. **5.** Applied to various contrivances for bearing and moving heavy things, parts of machinery &c.; e.g. **a** heavy frame on wheels on which cannon of various sizes are supported and transported, *gun-carriage*; **b** device for shifting the part of a typewriter which holds the paper from one position to another.

carriageable, adj. [1. kárijabl; 2. kǽridžəbl]. See prec. & **-able**. Of road, having a surface which permits of a carriage being driven along it. (Rare.)

carriage-dog, n. White and black or brown spotted Dalmatian, formerly chained to back axle of private carriage to prevent unauthorized persons from riding upon it.

carriage-drive, n. Road through private grounds, esp. one leading to the house.

carriage-folk, n. (vulg.) People who keep a private carriage; implying that they are in comfortable circumstances.

carriage-forward, adv. Tradesman's phrase meaning that the cost of carrying goods is to be paid on delivery.

carriage-free, adv. Cost of transport of goods paid by sender, not by recipient, and therefore 'free' so far as the latter is concerned.

carriage-horse, n. One broken to harness and used, or suitable, for drawing a carriage.

carriage-paid, adv. Qualifying *to send, sent* &c., implying that cost of delivery of goods is paid beforehand by sender.

carrick bend, n. [1. kárik bénd; 2. kǽrik bend]. Etymol. doubtful, perh. variant of **carack**. (naut.) Special kind of knot for joining two cables.

carrier, n. [1. kárier; 2. kǽriə]. **carry** & **-er**. **1. a** Person whose trade it is to carry goods of all kinds for hire from one place to another, and to distribute them to the persons to whom, or at the places to which, they are severally addressed; **b** specif., a trading concern, such as a railway or steamboat company, part of whose recognized business it is to carry goods. Phr. *common carrier*, one licensed to ply the trade. **2. a** Part of a machine which moves, and bears with it something which in the process of the work done by the machine requires to be shifted from one position to another; **b** support for luggage &c., attached to motor-car or bicycle. **3.** Person, or thing, acting as medium of transmission, (e.g. of disease germs): *milk is a recognized carrier of infection*; *certain persons are carriers of diseases, such as typhoid and diphtheria*.

carrier-pigeon, n. A variety of pigeon with special faculty for long flight, and for finding its way home from long distances, used to carry written messages.

carriole, n. [1. káriōl; 2. kǽrioul]. Fr., fr. Med. Lat. *carriola*, dimin. of *carrus*, 'two-wheeled waggon'. See **car**. **a** Light, open car for one (archaic); **b** Canadian sledge.

carrion, n. & adj. [1. káriun; 2. kǽriən]. M.E. *caroin, carion*, O. Fr. *caroigne*, Mod. Fr. *charoigne*, Low Lat. *caronia*, fr. Lat. *caro*, genit. *carnis*, 'flesh'. See **carnal**. **a** n. Putrefying animal carcass, rotten flesh; meat unfit for food; **b** adj., resembling, belonging to, carrion.

carrion-beetle, n. One of numerous sorts of beetles that feed upon dead animals.

carrion-crow, n. The black crow.

carronade, n. [1. kàrunád; 2. kǽrənéid], fr. Carron, in Scotland, where gun was first made. A short naval gun for throwing heavy shot.

carron-oil, n. [1. kárun óil; 2. kǽrən ɔ́il]. Said to be first used at Carron ironworks, in Scotland. A mixture of linseed-oil and lime-water, used for treating burns.

carrot, n. [1. kárut; 2. kǽrət]. Fr. *carotte*, fr. Lat. *carōta*, fr. Gk. *karōtón*. The suggestion of Boisacq that this Gk. word is derived fr. a suppositious **káros*, meaning 'head', fr. wh. another etymologist derives the vb. *karoûsthai*, 'to feel the head heavy', *kárōsis*, 'heaviness of head', &c., is not convincing. **a** An annual plant, *Daucus carota*, root of which is used as a vegetable; it is orange-red in colour, broad at the top and tapering, and of a sweetish taste; **b** pl. *carrots* (colloq.), red-haired person.

carroty, adj. [1. káruti; 2. kǽrəti]. Prec. & **-y**. Having colour of a carrot, reddish; applied especially to human hair of this colour.

carry (I.), vb. trans. & intrans. [1. kári; 2. kǽri]. M.E. *carien*, O. Fr. (Picard.) *carier*, cp. Fr. *charrier*, orig. 'transport in a car'; Low Lat. *carricāre*. See **car**. In the various meanings of the word in English, the senses of moving and supporting the weight of something, either combined, or singly, appear always to lurk, whether in the literal or figurative uses. **A.** trans. **1. a** To support the weight of something, and move it from one place to another while doing so: *to carry a box on one's shoulder*; *carry a basket in one's hand*; *carry a bundle in one's arms*. Phrs. *carry coals to Newcastle*, do something which is unnecessary; *carry one's bat* (at cricket), not to be out when innings is finished; *to carry weight*, of a race-horse, to be handicapped; *to carry sail*, of a ship; *to carry one's liquor like a gentleman*, without showing signs of intoxication; **b** specif., to cart hay from field after it is fully made: *the hay was cut and carried the same day*; **c** (of wind) to bear, waft along: *to carry a sound, smoke* &c. **2.** To bear about with one for use or ornament: *to carry a gun, stick, sword*. **3.** To support weight of something while remaining stationary: *the timbers carry the whole weight of the roof*. Phr. (of argument &c.) *to carry weight*, to be convincing, weighty. **4.** To maintain, hold, the body and limbs while standing or walking: *to carry oneself well, with dignity* &c.; *carry one's head on one side*. **5.** To convey from one place, or person, to another; **a** (non-material things) *to carry information, news, a message*; **b** to conduct, accompany, a person from one place to another: *he carried me to his lodgings* (obs.) **6.** To extend, prolong, in a given direction: *to carry a wall round a field*; *carry trellis work up round a window* &c. **7.** To move one's eye, shift one's range of vision: *to carry one's eye along a line* &c. **8.** (mil.) To gain, obtain possession of, by successful attack: *to carry an enemy's position, a fortress* &c.; (fig.) *to carry everything, all, before one*, be uniformly successful. **9. a** (of persons) To win over to one's own view by persuasion and argument: *to carry one's audience with one*; *I hope to carry you with me*; **b** (of opinions, proposals &c.) to succeed in commending these by persuading others that they are sound, obtain approval and support for them: *to carry a resolution* (*at a meeting*); *to carry one's point*. **10.** (of various mental processes) **a** To retain in the memory: *to carry something in one's head*; **b** to induce, impose, impress with: *his words carried conviction to his hearers*; **c** to bring along as a necessary consequence, involve, imply: *promotion carries with it higher pay*. **11.** (accounts, usually with *over*) To transfer (figures &c.) from one column to another. **B.** intrans. **1.** To perform act of carrying; chiefly in Phr. *to fetch and carry* (*for somebody*). **2. a** To traverse space, reach to a certain distance; (of sound) *his voice did not carry beyond the first few rows*; *the sound of the guns carried many miles*; **b** to cause to traverse space, be capable of propelling; (of guns) *our guns would not carry as far as the enemy ships*. **C.** with adv. *Carry away*, trans., **a** lit. to remove, e.g. a load of bricks &c.; **b** (of storm, wind, water, collision) to break off, remove forcibly from position (of ship's mast &c.); **c** (of action on, or through the emotions) to stir feelings of, deprive of cool judgement: *carried away by enthusiasm, by eloquence* &c. *Carry forward*, trans., **a** to advance, make progress with (an enterprise &c.); **b** (book-keeping) to transfer an item, entry, to next page, statement of accounts &c. *Carry off*, trans., **a** to take, lead, away, remove to another place, usually by force (prisoners, booty); **b** (of disease &c.) to remove from existence, kill; **c** to win (prize, honours &c.); **d** to make the best of: *to carry* (*a thing*) *off well*, to put a good face on a matter, show self-possession. *Carry on*, **a** trans., to pursue, continue, employ oneself in (a business, a discussion &c.); **b** intrans., (i.) to keep on, keep going (at work &c.); (ii.) (colloq.) to behave in an excited, angry, or flirtatious manner. *Carry out*, trans., to accomplish, continue to the end, complete (a scheme, threat, enterprise &c.). *Carry over*, trans. (Stock Exchange), to postpone date of settlement, hold till next selling-day. *Carry through*, trans., **a** to accomplish, complete: *carry an undertaking through*; **b** to support, sustain (in difficulties &c.): *his courage will carry him through*.

carry (II.), n., fr. prec. **a** Position of rifle or sword held vertically in front of right shoulder, esp. in Phr. *at the carry*; **b** flight, range of projectile from gun, or ball when hit by bat or club.

carryings-on, n. [1. kári ingz ón; 2. kǽri-iŋz ɔ́n]. (colloq.) Frivolous, slightly reprehensible behaviour.

carrying-trade, n. [1. kári-ing tråd; 2. kǽri-iŋ treid]. That consisting in the transport of goods, esp. by water.

cart (I.), n. [1. kart; 2. kāt]. O.E. *cræt*, M.E. *carte* &c. The latter may be fr. O.N. *kartr*. Etymol. doubtful. Celt. words, such as W. *kert*, Gael. *cairt*, may be borrowed fr. Engl.; perh. connected w. **crate**. **a** A two- or four-wheeled vehicle, drawn by one or more horses, for carrying loads; used of various vehicles, e.g. those used by tradesmen for distributing wares: *butcher's, baker's cart* &c.; by carriers for their trade; by coal-merchants: *coal cart*; by agricultural labourers for moving farm produce, calves &c. (see

wa(g)gon); Phrs. *to put the cart before the horse*, reverse natural order of things, transpose cause and effect &c.; *in the cart* (vulg. and colloq.), in a fix or awkward situation; **b** a light, two-wheeled horse-drawn carriage for conveying persons: *dog-cart* &c.

cart (II.), vb. trans. & intrans., fr. prec. **A.** trans. To carry, convey, in a cart: *to cart dung, hay* &c.; specif. **a** to carry crops to stack or barn; **b** (stag-hunting) to convey the deer to the meet. Phr. *cart about*, to carry, take, about with one (implying encumbrance). **B.** intrans. To drive a cart, work with a cart.

cartage, n. [1. kártij; 2. kátidž]. Prec. & **-age.** **a** Conveyance of goods by cart; **b** sum payable for such work.

carte, quarte, n. [1. kart; 2. kāt]. Fr. 'fourth'. One of the positions in fencing.

carte blanche, n. [1. kárt bláhnsh; 2. kát bláʃ]. Fr., 'blank paper'. See **card (II.)**. (lit.) A blank paper, form &c., entrusted to a person to fill up as he pleases; hence (fig.) *to give carte blanche*, full power of action, freedom of discretion, esp. in expenditure.

carte-de-visite, n. [1. kárt de vizḗt; 2. kát də vizít]. Fr., 'visiting card'. Special size of photograph, about $3\frac{1}{2} \times 2\frac{1}{4}$ in.

cartel, n. [1. kártel; 2. kátεl]. Fr., fr. Ital. *cartello*, fr. Lat. *charta*. See **charter** & **card (II.)**. Anything written or in writing; specif. **a** written agreement between belligerents as to exchange of prisoners; **b** written challenge to a duel; **c** also as in Germ. *kartel*, a voluntary combination of a loose kind between manufacturers of the same commodity, fixing prices, the pooling of orders &c. each business maintaining its independence.

carter, n. [1. kárter; 2. kátə]. **cart (II.)** & **-er.** Specif., one in charge of, and who drives, carts, and teams of horses; man who does the carting on a farm, as distinct from one who works on the land; one who drives heavy carts for tradesmen, esp. who conveys heavy merchandise in a cart between docks or railway stations and a merchant's warehouse, or who collects and distributes goods with a cart for firm of common carriers.

Cartesian, adj. & n. [1. kartḗzian, -tḗzhian; 2. kātíziən, -tíziən], fr. name of Fr. philosopher & mathematician, Descartes (1596–1650). **a** adj. Pertaining to Descartes and his philosophical and mathematical doctrines and methods; **b** n., follower of Descartes.

Cartesianism, n. [1. kartḗzianizm; 2. katíziənizəm]. Prec. & **-ism.** System and methods of Descartes.

cartful, n. [1. kártfool; 2. kátful]. **cart (I.)** & **-ful.** Amount that is usually carried in a cart, or that a cart will hold.

cart-horse, n., fr. **cart (I.)** & **horse.** One of a specially large, heavy, strong breed of horses, capable of drawing heavy loads. Phrs. *clumsy as a cart-horse*; *strong as a cart-horse.*

Carthusian, adj. & n. [1. karthúzian; 2. kaþjúziən]. Low Lat. *Cartusianus*, fr. Fr. Place-Name Chartreuse, where St. Bruno founded religious order of monks in 1086. **1.** adj. **a** Belonging to, connected with, the order founded by St. Bruno; **b** of, connected with *Charterhouse School.* **2.** n. **a** Member of St. Bruno's order of monks; **b** member, pupil, of *Charterhouse School*; *Old Carthusian*, former member.

cartilage, n. [1. kártilij; 2. kátilidž]. Fr., fr. Lat. *cartilāgo*, genit. *cartilāgin-(is)*, 'gristle', fr. same base as Lat. *crātis*, 'wicker-work, hurdle' &c.; cp. Gk. *kártallos, -on*, 'kind of basket', perh. also Gk. *krotṓnē*, 'excrescence on trees'. Orig. meaning 'firmly, securely woven or plaited', the base acquired the sense of 'hard, tough substance'; cp. further O. Slav. *krãtŭ*, 'firmly pressed, firm'. See **crate** & **hurdle.** **a** Strong, elastic, animal tissue, gristle; *temporary cartilage*, tissue in young children, animals, which later turns to bone; **b** specif., part of the body composed of cartilage: *the nasal cartilage* &c.

cartilaginoid, adj. [1. kàrtilájinoid; 2. kàtilǽdžinɔid]. See prec. & **-oid.** Resembling, composed of, cartilage

cartilaginous, adj. [1. kàrtilájinus; 2. kàtilǽdžinəs]. Fr. *cartilagineux*, Lat. *cartilāginōsus.* See prec. & **-ous.** **a** Resembling cartilage in texture; **b** composed of cartilage.

cart-ladder, n., fr. **cart (I.)** & **ladder.** Wooden framework fixed to sides of cart or waggon to increase its carrying capacity; esp. for hay, straw &c.

cart-load, n., fr. **cart (I.)** & **load.** **a** Amount of stuff which a cart can hold, and which the horse or team can draw at a time; **b** specif., used as a rough measure, for manure, gravel, straw &c.; the amount of one of these which can be put into a cart, and drawn in a single journey; **c** (colloq.), a large, undetermined quantity of anything. Phr. *to come down (on a person) like a cart-load of bricks*, to rebuke very severely.

cartographer, n. [1. kartógrafer; 2. kātɔ́grəfə]. See **card (II.)**, & **-graph(er).** Map-maker.

cartographic(al), adj. [1. kàrtōgráfikl; 2. kàtougrǽfikl]. See prec. & **-ic** & **-al.** Relating to maps and map-making.

cartography, n. [1. kartógrafi; 2. kātɔ́grəfi]. Fr. *cartographie*; fr. *carte*, 'map'. See **card (II.)**, **chart**, & **-graphy.** Art of making maps and charts.

cartology, n. [1. kartóloji; 2. kātɔ́lədži]. See prec. words & **-logy.** Art and science of constructing maps and charts.

cartomancy, n. [1. kártomànsi; 2. kátəmæ̀nsi]. Fr. *carte*, 'card', see **card (II.)** & **-mancy**, 'divination'. Art, or pretended art, of telling fortunes, and predicting future events, from the fall of playing-cards.

carton, n. [1. kárton; 2. kátən]. Fr. See **cartoon.** **a** Box made of cardboard; bandbox; **b** white disk attached to bull's eye of a target.

cartoon (I.), n. [1. kartóon; 2. kātún]. Fr. *carton*, 'pasteboard', hence various derived senses (see **1** below), fr. Ital. *cartone*, fr. *carta*, 'card', & augmentative *-one.* See **card (II.)**, **chart.** **1.** Drawing on strong paper, esp. a sketch, design for tapestry, mosaic work, or picture. **2.** A picture, caricature of a topical character in a newspaper &c., designed to express, or influence, public opinion, esp. on political questions.

cartoon (II.), vb. trans. & intrans., fr. prec. **a** trans. To portray in a cartoon; **b** intrans., to make a cartoon.

cartoonist, n. [1. kartóonist; 2. kātúnist]. Prec. & **-ist.** Person who draws cartoons, esp. in sense **2.** See above.

cartouche, n. [1. kartóosh; 2. kātúʃ]. Fr., fr. Ital. *cartoccio*, fr. *carta.* See **card (II.)**, **chart.** **1.** (archit.) A scroll-shaped ornament, e.g. **a** as top of capital of a column; **b** ornamental table bearing an inscription &c. **2.** (Egyptol.) Oval enclosing name, title &c. of a king on a monument.

cartridge, n. [1. kártrij; 2. kátridž]. Fr., fr. prec., wh. has same meaning, 'cartridge', in Fr. A case of metal, paper, linen &c., containing a charge for a firearm, or for blasting &c.: *ball-cartridge*, containing shot as well as explosive; *blank cartridge*, with explosive only.

cartridge-belt, n. One fitted with pockets for cartridges.

cartridge-clip, n. Device for holding a number of cartridges conveniently for use in magazine-rifle &c.

cartridge-paper, n. Stout, roughish paper used for making cartridge-cases; a kind of drawing-paper.

cart-track, n., fr. **cart (I.)** & **track.** Rough way through a field merely worn by carts passing, and not properly made as a road.

cartulary, n. [1. kártūlari; 2. kátjuləri]. Med. Lat. *cartularium.* See **card (II.)**, **chart**, **charter**, **chartulary.** Collection, or register, of charters and grants of land, held by persons or corporations; also of instruments conferring or confirming various rights and privileges to owners of such land; such collections are often compiled from the original documents, and may consist partly of originals and partly of copies.

cart-wheel, n., fr. **cart** & **wheel.** **a** Large heavy wheel (of large cart or waggon); **b** a sideways somersault: *to throw cart-wheels.*

cart-whip, n., fr. **cart** & **whip.** Long, heavy whip used by carters.

cart-wright, n., fr. **cart** & **wright.** One who makes, or repairs, carts. (Obsolesc. except as family name.)

carucate, n. [1. károokāt; 2. kǽrukeit]. Med. Lat. *carrucagium*, 'tax on plough, or plough-land', fr. *carrūca*, 'a plough', in Lat. 'a coach', cp. also Lat. *carracūtium*, 'two-wheeled cart', all fr. Lat. *carrus*, 'two-wheeled waggon for transporting burdens'. See **car.** (Engl. hist.) A mediaeval, variable measure of land, as a unit of taxation.

caruncle, n. [1. kárungkl; 2. kǽraŋkl]. Lat. *caruncŭlus*, 'little piece of flesh', dimin. form of *caro*, 'flesh'. See **carnal.** **1.** A fleshy excrescence, e.g. the comb or wattles of a bird. **2.** (bot.) Swollen part of seed-vessel, at the point where the seed joins the seed-coat.

carve, vb. trans. & intrans. [1. karv; 2. kāv]. O.E. *ċeorfan*, M.E. *cherven*, also *kerven*, w. [*k*] fr. Pret. pl., O.E. *curfon*, M.E. *curven*, or fr. P.P., O.E. & M.E. *corfen*, w. *k-* sound before *u* & *o*; O.H.G. *kerbēn*, 'engrave', cogn. w. Gk. *gráphein*, 'scratch, engrave, write', (see **graph**), Lett. *grebju*, 'scrape, cut'. **A.** trans. **1.** **a** To shape, form, a representation of something, produce a decoration, indentation, in some hard material (stone, wood &c.), by cutting or chiselling: *to carve a head out of stone*; to engrave an inscription: *carve one's name on a tree*; **b** to impart, by cutting or chiselling, decorations, designs, ornaments &c. to wood, stone &c., or to objects made of these: *to carve stone into strange shapes*; *to carve the head of a pillar*; *the leg of a chair.* **2.** To cut a joint of cooked meat into slices; to cut up and dismember poultry or game when cooked, at, or for, the table. **3.** (fig., of non-material things) To shape, mould, fashion, secure, esp. *to carve out a career for oneself.* **B.** intrans. To practise art of carving in any of above senses (**1** and **2**).

carvel. See **caravel.**

carver, n. [1. kárver; 2. kávə]. **carve** & **-er.** **1.** Person who carves wood &c.; **2.** **a** One who carves meat at table; **b** knife used for carving meat, also in pl., including fork and steel.

carving, n. [1. kárving; 2. káviŋ]. **carve** & **-ing.** **a** The art of cutting figures, designs &c., esp. in wood, ivory; **b** piece of carved work, carved design.

carving-fork, n. One used to hold meat while carving it, having a steel guard to protect the hand from being cut by the knife.

carving-knife, n. A long knife for carving meat at table.

caryatid, n. [1. kàriátid; 2. kæ̀riǽtid]. Lat. *caryātides*, fr. Gk. *karuátides*, priestesses in temple of Diana, at *Karúai*, Caryae, in Laconia. (archit.) A draped female figure in stone supporting an entablature; cp. *telamon.*

cascade, n. & vb. intrans. [1. kaskád; 2. kæskéid]. Fr., fr. Ital. *cascata*, formed fr. *cascare*, 'to fall', secondary vb. formed fr. Lat. *cāsum*, P.P. of *cadere*, 'fall'. See **cadence.** **1.** n. **a** Stream of water falling in a shower from a height; waterfall; **b** (fig.) something resembling this, e.g. soft folds of drapery, lace, &c. **2.** vb. (rare) **a** To fall in a shower, of water; **b** to fall in soft folds, of lace &c.

cascara sagrada, n. [1. káskara sagráhda; 2. káskara sagráda]; pop. [1. kaskáhra; 2. kæskárə]. Span., lit. 'sacred bark'. A laxative or mildly aperient drug, obtained from the bark of a Californian species of buckthorn.

case (I.), n. [1. kās; 2. keis]. M.E., fr. O. Fr. *cas*, fr. Lat. *cāsum*, 'that which has happened', P.P. of *cadere*, 'fall, fall out, happen'. See **cadence**, & cp. **chance.** **1.** Particular combination of circumstances, special condition of affairs: *his case is a peculiar one*; *we made an exception in your case*; *in evil case*. Phrs. *in case*, lest, if it should happen that; *in case of* (*fire, my not seeing you*), in the event of; *in this, that, case*, in such circumstances; *in any case*, anyhow, under any circumstances; *put* (*the*) *case* (*that*), supposing, assuming (that) (archaic). 2. Actual fact, existing state of affairs: *that is not the case*; *as the case stands*; *a hard case*, difficult, trying, circumstances. 3. Specific instance, example: *a clear case of murder*. Phr. *a case in point*, relevant to, illustrating, argument &c. 4. (specif. med.) **a** Occurrence of a disease in particular person: *a case of measles*; hence, **b** person suffering from a particular disease: *the worst cases are sent to the hospital*. 5. (legal) **a** Question to be decided, cause for trial; **b** a cause that has been tried and decided, and may be cited: *leading case*, one often cited as basis for decisions; **c** (fig.) *a case for conscience* &c., for conscience &c. to decide. 6. (from legal usage) Facts, evidence, arguments, in favour of one party: *the case for the defendant*; *to state one's case*; *to make out one's case*, prove that one is right; *to have a good case*. 7. (gram.) **a** A modification in the form of a noun, pronoun, or adjective, expressing its grammatical relation to another word in the sentence, shown usually by an inflection or inflectional ending. In English, the only case of the noun, strictly speaking, is the possessive; in pers. pron., possess. and acc. dat.; **b** the relation in which a noun or pronoun stands to another word in the sentence. See **case-relation**.

case (II.), n. M.E. *casse*, O. Fr. *casse*, Mod. Fr. *caisse* & (different dial. form) *châsse*, 'box for relics', fr. Lat. *capsa*, 'chest, box', fr. *capere*, 'take, receive, hold'. See **capsule**, **captive**, & cp. **capable**. General term for a box or bag used for keeping, storing, packing, and carrying things; also applied to various kinds of sheaths, and protective coverings and wrappers. 1. Various kinds of box or chest: **a** *packing case*, roughly made box for sending all kinds of goods by road, rail, or water; **b** *uniform case*, long tin box in which officers keep uniform, sword &c.; **c** *jewel case*, box lined with velvet, and specially fitted for jewellery; **d** *bookcase*, upright arrangement of shelves, often fitted with glass doors, for books; specif. **e** (printing) box, with compartments, containing type; *lower case*, that in which small letters are kept; *upper case*, that for capitals. 2. Various kinds of bag: **a** *dressing case*, bag fitted with brushes, combs, and bottles of materials for the toilet; **b** *suit-case*, flat, stiff leather travelling-bag; **c** *writing-case*, flat, folding portfolio of softish leather for carrying or keeping writing materials; **d** *pillow-*, *bolster-case*, linen or cambric bag for pillow &c. when in use. 3. Box together with that which it contains: specif., *case of wine*, box containing 1 dozen bottles. 4. Various kinds of sheath or protective covering: **a** outer, gold, silver &c. cover of a watch; **b** glazed tray, or a receptacle with glass top and sides for exhibiting objects of all kinds in a museum; glass cover for a clock: *glass case*; **c** wrapper of leather, silk &c. slipped over a bound book; the binding of a book; **d** sheath covering insect's wings when folded: *wing case*.

case (III.), vb. trans., fr. prec. To cover, enclose in, something: *case a wall with stone*; *cased in armour*.

case-ending, n. (gram.) Inflectional suffix expressing case-relation.

case-hardened, adj. [1. kā́s hàrdnd; 2. kéis hā́dnd]. **a** (of iron) Having a hard steel surface; **b** (fig., of persons) having sensibilities dulled, and nature made callous by experience of life.

casein, n. [1. kā́sēin; 2. kéisi-in], fr. Lat. *cāseus*, 'cheese'. See **cheese**. (chem.) A crumbling, acid substance, the basis of cheese.

case-knife, n. A knife usually carried, or kept, in a sheath.

case-law, n. Law based upon previously decided cases; distinguished from *statute-law*.

casemate, n. [1. kā́smāt; 2. kéismeit]. Fr., fr. Ital. *casamatta*. Perh. fr. Gk. *khásmata*, pl. of *khásma*, 'gulf', see **chasm**; pronunciation influenced by association w. *case*. **a** Bomb-proof vault in fortification, having embrasures for guns; **b** (in ships of war) enclosed space protected with armour in which the guns are mounted.

casement, casement window, n. [1. kā́sment; 2. kéismənt]. Fr., O. Fr. *enchassement*, 'frame'. See **chassis**, & **case** (II.) & **-ment**. Window made to open like a door, though not reaching to the ground, hung on hinges from sides of opening.

casement-cloth, n. A strong cotton material, used primarily for casement window curtains.

caseous, adj. [1. kā́seus; 2. kéisiəs]. Lat. *cāse-(us)* & *-ōsus*. See **cheese**. Composed of cheese; resembling cheese in texture.

case-relation, n. The grammatical relation in which a noun, or pronoun, or adjective stands towards some other word in the sentence, usually indicated in inflectional languages by a particular ending; in English (except in the case of the possessive) usually by position of word in the sentence.

caserne, n. [1. kazā́rn; 2. kæzə́ən]. Fr., fr. Ital. *cazerna*. Prob. fr. Lat. *quaterna*, fr. *quaternus*, 'four each', & thus orig. a small guard-house for four soldiers. See **quarter** & **four**. Building for housing troops; barracks.

case-shot, n. A quantity of shot enclosed in a metal case, or shell, for firing from cannon.

case-worm, n., fr. **case** (II.) & **worm**. See **caddis**. Larva which forms a protective case around its body.

cash (I.), n. [1. kash; 2. kæʃ]. Fr. *casse*, *caisse*, 'box, chest, treasury', fr. Lat. *capsa*. The word meant orig. 'chest for keeping money' & came to be applied to the money itself. See **capsule** & **case** (II.). Prob. confused in form & meaning w. **cash** (III.). **a** Money in form of coin or notes; **b** (colloq.) money in any form, wealth: *to be short of cash*; *ready cash*; *cash down*, payment on receipt of goods.

cash (II.), vb. trans., fr. prec. To give ready money in exchange for a cheque, bond &c.: *to cash a cheque*.

cash (III.), n. Tamil *cāsu*. Small coin used in East India and China, usually pierced with hole for stringing.

cash-account, n. (book-keeping) A record of transactions made in actual cash.

cash-box, n. A box for keeping notes, coin &c. in, esp. in a business establishment; money-box.

cashew, n. [1. kashōō; 2. kæʃú]. Fr. *acajou*, through Port. *acaju*, fr. Brazil. word *acajoba*. Cp. **cachou**. Brazilian tree producing kidney-shaped nuts.

cashier (I.), n. [1. kashḗr; 2. kæʃíə]. Fr. *caissier*, 'person in charge of the *caisse* or cash-box and its contents'. Engl. word, however, prob. independent formation fr. **cash** (I.), & **-ier**. A person in charge of the payments and receipts (cash) in a bank, merchant's office, shop &c.

cashier (II.), vb. trans. [1. kashḗr; 2. kəʃíə]. No connexion w. prec.; fr. Du. *kasseren*, loan-word fr. Fr. *casser*, 'break, shatter', fr. Lat. *cassāre*, 'bring to naught, annul', related to Lat. *cassus*, 'empty, void, futile', wh. is prob. fr. same base as Lat. *carēre*, 'to lack', see **caret**, & *castus*, 'pure', see **chaste**, & *castīgāre*, 'correct, chasten', &c., see **castigate**. There was another Lat. word *quatere*, 'strike, shatter', P.P. *quassus*, whence was formed a new vb. *quassāre*, 'shake, shatter'. These words had also the forms *cassus*, *cassāre*, & were confused in sense as in pronunciation w. those mentioned above. Thus Fr. *casser* still retains the meanings 'break' &c., & 'annul', cp. *cour de cassation*, *casser un jugement*, cp. Engl. **quash**. It may be noted that we also talk of *breaking* an officer in sense of 'dismissing', prob. through influence of the two meanings of *casser*. (only used of persons, and specif.) *To cashier an officer* (in army or navy), dismiss him from the service, deprive of military rank; a strong expression implying disgrace and dishonour.

cashmere, n. [1. káshmēr; 2. kæ̃ʃmiə], fr. country, the name of wh. is better spelt Kashmir, & accentuated w. chief stress on second syll., or equal stress on both sylls. Cp. **kerseymere**. 1. A fine, soft material woven from the wool of the Cashmere goat. 2. Soft, woven material imitating or resembling this.

cashmere-shawl, n., fr. prec. & **shawl**. Indian shawl made of cashmere, usually elaborately figured and richly coloured.

casing, n. [1. kā́sing; 2. kéisiŋ]. **case** (II.) & **-ing**. **a** That with, or in, which something is surrounded, enclosed, or covered; **b** specif., the wooden framework of a door or window.

casino, n. [1. kasḗnō; 2. kəsínou]. Ital., dimin. of *casa*, 'house'. See **chasuble**. A public place of amusement at a pleasure resort, devoted to theatrical performances, music, and often to gambling.

cask, n. [1. kahsk; 2. kāsk], fr. Span. *casco*, 'shell, rind, skull'. See **casque**. **a** A cylindrical wooden vessel made of staves bound by iron hoops and having flat ends; a barrel, esp. of vessel containing liquids, but also *cask of butter*; **b** a cask and its contents: *cask of whisky*; **c** a varying measure of capacity.

casket, n. [1. káhsket; 2. kā́skit]. Prob. not dimin. of *cask*, since the latter is not found before late 16th cent., while *casket*, 'box', occurs in the middle of 15th cent. It appears to be fr. Fr. *cassette*, & its deformation to be unexplained. The Fr. word is a dimin. of *casse*, 'box, chest', fr. Lat. *capsa*. See **capsule** & **case** (II.). A small box, with or without ornamentation, esp. one for jewels or other small but precious objects.

casque, n. [1. kahsk; 2. kāsk]. Fr., 'helmet', fr. Span. *casco*. See **cask**. The development of meaning seems to have been 'shell, rind', then 'the shell enclosing the brains, the skull, head', thence 'that which protected the head, headpiece, helmet'. The Span. *casco* is derived by Meyer-Lübke & others fr. Low Lat. *quassicāre*, *cassicāre*, 'to smash' &c. (q.v. under **cashier**), fr. Lat. *quassus*, P.P. of *quatere*, 'shake, shatter' &c. The connexion in meaning seems to be that *casco* was orig. 'something easily cracked or broken', whence a 'cask' on one hand, and 'the skull' on the other. (archaic and poet.) A helmet.

cassation, n. [1. kasā́shun; 2. kæséiʃən]. Fr., 'annulment of a sentence' &c. See **cashier** & **quash**. Annulment, quashing of a judicial decree, sentence, or judgement by a higher court &c., as by the *Cour de Cassation*, the highest Appeal Court in France.

cassava, n. [1. kasáhva; 2. kəsā́və]. Fr. *cassave*, fr. Haiti *casabi*. **a** A West Indian tree, from the root of which a kind of edible starchy flour is made; **b** flour from this root, whence a kind of bread or biscuit is made.

casserole, n. [1. káserōl; 2. kǽsəroul]. Fr., 'saucepan', Ital. *cazzuola*, Catalan *cassó*, 'pan', all fr. Gk. *kúathos*, 'wine-cup, bowl', connected w. Gk. *kuein*, 'to bear in the womb, be pregnant'; cogn. w. Scrt. *śvāyati*, 'swell, become strong'. Evidently the Gk. name for 'bowl' &c. was derived fr. the shape. A fireproof dish in which food is cooked and served. Phr. *en casserole*, (meat &c.) served in this way.

cassia, n. [1. kásia; 2. kǽsiə]. Lat. *casia*, *cassia*, 'tree with aromatic bark', fr. Gk. *kasia*, *kassía*, 'kind of cinnamon', fr. Heb. *qetsīā*. Genus of tropical plants, from one species of which senna is obtained.

cassia bark, n. Bark of lauraceous tree, *Cinnamomum cassia*, used in adulteration of real cinnamon.

cassock, n. [1. kásuk; 2. kǽsək]. Fr. *casaque*, fr. Ital. *casacca*, 'great-coat'; prob. derisive form, fr. *casa*, 'house'. For change of meaning see **chasuble**. Long, close-fitting garment with sleeves, buttoning up to the neck and reaching to the feet, worn by the clergy, under the surplice, or as ordinary walking dress, also by choristers and other officials in church; the lower clergy wear black cassocks as a rule, bishops, purple ones.

cassolette, n. [1. kàsolét; 2. kǽsəlét]. Fr., dimin. of *cassole*, itself dimin. of *casse*, 'pan'. See group of words under **casserole**. A vessel with a perforated lid, for holding or burning perfumes.

cassone, n. [1. kasṓnā; 2. kasṓne]. Ital., 'chest', see **case (I.)**. A marriage-chest, usually painted, carved, and gilded.

cassowary, n. [1. kásowari; 2. kǽsəwəri], fr. Malay *casuari*. Bird, something like an ostrich, but smaller and thicker built, found in Australia and New Guinea.

cast (I.), vb. trans. & intrans. [1. kahst; 2. kāst]. M.E. *casten*, fr. O.N. *kasta*; perh. cogn. w. Lat. *gest-(um)*, *gerere*, 'bear, carry about' &c. See **gerent** & **gesture**. **A.** trans. **1.** To propel through the air, esp. by means of the hand; throw. Phr. *to cast (something) in a person's teeth*, make it a ground for reproach. Various specific uses: **2.** To set, place, usually with violence: *cast ashore* &c. **3.** To throw in a particular direction or manner for some specific purpose; **a** (in fishing) *cast a fly*, throw artificial fly attached to line so that it falls lightly on the water; **b** *cast the lead*, measure depth of water; **c** *cast dice*; Phr. *the die is cast*, something irretrievably settled; **d** (of non-material things) *cast a look, glance &c. at*, direct towards; *to cast the blame on a person*, make him responsible. **4.** To let down, throw overboard, from a ship, while still retaining connexion with: *cast anchor, a net* &c. **5.** To shed, throw off, part of organism as a natural process: *a snake casts its skin*; *a stag casts its antlers* &c. **6.** To drop prematurely: *a tree casts its fruit, a cow its calf* &c. **7.** To dismiss, reject after examination: *a veterinary surgeon casts a horse for unsoundness*. **8.** To cause to fall, be immediate cause of: *cast a shadow, light &c. on person or thing*; (fig.) *cast a slur, aspersions, on a person's character* &c. **9.** To draw by chance: *cast lots*. **10.** To record, give: *cast a vote*. **11.** To form, shape, in a mould: *cast a statue, part for machine* &c. (in plaster, molten metal &c.). **12.** To reckon up, calculate value of: *cast accounts*; *cast a horoscope*. **13.** (theatr.) **a** To distribute the parts in a play to the actors; **b** to assign a part to: *to cast an actor for a certain part*. **14.** (legal) To condemn to pay damages in a lawsuit: *to be cast in, for, damages*. **15.** *Cast loose (a boat)*, unfasten connecting cable &c., detach. **B.** intrans. Specif., to throw a line, a fly, in fishing. **C.** With adverbs. *Cast about*, to devise, make plans, seek out: *cast about for means of escape*. *Cast aside*, to reject, abandon, throw away. *Cast away*, **a** to reject, throw aside; **b** to throw away, waste (one's fortune &c.); **c** to wreck (a ship). *Cast down*, **a** to overthrow; **b** (fig.) to depress, fill with dejection. *Cast in*: *cast in one's lot with*, to be prepared to share fortunes of. *Cast off*, **a** trans., to abandon, reject; **b** (fig.) to free oneself from (fetters &c.); **c** (in knitting) trans. & intrans., to finish off (stitches); finish off a piece of work. *Cast on*, trans. & intrans., to make first row of stitches on needle, in beginning a piece of knitting.

cast (II.), n. fr. prec. **1. a** The action of casting; single throw (of dice, line in fishing, net &c.); **b** piece of fine gut &c. fastened to end of fishing-rod, to which the fly, or hook with bait, is attached. **2.** Something that is shed, thrown off, rejected, by natural process, esp. (i.) skin shed by insect, snake &c.; (ii.) small mass of earth left on surface of ground by worms. **3.** The actors to whom the parts of a play are assigned: *a good, weak, cast*. **4. a** A model, figure, made by shaping material in a mould while soft or liquid; **b** characteristic quality: *cast of character, features* &c. **5.** Twist, wrong inclination; esp. *a cast in the eye*, slight squint **6.** Tinge of colour: *a slight cast of blue*.

Castalian, adj. [1. kastálian; 2. kæstéiliən]. **a** Belonging to Castalia, a fountain on Mount Parnassus, sacred to the Muses; hence, **b** poetic.

castanets, n. pl. [1. kàstanéts; 2. kæstənéts]. Fr. *castagnettes*, fr. Span. *castañetas*, fr. Lat. *castănea*, 'chestnut'. See **chestnut**. The name may be due either to fancied resemblance of the things to chestnuts in shape, or to their having been made of chestnut wood. Pair of small, flattish, but slightly hollowed pieces of ivory or hard wood, connected by a cord or ribbon, held by this to the thumb and clapped together by the middle finger in time to music.

castaway, n. [1. káhstawā; 2. kástəwei]. **cast (I.)** & **away**. **a** One who has been shipwrecked; **b** (fig.) an outcast, hardened sinner.

caste, n. [1. kahst; 2. kāst], fr. Port. *casta*, 'unmixed race; breed, race, strain', fr. *casto*, 'pure', hence 'well bred', fr. Lat. *castus*, 'pure' &c. See **chaste**. **1.** One of the hereditary social classes or groups of the Hindus. **2.** Exclusive social group or class generally. Phr. *to lose caste*, forfeit right to respect, or to social privileges.

castellan, n. [1. kástelan; 2. kǽstələn]. O. Fr. *castelain*, Lat. *castellānus*, 'belonging to a castle'. See **châtelaine** & **castle**. The warden, constable, or occupant of a castle.

castellated, adj. [1. kástelàted; 2. kǽstilèitid]. Low Lat. *castellātus*. See **castle** & **-ate**. **a** (of building) Provided with battlements, turrets &c.; built to look like a castle; machicolated; **b** (of a district) rich in castles.

caster, n. See **castor (II., III.)**.

castigate, vb. trans. [1. kástigât; 2. kǽstigèit], fr. Lat. *castīgātum*, P.P. of *castīgāre*, 'cleanse (fr. guilt), to correct, punish'. For **castiagere*, formed fr. *castus*, 'morally pure', see **chaste**, **chastise**, & *agere*, 'do, make' &c., see **act**. **1.** To chastise, punish severely, esp. by blows; also to reprove severely and harshly, to scold bitterly. **2.** To criticize adversely, make corrections in, emend (a literary work).

castigation, n. [1. kàstigáshun; 2. kæstigéiʃən]. Lat. *castīgātiōn-(em)*. See prec. & **-ion**. **1. a** Punishment, esp. a whipping; **b** sharp reproof, scolding. **2.** Emendation of literary work after critical examination.

castigatory, adj. [1. kástigāteri; 2. kǽstigeitəri]. See prec. & **-ory**. Corrective, disciplinary.

casting, n. [1. káhsting; 2. kástiŋ]. See **cast (I.)** & **-ing**. **a** The process of shaping metal by running it into moulds in a molten state; **b** piece of metal shaped by casting, esp. as part of a machine.

casting-net, n. A net that is cast or let down into the water and drawn in at once.

casting-vote, n. Decisive vote; specif., that cast or given on a division by the chairman of a meeting, in addition to his former vote, when the voting on both sides is equal.

cast iron (I.), n. [1. káhst ïern; 2. kást áiən]. Iron smelted in a blast-furnace, containing a large proportion of carbon, and not malleable; cp. *wrought iron*.

cast-iron (II.), adj. **a** Made of cast iron; **b** (fig.) unyielding, inflexible, inelastic: *cast-iron rules, constitution*.

castle, n. [1. káhsl; 2. kásl]. M.E. *castel*, found before Conquest in Late O.E., fr. Lat. *castellum*, 'citadel, fortress, stronghold', dimin. of *castrum*, 'fortified camp'. Various explanations of *castrum* have been suggested, of wh. the most convincing appears to be that of Walde, that it is connected w. Lat. *castrāre*, 'to cut' (see **castrate**), & means orig. 'a place, or building, cut off, separated'. For such transference of meaning cp. **thwaite**. **1.** Strongly fortified building or group of buildings, usually surrounded by a moat, as place of defence. Phr. *castle in the air, in Spain*, day dream, baseless hopes and plans. **2.** A large imposing house, either originally fortified or built in imitation of a castle, but with no present purpose of defence. **3.** A stronghold, place of refuge, giving security from attack, esp. in Phr. *an Englishman's house is his castle*. **4.** (Ireland) *The Castle*: **a** seat of the former viceregal government in Dublin; hence, **b** the viceregal household & government itself. **5.** (chess) Piece made like tower with battlements; also called *rook*.

castor (I.), n. [1. káhster; 2. kástə]. Through Lat. & Fr., fr. Gk. *kástōr*, 'beaver'. Etymol. unknown. **1.** Genus of rodent animals which includes the beaver family. **2.** Pungent oily substance obtained from the beaver, used in medicine and perfumery; castoreum. **3.** (obs.) Slang name for a beaver hat.

castor (II.), **caster**, n., fr. **cast (I.)** & **-or**, **-er**. Bottle, with perforated top, for sprinkling pepper, or sugar, upon food at table; extended to collection of bottles contained in cruet-stand, holding condiments.

castor (III.), **caster**, n., fr. **cast (I.)** in obs. sense 'to turn', & **-er**. Small wheel or roller made to revolve on central pin as well as to turn in any direction, fixed below the legs of heavy household furniture, esp. of arm-chairs and tables, to enable them to be moved along the floor without lifting.

castor (IV.), n. Etymol. doubtful. It is alsc called a 'chestnut', & may be corrupt. of O. Fr. *castanie*. A small callosity on the inner side of a horse's leg.

castoreum, n. [1. kahstṓrium; 2. kāstṓriəm]. Lat. See **castor (I.)**.

castor-oil, n. So called fr. supposed relation w. *castoreum*. See prec. Oil made from seeds of castor-oil plant, *Ricinus communis*, used as a purgative.

castrametation, n. [1. kástrametáshun; 2. kæstrəmitéiʃən]. Fr., fr. Lat. *castra*, 'camp' (see **castle**), & *mētāri*, 'measure off'. See base of this under **meter**. (archaeol.) The art of camp-planning; plan of a camp.

castrate, vb. trans. [1. kastrât; 2. kæstréit]. Lat. *castrāre*, P.P. *-ātum*, 'cut, geld'. Cp. Scrt. *śastrám*, 'knife', *śásati*, 'cuts'; prob. related to Lat. *cōs*, *cōtis*, 'whetstone'. See further under **castigate**, **castle**, **chasten**, **chaste**. **1.** To remove testicles, geld, emasculate. **2.** (fig.) To expurgate (book &c.).

castration, n. [1. kastráshun; 2. kæstréiʃən]. See prec. & **-ion**. **a** The act, or process, of castrating; **b** state of being castrated.

casual, adj. & n. [1. kázhooal; 2. kǽžuəl]. Fr. *casuel*, fr. Lat. *casuālis*, 'accidental, fortuitous', fr. *cāsus*, 'case, chance'. See **case (I.)** & **-al**. **1.** Happening by chance; accidental, unexpected: *casual visit, visitor, meeting, reference* &c. **2. a** Careless, without any definite intention: *casual glance, conversation, allusion*; **b** (colloq.) negligent, tending to leave things to chance, careless of, and indifferent to, convenience of others: *a very casual sort of person*. **3.** Irregular, occasional; esp. *casual labourer*, one who works at irregular intervals, taking any job that offers; *casual poor*, vagrants &c., occasionally in need of poor relief, esp. the vagrants who are dealt with in the *casual-ward* of a workhouse. **4. n.** A vagrant; (in pl.) the casual poor.

casually, adv. Prec. & **-ly**. In a casual manner; by chance, fortuitously; carelessly.

casualness, n. See prec. & **-ness**. The quality of being casual, esp. in colloq. sense (**casual, 2, b**).

casualty, n. [1. kázhooalti; 2. kǽžuəlti]. **casual** & **-ty**. **1.** A case of bodily injury, **a** as a result of accident, or **b** in battle &c., whether slight, serious, or fatal. **2.** (pl.) Number of killed or wounded in battle: *heavy casualties*; *the total casualties* &c.

casualty-list, n. A list of those killed or wounded in time of war.

casual-ward, n. The ward, rooms &c. in which casuals are dealt with in a workhouse.

casuist, n. [1. kázhūist; 2. kǽžjuist]. Fr. *casuiste*, fr. Lat. *cāsus* & **-ist**. See **case (I.)**. Person skilled in, or given to, casuistry, q.v.

casuistic(al), adj. [1. kàzhūístik(l); 2. kæžjuístik(l)]. Prec. & **-ic** & **-al**. In the manner of a casuist; pertaining to casuistry.

casuistically, adv. Prec. & **-ly**. In a casuistical manner, by casuistic arguments &c.

casuistry, n. [1. kázhūistri; 2. kǽžjuistri]. **casuist** & **-ry**. **1.** The art of applying general principles of conduct and morality to particular cases, determining precise bearing of former on latter, discovering and classifying the exceptions, and deciding how far in a given case an action can be justified and made to come under the rules laid down by Scripture, the Church, and society. **2.** (in disparaging sense) Disingenuous method of reasoning, over-subtlety, sophistry.

casus belli, n. [1. kā́zus bélī; 2. kéizəs bélai]. Lat. See **case** (I.) & **bellicose**. Action of foreign power, or political occurrence, between two nations, which justifies declaration of war.

cat (I.), n. [1. kat; 2. kæt]. O.E. *catt*, & in all Gmc. languages: Du. & Dan. *kat*, Swed. *katt*, Mod. Germ. *katze*, O.N. *köttr*; also W. *cath*, Ir. *cat*, Lat. *catus*, 'male cat', O. Slav. *kotŭka*, 'cat', Russ. *kot*, 'tom cat', Little Russ. *kitka* &c. The word must have passed as a loan-word, prob. fr. some non-Aryan tongue, into all these languages, but whence it came is unknown. **1. a** Small carnivorous animal remarkable for its activity, with soft fur, a long slender tail, and retractile claws, domesticated both in the East and West from the most ancient historical period; Phrs. *a cat may look at a king*, the humblest have their rights, even in the presence of the highest; *to bell the cat*, make a common enemy harmless (from fable); *care killed the cat*; *a cat-and-dog life*, with constant quarrels; *fight like Kilkenny cats*, with ferocity; *let the cat out of the bag*, reveal a secret; *not room to swing a cat*, very small space; *rain cats and dogs*, heavily; *wait for the cat to jump, see which way the cat jumps*, wait for expression of public opinion before deciding on course of action; *as many lives as a cat*; *active as a cat*; *to climb like a cat*; **b** (zool.) any animal of the genus *Felis*, e.g. lion, tiger, panther &c.: *the cats* (coll.); *Small Cats' House* (at the Zoo &c.); **c** small animal resembling cat, but of different species; see **civet-cat**, **polecat** &c.; **d** (fig., from uncertain temper of cat) spiteful female: *a regular old cat*. **2.** (naut.) Tackle for hoisting anchor to *cathead*, q.v. **3.** For **cat-o'-nine tails**, whip with nine lashes of knotted rope used by order of judge or magistrate for flogging certain types of criminal: *to give a dose of the cat*. **4.** A double tripod, always resting on three of its six feet, no matter how it is placed. **5.** (hist.) Movable tower or shelter for protection of besieging party.

cat (II.), vb. intrans. & trans., fr. prec. (colloq. and vulg.) To vomit violently. Cp. *as sick as a dog*.

cata-, **cath-**, pref. Gk. *katá*, prep., wh. in comp. becomes *kat-* before vowels, *kath-* before aspirated vowels. The force of the prep. & pref. in Gk. is 'down from, down to; against, in opposition to; over, throughout, along; according to' &c.; it is often merely intensive. Common in compounds borrowed as such fr. Gk., also used in new formations fr. Gk. elements. *Katá* represents Aryan **kmt-* &c., & the same base is found in Ir. *cēt*, W. *can(t)*, 'along, with, near'; Lat. *com-*, *cum-*, 'with' (see **com-**), & *contrā*, 'against'; perh. also Gmc. *ga-*, O.E. *ġe-* (unstressed). It has been suggested that the primitive sense was that of 'stopping, holding', & that the same base occurs in Goth. *hinþan*, 'catch, seize', fr. Aryan **ként-*, & *handus*, 'hand', fr. Aryan **kontús*; the pref., esp. in scientific terminology, is often spelt w. *k* as in Gk. orig.

catabasis, n. [1. katábasis; 2. kætǽbəsis]. Gk., 'a going down'. See **cata-** & **basis**. (med.) Stage from and in which a disease declines.

catabolism, also **katabolism**, n. [1. katábolizm; 2. kætǽbəlizəm], fr. **cata-**, & Gk. *bolḗ*, 'throw, cast', fr. *bállein*, see **ballistic**, & **-ism**. (biol. and physiol.) The breaking down or change of bodily tissues &c. from a more complex to a simpler form; destructive metabolism, contrasted with *anabolism*.

catachresis, n. [1. kàtakrḗsis; 2. kætəkrísis]. Gk. *katakhrēsis*, 'misuse of a word'; fr. **cata-** & *khrēsis*, 'use, employment', connected w. *khráomai*, 'make use of', *khrḗ*, 'it is necessary', fr. Aryan base **g'hers*, 'shortness, lack', cp. also Scrt. *hrásati*, 'diminish'; O. Ir. *gair*, 'short'. **a** The wrong use, misapplication, of a word, esp. by a mixing of metaphors; **b** a change in the form of a word, due to popular etymology.

catachrestic, adj. [1. kàtakréstik; 2. kætəkrístik]. Gk. *katakhrēstikós*, fr. prec. (of sense, use, of a word). Forming an example of catachresis; misapplied.

cataclasm, n. [1. kátaklàzm; 2. kǽtəklæzəm]. Gk. *katáklasma*, 'breakage'. See **cata-**. The second element is fr. *klásma*, 'fragment', Gk. *kláō*, 'break in pieces', cp. also *klásis*, 'a breaking', *kladarós*, 'fragile'; Lat. *clādēs*, 'disaster, loss, destruction', also *clāva*, 'club', fr. **cladiva*; O. Ir. *claidef*, W. *cleddyf*, 'sword'; Russ. *klasti*, 'castrate'. See **clado-**. Violent rending asunder, disruption.

cataclasmic, adj. [1. kàtaklázmik; 2. kætəklǽzmik]. Prec. & **-ic**. Of the nature of a cataclasm.

cataclysm, n. [1. kátaklìzm; 2. kǽtəklìzəm]. Gk. *kataklusmós*, 'a deluge, flood'. See **cata-**. Second element is connected w. Gk. *klúzō*, 'wash, dash against, break over'; cp. also *klúsma*, 'liquid used for washing out', *klúdōn*, 'wave, surge'. Cp. further the cognates, Lat. *cloāca*, earlier *clovāca*, 'sewer, drain', & O. Lat. *cluere*, 'to purge'; Goth. *hlutrs*, 'pure', O.E. *hlūttor*, O.H.G. *hlūttar*, 'pure, clear'. **1. a** An overwhelming deluge; esp. **b** (geol.) violent upheaval which produces sudden changes in surface of the earth. **2.** (fig.) Sudden, revolutionary, social or political event which sweeps away old landmarks and introduces violent changes in the structure of society and government.

cataclysmal, **cataclysmic**, adj. [1. kàtaklízmal, -mik; 2. kætəklízməl, -mik]. Prec. & **al-** & **-ic**. Of the nature of a cataclysm; having reference to destructive upheavals. Specif., (geol.) *cataclysmal theory*, doctrine that the configuration of the earth's crust was shaped by a series of violent upheavals, and sudden changes, and not by the gradual action of rivers, the atmosphere &c.

cataclysmist, n. [1. kàtaklízmist; 2. kætəklízmist]. Prec. & **-ist**. One who holds the *cataclysmal theory* of the earth.

catacomb, n. [1. kátakōm; 2. kǽtəkoum]. Fr. *catacombe*, L. Lat. *catacumba*, prob. formed fr. Gk. *katá* (see **cata-**) & *kúmbē*, 'hollow of a vessel, a bowl'. Orig. meaning was apparently 'something curved', then 'cup' &c., 'cup-shaped thing', that is, 'hollowed-out cavity', & further something shaped like an inverted cup or bowl, hence Engl. **hump**, wh. word in Norw. means a 'little hill'. In Celt. *kum*, W. *cwm* is 'valley'. See **coombe**. **1.** (commonly in pl.) An underground gallery or series of such, with recesses hollowed out in the sides to receive the bones of the dead; a subterranean cemetery. Specif., *the Catacombs*, such galleries in Rome, which formed a refuge for the early Christians.

catadromous, also **katadromous**, adj. [1. katádromus; 2. kætǽdrəməs], fr. **cata-** & Gk. *drómos*, 'a running, course', & **-ous**. See **dromedary**. Of fish, returning to the sea or to lower part of a river to spawn, contrasted with *anadromous*.

catafalque, n. [1. kátafàlk; 2. kǽtəfælk]. Fr., fr. Ital. *catafalco*. Etymol. unknown. The suggested connexion w. Fr. *échafaud*, 'scaffold' is very unconvincing, & the etymol. of this is equally doubtful. Wooden stand, sometimes elaborately draped and decorated, upon which a coffin rests while the deceased is lying in state, or while part of the Burial Service is being said in church.

Catalan, adj. & n. [1. kátalan, kàtalán; 2. kǽtələn, kætalǽn]. **a** adj. Belonging to Catalonia, in eastern Spain; **b** n., native, language, of Catalonia.

catalectic, adj. [1. kàtaléktik; 2. kætəléktik]. Gk. *katalēktikós*, of a verse, 'lacking the last foot', fr. *katalégein*, 'to stop, leave off'. See **cata-**. Gk. *légein*, 'leave off, cease from', is related to Gk. *lagarós*, 'slack, weak', wh. is cogn. w. Lat. *laxus*, 'wide, loose, slack', see **lax**, & further w. O.E. *slæc*, see **slack**. (pros.) Lacking the last syllable of the last foot; (by extension) imperfect in any foot.

catalepsy, also **catalepsis**, n. [1. kátalepsi, kàtalépsis; 2. kǽtəlepsi, kætəlépsis]. Gk. *katálēpsis*, 'seizure': see **cata-**; cp. *lēpsomai*, fut. of *lambánō*, 'I grasp, seize, take hold of', q.v. under **epilepsy**. Cognates in other Aryan languages seem to be lacking. (med.) Condition attended by unconsciousness, loss of sensation, and rigidity of the muscles, as in epilepsy, and certain kinds of trance; a fit.

cataleptic, adj. & n. [1. kàtaléptik; 2. kætəléptik], fr. Gk. *katalēptikós*. See prec. **a** adj. Characteristic of, subject to, catalepsy: *a cataleptic trance*; **b** n., person in a state of catalepsy.

catalogue (I.), n. [1. kátalòg; 2. kǽtəlɔ̀g]. Fr., fr. Gk. *katálogos*, 'counting up, enrolment; list of persons liable for military service'. See **cata-** & **logic**. A list, or register, of names of objects, property &c., methodically arranged on some specific principle, alphabetic or other: *catalogue of books, pictures, articles for sale* &c.

catalogue (II.), vb. trans., fr. prec. **a** To make a catalogue of: *to catalogue books, wines* &c.; **b** to enter in a catalogue.

cataloguer, n. [1. kátaloger; 2. kǽtəlɔgə]. Prec. & **-er**. Maker of a catalogue.

catalogue raisonné, n. [1. kátalog rāzónā; 2. kǽtəlog rezóne]. Fr. A catalogue of books, pictures &c., arranged according to subjects, together with explanatory or descriptive notes to each item.

catalpa, n. [1. katálpa; 2. kətǽlpə], fr. language of Carolina Indians. American tree with large trumpet-shaped flowers.

catalysis, n. [1. katálisis; 2. kətǽlisis]. Gk. *katálusis*, 'putting-down, dissolving' fr. **cata-** & *lúein*, 'loose, loosen'. See cognates under **loose**; originally meaning dissolution. A chemical change brought about in a substance by an agent which itself remains unchanged.

catalyst, n. [1. kátalist; 2. kǽtəlist]. See prec. A catalytic agent or catalyzer.

catalytic, adj. [1. kàtalítik; 2. kætəlítik]. See **catalysis** & **-ic**. Producing catalysis: *a catalytic agent*.

catalyze, vb. trans. [1. kátalīz; 2. kǽtəlaiz]. See prec. & **-ize**. To change by catalysis.

catalyzer, n. [1. kátalīzer; 2. kǽtəlaizə]. Prec. & **-er**. A catalytic agent, a catalyst.

catamaran, n. [1. kàtamarán; 2. kætəmərǽn]. Tamil *kattu*, 'binding', & *maram*, 'wood'; applied to raft of logs. **1.** A raft of logs lashed together. **2.** Boat formed of two hulls held together by bridge or framework, and propelled either by paddles, sails, or steam. **3.** Cross-grained woman.

catamite, n. [1. kátamīt; 2. kǽtəmait]. Lat. *catamītus*, corrupt form of Gk. *Ganumḗdēs*, Ganymede, Jupiter's cup-bearer. Person who serves as a pathic in unnatural crime.

catamount, **catamountain**, n. [1. kátamount, kàtamóuntin; 2. kǽtəmaunt, kætəmáuntin], fr. 'cat of the mountain'. **a** The European wild cat; **b** popular name of the North American lynx.

cataphract, n. [1. kátafrakt; 2. kǽtəfrækt]. Lat., fr. Gk. *kataphráktēs*, 'coat of mail', fr. *katáphraktos*, 'covered up'; see **cata-**, & cp. Gk. *phrássō*, fr. **phrak-jō*, 'fence round, defend' &c., & *phrágma*, 'defence'. The base is connected w. Lat. *farcīre*, 'fill full, stuff', & *frequens*, q.v. under **frequent**. **a** Coat of mail, suit of armour; esp. ancient Eastern scale armour; **b** soldier wearing such armour.

cataplasm, n. [1. kátaplàzm; 2. kǽtəplæ̀zəm]. Fr. *cataplasme*, 'poultice', Gk. *katáplasma*, 'plaster', fr. *katá* & *plásma*, fr. *kataplássō*, 'smear over, spread'. See **cata-** & **plasm**. A poultice.

catapult (I.), n. [1. kátapùlt; 2. kǽtəpàlt]. Lat. *catapulta*, 'war-engine for hurling stones', fr. Gk. *katapéltēs*. See **cata-**. The second element is cogn. w. Gk. *pállein*, 'brandish, swing, whirl' &c., *palmós*, 'a quivering', *paltón*, 'anything hurled; dart, javelin'; further Gk. *pelemízō*, 'swing, shake, tremble'. **1.** Ancient military engine for throwing darts, spears, stones &c. **2.** A forked stick with elastic attached to the ends of the forks, used by boys for propelling small stones, leaden bullets &c.

catapult (II.), vb. trans. & intrans. fr. prec. To shoot with a catapult.

cataract, n. [1. kátaràkt; 2. kǽtəræ̀kt]. Lat. *catar(r)acta*, 'waterfall', fr. Gk. *kataráktēs*, 'precipitous; a waterfall'; cp. *katarrégnūmi*, 'tear in pieces', also in pass., 'fall, rush down, gush out'. Other Gk. cognates of *rhégnūmi* are *rhṓx*, genit. *rhōg-ós*, 'cleft, narrow passage', *rhōgás*, 'rent, ragged'. Cp. O.E. *wrecan*, 'drive, push, expel', *wracu*, 'cruelty' &c., *wræc*, 'exile'. See further **wrack**, **wretch**. **1. a** A large volume of water falling sheer from a height; cp. *cascade*; hence **b** any rush or downpour of water (rain &c.). **2.** A disease of the eye, in which the crystalline lens becomes opaque, and partial or total blindness is caused. **3.** Hydraulic controller or brake in a pumping engine.

catarrh, n. [1. katáhr; 2. kətā́]. Fr. *catarrhe*, fr. Lat. *catarrhus*, fr. Gk. *katárroos*, 'cold in the head', fr. **cata-**, 'down', & *rhóos*, 'stream', vb. *rhéin*, 'to flow, pour'. See **rheum** & **stream**. **a** Inflammation of the mucous membrane; **b** popularly, a cold, a chill.

catarrhal, adj. [1. katáhral; 2. kətā́rəl]. Prec. & **-al**. Caused by, accompanied by, inflammation of the mucous membranes.

catarrhine, adj. & n. [1. kátarīn; 2. kǽtərain]. Gk. *katárrhīs*, 'with hanging, or curved, nose', *katá*, 'down', see **cata-**, & *rhīs*, genit. *rhinós*, 'nose'; fr. base **srēi-*, **sri-*, 'flow', as in Gk. **rhéō*, 'to flow', Scrt. *sárati*, 'flow'. See **rheum**. (zool.) Applied to a division of family of Primates, which includes the gorilla, orang-utan, and chimpanzee; lit., as in Greek word above, implying that the nose is formed, as in man, with nostrils downwards, instead of straight and outwards, as with other groups of monkeys.

catastrophe, n. [1. katástrofi; 2. kətǽstrəfi]. Lat. *catastropha*, fr. Gk. *kastrophḗ*, 'overturning, overthrowing'. Cp. *katastréphein*, 'to upset, overturn'; also 'dénouement in a drama'. See **cata-** & **strophe**. **1.** Sudden and overwhelming event which upsets, and makes a break with, what has gone before; **a** (in human affairs) a disaster, sudden irrevocable calamity; **b** (geol.) a sudden, violent change in configuration of the earth's surface; a cataclysm. **2.** (specif., drama) Culminating point; final, decisive event in a tragedy.

catastrophic, adj. [1. kàtastrófik; 2. kæ̀təstrɔ́fik]. Prec. & **-ic**. Pertaining to, caused by, a catastrophe; having character of great and sudden disaster.

catastrophism, n. [1. katástrofizm; 2. kətǽstrəfizəm]. **catastrophe** & **-ism**. Old doctrine that the geological features of the earth's surface were produced by sudden upheavals rather than by the gradual action of natural forces; cp. *cataclysm*.

catastrophist, n. [1. katástrofist; 2. kətǽstrəfist]. See prec. & **-ist**. One who holds doctrine of catastrophism.

catawba, n. [1. katáwba; 2. kətɔ́bə]. Name of a river in U.S.A. **a** A kind of grape, light red in colour, grown in U.S.A.; **b** a strong-flavoured wine made from this grape.

catbird, n. [1. kátbërd; 2. kǽtbʌd]. **cat** & **bird**. North American thrush, named from its cry.

catboat, n. [1. kátbōt; 2. kǽtbout]. A small sailing-boat, usually having a centre-board, and a single mast stepped well forward.

catcall, n. [1. kátkawl; 2. kǽtkɔ̄l]. **a** A noisy cry or whistle, esp. one uttered by vulgar ruffians as an expression of impatience, disapproval &c. at a theatre, or as a stupid insult to a public speaker; **b** an instrument for producing a noisy, shrill, discordant sound.

catch (I.), vb. trans. & intrans. [1. kach; 2. kætʃ]. M.E. *cacchen*, fr. O. Fr. (Picard.) *cachier*, dialectal variant of O. Fr. *chacier*, q.v. under **chase** (I.); L. Lat. *captiāre*, fr. Lat. *capere*, 'seize, take'. See **captive**. **A.** trans. **1.** To pursue and seize, so as thereby to hinder progress, get hold of: *the dog went after a rabbit but didn't catch it*; **a** to seize, take, by means of a snare, trap &c. (fish, butterfly &c.). Phr. (fig.) *to catch a crab* (in rowing), see **crab**; *catch a Tartar*, obtain something which is difficult to deal with or use; **b** (fig.) *to catch a person*, put into a dilemma. **2.** To overtake, come up with: *I caught him before he had gone far*. **3.** To strike suddenly, impinge upon: *wind catches a sail*. **4.** To be in time for, and avail oneself of: *catch a train, the post* &c. **5. a** To intercept motion of, by grasping, laying hold of, forming receptacle for: *to catch a ball, water in a basin* &c. Colloq. Phr. *catch it*, incur blame, punishment, receive a scolding; **b** (by transf., cricket) *to catch* (*batsman*), *catch out*, put out by catching ball before it strikes the ground; **c** to take hold of, detain by holding; arrest, entangle: *the boat was caught in the reeds; the nail caught her dress*; **d** to allow to be caught, be entangled with, strike against: *catch one's finger in a door, one's foot in a hole, one's coat on a hook* &c.; **e** *catch breath*, cause to choke or gasp. **6. a** To be infected with (a disease, a cold &c.); **b** to receive by communication: (of inflammable substances) *catch fire*; **c** (fig., of non-material things) *catch the prevailing enthusiasm*. **7.** To discover, detect: *to catch a person in the act, catch him at* (*something*). Colloq. Phr. *catch me doing that!*, there's no fear of my doing such a thing. **8.** (of the senses) To receive a momentary impression from, seize (something fleeting): *catch a glimpse, catch sight of* &c.; *catch the eye of*, attract attention of; *catch the Speaker's eye*, of member of House of Commons, to be called on by the Speaker to address the House. **9.** (of the mind) To grasp, take in, understand: *catch a person's meaning, the drift of an argument, an idea*. **B.** intrans. **1.** To become fastened, entangled, so as to be stopped or hindered in motion: *the lock won't catch; the line caught in the trees*. **C.** With adv. & prep. *Catch at*, **a** (of material things) make a movement towards as though to grasp, snatch at: *catch at a floating leaf*; Phr. *catch at straws*; see **straw**; **b** (of non-material things) to adopt with eagerness (an idea, proposal &c.). *Catch on* (intrans., colloq.), **a** to understand, apprehend: *catch on to an idea, meaning*; **b** to become popular, take the general fancy: *a song, fashion, that has caught on*. *Catch up*, **a** overtake, draw level with: *catch a person up in walking, riding, amount of work done* &c.; **b** to check by sudden interruption (a speaker, a person's words &c.); **c** to snatch, pick up suddenly and swiftly (a stick, one's hat &c.); **d** to loop up and hold in place (draperies by buckle &c.).

catch (II.), n., fr. prec. **1.** The act of catching; specif. **a** (cricket) act of catching ball (see (I.) 2); hence, **b** a sudden check, stoppage, break (in one's voice, breath). **2.** Something that catches; specif. **a** mechanical device to check motion, hold something in fixed position, e.g. *the catch of a window, of box-lid* &c.; **b** (fig.) device to entrap, perplex; artful trick: *this question has a catch in it*. **3.** Something caught; specif. **a** amount of fish &c. caught on one occasion, or in a given period: *a good, poor, catch*; **b** (colloq.) thing or person worth getting possession of: *the catch of the season* (in marriage); *not much of a catch*. **4.** (mus.) A round for three or more voices, in which each singer begins a line behind the preceding one, so arranged that the parts of the singers all harmonize.

catch-drain, n. A ditch cut on a slope, hill-side, to catch the drainage and prevent its flowing farther down.

catch-fly, n. One of several plants of the genus *Silene*; they give out a sticky fluid from their stems which catches insects.

catching, adj. [1. káching; 2. kǽtʃiŋ]. Pres. Part. of **catch** (I.). **a** (of disease, usually predic.) Infectious, liable to be communicated; **b** having attractive qualities; taking (of an air &c.).

catchment, n. [1. káchment; 2. kǽtʃmənt]. **catch** (I.) & **-ment**. Drainage of a river, esp. *catchment-area, -basin*, land drained by a river or system of rivers.

catchpenny, adj. [1. káchpèni; 2. kǽtʃpèni]. Of no real value, but intended to catch the public fancy; made to sell readily; showy.

catchpoll, -pole, n. [1. káchpōl; 2. kǽtʃpoul]. M.E. *cacchepol*, O. Fr. *chacepol*, Med. Lat. *chassipullus*, lit. 'chase-chicken'. See **catch**, **chase**, **poult**. Sheriff's officer, person employed to make arrests (esp. for debt).

catch-title, n. Abbreviated but expressive form of a book title, used in lists.

catchweed, n. [1. káchwēd; 2. kǽtʃwīd]. Goosegrass (from the clinging prickles on its seeds, leaves, and stem).

catchword, n. [1. káchwërd; 2. kǽtʃwʌd]. **a** A word or phrase so placed or printed as to attract attention, e.g. first word of a section of a dictionary &c.; first word of a page, in old books printed at foot of preceding page; **b** temporarily popular, often meaningless, phrase, in politics &c.; **c** actor's cue.

catchy, adj. [1. káchi; 2. kǽtʃi]. **catch** (I.) & **-y**. (colloq.) **1.** Taking the fancy, attractive; easy to pick up (of a tune &c.). **2.** Full of pitfalls and difficulties likely to hinder or entangle: *a catchy bit of work* &c.

cate(s), n. [1. kāt(s); 2. keit(s)]. For *acate*, cp. O. Fr. *acat*, *achat*, 'purchase, something bought'. See **cater** (II.), **caterer**. (archaic, usually in pl.) Food, esp. of a rich and delicate kind.

catechesis, n. [1. kàtekḗsis; 2. kæ̀tikísis]. Gk. *katḗkhēsis*, 'oral instruction'. See **catechize**. Instruction by word of mouth, esp. for catechumens.

catechetic(al), adj. [1. kàtikétik(l); 2. kæ̀tikétik(l)]. See prec. Pertaining to catechesis.

catechetics, n. [1. kàtekétiks; 2. kæ̀tikétiks]. Practice and art of catechesis.

catechism, n. [1. kátekìzm; 2. kǽtikìzəm]. Lat. *catechismus*, fr. Gk. See **catechize**. **a** Instruction by means of question and answer; hence, **b** set form of instruction of this kind, written or printed, esp. on religious doctrine; specif., *the Catechism, the Church Catechism*, in the Book of Common Prayer, embodying doctrines of Church of England; *Longer and Shorter Catechisms*, embodying the doctrines of Presbyterians; **c** any succession of questions. Phr. *to put a person through a, his, catechism*, question him closely.

catechist, n. [1. kátekist; 2. kǽtikist]. See **catechize** & **-ist**. One who instructs by questioning; one who teaches *the Catechism*.

catechize, vb. trans. [1. kátekīz; 2. kǽtikaiz]. L. Lat. *catēchizāre*, fr. Gk. *katēkhízein*, fr. *katēkhéō*, 'teach by word of mouth, instruct', fr. *katá* (see **cata-**) & *ēkhein*, 'to sound, ring' &c. See **echo**. **a** To instruct by systematic questioning for which definite answers are prepared, esp. in religious doctrines; **b** to examine by searching questions.

catechu, n. [1. kátichōō; 2. kǽtitʃū]. Malay *kāchū*. See **cashew**. A strong astringent obtained from several East Asiatic plants.

catechumen, n. [1. kàtekúmen; 2. kæ̀tikjúmən]. Lat. *catēchūmenus*, fr. Gk. *katēkhoúmenos*, 'instructed'. See **catechize**. **a** A convert, neophyte, or novice receiving religious instruction prior to baptism; esp. in the Early Church; **b** one undergoing elementary instruction of any kind.

categorical, adj. [1. kàtegórikl; 2. kætigɔ́rikl]. See **category**, & **-ic** & **-al**. **a** Of, belonging to, a category; **b** unconditional, not relative, without qualification, absolute, positive (of statement &c.).

categorically, adv. Prec. & **-ly**. Unconditionally, without qualification.

category, n. [1. kátegori; 2. kǽtigəri]. Lat., fr. Gk. *katēgoría*, 'accusation', lit. 'statement made in the assembly', fr. *katá-* (see **cata-**) & *agorá*, 'market-place, assembly', cp. *agoráomai*, 'to meet, speak in debate', *agoreúō*, 'harangue, assert', *agorázō*, 'buy or sell in market-place', *ageírō*, 'collect, gather together', also *gárgara*, 'heaps, plenty'. The base in all these is **ger-*, **gor-* &c., 'crowd', & occurs in different form in Lat. *grex*, base *greg-*, 'flock, drove, swarm', q.v. under **gregarious**. **a** Specif., one of the fundamental classes in one of which all objects of knowledge can be included; e.g. substance, quantity, quality, place, time &c.; **b** generally, a class, division, mode of grouping, based on consideration of certain attributes enumerated for purposes of a given argument.

catena, n. [1. katḗna; 2. kətínə]. Lat., 'chain'. See **chain**. A chain, or closely connected series of events, statements &c.

catenarian, adj. [1. kàtenárian; 2. kætinɛ́ərian]. Lat. *catēnārius*. Prec. & *-ārius*, see **-ary** & **-an**. Pertaining to a chain; pertaining to a catenary.

catenary, n. [1. katḗnari; 2. kətínəri]. See prec. Curve which a flexible chain assumes if suspended by both its ends, each at the same level.

catenate, vb. trans. [1. kátinàt; 2. kǽtineit]. Lat. *catēnāt-(um)*, P.P. type of *catēnāre*. See **catena**. To link together, connect as in a series of links.

cater (I.), n. [1. kā́ter; 2. kéitə]. Fr. *quatre*, Lat. *quatuor*, 'four'. See **quarter**. (obs.) The four of a suit at cards, or on dice.

cater (II.), vb. intrans., fr. n., now obs., *catour*, 'buyer', fr. O. Fr. (Nthn.) *acatour*, O. Fr. *achatour*, cp. Mod. Fr. *acheter*, 'buy'; Low Lat. *accaptāre*, formed fr. *accipere*, 'take, accept, receive, buy'. See **accept**. **a** (lit.) To act as 'cater' or buyer; hence, to provide food for: *to cater for a school feast*; **b** furnish what is required or desired, esp. as ministering to amusement, pleasure &c.: *to cater for one's enjoyments.*

cateran, n. [1. kā́teran; 2. kéitərən]. Low Lat. *caterānus*, fr. Gael. *ceathairne*, 'common people'. Cp. **kern**. Highland robber; member of a clan who is not a duniwassal.

cater-cousin, n. **cater (I.)** & **cousin**. (archaic) Intimate friend; originally *quarter-cousin*, meaning distant or fourth cousin.

caterer, n. [1. kā́terer; 2. kéitərə]. New formation fr. old *catour*, wh. itself meant 'buyer', & **-er**. Such doubling of the suff. is common in old names of occupations. Cp. *poulter-er*, *fruiter-er* &c. One who caters; specif., one who provides meals and service from outside, at private houses, clubs &c.

caterpillar, n. [1. káterpìlar; 2. kǽtəpilə]. L.M.E. *catyrpel*, fr. dialectal variant of O. Fr. *chate pelouse*, lit. 'hairy cat'; see **cat**. The second element is fr. Lat. *pilōsus*, 'hairy', fr. *pilus*, 'hair'; cp. also Lat. *pīleus*, *pilleus*, 'cap made of felt'. See further on this under **pile (VII.)** (of a carpet) & **felt (I.)**. The form in Engl. has possibly been modified through association of second element w. **pill (III.)**, 'to rob'. **1.** Creature somewhat resembling a worm, but possessing several pairs of legs, strong jaws, and short antennae, hatched from the eggs of butterflies, moths, and several kinds of flies. Caterpillars mostly live on leaves, and, on attaining their full development, (sometimes) surround themselves with a cocoon, and pass into chrysalis stage, whence, in time, the butterfly, moth, or fly emerges. **2.** Machine, such as a tractor, tank &c., in which the wheels move inside a continuous flexible band, enabling it to move over rough, boggy, or sandy ground &c.

caterwaul, vb. intrans. & n. [1. káterwawl; 2. kǽtəwɔ̄l]. M.E. *caterwawen*. Influenced by **wail**. **a** vb. To utter a shrill, discordant cry or shriek like that of a cat; **b** n., the discordant screaming or shrieking of a cat.

cat-eyed, adj. Able to see in the dark, like a cat.

catfish, n. [1. kátfish; 2. kǽtfiʃ]. One of several varieties of fish, so called from fancied resemblance to a cat in ferocity, and in having barbels which slightly resemble a cat's whiskers.

catgut, n. [1. kátgut; 2. kǽtgat]. First element doubtful; suggested fr. *kit*, 'small fiddle'. A tough, elastic cord made from the twisted intestines of sheep &c., used for the strings of musical instruments, tennis-rackets &c., and for sutures in surgical operations.

catharsis, n. [1. kathársis; 2. kəþásis]. Gk. *kátharsis*, 'cleansing, purification'. Cp. vb. *kathaírō*, 'I cleanse', *katharós*, 'pure, clean'. Connexion of this group of words w. Lat. *castus*, 'morally pure' (see **chaste**), is questioned by some on the ground that the latter is used only in moral sense. Other suggestions have been made, but appear purely speculative and not well grounded. **1.** (med.) Purgation of, and through, any passage in the body. **2.** (fig.) Emotional relief afforded by art, esp. by the drama.

cathartic, adj. & n. [1. kathártik; 2. kəþátik]. Gk. *kathartikós*, 'fit for cleansing'. See prec. (med.) **a** adj. Having purgative, cleansing properties; **b** n., purgative medicine.

cathead, n. [1. kát-hed; 2. kǽthed]. See **cat (I.)**, n., & **head**. (naut.) A wooden, or iron, projection from the bow of a ship, to which the anchor is attached when hoisted.

cathedral, n. & adj. [1. kathḗdral; 2. kəþídrəl]. L. Lat. *cathēdrālis*, fr. Gk. *kathédra*, lit. 'something to sit down upon, a seat', & Lat. adj. suff. *-ālis*, see **-al**. Thus Lat. (*ecclēsia*) *cathedrālis* is lit. 'a church with the seat, or throne', i.e. of the Bishop. See **cata-**, & the base **sed-*, whence Gk. *hédra*, *hédos*, 'seat, chair' &c., under **seat**, **sit**. Orig. an adj., & = *cathedral church*. **1.** n. The chief church of a diocese, containing the Bishop's official throne. **2.** adj. **a** Ranking as a cathedral: *cathedral church*; **b** containing a cathedral: *cathedral town*; **c** belonging to a cathedral: *cathedral choir.*

Catherine - wheel, n. [1. kátherin wḗl; 2. kǽþrin wíl], fr. name of St. Catherine of Alexandria, who was tortured upon a spiked wheel. **1.** (archit.) *Catherine-wheel window*, circular window with divisions arranged like spokes of a wheel. **2.** Firework in form of a wheel which revolves when lighted, and produces effect of continuous circle of fiery sparks. **3.** A somersault made sideways.

catheter, n. [1. kátheter; 2. kǽþitə]. Gk. *kathetḗr*, 'something let down into; surgical implement for emptying bladder'; fr. *katá*, 'down', see **cata-**, & a base **het-* connected with Gk. vb. *híēmi*, 'send, put' &c. See further under **jactitation**. Surgical instrument in form of a slender hollow tube with rounded end, used for introducing into one of the passages of the body, for purposes of dilation, or to draw off fluid, e.g. from the bladder.

cathode, **kathode**, n. [1. káthōd; 2. kǽþoud]. Gk. *káthodos*, 'way down, descent', fr. *katá*, 'down' (see **cata-**), & *hodós*, 'road, way', wh. is cogn. w. O. Slav. *chodu*, 'step', *choditi*, 'to go, walk' (fr. *-sod-*, w. change fr. *s-* to *ch*, back, open, voiceless cons., after a pref. *pri-* &c.); Scrt. *ā-sad*, 'approach, reach'. See **hodometer**. The base **sed-*, 'go', is identical w. **sed-*, 'sit', the primitive meaning being 'to place', whence, on the one hand, 'to place the foot on the ground, to walk', &, on the other, 'to place oneself in a seat' &c. See **sit**. Negative electrode in a battery; that by which the current leaves; (in wireless) the element of a thermionic valve, from which electrons are emitted, usually the filament. See **anode**. *Cathode rays*, negative, luminous discharge in a vacuum tube, having power of penetrating objects, X- or Röntgen-rays.

catholic (I.), adj. [1. kátholik; 2. kǽþəlik]. Gk. *katholikós*, 'general, universal', cp. *kath' hólou*, adv., 'on the whole, in general', fr. *katá*, 'according to', see **cata-**, & *hólos*, 'entire, whole, complete'. Gk. *hólos* has no connexion w. *whole*, but is fr. **solwos*, & cogn. w. Lat. *salvus*, 'safe, sound, unharmed', & *solidus*, 'firm, compact' &c. (see **solid**, **safe**); Scrt. *sarvátat-*, 'integrity, perfection'. Cf. further, Homeric *oûle*, 'hail!', & Lat. *salve*, in same sense of greeting. **1. a** Universal, embracing all men, of general interest; Phr. *The Catholic Epistles*, those addressed by the apostles to the whole Christian Church; **b** broad-minded, comprehensive, liberal: *catholic in one's tastes*; *catholic sympathies* &c. **2.** Specif. (eccles.), **a** pertaining to the Universal Christian Church as a whole: *Catholic faith* &c.; **b** sometimes used in reference to the Church of Rome in distinction to the Reformed, or Protestant, Churches; **c** applied to themselves by members of the section of Church of England farthest removed from Protestantism.

Catholic (II.), n. **a** As used by a member of Church of Rome, *Catholic* means a Roman Catholic only, to the exclusion of all other Christians; **b** as used by members of definitely Protestant bodies, the word means a Roman Catholic as distinguished from a Protestant or member of one of the Reformed Churches; **c** as used by members of that section of the Church of England which is farthest from Protestantism in belief and practice, the word means a person who holds the essential doctrines of the Christian Church as conceived of before the Reformation, and thus includes Roman Catholics, Greek Orthodox Catholics, and Anglo-Catholics, (i.e. members of the Church of England who adhere to the ancient doctrines and practice of the early Church as they conceive them to have existed).

Catholicism, n. [1. kathólisìzm; 2. kəþɔ́lisizəm]. **catholic** & **-ism**. **1.** The system of doctrine and practice adhered to by Catholics. **2.** Act of adhering to Catholic doctrine and practice.

catholicity, n. [1. kàtholísiti; 2. kæþəlísiti]. **catholic (I.)** & **-ity**. **1.** Catholic character, universality. **2.** Comprehensiveness, quality of being liberal, of having broad sympathies and interests. **3. Catholicism, 1.**

catholicize, vb. trans. [1. kathólisiz; 2. kəþɔ́lisaiz]. **catholic (I.)** & **-ize**. To give catholic character to; convert to Catholicism.

catholicly, **catholically**, adv. [1. kátholikli, kathólikali; 2. kǽþəlikli, kəþɔ́likəli]. See **catholic**, **-al**, & **-ly**. In a catholic manner, in accordance with Catholic doctrine.

catholicon, n. [1. kathólikon; 2. kəþɔ́likən]. Gk. *katholikón*, neut. adj. See **catholic (I.)**. **1.** Remedy for all diseases, panacea. **2.** (obs.) A general treatise; formula of general application. **3.** Church of a bishop in the Greek or Orthodox Church.

Catholikos, n. [1. kathólikos; 2. kəþɔ́likəs]. Gk. See prec. Title of the Patriarch of the Armenian Church.

cat-ice, n. As only able to bear a cat or other small animal. Thin, brittle, white ice formed over shallow pools, from which the water has afterwards receded.

catkin, n. [1. kátkin; 2. kǽtkin]. Lit. 'little cat', fr. supposed resemblance to a cat's tail. The downy flower-spike or ament of the hazel, willow &c.

cat-lap, n. See lap (III.). (vulg.) Very weak, ill-made tea, slops.

catlike, adj. [1. kátlīk; 2. kǽtlaik]. Resembling a cat, i.e. lithe and active; or something pertaining to a cat (disposition, tread &c.), soft, stealthy, noiseless.

catling, n. [1. kátling; 2. kǽtliŋ]. **cat** & **-ling**. **1.** (rare) A little cat. **2.** (surg.) A delicate amputating-knife. **3.** Catgut.

cat mint, also **cat nip**, n. A herbaceous aromatic plant, of the mint family, with a tall spike of small blue flowers, very attractive to cats.

cat-o'-nine-tails, n. [1. kàtonīntālz ; 2. kǽtənáinteilz]. See **cat (I.)**. Whip with nine lashes.

catoptric, adj. [1. katóptrik ; 2. kətɔ́ptrik]. Gk. *katoptrikós*, 'pertaining to a mirror', fr. *kátoptron*, 'mirror'. See **cata-** & **optic**. Pertaining to, produced by, reflection of light.

catoptrics, n., fr. prec. The study of the reflection of light.

cat's-cradle, n. A child's game, played with piece of string looped over the fingers to form geometrical designs and transferred from the fingers of one player to those of another.

cat's-eye, n., fr. supposed resemblance in the way it reflects light. A kind of semi-precious stone of yellowish brown colour; a variety of quartz or chrysoberyl.

cat's-foot, n. Ground-ivy.

cat's-meat, n. **a** Horse-flesh, offal &c. sold in towns, in small slices stuck on skewers, as food for cats; **b** (derisively) poor, unappetizing meat; *cat's-meat-man*, itinerant hawker of cat's meat.

cat's-paw, n. **1.** A person used by another as an unsuspecting agent, or tool, esp. in nefarious dealings; from fable of monkey which used cat's paw to draw hot chestnuts from the fire. Phr. *to make a cat's-paw of a person.* **2.** (naut.) A light breeze, just strong enough to ruffle the water.

cat's-tail, n. **a** Variety of the plant bugloss; **b** also name of various grasses, as timothy grass, or the horsetail.

cat's whisker, cat-whisker, n. Fine, coiled, movable contact wire in a crystal set for wireless.

cattle, n. [1. kátl ; 2. kǽtl]. M.E., fr. O. Fr. *catel*, 'property'; dialectal variant of **chattel**; fr. Low Lat. *captatale*, fr. *capitale*, 'property', orig. 'chief possessions'. See **capital.** Original meaning survives in *chattel.* **a** Bovine animals (esp. when domesticated), contrasted with sheep; *black cattle*, small breeds of oxen from Scotland and Wales; **b** also wild oxen, buffaloes &c.; **c** (contemptuously) human beings.

cattle-lifter, n. [1. kátl lìfter; 2. kǽtl lìftə]. See **lift (I.)**. One who steals cattle.

cattle-pen, n. See **pen (III.)**. Small enclosure for cattle.

cattle-plague, n. Infectious disease attacking cattle; murrain, esp. rinderpest.

cattle-truck, n. Special railway-truck, closed to about height of animal's head, and open above, for carrying cattle.

Caucasian, adj. & n. [1. kawkázhiun; 2. kɔ̄kéižiən]. Orig. of the races inhabiting the Caucasus; now less specialized. **a** adj. Belonging to the white race of human beings; **b** n., a member of the white race.

caucus, n. [1. káwkus; 2. kɔ̄kəs]. Origin unknown; orig. an American political slang term. **a** Small body of members of an administrative or legislative body, or of a political party within such a body, who meet privately, determine policy, and endeavour to force this upon their party, or upon the body as a whole; **b** any group of persons who, being members of any public body, arrange policy and details of business privately among themselves before consulting the whole body.

caudal, adj. [1 káwdl; 2. kɔ̄dl]. Lat. *cauda*, 'tail', & *-ālis*, see **-al.** Etymol. undetermined. Pertaining to, near, the tail; resembling a tail: *caudal appendage*, tail.

caudate, adj. [1. káwdāt; 2. kɔ̄deit]. Prec. & **-ate.** Having a tail.

caudle, n. [1. káwdl; 2. kɔ̄dl]. O. Fr. *caudel*, dimin. of L. Lat. *calidum*, 'hot drink', Lat. *calidus*, 'hot', cp. *calēre*, 'grow hot'. See **calenture, cauldron. a** Hot sweet drink, esp. one of spiced wine or ale; **b** hot drink for invalids.

caught, vb. [1. kawt; 2. kɔ̄t]. Pret. & P.P. of **catch**, wh. is a Fr. loan-word: M.E. *cauhte*, is on the anal. of M.E. *lazte*, *lauhte*, fr. *lacchen*, 'to catch', O.E. *læccan*, *læhte*, see **latch (I.)**.

caul, n. [1. kawl; 2. kɔ̄l]. O. Fr. *cale*, 'small cap'; etymol. doubtful. **1.** Membranous bag enclosing the foetus, sometimes enveloping the head of a newly born child; this was formerly regarded as a lucky omen, and the caul itself preserved as a charm against drowning. **2.** A cap or net covering the back of the head.

cauldron, caldron, n. [1. káwldrun; 2. kɔ̄ldrən]. M.E., fr. O. Fr., dialectal variant of **chaldron**, cp. O. Fr. *chalderon*, Fr. *chaudron*, Ital. *calderone*, fr. Lat. *caldārium*, 'that which serves for heating'. Connected w. Lat. *cal(i)dus*, 'hot'. This word is prob. cogn. w. O.H.G. *lao*, Mod. Germ. *lau*, 'warm', for O.H.G. *hlāo*, cp. O.E. *hlēo*, 'shelter, warm place'; also w. Lith. *szylù*, *szílti*, 'to become warm'. See **calm, lee (I.)**, & **lukewarm.** Large cooking-vessel, or saucepan of iron or copper.

caulescent, adj. [1. kawlésent; 2. kɔ̄lésənt]. Formed fr. Lat. *caulis*, 'stalk', see **cauline**, w. ending as in *arborescent* &c. (bot.) Having a visible stalk or stem.

cauliflower, n. [1. kóliflòuer; 2. kɔ́liflàuə]. *Collyflory* in 16th cent. The first element is O. Nthn. Fr. *col*, 'cabbage', of wh. O. Fr. *chol*, Mod. Fr. *chou*, is a dialectal variant, fr. Lat. *caulis* &c., 'stalk'; see next word & cp. **cole** & **flower.** The earlier *flory* is the P.P. of O. Fr. *florir*, 'put forth flowers'. Variety of cabbage, with a white, fleshy flower-head, eaten as a vegetable.

cauline, adj. [1. káwlīn; 2. kɔ̄lain], fr. Lat. *caulis*, 'stem, stalk', cogn. w. Gk. *kaulós*, 'stem'; related to Lat. *cavus*, 'hollow' (see **cave**), & to Goth. *-hulōn*, 'to hollow', O.H.G. *hol*, O.E. *holh*, *hol*, 'cave, den, hollow' &c. Orig. meaning 'hollow stem'. See **hollow.** (bot.) Pertaining to, growing on, a stem.

caulk, vb. trans. [1. kawk; 2. kɔ̄k]. Orig. 'to tread', cp. M.E. *cauken*, fr. O. Fr. *cauquer*, Lat. *calcāre*, 'tread', fr. *calx*, 'shoe'. See **calceolaria.** To make water-tight, stop up seams between boards of a boat by packing with mixture of tow and oakum and pitch.

caulker, n. [1. káwker; 2. kɔ̄kə]. Prec. & **-er. a** Man who caulks ships; **b** tool for doing this.

causable, adj. [1. káwzabl; 2. kɔ̄zəbl]. **cause** & **-able.** Capable of being caused.

causal, adj. [1. káwzal; 2. kɔ̄zəl]. **cause** & **-al.** Relating to, expressing, serving as, a cause.

causality, n. [1. kawzáliti; 2. kɔ̄zǽliti]. See prec. & **-ity. a** The state or condition of being a cause; the active principle of a cause; **b** the relation between cause and effect.

causally, adv. See prec. & **-ly.** As a cause; by cause and effect.

causation, n. [1. kawzáshun; 2. kɔ̄zéiʃən]. See **cause** & **-ation. a** The action of causing; **b** that which produces an effect.

causative, adj. [1. káwzativ; 2. kɔ̄zətiv]. See prec. & **-ive. a** Serving as a cause, producing an effect; **b** (gram.) expressing cause.

causatively, adv. Prec. & **-ly.** As a cause; to express cause.

cause (I.), n. [1. kawz; 2. kɔ̄z]. M.E., fr. O. Fr. *cause*, fr. Lat. *causa*, 'cause, reason, purpose, motive'. Prob. fr. **caud-ta*, & connected w. Lat. *cūdere*, 'strike, beat, knock'. Cogn. w. Lith. *kduti*, 'strike, struggle'; O. Slav. *kyjī*, 'hammer'; cp. O.E. *hēawan*, 'cut, strike'. See **hew, concussion. 1.** The force, or agent, that produces an effect; condition from which something results: *infection is a cause of many diseases*; *drunkenness is a cause of crime.* **2.** A reason, motive, ground: *cause for complaint*; adequate reason, esp. *to show cause.* **3.** Object to which the efforts and interests of a person or body of people are directed: *in the cause of science*; *in a good cause.* **4.** Law-suit, action in a court of law; hence case, arguments, evidence &c. in favour of one party in a law-suit, dispute &c.: *to plead a, one's, cause.*

cause (II.), vb. trans., fr. prec. To be the cause of, bring about, effect.

cause célèbre, n. [1. kōz sālábr; 2. kóuz seilébr]. Fr., 'celebrated case'. Law-suit which attracts much public notice.

causeless, adj. [1. káwzles; 2. kɔ̄zlis]. **cause (I.)** & **-less. a** Not produced by any apparent cause; **b** groundless, without adequate motive: *causeless anger.*

causelessly, adv. Prec. & **-ly.** Unjustifiably, on insufficient grounds.

cause list, n. [1. káwz list; 2. kɔ̄z list]. List of cases coming on for trial.

causerie, n. [1. kōzerē; 2. kóuzəri]. Fr., lit. 'conversation, talk', fr. *causer*, 'to talk'. A discursive, conversational article, in a periodical, newspaper &c., on any matter of discussion, e.g. a literary or dramatic subject.

causeway (I.), n. [1. káwzwā; 2. kɔ̄zwei]. Earlier *causey*, as in provinc. dials., fr. M.E. *causé*, fr. O. Fr. variant *causié*, of *chaucié*, Mod. Fr. *chaussée*, fr. Lat. *(via) calciāta*, 'a way made by being trodden', P.P. of *calciāre*, lit. 'to put shoes on', fr. *calx*, 'heel'. See **calceolaria. a** A raised path or road constructed across wet or marshy ground; **b** a raised footpath at the side of a road.

causeway (II.), vb. trans., fr. prec. To build a causeway across.

caustic (I.), adj. [1. káwstik; 2. kɔ̄stik]. Fr. *caustique*, Lat. *causticus*, fr. Gk. *kaustikós*, 'capable of burning, corrosive', fr. base **kaw-*, 'burn, shine', cp. Gk. *kaiō*, 'I burn, set on fire', for **kaw-jō*; cogn. w. Goth. *hauri* for **hurja*, 'burning coals'; O. Slav. *kuritĕ*, 'smoke'. Further, prob. cogn. w. O.E. *heorþ*, see **hearth**, & Lat. *carbō*, see **carbon. 1. a** Having the power of burning, or eating away, by chemical action, corrosive; **b** (fig.) biting, bitter, satirical, stinging: *caustic remarks*; *a caustic tongue.* **2.** (phys.) *Caustic curve*, one formed by rays of light reflected or refracted from a curved surface.

caustic (II.), n., fr. prec. **1.** (med.) Corrosive substance, esp. *lunar caustic*, nitrate of silver. **2.** (phys.) A caustic curve. See prec. **2.**

caustically, adv. [1. káwstikali; 2. kɔ̄stikəli]. **caustic (I.)** & **-al** & **-ly.** In a biting, sarcastic, manner.

causticity, n. [1. kawstísiti; 2. kɔ̄stísiti]. See prec. & **-ity.** The quality of being caustic (in lit. and fig. senses).

cautelous, adj. [1. káwtelus; 2. kɔ̄tiləs]. Lat. *cautēla*, 'caution', & *-ōsus*, see **-ous**, cp. Fr. *cauteleux.* See etymol. of base under **caution** & **cave (III.)**. Cunning, crafty, deceitful (rare and archaic.)

cauterization, n. [1. kàwterīzáshun; 2. kɔ̄tərаizéiʃən]. **cauterize** & **-ation. a** The act of cauterizing; **b** state or process of being cauterized.

cauterize, vb. trans. [1. káwterīz; 2. kɔ̄təraiz]. Fr. *cautériser*, fr. Gk. *kautēriázein*, 'to scar with a hot iron', cp. *kautḗr*, 'burner, branding-iron'; fr. base **kaw-*, 'burn', q.v. under **caustic. a** (med.) To burn, sear, with caustic substance, or with a hot iron, so as to destroy infection or dead tissue. Hence **b** (fig.) to deaden the feelings of, make callous.

cautery, n. [1. káwteri; 2. kɔ̄təri]. Lat. *cautērium*, Gk. *kautḗrion*, 'branding iron', fr. *kautḗr*, 'burner'. See **cauterize. a** Means employed, whether hot iron or chemical substance, to cauterize morbid tissues; **b** process of burning or searing of morbid tissues with a hot iron or a caustic substance.

caution, n. [1. káwshun; 2. kɔ̄ʃən]. Fr., fr. Lat. *cautiōn-(em)*, 'wariness, heedfulness'. Same base as in Lat. vb. *cavēre*, 'to be on one's guard, take heed' &c. See **cave (III.)**. **1.** Carefulness, prudence, care for safety, absence of recklessness: *to proceed with caution.* **2.** Warning, admonition to be wary; reproof which includes blame for past conduct, and warning for the future. **3.** (vulgar slang) Something, esp. a person, which is surprising by reason of unexpectedness, uncommonness or eccentricity; droll thing or person; (in unfavourable sense) person or thing which one should be on one's guard against.

cautionary, adj. [1. káwshuneri; 2. kɔ́ʃənəri]. Prec. & **-ary**. Serving, intended to serve, as a warning; specif., *cautionary tale*, one written to frighten people from wickedness by displaying its awful results to the perpetrator.

caution money, n. Sum of money deposited by a person on becoming member of a society, esp. of a college at one of the older universities &c., as security against debts which may be incurred.

cautious, adj. [1. káwshus; 2. kɔ́ʃəs], fr. Lat. *cautus*, 'careful'. See **caution** & **-ous**. **a** (of persons) Having, or showing, caution; prudent, careful to avoid danger, afraid of making mistakes, slow to accept any statement without full proof, and to take action of any kind until results can be foreseen; **b** (of human action) characterized by, exhibiting, caution, prudence, wariness.

cautiously, adv. Prec. & **-ly**. In a cautious manner; with care, prudence.

cautiousness, n. See prec. & **-ness**. **a** Quality of mind natural to cautious person; **b** characteristic of action of which caution is the mainspring.

cavalcade, n. [1. kàvalkád; 2. kæ̀vəlkéid]. Fr., fr. Ital. *cavalcado*, fr. *cavalcāre*, 'to ride on horseback', Low Lat. *caballicāre*, formed fr. *caballus*, 'horse'. See **cavalry** & **chivalry**. A body of horsemen; procession of riders, carriages &c.; esp. ceremonial procession of horsemen.

cavalier (I.), n. [1. kàvalḗr; 2. kæ̀vəlíə]. Fr., 'rider on horseback', variant of **chevalier**; see also **cavalry**. **1**. A horseman; esp. poet. in Phr. *gallant cavalier* &c., gay, dashing soldier. **2**. A gentleman, acting as escort to a lady, or as partner at a ball &c. (archaic). **3**. Specif., member of the king's party in the wars between King Charles I. and Parliament.

cavalier (II.), adj. fr. prec. (of persons and manners) Careless, free and easy, independent; supercilious, showing a thoughtless and selfish arrogance.

cavalierly, adv. Prec. & **-ly**. In a careless, arrogant manner.

cavalry, coll. n. [1. kávalri; 2. kǽvəlri]. Fr. *cavallerie*, Ital. *caballaria*, fr. Lat. *caballus*, 'poor horse, sorry nag'. The origin of this word, wh. has replaced *equus* in all the neo-Lat. languages, is doubtful, & much disputed. Gk. *kabállēs* (w. same meaning) has prob. a common origin, as has Gaul. *Caballos*, proper name. It is supposed that these are all borrowed fr. a N.E. European language. O. Slav. has *kobyla*, 'mare'. The Celt. languages have borrowed the word fr. Lat., cp. M. Ir. *cafall*, Bret. *caval*, W. *ceffyll*. See also **chivalry**. Horse soldiers; body of troops who fight on horseback.

cavalry bone, n. Hard swelling, due to constant pressure, on inside of thigh of habitual riders.

cavalry-man, n. Member of a cavalry corps.

cavatina, n. [1. kàvatḗna; 2. kæ̀vətínə]. Ital. Origin doubtful. (mus.) Originally a song of an operatic character, but simpler than an aria; now very vaguely used.

cave (I.), n. [1. kāv; 2. keiv]. Fr., fr. Lat. *cavus*, 'hollow', for **covus*; cogn. w. Gk. *koîlos*, 'hollow', fr. **kowilos*. Cp. also Gk. *kúar*, 'a hole', & see **codeine**. Further cognates are Scrt. *śváyatē*, 'to swell, puff out', O. Ir. *cūa*, 'pit', Bret. *kéô*, 'cave'; see also **cauline, hollow**. **1**. Partly enclosed hollow space, or chamber, under the ground, whether produced by natural forces, or artificially, usually having an opening, sometimes horizontal, communicating with outer air. Caves often extend backwards from a horizontal opening in exposed surface of a cliff, and it is lateral extension, in any direction, which is characteristic of a cave and distinguishes it from a pit. **2**. Section of a political party which secedes from main group, from *cave of Adullam*, in 1 Sam. xxii.

cave (II.), vb. trans. & intrans., fr. prec. **a** trans. To make a hollow in, hollow out (hardly ever used); **b** intrans., to fall in, subside into a hollow, hardly ever used except in combination, *cave in* (i.) to subside, of ground &c., and (ii.) (fig., more frequent) to abandon resistance, acquiesce in terms demanded by opponent; give up, give in.

cave (III.), interj. [1. kā́vi; 2. kéivi]. Lat. imperat. sing. fr. *cavēre*, 'to beware, be on one's guard, take care', fr. **covēre*. Cp. Gk. *koéō* for **kowjō*, 'mark, perceive'; cogn. w. Goth. *hiwi*, 'form, appearance', O.E. *hīw*, 'form' &c. (see **hue**); also, w. *-s-* addition, Goth. *hausjan*, O.E. *hīeran*, Mod. Engl. **hear**, Gk. *akoúō*, 'I hear', see **acoustic** & **custody**. For another form **skēw-* of this base, see **show, sheen.** (schoolboy slang) Look out! word of warning given on approach of a master. Phr. *to keep cave*, to act as sentry and give notice of approach of a master or person in authority, when some mischief is in the wind.

caveat, n. [1. kā́viàt; 2. kéiviæ̀t], lit. 'let him beware'. Lat. 3rd pers. pres. subj. of *cavēre*. See prec. **a** (legal). Notice issued by an interested party that no action is to be taken, e.g. in proving a will, until he (the party) has been heard. Phr. *to enter a caveat*; hence **b** a warning, protest.

cave-bear, n. Extinct variety of bear, whose bones are found in caves in Europe associated with those of the mammoth and of palaeolithic man.

cave-dweller, n. One living in a cave, esp. prehistoric inhabitant of Europe.

cave-man, n. Prehistoric and primitive human being whose remains and implements are found in caves in Europe, associated with bones of the mammoth and other extinct animals; fig., person of primitive and violent instincts, impulses, and passions.

cavendish, n. [1. kávndish; 2. kǽvndiʃ]. Origin unknown. Strong tobacco, generally dark in colour, mixed with molasses, and pressed into cakes.

cavern, n. [1. kávern; 2. kǽvən]. Fr. *caverne*, Lat. *caverna*, related to *cavus*, 'hollow'. See **cave** (I.). Another name for cave; a natural underground hollow.

cavernous, adj. [1. kávernus; 2. kǽvənəs]. Prec. & **-ous**. **a** Pierced by, containing, caverns; **b** resembling a cavern, deeply hollowed out; often (fig.) *cavernous cheeks* &c.; **c** (of sounds) as if produced in a hollow place.

caveson, n. [1. kávesun; 2. kǽvisən]. Fr. *caveçon*, fr. Ital. *cavezzone*, 'head-piece', Low Lat. *capitium*, 'head-covering, hood', fr. *caput*, 'head'. See **capital** (I.), & **chief**. A head-piece, with a nose-band and cheek-strap of leather, but no bit, having a strong ring to which a line is fastened; used in breaking and schooling horses.

caviar, caviare, n. [1. káviahr; 2. kǽviā]. Fr., fr. Turk. *khavyār*. The salted roe of the sturgeon, imported from Russia and eaten as a relish. Phr. *caviar to the general*, something that appeals only to a cultivated taste.

cavicorn, n. [1. kávikorn; 2. kǽvikɔ̄n]. Lat. *cavus*, 'hollow', see **cave** (I.). & *cornu*, 'horn'. See **corn** (III.). One of the group of ruminants having horns which are hollow and not shed periodically, e.g. the ox tribe.

cavil (I.), vb. intrans. [1. kávil; 2. kǽvil]. O. Fr. *caviller*, fr. Lat. *cavillāri*, 'to make captious objections'; cp. Lat. *cavilla*, 'a jest', *cavillātio*, 'quibbling, wrangling'. All these are prob. for **calv-*, cp. *calvāri*, 'devise tricks, deceive', & *calumnia* for **caluomnia*. See **calumny**. To raise frivolous objections, quibble, find fault unnecessarily; esp. *cavil at*.

cavil (II.), n., fr. prec. A captious argument, unnecessary objection.

caviller, n. [1. káviler; 2. kǽvilə]. **cavil** (I.) & **-er**. One who cavils, or finds fault unnecessarily; a captious critic.

cavity, n. [1. káviti; 2. kǽviti], fr. Fr. *cavité*. See **cave** (I.) & **-ity**. **a** Hollow space, cup-shaped depression in a solid body such as a rock, the earth &c.; **b** internal hollow chamber in the body, e.g. *the abdominal cavity*; *the mouth cavity* (formed by roof of mouth and the cheeks); **c** external depression on surface of body formed by projection of surrounding bones or soft tissues, *cavities in the neck* (formed by projection of collar-bone) &c.

cavort, vb. intrans. [1. kavórt; 2. kəvɔ́t]. Facetious word, apparently a blending of forms & meanings of *career, curvet, & snort.* (colloq.) To prance about, in a violent, unrestrained, noisy manner.

cavy, n. [1. kā́vi; 2. kéivi]. Fr. *cavié*, fr. native Brazil. *cabiai*. Small tailless rodent, of South America, such as the guinea-pig &c.

caw (I.), n. [1. kaw; 2. kɔ̄]. Imit. Found also in Du. *kaauw*, 'jackdaw', Dan. *kaa*; **chough** is perh. related. The cry of the rook or crow.

caw (II.), vb. intrans., fr. prec. To utter the cry of a rook &c.

Caxton, n. [1. kákstun; 2. kǽkstən]. From name of printer (1422 ?–91). **a** Book printed by William Caxton; **b** (typog.) type resembling that used by Caxton.

cay, n. [1. kā; 2. kei]. Old spelling of **quay.** Small island of sand or coral, near the mainland, cp. **key** (III.).

cayenne, n. [1. kāén; 2. kèi(j)én]. Modern spelling for Brazil. *kyýnha*. Very hot red pepper made from capsicums, also *cayenne pepper*.

cayman, caiman, n. [1. kā́man; 2. kéimən]. Span. *caiman*, prob. fr. Carib name *acayouman*. A South and Central American variety of alligator.

-ce, suff. found in abstract nouns, representing Lat. *-tia*, chiefly in forms fr. Pres. Part.: *indigence, reticence* &c.

cease (I.), vb. intrans. & trans. [1. sēs; 2. sīs]. M.E. *cessen*, so also in 16th cent., Fr. *cesser*, fr. Lat. *cessāre*, 'delay, loiter', freq. formed fr. *cessum*, P.P. of *cēdere*, 'go, walk to; go away, yield, withdraw'. Walde considers that the two meanings of *cēdere* can hardly be derived fr. the same orig. source, & suggests that the former is fr. base **sed-*, 'go' (see discussion under **cathode**), while the latter ('yield' &c.) he derives fr. base **kezd-*, as in O. Ir. *cēt*, 'permission', & in Zend *syazd-*, 'yield to, give way' &c. **A**. intrans. **a** To stop, desist from; esp. followed by *from*: *cease from troubling*; **b** to come to an end, stop: *the rain has ceased*; *all payments have ceased.* **B**. trans. To discontinue, leave off (one's own action): *cease talking*; *cease work* &c. Phr. (mil. command) *cease fire!*, stop firing; (of a bank) *to cease payment*, be unable to meet obligations.

cease (II.), n., fr. prec. Obs. except in Phr. *without cease*, without stopping, incessantly. Now replaced by vbl. n. *ceasing*.

ceaseless, adj. [1. sḗsles; 2. síslis]. **cease** (II.) & **-less**. (of action) Continuing without pause, continuous, uninterrupted.

ceaselessly, adv. Prec. & **-ly**. Without intermittence, continuously.

cecity, n. [1. sḗsiti; 2. sísiti]. Fr. *cécité*, fr. Lat. *caecus*, 'blind' & *-itāt-* (see **-ity**). Cp. the cognates O. Ir. *caech*, W. *coeg*, 'one-eyed'; Goth. *haih-s*, 'half-blind, one-eyed', Scrt. *kēkaraś*, 'squinting'. Walde rejects the attractive suggested derivation fr. **kwaikos*, 'single-eyed', fr. *quai-*, 'single' (see **celibate**) & *oq-*, 'eye' (see **ocular**), on account of the back consonants in the languages other than Latin. (rare) Blindness; usually of moral state.

cedar, n. [1. sḗdar; 2. sídə]. O.F. *cedre*, borrowed fr. Lat. *cedrus*, fr. Gk. *kédros*. The base is prob. **ked-*, **kod-*, 'roast, scorch', cp. Gk. *kodomeúein*, 'to roast barley', Scrt. *khadikā*, 'roasted grain'; O. Slav. *čadŭ*, 'smoke', *čaditi*, 'to smoke, fumigate' &c.: in this case *cedar* orig. meant 'wood for fumigating'. **a** Evergreen cone-bearing tree, with spines, possessing fine fragrant wood; Cedar of Lebanon, Deodar &c.; **b** one of various trees resembling the cedar.

cedarn, n. [1. sḗdarn; 2. sídən], fr. prec. (poet.) Pertaining to, made of, cedar-wood.

cedar-wood, n. The aromatic wood of the cedar tree.

cede, vb. trans. [1. sēd; 2. sīd]. Fr. *céder*, fr. Lat. *cēdere*, q.v. under **cease**. **a** To yield, surrender, transfer rights in: *to cede territory*; **b** to grant, admit; *to cede a point in discussion* &c.

cedilla, n. [1. sidíla; 2. sidílə]. Literally 'a little *z*', fr. name of Gk. letter *zēta*, Span. *çedilla*, Ital. *zediglia*, fr. Gk. ζ, 'zēta', & dimin. suff. Graphic symbol in form of a small hook (ʒ), placed under letter *c*, thus: *ç*, to indicate that it has a sound other than that of *k* [k], in French that of *s*, in Spanish that of *th* [þ].

cee-spring, **C-spring**, n. [1. sḗ spríng; 2. sí spríŋ]. Spring on which carriages are hung, having somewhat the shape of the letter C.

ceil, vb. trans. [1. sēl; 2. sīl]. M.E. *ceelen*, also *ciel*, *seile*, *syle*, 'hang with a canopy'. See **ceiling**. To line with plaster or boards the inner side of (roof of house or room).

ceiling, n. [1. sḗling; 2. sílíŋ]. Early Mod. Engl. *seeling*, *ceeling* &c., fr. Fr. *ciel*, 'canopy of a bed', as in Mod. Fr.; fr. Lat. *caelum*, 'heaven', fr. earlier **caidslom*, fr. **quait-*, 'clear, glowing'. Cp. O.N. *heið*, 'clear sky'; O.E. *hādor*, O H.G. *heitar*, 'clear, shining, cloudless'. Cp. also Goth. *heitō*, 'fever', & O.H.G. *heiz*, 'hot', O.E. *hāt*; see **hot**. Cp. also Scrt. *čitráš*, 'glorious', & *kētúš*, 'brightness, light'. **a** The layer of lath and plaster placed below the inner side of the roof of a house. The ceiling may either follow exactly the line of the roof, or it may be flat, leaving a space between its upper surface, and the inside of the roof; **b** the lining of the upper side of a room, made as a rule of plaster attached to laths fastened to the lower side of the timber work supporting floor above; **c** in aeronautics, highest altitude attainable by aircraft under specified conditions.

celadon, n. [1. séladun; 2. séladən]. Fr. *céladon*; origin doubtful. A light greyish-green or pale sea-green colour.

celandine, n. [1. sélandīn; 2. séləndain], fr. Fr. *celidoine*, 'swallow-wort', Lat. *chelīdonium*, fr. Gk. *khelīdónion*, fr. *khelīdṓn*, 'the swallow', wh. is fr. base **ghel-*, 'to sound'; cp. Gk. *kikhlē*, 'thrush', redupl. form, for **khekhel*; fr. the same base are derived O.H.G. *gellan*, 'shriek', O.E. *ġiellan*, 'to yell'; also O.E. *galan*, 'sing, sound'. Cp. **yell**, & *-gale* in **nightingale**. The first *n* in *celandine* is intrusive; cp. that of *messenger*, fr. *messagere*. Name of two wild plants with yellow star-shaped flower; **a** *the Greater Celandine*, or swallow-wort, supposed to flower with the arrival of swallows, belonging to the poppy family; and **b** *Lesser Celandine*, a species of ranunculus.

-cele, suff. [1. sēl; 2. sīl], fr. Gk. *kḗlē*, 'tumour, swelling', in med. terminology as *hydrocele* &c, cogn. w. O.E. *hēala*, O.N. *haull*, O.H.G. *hōla*, 'hernia'.

celebrant, n. [1. sélibrant; 2. sélibrənt], fr. Lat. *celebrant-(em)*, Pres. Part. of *celebrāre*. See **celebrate**. The priest who performs the central part of eucharistic service, who consecrates the elements and offers the sacrifice.

celebrate, vb. trans. & intrans. [1. sélibràt; 2. sélibrèit], fr. Lat. *celebrāt-(um)*, P.P. type of *celebrāre*, 'to frequent; practise often, repeat; solemnize; honour, praise; make known, publish abroad'; cp. further *celeber*, 'crowded, much frequented; renowned'; *celebrātio*, 'concourse, festival'; fr. base **kel-*, 'drive'; cogn. w. Gk. *kéllō*, 'I drive on, push', *keleúō*, 'I exhort, beseech urgently', & *kélomai*, 'urge on, cheer'. Various other words are cited as cognates by Walde & Boisacq, fr. several languages, but their connexion in meaning is even more doubtful & obscure than that of those just mentioned. **A.** trans. **a** To perform the ceremony of, in a public and solemn manner: specif., *to celebrate Mass, the Eucharist*, consecrate and offer; **b** to observe in a special manner, distinguish, do honour to, by public ceremonies, festivities: *to celebrate a victory, a feast of the Church, an occasion*; **c** to speak, write of, with praise and approbation, as deserving of fame, commend highly: *to celebrate a hero in song*. **B.** intrans. (of a priest) To perform ceremony of consecration &c., at the Eucharist.

celebrated, adj. [1. sélibrāted; 2. sélibreitid], fr. P.P. of prec. **a** Proclaimed abroad, spoken of with praise and commendation; **b** famous, well known (in bad sense as well as good): *a celebrated painter*; *a celebrated trial*.

celebration, n. [1. sèlibráshun; 2. sèlibréiʃən]. Lat. *celebrātiōn-(em)*, 'concourse; festal observance', fr. P.P. type *celebrāt-(um)*, of *celebrāre*. See **celebrate** & **-ion**. **a** Act of observing, and commemorating, by public ceremonies, an occasion or event which gives rise to feelings of joy and thankfulness; the ceremonies and festivities themselves; **b** specif., act of celebrating at the Eucharist; the service itself.

celebrity, n. [1. selébriti; 2. silébriti]. Fr. *célébrité*, 'fame' &c., fr. Lat. *celebritāt-(em)*, 'multitude; festal celebration; renown'. See **celebrate** & **-ity**. **a** Fame, renown, widespread recognition and applause; **b** person who enjoys these, a well-known person, public character.

celeriac, n. [1. séleriak; 2. séləriæk]. Cp. **celery** & **-ac**. Biennial plant resembling celery in appearance and flavour, cultivated for its turnip-shaped root, which is eaten as a vegetable.

celerity, n. [1. seléritі; 2. siléritі]. Fr. *célérité*, fr. Lat. *celeritāt-(em)*, 'swiftness', fr. Lat. *celer*, 'swift'. Possibly fr. base **kel-*, 'drive', as in **celebrate**, or fr. a base **(s)kʻel-*, 'to leap, run', as in Gk. *kélēs*, 'race-horse', also 'small, light, fast boat'; cp. further Scrt. *šalati*, 'hastens', *šalabhaš*, 'grasshopper'; Lith. *szùlys*, 'gallop'. Walde compares also M.H.G. *schel*, 'springy'. Cp. further **hold (I.)**. Rapidity, promptness of movement, or action; esp. of living things. Cp. different usage of *velocity*.

celery, n. [1. séleri; 2. séləri], fr. Fr. *celeri*, fr. Ital. *seleri* for older *seleni*, pl. of *seleno*, 'parsley', fr. Lat. *selīnon*, loan-word fr. Gk. *sélīnon*, 'wild parsley'. Sommer, cit. Boisacq, suggests derivation fr. base **swel-* 'roll, roll up', & compares *eileós*, 'twist in the gut', *eiléō*, 'roll, twist up tight' &c.; also Gk. *hélinos*, 'tendril of a vine', *hélix*, 'anything twisted, tendril', see **helix**. The application to the wild parsley wd. arise fr. this being used for twisting into crowns. The derivation is quite speculative; the initial *s-* in *sélīnon* is unexplained. Garden plant, whose highly flavoured stems are blanched and used as a vegetable, *Apium graveolens*.

celesta, n. [1. selésta; 2. siléstə]. See **celestial**. (mus.) Small keyboard instrument with bell-like tone.

celeste, n. [1. selést; 2. silést]. Fr., fr. Lat. *caelestis*, 'heavenly'. See next word. **1.** Sky-blue colour. **2.** One of the stops of an organ (also *voix celeste*).

celestial, adj. [1. seléschal; 2. siléstʃəl]. Lat. *caelestis*, 'pertaining to the sky, heavenly, divine', fr. *caelum* & **-al**, see **ceiling**. **1. a** Pertaining to the heavens or sky; contrasted with *terrestrial*: *a celestial map*; *celestial body*; **b** heavenly, divine, with qualities worthy of a divine origin; hence, exquisitely beautiful; extremely virtuous or benevolent: *celestial goodness* &c.; **c** like the sky in colour: *celestial blue*. **2.** A Chinaman.

Celestial empire, n. China; translation of native name.

celestially, n. [1. seléschali; 2. siléstʃəli]. **celestial** & **-ly**. In a heavenly manner.

celibacy, n. [1. sélibasi; 2. sélibəsi]. Formed as if fr. Lat. **caelibātia*, abstract n. fr. *caelebs*, 'unmarried'. See **celibate**. The unmarried state, esp. that of one under a vow.

celibatarian, adj. & n. [1. sèlibatárian; 2. sèlibətéəriən]. **celibate** & **-arian**. **a** adj. Advocating, practising, celibacy; **b** n., an advocate of celibacy; a celibate.

celibate, adj. & n. [1. sélibat; 2. sélibit]. Lat. *caelebs*, 'unmarried', & **-ate**. Prellwitz, cit. Walde, derives this word fr. **kailo*, 'alone' & **bhu*, 'being', that is 'living, existing for, and by, oneself'. Cogn. w. first element are Scrt. *kévalaš*, 'belonging exclusively to a single person', hence 'alone' & 'whole, complete'; Lett. *kails*, 'alone, bare'; further Goth. *hails*, O.E. *hāl*, 'whole' &c.; see **whole**. For **bhu-* see **be**. **1.** adj. **a** Unmarried; **b** vowed to a single life. **2.** n. Person who has taken a vow to remain single, or who does in effect remain unmarried.

cell, n. [1. sel; 2. sɛl]. M.E. *celle* (of a monk or nun); fr. Lat. *cella*, 'store-room, granary; bee's cell; mean apartment, hut, cot', cogn. w. Gk. *kalía*, 'wooden house, hut, cabin, cot; granary; bird's nest'; Scrt. *šālā*, 'hut, house, chamber'; also cogn. w. O.E. *heall*, 'hall', in ancient sense of 'residence' &c., O.H.G. & O.S. *halla*. The root meaning seems to be 'hiding-place, refuge', cp. Lat. *cēlāre*, 'hide, keep secret, conceal', & *occulere*, 'cover, conceal'; Goth. & O.H.G. *huljan*, 'to hide, cover', also Goth. *hulistr*, 'veil, covering', O.E. *heolstor*, 'that which veils, hiding-place, darkness'. See **hall**, **helm (II.)**, **occult**. **1.** A small room, small house; part of larger chamber separated off by dividing partition. Various specific meanings: **a** a room for one person in a monastery, nunnery; **b** hermit's one-roomed dwelling; **c** small monastery or nunnery dependent on a larger house; **d** small compartment in a prison in which a single prisoner is kept. Phr. *condemned cell*, for a person sentenced to death; **e** (poet.) the grave, '*Each in his narrow cell for ever laid*' (Gray); **f** a small cavity or compartment in larger enclosed space, e.g. *the cell of a honeycomb*; *cells of the brain*. **2.** (elect.) A single component part of a galvanic battery. **3.** (biol.) The smallest vital element of an organism, unit of living tissue, consisting of a mass of protoplasm, surrounded by a membrane and containing a nucleus.

cella, n. [1. séla; 2. sélə]. Lat., 'cell'. See prec. word. (class. archit.) The inner sanctuary or shrine of a temple.

cellar, n. [1. sélar; 2. sélə]. O. Fr. *celier*, fr. Lat. *cellārium*, neut. adj., 'pertaining to a store-room', fr. *cella*, q.v. under **cell**. **1.** That part of a house constructed in the foundations, below level of ground, often having vaulted roof supporting ground-floor of the house, and sometimes outer windows communicating with the air; **a** the whole of this underground basement: *to have one's house built on cellars*; **b** specif., applied to certain compartments within the basement, esp. that shut off as a store-house for wine, *wine-cellar*: *plenty of wine in the cellar*; **c** the contents of the wine-cellar: *to keep a good cellar*, i.e. to have good wine in abundance; *a small cellar*, small stock of wine; **d** place below ground for storing coal in town houses; usually called *coal-cellar*. **2.** Extended use: **a** a place for bins for wine, in small houses, constructed in some corner or cupboard above ground; **b** covered place in yard, for storing coal; more properly *coal-shed*.

cellarage, n. [1. sélarij; 2. sélərídʒ]. Prec. & **-age**. **1.** Space occupied by cellars; holding capacity of these; the cellars of a house considered collectively: *the house contains excellent cellarage*. **2. a** The storing of other persons' goods in a cellar; **b** charge made for such storage.

cellarer, n. [1. sélarer; 2. sélərə]. **cellar** & **-er**. Officer in a monastery, or college, in charge of the cellars and their contents; also of some kinds of provisions.

cellaret, n. [1. sèlarét; 2. sèlərét]. **cellar** & **-et**, dimin. suff. A cabinet in a dining-room, with bins and doors, to hold wine brought up from cellar, decanters &c.; sometimes with a flat top used as a kind of sideboard.

celliform, n. [1. séliform; 2. sélifōm]. See **cell** & **-form**. Having the appearance of a cell.

'cello, n. [1. chélō; 2. tʃélou]. Shortened form of *violoncello*, q.v.

cellular, adj. [1. sélūlar; 2. séljulə]. **cellule** & **-ar**. Containing cells; consisting of cells: *cellular tissue* &c.

cellularity, n. [1. sèlūláriti; 2. sèljulǽriti]. Prec. & **-ity**. Condition of being cellular.

cellulate, cellulated, adj. [1. sélūlāt, -ed; 2. séljuleit, -id]. Prec. & **-ate** (& **-ed**). Composed of cells.

cellule, n. [1. sélūl; 2. séljūl]. Fr., fr. Lat. *cellula*, 'small store-room or apartment'; dimin. of *cella*, q.v. under **cell**. (lit.) Small cell; ordinarily used simply for *cell*.

celluloid, adj. & n. [1. sélūloid; 2. séljulɔid]. **cellule** & **-oid**. **1.** adj. Having the form of cells. **2.** n. A highly inflammable substance made by treating cellulose with a solvent, such as camphor &c., used as a substitute for ivory, tortoise-shell &c., and also in the making of photographic films.

cellulose (I.), adj. [1. sélūlōs; 2. séljulous]. **cellule** & **-ose**. Composed of cells.

cellulose (II.), n., fr. prec. (chem.) The starch-like carbohydrate substance, of which the walls or cell framework of plants are composed, used in the making of paper, artificial silk, explosives &c.

Celt (I.), n. [1. kelt, selt; 2. kɛlt, sɛlt], also **Kelt**. Fr. *Celte*, Lat. *Celta*, Gk. *Keltoi*. A member of an Aryan-speaking race, including the ancient Gauls, formerly inhabiting a considerable part of Western Europe; from it are descended the Scotch Gaels, Irish, Manx, Welsh, Cornish, and Bretons.

celt (II.), n. [1. selt; 2. sɛlt]. The Lat. word *celtis* is not found before the Vulgate form *celte* abl., where it is supposed by some to be a false reading for *certe*, 'surely' (O.E.D.). This seems too clever. In an early Engl. Gloss. *celtem* is rendered by Engl. *chisel*. Walde casts no doubt upon authenticity of word, but merely suggests that it is a late loan-word. Name given by archaeologists to a prehistoric cutting-implement of stone or bronze.

Celtic, Keltic, adj. & n. [1. kéltik; 2. kéltik]. **Celt** (I.) & **-ic**. **a** adj. Pertaining to the Celts; **b** n., the language of the Celts.

celticism, n. [1. kéltisizm; 2. kéltisizəm]. Prec. & **-ism**. **a** The state of being a Celt; Celtic customs &c.; **b** a Celtic expression, idiom; e.g. Irish-English: *I'm after having my dinner*, meaning, I've just had it.

Celticize, vb. trans. & intrans. [1. kéltisīz; 2. kéltisaiz]. See prec. & **-ize**. To make, become, Celtic.

Celtologist, n. [1. keltólojist; 2. kɛltɔ́lədʒist]. **Celt** (I.), & **-logy** & **-ist**. A student of, authority on, the archaeology, history, art, and language of the Celtic peoples.

celtomaniac, n. [1. kèltōmániak; 2. kèltouméiniæk]. **Celt** (I.) & **maniac**. Person obsessed with the importance and interest of Celtic language, art, poetry &c.

cement (I.), n. [1. semént; 2. simént]. Fr., fr. Lat. *caementum*, 'rough stone, as cut fr. the quarry; stone chippings'. The Lat. word is for **caedmentum*, the first syll. being cogn. w. Lat. vb. *caedere*, 'to cut, hew, lop'; cp. also *caelum*, fr. **caed-lom*, 'sculptor's chisel'; all cogn. w. Scrt. *khidáti*, 'thrusts, tears'. **1.** Any compound substance, esp. in form of lime or other stone, ground to fine powder, mixed with water, and applied while moist or soft, and rapidly becoming very hard; e.g. material used a by builders to cover floors, walls &c.; **b** by dentists to stop teeth; *hydraulic cement*, kind that sets under water; *Portland cement*, a hydraulic cement composed of lime and clay. **2.** Any substance used to stick things together, applied while soft and drying hard; **a** material used by builders instead of ordinary mortar to bed stones in and bind them together, or mixed with sand and gravel to form concrete, q.v.; **b** adhesive material used to mend small articles of glass, china &c.; hence (fig.) **c** that which serves to unite persons, parties &c.; a link, bond of union. **3.** (anat.) The bony covering of the root and neck of a tooth.

cement (II.), vb. trans., fr. prec. **1. a** To cover with, join by means of, cement; **b** (fig.) to unite closely, cause to become firmer: *cement a friendship, union* &c.

cementation, n. [1. sèmentáshun; 2. sìmɛntéiʃən]. Prec. & **-ation**. **1.** The act of cementing; state, or process, of being cemented. **2.** A process in steel-making, the iron being heated in powdered charcoal.

cemetery, n. [1. sémeteri; 2. sémitri]. In early Mod. Engl., fr. L. Lat. *coemētērium*, fr. Gk. *koimētḗrion*, 'a sleeping-place'; cp. *koimáō*, 'I lull to sleep, put to bed'. These words are connected w. Gk. *keîmai*, 'lie down, lie asleep', & a large number of words in Gk.: *koítē*, 'place to lie, bed', *koítos*, 'sleeping, sleep' &c. Outside Gk. the base **k̑oi-*, **k̑ei-*, **k̑i-* appears in Goth. *haims*, 'village', O.E. *hām* (see **home, hide**, of land), & Lat. *cīvis*, 'citizen' (see **city, citizen**). An enclosed piece of consecrated ground for the burial of the dead, distinct from a churchyard in that it has no parish church attached, and is usually outside a town or village.

cenobite, coenobite, n. [1. sénōbīt; 2. sínoubait]. L. Lat. *coenobīta*, 'member of a social fraternity', fr. L. Gk. *koinóbion*, 'convent', lit. 'place where people live in common', fr. *koinó-(s)*, 'shared in common', & *bíos*, 'life'. See **biology**. The first element is perh. fr. **kom-jos*, & cogn. w. Lat. *cum*, 'with', see **com-**. Monk who lives common social life with other monks in a monastery; in opposition to an *anchorite*, q.v.

cenotaph, n. [1. sénotaf, -tahf; 2. sénɔtæf, -tāf]. M. Fr. *cénotaphe*, Lat. *cenotaphium*, fr. Gk. *kenotáphion*, fr. *kénos*, 'empty', & *táphion*, neut. of *táphios*, 'belonging to a grave', fr. *táphos*, 'burial, tomb'. The only cognate of *kénos*, outside Gk. given by Boisacq, is Armen. *sin*, 'empty', & the etymol. of *táphos* is equally obscure, save that it is related to Gk. *táphros*, 'a ditch'. (lit.) Empty tomb. Monument, sometimes in the form of a tomb, raised to the memory of a dead person, and containing statement of his name, age, and achievements &c., though it does not contain his body. Specif., *The Cenotaph*, monument in Whitehall, London, in honour of those who fell in the Great War (1914–18).

cense, vb. trans. [1. sens; 2. sɛns]. See **censer**. To swing censer towards person or thing, as a ceremonial observance during celebration of Eucharist, so that the smoke from the incense envelops and perfumes him or it.

censer, n. [1. sénser; 2. sénsə]. O. Fr. *encensier*, Mod. Fr. *encensoir*, former fr. L. Lat. *incensārium*, fr. Lat. *incensum*, 'that which is burnt', P.P. of *incendere*, 'set fire to, kindle, burn', formed fr. *candēre*, 'to glow, be hot'. See this under **candid, candle**; see also **incense**. Vessel with perforated lid in which incense is burnt, carried by a chain, and swung so as to spread the fumes, for purposes of purification, and as a symbolical ceremonial act in church, esp. during celebration of the Eucharist; a thurible.

censor (I.), n. [1. sénser; 2. sénsə]. Lat., in sense **1** below; fr. *censēre*, 'to reckon, assess; to estimate, value; deem, judge, be of opinion' &c.; cp. Scrt. *śāsáyati*, 'informs, makes known'. Relation of other words suggested as cognates is very doubtful, but see **cosmos**. **1.** (hist.) One of two magistrates in ancient Rome, who dealt with the rating of citizens, and with public morals. **2.** One of several officials who prevent **a** the publication of immoral books, or libellous and improper articles in the press, or performance of immoral plays &c.; or **b** (esp. in time of war) the publication through the press of news likely to be of service to the enemy, or to depress unduly the public morale, and the transmission, through private correspondence, of military and political secrets which by design or accident may fall into enemy hands. **3.** Official at Oxford who looks after discipline among non-collegiate students.

censor (II.), vb. trans., fr. prec. To examine books, plays, correspondence &c. with a view to suppressing anything unsuitable for publication, for public performance, or for transmission by letter.

censorial, adj. [1. sensórial; 2. sɛnsɔ́riəl]. **censor** & **-ial**. Pertaining to a censor, or to his office.

censorious, adj. [1. sensórius; 2. sɛnsɔ́riəs], fr. Lat. *censōrius*. See **censor** (I.) & **-ous**. **a** (of persons) Severely critical, inclined to assume the position of a censor, or of one having authority to judge, and pronounce, especially with disapproval, upon the abilities, morals, and manners of others; **b** (of disposition, manner) exhibiting above characteristics.

censoriously, adv. Prec. & **-ly**. In a censorious manner.

censoriousness, n. See prec. & **-ness**. Censorious habit of mind and expression.

censorship, n. [1. sénsership; 2. sénsəʃip]. **censor** (I.) & **-ship**. **a** The office, powers, of a censor; **b** tenure of this.

censurable, adj. [1. sénshurabl; 2. sénʃərəbl]. **censure** (I.) & **-able**. Deserving of blame or censure, liable to be censured.

censure (I.), vb. trans. [1. sénshur; 2. sénʃə]. Fr. *censurer*, fr. Lat. *censūra*, 'judgement, criticism', fr. *census*, 'rating of property' &c.; connected w. Lat. *censēre*, 'count, reckon' &c., & **censor**. To criticize adversely, blame, express disapproval of.

censure (II.), n. Fr., fr. Lat. *censūra*. See prec. Blame, expression of disapproval, reprimand: *vote of censure*, one passed in parliament, or at a public meeting, condemning a person, party, or government.

census, n. [1. sénsus; 2. sénsəs]. Lat., 'rating of property; lists of citizens compiled by the censors'. See **censor** (I.). Official, periodical numbering of the population of a state, together with collection of statistics concerning sex, age, occupation &c.

census-paper, n. A form on which particulars required for a census are entered.

cent, n. [1. sent; 2. sɛnt]. Fr., fr. Lat. *centum*, '100'. Cogn. w. Gmc. *hund-*, as in **hundred**. **1.** Used in *per cent* for Latin *per centum*, by the hundred, for every hundred, in stating proportions, rate of interest &c.; *3 per cents*, government securities yielding this rate of interest; *cent per cent*, a hundred for every hundred, used generally to imply extortionate rate of interest. **2.** (in U.S.A.) **a** Hundredth part of a dollar; **b** name of coin of this value.

cental, n. [1. séntl; 2. séntl], fr. Lat. *cent(um)*, see prec., & **-al** on anal. of **quintal**. A weight of 100 lb., used in measuring corn.

centaur, n. [1. séntōr; 2. séntɔ̄]. Fr. *centaure*, fr. Gk. *Kéntauros*, member of a savage race in ancient Thessaly; later popularly believed to be monsters, half-man, half-horse. Etymol. doubtful, but perh. fr. *kentéō*, 'I prick, goad', see **centre**, & **auro-*, 'horse', as in Gk. *auribátās*, 'quick-moving'. **1. a** (Greek mythol.) Fabulous monster, having half of the body, the arms, and head of a man, joined to the body and legs of a horse; hence, **b** a skilled horseman, one who sits a horse as though he were part of it. **2.** (cap., also in Lat., *Centaurus*) The name of a constellation of the southern hemisphere: *alpha Centauri*, the nearest of the stars.

centaury, n. [1. séntōri; 2. séntɔ̄ri]. M.E. *centaurie*, fr. Lat. *centaurēum*, fr. Gk. *kentaúreion*, neut. adj., 'belonging to the centaurs', so called because these monsters were supposed to have first discovered the medicinal properties of the plant. One of several varieties of plants, esp. **a** a medicinal herb of the gentian family; **b** the knapweed.

centenarian, adj. & n. [1. sèntenárian; 2. sèntinéəriən]. Lat. *centēnārius*, 'relating to number 100', fr. *centēni*, 'a hundred each', & *-ārius*. See **cent**, & **-ary** & **-an**. **a** adj. A hundred years old; **b** n., a person who has reached the age of 100 years.

centenary, adj. & n. [1. sentḗnari; 2. sentínəri]. Lat. *centēnārius*, same meaning as Engl. word, fr. *centum*, '100'. See **cent**. **1.** adj. Pertaining to the number 100, to a period of a hundred years. **2.** n. **a** A period of a hundred years; **b** the hundredth anniversary; celebration of this.

centennial, adj. & n. [1. senténial; 2. sinténiəl]. Lat. *centum*, '100', see **cent**, & *-ennis*, form of *annus*, 'year' used in composition, & **-al**; cp. *bi-ennial*. See **annual**. **1.** adj. **a** Having lived or lasted for a hundred years; **b** occurring once during, or at the end of, a period of a hundred years. **2.** n. **a** The hundredth anniversary, centenary; **b** the celebration of the centenary.

centennially, adv. Prec. & **-ly**. Once in every hundred years.

centesimal, adj. [1. sentésimal; 2. sintésiməl], fr. Lat. *centēsima*, 'hundredth part', fr. *centum*. See **cent** & **-al**. Based on mode of reckoning by multiples of 100 or of $\frac{1}{100}$.

centi-, pref., form of Lat., *centum* 100 used in composition. See **cent** & **hundred**.

centigrade, adj. [1. séntigrād; 2. séntigreid]. **centi-** & **grade**. (of the thermometer of Celsius) Divided into 100 degrees, freezing-point being 0° and boiling-point 100°: *centigrade thermometer*; *50° centigrade*.

centigramme, n. [1. séntigram; 2. séntigræm]. See **centi-** & **gramme**. (metric system) The hundredth part of a gramme (in weight).

centilitre, n. [1. séntilēter; 2. séntilītə]. Fr. See **centi-** & **litre**. Measure of capacity, one hundredth part of a litre.

centillion, n. [1 sentílyun; 2. sintíljən]. **centi-** w. suff. on anal. of **million**, as in **billion**. The hundredth power of a million.

centime, n. [1. sontēm; 2. sãtīm]. Fr., fr. O. Fr. *centisme*, fr Lat. *centēsimus*, 'hundredth' (part &c., see **centesimal**. **a** The hundredth part of a franc; **b** a coin of this value in France, Switzerland &c.

centimetre, n. [1. séntimēter; 2. séntimītə]. **centi-** & **metre**. (in metric system) One hundredth part of a metre.

centipede, n. [1. séntipēd; 2. séntipīd]. Fr., fr. Lat. *centipeda*, 'many-footed insect'. **centi-**, '100', & *ped-(em)*, *pēs*, 'foot'. See **pedal**. Crawling insect, of varying size, with a long, slender, many-jointed body and a pair of legs to each joint.

centner, n. [1. séntner; 2. séntnə]. Germ., fr. Lat. *centēnārius*. See **centenary**. A German measure of weight, about 1 cwt.

cento, n. [1. séntō; 2. séntou]. Lat., 'thick cloth, composed of many pieces sewn together, patchwork', fr. Gk. *kéntrōn*, 'patched dress', late meaning, earlier 'spur-galled jade'; cp. also *kánthā*, 'patched dress'. Connected w. base in Gk. *kentéō*, 'I prick, goad'. The sense of 'patching' must be derived fr. the idea of much pricking with a needle. See **centre**. A literary or musical composition made up of passages from the works of various writers or composers; a patchwork composition.

central, adj. [1. séntral; 2. séntrəl]. **centre** & **-al**. **a** (lit.) Occupying position at or in the centre, forming the centre, pertaining to the centre; **b** (specif., of locality) near important centres, hence, easy of access, convenient for business or pleasure. *our district is very central*; **c** hence (fig.) occupying a position in or on which intellectual or emotional interest is concentrated, hence principal, important, cardinal *central figure in a picture, play* &c.; *central idea* &c.

centralism, n. [1. séntralizm; 2. séntrəlizəm]. Prec. & **-ism**. The policy or system of centralizing government, organization &c.

centralist, n. [1. séntralist; 2. séntrəlist]. See prec. & **-ist** One who upholds the centralization of government &c.

centrality, n. [1. sentráliti; 2. sintræliti]. **central** & **-ity**. The state of being central.

centralization, n. [1. sèntralīzáshun; 2. sèntrəlaizéiʃən]. **centralize** & **-ation**. The act of centralizing, of bringing under single control &c.; state or process of being centralized.

centralize, vb. trans. [1. séntralīz; 2. séntrəlaiz]. **central** & **-ize**. To bring to the centre, concentrate in a single point &c.; esp. to organize some form of administration so as to make it dependent on a single centre of control, e.g. at the capital of a country, at the headquarters of a company &c.

centrally, adv. [1. séntrali; 2. séntrəli]. **central** & **-ly**. In the centre; in central position; with regard to the centre.

centralness, n. [1. séntralnes; 2. séntrəlnis]. **central** & **-ness**. State, condition, position, of being central in any sense.

centre (I.), n. [1. sénter; 2. séntə]. Fr., fr. Lat. *centrum*, fr. Gk. *kéntron*, 'point, prickle, spike; ox-goad; incentive to action; point round which a circle is described', fr. base in *kentéō*, 'prick, goad, wound'; cogn. w. W. *cethr*, 'nail'; O.H.G. *hantag*, 'sharp'. (in lit. and gen. sense) The middle point. **1.** **a** (specif., geom.) A point equidistant from the extremities of a line, plane figure, or solid body; or from any part of circumference of a circle; **b** (in wider sense) point farthest from the outside, from the boundaries, point mid-way between the extremities: *the centre of the town*. **2.** Person or object occupying a middle position; as the middle player in the forward line at hockey and association football; specif. **a** (mil.) main body of troops, holding the front between the wings; **b** (polit., usually cap.) party holding moderate views between two extremes of political doctrine, and (in some legislative assemblies, e.g. French) the party sitting in the centre of the Chamber. **3.** (physics) That point in a body on which some particular activity or phenomenon depends; (used specif. in many phrs.) e.g. *centre of gravity*, that point in a body, about which the whole weight is evenly balanced; *centre of oscillation*; *storm-centre*, the point towards which the wind blows in a cyclone; hence (fig.) main point of disturbance, upheaval &c. **4.** (fig.) **a** A place at which important events occur, or where important and essential activities are carried out: *a centre of trade, of government, of intrigue, agitation, amusement* &c.; **b** person who, activity which, invites attention, concentrates, and attracts intellectual or emotional interest: *centre of interest, attraction*. **5.** (archit.) Centreing.

centre (II.), vb. trans. & intrans., fr. prec. **A.** trans. **a** To place in the centre, take as central point of; hence **b** (fig.) to concentrate: *to centre one's affections, hopes, on, or in some one, something*. **B.** intrans. To be concentrated, come to a point, be fixed, converge; usually with prep.: *centre in*; *centre round* (generally condemned as inaccurate): *the interest centres in*; *the discussion centred round one point* &c.

centre-bit, n. A tool for boring, turning on a central point.

centre-board, n. A plate of wood or metal that can be lowered vertically from bottom of boat to act as a keel and give steadiness and stability.

centreing, centering, n. [1. séntering; 2. séntəriŋ]. **centre (I.)** & **-ing**. (archit.) A temporary structure or framework of timber used in building a dome, vault or arch.

centre-piece, n. An ornament designed to be placed in the middle of a table &c.

centric, centrical, adj. [1. séntrik(l); 2. séntrik(l)]. **centre (I.)** & **-ic** & **-al**. Placed at the centre, central; formed about a centre.

centrically, adv. Prec. & **-ly**. Centrally.

centricity, n. [1. sentrísiti; 2. sentrísiti]. Prec. & **-ity**. The quality of being centric.

centrifugal, adj. [1. sentrífūgal; 2. sentrífjugəl], fr. Lat. *centr-(um)*, 'centre', & *fug-(ere)* 'to fly from'. See **centre (I.)** & **fugacious** & **-al**. **a** Tending to fly from the centre; opposed to *centripetal*; *centrifugal force*, causing a body revolving about a centre to tend to fly off from its curved path: hence **b** (of machine &c.) using centrifugal force; **c** (bot.) of flower-cluster of which the flower at the apex opens first.

centrifugally, adv. Prec. & **-ly**. In a centrifugal manner.

centripetal, adj. [1. sentrípetal; 2. sentrípətəl, sentripítəl]. See prec., & Lat. *pet-(ere)*, 'to seek', see **petition**, & **-al**. **a** Tending towards the centre, opposed to *centrifugal*; *centripetal force*, tendency of a body revolving about a centre to fly towards the attracting point; opposed to, and counteracting the effect of, *centrifugal force*; hence **b** (of machine &c.) using centripetal force; **c** (bot.) of flower-cluster of which the lower flowers open first.

centripetally, adv. Prec. & **-ly**. In a centripetal manner.

centro-, pref. Form of Lat. *centrum*, used in compounds. See **centre (I.)**.

centumvir, n. [1. sentúmver; 2. sentámvə]. Lat. *centum*, '100', see **cent**, & *vir*, 'man', see **virile**. (Rom. hist.) One of a body or court of one hundred judges or jurors who tried civil cases.

centuple, adj. & vb. trans. [1. séntūpl; 2. séntjupl]. Fr., fr. Lat. *centuplex*, 'hundredfold', fr. *centum*, '100', see **cent**, & base *plec-*, *plic-*, cp. Lat. *plicāre*, 'to fold', & *plectere*, 'to plait, interweave'; cogn. w. Gk. *plékō*, 'plait'; Goth. *flahta*, 'plaiting of the hair', O.H.G. *flehtan*, 'plait' &c. See **plait**. The base is prob. an amplified form of **pel-*, 'to fold'. See **fold (I.)**. **1.** adj. A hundred times as large. **2.** vb. To multiply a hundredfold.

centuplicate (I.), adj. & n. [1. sentúplikat; 2. sintjúplikit], fr. Lat. *cent-*, '100', see **cent**, & *plicāt-(um)*, P.P. type of *plicāre*, 'to fold'. See **centuple**, cp. **duplicate**. **a** adj. Increased a hundredfold, copied a hundred times; **b** n., a hundred copies, esp. in Phr. *in centuplicate*.

centuplicate (II.), vb. trans. [1. sentúplikāt; 2. sintjúplikeit], fr. prec. To multiply by a hundred, make a hundred copies of.

centurion, n. [1. sentúriun; 2. sentjúəriən]. Lat. *centuriōn-(em)*, 'commander of a body of 100 men', cp. *centuria*, 'division of a hundred things of the same kind', fr. *centum*, '100'. See **cent**. An officer commanding a body of a hundred men in the Roman army. See **century, 1**.

century, n. [1. sénchuri; 2. séntʃəri]. Lat. *centuria*, 'parcel, or division of a hundred things of one kind'. See prec. & **cent**. **1.** (anct. hist.) A body of infantry in the Roman army, consisting originally of 100 men, and forming the sixtieth part of a legion. **2.** One of the periods of a hundred years reckoned backwards or forwards from a given epoch, esp. from the beginning of the Christian era: *the 19th century* (1801 to 1900 A.D. &c.); *fourth century* B.C. **3.** A hundred consecutive years, a centenary: *many centuries old*. **4.** A hundred things of the same kind, considered collectively; specif., (cricket) a hundred runs.

century plant, n. The Mexican agave or American aloe, supposed to flower once in a hundred years.

ceorl. See **churl**.

cephalic, adj. [1. sefálik; 2. sifælik], fr. Gk. *kephalḗ*, 'head' & **-ic**. In spite of its apparent resemblance to Lat. *caput*, 'head', O.E. *heafola*, *hēafod* &c., the Gk. word is prob. unrelated to these, & is prob. for Aryan **ghebhal-*, & cogn. w. Goth. *gibla*, 'pinnacle', O.H.G. *gibil*, 'gable, face of a house', Mod. Germ. *giebel*, 'gable'; O.H.G. *gebal* means 'skull'. The orig. sense was 'apex, highest point'. See **gable**; also **capital** & **head**. Connected with, relating to, the head. Esp. in expression *cephalic index* (anthropol.) which refers to the proportion of the length of the head to its breadth, considered as an indication of race. See also **brachycephalic**, & **dolichocephalic**.

cephalo-, pref. Form of Gk. *kephalḗ*, 'head', used in composition. See **cephalic**.

cephalopod, n. [1. séfalopòd; 2. séfələpɔ̀d]. Prec. & Gk. *pod-*, stem of *poús*, genit. *podós*, 'foot', cogn. w. **foot**, Lat. *ped-*, see **pedal**. Class of molluscs with tentacles on the head, including the octopus, cuttlefish, squid &c.

cephalothorax, n. [1. sèfalothṓraks; 2. sèfələþɔ̄ræks]. **cephalo-** & **thorax**. (anat.) The head and thorax, of spiders and crustaceans, considered as united.

-cephalous, suff. See **cephalic** & **-ous**. Used to form compound words as *brachycephalous*, *dolichocephalous*.

ceramic, keramic, adj. [1. serámik, kerámik; 2. sirǽmik, kirǽmik]. Gk. *keramikós*, 'made of earthenware, clay', fr. *kéramos*, 'potter's clay; pottery, tile'. From base **kʷer-*, or *kʷer-*, wh. seems to have meant both 'to burn', & 'to mix'; cp. in former sense Lat. *cremāre*, 'to burn', see **cremate**, & O.E. *heorþ*, see **hearth**; in latter, Gk. *keránnūmi*, 'blend, mix'; Scrt. *śrīnāti*, 'blend, mix', also 'bake, roast'; O.E. *hrēran*, 'touch'; *kéramos* may therefore have meant orig. either 'burnt, baked clay', or 'mixed, worked clay'. Pertaining to pottery, concerned with the art of manufacturing and ornamenting it.

ceramics, n., fr. prec. The art of making pottery &c. of clay.

cerastes, n. [1. serástēz; 2. sirǽstīz]. Lat., fr. Gk. *kerástēs*, 'horned; the horned serpent', fr. *kéras*, 'horn'. See **keratin**. The horned viper of North Africa and Syria.

cerato-, kerato-, pref. Horny, cartilaginous, fr. Gk. *kérat-os*, *kéras*, 'horn', see prec., used to form compounds.

Cerberus, n. [1. sérberus; 2. sə́bərəs]. Gk. *Kérberos*. (class. mythol.) The three-headed dog that guarded the entrance to the infernal regions. Phr. *a sop to Cerberus*, an offering or action to propitiate an opponent &c.

cere, n. [1. sēr; 2. siə], fr. Lat. *cēra*, 'wax'; cogn. w., or loan-word fr., Gk. *kērós*, 'beeswax', *kēríon*, 'honey-comb'. Cp. also Lith. *korỹs*, 'honey-comb', Lett. *kárites*, 'honey in the comb'. Some authorities relate the word, as also second elements of *sincērus*, 'pure', & *prōcērus*, 'tall, high', to Lat. *crescere*, 'to grow, increase'. See further **crescent, sincere.** At this rate *cēra* &c. was 'something grown, or formed'. (ornith.) The wax-like skin covering base of the beak in some birds.

cereal, adj. & n. [1. séreal; 2. síəriəl]. Lat. *Cereālis*, 'pertaining to *Cerēs*, goddess of corn and plenty, pertaining to corn itself', fr. *Cerēs* & *-ālis*, see **-al.** The name of the goddess has been explained in two ways; either as fr. the idea of growth, creation, in wh. case connected w. *creāre*, *crescere*, see **create, crescent**, or fr. that of plenty, in wh. case connected w. Gk. *kóros*, 'plenty, satiety', *korénnūmi*, 'to satisfy, glut', & perh. also O.H.G. *hirsi*, Mod. Germ. *hirse*, 'millet, grain'. **a** adj. Of, pertaining to, grain used for human food; to plants producing edible grain; **b** n., one of the varieties of plant producing edible grain, such as wheat, barley, maize, rye &c.

cerebellum, n. [1. sèrebélum; 2. sèribéləm]. Lat. dimin. of **cerebrum.** Hinder part of the brain in vertebrates, situated below and behind the hemispheres of the cerebrum.

cerebral, adj. [1. sérebral; 2. séribrəl]. Fr., fr. Lat. *cerebrum*, 'brain', & **-al.** See **cerebrum. a** Pertaining to the brain: *cerebral haemorrhage*, bleeding in the brain; **b** (phon.) *cerebral consonants*, expression due to misunderstanding of word used by Indian grammarians, and applied in Sanscrit philology to consonants formed with an inversion of the tip of the tongue; better called *point-inverted* consonants.

cerebration, n. [1. sèrebrā́shun; 2. sèribréiʃən], fr. Lat. *cerebrum*, 'brain', see **cerebrum**, & **-ation.** Action, working, of the brain, whether conscious or not.

cerebro-, pref. Form of Lat. **cerebrum**, used in compounds, e.g. *cerebro-spinal meningitis*, meningitis affecting the cerebral and spinal membranes, often taking an epidemic form.

cerebrum, n. [1. sérebrum; 2. séribrəm]. Lat. 'brain', fr. **cerasrom*. Cp. Scrt. *śiraś*, 'head, point', *śiršan*, 'head'; Gk. *kárā*, 'head, top, summit of anything', also *kárēnon*, 'head, mountain peak', for **karas-non*, & rare *karárā*, for **karasra*, 'head'. More remote are Gk. *krānion*, 'skull', see **cranium**, & O.H.G. *hirni*, 'brain', Mod. Germ. *gehirn* &c. See also **coryphaeus** & **cervical.** The main part of the brain, consisting of two hemispherical masses, filling the upper cavity of the skull, above, and in front of cerebellum.

cerecloth, n. [1. sérkloth; 2. síəklɔþ]. See **cere** & **cloth.** A wax-coated shroud, in which the embalmed bodies of the dead are wrapped.

cerement, n. [1. sérment; 2. síəmənt]. Fr. *cirement*, cp. *cire*, 'wax'. See **cere.** Waxed winding-sheet for the bodies of the dead; hence (usually pl.) simply grave-clothes.

ceremonial, adj. & n. [1. sèremṓnial; 2. sèrimóuniəl], fr. **ceremony** & **-al. 1.** adj. **a** Pertaining to, accompanied by, ceremony, formal rites: *ceremonial usage, observances* &c.; **b** specif. (eccles.) *ceremonial use*, use of some piece of ritual in, and as part of, religious service, esp. as conveying symbolical meaning and expressing a doctrine: *ceremonial use of incense.* **2.** n. Set of observances and rites, consisting of a series of dignified bodily movements, gestures, and other acts, carried out by those taking part, expressive of, or symbolizing, reverence and respect, upon an important and solemn occasion, such as a religious service, or public state function.

ceremonialism, n. [1. sèremṓnializm; 2. sèrimóuniəlizəm]. Prec. & **-ism.** Practice of, regard for, forms and ceremonies.

ceremonialist, n. [1. sèremṓnialist; 2. sèrimóuniəlist]. See prec. & **-ist.** One who attaches great (or exaggerated) importance to forms and ceremonies.

ceremonially, adv. [1. sèremṓniali; 2. sèrimóuniəli]. **ceremonial** & **-ly.** By way of, as forming part of, ceremonial; as forming essential part of service &c. in which ceremonial is used.

ceremonious, adj. [1. sèrimṓnius; 2. sèrimóuniəs]. **ceremony** & **-ous. a** (of persons) Observant of ceremony; possessing a stately, formal manner; excessively addicted to conventional formalities, over-punctilious; **b** (of a public function) characterized by, accompanied by, formal rites and ceremonies: *a ceremonious reception, welcome* &c.; **c** (of a person's manner) marked by formality or mannerism.

ceremoniously, adv. Prec. & **-ly.** With much ceremony, in a ceremonious manner.

ceremoniousness, n. See prec. & **-ness.** The quality of being ceremonious.

ceremony, n. [1. séremuni; 2. sériməni]. Fr. *cérémonie*, fr. Lat. *caerimōnia*, 'religious usage, sacred ceremony; reverence, awe, manifested in external acts'; cogn. w. Scrt. *čáyati*, 'honours, reverences', O. Slav. *čěna*, 'honour'. Various attempts have been made by several scholars to identify more closely the Aryan base fr. wh. these words are derived, but none is at all conclusive. **1. a** (often in pl.) External act or gesture, or series of such, expressive of reverence or veneration, used upon solemn occasions, or to give dignity and orderliness to a public function; ceremonial: *the king was crowned with all due ceremony*; **b** the service or public function itself at which ceremonies are used: *the royal wedding was an impressive ceremony. Master of Ceremonies*, one who superintends and directs proceedings at a public function. **2.** abstract n. Social convention, formality, polite and stately observances used in social intercourse, esp. among strangers, or with persons of high social or official standing: *I am treating you as a friend and without ceremony.* Phr. *to stand* (*up*)*on ceremony*, show frigid formal politeness, be very observant of etiquette.

ceriph, serif, n. [1. sérif; 2. sérif]. Prob. fr. Du. *schreef*, 'dash, stroke, scratch', fr. *schrijve*, 'to write', fr. Lat. *scrībere.* See **scribe.** A fine stroke in a written or printed letter, esp. a horizontal stroke at the top or bottom of a printed capital.

cerise, adj. & n. [1. serḗz; 2. səríz]. Fr., 'cherry'. See **cherry.** Cherry-colour, a clear red.

cerium, n. [1. sérium; 2. síəriəm]. Discovered in 1803, about the same time as the asteroid Ceres, and named after it. A rare, greyish, metallic element.

cernuous, adj. [1. sérnūus; 2. sə́njuəs], fr. Lat. *cernuus*, 'with face towards the earth'. Prob. related to **cerebrum.** Cp. cogn. Gk. *kára*, 'head', also 'brim of a cup'. (bot., of flowers &c.) Having the bell or cup of the blossom hanging downwards, pendent.

cero-, pref. Form of Lat. *cēra* or Gk. *kērós*, 'wax', used in composition. See **cere.**

cerograph, n. [1. sérograhf; 2. síərəgrāf]. Literally 'wax writing'. See **cero-** & **graph.** An engraving, or writing, on wax spread on a copper plate, afterwards treated with acid which eats away the exposed lines in the copper, thus forming a plate from which impressions are taken.

cerography, n. [1. sērógrafi; 2. siərɔ́grəfi], fr. prec. & **-y.** Art or process of making cerographs.

ceroplastic, adj. [1. sèroplástik; 2. siərəplǽstik]. Gk., 'pertaining to moulding in wax', fr. *kēróplastos*, 'moulded in wax', *kēroplástēs*, 'modeller in wax', fr. *kērós*, 'wax', & *plássō*, 'mould, model'. See **cero-** & **plastic. a** Pertaining to wax-modelling; **b** modelled in wax.

ceroplastics, n., fr. prec. The art of modelling in wax.

certain, adj. [1. sértn, sértin; 2. sə́tn, sə́tin]. M.E. & O. Fr. *certein*, fr. Lat. *certus*, 'determined, resolved, sure', formed w. different suff., Lat. *-ānus*; see **-an, -ain.** Connected w. Lat. *cernere*, P.P. *crētum*, 'to distinguish, discern, see distinctly; understand; decide'. Cp. further the group of cognates in Gk., *kritós*, 'picked out, chosen, excellent', *krités*, 'judge, arbiter', *krínō*, 'separate, put apart, pick out, decide, judge' &c.; see **critic.** From same base comes Lat. *crībrum*, 'sieve', O.E. *hridder, hriddel*, 'sieve'; see **riddle (IV.).** The present sense of *certain* has been reached through the stages 'well separated, sifted, apprehended, considered, judged, decided'; hence the further development of ideas, 'well assured, indubitable'. See **discern, discrete, decree. 1. a** (of state of mind, pred.) Sure, positive, not doubtful, convinced: *to be certain of one's facts*; *certain that one is right*; *to feel certain.* Colloq. Phr. *not to know for certain*, with complete knowledge; *to make certain of*, reach a position of certainty, ascertain, assure oneself of; **b** (of non-material things) sure, well established, to be accepted without hesitation: *the fact is certain*; *it is certain that*; *certain evidence*; **c** (of future events, actions, processes) inevitable, sure to happen, bound to come, to be expected without doubt; reliable; well-secured, well-founded: *to face certain death*; *a certain cure for dyspepsia*; *a certain hope of everlasting life.* **2.** (attrib.) Definite, agreed upon, fixed: *at a certain place*; *on a certain day*; *a certain rate of pay.* **3.** (attrib.) Not stated in explicit terms or named specifically, but assumed to be known, or agreed upon: *a certain person*; *under certain conditions.* **4.** Appreciable, not inconsiderable, to be reckoned with: *after a certain age one cannot bear a sudden strain*; *to have a certain hesitation in agreeing* &c.; *there was a certain coldness in her manner*; *to a certain extent.* **5.** Unerring, under complete control, unfailing, accurate, and unhesitating: *his aim was certain*; *his touch on the piano was not very certain*; *his information was by no means certain.*

certainly, adv. [1. sértnli; 2. sə́tnli]. Prec. & **-ly. a** Undoubtedly, beyond all doubt, with certainty: infallibly: *it is certainly* *warmer*; *he will certainly be killed*; *I will certainly call upon him*; **b** (expressing agreement with what another has said) *it is certainly the case that . . . but . . .*; **c** (as permissive formula) *may I take a holiday to-day? Certainly* = Yes, by all means &c.

certainty, n. [1. sértnti; 2. sʌ́tnti]. **certain** & **-ty**. **1.** The state of being certain, **a** (subjectively) assurance, positive knowledge, conviction: *this at least may be said with certainty*; **b** (objectively) inevitableness: *the certainty of failure damped men's spirits*. **2.** That which is certain; something positively known or believed to have happened, or to be about to happen: *his success was a certainty from the first*; *I know this for a certainty*. **3.** Security arising from solid evidence of permanence in a particular order of things: *the position of a cabinet minister in some countries is not one of safety and certainty*.

certes, adv. [1. sértiz; 2. sʌ́tiz]. M.E., fr. O. Fr., fr. Lat. *a certis*, 'from certain grounds', fr. *certus*. See **certain**. (archaic) Certainly, assuredly, truly.

certifiable, adj. [1. sértifiabl; 2. sʌ́tifaiəbl]. **certify** & **-able**. That can be certified; specif., showing signs of insanity and liable to be legally certified as insane.

certificate (I.), n. [1. sërtífikat; 2. sʌtífikit], Med. Lat. *certificātum*, P.P. of *certificāre*, 'certify'. See **certify**. A document issued by authority, containing formal statement, or declaration of a fact, esp. e.g. of a person's proficiency in anything, success in an examination, ownership of property &c.: *certificate of birth*, stating date, & attesting fact of registration; *certificate of baptism*, stating that this has been performed; *bankrupt's certificate*, legal discharge; *health certificate*, declaration that person is not suffering from, nor has been exposed to risk of, infectious disease &c.

certificate (II.), vb. trans., fr. prec. To grant a certificate to, license for particular purpose by a certificate: *certificated teacher*, holding qualification from Board of Education.

certification, n. [1. sêrtifikáshun; 2. sʌtifikéiʃən]. Prec. & **-ion**. The act of certifying; state of being certified.

certify, vb. trans. & intrans. [1. sértifī; 2. sʌ́tifai]. Fr. *certifier*, fr. L. Lat. *certificāre*, fr. *certi-*, 'sure', fr. *certus*, & form of *facere*, 'to make, do' &c. See **certain** & **fact**. **A.** trans. **1.** To assure, make certain, give definite information to: *to certify a person of something* (archaic). **2.** To give a certificate in testimony of, attest in a written document: *to certify a person as insane*. **3.** Specif., to certify as insane: *he ought to be certified*. **B.** intrans. To make formal statement of, testify to a fact: *I believe it to be true, but I am not able to certify to that effect*.

certiorari, n. [1. sèrshiōráhri; 2. sʌʃiōrári]. L. Lat. infin. pass. of *certiorāre*, 'to make certain, certify', fr. *certior*, compar. of *certus*. See **certain**. (law) Usually *writ of certiorari*, writ, issuing from superior court, removing a case from a lower court or calling for records of trial, for correction of errors &c.

certitude, n. [1. sértitūd; 2. sʌ́titjūd]. Fr., fr. L. Lat. *certitūdo*, 'certainty', on anal. of *amplitūdo* &c. See **certain** & **-tude**. Mental conviction, positive assurance, freedom from doubt.

cerulean, adj. [1. seroōlian; 2. sirūliən]. Lat. *caeruleus*, 'dark blue, like the sky', for **caeluleus*, fr. *caelum*, 'the sky, the heavens'. See **ceiling**. (of colour) Deep, clear blue, sky-blue.

cerumen, n. [1. seroōmen; 2. sirūmən], fr. Lat. *cēra*, 'wax', see **cere**, & *-umen*, on anal. of **albumen**. Wax-like substance secreted by glands in the external ear.

ceruse, n. [1. séroōs; 2. siərūs]. Lat. *cērussa*, 'white lead', as used by painters; said to be a loan-word fr. Gk. **kēróessa*, 'wax-like', fr. Gk. *kērós*, 'wax', cogn. w. Lat. *cēra*, q.v. under **cere**. A white paint made from lead, used as a cosmetic.

cervical, adj. [1. sërvíkl, sérvikl; 2. sʌváikl, sʌ́vikl]. Lat. *cervīc-(em)*, 'neck, back of the neck, with parts touching it', & **-al**. *Cervix* is for **cers-vīc-s*, the first syll. being same as that in **cerebrum**, **cernuous**, meaning 'head', & the second syll. prob. fr. Lat. *vīc-*, 'bind', as in P.P. of *vincīre*, 'bind'; fr. this base comes also Lat. *vicia*, q.v. under **vetch**. Cp. next word. Pertaining to, situated in, the neck; esp. *cervical vertebrae*, joints of the neck.

cervine, adj. [1. sérvīn; 2. sʌ́vain]. Lat. *cervus*, 'stag, deer', & **-ine**. *Cervus* means orig. 'horned animal', cp. Gk. *kéras*, 'horn', Lat. *cornu* (see **corn** on the foot), & Gk. *keróeis*, 'horned', for **kerwo-*, & Zend *srvara*, 'horned'; further, O.H.G. *hiruz*, O.E. *heorot*, 'stag', fr. **hirut-* (see **hart**); O. Slav. *srŭna*, 'roe-deer'. See **coryphaeus** & **horn**. Pertaining to the deer family; like a deer.

cess, n. [1. ses; 2. ses]. For earlier *sess*, fr. **assess**. A tax, rate (obs. in England). In Ireland the Phr. *bad cess to you!*, bad luck to you, confound you!, is common as a mild malediction.

cessation, n. [1. sesáshun; 2. siséiʃən]. Lat. *cessātiōn-(em)*, 'tarrying, delaying', formed fr. *cessātum*, P.P. of *cessāre*, 'give way, delay'. See **cease**. Stoppage, pause, discontinuance (whether temporary or final).

cesser, n. [1. séser; 2. sésə]. O. Fr. infin. See **cease**. (legal) Discontinuance, coming to an end of services, payment, liability.

cession, n. [1. séshun; 2. séʃən]. Lat. *cessiōn-(em)* (legal term), 'giving up, surrendering', fr. P.P. *cessum* of *cēdere*. See **cede**. The act of ceding, formal surrender, giving up: *cession of territory, of rights* &c.

cessionary, n. [1. séshunari; 2. séʃənəri]. Med. Lat. *cessiōnārius*. See **cession** & **-ary**. One to whom property &c. is legally transferred; an assign.

cess-pit, **cess-pool**, n. [1. sés pit, pōōl; 2. sés pit, pūl]. Not an old word in Engl., & often spelt *sess-*. Either fr. Lat. *secessus*, 'retiring place, latrine', cp. Ital. *cesso*, 'privy', fr. *secēdere*, 'go aside, withdraw' (see **secede** &c.), or for *recess-*, as Skeat thinks more prob. Cavity in the ground, usually covered in, into which drainage from a house or stables runs; part of the liquid usually drains off through an overflow-pipe, while the solid matter collects in the pit, whence it is pumped or otherwise extracted periodically.

cestoid, n. [1. séstoid; 2. séstɔid]. Gk., 'girdle-like', fr. *kestós*, 'girdle', & **-oid**, 'like'. Orig. meaning of *kestós* is 'embroidered, worked', connected w. *kentéō*, 'to prick, stab, pierce'. See **centre** (I.). (zool.) Flat, intestinal worm; tape-worm.

cestui que trust, n. [1. sétikwe; 2. sétikwe]. A.-Fr. law term, lit. 'that one who trusts'. (law) The beneficiary of a trust, the equitable beneficial owner, for whom the legal owner or trustee acts.

cestus (I.), n. [1. séstus; 2. séstəs]. Lat., earlier *caestus*, 'strap of bull's hide loaded with iron or lead, wound around the hands and arms of pugilists'. For **caed-stos*, 'striking weapon', fr. base of *caedere*, 'strike, kill', see *caed-*, as first syll. of *caementum*, under **cement**.

cestus (II.), n. Gk. *kestós*, 'girdle'. See **cestoid**. **a** (class. antiq.) The girdle of Aphrodite or Venus; **b** (zool.) genus of ribbon-like jelly-fish; also known as the Venus' girdle.

cetacean, adj. & n. [1. setáshun; 2. sitéiʃən]. Formed fr. Lat. *cētus*, 'large fish, whale', fr. Gk. *kētos*, 'sea monster, huge fish, whale'; an isolated word w. no well-established relations, cp. **spermaceti**, & **-acean**. **a** adj. Pertaining to the whale family; **b** n., a member of the group of sea mammals which includes whales, porpoises &c.

cetaceous, adj. [1. setáshus; 2. sitéiʃəs]. Lat. *cētus*, as in prec., & **-aceous**. Belonging to whale family.

ceteosaur, **ceteosaurus**, n. [1. séteosōr, seteosórus; 2. sítiəsɔ̄, sitiəsɔ́rəs]. Lat. *cētus*, 'whale', as in prec., & Gk. *saûros*, 'lizard'. See **saurian**. Huge fossil lizard.

ceteris paribus, adv. [1. séteris páribus; 2. sítəris pǽribəs]. Lat., abl. pl. See **etcetera** & **par**. Other conditions being equal.

Chablis, n. [1. sháblē; 2. ʃǽblī]. Name of Fr. town on the Serein, in Dept of Yonne. Light, sweetish white Burgundy wine named after above town.

chaconne, n. [1. shakón; 2. ʃakɔ́n]. Fr., fr. Span. *chacona*. **a** A slow, stately, Spanish dance; **b** music for this, or movement in ¾ time suitable for such.

chaeto-, pref., fr. Gk. *khaítē*, 'hair', cogn. w. Zend *gaēsa*, O. Ir. *gāissit*, 'hair', used to form scientific compounds, denoting presence of or resemblance to hairs, or bristles, or setae; as *Chaetopoda* [1. kētópoda; 2. kītɔ́pədə], class of segmented worms, having paired bristles, or setae, at the segments, used as means of movement; also *-chaeta*, as suff., as *Spirochaeta*, class of bacteria, of coiled, hair-like appearance.

chafe, vb. trans. & intrans. [1. chāf; 2. tʃeif]. M.E. *chaufen*, 'to warm', O. Fr. *chaufer*, Mod. Fr. *chauffer*, 'to warm', fr. Lat. *calefacere*, 'make warm, heat', fr. *calēre*, 'glow with heat', (for base see under **calorescence**, **caloric** &c.), & *facere*, 'make'. See **fact**. Cp. **calefacient**. **A.** trans. **1.** To rub (a limb, member) for purpose of restoring warmth or sensation. **2.** To rub so as to make sore, to gall: *a collar chafes a horse's neck* &c. **B.** intrans. **1.** Of one body against another: **a** to rub against; **b** to become sore from friction. **2.** (fig.) To become excited, restive, feel impatience, irritation, of mind: *to chafe under restraint, insult* &c.

chafer, n. [1. cháfer; 2. tʃéifə]. O.E. *ċeafor*, 'beetle'; cp. O.H.G. *kevar*, Mod. Germ. *käfer*, prob. fr. same base, w. different grade, as M.H.G. *kiven*, 'to gnaw', & connected w. **chaff**, & O.E. *ceafl*, 'jaw', q.v. under **jowl**. Applied to various winged beetles, esp. to the *cock-chafer*, q.v.

chaff (I.), n. [1. chahf; 2. tʃāf]. O.E. *ċeaf*, O.H.G. &c., *kaf*. Prob. fr. same base as **chafer**, & meaning orig. 'gnawings', i.e. 'something reduced to small fragments'. **1.** Husk of grain; chopped hay or straw. **2.** (fig.) Worthless imitation of the reality, esp. in Phrs. *to offer chaff for grain* (fig.); *too old a bird to be caught with chaff*, experienced and not easily deceived. **3.** (fig., extended meaning of **2.**) Good-natured teasing, or pleasantry, banter.

chaff (II.), vb. trans., fr. prec. **1.** To reduce to chaff, cut hay or straw fine for fodder (not much used). **2.** To tease, make fun of good-naturedly; to banter.

chaff-cutter, n. See **chaff** (I.) & **cutter**. Instrument fitted with revolving knives turned by a handle, for cutting up hay and straw, which are fed in from behind, for fodder.

chaffer (I.), n. [1. cháfer; 2. tʃǽfə]. M.E. *chaffare*, earlier *chapfare*, compound fr. O.E. *ċēap*, 'price, bargain', see **chapman**, & **cheap**, & O.E. *faru*, 'going, proceedings'. See **fare**. Orig. meaning 'goings-on about price, bargaining'. Bargaining, discussion, esp. mean, petty negotiations about price.

chaffer (II.), vb. intrans., fr. prec. In M.E. To bargain, haggle over prices in a mean manner.

chaffinch, n. [1. cháfinch, cháhfinch; 2. tʃǽfintʃ, tʃáfintʃ]. O.E. *ċeaffinċ*. See **chaff** & **finch**. Small, common British bird, the male of which is brightly coloured, *Fringilla coelebs*.

chafing-dish, n. [1. cháfing dish; 2. tʃéifiŋ diʃ]. See **chafe** & **dish**. Vessel of metal with spirit-lamp, or other means of heating, below it, and a lid, for heating or cooking food on the table.

chafing-gear, n. Any contrivance, on board ship, for prevention of chafing or friction of ropes &c., as mats, strips of rope or yarn &c.

chagrin (I.), n. [1. shágrin; 2. ʃǽgrin]. Fr., 'grief'. Perh. same word as **shagreen**, in wh. sense the Fr. word is also used; if so, the sense is metaphorical, fr. use of shagreen as an abrasive. Mortification, annoyance, disappointment.

chagrin (**II.**), vb. trans., fr. prec. [1. shagrḗn; 2. ʃəgrín]. To cause mortification and disappointment to; wound feelings of, esp. in P.P.: *to feel chagrined at, by.*

chain (**I.**), n. [1. chān; 2. tʃein]. O. Fr. *chaeine*, Fr. *chaîne*, fr. Lat. *catēna*, 'chain, fetter', the base of wh., *cat-*, 'confine', occurs also in Lat. *cassis* (*-es* pl.), fr. **cat-sis*, 'hunter's net, snare, toils'; prob. cogn. w. O.E. *heaþorian*, fr. **haþ-*, 'restrain, confine'. **1. a** Series of round, or oval, metal links connected together; **b** specif., *door chain*, chain for securing a door, not detachable from outside; **c** small chain for attaching watch to the clothing; **d** (fig., in plural) chain thought of as means of restraining liberty of a prisoner, hence, prison, imprisonment: *to be in chains.* **2.** Connected series or sequence **a** (of visible objects) *chain of mountains*; **b** (of non-material things) *chain of events, of thoughts, causes* &c. **3. a** Linked metal rod for measuring land; **b** measure of this, i.e. 66 feet. **4.** (naut., in plural) Iron plates, or links, bolted to side of vessel, to which the stays and lower shrouds are fastened, also *chain-wales.* See **channel** (**III.**).

chain (**II.**), vb. trans., fr. prec. **1.** To fasten **a** chain or chains to; to confine, make fast, with a chain: **a** *chain up a dog*; **b** *chain the door*; **c** *chain a prisoner to the wall.* **2.** (fig.) **a** To unite closely to: *chained to a drunken husband*; **b** to restrain freedom of: *chained to the desk*, bound to one's work.

chain-belt, n. Continuous belt of links passing over cogged wheels and geared, to transmit motion, in machinery.

chain-bridge, n. Suspension bridge, swung on, and by, chains.

chain-gang, n. Gang of convicts, prisoners &c., chained together.

chainless, adj. [1. chā́nles; 2. tʃéinlis]. **chain** & **-less.** Without chains.

chain-lightning, n. Very vivid and closely zigzagged forked lightning.

chain-mail, n. Flexible armour made of interlaced steel links.

chain-plates, n. pl. (naut.) The chains, channels.

chain-pump, n. A form of pump, consisting of an endless chain fitted with a series of buckets or dishes, working in a shaft or tube.

chain-stitch, n. **a** A fancy sewing stitch; **b** a loop stitch made by a sewing-machine, as contrasted with *lock-stitch.*

chain-stores, n. (Am. usage) Series, group, of multiple, retail shops owned by one company or firm.

chain-wale, n. See **channel** (**III.**).

chair (**I.**), n. [1. chār; 2. tʃeə]. M.E., fr. O. Fr. *chaiere*, Mod. Fr. *chaire*, 'pulpit', fr. Gk. *kathédra*, 'seat, chair, pulpit', fr. *katá*, 'down', & *hédra*, 'seat' (cp. **cathedral**). The Gk. base *hed-*, 'sit', is for **sed-*, q.v. under **sedentary**, **sit.** **1. a** A single seat with a back and usually four legs; sometimes with supports for the arms: *armchair*; **b** portable covered seat for conveying a passenger through the streets, also *sedan chair*; **c** small carriage on wheels to seat one person, drawn by a man, also *Bath chair.* **2.** Professorial post at a University: *Chair of Latin, History* &c. **3. a** Seat occupied by the Speaker in House of Commons, or by person presiding at an organized public or private meeting or discussion: *to take the chair*, to preside; **b** the office, status, dignity, and jurisdiction of one who presides; the person presiding at public or other meeting: *to respect, obey, the chair.* **4.** Steel block, or clutch, which supports railway line, keeps the rail in position, and attaches it to the sleeper.

chair (**II.**), vb. trans., fr. prec. To carry a person publicly in a chair in triumph, to celebrate his success in some achievement.

chairman, n. [1. chā́rman; 2. tʃéəmən]. **1. a** Person who presides, or takes the chair at a meeting of a deliberative or executive body; **b** principal director of a commercial undertaking, bank &c. *Chairman of Committees*, in House of Lords and of Commons, person chosen to preside when House is in Committee, taking place of Lord Chancellor or Speaker. **2.** One who draws a Bath chair; one of the bearers of a sedan chair.

chairmanship, n. [1. chā́rmanship; 2. tʃéəmənʃip]. Prec. & **-ship.** Office, tenure of office, of a chairman.

chaise, n. [1. shāz; 2. ʃeiz]. Fr., 'a chair, seat'; variant of **chair.** Name applied to any of several types of small, light, low travelling-carriages, in England generally having four wheels, and having no box for driver, and drawn by one or two ponies.

chaise longue, n. [1. shāz longg; 2. ʃēz lɔ̃g]. Fr. Long low couch with back and armrests, with a seat long enough to support sitter's legs.

chakra, n. [1. cháhkra; 2. tʃákra]. Scrt. *čakrá*, 'circle, wheel'. Cogn. w. Gk. *kúklos*, 'circle', q.v. under **cycle**, & w. Engl. **wheel.** Metal disk with sharp edges formerly used by the Sikhs as a missile in battle.

chalcedony, n. [1. kalséduni; 2. kælsédəni], fr. Chalcedon, town in Asia Minor. Variety of quartz; under the name are included several semi-precious stones such as cornelian, onyx, jasper, sard, cat's eye &c.

chalcography, n. [1. kalkógrafi; 2. kælkógrəfi]. Gk., fr. *khalkós*, 'copper, brass', wh. is perh. related to Engl. **gold**, meaning orig. 'red metal', & *graphṓ*, 'write', see **graph.** Art of engraving on copper or brass.

chaldron, n. [1. cháwldrun; 2. tʃɔ́ldrən]. O. Fr.; Mod. Fr. *chaudron*, 'kettle'. Variant of **cauldron.** Measure for coals = 36 bushels.

chalet, n. [1. shálā; 2. ʃælei]. Swiss patois word for wooden cabin or house, fr. O. Fr. *chastel-et*, dimin. of *chastel*, Mod. Fr. *château.* See **castle.** Wooden house of type found in mountain districts of Switzerland; rather loosely applied in English either **a** to a reproduction of a Swiss house, or **b** to any summer dwelling, or garden house built of wood and more or less fancifully ornamented.

chalice, n. [1. chális; 2. tʃælis]. O. Fr. fr. Lat. *calic-em.* See **calyx.** **a** Drinking cup; specif. **b** the cup used in celebration of the Eucharist; **c** (poet.) anything shaped like a cup, e.g. bell of a flower.

chalk (**I.**), n. [1. chawk; 2. tʃɔ̄k]. O.E. *čealc*, 'lime', borrowed fr. Lat. *calx*, 'lime' &c. See **calcareous.** **1.** Soft fossiliferous limestone, usually white or greyish in colour. Phrs. *not to know chalk from cheese*, an inferior, from a good thing; *as like as chalk and cheese*, quite unlike. **2.** Material made up of, or resembling chalk, esp. when shaped into pencils for writing on blackboard, or for crayon drawing. **3.** Mark made with chalk, esp. to indicate a score in a game. Phr. *better by a long chalk*, much better, in reference to this; **b** amount of money owing.

chalk (**II.**), vb. trans., fr. prec. **a** To mark with chalk; *chalk up*, write up score, in a game, or in public-house, with chalk; **b** rub, whiten, with chalk.

chalk-stone, n. **a** Lump of chalk; **b** (med.) rheumatic concretion or deposit in the joints.

chalky, adj. [1. cháwki; 2. tʃɔ́ki]. **chalk** (**I.**) & **-y.** Resembling chalk in colour or texture; consisting of chalk; covered or bedaubed with chalk.

challenge (**I.**), n. [1. chálenj; 2. tʃælindž], in M.E., A.-Fr. *chalenge*, O. Fr. *chalonge*, fr. Lat. *calumnia.* See **calumny.** Originally an accusation, reproach. **1.** Summons by a sentry to a person to prove his identity by giving secret pass-word. **2.** Summons, provocation, **a** to fight a battle, or a duel; **b** to engage in a contest of skill, strength, speed &c. with another party: *a challenge to a game, match, round of golf* &c. **3.** Provocation, incitement, to prove one's worth, courage, taste, skill &c., through a calling in question of these. **4.** (law) Objection, exception taken to a juror, on formation of the panel.

challenge (**II.**), vb. trans. M.E. *chalengen*, A.-Fr., fr. Lat. *calumniāre*, 'accuse' &c. See **calumniate.** **1.** To call upon to prove one's identity, as a sentry does. **2.** To summon, invite, to a contest of any kind, specif. **a** defy, provoke to fight; **b** to invite to a game or match. **3. a** To incite, provoke, to show one's mettle, character, worth; **b** to call in question, cast doubt upon: *to challenge a man's right to vote* &c. **4.** (law) To object, take exception, to a juror on formation of the panel.

challengeable, adj. [1. chálenjabl; 2. tʃælindžəbl]. Prec. & **-able.** Able to be challenged.

challis, n. [1. shāli(s); 2. ʃæli(s)]. Fr., 'stuff made of goat's hair'. Origin unknown. Soft fabric of wool or silk.

chalybeate, adj. [1. kalíbiat; 2. kælíbiət]. Coined fr. Gk. *khálups*, stem *khálub-*, 'steel', fr. *Khálubes*, name of ancient people of Pontus, Asia Minor. (of water, and springs) Impregnated with iron.

cham, n. [1. cham; 2. tʃæm]. Obs. form of **khan.** (archaic) Only in the *Great Cham* of Tartary, also applied to Dr. Johnson as the autocrat of literature in his age.

chamade, n. [1. shamáhd; 2. ʃæmā́d]. Fr., fr. Port. *chamada*, fr. *chamar*, 'to cry out', fr. Lat. *clamāre*, 'shout, cry out'. See **clamant, clamour.** (mil.) Signal made by drum or trumpet, for parley or retreat.

chamber (**I.**), n. [1. chā́mber; 2. tʃéimbə]. In M.E.; O. Fr. *chambre* &c., fr. Lat. *camera*, 'vault, arched roof'. See **camera.** **1.** A room, apartment in a house; enclosed apartment of any kind. **2. a** Specif., ante-room to apartments of the King or other great personage; hence, *Groom of the Chamber(s)*; **b** specif., in pl., private room of a judge, at law court: *the case was heard before a judge in chambers.* **3. a** Hall, great apartment used for meetings of national, or other legislative assembly; **b** one of the two 'houses', *upper, lower chamber*, into which most legislative bodies are divided; **c** the body of persons composing such an assembly: *Chamber of Commerce*; *Chamber of Deputies* (France) &c. **4. a** Hollowed-out space (in ground, rock &c.); cavity, enclosed division, compartment; **b** specif., a compartment in a cannon or smaller fire-arm which holds the charge: *revolver with six chambers.* **5.** Euphemistic for a domestic utensil, for *chamber-pot.* **6.** (in pl.) *Chambers*, **a** private rooms, or office in which a barrister interviews clients, and transacts business other than pleading, e.g. in Inns of Court &c.; *Chamber counsel*, barrister who gives advice in private but does not plead in court; **b** set of rooms in large building, for bachelors living alone.

chamber(**II.**), vb. trans., fr. prec. To make a hollow, or cavity; specif., to hollow out, by pressing or moulding a saddle, or a boot, to relieve pressure on a horse's shoulder, or on foot.

chamber concert, n. Concert of music suitable for a room but not for large hall &c.

chambering, n. [1. chā́mbering; 2. tʃéimbəriŋ]. **chamber** (**I.**) & **-ing.** (archaic) Frequenting of ante-rooms, hence, licentious behaviour.

chamberlain, n. [1. chā́mberlin; 2. tʃéimbəlin]. M.E. *cha(u)mberlein*; O. Fr. *chambrelenc*, Mod. Fr. *chambellan*, cp. Ital. *camerlengo.* The word is fr. an O.H.G. source, cp. O.H.G. *chamarlinc, -ling*, & is a hybrid fr. Lat. *camera*, see **camera**, & Gmc. suff. **-ling.** **1.** Officer having charge of private apartments of a monarch, hence later, a high court official. See *Lord Chamberlain.* **2.** Chief steward or factor on estates of a great nobleman, esp. in Scotland.

chamber-maid, n. Housemaid at a hotel or inn.

chamber music, n. Vocal or instrumental music suitable for performance before a small audience, in moderate-sized **apartment**, but not in a theatre &c.

chameleon, n. [1. kaméliun; 2. kəmfliən]. Lat. *chamaeleon*, fr. Gk. *khamailéōn*, lit. 'ground lion', fr. *khamai*, 'on the ground', q.v. under **humus**, & *léōn*, 'lion'. **1.** Genus of lizards found in Africa and Madagascar, possessing long tongue, prehensile tail, and the power of rapidly changing its colour according to its surroundings. **2.** (fig.) The name of the chameleon is used as symbolic of inconstancy.

chamfer (I.), n. [1. chámfer; 2. tʃǽmfə]. 16th cent., *chamfre*, fr. Fr. *chanfrein*, O. Fr. *chanfraindre*, 'bevel off', fr. *chant*, 'edge', & *fraindre*, 'break', Lat. *frangere*, 'to break'. See **cant (II.) & fracture.** Flat surface produced by cutting or paring off an angle formed by two surfaces in stone or wood.

chamfer (II.), vb. trans., fr. prec. To cut a chamfer, by bevelling off angle where two surfaces of stone or wood meet.

chamois, n. [1. shámwah; 2. ʃǽmwa]. Fr.; word derived fr. some dialectal type of M.H.G. *gamuz*, Mod. Germ. *gemse*; oldest form *camox*, prob. survival of a pre-Romance Alpine word. Small ruminant, horned animal, found in mountains of S. Europe and W. Asia; resembling a deer in build and agility, the chamois partakes also of the character of the goat.

chamois (leather), n. [1. shámi; 2. ʃǽmi]. Soft pliable leather, originally made from skin of chamois; now, also from that of the sheep, goat &c.

champ, vb. intrans. & trans. [1. champ; 2. tʃæmp]. Perh. Scand., cp. Swed. dial. *kämsa*, 'chew with difficulty'. **A.** intrans. **a** To bring teeth together repeatedly and noisily, as a horse does when eating; **b** (fig.) to gnash the teeth with excitement, rage, disappointment &c.; to show restlessness caused by these emotions. **B.** trans. **a** To munch food (of horses): *to champ their oats*; **b** to bite down repeatedly upon something: *the horses were champing their bits.*

champagne, n. [1. shàmpā́n; 2. ʃæmpéin], fr. name of province in east of France. French wine made in Champagne district, usually pale gold in colour, and highly sparkling, but *still champagne*, and *red champagne*, also exist.

champaign, n. [1. chámpān, shámpān; 2. tʃǽmpein, ʃǽmpein]. O. Fr. *champaigne*, Mod. Fr. (different dialect) *campagne*, 'open country', fr. Lat. *campānia*. See **campagna & campaign.** Open expanse of flat unenclosed country.

champak, n. [1. shámpak; 2. ʃǽmpæk]. Hind.; Scrt. *campaca*. An East Indian tree, belonging to the Magnolia family, with beautifully grained wood and very fragrant yellow flowers.

champertor, n. [1. chámpertōr; 2. tʃǽmpətɔ̄]. See **champerty.** Person who enters into a bargain with one of the parties to a lawsuit, of a kind known as **champerty.**

champertous, adj. [1. chámpertus; 2. tʃǽmpətəs]. See next word & **-ous.** Of, pertaining to, the nature of champerty: *a champertous bargain.*

champerty, n. [1. chámperti; 2. tʃǽmpəti]. Fr. *champart*, 'division of land rent', Lat. *campi partitio*, lit. 'dividing of the land', or of spoils in a litigation. See **camp & part.** Bargain with one of the parties in a litigation, whereby he who makes the bargain (*champertor*) agrees to bear the costs of the suit in return for sharing the profits in the object sued for, if they win their case. Champerty is an offence at law. Cp. *maintenance.*

champion (I.), n. & adj. [1. chámpiun; 2. tʃǽmpiən]. M.E., fr. O. Fr. *champiun*, fr. L. Lat. *campiōn-(em)*, 'fighter', lit. 'one who takes the field', fr. Lat. *campus*, 'field, field of battle'. See **camp.** O.E. *cempa*, 'warrior', fr. Gmc. **kampja*, is an exact cogn., though the base **kamp-* is an early loan-word fr. Lat. Cp. Germ. *kämpfen*, 'to fight', *kampf*, 'battle'. **1. a** Originally one who took part in a contest, esp. in single combat, to defend his own or another's honour, or to uphold a cause: *champions in a joust or tournament*; *the seven champions of Christendom*; **b** specif., *King's Champion*, hereditary officer (Dymoke of Scrivelsby), who at coronation of a British king bids defiance to the king's enemies, and challenges all such to single combat with him. **2. a** One who has an acknowledged superiority in courage, strength, and skill in use of arms; **b** now, somewhat degraded from the chivalric ideal, one who excels in fisticuffs: *the featherweight champion*; expert in cricket, tennis, chess &c. **3.** Advocate, defender of a person or cause, chiefly in war of words: *a champion of the oppressed, of tariff reform, prohibition* &c. **4.** Anything which wins first prize in a show or exhibition; variously applied to bulls, horses, dogs &c.; also to all kinds of vegetables &c. **5.** Also attrib.: *champion chess-player, champion bull* &c.

champion (II.), vb. trans., fr. prec. To act as champion, advocate, protector, of person or cause; to uphold, defend: *to champion the cause of enriching the poor by taking from the rich.*

championship, n. [1. chámpiunship; 2. tʃǽmpiənʃip]. **champion (I.) & -ship. a** Act of upholding, protecting, advocating: *his championship of Protection lost him his office*; **b** state, condition, of being a champion: *the championship of the ring, of the cattle world* &c.

champlevé, adj. [1. shahnlevā; 2. ʃãləve]. Fr., 'raised field'. Of kind of enamel work, in which the metal ground is scooped out into hollows leaving a metal ridge or bar outlining the pattern; the paste is then poured into these and fired; opposed to *cloisonné.*

chance (I.), n. [1. chahns; 2. tʃāns]. M.E. *cheance* &c., fr. O. Fr., fr. L. Lat. *cadentia*, 'falling, esp. of dice'. See **cadence, cadency. 1.** Events as they happen, course of events, way things occur: '*the changes and chances of this mortal life*'. **2.** Various senses implying happening of events without any cause that can be ascertained, foreseen, or controlled; **a** undesigned, unforeseen, unforeseeable occurrence, accidental circumstance, fortune, luck: *to be present by the merest chance*; *to leave things to chance*; *a game of chance*, reverse of one of skill. Phr. *by chance*, casually, by accident; **b** probability, likelihood, of something happening: *a good, slender, chance of success*; **c** possibility, barest possibility: *just a chance that I may be there, not the least chance.* Phrs. *on the (off) chance*, in case; *to take one's chance of*, trust to luck and run whatever risk there may be; **d** favourable opportunity, propitious occasion: *the chance for which one had been waiting*; *the chance of a lifetime.* Phr. *the main chance*, opportunity of making a profit.

chance (II.), adj., fr. prec. Coming, happening, by chance; accidental, casual, fortuitous: *a chance meeting*; *chance acquaintance*; *chance resemblance, occurrence* &c.

chance (III.), vb. intrans., fr. **chance** (I.). **1.** (impers.) To come about, to pass, happen, fall out, without design or preparation: *it chanced that I was at home when he called.* **2.** To do something, experience something, by accident: *I chanced to see, to meet, him.* **3.** *Chance upon*, meet, find, come across, unexpectedly, light on by accident. **4.** (also trans., colloq.) To risk: *to chance an accident*; *let's chance it.*

chancel, n. [1. cháhnsl; 2. tʃánsl]. O. Fr. *chancel*, Lat. *cancelli*, 'cross-bars, lattice', from the chancel being formerly separated from rest of the church by a lattice or screen. See **cancel.** That part of a Christian church, usually at the east end, in which the choir and clergy sit, and at upper extremity of which the altar stands.

chancel aisle, n. Aisle passing on either side of, or around chancel.

chancel arch, n. Arch crossing chief entrance to chancel from the nave.

chancellery, n. [1. cháhnsleri; 2. tʃánsləri]. Fr. *chancellerie*, L. Lat. *cancellāria*, fr. Lat. *cancellārius*. See **chancery & chancellor. 1. a** The position of a chancellor; **b** the court or department over which he presides; **c** specif., office of chief secretary of an embassy: *news to disturb the chancelleries of Europe*, i.e. the diplomatists. **2.** Building or apartment in which office of a chancellor is situated.

chancellor, n. [1. cháhnseler; 2. tʃánsilə]. M.E. *chanceler*, Fr. *chancelier*, L. Lat. *cancellārius.* The Roman chancellor was an officer who kept the records, and whose place was near the *cancelli* or 'lattice work', which screened off the judge's seat. See **cancel, chancel.** Name given to various great officials in this country and abroad. Specif. **1. a** *Lord* (*High*) *Chancellor* of England, the chief judge, who also presides at sessions of the House of Lords; **b** *Chancellor of the Exchequer*, chief finance minister of the Crown, head of the Treasury; **c** *Chancellor of the Duchy of Lancaster*, member of the Cabinet, representing the King as Duke of Lancaster. **2.** *Chancellor of the Diocese*, a law official appointed by the bishop to advise him on points of ecclesiastical law, hear cases in ecclesiastical court of the Diocese and grant faculties. **3.** *Chancellor of a university*, head of a university, generally represented in this country by the *Vice-Chancellor*, who resides continually, acts as chief executive officer, and presides at meetings of the legislative bodies of the university. **4.** Chief secretary of British embassies at foreign courts. **5.** Name of chief Minister of State in Germany and Austria.

chancellorship, n. [1. cháhnselership; 2. tʃánsiləʃip], fr. prec. & **-ship.** Office or tenure of the office of chancellor.

chance-medley, n. [1. cháhns médli; 2. tʃáns médli], fr. A.-Fr. law term *chance medlee*, 'mixed chance'. See **chance & meddle.** An old term for a sudden affray or encounter leading to homicide; hence such a homicide; practically equivalent to modern manslaughter.

chancery, n. [1. cháhnseri; 2. tʃánsəri]. Variant of **chancellery.** Branch of the High Court dealing with equity cases; the Lord Chancellor is the head of the Court of Chancery, but the presiding judge is the Master of the Rolls. Phr. *in chancery* (law). **a** In course of being heard in court of chancery; **b** under control of Lord Chancellor, e.g. *a ward in Chancery*; **c** (fig., in boxing) *in chancery*, refers to the head of one of the combatants, when securely held under the arm of the other, so that the former is at the latter's mercy; from the difficulty formerly existing of escaping from the old court of chancery owing to its dilatoriness.

chancre, n. [1. shángker; 2. ʃǽŋkə], Fr. form of **canker.** (med.) Form of venereal ulcer, esp. the primary sore and infective source of syphilis.

chancroid, n. [1. shángkroid; 2. ʃǽŋkrɔid]. Prec. & **-oid.** (med.) Sore resembling a chancre, but differing from it in being purely local.

chancrous, adj. [1. shángkrus; 2. ʃǽŋkrəs], fr. **chancre & -ous.** (med.) Having nature of a chancre.

chancy, adj. [1. cháhnsi; 2. tʃánsi], fr. **chance (I.) & -y.** Having the nature of chance; uncertain, hazardous, risky.

chandelier, n. [1. shàndelḗr; 2. ʃændəlíə]. Fr., fr. Lat. *candēlārius*, 'candle-maker', fr. *candēla*, 'candle'. See **candle & chandler.** Branched support for lights, originally for candles, but by extension of meaning applied to similarly shaped bracket, suspended from the ceiling, for gas or electric lights.

chandler, n. [1. cháhndler; 2. tʃándlə]. M.E. *chandeler*; same word as prec., w. retention of old meaning. Maker or seller of candles; dealer in candles, soap, oil, paints &c. Often with qualifying word: *tallow chandler*, dealer in candles, wax &c.; *ships' chandler*, dealer in stores and provisions for ships.

change (I.), vb. trans. & intrans. [1. chānj; 2. tʃeindž]. M.E. *cha(u)ngen*, fr. O. Fr.

changier, fr. Low Lat. *cambiāre*, Lat. *cambīre*, 'exchange, barter'. A Celt. loan-word; cp. M. Ir. *cimb*, 'tribute'. **A.** trans. **1.** To take instead of, substitute one thing for, another, put, adopt, a thing in place of another: *to change one's clothes, one's diet, habits, address* &c. Phrs. *to change countenance*, appear disconcerted; *change one's mind*, alter opinions, or plans; *change one's tune, note*, in speaking, pass from civility to insolence or vice versa; express different views from those formerly stated; *change sides*, go over to other side (lit. and fig.); *change step*, alter order in which feet are advanced. **2.** To cause to become different in any respect, cause to pass from one state into another, convert one thing into another: *railways have changed the face of the country; grief had changed his hair from black to white; conjurers change watches into rabbits at will.* **3.** Specif. **a** to give or receive money of larger or smaller denomination in place of that one has: *to change a five-pound note for gold*; **b** to give cash in exchange for a written draft or order: *to change a cheque, a postal order* &c. **4.** Followed by *with*, give something up to a person on receiving something equivalent from him: *to change seats with a person.* **5.** (in specific sense) To quit a railway train, or carriage, steamboat, or other conveyance, in order to enter another: *to change trains, boats* &c. **B.** intrans. **1.** To grow, become, different: *times change; he had changed greatly since last I saw him; our weather seems to change from day to day.* **2. a** (of the moon) To pass from one phase to another; **b** (of tides) to pass from ebb to flow, or vice versa. **3.** (absolutely) To quit a train, carriage &c., and enter another: *we shall have to change at Crewe; all change!* **4.** To take off clothes one is wearing, and put on different ones: *you have just time to change before dinner.*

change (II.), n. Fr., fr. Low Lat. *cambium*, 'exchange'. See **change** (I.) & **cambion. 1.** Substitution of one thing for another; alteration in sequence of events; variety, novelty: *a change of clothes; change of air; to be fond of change; to breakfast at 8 o'clock for a change.* Specif., a temporary visit to a different place: *you need a change; to go away for a change.* **2.** Alteration, modification, passing from one state or condition to a different one: *I have noticed a great change in him lately; my opinions have undergone a change; a change in the weather.* Specif. uses: *change of life*, climacteric, menopause in women; *change of voice*, alteration of a boy's voice to that of a man, at puberty. **3. a** Money, coins, of lower denomination, given for that, or those, of a higher: *to give one change for half-a-crown; small change*; **b** (by extension) small money: *to have no change about one.* Phr. *to get no change out of a person*, gain no advantage over him, get no information from him. **4.** Place where merchants and financiers publicly transact business, exchange; often written *'Change*; *to be, go, on 'Change.* **5.** Series of chimes, order in which bells are rung. Phr. (fig.) *to ring the changes (on)*, state same thing in many different ways. **6.** New phase of the moon, or tide.

changeability, n. [1. chānjabíliti; 2. tʃèin(d)žəbíliti]. See next word & **-ity.** Liability, tendency to change, quality of being changeable.

changeable, adj. [1. chānjabl; 2. tʃéin(d)žəbl]. **change** (I.) & **-able.** **a** Liable, prone, to change; variable, fickle; **b** capable of being changed.

changeableness, n. Prec. & **-ness.** Changeability.

changeful, adj. [1. chānzhfool; 2. tʃéinžful]. **change** (II.) & **-ful.** Constantly changing; inconstant.

changefulness, n. Prec. & **-ness.** Variability, inconstancy.

changeless, adj. [1. chānzhles; 2. tʃéinžlis]. **change** (II.) & **-less.** Unchanging, not liable to change; constant, immutable.

changelessness, n. Prec. & **-ness.** Quality of being invariable; immutability.

changeling, n. [1. chānzhling; 2. tʃéinžliŋ]. **change** (I.) & **-ling.** Creature, in human or animal form, supposed to be left by the fairies in place of one which they have stolen; often applied to a dwarfish, ill-favoured person or animal.

channel (I.), n. [1. chánel; 2. tʃǽn(ə)l]. M.E., fr. O. Fr. *chanel*; variant of **canal. 1.** Groove or hollow passage, for liquids; specif. **a** natural or artificial hollowed bed of a river or other flow of water; **b** passage in which river or body of water runs; **c** body of water joining two seas, specif. *the Channel*, between North Sea and Atlantic. **2. a** Passage, duct, tube, through which any liquid passes; **b** (fig.) means of access, communication; means or medium whereby non-material things are conveyed: *channel of information, news, knowledge* &c.

channel (II.), vb. trans., fr. prec. To cut, wear, hollow out, form, a channel.

channel (III.), n. For **chain-wale.** See **chain** (I.), 4, & **wale.** Cp. **gunnel.** (Usually in pl.). Massive pieces of wood, or metal, bolted to ship's sides; they keep the shrouds, or ropes, that support the masts, which are fastened to them, clear of the gunwale.

chant (I.), n. [1. chahnt; 2. tʃānt]. Fr., Lat. *cantus*, 'song'. See **cant** (I.). **a** Song; specif., melody to which the church canticles are sung; **b** the various sacred hymns and canticles sung to such a melody.

chant (II.), vb. trans. & intrans. Fr. *chanter*, 'to sing', fr. Lat. *cantāre.* See prec. **1.** trans. **a** To sing a chant; **b** to sing any song; **c** to celebrate in poetry; **d** to tell over and over again: *to chant a person's praises.* **2.** intrans. **a** To sing a chant; **b** to utter in a musical monotone.

chantage, n. [1. sháhntahzh; 2. ʃãtāž]. Fr. Cp. slang phrase *faire chanter*, 'to make a person pay'. Blackmail.

chanter, n. [1. cháhnter; 2. tʃántə]. Fr. *chanteur*, Lat. *cantor*, 'singer'. See **chant** (I.). Pipe of a bagpipe, with holes upon which, by fingering, the notes are produced.

chantey, chanty, also **shanty**, n. [1. shánti; 2. ʃǽnti]. Supposed corrupt. of Fr. *chanter*, 'to sing'. See **chant.** Rhythmical song, sung by sailors in time with the motions incidental to their work, e.g. turning a windlass &c.

chanticleer, n. [1. cháhntiklēr; 2. tʃántikliə]. M.E. (Chaucer), fr. O. Fr. *chantecler.* See **chant** & **clear.** Name for the barnyard cock, from his loud crowing.

chantress, n. [1. cháhntres; 2. tʃántris]. Fr. *chanteresse.* Cp. **chanter.** Female singer.

chantry, n. [1. cháhntri; 2. tʃántri]. O. Fr. *chanterie*, 'singing'. See **chant.** Chapel, altar, or part of a church where masses were sung for repose of the founder's soul.

chaos, n. [1. kāos; 2. kéiɔs]. Lat. *chaos*; fr. Gk. *kháos*, 'gulf, unorganized primordial matter', fr. same base as Gk. *khaínō*, 'I yawn'. Etymologists derive these words fr. an Aryan base **g̑heu-*, **g̑hou-* &c., whence also O.H.G. *goumo*, Mod. Germ. *gaumen*, 'palate' (of the mouth), O.E. *gōma*, 'gum' (of the teeth), see **gum** (I.). **1.** The formless void, bottomless abyss, prior to creation. **2.** Utter confusion, disorder, absence of ordered arrangement; muddle, whether in material, mental, or spiritual affairs.

chaotic, adj. [1. kāótik; 2. keiɔ́tik], fr. prec. on anal. of **erotic**, fr. Gk. *érōs.* Greatly disordered, confused, intermingled in hopeless confusion.

chaotically, adv. [1. kāótikali; 2. keiɔ́tikəli]. Prec. & **-al** & **-ly.** In a chaotic state or manner.

chap (I.), vb. trans. & intrans. [1. chap; 2. tʃæp]. In M.E. Connected with **chip** & **chop. 1.** trans. (said of frost, cold &c.) To cause cracks or slits, roughness and soreness, in exposed parts, such as the face, backs of the hands &c. **2.** intrans. (of the hands &c.) To split, become rough and sore from exposure to frost and cold.

chap (II.), **chop**, n. The M.E. word is *chaft*, cp. O.N. *kjaptr*, neither of wh. can be the direct ancestor of *chap.* (gen. in pl.) The **jaws**, esp. of an animal; for human beings *chops* is more usual, though the word is rare and vulgar. *Bath chap*, salted pig's cheek.

chap (III.), n. Shortened form of **chapman.** (colloq. and familiar) Male person, boy or man: *a good, nice, chap; old chap, my dear chap*, familiar and affectionate modes of address.

chaparajos, n. pl. [1. chaparáh-hōs; 2. tʃaparáhous]. Span. (Mexican), fr. **chaparral.** Sheepskin or leather overalls used by Western cowboys to protect the legs from the thorns of the chaparral, often abbreviated as *chaps.*

chaparral, n. [1. chaparál; 2. tʃaparál]. Span., 'evergreen oak'. Dense, thorny bush or scrub of Mexico and S.-W. United States of America.

chap-book, n. For first element see **chapman.** Small book, tract, or pamphlet, usually containing tales or ballads of a popular character, formerly sold by chapmen or pedlars.

chape, n. [1. chāp; 2. tʃeip]. Variant of **cape** (I.), fr. L. Lat *cāpa*, 'cope, cape'. Originally a covering, now rare and in varying senses: **a** metal point protecting end of scabbard; **b** metal mounting at top of scabbard which bears ring for attaching to belt; **c** back part of a buckle by which it is fastened to strap.

chapel, n. [1. chápl; 2. tʃǽpl]. M.E., fr. O. Fr. *chapele*, Low Lat. *capella, cappella*, 'cloak, hood', later 'sanctuary containing relics', orig. the cloak of St. Martin of Tours; dimin. of Low Lat. *cappa*, 'cap', or *cāpa*, 'cloak', closely related words, ultimately fr. *caput*, 'head', & meaning 'head-covering'. See **cap** & **cape. 1.** Place of Christian worship, subordinate to a larger **church**; **a** part of a church provided with an altar and specially dedicated; **b** small separate place of worship other than a cathedral or **parish** church, often situated in outlying part of a parish, and served by the parish clergy: *a chapel of ease; Lady-chapel*, one attached to a cathedral &c., dedicated to the B.V.M. **2.** Private, consecrated place of worship attached to a college, hospital, large private house, or castle, and usually extra-diocesan: *chapel royal*, one officially connected with the sovereign. **3.** Place of worship of a denomination other than the Church of England, esp. **a** one belonging to a Protestant nonconformist body; **b** a Roman Catholic place of worship. **4.** Specif., Protestant nonconformity in contrast to the Established Church: *to give up church and attend chapel*, to abandon the Church of England for nonconformity; *chapel folk*, nonconformists. **5.** (in Oxford and Cambridge) A service in the college chapel, a certain number of which all undergraduates must attend each term: *to keep a chapel*, or *chapels.* **6.** Printing-office; association or meeting of journeymen printers. (So called because the first printers carried on their work in a chapel near, or belonging to, Westminster Abbey.)

chapelle ardente, n. [1. shapél ardáhnt; 2. ʃapɛl ardãt]. Fr. Chapel, room, lighted with candles or torches, prepared for the lying in state of a sovereign &c.

chapelry, n. [1. chápelri; 2. tʃǽp(ə)lri]. Fr. *chapelerie.* See **chapel** & **-ry.** District served by a chapel.

chapel text, n. (typog.) Ornate style of type, somewhat resembling *church text* but lighter.

chaperon (I.), n. [1. sháperōn; 2. ʃǽpəroun]. Fr. 'a hood', used in this sense in M.E. The mod. sense seems to have grown fr. the idea of 'a protection', & then 'a protector'. A female attendant, friend, or parent, who accompanies daughter or younger lady to parties of pleasure, balls &c. to play propriety, and afford protection. Originally (Todd's *Johnson*) applied to a lady's male attendant or cavalier at a public assembly.

chaperon (**II.**), vb. trans., fr. prec. To act as a chaperon to a young lady; to accompany a young lady on a visit to, or on a party of pleasure with, one of the opposite sex.

chap-fallen, adj. [1. cháp fawlen; 2. tʃǽp fōlən]. See **chap** (**II.**) & **fallen.** With drooping, fallen jaws; (now only fig.) depressed, dispirited, abashed.

chapiter, n. [1. chápiter; 2. tʃǽpitə]. Fr. *chapitre.* See **chapter.** (archit.) Head, or capital, of a column.

chaplain, n. [1. cháplin; 2. tʃǽplin]. M.E., fr. O. Fr. *chapelein*, Low Lat. *capellānus*, 'one connected with a chapel'. See **chapel. 1.** Ecclesiastic who is attached to a chapel; specif., the clergyman officially appointed to minister in the chapel of a college, hospital, prison &c., or in private chapel of a nobleman &c.; a private priest and spiritual adviser; one who conducts religious services for a society (Free Masons' Lodge &c.). **2.** Clergyman officially appointed to minister in the army (*regimental chaplain* &c.), or in the navy, where he is attached to a ship or naval institution ashore.

chaplaincy, n. [1. cháplinsi; 2. tʃǽplinsi]. Preo. & **-cy. a** The office of a chaplain; **b** duration of this office.

chaplet, n. [1. cháplet; 2. tʃǽplit]. M.E. & O. Fr. *chapelet*, 'head-dress', O. Fr. *chapel*, fr. Low Lat. *capellum* (cp. Mod. Fr. *chapeau*, 'hat'), & dimin. **-et.** See **cap, cape, chape. a** Wreath, string of beads, band, worn round the head; **b** a rosary; **c** necklace.

chapman, n. [1. chápman; 2. tʃǽpmən]. O.E. *čēapmann*, 'merchant, pedlar', fr. *čēap*, 'price, bargain, commercial transaction'. See **cheap** & **man**, & cp. Germ. *kaufmann*, 'merchant'. Dealer, trader; hawker, pedlar. (No longer used except as a deliberate archaism, but common as a surname.)

chapped, adj. [1. chapt; 2. tʃæpt]. P.P. of **chap** (**I.**). (of skin, of hands &c.) Cracked, split, and sore from exposure to cold winds &c.

chaps, n. pl., colloquial abbreviation of **chaparajos.**

chapter, n. [1. chápter; 2. tʃǽptə]. M.E. *chapiter*, O. Fr. *chapitre*, variant of *chapitle*, fr. Lat. *capitulum*, 'head of a column', dimin. of *caput*, 'head'. See **capital. 1. a** Main division of a book or treatise; hence, **b** anything considered as an independent part of what is being discussed or considered; topic, subject: *enough on that chapter*; **c** episode, important stage in history or human life: *a sombre chapter in human affairs.* Phrs. *chapter of accidents*, series of disasters; *to, till, the end of the chapter*, (fig.) to the end; *chapter and verse*, exact, detailed reference. **2. a** Governing body of a cathedral or collegiate church, consisting of the canons, presided over by the dean; **b** a meeting of such a body, or of members of a monastic or knightly order.

chapter house, n. Room attached to a cathedral, in which the chapter meets.

char (**I.**), n. [1. char; 2. tʃā]. O.E. *čierr*, 'time, occasion', connected w. O.E. *čierran*, 'to turn'; cp. O.H.G. *keran*, 'turn'. See **churn.** A job of work, a duty, task which has to be done. (Not in common use, but common in U.S.A. in variant form **chore.**)

char (**II.**), vb. trans. & intrans. O.E. *čierran*, M.E. *cherren.* See prec. & **chare. 1.** trans. To scrub and clean (a house, building) as a charwoman does: *to char the house thoroughly.* **2.** intrans. To act as charwoman, do rough cleaning and tidying of houses; usually applied to action of temporary worker who comes in by the day: *to go out charring.*

char (**III.**), vb. trans. & intrans. Origin uncertain. Any connexion w. Fr. *charbon*, 'coal', is very doubtful; word is later than **charcoal. 1.** trans. (esp. of action of fire on wood) To burn, so as to render black, scorch, blacken surface of; reduce to charcoal. **2.** intrans. (of wood subjected to heat) To show signs of beginning to burn, to become scorched and blackened.

char (**IV.**), n., fr. Gael. *ceara*, 'red, blood-coloured'. A species of trout, with small scales and a red belly, found in Welsh hill-streams.

char-à-banc, n. [1. shár a bang; 2. ʃǽr ə bæŋ, ʃǽrəbã], fr. Fr. *char-à-bancs*, 'waggon with benches', pl. *chars-à-bancs.* See **car** & **bench.** Often in Mod. Engl. *charabanc*, pl. *charabancs*, pronounced [ʃǽrəbæŋz, -bãz]. Long-shaped public conveyance, now generally having a series of seats placed across its length, and driven by a petrol engine: *motor char-a-banc.*

character (**I.**), n. [1. kárikter; 2. kǽriktə]. Lat. *charactēr*, 'instrument for branding, mark; character, style', fr. Gk. *kharaktḗr*, 'engraved mark, imprint, mark', cp. *khárak-s*, 'stake', *kharássein*, 'to sharpen, carve, split, engrave'. **1. a** Mark or symbol, engraved or written; **b** alphabetical or graphic symbol, letter; **c** alphabet as a whole, typical mode of writing: *the Greek character.* **2.** (eccles.) Mark impressed upon human soul by the sacraments of baptism, confirmation, and holy orders. **3.** Distinguishing mark, essential quality, individual peculiarity; **a** (mental and moral attributes) the sum or aggregate of moral traits, idiosyncrasies, features, qualities which distinguish an individual or a race; personality: *a man of fine, strong, noble, character*; *the character of savage races is difficult to understand*; **b** (biol., in organic nature) an essential, typical, distinctive physical peculiarity, either inherited or acquired, marking either an individual or a species: *can acquired characters be inherited?*; **c** distinctive essential quality, nature, in material or non-material things: *the character of the country was gently undulating*; *the character of English institutions.* **4.** Specif., a good, strong character, moral backbone, stamina: *a man of character, of no character.* **5. a** A well-known person: *a public character*; **b** one of marked individuality, or eccentricity: *quite a character*; **c** *a bad character*, a notorious, or infamous, person. **6.** Description of a person's character, abilities, aptitudes, habits (esp. of a servant); a testimonial: *I gave my butler an excellent character when he left*; *to engage a servant without a character.* **7.** Reputation: *to bear a good character among one's acquaintance*; *to gain the character of a miser.* **8. a** Fictitious personages depicted in a novel or play; **b** portrayal of such by an actor on the stage. Phr. *in character* (lit. and fig.), appropriate(ly). **9.** Position, capacity, guise: *to come in the character of a friend.*

character (**II.**), vb. trans., fr. prec. To characterize, describe character of. (Rare.)

character actor, actress, n. One who plays, and excels in, the part of strongly marked, eccentric personages.

characteristic, adj. & n. [1. kàrakterístik; 2. kæ̀rəktərístik]. Fr. *caractéristique*, fr. Gk. *kharaktēristikós.* See **character** & **-ic. 1.** adj. Belonging to, forming constituent element in, and serving to display, the character, essential nature, of a person or thing; typical. **2.** n. Strongly marked, individual feature or trait of mind or body (in persons); typical, distinctive mark or quality (in things).

characteristical, adj. [1. kàrakterístikl; 2. kæ̀rəktərístikl]. Prec. & **-al.** Same as **characteristic, 1.** (Less commonly used.)

characteristically, adv. Prec. & **-ly.** In such a manner as to exhibit characteristics; typically.

characterization, n. [1. kàrakterizáshun; 2. kæ̀rəktəraizéiʃən]. See next word & **-ation.** Act of characterizing (in all senses).

characterize, vb. trans. [1. kárakterīz; 2. kǽrəktəraiz]. Fr. *caractériser*, fr. Gk. *kharaktērízein*, 'engrave'. **1.** To draw character of, describe. **2. a** To mark, be characteristic of, exhibit character of; **b** to give character to, mark with distinguishing feature.

characterless, adj. [1. kárakterles; 2. kǽrəktəlis]. **character** (**I.**) & **-less. a** Without character or individuality; **b** without a character, testimonial &c.

character part, n. That of a personage in a drama marked by strong or eccentric personality.

character sketch, n. Short theatrical performance which depicts a highly individual, eccentric, or fantastic character or characters.

charade, n. [1. sharáhd; 2. ʃərā́d]. Fr., fr. Provenç. *charrado*, 'conversation'. Origin unknown. Enigma which consists in guessing a word, indications of the whole, and of the various syllables of which are given either by descriptions, often in verse, or by dramatic representation.

charcoal, n. [1. chárkōl; 2. tʃā́koul]. See **char** (**III.**); Skeat points out that the word is earlier than **char**; suggested source may be *chare*, 'to turn'. See **char** (**I.**) & cp. **ajar.** Form of carbon; porous residuum obtained esp. by burning wood or other vegetable matter, but also from animal matter, used as fuel for certain purposes.

charcoal burner, n. One employed in manufacture of charcoal by burning wood.

chare, n. & vb. intrans. [1. chār; 2. tʃɛə]. Same as **char** (**II.**). **a** n. A job; **b** vb., to do odd jobs &c. (Rarely used.)

charge (**I.**), vb. trans. & intrans. [1. charj; 2. tʃādž], in M.E., fr. O. Fr. *chargier*, Low Lat. *carricāre*, 'to put a load on', fr. Lat. *carrus*, 'waggon'. See **car, cargo, cark. A.** trans. **1. a** To load (a fire-arm); **b** to store electricity in (battery); **c** to fill (a glass), esp. with wine preparatory to drinking a toast; **d** to burden (one's mind) with, commit to memory: *to charge one's memory.* **2.** To enjoin, lay as an injunction, command, exhort earnestly: *I charge you strictly not to forget what you are told.* Phr. (of a judge) *to charge a jury*, give directions to. **3.** To accuse (a person) of an offence, whether grave or trivial; impute to: *to charge a prisoner with murder*; *to charge an editor with carelessness.* **4.** To demand (a certain sum) in payment for goods delivered or services rendered; set a price upon: *to charge three shillings a dozen for eggs.* **5.** To entrust, commit something to a person's care, protection, make (a person) responsible for performance of a duty: *to be charged with an important mission.* **6.** (mil., of troops) To rush swiftly and violently against (the enemy), esp. to fling weight of mounted or unmounted men, armed with lances or bayonets, against him. **B.** intrans. **1.** To make a charge (see **6** above). **2.** To demand a price: *he charges too high.*

charge (**II.**), n. Fr. See prec. Orig. a load; all the present meanings are secondary & fig. except No. **1. 1. a** Amount of powder, or of powder and shot, used in a single discharge of a fire-arm; **b** amount of electricity stored in a battery. **2.** (her.) Any figure borne on a shield; a bearing. **3.** Price demanded for, cost of, an article, or service rendered. **4.** Burden, tax, payment, due on property or income: *a first charge on an estate.* **5.** Task imposed upon a person as a duty, esp. that of care, guardianship, of a person or thing; responsibility, trust: *in charge of a horse*; *to put something under a person's charge.* Phr. *to take charge of*, assume care, direction, of. **6.** That entrusted to one's care and protection: *young charges*, children one is taking care of. **7. a** Order, command, mandate; **b** an official exhortation: *a judge's charge* (*to the jury*); *a bishop's charge to his clergy.* **8.** Accusation, imputation of guilt or responsibility: *to bring a charge of theft against . . .* **9. a** Sudden attack in which troops are hurled at the enemy in the hope that the weight of men, horses, and weapons will dislodge him from a position, or break his line; **b** manœuvre in football in which a player puts himself into violent contact with an opponent with a view to stopping him, or depriving him of the ball; **c** fierce rush made by an animal, esp. a bull, when attacking.

chargeable, adj. [1. chárjabl; 2. tʃā́džəbl]. **charge** (**I.**) & **-able. a** Liable to be charged, payable; **b** liable to be accused.

chargé d'affaires, n., Engl. pronunciation. [1. shárzhā dafár; 2. ʃā́žei dæfɛ́ə]. Fr. Person below rank of an ambassador, entrusted with a diplomatic mission from one small court to another, or at or from a minor state; one acting as deputy for superior minister, ambassador &c.

charger (**I.**), n. [1. chárjer; 2. tʃádʒə]. M.E. *chargeour*, O. Fr. *chargeoir*, 'dish for carrying things'. See **charge** (**I.**). Large, flat dish.

charger (**II.**), n. **charge** (**I.**) & **-er.** An officer's battle or parade horse.

charily, adv. [1. chárili; 2. tʃéərili]. See **chary** & **-ly.** **a** Reluctantly; **b** cautiously.

chariness, n. [1. chárines; 2. tʃéərinis]. **chary** & **-ness.** Caution; sparingness, thriftiness.

chariot (**I.**), n. [1. chàriut; 2. tʃǽriət]. Fr. The M.E. form was *charette*, fr. O. Fr., wh. was the type *pronounced* as late as the 18th cent. Both words are fr. Fr. *char*, 'wagon' &c. See **car, carry. 1.** Name given to the two-wheeled car of the ancients, used in triumphal processions, in battle, and for races. **2.** (archaic) Light, four-wheeled private carriage; a state coach.

chariot (**II.**), vb., fr. prec. (poet.) To drive in a chariot; to convey as in a chariot.

charioteer, n. & vb. [1. chàriutḗr; 2. tʃæ̀riətíə]. Prec. & **-eer. 1.** Driver of a chariot; (poet., facet., or high-flown) a driver of any vehicle. **2.** To act as charioteer; drive person in a chariot; to convey in any sort of vehicle.

charitable, adj. [1. cháritabl; 2. tʃǽritəbl]. M.E., fr. O. Fr. See **charity** & **-able. 1.** Possessing and showing forth by conduct the Christian virtue of charity and love. **2. a** (of persons) Kind, benevolent, tending to put best interpretation on the actions of others; **b** specif., given to good works, generous to the poor and afflicted; **c** (of institutions) founded and existing for the purpose of relieving suffering, assisting the poor by services or money.

charitableness, n. Prec. & **-ness.** Quality of being charitable; benevolence, generosity of mind.

charitably, adv. [1. cháritabli; 2. tʃǽritəbli]. See prec. & **-ly.** In a charitable manner.

charity, n. [1. cháriti; 2. tʃǽriti]. M.E. *charité*, O. Fr. *charitet*, fr. Lat. *cāritāt-(em)*, 'affection', fr. Lat. *cārus*, 'dear, precious, high priced'. This base in Lat. & Fr. has acquired a more spiritual meaning than it orig. possessed, to judge by the cognates in other Aryan languages, wh. expressed for the most part simply 'desire' & associated ideas; the Gmc. languages have appropriated the base to the lowest uses: Lett. *kārs*, 'full of desire', O. Ir. *cara*, 'friend', *caraim*, 'I love'; Goth. *hōrs*, 'adulterous', O.H.G. *huorra*, O.E. *hōr*, 'whore'. See also **caress. 1.** Christian love; **a** love of man to God; **b** human love to fellow-men. **2.** Benevolence of disposition, esp. a disposition to judge favourably and tolerantly of men's actions and motives; tendency to put kindest interpretation on these. **3.** Benevolence, liberality, generosity in giving to the poor, for the relief of suffering &c. **4. a** Act of benevolence and liberality in almsgiving; **b** that which is given for benevolent purposes. **5.** (pl. *charities*) Public works of benevolence, organizations for relief of poverty and suffering: *to leave money to charities. Charity Commissioners,* official body appointed by the state for control of public charities; *charity school,* one for poor children, supported by endowments and gifts.

charivari, n. [1. shàriváhri; 2. ʃæ̀rivári]. Fr. Etymol. unknown. **1.** Rough, harsh music; hubbub of various discordant sounds. **2.** Name of a French comic paper, and thus second title of 'Punch'.

charlatan, n. [1. shárlatan; 2. ʃálətən]. Fr., fr. Ital. *ciarlatano*, cp. *ciarlare*, 'to jabber, prate'. Impostor; one who lays claim to knowledge and skill which he does not possess; a quack, empiric, unqualified and untrained practitioner of a skilled profession.

charlatanism, n. [1. shárlatanizm; 2. ʃálətənizəm]. Prec. & **-ism.** Practice of a charlatan; quackery.

charlatanry, n. [1. shárlatanri; 2. ʃálətənri]. See prec. & **-ry.** Charlatanism.

Charles's Wain, n. [1. chárlziz wān; 2. tʃálziz wéin]. O.E. *Carles-wæġn.* The seven bright stars of the constellation Ursa Major or the Great Bear, also called the Plough; Charles is Charlemagne, who was identified with King Arthur, and thus connected with *Arcturus*, the bright star in Boötes.

charley, n. [1. chárli; 2. tʃáli]. (obs.) Old-fashioned slang name for a night-watchman.

charlock, n. [1. chárlok; 2. tʃálɔk]. O.E. *ċerlic.* Origin unknown; the second element may possibly be a weakened form of O.E. *lēac*, 'leek' &c., wh. has gen. sense of 'vegetable', as in *lēac-tūn*, 'kitchen-garden'. Wild, or field, mustard, *Brassica arvensis.*

charlotte, n. [1. shárlot; 2. ʃálɔt]. Fr., fr. the woman's name. A pudding of stewed apples covered with bread-crumbs and baked, usually *apple charlotte.*

charlotte russe, n. [1. shárlot ro͞os; 2. ʃálɔt rūs]. Fr. Pudding made of whipped cream and sponge cakes.

charm (**I.**), n. [1. charm; 2. tʃām]. O.E. *ċierm, ċerm,* M.E. *chirm,* 'clamour, shout'; cp. O.S. *karm,* 'cry of woe'; cogn. w. O. Ir. *gairm,* 'cry'; Lat. *garrīre,* 'to chatter'; see **garrulous.** (archaic) Song of birds (used by Milton).

charm (**II.**), n. Fr. *charme,* Lat. *carmen,* 'song', prob. cogn. w. Gk. *kērux,* 'herald', q.v. under **caduceus. 1.** Song or chant having, or supposed to have, occult power for good or evil; incantation. **2.** Spell, occult influence exerted by an incantation. Phr. (of a remedy &c.) *to act like a charm.* **3. a** Material object possessing occult powers, supposed to bring good fortune to possessor or wearer, preserving him from accident and death; **b** any small object worn on the person for ornament, or in memory of the giver. **4.** Quality of delighting and enchanting, esp. in an indefinable way; attractiveness, fascination: *charm of manner; charm of style.*

charm (**III.**), vb. trans. & intrans., fr. prec. **A.** trans. **1. a** To exert magic influence, put a charm or spell upon (obs.); **b** to influence, produce an effect as though by magic spells: *to charm away pain, grief* &c; *charm (one) asleep;* **c** to tame or train (a snake). **2.** To delight, cause pleasure to, bewitch, enchant. Phr. *I shall be charmed to see you tomorrow* (polite formula) = shall be glad &c. **B.** intrans. To exercise an attractive influence, cause delight: *goodness often charms more than mere beauty.*

charmer, n. [1. chármer; 2. tʃámə]. Prec. & **-er. a** One who charms snakes; **b** a fascinating person, esp. an attractive woman.

charming, adj. [1. chárming; 2. tʃámiŋ], fr. Pres. Part. of **charm** (**III.**). Delightful, attractive, fascinating.

charmingly, adv. Prec. & **-ly.** In a bewitching, attractive manner; agreeably: *to sing, speak, charmingly.*

charnel-(house), n. [1. chárnel (hòus); 2. tʃánəl (hàus)]. Fr., fr. L. Lat. *carnāle,* 'graveyard', neut. of Lat. *carnālis,* adj. See **carnal.** *Charnel,* orig. an adj., is used as a n. in M.E. Vault where dead bodies or bones are stored; (by extension) applied to any place in which there are dead bodies or signs of death.

charpoi, n. [1. chárpoi; 2. tʃápɔi]. Hind. *chārpāi,* fr. *chār,* 'four', & *pāi,* 'foot'. Common light Indian bedstead.

charqui, n. [1. chárkē; 2. tʃákī]. Span., fr. native Peruvian word. Beef cut into strips and dried in the sun; often corrupted to 'jerked' beef.

chart (**I.**), n. [1. chart; 2. tʃāt]. O. Fr. *carte,* Lat. *carta.* See **card** (**II.**) & **charter. a** Seaman's sea-map, showing outlines of coasts, depth of water &c.; **b** graphic method of representing some fluctuating quantity, e.g. temperature, population, death-rate &c.

chart (**II.**), vb. trans., fr. prec. To make a chart or sea-map of (part of the ocean).

charter (**I.**), n. [1. chárter; 2. tʃátə]. O. Fr. *chartre,* fr. Lat. *chartula,* 'little paper, bill', dimin. of *carta.* See **card** (**II.**). Document granting rights, privileges, one conveying ownership of land, by sovereign or supreme governing body, to an individual or a corporation; e.g. a document constituting a place a borough &c.: *the Great Charter,* Magna Charta, obtained from King John in 1215; *the People's Charter,* see **chartism.**

charter (**II.**), vb. trans., fr. prec. **1.** To let, or hire (a vessel) by *charter-party,* q.v. **2.** (colloq.) To hire something, esp. a vehicle: *to charter a cab, taxi* &c.

chartered, adj. [1. chárterd; 2. tʃátəd]. P.P. of prec. **1.** Endowed with, created by, royal charter: *chartered accountant, chartered company* &c. **2.** Licensed, esp. in Phr. *chartered libertine,* one to whom considerable freedom of conduct is permitted by common consent.

charterer, n. [1. chárterer; 2. tʃátərə]. **charter** (**II.**) & **-er.** Person who charters a ship.

Charterhouse, n. [1. chárterhous; 2. tʃátəhaus]. Engl. name formed by popular etymol. fr. Fr. *Chartreuse,* Carthusian monastery. **a** Carthusian monastery; **b** specif., *the Charterhouse,* charitable foundation of 1611, on site of old Carthusian monastery, providing asylum for old men, and school for boys; the latter now removed from London.

charter-party, n. Fr. *chartre, charte partie,* 'divided charter', see **charter** (**I.**); fr. a form made in duplicate on same sheet, wh. is divided. Specif., mode of agreement between shipowner and merchant concerning hire and use of ship and transportation of cargo.

chartism, n. [1. chártizm; 2. tʃátizəm]. See **charter** & **-ism.** Form of radicalism prevalent in England, 1836–48; so named from the *People's Charter,* which embodied the aims and demands of the movement.

chartist, n. [1. chártist; 2. tʃátist]. See prec. & **-ist.** Supporter of chartism.

chartreuse, n. [1. shartrḗz; 2. ʃātrə́z]; Fr. [ʃartrøz]. Fr., fr. *La Grande Chartreuse,* chief house of the Carthusians, near Grenoble. **1.** A Carthusian monastery; in English corrupted to *Charterhouse.* **2.** Name given to a sweet, powerful, syrupy liqueur made at the Carthusian monastery: *green, white, chartreuse.*

chartulary, n. [1. chártūlari; 2. tʃátjuləri]. See **cartulary.**

charwoman, n. [1. chárwòoman; 2. tʃáwùmən]. See **char** (**I.**) & **woman.** Woman who works by the day at rough housework, scrubbing, cleaning &c.

chary, adj. [1. chári; 2. tʃéəri]. O.E. *ċeariġ,* 'anxious, sad', fr. *ċearu, caru.* See **care** (**I.**). **a** Careful, cautious: *to be chary of giving offence;* **b** reticent, unwilling to spare or give; parsimonious: *to be chary of one's favours.*

Charybdis, n. [1. karíbdis; 2. kəríbdis]. Gk. Name of whirlpool off coast of Sicily. For fig. use see **Scylla.**

chase (**I.**), vb. trans. [1. chās; 2. tʃeis]. O. Fr. *chacier,* fr. Low Lat. *captiāre*; dialectal variant of **catch. 1. a** To pursue, run after, try to catch (does not imply overtaking): *to chase a prisoner;* **b** to cause to run away by pursuit; drive away, expel: *the dog chased the cat out of the garden;* **c** (fig.) to dispel, banish: *joy chased all fear from her mind.* **2.** To hunt: *to chase the boar* (rather rare now in this sense).

chase (**II.**), n., fr. prec. **1.** Act of pursuing an animal (fox, stag, boar) with design of killing it; specif., hunting: *lovers of the chase.* **2.** Specific act of pursuit for purpose of capturing: *the chase after the murderer lasted several hours.* Phr. *to give chase,* to run after, pursue. **3.** Tract of open country in which game is bred and is, or was, hunted, often privately owned. Contrasted with a *forest* or a *park,* qq.v. **4.** A right or liberty to hunt over certain tract of country, and to preserve game and beasts of the chase therein. **5.** That which is being pursued; specif. **a** hunted animal; **b** ship running away from another. **6.** A stroke in the game of (court or royal) tennis.

chase (**III.**), vb. trans., for *enchace*, O. Fr. *enchasser*, 'to enshrine, set' (of ornaments &c.); fr. *chasse*, 'shrine for a relic'; dialectal variant of *caisse*. See **case** & **capsule.** To engrave by way of ornament: *richly chased plate.*

chase (**IV.**), n. Fr. *châsse*. See prec. Hollow or groove cut for reception of something; **a** part of a gun which receives the charge; **b** channel cut in a wall for a pipe to lie in, or trench cut for a drain-pipe &c.

chase (**V.**), n. See prec. (print.) Iron frame for holding columns or pages of type.

chaser, n. [1. chā́ser; 2. tʃéisə]. **chase** (**I.**) & **-er.** Gun, at bow or stern of ship, for use in chasing or being chased: *bow-, stern-chaser.*

chasm, n. [1. kazm; 2. kǽzəm]. Gk. *khásma*, 'yawning hollow, gulf', connected w. *khaínein*, 'to gape'. See **chaos. a** Broad, deep fissure in the earth; **b** a deep abyss; **c** (fig.) wide difference in opinions, feelings, tastes, between persons; **d** a gap, break, interruption of continuity.

chasse, n. [1. shas; 2. ʃæs]. Fr., 'chase'; also, though now rarely, in Engl. sense. Glass of liqueur taken immediately after cup of coffee.

chassé, n. & vb. intrans. [1. shásā; 2. ʃǽsei]. Fr., 'hunt'. See **chase** (**I.**). **1.** n. Rapid gliding step in dancing, esp. when the male partner holds the lady straight in front of him and pushes her before him, so that she runs backwards. **2.** vb. To dance with this step.

chassepot, n. [1. sháspō; 2. ʃǽspou]. Inventor's name. The French breech-loading rifle of the war of 1870.

chasseur, n. [1. shasĕr; 2. ʃæsə́]. Fr., 'hunter, huntsman'. **1.** Name of various light infantry or cavalry regiments of the French army, as *Chasseurs Alpins, Chasseurs d'Afrique* &c. **2.** A page-boy, messenger, in a French hotel or restaurant.

chassis, n. [1. shásē; 2. ʃǽsī]. Fr. *châssis*, 'frame, framework', Lat. *capsus*, 'body of a coach or waggon', fr. *capio*, 'take, receive'. See **capsule** & **captive.** Framework; specif., framework, wheels, and machinery upon which a gun-carriage or the body of a motor-car is mounted.

chaste, adj. [1. chāst; 2. tʃeist]. Fr., fr. Lat. *castus*, 'clean, unpolluted, continent, chaste'; prob. related to Lat. *castīgāre*, 'cleanse, punish', *castrāre*, 'to cut, castrate', & *carēre*, 'to be without, lack'. Cp. Scrt. *śásati*, 'cuts'. Cp. **caries** & **castrate. a** Pure in thought and word; pure in body, continent, refraining from impurity of any kind; **b** (of style, ornament &c.) restrained, free from extravagance and barbarism; simple.

chastely, adv. Prec. & **-ly.** In a chaste manner.

chasten, vb. trans. [1. chā́sn; 2. tʃéisn]. M.E. *chastien* &c., fr. O. Fr. *chastier*, Mod. Fr. *châtier*, 'punish', fr. Lat. *castīgāre* (see **castigate** & **chaste**) & Engl. suff. **-en. a** To punish, inflict pain upon, in order to correct and reclaim; **b** to restrain, subdue, reduce, a person's fervour, or high spirits.

chastened, adj. [1. chā́snd; 2. tʃéisnd], fr. P.P. of prec. Subdued, disciplined, saddened, and reduced to submissiveness by punishment or bitter experience.

chasteness, n. [1. chā́stnes; 2. tʃéistnis]. **chaste** & **-ness.** Condition of being chaste, esp. of style, design &c., severe simplicity, absence of meretricious ornament.

chastise, vb. trans. [1. chastī́z; 2. tʃæstáiz]. M.E. *chastisen*, fr. *chasti-(en)* &c., & **-ise.** See **chasten. a** To punish severely by beating; **b** to administer severe reproof, reprimand, to.

chastisement, n. [1. chástizment; 2. tʃǽstizmənt]. Prec. & **-ment. a** Act of inflicting punishment, of chastising; **b** the undergoing, suffering, of punishment.

chastity, n. [1. chástiti; 2. tʃǽstiti]. M.E. & O. Fr. *chastetē*, Lat. *castitāt-(em)*, 'purity of body'. See **chaste** & **-ity.** Purity, **a** (of body) continence, abstinence from unpermitted sexual indulgence; **b** complete abstinence from sexual intercourse; virginity: *priestly vows of chastity*; **c** purity, sensitive delicacy of thought and feeling; **d** (of style) severe simplicity; same as **chasteness.**

chasuble, n. [1. cházūbl; 2. tʃǽzjubl]. Med. Lat. *casubula*, lit. 'little house', dimin. of Lat. *casa*, 'cottage; hooded garment forming a covering like a little house'. Cp. **cassock.** *Casa* is perh. a dial. form of the base **kat-*, 'to protect, cover'; ultimately connected w. **hat.** Vestment worn over the alb by celebrant at the Mass. It is made of silk or linen, is in the form of a kind of cloak, oval in shape, with an opening in the middle for the head, and generally has a large Y-shaped cross, besides other embroideries, upon it.

chat (**I.**), vb. intrans. [1. chat; 2. tʃæt]. Short for **chatter.** To talk, converse, with another person in an informal, familiar manner, esp. upon light topics; to indulge in small talk.

chat (**II.**), n., fr. prec. **a** (with indef. art.) Light, familiar, easy, friendly talk, or conversation: *to have a chat*; **b** an informal address or popular lecture; **c** (without art.) chatter, futile babbling talk; specif., impudence, impertinence: *let me have none of your chat* (colloq. and vulg.).

chat (**III.**), n., fr. **chat** (**I.**). Name of several species of birds of thrush family: *stonechat, whinchat.*

château, n., pl. **-x** [1. shahtō; 2. ʃato]. Fr., fr. O. Fr. *chastel*, L. Lat. *castellum.* See **castle. 1.** A castle in France, also large country-house or mansion. **2.** Also, attrib. (of French wines) as produced on a private estate or *château*, as *Château Yquem* &c.

châtelaine, n. [1. shátelān; 2. ʃǽtəlein]. Fr., 'the mistress of a *château*', that is, a castle, or country-house. **1.** Used more or less in above sense; lady of the house, hostess. **2.** Ornamental chain hanging from a woman's belt, to which keys, seals &c. are attached. (Name due to association of the mistress of a house with keys of store-cupboards &c.)

chati, n. [1. shátē, chátē; 2. ʃǽtī, tʃǽtī]. Connected w. Lat. *catus*, Fr. *chat* &c. South American tiger-cat.

chatoyant, adj. & n. [1. shatwóiant; 2. ʃætwóiənt]. Fr., Pres. Part. of *chatoyer*, 'to shine like the eye of a cat', fr. *chat*, 'cat', fr. L. Lat. *catus*, see **cat. 1.** adj. Shining with a changeable colour or lustre, like the eye of a cat, or the cat's-eye. **2.** n. Stone, such as the cat's-eye, with this lustre.

chattel, n. [1. chátl; 2. tʃǽtl]. M.E. *chatel*, fr. O. Fr., dialectal variant of **cattle. a** An article of property; (in pl.) goods, possessions. Phr. *goods and chattels*; **b** (law) applicable to property of all and every kind except real estate, including money and plate, and rights in land less than freehold, which are termed *chattels-real*, as leaseholds; *chattel-mortgage*, mortgage on personal property as security for a debt.

chatter (**I.**), vb. intrans. [1. cháter; 2. tʃǽtə]. M.E. *chateren.* Prob. of imitative origin. **1. a** (of persons) To talk excessively, continuously and rapidly; **b** to talk in an idle, futile manner, esp. on trivial subjects; **c** to talk unwisely and widely, and upon subjects which were better kept private; hence to divulge secrets or confidences, to blab. **2. a** (of birds) To utter rapid, shrill cries of anger and excitement, other than song (esp. of jays, magpies, starlings); **b** (of monkeys) to utter rapid squeaks or semi-articulate sounds; **c** (of a rapidly flowing brook) to make a rippling, babbling sound; **d** to rattle, as of loose parts of machinery. **3.** (of the teeth) To produce series of clicking, rattling sounds, as when the lower jaw trembles with cold, fear, or other strong emotion. Often partially fig.: *his teeth chattered*, he was trembling, was frightened.

chatter (**II.**), n., fr. prec. **a** Idle, empty, noisy talk; **b** rapid cries of jays, magpies &c. or of monkeys; the sound of a brook rippling over stones &c.; rattle of machinery.

chatterbox, n. [1. cháterboks; 2. tʃǽtəbɔks]. Prec. & **box** (**I.**). Excessively talkative person, esp. one given to continuous vapid talking.

chatterer, n. [1. cháterer; 2. tʃǽtərə]. **chatter** (**I.**) & **-er.** One who chatters (in any sense).

chatty (**I.**), adj. [1. cháti; 2. tʃǽti]. See **chat** (**I.**) & **-y.** (in favourable sense) **a** Fond of, given to, familiar, friendly talk; **b** (soldiers' slang) verminous, lousy.

chatty (**II.**), n. Tamil *shāti.* Anglo-Indian term for an earthenware water-pot or water-cooler.

chauffer, n. [1. cháwfer; 2. tʃɔ́fə]. Fr. *chauffoir*, 'a heater', in various specific senses. See **chafe.** Small portable stove.

chauffeur, n. [1. shōfĕr; 2. ʃoufə́]. Fr., lit. 'one who heats', specif. 'a stoker, fireman'; the Fr. term in Engl. sense is *mécanicien.* See **chafe.** Man who drives and attends to a motor-car, generally applied to a private servant.

chaussée, n. [1. shōsā; 2. ʃousei]. Fr. See **causeway.** A paved road, highway.

chauvinism, n. [1. shṓvinizm; 2. ʃóuvinizəm]. Fr. *chauvinisme*, fr. Nicolas Chauvin, a Napoleonic soldier, notorious for extravagant expressions of loyalty. Term applied contemptuously after Napoleon's fall. Attitude of mind which is unwilling to admit the possibility of faults in one's own country and people, or much good in any other; perverted, blind patriotism.

chauvinist, n. [1. shṓvinist; 2. ʃóuvinist]. See prec. & **-ist.** Person affected by chauvinism.

chaw, vb. trans. [1. chaw; 2. tʃɔ̄]. Variant of **chew.** (vulg. and colloq.) To munch, masticate (food) coarsely and noisily. *Chaw up* (fig.), to defeat utterly an enemy or opponent in a game; to injure badly, e.g. in a battle, railway accident &c.

chaw-bacon, n. A vulgar, clumsy, rustic clown.

cheap, adj. & adv. [1. chēp; 2. tʃīp]. O.E. *ċēap*, n., 'a price, bargain', M.E. *chēp*, also a n. The present adj. sense arose fr. the M.E. phrase *biggen gōd chēp*, 'to buy at a good, favourable price', i.e. 'cheap'. Cp. Fr. (*à*) *bon marché.* The O.E. vb. is *ċēapian*, 'buy', & the word occurs also, in same sense, as *choufōn* in O.H.G., O.N. *kaupa*, Goth. *kaupōn*, 'to trade'. O.H.G. has *choufo*, 'a huckster' (cp. Germ. *kaufmann*, 'merchant'), & this is prob. the orig. sense of the word in Gmc. It is now again thought by etymologists, though this was earlier disputed, that the base is a loan fr. Lat., cp. *caupō*, 'huckster, petty tradesman, innkeeper'. The origin of this word is still disputed, but Walde connects it w. Lat. *cūpa*, 'tub, cask' (w. different gradation), in wh. case the earliest sense of *caupō* was 'one having to do with casks', whence the other meanings were derived. See further under **cup** & **hive. 1. a** Of low price, relative to value of article purchased; **b** of small value, worthless, bad: *cheap clothes are useless.* Phrs. *dirt cheap*, very cheap; *to hold something cheap*, set little value upon it; *make oneself (too) cheap*, be too accessible, allow undue familiarity; *on the cheap*, cheaply. **2.** (of works of art) Characterized by obvious, facile effects; meretricious. **3.** adv. Cheaply: *to buy, get, make, something cheap.*

cheapen, vb. trans. [1. chḗpen; 2. tʃípən]. Prec. & **-en. a** (archaic and rare) To bargain, haggle, for; **b** to make cheap, cut down price.

cheap-jack, n. Travelling dealer in cheap, inferior wares.

cheaply, adv. [1. chḗpli; 2. tʃípli]. **cheap** & **-ly.** Inexpensively; at, for, a small price.

cheapness, n. [1. chḗpnes; 2. tʃípnis]. See prec. & **-ness.** Condition of being cheap, smallness of price.

cheat (**I.**), n. [1. chēt; 2. tʃīt]. For **escheat.** M.E. *chēte*, 'confiscation'. **a** Deception, fraud, swindle, dishonest trick; **b** person who practises fraud; a swindler, trickster.

cheat (**II.**), vb. trans. & intrans., fr. prec. **A.** trans. **1.** To swindle, deceive, in order to obtain some advantage from, practise a trick, dishonesty, upon: *you've been cheated.* Also *to cheat* (a person) *of something, or out of something,* to obtain something from him by fraud; defraud of, deprive of, by a trick: *he has cheated me (out) of my property.* **2.** To escape by skill or good fortune: *to cheat the gallows.* **3.** To beguile, cause to forget tedium, fatigue, sorrow &c.: *to cheat time, the journey* &c. **B.** intrans. To practise deceit, fraud, trickery &c.: *to cheat at cards.*

check (I.), n. [1. chek; 2. tʃɛk]. M.E. *chek.* Term in chess, also 'defeat', O. Fr. *eschec,* fr. Arab. *shāq,* fr. Pers. *shāh,* 'king', introduced w. the game of chess. In Chaucer, an exclamation meaning 'beware', on analogy of chess: '*therewith Fortune seyde "chek here", And "mate" in the mid pointe of the chekkere*'. The various meanings in Fr. & Engl. all start fr. that in chess. **1.** Exclamation of warning at chess that opponent's king is threatened. **2.** Anything which hinders, retards, interrupts, limits, action, delays, progress, interferes with plans, hopes &c.; a rebuff, set-back; specif. **a** (mil.) slight reverse in attack; **b** (hunting) interruption to run of hounds by loss of scent; also in various specific applications to mechanical contrivances. **3. a** Control, supervision: *to keep in check*; **b** means of securing accuracy or honesty: *to keep a check on one's statements*; **c** specif., ticket, or other token, to prove identity, or ownership; e.g. for hats and coats at a theatre; for seat in a public conveyance &c. Phr. *to hand in one's checks,* (fig.) to die. **4.** (extension of **3.**) Usually *cheque,* q.v., printed or engraved form to be filled in and signed, for drawing money from bank; *to draw, write, a check.* **5. a** Pattern in squares, roughly resembling a chess-board; **b** cloth woven with such a pattern.

check (II.), vb. trans. & intrans., fr. prec. **A.** trans. **1.** (chess) To threaten the king. **2. a** To retard, restrain, hamper, delay progress, movement, material or non-material; **b** to warn, admonish, reprove (person) regarding an action (provinc.). **3.** To test, provide means for ensuring accuracy or honesty of: *to check statements, accounts, figures, references* &c. **B.** intrans. **a** To come to a sudden halt, specif., (of hounds who lose the scent) to pause in a run; **b** *check at,* resent, take offence at (rare).

checker (I.), n. [1. chéker; 2. tʃékə]. See **chequer. 1.** Chequer pattern. **2.** (pl.) The game of draughts, now American usage.

checker (II.), vb. See **chequer.**

checkmate, interj., n., & vb. trans. [1. chékmāt; 2. tʃékméit]. Arab. *shāh māta,* 'the king is dead' in chess. **1.** (chess) Exclamatory warning or announcement that the opponent's king is finally out of action owing to one's move. Now usually *mate!* **2.** n. **a** The act of putting opponent's king out of action; condition of the king thus affected; **b** (fig.) complete rebuff, defeat, frustration. **3.** vb. trans. **a** (chess) To put opponent's king finally out of action; **b** (fig.) to thwart, circumvent (a person or his action); frustrate (an attempt).

check-weigher, n. [1. chék wāer; 2. tʃék weiə]. **check** (II.) & **weigh** & **-er.** Man who, on behalf of the coal-miners, checks the weight of coal when it comes to the surface of the mine.

checky, chequee, checquy, adj. [1. chéki; 2. tʃéki]. Fr. See **check** (I.). (her., of field) Divided into squares of alternate tinctures.

Cheddar, n. [1. chédar; 2. tʃédə]. Name of place in Somerset. Kind of cheese.

cheek (I.), n. [1. chēk; 2. tʃīk]. O.E. *ċēace,* also *ċēoce,* M.E. *chēke,* cp. Du. *kaak.* **1. a** Side of human face from below eye and ear to chin and angle of jaw; **b** (in animals) corresponding part of head and jaw. Phrs. *cheek by jowl,* close together; *to one's own cheek,* for one's own exclusive use. **2.** (colloq.) Impudence, presumption, effrontery; behaviour or language unbefitting the relative character and status of the person using these, and those of the person to whom they are used. Cp. use of *face* in somewhat similar sense. Phr. *to have the cheek to* (*do, say* &c.), be so impudent as to.

cheek (II.), vb. trans., fr. prec. (colloq.) To speak impudently, rudely, pertly, to; to insult, address with disrespect.

cheekily, adv. [1. chékili; 2. tʃíkili]. **cheeky** & **-ly.** In a cheeky manner; impudently.

cheekiness, n. [1. chékines; 2. tʃíkinis]. **cheeky** & **-ness.** Impudence.

cheeky, adj. [1. chéki; 2. tʃíki]. **cheek** (I.) & **-y.** (colloq.) Impudent, displaying cheek.

cheep, vb. intrans. & trans. [1. chēp; 2. tʃīp]. Imitative. **a** intrans. To utter weak, shrill notes, to pipe (of young birds); to squeak shrilly (of mice or young rats); **b** trans., to utter with a cheeping sound.

cheeper, n. [1. chéper; 2. tʃípə]. Prec. & **-er.** **a** Young bird, esp. young partridge or grouse; **b** very young child.

cheer (I.), n. [1. chēr; 2. tʃiə]. M.E. *chēre,* 'countenance', O. Fr. *chiere, chere,* fr. L. Lat. *cāra,* 'face', the origin of wh. is uncertain; its relation to Gk. *kárā,* 'head', is by no means clear. Already in Chaucer the various uses of the word occur fr. wh. the present-day differentiation of meaning can be traced, namely, 'face, look, mien'; *good chere* in sense of 'mirth', & *greet chere* in much the same sense. The sense 'mirth, joy' &c. arose first in the phr. *good cheer,* 'happy countenance, or expression'; the sense of 'entertainment, food, and drink' seems a specialized development fr. the same starting-point. **1.** State of mind, mood, spirits: *to be of good cheer, of sad cheer* &c. Phr. *what cheer?* **2.** Entertainment, fare; often *good cheer; Christmas cheer; to enjoy good cheer.* **3.** Encouragement, inspiriting words: *words of cheer.* **4.** Applause, shout(s) expressing approval, triumph, delight: *to give a cheer; three cheers for the visitors!*

cheer (II.), vb. trans. & intrans. See prec. **A.** trans. **1.** To inspire with hope, joy, gladness; render more happy, raise spirits from despondency; to encourage, enliven, gladden. Also *to cheer up,* in some senses, but generally implying specific raising of spirits. **2. a** To applaud vocally, express approval, congratulation, good wishes, triumph, by loud shouts: *the speaker was lustily cheered; the House cheered the news of peace;* **b** also with *on,* to encourage, urge on with shouts: *the crowd cheered the Oxford crew (on) to victory.* Phr. *to cheer to the echo.* **B.** intrans. **1.** Always followed by *up,* to become happier, pass from state of depression to more joyful frame of mind: *he cheered up wonderfully at the news.* Phr. *cheer up!,* don't be depressed. **2.** To utter cheers, give shouts of applause or triumph &c.: *the audience stood up and cheered as the king entered.*

cheerful, adj. [1. chḗrfool; 2. tʃíəfəl]. **cheer** (I.) & **-ful. 1. a** (of persons) Happy, contented, in good spirits: *a cheerful old soul;* **b** (of things) tending to render happy; inspiriting, bright: *a cheerful room, the cheerful day;* **c** exhibiting, arising from, happiness, good spirits: *cheerful conversation, song* &c. **2.** Ironical, the reverse of happy; deplorable, miserable, reprehensible: *that's a cheerful remark; he must be a cheerful sort of man to treat his wife so badly!*

cheerfully, adv. Prec. & **-ly.** In a cheerful manner; with pleasure; without compunction.

cheerfulness, n. See prec. & **-ness.** Condition of being cheerful, good spirits.

cheerily, adv. [1. chḗrili; 2. tʃíərili]. **cheery** & **-ly.** In a cheery manner; merrily.

cheeriness, n. See prec. & **-ness.** State of being cheery; act of exhibiting lively spirits.

cheerless, adj. [1. chḗrles; 2. tʃíəlis]. **cheer** (I.) & **-less.** Devoid of cheerfulness, dismal, depressing, gloomy.

cheerlessly, adv. Prec. & **-ly.** Dismally, gloomily.

cheerlessness, n. See prec. & **-ness.** Misery, gloom, absence of cause for, or source of, joy or pleasure.

cheery, adj. [1. chḗri; 2. tʃíəri]. **cheer** (I.) & **-y.** In good spirits, lively, merry, genial.

cheese (I.), n. [1. chēz; 2. tʃīz]. O.E. *ċēse,* O.H.G. & O.L.G. *kāsi,* an early W. Gmc. loan-word fr. Lat. *cāseus,* 'cheese'; prim. W. Gmc. type **kāsjō.* The Lat. word is believed to be fr. earlier **kwatsō,* & cogn. w. O. Slav. *kvasŭ,* 'yeast', Russ. *kvass,* 'a sour malted drink'; cp. further Scrt. *kváthati,* 'cooks, boils'; Goth. *hwaþō,* 'foam', & *hwaþjan,* 'to foam'. The fundamental meaning seems to be the bubbling & foaming associated w. fermentation or the growing sour of certain substances. **1.** Consolidated milk curd used as food. **2.** Certain preparations resembling cheese in consistency, e.g. pomace cake; confection of quinces.

cheese (II.), n. Orig. an Anglo-Indian word, fr. Hind. *chīz,* 'thing', & arising fr. such a phrase as such and such is 'the real chīz', that is, the real thing. (vulg. slang, obs.) The correct thing: *quite the cheese.*

cheesecake, n. [1. chḗzkāk; 2. tʃízkeik]. Cake containing sweet mixture of sugar, butter, and lemon.

cheese-cloth, n. Loosely woven cotton material used in squeezing cheese curds.

cheese-mite, n. A small mite, infesting cheese.

cheesemonger, n. [1. chḗzmungger; 2. tʃízmaŋgə]. See **monger.** One who sells cheese, butter, eggs &c.

cheese-paring, n. & adj. **1.** n. **a** Thin portion of cheese rind which has been removed from the cheese; **b** (fig.) miserliness, stinginess, grudging spirit. **2.** adj. Miserly, stingy: *cheese-paring habits, policy.*

cheesy, adj. [1. chḗzi; 2. tʃízi]. **cheese** (I.) & **-y.** Having consistency or taste of cheese.

cheetah, n. [1. chḗta; 2. tʃítə]. Hind. *chītā;* Scrt. *chitta,* 'spotted, variegated'. One of the cat tribe, of S. Asia and Africa, known also as the *hunting leopard,* since it can be tamed and trained to hunt the antelope. The cheetah has a tawny skin, thickly spotted with black, and a very long tail; the claws, unlike those of the true cats, are very slightly retractile.

chef, n. [1. shef; 2. ʃef]. Fr., 'head', specif., a head man-cook. See **chief.** Head cook in large house, college, club, or restaurant.

chef-d'œuvre, n. [1. shā dḗvr; 2. ʃei dʌ́vr]. Fr. Masterpiece.

cheiro-, pref., 'hand'; form used in compounds, also **chiro-,** fr. Gk. *kheír,* 'hand', wh. stands for **kherj-,* or **khersj-,* cp. Scrt. *hárati,* 'he takes', & *háras-,* 'seizing'. The Aryan base was **gʷher-,* 'to seize'.

Cheiroptera, n. [1. kīróptera; 2. kairɔ́ptərə], fr. **cheiro-** & Gk. *ptéron,* 'wing', see **ptero-.** The natural order of flying mammals, which includes the bats, flying-foxes &c.

Cheka, n. [1. chā́ka; 2. tʃéka]. Russ. Names of initial letters (*ch, k*) of *Chrezvychainaya Komissiya,* 'Extraordinary Commission'. Political branch of Russian secret police; now **Ogpu.**

chela (I.), n. [1. chḗla; 2. tʃílə]. Hind. *chelā,* 'servant', also 'slave, household retainer; follower, pupil', specif., a Buddhist novice or disciple. In Anglo-Indian usage it came to mean 'a special battalion made up of prisoners and convicts'. (Yule and Burnell.)

chela (II.), n., pl. **-ae** [1. kḗla, -ē; 2. kílə, -i], fr. Gk. *khēlḗ,* 'fork, animal's pincer, claw'. The base is prob. the same as that in *khaínein,* 'to gape', q.v. under **chaos.** (zool.) The claw-like pincer of crabs, lobsters &c., also of spiders.

cheliform, adj. [1. kḗliform; 2. kílifɔ̄m]. See **chela** (II.) & **-form.** Having a movable joint or segment as in the pincer or claw of a crab &c.

Chellean, adj. [1. shélean; 2. ʃélian]. Fr., fr. Chelles, France, where earliest discoveries were made. Belonging to a primitive early palaeolithic culture or period in Europe contemporary with the elephant, cave-bear, rhinoceros &c., as evidenced by certain flint implements; it preceded the *Acheulian* and *Mousterian* ages.

chelonian, adj. & n. [1. kelṓnian; 2. kilóuniən], fr. Gk. *khelṓnē*, 'tortoise'. Cp. O. Slav. *žely*, 'tortoise'. (zool.) **a** adj. Belonging to the class or order *Chelonia*, of reptiles, which includes the turtles and tortoises; **b** n., a turtle or tortoise.

chemical, adj. & n. [1. kémikl; 2. kémikl]. Earlier *chemic*, abbreviated fr. **alchemic**, cp. Fr. *chimique*, & **-al**. **1.** adj. Relating to, made by, chemistry. (*Chemic* is now obs., except in poetry, and is sometimes used instead of *alchemic* in sense of 'false, not real'.) **2.** n. (often in pl.) Substance used in chemistry, or obtained by chemical process.

chemicalize, vb. trans. [1. kémikalīz; 2. kémikəlaiz]. Prec. & **-ize**. To treat with chemicals.

chemically, adv. [1. kémikali; 2. kémikəli]. **chemical** & **-ly**. **a** According to chemistry and its principles, laws &c.; **b** by chemical processes, manufacture &c.

chemin de fer, n. [1. shemán de fắr; 2. ʃəmǣ də fɛ̄r]. Fr., lit. 'iron road', hence 'railway'. A gambling game, a form of baccarat.

chemise, n. [1. shemḗz; 2. ʃəmíz]. In M.E., fr. Fr., fr. L. Lat. *camisia*, 'linen shirt, nightgown'. The word is of Gaulish origin, though O. Ir. *caimmse*, 'shirt', is reborrowed fr. Lat. There are several genuine cognates: Scrt. *śāmulyàm*, 'woollen shirt', O.H.G. *hemidi*, Mod. Germ. *hemd*, 'shirt'. Woman's undergarment, shift.

chemisette, n. [1. shèmizét; 2. ʃèmīzét]. Fr., dimin. of prec. Kind of bodice worn by women.

chemist, chymist, n. [1. kémist; 2. kémist]. Some good old-fashioned speakers still say [1. kímist; 2. kímist], esp. in sense **2**. Shortened form of **alchemist**. **1.** Student of, expert in, chemistry. **2.** (popular usage) Person who sells drugs and compounds medicines; an apothecary.

chemistry, n. [1. kémistri; 2. kémistri]. Prec. & **-ry**. Branch of natural science which deals with the composition of substances, and of the processes by which they are formed.

chenille, n. [1. shenḗl; 2. ʃəníl]. Fr., 'caterpillar', fr. fancied resemblance of material to this. Tufted cord of silk, wool &c., used for trimming and embroidery.

cheque, n. [1. chek; 2. tʃek]. See **check (I.), 4**, properly the counterfoil to the orig. draft, kept as a 'check' by drawer. **a** A form of bill of exchange, drawn on a banker and payable on demand; a draft ordering a bank to pay, out of funds standing to the drawer's credit at the bank, a sum stated on the draft to a person or his order or to bearer; **b** engraved, printed paper form for drawing money in this way from a bank.

cheque book, n. Collection of cheques bound together in paper cover with counterfoils attached.

chequer (I.), n. [1. chéker; 2. tʃékə]. O. Fr. *eschekier*, Lat. *scaccārium*, 'chess-board'. See **exchequer** & **check**. Pattern resembling squares of a chess-board, alternately black and white, or in other alternating colours.

chequer (II.), vb. trans., fr. prec. **1.** To mark or emblazon with chequer pattern. **2.** (fig.) **a** To form patches of alternate light and shade (as sunlight shining through foliage of a tree); to variegate; **b** to produce diversity, destroy uniformity, differentiate, esp. of life and experiences: *a chequered fortune, lot, career* &c., i.e. marked by changes, esp. from good to bad fortune &c.

cherish, vb. trans. [1. chérish; 2. tʃériʃ]. M.E. *cherischen*, O. Fr. *cheris-*, fr. *cherir*, 'hold dear'; cp. Fr. *cher*, Lat. *cārus*, 'dear'. See **caress** & **charity**. **1. a** To hold dear, set a high value upon; to show solicitude for, take care of; **b** (of non-material things) to dwell on with satisfaction, affection, and regret: *to cherish the memory of departed friends*. **2.** (fig.) To keep in the mind, memory, or heart; foster: *to cherish hopes*; *cherish a grudge against*.

cheroot, n. [1. sheroo͞t; 2. ʃirút]. Tamil word meaning 'a roll'. Kind of cigar, generally Indian, not closed by the covering leaf nor pointed at one end, but open at both ends, one being rather smaller than the other.

cherry, n. [1. chéri; 2. tʃéri]. M.E. *cheri* &c.; analogical sing. for *cheris*, *-s* being regarded as pl. ending; O. Fr. *cherise*, dialectal variant of *cerise* as in Mod. Fr., fr. Low Lat. **ceresia*, Lat. *cerasus*, 'cherry tree', fr. Gk. *kérasos*; word fr. Asia Minor, perh. related to Gk. *kéras*, 'horn', see **keratin**, & so called fr. hardness of the wood. **1.** n. **a** Name of many varieties of fruit, purple, red, or yellow and red, with very sweet juicy flesh and a small stone, and growing in clusters at the end of longish stalks; **b** the tree which bears these fruits. **2.** adj. Cherry-coloured, red: *cherry ribbon, cherry lips* &c.

cherry brandy, n. Sweet kind of liqueur made by steeping cherries in brandy.

cherry-pie, n. Popular name for heliotrope, from its smell.

chersonese, n. [1. kḗrsunēz; 2. kə́səniz]. Gk. *khersónēsos*, 'peninsula', fr. *khérsos*, 'dry, firm' (of land), & *nēsos*, 'island'. The first element is cogn. w. Lat. *horreo*, 'stand erect, become stiff' (see **horrid**), the second is connected w. Gk. *nḗ-kho*, 'swim', cogn. w. Lat. *natāre*, 'swim'. See **natation**. A peninsula, esp. the Thracian Chersonese, modern Gallipoli.

chert, n. [1. chĕrt; 2. tʃʌ̄t]. Origin unknown. Kind of quartz, resembling flint.

cherub, n. [1. chérub; 2. tʃérəb]. Heb. *kerūb*, pl. *-im*. **1.** (bib.) Winged supernatural being mentioned in the Bible, whose appearance and functions are variously described. **2.** Pictorial representation of a cherub, usually depicting a chubby child with wings on his shoulders, appearing out of a cloud. **3.** Human being, esp. a child, with rosy, chubby face and innocent expression as in pictures of cherubs.

cherubic, adj. [1. cheroo͞bik; 2. tʃərúbik]. Prec. & **-ic**. Like a cherub; applied to a person with rosy face and happy innocent expression.

chervil, n. [1. chĕrvil; 2. tʃʌ́vil]. O.E. *ċerfille*, fr. Lat. *chaerephyllum*, fr. Gk. *khairéphullon*. Garden plant whose leaves are used for flavouring.

Cheshire cat, n. [1. chésher kát; 2. tʃéʃə kǽt]. Only in Phr. '*to grin like a Cheshire cat*', to grin very broadly and frequently.

chess, n. [1. ches; 2. tʃes]. M.E. *ches*, O. Fr. *esches*, pl. of *eschec*. See **check (I.)**. Game of skill played with 32 pieces known as *chessmen*, upon a board, *chess-board*, marked in alternate squares of white and black.

chessel, n. [1. chésel; 2. tʃésəl], fr. **cheese**; suff. of doubtful origin. Mould used in cheese-making.

chest, n. [1. chest; 2. tʃest]. M.E. *chest, chist*, O.E. *ċest*, fr. Lat. *cista*, fr. Gk. *kistē*, 'basket'. Origin unexplained. **1. a** A box, coffer with a lid and strong lock, esp. one of some size for storing or transporting property: *linen chest*, for storing household linen; *plate chest*; **b** specif., box of a certain capacity, e.g. *chest of tea* = 108 lb.; *chest of drawers*, set of drawers arranged in several tiers, all contained in a single chest, the front of which is formed by the fronts of the drawers. **2.** Place or office where money of an institution is kept, where its financial business is transacted and its accounts prepared; treasury: *The Oxford University Chest*; *military chest*. **3. a** Front part of the body extending from base of the neck to where the lowest ribs spring from the breast-bone, containing the heart and lungs; the thorax; **b** the corresponding part in large animals, such as the horse; **c** by extension, the organs contained in the chest, esp. the lungs: *a cold on the chest*; *a weak chest*; *chest note*, deep note, one in lowest register of the voice; *chest voice*, voice produced so as to use lowest and most resonant notes.

-chested, adj. [1. chésted; 2. tʃéstid], fr. **chest, 3**. Having a chest of particular character: *hollow-, broad-, deep-, flat-chested* &c.

chesterfield, n. [1. chésterfēld; 2. tʃéstəfīəld], fr. one of the Earls of Chesterfield. **a** Kind of long-skirted overcoat; **b** kind of deep, well-stuffed sofa with two upright ends.

chestnut, n. [1. chés(t)nut; 2. tʃés(t)nət, -nat]. Properly *chesten nut*, M.E. *chestein*, O. Fr. *chastaigne*, Lat. *castanea*, fr. Gk. *kástanon*, fr. pl. n. *Kasthanaia*, city in Pontus. **1.** Also *chestnut tree*, one of two kinds of tree, the nuts being contained in a thick, prickly husk, within which is the thin, bright-brown, polished skin or shell which covers them; *Horse chestnut, Aesculus hippocastanum*, with bitter uneatable fruit; *Spanish*, or *sweet, chestnut, Castanea sativa*, with edible fruit. **2. a** A deep but bright reddish-brown colour, as of the skin of a chestnut; **b** horse of this colour; **c** attrib. or adj., coloured thus: *a chestnut horse* &c. **3.** (colloq.) An old, well-worn joke or anecdote which everybody knows.

cheval-, chevaux-de-frise, n. [1. shevál, shevṓ de frḗz; 2. ʃəvǽl, ʃəvóu də fríz]. Fr., lit. 'Friesland horse, cavalry'. Series of iron spikes projecting in several directions, set in a timber beam, or in iron, used as an obstacle to troops in storming fortifications; also placed along the top of wall or railings to prevent persons from climbing these.

cheval glass, n. [1. shevál glàhs; 2. ʃivǽl glās]. Fr. *cheval*, 'horse, frame'. Long mirror for reflecting the whole of the person, hung on upright frame and adjustable to any angle.

chevalier, n. [1. shèvalḗr; 2. ʃèvəlíə]; or Fr. [1. sheválya; 2. ʃəvalje]. Fr. See Engl. **cavalier, chivalry**. The Anglicized pronunciation now only used in Phr. *the young Chevalier*, referring to the Young Pretender. The Old Pretender was *le Chevalier de St. Georges*, and also called *the Chevalier*. In its French pronunciation the word is used of knights of several Foreign Orders, such as those of the Légion d'Honneur.

cheveril, n. [1. shéveril; 2. ʃévəril], fr. O. Fr. *chevrel*, dimin. of *chièvre*, 'goat'. See **chevron**. Soft, flexible leather made of the skin of a kid.

chevet, n. [1. shevā́; 2. ʃəvéi]. Fr., fr. O. Fr. *chevez*, fr. L. Lat. *capitium*, fr. Lat. *caput*, 'head', cp. **chef** & **chief**. (archit.) The apsidal east end of the choir or chancel of a French Gothic church, with radiating chapels.

chevin, n. [1. chévin; 2. tʃévin]. Etymol. unknown. The chub.

cheviot, n. [1. chéviut; 2. tʃéviət], fr. Cheviot Hills. Cloth made from wool of Cheviot sheep.

chevron, n. [1. shévrun; 2. ʃévrən]. Fr., 'rafter', also in Engl. sense. O. Fr. *chevron* means 'kid', the primitive sense, but also 'rafter', fr. Lat. *caper*, 'goat', *capra*, 'she-goat', Fr. *chèvre*, 'goat'. The connexion of meaning between 'kid' & 'rafter' is not obvious. The later meanings are due to the resemblance in shape between the her. chevron & the angle formed by two rafters meeting, or, as Skeat suggests, the direct connexion may be w. the gable-like peak of a saddle. See **caper**. A figure like an inverted V; **a** (her.) one of the honourable ordinaries; **b** strip of cloth of this shape worn on sleeve of military or police uniform to indicate rank or other distinction; **c** *chevron moulding*, (Norm. archit.) one in form of a series of chevrons.

chevrotain, n. [1. shévrotān; 2. ʃévrətein]. Fr., dimin. fr. O. Fr. *chevrot*, 'goat'. See **chevron**. A very small ruminant animal, genus *Tragulus*, of East Indies and Malaya &c.; the mouse-deer.

chevy. See **chivy**.

chew (I.), vb. trans. & intrans. [1. choo͞; 2. tʃū]. O.E. *ċēowan*, M.E. *chēwen*, cp. O.H.G. *kiuwan*, Mod. Germ. *kauen*; further, O. Slav. *živati*, 'to chew'; Lat. *gingīva* (whence Fr. *gencive*), 'gum' (in wh. the teeth are rooted), is fr. a redupl. form of this base. **1.** trans. **a** To grind, break up with the teeth, as food, tobacco &c., to masticate; **b** to ponder, turn, something over in the mind. Phrs. *to* *chew the cud,* action of ruminant animals; (fig.) to turn over in the mind, ponder; *to bite off more than one can chew,* undertake, attempt, more than one can accomplish. **2.** intrans. **a** To perform action of chewing; **b** to think over; also *chew on.*

chew (**II.**), n., fr. prec. **a** Act of chewing: *three chews to every mouthful*; **b** thing for chewing, thing chewed: *a chew of tobacco.*

chewing gum, n. [1. chōōing gùm; 2. tʃúiŋ gàm]. Preparation of various gums, esp. *chicle,* sweetened and flavoured, used for chewing, a habit originating in the U.S.A.

Chianti, n. [1. kiánti; 2. kiǽnti]. Ital. Name of wine-growing district in Tuscany. Red, rather astringent, Italian wine.

chiaroscuro, n. [1. kyáhroskōōrō; 2. kiárɔskûrou]. Ital., lit. 'clear-dark'. See **clear** & **obscure. a** Effect of light falling on objects, in nature, whereby some, or parts of some, are brightly illuminated, while others are less so, or in varying degrees of shade; **b** treatment of these effects in pictorial art; **c** use of strong contrasts of light and shade in art, or of contrast generally in literature.

chiasmus, n. [1. kīázmus; 2. kaiǽzməs]. Gk. *khīasmós,* 'placing crosswise'; fr. *khīázein,* 'to form letter χ', fr. *khi,* name of Gk. letter. Inversion of word order when the same word or phrase is repeated in the sentence.

chibouk, chibouque, n. [1. shibōōk; 2. ʃibûk]. Fr. *chibouque,* fr. Turk. *chibuq.* Turkish pipe with amber mouthpiece and long wooden stem.

chic, adj. & n. [1. shik, shēk; 2. ʃik, ʃīk]. Fr., only as n. Etymol. unknown. (colloq.) **a** adj. Possessing qualities of smartness, daring novelty, charm; having style; **b** n., style, charm, good form.

chicane, n. & vb. intrans. [1. shikā́n; 2. ʃikéin]. Fr. Origin doubtful. **1.** n. **a** Verbal subterfuge, quibble, pettifogging argument; **b** (in bridge) score allowed to player who holds no trumps. **2.** vb. To make use of chicanery. (Rare.)

chicanery, n. [1. shikā́neri; 2. ʃikéinəri]. Fr. *chicanerie.* See prec. Disingenuous argument, used to puzzle and perplex; sophistry, quibble, pettifogging.

chick, n. [1. chik; 2. tʃik]. Shortened form of **chicken. a** Young bird newly hatched, esp. of domestic fowls (not used of young ducks); **b** by extension, of young children.

chickabiddy, n. [1. chikabìdi; 2. tʃikəbìdi]. **a** Child's name for a chicken; **b** affectionate, playful name for a child.

chicken, n. [1. chíkin; 2. tʃíkin]. O.E. *ċicen, ċycen,* M.E. *chiken.* Possibly related to **cock,** fr. different gradation form, W. Gmc. **kaukin-* or **kiukin-,* the *-in-* being a dimin. suff. **1.** **a** Young bird of any species; **b** specif., domestic fowl; **c** the flesh of this. Phrs. *to count one's chickens before they are hatched,* be too sanguine of one's chances; *Mother Carey's chicken,* sailor's name for the Stormy Petrel. **2.** (fig.) Very young person; esp. in negative Phr.: *she's no (longer a) chicken,* no longer young.

chicken-breasted, adj. [1. chíken brésted; 2. tʃíkin bréstid]. Having an undue projection of breast-bone.

chicken cholera, n. Virulent, contagious disease of domestic fowls.

chicken-hazard, n. Game of hazard with very small stakes.

chicken-hearted, adj. Timid, cowardly.

chicken-liver, n., **-ed,** adj. [1. chíkin lìver(d); 2. tʃíkin lìvə(d)]. **a** n. Spiritless, cowardly person; **b** adj., cowardly &c.

chicken-pox, n. Disease, known medically as *Varicella,* resembling mild form of smallpox, chiefly affecting children.

chickling, n. [1. chíkling; 2. tʃíkliŋ]. **chick** & **-ling,** dimin. Small chicken.

chick-pea, n. Also *chich-pea,* Fr. *chiche,* fr. Lat. *cicer,* 'vetch'. The word is supposed to show reduplication, & to be cogn. w. Gk. *kriós,* 'kind of vetch'. Cp. also Scrt. *šišna,* 'pea'. The Engl. form prob. influenced by *chick.* Dwarf pea.

chick-weed, n. **chick** & **weed.** Wild creeping plant with small white flowers which is liked by birds.

chicle, n. [1. chíkl, chíklē; 2. tʃíkl, tʃíklī]. Span.-Amer. word. A gummy substance obtained from various C. and S. American trees, used esp. for making chewing gum.

chicory, n. [1. chíkuri; 2. tʃíkəri]. 16th cent. *cykorie,* fr. Fr. *cicorée,* now *chicorée,* Lat. *cichorium,* fr. Gk. *kīkhórion,* also as neut. pl. *kīkhoría.* See **succory.** Plant with blue flower, the root of which is dried, ground, and mixed with, or substituted for, coffee.

chide, vb. intrans. & trans. [1. chīd; 2. tʃaid]. O.E. *ċīdan.* Cognates are unknown. **1.** intrans. To complain angrily, wrangle, express angry disapproval. **2.** trans. To reprove, scold, find fault with.

chidingly, adv. [1. chídingli; 2. tʃáidiŋli], fr. Pres. Part. of prec. & **-ly.** Complainingly, reprovingly.

chief (**I.**), n. [1. chēf; 2. tʃīf]. M.E. *chief, chēf,* fr. O. Fr. *chef,* 'head', cp. Ital. *capo,* fr. L. Lat. *capum,* 'head', fr. Lat. *caput.* See **capital. 1.** Headman, leader, commander, of a body of men; specif., hereditary head of a Highland clan; *-in-chief,* in supreme position, as *commander-in-chief.* **2.** (her.) **a** The upper part of the shield; **b** mark consisting of a band occupying a third of the shield, from the top.

chief (**II.**), adj., fr. prec. **1.** Having supreme office of its kind, principal official: *Chief Justice, chief priest.* **2.** Principal, most important, holding first place: *chief thought in one's mind; chief points of an argument.*

chiefly, adv. & adj. Prec. & **-ly. a** adv. In the first place, principally, most of all; **b** adj., belonging to, connected with, a chief.

chieftain, n. [1. chéftin; 2. tʃíftin]. M.E. *chēvetein* &c. O. Fr. *chevetain,* fr. Low Lat. *capitān(e)us.* See **captain.** The first element of present form is influenced by **chief. 1.** Leader, esp. of a band of brigands and such-like. **2.** Specif., hereditary head of a Highland clan, chief.

chieftaincy, n. [1. chéftinsi; 2. tʃíftinsi]. Prec. & **-cy.** Position of a chieftain.

chieftainess, n. [1. chéftines; 2. tʃíftinis]. See prec. & **-ess.** Wife of chieftain; female chief.

chieftainship, n. [1. chéftinship; 2. tʃíftinʃip]. **chieftain** & **-ship.** Chieftaincy.

chiff-chaff, n. [1. chífchaf; 2. tʃíftʃæf]. Imitative. Popular name of a warbler related to the willow wren.

chiffon, n. [1. shéfon; 2. ʃífɔ̃]. Fr., fr. *chiffe,* 'rag'; pl. 'clothes'. A thin, gauzy material used in women's dresses.

chiffonier, n. [1. shifunḗr; 2. ʃifəníə]. Fr., 'rag-picker', also 'cupboard for small articles'. See prec. & **-ier.** Article of furniture rather lower than a sideboard, often having a marble top, and being otherwise ornamented, containing a cupboard, and sometimes also shelves for ornaments on either side.

chignon, n. [1. shényon; 2. ʃínjɔ̃]. Fr. 'back of the neck; hair worn in coils on top, or at back, of head'. Variant of *chaînon,* 'little chain', fr. the vertebrae of the neck. See **chain.** Style of hairdressing in women, consisting of a coil of hair at back of the head descending on to nape of the neck.

chigoe, n. [1. chígō; 2. tʃígou]. West Indian word. Flea which burrows into the skin, esp. of the foot, and causes sores. Popularly known as 'jigger'.

chilblain, n. [1. chílblān; 2. tʃílblein]. **chill** & **blain.** Painful and highly irritable swelling in the flesh, esp. on the ears, hands, and feet, caused by exposure to cold, and bad circulation.

child, n. [1. chīld; 2. tʃaild], pl. **children** [1. chíldren; 2. tʃíldrən]. O.E. *ċild,* 'child; young noble, or prince', M.E. *chīld,* pl. *childre(n)*; connected w. Goth. *kilþei,* 'womb', & Scrt. *jatháram* for **jalth-,* 'belly'. For remoter relationships, see under **calf. 1.** Young human being of either sex; **a** of unborn infant: Phr. *with child,* pregnant; **b** of boy or girl before period of youth and puberty: '*While still a child, nor yet a fool to fame*' (Pope). Phr. *child's play,* simple, easy task; **c** foolish, or simple, person; said of one who is either undeveloped mentally, or who is inexperienced in the ways of the world: *declared he was only a child in such matters.* **2. a** Offspring, son or daughter, of a man or woman: '*like as a father pitieth his own children*'; **b** descendant, esp. from remote ancestor: *child of Abraham, children of Israel,* Jew(s); **c** follower, disciple, servant: *a child of God, of the Devil*; **d** (i) one sprung from particular race, class, country; (ii) one intimately associated with, and sharing characteristics of, a period, school of thought or movement: *a child of the people, of the desert; child of sin, of light; child of the age, of the Revolution* &c. **3.** (fig.) Product of mental effort, imagination &c.: *his books were the children of his brain.* **4.** (archaic) Survival of O.E. second sense, young man of noble birth: *Child(e) Harold, Child Roland.*

child-bearing, n. Act of bringing forth children; process of bringing forth children, parturition (only of human beings).

childbed, n. [1. chíldbed; 2. tʃáildbed]. **child** & **bed.** The actual state of bringing forth a child; labour: *to die in childbed.*

childbirth, n. [1. chíldbërth; 2. tʃáildbʌ̄þ]. **child** & **birth. a** Parturition; **b** rate of production of children in a country or area: *statistics of childbirth.*

Childermas (day), n. [1. chíldermas (dā́); 2. tʃíldəməs (déi)]. O.E. *ċildramæsse dæġ.* **child** & **Mass** (**I.**). Holy Innocents' Day, December 28.

childhood, n. [1. chíld-hood; 2. tʃáildhud]. **child** & **-hood.** Period of human life between birth and puberty. Phr. *second childhood,* extreme old age, dotage.

childish, adj. [1. chíldish; 2. tʃáildiʃ]. **child** & **-ish. a** Pertaining to, suitable to, a child: *childish sports*; **b** simple, foolish, ill-considered, ineffective, futile: *a childish attempt, idea, answer, argument* &c.

childlike, adj. [1. chíldlīk; 2. tʃáildlaik]. **child** & **-like.** (in favourable sense) Innocent, simple-minded, ingenuous, frank, candid.

Chile saltpetre, n. [1. chíli sawltpḗter; 2. tʃíli sɔ̄ltpítə]. Sodium nitrate, found in Chile and Peru, and used as a fertilizer &c.

chili. See **chilli.**

chiliad, n. [1. kíliad; 2. kíliæd]. Gk. *khīliás,* genit. *khīliád-(os),* 'a thousand', fr. *khīlioi,* adj., 'thousand', for **khesloi,* cp. Scrt. *sa-hásra-m,* 'thousand', fr. **se-kheslo-.* **a** A thousand; **b** a thousand years.

chiliasm, n. [1. kíliazm; 2. kíliæzəm]. Gk. *khīliasmós.* See prec. Doctrine of millennium.

chiliast, n. [1. kíliast; 2. kíliæst]. Gk. *khīliastḗs.* Believer in doctrine of millennium.

chiliastic, adj. [1. kiliástik; 2. kiliǽstik]. Prec. & **-ic.** Pertaining to doctrine of millennium.

chill (**I.**), n. [1. chil; 2. tʃil]. O.E. (W.S.) *ċiele, ċile,* fr. **ċeali,* fr. **kæli-,* Gmc. base **kal-,* q.v. under **cold, cool. a** Cold, sensation of insufficient heat: *a chill in the air*; Phr. *to take the chill off,* to warm slightly (usually of liquids); **b** inflammatory illness, or indisposition caused by exposure to cold, a draught, damp &c.: *to catch a chill* &c.; **c** (fig., of manner, moral atmosphere) austerity, unfriendliness, absence of cordiality &c.; **d** dismal, depressing influence caused by this: *he cast a chill upon their gaiety.*

chill (**II.**), adj., fr. prec. **a** Cold to the touch, lacking warmth; **b** (fig., of manner and moral atmosphere) frigid, austere, depressing.

chill (**III.**), vb. trans. & intrans. **1.** trans. **a** To render cold, reduce temperature of; depress spirits (lit. and fig.); **b** specif., to strike cold into, subject to excessive cold, render ill with cold: *chilled to the bone*; **c** specif., to freeze food so as to preserve it; **d** to toughen or harden iron and steel. **2.** intrans. To become cold, lose warmth, undergo fall in temperature.

chilli, n. [1. chíli; 2. tʃíli]. Mexican word. Dried fruit of capsicum, used as condiment. *Chilli pepper*, kind of cayenne.

chilliness, n. [1. chílines; 2. tʃílinis]. **chilly** & **-ness**. Coldness, state of being chilly (lit. and fig.).

chilling, adj. [1. chíling; 2. tʃíliŋ], fr. Pres. Part. of **chill (III.)**. **a** Producing sense of cold; producing, tending to cause, a chill; **b** (fig.) depressing, casting a gloom, or loss of exhilaration by repellent, austere manner.

chilly, adj. [1. chíli; 2. tʃíli]. **chill (I.)** & **-y**. Rather cold, unpleasantly lacking in warmth: *to feel chilly*; *a chilly room*; *chilly manner*.

Chiltern Hundreds, n. [1. chíltern húndredz; 2. tʃíltən hándrədz], fr. *the Chilterns*, hills in Buckinghamshire. An old manorial office, held from the Crown, considered to be an 'office of profit', and therefore disqualifying a Member of Parliament from retaining his seat, and thus, by a legal fiction, enabling him to resign from Parliament, whence Phr. *to accept, apply for, the Chiltern Hundreds*, to resign seat in House of Commons.

chime (I.), n. [1. chīm; 2. tʃaim]. M.E. *chymbe, chīme* &c., 'chime, cymbal', O. Fr. *chimble* &c., fr. Lat. *cymbalum*. See **cymbal**. **a** Set of bells in church tower &c. tuned for ringing together in sequence; **b** musical sequence of sounds produced by such a set of bells (often pl.); **c** musical or rhythmic sound from instrument of music. Phr. *in chime*, in tune, in harmony; (fig.) in agreement.

chime (II.), vb. trans. & intrans., fr. prec. **1.** trans. To ring chimes on (a set of bells). **2.** intrans. **a** (of bells or a clock) to sound as a chime; Phr. *chime in*, break suddenly into a conversation; **b** (fig.) to harmonize with, respond to, be in agreement with; also *chime in with*, suit, be in accordance with (plans &c.).

chime (III.), **chimb**, n. O.E. *ćimb-*, in *ćimbstāne*, 'stone into which pillar is fitted', *ćimb-iren*, 'clamp'. Etymol. doubtful. Projecting rim at each end of a cask.

chimera, chimæra, n. [1. ki-, kīméra; 2. ki-, kaimíərə]. Fr. *chimère*, Gk. *khímaira*, lit. 'she-goat', also a monster, with lion's head, goat's middle, and serpent's tail; cp. *khímaros*, 'he-goat', orig. 'a yearling, creature of one winter', connected w. Gk. *kheíma*, 'winter, storm'; cp. Scrt. *himaś*, 'cold, winter'; cp. further Engl. dial. *gimmer lamb*, O.N. *gymbr*, 'ewe-lamb of one year'. See further cognates under **hibernal, hibernate**. **1.** In Gk. sense in Milton, '*hydras and chimæras dire*'. **2.** Hence, a bogey, a fancied horror which has no existence.

chimere, n. [1. shimḗr; 2. ʃimíə]. O. Fr. *chamarre*, Fr. *simarre*, 'magistrate's robe'. Origin unknown. Long black robe, open in front, worn by bishops over the rochet, the large sleeves of which come through openings in the sides.

chimney, n. [1. chímni; 2. tʃímni], fr. O. Fr. *cheminee*, fr. Low Lat. *camīnāta*, 'fire-place', fr. Lat. *camīnus*, 'forge, hearth', cp. Gk. *kámīnos*, 'oven', conn. w. *kamárā*, 'vault', q.v. under **camera**. **1.** Hollowed space in wall of house or other building passing from a fire-place upwards through the roof, and often projecting above this, which acts as a vent for smoke and fumes from fire. Phr. *to smoke like a chimney*. **2.** Tall tower-like structure in connexion with factory, furnace which causes draught for this and carries off smoke and fumes. **3.** Funnel-shaped structure in steam-engine or steamship which carries off smoke and steam from fires and boilers. **4.** Glass tube which protects flame of an oil lamp and regulates draught. **5.** Natural opening shaped like a chimney; **a** vent of a volcano; **b** narrow opening or cleft in mountain or rock.

chimney-corner, n. Large recess with seats in old-fashioned fireplace, formed by lowest part of chimney.

chimney-piece, n. Moulding or decorative structure placed across top, and on either side of the opening of a fireplace, often having a shelf at the top, and carved or ornamented.

chimney-pot, n. **a** Large tube of earthenware or metal, a few feet in height, fastened to the upper end of chimney whence it projects above roof of house, and serves to promote draught and to carry smoke away from house; **b** shiny silk hat of cylindrical form, so called from shape; a top hat; also *chimney-pot hat*.

chimney-stack, n. **a** (more used in U.S.A. than in England) Structure on roof of house containing the vents of several chimneys, from which the chimney-pots rise; **b** tall isolated chimney of factory, steam engine &c.

chimney-sweep(er), n. Person whose trade it is to remove soot from chimney.

chimpanzee, n. [1. chìmpanzḗ; 2. tʃìmpənzí]. W. Afr. name. Arboreal African anthropoid ape, smaller and less fierce than gorilla.

chin, n. [1. chin; 2. tʃin]. O.E. *ćin*; cp. O.N. *kinn*, Goth. *kinnus*, 'cheek', O.S., O.H.G. *kinni*, 'cheek', Mod. Germ. *kinn*, 'chin'; cogn. w. Lat. *gena*, 'cheek'; Gk. *génus*, 'lower jaw', *géneion*, 'chin, lower part of face'; Scrt. *hanuś*, 'jaw'; O.W. *gin*, 'mouth'. Cp. also Gk. *gnáthos*, 'jaw', q.v. under **gnathic**. Projecting front part of lower jaw below the mouth.

china, n. & adj. [1. chína; 2. tʃáinə], fr. name of country. **1.** n. **a** Fine porcelain ware made in China; **b** (general term) any kind of crockery or earthenware: *glass and china*. **2.** adj. Made of porcelain in specific or general sense: *china cup, basin* &c.

China aster, n. A garden flower resembling a chrysanthemum.

China bark, n. Quinine.

China clay, n. Kaolin.

Chinaman, n. [1. chínaman; 2. tʃáinəmən], irregular formation. Native of China, a Chinese.

chinchilla, n. [1. chinchíla; 2. tʃintʃílə]. Span. dimin. of *chinche*, 'bug', Lat. *cīmic-em*, acc. of *cīmex*, cogn. w. Scrt. *śyāmaś*, 'dark grey'. So named from supposed resemblance in smell between the insect and the animal. **a** Rodent of Peru, about the size of a large squirrel; **b** the soft, grey fur of this animal.

chin-chin, n. [1. chínchín; 2. tʃíntʃín]. Chinese *ts'ing-ts'ing*, 'please-please'; the phrase in pidgin-Engl. is equiv. to 'thank you, adieu'. **a** A polite salutation; **b** ceremonious conversation.

chin-deep, adj. **a** Reaching to the chin (of water &c.); **b** (of persons) in water to the chin; **c** (fig.) deeply immersed in business.

chine (I.), n. [1. chīn; 2. tʃain]. Cp. O.E. *ćine*, 'fissure', connected w. *ćīnan*, 'to gape, crack'. The mod. word presupposes earlier *ī* as in O.E. vb. Small deep, narrow valley in Hants and Isle of Wight.

chine (II.), n. M.E. *chȳne*, 'back', fr. O. Fr. *eschine*, wh. is prob. a H.G. loan-word; cp. O.H.G. *scina*, 'needle, prickle, splinter'; cogn. w. **shin**. For development of meaning cp. Lat. *spīna*, 'thorn, prickle, fish bone, spine of sea-urchin, spine, back', see **spine**. **a** Backbone, of an animal, esp. as a joint of meat; **b** ridge, spine, of a rock, or ice formation, arête.

Chinee, n. [1. chínḗ; 2. tʃáiní]. Formed fr. *Chinese*, wh. was supposed to be a pl. (vulg. and colloq.) A Chinese.

Chinese, n. & adj. [1. chínḗz; 2. tʃáiníz]. **China** & **-ese**. **a** n. A native of China; the language of China; **b** adj., belonging to, coming from, China.

Chinese lantern, n. One made of paper, containing a candle, and made to fold up; often used for decoration at night in open air.

Chinese white, n. White, zinc paint.

chink (I.), n. [1. chingk; 2. tʃiŋk]. Only since 16th cent. Same meaning as **chine (I.)**. Origin doubtful. A slit, narrow opening, crack, esp. one which lets light, a draught &c. through.

chink (II.), n. & vb. intrans., imitative. **1.** n. **a** Clinking, tinkling sound as of coins dropped one upon another, or of small metal objects lightly rubbing together; **b** (colloq.) money. **2.** vb. To make a noise as of coins or other pieces of metal knocking together.

Chink (III.), n. (vulg. and colloq.) A Chinese.

Chinook, n. [1. chinóök; 2. tʃinúk]. N. Amer. Indian. **1.** **a** North American Indian group of tribes on north-west coast; **b** their language; **c** member of such tribes. **2.** A patois or dialect of a mixture of French and Chinook. **3.** A warm, dry wind from the Rocky Mountains.

chintz, n. [1. chints; 2. tʃints]. Formerly a pl. fr. sing. *chint*; Hind. *chīnt*, 'spotted cotton cloth'. A kind of cotton cloth or calico printed or stamped with bright-coloured patterns; much used in upholstering.

chip (I.), n. [1. chip; 2. tʃip]. Perh. variant of **chop**. **1.** **a** Thin shaving or splinter of wood hacked or split off larger block; Phrs. *as dry as a chip*, very dry; *a chip of the old block*, a true representative, for good or ill, of parent or family; **b** small portion of some brittle substance, such as stone, glass, or crockery knocked off edge of a vessel; **c** the jagged, dinted place left in glass or crockery by such an injury: *there's a chip out of this cup*; *a chip in the edge of the cup*; **d** the act of making chips, or reducing to chips. **2.** **a** (gen. in pl., coll.) Thin slice of apple or other hard fruit, dried and preserved; **b** thin shaving of potato fried till it becomes dry and brittle: *fish and chips*.

chip (II.), vb. trans. & intrans., fr. prec. **1.** trans. **a** To knock or cut chips out of: *to chip the edge of a knife, of a tea-cup* &c.; **b** to make potatoes into chips, by slicing and frying: *chipped potatoes*. **2.** intrans. To be liable to be chipped: *this china chips very easily*. **3.** *Chip in* (colloq.), to take a sudden part in, a conversation, debate, fight &c.

chip basket, n. Light fragile basket for gathering flowers or fruit, made of thin shavings of wood plaited.

chip hat, n. Hat made of coarse straw.

chipmunk, chipmuck, n. [1. chípmungk, -muk; 2. tʃípmaŋk, -mak], fr. Amer.-Indian name. Small striped American squirrel.

Chippendale, adj. [1. chípendāl; 2. tʃípəndeil]. From Thomas Chippendale, died 1779, a celebrated maker and designer of furniture. (of furniture) Made by, or from designs of, or according to general style of, Thomas Chippendale.

chippy, adj. [1. chípi; 2. tʃípi], fr. **chip (I.)** & **-y**. **a** Resembling or abounding in chips; having chips knocked out (as a knife blade); **b** (colloq. slang) unwell, indisposed, esp. from over-indulgence in drink.

chiro-. See **cheiro-**.

chirograph, n. [1. kírograhf; 2. káirəgrāf]. Fr. *chirographe*, Gk. *kheirógraphon*, 'document written by hand'. Prec. & **-graph**. Legal instrument formally written or signed.

chiromancer, n. [1. kíromanser; 2. káirəmænsə]. See next word. Palmist.

chiromancy, n. [1. kíromansi; 2. káirəmænsi]. **chiro-**, 'hand', & **-mancy**, 'divination'. Art of telling a person's character, abilities, and fortune by the lines in his hand; palmistry.

chiromantic, adj. [1. kìromántik; 2. kàirəmǽntik]. See prec. & **-ic**. Relating to chiromancy.

chiropodist, n. [1. kìrópodist; 2. kairɔ́pədist]. See **chiro-** & **-pod** & **-ist**. Person skilled in the care of the feet, esp. in treatment of corns, cutting of toe-nails &c.

chiropody, n. [1. kīrópodi; 2. kairɔ́pədi], fr. first two elements of prec. & **-y**. The art, or trade, of the chiropodist.

chiroptera. See **cheiroptera**.

chirp, vb. trans. & intrans. & n. [1. chěrp; 2. tʃɜ̄p]. No history, but resembles several other imitative words. Cp. O.E. *ćearcian*, 'creak'. **1.** vb. **a** trans. To utter with shrill, piping note of birds: *to chirp a song*; **b** intrans., to utter shrill, piping note; **c** (fig.) to speak in a shrill, cheerful voice (said of rather futile persons with poor voices). **2.** n. Single cry or note of a bird: *a series of chirps.*

chirpy, adj. [1. chĕrpi; 2. tʃʌ́pi]. Prec. & **-y.** Cheerful, lively, brisk.

chirr, n. & vb. intrans. [1. chĕr; 2. tʃʌ̄]. Imitative. **a** n. The shrill, dry, rasping sound made by crickets and grasshoppers; or of dry reeds rubbing against each other &c.; **b** vb., to make this sound.

chirrup, vb. intrans. & n. [1. chírup; 2. tʃírəp]. Variant of **chirp. a** vb. To make a series of chirps, to twitter; to make a clicking sound to a horse &c.; **b** n., the sound itself.

chirurgeon, n. [1. kīrĕrjun; 2. kairʌ́dʒən]. M.E. *cirurgian*, fr. O. Fr. *cirurgien*, Mod. Fr. *chirurgien*, Low Lat. **chīrurgiānus*, fr. *chīrurgicus* (cp. *chīrurgia* under **chirurgery**), loan-word fr. Gk. *kheirourgós*, 'working by hand; hand-worker, surgeon'. See **cheiro-**. The second element is a form of the base *érgon*, 'action, work'; see **erg** & **work**, & cp. **surgeon.** A surgeon, which word, an early variant, has entirely superseded the longer word in English.

chirurgery, n. [1. kīrĕrjeri; 2. kairʌ́dʒəri]. O. Fr. *cirurgie*, Mod. Fr. *chirurgie*, L. Lat. *chīrurgia*, fr. Gk. *kheirourgia*, 'a working by hand, practice of a handicraft, trade'. See prec. & cp. **surgery.** (archaic) Surgery.

chirurgic(al), adj. [1. kīrĕrjik(l); 2. kairʌ́dʒik(l)]. Cp. Gk. *kheirourgikós*; see prec. & **-al.** (archaic) Pertaining to surgeons or surgery; survives in name of a society.

chisel (I.), n. [1. chízl; 2. tʃízl]. In M.E., fr. O. Nthn. Fr., Mod. Fr. *ciseau*, L. Lat. *cisellus* for *caesellus*, fr. *caes-*, P.P. type of Lat. *caedere*, 'to cut', q.v. under **cement.** Tool with rectangular cutting edge, used for cutting, dressing, and carving hard substances such as stone, bone, wood, and metal; held by the handle and often driven by a mallet.

chisel (II.), vb. trans., fr. prec. **1. a** To cut or dress or carve with a chisel; **b** (fig.) to give finish and refinement to literary work, to polish and perfect style. **2.** (fig. slang) To cheat, swindle, use sharp practice in a bargain; often, *to chisel one out of something.*

chiselled, adj. [1. chízeld; 2. tʃízəld], fr. P.P. of prec. (fig.) Highly wrought, perfected, clear-cut, well-shaped. Phr. *chiselled features.*

chit (I.), n. [1. chit; 2. tʃit]. O.E. *ċīþ*, 'germ, shoot, sprout'. A sprout from a root or seed.

chit (II.), vb. intrans., fr. prec. To shoot, sprout, as seed potatoes in late spring, or corn left too long on the ground after being cut.

chit (III.), n. Perh. variant of *kit(ten).* **a** (provinc. Engl.) A young animal; **b** an immature young person; esp. in Phr. *a chit of a girl.*

chit (IV.), n. Anglo-Indian word, also *chitty*; Hind. *chitthi*, 'note, letter, certificate given to a servant' &c., Scrt. *chitra*, 'spotted, black and white'. Cp. **cheetah.** (chiefly used in army and navy) **a** A short letter or note; **b** memorandum of small sum owing for drink &c.; **c** report on an officer by a superior.

chit-chat, n. [1. chít chat; 2. tʃít tʃæt]. Redupl. form of **chat.** Gossip; light, trivial talk.

chitin, n. [1. kítin; 2. káitin]. Gk. *khitṓn*, 'under garment, frock, tunic'. Semit. loan-word, cp. Heb. *ketōnet*, 'close-fitting garment'. Hard substance which covers the bodies externally, of certain invertebrates, such as beetles, lobsters &c., forming what is popularly called the shell.

chitinous, adj. [1. kítinus; 2. káitinəs]. Prec. & **-ous.** Of the nature of chitin.

chiton, n. [1. kíton; 2. káitən]. Gk. *khitṓn.* See **chitin. a** The garment, or tunic, worn by both sexes in ancient Greece, varying in shape, length, and manner of adjustment; **b** (zool., cap.) genus of molluscs, resembling the limpets.

Chittagong wood, n. [1. chítagong wood; 2. tʃítəgɔŋ wud], fr. name of a town in E. Bengal, also, more correctly, spelt *Chatgānw* (Yule and Burnell). Hard, finely grained wood, resembling mahogany.

chitterling(s), n. [1. chíterling(z); 2. tʃítəliŋ(z)]. Etymol. doubtful. Smaller intestines of a pig, used as food.

chivaleresque, adj. [1. shivàlerésk; 2. ʃivæ̀lərésk]. Fr. *chevaleresque.* See **chivalry,** & **-esque.** Having spirit of chivalry.

chivalrous, adj. [1. shívalrus; 2. ʃívəlrəs]; formerly, & more correctly [1. chívalrus; 2. tʃívəlrəs]. O. Fr. *chevalereus* &c., fr. **chevalier,** & adj. suff. fr. Lat. *-ōsus.* See **cavalier** & next word. **1.** Belonging to, connected with, the institution of chivalry. **2.** Possessing the moral qualities and manners of an ideal knight, hence, courageous, gallant, and generous; habitually given to protecting the weak, poor, and mean, and withstanding those who use their strength oppressively.

chivalry, n. [1. chívalri, shívalri; 2. tʃívəlri, ʃívəlri]. M.E. *chivalerie*, O. Fr. *chevalerie*, 'knighthood'. An early loan-word fr. O. Fr., hence the pronunciation w. initial [tʃ] is historical, the other based on the supposition that the word is fr. Mod. Fr. A dialectal doublet of **cavalry. 1.** The system and institution of knighthood, including the laws, customs, rules, and manners which distinguished it: *the laws of chivalry.* **2.** The body of members of the orders of knighthood; a body of knights: *the whole chivalry of France*; '*With al the chirche and al the chivalrie*' (Chaucer). **3. a** The characteristic qualities of temper, character, manners, and behaviour of the ideal knight, esp. courage, loyalty, generosity, courtesy; **b** specific exhibition of these qualities in word or deed.

chive, n. [1. chīv; 2. tʃaiv]. Cp. Fr. *cive*, fr. Lat. *cēpa*, *cēpe*, 'onion', prob. Gk. loan-word, though the Gk. n. is not found. It is suggested by Walde that a Gk. *kēpē* existed, perh. connected w. *kapúō*, 'breathe out', fr. its pungency. Plant of onion tribe used for flavouring.

chivied, adj. [1. chívid; 2. tʃívid], fr. P.P. of next word. (chiefly pred.) Worried, harassed, esp. by constant orders and instructions, or by having too many and various jobs on hand.

chivy, n. & vb. trans. [1. chívi; 2. tʃívi]. Prob. fr. *Chevy Chase.* Spelt *chevy* in some dictionaries, but never now so pronounced. **1.** n. Game somewhat resembling prisoners' base, which consists in chasing players who come out of base. **2.** vb. trans. **a** To chase rapidly from place to place; run after and cause to move on; **b** (fig.) to harass by giving constant orders, and entrusting with fresh tasks; to nag in a fussy manner.

chlamydo-, pref. Word used in scientific terminology, meaning 'mantle', see next word, e.g. *chlamydospore*, of certain fungi.

chlamys, n. [1. klámis; 2. kléimis]. Gk. *khlamús*, genit. *khlamúd-(os)*, 'mantle'; etymol. doubtful. A cloak, or mantle, fastened at the shoulder, worn out of doors by the ancient Greeks.

chloral, n. [1. klóral; 2. klɔ́rəl]. Derived fr. *chlor-* in **chlorine** & *al-* in **alcohol**; cp. Gk. *khlōrós*, 'light green'; perh. cogn. w. base found in **gold. a** Liquid with strong smell and bitter taste, obtained from chlorine by action of alcohol. **b** a compound of chloral and water, *chloral hydrate*, used as hypnotic &c.

chlorate, n. [1. klórāt; 2. klɔ́reit]. See **chloral** & **-ate.** A salt of chloric acid: *potassium chlorate.*

chloric, adj. [1. klórik; 2. klɔ́rik]. See **chloral** & **-ic.** Pertaining to, obtained from, chlorine: *chloric acid.*

chloride, n. [1. klórīd; 2. klɔ́raid]. See prec. & **-ide.** Compound of chlorine and another element: *sodium chloride*, common salt.

chlorine, n. [1. klórēn; 2. klɔ́rīn]. See prec. & **-ine.** A non-metallic element, a heavy, yellowish-green, ill-smelling gas, very poisonous, used as a disinfectant, for bleaching &c., and as a poison-gas in the Great War.

chloroform, n. & vb. trans. [1. klóroform; 2. klɔ́rəfōm]. Fr. See **chloral** & **formic. 1.** n. Colourless volatile liquid, used as an anaesthetic. **2.** vb. To dose with chloroform, to administer this as an anaesthetic.

chlorophyll, n. [1. klórofil; 2. klɔ́rəfil]. Gk. *khlōr-*, 'pale green' (see **chloral**), & *phúllon*, 'leaf', see **phyllo-.** Green colouring matter in leaves, grass &c.

chlorosis, n. [1. klorósis; 2. klɔróusis]. Gk. *khlōrós*, 'pale green' (see **chloral**), & **-osis**, formative suff. expressing pathological condition. **a** Complaint to which young women are liable, a kind of anaemia, formerly called 'green sickness' on account of its effect on the complexion; **b** (bot.) form of etiolation in plants in which green parts lose their colour, owing to lack of nutriment.

chock, n. & vb. trans. [1. chok; 2. tʃɔk], fr. O. Fr. *choque*, 'log'; etymol. unknown. **1.** n. Wooden block, or wedge, used to prevent a cask from rolling, or to support a boat on deck of a ship. **2.** vb. To make secure with chocks.

chock-a-block, adj. & adv. [1. chókablók; 2. tʃɔ́kəblɔ́k]. **a** (naut.) Hoisted so high as to touch the blocks of the tackle; hence, **b** (fig.) jammed together, packed tight.

chock-full, adj. & adv., also **choke-full.** Connexion w. *choke* doubtful. Very full, full to the brim, to utmost capacity.

chocolate, n. [1. chókolit; 2. tʃɔ́kəlit]. Span., fr. Mexican *chocolatl.* First used in Engl. in early 17th cent. No connexion w. **cacao. a** Sweetmeat in form of a hard paste, made from beans of cacao plant, ground down, sweetened, and otherwise flavoured; **b** sweet drink made by dissolving this in hot water; **c** the colour, dark brown, of chocolate.

choctaw, n. [1. chòktáw; 2. tʃɔ̀ktɔ́]. **a** (cap.) Name of a civilized North American Indian tribe; **b** name given to a particular step in figure skating.

choice (I.), n. [1. chois; 2. tʃɔis]. M.E., fr. O. Fr. *chois*, Mod. Fr. *choix*, fr. O. Fr. *choisir*, 'choose', cp. O. Ital. *ciausire*; Gmc. loan-word, cp. Goth. *kausjan*, 'prove, test', derived fr. str. vb. *kiusan*, 'choose' &c. With this O.E. *ċēosan*, 'choose', is cogn. See **choose. 1.** Act, or process, of selecting, or deciding between, several alternatives; selection, decision by judgement or feeling that one prefers one thing to another: *to make a choice*; *the lady of one's choice.* **2.** Opportunity or right to make a selection: *to offer, allow, a choice.* Phrs. *Hobson's choice*, no alternative; *to have no choice in the matter*, to be compelled to act in a certain way; also, not to care which one has; *by choice*, by preference. **3.** Something specially selected, the fine flower, best procurable: *here are the best I can find, the choice of the whole garden.* **4.** Collection of persons or objects from which one may choose; field of selection: *a wide, a poor, an insufficient, choice.*

choice (II.), adj. Most prob. fr. prec. M.E. *chīse* & *chūse*, 'elegant, loving', are dialectal variants of O.E. *ċīes*, *ċȳs*, 'fastidious', fr. **ciusi-*, or **ċēasi-*, cp. O.E. *ċēos-*; Pret. *ċēas*, 'choose', may conceivably have influenced the meaning, but the only M.E. form wh. cd. be confused w. M.E. *chois* (see prec.) is S.W. *chīse*, whereas we shd. expect *chēse* in S.E. Midl., fr. wh. Standard Engl. is derived. **a** (of things) Carefully picked, specially good, of high excellence: *the choicest fruit and flowers*; **b** (of persons) fastidious, dainty, nice, particular: *somewhat too choice in the selection of acquaintances.*

choicely, adv. Prec. & **-ly.** Carefully, discriminatingly.

choiceness, n. See prec. & **-ness.** Quality of being choice in both senses.

choir (I.), n. [1. kwīr; 2. kwáiə]. Formerly spelt **quire.** M.E. *quer*, O. Fr. *cuer*, Mod. Fr. *chœur*, fr. Gk. *khorós.* See **chorus. 1. a** Band of singers trained to sing together, esp. in church; **b** any body of persons who meet under direction of a conductor to perform vocal music; a choral society. **2.** That part of a church designed for the singers.

choir (II.), vb. trans. & intrans., fr. prec., formerly **quire**. (chiefly poetic) **1.** trans. To sing songs together as a choir; esp. of birds, angels. **2.** intrans. To sing together in chorus: '*Still quiring to the young-eyed cherubins*' (Shakespeare).

choir-screen, n. Screen of carved woodwork, or ornamented iron, which separates the choir of a church from the nave.

choke (I.), vb. intrans. & trans. [1. chōk; 2. tʃouk]. Cp. M.E. *chēken*, *chōken*, the history of wh. is obscure. **A.** intrans. **1.** To experience a violent spasm of the windpipe and temporary disability to breathe, caused by the introduction of liquid or solid matter into the windpipe, or of smoke or acrid fumes into the lungs. **2.** (fig.) To become momentarily speechless owing to strong emotion: *to choke with anger*. **B.** trans. **1. a** To cause to choke: *every mouthful he swallowed nearly choked him*; **b** (of action of persons) to throttle, cause suffocation to, a person by seizing him by the throat and compressing it. **2.** Also *choke up*, to block, fill up, partially or completely, a passage or vent which should be free: *the chimney was nearly choked* (*up*) *with soot, the drain-pipe with rubbish, the ventilator with dust* &c. **3.** (followed by advs.) *Choke up*, **a** to reduce space in: *the house was choked up with useless pieces of furniture*; **b** to stifle: *young plants choked up with weeds*. *Choke off*, **a** to kill by choking; **b** (fig.) to discourage, dash, get rid of (a person), by harshness and severity: *half-hearted supporters were soon choked off by the conditions imposed*; *choke down*, to swallow, repress, stifle: *to choke down one's emotion, indignation, sobs* &c.

choke (II.), n., fr. prec. **a** The act or process of choking (intrans.); **b** narrowed part of gun, see **choke-bore**.

choke-bore, n. A sporting gun tapered to smaller diameter a short distance behind muzzle; also attrib.: *choke-bore gun*.

choke-damp, n. Poisonous gas which accumulates in disused pits and mines.

choke-pear, n. **a** Pear with bitter astringent taste; **b** (fig., archaic) something hard to answer, disconcerting fact; a facer.

choker, n. [1. chōker; 2. tʃóukə]. See **choke** (I.) & **-er**. Something which chokes; facetiously applied to a necktie; chiefly *white choker*.

choking, adj. & vbl. n. [1. chōking; 2. tʃóukiŋ], fr. **choke** (I.), & **-ing**. **a** adj. Disposing one to choke, making one feel that one is being choked: *a choking sensation*; **b** n., the act and fact of choking: *a choking in the throat*.

choky (I.), adj. [1. chōki; 2. tʃóuki], fr. **choke** (II.) & **-y**. **a** Disposing one to choke; **b** having tendency to choke, esp. from strong emotion.

choky (II.), n. Anglo-Indian word, Hind. *chaukī*, connected prob. w. Scrt. *ćatur*, 'four'; orig. perh. a shed resting on four posts, whence, specif., 'a police station, lock-up', also a station of palankeen bearers, horses &c. (slang) Prison, chiefly *in choky*, in jail.

cholagogue, n. [1. kólagog; 2. kɔ́ləgɔg], fr. Gk. *kholḗ*, 'bile', see **choler**, & *-agōgós*, 'leading, expelling'; for the latter cp. **demagogue**. (med.) Drug, medicine, which expels or helps to free the system of bile.

choler, n. [1. kóler; 2. kɔ́lə]. M.E. & O. Fr. *colere*, 'wrath', Gk. *kholéra*, fr. *kholḗ*, 'gall, bile', *khólos*, 'bile, wrath'. The base **ghel-*, **ghol-*, was widespread among the Aryan languages in the literal sense of 'bile'; Lat. *fel*, gen. *fellis* (Fr. *fiel*), 'gall'; O. Slav. *žlŭčĭ*, Russ. *želčĭ*, 'bile'; O.S., O.H.G. *galla*, O.E. *ġealla*, 'gall'. The base is the same as that in **yellow**, & 'gall' &c. in the above cognates meant orig. 'yellow liquid'. **a** Originally, in mediaeval philosophy, one of the four humours which resided in the body and influenced the spirits; **b** in English the word has the secondary sense of anger, wrath.

cholera, n. [1. kólera; 2. kɔ́lərə]. Gk., a disease of the bile in wh. the humours of the body were violently discharged in vomiting & purging. See **choler**. **a** *Asiatic or malignant cholera*, a specific disease, attacking the bowels, generally fatal, characterized by violent purging, vomiting, and collapse, endemic in the East and epidemic elsewhere; **b** a bilious, non-epidemic and rarely fatal, summer disease, with vomiting and diarrhoea, also called *European* or *summer cholera*.

choleraic, adj. [1. kòleráik; 2. kɔ̀ləréi-ik]. Prec. & **-ic**. Related to, proceeding from, or resembling cholera.

choleric, adj. [1. kólerik; 2. kɔ́lərik]. In Chaucer; Fr. *cholérique*, Lat. *cholericus*, Gk. *kholerikós*, 'wrathful'. See **choler** & **-ic**. Irascible, hasty in temper, given to fits of anger.

choliamb, n. [1. kóliamb; 2. kɔ́liæmb]. Gk. *khōlíambos*, lit. 'lame, halting iambic'. See **iambic**. The etymol. of Gk. *khōlós*, 'lame', is doubtful. (Gk. pros.) An iambic verse having a spondee in last place instead of an iambus.

choliambic, adj. [1. kòliámbik; 2. kɔ̀liǽmbik], fr. prec. & **-ic**. Of the nature of, containing, a choliamb.

chondri-, chondro-. Prefixes occurring in technical scientific terms; the meaning is gen. 'cartilage', but occasionally 'granule' (e.g. *chondrule*), fr. the primary meaning of Gk. *khóndros*, wh. is 'corn, grain, groat'; the secondary meaning is 'cartilage'. The word is for earlier **khróndros* & is cogn. w. Lat. *frendō*, 'gnash the teeth', Lith. *grendu*, 'rub', & O.E. *grindan*, q.v. under **grind**.

choose, vb. trans. & intrans. [1. chōōz; 2. tʃūz]. O.E. *ċēosan*, M.E. *chēsen*, *chūsen*. The mod. form presupposes a M.E. type *chōsen* fr. an O.E. *ċ(e)ōsan*. The Gmc. cognates are O.S., O.H.G. *kiusan*, Goth. *kiusan*, O.N. *kjōsa*; cp. further Lat. *gustāre*, 'taste, partake of, enjoy' (see **gust, disgust**), Gk. *geúō* for **geus-ō*, 'taste', Scrt. *juṣā́te*, 'he enjoys, tastes'. See **choice** (I.). **A.** trans. **1.** To pick out, select, exercise choice in favour of, prefer: *to choose a house, a wife*. **2.** To elect by selection to an office or post: *who will be chosen Speaker?* Phr. *not much, nothing, to choose between them*, both equally good, or bad. **3.** (followed by infin.) To decide, be pleased, implying a certain degree of wilfulness: *if you choose to go you must*; *he didn't choose to obey orders*. **B.** intrans. To exercise choice, make an act of selection: *to choose between duty and inclination*.

chop (I.), vb. trans. & intrans. [1. chop; 2. tʃɔp]. The word has no history in English beyond a few centuries; origin doubtful. **A.** trans. **1. a** To cut by striking with knife or hatchet; to hack: *to chop wood*, cut it into small short pieces for burning; **b** (gen.) to cut by rapid, sudden blows or strokes, to cut roughly. **2.** *Chop up*, to cut into small pieces by chopping. **3.** *Chop off*, to separate one thing from another, or part from whole, by chopping. **4.** *Chop down*, to remove, cause to fall, by chopping, to fell: esp. *chop a tree down*. **5.** (fig.) *To chop words, logic*, bandy words, arguments. **B.** intrans. *To chop about, round*, (esp. of wind) to change direction suddenly. Phr. *to chop and change about*, keep altering one's plans, opinions, or occupations.

chop (II.), n., fr. prec. **1.** Act of chopping: *take a chop at it*. **2.** Something chopped off; specif., thick piece of pork or mutton: *pork chop* &c.

chop (III.), n. See **chap** (II.). (gen. pl.) *Chops*, **a** the jaws; **b** entrance of valley or channel; rare, except *chops of the Channel*, entrance to English Channel from Atlantic.

chop (IV.), n. Anglo-Indian word, fr. Hind. *chhāp*, 'seal or stamp', fr. vb. *chhāpnā*, 'to print (books)'. *Chop* is said by Yule and Burnell to be hardly used in Anglo-Indian now in sense of stamp or seal, but passed from the pidgin-English of the ports back to India and England in slang phrase *first chop*, first brand or quality, hence first rate.

chop-chop, adv. & interj. [1. chóp chóp; 2. tʃɔ́p tʃɔ́p]. Pidgin-Engl., fr. Chinese *kwai-kwai*, 'quick, quick'.

chopine, n. [1. chopḗn; 2. tʃɔpín], for *chapine*, fr. O. Fr. & Span. *chapin*; etymol. doubtful. A thick-soled, high-heeled shoe worn in wet weather &c. by women in 17th cent., esp. in Venice; a form of patten.

chopper, n. [1. chóper; 2. tʃɔ́pə]. **chop** (I.) & **-er**. One who, that which, chops. Specif., a class of heavy short-handled striking and cutting tools variously adapted for chopping wood, bones of meat &c.

choppy, adj. [1. chópi; 2. tʃɔ́pi], fr. **chop** (I.) & **-y**. **a** (of wind) Constantly changing; **b** (of the sea, or lake) agitated by small, rather violent waves; rough.

chopstick, n. [1. chópstik; 2. tʃɔ́pstik]. Chinese pidgin-Engl. **chop-chop**, 'quick', & **stick**. Thin piece of wood or ivory of which a pair, held in one and the same hand, serve the Chinese to lift food to the mouth.

chop suey, n. [1. chóp sōōi; 2. tʃɔ́p súi], fr. Chin. *shap sui*. A Chinese dish of small pieces of fried meat, onions, and other vegetable, served with rice and flavoured with sesame oil.

choragus. See **choregus**.

choral, adj. [1. kṓral; 2. kɔ́rəl]. Med. Lat. *choralis*, fr. Gk. *khorós*. See **chorus** & **choir** & **-al**. **a** Belonging, related, to a choir: *choral practice*; **b** sung by a choir: *choral service, Choral Eucharist*.

chorale, n. [1. koráhl; 2. kɔrā́l]. Same as prec., but spelt & pronounced as a foreign word. Sacred hymn sung by choir and congregation in unison; common type of hymn in German Lutheran churches.

chord (I.), n. [1. kord; 2. kōd]. Lat. *chorda*, 'gut, string of a musical instrument, rope', fr. Gk. *khordḗ*, 'intestine, string of gut, lyre-string'; cp. Alban. *zore*, 'entrails', Lat. *haru-* in *haruspex*, 'soothsayer who foretold future by contemplating entrails of victims', also Lat. *hīra*, 'empty gut', & prob. *hernia*, 'rupture'. See **hernia, cord**. **1. a** String of a harp, lyre &c. (now only poet.); **b** (geom.) a right line joining the extremities of the arc of a circle. **2.** Certain structures in the body resembling, or supposed to resemble, string of instrument: *spinal chord, vocal chord(s)*. **3.** Combination of musical notes which sounded simultaneously produce harmony. Phr. (fig.) *to strike a familiar, the right, chord*, call up by allusion some memory of the past.

chord (II.), vb. trans., fr. prec. Put strings (chords in old sense) into a musical instrument. (Rarely used.)

chore, n. [1. chōr; 2. tʃɔ̄]. Same as **char** (I.). A job of work, task (an American usage).

chorea, n. [1. korḗa; 2. kɔríə]. Gk. *khoreía*, 'choral dance'. See **chorus**. Disease of the nerves attended with involuntary twitchings; St. Vitus' dance.

choregraphic &c. See **choreographic**.

choregus, choragus, n. [1. kōrḗgus, -águs; 2. kɔrígəs, -éigəs]. Gk. *khorēgós*, fr. *khorós*, '**chorus**', q.v., & *-ág(ein)*, 'to lead', q.v. under **agent**. **a** (Gk. antiq.) The leader of the chorus, i.e. the citizen who provided and paid the expenses of training &c. of the chorus, both tragic and comic, for the Athenian festival of Dionysus; **b** title of the deputy of the Professor of Music at Oxford University.

choreograph(**er**), n. [1. kóreograhf, kòreógrefər; 2. kɔ́riougrāf, kɔ̀riɔ́grəfə]. See next word. One who devises or designs a ballet.

choreographic, adj. [1. kòreōgráfik; 2. kɔ̀riougrǽfik]. Gk. *khoreía*, 'dance', see **chorus**, & **graphic**. Pertaining to designing of ballet.

choreography, n. [1. kòreógrafi; 2. kɔ̀riɔ́grəfi]. See prec. & **-y**. Art of denoting a dance by graphic signs, as music by notes, or speech by letters.

chori-, pref., fr. Gk. *khōri*, *khōris*, 'separate, apart', cogn. w. Gk. *khōrízō*, 'separate', *khêros*, 'bereaved, widowed', *kēroûn*, 'to make desolate', *khē-tos*, 'lack, want', Scrt. *jáhāti*, 'abandon'. Base **ghē-*, **ghō-*, **ghə-*, prob. same as in Gk. *kháos* (see **chaos**), Lat. *hiāre*, 'yawn', see **hiatus**.

choriamb, n. [1. kóriamb; 2. kóriæmb]. Gk. *khoriambos*. See **chorus** & **iamb**. Four-syllabled foot of which first and last are long, the other two short.

choriambic, adj. [1. kòriámbik; 2. kòriǽmbik], fr. prec. & **-ic**. Of, containing, a choriamb.

chorion, n. [1. kórion; 2. kórion]. Gk. *khórion*, 'skin, leather', also 'after-birth'. It is doubtful whether Lat. *corium*, 'hide, leather', whence Fr. *cuir*, is an independent word, or borrowed fr. the Gk. Other cognates are Scrt. *khittiš*, 'skin', O. Slav. *(s)kora*, 'rind', O.E. *he(o)rþa*, 'deer-skin', & further Goth. *hairþra*, O.H.G. *herda*, O.E. *hreþer*, 'bowels, vitals', lit. 'something enfolded in skin or membrane' (?); cp. Mid. Ir. *scairt*, 'membrane round the bowels'. See **cortex**. (anat.) The membrane which encloses the unborn child in the womb.

choripetalous, adj. [1. kòripétalus; 2. kòripétələs]. See **chori-** & **petal** & **-ous**. (bot.) Having separate petals.

chorist, n. [1. kórist; 2. kórist]. See **chorus**, & **-ist**. A chorister, member of a choir.

chorister, n. [1. kórister; 2. kóristə]. Prec. & **-er**. Cp. formation of **barrister**. One who sings in, a member of, a church choir.

choroid, adj. & n. [1. kóroid; 2. kóroid]. See **chorion** & **-oid**. Resembling the chorion in character, that is, in being an enveloping membrane, esp. applied to that enclosing eye-ball: *choroid membrane*; *the choroid (of the eye)*.

chorology, n. 1. [koróloji; 2. kōrólədži]. Gk. *khṓra*, 'open space, place, land', & **-logy**; *khṓra* is fr. base **ghē-*, **ghō-* &c., 'open, separate' &c., see **chori-**. Study of the distribution of organisms upon the earth's surface.

chortle, vb. intrans. & n. [1. chórtl; 2. tʃótl]. Coined by Lewis Carroll. Apparently a mixture of *chuckle* & *snort*. **a** vb. To chuckle exultantly; to exult, triumph; **b** n. triumphant chuckle.

chorus (I.), n. [1. kórus; 2. kórəs]. Gk. *khorós*, 'dance in a ring, circular dance; festive dance, e.g. in honour of the gods; band of dancers and singers; troop, band of persons; place for dancing'. The etymol. of this word is not quite certain. Some think its first meaning was 'place for a dance', & identify the first syll. w. that in Gk. *khórtos*, Lat. *hortus*, 'enclosed place, court, garden', & w. O. Ir. *gort*, 'cornfield', Goth. *gard-s*, 'house' &c.; see **horticulture, court, garden, yard**. Others, again, think the starting-point is the idea of movement, & connect it w. Scrt. *ghūrṇati*, 'totter', Lith. *žer̃gti*, 'to spread open the legs', also Lith. *žirgus*, 'horse', i.e. 'the galloping animal'. **1.** Group of singers who assisted in, and interpreted the action in, Greek drama. **2.** The words sung by the chorus of singers. **3. a** Body of persons who sing together those parts of operas or musical drama not sung by the soloists; **b** the parts of the piece sung by these persons. **4.** Part of a song recurring at intervals, as a refrain, sung by a number of persons together. **5.** (fig.) **a** Cries or utterances made simultaneously by a number of persons; or opinions uttered, publicly, e.g. in the press, by a number of persons at the same time, or bearing on the same subject: *a chorus of protest, abuse* &c.; **b** remarks, chiefly by way of approval, uttered at intervals, like a recurring refrain, by one or more persons, while another is speaking.

chorus (II.), vb. trans., fr. prec. To sing or utter in chorus (lit. and fig.).

chose (I.), vb. [1. chōz; 2. tʃouz]. Pret. of **choose**; M.E. *choos*, fr. the P.P. type; see **chosen**. Cp. O.E. Pret. *ċēas*, M.E. *chēs*.

chose (II.), n. [1. shōz; 2. ʃouz]. Fr., 'thing, piece of property', fr. Lat. *causa*. See **cause**. (law) Only in *chose in action*, right to anything, as a debt, recoverable by action; the subject of such right; *chose in possession*, personal property actually in possession.

chosen, adj. [1. chṓzn; 2. tʃóuzn], fr. P.P. of **choose**. O.E. *coren*, M.E. *chōsen*, w. initial & medial consonants generalized fr. Inf. & Pret. S. Specially selected, picked out; hence, favourite: *chosen studies, occupation* &c.; specif., *the chosen people*, Jews.

chough, n. [1. chuf; 2. tʃaf]. Origin very doubtful; form unexplained. Red-legged, red-beaked crow, esp. *Cornish chough*, *Pyrrhocorax graculus*, now nearly extinct.

chouse, vb. trans. & n. [1. chous; 2. tʃaus]. Turk. *chāush*, formerly 'sergeant-at-arms, herald' &c., hence, an agent in diplomatic or other business; the derived unfavourable sense fr. Turkish agents sometimes being guilty of sharp practice or worse. **1.** vb. To swindle, cheat out of; used in this sense (spelt *chiause*) early in 17th cent. **2.** n. Formerly (17th cent.) of persons: a cheat, rogue; now only of actions: swindle, disappointment.

chow, n. [1. chou; 2. tʃau]. Prob. fr. next word. **1.** (Austral. slang) A Chinese. **2.** A variety of Chinese dog, with thick coat and curled tail and pointed muzzle; the special distinctive mark is its black tongue.

chow-chow, n. [1. chóu chou; 2. tʃáu tʃau]. Pidgin-Engl. Chinese pickles or preserves.

chowder, n. [1. chóuder; 2. tʃáudə], fr. Fr. *chaudière*, 'kettle, pot'. See **cauldron**. A dish of stewed fish, pork, clams, biscuits, onions &c., originally a Newfoundland fisherman's dish.

chrematistic, adj. [1. krèmatístik; 2. krìmətístik]. Gk. *khrēmatistikós*, 'of, or for, money', cp. *khrêma*, 'thing that one needs', in pl. *khrēmata*, 'goods, money', & *khráō*, 'give what is needful', *khré*, 'it is necessary', like Fr. *il faut*; fr. a base **gher-*, expressing 'shortness, lack', cp. Scrt. *hrásati*, 'decrease', O. Ir. *gair*, 'short'. Connected with, occupied in, the gaining of wealth.

chrematistics, n., fr. prec. Science of wealth, branch of political economy.

chrestomathy, n. [1. krestómathi; 2. krestóməþi]. Fr., fr. Gk. **khrēsto-mátheia*, fr. *khrēstós*, 'useful' (see prec.) & *math-*, 'learning', as in *matheîn*, 'learn' &c., see **mathematics**. Collection of literary passages with notes, used in the study of a language or as specimens of literature.

chrism, n. [1. krízm; 2. krízəm]. Already in O.E. *crisma*, 'holy oil, used in anointing', fr. Gk. *khrisma*, 'something smeared on, unguent', cp. Gk. *khríō*, 'anoint with oil', fr. base **gherei-*, 'rub', seen also in Lat. *friāre*, 'to rub, crumble to pieces' (see **friable**), *fricāre*, 'rub' (see **friction**). Cp. **cream**. Consecrated oil used in extreme unction, and other sacraments of the Christian Church.

chrismal, adj. [1. krízmal; 2. krízməl]. Prec. & **-al**. Connected with the chrism.

chrisom, n. [1. krísum; 2. krísəm]. Variant of **chrism**. Baptismal robe of infants, symbolical of innocence; used as a shroud for infants who die within a month of baptism; in origin a cloth to keep the chrism from the face.

Christ, n. [1. krīst; 2. kraist]. Gk. *khristós*, 'anointed one', fr. *khríō*, 'rub, anoint', see **chrism**. Transl. of Heb. word, see **Messiah**. **1.** The Lord's Anointed; the expected Jewish Messiah: '*Art thou the Christ?*' **2.** Title of the Saviour as being the Messiah; used as name of the Saviour.

Christ-cross. See **criss-cross**.

christen, vb. trans. [1. krísn; 2. krísn]. O.E. *crīstnian*, 'baptize', fr. *cristen*, 'Christian' (*-en*= Lat. *-ān(us)*, see **-an**) & vbl. suff. *-ian*. **a** To make a Christian by baptism, to baptize; **b** to give a name to in baptism: *to be christened John after one's father*; **c** (extended use) to give a name to generally, give nickname to: *he was christened the Snake by his contemporaries*.

Christendom, n. [1. krísendum; 2. krísəndəm]. O.E. *crīsten* (see prec.) & **-dom**. New formation. The whole body of baptized persons, who acknowledge Christ; all Christians.

christening, n. [1. krísning; 2. krísniŋ], fr. O.E. *crīsten*, 'Christian', & vbl. n. suff. *-ung*, **-ing**. Act and ceremony of administering baptism; baptism itself: *several christenings took place to-day*; *the christening of the infant was duly performed*.

Christhood, n. [1. krīst-hood; 2. kráisthud]. **Christ** & **-hood**. Personality of, fact of being, the Christ.

Christian, n. & adj. [1. krísChan, krístian; 2. kristʃən, krístjən]. Lat. *christiānus*. **Christ** & **-ian**. **1.** n. **a** One who, being baptized, holds the faith of Christ; one who professes, or is assumed to do so, the religion and doctrines taught by Jesus Christ and His Church, and who adheres to the code of conduct enjoined by them; **b** (colloq.) a human being contrasted with one of the lower animals; a decent person; esp. in phr. *why can't you behave like a Christian?* **2.** adj. **a** Belonging to, professing doctrines of, the Church of Christ, or of Christians: *the Christian Church, religion, beliefs* &c., *Christian men, Christian hearts*; **b** characteristic of Christians or Christianity, in accordance with Christ's teachings; humane, charitable, kind: *a true Christian act*.

Christian era, n. The period extending from and beginning with the birth of Christ, distinguished by the letters A.D., *Anno Domini*, 'in the year of our Lord', before the number of the year.

Christianity, n. [1. krìstiániti; 2. krìstiǽniti]. Lat. *Christiānitāt-(em)*. See **Christian** & **-ity**. **a** The religion of Christ and His Church; **b** a particular Christian religious system or organization: *Eastern, Western, Christianity*; **c** state of mind and faith characteristic of a Christian.

christianization, n. [1. krístianīzáshun; 2. krístjənaizéiʃən]. Next word & **-ation**. Act or process of Christianizing.

christianize, vb. trans. [1. krístianīz; 2. krístjənaiz]. **Christian** & **-ize**. To convert to Christianity, imbue with Christian spirit and principles.

Christianlike, adj. [1. kríschanlīk; 2. krístʃənlaik]. Having character and habits of a Christian.

Christian name, n. A name given to a person, by his godparents, at his baptism.

Christian Science, n. Name of a religious system and Church, founded by Mrs. Mary Baker Eddy, in America, based on theory that disease and sin are subjective, and arise from mental error, and that the mind is the sole cause; *Christian Scientist*, believer in Christian Science.

Christian year, n. The year as observed by Christian Churches, divided into seasons and days, in which the chief events of the Saviour's Life on earth, His Birth, Temptation, Crucifixion, Resurrection, and Ascension, and other important events and persons connected with the Church are commemorated.

Christlike, adj. [1. krístlīk; 2. kráistlaik]. Resembling the Saviour in character.

Christmas, n. [1. krísmas; 2. krísməs]. O.E. *Crīstes mæsse*, **Christ** & **Mass (I.)**. Festival of birth of Christ; **a** the actual day, Dec. 25th; or **b** the season from this day till end of year. *Christmas box*, present given at Christmas; *Christmas card*, ornamental card with text or motto, sent out at Christmas; *Christmas Day*, Dec. 25th, on which the festival is celebrated; *Christmas Eve*, Dec. 24th; *Christmas-time, -tide*, season of Christmas.

Christmas rose, n. Ranunculaceous plant, *Helleborus niger*, which blooms round about Christmas-time.

Christmas tree, n. Evergreen tree, usually a fir, supported in upright position in pot or tub indoors, hung with decorative, glittering festoons and other ornaments, and illuminated with candles attached to the branches, presents for the household being suspended on, or grouped round, the tree, which is lighted up on Christmas Eve or Christmas Day.

Christological, adj. [1. kristolójikl; 2. kristəlódžikl]. See next word & **-logical**. Pertaining to Christology.

Christologist, n. [1. kristólojist; 2. kristóladžist]. See next word & **-ist.** Student of, authority on, Christology.

Christology, n. 1. kristóloji; 2. kristóladži]. Gk. *khristo-*. See **Christ** & **-logy.** a Branch of theology which deals with the doctrine of Christ's personality and attributes; b body of doctrine on these.

Christophany, n. [1. kristófani; 2. kristófani]. Gk. *khristo-*, see **Christ**, & *phainein*, 'show, appear', see **phenomenon**, & **-y.** Appearance or all the appearances of Christ after His Resurrection.

Christ's-thorn, n. [1. krísts thórn; 2. kráists þɔ̄n]. Prickly shrub of Palestine, from which the Saviour's crown of thorns is reputed to have been made.

Christy minstrels, n. [1. krísti mínstrelz; 2. krísti mínstrəlz]. From first producer's name. Troupe of singers and banjoists with blackened faces.

chromatic, adj. [1. krōmátik; 2. kroumǽtik]. Gk. *khrōmatikós*, 'relating to colour', used metaphorically, 'florid, elaborate, artificial', & as a technical term in ancient music. See **chrome.** 1. Relating to, containing (bright) colour: *chromatic printing*, from variously coloured blocks. 2. (music) Of notes, not occurring in major or minor key, indicated by sharps, flats, or naturals foreign to the key signature: *chromatic scale.* 3. (biol.) Capable of receiving colour from staining agents.

chromatically, adv. [1. krōmátikali; 2. kroumǽtikəli], fr. prec. & **-al** & **-ly.** In a chromatic manner; in chromatic scale.

chromatics, n. pl. [1. krōmátiks; 2. kroumǽtiks]. See prec. Science of colours.

chromatin, n. [1. krómatin; 2. króumətin], fr. Gk. *khrōmat-*, 'colour'. See **chrome.** Form of protoplasm found in nuclei of cells, capable of being stained.

chromat(o)-, chromo-, prefs. Forms of Gk. *khrōma*, genit. *khrōmatos*, 'colour' &c., used in compounds. See **chrome.**

chromatism, n. [1. krṓmatizm; 2. króumətizəm]. Prec. & **-ism.** a Form of colour-blindness; b abnormal colouration in green parts of plants.

chromatophore, n. [1. krṓmatofōr; 2. króumətəfɔ̄]. See prec. & **-phore.** (biol. and zool.) A pigment cell.

chromatoscope, n. [1. krṓmatoskōp; 2. króumətəskoup]. **chromato-** & **scope.** Device for combining different coloured light-rays so as to form compound colours.

chromatrope, n. [1. krṓmatrōp; 2. króumətroup]. Gk., 'colour wheel'. See **chrome** & **trope.** Instrument for producing kaleidoscopic effects of colour by revolving two coloured disks one in front of the other.

chrome, n. [1. krōm; 2. kroum], also **chrome yellow.** Gk. *khrôma*, 'surface of a body', esp. 'human body, the skin'; then 'colour of the skin, complexion; colour generally'. connected w. Gk. *khroiá*, 'surface of body, skin, body itself, colour of skin, complexion, colour of a thing', also *khroízein*, 'to graze the surface'; *khroós, khrṓs*, 'skin, body, flesh'. All fr. base **gh(e)rew-*, **gh(e)rōw-* &c., allied to base **gherei-* &c., 'to rub', seen in Gk. *khríō*, 'rub, anoint'. See **chrism.** A yellow pigment; the yellow colour. Also *chrome green, red* &c. pigments from various compounds of *chromium.*

chrome steel, n. A fine alloy of steel and chromium.

chromic, adj. [1. krṓmik; 2. króumik]. **chromium** & **-ic.** Of chromium.

chromium, n. [1. krṓmium; 2. króumiəm]. See **chrome.** A greyish white, brittle, metallic element.

chromo-. See **chromato-.**

chromograph, n. [1. krṓmograhf; 2. króuməgrāf], fr. **chromo-** & **graph.** Apparatus for reproducing writing from an impression made by aniline dye on gelatine.

chromo-lithograph, n. [1. krṑmōlíthograhf; 2. kròumoulíþəgrāf]. **chromo-** & **lithograph.** Coloured picture printed from stone.

chromosome, n. [1. krṓmosōm; 2. króuməsoum]. Gk. (mod. coinage), fr. **chromo-**, & *sôma*, 'body', see **somatic.** Minute body developed out of the chromatin, q.v., existing in definite number in the germ-cells of animal species.

chromosphere, n. [1. krṓmosfēr; 2. króuməsfiə]. **chromo-** & **sphere.** The outer incandescent gaseous envelope of the sun, visible at a total eclipse.

chronic, adj. [1. krónik; 2. krɔ́nik]. Gk. *khronikós*, 'concerning time', fr. *khrónos*, 'time', cp. also *khrónios*, 'after a long time, lasting long, late, delaying'; etymol. uncertain. Boisacq hesitatingly suggests base **gher-*, 'wear out, down', an expanded form of wh. appears in **chrism.** a Lasting for a long time, continuing, inveterate; generally in unfavourable sense; b specif. (of disease &c.) one which lasts, with slowly developing symptoms of moderate intensity, contrasted with *acute*; hence c (colloq. slang) tedious, bad: esp. *something chronic.*

chronically, adv. [1. krónikali; 2. krɔ́nikəli]. Prec. & **-al** & **-ly.** In a chronic manner; persistently, continually.

chronicity, n. [1. kronísiti; 2. krɔnísiti]. **chronic** & **-ity.** (med.) State, condition, of being chronic or lasting.

chronicle, n. & vb. trans. [1. krónikl; 2. krɔ́nikl]. M.E. *cronicle*, Fr. *chronique*, through Lat. *chronica*, fr. Gk. *tà khroniká*, 'annals', neut. pl. of *khronikós.* See **chronic.** 1. n. a Systematic historical record of events in order of time; b loosely, any narrative, letter &c. containing news of persons and events &c.; c specif., *Chronicles*, two historical books of the Old Testament. 2. vb. To tell, narrate in a chronicle, to register (events, dates).

chronicler, n. [1. krónikler; 2. krɔ́niklə]. Prec. & **-er.** Writer, compiler, of chronicles.

chronique scandaleuse, n. [1. kronēk skahndalēz; 2. kronīk skādaløz]. Fr., 'scandalous chronicle'. Gossip, more or less scandalous, about people's private affairs and conduct.

chrono-, pref. Form of Gk. *khrónos*, 'time', used in compounds. See **chronic.**

chronogram, n. [1. krónogram; 2. krɔ́nəgræm]. Prec. & **-gram.** Inscription in which certain letters, usually made conspicuous, stand also for Roman numerals, their numerical values added together making the date which it is desired to record.

chronograph, n. [1. krónograhf; 2. krɔ́nəgrāf]. Gk., **chrono-** & **-graph.** Instrument for measuring minute fractions of time, and recording to fraction of a second the precise time at which an event takes place.

chronologic(al), adj. [1. krònolójik(l); 2. krɔ̀nəlɔ́džik(l)]. **chrono-** & **-logy** & **-ic** & **-al.** See **chronology.** According to the principles of chronology; in order of time.

chronologically, adv. [1. krònolójikali; 2. krɔ̀nəlɔ́džikəli]. Prec. & **-ly.** In order of time.

chronologist, n. [1. kronólojist; 2. krənɔ́lədžist]. See prec. & **-ist.** Student of, expert in, science of chronology.

chronologize, vb. trans. [1. kronólojīz; 2. krənɔ́lədžaiz]. **chronology** & **-ize.** To arrange (narrative or list of events &c.) in chronological order.

chronology, n. [1. kronóloji; 2. krənɔ́lədži]. Fr. *chronologie*, fr. Gk. See **chrono-** & **-logy.** a Science of measuring time by fixed periods, or of assigning the precise dates of events; b statement embodying results of study of the dates at which events happened; c a table or list of dates.

chronometer, n. [1. kronómeter; 2. krənɔ́mitə]. See **chrono-** & **meter.** Instrument usually much like a watch in size and shape, for measuring time with particular exactitude, differing from ordinary timepiece in having a device for compensating for changes of temperature.

chronometry, n. [1. kronómetri; 2. krənɔ́mitri]. Prec. & **-y.** Scientific measurement of time.

chronopher, n. [1. krónofer; 2. krɔ́nəfə]. **chrono-** & base **pher-* of Gk. *phérein*, 'to bear', see **-phore.** Electrical apparatus used in broadcasting time signals by wireless.

chronoscope, n. [1. krónoskōp; 2. krɔ́nəskoup]. **chrono-** & **scope.** Instrument for the measurement of minute intervals of time, as of speed of light.

chrysalid, adj. & n. [1. krísalid; 2. krísəlid]. See following word. a adj. Pertaining to a chrysalis; b n. a chrysalis.

chrysalis, n. [1. krísalis; 2. krísəlis]. Gk. *krūsallis*, genit. *-ídos*, 'golden-coloured sheath of butterflies', fr. *khrūsós*, 'gold'; Semit. loan-word fr. Phoen.-Hebr. *hārūz*, cp. Aramaic *hara*, 'yellow'. Membranous sheath within which the larva (caterpillar) of moths, butterflies &c. develops into the final stage, and from which the complete moth, butterfly &c. emerges.

chrysanthemum, n. [1. krisánthemum; 2. krisǽnþiməm]. Gk. *khrūsánthemon*, 'gold flower, corn-marigold', fr. *khrūsós*, 'gold', see prec. word, & *ánthemon*, 'flower', q.v. under **anther, anthology.** One of a large number of species of perennial flowering plants, some of which are specially cultivated for their elegance of form and richness and variety of colour; they have long slender petals, in some varieties sparsely set, in others very thickly, so that the bloom resembles the head of a mop, and attains 9 or 10 inches in diameter.

chryselephantine, adj. [1. krìselefántīn; 2. krìselifǽntain]. Gk. *khrūsós*, 'gold', see prec. words, & *elephántinos*, 'made of ivory', fr. *eléphas*, 'ivory, elephant'. See **elephant.** Overlaid with gold and ivory; of a type of ancient Greek sculpture, made of wood upon which plates of gold were affixed, for the drapery and hair, of ivory for the flesh.

chrysoberyl, n. [1. krísōbéril; 2. krísoubéril]. Gk. *khrūso-*, 'gold', see **chrysalis**, & *bérullos*, see **beryl.** Semi-precious stone used in jewellery; generally yellow, green, or brown.

chrysolite, n. [1. krísolīt; 2. krísəlait]. Gk. *khrūsólithos*, fr. *khrūso-*, 'gold', see **chrysalis**, & *líthos*, 'stone', see **lithia, lithotomy** &c. Olive-coloured semi-precious stone; called also *olivine* and *peridot.*

chrysoprase, n. [1. krísoprāz; 2. krísəpreiz], fr. Gk. *khrūsóprasos*, fr. *khrūso-*, 'gold', see **chrysalis**, & *práson*, 'leek', cogn. w. Lat. *porrum* 'leek'. An apple-green variety of chalcedony.

chthonian, -ic, adj. [1. thónian, thónik; 2. þóuniən, þɔ́nik], fr. Gk. *khthónios*, 'of the earth', fr. *khthonós*, genit. of *khthṓn*, 'the earth'. See **autochthon.** Of, pertaining to, the gods of the earth or of the underworld, as contrasted with those of Olympus, usually applied to the more primitive deities of ancient Greece &c.

chub, n. [1. chub; 2. tʃab]. Origin unknown. Freshwater fish of carp family, about 15 inches long, with thick body and coarse flesh, common in Europe and Asia. Also and earlier called **chevin**, which is of French origin.

chubbiness, n. [1. chúbines; 2. tʃábinis]. **chubby** & **-ness.** Condition of being chubby.

chubby, adj. [1. chúbi; 2. tʃábi]. Etymol. doubtful; perh. fr. **chub.** (of persons) Fat, round and short, stumpy; esp. *chubby cheeks, face*, plump and healthy-looking.

chuck (I.), vb. trans. [1. chuk; 2. tʃak]. Earlier *chock*, fr. Fr. *choquer.* 1. a To jerk something out of the hand, throw, hurl; b (fig.) to discontinue some action or task; give up, abandon, persons: *to chuck it*; *to chuck one's friends.* See *chuck up, away.* Phr. *chuck it*, stop making a nuisance of yourself. 2. Give a gentle, glancing, upward blow, playful or amorous: esp. *to chuck under the chin.* 3. (followed by various preps. or advs.) *Chuck away*, dispense thoughtlessly; to lose, waste (time, money, one's opportunities, &c.) *Chuck out*, a specif., to eject forcibly from a room, theatre &c.; **b** (colloq.) throw out a bill in parliament, or a motion at a meeting. *Chuck up*, abandon, relinquish: *chuck up one's job, salary* &c. Phr. *chuck up the sponge*, (fr. boxing-ring) indicate that one is giving in, abandoning hope of success &c.

chuck (**II.**), n., fr. prec. Action of chucking in various senses. Phr. (vulgar and colloq.) *to give a person the chuck*, dismiss suddenly, generally with ignominy, expel, break off relations with.

chuck (**III.**), vb. intrans. & interj. Imitative. **a** To make a clicking noise with the tongue as to a horse &c.; **b** *chuck, chuck!*, cry made to attract attention of, or call, animals or poultry.

chuck (**IV.**), n. Same as **chock**, n. Device for holding a tool in a lathe, or for holding wood which is to be turned, or cut, in the desired position.

chuck-farthing, n. Game in which small coins were chucked at a mark, and then into a hole, the successful player keeping those which he got into the hole.

chuckle, vb. intrans. & n. [1. chúkl; 2. tʃákl]. Imitative. **1.** vb. **a** To laugh softly, esp. in a way indicative of quiet mirth, satisfaction, or exultation: *to chuckle at, over, something*; *chuckle to oneself*; **b** (fig.) to feel satisfaction, have sense of triumph, gloat: *he must be chuckling at his success.* **2.** n. Low, suppressed laugh of satisfaction or triumph.

chuckle-head, n., fr. obs. *chuckle*, 'stupid, thick'. See **chuck** (**IV.**). A stupid, dull, person.

chuckle-headed, adj. Prec. & **-ed**. Muddle-headed, having a confused mind which leads to misapprehension of facts, and consequent foolish action.

chuddar, n. [1. chúdar; 2. tʃádə]. Hind. *chadar.* A square sheet of cloth worn in India by women as a shawl or head covering.

chukker, n. [1. chúker; 2. tʃákə]. Hind., 'a round'. One of the periods of play into which a game of polo is divided.

chum, n. & vb. intrans. [1. chum; 2. tʃam]. Origin unknown; first in late 17th cent. **1.** n. **a** An intimate, particular friend; **b** (in colonies) used for a close associate, partner, or participant in some undertaking or piece of business; **c** one who shares room or dwelling-house; esp. of young men at universities. **2.** vb. *Chum with, together*, to live together, share common rooms and life; *chum up* (*with*), to become friendly, or intimate, with.

chummy, adj. [1. chúmi; 2. tʃámi]. Prec. & **-y**. Friendly, intimate (said esp. of two persons).

chump, n. [1. chump; 2. tʃamp]. Etymol. doubtful. **a** A thick block of wood; **b** thick piece of meat, esp. mutton: *chump chop*; **c** (fig.) thick-headed, stupid person, a fool.

chunk (**I.**), n. [1. chungk; 2. tʃaŋk]. Etymol. doubtful. Thick, solid block, or lump, clumsily cut piece, e.g. of *wood, meat* &c.

chunk (**II.**), vb. intrans. Imitative. To make a thumping noise, as of machinery.

chunking, adj. & n. [1. chúngking; 2. tʃáŋkiŋ]. **chunk** & **-ing**. **a** adj., fr. **chunk** (**I.**) Large, thick, solid, and clumsy: (colloq.) *a chunking piece of beef*; **b** n., fr. **chunk** (**II.**), noise made by slow movement of heavy machinery.

chupatty, n. [1. choopáti; 2. tʃupǽti]. Anglo-Indian, Hind. *chapātī*, 'unleavened bread'. Flat cake, or scone, of flour and water, the native bread.

chuprassie, n. [1. choóprási; 2. tʃuprǽsi]. Anglo-Indian, fr. Hind. *chaprāsī*, 'bearer of a *chaprās*', or badge-plate, inscribed with the name of the office to which bearer is attached. The *chaprāsī* is an office-messenger, bearing such a badge on a cloth or leather belt. The term belongs to the Bengal Presidency. (Yule and Burnell.)

church (**I.**), n. [1. chěrch; 2. tʃʌtʃ]. O.E. *ċiriċe*, M.E. *chirche, churche*, O.H.G. *chirihha*, O. Du. & O.S. *kirika*, O.N. *kirkja* (borrowed fr. O.E.). All these are fr. an early W. Gmc. loan fr. Gk. *kuriakón*, 'Lord's house'; cp. *kuriakḗ*, 'Lord's Day', fr. *kúrios*, 'lord, master', q.v. under **kyrie**. **1.** **a** A building specially built, and set apart for the conduct of public religious worship; now used only of building devoted to Christian worship; **b** specif., (in England) a building devoted to the services of the Church of England, whose incumbent is a priest of this church, contrasted with a *chapel*, used by other denominations; **c** religious service or worship conducted in a church: *church begins at 11 o'clock*; *to attend church.* Phr. *at church*, in act of attending service. **2.** **a** Formal organization for the maintenance and dissemination of religious truth, having a definite form of government and various orders of officers, whose main functions are the preservation and teaching of sound doctrine in matters of faith and morals, the guardianship of traditions and mysteries, and the due performance of prescribed rites and ceremonies. The word is chiefly applied to the Church of Christ: *the Western, Eastern, Church* &c.; but is also extended to the religious organization of the Hebrews: *the Jewish Church*; **b** specif., the organization of the Established Church in England or of Scotland; **c** organization of other Christian bodies: *the Free Churches*; *the Presbyterian Church* &c. **3.** **a** The body of persons who are members of any given church; **b** more generally the whole body of Christians throughout the world. **4.** The clerical profession: *to enter the Church*, take orders, become a clergyman; *the Church, the Law, and other liberal professions.*

church (**II.**), vb. trans., fr. prec. **a** To bring into, make a member of, the Church, restore to privileges of a member of the Church; **b** specif., to perform the ceremony of *churching* a woman in church, who comes to render thanks for safe delivery from childbirth: *the mother was churched and her baby christened on the same day.*

church door, n. Specif., the outer door of main entrance to a church, to which, by law, certain public notices have to be affixed as a means of publication.

churching, n. [1. chěrching; 2. tʃʌtʃiŋ]. The ceremony performed over a woman who has given birth to a child, called in Prayer Book, *the churching of women.* See **church** (**II.**).

churchman, n. [1. chěrchman; 2. tʃʌtʃmən]. **a** An ecclesiastic, bishop, priest, or deacon (archaic); **b** (in England) a member of the Established Church as distinct from a dissenter: *a good churchman.*

church rate, n. Rate assessed on houses or lands for maintenance of the church of the parish.

church scot, n. See **scot** (**I.**). Contribution towards support of clergy formerly collected from parishioners.

church text, n. (typog.) Old English, or black-letter, type, so called because this form of lettering was used in ecclesiastical work on church windows, monuments &c.

churchwarden, n. [1. chěrchwórden; 2. tʃʌtʃwɔ́d(ə)n]. **church** & **warden**. **a** One of two officers appointed annually, for one year, in each parish, one nominated by the incumbent: *rector's, vicar's, churchwarden*; the other elected at Easter Vestry; their duties are to be responsible for upkeep of fabric of church, excluding the chancel, and to take charge, for benefit of parish, of monies collected in church other than *offertories*; **b** clay tobacco pipe with long stem.

churchwoman, n. [1. chěrchwooman; 2. tʃʌtʃwumən]. Woman member of Established Church, in contrast to a dissenter.

churchy, adj. [1. chěrchi; 2. tʃʌtʃi]. **church** & **-y**. (colloq., of persons) Devoted to the Church, its hierarchy, forms, and ceremonies; obsessed by these, given to dwelling upon them in and out of season; inclined to exalt the authority of Established Church in distinction to that of Nonconformist religion.

churchyard, n. [1. chěrchyard; 2. tʃʌtʃjád]. **church** & **yard**. Enclosed piece of consecrated ground surrounding a church, used for burials, as contrasted with *cemetery*. *N.B.* Accentuation of *St. Paul's Churchyard* [1. sant páwlz chěrchyárd; 2. sən pɔ̄lz tʃʌtʃjád].

churinga, n. [1. chooríngga; 2. tʃuríŋgə]. Native Australian word. Totemistic amulet of the Australian aborigines.

churl, n. [1. chěrl; 2. tʃʌl]. O.E. *ċeorl*, 'man of low degree', contrasted w. *eorl*, 'nobleman', also 'man, male', M.E. *cherl, chŭrl*, fr. wh. latter, Western, type the present-day form is derived; O.H.G. *karal*, M.H.G. *karl*, Mod. Germ. *kerl*, 'fellow', &c., influenced by L. Germ. *kerel.* The origin is obscure. **a** Peasant, rustic, bumpkin (archaic or obs.); **b** man of illiberal, ungracious manners and character; a surly, rude, mean, cantankerous fellow.

churlish, adj. [1. chěrlish; 2. tʃʌliʃ]. Prec. & **-ish**. Boorish, ungracious, lacking in courtesy; selfish, mean.

churlishly, adv. Prec. & **-ly**. In a churlish manner.

churn (**I.**), n. [1. chěrn; 2. tʃʌn]. O.E. *ċyren*, fr. **ċiren*, M.E. *chirne.* The Scand. languages have cognates, O.N. *kirna* &c. Etymol. doubtful. Some suggest relationship w. **corn** & **kernel**. Possibly connected w. O.E. *ċierran*, 'to turn', in wh. case the O.E. form wd. be for **ċierin*, fr. **ċearin*, fr. **ċærin-*, fr. W. Gmc. base **kar-*. Could this have remote relationship w. base in Lat. *ger-ere*, 'carry' &c., q.v. under **gerent**? See **char** (**I.**). Contrivance for making butter, consisting of a vessel in which cream is shaken, beaten, or stirred.

churn (**II.**), vb. trans. & intrans., fr. prec. **1.** trans. **a** To agitate (cream) in a churn in butter-making; **b** (fig. or extended use) to stir, agitate, violently, esp. liquid of any kind, until froth or foam is formed: *the wind churned the waters to foam.* **2.** intrans. To make butter by using a churn: *we churn twice a week.*

churning, n. [1. chěrning; 2. tʃʌniŋ]. Prec. & **-ing**. **a** Act of using a churn; process of making butter by this means; **b** (also in fig. use), agitation, violent stirring up of water &c.

chute, n. [1. shoot; 2. ʃut]. Fr., 'a fall'. Confused w. **shoot** (**II.**). **a** Channel by which water falls suddenly to a lower level; **b** a steep, inclined, hollow track down a hill, by which logs descend to the valley; any inclined slope or passage for sliding heavy things down.

chutney, n. [1. chútni; 2. tʃátni]. Hind. *chatnī.* A strong, hot, sweet-tasting pickle or relish, made of fruits and condiments.

chyle, n. [1. kīl; 2. kail]. Gk. *khūlós*, 'juice', connected w. Gk. *kéō*, 'pour', fr. **khew-*. Cp. Gk. *khúsis*, 'effusion', Lat. *fūdi*, perf. of *fundo*, 'pour', & Gmc. base **geut*, **gut-* &c., 'pour', as in O.E. *ġēotan*, q.v. under **ingot**. A lymphatic juice by means of which fatty substance is passed into the blood-stream.

chyme, n. [1. kīm; 2. kaim]. Gk. *khumós*, 'juice', fr. base *khu-*, 'pour', as in **chyle**, w. different formative suff. Food in process of digestion in the intestines.

chymist, n. Archaic, obsolesc. form of **chemist**.

ciborium, n. [1. sibórium; 2. sibɔ́riəm]. Lat., 'drinking-cup', fr. Gk. *kibṓrion*, 'fruit of Egyptian water-lily; cup made from, or having form of, this fruit'. Origin very obscure. The word is not found in Egyptian. Boisacq suggests tentatively, a connexion w. Gk. *kibōtós*, 'box, chest', the origin of wh. is equally doubtful. Some have proposed to derive it fr. a Semitic source; but the etymol. of both words remains a mystery. Is later association w. Lat. *cibārium*, neut. of *cibārius*, 'pertaining to food', fr. *cibus*, 'food' &c., possible? The word is only in ecclesiastical use, or in reference to church architecture. The meanings are somewhat highly differentiated; presumably the cup, or chalice, is the starting-point, & the other meanings are secondary, & associated w. this. **1.** Covered chalice for reserving the

Blessed Sacrament. **2.** Pendant tabernacle or receptacle for the pyx, or vessel in which the Host is kept. **3. a** Canopy over altar in early churches, supported on four columns, and furnished with curtains which were drawn at the consecration, cp. *baldachin*; **b** the arch below which the altar stands.

cicada, n. [1. sikáda ; 2. sikéidə]. Lat. *cicāda*, 'cricket', cp. Span. & Port. *cigarra*, Ital. *cicala*, Fr. *cigale*; perh. connected w. Lat. *calāre*, 'call out', cogn. w. Gk. *kaléō*, 'call, summon'. This base is dealt w. under **clamour, claim** &c. See also **low (I.)**. If *cicāda* belongs to this group it shows change fr. *l* to *d*, an inversion of that in *lacrima* for older *dacruma*. See **lacrimatory**. A kind of homopterous insect with transparent wings and a loud chirp.

cicatrice, cicatrix, n. [1. síkatris, sikátriks; 2. síkətris, sikéitriks]. Lat. *cicātrix*, 'scar', the origin of wh. is not satisfactorily explained. **a** A mark left on skin by a wound when it has healed; a scar; **b** (bot.) scar on stem &c. of a plant, when something growing from it (e.g. a leaf) has fallen away.

cicatricial, cicatricose, adj. [1. sìkatríshal, sikátrikōs; 2. sìkətríʃəl, sikǽtrikous]. Prec. & **-al, -ose**. Having the form of, resembling, a cicatrice or scar.

cicatrization, n. [1. sìkatrīzáshun; 2. sìkətraizéiʃən]. See next word & **-ation**. Formation of a scar, healing up of a wound.

cicatrize, vb. trans. & intrans. [1. síkatrīz; 2. síkətràiz]. Lat. *cicatr-*, see **cicatrix**, & Gk. suff. **-ize**. **a** trans. To cause to heal, make new skin to form over wound; **b** intrans. (of a wound) to heal, form a scar.

cicely, also **seseli**, n. [1. sísili; 2. sísili]. Lat., fr. Gk. *séselis*, influenced by Engl. female name. Wild umbelliferous plant of various kinds, e.g. Sweet Cicely, *Myrrhis odorata*.

cicerone, n., pl. **ciceroni** [1. chicheróne, -ē; 2. tʃitʃəróuni, -ī]. Ital., 'a guide', in derision fr. *Cicero*, the great orator; form, as usual in Ital., derived fr. Lat. abl. A guide, one who leads sightseers round, and discourses on the history &c. of the places and objects of interest visited.

Ciceronian, adj. [1. sìserónian; 2. sìsəróuniən]. See prec. & **-ian**. (of liter. and oratorical style) Resembling that of Cicero, eloquent.

cicisbeo, n. [1. chichizbáō; 2. tʃitʃizbéiou]. Ital. The professed lover of a married woman.

-cide, suff. **a** Lat. *-cīda*, as in *frātricīda*, 'murderer of a brother'; also **b** *-cīdium*, 'murder', as in *parricīdium*, 'murder of one's father or parents'; fr. form of *caedere*, 'strike, kill', used in composition, cp. *occīdere*, 'strike down, slay'. No distinction is made in Engl. in form between the two functions, so that *regicide* means both 'murder of a king', & 'the murderer of a king'.

cider, n. [1. síder; 2. sáidə]. M.E. *cyder, syder, sicer*, fr. O. Fr. *cisdre, sisdre*, earlier *sisre*, fr. L. Lat. *cicera*, 'strong drink', fr. Gk. *síkera*, fr. Heb. *shēkar*, 'strong drink'. Drink made of fermented apple-juice.

cider-cup, n. Summer drink made of a mixture of cider, liqueur, soda-water &c.

cider-press, n. Apparatus for crushing apples and extracting the juice to make cider.

ciel, cieling. See **ceil, ceiling.**

cigar, n. [1. sigár; 2. sigā́]. Earlier (18th cent.) *segar*, Span. *cigarro*, supposed to be fr. *cigarra*, 'grass-hopper', fr. fancied resemblance to body of this insect. See **cicada.** Cylindrical shaped roll of tobacco-leaves, for smoking.

cigarette, n. [1. sìgarét; 2. sìgərét]. Fr., dimin. of **cigar.** A small roll of finely cut tobacco, enclosed in thin sheet of paper.

cigarette-holder, n. Small tube of meerschaum, amber, ivory &c., one end of wh. is fitted so as to hold a cigarette, while the other is held in the mouth.

cigar-shaped, adj. Shaped like a thin cylinder with tapering ends.

cilia, n. [1. sília; 2. síliə]. Lat. pl. of *cilium*, 'eyelid, eye-brow'. Perh. fr. same base as *cēlare*, 'hide'. See **conceal. 1.** The eyebrows, eyelashes. **2.** Fine hairs on plants and on surface of certain kinds of simple animal organisms.

ciliary, adj. [1. síliari; 2. síliəri]. See prec. & **-ary.** Pertaining to the eyelashes, or eyelids, or to hair-like appendages in animals or plants.

ciliate, ciliated, adj. [1. síliat, síliāted; 2. síliət, silieitid]. See **cilia** & **-ate.** (bot. and zool.) Possessing cilia.

cilice, n. [1. silis; 2. sílis]. The word occurs as *cilic* in O.E. & means 'hair-cloth', but in so far as it exists at all in Engl. at the present time, it is direct fr. Fr. & fr. Lat. *Cilicium*, 'cloth of Cilician goat's hair, used by soldiers & seamen', & this is fr. Gk. *Kilíkion*, from name of the country. **a** Cloth woven of hair; **b** a garment of hair-cloth.

Cimmerian, adj. [1. simérian; 2. simériən], fr. Lat. *Cimmerii*, fr. Gk. *Kimmérioi*, a mythical people mentioned by Homer, who dwelt in the farthest West, & were supposed to live in perpetual mists & darkness. For suff., see **-an.** In Phr. *Cimmerian darkness*, one which is profound and continual.

cinch, n. & vb. trans. [1. sinch; 2. sin(t)ʃ]. Span. *cincha*, vb. *cinchar*, 'girdle, girth', fr. Lat. *cingula*, 'girdle, belt', fr. base *cing-* as in *cingere*, 'gird'. See **cincture. 1.** n. **a** Girth of a saddle; **b** (Am. slang) a firm hold on anything; certainty. **2.** vb. trans. To tighten (the girths of a saddle).

cinchona, n. [1. sinkóna; 2. sinkóunə]. Named after Countess (or Duchess) of Chinchon, who introduced the drug into Spain in 1638. **a** A South American evergreen tree, from which come quinine and Peruvian bark; **b** the bark of this tree; **c** the drug obtained from it.

cinchonaceous, adj. [1. sìnkonáshus; 2. sìnkənéiʃəs]. Prec. & **-aceous.** Pertaining to cinchona.

cinchonism, n. [1. sínkonizm; 2. sínkənizəm]. See prec. & **-ism.** Physical condition caused by overdose of cinchona, characterized by temporary deafness and giddiness.

cincture (I.), n. [1. síngkchur; 2. síŋktʃə], fr. Lat. *cinctūra*, 'a girdle', formed fr. *cinct-(um)*, P.P. type of *cingere*, 'to gird, bind round'. Cogn. w. Scrt. *káñcate*, 'he binds', & *káñcī*, 'girdle'; according to Walde, Lat. *cancelli*, 'lattice' (see **cancel, chancel** &c.), is distinct fr. this base. **1.** A belt, girdle; specif., band or cord of stuff or silk, worn by ecclesiastics over the alb, with proper colour for the season and having tassels of gold, green, violet, or black according to rank. **2.** Something that encircles, encloses; specif. (archit.) a ring, of carved stone &c. round a column.

cincture (II.), vb. trans., fr. prec. To put a girdle, or enclosure, round.

cinder, n. [1. sínder; 2. síndə]. O.E. *sinder*, 'cinder, dross', M.E. *sindir, cyndir*, O.H.G. *sintar*, the etymol. of wh. is not traced. *Cinder* has been associated owing to similarity of form & meaning w. Fr. *cendre*, fr. Lat. *ciner-(em)*, w. wh. it has nothing to do. See **cinerary.** Hard, crumbly substance which remains after the inflammable quality of coal, coke, wood has been destroyed by burning but when they have not yet been reduced to ashes. Phr. *to burn to a cinder* (of food), cook too much, render black, dry up.

Cinderella, n. [1. sinderéla; 2. sindərélə]. Lit. 'little girl who cleans the hearth'; **cinder** & dimin. suff. *-ella*; cp. Fr. *Cendrillon*, heroine of well-known fairy-tale. A beauty in humble disguise or surroundings.

cinderella-dance, n. Small, informal dancing-party which ends at midnight. So called from the fairy story in which the heroine's fine clothes turned to rags at midnight.

cinder-path, n. A path laid with small cinders, tightly rolled down, used as running-track, or in a garden.

cinder-sifter, n. A sieve for separating cinders from ashes.

cindery, adj. [1. sínderi; 2. síndəri]. **cinder** & **-y. a** Resembling cinders; **b** full of cinders.

cinema, n. [1. sínema; 2. sínimə]. Colloq. form of **cinematograph.** Usual name for theatre in which moving pictures are shown.

cinematograph, kinematograph, n. now usually [1. sìnemátograhf; 2. sìnimǽtəgrāf]; the attempt to establish [kainímətəgrāf] failed. Newly coined word fr. Gk. *kīnēmat-*, 'motion', see **kinematic**, & **graph.** Literally 'motion picture'. Apparatus by means of which a continuous series of photographs taken every few fractions of a second, and thus recording the continuous series of positions involved in any natural or mechanical movement, are highly magnified and thrown by a strong light upon a screen. The result is a picture in which all the movements of living beings, of the sea, of objects shaken by the wind, and the movements of machines &c., appear to be reproduced in a perfectly natural manner.

cineraria, n. [1. sìneráría; 2. sìnəréəriə]. Lat. *cinerārius*, 'of ashes', fr. *cinis*, q.v. under **cinerary.** So called fr. colour of down on the leaves. A genus of South African plants of the aster family, with brightly coloured flowers, cultivated in England, esp. as hothouse plant.

cinerarium, n. [1. sìnerárium; 2. sìnəréəriəm]. Lat., fr. *cinis*, 'ash'. See next word. (Rom. archaeol.) A recess in a sepulchral monument &c., for a cinerary urn.

cinerary, adj. [1. sínerari; 2. sínirəri]. Lat. *cinerārius*, 'of ashes, belonging to ashes', fr. *cinis*, acc. *ciner-em*, 'ash', cogn. w. Gk. *kónis*, 'dust, dust of ashes'. Perh. related to Gk. *knên*, 'scratch, scrape'. Others connect w. the base *(*s*)*kaid-*, 'shine, glow' as in *caelum*, 'heaven', q.v. under **ceiling**, in wh. case *cinis* meant, not primarily 'dust', but 'glowing ash'. Pertaining to, holding, ashes; *cinerary urn*, one in which the ashes of the cremated dead are preserved.

cinereous, adj. [1. sinérius; 2. siníəriəs], fr. prec., Lat. *cinereus*, 'ashy', fr. *ciner-(em)*. See **cinerary.** Of the colour of ashes, ashen grey.

Cingalese, adj. & n. [1. singgaléz; 2. siŋgəlíz]. Scrt. *sinhalas.* **a** adj. Belonging to Ceylon; **b** n., (i.) native of; (ii.) native language of, Ceylon.

cingulum, n. [1. sínggūlum; 2. síŋgjuləm]. Lat., 'girdle'. See **cincture.** A girdle or belt; **a** (eccles.) a cincture, q.v.; **b** (surg.) belt.

cinnabar, n. & adj. [1. sínabàr; 2. sínəbā]. M.E. *cinnaber*, Lat. *cinnabaris*, fr. Pers. *zinjarf*, 'red lead'. **1.** n. **a** A reddish mineral substance, sulphide of mercury; **b** the red pigment obtained from cinnabar; vermilion. **2.** adj. Having colour of cinnabar, vermilion coloured.

cinnamon, n. & adj. [1. sínamun; 2. sínəmən]. Low Lat. *cinnamōmum*, fr. Gk. *kinámōmon*, fr. a Heb. form, wh. according to Skeat is not of Semitic origin but found in Malay. **1.** n. **a** Spice made from bark of a Ceylon laurel; **b** the tree itself; **c** the colour of cinnamon, yellowish brown. **2.** adj. Having the colour of cinnamon; also *cinnamon-coloured.*

cinnamon-stone, n. Orange-brown variety of garnet.

cinq(ue), n. [1. singk; 2. siŋk]. Fr., fr. Lat. *quinque.* See **quinqu(e)-.** The five on dice, or in cards.

cinquecentist, n. [1. chìngkwichéntist; 2. tʃiŋkwitʃéntist]. Ital. *cinquecentisto.* An Italian artist of the cinquecento.

cinquecento, n. [1. chìngkwichéntō; 2. tʃiŋkwi(t)ʃéntou]. Ital., 'five hundred', but here used for 'fifteen hundred', *mil*, 'thousand', being omitted. Cp. Fr. *mil cinq cents.* Italian art of later 16th cent., characterized by return to classical models.

cinquefoil, n. [1. síngkfoil; 2. síŋkfɔil]. O. Fr., fr. Lat. *quinque-folium*, fr. *quinque*, '5', & *folium*, 'leaf'. See **quinque** & **folio. a** (bot.) Plant of Potentilla genus, the leaves of which are composed of five leaflets; b (archit.) ornament with five cusps in a circular window, or arch &c.

cinque-pace, n. [1. síngkpās; 2. síŋkpeis]. See **cinque** & **pace** (I.). Dance of lively character, also called *galliard*, the rhythm of which is regulated by five beats.

Cinque Ports, n. [1. síngk ports; 2. síŋk pɔ̄ts]. A group of towns (originally five) on the south-east coast of England, which enjoyed certain privileges on condition of providing warships.

cipher, cypher (I.), n. [1. sífer; 2. sáifə]. M.E. *siphre*, O. Fr. *cifre*, Mod. Fr. *chifre*, 'figure'; fr. Span. *cifra*, 'O', fr. Arab. *sifr*, 'empty thing, a cipher'. **1. a** (in numerical notation) The symbol 0, representing zero; the absence of number; when placed to the right of a figure it multiplies it by 10; when placed to the right of the decimal point, it divides the following figures by 10; **b** (fig.) a person or thing of no importance or value. **2. a** A method of secret writing, intelligible only to those having a key to it; **b** a key to a particular form of secret writing. **3.** A monogram, two or more letters interlaced to form one character. **4.** An organ-note that continues to sound when pressure is removed from the key, owing to a faulty valve.

cipher, cypher (II.), vb. trans. & intrans., fr. prec. **A.** trans. **1.** To calculate, work arithmetically (also *cipher out*). **2.** To write in secret writing. **B.** intrans. **1.** To do arithmetic, work with figures. **2.** (of an organ-note) To sound, though not pressed.

cipolin, n. [1. sípolin; 2. sípəlin]. Ital. *cipolino*, dimin. of *cipolla*, 'onion', fr. Lat. *cēpa*, *caepa*, 'onion'. See **chive**. Green Italian marble, with greenish and white streaks.

circa, adv. & prep. [1. sérka; 2. sʌ́kə]. Lat. 'round about, near to, nearly'. See **circum-** & **circus**. About, approximately. Sometimes abbreviated as *c*.

Circe, n. [1. sérsē; 2. sʌ́si]. Gk. *Kírkē*. **a** (Gk. mythol.) Name of a sorceress, in the *Odyssey*, who changed men into swine; **b** (by transf.) a temptress, dangerously fascinating woman.

Circean, adj. [1. sersēan; 2. sʌsíən]. Prec. & **-an.** Having Circe's qualities, dangerously fascinating; pleasing but noxious: *Circean charms, spells* &c.

circinate, adj. [1. sérsināt; 2. sʌ́sineit]. Lat. *circinātum*, P.P. of *circināre*, 'make round', cp. *circinus*, 'pair of compasses', Gk. *kírkinos*, & Lat. *circus*, 'ring, hoop, circle'. See **circus.** (bot., of leaves, esp. of ferns &c.) Having the tip rolled up inwards, so that this forms centre of the round.

circle (I.), n. [1. sérkl; 2. sʌ́kl]. Lat. *circulus*, 'small ring, circular figure, circle'. Dimin. of **circus.** The O.E. borrowed the word as *čircul*, but this wd. give *chircle* in Mod. Engl. & has nothing to do w. the present form; the M.E. *cercle* is fr. Fr.; so that *circle* is a new, direct borrowing fr. the Lat. **1.** (geom.) **a** Space enclosed by a curved line, every point in which is equidistant from the centre; perfectly round plane figure. Phr. *to square the circle*, to find a square of the same area as a given circle; hence fig. to attempt the impossible; **b** circle on surface of a sphere, e.g. of earth: *Arctic Circle*. **2.** An object similar in shape to a circle, **a** a ring; **b** series of objects arranged to form a circle: *a circle of trees*; *to dance in a circle*; *stone circle*, (archaeol.) prehistoric ring of upright stones; **c** specif., parts of a theatre: *dress circle*; *upper circle* &c. **3.** A number, group, of people associated, bound together, **a** by common interests, occupations &c.: *a large circle of friends*; **b** by inclusion in the same social class: *the upper circles* &c. **4.** A complete system or series; recurring succession of events &c.; cycle: *the circle of the seasons*; *circle of the sciences*. Phr. *to argue in a circle*, to assume the conclusion as a proof of the premises, and to use the premises to prove the conclusion; *vicious circle*, (i.) argument in a circle; (ii.) a succession of events, reacting upon each other. **5.** (fig., of non-material things, as ideas, experiences) Range, reach, what has come within and is bounded by, a person's knowledge: *a wide circle of interests, ideas*.

circle (II.), vb. trans. & intrans., fr. prec. **1.** trans. To go right round, pass round: *the moon circles the earth*. **2.** intrans. To move, fly in a circle (of birds, aeroplanes); also *circle round*; specif. **a** (of wine &c.) be passed round; **b** (mil., of a line of cavalry) wheel, swing round.

circlet, n. [1. sérklet; 2. sʌ́klit]. Dimin. of **circle** (I.); see **-et.** A small circle, ring, fillet: *circlet of flowers*; (poet.) *small circlet of gold*, finger ring.

circlewise, adv. [1. sérklwīz; 2. sʌ́klwaiz]. **circle** & **-wise.** In a circle, forming a ring.

circuit, n. [1. sérkit; 2. sʌ́kit]. Lat. *circuitus*, also *circumitus*, 'going round, revolution, path traversed in going round, detour'; fr. P.P. type of *circu(m)īre*, **circum-**, 'round', & *īre*, 'go'. For base *i-*, 'go', see **itinerant.** **1.** A going round, going from place to place; space traversed in such a journey: *a country postman has a long circuit*; *the circuit of the globe*, distance, journey round. **2.** Specif. **a** the series of towns at which Assizes are held: *Judges often go on circuit*; *the Northern Circuit*; **b** the barristers who practise on a particular circuit: *he joined the Western Circuit*.

circuitous, adj. [1. serkûitus; 2. səkjûitəs]. Lat. *circuitus*, P.P. of *circuīre*, 'to go round', & fig., 'to express by circumlocution'. See prec. & **-ous.** (lit. and fig.) Round about, leading to a given point, or position, by devious paths, reverse of direct: *a circuitous route, mode of approach* &c.; also, *circuitous argument, mode of reasoning* &c.

circuitously, adv. Prec. & **-ly.** In a circuitous, indirect manner; by a roundabout route.

circuitousness, n. See prec. & **-ness.** The quality of being circuitous; habit of thinking, arguing, in circuitous manner.

circular (I.), adj. [1. sérkūlar; 2. sʌ́kjulə]. Lat., fr. *circulus*, 'circle' &c., & adj. suff. **-ar.** See **circle** & **circus.** **1.** Round, having form, being in form, of a circle; forming part of a circle. **2. a** Moving in a circle, turning round; **b** traversing, or involving passing round, given route, or circuit: *circular tour*; *circular ticket*, one issued for such a tour; **c** passing, travelling in a circle completely round an area: *circular railway*, one running round a town &c. **3.** (of documents) Addressed and sent round to a number of persons: *circular letter*; *circular note*, one used by travellers, which can be exchanged for cash at any of several places, esp. different foreign banks.

circular (II.), n., fr. prec. Document, generally a tradesman's advertisement, or a notice of any kind, of which many copies are issued at the same time and sent round to a number of people.

circularity, n. [1. serkūláriti; 2. sʌkjulǽriti]. See prec. & **-ity.** The state of being circular in shape; roundness.

circularize, vb. trans. [1. sérkūlarīz; 2. sʌ́kjuləraiz]. **circular** (II.) & **-ize.** To send circulars to; give notice to, by means of circulars.

circularly, adv. [1. sérkūlarli; 2. sʌ́kjuləli]. **circular** (I.) & **-ly.** In a circular manner, with a circular motion.

circulate, vb. intrans. & trans. [1. sérkūlāt; 2. sʌ́kjuleit], fr. P.P. of Lat. *circulāri*, 'form a circle', fr. *circulus*, 'circle'. See **circle** (I.). **A.** intrans. **1.** To move, pass round, or by, a certain way and return to starting-point: *blood circulates in the body*. **2.** (of material and non-material things) To move, pass freely, from one person or place to another, pass round, change hands, pass from hand to hand in a company: *the wine circulated freely*; *news, rumour, circulates rapidly*; *when trade is good money circulates*. **3.** (maths., of decimal) To recur. **B.** trans. (of material and non-material things) To send round, cause to circulate, pass from one person or place to another: *to circulate the wine, the bottle*; *to circulate a report*.

circulating library, n. [1. sérkūlāting líbrari; 2. sʌ́kjuleitiŋ láibrəri]. **a** Institution which hires or lends out books, to be kept for a specified time, to a number of readers in succession; **b** the collection of books so lent; **c** the building or apartment where the books are stored, and whence they are borrowed.

circulation, n. [1. serkūláshun; 2. sʌkjuléiʃən]. **circulate** & **-ion.** **1.** Process of circulating; **a** specif., flow of the blood through the vessels of the body, or of sap through veins of plants: *Harvey discovered the circulation of the blood*; *to have a good, bad circulation*; **b** process of passing, being handed, or transmitted, from one person to another; of being sent from place to place (of material and non-material things): *circulation of books, newspapers*; *circulation of rumours, news* &c. **2.** Fact of being (much) circulated: *the circulation of the evening papers is surprising*, a large number are sold. **3.** Condition of being circulated, of being passed from one person to another, of being in use, and obtainable for circulation: *the book is no longer in circulation*; *many forged notes are in circulation*; *withdrawn from circulation* (of books, coinage &c.) **4.** Movement, flow, of water through pipes; passage, to and fro wafting of air through a house &c.

circulative, adj. [1. sérkūlativ; 2. sʌ́kjulətiv]. **circulate** & **-ive.** Inclined to circulate; tending to promote circulation.

circulator, n. [1. sérkūlātur; 2. sʌ́kjuleitə]. See prec. & **-or.** One who circulates, distributes, or spreads: *circulator of rumours, news, infection* &c.

circulatory, adj. [1. sérkūlaturi; 2. sʌ́kjulətəri]. Lat. *circulātōrius*. See **circulate** & **-ory.** Pertaining to the circulation of the blood, of sap, water, or air.

circum-, pref. Lat. adv. & prep., acc. of **circus.** 'All around; in neighbourhood; about, among.' In composition *-m* dropped in *circuitus* &c.; cp. **circuit** & see etymol. under **circus.** Used in many Lat. compounds, & in some fr. Fr., instead of Fr. *circon-*.

circumambient, adj. [1. serkumámbient; 2. sʌkəmǽmbiənt]. **circum-** & **ambient.** Lying around, surrounding on all sides, completely enclosing.

circumambulate, vb. trans. & intrans. [1. serkumámbūlāt; 2. sʌkəmǽmbjuleit]. **circum-** & P.P. type of Lat. *ambulāre*, 'walk, go to and fro'. See **amble.** **1.** trans. To walk round (a piece of ground &c.). **2.** intrans. **a** To walk about, walk round; hence, **b** (fig.) to approach a subject indirectly, avoid straightforward statement.

circumambulation, n. [1. serkumàmbūláshun; 2. sʌkəmæ̀mbjuléiʃən]. Prec. & **-ion.** (lit. and fig.) The act of circumambulating; state of being circumambulated.

circumambulatory, adj. [1. serkumámbūlaturi; 2. sʌkəmǽmbjulətəri]. See prec. & **-ory.** Walking, going round; avoiding the main issue, indirect, roundabout.

circumbendibus, n. [1. serkumbéndibus; 2. sʌkəmbéndibəs]. Facetious concoction fr. **circum-** & Engl. **bend** & *-ibus*, Lat. abl. pl. A long, circuitous way round; circumlocution.

circumcise, vb. trans. [1. sérkumsīz; 2. sʌ́kəmsaiz]. O. Fr. *circonciser*, fr. Lat. *circumcīs-(um)*, 'cut around', fr. **circum-** & P.P. type *cīs-(um)*, of *-cīdere*, form of *caedere*, 'cut', used in composition. See **cement.** **a** To cut off the foreskin of, esp. as religious rite of the Jews, and other Semitic races, as symbolical of casting away sin; **b** (fig., in Bib. language) to purify, do away sinfulness of.

circumcision, n. [1. serkumsízhun; 2. sʌkəmsíʒən], fr. Lat. *circumcīsiōn-(em)*. See prec. & **-ion.** **1.** The act, rite, of circumcising, state of being circumcised. **2.** (eccles.) The festival commemorating the circumcision of

Christ, kept on Jan. 1st. 3. (Bib., fig.) Purification of the spirit. 4. (Bib.) The Jewish people, as a circumcised race: *the people of the circumcision.*

circumference, n. [1. sĕrkúmferens; 2. sǝkámfǝrǝns]. Lat. *circumferentia*, formed fr. Pres. Part. *circumferent-(em)* of *circumferre*, 'carry round', fr. **circum-** & *ferre*, 'to bear' &c. See **bear** (I). a Boundary of a circle; b measurement of the circumference, distance round.

circumferential, adj. [1. sĕrkùmferénshal; 2. sǝkàmfǝrénʃǝl]. See prec. & **-ial**. Pertaining to the circumference.

circumflex, n. [1. sĕrkumflèks; 2. sǝ́kǝmflèks], fr. Lat. *(syllaba) circumflexa*, P.P. of *circumflectere*, 'to turn back'. See **circum-** & **flex** (I.). 1. Mark or accent, written (⁀) in Greek, (^) in French &c. 2. a This mark, in Greek, probably expressed a composite tone, a rise and then a fall, and in this sense the expression *circumflex accent* (indicated by (∧)) is generally used by phoneticians and philologists; b in French the mark is purely graphic at the present time, and merely marks the loss of a sound—generally *s*.

circumflexion, n. [1. sĕrkumflékshun; 2. sǝkǝmflékʃǝn]. Prec. & **-ion**. A bending, twisting, round.

circumfluence, n. [1. sĕrkúmflooens; 2. sǝkámfluǝns], fr. Lat. *circumfluentia*, fr. *circumfluent-(em)*, Pres. Part. of *circumfluere*, 'to flow round', & *-ia*. See **circum-** & **fluency**. A flowing round.

circumfluent, adj. [1. serkúmflooent; 2. sǝkámfluǝnt]. **circum-** & **fluent**. Flowing round, encompassing on all sides.

circumfuse, vb. trans. [1. sĕrkumfúz; 2. sǝkǝmfjúz], fr. P.P. *circumfūs-(um)*, of Lat. *circumfundere*, 'to pour around'. See **circum-** & **fuse**. To pour (air, light, liquid &c.) round, surround with (fluid), bathe with or in; also fig.

circumfusion, n. [1. sĕrkumfúzhn; 2. sǝkǝmfjúžn]. See prec. & **-ion**. The act or process of circumfusing; state or process of being surrounded (with fluid).

circumgyrate, vb. intrans. [1. sĕrkumjírāt; 2. sǝkǝmdžáiǝrèit]. **circum-** & **gyrate**. To turn round, revolve, rotate; go round in a circle.

circumgyration, n. [1. sĕrkumjīrā́shun; 2. sǝkǝmdžairéiʃǝn]. Prec. & **-ion**. The act of revolving, rotation; circular movement.

circumjacent, adj. [1. sĕrkumjā́sent; 2. sǝkǝmdžéisǝnt]. Lat. *circumjacent-(em)*, Pres. Part. of *circumjacēre*, 'to lie around, border upon'. See **circum-** & **jet** (III.), also **deject** &c. Lying around, near, bordering on.

circumlittoral, adj. [1. sĕrkumlíteral; 2. sǝkǝmlítǝrǝl]. **circum-** & **littoral**. Lying along, close to, the shore.

circumlocution, n. [1. sĕrkumlōkúshun; 2. sǝkǝmloukjúʃǝn]. Lat. *circumlocūtiōn-(em)*, 'talking round'. See **circum-** & **locution**. a A talking round; roundabout manner of stating, or discussing, a question; b a specific instance of this: *Circumlocution Office*, name invented by Dickens ('Little Dorrit') for a government department which pays more attention to red tape than to the dispatch of business.

circumlocutional, adj. [1. sĕrkumlokúshunal; 2. sǝkǝmlǝkjúʃǝnǝl], fr. prec. & **-al**. a (of persons) Given to roundabout ways of speaking, wordy; b (of a sentence, speech, manner of speaking) roundabout, not direct.

circumlocutionary, adj. [1. sĕrkumlokúshunari; 2. sǝkǝmlǝkjúʃǝnǝri], fr. **circumlocution** & **-ary**. Circumlocutional.

circumlocutory, adj. [1. sĕrkumlókūturi; 2. sǝkǝmlókjutǝri], fr. Lat. **circum-** & *locūt(us)*, P.P. of *loqui*, 'to speak', (see **locution**) & **-ory**. Exhibiting circumlocution, roundabout.

circumnavigable, adj. [1. sĕrkumnávigabl; 2. sǝkǝmnǽvigǝbl]. **circum-** & **navigable**. Capable of being sailed round.

circumnavigate, vb. trans. [1. sĕrkumnávigāt; 2. sǝkǝmnǽvigeit], fr. Lat. *circumnāvigāt-(um)*, P.P. type of *circumnāvigāre*, 'to sail round'. See **circum-** & **navigate**. To sail round (esp. the world, globe &c.).

circumnavigation, n. [1. sĕrkumnàvigā́shun; 2. sǝkǝmnæ̀vigéiʃǝn]. Prec. & **-ion**. The act of sailing round (esp. of the world).

circumnavigator, n. [1. sĕrkumnávigāter; 2. sǝkǝmnǽvigeitǝ]. **circum-** & **navigator**. One who sails right round something; specif., one who has sailed round the globe.

circumnutation, n. [1. sĕrkumnūtā́shun; 2. sǝkǝmnjūtéiʃǝn], fr. **circum-** & **nutation**. (bot., of plant-tendrils) Lit. 'a nodding round', turning in all directions.

circumoral, adj. [1. sĕrkumóral; 2. sǝkǝmɔ́rǝl]. See **circum-** & **oral**. Near, round, the mouth.

circumpolar, adj. [1. sĕrkumpólar; 2. sǝkǝmpóulǝ]. **circum-** & **polar**. a (geog.) Near, round, the North or South Pole: *circumpolar ocean* &c.; b (astron.) of stars, moving round the celestial poles, without going below horizon: *circumpolar motion*.

circumscissile, adj. [1. sĕrkumsísil; 2. sǝkǝmsísail], fr. Lat. *circumscissum*, P.P. of *circumscindere*, 'to strip off, tear round', fr. **circum-** & *scindere*, 'to cut, tear' &c., & **-ile**. See **scissile**. (bot., of seed-vessels) Opening along a transverse circular line.

circumscribe, vb. trans. [1. sĕrkumskríb; 2. sǝkǝmskráib], fr. Lat. *circumscrib-(ere)*, 'to draw a line round, enclose in a circle; (fig.) to limit, define; restrain'; fr. **circum-**, 'around', & *scribere*, 'to write, draw', see **scribe**. a To draw a line round, mark the boundary of; enclose within bounds; hence, b (fig.) to limit, restrict, set bounds to, confine within limits: *circumscribe one's power of action, interests, experience* &c.

circumscription, n. [1. sĕrkumskrípshun; 2. sǝkǝmskrípʃǝn], fr. Lat. *circumscriptiōn-(em)*, acc. of *circumscriptio*, 'the act of encircling; a circle; a limit, boundary'; fr. **circum-** & *script-(um)*, P.P. of *scribere*, 'to write, draw', & **-ion**. See **description, script, scripture** &c. 1. (lit. and fig.) The act or process of outlining, defining, setting limits; condition of being limited, defined, restricted. 2. That which is inscribed round anything, specif., title, inscription, round a coin &c.

circumsolar, adj. [1. sĕrkumsṓlar; 2. sǝkǝmsóulǝ]. **circum-** & **solar**. Revolving round, situated near, the sun.

circumspect, adj. [1. sĕrkumspèkt; 2. sǝ́kǝmspèkt], fr. Lat. *circumspect-(um)*, P.P. of *circumspicere*, 'to look about, look round'; (fig.) 'to be cautious, take heed'; fr. **circum-** & *specere, spicere*, 'to look'. See **special, species, spy** &c. Only used of moral qualities (of persons and their actions). a Attentive, observant, heedful of conduct and behaviour, decorous; also b careful in forming judgements and decisions, prudent, cautious.

circumspection, n. [1. sĕrkumspékshun; 2. sǝkǝmspékʃǝn]. See prec. & **-ion**. Lit., a looking round, but generally used in moral sense of attention, observation, esp. to conduct, action, and behaviour; hence, a prudence, caution; b decorum, propriety.

circumspective, adj. [1. sĕrkumspéktiv; 2. sǝkǝmspéktiv], fr. **circumspect** & **-ive**. a Cautious, prudent, vigilant; b sometimes in lit. sense, looking round, observing, noting everything: '*All sly, slow things with circumspective eyes*' (Pope, 'Ess. on Man', iv. 226).

circumspectly, adv. [1. sĕrkumspèktli; 2. sǝ́kǝmspèktli], fr. **circumspect** & **-ly**. In a circumspect manner, prudently, cautiously; decorously.

circumstance, n. [1. sĕrkumstans; 2. sǝ́kǝmstǝns]. M.E. *circumstance, -staunce*, fr. O. Fr., fr. Lat. *circumstantia*, 'the act of surrounding; (fig.) condition, attribute, circumstances', fr. *circumstant-*, stem of Pres. Part. of vb. *circumstāre*, 'to surround, encompass' (lit. and fig.), fr. **circum-** & *stāre*, 'to stand', see **stand, stance**. 1. a (usually in pl.) External factor relating to an act, attendant condition (of place, time, previous events, etc.): *to know all the circumstances of a case*; *the circumstances were peculiar*; *an unforeseen circumstance*; Phrs. *in, under the circumstances*, such being the case; *under, in, no circumstances*, never; *it depends on circumstances*, on how matters stand; hence, b an incident, event, fact, detail: *to omit no essential circumstance in a report*; *to be unaware of a particular circumstance*. 2. (pl.) Degree of worldly prosperity or reverse, financial condition: *in reduced, flourishing, circumstances*. 3. Formality, splendid ceremony; esp. in Phr. *pomp and circumstance*.

circumstanced, adj. [1. sĕrkumstanst; 2. sǝ́kǝmstǝnst], fr. prec. & **-ed**. In a particular situation, relative position, placed in certain circumstances: *to be awkwardly circumstanced*.

circumstantial, adj. [1. sĕrkumstánshal; 2. sǝkǝmstǽnʃǝl]. See prec. & **-ial**. 1. Displaying all the circumstances, detailed, minute: *a circumstantial account of what happened*. 2. *Circumstantial evidence*, that which is not positive, or direct, evidence of a particular fact, but consists of proof of a number of other facts, the cumulative effect of which is to establish a strong presumption of the particular main fact.

circumstantiality, n. [1. sĕrkumstànshiáliti; 2. sǝkǝmstæ̀nʃiǽliti], fr. prec. & **-ity**. The quality of being circumstantial in either sense.

circumstantially, adv. [1. sĕrkumstánshali; 2. sǝkǝmstǽnʃǝli], fr. **circumstantial** & **-ly**. In a circumstantial manner; specif. a in detail, minutely; b indirectly, inferentially, by reference to other established facts: *circumstantially proved* (of a fact sought to be proved by evidence).

circumvallate, vb. trans. [1. sĕrkumválāt; 2. sǝkǝmvǽleit], fr. Lat. *circumvallāt-(um)*, P.P. type of *circumvallāre*, 'to build a wall round' (mil.); fr. **circum-** & *vallāre*, 'to entrench, surround, with a *vallum*, or rampart; (fig.) defend, strengthen'. See **vallum** & **wall**. To build a rampart round.

circumvallation, n. [1. sĕrkumvalā́shun; 2. sǝkǝmvǝléiʃǝn], fr. prec. & **-ion**. a Act or process of constructing a rampart round; b an encircling rampart.

circumvent, vb. trans. [1. sĕrkumvént; 2. sǝkǝmvént], fr. Lat. *circumvent-(um)*, P.P. of *circumvenīre*, 'to surround (in a hostile manner); beset; (fig.) to oppress; defraud'. See **circum-** & **vent** & **venue**. a (of persons) To frustrate, outwit, prevent from doing something; b (of plans, designs &c.) to prevent something happening, stop, hinder, render of none effect.

circumvention, n. [1. sĕrkumvénshun; 2. sǝkǝmvénʃǝn], fr. Lat. *circumventiōn-(em)*, acc. of *circumventio*, 'the act of defrauding', fr. *circumvent us*. See prec. & **-ion**. The act of circumventing, outwitting, hindering, preventing action; process of being circumvented.

circumventive, adj. [1. sĕrkumvéntiv; 2. sǝkǝmvéntiv]. See prec. & **-ive**. Tending to circumvent or outwit.

circumvolution, n. [1. sĕrkumvolū́shun; 2. sǝkǝmvǝljúʃǝn], fr. Lat. *circumvolut-(um)*, P.P. type of *circumvolvere*, 'to roll round, revolve', fr. **circum-** & *volvere*, 'to roll', & **-ion**. See **devolve, volume, volute, whelm**. a The act of rolling round, winding, coiling; state of being coiled, wound, rolled up; b something rolled up, a coil.

circus, n. [1. sĕrkus; 2. sǝ́kǝs]. Lat. *circus*, 'a ring; specif., a round, or oval, enclosure for games'; prob. genuine Lat. word, & not borrowed fr. Gk. *kírkos, kríkos*, 'a ring'. Prob. a redupl. form of base in Lat. *curvus*, 'crooked, bent'. See **curve**. 1. a A circular enclosure, surrounded with tiers of seats, for the exhibition of equestrian, athletic &c. performances; b a show consisting of performing animals, horses &c., or feats of horsemanship and agility, and humorous interludes by clowns and acrobats: *travelling* *circus*, one including above, and generally also wild beasts in cages. 2. A rounded open space in a town, with streets radiating from it: *Oxford, Piccadilly, Circus* &c.

cire-perdue, adj. & n. [1. sēr perdū; 2. sīr perdy]. Fr., lit. 'lost wax'. **a** adj. Of, denoting a process of casting objects in bronze, the clay model being coated with wax, on which the finishing work is done; the whole is covered with a paste and clay envelope and baked, when the wax melts, leaving a hollow mould for the casting; **b** n., bronze object made by this process.

cirque, n. [1. sërk; 2. sǣk]. Fr., fr. Lat. **circus.** (poet.) Amphitheatre, arena.

cirrhosis, n. [1. sirṓsis; 2. siróusis], fr. Gk. *kirrhós*, 'tawny', & **-osis.** Cp. Lith. *szirvas*, 'grey'. Disease of the liver, chiefly caused by excess of alcohol.

cirri-, cirro-, prefs. used for Lat. *cirrus*, 'curl, ringlet, tuft of hair'. See **cirrus.**

cirriferous, adj. [1. siriferus; 2. sirífərəs], fr. **cirri- & -ferous.** (bot.) Having curling tendrils.

cirriform, n. [1. síriform; 2. sírifōm]. See **cirri- & -form.** Having shape of a curl, or tendril.

cirriped, cirripede, n. [1. síripèd, -pēd; 2. síripèd, -pīd], fr. **cirri-** & Lat. *ped-*, stem of *pēs*, 'foot'. See **pedal & foot.** A member of an order of crustaceans, including barnacles &c., having legs in form of a curl.

cirro-, see **cirri-.**

cirro-cumulus, n. [1. sirōkū́mūlus; 2. sìroukjū́mjuləs]. See prec. & **cumulus.** A cloud formation of small fleecy clouds, *cirri*, arranged in groups or masses.

cirrose, adj. [1. sirṓs; 2. siróus], fr. **cirri- & -ose.** (bot. and zool.) **a** Having appendages like locks of hair; **b** resembling a curl, lock of hair.

cirro-stratus, n. [1. sirō strā́tus; 2. sìrou stréitəs]. See **cirro- & strata.** Cloud formation of small fleecy clouds arranged in belts or strata.

cirrous, adj. [1. sírus; 2. sírəs]. See **cirro- & -ous.** Cirrose.

cirrus, n. [1. sírus; 2. sírəs]. Lat., 'a curl, ringlet, lock, tuft of hair; hence anything resembling a curl, e.g. a tuft of feathers, tendrils of a plant' &c. The etymol. is doubtful, but there is perh. relationship w. **circus & curve. 1. a** (bot.) A tendril; **b** (zool.) a thread-like appendage, serving as means of locomotion, organ of touch &c. **2.** (meteor.) A kind of cloud, having the appearance of straggling locks of hair or fleeces.

cis-, pref. Lat. *cis*, 'on this side of'; cogn. w. Lat. *citrā*, 'on this side of'; *citrō*, 'to this side'; the base **ki-*, Gmc. **hi-*, is found also in Goth. *hidrē*, O.E. *hiðer*. See **hither.**

cisalpine, adj. [1. sisálpīn; 2. sisǽlpain], fr. **cis- & Alpine.** On this, that is, the Roman, side of the Alps.

cisatlantic, adj. [1. sisatlántik; 2. sisətlǽntik]. On this (the European) side of the Atlantic.

cist, n. [1. sist; 2. sist], fr. Lat. *cista*, 'a chest, box of wood, twigs &c., esp. that used for the sacred utensils in religious festivals', loan-word fr. Gk. *kistē*, 'woven basket', wh. is prob. cogn. w. Gk. *koitis*, 'box, basket'. Cp. **chest. 1.** (Gk. antiq.) A casket, esp. that which held the sacred utensils used in the Eleusinian mysteries. **2.** Primitive tomb consisting of a stone coffin, or cavity lined and covered with slabs of stone.

Cistercian, adj. & n. [1. sistérshan; 2. sistə́ʃən]. **a** adj. Of, belonging to, an order of monks, a branch of the Benedictines, founded at *Cîteaux* (*Cistercium*), France, in 1098 by St. Bernard of Clairvaux; **b** n., monk of this order.

cistern, n. [1. sístern; 2. sístən]. M.E. *cisterne*, fr. O. Fr. *cisterne*, fr. Lat. *cisterna*, 'a reservoir for water', fr. Lat. *cista*, 'a chest' &c., see **cist**, & *-ern*, as in *caverna, taberna*; cp. **cavern, tavern. a** An artificial receptacle for storing water; water-tank; esp. one at the top of a house for supplying the building with water; **b** a natural reservoir, pond &c.

cistus, n. [1. sístus; 2. sístəs], fr. Gk. *kisthos, kistos*, 'a kind of flowering shrub'; the name is perh. of Asiatic origin. Either borrowed fr. a common source, or an early independent borrowing, is O. Frankish (also Du.) *heester*, 'beech tree', whence Fr. *hêtre*, 'beech'. A genus of flowering shrubs; the rock-rose.

cit, n. [1. sit; 2. sit]. Contraction of **citizen,** used in 17th & 18th cents., now obsolete.

citable, adj. [1. sítabl; 2. sáitəbl], fr. **cite & -able.** That may be cited.

citadel, n. [1. sítadl; 2. sítədl], fr. Fr. *citadelle*, fr. Ital. *cittadella*, dimin. of *cittàde*, 'city', Mod. Ital. *città*, fr. Lat. *cīvitāt-e*, abl. of *cīvitas*, 'city'. See **city. a** A fortress protecting a town; the chief point of defence in a fortified town; hence **b** (fig.) a place of refuge, retreat.

citation, n. [1. sit-, sītā́shun; 2. sit-, saitéiʃən]. M.E. fr. Fr. *citation.* See **cite & -ation. 1.** A summons to appear in a court of law. **2. a** The act of citing, quoting, referring to (a passage, book, previous case &c.); **b** passage cited.

cite, vb. trans. [1. sīt; 2. sait], fr. Fr. *citer*, fr. Lat. *citāre*, 'to put into motion, stimulate'; (fig.) 'to call urgently, summon'; esp. in legal sense; formed fr. *cit-(um)*, P.P. type of *ciēre*, 'to put in motion, shake, rouse up; invoke'; cp. also Lat. *cito*, 'quickly', Gk. *kiō*, 'go'; & w. different vowel grade, Goth. *haitan*, O.H.G. *heizan*, 'order, call by name'. The orig. meaning of the base is apparently 'quick motion', then 'to rouse to action', then both in Lat. & Gmc., 'to rouse by means of the voice', hence 'to call, command', w. the derived meaning 'to call by name, give a name to'. See **hight,** & for survival of a primitive meaning, **hie,** vb., fr. O.E. *hīgian*, 'hasten' &c. **1.** To summon, command to appear, before a tribunal. **2. a** To quote a passage from an authority, or authority himself; **b** to bring forward, mention as example or authority.

cither(n), cittern, n. [1. síther(n), sítern; 2. síþə(n), sitən], Shakesp. *cittern*; O. Fr. has *guiterne*, q.v. under **guitar,** a variant. The *-n* is not orig. part of the word; cp. O.E. *cytere*, wh. together w. above forms, is fr. Lat. *cithara*, 'lute', fr. Gk. *kithára*, wh. is prob. borrowed fr. an Asiatic language. (archaic, chiefly poet.) A musical stringed instrument, like a lute, a zither; the word is rather loosely applied to many instruments of this type.

citizen, n. [1. sítizen; 2. sítizən]. M.E. *citezein*, fr. O. Fr. *citeain*, fr. *cité* & *-ain* = **-an.** The suggestion that this word in Engl. owes its *-z-* to anal. of *denizen*, wd. be plausible were the latter not a comparatively rare word, & the former very common. See **city, civil. 1.** An inhabitant of **a** a specific town or city; **b** inhabitant of a state; **c** a dweller in a city as opposed to one living in the country; city dweller. Phr. *citizen of the world*, a cosmopolitan. **2. a** Member of a city community, enjoying rights and privileges as a burgess and bound by duties of loyalty; **b** person occupying same position in regard to a state, or country; one native to, or naturalized in, a country; opposed to a foreigner, or alien.

citizenship, n. [1. sítiznship; 2. sítizənʃip]. Prec. & **-ship. a** The status of a citizen; **b** the duties and privileges pertaining to it; **c** the state of being a citizen.

citole, n. [1. sitṓl; 2. sitóul]. O. Fr., fr. same stem as **cittern.** (obs., poet.) Kind of lute or dulcimer: '*Citterns and citoles*' (Rossetti).

citrate, n. [1. sítrat; 2. sítr(e)it]. See **citric & -ate.** (chem.) A salt of citric acid.

citric, adj. [1. sítrik; 2. sítrik], fr. Lat. base *citr-(us)*, 'citron', & **-ic.** See **citron.** Pertaining to, derived from, the citron, or from fruits of the same genus, e.g. lemons, limes &c.; esp. *citric acid.*

citrine, adj. [1. sítrin; 2. sítrin], fr. Fr. *citrin*, fr. Lat. *citr-(us)*, see **citron, & -ine.** Pale greenish-yellow, lemon-coloured.

citron, n. [1. sítrun; 2. sítrən], fr. Fr. *citron*, fr. Ital. *citrone* (see **-oon**), fr. Lat. *citr-us*, 'citron-tree', fr. Gk. *kitron*. Origin unknown. **a** A kind of fruit resembling the lime and lemon, but larger and less acid; **b** the tree bearing this fruit; **c** *citron colour*, pale yellow.

Citrus, n. [1. sítrus; 2. sítrəs]. Lat. See prec. (bot.) The genus of shrubs or trees which bear fruit like the citron, including the orange, lemon &c.

cittern, see **cither(n).**

city, n. [1. síti; 2. síti]. M.E. *cite*, fr. O. Fr. *cité*, fr. Lat. *cīvitāt-em*, acc. of *cīvitas*, 'a community of citizens, the state', fr. *cīvi-s*, 'member of a community, citizen' & *-tas* (see **-ty**). See **civil. 1.** A town of considerable size and importance. Phrs. *Celestial City*, heaven; *Eternal City, City of the Seven Hills*, Rome; *City of Refuge* (Bib.), one of the six cities of Palestine to which persons guilty of murder might flee for safety; hence, a sanctuary, place of shelter. **2.** (in England) A town, borough, raised to a position of importance by royal charter; esp. one which is also an episcopal see. **3.** The originally fortified centre of a city. Specif., *the City*, the original municipal centre of London, governed by the Lord Mayor and Corporation, the banking and commercial centre of England and the British Empire. Phr. *city man*: one engaged in finance, commerce &c., in the city. *City Company*, a body representing one of the trade-guilds. **4.** One of the ancient Greek republics, *a city-state.*

cityward(s), adv. [1. sítiward(z); 2. sítiwəd(z)], fr. **city & -ward(s).** Towards the city.

civet, n. [1. sívit; 2. sívit], fr. Fr. *civette*, fr. Arab. *zabad*. **1.** Also *civet-cat*, a small carnivorous quadruped, *Viverra civetta*, found in Asia and Africa, between a fox and a weasel in size, and of a brownish grey colour. **2.** A substance with a strong musky smell, obtained from the anal glands of the civet-cat, used in manufacture of perfume.

civic, adj. [1. sívik; 2. sívik], fr. Lat. *cīvic-(us)*, 'pertaining to citizens', fr. *cīvis*, 'citizen', & **-ic.** See **civil.** Pertaining to a citizen, to citizenship. *Civic crown*, (Rom. antiq.) a crown of oak-leaves, given as an honour to a soldier who saved the life of a fellow-citizen in battle.

civics, n. [1. síviks; 2. síviks]. The organized and systematic study of the duties and privileges of citizenship, and of the well-being, and suitable planning, of cities.

civil, adj. [1. sívil; 2. sívl, sívil]. Lat. *cīvilis*, 'pertaining to a citizen, to political rights of citizens, to public life; affable, polite', fr. base *civ-* as in *cīvitātem*, 'city'. *cīvis*, 'citizen'. All these derived fr. base **k̑ei(w)-*, **k̑oi(w)-* &c. 'to lie, settle down', wh. occurs in first element of Goth. *heiwa-frauja*, 'master of a house', O.E. *hīwa*, 'member of a family', *hīwen*, 'household', O.H.G. *hīwo*, 'husband'; further O.E. *hīgid*, 'hide of land', originally 'as much land as would support a family', see **hide (IV.).** See further **home, & city, civic, quiet. 1. a** Of, connected with, pertaining to, based on, organized human society, or connected with citizens in widest sense: *civil administration, rights, liberties, life* &c.; **b** connected with citizens of same state, individuals who are members of a single political unit: *civil war*, i.e. war between factions in same country. **2.** Specif., having to do, concerned with, such citizens as do not belong to any of the fighting services, as opposed to, contrasted with, military, naval &c.; or with activities and affairs of a state, other than military or naval: *to leave the army and enter civil life; military organization is hampered by an inefficient civil government.* **3. a** Urbane, affable, polite; considerate, obliging; complimentary: *it was very civil of him to take so much trouble on my behalf; I must say something civil to him*; **b** (of inferiors) respectful: *a very civil tradesman.* Phr. *to keep a civil tongue in one's head*, to refrain from insolence, be polite. For development of this meaning of *civil,* which existed already in Lat., cp. *urbane*. *Civil case*, action at law concerned with private rights and wrongs, not involving criminal actions; *Civil Court*, court of law where *civil cases* are tried; *civil engineer*, one whose work is not primarily concerned with purely mechanical branches of the profession; one who plans and superintends the construction of bridges, canals, docks, reservoirs, roads, railways, tunnels &c.; *Civil Law*, system of laws enacted by a state to regulate the affairs and interests of its citizens, specif., Roman law; *Civil List*, grant by parliament for the maintenance of the Royal Household; *Civil Servant*, person employed in any public office or service of the state, other than the fighting services; *Civil Service*, applied to all public state departments and services except the army, navy, and air force: *Home Civil Service*, British Treasury, Post Office &c., contrasted with *Indian, Sudan, Civil Service*.

civilian, adj. & n. [1. sivílyan; 2. sivíljən], fr. O. Fr. *civilien*, fr. Lat. *cīviliānus*. See **civil** & **-an**. **1.** adj. Relating to, belonging to, civil life, that is, not naval or military: *civilian professions, clothes* &c. **2.** n. (from prec.) **a** Person employed in, occupied with, *civil life*, as contrasted with a soldier, naval man &c.; **b** specif., a member of the *Civil Service*; esp. one holding judicial, or administrative appointment under government in India, the Sudan; **c** one learned in the Civil Law.

civility, n. [1. sivíliti; 2. sivíliti], fr. O. Fr. *civilité*, 'citizenship', fr. Lat. *cīvīlitāt-(em)*, acc. of *cīvīlitas*, 'art of government; politics'; also 'courteousness, affability', fr. *cīvīlis*. See **civil** & **-ity**. **a** Politeness, courtesy; obliging, serviceable behaviour to, or treatment of, another in word or deed: *to treat a person with, show him, the utmost civility*; **b** a specific polite, kind, attentive act, or complimentary utterance: *I am grateful for your civility in taking so much trouble*; *to exchange civilities*.

civilization, n. [1. sìvilīzáshun; 2. sìvilaizéiʃən], fr. **civilize** & **-ation**. **1.** The act of civilizing; the state or process of being civilized. **2. a** State of social, moral, intellectual, and industrial development; culture; esp. one in which an advanced stage has been reached; contrasted with *barbarism*; **b** type of culture characteristic of particular nation or race: *ancient Irish civilization*. **3.** Tract of the earth's surface over which highly developed civilization extends: *beyond the bounds of civilization*.

civilize, vb. trans. [1. sívilīz; 2. sívilaiz], fr. **civil** & **-ize**. **1.** To bring from a state of barbarism to one of civilization, to introduce and foster social and moral improvement among: *savages have often been civilized by missionaries*. **2.** (extended use) To improve the morals or manners of; render more polished, impart social arts and graces to, refine: *many a rough, ill-mannered clown has been civilized by his wife*.

civilized, adj. [1. sívilīzd; 2. sívilaizd]. P.P. of prec. **1.** Possessing civilization; highly developed in social organization, in the arts and sciences; contrasted with *savage* or *barbarous*. **2.** Conversant with manners and modes of thought of good society; well-bred; highly cultivated.

civilizing, adj. [1. sívilīzing; 2. sívilaiziŋ], fr. Pres. Part. of **civilize**. Tending to civilize, to promote civilization: *religion exerts a civilizing influence*.

civilly, adv. [1. sívili; 2. sívili], fr. **civil** & **-ly**. **1.** In relation to the community, to the government (rare). **2.** In a civil manner, politely, courteously.

civism, n. [1. sívizm; 2. sívizəm]. Fr. *civisme*. See **civil** & **-ism**. Principles, laws of good citizenship.

clachan, n. [1. klághan; 2. klǽχən]. Gael. fr. *clach*, 'stone'. Scottish name for a village.

clack (**I.**), n. [1. klak; 2. klæk]. M.E. *clacke, klakke*. Prob. imitative. Cp. O.E. *clacu*, 'strife', *clacian*, 'hasten'. **1.** A sharp, non-resonant sound, like that made by striking one wooden object against another. Hence **2**, noisy talk, clatter of tongues (provinc.). **3.** Also *clack-valve*, a valve shutting with a sharp clack when raised.

clack (**II.**), vb. intrans. M.E. *clacken, clake*. Cp. prec. **1.** To make a sharp, abrupt sound, as that of wood when struck. Hence **2**, to chatter noisily.

clad, adj. [1. klad; 2. klæd], fr. P.P. of **clothe**. M.E. *clad, cladde*, O.E. *clāðod*, P.P. of *clāðian*, 'to clothe'. See **clothe**. **a** Having clothes on, dressed, as distinct from *naked, undrest*: *he was up and fully clad by 6 o'clock*; **b** arrayed, dressed, in particular manner: *clad in splendid uniform, in rags* &c.

clado-, pref. fr. Gk. *kládos*, 'sprout, shoot', used to form various scientific words, e.g. *cladophora*, a genus of algae. *Klados* prob. meant orig. 'branch lopped off', fr. the base **kʷel-*, **kʷl-*, 'to strike, cut', seen in Lat. *clādēs*, 'disaster', see **callosity**, Gk. *kláō*, 'break in pieces,' see **cataclasm**. See also **claviform**.

claim (**I.**), vb. trans. & intrans. [1. klām; 2. kleim]. M.E. *claimen*, fr. O. Fr. *claime*, pres. ind. of *clamer*, fr. Lat. *clāmāre*, 'to call, cry out, declare'. This vb. is fr. another form of the base fr. wh. comes also Lat. *calāre*, 'to call out', Gk. *kaléō*, wh. have no connexion w. **call**, but are cogn. w. O.E. *hlōwan*, 'roar' &c., cp. **low** (**I.**). See also **calends**, **clamour**, **clarify**, **clear**. **A.** trans. **1.** To assert one's right to, demand to have, apply for, as a right: *to claim a reward, the crown, damages* (*in law*), *the protection of the law*. **2.** To demand the recognition of (an alleged fact): *to claim the victory*; *claim to have won the victory*. **3.** To assert one's ownership of something lost and found, and demand that it shall be restored to one: *the police found a watch, which was afterwards claimed by several persons*. **4.** (of things) To call for, demand, deserve: *to claim attention*. **B.** intrans. (law) **a** To make a claim for damages in law; **b** *claim against* (*a person*), assert that one has been injured by, and bring an action at law against him: *unless he pays up I shall claim against him*.

claim (**II.**), n. M.E., fr. O. Fr. *claime*. See prec. **1.** The act of claiming, a demand, application, for something to which one has a real or supposed right. Phrs. *to lay claim to*, assert one's right to obtain; *set up a claim to*; *put in a claim for*, attempt to establish one's right to obtain. **2.** A right, something to which one is entitled; a right to demand: *to have a claim, no claim, on* (*a person*, or *his charity* &c.). **3.** That which is claimed, esp. piece of land allotted to and taken possession of by settler, miner (in a gold-field &c.). Phr. *to stake out a claim*, mark out boundaries of such an allotment, in proof of ownership; also fig., of non-material things, of discovery.

claimable, adj. [1. klāmabl; 2. kléiməbl]. **claim** (**I.**) & **-able**. Able to be claimed.

claimant, n. [1. klāmant; 2. kléimənt], fr. O. Fr., Pres. Part. of *clamer*. See **claim** (**I.**). **a** (law) Person who brings an action in law, to recover damages, or to have wrongs righted; **b** one who makes a claim, who demands something as a right, esp. in a public, official manner: *a claimant for the crown*.

clairaudience, n. [1. klāráwdiens; 2. klɛərɔ́diəns]. See next word & first element in **audible**. Clear hearing; supposed faculty of hearing sounds not naturally audible, as by spiritualistic mediums &c.

clairvoyance, n. [1. klārvóians; 2. klɛəvɔ́iəns]. Fr., 'clear seeing, sight'. See next word. Second sight; power of seeing, as in a mental picture, objects and events which are hidden from the bodily eyes.

clairvoyant, adj. & n. [1. klārvóiant; 2. klɛəvɔ́iənt]. Fr., fr. *clair* & *voyant*, Pres. Part. of *voir*, 'to see'. See **clear**, **vision**, **view**. **1.** adj. **a** Connected with clairvoyance; **b** having faculty of second sight. **2.** n. Person possessing faculty of second sight.

clam, n. [1. klam; 2. klæm]. Orig. something cold & sticky. See **clammy**. Perh. O.E. *clām*, 'mud, paste', w. early shortening of vowel, & connected ultimately w. **clay**. See *-glom-* in **agglomerate**, also **glue**, **glutinous**. Edible bivalve shell-fish of various kinds. (Word chiefly used in America.)

clamant, adj. [1. klāmant; 2. kléimənt], fr. Lat. *clāmant-(em)*, acc. of *clāmans*, Pres. Part. of *clāmāre*, 'to cry aloud'. See **claim**. **a** Making urgent entreaties, clamouring, insistent; **b** (of non-material things) demanding, deserving, to be examined and attended to: *clamant injustice*.

clamber, vb. intrans. & n. [1. klámber; 2. klǽmbə]. M.E. *clambren, clameren*, 'to climb; cluster round'; cp. Mod. Germ. *sich klammern an*, 'grasp, cling to'. Prob. conn. w. **climb**, cp. O.E. Pret. *clamb*. **1.** vb. Generally *clamber up*, to climb with difficulty, or clumsily. **2.** n. A laborious climb.

clammily, adv. [1. klámili; 2. klǽmili], fr. next word & **-ly**. In a cold, damp, sticky manner.

clammy, adj. [1. klámi; 2. klǽmi], fr. M.E. *clam*, 'sticky', cp. O.E. *clām*, 'mud', & **-y**. See **clam** & words there referred to. Cold and sticky; moist and cold to the touch.

clamorous, adj. [1. klámurus; 2. klǽmərəs], fr. **clamour** & **-ous**. **a** (of persons) Noisy, vociferous; uttering loud, angry complaints or threats; **b** (of cries, utterances) loud, confused, insistent, filled with menace; **c** (poet. and fig., of inanimate things) giving forth continuous, confused sound: *clamorous hammers in the forge*; *clamorous brook*.

clamorously, adv. Prec. & **-ly**. In a clamorous manner, with clamour.

clamour (**I.**), n. [1. klámur; 2. klǽmə]. M.E., fr. O. Fr., fr. Lat. *clāmor*, 'a loud cry'. See **claim**. A loud, confused, esp. hostile outcry, as of an angry crowd; loudly expressed, angry complaint.

clamour (**II.**), vb. intrans. & trans., fr. prec. **1.** intrans. **a** To make a loud, confused noise; **b** *to clamour for*, demand loudly and insistently; **c** *clamour against*, complain loudly of, make hostile and threatening complaints about a person or thing. **2.** trans. **a** *Clamour down*, to shout person down, silence by clamour; **b** *clamour out*, to utter, express with shouts.

clamp (**I.**), n. [1. klamp; 2. klæmp]. Prob. related to O.E. *clamm*, 'fetter, bond', but cp. the related words, Du. *klamp*, 'a clamp, heap', *klampen*, 'to grapple', & similar words in Dan. & Swed. The central idea in all these words is 'to bind, fasten, stick together', therefore we may prob. compare **clam**, **clammy**, **clay** &c. **1.** Applied to various devices for holding things together, bracing, clasping, strengthening &c.; e.g. piece of metal fastened by rivets or screws holding two pieces of wood together; metal bar with thread at either end to which nuts or flat pieces of wood or iron are screwed, to strengthen, or hold together that through which the rod passes. **2.** A pile of bricks or potatoes; esp. heap of potatoes covered with straw and earth stored for the winter.

clamp (**II.**), vb. trans., fr. prec. **1.** To bind together by means of a clamp or clamps; to fasten firmly together. **2.** (of potatoes) To put them into a pile and cover with straw and earth.

clan, n. [1. klan; 2. klæn], fr. Gael. *clann*, 'family, descendants'. (in Scottish Highlands) A group of families assumed to be descended from a common ancestor, under, or formerly under, the patriarchal leadership of an hereditary chieftain; hence, **a** (in wider sense) a family; connected group of families; tribe; **b** a group of people united by some common interest; a party, set.

clandestine, adj. [1. klandéstin; 2. klændéstin], fr. Lat. *clandestīnus*, 'secret, clandestine', formed fr. *clam*, adv. & prep., 'secret, unknown', on anal. of *intestīnus* (see **intestine**); *clam* is fr. base **k̑ĕl-* &c. as in *cēlāre*, 'to hide', w. adv. suff. *-am*, like *cōram*, 'in presence of' (see **coram populo**), or *palam*, 'publicly', fr. **pel-*, 'spread out', cp. *plānus*, 'level, flat' (see **plain (I.)**). Secret, surreptitious, guiltily secret, purposely hidden.

clandestinely, adv. Prec. & **-ly**. In a secret, underhand manner.

clang (I.), vb. intrans. & trans. [1. klang; 2. klæŋ]. Most dictionaries derive the word fr. Lat. *clang-ere*, 'to resound, clang', but it seems more probable that they are independent, imitative words. O.H.G. & O.L.G. *klank, clanc*, Mod. Germ. *clang*, 'sound', are clearly the same as the Engl. word, & all these are, moreover, related to Germ. *klingeln*, 'to tinkle', & Engl. **clink**, wh. show the normal Gmc. gradation w. *clang*. It is prob. safer to regard all these as true Gmc. words. They might be re-invented among different races & at varying periods to express differing qualities of sound. **a** intrans. To make a loud resonant sound, as of metal when struck (esp. of large bell, armour &c.); **b** trans., to cause (a bell &c.) to clang.

clang (II.), n., fr. prec. A loud metallic ring.

clangorous, adj. [1. klánggurus; 2. klǽŋgərəs], fr. next word & **-ous**. Making a clanging sound.

clangour, n. [1. klánggur; 2. klǽŋgə], fr. Lat. *clangor*, 'a noise, clang', fr. *clangere*, 'to resound, clang', & **-or**. This, wh. is apparently a pure Lat. word, is naturally associated in most minds w. **clang**, wh. has an identical meaning. If the latter be, as is suggested, independent of Lat. *clangere*, its existence in Engl. wd. facilitate the adoption of *clangour*, wh. wd. be intelligible to all. Or this word may have nothing to do w. the Lat. n., but may have been formed fr. *clang*, w. a suff. on the anal. of *clamour*. A repeated loud metallic sound, continued clanging.

clank (I.), vb. intrans. & trans. [1. klangk; 2. klæŋk]. Prob. a mere variant of **clang**, w. slight differentiation of meaning. **a** intrans. (esp. of chain &c.) To make a sharp ringing sound; **b** trans., to cause metal to sound by striking it; esp. *to clank chains*.

clank (II.), n. See prec. A sharp metallic sound, as of metal when struck (implying less resonance than *clang*).

clannish, adj. [1. klánish; 2. klǽniʃ], fr. **clan** & **-ish**. **1.** Pertaining to, characterizing, a clan. **2.** (of individual members of a group or family) Having the spirit and feelings which animate members of the same clan towards each other; hence, inclined to support and help each other, and to be bound together by ties of common interest, affection, and social intercourse, to exclusion of others: *the Scotch are notoriously clannish.*

clannishly, adv. Prec. & **-ly**. In a clannish manner.

clannishness, n. See prec. & **-ness**. The quality of being clannish.

clanship, n. [1. klánship; 2. klǽnʃip], fr. **clan** & **-ship**. **a** Membership of a clan; **b** devotion to one's clan.

clansman, n. [1. klánzman; 2. klǽnzmən]. See **clan** & **man**. Hereditary member of a clan.

clap (I.), vb. trans. & intrans. [1. klap; 2. klæp]. M.E. *clappen*, O.E. *clæppan*; cp. O.N. *klappa*; O.H.G. *klapfen, klaphōn*, Mod. Germ. *klopfen*. **A.** trans. **1. a** To strike together sharply (esp. one's hands, as a sign of approval, as a signal &c.); hence, **b** (with transferred meaning) to express approval of by clapping hands, applaud: *to clap a performance, performer*; **c** to strike lightly, slap with open hand, in a friendly way: *to clap a person on the back.* **2.** (expressing various rapid, forcible movements; followed by *to, on*) *clap spurs to one's horse*; *clap a hat on one's head*; *to clap the lid of a box to*; *to clap on sail* &c. Colloq. Phr. *to clap eyes on*, see, catch sight of. **B.** intrans. To strike hands together as sign of applause; *the crowd cheered and clapped.*

clap (II.), n. M.E. *clap*; cp. M. Du. *klap*, & see prec. **a** A sudden noise caused by two objects striking together (esp. the palms of the hands, as applause &c.); **b** loud, sudden noise as of explosion; esp. *clap of thunder.*

clap (III.), n. Origin doubtful. (vulgar) Gonorrhoea.

clapboard, n. [1. klápbord; 2. klǽpbɔ̄d]. Cp. L.G. *klappholt*, 'stave of cask'. **a** A stave or split oak board, used for making barrels or casks; **b** in U.S.A., a wooden board with one side thicker than the other, used for weather-boarding of houses.

clap-net, n., fr. **clap** (I.) & **net**. A net with jointed rim for catching birds &c., made to close suddenly by clapping the two portions of rim together.

clapper, n. [1. kláper; 2. klǽpə]. M.E. *clapper, cleper*, fr. **clap** (I.) & **-er**. That which claps, strikes; specif. **a** the metal tongue of a bell; **b** rattle for scaring birds.

clapperclaw, vb. trans. [1. kláperklàw; 2. klǽpəklɔ̀], fr. prec. & **claw**. (lit. and fig.) To attack spitefully.

claptrap, n. [1. kláptrap; 2. klǽptræp], fr. **clap** (I.) & **trap**. Empty, plausible, ostentatious language, designed to attract and win popular approval.

claque, n. [1. klak; 2. klæk]. Fr., fr. *claquer*, 'to clack'; cp. **clique**. Set of persons hired to applaud at a play &c.; hence, any organized, hired body of supporters at a public meeting &c.

clarabella, n. [1. kláhrabéla; 2. klárəbélə], fr. Lat. *clāra*, fem. of *clārus*, 'clear', & *bella*, fem. of *bellus*, 'pretty'. See **clear, beauty**. The name of an organ-stop.

clarence, n. [1. klárens; 2. klǽrəns]. Closed, four-wheeled carriage resembling a brougham; named after Duke of Clarence (William IV.).

Clarencieux, n. [1. klárensū; 2. klǽrənsjū], fr. *Clarence* (ducal title of Lionel, third son of Edward III., fr. Clare, in Suffolk) & O. Fr. *-eux*, adj. suff. Title borne by one of the Kings-of-Arms at the Heralds' College, having jurisdiction south of the Trent.

clarendon, n. [1. klárendun; 2. klǽrəndən], fr. the Clarendon Press, Oxford. (typog.) A kind of bold-faced type.

claret, n. [1. kláret; 2. klǽrət]. M.E. *claret, claré, clarry*, fr. O. Fr. (*vin*) *clareté, claré*, fr. Lat. *clārātum*, 'made clear', P.P. of *clārāre*, fr. *clārus*, 'clear, bright'. See **clarify**. **1. a** Originally a clarified wine, now applied in England to red wine of Bordeaux; **b** (colloq. slang) blood; esp. in Phr. *to tap a person's claret*, make his nose bleed. **2.** The colour of this wine, a purplish red.

claret-cup, n., fr. prec. & **cup**. A drink made of claret mixed with liqueur and soda water, together with lemon and spices, generally sweetened and iced.

clarification, n. [1. klàrifikáshun; 2. klæ̀rifikéiʃən], fr. Lat. *clārificātiōn-(em)*, acc. of *clārificātio*, 'glorification' (eccles. Lat.). See **clarify, -ation**. The act of clarifying, clearing up, making bright; state or process of being clarified.

clarify, vb. trans. & intrans. [1. klárifī; 2. klǽrifai]. M.E. *clarifien*, fr. O. Fr. *clarifier*, fr. Lat. *clārificāre*, 'to make illustrious', fr. *clārus*, 'clear, bright, shining; (of sound) loud, distinct; plain, manifest, intelligible', & form of *facere*, 'to make', used in composition (see **fact, -fy**). *Clārus* must orig. have referred to sound, w. the meaning 'loud, resonant', & belongs to the group of words, Lat. *calāre*, 'cry out', *clāmāre*, 'shout' &c., *clāmor*, 'loud cry, shout' &c., discussed under **claim**; cp. **clear**. **1.** trans. **a** To make clear, to strain impurities from (liquids or semi-liquids); **b** (fig., of mind, ideas, feelings &c.) to make intelligible, distinct, plain, to remove obscurity, confusion &c., from. **2.** intrans. (lit. and fig.) To become clear, be freed from obscurities, impurities &c.

clarinet, n. [1. klàrinét, klárinèt; 2. klæ̀rinét, klǽrinèt], fr. Fr. *clarinette*, dimin. of O. Fr. *clarine*, fr. Lat. *clārus*, 'loud and clear'. See **clarify**. **1.** Wood-wind instrument, consisting of a slender tube, with a single reed mouth-piece at one end and bell-shaped opening at the other, played by the fingers on holes and keys. **2.** Organ-stop producing a note resembling that of the clarinet.

clarinettist, n. [1. klàrinétist; 2. klæ̀rinétist], fr. prec. & **-ist**. A player of the clarinet.

clarion, n. & adj. [1. klárìun; 2. klǽriən]. M.E. *clarioun*, fr. O. Fr. *clarion*, 'a kind of trumpet', fr. L. Lat. *clāriōn-(em)*, acc. of *clārio*, fr. Lat. *clārus*, 'clear'. See prec. **1.** n. **a** (chiefly poet.) A kind of trumpet with a narrow tube, producing a clear ringing note; **b** an organ-stop producing a similar tone; **c** the sound produced by the clarion; any clear ringing note resembling it. **2.** adj. (of sounds) Clear, ringing, appealing; chiefly in literary usage: *clarion note*; *clarion voice* &c.

clarionet, n. [1. klàriunét; 2. klæ̀riənét]. Blend of **clarion** & **clarinet**. A clarinet.

clarity, n. [1. kláriti; 2. klǽriti]. M.E. *clarete*, O. Fr. *clarté*, fr. Lat. *clāritāt-(em)*, acc. of *clāritas*, 'brightness, clearness; splendour, celebrity', fr. *clārus*, 'clear'. See **clear** & **-ty**, also **clarify**. **a** (chiefly fig., of ideas, style &c.) Clearness, lucidity, freedom from obscurity; **b** (also lit., of sounds) resonance, distinctness, purity of tone.

clarkia, n. [1. klárkia; 2. klákiə]. Named after an American explorer. A herbaceous, annual garden plant, allied to the willow-herb and fuchsia, cultivated for its bright flowers.

clary, n. [1. klári; 2. kléəri], fr. O. Fr. *sclarée*, fr. Low Lat. *sclarea*; etymol. obscure. A pot herb of the sage family; one variety is cultivated for its ornamental leaves.

clash (I.), vb. intrans. & trans. [1. klash; 2. klæʃ]. Cp. Mod. Germ. *klatschen*, Du. *kletsen*. Imitative. **A.** intrans. **1.** To strike together so as to produce a loud, confused, ringing sound (esp. of arms, bells &c.). **2. a** To come into collision, strike together suddenly, to shock; **b** (fig., of several events fixed to take place at given time) to coincide in time, interfere with each other: *your lecture tomorrow clashes with mine.* **3. a** (fig., of opinions, temper &c.) To be in disagreement, come into conflict, be opposed, irreconcilable; **b** (colloq., of colours) fail to harmonize, be discordant. **B.** trans. To cause to clash, strike together noisily.

clash (II.), n., fr. prec. **1.** A loud, confused, ringing sound, produced by the sudden contact of two, esp. metallic, objects: *the clash of arms, bells* &c. **2.** (fig.) Conflict, disagreement, opposition: *clash of opinions, views* &c.

clasp (I.), vb. trans. & intrans. [1. klahsp; 2. klāsp]. M.E. *claspen, clapsen*; there is no traceable history of the word, wh. appears only in M.E. **A.** trans. **1.** To fasten with a clasp: *to clasp a bracelet round one's wrist* &c. **2. a** To fold tightly with the arms, embrace; **b** to grasp firmly, grip, with the hand. Phrs. *to clasp one's hands*, press tightly together, interlock fingers, in token of supplication, despair, or similar emotion; *to clasp another's hand*, shake hands cordially; **c** (of climbing plants) to twine round, encircle, adhere to with tendrils. **B.** intrans. To perform action of clasping: *we met and clasped*, shook hands.

clasp (II.), n. M.E. *claspe*, fr. prec. **1.** Apparatus provided with a hook, tongue, bolt, or other device, for fastening two things together, e.g. the ends of a belt, the covers of a book, the two parts of a window &c. **2.** A firm hold, grasp, grip, embrace. **3.** A bronze or silver bar affixed to ribbon of a military medal, to commemorate a particular battle in a campaign.

clasp-knife, n. One with blade, or blades, made to shut into the handle.

class (I.), n. [1. klahs; 2. klās]. Fr. *classe*, fr. Lat. *classis*, 'army, fleet; class, division; division of Roman people'. The nearest cogn. is Gk. *klēsis*, 'a calling into court, legal summons; invitation' (to a feast &c.). The fundamental meaning of the Lat. word seems to be 'host, multitude of persons called, or summoned together', hence, 'a group of people'. The starting-point is the base *kel-, *kl- &c., 'to call, shout' &c., wh. appears w. highly differentiated form & meaning in a large number of words in Lat. & Gk., e.g. *calāre*, 'to call', Gk. *kaléō* &c. Cp. **claim, clear, & clarify. 1.** In most general sense, division, group, category; whence kind, sort, type: *a good class of man*; *a poor class of house.* In various senses arising from notion of grouping together according to some definite principle. **2.** (nat. sc.) Order, group, category of organisms &c., which have some essential character or feature in common: *class of animals, of plants, of rocks* &c.; specif., the division or group ranking next below a phylum. **3.** (school and university) **a** Group, collection, assemblage of pupils who learn in common, are taught the same things at the same time: *to be top of the class*; *to take a class of beginners*; **b** category into which candidates are placed according to their degree of success in examination for honours in a university: *to obtain a First Class.* Phr. *to obtain, get, a class*, take honours, as distinguished from pass examination; **c** systematic teaching given in a class, course of instruction: *to take classes in cookery.* **4.** Rank, position, standing in society; social division: *the upper, middle, and lower classes*; *working class.* Phr. *the classes*, upper classes, as contrasted with *the masses.* **5.** Particular degree of approximation to, conformity with, a fixed standard of excellence, merit, beauty, usefulness &c.: *as an orator he was not in the same class with the Prime Minister*; *the best class of hotel.* Phr. *in a class by itself*, of unapproachable merit; (colloq.) *no class*, having no merit, very inferior. **6. a** Distinction in style and quality of accommodation in railway carriages, steamers &c.; **b** compartment, cabin &c. of such description. **7.** Categories into which the management of exhibitions, shows &c. place animals, produce &c. according to principles of classification, more or less arbitrary, decided on by them: *there were several very interesting classes of hunters and carriage horses.*

class (II.), vb. trans., fr. prec. **a** To put into a class, classify, arrange; assign place in a class; hence, **b** to estimate at true value, size up: *to be unable to class a person*; **c** specif., to put (a candidate) into one of the classes at any university honour examination: *he obtained a degree, but was not classed.*

classic (I.), adj. [1. klásik; 2. klǽsik]. Cp. **classical.** Fr. *classique*, fr. Lat. *classicus*, 'relating to the classes of the Roman people; relating to the army or navy'; see prec. & **-ic.** The Engl. word has a very faint connexion w. the Lat. & may be regarded as a fresh creation fr. old material. **1. a** Of the highest excellence, of recognized and undisputed merit: *long before his death, Tennyson's poetry had become classic*; **b** in accordance with the highest canons of excellence: *classic taste.* **2.** Pertaining to, in accordance with, standards of ancient Greek and Roman literature and culture: *classic style*, simple, austere. **3.** Connected with, having associations with, great literature or great writers: *the English Lake district is classic ground for students of Wordsworth and Coleridge.* **4.** Important, famous, having great traditions: in Phr. *classic races*, the five great horse races for three-year-olds, viz., *the Derby, Oaks, St. Leger, Two Thousand* and *One Thousand Guineas.*

classic (II.), n., fr. prec. **1. a** Writer, painter &c. of established and undisputed excellence; **b** specif., an ancient Greek or Latin author. **2.** A scholar, special student, highly skilled and deeply versed in the languages, literatures, and culture of ancient Greece and Rome: *a first-rate classic.* **3.** One whose taste and style are modelled on the ancient writers of Greece and Rome; contrasted with *romantic.* **4.** (in pl.) *The classics*, specif., the ancient languages of Greece and Rome, Greek and Latin.

classical, adj. [1. klásikl; 2. klǽsikl]. **classic & -al.** This word overlaps with **classic** (I.) in respect of some of its usages, while in others it shows some differentiations of meaning. **1.** Of the highest excellence, commonly acknowledged as possessing such; esp. of musical composition, conforming to the best-informed critical taste, representing the most highly elaborated forms, as *sonata, fugue* &c.; contrasted with *popular music.* **2.** Specif. **a** pertaining to, connected with, the ancient culture of Greece and Rome, esp. the language and literature: *classical studies*; *classical art*; *classical literature*; *the classical languages*; *classical tradition*; **b** (of persons) devoted to, deeply versed in, the ancient Greek and Latin culture, languages and literatures: *classical scholar, student, teacher.* **3.** Animated with, exhibiting spirit of, based on, the standards of art which prevailed in ancient Greece and Rome; restrained, severe: *his tastes were strictly classical*; *a building in the classical style*; *a poem conceived on classical lines.* In the Phr. *classical architecture*, the former word might be used of that of a modern building in sense **3**, as well as of an ancient one according to **2, a**, above.

classicalism, n. [1. klásikalizm; 2. klǽsikəlizəm]. Prec. & **-ism. 1. a** Habit of mind formed by prolonged study of, and devotion to, the classical traditions; **b** practice of exhibiting the classical spirit and taste in writing &c. **2.** Greek or Latin idiom introduced into another language.

classically, adv. [1. klásikali; 2. klǽsikəli]. **classical & -ly.** In a classical manner; after the style of classical writers or artists.

classicism, n. [1. klásisizm; 2. klǽsisizəm]. **classic & -ism. 1. a** Adherence to classical principles and taste in art and literature; **b** observance of these in practice. **2.** Scholarship in the ancient languages of Greece and Rome. **3.** Idiom from Greek or Latin introduced into another language.

classicist, n. [1. klásisist; 2. klǽsisist]. **classic & -ist.** Adherent of classical taste, follower of classical models.

classicize, vb. trans. & intrans. [1. klásisīz; 2. klǽsisaiz]. **classic & -ize. 1.** trans. To make classic, approximate to classical models (in style &c.). **2.** intrans. To affect a classical manner in style.

classifiable, adj. [1. klásifīabl; 2. klǽsifaiəbl]. **classify & -able.** Capable of being classified.

classification, n. [1. klāsifikāshun; 2. klǽsifikéiʃən]. See **classify & -ation. 1.** Act or process of classifying, i.e. of arranging things and ideas in groups and classes according to a systematic principle: *the classification of speech sounds has interested grammarians from early times.* **2.** Result of act or process of classifying; the groups and categories in which things are arranged in accordance with a particular principle: *Sweet's classification of speech sounds is regarded by many phoneticians, not only as the most accurate yet proposed, but also as the simplest.*

classificatory, adj. [1. klásifikāteri; 2. klǽsifikeitəri]. See prec. & **-ory.** Of the nature of, connected with, classification.

classify, vb. trans. [1. klásifī; 2. klǽsifai]. Fr. *classifier*, Lat. *classi-*, see **class** (I.), & **-fy.** To arrange in classes, groups, categories, according to a systematic principle, assigning to the same class those things which possess certain features or properties in common.

class list(s), n. **class** (I.) & **list.** List of names published by authority of a university showing which class the candidates in an honours examination have severally obtained.

classman, n. [1. kláhsman; 2. klā́smən]. **class** (I.) & **man.** Candidate who, as a result of a university honours examination, has been put into a class; contrasted with *passman.*

classy, adj. [1. kláhsi; 2. klā́si]. **class** (I.) & **-y.** (vulg. slang) Belonging to, in, a good class; hence superior.

clastic, adj. [1. klástik; 2. klǽstik], fr. Gk. *klastós*, 'broken in pieces', fr. *kláein*, 'to break'. See second element in **cataclasm & -ic.** (geol.) Composed of fragments, fragmental: *clastic rocks*, conglomerates, sandstones &c.

clatter (I.), vb. intrans. & trans. [1. kláter; 2. klǽtə]. O.E. *clatrian.* Imitative word. **1.** intrans. To make a hard, dull noise, or rapid series of such noises, as of a quantity of crockery being put down noisily, or banged together, or of revolving part of machinery which strikes against something at intervals. **2.** trans. To cause to clatter, cause hard objects to give out a dull noise by knocking them together, or against some other hard substance: *to clatter the glass and china*; *clatter about*, to walk about in a rapid, noisy manner, as with hob-nailed boots on a pavement; *clatter along*, to run in heavy boots, or gallop on a horse, along a hard road, making a loud, rattling noise.

clatter (II.), n., fr. prec. The O.E. n. is *clatrung*, 'chattering'. **a** Continuous series of hard, dull, harsh noises, as caused by hard objects knocking together, being flung about, by rattle of revolving machinery, or by a horse's hoofs repeatedly striking hard road; **b** confused, noisy chattering and laughing, esp. of a crowd of people: *clatter of tongues, of noisy laughter.*

clause, n. [1. klawz; 2. klɔ̄z]. Fr. & M.E., fr. Lat. *clausum*, P.P. of *claudere*, 'to shut, enclose', q.v. under **close** (I.) & **conclude.** The Lat. equiv. in rhetoric to *clause* was *clausula*, a dimin. of *clausum.* See also **clavicle, cloister. 1.** (gram.) A short sentence; part or division of a main sentence, forming a grammatical unity in itself, but not necessarily a complete, logical, or grammatical sentence. **2.** A single article, stipulation, or condition in a formal legal instrument, such as a treaty, statute, will &c.

claustral, adj. [1. kláwstral; 2. klɔ̄strəl], fr. Lat. *claustra*, neut. pl. of *claustrum* (rare), 'lock, bolt, bar; barrier', & **-al**, fr. base *claud-*, 'shut', q.v. under **close.** Connected with, pertaining to, resembling, a cloister: *claustral rule.*

claustration, n. [1. klawstrā́shun; 2. klɔ̄stréiʃən]. Formed as though fr. *claustrāt-, P.P. type of *claustrāre, see prec., & **-ion.** Act of shutting up in, confining to, a cloister, or monastery; act of confining rigorously as though in a cloister.

claustrophobia, n. [1. klàwstrōfóbia; 2. klɔ̀strouf óubiə]. Hybrid word formed fr. Lat. *claustrum*, see **claustral**, & Gk. *phóbos*, 'fear', see **-phobia & -phobe.** Morbid fear or dislike of enclosed places.

clavate, adj. [1. klā́vāt; 2. kléiveit], fr. Lat. *clāva*, 'club'. See **claviform & -ate.** (bot.) Shaped like a club.

clavecin, n. [1. klávesin; 2. klǽvəsin]. Fr. See next word. An early form of harpsichord.

clavichord, n. [1. klávikord; 2. klǽvikɔ̄d]. Med. Lat. *clavichordium*, fr. *clāvis*, 'key', & *chorda*, 'string'. See **clavicle & chord.** Early predecessor of the piano; a musical instrument consisting of metal strings stretched horizontally, which were struck from below by small hammers, or tangents, worked from a short keyboard.

clavicle, n. [1. klávikl; 2. klǽvikl], fr. Lat. *clāvicula*, 'small key', also 'tendril of a vine', dimin. of *clāvis*, 'key'. This word is closely related to *clāvus*, 'nail', & both are fr. the base seen in Lat. *claudere*, 'to shut', see **clause & close** (I.). *Clāvis* meant orig. 'a means of shutting, fastening' (a door &c.), & was prob. some form of pin or peg, not greatly differing in form fr. a nail. The secondary meaning 'tendril' was prob. derived fr. the habit of tendrils to 'enclose or encompass' stems &c. The anatomical application of *clavicle* is not very obvious. (anat.) Collarbone, the small bone which connects the sternum or breast-bone with the point of the shoulder.

clavicular, adj. [1. klavíkūlar; 2. klævíkjulə]. Lat. *clāvicula*, see prec., & **-ar**. Connected with the collar-bone.

claviform, adj. [1. kláviform; 2. klǽvifōm]. Lat. *clāva*, 'knotty stick, club', & **-form.** *Clāva* may be compared w. Lat. *clādēs*, 'disaster, injury, defeat'; cp. Gk. *klādos*, 'branch'. The orig. meaning of the base was 'strike, injure, cut' &c. *Clāva* & *klādos* meant perh. first of all 'piece of wood hacked off the tree'; *clādes* having the sense of our 'blow' in fig. meaning. See **clado-**. In the form of a club, i.e. having a knob at one end.

claw (I.), n. [1. klaw; 2. klō]. O.E. *clāwu*, 'hoof, claw, pincers', M.E. *clawe*, still applied in early 13th cent. to the hoof of the ox; cognates are found in many Gmc. languages, cp. O.H.G. *klāwa*, Mod. Germ. *klaue*, O.N. *klō*. The Aryan base **glew-* &c., wh. is supposed to mean 'to roll up, form a ball', & the related base **gloi-*, **glei-* &c., 'stick together' &c., have according to the etymologists been extraordinarily prolific. Some of the words derived fr. these are discussed under **glue, glutinous, globe**, wh. are Lat.; others under **clod, clot, clay, cleave** (II.), wh. are English words of Gmc. origin. The orig. sense of O.E. *clāwu* was apparently 'something curled up', which is not inapplicable to a bird's, or animal's, claws or talons; the allied idea of a 'ball' is perh. the starting-point in its use to describe an animal's hoof. The idea of 'adhering to, seizing', may perh. have been present in the designation of talons. **1.** The sharp, (often) prehensile nails, or talons, of animals of the cat and dog tribe, or of birds. **2.** Things resembling animals' claws, e.g. **a** the human fingers and nails, esp. when long and slender; **b** a tool so shaped, e.g. end of a hammer made for drawing nails. Phr. *to get one's claws into a person*, (fig.) to attack maliciously and fiercely, injure deliberately. **3. a** The pincer-like appendages of lobsters and crabs; **b** pair of steel hooks made to close for gripping and holding things.

claw (II.), vb. trans., fr. prec. **a** (of animals) To seize with the claws; to stick the claws into; scratch, scrape with claws; **b** (fig., of human beings) to seize eagerly, and greedily, with the hand, snatch at: *claw hold of*, seize with claws, or hands.

claw-hammer, n. One with one end of head bent, made thin, and divided by V-shaped opening for extracting nails; *claw-hammer coat*, evening dress-coat, swallow-tail coat.

clay (I.), n. [1. klā; 2. klei]. O.E. *clǣġ*, M.E. *clei, clai* &c. One of the numerous words fr. Aryan base **gloi-*, **glei-*, **gli-*, Gmc. **klai-* &c. meaning 'to stick to, bind, adhere'. O.E. *clǣġ* is fr. Gmc. **klai-gi* (cp. O.E. *clām*, fr. **klai-m*, 'mud'), Aryan **gloi-*, & is therefore cogn. w. Gk. *gloia*, 'glue', & *gloiós*, 'anything sticky or clammy', & w. Lat. *glū-ten*, 'glue', & *glūs*, gen. *glūtis*, 'glue', in wh. *glū-* is fr. earlier **gloi-*; cp. **glue.** See further **cleave** (II.), **glebe, globe,** & the cogn. words mentioned under **claw** & **clammy. 1.** Sticky, tenacious earth, plastic and hardening when baked, as brick, pottery &c. **2.** (fig.) **a** Human flesh: *a man of common clay*; **b** (poet.) the human body when dead; equivalent to *ashes, bones*: *dead and turned to clay*; *the kindly earth will soon hide our clay.* **3.** A clay pipe: *smoking a short clay.*

clay (II.), vb. trans., fr. prec. To cover, smear, bedaub with clay.

clayey, adj. [1. klāi; 2. kléi-i]. **clay** (I.) & **-(e)y. a** Consisting of, abounding in, clay: *a clayey soil*; **b** having a clammy consistency like clay.

claymore, n. [1. klāmōr; 2. kléimō]. Gael., lit. 'big sword', fr. *claidheamh*, 'sword', & *mor*, 'great'. Cp. W. *cledyff*, 'sword', q.v. under **cataclasm**, & W. *mawr*, 'great', cogn. w. O.E. *mǣre*, 'famous, illustrious', & *māra*, 'more'. See **more.** Ancient Scottish two-edged broadsword, esp. one used formerly by the Highland clans.

clay-pigeon, n. A disk of baked clay, sprung from a trap, to take the place of a live pigeon, in pigeon-shooting.

clean (I.), adj. [1. klēn; 2. klīn]. O.E. *clǣn(e)*, 'clear, open; clean; morally pure', fr. W. Gmc. **klaini*, found also in O.H.G. *kleini, chleini*, 'shining, neat, clean, careful, small'. Mod. Germ. *klein*, 'small', O.S. *klēni*, 'neat, small'. The apparent gulf in meaning between the Engl. & Germ. words, at the present day, is largely bridged by the meanings given above for the O.E. & O.H.G. forms. The starting-point of meaning was prob. 'bright', fr. wh. to 'clean' in modern sense is a natural development; Germ., on the other hand, has developed the meaning further, to 'careful, neat, small'. We today associate the last two words & their meanings together. The base **ĝel-*, **ĝl-*, 'bright', occurs in Lat. *galbus*, 'yellow', a Gaulish loan-word, cogn. w. Ir. *glan*, 'clean'; further Gk. *glēnos*, 'bright object, wonder'. The Gk. *geláō*, 'I laugh', *gelānés*, 'smiling, joyful', are fr. same base, showing transference of the idea, 'brightness, radiancy', to a spiritual state, whence the further change of meaning, 'brightness, cheerfulness of mind, mirth, laughter'. The above is accepted by most etymologists, but Kluge goes a step farther & connects the base **gel-* w. that in Gk. *gloiós* &c., 'sticky, greasy' (see **clay, clammy, glue** &c.), & suggests that *clean* & the other Gmc. words meant first of all 'bright and shining from grease'. **1. a** Free from dirt, dust, filth, or impurities of any kind: *to keep oneself, one's house, clean*; **b** specif., physically chaste, pure, continent: *to lead a clean life*; **c** free from moral defilement or blemish; **d** (surg.) free from infective matter, microbes &c., non-septic: *surgically clean*; **e** free from raggedness, having no rough edges, smooth, clear: *a sharp knife makes a clean cut.* Phrs. *to make a clean sweep of*, get rid of entirely; *to have clean hands in the matter* (fig.), be innocent, free from blame; *to make a clean breast of*, to make complete confession of, acknowledge frankly; *to show a clean pair of heels*, to run away from, to escape. **2.** Habitually clean, having clean habits, not given to being dirty or making things dirty: *to be clean in one's person*; *a very clean dog in the house.* **3.** Newly cleaned, just washed, unused, fresh, unsoiled: *to put clean sheets on the bed*; *clean linen*; *put on a clean collar.* **4.** (of paper, slate &c.) Free from writing or printing, unwritten on, fresh, new: *a clean page*; *a clean sheet of paper.* Phr. *a clean record*, with no bad marks or charges. **5.** Symmetrical, shapely, well-proportioned, trim: *clean limbs*; *a clean figure, ankle* &c. **6.** (of physical actions) Dexterous, skilful, well-finished, neat: *a clean stroke, blow*; *clean ball* (at cricket) &c.

clean (II.), vb. trans., fr. prec. **1.** To render clean, remove dirt, filth, dust. A stronger word, usually, when applied to persons, than *wash*; *to clean one's nails, to clean one's hands*, implying removal of considerable dirt; on the other hand, *to clean one's teeth* is equivalent only to *brush, wash, one's teeth.* Applied to other things than the human person, *clean* is more or less colourless, but conveys various shades of meaning, thus: *to clean a house, a room*, sweep and dust it; *to clean a window*, remove dirt by washing, and polish; *clean a picture*, remove dust and dirt which have stuck to it; *clean the silver-plate*, brighten it; *clean a floor*, scrub it; *clean boots*, remove mud, and polish; *clean a stable*, remove filth, and sweep, and so on. **2.** (in various senses, when followed by prepositions or adverbs) *Clean down*, to sweep down (walls &c.); brush down (a horse). *Clean out*, **a** remove dirt and dust from inside a room, receptacle &c.; **b** (colloq.) to exhaust financial resources of: *his betting losses have cleaned him out*; **c** to purge. *Clean up*, **a** to remove dirt and rubbish &c., esp. from floor, make tidy; **b** (fig.) to reduce (affairs, arrears of work &c.) to order, put in order; finish up a job left uncompleted.

clean (III.), adv., fr. **clean** (I.). O.E. *clǣne*, 'entirely'. **1.** Entirely, completely: *I clean forgot to ask*; *to throw a stone clean over the house.* **2.** (direct fr. **clean** (I.) adj.) **a** In a manner free from dirt: *to scrub the floor clean*; **b** exactly, neatly: *to be hit clean in the eye.* (This usage is almost that of the old adv. **1.**)

clean-cut, adj. [1. klénkut, klénkút; 2. klínkat, klinkát]. **a** Clearly, sharply, defined; well-moulded, clear-cut: *clean-cut features*; **b** (fig.) clear, free from obscurity, not dubious; definite: *a clean-cut scheme.*

cleaner, n. [1. kléner; 2. klínə]. **clean** (II.) & **-er. a** Person who cleans; specif., one who cleans clothes by some chemical process; **b** mechanical device for cleaning.

clean-handed, adj. **clean** (I.) & **handed.** (only fig.) Free from reproach or blame; innocent; upright.

clean-limbed, adj. **clean** (I.) & **limbed.** Having shapely, well-proportioned limbs.

cleanliness, n. [1. klénlines; 2. klénlinis]. **cleanly** (I.) & **-ness. a** Habit of being clean; **b** condition of being clean.

cleanly (I.), adj. [1. klénli; 2. klénli]. O.E. *clǣnlīce*, 'pure'. See **clean** (I.). The shortening of the vowel is a late O.E. process, and took place before the combination of consonants *-nl-*. Of clean habits; clean, pure.

cleanly (II.), adv. [1. klénli; 2. klínli]. This is a new formation fr. *clean*, w. addition of the ordinary adv. suff. Had the word been derived fr. the O.E. *clǣnlīce*, adv., the vowel wd. have been shortened as in prec. word, q.v. In a clean manner; purely, chastely: *to work cleanly*; *to live cleanly.*

cleanness, n. [1. klén-nes; 2. klín-nis]. O.E. *clǣnnes*, 'purity'. The direct survival of the O.E. word wd. have had a short vowel in first syll., through the influence of the *-nn-*. Our present pronunciation is due to the anal. of the adj. *clean.* **a** State of being clean, in any sense; **b** quality of being clean.

cleanse, vb. trans. [1. klenz; 2. klenz]. O.E. *clǣnsian*, M.E. *clensen.* See **clean** (I.) & **cleanly** (I.). The vowel was shortened in late O.E. before *-ns-*. To clean, purify thoroughly, remove dirt and impurity from; in various specif. senses, lit. and fig. **a** To remove source of infection: *surgeons cleanse their hands before an operation*; **b** to clean ceremonially: *the priest cleanses the vessels after Mass*; **c** to purge medicinally: *to cleanse the system*; **d** to free from moral pollution: *to cleanse the soul from sin.*

cleansing, n. & adj. [1. klénzing; 2. klénziŋ]. Prec. & **-ing. a** n. Act or process of cleansing or of being cleansed; **b** adj., fr. Pres. Part. of *cleanse*, tending to cleanse, having the property of rendering clean: *soap and hot water are very cleansing*; *cleansing fires* (esp. in moral sense).

clean-up, n. [1. klén úp; 2. klín áp]. **a** Act or process of cleaning up; **b** specif., the collection of stores, ammunition &c., left behind by troops on the move.

clear (I.), adj. [1. klēr; 2. kliə]. M.E. *clēr(e)*, fr. O. Fr. *cleir, cler* &c., 'pure, bright', fr. Lat. *clārus*, 'bright, shining; loud; plain, intelligible'. The etymol. of this Lat. word is discussed under **clarify.** See also **claim, clamour** &c. General meaning bright, plain, distinct; applied literally to sensations of sight and hearing, and also figuratively to things of the mind. **1.** (of sound) **a** Ringing, resonant, audible, pure, reverse of *husky, hoarse*: *clear note of the trumpet*; *a clear tone*; *clear voices of children*; **b** (of mode of speech, articulation, pronunciation) distinct, well-articulated, capable of being easily distinguished by the ear; reverse of *thick, indistinct*: *he had a loud, strong voice, but his utterance was far from clear*; *in spite of a poor, weak voice, his delivery was clear and distinct.* **2.** (of visual impressions) **a** (light, or luminous objects) Bright, free from cloudiness or mist: *a clear sky*; *clear light from heaven*; *a clear fire*, b (of things seen) distinct, easily seen, making sharp, vivid impression on the eye; contrasted with *dim, indistinct, blurred*: *a clear outline*; *a clear reflection in the water*; *a clear photograph*; Phr. *as clear as day*, bright and distinct; c (of the eye, sight) penetrating, capable of seeing distinctly: *my power of seeing is still clear.* 3. (of consistency of transparent substances, esp. liquids, as judged by the eye) Bright, translucent, free from cloudiness, as of solid particles held in suspension: *old port will not be clear unless it is carefully decanted*; *the clear waters of the lake.* 4. a Free from obstruction, hindrance, danger; unimpeded: *our Navy kept the seas clear of enemy vessels*; *a clear passage*; *roads clear of traffic*; Phrs. *the coast is clear* (fig.), no difficulty, hindrance; *to keep clear of*, avoid; b free(d) from, quit of: *clear of debt*; *clear of worry* &c.; c entire, with nothing subtracted, intact: *a clear month*; *two clear days*; *a hundred pounds clear profit.* 5. (fig., of character, conduct &c.) Free from imputation of evil or guilt, devoid of sinister motives &c.: *clear from suspicion*; *clear of all bad intentions.* 6. (fig., of states of mind, ideas, understanding, expression of ideas &c.) a Free from obscurity or dubiety; easy to be apprehended, grasped, by the intellect, plain to the intelligence: *a clear statement*; *clear style*; *to make things clear*; *it is quite clear what he is driving at*; b (of things) certain, unmistakable; (of persons) positive, confident, sure: *it is clear you have been swindled*; *I am quite clear what I ought to do.* Phrs. *to see one's way clear* (fig.), have no difficulty: *to be clear in one's (own) mind*; *to have a clear head.*

clear (II.), vb. trans. & intrans., fr. prec. **A.** trans. 1. To render clear, free from cloudiness, oppressiveness &c.: *thunder has cleared the air.* Phr. *to clear the air* (fig., of moral atmosphere), get rid of misunderstanding, ill-feeling, so as to make situation easier and pleasanter. 2. a To render free from, remove obstructions, hindrances, encumbrances from: *to clear the road of traffic*; *clear the pavement of snow*; *clear the decks for action*, also fig.; Phr. *to clear the way* (fig.), prepare for future action by removing difficulties; b get rid of, banish from: *to clear the city of undesirables*; c specif., to get rid of obstacles in throat, or hoarseness of voice, by coughing: *to clear one's throat*; d (of mental process) to do away with, banish from: *to clear one's mind of doubts, suspicions* &c.; c (tradesman's expression) to get rid of superfluous or antiquated stock by selling at reduced price: *must be cleared*; *great reductions in order to clear.* 3. To free from suspicion, or imputation of guilt, from guilt: *to clear one's character*; *clear oneself from a charge*; *clear one's conscience.* 4. To prevent from becoming entangled; disentangle; esp. of *a fishing line, lash of a whip* &c. 5. To pass an obstacle without collision: *my car only just cleared the lorry in the lane.* 6. To leap over without touching: *to clear a hedge, a five-bar gate* &c. 7. To make an absolute profit of so much: *to clear £50.* Phr. *to clear expenses*, make enough over a transaction to pay expenses. **B.** intrans. 1. To become clear, cloudless: *the sky, weather, is clearing.* 2. (of liquids &c.) To become free from suspended particles of matter; become bright, limpid: *the wine will clear if the sediment is allowed to settle.* 3. (of shipping) To fulfil all conditions required by port authorities, by paying dues &c., before leaving. 4. (colloq. slang) To go away, leave; for *clear out.* **C.** Followed by adverbs or prepositions. *Clear away*, 1. trans., a to remove (obstructions &c.); b specif., to remove plates &c. from table after a meal: *please clear away the tea-things*; *you can clear away now*; c (of non-material things) to remove, get rid of: *clear away doubts, difficulties* &c.; 2. intrans., to dissipate, pass off, vanish: *the thunder has, clouds have, cleared away.* *Clear off*, 1. trans., a to complete, bring to finish, wipe out: *to clear off arrears of work*; b drive out, expel: *to clear bad workmen off one's place*; 2. intrans., a (of rain, clouds &c.) see *clear away* 2; b (slang) to take one's leave, depart: *just clear off at once.* *Clear out*, 1. trans., a to remove dirt, obstruction from inside of anything: *clear out a drain, pigstye* &c.; b (colloq. slang) to exhaust one's supply of money, leave one penniless: *that loss has cleared me out completely*; 2. intrans. (colloq. slang) to go away, take one's leave abruptly: *I must clear out at once, the house is unhealthy.* *Clear up*, 1. trans., a to put a muddle straight, reduce confusion to order, make (a room &c.) tidy: *clear up this litter before you go away*; b (fig.) to solve, explain (a mystery &c.); 2. intrans. (of weather) to become fine(r), brighter &c.

clear (III.), adv., fr. **clear** (I.). Without let or hindrance, without impediment, completely, clean: *to get clear away, off.*

clearage, n. [1. klḗrij; 2. klíəridž]. **clear** (I.) & **-age**. Act of clearing; a clearance.

clearance, n. [1. klḗrans; 2. klíərəns]. **clear** (I.) & **-ance**. Act or process of clearing (in various senses); a removal, riddance, of obstruction and encumbrances: *to make a clearance of one's old clothes*; b cutting down of wood over considerable area, esp. of a large tract in a forest so cleared, so as to open up and put into cultivation; c expulsion of inhabitants from all the houses in a village, by the landlord, e.g. as formerly in the Highlands of Scotland, in order to afforestate area; d act of paying dues and fulfilling all obligations by a ship at a port, prior to departure; e space left clear between two objects passing each other or between a moving object and that through which it passes: *the canal leaves a clearance of ten feet for the largest vessels afloat*; *clearance sale*, system adopted by shopkeepers at certain seasons of the year of selling out their old stock at reduced prices, in order to make room for new stock.

clear-headed, adj. (fig.) Having a clear mind, free from confusion of thought.

clearing, n. [1. klḗring; 2. klíəriŋ]. **clear** (II.) & **-ing**. 1. Tract of land cleared of wood or forest. See **clearance, b.** 2. Commercial method of exchanging cheques, settling accounts &c. between different banks and business firms.

clearing-house, n. Central office and system by which cheques of different banks are exchanged and accounts made up.

clearly, adv. [1. klḗrli; 2. klíəli], fr. **clear** (I.) & **-ly**. In a clear manner (in various senses): a brightly, radiantly: *the sun shone clearly*; b distinctly, plainly perceptible to the sight: *to see clearly*; c with a ringing sound, not husky or muffled: *to sing clearly*; d with distinct articulation, so that the words can be heard: *to speak clearly*; e in a condition free from cloudiness, in state of translucence, brightly: *the river ran clearly*; f (of intellectual things) in a manner plain to the intellect, easily to be understood, free from obscurity: *to state one's case clearly.*

clearness, n. [1. klḗrnes; 2. klíənes], fr. **clear** (I.) & **-ness**. The quality of being clear, in all senses.

clear-starch, vb. trans. & intrans. a trans. To stiffen (linen &c.) with colourless starch; b intrans., to practise this art.

clear-starching, n. Act and process, trade, of stiffening material with colourless starch.

clearstory. See **clerestory.**

cleat (I.), n. [1. klēt; 2. klīt]. Not found in O.E., but wd. be **clēat*, fr. Gmc. **klaut-*; M.E. *clēte*, 'wedge'. Cogn. w. Du. *kloot*, 'ball', Germ. *klotz*, 'lump'. See further under **clod** & **clot.** Device for preventing a rope from slipping, consisting of a horizontal piece of wood or iron either with projecting ends round which rope is hitched, or with two holes through which rope is threaded, passing upwards through one and downward through the other.

cleat (II.), vb. trans., fr. prec. To fasten by means of a cleat.

cleavable, adj. [1. klḗvabl; 2. klívəbl]. **cleave** (I.) & **-able.** Capable of being cloven apart, divided.

cleavage, n. [1. klḗvij; 2. klívidž]. **cleave** (I.) & **-age.** 1. a (of material things) Act of splitting or cleaving; b condition of being divided or split; c place in anything where there is a cleft or fissure. 2. (of non-material things) Disruption, division, separation, lack of agreement between persons, or in their opinions &c.: *a cleavage in a community, in regard to policy, views* &c.

cleave (I.), vb. trans. & intrans. [1. klēv; 2. klīv]. O.E. *clēofan*, 'split, cleave', M.E. *clēven*; orig. a strong vb., now both strong & weak. Pret. *clove* & *cleft*, P.P. *cloven* & *cleft.* Germ. cognates, O.H.G. *chlioban*, Mod. Germ. *klieben*, O.N. *kljūfa*, fr. Gmc. base **kleub-*, **klaub-*, **klub-*; cogn. w. Lat. *glūbere*, 'peel, strip bark off', fr. **gleubh-*, & *glūma*, 'husk, shell', fr. **gleubh-ma*; further, Gk. *glúphō*, 'I hollow out, engrave, carve', see **glyph**, *gluphis*, 'notch in an arrow for the string'. The further, remoter connexion w. a base **gel-*, 'to roll up in a ball', wh. Walde suggests, may appear fanciful, but is not absolutely impossible. The line of development of meaning, at this rate, wd. be 'to unroll a ball, peel the skin off a round thing, e.g. the rind off a fruit', whence 'to break up, divide, split' generally. For this other base see **claw, clot, globe.** 1. trans. To divide by force, either by a powerful blow, or by a slashing stroke from a sharp cutting edge; to split; to cut in two; make a fissure, chasm, in the ground: *to cleave a block of wood in two*; *to cleave an apple in two with a knife*; *to cleave a man's head open with a sword*; *the earthquake has cleft great chasms in the rocks.* 2. intrans. To come apart, split in two, fall open: *green wood cleaves more easily than dry.*

cleave (II.), vb. intrans. O.E. *clifian, cleofian*, 'stick, adhere', M.E. *clēven*; O.H.G. *chlēben*, Mod. Germ. *kleben*, 'stick'. This is fr. Gmc. **klī(b-)*, **klai(b-)*, **kli(b-)*, Aryan **glei-*, **gloi-* &c., & belongs to the group of words discussed under **clammy, clay, glebe, glue, agglutinate** &c. Orig. weak, *cleave* is now usu. strong in Pret. by confusion w. **cleave** (I.). a To stick, adhere, become attached to, as of *clay to boots* &c.; Phr. *his tongue clove (clave) to the roof of his mouth*, he was in a state of agitation and fear; b (fig.) to unite oneself to, have attachment for, adhere to: *a man shall leave his father and mother and cleave to his wife.* (Archaic in both senses.)

cleaver (I.), n. [1. klḗver; 2. klívə]. **cleave** (I.) & **-er.** He who, that which, splits, cleaves; specif., a heavy, short-handled chopper for cutting up carcases.

cleaver(s) (II.), n., fr. **cleave** (II.) & **-er.** That which sticks; specif., pl. goose-grass, with sticky, hairy leaves that stick to clothes and animals' coats.

cleek, n. [1. klēk; 2. klīk]. Nthn. form of **clutch.** Large hook or crook for seizing hold of things; specif., an iron-headed club, used in golf, with narrow, straight face.

clef, n. [1. klef; 2. klɛf]. Fr., fr. Lat. *clāvis*, 'key'. See **clavicle.** a Sign of pitch used in musical notation; three clefs are used, indicating respectively bass, medium, and treble; b the ranges of pitch indicated by the symbols.

cleft (I.), n. [1. kleft; 2. klɛft]. Not found in O.E., but in M.E., as *clift*; prob. a S.E. dialectal type of an O.E. **clyft*, fr. **klufti-*; cp. Mod. Germ. *kluft*, 'fissure, chasm', fr. base **klub-*, as in O.E. *clufon*, Pret. pl. of *clēofan*, q.v. under **cleave** (I.). Opening, division, result of cleaving; now chiefly a fissure, chasm, opening in the ground or a rock.

cleft (II.), vb. Pret. & P.P. of **cleave** (I.). M.E. *cleft(e)*, a new wk. formation. Cp. O.E. Pret. *clēaf*, M.E. *clēf.* See also **clove, cloven.**

cleft-palate, n. P.P. of **cleave** (I.) & **palate.** Congenital defect of the roof or palate of the mouth, the two halves not being properly joined together.

cleg, n. [1. kleg; 2. klɛg], fr. O.N. *cleggi*. (provinc.) A horse-fly.

cleistogamic, adj. [1. klīstōgámik; 2. klàistougǽmik], fr. Gk. *kleistós*, 'shut', & *gamikós*, 'connected with a wedding'. For former see **close** (I.), & for the latter **-gamy.** (bot.) Having flowers that do not open, and are self-fertilizing.

clem, vb. trans. [1. klem; 2. klɛm]. Cp. Du. & Germ. *klemmen*, 'to pinch', & cp. **clamp.** (N. and Scots dial.) To starve, pinch, as with hunger, cold &c.

clematis, n. [1. klématis; 2. klémətis]. Lat., fr. Gk. *klēmatís*, 'brushwood, faggot-wood', fr. *klêma*, genit. *klémat-os*, 'twig, shoot, for grafting, slip', esp. 'vine-twig'. These belong to the base seen in Gk. *kláō*, 'I break, break off'; cp. Lat. *clāva*, 'a club', & discussion of etymol. under **claviform.** See also **holt**, 'woodland'. One of large group of trailing, climbing, ornamental plants with bright-coloured flowers, varying in size, colour, and form according to species.

clemency, n. [1. klémensi; 2. klémənsi]. Cp. Fr. *clémence*, 'mildness, mercy', fr. Lat. *clēmentia*, 'calmness, mildness of weather', also of disposition. See **clement. a** (of weather) Calmness, mildness, warmth; **b** (fig., of human character and habits) gentleness, forbearance; leniency (towards offenders).

clement, adj. [1. klément; 2. klémənt]. Fr., fr. Lat. *clēment-(em)*, in same senses as Engl. Connected w. base **kʹlin-* &c., 'slope, incline towards', as in Lat. *clīnāre*, Gk. *klínō*, 'slope' &c., q.v. under **clinical**; see also Gmc. form of same base, **hli(n)-* &c., under **lean** (II.), **lid, ladder.** Mild, calm, soft (of weather); gentle, indulgent, forbearing (of human beings).

clench, vb. trans. & intrans. [1. klensh; 2. klɛnʃ]. See also **clinch.** Not in O.E., but as *clenchen* in M.E. This has all the appearance of an Engl. word & wd. presuppose a Gmc. type **klankjan*, wh. was prob. the same base as **clank** & **clink.** These are words imitative of sound caused by striking metal &c., so that **clinch** & **clench**, meaning 'to fix, fasten', must orig. have meant 'to secure, make fast, by striking', e.g. by driving home a nail. All these words are prob. further connected w. **cling. 1.** General sense, to make fast, firm, to secure, tighten &c. Specif. **a** to make a bolt, rivet, or nail secure from slipping or pulling out by bending over or flattening the ends when in position; **b** to close fingers tightly inwards and fold the thumb firmly over them outside: *to clench one's fist*; **c** to set the jaw tight, with upper and lower teeth brought firmly together, and held in this position by bracing muscles of the jaw: *to clench one's teeth, jaws*; (also fig.) to adopt firm determination; **d** intrans.: *his hands, teeth, clenched.* **2.** (fig., more often **clinch**, in this sense) To settle definitely, conclude, beyond possibility of undoing: *to clench a bargain, argument* &c.

clepsydra, n. [1. klépsidra; 2. klépsidrə]. Gk. *klepsúdra*, 'water-clock', fr. *kléptō*, 'I steal' (see first element in **kleptomania**), & *húdōr*, 'water' (see **hydro-**). Device for measuring passage of time by means of a graduated flow of water, through an aperture in a bowl &c.

clerestory, clearstory, n. [1. klḗrstōri; 2. klíəstɔ̄ri]. **clear** & **storey.** Upper row of windows above the roofs of the aisles in large churches and cathedrals, esp. of Gothic style; contrasted with the *blind-storey*, or *triforium.*

clergy, n. [1. klérji; 2. klə́dži]. M.E., fr. O. Fr. *clergie* &c., 'clerkship, learning', & 'clergy' in mod. sense, fr. L. Lat. *clēricātus.* See **clerk, cleric. 1.** Body of ordained ministers of religion in the Church of England, Church of Scotland, the Roman and the Greek Churches, including bishops, priests, and deacons; extended also to ministers of other Christian denominations. *Benefit of clergy*, right formerly claimed by, and granted to, one in holy orders accused of felony, to be tried before an ecclesiastical court; afterwards extended to all who could read. Phr. *to plead one's clergy*, to plead that one is entitled to benefit of clergy. **2.** Learning (obs.).

clergyable, adj. [1. klérjiabl; 2. klə́džiəbl]. Prec. & **-able.** Admitting to, entitled to, benefit of clergy.

clergyman, n. [1. klérjiman; 2. klə́džimən]. One in holy orders; specif., an ordained minister of the Church of England, for whom, until recently, it was the universal term; now, in some circles, giving place to *priest.* Not normally used of bishops. *Clergyman's sore throat*, inflammation of the larynx and vocal chords, which attacks those who have to use their voices frequently in public; generally caused by imperfect voice production.

cleric, n. [1. klérik; 2. klérik]. L. Lat. *clēricus*, fr. Gk. *klērikós*, 'belonging to the clergy'; an adj. derived fr. *klêros*, 'lot, portion, inheritance', applied to Christian clergy fr. the notion that the Lord was their portion. The word was borrowed fr. Lat. already in O.E. in the forms *clēric, clīroc* &c., but was prob. reborrowed later; see **clerk.** Gk. *klêros* is related to *kláō*, 'cut, break off'; cp. **clematis** & **claviform.** Any person in holy orders; of rather wider application than *clergyman*, since it is applicable to one of any rank in the hierarchy.

clerical, adj. & n. [1. klérikl; 2. klérikl]. L. Lat. *clēricālis*, fr. prec. & **-al. 1.** Connected with the clergy: *clerical garments.* **2.** Attached to the clergy; favourable to the influence of the clergy in political affairs. **3.** Pertaining to writing and copying: *clerical work in an office*; *a clerical error.* **4.** n. Member of clerical party, one favourable to the domination of the clergy.

clericalism, n. [1. klérikalizm; 2. klérikəlizəm]. Prec. & **-ism. a** State of mind, system, favourable to domination of the clergy; **b** undue, exaggerated, influence exerted by the clergy.

clericalist, n. [1. klérikalist; 2. klérikəlist]. **clerical** & **-ist.** One who supports clericalism.

clerk (I.), n. [1. klark; 2. klāk]. Same as **cleric**, but prob. descendant of the word as borrowed in O.E. *clēric, clērc*, M.E. *clerk(e).* **1.** A clergyman (archaic); legal Phr. *clerk in holy orders*, official description of a clergyman of the Church of England. **2.** A learned man, scholar (archaic or historical). **3. a** Term applied to various types of official in Government service: *clerk of the House of Lords, House of Commons*; **b** (law) *clerk of Arraigns, Assize*, barrister with permanent duties in a criminal court. Phr. *clerk of the weather*, fictitious official supposed to control the weather. **4.** Minor (lay) official connected with a parish church, one of whose duties was formerly to lead the responses: *parish clerk.* **5.** Person employed in a commercial or business office, generally in a humble capacity, his duties being to copy documents, add up accounts &c.: *bank clerk*; *correspondence clerk.*

clerk (II.), vb. intrans., fr. prec. To act as a clerk.

clerkdom, n. [1. klárkdum; 2. klákdəm]. **clerk** (I.) & **-dom. a** Rank, status, of a clerk; **b** social grade composed of clerks.

clerkly, adj. [1. klárkli; 2. klákli]. **clerk** (I.) & **-ly. a** Pertaining to a clergyman; clerical (archaic); **b** pertaining to a scholar; esp. *a clerkly hand*, good penmanship.

clerkship, n. [1. klárkship; 2. klákʃip]. **clerk** (I.) & **-ship. a** Position, status, of a clerk; **b** occupation of a clerk.

clever, adj. [1. kléver; 2. klévə]. The etymol. of this typical Engl. word is very obscure. The form *cliver*, 'quick at seizing', is found in early M.E., & this is prob. connected w. **cleave** (II.). If this is so, the transference of meaning fr. bodily to mental grasping or understanding is not violent. On the other hand, connexion of *clever* (though not of M.E. *cliver*) w. **cleave** (I.) is equally possible, & the development of meaning, 'divide, distinguish, discriminate' &c., is an obvious one. Cp. **discriminate**, & O.E. *(ġe)scād*, 'separation, discrimination, understanding', fr. *scādan*, 'to divide, distinguish between'. **1.** (of mental qualities) **a** Intelligent, capable of understanding, quick, able to learn (contrasted with *stupid*); **b** generally competent, ingenious; **c** (of human action or its products) evincing ability, intelligence, ingenuity, skill on part of performer: *a clever move, speech, book, piece of work* &c.; **d** (in unfavourable sense) showy but shallow, pert, superficial. **2.** (of bodily qualities) **a** Possessing, exhibiting, dexterity and skill; dexterous, neat, adroit, highly skilful: *a clever conjurer, player on the banjo*; *a clever catch at cricket clever stroke at golf*; **b** specif. (of a horse), a good jumper, safe and certain across country.

cleverish, adj. [1. kléverish; 2. klévəriʃ]. Prec. & **-ish. a** Rather, moderately, clever; **b** decidedly, remarkably, clever.

cleverly, adv. [1. kléverli; 2. klévəli]. **clever** & **-ly.** In a clever manner.

cleverness, n. [1. klévernes; 2. klévənis]. **clever** & **-ness.** State, quality, of being clever.

clevis, n. [1. klévis; 2. klévis]. Connected w. **cleave** (II.). U-shaped piece of iron with a pin passing through the open ends, used for making fast tackle to pole of a waggon, plough &c.

clew, n. & vb. trans. [1. kloo; 2. klū]. O.E. *clīwen*, 'ball of thread, anything in the shape of a ball'. Same word as **clue**, though differentiated in spelling & meaning. In M.E. *clue, clewe, of threde.* Cp. O.H.G. *chliuwi* &c. in same sense. Derived fr. base **glew-* &c., 'draw together, roll up into something like a ball'. See the words referred to under etymol. of **claw**, also **globe, & agglomerate**; see also **clue. 1.** n. **a** Ball of yarn or thread &c.; **b** after, lower corner of a sail; loop at corner of a sail; **c** combination of cords with which hammock is suspended. **2.** vb. **a** *Clew up*, to roll up into a ball; **b** *to clew up a sail*, to haul it up to the yard ready for furling. Phr. (naut.) *clew up*, intrans., finish off a job of work.

clew garnet, n. Rope by which a sail is hauled up to the yards for furling.

cliché, n. Anglicized pronunciation [1. kléshā; 2. klíʃei]. Fr., 'stereotype reproduction of picture or writing; stereotyped expression', P.P. of *clicher*, 'to stereotype'. Verbal formula, stereotyped expression, set, hackneyed phrase, catch-word.

click (I.), vb. intrans. & trans. [1. klik; 2. klik]. Imitative word; occurs as *klikken* in E. Fris. Cp. **clack. 1.** intrans. To make a slight cracking, snapping, dull noise, **a** with tongue against roof of mouth; **b** as of a lock or catch, gun-cock &c., working on a spring, snapping into position. **2.** trans. **a** To use (one's tongue) against roof of mouth so as to produce clicking sound: *to click one's tongue*; **b** to cause (a mechanical, spring-driven device) to make such a sound in shooting into position: *to click a bolt* &c.; hence, **c** to shut or open (door, window-catch &c.) so that the sound is made: *to click the door (to).* Phr. *to click one's heels (together)*, bring them together with a snap, esp. when about to bow to someone.

click (II.), n., fr. prec. Thin, rapid, snapping sound. See prec. Specif., sound which forms essential part of some South African languages, made by sucking the air between tongue and roof of mouth: *Kaffir clicks* &c.

click beetle, n. Any of several coleopterous insects, of tropical America, family *Elateridae*, emitting light, popularly known as *firefly.*

client, n. [1. klíent; 2. kláiənt]. Fr., fr. Lat. *client-(em)*, 'adherent, retainer, follower'. Prob. fr. base **kʹli-* &c., 'slope towards, lean on' &c., in sense of 'one who leans on another, dependent'. See this base & the other form **kʹlin-* &c. under **acclivity,**

climax, clinical, decline, lean (**II.**) **ladder. 1.** (Roman hist.) One of an inferior class, that of the Plebeians, who were the dependents of the patrician families, or of an individual member of one of these. **2. a** One who employs another professionally, as adviser, or agent in his affairs; esp. one advised by a solicitor, or represented in a law court by a barrister: *a lawyer's clients*; **b** (more rarely) a tradesman's customer.

clientage, n. [1. klíentij; 2. kláiəntidž]. Prec. & **-age.** Body of clients, supporters; clientèle.

cliental, adj. [1. kliéntal; 2. klaiéntəl]. See prec. & **-al.** Pertaining to, being in relation of, a client.

clientèle, n. [1. kléahntél, -tál; 2. kliãtél, kliãtéil]. Fr. See **client.** Persons employing tradesman, patronizing hotel, place of amusement &c.; whole body of such customers or patrons: *it is good business to try to satisfy the usual clientèle.*

clientless, adj. [1. klíentles; 2. kláiəntlis]. **client** & **-less.** Deprived of, without, clients.

clientship, n. [1. klíentship; 2. kláiəntʃip]. **client** & **-ship.** Position, status, of a client.

cliff, n. [1. klif; 2. klif]. O.E. *clif*, O.S. & O.N. *klif.* Origin doubtful. Connexion w. **cleave** (**II.**), wh. has been suggested, appears improbable. Steep, precipitous surface of rock, esp. lofty rocky edge of land facing sea.

climacteric, n. & adj. [1. klīmaktérik; klimákterik; 2. klaimæktérik; klaimǽktərik]. Gk. fr. *klīmaktḗr*, 'rung of a ladder', & **-ic**, fr. *klímax*, 'ladder'. See **climax. 1.** n. **a** Some great, decisive, and crucial stage, or period, in life of individual, or history of nations; **b** some great and decisive event happening at such a period; **c** specif., period of life at which the human constitution undergoes a fundamental change with the approach of old age, esp. the time of the menopause in women. Phr. *grand climacteric*, generally the 63rd year of human life. **2.** adj. Connected with, pertaining to the, or a, climacteric: *climacteric changes.*

climactic, adj. [1. klīmáktik; 2. klaimǽktik]. Irregular formation fr. **climax** & **-ic.** Pertaining to a climax.

climate, n. [1. klímit; 2. kláimit]. Fr. *climat*, Gk. *klímat-os* (gen. of *klíma*), 'slope, region of the earth, climate'. See **climax. a** Habitual, average, condition of the atmosphere with regard to temperature, sunshine, wind, rainfall &c.; **b** region of the earth considered as exhibiting certain atmospheric conditions: *to winter in Africa or some other warm climate.*

climatic, adj. [1. klīmátik; 2. klaimǽtik]. Prec. & **-ic.** Pertaining to, connected with, the climate.

climatographical, adj. [1. klīmatográfikl; 2. klaimætəgrǽfikəl]. Next word & **-ic** & **-al.** Pertaining to the study of climate.

climatography, n. [1. klīmatógrafi; 2. klaimətɔ́grəfi]. See **climate** & **-graphy.** Study of, description of, climates.

climatologist, n. [1. klīmatólojist; 2. klaimətɔ́lədžist]. See **climate** & **-logist.** Student of, expert in, climatology.

climatology, n. [1. klīmatóloji; 2. klaimətɔ́lədži]. See **climate** & **-logy.** Scientific study of climatic conditions, their causes, and distribution.

climax, n. [1. klímaks; 2. kláimæks]. Gk., 'ladder, flight of steps', lit. 'something sloping, leading up'. The base **k'li-*, **k'lin-* &c., occurs in many formations in the various branches of Aryan speech, is enormously prolific, & undergoes numerous differentiations of meaning. From the same base, though w. different formative elements associated w. it, comes **ladder**, O.E. *hlǣdder*, fr. Gmc. **hlaid-*, Aryan **k'loit-*; cp. Gk. *klītús*, 'slope, hill-side', w. different vowel gradation; cp. also Gk. *klínō*, 'slope, slant, incline'. See further under **clinical** & words referred to under **client.** Originally a series, now chiefly the final stage, or object in such: **a** the last, and most important, in a series of events of which this is the outcome; **b** culminating point in an argument or statement; **c** highest point, apex (lit. and fig.).

climb (**I.**), vb. trans. & intrans. [1. klīm; 2. klaim]. O.E. *clīmban* (strong vb.), O.H.G. *chlimban.* Prob. related to the large group of words such as **clam, clammy**; more remotely w. **cleave** (**II.**), & the other words there referred to; cp. further O.E. *clamm*, 'grasp, grip, bond, fetter' &c. The basal idea is 'grip, stick on to, grasp' &c. See **clamber. A.** trans. **1. a** To pull and propel oneself upwards on something, by an effort, esp. using hands and feet: *to climb a tree, a rope* &c.; **b** to walk up a steep incline, to scale flight of stairs, ladder &c.: *to climb a hill, mountain* &c.; also *climb up.* **2.** (of plants) To grow up or along something, holding by means of tendrils: *the clematis has climbed the trellis.* **3.** To mount gradually as though with effort: *the sun has climbed the sky.* **4.** (fig.) To rise in the world, attain important position by exerting effort: *to climb the path of fame*; *climb the heights of power.* **B.** intrans. **1.** To get higher up, raise oneself, ascend, by using effort, using hands and feet: *sailors and monkeys are supposed to climb well.* Phr. *to climb like a monkey, like a goat, a cat.* **2.** (of plants) To grow upwards or along, clinging by tendrils: *many roses will not climb, but have to be carefully trained up a wall.* **3.** (fig.) To rise in life, in society, by dint of effort, to exert considerable energy to this end: *to climb to power, into society* &c. **C.** (with prep. and adv.) *Climb down*, to descend, come down, laboriously, with effort; lower oneself, using hands and feet. Phr. *to climb down* (fig.), abandon position, give up one's point, abate one's claims. *Climb up*, to ascend with an effort; pull oneself upwards.

climb (**II.**), n. fr. prec. The act or effort of climbing: *a hard, difficult climb.*

climbable, adj. [1. klímabl; 2. kláiməbl]. **climb** (**I.**) & **-able.** Capable of being climbed.

climb down, n. [1. klím dóun; 2. kláim dáun]. See **climb** (**I.**) & **down.** Descent, esp. (fig.) giving up of point in argument &c.

climber, n. [1. klímer; 2. kláimə]. **climb** (**I.**) & **-er.** Various senses: **a** person who climbs (trees, mountains, ropes &c.); **b** plant which grows upwards, attaching itself by tendrils or suckers; **c** (fig.) person who strives for social advancement.

clime, n. [1. klīm; 2. klaim]. Variant of **climate,** fr. Lat. form *clima.* (poet.) Region of the earth, generally as thought of in relation to its climate: *to seek a milder clime.*

clinch (**I.**), vb. trans. [1. klinsh; 2. klinʃ]. Variant of **clench.** Showing change of *e* to *i* before *nch.* **a** To make fast, fix, rivet, esp. by turning over ends of nails or bolts when in position, so that they cannot draw out; **b** (fig.) to decide, establish firmly: *to clinch an argument, bargain* &c.

clinch (**II.**), n., fr. prec. Something which fastens, fixes, holds fast; **a** a grip, lock (boxing and wrestling); **b** device for fastening or clinching nail or bolt; **c** portion of mortar projecting from between laths of a wall, to which plaster is fixed.

clincher, n. [1. klínsher; 2. klínʃə]. **clinch** (**I.**) & **-er. 1.** Person who, thing which, clinches; specif., workman who clinches bolts &c.; device or tool for clinching or clenching (nails, bolts &c.). **2.** (colloq.) A final, unanswerable, decisive argument.

cling, vb. intrans. [1. kling; 2. kliŋ]. O.E. *clingan*, 'shrivel, contract', M.E. *clingen*, 'become stiff (with blood), stick together'. Cp. Dan. *klinge*, 'to cluster'. Related remotely to **clench, climb, cleave.** These words in Engl. have formally nothing in common beyond the two first consonants. These must, however, be regarded as the 'vanishing' grade of an Aryan base **kel-*; the remaining parts of the various words are the result of combination w. different formative elements. Followed by *to*, when followed by a n. **1. a** To adhere, stick to; remain attached to, esp. by throwing arms round, twining round, or grasping with tendrils: *clay clings to the boots*; *creeper, ivy, clings to the wall*; *the child clung to its mother*; *the tiger clung to its prey* &c.; **b** (of odours &c.) to pervade, hang about or around, remain attached to: *the scent of cigar smoke clings to curtains for some time.* **2.** To keep close to, remain near (in motion), follow line of: *the vessel clung to the coast*; *when walking in a fog it is best to cling to the houses.* Cp. *hug* in this sense. **3.** (fig.) To set one's affections, wishes, hopes, firmly on, remain attached to by bonds of affection, be unwilling to part from, dwell on in memory; lean on for moral support: *to cling to one's hopes, memories, friends, one's home* &c.; *to cling to religion.*

clinging, adj. [1. klínging; 2. klíŋiŋ], fr. Pres. Part. of prec. Apt to cling, in all senses; tenacious.

clingy, adj. [1. klíngi; 2. klíŋi]. **cling** & **-y.** Adhesive, sticky; also (fig.) clinging.

clinic, n. [1. klínik; 2. klínik], fr. Fr. *clinique*, n., see next word. **1. a** Teaching of medicine and surgery in hospital &c., to students, by practical demonstration in the wards, operating theatre &c.; **b** class of students so taught. **2.** Institution, organization outside a hospital for medical or surgical examination, treatment of patients attending it, as for elementary school children &c.

clinical, adj. [1. klínikl; 2. klínikl]. More rarely **clinic** (in eccles. sense). Gk. *klinikós*, adj., fr. *klínē*, 'bed, couch'; connected w. Gk. *klínō*, 'cause to slope, slant; cause to recline'; in pass. 'to lean, support oneself against; lie down'. This is one of the most fertile bases, & occurs in various forms in most Aryan languages in a host of words, w. extraordinary differentiations of meaning & combined w. different elements. The basal meaning is 'to bend, slope', as in Lat. *dēclīnāre*, 'bend, turn aside from'; also Lat. *clīnātus*, 'bent'. **Clīnāre*, 'to bend, turn' &c., does not occur uncompounded. The Aryan base **k'lin-* w. the grades **k'loin-*, **k'lein-*, represented in Gmc. by **hlin-*, **hlain-*, **hlīn-* occur in the following words: O.E. *hlinian* (& *hleonian*), 'recline, lie', *hlin-bedd*, 'couch'; O.S. *hlinōn*, O.H.G. *hlinēn*, 'lie' &c.; Goth. *hlains*, 'hill, slope'; O.E. *hlǣnan*, fr. **hlainjan*, 'to cause to lean', O.H.G. *leinen.* See further fr. same base the words of Lat. origin, **clement, decline** &c., **declivity**; the words fr. Gk., **climate, climax**; words in **clino-**; the Engl. words of Gmc. origin: **lean** (**II.**); **lee**, 'shelter'; **ladder, lid.** Literally, pertaining to a bed, hence pertaining to a sick-bed, pertaining to, used in, illness. **1.** (med.) *Clinical instruction*, that given to medical students at bedside of patients; *clinical thermometer*, one used for taking temperature of sick persons. **2.** (eccles.) *Clinical conversion*, one made on sick-bed, or death-bed.

clinically, adv. Prec. & **-ly.** By clinical examination or instruction; at bedside of patient &c.

clink (**I.**), vb. intrans. & trans. [1. klingk; 2. kliŋk]. This word belongs to same group as **clank.** Used of a bell in M.E. Cp. also E. Fris. & Du. *klinken*, O.H.G. & Mod. Germ. *klingen*, 'ring, sound (like a bell)'. **click** & **clack** also connected, but imply less resonant sound. All these are imitative. **1.** intrans. To give forth a slight, rather harsh, shrill, tinkling, ringing sound, as of light pieces of metal, glass &c., knocking together. Contrasted with *clank*, which implies a louder, deeper sound caused by the shock of heavy metal objects: *glasses, money, coins* &c., *clink.* **2.** trans. To cause to clink, by striking resonant objects together: *to clink one's money in one's pocket* &c. Phr. *to clink glasses*, by striking gently together, esp. in drinking a person's health.

clink (**II.**), n., fr. prec. **1.** Slight, ringing, metallic sound. See preceding word. *The clink of money, of glasses* &c. **2.** (slang) Prison cell, prison (in allusion to sound of lock or bolt); *in clink*, in jail.

clinker, n. & vb. intrans. [1. klíngker; 2. klíŋkə], fr. **clink** (I.) & **-er**, fr. sound given forth when struck together. **1.** n. **a** Very hard-burnt brick; **b** hard, vitrified matter produced in furnaces by fusion under great heat; refuse of coal or coke. **2.** (colloq. slang) Something very fine, best of its kind, a paragon (from notion of good money 'ringing true'): *a regular clinker.* **3.** vb. To become fused into clinkers.

clinker-built, adj. First element a variant of **clincher.** (of boats and ships) Having outer boards or plates overlapping, and fastened by clinched nails, contrasted with *carvel-built*, see **caravel.**

clinking, adj. [1. klíngking; 2. klíŋkiŋ], fr. Pres. Part of **clink** (I.). **a** Giving forth tinkling, ringing sound; **b** (fig., colloq.) first-rate, splendid, tip-top.

clino-, pref., used in modern compounds, meaning 'slope, slant, angle'. More likely fr. Lat. than Gk., though it might come fr. either, as compounds in latter language w. *klino-* refer to a bed, e.g. *klino-kharés*, 'bed-loving'. This meaning is characteristically Gk. & does not occur in connexion w. this base in Lat. See further under **clinical.**

clinometer, n. [1. klīnómeter; 2. klainɔ́mitə], fr. prec. & **-meter.** Instrument for measuring angles of slopes.

clinometric, adj. [1. klīnōmétrik; 2. klàinoumétrik]. Next word & **-ic.** Pertaining to clinometry.

clinometry, n. [1. klīnómetri; 2. klainɔ́mitri]. **clinometer** & **-y.** Art of using clinometer.

clip (I.), vb. trans. & intrans. [1. klip; 2. klip]. O.E. *clyppan*, 'to embrace, love', M.E. *clippen*, 'embrace, fondle', O.N. *klýpa*, 'pinch, squeeze'. The nearest cogn. in form & meaning are Lith. *glébiu*, 'I embrace, take in my arms', *glóbiu*, 'I embrace, wrap round', orig. 'press, hold tight'. It is remarkable that languages so widely separated & differentiated as O.E. & Lith. shd. have specialized this word for the same precise use. The remoter cognates are innumerable words in various languages derived fr. Aryan base **gel-* &c., 'to adhere, stick, roll up in a ball' &c. See **glebe**, fr. Lat. *glēba*, 'lump of earth, land', **globe, glue**; & further **clammy, clay, cleave** (II.) & words there referred to. **1.** To embrace with the arms, hug (archaic). **2.** To grip tight, hold fast, keep together by squeezing (chiefly of mechanical devices); often *clip hold.*

clip (II.), n. O.E. *clypp*, 'an embrace'. See prec. Term for various mechanical devices for holding separate things together, either by means of a screw, a spring, or by squeezing between two parts of same piece of metal which have been tightly pinched together.

clip (III.), vb. trans. Perh. related to **clap** (I.), possibly connected w. **clip** (I.), expressing idea of nipping off, by pinching. To cut off, snip off the ends of (hair, twigs &c.), with scissors or shears; specif. **a** to trim, cut, a hedge or shrub into shape; **b** to cut the straggling ends of grass at edge of a lawn; **c** to shear the fleece off a sheep; **d** to cut a horse's coat close with special instrument (see **clipper**); **e** to cut off the edge of coins. Phrs. *to clip (a person's) wings*, hinder, restrict his activities, render powerless; *to clip one's words*, to utter with imperfect articulation, shortening, slurring over final sounds of words.

clip (IV.), n., fr. prec. **a** Act of clipping; **b** that which is clipped off; specif., all the wool from a sheep, or number of sheep, removed at one shearing.

clipper, n. [1. klíper; 2. klípə]. **clip** (III.) & **-er.** **1.** **a** One who clips; **b** in pl., *clippers*, instrument for clipping, esp. instrument worked by one or both hands for clipping horses' coats &c., with sharp, cutting, teeth upon opposed blades. **2.** (naut.) Sailing vessel with sharp bow, designed for fast sailing. **3.** (slang) Some person who, or thing which, is very excellent and highly admired and approved of.

clipping, adj. & n. [1. klíping; 2. klípiŋ]. **clip** (III.) & **-ing.** **1.** adj. (slang) Excellent, first-rate. **2.** n. That which is clipped off; specif. **a** ends of grass, or twigs &c.; **b** isolated paragraphs cut out of a newspaper; **c** newspaper column containing odds and ends of miscellaneous information or news.

clique, n. [1. klēk; 2. klīk]. Fr., prob. connected w. *cliqueter*, 'make a noise, click', & *claque*, 'band of persons paid to applaud'; a *clique* in origin apparently meant a noisy gang, or a group of persons who applauded each other. Group or circle of persons closely united by common tastes and interests, or traditions, who form a close society, set, or caste, all the members of which support and help each other, and exclude others from their company; a coterie.

cliqu(e)y, adj. [1. klḗki; 2. klíki]. Prec. & **-y.** Consisting of cliques; tending to form cliques; inclined to belong to a clique, exclusive, cliquish.

cliquish, adj. [1. klḗkish; 2. klíkiʃ]. See prec. & **-ish.** Tending, inclined to form cliques.

cliquishly, adv. Prec. & **-ly.** In a cliquish manner.

cliquishness, n. See prec. & **-ness.** State, condition, of being cliquish.

clistogamic. See **cleistogamic.**

clitoris, n. [1. klítoris; 2. klítəris]. Gk. *kleitorís*, fr. base **klew-* &c., seen in **cleistogamic** & **close** (I.). (anat.) Rudimentary organ, in females, resembling the male sexual organ.

cloaca, n. [1. klōā́ka; 2. kloueíkə]. Lat., 'an artificial sewer in ancient Rome which carried the sewage into the Tiber; sewer, drain', fr. earliest Lat. *clovāca*, derived fr. base meaning 'to wash out, purge, purify', hence 'something which carries off impurities'. Cp. O. Lat. *cluō*, 'purge', Gk. *klúzō*, 'wash over, wash away, wash out', nearly connected w. wh. is Gk. *klúsma*, 'liquid used for washing out', as in *kata-klusmós*, 'deluge' (see **cataclysm**) & *klustḗr*, 'syringe' (see **clyster**). In Gmc. fr. this base, we have Goth. *hlūtrs*, 'pure', O.H.G. *hlūttar*, O.E. *hlūttor*, 'pure, clear', of sounds, & liquids; Lith. *szlúta*, 'broom', & *szlú-ju*, 'I clean, sweep out'. **1.** **a** A sewer; **b** a privy; **c** (fig.) a centre of moral impurity and obscenity. **2.** (anat.) Cavity or chamber, in birds, reptiles, fishes &c., into which the intestines, urinary organs &c. discharge their contents.

cloacal, adj. [1. klōā́kal; 2. kloueíkəl], fr. prec. & **-al.** Pertaining to a drain, to a privy, or intestinal chamber in birds &c.

cloak (I.), n. [1. klōk; 2. klouk]. M.E., fr. O. Fr. *clōke*; also *cloque*, & *cloche*, in O. Fr.; fr. L. Lat. *clocca*, 'bells', the same word as **clock.** *Cloak* orig. meant 'a bell-shaped mantle'. **1.** A garment in the form of a robe or mantle, without sleeves, covering the back and chest and usually descending to, or below, the knees. **2.** That which covers, or conceals something, esp. in a moral sense; disguise, mask: *to use religion as a cloak for wickedness.*

cloak (II.), vb. trans., fr. prec. **1.** To cover with a cloak, or as with a cloak. **2.** To conceal, hide, in moral sense: *he cloaks his ignorance under a confident, assured manner.*

cloak-room, n. **cloak** & **room.** **a** Room where coats and other outdoor garments are left in a private house, club, theatre, hotel &c.; **b** office in a railway station where passengers' luggage and parcels of all kinds are deposited and taken care of until they are claimed. *Cloak-room ticket*, one issued to persons depositing property in a cloak-room to facilitate identification.

cloche, n. [1. klōsh; 2. klouʃ]. Fr., 'a bell'. See **cloak** & **clock.** Bell-shaped protection for plants in a garden, made of glass; *cloche hat*, woman's bell-shaped, close-fitting hat.

clock (I.), n. [1. klok; 2. klɔk]. A variant of **cloak** (I.). Orig. 'a bell'. The form *clugga*, 'bell', fr. L. Lat. *clocca*, 'bell', the source of O. Fr. *cloque*, *cloche* &c., is found already in O.E. The word is prob. of Celt. origin, cp. Ir. *clog*, W. *cloch*, 'bell'. Device, of various designs and sizes, for measuring time, but, however small, distinct from a *watch*, in not being intended for carrying on the person. The motive power of a clock may be derived from water, or electricity, from weights which as they descend cause the cogged wheels to revolve, or, as in a watch, from an expanding spring. Clocks also have either a pendulum or a balance; archaic Phr. *what of the clock?*, what time is it; now *o'clock*: *what o'clock is it? it is 10 o'clock* &c.

clock (II.), vb. intrans. & trans., fr. prec. (of workmen &c.) With *in*, *out*, **a** intrans., to register one's time of beginning or ceasing work, by various mechanical devices, combined with a clock, at entrance of factory &c.; **b** trans. to register (workman's) arrival or departure by such means.

clock (III.), n. Origin doubtful. Embroidered ornament on sock or stocking, running from foot some way up the ankle.

clock-face, n. Disk or dial on front of a clock, upon which are the hands and the figures denoting the hours.

clocking, adj. [1. klóking; 2. klɔ́kiŋ]. Variant of **cluck** & **-ing.** *Clocking hen*, one sitting, or wanting to sit, on eggs; broody; from noise made by hens in this condition when disturbed.

clockwise, adj. & adv. **clock** (I.) & **-wise.** Moving as in the direction of the hands of a clock; *counter-clockwise*, in the opposite direction.

clock-work, n. Mechanism of, or like that of, a clock, i.e. worked by expanding spring. Phr. (*to go*) *like clock-work*, with the utmost regularity and order. Also attrib.: *clock-work toys*, mechanical toys.

clod, n. [1. klod; 2. klɔd]. M.E. *clodde*, variant of **clot.** **1.** **a** Lump of earth, firmly cohering mass of earth or clay, as from newly broken ground; **b** (fig.) man's mortal body when dead, as distinct from his soul; lifeless clay: *mighty kings, great captains, immortal poets, all become mere clods at the last.* **2.** (fig.) A slow-witted, inert, dull, stupid person.

cloddish, adj. [1. klódish; 2. klɔ́diʃ]. Prec. & **-ish.** (fig.) Like a clod; dull, stupid, clumsy.

cloddy, adj. [1. klódi; 2. klɔ́di]. **clod** & **-y.** Full of clods, lumpy, as of newly broke or ill-dug ground.

clod-hopper, n. [1. klód hòper; 2. klɔ́d hɔ̀pə]. A country bumpkin; from idea that his walk resembles that of one jumping over clods; hence, a clumsy, awkward, loutish, ill-bred man or boy.

clod-poll, n. **clod** & **poll** (I.). Thick-headed, stupid, doltish male person.

clog (I.), n. [1. klog; 2. klɔg]. M.E. *klogge*, 'block of wood', prob. Scand., cp. Norw. *klugu*, 'hard, knotty log of wood'. Perh. ultimately related to **clod, clot** &c., **clew**, 'ball', & **clip** (I.) **1.** **a** Block of wood fastened to animal's leg to impede movement, and prevent straying (rare in good English); **b** an impediment caused by accumulation of dirt &c. in machinery; **c** (fig.) a hindrance, encumbrance. **2.** Wooden-soled outer shoe, formerly worn in wet weather by many, now chiefly confined to industrial classes in North of England.

clog (II.), vb. trans. & intrans., fr. prec. **A.** trans. **1.** **a** To act as an impediment to, to hamper, hinder, restrain (any form of activity): *to clog one's movements*; **b** specif., to hinder, impede free movement of by forming coagulated mass, and adhering to, cause to jam; render heavy: *the machinery gets clogged by thick oil and dirt*; *sawdust clogs the teeth of the saw*; *boots clogged with mud*; **c** to choke up, obstruct passage: *the pipe is clogged with frozen snow.* **2.** (fig., of mental processes) To render slow, paralyse: *his brain is clogged with useless facts.* **B.** intrans.

a To become clogged, hampered, obstructed: *this pipe is so small that it clogs very easily*; *a saw clogs very soon with damp wood*; **b** to act as a clog, get into a condition likely to cause clogging: *oil soon clogs in cold weather*.

clog almanac, n. An old form of almanac, in which the figures, of dates &c., are notched on a piece of wood.

clog-dancing, n. Step dancing in clogs, beating time to music.

clogging, n. [1. klóging; 2. klɔ́giŋ]. See **clog (II.)** & **-ing**. Act or process of becoming a clog: *machinery must be cleaned and oiled to prevent clogging*.

cloggy, adj. [1. klógi; 2. klɔ́gi]. **clog (I.)** & **-y**. Liable to clog; full of lumps &c., likely to cause clogging.

cloisonné, adj. & n. [1. kloizónā; 2. klɔizɔ́nei]. Fr., fr. *cloison*, 'a partition', fr. Low Lat. *clōsiōn-(em)*, for *claus-*, fr. P.P. type of *claudere*, 'shut, enclose'. See **claustral, cloister, close (I.)**. **a** adj. Generally *cloisonné work*, copper or other material, overlaid with enamel, the design on which is outlined by fine metallic lines, which are the edges of thin metal bands forming partitions, and as it were moulds, for the forms and colours of the pattern; cp. *champlevé*; **b** n., work ornamented in this way.

cloister (I.), n. [1. klóister; 2. klɔ́istə], in M.E., fr. O. Fr. *cloistre*, fr. Lat. *claustrum*, 'lock; place that is shut up'. See **claustral** & **close (I.)**. **1.** Establishment where monks or nuns live a retired life, under strict vows, in practice of religion and pious works. **2.** (archit.) Covered way, generally running round a quadrangle, in a monastic or collegiate building, usually with a vaulted roof, which is supported on pillars at intervals on the inner side, this side being open, the other formed by the outer walls of the building.

cloister (II.), vb. trans., fr. prec. **a** To confine in a cloister, or monastery; hence **b** to withdraw from society and cause to lead a retired life; (often reflex.) *to cloister oneself*, shut oneself up, refrain from social intercourse.

cloistered, adj. [1. klóisterd; 2. klɔ́istəd], fr. P.P. of prec. **a** Shut up in a cloister; **b** living solitary, retired from the world; **c** (of buildings) provided with cloisters.

cloistral, adj. (rarely n.) [1. klóistral; 2. klɔ́istrəl], fr. **cloister (I.)** & **-al**. **a** Pertaining to a cloister or to a monastery; **b** confined in a monastery; **c** as though confined in a monastery; lonely, retired.

clonic, adj. [1. klónik; 2. klɔ́nik]. Gk. See **clonus** & **-ic**. (med.) Pertaining to clonus.

clonism, n. [1. klónizm; 2. klɔ́nizəm]. **clonus** & **-ism**. (med.) Condition of being afflicted with clonus.

clonus, n. [1. klṓnus; 2. klóunəs]. Gk. *klónos*, 'any violent motion; tumult', cp. *klonéō*, 'confound, agitate, distract'; developed fr. base **kel-*, 'move violently and swiftly', as in Gk. *keleúō*, 'set in movement, urge on', *késllō*, 'drive on, run (a ship) ashore'; cogn. w. Lat. *celer*, 'swift'. See **celerity, accelerate**. (med.) Series of violent muscular spasms.

close (I.), adj. & adv. [1. klōs; 2. klous]. O. Fr., *clos*, P.P. of *clore*, 'enclose', fr. Lat. *clausum*, P.P. of *claudere*, 'shut' &c., connected w. Lat. *clāvis*, 'key', orig. prob. 'a bar, or peg of wood' (see **clavicle** & **clef**); also *clāvus*, 'nail, pin'. Cp. further the group of Gk. words, *kleis*, 'thing for barring a door, bolt', for **klewis*, *klāis* for **klawis*, 'key', *kleiō* for **klew-jō*, 'shut up close, keep fast', *kleistós*, 'that can be shut'. Another near cogn. is O. Slav. *ključiti*, 'to shut up'. A variant of this base, w. initial *s*, is **(s)klewt-*, **sklut-*, whence Gmc. **sleut-*, **slut-* &c., in O.H.G. *sliozan*, Mod. Germ. *schliessen*, O. Fris. *sluta*, 'to shut', O.S. *slutil*, O.H.G. *sluzzil*, 'key', Mod. Germ. *schlüssel*. See also **clause, claustral, cloister**. **1.** Shut, closed, not open; now obs. in this literal sense except in a few phrases: *Close Rolls*, compared with *Patent Rolls*; (her., of a helmet) with visor down; (in extended sense) *close time, season*, esp. one during which game may not be shot, or (salmon) caught. **2.** **a** Withdrawn from observation, secluded: *to keep oneself close*; **b** well-guarded, confined: *to be kept a close prisoner*; *in close confinement*; **c** (of persons) reticent, reserved, reverse of frank; **d** niggardly, parsimonious, stingy; **e** (of money) difficult to obtain, scarce. **3.** **a** Restricted, narrow, lacking space: *close quarters*; **b** restricted to certain classes, not open to all: *a close scholarship, competition*; **c** with sense of severity, keenness: *to press a man close*, treat rigorously. **4.** **a** Near, adjacent to, in proximity to; followed by *to*: *close to the station*; **b** (fig.) near to the heart, intimate: *a close friend*; **c** evenly, nicely, balanced: *a close contest*. Phrs. *to run a man close*, be nearly even with him; *a close thing*, nearly a failure or disaster, *close shave*, narrow escape from accident, nearly a collision; *close to the wind*, (naut.) with head directed nearly to point from which wind blows; (also fig.) just avoiding illegality. **5.** **a** Dense, having constituent elements near together; tightly packed, serried, tightly woven: *close contact*; *to sit close*; *a close material*; *close texture*; *close order*, (mil.) without spaces between men in line; **b** (fig.) pregnant, full of thought and meaning; compact: *close statement, argument*. **6.** Nicely and accurately adjusted, or adapted to; following nearly, approximating to; (in various shades of meaning, lit. and fig.); **a** accurate, careful: *close copy*; **b** thorough, searching: *close investigation*; **c** concentrated, careful: *close attention, management*; **d** down to level of roots: *to cut a lawn close*; *a close shave* (with razor). **7.** Oppressive, heavy; specif. **a** (of weather) sultry, stifling, thundery, very hot; **b** (of rooms) stuffy, airless, ill ventilated. **8.** (phon.) *Close vowel*, term used vaguely and without precision to mean **a** a vowel uttered with but a slight aperture between tongue and palate; **b** one uttered with the tongue tense and muscularly braced and hard.

close (II.), n. [1. klōs; 2. klous]. O. Fr. *clos*. See prec. An enclosure; specif. **a** small field or paddock enclosed by walls, usually adjacent to a house, or a village; **b** open space, wholly or partially enclosed by buildings, in neighbourhood of a cathedral, round which are often situated the deanery, houses of canons &c.; **c** (in Scotland) any passage, entry, or wynd leading from the street to an inner court or to a common stair in a tenement.

close (III.), vb. trans. & intrans. [1. klōz; 2. klouz]. M.E. *clōsen*, fr. P.P. type *clos* of O. Fr. *clore*, 'to shut', fr. Lat. *clōdere*, *claudere*, q.v. under **close (I.)**. The difference in the final consonants of **close (I., II.)** on one hand, & **close (III., IV.)** on the other, is due to the fact that in M.E. the *-s* of the former was final in nom. & acc., whereas in the latter, *-s-* was followed by *-e(n)* of inf. & was thus pronounced as [z]. **A.** trans. **1.** Applied to a variety of actions and movements, implying some form of shutting, filling up an open space, obstructing entrance or exit, excluding light, bringing together separable parts of something, returning some movable part of a thing to a position which covers, stops an opening, and so on: *to close a door, gate, window*; *close shutters, blinds*; *close a box*, cover with lid; *close a drawer*, push back into place; *close a hole*, stop it up; *close one's mouth, lips, eyes* &c., bring lips together, lower eyelids; *close a shop*, exclude customers (for the night &c.); withdraw from the business. Phrs. and special uses: *close the door on*, (fig.) prevent further discussion; *close a man's eye*, hit it so that it swells; *to close (one's parent's) eyes*, attend on deathbed; *to have one's eyes closed*, be unable, unwilling, to see; *his eyes are closed*, he is dead; *my mouth is closed*, I cannot, must not, speak; *to close one's purse to*, refuse money; *close the ranks*, fill up spaces between men in line, by setting them close together; (also fig.) increase zeal of, organize better, the adherents of a cause. **2.** To complete, bring to an end, terminate, conclude, finish off: *to close one's career*; *close a speech, labours* &c. Phrs. *that chapter is closed*, episode concluded; not to be discussed; *to close a discussion*, as chairman, declare it ended, or sum it up and bring to an end; *to close an account* (with a tradesman), pay one's bill and withdraw custom. **B.** intrans. **1.** **a** To go through process of closing (in various senses), be capable of being closed, allow itself to be closed: *the window won't close*; *the door closes easily, of itself*; '*Her tired eyelids closed*' (Hood); **b** (of flowers) to curl up, roll up, bring petals together: *many flowers close at night*; **c** (of fractures, wounds) unite, cicatrize. **2.** To draw to, come to, reach, an end: *the day, life, will close at last*; *the speech closed abruptly*. **C.** Followed by prepositions and adverbs. *Close about*, to surround, envelop: *the mists closed about him*. *Close in*, **a** to draw near and surround, for an attack: *the enemy now closed in* (also followed by *on, upon*); **b** draw on, approach, encircle (of night, darkness, mist &c.). *Close round*, to envelop, surround. *Close up*, intrans., **a** (of persons in a line or group) to draw nearer together; **b** (of a wound) to unite, heal up; **c** trans., to shut up completely, stop: *the old well has been closed up*. *Close with*, intrans., **a** to rush towards, in order to attack; come to grips with; **b** (fig.) (i.) to strike bargain with (a person), agree with, as to terms; (ii.) to accept (terms, offer, bargain).

close (IV.), n. [1. klōz; 2. klouz], fr. prec. **a** Completion, conclusion, ending, end: *a fitting close to a strenuous life*; *the discourse in due time reached its close*. Phr. *bring to, draw to, a close*, finish; bring, come to, an end; **b** (music) cadence, final part of a melody &c.

close-fisted, adj. [1. klṓs físted; 2. klóus fístid]. **close (I.)** & **fist** & **-ed**. Unwilling to part with money; stingy, miserly.

close-grained, adj. [1. klṓs grā̀nd; 2. klóus grèind]. See **grain (I.)** & **-ed**. Having a dense grain (of wood).

close-hauled, adj. [1. klṓs háwld; 2. klóus hɔ̀ld]. See **haul (I.)**. Having yards braced up tight (of ship, rigging), so that the vessel sails close to the wind.

closely, adv. [1. klṓsli; 2. klóusli]. **close (I.)** & **-ly**. In a close manner. See various senses of **close**, esp. **a** tightly; **b** carefully, narrowly: *to watch closely*.

closeness, n. [1. klṓsnes; 2. klóusnis]. See prec. & **-ness**. Quality of being close in various senses; specif. **a** oppressiveness, stuffiness; **b** intimacy: *closeness of our friendship*; **c** stinginess.

closet, n. [1. klózit; 2. klɔ́zit]. O. Fr., dimin. of *clos*, 'enclosure'. See **close (II.)**. **1.** **a** A small chamber or apartment, esp. one leading out of a larger room; a private room; Phr. *of the closet*, of theories &c. formed without knowledge or experience of realities; **b** a cupboard: *jam closet*. These uses now obsolescent and commonly avoided because of ambiguity due to association of the word with the meaning now most usual, i.e. **2.** A privy; for *water-closet*.

closeted, adj. [1. klózited; 2. klɔ́zitid]. Prec. & **-ed**. In Phrs. *to be closeted with someone*; *to be closeted together*, in private room, engaged in confidential talk.

close-up, n. [1. klṓs up; 2. klóus ap]. Cinematograph picture taken close to the object.

closure (I.), n. [1. klṓzhur; 2. klóužə]. Ad. fr. Fr. *clôture*, on anal. of *to close*. Means of securing an immediate vote on a measure before Parliament, and bringing debate to a close, by moving, and carrying, motion 'that the question be now put'.

closure (II.), vb. trans., fr. prec. To close (debate in Parliament) by applying the closure.

clot (I.), n. [1. klot; 2. klɔt]. O.E. *clott*, 'lump', cp. Du. *kloot*, 'ball', Mod. Germ. *kloss*, 'clod', & *klotz*, 'block'; fr. Aryan base meaning 'to stick, adhere', & 'to roll up' &c., discussed under **cleave (II.), claw, glue** &c. Coagulated, thickened, partially solidified mass, esp. of blood.

clot (II.), vb. trans. & intrans., fr. prec. **a** trans. To cause to clot; **b** intrans., to assume the form of clots, become coagulated.

cloth, n. [1. klawth, kloth; 2. klōþ, klɔþ]; pl. **cloths** [1. klawdhz, kloths; 2. klōðz, klɔþs]; also **clothes**, now a separate word. O.E. *clāþ*, 'cloth, a cloth'. Not widely spread in Gmc. languages; not found in O.H.G., but Mod. Germ. *kleid*, 'garment', & Du. *kleed*, have true W. Gmc. forms; O.N. has *klæði*, Dan. *kläde*, 'cloth'. The base has not been identified outside Gmc. **1. a** Soft, usually pliable fabric, woven from wool, hair, cotton, or silk, linen, fibre &c.; **b** specif., woollen cloth; **c** (i.) black cloth worn by clergy, hence (ii.) the clergy themselves: *gentlemen of the cloth*; also (iii.) the rank, sacred character of a clergyman: *to respect a man's cloth*; **d** *cloth of gold*, woven of gold threads; *cloth of estate*, richly woven, embroidered cloth used for canopy and background of a king's throne; *American cloth*, fabric of cotton &c. coated and varnished, so as to imitate leather. **2.** Various articles made of woven, esp. of cotton, or linen, fabric; **a** piece of this cut square and hemmed for dusting, cleaning furniture &c.; a duster; **b** large, often figured, finely woven strip of linen &c. put upon a table at meal-time, *table cloth (a, the, cloth)*. Phr. *to lay the cloth*, put table-cloth on for a meal.

clothe, vb. trans. [1. klōdh; 2. klouð]. O.E. *clāþian*, fr. *clāþ*. See prec. The Pret. & P.P. *clad* are still current in literary style, but *clothed* is more common colloquially. See **clad. 1.** To put on wearing apparel, cover with garments; to dress; esp. *clothe oneself*; **a** to put clothes on naked body, don, assume, clothes: *you had better get up and clothe yourself*; **b** to put on specific set of garments: *he had clothed himself in his best.* (In these senses the word has been ousted in colloquial usage by *to dress.*) **2.** To provide, supply (others), with wearing apparel: *to clothe one's wife and family.* **3.** (fig.) To cover as with a garment; **a** (of persons) to endow, invest with, assign non-material qualities to: *the ambassador was clothed with full powers*; *clothed with righteousness, authority*; **b** (of inanimate nature) to throw over, surround, cover with: *the sun clothed the hill with light*; *spring clothes the land with verdure.* **4.** To embody, express (thoughts and ideas): *to clothe one's thoughts in suitable language.*

clothes, n. pl. [1. klōz, klōdhz; 2. klouz, klouðz]. The pronunciation [klouz] is usual in familiar speech, & is already indicated in the rhymes of Donne, Swift, Pope, & Goldsmith; fr. O.E. *clāþas*, pl. of *clāþ*, q.v. under **cloth. 1.** Garments, wearing apparel, raiment, designed to cover, protect, and adorn the human body. **2.** Coverings, including sheets, blankets, quilts, used upon a bed. Also *bed-clothes.*

clothes-basket, n. Basket in which clothes are sent to and from the laundry.

clothes-horse, n. Wooden frame for airing clothes before a fire.

clothes-line, n. Thin rope stretched between posts upon which newly washed clothes and linen are hung to dry in the open air.

clothes-moth, n. Small, pale-brown moth, genus *Tinea*, whose caterpillar feeds upon woollen fabric.

clothes-peg, n. Wooden forked clip for fastening articles to a clothes-line.

clothier, n. [1. klṓdhier; 2. klóuðiə]. **cloth & -ier.** Formerly a maker of cloth (obs.). Tradesman who supplies cloth for suits, and makes suits; a tailor; one who sells clothes of all kinds.

clothing, n. [1. klṓdhing; 2. klóuðiŋ]. **clothe & -ing.** Wearing apparel generally: *an article of clothing*, a garment.

cloth measure, n. One applied formerly to cloth, composed of ells, quarters, and nails.

cloth yard, n. **a** Rod used formerly for measuring cloth; **b** now the yard of 3 feet (36 inches); **c** also the length of the arrow used with the long-bow, hence the arrow itself.

clotted, adj. [1. klóted; 2. klɔ́tid], fr. P.P. of **clot** (II.). **a** Formed into clots, coagulated, esp. of blood; **b** stuck together, as *hair*, by blood or filth; **c** special use, *clotted cream*, thickened and solidified by boiling; also *Devonshire cream.*

clôture, n. Fr. Same as **closure.**

cloud (I.), n. [1. kloud; 2. klaud]. O.E. *clūd*, 'rock, mass of rock'; in Early M.E. *cloud* is still used in this sense, but subsequently applied in present sense, thus displacing O.E. *wolcen*, see **welkin**, & M.E. *skie*, fr. O.N. *ský*, see **sky**. *Cloud* in the old sense survives in *Cloud End*, Cheshire, 'termination of the Biddulph Moor hill range' (Bartholomew's 'Gazetteer'). The orig. meaning of the word was simply 'mass', & it is fr. same base as **clot, clod, cleave (I.), & clew. 1.** Mass of vapour, specif. **a** one formed in the sky; **b** any mass of vapour or of something resembling vapour in appearance: *cloud of steam, smoke, dust* &c.; *cloud of flies*; **c** darker veining, marking in marble, amber &c.; **d** (fig.) great multitude: *cloud of witnesses.* **2.** (in pl.) The sky itself, upper atmosphere: *to sail up into the clouds.* Phr. *to have one's head in, to be in, the clouds*, to be preoccupied with one's thoughts; unpractical and inattentive to mundane matters. **3.** (fig.) Anything which darkens, obscures, dims, sullies, casts shadow or blight, in spiritual sense: *a cloud on one's happiness, spirits, reputation*; *the cloud of war.* **4.** A soft, fleecy, woollen wrap for the head and neck used by women.

cloud (II.), vb. trans. & intrans., fr. prec. **1.** trans. (lit. and fig.) **a** To make dark, obscure; overshadow, dim as by intervention of a cloud; mar, spoil: *the weather, brightness of the day, has been clouded*; *to cloud the spirits, happiness, intellect*; **b** to mark with darker streaks of colour: *clouded marble, amber* &c.; *clouded tiger, leopard*, a wild forest cat of Borneo and S.E. Asia with coat striped and clouded with dark patches. **2.** intrans. To become overcast, cloudy, dark with clouds: *the sky has clouded.* Also *cloud over.*

cloudberry, n. [1. klóudberi; 2. kláudberi]. Species of wild raspberry.

cloud-burst, n. Sudden, violent downpour of water from the sky; abnormally heavy, sudden rain.

cloud-capped, adj. [1. klóud kapt; 2. kláud kæpt]. (of mountain peaks, high spires &c.) Covered, enshrouded, by cloud.

cloudiness, n. [1. klóudines; 2. kláudinis]. **cloudy & -ness. a** Condition of being cloudy; **b** visual, mental, or intellectual dimness, obscurity, dullness: *cloudiness of sight, of understanding.*

clouding, n. [klóuding; 2. kláudiŋ]. Veining, streaking, in stone of different shade from main mass; variegation.

cloudland, n. [1. klóudland; 2. kláudlænd]. Region of dreams, visions, and speculation.

cloudless, adj. [1. klóudles; 2. kláudlis]. **cloud (I.) & -less.** Free from clouds, clear, bright (lit. and fig.).

cloud-ring, n. Permanent belt of cloud at the equator.

cloudy, adj. [1. klóudi; 2. kláudi]. **cloud (I.) & -y. 1.** Covered with, full of, cloud or clouds; consisting of cloud. **2. a** (of vision and things seen) Dim, indistinct: *eyes cloudy with sleep*; *cloudy picture*; **b** (of mind) lacking clearness and precision; **c** (of liquids) not clear, thick, turgid. **3.** Marked with veins, as marble, variegated.

clough, n. [1. kluf; 2. klaf]. Presupposes an O.E. **clōh*, wh. is not found, but wd. come fr. Gmc. **klanχ*, cogn. w. Germ. dial. *klinge*, 'valley'. Cp. Scots *cleuch*. Perh. connected w. **clang, clink**, & other words expressing sound, from prevalence of echoes, or from noise of stream flowing through. (provinc.) Small valley, or cleft in a hill; a ravine.

clout (I.), n. [1. klout; 2. klaut]. O.E. *clūt*, 'piece of cloth, patch', also 'metal plate'. Cogn. w. **clot** (I.). **1.** A rough, coarse piece of cloth, esp. one used for cleaning, *dish clout*; generally in contemptuous sense: *a filthy clout* &c. **2.** Bull's eye of an archery target. **3.** (colloq. and vulg.) A blow, crack, esp. *clout on the head.*

clout (II.), vb. trans. O.E. *clūtian*, 'to patch'. See prec. **1.** To patch roughly (esp. of boots and shoes). **2.** (colloq. and vulg.) To strike roughly, esp. in Phr. *to clout his head for him.* Perhaps originally to strike with a clout of metal.

clove (I.), n. [1. klōv; 2. klouv]. M.E. *clow*, fr. O. Fr. *clou*, 'nail', fr. Lat. *clāvus*, 'nail', q.v. under **clavicle & close (I.)**. Fr. *clou de girofle*, 'nail of clove plant', fr. its resemblance to a nail. The present form is due to influence of Ital. *chiovo*, 'clove', or by confusion w. **clove (II.)**. Dried, unexpanded flower-bud, of tree or bush (*clove-tree*), grown in the Moluccas or Spice Islands, with hot, pungent flavour; much used for flavouring in cooking.

clove (II.), n. O.E. *clofe*, 'bulb, tuber of a plant', fr. W. Gmc. **kluf-*, same base as O.E. *clēofan*, 'split, divide', q.v. under **cleave (I.)**. Small bulb which has budded off from a larger one, as of garlic, shallot.

clove (III.), vb. Pret. of **cleave (I.)**, fr. P.P. type **cloven.** Cp. also **cleft.**

clove (IV.), vb. Pret. of **cleave (II.)**, orig. a weak vb. The new Pret. is on the anal. of prec.

clove-hitch, n., fr. **cleave (I.)**. Kind of hitch in a rope, made on a spar, or another rope.

cloven, adj. [1. klṓven; 2. klóuvən], fr. P.P. of **cleave (I.)**. O.E. *clofen*, M.E. *clōven.* This is fr. the same vowel-grade as **clove (II.)**. Divided, separated, into two parts, as the hoofs of ruminant animals; chiefly in *cloven foot, cloven hoof.* Phr. *to show the cloven hoof*, allow one's real (bad) character to be seen, in spite of disguise; in reference to popular conception of physical characteristics of the devil.

clove-nutmeg, n. Tree grown in Madagascar, *Ravensara aromatica*, with aromatic leaves and fruit like a nutmeg.

clove pink, n. A variety of pink with strong perfume.

clover, n. [1. klṓver; 2. klóuvə]. O.E. *clǣfre*, M.E. *clāver, clōver*; cp. Du. *klaver*, Swed. *klöfver*. Low-growing plant, variety of trefoil, with strong-scented pink or white flowers; cultivated as fodder for cattle. Phr. *to be, live, in clover*, in great luxury.

clown (I.), n. [1. kloun; 2. klaun]. Scand. Cp. O.N. *klunni*, 'clumsy, boorish fellow'. **1. a** A rustic; clumsy, ill-bred lout; person of coarse manners; **b** a buffoon; a fellow who indulges in rough horse-play, and coarse jests. **2.** The buffoon in a circus or pantomime, who affects great simplicity, together with a certain good-natured cunning, and plays off practical jokes on other characters.

clown (II.), vb. intrans., fr. prec. Generally *to clown it*, to play the clown.

clownish, adj. [1. klóunish; 2. kláuniʃ]. **clown (I.) & -ish.** Like a clown; rough, boorish, clumsy, ill-bred.

clownishness, n. Prec. & **-ness.** Behaviour, or character, of a clown; rough, ill-timed horse-play; rudeness.

cloy, vb. trans. [1. kloi; 2. klɔi]. Skeat traces history of word fr. M. Fr. *enclouer*, & a by-form, *encloyer*, 'to nail up, fasten'; & cites *accloyed, cloyed*, as a term used by farriers for a horse injured by a nail. The Fr. vb. is fr. *clou*, 'nail', Lat. *clāvus*; see **clove (I.) & close (I.)**. The present sense is therefore secondary, & derived fr. the idea of stopping up, numbing, the taste. (of physical or mental appetite) To satiate, surfeit, glut with sweetness or pleasure, cause to grow weary of: *too many sweets cloy the palate*; *the music of the great poets delights but never cloys the taste.*

club (I.), n. [1. klub ; 2. klab]. Scand., M.E. *clubbe*, O.N. *klubba*, *klumba*, 'club, thick stick'; also Swed. *klubba*, *klubb*, 'club, block'. Variant of **clump**, & further connected w. **cleave (II.)**, **clew, clod, clot, glue**, together w. cognates cited. The basal idea is 'ball, knob, lump'. **1. a** Thick wooden stick with lump at one end; **b** stick with knob or head at one end used in games such as golf and hockey. **2.** (in pl.) A suit at cards bearing image of a trefoil: *king &c. of clubs*; any card of this suit: *a small club*. **3. a** Knot or group of persons possessing common or similar tastes, interests, or occupations, social, political, convivial, sporting (or lack of these) who unite as an organized society, with rules, a president, specified times of meeting, and routine procedure when they meet; **b** similar group of persons whose aims are mainly social, and who unite to own or rent a house with special rooms for reading, recreation, and meals, where members meet at such hours as they please; **c** the place in which societies (as in **a**) meet; the premises owned and used by those described in **b**.

club (II.), vb. trans. & intrans., fr. prec. **1.** trans. **a** To chastise with a club, or something resembling a club: *to club a person to death*; *to club a person with a rifle butt*; **b** to use as a club; *to club a rifle*, use the butt-end. **2.** intrans. To unite for a common purpose, combine forces and means to effect common end; generally *club together*.

clubbable, adj. [1. klúbabl; 2. klábəbl]. Prec. & **-able**. Suitable for, fond of, society as found in a club; hence (in general sense) sociable, fond of friendly conversation and social intercourse.

clubbed, adj. [1. klubd; 2. klabd]. **club (I.)** & **-ed**. Shaped like a club; specif., of certain malformations of vegetables and fruit.

clubfoot, n. [1. klúbfóot; 2. klábfút]. Ill-developed, distorted foot, a congenital deformity.

club law, n. Violence.

clubman, n. [1. klúbman; 2. klábmæn]. **a** A member of a social club; **b** an American journalistic term for a 'man about town.'

club moss, n. Kind of moss, *Lycopodium*, with erect club-shaped spore-cases.

club-root, n. Disease of cabbage tribe, consisting of growth of swellings on the root.

club-shaped, adj. Having a thick knob at one end.

cluck (I.), vb. intrans. [1. kluk; 2. klak]. Imitative, but cp. Du. *klukken*, Dan. *klukke*. Perh. associated, in the mind, w. **clutch (III.)** (of eggs). **a** (of a hen) To make a characteristic sound to call chickens together; **b** to utter the shrill, petulant cry of a broody hen when disturbed.

cluck (II.), n., fr. prec. **a** Sound of a hen calling chickens; **b** noise made by broody hen.

clue, n. [1. kloo; 2. klū]. See **clew.** Guide to solution of a puzzle or mystery, group or series of facts which leads up to the explanation of this.

Clumber, n. [1. klúmber; 2. klámbə], fr. name of place where the animals were bred. Stocky breed of spaniel with short legs: *Clumber spaniel.*

clump (I.), n. [1. klump; 2. klamp]. Dan. & Swed. *klump*, 'a lump'. Cogn. of **club (I.)**, **clod, clot (I.)**. **1.** A lump, shapeless mass of earth or wood. **2.** Isolated group of trees in open field or park. **3.** Thick piece of leather fastened to outside of sole of boot or shoe. **4**: Sound of heavy footfalls (imitative).

clump (II.), vb. trans. & intrans. See prec. **1.** To group, mass, together. **2.** To put extra piece of leather on (sole of boot). **3.** To walk, tread, with heavy footfalls.

clumpy, adj. [1. klúmpi; 2. klámpi]. **clump (I.)** & **-y**. **a** Full of clumps; **b** like, abounding in, clumps (of trees &c.).

clumsily, adv. [1. klúmzili; 2. klámzili]. **clumsy** & **-ly**. In a clumsy manner.

clumsiness, n. [1. klúmzines; 2. klámzinis]. **clumsy** & **-ness**. Quality of being clumsy.

clumsy, adj. [1. klúmzi; 2. klámzi]. M.E. *clumsen*, 'to be benumbed', Scand.; cp. Swed. *klummsen*, 'benumbed'. Connected w. base in O.E. *clamm*, 'fetter, bond', & *clemman*, 'to contract'. See **clammy, clamp**, & words there referred to. Awkward, lacking in grace; **a** (of persons) lacking grace, ease, dexterity, of movement or action; loutish; **b** (of action) badly controlled, lumbering, unskilful; **c** (of mental processes) slow-moving, inexact, lacking nimbleness and readiness; **d** (of style) inelegant, lacking smoothness, directness, neatness; **e** (of manner and behaviour) lacking habit of polite usage; ill-bred, rough, gauche, tactless.

clung, vb. [1. klung; 2. klaŋ]. Pret. & P.P. of **cling**; fr. M.E. P.P. type *clunge(n)*, O.E. *clungen*; cp. O.E., M.E. Pret. *clang*.

cluster (I.), n. [1. klúster; 2. klástə]. O.E. *clūstor*, 'lock, barrier, confinement', borrowed fr. Lat. *claustrum*, 'lock, barrier, defence'. See **claustral.** Number of similar objects naturally or fortuitously grouped together in close proximity to each other; **a** bunch of fruit, flowers &c.: *cluster of currants*; **b** crowd, multitude, of persons: *clusters of spectators*; **c** mass of bees, stuck together when swarming: *bees in a cluster.*

cluster (II.), vb. intrans., fr. prec. **1. a** (of fruit, flowers) To grow in clusters; **b** (of persons &c.) come together, congregate in clusters. **2.** *Cluster round* **a** (of growing things) to grow, spring, in clusters: *roses clustered round the windows*; *curls clustered round her head*; **b** (of persons &c.) to press, throng round in crowds; **c** (of mental things) to be associated with, arise in the mind in large numbers in connexion with: *memories of the past cluster round the spot.*

clustered, adj. [1. klústerd; 2. klástəd], fr. P.P. of **cluster (II.)**. Growing in, grouped into, clusters. *Clustered column*, one having appearance of, or consisting of, a number of slighter columns united.

clustery, adj. [1. klústeri; 2. klástəri], fr. **cluster (I.)** & **-y.** Inclined to grow in clusters; in clusters.

clutch (I.), vb. trans. & intrans. [1. kluch; 2. klatʃ]. O.E. *clyććan*, 'bring together, clench', fr. Gmc. base **kluk-*, 'seize'. Prob. connected ultimately w. **claw** & words there mentioned. Cp. **clutch (II.)**. To seize suddenly and convulsively; grip, grasp with the hand. Phr. (fig.) *to clutch at a straw*, use any help available when in difficulties.

clutch (II.), n. M.E. *clucche*. See **clutch (I.)**. **1.** Act of gripping, seizing, grasping; a rapid snatch, grab: *to make a clutch at.* **2.** Grip, grasp, firm hold: *in the clutch of fate.* Phr. (fig.) *to get into, out of, a person's clutches*, into, out of, his power. **3.** Device for coupling and uncoupling engine with driving gear and driving wheels.

clutch (III.), n. Earlier *cletch*, fr. O.N. *klekja*. Origin doubtful, cp. **cluck (I.)**. **a** The set of eggs, usually 13, put under a hen for her to hatch at one time; **b** the chicks from these when newly hatched.

clutter (I.), n. [1. klúter; 2. klátə], fr. same base as **clot (I.)**. Originally, a clotted mass; confusion, disorder, muddle.

clutter (II.), vb. trans., fr. prec. To make confused, put into disorder; choke up, clog. Also *clutter up.*

Clydesdale, n. [1. klídzdāl; 2. kláidzdeil], fr. place-name, Scotland. Heavy, powerful breed of cart horse. *Clydesdale terrier*, a breed of Scotch terrier, related to the Skye terrier, with silky hair.

clypeus, n. [1. klípeus; 2. klípiəs]. Lat., also *clipeus, clupeus*, 'round shield'; cogn. w. Gk. *kalúptō*, 'envelop, cover', & *kalúbē*, 'hut, cabin'. Perh. connected w. Lat. *clepo*, 'steal'. See **kleptomaniac** & **lift**, 'to steal'. (archaeol.) Large round shield, with convex outer, and concave inner, face.

clyster, n. [1. klíster; 2. klístə]. Fr. *clystère*, fr. Gk. *klustḗr*, 'syringe'. See discussion of the base, meaning, 'to wash out', under second element of **cataclysm**, & **cloaca.** An enema, injection into lower bowel.

co-, pref. Lat., form of prep. *cum*, used before vowels; also used to make new compounds in Engl., before vowels & any consonant, expressing joint action or operation, reciprocity, association &c.; sometimes written w. hyphen in new & unfamiliar compounds, or w. diaeresis on vowel immediately following if an *o-*, *co-ordinate, coördinate, coordinate*, the first being best. For etymol. & force in Lat. compounds see **com-.**

coach (I.), n. [1. kōch; 2. koutʃ], fr. Fr. *coche*; Hungarian word, *kocsi* [1. kŏchi; 2. kōtʃi], fr. place-name Kocs [kōtʃ] in Hungary. **1. a** Large obsolete closed travelling carriage with four wheels, two seats inside, a box outside for driver, and doors, with windows, in the sides; **b** term applied to various modifications of this, esp. to one with seats inside and out, generally drawn by four horses and formerly employed in carrying travellers and mails before railways: *stage-coach*; also *mail-coach, state-coach* (esp. for the king). Phrs. *slow-coach*, person slow in movements, action, or understanding; *drive a coach and four through an Act of Parliament*, get round its provisions; *hackney-coach*, cab plying for hire. **2.** (extended usage) Carriage on a railway, divided into several compartments, the *coach* being the whole unit so divided. **3.** Instructor, tutor, teacher, **a** one employed to help students with intellectual work, esp. in preparing for an examination; **b** one who prepares individuals or teams in games, athletics, rowing &c., corrects faults of style, superintends practice &c.: *Dr. Bourne acted as the Oxford coach for the boat-race on many occasions.*

coach (II.), vb. trans. & intrans., fr. prec. **A.** trans. **1.** To drive one in, or provide one with, a coach. **2.** To prepare (persons) for examinations or athletic contests; superintend studies or practice. **B.** intrans. **1.** To use a coach for travelling; drive a coach: *to coach from London to Brighton.* **2.** To act as tutor or coach: *to coach for a living.*

coach-box, n. Driver's seat, when separate from others, in any kind of coach or carriage.

coach dog, n. Carriage dog.

coachful, n. [1. kóchfool; 2. kóutʃful]. **coach (I.)** & **-ful.** All the occupants of a coach at one time.

coach-horn, n. A long straight horn of brass or copper, with belled end, used for sounding simple calls; post-horn.

coachman, n. [1. kóchman; 2. kóutʃmən]. **1. a** Driver of any kind of vehicle for passengers or mails; specif. **b** servant employed to drive a private carriage and superintend management of stables. **2.** Artificial fly used in trout-fishing, with a peacock-green body and brown hackles.

coachmanship, n. [1. kóchmanship; 2. kóutʃmənʃip]. Prec. & **-ship.** Degree of skill as driver of a vehicle.

coadjutor, n. [1. kōajóotor; 2. kouædžútə]. Lat. **co-** & *adjūtor*, 'helper, promoter; deputy, assistant', fr. *ad-jūtāre*, 'help', fr. *juvāre*, 'to assist, aid', wh. is cogn. w. Scrt. *yuváti*, 'binds, makes fast', & *yu-ś*, 'companion'. Cp. further **join, junction, yoke.** Assistant: *bishop's coadjutor*, one appointed to assist a diocesan.

co-administrator, n. [1. kóadmínistrāter; 2. kóuədmínistreitə]. **co-** & **administrator.** One who administers jointly with another.

coagulate, vb. intrans. & trans. [1. kōágūlāt; 2. kouǽgjuleit]. Formed fr. Lat. *coāgulāt-(um)*, P.P. type of *coāgulāre*, itself formed fr. *coāgulum*, 'means of coagulation'. **co-**, 'together', & Lat. *agere*, 'bring' &c. See **agent. 1.** intrans. (of liquids) To become partially solid; to clot, curdle. **2.** trans. To cause to coagulate.

coagulation, n. [1. kōagūláshun; 2. kouægjuléiʃən]. Prec. & **-ion. a** Process of coagulating; **b** condition of being coagulated.

coaita, n. [1. kōĭta; 2. kouáitə]. Native Brazil. name. The South American spider-monkey.

coal (**I.**), n. [1. kōl; 2. koul]. O.E. *col*, M.E. *cōle*; O.H.G. *cholo*, Mod. Germ. *kohle*. Perh. connected w. Scrt. *jval*, 'to burn'. **1. a** Solid combustible material of vegetable origin, consisting largely of carbon, occurring in fossil state, generally found beneath the ground, used for heating and in manufacture of gas; **b** a piece of coal, esp. one in process of combustion: *a hot coal fell on the carpet.* Phr. *as black as a coal.* **2.** (in pl., coll.) Lumps of coal ready for use: *to lay in coals for the winter.* Phrs. *to carry coals to Newcastle*, do something superfluous; *heap coals of fire on one's head*, reward evil with good; *to call a person over the coals* (*for* something), blame, scold.

coal (**II.**), vb. intrans. & trans., fr. prec. **1.** intrans. To take in a supply of coal, esp. of steamships and engines: *to coal at Gibraltar, at Swindon.* **2.** trans. To supply with coal, esp. to put coal into bunkers of steamship or locomotive.

coal-bed, n. Stratum of coal.

coal-black, adj. Black as coal, jet-black.

coaler, n. [1. kóler; 2. kóulə]. **coal** (**II.**) & **-er**. **a** Ship for supplying others with coal; **b** person employed in coaling.

coalesce, vb. intrans. [1. kòalés; 2. kòuəlés], fr. Lat. *coalescere*, 'to grow together, unite, become consolidated' (lit. and fig.), fr. **co-** & *alescere*, inceptive vb. fr. *alere*, 'to rear, support, maintain'. See **aliment** & **Alma Mater**. **1. a** To grow together, unite, as parts of a broken bone; **b** (of separate elements), to come together, unite, fuse into single body or mass. **2.** (fig., of persons and personalities) To intermingle easily; agree, assimilate.

coalescence, n. [1. kòalésens; 2. kòuəlésəns]. Lat. *coalescentia*. See next word & **-ce**. Process of coalescing.

coalescent, adj. [1. kòalésent; 2. kòuəlésənt]. Lat. *coalescent-(em)*, Pres. Part. of *coalescere*. See **coalesce**. Growing together.

coal-field, n. Region in which coal strata are found.

coal-fish, n. The black pollack, *Gadus virens*.

coal-gas, n. Mixture of gases produced by the burning and distillation of coal, used for lighting and heating.

coal-heaver, n. One who carts and carries coal, esp. one who brings it to private houses.

coal-hole, n. **a** Underground cavity or cellar in which coal is stored; **b** applied also to receptacle for coal above ground; **c** hole in street in towns through which coal is shot into the cellar.

coaling, n. [1. kóling; 2. kóuliŋ]. **coal** (**II.**) & **-ing**. Process of taking in, or putting coal into, bunkers of ship or locomotive.

coaling-station, n. Port where large supplies of coal are stored for steamships.

coalition, n. [1. kòalíshun; 2. kòuəlíʃən], fr. Lat. *coalit-(um)*, P.P. of *coalescere*, see **coalesce**, & **-ion**. **a** Act or process of fusion; **b** temporary union of forces by political parties for particular purpose, on the understanding that neither party abandons its distinctive principles.

coalitional, adj. [1. kòalíshunal; 2. kòuəlíʃənəl]. Prec. & **-al**. Pertaining to (a) coalition.

coalitionist, n. [1. kòalíshunist; 2. kòuəlíʃənist]. See prec. & **-ist**. One who favours or supports a political coalition.

coal-measure, n. (geol.) System of carboniferous strata; coal bed.

coal-mine, n. Mine from which coal is dug; coal-pit.

coal-pit, n. Excavation from which coal is dug; generally, all the group of associated works and workings connected with the digging of coal in a given place; coal-mine.

coal-scuttle, n. Vessel for holding and carrying coal for domestic use.

coal-tar, n. Tar obtained as a by-product in manufacture of gas from bituminous coal, the source of aniline dyes, disinfectants, benzene, creosote &c.

coal tit(**mouse**), n. European titmouse, so called from black on head and throat.

coaly, adj. [1. kóli; 2. kóuli]. **coal** (**I.**) & **-y**. Like coal; black; containing coal.

coaming, n. [1. kóming; 2. kóumiŋ]. Origin doubtful. Raised edge round outside of an opening such as a trap-door, or a ship's hatches, to keep out water.

coarse, adj. [1. kors; 2. kōs]. Origin doubtful. Variously applied in literal and figurative senses, meaning reverse of fine or delicate; hence, rough, thick, harsh, rude. **1.** (of quality) Common, rough, inferior: *coarse clothes, furniture, food* &c. **2.** (of texture) **a** (of fabrics) Rough, not finely and densely woven: *coarse cloth*; *a coarse mesh*; **b** (of powder-like substances, earth, meal &c.) having large particles; lumpy, not finely ground or pulverized: *coarse sand, oatmeal* &c. **3.** (of non-material things) **a** Lacking in refinement, delicacy, subtlety: *coarse methods, manners*; *coarse voice*; *coarse mind, intelligence*; **b** verging on impropriety, ribaldry, or obscenity; crude, gross: *coarse language, jokes.*

coarse-grained, adj. [1. kórs grānd; 2. kōs greind]. **a** Having coarse texture or grain; **b** (fig., of spiritual things) crude, gross; not delicate or subtle.

coarsely, adv. [1. kórsli; 2. kōsli]. **coarse** & **-ly**. (lit. and fig.) **a** Not finely, delicately; **b** roughly, crudely, grossly.

coarsen, vb. trans. & intrans. [1. kórsen; 2. kōsən]. **coarse** & **-en**. **a** To make coarse; **b** to become coarse, esp. in appearance and manners.

coarseness, n. [1. kórsnes; 2. kōsnis]. **coarse** & **-ness**. Property or quality of being coarse (lit. and fig.).

coast (**I.**), n. [1. kōst; 2. koust]. M.E., fr. O. Fr. *coste*, Mod. Fr. *côte*, 'rib; coast', fr. Lat. *costa*, 'rib, side; wall'. Cogn. w. O. Slav. *kostĭ*, 'bone'; further connexions dubious. Engl. & Fr. meaning perh. derived fr. 'ribs of rock by seashore'. Edge of the land at seashore; seashore and area adjacent to it. Phrs. *the coast is clear*, nothing, no one, in the way; *on the coast*, at the seaside.

coast (**II.**), vb. intrans., fr. prec. **1.** To go, in boat or ship, along the coast, from port to port, esp. to trade with coastal ports. **2. a** To slide down a snowy or ice-covered slope on a sledge or toboggan; **b** to go downhill on a bicycle without using pedals.

coastal, adj. [1. kóstal; 2. kóustəl]. **coast** (**I.**) & **-al**. Connected with, at, the coast.

coaster, n. [1. kóster; 2. kóustə]. **coast** (**II.**) & **-er**. **a** Vessel engaged in coastal trade; **b** silver tray for sliding wine decanters along a table.

coast-guard, coast-guardsman, n. One of a body of men, recruited from the Navy, who keep a look-out on the coast, and notify the passing of vessels, occurrence of wrecks &c., and assist the Customs officials, formerly under the Admiralty, now transferred to Board of Trade.

coast-line, n. **a** Outline of a coast seen from the sea; **b** contour of a coast.

coast waiter, n. Customs official who deals with shipping of goods in coasting trade.

coastwise, adj. & adv. [1. kóstwīz; 2. kóustwaiz]. **coast** (**I.**) & **-wise**. **a** adj. (of trade, and shipping) Going along the coast from port to port; as distinct from *over-seas* or *cross-channel*: *coastwise business, traffic* &c.; **b** adv., along the coast: *to sail coastwise.*

coat (**I.**), n. [1. kōt; 2. kout]. M.E. *cōte*, fr. O. Fr. *cote*, fr. L. Lat. *cota*, 'garment, tunic'; Mod. Fr. *cotte*, prob. new borrowing fr. Ital *cotta*, both fr. L. Lat. **cotta**, 'tunic'. The word was also borrowed into O.H.G. as *chozzo*, 'coarse tunic', & into O.S. as *kot.* None of the authorities throw any light on origin of the Lat. word. Is it possibly itself a loan-word fr. a Gmc. source, meaning 'hut, small house', as in O.E. *cot*? For change of meaning involved, cp. **chasuble.** In pl. *coats*, formerly denoting a child's or woman's petticoats (obs.). **1.** Garment with sleeves, of varying length, usually buttoned up the front; specif. **a** garment worn by men over the waistcoat, as part of a suit of outer clothes; a jacket; **b** similar garment made much longer, and worn outside the coat belonging to a suit, *greatcoat, overcoat*; **c** similar garments worn by women; esp. *coat and skirt*; **d** sleeved garment buttoning in front, and worn over other clothes by children. Phrs. *to take off one's coat*, prepare to fight; *take off one's coat to the work*, set about it vigorously; *to cut one's coat according to one's cloth*, make efforts, form plans, in proportion to one's means; *dust a man's coat* (*for him*), give him a thrashing; *wear the king's coat*, be dressed in uniform, i.e. be a soldier; *to turn one's coat*, go over to the other side or cause, esp. in politics. **2.** Sleeved body protection of chain mail worn formerly as part of a suit of armour: *coat of mail.* **3.** (her.) For *coat of arms*, see **arm** (**II.**) **2.** **4.** The external hairy, furry, or woolly covering of animals: *the horse's coat needs clipping.* **5. a** (anat.) Membrane covering or lining an organ of the body: *coats of the stomach*; **b** (hort.) tough outer skin of bulbs &c. **6.** Layer, film, of something spread, smeared, or applied to surface of an object, or settling upon it so as to cover the surface: *coat of paint, varnish, plaster*; *coat of dirt, dust.*

coat (**II.**), vb. trans., fr. prec. To cover as with a coat: *to coat wood with paint.*

coat-armour, n. Heraldic shield, escutcheon of individual or family, bearing crests and charges to which he or it is entitled.

coat-card, n. A court card, playing card with the coated figure of king, queen, or knave.

coatee, n. [1. kōté; 2. koutí]. **coat** (**I.**) & **-ee**. Short, close-fitting coat worn by women or children.

coati, n. [1. kōáhti; 2. kouáti]. Native Brazilian name. Small racoon-like mammal, of South and Central America, genus *Nasua*, with flexible snout and long tail.

coating, n. [1. kóting; 2. kóutiŋ]. **coat** (**II.**) & **-ing**. **a** Something painted on, or applied as, a coat (in sense **6**); **b** material suitable for making coats (tradesman's word).

coax (**I.**), vb. trans. & intrans. [1. kōks; 2. kouks]. Suggested etymologies appear to be counsels of despair. The word (n.) was spelt *cokes* in 16th cent., & had sense of 'dupe'. **a** trans. To use friendly efforts to persuade a person to do something, by flattery, entreaty, humouring; to wheedle, cajole; generally used in inoffensive sense: *to coax a child to take his medicine*; **b** intrans. to exercise the art of coaxing.

coax (**II.**), n. fr. prec. Person who practises coaxing; a pleasant-spoken, plausible, persuasive person.

coaxal, -ial, adj. [1. kòáksal, -ial; 2. kòuǽksl, -iəl]. **co-** & **axis** & **-al**. (maths.) Having a common axis.

coaxing, n. [1. kóksing; 2. kóuksiŋ]. **coax** (**I.**) & **-ing**. The act and process of persuading by cajolery.

cob, n. [1. kob; 2. kəb]. Origin unknown. **1.** Smallish, thick-set, stocky horse. **2.** Male swan. **3. a** Lump of ore, or esp. of coal, of moderate size (chiefly a trade word); cp. *cobnut*, small round nut; **b** lump of clay mixed with straw, used in building cottages in some districts where stone and brick are costly. **4.** Head of Indian corn, usually *corncob.*

cobalt, n. [1. kóbawlt, kobáwlt; 2. kóubōlt, kəbōlt]. Germ. *kobalt.* Prob. fr. Germ. **kobold**, 'sprite haunting mines'. See this word, & for transference of meaning cp. **nickel.** **a** Reddish-white metallic element found with nickel; **b** pigment made from a compound of this. See next word.

cobalt blue, n. Pigment of dark-blue colour made from a compound of cobalt.

cobble (**I.**), n. & vb. trans. [1. kóbl; 2. kóbl]. Cp. **cob, 3, a.** **1.** n. Rounded stone about the size of human fist, used for paving streets in old towns. **2.** vb. To pave with cobbles.

cobble (**II.**), vb. trans. & n. Perh. connected w. prec., 'to do lumpy work'. **1.** vb. To mend or make, sew, in a rough, clumsy manner; esp. *to cobble boots and shoes*, mend and patch. **2.** n. Clumsily done piece of sewing, patching, mending.

cobbler, n. [1. kóbler; 2. kɔ́blə], fr. prec. & **-er**. **1. a** One who mends boots and shoes as a trade; **b** (facetious) bootmaker, esp. one in small way of business. **2.** Clumsy, bad workman of any kind. **3.** Iced drink made of wine, sugar, lemon; *sherry cobbler*.

cobbler's wax, n. Sticky, wax-like compound used by cobblers for stiffening and preserving thread.

cobbling, n. [1. kóbling; 2. kɔ́bliŋ]. **cobble** (**II.**) & **-ing**. The work of a cobbler: *cobbling done here.*

cobby, adj. [1. kóbi; 2. kɔ́bi]. **cob** & **-y**. Like a cob, **1**, in build; shortish, thick-set, stocky; of horses and persons.

Cobdenism, n. [1. kóbdenizm; 2. kɔ́bdənizəm], fr. Richard Cobden (1804–65) & **-ism**. Political and economic principles advocated by Cobden, esp. free trade.

Cobdenite, n. [1. kóbdenīt; 2. kɔ́bdənait]. Prec. & **-ite**. Adherent of Cobdenism; esp. a convinced believer in free trade in all circumstances.

co-belligerent, n. [1. kōbelíjerent; 2. kòubɛlídžərənt]. **co-** & **belligerent**. Power associated with another in carrying on a war.

coble, n. [1. kṓbl, kóbl; 2. kóubl, kɔ́bl]. Cp. Bret. *caubal*, W. *ceubal*. Flat-bottomed boat with lug sail, used for fishing.

cob-loaf, n. **cob 3**, **a**, & **loaf**. Small rounded loaf, with flat bottom, not baked in a tin.

cob-nut, n. **cob 3**, **a**, & **nut**. Variety of hazel-nut.

cobra, n. [1. kṓbra; 2. kóubrə]. Port. *cobra di capello*, 'snake with a hood'; *cobra*, fr. Lat. *colubra*, 'female adder', *coluber*, 'serpent, snake, adder', cp. Fr. *couleuvre*. The Lat. word is for **corubra* &c., fr. base **ker-*, 'bend, twist', as in Lat. *curvus*, 'bent'. See **curve** & **circus**. **a** Venomous snake, *Naja*, with movable skin, resembling a hood, on its neck; found in India and other parts of Asia; **b** also allied kind, of Africa.

cobriform, adj. [1. kṓbriform; 2. kóubrifɔ̄m]. Prec. & **form** (**I.**). Allied to the cobra.

coburg, n. [1. kṓbĕrg; 2. kóubāg], fr. Germ. town. **a** Thin fabric of worsted and cotton or silk, used for women's dresses; **b** also a kind of fancy bread, light and rather sweet.

cobweb, n. [1. kóbweb; 2. kɔ́bwɛb]. M.E. *copweb*, wh. is for *attercop-web*, *ātor* being O.E. for 'poison', & *āttorcoppe*, 'spider', occurring in O.E., & *attercop* in M.E. The origin of this *cop* is unknown; it is found in same meaning in earlier Du. See **web**. **1. a** Network of thin threads spun by a spider from its own body to catch flies and small winged insects; **b** a single thread of this, often used for locating an object, in telescopes. **2.** Any very thin, unsubstantial, gauzy fabric; esp. of thin shawls, or lace. **3.** (fig.) As symbol of the obscuring of mental processes which have become inactive from disuse, or by prolonged concentration upon a single subject of study: *to blow the cobwebs from one's brain.*

cobwebby, adj. [1. kóbwebi; 2. kɔ́bwɛbi]. Prec. & **-y**. **a** Covered with, abounding in, cobwebs; **b** resembling these in texture and substance; light, filmy.

coca, n. [1. kṓka; 2. kóukə]. Peruvian word. South American plant; a decoction made from its leaves is used as a nerve tonic, and the dried leaves mixed with lime are chewed.

cocaine, n. [1. kōkā́n; 2. koukéin]. Prec. & **-ine**. Alkaloid poisonous substance obtained from coca plant, used as a local anaesthetic; also, in powdered form, snuffed up the nose by drug-takers, as an intoxicant and stimulant.

cocainism, n. [1. kōkā́nizm; 2. koukéinizəm]. Prec. & **-ism**. **a** Addiction to cocaine, as a drug; **b** poisoning by cocaine.

coccus, n., pl. **cocci** [1. kókus, kóksī; 2. kɔ́kəs, kɔ́ksai]. Latinization of Gk. *kókkos*, 'kernel, berry'. Etymol. unknown. **1.** One of many species of disease-causing bacteria, spherical in shape. **2.** (entom.) Any member of the family *Coccidae* or scale insects, such as the cochineal insect &c.

coccygeal, adj. [1. koksíjeal; 2. kɔksídžiəl], fr. Gk. *kókkūg-(os)*, base of *kókkux*. See next word & **-al**. (anat.) Of, pertaining to, the coccyx.

coccyx, n. [1. kóksiks; 2. kɔ́ksiks]. Lat., fr. Gk. *kókkux*, 'a cuckoo'; fr. supposed resemblance in shape of the bone to a cuckoo's bill. The Gk. word is imitative; cp. **cuckoo**. (anat.) The vertebrae at the base of the spine in man and some of the apes, corresponding to the root of the tail in other animals.

cochin-china, n. [1. kòchin chína; 2. kɔ̀tʃin tʃáinə], fr. country. Breed of domestic fowl with feathered legs.

cochineal, n. [1. kòchinḗal; 2. kɔ̀tʃiníəl]. Fr. *cochenille*, fr. Span. *cochinilla*, dimin. fr. Lat. *coccinus*, 'scarlet', fr. *coccum*, 'berry', fr. Gk. *kókkos*. See **coccus**. Bright scarlet dye made from dried bodies of insects called *coccus cacti*, found in Central America; formerly believed to be seeds, which they greatly resemble.

cochlea, n. [1. kóklea; 2. kɔ́kliə]. Lat. *coc(h)lea*, fr. Gk. *kokhliās*, 'snail', hence 'spiral in form of snail-shell'; prob. fr. **kogkhl-*, & thus connected w. *kógkhos*, 'shell', see **conch**. (anat.) A spiral division of the inner ear.

cochleare, n. [1. kòkleā́re; 2. kɔ̀kliéəri]. Lat. *coc(h)lear*, 'spoon', prob. dissimilated fr. **cocleāli* (see prec. & **-al**), perh. so named, according to Boisacq, because the pointed end was used to extract snails from their shells. (med.) A spoonful; the abbreviated form *cochle.* is used in writing prescriptions.

cock (**I.**), n. [1. kok; 2. kɔk]. Early in O.E. as *cocc*; cp. O. Fr. *coc*, Mod. Fr. *coq*, L. Lat. *coccus*, prob. of imitative origin, fr. cry of bird, like **cuckoo**. **1. a** The male of domestic fowl; **b** male of other birds, when used with explanatory context, as *the cock bird of this species* &c.; **c** in combination as name of birds e.g. *woodcock*, *peacock* &c.; also *cock of the woods*, the capercailzie; Phrs. *that cock won't fight*, that scheme, plan &c., will not succeed, won't answer; *old cock*, familiar, affectionate mode of address, old boy &c.; *cock-and-bull story*, fantastic yarn that no one can believe; **d** used in various senses, esp. in phrases, all based on the strutting and swaggering of a cock before his hens, or his pugnacious and dominating character; *cock of the school*, boy of dominating character; *cock of the walk*, *dunghill*, leading, ruling spirit in a body of men; *live like a fighting cock*, luxuriously. **2. a** Tap and spout; various objects supposed to resemble cock's head and comb: *watercock* &c.; **b** hammer of a gun: *at half-cock* &c.; **c** weather vane; generally *weather-cock*.

cock (**II.**), vb. trans. & intrans., fr. prec. **A.** trans. **1. a** To bring the hammer of a fire-arm into position for firing: *to cock one's pistol* &c.; **b** to turn back, or up, the brim of a hat (formerly); now to set a hat jauntily on side of the head (either from idea of pulling back, as in cocking a gun, or from that of swaggering like a cock); **c** to turn organs of sight or hearing towards something, ready for looking or listening: *to cock the ears*, to prick them (of a dog, or facetiously, of a man), to listen; *to cock one's eye at something* (colloq.), to glance at. **B.** intrans. To swagger or strut like a cock (rare). **C.** (with prep.) *Cock up*, **a** to turn up, put up; **b** specif. (boys' slang at Charterhouse School), to administer corporal punishment to, with an ash-rod. (Act of a monitor upon a junior boy for breach of discipline.)

cock (**III.**), n., fr. **cock** (**II.**). **a** Smart, rapid, upward turn or movement: *cock of the eyes, ears*; **b** result of such a turn, a jaunty, sideways position: *a cock in a hat brim.*

cock (**IV.**), n. & vb. trans. Cp. Dan. *kok*, 'hay-cock', & O.N. *kōkkr*, 'lump, ball'. **1.** n. Pile of hay, raked together ready for carting. **2.** vb. To put, or pile up (hay), into cocks.

cockabundy, n. [1. kókabúndi; 2. kɔ́kəbándi]. W. *coch a bon dhu*, 'red with black body'. Artificial fly used in trout-fishing.

cockade, n. [1. kokā́d; 2. kɔkéid], fr. Fr. *cocarde*, fr. *coq*, 'cock', fr. resemblance to comb of a cock. See **rosette** (**I.**). Kind of ornamental device or rosette, worn in the hat by men-servants of military and naval officers, or of others holding office under the Crown.

cock-a-doodle-doo, n. [1. kókadōōdldṓō; 2. kɔ́kədúdldú]. Imitative word. **a** Childish imitation of cry of a cock; **b** name for cock itself.

cock-a-hoop, adj. [1. kókahṓōp; 2. kɔ̀kəhúp]. **a** Elated, exultant, as with success; **b** (in bad sense) self-satisfied, arrogant, hubristic.

cock-a-hoopness, n., fr. prec. & **-ness**. Condition of being cock-a-hoop.

cockaigne, n. See **cockayne**.

cocka-leekie, n. See **cocky-leekie**.

cockalorum, n. [1. kòkalṓrum; 2. kɔ̀kəlɔ́rəm]. Sham Latin. A young cock, esp. applied to a young, perky, rather conceited little man.

cockatoo, n. [1. kòkatṓō; 2. kɔ̀kətú]. Malay *kakatúa*, influenced by **cock** (**I.**). Crested parrot.

cockatrice, n. [1. kókatrīs, -is; 2. kɔ́kətrais, -tris]. M.E. *cocatryse* &c., fr. O. Fr. *cocatrice*, 'ichneumon', &, by confusion w. *cocodrille*, also 'crocodile'. The O. Fr. is fr. L. Lat. *cŏcātric-(em)* for *calcātric-(em)*, lit. 'the tracker', fr. *calcāre*, 'to tread', a translation of Gk. *ikhneúmōn*, wh. tracked out & devoured crocodiles' eggs. See **caulk** & **calceolaria**. **1.** Fabulous reptile whose glance was venomous, supposed to be hatched by some reptile from the egg of a cock; a basilisk. **2.** (her.) Creature having head, wings, and legs of a cock, with a serpent's body and tail. **3.** (fig.) A seductive, designing woman.

cockayne, cockaigne, n. [1. kokā́n; 2. kɔkéin]. O. Fr. *coquaigne*, perh. connected w. Lat. *coquere*, 'to cook', see **cook**; Mod. Fr. *pays de cocagne*, perh. lit. 'land of cakes'. **a** Imaginary land of plenty and delights; **b** (facetious) *the land of Cockayne*, place where cockneys live, London.

cock-boat, n. The first element is derived by Skeat & Diez ultimately fr. Lat. *concha*, 'shell'. See **conch**. O. Fr. has *coque*, 'kind of boat'; cp. also Ital. *cocca*, Span. *coca*, 'boat'. A doublet *cog(ge)* fr. Scand. sources is found in M.E. O.N. has *kuggr* & Dan. *kog*, 'a boat', prob. early independent borrowings fr. Lat. Small boat attached to a ship.

cockchafer, n. [1. kókchāfer; 2. kɔ́ktʃeifə]. **cock** (**I.**) (expressing size ?) & **chafer**. Large, winged beetle, pale brown in colour, which flies by night, in summer-time, with a loud humming of its wings.

cock-crow, n. See **cock** (**I.**) & **crow** (**III.**). In O.E. *hancred*, 'cock crow', is used in the sense of *the early hours*, the second element being derived fr. *crāwan*, 'to crow'. The hour at which cocks begin to crow; the early hours, dawn.

cocker (**I.**), vb. trans. [1. kóker; 2. kɔ́kə]. Found in sense of 'to pamper' in 15th cent. Skeat adduces early Dan. *kokre*, 'to call often, as a cock or hen does', also Norw. *kokla*, (1) 'to cackle', (2) 'to pet, pamper'. Doubtless the word is derived fr. a Norse word used in above senses, but not, as Skeat suggests, fr. the idea of calling *chickens*, to feed them constantly, hence to pamper, since this office is performed by the hen. On the other hand, the cock does call the hens when he finds a tit-bit, & the sense is no doubt derived fr. the cock pampering his wives in this way. *To cry cok* in M.E. is to call constantly as a cock does. To pamper, cosset, indulge (children). Also *cocker up*, feed up with dainties.

Cocker (II.), n. Proper name; Edward Cocker (1631–75), a celebrated teacher of arithmetic in London, whose book on this subject went through a hundred editions. Only in phrase *according to Cocker*, in order, correct, as it should be, orthodox.

cockerel, n. [1. kókrel; 2. kɔ́krəl]. Dimin. of **cock** (I.). A young cock, from the time it is hatched, until about a year old.

cocker spaniel, n. Moderate-sized spaniel, of various colours, black and white, black and tan, liver, red &c., bred for retrieving game, and as a pet.

cocket, n. [1. kóket; 2. kɔ́kit]. Origin doubtful. **a** Seal of King's custom house; **b** kind of leavened bread.

cock-eyed, adj., fr. **cock** (II.). **1.** (colloq. slang) Squinting, having crooked eyes. **2.** Generally, crooked, slanting, out of the straight line; also often *cockeye*: *the pictures are hung all cockeye*; (of a crooked, badly made person) *to be built cockeye(d)*.

cock-fight, n. **cock** (I.) & **fight** (I.). Organized contest between gamecocks, which used to have long steel spurs fastened to their feet.

cock-fighting, n. Prec. & **-ing**. Practice, sport, of setting gamecocks to fight.

cockle (I.), n. [1. kókl; 2. kɔ́kl], also **corn-cockle**. O.E. *coccel*, 'tares' &c., perh. dimin. of Lat. *coccum*, 'berry'. See **cochineal**. Any of various plants which grow in cornfields, including the corn cockle.

cockle (II.), n. M.E. *cokel*, Fr. *coquille*, dimin. of *coq*, 'shell', fr. Lat. *concha*. See **conch**. Edible bivalve with shells somewhat in the shape of a heart. Phr. *to warm the cockles of one's heart*, cheer, hearten one, physically and morally. (Connexion is obscure.)

cockle (III.), vb. intrans. & trans. Perh. fr. ridges on cockle-shell? **1.** intrans. To wrinkle or pucker, become warped. **2.** trans. To cause to wrinkle &c.

cockle-shell, n. See **cockle** (II.) & **shell**. **1. a** One of the shells of a cockle; **b** any shell of approximately this shape, esp. one formerly carried by pilgrims to the Holy Land. **2.** A very light, fragile, boat.

cock-loft, n. **cock** (I.) & **loft**. **a** Originally a place where cocks roosted; **b** (derisively) a small garret or attic, esp. one just under the roof; any small room in an upper storey approached by a steep, narrow stair.

cockney, n. & adj. [1. kókni; 2. kɔ́kni]. M.E. *cokeney*, used for 'egg'; *coken-*, is a gen. pl., for O.E. *-ena*; the last syll. is M.E. *ēy*, 'egg', O.E. *ǣg*. See **egg**. The word, therefore, means lit. 'cock's egg', a term still applied to small yolkless eggs. Hence it was used as a term of reproach, meaning orig. an effeminate, foolish person, also, a spoilt child. See Skeat on this word. Prob. the term was applied to townsmen as representing the view of country dwellers. **1.** n. **a** One born in London, traditionally within the sound of Bow Bells, and passing his life there; **b** specif., a vulgar person from London, esp. one with a London accent, and possessing certain characteristics of mind and manners which are supposed to be typical of Londoners; **c** a vulgar, presuming, trivial fellow from a town. **2.** adj. Belonging to, connected with, cockneys in any sense: *a cockney accent, manner* &c.

cockneydom, n. [1. kóknidum; 2. kɔ́knidəm]. Prec. & **-dom**. District inhabited, social circles frequented, by cockneys.

cockneyism, n. [1. kókni-izm; 2. kɔ́kni-izəm]. **cockney** & **-ism**. A characteristic vulgarism belonging to the speech of Londoners, e.g. *plate* pronounced very like *plight* [plait], or *house*, pronounced [hæus].

cockpit, n. [1. kókpit; 2. kɔ́kpit]. **cock** (I.) & **pit** (I.). **1.** Small enclosure or arena, with raised border, used in cock-fighting. **2.** Quarters of junior officers, below deck, in an old man-of-war, used in battle for the wounded. **3.** The scene of any considerable contest: *Flanders has been called the cockpit of Europe*. **4.** Small space in an aeroplane for accommodation of pilot, or passenger.

cockroach, n. [1. kókrōch; 2. kɔ́kroutʃ], fr. Span. *cucaracha*, 'woodlouse, kind of centipede'. Offensive insect of the *Blattidae* family, which infests houses, of which the domestic *black beetle* is a variety; it attacks any kind of food; the male is winged, the female wingless, and both run rapidly.

cock robin, n. **a** Male of the robin; **b** applied to a small, bright-eyed, alert, perky man.

cockscomb, n. [1. kókskōm; 2. kɔ́kskoum]. **cock** (I.) & **comb**. See also **coxcomb**. **1.** The fleshy red crest on the head of a cock. **2.** Large red, feathery flower, supposed to resemble above in shape and colour.

cockshy, n. [1. kókshī; 2. kɔ́kʃai]. **cock** (I.) & **shy** (IV.). **1.** Ancient game, which consisted of throwing sticks at gamecocks tied to stakes. **2.** Game, practised at fairs and shows, of throwing a stick, or ball, at coco-nuts &c., balanced on stands, those knocked off being handed as a prize to the persons who hit them. **3. a** A throw, shy, shot, at coco-nuts &c., at a fair; **b** a shy at any object taken as a mark or target; **c** object at which one shies.

cock sparrow, n. **cock** (I.) & **sparrow**. **a** Male of the sparrow; **b** small, insignificant-looking little man who gives himself certain airs of importance.

cock-sure, adj. **cock** (I.) & **sure**. (formerly) Perfectly certain or assured (of something); now generally **a** (of a habit of mind) self-confident, overweeningly sure of one's own judgement, convinced that one is right; **b** (of event &c.) certain to happen.

cocksureness, n. Prec. & **-ness**. Excessive self-confidence.

cocksy. See **coxy**.

cocktail, n. [1. kóktāl; 2. kɔ́kteil]. **cock** (II.) & **tail**. **1. a** Horse which is nearly, but not quite thoroughbred; **b** vulgar, ill-bred person raised above his station. **2.** American short drink, or appetizer, of various kinds, but always consisting of spirit, whether gin or not, bitters, and various flavourings, and often iced.

cock-up, n. [1. kókup; 2. kɔ́kap]. (typog.) Letter or figure in abbreviations lifted above the alignment, as in M^{rs}., x^2 &c.

cocky, adj. [1. kóki; 2. kɔ́ki]. **cock** (I.) & **-y**. See variant **coxy** w. slight difference of meaning. Bumptious, conceited, inclined to swagger.

cocky-leekie, n. [1. kókilēki; 2. kɔ́kilīki]. **cock** (I.) & **leek**. Soup made of a fowl, generally an old cock, or hen, boiled down with leeks.

cockyolly bird, n. [1. kòkióli bērd; 2. kɔ̀kiɔ́li bə̄d]. Baby name for a bird.

coco (also by confusion w. next word, **cocoa**), n. [1. kōkō; 2. kóukou], or when hyphened w. another word [kóukə]; fr. Port. *coco*, 'grimace', fr. resemblance of nut to a monkey's face. A tropical palm tree and its fruit; chiefly in compounds, as *coco-nut, coco-palm*.

cocoa, n. [1. kōkō; 2. kóukou]. Anglicized form of **cacao**. **a** Fine powder made from the ground seeds of the cacao plant; **b** drink made from this, with the addition of hot water, sugar, and milk.

cocoa bean, n. Seed of cacao plant, from which the substance known as cocoa, and also chocolate, is made.

cocoa nib, n. Cocoa-bean with husk removed.

cocoa powder, n. Kind of gunpowder, so called from its colour.

coco-nut, n. See **coco** & **nut**. **a** Large nut with hard shell, surrounded by fibrous husk, and thick hard white hollow kernel with characteristic taste, filled with milky juice, *coco-nut milk*; **b** (vulg.) human head.

coco-nut tree, n. The coco-palm.

cocoon, n. [1. kokōōn; 2. kəkūn, kəkún]. Fr. *cocon*, formed fr. *coque*, 'shell of eggs'. See **cock-boat** & **conch**. Outer envelope of silk, or silk-like thread, which a caterpillar spins round itself at the end of this stage of its existence, and within which it develops into the final stage, and whence it emerges as a butterfly, moth &c.

coco-palm, n. Tree with pinnate leaves, growing freely in the tropics, upon which coco-nuts grow.

cod (I.), n. [1. kod; 2. kɔd]. In M.E. Only found in Engl. Etymol. unknown. Connexion w. **cod** (II.) hardly possible, though suggested by Skeat. Large sea fish, genus *Gadus*, esp. *G. morrhua*, with soft fins and firm, but flaky, rather tasteless flesh. Also *cod-fish*.

cod (II.), n. O.E. *codd*, 'bag, shell, husk, skin of a grape', M.E. *cod, codde*, 'pod, husk of leguminous plants', also 'scrotum'; cp. also O.N. *kuðri*, 'scrotum of animals', Swed. dial. *kudde*, 'pod', & Jutland dial. *kodde*, 'pod, scrotum'. In 15th cent. *cod* is used in Engl. for 'pillow', cp. O.N. *koddi*, 'pillow'. All these words are cogn. w. Goth. *qiþus*, 'womb', O.E. *cwiþ, cwiþa*, 'womb'. The latter words go back to Aryan *g^w*ét-*, Gmc. **kwiþi, -u*; *codd* &c. go back to Gmc. **kuððá-*, fr. Aryan *g^w*ətó*. A further cogn. fr. an Aryan *g^w*ot-* type is Lat. *botulus*, 'sausage', w. Umbrian *b-* for *g^w-. See **botulism**. The orig. meaning of the base is prob. 'to swell out'. This word is now obsolete in English, apart from provincial dialects, except perhaps in *peasecod*, shell or pod of peas, but is of frequent occurrence in 16th and 17th cent. literature in general sense of bag, and in the other M.E. meanings given above. See **cod-piece**.

cod (III.), vb. trans. Etymol. doubtful. (slang) To hoax, play tricks on; to swindle, cheat.

coddle, vb. trans. [1. kódl; 2. kɔ́dl]. Prob. a form of **caudle**. Take excessive care of, treat as though frail and delicate, esp. by feeding choicely, and protecting from cold and damp; to pamper, cosset.

code (I.), n. [1. kōd; 2. koud]. Fr., fr. Lat. **codex**, 'book' &c. **1.** Systematic body of laws compiled by authority of the state. **2.** Set of accepted manners and morals current in a given section of society: *code of honour*. **3. a** Set of conventional symbols used in transmitting messages by flags, telegraph, heliograph &c.: *Morse code* &c.; **b** agreed system of letters or words used in very secret or private communications, in which a letter or word is put for one quite different.

code (II.), vb. trans. To put a message into the symbols of a code, 3.

codeine, n. [1. kōdiēn; 2. kóudiīn]. Gk. *kṓdeia*, 'poppy-head', & **-ine**. Cp. Gk. *kôos*, 'cavern, burrow', *koîlos* (fr. **kowil-*), 'hollow'; fr. base **kow-*, **kew-*, 'hollow', seen also in **cave** (I.). Alkaloid derived from opium, used as a narcotic &c.

codex, n. [1. kōdeks; 2. kóudɛks]. Lat., also *caudex*, 'trunk of a tree, block of wood, writing-tablet, ledger' &c. Orig. 'tree which has been felled'; connected w. *cūdere*, 'strike, beat, pound' &c.; the base **kow-* is found in Gmc. as **haw-*, cp. O.E. *hēawan*, 'hew' &c. See further under **hew, hay**. A manuscript, or manuscript volume; applied especially to an ancient manuscript of the Scriptures, or of a classical author.

codger, n. [1. kójer; 2. kɔ́dʒə]. Variant of **cadger**. (colloq. and facetious) A queer old fellow; chiefly *an old codger*.

codicil, n. [1. kódisil; 2. kɔ́disil]. Fr. *codicille*, fr. Lat. *cōdicillus*, dimin. of **codex**, 'small tree-trunk; small writing tablet; a short writing, petition &c.; addition to a will'. An addition to a will, modifying its provisions in some particular; a codicil must be formally signed and witnessed in the same way as the main body of the will.

codicillary, adj. [1. kòdisíleri; 2. kɔ̀disíləri]. Prec. & **-ary**. Connected with, of the nature of, a codicil.

codification, n. [1. kōdifikáshun; 2. kóudifikéiʃən]. See **code** (I.) & **-fication**. **a** Act or process of putting laws in form of a code; **b** result of such act.

codify, vb. trans. [1. kōdifī; 2. kóudifai]. **code** & **-fy**. To reduce laws to the form of a code.

codling (**I.**), n. [1. kódling; 2. kɔ́dliŋ]. **cod** (**I.**) & **-ling**. **a** Young cod; **b** a small kind of cod.

codling (**II.**), n. M.E. *querdling*; *quadlin* in Bacon. Skeat cites Ir. *cueirt*, 'apple tree'. The suff. in any case is Engl. **-ling**. Cooking apple, generally of inferior quality, and rather tapering towards the apex.

codlin(g) moth, n. Small moth which lays its eggs in the eye of an apple, pear, or quince, and whose grub when hatched out eats its way into, and destroys the fruit.

cod-liver oil, n. [1. kódliver óil; 2. kɔ́dlivər ɔ́il]. Oil, the source of which is suggested by its name, used as tonic and nutriment for the weak and sickly.

codpiece, n. [1. kódpēs; 2. kɔ́dpīs]. See **cod** (**II.**) & **piece**. (archaic) Part of a man's attire; formerly, an appendage, more or less in form of a bag, often highly ornamented, worn in front of the breeches.

co-ed, n. [1. kő éd; 2. kóu éd]. Abbr. of next word. (slang, U.S.A.) Girl student at a school &c., where co-education is practised.

co-education, n. [1. kőedūkáshun; 2. kóuɛdjukéiʃən]. **co-** & **education**. System of educating children of both sexes in the same school and class.

co-efficient, adj. & n. [1. kȯefíshent; 2. kòuifíʃənt]. **co-** & **efficient**. **a** adj. Combining with something else to produce result; **b** n., that which combines, is united with some other factor or factors to produce a given result; the word has special and specific applications in mathematics and physics.

coel(o)-, pref. Form used in composition; fr. Gk. *koîlos*, 'hollow', for **kowilos*, cogn. w. Lat. *cavus*, 'hollow'. See **cave** & **codeine**.

coelenterate, adj. & n. [1. sēlénterāt; 2. sīléntəreit]. **coelo-** & Gk. *énteron*, 'intestine', see **enteric** & **-ate**. (zool.) **a** adj. Of, pertaining to, the *Coelenterata*, the group of marine invertebrates which includes the jelly-fish, sea-anemones, corals &c., so-called as having a single body-cavity or *coelenteron*; **b** n., member of this group.

coeno-, ceno-, pref. Form used in composition; fr. Gk. *koinós*, 'common, public'; the word is possibly, though not certainly, connected w. Lat. *com*, *cum*, 'together with' &c. See **com-**.

coenobite, n. [1. sḗnōbīt; 2. sínoubait]. L. Lat. *coenobīta*, 'member of a social fraternity'; cp. *coenobium*, 'member of a monastery', fr. Gk. *koinóbion*, in same sense, fr. *koinó-*, 'common', see prec., & *bios*, 'life', see **biology**. One living in a conventual establishment, or similar institution; member of a community sharing a common life.

coenobitic(al), adj. [1. sēnōbítik(l); 2. sìnoubítik(l). Prec. & **-ic** & **-al**. Pertaining to a coenobite: *the coenobitic life*.

co-equal, adj. [1. kőḗkwal; 2. kòuíkwəl]. Lat. *coaequālis*, 'equal'. **co-** & **equal**; *coaequāre* means 'to put on same level, equalize'. (chiefly theological) Having complete equality.

co-equality, n. [1. kőēkwóliti; 2. kóuīkwɔ́liti]. Complete equality.

co-equate, vb. trans. & intrans. [1. kȯikwāt; 2. kóuikwéit]. **co-** & **equate**. Lat. *coaequātum*, P.P. of *coaequāre*, 'equalize'. **a** trans. To make completely equal to something else; **b** intrans., to become completely equal to something else.

co-equation, n. [1. kȯikwáshun; 2. kóuikwéiʃən]. Prec. & **-ion**. **a** Act of making equal; **b** process of becoming equal; **c** fact of being equal.

coerce, vb. trans. [1. kőḗrs; 2. kouə́s]. Lat. *co-ercēre*, 'to shut up together, confine'; (fig.) 'confine, restrain, limit, repress; punish', fr. **co-** & *arcēre*, 'to shut up, enclose', cogn. w. *arca*, 'chest, coffer'. See **ark**. **a** To compel (a person) by exercise of authority or force, to act in a certain way, or to abstain from a given action, to constrain; usually with *into*: *to coerce a person into an agreement, silence* &c.; **b** (more rarely) to secure, obtain by compulsion: *to coerce acquiescence*.

coercible, adj. [1. kōḗrsibl; 2. kouə́sibl]. Prec. & **-ible**. Liable to be, capable of being, coerced.

coercion, n. [1. kōḗrshun; 2. kouə́ʃən]. **coerce** & **-ion**. Act, or process of compelling, constraining by force; esp. of system of government in which various liberties are suspended.

coercive, adj. [1. kōḗrsiv; 2. kouə́siv]. **coerce** & **-ive**. Pertaining to, characterized by, coercion: esp. *coercive methods, measures* &c.

coercively, adv. Prec. & **-ly**. By the exercise of coercion.

coerciveness, n. See prec. & **-ness**. Quality of being coercive.

co-essential, adj. [1. kȯesénshal; 2. kòuisénʃəl]. **co-** & **essential**. Having one and the same nature or essence.

co-eternal, adj. [1. kȯetérnal; 2. kòuitə́nl]. **co-** & **eternal**. Equally eternal, chiefly a theological use.

coeval, adj. [1. kȯḗval; 2. kòuívəl]. **co-** & Lat. *aevus*, 'age', & **-al**; *aevus* is cogn. w. Engl. **aye**, **ever**, also **age**. Having the same age; existing during same period (esp. of a remote period).

co-executor, n. [1. kȯegzékūter; 2. kòuɛgzékjutə]. **co-** & **executor**. One who is an executor jointly with another.

co-executrix, n. [1. kȯegzékūtriks; 2. kòuɛgzékjutriks]. Fem. of prec.

co-exist, vb. intrans. [1. kȯegzíst; 2. kòuigzíst]. **co-** & **exist**. **a** To exist at same time as; **b** to exist in association with. (Sometimes *coexist with*, or *together with*.)

co-existence, n. [1. kȯegzístens; 2. kòuigzístəns]. Prec. & **-ence**. Existence at same time as, or in association with.

co-existent, adj. [1. kȯegzístent; 2. kòuigzístənt]. **co-** & **existent**. Existing at same time as, or together with.

co-extensive, adj. [1. kȯexténsiv; 2. kòuiksténsiv]. **co-** & **extensive**. Having equal extension in time or space.

coffee, n. [1. kófi; 2. kɔ́fi]. Turk. & Arab. *qahveh*. **1.** **a** Evergreen shrub growing originally indigenous in Abyssinia and now cultivated in Arabia, W. Africa, Ceylon, Java, and Brazil &c., with pulpy berries containing hard aromatic seeds; **b** pungent drink made from a decoction of these seeds ('beans') roasted and ground fine. *Black coffee*, this drink made strong and undiluted with milk.

coffee-bean, n. The seed of coffee plant, whence the drink is made.

coffee-berry, n. **a** The fruit of coffee plant which contains the seeds; **b** (more commonly) the coffee bean.

coffee-cup, n. Small cup, usually of delicate china, from which coffee is consumed.

coffee-house, n. House of public entertainment where coffee and other non-alcoholic drinks are consumed; formerly a place of resort for literary men, used as a kind of club.

coffee-mill, n. Contrivance for crushing or grinding the roasted coffee beans by turning a handle which sets small rollers in motion.

coffee-pot, n. Vessel of silver, earthenware &c., in which the drink coffee is made or served.

coffee-room, n. Room in an inn or old-fashioned hotel in which public meals are served; hotel dining-room.

coffer (**I.**), n. [1. kófer; 2. kɔ́fə]. Variant of **coffin**. M.E., fr. O. Fr. *coffre*, 'box', fr. Gk. *kóphinos*, 'a basket'. **a** Strong chest or box, esp. one for storing valuables, specif., money-box; **b** panel in ceiling, deeply recessed and ornamented; **c** a coffer-dam.

coffer (**II.**), vb. trans., fr. prec. To enclose in a coffer.

coffer-dam, n. Enclosed space on river-bed &c. from which water has been pumped, and which is filled with clay &c. tightly rammed down; used in making foundations for piers of a bridge &c.; a caisson.

coffin (**I.**), n. [1. kófin; 2. kɔ́fin]. M.E., fr. O. Fr. *cofin*, Lat. *cophinus*, fr. Gk. *kóphinos*, 'basket'. The etymol. of Gk. word is very doubtful; it is possibly non-Aryan. **1.** Receptacle or case, formerly of stone or metal, now usually of wood, in which the bodies of the dead are buried. Phr. *a nail in one's coffin*, action, or event, which has disastrous effect on one's health, future career. **2.** Coffin-bone of a horse.

coffin (**II.**), vb. trans., fr. prec. To place in a coffin.

coffin-bone, n. Bone inside horse's hoof, corresponding to a finger or toe in other mammals.

coffin-joint, n. That just above coronet in horse's foot.

coffin-plate, n. Metal plate attached to lid of a coffin, bearing name, date of death &c. of the dead within.

coffin-ship, n. Ship so unsound and unseaworthy as to make it seem probable that those who sail in her will perish at sea.

coffle, n. [1. kófl; 2. kɔ́fl]. Arab. *qafilah*, 'caravan'. String of beasts, e.g. camels, fastened together; a caravan.

cog (**I.**), n. [1. kog; 2. kɔg]. Scand. Cp. Dan. *kogge*. One of a series of tooth-like projections on rim of a wheel, a cam for transmitting motion.

cog (**II.**), vb. trans. & intrans. Origin unknown. **a** To manipulate fraudulently the fall of dice; hence, **b** to cheat, swindle, act fraudulently.

cog (**III.**), n. Scand. Cp. O.N. *koggi*, *koggr*; see **cock-boat**. Small fishing-boat.

cogency, n. [1. kṓjensi; 2. kóudʒən(t)si], fr. **cogent** & **-cy**. Condition of being cogent; (of arguments, reasons &c.) convincing force.

cogent, adj. [1. kṓjent; 2. kóudʒənt]. Lat., fr. *cōgent-(em)*, Pres. Part. of *cōgere*, 'to drive together; compel', fr. **co-** & *agere*, 'to drive'. See **agent**, **act** &c. Chiefly **a** (of non-material force) impelling, appealing to, the mind, so as to influence it powerfully; persuasive, convincing: *cogent reasons, arguments* &c.; also **b** (facetiously) of actual physical compulsion: *the policeman's hand on his shoulder was a cogent reason for his departure.*

cogently, adv. Prec. & **-ly**. In a cogent manner.

cogged, adj. [1. kógd; 2. kɔ́gd]. P.P. of **cog** (**II.**) in mistaken sense. (of dice) Loaded for purpose of cheating.

cogitable, adj. [1. kójitabl; 2. kɔ́dʒitəbl]. Lat. *cōgitābilis*, fr. *cōgitāre*, 'ponder, reflect upon'. See **cogitate**. Thinkable, capable of being made subject of thought.

cogitate, vb. intrans. (rarely trans.) [1. kójitāt; 2. kɔ́dʒiteit]. Lat., fr. *cōgitāt-(um)*, P.P. of *cōgitāre*, 'ponder deeply, reflect upon' &c., fr. **co-** & *agitāre*, 'put in constant or frequent motion; toss about, shake up and down' &c.; (fig.) 'turn over in the mind'. See **agitate**. **a** intrans. To think deeply; ponder, ruminate, plan; **b** (rarely) trans., to think out, devise: *to cogitate a scheme.*

cogitation n. [1. kòjitáshun; 2. kɔ̀dʒitéiʃən]. Prec. & **-ion**. **a** Act of cogitating; **b** (esp. in pl.) the results of this; thought, plans.

cogitative, adj. [1. kójitātiv; 2. kɔ́dʒitèitiv]. **cogitate** & **-ive**. **a** Having faculty of thought; **b** inclined, given, to cogitation; pensive.

cogitatively, adv. Prec. & **-ly**. In a pensive manner.

cognac, n. [1. kṓnyak; 2. kóunjæk]. Fr. Place-Name. Brandy, distilled from wine, made at Cognac; (loosely) brandy in general.

cognate (**I.**), adj. [1. kógnāt; 2. kɔ́gneit]. Lat. *cognātus*, 'related by birth; kindred, connected, similar', fr. **co-** & *(g)nātus*, 'born', P.P. of *nascor*, 'to be born'. See **natal** & **nascent**. **1.** Sprung from a common stock, having common ancestor, related by blood. (In this literal sense, applicable to men and animals, the word is far less used than in the derived and figurative senses.) **2.** Having common source or origin; **a** (of languages) derived from the same original language, sprung from the same primitive mother tongue: *English and Dutch are cognate languages, both belonging to the Germanic family*; *the Germanic, Celtic, Slavonic, Italic,*

Hellenic, and Indian families of language are cognate, being all derived from Primitive Aryan, the mother tongue of them all; **b** (of words) derived from the same 'root' or base; or from same complete word in the mother tongue: *Greek* patēr, *Latin* pater, *English* father, *are unmistakably cognate*; **c** (of things of the mind) having affinity, close resemblance, much in common: *cognate ideas, tastes*; *physics and astronomy are cognate sciences.*

cognate (II.), n. **1.** (law) Person having blood-relationship to another. **2.** Anything closely related to, having common origin with, or resembling, another; (specif. of languages and words, see (**I.**), **2, a** and **b**): *Latin* vīvus, *Greek* bíos, '*life*', *and English* quick, '*alive*', *are cognates.*

cognation, n. [1. kognā́shun; 2. kɔgnéiʃən]. **cognate (I.)** & **-ion.** Blood-relationship.

cognition, n. [1. kognishun; 2. kɔgniʃən]. Lat. *cognitiōn-(em)*, 'a becoming acquainted with, acquiring of knowledge; knowledge; a conception, notion, idea', fr. *cognitum*, P.P. of *cognoscere*, 'to understand, learn' &c., fr. **co-** & *gnoscere*, 'to know'. See **cognoscible. a** Fact of knowing; knowledge; **b** mental process whereby consciousness is acquired of what is perceived by the senses, or conceived by the mind.

cognitive, adj. [1. kógnitiv; 2. kɔ́gnitiv]. Lat. *cognit-*, see prec., & **-ive.** Connected with, belonging to, cognition.

cognizable, adj. [1. kógnizabl, kognízabl; 2. kɔ́gnizəbl, kɔgnáizəbl]. (Latter pronunciation due to influence of **cognize.**) See this word & **-able.** Capable of being known, cognoscible.

cognizance, n. [1. kógnizans; 2. kɔ́gnizəns]. The Lat. word is *cognoscentia*, wh. has been remodelled on anal. of **cognize** & **-ance. 1.** Fact of being aware, conscious recognition; range or sphere of knowledge: *within one's cognizance*; *to have cognizance of.* Phr. *to take cognizance of*, to notice, to become consciously aware of, esp. officially. **2.** (her.) Distinctive badge, coat of arms &c.

cognizant, adj. [1. kógnizant; 2. kɔ́gnizənt]. Next word & **-ant.** Aware of, informed of, in the condition of having perceived and apprehended (followed by *of*).

cognize, vb. trans. [1. kogníz; 2. kɔgnáiz]. The base is fr. Lat. *cognoscere.* See **cognoscible**, w. Gk. suff. **-ize.** Take, have, cognizance of, know, recognize.

cognomen, n. [1. kognṓmen; 2. kɔgnóumen]. Lat. *cognōmen*, 'a Roman family name; a name', fr. **co-** & *nōmen*, 'name'. See **nominal.** The *-g-* is due to confusion of the word for name w. an entirely different word *gnōmen, fr. Gk. *gnôma*, 'mark, token', fr. base *gnō-, 'to know', q.v. under **gnostic, cognoscible, know.** Family name, surname; appellation.

cognoscente, n., pl. **-enti** [1. kònyōshénte, -ē; 2. kɔ̀njouʃénte, -ī]. Ital. (lit.) One who knows; a connoisseur of art &c.

cognoscible, adj. [1. kognósibl; 2. kɔgnɔ́sibl]. Lat. *cognoscibilis*, 'knowable', fr. *cognoscere*, 'investigate, understand, learn, know', & *-ibilis*, q.v. under **-ible.** The vb. is fr. **co-** & *noscere*, earlier *gnoscere, 'become acquainted with, learn, know'; the base is *-gnō-* &c., & fr. the various forms of it come Lat. *i-gnōrāre*, 'be ignorant' (see **ignore**); Gk. *gnṓskō*, 'know', see **gnostic**; Goth. *kunnan*, Engl. *cunnan*, 'to be able' (see **can, ken**); O.E. *cnāwan*, 'know' (see **know**). Able to be known, cognizable.

cognovit, n. [1. kògnṓvit; 2. kɔ̀gnóuvit]. Lat., 'he has acknowledged', 3rd pers. sing. of perf. of *cognoscere.* See prec. (law) Document signed by defendant in a civil action brought against him, in which to save time and expense of defending, he admits liability, thus authorizing judgement being entered against him.

cogwheel, n. [1. kógwēl; 2. kɔ́gwīəl]. **cog (I.)** & **wheel.** Wheel furnished with cogs.

cohabit, vb. intrans. [1. kōhábit; 2. kouhǽbit]. Lat. *cohabitāre*, 'dwell in, have possession of, a place', fr. **co-** & *habitāre*, 'to have possession of, inhabit'. See **habit.** To live with, to live together; generally specif., to live together as man and wife (followed by *with*, or absolutely).

cohabitation, n. [1. kòhabitā́shun; 2. kòuhæbitéiʃən]. Prec. & **-ation.** Act or fact of cohabiting.

co-heir, n. [1. kṓ ā́r; 2. kóu ɛ́ə]; fem. **co-heiress** [1. kṓ ā́res; 2. kóu ɛ́əris]. **co-** & **heir, -ess.** Joint heir or heiress; one who is heir along with another.

cohere, vb. intrans. [1. kōhḗr; 2. kouhíə]. Lat. *co-haerēre*, 'to stick, cling together', fr. **co-** & *haerēre*, 'to stick, cling, be close'. The latter vb. may be fr. a base *ghēis- &c., & the suggestion has been made that Goth. *us-gaisjan*, 'to terrify', & *us-geisnan*, 'to become terrified', as though orig. 'to become stiff with horror', are also fr. this base. If so, then Engl. **ghost, ghastly**, are cognates. The difference of meaning, however, makes the proposed etymol. doubtful; cp. **adhere. 1.** To remain united, stick together as parts of a single mass. **2.** (fig., of non-material things) To be united by common principle; remain a unity; be logically consistent.

coherence, -cy, n. [1. kōhḗrens(i); 2. kouhíərəns(i)]. Prec. & **-ence, -cy.** A sticking, cleaving, together (gen. in fig. sense); **a** logical consistency; **b** clearness of utterance; **c** clearness, intelligibility, in expression of ideas. Contrast this with *cohesion.*

coherent, adj. [1. kōhḗrent; 2. kouhíərənt]. Lat. *cohaerent-(em)*, Pres. Part. of *cohaerēre*, 'stick together'. See **cohere. 1.** Having the property of sticking together, remaining in union (of particles which compose solid or fluid bodies). **2.** (fig.) **a** (of mental processes) Logically consistent, consequent, clear: *coherent thought, reasoning* &c.; **b** (of verbal utterance of thought) properly articulated, clearly uttered; hence, **c** intelligible.

coherently, adv. Prec. & **-ly.** In a coherent manner; consistently; intelligibly.

coherer, n. [1. kōhḗrer; 2. kouhíərə]. **cohere** & **-er.** Device for detecting radiated ether waves in wireless.

co-heritage, n. [1. kòhéritij; 2. kòuhéritidž]. **co-** & **heritage.** Heritage to which one person is heir together with another.

co-heritor, n. [1. kòhériter; 2. kòuhéritə, -ɔ̄]. **co-** & **heritor.** Co-heir.

cohesion, n. [1. kōhḗzhun; 2. kouhížən]. Fr., fr. Lat. *co-haesiōn-(em)*, formed fr. type in *cohaesum*, P.P. of *co-haerēre*, & **-ion.** See **cohere.** Act or condition of cohering, esp. **a** in physical sense, sticking together, state of union (of the particles of a mass); also **b** (fig.) spiritual unity, harmony, agreement: *the Conservative Party lacked cohesion.*

cohesive, adj. [1. kōhḗsiv; 2. kouhísiv], fr. Lat. base *co-haes-*, as in prec., & **-ive.** Tending to, promoting, cohesion; inclined to cohere (in lit. and fig. senses).

cohesiveness, n. Prec. & **-ness.** The property, or condition, of cohering, of being cohesive.

cohort, n. [1. kṓhort; 2. kóuhɔ̄t]. Lat. *co-hort-(em)*, acc. of *cohor-s*, 'enclosed place, yard', hence, 'a body of soldiers guarding a fortified enclosure'; specific name in ancient Rome for a division of soldiers composing tenth part of a legion; fr. **co-** & the base in Lat. *hortus*, 'enclosed place for plants, a garden' (see **horticulture**); cp. Gk. *khórtos*, 'courtyard, feeding-place', & *khortázō*, 'fatten cattle at the stall'; (both words have basal idea of 'enclosing'.) The Aryan base is *g̑herd-, *g̑hord- &c., 'to enclose. See further **court, garden, garth, gird, yard (II.). a** Roman sense as above; **b** a body of troops, army (often in pl.).

coif, n. [1. koif; 2. kɔif]. M.E., fr. O. Fr. *coif(e)*, fr. Low Lat. *cofia, cofea*, 'cup'; a borrowing fr. O.H.G. *chuppha*, 'cap worn under a helmet', M.H.G. *kuffe, kupfe*, wh. is a dimin. of the O.H.G. *kopf*, 'cup', also 'head'; The word *cuppe*, 'cup', occurs in O.E., & it, together w. the H.G. word, is itself an early borrowing fr. Lat. *cūpa*, 'drinking vessel'. See **cup.** Head-dress consisting of a close-fitting cap, or hood. The cap formerly worn under a helmet was called a coif, likewise a white cap worn in England by serjeants-at-law, which later became a mere black patch of cloth fastened to the top of the wig.

coiffeur, n. [1. kwahfḗr; 2. kwāfā́]. Fr. Hair-dresser.

coiffure, n. [1. kwáhfūr; 2. kwā́fjuə]. Fr., 'head-dress, hairdressing'. Mode of dressing the hair in women.

coign, quoin, n. [1. koin; 2. kɔin], fr. O. Fr. *coign*, Mod. Fr. *coin*, 'corner', fr. Lat. *cuneus*, 'wedge'. The suggested equation of this word w. O. Ir. *cenn*, W. *penn*, 'head, point' &c., is rejected by Walde. See **cuneate.** (archit.) **a** The external angle of wall or other building; **b** a dressed ashlar of which coigns are built. See **quoin.** Apart from above special use, the word occurs chiefly in *coign of vantage*, a favourable position for seeing what is going on.

coil (I.), vb. trans. & intrans. [1. koil; 2. kɔil]. O. Fr. *coillir*, 'collect', Mod. Fr. *cueillir*, 'gather, pluck', fr. Lat. *colligere*, 'gather, pick up, draw together'. See **collect (II.). 1.** trans. To wind or gather up in cylindrical or spiral folds, as: *to coil a rope.* **2.** intrans. To wind round, turn in upon itself as though coiled: *a rope coils round a mast, a serpent round a tree* &c.

coil (II.), n., fr. prec. **1. a** A series of circular folds, as of a rope when coiled; **b** any one of such folds. **2.** (elect.) Device consisting of a number of turns of insulated wire carrying a current and producing various electric and magnetic phenomena, as in electric bells, dynamo &c.; see **inductance.**

coil (III.), n. Origin unknown. (archaic) Tumult, confusion, bustle: '*I am not worth this coil that's made of me*' (Shakespeare); '*this mortal coil*' (Shakespeare), the turmoil of earthly life.

coin (I.), n. [1. koin; 2. kɔin]. Doublet of **coign**, fr. Lat. *cuneus*, 'wedge'; the Fr. word meant also 'stamp'. **a** Piece of metal (rarely another substance) officially stamped and used as money; **b** (colloq.) money collectively: *to have plenty of coin.* Phrs. *to pay a man back in his own coin*, treat him as he has treated oneself; *false coin*, bad money, also (fig.) an imitation, fraud.

coin (II.), vb. trans., fr. prec. O. Fr. *coignier*, Mod. Fr. *cogner*, 'strike'. **a** To stamp, make coins, to mint; **b** to invent, give currency to, new word or expression. Phr. *to be coining money*, make large profits, grow rich.

coinage, n. [1. kóinij; 2. kɔ́inidž]. **coin (I.)** & **-age. a** Act of minting or stamping money; **b** that which is minted, coins collectively, current in a given country and age; **c** act of inventing new word or expression; word &c. thus made.

coincide, vb. intrans. [1. kòinsíd; 2. kòuinsáid], fr. Lat. **co-** & *incidere*, 'to fall upon, light upon', (also fig.) 'to fall out, befall, happen' (see **incident**), fr. **in-** & *cadere*, 'to fall'; see **cadence. 1.** (of space) To occupy the same amount, to correspond in area, position, or outline: *a tracing if accurate necessarily coincides with the drawing from which it is made*; *the back-gardens of all houses in the street coincide with each other in size.* **2.** (of time) To happen at the same period; happen during, take up, the same period of time: *the death of Chaucer may be said to coincide with the end of the Middle English period of the language*; *payment of an annuity coincides with the lifetime of the annuitant.* **3.** (fig., of mental and moral acts and states) To agree, be in harmony with, concur, show exact correspondence: *our tastes and habits exactly coincide.* **4.** (of weight, amount, number &c.) To be equal or equivalent to, be adequate: *his income hardly coincided with his expenditure*; *our resources coincide with our requirements.*

coincidence, n. [1. kōínsidens; 2. kouínsidəns]. Fr., as fr. Lat. *coincident-* & *-ia.* See **coincident. 1.** Fact, or condition, of coinciding, in any sense: *coincidence of space, time, amount, wishes* &c. **2.** Noteworthy event, circumstance, or series of such, which occurs in conjunction, or synchronously, with others, and is of such a character as to suggest a connexion of cause and effect, although apparently no connexion of the kind exists.

coincident, adj. [1. kōinsident; 2. kouínsidənt]. **co-** & Lat. *incident-(em)*, Pres. Part. of *incidere*, 'happen, fall out'. See **coincide**. Coinciding; happening at same time; agreeing with: *his mother's death was coincident with his birth*; *what has occurred is coincident with my hopes*.

coincidental, adj. [1. kòinsidéntl; 2. kòuinsidéntl]. Prec. & **-al**. Exhibiting coincidence; coincident.

coincidentally, adv. Prec. & **-ly**. As, by way of, (a) coincidence.

coiner, n. [1. kóiner; 2. kóinə]. **coin (II.)** & **-er**. One who coins; specif., a maker of false money.

co-instantaneous, adj. [1. kṓ instantáneus; 2. kóu instəntéinjəs]. **co-** & **instantaneous**. Happening at precisely the same moment.

coir, n. [1. koir; 2. kóiə]. Malayalam *kayar*, 'cord'. Fibre made from the husk of the coco-nut, used for door-mats, cables &c.

coition, n. [1. kōíshun; 2. kouíʃən]. Lat. *coitiōn-(em)*, 'coming together', fr. **co-** & **it-io*, fr. vb. *īre*, 'to go'. See **iterate**, **itinerant**. Sexual intercourse.

coitus, n. [1. kṓitus; 2. kóuitəs]. Lat. See prec. Coition.

coke, n. & vb. trans. [1. kōk; 2. kouk]. Etymol. doubtful; used in sense of 'cinder' in 17th cent. **1.** n. Coal from which a large part of the gas has been extracted by heating in an oven or retort, leaving a rough, light, brittle substance, used for heating. **2.** vb. To turn (coal) into coke.

coke-oven, n. Oven in which coal is heated to produce coke.

coker-nut, n. [1. kṓker nut; 2. kóukə nat]. Vulgarism for **coco-nut**, in sense of a sweet-meat flavoured with this.

col, n. [1. kol; 2. kɔl]. Fr., 'the neck, a pass', fr. Lat. *collum*, 'neck', wh. is for **colsom*, w. wh. cp. O.E. *heals*, 'neck', O.H.G. & Mod. Germ. *hals*. See **collar**. Depression in a mountain range or chain, affording a pass from one valley to another.

col-, pref. Form of **com-** occurring before *l-*.

cola, kola, n. [1. kóla; 2. kóulə]. W. Afr. Tree bearing a seed (*cola-nut*), used as tonic.

colander, n. See **cullender**.

colcannon, calecannon, n. [1. kol-, kāl-kánun; 2. kɔl-, keilkǽnən]. First element **cole** or **cale**, second element unknown. Favourite dish in Ireland, made of potatoes, cabbage, and onions boiled together.

colchicum, n. [1. kólchikum; 2. kɔ́ltʃikəm]. Lat., fr. Gk. *kolkhikón*, neut. adj., fr. Place-Name *Colchis*. **a** Plant known as autumn crocus, or meadow saffron; **b** narcotic drug obtained from corm, or seeds, of this; used for rheumatism and gout.

colcothar, n. [1. kólkothar; 2. kɔ́lkɔþā]. Arab. *qolqotār*. Red oxide of iron, used in polishing glass and cleaning metals.

cold (I.), adj. [1. kōld; 2. kould]. O.E. (Anglian) *cāld*, O.H.G. *kalt*, Goth. *kalds*, O.N. *kaldr*, Lat. *gelidus*, 'very cold, icy', connected w. Lat. *gelāre*, 'cause to freeze' (see **gelid**), further connected w. Lat. *glaciēs*, 'ice' (see **glacial**). The Aryan base is **gel-*, **gl-* &c., 'to freeze'. Cp. further O. Slav. *žledica*, 'frozen rain'. O. Slav. *golotĭ*, 'ice', & Gk. *khálaza*, 'hail', must be fr. an Aryan **ghel-* &c. See further **cool, chill**. **1. a** Lacking heat or warmth, of low temperature, as tested by human touch or sensations: *to be cold*; *to feel cold*; *a cold day, room, bed* &c.; *cold hands, feet, nose* &c. Phrs. *as cold as ice, as a stone*, very cold; *as cold as charity* (ironical); *cold steel*, sword, bayonet &c.; (*to have*) *cold feet*, (colloq.) be frightened; *to make one's blood run cold*, (fig.) horrify, terrify; *in cold blood*, without excitement, while unstirred by passion; *a cold scent* (hunting), faint; **b** naturally lacking heat, or having lost it: *a glass of cold water*; *a cold bath*; *cold meat*. Phrs. *to throw cold water on*, to discourage; *hardly cold in one's grave*, not long dead. **2. a** (of temperament, emotions, and expression of these) Unexcitable, calm, frigid, unstirred: *cold in manner*; *a cold heart*; **b** lacking in cordiality, unfriendly: *a cold greeting, reception*; **c** (of the intellect) calm, unruffled, unclouded by passion: *cold reason*; *to take a cold survey of the situation*. **3.** Suggestive of cold, e.g. (of colours) faint, lacking in brilliance and glow.

cold (II.), n., fr. prec. **1. a** (popularly) A relative term implying a condition of the atmosphere or of a body which produces to the human touch a sensation of absence of heat; **b** (absolutely) a low temperature, as due to frost, presence of ice or snow: *the cold has got into the ground*; *to feel the cold*. **2.** *A cold*, popular name for catarrh; inflammation of the mucous membrane of the nose and throat; *to catch, take, cold, have a cold*; *a cold in the head, nose* &c.

cold-blooded, adj. [1. kṓld blúded; 2. kóuld bládid]. **1. a** Specif. (of fishes, reptiles &c.), having cold blood; **b** (of human beings) sensitive to cold, chilly, esp. from bad circulation. **2.** (fig., of persons and actions) **a** Lacking passion, enthusiasm, sensibility; hence, **b** lacking pity, cruel, merciless: *cold-blooded murder*.

cold-bloodedly, adv. Prec. & **-ly**. In a cold-blooded manner.

cold-bloodedness, n. See prec. & **-ness**. State, quality, of being cold-blooded.

cold-chisel, n. One with strong, hard edge, used for cutting unheated metal.

cold cream, n. Soothing ointment made of wax or spermaceti, rose water, oil of almonds &c.

cold-drawn, adj. Drawn without application of heat; of steel tubing, oil &c.

cold frame, n. Glass-covered frame not heated by a hotbed or otherwise, in which young plants are put to harden off.

cold-hammer, vb. trans. To hammer metal without heating it.

cold-hearted, adj. (fig.) Wanting feeling and affection.

cold-heartedly, adv. Prec. & **-ly**. In a cold-hearted manner.

cold-heartedness, n. See prec. & **-ness**. Condition of being cold-hearted.

coldish, adj. [1. kṓldish; 2. kóuldiʃ]. **cold (I.)** & **-ish**. **a** Rather cold; **b** fairly cold, very cold.

coldly, adv. [1. kṓldli; 2. kóuldli]. **cold (I.)** & **-ly**. In a cold manner (lit. and fig.): *the wind blows coldly*; *to treat, receive, a person coldly*; *consider coldly*, i.e. without excitement, calmly.

coldness, n. [1. kṓldnes; 2. kóuldnis]. **cold (I.)** & **-ness**. The property of being cold in any sense: *the coldness of the weather, water* &c., *of one's reception*; *coldness of heart*.

cold-pig, n. (colloq.) Drenching a sleeping or sleepy person with cold water to rouse him.

cold-short, adj. Prob. fr. Swed. *kallskör*, 'cold brittle'; the neut. is *-skört*, wh. has been confused w. *short*, both in form & meaning. Cp. *shortbread, short pastry* &c. (of iron) Brittle in its cold state.

cold-shoulder, n. & vb. trans. For origin see **shoulder (I.)**. **1.** n. Rebuff, deliberate indifference, neglect, or snub: *to give a person the cold-shoulder*. **2.** vb. To rebuff, neglect, snub, avoid deliberately: *to cold-shoulder a person*.

cold-storage, n. **a** The storage, keeping, preservation of meat, fish, fruit &c. in refrigerating chambers; **b** building with refrigerating apparatus for this.

cole, n. [1. kōl; 2. koul]. O.E. *cāl*, *cāwl*, M.E. *cōl*, fr. Lat. *caulis*, *cōlis*, 'stem of a plant, esp. of cabbage'. The word is connected w. *cavus*, 'hollow'. See **cauliflower** & **cauline**, & cp. **kale (kail)**. General name for all kinds of *Brassica* or cabbage; usually in compounds as *cole-wort*, cabbage cut before head is firm. Cp. *sea-kale*.

colectomy, n. [1. koléktumi; 2. kɔléktəmi], fr. **colon** & Gk. *ektomia*, 'cutting out'. See **ex-** & **-tomy**. (surg.) Removal, excision, of a part of the colon.

Coleoptera, n. pl. [1. kòleóptera; 2. kɔ̀liɔ́ptərə], fr. Gk. *koleós*, 'sheath', & *pterón*, 'wing'. Lat. *culleus*, 'leather bag', is prob. borrowed fr. Gk., likewise Lith. *kulìs*, 'bag'. The second element is fr. base **pet-*, 'to go, fly'. See **ptero-** & **feather**. Lit. 'sheath-winged'. Order of insects commonly known as beetles; the main characteristic, as implied by the scientific name, is that the fore-wings form sheaths for the hind-wings when folded.

coleopterous, adj. [1. kòleópterus; 2. kɔ̀liɔ́ptərəs]. Prec. & **-ous**. Of, belonging to, the Coleoptera.

colibri, n. [1. kólēbrē; 2. kɔ́librī]. Fr. & Span., fr. native W. Indian (Caribbean) word. A humming-bird.

colic, n. [1. kólik; 2. kɔ́lik], fr. Fr. *colique*, fr. Lat. *colicus*, fr. Gk. *kólikos*, adj., fr. *kólon*, 'large intestine'. See **colon**. Severe griping pain in the abdomen, esp. of a paroxysmal character, which may arise from many different causes.

colicky, adj. [1. kóliki; 2. kɔ́liki]. Prec. & **-y**. **a** Of the nature of, resembling, colic; **b** liable to cause colic.

colitis, n. [1. kolítis; 2. kəláitis]. Gk. *kólon*, 'large intestine'. See **colon** & **-itis**. (med.) Inflammation of membrane of the large intestine.

collaborate, vb. intrans. [1. koláberàt; 2. kəlǽbərèit]. Lat. *collabōrāt-(um)*, P.P. type of *collabōrāre*, 'to work with'. See **col-** & **labour**. (absol., or followed by *with* before name of person) To work together with another to a common end; to share the labour of given tasks (gen. of artistic and intellectual work).

collaboration, n. [1. kolàboráshun; 2. kəlǽbəréiʃən]. Prec. & **-ion**. The act or process of collaborating: *to work in collaboration with* (person).

collaborator, n. [1. koláborātur; 2. kəlǽbəreitə]. **collaborate** & **-or**. One who collaborates with another in his work.

collagen, n. [1. kólajen; 2. kɔ́lədžen], fr. Gk. *kólla*, 'glue', & **-gen**. See **genesis**. The first element is cogn. w. M.L.G. *helen*, 'to stick'; O. Slav. *klěj*, 'glue'. (physiol.) Gelatinous substance which forms one of the chief constituents in connective tissues of the animal body.

collapse (I.), n. [1. koláps; 2. kəlǽps], fr. Lat. *collapsum*, P.P. of *collābi*, 'to fall in ruins, sink down in a swoon, or in death', fr. **col-** & *lābi*, 'to fall'. See **lapse**. (The fundamental meaning is *falling* or *breaking down*. All the meanings, chiefly fig., are related to this idea.) **1.** (of material things) The fact or process of falling down, falling in, falling away, breaking down, as result of strain or pressure from above, or to sides: *collapse of a tent, hammock, chair, seat, roof, tower* &c. **2.** (fig.) A breaking down, crumbling away: *collapse of plans, schemes, negotiations, hopes* &c. **3.** (of persons) **a** A sudden decline or breakdown, esp. in health; sudden or complete mental or physical breakdown through ill-health, loss of nervous or muscular power &c.; prostration; specif., sudden failure of heart or other vital organs, esp. just before death; **b** (fig.) a sudden loss of moral strength or courage, a giving way, yielding to misfortune, difficulties &c. **4.** (fig.) A sudden loss of stability, success, security &c.: *collapse of a ministry, bank, money-market* &c.

collapse (II.), vb. intrans. fr. prec. **1.** (of material things) To fall down, fall in, tumble to pieces, crumble away, as e.g. *a roof, building, scaffolding* &c. **2.** (fig., of non-material things) To break down suddenly, come to nothing, fail (of plans, hopes &c.). **3.** (of persons) **a** To fall down, esp. as result of a blow, strain; **b** to break down suddenly in health and physical strength; specif., to experience sudden failure of the heart or other vital organs, as shortly before death; **c** to break down in moral stamina, be unable to offer further resistance to danger and difficulties. **4.** (fig.) To decline suddenly from success or prosperity; to fail, come to grief, e.g. of schemes, enterprises, commercial undertakings &c.

collapsible, adj. [1. kolápsibl; 2. kəlǽpsibl]. Prec. & **-ible**. Capable of collapsing or being folded up, as for packing, carrying &c.: *collapsible boat, chair* &c.

collar (I.), n. [1. kólar; 2. kɔ́lə]. In M.E., fr. A.-Fr. *coler*, O. Fr. *colier*, fr. Lat. *collāre*, 'band for the neck', fr. *collum*, 'neck'. See **col.** The base is **kʷel-*, **kʷol-*, 'to turn, turn round', see **colony**. **1.** General meaning, something encircling the neck; specif. **a** article of male attire, usually of linen, worn round the neck, fastened to, or part of, the shirt; **b** that part of a garment which surrounds the neck, e.g. of coat, dress; neck-band of shirt; **c** neck-chain forming part of insignia of order of knighthood: *collar of SS.*, chain of interlaced letter S, worn by the Lord Chief Justice of England; **d** ornamental circlet worn by women, of gold, often set with jewels; necklet: *collar of pearls*; **e** band of leather or metal placed round neck of dog or other animal for purposes of restraint or identification; Phr. *to slip the collar*, get it off; **f** part of harness worn round neck by horse or other draught animal, to which the traces are fastened, and which takes strain of the weight which is drawn; Phrs. *against the collar*, (lit. and fig.) implying continuous strain; *collar-work* (of horse), pulling weight uphill, (fig.) continuous strain. **2.** Encircling band connecting two parts (rods) of a machine; projecting outer part of drain-pipe covering end of the next length &c. **3.** (zool.) Any marking or stripe round neck of an animal, bird, reptile &c. resembling a collar. **4.** (bot.) Part of plant immediately above the root, usually just above the ground. **5.** (wrestling and Rugby football) The act of laying hold of an opponent; a tackle, or grip.

collar (II.), vb. trans. fr. prec. **1.** To put a collar on (rare). **2. a** To seize by the collar, to capture: *a policeman collars a thief*; specif. (Rugby football), to lay hold of an opponent, who has the ball, and stop his progress; **b** (colloq.) to seize hold of, get control of, something; to take or appropriate for oneself. **3.** To roll and tie up (meat &c.) before cooking; esp. *collared head, brawn* &c.

collar-beam, n. Beam bearing two rafters.

collar-bone, n. The clavicle.

collaret(te), n. [1. kolarét; 2. kɔlərét]. Fr. *collerette*, dimin. of **collar**. Piece of lace or fur worn round the neck by women.

collate, vb. trans. [1. kolā́t; 2. kəléit], fr. Lat. *collātum*, used as P.P. of *conferre*, 'to bring together', fr. **col-** & *lātum*, wh. stands for **tlātum*, fr. base **tel-*, **tol-* &c., q.v. under **tolerate, thole.** To bring together for the purpose of comparison. **1.** To examine a text or MS. critically and compare it with others. **2.** To examine, and place in order, the sheets of a book; verify order of sheets by the signatures. **3.** To present and institute (a clergyman) to a benefice.

collateral (I.), adj. [1. koláteral; 2. kəlǽtərəl]. See **col-** & **lateral**. **1.** Accompanying, existing alongside of, an event, or fact, but secondary, subordinate, to it; *collateral circumstance, evidence* &c.; *collateral security*, security for a loan &c. in addition to the principal security. **2.** (of descent) Derived from common ancestor, but through different sons or daughters; descended from and through parallel lines: *collateral descent, relationship* &c.

collateral (II.), n. fr. prec. **a** Person standing in collateral relationship to another; **b** persons descended from common ancestor through different lines; **c** collateral security.

collaterally, adv. [1. koláterali; 2. kəlǽtərəli]. **collateral** (I.) & **-ly**. In a collateral manner; **a** of occurrences: *to happen collaterally*; **b** of relationship: *to be descended collaterally from* (person).

collation, n. [1. kolā́shun; 2. kəléiʃən], fr. Lat. *collātiōn-(em)*. See **collate** & **-ion**. **1. a** Act or process of collating a text or book; **b** act of collating to a benefice. **2.** (in sense of something brought together, prepared) A repast, esp. a light and delicate one.

collator, n. [1. kolā́ter, -ōr; 2. kəléitə, -ɔ̄]. **collate** & **-or.** One who collates in any sense.

colleague, n. [1. kólēg; 2. kɔ́līg], fr. Fr. *collègue*, fr. Lat. *collēga*, 'one chosen at same time as another; associate', fr. **col-** & *leg-*, 'pick out, select' &c. See **lecture**, further **college, collect** (II.). **a** One associated with another, or others, in any duty or occupation, esp. of an official character; person who with others holds an office under the same authority; thus a minister of the Crown is the colleague of the other ministers, a professor at a university is the colleague of other professors at the same university and so on, and one will speak of another as *my colleague so-and-so*; **b** applied also, perhaps in imitation of foreign practice, to persons who are members of the same profession though otherwise in no way connected, e.g. a London surgeon might speak of Edinburgh surgeons as *colleagues*. Less commonly used of persons associated in purely business pursuits.

collect (I.), n. [1. kólekt; 2. kɔ́lekt], fr. Fr. *collecte*, fr. Lat. *collectum*, P.P. of *colligere*, 'gather, assemble, put together'; Engl. use perh. fr. idea that essential things are gathered up & summarized. See **collect** (II.). Short prayer in Church of England Prayer Book, one of those specially appointed to be read on particular days, during certain seasons, or on specified occasions: *the collect for the day, for peace, for the king* &c.

collect (II.), vb. trans. & intrans. [1. kulékt; 2. kəlékt], fr. Lat. *colligere, collectum*, fr. **col-** & *legere*, 'to choose'. See **lecture**. **A.** trans. To assemble or bring together. **1.** To gather (persons) together into a body or into one place. **2. a** To pick up, gather (scattered things), and put (them) together into one place: *to collect the waste-paper lying about*; *to go out and collect the eggs*; **b** to gather, bring, (things) together as specimens: *to collect books, stamps, birds' eggs* &c.; **c** to gather together, amass (facts &c.): *to collect evidence, information, material for a dictionary* &c. **3.** To obtain (money) from a number of scattered sources, by solicitation: *collect taxes, rent, contributions for a hospital* &c. **4.** To arrange one's thoughts and ideas; recover by deliberate effort from shock of surprise &c.: *collect one's thoughts, energies, courage* &c.; *to collect oneself*. **5.** To gather, infer, conclude something, from what has been said. **B.** intrans. **1.** (of living things) To come, gather, flock, together: *a crowd of idlers, flock of starlings &c. has collected*. **2.** (of inanimate things) To accumulate, become heaped up: *dust and rubbish soon collect*; *water collects in hollows*.

collectanea, n. [1. kòlektáhnea, -ā́nea; 2. kɔ̀lektánīə, -éiniə]. Neut. pl. of Lat. *collectāneus*, adj., 'gathered, collected, together'. **collect** (II.) & *-āneus*, Engl. **-an**. Collection of passages from works of an author, or of several authors; anthology, miscellany.

collected, adj. [1. kulékted; 2. kəléktid], fr. P.P. of **collect** (II.), **A, 4.** Cool, self-possessed, having complete control of oneself, not distracted: esp. *calm and collected*.

collectedly, adv. Prec. & **-ly**. In a calm, self-possessed manner.

collectedness, n. See prec. & **-ness**. State of being collected.

collection, n. [1. kulékshun; 2. kəlékʃən]. Lat. *collectiōn-(em)*, 'a gathering together', fr. *collect-*, as in P.P. of *colligere*, & -ion. See **collect** (II.). **1.** The act of gathering together; an assemblage or crowd of people. **2.** Money given voluntarily and collected for charity; specif., money collected at a church service or at a meeting &c.: *a collection will be made after the service*. **3.** Process or fact of accumulation of a material things: water, dust, papers &c.; **b** act of collecting facts, evidence &c. **4.** Group of things collected and preserved on account of their beauty, rarity, or value: *a collection of books, art treasures, stamps, birds' eggs* &c. **5.** (in pl.) Terminal examination of undergraduates held at Oxford colleges.

collective, adj. [1. kuléktiv; 2. kəléktiv]. **collect** (II.) & **-ive**. **1.** (of a number of individuals) Viewed as a whole, taken all together, considered as a unity: *the collective body of the university*. **2.** Belonging to, emanating from, characteristic of, representing, a whole body, group, society of persons: *collective property*; *the collective wishes of the community*; *collective opinion*. **3.** (gram.) *Collective noun*, one whose form is singular, but which expresses a number of individuals: *to catch fish*; *feed cattle*; *shoot snipe*; *herd of swine* &c.

collectively, adv. Prec. & **-ly**. In a collective manner, as a whole, as a single body: *to harangue the crowd collectively*.

collectivism, n. [1. kuléktivizm; 2. kəléktivizəm]. **collective** & **-ism**. Political or social theory, identical with socialism, but which does not include revolution, based on collective ownership of means of production and exchange under the State.

collectivist, n. [1. kuléktivist; 2. kəléktivist]. **collective** & **-ist**. Adherent of collectivism.

collector, n. [1. kuléktur; 2. kəléktə], fr. **collect** (II.) & **-or**. **1.** One who collects (in many specific senses); **a** one who makes a collection of objects of beauty, rarity, value &c., e.g. pictures, curiosities, gems &c.; **b** one whose official duty it is to collect tickets, taxes, rates &c.: *ticket-collector* (on railway &c.); *rent-, tax-collector* &c. **2.** Device for collecting electricity in an electric machine; for collecting waves sent by wireless. **3.** (Indian Civil Service) Head administrative official in a district of an Indian Province, called also Deputy-Commissioner.

collectorship, n. [1. kulékturship; 2. kəléktəʃip]. Prec. & **-ship**. Office of collector in Indian Civil Service.

colleen, n. [1. kólēn; 2. kɔ́līn]. Ir. *cailín*. A girl; also *colleen bawn* [1. bawn; 2. bɔ̄n], 'pretty girl', Ir. *bān*, 'white'.

college, n. [1. kólij; 2. kɔ́lidž], fr. Fr. *collège*, fr. Lat. *collēgium*, 'union or association of persons in any office or for any purpose; body of persons living by common rules, guild, brotherhood', fr. *colligere*, 'to gather together'. See **collect** (II.). **1.** See meaning of Latin *collegium* above, which has the basal sense of English word; the old sense is retained in *College of Cardinals*, or *Sacred College*, the papal council and electors; *College of Surgeons, of Heralds* &c. **2.** More specif. **a** a self-governing educational institution of varying kinds, with a status ranging from that almost of a university (*University College*) to a school for boys or girls (*Winchester College* &c.); **b** a *college* at Oxford and Cambridge is an educational institution for members of these universities, which combines a position of great independence in its own affairs with that of being an integral part of the university. **3.** The building, or group of buildings, in which a college in any of above senses is housed.

colleger, n. [1. kólijer; 2. kɔ́lidžə]. Prec. & **-er**. One who holds a scholarship at Eton, as distinct from an oppidan.

collegian, n. [1. kolḗjian; 2. kəlídžiən]. **college** & **-ian**. Member of a college (chiefly used by persons who are not members of a college).

collegiate, adj. [1. kolḗjiat; 2. kəlídži-it], fr. Lat. *collēgiātus*. See **college**. Connected with, having character and status of, a college: *collegiate life*; *collegiate institution*.

collegiate church, n. One which, though not a cathedral, has a College, or Chapter of Canons, and a Dean or (in Scotland sometimes) a Provost.

collet, n. [1. kólet; 2. kɔ́lit]. Fr., 'little collar', dimin. of **col**, 'neck', fr. Lat. *collum*, 'neck'. Small metal band; specif., the part of a ring which holds the stone.

collide, vb. intrans. [1. kolíd; 2. kəláid], fr. Lat. *collīdere*, 'dash together', fr. **col-** & *laedere*, 'strike, hurt'. See **lesion**. **a** (of solid, rapidly moving objects) To come into violent contact with, run into, dash against (followed by *with*, or absol.); **b** (of moral impact) to clash, be in conflict, be mutually antagonistic (of wills, aims, purposes.

collie, n. [1. kóli; 2. kɔ́li]. Perh. fr. Gael. *cuilean*, 'a whelp'. Scotch sheep-dog, with long hair, a pointed nose, and a bushy tail.

collier, n. [1. kólier; 2. kɔ́liə]. M.E. *colyer*. See **coal** & **-ier**. **1.** Man who digs coal out of the pit; coal-miner. **2. a** Ship employed in carrying coal; **b** sailor on such a ship.

colliery, n. [1. kólieri; 2. kɔ́liəri]. Prec. & **-ry**. Place where coal is dug and brought to the surface; a coal-mine; applied also to all the workings in one district under single management, together with buildings and apparatus.

colligate, vb. trans. [1. kóligāt; 2. kɔ́ligeit], fr. Lat. *colligāt-(um)*, P.P. type of *colligāre*, 'to bind together', fr. **col-** & *ligāre*, 'to bind'. See **ligature**. To bind together, connect; esp. to connect isolated facts and bring them under a general principle.

colligation, n. [1. kòligā́shun; 2. kɔ̀ligéiʃən]. See prec. & **-ion**. Act of binding together; esp. process of colligating facts.

collimate, vb. trans. [1. kólimāt; 2. kɔ́limeit], fr. Lat. *collīmāt-(um)*, P.P. type of *collīmāre* for *collīneāre*, 'to bring into line with', fr. **col-** & *līnea*, 'a line'. See **line (I.)**. To make parallel to a given line; specif., to adjust the line of sight in a telescope &c.

collimation, n. [1. kòlimā́shun; 2. kɔ̀liméiʃən]. Prec. & **-ion**. Adjustment of the line of sight.

collimator, n. [1. kólimāter; 2. kɔ́limeitə]. **collimate** & **-or**. A small telescope attached to larger one for securing precision of collimation of latter.

collinear, adj. [1. kolínear; 2. kəlíniə]. See **col-** & **linear**. In the same straight line.

collision, n. [1. kolízhun; 2. kəlížən]. Lat. *collīsiōn-(em)*, *collīs-(um)*, P.P. of *collīdere*, & **-ion**. See **collide**. **1. a** Act or process of colliding, violent impact of two bodies; **b** specif., such an impact between moving trains, ships, carriages &c. **2.** (fig.) Clash of conflicting interests, passions, motives &c. Phr. *to come into collision with*, find oneself opposed by.

collision-mat, n. (naut.) One to cover a hole in ship's side caused by collision &c.

collocate, vb. trans. [1. kólokāt; 2. kɔ́ləkeit], fr. Lat. *collocāt-(um)*, P.P. of *collocāre*, 'place together, arrange', fr. **col-** & *locāre*, 'to place'. See **locate**. To place, place together, arrange.

collocation, n. [1. kòlokā́shun; 2. kɔ̀ləkéiʃən]. Prec. & **-ion**. **a** Act of placing together, putting in association or juxtaposition; **b** anything grouped or placed together with something else, grouping, arrangement, in relation to something else: (esp. fig.) *collocation of words, ideas* &c.

collocutor, n. [1. kolókūtur; 2. kəlɔ́kjutə], fr. Lat. *colloqui*, *collocūtus*, fr. **col-**, & *locūtum*, P.P. of *loqui*, 'to speak'. See **locution**. One who takes part in dialogue or conversation.

collodion, n. [1. kolódion; 2. kəlóudiən], fr. Gk. *kollṓdēs*, 'like glue', fr. *kólla*, 'glue', & **-ode**. Cp. **collagen**. Tough, elastic substance, in form of liquid which dries rapidly, made from gun-cotton, dissolved in ether, used for photographic films, and for coating abrasions &c. in surgery.

collodionize, vb. trans. [1. kolódionīz; 2. kəlóudiənaiz]. Prec. & **-ize**. To coat with collodion.

collogue, vb. intrans. [1. kológ; 2. kəlóug]. Fr. *colloque*, 'conversation', fr. Lat. *colloquium*, fr. *colloqui*, 'talk together', fr. **col-** & *loqui*, 'speak'. See **locution**. The final *g* is due to influence of *dialogue*. To discuss, converse, with another in privacy and confidence.

colloid, adj. & n. [1. kóloid; 2. kɔ́lɔid], fr. Gk. *kólla*, 'glue', & **-oid**. See **collodion**. **1.** adj. Having consistency of glue; sticky, gelatinous. **2.** n. Substance having these characteristics; specif. (chem.) non-crystalloid state of substance in suspension in water or alcohol which does not diffuse through a parchment or collodion membrane.

colloidal, adj. [1. kolóidal; 2. kəlɔ́idəl]. Prec. & **-al**. Of the nature of a colloid.

collop, n. [1. kólop; 2. kɔ́ləp]. Etymol. unknown. **a** (in Dryden and dictionaries) Slice of meat (hardly current now in England); **b** (in Scotland) meat coarsely minced and then cooked: *minced collops*.

colloquial, adj. [1. kolṓkwial; 2. kəlóukwiəl]. See **colloquy** & **-al**. **1.** (of speech and modes of expression) **a** Pertaining to, connected with, used in, uttered speech or conversation: *a colloquial knowledge of, practice in, a language*; hence, **b** characteristic of, current, used, in familiar conversation; (with implication of not being used in lofty, or literary, style). **2.** (of persons) Given to using colloquial words and turns of phrase.

colloquialism, n. [1. kolṓkwializm; 2. kəlóukwiəlizəm]. Prec. & **-ism**. Word or expression usual in familiar conversation, but avoided in formal or elevated style.

colloquialist, n. [1. kolṓkwialist; 2. kəlóukwiəlist]. **colloquial** & **-ist**. (rare) **a** Conversationalist; **b** one given to colloquialism.

colloquialize, vb. trans. [1. kolṓkwialīz; 2. kəlóukwiəlaiz]. See prec. & **-ize**. To render colloquial.

colloquially, adv. [1. kolṓkwiali; 2. kəlóukwiəli]. **colloquial** & **-ly**. **a** Orally, as uttered in spoken language: *to know a language colloquially*, so as to speak it; **b** after the manner of familiar conversation.

colloquist, n. [1. kólokwist; 2. kɔ́ləkwist]. See **colloquy** & **-ist**. Speaker in a colloquy.

colloquy, n. [1. kólokwi; 2. kɔ́ləkwi], fr. Lat. *colloquium*, 'conversation', fr. **col-** & *loqui*, 'to speak'. See **locution**. A formal conversation, debate, conference.

collotype, n. [1. kólotip; 2. kɔ́lətaip], fr. Gk. *kólla*, 'glue', see **collagen**, & **type**. Photographic print made directly from colloid film.

collude, vb. intrans. [1. kolū́d; 2. kəljū́d], fr. Lat. *collūdere*, 'play together, act in collusion', fr. **col-** & *lūdere*, 'to play'. See **ludicrous**. (archaic) To act in collusion.

collusion, n. [1. kolū́zhun; 2. kəljū́žən], fr. Lat. *collūsiōn-(em)*, 'secret understanding', fr. *collūs-(um)*, P.P. of *collūdere*, & **-ion**. See prec. Fraudulent manœuvre in which, by preconceived arrangement, two or more persons play into each other's hands for the purpose of getting the better of a third party in a negotiation or transaction, the parties *in collusion* appearing as indifferent to, or actually opposed to, each other.

collusive, adj. [1. kolū́siv; 2. kəljū́siv]. Lat. *collūs-*, see prec., & **-ive**. Of the nature of, characterized by, arranged in, collusion.

collusively, adv. Prec. & **-ly**. In the manner of collusion.

collywobbles, n. pl. [1. kóliwòblz; 2. kɔ́liwɔ̀blz]. (colloq. and facetious) Any pain, discomfort, or looseness in the bowels or abdomen.

colocynth, n. [1. kólosinth; 2. kɔ́ləsinþ]. Lat. *colocynthis*, fr. Gk. *kolokúnthis*, 'the wild gourd'. Etymol. uncertain. A purgative drug obtained from the bitter pulp of the fruit of a wild gourd, *coloquintida*, the bitter apple.

Cologne, see **Eau de Cologne**.

colon (I.) n. [1. kṓlon; 2. kóulən]. Lat., fr. Gk. *kólon*, 'the large intestine'. Etymol. doubtful. (anat.) That part of the larger intestine which extends from the caecum to the rectum.

colon (II.), n. [1. kṓlun; 2. kóulən]. Lat. *cōlon*, fr. Gk. *kôlon*, 'a limb, part'. (in writing or printing) A punctuation mark (:), on the whole, corresponding in uttered speech, to a pause longer than that implied by a semi-colon, but shorter than that indicated by a full-stop. A colon is used after a part of a sentence which is complete in itself in construction, and when the sense of what follows arises naturally from the former; in introducing an example, argument, quotation; after such words as, *as follows, namely, for example, so-and-so says*, and so on; after words indicating a new stage in an argument, as, *to sum up*, &c.

colonel, n. [1. kĕ́rnel; 2. kʌ́nəl]. The spelling is from the present Fr. *colonel*, or Ital. type, *colonello*; the pronunciation, however, is fr. the type *coronel*, the older form, used in 16th cent. fr. an older Fr. type. *Colonello* is dimin. of *colonna*, 'column', & derived fr. the first company of a regiment of infantry being called '*la compagnie colonelle*, or *la colonelle*'; the commander of the regiment apparently got his title from his place with or near this company. *Coronel*, on the other hand, appears to be fr. Lat. *corōna*, 'crown', & dimin. suff. *-el*, a crown being the badge of this rank. The pronunciation of this word as [karnəl] (w. *r*) in Scotland & Ireland, shows that in spite of the present spelling, *coronel* is the type fr. wh. it is derived. Officer in command of a regiment; or, usually lieutenant-colonel of a battalion.

colonel commandant, n. Officer commanding a brigade; the old title, *brigadier*, is now in use again.

colonelcy, n. [1. kĕ́rnlsi; kʌ́nlsi]. **colonel** & **-cy**. Office, rank, or commission of colonel.

colonial, adj. & n. [1. kolṓnial; 2. kəlóuniəl]. **colony** & **-al**. **1.** adj. **a** Pertaining to, connected with a colony or colonies. *Colonial Office*, department of state in charge of the colonies; **b** characteristic of the colonies, or their inhabitants, esp. of differences of speech, manners, habits &c., between them and those who have always lived in the British Isles. **2.** n. Inhabitant, subject, of a colony; esp. a British Colony.

colonialism, n. [1. kolṓnializm; 2. kəlóuniəlizəm]. Prec. & **-ism**. A trait of colonial life, manners, speech &c.

colonially, adv. [1. kolṓniali; 2. kəlóuniəli]. **colonial** & **-ly**. From point of view of, after manner of, a colonial.

colonist, n. [1. kólonist; 2. kɔ́lənist]. **colony** & **-ist**. Settler in, or inhabitant of, a colony, esp. an original settler or founder of a colony.

colonization, n. [1. kòlonīzā́shun; 2. kɔ̀lənaizéiʃən]. **colonize** & **-ation**. Act or process of founding, establishing, developing, a colony or colonies.

colonize, vb. trans. & intrans. [1. kólonīz; 2. kɔ́lənaiz]. **colony** & **-ize**. **A.** trans. **1.** To settle in a country, usually an undeveloped one, remote from one's own, and develop its agricultural and other resources: *the British and Dutch colonized South Africa.* **2.** To place, settle, (persons) in a colony, with a view to getting rid of them from the old country, and in the hope that they will be more useful in the new: *we are urged by some to colonize our criminals and undesirables.* **B.** intrans. **a** To become a settler and founder of a colony; **b** to settle in a colony already established; go to a colony to live.

colonizer, n. [1. kólonīzer; 2. kɔ́lənaizə]. Prec. & **-er**. One who helps to found and develop a colony; one who settles in a colony.

colonnade, n. [1. kòlonā́d; 2. kɔ̀lənéid]. Fr., fr. Ital. *colonnata*, on anal. of other words in **-ade** (*arcade* &c.). See **column**. **a** A series or row of columns placed at regular intervals; **b** a double row, avenue, of trees &c.: '*The poplars are felled, farewell to the shade, and the whispering sound of the cool colonnade*' (Cowper).

colonnaded, adj. [1. kòlonā́ded; 2. kòlənéidid]. Prec. & **-ed**. Provided with a colonnade.

colony, n. [1. kóloni; 2. kóləni], fr. Lat. *colōnia*, 'landed estate, farm; settlement, colony', fr. *colōnus*, 'cultivator of the ground, husbandman, farmer', fr. *colere*, 'to till, tend, take care of (the soil); dwell, inhabit'. The base is **kʷel-*, 'turn, revolve', & the sense of *colere* is apparently derived fr. the idea of 'turning one's hand to, getting busy on, a piece of work', or possibly fr. 'turning up' the ground with a plough. The base is a fertile one; fr. the idea of cultivating soil follows that of settling on & inhabiting it, as in Lat. *incola*, 'inhabitant', *incolāre*, 'to inhabit'; further Lat. *inquilīnus*, 'residing in a city'; fr. same base comes also Lat. *collum*, 'neck', that wh. turns the head, see **col**. The orig. idea of turning is more obviously preserved in Gk. *kúklos*, 'ring, circle, circular motion', fr. **kʷəkʷlo-* (with reduplication) & Gk. *pólos*, 'pivot, axis', also 'land turned up with a plough'; see **cult**, **cycle**, & **pole** (**II.**); O.E. *hweol* (fr. **hwehwol-*). See **wheel**. (Used both of the geographical area and of those who inhabit it.) **1.** A geographical area, usually in a primitive state of cultivation and thinly populated, which is settled by people from a distant country who cultivate the ground and develop all the resources of the country, ultimately building cities, creating an advanced condition of civilization, and sometimes founding an independent, or largely self-governing state; in the British Empire, the word *Dominion* is the general term for the self-governing states, and *Colony*, for the *Crown Colonies* &c.: *the Secretary of State for Dominion Affairs and the Colonies.* **2.** (anct. hist.) **a** (Gk. hist.) An independent city state, founded by emigrants from a mother city; **b** (Rom. hist.) settlement of Roman citizens, usually veteran soldiers, in a conquered country. **3.** The band of persons who found, create, and develop the new state; those descended from them, and those who subsequently migrate to it. **4.** Group of people of the same, foreign, race or nationality living in a town or area, esp. such a group of aliens occupying a special quarter of a city: *the Italian colony in Soho*; *the Jewish colony in Park Lane* &c. **5.** (nat. sc.) **a** Group of related organisms occurring in close association, e.g. *colony of cells*; *colony of plants*, group more or less isolated from others; **b** assemblage of fossils occurring for some reason in a different formation from that to which they normally belong.

colophon, n. [1. kólofōn, -fon; 2. kóləfoun, -fən]. L. Lat., fr. Gk. *kolophṓn*, 'the summit, finish, end, finishing stroke'. Supposed to be fr. **kʷoln̥bhos*, & connected w. Lat. *collis*, 'hill', wh. is fr. **colnis*, cogn. w. Engl. **hill** & **hall**. See **column**. (in early printing) The device or tailpiece, often highly ornamented; the inscription at the end of a book giving information now put on the title-page (name of book, place, and date of publication &c.).

colophony, n. [1. kolófuni; 2. kəlófəni], fr. *Colophon* in Lydia; the Gk. being *Kolophōnía rhētínē*, 'resin or gum from Colophon'. Common rosin, or resin, made from the exudation of coniferous trees.

coloquintida, n. [1. kòlokwíntida; 2. kòləkwíntidə]. Variant of **colocynth**; fr. Gk. acc. *kolokunthída*.

Colorado beetle, n. [1. kòloráhdō bḗtl; 2. kòlərā́dou bítl]. Named after state in U.S.A. Yellow beetle with black stripes, very destructive to potatoes; potato bug.

colo(u)ration, n. [1. kuluráshun; 2. kaləréiʃən]. Fr., fr. Lat. *colōrāt-(um)*, P.P. of *colōrāre*, 'to colour, paint, tinge', see **colour**, & **-ion**. **a** Act of colouring; **b** condition of being coloured; **c** arrangement and combination of colours, whether natural or the result of artistic effort.

coloratura, n. [1. kòloratóora; 2. kòlərātúrə]. Ital., 'coloration'. See prec. (mus.) Florid variations or ornaments in playing or singing.

colorific, adj. [1. kulurífik; 2. kalərífik], fr. Fr. *colorifique*, Lat. base *colōri-*, see **colour**, & **-fic**. **a** Connected with, producing, colour; **b** highly coloured.

colorimeter, n. [1. kolorímeter; 2. kələrímitə], fr. Lat. base *colōri-*, 'colour', see **colour**, & **meter**. Apparatus for measuring depth of colour in a liquid by comparison with the tint of a standard solution.

colossal, adj. [1. kolósal; 2. kəlósəl]. **colossus** & **-al**. **1.** Like a colossus; gigantic, huge (of material and non-material things). **2.** (colloq., not common) Remarkable, splendid, fine.

colossus, n. [1. kolósus; 2. kəlósəs]. Lat., fr. Gk. *kolossós*, 'gigantic statue', also simply 'statue'. Origin obscure. **a** Gigantic statue of Apollo at the entrance of the harbour at Rhodes; hence, any gigantic statue; **b** a huge, hulking, human being.

colotomy, n. [1. kolótumi; 2. kəlótəmi], fr. **colon** (**I.**) & **-tomy**. An opening or incision into the colon.

colour (**I.**), n. [1. kúlur; 2. kálə], fr. O. Fr. *colór*, fr. Lat. *color*, genit. *colōr-is*, 'colour of the skin, complexion; colour in general, tint, hue; outward show, appearance; colouring'; connected w. Lat. *cēlāre*, 'hide, keep secret'; also w. *cella*, 'store-room' &c., see **cell**, further w. Goth. *hulistr*, 'veil', & *huljan*, 'to hide'; O.E. *heolstor*, 'hiding-place; darkness', & *helan*, 'hide, conceal'; also O.H.G. *hulsa*, 'husk'. See **conceal**. **1. a** Visual sensations produced upon the retina by light-waves of different length; **b** specif., sensation of this kind produced by light-waves of given length as reflected by objects of nature, or by reproductions of these in art; hue, tint; Phrs. *dress in colours*, wear bright coloured clothes, as distinct from black; *to see the colour of one's money*; *to take one's colour from a person*, imitate him, affect to think as he does; **c** (in black and white drawing), contrast of light and shade. **2. a** Colour produced by pigments through skill of an artist (painter); his method, and degree of skill in using this so as to produce an effect in a picture: *Velasquez was as great in colour as in form*; **b** (in pl.), *the colours*, paints; Phrs. *to lay on the colours*; (fig.) *lay on the colours too thickly*, describe in extravagant terms; *paint in bright, dark, colours*, describe favourably, unfavourably. **3.** Tint of the human complexion, esp. red or pink colour in the cheeks: *to have very little colour, too much colour.* Phrs. *to change colour*, grow red or pale; *lose colour*, become pale; *high colour*, red complexion; *off colour*, not in full vigour, out of spirits; *gentleman, lady, of colour*, (facetious) negro, negress. **4.** Appearance of reality or truth, verisimilitude: *some colour of truth.* Phrs. *under colour of*, under pretext of; *to give, lend, colour to*, make probable; *to give a false colour to*, pervert, twist (a statement, act, &c.). **5. a** (fig., of persons) Intensity of character, vividness of personality; individuality; **b** (of literary work) spirit, zest, picturesqueness, atmosphere, interest; *local colour*, details of description which heighten effect of reality by completing impression given of a scene, place, period; **c** (mus.) tone, quality, variety of expression. **6. a** (pl.) Coloured ribbons, dresses &c., esp. those distinctive of a party, club, school &c.; coloured jacket distinguishing owner of horse worn by jockeys when riding in a race: *the King's colours were borne to the winning-post.* Phr. *to get one's colours*, get into the first eleven, rowing team &c.; **b** (often in pl.) flag of ship or infantry regiment: *to salute the colours*; *trooping of the colours*; *King's colour*, the Union flag; *regimental colour*, that bearing the battle honours of the regiment; *to join the colours*, enlist. (fig.) Phrs. *to stick to one's colours*, to adhere to one's party, opinions &c.; *come off with flying colours*, make a great success of anything; *nail one's colours to the mast*, form and announce a decision, opinion &c., and stick to it; *lower one's colours*, abate one's demands, abandon position; *desert one's colours*; *in one's true colours*, as one is.

colour (**II.**), vb. trans. & intrans., fr. prec. **A.** trans. **1.** To overlay, or imbue, with pigment, colour, to paint, stain, tint: *to colour a picture, wall*; specif., *a pipe*, stain it with nicotine by smoking it. **2.** (fig., of non-material things) **a** To distort, pervert, deliberately from malice, or unconsciously from prejudice (a report, description, statement &c.); **b** to exaggerate, heighten, add some emotional quality to (a story, account &c.); **c** to influence deeply, permeate, for good or ill: *his whole thought was coloured by innate benevolence*; *one's point of view is necessarily coloured by past experience.* **B.** intrans. To acquire colour, become coloured; specif. **a** (of persons) to blush, become pink in the face, esp. from emotion; also *to colour up*; **b** of fruits, grain, when ripening; **c** (of a tobacco-pipe) become brown from being impregnated with nicotine: *this pipe is colouring nicely.*

colourable, adj. [1. kúlurabl; 2. kálərəbl]. **colour** (**II.**) & **-able**. **a** Capable of receiving colour, of being coloured (rare); **b** having a fair appearance, specious, plausible; esp. in Phr. *colourable imitation.*

colourably, adv. Prec. & **-ly**. In a plausible, specious manner.

colouration, see **colo(u)ration.**

colour-blind, adj. Incapable, through defect in the eyes, of distinguishing between certain colours, esp. between red and green.

colour-blindness, n. Prec. & **-ness**. Defect of vision which makes the sufferer incapable of distinguishing between colours; Daltonism.

coloured, adj. [1. kúlerd; 2. káləd]. **colour** (**I.**) & **-ed**. Having colour, often in compounds: *cream-coloured*, *flesh-coloured* &c. Phr. *coloured man*, negro.

colouring, n. [1. kúluring; 2. káləriŋ]. **colour** (**I.**) & **-ing**. **1.** Substance used to give colour; also *colouring matter.* **2. a** Style in which, degree of skill with which, an artist uses colours: *X's colouring is quite elementary*; **b** manner in which a thing is coloured: *colouring of a picture* &c. **3.** Colour of human complexion, usually including hair and eyes: *she had ugly features but attractive colouring.*

colourless, adj. [1. kúlurles; 2. káləlis]. **colour** (**I.**) & **-less**. **1.** Without vivid or distinctive colour, washed-out; **a** (of sky) dull, gloomy; **b** (of liquids) clear like water; **c** (of human complexion) pale, pallid, white. **2.** (fig.) Lacking character, vividness, individuality; non-committal, insipid: *a colourless person*; *a colourless speech.*

colourlessly, adv. Prec. & **-ly**. In colourless manner; (fig.) inertly, without spirit.

colourlessness, n. See prec. & **-ness**. Quality of being colourless.

colourman, n. [1. kúlurman; 2. káləmən]. Shopkeeper who deals in paints &c., usually *oil and colourman.*

colour-process, n. Process of reproducing prints &c. in colours by means of photography through coloured screens.

colour-sergeant, n. Senior sergeant in a company of a battalion, attached to the officers bearing the colours on parade.

coloury, adj. [1. kúluri; 2. káləri]. **colour** (**I.**) & **-y**. (trade term) Having such a colour as denotes good quality in a particular article.

colporteur, n. [1. kòlportḗr; 2. kòlpō(r)tə́(r)]. Fr., 'hawker'. See **col**, 'neck', & **port**, 'to carry'. Lit., one who carries things slung round his neck. Itinerant seller of books; specif., one who hawks cheap Bibles, or distributes Bibles &c. for a society.

colt (**I.**), n. [1. kōlt; 2. koult]. Etymol. doubtful. **1.** Young horse, from the time he leaves his dam up to the age of four or five. **2. a** (i.) A gay, noisy, inexperienced youth; (ii.) a green, awkward, rough lout of a boy; **b** a young cricket professional in his first season. **3.** (naut.) A rope's end (used for thrashing); as vb. trans., to thrash, beat.

colt (II.), n. A revolver, pistol, of type invented by Samuel Colt, or made by the American company of that name.

coltish, adj. [1. kóltish; 2. kóultiʃ], fr. **colt** (I.) & **-ish**. Like a colt, frisky; wanton.

coltishly, adv. Prec. & **-ly**. In a coltish manner; like a colt.

colt's-foot, n. [1. kóltsfoot; 2. kóultsfut]. Plant, *Tussilago*, with large leaves and yellow flowers; extract from this used as a medicine for coughs and asthma.

colubrine, adj. [1. kólūbrīn; 2. kóljūbrain]. Lat. *colubrīnus*, fr. *coluber*, 'snake'. See **cobra**. (zool.) Pertaining to, of a genus, *Coluber*, of non-poisonous snakes.

columbarium, n. [1. kolumbárium; 2. kɔlɔmbéəriəm]. Lat. fr. *columba*, 'dove'. See **columbine**. a Dove-cot, pigeon-house; b a chamber, with niches for receiving dead bodies, in the Catacombs.

columbine (I.), n. [1. kólumbīn; 2. kɔ́lɔmbain], fr. Fr. *colombine*, fr. L. Lat. *columbīna*, 'dove-like', fr. Lat. *columba*, 'dove'; possibly so called fr. its colour. The word is supposed to be connected w. Gk. *kelainós*, 'black, dark', & Scrt. *kalánkaš*, 'spot', *kalmášaš*, 'variegated, spotted'. O. Slav. *golqbĭ*, 'dove', Russ. *gólubj* is the same word; Russ. *golubyj*, 'blue', is primarily 'dove-colour'. Herbaceous, perennial plant, genus *Aquilegia*, with bright flowers supposed to resemble a group of pigeons.

Columbine (II.), n., fr. female name of same origin as prec. Sprightly female companion of Harlequin in a pantomime.

column, n. [1. kólum; 2. kɔ́lɔm]. Lat. *columna*, 'pillar', related to Lat. *columen*, 'height, summit, peak; gable; prop', *collis*, 'hill', & *culmen*, 'top, highest point, gable' (see **culminate**); further, cogn. w. Lat. *celsus*, 'high, lofty, tall', & *-cellere* (only in compounds, *excellere*, 'rise', see **excel**); outside Lat. the base is copiously represented in Gmc., Goth. *hallus*, 'rock', O.E. *heall*, see **hall**; O.E. *holm*, 'high sea', O.E. *hyll*, see **hill**; in Gk. *kolōnós*, 'hill', & *kolophṓn*, 'top, end', see **colophon**. **1.** (archit.) A pillar, shaft, tall support, usually of stone, slender in proportion to its height, carrying weight of arch, beam, girder &c. **2.** Any of various objects shaped like a column: as **a** *column of water, smoke*; **b** (anat.) *spinal column*, which supports upper part of the body. **3. a** Vertical division of page of a book or newspaper; **b** set of figures arranged in short lines one below the other on a sheet of paper &c. **4.** (mil. & naval) Formation in which the elements are placed one behind the other, instead of being abreast, and forming a line.

columnar, adj. [1. kolúmnar; 2. kɔlámnə]. Lat. *columnāris*. See prec. & **-ar**. Pertaining to, formed in, a column or columns; like a column in shape: *columnar structure, formation* &c.

columned, adj. [1. kólumd; 2. kɔ́lɔmd]. **column** & **-ed**. Provided with columns; columnar.

columniform, adj. [1. kolúmniform; 2. kɔlámnifɔ̄m]. **column** & **-form**. In the form of a column.

colure, n. [1. kólūr; 2. kóuljɔ̄], fr. Gk. *kólouros*, 'docked, truncated', fr. *kólos*, 'cut off', cogn. w. **clado-**, & *ourá*, 'tail, point', see **uro-** (II.). One of two imaginary circles which intersect at the poles.

colza, n. [1. kólza; 2. kɔ́zə], fr. Du. *koolzaad*, lit. 'cabbage-seed, rapeseed'. See **cole**. **a** Rapeseed; **b** oil made from rapeseed, used in lamps.

com-, pref. See also **co-**, **con-** & **col-**. Old form, & only one used in compounds, of Lat. *cum*, 'with' &c. The force in compounds is (1) union, combination, as in *con-currere*, 'run together'; (2) completeness, *com-edere*, 'to eat up', *con-tundere*, 'hammer to pieces'; *con-ficere*, 'make an end of doing, finish off' &c. As regards the relations of the word outside Lat., it seems probable that the common Gmc. pref., Goth. *ga-*, O.E. *ġe-*, is identical, the initial voiced consonant being derived fr. earlier χ or *h*, in an unstressed position. The identity of Lat. *com-* w. this is made probable by such old compounds as Lat. *commūnis* (fr. **kommoinos*), 'common', Goth. *gamains*, O.E. *ġemǣne*, 'common'. It has been suggested that the orig. meaning of the base is 'to seize, grip, hold together'. Cp. further the prepositions, O. Ir. *com*, 'with', O. Slav. *sŭ*, 'with', &, in spite of the difference of meaning, Gk. *katá*, 'down'. A further suggestion of some interest is that the base **k̑em-*, **k̑om-* &c. fr. wh. these words come, is that in Goth. *fra-hinþan*, 'seize, take captive', & Goth. *handus*, O.E. *hand*, 'hand', orig. 'the grasper'; & further that in this primitive sense the same base lurks also in Lat. *decem*, 'ten', wh. according to this view wd. come fr. an orig. **duo kem-*, or some such form, meaning 'two hands' (of five fingers each). See **hand, December, ten.**

coma (I.), n. [1. kóma; 2. kóumə]. Gk. *kôma*, genit. *kṓmatos*, fr. **kōima-*, cp. *koimáō*, 'I put to sleep', connected w. *keimai*, 'lie down', & a large group of words in Gk. & other languages. See **civil**, **hide** (IV.) (of land), **home**. State of profound insensibility, resembling a deep sleep, caused by disease or serious injury.

coma (II.), n. Lat., fr. Gk. *kómē*, 'hair of the head'. The etymol. is unknown, & the earlier proposal to derive fr. **kosma-* & connect w. O. Slav. *kosmŭ*, 'hair of the head'; Lith. *kasa*, 'plait of hair'; O.N. *haddr* (for **hazd-*), 'woman's hair'; O.E. *heord(an)*, 'hards, or fibres of flax', is now rejected. **1.** (bot.) Tuft of hairs at end of some seeds. **2.** (astron.) Nebulous mass forming 'head' of a comet.

comate, adj. [1. kómāt; 2. kóumeit]. Prec. & **-ate**. (bot.) Hairy.

comatose, adj. [1. kómatōs; 2. kóumətous]. *comat-* & **-ose**. See **coma** (I.). In a state of profound insensibility or coma.

comb (I.), n. [1. kōm; 2. koum]. O.E. *cāmb*, O.H.G. *chamb*, Mod. Germ. *kamm*, O.N. *kambr*. Cp. Gk. *gomphios*, 'grinder-tooth, tooth of a key', & Gk. *gómphos*, 'wedge-, (tooth-) shaped bolt, or nail', & *gamphēlai*, 'jaws of a beast'; Scrt. *jambhaš*, 'tooth', in pl. 'row of teeth'; Lith. *žambas*, 'edge of a beam', O. Slav. *ząbŭ*, 'tooth'. **1.** Instrument with teeth **a** for arranging the hair; **b** for holding it in position; **c** similar instrument for preparing and cleaning wool, flax &c. **2.** Crest of cock. Phr. *to cut the comb of*, to humiliate. **3.** Crest of a wave. (Rare.) **4.** Group of wax cells constructed by bees for storing honey: *honey-comb*; similar group of cells made by wasps.

comb (II.), vb. trans. & intrans., fr. prec. **1.** trans. To arrange, smooth (the hair); clean, unravel (wool, flax &c.), by means of a comb. **2.** intrans. (of a wave) To curl over, to break, with white foam.

combat (I.), vb. trans. & intrans. [1. kúmbat; 2. kámbət], fr. Fr. *combattre*, 'to fight'. See **com-** & **batter** (I.). **1.** trans. (chiefly fig., of non-material things) To contest, oppose, strive, fight against: *to combat a tendency, opinion, movement* &c. **2.** intrans. To practise opposition, be in habit or act of contesting &c., followed by *with, against, for.*

combat (II.), n. Fr. See prec. (of physical and spiritual action) **a** A contest, fight, struggle; **b** strife, struggle in general: *to love combat.* Phr. *single combat*, fight between two opponents only.

combatant, adj. & n. [1. kúmbatant; 2. kámbətənt]. Fr. *combattant*, Pres. Part. of *combattre*. See **combat** (I.). **1.** adj. Engaged in fighting; esp. (mil.) *combatant officer*, one whose business is to lead and direct operations in the field, as opposed to administrative and other branches. **2.** n. One engaged in physical or moral conflict; a party in a fight. (Applied to individuals and to a military force as a whole.)

combative, adj. [1. kúmbativ; 2. kámbətiv]. **combat** (II.) & **-ive**. Addicted to, fond of, fighting, whether in physical or figurative sense; pugnacious.

combatively, adv. Prec. & **-ly**. Pugnaciously, as though inviting a conflict.

combativeness, n. See prec. & **-ness**. Quality of being combative; tendency to, love of, conflict.

combe, n. [1. kōōm; 2. kūm]. See **coombe**. Small valley.

comber, n. [1. kómer; 2. kóumə]. **comb** (II.) & **-er**. **1.** Machine for combing wool and flax. **2.** A large wave, breaking on a beach, reef &c. Cp. *beachcomber*.

combination, n. [1. kòmbināshun; 2. kɔ̀mbinéiʃən]. **combine** & **-ation**. **1.** Act, or process, of combining. **2.** Result of combination; union, uniting, amalgamation of two or more things or persons; in various specific senses: **a** (of persons) for a political or commercial purpose; (in good sense) league, party, company; (in bad sense) cabal, gang, ring &c; **b** (math.) various groups in which numbers or their equivalents may be arranged. **3.** (in pl.) *Combinations*, tight-fitting undergarment consisting of a vest with coverings for the lower limbs attached.

combination-room, n. A common-room (q.v.) at Cambridge University.

combinative, adj. [1. kómbinativ; 2. kɔ́mbinətiv]. **combine** & **-ative**. **1.** Connected with, result of, combination; specif., philology, *combinative sound change*, one which results from reciprocal influence of several sounds in combination, or from effects of varying stress or intonation; *combinative factor*, one which produces such a change. **2.** (of persons) Able to combine ideas, facts &c., and make something of them.

combine (I.), vb. trans. & intrans. [1. kumbín; 2. kəmbáin]. fr. L. Lat. *combīnāre*, fr. **com-** & *bīn(i)*, 'two-apiece; two; a pair', for **dwīni*, connected w. *duo*, 'two'. See **bi-**, **bis**. **A.** trans. **1.** General meaning, to join two or more (material or non-material) things together, bring them into a close union so as to form a unity: *to combine several fields and form a park*; *to combine intelligence and learning with good manners*, to exhibit all these qualities; *to combine the characters of soldier and Christian*, to be both of these; *combine the office of head of a college with that of a professor*, to hold both offices; *to combine forces.* **2.** (specif. chem.) To unite two or more (different substances) in such proportions as to form a compound. **B.** intrans. To unite, mix; form a unity, compound, or harmonious whole: *oil and water, Bolshevists and Tories, do not readily combine.*

combine (II.), n. [1. kómbīn; 2. kɔ́mbain], fr. prec. Combination; specif., union of persons or trading companies in a commercial enterprise; alliance of persons or parties for political purposes.

combing(s), n., gen. in pl. [1. kómingz; 2. kóumiŋz]. **comb** (II.) & **-ing**. Material collected in a comb; specif. (in pl.) hair removed from the head by a comb, and remaining between the teeth of the latter.

combustibility, n. [1. kumbùstibíliti; 2. kəmbàstibíliti]. **combustible** & **-ity**. Quality of burning, of taking fire, easily.

combustible, adj. [1. kumbústibl; 2. kəmbástibl]. Fr., fr. L. Lat. *combustibilis*, fr. Lat. *combust-(um)*, P.P. of *combūrere*, 'to burn up', & **-ible**. See **combustion**. Liable to burn, to take fire, to spring suddenly into flame.

combustion, n. [1. kumbúschun; 2. kəmbástʃən], fr. L. Lat. *combustiōn-(em)*, fr. Lat. *combust-(um)*, P.P. of *combūrere*, 'to burn up'. This vb. is for *co-amb-ūrere*; owing to the contraction, the compound was considered as though fr. *com-* & **būrere* &c., so much so that the words *bustum*, 'place where corpses were burnt', hence 'tomb', as well as *bustar* & *bustio*, were formed fr. it. The vb. *ūrere* (for **ūsere*), 'to burn', P.P. *us-tum*, fr. base **us-*, **eus-*, **aus-*, 'burn, glow', occurs in Lat. *aurōra*, fr. **ausōza*, 'dawn' (see **aurora**); Gk. *heúō*, 'singe', fr. **eusō*; Scrt. *ṓšati*, 'burns', & *uš-na*, 'hot'; in Gmc. we have O.H.G. *usil-var*, 'yellow' (flame-colour); O.N. *usli*, O.E. *ysle*, 'glowing ash, ember'. By the side of **eus-* &c., a form **ewes-* existed, wh. occurs in the name of the volcano *Vesuvius*, perh. also in **Vesta**. Goth. *wis*, 'a calm', lit. 'warm weather', is prob. fr. this base. For development of meaning see **calm**. **a** Process of burning; **b** specific instance of this. Phr. *spontaneous combustion* (popularly), bursting into flame, and burning without any assignable reason; also (actually) bursting into flame from ascertainable, natural, chemical causes, without human agency.

come, vb. intrans. [1. kum; 2. kam]. O.E. *cuman* (for *cwiman* through *cweoman* ?), M.E. *cumen*, *cōmen*; common Gmc., O.S. *cuman*, O. Fris. *cuma*, O.H.G. *kuman*, *koman*, also *queman*; O.N. *koma*; Goth. *qiman*; fr. Gmc. **kwim-*, **kwum-*, Aryan **gʷem-*, **gʷm-* &c. Cp. Lat. *venio*, fr. **gwemjo*; see **venue**; Gk. *bainō*, fr. **gʷm̥-jō*; see **basis**; Scrt. *gámati*, 'he goes', *gamjati*, 'causes to come, brings' &c. The base orig. expressed the related, but different, ideas 'go' & 'come'. Most general meaning, to move nearer, approach; with considerable differentiation. **A.** (chiefly independent) **1. a** (of the speaker) To move towards the person whom he addresses, or to the place in which this person is, or will be: *I will come to you, to London while you are there*; *I will come and see you*; **b** (of person addressed) to move towards, or into presence, or vicinity, of speaker; or to the place in which he is: *come here*; *you must come to me in Oxford*; *come nearer*; *come to my house*; **c** to accompany speaker, move in any direction or to any place along with him, in his company: *will you come with me to India?*; *come along*; *are you coming my way?* **2. a** To arrive at, reach, appear at, place where speaker is, or where some action referred to is taking place: *he hasn't come yet*; *he won't come till late*; *the doctor comes (here) every day*; *in the middle of the battle, help came*; *one shot came after another*; *no stranger ever comes to that place*; **b** to arrive from a distance at some nearer point: *he never came home all night*; *he came to Abingdon at the end of the first day*. Phrs. *to come home to*, to impress forcibly, appeal to; *come to hand*, arrive (esp. of letters); *come to life*, regain consciousness; *come to terms*, reach agreement; *come to the scratch*, be ready to fulfil one's bargain, to take action. **3.** (of events) **a** To happen, come about, take place, befall, occur: *to be ready for whatever comes*; **b** to occur, befall (as something unforeseen); turn out; (of persons) to behave in unexpected way, turn out to be of such a character: *how did it come that you quarrelled?*; *how did you come to be such a fool?* Phrs. *to come true*, fulfil prediction; *everything comes to him who waits*; *come to pass*, happen. **4.** (of natural phenomena) To appear, develop, reach natural stage of growth and maturity: *bud, flower, and fruit come each year*; *the seeds don't come true (to type)*. **5.** (of times and seasons) To recur, appear in natural sequence: *summer comes every year*; *old age comes soon enough*. **6. a** To happen as result of, be due to, be caused by: *this comes of disobedience*; **b** to spring from, be physically descended from: *to come of sound stock, of a good family*; **c** (of persons) to be born, originate in or at, proceed from: *I come from Dorset*; (of things) be derived from, emanate from, originate with: *caviare used to come from Russia*; *his money comes from his wife*; **d** to pass into one's possession: *his fortune came to him from his father*. **7. a** To reach, amount to, a certain figure, amount, price, as result of addition of separate figures, amounts &c.: *this sum comes to 300*; *your bill comes to £5*; *altogether your winnings come to a nice lot of money*; **b** (fig.) to amount to, be equivalent to: *what you say comes to this*. **8. a** (of emotions, mental activities, ideas &c.) To arise, take shape, in the mind, develop, become actual: *love will come in time*; *the inspiration never came*; Phr. *to come into one's head*, occur to one; **b** (of material things) to form, assume character, bulk, or consistency: *after much planning and planting my garden is coming just as I wanted it*; *the butter came very quickly today* (in churn). **9.** To pass, enter, into a particular state, relation, use: *to come into use, favour*; *come into conflict, into play* &c. Phrs. *to come to blows*, quarrel and fight; *come to grief*, be injured by an accident, ruined by failure of enterprises &c.; *to come to no good*, to go wrong, end disastrously; *to come a cropper*, have a heavy fall (also fig.) **10.** To stand in certain place or order (in time or space): *after Anne comes George I.*; *Revelation comes at the end of the Bible*; *next to Oxfordshire, southwards across the Thames, comes Berkshire*. **11.** (with adv. use of n.) To behave as though one had a certain character, or occupied a particular position, and overdo it; act the part of, assume the airs of, a certain rôle: *to come the great man*; *to come the swell*; *he comes the admiral too much in private life*. **12.** In reference to future points of time, equivalent to *when it comes*: *he will be fifty come midsummer*; *a year ago come Christmas* (archaic or provinc.). **13.** (in imperat., as interj.) With intention of rousing, attracting, attention, expostulating mildly &c.: *come, tell me what it's all about*; *come, come, you shouldn't speak like that!* **B.** Followed by prepositions or adverbs with special meanings. *Come about*, **a** to happen, arise, come to pass; **b** (of wind) to change round. *Come across*, to meet accidentally, unexpectedly (a person); to find, happen upon (a thing). *Come after*, **a** to seek, make efforts to obtain: *to come after a situation*; **b** to follow (in time or place); **c** to succeed: *to come after one's father* (in an estate). *Come along*, **a** to pass, take one's way along: *to come along the road*; **b** to agree with, agree to adopt proposed plan: *we explained our proposal, but he would not come along*. *Come at*, **a** to arrive at, reach, with hostile intent: *just let me come at you!*; **b** to make a rush at, attack: *the bull came at me with his head down*; **c** to obtain, attain to, gain: *to come at the knowledge of so-and-so*. *Come away*, to give way, detach itself, tear, break: *the handle came away in her hand*. *Come back*, **a** to return: *to come back home*; *come back to power*; **b** to return to one's memory: *the tune comes back to me now*. *Come by*, to obtain possession of, get hold of: *good servants are very hard to come by now*; *how did you come by your library?* *Come down*, **a** to lose position, caste, fortune &c.: *to come down in the world*; **b** (colloq.) to pay down, give money: *he came down very handsome(ly) when I was hard up*; **c** descend by tradition or inheritance: *the custom has come down to us from our prehistoric ancestors*. *Come down on*, to treat with severity, censure, upbraid: *to come down on a man for his carelessness*. *Come forward*, to present oneself, offer help, services &c.: *when England was in danger, all patriotic men came forward at once to help in any way they could*. *Come in*, **a** to come into the house from out of doors, into a room from passage: *ask him to come in*; **b** (of politics) assume, obtain power, office &c.: *the Coalition came in with a big majority*; **c** to arrive: *what time does the train come in?*; *the horse came in third*; **d** become fashionable, come into use: *short skirts for women came in towards the close of the war*; **e** come to fruition, mature, come into season: *early potatoes came in very late last year*; *these apples don't come in till February*; **f** serve a purpose, be useful: *odds and ends that will come in some day*; also *to come in useful*. *Come into*, **a** enter into an agreement, agree to join, support: *to come into a scheme*; **b** to inherit: *to come into a nice income*. *Come near*, to approach, or equal, in merit or quality: *modern poets cannot come near the old masters as makers of verbal music*. *Come off*, **a** (of events) to happen, esp. after delay or uncertainty, reach successful conclusion: *everything came off satisfactorily*; *the marriage never came off after all*; **b** (of persons) to acquit oneself: *to come off with flying colours*. *Come on*, **a** (of actors) to appear; make entry on to the stage; **b** to make progress, develop (lit. and fig.): *the crops are coming on nicely*; *he is coming on well in his studies*; **c** to advance towards and attack: *the enemy came on furiously*; **d** (of attack, of disease, pain &c.): *a terrible spasm of pain came on just before he died*; **e** to arise, be put forward for discussion, or hearing, in a court of law: *my case comes on before the judge tomorrow*. *Come out*, **a** to be made public, be published, be put on the market: *a play, book, new fashion comes out*; **b** to be divulged, made manifest, discovered: *the secret came out very inconveniently*. *Come out with*, to blurt out, disclose, utter: *to come out with the whole story, a horrible oath*. *Come round*, **a** to coax, wheedle, overcome scruples of: *you can't come round me with such yarns*; **b** to recover consciousness, regain strength: *to come round after a fainting-fit, a serious illness* &c.; *he took a long time to come round*; **c** (fig.) to change one's opinions, adopt a point of view: *to come round to another's way of thinking*. *Come to* [1. kùm tóō; 2. kàm tú], to regain consciousness: *it was many hours before he came to after being wounded*. *Come under*, **a** to pass, be under jurisdiction of; **b** to fall, be in, belong to, a certain category. *Come up*, **a** (of plants) to spring, show above ground: *the corn hasn't come up yet*; **b** arise, be put forward for discussion and debate; to be suggested by what has been said, and be discussed: *to come up in conversation*. *Come up to*, **a** to equal, be of same degree of excellence as: *his new book doesn't come up to the last*; **b** reach, extend to in height: *she hardly came up to her husband's elbow*. *Come up with*, to catch up, overtake, person or thing, moving forward, ahead of one.

come and go, n. [1. kúm and gṓ; 2. kám ənd góu]. Movement to and fro, passing backwards and forwards.

come-at-able, adj. [1. kùmátabl; 2. kàmǽtəbl]. **come, at, & -able.** **a** (of persons) Accessible, approachable, easy to get on with, willing to tolerate social intercourse; **b** (of places) easy to reach, not remote or without means of access.

come-back, n. [1. kúmbak; 2. kámbæk]. See **come & back.** (colloq.) A return to power, popularity &c., after retirement.

comedian, n. [1. kumēdian; 2. kəmídiən], fr. Fr. *comédien*, fr. **comedy** & **-an. 1.** An actor in comedy, comic actor: *low comedian*, actor of light (low) comedy. **2.** (fig.) An irresponsible person, who behaves in a foolish, futile manner, like a character in a farce; one who cannot be taken seriously.

comedienne, n. [1. kòmedién; 2. kɔ̀mɛdién]. Fr. An actress in comedy.

comedietta, n. [1. kòmādiéta; 2. kɔ̀mɛdiétə]. Ital., dimin. of *comedia*, 'comedy'. Short comedy.

comedo, n., pl. **comedones** [1. kómēdō; 2. kɔ́mīdou]. Lat., 'glutton', fr. *comedere*, 'to eat greedily, consume', fr. **com- &** *edere*, 'eat'. See **edible.** (med.) A blackhead on the face, chest &c., due to blocking of the sebaceous ducts.

come-down, n. [1. kúmdoun; 2. kámdaun]. See **come & down.** A downfall, set-back, change for the worse in one's circumstances; something that is humiliating: *it's rather a come-down for him to serve behind a counter*.

comedy, n. [1. kómidi; 2. kɔ́midi], fr. Fr. *comédie*, fr. Lat. *cōmoedia*, fr. Gk. *kōmōidia*, 'mirthful spectacle', fr. *kṓmos*, 'banquet, merrymaking, revel', & *ōidḗ*, 'song, lay'. The first element is perh. connected w. Lat. *cibus*, 'food'; for second element see **ode. 1.** That branch of drama which deals with humorous, familiar events, passions, and motives, and which exhibits characters speaking the language of everyday life. Comedy has usually a certain element of exaggeration and caricature in the treatment of character. **2.** A gay, humorous play which deals with life and character on above lines. Phr. *as good as a comedy. Musical comedy*, a humorous play (frequently a burlesque) with music, songs, dancing &c. **3.** Any comic or amusing incident or event in real life which reveals the interplay of human characters and motives. **4.** A serious composition which treats human life after the manner of a comedy, but which aims at depicting human life and character in accordance with truth, without leaving a sense of tragedy: *Dante's 'Divine Comedy'*.

comeliness, n. [1. kúmlines; 2. kámlinis]. **comely** & **-ness.** **a** Beauty of person, handsomeness; orderliness, appropriateness of arrangement; **b** moral beauty, seemliness.

comely, adj. [1. kúmli; 2. kámli]. O.E. *cȳm(e)līc*, 'beautiful, splendid', fr. **kūmi-*; cp. O.H.G. *kūmi*, 'weak', & *kūmo*, 'with difficulty, hardly, scarcely', whence Mod. Germ. *kaum*, 'scarcely'; further, O.H.G. *chūmōn*, *kūmen*, 'lament', & O.S. *kūmian*, 'bewail' &c. The word meant first 'feeble, weak', then 'delicate, fine, beautiful'. Outside Gmc. the word is perh. connected w. Gk. *goáō*, 'weep, lament, wail', & *góos*, 'lamentation', wh. wd. further bring it into relation w. O.E. *ċīeġan*, fr. **kaujan*, 'cry out', & w. O. Slav. *govoriti*, Russ. *govoritĭ*, 'to speak'. **a** Beautiful in person, handsome, well-proportioned, pleasing to the eye; **b** (fig., of moral beauty) seemly, fitting, decent (archaic).

comer, n. [1. kúmer; 2. kámə], fr. **come** & **-er.** One who comes; chiefly in Phrs. *first comer*, first arrival; *all comers*, all who present themselves for particular purpose.

comestible, adj. & n. [1. kuméstibl; 2. kəméstibl]. Fr., fr. L. Lat. *comestibilis*, fr. *comest-(um)*, P.P. of *comedere*, 'to eat up', fr. **com-** & *edere*, 'to eat'. See **edible.** **1.** adj. Fit to be eaten; pertaining to food. **2.** n. Food-stuff, thing(s) to eat (usually in pl.).

comet, n. [1. kómet; 2. kómit], fr. Lat. *comētes*, 'comet', fr. Gk. *komḗtēs*, 'long-haired', fr. *kómē*, 'hair'. See **coma (II.).** In O.E. a comet was called *feaxode-steorra*, 'hairy, long-haired, star'; for O.E. *feax*, 'hair', see **ctenoid.** Luminous heavenly body with a nucleus and a tail, appearing periodically at long intervals, and moving in an eccentric orbit; the nature and origin of the tail is disputed by astronomers.

cometary, adj. [1. kómitari; 2. kómitəri]. Prec. & **-ary.** Pertaining to or resembling a comet.

cometic, adj. [1. kométik; 2. kəmétik]. **comet** & **-ic.** Cometary.

comfit, n. [1. kúmfit; 2. kámfit], fr. Fr. *confit*, P.P. of O. Fr. *confire*, 'to preserve, to make into a sweetmeat', fr. Lat. *confectum*, P.P. of *conficere*, 'prepare', fr. **com-** & *facere*, 'to make'. See **confection** & **fact.** Sugar-plum.

comfort (I.), vb. trans. [1. kúmfort; 2. kámfət], fr. O. Fr. *conforter*, fr. L. Lat. *confortāre*, 'strengthen, fortify', fr. **com-** & *fortis*, 'strong'. See **force, fort.** **a** To bring ease of mind, consolation, to one suffering from grief; **b** to reassure, encourage, one in anxiety or perplexity.

comfort (II.), n., fr. prec. **1.** (of mental sensations and conditions) **a** Consolation in sorrow, anxiety &c.; **b** relief from sorrow &c., as result of such consolation; **c** the person or thought which gives or produces such relief: *he was a great comfort to his parents in old age.* **2.** (of physical sensations and conditions) **a** a bodily ease, well-being, repose; freedom, relief, from pain: *to be fond of comfort*; **b** ease of circumstances, pleasant, cheerful, sheltered conditions of life, sufficiency, luxury: *to live in comfort.*

comfortable, adj. [1. kúmfortabl; 2. kámfətəbl]. Prec. & **-able.** (chiefly of physical conditions) **a** Possessing, promoting, tending to, comfort: *a comfortable chair*; **b** (of persons) in a state of physical comfort, free from pain, easy: *to feel comfortable*; **c** (of conditions of life) adequate, sufficient for one's wants: *a comfortable income*; **d** (of houses) convenient, well-appointed: *comfortable lodgings*; **e** giving spiritual or moral comfort: '*Hear what comfortable words*' &c. (Communion Service).

comfortably, adv. Prec. & **-ly.** **a** In a comfortable manner, in all senses; **b** (also applied to fit) easily, conveniently, in a well-adjusted manner: *the key fits the lock quite comfortably*; *the drawer goes in and out comfortably.*

comforter, n. [1. kúmforter; 2. kámfətə]. **comfort (II.)** & **-er.** **1.** **a** One who comforts; **b** specif., *the Comforter*, the Holy Ghost. Phr. *Job's comforter*, one who professes to comfort, but in reality depresses. **2.** **a** A woollen scarf for the neck; **b** a dummy teat, used to quiet babies.

comfortless, adj. [1. kúmfortles; 2. kámfətlis]. **comfort (II.)** & **-less.** **a** (of things) Lacking conditions and means of, arrangements for, comfort; not promoting comfort; **b** (of persons) uncomforted, miserable.

comfrey, n. [1. kúmfri; 2. kámfri]. O. Fr. *cunfirie*, *cumfirie* &c., Low Lat. *conferia*, either fr. Lat. *confervēre*, 'to boil together; to heal', see **fervent**, or fr. *confirmāre*, 'to strengthen', see **confirm.** (bot.) Common plant of the borage family, with hairy leaves and purple or white flowers, the root and leaves of which are used medicinally.

comic, adj. [1. kómik; 2. kómik], fr. Lat. *cōmicus*, fr. Gk. *kōmikós*, fr. *kômos*, 'banquet, revel'. See **comedy.** **1.** Pertaining to comedy as opposed to tragedy: *comic writers.* **2.** Having the elements of comedy; intended to amuse (though not always succeeding): *comic song*, absurd, ludicrous song.

comical, adj. [1. kómikl; 2. kómikl]. Prec. & **-al.** Amusing, provoking laughter and merriment; freakish, quaintly humorous.

comicality, n. [1. kòmikáliti; 2. kòmikǽliti]. Prec. & **-ity.** **a** Quality of being comical and amusing; **b** a comical person.

comically, adv. [1. kómikali; 2. kómikəli]. **comical** & **-ly.** In a comical manner.

comity, n. [1. kómiti; 2. kómiti]. Fr. *comité*, fr. Lat. *cōmitāt-(em)*, 'courtesy, friendliness', fr. *cōmis*, 'courteous, affable, kind', earlier *cosmis*, prob. fr. **co-** & **smi-s*, fr. base **smei-*, 'to smile', cp. Scrt. *smáyati*, 'smiles', also Lat. *mīrus*, 'wonderful, admirable', *mīrāri*, 'marvel at, admire', fr. **smī-*, the same base as in Engl. **smile.** See also **admire.** Courtesy, urbanity of manners. Phr. *comity of nations*, courtesy and recognition extended by one nation to the laws, customs, institutions of others. Such expressions as *to be received into, excluded from, the comity of nations*, often met with in the press, political speeches &c., are wrong and due to an ignorant confusion of word with Latin *comes*, 'companion', as if *comity* meant 'company'.

comma, n. [1. kóma; 2. kómə]. Gk. *kómma*, 'something struck or cut, impression on a coin; clause in a sentence', for **kopma*, connected w. Gk. *kóptein*, 'to cut, strike', cogn. w. Gk. *kopis*, 'knife'; O. Slav. *kopati*, 'to dig', *kopije*, 'lance', & possibly also w. Gk. *kápōn*, Lat. *capōn-(em)*, 'castrated cock'. See **capon.** Punctuation mark (,) indicating the least possible separation between words in, or parts of, a sentence, and corresponding to very slight pause in uttered speech. *Inverted commas* (' '), placed before and after quotations &c.; *comma bacillus*, micro-organism shaped like a comma, the cause of Asiatic cholera; *comma butterfly*, a rare British butterfly, with white comma-like marks on the hind wings.

command (I.), vb. trans. & intrans. [1. komáhnd; 2. kəmánd], fr. Fr. *commander*, fr. L. Lat. *commandāre*, fr. Lat. **com-** & *mandāre*, lit. 'to put, give, into one's hand', fr. *manus*, 'hand', & *dare*, 'give'; hence, 'to commit to one's charge, to order, command'. See **mandate, manual** &c. **A.** trans. **1.** **a** (of persons) To order peremptorily, and with authority so as to secure obedience; to charge, bid: *to command a person to do something*; *I don't request, I command you to do it*; **b** (of things) to require authoritatively, enjoin: *to command silence.* **2.** To have authority over, lead; to direct and control: *to command a battalion, ship* &c. **3.** **a** To control, be master of (states of mind and emotion): *to command oneself, one's temper* &c.; **b** to have at one's disposal: *to command the services of.* Phr. (polite or ironical formula), *yours to command*; **c** (mil.) to dominate (a position), hold, have, under fire; **d** to have within one's field of vision, to dominate, as from superior height, overlook: *to command a view.* **4.** **a** (of persons) To deserve and get; evoke, compel: *to command respect, sympathy* &c.; **b** (of things for sale) to bring in, fetch: *to command a good price.* **B.** intrans. To be in authority, exercise supreme power or influence: *who commands here?*

command (II.), n. Fr. *commande.* See prec. **1.** **a** Authority and power to command, and to give orders which must be obeyed: *to be in command*; **b** act in exercise of such authority and power; a peremptory order: *you have my command to retreat*; Phr. *word of command*, set form of words embodying an order for particular movement of troops; **c** position of possessing such authority over persons: *to take command of a division* &c. **2** **a** Power or ability to control, govern, regulate: *command of one's emotions, passions, movements, faculties, language* &c.; **b** power to possess and use: *command of money*; **c** fact of possession, dominance &c.: *to get command of a military position.*

commandant, n. [1. kòmandáhnt; 2. kòmənd́ánt]. Fr., lit. 'the one commanding'. Pres. Part. of *commander.* See prec. Officer in command, esp. governor of a fortified town or naval station, of Royal Military College at Sandhurst &c.

commandeer, vb. trans. [1. kòmandḗr; 2. kòməndíə], fr. Du. *kommandeeren*, used by Boers in sense of taking by force, food, arms, or whatever was required in time of war. **1.** To force into military service, to conscript. **2.** **a** To take possession of (property) for military purposes, an act performed by authority of government or of military commander, receipts being given and payment subsequently made; **b** (colloq.) to take, appropriate (anything) to one's own use.

commander, n. [1. komáhnder; 2. kəmándə]. **command (I.)** & **-er.** One who commands; a chief, leader, esp. **a** (mil.) the officer in command of any military unit, from a platoon upwards; **b** (nav.) naval officer in rank between captain and lieutenant-commander; **c** member of one of the classes in certain orders of knighthood. *Commander of the Faithful*, title of the Caliph of Islam. *Commander-in-chief*, a officer in chief command of a whole force of the British army in the field in a given place. The office has been abolished for the army as a whole; **b** admiral in chief command of a naval station.

commandership, n. [1. komáhndership; 2. kəmándəʃip]. **commander** & **-ship.** The office of a commander.

commandery, n. [1. komáhnderi; 2. kəmándəri], fr. Fr. *commanderie.* See **command** & **-ery.** A provincial, subordinate community of Knights Hospitallers, corresponding to a *preceptory*, q.v., of the Templars.

commanding, adj. [1. komáhnding; 2. kəmándiŋ]. **command (I.)** & **-ing.** **1.** Exercising authority: (mil.) *commanding officer.* **2.** Controlling, dominating, by wisdom, weight, force of character, position, dignity of appearance &c.; impressive: *a commanding presence, influence, speech.* **3.** (of a mountain or hill &c.) Dominating by reason of its position and loftiness : *a commanding eminence.*

commandment, n. [1. komáhndment ; 2. kəmándmənt]. Fr. *commandement.* **command (I.) & -ment.** A peremptory order given by authority ; an edict, charge, precept ; specif., a law of God, one of the divisions of the decalogue, *Ten Commandments.*

commando, n. [1. komáhndō ; 2. kəmándou]. Du. term, naturalized during the Boer War. A body of armed burghers, raised for military service among the Boers.

comme il faut, as adj. [1. kòm ēl fō ; 2. kòm il fóu]. Fr., lit. 'as it ought to be' ; 'well-bred, proper '. *To be, not to be, quite comme il faut.* Not quite in French sense, and used less of persons, in English, than of conduct ; expresses idea of good form, the correct thing.

commemorable, adj. [1. komémurabl ; 2. kəmémərəbl], fr. Lat. *commemorābilis*, **com- & memorable.** Worthy to be commemorated.

commemorate, vb. trans. [1. komémurāt ; 2. kəmémərəit], fr. Lat. *commemorāt-(um)*, P.P. of *commemorāre*, ' to recall to memory ', fr. **com-** & *memorāre*, to ' bring to remembrance, to mention ', fr. *memor*, ' mindful of '. See **memory. 1.** (of persons) To preserve the memory of a person or event by some formal means ; to honour the memory of by solemn celebration. **2.** (of things, statues, inscriptions &c.) To serve as a reminder of, recall, and do honour to memory of.

commemoration, n. [1. komèmuráshun ; 2. kəmèməréiʃən]. **commemorate & -ion. a** The act of commemorating ; **b** solemn or merry function, any kind of public celebration in honour of the memory of persons or events. Specif. **c** (at Oxford Univ.) *Commemoration (Day)*, that on which founders are commemorated, honorary degrees conferred on distinguished persons, and prize poems, essays &c., read in public. Abbrev. Commem.

commemorative, adj. [1. komémurativ ; 2. kəmémərətiv]. **commemorate & -ive.** Pertaining to, in nature of, a commemoration ; tending to commemorate.

commemorator, n. [1. komémurātor ; 2. kəmémərəitə]. Lat. **commemorate & -or.** One who commemorates.

commemoratory, adj. [1. komémuraturi ; 2. kəmémərətri]. See prec. & **-ory.** Commemorative.

commence, vb. trans. & intrans. [1. kuméns ; 2. kəméns], fr. Fr. *commencer*, fr. Lat. **com-** & *initiāre*, ' to begin ', fr. *initium*, ' beginning '. See **initiate.** (The word has now fallen to vulgar use, and fastidious speakers more often use *begin* instead.) **A.** trans. To begin, start, enter upon : *to commence a meal* ; *to commence a law-suit* &c. **B.** intrans. **1.** To have, make, a start or beginning (of things and persons respectively), originate, start. **2.** (archaic) To begin to be, become, start as : *to commence schoolmaster, author* &c.

commencement, n. [1. kuménsment ; 2. kəménsmənt]. **commence & -ment. 1. a** The act, or process, of commencing ; beginning, origin ; **b** time at which anything begins : *at the commencement of spring* &c. **2.** Specif. (Cambridge Univ. and Trinity College, Dublin) the day on which the degrees of master and doctor are conferred.

commend, vb. trans. [1. kuménd ; 2. kəménd], fr. Lat. *commend-āre*, ' to commit to one for preservation, to entrust to one's charge ; to command, recommend ', fr. **com-** & *mandāre* ; same word as **command**, w. differentiation of meaning. **1. a** To give in charge, entrust : *to commend one's soul to God* ; **b** to recommend, introduce with favourable mention : *to commend a person to the notice of another.* **2. a** (of persons) To speak favourably of, to praise : *to commend one for his good work* ; *to be highly commended* ; **b** (of things, reflex.) to create a favourable impression, attract : *this proposal does not commend itself to me.* **3.** In greetings sent by one person to another, to remind of, mention favourably (archaic) : '*Commend me to my brother Cassius*' (Shakespeare). Phr. (facetious and ironical) *commend me to a decayed country parson for a dull dog.*

commendable, adj. [1. kuméndabl ; 2. kəméndəbl]. **commend (I.) & -able.** Worthy to be commended, deserving praise.

commendably, adv. Prec. & **-ly.** In a commendable or praiseworthy manner.

commendam, n. [1. kuméndam ; 2. kəméndæm]. Med. Lat. *in commendam depositum*, ' placed in trust ', fr. Lat. *commendātam*, P.P. acc. fem. of *commendāre.* See **commend.** (eccles.) Grant of revenues of a benefice to a bishop or layman in absence of a regular incumbent ; a practice forbidden since 1836 : *to hold a benefice in commendam.*

commendation, n. [1. kòmendáshun ; 2. kòmendéiʃən], fr. L. Lat. *commendātiōn-(em).* **commend & -ation.** The act of commending ; praise, approbation.

commendatory, adj. [1. koméndaturi ; 2. kəméndət(ə)ri]. **commend & -ate & -ory. 1. a** Serving to commend ; expressing approval ; **b** presenting to favourable notice or reception : *a commendatory letter* ; *commendatory verses* &c. **2.** (eccles.) Holding a benefice *in commendam.* See **commendam.**

commensal, n. & adj. [1. koménsl ; 2. kəménsl], fr. Med. Lat. *commensālis*, fr. **com-** & Lat. *mensa* & **-al.** *Mensa*, ' table, table for meals, the food itself ', is formed fr. P.P. type of *mētior*, ' measure ', prob. fr. idea of ' measuring, dividing, sharing out ' the food. See **measure. 1.** n. **a** One who dines at the same table as others ; a table companion ; **b** (biol.) a form of parasite ; one that lives on or is attached to another, as host, and shares its food &c. but does not get this from the host itself and is not strictly a parasite. **2.** adj. Sharing food of, parasitic in above sense.

commensalism, n. [1. koménsalizm ; 2. kəménsəlizəm]. Prec. & **-ism.** The state of being commensal.

commensurability, n. [1. komènsūrabíliti ; 2. kəmènsjərəbíliti]. Next word & **-ity.** Quality of being commensurable.

commensurable, adj. [1. koménsūrabl ; 2. kəménsjərəbl]. See **commensurate & -able. a** Capable of being measured, or judged, by the same standard ; **b** proportionate to, suitably proportioned.

commensurably, adv. Prec. & **-ly.** Proportionally.

commensurate, adj. [1. koménsūrāt ; 2. kəménsjərəit]. Lat. **com-** & *mensūra*, ' measure ' (see **mensuration**), & **-ate.** Lat. has *commensum*, P.P. of *commētior*, ' measure with, or by, something, to proportion '. Proportioned to, in proper proportion with, adapted to capacity of : *a dinner commensurate with one's appetite.*

commensurately, adv. Prec. & **-ly.** Proportionally.

commensurateness, n. See prec. & **-ness.** Fact, state, of being commensurate.

comment (I.), n. [1. kóment ; 2. kóment]. Lat. *commentum*, ' invention, fabrication, fiction ; mechanical contrivance ', P.P. of *comminiscor*, ' contrive, devise, fabricate ', fr. **com-** & base **ment-*, ' mind '. See **mental, mind. a** A remark, observation, made and uttered upon any subject, in conversation or writing, expressing some view or opinion upon what is happening or being said ; **b** specif., learned note of an explanatory character, made by editor of a literary or learned work, designed to make the author's meaning more intelligible, supplement gaps in his knowledge &c.

comment (II.), vb. intrans. [1. kóment ; 2. kóment], more rarely [1. komént ; 2. kəmént]. See prec. **1.** To refer to something that is said or has happened, expressing a view of some sort. **2.** To write notes, intended to be explanatory, supplementary &c. upon a text or book.

commentary, n. [1. kómentari ; 2. kóməntəri]. Lat. *commentārium.* See prec. & **-ary. a** Collection of critical remarks upon text, or author, either as separate treatise, and independent of the work, or scattered throughout the book ; the latter is called *running commentary* ; **b** persistently and continuously uttered series of remarks upon events, or upon another's statements : *to keep up a running commentary on a speech* &c.

commentation, n. [1. kòmentáshun ; 2. kòmentéiʃən], fr. Lat. *commentātiōn-(em).* See **comment (II.) & -ation.** Act of making comments (on texts &c.) ; annotation.

commentator, n. [1. kómentàtur ; 2. kómentèitə]. **comment & -ate & -or.** Writer of a commentary, of annotations.

commerce, n. [1. kómërs ; 2. kómʌs]. Fr., fr. Lat. *commercium*, ' legal capacity to buy and sell ; trade, traffic ', fr. **com-** & *merx*, acc. *mercem*, ' merchandise '. See **market, merchant. 1.** The business of buying and selling, exchanging and distributing goods of all kinds (used esp. of large transactions) ; also of financial business involved in this traffic ; *Chamber of Commerce*, organization for promotion and regulation of trade and commerce in a particular town or district. **2. a** Social intercourse and dealing generally : *to have but little commerce with one's neighbours* ; **b** (archaic, rare) sexual relations.

commerce-destroyer, n. Armed vessel designed for destruction and capture of an enemy's merchant vessels in time of war.

commercial, adj. & n. [1. kumérshal ; 2. kəmʌ́ʃl]. **commerce & -ial. 1.** adj. Connected with, having character of, adapted to, commerce : *commercial pursuits, man, education* &c. **2.** n. (colloq.) A commercial traveller.

commercialism, n. [1. kumérshalizm ; 2. kəmʌ́ʃəlizm]. Prec. & **-ism.** State of mind, habit of thought which regards everything from point of view of commerce or material profit and loss, and is blind to other aspects of human life and activity.

commercialist, n. [1. kumérshalist ; 2. kəmʌ́ʃəlist]. See prec. & **-ist.** One suffering from commercialism.

commercialize, vb. trans. [1. kumérshalīz ; 2. kəmʌ́ʃəlaiz]. **commercial & -ize. a** To turn a transaction unconnected with commerce into a matter of profit and loss ; **b** to put on the market, render an object of commerce.

commercially, adv. [1. kumérshali ; 2. kəmʌ́ʃəli]. **commercial & -ly.** From point of view of commerce, as a business matter.

commercial room, n. One at an inn, devoted to commercial travellers, in which they take their meals, or can interview their clients.

commercial traveller, n. Person employed by manufacturer, or wholesale dealer, to travel about the country and commend goods and merchandise to those (smaller traders and shopkeepers) who deal direct with the consumer ; the traveller shows specimens (' samples ') of the things his employers have to sell, and tries to induce those whom he visits to buy them.

commination, n. [1. kòmináshun ; 2. kòminéiʃən]. Fr., fr. Lat. *comminātiōn-(em)*, ' a threatening ', fr. *comminārī*, fr. **com-** & *minārī*, ' to threaten '. See **minatory. a** Threatening, denunciation of punishment or vengeance, esp. divine vengeance ; **b** specif., *commination service*, one said on Ash Wednesday in the Church of England, in which God's curse is pronounced against certain sins.

comminatory, adj. [1. kóminaturi ; 2. kóminətəri]. Lat. *comminăt-* (see prec.) & **-ory.** Threatening, denunciatory.

commingle, vb. trans. & intrans. [1. komínggl ; 2. komíŋgl]. See **com- & mingle.** To intermingle, mix together.

comminute, vb. trans. [1. kóminūt ; 2. kóminjūt], fr. Lat. *comminūtum*, P.P. of *comminuere*, ' to separate into small parts, break into pieces ', fr. **com-** & *minuere*, ' to make small, lessen ', cp. *minor*, ' less '. See **minute (I.), minish** &c. **a** To divide, split up into small particles (of ore) ; **b** divide into portions (of an estate &c.).

comminuted, adj. [1. kòminúted; 2. kòmìnjútid]. P.P. of prec. (surg.) *Comminuted fracture*, one in which the bone is splintered, or smashed to pieces.

comminution, n. [1. kòminúshun; 2. kòmìnjúʃən]. **comminute** & **-ion**. **a** Act or process of comminuting; **b** gradual lessening and wearing away.

commiserate, vb. intrans. & trans. [1. kumízerāt; 2. kəmízəreit], fr. Lat. *commiserāt-(um)*, P.P. of *commiserāri*, 'to bewail', fr. **com-** & *miserāri*, 'to pity, deplore', fr. *miser*, 'wretched'. See **miser, misery**. To feel and express compassion, sympathy, with a person, in sufferings, misfortune &c.: *to commiserate with (a person)*; *commiserate a misfortune*.

commiseration, n. [1. kumìzeráshun; 2. kəmìzəréiʃən]. Prec. & **-ion**. Pity, compassion, for the sufferings or distresses of others.

commissar, see **commissary, 4.**

commissarial, adj. [1. kòmisárial; 2. kòmiséəriəl]. See **commissary** & **-al**. Pertaining to a commissary.

commissariat, n. [1. kòmisáriat; 2. kòmiséəriət]. Fr., 'body of commissaries'. See **commissary** & **-ate**. (mil.) **a** Department of an army charged with the supply of provisions; **b** food supply itself.

commissary, n. [1. kómisari; 2. kómisəri], fr. Low Lat. *commissārius*, 'person in charge', fr. Lat. *commiss-(um)*, P.P. of *committere*, 'make over, entrust, give in charge', & **-ary**. See **commit**. **1.** One to whom any charge, duty, or office is entrusted by authority; **a** deputy, delegate. **2.** Specif. (eccles.) representative of a bishop deputed by him to exercise his jurisdiction in certain circumstances, or in parts of his diocese. **3.** (obs.) Officer in charge of commissariat or supply services of an army. **4.** (also *commissar*, chiefly a Russian Soviet usage) Person in charge of a special state department, a commissioner.

commissary court, n. Ecclesiastical court of a bishop's commissary, in diocese of Canterbury, same as *Consistory Court*.

commission (**I.**), n. [1. kumíshun; 2. kəmíʃən]. Lat. *commissiōn-(em)*, 'letting together; beginning of a fight or game', fr. *commiss-(um)*, P.P. type of *committere*, the first meaning of wh. is 'to let together, join, unite'. The Engl. meanings of *commission* are due to one of the many derived meanings, 'entrust' &c., in close relation w. our uses of **commit**. See **mission**. **1. a** Formal document authorizing a person or persons to act in a certain way, perform certain functions, hold certain offices &c.; **b** specif., warrant signed by the king, conferring a certain military or naval rank (usually the lowest, on his joining the army &c.) upon a person, and entitling him to enjoy and exercise the authority belonging to that rank in the British Army, Navy, or Air Force; **c** authority, power to act, as conveyed by a formal warrant, esp. as a magistrate: *commission of the peace*. **2. a** Authorization to act for another, in purchasing something on his behalf, or otherwise as his agent; **b** payment made for such service (e.g. *an auctioneer's commission* for selling, or buying in, something on one's behalf); **c** small services rendered, purchases made, messages delivered, small business transacted by a person as a favour to another: *I have one or two commissions for you if you are going into town*. **3.** Body of persons entrusted by the State with the duties and powers of holding an inquiry, issuing a report, and sometimes with power to act on their opinions: *Royal Commission*. Phr. *in commission*, vested in, entrusted to, a body of commissioners, of an office of state during temporary vacancy. *Commission of array*, method of raising soldiers, employed in England from 13th to 17th cents., whereby an official was commissioned by the sovereign to raise so many men in each district. **4.** Act of carrying out, perpetrating, an action (usually in bad sense): *the commission of murder*.

commission (**II.**), vb. trans., fr. prec. **1.** To give a commission to (in various senses). **2.** Specif., to give authority to naval officer to command, man, arm, and prepare for sea a ship of war.

commissionaire, n. [1. komìshunár; 2. kəmìʃənéə]. Fr., **commisioner**. **1.** A person in uniform who acts as door porter in large shops and offices &c. **2.** Specif., one of a body of old soldiers of good character, *the Corps of Commissionaires*, organized for such services.

commissioned, adj. [1. kumíshund; 2. kəmíʃənd]. **commission** (**II.**) & **-ed**. Having, holding, provided with a commission, esp. in military sense: *commissioned officer*, one (from second lieutenant upwards) holding H.M. commission, as distinct from a *non-commissioned officer*.

commissioner, n. [1. kumíshuner; 2. kəmíʃənə]. **commission** (**II.**) & **-er**. **1. a** A member of a commission, esp. a Royal Commission; **b** person appointed to act by himself in investigating or deciding some difficult question of law or government. **2.** Specif., a high officer in the Indian Civil Service, in charge of a large district of a province. **3.** *High Commissioner*; **a** chief representative of a self-governing British Dominion in England; **b** representative of the king at the General Assembly of the Church of Scotland.

commissionership, n. [1. kumíshunership; 2. kəmíʃənəʃip]. Prec. & **-ship**. Office of a commissioner.

commissure, n. [1. kómisūr; 2. kómisjuə]. Fr., fr. Lat. *commissūra*, 'joint, seam', fr. *commiss-*, as in P.P. of *committere*. See **commit** & **commission**. (anat.) Junction between two parts or organs of the body, or between two parts of the same organ.

commit, vb. trans. [1. kumít; 2. kəmít], fr. Lat. *committere*, lit. 'put, join together'; hence, 'to go to work, act; to do wrong, perpetrate; make over, entrust', fr. **com-** & *mittere*, 'to send' &c. See **missile** & **mission**. **1.** To entrust, consign, give into keeping; (in various senses) **a** bestow, put away in: '*We commit his body to the ground*'; **b** (law) to send for trial before higher tribunal: *to commit a prisoner for trial*; **c** to put into custody: *commit a person to jail*; **d** to entrust to guardianship and keeping, commend: *to commit one's soul to God, to God's mercy*; **e** to send (a bill, question for report &c.) to a committee. Phrs. *to commit to memory*, impress upon memory, memorize, learn by heart; *commit to paper, writing*, to write down. **2.** To pledge, engage, bind morally or legally: *to commit oneself (or others) to a particular action*. **3.** To carry out, perpetrate, an act (always in bad sense): *to commit sin, a crime, an offence* &c.

commitment, n. [1. kumítment; 2. kəmítmənt]. **commit** & **-ment**. **a** That to which one is committed, pledged; **b** financial liability which has been entered into.

committable, adj. [1. kumítabl; 2. kəmítəbl]. **commit** & **-able**. **a** (of persons) Liable to be committed to prison or for trial; **b** (of offences) of such a character as to permit committing perpetrator for trial.

committal, n. [1. kumítal; 2. kəmítəl]. **commit** & **-al**. **a** Act of committing (an offence); **b** act of pledging, involving oneself in particular action &c.; **c** act of consigning, entrusting in various senses; **d** committing to prison of a person by order of a court.

committee, n. [1. kumíti; 2. kəmíti], fr. A.-Fr. *comité*. See **commit** & **-ee**. **1.** Group of persons appointed to consider, and report on, specific questions referred to them; esp. a number of members of a larger body appointed by this, jointly to do certain business, draft a scheme, or generally to prepare some items of business for consideration of body which appoints them: *standing committee*. **2.** Specif. (English Houses of Parliament) either house *goes into, resolves itself into, Committee*, in order to consider any bill in detail. **3.** (law) [1. kòmitḗ; 2. kòmitī]. Person to whom the charge of another, esp. a lunatic and his estates &c., is legally entrusted.

committee English, n. Style often adopted by committees in their reports, or by official bodies, which consists of a number of set formulae and clichés, and from which all individuality and emotion are eliminated.

commix, vb. trans. & intrans. [1. komíks; 2. kəmíks]. **com-** & **mix**. To mix, blend (archaic).

commixtion, n. [1. komíkschun; 2. kəmíkstʃən]. Also **commixture**. Prec., w. *-t-*, as from *mixt*, & **-ion**. (eccles.) Act of putting a small particle of the Host into the chalice by the priest at Mass, to be consumed by him together with the wine. Cp. *intinction*.

commixture, n. [1. komíkschur; 2. kəmíkstʃə]. **com-** & **mixture**. **1. a** Act of mixing; **b** things blended together. **2.** (eccles.) Commixtion.

commode, n. [1. kumṓd; 2. kəmóud]. Fr., fr. Lat. *commodus*, lit. 'measured with', hence, 'well-adapted, suitable, convenient', fr. **com-** & *modus*, 'standard by which anything is measured; a measure'. See **mode**. **1.** Chest of drawers. **2.** (also *night-commode*) Small portable privy for use in bedroom.

commodious, adj. [1. kumṓdius; 2. kəmóudiəs], fr. Fr. *commodieux*, fr. L. Lat. *commodiōsus*. See prec. & **-ous**. Having ample room, spacious, esp. of *houses, apartments* &c.

commodiously, adv. Prec. & **-ly**. In a roomy, convenient manner.

commodiousness, n. See prec. & **-ness**. Quality of being commodious.

commodity, n. [1. kumóditi; 2. kəmóditi]. Fr. *commodité*, fr. Lat. *commoditāt-(em)*, fr. *commodus*. See **commode**. Something adapted for use and convenience, hence, an article of commerce of any kind; anything that is for sale, esp. in pl., *commodities*, goods, merchandise, produce.

commodore, n. [1. kómodōr; 2. kómədō]. Earlier *commandore*, fr. L. Lat. *commandātor*, 'commander'. See **command** & **-ate** & **-or**, **1.** Captain in Royal Navy, discharging duties rather more important than those usually undertaken by a captain; e.g. *the commodore of a squadron*. *Commodore* is not a rank, and is only borne as a courtesy title, thus resembling *brigadier-general*. **2.** Term applied to senior captains of merchant-fleet, and to the president of yacht squadrons &c.

common (**I.**), adj. [1. kómun; 2. kómən], fr. Fr. *commun*, fr. Lat. *commūnis*, O. Lat. *commoinos*, 'shared together, common to all'; fr. **com-** & *mūnus*, O. Lat. *moinos*, 'service, office, function, duty'. The compound is apparently a very old one, since the corresponding form is found in Gmc.; Goth. *gamáins*, O.E. *gemǣne* (see **mean** (**III.**)), O.H.G. *giméini*, 'common', Mod. Germ. *gemein*. For identity of **com-** & Gmc. **ga-* see etymol. of former; for etymol. of *mūnus, mūnia*, see **municipal**. **1.** General, shared equally by several or many individuals, or by all members of a group; **a** used by, accessible to, at disposal of, all or many: *common high road; common interests, advantage; Book of Common Prayer; common law*, unwritten law of England, based on immemorial custom and usage; Phrs. *common woman*, prostitute; *common table*, one at which all dine; *common land*, that in which all members of community have rights of pasturage; **b** (i) having same source, origin: *common descendants*; (ii) being the source, origin &c. of all members of a group: *common ancestor, common mother tongue*; Phr. *our common humanity*; **c** participated in as joint pledge, involving equal obligations on all: *common agreement, treaty, undertaking*. Phrs. *to make common cause*, take joint action; *by common consent*. **2. a** Widespread, usual, generally current: *common coin of the realm; the common daisy*; '*the trivial round, the common task*'; Phrs. *common or garden*, very familiar, everyday; *common* *honesty,* mere, average, honesty; *common sense,* ordinary intelligence, practical sense; **b** of frequent occurrence: *a common experience, event, accident*; **c** ordinary, undistinguished by rank: *the common people, a common soldier*; *the common man,* plain, average citizen; **d** (of non-material things) known to all, current, in everyone's mouth: *common knowledge, talk, rumour, report.* **3.** In disparaging or unfavourable sense: **a** (of persons and their behaviour &c.) vulgar, lacking distinction or refinement; ill-bred, plebeian; characteristic of coarse, uncultivated persons, esp. of those unacquainted with usages of good society: *common manners, accent, appearance*; **b** (of material things, esp. commodities) ill-made, shoddy, lacking style, or exhibiting bad style: *common clothes, furniture, decoration*; *common make of goods* &c. **4. a** (gram.) *Common noun,* one applicable to any member of a group, distinguished from *proper noun*; **b** (math.) belonging to several quantities: *common factor.*

common (II.), n., fr. prec. **1.** An unenclosed tract of land accessible to the public, on which certain types of tenants have rights of feeding cattle, geese &c.; a common is not the property of the lord of the manor, or other individual. **2.** (law) A person's right in or over another's land: *right of common*; *common of pasturage, common of piscary* &c. **3.** (pl. *commons*) The common people of the realm; specific branch of the legislature, those who are neither princes of the blood nor peers: *House of Commons,* the assembly of elected representatives of the people; chamber in which these transact the business of Parliament.

commonable, adj. [1. kómunabl; 2. kómənəbl], fr. **common (II.)** & **-able.** (of cattle &c., such as plough and manure the land). Allowed to pasture on common land.

commonage, n. [1. kómunij; 2. kómənidž], fr. **common (II.)** & **-age.** Cp. O. Fr. *communage.* **1.** The right of pasturing on a common. **2.** The commons of the realm.

commonalty, n. [1. kómunalti; 2. kómənəlti], fr. O. Fr. *communalté,* fr. *communal,* fr. Lat. *commūnālis.* **common (I.)** & **-al** & **-ty.** The common people, the commons.

commoner, n. [1. kómuner; 2. kómənə]. **common** & **-er. 1.** One of the common people (below the rank of peer). **2. a** One who is not a peer; **b** a member of the House of Commons (rare); esp. *the great Commoner,* William Pitt the elder. **3.** One having right of common (see **common (II.)**). **4.** (Oxford Univ.) An undergraduate member of the university who is not on the foundation of his college; one who is neither fellow, scholar, nor exhibitioner.

commonly, adv. [1. kómunli; 2. kómənli]. **common (I.)** & **-ly.** In most senses of *common,* esp. usually, ordinarily, as a rule.

commonness, n. [1. kómunnis; 2. kómənnis]. See prec. & **-ness.** The state of being common; specif., vulgarity, lack of breeding, want of familiarity with best usage in manners, speech &c.

commonplace, n. & adj. [1. kómunplās; 2. kómənpleis]. See **common (I.)** & **place,** & cp. Lat. *loci commūnes,* 'common topics', & Fr. *lieu commun,* 'common place'. **1.** n. **a** Anything common, ordinary, or trite, esp. a trite or obvious remark, a platitude; **b** *the commonplace,* triteness, lack of interesting and striking qualities, matter-of-factness. **2.** adj. Lacking originality, trite, ordinary.

commonplace-book, n. Book in which are entered passages and poems, remarks, epigrams &c., original, or borrowed from the works of others.

commonplaceness, n. [1. kómunplàsnes; 2. kómənplèisnis]. Quality of being commonplace.

common room, n. A room or set of rooms at a college, esp. at Oxford University, for the social and business use of the Fellows, usually *senior common room*; *junior common room,* similar room or rooms for the use of undergraduates.

commons, n. pl. [1. kómunz; 2. kómənz]. See **common (I.) 1.** The common people (see **common (II.), 3**). **2. a** Provisions to be shared in common; hence, allowance of food, rations. Phr. *short commons,* insufficient food; **b** (Oxford and Cambridge) portion of food supplied at a fixed charge: *a commons of bread, butter, beer* &c.; **c** company eating at a common table; survives only in *Doctors' Commons,* q.v.

Common Serjeant, n. Law officer of City of London who sits as judge at Central Criminal Court, and in Lord Mayor's Court.

commonwealth, n. [1. kómunwelth; 2. kómənwelþ], fr. **common (I.)** & **wealth. 1.** An independent political community; the body politic, the state: *for the good of the commonwealth.* **2.** A republic; specif. (cap.) period during which Cromwell was Protector. **3.** (cap.) Title granted to Federated States of Australia.

commotion, n. [1. kumóshun; 2. kəmóuʃən], fr. Lat. *commōtiōn-(em),* 'violent movement, disturbance, excitement', fr. *commōt-(um),* P.P. of *commovēre,* 'to move violently, disturb, stir', fr. **com-** & *movēre,* 'to move'. See **motion.** Violent motion, agitation, tumult, disturbance: **a** (in nature) *commotion of the waves* &c.; **b** (in polit. and social affairs) riot, rising, noisy fuss; **c** (of the mental or physical organism) excitement, upset: *commotion of the nerves, spirits* &c.

communal, adj. [1. kómūnal; 2. kómjunəl], fr. L. Lat. *commūnālis,* fr. *commūna,* fr. Lat. *commūnis.* See **common (I.). 1.** Belonging to the community; common, public: *communal property.* **2.** Specif. (India) of the different religious or racial communities, in a district, esp. of Hindu and Moslem: *communal voting, elections* &c.; *communal disturbances* &c.

communalism, n. [1. kómūnalizm; 2. kómjunəlizəm]. Prec. & **-ism.** System in which communes, or small political unities, have considerable legislative powers delegated by the central government.

communalist, n. [1. kómūnalist; 2. kómjunəlist]. **communal** & **-ist.** One who lives under, or who favours, communalism.

communalistic, adj. [1. kòmūnalístik; 2. kòmjunəlístik]. Prec. & **-ic.** Connected with, characterized by, communalism.

communalization, n. [1. kómūnalīzáshun; 2. kómjunəlaizéiʃən]. Next word & **-ation.** Transference of property to a community.

communalize, vb. trans. [1. kómūnalīz; 2. kómjunəlaiz]. **communal** & **-ize.** To make over to, vest (property) in, a community.

commune (I.), n. [1. kómūn; 2. kómjūn]. Fr., fr. L. Lat. *commūna,* fr. Lat. *commūnis.* See **common (I.). 1.** (in France and some other countries as Belgium, Italy, Spain) A small political unit, district, under the government of a mayor and a municipal council, with considerable degree of independence of central government. **2.** Specif., *Paris Commune,* municipality of Paris, which, in 1792 and 1871, overrode and overthrew the supreme government of the country, bringing about revolution and terrorism.

commune (II.), vb. intrans. [1. kómūn; 2. kómjūn]; more rarely [1. kumū́n; 2. kəmjū́n], fr. Fr. *communier,* fr. Lat. *commūnicāre.* See **communicate.** (followed by *with*) To hold intimate and familiar converse.

communicability, n. [1. kumūnikabíliti; 2. kəmjūnikəbíliti]. Next word & **-ity. 1.** Capacity, capability, of being communicated. **2.** The quality of frankness, openness of speech, communicativeness.

communicable, adj. [1. kumū́nikabl; 2. kəmjū́nikəbl], fr. L. Lat. *commūnicābilis,* fr. Lat. *commūnicāre.* See **communicate.** Capable of being communicated, transferred, imparted **a** from one mind to another (of thoughts, states of mind &c.); **b** (of material things, esp. of disease) transmissible, capable of being handed on.

communicant, adj. & n. [1. kumū́nikant; 2. kəmjū́nikənt], fr. Lat. *commūnicant-(em),* Pres. Part. of *commūnicāre.* See **communicate. 1.** adj. Communicating, esp. (anat.) *communicant with* (of nerves and arteries). **2.** n. **a** Specif., one who communicates at the celebration of Holy Communion; **b** one who imparts information.

communicate, vb. trans. & intrans. [1. kumū́nikāt; 2. kəmjū́nikeit], fr. Lat. *commūnicāt-(um),* P.P. of *commūnicāre,* 'to share with others, have in common; impart', fr. *commūnis,* 'common to several'. See **common (I.). A.** trans. **1.** To impart, transmit, hand on, to another, or to others (always non-material things): *to communicate news, opinions, ideas* &c. **2.** To pass on, transmit (a disease). **B.** intrans. **1.** (followed by *with*) To hold social intercourse with; to impart, or interchange, thoughts, ideas, opinions &c. by speech or writing: *to communicate with one's friends*; *communicate by telegram.* **2.** (of spaces, rooms, houses) To be connected with each other by means of a passage, opening, or other mode of access: *this garden communicates with the next by a gate*; *three rooms communicating,* adjoining each other and having doors between. **3.** Specif., to receive the Sacrament at Holy Communion.

communication, n. [1. kumūnikáshun; 2. kəmjūnikéiʃən], fr. Lat. *commūnicātiōn-(em).* See **communicate** & **-ion. 1.** The act of communicating; the imparting or interchange of ideas, opinions, sentiments &c.; correspondence: *to be in communication with.* **2.** That which is communicated, a letter, a message, information imparted by speech, writing &c.: *to receive a communication.* **3. a** A means of communicating: *communication between England and Iceland is rather slow*; *there is no direct communication between the two wings of the house*; **b** specif. (mil.) means of communication of every sort between an army in the field and its base, e.g. roads, railways, bridges, telegraph wires &c.; known collectively as *lines of communication.*

communication-cord, n. Cord running through railway carriages, by pulling which passengers can communicate with the guard while the train is travelling.

communicative, adj. [1. kumū́nikativ; 2. kəmjū́nikətiv]. **communicate** & **-ive.** Inclined to communicate; ready to converse with, and to impart information to others; talkative, reverse of *reserved.*

communicatively, adv. Prec. & **-ly.** Freespokenly.

communicativeness, n. See prec. & **-ness.** Quality or habit of being communicative.

communicator, n. [1. kumū́nikātur; 2. kəmjū́nikeitə]. **communicate** & **-or.** Person who, thing which, communicates; specif., part of telegraph instrument; contrivance on trains for calling guard.

communion, n. [1. kumū́nyun; 2. kəmjū́njən], fr. Lat. *commūniōn-(em),* 'fellowship, a common share or interest', fr. *commūnis,* see **common (I.)** & **-ion. 1. a** Common participation in something; **b** fellowship, close and intimate relations between two or more persons; **c** intimate, heart-searching introspection: *to hold communion with oneself*; **d** specif., organized religious body holding the same specific tenets, and having the same hierarchy: *religious communion*; *to be of the same communion.* **2.** (cap.) **a** Celebration of the Eucharist, at which the people communicate: *to go to Communion*; **b** specif., individual act of partaking: *to make one's Easter Communion.*

Communion cup, n. That which contains the wine at Holy Communion, a chalice.

communionist, n. [1. kumū́nyunist; 2. kəmjū́njənist]. **communion** & **-ist.** One who holds a specific and strict theory regarding Holy Communion.

Communion service, n. **a** A celebration of Holy Communion; **b** the prescribed order, or office, for this.

Communion table, n. Altar at which Holy Communion is celebrated.

communiqué, n. [1. komū́nikā; 2. kəmjū́nikei]. Fr., P.P. of *communiquer*, lit. 'something communicated'. See **communicate**. Official bulletin, or statement, containing information on a matter of public concern.

communism, n. [1. kómūnizm; 2. kómjunizəm], fr. Fr. *communisme*, fr. *commun* & **-ism**. See **common (I.)**. Theory that all should possess and enjoy property in common, and that individual ownership should be abolished; the most extreme form of socialism, as established in Russia, under the 'Soviet' system of government; the so-called 'Dictatorship of the Proletariat'.

communist, n. & adj. [1. kómūnist; 2. kómjunist]. See prec. & **-ist**. **a** n. One who holds the doctrine of communism; **b** adj., communistic.

communistic, adj. [1. kòmūnístik; 2. kòmjunístik]. **communist** & **-ic**. Pertaining to communism and communists; pervaded by, based on, according to, communism.

communitarian, n. [1. kòmūnitárian; 2. kòmjūnitéəriən]. **community** & **-arian**. Member of a community practising communism.

community, n. [1. kumū́niti; 2. kəmjū́niti], fr. Lat. *commūnitāt-(em)*, 'fellowship', fr. *commūnis*. See **common (I.)** & **-ity**. **1. a** A society of people living in proximity to each other, in one locality, under same conditions of life, and having some common bond of organization, political or religious, which makes them a more or less closely knit unit; **b** a society of people with common interests, occupations, or fads, who live a common life; (by extension) **c** *the community*, the public. **2. a** Sharing by all alike, common possession or enjoyment: *community of goods, wealth* &c.; **b** possession of a common character or nature: *community of race, religion* &c.

communization, n. [1. kòmūnīzáshun; 2. kòmjunaizéiʃən]. See next word & **-ation**. Act of rendering anything common property.

communize, vb. trans. [1. kómūnīz; 2. kómjunaiz], fr. Lat. *commūn-(is)*, see **common (I.)**, & **-ize**. To make into common property; to make public.

commutable, adj. [1. kumū́tabl; 2. kəmjū́təbl], fr. Lat. *commūtābilis*, 'subject to change, changeable', fr. *commūtāre*, see **commute**, & **-able**. Capable of being commuted.

commutation, n. [1. kòmūtáshun; 2. kòmjutéiʃən], fr. Lat. *commūtātiōn-(em)*, 'a changing', fr. *commūtāre*, see **commute** & **-ation**. **1.** The act of commuting, exchanging, or substituting one thing for another, esp. the substitution of one kind of payment for another, or money for service owed, &c.: *commutation of tithes*. **2.** (law) A reduction of the penalty imposed by sentence of a judge, esp. *commutation of the death penalty* (to penal servitude for life).

commutative, adj. [1. kumū́tativ; 2. kəmjū́tətiv]. See prec. & **-ive**. Pertaining to substitution; interchangeable, mutual.

commutator, n. [1. kómūtātur; 2. kómjuteitə]. See prec., **commute**, & **-or**. Device for altering direction or polarity of electric current; in a dynamo it converts alternating into direct current and collects it.

commute, vb. trans. [1. kumū́t; 2. kəmjū́t], fr. Lat. *commūtāre*, 'to change entirely; to exchange (in trade)', fr. **com-** & *mūtāre*, 'to change'. See **mutable**. To exchange, substitute; **a** one kind or mode of payment for another: *to commute a pension* &c.; **b** one punishment for another, a lesser for a greater: *to commute the death penalty* (to imprisonment for life).

commuter, n. [1. kumū́ter; 2. kəmjū́tə]. Prec. & **-er**. **a** Commutator; **b** (in U.S.A.) a season-ticket holder.

comose, adj. [1. kómōs; 2. kóumous], fr. Lat. *comōsus*, fr. *coma*, 'hair', fr. Gk. *kómē*, 'hair'. See **coma (II.)** & **-ose**. (bot.) Hairy.

compact (I.), n. [1. kómpakt; 2. kómpækt], fr. Lat. *compactum*, 'an agreement', fr. *compactum*, P.P. of *compaciscor*, 'I make an agreement with', fr. **com-** & *paciscor*, 'make a bargain'. See **pact**. Agreement, bargain, understanding between parties.

compact (II.), adj. [1. kumpákt; 2. kəmpǽkt], fr. Lat. *compact-(um)*, P.P. of *compingere*, 'to fix or fasten together, unite', fr. **com-** & *pangere*, 'to fasten, fix'. This vb. is fr. same base as *paciscor*, 'settle, fix up', the latter expressing 'fixing, settlement', of non-material things, the former of material things also. See **impinge, impact, pact**, & **pax**. **1. a** Closely and firmly, tightly, put together; hence, **b** lying within small compass, fitting neatly together; **c** dense, firm (in texture), solid; **d** (fig., of persons) well-knit. **2.** (of style) Concise, condensed, terse.

compacted, adj. [1. kumpákted; 2. kəmpǽktid], fr. obs. vb. *compact*. See prec. Closely stowed, firmly packed together: *compacted earth* &c.; '*A box where sweets compacted lie*' (Geo. Herbert).

compactly, adv. [1. kumpáktli; 2. kəmpǽktli]. **compact (II.)** & **-ly**. **a** In a compact, closely packed condition; **b** succinctly, tersely.

compactness, n. [1. kumpáktnes; 2. kəmpǽktnis]. **compact (II.)** & **-ness**. Quality of being compact.

compages, n. [1. kompájēz; 2. kəmpéidʒīz]. Lat., 'fastening, joint, fabric, framework', fr. **pag-*, base of *pangere*. See **compact (II.)**. Framework, structure of many parts joined together.

compaginate, vb. trans. [1. kumpájināt; 2. kəmpǽdʒineit], fr. L. Lat. *compāgināt-(um)*, P.P. of *compāgināre*, fr. Lat. *compāgo*, genit. *compāginis*, 'fastening, connexion'. Cp. prec. To join or fit together.

compagination, n. [1. kumpàjináshun; 2. kəmpæ̀dʒinéiʃən]. See prec. & **-ion**. (obs.) Something fixed together.

companion (I.), n. [1. kumpányun; 2. kəmpǽnjən], fr. O. Fr. *compainon*, Mod. Fr. *compagnon*, formed w. suff. **-ion**, fr. Low Lat. *compānies*, 'company taking meals together', fr. **com-** & *pānis*, 'bread'. For etymol. of the last see **panification**, also **food**. **1. a** One who is associated with, supports and accompanies, another, on a journey, expedition, or enterprise: *the companions of the Conqueror*; *companion-in-arms*; **b** associate, confederate in, sharer of: *companion in crime*; *companion of his misery* &c.; **c** permanent associate, friend, mate, spouse: *a faithful companion for forty years*; **d** one being, or found, casually, and fortuitously, in another's company: *my companion in the railway-carriage was a total stranger to me*; **e** sociable, friendly, cheerful, amiable person, esp. one who shares another's tastes and interests: *a first-rate companion*; *a poor companion*; *not much of a companion*. **2.** Specif., a woman who lives with another at the latter's charge, as friend and helper in the household. **3.** (cap.) a Member of lowest grade of an order of knighthood: *Companion of the Bath* &c.; **b** member of a grade in orders, which have lower grades, as *Companion of British Empire*. **4.** A thing that matches another, the other of a pair: *companion vase, portrait* &c. **5.** (fig.) Title of handbook, esp. of an educational or religious type, a guide: '*The Young Sugar-Broker's Companion*'.

companion (II.), n. Ital. (*camera della*) *compagna*, 'store-room', also Du. *kompanje*. See prec. (naut.) Framing or skylight on quarter-deck through which light passes to the cabins &c. below.

companion (III.), vb. trans. See **companion (I.)**. To act as companion to, accompany.

companionable, adj. [1. kumpányunabl; 2. kəmpǽnjənəbl]. **companion (I.)** & **-able**. Suitable to be, having qualities of, a good companion; sociable, easy to get on with.

companionableness, n. Prec. & **-ness**. Quality of being companionable.

companionably, adv. **companionable** & **-ly**. In a sociable, friendly manner.

companion-hatch, n. Covering of companion-way.

companion-hatchway, n. Opening in deck of a ship leading below.

companion-ladder, n. One leading down companion hatchway.

companionship, n. [1. kumpányunship; 2. kəmpǽnjənʃip]. **companion (I.)** & **-ship**. **1. a** Friendly, intimate association, social fellowship: *to enjoy the companionship of a person*; **b** (cap.) rank of Companion of an Order of Knighthood. **2.** (print.) Group of compositors working under a foreman.

companion-way, n. **companion (II.)** & **way**. Staircase leading from deck of a ship to cabins &c. below.

company, n. [1. kúmpani; 2. kámpəni], fr. O. Fr. *compainie*, fr. L. Lat. *compānia*. See **companion (I.)**. **1. a** The state of being associated, gathered together, or assembled, with others in friendly social intercourse; Phrs. *to keep, bear, a person company*, remain with for companionship; *to part company (with)*, discontinue association; **b** group of persons so assembled; specif., number of persons invited for a festal occasion, guests, a party: *to have company present*; *to see a great deal of company*; **c** social gifts and qualities, capacity for companionship: *to find a person poor company*; *to like his company*. **2. a** Any collection or gathering of persons; esp. with common purpose or bond: '*the glorious company of the Apostles*'; **b** specif. (military unit) one fourth of a battalion, commanded by a major or captain; (also attrib.) *company commander*; *company sergeant-major* &c. **3.** Habitual associates: *to keep good, bad, company*; *get into bad company*. Phr. *to err in good company*, to share views held by persons of repute. **4. a** Association of persons formed for trading purposes: *East India Company*; *joint stock and limited liability company*; **b** party of actors playing together under common management: *a theatrical company*; **c** the crew, hands, on a ship: *ship's company*.

comparability, n. [1. kòmparabíliti; 2. kòmpərəbíliti]. Next word & **-ity**. (rare) Comparison.

comparable, adj. [1. kómparabl; 2. kómpərəbl], fr. Lat. *comparābilis*. See **compare (I.)** & **-able**. Able or fit to be compared (*with* or *to*); as **a** having certain points of resemblance; or, **b** having the same degree, or kind, of merit. Phr. *this is not at all comparable to (with) that*, is not nearly so good.

comparative, adj. [1. kumpárativ; 2. kəmpǽrətiv], fr. Lat. *comparātīvus*, 'suitable for or pertaining to comparison', fr. *comparāt-(um)*, P.P. of *comparāre*. See **compare (I.)** & **-ive**. **1. a** Involving, based on comparison, esp. on the comparison of resemblances and differences in a particular branch of study or science: *comparative philology*; *comparative anatomy*; **b** having the power of making comparisons: *the comparative faculty*. **2.** Judged by comparison, relative to something else, not absolute, qualified by comparison with some other thing or state; hence moderate: *comparative merits*; *in comparative comfort*; *with comparative ease*. **3.** (gram.) *Comparative degree* of an adjective, or adverb, form with suffix *-er*, or the uninflected form preceded by *more*: *healthier, more generous*, expressing an enhancement of the quality expressed by simple, positive form of adj. &c. Also as n.: *the comparative*.

comparatively, adv. Prec. & **-ly**. To a degree estimated by comparison with something else; relatively, by comparison: *comparatively well done*, it might have been worse done; *comparatively clever, rich* &c., clever compared to a stupid person, rich compared with a poor one &c.

compare (I.), vb. trans. & intrans. [1. kumpā́r; 2. kəmpéə]. Fr. *comparer*, fr. Lat. *comparāre*, 'to put together (lit.), to bring together, match, compare', fr. **com-**, & *pār*, 'equal'. See **par, peer**, n. **A.** trans. **1.** To put or bring together two or more persons or things, in fact or in thought, and contrast them, in order to discover and note points of resemblance and of difference; followed by *with*: *I have compared these handwritings and find no resemblance between them*; *to compare a translation with the original*. Phr. *not to be compared with*, nothing like so good. **2.** To observe and express the resemblance of one thing to another; to represent as similar; followed by *to*: *Milton's verse has been justly compared to organ-notes*. **3.** (gram.) To inflect an adjective or adverb so as to form the comparative and superlative degrees: *compare 'good'*. **B.** intrans. To be capable, or worthy of comparison with, be regarded as having similar or equal qualities or merits with: *few writers can compare with Scott as creators of romance*. Phr. *imported meat does not compare with English*, is not nearly so good.

compare (**II.**), n., fr. prec. Same as **comparison, 4.** (archaic or poet.) Found chiefly in such phrases as *beyond, without, past, compare*; *lovely beyond compare*, so lovely that none can equal, none can be compared with (*her* &c.).

comparison, n. [1. kumpárisun; 2. kəmpǽrisən], fr. O. Fr. *comparaison*, fr. Lat. *comparātiōn-(em)*, 'a bringing together, comparison', fr. *comparāre*. See **compare** (**I.**) & **-ion**. **1.** The act of comparing: *to make, establish, a comparison between*. Phr. *in comparison with*, compared with, if a comparison be made. **2.** Statement, expression, of a likeness perceived between one person or thing and another; simile, illustration. Phr. *comparisons are odious*. **3.** Relative likeness, resemblance, degree of merit, between two persons or things. **4.** Possibility of comparison; existence of such degree of resemblance or equality between two persons or things as to warrant comparison: *there is no comparison between. . .* **5.** (gram.) Act of inflecting adj. and adv. to form comparative and superlative degrees.

compartment, n. [1. kumpártment; 2. kəmpátmənt], fr. Fr. *compartiment*, fr. Low Lat. *compartiment-(um)*, fr. Lat. *compartīri*, 'to divide something with one, to share', fr. **com-** & *partīri*, 'to share, divide', fr. *part-(em)*, 'part'. See **part**. Part of anything separated off from the rest by partitions of any kind: specif. **a** division in a railway carriage forming complete unity, with doors, and windows, and seats for limited number of persons; **b** *watertight compartment* in a ship, one capable of being completely closed so as to form an air-chamber if water penetrates to other parts of vessel; Phr. *to be, live &c. in watertight compartments*, shut off from, unrelated to, other persons or things; **c** division of the brain containing localized centres of sensation, or of control of movements &c.; **d** (fig.) group of ideas, facts &c., existing or retained in the mind apart from and unrelated to, others.

compass (**I.**), n. [1. kúmpas; 2. kámpəs], fr. Fr. *compas*, fr. L. Lat. *compassus*, 'pair of compasses', fr. **com-** & *passus*, 'step'. See **pace** & **pass**. **a** Circuit, circumference, boundary or enclosing line: *to fetch a compass*, go round; hence, bounds, reach, extent, range, in various senses; esp. **b** (fig., of time and space) *within the compass of a lifetime*; **c** range of mental or physical powers: *a feat beyond my compass*; **d** due limits, moderate bounds: *to keep one's desires &c. within compass*; **e** (mus.) range of voice; range demanded of the voice in a song.

compass (**II.**), n. See prec. **a** *Mariner's compass*, instrument provided with magnetic needle on a pivot which always points north, and which hence enables the relative position of the other *points of the compass* to be found; **b** *compasses* (pair of), instrument with two legs, connected at the top by a movable joint, used for describing circles, measuring distances between points &c.

compass (**III.**), vb. trans., fr. Fr. *compasser*, 'to measure, contrive'. See **compass** (**I.**) **1.** To stretch round, go round; to enclose, encircle, hem in. Obsolete in this sense, and superseded by *encompass*; except in P.P. (archaic) *compassed about*, surrounded. **2.** To attain, accomplish: *to compass one's purpose* &c. **3.** (in bad sense) To plot, scheme for, design, contrive, scheme to bring about: *to compass the death of*.

compassable, adj. [1. kúmpasabl; 2. kámpəsəbl], fr. **compass** (**III.**) & **-able**. Capable of being compassed; attainable.

compassion, n. [1. kumpáshun; 2. kəmpǽʃən], fr. Fr. *compassion*, fr. Eccles. Lat. *compassiōn-(em)*, 'fellow-feeling, sympathy'. See **com-** & **passion**. Sympathy, pity with desire to help, relieve, or spare. Phr. *to have, take, compassion upon*, pity and help.

compassionate (**I.**), adj. [1. kumpáshunat; 2. kəmpǽʃənit]. **com-** & **passionate**. Filled with compassion, sympathetic, full of pity, tender-hearted.

compassionate (**II.**), vb. trans. [1. kumpáshunāt; 2. kəmpǽʃəneit]. **compassion** & **-ate**. To regard or treat with compassion, take pity upon.

compassionately, adv. [1. kumpáshunatli; 2. kəmpǽʃənitli]. **compassionate** (**I.**) & **-ly**. In a tender-hearted, pitying manner.

compassionateness, n. See prec. & **-ness**. Compassionate habit of mind, habitual compassion.

compass-plane, n. **compass** (**I.**) & **plane** (**II.**). Carpenter's plane with convex under side for planing round surfaces.

compass-saw, n. See prec. & **saw** (**III.**). Fine saw for cutting curves.

compatibility, n. [1. kumpàtibíliti; 2. kəmpæ̀tibíliti]. See **compatible** & **-ity**. State of being compatible; capacity for existing alongside something else, or of agreeing with someone else: *compatibility of two statements*, possibility of both being true; *compatibility of temper*, possibility of agreement.

compatible, adj. [1. kumpátibl; 2. kəmpǽtibl]. Fr., fr. Med. Lat. *compatibilis*, fr. L. Lat. *compatior*, 'I suffer with, feel pity', fr. **com-** & Lat. *patior*, 'I suffer', q.v. under **patient**. Able to coexist with, not incongruous, consistent (with).

compatibly, adv. Prec. & **-ly**. (followed by *with*) In a compatible manner, agreeably with.

compatriot, n. [1. kumpátriut; 2. kəmpǽtriət], fr. Fr. *compatriote*. See **com-** & **patriot**. One having the same native country as another; fellow-countryman.

compeer, n. [1. kómpēr; 2. kómpiə]. M.E. *compér*, Fr. *compair*, fr. Lat. *compār*, 'equal to another'. **com-** & Lat. *pār*, 'equal'. See **peer**. An equal, in standing and age, esp. such when associated with one; a comrade.

compel, vb. trans. [1. kumpél; 2. kəmpél], fr. Lat. *compellere*, 'to drive together; force, constrain', fr. **com-** & *pellere*, 'to push, strike; drive, impel'; the P.P. is *pulsum*, wh. form of the base occurs also in Lat. *pulsāre*, 'beat, strike, set in violent motion', & *pulsus*, 'a pushing, beating', see **pulsate**, **pulse** (**I.**); the base is found in Gmc. in O.E. *fealdan*, 'to fold' &c., see **fold** (**I.**), in **felt** (**I.**) (made by pressing), & in the second element of **anvil**. **1.** To force, constrain, oblige (a person), by physical or moral force, to do as one wishes. **2.** To obtain, secure, by physical or moral authority; to enforce: *to compel submission, obedience, silence* &c. **3.** To cause to submit or yield, to bring into subjection: *to compel a person to one's will*.

compellable, adj. [1. kumpélabl; 2. kəmpéləbl]. Prec. & **-able**. Capable of being compelled.

compelling, adj. [1. kumpéling; 2. kəmpéliŋ], fr. Pres. Part. of **compel**. That which compels; esp. of moral suasion, irresistible, winning: *a compelling force*; (fig.) *compelling manner, smile* &c.

compellingly, adv. Prec. & **-ly**. In a compelling manner.

compendious, adj. [1. kumpéndius; 2. kəmpéndiəs], fr. Lat. *compendiōsus*, 'abridged, short', fr. *compendi-(um)*, see **compendium** & **-ous**. Containing much matter in a small space; full but concise.

compendiously, adv. Prec. & **-ly**. Concisely, briefly.

compendiousness, n. See prec. & **-ness**. Fullness combined with conciseness.

compendium, n. [1. kumpéndium; 2. kəmpéndiəm], pl. *-ums*, learned pl. *-a*. Lat., lit. 'a weighing together; a laying up, storing'; hence, 'a saving (of space &c.), a shortening', fr. **com-** & *pendere*, 'to weigh', orig. 'to hang for weighing', & fr. same base as *pendēre*, 'to hang'. See **pendant**. As in the adj. *compendious*, the joint ideas of abridgement, and fullness are expressed in the n., so that it may mean a summary (in treatise form) of knowledge &c., with either the idea of completeness, or that of conciseness uppermost; the word may therefore be said to mean **a** an epitome; **b** a comprehensive account, or treatise; **c** a treatise both comprehensive and concise.

compensate, vb. trans. & intrans. [1. kómpensāt; 2. kómpinseit], fr. Lat. *compensāt-(um)*, P.P. type of *compensāre*, 'to weigh together, to weigh one thing against another, to counterbalance', fr. **com-** & *pensāre*, freq. of *pendere*, 'to weigh'. See prec. & **pensive**. **A.** trans. **1.** To give an equivalent to in return for (esp. for injury, loss &c.); make up to a person for a loss &c.; counterbalance a loss with gift or payment: *to compensate a soldier for disablement*; *compensate one for loss of time* &c. **2.** (mechan.) To counteract variation of movement &c., as of a pendulum, balance of a watch &c. **B.** intrans. (of actions or circumstances) To make amends, make up for; esp. in such phrases as: *nothing can compensate for the loss of a mother*.

compensation, n. [1. kòmpensáshun; 2. kòmpinséiʃən], fr. Lat. *compensātiōn-(em)*, lit. 'a weighing together, a balancing of accounts, a rendering of an equivalent,' fr. *compensāre*. See **compensate** & **-ion**. **1. a** Act of compensating: *to make compensation for* &c.; **b** something given to make up for, to counterbalance, loss, injury &c.: *he received £100 a year as compensation for the loss of his eye*. **2.** (mechan.) Process of counteracting variation.

compensational, adj. [1. kòmpensáshunal; 2. kòmpinséiʃənəl]. Prec. & **-al**. Of the nature of compensation; as, by way of, compensation.

compensative, adj. [1. kómpensàtiv; 2. kómpinsèitiv]. **compensate** & **-ive**. Pertaining to compensation.

compensator, n. [1. kómpensàtur; 2. kómpinsèitə]. **compensate** & **-or**. Mechanical device for neutralizing or counteracting deviations from required speed or direction of movement in parts of a machine.

compensatory, adj. [1. kompénsaturi; 2. kəmpénsətəri]. Prec. & **-y**. **a** Affording compensation: *compensatory payment* &c.; **b** specif., *compensatory lengthening*, term in general use in philology, denoting a lengthening of a vowel or consonant which is observed to take place when some sound has been lost; e.g. the long vowel in O.E. *tōþ*, 'tooth', is said to be due to *compensatory lengthening*, on the loss of nasality of the vowel, the earlier form being **tǫþ*. The term is apt to mislead as to the nature of the process, since it introduces an erroneous idea of amends deliberately made to the vowel for some injury which it has suffered.

compete, vb. intrans. [1. kumpḗt; 2. kəmpít], fr. Lat. *competere*, 'to strive together for' (post-class. meaning), fr. **com-** & *petere*, 'to go, travel, fly; go towards; attack; demand', & finally 'to seek'. The base **pet-* in its primary sense 'go, fly', has numerous derivatives; see in particular **pen** (**III.**) (fr. **petsna*); **feather**; the Gk. pref. **ptero-**; &, fr. a secondary meaning, **petition**. **1.** Followed by *with*: **a** (of persons) to pit oneself against another or others, engage in a contest with, be a party together with another or others in an attempt to gain possession of something which both or all want: *to compete with others or another for a prize, for the hand of a lady, for mastery* &c.; **b** (of things) to be so near in quality to something else, or so like it in kind, as to make it uncertain which is preferable: *a new dictionary must be very good if it is to compete with the many already in the market.* **2.** Used absolutely: **a** (of persons) to engage in, enter into a contest to obtain something: *the prize was open to all, but few competed*; **b** (of things) to come up to approximately the same standard of merit, be of same kind, challenge comparison with each other and claim preference: *these two books though on the same subject are addressed to such different publics that they do not compete at all.*

competence, -cy, n. [1. kómpetens(i); 2. kómpitəns(i)], fr. Fr. *compétence*, fr. Lat. (post-class.) *competentia*, 'agreement', fr. Lat. *competere* (class. meaning), 'to coincide, agree, to be capable, competent'. See prec. **1. a** Adequacy, sufficiency, of intellect, or skill, to perform a particular task or duty: *I doubt his competence for such a post*; **b** intellectual ability, or manual skill in general: *a well-meaning fellow but with no great competence in any direction.* **2.** Adequacy of means of livelihood: *to enjoy a modest competence.* **3.** (law) Legal authority or jurisdiction.

competent, adj. [1. kómpetent; 2. kómpitənt], fr. Fr. *compétent*, Lat. *competent-(em)*, Pres. Part. of *competere*. See **competence. 1.** (of persons) Capable, well qualified for what one undertakes: *a competent teacher* &c. **2.** (of mental attainments) Adequate, sufficient, fulfilling all requirements: *a competent knowledge.* **3.** (law) **a** (of a judge, or court) Legally authorized, having jurisdiction: *Ecclesiastical Courts are not competent to deal with criminal cases*; **b** (of acts) permissible, legally allowable: *it is perfectly competent for me to refuse to consider such a point at all.*

competently, adv. Prec. & **-ly.** In a competent manner.

competition, n. [1. kòmpetíshun; 2. kòmpitíʃən], fr. L. Lat. *competītiōn-(em)*, (i.) 'an agreement', (ii.) 'rivalry' (fr. different meanings of *competere*). See **compete** & **competence. 1. a** The act of competing; friendly strife, rivalry, between persons for an object which both want: *to be in competition with others for a prize* &c.; **b** (of things) state of making rival claims to superiority of any kind: *great competition for public favour exists between various makes of matches.* **2.** A contest, trial of strength, skill, knowledge, between two or more rivals; a match or series of matches: *boxing competition, chess competition* &c. Phr. *competition-wallah*, Anglo-Indian term for a person who secures an appointment, esp. in Indian Civil Service, by competitive examination.

competitive, adj. [1. kumpétitiv; 2. kəmpétitiv], fr. Lat., P.P. type *competīt-(um)* & **-ive.** See **compete.** Of or pertaining to competition; based on competition, by competition: *competitive examination.*

competitively, adv. Prec. & **-ly.** By, in, competition.

competitor, n. [1. kumpétitur; 2. kəmpétitə], Lat. *competītor.* See **competitive** & **-or.** One who competes; a rival; a claimant.

compilation, n. [1. kòmpiláshun; 2. kòmpiléiʃən]. Fr., fr. Lat. *compīlātiōn-(em)*, 'a pillaging, plundering', fr. *compīlāre.* See **compile** & **-ation. 1.** The act or process of compiling. **2.** That which is compiled; mass of material brought together from many sources; esp. a book composed of material taken from others: *a dictionary is largely a compilation from the works of others.*

compile, vb. trans. [1. kumpíl; 2. kəmpáil], fr. Lat. *compīlāre*, 'to plunder, pillage', (fig.) 'to plagiarize', fr. **com-**; for second element see **pillage.** In sense of 'bring together', prob. influenced by **pile,** 'heap'. To collect together from various sources, **a** in general sense; **b** to put together, in a more or less new form, literary, historical, and other material already existing in scattered works: *to compile a dictionary, guide-book, an anthology* &c.

complacence, -cy, n. [1. kumplásens(i); 2. kəmpléisəns(i)], fr. Med. Lat. *complacentia* (Fr. *complaisance*), fr. Lat. *complacent-(em)*, Pres. Part. type of *complacēre*, 'to please', fr. **com-** & *placēre*, 'to please'. See **placate,** fr. cogn. *placāre*, 'appease'. **a** Quiet, tranquil satisfaction, unruffled serenity of mind; **b** self-satisfaction.

complacent, adj. [1. kumplásent; 2. kəmpléisənt], fr. Lat. *complacent-(em)*, Pres. Part. type of *complacēre*, 'to please'. See **complacence.** Self-satisfied.

complacently, adv. Prec. & **-ly.** In a complacent manner.

complain, vb. intrans. [1. kumplán; 2. kəmpléin], fr. Fr. *complaindre*, fr. L. Lat. *complangere*, 'to beat the breast, bewail', fr. **com-** & Lat. *plangere*, 'to strike, beat, beat the breast or head as a sign of grief, to lament'. See **plain (IV.)** & **plaint. 1.** To utter expressions of discontent, dissatisfaction, objection, regret, pain &c.; to utter a grievance, to blame, find fault, to grumble: *to be always complaining.* **2.** *Complain to*, address a complaint to someone. **3.** *Complain of*, **a** make an accusation against a person; **b** (of things) to find fault with, grumble at, declare that one is annoyed by: *to complain of the beds, the food* &c.; **c** specif., to declare that one is suffering from a disease or pain: *to complain of indigestion.*

complainant, n. [1. kumplánent; 2. kəmpléinənt]. Prec. & **-ant. 1.** One who complains. **2.** (law) The person who complains, who brings the action in a law case.

complaint, n. [1. kumplánt; 2. kəmpléint], fr. Fr. *complainte.* See **com-** & **plaint** & **complain. 1.** Expression of resentment, discontent, regret &c.; utterance of grievance; murmuring; fault-finding: *to be full of complaints about one's food.* **2.** Formal accusation: *to lodge, make, a complaint against a person.* **3.** Cause, subject, ground, of resentment, discontent &c.; a grievance: *to have no complaint to make.* **4.** Bodily ailment, disease: *that common complaint, a cold.*

complaisance, n. [1. kumplázans; 2. kəmpléizəns]. Fr. See **complacence.** Easy-going habit of mind, desire to please, or to oblige; courtesy, civility.

complaisant, adj. [1. kumplázant; 2. kəmpléizənt]. Fr. See prec. & **complacent. a** Disposed to please, courteous; **b** yielding to the wishes of others, accommodating, compliant.

complement (I.), n. [1. kómpliment; 2. kómplimənt], fr. Lat. *complēmentum*, 'that which fills up or completes', fr. *complēre*, 'to fill up'. See **complete (II.). 1.** That which fills up or completes; that which is required to make up a deficiency, to make something else perfect or complete. **2.** (gram.) *Complement of the predicate*, word or words completing the predicate. **3.** (of men, provisions &c.) Number, quantity, amount, required to fill or make complete; full allowance; specif. (navy) the full number of officers and men allowed to a ship. **4.** (math.) *The complement of an angle*, its deficiency from 90°, the amount by which it falls short of 90°. Cp. *supplement.*

complement (II.), vb. trans. [1. kómpliment; 2. kómpliment], fr. prec. To make complete, form a complement to.

complemental, adj. [1. kòmpliméntal; 2. kòmpliméntəl], fr. **complement (I.)** & **-al.** Serving as a complement.

complementally, adv. Prec. & **-ly.** By way of, as, complement.

complementary, adj. [1. kòmpliméntari; 2. kòmpliméntəri], fr. **complement (I.)** & **-ary.** Serving as a complement, helping to constitute a whole. Specif. (opt.) *complementary colour*, that which combined with a given colour produces white.

complete (I.), adj. [1. kumplét; 2. kəmplít], fr. Lat. *complēt-(um)*, P.P. type of *complēre*, 'to fill up'. See **complete (II.). 1. a** Filled up, entire, perfect, with no part or element lacking: *a complete set*; **b** various extended uses: *a complete stranger*, one altogether, entirely, strange; *a complete ass*, a thoroughgoing fool (cp. *perfect* in same sense); *complete surprise* &c. **2.** Finished, brought to an end, brought to a state of perfection or fulfilment: *my work is now complete.* **3.** Accomplished, consummate: *complete master of fence* &c.

complete (II.), vb. trans., fr. Lat. *complētum*, P.P. of *complēre*, 'to fill up', fr. **com-** & *plēre*, 'to fill'. For account of base **plē-* see **plenum**; **full. 1.** To finish, bring to an end or to a state of fulfilment: *to complete a task*; *the builders have completed the house.* **2.** To make whole, make perfect: *this good news completes my happiness.*

completely, adv. [1. kumplétli; 2. kəmplítli], fr. **complete (I.)** & **-ly.** To a complete degree; entirely, thoroughly, utterly.

completeness, n. See prec. & **-ness.** The state or quality of being complete; thoroughness, perfection.

completion, n. [1. kumpléshun; 2. kəmplíʃən], fr. Lat. *complētiōn-(em)*, 'a filling; a fulfilment', fr. *complēre.* See **complete (II.)** & **-ion.** Act or process of completing; stage of being completed: *the completion of a task, plan, an undertaking, an education*; *to reach completion.*

complex (I.), adj. [1. kómpleks; 2. kómpleks], fr. Lat. *complex-(um)*, P.P. type of *complecti*, 'to fold or twine together; to clasp around, encircle; to comprise, include', fr. **com-** & *plex-(um)*, P.P. type of *plectere*, 'to plait, interweave, twist'; cp. also Lat. *plicāre*, 'fold, wind together'. These are all fr. **plek'-*, 'fold', a variant of the base **pel-*, 'strike, press' &c. See **compel,** also **ply (I.),** & **plait (II.). 1.** Composite, complicated, consisting of two or more closely connected or interwoven parts, elements, strands &c.; not simple: *complex machinery*; but chiefly of non-material things, intricate, difficult to understand in all bearings: *complex argument, idea, conception* &c. **2.** (gram.) *A complex sentence*, one containing a principal clause and one or more subordinate clauses.

complex (II.), n. Lat. *complexus*, 'an embrace, encompassing'. See prec. **1.** A whole made up of interwoven, interconnected parts, elements &c. **2.** (psycho-analysis) Collection of ideas, chiefly emotional, repressed and therefore subconscious, and resulting in an abnormal mental condition, which, by questioning &c., can be brought to the consciousness and explained, especially by elucidation of their origin and reason of repression.

complexion, n. [1. kumplékshun; 2. kəmplékʃən]. Fr., fr. Lat. *complexiōn-(em)*, 'combination, close connexion', fr. *complexus* & **-ion.** See **complex (I.). 1. a** Originally the combination of humours in certain proportions, which were supposed to determine the temperament and bodily habit; hence, **b** the temperament, bodily habit, constitution itself. (Obsolete now in these senses, which occur, however, in our older literature.) Now limited to the colour and texture of the face (sometimes including those of hair and eyes): *a pink-and-white complexion*; *good, bad, sallow* &c. *complexion.* **3.** (fig.) General appearance, character, condition, of outward affairs: *the matter wears a strange complexion*; *what you say puts a very different complexion on the incident.*

complexity, n. [1. kumpléksiti; 2. kəmpléksiti]. **complex (I.)** & **-ity.** State or quality of being complex; intricacy.

complexly, adv. [1. kómpleksli; 2. kómpleksli]. See **complex (I.)** & **-ly.** In a complex manner; intricately.

compliance, n. [1. kumplíans ; 2. kəmpláiəns]. **comply** & **-ance**. **1**. The act of complying *with* ; a yielding to a request, wish, desire, proposal &c. **2**. A disposition to yield or give way to others ; complaisance ; submission ; (often in bad sense) subservience : *base compliance* &c.

compliancy, n. [1. kumplíansi ; 2. kəmpláiənsi]. Prec. & **-y**. Complaisance.

compliant, adj. [1. kumplíant ; 2. kəmpláiənt]. See **comply** & **pliant**. Ready to comply, to fall in with another's wishes &c., yielding, submissive. Used by Milton in sense of flexible, easily bent : *compliant boughs*.

complicacy, n. [1. kómplikasi ; 2. kómplikəsi]. See **complicate** & **-cy**. The state or quality of being complex or intricate.

complicate (I.), vb. trans. [1. kómplikāt ; 2. kómplikeit], fr. *complicāt-(um)*, P.P. of Lat. *complicāre*, 'to fold together', fr. **com-** & *plicāre*, 'to fold'. See **complex** (I.). To make complex, intricate, involved ; produce awkward combination of circumstances ; esp. *to complicate matters*, add new element of difficulty.

complicate (II.), adj., fr. Lat. *complicātum*, P.P. of *complicāre*. See prec. **1**. Complex, involved, intricate (rare, usually *complicated*). **2**. (bot.) Conduplicate.

complicated, adj. [1. kómplikāted ; 2. kómplikeitid], fr. P.P. of **complicate** (I.). Consisting of parts or elements intricately combined, complex ; difficult to analyse, solve, or understand : *a complicated machine, puzzle* ; *a complicated business* &c.

complication, n. [1. kòmplikáshun ; 2. kòmplikéiʃən]. **complicate** (I.) & **-ion**. **1**. The act or process of complicating ; **a** state of being complicated ; a number of things (facts, events &c.) or parts mixed up or involved in an intricate or a confusing manner ; tangle ; also **b** mental and moral confusion. **2**. Specif. (med.) a fresh element, symptom, or disease which arises during illness, and makes this more difficult to treat.

complicative, adj. [1. kómplikativ ; 2. kómplikətiv]. **complicate** (I.) & **-ive**. Tending to complicate.

complicity, n. [1. kumplísiti ; 2. kəmplísiti], fr. Fr. *complicité*, fr. L. Lat. *complici-*, stem of *complex*, 'one mixed up with another, participant, confederate', & **-ty**. See **complex** (I.) & **complicate**. The act or state of being concerned with another in an action (usually in bad sense) ; state of being an accomplice ; partnership in crime &c. : *complicity in wickedness*.

compliment (I.), n. [1. kómpliment ; 2. kómplimənt]. Fr. *compliment*, fr. Ital. *complimento*, 'fulfilment of duties of politeness' &c. Variant of **complement**. **1**. **a** An expression of polite admiration ; urbane, flattering tribute to a person ; **b** a courteous act, expressing admiration and esteem : *to pay a compliment* ; *to do a person the compliment of inviting him* &c. ; *I take it as a compliment to be asked to speak*. Phr. *left-handed compliment, doubtful compliment*, one that contains an element of irony or malice. **2**. Polite, formal greeting, ceremonious expression of regard &c. : *to send one's compliments to a person* ; *give him my compliments* ; *the compliments of the season* (at Christmas &c.).

compliment (II.), vb. trans. [1. kómplimènt ; 2. kómplimènt], fr. prec. To pay a compliment to ; to express admiration, esteem, respect &c. for a person or his (her) achievements ; to flatter ; to congratulate a person on an achievement, quality &c. : *to compliment a lady on her appearance, a man on his courage, speech* &c.

complimentary, adj. [1. kòmpliméntari ; 2. kòmpliméntəri]. **compliment** (I.) & **-ary**. **a** (of uttered expressions) Expressing civility, regard, admiration &c. ; conveying, containing, compliments ; **b** (of persons) given to paying compliments : *to be too complimentary*, flattering, expressing admiration ; *to be complimentary about a person's work* &c. Special uses : *a complimentary dinner*, one held as a compliment to a person, to show regard or admiration for him ; *complimentary tickets* (for theatre &c.), sent gratis by manager.

complin(e), n. [1. kómplin ; 2. kómplin]. The *-n* unexplained, unless it be due to influence of **mat(t)ins**. M.E. & Fr. *complie*, fr. Lat. *complēta* (*hōra*), 'completed'. Often *complins*, wh. lends some strength to the suggested influence of *mat(t)ins*. The last service in the day in the Christian Church.

complot, n. [1. kómplot ; 2. kómplɔt]. Fr. See **com-** & **plot**. (archaic) A plotting together, conspiracy.

compluvium, n. [1. komplóōvium ; 2. kəmplúviəm]. Lat. See **com-** & **pluvial**. (class. archit.) The opening over the atrium of a Roman house, admitting light and air.

comply, vb. intrans. [1. kumplí ; 2. kəmplái], fr. Ital. *complire*, fr. Lat. *complēre*, 'to fill up'. See **complete**. The meaning has been affected by **ply** & **pliant**. **1**. (followed by *with*) **a** To adopt a course of action at the wish, or command, of another : *to comply with one's request* ; **b** to act in conformity with : *to comply with the rules*. **2**. (used absolutely) To yield, consent, agree : *threats, commands, entreaties were useless* ; *he would not comply*.

compo, n. [1. kómpō ; 2. kómpou]. Abbreviation of **composition**. Term applied by builders and tradesmen to various patent plasters &c.

component, adj. & n. [1. kumpónent ; 2. kəmpóunənt], fr. Lat. *compōnent-(em)*, Pres. Part. of *compōnere*, 'to put together', fr. **com-** & *pōnere*, 'to put, place'. See **compound** (II.). **1**. adj. Composing, constituting, forming part of, a whole ; esp. *component part*. **2**. n. Constituent element, ingredient, or part.

comport, vb. trans. & intrans. [1. kumpórt ; 2. kəmpɔ́t], fr. Fr. *comporter*, 'to admit of, allow, endure', *se comporter*, 'behave', fr. Lat. *comportāre*, 'to carry, bear, or bring together', fr. **com-** & *portāre*, 'to carry, bear'. See **port** (IV.). **1**. trans. (reflex.) To behave, conduct, *oneself* : *to comport oneself decently*. **2**. intrans. To be compatible with, be fitting, agree, accord with.

comportment, n. [1. kumpórtment ; 2. kəmpɔ́tmənt]. Prec. & **-ment**. Behaviour, demeanour, deportment ; (rare, and usually replaced by *deportment*).

compose, vb. trans. [1. kumpóz ; 2. kəmpóuz], fr. Fr. *composer*, cp. Lat. *compos-(itum)* &c., P.P. of *compōnere*, 'put together ; draw up, write'. See **com-** & **pose** (I.), also **depose** (I.). **1**. (of constituent parts or elements, material and non-material) To make up, constitute, result in, form by being put together : *colours and forms properly arranged compose a picture* ; *mere facts, baldly stated, do not compose a good book*. **2**. **a** To put words together so as to form sentences ; construct, create, literary work in prose or verse, to write as author : *to compose a poem, a sermon* &c. ; **b** (mus.) to create and put into musical form : *to compose an opera* ; (absol.) to engage in, practise, musical composition : *he is not only a teacher of music, he composes*, i.e. writes music ; **c** (of artistic work generally) to think out a design, arrange a scheme of colour or form : *to compose a picture*, i.e. plan it out, as distinct from painting it. **3**. (print.) To set up (type) ; set up in type (a piece of printing). **4**. **a** To calm, allay, settle, adjust : *to compose a dispute* ; **b** *to compose oneself*, restrain excitement, recover calmness ; **c** (of mental or emotional states) to arrange, put in order ; restore from confusion, or excitement, to a condition of repose &c., suitable to a particular purpose : *to compose one's thoughts, mind* ; **d** (of dead body) to arrange in decent position : *'By foreign hands thy decent limbs composed'* (Pope) ; restore (the features) to calm expression : *to compose one's features*.

composed, adj. [1. kumpózd ; 2. kəmpóuzd], fr. P.P. of prec. Calm, in mind and bearing, self-possessed, tranquil, free from agitation of mind.

composedly, adv. [1. kumpózedli ; 2. kəmpóuzidli]. Prec. & **-ly**. In a composed manner, calmly, without agitation.

composedness, n. [1. kumpózednes ; 2. kəmpóuzidnis]. See prec. & **-ness**. Composure.

composer, n. [1. kumpózer ; 2. kəmpóuzə]. **compose** & **-er**. **a** One who composes ; specif. **b** one who composes music.

composing, adj. [1. kumpózing ; 2. kəmpóuziŋ], fr. Pres. Part. of **compose**. Tending to compose, soothe, or calm, mind or body ; specif., *composing medicine, draught* &c., a sedative.

composing-stick, n. Compositor's tray in which he arranges the type in lines, with open side and adjustable end.

composite (I.), adj. [1. kómpozit ; 2. kómpəzit], fr. Lat. *composit-(um)*, P.P. of Lat. *compōnere*, 'to put together'. See **component** & **compose**. **1**. Made up of various distinct parts or elements ; specif. (of candles) made of stearine or stearic acid. **2**. (archit.) Exhibiting several styles blended, specif. (of an order) blending the Ionic and the Corinthian orders. **3**. (bot.) Belonging to the order *Compositae*, in which the florets are clustered together to form a single head, as in the daisy, tansy &c.

composite (II.), n., fr. prec. **1**. **a** A thing made up of various parts ; **b** specif., composite candle. **2**. (bot.) Flower belonging to order *Compositae*.

composition, n. [1. kòmpozíshun ; 2. kòmpəzíʃən]. Fr., fr. Lat. *compositiōn-(em)*, 'a putting together', fr. *composit-(um)*, P.P. type of *compōnere*. See **component, compose**. **1**. Act of putting together ; composing, construction, of various kinds ; **a** the building or fusion of separate words into a compound word ; **b** the construction of sentences ; the art or practice of writing ; **c** the art or practice of composing a piece of music ; **d** (print.) setting up of type. **2**. The thing composed ; **a** a piece of music or writing, a literary or artistic production ; used specif. of an essay, translation &c. done as an educational exercise ; **b** a compound, mixture of substances, made to represent a real or simple substance. **3**. Arrangement, grouping of the parts, of a work of art so as to produce the best effect : *the composition of a picture*. **4**. The constituent parts or elements of which anything is made up, formed, composed : **a** (of material things) *the composition of a pudding, of soils, gases* &c. ; **b** mental and moral constitution : *not a spark of generosity in his composition*. **5**. **a** Agreement to terms or conditions for settlement of a dispute or cessation of hostilities ; the terms of settlement ; a compromise ; **b** legal agreement with creditors to pay so much less than is actually due.

compositive, adj. [1. kumpózitiv ; 2. kəmpózitiv]. **composite** & **-ive**. **a** Capable of forming constituent part, of being compounded ; **b** connected with, involving, composition.

compositor, n. [1. kumpózitur ; 2. kəmpózitə]. Lat., 'one who orders, arranges, disposes' ; see **composite** (II.) & **-or**. (print.) One who sets up type.

compos mentis, adj. [1. kómpos méntis ; 2. kómpos méntis]. Lat., 'having power over the mind', fr. *compos, compot-is*, fr. **com-** & **pot-*, see **potent**, & *mens, mentis*, 'mind', see **mental**. (law) In one's right mind, sane ; also in Phr. *non-compos*, insane.

compost (I.), n. [1. kómpost ; 2. kómpɔst]. O. Fr. *composte*, fr. Lat. *composit-(um)*, P.P. of *compōnere*. See **component** & **compose**. A composition, mixture ; specif., a fertilizing mixture, manure for soils.

compost (II.), vb. trans. See prec. To treat with compost, put compost into.

composure, n. [1. kumpózhur ; 2. kəmpóuʒə], fr. **compose** & **-ure**. Calmness, tranquillity, serenity ; peace of mind, expressed by calm manner and demeanour.

compotation, n. [1. kòmpōtáshun; 2. kòmpoutéiʃən]. **com-** & **potation.** A drinking or tippling together.

compote, n. [1. kómpōt; 2. kómpout]. Fr., fr. O. Fr. *composte.* See **compost (I.).** Stewed fruit in syrup.

compound (I.), vb. trans. & intrans. [1. kumpóund; 2. kəmpáund]. M.E. *compounen,* 'to mix', fr. Lat. *compōnere.* See **component, compose.** The final *-d* is excrescent as in *sound,* & as in the now vulgar *gownd.* **A.** trans. **1.** To form or make up a composite whole by putting together parts, elements, ingredients &c.; to mix ingredients: *to compound a medicine.* **2. a** To settle, adjust, by agreement; **b** to discharge an obligation, debt &c., on terms different from those originally stipulated; esp. (i.) to settle a subscription &c. by paying a lump sum instead of paying by instalments; (ii.) to discharge a debt by partial payment. **3.** (law) To forbear prosecution, condone an offence for money, esp. in the Phr. *to compound a felony.* **B.** intrans. To perform the acts mentioned in **2** above: *to compound with one's creditors.*

compound (II.), adj. & n. [1. kómpound; 2. kómpaund], for *compouned,* P.P. of prec. **1.** adj. Made up of several ingredients, parts, or elements; not simple: *compound word,* one composed of two or more words; *compound interest,* interest on interest accruing from capital: *compound householder,* one whose rates, by agreement with landlord, are included in rent and paid by landlord. **2.** n. Anything composed of a mixture of elements, parts; a compound substance.

compound (III.), n. Prob. fr. Malay. *kampong.* (in India, China &c.) An enclosure in which a house or factory stands, esp. the walled or fenced enclosure round a European house.

comprador, n. [1. kómpradōr; 2. kómprədō]. Port. 'buyer', fr. L. Lat. *comparātōr-(em),* fr. Lat. P.P. *comparāt-(um)* & **-or.** See **compare.** (in China or Japan) Native factotum or agent employed in a European bank or commercial office.

comprehend, vb. trans. [1. kòmprehénd; 2. kòmprihénd], fr. Lat. *comprehendere,* 'to seize, grasp' (lit. and fig.), fr. **com-** & *prehendere,* 'to seize'. See **prehensile. 1.** To take in, embrace, include, within a certain compass or scope, comprise. **2.** To grasp with the intellect, to understand: *to comprehend a question, meaning.*

comprehensibility, n. [1. kómprehènsibíliti; 2. kómprihènsibíliti]. Next word & **-ity.** Quality of being comprehensible.

comprehensible, adj. [1. kòmprehénsibl; 2. kòmprihénsibl], fr. Lat. *comprehensibilis,* fr. *comprehens-(um),* P.P. of *comprehendere,* & **-ible.** See prec. Capable of being understood; intelligible.

comprehensibly, adv. Prec. & **-ly.** In a comprehensible manner.

comprehension, n. [1. kòmprehénshun; 2. kòmprihénʃən], fr. Lat. *comprehensiōn-(em),* 'a seizing (fig.), perception', fr. *comprehens-(um),* P.P. of *comprehendere,* & **-ion.** See **comprehend. 1.** The act or result of grasping facts, ideas &c. with the mind; the power or faculty of comprehending; understanding. **2.** The act or state of taking in, comprising, or including; inclusion.

comprehensive, adj. [1. kòmprehénsiv; 2. kòmprihénsiv], fr. Lat. *comprehens-* (see prec.) & **-ive.** See **comprehend.** Comprehending, embracing, or including, a great number of objects or a wide range of thoughts, ideas &c.; wide in scope, including a great deal (lit. and fig.): *a comprehensive term; a comprehensive survey; a comprehensive church.*

comprehensively, adv. Prec. & **-ly.** In such a manner as to comprehend, include.

comprehensiveness, n. See prec. & **-ness.** Faculty, quality, of being comprehensive.

compress (I.), vb. trans. [1. kumprés; 2. kəmprés], fr. O. Fr. *compresser,* fr. L. Lat. *compressāre,* fr. Lat. *compress-(um),* P.P. of *comprimere,* 'to press or squeeze together', fr. **com-** & *premere,* 'to press'. See **press (I.). a** To put pressure upon, press or squeeze together; to press or squeeze into smaller space (of solid matter, air, gases); **b** (fig., of non-material things) to pack densely, condense so as to cause to occupy a relatively short time or space: *experience of a lifetime compressed into a short period; to compress one's thoughts, language, style.*

compress (II.), n. [1. kómpres; 2. kómpres], fr. Fr. *compresse,* fr. Lat. *compressus.* See prec. (surg.) **a** Soft pad of folded material for bringing pressure to bear on any part of the body, esp. an artery; **b** a wet bandage, covered with oil-silk, applied to inflamed part of the body.

compressed, adj. [1. kumprést; 2. kəmprést], fr. P.P. of **compress (I.). a** Pressed together: *compressed lips;* **b** reduced in size or volume, condensed: *compressed air,* reduced in volume by pressure; **c** (fig., of thought, style &c.) made concise; terse.

compressibility, n. [1. kumprèsibíliti; 2. kəmprèsibíliti], fr. next word & **-ity.** Capacity for undergoing compression.

compressible, adj. [1. kumprésibl; 2. kəmprésibl], fr. **compress (I.)** & **-ible.** Capable of being compressed, soft and yielding.

compression, n. [1. kumpréshun; 2. kəmpréʃən], fr. Lat. *compressiōn-(em),* 'a pressing together', fr. P.P. type of *comprimere,* & **-ion.** See **compress (I.). a** (lit.) The act of compressing or state of being compressed; condensation; **b** (also fig.) of expression of thought in language uttered or written.

compressor, n. [1. kumprésur; 2. kəmprésə]. **compress (I.)** & **-or.** Anything serving to compress; specif., e.g. **a** a muscle; **b** mechanical device for compressing air.

comprise, vb. trans. [1. kumpríz; 2. kəmpráiz], fr. Fr. *compris,* P.P. of *comprendre,* fr. Lat. *comprehendere, comprendere.* See **comprehend.** To include, contain, consist of, be composed of: *'Who's Who' comprises biographical notices of persons both famous and obscure.*

compromise (I.), n. [1. kómpromīz; 2. kómprəmaiz], fr. Fr. *compromis,* fr. *compromettre,* fr. Lat. *comprōmissum,* 'a mutual engagement to abide by the award of an arbiter', P.P. of *comprōmittere.* See **com-** & **promise. a** Arrangement reached between parties in a dispute of any kind, in which each side gives up something, and makes concessions in the direction of the other side's claim, opinions, principles &c.; **b** in ordinary affairs, a mutual working agreement between parties whereby each, as a rule, surrenders something which he considers important, so that neither is satisfied.

compromise (II.), vb. trans. & intrans. See prec. **A.** trans. **1.** To settle (dispute, differences) by mutual concessions: *to compromise a lawsuit.* **2. a** To imperil the safety, jeopardize interests of, by rashness or folly: *the position of the whole army was gravely compromised by premature activity;* **b** to bring under suspicion, incur risk of scandal, by indiscreet conduct: *to compromise one's own, or another's, reputation;* **c** (also reflex.) *to compromise oneself,* incur suspicion, place oneself in an ambiguous position. **B.** intrans. To make a compromise, to make a settlement by mutual concessions: *we shall have to compromise on this point, or lose everything.*

comptroller, n. [1. kontrṓler; 2. kəntróulə]. See **controller.** Official spelling for *controller,* q.v., in certain titles, esp. *comptroller of accounts,* an official who examines the accounts of collectors of public money.

compulsion, n. [1. kumpúlshun; 2. kəmpálʃən]. Fr., fr. Lat. *compulsiōn-(em),* fr. *compuls-(um),* P.P. type of *compellere,* 'to drive, force'. See **compel.** The difference of vowel is the result of the Aryan process known as gradation. The act of compelling; constraint imposed by physical force, threats, or by legal or moral authority; coercion: *to act under compulsion.*

compulsive, adj. [1. kumpúlsiv; 2. kəmpálsiv]. Lat. *compuls-* (see prec.) & **-ive.** Of the nature of, implying, compulsion: *compulsive action; a compulsive measure.*

compulsively, adv. Prec. & **-ly.** By, under, compulsion.

compulsorily, adv. [1. kumpúlsurili; 2. kəmpálsərəli]. Next word & **-ly.** On account of compulsion.

compulsory, adj. [1. kumpúlsuri; 2. kəmpálsəri]. Lat. *compuls-* & **-ory.** See **compulsion. 1.** (of actions) Enforced by compulsion: *compulsory payment, education* &c. **2.** (of agent) Compelling, exercising compulsion; coercive: *compulsory measures.*

compunction, n. [1. kumpúngkshun; 2. kəmpáŋkʃən], fr. Lat. *compunctiōn-(em),* fr. *compunct-(um),* P.P. type of *compungere,* & **-ion,** 'to prick, sting', fr. **com-** & *pungere,* 'to prick'. See **puncture, pungent, point. a** Qualm of conscience, regret, for wrong done in the past; hesitation, scruple, concerning action in process of being, or about to be, done; **b** also in much weaker sense of more or less trifling hesitation, regret, or scruple concerning an action which at worst is an error of judgement, involving no moral wrong: *he ate up the whole pie without the slightest compunction.*

compunctious, adj. [1. kumpúngkshus; 2. kəmpáŋkʃəs]. See **compunction** & **-ous.** Causing compunction, pricking or stinging of the conscience: *'That no compunctious visitings of nature Shake my fell purpose'* (Shakespeare).

compunctiously, adv. Prec. & **-ly.** With compunction.

compurgation, n. [1. kòmpërgáshun; 2. kòmpāgéiʃən], fr. Lat. *compurgātiōn-(em),* fr. *compurgāre,* 'to purify wholly', fr. **com-** & *purgāre,* 'to make clean, purify'. See **purge** & **-ation.** (legal hist.) Complete purging and doing away of an offence with which a person was charged by the oath of *compurgators* who solemnly swore that he was innocent. The older name for this process was *wager of law;* abolished in 1833.

compurgator, n. [1. kómpërgātōr; 2. kómpāgeitō]. Med. Lat. See prec. & **-or.** (legal hist.) One who under Anglo-Saxon law took an oath that an accused person was innocent of the crime charged against him.

computable, adj. [1. kumpū́tabl; 2. kəmpjū́təbl]. **compute** & **-able.** Capable of being reckoned.

computation, n. [1. kòmpūtáshun; 2. kòmpjūtéiʃən], fr. Lat. *computātiōn-(em),* fr. *computāt-(um),* P.P. of *computāre.* See **compute. 1.** The act or process of computing or reckoning. **2.** The result of reckoning, the amount computed, a totting-up, estimate.

computative, adj. [1. kumpū́tativ; 2. kəmpjū́tətiv]. Lat. *computāt-* (see prec.) & **-ive.** Given to computation.

compute, vb. trans. & intrans. [1. kumpū́t; 2. kəmpjū́t], fr. Lat. *computāre,* 'to sum up, reckon', fr. **com-** & *putāre,* 'to think'. See **putative. 1.** trans. To determine by calculation; to count, reckon, estimate, the number, amount &c. **2.** intrans. To make calculation, reckon.

comrade, n. [1. kómrad; 2. kómrid], fr. Fr. *camarade,* Span. *camarada,* 'a chamber-fellow', fr. Lat. *camara, camera,* 'a vault', fr. Gk. *kamára,* 'anything with a vaulted or arched covering'. See **camera, chamber.** Companion, mate, associate.

comradeship, n. [1. kómradship; 2. kómridʃip]. Prec. & **-ship. a** Condition of being a comrade; **b** friendly relation existing among comrades; **c** companionship, fellowship.

Comtism, n. [1. kómtizm; 2. kómtizəm], fr. Auguste Comte, French philosopher, d. 1857, founder of the system. Positivism.

Comtist, n. [1. kómtist; 2. kómtist]. Prec. & **-ist.** Positivist.

con-, pref. Form of **com-**, used before all consonants except *b* & *p, l, m* & *r.*

con (I.), vb. trans. [1. kon; 2. kən]. Variant of **can (I.)**, wh. in O.E. appears as *cann* & *conn.* The meaning is derived fr. that found also in

O.E. by the side of 'am able'. The infin. *cunnan* means 'to be able', & 'to know'. To peruse, scrutinize, examine carefully; to study in order to learn by heart; commit to memory: *to con a lesson*; often *to con over.*

con (II.), vb. trans., fr. *cond*, fr. Fr. *conduire*, 'lead, guide', Lat. *condūcere*. See **conduct.** (naut.) To direct the course of (a ship). See also **conning-tower.**

con (III.). Ital. prep., 'with', fr. Lat. **com-**. Used in music in such phrases as *con espressione*, 'with expression' &c., or, gen., as *con amore*, 'with enthusiasm, eagerly'.

con (IV.), adv. & n. Abbr. of Lat. *contrā*, 'against'. **a** adv., *pro and con*, 'for and against'; **b** n., vote, argument, against: *the pros and cons.*

conacre, n. [1. kónāker; 2. kɔ́neikə]. For *cornacre.* See **corn** & **acre.** In Ireland, the subletting of small portions of a farm, already tilled, for a single crop.

conation, n. [1. kōnā́shun; 2. kounéiʃən], fr. Lat. *cōnātiōn-(em)*, 'endeavour, effort', fr. *cōnāt-(um)*, P.P. of *cōnāri*, 'to attempt, try, endeavour'. Prob. fr. **cowen-*, fr. **co-**, the base **wen-* &c., 'to wish, strive', q.v. under **win.** (psychol.) Faculty or power of directing the will to effort, physical or mental.

conative, adj. [1. kṓnativ; 2. kóunətiv]. See prec. & **-ive.** Of, tending to, conation.

concatenate, vb. trans. [1. kònkátināt; 2. kɔ̀nkǽtineit], fr. Lat. *concatēnāt-(um)*, P.P. type of *concatēnāre*, fr. **con-** & *catēna*, 'a chain; series of events linked together'. See **catenary** & **chain.** (fig., of events) To link together, to unite as in a series of links, or chain.

concatenation, n. [1. kunkàtinā́shun; 2. kənkæ̀tinéiʃən]. Prec. & **-ion.** (chiefly fig.) **a** Act or process of concatenating; **b** series, group, combination, of events, happening in succession, and apparently causally connected; *concatenation of events, circumstances.*

concave, adj. & n. [1. kónkāv; 2. kɔ́nkeiv], fr. Lat. *concavus*, 'hollow, arched, curved'. See **con-** & **cave.** Hollow, curved inwardly.

concavely, adv. Prec. & **-ly.** In concave shape or form.

concavity, n. [1. kònkáviti; 2. kɔ̀nkǽviti]. See prec. & **-ity.** Curved, vaulted surface, considered from inside.

concavo-, pref. [1. konkā́vō; 2. kənkéivou], fr. **concave**, in compounds, as *concavo-convex*, of surfaces, concave on one side, convex on the other.

conceal, vb. trans. [1. kunsḗl; 2. kənsíəl], fr. O. Fr. *conceler*, fr. Lat. *concēlāre*, fr. **con-** & *cēlāre*, 'to hide', fr. Aryan base **kel-*, 'hide, cover', cogn. w. O.E. *helan*, 'hide' &c. See **cell, colour,** also **hall, holster.** **a** To hide, cover, keep from sight (of material objects); (reflex.) *to conceal oneself*; **b** to withhold knowledge of, to keep secret (facts, information &c.): *to conceal the truth.*

concealment, n. [1. kunsḗlment; 2. kənsíəlmənt]. Prec. & **-ment.** **1. a** The act of concealing, hiding, or keeping secret (material and non-material things), esp. as deliberate and wilful act: *concealment of birth*, a criminal offence; **b** state of being concealed: *to remain in concealment.* **2.** A hiding-place; a retreat or shelter from observation.

concede, vb. trans. [1. kunsḗd; 2. kənsíd], fr. Lat. *concēdere*, 'to go away, to give way, yield', fr. **con-** & **cede.** **1.** To surrender, grant; admit to be true, let pass undisputed: *to concede a point in argument.* **2.** To grant, as a right or privilege.

conceit (I.), n. [1. kunsḗt; 2. kənsít]. M.E. *conceite*, formed fr. **conceive**, on anal. of **deceit**; also influenced by **concept.** **1. a** (rare, archaic) Form of *concept*; **b** fanciful and rather trivial idea or notion; a quaint, humorous, or witty fancy: *poetry full of artificial conceits.* **2. a** Personal judgement, opinion, esp. in the phrase *in one's own conceit*: *wise in his own conceit*; **b** exaggeratedly favourable opinion of oneself or one's belongings: *to be full of conceit.* Phr. *to be out of conceit with*, to be no longer pleased with.

conceit (II.), vb. trans., fr. prec. Formerly used in sense of to imagine, suppose, which is now obs.; survives in P.P. as a rare literary archaism in sense of conceive (mentally), produce by imagination, imagine: *a well-conceited play* &c.

conceited, adj. [1. kunsḗted; 2. kənsítid]. **conceit** (I.) & **-ed.** Filled with exaggerated sense of one's own merits and importance; vain.

conceitedly, adv. Prec. & **-ly.** In a conceited manner.

conceivability, n. [1. kunsḕvabíliti; 2. kənsìvəbíliti]. **conceivable** & **-ity.** Possibility of being thought of, or imagined; hence probability, possibility, likelihood.

conceivable, adj. [1. kunsḗvabl; 2. kənsívəbl]. **conceive** & **-able.** Capable of being mentally conceived; capable of being understood by the mind; credible, possible.

conceivableness, n. Prec. & **-ness.** Conceivability.

conceivably, adv. [1. kunsḗvabli; 2. kənsívəbli]. **conceivable** & **-ly.** According to what can be conceived by the mind.

conceive, vb. trans. & intrans. [1. kunsḗv; 2. kənsív]. M.E. *concēven*, fr. O. Fr. *conceivre, conceveir*, fr. Lat. *concipere*, 'to take to oneself, take in, perceive, conceive, understand', fr. **con-** & *capere*, 'to take', q.v. under **captive.** **A.** trans. **1.** (physiol.) To generate by process of conception, become pregnant with: *to conceive a child.* **2. a** To take into, form, in the mind: *to conceive an affection, a dislike for* &c.; **b** to devise, form: *conceive an idea, purpose* &c.; **c** to apprehend, grasp, understand, take in full meaning of: *I conceive you, your meaning* (archaic); **d** to formulate in the mind, think out, and express: *a badly conceived scheme.* **B.** intrans. **1.** (physiol.) To carry out process of conception. **2.** To grasp with the mind, understand: *I cannot conceive what he means.* **3.** To imagine, suppose, be under the impression (that): *I conceive that an unselfish devotion to one's country is the first of civic virtues.*

concelebrate, vb. intrans. [1. kònsélebrāt; 2. kɔ̀nsélibreit]. See **con-** & **celebrate.** To celebrate Mass together. See next word.

concelebration, n. [1. kònselebrā́shun; 2. kɔ̀nselibréiʃən]. **con-** & **celebration.** Celebration of Eucharist at which two or more priests take part; in Latin Church, a newly ordained priest and the bishop.

concentrate, vb. trans. & intrans. [1. kónsentrāt; 2. kɔ́nsəntreit]. **con-** & Lat. *centrum*, 'centre', see **centre**, & **-ate.** **A.** trans. **1.** (of material things) To bring together to, or direct towards, a single place or centre; to unite into one body or force: *to concentrate a military force.* **2.** (of non-material things) To devote, direct, to a single object or purpose: *to concentrate one's attention, one's effort* &c. **3.** (chem.) To increase the strength of a liquid or ore by reducing its volume, to condense; to intensify in strength, or to purify, by getting rid of foreign material: *to concentrate acid by evaporation.* **B.** intrans. **a** To converge towards, meet in, common centre, to consolidate in a place: *the troops concentrated at Southampton*; **b** (followed by *on, upon*) to fix efforts and attention on single point or object, to devote oneself chiefly or exclusively to: *to concentrate upon a particular subject of study, a single purpose* &c.

concentrated, adj. [1. kónsentrāted; 2. kɔ́nsəntreitid]. P.P. of prec. **a** (mil.) *Concentrated fire*, firing directed upon a particular point; **b** (chem.) produced by concentration.

concentration, n. [1. kònsentrā́shun; 2. kɔ̀nsəntréiʃən]. **concentrate** & **-ion.** **1.** Act or process of concentrating (in any sense): *power of concentration.* **2.** Anything concentrated: *concentration of troops, of energy.*

concentrative, adj. [1. konséntrativ, kónsentrā̀tiv; 2. kənséntrətiv, kɔ́nsəntrèitiv]. **concentrate** & **-ive.** Tending to concentrate, characterized by concentration.

concentrativeness, n. Prec. & **-ness.** State of being concentrative.

concentrator, n. [1. kónsentrātur; 2. kɔ́nsəntreitə]. **concentrate** & **-or.** One of various mechanical devices, e.g. ring of wire round cartridge case to prevent too much spreading of the shot.

concentre, vb. trans. & intrans. [1. konsénter; 2. kənséntə], fr. Fr. *concentrer.* See **con-** & **centre.** **a** trans. To draw, bring, together at a common centre or focus; cp. Milton, 'Paradise Lost': '*In thee concentering all their precious beams*'; **b** intrans., to come together, meet, in, or have a common centre or focus; formerly for *concentrate.*

concentric, adj. [1. kònséntrik; 2. kɔ̀nséntrik], fr. Fr. *concentrique.* See prec. & **-ic.** (of circles, spheres &c.) Having a common centre.

concentrically, adv. [1. kònséntrikali; 2. kɔ̀nséntrikəli]. Prec. & **-al** & **-ly.** In a concentric manner, with a common centre.

concentricity, n. [1. kònsentrísiti; 2. kɔ̀nsəntrísiti]. **concentric** & **-ity.** State of being concentric.

concept, n. [1. kónsept; 2. kɔ́nsept], fr. Lat. *concept-(um)*, P.P. of *concipere*, 'take in by the mind, perceive, understand'. See **conceive.** (philos.) Any idea; a general notion.

conception, n. [1. kunsépshun; 2. kənsépʃən]. Fr. *conception*, fr. Lat. *conceptiōnem*, 'a comprehending; conception of offspring', fr. *concept-(um)*, P.P. type of *concipere.* See **conceive.** **1. a** (physiol.) Process of the fertilization of the ovum, and the beginning of the growth of the embryo in the womb; **b** fact of being conceived; *Immaculate Conception*, doctrine that the B.V.M. was not conceived in sin. **2.** The act or faculty of forming ideas &c. in the mind: *great powers of conception.* **3.** The thing conceived; idea, notion, picture &c. formed of something by the mind; a plan or invention of the mind: *a great, a clever, conception*; *an actor's conception of his part.* Phr. *to have no conception of.*

conceptive, adj. [1. kunséptiv; 2. kənséptiv]. **concept** & **-ive.** Pertaining to conceiving; capable of conceiving.

conceptual, adj. [1. kunsépchooal; 2. kənséptʃuəl]. Lat. *conceptu-(s)*, 'a taking, gathering; conception of offspring', see **concept**, & **-al.** Pertaining to conception (in physical and psychol. senses); pertaining to concepts.

conceptualism, n. [1. kunsépchooalìzm; 2. kənséptʃuəlìzəm]. **conceptual** & **-ism.** Mediaeval philosophical doctrine concerning the reality of things perceived by the senses, asserting that universals have reality, but only in the mind, cp. *nominalism* and *realism.*

conceptualist, n. [1. kunsépchooalist; 2. kənséptʃuəlist]. **conceptual** & **-ist.** Believer in doctrine of conceptualism.

concern (I.), vb. trans. [1. kunsérn; 2. kənsə́n], fr. Fr. *concerner*, fr. L. Lat. *concernere*, 'to regard, have regard to', in class. Lat., 'to mix together as in a sieve', fr. **con-** & *cernere*, 'to sift'; (fig.) 'to distinguish, observe, perceive, see distinctly'. The orig. base is **ker-*, **kri-* &c., 'to separate out, distinguish', & occurs in several languages in both lit. & fig. sense; cp. Lat. *crībrum*, 'sieve', cp. **cribriform**; *certus*, 'well-separated, distinguished, perceived', see **certain**; in Gk. *krī́nō*, 'distinguish, judge', *krités*, 'judge', see **critic, crisis**; in O.H.G. *rītera*, 'coarse sieve', O.E. *hrīdder, hrīddel*, 'sieve'. See **riddle** (III.). **1. a** To relate to, have reference to, have connexion with; to be of importance to, apply to, affect the interest of: *attend to what concerns you*; **b** to affect the mind painfully, cause anxiety to: *to be concerned about the future* &c., i.e. filled with concern, anxiety, misgiving. **2.** (reflex., followed by *with, in, about*) To interest oneself in, occupy oneself with, take trouble about a matter: *to concern oneself about one's own affairs*; *concern oneself with public work* &c.

concern (II.), n., fr. prec. **1. a** That which concerns or relates to one, something which affects one, something which is part of one's business: *it's no concern of mine*; (pl.) *one's own concerns*, one's own particular business; **b** interest, share *in*: *to have a concern in a business* &c. **2.** Anxiety, misgiving: *to feel concern about*; *to see with concern*. **3.** Business, group of activities: *a flourishing concern*.

concerned, adj. [1. kunsĕrnd; 2. kənsə́nd], fr. P.P. of **concern (I.)**. **1. a** Occupied with, busy with, employed in: *to be concerned in writing a book* (see **concern (I.), 2**); **b** involved in, affected by (often in bad sense): *concerned in the crime*; *I am not concerned*, it doesn't affect me. **2.** Troubled, worried, anxious: *a concerned air*; *to be much concerned about*.

concerning, prep. [1. kunsĕrning; 2. kənsə́niŋ], fr. Pres. Part. of **concern (I.)** In regard to, with relation to, regarding, about.

concernment, n. [1. kunsĕrnment; 2. kənsə́nmənt]. **concern (I.)** & **-ment**. **1.** (rare in all senses) That in which one is concerned or interested. **2.** Importance, moment: *a matter of concernment*. **3.** State of being concerned or occupied; participation. **4.** Anxiety, solicitude, concern.

concert (I.), n. [1. kónsert; 2. kɔ́nsət]. Fr. *concert*, fr. Ital. *concerto*, fr. *concertare*, 'arrange, agree, accord', cp. also Fr. *concerter* in same senses. Skeat suggests derivation fr. Lat. *concertāre*, 'dispute, contend' (**con-** & *certus*, see **certain**), through intermediate sense of 'arrange dispute, bargain, agree', cp. Span. *concertar*, 'bargain'. This has verisimilitude but is questioned by some. **1.** Agreement of persons or movements; accordance, concord, unison, harmony: *to act in concert*; *to proceed in concert* &c.; the *Concert of Europe*, of agreement between the European powers, as before the Great War, esp. on matters concerning the Balkans, Near East &c. **2.** Specif. (mus.) musical entertainment at which vocalists and instrumentalists perform either singly or in combination: *concert grand*, a grand piano of largest size and powerful tone for use at concerts; *concert-pitch* (tuning of musical instruments), rather higher than usual.

concert (II.), vb. trans. [1. kunsĕrt; 2. kənsə́t], fr. Fr. *concerter*, fr. Ital. *concertare*, 'to accord together'. See prec. To devise plans &c., together, agree in common, arrange by mutual agreement.

concerted, adj. [1. kunsĕrted; 2. kənsə́tid], fr. P.P. of prec. **1.** Planned or arranged in common by several parties, agreed to by those so acting: *to take concerted action*. **2.** (mus.) Arranged in parts for voices or instruments.

concertina, n. [1. kònsertḗna; 2. kɔ̀nsətínə]. Invented word fr. **concert (I.)**. (mus.) Portable musical wind instrument furnished with a bellows worked by the hands, the notes of which are produced by fingering keys.

concerto, n. (Engl. imitation of Ital.) [1. konchártō; 2. kəntʃéətou]. Ital. See **concert (I.)**. (mus.) Musical composition for solo instrument with orchestral accompaniment.

concession, n. [1. kunséshun; 2. kənséʃən]. Fr., fr. Lat. *concessiōn-(em)*, fr. *concess-(um)*, P.P. type of *concēdere*, see **concede**, & **-ion**. **1.** Act of yielding or conceding what is asked. **2. a** Anything so yielded or granted: *a concession to public opinion*; **b** specif., a privilege or property granted by a government: *a concession of land, rights to trade* &c.

concessionaire, n. [1. kunsèshunár; 2. kənsèʃənéə], or as Fr. Fr. Person to whom concession is made; esp. one granted mining, trading, or such rights, by a government.

concessive, adj. [1. kunsésiv; 2. kənsésiv], fr. Lat. *concessīvus*. See **concession** & **-ive**. **1.** Implying concession. **2.** (gram.) Expressing concession: *concessive clause*, a subordinate adverbial clause introduced by the conjunctions *though*, *although* &c.

concettism, n. [1. konchétizm; 2. kəntʃétizəm]. See **concetto** & **-ism**. The use of fanciful or ingenious turns of expression in literary style.

concetto, n., pl. **concetti** [1. konchétō, -ē; 2. kəntʃéttou, -i]. Ital., fr. Lat. *concepto*, dat. of *conceptum*. See **conceit** & **concept**. A fanciful turn of expression, a conceit.

conch, n. [1. kongk; 2. kɔŋk], fr. Lat. *concha*, 'shell', fr. Gk. *kógkhē*, *kógkhos*, cogn. w. Scrt. *čankhás*, & Lett. *senze*, 'mussel'; also Lat. *congius*, 'a liquid measure', wh., however, may be borrowed fr. Gk. *kógkhē*. **1. a** Large marine shell, now esp. a spiral univalve shell; **b** (Roman myth.) shell used by the Tritons as a trumpet. **2.** (archit.) Dome of semicircular apse, from its shape.

concha, n. [1. kóngka; 2. kɔ́ŋkə]. Lat., 'a shell'. See prec. **1.** The outer part of the ear, esp. the central cavity of the outer ear. **2.** (archit.) conch.

conchiferous, adj. [1. kòngkíferus; 2. kɔ̀ŋkífərəs]. See prec. & **-ferous**. **a** (zool.) Having a shell; **b** (geol.) shell-bearing.

conchoid, n. [1. kóngkoid; 2. kɔ́ŋkɔid]. **conch** & **-oid**. **1.** (math.) A plane curve, for trisecting a plane angle. **2.** (geol., mineral.) A conchoidal surface.

conchoidal, adj. [1. kongkóidl; 2. kɔŋkɔ́idl]. Prec. & **-al**. (geol., mineral.) Having a surface fracturing with depressions like one valve of a bivalve shell or conch.

conchological, adj. [1. kòngkolójikl; 2. kɔ̀ŋkəlɔ́dʒikl]. **conchology** & **-ic** & **-al**. Pertaining to conchology.

conchologist, n. [1. kòngkólojist; 2. kɔ̀ŋkɔ́lədʒist]. **conchology** & **-ist**. Student of conchology; collector of shells.

conchology, n. [1. kòngkóloji; 2. kɔ̀ŋkɔ́lədʒi], fr. Gk. *kóngkhos*, see **conch**, & **-logy**. Science or study of shells and mollúscs.

concierge, n. [1. kónsiărzh; 2. kɔ̃siɛəʒ]. Fr. Origin unknown. (in France) **a** Doorkeeper, janitor, head-porter, of hotels, public offices &c.; **b** person in charge of a set of apartments, lodgings, or flats.

conciliar(y), adj. [1. konsíliar(i); 2. kənsíliə(ri)], fr. Lat. *concilium*, 'meeting, assembly, council'. See **council** & **-ar**. Pertaining to an ecclesiastical council.

conciliate, vb. trans. [1. kunsíliāt; 2. kənsílieit], fr. Lat. *conciliāt-(um)*, P.P. type of *conciliāre*, 'to bring together, make friendly, win over', fr. *concilium*, 'a meeting, assembly'. See **council**. **a** (of persons) To overcome the indifference or hostility of, pacify, mollify, propitiate; to gain the esteem, good-will, or favour of, win over; **b** (of apparently incongruous things) to make compatible, reconcile (archaic).

conciliation, n. [1. kunsìliáshun; 2. kənsìliéiʃən]. Prec. & **-ion**. The act of conciliating; adjustment of differences &c.: *court of conciliation*.

conciliative, adj. [1. kunsíliativ; 2. kənsíliətiv]. **conciliate** & **-ive**. Conciliatory.

conciliator, n. [1. kunsíliātur; 2. kənsílieitə]. **conciliate** & **-or**. One who conciliates, a peacemaker.

conciliatory, adj. [1. kunsíliaturi; 2. kənsíliət(ə)ri]. Prec. & **-y**. Tending, inclined, to conciliate; conciliative: *conciliatory measures, manner* &c.

concinnity, n. [1. konsíniti; 2. kənsíniti], fr. Lat. *concinnitāt-(em)*, 'fitness, elegance, neatness', fr. *concinnus*, 'well-adjusted, neat, elegant'; etymol. obscure. Harmony, elegance, or neatness of literary style or of discourse.

concise, adj. [1. kunsís; 2. kənsáis], fr. Lat. *concīsus*, 'divided, concise', P.P. of *concīdere*, 'to cut to pieces', fr. **con-** & *caedere*, 'to cut', q.v. under **caesura**, **cement**. Brief but expressive, terse, pithy (of speech, style of writing &c.); (also of persons) given to concise expression.

concisely, adv. Prec. & **-ly**. In a concise manner.

conciseness, n. See prec. & **-ness**. The quality of being concise, terseness in speaking or writing.

concision, n. [1. kunsízhun; 2. kənsíʒən], fr. Lat. *concīsiōn-(em)*, 'separation into divisions', fr. *concīs-(um)* & **-ion**. See **concise**. **1.** A division, schism, faction. **2.** Conciseness.

conclave, n. [1. kónklāv; 2. kɔ́nkleiv]. Fr., fr. Lat. *conclāve*, 'a room that can be locked up', fr. **con-** & *clāvis*, 'a key'. See **clavicle**. **1. a** The apartments which form the meeting-place of cardinals of the Roman Catholic Church for election of Pope; **b** the assembly of cardinals for this purpose. Hence **2.** Any private or secret assembly: *to sit in conclave*, to be engaged in a secret meeting.

conclude, vb. trans. & intrans. [1. kunklóod; 2. kənklúd], fr. Lat. *conclūdere*, (i.) 'to shut up together', (ii.) 'to end, close', fr. **con-** & *claudere*, 'to shut'. See **claustral** & **close (I.)**. **A.** trans. **1.** To bring to an end, close, finish: *to conclude a speech, argument* &c. **2.** To bring about as a result, to effect, settle, arrange: *to conclude a treaty, bargain* &c. **3.** To draw an inference, argue, consider as proved by what has gone before: *from what you say I conclude that* &c. **B.** intrans. To come to an end: *the meeting concluded in uproar*.

conclusion, n. [1. kunklóozhun; 2. kənklúʒən]. Fr., fr. Lat. *conclūsiōn-(em)*, fr. *conclūs-(um)*, P.P. type of *conclūdere*, & **-ion**. See **conclude**. **1. a** Act of concluding or ending; Phr. *in conclusion*, lastly; **b** end, termination, close. **2.** Final result, outcome, upshot: *the conclusion of the whole matter*. **3.** Arrangement, settling: *the conclusion of peace, of a treaty* &c. **4.** Something believed in consequence of investigation or thought, reasoned judgement, inference, deduction. Phrs. *to draw conclusions, to come to a conclusion* &c., infer; *foregone conclusion*, something already decided on and not to be altered by argument &c.; *to try conclusions with*, pit oneself against. **5.** (log.) The proposition deduced from the premises of a syllogism.

conclusive, adj. [1. kunklóosiv; 2. kənklúsiv]. Fr. *conclusif*, Lat. *conclūs-* (see prec.), & **-ive**. That which settles, decisive, convincing, final: *conclusive evidence, proof*.

conclusively, adv. Prec. & **-ly**. Decisively, finally; convincingly.

conclusiveness, n. See prec. & **-ness**. Quality of being final and decisive.

concoct, vb. trans. [1. kunkókt; 2. kənkɔ́kt], fr. Lat. *concoct-(um)*, P.P. type of *concoquere*, 'to cook together', fr. **con-** & *coquere*, 'to cook'. See **cook (I.)**. **a** To invent or prepare by mixing together different ingredients of food or drink: *to concoct a new dish*; hence, **b** (fig.) to devise, plan, invent, make up: *to concoct a story, a plot* &c.

concoction, n. [1. kunkókshun; 2. kənkɔ́kʃən]. **concoct** & **-ion**. **1.** Act of concocting (lit. and fig.). **2.** That which is concocted (lit. and fig.).

concoctive, adj. [1. kunkóktiv; 2. kənkɔ́ktiv]. See prec. & **-ive**. (obs.) Pertaining to concoction. Used by Milton in sense of tending to ripen, maturing: '*concoctive heat*'.

concolorous, adj. [1. kònkúlurus; 2. kɔ̀nkálərəs]. See **con-** & **colour** & **-ous**. (nat. hist.) Uniform in colour, esp. of the wings of certain butterflies and moths.

concomitance, -cy, n. [1. konkómitans(i); 2. kənkɔ́mitəns(i)], fr. L. Lat. *concomitantia*. See **concomitant**. **1.** Accompaniment, coexistence. **2.** Specif. (eccles.) the existence of the whole of both the body and blood of Christ in each element of the Eucharist.

concomitant, adj. & n. [1. kunkómitant; 2. kənkɔ́mitənt], fr. **con-** & *comitant-(em)*, Pres. Part. of *comitāri*, 'to accompany', fr. *comit-(em)*, *comes*, 'companion'. See **count (III.)**. **1.** adj. Going together with, accompanying: *concomitant circumstances*. **2.** n. An accompanying thing, an accompaniment, an attendant fact or circumstance: *a bad temper is often a concomitant of indigestion*.

concomitantly, adv. Prec. & **-ly**. As an accompaniment, together with.

concord, n. [1. kóngkord; 2. kóŋkōd], fr. Fr. *concorde*, fr. Lat. *concordia*, 'an agreement together, union, harmony', fr. *concors*, adj., 'of the same mind', fr. **con-** & *cor, cordis*, 'heart'. See **cordate**. **1.** Moral agreement, harmony, between persons in opinions, views, interests &c.; agreement between things, suitability. **2.** (mus.) Pleasing combination, harmony, of tones heard simultaneously: '*Concord of sweet sounds*' (Shakespeare). **3.** (gram.) Syntactic agreement between words in person, number, gender, and case.

concordance, n. [1. kunkórdans; 2. kənkṓdəns]. Fr., fr. L. Lat. *concordantia*. See **concordant**. **1.** Agreement, harmony, concord: *to be in concordance; in concordance with your wishes* &c. **2.** Specif., a book which gives an index of, and references to, the principal words used in a work, or by an author, alphabetically arranged, and with full context cited: *a concordance of Shakespeare, of the Bible* &c.

concordant, adj. [1. kunkórdant; 2. kənkṓdənt], fr. Lat. *concordant-(em)*, Pres. Part. of *concordāre*, 'to be of one mind, to agree together', fr. *concors*. See **concord**. Agreeing, harmonious, consistent, consonant (followed by *with*, or absol.).

concordantly, adv. Prec. & **-ly**. In concordance, in agreement, consistently.

concordat, n. [1. kònkórdat; 2. kònkṓdæt]. Fr., fr. Lat. *concordātum*, P.P. of *concordāre*. See **concordant**. **a** (eccles. hist.) A formal agreement between the Pope and any secular government for the settlement and control of ecclesiastical affairs; **b** a friendly agreement which settles disputed points between individuals or parties.

concourse, n. [1. kóngkors; 2. kóŋkōs], fr. Fr. *concours*, fr. Lat. *concursus*, 'a running together', fr. *concurs-(um)*, P.P. type of *concurrere*, 'to run together', fr. **con-** & *currere*, 'to run', q.v. under **course, courier**. **1.** A running or moving together, a confluence of things. **2.** An assembly of persons, a crowd, throng.

concrescence, n. [1. konkrésens; 2. kənkrésəns], fr. Lat. *concrescentia*, fr. *concrescent-(em)*, Pres. Part. of *concrescere*, 'to grow together'. See **concrete**. A growing together, coalescence; a growing together of cells or other organisms.

concrete (I.), adj. [1. kónkrēt; 2. kónkrīt], fr. Lat. *concrētus*, 'grown together', P.P. of *concrescere*, 'to grow together', fr. **con-** & *crescere*, 'to grow'. See **crescent**. **1.** Formed into one mass; hence, existing in material form, having a real existence; real: *a concrete fact*. **2.** (gram., of a noun) Denoting a thing, not a quality, state, or action; reverse of *general* or *abstract*. **3.** Made of concrete, see **concrete (II.), 2**.

concrete (II.), n., fr. prec. **1.** A concrete thing. See **concrete (I.), 1**. **2.** Composition of gravel or sand and cement, used in building.

concrete (III.), vb. trans. & intrans. See **concrete (I.)**. **1.** [1. kunkrḗt; 2. kənkrī́t]. **a** trans. To bring or unite together into a mass, cause to coalesce; **b** intrans., to grow together; coalesce, become concrete. **2.** [1. kónkrēt; 2. kónkrīt] To cover with concrete, as a pavement &c.

concretion, n. [1. kunkréshun; 2. kənkríʃən]. See **concrete (I.)** & **-ion**. **1.** The process of growing together, coalescence. **2.** A mass formed by the union of various parts adhering to one another, a concrete mass; (esp. geol.) a mass formed of solid particles. **3.** Specif. (pathol.) a calculus formed in a cavity of the body; stone: *calcareous concretion*.

concretionary, adj. [1. kunkréshunari; 2. kənkríʃənəri]. Prec. & **-ary**. **1.** Pertaining to, or formed by, concretion. **2.** Containing concretions; (geol.) *concretionary deposits*, chemically formed deposits, generally from springs containing lime or flint.

concretive, adj. [1. kunkrḗtiv; 2. kənkrī́tiv]. **concrete (I.)** & **-ive**. Tending to concretion.

concubinage, n. [1. kongkū́binij; 2. kəŋkjū́binidž]. See **concubine** & **-age**. **a** Cohabitation of a man and a woman without marriage; **b** condition of a concubine.

concubinal, adj. [1. kongkū́binal; 2. kəŋkjū́binəl]. **concubine** & **-al**. Pertaining to concubinage or to concubines.

concubinary, adj. [1. kongkū́binari; 2. kəŋkjū́binəri]. Next word & **-ary**. Connected with concubinage; born from such a connexion.

concubine, n. [1. kóngkūbīn; 2. kóŋkjubain]. Fr., fr. Lat. *concubīna*, fr. *concubere*, 'to lie with', fr. **con-** & *cubāre*, 'to lie, lie down'. This vb. appears to be fr. a base meaning 'to bend, curve' &c., as in Lat. *cubitum*, 'elbow', fr. Gk. *kúbiton*, cogn. w. Goth. *hups*, O.E. *hype*, O.H.G. *huf*, q.v. under **hip (I.)**, & Gk. *kūphós*, 'bent, crooked'. See **cube** & **cubicle**. A woman who lives with a man outside lawful wedlock.

concupiscence, n. [1. konkū́pisens; 2. kənkjū́pisəns]. Fr., fr. Lat. *concupiscentia*, fr. *concupiscere*, 'to long for, desire', fr. **con-** & *cupere*, 'to desire'. See **cupidity**. Sexual desire, lust.

concupiscent, adj. [1. konkū́pisent; 2. kənkjū́pisənt], fr. Lat. *concupiscent-(em)*, Pres. Part. of *concupiscere*, see prec. Inflamed by sexual passion, ardently desirous.

concur, vb. intrans. [1. kunkér; 2. kənkə́], fr. Lat. *concurrere*, 'to run together; to happen at same time', fr. **con-** & *currere*, 'to run'. See **course, courier**. **1.** To meet in one point, to coincide, happen together (of circumstances &c.): *everything concurred to make him happy*. **2.** To agree, be of same opinion: *all will concur in this opinion with the speaker, in condemning the practice*.

concurrence, n. [1. kunkúrens; 2. kənkárəns]. **concur** & **-ence**, & see next word. Agreement or union in action or opinion (gen. the latter); assent.

concurrent, adj. & n. [1. kunkúrent; 2. kənkárənt], fr. Lat. *concurrent-(em)*, Pres. Part. of *concurrere*. See **concur**. **1.** adj. **a** Running together, meeting at single point: *concurrent lines*; **b** acting together; **c** agreeing together in opinion; **d** existing and taking effect at same time. **2.** n. That which concurs, a concurrent circumstance, a joint or contributory cause.

concurrently, adv. Prec. & **-ly**. With concurrence, unitedly; at same time; in agreement.

concuss, vb. trans. [1. kunkús; 2. kənkás], fr. Lat. *concuss-(um)*, P.P. type of *concutere*. See next word. **1.** To shake, stir, agitate (usually fig.). **2.** To cause concussion (of brain) to, to render unconscious by a blow on the head; usually in P.P. *concussed*.

concussion, n. [1. kunkúshun; 2. kənkáʃən], fr. Lat. *concussiōn-(em)*, 'a shaking', fr. *concuss-(um)*, P.P. type of *concutere*, 'to shake violently', fr. **con-** & *quatere*, 'to shake'. See **quash**. **1.** Agitation, commotion, shock, caused by violent collision of two bodies: *concussion of the air*. **2.** Specif. (med.) injury to an organ caused by heavy blow, fall &c.; esp. *concussion of the brain*.

concussive, adj. [1. kunkúsiv; 2. kənkásiv]. See prec. & **-ive**. Tending, likely, to concuss or render unconscious.

condemn, vb. trans. [1. kundém; 2. kəndém], fr. Lat. *condemnāre*, 'to sentence, doom; accuse, blame', fr. **con-** & *damnāre*, 'condemn'. See **damn**. **1.** To disapprove of, censure, blame, reprove, upbraid: *to condemn a person for his conduct; to condemn conduct, behaviour*. **2.** **a** To pronounce unfit for use: *to condemn meat as unfit for human food* &c.; **b** to pronounce forfeited (of ships, cargo &c.). **3.** **a** To pronounce legal judgement against, inflict legal penalty on, to doom: *to condemn a man to death, to imprisonment* &c.; Phr. *condemned cell*, that in which person under sentence of death is placed; **b** to find guilty, convict a person of crime charged against him: *in spite of the evidence he was not condemned*; **c** (fig., of a physician) to pronounce a person to be suffering from mortal illness: *he recovered, though several doctors had condemned him*; **d** (fig.) to give appearance of guilt: *his shifty looks were enough to condemn him, apart from the other facts*.

condemnable, adj. [1. kundémnabl; 2. kəndémnəbl], fr. Lat. *condemnābilis*. See prec. & **-able**. Blamable, culpable.

condemnation, n. [1. kòndemnā́shun; 2. kòndemnéiʃən], fr. Lat. *condemnātiōn-(em)*. See prec. & **-ation**. **1.** The act of condemning; censure, blame: *to incur one's condemnation*. **2.** **a** Judicial conviction; act (by a judge) of adjudging guilty and of dooming to punishment &c.; **b** fact of being judicially condemned (of an accused person).

condemnatory, adj. [1. kundémnaturi; 2. kəndémnətəri]. Lat. *condemnātor*, 'an accuser'. See prec. & **-ory**. Expressing or implying condemnation: *condemnatory statement*.

condensability, n. [1. kundènsabíliti; 2. kəndènsəbíliti]. See next word & **-ity**. The quality of being condensable.

condensable, adj. [1. kundénsabl; 2. kəndénsəbl]. **condense** & **-able**. Capable of being condensed.

condensation, n. [1. kòndensā́shun; 2. kòndenséiʃən]. See next word & **-ation**. The act of condensing or state of being condensed; in various senses: **a** of chemical or physical processes; reduction to a denser state, as of gases to a liquid form, steam to water &c.; **b** (fig.) abbreviation, compression, putting tersely (of ideas &c., as expressed in words).

condense, vb. trans. & intrans. [1. kundéns; 2. kəndéns], fr. Lat. *condensāre*, fr. **con-** & *densāre*, 'to make dense, press together'. See **dense**. **A.** trans. **1.** To make dense, make compact; to compress into a smaller compass; to abridge. **2.** (chem. and phys.) **a** To reduce into a denser form (by pressure, cold &c.); esp. to reduce from gas or vapour to liquid; **b** (fig.) to compress one's words, put what one has to say in small space; **c** (of rays of light) to concentrate, intensify. **B.** intrans. To be reduced into a denser form; to become more compact.

condenser, n. [1. kundénser; 2. kəndénsə]. Prec. & **-er**. Person who, thing which, condenses; in various purely technical senses, as for reducing gas &c. to liquid state, for concentrating rays of light &c.; specif. (elect.) apparatus consisting of two or more conducting plates separated by a non-conducting substance, known as a dielectric (q.v.); its function is to receive and retain an electric charge from an alternating current, the charge being in proportion to its capacity.

condescend, vb. intrans. [1. kòndesénd; 2. kòndisénd], fr. Fr. *condescendre*, fr. L. Lat. *condescendere*, fr. **con-** & *descendere*, 'to stoop'. See **descend**. **1.** **a** (in good sense) To behave with humility, by consenting to perform offices, or accept positions, of a more lowly character than those to which one is entitled by one's merits, attainments, rank &c.; *the Saviour condescended to dwell as a man among men*; **b** (in unfavourable sense) to stoop to unworthy actions, to lower oneself, demean oneself, by undignified or low conduct: *to condescend to accept bribes; to condescend to trickery*. **2.** To behave with affability in one's social relations with inferiors, although retaining, and to some extent expressing in manner, a full consciousness of superiority: *the great man seemed to be condescending all the time he was speaking to his guests*.

condescending, adj. [1. kòndesénding; 2. kòndiséndiŋ], fr. Pres. Part. of prec. Showing condescension; (in good sense) modest and humble, with courtesy and geniality towards inferiors; (in unfavourable sense) affable with a suggestion of conscious superiority; patronizing: *a haughty and condescending manner*.

condescendingly, adv. Prec. & **-ly**. In a condescending manner.

condescension, n. [1. kòndesénshun; 2. kòndisénʃən], fr. Lat. *condescensiōn-(em)*, fr. *conde-*

scens-(um), P.P. type of *condescendere*, & **-ion.** See **condescend.** The act of condescending; (in good sense) affability, graciousness, courtesy to inferiors; (in unfavourable sense) a manner which betrays consciousness of being superior to one's surroundings.

condign, adj. [1. kundín; 2. kəndáin], fr. Fr. *condigne*, fr. Lat. *condignus*, 'wholly deserving, worthy', fr. **con-** & *dignus*, 'worthy'. See **dignity.** Deserved, adequate; esp. suitable, adapted, to a fault or crime: chiefly, *condign punishment.*

condignly, adv. Prec. & **-ly.** Deservedly, adequately.

condiment, n. [1. kóndiment; 2. kɔ́ndimənt], fr. Lat. *condīmentum*, 'spice, seasoning', fr. *condīre*, 'to preserve, pickle, spice'. Origin obscure. Very doubtfully connected w. Gk. *ténthēs*, 'a dainty feeder', fr. base *kʷendh-. The obvious connexion is w. *condere*, 'put together, store up' &c., but the difference of conjugation raises doubts. Seasoning for food, anything spicy, high-flavoured or pungent, used as a relish, as mustard, pepper &c.

condition (I.), n. [1. kundíshun; 2. kəndíʃən], fr. Lat. *conditiōn-(em)* for *condiciōn-(em)*, 'stipulation, agreement; situation, rank; circumstances', connected w. *condīcere*, P.P. *-dictum*, 'agree upon' &c., fr. **con-** & *dīcere*, 'point out, tell' &c., as in **indicate** &c. See **diction.** **1.** State or manner of being; state in which a person or thing exists, esp. in regard to external circumstances, and to health, strength &c.: *the house, the man's person, was in a horrible condition.* Phrs. *in good condition*, (of food) fit to eat; (of persons or animals) healthy, plump, strong: *in, out of, condition*, in good, bad, health. **2.** Rank, position, estate, station: *humble condition of life.* Phrs. *to change one's condition*, specif., to marry; *a man of condition*, man of rank. **3.** (in pl.) External circumstances, limiting factors, concomitants: *under existing, favourable, conditions.* **4.** A stipulation, something imposed as a provision, or restriction, essential qualification in an agreement, failing the fulfilment of which something else will not take effect: *to impose conditions*; *to make it a condition that*; *the conditions are very severe* &c. Phr. *on condition*, provided (that).

condition (II.), vb. trans., fr. prec. **1. a** (rare) To impose conditions, stipulate; **b** to produce a certain state or condition; to determine: *the circumstances which condition our lives.* **2.** To bring into good condition or state of health (of horses, cattle &c.).

conditional, adj. [1. kundíshunal; 2. kəndíʃənəl]. **condition (I.)** & **-al.** **1.** Containing or depending upon a condition or conditions, not unqualified: *a conditional promise*; *a promise conditional on circumstances being favourable.* **2.** (gram.) *Conditional clause*, one expressing a condition.

conditionally, adv. Prec. & **-ly.** With, under, conditions, with qualifications.

conditioned, adj. [1. kundíshund; 2. kəndíʃənd]. **condition (I.)** & **-ed.** **1.** Placed under, subject to, certain conditions, restrictions, modifying factors, or circumstances: *the degree of happiness we enjoy is conditioned partly by our temperament, partly by external circumstances.* **2.** In a specific state of bodily or moral condition: *ill-conditioned*; *well-conditioned.*

condolatory, adj. [1. kundṓlatri; 2. kəndóulətri], fr. **condole**, w. adj. suff. on anal. of **consolatory**, the base of former being in Lat. *condolē-*, see next word. Condoling, expressing condolence.

condole, vb. intrans. [1. kundṓl; 2. kəndóul], fr. Lat. *condolēre*, 'to suffer severe pain; suffer with another', fr. **con-** & *dolēre*, 'to grieve, suffer'. See **dole (III.).** To express sympathy with, lament in company with another, as for a common sorrow or loss.

condolence, n. [1. kundṓlens; 2. kəndóuləns]. Fr., fr. Lat. *condolent-(em)*, Pres. Part. of *condolēre*, & *-ia.* See **condole** & **-ence.** Expression, exhibition, of sympathy with another in sorrow &c.: (often in pl.) *present my condolences to* &c.

condominium, n. [1. kòndōmínium; 2. kɔ̀ndoumíniəm], fr. **con-** & *dominium.* See **dominion.** Joint rule or sovereignty, as over a state shared by two or more powers.

condonation, n. [1. kòndōnā́shun; 2. kɔ̀ndounéiʃən], fr. Lat. *condōnātiōn-(em)*, 'giving away'. See **condone** & **-ation.** The act of condoning, overlooking, an offence against one; specif., of offences against marriage vow, by injured party.

condone, vb. trans. [1. kundṓn; 2. kəndóun], fr. Lat. *condōnāre*, 'to give up, pardon, forgive', fr. **con-** & *dōnāre*, 'to give'. See **donate.** To overlook, forgive (an offence &c.); specif. (law) of matrimonial infidelity.

condor, n. [1. kóndor; 2. kɔ́ndə]. Span., fr. Peruvian *cuntur.* A large American vulture found in the Andes.

condottiere, n. [1. kòndotyā́rā; 2. kɔ̀ndətjérɛ]. Ital., fr. *condotto*, fr. Lat. *conduct-(um)*, P.P. type of *condūcere*, in sense of 'to hire', see **conduct**, & suff. fr. Lat. *-ārius*, see **-ary.** Captain of a band of military adventurers and mercenaries in the Late Mediaeval period.

conduce, vb. intrans. [1. kundū́s; 2. kəndjū́s], fr. Lat. *condūcere*, 'to bring together, to contribute (to)', fr. **con-** & *dūcere*, 'to lead'. See **duct** & cp. **conduct (II.).** (chiefly of events, circumstances, actions) To help to produce, tend to bring about, promote: *the possession of wealth often conduces to happiness*; *revolution generally conduces to much subsequent misery.*

conducive, adj. [1. kundū́siv; 2. kəndjū́siv]. Prec. & **-ive.** Tending to promote, contributive to: *conducive to health.*

conducively, adv. Prec. & **-ly.** In a conducive manner.

conduciveness, n. See prec. & **-ness.** Tendency to conduce or contribute to.

conduct (I.), n. [1. kóndukt; 2. kɔ́ndəkt]. L. Lat. *conductus*, 'defence, protection, escort', fr. P.P. of *condūcere*, 'lead, draw together', fr. **con-** & *dūcere*, 'lead' &c. See **duke**, **duct**; cp. **conduit.** **1.** The act or method of conducting; direction, guidance, management: *the conduct of a war, of a business* &c. **2.** Escort, guide, convoy (obs. except in Phr. *safe-conduct*). **3.** Manner of carrying, managing, ruling, oneself from a moral point of view; behaviour: *good, bad, conduct* &c.

conduct (II.), vb. trans. & intrans. [1. kundúkt; 2. kəndákt], fr. Lat. *conduct-(um)*, P.P. type of *condūcere.* See prec. **1.** To lead, guide, escort: *to conduct a person to a seat, a party up a mountain.* **2. a** To direct, manage, carry on: *to conduct a campaign* &c.; **b** specif. (mus.) to direct performance, by indicating time, expression &c., both of players and music itself: *to conduct an orchestra*; *conduct an opera*; (also absol.) *he conducts at all the chief concerts.* **3.** (reflex.) *To conduct oneself*, to behave. **4.** (phys.) **a** trans. To serve as a medium for, to transmit (heat, electricity &c.); **b** intrans., to act as a conductor (of heat, electricity &c.).

conductibility, n. [1. kundùktibíliti; 2. kəndàktibíliti]. See next word & **-ity.** (phys.) Capacity of conducting (a current, heat &c.).

conductible, adj. [1. kundúktibl; 2. kəndáktibl]. **conduct (II.)** & **-ible.** **a** Capable of conducting (heat &c.); **b** capable of being conducted.

conduction, n. [1. kundúkshun; 2. kəndákʃən], fr. Lat. *conductiōn-(em)*, 'bringing together'. See **conduct (II.)** & **-ion.** **a** (phys.) Transmission, conductivity (of heat &c.); **b** transmission of, act of conducting, liquid through a channel.

conductive, adj. [1. kundúktiv; 2. kəndáktiv]. **conduct (II.)** & **-ive.** Having the quality or power of conducting (heat &c.).

conductivity, n. [1. kònduktíviti; 2. kɔ̀ndaktíviti]. Prec. & **-ity.** Property of transmitting (heat, electric current &c.).

conductor, n. [1. kundúktur; 2. kəndáktə]. L. Lat., 'a carrier, transporter', fr. Lat., 'one who hires (a thing), a farmer, lessee'. See **conduct (II.).** Some of the senses through Fr. *conducteur.* (of persons) **1.** A leader, guide. **2.** A manager, director (esp. mus.), the director of an orchestra. **3.** Official, generally a ticket-collector, in charge of public street conveyance, tram &c. (of things) **4.** (phys.) A substance or body having special property of transmitting (heat, electricity &c.): *wood is a bad conductor.* Cp. *lightning-conductor.*

conductorship, n. [1. kundúkturship; 2. kəndáktəʃip]. Prec. & **-ship.** Office of conductor in senses **1**, **2**, or **3**, esp. **2.**

conduit, n. [1. kúndit; 2. kándit]. Variant of **conduct (I.).** Fr., fr. L. Lat. *conductus*, 'escort, conduit'. A natural or artificial channel which conveys water or other liquid; an aqueduct, canal &c.

conduplicate, adj. [1. kondū́plikat; 2. kəndjū́plikit]. **con-** & **duplicate.** (bot.) Doubled and folded together lengthwise, of petals and leaves.

condyle, n. [1. kóndil; 2. kɔ́ndil]. Fr. *condyle*, fr. Lat. *condylus*, fr. Gk. *kóndulos*, 'knuckle', cogn. w. Scrt. *kandaš*, 'bulb', *kandúkaš*, 'ball'. (anat.) Ball at the end of a bone which forms joint with socket of another bone.

condyloid, adj. [1. kóndiloid; 2. kɔ́ndilɔid]. **condyle** & **-oid.** (anat.) Shaped like a condyle.

cone, n. [1. kōn; 2. koun], fr. Lat. *cōnus*, fr. Gk. *kōnos*, (i.) 'a pine-cone, fir-cone', (ii.) 'the cone or peak of a helmet', cogn. w. Scrt. *šānaš*, Lat. *cōs*, O.E. *hān*, 'whetstone', see **hone**, Scrt. *šitáš*, 'sharp'. **1.** A solid body with circular base, tapering to a point or apex; anything having this shape, such, specif., as the signal hoisted as warning of bad weather; similarly shaped part in couplings, bearings &c.; specif., the fruit of conifers, such as the fir, pine &c. **2.** (geom.) A surface described by a moving straight line, *generator*, passing through a fixed point, *vertex*, intercepted by a fixed curve, *directrix.* See **conics.**

coney, n. See **cony.**

confab, n. [1. kónfab; 2. kɔ́nfæb]. Abbr. fr. **confabulation.** (colloq.) Familiar, intimate, talk or discussion.

confabulate, vb. intrans. [1. konfábūlāt; 2. kənfǽbjuleit], fr. Lat. *confābulāt-(um)*, P.P. type of *confābulārī*, 'to converse together', fr. **con-** & *fābulārī*, 'to speak', fr. *fābula.* See **fable.** To talk, discuss, argue, familiarly and intimately together.

confabulation, n. [1. kunfàbūlā́shun; 2. kənfæ̀bjuléiʃən]. Prec. & **-ion.** Familiar discussion.

confabulatory, adj. [1. kunfábūlatri; 2. kənfǽbjulətri]. See prec. & **-ory.** Pertaining to, of the nature of, confabulation.

confection, n. & vb. trans. [1. kunfékshun; 2. kənfékʃən]. Fr., fr. Lat. *confectiōn-(em)*, fr. *confect-(um)*, P.P. type of *conficere*, 'to make up together, to prepare', fr. **con-** & *facere*, 'to make'. See **fact.** **1. n. a** A preparation of fruits &c. with sugar; a sweetmeat, preserve; **b** an elaborate, fashionable woman's garment. **2.** vb. To make, prepare, as sweetmeats, costumes &c.

confectionary, adj. [1. kunfékshunri; 2. kənfékʃənri]. Prec. & **-ary.** Of the nature of a confection.

confectioner, n. [1. kunfékshuner; 2. kənfékʃənə]. **confection**, vb., & **-er.** One who makes and sells sweetmeats, cakes, pastry &c.; a pastrycook.

confectionery, n. [1. kunfékshunri; 2. kənfékʃənri]. Prec. & **-ry.** Sweet pastry, cakes, jellies, and sweetmeats of all kinds.

confederacy, n. [1. kunféderasi; 2. kənfédərəsi]. See **confederate** & **-cy.** **1.** A league, alliance. **2. a** Body of confederate persons, often in sense **3**; **b** body of separate states united for certain purposes, each having more independence than in a 'federal' state, esp. used of the Southern States in the American Civil War. **3.** Conspiracy, collusion of two or more persons to commit an unlawful act.

confederate (I.), adj. [1. kunfédérat; 2. kənfédərit], fr. Lat. *confoederātus*, fr. **con-** & *foederātus*, 'leagued together', fr. *foedus*, *foederis*, 'a league, treaty'. See **federal.** **1.** United in a confederacy or league; banded together by treaty. **2.** (Am. hist.) *The Confederate States of America*, those of the South which seceded from the Union (1860–1865).

confederate (II.), n., fr. prec. **1. a** Person or nation united with others in a confederacy or league; ally; **b** (usually in bad sense) a companion, an accomplice, in crime. **2.** (Am. hist.) An adherent to the cause of the Confederate States.

confederate (III.), vb. trans. & intrans. [1. kunfédérāt; 2. kənfédəreit]. See prec. **1.** trans. To bring into alliance or confederacy; (also reflex.) to ally oneself with. **2.** intrans. To come into alliance with; to form a confederacy.

confederation, n. [1. kunfèderáshun; 2. kənfèdəréiʃən]. See **confederate** & **-ion. a** Act of confederating; **b** a league, alliance (esp. of princes, nations, states); a confederacy.

confer, vb. trans. & intrans. [1. kunfér; 2. kənfʌ́], fr. Lat. *conferre*, 'to bring together, contribute, consult, bestow', fr. **con-** & *ferre*, 'to bring, bear'. See **-ferous** & **bear** (I.). **1.** trans. **a** To grant, bestow (a title, benefit, favour &c. upon a person); **b** to compare, collate (archaic except in imperat.): *confer remarks on next page* &c., usually abbreviated *cf.* **2.** intrans. (followed by *with*) To consult, deliberate, discuss with, talk over business with: *to confer with one's advisers* &c.

conference, n. [1. kónferens; 2. kɔ́nferens], fr. Fr. *conférence*, fr. Med. Lat. *conferentia*. Prec. & **-ence.** Formal deliberation in common with others, interchange of opinions, discussion.

conferment, n. [1. kunférment; 2. kənfʌ́mənt]. **confer** & **-ment.** The act of bestowing (a title, degree, gift, privilege, favour &c.).

conferrable, adj. [1. kunférabl, kunférabl; 2. kənfʌ́rəbl, kənférəbl]. **confer** & **-able.** Capable of being conferred.

confess, vb. trans. & intrans. [1. kunfés; 2. kənfés], fr. Fr. *confesser*, Low Lat. *confessāre*, formed fr. Lat. *confess-(um)*, P.P. type of *confitēri*, 'to confess', fr. **con-** & *fatēri*, 'to confess, acknowledge'; fr. Lat. base *fă-*, 'to speak', q.v. under **fame. 1.** trans. **a** To acknowledge, own, admit: *to confess a fault, crime* &c.; *to confess that one has done something amiss*; **b** (colloq. with weakened meaning) as *I confess I was surprised to hear it*; **c** (i.) (of a penitent) to make formal admission of (sins) to a priest; (ii.) (of a priest) to hear confession of: *to confess a penitent.* **2.** intrans. **a** To make an admission of guilt: *he confessed before he was hanged*; **b** specif. (eccles.) to declare and enumerate one's sins to a priest in order to receive sacramental absolution: *to confess regularly before hearing Mass.*

confessant, n. [1. kunfésant; 2. kənfésənt], fr. Fr. *confessant*, Pres. Part. See **confess.** One who makes confession to a priest. (Rare.)

confessed, adj. [1. kunfést; 2. kənfést], fr. P.P. of **confess.** Admitted, avowed, evident: *a confessed thief.* Phr. *to stand confessed as*, be revealed.

confessedly, adv. [1. kunfésedli; 2. kənfésidli]. Prec. & **-ly.** By (general) admission, confession.

confession, n. [1. kunféshun; 2. kənféʃən]. Fr. *confession*, fr. Lat. *confessiōn-(em)*. See **confess** & **-ion. 1.** Acknowledgement, avowal, admission. **2. a** Acknowledgement of belief; profession of faith, declaration of religious creed, doctrine &c.: *confession of faith*; **b** a particular creed or religion. **3.** Specif. (eccles.) the act of confessing sins to a priest in order to receive absolution; **a** in church, in common with others, as a congregation: *public confession*; **b** alone, in private: *auricular confession*; *to go to confession*; (of a priest) *to hear confession*; **c** any one of several forms of public confession in the Book of Common Prayer: *the Confession.* **4.** (law) In *confession and avoidance*, plea admitting certain facts but alleging others which traverse them.

confessional, adj. & n. [1. kunféshunal; 2. kənféʃənəl], fr. prec. & **-al. 1.** adj. Pertaining to a confession of faith. **2.** n., **a** enclosed place screened off from rest of church, in which priest hears confessions; **b** system and practice of confession to a priest.

confessionary, adj. & n. [1. kunféshunari; 2. kənféʃənəri]. **confession** & **-ary. a** adj. Pertaining to auricular confession; **b** n., confessional.

confessionist, n. [1. kunféshunist; 2. kənféʃənist], fr. Fr. *confessioniste.* **confession** & **-ist.** Adherent of a certain creed or confession.

confessor, n. [1. kunfésur, kónfesōr; 2. kənfésə, kɔ́nfesɔ]. **confess** & **-or. 1. a** One who confesses; **b** specif. (eccles.) one who suffers persecution or death for his religion. **2.** A priest who has a mission to hear confession, and give absolution.

confetti, n. pl. [1. konféti; 2. kənféti]. Ital. *confetto*, pl. *confetti*, 'sweetmeat'. See **confection.** Small round pieces, originally of plaster, now of coloured paper, used by revellers at carnivals to pelt each other, or thrown at departing bridal pair after a wedding.

confidant, n. (fem. **confidante**) [1. kònfidánt; 2. kɔ̀nfidǽnt]. **confide** & **-ant.** One to whom another confides his most intimate affairs and thoughts; a trusted bosom friend.

confide, vb. intrans. & trans. [1. kunfíd; 2. kənfáid], fr. Lat. *confīdere*, 'to trust', fr. **con-** & *fīdere*, 'to trust'. See **fidelity. 1.** intrans. (followed by *in*) **a** To entrust secrets, intimate affairs to, take into one's confidence; **b** to put trust in, rely upon (rare). **2.** trans. **a** To tell, impart, as a secret: *confide one's troubles to a friend*; **b** to hand over, entrust to, give into keeping of: *to confide a task to a person's charge.*

confidence, n. [1. kónfidens; 2. kɔ́nfidəns], fr. Lat. *confidentia.* See prec. & **-ence. 1. a** Feeling of certainty, strong hope, or conviction that circumstances are as one wishes; belief that a person may be trusted, relied on: *to have confidence in the future*; *to place every confidence in a person's honesty, skill, judgement* &c.; **b** similar feeling about oneself and one's abilities, self-reliance: *to be poor but full of confidence*; *self-confidence.* **2.** Something told, confided, to another as a secret, something which a person wishes to keep private: *I have no wish to hear confidences.* **3.** Act of confiding, trusting, or state of mind in which trust and reliance are felt and exhibited. Chiefly in Phrs. *to take a person into one's confidence*, tell him a secret; *to tell something in confidence*, as a secret; *in strict confidence*, not to be revealed on any account.

confidence man, n. One who practises the confidence trick.

confidence trick, n. Swindle worked by practising on the confidence or trust of credulous and not too scrupulous persons.

confident, adj. [1. kónfident; 2. kɔ́nfidənt]. Lat. *confīdent-(em)*, Pres. Part. of *confīdere*. See **confide. 1.** (of persons) **a** Having feeling of certainty, convinced, fully persuaded, esp. that circumstances are favourable: *confident of success*; *confident that everything will go well*; (but also gen.) *confident one is mistaken*; **b** (transferred from feelings to the objects or circumstances which provoke them): '*Never glad, confident morning again*' (Browning); **c** (of non-material things) exhibiting, expressing, inspired by confidence: *a confident manner, confident smile*; *a confident attack* &c. **2. a** Having confidence in one's own abilities, skill &c.; self-reliant; **b** overweeningly confident in oneself, cocksure, conceited: *a very confident, uppish young man.*

confidential, adj. [1. kònfidénshal; 2. kɔ̀nfidénʃəl]. Prec. & **-ial. 1. a** Communicated in confidence, secret: *a confidential communication*; **b** (of persons) inclined to impart confidences, to take another into confidence: *to become confidential with strangers.* **2.** Enjoying confidence; entrusted with secrets, trustworthy: *confidential clerk, servant* &c.

confidentially, adv. Prec. & **-ly. a** In confidence, under promise of secrecy: *to tell something confidentially*; **b** privately, intimately, in such a way as to show confidence, or by way of imparting confidences: *to speak confidentially to a person.*

confidently, adv. [1. kónfidentli; 2. kɔ́nfidəntli]. **confident** & **-ly.** With confidence, assurance, in a confident manner.

configuration, n. [1. kunfìgūráshun; 2. kənfìgjəréiʃən], fr. Lat. *configūrātiōn-(em)*. See **configure** & **-ation. 1.** Relative disposition of inequalities of surface, contour; figure, form, shape. **2.** (astrol.) Relative position or aspect of planets.

configure, vb. trans. [1. kunfígur; 2. kənfígə], fr. Lat. *configūrāre*, 'to form from, or after, something', fr. **con-** & **figure.** To shape, give contour or configuration to.

confine (I.), n. [1. kónfīn; 2. kɔ́nfain], fr. Fr. *confins*, pl., fr. Med. Lat. *confines*, pl. adj., fr. Lat. **con-** & *fīnis* (pl. *fīnes*), 'end, limit, boundary'. See **final.** (usually pl.) **a** Boundary, border, limit: *within the confines of his kingdom*; **b** (fig.) borderland between different feelings, ideas &c.

confine (II.), vb. trans. & intrans. [1. kunfín; 2. kənfáin], fr. Fr. *confiner*, 'to border on', fr. Ital. *confinare*, fr. Lat. *con-* & *fīnis.* See **confine** (I.). **1.** trans. **a** (followed by *to*) To keep or restrain within limits; to restrict, limit (esp. oneself *to* something): *to confine oneself, one's remarks, to*; **b** (followed by *within, in*) to keep shut up within limits, to imprison: *to confine a prisoner in a cell.* Phr. *to be confined to one's room*, unable to leave it from illness; *confined to barracks*, as punishment of soldier for breaches of discipline &c. **2.** intrans. (obs.) *To confine with*, to have common boundaries, be adjacent to, border on, touch.

confined, adj. [1. kunfínd; 2. kənfáind], fr. P.P. of prec. **1. a** (of space) Limited, narrow, oppressively small and restricted: *room in so small a house was very confined*; **b** (fig., of spiritual restrictions) hampered, fettered: '*cabin'd, cribb'd, confined*'. **2.** (specif. of women) To be in act of giving birth to a child: *to expect to be confined on such a date*, expect child to be born then; *about to be confined*, going to have a child. **3.** Constipated.

confinement, n. [1. kunfínment; 2. kənfáinmənt], fr. **confine** & **-ment. 1. a** State in which liberty and power of movement are hindered or prevented: *to live in confinement*; *to be placed under confinement*; specif., to be put in prison or in a lunatic asylum; *close confinement, solitary confinement*, imprisonment under conditions of complete separation from others; **b** (fig.) sensation of being kept in, restricted in action &c. by surroundings, or conditions of life: *to feel the confinement of an office.* **2.** (specif. of women) The giving birth to a child, delivery.

confirm, vb. trans. [1. kunférm; 2. kənfʌ́m], fr. O. Fr. *confermer*, Fr. *confirmer*, fr. Lat. *confirmāre*, 'to make firm', fr. **con-** & *firmāre* 'to make firm', fr. *firmus*, see **firm** (I.). **1.** To make firm; to establish more firmly; **a** (of persons) to encourage, make more determined and resolute, add conviction to: *to confirm a person in his decision, opinions* &c.; **b** (of opinion, purpose, determination &c.) to fortify, fix more firmly: *later events served to confirm his previous determination*; **c** (of statements, rumour, evidence) to render certain, corroborate: *the reported disaster is now confirmed.* **2.** To ratify, sanction, make valid: *to confirm a treaty, an appointment* &c. **3.** (eccles., of a bishop) To admit to privileges of Holy Communion by imposition of hands in Confirmation.

confirmation, n. [1. kònfermáshun; 2. kònfəméiʃən], fr. Lat. *confirmātiōn-(em)*. See prec. & **-ation**. **1.** Act or process of confirming, esp. in sense of **confirm, 1, c**; corroboration, making more certain: *confirmation of one's statements, hopes, promises, news* &c. **2.** (eccles., cap.) Laying of hands by a bishop on such as are of age to reaffirm for themselves the promises made for them by their god-parents at baptism; rite essential to the admission of baptized persons to Holy Communion.

confirmative, adj. [1. kunférmativ; 2. kənfə́mətiv]. See prec. & **-ive**. Tending to confirm, strengthen, corroborate.

confirmatively, adv. Prec. & **-ly**. In a confirmative manner.

confirmatory, adj. [1. kunférmaturi; 2. kənfə́mətri]. See prec. & **-ory**. Confirmative.

confirmed, adj. [1. kunférmd; 2. kənfə́md], fr. P.P. of **confirm**. Settled, fully established, inveterate: *a confirmed invalid, bachelor, drunkard* &c.

confirmee, n. [1. kònfermḗ; 2. kònfəmí]. **confirm** & **-ee**. Candidate for confirmation by the bishop.

confiscable, adj. [1. kónfiskabl; 2. kónfiskəbl]. See **confiscate** & **-able**. Liable to be confiscated.

confiscate, vb. trans. [1. kónfiskāt, kónviskāt; 2. kónfiskeit, kónviskeit], fr. Lat. *confiscāt-(um)*, P.P. of *confiscāre*, 'to lay up in a chest; to seize on for public treasury', fr. **con-** & *fiscus*, 'basket, purse, treasury'. See **fisc**. To seize, appropriate, take (property) from owner with legal authority, or by superior strength; specif., to appropriate property to purposes of the State, or, as a penalty, with sanction of the State and without compensation.

confiscation, n. [1. kònfiskáshun; 2. kònfiskéiʃən], fr. Lat. *confiscātiōn-(em)*, 'forfeiting, confiscation'. See **confiscate** & **-ion**. The act or process of confiscating; specif., appropriation of property by the State without compensation.

confiscator, n. [1. kónfiskāter; 2. kónfiskeitə]. Lat. **confiscate** & **-or**. One who confiscates.

confiscatory, adj. [1. kònfiskáturi; 2. kònfiskéitəri]. See prec. & **-y**. Of the nature of, connected with, confiscation.

confiteor, n. [1. konfítēōr; 2. kənfítiɔ]. Lat., 'I confess', fr. *confitēri*. See **confess**. (eccles.) The Confession, **3, c**.

conflagration, n. [1. kònflagráshun; 2. kònflagréiʃən], fr. Lat. *conflāgrātiōn-(em)*, 'a burning', fr. *conflāgrāre*, 'to be in flames, to burn up', fr. **con-** & *flāgrāre*, 'to flame, blaze, burn'. See **flagrant**. A great fire.

conflate, vb. trans. [1. kunflát; 2. kənfléit], fr. Lat. *conflāt-(um)*, P.P. type of *conflāre*, 'to blow together', fr. **con-** & *flāre*, 'to blow'. See **afflatus** & **blow (I.)**. **a** To blow together; to fuse or bring together; to join or weld together; **b** to run together two readings of a text, and so produce composite reading.

conflation, n. [1. kunfláshun; 2. kənfléiʃən]. fr. Lat. *conflātiōn-(em)*. See prec. & **-ion**. A fusing together, fusion, esp. of two readings.

conflict (I.), n. [1. kónflikt; 2. kónflikt], fr. Lat. *conflictus*, 'a striking together; strife, contest'. See **conflict (II.)**. **1.** Physical struggle, fight, contest, between individuals, parties, armies. **2.** Strife of opinions, principles, desires &c.; a quarrel: *a wordy conflict.* **3.** Strong difference or opposition between statements, opinions, interests &c.; disagreement, contradiction, disparity: *a conflict of evidence, of feelings.*

conflict (II.), vb. intrans. [1. kunflíkt; 2. kənflíkt], fr. Lat. *conflict-(um)*, P.P. type of *confligere*, 'to strike against or on, to strike or bring together, to contend, fight', fr. **con-** & *fligere*, 'to strike'; perh. cogn. w. Goth. *bliggwan*, 'beat, kill'; more certainly w. O. Slav. *blizná*, 'scar, wound'; cp. **afflict, profligate**. **1.** To contend, struggle, fight, strive (rare or obs.). **2.** To clash with, be incompatible, irreconcilable, at variance with, be opposed to: *my interests conflict with yours*; *conflicting accounts, opinions* &c. (See also next word.)

conflicting, adj. [1. kunflíkting; 2. kənflíktiŋ], fr. Pres. Part. of prec. (gen. fig.) Incompatible, tending in different and opposite directions: *a prey to conflicting emotions.*

confluence, n. [1. kónflooens; 2. kónfluəns], fr. Lat. *confluentia*, 'a flowing together', fr. *confluent-(em)*, Pres. Part. type of *confluere*, 'to flow together', fr. **con-** & *fluere*, 'to flow'. See **fluent, fluid**. **1.** A flowing together; place where two streams meet. (Cp. German place-name *Coblentz.*) **2.** (fig.) The act of coming, meeting, together; hence, a crowd, concourse.

confluent (I.), adj. [1. kónflooent; 2. kónfluənt], fr. Lat. *confluent-(em)*, Pres. Part. of *confluere*. See **con-** & **fluent**. **1.** Flowing together, uniting (esp. of rivers and streams, but also (more rarely) of roads). **2.** Specif. (med.) running together: *confluent small-pox* (in which the pustules unite and cover large areas of the skin).

confluent (II.), n., fr. prec. **a** A stream which unites with another; **b** a tributary, an affluent.

conflux, n. [1. kónfluks; 2. kónflaks]. See **con-, flux**, & cp. **confluence**. Confluence, esp. of people or things.

conform, vb. trans. & intrans. [1. kunfórm; 2. kənfɔ́m], fr. Fr. *conformer*, fr. Lat. *conformāre*, 'to fashion, shape symmetrically', fr. **con-** & *formāre*, 'to form'. See **form (II.)**. **1.** trans. (only fig., of non-material things) To give same form to, shape in accordance with a model, adapt: *to conform one's manners to those of one's associates.* **2.** intrans. (followed by *to*) **a** (of material things) To be adapted to shape of, follow contour of &c.: *a coat must conform to the figure of the wearer*; **b** (fig.) to be in harmony or agreement with; comply, be obedient, submit to: *to conform to the rules*; **c** (Engl. eccles. hist.) to comply with the usages of the Established Church, obey *Act of Uniformity.*

conformability, n. [1. kunfòrmabíliti; 2. kənfɔ̀məbíliti]. **conformable** & **-ity**. Condition of being conformable.

conformable, adj. [1. kunfórmabl; 2. kənfɔ́məbl], fr. **conform** & **-able**. **1.** (followed by *to*, more rarely by *with*) Corresponding, according with; consistent, suitable to. **2.** Submissive, compliant, tractable: *conformable to another's will.*

conformably, adv. Prec. & **-ly**. In accordance with.

conformation, n. [1. kònformáshun; 2. kònfɔméiʃən], fr. Lat. *conformātiōn-(em)*, 'a symmetrical forming or fashioning'. See **conform** & **-ation**. **1.** The act of conforming or of producing conformity (obs. or rare). **2.** Manner in which a thing is formed, or shaped; arrangement and shape of parts.

conformist, n. [1. kunfórmist; 2. kənfɔ́mist]. **conform** & **-ist**. One who conforms; specif. (cap.) one who conforms to the religious usages of the Established Church of England; contrasted with *Dissenter* or *Nonconformist.*

conformity, n. [1. kunfórmiti; 2. kənfɔ́miti]. See **conform** & **-ity**. **1. a** Correspondence with, in outward shape, in manner, character, principles &c.; **b** agreement, congruity; **c** compliance. Phr. *in conformity with your orders* &c. **2.** (Engl. eccles. hist.) Compliance with the usages of the Established Church as distinguished from nonconformity or dissent.

confound, vb. trans. [1. kunfóund; 2. kənfáund], fr. O. Fr. *confondre*, fr. Lat. *confundere*, *confūsum*, 'to pour together', fr. **con-** & *fundere*, 'to pour'. See **fuse**. **1. a** (of ideas) To mix up, confuse; **b** to mistake one person or one thing for another: *I always confound him with his brother.* **2. a** To throw into confusion, disorder, perplexity, or dismay; (Bib.) to abash, put to shame: '*Let me never be confounded*' ('Te Deum'); hence, **b** to defeat, overthrow (esp. fig., of plans, hopes &c.): '*Confound their politics*' ('National Anthem'); **c** (colloq.) *confound it!*; *confound you!*, a mild expletive.

confounded, adj. [1. kunfóunded; 2. kənfáundid], fr. P.P. of prec. **1.** Confused, perplexed (rare). **2.** (colloq.) A mild expletive expressing slight annoyance: *I've been waiting a confounded long time*; *here's your confounded hat, now be off.*

confoundedly, adv. Prec. & **-ly**. (colloq.) As intensive, equivalent to *very, extremely*, &c.; generally, though not always, expressing disapprobation: *confoundedly annoying, cold* &c.; *a confoundedly good dinner.*

confraternity, n. [1. kònfratérniti; 2. kònfrətə́niti]. See **con-** & **fraternity**. An organized society, association; a brotherhood (esp. a religious body).

confrère, n. [1. kónfrār; 2. kónfreə]. Fr. See **con-** & **friar**. Fellow-member of a society, associate in profession, office, or business; a colleague.

confront, vb. trans. [1. kunfrúnt; 2. kənfránt], fr. Fr. *confronter*, fr. **con-** & Lat. *frons, frontis*, 'forehead, front'. See **front**. **1. a** (of persons or other living beings) To stand in front of, and gaze at fixedly and resolutely; often with sense of defiance, threat, hostility: *two queer-looking men confronted me*; **b** to present unflinching face to, offer bold, resolute resistance to, to face bravely and calmly: *to confront danger, death.* **2.** (followed by *with*) **a** To place before, bring into presence of (esp. of persons) *to confront a man with his accusers, with evidence of guilt* &c.; **b** (in pass.) to be faced by, find oneself faced and opposed by: *I am confronted with many difficulties.*

confrontation, n. [1. kónfruntáshun; 2. kònfrantéiʃən]. Prec. & **-ation**. Act of confronting (rare, hardly an English term). In special French sense, act of confronting an accused person with witnesses against him.

Confucian, adj. & n. [1. kunfúsian; 2. kənfjúsiən], fr. *Confucius*, the Latinized form of Chinese *Kung-Fû-tsze*, founder of Chinese system of ethics, 551–478 B.C. **1.** adj. Pertaining to Confucius. **2.** n. A follower of Confucius.

Confucianism, n. [1. kunfúsianizm; 2. kənfjúsiənizəm]. Prec. & **-ism**. System of philosophy and ethics propounded by the Chinese Confucius.

Confucianist, n. [1. kunfúsianist; 2. kənfjúsiənist]. See prec. & **-ist**. Follower of Confucianism.

confuse, vb. trans. [1. kunfúz; 2. kənfjúz]. Fr. *confuser*, fr. Lat. *confūs-(um)*, P.P. type of *confundere*. See **con-** & **fuse**. **1. a** To put into disorder, mix up (esp. the mind, ideas &c.): *too many new objects merely confuse one's ideas*; **b** to mistake one thing for another, to fail to distinguish between: *you are confusing two perfectly different things.* **2.** (in pass.) **a** (of the mind) *To become confused*, to be bewildered, perplexed, disconcerted; **b** (of statements, expression of ideas) muddled, lacking in clearness, obscure: *a confused account, statement* &c.

confusedly, adv. [1. kunfúzedli; 2. kənfjúzidli], fr. P.P. of prec. & **-ly**. In a muddled, obscure manner.

confusedness, n. [1. kunfúz(e)dnes; 2. kənfjúz(i)dnis]. See prec. & **-ness**. State of being confused.

confusion, n. [1. kunfúzhun; 2. kənfjúʒən]. Lat. *confūsiōn-(em)*, 'a mixing, combining; disorder, confusion'. See **confuse** & **-ion**. **1.** (of material things) Disorder, disarray, muddle, lack of orderly arrangement: *to leave one's papers in confusion*; (also fig. of non-material things) *to leave one's affairs in confusion*, unsettled. **2.** (of the mind and mental processes) **a** Muddle, perplexity, lack of clearness: *confusion of mind, thought, ideas* &c.; **b** embarrassment, shame: Phr. *covered with confusion.*

confutation, n. [1. kònfūtáshun; 2. kònfjutéiʃən]. Next word & **-ation**. Act or process of confuting.

confute, vb. trans. [1. kunfût; 2. kənfjút], fr. Lat. *confūtāre*, 'to repress a boiling liquid; check, suppress; put down by words, silence, disprove', see **batter (I.)**, **beat (I.)**. **a** To prove by argument that a person is wrong, convict of error; **b** to disprove a statement by irrefragable, unanswerable, evidence.

congé, n. [1. kónzhā; 2. kɔ̃žei]. Fr., 'permission, leave of absence, dismissal', fr. Lat. *commeātus*, 'a going to and fro at will; leave of absence', fr. **con-** & *meātus*, 'a going, motion, course'. See **meatus**. **1.** Abrupt and unceremonious dismissal. Phr. *to give (a person) his congé*. **2.** Specif., *congé d'élire* [1. kónzhā dālḗr; 2. kɔ̃žei deilíə], lit. 'leave to choose', the Royal authority issued to a Chapter for the election of a bishop.

congeal, vb. trans. & intrans. [1. kunjḗl; 2. kəndžíəl], fr. Fr. *congeler*, fr. Lat. *congelāre*, 'to cause to freeze; to freeze up', fr. **con-** & *gelāre*, 'to freeze' (trans. & intrans.), fr. *gelu*, 'frost, cold'. See **gelid**. **1.** trans. To freeze; to change from fluid to solid through cold, to solidify; to coagulate (often fig.) *his very blood was congealed* (through fear). **2.** intrans. To become hard or coagulated from cold &c; to freeze, to become chilled (lit. and fig.).

congealable, adj. [1. kunjḗlabl; 2. kəndžíləbl]. Prec. & **-able**. Capable of being congealed.

congealment, n. [1. kunjḗlment; 2. kəndžíəlment], fr. **congeal** & **-ment**. Process of congealing.

congee, n. [1. kònjḗ; 2. kɔ̀ndzí]. M.E. *congye*, fr. O. Fr. *congiez*. See **congé**. (archaic) Formal bow, greeting, salute; esp. parting bow or curtsey: *to make one's congees*, to take leave.

congelation, n. [1. kònjelā́shun; 2. kɔ̀ndželéiʃən], fr. Lat. *congelātiōn-(em)*, fr. *congelāt-(um)*, P.P. type of *congelāre*. See **congeal**. **a** Process of congealing or freezing; **b** state of being congealed; **c** that which is congealed.

congener, n. [1. kunjḗner; 2. kəndžínə]. Lat., 'of same race or kind', fr. **con-** & *genus*, genit. *generis*, 'kind, species'. See **genus**. A thing or person related to another in race, kind, character.

congeneric(al), adj. [1. kònjenérik(l); 2. kɔ̀ndženérik(l)]. Prec. & **-ic** & **-al**. Of the same genus, kind, nature, race &c.

congenerous, adj. [1. kònjénerus; 2. kɔ̀ndžénərəs], fr. **congener** & **-ous**. **a** Of the same genus, nature, or kind; **b** performing similar function; acting in concert with.

congenial, adj. [1. kunjḗnyal; 2. kəndžínjəl]. See **con-** & **genial**. **a** (of two or more persons) Having the same nature, tastes, disposition &c.; sympathetic: *to meet those congenial to one*; *in congenial society*; **b** (of things in relation to persons) suitable, suited, propitious to: *a climate congenial to health*; agreeable, adapted to: *work congenial to one, to one's tastes*.

congeniality, n. [1. kunjḕniáliti; 2. kəndžìniǽliti]. Prec. & **-ity**. State or quality of being congenial.

congenially, adv. [1. kunjḗnyali; 2. kəndžínjəli]. **congenial** & **-ly**. In a congenial manner.

congenital, adj. [1. kunjénital; 2. kəndžénitəl], fr. Lat. *congenitus*, 'produced together with', fr. **con-** & P.P. of *gignere*, 'to beget', & **-al**. See **genital**, adj. Born with one; possessed, belonging to one, from birth; used esp. of defects, diseases &c.: *congenital idiocy*.

congenitally, adv. Prec. & **-ly**. From birth: *congenitally blind* &c.

conger, n. [1. kóngger; 2. kɔ́ŋgə], fr. O. Fr. *congre*, fr. Lat. *conger*, & *congrus*, 'sea-eel', fr. Gk. *góggros*, 'growth on trees; conger', cogn. w. Gk. *gráō*, 'I eat, gnaw', & *grástis*, 'green forage', Lat. *grāmen*, fr. **grasmen*, 'grass, forage', & O.E. *græs* &c. See **grass**. Large species of marine eel, also *conger-eel*.

congeries, n. [1. konjḗriz; 2. kəndžíəriz]. Lat., 'that which is brought together, pile, heap', fr. *congerere*, 'bring, carry together', fr. **con-** & *gerere*, 'bear', fr. earlier **gesere*. See **gerent**. A collection of separate bodies or parts into one mass; a heap, pile.

congest, vb. trans. [1. kunjést; 2. kəndžést], fr. Lat. *congest-(um)*, P.P. type of *congerere*, 'to bring together, heap up', fr. **con-** & *gerere*, 'to bear, carry'. See prec. **1.** To collect into a mass, to bring, crowd, together; to overcrowd, load, glut. **2.** Specif. (med.) to affect with congestion.

congested, adj. [1. kunjésted; 2. kəndžéstid], fr. P.P. of prec. **1.** (med., of organs of the body) Overcharged with blood, clotted up. **2.** Overcrowded, pressed, crowded together (of places, streets &c., also of population), esp. of agricultural districts, where the holdings are too small and the land too poor to support the population.

congestion, n. [1. kunjéschun; 2. kəndžéstʃən], fr. Fr., fr. Lat. *congestiōn-(em)*, 'a heaping up, accumulation'. See **congest** & **-ion**. **1.** (med.) An excessive and abnormal accumulation of blood in any organ of the body: *congestion of the lungs, brain* &c. **2.** Overcrowding (of population, traffic &c.).

congestive, adj. [1. kunjéstiv; 2. kəndžéstiv], fr. **congest** & **-ive**. (med.) Pertaining to congestion; indicating, attended with, congestion: *congestive appearance, symptoms* &c.

conglobate (I.), vb. trans. [1. konglṓbāt; 2. kənglóubeit], fr. Lat. *conglobāt-(um)*, P.P. of *conglobāre*, 'to gather into a ball', fr. **con-** & *globāre*, 'to make into a ball'. See **globe**. To form into a ball.

conglobate (II.), adj. [1. konglṓbat; 2. kənglóubit], fr. Lat. *conglobātus*, P.P. of *conglobāre*. See prec. Formed into a globe, ball, or round mass.

conglobation, n. [1. kònglōbā́shun; 2. kɔ̀nglоubéiʃən], fr. Lat. *conglobātiōn-(em)*, 'a heaping, gathering, or crowding together'. See prec. & **-ion**. Process of forming into a round mass.

conglobe, vb. trans. & intrans. [1. kunglṓb; 2. kənglóub]. See **conglobate**. To conglobate.

conglomerate (I.), adj. & n. [1. kunglómerāt; 2. kənglɔ́məreit], fr. Lat. *conglomerāt-(um)*, P.P. type of *conglomerāre*, 'to roll together', fr. **con-** & *glomerāre*, 'to wind up, form into a ball', fr. *glomus, glomeris*, 'a ball of yarn'. See **agglomerate (I.)**. **1.** adj. Composed of a number of separate objects, elements, or parts, stuck or heaped together. **2.** n. **a** A mass or pile of things heaped together; **b** specif. (geol.) a rock formed of shingle or small fragments, embedded in a matrix of finer material.

conglomerate (II.), vb. trans. & intrans. See prec. To gather together or collect into a mass (lit. and fig.).

conglomeration, n. [1. kunglòmerā́shun; 2. kənglɔ̀məréiʃən]. Prec. & **-ion**. **1.** **a** The act or process of collecting separate objects or elements into a mass; **b** the state of being piled, massed together. **2.** Collection of separate objects of various kinds, or from different sources, gathered or heaped together into a mass or pile.

conglutinate, vb. trans. & intrans. [1. kunglṑotināt; 2. kənglútineit], fr. Lat. *conglūtināt-(um)*, P.P. of *conglūtināre*, 'to glue together', fr. **con-** & *glūtināre*, 'to glue', fr. *glūten, glūtinis*, 'glue'. See **glue**, **gluten**. **1.** trans. To glue or stick together; to cause to adhere, unite or grow together (of bones). **2.** intrans. To stick together; to unite or grow together.

conglutination, n. [1. kunglòotinā́shun; 2. kənglùtinéiʃən], fr. Lat. *conglūtinātiōn-(em)*. Prec. & **-ion**. Process of conglutinating.

congo, congou, n. [1. kónggō; 2. kɔ́ŋgou]. Chinese. Black China tea.

congratulant, adj. [1. kungráchoolant; 2. kəngrǽtʃulənt], fr. Lat. *congrātulant-(em)*, Pres. Part. of *congrātulāri*. See next word. Expressing congratulation, congratulatory.

congratulate, vb. trans. [1. kungráchoolāt; 2. kəngrǽtʃuleit], fr. Lat. *congrātulāt-(um)*, P.P. type of *congrātulāri*, 'to wish joy warmly', fr. **con-** & *grātulāri*, 'to wish joy', fr. *grātus*, 'pleasing'. See **grateful** & **grace (I.)**. To wish joy to, express to another one's own satisfaction at his happiness, success, good fortune &c.; in such constructions as: *I congratulate you*; or *I congratulate you on your engagement*.

congratulation, n. [1. kungràchoolā́shun; 2. kəngrætʃuléiʃən]. **congratulate** & **-ion**. Expression of good wishes on another's good fortune, success &c.

congratulatory, adj. [1. kungráchoolatri; 2. kəngrǽtʃulətri]. See **congratulate** & **-ory**. Expressing congratulations: *a congratulatory speech, message* &c.

congregate, vb. trans. & intrans. [1. kónggregāt; 2. kɔ́ŋgrigeit], fr. Lat. *congregāt-(um)*, P.P. type of *congregāre*, 'to flock together', fr. **con-** & *gregāre*, fr. *greg-*, base of *grex*, 'flock, herd'. See **gregarious**. **1.** trans. (not frequent) To collect, bring together. **2.** intrans. To flock together, assemble, come together at same time and place.

congregation, n. [1. kònggregā́shun; 2. kɔ̀ŋgrigéiʃən], fr. Fr. *congrégation*, fr. Lat. *congregātiōn-(em)*, 'an assembling together; a society, association'. **congregate** & **-ion**. **1.** An assembly or gathering of persons, esp. **a** a body of people assembled in a church for religious service; **b** general body of worshippers at a particular church or chapel. **2.** Various specific senses, usually cap.: **a** (Oxford University) body composed of all resident masters and doctors engaged in teaching, or occupying certain offices in the university; **b** (Jewish hist.) *the Congregation*, whole assembly of the Jewish people; **c** (R.C. Ch.) applied to various religious orders and associations; specif., one of the Committees of cardinals in charge of a department of the Vatican.

congregational, adj. [1. kòngregā́shunal; 2. kɔ̀ŋgrigéiʃənəl]. See prec. & **-al**. **1.** Of, or pertaining to a congregation: *congregational worship*. **2.** Pertaining, adhering to, Congregationalism: *Congregational chapel*.

Congregationalism, n. [1. kònggregā́shunalizm; 2. kɔ̀ŋgrigéiʃənəlizəm]. See prec. & **-ism**. A system of nonconformist church government in which each church and congregation is independent in the management of its own affairs.

Congregationalist, n. [1. kònggregā́shunalist; 2. kɔ̀ŋgrigéiʃənəlist]. **congregational** & **-ist**. Adherent of Congregationalism.

congress, n. [1. kónggres; 2. kɔ́ŋgres], fr. Lat. *congressus*, 'a friendly meeting together', fr. *congressus*, P.P. of *congredi*, 'to go, come, or meet together', fr. **con-** & *gradi*, 'to go, step', fr. *gradus*, 'a step'; see **gradus**. **1.** A gathering together, an assembly, a conference; specif., a formal meeting for discussion of questions of common interest between envoys or delegates representing different governments or learned bodies &c.: *the congress of Vienna*; *a church, university, medical, congress*. **2.** Specif. (cap.) the national legislative body of the United States of America, or of a S. or C. American republic.

congressional, adj. [1. konggréshunal; 2. kəŋgréʃənəl]. Lat. *congressiōn-(em)*, 'a coming together, meeting', fr. *congress-*, as in P.P. of *congredi*, & **-ion** & **-al**. See prec. Of, or pertaining to, a congress, esp. to the Congress of the U.S.A.: *congressional debates* &c.

Congress-man, n. A member of Congress in the U.S.A.

Congreve, adj. & n. [1. kónggrēv; 2. kɔ́ŋgriv]. For *Congreve rocket*, fr. Sir William Congreve, the inventor. Powerful type of rocket.

congruence, -cy, n. [1. kónggrooens(i); 2. kɔ́ŋgruəns(i)], fr. Lat. *congruentia*, 'agreement, harmony'. See **congruent**. **1.** Suitability of one thing to another; correspondence, agreement. **2.** Specif. (math.) relation between two numbers which, when divided by a third number, the *modulus*, give the same remainder.

congruent, adj. [1. kónggrooent; 2. kɔ́ŋgruənt], fr. Lat. *congruent-(em)*, 'agreeing', Pres. Part. of *congruere*, 'to come together, coincide, agree'. See **con-**; the second element is identical w. *ruere*, 'to fall with violence, rush down', fr. **ghru-*, & cogn. w. *ruīna*, 'a rushing down, a fall'. See further under **ruin**. a Suitable, agreeing with; b (math.) having congruence.

congruity, n. [1. konggróoiti; 2. kɔŋgrúiti], fr. Lat. *congru-*, as in *congruus*, 'agreeing, fit, suitable' &c., & **-ity**. See prec. State or quality of being congruous, agreement between things, fitness.

congruous, adj. [1. kónggroous; 2. kɔ́ŋgruəs], fr. Lat. *congru-(us)*, 'agreeing, fit, suitable; concordant', & **-ous**. See **congruent**. Suitable, conformable, consistent.

congruously, adv. Prec. & **-ly**. In a congruous manner.

conic, adj. & n. [1. kónik; 2. kɔ́nik]. **cone** & **-ic**. (math.) a adj. Concerned with the properties of cones: *conic sections*; b n., in pl., *conics*, the theory and doctrine of cones.

conical, adj. [1. kónikl; 2. kɔ́nikl]. Prec. & **-al**. Shaped like a cone, broad at the base and tapering towards the apex.

conifer, n. [1. kōnifer; 2. kóunifə]. Lat., 'cone-bearing'. See next word. (bot.) A cone-bearing tree or shrub, as pine, fir, yew, cypress &c.

coniferous, adj. [1. kòníferus; 2. kòunífərəs]. See **cone** & **-ferous**. Cone-bearing (of trees, such as pines, firs &c.).

coniform, adj. [1. kōniform; 2. kóunifɔ̄m]. **cone** & **form**. Having the form of, shaped like, a cone.

conine, n. [1. kōnīn; 2. kóunain], fr. Lat. *cōnīum*, fr. Gk. *kṓneion*, 'hemlock', perh. related to *kōnos*, 'cone', see **cone**, & so called fr. the shape of its leaves, & **-ine**. A poisonous alkaloid obtained from hemlock.

conjecturable, adj. [1. kunjékchurabl; 2. kəndžéktʃərəbl], fr. **conjecture (II.)** & **-able**. Capable of being conjectured.

conjectural, adj. [1. kunjékchural; 2. kəndžéktʃərəl], fr. Lat. *conjectūrālis*. See **conjecture (I.)** & **-al**. Arrived at by conjecture, not based upon certain and complete knowledge.

conjecturally, adv. Prec. & **-ly**. In the manner of, by, conjecture.

conjecture (I.), n. [1. kunjékchur; 2. kəndžéktʃə], fr. Lat. *conjectūra*, 'an inference, conclusion', fr. *conject-(um)*, P.P. type of *conjicere*, lit. 'to throw together; to infer, conclude', fr. **con-** & *jacere*, 'to throw'. See **jactitation** & **jet (III.)**. Inference based on evidence which is not complete; a guess, the truth of which at the moment is not fully confirmed. *Conjecture* is used both of an inference which is supported by a considerable amount of evidence, and of one which has very little in support of it. Specif., of an emendation to a text. Phr. *to hazard a conjecture.*

conjecture (II.), vb. trans. & intrans., fr. prec. 1. trans. a To guess, surmise, something; b (in textual criticism) to propose a reading. 2. intrans. To make a conjecture, guess.

conjoin, vb. trans. & intrans. [1. kunjóin; 2. kəndžóin]. M.E. *conjoinen*, fr. O. Fr. *conjoign-*, fr. *conjoindre*, fr. Lat. *conjungere*, 'to join together'. See **con-** & **join**. To join together, unite.

conjoined, adj. [1. kunjóind; 2. kəndžóind]. Prec. & **-ed**. a Joined together, occurring together (of events, circumstances &c.); b specif. (her.) joined together, touching, overlapping, e.g. of two heraldic animals united by a single head.

conjoint, adj. [1. kunjóint; 2. kəndžóint]. Fr., P.P. of *conjoindre*. **con-** & **joint**. See **conjoin**. United, associated, in conjunction: *conjoint action.*

conjointly, adv. Prec. & **-ly**. Jointly, together, in common, in association.

conjugal, adj. [1. kónjoogal; 2. kɔ́ndžugəl]. Fr. fr. Lat. *conjugālis*, 'relating to marriage', fr. *conjug-*, base of *conjux*, 'spouse', & **-al**. Cp. Lat. *jugum*, 'yoke', & **join**. Pertaining to marriage and the marriage state: *conjugal rights, relations* &c.

conjugality, n. [1. kònjoogáliti; 2. kɔ̀ndžugǽliti]. Prec. & **-ity**. The conjugal state, state of marriage; used by Milton.

conjugally, adv. [1. kónjoogali; 2. kɔ́ndžugəli]. **conjugal** & **-ly**. As husband and wife, in a conjugal manner.

conjugate (I.), vb. trans. & intrans. [1. kónjoogāt; 2. kɔ́ndžugeit], fr. Lat. *conjugāt-(um)*, P.P. type of *conjugāre*, 'to join together, unite', fr. **con-** & *jugāre*, 'to join, yoke, marry', fr. *jugum*, 'yoke', see **join, jugate**. a trans. (gram.) To inflect (a verb), to enumerate the forms of the various voices, moods, tenses, persons, numbers of a verb; b intrans. (of a vb.), to possess such-and-such inflexions, be conjugated.

conjugate (II.), adj. See prec. Joined, united.

conjugation, n. [1. kònjoogáshun; 2. kɔ̀ndžugéiʃən]. Lat. *conjugātiōn-(em)*, 'a joining; etymological relationship of words; conjugation' in present gram. sense. See **conjugate** & **-ion**. (gram.) a Inflexion of verbs; b one of several categories into which verbs are classified according to the particular mode of inflexion to which they are severally subject.

conjugational, adj. [1. kònjoogáshunal; 2. kɔ̀ndžugéiʃənəl]. Prec. & **-al**. Pertaining to the conjugation of verbs.

conjunct, adj. [1. konjúngkt; 2. kəndžʌ́ŋkt], fr. Lat. *conjunct-(um)*, P.P. of *conjungere*. See **conjoin**. United, joined with another, combined (archaic).

conjunction, n. [1. kunjúngkshun; 2. kəndžʌ́ŋkʃən]. Lat. *conjunctiōn-(em)*. See **conjunct** & **-ion**. 1. The act of conjoining, or the state of being conjoined; union, association, connexion: *in conjunction with*, together with. 2. (astrol. and astron.) Supposed propinquity of two heavenly bodies; meeting or passing, presence in same part of the heavens, of two bodies. 3. Combination, occurrence at the same time, coincidence in effect, of several events and circumstances. 4. (gram.) An indeclinable, connecting particle which joins together the parts and divisions of sentences; esp. the words *and, but.*

conjunctional, adj. [1. kunjúngkshunal; 2. kəndžʌ́ŋkʃənəl]. Prec. & **-al**. Of the nature of, having force of, a conjunction.

conjunctionally, adv. Prec. & **-ly**. As a conjunction.

conjunctiva, n. [1. kònjungktíva; 2. kɔ̀ndžaŋktáivə]. Neo-Lat. See **conjunctive**. (anat.) The mucous membrane covering the inner surface of the eyelids and front of the eyeball.

conjunctive, adj. [1. kunjúngktiv; 2. kəndžʌ́ŋktiv], fr. Lat. *conjunctīvus*, 'serving to connect'. **conjunct** & **-ive**. 1. Serving to join or unite: *conjunctive tissue.* 2. (gram.) Serving as a conjunction.

conjunctively, adv. Prec. & **-ly**. a By a conjunction; b conjointly.

conjunctivitis, n. [1. kunjùngktivítis; 2. kəndžʌ̀ŋktiváitis]. See **conjunctiva** & **-itis**. (med.) Inflammation of the conjunctiva.

conjunctly, adv. [1. konjúngktli; 2. kondžʌ́ŋktli]. **conjunct** & **-ly**. Jointly; adjoined together.

conjuncture, n. [1. kunjúngkchur; 2. kəndžʌ́ŋktʃə], fr. Fr. *conjoncture*, fr. L. Lat. *conjunctūra*. See **con-** & **juncture**. Combination of circumstances or events.

conjuration, n. [1. kònjooráshun; 2. kɔ̀ndžuréiʃən], fr. Lat. *conjūrātiōn-(em)*, lit. 'a swearing together, a conspiracy, plot'. **conjure** & **-ation**. a Solemn invocation; b incantation, spell, charm.

conjure (I.), vb. trans. [1. konjóor; 2. kɔndžúə, kəndžɔ̄]. Fr. *conjurer*, 'to beg, entreat, with insistence', fr. Lat. *conjūrāre*, 'to swear together, combine together by an oath; to conspire'. **con-** & *jūrāre*, 'to swear on oath'. See **jury**. To beg with insistence, make solemn appeal to, to entreat, ask earnestly, implore, beseech (a person) to do something: *I conjure you to grant my request, not to act in this way* &c. (Formerly used in this sense with stress on first syll.). Cp. Shakespeare, '*I conjure you by that which you profess*'.

conjure (II.), vb. intrans. [1. kúnjur; 2. kʌ́ndžə]. Same as prec., w. shifting of stress. 1. To exercise magical arts, practise sorcery. (obs.) Cp., however, Phr. *a name to conjure with*, with which to perform wonders. 2. To perform tricks of sleight-of-hand or legerdemain, to juggle (derived from 1). *Conjure up*, a to call up, cause to appear by exercise of magic, the spirits of the dead, genii &c.; b (fig.) to call up a mental picture of objects or events, in oneself by exercise of imagination, or in others by vivid description and suggestion: *to conjure up visions of the past* &c.

conjurer, conjuror, n. [1. kúnjurer; 2. kʌ́ndžərə]. Prec. & **-er** & **-or**. 1. One who practises magical arts (obs., except in fig. sense of one who manages to do difficult and wonderful things): *he was such a persuasive speaker, that he seemed a veritable conjurer.* 2. One who performs tricks of sleight-of-hand or legerdemain; one who produces illusions of a mystifying or amazing kind: *a professional, an amateur, conjurer.*

conjuring, n. & adj. [1. kúnjuring; 2. kʌ́ndžəriŋ]. Prec. & **-ing**. 1. vbl. n. Act of performing sleight-of-hand tricks: *this is very clever conjuring.* 2. adj. (from Pres. Part.) Based on, having character of, sleight-of-hand: *a conjuring trick.*

conk, n. [1. kongk; 2. kɔŋk]. Same as **conch**. (vulg. slang) Nose.

connate, adj. [1. kónāt; 2. kɔ́neit]. Variant of **cognate**, Lat. **con-** & *nātus*, 'born'. See **natal**. a Born with, acquired at or by birth, inborn (of qualities); b born at same time, produced together.

connatural, adj. [1. kònáchural; 2. kɔ̀nnǽtʃrəl]. Fr. *connaturel*. **con-** & **natural**. a Inborn; b of like nature.

connect, vb. trans. & intrans. [1. kunékt; 2. kənékt], fr. Lat. *connectere*, 'to bind together', fr. **con-** & *nectere*, 'to bind'; cp. perh. Scrt. *náhyati*, 'he binds'. See **nexus, net, needle**. A. trans. 1. To join or fasten together, to unite or link together; a (of material things) *to connect a bit with a bridle by a strap*; *two banks of a river by a bridge*; b (of mental process) to show historical or causal relation between events: *to connect the downfall of Charles I. with his character and behaviour*; c to associate, relate together in the mind: *we connect the suffix -ed with the idea of past action.* B. intrans. a (of material things) To join on to, unite with, fit into or together, be adapted for joining on to: *the two ends of the pipe connect with the collar*; Phr. *this train connects with another at Bletchley*, runs in connexion with; b specif. (of actions or events) to link up, be planned to happen or to take place in relation; c (of mental processes, or expression of these) to follow naturally, form logical sequence, be in proper logical relation to: *this sentence does not seem to connect with the context.*

connected, adj. [1. kunékted; 2. kənéktid], fr. P.P. of prec. 1. Joined, united, esp. joined in logical sequence, coherent: *connected account.* 2. a Associated, united in relationship with others: *connected by marriage with*; Phr. *well connected*, of good family; b participant in, involved in, occupation, action &c.: *connected with an undertaking, with a crime* &c.

connectedly, adv. Prec. & **-ly**. (of thinking, speaking, writing) In a connected, logical manner.

connectedness, n. See prec. & **-ness**. Quality of being connected (in thought &c.).

connective, adj. [1. kunéktiv; 2. kənéktiv]. **connect** & **-ive**. Serving to connect, acting as means of connexion. *Connective tissue*, a wide term including all the tissues which enclose and connect the various organs of the body.

connectively, adv. Prec. & **-ly.** In a connective manner, by connexion.

connexion, connection, n. [1. kunékshun; 2. kənékʃən], fr. Lat. *con(n)exiōn-(em)*, 'a binding together, close union; conclusion, logical sequence; a sentence', fr. *connex-(um)*, P.P. type of *connectere*, & **-ion.** See **connect.** The spelling w. *x* is historically correct, & is based on the Lat.; the other, due to the influence of *connect*, is also common. **1.** Relation, association: **a** (causally, of events, actions &c.) *the connexion between crime and insanity*; **b** (of relation in thought and logic) *connexion between ideas*; Phr. *in this connexion*, with reference to what is being discussed or considered; **c** specif. (of trains, boats &c.) correspondence in hours of arrival and departure: *to run in connexion*, so as to meet, catch; *a good connexion of trains* &c. **2. a** (of personal and social relations) Association, intimacy, union, bond of union: *to live in close connexion with members of one's profession*; Phrs. *to form useful connexions*, to make powerful friends; *to form a connexion*, often said of intimacy between a man and a woman; **b** specif., sexual union; Phr. *to have connexion with*; **c** a relative, member of one's family (by blood or marriage). **3. a** Body of persons associated in a religious organization: *the Methodist Connexion*; **b** body of clients, customers of a business undertaking. Phr. *to establish a connexion*, form a clientèle. **4.** Anything which connects: *hot water connexions*, pipes &c.

conning-tower, n. [1. kóning tòur; 2. kóniŋ tàuə]. Pres. Part. of **con (II.).** The armoured, protected station in a warship from which the steering &c. is directed.

conniption fit, n. [1. kanípshun fit; 2. kənípʃən fìt]. Origin unknown. (slang, U.S.A.) A fit, paroxysm, of anger, hysteria &c.

connivance, n. [1. kunívans; 2. kənáivəns], fr. Fr. *connivence*, fr. Lat. *connīventia.* See **connive** & **-ance.** Tacit assent to, acquiescence in, the wrong-doing of another.

connive, vb. intrans. [1. kunív; 2. kənáiv], fr. Lat. *connīvēre*, 'to close the eyes; to blink; to leave a crime unnoticed, overlook errors', fr. **con-**, & *nīvēre*, 'to close the eyes; to blink; to leave a crime unnoticed', wh., however, only occurs uncompounded in *nīvens*, 'winking'. The base is **knīgʷ-*, cogn. w. Goth. *hneiwan*, 'to bend downwards, incline', & *hnaiws*, 'humble'; O.H.G. *hneigen*, Mod. Germ. *neigen*, 'to bend down, incline'. Lat. *nictāre*, 'to move the eyelids up and down', is fr. same base, for **nig-tāre.* The orig. meaning is 'to move, to move downwards', the Lat. sense being specialized. See **nictitate.** Generally *connive at*, to leave error or wrongdoing in another unnoticed; to pass over bad behaviour or crime in silence, to acquiesce in. The word implies tacit and approving assent to another's wrong-doing, or actual encouragement and assistance. The English Phr. *to wink at, keep one's eyes closed to, a fault* &c., exactly corresponds with original Latin meaning.

connivent, adj. [1. kunívent; 2. kənáivənt]. Lat. *connīvent-(em)*, Pres. Part. of *connīvēre.* See prec. Used in lit. sense. (biol., of parts of animals and plants) Inclining towards each other, converging.

connoisseur, n. [1. kònisér; 2. kònisə́]. Fr., fr. L. Lat. *cognoscitōr-(em)*, fr. *cognoscere*, 'to get to know, become acquainted with'. See **cognoscible.** (lit.) One who knows; one having special or expert knowledge, esp. in artistic matters, or things involving aesthetic taste: *a connoisseur in pictures, music, wine* &c.

connotate, vb. trans. [1. kónotāt; 2. kónəteit], fr. Lat. **con-** & *notāt-(um)*, P.P. type of *notāre*, 'to mark'. See **connote.** To connote.

connotation, n. [1. kònotáshun; 2. kònətéiʃən]. Prec. & **-ion.** Implication; specif. (logic) sum total of qualities or attributes implied by a term, cp. *denotation.*

connotative, adj. [1. konṓtativ; 2. kənóutətiv]. **connotate** & **-ive.** Having connotation.

connote, vb. trans. [1. konṓt; 2. kənóut], fr. Lat. *connotāre*, 'to mark together', fr. **con-** & *notāre*, 'to mark', fr. *nota*, 'a mark'. See **con-** & **note.** (of words) To suggest, indicate, imply; to include in the meaning; imply in addition to the primary meaning; (popularly) to mean.

connubial, adj. [1. kunúbial; 2. kənjúbiəl], fr. Lat. *connūbiālis*, 'pertaining to marriage', fr. *connūbium*, 'marriage', fr. **con-** & *nūbere*, 'to marry'. The etymological connexion between this vb. & *nūbes*, 'cloud, veil', is now denied, in wh. case the word does not mean 'to cover with a veil' as a bride, as was formerly taught. See **nuptial. a** Of, connected with, the marriage state, conjugal; **b** connected with spouses.

connubiality, n. [1. kunūbiáliti; 2. kənjūbiǽliti]. Prec. & **-ity.** State of being connubial; something characteristic of the marriage state.

connubially, adv. [1. kunúbiali; 2. kənjúbiəli]. See prec. & **-ly.** In the manner of married persons.

conoid, adj. & n. [1. kṓnoid; 2. kóunɔid], fr. Gk. *kōnoeidḗs*, 'cone-shaped'. See **cone** & **-oid. a** adj. Resembling a cone, cone-shaped; **b** n., cone-shaped object.

conquer, vb. trans. & intrans. [1. kóngker; 2. kɔ́ŋkə], fr. O. Fr. *conquerre*, Fr. *conquérir*, fr. Lat. *conquīrere, conquaerere*, 'to seek, search out with care', L. Lat. 'to conquer', fr. **con-** & *quaerere*, 'to seek'. See **query. A.** trans. **1. a** To overcome by force, deprive of power of resistance, overpower, defeat: *to conquer the enemy, a people* &c.; **b** to subjugate, overrun and take possession of *a country, land* &c. by force; to gain or acquire by force. **2.** (fig., of non-material things) To subdue, overcome, get the better of: *to conquer bad habits, passions, difficulties* &c. **B.** intrans. To gain the victory, to prevail: '*To conquer or to die*'.

conquerable, adj. [1. kóngkerabl; 2. kɔ́ŋkərəbl]. Prec. & **-able.** Capable of being conquered.

conqueror, n. [1. kóngkerer; 2. kɔ́ŋkərə]. See prec. & **-or. a** One who conquers; **b** specif. (Engl. hist.) *The Conqueror*, William of Normandy.

conquest, n. [1. kóngkwest; 2. kɔ́ŋkwest]. M.E., fr. A.-Fr. *conquiste*, Low Lat. *conquīsita*, fem. of P.P. of *conquīrere.* See **conquer. 1. a** The act or process of conquering, defeating, subjugating, chiefly used of a country and its inhabitants; **b** specif., *The Conquest*, that of England by the Normans in 1066; **c** (feudal law) acquisition of property by purchase. **2.** That which is conquered or acquired by conquest: *the conquests of Napoleon.* **3. a** The act or process of gaining the affections, capturing the favour or fancy of a person; Phr. *to make a conquest of*, win the affections &c. of; **b** person whose affections or favour are captured.

consanguine, adj. [1. konsánggwin; 2. kənsǽŋgwin]. See next word. Consanguineous.

consanguineous, adj. [1. kònsanggwíneus; 2. kònsæŋgwíniəs], fr. Lat. *consanguine-(us)*, fr. **con-** & *sanguin-(is)*, 'blood'. See **sanguine** & **-ous.** Having the same blood, belonging to same family, related by descent.

consanguinity, n. [1. kònsanggwíniti; 2. kònsæŋgwíniti], fr. Fr. *consanguinité*, fr. Lat. *consanguinitāt-(em).* **consanguine** & **-ity.** Relationship by blood and common descent.

conscience, n. [1. kónshens; 2. kɔ́nʃəns]. Fr., fr. Lat. *conscientia*, 'consciousness, knowledge, feeling, sense; sense of right and wrong, moral sense', fr. *conscient-(em)*, Pres. Part. of *conscīre*, 'to be conscious of', fr. **con-** & *scīre*, 'to know'. See **science.** The knowledge of one's own thoughts and actions as right or wrong; the moral faculty of distinguishing right from wrong; sense of right and wrong: *a good, clear, bad, guilty, conscience.* Phrs. (colloq.) *in all conscience*, surely; (colloq.) *to have the conscience to*, be so callous as to; (vulg. slang) *my conscience!*, meaningless exclamation; (law) *conscience clause*, one granting exemption from provisions of an Act &c. on ground of conscientious scruples, esp. in religious matters. *Conscience money*, money paid in discharge of a claim (esp. income-tax) formerly evaded. *To make a matter of conscience*, to act according to the promptings of conscience; to have scruples about.

conscienceless, adj. [1. kónshensles; 2. kɔ́nʃənslis], fr. prec. & **-less. a** (of persons) Lacking conscience, unscrupulous; **b** (of actions) evincing lack of scruples on part of him who commits them.

conscientious, adj. [1. kònshiénshus; 2. kònʃiénʃəs], fr. Fr. *consciencieux, -euse*, fr. L. Lat. *conscientiōsus*, fr. Lat. *conscient-*, Pres. Part. stem. See **conscience** & **-ous. 1.** (of persons) Having keen sense of moral obligations, power of discriminating between right and wrong, and strong bias towards the former, obedient to the dictates of conscience; scrupulously, punctiliously, honest and upright. *Conscientious objector*, in the Great War, one who claimed exemption from military service by alleging moral scruples against fighting for his country against her enemies. **2.** (of actions, conduct &c.) Characterized, animated by, expressing, a lively regard for the dictates of conscience, exhibiting strong sense of duty.

conscientiously, adv. Prec. & **-ly.** In a conscientious manner.

conscientiousness, n. See prec. & **-ness.** The quality of being conscientious.

conscious, adj. [1. kónshus; 2. kɔ́nʃəs], fr. Lat. *conscius*, 'knowing, aware of', w. change of suff. to *-ōsus.* See **conscience** & **-ous. 1.** Having the faculty of knowing that one can know, think, and feel; having the power of thought: *man is a conscious being.* **2. a** Possessing knowledge of (whether derived from sensuous impressions or moral experience), alive to, aware of, cognizant of: (followed by *of* before a n.) *conscious of his own merits, guilt, folly* &c.; *conscious of pain, cold, discomfort* &c.; (followed by *that* before a vb.) *conscious that his strength was failing, that he had been a fool*; **b** (pred.) in possession of one's mental faculties, awake, alert: *he was conscious to the last.*

consciously, adv. Prec. & **-ly.** In a conscious manner; with knowledge of one's own thoughts or actions.

consciousness, n. See prec. & **-ness. 1.** The state of being conscious; **a** state possessed by all sentient beings of being able to perceive and feel: *we do not credit stones with consciousness*; **b** the whole body of perceptions, thoughts, and feelings possessed by any organism, esp. by man: *such things as speculations on man's destiny hardly enter the consciousness of savages.* **2. a** Perception of, capacity for perceiving, external objects through the senses, and thought and ideas by the mind; awareness of external circumstances and of mental processes, knowledge: *consciousness of a person's presence, of what is going on*; *consciousness of danger, of evil, of guilt* &c.; **b** possession of one's mental faculties, power to take in through the senses, and to understand; knowledge of one's existence and of that of external world: *to lose consciousness*, become unconscious; *regain, recover, consciousness*, after temporary loss through illness or injury.

conscribe, vb. trans. [1. kunskríb; 2. kənskráib], fr. Lat. *conscrībere.* See next word. To enlist soldiers &c. by *conscription.* (obs.) Replaced by *conscript.*

conscript (I.), adj. & n. [1. kónskript; 2. kɔ́nskript], fr. Lat. *conscript-(um)*, P.P. of *conscrībere*, 'to write together; to enrol, enlist', fr. **con-** & *scrībere*, 'to write'. See **scribe. 1.** adj. **a** Enrolled by conscription; compelled by law to serve the State, esp. as a fighting man; **b** (Rom. antiq.) *conscript fathers*, the senators of ancient Rome. **2.** n. A person compulsorily enrolled to serve the State, esp. as a soldier or sailor, contrasted with one who enlists voluntarily.

conscript (II.), vb. trans. [1. kunskrípt; 2. kənskrípt], fr. prec. To enrol by compulsion for State service, esp. one of the fighting services.

conscription, n. [1. kunskrípshun; 2. kənskrípʃən]. Prec. & **-ion.** System of enlisting men compulsorily for State service, esp. for the army or navy.

consecrate (I.), adj. [1. kónsekrāt; 2. kɔ́nsikreit], fr. Lat. *consecrāt-(um)*, P.P. type of *consecrāre*, 'to dedicate, consecrate', fr. **con-** & *sacrāre*, 'to set apart as sacred', fr. *sacer*, 'holy, sacred'. See **sacred.** Consecrated, devoted, dedicated, sacred.

consecrate (II.), vb. trans. See prec. **1.** (general sense) To set apart as sacred; dedicate, devote, to some use, purpose, or person: *to consecrate one's life, talents, energies &c. to some object*; '*Rose Aylmer . . . a night of memories and sighs I consecrate to thee*' (Landor). **2.** Specif. (eccles.) to perform one of the spiritual functions of a bishop; **a** to set apart a man as, and make him, a bishop or archbishop, by imposition of hands and utterance of prescribed words, '*Receive thou the Holy Ghost* &c. . . . *for the office of bishop*' &c.; **b** to dedicate some object (a building, place, oil &c.) to the service of God, and impart to it a sacred character, by prescribed words and acts. **3.** To render holy, sanctify, hallow: '*Principles consecrated by time*' (Burke).

consecration, n. [1. kònsekráshun; 2. kɔ̀nsikréiʃən], fr. Lat. *consecrātiōn-(em)*, see prec. & **-ion.** Act or process of consecrating in any sense; **a** devotion, dedication, of anything to a purpose &c.: *the consecration of one's life to study* &c.; **b** act by which, and ceremony at which, a bishop consecrates persons or things in specific sense: *the consecration of bishops*; **c** process of making sacred or venerable: *the place had undergone a kind of consecration from the continuous presence of great men during long ages.*

consecrator, n. [1. kónsekrātur; 2. kɔ́nsikreitə]. **consecrate (II.)** & **-or.** One who consecrates.

consecratory, adj. [1. kónsekrāturi; 2. kɔ́nsikreitəri]. See prec. & **-ory.** Pertaining to the act of consecration, dedicatory.

consectary, n. [1. kunséktari; 2. kənséktəri], fr. Lat. *consectārium*, 'that which follows logically, a conclusion, inference', fr. *consectāri*, 'to follow after eagerly', fr. **con-** & *sectāri*, 'to follow eagerly', freq. of *sequi*, 'to follow', & **-ary.** See **sequel, sociable.** (rare) Something which follows logically from something else; a corollary.

consecution, n. [1. kònsekúshun; 2. kɔ̀nsikjúʃən], fr. Lat. *consecūtiōn-(em)*, 'an effect, consequence', fr. *consequi*, 'to follow'. See **consequent. a** A following or sequel; logical sequence; sequence of events; **b** (gram.) sequence of words, tenses &c.

consecutive, adj. [1. kunsékūtiv; 2. kənsékjutiv]. Lat. *consecūt-(um)*, P.P. type of *consequi*, 'to follow', & **-ive.** See **sequel, sociable. 1.** Following in regular order, successive, following without an interval or break. **2.** (gram.) Expressing the idea of consequence: *consecutive clause.*

consecutively, adv. Prec. & **-ly.** In a consecutive manner, following continuously, without break.

consecutiveness, n. See prec. & **-ness.** Property of following in natural succession; esp. of logical sequence in ideas or expression.

consenescence, n. [1. kònsenésens; 2. kɔ̀nsenésəns]. See **con-** & **senescence. a** Process of growing old together; **b** general decay through old age.

consensual, adj. [1. kònsénsūal; 2. kɔ̀nsénsjuəl]. Next word & **-al. 1.** (physiol., of involuntary movement) Accompanying, correlated with, voluntary movement. **2.** (law, of contracts &c.) Made by mutual consent.

consensus, n. [1. kunsénsus; 2. kənsénsəs]. Lat., 'agreement, unanimity', fr. *consens-(um)*, P.P. type of *consentīre*. See next word. Agreement, unanimity, in feeling, opinion.

consent (I.), vb. intrans. [1. kunsént; 2. kənsént], fr. O. Fr. *consentir*, fr. Lat. *consentīre*, 'to feel together, to agree with; determine in common', fr. **con-** & *sentīre*, 'to feel'. See **sense.** (followed by *to* before a n., or by infin.) **a** To agree not to resist, or prevent: *to consent to a suggestion, proposal*; **b** to acquiesce in, agree to, permit: *to consent to another's action*; **c** to be willing to undertake, agree to do: *to consent to give a lecture.*

consent (II.), n., fr. O. Fr. *consente*. See prec. **1.** (of a number of persons) Agreement, community of feeling and opinion, unanimity: *Sir Joshua was by common, general, consent the first English painter of his day.* **2.** (of one person) Assent, acquiescence, leave, permission: *nothing can be settled finally without my consent*; *to obtain a person's consent*; *to withhold one's consent.* Phrs. *silence gives consent*; (legal) *age of consent*, that at which consent is held valid by the law.

consentaneity, n. [1. kònsentanéiti; 2. kɔ̀nsentəníiti]. Lat. *consentāne-(us)* & **-ity.** See **consentaneous.** Quality of being consentaneous.

consentaneous, adj. [1. kònsentáneus; 2. kɔ̀nsentéinjəs], fr. Lat. *consentāne-(us)*, 'agreeing, suited, fit', fr. *consentīre*, & **-ous.** See **consent** (I.). Agreeable or accordant *to*, suited *to*, consistent *with.*

consentaneously, adv. Prec. & **-ly.** In accordance with; consistently with.

consentaneousness, n. See prec. & **-ness.** Quality or state of being consentaneous.

consentient, adj. [1. kunséntient; 2. kənsénʃiənt], fr. Lat. *consentient-(em)*, Pres. Part. of *consentīre.* See **consent (I.).** Agreeing; disposed to acquiesce or consent.

consequence, n. [1. kónsekwens; 2. kɔ́nsikwəns], fr. Fr. *conséquence*, fr. Lat. *consequentia.* See **consequent** & **-ce. 1.** Event which follows upon something else which is, or appears to be, the cause; a result, outcome of what has gone before: *the consequences of an action.* Phr. *in consequence* (*of*), as a result (of). **2.** Something which follows logically from a train of reasoning, or statement; logical result, conclusion: *it follows as a logical consequence that . . .* **3.** Importance, consideration, value: *of no consequence*, not important; Phr. *person(s) of consequence*, of social (or other kind of) importance.

consequent (I.), adj. [1. kónsekwent; 2. kɔ́nsikwənt], fr. Fr. *conséquent*, fr. Lat. *consequent-(em)*, Pres. Part. of *consequi*, 'to follow', fr. **con-** & **sequent.** Cf. **consecutive.** Following as a result **a** of events and actions; **b** of logical reasoning.

consequent (II.), n., fr. prec. That which follows, or results from, a cause; the natural effect of what has gone before.

consequential, adj. [1. kònsekwénshal; 2. kɔ̀nsikwénʃəl]. Prec. & **-ial. 1.** Following as a consequence, on what has gone before, resultant: *consequential alterations in wording of a document*, those made necessary by others already made; (law) *consequential damages*, those incidental to the whole case, and arising out of it, though not those directly claimed. **2.** (of persons) Assuming and displaying an air of consequence; self-important, pompous.

consequentially, adv. Prec. & **-ly. 1.** Arising as a consequence, because consequential, **1. 2.** In a self-important, pompous manner.

consequently, adv. & conj. [1. kónsekwentli; 2. kɔ́nsikwəntli]. **consequent (I.)** & **-ly.** As a consequence; therefore.

conservancy, n. [1. kunsérvansi; 2. kənsə́vənsi]. See **conserve (I.)** & **-ancy. a** Body of persons appointed by authority to control and protect forests or water-ways, to ensure rivers against pollution &c.; esp. *Thames Conservancy*; **b** official control and preservation of forests and rivers.

conservation, n. [1. kònservāshun; 2. kɔ̀nsəvéiʃən], fr. Lat. *conservātiōn-(em)*, 'a keeping, preserving', fr. *conservāre.* See **conserve (I.)** & **-ation. a** The act or process of conserving, preservation; **b** specif., conservancy, official protection, superintendence of forests or rivers; **c** specif. (phys.) *conservation of energy*, doctrine that total amount of energy in the universe can neither be increased nor diminished, though it be constantly transformed from one form of energy into another.

conservatism, n. [1. kunsérvatizm; 2. kənsə́vətizəm]. See next word & **-ism. a** Disposition, tendency, to preserve or maintain what is established; opposition to sudden, ill-considered change; **b** (specif., of political doctrine) principles of the Conservative party.

conservative, adj. [1. kunsérvativ; 2. kənsə́vətiv], fr. Fr. *conservatif, -ive*, fr. Lat. *conservāt-(um)*, P.P. type of *conservāre*, & **-ive.** See **conserve (I.). 1. a** Having power to preserve; tending to preserve; **b** attached to, desirous of preserving, existing conditions against sudden innovation; unwilling to change habits and mode of life: *the British working man is thoroughly conservative in his habits.* **2.** (specif., of political doctrine) Solicitous to preserve the institutions and traditions of the past, where experience has proved their value, opposed to wanton destruction of institutions, to rash change or sudden innovation; *Conservative party*, English political party favouring the maintenance of existing institutions and forms of government. **3.** Popular use, *conservative estimate*, a moderate or cautious estimate, purposely low.

conservative (II.), n. A preservative, that which preserves from injury or change. **a** Person who is conservative in tastes and habits; **b** (cap.) one holding political doctrine of conservatism; member of the Conservative party.

conservatoire, n. [1. konsárvatwar; 2. kɔ̃séəvətwā] (Engl.-Fr. pronunciation). Fr., fr. Low Lat. *conservātōrium*, 'place for conserving and fostering'. Variant of **conservatory.** Public academy where instruction is given in music and other arts in France.

conservator, n. [1. kónservātur, konsérvatur; 2. kɔ́nsəveitə, kənsə́vətə]. Lat., 'protector'. See **conserve (I.)** & **-ate** & **-or. a** A preserver, protector; **b** official guardian, keeper (of a museum &c.); **c** member of a conservancy.

conservatory, n. [1. kunsérvaturi; 2. kənsə́vətri]. Variant of *conservatoire*, fr. Low Lat. *conservātōrium.* See next word. A glass house in which young, tender, or exotic plants are reared and protected from the weather; one in which plants are grown and matured earlier than under purely natural conditions.

conserve (I.), vb. trans. [1. kunsérv; 2. kənsə́v], fr. Fr. *conserver*, fr. Lat. *conservāre*, 'to keep in existence, preserve', fr. **con-** & *servāre*, 'to save, keep, protect'; see **serve, serf**; prob. cogn. w. Goth. *saurga*, 'sorrow, grief', see **sorrow.** To keep safe, to keep, protect, preserve, esp. from waste, loss &c.: *to conserve one's strength, health* &c.

conserve (II.), n., fr. prec. Fr., 'preserved fruit, jam'. (often in pl.) Preserved, candied fruit; jam.

consider, vb. trans. [1. kunsíder; 2. kənsídə], fr. Fr. *considérer*, fr. Lat. *considerāre, -ātum*, 'to look at closely; think of attentively', perh. orig. a term of astrol. or augury, fr. **con-** & *sīdus, sīderis*, 'star', q.v. under **sidereal. 1.** To turn over in the mind, contemplate carefully, reflect, meditate upon: *to consider a matter in all its aspects*; also absol.: *consider carefully before coming to a decision.* **2. a** (of events, circumstances &c.) To have regard to, reckon with, take into consideration: *there are many points in the argument which have not been considered.* Phr. *all things considered*, taking everything into account; **b** (of persons) to show solicitude, consideration for, pay regard to: *to consider others, the feelings, susceptibilities &c. of others.* **3. a** To regard as, deem, set down as: *to consider a man (to be) a fool, very clever* &c.; **b** to hold, be of opinion, come to the conclusion: *to consider that one has been badly treated.*

considerable, adj. [1. kunsíderabl; 2. kənsídərəbl]. Prec. & **-able. 1.** (of persons)

Worthy of being considered, noteworthy, important, distinguished: *to become a considerable personage.* **2.** (of size, measure, distance, number, amount) Rather large; *a considerable weight,* heavy; *considerable distance,* a long way; *considerable expense,* great cost.

considerably, adv. Prec. & **-ly.** Much, a great deal: *considerably larger; considerably less,* much less.

considerate, adj. [1. kunsíderat; 2. kənsídərit]. **consider** & **-ate.** Thoughtful for, solicitous, regardful of, given to considering, the feelings of others.

considerately, adv. Prec. & **-ly.** In a considerate manner.

considerateness, n. See prec. & **-ness.** Thoughtfulness for others.

consideration, n. [1. kunsìderáshun; 2. kənsìdəréiʃən], fr. Fr. *considération,* fr. Lat. *consīderātiōn-(em)* 'contemplation, reflection'. **consider** & **-ation. 1.** Act of considering; careful deliberation, pondering, meditation, reflection: *to bestow anxious consideration upon; to give (a problem &c.) one's careful consideration.* **2.** Fact or thing regarded as being the cause of, or as furnishing a motive for, an action: *several considerations have weighed with me in coming to a decision; on, under, no consideration could I consent; in consideration of,* taking into account: *in consideration of previous good conduct.* **3. a** Compensation, reward, bribe: *the kind of man who would do anything for a consideration;* **b** (law) in full *valuable consideration,* act, such as a payment, forbearance from doing something, or promise to do or forbear, offered and accepted as inducement for making a contract; the essential condition of all contracts except those under seal. **4.** Thoughtfulness, tender solicitude for others; thoughtful regard for: *to show great consideration for one's friends.*

considered, adj. [1. kunsíderd; 2. kənsídəd]. P.P. of **consider.** Well thought out, deliberated, thoroughly pondered, weighed, reflected upon: *to give a considered opinion, judgement.*

considering, prep. [1. kunsídering; 2. kənsídəriŋ], fr. Pres. Part. of **consider.** In view of, taking into account, making allowance for: *a hearty old man considering his years;* (colloq.) *that's not so bad considering* (sc. 'the circumstances').

consign, vb. trans. [1. kunsín; 2. kənsáin], fr. Fr. *consigner,* fr. Lat. *consignāre,* 'to mark with a seal, attest', fr. **con-** & *signum,* 'a seal or stamp'. See **sign. 1.** To hand over, deliver over, commit, entrust: *to consign a letter to the post; consign something to a person's care; to consign one's soul to God;* (fig.) *to consign something or someone to the Devil.* **2.** (commerc. usage) To transmit, send goods specifically addressed, to be delivered to a person or trading company.

consignable, adj. [1. kunsínabl; 2. kənsáinəbl], fr. **consign** & **-able.** Capable of being consigned, esp. in commercial sense.

consignation, n. [1. kònsìnáshun; 2. kɔ̀nsainéiʃən]. Lat. *consignātiōn-(em),* 'a written proof', fr. *consignāt-(um)* P.P. type of *consignāre,* & **-ion.** See **consign.** Act of consigning goods.

consignee, n. [1. kònsìné; 2. kɔ̀nsainí], fr. **consign** & **-ee.** Person to whom anything, esp. goods, is consigned.

consignment, n. [1. kunsínment; 2. kənsáinmənt], fr. **consign** & **-ment. a** The act of consigning; **b** thing consigned, esp. (tradesmen's word) collection of goods for trading, sent to, and received by a trader: *a new consignment of autumn hats.*

consignor, n. [1. kònsìnór; 2. kɔ̀nsainɔ́]. **consign** & **-or.** One who consigns; esp. in commercial sense.

consilience, n. [1. kunsíliens; 2. kənsíliəns]. See **consilient.** Act or fact of concurring, coinciding; concurrence.

consilient, adj. [1. kunsílient; 2. kənsíliənt]. This compound not found in class. Lat., but evidently made on anal. of *resilīre,* 'to spring back' (see **resilient**), fr. **con-** & *salīre,* 'to leap', q.v. under **salient.** Coincident, concurring.

consist, vb. intrans. [1. kunsíst; 2. kənsíst], fr. Lat. *consistere,* 'to make to stand, to stop', fr. **con-** & *sistere,* 'to place' &c., a redupl. form of *stāre,* P.P. *sta-tum,* 'to stand'. See **stand (I.)** & **state (I.). 1. a** (followed by *of*) To be composed of, be made up of, to have as parts or elements: *most books consist of several chapters; man consists of body, soul, and spirit; our dinner consisted of three courses only;* **b** (followed by *in*) to comprise, contain, as an essential ingredient or element: *happiness consists largely in being easily pleased.* **2.** (followed by *with*) To be capable of existing with, or alongside of, to be congruous with: *great learning sometimes consists with remarkable obtuseness.*

consistence, -cy, n. [1. kunsístens(i); 2. kənsístəns(i)]. Prec. & **-ence, -cy. 1. a** Degree of density, mode in which the elements are arranged: *the consistency of a pudding, of a liquid;* **b** a dense consistency, solidity: *train oil has much greater consistence than petrol.* **2.** (always *consistency*) Quality of being consistent; **a** (of persons) consequence, capacity of a congruous line of thought, logicality; **b** (of mental processes and their expression) congruity, relevancy, logical sequence.

consistent, adj. [1. kunsístent; 2. kənsístənt]. **consist** & **-ent. 1.** (of actions, thoughts &c.) Congruous, agreeing with itself or with something else, compatible, in accordance with. **2.** (of persons) Acting and living in accordance with professed principles.

consistently, adv. Prec. & **-ly.** In a consistent manner.

consistory, n. [1. kunsísturi; 2. kənsístəri], fr. Fr. *consistoire,* fr. L. Lat. *consistōrium,* 'a place of assembly, place where the council of the Roman Emperor met, the council itself'. See **consist** & **-ory.** (eccles.) **a** Ecclesiastical tribunal or court, composed of the Pope and cardinals; the College of Cardinals; **b** bishops' ecclesiastical court of a diocese, in English Church; **c** (Presbyterian Church) body of presbyters, the court next above kirk-session.

consociate, vb. trans. & intrans. & n. [1. kunsóshiāt; 2. kənsóuʃieit], fr. Lat. *consociāt-(um),* P.P. type of *consociāre,* 'to associate with', fr. **con-** & *sociāre,* 'to associate', fr. *socius,* 'a companion'. See **social. a** vb. To associate, bring into alliance, unite; **b** n., an associate. (Rare.)

consolable, adj. [1. kunsólabl; 2. kənsóuləbl]. **console** & **-able.** Capable of being consoled, comforted.

consolation, n. [1. kònsoláshun; 2. kɔ̀nsəléiʃən]. Fr., fr. Lat. *consōlātiōn-(em).* See **console (I.)** & **-ation. 1.** The act or fact of consoling, of affording relief in grief or disappointment. **2.** Something, some act, which affords moral comfort; mitigating fact or circumstance; fact, source, of solace, in grief or disappointment: *religion was his chief consolation in affliction.* Phr. *consolation race,* in which those previously unsuccessful compete; *consolation prize,* given to a competitor who has just missed success.

consolatory, adj. [1. kunsólaturi; 2. kənsɔ́lətəri]. See prec. & **-ory.** Tending to console, of a kind which gives consolation.

console (I.), vb. trans. [1. kunsól; 2. kənsóul], fr. Fr. *consoler,* fr. Lat. *consōlāri,* 'to comfort greatly', fr. **con-** & *sōlāri,* 'to comfort'. See **solace.** To bring moral comfort to, make amends for, provide means of mitigation in, grief, disappointment, loss.

console (II.), n. [1. kónsōl; 2. kɔ́nsoul]. Fr., 'a bracket', esp. in archit. Origin doubtful. (archit.) A bracket supporting a shelf, cornice, window-head &c., often in form of a highly carved scroll, and forming part of a general design.

console table, n. One whose top is supported on consoles or carved scrolls; esp. a narrow table with such supports, and curved legs, placed as a fixture between windows, or beneath a mirror.

consolidate, vb. trans. & intrans. [1. kunsólidāt; 2. kənsɔ́lideit], fr. Lat. *consolidāt-(um),* P.P. type of *consolidāre,* 'to make firm; to make thick', fr. **con-** & *solidus,* 'firm, solid'. See **solid. A.** trans. **1. a** To make strong and solid; (esp. fig. of non-material things) to establish firmly, assure stability of: *to consolidate one's power, influence, position in society* &c.; **b** (specif. mil.) to make (a position) safer and easier to hold, strengthen. **2.** To unite, combine, several things, hitherto distinct and separate, into one (of territories, estates, companies, debts, legal actions). **B.** intrans. To become firm; to pass from a liquid to a solid condition.

consolidated, adj. [1. kunsólidāted; 2. kənsɔ́lideitid], fr. P.P. of prec. Specif. **a** *consolidated annuities,* government securities funded, first in 1751, at 3%, now at 2½%, usually known as *consols;* **b** *Consolidated Fund,* fund established in 1787, into which the main part of the revenue is paid, and out of which are paid interest on national debt and charges other than *supply* charges, voted annually.

consolidation, n. [1. kunsòlidáshun; 2. kənsɔ̀lidéiʃən]. Lat. *consolidātiōn-(em),* 'an establishing of ownership'. See **consolidate** & **-ion.** Act or process of consolidating.

consols, n. pl. [1. kunsólz, kónsolz; 2. kənsɔ́lz, kɔ́nsəlz]. Short for *consolidated annuities.* British Government stock: *to put all one's money in consols.*

consommé, n. [1. konsómā; 2. kɔ̃sɔ́mei]. Fr., P.P. of *consommer.* See **consummate.** A clear, rich meat broth or soup.

consonance, n. [1. kónsonans; 2. kɔ́nsənəns]. Fr. *consonance,* fr. Lat. *consonantia.* See next word. Agreement, congruity.

consonant (I.), adj. [1. kónsonant; 2. kɔ́nsənənt]. Fr., fr. Lat. *consonant-(em),* Pres. Part. of *consonāre,* 'to sound with, to harmonize', fr. **con-** & *sonāre.* See **sonant.** Agreeing, consistent, in keeping with.

consonant (II.), n., fr. prec. The name is due to the erroneous view that a consonant can only be sounded along w. a vowel. **1.** (phon.) A sound in speech, produced either **a** by a complete momentary stoppage of the air-stream in some part of the mouth-cavity, or by the lips, as it passes from the lungs, or **b** by a partial stoppage or constriction, sufficient to produce a distinct and perceptible friction. Those sounds accompanied by complete stoppage are called *stops;* those occurring during constriction of the mouth-passage are variously called *open consonants, fricatives, spirants,* or *continuants.* **2.** (popularly) A letter or symbol which expresses a consonantal sound.

consonantal, adj. [1. kònsonántl; 2. kɔ̀nsənǽntl]. Prec. & **-al.** Resembling, having the nature and character of, a consonant.

consort (I.), n. [1. kónsort; 2. kɔ́nsɔ̄t]. Fr., fr. Lat. *consort-(em), consors,* 'sharer, comrade', fr. **con-** & *sort-(em),* 'lot, condition'. See **sort. 1. a** Dignified term for spouse of either sex, esp. of spouse of a royal personage; **b** specif., the spouse of a reigning monarch, who may be given the title of *king-consort, queen-consort.* **2.** A ship sailing in company with another for mutual protection.

consort (II.), vb. intrans. [1. kunsórt; 2. kənsɔ́t], fr. prec. **a** (followed by *with*) To associate with, frequent company of; **b** to be congruous, to go well with, be in keeping with: *pride does not consort well with poverty.*

consortium, n. [1. konsórtium; 2. kənsɔ́tiəm]. Lat., 'fellowship, partnership'. See **consort (I.).** An agreement between several powers or national banking interests to give joint financial assistance to another power.

conspecific, adj. [1. kònspesífik; 2. kɔ̀nspesífik]. **con-** & **specific.** Having, belonging to, same species.

conspectus, n. [1. kunspéktus; 2. kənspéktəs]. Lat., 'look, view, power of seeing', fr. *conspect-(um),* P.P. type of *conspicere,* 'to look at'.

See **con-** & **species**. **a** General view, comprehensive survey; **b** a summary, synopsis.

conspicuity, n. [1. kònspikū́iti; 2. kònspikjū́iti]. See next word & **-ity**. Quality of being conspicuous.

conspicuous, adj. [1. kunspíkūus; 2. kənspíkjuəs], fr. Lat. *conspicu-(us)*, fr. *conspicere*, 'to look at', & **-ous**. See **con-** & **species**. **1.** Clearly visible, easily seen, standing out from surroundings: *a conspicuous landmark*; *several conspicuous errors*. Phr. *conspicuous by absence*, calling attention by not being where expected. **2.** (of persons) Remarkable, attracting attention; **a** by reason of beauty, outstanding qualities of character or intellect: *conspicuous among a distinguished company*; **b** by some eccentricity of appearance or behaviour: *to make oneself conspicuous*, to behave strangely, noisily &c.

conspicuously, adv. Prec. & **-ly**. In a conspicuous manner.

conspicuousness, n. See prec. & **-ness**. Quality of being conspicuous (in any sense).

conspiracy, n. [1. kunspírasi; 2. kənspírəsi]. M.E., fr. Lat. *conspīrāt-(um)*, P.P. type of *conspīrāre*, see **conspire**, & **-acy**. Lat. *conspīrātio* means 'a breathing together, agreement, unanimity', hence 'plot' &c. **1.** The act of conspiring, agreeing to act in common; (gen. for a bad purpose): '*sedition, privy conspiracy, and rebellion*'. **2.** An agreement between two or more persons to act in common to effect some unlawful purpose, a plot: *the Gunpowder Conspiracy*. Phr. *conspiracy of silence*, (innocent sense) agreement not to comment on or discuss something, esp. publicly; (bad sense) determination to hush up what ought to be revealed.

conspirator, n. [1. kunspíratur; 2. kənspírətə], fr. Fr. *conspirateur*, fr. Lat. *conspīrāt-(um)*, P.P. type of *conspīrāre*, & **-or**. See next word. One who conspires, person taking part in a conspiracy.

conspire, vb. intrans. & trans. [1. kunspī́r; 2. kənspáiə], fr. Fr. *conspirer*, fr. Lat. *conspīrāre*, lit. 'to breathe together, harmonize, agree; act in concert; to plot together', fr. **con-** & *spīrāre*, 'to breathe, blow'. See **spirant, spirit**. **1.** intrans. To join with another, or with others, in secret, to devise means for effecting, and to effect, a particular purpose; esp. a crime, and, specif., treason against a person or institution: *to conspire against the throne, the State*. **2.** trans. (rare) To plot together to bring about, devise: *to conspire a crime*.

conspue, vb. trans. [1. kunspū́; 2. kənspjū́], fr. Fr. *conspuer*, fr. Lat. *conspuere*, 'to spit on', fr. **con-** & *spuere*, 'to spit', see **sputum**. (very rare) To express strong dislike, detestation of a person or policy, and demand disappearance of former from power and abandonment of latter.

constable, n. [1. kúnstabl; 2. kánstəbl]. M.E., fr. O. Fr. *conestable*, fr. Low Lat. *comes stabuli*, 'count of the stable', fr. *stabulum*, 'stable'. See **count (III.)** & **stable (II.)**. **1.** Policeman; also *police constable*. *Special constable*, one sworn in by the justices of the peace to act on special occasions. Phr. *to outrun the constable*, get into debt. **2.** Special uses: **a** *Constable of France*, chief officer of the household under the early French kings; later, commander-in-chief of the army; **b** *High Constable of England*, a high officer of State, whose office, abolished in 16th cent., has been revived temporarily on special occasions; **c** *Chief Constable*, head of the police in a city or a county.

constabulary, adj. & n. [1. kunstábūlari; 2. kənstǽbjuləri], fr. Low Lat. *constabulārius*. See prec. & **-ary**. **1.** adj. Connected with, consisting of, constables: *constabulary force*. **2.** n. Organized body of police of a city &c.

constancy, n. [1. kónstansi; 2. kónstənsi], fr. Lat. *constantia*, 'steadfastness, firmness', fr. *constāre*. See next word. Firmness, steadfastness: **a** of purpose, **b** of affections esp. between the sexes.

constant (I.), adj. [1. kónstant; 2. kónstənt], fr. Lat. *constant-(em)*, Pres. Part. of *constāre*, 'to stand firm', fr. **con-** & *stāre*, 'to stand'. See **stand (I.)** & **state (I.)**. **1. a** Continuous, unceasing, continuing: *constant trouble, noise, complaints*; **b** (esp. of external conditions) unvarying, lasting unchanged: *it is important in scientific experiments that all the conditions should be constant*. **2. a** (of the mind, will, purpose) Firm, steadfast, well established, resolute, determined; **b** (of affections and inclinations, esp. between the sexes) enduring, firmly fixed, unswerving, faithful; contrasted with *fickle*: *a constant lover, wife* &c.; **c** (also in relation to other objects) *constant in one's devotion to learning*.

constant (II.), n., fr. prec. (math. and phys.) A term, quantity, or factor which does not vary.

Constantia, n. [1. kunstánshia; 2. kənstǽnʃiə]. Kind of wine, fr. name of a place near Cape Town, South Africa.

constantly, adv. [1. kónstantli; 2. kónstəntli]. **constant (I.)** & **-ly**. **a** Continually, continuously: *to be constantly employed at one job*; **b** frequently, at repeated intervals: *I am constantly being asked to recommend books on philology*.

constellate, vb. trans. & intrans. [1. kónstelāt; 2. kónsteleit], fr. Lat. *constellātus*, 'studded with stars', fr. **con-** & *stella*, 'a star', & **-ate**. See **stellar**. To form into a constellation, to cluster.

constellation, n. [1. kònstelā́shun; 2. kònsteléiʃən], fr. Lat. *constellātiōn-(em)*. Prec. & **-ion**. **1.** (astrol.) Grouping of the stars at a person's birth, which was supposed to influence his life and fortunes. **2.** (astron.) **a** A group of fixed stars, formerly believed to have some relation to, and named after, a mythological personage or animal; **b** part of the heavens in which such a group occurs; **c** (fig.) group of distinguished persons, as: *a constellation of genius* &c.

consternation, n. [1. kònsternā́shun; 2. kònstənéiʃən], fr. Lat. *consternātiōn-(em)*, 'dismay, alarm', fr. *consternāt-(um)*, P.P. type of *consternāre*, 'to stretch upon the ground, overcome; overwhelm with terror, to perplex'. Not fr. *con-* & *sternere*, 'to strew', q.v. under **stratum**. The source of *-sternāre* is doubtful, but it is perh. cogn. w. Gk. *ptúromai*, 'be scared', & O.H.G. *stornēn*, 'to be thunderstruck'. Surprise and alarm, dismay; horror arising from realization of danger or evil.

constipate, vb. trans. [1. kónstipāt; 2. kónstipeit], fr. Lat. **con-** & *stīpātum*, P.P. of *stīpāre*, 'to pack, press, stuff, cram'; cogn. w. Gk. *stiphos*, 'a heap firmly pressed together', Scrt. *styáyatē*, 'becomes hard', & more remotely w. Goth. *stains*, 'stone' &c. See **stipend** & **stone**. To render the bowels sluggish or costive. (Chiefly in P.P.).

constipation, n. [1. kònstipā́shun; 2. kònstipéiʃən], fr. Lat. *constīpātiōn-(em)*. Prec. & **-ion**. Condition of inactivity of the bowels, in which defaecation is irregular and difficult.

constituency, n. [1. kunstítūensi; 2. kənstítjuənsi]. See next word & **-ency**. **1. a** Body of persons who have votes for a parliamentary candidate in a given borough or parliamentary area; **b** place &c. represented in Parliament. **2.** Body of customers, clients &c.

constituent (I.), adj. [1. kunstítūent; 2. kənstítjuənt], fr. Lat. *constituent-(em)*, Pres. Part. of *constituere*. See **constitute**. **1.** Forming part of, being an element in, helping to compose, whole; component. **2.** (of electors to Parliament &c.) Having power to elect. **3.** Having power to make or revise a constitution: *constituent assembly*.

constituent (II.), n., fr. prec. **1.** That which constitutes a formative element; composing part. **2. a** One of the body of electors to Parliament; **b** a resident voter in a parliamentary district.

constitute, vb. trans. [1. kónstitūt; 2. kónstitjūt], fr. Lat. *constitūt-(um)*, P.P. type of *constituere*, 'to place or set together, establish, construct', fr. **con-** & *statuere*, 'to cause to stand, to place, set up'. See **stand (I.)** & **state (I.)**. **1.** To appoint to, give authority to hold (an office or function), make: *the issue of a writ or patent constitutes a man a peer*. **2. a** To set up by authority, establish: *to constitute an acting committee*; **b** to enact, bring into force (a law &c.). **3.** To compose, make up, go to the making of, form (esp. in non-material sense): *her vivacity constitutes her main charm*; *I am not so constituted that I can accept insults lying down*.

constitution, n. [1. kònstitū́shun; 2. kònstitjū́ʃən]. Fr., fr. Lat. *constitutiōn-(em)*, 'constitution, disposition, nature'. See prec. & **-ion**. **1.** The act or process of constituting, appointing, establishing, enacting &c. **2.** Structure, fabric; mode in which, aggregate of elements of which, anything is composed. **3. a** The sum of bodily qualities and functions in an individual, esp. those inherited from his forbears, which determine his general health, power of resisting disease, prospects of reaching old age &c.: *a good, strong, poor* &c. *constitution*; **b** sum of intellectual and spiritual characteristics which determine an individual's general moral character and mental powers: *the constitution of one's mind and character*. **4.** (polit.) **a** The body of written laws, and unwritten customs, embodying the principles which underlie and determine the mode of government of a nation, State, or society; **b** mode of organization of a society, institution, association. **5.** (hist.) Decree, ordinance, enacted by authority, esp. one governing ecclesiastical matters: *the Constitutions of Clarendon*.

constitutional (I.), adj. [1. kònstitū́shunal; 2. kònstitjū́ʃənəl]. Prec. & **-al**. **1.** Inherent in, arising from, connected with, affecting, the physical or mental constitution: *a constitutional weakness, ailment, peculiarity* &c. **2.** Pertaining to, derived from, in accordance with, the constitution of a State, society &c.: *constitutional powers*; *constitutional government, law*; *constitutional monarch*, one who rules subject to and whose powers are limited by the constitution.

constitutional (II.), n., fr. prec. A walk, exercise, esp. for the sake of one's health.

constitutionalism, n. [1. kònstitū́shunalizm; 2. kònstitjū́ʃənəlizəm]. **constitutional (I.)** & **-ism**. **a** System of government by a constitution; **b** adherence in practice to the principles of a constitution; **c** doctrine that constitutional government is the best form.

constitutionalist, n. [1. kònstitū́shunalist; 2. kònstitjū́ʃənəlist]. See prec. & **-ist**. **a** One who adheres strictly to the principles of a given constitution; **b a** believer in constitutionalism.

constitutionalize, vb. trans. [1. kònstitū́shunalīz; 2. kònstitjū́ʃənəlaiz]. See prec. & **-ize**. To give a political constitution to, make constitutional.

constitutionally, adv. [1. kònstitū́shunali; 2. kònstitjū́ʃənəli]. **constitutional** & **-ly**. In accordance with the or a (political) constitution.

constitutive, adj. [1. kónstitūtiv; 2. kónstitjūtiv]. **constitute** & **-ive**. Having power to constitute, establish, enact; constituent.

constrain, vb. trans. [1. kunstrā́n; 2. kənstréin]. M.E. *constreinen*, fr. O. Fr. *constreindre*, fr. Lat. *constringere*, 'to draw or bind together; to fetter, restrain', fr. **con-** & *stringere*, 'to bind, tie'. See **strain (I.)**. **a** To bring influence, pressure, force, to bear upon a person; use compulsion towards a person in order to get him to do something; **b** (in pass.) *to be, feel, constrained to*, to be, feel, compelled.

constrained, adj. [1. kunstrā́nd; 2. kənstréind]. P.P. of prec. (of manner) Embarrassed, self-conscious; reverse of easy: *a constrained manner*.

constrainedly, adv. [1. kunstrā́nedli; 2. kənstréinidli], fr. prec. & **-ly**. In a constrained manner.

constraint, n. [1. kunstrānt; 2. kənstréint], fr. O. Fr. *constreinte*. See **constrain**. **1**. Compulsion: *to act under constraint*. **2**. Self-consciousness, awkwardness of manner, embarrassment: *to feel, show, constraint*.

constrict, vb. trans. [1. kunstríkt; 2. kənstríkt], fr. Lat. *constrict-(um)*, P.P. type of *constringere*. See **constrain**. To draw together, contract, compress, cramp.

constricted, adj. [1. kunstríkted; 2. kənstríktid]. P.P. of prec. **a** Narrowed, drawn together; **b** (of moral conditions) cramped, limited: *a constricted outlook*.

constriction, n. [1. kunstríkshun; 2. kənstríkʃən]. See **constrict** & **-ion**. **a** Compression, drawing together; **b** sensation of tightness: *constriction of the chest*.

constrictive, adj. [1. kunstríktiv; 2. kənstríktiv]. See prec. & **-ive**. Tending to constrict.

constrictor, n. [1. kunstríkter; 2. kənstríktə]. See prec. & **-or**. **1**. (anat.) Muscle that constricts, narrows, or closes an orifice, or which compresses an organ of the body. **2**. Serpent which kills its prey by crushing it in its folds; cp. *boa constrictor*.

constringe, vb. trans. [1. kunstrínj; 2. kənstrín(d)ž], fr. Lat. *constringere*. See **constrain**. To constrict, contract; to cause to contract.

constringency, n. [1. kunstrínjensi; 2. kənstrín(d)žənsi]. See next word & **-cy**. Act or process of constringing.

constringent, adj. [1. kunstrínjent; 2. kənstrín(d)žənt]. Lat. *constringent-(em)*, Pres. Part. of *constringere*. See **constrain**. Tending to constrict, causing constriction.

construct, vb. trans. [1. kunstrúkt; 2. kənstrákt], fr. Lat. *construct-(um)*, P.P. type of *construere*, 'to heap or pile together, to build', fr. **con-** & *struere*, 'to pile up, build'. See **structure**. **a** (of material things) To put and fit together separate objects, elements, materials in such a manner, and according to such a design, as to produce a new thing, having a definite shape, and adapted for a desired purpose; to build, form: *to construct a house, shed, bridge, engine* &c.; **b** (of non-material things) to design, plan out, frame, make, some rational and coherent unity from a number of thoughts and ideas: *to construct a theory, an argument, a sentence, the plot of a novel or play* &c.

construction, n. [1. kunstrúkshun; 2. kənstrákʃən], fr. Lat. *constructiōn-(em)*, 'a joining together; a building; fit connexion in discourse'. **construct** & **-ion**. **1**. The act or process of constructing: *the construction of a bridge is a slow process*. **2**. Some material thing constructed or built: *a flimsy, solid, beautiful, construction*. **3**. (gram.) Syntactic arrangement and relation of words in a sentence: *the ablative absolute construction in Latin*. **4**. Interpretation, explanation, meaning: esp. *to put a good, bad, construction on (words, conduct* &c.).

constructional, adj. [1. kunstrúkshunal; 2. kənstrákʃənəl]. Prec. & **-al**. Relating to, arising from, the mode of construction: *a constructional defect* (in a building, play &c.).

constructive, adj. [1. kunstrúktiv; 2. kənstráktiv]. **construct** & **-ive**. **1**. **a** (of persons) Able to construct, possessing faculty of construction; **b** (of things) resulting from construction, displaying ability to construct on part of the maker; **c** (of mental action) tending to build up something new; formative, creative. **2**. Pertaining to the structure of a building; structural. **3**. Not directly expressed, but depending on interpretation and inferences based on this; *constructive crime*, an act held to imply criminality, and the commission of a crime, though not in itself a criminal act.

constructively, adv. Prec. & **-ly**. In a constructive manner.

constructor, n. [1. kunstrúkter; 2. kənstráktə]. **construct** & **-or**. One who constructs.

construe, vb. trans. & intrans. [1. kunstrōō; 2. kənstrû]. M.E. *construe*, fr. Lat. *construere*, 'to build up, set in order', is used in present-day sense; *to construe a clause*, occurs in 'Piers Plowman'. A doublet of **construct**. **1**. trans. **a** To analyse a clause or sentence closely, so as to bring out the syntactic structure; **b** to do this for a foreign language by rendering its constructions into a more familiar language; to translate. **2**. intrans. **a** To carry out the process of construing: *he knows his Latin grammar indifferently, and cannot construe easily*; **b** to admit of this process; to be capable of being construed: *the sentence does not construe*. **3**. (fig.) trans. To place an interpretation upon words or actions, understand them to have a certain meaning: *a quite innocent remark was unfairly construed and aroused suspicion*.

consubstantial, adj. [1. kònsubstánshal; 2. kɔ̀nsəbstǽnʃəl]. **con-** & **substantial**. Having the same substance. Theological expression used especially of the Persons of the Holy Trinity.

consubstantiality, n. [1. kònsubstanshiáliti; 2. kɔ̀nsəbstænʃiǽliti]. Prec. & **-ity**. State of being consubstantial.

consubstantiate, vb. intrans. & trans. [1. kònsubstánshiāt; 2. kɔ̀nsəbstǽnʃieit]. **con-** & **substantiate**. **a** To unite; **b** to cause to unite in one common substance.

consubstantiation, n. [1. kònsubstanshiáshun; 2. kɔ̀nsəbstænʃiéiʃən]. Prec. & **-ion**. (theol.) The doctrine that after consecration of the elements in the Eucharist, the substance of these exists alongside of that of Christ's body and blood.

consuetude, n. [1. kónswitūd; 2. kɔ́nswitjūd]. O. Fr., Mod. Fr. *consuétude*, fr. Lat. *consuētūdo, consuētūdinis*, 'custom', fr. *consuēt-(um)*, P.P. type of *consuēscere*, 'to accustom, to be accustomed', fr. **con-** & *suēt-(um)*, P.P. of *suēre, suēscere*, 'to be wont, to accustom oneself', & **-tude**. The vb. meant orig. 'to make one's own', fr. a base **swĕ-* &c., 'own', cp. Gk. *éthos*, 'custom, habit', fr. **swedh-*; Lat. *suēsco* may actually be fr. **swedh-ko*. Cp. further Lat. *sodālis*, fr. **swedhālis*, 'mate, companion, intimate', & Goth. *swēs*, 'own', adj., O.E. *swǣs*, 'own, own dear' &c., & Lat. *suus*, 'own', fr. **sovos*, O. Slav. *swoji*, 'one's own'. See also **sui**, & cp. **desuetude**. Custom, usage, habit.

consuetudinary, adj. & n. [1. kònswitūdinari; 2. kɔ̀nswitjūdinəri]. Lat. *consuētūdinārius*. See prec. & **-ary**. **1**. adj. Customary: *consuetudinary law*. **2**. n. A manual of customary observances, ritual &c.

consul, n. [1. kónsl; 2. kɔ́nsl]. Lat. The etymol. is very uncertain, but the word is perh. connected w. *consilium*, 'a council', see **counsel** & **consult**. **1**. (Roman hist.) The title of the two chief magistrates of the Roman Republic, elected annually. Hence, **2**. (Fr. hist.) the title of the three chief magistrates of the French Republic (1799–1804). **3**. A person appointed by a State to look after matters connected with its commercial affairs, and those of its subjects, in a foreign country.

consular, adj. [1. kónsūlar; 2. kɔ́nsjulə], fr. Lat. *consulāris*. Of or pertaining to a consul, or a consul's duties.

consulate, n. [1. kónsūlat; 2. kɔ́nsjulit], fr. Lat. *consulātus*, 'the office of consul'. **1**. **a** Office of a consul; **b** period of tenure of a consular post; **c** house, or building, in which a consul conducts his official business; often a consul's residence. **2**. Specif., period during which consular government lasted in France (1799–1804).

consulship, n. [1. kónslship; 2. kɔ́nslʃip]. See **consul** & **-ship**. **a** The post of consul; **b** period during which this is held.

consult, vb. trans. & intrans. [1. kunsúlt; 2. kənsált], fr. Lat. *consultāre*, 'reflect, consider maturely, take counsel, deliberate; pay regard to', fr. *consult-(um)*, P.P. of *consulere*, 'to consider, reflect, take counsel; to ask the opinion or advice of'. Walde suggests that the word orig. meant 'to assemble, bring together', & that the sense of 'to consider' arose fr. the use of the Phr. *consulere senātum*, 'to summon the senate'. If this be so, the vb. *consulere* is fr. **con-** & the base seen in Gk. *helein*, 'to take', O. Ir. *selb*, 'possession', Goth. *soljan*, 'to give'; see **sell**, & cp. **consul**. **1**. trans. **a** To seek information or advice from (a person or other source of information): *to consult a doctor, one's friends, a dictionary* &c.; **b** to consider, pay regard to, show solicitude for: *to consult one's own interests, the feelings, convenience, of oneself or another*. **2**. intrans. To deliberate, confer, with another: *I can't decide finally until I have consulted about the matter*.

consultant, n. [1. kunsúltant; 2. kənsáltənt], fr. Lat. *consultant-(em)*, Pres. Part. of *consultāre*. See **consult**. **1**. One who consults another. **2**. A consulting physician.

consultation, n. [1. kònsltáshun; 2. kɔ̀nsltéiʃən], fr. Lat. *consultātiōn-(em)*, 'deliberation, consideration; an inquiry', fr. *consultāre*. See **consult** & **-ation**. **1**. The act of consulting. **2**. Deliberation; a meeting of two or more persons to deliberate on a matter; a conference, e.g. of doctors upon a puzzling case.

consultative, adj. [1. kunsúltativ; 2. kənsáltətiv], fr. Lat. *consultāt-(um)*, P.P. type of *consultāre*, & **-ive**. Having function of giving advice when consulted; advisory: *a consultative committee*.

consulting, adj. [1. kunsúlting; 2. kənsáltiŋ], fr. Pres. Part. of **consult**. (of persons) Possessing expert scientific or technical knowledge, and acting in advisory capacity in different cases which require special handling and treatment: *consulting surgeon, engineer*.

consume, vb. trans. & intrans. [1. kunsûm; 2. kənsjûm], fr. Lat. *consūmere*, 'to take up, use up; eat, devour; waste, squander, destroy'; **con-**, & *sūmere*, 'to take up, lay hold of,' wh. is itself fr. **subs-emere*, 'to take, receive, obtain', q.v. under **sub-** & **exempt**. **A**. trans. **1**. **a** To do away, destroy, cause to disappear (material objects): *the flames consumed the whole building*; **b** (fig.) to squander, waste, fritter away, use up: *to consume one's fortune, one's life, time*. **2**. To take to oneself, receive into one's system, eat, devour: *he consumed the best part of a leg of mutton at a sitting*. **3**. (of action on mind and feelings) To penetrate deeply, possess entirely, absorb the mental or emotional faculties (esp. in pass. constructions): *to be consumed with envy, hatred, excitement* &c. **B**. intrans. (gen. followed by *away*) To waste away, undergo dissolution or destruction: *to consume away with grief*.

consumedly, adv. [1. kunsûmedli; 2. kənsjûmidli]. Prec. & **-ed** & **-ly**. To an extreme or excessive degree (archaic).

consumer, n. [1. kunsûmer; 2. kənsjûmə]. **consume** & **-er**. One that consumes; specif. (econ.) one who uses economic material; contrasted with *producer*.

consummate (I.), vb. trans. [1. kónsumāt; 2. kɔ́nsəmeit], fr. Lat. *consummāt-(um)*, P.P. type of *consummāre*, 'to accomplish, finish, complete, make perfect', fr. **con-** & *summus*, 'highest, topmost, utmost'. See **summit**. **a** To bring to completion or perfection, to accomplish, complete, finish; **b** specif., to complete (marriage) physically.

consummate (II.), adj. [1. kunsúmat; 2. kənsámit], fr. Lat. *consummātum*, P.P. of *consummāre*. See prec. Brought to the last point of perfection, complete: *consummate skill, taste* &c.; *a consummate master of his craft* &c.

consummately, adv. Prec. & **-ly**. Completely, perfectly; to a point of perfection.

consummation, n. [1. kònsumáshun; 2. kɔ̀nsəméiʃən], fr. Lat. *consummātiōn-(em)*, 'an ending, completing'. See **consummate** (I.) & **-ion**; cp. Fr. *consommation*. **a** Completion (of a work); attainment (of object desired and aimed at); **b** specif., physical completion of a marriage.

consummative, adj. [1. kónsumātiv; 2. kónsameitiv]. See prec. & **-ive.** Serving, tending, to consummate.

consumption, n. [1. kunsúmpshun; 2. kənsámpʃən], fr. Lat. *consumptiōn-(em)*, 'a consuming, wasting', fr. Lat. *consumpt-(um)*, P.P. of *consūmere.* See **consume. 1. a** Act or process of consuming; **b** the amount consumed: *the consumption of beer in Great Britain is enormous*; **c** specif. (econ.) the usage of articles of industry or commerce; amount of such articles used; contrasted with *production.* **2.** Tubercular disease, esp. of the lungs; phthisis.

consumptive, adj. & n. [1. kunsúmptiv; 2. kənsámptiv]. Lat. base *consumpt-.* See prec. & **-ive. 1.** adj. **a** Tending to consume, destructive; **b** liable to, suffering from, tubercular disease, esp. of the lungs. **2.** n. Person suffering from tubercular disease.

contabescence, n. [1. kòntābésens; 2. kònteibésəns]. Lat. *contābescent-(em)*, Pres. Part. of Lat. *contābescere*, 'to waste away', fr. *con-* & *tābescere*, 'to melt, waste away', fr. *tābes*, 'a wasting away; putrefaction'. See **con-** & **tabes. a** A wasting away; **b** specif. (bot.) suppression of the pollen in flowers through disease of the stamens.

contabescent, adj. [1. kòntābésent; 2. kònteibésənt]. See prec. Affected by contabescence.

contact, n. [1. kóntakt; 2. kóntækt]. Lat. *contactus*, 'a touching, a touch'. **con-** & **tact. 1.** Condition in which two things touch, or are in close proximity to each other: *to bring fire into contact with gunpowder is dangerous.* **2.** (of mental relations) **a** Friendly communication, sympathy, rapport: *to be brought into contact with other minds*; **b** hostile, unfriendly meeting, clash of interests, opinions, collision &c.: *to come into contact with opposing tendencies* &c. **3.** Various special uses: **a** (mil., of bodies of troops) contiguity, communication; **b** (elect.) junction, close proximity, of two conductors, or ends of a conducting wire, sufficient to allow passage of electric current; **c** (math.) meeting of two curves or surfaces.

contagion, n. [1. kuntā́jun; 2. kəntéidžən], fr. Fr., Lat. *contāgiōn-(em)*, 'a touching, an infection'. The Lat. base *tāg-* is connected w. the vb. *tangere*, 'to border on, touch'. See **tangent, contingent,** & cp. **contiguous. 1. a** Process of communicating a disease from one person to another by contact; **b** disease so communicated. **2.** (fig.) Moral influence which spreads from one person to another and affects a large number (usually in bad or derogatory sense).

contagious, adj. [1. kuntā́jus; 2. kəntéidžəs]. Lat. *contāgiōsus*, fr. base *contāgi-* & adj. suff. See prec. & **-ous. 1. a** (of diseases) Communicable by contact; **b** (of persons) in a condition which renders one liable to communicate disease. **2.** (fig., of any moral influence or emotion, good or bad) Catching, liable to spread from one person to another: *example, whether good or ill, is contagious*; also of *enthusiasm, laughter, gloom, mirth, religious fervour* &c.

contagiously, adv. Prec. & **-ly.** In a contagious manner; by, through, contagion.

contagiousness, n. See prec. & **-ness.** Fact or condition of being contagious, in good or bad sense (lit. and fig.).

contain, vb. trans. [1. kuntā́n; 2. kəntéin]. M.E. *contéinen*, fr. O. Fr. *contenir*, Lat. *continēre*, 'hold, bind together; contain, comprise; keep within, keep in a place, confine, restrain'. **con-** & *tenēre*, 'to hold'. See **tenable. 1. a** To hold within a fixed space or fixed limits, to enclose: *the nest contained six eggs*; **b** to have as a part or element, to be made up of, comprise, include: *the blood contains several chemical substances*; *the book contains a good bibliography.* **2. a** To have capacity for, to be able to hold: *this jug will contain a quart*; *my house cannot contain all my books*; **b** (of measures) to be equivalent to: *a gallon contains four quarts.* **3.** (reflex.) *to contain oneself*, to restrain oneself, keep one's feelings under control, within the bounds of convention or decorum. **4.** (geom.) To enclose, bound (a figure or angle). **5.** (arith. and alg.) To be divisible by (a number), usually without a remainder.

container, n. [1. kuntā́ner; 2. kəntéinə]. Prec. & **-er.** That which contains; vessel, box &c. which holds or contains something else.

contaminate, vb. trans. [1. kuntáminät; 2. kəntǽmineit], fr. Lat. *contāmināt-(um)*, P.P. of *contāmināre*, 'to bring into contact, to mingle, to defile, pollute', fr. *contāmen*, 'contamination', wh. stands for **contāg-men*, fr. **con-** & base *tāg-* (see **contagion** & **tangent**) & formative suff. To exert a bad, corrupting influence upon, render impure, by addition of unclean matter; cause decay, deterioration, disease, by contact; (of physical and moral influence): *to contaminate a river with sewage, milk, by putting it in dirty vessels*; *to contaminate a person's morals by evil example* &c.

contamination, n. [1. kuntàminā́shun; 2. kəntæ̀minéiʃən], fr. Lat. *contāminātiōn-(em)*. Prec. & **-ion. 1. a** Act or process of contaminating; **b** state of being contaminated; **c** that which contaminates. **2.** Specif. (extended application) of texts, records, narratives &c., alteration from original form by influence of later versions, traditions &c.

contango, n. [1. kuntánggō; 2. kəntǽŋgou]. Prob. sham Lat., 'I refrain, postpone'; cp. Span. *contengo*, 'I refrain, check progress of something'. Cp. **contain.** (Stock Exchange) Interest paid by buyer of stock to seller, on condition of which the former is allowed to postpone completion of purchase; *contango day*, the second day before settling-day.

contemn, vb. trans. [1. kuntém; 2. kəntém], fr. Lat. *contemnere*, 'to despise, scorn', fr. **con-** & *temnere*, 'to slight, scorn, disdain'; cp. O. Fr. *contemner.* The base is possibly cogn. w. O.H.G. *stampfōn*, 'trample'. See **stamp (I.).** To despise, hold in contempt.

contemplate, vb. trans. & intrans. [1. kóntemplāt, kuntémplāt; 2. kóntempleit, kəntémpleit], fr. Lat. *contemplāt-(um)*, P.P. type of *contemplāri*, 'to look upon, observe, consider', fr. *templum*, 'an open place for observation marked out by the augur'. See **con-** & **temple (I.). A.** trans. **1.** To look at intently, gaze upon thoughtfully. **2.** To examine mentally, turn over in the mind, reflect deeply upon, consider: *to contemplate a problem.* **3. a** To have in view as an end or intention; to intend, purpose: *to contemplate resigning at once*; **b** to look forward to, expect: *I do not contemplate any opposition from him.* **B.** intrans. To engage in contemplation, meditate, ponder deeply, muse.

contemplation, n. [1. kòntemplā́shun; 2. kòntempléiʃən]. Fr., fr. Lat. *contemplātiōn-(em)*. See prec. & **-ion. 1.** The act of gazing upon or looking attentively at: *Wordsworth derived his chief inspiration from the contemplation of mountain scenery.* **2.** Continuous fixing of the mind upon a subject; meditation, thought; specif., *spiritual contemplation.* **3. a** The act of looking forward to an event or expecting that an event will happen; expectation; **b** act of forming an intention, or plan of action: *to have something in contemplation.*

contemplative, adj. [1. kóntemplātiv, kuntémplativ; 2. kóntempleitiv, kəntémplətiv]. **contemplate** & **-ive.** Meditative, thoughtful; *contemplative life*, passed in meditation; specif., in religious meditation and prayer.

contemplatively, adv. Prec. & **-ly.** In a contemplative manner.

contemplativeness, n. See prec. & **-ness.** Contemplative state or habit of mind.

contemporaneity, n. [1. kuntémporanḗiti; 2. kəntémpərəníiti]. See next word & **-ity.** State of being contemporaneous.

contemporaneous, adj. [1. kuntèmporā́neus; 2. kəntèmpəréiniəs], fr. Lat. *contemporāne-(us)* & **-ous, fr. con-** & *tempus, temporis*, 'time'. See **temporal (I.).** (chiefly of events) Existing, occurring, at the same time; (followed by *with*, or absolutely).

contemporaneously, adv. Prec. & **-ly.** At the same time as.

contemporaneousness, n. See prec. & **-ness.** Fact or condition of being contemporaneous.

contemporary (I.), adj. [1. kuntémporari; 2. kəntémpərəri]. **con-** & **temporary. 1.** (of persons) Living, existing; (of events) occurring, at the same time; contemporaneous. **2.** Arising, made, at the same period: *contemporary accounts.*

contemporary (II.), n., fr. prec. **1. a** One who lives during the same time as another; **b** one having the same age as another. **2.** Specif., a newspaper, magazine &c. published during the same period or on same day as another.

contemporize, vb. trans. & intrans. [1. kuntémporīz; 2. kəntémpəraiz]. See **contemporary (I.)** & **-ize. 1.** trans. To make contemporary, make to coincide in time. **2.** intrans. To happen, exist, at the same time.

contempt, n. [1. kuntémpt; 2. kəntémpt]. Lat. *contemptus*, 'scorn' &c., formed fr. P.P. of *contemnere*, 'to despise'. See **contemn. 1. a** The emotion raised in the mind by that which is despicable, mean, and low: *to feel contempt for*; *an object of contempt.* Phr. *familiarity breeds contempt*; **b** act of possessing and evincing this feeling: *to deserve the contempt of all decent men.* **2.** The condition of provoking contempt, of being contemned; disgrace: *to bring, fall into, live in, contempt.* **3.** Specif. (law), disregard, disrespect shown for, open flouting of the dignity, or of the rules and pronouncements, of a body of established and recognized legal authority: *contempt of court.*

contemptibility, n. [1. kuntèmptibíliti; 2. kəntèmptibíliti], fr. next word & **-ity.** The quality of being contemptible.

contemptible, adj. [1. kuntémptibl; 2. kəntémptibl], fr. Lat. *contemptibilis*, 'worthy of scorn'. See **contempt** & **-ible.** Worthy of, deserving, provoking, contempt; despicable, mean.

contemptibleness, n. Prec. & **-ness.** State, quality, of being contemptible.

contemptibly, adv. [1. kuntémptibli; 2. kəntémptibli]. See prec. & **-ly.** In a manner deserving and provoking contempt.

contemptuous, adj. [1. kuntémptūus; 2. kəntémptjuəs]. **contempt** & **-ous. a** (of persons) Feeling, showing, contempt; disdainful; **b** (of manner, verbal utterance, written remarks &c.) expressing contempt.

contemptuously, adv. Prec. & **-ly.** In a contemptuous manner; disdainfully, scornfully.

contemptuousness, n. See prec. & **-ness.** The feeling of contempt, fact of being contemptuous.

contend, vb. intrans. [1. kunténd; 2. kənténd], fr. Lat. *contendere*, 'to stretch, strive', fr. **con-** & *tendere*, 'to stretch'. See **tend (II.). 1.** To engage, take part, in a struggle, or contest of any kind; **a** (followed by *with* before name of person, and *for* before the name of the object contended for): *our troops contended with the enemy for the hill*; generally, **b** (of struggle, or contest in words, or by efforts other than physical) to vie with, compete with: *to contend with others for a prize*; or **c** (of wordy strife) to argue, discuss, debate: *the minister contended vigorously against the opponents of the bill*; **d** to engage in angry discussion, to quarrel: *to be fond of contending about everything.* **2.** To be opposed by, struggle against, endeavour to overcome, esp. in such Phrs. as: *to have much to contend with*; *to have many difficulties to contend with* &c. **3.** To maintain, argue, that, affirm as a fact or principle (followed by *that*): *I contend that national defence is one of the first duties of a government.*

content (I.), n. [1. kuntént; 2. kəntént], more rarely [1. kóntent; 2. kóntent], fr. Lat. *content-(um)*, P.P. of *continēre*, 'to contain'.

See **contain.** **1.** **a** (usually in pl., of material things) That which is contained; that which is inside, and held by, a receptacle or vessel of any kind: *the contents of the bag, bottle* &c.; **b** (of non-material things) the topics, subjects, dealt with in a treatise or other document; in a discourse &c.: *the contents of many sermons are very slight*; *the contents of a book*; *table of contents*, list of matters treated in a document of any kind (often [kóntents; kóntɛnts] in this sense. See also **2** below). **2.** (in sing.) [kóntent; kóntɛnt] (of non-material things) **a** Essential elements; real meaning: *the content of a proposition, statement* &c.; **b** (philos.) the sum of the characteristics which are united in an idea or concept. **3.** Holding capacity of a vessel. **4.** (geom.) Space or area, volume of matter, bounded by, or confined within, a certain space: *linear, solid, content(s)*.

content (II.), adj. [1. kuntént; 2. kəntént]; see also **contented.** Fr., fr. Lat. *contentus*, P.P. of *continēre*. See prec. The orig. sense is 'bounded in one's desires', hence 'satisfied'. **1.** (only used pred.) Satisfied, served, provided for, according to one's desires; pleased with one's lot and circumstances; not desiring more: *content with very little, with what one has*; *to be quite content.* **2.** **a** Willing, well pleased: *I should be content to stay here all the year*; **b** (*House of Lords*) *content* is used by their Lordships to signify agreement, corresponding to *aye* in House of Commons.

content (III.), n. [1. kuntént; 2. kəntént]. See prec. **a** State of being content, satisfied, with one's possessions and condition: *to live in peace and content*; **b** satisfaction; Phr. *to one's heart's content*, as much as one wants, to the limit of one's desires; **c** *contents*, in the House of Lords are those who vote for a measure.

content (IV.), vb. trans. [1. kuntént; 2. kəntént], fr. Fr. *contenter*, L. Lat. *contentāre*, fr. Lat. *contentus*. See **content** (II.). **1.** To give content to, make contented; to satisfy. **2.** (reflex.) *Content oneself* (*with*), **a** to accept something as sufficient, make it do: *to content oneself with dry bread*; **b** to do nothing more than: *to content oneself with looking on.*

contented, adj. [1. kunténted; 2. kənténtid], fr. P.P. of prec. Content, satisfied; having the feeling that something is adequate: '*Contented if he might enjoy The things which others understand*' (Wordsworth).

contentedly, adv. Prec. & **-ly.** In a contented manner.

contentedness, n. See prec. & **-ness.** Contented state of mind.

contention, n. [1. kunténshun; 2. kənténʃən]. Fr., fr. Lat. *contentiōn-(em)*, 'stretching, striving, strife', fr. *content-(um)*, P.P. type of *contendere*. See **contend** & **-ion.** **1.** Wordy strife, quarrel, altercation; controversy; Phr. *bone of contention*, cause, subject, of dispute. **2.** Something contended in an argument; a point maintained; disputed point: *his contention was that* &c.

contentious, adj. [1. kunténshus; 2. kənténʃəs], fr. Fr. *contentieux*, Lat. *contentiōsus*, 'pertaining to contention, headstrong, obstinate'. See prec. & **-ous.** **1.** **a** (of persons) Given to argument; disputatious, quarrelsome; **b** (of subjects of, questions for, discussion &c.) likely to provoke controversy and difference of opinion; involving contention: *a contentious point, clause* &c.

contentiously, adv. Prec. & **-ly.** In a contentious, argumentative manner.

contentiousness, n. See prec. & **-ness.** Condition of, liability to cause, contention; contentious habits.

contentment, n. [1. kunténtment; 2. kənténtmənt]. **content** (IV.) & **-ment.** **a** Act of contenting; **b** state of being contented.

conterminal, adj. [1. kòntérminal; 2. kòntə́minəl]. **con-** & **terminal.** Having a common boundary.

conterminous, adj. [1. kòntérminus; 2. kòntə́minəs]. Lat. *conterminus*, 'bordering upon, neighbouring', & **-ous.** See **con-** & **terminus.** (followed by *with*) Having a common boundary, adjacent.

conterminously, adv. Prec. & **-ly.** Adjacently.

contest (I.), vb. trans. & intrans. [1. kuntést; 2. kəntést], fr. Fr. *contester*, 'to call to witness, argue, gainsay', fr. Lat. *contestāri*, 'to call to witness', esp. *contestāri lītem*, 'to enter on a lawsuit by calling witnesses, to bring an action', fr. *con-* & *testāri*, 'to be a witness', fr. *testis*, 'a witness'. **con-** & **test** (I.). **A.** trans. **1.** **a** To dispute, argue, call in question: *to contest a point, statement* &c.; specif. **b** (law) to make a subject of litigation, go to law about; to defend (a suit). **2.** **a** (mil.) To fight for, struggle against hostile force in order to gain, or maintain a position: *to contest every inch of ground*; **b** (fig., of any kind of struggle for a desired object) to dispute, try to gain: *to contest a prize, match* &c.; **c** (politics) *to contest a seat, an election*, to endeavour to get elected to parliament against another candidate. **B.** intrans. (followed by *with*) To contend, strive, vie with (rare).

contest (II.), n. [1. kóntest; 2. kóntɛst], fr. prec. **a** A debate, dispute, controversy; **b** any struggle, strife, or encounter, friendly or hostile, for victory, superiority &c.

contestant, n. [1. kuntéstant; 2. kəntéstənt]. Fr. See **contest** (I.) & **-ant.** A party in a contest.

contestation, n. [1. kòntestáshun; 2. kòntɛstéiʃən]. Fr., 'a contesting', fr. Lat. *contestātiōn-(em)*, 'testimony'. **contest** (I.) & **-ation.** Act or process of contesting; controversy: *in contestation*, in dispute.

context, n. [1. kóntekst; 2. kóntɛkst]. Fr., fr. Lat. *contextus*, 'a joining or putting together, connexion', fr. P.P. of *contexere*, 'to weave, join together, connect'. See **con-** & **text.** The parts of a written document, which come immediately before and after a particular passage, so closely connected in meaning with it that its sense is not clear apart from them.

contextual, adj. [1. kòntékstūal; 2. kòntékstjuəl]. Lat. *contextu-* (see prec.) & **-al.** Connected with the context.

contextually, adv. Prec. & **-ly.** In connexion with, with reference to, the context.

contexture, n. [1. kuntékschur; 2. kəntékstʃə]. Fr. See **con-** & **texture.** **a** Mode of putting parts of a thing together, structural character; **b** something put together, interwoven; a fabric.

contiguity, n. [1. kòntigúiti; 2. kòntigjúiti]. L. Lat. *contiguitāt-(em)*, formed fr. *contiguus*, 'touching, adjoining'. See **contiguous** & **-ity.** **1.** **a** State of being contiguous; contact, nearness, proximity; **b** a continuous, unbroken, stretch: '*Some boundless contiguity of shade*' (Cowper). **2.** (psychol.) Association of ideas.

contiguous, adj. [1. kuntígūus; 2. kəntígjuəs], fr. Lat. *contigu-*, as in *contiguus*, 'touching, neighbouring', & **-ous.** Prob. connected w. Lat. *tignum*, 'a beam', & meaning 'joined together, as by beams'. On the other hand, Lat. *contingere*, 'to touch, seize', wh. has a perf. *contigi*, & wh. is usually given as connected w. the above adj., appears to differ considerably in meaning. See under **contingent, tangent.** The form *tignum* may be fr. **tegnom*, & is perh. connected w. the base **steg-* &c. seen in **stake** &c. In contact, touching, near by, next to, adjoining.

contiguously, adv. Prec. & **-ly.** In close proximity, near.

continence, n. [1. kóntinens; 2. kóntinəns]. Fr. *continence*, fr. Lat. *continentia.* See next word & **contain.** **a** Self-restraint, moderation: *continence in speech*; **b** specif., self-restraint in regard to the sexual act.

continent (I.), adj. [1. kóntinent; 2. kóntinənt], fr. Lat. *continent-(em)*, Pres. Part. of *continēre*, 'to hold together, repress'. See **contain.** **a** Practising self-restraint in word and act, moderate; **b** specif., chaste.

continent (II.), n. [1. kóntinent; 2. kóntinənt]. Same origin as prec. **1.** **a** A continuous stretch of land, of very large extent; mainland, as distinct from outlying islands; **b** specif. (phys. geog.) one of the main divisions of land on the globe, as Europe, Asia, Africa &c. **2.** *The Continent*, the mainland of Europe, as distinguished from the British Isles.

continental, adj. & n. [1. kòntinéntl; 2. kòntinéntl]. Prec. & **-al.** **1.** adj. **a** Of, pertaining to, characteristic of, a continent; **b** belonging to, or characteristic of the continent of Europe, as contrasted with the British Isles; foreign, non-English, non-British. **2.** n. An inhabitant of the Continent or mainland of Europe as distinct from an Englishman; a foreigner.

continentalism, n. [1. kòntinéntalizm; 2. kòntinéntəlizəm]. Prec. & **-ism.** Manner, mode of thought and conduct, of the inhabitants of the continent of Europe, contrasted with British habits.

continentalist, n. [1. kòntinéntalist; 2. kòntinéntəlist]. **continental** & **-ist.** Person who favours continental ways and habits.

continentally, adv. [1. kòntinéntali; 2. kòntinéntəli]. **continental** & **-ly.** **a** As a continent; **b** after the manner of a continental, in a foreign way as contrasted with the British manner.

continently, adv. [1. kóntinentli; 2. kóntinəntli], fr. **continent** (I.) & **-ly.** In a continent, temperate manner; chastely.

contingency, n. [1. kuntínjensi; 2. kəntín(d)žənsi]. See **contingent** & **-ency.** **a** Possibility of occurrence; **b** something which may or may not happen, the occurrence of which is looked forward to as a possibility; **c** event, or conditions, dependent upon something else which may or may not happen.

contingent (I.), adj. [1. kuntínjent; 2. kəntíndžənt], fr. Lat. *contingent-(em)*, Pres. Part. of *contingere*, 'to touch, take hold of; border upon; to affect; be related to; happen', fr. **con-** & *tangere*, 'to touch'. See **tangent.** **1.** Of uncertain occurrence; possible. **2.** **a** Dependent on, subject to, something else; conditional; **b** (law) dependent for effect on some other event that may or may not happen, or conditions which may or may not arise: *contingent remainder, legacy.*

contingent (II.), n. fr. prec. **1.** A contingency. **2.** That which falls to one's share; a suitable proportion; hence, a quota of troops, ships &c.

contingently, adv. [1. kuntínjentli; 2. kəntíndžəntli]. **contingent** (I.) & **-ly.** Conditionally.

continual, adj. [1. kuntínūal; 2. kəntínjuəl]. M.E., fr. O. Fr. *continuel.* See **continue** & **-al.** **a** Occurring intermittently over a considerable period; frequently repeated, occurring in rapid succession, occurring as a series, but with breaks between each occurrence: *continual bouts of toothache, attacks of gout* &c.; **b** also used, more rarely, in sense of continuous.

continually, adv. Prec. & **-ly.** **a** Repeatedly; **b** uninterruptedly.

continuance, n. [1. kuntínūans; 2. kəntínjuəns]. **continue** & **-ance.** **1.** **a** A going on; duration, unbroken course (of an action or a process): *a continuance of strife, of bad weather*; **b** a remaining of or in the same conditions: *a continuance of famine, of,* or *in, prosperity, happiness*; **c** a remaining in the same place: *continuance in one's old home* &c.; **d** an unbroken period of time: *an arrangement which is for a continuance.* **2.** Continuation, succession (archaic).

continuant, n. [1. kuntínūant; 2. kəntínjuənt], fr. Lat. *continuant-(em)*, Pres. Part. of *continuāre.* See **continue.** (phon.) Name given by some phoneticians to consonant sounds formed by narrowing, but not completely closing, the air-passage, so that the air-stream passes, and the sound can be prolonged, as long as the breath lasts, e.g. **z, s, f, v** &c. Also called *open consonant*; contrasted with *stop consonant.*

continuation, n. [1. kuntìnūáshun; 2. kəntìnjuéiʃən]. Lat. *continuātiōn-(em)*, 'an unbroken series', fr. *continuāt-(um)*, P.P. type of *continuāre*, & **-ion.** See **continue.** **1. a** Act of continuing; **b** state of being continued. **2.** Unbroken existence, prolongation, continuance; **a** (of action) *the further continuation of misrule must be prevented*; **b** (of a state, system &c.) *the continuation of the good health of the army must be secured*; *the continuation of the monarchy in the direct line.* **3. a** Resumption, carrying further towards completion after an interruption: *the continuation of the subject will be proceeded with in the next lecture*; **b** the part of anything which follows the earlier instalments and forms part of the completion; sequel, further instalment: *the next number of the magazine will contain a continuation of the story.* **4.** Something added to another thing as an extension or prolongation, e.g. *to build a continuation to a room*; *the continuations of riding breeches*, that part below the knee which is worn inside the boots or gaiters.

continuative, adj. [1. kuntínūativ; 2. kəntínjuətiv], fr. Lat. *continuātīvus*, 'serving to connect the discourse'. See prec. & **-ive.** Expressing continuance; specif. (gram.) serving to connect the parts of a sentence.

continue, vb. intrans. & trans. [1. kuntínū; 2. kəntínju], fr. Lat. *continuāre*, 'to make continuous, to join, connect', fr. *continu-(us)*, 'holding together, unbroken', fr. *continēre*, 'to hold together, bind, connect', fr. **con-** & *tenēre*, 'to hold'. See **tenable. A.** intrans. **1.** To go on, extend, be prolonged, reach: *this path continues for miles.* **2.** To remain in existence, last, persist; **a** (of a state or condition) *lawlessness continued for years*; **b** (of an action or process) to be carried out during a period of time, to be prolonged: *the king's reign continued*; (of persons) **c** to persist in, maintain, a course of action or line of conduct: *to continue in the faith of one's fathers, in well-doing*; **d** to remain at or in a place, position, office &c.: *to continue in power, in command, at one's post* &c.; **e** to remain in a frame of mind, or state of body: *to continue obdurate*; *continue ailing.* **3.** (of persons and things; followed by an infin.) To keep up certain course of action or movement unbrokenly, or repeatedly at frequent intervals; to go on doing something: *he continued to live at home*; *he continued to cause his parents great anxiety*; *the door continued to bang all night.* **B.** trans. **1. a** To keep on with, prolong duration of anything: *his father continued his allowance for several years*; **b** to pursue farther, extend: *to continue one's walk for several miles.* **2.** To take up again, and go on doing, something the carrying on of which has been interrupted; to resume: *to continue one's remarks from where one left off*; *to continue a story in the following number of a magazine.* **3.** To allow to remain, retain, in a post: *to continue an old servant in office.*

continuity, n. [1. kòntinūiti; 2. kɔ̀ntinjūiti]. Lat. *continuitāt-(em)*; cp. Fr. *continuité.* See prec. & **-ity. a** Quality or state of being continuous; **b** unbroken series, succession; **c** close proximity in space, cohesion; **d** close relationship, logical sequence, of ideas.

continuous, adj. [1. kuntínūus; 2. kəntínjuəs], fr. Lat. *continuus*, 'joining or connecting with something, hanging together (in space or time), uninterrupted, unbroken'. See **continue** & **-ous. a** (of events) Occurring in an unbroken sequence: *a continuous series of calamities*; **b** (of actions or processes) going on without intermission or cessation: *continuous laughter, coughing*; *continuous development, eruption* &c.

continuously, adv. Prec. & **-ly.** In a continuous manner, without cessation.

continuousness, n. See prec. & **-ness.** State or fact of being continuous.

continuum, n. [1. kontínūum; 2. kəntínjuəm]. Lat. neut. form of *continuus*, see **continuous.** A whole, the structure of whose parts is continuous and not atomic; see also **space-time.**

contline, n. [1. kóntlīn; 2. kɔ́ntlain]. Etymol. obscure. Space **a** between the strands of a rope; **b** between casks stowed side by side.

contorniate, n. & adj. [1. kòntórniāt; 2. kɔ̀ntɔ́nieit], fr. Ital. *contorniato*, P.P. of *contorniare*, 'to make a circuit or outline', fr. *contorno*, 'circuit, outline'. See **con-, tour** & **turn.** (numis.) **a** n. Bronze medal with a deep furrow round the edge; **b** adj., having a furrow of this kind.

contort, vb. trans. [1. kuntórt; 2. kəntɔ́t], fr. Lat. *contort-(um)*, P.P. type of *contorquēre*, 'to twist'. See **con-** & **tort.** To twist, pull awry, to distort; **a** (esp. of muscular action) *to contort one's features, limbs* &c.; **b** (fig.) to wrest a word or expression from its ordinary meaning.

contorted, adj. [1. kuntórted; 2. kəntɔ́tid], fr. P.P. of prec. Unnaturally twisted; twisted, pulled, awry.

contortion, n. [1. kuntórshun; 2. kəntɔ́ʃən], fr. Lat. *contortiōn-(em)*, 'a whirling round, intertwining'. **contort** & **-ion.** The act of contorting; twisting awry, distortion, esp. of face or body.

contortionist, n. [1. kuntórshunist; 2. kəntɔ́ʃənist]. Prec. & **-ist.** An acrobat who twists his body and limbs into unnatural postures.

contour (**I.**), n. [1. kóntōōr; 2. kɔ́ntuə]. Fr., 'outline', fr. *contourner.* See **con-** & **tour. a** The outline of a surface; **b** lines or colours representing this on a map or painting. Also attrib. *Contour line*, a line, esp. one drawn or shaded on a map, connecting the points of a surface having the same elevation, as of a mountain. *Contour map*, one which shows contours of surface of a given area.

contour (**II.**), vb. trans., fr. prec. **a** To indicate a contour of, by lines, shading, or colour; **b** to serve as a contour for.

contourné, adj. [1. kòntōōrnā; 2. kɔ̀ntúənei]. Fr., P.P. of *contourner*, 'to turn, twist'. Cp. **contour.** (her.) Turned about (of an animal facing sinister side of shield).

contra-, pref. Lat., 'over against, facing'. In compounds expresses hostile opposition. From **con-**, w. compar. suff., as in Lat. *alter*, fr. *alius* 'other', cp. **-ther.** Against; (mus.) opposite to.

contra, adv., prep. & n. [1. kóntra; 2. kɔ́ntrə]. See prec. **a** adv. To the contrary: *pro and contra*; **b** prep., against, in opposition to; **c** n., a contrary vote, opinion &c.: *pros and contras.* Gen. abbrev. *con.*

contra-account, n. **a** Opposite, credit side of an account; **b** account, bill which can be set against another's account or bill.

contraband, n. & adj. [1. kóntraband; 2. kɔ́ntrəbænd]. Fr. *contrebande*, Ital. *contrabando*, fr. **contra-** & *bando*, 'ban, edict'. See **ban** (**II.**). **1.** n. **a** Illicit trading, smuggling; **b** goods bought or sold in contravention of excise laws; **c** *contraband of war*, goods which during war time may not be supplied by neutrals to belligerents. **2.** adj. Forbidden by law; (of merchandise) *contraband goods, trade.*

contrabandist, n. [1. kóntrabandist; 2. kɔ́ntrəbændist], fr. Span. *contrabandista*, cp. prec., & **-ist.** A trafficker in contraband goods, a smuggler.

contrabass, n. [1. kóntrabās; 2. kɔ́ntrəbeis]. See **contra-** & **bass** (**I.**). (mus.) Largest and deepest-toned instrument of the viol kind; double-bass.

contraception, n. [1. kòntrasépshun; 2. kɔ̀ntrəsépʃən]. Formed fr. **contra-** & **conception.** Practice, method, of preventing or avoiding conception; birth control.

contraceptive, adj. & n. [1. kòntraséptiv; 2. kɔ̀ntrəséptiv]. See prec. & **-ive. a** adj. Preventing conception; **b** n., device, drug &c. for preventing conception.

contract (**I.**), n. [1. kóntrakt; 2. kɔ́ntrækt]. O. Fr. *contract*, Fr. *contrat*, Lat. *contractus*, 'an agreement', fr. P.P. of *contrahere*, 'to draw together, to conclude a bargain' &c. See **con-** & **tract. 1. a** An agreement of a solemn and binding character between two (or more) parties or states &c. to do or not to do something; **b** a bargain or compact (in business matters &c.) respecting work to be done, goods to be supplied &c., at a fixed price &c.; **c** the work carried out under a contract; **d** any agreement, undertaking, promise &c. between private persons. **2.** Specif. **a** a formal act whereby two persons enter upon marriage relation; **b** betrothal. **3.** Document embodying the terms of an agreement or contract. **4.** Also *contract bridge*, a form of the game of bridge, a modification of *auction bridge.*

contract (**II.**), vb. trans. & intrans. [1. kuntrákt; 2. kəntrǽkt], fr. Lat. *contract-(um)*, P.P. type of *contrahere*, 'to draw together, collect; draw close, tighten; shorten, abridge, contract; draw in, restrain'. See prec. For further meanings in Lat. see next word. **A.** trans. **1. a** To draw up, brace, tighten: *to contract a muscle*; **b** to cause to wrinkle, to knit together: *to contract one's forehead, eyebrows* &c. **2.** To limit, reduce in size or length; **a** to abridge, put into smaller compass: *to contract what one has to say into a short space* (rare or obs.); **b** to narrow, cause to shrink, diminish mental capacity: *to contract one's mind, faculties, by disuse*; **c** (gram.) to shorten, abbreviate, a word by leaving out letter or syllable, a sentence by omission of a word. **3. a** To take, acquire, catch: *to contract a disease, a habit*; **b** to incur, become liable for: *to contract debts, responsibilities.* **B.** intrans. To draw together, shrink, become smaller in bulk, more compact (opposite of *swell, dilate*): *wood contracts as it dries*; *the heart contracts by muscular action.*

contract (**III.**), vb. trans. & intrans. Same as prec. in origin, but almost completely isolated fr. it in meaning, being connected w. **contract** (**I.**), its usage being derived fr. a further sense of Lat. *contrahere* (P.P. *contractum*), 'to make a contract, conclude a bargain'. **1.** trans. To enter into relations with another person, state &c., which are **a** based upon a formal contract, e.g.: *to contract an alliance, a marriage* (*with*); **b** (i.) to establish a bond of union with another person based upon agreement in feeling, tastes &c.; (ii.) to establish, strike up: *to contract a friendship for* or *with a person*; (iii.) (in pass.) *to be contracted to*, to be betrothed to. **2.** intrans. To enter into an agreement, make a contract or bargain to do something: *to contract to allow goods to pass into a country on certain terms*; *to contract to build a bridge for ten thousand pounds. Contract out of* (*an agreement* &c.), to free oneself from its terms, undertakings, and restrictions.

contracted, adj. [1. kuntrákted; 2. kəntrǽktid], fr. P.P. of **contract** (**II.**). **a** Drawn together, wrinkled: *a contracted brow*; **b** (gram.) shortened, by omission of letters or syllables; **c** (of the mind, ideas, &c.) narrow, limited, illiberal.

contractile, adj. [1. kuntráktīl; 2. kəntrǽktail], fr. **contract** (**II.**) & **-ile. a** Tending to contract, having the power of contracting, capable of contraction; producing contraction: *contractile tissue* &c.; **b** specif. (of wings of insects) capable of being folded close to the body.

contractility, n. [1. kòntraktíliti; 2. kɔ̀ntræktíliti]. Fr. *contractilité.* See prec. & **-ity.** The quality or power of contracting or shrinking, esp. of living muscle &c.

contraction, n. [1. kuntrákshun; 2. kəntrǽkʃən], fr. Lat. *contractiōn-(em)*, 'a drawing together'. See **contract** (**II.**) & **-ion. 1. a** Process of contracting, shrinkage: *contraction of iron in cold*; **b** shortening, drawing up of a muscle &c.; of the eyebrows; **c** shortening of a word by omission of syllable or syllables, or of letters in written form; **d** form of word so shortened. **2.** Process **a** of acquiring disease &c.; **b** of incurring liabilities &c.

contractive, adj. [1. kuntráktiv ; 2. kəntrǽktiv]. **contract (II.)** & **-ive.** Tending to contract, having the function of contracting.

contractor, n. [1. kuntrákter ; 2. kəntrǽktə]. **1.** (fr. **contract (III.)** & **-or**). **a** One who makes, enters into, a contract; specif. **b** one who contracts to carry out building or engineering operations &c. on specified terms; **c** one who undertakes to supply goods according to terms of a contract: *army clothing contractor* &c. **2.** (fr. **contract (II.)**, physiol.) Muscle that contracts.

contractual, adj. [1. kuntráktūal ; 2. kəntrǽktjuəl]. **contract (I.)** & **-al.** Cp. Fr. *contractuel.* Having the character of a legal contract.

contracture, n. [1. kuntráktūr ; 2. kəntrǽktjə], fr. Lat. *contractūra*, 'a drawing together', (esp. in archit.) 'a contracting of a pillar'. Cp. Fr. *contracture.* See **contract (II.)** & **-ure. 1.** (med.) A state of permanent contraction of the muscles. **2.** (archit.) Tapering of a column.

contradict, vb. trans. [1. kòntradíkt ; 2. kɔ̀ntrədíkt], fr. Lat. *contrādict-(um)*, P.P. of *contrādīcere*, 'to speak against'. See **contra-** & **diction. 1. a** To deny the truth of, assert the opposite of, a statement: *to contradict a report, statement* &c.; **b** to assert the contrary of what a person says; to gainsay him, to deny the words of (a person). **2.** (of what is asserted) To be inconsistent with, opposed to: *the two accounts contradict each other.*

contradiction, n. [1. kòntradíkshun ; 2. kɔ̀ntrədíkʃən], fr. Lat. *contrādictiōn-(em)*, 'a reply, counter-argument'. See **contra-** & **diction. 1. a** Act of contradicting; **b** an assertion which contradicts another; denial, opposition. **2.** Inconsistency, incompatibility, fact of being contradictory (of acts, occurrences, statements). Phr. *contradiction in terms*, statement which contradicts itself.

contradictious, adj. [1. kòntradíkshus ; 2. kɔ̀ntrədíkʃəs]. **contradict** & **-ious. a** (of persons) Fond of contradicting, inclined to contradict, captious; **b** (of style of conversation) full of contradiction, of denial of truth of statements made by others.

contradictiously, adv. Prec. & **-ly.** In a contradicting, cavilling manner.

contradictiousness, n. See prec. & **-ness.** Fact or state of being contradictious.

contradictorily, adv. [1. kòntradíkturili ; 2. kɔ̀ntrədíktərili]. **contradictory** & **-ly.** In a contradictory manner.

contradictoriness, n. [1. kòntradíkturines ; 2. kɔ̀ntrədíktərinis]. Next word & **-ness.** Quality of being contradictory.

contradictory, adj. & n. [1. kòntradíkturi ; 2. kɔ̀ntrədíktəri], fr. L. Lat. *contrādictōrius*, 'containing an objection or contradiction'. See **contradict** & **-ory. 1.** adj. Tending to contradict; containing, involving, contradiction; logically opposed, or inconsistent: *contradictory statements.* **2.** n. **a** An assertion, proposition, which denies; **b** a thing which is opposed to another.

contradistinction, n. [1. kòntradistíngkshun ; 2. kɔ̀ntrədistíŋkʃən]. **contra-** & **distinction.** Distinction by contrast; esp. in Phr. *in contradistinction from.*

contradistinguish, vb. trans. [1. kòntradistínggwish ; 2. kɔ̀ntrədistíŋgwiʃ], fr. **contra-** & **distinguish.** To distinguish things from one another by contrasting them.

contralto, n. & adj. [1. kuntráhltō ; 2. kəntrǽltou]. **contra-** & **alto. 1.** n. (mus.) **a** The part sung by the highest male or lowest female voices (usually the latter); between tenor and soprano; **b** female voice of deep tone and quality; **c** woman with a voice of this kind. **2.** adj. (mus.) Of or pertaining to, having quality of, contralto: *contralto voice.*

contraposition, n. [1. kòntrapōzíshun ; 2. kɔ̀ntrəpouzíʃən], fr. **contra-** & **position. 1.** Opposition, contrast, antithesis. **2.** (log.) Also called immediate inference, e.g. *every Jew is an Oriental, therefore no non-Oriental is a Jew.*

contraption, n. [1. kuntrápshun ; 2. kəntrǽpʃən]. Manufactured word. (colloq.) A contrivance; a new-fangled device (term of contempt).

contrapuntal, adj. [1. kòntrapúntal ; 2. kɔ̀ntrəpʌ́ntəl], fr. Ital. *contrappunto*, 'counterpoint', & **-al.** See **counterpoint.** (mus.) Pertaining to, according to, counterpoint.

contrapuntist, n. [1. kòntrapúntist ; 2. kɔ̀ntrəpʌ́ntist], fr. Ital. *contrappuntista.* See prec. & **-ist.** (mus.) One skilled in counterpoint.

contrariant, adj. [1. kontráriant ; 2. kəntréəriənt], fr. O. Fr., fr. L. Lat. *contrāriant-(em)*, Pres. Part. of *contrāriāre*, 'to oppose', fr. Lat. *contrārius.* See **contrary.** Opposed, contrary to. (Rare.)

contrariety, n. [1. kòntraríeti ; 2. kɔ̀ntrəráiəti], fr. O. Fr. *contrarieté*, fr. L. Lat. *contrārietāt-(em)*, 'opposition', fr. *contrārius.* See **contrary. a** Opposition, antagonism; **b** an inconsistency, discrepancy.

contrarily, adv. [1. kuntrárili ; 2. kəntréərili], fr. **contrary (I.) 5** & **-ly.** (colloq.) In a contrary manner, perversely.

contrariness, n. [1. kuntrárinis ; 2. kəntréərinis]. See prec. & **-ness.** (colloq.) Perverseness, perversity.

contrarious, adj. [1. kuntrárius ; 2. kəntréəriəs], fr. O. Fr. *contrarios*, L. Lat. *contrāriōsus*, fr. *contrārius.* See **contrary** & **-ous.** (archaic or obsolesc.) **a** (of persons) Contrary, perverse; **b** (of things) adverse, unfavourable.

contrariwise, adv. [1. kóntrariwīz ; 2. kɔ́ntrəriwaiz]; popularly [1. kuntráriwīz ; 2. kəntréəriwaiz], fr. next word & **-wise. a** On the contrary, on the other hand; **b** in the opposite direction, manner; conversely; **c** perversely, contrarily.

contrary (I.), adj. [1. kóntrari ; 2. kɔ́ntrəri], fr. O. Fr. *contrarie*, fr. Lat. *contrārius*, (of places) 'lying over against, opposite'; (of other objects) 'opposed'. See **contra-** & **-ary. 1.** In opposition to; contradicted by; having an opposite tendency or character: *contrary to all experience*; *contrary to custom and tradition.* **2. a** Opposed to one's interests: *contrary to one's hopes, wishes* &c.; **b** unfavourable: *contrary weather* &c. **3.** Opposite in direction. **4.** (log.) *Contrary propositions*, those which are mutually exclusive; *contrary terms*, extreme opposites within the same class, e.g. *hot and cold.* **5.** (colloq.) [1. kuntrári ; 2. kəntréəri]. Perverse; cantankerous; given to making difficulties (of persons and their dispositions).

contrary (II.), n. fr. prec. **1.** *The contrary*, the exact opposite. Phrs. *on the contrary*, on the other hand (esp. emphasizing a denial); *to the contrary*, to the opposite effect (contradicting something that has been said, assumed, arranged &c.): *unless I hear to the contrary.* **2.** Object, fact, or quality that is the exact opposite of something else (often in pl.). Phr. *by contraries*, by way of opposition; contrary to expectation. **3.** (log.) A contrary term or proposition.

contrary (III.), adv. See prec. In opposition to, against: *to act, go, contrary to one's interests* &c.

contrast (I.), vb. trans. & intrans. [1. kuntráhst ; 2. kəntrǽst], fr. Fr. *contraster*, Ital. *contrastare*, 'to oppose', fr. Lat. *contrā* (see **contra-**) & *stāre*, 'to stand'. See **stand (I.)**, **state (I.). 1.** trans. To compare objects or ideas with others in such a way as to put into relief the differences in quality or character exhibited severally by the things or ideas compared. The word is often used rhetorically to indicate that one thing compares unfavourably with another: *contrast the character of Charles I. with that of Cromwell!* **2.** intrans. To form a contrast, to show a distinct difference when compared with something else: *the bright green of the larch in spring contrasts agreeably with the sombre green of the yew.*

contrast (II.), n. [1. kóntrahst ; 2. kɔ́ntrāst]. Fr. *contraste*, fr. Ital. *contrasto.* See prec. **a** Differences observable between objects or ideas when these are compared; **b** the objects &c. which exhibit such differences; **c** act of contrasting, of placing side by side objects or qualities in such a way as to cause the differences between them to tell. *Contrast* is often established between objects or qualities belonging to some general class, e.g. colours, sensations &c.

contrate, adj. [1. kóntrāt ; 2. kɔ́ntreit]. See **contra-** & **-ate.** (lit.) Opposite; specif. (horol.) designating one of the wheels in the works of a watch, which has the teeth at right angles to its surface.

contravallation, n. [1. kòntravaláshun ; 2. kɔ̀ntrəvæléiʃən], fr. Fr. *contrevallation*; fr. **contra-** & Low Lat. *vallātiōn-(em)*, 'an intrenchment', akin to *vallāre*, 'to surround with a rampart', cp. *vallum*, 'a rampart', see **vallum**, orig. an earth wall set with palisades; also *vallus*, 'a stake'; all cogn. w. Goth. *walus*, 'a staff', & ultimately w. O.E. *weall*, q.v. under **wall.** Series of trenches or other fortifications thrown up round a beleaguered place by the besieging force.

contravene, vb. trans. [1. kòntravḗn ; 2. kɔ̀ntrəvín]. Fr. *contrevenir*, L. Lat. *contrāvenīre*, 'to oppose', fr. **contra-** & *venīre*, 'to come'. The latter is for older *g^w*emjō-* & is cogn. w. Goth. *kwiman*, O.E. *cuman.* See **venue** & **come. 1.** To go against, act contrary to, infringe: *contravene a law* &c. **2. a** To oppose, attack, contradict, dispute (a statement, principle); **b** to conflict with (of facts or events).

contravention, n. [1. kòntravénshun ; 2. kɔ̀ntrəvénʃən], fr. **contra-** & *vent-(um)*, P.P. of *venīre*, 'to come' & **-ion.** See prec. Act of contravening; infringement, violation.

contretemps, n. [1. kóntrtom ; 2. kɔ́ntrətã]. Fr., 'mishap', fr. *contre* (Lat. **contra-**) & *temps*, 'time'. See **tempus.** An unlucky or untoward accident; an inopportune or embarrassing occurrence, a hitch.

contribute, vb. trans. & intrans. [1. kuntríbūt ; 2. kəntríbjūt], fr. Lat. *contribūt-(um)*, P.P. type of *contribuere*, 'to bring together, to add, join'. See **con-** & **tribute. A.** trans. **1.** To give, furnish, money, supplies, or other help, esp. to a common fund for charitable, pious, patriotic purposes &c.: *to contribute time and money to relieving the poor.* **2. a** To furnish, supply, help of an intellectual kind: *to contribute suggestions, ideas*; **b** to add to knowledge by research: *to contribute new information.* **3.** To write and get ready (literary productions) for the press: *to contribute articles to scientific journals.* **B.** intrans. **1.** (of persons) *To contribute to*, to give to a common stock, fund &c. **2.** *To contribute to a newspaper* &c., to write articles &c. for publication in it. **3.** To have a share in, help to bring about, be partly responsible for: *drink contributed to his downfall.*

contribution, n. [1. kòntribúshun ; 2. kɔ̀ntribjúʃən]. Fr., fr. Lat. *contribūtiōn-(em).* See prec. & **-ion. 1. a** The act of contributing; **b** that which is contributed (in all senses). **2.** Tax imposed for support of an army, esp. on inhabitants of occupied territory for maintenance of army in the field. Phr. *to lay under contribution*, subject to such a tax.

contributor, n. [1. kuntríbūter ; 2. kəntríbjutə]. See **contribute** & **-or.** One who contributes; **a** by giving money &c. for a specific object; **b** by sending articles to journals; specif., one who habitually writes for the same journal.

contributory, adj. [1. kuntríbūteri ; 2. kəntríbjutəri]. **contribute** & **-ory. a** Connected with contribution, or contributors; **b** having character of a contributor, or a contribution; **c** based on, involving, contributions: *a contributory scheme of insurance*, one to which the beneficiaries contribute.

contrite, adj. [1. kóntrīt ; 2. kɔ́ntrait]; archaic and poet. [1. kuntrít ; 2. kəntráit], fr. Fr. *contrit*, Lat. *contrītus*, 'bruised', P.P. of *conterere*, 'to grind, bruise'. See **con-** & **trite. 1.** Broken in spirit, having a sense of sin; deeply sorrowful for sin, penitent: '*A contrite heart*' (Psalm li.). **2.** (of actions) Showing a contrite spirit, proceeding from remorse for sin.

contritely, adv. Prec. & **-ly**. In a contrite manner or spirit; with contrition.

contriteness, n. See prec. & **-ness**. Contrition, state in which contrition is felt.

contrition, n. [1. kuntríshun; 2. kəntríʃən]. Fr., fr. Lat. *contrītiōn-(em)*, 'a grinding'. See prec. & **-ion**. State of being contrite; genuine sorrow for sin as displeasing to God; contrasted with the inferior state of *attrition*.

contrivance, n. [1. kuntrívans; 2. kəntráivəns]. Next word & **-ance**. **1.** Act of contriving, planning, devising: *by his contrivance*. **2.** A thing contrived; **a** a plan, artful scheme, project, artifice, device; **b** an invention, mechanical device.

contrive, vb. trans. & intrans. [1. kuntrív; kəntráiv], M.E. *controve, -troeve, -treve*, fr. O. Fr. *controver*, Fr. *controuver*, fr. *con-* & O. Fr. *trover*, 'to find'. See **con-** & **trover**. **1.** trans. To fashion, make by using ingenuity or skill; to invent, devise, plan: *to contrive a hidden post of observation*; *to contrive a mask against poison gas*. **2.** intrans. To bring about, effect, manage to do, something; **a** (implying achievement after effort) *he contrived to arrive in time after all*; **b** (implying misdirected effort) *he contrived to make a mess of the whole thing*; **c** specif. (colloq.) to manage household affairs cleverly and economically; Phr. *to cut and contrive*, to make a small income suffice by careful management; **d** to scheme, plan.

control (I.), n. [1. kuntról; 2. kəntróul], fr. Fr. *contrôle* for *conterolle*, 'copy of a roll, a counter register, scrutiny', fr. Lat. **contra-** & *rotulus*, 'a roll'. See **roll (I.)** **1.** (of moral influence) **a** Power, authority to direct and govern; superintendence: *parental control*; **b** restraint, discipline, means of restraint, check, curb: *beyond control, out of control*; **c** physical and mechanical guidance, direction &c. of machines, e.g. pl., *controls*, means whereby machines are directed. **2.** A standard for comparing and testing, means of checking and verifying inferences deduced from experiment; also attrib.: *a control experiment*. **3.** (spirit.) A spirit supposed to direct the utterances and actions of the medium.

control (II.), vb. trans., fr. Fr. *contrôler*, fr. O. Fr. *conteroller*, 'to keep copy of roll of accounts', fr. *contrôle*, 'counter register'. See prec. **1.** To check, regulate, esp. of financial affairs, e.g. *expenditure, payments, accounts* &c. **2.** To dominate, command; curb, hold in check; **a** *oneself and others*; **b** *passions, thoughts, emotions* &c. **3.** To test, verify, by comparison with recognized authority or standard. (French usage, hardly fully naturalized, though used in English.)

controllable, adj. [1. kuntrólabl; 2. kəntróuləbl]. Prec. & **-able**. Able to be controlled.

controller, also **comptroller**, n. [1. kuntróler; 2. kəntróulə]. See prec. & **-er**. The alternative spelling is due to confusion w. Fr. *compter*, 'to reckon', & obs. Fr. *compte*, n.; see **count (I.)**. **1.** One who controls; specif., person who regulates expenditure, esp. a public official who does this for the army, navy, king's household &c. **2.** Mechanical device for regulating speed, movements &c. of machines.

controllership, n. Prec. & **-ship**. The office of a controller.

controversial, adj. [1. kòntrovérshl; 2. kòntrəvə́ʃəl], fr. L. Lat. *contrōversiālis*, 'pertaining to controversy'. See **controversy** & **-al**. **a** Relating to, subject to, liable to provoke, controversy: *a controversial matter, clause, speech* &c.; **b** (of persons) fond of, given to, controversy; disputatious.

controversialism, n. [1. kòntrovérshalizm; 2. kòntrəvə́ʃəlizəm]. Prec. & **-ism**. Habit of controversy; controversy.

controversialist, n. [1. kòntrovérshalist; 2. kòntrəvə́ʃəlist]. See prec. & **-ist**. One given to, or who engages in, controversy.

controversially, adv. [1. kòntrovérshali; 2. kòntrəvə́ʃəli]. **controversial** & **-ly**. In a controversial manner.

controversy, n. [1. kóntroversi; 2. kóntrəvəsi], fr. Lat. *contrōversia*, 'a civil lawsuit, dispute', fr. *contrōversus*, 'turned against, disputed', fr. *contrō-* (cp. **contra-**) & *versus*, P.P. of *vertere*, 'to turn', q.v. under **verse, version**. **a** (preceded by indef. art.) Dispute, debate, discussion, upon some question regarding which differences of opinion exist, the ultimate facts not being decisively ascertained; **b** discussion, argument generally; also in sense of heated dispute, quarrel. Phr. *beyond controversy*, indisputable, no longer subject of discussion, certain.

controvert, vb. trans. [1. kóntrovert, kòntrovért; 2. kóntrəvə̄t, kòntrəvə́t]. See prec. **a** To dispute, bring arguments against (persons or statements); **b** to deny (statements, arguments).

contumacious, adj. [1. kòntūmáshus; 2. kòntjuméiʃəs], fr. Lat. *contumāc-(em)* &c., 'insolent, unyielding, obstinate', esp. 'refusing to appear in a court of law in obedience to a lawful summons', & **-ious**; **con-** & base *tum-* as in Lat. *tumēre*, 'to swell'. See **tumid**. Resisting authority, obstinate, stubborn, disobedient; esp. regardless of orders of a judicial court.

contumaciously, adv. Prec. & **-ly**. In a contumacious manner.

contumaciousness, n. See prec. & **-ness**. Contumacy.

contumacy, n. [1. kóntūmasi; 2. kóntjuməsi], fr. Lat. *contumācia*, 'obstinacy', esp. 'obstinate disobedience to a judicial order'. See **contumacious**. Quality or state of being contumacious; stubborn and perverse resistance to authority; esp. wilful disobedience to the orders of a court of law.

contumelious, adj. [1. kòntūmélius; 2. kòntjumíliəs], fr. O. Fr. *contumelieus*, Lat. *contumēliōsus*, 'full of abuse, insolent'; see **contumely** & **-ous**. Insolent and abusive.

contumeliously, adv. Prec. & **-ly**. In a contumelious manner.

contumely, n. [1. kóntūmeli; 2. kóntjumili], fr. O. Fr. *contumelie*, Lat. *contumēlia*, 'abuse'; connected w. *contumacia*. See **contumacy**. **a** Haughty, contemptuous insolence, in speech or manner: '*The proud man's contumely*' (Shakespeare); **b** reproach, disgrace.

contuse, vb. trans. [1. kuntúz; 2. kəntjúz], fr. Lat. *contūs-(um)*, P.P. type of *contundere*, 'to beat, bruise', fr. *con-* & *tundere*, 'to beat, thump', q.v. under **stint (I.)** & cp. **toil (II.)**. To bruise without breaking the skin.

contusion, n. [1. kuntúzhun; 2. kəntjúžən], fr. Lat. *contūsiōn-(em)*, 'a crushing, bruising'. Prec. & **-ion**. (med.) **a** Process of causing a bruise; **b** condition of being bruised; **c** a bruise.

conundrum, n. [1. kunúndrum; 2. kənándrəm]. Origin unknown. **a** A riddle, puzzle; **b** a puzzling question, one which is difficult or impossible to answer; a problem.

convalesce, vb. intrans. [1. kònvalés; 2. kònvəlés], fr. Lat. *convalescere*, 'to regain health', fr. *con-* & *valescere*, 'to grow strong', incept. of *valēre*, 'to be strong, be well'. See **con-** & **valiant**. To recover gradually from effects of illness or disease; to get better.

convalescence, n. [1. kònvalésens; 2. kònvəlésəns]. Fr., fr. Lat. *convalescentia*, 'a regaining of health'. See prec. **a** Process of gradually recovering health and strength after illness; **b** bodily condition during this process.

convalescent, adj. & n. [1. kònvalésent; 2. kònvəlésənt], fr. Lat. *convalescent-(em)*, Pres. Part of *convalescere*. See **convalesce**. Cp. Fr. *convalescent*. **1.** adj. **a** Recovering from illness, partly restored to health and strength: *convalescent patient*; **b** of or pertaining to convalescence or convalescents: *a convalescent hospital*, a hospital for convalescents. **2.** n. A person recovering from illness.

convection, n. [1. kunvékshun; 2. kənvékʃən], fr. Lat. *convectiōn-(em)*, 'a carrying or bringing together', fr. *convect-(um)*, P.P. type of *convehere*, 'to carry or bring together', fr. **con-** & *vehere*, 'to carry'. See **vehicle** & **-ion**. Process of transmitting; specif., mode of transmitting heat or electricity by the movement of heated or electrified bodies, such as liquids or gases. Distinct from *conduction* or *radiation*.

convective, adj. [1. kunvéktiv; 2. kənvéktiv]. See prec. & **-ive**. **a** Having the power of conveying; **b** connected with convection.

convenance, n., semi-Fr. pronunciation [1. konvenahns; 2. kɔ̃vənɑ̃s]. Fr. (gen. pl.) [1. konvenahnsiz; 2. kɔ̃vənɑ̃siz]. The accepted principles of manner and conduct; propriety in these; conventional respectability.

convene, vb. trans. & intrans. [1. kunvén; 2. kənvín], fr. Lat. *convenīre*, 'to come together, assemble'. **con-** & *venīre*, 'to come', q.v. under **venue** & the Engl. cogn. **come**. **1.** trans. **a** To cause to come, call, together, summon, convoke; esp. *to convene a meeting, council* &c.; **b** to summon (a person) before a tribunal. **2.** intrans. To come together, assemble.

convener, n. [1. kunvéner; 2. kənvínə]. Prec. & **-er**. One who convenes; specif., member of a committee or deliberative body who is specially appointed to fix dates of meetings, and to issue notices of meetings.

convenience, n. [1. kunvéniens; 2. kənvíniəns], fr. Lat. *convenientia*, 'agreement, fitness, suitableness'. See **convenient** & **-ce**. **1.** The quality of being convenient; conformity to one's wishes and requirements; suitability. **2.** Personal comfort, well-being, freedom from discomfort; material advantage; condition favourable and suitable to one; Phr. *at one's (own) convenience*, where and how one chooses; *to suit, await, a person's convenience*, consult his wishes as to manner, time, place &c.; *a marriage of convenience*, one affording material advantage. **3.** Convenient state or condition of things; an advantage: *it is a great convenience to have a doctor so near*. **4.** **a** Any useful appliance or utensil suited to one's needs; specif., a privy; **b** (pl.) material comforts: *a house full of conveniences of every sort*. Phr. *to make a convenience of a person* or *his property*, to use him or it to suit one's own purposes and so as to trespass on his kindness, &c.

convenient, adj. [1. kunvénient; 2. kənvíniənt], fr. Lat. *convenient-(em)*, 'suitable', Pres. Part. of *convenīre*, 'to be suitable', lit. 'to come together', hence, to occur opportunely with some other event. See **con-** & **venue** & **come**. **a** Suitable, possessing, exhibiting, the conditions which promote comfort, ease, freedom from trouble and difficulty of any sort; easy to use, suitable, well adapted for use: *convenient time, house, tool, method, place* &c.; **b** suited to a particular season and set of circumstances, hence, seemly, proper, pertinent: '*To do those things which are not convenient*' (Rom. i. 28) (archaic).

conveniently, adv. Prec. & **-ly**. In a convenient way, opportunely.

convent, n. [1. kónvent; 2. kónvənt]. Lat. *conventus*, 'a coming together, assembly', fr. P.P. type of *convenīre*. See **convene**. The A.-Fr. form *covent*, cp. Fr. *couvent*, survives in *Covent Garden*. **1.** A community of monks or nuns, generally the latter, living according to a rule, under a superior, and devoting themselves to a religious life, education of the young &c. Phr. *to go into a convent*, to become a professed nun. **2.** Building or set of buildings occupied by such a community.

conventicle, n. [1. kunvéntikl; 2. kənvéntikl], fr. Lat. *conventiculum*, 'small assembly, place of meeting'; dimin. of *conventus*. See prec. **1.** Formerly, a prohibited meeting of a religious sect other than the Church of England, esp. of Puritan Nonconformists in England, and of Covenanters in Scotland. **2.** Small building used for religious services by Nonconformists; (generally used contemptuously).

convention, n. [1. kunvénshun; 2. kənvénʃən]. Fr., fr. Lat. *conventiōn-(em)*, 'an assembly, a meeting; an agreement, compact', Fr. *convent-(um)*, P.P. type of *convenīre*. See **convene** & **-ion**. **1.** **a** Formal meeting of delegates and representatives to discuss and transact political, religious, or other public affairs; **b** (specif., Engl. hist.) the meetings of parliament in 1660 and 1688, which assembled without the king's writ or summons. **2.** Formal agreement or compact between sovereigns or states. **3.** **a** Generally accepted standard of conduct and behaviour; common consent and agreement, embodied in fixed usage and custom; **b** custom and usage, rule of conduct, or manners, based on, and embodying this general concurrence of opinion; **c** (pl.) accepted, standard leads, method of play, as at bridge and other card games.

conventional, adj. [1. kunvénshunal; 2. kənvénʃənəl], fr. Lat. *conventiōnālis*, 'of or pertaining to an agreement'; prec. & **-al**. Connected with, governed by, convention; specif.: **a** (of persons) depending upon convention, habitually shaping conduct, manners, opinions, ideas &c., in accordance with the fixed standards of convention; bound and limited by these; **b** (of human action) directed, dictated, by convention; arising from desire to conform to accepted standards rather than from natural impulses; **c** (of art &c.) based on the standards of the schools, following accepted methods in technique, design &c.; not spontaneous and original.

conventionalism, n. [1. kunvénshunalizm; 2. kənvénʃənəlizəm]. Prec. & **-ism**. Adherence to conventional practice in opinions, conduct, behaviour &c.

conventionalist, n. [1. kunvénshunalist; 2. kənvénʃənəlist]. **conventional** & **-ist**. One who follows convention in conduct &c., or in artistic practice.

conventionality, n. [1. kunvènshunáliti; 2. kənvènʃənǽliti]. **conventional** & **-ity**. **a** Adherence to convention, esp. in social formalities; **b** specific exhibition of such adherence.

conventionalize, vb. trans. [1. kunvénshunalīz; 2. kənvénʃənəlaiz]. **conventional** & **-ize**. To make conventional; in art, to portray according to conventional rules &c.; to follow convention in treatment.

conventionally, adv. [1. kunvénshunali; 2. kənvénʃənəli]. **conventional** & **-ly**. In a conventional manner.

conventionary, adj. [1. kunvénshunari; 2. kənvénʃənəri]. **convention** & **-ary**. Acting under a convention or contract; based on terms laid down in a special agreement; esp. of certain kind of land tenure, and tenants holding under this.

conventual, adj. & n. [1. kunvénchooal; 2. kənvéntʃuəl], fr. Med. Lat. *conventuālis*, 'of or pertaining to a convent'. See **convent** & **-al**. **1.** adj. Of, pertaining to, characteristic of, a convent; specif. (cap.) connected with a branch of the Franciscans. **2.** n. A member or inmate of a convent; specif. (cap.) member of branch of Franciscans.

converge, vb. intrans. & trans. [1. kunvě̂rj; 2. kənvə́dž]. Lat. *convergere*, 'to incline towards one another'. **con-** & **verge (II.)**. **1.** intrans. (of lines, roads &c.) To come nearer and nearer together, and finally to meet at a given point. Also (fig., of ideas, actions) to be directed towards single point. **2.** trans. To cause to converge.

convergence, -cy, n. [1. kunvě̂rjens(i); 2. kənvə́džəns(i)]. Prec. & **-ence, -cy**. Process, or fact of converging.

convergent, adj. [1. kunvě̂rjent; 2. kənvə́džənt]. **converge** & **-ent**. Converging, tending to converge.

conversable, adj. [1. kunvě̂rsabl; 2. kənvə́səbl]. **converse (I.)** & **-able**. **a** Easy in conversation, easy and pleasant to talk to; **b** fit for, suitable for, marked by, conversation or social intercourse: '*The evening was quiet and conversable*' (Jane Austen).

conversableness, n. Prec. & **-ness**. Quality of being conversable.

conversably, adv. See prec. & **-ly**. In a conversable manner.

conversance, -cy, n. [1. kónversans(i); 2. kónvəsəns(i)]. See next word & **-ance** & **-cy**. State of being accustomed; familiarity, acquaintance; (followed by *with*).

conversant, adj. [1. kónversant; 2. kónvəsənt], fr. Lat. *conversant-(em)*, Pres. Part. of *conversāre*, 'to turn round, over, frequently', in pass. 'to live with', see **converse (I.)**. Having familiar association with, knowledge of, being acquainted with, informed concerning: *conversant with a subject*, more rarely, *with a person.*

conversation, n. [1. kònversáshun; 2. kònvəséiʃən]. Fr., fr. Lat. *conversātiōn-(em)*, 'frequent abode in a place, intercourse, conversation'. See **converse** & **-ation**. **1.** Familiar communication with another in speech; talk. **2.** Familiar association, social intercourse (archaic and lit.). **3.** *Criminal conversation* (crim. con.), sexual association, as ground for divorce, under the old ecclesiastical law.

conversational, adj. [1. kònversáshunal; 2. kònvəséiʃənəl]. Prec. & **-al**. **1.** (of persons) Fond of conversation; ready and willing to converse. **2.** Connected with conversation; appropriate to conversation; colloquial: *conversational style.*

conversationalist, n. [1. kònversáshunalist; 2. kònvəséiʃənəlist]. Prec. & **-ist**. One addicted to conversation; a ready, interesting, amusing talker.

conversationally, adv. [1. kònversáshunali; 2. kònvəséiʃənəli]. **conversational** & **-ly**. **a** In a manner suitable to conversation, colloquially; **b** in conversation.

conversazione, n. [1. kònversatsióni; 2. kònvəsætsióuni]. Ital., 'conversation'. Evening party, esp. social gathering in the evening, one given by, or for, a learned society, or for party of distinguished visitors.

converse (I.) vb. intrans. [1. kunvě̂rs; 2. kənvə́s], fr. Fr. *converser*, fr. Lat. *conversāri*, 'to associate with', fr. *con-* & *versāri*, orig. 'to be turned', hence, 'to live, remain', fr. *versāre*, 'to turn often', intens. of *vertere*, 'to turn'. See **con-** & **version**. **a** To talk, have conversation with a person; **b** *converse with* (person), to hold social intercourse with, frequent society of (archaic or liter.).

converse (II.) n. [1. kónvěrs; 2. kónvəs], fr. prec. (archaic or poet.) **a** Familiar discourse, conversation; **b** familiar social intercourse.

converse (III.), adj. & n. [1. kónvěrs; 2. kónvəs], fr. Lat. *conversus*, P.P. of *convertere*, 'to turn about, turn towards'. See **convert**. **1.** adj. Reversed in order or relation; opposite, contrary. **2.** n. Something related to another thing in a converse manner; **a** that which is exactly opposite in character to something else; **b** a statement produced by transposition of the antithetical terms of another statement: *he is rich but not happy*, is the converse of *he is happy but not rich.*

conversion, n. [1. kunvě̂rshun; 2. kənvə́ʃən]. Fr., fr. Lat. *conversiōn-(em)*, 'a turning round'. See **con-** & **version**; also **convert (I.)**. **1.** Process of converting, alteration, changing, turning; **a** from one physical state or condition to another: *the conversion of a solid into a liquid*; **b** from one spiritual or intellectual state, from one set of opinions, beliefs &c., to another: *the conversion of the Tory party from Free Trade to Protection was not yet an accomplished fact*; specif. **c** change of religion, act of changing over, or being changed from one religion to another: *the conversion of St. Paul, conversion of the Jews* (*to Christianity*); change from heathendom to Christianity: *conversion of the heathen*; **d** (gen. theol. usage) awakening of the soul and spiritual faculties to a sense of religion in general, and to realization of God. **2.** (law) Appropriation of property belonging to another: *conversion of public money to one's own use.*

conversive, adj. [1. kunvě̂rsiv; 2. kənvə́siv]. Fr. *conversif*, fr. Lat. *convers-(um)*, P.P. type of *convertere*, see **convert** & **-ive**. **a** Causing, having function of conversion; **b** specif. (gram.) of Hebrew conjunction *wa* written with the letter *waw* to convert a future into a past sense: *waw conversive.*

convert (I.), vb. trans. [1. kunvě̂rt; 2. kənvə́t]. Fr. *convertir*, fr. Lat. *convertere*, 'to turn round'. See **con-** & **version**. **1.** To change, transmute, a thing: **a** from one physical state to another: *to convert water into steam*; **b** from one character or use to another: *to convert a stable into a pigsty*; *convert a number of fields into a park*; **c** specif. (finance) to change a form of security into one of another kind of equivalent value. **2.** **a** To affect a spiritual or intellectual change, cause to alter opinions, religious and moral beliefs &c., persuade to adopt new opinions and beliefs &c.: *to convert a Free Trader to Protection*; *to convert a Jew to Christianity*; *a Roman Catholic to Protestantism, a heathen to belief in God*; **b** to awaken from indifference to a sense of religion, to turn from sin to righteousness. Phr. *to become converted*, to receive spiritual light &c. **3.** (law) To appropriate property from its owner's use to one's own. **4.** Various specific and technical senses implying alteration, adaptation &c., of material objects and substances to different character or use.

convert (II.), n. [1. kónvěrt; 2. kónvət], fr. prec. A person converted from one set of opinions, practice, party, religious creed &c., to another; esp. one converted to a different form of religion, or to a religion of any sort from none at all.

convertibility, n. [1. kunvě̂rtibíliti; 2. kənvə̀tibíliti]. **convertible** & **-ity**. State or quality of being convertible.

convertible, adj. [1. kunvě̂rtibl; 2. kənvə́tibl]. Fr., fr. L. Lat. *convertibilis*. See **convert (I.)** & **-ible**. Capable of being converted in any sense.

convex, adj. [1. kónveks; 2. kónvεks], fr. Lat. *convexus*, 'vaulted, arched', fr. **con-** & base in *vehere*, 'to draw' &c. See **vehicle**. This is the old etymol. in favour of wh. Walde rejects several more recent & attractive suggestions. Having the surface curving outwards. Reverse of *concave.*

convexity, n. [1. kunvéksiti; 2. kənvéksiti]. Lat. *convexitāt-(em)*, cp. Fr. *convexité*, fr. prec. & **-ity**. State or quality of being convex.

convexly, adv. [1. kónveksli, kunvéksli; 2. kónvεksli, kənvéksli]. **convex** & **-ly**. Curving outwards.

convexo-, pref. [1. kunvéksō; 2. kənvéksou]. Form of *convex* used in compounds; *convexo-concave* &c.

convey, vb. trans. [1. kunvā́; 2. kənvéi], fr. O. Fr. *conveier, convoier*, 'to escort', Fr. *convoyer*, Ital. *conviare*, fr. Lat. *con-* & *via*, 'a way'. See **con-**, **via (I.)**, & cp. **voyage**. **1.** To carry, transport, from one place to another. **2.** To serve as a means of conveying, conducting; to transmit (esp. sound, smell &c.): *a pipe conveys the hot water from the boiler to the bath.* **3.** (fig., of non-material things) To impart, communicate, make known: *to convey meaning, ideas, information* &c. **4.** (law) To make over formally, esp. of real property, by a conveyance.

conveyance, n. [1. kunvā́ans; 2. kənvéiəns]. Prec. & **-ance**. **1.** Act or process of carrying, in all senses. **2.** The object or means whereby a person or thing is conveyed; a vehicle of any kind; hence, specif., a carriage. **3.** (law) **a** The transfer of real property or title; **b** legal document or deed by which the property or title is conveyed.

conveyancer, n. [1. kunvā́anser; 2. kənvéiənsə]. Prec. & **-er**. Lawyer who draws up documents for the conveyance of property.

conveyancing, n. [1. kunvā́ansing; 2. kənvéiənsiŋ]. **conveyance** & **-ing**. (law) **a** The business of a conveyancer; **b** that branch of law which deals with titles to property and their conveyance.

conveyer, n. [1. kunváer; 2. kənvéiə]. **convey** & **-er**. One who, that which, conveys; specif., any mechanical device or apparatus for moving heavy weights, large quantities of goods &c., as a *coal-conveyer*.

convict (**I.**), n. [1. kónvikt; 2. kɔ́nvikt], fr. Lat. *convictus*, P.P. of *convincere*, 'to prove guilty'. See **convince**. **a** Person found guilty, convicted, of a crime by a court of justice; **b** such a person undergoing penal servitude.

convict (**II.**), vb. trans. [1. kunvíkt; 2. kənvíkt]. See prec. **a** To prove, find, guilty of a crime, formally, after trial in a court of law; **b** (fig.) to bring guilt home to one, to convince of wrongdoing, esp. in such a phrase as: *to be convicted of sin, by one's conscience*.

conviction, n. [1. kunvíkshun; 2. kənvíkʃən], fr. Lat. *convictiōn-(em)*. See **convict** (**II.**) & **-ion**. **1.** Act of convicting, proving or finding guilty of a crime: *the conviction of the prisoner was expected*. **2.** Act of convincing or bringing certainty to the mind; hence, settled opinion, assured belief; specif., *conviction of sin*, by one's own conscience.

convictive, adj. [1. kunvíktiv; 2. kənvíktiv]. See **convict** (**II.**) & **-ive**. Tending to convict or convince.

convince, vb. trans. [1. kunvíns; 2. kənvíns], fr. Lat. *convincere*, 'to overcome, beat down in argument; to prove wrong, convict of crime; to prove, show clearly, esp. to prove (statement &c.), wrong', fr. **con-** & *vincere*, 'to conquer, overcome, defeat; to get the better of, outdo, prevail over; win, gain; to demonstrate conclusively'. See discussion of Lat. base *vinc-*, *vic-*, under **vincible** & **victor**. **1.** To bring certainty to the mind by proof or argument, to create, establish, conviction in the mind; overcome by demonstration; satisfy the reason that something is or is not true, exists or does not exist: *to convince a person that one is sincere*, or *of one's sincerity*; *to convince a person that there is no danger, of the safety of travelling by aeroplane* &c., *of the truth of Christianity*; *to convince oneself of the wisdom of a course of action* &c. **2. a** To persuade, prove to, a person that he is wrong: *to convince a man of error*; **b** to excite, create, moral conviction in the mind of another: *to convince a man of sin*.

convincible, adj. [1. kunvínsibl; 2. kənvínsibl]. Prec. & **-ible**. **a** Able to be convinced; **b** open to conviction.

convincing, adj. [1. kunvínsing; 2. kənvínsiŋ], fr. Pres. Part. of **convince**. Carrying conviction, compelling belief: *a convincing argument*; *a convincing speaker* &c.

convincingly, adv. Prec. & **-ly**. In a convincing manner.

convincingness, n. See prec. & **-ness**. The property, quality, of being convincing.

convivial, adj. [1. kunvívial; 2. kənvíviəl], fr. Lat. *convīviālis*, 'festal, pertaining to a feast', fr. *convīvi-(um)*, 'a feast', fr. **con-** & *vīvere*, 'to live', q.v. under **vivacious** & **vital**. **a** Of or relating to a feast or a merry-making; **b** (of persons) festive, sociable, jovial, fond of merry-making; **c** betraying effects of excessive merry-making; slightly intoxicated.

convivialist, n. [1. kunvívialist; 2. kənvíviəlist]. Prec. & **-ist**. A convivial person.

conviviality, n. [1. kunviviáliti; 2. kənviviǽliti]. **convivial** & **-ity**. Feasting, merry-making, sociable jollification.

convivially, adv. [1. kunvíviali; 2. kənvíviəli]. **convivial** & **-ly**. In a convivial manner.

convocation, n. [1. kònvōkáshun; 2. kɔ̀nvoukéiʃən], fr. Lat. *convocātiōn-(em)*. See **convoke** & **-ation**. **1.** The act of calling together: *the convocation of Parliament*. **2.** An assembly of persons, formally called together to transact public business. Specif. (cap.) **a** (Ch. of Engl.) synod of the clergy of the province of Canterbury or of York; **b** term applied to specific legislative bodies of the Universities of Oxford and Durham; **c** (freemasonry) Chapter meeting of Royal Arch Masons: *Grand Convocation*, a meeting of Grand Chapter.

convocational, adj. [1. kònvōkáshunal; 2. kɔ̀nvoukéiʃənəl]. Prec. & **-al**. Of, pertaining to, a convocation or to Convocation.

convoke, vb. trans. [1. kunvók; 2. kənvóuk], fr. Fr. *convoquer*, fr. Lat. *convocāre*, 'to call together', fr. *con-* & *vocāre*, 'to call'. See **con-** & **vocal**, **vocation**. To call together, to summon to assemble; esp. to summon by authority a formally constituted body.

convolute, adj. [1. kònvolût; 2. kɔ̀nvəljût], fr. Lat. *convolūt-(um)*, P.P. of *convolvere*, 'to roll together, roll round'. See **con-** & **volute**. (of flowers and leaves; also of whorls of shells) Rolled or wound up.

convoluted, adj. [1. kònvolûted; 2. kɔ̀nvəljûtid], fr. P.P. of prec. (zool.) Coiled, twisted, e.g. of a ram's horn &c.

convolution, n. [1. kònvolûshun; 2. kɔ̀nvəljûʃən]. See **convolute** & **-ion**. **1.** A rolling, coiling, or twisting together. **2.** Fold, coil, whorl; something having folds or coils.

convolve, vb. trans. & intrans. [1. kunvólv; 2. kənvɔ́lv], fr. Lat. *convolvere*, *-volūtum*, 'to roll'. See **con-** & **volute**. **a** trans. To roll up together, intertwine; **b** intrans., to writhe about, intertwining one, or one part, with another.

convolvulus, n. [1. kunvólvūlus; 2. kənvɔ́lvjuləs]. Lat., 'bindweed', lit. 'twisting thing'; dimin. fr. *convolvere*. See prec. (bot.) Bindweed; plant with white, pink, or blue flowers and long, climbing, tough, elastic stems which twine up the stems of other plants in a tangled mass and tend to throttle them.

convoy (**I.**), vb. trans. [1. kunvói; 2. kənvɔ́i], fr. Fr. *convoyer*, O. Fr. *convoier*, *conveier*; dialectal variant of **convey**. To accompany in order to protect; (esp. of a warship) to escort a merchantman or other non-fighting ship on a voyage in war-time.

convoy (**II.**), n. [1. kónvoi; 2. kɔ́nvɔi]. See prec. **a** A warship which convoys a merchantman &c.; **b** the ship convoyed.

convulse, vb. trans. [1. kunvúls; 2. kənváls], fr. Lat. *convuls-(um)*, P.P. type of *convellere*, 'to tear up, pull up, shake', fr. **con-** & *vellere*, 'to pluck, pull, twitch', see **vellicate**. The base **vel-* is prob. cogn. w. Lat. *volnus*, *vulnus*, 'a wound' (see **vulnerable**), & w. Lat. *voltur*, *vultur* (see **vulture**). **1.** To shake, agitate, violently; **a** (of physical disturbance) *the ground was convulsed by an earthquake*; **b** (fig., of emotional or political excitement and agitation) to disturb violently, cause unrest in: *the wretched country was convulsed with civil strife*. **2.** To cause sudden and violent contractions or spasms of nerves and muscles; **a** from pain, disease &c.: *to be convulsed with toothache, colic* &c.; **b** by powerful emotion: *to be convulsed with laughter, anger* &c.

convulsion, n. [1. kunvúlshun; 2. kənválʃən]. Lat. *convulsiōn-(em)*; see prec. & **-ion**. Violent and sudden agitation, disturbance, commotion &c.; **a** *convulsion of nature*, e.g. an earthquake, volcanic eruption &c.; **b** series of spasmodic movements of the body, caused either by physical disease, affecting nerves and muscles, or by emotional excitement: *to fall into a fit of convulsions*; *a convulsion of laughter, mirth* &c.; **c** social and political uproar, turmoil: *civil convulsions and riots*.

convulsive, adj. [1. kunvúlsiv; 2. kənválsiv]. Fr. *convulsif*; see **convulse** & **-ive**. Attended with, exhibiting, having character of, convulsions of any kind: *convulsive movements*; *convulsive laughter* &c.

convulsively, adv. Prec. & **-ly**. In a convulsive manner, with convulsive movements.

cony, **coney**, n. [1. kóni; 2. kóuni]. M.E. *coning*, *conig*, *coni*, O. Fr. *connin*, *conin*, *connil*, fr. Lat. *cunīculus*, 'rabbit'; prob. an Iberian word. The animal became known to the Romans through the Spaniards. **1.** A rabbit (archaic). **2.** (Bib.) Small short-eared, ungulated animal of Palestine and Syria, the hyrax, living in clefts of rocks. **3.** (also *cony-seal* &c.) Trade name for various imitation furs made from dyed rabbit-skin.

cony-catch, vb. trans. Prec. & **catch**. (obs.) To deceive, cheat.

cony-catcher, n. Prec. & **-er**. (obs.) A cheat.

coo (**I.**), vb. intrans. & trans. [1. kōō; 2. kū]. Of imitative origin. **1.** intrans. **a** (of doves and pigeons) To utter a soft, characteristic, murmuring cry or sound; **b** (of babies) to utter a sound expressive of satisfaction, somewhat resembling that made by doves; **c** (of grown persons) to speak softly and caressingly. Phr. *to bill and coo*, to make love by soft words and caresses. **2.** trans. To say or utter cooingly: *to coo one's words caressingly*.

coo (**II.**), n., fr. prec. The gentle, liquid sound made by doves or pigeons; any similar sound uttered by human beings.

cooee, **cooey**, n. & interj. [1. kōōē; 2. kū-í]. Of imitative origin. Cry or call used by white men in Australia; adopted from the aborigines.

cook (**I.**), n. [1. kook; 2. kuk]. O.E. *cōc*, borrowed fr. Low Lat. *cocus*, Lat. *coquus*. An early loan-word w. subsequent lengthening of vowel. The word must have been borrowed in W. Gmc.; cp. O.H.G. & Mod. Germ. *koch*, wh., however, has the orig. short vowel. Lat. *coquus* & *coquere*, vb., go back to earlier **quequo-*, wh. stands for Aryan **pekʷo-* (w. *q* by assimilation of first to second cons., cp. *quinque*, 'five', fr. **penkʷe-*, see **quinque-**); Scrt. *pácati*, 'he cooks, bakes', *pakvás*, 'cooked, ripe'; O. Slav. *pekq*, 'I bake, roast', & *pekŭ*, 'heat'. Cp. also Gk. *péssō*, 'I soften, ripen, boil, cook, digest', fr. **pekʷjō*; see the Gk. base under **peptic**, **pepsis**. See also **concoct**, **decoct**. One who prepares food for the table, esp. by baking, roasting, boiling it &c.

cook (**II.**), vb. trans. & intrans., fr. prec. **A.** trans. **1.** To prepare food for the table by subjecting it to heat in various ways. Phr. (fig.) *to cook one's goose*, settle his affair, spoil his plans. **2.** (fig.) To concoct; to prepare something fraudulently for any purpose; to falsify, tamper with, fake: *to cook accounts*; also *cook up* (*a story, account* &c.). **3.** To subject to great heat: *to be cooked alive in the tropics*. **B.** intrans. To undergo the process of cooking: *some early apples cook quite well in August*.

cooker, n. [1. kóoker; 2. kúkə]. **cook** (**II.**) & **-er**. **1.** An apparatus, esp. a stove, for cooking food. **2.** Varieties of fruit, esp. of apples, pears, plums, which are grown for cooking; contrasted with *dessert apples* &c.

cookery, n. [1. kóokeri; 2. kúkəri]. **cook** & **-ery**. The art or practice of cooking. Also attrib.: *cookery-book*, one containing instructions for preparing food.

cook-house, n. An outdoor or detached kitchen, as in a camp &c.

cook-shop, n. One where food is cooked and sold; an eating-house.

cooky, n. [1. kóokie; 2. kúki]. **cook** & **-y**, but cp. Du. *koekje*, dimin. of *koek*, 'cake'; see **cake**. A small, thin, sweet cake, esp. a home-made cake of this sort. (A Scottish & American usage.)

cool (**I.**), adj. [1. kōōl; 2. kūl]. O.E. & M.E. *cōl*, fr. same base as **cold**, w. different vowel grade. See also **gelid**. (general sense) Having a degree of temperature higher than *cold* and lower than *warm*; moderately cold. **1. a** Contrasted with excessive heat, giving a pleasurable sensation of freshness and absence of warmth: *a cool evening after a hot day*; *the house is nice and cool*; **b** having lost excessive heat, having sunk to a degree of temperature bearable to the touch: *the coffee isn't cool enough to drink yet*; *don't touch the iron till it has got cool*; (of the human body) **c** not excessively hot; of a normal temperature, contrasted with the heat of fever: *the fever has left him, and he is quite cool*; **d** not too hot to be pleasant; contrasting comfortably and agreeably with extreme heat: *sit in the shade and get, keep, cool*. **2.** Not tending to induce sensation of warmth, tending to promote pleasantly low temperature of the body; having an appearance suggesting this: *a cool frock, hat* &c. **3.** (fig., of moral or emotional condition) **a** Not ardent or passionate; moderate; apathetic; lacking cordiality: *cool in one's affections*; *rather a cool wooer*; *a cool reception*; **b** not excited; calm, unruffled, unperturbed, deliberate, collected: *cool amid dangers and difficulties*; *a cool head*; **c** displaying inadequate attention to conventional propriety; lacking deference and consideration for others, casual; calmly impudent, deliberately audacious: *I call that pretty cool behaviour*; *he's a little bit too cool for me.* Phrs. *a cool customer*; *a cool fish*; *cool cheek*, great impudence. **4.** (colloq., of a sum or amount) Stated deliberately, in its entirety, with no deductions or qualifications: *to lose a cool thousand*; *a cool twenty miles farther.* **5.** (hunting, of scent) Weak, faint.

cool (II.), n., fr. prec. Something that is cool, esp. cool air, place, time &c.; coolness: *in the cool of the evening*; *the cool of the forest* &c.

cool (III.), vb. intrans. & trans. O.E. *cōlian*, 'to grow cold'; 'to make cold' is *cēlan* in O.E., preserved as *keel* in some dialects. **1.** intrans. **a** (lit.) To grow cool, lose heat: *your porridge will soon cool in the draught*; **b** (fig.) to become less ardent, zealous, affectionate, angry &c.: *his affection for her had cooled*; *my anger has cooled*; also *cool down* in same sense. **2.** trans. **a** To make cool: *the rain has cooled the air*; Phrs. *keep your breath to cool your porridge*, don't waste your words; *to cool one's heels*, be kept waiting; **b** (fig.) to reduce ardour, enthusiasm, anger &c.: *that will cool your eagerness for you.*

cooler, n. [1. kōōler; 2. kúlə]. Prec. & **-er.** A vessel in which anything is cooled or kept cool: *wine, butter, cooler.*

cool-headed, adj. Calm, imperturbable, having clear, calm, judgement; not liable to be disconcerted or flustered.

coolie, cooly, n. [1. kōōli; 2. kúli]. Anglo-Indian. Perh. fr. *kōlī*, name of a race or caste in Western India who performed menial offices; on the other hand, in S. India *kūli* means 'hire, wages' in Tamil. Used among Europeans in India, Mesopotamia, China, and Straits Settlements &c. for a hired native servant, esp. a bearer or porter.

cooling card, n. [1. kōōling kard; 2. kúliŋ kād]. Prob. derived fr. an obs. card game. Something that dashes one's hopes and expectations (obs.).

coolly, adv. [1. kōōlli; 2. kúlli]. **cool** (I.) & **-ly.** In a cool manner, (in all senses).

coolness, n. [1. kōōlnes; 2. kúlnis]. See prec. & **-ness.** **1. a** State of being cool; **b** sensation of moderate cold. **2. a** Absence of ardour, enthusiasm &c.; specif. **b** absence of cordiality, esp. owing to difference of opinion; hence, disagreement, falling out: *there is a slight coolness between us.*

coolth, n. [1. kōōlth; 2. kūlþ]. **cool** (I.) & **-th**; new formation on anal. of **warmth**, etc. Coolness.

coomb, combe, n. [1. kōōm; 2. kūm]. O.E. *cumb*, perh. of Celt. origin; cp. W. *cwm*, perh. cogn. w. **cup**; see also **cymbal.** A deep, narrow valley; a valley on the side of a hill.

coon, n. [1. kōōn; 2. kūn]. For **racoon.** **a** A racoon; **b** a negro. *Coon song*, negro melody. Phr. (slang) *a gone coon*, a person who is done for, ruined, as good as dead.

coop (I.), n. [1. kōōp; 2. kūp]. M.E. *cōpe*, prob. loan-word fr. Lat. *cūpa*, 'cask, tub'. See **cup.** **a** Kind of wooden cage with back and sides of boarding and front of wooden bars, used esp. for sitting hens, or those with broods of chickens; **b** apparatus of wicker for catching fish; a pot.

coop (II.), vb. trans., fr. prec. **a** To put or keep (hens &c.) in a coop; **b** to confine (persons) within narrow bounds, in small stuffy room &c.: esp. *to coop up*; *coop in.*

cooper, n. & vb. trans. [1. kōōper; 2. kúpə]. M.E. *cowper*, prob. fr. Low Lat. *cūpārius*, see **coop** (I). **1.** n. One who makes and mends barrels and casks. **2.** vb. trans. To repair, patch up, casks &c.

cooperage, n. [1. kōōperij; 2. kúpəridž]. Prec. & **-age.** The work of a cooper; place where he works.

co-operate, vb. intrans. [1. kō óperāt; 2. kòu ópəreit], fr. **co-** & **operate.** **a** (of persons) To act together, work with another for, help to accomplish, a common purpose; **b** (of things) to combine in producing an effect.

co-operation, n. [1. kō operáshun; 2. kòu əpəréiʃən]. Prec. & **-ion.** **a** Act of co-operating, of working together to the same end; **b** (econ.) association of a number of persons for a common benefit, esp. in carrying on some branch of trade or industry &c., the profit being shared as dividend among the members.

co-operative, adj. [1. kō óperativ; 2. kòu ópərətiv]. **co-operate** & **-ive.** **a** connected with co-operation; **b** practising co-operation: *co-operative society.*

co-opt, vb. trans. [1. kō ópt; 2. kou ópt]. Lat. *co-optāre*, 'to choose, elect'. See **co-** & *optāre*, 'to desire, choose, demand'; connected w. Lat. *opīnus*, 'thinking', *opīniō*, 'opinion, conjecture', *opīnāri*, 'to suppose, deem'. See **opine, option.** To add a person who is not an ex-officio member to a committee, or other deliberative body, by election by the votes of those who are already members.

co-optation, n. [1. kō optáshun; 2. kòu əptéiʃən]. Prec. & **-ation.** The act of co-opting; position of being co-opted.

co-ordinate (I.), adj. & n. [1. kō órdinat; 2. kou ɔ́dinət]. Lat. *co-ordināt-(um)*, P.P. of *co-ordināre*, 'set in order, regulate'. See **co-** & **ordain.** **1.** adj. **a** Having equal rank, order, with, not subordinate to; **b** specif. (gram.) of clauses of a compound sentence; cp. *subordinate.* **2.** n. **a** A co-ordinate thing; **b** (math.) any one of a system of magnitudes used in determining position of a point.

co-ordinate (II.), vb. trans. [1. kō órdināt; 2. kou ɔ́dineit]. See prec. **1.** To make co-ordinate; to bring into logical and organic relation (of ideas &c.). **2.** To bring into such relation that all the things co-ordinated take part in a common action; to adjust, cause to harmonize: *co-ordinate hand and eye.*

co-ordinately, adv. [1. kō órdinatli; 2. kou ɔ́dinətli]. **co-ordinate** (I.) & **-ly.** In a co-ordinate manner.

co-ordination, n. [1. kō ordináshun; 2. kòu ɔdinéiʃən]. **co-ordinate** (II.) & **-ion.** The act of co-ordinating, or state of being co-ordinate.

co-ordinative, adj. [1. kō órdinātiv; 2. kou ɔ́dineitiv]. **co-ordinate** (II.) & **-ive.** Tending to co-ordinate.

coot, n. [1. kōōt; 2. kūt]. M.E. *cōte*; cp. Du. *koet.* Etymol. doubtful. Water-bird of rail family, *Fulica atra*, much resembling a duck, having a white spot on the head; hence name *bald coot*, and Phr. *as bald as a coot.*

cop (I.), n. [1. kop; 2. kɔp]. O.E. *copp*, 'summit', cogn. w. Germ. *kopf*, 'head', O.H.G. *kopf* & *chupf*, 'cup'; prob. derived ultimately fr. Lat. *cūpa*, 'tub, cask'. See **cup.** The word has developed considerable diversity of meaning. Orig. 'a hollow vessel, a drinking vessel', & hence, 'a round thing', w. special application, on the one hand 'a head', on the other 'rounded top of a hill, a hill'. In Engl. Place-Names, *copt-*, *copped-* means 'pollarded, having had the head cut off'; e.g. *Copthorn*, earlier *copped thorn.* Cp. O.E. *coppede*, in same sense, used of trees. **1. a** A mound of earth thrown up in excavating; **b** a small hill. **2.** Round mass of thread or yarn, wound on a spindle.

cop (II.), vb. trans. Origin uncertain. (vulg. slang) **a** To catch, arrest; to detect in the act of committing an offence. Phr. *to cop (him, her &c.) at it*; **b** in Phr. *to cop it* (schoolboy slang), to catch it, i.e. to receive punishment.

cop (III.), n. fr. prec. (vulg. slang) **1.** Act of detecting or catching. Phr. *a fair cop*, said by criminals when caught and arrested in the act of committing an offence. **2.** A policeman. See **copper** (III.).

copaiba, n. [1. kopíba; 2. kɔpáibə]. Span., fr. Brazil. *cupauba.* An oily resin obtained from the copaiva and other tropical trees found in S. America, and in West Indies; used medically in diseases of mucous membranes.

copaiva, n. [1. kopíva; 2. kɔpáivə]. See prec. (bot.) Genus of South American trees yielding copaiba.

copal, n. [1. kōpal; 2. kóupəl]. Mexican *copalli*, 'resin'. A resin used in varnish, obtained from living S. or Central American trees, or dug up in fossil condition.

coparcenary, n. [1. kōpársenari; 2. kòupásinəri]. **co-** & **parcenary.** Inheritance by descent of lands by two or more persons in common; co-heirship, as by co-heiresses, on an intestacy, or under a custom, as of gavelkind.

coparcener, n. [1. kōpársener; 2. koupásinə]. **co-** & **parcener.** Joint heir or heiress of an estate in coparcenary.

copartner, n. [1. kōpártner; 2. kòupátnə]. **co-** & **partner.** **a** A fellow-partner; **b** specif., employé having a share in the profits of a business or industry in addition to his salary or wages.

copartnership, n. [1. kōpártnership; 2. kòupátnəʃip], fr. prec. & **-ship.** **a** Condition of being associated with another or others in trade or business; **b** system of trading in which the employés of a firm have a share of the profits.

copartnery, n. [1. kōpártneri; 2. kòupátnəri]. **copartner** & **-y.** (rare) Copartnership.

cope (I.), n. [1. kōp; 2. koup]. M.E. *cope*, Med. Lat. *cōpa*, also *cappa.* See **cape** (I.). **1.** (eccles.) Vestment resembling a long cloak, without sleeves or armholes, worn by the clergy of a cathedral on ceremonial occasions, in processions &c., and by a bishop when visiting the cathedral of his diocese. **2.** (fig.) Something which covers like a cope; hence, the arch of the sky, canopy of heaven: *the cope of heaven.* **3.** Coping, q.v.

cope (II.), vb. trans. & intrans., fr. prec. **1.** trans. **a** To dress in a cope or cloak; **b** (archit.) to put a coping on (a wall &c.). **2.** intrans. To hang or arch over like a coping (obs.).

cope (III.), vb. intrans., fr. O. Fr. *couper, colper*, 'to strike', Fr. *couper*, 'to cut', fr. O. Fr. *coup, colp*, 'blow', Fr. *coup.* See **coup.** (always followed by *with*) To deal successfully with a difficult situation, or with a violent and unruly person: *to cope with a difficulty*; *cope with a crowd.*

copeck, n. [1. kópek; 2. kɔ́pek]. Russ. *kopieika.* Perh. dimin. of *kopie*, 'lance', applied to the coin fr. the fact that it bore a figure of Ivan IV. holding a lance. The Slav. words for 'lance' are cogn. w. Gk. *kopis*, 'sacrificial knife' &c., & *kópanon*, 'sword', *kóptō*, 'strike, cut', q.v. under **comma.** On the other hand, *kopieika* is possibly a Mongol word. Russian copper coin, the hundredth part of a rouble.

copepod, n. [1. kōpepod; 2. kóupipɔd], fr. Gk. *kōpē*, 'handle of an oar, haft of sword' (q.v. under **captive**), & **-pod.** (zool.) A minute marine crustacean, order *Copepoda*, forming a great part of the *plankton* of the ocean.

coper (I.), n. [1. kōper; 2. kóupə], fr. Du. *koopen*, 'to buy, bargain', wh. is cogn. w. O.E. *cēapian*, w. same meaning. See **cheap.** Gen. *horse-coper*, a horse-dealer, esp. one of doubtful honesty.

coper (II.), n., fr. Du. *kooper*, 'trading vessel'. See prec. word. A vessel stocked with grog and supplying it to the North Sea fishermen while afloat.

Copernican, adj. [1. kōpérnikan; 2. koupə́nikən]. (astron.) *Copernican system* or *theory*, that propounded by Copernicus (1473–1543), who first taught that the sun is the centre round which the earth and other planets revolve.

copestone, n. [1. kṓpstōn; 2. kóupstoun]. **cope (I.)** & **stone**. More gen., coping-stone, q.v.

coping, n. [1. kṓping; 2. kóupiŋ]. **cope (I.)** & **-ing**. (archit.) **a** Covering course of a wall, or parapet, sloped, and projecting to carry off water; **b** ledge, overhanging top, of a wall, to give protection to wall-fruit.

coping-stone, n. Prec. & **stone**. **a** Course of stones along the ridge of a roof; **b** (fig.) final, and completing act in a piece of work; climax of an achievement; finishing stroke, crowning touch.

copious, adj. [1. kṓpius; 2. kóupiəs], fr. Lat. *cōpiōsus*, 'well supplied, plentiful', fr. *cōpia*, 'plenty, abundance', fr. **co-** & *ops*, genit. *opis*, 'power, might, wealth', wh. is cogn. w. Lat. *opus*, 'work, labour, exertion', & **-ous**. See **opera** & **optimism**; cp. **copy**. **1.** (of material things) Plentiful, abundant in amount or quantity: *a copious repast*; *copious harvest*. **2.** (of non-material things) **a** Full, abundant: *copious material, notes* (e.g. for a book, speech &c.); *copious information*; **b** (of expression, diction, style) exuberant, profuse (often with sense of excess): *a copious vocabulary*; *copious eloquence*; **c** (of persons) *a copious writer, preacher* &c.

copiously, adv. Prec. & **-ly**. In a copious manner.

copiousness, n. See prec. & **-ness**. Quality of being copious, **a** abundance, plenty, exuberance; **b** excess of quantity, too great fullness and abundance.

copper (I.), n. & adj. [1. kóper; 2. kɔ́pə]. O.E. *copor*, fr. L. Lat. *cuper*, Lat. *cuprum*. Earlier *aes cuprium*, 'Cyprian brass', Gk. *kúprion*, (Cyprus being a chief source of copper for the ancients); borrowed fr. Lat. in W. Gmc. period, cp. O.H.G. *kupfar*, Mod. Germ. *kupfer*. **1.** n. **a** A reddish malleable ductile metal which is a good conductor of heat and electricity; **b** a coin of small value made of copper or of bronze, e.g. a penny, halfpenny, or farthing; **c** a large vessel made of copper, esp. one used for boiling clothes in a laundry. **2.** adj. Made of copper: *a copper kettle* &c.

copper (II.), vb. trans., fr. prec. To cover with sheets of copper.

copper (III.), n., fr. **cop (II.)** & **-er**. (slang) A policeman; lit. 'one who cops or catches'.

copperas, n. [1. kóperas; 2. kɔ́pəræs]. M.E. *coperose*, cp. Fr. *couperose*; fr. Lat. *cupri-* (as in *cupri-um*) & *-ōsum*, adj. suff. See **copper (I.)** & **-ose**. (chem.) Sulphate of iron, green vitriol.

copper beech, n. Variety of beech tree with copper-coloured foliage.

copper-bit, n. Soldering tool with a copper point.

copper-bottomed, adj. [1. kóper bótumd; 2. kɔ́pə bɔ́təmd]. (of ships) Having a bottom sheathed with copper; (hence by transf.), thoroughly seaworthy, sound; also fig.

copperhead, n. [1. kóperhed; 2. kɔ́pəhed]. A poisonous North American snake.

copper-nose, n. A red nose caused by excessive drinking.

copperplate, n. & adj. [1. kóperplāt; 2. kɔ́pəpleit]. **1.** n. **a** Plate of polished copper on which a picture, design, or writing is engraved or etched; **b** impression from this: Phr. *to write like copperplate*, very neatly, forming every letter perfectly. **2.** adj. Resembling an impression from a copperplate; beautifully formed, esp. of writing.

copper-smith, n. A worker in copper, one who manufactures copper utensils.

coppery, adj. [1. kóperi; 2. kɔ́pəri]. **copper (I.)** & **-y**. Like copper, esp. in colour or taste.

coppice, n. [1. kópis; 2. kɔ́pis]. O. Fr. *copeis*, 'cut wood', fr. L. Lat. *colpecia*, cp. L. Lat. *colpus*, 'a stroke', fr. Gk. *kólaphos*, wh. is connected w. Gk. *kláō*, 'smash, break'. Possibly related to Lat. *culpa*, 'a fault'. See **cataclasm, culpable**, also **copse** & cp. **coup**. A wood of small trees, with underwood, which is cut periodically.

copra, n. [1. kópra; 2. kɔ́prə]. Malayalam *koppara*, 'coco-nut', through Port. Kernel of the coco-nut, broken up and dried in the sun, and exported to Europe for the sake of the oil which is extracted by pressure, and used in manufacture of margarine, candles, and soap.

copro-, pref. Form of Gk. *kópros*, 'dung', used in composition. Cp. Scrt. *čakṛt*, 'manure'.

coprolite, n. [1. kóprōlīt; 2. kɔ́proulait]. Prec. & **-lite**, 'stone'. Fossil dung.

coprology, n. [1. koprólọji; 2. kɔprɔ́lədži]. **copro-** & **-logy**. Treatment of obscene subjects in literature or painting.

coprophagous, adj. [1. koprófagus; 2. kɔprɔ́fəgəs]. **copro-** & **-phagous**, 'eating'. Dung-eating; of class of beetles.

copse, n. [1. kops; 2. kɔps]. Another form of **coppice**. A coppice.

copsewood, n. [1. kópswood; 2. kɔ́pswud]. Small wood cut from a copse.

copsy, adj. [1. kópsi; 2. kɔ́psi]. **copse** & **-y**. **a** Covered with copse; **b** like a copse.

Copt, n. [1. kopt; 2. kɔpt], fr. Coptic *Kuptaios*, fr. Gk. *Aigúptios*, 'Egyptian'. Egyptian Christian.

Coptic, adj. & n. [1. kóptik; 2. kɔ́ptik]. Prec. & **-ic**. **a** adj. Pertaining to the Copts; **b** n., the language of the Copts.

copula, n. [1. kópūla; 2. kɔ́pjulə]. Lat. *cōpula*, 'that which binds together, a band, link', for earlier **co-apula*. For pref. see **co-**; the second element is a dimin. fr. Lat. *ap-*, 'to join', see **apt**. **1.** (gram. and log.) The word, generally a form of verb *to be*, which connects subject and predicate. **2.** (anat.) A connecting bone, cartilage &c.

copulate, vb. intrans. [1. kópūlāt; 2. kɔ́pjuleit], fr. Lat. *cōpulāt-(um)*, P.P. type of *cōpulāre*, 'to fasten or bind together', fr. *cōpula*. See prec. To join; used especially of sexual union.

copulation, n. [1. kòpūlā́shun; 2. kɔ̀pjuléiʃən]. Lat. *cōpulātiōn-(em)*, fr. prec. & **-ion**. **a** Act or process of uniting, joining together; esp. **b** sexual union.

copulative, adj. & n. [1. kópūlativ; 2. kɔ́pjulətiv]. Fr. *copulatif, -ive*, fr. Lat. *cōpulātīvus*. See **copulate** & **-ive**. **1.** adj. **a** (gram.) Having function of connecting, (of conjunctions and certain intrans. verbs); **b** relating to, connected with, sexual union. **2.** n. A copulative word.

copulatory, adj. [1. kópūlaturi; 2. kɔ́pjulətri]. **copulate** & **-ory**. Pertaining to copulation.

copy (I.), n. [1. kópi; 2. kɔ́pi], fr. Fr. *copie*, fr. Lat. *cōpia* (see **copious**), 'abundance, plenty, power, ability, opportunity, means'. Our sense is fr. the last mentioned, in Phr. *dare cōpiam legendi*, 'to give means of reading'. **1. a** An imitation or reproduction of anything: *copy of a picture, another's style* &c.; **b** transcript of an original document: *copy of a letter*. Phr. *rough copy*, first draft of a document; *fair copy*, final form of a document transcribed from former. **2.** One of a number of specimens of the same book, or other published document: *a copy of 'Paradise Lost'*; *to have several copies of a book*. **3.** (law) Transcript of manorial roll, recording the admissions of tenants to land, under the tenure known as *copyhold* (q.v.). **4.** That from which a copy or reproduction is made; a model: *to write, paint, from a copy*. **5. a** Manuscript sent to be printed: *the printers demand copy at once*; **b** anything, a story or event, suitable to form subject-matter for an author or journalist.

copy (II.), vb. trans. & intrans., fr. Fr. *copier*, fr. L. Lat. *cōpiāre*. See prec. **A.** trans. **1.** To make a copy, or transcript of (a document &c.). **2.** To reproduce by imitation the work of another: *to copy a picture*. **3.** To imitate (a person) in manner, behaviour, speech &c.; to take a person as a model and example. **4.** To imitate the manners and behaviour of another: *copy his virtues but not his follies*. **B.** intrans. (with *from* or absol.) To make a copy; to imitate.

copy-book, n. One containing letters, words, sentences engraved to serve as models for persons learning to write, having spaces between the lines in which the imitation of what is engraved is written below it. Phr. *copy-book morality, maxim*, trite, superficial teaching such as used to be found in copy-books.

copyhold, n. [1. kópihōld; 2. kɔ́pihould]. **copy (I.)** & **hold (II.)**. (law) **a** Tenure of land on a manor 'at the will of the lord and according to the custom of the manor'. So called because the conditions under which the land was held were laid down, and copied in the manor rolls; **b** land held in this way.

copyholder, n. [1. kópihōlder; 2. kɔ́pihouldə]. Prec. & **-er**. **1.** (law) Tenant of land by copyhold. **2.** Assistant of a printer's reader, who holds the MSS., while reader corrects proof.

copyist, n. [1. kópiist; 2. kɔ́piist]. **copy (I.)** & **-ist**. **a** A copier, transcriber; **b** one who imitates another, esp. a slavish imitator without initiative of his own.

copyright, n., adj., & vb. trans. [1. kópirīt; 2. kɔ́pirait]. **copy (II.)** & **right**. **1.** n. The exclusive right of an author, artist, composer, or his assignees, to reproduce his works, whether literary, dramatic, pictorial, or musical, in a material form, during a certain period, fixed by law. **2.** adj. Subject to, protected by, copyright. **3.** vb. To protect (a literary or artistic work) by copyright.

coquet, vb. intrans. [1. kōkét; 2. koukét], fr. Fr. *coqueter*, lit. 'to behave like a cock, to swagger, strut', fr. *coq*, 'a cock'. See **cock (I.)**. **1.** (of women) To act towards the other sex in such a way as to attract, and gain admiration; to flirt (followed by *with*, or, more rarely, absolutely). **2.** (fig., followed by *with*) To pay superficial and brief attention to an idea, proposal, subject &c., concern oneself with it temporarily, as a matter of only passing interest, without considering it seriously; to dally.

coquetry, n. [1. kṓketri; 2. kóukitri], fr. Fr. *coquetterie*. See prec. & **-ry**. **a** Behaviour of a flirtatious, alluring kind, designed to win admiration; light conduct dictated by vanity and love of admiration; **b** affected gaiety, facile prettiness of appearance, such as that displayed by a coquette.

coquette, n. [1. kōkét; 2. koukét]. Fr. See **coquet**. **a** Woman who tries to attract the other sex from vanity and love of admiration; a female flirt; **b** crested humming-bird.

coquettish, adj. [1. kōkétish; 2. koukétiʃ]. Prec. & **-ish**. **a** Exhibiting coquetry; having the manner and air of a coquette; **b** smartly attractive, engagingly pretty.

coquettishly, adv. Prec. & **-ly**. In a coquettish manner; smartly, attractively.

coquito, n. [1. kōkḗtō; 2. koukítou]. Span., dimin. of *coco* (palm). Palm tree which grows in Chile, the sap and seeds of which are sweet and edible.

cor-, pref. Form of **com-** used in compounds when the second element begins w. *r-*.

coracle, n. [1. kórakl; 2. kɔ́rəkl], fr. W. *cwrwgl*, dimin. of *corwg, cwrwg*, 'trunk, carcase, boat'. Cp. also Gael. *curach*, 'boat of wicker-work'. Primitive type of boat, still used on lakes and rivers in Ireland and Wales, consisting of a wicker framework covered with hide &c.

coracoid, adj. [1. kórakoid; 2. kɔ́rəkɔid], fr. Gk. *korakoeidḗs*, 'shaped like the beak of a crow', fr. *kórax, kórak-(os)*, 'crow', & **-oid**; *kórax* is fr. Aryan **kornk-s*, cp. Lat. *corn-ix*, 'crow'. The word is prob. of imitative origin & cogn. w. O.E. *hrōc*, 'rook', O.H.G. *hruoh*. The base, w. different formative element, is seen also in Lat. *crepō*, 'crack, creak, clatter' &c. See **corbel** & **crepitate**. (anat. and zool.) *Coracoid bone*, pertaining to a process or bone of the shoulder girdle of vertebrates, extending from the shoulder-joint towards the breast-bone; it is well developed in birds and most reptiles; in man and other mammals it is only a rudimentary process, *coracoid process*. So called from fancied resemblance in shape to a crow's beak.

coral, n. & adj. [1. kóral; 2. kórəl], fr. O. Fr. *coral*, Fr. *corail*, fr. Lat. *corallum*, *coralium*, fr. Gk. *korállion*, borrowed fr. Heb. *gōrāl*, 'a small stone'. **1.** n. **a** Marine polyp or zoophyte related to the sea-anemones, found in tropical seas, which extracts the lime from the water and builds up a limy substance, which acts as a skeleton or support, within or around itself; **b** white or red hard substance formed by the coral organism, which assumes various fantastic and often beautiful forms, according to the shape of the organism which secretes it; many corals are hard and of dense texture, and are capable of being carved and polished to make personal ornaments; **c** piece of polished coral specially shaped and adapted for babies to bite on when cutting teeth; **d** ovaries of a lobster which, when boiled, resemble red coral in colour and to some extent in texture. **2.** adj. **a** Made of coral; **b** like coral (red or pink) in colour.

coral-island, n. Island, as in Pacific, formed of coral.

corallin, n. [1. kóralin; 2. kórəlin], fr. **coral** & **-in.** Poisonous dyestuff (red or yellow) made from phenol and oxalic and sulphuric acids. Named from resemblance of red corallin to red coral in colour.

coralline (I.), n. [1. kóralin, kóralīn; 2. kórəlin, kórəlain], fr. **coral** & **-ine.** Coral-like seaweed or animal.

coralline (II.), adj. [1. kóralīn; 2. kórəlain]. Made of, resembling, (red) coral in colour.

corallite, n. [1. kóralīt; 2. kórəlait]. **coral** & **-lite.** **a** A fossil coral; **b** (zool.) coral skeleton of a single polyp.

coralloid, adj. [1. kóraloid; 2. kórələid]. **coral** & **-oid.** Like coral in form and appearance: *coralloid root*, one branching like coral.

coral-reef, n. One slowly built up by the activities of the coral organism.

coral snake, n. A small venomous snake, *Elaps*, of America, of bright coral-red colour with black markings.

coral-tree, n. Name of some East and West Indian trees with bright coral-red flowers and seeds.

cor anglais, n. [1. kór ónglā; 2. kɔ̄r ã́glei]. Fr., 'English horn'. (mus.) The English horn or tenor oboe.

coranto, n. [1. korántō; 2. kəræ̃ntou]. Span., lit. 'running'; cp. Fr. *courante*. See **current.** **a** A lively dance in triple time; **b** music for this.

corban, n. [1. kórban; 2. kɔ̄bæn]. Heb. *qorbān*, 'offering (to God)', cogn. w. Arab. *qurbān*, 'victim, sacrifice'. (Bib.) Something dedicated to God as an offering and therefore not to be used for other purposes.

corbel, n. & vb. trans. [1. kórbl; 2. kɔ̄bl]. O. Fr. *corbel*, Fr. *corbeau*, 'raven', fr. Low Lat. *corbellum* (*b* for *v*), dimin. of Lat. *corvus*, 'raven', w. wh. is cogn. O.E. *hræfn*, 'raven', O.H.G. *hraban*, O.N. *hrafn*; further, O. Slav. *svraka*, Russ. *soróka*, 'magpie'. The base of all these is Aryan **kor-*, **kr-*, 'creak' &c., q.v. under **coracoid.** See also **raven.** **1.** n. (archit.) a Support or bracket of stone projecting from the face of a wall to carry some structural feature; **b** short timber placed lengthwise under a girder or beam; also called *corbel-block*. **2.** vb. (archit.) To furnish with a corbel or corbels; to support by a corbel.

corbel arch, n. (archit.) Span of masonry made by projecting each successive course until the two opposing top ones are joined by a cap-stone.

corbelling, n. [1. kórbeling; 2. kɔ̄bəliŋ]. **corbel** & **-ing.** Corbel work, series of corbels.

corbel table, n. (archit.) Row of corbels supporting a parapet or cornice, usually having a small arch between each pair of corbels.

corbie, n. [1. kórbi; 2. kɔ̄bi]. In M. Scots, fr. O. Fr. *corbin*, 'raven', dimin. of O. Fr. *corb*, fr. Lat. *corvus*. See **corbel.** (Scots) A raven; carrion-crow.

corbie-steps, n. pl. (archit.) Series of step-like projections on either side of gable.

cord (I.), n. [1. kord; 2. kɔ̄d]. M.E. *corde*, fr. Fr., fr. Lat. *chorda*, fr. Gk. *chordḗ*, 'gut, string of musical instrument'. See **chord.** **1.** Thick string or thin rope. **2.** (anat.) Applied to various structures which resemble cords, e.g. *spinal*, *spermatic*, *cord* &c.; *vocal cords* &c. **3.** Cord-like rib on cloth; ribbed fabric, esp. in corduroy; *cords* (pl.), breeches made of such cloth. **4.** A measure (128 cub. ft.) of wood cut for fuel; formerly measured with a cord.

cord (II.), vb. trans., fr. prec. To bind, fasten, with cord or rope; esp. *to cord a box*. Also *to cord up* (*a box* &c.).

cordage, n. [1. kórdij; 2. kɔ̄didž]. Fr. *cordage*. Prec. & **-age.** Collection of cords or ropes; systematized group of cords, esp. those of a ship's rigging.

cordate, adj. [1. kórdāt; 2. kɔ̄deit]. Lat. *cord-(is)*, *cor*, 'heart', & **-ate.** The base **k̑or-*, **k̑er-*, 'heart', is found in several branches of Aryan speech. Cp. Gk. *kardiā*, O. Ir. *cride*, O. Slav. *srŭdĭce* (fr. Aryan **k̑r̥d-*), cp. also Goth. *hairtō*, O.E. *heorte*, q.v. under **heart**; Lat. *crēdere*, 'to believe', is also fr. same base; see **creed.** Heart-shaped (of a leaf, shell &c.).

corded, adj. [1. kórded; 2. kɔ̄did], fr. P.P. of **cord** (II.). **a** Bound, tied up with cords; **b** made of, provided with, cords; **c** (of cloth &c.) ribbed.

Cordelier, n. [1. kórdeliā; 2. kɔ̄dəliei]. Fr., fr. *cordelle*, 'small cord', dimin. of *corde*, 'rope', & **-ier.** See **cord** (I.). **1.** **a** (eccles. hist.) Franciscan friar, from his girdle of knotted cord; **b** a political club, during the French Revolution, meeting in the Church of the Cordeliers in Paris. **2.** Rope-making machine.

cordial (I.), adj. [1. kórdial; 2. kɔ̄diəl], fr. L. Lat. *cordiālis*, fr. Lat. *cord-(is)*, *cor*, 'heart', q.v. under **cordate,** & **-ial.** **1.** Connected with the heart considered as the seat of life, or of the affections and feelings, hence, **a** vital: '*Cordial spirits*' (Milton) (obs.), and **b** having quality of reviving, giving fresh life and strength: *cordial medicine, drink* &c. **2.** (of manner, states of mind, feelings, and expression of these) **a** Hearty, friendly, cheerful: *a cordial smile, welcome, grasp of the hand* &c.; **b** deeply and strongly felt, sincere: *cordial liking, dislike* &c.

cordial (II.), n., fr. prec., **1, b.** **a** A medicine or drug which stimulates the heart's action; **b** a warming, invigorating drink, esp. one of aromatic spirit.

cordiality, n. [1. kòrdiáliti; 2. kɔ̄diæ̀liti]. Prec. & **-ity.** **a** Warm, strong feeling, esp. of liking, approval, affection; **b** expression of such feeling in manner, actions, or words.

cordially, adv. [1. kórdiali; 2. kɔ̄diəli]. **cordial** (I.) & **-ly.** In a cordial manner; heartily, sincerely; emphatically: *to approve, dislike* &c. *cordially*.

cordillera, n. [1. kòrdilyára; 2. kɔ̄diljéərə]. Span., fr. *cordilla*, dimin. of *cuerda*, 'rope, cord'. See **cord** (I.) Any one of a system of parallel mountain ranges, esp. of such in S. and Central America &c.

cordite, n. [1. kórdīt; 2. kɔ̄dait], fr. **cord** (I.) & **-ite.** So called from its appearance. A smokeless explosive, composed principally of nitroglycerin and gun-cotton.

cordon, n., Engl. pronunciation [1. kórdon; 2. kɔ̄dən, kɔ̄dɔ̃]. Fr., fr. *corde*. See **cord** (I.). **1.** Course of stone projecting from surface of a wall, string course; specif. (fort.) projecting coping of the scarp-wall of a fortification. **2.** **a** (mil.) Chain or circle of military posts to prevent passage into or out of a particular place or area; **b** a continuous circle of persons entirely surrounding or screening a place or person: *cordon of police*; **c** *sanitary cordon*, guards preventing ingress to or egress from an infected area. **3.** Broad ribbon of an Order (esp. a foreign Order) worn across the shoulder. **4.** (hort.) Fruit tree (esp. apple-, pear-, gooseberry-) with all its branches pruned back to a single stem, from which the fruit buds grow; usually trained against a wall or supported by a wire frame.

cordon bleu, n. [1. kórdon blē; 2. kɔ̄dɔ̃ blø]. **a** The blue ribbon worn formerly by the knights of the Holy Ghost, the highest Order in France under the Bourbons; hence, **b** a person of eminence or distinction; applied facetiously to a first-class cook.

cordovan, n. [1. kórdōvan; 2. kɔ̄douvən], Span. *Cordovano*, adj., 'of Cordova'. **a** adj. Belonging to Cordova, esp. *cordovan leather*; **b** n., the leather itself.

corduroy, n. & adj. [1. kórduroi; 2. kɔ̄dərɔi]. Prob. fr. Fr. *corde du roi*, 'king's cord'. **1.** n. **a** A kind of coarse, tough, ribbed cotton stuff, with a pile like velvet, used chiefly for making trousers for labourers; **b** (pl.) breeches, trousers, made of corduroy. **2.** adj. Made of corduroy.

corduroy road, n. In U.S.A., road with logs laid across it for use in marshy ground.

cordwain, n. [1. kórdwān; 2. kɔ̄dwein]. Variant of **cordovan.** Spanish leather, formerly used in making shoes.

cordwainer, n. [1. kórdwāner; 2. kɔ̄dweinə]. 15th cent. *cordwaner*, O. Fr. *cordoanier*, 'a shoemaker', cp. Fr. *cordonnier*, lit. 'a worker in Cordovan leather'. Chaucer has *Cordevane* as name of the leather, cp. M.E. *Cordouan*, *Cordewan*. Member of ancient trade guild, the *Cordwainers' Company*, one of the London Livery Companies.

core (I.), n. [1. kōr; 2. kɔ̄]. O. Fr. & Mod. Fr. *cor*, 'a horn', also 'corn on the foot'. Lat. *cornu* (see **corn** (III.)), but associated later w. O. Fr. *coer*, Mod. Fr. *cœur*, 'heart'. See **cordate.** **1.** Central or innermost part of a thing: *core of a rope*, central strand; *core of rock*, part removed by boring; *core of an abscess*, *corn*, central hard part &c. **2.** The hard central portion in certain fruits (apple, pear, quince &c.) containing the pips or seeds. **3.** Various technical usages from **1**, as **a** (elect.) a bar of soft iron, as an intensifier in an induction coil; **b** (founding) internal mould. **4.** (fig.) The inmost part, heart; substance, pith, gist of a subject &c.: *true to the core*; *rotten at the core*; *the very core of a subject*.

core (II.), vb. trans., fr. prec. To take out the core of: *to core an apple*.

co-relation. See **correlation.**

co-religionist, n. [1. kō relíjunist; 2. kóu rilídžənist]. **co-** & **religion** & **-ist.** One of the same religion.

Coreopsis, n. [1. kòreópsis; 2. kɔ̀riɔ́psis], fr. Gk. *kóris*, 'bug', (perh. cogn. w. **acarid**), & *ópsis*, 'sight, appearance' (see **optic**), fr. shape of seed. A genus of brightly coloured flowering plants of the aster family.

co-respondent, n. [1. kō respóndent; 2. kòu rispɔ́ndənt]. **co-** & **respondent.** (law) Man charged with committing adultery with another's wife (the *respondent*) in a divorce suit.

corf, n. [1. korf; 2. kɔ̄f], fr. Du. *korf*, cp. Germ. *korb*, 'basket', both loan-words fr. Lat. *corbis*, 'basket', itself prob. a Celt. loan-word; cp. M. Ir. *corb*, 'carriage, waggon', orig. one w. a wicker body. Perh. ultimately cogn. w. Lat. *curvus* (see **curve**) & *crātis*, 'wicker-work'. See **crate, cart, cradle.** **1.** Floating cage or basket for keeping fish alive in water. **2.** Large basket formerly used for hauling up coal from the mine to the pit-head.

coriaceous, adj. [1. kòriáshus; 2. kɔ̀riéiʃəs], fr. Lat. *coriaceus*, 'of leather', fr. *corium*, 'leather', on wh. see **corium, cortex.** Consisting of or resembling leather; leathery, tough.

coriander, n. [1. kòriánder; 2. kɔ̀riæ̃ndə], fr. Fr. *coriandre*, fr. Lat. *coriandrum*, fr. Gk. *koriannon*, *koriandron*. (bot.) Umbelliferous plant the aromatic fruits (known as seeds) of which are used medicinally as a digestive.

Corinthian, adj. & n. [1. kurínthian; 2. kərínþiən], fr. Gk. Place-Name Corinth & **-ian.** **1.** adj. **a** Of, pertaining to, Corinth; **b** specif., *Corinthian column*, one of the three types, in ancient Greek architecture, having slender, fluted shaft and capital decorated with carved acanthus leaves. 2. n. a Inhabitant of Corinth; b specif., pl. *Corinthians*, St. Paul's Epistles to the Corinthians; c (obs.) a gay spark, man about town.

Corinthianesque, adj. [1. kurìnthianésk; 2. kərìnþiənésk]. Prec. & **-esque.** (archit.) Resembling the Corinthian style.

corium, n. [1. kórium; 2. kɔ́riəm]. Lat., 'hide, leather', cogn. w. Lat. *cortex*, 'bark'; outside Lat. the base is found in various words in Gmc. & Slav., e.g. O.E. *hǽr*, 'hair' (see **hair**), & *heorþa*, 'deer-skin'; the orig. meaning seems to have been 'hide, thick skin'; fr. *corium* comes Fr. *cuir*, 'leather'. The base is ultimately **kʷer-*, 'to make, shape'. See **cortex** & **cuirass.** a Body armour of overlapping leather flaps; b (anat.) lower, vascular layer of skin covering the body.

cork (I.), n. [1. kork; 2. kōk]. Span. *corcho*, prob. through Arab. fr. Lat. *quercus*, 'oak'; cp. Span. & Port. *alcorque*, 'shoe with cork sole'. According to Meyer-Lübke the word has no connexion w. Lat. *cortex*, 'bark, rind' (of trees and plants). 1. a Specif., name given to the outer bark of the cork oak, species of evergreen or holm oak, *Quercus suber*, a light, tough, elastic substance used for a large number of purposes; b (bot.) applied to bark of trees and outer protecting covering of the stems of woody plants. 2. (preceded by def. or indef. art.) Portion of this substance cut into suitable shape and size to form a stopper for wine, medicine, and other bottles. *Burnt cork*, charred cork used for blackening the face in theatricals &c.

cork (II.), adj., fr. prec. Made of cork: *a cork carpet, cork sole* &c.

cork (III.), vb. trans., fr. **cork** (I.). 1. To place a cork in a bottle; stop up by means of a cork. 2. To impart taste of cork (to wine); chiefly in P.P. See **corked.** 3. To blacken (the face &c.) with burnt cork: *to cork one's face, eyebrows* &c.

corkage, n. [1. kórkij; 2. kɔ́kidž]. **cork** & **-age.** 1. Process of corking or uncorking of bottles. 2. Charge made by innkeepers on every bottle of wine or spirits purchased elsewhere than in the hotel, opened and consumed by guests in the hotel.

corked, adj. [1. korkt; 2. kōkt]. **cork** (I.) & **-ed.** 1. (of bottles &c.) Stopped with a cork. 2. (of the face and hands &c.) Blackened with burnt cork. 3. (of wine) Having taste derived from the cork, esp. when this is decayed.

corker, n. [1. kórker; 2. kɔ́kə]. **cork** (III.) & **-er.** (slang and colloq.) 1. Argument, circumstance, which appears to settle a question and to put a stop to further discussion. 2. An audacious, vivid person, who startles and impresses, whether favourably or the reverse, by his personality. 3. A daring, preposterous lie.

corkscrew, n. & adj. [1. kórkskrōō; 2. kɔ́kskrū]. 1. n. Instrument for drawing corks from bottles, consisting of a piece of steel twisted into a spiral, sharply pointed at one end and having a handle projecting at right angles on both sides of the other end. 2. adj. Twisted into a spiral like a corkscrew: *corkscrew curls*; *a corkscrew path.*

corkwood, n. [1. kórkwood; 2. kɔ́kwud]. The light, porous, buoyant wood of the evergreen *corkwood tree*, a native of Central America.

corky, adj. [1. kórki; 2. kɔ́ki]. **cork** (I.) & **-y.** 1. Like cork: *a corky taste.* 2. (colloq.) Vivacious, buoyant, skittish.

corm, n. [1. korm; 2. kōm], fr. Gk. *kormós*, 'the trunk of a tree with the boughs lopped off', fr. different gradation of the base in *keirō*, 'I cut off', for **ker-jō*. The base occurs w. variously differentiated meaning in Lat. *carō, carn-*, 'flesh', see **carnal**, & in **cortex**, **corium.** (bot.) A solid bulb, that is, a subterranean plant stem which bears buds at the summit, while roots sprout from its base. A corm is of different structure from the true (tunicated) bulb, which consists of a number of fleshy overlapping scales.

cormo-, pref., fr. Gk. *kormós*, 'trunk', see prec.; used in scientific terminology to indicate the principal line of descent.

cormorant, n. [1. kórmurant; 2. kɔ́mərənt], fr. Fr. *cormoran*, fr. Lat. *corvus marīnus*, 'sea-raven'. See **corvine** & **marine.** A large, voracious sea-bird found round coasts of Britain, and most parts of the world; hence (fig.), a greedy person, a glutton.

corn (I.), n. [1. korn; 2. kōn]. In O. & M.E., & all Gmc. languages, O.H.G. & Mod. Germ. *korn*, Du. *koren*, O.N. *korn*, Goth. *kaurno*, all fr. Gmc. **kurna-*, fr. Aryan **ǵṝno-*, **ǵeren-* &c., wh. meant 'to grow old, to mature', or something of the kind, cp. Gk. *gérōn*, 'old man', *gêras*, 'old age', Scrt. *jíryati*, 'becomes rotten, old' &c. Closely cogn. w. *corn*, are Lat. *grānum*, 'grain, small kernel' (see **grain** (I.)), O. Slav. *zrŭno*, 'corn', Lith. *žírnis*, 'a pea'. See also **kernel.** 1. a (coll.) Seeds of cereal plants (wheat, barley, rye, oats, maize); grain; b specif., oats, esp. as food for horses; c in English usage, when applied to human food, wheat; in American usage, maize. 2. A single seed, a grain, of wheat, barley &c.; also a grain of pepper. 3. Cereal plants of any kind when growing, or after being cut, including the stalks and ears, before the grain is separated out: *to cut the corn*; *a field of corn*; *sheaf of corn.*

corn (II.), vb. intrans., fr. prec. a (of cereals) To form grain, undergo swelling of the ear; also *to corn up*; b to sow land with, put into, corn.

corn (III.), n., fr. O. Fr. *corn*, Mod. Fr. *cor*, 'hard swelling', fr. Lat. *cornu*, 'a horn', exactly cogn. w. O.E., O.H.G. *horn*, Goth. *haurn* (see **horn**); cp. further Scrt. *śṛṅga-m*, 'horn'. a Hardened and thickened skin, often causing painful swelling, esp. on a toe; Phr. (fig.) *to tread on a person's corns*, offend him by saying something contrary to his opinions and prejudices; *corn-plaster*, a plaster to cure corns; b painful affection on forefoot of horse, due to bruising of the soft tissues.

corn (IV.), vb. trans. Perh. fr. **corn** (I.) meaning to sprinkle with salt, peppercorns &c. To preserve meat by pickling and salting: *corned beef*, beef so preserved and canned.

corn-beetle, n. Small beetle which infests corn in the store.

cornbrash, n. [1. kórnbrash; 2. kɔ́nbræʃ]. Coarse chalky soil, so called from its corn-growing qualities.

corn-chandler, n. Retail dealer in corn, oats, hay &c.

corn-cob, n. a Head, cob, of Indian corn or maize upon which the grains grow; b pipe of which the bowl is made of a corn-cob.

corn-cockle, n. Weed with purplish red flowers, a species of campion, which grows among the corn.

corncrake, n. [1. kórnkrāk; 2. kɔ́nkreik]. A common European bird, *Crex pratensis*, of the rail family, which frequents cornfields, the male of which has a loud harsh cry which he utters continuously for hours at night; also called *land-rail.*

cornea, n. [1. kornéa; 2. kōníə]. Fem. of Lat. *corneus* (adj.), 'horny', fr. *cornu*, 'horn'. See **corn** (III.). Tough outer membrane protecting the eyeball.

cornel, n. [1. kórnel; 2. kɔ́nəl]. O. Fr. *cornille*, L. Lat. *cornolium*, 'cornel tree'. So called fr. hardness of the wood, fr. Lat. *cornu*, 'horn'. See **corn** (III.). Tree with very hard wood, such as the dogwood tree.

cornelian, n. [1. kornélian; 2. kōníljən]. Fr. *corneline*, fr. Lat. *cornu*, 'horn'. See prec. Variety of reddish brown or white chalcedony, a semi-precious stone; the name is derived from transparent, supposed horny appearance when the stone is broken.

corneous, adj. [1. kórneus; 2. kɔ́niəs], fr. Lat. *corneus*, 'horny'. See **corn** (III.) & **-ous.** Horny, horn-like.

corner (I.), n. [1. kórner; 2. kɔ́nə]. O. Fr. *cornier*, L. Lat. *cornerium*, fr. Lat. *cornu*, 'horn', in sense of a point. See **corn** (III.). 1. Meeting-place of two converging lines, sides, or surfaces; edge, angle: *corner of a street, house, table* &c. Phr. *to turn the corner*, to pass round the corner into another street; (fig.) to pass a crisis safely; *to cut off a corner*, to take a short cut. 2. Enclosed angle formed by meeting walls of a room, sides of a box &c.: *to stand, put a child, in the corner* (of a room), as a punishment; *to drive* (*a person*) *into a corner* (fig.), put him into a difficult, or embarrassing position; *a tight corner*, awkward situation. 3. A hidden, remote, out-of-the-way place: *a dark, odd corner.* Phr. (fig.) *hole-and-corner* (*transaction*), underhand, 'shady'. 4. Quarter, region, part: *the four corners of the earth.* 5. Specif. a (commerc.) method of controlling prices of an article of commerce by purchasing, and holding, all the available supply: *a corner in wheat* &c.; b (Assoc. football) corner-kick.

corner (II.), vb. trans., fr. prec. 1. To force or drive into a corner, (lit. and fig.) bring to bay, put in awkward position. 2. To make a corner in an article of commerce. See prec. 5.

cornered, adj. [1. kórnerd; 2. kɔ́nəd], fr. P.P. of prec. Placed in difficult position, brought to bay.

corner-kick, n. (Assoc. football) Kick from the corner, allowed when the ball has been kicked by opponent over his own goal line.

corner-man, n. Performer who sits at the end, and plays a prominent part, in a troupe of nigger minstrels.

corner-pins, n. Skittle pins numbered 7 and 10.

corner-stone, n. a Stone forming a corner of the foundation of a building; b (fig.) something indispensable, of primary importance; basis: *the corner-stone of a philosophical system.*

cornet, n. [1. kórnet; 2. kɔ́nit]. O. Fr. dimin. of *corn*, 'horn'. See **corn** (III.). 1. (mus.) a Brass wind-instrument of the trumpet class with valves or pistons; also *cornet-à-pistons*; b person who plays this instrument in an orchestra; c *solo cornet, echo cornet*, names of organ stops. 2. Cone-shaped paper wrapper; also, cone-shaped wafer for holding ice-cream. 3. (mil.) Generally *cornet of horse*, formerly fifth commissioned officer in cavalry troop who carried the colours (obs.).

cornetcy, n. [1. kórnetsi; 2. kɔ́nitsi]. Prec. & **-cy.** (mil., obs.) The commission or rank of a cornet.

corn-exchange, n. Place where corn-dealers transact their business.

corn-field, n. One in which corn is growing.

corn-flour, n. Finely ground meal made from maize, rice, or other kinds of grain.

corn-flower, n. Any of several varieties of plants which grow among corn, esp. a blue-flowered kind, *Centaurea cyanus*, often cultivated.

cornice, n. [1. kórnis; 2. kɔ́nis]. Fr., fr. Ital.; prob. derived fr. Lat. *corōna*, 'crown, cornice'. See **corona.** 1. (archit.) a Carved moulding round top of a building; b moulding, generally of plaster, round walls of a room below the ceiling. 2. (mountaineering) Layer of snow overhanging crest of a ridge.

corniced, adj. [1. kórnist; 2. kɔ́nist], fr. prec. & **-ed.** Having a cornice.

corniferous, adj. [1. kornífferus; 2. kōnífərəs], fr. Lat. *cornifer*, 'having or bearing horns'. **corn** (III.) & **-ferous.** (of geol. epoch) Producing or containing hornstone, or horn-like nodules of chert which occur in the limestone.

Cornish, adj. & n. [1. kórnish; 2. kɔ́niʃ]. 1. adj. Of, coming from, Cornwall; pertaining to Cornwall, its inhabitants, or the Celtic dialect formerly spoken there. 2. n. Celtic dialect spoken in Cornwall till the eighteenth century.

corn law(s), n. Law or group of laws regulating trade in corn, specif. those, repealed in 1846, which imposed very heavy duty on importation of corn.

cornopean, n. [1. kornṓpean; 2. kənóupiən]. Another name for the musical instrument usually known as the cornet, q.v.

cornstalk, n. [1. kórnstawk; 2. kɔ́nstɔk]. **a** A stalk of corn, as of wheat or maize; **b** (colloq.) an Australian, esp. used of Australian cricketers, *the Cornstalks*.

cornstone, n. [1. kórnstōn; 2. kɔ́nstoun]. See **corn** (**I.**) & **stone**. (geol.) Variety of red and green limestone occurring as the base of Old Red Sandstone.

cornucopia, n. [1. kòrnūkṓpia; 2. kɔ̀njukóupiə]. L. Lat. *cornūcōpia*, fr. Lat. *cornu cōpiae*, 'horn of plenty'. See **corn** (**III.**) & **copious**. **1.** (class. mythol.) The horn of the goat Amalthea, which suckled Zeus. Hence **2. a** ornament in moulding and sculpture &c., representation in painting, representing a goat's horn with fruit, flowers, and corn flowing from it; **b** (fig.) abundance, plenteousness, overflowing supply.

cornute(d), adj. [1. kornū́t(id); 2. kənjū́t(id)], fr. Lat. *cornūtus*, 'horned', fr. *cornu*, 'horn'. See **corn** (**III.**). **a** Having horns; **b** horn-shaped.

corolla, n. [1. koróla; 2. kərɔ́lə], fr. Lat. *corolla*, 'little crown', fr. **corōn-la*, fr. *corōna*, 'a crown', w. dimin. suff. See **corona**. (bot.) The cup-like form composed by the inner series of leaves, or petals of a flower.

corollary, n. [1. korólari; 2. kərɔ́ləri], fr. Lat. *corollārium*, 'money paid for a garland; a gift, gratuity'; in later philos. writings, 'a deduction'. See prec. & **-ary**. **a** An additional inference which follows as a natural sequence from a proposition which has already been proved; **b** natural consequence, result.

corona, n. [1. korṓna; 2. kəróunə]. Lat., 'crown', borrowed fr. Gk. *korṓnē*, 'anything bent or curved'; cp. also Gk. *korōnis*, adj. 'crooked', & as n. 'anything curved; a wreath'; cogn. w. Lat. *curvus*, 'bent, curved' &c. See **curve**. **1. a** Luminous circle round or near sun or moon; **b** luminous envelope surrounding the sun; seen in total eclipse round the edge of the disk of the moon. **2. a** Circlet suspended from roof of a church to hold tapers; **b** (archit.) the flat, vertical part of a large cornice. **3.** (anat.) **a** Upper surface of the skull; **b** the crown of a tooth.

coronach, n. [1. kóronagh; 2. kɔ́rənəχ]. Gael., fr. *comh*, 'with, together', & *ra(i)nach*, 'wailing, shrieking'. **a** (among Scotch Highlanders) A dirge, lament for the dead, sung, or played on the bagpipes; **b** (among the Irish) keening, or wailing uttered at funerals.

coronal (**I.**), n. [1. kóronal; 2. kɔ́rənəl], fr. L. Lat. *corōnālis*, adj. See **corona** & **-al**. **a** A circlet (of gold, gems &c.) for the head; diadem; **b** a wreath, garland (of flowers &c.), for the head.

coronal (**II.**), adj. [1. kóronal, korṓnal; 2. kɔ́rənəl, kəróunəl]. Same as prec. **1.** (astron.) Of or pertaining to a crown or corona, q.v. **2.** (phon.) Old name for sounds uttered with the tip of the tongue turned upwards and backwards, better called *inverted sounds*, e.g. the *r*-sound in many provincial dialects of the south of England. **3.** (anat.) Of, pertaining to, the corona of the skull, esp. *coronal suture*, separating the frontal bone from the parietal bones.

coronate, vb. trans. [1. kóronāt; 2. kɔ́rəneit], fr. Lat. *corōnātus*, P.P. of *corōnāre*, 'to crown', fr. *corōna*, 'a crown'. See **corona**. To place crown on head of; to crown.

coronated, adj. [1. kóronāted; 2. kɔ́rəneitid]. Prec. & **-ed**. Crowned, having a crown, esp. of birds &c., crested.

coronation, n. [1. kòronā́shun; 2. kɔ̀rənéiʃən]. **coronate** & **-ion**. The act or ceremony of crowning a sovereign; *coronation-oath*, that taken by a sovereign at coronation, promising fidelity to the laws and constitution of his country.

coroner, n. [1. kóroner; 2. kɔ́rənə], formerly [1. króuner; 2. kráunə]. A.-Fr. *corouner*, fr. O. Fr. *corone*, 'crown' & **-er**. See **crown**. **1.** (legal hist.) An officer charged with keeping records of crown pleas in a county, and looking after revenue thence accruing, also of private property of the crown; now only surviving in duty of the present-day coroner to make inquiry in cases of treasure trove. **2.** An officer of a county or borough whose business is to hold an inquiry or inquest as to the cause of death of persons who have died, as the result of a crime, or accident, or, as it is supposed, from other than natural causes.

coronership, n. [1. kóronership; 2. kɔ́rənəʃip]. Prec. & **-ship**. **a** Office of a coroner; **b** period of holding such office.

coronet, n. [1. kóronet; 2. kɔ́rənet], fr. O. Fr. *coronette*, dimin. of *corone*, 'crown', fr. Lat. *corōna*. See **corona**. **1.** A small crown worn by persons of various rank in the peerage, and by princes of the blood other than the sovereign himself. **2. a** Ornamental female head-dress, in form of a coronet, often of gold and jewels; **b** (poet.) chaplet, or garland for the head. **3.** Horny, upper part of horse's foot where the hoof joins the skin.

coroneted, adj. [1. kóroneted; 2. kɔ́rənetid]. Prec. & **-ed**. Wearing a coronet; belonging to the peerage.

coronoid, adj. [1. kóronoid; 2. kɔ́rənɔid], fr. Gk. *korṓnē*, 'crow', cp. **coracoid** & **-oid**. (anat.) Curved, shaped like a crow's beak (used of processes in the bones of the lower jaw, or of the forearm below the elbow).

corozo, n. [1. korṓzō; 2. kəróuzou]. South American word. South American tree, bearing *corozo-nut*, from which vegetable ivory is made.

corporal (**I.**), adj. [1. kórporal; 2. kɔ́pərəl], fr. Lat. *corporālis*, fr. Lat. base *corpor-*, 'body'. See **corpus**. Of, or connected with the human body: *corporal punishment*, bodily pain, esp. by whipping, deliberately inflicted.

corporal (**II.**), n., also **corporas**, fr. L. Lat. *corporālis* (*palla*), 'body cloth'. See prec. (eccles.) Fine linen cloth covering the altar during Mass, upon which the consecrated elements are placed, and with which they may be covered; communion cloth. Hence, (archaic) *corporal oath*, esp. one solemn one sworn upon the corporal cloth or other sacred object.

corporal (**III.**), n., fr. Fr. *caporal*, Ital. *caporale*, fr. *capo*, fr. Lat. *caput*, 'head'. See **capital** (**I.**) **1.** (mil.) Lowest non-commissioned officer, ranking immediately below sergeant and above a lance-corporal. *Corporal of horse*, sergeant in the Household cavalry; *corporal-major*, sergeant-major in the same. Phr. *The Little Corporal*, nickname of Napoleon. **2.** (nav.) *Ship's corporal*, petty officer who assists the master-at-arms.

corporality, n. [1. kòrporáliti; 2. kɔ̀pərǽliti], fr. L. Lat. *corporālitāt-(em)*, abstract n., fr. *corpor-*, 'body'. See **corporal** (**I.**) & **-ity**. State of having a body, material existence; bodily substance.

corporate, adj. [1. kórporat; 2. kɔ́pərit], fr. Lat. *corporātus*, 'embodied', P.P. of *corporāre*, 'to form into a body', fr. *corpor-(is)*, 'body'. See **corpus**. **a** Of a number of persons, legally united in a body, for transaction of business, and forming a single entity in law: *a corporate body*; **b** shared by all members of a body regarded as a single unity, e.g. members of a committee, of a cabinet &c.: *corporate responsibility*; **c** of, belonging to, a corporation or group of persons united as above: *corporate property*.

corporation, n. [1. kòrporā́shun; 2. kɔ̀pəréiʃən], fr. L. Lat. *corporātiōn-(em)*, 'an assuming of a body, incarnation', fr. *corporāt-(um)*, P.P. of *corporāre*, 'to form into a body, furnish with a body', & **-ion**. See **corpus**. **1. a** Combination or group of persons regarded for legal purposes as a unit; **b** specif., civic authority, body of persons elected to carry on the public business of a city or town; a city council, consisting of Mayor, aldermen and councillors; **c** (U.S.A.) limited liability or joint-stock company. **2.** (colloq.) Large and prominent abdomen.

corporative, adj. [1. kórporativ; 2. kɔ́pərətiv], fr. L. Lat. *corporātīvus*, adj., 'pertaining to the forming of a body'. See **corporate** & **-ive**. Belonging to, connected with, a corporation.

corporator, n. [1. kórporātur; 2. kɔ́pəreitə], **corporate** & **-or**. Member of a corporation.

corporeal, adj. [1. korpóreal; 2. kɔpɔ́riəl], fr. Lat. *corporeus*, 'belonging to the body', fr. *corpus*, 'body', see **corpus**, & **-al**. **a** Connected with a body or with material nature; bodily, physical, as opposed to spiritual; **b** specif. (law) *corporeal hereditament, property*, something tangible, as land, bullion &c., as distinct from rights over land &c.

corporeality, n. [1. kòrpōreáliti; 2. kɔ̀pɔriǽliti]. Prec. & **-ity**. The state of being corporeal; corporeal existence.

corporeally, adv. [1. korpóreali; 2. kɔpɔ́riəli]. See prec. & **-ly**. In bodily form, in the body.

corporeity, n. [1. kòrporḗiti; 2. kɔ̀pɔríiti]. Lat. *corpor-* (see **corpus**) & **-ity**. Existence in the body, material existence.

corposant, n. [1. kórpōzant; 2. kɔ́pouzænt], fr. Port. *corpo santo*, 'holy body', fr. Lat. *corpus sanctum*, or = *corpus sancti*, 'body of a saint'. Luminous electrical discharge observable sometimes in stormy weather at the top of flagstaffs, ships' masts, or trees: also called *St. Elmo's fire*.

corps, n. [1. kōr; 2. kɔ], pl. [1. kōrz; 2. kɔz]. Fr. *corps*, fr. Lat. *corpus*, 'body'. See **corpus**. Body of persons associated in some way. Specif. **1.** (mil.) **a** the largest tactical unit of an army, consisting of two or more divisions; in Fr. *corps d'armée*, army corps; **b** separate department or branch of the army; as, *Army Service Corps*, branch that has charge of commissariat; *Army Ordnance Corps*; *Army Veterinary Corps* &c. **2.** Applied to various groups of persons: **a** *corps de ballet*, the dancers in a ballet collectively; **b** *Corps Diplomatique*, all persons associated with an embassy or legation in a foreign country; the diplomatic service generally, ambassadors, minister plenipotentiary, attachés, secretaries of legation &c.

corpse, n. [1. korps; 2. kɔps]. Variant of **corps**. M.E. *corps*, fr. O. Fr., fr. Lat. **corpus**. The pronunciation shows earlier borrowing than **corps**, wh. has approximately the Mod. Fr. sounds; variant is **corse**. Dead body, usually of a human being. Still applied by Spenser to the living body. *Corpse-candle*: **a** luminous appearance sometimes seen in churchyards and marshy places; **b** thick candle lighted and placed near a dead body coffined, or laid out for burial.

corpulence, n., also **corpulency** [1. kórpūlens(i); 2. kɔ́pjuləns(i)]. Fr., fr. Lat. *corpulentia*, 'grossness or fleshiness of body', fr. *corpus*, 'body'. See **corpus**. Excessive stoutness of body, fatness; obesity.

corpulent, adj. [1. kórpūlent; 2. kɔ́pjulənt]. Fr., fr. Lat. *corpulentus*, 'fleshy, fat'. See prec. (of persons only) Having great or excessive bodily bulk; stout, fat, obese.

corpus, n. [1. kórpus; 2. kɔ́pəs]. Lat., 'body', base *corpor-*, fr. **corpos-*, genit. *corporis*. Cogn. w. Scrt. *kṛp-*, 'form, beauty'; Gk. *prapis*, gen. in pl., *prapides*, 'diaphragm, heart, intelligence', for **kʷṛp-*; in Gmc. cp. O.H.G. *href*, O.E. *hrif*, 'womb, abdomen' (see **midriff**). The whole group is perh. connected w. Aryan base **kʷer-*, 'to shape, form, make', cp. Scrt. *karṓti*, 'he makes'. See **corium** & **create**. **1. a** Dead body of man or animal (rare); **b** (anat.) part of an organ of the body, having a solid and more or less homogeneous structure. **2.** Collection of writings or documents, esp. the whole collection of writings of a particular country, age, or type: *the corpus of Latin poetry*; *corpus of English Common Law*. **3.** The principal or capital sum of a fund, as distinct from the interest. **4.** (law) *Corpus delicti* [1. dilíktī; 2. diliktai]. Lat., 'body of the crime', the essential acts and facts which constitute a crime and breach of the law.

Corpus Christi (Day), n. [1. kórpus krístī; 2. kɔ̄pəs kristai]. Lat., 'Body of Christ'. Festival in honour of the Eucharist, held on the Thursday after Trinity Sunday, when the Host is carried in procession.

corpuscle, n. [1. kórpusl; 2. kɔ̄pəsl], or **corpuscule** [1. korpúskūl; 2. kɔ̄páskjul], fr. Lat. *corpusculum*, 'a little body', dimin.; see **corpus** & **-cule**. Minute body, atom, particle; specif. **1.** (biol.) a small particle of protoplasm having a specific structure and function; esp. **b** a constituent particle of the blood: *the red, white corpuscles.* **2.** (phys.) An atom of electricity; electron.

corpuscular, adj. [1. korpúskūlar; 2. kɔ̄páskjulə]. Prec. & **-ar**. Consisting of corpuscles, connected with corpuscles.

corral, n. & vb. trans. [1. koráhl; 2. kərál]. Span., fr. *corro*, 'circle', fr. Lat. *currere*, 'to run'. See **courier, course. 1.** n. Pen or enclosure for horses, cattle &c.; enclosure for capturing wild animals; defensive enclosure formed hastily of waggons and camp equipment; cp. **kraal. 2.** vb. To confine in a corral; to make a corral for.

correct (I.), adj. [1. kurékt; 2. kərékt], fr. Lat. *correct-(um)*, P.P. type of *corrigere*, 'to make straight, set right', fr. *con-* & *regere*, 'to lead straight'. See **cor-** & **rectum** & words referred to there. **1.** In accordance with facts, or reasoning; true, accurate, exact, right: *correct statement, inference, calculation* &c. **2.** In accordance or conformity with a recognized and accepted standard of rules, customs, morals, manners, behaviour, taste, dress &c. Phr. *to do, to say, the correct thing*, do or say something suitable to the circumstances, say what is expected.

correct (II.), vb. trans., fr. prec. Generally, to set right, make correct. Specif. **1.** (of products of human activity) to set right, improve by removing errors and making accurate: *to correct a translation; to correct mistakes, blunders, in an exercise, a book, a printer's proof* &c. **2. a** To reprove, admonish (persons), point out errors of &c.; censure with view to improvement: *to correct a child for disobedience* &c.; **b** to punish for errors, misconduct &c. **3.** (of diseases or physical defects) To counteract, neutralize, cure: *to correct acidity in the system; to correct curvature in a child's spine* &c. **4.** (of mechanical devices, instruments &c.) To alter or adjust, modify action of, so as to bring into accordance with required standard: *to correct the timing of a watch* &c.

correction, n. [1. kurékshun; 2. kərékʃən]. Fr., fr. Lat. *correctiōn-(em)*, 'a making straight, improvement, correction'. **correct (I.)** & **-ion**. Act or process of correcting (in all senses). Phrs. *to speak under correction*, with consciousness that what one says may not be quite accurate; *house of correction*, a prison or bridewell.

correctional, adj. [1. kurékshunal; 2. kərékʃənəl]. Prec. & **-al**. Of, pertaining to, correction; tending to correct.

correctitude, n. [1. koréktitūd; 2. kəréktitjūd]. Fr. Not fully naturalized in English. Use perh. due to influence of *rectitude*. Correctness of conduct.

corrective, adj. & n. [1. kuréktiv; 2. kəréktiv], fr. Fr. *correctif*. See **correct** & **-ive. 1.** adj. Tending to correct; serving to neutralize or mitigate what is pernicious, to rectify what is amiss. **2.** n. Thing which does this, a corrective agent.

correctly, adv. [1. kuréktli; 2. kəréktli]. **correct (I.)** & **-ly**. In a correct manner; **a** accurately, without any mistake; **b** in accordance with a standard of conduct, style, taste &c.: *to behave, speak, correctly.*

correctness, n. [1. kuréktnes; 2. kəréktnis]. See prec. & **-ness**. State of being correct; **a** accuracy, exactness; **b** conformity to a standard.

corrector, n. [1. kuréktur; 2. kəréktə]. Lat. See **correct (II.)** & **-or**. One who, or that which, corrects in any sense; specif. **a** one who punishes for correction; **b** *corrector of the press*, a proof-reader.

correlate (I.), vb. intrans. & trans. [1. kórelāt; 2. kɔ́rileit]. **cor-** & **relate. 1.** intrans. (followed by *to*) To have a mutual relation. **2.** trans. (followed by *with*) To put a thing in relation with another, to connect together by showing mutual relation.

correlate (II.), n., fr. prec. Either of two reciprocally related things, esp. one of such things as are so connected that one directly implies the other.

correlation, n. [1. kòreláshun; 2. kɔ̀riléiʃən]. **correlate (I.)** & **-ion. a** Mutual or reciprocal relation; **b** act or process of showing existence of such relation between things.

correlative, adj. & n. [1. kōrélativ; 2. kourélətiv]. **correlate** & **-ive. 1.** adj. **a** Having, or involving, reciprocal relation; **b** (gram.) having and expressing a mutual relation; applied to certain pairs of words and expressions, commonly used together, such as *either — or* &c. **2.** n. A correlative word or thing.

correlatively, adv. Prec. & **-ly**. By, in correlation; reciprocally.

correspond, vb. intrans. [1. kòrespónd; 2. kɔ̀rispɔ́nd]. See **cor-** & **respond. 1. a** (followed by *with* or *to*) To be in conformity, or agreement with; to equal, come up to; to fit, suit: *the reality does not always correspond with one's expectations; the description did not correspond with the thing itself; the house exactly corresponds to my requirements;* **b** to be equivalent to, represent: *the broad lines on the map correspond to roads.* **2.** (followed by *with* and *name of person*) To communicate with, in writing, write letters to, esp. habitually. Also absol.: *we rarely meet though we correspond regularly*, i.e. write to each other.

correspondence, n. [1. kòrespóndens; 2. kɔ̀rispɔ́ndəns]. Fr. See prec. & **-ence. 1.** (of things) Fact or condition of agreeing, being in conformity with, or of being equivalent to, something else: *phonetic notation implies as great a correspondence between sound and symbol as possible.* **2. a** Communication between persons, esp. when habitual, by means of writing; **b** the total number of letters that one habitually writes and receives: *to have a large, regular correspondence;* **c** the letters exchanged between two or more persons, esp. when collected for publication. *Correspondence column*, one reserved in a newspaper for letters to the editor.

correspondent (I.), n. [1. kòrespóndent; 2. kɔ̀rispɔ́ndənt]. **cor-** & **respondent. 1. a** One who writes letters to another; specif. **b** a person paid to write regularly to a newspaper contributing information, criticism on some particular subject, or from some particular place or scene of action &c.; **c** one who writes occasionally to the editor of a newspaper, without payment, in order to make public a personal view, to ventilate a grievance, or make suggestions which he believes to be of value on a matter of public interest &c. **2.** (commerc.) A person or firm having regular business relations with another.

correspondent (II.), adj. Same as prec. Corresponding.

corresponding, adj. [1. kòrespónding; 2. kɔ̀rispɔ́ndiŋ], fr. Pres. Part. of **correspond. 1.** Standing in a similar relation, agreeing with, being equivalent to. **2.** Carrying on a correspondence by letters: *a corresponding member* (of a learned society &c.), an honorary, non-resident member who is not a member of governing body.

corridor, n. [1. kóridōr; 2. kɔ́ridɔ̄]. Fr., fr. Ital. *corridore*, Span. *corredor*, 'a runner', hence, 'a long running line, a gallery'; fr. Lat. *currere*, 'to run'. See **courier** &c. **1. a** Long passage in large building (as hotel, school &c.) from which rooms open; **b** narrow passage from end to end of a railway coach, into which the compartments open; hence, *corridor train*, a train whose coaches are connected so that the corridor is continuous. **2.** (polit. geog.) A narrow strip of country passing through a foreign state, either neutralized or belonging to another state, as from an inland state to a seaport; as *the Danzig Corridor*, from Poland, through Germany to that port.

corrie, n. [1. kóri; 2. kɔ́ri]. Gael. *coire*, 'cauldron'; cogn. w. Scrt. *čarúš*, O.E. *hwer*, O.N. *hverr*, 'kettle', Goth. *hwairnei*, 'cranium'. (Scots) Hollow in the side of a mountain; a small valley.

corrigendum, n. [1. kòrijéndum; 2. kɔ̀ridžéndam]. Lat., 'to be corrected', fr. *corrigere*. See **correct (I.)**. Something to be corrected; esp. in a printed book; (gen. in pl.) *corrigenda*, list of corrections of errors in the text, printed after completion of printing of book itself, and added before publication.

corrigible, adj. [1. kórijibl; 2. kɔ́ridžibl], fr. L. Lat. *corrigibilis*, fr. Lat. *corrigere*, 'to correct'. See prec. **a** (of errors) Capable of being, liable to be, corrected; **b** (of persons) submitting to correction.

corrival, n. [1. kòríval; 2. kòuráivəl]. **cor-** & **rival**. A rival; competitor.

corroborant, adj. & n. [1. koróborant; 2. kərɔ́bərənt], fr. Lat. *corrōborant-(em)*, Pres. Part. of *corrōborāre*. See next word. **1.** adj. **a** Tending to corroborate; confirmatory; **b** (med.) invigorating, tonic. **2.** n. **a** Fact which corroborates; **b** tonic medicine.

corroborate, vb. trans. [1. koróborāt; 2. kərɔ́bəreit], fr. Lat. *corrōborāt-(um)*, P.P. type of *corrōborāre*, 'to strengthen', fr. **cor-** & *rōborāre*, 'to strengthen', fr. *rōbur*, 'hard wood, oak; strength'. See **robust**. To strengthen, make more certain, bear out, confirm, a statement, theory &c., by producing or discovering fresh evidence in support of it.

corroboration, n. [1. koròboráshun; 2. kərɔ̀bəréiʃən]. Fr., fr. Lat. See prec. & **-ion. a** The act of corroborating; **b** that which corroborates; confirmation of statement, theory, suspicion by additional facts.

corroborative, adj. [1. koróborativ; 2. kərɔ́bərətiv]. Fr. *corroboratif*. **corroborate** & **-ive**. Tending to corroborate, confirmatory.

corroborator, n. [1. koróborātur; 2. kərɔ́bəreitə]. **corroborate** & **-or**. One who corroborates.

corroboratory, adj. [1. koróborāturi; 2. kərɔ́bəreitəri]. **corroborate** & **-ory**. Corroborative.

corroboree, n. [1. koróborē; 2. kərɔ́bəri]. Native word. Festivity held by Australian aborigines, on moonlit nights, consisting of dances representing deeds of war and the chase, and events of tribal history.

corrode, vb. trans. & intrans. [1. koród; 2. kəróud]. Fr. *corroder*, fr. Lat. *corrōdere*, 'to gnaw to pieces', fr. **cor-** & *rōdere*, 'to gnaw'. See **rodent** & **rat. 1.** trans. **a** To eat away gradually, as though by gnawing, to wear away (used of action of rust, acids &c.); **b** (fig.) of evil passions, sorrow &c.: *corroding hate, care* &c. **2.** intrans. To wear, waste away, to diminish through action of rust, or chemical agents.

corrosion, n. [1. korózhun; 2. kəróužən]. Fr., fr. L. Lat. *corrōsiōn-(em)*, fr. *corrōs-(um)*, P.P. type of *corrōdere*. See prec. & **-ion**. Process or action of corroding, or being corroded, gradual eating away, esp. by chemical action (also fig.).

corrosive, adj. & n. [1. korósiv; 2. kəróusiv]. Lat. *corrōs-(um)* & **-ive**. See prec. **1.** adj. Tending to corrode, producing corrosion (lit. and fig.); *corrosive sublimate*, bichloride of mercury, a poisonous but powerful antiseptic. **2.** n. A corroding substance or agent.

corrosively, adv. Prec. & **-ly**. By a process of corrosion, as though by corrosion.

corrosiveness, n. See prec. & **-ness**. The property of corroding or being corrosive.

corrugate, vb. trans. & intrans. [1. kórūgāt; 2. kɔ́rjugeit], fr. Lat. *corrūgāt-(um)*, P.P. type of *corrūgāre*, fr. **cor-** & *rūgāre*, 'to wrinkle', fr. *rūga*, 'a wrinkle', q.v. under **rugose**;

see also **rough.** **1.** trans. To cause to form into wrinkles or folds, to make wrinkles in, esp. *to corrugate the brows, forehead.* **2.** intrans. To form into wrinkles, become wrinkled.

corrugated, adj. [1. kórūgāted ; 2. kórjugeitid]. Prec. & **-ed.** Formed into folds or furrows, bent into ridges : *corrugated iron*, galvanized sheet iron bent into a series of parallel and alternate ridges and grooves, used for roofing &c. ; *corrugated paper, cardboard*, paper or cardboard with corrugations, used for packing fragile articles.

corrugation, n. [1. kòrūgā́shun ; 2. kòrjugéiʃən]. **corrugate & -ion.** **a** Ridges and furrows running parallel as in corrugated iron &c. ; **b** wrinkles in forehead &c.

corrugator, n. [1. kórūgātur ; 2. kórjugeitə]. **corrugate & -or.** (anat.) The small muscle which contracts the brow into wrinkles in frowning.

corrupt (I.), adj. [1. kurúpt ; 2. kərápt], fr. Lat. *corruptus*, P.P. of *corrumpere*, 'to destroy, corrupt', fr. **cor-** & *rumpere*, 'to break', q.v. under **rupture. 1. a** Changed from a sound to a putrid state ; putrid, rotten ; **b** tainted, vitiated, unhealthy : *corrupt air* ; **c** (law) *corrupt in blood*, having lost all civil rights, and become outlaw by attainder of treason or felony. **2.** (of persons) **a** Having a perverted character ; morally debased, depraved, vicious &c. ; **b** bribable, in the habit of accepting bribes ; given to acting from interested motives and not from principle, or according to justice ; **c** (of action) *corrupt practices*, bribery. **3. a** (of languages) Not pure ; mixed with other languages, or having lost standard of correctness and elegance ; **b** (of liter. texts, manuscripts) defective, not genuine ; changed from original state ; overlaid with later, unauthorized additions and alterations.

corrupt (II.), vb. trans. & intrans., fr. prec. **A.** trans. To make corrupt (in various senses). **1. a** To cause to become rotten, render putrid ; **b** to consume, cause to consume away ; corrode : '*Where moth and rust doth corrupt*' (Matt. vi. 19). **2.** (of moral action) **a** To contaminate, pollute, debase : *to corrupt the manners, character* &c. ; (proverb) *evil communications corrupt good manners* ; **b** to destroy the integrity of, by bribery. **3.** (law) To render corrupt in blood (see **corrupt (I.) 1, c). 4.** (of liter. texts &c.) To falsify, by introducing non-original matter. **B.** intrans. To become corrupt or rotten (lit. and fig.).

corruptible, adj. & n. [1. kurúptibl ; 2. kəráptibl]. Lat. *corruptibilis.* **corrupt (II.) & -ible. 1.** adj. Capable of becoming corrupted, liable to corruption (in various senses) ; perishable ; bribable. **2.** n. That which is corruptible, specif., the human body : '*This corruptible must put on incorruption*' (1 Cor. xv. 53).

corruptibility, n. [1. kurùptibíliti ; 2. kəràptibíliti]. Prec. & **-ity.** Liability, proneness, to corruption (in various senses).

corruptibly, adv. [1. kurúptibli ; 2. kəráptibli]. **corruptible & -ly.** In a corruptible manner.

corruption, n. [1. kurúpshun ; 2. kərápʃən], fr. Lat. *corruptiōn-(em).* **corrupt (II.) & -ion. 1.** Physical decay, decomposition, putrefaction : *the corruption of the body.* **2. a** Moral deterioration, depravity ; **b** use of corrupt practices ; bribery. **3. a** Debasement or perversion of language, style &c. from its purity and simplicity ; **b** falsification of a text or manuscript. **4.** (law) *Corruption of blood*, rendering of a person outlaw by attainder of treason or felony.

corruptive, adj. [1. kurúptiv ; 2. kəráptiv]. **corrupt (II.) & -ive.** Tending to corrupt.

corruptly, adv. [1. kurúptli ; 2. kəráptli]. **corrupt (I.) & -ly.** In a corrupt manner.

corruptness, n. [1. kurúptnes ; 2. kəráptnis]. See prec. & **-ness.** State or quality of being corrupt.

corsac, -ak, n. [1. kórsak ; 2. kɔ́sæk]. Turki word. A small yellowish fox of Central Asia.

corsage, n. [1. kórsahzh, kórsij ; 2. kɔ́sāž, kɔ́sidž]. Fr., fr. O. Fr. *cors*, Fr. *corps*, 'body', see **corps, corpus, & -age.** Bodice of a woman's dress.

corsair, n. [1. kórsār ; 2. kɔ́sɛə], fr. Fr. *corsaire*, fr. Ital. *corsare*, lit. 'a runner, one who makes incursions', fr. L. Lat. *corsārius, cursārius*, fr. Lat. *cursus*, 'a running, a course, voyage', fr. *currere*, 'to run'. See **course & courier. a** A Barbary pirate, a privateer ; **b** a privateering vessel.

corse, n. [1. kors ; 2. kōs]. Variant of **corpse.** (poet.) Corpse.

corset, n. [1. kórset ; 2. kɔ́sɛt]. Fr. *corset*, dimin. of O. Fr. *cors*, Fr. *corps*, 'body'. See **corps & corpus.** Close-fitting garment, stiffened with whalebone, and adapted to the figure, worn by women under the bodice ; more popularly, stays.

corslet, corselet, n. [1. kórslet ; 2. kɔ́slit]. Fr. *corselet*, dimin. of O. Fr. *cors*, Fr. *corps*, 'body'. See **corpus.** Tight-fitting coat of armour protecting the body.

cortège, n. [1. kortázh ; 2. kōtéiž]. Fr., 'procession', fr. Ital. *corteggio*, fr. *corte*, 'court'. See **court.** A train of attendants on a great person on ceremonial occasions ; ceremonial procession.

cortes, n., Anglicized as [1. kórtez ; 2. kɔ́tez]. Span., pl. of *corte*, 'court'. Name of Spanish and Portuguese legislative assembly of two chambers.

cortex, n. [1. kórteks ; 2. kɔ́tɛks], pl. **cortices** [1. kórtisēz ; 2. kɔ́tisīz]. Lat., 'bark of a tree' ; fr. Aryan base *$k^{w}er$- &c., as in Lat. **corium**, 'hide' &c. The fundamental meaning of the base is 'to cut, strip', & both the above Lat. words meant orig. 'something stripped off', whence later 'bark' & 'skin' respectively. For relation of meanings cp. Gk. *dérma*, 'skin', the first syll. of wh. is cogn. w. Goth. *ga-tairan*, O.E. *teran*, Mod. Engl. 'to tear'. See **tear (I.). a** (bot.) The bark or rind of a tree ; **b** (anat.) outer covering, structure, of an organ, esp. the outer layer of grey matter of the brain.

cortical, adj. [1. kórtikl ; 2. kɔ́tikl]. See prec. Lat. stem *cortic-* & **-al.** Pertaining to, of the nature of, a cortex.

corticate(d), adj. [1. kórtikāt(ed) ; 2. kɔ́tikeit(id), fr. Lat. *corticātus*, 'covered with a bark'. See prec. & **-ate.** Provided with, resembling, a cortex.

corundum, n. [1. korúndum ; 2. kərándəm], fr. Tamil *kurand*, 'ruby'. (min.) Very hard mineral of same class as the ruby and sapphire ; used in grinding and polishing.

coruscate, vb. intrans. [1. kóruskāt ; 2. kórəskeit], fr. Lat. *coruscāt-(um)*, P.P. type of *coruscāre*, 'to thrust or push with the horns ; to vibrate, shake, wave ; to flash, gleam, glitter' ; cp. also adj. *coruscus*, 'vibrating, tremulous ; flashing, glittering'. Gk. *korúptō*, 'butt with the head', belongs to a different base (cp. Gk. *kórus*, 'helmet, head', q.v. under **cerebrum**), but has prob. influenced the meaning of Lat. vb. The genuine cognates are prob. O.N. *horskr*, O.S. & O.H.G. *horsc*, 'sudden, rapid', O.E. *horsć*, 'brisk'. To sparkle, flash, scintillate (lit., of stars, jewels, gems &c. ; fig., of wit &c.).

coruscation, n. [1. kòruskā́shun ; 2. kòrəskéiʃən], fr. Lat. *coruscātiōn-(em)*, 'a glittering, flash' (post-class.). See prec. & **-ion.** A sudden flash or gleam of light ; glitter, sparkle, of light, or of wit.

corvée, n. [1. korvā́ ; 2. kōvéi]. Fr., 'labour performed by a vassal for his lord, under the feudal system' ; hence, 'wearisome, uncongenial work', Low Lat. *corvada*, earlier *corrogāta (opera)*, P.P. of Lat. *corrogāre*, 'bring together by entreaty ; collect'. See **cor- & rogation. a** Unpaid, enforced, statutory labour performed by peasants on roads &c., as in France, till 1776 ; also formerly in Egypt ; **b** a hard, tedious, unwillingly performed duty.

corvette, n. [1. korvét ; 2. kōvét]. Fr., fr. Port. *corveta*, or Span. *corbeta*, fr. Lat. *corbita*, 'a slow-sailing ship of burden' ; fr. *corbis*, 'a basket', wh. is prob. borrowed fr. Celt., cp. M. Ir. *corb*, 'basket' ; orig. 'plaited wicker-work'. See **corf, crate & curve.** (naut.) A war vessel with flush deck and one tier of guns, ranking below a frigate.

corvine, adj. [1. kórvīn ; 2. kɔ́vain]. Lat. *corvīnus*, adj., fr. *corvus*, 'a raven', ultimately an imitative word, cp. the cognates Gk. *kórax*, 'raven', see **coracoid**, & further O.E. *hrōc*, O.H.G. *hruoh*, see **rook** ; & O.H.G. *hraban*, O.E. *hræfn*, see **raven.** Cp. also **corbie.** Of or pertaining to the raven or crow or to this family of birds.

Corybant, n. [1. kóribant ; 2. kóribænt]. Lat. *corybas*, fr. Gk. *korúbas.* (Gk. mythol.) (pl. *Corybantes*) One of the attendants of Cybele ; also one of the priests of Cybele, who engaged in wild orgies and dances.

Corybantian, adj., also **Corybantic, Corybantine** [1. kòribántian, -ik, -in ; 2. kòribæntiən, -ik, -ain]. Pertaining to the Corybantes or their rites ; hence, wild, frenzied.

Corydon, n. [1. kóridon ; 2. kóridən]. Lat. *Corydon*, fr. Gk. *Korudṓn*, name of a shepherd in the Idylls of Theocritus & Virgil's Eclogues. Traditional name for a shepherd in pastoral poetry ; hence, a young rustic swain.

corymb, n. [1. kórimb ; 2. kórimb], fr. Lat. *corymbus*, fr. Gk. *kórumbos*, 'a cluster (of fruit or flowers)'. Etymol. doubtful. (bot.) Type of inflorescence in clustered flowers in which the lower pedicels (stalks of each single flower) are much longer than the upper ones.

corymbose, adj. [1. kórimbōs ; 2. kórimbous]. Prec. & **-ose.** (bot.) Pertaining to or resembling a corymb.

coryphaeus, n. [1. kòrifḗus ; 2. kòrifíəs]. Lat. *coryphaeus*, fr. Gk. *koruphaîos*, 'leader, chief', fr. *koruphḗ*, 'head, top, summit', cp. Gk. *kórus*, 'head', cogn. w. Lat. *cerebrum*, 'brain', *cervus*, 'stag', & *cervix*, 'neck'. See **cerebrum, cervical, cervine.** The leader of the chorus in the Greek drama ; hence, now, the leader of a chorus.

coryphée, n. [1. kórifā ; 2. kórifei]. Fr. See prec. A leading dancer in a *corps de ballet.*

coryza, n. [1. korīza ; 2. kəráizə]. Lat. *coryza*, fr. Gk. *kóruza*, 'a cold in the head, catarrh', fr. *kórus*, 'helmet, head'. See **coryphaeus.** (med.) Cold in the head ; nasal catarrh.

cos (I.), n. [1. kos ; 2. kɔs], fr. Gk. *Kṓs*, Cos, one of the Ægean Islands, now Stanchio. Name of several kinds of lettuce said to have been introduced from Cos.

cos (II.), n. Abbreviation of **cosine.**

cosecant, n. [1. kōsékant ; 2. kousékənt]. **co- & secant.** (math.) Secant of complement of an angle. (Abbreviated to *cosec.*)

coseismal, coseismic, adj. & n. [1. kōsízmal, -ik ; 2. kousáizməl, -ik]. See **co- & seismal. 1.** adj. Indicating line or area along, or over, which earthquake shocks are experienced with equal intensity. **2.** n. Line or area where these conditions occur.

co-signatory, adj. & n. [1. kō sígnaturi ; 2. kou sígnətəri]. **co- & signatory. a** adj. Signing jointly with another or others ; **b** n., one who signs a document (treaty, agreement &c.) along with another or others.

cosily, adv. [1. kṓzili ; 2. kóuzili]. See **cosy & -ly.** In a cosy, snug, convenient, or comfortable manner or position.

cosiness, n. [1. kṓzines ; 2. kóuzinis]. See prec. & **-ness.** State or quality of being cosy, snug, and comfortable.

cosine, n. [1. kṓsīn ; 2. kóusain], fr. **co- & sine.** (trig.) Sine of the complement of an angle.

cosmetic, adj. & n. [1. kozmétik ; 2. kɔzmétik], fr. Gk. *kosmētikós*, 'well-arranged', fr. *kosméō*, 'I order, arrange, adorn', fr. *kósmos*, 'order ; an ornament, decoration'. See **cosmos. a** adj. Designed to beautify the complexion or hair ; **b** n., substance in form of a lotion, ointment, or powder applied to the skin or hair with the object of improving their appearance.

cosmic, adj. [1. kózmik; 2. kɔ́zmik], fr. Gk. *kosmikós*, 'connected with the world'. See **cosmos** & **-ic**. **a** Pertaining to the universe or cosmos as a whole; to its laws and order: *cosmic philosophy*, that concerned with the evolution of the universe; hence, **b** harmonious, orderly; opposed to *chaotic*; **c** conveying a sense of vastness; universal, grandiose.

cosmical, adj. [1. kózmikl; 2. kɔ́zmikl]. Prec. & **-al.** Cosmic.

cosmically, adv. Prec. & **-ly.** According to the laws of the universe.

cosmism, n. [1. kózmizm; 2. kɔ́zmizəm]. See **cosmos** & **-ism.** The theory and philosophy of the evolution of the universe.

cosmist, n. [1. kózmist; 2. kɔ́zmist]. See prec. & **-ist.** Student of cosmism.

cosmo-, pref. Form of Gk. *kósmos*, 'universe', used in composition. See **cosmos.**

cosmogonic(al), adj. [1. kòzmogónik(l); 2. kɔ̀zməgɔ́nik(l)]. **cosmogony** & **-ic** & **-al.** Pertaining to cosmogony.

cosmogonist, n. [1. kozmógunist; 2. kɔzmɔ́gənist]. Next word & **-ist.** Student of cosmogony.

cosmogony, n. [1. kozmóguni; 2. kɔzmɔ́gəni]. See **cosmo-** & **-gony.** **a** The origin of the universe, manner in which it came into existence; **b** a theory, or account, of this process.

cosmographer, n. [1. kozmógrəfer; 2. kɔzmɔ́grəfə]. See **cosmography** & **-er.** One concerned with cosmography.

cosmographic(al), adj. [1. kòzmográfik(l); 2. kɔ̀zməgrǽfik(l)]. **cosmography** & **-ic** & **-al.** Pertaining to cosmography.

cosmography, n. [1. kozmógrafi; 2. kɔzmɔ́grəfi]. See **cosmo-** & **-graphy.** **a** Description of the universe, or world as a whole, in all its parts; **b** science which treats of these and of the interrelations of each.

cosmological, adj. [1. kòzmolójikl; 2. kɔ̀zməlɔ́dʒikl]. **cosmology** & **-ic** & **-al.** Pertaining to cosmology.

cosmologist, n. [1. kozmólojist; 2. kɔzmɔ́lədʒist]. Next word & **-ist.** One concerned with, versed in, cosmology.

cosmology, n. [1. kozmóloji; 2. kɔzmɔ́lədʒi]. See **cosmo-** & **-logy.** Metaphysical speculation regarding the nature of the universe as an ordered whole, formed upon a definite plan.

cosmoplastic, adj. [1. kòzmoplástik; 2. kɔ̀zməplǽstik]. See **cosmo-** & **plastic.** Pertaining to the plastic, formative force which moulds the universe.

cosmopolitan, adj. & n. [1. kòzmopólitan; 2. kɔ̀zməpɔ́litən], fr. **cosmo-** & Gk. *polítēs*, 'citizen', fr. *pólis*, 'city'. See **political.** **1.** adj. **a** Common to all parts of the world; **b** at home all over the world; free from narrow provincial or national bias, prejudice, or other limitations. **2.** n. One who is at home everywhere; a citizen of the world.

cosmopolitanism, n. [1. kòzmopólitanizm; 2. kɔ̀zməpɔ́litənizəm]. Prec. & **-ism.** The condition, character, of a cosmopolitan.

cosmopolitanize, vb. trans. & intrans. [1. kòzmopólitaniz; 2. kɔ̀zməpɔ́litənaiz]. **cosmopolitan** & **-ize.** To make, or become, cosmopolitan.

cosmopolite, n. & adj. [1. kozmópolīt; 2. kɔzmɔ́pəlait], fr. Gk. *kosmopolítēs*. See **cosmopolitan.** Cosmopolitan.

cosmopolitism, n. [1. kòzmopólitizm; 2. kɔ̀zməpɔ́litizəm]. Prec. & **-ism.** Cosmopolitanism.

cosmopolitical, adj. [1. kòzmōpolítikl; 2. kɔ̀zmoupəlítikl], fr. **cosmo-** & **political.** Connected with universal politics.

cosmorama, n. [1. kòzmoráhma; 2. kɔ̀zmərámə], fr. **cosmo-** & Gk. *hórāma*, 'that which is seen, a view, spectacle', fr. *horáō*, 'I see'. Gk. *hor-* is fr. Aryan **wor-*, 'to see', & is cogn. w. O.E. *wær*, 'observant, cautious' &c. See **ware (II.)**, **wary** &c. An exhibition of views of different parts of the world seen by means of mirrors and lenses.

cosmoramic, adj. [1. kòzmorámik; 2. kɔ̀zmərǽmik]. Prec. & **-ic.** Pertaining to a cosmorama.

cosmos, n. [1. kózmos; 2. kɔ́zməs], fr. Gk. *kósmos*, 'good order, decency, set form, government', hence 'the world or universe' viewed as an ordered and orderly system. Cp. *kosméō*, 'I order, arrange; rule, govern; adorn, embellish' &c.; *kósmios*, 'well-ordered, regular', fr. base **kˆons-*, perh. cogn. w. Goth. *hansa*, O.E. *hōs*, 'company, band', orig. 'an ordered, well-arrayed band'; & perh. w. Lat. *censēre*, 'reckon, take into account, think'. See **censor, Hanse.** **1.** The world or universe as a perfect and well-ordered whole, as opposed to *chaos*. **2.** Hence, any harmonious and well-ordered system.

Cossack, n. [1. kósak; 2. kɔ́sæk]. Russ. *kosák*, of Central Asian origin, fr. *kazzâk*, 'adventurer, vagabond'; Turkish *qazzaq*, 'a predatory horseman, a free-booter'. Race of mixed Tartar and Slavonic origin, having a military organization and supplying cavalry to the Russian army under the Empire.

cosset, vb. trans. [1. kóset; 2. kɔ́sit]. Perh. fr. O.E. *cot-sǣta*, 'cottage-dweller'. See **cot (I.)** & **sit.** Used formerly as a n., applied to a pet lamb reared by hand & not by its dam. To fondle, pet, pamper.

cost (I.), vb. intrans. [1. kawst, kost; 2. kōst, kɔst], fr. O. Fr. *coster, couster*, fr. Lat. *constāre*, lit. 'to stand together; to stand at'; hence, 'to cost'; fr. **con-** & *stāre*, 'to stand', q.v. under **state (I.)** & **stand (I.).** **1. a** To cause or involve the expenditure of money, the payment of a certain price, in order to obtain possession or use of: *to cost five pounds, a lot of money, too much* &c.; **b** to involve expenditure of mental effort: *to cost much careful thought.* **2.** (of action or conduct) **a** To result in the loss of something: *to cost a man his life, fortune, peace of mind, health* &c.; **b** to result in some misfortune, injury, disadvantage: *to cost many sleepless nights, anxious moments* &c. **3.** (commerc.) To estimate cost of producing an article.

cost (II.), n., fr. prec. **1.** Price to be paid for a thing in order to purchase it; the price paid for a thing purchased. Phr. *cost price*, actual price of production, or that at which a commodity can be bought wholesale; opposed to *sale price.* **2.** (pl., law) Expenses of a law-suit. **3.** (fig.) Expenditure or sacrifice of time, labour, energy, money, health &c., in order to obtain or achieve something; hence, loss, detriment, suffering: *at great cost of life*; *at a heavy cost.* Phrs. *at all costs*, no matter what the cost may be; *to count the cost*, weigh all circumstances; *at the cost of*, at the expense of; *to one's cost*, to one's loss or detriment.

costal, adj. [1. kóstal; 2. kɔ́stəl], fr. L. Lat. *costālis*, fr. Lat. *costa*, 'a rib', & **-al**; cp. O. Fr. *coste*, Mod. Fr. *côte*; the only certain cogn. is O. Slav. *kosti*, 'bone', & various related forms in Slav. languages. Of or pertaining to the ribs or region of the body enclosed by or near them.

costard, n. [1. kústard; 2. kástəd]. Perh. connected w. O. Fr. *coste*, 'rib', see prec., in reference to the ridges on the surface. **1.** A large English variety of apple. **2.** (archaic and humorous) The head.

costate, adj. [1. kóstāt; 2. kɔ́steit], fr. Lat. *costātus*, 'having ribs', fr. *costa*, 'a rib', & **-ate.** See **costal.** Having ribs, ribbed, marked with rib-like ridges.

costean, vb. intrans. [1. kostḗn; 2. kɔstín], fr. Corn. *cothas stean*, 'dropped tin'. See **stannary.** (min.) To bore through soil down to underlying rock, to determine existence, or course, of a mineral deposit.

coster, n., short for **costermonger** [1. kóster-(mungger); 2. kɔ́stə(maŋgə)]. Orig. *costard-monger*, 'fruit-seller'. See **costard** & **monger.** One who sells fruit and vegetables &c., by hawking them in a barrow through the streets.

costive, adj. [1. kóstiv; 2. kɔ́stiv], fr. O. Fr. *costivé*, fr. Lat. *constipātus*, P.P. of *constīpāre*, 'to press closely together'. See **constipate.** **a** Constipated, having difficulty in evacuating the bowels; **b** (fig., of mental state) unable to express thoughts and feelings; barren, jejune; excessively reserved in manner.

costiveness, n. See prec. & **-ness.** State of being costive.

costliness, n. [1. káwstlines, kóstli-; 2. kɔ̄́stlinis, kɔ́stli-]. **costly** & **-ness.** The state or quality of being costly, dear in price.

costly, adj. [1. káwstli, kóstli; 2. kɔ̄́stli, kɔ́stli]. **cost (II.)** & **-ly.** **a** Of great cost, expensive, dear in price; hence **b** valuable, splendid, gorgeous.

costmary, n. [1. kóstmāri; 2. kɔ́stmɛ̀əri]. O.E. *cost*, fr. Lat. *costos*, Gk. *kóstos*, 'oriental aromatic plant', & *Mary* (the Virgin). Garden plant with star-shaped flowers, with aromatic leaves, used as a pot-herb, and formerly for flavouring ale.

costume (I.), n. [1. kóstūm; 2. kɔ́stjūm]. Orig. 'customary dress', fr. O. Fr., through Ital., fr. Lat. *consuētūdo, consuētūdinis*, 'custom'. See **custom.** **1. a** Style, fashion, or mode of dress peculiar to a people, nation, class, period &c.: *Highland costume*; *academic costume* &c. **b** clothes or garments generally, esp. such as are worn externally: *her costume was simple and expensive.* **2.** Dress worn by actors in a play representing the life of a former period of history: *a costume-piece*, a dramatic production in which the costumes are a reproduction of the dress of the period portrayed; *a costume ball*, a fancy-dress ball. **3.** Now used chiefly of women's dress, specif., a dress designed as a unity, e.g. coat and skirt of the same material.

costume (II.), vb. trans., fr. prec. To dress, provide with a costume.

costumier, n. [1. kostūmier; 2. kɔstjúmiə], fr. Fr. *costumier.* Prec. & **-ier.** Tradesman who makes, designs, and supplies costumes. Tradesman's word for dressmaker.

cosy, adj. & n. [1. kṓzi; 2. kóuzi]. Perh. fr. Norw. *koselig*, w. much the same meaning. **1.** adj. Comfortable, snug. **2.** n. Also *tea-cosy*, thickly lined covering put over a teapot to keep it hot.

cot (I.), n. [1. kot; 2. kɔt]. O.E. & M.E. *cot*, 'cottage, house, dwelling'. History and origin unknown. **a** A small shelter or hut; *sheep-cot* &c.; **b** (poet.) humble dwelling, cottage.

cot (II.), vb. trans., fr. prec. To put (sheep) in a cot.

cot (III.), n. [1. kot; 2. kɔt]. Hind. *khat*, 'light bed'. **1.** (Anglo-Ind.) A light bedstead. **2.** (naut.) Bed swung from the beams, for officers and sick persons. **3. a** A small bed for a child, larger than a cradle; **b** bed in children's hospital.

cot (IV.), n. Abbr. of cotangent.

cotangent, n. [1. kṓtánjent; 2. kóutǽndʒənt], fr. **co-** & **tangent.** (maths.) Tangent of complement of an angle.

cote, n. [1. kōt; 2. kout], fr. M.E. *cōte* &c., inflected form of **cot (I.).** A shelter, shed &c. for domestic animals or birds: as, *a dove-cote* &c.

co-temporary, adj. & n. [1. kṓ témporari; 2. kóu témpərəri]. Contemporary.

co-tenant, n. [1. kṓ ténant; 2. kóu ténənt]. See **co-** & **tenant.** A joint tenant.

coterie, n. [1. kóterē; 2. kóutərī]. Fr., 'association of villagers or country people', fr. *cotier*, 'cottar'. See **cot (I.).** **a** A circle, set, group of people associated by some common interest, sympathies, tastes &c.; **b** a social clique.

co-terminous, adj. [1. kṓ tḗrminus; 2. kóu tə́minəs]. Conterminous.

cothurnus, n. [1. kōthérnus; 2. kouþə́nəs]. Lat. *cothurnus*, fr. Gk. *kóthornos.* Etymol. unknown. The high boot or buskin worn by tragic actors on the Athenian stage and later on the Roman stage: hence (fig. and poet.) tragedy, or lofty style suitable for this.

co-tidal, adj. [1. kṓ tídal; 2. kóu táidl]. See **co-** & **tidal.** *Co-tidal line*, a line on a map showing the places along the coast at which the high-water mark is reached at one and the same time.

cotillion, n. [1. kotílyun; 2. kɔtíljən], fr. Fr. *cotillon*, 'a petticoat'; also a dance. **a** A lively dance, the chief interest in which is the method of choosing partners by men and women alternately, which is done by various ingenious devices; **b** the music for such a dance.

cotoneaster, n. [1. kotōniáster; 2. kɔtóuniǽstə], fr. Lat. *cotōnea*, 'quince'. (bot.) Genus of small trees or shrubs, allied to medlar and hawthorn, with pink flowers and clusters of bright yellow or red berries.

co-trustee, n. [1. kṓ trustḗ; 2. kóu trastí]. Joint trustee.

cotta, n. [1. kóta; 2. kɔ́tə]. L. Lat., 'tunic'. See **coat.** (eccles.) Short surplice, sleeveless or with short sleeves.

cottage, n. [1. kótij; 2. kɔ́tidž]. In M.E., fr. Med. Lat. *cottagium*. See **cot** (I.) & **-age. 1.** The small house of a villager or labourer. **2.** A small country or suburban house of superior kind; *cottage loaf*, a loaf of bread consisting of two round parts, the smaller on the top of the larger; *cottage piano*, a small upright piano; *cottage pie*, minced meat, covered with a layer of mashed potatoes and baked in a pie-dish.

cottager, n. [1. kótijer; 2. kɔ́tidžə]. **cottage** & **-er. a** A person who dwells in a cottage; **b** specif., one of the humbler, working-class, inhabitants of a village.

cottar, n. [1. kóter; 2. kɔ́tə], fr. Med. Lat. *cotārius*, fr. *cota*, fr. **cot** (I.). **1.** A cottager; specif., a Scotch peasant attached as permanent labourer on a farm and living in a cottage on the farm. **2.** One holding land by a peculiar tenure, a cottier, q.v.

cotter, n. [1. kóter; 2. kɔ́tə]. Origin unknown. Wedge, bolt &c. for securing parts of machinery: *cotter-pin*, pin to keep cotter in position.

cottier, n. [1. kótier; 2. kɔ́tiə]. **cot** (I.) & **-ier.** A cottager; specif., an Irish peasant holding a cottage under *cottier tenure*. *Cottier tenure*, that by which land, or a house, falls to the highest bidder of those competing for it.

cotton (I.), n. [1. kótn; 2. kɔ́tn], fr. Fr., fr. Span. *coton*, fr. Arab. *qutun*. **1. a** Plant of mallow family, genus *Gossypium*, grown in many parts of Asia, Africa, and America; **b** the soft, downy, seed hairs of this which are long and strong, and being used for a large number of purposes in the manufacture of textiles, are a most important article of commerce. **2. a** Yarn or thread made from these hairs; **b** specif., thread of this kind used for sewing: *a needle and cotton*, needle threaded with cotton, ready for sewing. **3.** Cloth of various kinds, woven from cotton thread.

cotton (II.), adj., fr. prec. Made of cotton.

cotton (III.), vb. intrans., fr. **cotton** (I.), lit. 'to adhere together like cotton'. **a** To take to, take a fancy to a person, feel in sympathy with, become friendly with him: *I don't cotton to him at all*, am not favourably impressed, don't like him; Phr. *to cotton up to*, become friends with &c.; **b** to be favourably impressed with a proposal, idea &c., to accept it as sound, be prepared to adopt it.

cotton-cake, n. Cake, used as cattle food, made from compressed cotton-seed, after extraction of the oil.

cotton-gin, n. Device for separating the seeds from the cotton hairs.

cotton-grass, n. A species of sedge, the fruit of which contains long, white, silky hairs, resembling those of cotton plant.

cottonocracy, n. [1. kòtn-ókrasi; 2. kɔ̀tn-ɔ́krəsi], fr. **cotton** (I.), on anal. of *aristocracy*. The leaders, the wealthy members, of the cotton industry in Lancashire.

Cottonopolis, n. [1. kòtn-ópolis; 2. kɔ̀tn-ɔ́pəlis]. Manchester, as centre of the cotton trade.

cotton-plant, n. Plant which bears cotton, genus *Gossypium*.

cotton-press, n. A machine for pressing cotton into bales.

cotton-seed, n. Seed of the cotton-plant, yielding oil and cotton-cake.

cotton-spinner, n. Manufacturer of cotton yarn.

cotton-tail, n. American rabbit, with a white, downy tail.

cotton waste, n. Remnants left from manufacture of cotton used for making inferior cloth.

cotton-wood, n. A species of poplar found in North America.

cotton-wool, n. Downy mass consisting of the hairs of the cotton-plant after cleansing and removal of seeds; used in packing fragile articles, and, when treated with antiseptics, for surgical dressings.

cottony, adj. [1. kótuni; 2. kɔ́təni]. **cotton** (I.) & **-y. a** Downy, having texture and appearance of cotton hairs, or cotton-wool; **b** (of woollen cloth) of inferior quality, resembling cotton rather than wool in texture and touch.

cotton yarn, n. Thread spun from cotton hairs, ready for weaving.

cotyledon, n. [1. kòtilḗdun; 2. kɔ̀tilídən]. Lat., fr. Gk. *kotulēdṓn*, 'a cup-like hollow, socket; navelwort', fr. *kotúlē*, 'a small cup'; cogn. w. Scrt. *čatvālaš*, 'cavity', Lat. *catillus*, dimin. of *catīnus*, 'deep vessel for cooking, pot, dish'; fr. the Lat., Gmc. **katil-*, Goth. *katils*, 'kettle', was borrowed, fr. wh. Gmc. type comes also O.E. *ċietel* &c. (see **kettle**); O. Slav. *kotulu*, 'cauldron', was borrowed fr. Gmc. sources. (bot.) **a** The first leaf or leaves found in a plant developing from seed; **b** (cap.) large genus of herbaceous plants, natives particularly of S. Africa, much cultivated as bedding plants on account of their bright flowers.

cotyledonous, adj. [1. kòtilḗdunus; 2. kɔ̀tilídənəs]. Prec. & **-ous.** Having cotyledons.

cotyloid, adj. [1. kótiloid; 2. kɔ́tiloid], fr. Gk. *kotúlē*, 'cup' (see **cotyledon**) & **-oid.** Cup-shaped; specif., of a deep joint-cavity, e.g. that of hip-bone.

couch (I.), n. [1. kouch; 2. kautʃ]. Fr., fr. vb. *coucher*, 'to lie, to lay'. See **couch** (II.). **1. a** An article of furniture on which a person may lie down to rest or sleep; a kind of sofa; **b** (chiefly poet. or liter.) a bed: *to retire to one's couch*; *a couch of pain, fever*, &c.; **c** any place of rest for man or beast, as a grassy bank; the lair of a wild animal &c. **2.** Various specific and technical uses: **a** (malting) mass or heap of grain, piled or spread out to germinate; **b** (painting) preliminary coat of colour or size &c.

couch (II.), vb. trans. & intrans., fr. Fr. *coucher*, O. Fr. *colchier*, 'to lie down'; cp. Ital. *colcare*, fr. Lat. *collocāre*, 'to place, station, arrange, dispose'. See **collocate. A.** trans. **1.** (pass.) To lay (oneself) down, only in P.P.: '*. . . where couched at ease, the white kine glimmer*' (Tennyson, 'In Memoriam'). **2.** To bring, put (a lance, spear) into the position suitable for attack. **3.** To put (a thought, request, refusal) into words, written or uttered: *a demand couched in arrogant style*; *to couch one's refusal in polite terms*. **4.** (surg.) To perform operation on cataract in the eye by pushing down the crystalline lens with a needle. **B.** intrans. **1.** To lie down, make one's bed or lair: '*Ere we own a usurper we'll couch with the fox*' (Scott). **2.** To crouch ready for springing; lie in hiding, lie in ambush.

couch (III.), n. Couch-grass, q.v.

couchant, adj. [1. kóuchant; 2. káutʃənt]. Fr. Pres. Part. of *coucher*. See **couch** (II.). (her.) Lying down with head up: *a lion couchant*.

couch-grass, n. Variant of **quitch.** Weed in form of coarse grass, with creeping roots.

cougar, n. [1. kōōgar; 2. kū́gə]. Fr. *couguar*, fr. native (Brazil.) *guaçu ara*. Large tawny quadruped, *Felis concolor*, of the cat tribe, resembling a jaguar, but smaller and without spots, found in parts of America; the *puma*.

cough (I.), vb. intrans. [1. kawf, kof; 2. kɔ̄f, kɔf]. M.E. *cohen* &c., O.E. *cohhetan*; cp. Mod. Germ. *keuchen*, M.H.G. *kūchen*, 'to pant'. Origin doubtful. To make a sudden noise caused by a spasm of the vocal chords, or by forcibly driving air through the vocal chords; to clear the throat or upper air-passage by this means. *Cough out*, trans., to eject, get rid of phlegm, or other foreign substance from throat by means of coughing. *Cough up*, trans., **a** to throw up phlegm &c. from air-passages by means of coughing; **b** (fig., vulg.) to blurt out something, utter some statement with a certain reluctance.

cough (II.), n., fr. prec. **a** (single action) A spasm of the vocal chords, caused by disease, or temporary irritation, accompanied by a sudden and violent expulsion of air from the lungs; also deliberate action of clearing throat by driving air forcibly through the vocal chords: *to give a slight cough*; **b** permanent or temporary affection of the lungs, or mucous membrane of throat, or oesophagus, which results in frequent fits of coughing: *to have a bad cough*. Phr. (colloq.) *churchyard cough*, very severe one.

cough-drop, n., also **cough-lozenge.** One with medicinal properties, taken to relieve a cough.

could, vb. [1. kood; 2. kud]. Past tense of **can,** O.E. *cūþe*, M.E. *coude*; the *l* was introduced into the spelling (& even into the pronunciation of 16th & early 17th cent.) through the anal. of *should* & *would*.

coulisse, n. [1. kōōlḗs; 2. kūlís]. Fr., 'passage' &c., fr. *couler*, 'flow, glide'. See **percolate.** Space at the back, and at the sides of the scenes on stage of a theatre.

couloir, n. [1. kōōlwar; 2. kū́lwā]. Fr., 'a strainer', fr. *couler*, 'flow', see prec. Mountain gully. (From supposed resemblance in shape to a strainer.)

coulomb, n. [1. kōōlóm; 2. kūlɔ́m], fr. name of the French scientist, C. A. de Coulomb (1736–1806). (elect.) Unit of quantity in electrical measurements, being the quantity transferred by one ampere in one second.

coulter, also **culter**, n. [1. kṓlter; 2. kóultə]. O.E. *culter*, fr. Lat. *culter*, 'a ploughshare, a knife', fr. Aryan base **kel-*, 'strike, cut' &c.; cp. Lat. *per-cellere*, 'beat down, upset, strike', also *clādes*, 'slaughter' &c., see **cataclasm** & words there referred to; perh. O.E. *holeġn*, **holly,** is fr. same base, meaning 'that which stabs, pricks'. Blade, fastened in front of the share of a plough, which makes vertical cut in the furrow slice.

coumarin, n. [1. kōōmarin; 2. kū́mərin]. Fr. *coumarine*, fr. native name in Guiana. A crystalline substance with vanilla flavour obtained from the seeds of the Tonka bean.

council, n. [1. kóunsl, kóunsil; 2. káunsl, káunsil]. O. Fr. *cuncile*, fr. Lat. *concilium*, 'a calling together, meeting, public assembly for political purposes'; cp. Lat. *conciliāre*, 'call together, bring together, unite, connect' (see **conciliate**), fr. **con-** & base seen in Lat. *calāre*, 'call out, convoke'. See **clamour, claim, clear, class.** Formerly confused w. **counsel,** fr. O. Fr. *cunseil*, wh. is quite unconnected. (gen. sense) A body of persons convoked by authority for deliberative or executive functions. Various specific uses, e.g.: **a** (eccles.) assembly of Bishops of the whole Church, formerly convoked by Pope and Emperor, to discuss and define the doctrine of the Christian Church: *General, Ecumenical, Council*; **b** body of persons elected to represent a diocese, or parish, and to discuss matters connected with the well-being of the Church; **c** (constitut. hist.) applied to important deliberative and consultative bodies variously constituted, and having different specific functions in different states: *Privy Council, Council of State* &c.; **d** (county and municipal) body of persons elected to carry on the business of a county, city, district &c.; **e** *council of war*, conference of generals in the field, called by commander-in-chief, generally in emergencies, to deliberate upon strategic and tactical problems; (also fig.) discussion of plan of action in ordinary life.

council-board, n. The table at which the president of a council sits; a council in session.

council-chamber, n. The room in which a council transmits its business.

councillor, n. [1. kóunselur, kóunsilur; 2. káunsələ, káunsilə]. Prec. & **-or.** A member of a council, esp. of a town or county council.

counsel (I.), n. [1. kóunsl; 2. káunsl]. O. Fr. *cunseil, counseil*, fr. Lat. *consilium*, 'deliberative assembly; deliberation, plan, design; advice, counsel; sagacity, wisdom'; cp. also derived vb. *consiliāri*, 'to take counsel, consult'. Opinions are divided as to the origin of the element *-sil-* in this word; Walde connects it w. the second element in **consul** & **consult** (Lat. *consulere, consultāre*), & further w. Gk. *heleîn*, 'to take'. Others connect w. the base *sal-*, as in Lat. *saltus*, 'a leap, bound', *saltāre*, 'to jump, dance' &c., see **salient.** Others again regard it as a variant of **considium*, fr. the base **sed-*, 'sit', q.v. under **sedentary.** This suggests that the meaning of *consilium* was, primarily, 'coming together, assembly', & only secondarily 'consultation' &c. of the persons assembled. See **council. 1. a** Consultation: *to take counsel with*, to consult; **b** advice, result of consultation: *to give good counsel.* Phrs. *to keep one's own counsel*, to keep one's plans to oneself; *counsel of perfection*, excellent advice which cannot be followed, good plan which cannot be carried out. **2.** (law) **a** A legal adviser, barrister, advocate; **b** (coll.) body of legal advisers, barristers who conduct and plead in a trial or lawsuit; *King's Counsel* (abbr. K.C.), a barrister officially appointed as Counsel to the Crown, who takes precedence of other barristers.

counsel (II.), vb. trans. Fr. *conseiller*, fr. Lat. *consiliāri*, 'to take counsel, to give counsel'. See prec. **a** To advise, give advice to (a person), recommend him to do something (absol. or followed by infin.); **b** to advise, recommend, urge, adoption of a certain line of action, attitude of mind &c.: *to counsel instant action, delay, prudence* &c.

counsellor, n. [1. kóunselur; 2. káunsələ]. Prec. & **-or.** Cp. Fr. *conseiller*, fr. Lat. *consiliārius*, 'a counsellor, adviser'. **a** An adviser; one habitually consulted regarding action, conduct, policy; **b** barrister, counsel. (An Irish and American usage.)

count (I.), vb. trans. & intrans. [1. kount; 2. kaunt], fr. O. Fr. *conter*, Mod. Fr. *compter*, 'to count, reckon', fr. Lat. *computāre*, 'to reckon'. See **compute. A.** trans. **1. a** To name the numerals in order up to and including a specified numeral: *to count twenty*; **b** to reckon, arrive at, the total number of objects or names before one by naming a numeral in connexion with each: *to count the number of words in a dictionary*; **c** to reckon up, calculate, arrive at, an amount: *to count one's money, receipts, losses*; **d** to check by counting, to find out whether the number of things is complete, take stock: *to count one's luggage on arrival*; *to count the plate and valuables.* **2.** To take into account, take account of, include in one's reckoning: *I have forty hens, counting this year's pullets*; *there are ten guests, not counting members of the family.* **3.** To consider, esteem, account: *to count oneself fortunate*; *to count one's life of no importance.* **B.** intrans. **1. a** To enumerate; repeat the numerals in order: *he can't even count properly*; **b** to carry out process of numbering articles: *I don't know how many I have, I didn't count*; **c** (mus.) to keep correct time by counting. **2.** To be included in a reckoning: *a soldier's pension is not allowed to count in fixing his wages.* **3.** To possess value, be of account, amount to something (lit. and fig.): *every little counts*; *he is a person who simply doesn't count.* **C.** Followed by a preposition or adverb. *Count for*, **a** to be reckoned as: *that ought to be counted for righteousness*; **b** to be worth, amount to: *mere cleverness without sound principles counts for very little. Count in*, to include in one's enumeration or estimate: *an income of £1000 counting in extra fees. Count on, upon*, to rely upon, expect confidently: *to count on a person for help*; *to count on inheriting a fortune. Count out*, **a** (Parliament) to declare a sitting adjourned on discovery by counting that a quorum of members is not present; **b** (boxing) declare a combatant beaten who fails to rise within a given number of seconds after being knocked down.

count (II.), n., fr. O. Fr. *conte*, fr. L. Lat. *computum.* See prec. & **compute. 1. a** Act or process of numbering or reckoning, as: *to take count of votes* &c.; **b** (archaic) sum total: *his count of years.* Phr. (boxing) *to take the count*, to be counted out, to fail to rise within ten seconds of being knocked down and so to lose the fight. **2.** Regard, notice, account: *to take no count of.* **3.** (law) Each particular charge in an indictment which states a ground for prosecution.

count (III.), n. Formerly often *county.* M.E. *counte*, fr. Fr. *comte*, fr. Lat. *comitem*, acc. of *comes*, lit. 'one who goes with another, a companion; one of the suite of a proconsul or propraetor', later 'one of the imperial court', Lat. **com-** & base *it-*, 'go', fr. *īre*, 'go'. See **iterate.** A title of nobility conferred in England on foreigners who hold, or allege that they hold, in their own countries the title of *comte, conte, graf* &c. The nearest English title is *earl. Count Palatine*; see **Palatine.**

countenance (I.), n. [1. kóuntenans; 2. káuntinəns]. Fr. *contenance*, 'demeanour', fr. Lat. *continentia*, 'a holding in, self-control', fr. *continēre*, 'to hold in'. See **contain.** *Countenance* is lit. 'the manner of holding, bearing, oneself'. **1. a** The face, including look or expression and cast of features; esp. sum total of these as expressing mental or moral qualities: *an expressive countenance*; Phrs. *to change (one's) countenance*, change expression from some emotion (anger, pity, dismay &c.); *to keep one's countenance*, maintain one's composure, esp., refrain from laughing; hence, **b** the mental or emotional state shown by expression of features: *to put a person out of countenance*, to disconcert him; *to lose countenance*, lose composure. (The word seems never to express the mere face and features of flesh alone apart from the moral attributes of which these are the index. One could not say, 'I struck him on the countenance'.) **2.** Favour, support, aid, encouragement: *to give, lend, countenance (to a person, scheme* &c.).

countenance (II.), vb. trans., fr. prec. **a** (of actions) To sanction, approve, permit without protest, tolerate; **b** (of persons) to lend support to, approve.

counter (I.), n. [1. kóunter; 2. káuntə]. Fr. *comptoir*, fr. *compter.* See **count** (I.). **a** Long slab or table of wood in a bank, behind which the bank officials sit, stand, and work, and over which they hand money, or receive it; **b** a similar structure in a shop, upon which articles for sale are exhibited, and from behind which the shop-assistants hand them to those who buy. Phr. *to serve behind the counter*, to be a shopkeeper or shop-assistant.

counter (II.), n., fr. **count** (I.) & **-er.** Small thin disk or square of ivory, mother-of-pearl, or metal, used for scoring, or as equivalent of money, in card and other games.

counter (III.), adv. & adj., fr. Fr. *contre*, fr. Lat. *contrā*, 'over against, facing, opposite to; in reply; against, contrary to'. See **contra-. a** adv. In the opposite direction, against; (now chiefly in moral sense) *counter to one's inclinations* &c; **b** adj., (on anal. of *counterchange* &c.) opposed to, opposite to.

counter (IV.), n., fr. prec. **a** Parry in fencing; **b** blow given while warding off one in boxing.

counter (V.), vb. trans. & intrans., fr. prec. **a** trans. To reply to an attack by some movement which is more than a mere parry; to make a counterstroke; specif. (boxing) to give a blow at the moment of parrying one; **b** intrans., to make the act of countering: *to counter with the right.*

counter (VI.), n. Line of derivation in each meaning difficult. See **counter (III.)** & **counter-**, pref. **1.** Part of a horse's breast between shoulders and lower part of neck. **2.** Arched, curved part of the stern of a ship. **3.** The piece of leather at the back or heel of a boot or shoe.

counter-, pref., fr. Fr. *contre-*, fr. Lat. *contrā*, wh. in compounds gen. expresses hostile opposition (see **contra-**). *Counter-* is a living pref., but may also represent Fr. *contre-* in old compounds. It expresses: action hostile to, or neutralizing another action, rivalry &c.; correspondence, e.g. *counterpart*; substitution, e.g. *counterfeit* &c.

counteract, vb. trans. [1. kòunterákt; 2. kàuntərǽkt]. See **counter-** & **act.** (of both material and moral action) To act in opposition, have contrary effect to, defeat, hinder, neutralize, mitigate: *to counteract effects of a drug* &c.; *counteract a person's influence.*

counteraction, n. [1. kòunterákshun; 2. kàuntərǽkʃən]. **counter-** & **action.** Action in opposition; hindrance.

counteractive, adj. & n. [1. kòunteráktiv; 2. kàuntərǽktiv]. **counter-** & **active. a** adj. Tending to counteract; **b** n., something which counteracts.

counter-agent, n. [1. kòunter ájent; 2. kàuntər éidʒənt]. **counter-** & **agent.** Agent or force that counteracts.

counter-approach, n. [1. kóunter apróch; 2. káuntər əpróutʃ]. **counter-** & **approach.** Advance defences to check besiegers of fortress &c.

counter-attraction, n. [1. kóunter atrákshun; 2. káuntər ətrǽkʃən]. An attraction which competes with, and diminishes the force of, another.

counterbalance, n. & vb. trans. [1. kòunterbálans; 2. kàuntəbǽləns]. See **counter-** & **balance. a** n. A weight that balances another; (fig.) any force or influence of equal strength with another; **b** vb., to weigh against with an equal weight; to oppose with equal power or effect; to compensate for.

counterblast, n. [1. kóunterblàhst; 2. káuntəblàst]. See **counter-** & **blast** (I.). A forcible denunciation of a person or thing, esp. with object of weakening influence.

counterchange, n. & vb. trans. [1. kóunterchànj; 2. káuntətʃèindʒ]. **counter-** & **change. 1.** n. Exchange, alternation (rare). **2.** vb. **a** To cause to change places; to interchange. **b** To chequer, diversify, esp. in heraldry.

counterchanged, adj. [1. kóunterchànjd; 2. káuntətʃèindʒd], fr. P.P. of prec. (her.) Having metal and colour reversed.

countercharge, n. & vb. trans. [1. kóunterchàrj; 2. káuntətʃàdʒ]. See **counter-** & **charge. 1.** n. **a** A retaliatory attack or onslaught; **b** an accusation in opposition to another, a charge against the accuser. **2.** vb. **a** To charge in opposition to a charge (of cavalry &c.); **b** to accuse in return, to make an accusation against an accuser: *he charges me with bribery, I countercharge him with slander.*

countercheck, n. [1. kóunterchèk; 2. káuntətʃèk]. See **counter-** & **check.** A restraining or opposing check; a check upon a check.

counter-claim, n. & vb. [1. kóunter klàm; 2. káuntə klèim]. **counter-** & **claim. 1.** n. (law) A claim made by the defendant in an action as an offset of claim made against him. **2.** vb. To bring a counter-claim, *for* (an amount), *against* (a person).

counter-clockwise, adv. [1. kóunter klókwiz; 2. káuntə klɔ́kwaiz]. In the opposite direction of clockwise.

counterfeit (I.), adj. & n. [1. kóunterfēt; 2. káuntəfit], fr. Fr. *contrefait*, P.P. of *contrefaire*, 'to counterfeit', fr. *contre* (Lat. *contrā*), 'against', & *faire* (Lat. *facere*), 'to do, make'. See **counter-** & **fact. 1.** adj. **a** Made in imitation of something else with intent to deceive by passing it off as genuine; esp. of coins, antiques, writings &c.; **b** assuming the appearance of, spurious, imitated, feigned (of persons, qualities &c.): *counterfeit virtue, grief* &c. **2.** n. **a** A thing made to resemble, or which resembles, something else; a forgery; **b** one who pretends to be what he is not; an impostor, cheat.

counterfeit (II.), vb. trans., fr. prec. **1. a** To imitate, reproduce by mimicry: *to counterfeit another's voice, manner* &c.; **b** (of persons) to simulate, make pretence of: *to counterfeit sorrow.* **2.** To make something in imitation of (something else) with intent to defraud; to forge: *to counterfeit coins, handwriting* &c.

counterfeiter, n. [1. kóunterfèter; 2. *káuntə*fìtə]. Prec. & **-er**. One who counterfeits, esp. coins, bank-notes &c.

counterfoil, n. [1. kóunterfoil; 2. *káuntəfɔil*]. See **counter-** & **foil**. That part of a bank cheque, postal order, receipt &c., containing a note of date, amount, name of payee, retained when the cheque &c. is detached.

counterfort, n. [1. kóunterfort; 2. *káuntəfɔ̄t*], fr. Fr. *contrefort.* See **counter-** & **fort**. A buttress supporting a wall, terrace &c.

counter-irritant, n. [1. kóunter íritant; 2. *káuntə íritənt*]. **counter-** & **irritant**. (med.) Substance applied to the skin to produce irritation and blistering in order to relieve inflammation elsewhere, and more deeply seated.

counter-irritation, n. [1. kóunter iritáshun; 2. *káuntə iritéiʃən*]. **counter-** & **irritation**. Effect of counter-irritant.

counter-jumper, n. [1. kóunter jùmper; 2. *káuntə džàmpə*]. **counter (I.)**, **b**, & **jump**. (colloq.) One who serves behind the counter of a shop; shop-assistant.

countermand, vb. trans. & n. [1. kòunter-máhnd; 2. *kàuntəmánd*]. See **counter-** & **mandate**. **1.** vb. To revoke, cancel, an order. **2.** n. Order revoking or cancelling a previous order.

countermarch, n. & vb. intrans. [1. kóunter-màrch; 2. *káuntəmàtʃ*]. **counter-** & **march**. (mil.) **1.** n. March of a body of troops, backwards, over ground over which it has advanced; retrogression. **2.** vb. To march backwards or in reverse order.

counter-mark, n. [1. kóunter màrk; 2. *káuntə màk*]. Fr. *contremarque.* See **counter-** & **mark (I.)**. **1.** Second mark placed on goods as extra proof of genuineness &c., or security against fraud. **2.** Specif., hall mark on plate, in addition to maker's mark.

countermine, n. & vb. trans. & intrans. [1. kóuntermìn; 2. *káuntəmàin*]. **counter-** & **mine (II.)**. **1.** n. **a** (mil.) A mine made to meet and destroy an enemy mine; **b** (nav.) a mine or torpedo sunk to explode the enemy's mines; **c** (fig.) plot to circumvent another plot. **2.** vb. To make, direct, a countermine (against enemy mine).

counter-paly, adj. [1. kóunter páli; 2. *káuntə péili*]. **counter-** & **paly (I.)** (her.) Paly, divided fesswise with tinctures alternating or countercharged.

counterpane, n. [1. kóunterpān, -pin; 2. *káuntəpein, -pin*]. O. Fr. *contrepoincte* for *cuilte-*, fr. Lat. *culcita*, 'bed, cushion, pillow, mattress', & *puncta*, 'pricked', meaning 'embroidered' (see **quilt** & **point**), but confused w. Fr. *contre-*, see **contra-**, & *pan*, 'cloth, skirt' (fr. Lat. *pannus*, 'piece of cloth', q.v. under **pane**), owing to counterpanes being often made in squares of different colours. Lat. *culcita* is cogn. w. Scrt. *kūrcáš*, 'bundle'; other cognates are doubtful. Outer covering for a bed, placed over the bedclothes.

counterpart, n. [1. kóunterpart; 2. *káuntəpāt*]. **counter-** & **part (I.)**. **1. a** Thing, exactly corresponding to another, esp. by possessing certain complementary qualities which supplement it; **b** the corresponding part of an indenture; a duplicate, copy of a document &c. **2.** Person exactly resembling another, or performing similar, or corresponding functions.

counter-passant, adj. [1. kóunter pásant; 2. *káuntə pǽsənt*], fr. Fr. *contre-passant.* **counter-** & **passant**. (her.) Going in different directions (of two animals on a shield).

counterplot, n. & vb. intrans. [1. kóunterplòt; 2. *káuntəplɔ̀t*]. See **counter-** & **plot**. **a** n. A plot to defeat another plot; **b** vb., to form a counterplot.

counterpoint, n. [1. kóunterpòint; 2. *káuntəpɔ̀int*], fr. O. Fr. *contrepoint.* **counter-** & **point (I.)**. (mus.) **a** (in mediaeval music) Addition of notes to a given melody, note against note; **b** (in modern music) free part-writing.

counterpoise (I.), n. [1. kóunterpòiz; 2. *káuntəpɔ̀iz*], fr. O. Fr. *contrepois.* See **counter-** & **poise**. **1. a** A weight that balances another; **b** (fig.) a counterbalancing force; power, influence, which largely neutralizes another; an equal force or power acting in opposition. **2.** State of equilibrium.

counterpoise (II.), vb. trans., fr. prec. To act as a counterpoise to (lit. and fig.).

counter-reformation, n. [1. kóunter rèformáshun; 2. *káuntə rèfəméiʃən*]. **counter-** & **reformation**. Movement directed against a reformation, which seeks to destroy it and its effect; specif., that of the Papacy, in answer to the Protestant Reformation.

counter-revolution, n. [1. kóunter rèvolúshun; 2. *káuntə rèvəljúʃən*]. **counter-** & **revolution**. Political movement directed against a revolution which has taken place, or against revolutionary tendencies.

counterscarp, n. [1. kóunterskàrp; 2. *káuntəskàp*]. Fr. *contrescarpe.* **counter-** & **scarp**. (fort.) The outer slope or wall of a ditch.

countersign, n. & vb. trans. [1. kóuntersìn; 2. *káuntəsàin*]. **counter-** & **sign (I.)**. **1. a** (mil.) A secret word or phrase given to a sentry, as means of identification, password; **b** (Freemasonry) secret sign given on receiving one from another mason. **2.** vb. To put signature to (a document already signed by someone else).

countersink, vb. trans. [1. kóuntersìngk; 2. *káuntəsìŋk*]. See **counter-** & **sink**. To sink the head of a screw, bolt &c., level with surface of wood by bevelling away outer edges of the hole in which the screw is fixed.

counter-tenor, n. [1. kóunter ténur; 2. *káuntə ténə*]. **counter-** & **tenor**. **a** A high tenor voice; **b** the part sung by such a voice, between treble and tenor.

countervail, vb. trans. & intrans. [1. kóunter-vàl; 2. *káuntəvèil*], fr. O. Fr. *contrevaloir*, fr. Lat. *contrāvalēre*, 'to be effective against'. See **counter-** & **valiant**. **1.** trans. To counterbalance. **2.** intrans. To have equal or compensating effect or power against, esp. *countervailing duties*, in a tariff.

counterweigh, vb. trans. [1. kóunterwā; 2. *káuntəwéi*]. **counter-** & **weigh**. To counterbalance.

counterweight, n. [1. kóunterwàt; 2. *káuntəwèit*]. **counter-** & **weight**. A weight equivalent to another; a counterbalance.

counterwork, n. [1. kóunterwĕrk; 2. *káuntəwàk*]. **counter-** & **work**. (fort.) Rampart, ditch &c., raised to oppose a similar work on part of the enemy.

countess, n. [1. kóuntes; 2. *káuntis*]. M.E., fr. O. Fr. *cuntesse.* See **count (III.)**. **a** (English title) Wife or widow of an earl; lady to whom an earldom has descended; **b** (foreign) wife, widow, or daughter of a count.

counting-house, n. [1. kóunting hòus; 2. *káuntiŋ hàus*], fr. **count (I.)** & **house**. Office in which the financial business of a mercantile firm, large shop &c., is transacted.

countless, adj. [1. kóuntles; 2. *káuntlis*]. **count (II.)** & **-less**. Too numerous to count, hence, very numerous.

countrified, adj. [1. kúntrifid; 2. kántrifaid]. As if fr. P.P. of a vb. *to countrify*, wh. is hardly used. **country** & **-fy** & **-ed**. Accustomed to the country, and imbued with the ways and habits, and outlook of one who lives in the country; opposed to *townified* or *suburban.*

country, n. [1. kúntri; 2. kántri]. M.E., fr. O. Fr. *cuntré*, fr. Low Lat. *contrāta*, 'land lying over against', fr. Lat. *contrā.* See **contra-**. **1. a** Land, territory, with definite boundaries, with distinctive name, occupied by a particular race, or nation; *the countries of Europe*; *the wine of the country*; **b** the population of such an area, the nation as a whole: *the country would never countenance a war of aggression.* Phr. *to go to the country*, hold a general election. **2.** Native land, country of one's birth: *Nelson's last words were, 'God and my country'*; *to fight for king and country.* **3. a** Tract, area, of land, esp. considered with reference to its physical and geographical features, type of soil, character of landscape &c.: *fine, undulating, wooded, country*; *good hunting country*; *unknown, unfamiliar, country* &c.; **b** (fig.) province of knowledge, range of ideas &c.: *this subject is quite unknown country to me.* **4.** Rural district, continuous area of land which is open, not built over; contrasted with *town* or *suburbs*: *to live in the country*; *to leave the country and move into the town*; *life in the country is utterly different from that of a town.*

country cousin, n. One unaccustomed to towns and town life, who is struck with wonder by all he sees in town, and feels bewildered by the novelty of his surroundings.

country-dance, n. Rural dance, generally one in which men and women stand in circles, in squares, or in rows facing one another.

country gentleman, n. Landed proprietor, squire, who lives on his estates; usually one given up to rural pursuits and business.

country-house, n. One in the country, surrounded by grounds, gardens, park &c.

countryman, n. [1. kúntriman; 2. kántrimən]. **a** A country dweller, esp. of humbler classes; **b** a compatriot.

country party, n. Political group representing agricultural, as against industrial interests.

country-seat, n. House and demesne, of some size; residence of landowner.

countryside, n. [1. kúntrisìd; 2. kántrisàid]. Rural district, neighbourhood.

countrywoman, n. [1. kúntriwòoman; 2. kántriwùmən]. **a** Woman living in the country, esp. of humbler classes; **b** a compatriot.

county (I.), n. [1. kóunti; 2. *káunti*], fr. O. Fr. *cunté*, fr. Lat. *comitātus*, 'an escort, retinue, the imperial retinue, court, a company'. Cp. *comitāri*, 'to accompany'. See **count (III.)**. **1. a** The domain of an earl or count; **b** an earl or count himself: cp. Scott's ballad '*County Guy*' (archaic). **2.** A territorial division of a State or kingdom for administrative purposes, a shire: *home counties*, the six counties nearest to London. *County Palatine.* See **palatine**. **3. a** The inhabitants of a county; **b** county families.

county (II.), adj., fr. prec. Of or pertaining to a county.

county borough, n. One of over 50,000 inhabitants, now ranking as an administrative county.

county council, n. Elected public body which administers county business.

county court, n. & vb. trans. **a** n. A local civil court, with jurisdiction usually limited to amounts not exceeding £100; mainly used for collection of debts; **b** vb., to sue (person) in a county court.

county family, n. One with inherited territorial possessions, and a residential seat in a county.

county town, n. The chief town in a county; one in which county business is transacted.

coup, n. [1. kōō; 2. kū]. Fr., 'a stroke, blow,' fr. Low Lat. *colpus*, fr. Lat. *colaphus*, fr. Gk. *kólaphos*, 'a blow with the fist, a box on the ear'; cp. Gk. *koláptein*, 'to hew, cut' &c.; prob. belong to the same group as Lat. *clāva*, 'club', see **claviform**; further related to Lat. *culpa*, 'fault, crime'. See **coppice** & **culpable**. A successful stroke of business, a lucky move: *to make, pull off, a great coup. Coup d'état,* (polit.) a sudden change in the political affairs of a country, effected by unconstitutional methods. *Coup de grâce,* finishing stroke (lit. and fig.). *Coup de main,* a surprise attack. *Coup d'œil,* a glance, a rapid general survey. *Coup de théâtre,* a theatrical hit; hence, any showy or sensational trick or surprise.

coupé, n. [1. kṓōpā; 2. kúpei]. Fr., P.P. of *couper,* 'to cut', used as a n. **1. a** A four-wheeled closed carriage for two, with a box outside for the coachman; **b** closed two-seater motor-car. **2.** A half-compartment at the end of a railway carriage with seats on one side only.

couple (I.), n. [1. kúpl; 2. kápl]. Fr., O. Fr. *cople,* fr. Lat. *cōpula,* 'a band, bond'. See **copula**. **1.** A short thong for holding two dogs together, esp. for hunting. Phr. (lit. and fig.) *to go, hunt, run, in couples.* **2. a** Two things or persons of the same class or kind: *a couple of pears; couple of parsons* &c.; specif. **b** two persons closely associated in interests and occupation, esp. when found together: *a couple of rogues, couple of players.* **3.** Specif. **a** a married pair: *a good old couple;* **b** an engaged pair; **c** a pair of partners in a dance.

couple (II.), vb. trans. & intrans., fr. Fr. *coupler,* O. Fr. *copler,* fr. Lat. *cōpulāre.* See prec. **A.** trans. **1.** (lit.) To join, link, fasten together; to connect (railway carriages &c.) together. **2. a** To unite or join (two persons in marriage); **b** to mate (two animals) together. **3. a** To associate things or ideas together in the mind or in speech: *to couple the name of Oxford with the idea of learning;* **b** to associate (the names of) two persons together in the mind, to attribute to them close relations or attachment: *it is not fair to couple his name with that of Miss Z.* **B.** intrans. **a** To come together, to unite, join; **b** (of animals) to perform the sexual act; **c** to marry.

coupled, adj. [1. kúpld; 2. kápld], fr. P.P. of prec. Joined together; in various senses: (of hounds) fastened together by a thong; (of persons) married &c.; specif. (archit.) *coupled columns,* those placed near together in groups of two.

coupler, n. [1. kúpler; 2. káplə]. **couple** (II.) & **-er**. **a** One who or that which couples; **b** mechanical device for connecting things.

couplet, n. [1. kúplet; 2. káplit]. Fr., dimin. of *couple.* See **couple** (I.). Two lines of verse of the same length, united by rhyme; *heroic couplet,* one of ten syllables to each line.

coupling, n. [1. kúpling; 2. kápliŋ]. **couple** (II.) & **-ing**. **1.** Act of joining together. **2. a** Contrivance for connecting parts of machinery; **b** specif., link(s) connecting two railway carriages.

coupon, n. [1. kṓōpon; 2. kúpɔ̃]. Fr., 'piece cut off', fr. *couper,* 'to cut'; see **coup**. Detachable portion of a sheet of paper or cardboard. Used in various specific senses, e.g.: **a** one detached from a bond, entitling holder to interest at proper time; **b** a ticket entitling holder to place in a theatre &c.; **c** part of a newspaper advertisement to be cut off and used as a form of entry for competition, application for free sample or specimen of goods advertised &c.

courage, n. [1. kúrij; 2. káridž]. M.E., fr. O. Fr., also in Mod. Fr. In M.E. the word means 'heart' as the seat of emotions & affections, as well as having present meaning. O. Fr. *cœur,* fr. Lat. *cor,* 'heart', see **cordate, cordial,** & **-age**. That quality of mind which enables one to face dangers, difficulties, threats, pain &c., without fear; bravery, boldness, intrepidity, pluck. Phrs. *to take, pluck up, muster up, lose, courage; courage of one's convictions;* (colloq.) *Dutch courage,* that produced by strong drink, therefore not genuine or lasting.

courageous, adj. [1. kurā́jus; 2. kəréidžəs], fr. O. Fr. *corageus.* Prec. & **-ous**. (of persons and actions) Possessing, showing, giving proof of courage, the reverse of cowardly; brave, plucky, fearless.

courageously, adv. Prec. & **-ly**. In a courageous manner.

courageousness, n. See prec. & **-ness**. Courage.

courier, n. [1. kṓōrier; 2. kúriə]. Fr.; M.E. *courour,* 'runner', O. Fr. *coreor,* Low Lat. *curritōrem,* fr. Lat. *currere,* 'to run', fr. **curs-*, cp. P.P. *cursum;* cogn. w. O.E. **hors* (fr. *hros*), O.H.G. *hros,* 'horse'. See **horse**. Base means 'to move swiftly'. **a** Person employed to arrange all the details of journey, esp. for those travelling abroad, who accompanies the traveller or party, and takes tickets and seats, looks after luggage, secures rooms in hotels &c.; **b** an express messenger; **c** name given to several newspapers.

course (I.), n. [1. kors; 2. kɔ̄s]. (i.) Fr. *cours,* fr. Lat. *cursus, -ūs,* 'a running, course, journey &c'; (ii.) Fr. *course* (fem. n.), fr. Lat. *cursus,* P.P. of *currere,* 'to run'. See prec. **1. a** The act or process of moving from one point to another; continuous moving onward, progress, onward trend: *the course of life;* **b** (of time) passage, duration: *in the course of a year.* Phr. *in due course,* at the proper, natural time or season. **2. a** The path that is traversed, channel, line, along which onward movement (esp. of water) takes place: *watercourse, course of a river; the stars in their courses;* **b** specially marked out and prepared ground for running competitions: *race-course;* or for certain games: *golf course* &c. **3.** Specif., line of movement followed in a journey or voyage, direction: *a ship's course; your proper course is from London to Dover, and so on.* **4.** Mode of action, conduct, behaviour. **5.** A connected series of acts or events, implying gradual progress in treatment, which together form a unity: *a course of lectures, of instruction;* continuous concentration of the mind for the purpose of learning: *course of study.* **6.** Each division of, kind of food, dish, served at a meal: *a dinner of five courses.* **7.** (fig.) **a** The natural process and path or line of development: *the course of a disease; the course of true love; the course of an argument;* **b** orderly or customary sequence of events, as *the course of nature;* Phrs. *in due course,* in the natural, legal, or proper order; *a matter of course,* the natural thing; *of course,* in the regular order, as was to be expected; naturally. **8.** (archit.) A continuous layer of stones or bricks on same level, along a surface of building. **9.** (naut.) **a** One of the sails that hang from the lowest yards of a ship; **b** a point of the compass.

course (II.), vb. trans. & intrans. **1.** trans. **a** To hunt, pursue closely; specif. **b** to follow game with hounds, esp. hares with greyhounds, by sight and not by scent; **c** (poet.) to traverse: '*The bounding steed courses the dusty plain*' (Pope). **2.** intrans. **a** To run swiftly, race: *the blood courses through the veins;* **b** to take part in coursing.

courser, n. [1. kórser; 2. kɔ̄sə]. Fr. *coursier,* fr. Low Lat. *cursārius.* See **course** (II.) & **courier**. (poet.) A swift, spirited horse, a war-horse; a horse generally.

coursing, n. [1. kórsing; 2. kɔ̄siŋ]. **course** (II.) & **-ing**. The sport of chasing game, esp. hares, with hounds that hunt by sight instead of by scent.

court (I.), n. [1. kort; 2. kɔ̄t]. M.E. *curt, court,* fr. O. Fr. *cort, court,* fr. Lat. *cort-em,* fr. *co-hort-em,* 'enclosure, yard, pen' &c., fr. **co-** & the base seen in Lat. *hortus,* 'garden'; Gk. *khórtos,* 'feeding-place'; cogn. w. Goth. *gards,* 'house', O.E. *geard,* 'fence, enclosure, dwelling' (see **yard** (II.)); also w. O.E. *gyrdel,* 'belt' (see **girdle**). See further under **cohort, hortus siccus**. **1. a** Unroofed space, partially or entirely enclosed by walls or buildings, and often paved; a courtyard; **b** paved yard enclosed by small houses, esp. one in poor part of a town. **2.** A large mansion, stately and important dwelling, originally one with a large entrance court-yard. **3. a** Space roofed, enclosed, and marked for tennis or racquets; **b** one partially enclosed with walls for the game of fives; **c** lawn, measured and marked out for lawn tennis; **d** one of the subdivisions in this. **4. a** Household of a sovereign; **b** sovereign and his family, the officials and other persons who compose his household; **c** state gathering of the sovereign, great officers of State, the notables, and others who come to pay their respects to the sovereign: *to hold a court; go to, be presented at, court.* **5. a** Place, building, hall, where justice is officially administered, or where inquests and inquiries are held by judges, civil, military, or ecclesiastical, or by magistrates, coroners &c.: *law court; police court* &c.; **b** assembly of judges, magistrates &c., or a single one of such persons, sitting in discharge of their or his judicial functions: *decision of the court; contempt of court.* Phr. (fig.) *to put oneself out of court,* to behave or speak in such a way that one is not considered entitled to a hearing. **6.** Assiduous attention, deferential homage, ingratiating courtesy bestowed upon **a** a person of either sex with a view to enlisting his or her favour and interest; **b** specif., by a man upon a woman in order to engage her affections: *to pay (one's) court to.*

court (II.), vb. trans., fr. prec. **1. a** (of persons) To pay court to, to treat with particular respect and deference in order to secure favour and esteem; **b** specif. (of a man) to woo, seek to win affections of (a woman); **c** to try to gain (esteem, regard &c.), seek by deference or flattery: *to court a person's approbation;* **d** (fig.) to take the best way to get, to behave, act, in such a way that one will probably meet, be overtaken by (gen. of something unfavourable): *to court a rebuff; to court disaster, defeat* &c.

court-baron, n. (legal hist.) A manorial court, having jurisdiction over the tenants, esp. the copyholders.

court-card, n. Formerly *coat-card.* The king, queen, or knave of any suit in playing cards.

court-dress, n. Dress worn at a court of the sovereign.

courteous, adj. [1. kórtius, kértius; 2. kɔ̄tjəs, kɔ̄tiəs, kə́tiəs]. M.E. *cortais, corteis, cortois,* or, w. change of suff., *corteous,* fr. O. Fr. *curteis, corteis,* Mod. Fr. *courtois.* **court** (I.) & **-ous**. (lit.) Having the bearing and manners of a king's court; hence, **a** (of persons) having manners at once dignified, urbane, and considerate; polite, with deference and good breeding; **b** (of manners, speech &c.) evincing, expressing, these qualities.

courteously, adv. Prec. & **-ly**. In a courteous manner.

courteousness, n. See prec. & **-ness**. Exhibition of courteous behaviour.

courtesan, -zan, n. [1. kòrtezán; 2. kɔ̄tizǽn], fr. Fr. *courtisane,* fr. Ital. *cortigiana* or Span. *cortesana.* See **court** (I.). Woman who sells her favours.

courtesy, n. [1. kórtisi, kértisi; 2. kɔ̄tisi, kə́tisi], fr. M.E. *cortaisie, corteisie, courtesie,* fr. O. Fr. *curteisie, cortoisie,* Mod. Fr. *courtoisie.* **courteous** & **-y**. **1.** The politeness which springs from good breeding and kindness of heart, courteous behaviour or disposition. **2.** Favour, indulgence, acquiescence, as distinct from strict legal right: *by the courtesy of. Courtesy title,* one assumed, according to custom, by a person and conceded to him by use and wont, to which he has no strict legal right, e.g. second and lower title of father, by eldest sons of dukes, marquises, and earls; *honourable,* by all children of viscounts and barons, and so on.

court-guide, n. Directory, originally containing the names of those who had been presented at court, now of the more wealthy classes of a town or district, or of those living in the better parts of these.

court-hand, n. Special form of handwriting, used in legal documents, official records &c.

courtier, n. [1. kórtier; 2. kɔ̄tiə]. **court (I.) & -ier.** **a** One habitually associated personally with a sovereign or other royal personages, who is accustomed to the ways and manners of courts; **b** one having the ingratiating and deferential manners supposed to be characteristic of courtiers.

court-leet. See **leet.**

courtliness, n. [1. kórtlines; 2. kɔ̄tlinis]. **courtly & -ness.** The quality of being courtly; dignity and urbanity of manner and bearing.

courtly, adj. [1. kórtli; 2. kɔ̄tli]. **court (I.) & -ly.** **a** (of persons) Dignified, stately, in manner and bearing; **b** (of manners) exhibiting a polished dignity.

court-martial, n. & vb. trans. **court (I.) & martial.** **1.** n. Trial of a sailor or soldier of any rank, conducted by naval or military authorities, for offences against naval or military law. **2.** vb. To try by court-martial.

court-plaster, n. **court (I.) & plaster.** So called from being formerly used by court ladies to make patches for the face. Kind of protective sticking-plaster applied to cuts &c.

courtship, n. [1. kórtship: 2. kɔ̄tʃip]. **court (I.) & -ship.** **a** Process of wooing or courting a woman with a view to matrimony; **b** period during which the process lasts.

courtyard, n. [1. kórtyard, kortyárd; 2. kɔ̄tjād, kɔ̄tjắd]. **court (I.) & yard.** Large paved space forming approach to a castle or large mansion, having an entrance gate, and enclosed partly by the building itself, partly by other walls built for the purpose.

cous-cous, n. [1. kōōs kōōs; 2. kūs kūs]. Arab. *kuskus.* A North African dish of meat and steamed flour, esp. semolina, seasoned with herbs.

cousin, n. [1. kúzn; 2. kázn]. Fr., fr. Lat. *consōbrīnus*, 'the child of a mother's sister, a cousin by the mother's side; a cousin' (in any degree); **con-** & *sōbrīnus*, 'a cousin by the mother's side'. This word is fr. earlier **swesrīnos*, fr. **swesor-*, 'sister', wh. normally becomes *soror* in Lat., & adj. suff. *-ino-*. Cp. exactly similar formation in O. Slav. *sestrinŭ*, 'pertaining to a sister', wh. goes back to **swesrin-*. See further under **sister.** **1. a** The child of an uncle or aunt: *first cousin, cousin german*; *second cousin*, the child of a parent's first cousin; *first cousin once removed*, the child of a first cousin; **b** a more or less remote kinsman, or kinswoman, by blood or marriage. Phr. *to call cousin with*, recognize kinship with. **2.** Title used by a sovereign in writing to, or naming in a formal document, another sovereign, or a peer of his own country.

cousinhood, n. [1. kúznhood; 2. káznhud]. **cousin & -hood.** Cousinship.

cousinly, adj. [1. kúznli; 2. káznli]. **cousin & -ly.** Like or pertaining to that of a cousin: *cousinly affection.*

cousinship, n. [1. kúznship; 2. káznʃip]. **cousin & -ship.** The relation of cousins.

couvade, n. [1. kōōváhd; 2. kūvắd]. Fr., 'a brood'. See **covey.** Custom practised by some primitive peoples, whereby, when the wife is lying in, the husband also lies up and feigns delicate health.

cove (I.), n. [1. kōv; 2. kouv]. O.E. *cofa*, 'a chamber', M.E. *cōue*, 'den'; cp. O.N. *kofi*, 'shed', & O.H.G. *koben*, 'cabin, pigsty'. Origin of these uncertain. **1.** A small sheltered bay; a sheltered recess in cliffs by the seashore. **2.** (archit.) A concave moulding, arch, esp. of ceiling or inner roof.

cove (II.), vb. trans., fr. prec. (archit.) To arch over, build in a concave form; to slope inwards.

cove (III.), n., fr. Gipsy *kova*, 'thing, creature'; orig. a remote demons. (slang) Applied familiarly to a male person of any age, equivalent to *fellow, chap*: *a rum cove*, queer fellow.

coved, adj. [1. kōvd; 2. kouvd], fr. P.P. of **cove (II.).** (archit.) Provided with, in form of, a cove: *a coved roof, ceiling.*

coven, n. [1. kúven; 2. kávən]. O. Fr. *covent*, 'assembly', lit. 'a coming together'. See next word. An assembly or gathering of witches, esp. to celebrate a Sabbath.

covenant (I.), n. [1. kúvenant; 2. kávinənt], fr. O. Fr. *covenant*, fr. *covenir*, Mod. Fr. *convenir*, 'to agree', fr. Lat. *convenīre.* See **convene, convenient.** **1.** A solemn and binding undertaking to do something or get something done. Various specific uses: **2.** (law) A contract sealed and delivered containing a definite undertaking; a particular clause in a contract in which an undertaking is given. **3.** (Bib.) The promise of God to the Jews: *land of the covenant*, Canaan. **4.** (hist.) *The Solemn League and Covenant*, an agreement signed in 1643 between the Scots and the English Parliament, for the preservation of Presbyterianism.

covenant (II.), vb. intrans. & trans., fr. prec. **a** intrans. To make a covenant; **b** trans., to grant or promise by covenant.

covenanted, adj. [1. kúvenanted; 2. kávinəntid], fr. P.P. of prec. **a** Bound by; **b** secured by, a covenant.

Covenanter, n. [1. kúvenanter; 2. kávinəntə]. **covenant (II.) & -er.** Adherent of the Solemn League and Covenant.

Coventry, n. [1. kóventri, kúventri; 2. kɔ́vəntri, kávəntri]. A town in Warwickshire; origin of Phr. unknown. *To send to Coventry*, to refuse to speak to, or hold social intercourse with; to ostracize.

cover (I.), vb. trans. [1. kúver; 2. kávə]. M.E. *coueren, keueren, kiueren*, fr. O. Fr. *covrir, cuvrir*, Mod. Fr. *couvrir*, fr. Lat. *cooperīre*, 'to cover wholly, overwhelm', fr. **co-** & *operīre* for **ob-verīre* 'to cover, cover over'. This word is an old compound fr. *ob* (see **ob-**), 'against, over', & base **wer-*, 'to shut, cover over, protect' &c. See **aperient.** This base occurs in Lat. *vestibulum*, 'enclosed space' &c. (see **vestibule**), & in the Scrt. compounds *apa-vṛnōti*, 'he uncovers, opens', & *api-vṛnōti*, 'covers, shuts'; further, in O. Slav. *vrěti*, 'to shut', Goth. *warjan*, 'to ward off, forbid', O.H.G. *werjan*, O.E. *werian*, 'guard, protect', & O.E. *wēr*, 'a weir, dam'; see **weir.** **A. 1. a** To place, draw, stretch, one substance or thing over, or in front of, another: *to cover a wall with paper, the seat of a chair with leather* &c.; **b** to superimpose one thing upon another so that it exactly corresponds with it in extent: *as much as will cover a sixpence*; **c** to spread, extend over, lie upon: *floods, snow, covered the ground.* **2. a** To place something over or in front of another so as to afford protection: *to cover a rick of hay with a rick-sheet*; *to cover one's head*; (fig.) *to cover the retreat of an army*; Phrs. *pray be covered*, put your hat on; *to remain covered*, to keep one's hat on; **b** to protect from a blow or injury by standing, or placing oneself in front of another: *he covered his wife from the assassin's blows with his own body.* **3. a** To conceal by covering: *to cover one's face with one's hands*; *cover one's bare shoulders with a shawl*; Phr. *to cover one's tracks*, (lit.) to conceal one's footprints; (fig.) conceal one's actions, whereabouts &c.; **b** (fig., of non-material things) to dissemble, hide, pass off: *to cover one's shame, confusion, annoyance* &c. **4.** To protect financially, be sufficient to meet one's liabilities: *to cover one's expenses*; be security for: *to cover an overdraft*; to protect by insurance: *my policy covers me against loss from fire*; *my loss is covered by insurance.* **5. a** To traverse in space, go a certain distance, travel: *to cover a distance, so many miles*; **b** (fig.) to include in one's treatment of a subject, take in, deal with, pass in review: *his studies covered a wide field*; *this book covers the subject adequately.* **6.** To sprinkle thickly, coat, splash, bedaub: *you are covered with dust*; *a passing motor covered me with mud.* **7.** (usually in pass.) *To be covered with*; **a** to abound in, have a great number or amount of: *trees covered with fruit*; *a face covered with freckles, pimples* &c.; (fig.) *covered with blushes*; **b** to have as a natural coat or marking: *young chicks are covered with down*; *cats are covered with fur*; *the breast of a thrush is covered with speckles*; **c** to swarm with, be infested with: *covered with flies, blackbeetles* &c.; **d** (fig., of non-material things) to overwhelm, overcome: *covered with shame, confusion* &c. **8.** (reflex.) *To cover oneself with*, to be involved in, to acquire, bring upon oneself; *to cover oneself with glory, with ignominy* &c. **9.** (of remarks, instructions, clauses, provisions &c.) To be adequate to, allow, provide for, take cognizance of: *the rules are supposed to cover all cases*; *the circumstances are covered by this clause.* **10.** To point a firearm at, keep under the range of a firearm: *to cover with a revolver* &c. **11.** (of stallions) *To cover a mare*, copulate with. **12.** (of a sitting hen) *To cover eggs*, to sit upon in such a way as to hatch. **B.** Followed by an adverb. *Cover in* (a hole in ground &c.), to fill in with earth. *Cover over*, to overspread so as to cover completely: *to cover over a hole in the roof.* *Cover up*, to cover thoroughly, wrap up.

cover (II.), n., fr. prec. **1.** Anything specially made or adapted **a** to envelop, or act as a covering or casing for something: *cover for a chair*; **b** something made to fit on to the top of a vessel and close it; a lid: *a cover for saucepan, kettle* &c.; **c** something made to fit over another thing to preserve it from dust, a case &c., or to keep contents of a vessel hot: *a glass cover* (e.g. for a stuffed bird); *a cover for a book, in paper covers*; *a metal cover* (for a dish or plate). Phrs. *under the same cover*, of several letters &c. placed and sent in same envelope; *from cover to cover* (of books), from first to last page. **2.** Place laid for a person at a meal, including knives, forks, spoons, napkin, glasses. **3.** Anything which protects and hides, **a** (troops) wood, hollows in the ground, rocks &c.; **b** (game, foxes &c.) woodland, plantations, gorse bushes &c.; **c** anything which obscures vision: *under cover of darkness, night, clouds of smoke.* **4.** (fig.) Pretence, disguise: *under cover of friendship.* **5.** (commerc.) Sum of money deposited as guarantee or security for possible loss through fall in prices. **6.** (cricket) Cover-point.

covered-way, n. [1. kúverd wā́; 2. kávəd wéi]. **a** Roofed passage in the open, corridor, with sides open to the air; **b** (fort.) protected corridor or way below the top of the counterscarp.

covering, n. [1. kúvering; 2. kávəriŋ]. **cover (I.) & -ing.** Anything which covers or protects: *trees provided a leafy covering* &c.; sheath, case: *membranous covering of the lungs.*

covering letter, n. One sent along with another document, often in less formal terms than this, which it accompanies by way of introduction or explanation.

covering party, n. (mil.) Detachment of soldiers sent to protect others while at work digging trenches, wiring &c.

coverlet, n. [1. kúverlet; 2. kávəlit]. M.E. *couerlyte*, fr. A.-Fr.; cp. Mod. Fr. *couvrelit*, fr. *couvrir*, see **cover (I.)**, & *lit*, fr. Lat. *lectus*, 'bed'. For the base **lek-* &c., see **lie (I.), lay (I.), lair.** The outermost covering of a bed; a counterpane.

coverlid, n. Variant of prec.

cover-point, n. (cricket) **a** Position behind point; **b** fielder occupying this position.

covert (I.), n., gen. pronounced [1. kúver; 2. kávə], but sometimes w. final *-t.* In M.E. fr. O. Fr., the P.P. of *covrir*; means 'covered place'. See **cover (I.) & (II.).** **1.** A shelter, esp. a wood, thicket &c., which shelters game, foxes &c. Phrs. *to draw a cover(t)*, search cover(t) for game or a fox; *break. cover(t)* (of game &c.), to come out from a covert. **2.** Feather of bird: *wing-, tail-covert.*

covert (II.), adj. See prec. Always pronounced w. final *-t*. **1.** (only fig., of non-material things) Veiled, partly hidden, but implied, disguised; (reverse of *overt*): *a covert threat, sneer, glance.* **2.** (law) In phr. *feme covert*, a married woman; lit. one covered or protected by her husband.

covert-coat, n. **covert** (I.) & **coat.** Light overcoat.

covertly, adv. [1. kúvertli; 2. kávətli]. See **covert** (II.) & **-ly.** In a shy, cautious, surreptitious manner.

coverture, n. [1. kúverchur; 2. kávətʃə]. O. Fr. **a** Covering, shelter (obs.); **b** (law) The status of a married woman. See **covert** (II.), **2.**

covet, vb. trans. [1. kúvet; 2. kávit]. M.E. *coueiten*, A.-Fr. *coueiter*, Mod. Fr. *convoiter* (w. *n*, as though fr. *con-*), fr. Low Lat. *cupidāre*, formed fr. Lat. *cupidus*, 'eager, desirous', fr. *cupere*, 'to desire'. See **Cupid.** To hanker after, desire ardently, wish to possess; esp. to desire unlawfully something which is unattainable, or another person's property.

covetable, adj. [1. kúvetabl; 2. kávitəbl]. Prec. & **-able.** That may be coveted or desired.

covetous, adj. [1. kúvetus; 2. kávitəs]. **covet** & **-ous.** **a** Having a tendency to covet, the habit of coveting; **b** filled with desire for something (in innocent and bad sense); **c** anxious to have more than one is entitled to; avaricious, greedy, grasping.

covetously, adv. Prec. & **-ly.** In a covetous manner.

covetousness, n. See prec. & **-ness.** The state, or habit, of being covetous.

covey, n. [1. kúvi; 2. kávi], fr. O. Fr. *covée*, Mod. Fr. *couvée*, 'a brood', fr. O. Fr. *cover*, Fr. *couver*, 'to sit or brood on, to hatch', fr. Lat. *cubāre*, 'to lie down'. See **concubine, cubicle.** **a** Brood of young partridges; **b** (facet.) family of children, set of persons.

covin, n. [1. kúvin; 2. kávin]. M.E. *covin(e)*, 'a trick, a sleight', fr. A.-Fr. & O. Fr. *covin*, *covine*, fr. Med. Lat. *convenium*, 'convention, agreement'. See **convene, convenient, convention, covenant.** (law) Unlawful collusive agreement, conspiracy between two or more persons to the prejudice of another.

coving, n. [1. kōving; 2. kóuviŋ], fr. **cove** (I.) & **-ing.** (archit.) **a** A cove or series of coves; arched roof of a building; **b** curved sides of a fireplace.

cow (I.), n. [1. kou; 2. kau]. O.E. *cū*, M.E. *cow*; O.H.G. *kuo*, Mod. Germ. *kuh*, O.N. *kýr*; cogn. w. Scrt. *gāuš*, 'ox', Gk. *boûs*, Lat. *bōs*, 'ox' (see **bovine**), all fr. Aryan **gʷōu-*. The Lat. form is Umbrian; the true Lat. wd. be **vōs*. Cp. O. Slav. *govędo*, 'ox'; O. Ir. *bō*, 'cow'. **1. a** The female of any animal of the ox tribe; specif. **b** familiar domestic female of this kind, usually kept for its milk. **2.** Female of various other animals the male of which is called the *bull*, e.g. the moose, elephant, rhinoceros, whale, seal, walrus &c.

cow (II.), vb. trans. Scand., cp. O.N. *kuga*, 'to tyrannize over'. To take the spirit out of, to subdue, frighten, by threats or violence.

coward, n. & adj. [1. kóuard; 2. káuəd], fr. O. Fr. *couard, coard, coart*, fr. *coe, coue*, 'tail' & **-ard**; cp. Ital. *codardo*, fr. *coda*, 'tail', fr. Lat. *cauda*. Prob. orig. one who turns tail, or shows his tail. See **caudal.** **1.** n. One who lacks courage; a craven, poltroon. **2.** adj. **a** Destitute of courage, faint-hearted, pusillanimous; **b** (her.) of a lion borne on a shield with his tail between his legs.

cowardice, n. [1. kóuardis; 2. káuədis]. O. Fr. *couardise*. Prec. & **-ice.** Lack of courage, faint-heartedness, pusillanimity.

cowardliness, n. [1. kóuardlines; 2. káuədlinis]. Next word & **-ness.** Cowardice.

cowardly, adj. & (rarely) adv. [1. kóuardli; 2. káuədli]. **coward** & **-ly.** **1.** adj. **a** (of persons or animals) Lacking courage; **b** (of words, actions &c.) befitting a coward, proceeding from fear of danger &c., mean; **a** *cowardly lie; cowardly conduct.* **2.** adv. Like a coward.

cowbane, n. [1. kóubān; 2. káubein]. See **cow** (I.) & **bane.** Water hemlock.

cowboy, n. [1. kóuboi; 2. káubɔi]. One in charge of cows; specif. (U.S.A., Canada &c.) a cattle herder, a mounted employee of a ranchman in charge of grazing cattle.

cow-catcher, n. [1. kóu kàcher; 2. káu kæ̀tʃə]. (U.S.A.) A strong frame fixed in front of a railway engine for picking up, or removing obstructions from the line.

cower, vb. intrans. [1. kóuer; 2. káuə]. M.E. *coueren*, in present sense. fr. O.N. *kūra*, 'to doze, lie quiet'. **a** To crouch, sit huddled up, esp. as from cold, misery, or fear; **b** (fig.) to shrink tremblingly, and fearfully, from another's anger, threats, blows &c.

cow-heel, n. Dish consisting of the foot of a cow or ox, stewed down with onions and other seasoning.

cowherd, n. [1. kóuhērd; 2. káuhəːd]. One who tends or herds cows at pasture.

cow-hide, n. Leather made of the hide of a cow; also, a whip made of this.

cow-house, n. Shed or stable in which cows are kept when not out at grass.

cowish, adj. [1. kóuish; 2. káuiʃ]. **cow** (I.) & **-ish.** Like a cow, heavy, slow, and clumsy in movement.

cowl (I.), n. [1. koul; 2. kaul], fr. O.E. *cugele, cūle*, 'hood', loan-word fr. Lat. *cucullus*, 'hood', the origin of wh. is doubtful. **1.** Hood fixed to long outer garment worn by monks, which can be drawn over the head. **2.** Device of metal, shaped like a cowl, fixed on the top of a chimney-pot, to increase draught, and prevent smoke coming back into the house.

cowl (II.), n. M.E., fr. O. Fr. *cuvel*, dimin. of *cuve*, 'tub', fr. Lat. *cūpella*, dimin. of *cūpa*, 'a tub, cask, vat'. See **cup, cupel, cupola.** (archaic and rare) A large tub for carrying water, esp. one borne on a pole between two persons.

cowlike, adj. [1. kóulīk; 2. káulaik]. **cow** (I.) & **-like.** Resembling a cow, esp. in being fat, and having large, mild eyes.

cowl-staff, n. M.E. *cuuel-staf*. **cowl** (II.) & **staff.** (archaic and rare) Pole on which a cowl for water is carried.

cow parsley, n. Wild chervil.

cow parsnip, n. Wild parsnip.

cow-pox, n. Disease consisting of small pustules on cows' udders, the matter from which, when applied to a scratch on a human being, gives him a mild form of the disease, and renders him immune from small-pox; the medical term is *Vaccinia*.

cow-puncher, n. [1. kóu pùncher; 2. káu pàntʃə]. (colloq.) Man who herds cattle, esp. at docks when they are landed from a ship.

cowrie, cowry, n. [1. kóuri; 2. káuəri]. Hind. *kaurī*. Small shell used instead of a coin in Western Africa and in parts of Southern Asia.

cowshed, n. [1. kóushed; 2. káuʃed]. Cow-house.

cowslip, n. [1. kóuslip; 2. káuslip], fr. O.E. *cū-slyppe*, 'cow-dung', fr. *cū*, 'cow' & *slyppe*, 'slime', fr. **slupj-*; cp. **slop** (I.). Common plant of primrose family, *Primula veris*, bearing sweet-smelling yellow flowers in clusters, and growing freely in English meadows and pastures in early summer.

cox, n. & vb. trans. [1. koks; 2. kɔks]. For **coxswain.** **a** n. Person who steers a racing boat; **b** vb., to act as cox, steer racing boat.

coxa, n. [1. kóksa; 2. kɔ́ksə]. Lat., 'hip'; cogn. w. Scrt. *kákša*, 'armpit', O.H.G. *hahsa*, 'bend of the knee'; see **cuisse.** Hip-joint, specif., first segment of the leg of an insect.

coxal, adj. [1. kóksal; 2. kɔ́ksəl]. Prec. & **-al.** Of, pertaining to, the coxa.

coxcomb, n. [1. kókskōm; 2. kɔ́kskoum]. For *cock's comb*. See **cock** (I.) & **comb** (I.). **1.** Red cap of a professional jester, with notched ridge like the comb of a cock. **2.** A foppish, conceited, swaggering fellow.

coxcombical, adj. [1. kòkskṓmikl; 2. kɔ̀kskóumikl]. Prec. & **-ic** & **-al.** Resembling, characteristic of, a coxcomb; conceited, foppish.

coxcombry, n. [1. kókskōmri; 2. kɔ́kskoumri]. **coxcomb** & **-ry.** **a** The behaviour of a coxcomb; conceit, affectation; **b** specific example of this; foppishness.

coxswain, n. [1. kókswān, kóksn; 2. kɔ́kswein, kɔ́ksn], fr. earlier *cockswain*, fr. *cock* (see **cockboat**) & **swain.** Cp. **boatswain.** **a** Sailor in charge of a ship's boat and crew, who generally steers; **b** one who steers a racing boat, usually abbreviated **cox.**

coxy, adj. [1. kóksi; 2. kɔ́ksi]. Variant of **cocky.** (schoolboy's word) Cheeky, giving oneself airs of importance unjustified by one's position and achievements; conceited.

coy, adj. [1. koi; 2. kɔi], fr. O. Fr. *coi, coy, coit*, fr. Lat. *quiētus*, **quiet.** Shy, modest, retiring, demure; affecting to repel advances.

coyly, adv. Prec. & **-ly.** In a coy manner.

coyness, n. See prec. & **-ness.** The quality of being coy; shyness, modesty, reserve of manner.

coyote, n. [1. koiyṓti, kóiyōt; 2. kɔióuti, kɔ́iout]. Mex. *koyotl*. North American prairie-wolf, *Canis latrans*.

coypu, n. [1. kóipōō; 2. kɔ́ipū]. Native name. South American water rodent, *Myocastor*, with valuable fur, known as *nutria*.

coz, n. [1. kuz; 2. kaz]. Abbreviation of **cousin.** (archaic and obs.)

cozen, vb. trans. & intrans. [1. kúzn; 2. kázn]. Cp. Fr. *cousiner*, 'to claim relationship for advantage'. See **cousin.** (archaic) **a** trans. To come the cousin, pretend to be a relative, in order to get something out of a person; hence, to cheat, defraud, deceive; to beguile, hoodwink (a person); **b** intrans. To act deceitfully, to cheat.

crab (I.), n. [1. krab; 2. kræb]. O.E. *crabba*, M.E. *crabbe*; w. cognates in most Gmc. tongues, O.N. *krabbi*, Swed. *krabba*; Mod. Germ. *krabbe*; related to O.H.G. *krebiz*, Mod. Germ. *krebs*, 'a crab'. See **crayfish.** **1. a** Popular name for short-tailed crustacean of which there are many varieties. The common crab is flat and rounded in shape, reddish-brown in colour, with powerful pincer-like claws; Phr. *to catch a crab*, to thrust one's oar so deeply into the water in rowing that one cannot get it out in time for the next stroke; **b** species of body louse. **2.** (astron.) *The crab*, Cancer, one of the signs of the zodiac. See **cancer.** **3.** One of various machines with claws for seizing and hoisting heavy weights. **4.** (pl., rare or obs.) Lowest throw at dice. **5.** (colloq.) Disadvantage, drawback.

crab (II.), vb. trans., fr. prec. Cp. Fris. & Du. *krabben*, 'to scratch, claw, behave like a crab'. **a** To speak ill of, find fault with, pick holes in, disparage (a person or thing); **b** to carp at, object to, try to thwart (an action).

crab (III.), n. In M.E. Perh. connected w. prec., referring to the sourness and griping qualities of the fruit. There is, however, an Engl. dial. word *scrab*, & Swed. dial. *skrabba*, 'crab apple'. **a** A small, sour, wild apple; **b** the tree producing this fruit.

crab-apple, n. **crab** (III.) & **apple.** Fruit of the crab.

crabbed, adj. [1. krábid; 2. kræ̀bid], fr. P.P. of **crab** (II.), or **crab** (III.) & **-ed.** **a** (of persons, speech, expression &c.) Cross-grained, harsh, bitter, disagreeable; **b** (of handwriting, style &c.) cramped, awkward, stiff; difficult to read.

crabbedly, adv. Prec. & **-ly.** In a crabbed manner.

crabbedness, n. See prec. & **-ness.** Quality of being crabbed.

crablike, adj. [1. kráblīk; 2. kræ̀blaik]. **crab** (I.) & **-like.** Like a crab; esp. *crab-like motion, gait* &c., devious, circuitous, zigzag.

crab-louse, n. See **crab** (I.) & **louse.** Species of body louse.

crab-pot, n. Wicker basket, buoyed and anchored in the sea, for catching crabs.

crab's eye, n. Calcareous mass found in stomach of crayfish, used medicinally.

crack (I.), vb. trans. & intrans. [1. krak; 2. kræk]. O.E. *cracian*, 'to resound', M.E. *cracken* &c. Imitative, connected w. **creak**, **croak**. **A.** trans. **1.** To cause a narrow aperture, fissure, split, esp. in a brittle substance such as glass, china &c., not sufficient to cause complete separation of parts. **2. a** To break by a sudden sharp blow: *to crack a skull, an egg-shell*; **b** to fracture by continuous pressure: *to crack a nut.* Fig. uses: *to crack a joke*, make a joke, exchange pleasantries with another; *crack a bottle* (of wine), to open it and drink the contents; (slang) *to crack a crib* to break into a house, to commit burglary; *to crack up* (a person or thing), praise highly. **3.** To cause to make a loud report, esp. *to crack a whip.* **4.** To treat (crude petroleum) to a process of destructive distillation increasing its illuminating and other powers. **B.** intrans. **1. a** To break or split suddenly; **b** (of brittle substances, glass, ice &c.; of plaster when drying) to open into fissures, spring apart, leaving narrow aperture. **2.** To make a sudden sharp, explosive noise (of a rifle or whip). **3.** (of the voice) **a** To break suddenly, become dissonant; **b** (specif., of male voices) to begin to undergo the change which occurs at puberty. **4.** *Crack up* (colloq.) To show signs of wear, old age, decay (of persons, health &c.).

crack (II.), n., fr. prec. **1. a** A split, chink, fissure, narrow opening or cleavage: *crack in the ground, in wood* &c.; **b** slight split, partial separation of parts, a flaw in a brittle substance, caused by a blow &c., sometimes accompanied by a thin line along the course of injury on the surface, sometimes without visible signs of breakage: *a crack in a basin.* **2.** A sharp, shrill, sudden noise, report: *the crack of a whip, of a rifle.* Phr. *crack of doom*, sound which will arise from the final destruction of earthly things; hence the end of the world, day of judgement. **3.** Sudden, sharp blow: *a crack on the head.*

crack (III.), adj., fr. prec. Of the highest quality, possessing superior skill or great reputation, first-rate: *a crack polo player*; *a crack regiment.*

crack-brained, adj. **a** (of persons) Mad, crazy; foolish, weak-minded; **b** (of conduct, plans &c.) ill-judged, ill-considered, senseless.

cracked, adj. [1. krakt; 2. krækt]. **crack** (I.) & **-ed. 1.** (of material objects) Having a crack or cracks, split, broken, having a flaw, e.g. of a bell, and the sound resulting from such a defect. **2.** (of the voice) Broken, harsh. **3.** (colloq., of persons) Rather mad, slightly deranged mentally, foolish.

cracker, n. [1. kráker; 2. krǽkə]. **crack** (I.) & **-er. 1. a** A small firework which explodes with a sharp crack or a series of cracks, when lighted and thrown down; **b** one enclosed in bright-coloured paper which explodes with a loud but harmless noise when the ends are pulled. **2.** (introduced from U.S.A.) A thin, crisp crackly biscuit. **3.** (pl.) *Crackers*, or nut-crackers, q.v.

crackjaw, adj. [1. krákjaw; 2. krǽkdžō]. (colloq., of words) Difficult or awkward to pronounce.

crackle (I.), vb. intrans. [1. krákl; 2. krǽkl]. Freq. of **crack** (I.) & **-le.** To give forth a series of slight, rapid cracking sounds, to sputter, as a fire in frosty weather, or as light, inflammable substance when thrown on a fire; also used of distant rifle-fire &c.

crackle (II.), n., fr. prec. **a** Rapid succession of sharp, slight cracking sounds; **b** surface, as of porcelain or glass-ware, with appearance of a network of small cracks.

crackling, n. [1. krákling; 2. krǽkliŋ]. **1.** Same as **crackle** (II.): '*the crackling of thorns under a pot*'. **2.** The crisp, browned outer skin and underlying layer of fat of roast pork.

cracknel, n. [1. kráknel; 2. krǽknəl]. In 15th cent. Engl., meaning the crust of bread. Perh. a distortion of Fr. *craquelin*, connected w. *craquer* & **crack.** A kind of thick, puffy, dry, crumbly biscuit.

cracksman, n. [1. kráksman; 2. krǽksmən]. **crack** (I.) & **man.** A burglar. See *to crack a crib* under **crack** (I.).

-cracy, suff. [1. krasi; 2. krəsi]. Fr. *-cracie*, fr. Gk. *-kratia*, fr. *krátos*, 'strength, might, power, rule'; cp. *kratein*, 'to be strong, rule over, subdue'. The base *krat-* is cogn. w. Goth. *hardus*, O.E. *heard*, 'hard, brave'. See **hard.** Suffix indicating rule, government, as *aristocracy, democracy, plutocracy* &c.

cradle (I.), n. [1. krā́dl; 2. kréidl]. O.E. *cradol*, M.E. *crādel.* The word is peculiarly Engl. in its form & meaning. It is, however, allied to O.H.G. *kratto*, 'basket', Mod. Germ. *kratte.* The origin of this Gmc. base is uncertain; some authorities consider it as a loan fr. Lat. *crātis*, 'wicker-work, hurdle'. See **crate** & **cart. 1. a** An infant's bed, made with high sides and sometimes mounted on rockers; Phr. *the cradle of the deep*, the sea, from its motion; (fig.) **b** time when one occupied a cradle, hence, infancy; Phr. *from, in, the cradle*, during, from, infancy or early childhood; **c** the place in which anything comes into existence, where its earliest developments are fostered; place of origin: *it was long disputed whether the cradle of Aryan speech was Europe or Asia.* **2.** Applied to various objects supposed to resemble a cradle in shape, motion, or usage: e.g. **a** (naut.) a framework of timbers or iron for supporting a ship during construction or repairs; **b** a kind of basket, attached to a line, used for bringing people ashore from a wrecked ship; **c** (med.) a frame to keep the bedclothes from pressing upon a wounded limb; **d** (min.) device for washing earth from gold by rocking.

cradle (II.), vb. trans., fr. prec. **1.** (chiefly poet.) **a** To place or rock (a child) to sleep in a cradle; **b** (fig.) to rear, train, from or during infancy; **c** to lull to rest as in a cradle: *to cradle a child in one's arms.* **2.** (min.) To wash (auriferous earth) in a cradle. See **cradle** (I.), **2 d.**

craft, n. [1. krahft; 2. krāft]. O.E. *cræft*, 'skill, cunning; strength, power; trade, profession', O.S. & O.H.G. *kraft*, 'power' &c. Connexions outside Gmc. are uncertain. **1.** The old sense of skill, or power in general, is obsolete; the meaning is now specialized in two directions; **a** cunning, deceit, guile; mental ability maliciously or dishonestly used: '*the craft and subtlety of the devil or man*'; **b** special skill or dexterity as displayed in some particular art, or manual work: *a fine specimen of the builder's craft.* Hence, **2. a** a trade or employment demanding highly trained manual dexterity, but not necessarily aesthetic perception, and thus distinguished from an *art* on one hand, and from unskilled labour on the other: *to learn the craft of a wood-carver*; **b** the members, collectively, of a skilled trade, esp. when organized as a guild or brotherhood; specif. **c** *the craft*, the body of Freemasons. **3.** A boat or vessel of any kind. *Craft* is used collectively without pl. suff.: *the harbour was full of all manner of craft.*

-craft, fr. prec. Suffix denoting skill, art, occupation, e.g. *statecraft, witchcraft, priestcraft, handicraft* &c.

craftily, adv. [1. kráhftili; 2. krā́ftili]. **crafty** & **-ly.** In a crafty manner; deceitfully, cunningly.

craftiness, n. [1. kráhftines; 2. krā́ftinis]. **crafty** & **-ness.** The quality of being crafty.

craftsman, n. [1. kráhftsman; 2. krā́ftsmən]. **a** One who exercises a skilled trade or craft; **b** a highly skilled manual worker; (by extension) **c** an artist.

craftsmanship, n. [1. kráhftsmanship; 2. krā́ftsmənʃip]. Prec. & **-ship.** Skilled manual work; often used specifically to denote work of high excellence and artistry.

craftsmaster, n. [1. kráhftsmáhster; 2. krā́ftsmāstə]. A highly skilled craftsman.

crafty, adj. [1. kráhfti; 2. krā́fti]. O.E. *cræftig*, 'skilled, powerful'. See **craft** & **-y.** Skilled in deception, subtly cunning and deceitful.

crag, n. [1. krag; 2. kræg]. In M.E.; of Celt. origin; cp. W. *craig*, 'rock', Ir. *carraig*, 'cliff, rock'. **a** Large, rough mass of rock, esp. one broken off from main body of cliff, and projecting; **b** specif. (geol.) bed, or deposit, of sand mixed with shells.

cragginess, n. [1. krágines; 2. krǽginis]. Next word & **-ness.** The state of being craggy.

craggy, adj. [1. krági; 2. krǽgi]. **crag** & **-y.** Abounding in crags.

cragsman, n. [1. krágzman; 2. krǽgzmən]. Expert climber of crags.

crake, n. & vb. intrans. [1. krāk; 2. kreik]. Imitative word, cp. M.E. *crāken*, 'to shriek'. **1.** n. **a** A small short-billed bird of the rail family which utters a harsh cry; the corn-crake; **b** the cry of this bird. **2.** vb. To utter this cry.

cram (I.), vb. trans. & intrans. [1. kram; 2. kræm]. O.E. *crammian*, 'to cram, stuff'; cp. also strong vb. *crimman*, 'to cram, insert', O.N. *kremia*, 'to press, squeeze'. These are all fr. the Aryan base **grem-*, 'press, grip' &c., wh. is believed to appear also in Lat. *gremium*, 'bosom' (see **gremial**), orig. that part of the body to wh. objects are pressed when seized by the arms so as to lift them. **A.** trans. **1. a** To squeeze, force, stuff, pack, objects tightly into a confined space: *to cram clothes into a bag* &c.; **b** to pack (food) into one's mouth, to eat to excess; **c** (fig.) to crowd (facts, or items of information) into the mind of another, esp. with a view to enabling him to pass an examination: *to cram a pupil for the army entrance exam.*; **d** often *cram up*, to learn a subject, or certain facts concerning it, by an intensive and hasty act of memory, esp. for a particular occasion, and without any intention of really mastering it by serious study; to get up facts superficially: *to cram (up) history for an exam.* **2.** Specif., to feed (poultry) by stuffing large quantities of food down their throats in order to fatten them for the table. **B.** intrans. **1.** To eat greedily and to excess; **b** (fig.) to fill the mind hastily with badly assimilated facts, esp. as in attempting to prepare for an examination. **2.** (fig. and slang) To make an untrue statement, tell a lie; chiefly in such Phrs. as *you are cramming.*

cram (II.), n., fr. prec. (fig. and slang) An untrue statement, a falsehood, a lie: *to tell a cram.* Cp. the Phrs. *to stuff up*; *to swallow anything.*

crambo, n. [1. krámbō; 2. krǽmbou]. Supposed to be derived fr. Lat. *crambē*, 'cabbage', in Phr. *crambē repetīta*, 'warmed up cabbage, an old story'. The word is ultimately fr. Gk. *krámbē.* This is connected w. Gk. *krámbos*, 'dry, parched, shrivelled', & meant orig. 'the wrinkled vegetable'. These words are cogn. w. O.H.G. *hrimfan*, 'to contract, wrinkle' &c., & O.E. *hrympel*, 'wrinkle'. See **rumple.** A parlour game in which the players attempt to find rhymes for a word proposed by one of them. *Dumb crambo*, game in which some of the players attempt to guess a word which the others select and illustrate by dumb show.

crammer, n. [1. krámer; 2. krǽmə]. **cram** (I.) & **-er.** One who crams; specif., a coach or tutor who prepares or crams candidates for examinations.

cramoisy, adj. & n. [1. krámezē; 2. krǽməzī]. Fr. *cramoisi.* See **crimson.** (archaic) Crimson; cloth of crimson.

cramp (I.), n. [1. kramp; 2. kræmp]. M.E. *crampe*, 'a spasm', fr. L. Germ. source, cp. O.S. *kramp* & O.H.G. *krampf*, 'bend, crooked thing', Mod. Germ., 'spasm, convulsion'; connected w. O.H.G. *krump*, 'crooked', Mod. Germ. *krumm.* Cp. **crimp** & **crumple.** Ultimately related to **curve** &c. Sudden, convulsive, muscular contraction, accompanied with great pain. Specif. **a** a form which attacks swimmers from exposure to cold; **b** *writer's cramp*, partial paralysis of the finger muscles, due to constant use.

cramp (II.), n. Same as prec. in origin; re-borrowed fr. Du. Kind of rivet, consisting of an iron bar with points turned up, let into masonry to increase its stability by binding it firmly together.

cramp (III.), vb. trans., fr. prec. (I. & II.). **1.** To affect with cramp. **2.** To fasten together with a cramp. **3.** (fig.) To restrict action; to cripple, confine, hamper, physical or mental activity.

cramped, adj. [1. krampt; 2. kræmpt], fr. P.P. of prec. **a** (of space) Restricted, limited; **b** (fig., of mental powers) lacking breadth, confined, contracted, narrow; **c** (of handwriting) badly shaped, ill-formed, difficult to read.

cramp-fish, n. The electric ray or torpedo fish.

cramp-iron, n. An iron cramp, used in masonry.

crampon, n. [1. krámpon; 2. krǽmpɔ̃]. Fr., connected w. **cramp** (I.). **a** A grappling-iron; **b** (pl.) iron spikes worn on shoes for climbing over ice.

cran, n. [1. kran; 2. kræn]. Origin unknown. Provincial word; measure for herrings, 37½ gallons.

cranage, n. [1. krānij; 2. kréinidž]. **crane** (I.) & **-age**. **a** Use of a crane; **b** price of hire of a crane.

cranberry, n. [1. kránberi; 2. krǽnbəri]. First element is **crane**; cp. Mod. Germ. *kranich-beere*. Small red acid berry growing on a low bush.

crane (I.), n. [1. krān; 2. krein]. O.E. *cran*, cp. O. Du. *kran*, O.H.G. *chran-ich*; cogn. w. Gk. *géranos* (cp. **geranium**), O. Slav. *žer-avi*; cp. Lat. *grūs*, 'crane', genit. *grū-is*; also Lat. *garrulus*, 'talkative, chattering', & *garrīre*, 'to chatter' (see **garrulous**). **1.** A tall, slender wading bird, *Grus communis*, with long legs, neck, and bill. **2.** (so named from fancied resemblance to the bird) A machine for raising heavy weights.

crane (II.), vb. trans. & intrans., fr. prec. **1.** To stretch out the neck to its full length (like a crane): *to crane the neck*. **2.** To raise weight by means of a crane.

crane-fly, n. The daddy-long-legs.

crane's bill, n. Species of wild geranium.

cranial, adj. [1. krānial; 2. kréiniəl]. **cranium** & **-al**. Of, or pertaining to, the cranium.

craniological, adj. [1. krāniolójikl; 2. krèiniəlɔ́džikl]. See **craniology** & **-ic** & **-al**. Connected with craniology.

craniologist, n. [1. krāniólojist; 2. krèiniɔ́lədžist]. See next word & **-ist**. Student of, authority on, craniology.

craniology, n. [1. krānióloji; 2. krèiniɔ́lədži]. See **cranium** & **-logy**. The science which deals with the shape, size, proportions, and other characteristics of (human) skulls, esp. as an indication of race.

craniometer, n. [1. krāniómeter; 2. krèiniɔ́mitə]. See **cranium** & **-meter**. Instrument for measuring skulls.

craniometry, n. [1. krāniómetri; 2. krèiniɔ́mitri]. Prec. & **-y**. The science of the measurement of skulls.

cranium, n., pl. **crania** [1. krānium, -ia; 2. kréiniəm, -iə]. Med. Lat., fr. Gk. *krānion*, 'the skull', connected w. Gk. *kárā*, 'the head, top, summit of anything'. The word is further connected w. Gk. *kéras*, 'horn', & Lat. *cerebrum*, 'brain' (see **cerebrum**), & w. O.H.G. *hirni*, 'brain', Mod. Germ. *hirn*. See further under **cervine, cervical**. That part of the animal bony skeleton which contains the brains; the skull.

crank (I.), n. [1. krangk; 2. kræŋk]. M.E. *cranke*, connected w. O.E. vb., *crincan* (also *cringan*), 'to bend, double up, sink down' (esp. in battle). The Pret. is *cranc*. See **crinkle** & **cringe**. Ultimate meaning is 'twist, turn'. **1.** Part of a machine projecting at right angles to a shaft, whereby motion is imparted to a wheel or disk. **2.** (fig.) Turn, twist; **a** (of wit or speech) a quaint conceit: '*Quips and cranks and wanton wiles*' (Milton); **b** a twist or kink in the mind, an eccentricity of thought, opinions, habits, behaviour; a fad; **c** a person having an odd eccentric mind or behaviour; a faddist.

crank (II.), adj., fr. prec. (of a building) Tottery, shaky, unsteady; (also fig., of persons) in poor health, frail.

crank (III.), vb. trans., fr. **crank** (I.). **a** To bend; **b** to fasten with a crank; to cause to move by means of a crank; (often with *up*) *to crank up an engine*.

crankily, adv. [1. krángkili; 2. krǽŋkili]. **cranky** & **-ly**. In a cranky manner.

crankiness, n. [1. krángkines; 2. krǽŋkinis]. Next word & **-ness**. Condition of being cranky (in any sense).

cranky, adj. [1. krángki; 2. krǽŋki]. **crank** (I.) & **-y**. **1.** (of machinery, buildings &c.) Out of order, out of gear; shaky, unsteady. **2.** (colloq., of persons) **a** In poor health, shaky; **b** cantankerous, cross; **c** eccentric, crazy, full of whims and fads. **3.** (of roads &c.) Full of twists and turns, tortuous.

crannog, n. [1. kránog; 2. krǽnɔg]. Ir. *crann*, 'a tree, beam', cp. W. *prenn*, 'tree-stump', fr. *k^wremn-*, whence also Gk. *prémnon*, 'tree-stump'. Ancient Irish or Scottish lake-dwelling.

cranny, n. [1. kráni; 2. krǽni]. M.E. *crāni*, 'chink', fr. Fr. *cran*, 'notch', fr. Romance *crēna*, fr. Lat. **crēna*. See **crenel**. A small opening, fissure, crevice, chink, crack in a rock or wall.

crape, n. [1. krāp; 2. kreip]. Fr. *crêpe*, O. Fr. *crespe*, 'curled', fr. Lat. *crispus*. See **crisp**. **a** A thin, gauze-like crimped material or cloth, of black silk, used for mourning garments; **b** band of this worn round hat or arm as sign of mourning.

craps, n. pl. [1. kraps; 2. kræps], fr. Fr. *crabs*, *craps*, 'game of dice'. (U.S.A.) A gambling game played with two dice.

crapulence, n. [1. krápūlens; 2. krǽpjuləns], fr. Lat. *crāpula*, 'drunkenness, debauch, and the consequent sickness', fr. Gk. *kraipálē*, 'a debauch, sickness, or headache resulting from a debauch'; etymol. doubtful. Sickness caused by excessive drinking; drunkenness.

crapulent, adj. [1. krápūlent; 2. krǽpjulənt], fr. Lat. *crāpulentus*, 'very much intoxicated', fr. *crāpula*. See prec. Connected with, arising from, crapulence.

crapulous, adj. [1. krápūlus; 2. krǽpjuləs], fr. L. Lat. *crāpulōsus*. See prec. words & **-ous**. Crapulent.

crash (I.), vb. intrans., rarely trans. [1. krash; 2. kræʃ]. Imitative, but perh. associated w. some Scand. word such as Swed. *krasa*, 'to break'. See **craze**. **A.** intrans. **1.** **a** To fall suddenly and violently, esp. with a loud noise; used of sudden falling in general, but particularly of fragile, brittle objects, crockery &c.; **b** specif. (of aircraft) to fall suddenly through engine failure, breaking of essential part of machinery &c.; **c** (fig.) to collapse, be ruined, come to serious grief: *the whole financial scheme crashed disastrously*. **2.** *Crash down*, to run, slide, descend rapidly with much noise: *the avalanche crashed down the mountain-side*. **3.** *Crash into* (of vehicles &c. in collision), to run into with violent, noisy impact: *the runaway engine crashed into the goods train*. **B.** trans. To cause to crash: *to crash an aeroplane* &c.

crash (II.), n., fr. prec. **1.** **a** A loud, sudden noise as of heavy, brittle objects falling and smashing; **b** a noise resembling this: *crash of thunder, of artillery* &c. **2.** **a** A noisy violent impact resulting from collision or fall; **b** specif., the sudden, accidental fall of aircraft. **3.** (fig.) **a** Ruin, failure, esp. in financial affairs; **b** sudden social ruin due to outbreak of a scandal.

crash (III.), n. Origin unknown. Coarse linen cloth.

crasis, n. [1. krāsis; 2. kréisis]. Gk. *krâsis*, lit. 'a mixing, blending', fr. base **k erā-*, as in Gk. *keránnūmi*, 'I mix'; cp. also Gk. *krātḗr*, 'bowl for mixing wine and water' (see **crater**); fr. this base come also Scrt. *śrīnāti*, 'mix, cook', *śrāyati*, 'cook, roast', & also O.E. *hrīnan*, 'to touch', & *hrēran*, 'stir, shake'. Contraction of two vowels, esp. of the last and first of two words in combination; e.g. Lat. *cōpia*, 'plenty', fr. *co-opia*; see **copious**.

crass, adj. [1. kras; 2. kræs], fr. Lat. *crassus*, 'solid, thick, dense, fat', fr. **krăt-to-*, fr. base **kerăt-* &c., 'twist together, plait', expanded fr. **ker-* &c., 'to bend', see **curve**; cp. Lat. *crātis*, 'basket-work'. See further on this base under **crate**. (of mental state) Gross, coarse; hence, utter, complete; esp. *crass ignorance*; *crass stupidity* &c.

crassitude, n. [1. krásitūd; 2. krǽsitjūd], fr. Lat. *crassitūdo*, 'thickness, density'. See prec. & **-tude**. Gross stupidity, denseness, obtuseness.

crassly, adv. [1. krásli; 2. krǽsli]. **crass** & **-ly**. In a grossly stupid manner; completely.

crassness, n. [1. krásnes; 2. krǽsnis]. See prec. & **-ness**. State, condition, of being crass; gross stupidity.

-crat, suff. [1. krat; 2. kræt]. See **-cracy**, as in *autocrat*, *plutocrat* &c.

cratch, n. [1. krach; 2. krætʃ]. M.E. *cracche*, *crecche*, fr. Fr. *crèche*, 'crib, manger'. Gmc. loan-word, O.H.G. (Frankish) *krippja*. See **crib**. A rack for fodder.

crate, n. [1. krāt; 2. kreit]. Lat. *crātis*, 'wicker-work, a hurdle'. The base **krāt-* &c. is found in Lat. *crassus*, 'thick' (see **crass**), & further in Goth. *haurds*, 'door' (orig., apparently, 'a wooden gate'), O.H.G. *hurt*, 'basket-work', O.E. *hyrdel*, 'hurdle'. See further under **hurdle**. A case or hamper of basket-work, or of light boarding, used for packing, carrying, or sending fragile objects, such as glass, crockery &c.

crater, n. [1. krāter; 2. kréitə]. Lat., 'bowl for mixing wine', fr. Gk. *krātḗr* (see **crasis**), 'a large bowl for mixing wine and water'. **a** Bowl-shaped mouth of a volcano; **b** (mil.) hole in the ground, somewhat resembling this in shape, caused by explosion of a mine or heavy projectile.

crateriform, adj. [1. krāteriform; 2. kréitərifɔ̄m]. Prec. & **-form**. Shaped like a crater.

cravat, n. [1. kravát; 2. krəvǽt]. Fr. *cravate*, orig. 'a Croat'. The word was applied to an article of dress worn by these people, some of whom were in French service in the 17th cent. Old-fashioned form of neck-tie, in form of a piece of lace, silk, linen &c., worn by men about the neck, folded flat and kept together by a brooch or pin.

crave, vb. trans. & intrans. [1. krāv; 2. kreiv]. L.O.E. *crafian*, M.E. *crāven*, fr. Scand., cp. O.N. *krefja*. Etymol. doubtful. **1.** trans. To ask humbly and insistently for, to beg, entreat, beseech, implore: *to crave one's pardon*. **2.** intrans. *Crave for*, to have a persistent and intense longing for.

craven, n. & adj. [1. krāven; 2. kréivən]. Etymol. doubtful. **a** n. A coward, a poltroon, one devoid of spirit and courage; **b** adj., cowardly, faint-hearted.

cravenly, adv. Prec. & **-ly**. In a craven, cowardly, manner.

craving, n. [1. krāving; 2. kréiviŋ]. **crave** & **-ing**. Intense and persistent longing, strong desire; passionate yearning: *a craving for pleasure, drink, affection* &c.

craw, n. [1. kraw; 2. krɔ̄]. M.E. *crawe*. The expected form **craga* is not found in O.E. Note, however, Du. *kraag*, 'neck, collar', & Mod. Germ. *kragen*, 'collar'; prob. cogn. w. Gk. *brókh-(thos)*, 'throat', wh. is fr. *g^wrokh-*, & *brókhein*, 'to gulp down'. Bird's crop.

crawfish, n. [1. krawfish; 2. krɔ̄fiʃ]. Variant of **crayfish**.

crawl (I.), vb. intrans. [1. krawl; 2. krɔ̄l]. Spelt *crall* in Spenser; prob. Scand., cp. O.N. *krafla*, 'to paw, scrabble with the hands',

Swed. dial. *kralla*, 'creep on hands and knees', & Dan. *kravle*, 'to creep'. **1. a** To creep, move by dragging the body along the ground (of worms &c.); **b** to move along on hands and knees (of young children); **c** to move by wriggling the body along the earth (of human beings trying to avoid observation, or passing through steep or otherwise difficult ground). **2.** To move about slowly and feebly; often *crawl about*, applied to the weak, uncertain gait of sick or infirm persons. **3.** (fig.) To abase oneself before another, to act in a servile manner in order to curry favour. **4.** To abound in, swarm with, crawling things: *the ground was simply crawling with insects.* **5.** To have a tickling sensation in the surface of the skin, as though crawling things were moving on it.

crawl (II.), n., fr. prec. **a** The act of crawling; **b** a slow or feeble pace: *to go at a crawl*, to walk, drive &c. very slowly; **c** a racing stroke in swimming with head kept low in the water.

crawler, n. [1. kráwler; 2. krɔ́lə]. **crawl (I.)** & **-er**. **a** Person or animal that crawls; **b** (fig.) a servile, abject time-server or flatterer; **c** (pl.) baby's overalls used for crawling about on the floor.

crawly, adj. [1. kráwli; 2. krɔ́li]. **crawl (II.)** & **-y.** (colloq.) Having a creepy sensation on one's body.

crayfish, n. [1. kráfish; 2. kréifiʃ]. Adaptation of M.E. *crevis* &c., fr. O. Fr. *crevisse*, Mod. Fr. *écrevisse*, wh. is fr. O.H.G. *krebiz*, 'crab'. See **crab.** **a** A Fresh-water crustacean resembling a small lobster, found in streams; **b** the spiny lobster, the sea-crayfish.

crayon, n. & vb. trans. [1. krā́on; 2. kréiən]. Fr., 'pencil', orig. 'a chalk pencil', cp. Fr. *craie*, Lat. *crēta*, 'chalk', lit. 'Cretan earth'. **1.** n. **a** Thin short stick of soft, oily chalk, clay, or charcoal, used in drawing; **b** a drawing executed in this material; also *crayon drawing*; **c** carbon point in an electric lamp. **2.** vb. To draw with crayon.

craze (I.), vb. trans. [1. krāz; 2. kreiz]. M.E. *crāsen*, fr. Scand. source; cp. Swed. *krasa*, 'to break', *slå i krasa*, 'break to pieces'; Fr. *écraser*, 'to crush', is fr. same source. See **crash.** The orig. meaning, 'to shatter' &c., is now obs. Nearest survival in specific sense in **2.** **1.** To render insane, cause mental derangement in. **2.** To produce crackled effect in glaze of pottery.

craze (II.), n., fr. prec. **a** An exaggerated fondness, irrational enthusiasm: *a craze for stamp-collecting*; **b** a popular fashion, a rage: *aerial gliding was the latest craze.*

crazed, adj. [1. krāzd; 2. kreizd], fr. P.P. of **craze (I.)**. **1.** (of persons) **a** Insane; **b** greatly excited: *crazed about*, madly enthusiastic, exaggeratedly fond of. **2.** (of pottery glaze) Crackled.

crazily, adv. [1. krázili; 2. kréizili]. **crazy** & **-ly.** In a crazy manner.

craziness, n. [1. krázines; 2. kréizinis]. Next word & **-ness.** The state of being crazy; madness, folly.

crazy, adj. [1. krázi; 2. kréizi]. **craze (I.)** & **-y.** **1.** (of persons) **a** Mentally deranged, lacking balance; **b** excited, enthusiastic; **c** *crazy about*, rendered unreasonable by exaggerated fondness for. **2.** (of a structure) **a** Dilapidated, rickety, shaky, unsound: *a crazy building, ship* &c.; **b** *crazy pavement*, one formed of irregularly shaped pieces.

creak (I.), vb. intrans. & trans. [1. krēk; 2. krīk]. M.E. *crēken*. Imitative word, allied to O. Du. *kreken*, 'creak'. Cp. also **crack** & **croak.** **1.** intrans. To emit a shrill, dry, harsh, grating sound, like that of a piece of rusty metal, or other dry material, grating upon another piece; esp. of rusty hinges, ill-fitting gates, doors, new cheap boots &c. **2.** trans. To cause to creak: *to creak a chair.*

creak (II.), n., fr. prec. A sharp, harsh, dry noise, caused by friction of rusty metal, or any dry hard substance, moving upon another under pressure.

creakily, adv. [1. krḗkili; 2. kríkili]. See next word & **-ly.** With a creaking noise.

creaky, adj. [1. krḗki; 2. kríki]. **creak** & **-y.** Apt to creak, emitting a creaking noise.

cream (I.), n. [1. krēm; 2. krīm]. M.E. *crēme*, O. Fr. *cresme*, Mod. Fr. *crème*, Lat. *chrisma*, fr. Gk. *khrīsma.* See **chrism.** **1. a** The rich oily element in milk which rises to, and floats upon, the surface; the foundation of butter; **b** any substance resembling cream in consistency. **2.** A table dish containing or resembling cream in consistency, mixed with other ingredients and flavoured: *ice cream, chicken cream* &c. **3.** (fig.) The best, choicest part, fine flower, of anything, as: *the cream of society*; *the cream of the story, of the joke*, the climax, point. **4.** Colour resembling that of cream; specif., a horse of this colour.

cream (II.), vb. trans. & intrans., fr. prec. **1.** trans. **a** To remove the cream from (milk) by skimming. **2.** intrans. **a** (of milk) To form into a cream; **b** (of other liquids) to form into a thick foam or scum.

cream-cheese, n. **cream (I.)** & **cheese.** A soft rich cheese made of unskimmed milk and cream.

cream-coloured, adj. Of the colour of cream; yellowish white.

creamer, n. [1. krḗmer; 2. krímə]. **cream (II.)** & **-er.** Any kind of instrument for skimming cream off milk.

creamery, n. [1. krḗmeri; 2. kríməri], fr. Fr. *crèmerie.* **cream (I.)** & **-ery.** **a** An establishment where cream is separated from milk, and where butter is made from it; **b** shop where milk, cream, and butter are sold.

cream-laid, adj. Trade term for a smooth, glossy, cream-coloured paper.

cream of tartar, n. [1. krḗm uv tártar; 2. krím əv tátə]. So called because the crystals form on the surface of the liquid in process of purification. Purified and crystallized potassium bitartrate, used in medicine and cookery.

cream-wove, adj. Trade term for a cream-coloured wove paper.

creamy, adj. [1. krḗmi; 2. krími]. **cream (I.)** & **-y.** Resembling cream in consistency, texture, or colour.

crease (I.), n. [1. krēs; 2. krīs]. Etymol. doubtful. **1. a** A line, mark, or ridge made upon cloth or similar material by folding and pressing; a fold, rumple; specif. **b** straight ridge or fold deliberately made by pressing down the front of trousers. **2.** Line of whiting on a cricket pitch, which defines the position of the batsman or bowler.

crease (II.), vb. trans. & intrans. See prec. **1.** trans. To impart a crease or creases to cloth, whether by design or accident: **a** *to crease one's trousers* (deliberate); **b** *to crease one's clothes*, to make irregular lines, folds, wrinkles, in them by careless folding or wear. **2.** intrans. To fall into creases, become wrinkled: *this material creases very easily.*

creased, adj. [1. krēst; 2. krīst]. **crease (I.)** & **-ed.** Full of, covered with, creases; specif. **a** deliberately folded, as the front of trousers; **b** irregularly wrinkled and tumbled, as clothes &c. which have been badly folded.

create, vb. trans. [1. krēā́t; 2. kriéit], fr. Lat. *creāt-(um)*, P.P. type of Lat. *creāre*, 'to make, produce, create', lit. 'cause to grow', fr. Aryan base **ker-*, **kor-* &c., 'to grow', fr. wh. comes also Lat. **corpus,** & *crēscere*, 'to grow, arise, spring' &c. (see **crescent**); further cognates are Gk. *kóros*, 'stripling', *kórē*, 'maiden', lit. 'growing creatures'; in Gmc., Goth. *hairda*, O.H.G. *herta*, O.E. *heord*, 'herd' (see **herd**), & O.E. *hyrst*, O.H.G. *horst*, 'wood, thicket, growing wood'; see **hurst.** **1. a** (of the Divine act) To produce from nothing, call into being, cause existence of to begin: *God created all things*; **b** (of processes of nature and social causes) to bring about, cause to exist: *new forms of life are created by the forces of evolution.* **2.** (of human activity) **a** To produce, construct, something new and original in thought or imagination: *to create an epic, drama, system of philosophy* &c.; **b** specif. (of an actor) *to create a part, character*, conceive, and express it in action in an original way; **c** (of human material activity) to make, produce, as an organic whole, by bringing together materials already existing into proper order and relation: *to create an army, an empire, a cathedral* &c. (gen. used in this sense of work of some magnitude); **d** to bring into existence by legal action: *to create a peer, an office of State* &c.; **e** to confer a new status, dignity, rank, on a person: *to create a man a peer, baronet* &c. **3.** To give rise to, produce, cause to exist, or to become apparent, something not previously in existence; **a** (of non-material things) *to create a feeling of surprise, an awkward situation* &c.; **b** (of material things) *to create a sensation of cold, a painful itching* &c.

creatin(e), n. [1. krḗatin, -ēn; 2. kríətin, -īn], fr. Gk. *kreat-*, stem of *kréas*, 'flesh'. See account of base of this & its derivatives under **crude.** (chem.) A white crystalline substance found in the blood and soft tissues of vertebrates.

creation, n. [1. kreáshun; 2. kriéiʃən], fr. Fr. *création*, fr. Lat. *creātiōn-(em).* See **create** & **-ion.** **1. a** The act of creating or causing to exist; specif. (with cap.) the act of God in bringing the universe and life into existence; **b** all that God created, man and the whole universe: *the whole creation*, the whole universe, all living creatures. **2. a** The human mental act or process of producing a new work of thought or imagination: *the creation of great poetry*; **b** something produced by the operation of the human mind; specif., by the imagination of a poet or other artist: *a creation of genius*; **c** act of instituting or making an office, rank &c. by a legal decree: *the creation of a peerage* &c.; the rank &c. thus created: *his peerage was a creation of yesterday*; **d** (i.) act or process of making, producing, some new material thing: *the creation of an empire, a new city*; (ii.) specific use: act of designing an article of wearing apparel, and the garment designed: *the latest Paris creations*; **e** process of producing, giving rise to something, by the agency of natural or social forces: *the creation of new species by an evolutionary process*; *the creation of social unrest by economic conditions.*

creationism, n. [1. kreáshunizm; 2. kriéiʃənizəm]. Prec. & **-ism.** **1.** (theol.) The doctrine that the origin of species and that of matter is due to special acts of creation by God. **2.** (theol.) The doctrine that a new soul is created for every human being that is born.

creationist, n. [1. kreáshunist; 2. kriéiʃənist]. **creation** & **-ist.** An adherent of creationism.

creative, adj. [1. kreátiv; 2. kriéitiv]. **create** & **-ive.** **1.** Having the power to create (in varying senses): **a** of the Almighty; **b** of human beings; **c** of natural forces. **2.** Connected with, pertaining to, creation.

creatively, adv. Prec. & **-ly.** In a creative manner.

creativeness, n. See prec. & **-ness.** Quality or faculty of creating.

creator, n. [1. kreátur; 2. kriéitə]. Lat. See **create** & **-or.** **a** Specif., *the Creator*, God in His aspect of maker of the universe; **b** one who creates (in any sense).

creature, n. [1. krḗcher; 2. krítʃə]. M.E., fr. Fr., fr. L. Lat. *creātūra*, 'a thing created'. See **create** & **-ure.** **1.** (archaic) A created thing, as distinct from something self-existent: '*these thy creatures of bread and wine*'; *we are all God's creatures.* **2.** Specif., a living being; **a** a human being: *a good creature*; *a lovely creature* (woman); *a poor creature*, (i.) contemptible human being; (ii.) now gen. expressive of pity, patronage, contempt, and sense of superiority on the part of speaker: *poor creature*; **b** one of the lower animals: *dumb creatures.* **3.** One who from interested motives, or sense of obligation to another, is subservient to him, and entirely at his service for all purposes, good or bad; an unscrupulous tool of another. **4.** (humorous) *The creature*, strong spirits, esp. whisky. Often spelt *cratur*, from the Irish pronunciation. **5.** As adjective in *creature comforts*, material comforts and luxuries.

creaturely, adj. Prec. & **-ly.** Pertaining to creatures.

crèche, n. [1. krāsh; 2. kreiʃ]. Fr., 'cradle'. Variant of **cratch.** Public institution in which young children are cared for during the day while the mothers are at work.

credence, n. [1. krédens; 2. kríd*ə*ns], fr. Med. Lat. *crēdentia*, fr. Lat. *crēdent-(em)*, Pres. Part. of *crēdere*, 'to trust, believe'. See **creed. 1.** Belief, esp. reliance on the testimony of others: *to give credence to*, to believe. **2.** (eccles.) A small table in a church by the side of the altar on which the bread and wine are placed ready for the Eucharist. Also *credence table.*

credentials, n. pl. [1. kredénshalz; 2. kridénʃəlz]. See prec. & **-al.** Documents, written or other testimonials, which furnish evidence to others of a person's identity, genuineness, respectability of character, competence, knowledge, and other qualities necessary, to be established for his particular purpose.

credibility, n. [1. krèdibíliti; 2. krèd*i*bíl*i*ti]. See next word & **-ity.** State or quality of being credible.

credible, adj. [1. krédibl; 2. kréd*i*bl], fr. Lat. *crēdibilis*, 'worthy of belief', fr. *crēdere*, 'to believe', & **-ible.** See **creed. a** (of persons) Worthy to be believed; trustworthy; **b** (of statements) capable of being believed, possible to believe.

credibly, adv. Prec. & **-ly.** In a manner deserving, commanding, belief; from a reliable source: *to be credibly informed that* &c.

credit (I.), n. [1. krédit; 2. kréd*i*t]. Fr., fr. Lat. *crēditum*, 'what is believed', P.P. of *crēdere*, 'to believe'. See **creed. 1.** Belief, credence: *to give credit to a person's statements.* **2.** Personal honour, integrity, trustworthiness: *a man of the highest credit.* **3.** Some person, circumstance, quality, act, which reflects honour upon a person, and confirms or enhances his reputation: *he is a credit to his parents.* **4.** Reputation, prestige, honour, gained by acknowledged merit: *to have the credit of one's discoveries*; *to add to one's credit*; *to give a person credit for being a sensible man*; Phrs. *very much to his credit*; *to do one credit.* **5.** (commerc.) Trust and confidence based upon belief in a person's, a corporation's, or a state's promise to pay, in the future, within a certain time, and his or its ability to do so as being financially solvent: *to have unlimited credit*; *to purchase goods on credit.* **6. a** Sum standing in a person's favour in a banking account; **b** (book-keeping) that part or side of an account in which are entered all sums received in favour of the account; contrasted with *debit. Letter of credit*, banker's letter authorizing the agents in other places to make payments to holder, up to a certain sum.

credit (II.), vb. trans., fr. prec. **1.** To believe, attach credence to, accept as reliable (a person or statement). **2.** *To credit (a person) with* a quality, or with having done something; to give him the credit of possessing or doing it; to attribute or ascribe it to him. **3.** (book-keeping) To enter on the credit side of an account: *to credit an amount to a person*; *to credit a person with an amount*, to place it in his favour on credit side of the account.

creditable, adj. [1. kréditabl; 2. kréd*i*təbl]. Prec. & **-able.** Bringing credit, redounding to (a person's) honour: *a creditable performance*; *an action creditable to him who performed it.*

creditably, adv. Prec. & **-ly.** In a creditable manner, with credit, without disgrace.

creditor, n. [1. kréditer; 2. kréd*i*tə]. Lat., 'a truster, a lender'. **credit** (II.) & **-or. 1.** One to whom a debt is owing. **2.** (book-keeping) The credit side of an account, abbreviation *Cr.*

credo, n. [1. krḗdō; 2. krídou]. Lat., 'I believe'. See **creed. a** The Apostles' or the Nicene Creed, which in Latin begin '*credo*, 'I believe'; **b** a musical setting of the Creed.

credulity, n. [1. kredū́liti; 2. kridjū́l*i*ti], fr. Lat. *crēdulitāt-(em)*, 'trustfulness, easiness of belief', fr. *crēdulus.* See next word & **-ity.** Quality of mind which renders a person prone to believe what he hears without sufficient evidence; liability to be imposed upon; foolish, unjustified trustfulness.

credulous, adj. [1. kréjoolus, krédūlus; 2. krédžuləs, krédjuləs], fr. Lat. *crēdulus*, 'believing too easily, too confiding', fr. *crēdere*, 'to believe'. See **creed. a** (of persons) Ready to believe on slight evidence; easily imposed upon; **b** (of things) easily believed by the credulous (archaic and rare).

credulously, adv. Prec. & **-ly.** In a credulous manner.

credulousness, n. See prec. & **-ness.** Quality of being credulous.

creed, n. [1. krēd; 2. krīd]. O.E. *creda*, fr. Lat. *crēdo*, 'I believe', Scrt. has *śrad-dhā*, 'trust'. The word is possibly a compound of two Aryan bases, **k̂erd-*, **k̂rd-*, **k̂rēd-*, 'heart' (see **cordate** & **heart**), & **dhē-*, 'to place'. See **do. 1.** A brief formal summary of the essential articles of Christian faith or doctrine, esp. *the Apostles' Creed, Nicene Creed*, and the *Athanasian Creed*; Phr. *to know one's*, or *the Creed*, refers specifically to the Apostles' Creed. Hence, **2,** any formula, or system of religious or other beliefs or principles.

creek, n. [1. krēk; 2. krīk]. M.E. *cryke*, perh. of Scand. origin, cp. O.N. *kriki*, 'bay', Swed. *krik*, or fr. a L. Germ. source, cp. Du. *kreek*; Fr. *crique*, must be fr. the O.N. A narrow inlet of water, near the seashore, or in the bank of a river.

creel, n. [1. krēl; 2. krīəl]. Late M.E. *crelle*, 'basket', fr. O. Fr. *creil*, prob. L. Lat. *crāticulum*, dimin. of *crātis*, 'wicker-work'. See **crate.** A wicker basket for carrying fish.

creep (I.), vb. intrans. [1. krēp; 2. krīp]. O.E. *crēopan*, M.E. *crēpen*; O.N. *krjūpa*, Du. *kruipen.* The base has not been definitely identified outside Gmc., but it may be cogn. w. that in **griffin.** Cp. **cripple.** The general sense is the same as *crawl.* **1. a** To move along with the body near to the ground, go on hands and knees; said of progressive movements of babies, insects and small animals as mice, squirrels; also of some kinds of birds moving about on trees looking for insects; **b** (of plants) to grow along the ground, a wall, or other surface; as ivy, a vine &c. **2. a** To walk cautiously, stealthily, without making a noise: *to creep about on tiptoe*; **b** to move about feebly and shakily like a sick or old person. **3.** (fig.) **a** Esp. of time, age &c., to come on gradually and almost unobserved; followed by *upon*: *old age comes creeping upon one unnoticed*; **b** of other things which appear unobserved. **4.** (fig.) To fawn, cringe; to insinuate oneself by servile behaviour: *to creep into a person's favour.* **5.** To have a sensation as though insects were creeping over one, to feel creepy; (but gen. fig.) to shudder, feel fear, repugnance, horror &c., esp. in Phr. *to make one's flesh creep.* **6.** (naut.) To drag in deep water with a creeper.

creep (II.), n., fr. prec. **1.** (colloq. in pl.) *The creeps*, feeling of shrinking, shuddering horror. **2. a** (geol.) A gradual movement of loose rock material; **b** (min.) a slow rising of the floor of a gallery. **3.** An opening in a hedge &c., for animals to pass through.

creeper, n. [1. krḗper; 2. krípə]. **creep** (I.) & **-er. 1.** One that creeps, esp. an insect or reptile. **2.** Name of various small birds as *Tree Creeper, Wall Creeper* &c. **3.** (bot.) A plant which creeps along, or beneath, the ground or climbs up a wall by means of tendrils, as *the Virginia creeper.* **4. a** An instrument with iron hooks for dragging the bottom of a body of water; a grapnel, drag; **b** (pl.) spikes or nails fitted to boots for climbing or walking on ice.

creephole, n. [1. krḗphōl; 2. kríphoul]. **A** hole or retreat into which one may creep to hide.

creeping, adj. [1. krḗping; 2. krípiŋ], fr. Pres. Part. of **creep** (I.). **1. a** (of insects &c.) Moving with crawling movement: *creeping things*; **b** (of plants) tending to run along the ground: *creeping plants.* **2.** Slow, feeble: *a creeping gait, movement.* **3.** Fawning, cringing: *a creeping sycophant.*

creepy, adj. [1. krḗpi; 2. krípi]. **creep** & **-y.** Tending to give one the creeps; producing horror, fear, and disgust.

creepy-crawly, adj. [1. krḗpi kráwli; 2. krípi krɔ́li]. Creepy.

creese, n. See **kris.**

cremate, vb. trans. [1. kremā́t; 2. kriméit], fr. Lat. *cremāt-(um)*, P.P. type of *cremāre*, 'to reduce to ashes, consume by fire'. The word is amplified fr. base **ker-* &c., 'to burn', seen also in Lat. *carbo*, 'coal' (see **carbon**), & in Gk. *kéramos*, 'potter's clay, a tile' (see **ceramic**), *keránnūmi*, 'I mix, cook', *krātḗr*, 'bowl', & *krāsis*, 'a mixing'. See **crasis.** To burn up, consume entirely by fire, reduce to ashes, esp. to dispose in this way of a human body after death, in a specially constructed furnace. Used also of burning of rubbish and waste matter generally in an incinerator.

cremation, n. [1. kremā́shun; 2. kriméiʃən]. Lat. *cremātiōn-(em)*, 'a turning'. See prec. & **-ion.** Act, process, of cremating; specif., that of burning a human corpse.

cremationist, n. [1. kremā́shunist; 2. kriméiʃənist]. **cremation** & **-ist.** One who believes in cremating dead human bodies instead of burying them.

cremator, n. [1. kremā́tur; 2. kriméitə]. **cremate** & **-or. a** One who cremates; **b** special furnace for cremating.

crematorium, n. [1. krèmatṓrium; 2. krèmətɔ́riəm]. Invented Lat. word fr. **crematory. a** Public institution where human corpses are cremated; **b** one where refuse is consumed.

crematory, n. & adj. [1. krématuri; 2. krémətəri]. **cremate** & **-ory. a** n. A crematorium; **b** adj., pertaining to cremation.

crême de menthe, n. [1. krām de mónt; 2. kreim də mā́t]. Fr., lit. 'cream of mint'. A sweet, thick, greenish liqueur flavoured with peppermint.

Cremona, n. [1. kremṓna; 2. krimóunə]. An ancient and valuable make of violin, made at Cremona in Italy.

crenate(d), adj. [1. krenā́t(id); 2. krenéit(id)]. Ital. *crena*, 'a notch', & **-ate.** See **crenel.** Notched, indented, scalloped, esp. **a** (bot., of a leaf) Having its margin cut into even and rounded notches; **b** (physiol.) of shrunken blood corpuscles, having toothed edges.

crenation, n. [1. krenā́shun; 2. krenéiʃən]. Prec. & **-ion.** Condition of being crenate, esp. of leaves and blood corpuscles.

crenature, n. [1. krénachur; 2. krénətʃə]. **crenate** & **-ture.** A crenate formation.

crenel(le), n. [1. krénel; 2. krénəl]. O. Fr. *crenel*, fr. Med. Lat. *crenellum*, dimin. of Romance *crēna*, 'notch', fr. Lat. **crēna*, fr. base **ker-* 'to cut', wh. occurs also in Lat. *caro*, 'flesh', orig. 'piece of flesh, portion cut off'. See **carnal. a** One of the gaps between the raised parts in the castellation on a battlement; **b** any structure or ornament resembling these in form.

crenel(l)ate(d), vb. trans. & adj. [1. krénelāt(id); 2. krénəleit(id)]. Prec. & **-ate. a** vb. To furnish with crenels; **b** adj., having crenels.

crenellation, n. [1. krènelā́shun; 2. krènəléiʃən]. Prec. & **-ion. a** The act of crenellating; **b** crenellated work.

creole, n. & adj. [1. krḗōl; 2. krioul]. Fr., fr. Span. *criollo*, 'native of America or W. Indies'; word made by negroes; perh. contraction of Span. *criadillo*, dimin. of *criado*, 'educated, instructed, bred up', P.P. of *criar*, 'to create'. The sense was orig. 'little nurseling' (Skeat). See **create. 1. n.** Used in two different senses: a person of pure European descent born in the W. Indies or

Mauritius or S. American states; **b** a half-caste; person half negro, half European. **2.** adj. Belonging to, connected with, springing from, a creole in either sense.

creosote, n. [1. krēosōt; 2. kríəsout]. Word of mod. scientific manufacture, fr. Gk. *kréas*, genit. *kréōs*, 'flesh', see **crude**, & *sṓzō*, 'I save'. With the latter cp. Gk. *sōtḗr*, 'saviour', &, w. a different grade of vowel, *sáos*, 'safe'; fr. base **twə-*, **twō-*, **tewā-*, &c., 'to swell', hence 'to be strong'. See **tumid**. Oily, dark-brown, strongly smelling liquid, obtained from wood tar, and used as an antiseptic, and as a preservative for wood which is exposed to the weather.

crêpe, n. [1. krāp; 2. kreip]. Fr., **crape**. Dressmaker's word for certain fabrics which resemble crape; esp. *crêpe de chine*, a material of this kind made from silk.

crepitant, adj. [1. krépitant; 2. krépitənt], fr. Lat. *crepitant-(em)*, Pres. Part. of *crepitāre*. See next word. Having or making a crackling sound.

crepitate, vb. trans. [1. krépitāt; 2. krépiteit], fr. Lat. *crepitāt-(um)*, P.P. of *crepitāre*, 'to rattle, creak, crackle', freq. of *crepāre*, 'to creak'; the word is prob. of imitative origin fr. Aryan itself; cp. Lat. *cornix*, 'raven', *corvus*, 'crow', prob. fr. same base (see **corvine**); Scrt. *kṛpātē*, 'to lament'. See also under **raven, coracoid. 1.** To emit a series of sharp, frequent, crackling sounds; to crackle. Specif. **2.** (of certain beetles &c.) To discharge a defensive fluid accompanied by a slight explosive sound.

crepitation, n. [1. krèpitáshun; 2. krèpitéiʃən]. Prec. & **-ion. a** Crackling, creaking sound, esp. (med.) of sound made by ends of broken bone rubbing together, or of breathing as heard in pneumonia; **b** act of crepitating (see prec. **2**).

crepitus, n. [1. krépitus; 2. krépitəs]. Lat., 'rattling, clashing, creaking' &c. See **crepitate**. (med.) Sound made by sudden discharge of wind from the bowels.

crépon, n. [1. krépon; 2. krépɔ̃]. Fr. See **crape**. Crape of firm texture.

crept, vb. [1. krept; 2. krɛpt]. Pret. & P.P. of **creep**. M.E. *crepte*, new wk. form; cp. O.E. str. Pret. *crēap*, M.E. *crēp*.

crepuscular, adj. [1. krepúskūlar; 2. krəpáskjulə], fr. Lat. *crepusculum*, 'twilight, dusk', dimin. formation fr. *creper* (adj.), 'dusky'. The etymol. of the latter is doubtful, but if, as has been suggested, *cr-* is fr. *cn-*, then it might be connected w. Gk. *knéphas*, 'dark' the Lat. representing a dial. (Sabine) form w. *p* for Aryan *bh*. **a** Of, pertaining to, resembling, twilight; dim, glimmering; specif. **b** (of animals, as bats &c., and insects) active, flying, in the evening or just before the dawn.

crepuscule, n. [1. krépuskūl; 2. krépəskjūl]. Fr., fr. Lat. *crepusculum*, 'twilight'. See prec. Twilight.

crescendo, adv., adj., & n. [1. kreshéndō; 2. kriʃéndou]. Ital., Pres. Part. of *crescere*, 'to increase, grow', fr. Lat. See **crescent**. **a** (mus.) A direction signifying increase of loudness; **b** (fig., gen. as adv.) signifying increasing intensity of feeling or action. Abbreviation *cres(c)*.

crescent (I.), n. [1. krésent; 2. krésənt], fr. Lat. *crēscent-(em)*, 'growing, increasing'. Pres. Part. of *crēscere*, 'to grow'. This word is fr. base **ker-* &c., 'to grow'. See **create. 1.** The shape of the waxing or waning moon; properly, the moon in the first quarter, but applied to the moon in any stage which exhibits this shape. **2.** Anything curved in the shape of the moon in early or late stages: **a** (her.) a charge consisting of the figure of the increasing moon with the horns pointing upward; **b** the emblem of the Turkish Empire; hence (fig.) the Turkish power; **c** the Mohammedan religion contrasted with Christianity: Phr. the *Cross and the Crescent*; *Red Crescent*, Turkish and Moslem equivalent of the *Red Cross*. **3.** A row of houses built in a semicircle, or approximately in form of a crescent.

crescent (II.), adj. See prec. **a** Shaped like a crescent; **b** increasing in size, growing (poet.).

cresol, n. [1. krēsol; 2. krísəl], fr. **creosote** & **-ol.** (med.) A caustic liquid obtained by distillation of coal tar, an essential constituent of the antiseptic *lysol*, q.v.

cress, n. [1. kres; 2. krɛs]. O.E. *cærse, cresse*, & M.E. *cresse*; O.H.G. *kresso* (whence Fr. *cresson*), Mod. Germ. *kresse*, 'watercress'; Kluge suggests a connexion between the O.H.G. n. & *chresan*, 'to creep'. The name of various plants, with hot-tasting edible leaves; often used and referred to in combination with *mustard*, which is sown alongside of cress, the tender leaves of which are used together with it in salads &c.

cresset, n. [1. kréset; 2. krésit], in M.E., fr. O. Fr. *craisse*, 'grease', fr. Low Lat. *crassia*, fr. *crassus*, 'thick'. Cp. **crass**. An iron vessel for holding burning oil, pitch &c., hung aloft and used as a torch.

crest (I.), n. [1. krest; 2. krɛst]. M.E. fr. O. Fr. *creste*, fr. Lat. *crista*, 'tuft on the head of animals, cock's comb'. Connected w. Lat. *crīnis*, 'hair of the head', wh. is for **crisnis*, perh. also w. *crispus*, 'curly' (see **crisp** & **crinite**); Goth. *af- hrisjan*, 'to shake off', & O.E. *hrisian*, 'to rattle, creak'. **1. a** Tuft of hair or feathers on head of animal or bird; comb of a cock; **b** distinctive device, tuft, carving &c., anciently worn on a helmet; **c** (poet.) the helmet itself; **d** (her.) distinctive device (see **b**) borne above the shield on a coat of arms: *family crest*. **2.** The top, highest point, of a thing; **a** of a hill, mountain, wave; Phr. (fig.) *on the crest of the wave*, at the highest point, most favourable moment of one's fortunes; **b** the arched neck of a horse and the mane upon it; **c** (anat.) bony ridge at the top of the head of primitive races: *occipital crest*.

crest (II.), vb. trans. & intrans., fr. prec. **1.** trans. **a** To furnish, adorn, with a crest; **b** to mount to the top or crest of: *to crest a hill, wave* &c. **2.** intrans. To rise into, form, a crest; esp. of waves (rare and poet.).

crested, adj. [1. krésted; 2. kréstid]. Prec. & **-ed.** Having a crest (in all senses): *a golden-crested wren*; *crested notepaper* &c.

crestfallen, adj. [1. kréstfawlen; 2. kréstfōlən]. **crest** (I.) & **fall. a** (lit.) With drooping plume or crest; hence, **b** dejected, dispirited, depressed, and disappointed.

cretaceous, adj. [1. krētáshus; 2. krītéiʃəs], fr. Lat. *crētāceus*, adj., 'chalk-like', fr. *crēta*, 'chalk', & **-aceous**. See **crayon**. **a** Having the qualities of chalk; chalky; **b** abounding in, full of, chalk; specif. **c** (geol.) belonging to the last Mesozoic period or system between the Jurassic and Tertiary.

cretic, n. [1. krētik; 2. krítik], fr. Lat. *Crēticus* (sc. *pēs*), 'Cretan (foot)', fr. *Crēta*, 'Crete'. (class. pros.) Metrical foot consisting of a short syllable between two long ones.

cretification, n. [1. krètifikáshun; 2. krìtifikéiʃən]. See next word. Process of converting something into chalk.

cretify, vb. trans. [1. krētifī; 2. krítifai], fr. Lat. *crēta*, 'chalk' (see **crayon**), & **-fy**. To convert into chalk; to impregnate with salts of lime.

cretin, n. [1. krétin; 2. krétin]. Fr., *crétin*, dial. form fr. Lat. *christiānus*, **Christian**, hence, 'human being' in sense of 'just human'. **a** Person afflicted with cretinism; **b** an idiot, mean-spirited person.

cretinism, n. [1. krétinizm; 2. krétinizəm]. Prec. & **-ism**. Disease arising from deficiency of the thyroid gland, which results in stunted physical development, and idiocy, often accompanied by goitre and deformity.

cretonne, n. [1. kréton; 2. krétɔn]. Fr. *cretonne*, fr. Creton, a village in Normandy. A strong unglazed cotton cloth, having a pattern printed on it, used in upholstery.

crevasse, n. [1. krevás; 2. krɛvǽs]. Fr. See next word. A deep cleft, specif., in the ice of a glacier.

crevice, n. [1. krévis; 2. krévis]. M.E. & O. Fr. *crevace*, Mod. Fr. *crevasse*, fr. *crever*, 'to break, burst', fr. Lat. *crepāre*, 'to creak, crack'. See **crepitate**. A narrow opening, crack, split, chink, fissure in the earth, a rock, a building &c.

crew, n. [1. kroo; 2. krū], formerly *crue*, fr. O. Fr. *accrue, accreue*, 'augmentation, reinforcement', fr. P.P. of *accroître*, 'to increase', fr. Lat. *crēscere*; see **crescent. 1. a** The whole body of those employed in working a ship or boat; **b** (in restricted sense) excluding the officers of the ship: *officers and crew*. **2.** A group or company of persons associated, bound, seen together; (gen. in derogatory sense) gang, set, mob: *a noisy, disreputable crew*.

crewel, n. [1. krooel; 2. krūil]. Earlier *creeal*, *crule*, perh. fr. O. Fr. *escrouelle (de laine)*, 'shreds of wool', fr. Low Lat. *scrōfella*, Lat. *scrōfula*, 'pig'. See **scrofula**. The connexion in sense between the Fr. & Lat. words is not easy to see, though accepted by Meyer-Lübke. Worsted yarn for tapestry and embroidery.

crewel-work, n. Embroidery on canvas with coloured crewels.

crib (I.), n. [1. krib; 2. krib]. O.E. & M.E. *cribb*, O.S. *kribbia*, O.H.G. *krippha*, Mod. Germ. *krippe*, Swed. *krubba*, Dan. *krybbe*, 'crib, manger'. Cp. **cratch**. Relationships outside Gmc. doubtful. **1. a** A manger or rack for fodder; **b** a stall for oxen (archaic). **2.** A hut; a small room; a small house: *a snug crib*. **3.** A child's cot with high sides to prevent inmate from rolling out. **4.** A wicker basket, esp. a wicker salmon-trap. **5.** (min.) A heavy framework for shoring up sides of a mine-shaft. **6.** (cards) In cribbage, *the crib* comprises the cards given to the dealer to use in scoring and discarded for that purpose by the other players. **7.** (colloq.) A plagiarism; hence, a literal translation of a foreign or classical author, esp. one dishonestly used by schoolboys. **8.** (slang) A house, shop &c., esp. in thieves' cant: *to crack a crib*, break into, burgle, a house.

crib (II.), vb. trans. & intrans., fr. prec. **A.** trans. **1.** To confine within a small space, as in a crib; to cramp: *'Cabin'd, cribb'd, confined'* (Shakespeare). **2.** To furnish (a stall, stable, cowshed &c.) with cribs. **3.** (colloq.) To plagiarize literary work; to appropriate passages or ideas without acknowledgement from another's work: *to crib one's best things from others*. **B.** intrans. (esp. of schoolboys) **a** To make secret and dishonest use of literal translations of classical authors; **b** to copy a translation, exercise &c. from a schoolfellow and show it up as one's own: *to crib out of another's exercise book*.

cribbage, n. [1. kríbij; 2. kríbidž], perh. fr. **crib** (I.). A card game for two, three, or four players; the points made in this game are scored on a *cribbage board*, by pegs stuck into holes.

cribbing, n. [1. kríbing; 2. kríbiŋ]. **crib** (II.) & **-ing.** Action expressed by the vb. 'to crib'; specif., *crib-biting*.

crib-biting, n. (veter.) A habit among some horses of biting the manger or other object, at the same time sucking in air.

cribriform, adj. [1. kríbriform; 2. kráibrifōm], fr. Lat. *crībrum*, 'sieve', & **-form**. The Lat. n. is fr. base **ker-*, **krei-* &c., meaning 'to distinguish, separate out, discriminate, sift' &c. Cp. Lat. *cernere* (fr. **crin-*), 'distinguish', see **concern**, *certus*, 'certain', see **certain**; Gk. *krínō*, 'I separate, distinguish, decide, judge', *kritḗs*, 'judge'; see **critic**. Perforated like a sieve.

crick, n. & vb. trans. [1. krik; 2. krik]. Variant of **creek**, w. orig. meaning of 'bend, crook'. **1.** n. A sharp, painful wrench or strain in a muscle or joint. **2.** vb. To strain or wrench a joint or muscle so as to produce a crick: *to crick one's neck*.

cricket (I.), n. [1. kríket; 2. kríkit]. M.E., fr. O. Fr. *criquet*. Imitative; connected w. **creak**. A small brown winged insect, *Gryllus*, frequenting warm places near a hearth, which jumps and produces continuous shrill, grating noise by rubbing parts of the wings together. Phr. *as lively, merry, as a cricket.*

cricket (II.), n. O. Fr. *criquet*, 'a bat used in a ball game'. The word is a dimin. fr. L.G. sources; cp. M. Du. *krick*, 'crutch'. The Engl. cogn. of this is **crutch.** Outdoor game played with bats, ball, and wickets, between two sides of eleven players each. Phr. (colloq.) *not (quite) cricket*, (describing conduct) unsporting, not fair, not according to the received convention.

cricketer, n. [1. kríketer; 2. kríkitə]. Prec. & **-er.** Player of cricket.

cricoid, adj. & n. [1. kríkoid; 2. kráikoid], fr. Gk. *krikos*, 'ring', also *kirkos*; cogn. w. Lat. **circus**, & **-oid.** **a** adj. Pertaining to the ring-shaped cartilage of the larynx, which articulates with the lower horn of the thyroid cartilage; **b** n., this cartilage itself.

cried, vb. [1. krīd; 2. kraid]. M.E. *crīde, crīed.* Pret. & P.P. of **cry.**

crier, n. [1. krīer; 2. kráiə], fr. **cry** (I.), & **-er.** Cp. Fr. *crieur.* **1.** One who cries, esp. habitually (of a young child &c.). Specif. **2. a** an official who proclaims the orders, directions &c. in a court of justice; **b** official employed by a corporation to make public announcements, generally prefacing by the words *o-yes, o-yes*= A.-Fr. *oyez*, 'hear'. Also *town-crier.*

crime (I.), n. [1. krīm; 2. kraim]. M.E., fr. O. Fr., fr. Lat. *crīmen*, 'judicial decision, charge, crime'. The Aryan base **krēi-* &c. meant 'to sift out; to distinguish, to judge, to decide' &c. See **critic, crisis, concern, certain, decree. a** An act which is an offence against human law, of a grave character, and punishable by death, imprisonment, or fine; **b** (fig., popular usage) a foolish, ill-judged, useless action: *it would be an absolute crime to put a race-horse to do the work of a cart-horse.*

crime (II.), vb. trans. (mil. usage) To charge and convict (soldier) of a military offence, his name being entered on the *crime-sheet*, the record of such offences.

crimeless, adj. [1. krímles; 2. kráimlis]. **crime** (I.) & **-less.** Free from crime.

crimelessness, n. See prec. & **-ness.** State, condition, of being free from crime.

criminal (I.), adj. [1. kríminal; 2. kríminəl]. Lat. *crīminālis*, fr. *crīmen, crīminis*, 'crime'. See **crime** (I.). **1. a** (of action and conduct) Of the nature of crime, wicked: *criminal neglect; a criminal offence; criminal conversation*, adulterous sexual intercourse; **b** (of persons) guilty of crime. **2.** Connected with, directed against, crime: *a criminal action* (at law); *criminal law; criminal code* &c.

criminal (II.), n., fr. prec. One guilty of crime.

criminality, n. [1. krìminálíti; 2. krìminǽliti]. Fr. *criminalité*, fr. L. Lat. *crīminālitāt-(em).* See **criminal** (I.) & **-ity.** The quality or state of being criminal; guilt; guiltiness.

criminally, adv. [1. kríminali; 2. kríminəli]. **criminal** (I.) & **-ly. a** In a criminal manner, like a criminal; **b** according to criminal law: *to proceed against a person criminally.*

criminate, vb. trans. [1. kríminät; 2. kríminejt], fr. Lat. *crīmināt-(um)*, P.P. type of *crīmināri*, 'to bring a charge', fr. *crīmen.* See **crime** (I.). **a** To bring a charge of crime against; **b** to censure.

crimination, n. [1. krìminā́shun; 2. krìminéiʃən]. Lat. *crīminātiōn-(em)*, 'accusation'. Prec. & **-ion.** An accusation; strong censure.

criminative, adj. [1. kríminativ; 2. kríminətiv]. **criminate** & **-ive.** Tending to crimination.

criminatory, adj. [1. kríminaturi; 2. kríminətri]. Lat. *crīminātor*, 'accuser'; see **criminate** & **-ory.** Involving an accusation.

criminology, n. [1. krìminóloji; 2. krìminɔ́lədži]. Lat. *crīmen*, genit. *crīminis* (see **crime**), & **-logy.** The systematic study of crime and criminals.

criminous, adj. [1. kríminus; 2. kríminəs]. Lat. *crīminōsus*, 'faulty, blameworthy', fr. *crīmen*, 'crime'. See **crime** (I.) & **-ous.** Only in Phr. *criminous clerk*, a clergyman guilty of a heinous offence.

crimp (I.), n. & vb. trans. & intrans. [1. krimp; 2. krimp]. Etymol. unknown. **1.** n. Person on shore, usually the keeper of a lodging-house, who supplies sailors for ships which are short-handed, by various illegal means; also one who robs sailors when ashore by inducing them to spend money foolishly and get into his debt. **2.** vb. **a** trans. To supply (sailors, crew) for a ship by illegal means; **b** intrans., to practise the arts of a crimp.

crimp (II.), vb. trans. O.E. *crympan*, 'to curl', cogn. w. Du. *krimpen*, 'to shrink'. Cp. also **cramp & crumple. 1. a** To produce wrinkles or crinkles in cloth &c.; **b** to curl (the hair) artificially. **2.** To gash the flesh of a newly caught fish so as to make it more crisp when cooked: *crimped cod.*

crimping, n. [1. krímping; 2. krímpiŋ]. Prec. & **-ing.** Act, art, of imparting a frill or wave to the edge of linen articles, caps &c.

crimpy, adj. [1. krímpi; 2. krímpi]. **crimp** (II.) & **-y.** Frizzly, curly, wavy, esp. of the hair.

crimson, n., adj., & vb. trans. & intrans. [1. krímzun; 2. krímzən]. M.E. *crimosine* &c., O. Fr. *cramoisi(n)* (cp. **cramoisy**), Low Lat. *carmesīnus*, fr. Arab. & Pers. *quirmisī*, fr. Scrt. *kṛmi-*, 'worm, insect'. Applied to the colour because this is produced by the cochineal insect: cp. **carmine & kermes, vermi- & worm. a** n. A deep, slightly bluish, red colour; **b** adj., having, being of, this colour; **c** vb., to make, become, crimson in colour; specif. (intrans.) to blush.

crimson rambler, n. Descriptive name of a climbing, clustered rose.

cringe (I.), vb. trans. [1. krinj; 2. krindž]. Cp. O.E. *cringan, crinċġan*, 'to bend, sink down, fall' (esp. in battle). The word is connected w. **crinkle & crank.** To shrink, cower, as though in fear; hence, **a** to adopt a bodily attitude expressing fear or servility; **b** to behave to another in a servile, abject manner, betokening exaggerated and timid respect for him, and a lack of self-respect; to fawn, play the sycophant.

cringe (II.), n., fr. prec. The act of cringing, fawning &c.

cringing, adj. [1. krínjing; 2. kríndžiŋ], fr. Pres. Part. of **cringe** (I.). Abject, fawning, obsequious.

cringle, n. [1. kringgl; 2. kríŋgl]. L.G., E. Fris., & Du. *kringel*, 'a ring'; cp. O.N. *kringla*, 'orb, circle, ring', fr. old base meaning 'to bend'; connected w. **cringe, crinkle, crank** &c. (naut.) Metal ring or eyelet worked into the rope attached to a sail.

crinite, adj. [1. krínīt; 2. kráinait], fr. Lat. *crinīt-(um)*, P.P. of *crinīre*, 'to provide, cover, with hair', fr. *crīnis*, 'hair', wh. stands for **cris-nis*; this base occurs also in Lat. *crista*, 'tuft on the head of animals' (see **crest**), & means orig. 'something trembling, waving, shaking' &c. Outside Lat. the base occurs in Scrt. *krīdati*, 'he dances, plays' (for **krizd-*), & in Goth. *us-hrisjan*, 'to shake out', & O.E. *hrisian*, 'to shiver, shake' &c. Having hairs, hairy.

crinkle (I.), vb. intrans. & trans. [1. kríngkl; 2. kríŋkl]. Connected w. the group **crank, cringe. a** intrans. To become wrinkled, rumpled, undulated; **b** trans., to cause to wrinkle &c.

crinkle (II.), n., fr. prec. A wrinkle.

crinkly, adj. [1. kríngkli; 2. kríŋkli]. Prec. & **-y.** (of fabrics) Wrinkled, wavy; (of hair) twisting, curly.

crinkum-crankum, adj. & n. [1. kríngkum krángkum; 2. kríŋkəm krǽŋkəm]. See **crinkle & crank.** (colloq.) **a** adj. Full of twists and turns, tortuous (lit. and fig.); **b** n., something twisted.

crinoid, adj. & n. [1. krínoid; 2. krínɔid], fr. Gk. *krinon*, 'lily', the origin of wh. is unknown, & **-oid. a** adj. Lily-shaped; relating to a group of sea-urchins (also *crinoidal*); **b** n., a member of this group of animals.

crinoline, n. [1. krínolēn; 2. krínəlīn]. Fr., fr. Lat. *crīnis*, 'hair' (see **crinite**), & *lin*, fr. Lat. *līnum*, 'flax, a thread'; see **linum, linen. 1.** Device consisting of a light round steel frame and stiff fabric, originally of horse-hair, formerly used for producing a large bulging or swelling, in women's skirts. **2.** Framework of timber and wire-netting used as a protection against torpedoes on warships.

crio-, pref. meaning 'ram-headed', fr. Gk. *kriós*, 'a ram, battering-ram', cogn. w. Gk. *kéras*, 'a horn', & Homeric *keraós*, 'horned'. See **cerato- & hart.**

criosphinx, n. [1. kríōsfingks; 2. kráiousfiŋks]. Prec. & **sphinx.** Ram-headed sphinx.

cripple, n. & vb. trans. [1. krípl; 2. krípl]. O.E. *crўpel*, M.E. *crŭpel, crĭpel* &c., 'lame, paralysed person', fr. **krūp-il*, fr. base **kreup-*, as in O.E. *crēopan.* See **creep. 1.** n. A lame, or otherwise maimed, person; one who has lost the use of a limb; one who is disabled. **2.** vb. **a** To lame, to disable; **b** (fig.) to impair, weaken: *to cripple one's activities, usefulness* &c.

crippled, adj. [1. kripld; 2. kripld]. Prec. & **-ed.** Maimed, disabled; impaired.

crisis, n. [1. krísis; 2. kráisis], Lat., fr. Gk. *krisis*, 'a separating, putting apart, a decision', fr. *krinō*, 'I separate, decide, judge'. Same base in **crime, critic, cribriform, certain, riddle** (III.). **1.** The decisive moment, or stage, **a** in affairs, life, fate, politics; **b** turning-point in a disease. Hence, **2,** any difficult, dangerous, fateful situation, combination of circumstances: *financial crisis* &c.

crisp (I.), adj. [1. krisp; 2. krisp]. M.E. *crisp, crips*, 'curly'. Cp. Lat. *crispāre*, 'to curl, to set in trembling motion', fr. Lat. *crispus*, 'curled'. O.H.G. *hrespan*, 'to pluck', The base is perh. orig. the same as that in Lat. *crīnis*, 'hair'; see **crinite. 1. a** Curly, tightly curled (esp. of hair); **b** (bot.) curled or wrinkled (of cabbage leaves). **2.** Dry and brittle, liable to break easily: *crisp toast, biscuit* &c. **3.** (fig. uses) **a** (of style) Sharp, clear, incisive; **b** (of manners, utterance) brisk, decided; **c** lively, sparkling: *crisp repartee*; **d** inducing briskness, fresh and bracing: *crisp air.*

crisp (II.), vb. trans. & intrans., fr. prec. **A.** trans. **1.** To curl, to form into ringlets (of hair). **2.** To make (pastry, toast &c.) crisp. **B.** intrans. **1. a** To form into curls, or short, tight folds; **b** (of surface of water) to ripple. **2.** To become crisp (of toast &c.).

crispate, adj. [1. kríspāt; 2. kríspeit], fr. Lat. *crispātum*, P.P. of *crispāre*, 'to curl, wave'. See **crisp** (I.). Having a crisped, curled appearance.

crispation, n. [1. krispā́shun; 2. krispéiʃən]. Prec. & **-ion. 1.** Act of crisping or curling; state of being curled &c. **2.** A slight spasmodic contraction of the muscles or skin.

crisply, adv. [1. kríspli; 2. kríspli]. **crisp** (I. & **-ly.** In a crisp manner.

crispness, n. [1. kríspnes; 2. kríspnis]. See prec. & **-ness.** Quality of being crisp.

crispy, adj. [1. kríspi; 2. kríspi]. **crisp** (I.) & **-y. a** (poet.) Crisp, curly (of hair); **b** crisp, short (of crust, toast &c.).

criss-cross (I.), n. [1. krís kraws; 2. krís krɔ̄s]. For earlier *Christ-cross.* **1.** (archaic) Also *criss-cross row*, for Christ-cross row, name of a child's alphabet on a horn-book, from the cross which was placed at the beginning. **2.** A child's game, naughts and crosses, played on paper or slate, with squares made by drawing lines crossing each other. **3.** Mark made by crossing of two lines.

criss-cross (II.), adj., adv., & vb. trans., fr. prec. **1.** adj. Marked with crossed lines. **2.** adv. Cross-wise, in opposite directions. **3.** vb. To mark with crossed lines.

cristate, adj. [1. krístāt; 2. krísteit], fr. Lat. *cristātus*, 'having a crest or tuft', fr. *crista*, 'a tuft or crest on the head of animals'. See **crest.** Crested (of birds and animals).

criterion, n. [1. krītḗriun; 2. kraitíəriən]. Gk. *kritḗrion*, 'a means for judging', fr. *kritḗs*, 'a decider, judge', fr. *krínō*, 'I separate, decide'. See **critic.** A principle, means, standard, by which anything is judged; a test.

crith, n. [1. krith; 2. kriþ], fr. Gk. *krīthḗ*, 'barley-corn', also 'a small weight', etymol. doubtful. (phys.) Unit of weight for measuring gases.

critic, n. [1. krítik; 2. krítik]. Lat. *criticus*, fr. Gk. *kritikós*, adj., 'able to discern and decide'; cp. *kritēs*, 'judge', connected w. *krínō*, 'I pick out, separate, decide, judge, estimate'; cp. also Lat. *cernere*, 'to distinguish, perceive, understand, decide' (see **certain**), & *crībrum*, 'sieve'. See **cribriform, crime, crisis.** **1. a** One who forms and expresses a reasoned, balanced judgement on, or estimate of, a subject; specif., on works of art, or literature; **b** one whose profession is to write critical accounts of dramatic and musical performances, to review books &c.: *musical, dramatic, literary critic* &c.; **c** one skilled in judging, comparing, and emending ancient manuscripts, or other old and doubtful texts, distinguishing later corruptions from original matter &c.: *textual, biblical, critic.* **2.** One inclined to form severe, harsh, judgements of persons, actions, and things; one ready to find fault.

critical, adj. [1. krítikl; 2. krítikl]. Prec. & **-al.** **1. a** Pertaining to, based on, deliberate, reasoned, balanced, judgement: *a critical opinion, analysis* &c.; **b** connected with, based on, the work of textual critics: *a critical edition.* **2.** Fond of forming (generally harsh) judgements of men, actions &c.; censorious. **3. a** Indicating, pertaining to, a crisis or turning-point: *the critical moment*; hence, **b** fraught with risk, giving rise to anxiety: *in a critical condition* (of health). **4.** (phys. and math.) Marking a transition point of some character or property: *a critical angle*; *a critical curve* &c.

critically, adv. Prec. & **-ly.** In a critical manner.

criticism, n. [1. krítisìzm; 2. krítisìzəm]. **critic** & **-ism.** **1. a** The rules and principles which govern the methods of a critic; **b** the art of judging and estimating correctly the quality of works of art, literature &c.; **c** the work of a critic: *textual criticism*, scientific investigation, and analysis of texts, with a view to ascertaining the original form. **2.** A reasoned judgement, balanced estimate, esp. one in which defects are emphasized.

criticizable, adj. [1. krítisìzabl; 2. krítisàizəbl]. Next word & **-able.** Capable, worthy, of being criticized.

criticize, vb. trans. [1. krítisīz; 2. krítisaiz]. **critic** & **-ize.** **1.** To form and express a judgement on, to estimate, discuss as a critic. **2.** To censure, find fault with.

critique, n. [1. kritḗk; 2. kritík]. Fr., fr. Gk. *kritikḗ* (*tékhnē*), 'the critical art', fr. *kritikós.* See **critic.** **1.** A critical essay or review of a work of literature or art &c. **2.** The art of criticism.

croak, vb. intrans., rarely trans., & n. [1. krōk; 2. krouk]. O.E. has *crāc-ettan*, 'to croak'; cp. Swed. *kråka.* Of imitative origin & related to **creak, crow, crack.** **1.** vb. **a** To emit a loud, hoarse, dismal discordant cry or sound; specif., of frogs and ravens; **b** to take and express a dismal view of things, to foresee evil; **c** (colloq.) to die. **2.** n. The sound itself: *the raven's croak.*

croaker, n. [1. krṓker; 2. króukə]. Prec. & **-er.** **a** Animal or bird that croaks; **b** a person with harsh voice or cough; **c** a dismal, grumbling pessimist.

croaking, adj. & n. [1. krṓking; 2. króukiŋ]. **croak** & **-ing.** **1.** adj. **a** Given to emitting croaks: *a croaking frog*; **b** resembling a croak: *a croaking sound.* **2.** n. A croak: *the croaking of frogs.*

croceate, adj. [1. krṓseāt; 2. króusieit]. Lat. *croce-(us)*, 'saffron-coloured', & **-ate.** See **crocus.** Saffron-coloured.

crochet, n. & vb. trans. [1. krṓshā; 2. króuʃei]. Fr., 'a small hook', dimin. of *croche, croc*, 'hook', wh. is a Gmc. word, cp. O.N. *krōkr*, 'hook', see **crook (I.).** **1.** n. A kind of fancy-work, esp. in silk or wool, done with a small, ivory or metal hook. **2.** vb. To do work of this kind; to work (an article) with a crochet needle.

crochet-hook, n. Small ivory, bone, or steel hook for crochet work.

crocidolite, n. [1. krōsídolīt; 2. krousídəlait], fr. Gk. *krokís, krokídos*, 'flock, nap, pile of cloth', & **-lite**, 'stone'; cp. Gk. *krókē*, 'the woof, a thread', also *krékō*, 'I weave'; cogn. w. O.E. *hræġ(e)l*, 'garment' (see **rail (III.)**, & w. O.E. *hrēol*, 'reel', fr. **hreh-ul.* See **reel** (of cotton &c.). (mineral.) A blue or green fibrous mineral, silicate of iron and sodium; also known as *blue asbestos.*

crock (I.), n. [1. krok; 2. krɔk], fr. O.E. *croc, crocca*, 'earthenware pot', O.H.G. *chruac*, Mod. Germ. *krug*, 'jar, mug', O.N. *krukkr*; perh. of Celt. origin; cp. O. Ir. *crocan*, 'pitcher', W. *crochan*, 'a pot' &c. **a** An earthenware pot; **b** a broken piece of rough earthenware.

crock (II.), n. Etymol. doubtful; perh. fr. prec. **b** or related to **crack.** **a** An old or broken-down horse; (slang, of human beings) **b** a cripple; **c** an inefficient person, a poor creature.

crock (III.), vb. intrans. & trans. See prec. **1.** intrans. Usually *crock up*, (of horses or men) to become a crock. **2.** trans. **a** To break down (a horse); **b** to injure person's health, render him unfit for work; usually in P.P. *crocked.*

crockery, n. [1. krókeri; 2. krɔ́kəri], fr. **crock (I.)** & **-ery.** Collection of earthenware and china vessels, esp. for domestic use; pots and pans; applied colloquially and derisively to all kinds of china and porcelain.

crocket, n. [1. króket; 2. krɔ́kit]. Fr. *croquet*, dial. variant of **crochet.** (archit.) Small curved ornament on the side of a gable &c.

crocodile, n. [1. krókodīl; 2. krɔ́kədail]. M.E. *cokedrill*, fr. Low Lat. *cocodrillus*, fr. Gk. *krokódeilos*, earlier *krokodīlos*, 'lizard', fr. *krokó-drīlos*, fr. *krókē*, 'pebble', & *drīlos*, 'earth-worm', fr. the lizard's habit of basking on rocks in the sun. The first element is cogn. w. Scrt. *śarkara*, 'pebble' (see **sacchar-** & **sugar**); the etymol. of the second is doubtful. **1.** (zool.) A large thick-skinned, plated aquatic reptile with long tail and powerful jaws, some species of which is found in every continent but Europe, but usually of the African and Asiatic species; cp. *alligator* of America. Phr. *crocodile tears*, sham sorrow; from old belief that crocodiles wept while devouring their prey. **2.** (facetious) A girls' school, walking in couples.

crocodile bird, n. African bird resembling a plover, which feeds on the insect parasites of the crocodile.

crocodilian, adj. [1. krokodílian; 2. krɔkədíliən], fr. **crocodile** & **-ian.** Of, pertaining to, the *Crocodilia*, which includes crocodiles and alligators.

crocus, n. [1. krṓkus; 2. króukəs]. Lat. *crocus*, 'the crocus flower, saffron', fr. Gk. *krókos*, the colour 'saffron'; a Semitic word, cp. Heb. *karkōm.* Common plant growing from a bulb, with yellow, purple, or white flowers.

Croesus, n. [1. krḗsus; 2. krísəs]. Lat., fr. Gk. *Kroisos*, name of a king of Lydia, 6th cent. B.C., famous for his great wealth. A very rich man: *a regular Croesus.* Phr. *as rich as Croesus.*

croft, n. [1. krawft, kroft; 2. krōft, krɔft]. In O.E. & M.E.: cp. M. Du. *kroft*, 'field on the downs, high and dry land', Mod. Du., 'a hillock'; origin uncertain. **a** A small enclosed piece of arable or pasture land, usually adjoining a house; **b** a small farm.

crofter, n. [1. kráwfter; 2. krɔ́ftə]. Prec. & **-er.** One who owns and works a croft, or small farm, esp. in Scottish Highlands.

Cro-Magnon, adj. [1. krō mányon; 2. krou mǽnjɔ̃], fr. name of caves in Dordogne, France. (anthrop.) The name given to a race of late palaeolithic man, belonging to the Aurignacian period, tall and long-headed.

cromlech, n. [1. krómlek; 2. krɔ́mlek]. W., fr. *crom*, 'bent, inclined', & *llech*, 'flat flagstone'. An ancient prehistoric structure, a kind of sepulchral monument, consisting of a large flat stone laid as a roof across two or more other stones standing upright.

cromorna, n. [1. kromórna; 2. krəmɔ́nə], fr. Fr. *cromorne*, fr. Germ. *krummhorn*, 'crooked horn'. See **cramp** & **horn** (mus.) An organ reed-stop.

crone, n. [1. krōn; 2. kroun]. In M.E. (Chaucer). Perh. fr. O. Fr. *caroigne* (cp. **carrion**); cp. also O. Du. (fr. O. Fr.) *karonie, kronie*, 'an old ewe'. A hideous, withered, squalid, old woman.

crony, n. [1. krṓni; 2. króuni]. Perh. fr. Gk. *khrónios*, 'lasting', fr. *khrónos*, 'time'. See **chronicle.** An intimate and constant companion, an old friend.

crook (I.), n. [1. krook; 2. kruk]. M.E. *crōke*, fr. O.N. *krōkr*, 'hook, bend'; perh. connected w. **crutch.** **1. a** A shepherd's staff having a rounded, bent, top end; **b** anything shaped like this; **c** a bend, curve. Phr. *by hook or by crook*, by any means, fair or foul; somehow or other. **2.** (slang) One who lives by his wits; a professional swindler, or sharper.

crook (II.), vb. trans. & intrans., fr. prec. **a** To bend, curve, into the shape of a crook; **b** to catch with a crook.

crookback(ed), adj. [1. króokbak(t); 2. krúkbæk(t)]. Humpbacked. (Rare.)

crooked, adj. [1. króoked; 2. krúkid]. **crook (I.)** & **-ed.** Not straight; bent, curved, awry; specif. **a** (of persons) deformed, distorted; **b** (fig., in moral sense) dishonest, tortuous, reverse of straightforward: *crooked dealing.*

crookedly, adv. Prec. & **-ly.** In a crooked manner.

crookedness, n. See prec. & **-ness.** State of being crooked.

croon, vb. trans. & intrans. & n. [1. kro͞on; 2. krūn]. Cp. M. Du. *krōnen*, 'to murmur'. **a** vb. To hum or sing in a gentle undertone: *to croon a song*; *to croon to oneself*; **b** n., also *crooning*, low singing, or humming.

crop (I.), n. [1. krop; 2. krɔp]. O.E. *cropp*, 'sprout, bunch of flowers, ear of corn; crop of a bird; kidney'; O.H.G. *kropf*, 'growth on human body, craw of a bird'; O.N. *kroppr*, 'hunch, bump on the body'; Swed. *kropp*, Dan. *krop*, 'trunk of the body'. The root meaning appears to be 'something which sticks out, protuberance', hence, 'something which sticks out of the earth, which grows; the top of a growing plant', &c. The various senses in Engl. are mostly indigenous developments in our language, the starting-point of wh., however, is discernible in the meanings of the different forms in the other Gmc. languages. It is tempting to connect Gk. *bréphos*, 'new-born child, foetus, fruit of the womb', wh. is fr. earlier **gʷrebhos*; cp. Scrt. *gárbhaś*, 'womb'. The *ŏ* of the Gmc. words, however, presents difficulties, as this must go back to earlier *ŭ*, wh. is hard to account for, unless indeed we assume an Aryan **gʷr̥bbh-*, Gmc. **kurpp-*, whence w. metathesis, **kruppa-.* See further derivatives of Gmc. **kropp* under **croup(e)** & **crupper.** Cp. also **group.** **1.** The pouch in the gullet of birds, the craw. Phr. *neck and crop*, (colloq.) bodily, altogether, bag and baggage. **2.** The stock or handle of a whip; specif., a riding-whip with a short handle and a flat loop of leather to which a lash can be fastened; also *hunting-crop.* **3.** That which the earth produces as a result of each year's growth—grain, grass, vegetables, fruit, roots: *a crop of hay, of corn, of beans, of mangolds, of apples* &c. Collectively, *the crops*, the total yield of a season in every kind of growth of grain, grass, vegetables, fruit &c. **4.** (by extension) A group or collection of things; esp. **a** of things which grow on the body: *a crop of pimples, blisters* &c.; **b** of other things occurring together: *a crop of letters, bills, applications* &c. **5.** The entire tanned hide of an animal, esp. of a cow or steer. **6.** (new formation from vb.) Condition of the hair when cut very short: *a close crop.*

crop (II.), vb. trans. & intrans., fr. prec. **A.** trans. **1. a** To cut off; (of animals) to bite, nibble, off the tops of plants, herbage &c.: *to crop the young grass*; **b** to gather, pluck, reap (rare). **2.** To clip or cut short: esp. *to crop the hair*; *to crop the ears of a person*, to cut them off as a punishment; *to crop the ears, tail, of an animal.* **3.** To plant with seed so as to cause to produce a crop: *to crop a field with barley.* **B.** intrans. (of plants) To yield crop: *lucerne crops heavily. Crop up*, **a** (fig.) to come, appear, turn up, unexpectedly: *difficulties cropped up*; **b** (min. and geol., of a seam, rock &c.) to come to the surface, appear at the surface.

crop-eared, adj. [1. króp ērd; 2. krɔ́p iəd]. Having the ears cropped; also, having hair cut short to show the ears.

cropper, n. [1. króper; 2. krɔ́pə]. **crop (II.)** & **-er. 1.** Person or thing that crops. **2.** A pouter pigeon, one having a large crop. **3.** A plant which yields a crop; esp. in Phr. *a good, poor &c. cropper.* **4.** (colloq.) A heavy, crashing, fall. Phr. *to come a cropper*, (i.) have a heavy fall; (ii.) (fig.) to collapse; experience failure in an undertaking, business &c.; to undergo moral disaster.

croppy, n. [1. krópi; 2. krɔ́pi], fr. **crop (I.) 6** & **-y.** Person with short, cropped hair, applied to the Roundheads and later to the rebels in Ireland of 1798.

croquet (I.), n. [1. krṓkā, -i; 2. króukei, -i]. Fr., dial. variant of **crochet**, dimin. of *croc*, 'crook, hook'. **1.** A game played on a levelled lawn between one or more players a side, in which large wooden balls are driven with wooden mallets through a series of narrow iron hoops set in the ground. **2.** The act of croqueting a ball. See **croquet (II.)**.

croquet (II.), vb. trans., fr. prec. To drive away an opponent's ball in croquet, by placing one's own in contact with it and striking the former sharply with the mallet.

croquette, n. [1. krōkét; 2. kroukét]. Fr., fr. *croquer*, 'to crunch'. (cookery) Ball of meat, rice, potato &c., seasoned and fried brown and crisp.

crore, n. [1. krōr; 2. krɔ̄]. Anglo-Ind. word, fr. Hind. *karor*. One hundred lakhs, or ten million rupees.

crosier, crozier, n. [1. krṓzier, krṓzher; 2. króuziə, króužə]. M.E. *crocer, croyser* &c.; O. Fr. *crossier* was one who carried a *crosse* or bishop's staff, & the word has been transferred fr. the bearer to the staff itself. O. Fr. & Fr. *crosse*, though confused w. **cross (I.)** is not historically connected w. the latter, but is of Gmc. origin, see under **crutch**; the Gmc. **krukkja* meaning a bent staff. Further confusion in form has taken place w. Gmc. **krōk*, 'hook', q.v. under **crook (I.)**. **a** Pastoral staff of a Bishop, generally in the form of a shepherd's crook, and symbolical of his pastoral functions; **b** (fig.) the office, functions, authority of a bishop.

cross (I.), n. [1. kraws, kros; 2. krɔ̄s, krɔs]. O.E. *cros* occurs only in a rather late (10th cent.) document in Place-Name *Normannes cros*; the native & usual O.E. word was *rōd* (see **rood**), wh. has been displaced by the present word. M.E. commonly has *cros*. This form of the word prob. came through O.N. *kross*, fr. the O. Ir. type *cros*. The other old W. Gmc. languages have a different type: O.S. *krūzi*, M. Du. *crūsi*, Du. *kruis*; O.H.G. *krūsi*, M.H.G. *kriuze*, Mod. Germ. *kreuz*. All these, together w. the various forms in Romance languages, Ital. *croce*, Span. & Port. *cruz*, Fr. *croix*, are ultimately derived fr. Lat. *crux*, genit. *crucis*, 'cross'. Cp. **crux. 1. a** Structure of wood upon which martyrs and malefactors were executed by the ancients, usually consisting of an upright piece of timber with a shorter piece fastened near the top, at right angles, but sometimes lacking this; **b** specif., *the Cross*, that upon which the Saviour died. *The True Cross*, actual cross upon which Christ died. **2. a** Any model or pictorial representation (of which there are many recognized forms) of *Christ's Cross*, esp. as a symbol of Christ's death and its purpose; hence, specif. **b** Christianity as symbolized by the Cross: *the Cross versus the Crescent*; *the power of the Cross*; *a follower of the Cross.* **3.** (fig.) Affliction, suffering, trouble, misfortune: *to bear one's crosses.* **4. a** A staff surmounted by a cross, often of precious metal and highly decorated, carried in religious processions; **b** specif., that borne before an archbishop as a sign of his office; **c** *pectoral cross*, one made of gold worn by a bishop, suspended on his breast. **5.** A structure in the form of, or surmounted by, a cross: *a market cross*; *a boundary cross* &c. **6.** Insignia of an Order, in shape of a cross, of gold, silver, or other metal, often enamelled with various coloured designs, worn by members, esp. **a** one distinguishing orders of knighthood: *Grand Cross of Michael and George* &c.; or **b** a decoration for personal gallantry in war: *Victoria Cross*; *Military Cross* &c. **7. a** A line or stroke in ink, pencil &c., drawn at right angles through the upright part of a letter: *the cross of a t*; **b** a cross-shaped mark (+) put as a distinguishing mark on part of a sketch, plan &c.; **c** similar mark, as signature, used by those unable to write: *to make one's cross*, to sign with this mark. **8.** (astron.) *The Southern Cross*, a constellation. **9.** (derived from vb. **cross (II.)**, 7) A mingling of races, breeds, species; the product of such a mixture; a hybrid, mongrel: *a cross between a Malay and a Chinese, between a Leghorn and a Rhode Island Red* (fowl) &c.

cross (II.), vb. trans. & intrans., fr. prec. **A.** trans. **1. a** To put or lay across or over, to place crosswise: *to cross one's legs*, put one leg over the other; Phrs. *to cross swords with a person*, to fight with; (also fig.) to engage in argument with; *to cross a fortune-teller's palm with money*, to give him, or her, money; **b** to intersect: (of two roads) *to cross each other.* **2.** (reflex.) *Cross oneself*, to make the sign of the cross on one's forehead and breast. **3.** To draw a line or lines across: *to cross a t.* Phrs. (fig.) *to cross one's t's*, to be very exact and scrupulous in speech and conduct; *to cross off, cross out*, to cancel by drawing a line or lines across; *to cross a cheque*, to draw two parallel lines at right angles across the face of a cheque, often with words *& Co.* between them, to indicate that the cheque can only be paid through a bank; *to cross a letter*, write at right angles across what is already written. **4. a** To go, walk, across, pass over from one side to the other, traverse: *to cross a road, room, field, river, sea, the desert* &c.; Phrs. *to cross one's path*, to meet; (fig.) to be brought, come into personal relations with; *to cross a horse*, to ride; **b** to cause to pass over, to carry or take across (rare); **c** (fig.) *to cross one's mind* (of thoughts, ideas &c.), to occur to one. **5. a** (of persons) To meet and pass: *to cross each other on the road*; **b** (of letters written by two persons) to be written, and arrive, at same time: *your letter crossed mine*, or, *our letters have crossed each other in the post.* **6.** To thwart, obstruct, oppose (a person, another's will, plans). **7.** To mingle the breed or strain of animals, birds, plants; to interbreed. **B.** intrans. **1.** To move or pass over from one side to another: *to cross from Dover to Calais*; also *cross over.* **2.** (of letters) To meet and pass: *to cross in the post.* **3.** To interbreed, to become mixed in strain.

cross (III.), adj., fr. **cross (I.)**. **1.** Passing from side to side, placed across, transverse, intersecting: *cross stroke, beam* &c. **2.** Contrary, adverse, opposed *to* a purpose. **3.** (of persons) Irritated in mind, peevish, fretful, bad-tempered. Phr. *as cross as two sticks*, very cross, irritable.

crossbar, n. [1. kráwsbar; 2. krɔ́sbā]. Bar of wood fastened across one or more others, as between goal-posts at football &c.

crossbeam, n. [1. kráwsbēm; 2. krɔ́sbīm]. A girder; a transverse supporting beam.

cross-bearer, n. One who bears a cross, esp. in a religious procession.

cross-bench, n. One of the places in House of Commons occupied by members who vote with neither party. *Cross-bencher*, one sitting on the cross-benches; a neutral.

crossbill, n. [1. kráwsbil; 2. krɔ́sbil]. A kind of finch, with mandibles crossing each other.

crossbones, n. pl. [1. kráwsbōnz; 2. krɔ́sbounz]. Representation of two thigh-bones crossed, usually under one of a skull; in Phr. *skull and crossbones*, the symbol of death; also pirates' emblem.

crossbow, n. [1. kráwsbō; 2. krɔ́sbou]. An arbalest, a mediaeval weapon consisting of a bow fastened at right angles to a wooden stock, with a groove for the shafts, and a kind of trigger for releasing the bow-string.

crossbred, adj. [1. kráwsbred; 2. krɔ́sbrɛd]. Produced by mixing breeds, varieties &c.; mongrel.

crossbreed, n. **a** [1. kráwsbrēd; 2. krɔ́sbrīd]. A mixed strain (of men or beasts); **b** [1. kráwsbrēd; 2. krɔ́sbrīd] an individual produced from parents of different species or races; a hybrid.

cross-bun, n. Generally *hot cross-bun*, one marked with a cross, eaten on Good Friday.

cross-buttock, n. A throw in wrestling, made by using the hip as a lever.

cross counter, n. (boxing) A blow countering a lead to the head in which the countering right arm crosses the opponent's left.

cross-country, adj. Across the country or fields, not by the roads: *a cross-country race.*

crosscut, adj. [1. kráwskut; 2. krɔ́skat]. **a** *Crosscut saw*, one made for cutting across the grain; **b** cut across the grain.

crosse, n. (1. kraws, kros; 2. krɔ̄s, krɔs]. **Fr.**, fr. O. Fr. *croce, croc*, 'hook', see **crochet.** Long-handled racquet, used in the game of lacrosse, with which the ball is caught, carried, and thrown.

cross entry, n. (book-keeping) An entry transferring an amount to a different account.

cross-examination, n. Examination by a barrister in court of a witness on the other side; any severe questioning.

cross-examine, vb. trans. Specif. (of a counsel in court) to examine a witness who has been already examined by the counsel on the other side; to question closely.

cross-eyed, adj. Squinting, having eyes looking in different directions.

cross fire, n. (mil.) Firing directed on an objective from two or more points so that the lines of fire cross; (also fig.) of questions &c.

cross-grain, n. Grain in wood running across the regular grain.

cross-grained, adj. [1. kráws grānd; 2. krɔ́s greind]. **a** (of wood) Having the grain running transversely or irregularly; **b** (fig., of persons) perverse, cantankerous.

cross-hatch, vb. trans. To engrave or shade (a drawing) by means of a series of cross lines.

cross-hatching, n., fr. prec. Process of shading &c. by a cross-hatch.

cross-heading, n. A sentence, or short headline, inserted at intervals in a column of an article in a newspaper &c. to indicate the point, contents &c. of what follows.

crossing, n. [1. kráwsing; 2. krɔ́siŋ]. **cross (II.)** & **-ing. 1.** Act of passing across, traversing, anything; specif., sea-passage: *a good, a rough, crossing*; *the Channel crossing.* **2.** The point where two roads, railway lines, cross; *a level crossing*, place where a road runs across a railway line, being closed to traffic while trains are passing. **3.** Specially paved place where a street may be crossed, generally at point where two roads intersect each other. 4. The act of contradicting or thwarting (archaic).

crossing-sweeper, n. One who sweeps a street crossing.

cross-legged, adj. Having one leg crossed over another when sitting.

crosslet, n. [1. kráwslet; 2. krɔ́slit]. Dimin., fr. **cross** (I.) & **-let**. Small heraldic cross.

cross-light, n. Light coming from two or more different directions.

crossly, adv. [1. kráwsli; 2. krɔ́sli]. **cross** (III.) & **-ly**. Peevishly, ill-temperedly.

crossness, n. [1. kráwsnes; 2. krɔ́snis]. See prec. & **-ness**. Peevishness, bad temper.

crosspatch, n. [1. kráwspach; 2. krɔ́spætʃ]. (colloq.) A cross, bad-tempered person.

cross-purpose, n. Purpose which conflicts with, is inconsistent with, another: *to be at cross-purposes*, to have a misunderstanding with another person; to act or argue counter to one another (unintentionally and through misunderstanding).

cross-question, n. & vb. trans. **a** n. (rare) Question put in cross-examination; **b** vb., to cross-examine.

cross reference, n. One from one part of a book &c. to others, or another, where a particular question is further dealt with.

crossroad, n. [1. kráwsrōd; 2. krɔ́sroud]. **a** One which crosses another at right angles; **b** smaller road joining two main roads; pl. *crossroads* (used as sing.), the place where two roads intersect. Phr. (fig.) *at the crossroads*, decisive moment when one must settle what line of conduct &c. one will pursue.

cross-stitch, n. Kind of needlework consisting of stitches in which threads cross each other.

cross-trees, n. pl. (naut.) Horizontal timbers at mast-head, which serve to spread the shrouds that support the masts.

crosswise, adv. [1. kráwswīz; 2. krɔ́swaiz]. **cross** (I.) & **-wise**. **a** In the form of a cross; **b** across, athwart.

cross-word, n. A word written or printed so as to cross another word, having one letter in common with it at the point of intersection. *Cross-word puzzle*, puzzle based on an arrangement of such words, which are to be discovered from clues referring to numbered squares, each letter being inserted in a separate square.

crotch, n. [1. kroch; 2. krɔtʃ]. Prob. variant of **crutch**. Place **a** where a branch forks from a tree; **b** where the legs fork from the human trunk.

crotchet, n. [1. króchet; 2. krɔ́tʃit]. Fr., dimin. of *croc*, 'hook'. See **crochet**. **1.** (mus.) **a** A note having half time-value of a minim; **b** the symbol of this. **2.** A fad, fixed, perverse notion obstinately held; unreasoning whim.

crotchetiness, n. [1. króchetines; 2. krɔ́tʃitinis]. See next word & **-ness**. State of being crochety.

crotchety, adj. [1. krócheti; 2. krɔ́tʃiti]. Prec. & **-y**. (of persons) Full of crotchets or whims.

croton, n. [1. krṓtun; 2. króutən], fr. Gk. *krotṓn*, 'a sheep-tick', fr. shape of the seeds. Perh. connected w. Gk. *krotṓnē*, 'growth, lump', q.v. under **cartilage**. (bot.) A genus of strong-scented plants, from which a medicinal purgative oil of this name is obtained.

crouch (I.), vb. intrans. [1. krouch; 2. krautʃ]. M.E. *crouchen*, 'to bend', fr. O. Fr. *crochir*, 'to become bent, crooked', fr. *croche*, 'hook', a Gmc. loan-word; cp. O.N. *krōkr*, 'hook'. See **crook** (I.). **a** (of persons) To adopt a huddled-up attitude, in which the body is bent and the limbs drawn close together so as to occupy as small a space as possible, as though shrinking from observation, or to avoid a blow; **b** (of animals) to lie close to the ground in corresponding attitude, from fear, or when about to pounce upon prey. Also *crouch down*.

crouch (II.), n., fr. prec. Posture of one crouching.

croup, n. [1. kro͞op; 2. krūp]. Of imitative origin. Cp. Scots dial. *crowp*, 'to croak, cry out'. Connected w. **crow**, & prob. associated w. Scots *roup*, 'to call', fr. O.N. *hrōpa*, 'call out'. (med.) An inflammatory disease of the throat accompanied by a hard cough and difficulty in breathing; generally attacking children.

croup(e), n. [1. kro͞op; 2. krūp]. Fr. *croupe*, 'hind quarters'; of Gmc. origin. See **crop** (I.) & **crupper**. The hind quarters of a horse.

croupier, n. [1. kro͞opiā; 2. krúpiei]. Fr., fr. *croupe*, 'hind quarters', lit. 'one who rides on the croup', hence 'a servant, assistant.' See **croup(e)**. **1.** The person who presides at a gaming table and who rakes in, and pays out, money. **2.** Assistant chairman at a public dinner.

crow (I.), n. [1. krō; 2. krou]. O.E. *crāwe*, M.E. *crōwe*, 'a crow', fr. *crāwan*, 'to crow'. See **crow** (II.). Any of a large group of birds of the genus *Corvus* (including raven, rook, jackdaw &c.), which are entirely black and have loud harsh voices. Phrs. *as black as a crow*; *a white crow*, a rarity; *as the crow flies*, in a direct line; *to have a crow to pluck with* (*person*), an unpleasant matter to discuss and settle with him, a criticism to make.

crow (II.), vb. intrans. O.E. *crāwan*, M.E. *crōwen*, 'to crow like a cock'. Of imitative origin; cp. O.H.G. *kragilōn*, 'to chatter'; cogn. w. Lat. *graculus*, 'jackdaw', O. Slav. *grakati*, 'to croak'; further connected w. Lat. *garrīre*, 'to chatter'; see **garrulous**. Although historically connected w. the bird-name *crow*, this vb. has never been used in Engl. to express the cry of this bird. **1.** (of a cock) To utter the loud, shrill, characteristic cry. **2.** (of persons, fig.) **a** To express, by vocal utterance, the emotions of satisfaction and exultation, to triumph: *to crow over*, to exult, triumph over (anyone whom one has defeated physically or morally); **b** to feel and express jubilation at success of any kind. **3.** (of an infant) To utter a soft sound expressing pleasure or mirth.

crow (III.), n., fr. prec. The crowing of the cock: *cock-crow*, the dawn; also the joyful cry of an infant.

crowbar, n. [1. krṓbar; 2. króubā]. **crow** (I.) & **bar**. A stout iron bar, used as a lever, for prizing and lifting; so called from its pointed end, supposed to resemble a crow's beak.

crowberry, n. [1. krṓberi; 2. króubəri]. **a** A low shrub, growing on heaths, with black edible berries; **b** (U.S.A.) the cranberry.

crowbill, crow's-bill, n. [1. krṓ-, krṓz bil; 2. króu-, króuz bil]. Small forceps.

crowd (I.), n. [1. kroud; 2. kraud]. M.E. *crūd*. The O.E. *ġe-crod*, 'crowd, throng', is fr. same base, but is not the ancestor of the modern n., wh. is a later formation fr. the vb. See next word. **1. a** An assembly of persons large enough to produce a sense of considerable mass, casually gathered together without organized discipline or order; a multitude: (*large*) *crowds in the streets*; Phrs. *the crowd*, the multitude, the masses, the mob; *to go with, follow, the crowd*, to do what majority is doing; **b** a densely packed assembly, a throng, in which space is insufficient: *the audience was large, but there was no crowd.* **2.** (colloq.) A company of persons associated by a common tie; set, clique: *he belongs to a fast, extravagant crowd.* **3.** A large number of things in close proximity, or in one place; generally implying lack of order and arrangement: *a room littered with a crowd of books.* **4.** (naut.) *Crowd of sail*, a large number of sails hoisted at same time, on same ship; **b** large number of sailing-ships.

crowd (II.), vb. intrans. & trans. O.E. *crūdan*, 'to press forward, hasten' (esp. of a ship), M.E. *crūden*, *crouden*, 'to crowd, thrust, push'; cp. also M.E. *crūde*, 'barrow, handcart', & *croudewain* in same sense, & M. Du. *kruyden*, 'to push in a handcart'. The above show sufficiently the orig. meaning & make it clear that the chief mod. sense is secondary, though the word still retains some shade of the older meaning. The remoter origin, beyond Gmc., is obscure. **A.** intrans. **1. a** To collect in numbers so as to form a crowd; to throng: esp. *crowd together, round*; **b** to press forward in a mass; to flock: esp. *to crowd into* (*a room*), *through* (*a gate*) &c. **2.** (fig., of ideas, thoughts, images &c.) *To crowd in upon*, to come thick and fast; to rush into the mind. **B.** trans. **1.** To fill to excess; occupy (a place) by pressing or thronging together into it: *to crowd a church, street* &c. **2. a** To oppress, press upon, squeeze (persons) as in a crowd; **b** to cause an excessive number of persons or things to enter a place; to pack tight, fill to excess: *to crowd people into a room*; *to crowd a room with people, furniture*; *to crowd books into a box.* **3.** (naut.) *To crowd* (*on*) *sail*, to hoist a large number of sails so as to increase the speed of a vessel.

crowd (III.), n. M.E. *crowde*, 'a fiddle'; Celt., cp. W. *crwth*, 'a swelling, bulging thing; a fiddle'. (archaic) An old-fashioned, now obsolete, stringed instrument played with a bow, somewhat resembling a violin, but often without a neck.

crowded, adj. [1. króuded; 2. kráudid], fr. P.P. of **crowd** (II.). **1.** (of material conditions) **a** (of places) Filled to excess, packed with people: *crowded streets, church, house, room* &c.; **b** (of living things generally) pressed upon by a crowd, restricted in movement, lacking adequate room, inconveniently close together: *to feel crowded by one's audience*; *the beasts were too crowded in their small stable*; *trees rather crowded* &c.; **c** (of inanimate objects) encumbered, excessively filled or covered: *a room crowded with furniture*; *a table crowded with papers and books* &c. **2.** (of non-material conditions) **a** (of mental states) Oppressed by duties, responsibilities &c.; **b** (of periods of time) thronged, packed, with action, experience &c.: *a life crowded with adventure*; '*One crowded hour of glorious life*' (quoted by Scott, and until recently attributed to him).

crowder, n. [1. króuder; 2. kráudə], fr. **crowd** (III.) & **-er**. Player on a crowd; itinerant fiddler.

crowfoot, n. [1. krṓfoot; 2. króufut]. **crow** (I.) & **foot**. Name of various plants, of buttercup class, from shape of leaves.

crown (I.), n. [1. kroun; 2. kraun]. M.E. *croune* &c., fr. O. Fr. *corone*, *corune*, Fr. *couronne*, fr. Lat. *corōna*, 'garland, wreath, crown'; a loan-word fr. Gk. *korōnís*, 'anything curved, wreath'; cp. also Gk. *korṓnē*, 'tip of bow, to which bowstring was hooked', & *korōnós*, 'curved, bent; (of cows) having crumpled horns'. The word is fr. same base as Lat. *curvus*, 'bent', & *circus*, 'ring, circle', & the various groups of words related to these. See **circus** & **curve** (I.). **1. a** A wreath or garland for the head, esp. as symbol of victory; **b** (fig.) a reward, esp. that of heavenly bliss: *the martyr's crown*; '*a crown of life*'. **2. a** Head-dress of gold highly ornamented, and set with gems, worn on ceremonial occasions by emperors and kings; **b** regarded as the symbol of the kingly office and function: *to succeed to the crown, relinquish the crown*, to become, cease to be, king; **c** the king or queen, him or herself: *demise of the crown*, death of the king; **d** the supreme power and government in a monarchy: *an officer of the crown*; *a crown appointment.* **3.** Any representation, pictorial or other, of a royal crown, e.g. as a crest on note-paper, a carriage; badge of a major's rank; as mark indicating government property &c.; **4.** British silver coin, worth five shillings, formerly bearing image of royal crown. **5.** A size of paper (15″ × 20″) originally having royal crown as a watermark. **6.** Summit, highest point of achievement or development; most perfect state of anything: *the crown of one's labours*; *the crown of the year.* **7.** The top or highest part of a thing; specif. **a** the top of the skull or head; (by extension) the head: *to break a man's crown*; **b** the top of a hat; **c** (archit.) the highest part of an arch; **d** (anat.) that part of a tooth which projects beyond the gum; **e** (naut.) the end of the shank of an anchor where the arms join it.

crown (II.) vb. trans., fr. prec. **1. a** To place a crown upon a man's head, thus investing him with the kingly office: *to crown (person)*; *crown (him) king*; **b** to honour, reward, in allusion to the ancient crowning of victors with wreaths: *to crown a person with glory*. **2. a** To occupy the head of; to top, cap, surmount: *a hill crowned with wood*; *a tower crowned with a spire*; **b** (fig.) to put the finishing touch to: *the end crowns the work*. **3.** (draughts) To place one piece upon another, when it reaches a certain line on the board, to indicate that it is a 'king'. **4.** Specif. (dentistry) *to crown a tooth*, to cover it with gold or other material as a protection.

Crown Colony, n. One belonging to the British Empire which is governed direct from the Colonial Office.

crowner, n. [1. króuner; 2. kráunə]. See **coroner.** (archaic; now vulg., or provinc.) Coroner; as in Phr. *crowner's quest*, an inquest.

crown glass, n. Thick glass used for window panes, blown in a special manner, so as to leave a knot in the centre.

crown imperial, n. **a** An emperor's crown; **b** a species of tall garden lily.

crown-law, n. That of criminal prosecutions.

crown prince, n. Heir-apparent to a throne, esp. in North Europe (Sweden, Denmark &c. and formerly in Prussia and Bavaria).

crown princess, n. The wife of a crown prince.

crown-wheel, n. A wheel with cogs or teeth set in its rims at right angles to its plane, as in a watch.

crow-quill, n. A small steel pen used for fine writing, lithography, tracing &c.

crow's-foot, n. Various things shaped like the foot of a crow: specif. **1.** (mil.) a caltrop. **2.** Usually pl., *crow's-feet*, series of wrinkles, which diverge from outer corner of human eye in old age.

crow's-nest, n. A small protected platform on mast-head of a sailing vessel for the look-out man.

crozier. See **crosier.**

crucial, adj. [1. kro͝oshl, kro͝oshial; 2. krúʃl, krúʃiəl], fr. Lat. *cruci-* 'cross', & **-al.** See **crux.** Fr. *crucial*, used of surgical incisions, means 'cross-shaped'. **1.** (surg.) Cross-shaped: *crucial incision*. **2. a** Relating to final and supreme trial, or decision, decisive, critical: *crucial test*, *experiment* &c.; **b** of the nature of a crux; severe, difficult: *crucial period*, *question*.

crucian carp, n. [1. kro͝oshan kárp; 2. krúʃən káp]. Fr. *carousse*, fr. Lat. *coracīnus*, 'species of river fish', fr. Gk. *korakînos*, 'young raven', also 'a kind of perch' (fr. its colour), fr. *kórax*, 'crow'. See base **kor-*, 'croak', in **corvine, rook.** A species of carp.

cruciate, adj. [1. kro͝osiāt, kro͝oshiāt; 2. krúsieit, krúʃieit]. Formally might be fr. Lat. *cruciātum*, P.P. of *cruciāre*, 'to crucify, torture', fr. *crux*, 'cross' (see **crux**); but the word is prob. a new formation fr. *cruci-* & **-ate**, w. special meaning. Cross-shaped; specif. (bot.) having leaves or petals in the form of a cross.

crucible, n. [1. kro͝osibl; 2. krúsibl]. Low Lat. *crucibulum*, 'a hanging lamp', also 'a melting pot'. The etymol. is doubtful, but Skeat suggests *cruci-*, 'cross-shaped', fr. a type of lamp w. four wicks coming fr. arms in form of a cross. The suff. is doubtless on the anal. of Lat. *thuribulum*, 'censer' (see **thurible**). *Cruci-* here might possibly be a neo-Lat. word akin to Fr. *cruche*, 'earthenware pot' &c., wh. is fr. Gmc.; cp. O.N. *krukka*, 'pot', O.H.G. *kruog*, Mod. Germ. *krug*. See **crock (I.).** **a** A melting-pot of earthenware, platinum &c., for melting substances which require great heat to dissolve; *crucible steel*, a very fine, hard steel, used for making tools; **b** (fig.) a severe, searching test.

cruciferous, adj. [1. kro͝osíferus; 2. krūsífərəs], fr. L. Lat. *crucifer*, 'cross-bearing', & **-ous.** See **crux & -ferous.** (bot.) Belonging to the *Cruciferae*, a natural order of plants with flowers of four petals arranged as a cross, which includes the cabbage, turnip &c.

crucifix, n. [1. kro͝osifiks; 2. krúsifiks]. Fr., or direct fr. L. Lat. *crucifixus*, 'one fixed to the cross', fr. Lat. *crux*, stem *cruci-*, 'cross', & *fixus*, P.P. of *fīgere*, 'to fix'. See **crux & fix (I.).** A religious emblem consisting of sculptured or moulded figure of the Saviour upon the Cross.

crucifixion, n. [1. kro͝osifíkshun; 2. krūsifíkʃən], fr. L. Lat. *crucifixiōn-(em)*. **crucifix & -ion. 1. a** The act of crucifying or hanging a person upon a cross; specif., the crucifying of Christ; **b** a pictorial representation of this. **2.** The state of being crucified; death on a cross; specif., the death of Christ. **3.** (fig.) Great suffering or affliction.

cruciform, adj. [1. kro͝osiform; 2. krúsifōm]. Lat. base, *cruci-*, 'cross'. See **crux & -form.** Cross-shaped; esp. built in the form of a cross, as churches with transepts.

crucify, vb. trans. [1. kro͝osifī; 2. krúsifai]. Fr. *crucifier*, fr. Low Lat. **crucificāre* for *crucifīgere*, 'to fix to a cross'. See **crux & fix (I.)** **a** To fasten to a cross, to put to death by nailing to a cross; **b** (fig.) to subdue, mortify, by a severe, ascetic mode of life: esp. *to crucify the passions, evil desires* &c.

crude, adj. [1. kro͞od; 2. krūd], fr. Lat. *crūdus*, 'raw, hard; undigested (of food); unprepared, undressed (of hides &c.); harsh, cruel'; connected w. Lat. *cruor*, 'gore, thick blood', *crūdēlis*, 'cruel' &c. A large group of Gmc. words, of wh. O.E. *hrēaw*, 'raw' (see **raw**), is an example, are related; possibly also Gk. *kréas*, 'raw flesh', & Gk. *kruós*, 'icy', *krústallos*, 'ice'; see **crystal.** See also **cruel, crust. 1.** (of physical condition) **a** Rough, bitter to the taste (poet. and archaic): '*I come to pluck thy berries harsh and crude*' (Milton); **b** in a natural state, raw; not cooked; not refined or prepared for use: *crude flesh*; *crude salt, sugar* &c.; **c** (rare, of food) not digested; (of fruit &c.) unripe. **2.** (fig., of non-material things) **a** Ill-conceived, badly arranged, not thought out, immature: *crude theories, methods, statements*; **b** lacking finish or grace; unpolished: *crude manners*; **c** (of colours) harsh, garish, inharmonious; **d** undisguised, not softened down, bald, bare: *crude facts, necessities*.

crudely, adv. Prec. & **-ly.** In a crude manner.

crudeness, n. See prec. & **-ness.** Quality of being crude.

crudity, n. [1. kro͞oditi; 2. krúditi]. Fr. *crudité*, Lat. *crūditāt-(em)*, lit. 'indigestion'. See **crude & -ity. 1. a** The state or quality of being crude; rawness; **b** that which is crude. **2.** That which is crude, undigested, lacking finish or polish &c.

cruel, adj. [1. kro͞oel; 2. krúil]. Fr., fr. Lat. *crūdēlis*, 'hard, unmerciful, fierce', fr. *crūdus*. See **crude. 1. a** (of persons) Disposed, willing, to cause pain to others in body or mind, taking pleasure in giving pain to others; hard-hearted, unfeeling; **b** (applied to inanimate objects) causing pain and suffering: *a cruel wound, blow*. **2.** (of actions, words &c.) Designed to cause, causing, pain or distress. **3.** Exhibiting results of the cruelty of man or circumstances; hence, painful, distressing: *a cruel sight*; *cruel suffering*; *cruel fate*. **4.** As adverb, (colloq., and vulg.) as mere intens., a very, extremely: *cruel cold*, very cold; **b** excessively and badly; esp. in vulg. Phr. *I hurt myself something cruel*.

cruelly, adv. Prec. & **-ly.** In a cruel manner.

cruelty, n. [1. kro͞oelti; 2. krúilti], fr. O. Fr. *cruelté*, fr. Lat. *crūdēlitāt-(em)*, fr. *crūdēlis*. See **cruel & -ty. 1. a** The quality or state of being cruel or hard-hearted; inhumanity: *the cruelty of man*; **b** an act, or treatment, which springs from this quality of mind, and inflicts pain upon others; a cruel action: *he died by the cruelty of his enemies*. **2. a** Suffering not deliberately inflicted by man, but arising from natural circumstances: *the cruelty of his sufferings*; **b** severity of circumstances which causes suffering: *the cruelty of fate*.

cruet, n. [1. kro͞oit; 2. krúit]. A.-Fr., dimin. of O. Fr. *crue* &c., 'earthen pot'. Of Gmc. origin, cp. O.H.G. *kruog*, 'pitcher' &c. See **crock (I.). 1. a** A small glass bottle holding vinegar, oil &c. at table; **b** a collection of several of these, a cruet-stand. **2.** (eccles.) A small vessel for holding wine or water for use at the Eucharist.

cruet-stand, n. Small receptacle, of silver or baser metal, with a handle for lifting, designed to hold several cruets.

cruise (I.), vb. intrans. [1. kro͞oz; 2. krūz], fr. Du. *kruizen*, 'to cross, traverse', fr. *kruiz*, 'cross'. See **cross (I.) & crux.** To sail on the sea in a ship; esp. **a** to sail about from place to place on business or pleasure; **b** (of war-vessels) to traverse the seas in scouting for the enemy or in pursuit of the enemy's mercantile marine &c.

cruise (II.), n., fr. prec. **a** A sea voyage of any kind: *a long cruise*; *four years' cruise*; **b** a sea voyage from place to place, or in constantly changing directions, whether undertaken on business or pleasure; **c** sea voyage of a war-vessel for scouting, commerce destruction &c.

cruiser, n. [1. kro͞ozer; 2. krúzə]. **cruise (I.) & -er.** A war-vessel adapted for cruising; formerly a privateer, now a man-of-war less heavily armoured than a battleship and therefore having greater speed.

crumb (I.), n. [1. krum; 2. kram]. O.E. *crūma*, M.E. *crūme, crumme*; perh. cogn. w. Lat. *grūmus*, 'little heap, or hillock of earth'. With this Walde also compares O.H.G. *krouwōn*, 'to scratch with the nails', further Gk. *grūpós*, 'hooked, curved', esp. of the nose, see **griffin.** Boisacq also quotes Albanian *grimɛ*, 'crumb of bread'. The orig. idea expressed by the base is, according to Walde, 'scratching with the bent fingers', & according to Boisacq, 'to rub, wear away'. **1.** A very small piece rubbed or broken off something, esp. a small portion of bread; (of non-material things) a trifling amount: *a crumb of comfort*; *crumbs of information*. **2.** The soft, spongy part of bread inside the crust.

crumb (II.), vb. trans., fr. prec. **1.** To break, rub into crumbs (of bread). **2.** (cookery) To cover, dress, or thicken with crumbs.

crumb brush, n. Curved brush for sweeping crumbs off a tablecloth.

crumb cloth, n. One spread over a carpet, esp. under a dining-table to preserve the carpet.

crumble, vb. trans. & intrans. [1. krúmbl; 2. krámbl]. Freq. fr. **crumb. 1.** trans. To rub or break into small morsels, reduce to crumbs: *to crumble one's bread*; also *crumble up*. **2.** intrans. **a** To fall into small pieces, decay: *crumbling walls* &c.; *bones long since crumbled to dust*; **b** (fig., of non-material things) to disintegrate, come to nothing, pass away, become ruined: *the great empires of the past have crumbled and fallen*; *my dearest hopes have crumbled to nothing*; also *crumble away*.

crumbly, adj. [1. krúmbli; 2. krámbli]. Prec. & **-ly.** Apt to crumble, easily crumbled, brittle, friable: *crumbly soil* &c.

crumby, crummy, adj. [1. krúmi; 2. krámi]. **crumb (I.) & -y. 1. a** Full of crumb, soft; **b** full of crumbs, soft. **2.** (vulg. and obs. slang, of women) Plump, well-covered.

crump, n. [1. krump; 2. kramp]. Imit. (army slang) A heavy, bursting shell.

crumpet, n. [1. krúmpet; 2. krámpit]. Earlier *crumpid*, as through P.P. of *to crump*, 'to make crisp'. Cp. **crimp. a** Sort of thin, sticky, doughy, flabby, unsweetened cake of flour; usually toasted and plentifully buttered and eaten hot; **b** (vulg. slang) the head, brain, esp. in Phr. *barmy on the crumpet*, foolish, crazy.

crumple, vb. trans. & intrans. [1. krúmpl; 2. krámpl]. Cp. O.H.G. *krump*, 'crooked', & see **cramp** & **crimp**. **1.** trans. **a** To roll, crush up roughly and carelessly, so as to make creases or folds: *to crumple one's clothes*; **b** *crumple up*, to roll or crush up by squeezing in the hand, esp. of a dry material such as paper; **c** (fig., applied to persons) to overwhelm, reduce to helplessness, overcome: *to crumple up an opponent.* **2.** intrans. **a** To become creased, fall into wrinkles: *this cloth crumples very easily*; **b** *to crumple up*, to fall, collapse, bend under a strain: *the wall, wings of an aeroplane, crumpled (up)*; *he simply crumpled up under the blows he received*; **c** to collapse, give way, be crushed, morally: *to crumple up under a mental shock* &c.

crunch (I.), vb. trans. & intrans. [1. krúnsh; 2. kran(t)ʃ]. Imitative word of same order as **scrunch**. **A.** trans. **1.** To crush, shatter, crack, chew up noisily with the teeth, esp. some hard, brittle substance, such as toast, biscuit, small bones &c. **2.** To grind hard dry ground under foot or wheel, so as to make crushing, crackling sound. **B.** intrans. To carry out action of chewing noisily; of treading heavily on gravel &c., or of bursting noisily through hard brittle material.

crunch (II.), n. See prec. **a** The act of crunching; **b** a crunching noise.

crupper, n. [1. krúper; 2. krápə]. M.E. *cropere*, O. Fr. *cropiere*, Fr. *croupière*. See **croup(e)**. **1.** That part of a horse's hind quarters between the saddle and the root of the tail. **2.** Leather strap in driving harness, from the back of the saddle, having a loop which passes under the horse's tail, to keep the saddle in position.

crural, adj. [1. kro͞oral; 2. krúərəl]. Lat. *crūrālis*, adj., fr. Lat. *crūr-*, base of *crūs*, genit. *crūr-is*, 'leg, shank, shin'. Etymol. uncertain. (anat.) Connected with, belonging to, the leg.

crusade, n. & vb. intrans. [1. kro͞osád; 2. krūséid], fr. Fr. *croisade*, Span. *cruzada*, Ital. *crociata*, fr. Med. Lat. *cruciata*, fr. P.P. of *cruciāre*, 'to mark with a cross'. See **crux** & **cross** (I.) & **-ate**. **1.** n. **a** Military expedition, undertaken by Christian kings and peoples in the Middle Ages, sanctioned by the Pope, with the object of recovering the Holy Sepulchre and Holy Land from the Mohammedans; **b** a holy war with a religious object; **c** any enterprise or agitation inspired by moral, religious, or political fervour, against a public scandal or abuse: *a crusade against drunkenness, Bolshevism* &c. **2.** vb. To take part in a crusade.

crusader, n. [1. kro͞osáder; 2. krūséidə]. Prec. & **-er**. One engaged in a crusade; specif., one who took part in the crusades of the Middle Ages.

cruse, n. [1. kro͞oz; 2. krūz]. M.E. *crūse* &c. Etymol. uncertain. Perh. fr. O.N. *krūs*, 'pot'. (archaic) A vessel (jar, pot, or cup) for holding water, oil, honey &c. Phr. *widow's cruse* (in allusion to 1 Kings xvii. 16), an inexhaustible source of supply.

crush (I.), vb. trans. & intrans. [1. krush; 2. kraʃ]. O. Fr. *croissir*, 'to break', fr. Gmc.; cp. O.N. *kreysta*, 'to squeeze, press'; Goth. *kriustan*, 'to gnash the teeth'; cp. also Goth. *krusts*, 'gnashing of teeth'. **A.** trans. **1. a** To compress, esp. something frail or brittle, with force between two resisting bodies, so as to shatter, break in, bruise: *to be crushed by a heavy waggon* &c.; *to crush a black beetle with the foot* &c.; **b** specif., to press, squeeze, so as to distort shape, alter natural consistency, or force out contents: *to crush grapes* (for wine), *nuts* (for oil), *corn* &c.; **c** to cause to become creased, impart wrinkles to (a dress, piece of fabric &c.); Phr. (obs.) *to crush a bottle of wine*, open and drink it. **2.** To pulverize by mechanical means, such as pounding or grinding: *to crush quartz.* **3.** (fig.) **a** To subdue, overcome, suppress (a rebellion, opposition &c.); **b** overwhelm completely, annihilate, destroy, reduce to impotence (a military force &c.); **c** (of moral effects) to disconcert, abash, render confused (of persons); to destroy, damp, extinguish (hopes, aspirations &c.). **B.** intrans. **1.** To become crushed: *silk crushes very easily.* **2.** (of a crowd of persons) To press, squeeze, flock in crowds into: *to crush into a small room.* **C.** Followed by adverbs. *Crush up*, **a** to reduce to powder: *to crush up sugar*; **b** to squeeze up into a ball in the hand: *to crush up a piece of paper. Crush down*, **a** to press down by weight: *to crush down growing plants*; **b** to pulverize, reduce to small particles: *crush down stone into cement*; **c** to suppress forcibly, put down: *to crush down opposition*; overwhelm by strong emotion.

crush (II.), n., fr. prec. **1.** The act of crushing. **2. a** A dense, tightly packed crowd of people; **b** specif. (colloq.) a crowded social gathering, a reception, large party.

crush-hat, n. (obsolesc.) One with folding springs, made to collapse and lie flat; an opera hat, gibus.

crushing, adj. [1. krúshing; 2. kráʃiŋ]. **crush** (I.) & **-ing**. In various senses, mostly fig. **a** Overwhelming, annihilating: *a crushing defeat*; **b** tending to disconcert, abash, silence: *a crushing answer, retort* &c.; **c** tending to prostrate, unnerve &c.: *a crushing sorrow.*

crush-room, n. (obsolesc.) Large room at a theatre, to which the audience may resort during intervals; foyer.

crust (I.), n. [1. krust; 2. krast]. M.E., fr. O. Fr. *crouste*, fr. Lat. *crūsta*, 'the hard surface of a body, the rind, shell, crust' &c.; cogn. w. a considerable group of Gk. words relating to ice, frost &c., cp. *krúos*, n., 'icy cold, chill, frost', *kruerós*, 'icy, chilling', *krūmós*, 'frost', *krustaínesthai*, 'to be congealed with cold, freeze'. The orig. sense of the n. would appear to be 'film of ice'. Cp. further O.E. *hruse*, 'the earth, ground', orig. 'crust of the earth'; O.H.G. *hroso*, 'crust, ice'. The remoter connexion of these words w. Lat. *cruor*, 'blood from a wound', *crūdus*, 'raw' &c. (see **crude** & **cruel**) is doubtful. See **crystal**. **1. a** The hard outer part of bread; a dry, hard piece of bread; **b** (fig.) bread considered as support of life, livelihood: *to earn one's crust*, one's living. **2.** Baked outer covering of a pie, made of flour, water and fat. **3.** The hard exterior surface, shell, or covering of anything; various specific uses; **a** a scab on the skin; **b** the outer portion of the globe: *the crust of the earth*; **c** hardened outer surface over a layer of snow; **d** a filmy deposit from wine formed on the inside of the bottle.

crust (II.), vb. trans. & intrans., fr. prec. **a** trans. To cover with a crust; **b** intrans., to form into a crust.

Crustacea, n. pl. [1. krustásia; 2. krastéiʃiə]. Neut. pl. of New Lat. *crustāceus*, adj., 'pertaining to the crust or shell', fr. Lat. *crūsta*, 'crust, shell'. See **crust** (I.). (zool.) Name of a large class of salt or freshwater animals, such as crabs, lobsters, shrimps, crayfish &c., all of which have a hard outer shell, and are segmented, many having a pair of forelimbs furnished with pincers.

crustacean, adj. & n. [1. krustáshan; 2. krastéiʃən]. Prec. & **-an**. **a** adj. Of or pertaining to the Crustacea; **b** n., an animal of this class.

crustaceology, n. [1. krùstāsiólọji; 2. kràsteiʃiólədži], fr. **Crustacea** & **-logy**. The study of crustaceans.

crustaceous, adj. [1. krustáshus; 2. krastéiʃəs]. See **crustacean** & **-ous**. **a** Crust-like; specif. **b** (zool.) crustacean.

crusted, adj. [1. krústed; 2. krástid]. **crust** & **-ed**. **a** Having, covered with, a crust; specif. **b** (of wine) having deposited a crust; **c** (fig.) ancient, venerable, hoary: *crusted habits.*

crustily, adv. [1. krústili; 2. krástili]. **crusty** & **-ly**. In a crusty manner.

crustiness, n. [1. krústines; 2. krástinis]. **crusty** & **-ness**. State of being crusty.

crusty, adj. [1. krústi; 2. krásti]. **crust** (I.) & **-y**. **1. a** Of the nature of crust, crust-like, hard; **b** (of bread) having a hard thick crust. **2.** (fig., of persons, manners &c.) Harsh, irritable, easily roused to anger.

crutch, n. [1. kruch; 2. kratʃ]. O.E. *cryċċ*, 'crutch, staff, crozier'; M.E. *crucche*; etymol. doubtful; perh. related to O.H.G. *kriochan*, Mod. Germ. *kriechen*, 'to creep'. **1. a** Device for enabling partially lamed persons to walk, consisting of a stout staff, with a padded cross-piece which goes under the arm so that the weight of the body can rest upon the crutch, which supports it and takes to some extent the place of the leg or legs; (often pl.) *pair of crutches*; **b** (fig.) a support, prop: *the crutch of my declining years.* **2.** One of several mechanical devices with forks (chiefly naut.) somewhat resembling a crutch. **3.** Fork, crotch.

Crutched Friars, n. [1. krúched fríerz; 2. krátʃid fráiəz]. Lit. 'crossed friars'. **a** A minor order, formerly in England (1244–1656), which bore the sign of the cross on its habit. Called also *Crouched Friars* and *Crossed Friars*; **b** ancient site of the monastery in London.

crux, n. [1. kruks; 2. kraks]. Lat. *crux*, genit. *crucis*, 'a cross', also 'torture, trouble'. See **cross** (I.). Prob. fr. same base as **curve** etc. Something difficult to explain, a hard question, knotty point, puzzle (cp. *crucial*).

cry (I.), vb. intrans. & trans. [1. krī; 2. krai]. M.E. *crīen*, O. Fr. & Mod. Fr. *crier*, fr. Lat. *quirītāre*, *-i*, 'to raise a plaintive cry, to wail, scream' &c. This word was derived in an anct. (popular) etymol. fr. *Quirītēs* (Romans in civil capacity), & its orig. meaning was said to be 'to invoke the help of' a Roman citizen. A more probable explanation is that wh. identifies the word w. *quirītāre*, *quirrītāre*, 'to squeak like a pig', regarding this as an imitative word, & connecting it w. Lat. *queri*, 'to complain, bewail', & *querulus*, 'full of complaints'. See **quarrel**, **querulous**. **A.** intrans. **1.** (of men and animals) To utter an inarticulate sound by means of the vocal organs; to make the sound characteristic of a baby, or of a particular animal. **2.** (of men) To utter words with a loud voice, in such a way as to attract attention, to call out: '*the voice of one crying in the wilderness*'; *to cry aloud*; '*No*', *he cried.* **3.** To express grief or pain by audible lamentation; to shed tears with or without sound; utter sobs, to weep. Phrs. (trans.) *to cry one's eyes, one's heart, out*, weep bitterly; *cry oneself to sleep*, weep until one falls asleep. **B.** trans. **1.** To advertise, announce, by calling out: *to cry one's wares*; *to cry the news all over the town* &c.; Phr. *to cry quits.* **2.** Various literary or obsolete Phrs.: *I cry you pardon, mercy* &c.; *to cry shame upon.* **C.** Followed by adverbs or prepositions. *Cry down*, trans., to disparage, belittle, decry. *Cry for*, trans., **a** to ask for, demand loudly, earnestly, with insistence; **b** to weep in order to obtain, until one obtains. *Cry off*, intrans., to retire, retreat from a bargain, decline to do something. *Cry out*, **a** trans., to call out, shout (names, words &c.); **b** intrans., to utter a loud cry. *Cry to, unto*, to call upon for help: *to cry to God*, pray to Him for help. *Cry up*, trans., to praise highly.

cry (II.), n., fr. prec. Used as n. *crī* in 13th cent. Engl. **1.** An inarticulate vocal sound, whether loud or soft; uttered **a** by human beings, esp. by young children; **b** by animals or birds as their characteristic call or note. Phr. *in full cry* (of a pack of hounds), yelping all together in pursuit of their quarry; (fig.) in hot pursuit. **2.** A loud sound made by the human vocal organs, whether articulate or the reverse, expressing pain, anger, fear, joy, or other emotion, or being a call for help. Phrs. *a far cry*, a long distance; an abrupt transition, great contrast; *within cry of*, within hearing; *to be deaf to a person's cries*, to disregard his entreaties, refuse to help him;

hue and cry, pursuit, clamour of public anger (lit. and fig.). **3.** (colloq.) The act of weeping, of shedding tears: *women love to have a good cry.*

cry-baby, n. A child who cries frequently, or on small provocation.

crying, adj. [1. krīing; 2. krái-iŋ], fr. Pres. Part. of **cry (I.)**. Clamant, demanding attention; notorious, esp. *a crying evil, shame.*

cryogen, n. [1. kríojen; 2. kráiədžen], fr. Gk. *krúos*, 'icy cold, frost' (see **crust**), & **-gen.** A refrigerant, freezing-mixture.

cryolite, n. [1. kríolīt; 2. kráiəlait], fr. Gk. *krúos.* See prec. & **-lite.** (mineral.) A fluoride of sodium and aluminium found in Greenland, much used in making soda, aluminium &c.

cryometer, n. [1. krīómeter; 2. kraiɔ́mitə]. See prec. & **meter.** (phys.) An instrument for measuring very low temperatures.

crypt, n. [1. kript; 2. kript], fr. Lat. *crypta*, 'a vault', fr. Gk. *krúptē*, 'vault, crypt', fr. *kruptós*, 'hidden', cp. *krúptein*, 'to hide'; this base shows an extension fr. **kʷru-* &c., wh. occurs in O. Slav. *kryti*, 'to hide, cover up', Mod. Russ. *krўt*, 'to cover' &c. An underground vaulted chamber, esp. one under a church, used as a chapel, or as a place of burial.

cryptic, adj. [1. kríptik; 2. kríptik], fr. Lat. *crypticus*, 'covered, concealed', fr. Gk. *kruptikós.* See prec. & **-ic. 1.** Secret, mystic: *a cryptic remark, utterance*, one containing hidden meaning. **2.** (zool.) Concealing, adapted for concealment: *cryptic colouring*, one rendering an animal invisible in its usual environment.

crypto-, pref. Form of Gk. *kruptós*, 'hidden, secret', used in compounds. See **crypt.**

cryptogam, n. [1. kríptōgam; 2. kríptougæm], fr. prec. & Gk. *gámos*, 'marriage'. See **-gamy.** (bot.) One of the group, Cryptogamia, of plants which have no external flowers and seeds, such as mosses, algae, fungi &c.; so called from the idea that the reproductive organs were secret, or hidden; the term is not one of modern classification.

Cryptogamia, n. pl. [1. krìptōgámia; 2. krìptougǽmiə]. See prec. (bot.) The group of cryptogams collectively.

cryptogamic, -ous, adj. [1. krìptōgámik, kriptógamus; 2. krìptougǽmik, kriptɔ́gəməs]. See prec. & **-ic** & **-ous.** (bot.) Pertaining to a cryptogam or to the group Cryptogamia.

cryptogram, n. [1. kríptōgram; 2. kríptougræm]. **crypto-** & **-gram.** Something written in a cipher; secret arrangement of words or letters.

cryptograph, n. [1. kríptōgrahf; 2. kríptougrāf]. **crypto-** & **graph.** Cryptogram.

cryptographer, n. [1. kriptógrafer; 2. kriptɔ́grəfə]. Prec. & **-er.** One who writes in cipher.

cryptographic, adj. [1. krìptōgráfik; 2. krìptougrǽfik]. **cryptograph** & **-ic.** Pertaining to cryptography.

cryptography, n. [1. kriptógrafi; 2. kriptɔ́grəfi]. **crypto-** & **-graphy.** The art of writing in cipher.

crystal (I.), n. [1. krístal; 2. krístəl], fr. O. Fr. *cristal*, Lat. *crystallum*, 'crystal, ice', fr. Gk. *krústallos*, 'ice, extreme cold, crystal', fr. *krúos*, 'icy cold, frost'. See **crust (I.). 1.** A form of clear, transparent, usually colourless quartz; a piece of this cut into an ornament. Phr. *as clear as crystal.* **2.** (chem. mineral.) **a** An inorganic body, having a definite internal structure, formed by the solidification of a chemical element; **b** structure resembling a crystal in form: *snow crystals* &c. **3.** (wireless) A detector for reception, made of a crystalline substance capable of rectifying oscillating currents. **4.** Glass-ware: *silver and crystal*, plate and glass.

crystal (II.), adj., fr. prec. Made of crystal; resembling crystal, clear, transparent: *crystal glass*, a very clear kind of glass used for drinking-vessels &c.

crystal-gazing, n. [1. krístal gāzing; 2. krístəl gèiziŋ]. Method of foretelling future events &c. by peering fixedly into a glass or crystal ball, wherein some believe that they can see images of objects, scenes of action. Cp. *scrying.*

crystalline, adj. [1. krístalīn; 2. krístəlain], fr. Lat. *crystallīnus*, fr. Gk. *krustállinos*, 'of crystal'; cp. Fr. *cristallin.* **crystal** & **-ine. a** Made of crystal; **b** (chem., mineral.) formed by crystallization; having the formation of a crystal; **c** resembling a crystal; **d** (anat.) *crystalline lens*, a lens-shaped body within the eye which focuses the rays of light.

crystallization, n. [1. krìstalīzā́shun; 2. krìstəlaizéiʃən]. **crystallize** & **-ation. a** The process of crystallizing; **b** a form or body resulting from this process.

crystallize, vb. intrans. & trans. [1. krístalīz; 2. krístəlaiz]. **crystal** & **-ize. 1.** intrans. **a** To form into a crystal, to take on the shape of crystals; **b** (fig., of non-material things) to take on definite shape, become clearly formed in the mind; esp. of ideas, plans &c. **2.** trans. **a** To cause to form into crystals; **b** (fig.) to clarify, make definite, give a form to; **c** to coat with crystals of sugar: *crystallized fruits.*

crystallographer, n. [1. krìstalógrafer; 2. krìstəlɔ́grəfə]. See next word & **-er.** Student of crystallography.

crystallography, n. [1. krìstalógrafi; 2. krìstəlɔ́grəfi], fr. Gk. *krústallo-(s)*, 'crystal', & **-graphy.** Study, science, of the structure and formation of crystals and crystalline substances.

crystalloid, adj. & n. [1. krístaloid; 2. krístəloid]. **crystal** & **-oid. a** adj. Like a crystal; **b** n., something having form or character of a crystal; specif., substances which are capable of passing, in solution, through membranes; contrasted with *colloid.*

ctenoid, adj. & n. [1. ktḗnoid; 2. ktínoid], fr. Gk. base *kten-*, as in *ktenós*, genit. of *ktéis*, 'comb', & **-oid.** This form stands for **kten-s*, & this for still earlier **pk̑ten-*, cp. Lat. *pecten*, 'comb'; the Gk. form shows complete loss of vowel in first syll., & the loss of initial *p-* before the two following consonants. Lat. has the vb. *pectere*, 'to comb', & Gk. *pektéō*, & *pékō*, in same sense. The orig. meaning is 'something with which to scrape wool', & of vb. 'to scrape, shear, or comb wool'. This is proved by the cognates, Gk. *pékos*, 'fleece, wool', *pókos*, 'tuft, lock of wool'; cp. further Scrt. *pakšmaláš*, 'having thick hair'; also O.H.G. *fahs*, O.E. *feax*, 'hair' (wh. survives in names *Fairfax, Colefax*). Lat. *pecus*, 'flock, cattle', Scrt. *páśu*, cogn. w. O.E. *feoh*, 'cattle, property' &c., are all fr. same base, without the *-t-* as formative element, & meant orig. 'woolly, hairy, creatures'. See **fee** & **pecuniary. 1.** adj. (lit.) Comb-like. Applied **a** to the scales of certain fish, *ctenoid scales*, whose edges have this form; **b** to fish having scales of this kind. **2.** n. Ctenoid fish.

cub (I.), n. [1. kub; 2. kab], prob. fr. or cogn. w. Ir. *cuib*, 'whelp'; cp. Gael. *cu*, 'dog'. See **canine. 1.** The young of the fox, a whelp; also of the bear, wolf, lion, tiger &c. **2.** (of young male human beings) An unpolished, raw, ill-mannered boy: *an idle, conceited cub*; also (playfully) young creature: *a mischievous young cub.* Phr. *an unlicked cub*, inexperienced, raw youth.

cub (II.), vb. intrans., fr. prec. **a** (of female foxes &c.) To bring forth young, produce cubs; **b** to hunt cubs, esp. those of the fox, at the beginning of the hunting season.

cubage, n. [1. kū́bij; 2. kjū́bidž]. **cube** & **-age. a** The cubic content of a solid; **b** the determination of this.

cubature, n. [1. kū́bachur; 2. kjū́bətʃə]. Fr. See **cube** & **-ate** & **-ure. a** Determination of cubic content; **b** cubic content, volume.

cubbing, vbl. n. [1. kúbing; 2. kábiŋ]. See **cub (II.)** & **-ing.** The hunting of fox cubs at beginning of the season. Also *cub-hunting.*

cubbish, adj. [1. kúbish; 2. kábiʃ]. **cub (I.)** & **-ish.** (gen. fig.) Resembling a cub; awkward, uncouth, ill-conditioned.

cubby, n. [1. kúbi; 2. kábi], fr. obs. or provinc. *cub*, 'a stall'. A snug place or cabin.

cubby-hole, n. Prec. & **hole.** A cubby.

cube, n. & vb. trans. [1. kūb; 2. kjūb]. Fr., fr. L. Lat. *cubus*, fr. Gk. *kúbos*, 'cube, die', fr. base meaning 'curve'; cp. Gk. *kúptein*, 'bend, stoop', *kúphos*, 'bent'; Goth. *hups*, O.E. *hype*, 'hip'; see **hip. 1.** n. **a** (geom.) A regular solid having six equal square sides; **b** anything shaped like a cube; specif., block of stone for paving; **c** (math.) the 3rd power; the product of a number multiplied by the square of that number; the product obtained by taking a number three times as a factor: *the cube of 3 is 27. Cube root*, the number or quantity that produces a given cube when raised to the 3rd power: *the cube root of 27 is 3.* **2.** vb. **a** To find the cube of (a number); to raise to the 3rd power; **b** to pave with cubes.

cubeb, n. [1. kū́beb; 2. kjū́beb]. Fr. *cubèbe*, through Ital. & Span. fr. Arab. *kabābah.* Aromatic berry, with medicinal properties, grown in tropics.

cubhood, n. [1. kúbhood; 2. kábhud]. **cub (I.)** & **-hood.** State or condition of being a cub.

cubic(al), adj. [1. kū́bik(l); 2. kjū́bik(l)], fr. Fr. *cubique*, fr. Lat. *cubicus*, fr. Gk. *kubikós.* **cube** & **-ic** & **-al.** Having the shape or mathematical properties of a cube: *cubic content; a cubic equation* &c.

cubicle, n. [1. kū́bikl; 2. kjū́bikl], fr. Lat. *cubiculum*, 'apartment for reclining or resting', for **cubit-lom*, base *cubit-*, 'lie', connected w. Lat. *cubitum*, P.P. of *cumbere*, 'to lay oneself down', *cub-āre*, 'lie down' &c. Prob. same base as in **cube, cubit**, wh. orig. meant 'to bend' &c., hence 'bend down in order to recline'. Small separate sleeping compartment, esp. one of a number, partitioned off from each other, and contained within a large dormitory.

cubiform, adj. [1. kū́biform; 2. kjū́bifɔ̄m]. See **cube** & **-form.** Having the shape of a cube.

cubism, n. [1. kū́bizm; 2. kjū́bizəm], fr. **cube** & **-ism.** Style of painting in which all form is expressed by rectangular figures or cubes.

cubist, n. [1. kū́bist; 2. kjū́bist]. Prec. & **-ist.** Painter who practises *cubism.*

cubit, n. [1. kū́bit; 2. kjū́bit], fr. Lat. *cubitum, cubitus*, 'elbow'; (also as measure of length) 'ell', cp. Gk. *kúbiton*, 'elbow', fr. base meaning 'to bend' &c. (discussed under **cube** & **cubicle**), the elbow being regarded either as something 'crooked' or 'bent', or as 'that upon which one leans or reclines'. Ancient measure of length, as taken from the elbow to the tip of the middle finger; roughly 18 to 22 ins. Cp. (Bib.) *to add a cubit to one's stature.*

cubital, adj. [1. kū́bital; 2. kjū́bitəl]. Prec. & **-al.** Lat. *cubitālis.* **1.** Of the length of a cubit. **2.** (anat. and zool.) Of or pertaining to the cubitus.

cubitus, n. [1. kū́bitus; 2. kjū́bitəs]. Lat. See **cubit.** The forearm or ulna.

cuboid, adj. & n. [1. kū́boid; 2. kjū́bɔid]. Gk. *kuboeidḗs.* See **cube** & **-oid. a** adj. Resembling a cube in shape; also *cuboidal*; **b** n., something having this form.

cucking-stool, n. [1. kúking stōōl; 2. kákiŋ stūl]. Perh. fr. Icel. *kūka*, 'to defecate', fr. resemblance to a close-stool. A chair or stool to which female scolds, or dishonest tradesmen were tied, and in which they were sometimes ducked in water.

cuckold, n. & vb. trans. [1. kóok-, kúkōld; 2. kúk-, kákould]. M.E. *cokewold* &c. Origin not clear. Perh. related to **cuckoo.** (archaic) **1.** n. A man whose wife is unfaithful to him. **2.** vb. **a** (of a man) To make (another) a cuckold by seducing his wife; **b** (of a married woman) to be unfaithful to (her husband).

cuckoldry, n. [1. kóok-, kúkōldri; 2. kúk-, kákouldri]. Prec. & **-ry.** Adultery.

cuckoo, n. [1. kóokōō; 2. kúkū]. Imitative of cry of the bird; found in many languages: Fr. *coucou*, Lat. *cuculus* (dimin.), Gk. *kókkux*

&c. Migratory bird with well-known typical note or cry, which reaches this country in early spring, and lays its eggs in the nests of small birds. Phr. *the cuckoo in the nest*, an intruder who ousts the true owners from home, diverts to himself the affection of parents from their children &c.

cuckoo-clock, n. A clock which strikes the hours with a sound like a cuckoo's note and the appearance at the same time of a small imitation cuckoo.

cuckoo-flower, n. (bot.) The lady's smock; a species of a wild orchis.

cuckoo-pint, n. See **pintle.** (bot.) The wake-robin or common arum.

cuckoo-spit, n. A frothy substance resembling spittle, excreted by several kinds of parasitic insects on plants, which envelops the larvae.

cucullate(d), adj. [1. kúkulāt(ed); 2. kjúkaleit(*id*)], fr. L. Lat. *cucullātus*, fr. Lat. *cucullus*, 'a hood'. See **cowl.** Hooded, cowled; specif. **1.** (bot., of leaves) having edges at base rolled inwards, forming a hood-shaped cavity. **2.** (zool., of insects) Having head &c. covered by a kind of hood.

cucumber, n. [1. kúkumber; 2. kjúkambə]. Fr. *concombre*, O. Fr. *cocombre*, fr. Lat. *cucumis*, genit. *cucumeris.* Prob. connected w. base seen in *cavus*, 'hollow', also 'full, round'; see **cave (I.).** The long succulent fruit of a trailing plant of gourd kind, cultivated as a salad and eaten in thin slices. Phr. *as cool as a cucumber*, (chiefly fig.) imperturbable.

cucurbit, n. [1. kūkĕrbit; 2. kjūkābit], fr. Lat. *cucurbita*, 'a gourd', Fr. *cucurbite.* See **cucumber. a** Gourd; **b** gourd-shaped flask, formerly used in distillation.

cucurbitaceous, adj. [1. kūkĕrbitáshus; 2. kjūkābitéiʃəs]. Prec. & **-aceous.** (bot.) Belonging to the gourds, including melons, cucumbers &c.

cud, n. [1. kud; 2. kad]. O.E. *cwidu, cudu.* Origin unknown. That portion of food which ruminating animals bring up into the mouth from the first stomach to chew at leisure; (fig.) *to chew the cud*, to turn a thing over in the mind, ponder.

cudbear, n. [1. kúdbār; 2. kádbeə]. Coined fr. name *Cuthbert*, after Cuthbert Gordon, who invented the dye late in eighteenth cent. Purple dye made from lichens.

cuddle, vb. trans. & intrans. & n. [1. kúdl; 2. kádl]. Origin unknown. **1.** vb. **a** trans. To hug, embrace fondly and closely; **b** intrans., to curl up in bed, warmly and comfortably. *Cuddle up (together)*, to nestle together. **2.** n. A hug.

cuddy (I.), n. [1. kúdi; 2. kádi]. Etymol. unknown. (naut.) A cabin in a ship where officers have meals.

cuddy (II.), n. Provinc., chiefly Scotch. Origin unknown; perh. fr. *Cuthbert.* A donkey.

cudgel (I.), n. [1. kújl; 2. kádžl]. O.E. **cyċġel*, M.E. *kuggel.* Origin doubtful. Gmc. type **kugil*; perh. allied to **cog (I.).** A stout, heavy stick; specif., short thick stick formerly used among rustics in contests. Phr. (fig.) *to take up the cudgels (for)*, assume defensive, esp. on behalf of another, or of a cause. *Cudgel play*, fighting, contest, with cudgels.

cudgel (II.), vb. trans., fr. prec. To thrash, belabour, with a stick. Phr. (fig.) *to cudgel one's brains*, use one's intelligence, esp. on difficult problem.

cue (I.), n. [1. kū; 2. kjū]. Perh. fr. name of letter *q* = *quando*, 'when'. **a** The last word or words of a speech of an actor in a play which serve as a signal to another actor to enter, or to begin his speech; **b** hence (fig.) hint, direction, lead. Phrs. *to give a person his cue*; *to take one's cue from a person*, give, accept, suggestion of what to do or say on given occasion.

cue (II.), n., fr. Fr. *queue*, 'tail', fr. Lat. *cōda* for *cauda*, 'tail', etymol. of wh. is uncertain. Cp. **caudal. 1.** Pigtail, esp. the tail or plait of hair formerly worn by men; more usually *queue.* **2.** Long straight tapering rod tipped with leather for striking the ball in billiards.

cueist, n. [1. kúist; 2. kjúist]. Prec. & **-ist.** (slang) A billiard-player.

cuff (I.), vb. trans. & n. [1. kuf; 2. kaf]. Cp. Swed. *kuffa*, 'to knock'. **a** vb. To strike, esp. on head or face, with the hand; to box a person's ears; **b** n., a blow, esp. on head, given with the open hand.

cuff (II.), n. Etymol. unknown. The lower part of the sleeve of a shirt or coat &c.; specif., a piece of linen attached to the lower part of a shirt-sleeve close to the hand, sometimes stiffened, fastened by links or buttons; similar band of stiffened linen worn round the wrist, separate from shirt, but temporarily attached to it.

cuirass, n. [1. kwirás; 2. kwirǽs], fr. Fr. *cuirasse*, orig. 'a leather breastplate', for O. Fr. *cuiriée*, influenced by Ital. *corazza* or Span. *coraza*, fr. Lat. *coriacea*, fem. adj. of *coriaceus*, 'of leather', fr. **corium** (whence Fr. *cuir*), 'hide, leather'. This word is fr. a very productive base, **ker-*, meaning 'hide newly stripped off, skin, dressed hide' &c.; the orig. meaning is 'cut, tear'. Cp. Scrt. *kr̥-ttiš*, 'hide, fleece', O.H.G. *herdo*, 'hide', O.E. *heorþa*, 'hide, leather'. See further **cortex, corpus.** Piece of armour, of leather, later of metal, protecting the back and breast.

cuirassier, n. [1. kwirasḗr; 2. kwiərəsíə]. Fr., fr. prec. & **-ier. a** Soldier wearing a cuirass; **b** specif., member of a (foreign) cavalry regiment in which cuirasses were worn.

cuisine, n. [1. kwizḗn; 2. kwizín]. Fr., 'kitchen, cooking', fr. Lat. *coquīna*, 'kitchen', fr. *coquere*, 'to cook'. See **cook, kitchen. a** Organization of the kitchen; **b** style, quality, of cooking: *an excellent cuisine.*

cuisse, cuish, n. [1. kwēs, kwish; 2. kwīs, kwiʃ]. Fr., 'thigh', fr. Lat. *coxa*, cogn. w. Scrt. *kakšaš*, 'arm-pit', O.H.G. *hahsa*, 'bend of the knee', Ir. *coss*, 'foot'. Possibly orig. meaning 'curved bone'; cp. Lat. *costa*, 'rib', perh. fr. **coxta*, & O. Slav. *kostĭ*, 'bone'. Cp. **coxa.** Protective armour for the thighs (usually pl.).

cul-de-sac, n. [1. kool de sak; 2. kyl də sak, kul də sæk]. Fr., lit. 'bottom of a bag'. **a** A street, passage, or position with only one open end; blind alley; **b** (fig.) a situation from which there is no escape or outlet.

-cule, dimin. suff. [1. kūl; 2. kjūl]. Fr., fr. Lat. *-culus, -cula, -culum*, as in *animalcule, molecule* &c.

culet, n. [1. kúlet; 2. kjúlit]. Fr., dimin. of *cul*, 'tail, bottom'. The flat base of a diamond of which the face is cut as a brilliant.

culex, n. [1. kúleks; 2. kjúleks]. Lat., 'gnat', cogn. w. Ir. *cuil*, 'gnat', & w. Scrt. *śūla*, 'spear, spit', cp. **cuneate. a** Genus of mosquitoes; **b** insect of this genus.

culinary, adj. [1. kúlinari; 2. kjúlinəri], fr. Lat. *culīnārius*, fr. *culīna*, 'kitchen', for **coq-slīna*, fr. base in *coquere*, 'cook', q.v. under **cook. a** Connected with the kitchen or with cooking: *culinary art* &c.; **b** fit, suitable, for cooking: *culinary vegetables.*

cull (I.), vb. trans. [1. kul; 2. kal], fr. O. Fr. *cuillir, coillir*, Mod. Fr. *cueillir*, 'to gather, pluck, pick', fr. Lat. *colligere.* See **collect. a** To pick out and gather, pluck, pick, esp. flowers; **b** (fig.) to select, collect, from among a number: *to cull the choicest lines from a poem.*

cull (II.), n., fr. prec. Something picked out; specif., animal picked out and separated from flock as being inferior to general standard, too old &c.

cullender, colander, n. [1. kúlender; 2. kálində], fr. Lat. *collant-(em), cōlant-(em)*, Pres. Part. of *cōlāre*, 'to strain'. See **percolate.** Metal vessel with perforated bottom, used in the kitchen as a strainer.

cullet, n. [1. kúlet; 2. kálit], fr. Fr. *collet*, 'a little neck'. Applied to the small pieces of glass at the neck of a bottle detached in blowing the glass. See **collet.** Broken or refuse glass for remelting.

cullion, n. [1. kúlyun; 2. káljən]. O. Fr. *coillon, couillon*, Mod. Fr. *couillon*, 'testicles', also term of low abuse; fr. *coil*, Mod. Fr. *couille*, 'scrotum, testicles', fr. Lat. *cōleus*, 'scrotum', ultimately connected w. *cutis*, 'skin', q.v. under **cuticle.** A low, base, mean-spirited rascal; a cowardly blackguard (obs. or liter.).

cully, n. & vb. trans. [1. kúli; 2. káli]. Abbr. of prec. **1.** n. **a** A person who is the dupe of another; **b** (slang) mate, pal. **2.** vb. To impose on, trick, cheat, deceive (rare or obs.).

culm (I.), n. & vb. intrans. [1. kulm; 2. kalm], fr. Lat. *culmus*, 'a stalk, stem' (esp. of grain), akin to *calamus*, 'a reed'; cp. further O. Slav. *slama*, Russ. *solóma*, 'straw'; O.H.G. *halm*, O.E. *healm*, 'stem' &c. See **haulm. a** n. (bot.) Jointed, hollow stem of grasses; **b** vb., to form, or grow into, a culm (very rare).

culm (II.), n. Etymol. unknown. **1.** Slack, dust of anthracite coal. **2.** (geol.) Form of shale or sandstone.

culminant, adj. [1. kúlminant; 2. kálminənt], fr. Lat. *culminant-(em)*, Pres. Part. of *culmināre.* See next word. At the highest point; specif., of a heavenly body, on the meridian.

culminate, vb. intrans. [1. kúlminăt; 2. kálmineit], fr. L. Lat. *culmināt-(um)*, P.P. of *culmināre*, fr. *culmin-(is)*, genit. of *culmen*, 'top, summit', fr. *columen*; cp. *columna*, q.v. under **column.** To reach the highest or uttermost point. **a** (astron., of the sun &c.) To reach its highest altitude; but chiefly **b** (fig., of development) *culminate in amount, volume, power* &c.

culmination, n. [1. kùlminā́shun; 2. kàlminéiʃən]. Prec. & **-ion. 1.** Act or fact of culminating. **2.** Highest point attainable, or attained; **a** (astron.) highest point reached by heavenly body, zenith; **b** (fig., in non-material things): *culmination of one's hopes, career, efforts* &c.

culpability, n. [1. kùlpabíliti; 2. kàlpəbíliti]. Lat. *culpābilitāt-(em)*, 'guilt'. See next word. Fact of being culpable; guilt, blameworthiness.

culpable, adj. [1. kúlpabl; 2. kálpəbl], fr. L. Lat. *culpābilis*, fr. *culpa*, 'fault'. Etymol. disputed, but perh. the orig. sense was 'blow' (as in Fr. *coup*, Ital. *colpo*), cp. Lat. *colaphus*, fr. Gk. *kólaphos*, 'blow with the fist', & Gk. *kolaptein*, 'to hew, cut'. See **coppice & coup.** Deserving blame or censure, blameworthy; reprehensible, criminal, esp. *culpable negligence.*

culpableness, n. Prec. & **-ness.** Culpability.

culpably, adv. See prec. & **-ly.** In a culpable or faulty manner.

culprit, n. [1. kúlprit; 2. kálprit], fr. A.-Fr. *cul-* (fr. *culpa*, 'guilt', see **culpable**), & *prist*, 'ready', indicating that prosecutor was ready to prove guilt of accused. **1.** A person guilty of a crime or offence; an offender. **2.** (law) One accused of a crime; the prisoner at the bar.

cult, n. [1. kult; 2. kalt], fr. Fr. *culte*, fr. Lat. *cultus*, 'culture, care; worship'; also P.P. of *colere*, 'to till, tend, take care of, to cherish, revere, worship'. See **colony. 1.** A system of religious belief and observance. **2.** Enthusiastic devotion or homage paid to a person, idea, or thing, esp. **a** intellectual homage paid to a person or his work by a body of admirers: *the cult of Browning*; **b** devoted attention to, enthusiastic, regular, pursuit of: *cult of athletics*; **c** a fad, craze, passing fancy, for some particular thing, a fashion: *the cult of the eye-glass.*

cultivable, adj. [1. kúltivabl; 2. káltivəbl], fr. L. Lat. *cultīv-*, as in *cultīvāre*, q.v. under **cultivate, & -able.** (of soil) Capable of being tilled.

cultivate, vb. trans. [1. kúltivāt; 2. káltiveit], fr. L. Lat. *cultīvāt-(um)*, P.P. of *cultīvāre*, fr. Lat. *cultīva (terra)*, 'tilled (land)'. See **cult & -ive. 1.** To till, work, break up (land), prepare it for crops. **2.** (fig.) **a** (of mental and moral qualities and powers) To improve, exercise, develop, refine, strengthen, enlighten: *to cultivate the mind, the moral sense*; **b** (of material and non-material things) to bestow particular attention upon, pursue, seek to obtain: *to cultivate a person's friendship, acquaintance*; *to cultivate the manners of a gentleman*; *to cultivate a moustache.*

cultivated, adj. [1. kúltivāted ; 2. káltiveitid], fr. P.P. of prec. **1.** (of soil) **a** Tilled, prepared for seed; **b** (of land) habitually worked, in a state of cultivation; contrasted with *pasture land* or *waste land*. **2.** (fig., of persons, mind, manners &c.) Highly trained and developed; polished, refined: *a cultivated man, mind; a cultivated taste.*

cultivation, n. [1. kùltiváshun ; 2. kàltivéiʃən]. **cultivate** & **-ion**. **1.** The act of cultivating (lit. and fig.): *engaged in the cultivation of the land, of the mind.* **2. a** (of land) Condition of being cultivated; **b** (fig.) polish, high state of development and refinement.

cultivator, n. [1. kúltivāter ; 2. káltiveitə], fr. **cultivate** & **-or**. **a** Person engaged in cultivating the land; **b** mechanical device for breaking up the land.

cultrate, adj. [1. kúltrāt ; 2. káltreit], fr. Lat. *cultrātus*, fr. *culter*, 'knife'. See **coulter** & **-ate**. Shaped like a pruning-knife; sharp-edged.

cultriform, adj. [1. kúltriform ; 2. káltrifōm], fr. Lat. *cultri-*, stem of *culter*. See prec. & **-form**. Cultrate.

cultural, adj. [1. kúlchural ; 2. káltʃərəl]. Next word & **-al**. Of, pertaining to, culture.

culture, n. [1. kúlchur; 2. káltʃə]. Fr., fr. Lat. *cultūra*, 'a cultivating; agriculture; care, culture'. See **cult** & **-ure**. **1.** Rearing of animals and plants; production of articles of commerce which are due to animal or vegetable activities or functions: *culture of silk, cotton* &c. **2.** Education, training; development of mental and bodily faculties and qualities. **3.** The result of mental training; refinement of taste, keenness and balance of intellect and judgement; elegance of manners.

cultured, adj. [1. kúlchurd ; 2. káltʃəd]. Prec. & **-ed**. Possessing culture, esp. of the mind.

culver, n. [1. kúlver ; 2. kálvə]. O.E. *culfre*, M.E. *colver, culver*, fr. Lat. *columba*, 'dove'. See **columbine** (I.). Wood-pigeon.

culverin, n. [1. kúlverin ; 2. kálvərin], fr. Fr. *coulevrine*, fr. *couleuvre*, 'snake', fr. Lat. *colubrīnus*, 'snake-like'. See **colubrine**. A long slender cannon for long-range firing, first used during the 16th cent.

culvert, n. [1. kúlvert ; 2. kálvət]. Late 18th cent. Origin uncertain. Large iron pipe, or channel of masonry, for conveying a flow of water under a roadway.

cumber, vb. trans. & n. [1. kúmber ; 2. kámbə], fr. O. Fr. *combrer*, fr. Low Lat. *cumbrus*, 'a heap', akin to Lat. *cumulus*, 'a heap'. See **cumulus**. **1.** vb. To hinder, trouble, or burden with something useless; to hamper: *to cumber oneself with a lot of luggage.* **2.** n. That which cumbers; encumbrance, hindrance.

cumbersome, adj. [1. kúmbersum ; 2. kámbəsəm]. **cumber** & **-some**. Burdensome, heavy; unwieldy, clumsy.

cumbersomely, adv. Prec. & **-ly**. In a cumbersome manner.

cumbersomeness, n. See prec. & **-ness**. Quality of being cumbersome.

cumbrous, adj. [1. kúmbrus ; 2. kámbrəs]. **cumber** & **-ous**. Heavy, clumsy, inconvenient, tending to cumber.

cumbrously, adv. Prec. & **-ly**. In a cumbrous manner.

cumbrousness, n. See prec. & **-ness**. Quality of being cumbrous.

cumin, cummin, n. [1. kúmin ; 2. kámin]. Lat. *cumīnum*, Gk. *kúminon*, fr. Heb. *kammōn*. An umbelliferous Eastern plant, with aromatic seeds, valuable as a carminative.

cummer, n. [1. kúmer ; 2. kámə]. Also in Scots, *kimmer*, fr. Fr. *commère*, 'godmother; gossip'. (Scots) A woman companion, gossip.

cummerbund, n. [1. kúmerbund ; 2. káməband]. Hind., fr. Pers. *kamarband*, 'loin-band'. (Anglo-Ind.) Piece of cloth or silk worn round the waist inside the clothes for warmth, or outside for ornament.

cumulate, vb. trans. & intrans. [1. kúmūlāt ; 2. kjúmjuleit], fr. Lat. *cumulāt-(um)*, P.P. type of *cumulāre*. See **accumulate** & **cumulus**. To accumulate. (Rarely used.)

cumulate(d), adj. [1. kúmūlāt(ed) ; 2. kjúmjuleit(id)]. Prec. & **-ed**. Heaped up.

cumulation, n. [1. kūmūláshun ; 2. kjùmjuléiʃən]. **cumulate** & **-ion**. Accumulation.

cumulative, adj. [1. kúmūlativ ; 2. kjúmjulətiv]. **cumulate** & **-ive**. Heaped up; increasing in strength, force, value &c., by successive additions: *cumulative proof, evidence* &c. Special uses: **a** *cumulative voting*, a system of voting in which each voter has as many votes as there are candidates, and can either give them all to one candidate or distribute them as he pleases; **b** *cumulative preference shares*, shares entitling the holder to arrears of interest before other shareholders receive interest on current year.

cumulatively, adv. Prec. & **-ly**. In a cumulation, by accumulation.

cumulo-stratus, n. [1. kúmūlō strátus; 2. kjúmjulou stréitəs]. See **cumulus** & **stratus**. A cloud in which the structure of the cumulus is mixed with that of the stratus, the cumulus being often flattened on top and overhanging its base.

cumulus, n. [1. kúmūlus ; 2. kjúmjuləs]. Lat., 'a heap'. The first syll. is cogn. w. Goth. *hauhs*, 'high', O.E. *hēah*. See **high**. Specif., one of the main classes of clouds in the form of rounded, piled-up masses.

cuneate, adj. [1. kúniāt ; 2. kjúnieit], fr. Lat. *cuneāt-(um)*, P.P. type of *cuneāre*, 'to drive in a wedge, to furnish with wedges, to form into the shape of a wedge', fr. *cuneus*, 'wedge', wh. is perh. cogn. w. O. Ir. *cenn*, W. *penn*, 'head, top of a hill', O. Slav. *kaniti*, 'to drive, goad on'. Cp. also **culex**, fr. base meaning 'point, spear' &c. Wedge-shaped.

cuneiform, adj. & n. [1. kúniform, kūnéiform; 2. kjúnifōm, kjūníifōm]. See prec., fr. Lat. *cuneus*, 'wedge', see prec. & **-form**. **a** adj. Wedge-shaped; specif., *cuneiform characters*, letters in which the old Assyrian and Babylonian inscriptions are written, so called from their shape; **b** n., as in *written in cuneiform.*

cunning (I.), n. [1. kúning ; 2. kániŋ]. M.E. *cunning, conning* &c., 'skill, experience, knowledge'; vbl. ns. fr. base *cun-*, 'to know', O.E. *cunnan*, 'to know, be able'. See **can** (I.), auxil., **con** (I.). **1.** (of physical qualities) Skill, dexterity; archaic except in such Phr. as *my hand has lost its cunning.* **2.** (of mental qualities) Slyness, astuteness, subtlety.

cunning (II.), adj., orig. Pres. Part. of *cunnan*, 'to know', w. normal substitution of **-ing** for earlier *-ende* &c. See prec. & **can** (I.), auxil. **1.** Skilful, dexterous: *a cunning workman* (archaic). **2.** Wily, designing, artful, crafty. **3.** (U.S.A., colloq.) Attractive, pretty, pleasant, nice.

cunningly, adv. Prec. & **-ly**. In a cunning manner, esp. craftily.

cup (I.), n. [1. kup ; 2. kap]. O.E. *cuppe*, fr. Low Lat. *cuppa*, 'cup', Lat. *cūpa*, 'vat, cask'; cp. Gk. *kúpē*, 'goblet'; also cogn. w. O.E. *hȳf*, 'beehive'. See **hive**. The fundamental sense of the base is 'to bend outwards, swell out, bulge' &c., and a large number of words in various Aryan languages have been connected w. it. See under **coop, coomb, cubit, cubicle** &c. **1. a** A small drinking vessel, esp. a vessel of gold, silver, pottery, porcelain &c.; specif., one of porcelain with a handle, used together with a saucer, for drinking tea, coffee, cocoa; cp. also *loving cup*; **b** the contents of such a cup; a cupful: *to drink two cups (of tea)*; **c** (specif. eccles.) the chalice containing the wine used at the Eucharist. Specif. Phr. *to withhold the cup* (from the laity), to communicate only in one kind. **2.** A rather large vessel, usually of silver or gold, given as a prize in racing, games, athletics: *to win the cup.* **3.** Transferred from *wine-cup*, to contents of this, wine; hence, excessive indulgence in this: *to be too fond of the cup.* Phr. *in one's cups*, intoxicated. **4.** (fig.) That which falls to one as one's portion in life, fate, experience: *a bitter cup; his cup (of happiness, misery &c.) was full.* **5.** Cup-shaped object, whether concave or convex; e.g. **a** a hollow in the ground, valley with hills all round; **b** (bot.) the calyx of a flower; the woody outer case of an acorn; **c** (anat.) the socket of certain bones.

cup (II.), vb. trans., fr. prec. (surg.) To perform the operation of cupping, q.v.

cupbearer, n. [1. kúpbārer ; 2. kápbèərə]. **cup** (I.) & **bearer**. Person charged with duty of serving wine at ceremonial banquets; esp. an officer in a prince's household.

cupboard, n. [1. kúburd ; 2. kábəd], fr. **cup** (I.) & **board**. The present pronunciation is old, & the word appears without a *p* in the early 16th cent. A set of shelves with doors in front of them, either in a recess in a wall, or as a separate piece of furniture with top and bottom, sides and back. *Cupboard love*, affection, or the show of it, which is not disinterested, but assumed from ulterior motives, esp. specif., demonstrativeness on part of a child who hopes to be rewarded by the gift of a sweetmeat or other delicacy—from the store-cupboard.

cupel, n. [1. kúpel ; 2. kjúpɛl], fr. Fr. *coupelle*, fr. Low Lat. *cūpella*, 'cup', Lat. *cūpella*, 'a small cask', dimin. of *cūpa*, 'cask'. See **cup**. A shallow vessel, used in assaying precious metals.

cupellation, n. [1. kùpeláshun ; 2. kjùpɛléiʃən]. Prec. & **-ation**. The process of assaying in a cupel.

cupful, n. [1. kúpfool ; 2. kápful]. **cup** (I.) & **-ful**. As much as a cup will hold, contents of a cup.

Cupid, n. [1. kúpid ; 2. kjúpid], fr. Lat. *Cupīdo*, 'the god of love', personification of *cupīdo*, 'desire, love', fr. type *cupidum*, fr. *cupere*, 'to desire'. Cp. O. Slav. *kypěti*, 'to boil'. The base is **kewēp-*, whence comes also Scrt. *kúpyati*, 'boil, bubble up, become agitated', & further, fr. different grade, Lat. *vapor*, 'steam', see **vapour**, & Gk. *kapnós*, 'smoke'; cp. also **hope**. **a** (Rom. mythol.) The god of love, the son of Venus; hence **b** a lovely little boy; **c** allegorical pictorial representation of Cupid as god of love, as a beautiful little boy, with wings and a bow and arrow; often in pl. *cupids*; **d** the passion of love.

cupidity, n. [1. kūpíditi ; 2. kjūpíditi], fr. Fr. *cupidité*, fr. Lat. *cupiditāt-(em)*, 'desire', fr. *cupidus*, 'longing, desirous'. See prec. Excessive desire, esp. for wealth and possessions; greed of gain, avarice.

cupola, n. [1. kúpola ; 2. kjúpələ]. Ital., fr. Low Lat. *cūpula, cuppula*, fr. *cūpa, cuppa*, 'cup'. Cp. Lat. *cūpula*, dimin. of *cūpa*, 'tub'. See **cup** (I.). **1.** (archit.) A rounded roof like an inverted cup, generally projecting and separate in structure from the other roofing; a small dome. **2.** A furnace for melting iron and other metals, also called *cupola furnace.* **3.** A dome-shaped revolving turret, which protects heavy guns on a warship. **4.** (anat.) A dome-shaped organ or process.

cupping, n. [1. kúping ; 2. kápiŋ]. **cup** (II.) & **-ing**. (surg.) The operation of drawing blood &c. to or through the surface of the skin, by forming a partial vacuum over a given area by means of a *cupping glass*, sometimes accompanied by scarification with minute lancets.

cupping-glass, n. Glass vessel in shape of a cup, used for forming a vacuum, into which a portion of the surface of the skin is drawn in the cupping operation.

cupreous, adj. [1. kúprius ; 2. kjúpriəs], fr. Lat. *cupreus*, fr. *cuprum*, 'copper', & **-ous**. See **copper**. Of or resembling copper.

cupric, adj. [1. kúprik ; 2. kjúprik]. Lat. *cupr-*, 'copper', see prec. & **-ic**. (chem., of certain compounds) Containing copper as bivalent element, as cupric oxide.

cupriferous, adj. [1. kūpríferus ; 2. kjūpríférəs], fr. Lat. *cuprum*, 'copper', see **copper**, & **-ferous**. (chem.) Containing copper.

cuprite, n. [1. kū́prīt; 2. kjū́prait]. See prec. & **-ite**. (mineral.) Red oxide of copper, ruby copper.

cuprous, adj. [1. kū́prus; 2. kjū́prəs]. See **cupric** & **-ous**. (chem.) Containing copper as univalent element, as cuprous oxide.

cupule, n. [1. kū́pūl; 2. kjū́pjūl]. Variant of **cupola**. **a** (bot.) A kind of small cup &c., surrounding the whole or the base of certain kinds of fruit, e.g. that of the acorn, of the hazel nut; **b** (zool.) A cup-shaped sucker; acetabulum.

cur, n. [1. kër; 2. kā]. Early M.E. *kur dogge, curre* &c., Scand.; cp. O.N. *kurra*, 'to grumble, murmur'; Mod. Swed. dial. *kurre*, 'house-dog'; so called fr. his growl. **1.** A dog of no particular breed, a mongrel; esp. a snappish, ill-tempered dog. **2.** (fig.) A low, mean-spirited, ill-bred, cross-grained fellow.

curability, n. [1. kūrabíliti; 2. kjùərəbíliti]. See next word & **-ity**. State, quality, of being curable.

curable, adj. [1. kū́rabl; 2. kjɔ́rəbl]. **cure (II.)** & **-able**. Able to be cured.

curaçao, -çoa, n. [1. kūrasṓ, -ṓa; 2. kjùrəsóu, -óuə]. The name of a Dutch island in the Caribbean Sea where this drink was first made. Spirituous, syrupy, sweet liqueur, with strong taste of orange.

curacy, n. [1. kū́rasi; 2. kjɔ́rəsi]. See **curate** & **-acy**. The office and occupation of a curate.

curare, curari, n. [1. kūráhri; 2. kjurári]. Native name, also *urare, wurali* &c. Poison obtained from bark of certain trees, having some of the properties of strychnine, used by the Indians of S. America for poisoning arrows.

curarine, n. [1. kūráhrēn; 2. kjurárīn]. Prec. & **-ine**. (chem.) An alkaloid extracted from curare.

curarize, vb. trans. [1. kūráhrīz; 2. kjuráraiz]. **curare** & **-ize**. To poison with curare.

curassow, n. [1. kū́rasō; 2. kjúərəsou], fr. Curaçao island. See above. Large crested South and Central American bird resembling a turkey.

curate, n. [1. kū́rat; 2. kjɔ́rit], fr. Low Lat. *cūrātus*, 'one who is charged with the care of souls', cp. Fr. *curé*, fr. Lat. *cūra*, 'care'. See **cure (I.)**. In the Church of England an assistant priest to an incumbent of a parish. Formerly called a *vicar*, which word is now usually applied to the incumbent himself, if he is not a *rector*, or a *curate-in-charge*. *Curate-in-charge*, here the word is used in its old sense, one in permanent charge of a parish, other than a rector or vicar. The term still survives in some parishes and designates a status equivalent to that of vicar.

curative, adj. & n. [1. kū́rativ; 2. kjɔ́rətiv], fr. Fr. *curatif, -ive*. See **cure (II.)** & **-ate** & **-ive**. **a** adj. Having the property of curing diseases or other ills; **b** n., means used as a cure of diseases &c.

curator, n. [1. kūrā́tur; 2. kjuréitə]. Lat., 'a manager, overseer, guardian, trustee'. See **cure** & **-ate** & **-or**. **1. a** One to whom care or charge of anything has been officially entrusted; esp. the keeper or custodian of a museum, public collection of pictures &c.; **b** specif. (in Oxford) one of several persons to whom the general management and supervision of some university institution or collection is entrusted by the university. **2.** (Scots law) A trustee, guardian, appointed by the Court of Session for a minor or person of defective mind.

curatorship, n. [1. kūrā́torship; 2. kjuréitəʃip]. Prec. & **-ship**. **a** The office of a curator; **b** period of such office.

curb (I.), n. [1. kërb; 2. kāb], fr. Fr. *courbe*, adj., fr. Lat. *curvus*, 'bent, curved'. See **curve**. **1. a** A chain or strap fastened to the bit, and passing under horse's chin, which presses upon this when the bridle reins are drawn tight, and acts from the leverage of the bit as an additional check; **b** (fig.) a check, restraint, form of discipline: *a curb to violence, to passion* &c. **2.** A hard swelling on the back part of a horse's hind leg, usually causing lameness. For architectural usage see **kerb**.

curb (II.), vb. trans., fr. prec. **a** To hold in (a horse) by means of a curb; **b** (fig.) to restrain, subdue, keep in check: *to curb one's temper, desires, tongue* &c.

curb roof, n. One with a double slope, the lower one being the steeper.

curbstone, n. See **kerb**.

curcuma, n. [1. kërkūma; 2. kákjumə]. Arab. *kurkum*. Plant with bright-coloured flowers and tuberous roots, which are used as a condiment in curry-powder; see **turmeric**.

curd, n. [1. kërd; 2. kād]. M.E. *crud* & *curd*, fr. base wh. occurs in O.E. *crūdan*, 'to press, crowd'. See **crowd**. The thick substance, the basis of cheese, which separates from milk under the action of any acid substance; distinguished from whey, the watery part of milk.

curdle, vb. intrans. & trans. [1. kërdl; 2. kādl]. Prec. & **-le**. **1.** intrans. **a** (of milk) To become separated into curd and whey by the action of acid; **b** to become thick like curd; **c** (fig., of the blood) to become congealed: *the sight made my blood curdle*. **2.** trans. **a** To cause (milk) to curdle by exposing to acid action; **b** (fig.) to cause the blood to curdle through fright &c.: *terror curdled his blood*.

curdy, adj. [1. kërdi; 2. kādi]. **curd** & **-y**. Like curd; full of curd.

cure (I.), n. [1. kyōr, kūr; 2. kjɔ̄, kjuə]. In M.E., fr. O. Fr., fr. Lat. *cūra*, 'care, trouble, attention; management, charge; medical attendance, healing, cure'. The O. Lat. is *coira-* (for the vb.), wh. points to Aryan *oi* as the vowel; *r* may be for *-s-*, in wh. case Lat. *cūr-* stands for **kois-*, wh. in Gmc. wd. be **hais-*, wh. possibly appears in Goth. *ushaists*, 'very poor, in great want', lit. 'uncared for'. Beyond this the etymol. is obscure. **1.** The pastoral care of souls; a spiritual charge: *to obtain, resign, a cure*. **2. a** (med.) A remedy for disease, a healing substance, or treatment which does away with the disease and restores health: *a certain cure for headaches, corns, coughs* &c.; *rest is the best cure for sprains*; **b** a course of medical treatment designed to heal and restore health: *to undergo a cure*; *the hot water, grape, cure* &c.; **c** act or process of healing a disease; fact of being cured: *no doctor would guarantee his cure*. **3.** (fig.) Remedy for, or against, moral and social evils: *a cure for unemployment, for homesickness, despondency* &c.

cure (II.), vb. trans. & intrans., fr. O. Fr. *curer*, 'to take care, to heal', Mod. Fr. 'to take care of, clean' (*curer les ongles* &c.), fr. Lat. *cūrāre*, 'to take care of; to heal'. See prec. The word has very largely taken the place of the older *heal*. **A.** trans. **1. a** To heal, make well, restore to health: *to cure a patient*; **b** to remove, provide a remedy for, disease or ill-health: *to cure disease, pain* &c. **2.** (fig.) **a** To provide a remedy for persons suffering from mental, moral, or social evils and ailments: *to cure a man of bad habits*; **b** to do away with the evils themselves: *to cure drunkenness, social discontent, mental worry* &c. **3.** To preserve from corruption by salting, drying, pickling: *to cure bacon, fish, hides* &c. **B.** intrans. To effect a cure in various senses: *to kill or cure*.

cure (III.), n. Perh. abbr. of *curious*. (obs. slang) A strange, eccentric, rather comical person; a queer fish.

curé, n. [Engl. 1. kū́rā; 2. kjúərei]; Fr. [kyre] 'a parish priest', fr. Low Lat. *cūrātus*, 'entrusted with a cure of souls'. See **curate**. A parish priest in France.

cureless, adj. [1. kū́rles; 2. kjɔ́lis]. **cure (I.)** & **-less**. Incurable, incapable of being cured.

curer, n. [1. kū́rer; 2. kjɔ́rə]. **cure (II.)** & **-er**. One who preserves meat, fish &c. by salting, drying &c.; esp. *bacon, fish, curer*.

curette, n. & vb. trans. [1. kūrét; 2. kjurét]. Fr., fr. *curer*, 'to cure'. See **cure (II.)**. **1.** n. A surgical instrument shaped like a small spoon with sharp edge, used in operations for cataract, removal of growths &c. **2.** vb. To operate on (person), remove (growths &c.), by means of the curette.

curfew, n. [1. kërfū; 2. káfjū]. M.E. *co(u)rfew* &c., lit. 'cover fire', A.-Fr. *coever-fu, curfeu*, O. Fr. *covre-feu*. See **cover** & **focus**. **a** (Engl. Med. hist.) The ringing of a bell at 8 P.M., or other fixed hour, as a signal to the inhabitants of a town &c. to extinguish all lights and cover fires; **b** the bell which gave the signal: '*The curfew tolls the knell of parting day*' &c. (Gray); **c** the hour at which the bell was rung.

curia, n. [1. kṓōria, kū́ria; 2. kū́ria, kjúəriə]. Lat., prob. an ancient compound fr. *co-*, 'together' (see **com-**), & *viro-*, 'man, men'. See **virile**. **1. a** Each of the tribal subdivisions which composed the political divisions of ancient Rome; **b** the Roman senate-house. **2.** The Papal court, in full *Curia Romana*, collectively, term for all the government departments of the Vatican. **3.** (hist.) The mediaeval judicial council or court of justice of the king: *the Curia Regis*.

curio, n. [1. kū́riō; 2. kjúəriou]. See next word. Object which presents some unusual and interesting features commending it to collectors, from its beauty, antiquity, or rarity.

curiosity, n. [1. kūriósiti; 2. kjɔ̀ri-, kjùəriɔ́siti]. M.E., 'carefulness', fr. O. Fr. *curioseté, curiosité*, fr. Lat. *cūriōsitāt-(em)*, 'desire of knowledge, curiosity'. See next word & **-ity**. **1. a** A desire to obtain knowledge, get fresh information, find out things, learn something new; **b** (in a derogatory sense) desire to find out things that do not concern one; inquisitiveness. **2.** *A curiosity*, a rare, strange, and interesting object; a curio.

curious, adj. [1. kū́rius; 2. kjɔ́riəs]. M.E., fr. O. Fr. *curios, curius*, fr. Lat. *cūriōsus*, 'careful, diligent; eager; inquisitive'. See **cure (I.)** & **-ous**. **1.** The older senses, **a** (of mental activities and attributes) careful; **b** (of things) showing the result of care and attention, highly wrought, are now largely obsolete in popular usage, though surviving in a few contexts; even in literary style they are distinctly archaic; **a** *curious research, inquiry*; *curious industry, attention, knowledge* &c.; **b** *curious design, workmanship* &c. Probably by many people the word in these connexions is understood in the sense of No. **2.** **2.** Of a rare or remarkable character; presenting exceptional features, arousing interest and attention, causing surprise; strange, odd, hard to explain: *a curious sight, spectacle, sound*; *a curious view to take*; *a curious coincidence*. Phr. *it's a (very) curious thing (that)* &c., it is strange, remarkable. (also of persons) Unlike most other people in appearance or character, hard to understand, odd, peculiar: *a curious fellow*; *a curious-looking man*. **3.** (of persons) **a** Anxious to know, desiring to be informed, anxious to find out things. Phr. *I am, should be, curious to know if* &c.; **b** (in bad sense) inquisitive, given to prying into matters which do not concern one: *curious neighbours*; *curious eyes*.

curiously, adv. Prec. & **-ly**. **a** In a curious manner; **b** (as simple intensive) to the point of strangeness, very: *she was curiously ugly*; *a curiously bad accent*.

curiousness, n. See prec. & **-ness**. **1.** (archaic or obs., see **curious**, **1**) Carefulness, skill, ingenuity, of design &c. **2.** The state of being exceptional, remarkable &c.; see **curious, 2.** **3.** Inquisitiveness. (Rare.)

curl (I.), n. [1. kërl; 2. kāl]. Not in O.E. M.E. has *crulle*, adj., 'curly'; cp. E. Fris. *krul, krulle*, 'a curl'. The present form, w. metathesis, is nearer to Scand. type, cp. Norw. & Dan. *kurle*, 'a curl'; prob. related to Mod. Fris. *krall*, 'closely twisted'; further connexions have not been identified. **1. a** A lock of hair which rolls up on itself and forms a little, spiral ringlet; **b** in pl., *curls*, curly hair; hair in general. **2.** Various applications to things suggesting a twist, spiral, or curl, in form: *curl of smoke, of a wave*; *curl of the lips*, scornful sneer. **3.** The state of being curled: *hair in curl.* **4.** Disease in potatoes in which the leaves curl up.

curl (II.), vb. trans. & intrans., fr. prec. **A.** trans. **1. a** To twist, roll, press into spirals or curls: *to curl the hair, moustache*; **b** to cause to roll over like a curl: *a light breeze curled the waves.* **2.** *Curl up*, **a** to roll something up by bending the edges; **b** (fig.) to render powerless; cause to collapse physically or mentally: *the blow completely curled him up.* **B.** intrans. **1.** To roll into, assume the form of, grow in, curls: *hair curling thick round the forehead.* **2.** *Curl up*, **a** to roll, coil up: *the leaves curl up in the frost*; **b** (of persons and animals) to roll up, lie bunched up for sleep; **c** to collapse, suffer severe shock. **3.** To assume shape of a curl or spiral (of smoke, waves &c.). **4.** To play at curling; see **curling** (I.).

curled, adj. [1. kĕrld; 2. kʌ̄ld], fr. P.P. of prec. **a** Having curls; curly, wavy; **b** specif., *curled hair*, horsehair prepared for stuffing cushions &c.

curler, n. [1. kĕrler; 2. kʌ́lə]. **curl** (II.) & **-er.** **a** Device for curling the hair; **b** specif., one who plays at the game of curling; see **curling** (I.).

curlew, n. [1. kĕrlū; 2. kʌ́ljū]. M.E., fr. O. Fr. *courlieu*, prob. imitative. Name of two birds with the same frequent, loud, shrill, characteristic cry; **a** a large wading bird of the snipe family, genus *Numenius*, with long, curved bill, frequenting estuaries and the seashore, but breeding on moors; a small species is known as *jack-curlew* or *whimbrel*; **b** an inland bird, the *stone-curlew* or 'thick-knee', genus *Oedicnemus*, with short bill, frequenting chalky downs.

curliness, n. [1. kĕrlines; 2. kʌ́linis]. **curly** & **-ness.** The state of being curly, or of having curly hair.

curling (I.), n. [1. kĕrling; 2. kʌ́liŋ]. **curl** (II.) & **-ing**, so called fr. the movement of the arm in swinging the curling stone. A Scotch game, like bowls, played on ice with special, heavy, round, flat, polished pieces of granite held by an iron or wooden handle.

curling (II.), adj., fr. Pres. Part. of **curl** (II.). **a** (of the hair) Inclined, tending, to curl; **b** used for curling (hair) &c. *Curling-irons, curling-tongs*, instruments for curling the hair.

curl-paper, n. Piece of paper in which a lock of hair is tightly rolled for several hours to make it curl into a ringlet.

curly, adj. [1. kĕrli; 2. kʌ́li]. **curl** (I.) & **-y.** **a** (of the hair) Curling, tending to curl; **b** (of persons) having curls; (of other objects) having a considerable curve: *a chair with curly legs.*

curmudgeon, n. [1. kurmújun; 2. kəmʌ́dʒən]. Etymol. unknown. In the first edition of his Dictionary Johnson doubtfully suggests as the origin of the word, *cœur méchant*, giving as the source of the suggestion 'an unknown correspondent'; Ash, the compiler of an English Dictionary a little later, misunderstood this & boldly explained the word as derived fr. 'Fr. *cœur*, "unknown", & *méchant*, "a correspondent"'! A churlish, cross-grained, surly, ill-tempered, cantankerous fellow.

curmudgeonly, adj. Prec. & **-ly.** Having the manners of a curmudgeon.

currant, n. [1. kúrant; 2. kárənt]. For 'raisins of Corauntz', Fr. *raisins de Corinthe.* **1.** A very small, sweet, dried grape from the Levant. **2.** Juicy fruit of several species of *Ribes*, known as *red, white, black, currants.*

currency, n. [1. kúrensi; 2. kárənsi], fr. Lat. *current-(em)*, Pres. Part. of *currere*, 'to run'. See **courier, course, curricle** & **-ency.** **1.** (lit.) A flowing, passage, state of flux (obs. and rare). **2.** State of being current; common habitual use, general acceptation: *the currency of a word or phrase*; *in common currency.* **3. a** That which circulates, specif., money, as coinage or notes, used as common medium of exchange, **coin of the realm**; **b** total amount of coinage or notes in circulation. **4.** Estimated value as commonly accepted: *to accept a person at his own currency.*

current (I.), adj. [1. kúrent; 2. kárənt], fr. O. Fr. *curant, corant*, Pres. Part. of *curre, corre*, fr. Lat. *current-(em)*, 'running, flowing', Pres. Part. of Lat. *currere*, 'to run'. See prec. & **courier, course.** **1. a** (of non-material things) Passing, handed on, from person to person: *current reports, rumours, opinions* etc.; **b** (of material objects) passing from hand to hand; in general or everyday use; in general circulation: *current money.* Phrs. *current coin*, (i.) money in daily use, legal tender; (ii.) (fig.) commonly accepted opinions &c.: *current beliefs, superstition.* **2. a** (of time) Now passing: *the current month* &c.; **b** belonging to the current time, present: *the current issue of a magazine* &c.

current (II.), n., fr. prec. **1. a** Continuous flow, or movement, of a body of water or air, or of part of such a body through the main bulk: *a strong current in the river*; *a violent current of air*; **b** flow of water or air in a particular direction: *which way is the current?*; **c** movement of electricity through or along a conducting body. **2.** (fig.) **a** (of time) Passing, passage onwards; **b** (of events, opinions) tendency, trend.

currently, adv. [1. kúrentli; 2. kárəntli]. **current** (I.) & **-ly.** In a current manner; commonly, generally.

curricle, n. [1. kúrikl; 2. kárikl]. See next word. A light open carriage, now obsolete, with two wheels, drawn by two horses abreast.

curriculum, n. [1. kuríkūlum; 2. karíkjuləm]. Lat., 'a race, race-course, chariot for racing', fr. *currere*, 'to run'. See **current** (I.). A fixed course of study, training &c. in a university or school.

currier, n. [1. kúrier; 2. káriə]. M.E. *coriour, curiour*, fr. O. Fr. *corier*, fr. Lat. *coriārius*, fr. *corium*, 'hide, leather'. See **cuirass, corium.** The M.E. form is by some derived fr. O. Fr. *conreeur*, fr. vb. *conreer*, 'to prepare', but although it may have been later confused w. this, it can hardly be separated fr. the Lat. words above cited. See **curry** (I.). One who dresses and curries tanned leather.

currish, adj. [1. kĕrish; 2. kʌ́riʃ]. **cur** & **-ish.** Like a cur; having the qualities of a cur; cross-grained, quarrelsome, churlish, ill-bred.

currishly, adv. Prec. & **-ly.** In a currish manner; churlishly.

currishness, n. See prec. & **-ness.** The qualities of a cur.

curry (I.), vb. trans. [1. kúri; 2. kári]. It seems probable that this word is a back-formation fr. the n. **currier.** On the other hand, O. Fr. has *conreder*, 'prepare', later *conreer, correier.* The latter was mixed up w. *courroyer*, 'to dress leather', fr. *corium*, 'leather', & *conreer* was also used in the same sense. It is impossible to separate **currier** fr. *corium*, & just as difficult to separate **curry** fr. the former. For origin of O. Fr. *conreer* see **com-** & the second element in **array.** **1.** To dress tanned leather. **2.** To rub down and dress (the coat of a horse &c.) with a curry-comb and brush. Phr. *to curry favour* (M.E., fr. O. Fr., *favel*, used by Latimer, 'a chestnut horse'), to seek to ingratiate oneself with a person by flattery &c.

curry (II.), n. & vb. trans., fr. Tamil *kari*, 'sauce'. **1.** n. Indian dish of stewed meat, fish, game &c., dressed with highly flavoured sauce made of various condiments. *Curry powder*, Indian preparation of turmeric and other hot and strong condiments used for making curry. **2.** vb. To turn into a curry, make a curry from: *to curry a fowl.*

curry-comb, n. See **curry** (I.) & **comb.** Semicircular strip of flexible metal, with teeth, held by a handle, used for scraping and cleaning horses' coats.

curse (I.), n. [1. kĕrs; 2. kʌ̄s]. L.O.E. (11th cent.) & M.E. *curs.* The origin is very doubtful; the connexion w. an old form of *cross* wh. has been suggested offers many difficulties. Weekley proposes to derive the word fr. O. Fr. *coroz*, or Norman *curuz*, 'wrath', Mod. Fr. *courroux.* The A.-Fr. form of the vb. is *curcier*, w. wh. cp. the L.O.E. *cursian.* The O. Fr. form is *couroucier*, wh. is fr. Low Lat. *corruptiāre*; see **corrupt.** **1.** The calling down, invoking, of divine or supernatural anger or vengeance, involving death, misfortune, destruction, upon a person or thing; malediction: *to call down, lay, a curse upon.* **2.** A blasphemous utterance, an impious word or expression; a profane exclamation expressing anger or malevolence; an oath, imprecation. **3.** A source, cause, of misfortune, misery, ruin: *he is a curse to his family*; *drink is a curse to many.* Phr. *curse of Scotland*, nine of diamonds.

curse (II.), vb. trans. & intrans. See prec. **A.** trans. **1. a** To call down divine or supernatural wrath or vengeance upon; to lay under a malediction, place under a ban; **b** (eccles.) to place under excommunication. **2.** To swear at, direct blasphemous, impious remarks to, express enmity towards; to complain of with violent expressions of resentment: *to curse the day one was born, one's own folly* &c. **3.** To bring misfortune, misery, ruin, upon; to afflict, torment; esp. in construction *to be cursed with.* **B.** intrans. To utter blasphemous impieties, give vent to profane swearing: *to curse and swear.*

cursed, adj. [1. kĕrsed; 2. kʌ́sid]. Prec. & **-ed.** **1. a** Deserving strong reprobation, execrable, hateful; **b** (used colloquially with very little significance, as an intens.) *a cursed nuisance*; **c** (colloq.) [1. kúsid; 2. kásid], perverse, contrary: *a cursed boy.* **2.** (archaic and obs., gen. **curst**) Malevolent, ill-tempered.

cursedly, adv. [1. kĕrsedli; 2. kʌ́sidli]. Prec. & **-ly.** In a cursed manner.

cursedness, n. [1. kĕrsednes; 2. kʌ́sidnis]. **cursed** & **-ness.** **1.** Fact, condition, of being cursed. **2.** (colloq. and facet.) [1. kúsidnes; 2. kásidnis]. Perversity, contrariness.

cursive, adj. & n. [1. kĕrsiv; 2. kʌ́siv], fr. Low Lat. *cursīvus*, fr. Lat. *currere, cursum*, 'to run'; cp. Fr. *cursif.* See **courier, current,** & **-ive.** **a** adj. (of handwriting in MSS.) *Cursive hand*, running hand, with the letters formed, curved, and connected by strokes; contrasted with *uncial*; **b** n., handwriting of this type.

cursorily, adv. [1. kĕrsorili; 2. kʌ́sərili]. **cursory** & **-ly.** Hastily, carelessly.

cursoriness, n. [1. kĕrsorines; 2. kʌ́sərinis]. See next word & **-ness.** The quality of being cursory.

cursory, adj. [1. kĕrsori; 2. kʌ́səri], fr. Low Lat. *cursōrius*, 'hasty', & adv. *cursōriē*, 'hastily', fr. *cursor*, 'a runner'. See **cursive, courier, current.** Hasty, hurried, passing; hence superficial, careless: *a cursory inspection, glance* &c.

curst, adj. [1. kĕrst; 2. kʌ̄st]. See **cursed.**

curt, adj. [1. kĕrt; 2. kʌ̄t], fr. Lat. *curtus*, 'shortened, mutilated, broken; mean; incomplete'. From base *(*s*)*ker-*, 'to cut'; connected w. Lat. *caro*, 'flesh, (orig.) slice of flesh', see **carnal**; Scrt. *kṛdhúš*, 'shortened, maimed'; O. Slav. *kratŭkŭ*, 'short'; cogn. w. O.H.G. *scurz*, 'short'. See **short.** Short, brief, truncated; (chiefly applied to verbal style, mode of address &c.) brief and incomplete to the point of discourtesy: *a curt answer.*

curtail, vb. trans. [1. kĕrtā́l; 2. kʌ̄téil]. Earlier (16th cent.) *cúrtall*; prob. influenced by Engl. *tail*, & supposed to have relation to docking a tail; possibly also, as Skeat suggests, by Fr. *tailler*, 'cut'. M. Fr. *curtault*, 'horse of middle size'; M. Ital. *cortaldo*, 'a horse without a tail', in wh. sense Florio uses Engl. *curtall.* The first element is Lat. *curtus*, 'short', see **curt**; the second, apparently fr. Gmc. *wald*, 'strength' &c., O.H.G. *walt*; see **wield.** **a** To abbreviate, cut short, shorten, make shorter than was originally intended; (chiefly of non-material things) *to curtail a lecture, speech, a holiday*

&c.; **b** to reduce, cut down: *to have one's pay curtailed.*

curtailment, n. [1. kĕrtálment; 2. kʌ̄téilmənt]. Prec. & **-ment.** The act or result of curtailing.

curtain (I.), n. [1. kĕrtin; 2. kʌ̄tin]. M.E. *curtin* &c., fr. L. Lat. *cortīna*, 'little court, enclosure', dimin. of Lat. *cort-*, as in *co(ho)r-s*, acc. *co(ho)rt-(em)*. See **court** (I.). **1.** Sheet of cloth, or other material, suspended so as **a** to keep out sun or draught, hung so as to draw over a window or door; **b** so as to draw round a bed; **c** so as to divide one part of a room from another. Phrs. *to draw a curtain over*, (fig.) to say no more about something, conceal it; *to lift the curtain*, (fig.) to reveal something, give information about it; *to draw the curtains*, draw them across a window &c., so as to hide it from the room, shut out light or draught. **2.** Sheet of heavy material, often fire-proof, raised and lowered by pulleys, to divide the stage in a theatre from the auditorium. Phrs. *the curtain rises*, the play, act &c. begins; (fig.) the story opens; *the curtain falls*, the play, act &c. ends; (fig.) the story ends, life comes to an end &c. **3.** Various things which cover or protect like a curtain, e.g.: *curtain of fire*, artillery barrage; *curtain of cloud, smoke* &c.; specif. also *curtain-wall*, that part of a rampart and wall, in fortification, which lies between two projecting towers or bastions.

curtain (II.), vb. trans., fr. prec. To cover, protect, by a curtain: *to curtain a window*; *curtain off*, to divide, shut off, by a curtain; *to curtain off part of a room, an alcove* &c.

curtain-lecture, n. Scolding given by a woman to her husband in private.

curtain-raiser, n. Short play performed while some of the audience are taking their seats, just before the opening of the principal play.

curtana, n. [1. kĕrtána, -áhna; 2. kʌ̄téinə, kʌ̄tánə], fr. Anglo-Lat. *curtāna (spada)*, 'curtailed (sword)'. See **curt.** Sword without a point carried in front of English sovereigns at their coronation as symbolical of mercy.

curtesy, n. [1. kĕrtesi; 2. kʌ̄təsi]. Variant of **courtesy.** (law) Life estate enjoyed by husband in lands of a deceased wife, when there has been issue: *tenant by curtesy.*

curtilage, n. [1. kĕrtilij; 2. kʌ̄tilidž]. O. Fr. *cortill-*, *curtillage*, fr. *cortil*, 'little court'. See **court** (I.) & **-age.** Portion of land immediately surrounding a dwelling-house, esp. one forming part of the same enclosure as the house.

curtle axe, n. [1. kĕrtl àks; 2. kʌ̄tl æks]. (archaic) Variant of **cutlass.**

curtly, adv. [1. kĕrtli; 2. kʌ̄tli]. **curt** & **-ly.** In a curt manner, abruptly (of speech &c.).

curtness, n. [1. kĕrtnes; 2. kʌ̄tnis]. **curt** & **-ness.** The quality of being curt.

curtsey, -sy, n. & vb. intrans. [1. kĕrtsi; 2. kʌ̄tsi]. Variant of **courtesy. 1.** n. Movement of the body implying recognition or respect, made by women and girls. **a** Consisting generally of a slight, jerky, momentary bending of the knees: *to drop a curtsey*; **b** in a more formal shape, as to royalty, a slow, sweeping movement, with a forward inclination of the body from the waist, together with flexion of the knees, a drawing backwards of the whole body, and a gradual rising to the upright position: *to make one's curtsey to the queen*, (of a woman) to be presented at court. **2.** vb. To make a curtsey.

curule, adj. [1. kūrōōl; 2. kjúərūl]. Lat. *sella curūlis*, chair inlaid with ivory used by the highest magistrates in ancient Rome. *Curūlis* is fr. *currus*, 'chariot, triumphal car' &c. See **curricle, courier, course.** Esp. in Phr. *curule chair*, magisterial or official seat.

curvature, n. [1. kĕrvachur; 2. kʌ̄vətʃə], fr. Lat. *curvātūra*, fr. *curvāt-*, as in P.P. of *curvāre*, 'to bend, curve' (see **curve**), & **-ture.** Act of curving; condition of being curved: *curvature of the spine* &c.

curve (I.), n. [1. kĕrv; 2. kʌ̄v], fr. Lat. *curvus*, 'bent, curved', cogn. w. O. Slav. *krivu*, 'crooked', Lith. *kreivas*, 'twisted, crooked', W. *corwynt*, 'eddy', & related to a large group of words fr. same base, **ker(e)-*, 'twist, turn', w. various formative elements. See further under **circus, crass, crate, crux, cart, crown, hurdle,** & perh. **crisp. 1.** (geom.) A line of which no part is straight. **2. a** A rounded bend, one which has no angles; **b** curved part of anything: *a curve in the road.*

curve (II.), vb. trans. & intrans. Lat. *curvāre.* See prec. **a** trans. To cause to bend, impart a curve to; **b** intrans., to assume the form of a curve.

curvet, n. & vb. intrans. [1. kĕrvét; 2. kʌ̄vét], fr. Ital. *corvetta*, dimin. of *corvo*, 'a curve', fr. Lat. *curvus*, see **curve** (I.). **1.** n. Graceful, bounding action of a horse, in which he raises both fore legs and leaps forward from the hind legs while the fore legs are still in the air. **2.** vb. (of a horse) To execute the motion of a curvet; (also of the rider) *curveting on a horse.*

curvi-, pref. Form of **curve** (I.), used in compounds.

curvilineal, -ar, adj. [1. kĕrvilíneal, -ar; 2. kʌ̄vilíniə(l)]. Prec. & Lat. *līnea*, 'line'. see **line.** Consisting of, bounded by, enclosed in, curving lines.

cuscus (I.), n. Variant of **cous-cous.**

cuscus (II.), n. [1. kúskus; 2. káskas], fr. Pers. *khas-khas.* Fibrous, scented root of an Indian grass, used for making fans, screens &c.

cuscus (III.), n. [1. kóoskoos; 2. kúskus]. Native Moluccan name. A genus of tree-living marsupials, Phalangers, of the East Indian Archipelago, with grey or spotted fur.

cushat, n. [1. kúshat; 2. káʃæt]. O.E. *cūscote*, 'wild pigeon, ring-dove', L.M.E. *cowschote.* Skeat suggests that the first element refers to the bird's note, and that the second means 'the shooter, darter', fr. *scēotan*, 'shoot'. See **shoot.** Wood-pigeon, ring-dove. (Archaic or poet.)

cushion (I.), n. [1. kóoshun; 2. kúʃən]. M.E. *quisschen*, fr. A.-Fr. *quissine*, O. Fr. *cuissin*, *coissin*, as though fr. Low Lat. *coxīnum*, fr. *coxa*, 'hip-bone'. Thus the word orig. meant a rest for the hips or thighs. See **coxa** & **cuisse. 1.** A bag or case of cloth or other fabric stuffed with some soft elastic material such as feathers, wool, horsehair &c., used to lie, sit, or kneel upon. **2.** Applied to various objects somewhat resembling this, either in shape or in function, by acting as pads, shock-receivers &c., e.g.: **a** a soft pad of any kind to fill out a space or support something, e.g. for a woman's hair; **b** the resilient, rubber lining of the inner sides of a billiard table; **c** the frog of a horse's hoof; **d** steam left in the cylinder of a steam engine acting as a buffer to the piston &c.

cushion (II.), vb. trans., fr. prec. **1.** To supply, fit with, cushions; to protect from shock or injury by means of cushions or padding. **2.** (billiards) To leave (a ball) against a cushion.

cushiony, adj. [1. kóoshuni; 2. kúʃəni]. **cushion** (I.) & **-y.** Resembling a cushion; soft.

cushy, adj. [1. kóoshi; 2. kúʃi]. Origin doubtful; said to be of Anglo-Indian origin, fr. Hind. *khashi*, 'pleasant'. (slang) Easy, soft, pleasant: *to find a cushy job.*

cusp, n. [1. kusp; 2. kasp], fr. Lat. *cuspis*, 'a point'. The relations of the word are very uncertain, but it may be cogn. w. O.E. *hosp*, 'contumely, insult', wh. is fr. Gmc. **huspa.* **1.** (archit.) A projecting point where two inner curves in Gothic tracery meet. **2.** (astron.) Either point of the crescent moon. **3.** (geom.) The point at which two branches of a curve have a common tangent. **4.** A sharp point, esp. that at the end of a leaf.

cuspidal, adj. [1. kúspidal; 2. káspidəl], fr. Lat. *cuspid-*, stem of *cuspis*, & **-al.** See prec. Ending in a cusp or point.

cuspidate(d), adj. [1. kúspidāt(ed); 2. káspideit(id)], fr. Lat. *cuspidātum*, P.P. of *cuspidāre*, 'to make pointed'. See prec. & **cusp.** Having a sharp or pointed end; esp. of leaves.

cuspidor, n. [1. kúspidōr; 2. káspidō], fr. Port. *cuspideira*, fr. *cuspir*, 'to spit'. American refined name for vulgar object, a spittoon.

cuss (I.), n. [1. kus; 2. kas]. Variant of **curse** (I.). Chiefly in vulgar Phr.: *not to care a cuss.*

cuss (II.), n. A person. Either short for **customer** (cp. *queer customer* &c.) or in sense of a cantankerous, shrewish person, same as prec., with sense as in *cursed.*

cussed, adj. [1. kúsed; 2. kásid]. See **cursed.** Perverse, contrary.

custard, n. [1. kústard; 2. kástəd]. Prob. a form of Lat. *crūstātum*, 'having a crust', M.E. *crustate*, *crustade*; cp. O. Fr. *croustade*, 'something covered with a crust'. See **crust.** A mixture of sweetened milk and eggs, cooked and eaten hot or cold with fruit &c. Also *baked custard* or *custard pudding.*

custard-apple, n. West Indian fruit with a soft yellowish pulp, *Anona.*

custodial, adj. & n. [1. kustódial; 2. kastóudiəl]. **custody** & **-al. a** adj. Relating to custody; **b** n., receptacle for relics.

custodian, n. [1. kustódian; 2. kastóudiən]. **custody** & **-an. a** One who has the care or custody of anything; **b** specif., the keeper of a public building &c.

custody, n. [1. kústodi; 2. kástədi], fr. Lat. *custōdia*, 'a keeping of guard, watch, guard, care', fr. *custōd-(em)*, 'a guardian'. The base is considered by Walde to be cogn. w. that in Gk. *akoúō*, 'I hear', fr. **a-kous-jō* (see **acoustic**), & Goth. *hausjan*, O.E. *hīeran*, 'to hear', see **hear** & **cave** (III.). **1.** Care, guardianship; duty of guarding, keeping, taking care of: *a father has the custody of his child.* **2.** Specif., guardianship of persons exercised by officers of the law, detention by the police, imprisonment: *to be in custody*, in charge of the police: *to take (a person) into custody*, to arrest.

custom, n. [1. kústum; 2. kástəm]. M.E. & O. Fr. *custume*, *costume* &c., fr. earlier *costumne*, fr. *costudne*, Lat. *consuētūdinem* (acc.), fr. **con-** & *suētu-*, as in P.P. of *suēscere* (for **swēdh-sk-*), 'to become accustomed', inchoative fr. *suēre*, 'to be accustomed, to be wont'; the fundamental sense is 'to follow one's own ways', cp. Lat. *suus* (fr. **swe-wos*), 'one's (his, her) own, belonging to oneself (himself &c.)', cp. **sui.** From the base **swe-* is derived also Gk. *éthos* (fr. **swedhos*), 'custom, usage, habit' (cp. **ethical**), *ēthos*, 'accustomed place, abode, habit' (cp. **ethos**); also Scrt. *swadhā*, 'custom, habit, habitual home', & in spite of the absence of *w*, Goth. *sidus*, O.E. *sidu*, O.H.G. *situ*, 'habit, custom, behaviour'. **1. a** Usual habit, established practice, use and wont; **b** any specific instance of this in individuals or communities. **2.** Support given to a trader by dealing with him, purchasing his goods: *to withdraw one's custom.* **3.** *Customs*, duties paid on foreign goods.

customable, adj. [1. kústumabl; 2. kástəməbl]. Prec. & **-able.** Liable to customs, taxable as an import.

customary, adj. & n. [1. kústumari; 2. kástəməri]. See prec. & **-ary. 1.** adj. **a** Usual, habitual, according to custom: *customary practice* &c.; **b** (of land and tenants, tenure) held by, holding according to, made legal by virtue of custom. **2.** n. Collection of customary laws, esp. of a manor.

customer, n. [1. kústumer; 2. kástəmə]. **custom** & **-er. a** One who deals (esp. habitually) with a trader, one who buys from a trader; **b** (colloq.) general, slightly derogatory, term for a person, equivalent to fellow, chap &c.; esp. in Phrs. *queer, awkward, rough, tough customer.*

custom-house, n. **a** Office where business connected with duties on imports is transacted; **b** (at a seaport) office where, in addition to above, vessels are cleared.

custos, n. [1. kústos; 2. kástəs]. Lat., 'keeper'. See **custody.** Keeper, guardian; esp. in Phr. *Custos Rotulorum*, 'keeper of Rolls', an important crown officer in a county, generally chosen from among the territorial magnates, who is responsible for the safe keeping of the county records and archives.

custumal, n. [1. kústūmal; 2. kástjuməl]. **custom** & **-al**. Same as customary, n., a collection of the customs of a manor.

cut (I.), vb. trans. & intrans. [1. kut; 2. kat]. M.E. *kutten, cutten, kitten, ketten*. Origin unknown. **A.** trans. **1.** To penetrate surface of with the edge of a sharp-bladed instrument, knife, scissors &c., and divide partially or wholly. Phr. *to cut the knot*, dispose of a difficulty hastily and by easiest means instead of by application of patience and skill; specif. **a** to sever and remove whole or a part, hew down: *to cut trees, timber, wood*; **b** to slice thinly, sever small pieces, carve: *to cut a joint of meat, a slice of cake, piece of cheese*; **c** to gash, slit, inflict a wound with a knife &c.: *to cut oneself, one's fingers*; *to cut one's throat*, sever jugular vein; **d** to break up, shape, pierce hard substance by hacking and splitting &c.: *to cut steps in a rock*; *cut a road through a hill* &c.; *to cut ice*; Phr. (fig.) *to cut no ice*, to accomplish nothing, be ineffective; **e** to slit, tear (paper) with a blunt-edged instrument: *to cut a book, the pages of a book* &c.; **f** to shape and polish a precious stone, bring it out of the rough: *to cut a diamond* &c. **2.** To mow, reap with a scythe, sickle, or mechanical device: *to cut the crops, hay, corn* &c. Phr. *cut and dried* (fig., of mental processes and their results), stereotyped, narrow, lacking initiative and vitality. **3.** To divide the stalks of (plants) with knife or scissors: *to cut flowers, roses*; *to cut asparagus, grapes* &c. **4.** To castrate (a male animal); chiefly in Phr.: *this pony ought to be cut*. **5. a** To chisel, carve, engrave a hard substance so as to mould and shape it: *to cut stone into various forms*; **b** impart certain shapes to hard material by chiselling it; to engrave, inscribe characters upon it; *to cut a device in marble*; *to cut one's name on a tree*; **c** (in P.P.) *well-cut features*, shapely, well formed. **6.** To shape cloth for wearing apparel with scissors; to form a garment out of cloth by cutting: *to cut a pattern*; *to cut a coat*. Phr. (fig.) *to cut one's coat according to one's cloth*, adapt one's desires to one's means. **7.** To strike a ball to the off in a particular way at cricket or tennis &c., with action as if cutting something with the bat. **8. a** To inflict, cause, pain resembling that of cutting to, by giving a smart blow with a whip, by cold &c.: *to cut a horse with a switch*; *the icy wind cut me to the bone*; **b** (fig.) to inflict, cause, mental pain to: *your reproach cuts me to the heart, the quick*. **9.** To refuse to acknowledge a person's acquaintance, refuse to recognize him on meeting, pretend not to know him: *to cut a man in the street*; *to cut him dead*, ignore him completely. **10.** To avoid, absent oneself from a place, or not to be present on an occasion, where and when one ought to be present: *to cut a lecture, a meeting, a service in church* &c. **11. a** To shorten, reduce in length by removing ends by trimming with scissors: *to cut one's hair*; **b** to shorten and pare: *to cut one's nails*; **c** to abbreviate, abridge, by striking out part: *to cut a newspaper article* &c.; **d** to reduce in amount: *to cut prices, rates*. **12.** *To cut one's teeth*, to undergo process of the teeth reaching that stage of growth when they pierce the gums and come into use. **13.** To execute, carry out, a lively movement; esp. *to cut a caper*; (fig.) *to cut capers*, to play tricks, behave in a lively, irresponsible, unreliable manner. Phrs. *to cut a poor figure*, create a bad impression, to come with discredit out of an affair; *to cut a dash*, be dashing, showy. **14.** *To cut the cards*, to divide pack by lifting off a portion from the top. Phrs. *cut for deal*, remove upper portion of pack and expose lowest card taken so as to decide who shall deal; *cut for partners*, do the same to decide who shall play whom. **15.** (of lines) To intersect, cross. **B.** intrans. **1. a** To perform the function of an edged tool, the operation of cutting; specif., to do this well, adequately, satisfactorily: *this knife* (or *razor*) *won't cut*; **b** to inflict pain resembling cutting, as of an icy wind; to give a smart stroke with a whip: *the wind cuts keenly*; *the lash cut like a knife*. **2.** (colloq.) **a** To depart hastily, run away: *I must cut*, go away, leave; Phrs. *cut!*, be off!; *to cut and run*, run away with speed; **b** to carve meat, help oneself to meat, in Phr. *cut and come again*, have another helping, eat heartily. **C.** Followed by various prepositions and adverbs. *Cut away*, **a** trans., to remove entirely by cutting: *to cut away dead wood from a tree, diseased tissue* &c.; **b** intrans. (colloq.), to run away, depart hurriedly, escape. *Cut at*, intrans., **a** to aim a sharp rapid stroke at, strike smartly, with sword or whip; **b** (fig.) to inflict moral injury, to tend to destroy, to sap: *that cuts at all my hopes*. *Cut down*, trans., **a** to fell (timber &c.); **b** to cause to fall, kill by striking with edge of a sword; **c** (fig.) to deprive of life, health &c., as by disease: *he was cut down in full strength by paralysis*; **d** to reduce in size or amount: *to cut down expenses*; *to cut down a curtain into two small ones* &c. *Cut in, into*, intrans., make a sudden entry, intervention: *cut into a conversation* &c. *Cut loose*, trans. & intrans.: **a** trans., to separate, sever connexion between by cutting: *to cut a boat loose from a ship*; (fig.) *cut oneself loose from*, discontinue relations, become independent: *to cut oneself loose from one's family*; **b** intrans., to free oneself from restraint; behave in irresponsible manner. *Cut off*, trans., **a** to remove, esp. the top or extremity of anything, by cutting: *to cut a man's head off*; **b** to interrupt a connexion suddenly, e.g. on a telephone; **c** to stop, discontinue, deprive of supplies of anything: *to cut off the gas at the meter*; *to cut off food, money* &c.; **d** to strike down, lay aside, kill, or injure severely, as by an accident, sudden illness &c.: *to be cut off in one's prime*; Phr. *to cut off with a shilling*, leave little or nothing to, by will. *Cut out*, trans., **a** to shape a garment by cutting its outline in cloth with scissors: *to cut out a dress*; **b** (fig.) to oust another from a position, show oneself his superior, be more successful than: *to cut out another in a lady's affections, in obtaining an appointment* &c.; **c** (nav.) to attack and seize a ship under enemy's guns, or in harbour. *Cut short*, trans., to interrupt, bring to a sudden close: *to cut short a person's remarks*; *cut short a career*. *Cut up*, trans. & intrans.: **1.** trans., **a** to cut to pieces, cut small: *to cut up a piece of meat*; **b** to criticize severely, point out all defects of: *to cut up a book, speech* &c.; **c** to cause severe mental suffering to, to afflict: *his son's death cut him up badly*; **2.** intrans., **a** to undergo process of being cut up: *this cloth will cut up into several suits*; **b** (colloq.) *to cut up well*, die worth a large fortune; Phr. *to cut up rough*, show strong displeasure, ill-temper.

cut (II.), P.P. of prec., used as adj. Various specif. uses, e.g.: *cut flowers*, such as have been cut or gathered for decoration; contrasted with *growing flowers* (in pots &c.); *cut glass*, that which has the surface incised, cut into facets, or otherwise decorated with designs engraved upon it; *cut horse*, a gelding, castrated horse; *cut sugar*, that which is cut into, and sold in cubes, instead of in the loaf; *cut tobacco*, such as has been sliced or shredded, contrasted with *cake tobacco*.

cut (III.), n., fr. **cut** (I.). **1. a** Result of cutting, a wound inflicted by an edged instrument, a gash: *a cut in the finger* &c.; **b** incision, mark, notch, scratch on a hard surface: *a cut on stone*; Phr. (fig.) *a cut above*, rather superior to, from idea of a mark made to indicate height, amount &c. **2. a** The action of cutting, a slashing stroke, smart blow with edge, lash, thin cane &c.: *to make a vicious cut with a sword, whip* &c.; **b** specif., a peculiar sharp mode of striking a ball at cricket, tennis &c. **3.** Something removed by cutting, **a** something cut, sliced, off: *a cut from the joint*; **b** yield of certain products obtained by cutting: *this year's cut of wool*; *a cut of timber*. **4.** Mode of fashioning, shaping, by cutting, style: **a** (of clothes &c.) *the cut of a coat*; *a garment of ancient cut*; **b** manner, type of a ship's rigging; Phr. (fig. and colloq.) *the cut of a person's rig*, general style of appearance, impression he conveys. **5. a** An engraved plate or block from which prints are made; **b** impressions taken from this. **6. a** Curtailment, abridgement, shortening, by striking out or omitting, passages from a literary work, newspaper article &c.; **b** reduction in amount, or sum: *a cut in prices*. **7.** Rebuff administered by refusal to recognize and greet a person on meeting, deliberate avoidance of a person, failure to acknowledge his acquaintance: *to give (a man) the cut direct*. **8.** (obs.) *To draw cuts*, to draw, cast lots, by drawing a straw from several of various lengths, held in the hand; Chaucer uses this phrase and also the word *cut(s)* in reference to the straws themselves. This is perhaps a different word from that here dealt with.

cutaneous, adj. [1. kūtâneus; 2. kjūtéiniəs]. Cp. Fr. *cutané*, 'relating to the skin'; fr. Lat. **cutis**, 'skin', & **-aneous**. Pertaining to the skin, on the skin: *cutaneous eruption*.

cutaway, adj. & n. [1. kútawā; 2. kátəwei]. **cut** & **away**. (obsolesc.) **a** adj. *Cutaway coat*, kind of tail coat, cut so as to slope sharply back from the waist; **b** n., *a cutaway*, this kind of coat.

cutcherry, **cutchery**, n. [1. kuchéri, kúcheri; 2. katʃéri, kátʃəri]. Hind. *kachahrī*. Anglo-Indian word. **a** Office of administration, court-house; **b** office of a planter.

cute, adj. [1. kūt; 2. kjūt], for **acute**. **1.** Having a sharp, lively, intellect; shrewd, sagacious, wary. **2.** (U.S.A., colloq.) Attractive, pretty.

cutely, adv. Prec. & **-ly**. In a cute manner.

cuteness, n. See prec. & **-ness**. Quality of being cute.

cuticle, n. [1. kūtikl; 2. kjūtikl]. Lat. *cutīcula*, 'thin external skin', dimin. of **cutis**. Epidermis, outer skin of animals and plants.

cuticular, adj. [1. kūtíkūlar; 2. kjūtíkjulə]. Prec. & **-ar**. Pertaining to, consisting of, cuticle.

cutis, n. [1. kūtis; 2. kjūtis]. Lat. *cutis*, fr. the base *(s)keut-, *(s)kut-, 'to cover, hide'. The base is a prolific one, & appears in many forms. Closely related to Lat. *cutis* are Gk. *kútos*, 'skin, cover', *skûtos*, 'leather'; O.E. *hȳd*, 'skin' (see **hide** (I.)); Lith. *kiaũtas*, 'husk'; O. Prussian *keuto*, 'skin'. Cp., w. different formative elements, Gk. *keúthein*, 'to hide' (fr. *keu-dh-); O.E. *hȳdan* (see **hide** (III.)), W. *cuddio*, 'to hide'; fr. *kut-so, O.E. *hūs* (see **house**), Lith. *kūtis*, 'stall'. Cp. further, Scrt. *skunáti*, 'covers'; Gk. *skúlon*, 'flayed skin'; M. Fr. *cūil*, 'concealment'; O.N. *skjōl*, 'shelter'; O. Fris. *skūl*, 'concealment'; O.H.G. *scūr*, 'eaves'. See also **obscure**, **scutum**, **sky**. (anat.) The derma, or inner skin, below the epidermis.

cutlass, n. [1. kútlas; 2. kátləs]. Earlier spelt *coutelace*; fr. Fr. *coutelas*, 'sword with a short, broad blade'; Ital. *coltellaccio*, 'large knife', fr. Lat. *cultellus*, 'small knife', dimin. of *culter*, 'knife'. See **coulter**. *Curtle axe* is a corrupt. of *cutlass*, due to confusion of *curtal*, 'docked' &c. (see **curtail**), w. the first two sylls., & of *axe* w. the last. A short, heavy sword, esp. used by seamen.

cutler, n. [1. kútler; 2. kátlə]. M.E. *cotelere*, fr. A.-Fr. *cotillere*, O. Fr. *cotelier*, Mod. Fr. *coutelier*, 'knife-maker', fr. Low Lat. *cultellārius*, 'soldier armed with a knife'; also 'maker of knives', fr. Lat. *cultellus*, 'knife'. See prec. & **coulter**. **a** A manufacturer of knives; **b** one who sells and repairs knives.

cutlery, n. [1. kútleri; 2. kátləri]. O. Fr. *coutelerie*. See prec. & **-y**. **a** Business of a cutler; **b** collection of knives and other articles of steel; specif., the knives &c. in use in a household: *plate and cutlery*.

cutlet, n. [1. kútlet; 2. kátlit]. O. Fr. *costelette*, lit. 'little rib', dimin. fr. *coste*, 'rib', Lat. *costa*, Mod. Fr. *côtelette*. See **costal**. Small rib bone with meat attached, small chop: *mutton cutlet*; *veal cutlet*, small slice of lean meat without any bone, usually served fried in egg and bread crumbs.

cut-off, n. [1. kút awf; 2. kát ōf]. See **cut (I.) C**, & **off**. That which cuts something off or shortens it, esp. device **a** in engine which shuts off steam from the cylinder during the piston-stroke; **b** in magazine rifle which prevents the automatic passing of cartridges into the breech chamber.

cut-out, n. [1. kút out; 2. kát *aut*]. See prec. & **out**. Device **a** for automatically stopping or cutting out an electric current when above a certain force, a circuit-breaker; **b** for shutting off the exhaust in a motor car &c.

cutpurse, n. [1. kútpërs; 2. kátpās]. (archaic, obsolesc.) A pickpocket; from a type of thieving formerly in vogue, when purses were hung by straps from the girdle, and were liable to be detached by cutting.

cutter, n. [1. kúter; 2. kátə]. **cut (I.)** & **-er**. **1. a** One who cuts, specif., *a tailor's cutter*, one who cuts out clothes; *glass-cutter* &c.; **b** machine or tool for cutting, e.g. *grass-cutter*, mowing machine; *paper-cutter*, paper knife &c. **2.** (naut.) A type of sailing vessel, rigged somewhat like a sloop, with a deep keel to ensure stability.

cut-throat, n. & adj. **a** n. One who cuts throats; a murderer, a bloodthirsty ruffian; **b** adj., murderous, cruel, ruffianly.

cutting (I.), vbl. n. [1. kúting; 2. kátiŋ]. **cut (I.)** & **-ing**. **1.** Act of, process carried out by, one who cuts: *the cutting of riding-breeches is a highly skilled work.* **2.** Something cut off, hewn out &c.; specif. **a** an excavation, a tunnel, channel, cut through a hill &c.: *railway cutting*, passage for trains cut through rock or earth to avoid excessive change of levels; **b** portion of a growing plant, cut off and struck in the earth to form a new plant; **c** excerpt from a newspaper, an article, notice &c., cut out, or snipped off to be preserved: *newspaper cutting*; *press cuttings.*

cutting (II.), adj., fr. Pres. Part. of **cut (I.)**. **1.** Able to cut, made for cutting: *the cutting edge of a knife.* **2. a** Inflicting a sensation of cutting, piercing: *a cutting wind*; **b** (fig.) tending to wound; liable, intended, to inflict pain of mind, stinging: *a cutting remark*; **c** keen, shrewd, penetrating: *a cutting glance.*

cuttingly, adv. Prec. & **-ly**. In a cutting manner, esp. in senses **2, a** and **b** above.

cuttle bone, n. [1. kútl bōn; 2. kátl boun]. See next word. Shelly internal bone of cuttle-fish, used as food for small cage birds; also ground fine and used as polishing powder.

cuttle-fish, n. [1. kútl fish; 2. kátl fiʃ]. The present form apparently borrowed fr. a H.G. source, cp. Mod. Germ. *kuttelfisch*. Late M.E. has *cotul* & *codul*, the latter being the genuine Engl. form fr. O.E. *cudule*. This is prob. cogn. w. Germ. *kutteln*, 'guts, bowels', L.G. *kütt*, & also w. O.E. *codd* (see **cod (II.)**), wh. is fr. the same base as Lat. *botulus*, 'a sausage', for **gʷot-*; see **botulism**. **a** Marine animal of the cephalopod class, having long tentacles, a sac from which a black fluid is squirted, known as 'sepia', and hard internal shelly bone; **b** (loosely) a squid, which has no internal bone.

cutty, adj. & n. [1. kúti; 2. káti], fr. **cut (I.)** & **-y**. **1.** adj. Cut short, short, originally a Scots or M. English usage: esp. *cutty pipe*, short clay pipe; *cutty stool*, stool in Presbyterian churches on which a woman under censure for immoral conduct was seated to receive admonition. **2.** n. A cutty pipe.

cutwater, n. [1. kútwawter; 2. kátwōtə]. **a** Forepart of a ship which cuts the water; **b** pointed part of a pier of a bridge facing upstream, dividing the stream so that it passes under the arches.

cutworm, n. [1. kútwërm; 2. kátwām]. Caterpillar which eats off young cabbage-plants.

-cy, suff. [1. si; 2. si], used to form abstract ns. Fr. *-tie*, Lat. *-cia*, *-tia*, or Gk. *-keia*, *-teia*, *-kia*, *-tia*. Used after ns. ending in *-n*, *captaincy*=**-ship**; after some ending in *-t*, *idiotcy*, also *idiocy*.

cyanate, n. [1. síanāt; 2. sáiəneit]. See next word & **-ate**. (chem.) A salt of cyanic acid.

cyanic, adj. [1. siánik; 2. saiǽnik], fr. Gk. *kúanos*, 'a dark-blue mineral substance'; origin unknown, prob. a loan-word. **a** Blue in colour; **b** specif., pertaining to, containing, cyanogen. *Cyanic acid*, volatile acid liquid, compound of oxygen and cyanogen.

cyanide, n. [1. síanīd; 2. sáiənaid]. See prec. & **-ide**. (chem.) A salt of hydrocyanic acid, usually known as 'prussic acid'; esp. *cyanide of potassium*, used in chemical extraction of gold from ore by the *cyanide process.*

cyano-, pref. Used in compounds (see **cyanic**), meaning 'blue', in chemical terminology.

cyanogen, n. [1. siánōjen; 2. saiǽnoudžen]. Prec. & **-gen**. (chem.) A poisonous gas, a compound radical of nitrogen and carbon, forming with hydrogen, *hydrocyanic acid.* See **cyanide**.

cyanosis, n. [1. sianṓsis; 2. saiənóusis]. See prec. & **-osis**. Pathological condition in which the surface of the body becomes blue through lack of aeration.

cycad, cycas, n. [1. síkad, -as; 2. sáikæd, -æs]. Etymol. doubtful; perh. for Gk. *kóikas*, acc. pl. of *kóix*, 'an Egyptian palm tree'. Kind of palm tree the trunk of which yields sago; also called *sago palm.*

cyclamen, n. [1. síklamen; 2. sikləmən]. Gk. *kuklā́minos*, through Med. Lat. See **cycle**. Plant with rounded, dark-green leaves and graceful flowers of various colours on slender, curved stalks.

cycle (I.), n. [1. síkl; 2. sáikl]. L. Lat. *cyclus*, fr. Gk. *kúklos*, 'a ring, round, circle', cogn. w. Scrt. *čakrá-*, 'wheel', both showing redupl. forms of base **kʷel*, 'turn, drive,' wh. is seen also in O.E. *hwēol*, fr. **hwehwla-*, & *hweogol*. See **cylinder** & **wheel** & words there referred to. **1. a** An interval of time within which a series of events or phenomena of regular recurrence takes place or appears: *the cycle of human life, of the seasons*; **b** an age, immense period of time: '*a cycle of Cathay*' (Tennyson). **2.** Group of poems (romances) connected with some central heroic figure or some great event: *the Arthurian cycle of Romances.* **3.** (colloq.) Abbreviation of *bicycle.*

cycle (II.), vb. intrans., fr. prec. **1.** To pass through a cycle; recur in cycles. **2.** To ride a bicycle.

cyclic, cyclical, adj. [1. síklik(l); 2. sáiklik(l)]. **cycle (I.)** & **-ic** & **-al**. **1.** Belonging to, recurring in, a cycle or cycles. **2.** Connected with a cycle of poems: esp. *cyclic poets*, epic poets, succeeding Homer, dealing with same subject as the 'Iliad'.

cycling, vbl. n. [1. síkling; 2. sáikliŋ]. **cycle (II.)** & **-ing**. Act of riding a bicycle.

cyclist, n. [1. síklist; 2. sáiklist]. **cycle (I.)** & **-ist**. One who rides a bicycle.

cyclo-, pref. Form of **cycle**, fr. Gk. *kúklos*, 'circle' &c., used in compounds. General meaning, round.

cycloid, n. & adj. [1. síkloid; 2. sáikloid]. **cycle (I.)** & **-oid**. **1.** n. A transcendental curve generated by the revolution of a circle along a straight line. **2.** adj. Circular, occurring in circles.

cycloidal, adj. [1. siklóidl; 2. saiklóidl]. Prec. & **-al**. Pertaining to a cycloid.

cyclometer, n. [1. siklómeter; 2. saiklɔ́mitə]. **cyclo-** & **meter**. **1.** Instrument for measuring circles. **2.** Instrument for recording the number of revolutions of a wheel.

cyclone, n. [1. síklōn; 2. sáikloun]. Gk. *kuklôn*, 'moving in a circle, whirling round', Pres. Part. of *kukló̄ō*, 'circle round, whirl', fr. *kúklos*, 'circle'. See **cycle (I.)**. A storm of wind rotating with violence round a calm centre; a tornado.

cyclonic, adj. [1. siklónik; 2. saiklɔ́nik]. Prec. & **-ic**. Connected with, arising from, a cyclone.

cyclop(a)edia, n. [1. siklōpḗdia; 2. saikloupídiə]. Gk. *kúklos*, 'circle' (see **cycle**), & *paideia*, 'bringing up of a child, education', fr. *paid-*, 'child, boy'; see **pedagogue**. Abbreviation of *Encyclopaedia*. **a** A work giving information upon all subjects and branches of knowledge; **b** one dealing with all branches and aspects of some particular department of knowledge.

cyclopaedic, adj. [1. siklōpḗdik; 2. saikloupídik]. Prec. & **-ic**. Relating to a cyclopaedia, having the character of a cyclopaedia, hence, all-embracing, universal: *cyclopaedic knowledge.*

Cyclopean, adj. [1. siklōpḗan, siklṓpean; 2. saikloupíən, saiklóupiən]. Lat. *Cyclōpēus*, fr. Gk. *Kuklṓpeios*, & **-an**. See **Cyclops**. **1.** Pertaining to, resembling, the Cyclops; gigantic, vast; esp. *Cyclopean task, labour* &c. **2.** (archit.) Pertaining to, referring to, a primitive style of construction in which enormous blocks of stone were used, fitted together without mortar; supposed to have been built by the *Cyclops.*

Cyclops, n. [1. síklops; 2. sáiklɔps]. Lat. (pl. *-ōpes*), fr. Gk. *kúklōps*, 'round eye', fr. *kúklos*, 'circle' (see **cycle**), & *ōps*, 'eye'. See **optic**. **1. a** One of a fabulous race of one-eyed giants supposed originally to have inhabited Sicily; **b** a person with only one eye. **2.** Minute crustacean, with a single large, median eye.

cyclostome, n. [1. síklōstōm; 2. sáikloustoum], fr. **cyclo-** & Gk. *stóma*, 'mouth'. See **stomach**. (zool.) Any one of a class, *Cyclostomata*, of fishes, of a low order of vertebrates, including the lampreys and hag-fishes.

cyclostyle, n. [1. síklōstīl; 2. sáikloustail]. **cyclo-** & **style**. Device for multiplying copies of a written document, consisting of a pen with a toothed wheel which makes small holes in the paper.

cyder. See **cider**.

cygnet, n. [1. sígnet; 2. sígnit]. Earlier *cignet*; Fr. *cygne*, Lat. *cygnus*, 'swan', fr. Gk. *kúknos*, 'swan', & dimin. suff. **-et**. The word orig. means 'the white bird', cp. Scrt. *çuciš*, 'brilliant, white'. A young swan.

cylinder, n. [1. sílinder; 2. sílində]. O. Fr. *cilindre*, fr. Lat. *cylindrus*, fr. Gk. *kúlindros*, 'roller, a roll'; cp. also Gk. *kulíndein*, 'to roll, roll along, to wallow', & *kullós*, 'curved, crooked, crippled'. Gk. *kul-* is fr. Aryan **kʷəl-*, the reduced grade of the base **kʷel-*, **kel-*, **kʷol-*, **kol-*, 'curve, turn' &c. This base occurs in a large number of words, cp. Lat. *colus*, 'distaff'; O. Slav. *kolo*, 'wheel'; Gk. *pólos*, fr. **kʷólos*, 'that on which something turns, pivot, axis' (see **pole (III.)**). The base is redupl. in Gk. *kúklos*, 'circle', fr. **kʷəkʷlos* (see **cycle**), & O.E. *hwēol*, 'wheel', fr. Gmc. **hwehwlo-*, Aryan **kʷekʷló-*. see **wheel**. **1.** A body of which both ends are circular and equal in size, having long and perfectly straight sides, so that the circle of one end is continued in a parallel direction towards that of the other end, a roller-shaped body. **2.** Any one of many objects having this form, esp. a chamber of this shape in which the piston works under the pressure of steam, explosion of gas &c.

cylindrical, adj. [1. silíndrikl; 2. silíndrikl]. Prec. & **-ic** & **-al**. Having shape of a cylinder.

cylindroid, n. & adj. [1. sílindroid; 2. sílindrɔid]. **cylinder** & **-oid**. **a** n. Object shaped like a cylinder; **b** adj., shaped like a cylinder.

cylix, n. [1. síliks, síliks; 2. sáiliks, síliks]. Gk. *kúlix*, 'drinking-cup'. Another grade of the first syll. is seen in Gk. *kálux*, 'cup, calyx of a flower', see **calyx**. The base **kel-*, **kol-* &c., means orig. 'hide, protect'. See **cell**; also **hall, occult**. Ancient Greek drinking-vessel in form of a shallow, flattish bowl, with two handles, set upon a short stem and foot.

cyma, n. [1. síma; 2. sáimə]. Gk. *kûma*, 'anything swelling or swollen, a wave'; connected w. Gk. *kueîn*, 'to become pregnant', & Lat. *cavus*, 'hollow'. See **cave (I.)** & cp. **cynic.** The moulding of a cornice formed in two curves with a hollow between.

cymar, n. [1. símar; 2. sáimā]. Fr. *simarre*, fr. Ital. *simarra*. Variant of **chimere.** **a** A woman's loose garment; **b** bishop's robe, chimere.

cymbal, n. [1. símbl; 2. símbl]. Fr. *cymbale*, Lat. *cymbalum*, fr. Gk. *kúmbalon*, fr. *kúmbē*, 'a hollow cup or vessel'; cogn. w. W. *cwm*, 'valley'. See **coomb(e)** & **cup.** (usually pl.) Thin, flattish, slightly hollowed plate of brass held in the hand and struck against another similar to it held in the other hand, when a harsh penetrating note is emitted; used as an accompaniment to other instruments in an orchestra.

cymbalo, n. [1. símbalō; 2. símbəlou]. Ital. *cim-*, *cembalo*. See prec. Stringed instrument played with hammers, a kind of dulcimer.

cymbiform, adj. [1. símbiform; 2. símbifōm]. Gk. *kúmbē*, 'hollow vessel; boat'. See under **cymbal** & **-form.** Shaped like a boat.

cymbocephalic, adj. [1. sìmbosefálik; 2. sìmbousifǽlik]. Next word & **-ic.** (lit.) Boat-headed; having a long boat-shaped skull.

cymbocephaly, n. [1. sìmbōséfali; 2. sìmbouséfəli]. Gk. *kúmbē*, 'boat' (see **cymbal**), & Gk. *kephalḗ*, 'head', see **cephalic.** Shape of skull consisting in retreating forehead, and great length.

cyme, n. [1. sīm; 2. saim], fr. Lat. *cyma*, 'young sprout of a cabbage', fr. Gk. *kûma*, 'anything swollen' &c. See **cyma.** Mode of blossoming in which several stalks, of varying lengths, each surmounted by a single flower, spring from a common stem; contrasted with *umbel.*

cymograph, **kymograph**, n. [1. kímograhf; 2. káiməgrāf], more rarely [1. símograhf; 2. sáiməgrāf]. See next word & **-graph.** Apparatus comprising a revolving cylinder on which curves or graphs representing electric waves &c. may be traced.

cymometer, n. [1. sīmómeter; 2. saimɔ́mitə], fr. Gk. *kûma*, 'wave'. See **cyma** & **-meter.** Instrument for measuring etheric waves in wireless telegraphy or telephony.

cymophane, n. [1. símōfān; 2. sáimoufein], fr. Gk. *kûma*, see prec., & *phain-(esthai)*, 'to appear'; see **phantasm.** An opalescent, wavy variety of chrysoberyl.

cymoscope, n. [1. símōskōp; 2. sáimouskoup]. See prec. words & **-scope.** Instrument, device, for detecting etheric waves in wireless telegraphy or telephony, a detector, whether crystal or thermionic valve.

Cymric, adj. [1. kímrik; 2. kímrik]. W. *Cymru*, Wales. Welsh.

cynanche, n. [1. sīnángkē; 2. sainǽŋkī], fr. Gk. *kunágkhē*, lit. 'dog's collar; sore throat'. See **quinsy.** General medical term for diseases affecting the throat, tonsils &c.

cynic, n. [1. sínik; 2. sínik]. Fr. *cynique*, fr. Lat. *cynicus*, fr. Gk. *kunikós*, lit. 'like a dog', fr. *kúōn*, genit. *kunós*, 'dog'; this is cogn. w. Scrt. *śvan-*, Lat. *canis* (see **canine**), Lith. *szũns*, Goth. *hunds*, O.E. *hund* (see **hound**). Some etymologists connect this word w. the base **k̑ew-* &c., 'to swell', either in the sense of 'powerful', as in Scrt. *śávīraš*, 'strong' &c., or in sense of 'young animal', cp. Scrt. *śíšuš*, 'young of an animal', Gk. *kúos*, 'foetus', & *kuein*, 'become pregnant', see **cyma** & **cave (I.).** With such an assumed transference of meaning cp. **bird.** Osthoff has suggested a connexion w. the base **pek̑-*, 'cattle', in a reduced form *(*p*)*k̑ u-*, w. the orig. sense of 'watch-dog, guardian of cattle'. See this base under **pecuniary.** **1.** (Cap.) Member of a school of Greek philosophers who taught that the essence of virtue was self-control. Later they came to be regarded as representing a gloomy revolt against current philosophy and social customs. **2.** A captious, sneering, fault-finding person, esp. one who attributes human conduct to low motives of self-interest.

cynical, adj. [1. sínikl; 2. sínikl]. Prec. & **-al.** Having the character and opinions of a cynic.

cynically, adv. Prec. & **-ly.** In a cynical manner.

cynicism, n. [1. sínisizm; 2. sínisizəm]. **cynic** & **-ism.** **a** Opinions of a cynic; **b** cynic's habit of mind; **c** particular expression of this.

cyno-, pref. Form of Gk. *kúōn*, 'dog', used in compounds, fr. the genit. type *kunó-*. See **cynic.**

cynocephalic, adj. [1. sìnosefálik; 2. sàinousifǽlik]. Prec. & **cephalic.** Dog-headed, dog-faced; esp. of baboons.

cynoglossum, n. [1. sínouglósum; 2. sáinouglɔ́səm], fr. **cyno-** & Gk. *glōssa*, 'tongue', see **gloss (I.).** One of a large class of flowering plants of the borage tribe.

cynosure, n. [1. sínōshoor, -sūr; 2. sínouʃɔ̄, -sjuə]. Gk. *kunósoura*, 'dog's tail', also name of the Little Bear, the constellation. See **cyno-.** For the second element, *ourá*, 'tail', see **uro- (II.).** **1.** The Little Bear. **2.** An object which draws attention, attracts notice and admiration: '*The cynosure of neighbouring eyes*' (Milton).

cypher, n. See **cipher.**

cy pres, adv., adj. [1. sē prā; 2. sí préi]. Fr., 'nearly, as nearly as may be'. (law) Applied to the construing of wills, esp. in cases of charitable trusts, where any verbal ambiguity exists, when this is equitably interpreted as near as possible, agreeably with the testator's intentions.

cypress (I.), n. [1. sípres; 2. sáiprəs]. M.E. *cipres*, O. Fr. *cypres*, fr. Lat. *cyparissus*, *cupressus*, fr. Gk. *kupárissos*, 'the cypress tree'. Prob. Semitic; perh. fr. Heb. *gōpher*, see **gopher (II.).** **a** Ornamental, pinaceous, coniferous, evergreen tree with dark foliage; **b** (poet.) this tree, or branch of it, as a symbol of mourning.

cypress (II.), n., also *cypress lawn.* M.E. *cipres*, 'fine gauze', also 'valuable cloth of gold, or other material'; O. Fr. *Cypres*, the island of Cyprus. A thin, fine cloth or crape.

Cyprian, n. [1. síprian; 2. síprien]. Lat. *Cyprius*, 'inhabitant of Cyprus', & **-an**, fr. Gk. *Kúpros*, 'Cyprus'. This island was the birthplace of Aphrodite, goddess of love, and famous for the rites of her worship. (obs.) A loose-living person, esp. a light woman.

cyprinid, n. [1. síprinid; 2. síprinid], fr. Gk. *kuprînos*, 'carp'. See **carp.** (zool.) Any fish of the family *Cyprinidae*, which includes the carps, barbels, chubs, tenches &c., having soft fins and living in fresh water.

Cypriote, n. [1. sípriōt; 2. sípriout]. See **Cyprian.** A native of Cyprus.

cypripedium, n. [1. sìpripḗdium; 2. sìpripídiəm]. New Lat., fr. Gk. *Kúpris*, 'Aphrodite, Venus' (see **Cyprian**), & *ped-(em)*, *pēs*, 'foot'; see **pedal.** (bot.) A genus of orchids, including 'lady's slipper' &c.

Cyrenaic, adj. & n. [1. sīrenáik; 2. sairənéiik]. fr. Gk. *Kūrēnaikós*, 'of Cyrene', town in N. Africa. **a** adj. Pertaining to the hedonistic school of philosophy, founded by Aristippus of Cyrene, 4th cent. B.C.; **b** n., member of this school.

Cyrillic, adj. & n. [1. sirílik; 2. sirílik], fr. St. Cyril. Applied to the alphabet, founded on the Greek, invented by St. Cyril, and used by the ancient Slavonic Church. The ancient liturgy and the remains of the gospels in what is variously called Old Church Slavonic, Old Bulgarian, are written in this alphabet, and modified forms of it are used in writing Mod. Russian and Bulgarian.

cyst, n. [1. sist; 2. sist]. Gk. *kústis*, 'the bladder, a bag, pouch'. This word is connected w. & derived fr. a variant of the base meaning 'cover, hide' &c., discussed under **cutis**, & the other words there referred to. **1.** (med.) A closed membranous sac within a tissue of the body, containing pus or morbid matter. **2.** A hollow cavity containing liquid secretion, not necessarily morbid.

cysti-, **cysto-**, pref. Forms of above used in compounds, often referring specifically to the urinary bladder.

cystic, adj. [1. sístik; 2. sístik]. **cyst** & **-ic.** **a** Pertaining to a cyst; **b** pertaining to the urinary bladder.

cystiform, adj. [1. sístiform; 2. sístifōm]. **cysti-** & **-form.** Having shape or character of a cyst.

cystitis, n. [1. sistítis; 2. sistáitis]. **cyst** & **-itis.** Inflammation of the bladder.

cystoid, adj. [1. sístoid; 2. sístɔid]. **cyst** & **-oid.** Resembling a cyst.

cystotomy, n. [1. sistótomi; 2. sistɔ́təmi]. **cysto-** & **-tomy.** Operation of cutting open the bladder, esp. for stone.

-cyte, suff. [1. sīt; 2. -sait], meaning *cell* in biol. sense, fr. Gk. *kútos*, 'hollow vessel, jar &c.; skin', see **cutis**, as *leucocyte*, *phagocyte* &c.

cyto-, pref. See prec.

cytology, n. [1. sītóloji; 2. saitɔ́lədži]. Prec. & **-logy.** (biol.) Study of the structure, functions, growth, and life history of cells.

cytoplasm, n. [1. sítōplazm; 2. sáitouplæzəm]. **cyto-** & **plasm.** The protoplasm of the cells of plants or animals.

czar, n. [1. zar, tsar; 2. zā, tsā]. Russ., fr. Lat. **Caesar.** Title of the Emperor of the Russians.

czardas, n. [1. zárdas, chárdahsh; 2. zā́dæs, tʃā́rdāʃ]. Hungarian. **a** National dance of Hungary; **b** music for this.

czarevitch, n. [1. záhrevich, tsahrā́vich; 2. zā́rə-, tsārévitʃ]. Russ., 'son of a czar'. The reigning czar's eldest son.

czarevna, n. [1. zahrévna, tsahrévna; 2. zārévnə, tsārévnə]. Russ. Czar's daughter.

czarina, n. [1. zahrḗna, tsahrḗna; 2. zārínə, tsarínə]. Through Germ. *czarin*, fr. Russ. Czar's wife, the Empress of Russia.

czaritza, n. [1. zahrítsa, tsahrítsa; 2. zārítsə, tsarítsə]. Russ. Form used in Russia. Empress of Russia.

Czech, **Czekh**, n. & adj. [1. chek; 2. tʃek]. Pol. form of Bohem. *Čech.* **1.** n. **a** A Bohemian; **b** Bohemian language. **2.** adj. Of, pertaining to, Bohemia, its inhabitants or language.

Czechoslovakia, n. [1. chékōslōvákia; 2. tʃékouslouvǽkiə]. Republican state formed of a union of the Czechs and Slovaks after the Great War.

D

D, d [1. dē; 2. dī], the fourth letter of the English and other languages, as in Phœnician, Greek, and Latin. For use in abbreviations see end of Dictionary. Specif. **a** (math.) a fourth unknown quantity; **b** (mus.) second note of the major scale; **c** (Roman numerals) D = 500, properly half of M = 1000, formerly written CIƆ; **d** the fourth of any series of objects: *vitamin D* &c.

dab (I.), vb. trans. [1. dab; 2. dæb]. M.E. *dabben*, 'slap, strike'. Scand., cp. Norw. *dabba*, 'tap with the foot'. Connected w. **dub** & **tap (III.).** **1.** To touch suddenly and lightly; give a series of slight, hesitating taps to; esp. with sponge, brush &c.: *to dab one's eyes with* *a handkerchief*, attempt to dry by repeated slight touches. **2.** *Dab on*, to put on moisture, paint &c. with a series of light, jerky strokes.

dab (II.), n. M.E. *dabbe*, fr. prec. **1.** Quick, light tap or blow. **2.** Something dabbed on: *dab of paint*, slight amount.

dab (III.), n. Etymol. unknown. A kind of small flat-fish or flounder.

dab (IV.), n. Etymol. unknown. (colloq.) A skilful, dexterous person; one learned in some particular subject: *a dab at tennis, at Greek.*

dabble, vb. trans. & intrans. [1. dábl; 2. dǽbl]. Freq. of **dab** (I.), cp. Du. *dabbelen.* **1.** trans. To dip in and out of water, splash about in water: *to dabble one's hands in the river.* **2.** intrans. **a** To dip one's hands or feet in and out of water, splash about; **b** (fig.) *dabble in*, to engage in (a study, pursuit &c.), half-heartedly, without going into it very deeply: *to dabble in Anglo-Saxon, in politics* &c.

dabbler, n. [1. dábler; 2. dǽblə]. Prec. & **-er.** One who dabbles; (esp. fig.) one who engages in a pursuit or studies a subject in a superficial, incomplete manner.

dabchick, n. [1. dábchik; 2. dǽbtʃik], fr. **dab** (I.) & **chick.** A kind of small water-bird, the Little Grebe.

da capo, adv. [1. dáh káhpō; 2. dȧ kȧpō]. Ital., 'from the head or beginning'. Musical direction, D.C., to repeat from the beginning.

dace, n. [1. dās; 2. deis]. M.E. *dar, darce*, fr. O. Fr. *dars, dart.* See **dart** (I.). A small river-fish, genus *Leuciscus*, belonging to the carp family.

dachshund, n. [1. dáks-hoond, dáhks-hoont; 2. dǽkshund, dákshunt], fr. Germ. *dachs*, 'badger', & *hund*, 'dog'. The first element, according to Kluge, is perhaps cogn. w. Lat. *texere*, 'to build' (see **textile**), the animal being named fr. its underground home. Lat. *taxus*, 'badger', is borrowed fr. Gmc. For the second element, see **hound.** A breed of dog with a long body, short crooked legs, a long muzzle and large, drooping ears.

dacoit, n. [1. dakóit; 2. dækóit]. Hind. *dākāit*, 'robber'. One of a gang of robbers (in India, Burma).

dacoity, n. [1. dakóiti; 2. dækóiti]. Hind. *dākāiti*, 'gang-robbery'. Robbery by armed bands (in India, Burma).

dacry-, dacryo-, pref. [1. dákri, dákriō; 2. dǽkri, dǽkriou]. Form fr. Gk. *dákruon*, 'tear' cogn. w. Lat. *lacrima*, see **lachrymal** & **tear.** Used in physiological terminology, as *dacryocyst*, cyst in a lachrymal gland &c., *dacryoma*, tumour of the same, &c.

dactyl, n. [1. dáktil; 2. dǽktil]. Gk. *dáktul-os*, 'a finger; a metrical foot, dactyl'; according to Boisacq, fr. **datkulos*, fr. **dn̥t-ku-los* (see **tooth**), w. sense of something pointed, projecting. Cp. M.H.G. *zint*, 'a spike, prong', O.H.G. *zinko*, fr. Gmc. **tent-ko.* A metrical foot, consisting of one long syllable followed by two short syllables, or one stressed followed by two unstressed.

dactylic, adj. & n. [1. daktílik; 2. dæktílik], fr. Gk. *daktulik-ós*, 'pertaining to a finger'. **dactyl** & **-ic. a** adj. Composed of, pertaining to, dactyls; **b** n., a dactylic verse.

dactylioglyph, n. [1. daktílioglif; 2. dæktíliəglif], fr. Gk. *daktúli-os*, 'finger-ring', fr. *dáktulos*, 'finger' (see **dactyl**), & *glúphō*, 'I engrave, carve', fr. Aryan **glubh-.* Cp. (fr. base w. different grade of vowel: **gleubh-*) Lat. *glūb-ere*, 'to flay'; *glūma*, 'shell, husk', fr. **glūbh-ma*; O.H.G. *klioban*, 'split, cleave', O.E. *clēofan.* See **cleave, glume. a** An engraver of rings; **b** the engraver's name inscribed on a ring.

dactyliography, n. [1. dàktilióɡrafi; 2. dæktilíɔgrəfi]. See prec. & **-graphy.** Art of engraving rings and precious stones.

dactylogram, n. [1. daktilogràm; 2. dæktíləgræm]. See **dactyl** & **-gram.** A finger-print.

dactylography, n. [1. dàktilógrafi; 2. dæktilɔ́grəfi]. See **dactyl** & **-graphy.** The use or study of finger-prints for purposes of identification.

dactylology, n. [1. dàktilóloji; 2. dæktilɔ́lədži]. See **dactyl** & **-logy.** The study or use of the finger-alphabet; communication of ideas by means of the fingers, for the deaf and dumb.

dactylorhiza, n. [1. dàktiloríza; 2. dæktilərάizə], fr. Gk. *dáktul-os*, 'finger' (see **dactyl**), & *rhiza*, 'a root'. See **rhizo-.** A disease attacking the roots of certain vegetables, esp. turnips, causing them to fork and harden; finger-and-toe disease.

dad, daddy, n. [1. dád, -i; 2. dǽd, -i]. Cp. W. *dad, tad*, 'father'. Father (a child's word).

daddy-long-legs, n. [1. dàdi lóng lègz; 2. dǽdi lɔ̀ŋ lègz]. A flying insect, with long thin legs and filmy wings, the crane-fly.

dado, n. [1. dádō; 2. déidou]. Ital. *dado*, 'die, cube, pedestal'. See **die** (I.). **a** The part of a pedestal between base and cornice; **b** the lower part of the walls of a room, when decorated differently from the upper part by being panelled, or differently coloured. The *dado* is usually separated from the upper part by a moulding.

daedal, adj. [1. dḗdl; 2. dídl], fr. Lat. *daedal-us*, fr. Gk. *daidalos*, 'cunningly wrought', fr. *daidállein*, 'to work, form, skilfully', formed by reduplication fr. base **dl̥-*, fr. **del-*, **dol-*, 'to cut' &c., whence also Scrt. *dálati*, 'bursts', *dalayati*, 'splits open', *dalam*, 'part'; Lat. *dolāre*, 'to chip, hew, cut out'; O. Ir. *delb*, 'figure, form'; Lith. *dalìs*, Russ. *dolji*, O. Prussian *dellieis*, 'part'; O.N. *talga*, 'cutting'; M.H.G. *zoll*, 'cylindrical piece of wood', *zol*, 'inch'. O.E. *tōl* is prob. fr. this base. See **tool.** Ingenious, skilfully made; highly elaborated, intricate; various.

daedalian, adj. [1. dēdálian; 2. dīdéilian], fr. Gk. *Daidalos* & **-ian.** See prec. Pertaining to, resembling the work of, Daedalus, the mythical architect who built the labyrinth for Minos, king of Crete; intricate, highly wrought.

daemon, n. [1. dḗmon; 2. dímən], fr. Gk. *daímōn.* See **demon.** In original Greek sense, a tutelary divinity, inspiring spirit: *the daemon of Socrates.*

daemonic, adj. [1. dēmónik; 2. dīmɔ́nik]. Prec. & **-ic.** Of, possessed, inspired by, a daemon.

daffodil, n. [1. dáfodil; 2. dǽfədil]. M.E. *affodille, affadille*, fr. Low Lat. *affodillus, asphodelus*, fr. Gk. *asphódelos*, 'a plant of the lily family'. The origin of the *d-* is obscure. The suggestion that it stands for *th* (the) is very improbable. See **asphodel. 1.** A bulb-rooted spring flower, wild and cultivated, usually yellow, or yellow and white; the narcissus. **2.** The colour of a daffodil, pale, bright, yellow.

daffodilly, daffadowndilly, n. [1. dàfodíli, dáfadòundíli; 2. dæfədíli, dǽfəddàundíli]. See prec. The daffodil.

daft, adj. [1. dahft; 2. dāft]. M.E. *daft*, 'mild, gentle; stupid', O.E. (*ġe*)*dæfte*, 'gentle, meek'; cp. O.E. *ġedafnian*, Goth. *gadaban*, 'be suitable, becoming'. For development of meaning, cp. **simple** & **silly.** See also **deft, fabric.** (provinc.) Foolish, weak-minded; mad.

dag, n. [1. dag; 2. dæg]. Origin doubtful. An old form of long pistol.

dagger, n. [1. dáger; 2. dǽgə]. M.E. *dagger*, lit. 'that which tears', fr. vb. *daggen*, 'to slit, tear in pieces'; cp. *dagge*, 'a strip of cloth', Fr. *dague*, 'dagger'. **1.** A weapon, consisting of a handle and a short, pointed, two-edged blade, used for stabbing. Phrs. *at daggers drawn*, on terms of hostility; *to look daggers at a person*, to look at with an expression of hatred and hostility. **2.** (typog.) A symbol of reference (†) shaped like a dagger.

daggle, vb. trans. [1. dágl; 2. dǽgl]. Scand. Cp. Swed. *dagg*, 'dew', & **-le.** See **dew.** To trail through mud and wet: '*Nor like a puppy, daggled through the town*' (Pope).

dago, n. [1. dágō; 2. déigou], fr. common Span. proper name *Diego* = James. Contemptuous term for a Spaniard, Portuguese, or Italian; also generally for a person of dusky complexion and dubious origin.

daguerrotype, n. [1. dagérotīp; 2. dəgérətaip], fr. name of inventor of process, Louis Daguerre (1789–1851). Portrait produced by an early method of photography, in which the picture is fixed on a chemically treated metal or glass plate.

dahabiah, dahabieh, n. [1. dàhhahbḗa; 2. dàhābíə]. Arab. *dahabīya.* A sailing-boat used on the Nile, chiefly for passengers.

dahlia, n. [1. dália; 2. déiljə], fr. A. Dahl, the name of a Swedish botanist. A composite herbaceous plant, a native of Mexico, now much cultivated in Europe, having brightly and variously coloured double or single flowers.

Dail Eireann, n. [1. dáwl áran; 2. dɔ̄l éərən]. Ir., 'Assembly of Ireland'. The lower house of Parliament in the Irish Free State.

daily, adj., adv., & n. [1. dāli; 2. déili]. M.E. *daili*, O.E. *dæġlīc.* **day** & **-ly. 1.** adj. & adv. Happening, appearing, every day: *a daily event*; *to happen daily.* Phr. *daily bread*, one's livelihood, way one earns one's living. **2.** n. A newspaper published every day.

daimio, n. [1. dímiō; 2. dáimiou]. Jap. & Chin. *dai*, 'great', *myo*, 'name'. Ancient hereditary noble of Japan.

daintily, adv. [1. dāntili; 2. déintili], fr. **dainty** & **-ly.** In a dainty, refined, fastidious, graceful manner.

daintiness, n. [1. dāntines; 2. déintinis]. See prec. & **-ness.** The quality of being dainty (in various senses).

dainty, adj. & n. [1. dānti; 2. déinti]. M.E. *deinté*, 'dignity, value', fr. O. Fr. *deinté, deintet*, fr. Lat. *dignitāt-(em).* See **dignity. 1.** adj. **a** (of persons or things) Refined, elegant, delicate, in appearance, taste &c.; **b** affectedly fastidious, esp. regarding choice of food. **2.** n. Something agreeable to the taste; choice morsel of food.

dairy, n. [1. dāri; 2. déəri]. M.E. *deierie*, fr. *deie*, 'dairymaid' & **-ery.** M.E. *deie*, fr. O.N. *deigja*, cogn. w. O.E. *dāg*, 'dough'. See **dough. a** The building or room in which milk and cream are kept and made into butter and cheese; **b** a shop for the sale of dairy produce.

dairy-farm, n. Farm devoted to the produce of milk and butter.

dairying, n. [1. dāri-ing; 2. déəri-iŋ], fr. **dairy** & **-ing.** The business of a dairy-farm.

dairymaid, n. [1. dārimàd; 2. déərimèid]. Woman in charge of, or working in, a dairy.

dairyman, n. [1. dāriman; 2. déəriman], **a** Man working in a dairy; **b** dealer in milk, cream, butter, and eggs.

dais, n. [1. dās; 2. deis]. M.E. *deis*, 'dais' (w. transferred meaning), fr. O. Fr. *deis*, 'table', fr. Low Lat. *discus*, 'table', fr. Lat. *discus*, 'a quoit, dish, disc'. See **disk.** A raised platform at one end of a room, esp. the high table in a dining-hall.

daisied, adj. [1. dázid; 2. déizid], fr. **daisy** & **-ed.** (of a meadow &c.) Having daisies growing in it, thickly dotted with daisies.

daisy, n. [1. dázi; 2. déizi]. O.E. *dæġesēġe*, M.E. *daies eie, daies īe*, 'the day's eye, daisy'. See **day, eye. 1. a** A small composite flower, genus *Bellis*, esp. the common daisy, *B. perennis*, with a yellow centre surrounded by white, pink-tipped petals, growing wild, esp. among grass; **b** one of several varieties of flower resembling the daisy, as the *Michaelmas daisy*, species of aster; *ox-eye daisy*, chrysanthemum. **2.** (slang) Something first-rate, capital, or charming.

daisy-chain, n. Garland, festoon, of daisies fastened together by inserting the stem of one through a slit in that of another.

daisy-cutter, n. (colloq., slang) **a** Horse which does not pick its feet up off the ground as it moves; **b** ball at cricket which keeps low on the ground.

dâk, dawk, n. [1. dawk; 2. dɔ̄k]. Hind. (in India) **a** Relays of men or horses for transport of mails or passengers; **b** post, mail.

dâk-bungalow, n. Travellers' rest-house in India.

dalai-lama, n. [1. dalī láhma; 2. dəlái lámə]. Tibetan. See **lama**. The Grand Lama; chief Buddhist priest of Tibet.

dale, n. [1. dāl; 2. deil]. M.E. *dāle*, O.E. *dæl*, 'a valley'. Cp. O.H.G. *tal*, O.N. *dalr*, Goth. *dal*. Cogn. w. Gk. *thólos*, 'a circular vault, dome'; *thálamos*, 'a room'; O. Slav. *dolŭ*, 'ditch'; Aryan **dhol-*, 'something bent; a bending'; whence 'a hollow; concave or convex surface'. See **dell**, **thalamus**. A valley; low ground between hills.

dalesman, n. [1. dálzman; 2. déilzmən], fr. prec. & **man**. **a** One who lives in a valley (esp. in N. of England); **b** specif., a small freeholder in the northern dales.

dalle, n. [1. dal; 2. dæl]. Fr., 'slab', pl. 'gutter, trough'. (Canada & U.S.A.) **a** A flat paving-stone; specif. **b** (pl.) a rapid as it flows over flat rocks.

dalliance, n. [1. dálians; 2. dæliəns]. M.E. *daliance*, *daliaunce*. See next word & **-ance**. **a** Childish, trifling, hesitating action; futile amusement; **b** amorous toying.

dally, vb. intrans. [1. dáli; 2. dæli]. M.E. *dalien*, A.-Fr. *dalier*, 'chat, pass time in social converse'; etymol. doubtful. **a** To trifle, behave in a futile manner, to linger, hesitate in action, delay; **b** to trifle, toy, interchange amorous caresses with; **c** (fig., of mental action) to consider, entertain: *to dally with an idea.*

Dalmatian, n. [1. dalmáshun; 2. dælméiʃən], fr. Dalmatia, on the eastern shore of the Adriatic, & **-an**. A kind of dog, white with black spots, formerly kept as a carriage-dog.

dalmatic, n. [1. dalmátik; 2. dælmǽtik]. M.E. *dalmatik*, fr. Fr. *dalmatique*, fr. Lat. *dalmatica (tunica)*, a long tunic of Dalmatian wool. A loose vestment with wide sleeves and open sides worn **a** by deacons at the celebration of Mass; **b** by bishops, under the chasuble; **c** by a king or emperor at his coronation.

dal segno, adv. [1. dal sényō; 2. dæl sénjou]. Ital., lit. 'from the sign'. Musical direction to go back to repeat from a sign.

daltonism, n. [1. dáwltonizm; 2. dɔ́ltənizəm], fr. the name of a chemist, John Dalton (1766–1844), who was colour-blind, & **-ism**. Colour-blindness.

dam (I.), n. [1. dam; 2. dæm]. M.E. *dam*, shortened form of **dame**. **a** (of animals) and **b** (archaic, fig., of persons) Mother.

dam (II.), n. Not in O.E., but widespread among Gmc. languages. M.E. *dam*. Cp. M.H.G. *tam*, O. Fris. & Mod. Du. *dam*, O.N. *damr*; cp. Goth. *faur-dammjan*, 'to shut off, stop up'. Skeat suggests connexion w. Gk. *thōmós*, 'heap', wh. is phonetically irreproachable. The last word is gen. believed to be cogn. w. O.E. *dōm*, 'judgement, dominion, glory, fame' &c. See **doom & deem**. The simplest form of the base is **dhē-* &c., 'set, place, make'. See **theme**. **a** An embankment, built across a river or stream to arrest its flow and raise its level in order to form a reservoir &c.; **b** water obstructed by a dam.

dam (III.), vb. trans., fr. prec. (lit. and fig.) To obstruct, confine by a dam; also *dam up.*

damage (I.), n. [1. dámij; 2. dǽmidž]. M.E. *damāge*, fr. O. Fr. *damage*. See **damn** & **-age**. **1. a** Harm, injury, hurt, to property, person, reputation; Phr. *to do damage*, break, spoil, things; (fig.) to cause trouble; **b** (colloq.) cost, price, amount to be paid for anything: *what's the damage?*; *I'll stand the damage*, will pay. **2.** (law, in pl.) Money claimed, or ordered by a court to be paid, as compensation for injury, libel &c.: *to claim, pay, damages.*

damage (II.), vb. trans., fr. prec.; cp. O. Fr. *damager*. **1. a** (of material things) To cause injury to, impair usefulness, diminish beauty of, lessen value, spoil: *to damage property*; *my luggage was damaged in transit*; *pictures damaged by fire* &c.; **b** (colloq., of human beings and their persons): *his nose was rather damaged by the blow*; **2.** (of non-material things, character, reputation &c.) To blacken, cause loss of, stain.

damageable, adj. [1. dámijabl; 2. dǽmidžəbl]. Prec. & **-able**. Capable of being damaged.

damascene (I.), n. [1. dàmasḗn; 2. dæ̀məsín]. See **damson**. A kind of small plum.

damascene (II.), vb. trans., fr. Fr., fr. Lat. *Damascēnus*, 'of Damascus'. See **damask**. To ornament steel or other metal, by incrusting or inlaying, with patterns in gold or silver wire, or by giving a wavy appearance, esp. to the blades of swords, resembling that of watered silk; chiefly in P.P. *damascened.*

damask (I.), n. [1. dámask; 2. dǽməsk], fr. place-name Damascus. **1.** A material of silk, linen &c., with a raised or flat pattern woven into it. **2.** Steel made in, or like that made in, Damascus, decorated by a pattern of wavy lines. **3.** The colour of the *damask rose.*

damask (II.), adj., fr. prec. **a** Made of damask in senses **1** or **2**: *damask cloth, steel*; **b** of the colour of a *damask rose*, rosy-pink.

damask (III.), vb. trans., fr. prec. To adorn with ornamental patterns like those of damask linen or steel.

damask rose, n. A pink rose brought originally from Damascus.

dame, n. [1. dām; 2. deim]. M.E. *dāme*, fr. O. Fr. *dame*, fr. Lat. *domina*, 'the mistress of a household', fem. of *domin-us*, 'lord'; prob. fr. a form **domen-*, fr. base *dom-* as in Lat. *dom-us*, 'a house'. See **dome**. **1. a** A lady, woman in authority, mistress of a household; now archaic as a title, except in such Phrs. as *Dame Nature*, *Dame Fortune* &c.; **b** (facetious) *an old dame*, old woman; **c** (archaic) a schoolmistress; formerly applied to a lady in charge of a house at Eton. **2.** The legal title of the wife of a baronet or knight; or (recently) of a woman who has personally received an order of knighthood; always with Christian name: *Sir George and Dame Alice X*; *Dame Ellen Terry* &c.

dame-school, n. A school for small children, kept by a woman.

dammar, n. [1. dámar; 2. dǽmā], fr. Malay *damar*. Resin used for varnishes, obtained from various East Indian and Australasian trees.

damn (I.), vb. trans. [1. dam; 2. dæm]. M.E. *damnen*, Fr. *damner*, fr. Lat. *damnāre*, 'to injure, cause loss to, condemn', fr. *damnum*, 'harm, loss', fr. **dapnom*, cogn. w. Gk. *dapánē*, 'cost, expense', Lat. *daps*, 'a feast, esp. a sacrificial feast'; Scrt. *dāpayati*, 'he distributes'; O.N. *tafn*, 'sacrificial animal'. Aryan base **dāp-*, **dəp-*, 'to distribute', extended fr. **dā(i)-*, **də(i)-*, **di-*, 'share, divide', wh. appears in Gk. *daiomai*, 'I share, take part in', *daitē*, 'meal, feast'; Scrt. *dáyatē*, 'to share', *dāti*, 'cuts, reaps'. The sense of injury & loss has developed fr. the idea of compulsory expenditure. Cp. **condemn** & see further under **time** & **demon**. **1.** To condemn or consign to eternal punishment. **2.** Interjectionally as an oath; expressing annoyance, disappointment, anger; **a** (absol.) *oh damn!*; **b** (followed by object) *damn it all*; *damn this dictionary* &c. Phr. *to know, do &c., damn all*, nothing at all; **c** to utter oaths, swear: *to curse and damn*. **3.** To ruin, destroy reputation, possibility of success of: *to damn a play, a person's prospects* &c.; '*damn with faint praise*' (Pope).

damn (II.), n., fr. prec. **a** An oath, consisting of utterance of the word; **b** swearing generally; **c** a trifling amount: *not to care a damn*; probably for *dime.*

damnable, adj. [1. dámnabl; 2. dǽmnəbl], fr. **damn (I.)** & **-able**. **a** Deserving damnation, detestable, horrible: *a damnable heresy*; **b** (colloq.) expressing disapproval, displeasure: *the dinner was damnable.*

damnably, adv. Prec. & **-ly**. **a** In a damnable manner, detestably; **b** (colloq., as mere intens.) very: *damnably hot*; *damnably sorry* &c.

damnation, n. & interj. [1. damnáshun; 2. dæmnéiʃən], fr. Lat. *damnātiōn-(em)*. See **damn (I.)** & **-ation**. **1. a** The act of condemning, state of being condemned, to eternal punishment; **b** ruin, destruction, confounding of hopes of success, condemnation (of a book, play, &c.). **2.** (interj.) Oath of same value as *damn!*

damnatory, adj. [1. dámnaturi; 2. dǽmnətəri], fr. Lat. *damnātōrius*, fr. *damnāt-(um)*, P.P. type of *damnāre*. See prec. & **-ory**. **a** Causing condemnation: *damnatory evidence* &c.; **b** uttering sentence of condemnation: *the damnatory clauses* (in the Athanasian Creed).

damned, adj. [1. damd; 2. dæmd], fr. P.P. of **damn (I.)**. **1.** Condemned to punishment or destruction; specif., *the damned*, souls undergoing eternal punishment; *the tortures of the damned*. **2. a** Odious, detestable, execrable; **b** (colloq.) as almost meaningless expletive: *none of your damned nonsense*. Also as adverb in approximately same sense: *a damn(ed) silly remark.*

damnific, adj. [1. damnífik; 2. dæmnífik], fr. Lat. *damnificus*, 'injurious, pernicious'. See **damnify** & **-ic**. Causing injury, harmful.

damnification, n. [1. dàmnifikáshun; 2. dæ̀mnifikéiʃən]. See next word & **-ation**. The act of injuring, causing loss to; the state of being injured.

damnify, vb. trans. [1. dámnifī; 2. dǽmnifai], fr. O. Fr. *damnifier*, fr. Lat. *damnificāre*, 'to injure'. See **damn (I.)** & **-fy**. (rare) To cause loss or damage to.

damning, adj. [1. dáming; 2. dǽmiŋ], fr. Pres. Part. of **damn (I.)**. Causing, tending to cause, condemnation: *damning evidence*; *a damning statement.*

Damocles, n. [1. dámoklēz; 2. dǽməklīz]. In Phr. *Sword of Damocles*, an ever-present, imminent, threatening danger, from story of Damocles, courtier of the tyrant Dionysius of Syracuse, over whose head at a feast a sword hung by a thread.

damosel, n. [1. dámozel; 2. dǽməzel]. (archaic, poet.) Variant of **damsel**.

damp (I.), n. [1. damp; 2. dæmp]. Cp. Du. *damp*, Germ. *dampf*, 'steam'. Further relations wh. might be suggested are very doubtful. **1.** Moisture, humidity, vapour. **2. a** Harmful exhalations rising from the ground; **b** specif., noxious gas in coal mines; *choke-damp*, *fire-damp*. **3.** (fig.) Depression, feeling of dejection, discouragement; esp. *to cast a damp over*, depress.

damp (II.), adj., fr. prec. Containing a small amount of moisture, slightly wet; often applied to superficial moisture.

damp (III.), vb. trans., fr. **damp (I.)**. **1.** To moisten, make slightly wet. **2. a** To hinder combustion of a fire by checking supply of air with ashes &c., often *damp down*; **b** (fig.) to depress, discourage: *to damp a person's spirits*. **3.** (mus.) To check vibration of (string of an instrument). *Damp off*, intrans., (of flowers and shoots &c. of plants) to perish, wither off from mildew.

damp-course, n. Layer of damp-proof material, as slate &c. in wall of a house, to prevent damp rising from the ground.

dampen, vb. trans. & intrans. [1. dámpen; 2. dǽmpən]. **damp (I.)** & **-en**. **1. a** trans. (rare or familiar) To make damp; **b** intrans., to become damp. **2.** (fig., of action on the mind) To cast a chill, blight over, depress (the spirits &c.).

damper, n. [1. dámper; 2. dǽmpə], fr. **damp (III.)** & **-er**. **1.** Anything which makes damp; specif. **a** pad or roller for wetting adhesive stamps; **b** (fig.) something which depresses the mind, spirits &c.: *to cast a damper on a party* &c. **2.** A sliding iron plate for closing or opening the flues of a stove, furnace &c., so as to regulate the combustion. **3.** A contrivance for checking the vibration of the wires of a piano &c.; usually consisting of a felt pad, applied by pressure on a pedal. **4.** (Austral.) A thinnish cake made of flour and water, cooked in hot ashes or before a fire.

dampish, adj. [1. dámpish; 2. dǽmpiʃ]. **damp (II.)** & **-ish**. Slightly damp.

damply, adv. [1. dámpli; 2. dǽmpli]. **damp (II.)** & **-ly**. In a damp state.

dampness, n. [1. dámpnes; 2. dǽmpnis]. **damp (II.)** & **-ness**. The state of being damp, humidity.

damp-proof, adj. Capable of resisting damp.

damsel, n. [1. dámzl; 2. dǽmzl]. M.E. *damisel*, O. Fr. *damisele*, Mod. Fr. *demoiselle*, 'young lady', fr. Low Lat. *dominicella*, dimin. of *domina*. See **dame**. A young girl, maiden.

damson, n. [1. dámzn; 2. dǽmzn]. M.E. *damasin* (*plumme*), O. Fr. *damascene*, 'plum of Damascus'. **a** A small, purple, very sour plum; **b** the tree bearing this kind of plum.

damson-cheese, n. Prec. & **cheese**. A preserve of solid consistency, without juice, made of damsons.

dan, n. [1. dan; 2. dæn]. See **don (I.)**, fr. Lat. *dominus*. (archaic, poet.) Master, sir: *Dan Chaucer*.

dance (I.), vb. intrans. & trans. [1. dahns; 2. dāns]. M.E. *dancen*, *dauncen*, fr. O. Fr. *danser*, fr. Gmc. source; cp. O.H.G. *dansōn*, 'to draw along, as in a dance'; cogn. w. Goth. (*at-*)*þinsan*, 'to draw towards'. Prob. fr. the Aryan base **tend-* &c., 'stretch', as in Lat. *tendere*, 'to stretch', P.P. *tensum*, 'stretched out', see **tense**, & *tenuis*, 'thin'. See **tenuis** & **thin**. **A.** intrans. **1. a** To move along, or leap, with a series of rhythmical steps and movements of the body, esp. to a musical accompaniment; **b** to spring lightly about with swift, buoyant, irregular movements, not according to any rhythm; to caper about: *to dance for joy*; *to dance with rage*, be furiously angry. **2.** (of light inanimate objects, of shadows &c.) To be moved, stirred, wafted into rapid, irregular motion: *leaves dancing in the wind*; *motes dancing in the sunbeams*; *shadows dancing on the grass* &c. **B.** trans. **1. a** To execute rhythmically steps of a particular kind: *to dance a jig*, *waltz*; **b** in Phr. *to dance attendance upon*, to give one's society constantly to, attend frequently and with solicitude. **2.** To lift up and down, swing, dandle: *to dance a child on one's knee*.

dance (II.), n., fr. prec. **1.** A series of rhythmical steps and movements of the body made in dancing. Phr. *to lead a person a dance*, to put difficulties in the way of, hinder by troublesome distractions; lead here and there in a vain pursuit. *Dance of death*, representation of death carrying off all classes of men, frequent in mediaeval art. *St. Vitus's dance*, nervous disorder, chorea, characterized by convulsive movements of the muscles. **2.** A particular form of dance, such as a waltz, fox-trot, quadrille &c.: *folk-dance* &c. **3.** A musical air, intended as an accompaniment to a dance. **4.** A social gathering, party of pleasure, organized for dancing.

dance-music, n. Music composed primarily as an accompaniment to dancing.

dancer, n. [1. dáhnser; 2. dā́nsə]. See **dance (I.)** & **-er**. One who dances; specif., a professional who executes elaborate and graceful steps, and movements of the body, as a public entertainment.

dancetty, dancetté, adj. [1. dahnséti; 2. dānséti]. As if fr. **dance (I.)**; but corrupt. of Fr. *denché*, 'indented', fr. *dent*, 'tooth'. See **dent-**. (her., of bars or fences) Indented.

dancing, n. [1. dáhnsing; 2. dā́nsiŋ]. **dance (I.)** & **-ing**. Art, practice, of dancing, or the dance: *ballet-dancing*, *step-dancing*.

dancing dervish, n. A dervish belonging to a particular order, Mevlevites, who practise a ritual whirling dance.

dancing-master, n. Teacher of dancing.

dandelion, n. [1. dándelīon; 2. dǽndilaiən], fr. Fr. *dent de lion*, lion's tooth', fr. the indented leaves. See **dent-** & **lion**. A common plant, *Taraxacum officinale*, considered by gardeners as a troublesome weed, with bright yellow composite flowers, deeply indented leaves, and hollow stems containing a bitter, milky juice.

dander, n. [1. dánder; 2. dǽndə]. Etymol. unknown. Temper, anger, in Phr. *to get one's dander up*, to rouse to anger.

dandiacal, adj. [1. dàndíakl; 2. dæ̀ndáiəkl]. See **dandy** & **-ac** & **-al**. Like a dandy, dandified.

Dandie Dinmont, n. [1. dándi dínmont; 2. dǽndi dínmənt], fr. name of a character in Scott's *Guy Mannering*. A breed of Scotch terriers with short legs and bluish-grey or yellowish rough hair.

dandify, vb. trans. [1. dándifī; 2. dǽndifai]. See **dandy** & **-fy**. To make up, dress out, like a dandy; make affected; esp. in. P.P.: *a dandified appearance*, foppish.

dandle, vb. trans. [1. dándl; 2. dǽndl]. Cp. Flemish *danderen*, 'to bounce a ball'; Ital. *dandolare*, 'dandle', & Fr. *dandiner*, 'walk with swaying or swaggering gait', are prob. fr. same Gmc. base. To rock, toss, dance up and down, and fondle (a child) in one's arms or on one's lap.

dandruff, n. [1. dándruf; 2. dǽndrəf]. Etymol. doubtful. Scurf, small scales of dead skin formed on the head among the hair.

dandy (I.), n. [1. dándi; 2. dǽndi]. Originally a Scots word. Perh. fr. name *St. Andrew*, pronounced [sən tǽndru] in Scotland. **a** A man who devotes an excessive amount of attention to his dress and personal appearance; a fop, a rather finicky, fastidious person; **b** (in favourable sense) a well- and carefully-dressed man.

dandy (II.), adj., fr. prec. Finely, foppishly dressed, smart.

dandy (III.), n. Perh. fr. **dandy (I.)**. **a** A kind of one-masted sloop; **b** light, two-wheeled spring cart.

dandy (IV.), n. Corrupted form of **dengue**.

dandy-brush, n. First element perh. **dandruff**. A brush with strong whalebone bristles, used to clean horses' coats.

dandyish, adj. [1. dándi-ish; 2. dǽndi-iʃ]. **dandy** & **-ish**. Like, pertaining to, a dandy.

dandyism, n. [1. dándi-izm; 2. dǽndi-izəm]. **dandy** & **-ism**. Excessive and fastidious solicitude for smartness of dress and appearance; foppishness.

Dane, n. [1. dān; 2. dein]. Dan. *Daner*, pl.; cp. O.E. *Dene*. **1.** A native of Denmark. **2.** (also *Great Dane*) A breed of large, smooth-coated dogs.

danegeld, n. [1. dā́ngeld; 2. déingeld]. See prec. & **yield**. (hist.) A tax on land, originally imposed in the 10th cent., as payment to the Danes, or to support a military force against them.

Danelaw, -lagh, n. [1. dā́nlaw; 2. déinlɔ̄]. O.E., fr. **Dane** & *lagu*, see **law**. (hist.) **a** Danish law as prevailing in England at Danish Conquest; **b** part of N.E. England under this law, after Treaty of Wedmore.

danger, n. [1. dā́njer; 2. déindžə], w. changed meaning fr. M.E. *danger*, 'power, control; resistance', O. Fr. *dangier*, 'power, domination', fr. Low Lat. **dominiārium*, 'power', fr. *dominus*, 'a master, lord'. See **dominate, dominie**. **1.** Exposure to risk of death, injury &c.; peril: *his life is in danger*; *the dangers of a journey*. **2.** Something involving risk of injury; menace, cause of peril: *a danger to health*, *to peace* &c. **3.** Position of signal giving warning of danger: *at danger*; (also attrib.) *danger-signal* &c.

dangerous, adj. [1. dā́njerus; 2. déindžərəs]. Prec. & **-ous**. **a** (of circumstances) Fraught with danger; unsafe, causing, or involving, risk, exposure to death, injury, &c.; perilous: *a dangerous illness*, *journey* &c.; **b** (of persons or animals) likely to do physical or moral injury; unreliable: *a dangerous man*, *dog* &c. Phr. *To look dangerous*, to appear angry, and to be about to make a disturbance.

dangerously, adv. Prec. & **-ly**. In a dangerous manner, so as to involve exposure to danger: *dangerously ill*; *dangerously near the edge*.

dangerousness, n. Prec. & **-ness**. The quality of being dangerous.

danger-signal, n. (lit. and fig.) A sign of danger, impending, or to be avoided.

dangle, vb. intrans. & trans. [1. dánggl; 2. dǽŋgl]. Scand., cp. Swed. dial. *dangla*, 'to swing', & in different grade, O.N. *dingla*, 'dangle, swing about'. **A.** intrans. **1.** To hang and sway loosely, as a weight at the end of a cord: *an eyeglass dangling from a ribbon*. **2.** *Dangle after*, to follow, hang about, hover round, to court in desultory fashion. **B.** trans. **a** To cause to hang and swing loosely: *to dangle a toy before a child*; **b** (fig.) to display as an attraction, tempt with: *to dangle bright prospects before a person*, *before his eyes*.

Danish, adj. & n. [1. dā́nish; 2. déiniʃ]. **Dane** & **-ish**. **a** adj. Belonging to Denmark; **b** n., the language of the Danes.

dank, adj. [1. dangk; 2. dæŋk]. M.E. *dank*, cp. Swed. *dänka*, 'to moisten', perh. connected with **damp**. Harmfully, disagreeably damp.

dankness, n. Prec. & **-ness**. The quality of being dank.

dap, vb. intrans. & trans. & n. [1. dap; 2. dæp]. Etymol. doubtful. **1.** vb. **a** (fishing) To allow the bait to fall or dip gently into the water; **b** (of ball) to bounce. **2.** n. Bounce of a ball.

Daphne, n. [1. dáfni; 2. dǽfni]. Gk. *dáphnē*, 'laurel'. Etymol. unknown. Genus of flowering shrubs, including the mezereon.

dapper, adj. [1. dáper; 2. dǽpə]. M.E. *daper*. Cp. Du. *dapper*, O.H.G. *tapfar*, 'firm, strong, brave'; fr. Gmc. **dap-*, 'closely knit, compact'; cogn. w. O. Slav. *dobrŭ*, Russ. *dobry*, 'good'. Aryan base **dhē-* &c., 'to make fitting, suitable, fit together'. See **deft** & **theme**. Neat and smart in appearance; active and smart of movement (usually applied to small persons).

dapple, vb. trans. [1. dápl; 2. dǽpl]. The suggested etymologies are mere ingenious shots. **a** To mark with spots or splodges of different colour, or shade of colour; generally in P.P. and applied to horses and deer; **b** (referring to spots of light and shade caused by sunlight coming through leaves); to variegate: *dappled shade*.

dapple-grey, adj. & n. M.E. *dappel-grai*; **a** adj. (of horses) Marked with a different shade of grey; **b** n., a horse of this colour.

darbies, n. pl. [1. dárbiz; 2. dā́biz]. Origin unknown. (slang) Handcuffs.

Darby and Joan, n. [1. dárbi and jṓn; 2. dā́bi ən(d) džóun]. An old, devoted, happy married couple; probably from characters in an 18th cent. poem.

dare, vb. intrans. & trans. [1. dār; 2. dɛə]. O.E. Pret.-Pres. *dear*(*r*), infin. *durran*; M.E. *dar*, 3rd sing. pres. of *durren*, 'dare'. Cp. O.H.G. (*ge*)*turren*; Goth. (*ga*)*daursan*; fr. Aryan base **dhrs*. Cp. Gk. *tharséō*, I am of good courage', *thársos*, 'boldness', fr. the same base; Scrt. *dhr̥ṣṇóti*, *dhárṣati*, 'to dare'; Lith. *drę̃sù*, I dare'; O. Slav. *drŭzŭ*, 'bold'. The present-day form is a new formation fr. the old Pret.-Pres. The form *he dare* (without *-s*) is a survival of the old Pret.-Pres. *He dares* is a new formation. **1.** intrans. To have the courage or audacity for some action, be brave enough to do something: *he daren't fight*; *he won't dare to deny it*. Phrs. *I dare say*, believe possible or probable; *don't you dare to touch me*, don't have the impudence to. **2.** trans. **a** To challenge, provoke to an action, implying that the challenged party cannot, or has not the courage to, do it: *I dare you to jump that stream*; **b** to attempt, venture to do; have courage for; to face: *he will dare any danger*.

dare-devil, n. See **dare** & **devil**. A bold, careless, reckless, foolhardy person.

daric, n. [1. dárik; 2. dǽrik], fr. Gk. *dāreikós*, as supposed to have been first coined by Darius the Great, or direct fr. Pers. *darā*, 'king'. Ancient Persian gold coin.

daring (I.), adj. [1. dā́ring; 2. déəriŋ]. Pres. Part. of **dare**. **a** (of persons) Having courage, brave; foolhardy: *a daring adventurer*; **b** (of actions) requiring courage on the part of those who perform them: *a daring attempt*; **c** impudent, audacious: *a daring robbery*.

daring (II.), n. See **dare** & **-ing**. Courage, audacity, intrepidity.

daringly, adv. **daring** (I.) & **-ly**. In a daring manner, boldly.

dark (I.), adj. [1. dark; 2. dāk]. O.E. *deorc*, M.E. *derk*; cp. O.H.G. *tarchanjan*, 'to hide'; the base, w. a different formative element, occurs also in O.E. *dierne*, 'secret, hidden', O.S. *darni*, O.H.G. *tarni*. See **darn** (I.). No certain cognates have been noted outside Gmc. **1.** Partially or wholly without light: *a dark night, room* &c. Hence, **a** (of colour) not reflecting light, verging towards black, sombre: *a dark dress*; *dark blue*; **b** (of colour of skin, eyes, and hair) not pale or fair, verging towards brown or black: *a dark complexion.* **2.** (fig.) Unillumined by intellectual or moral light. Phr. *Dark Ages*, the Middle Ages, esp. the early period from 6th cent. onwards. Specif. **a** hidden, not revealed, mysterious: *a dark secret*; Phrs. *to keep dark*, remain in hiding; *to keep a thing dark*, keep it a secret; *a dark horse* (in racing, and fig., of persons), of unknown or unexpected capabilities; **b** sinister, malevolent, evil: *dark deeds, thoughts* &c.; **c** gloomy, hopeless, sad: *dark days*; *to look on the dark side of things*; **d** not clear to the mind, obscure: *the meaning is still dark.*

dark (II.), n., fr. prec. Total or partial absence of light, darkness. **1. a** Absence of physical light: *to sit in the dark*; *afraid of the dark.* Phr. (fig.) *a leap in the dark*, an action of which one is unable to foresee the consequences; **b** dark colour (in a picture &c.). **2.** (fig.) A state of unenlightenment, ignorance: *to be in the dark about*, not to know, not to understand fully; *to keep a person in the dark*, to hide things from him, withhold information.

darken, vb. trans. & intrans. [1. dárken; 2. dākən]. **dark** (I.) & **-en**. **A.** trans. **a** (in physical sense) To make darker, obstruct or remove light from: *to darken a room* (by drawing down the blinds, putting out a light &c.); Phrs. *don't darken my door again*, don't come to my house &c.; *to darken counsel*, to make more perplexing, increase difficulty, confusion &c.; **b** (of colour) to give a deeper tone to; **c** (fig., of action on the mind) to sadden, depress, make gloomy: *my life is, days are, darkened by sorrow.* **B.** intrans. To become dark or darker.

darkish, adj. [1. dárkish; 2. dākiʃ]. **dark** (I.) & **-ish**. Rather dark.

dark-lantern, n. A lantern with a shutter for concealing, or letting out, the light as required.

darkle, vb. intrans. [1. dárkl; 2. dākl]. Recent back-formation fr. **darkling**, wh. was regarded as a Pres. Part. Often rather vaguely used. **a** To become dark, gloomy, overcast; **b** (in moral sense) to lour.

darkling, adv. & adj. [1. dárkling; 2. dākliŋ]. See **dark** & **-ling**. The word is one of a group of advs. formed w. the suff. *-ling*, wh. were formerly more numerous—*backling*, 'backwards', *flatling*, 'with the flat of the sword' &c., and cp. **grovelling**. **a** adv. In the dark: *to sit darkling*; '*Went darkling down the torrent of his fate*' (Johnson); **b** adj., growing dark, dusky, dim: *the darkling wood.*

darkly, adv. [1. dárkli; 2. dākli]. See **dark** (I.) & **-ly**. **1.** In a dark manner (in various senses, fig.): **a** *to look darkly at a person*, gloomily, malignantly; **b** *to answer darkly*, mysteriously, obscurely. **2.** (archaic) Imperfectly, indistinctly: '*for now we see through a glass darkly.*' (1 Cor. xiii. 12.)

darkness, n. [1. dárknes; 2. dāknis]. See **dark** & **-ness**. **1. a** The state of being without light, mental or physical obscurity; **b** blackness, duskiness of complexion &c. **2.** Specif., absence of the sun's light; night.

dark-room, n. A room specially darkened, by excluding all natural light, for the development of photographic plates and films.

darksome, adj. [1. dárksum; 2. dāksəm]. **dark** (I.) & **-some**. (poet.) Dark. **a** Devoid of physical light; **b** devoid of lightheartedness, or cause for this, dismal, sad: *the darksome time of sorrow.*

dark(e)y, n. [1. dárki; 2. dāki]. **dark** (I.) & **-y**. (colloq.) A negro.

darling, n. & adj. [1. dárling; 2. dāliŋ]. O.E. *dēorling*, M.E. *derling*. See **dear** & **-ling**. **1.** n. **a** Dearly, fondly, loved person; object of deep affection; much-favoured person, a favourite: *the darling of all hearts*; *the darling of fortune*; **b** term of endearment: *my darling!*; **c** a charming, lovable person, one who inspires affection: *a perfect darling.* **2.** adj. **a** Greatly beloved and cherished, very dear: *I have lost my darling child*; **b** (of hopes, aspirations) greatly desired, whose realization is ardently longed for: *my darling hope was to see him before he died.*

darn (I.), vb. trans. [1. darn; 2. dān]. Prob. O.E. *dernan, dyrnan*, M.E. *dernen*, 'to hide, conceal', fr. *derne, dyrne*, 'hidden, secret'. Cp. O.H.G. *tarnan*, 'to hide', & see **dark** (I.). To repair a hole in woven or knitted material, esp. in stockings and socks, by covering it with a network of threads at right angles to each other, drawn in and out of the material by means of a needle.

darn (II.), n., fr. prec. A repair effected by darning.

darn (III.), vb. trans. Milder form of **damn**, used as an oath.

darnel, n. [1. dárnel; 2. dānl]. M.E. *dernel.* Skeat suggests an etymol. fr. a base *dar-, dor-*, found in Walloon & Du. &c., cogn. w. Germ. *tor*, 'a fool', & signifying 'stupefying', & *nel*, fr. O. Fr. *nelle, nielle*, 'darnel', fr. Lat. *nigella*, 'plant with black seeds'. He cites also Swed. *dår-repe*, 'bearded darnel'. But this explanation is largely ingenious conjecture. A coarse weed found chiefly among corn, a kind of rye-grass.

darner, n. [1. dárner; 2. dānə]. See **darn** (I.) & **-er**. **a** A person who darns; **b** metal or wooden device put under a hole in a stocking &c. to facilitate its repair by darning.

darning, n. [1. dárning; 2. dāniŋ]. **darn** (I.) & **-ing**. **a** The act of repairing a hole by means of a darn; **b** material to be repaired by darns.

darning-needle, n. A long, large-eyed needle used in darning.

darrein, adj. [1. dárān; 2. dǽrein]. O. Fr., also *derrein*, fr. Lat. *de*, 'from', & *retro*, 'back, backward'. See **de-** & **retro-**. (law) In *darrein presentment*, the last presentation to an ecclesiastical benefice, as evidence of right of presentation.

dart (I.), n. [1. dart; 2. dāt]. M.E. *dart*, O. Fr. *dart, darz*, fr. a Gmc. source, cp. O.E. *daroþ*, 'javelin'. This word is connected w. O.E. *derian*, 'to injure'. **1. a** A pointed weapon to be thrown by the hand; **b** anything resembling this, for piercing and wounding. **2.** A sudden rapid forward movement, as resembling the flight of a dart.

dart (II.), vb. intrans. & trans. M.E. *darten*, 'to pierce with a dart', fr. prec. **a** intrans. To move like a dart, shoot forward suddenly and swiftly: *to dart forward*; *dart out*; *dart through the air*; used especially of rapid arrow-like flight of swallows, humming-birds, and of certain insects such as the dragon-fly; **b** trans., (lit. and fig.) to shoot out, send forward quickly and suddenly: *the sun darts its beams*; *to dart an angry look at a person.*

darter, n. [1. dárter; 2. dātə]. Prec. & **-er**. **1.** (pl.) A genus of birds allied to the pelicans and cormorants. **2.** The name of certain kinds of fish.

dartle, vb. intrans. [1. dártl; 2. dātl]. Freq. fr. **dart**; see **-le**. (rare) To dart about.

dartre, n. [1. dárter; 2. dātə]. Fr. *dartre*; of Celt. origin. A kind of skin eruption.

dartrous, adj. [1. dártrus; 2. dātrəs]. fr. prec. & **-ous**. Pertaining to, resembling, dartre.

Darwinian, adj. [1. darwínian; 2. dāwínjən], fr. Charles Darwin & **-ian**. Pertaining to Darwin and his theories.

Darwinism, n. [1. dárwinizm; 2. dāwinizəm]. See prec. & **-ism**. That theory of the origin and evolution of species by natural selection, propounded by Darwin in the 'Origin of Species' and other works.

dash (I.), vb. trans. & intrans. [1. dash; 2. dæʃ]. M.E. *daschen*, 'to rush; strike down', Scand.; cp. Dan. *daske*, 'to slap', Swed. *daska*, 'to beat'. **A.** trans. **1. a** To fling or hurl with violence: *to dash a person or thing to the ground.* Phr. *to dash off*, execute roughly and hastily (of writing, drawing, &c.); **b** (fig.) to destroy, shatter, frustrate: *his hopes were dashed.* **2.** (of liquids) **a** To sprinkle, splash: *dash water in a man's face*; *dashed with mud*; **b** to mix a small quantity of other liquid with: *milk dashed with brandy.* **3.** Mild oath, substituted for *damn.* **B.** intrans. To move, be moved, forward rapidly and violently; rush furiously: *to dash from the room*; *dash up to the door*; *sea dashing on the rocks.*

dash (II.), n., fr. prec. **1. a** A rapid and violent forward movement, a rush: *a dash for safety, for the goal* &c.; hence, **b** vigour, capacity for bold, spirited, rapid, resolute action: *this general has both skill and dash.* **2.** (of liquids) **a** The noise produced by the sudden striking of a liquid on a solid substance: *the dash of the rain on the windows* &c.; **b** (lit. and fig.) a small admixture: *whisky with a dash of water.* **3.** (in writing &c.) **a** A swift stroke of pen, pencil, or brush; specif. **b** a short horizontal line (—) used as a punctuation mark, usually to denote a pause or parenthesis. **4.** An ostentatious display, showy appearance. Colloq. Phr. *to cut a dash*, make a brilliant impression, play a prominent part in society by showy manners, appearance &c.

dash-board, n. **1.** A screen of wood, leather &c., in the front of a vehicle, to protect the interior, or the driver's box, from mud-splashes. **2.** Board in front of driver of motor car, pilot of an aeroplane, which carries various indicators, gauges &c.

dasher, n. [1. dásher; 2. dǽʃə]. **dash** (I.) & **-er**. **1.** One who cuts a dash. **2.** The revolving part of a churn which beats the cream.

dashing, adj. [1. dáshing; 2. dǽʃiŋ], fr. Pres. Part. of **dash** (I.). Bold, eager, and ready for action, spirited: *a dashing rider.*

dastard, n. [1. dástard; 2. dǽstəd]. L.M.E. *dastard*, 'stupid person'; the suff. is **-ard**, as in *sluggard* &c. The first element is possibly *dazed.* See **daze**. M. Du. has *daasaardt*, 'fool'. A coward; a mean-spirited fellow.

dastardliness, n. [1. dástardlines; 2. dǽstədlinis], fr. next word & **-ness**. The state of being dastardly.

dastardly, adj. [1. dástardli; 2. dǽstədli], fr. **dastard** & **-ly**. Cowardly, mean; brutal when it is safe to be so.

dasy-, pref. Form used in compounds, fr. Gk. *dasús*, 'rough, hairy; thick', according to Boisacq fr. **datús*, fr. Aryan **dn̥tu-s*; cp. Lat. *densus*, 'crowded, dense'. See **dense**.

dasymeter, n. [1. dasímeter; 2. dæsímitə]. Prec. & **-meter**. Instrument for measuring the density of gases.

dasypod, n. [1. dásipod; 2. dǽsipɔd]. **dasy-** & **-pod**; cp. Gk. *dasúpous*, 'the hairy-footed one, hare'. (zool.) Member of the family *Dasypodidae*, which includes the armadillo.

dasyure, n. [1. dásiūr; 2. dǽsijuə]. **dasy-** & Gk. *ourá*, 'tail', see **uro-** (II.). (zool.) Member of a genus, *Dasyurus*, of small tree and rock marsupials of Australasia, including the Tasmanian devil &c.

data, pl. n. [1. dāta; 2. déitə]. See **datum.** (pl.) Things certainly known, or taken as known, from which inferences can be drawn.

datable, adj. [1. dātabl; 2. déitəbl]. **date** (II.) & **-able.** Capable of being dated, of having a date assigned to it.

dataller. See **daytaller.**

date (I.), n. [1. dāt; 2. deit]. Fr., fr. Lat. *data*, 'things given, announced', P.P. of *dare*, 'give'. The base **dō-, *dă-* (fr. **də-*), **dē-*, 'give', is fairly widespread among the Aryan languages, but does not occur in Gmc. Cp. Gk. *dí-dō-mi*, 'I give', *dô-ron*, 'gift' &c.; Sert. *dá-dāti*, 'he gives', *dā-tram*, 'gift'; Lith. *dŭ-mi*, 'I give'; O. Slav. *dati*, 'to give' &c. In addition to the words given above, Lat. has *dōnum*, *dō(t)s*, 'marriage portion'; cp. *sacerdōs*, 'priest'. See **donation, dot** (III.), & **sacerdotal. 1.** Indication of day of week or month, and year, **a** upon a written document of any kind, on or in which it is written, signed, sent, delivered, or received: *the date on a letter*; **b** upon a coin, inscribed statue, picture &c. **2.** Given point of time; the day, month, or year, on or in which an event has taken, or will take place: *date of birth, of a battle* &c. Phr. *out of date*, obsolete, becoming obsolete; *up to date*, in accordance with the newest fashion, knowledge, improvements &c.; *to have a date with someone*, an appointment to meet.

date (II.), vb. trans. & intrans., fr. prec. **1.** trans. **a** To put a date to (letter, document, picture &c.); **b** assign a date to, estimate when a thing happened or when something was done, or made: *to date a document, piece of china, building* &c. **2.** intrans. Esp. *to date from, date back to*: to be traceable to a given time in the past, go back to, be coeval with: *these ideas date from before the war*; *his family dates back to the Conquest*.

date (III.), n. Fr. *datte*, Lat. *dactylus*, fr. Gk. *dáktulos*, 'finger'; a popular etymol. of a Semitic word, cp. Arab. *dagal*, 'kind of palm'. This was made plausible by a fancied resemblance of the fruit to fingers. See **dactyl. a** Eastern stone fruit of elongated shape, sweet taste and sticky consistency; **b** the tree which produces the fruit, the *date palm*.

dateless, adj. [1. dā́tles; 2. déitlis]. See **date** (I.) & **-less.** Not assignable to any particular date or period of time, unlimited, indefinite: '*Death's dateless night*' (Shakespeare).

date-line, n. **date** (I.) & **line.** Meridian or hypothetical line 180° from Greenwich, on each side of which the date of the day differs.

date-palm, n. See **date** (III.) & **palm.** African tree with a tall slender trunk and foliage at the top, which produces the date fruit.

dative, n. & adj. [1. dā́tiv; 2. déitiv]. Lat. *datīvus*, 'pertaining to the act of giving; given, appointed'. See **date** (I.) & **-ive.** (gram.) That case in inflected languages, or case-relation in others, in which the indirect object of a verb stands, or which follows certain prepositions.

datum, n. [1. dā́tum; 2. déitəm], P.P. (neut.) of Lat. *dare*, 'to give', fr. base **da-*. See **date** (I.) & also **donation, donor** &c. (usually in pl. *data*) Something known; facts known, given, or assumed, forming the basis of an argument, or from which inferences are drawn.

datum-line, n. Horizontal line or level, used in surveying, from which heights and depths of surfaces are reckoned.

datura, n. [1. dátūra; 2. dǽtjərə]. Hind. *dhatūrā*, Scrt. *dhattūra*. Plant, also called stramonium and thorn-apple; from one variety which grows in the Himalayas a poison is made, often criminally used in India to produce temporary madness in the victims.

daub (I.), vb. trans. & intrans. [1. dawb; 2. dōb]. M.E. *dauben*, 'to daub, plaster', O. Fr. *dauber*, fr. Lat. *dealbāre*, 'to whitewash, plaster', fr. *dē*, 'over', & *albus*, 'white'. See **de-** & **alb, albino. 1.** trans. **a** To smear, coat, overlay &c., with soft, sticky, moist substance, such as paint, clay, mud &c.: *to daub a hut with clay*; **b** to lay on paint unskilfully, paint (pictures) incompetently, without artistic talent. **2.** intrans. To paint unskilfully and inartistically.

daub (II.), n., fr. prec. **a** A covering, or splash of soft adhesive substance; **b** a badly executed, inartistically painted picture.

dauber, n. [1. dáwber; 2. dṓbə]. Prec. & **-er.** One who daubs; specif., an unskilful picture-painter.

daubster, n. [1. dáwbster; 2. dṓbstə]. **daub** (I.) & **-ster.** An inferior painter of pictures.

daughter, n. [1. dáwter; 2. dṓtə]. O.E. *dohtor*, M.E. *doughter, dohter* &c.; Common Gmc., cp. O.H.G. *tohtar*, Mod. Germ. *tochter*, O. Fris. *dochter*, O.N. *dottir*, Goth. *dauhtar*, identical w. Gk. *thugátēr*, Scrt. *duhitá*, Lith. *duktė̃*, O. Slav. *dŭšti*, O. Prussian *duckti*. The connexion of these words w. Scrt. *dṓgdhi*, 'to milk', according to wh. daughter was (not the 'milkmaid' but) the 'suckling', is now largely rejected. See on the other hand the etymol. of Lat. *fīlia*, 'daughter', *fīlius*, 'son', under **filial. 1.** A female child or offspring; a woman considered in relation to one or both of her parents. **2.** A female descendant: *a daughter of Abraham*, a Jewess. **3.** (fig.) **a** A woman considered as the intellectual or moral descendant of some person, or as the product of some event, period &c.: *a daughter of Eve*; *a daughter of the Revolution*; **b** something personified as female and considered in relation to its origin: *a daughter nation*; *daughter languages*.

daughterhood, n. [1. dáwterhòod; 2. dṓtəhùd]. Prec. & **-hood.** The condition, state, of being a daughter.

daughter-in-law, n. [1. dáwter in làw; 2. dṓtər in lṑ]. A son's wife.

daughterliness, n. [1. dáwterlines; 2. dṓtəlinis], fr. next word & **-ness.** The state of being daughterly.

daughterly, adj. [1. dáwterli; 2. dṓtəli]. See **daughter** & **-ly.** Pertaining to, proper to, a daughter: *daughterly affection*.

daunt, vb. trans. [1. dawnt; 2. dōnt]. M.E. *daunten*, O. Fr. *danter, donter*, fr. Lat. *domitāre*, 'to tame', freq. of *domāre*, 'to tame, vanquish'. See **tame. 1.** To subdue, reduce to silence, or passivity, by physical or moral ascendancy: *to daunt a bully with a look*. **2. a** To inspire with fear, terror, dismay: *completely daunted by the number of his enemies*; **b** to dishearten, disconcert, discourage: *daunted by the magnitude and difficulty of the task*; Phr. *nothing daunted*, not at all dismayed, or discouraged &c.

dauntless, adj. [1. dáwntles; 2. dṓntlis], fr. obs., M.E. *daunt*, 'a check, stoppage', see prec. & **-less. a** (of persons) Incapable of fear, of being frightened; courageous, intrepid: *a dauntless hero*; **b** (of character and its qualities) unshakable by danger, or threats; not accessible to, not impaired by, terror: *dauntless courage*.

dauntlessly, adv. Prec. & **-ly.** In a dauntless manner.

dauntlessness, n. See prec. & **-ness.** The quality of being dauntless.

dauphin, n. [1. dáwfin; 2. dṓfin]. Fr., derived fr. the Dauphiné & its lords, Counts of Vienne, in whose family it was a proper name, Latinized as *Delphinus*, 'dolphin', q.v. (hist.) The title of the eldest son of the King of France, from 1364, when the Dauphiné became an appanage of the Crown.

dauphiness, n. [1. dáwfines; 2. dṓfines]. Prec. & **-ess.** The wife of a dauphin.

davenport, n. [1. dávnpòrt; 2. dǽvnpɔ̀t]. Prob. fr. name of orig. maker. A small cabinet, with a hinged flap made to open and serve as a writing-desk.

davit, n. [1. dávit; 2. dǽvit]. A.-Fr. *daviot*, perh. orig. the name *David*, fr. O. Fr. type *Davi*, & **-et** (*-ot*). (naut.) **a** One of the two uprights, curved at the top, used on a ship for raising or lowering a boat over the side by means of pulleys and chains, and for holding a boat suspended over the deck; **b** a crane in the bow of ship for hauling in the anchor.

davy, n. [1. dā́vi; 2. déivi]. For **affidavit.** (vulg. slang) *To take one's davy*, to swear that. . .

Davy Jones's locker, n. [1. dā́vi jṓnzez lóker; 2. déivi džóunziz lɔ́kə]. Origin of name unknown. The sea considered as a grave: *to go to Davy Jones's locker*, to be drowned.

Davy-lamp, n. [1. dā́vi làmp; 2. déivi lǽmp], fr. the name of the inventor, Sir Humphry Davy (1778–1829). A miner's safety-lamp, in which the flame is protected by wire-gauze from coming into contact with fire-damp.

daw, n. [1. daw; 2. dō]. M.E. *dāwe*. Cp. O.H.G. *tāha*; cp. also M.H.G. *dāhele* & *tāle*, Mod. Germ. *dahle*, now *dohle*, 'jackdaw, chough'. A kind of crow, a jackdaw.

dawdle, vb. intrans. & trans. [1. dáwdl; 2. dṓdl]. Etymol. doubtful; prob. a provinc. dial. word; cp. provinc. *daddle*, 'totter like a baby'. Skeat connects the word w. O.N. *dauðr*, 'dead', & *dauði*, 'death'. See **death. a** intrans. To loiter, linger, waste time, spend too much time over doing something; **b** trans., *dawdle away* (one's time &c.): to waste in idleness, sloth, inaction.

dawdler, n. [1. dáwdler; 2. dṓdlə]. Prec. & **-er.** Slow, desultory person; one who spends unnecessary length of time over a job, slow worker, one who fritters away his time.

dawk. See **dâk.**

dawn (I.), vb. trans. [1. dawn; 2. dōn]. M.E. *dawnen*; also *dazien, dawen*; cp. O.E. *dagian*, 'dawn, become day'. The *-n-* in M.E. is prob. due to the influence of that in O.N. *dag-n-ing*, 'dawning'. The normal descendant of O.E. *dagian*, M.E. *dawen*, wd. be *daw*. See **day. 1.** (of the day, morning) To begin to grow light. Phr. (fig.) *a glad day dawned*, a good time began. **2.** (fig.) **a** (of non-material things) To begin to develop, appear, emerge into existence: *dawning intelligence, consciousness*; Phr. (impers.), *it has just dawned upon me, him* &c., I have just come to realize, it has just occurred to me; **b** (of material things) to show for first time, begin to appear: *a dawning moustache*.

dawn (II.), n., fr. prec. **a** Daybreak, beginning of day, first appearance of daylight. Phr. *the dawn of brighter days* &c., beginning of better things; **b** (fig., of non-material things) the beginning, first appearance of something, first sign of life and development: *the dawn of civilization, of the arts, of life, intelligence, hope, love* &c.

dawning, n. [1. dáwning; 2. dṓniŋ]. M.E. *dawening, daigening*, prec. & **-ing.** The O.E. form was *dagung*, whence M.E. *dawung*. **a** (in same senses as **dawn**) Process of growing light, first light of day; **b** the process of appearing, coming into existence; (in many fig. uses) *the dawning of a new era* &c.

day, n. [1. dā; 2. dei]. Common Gmc. O.E. *dæġ*, M.E. *dai, dei*; O.H.G. *tag*, O. Fris. *dei*, O.S. *dag*, O.N. *dagr*, Goth. *dags*; also, w. different grade, O.E. *dōgor*, O.N. *døgr*. Gmc. **dag-, *dōg-*, 'time during which the sun shines', fr. Aryan base **dhogʷh-, *dhōgʷh-, *dhegʷh-* &c., 'the shining, glowing, burning thing'. From the same base come Gk. *téphrā* for **thegʷhrā-*, 'ashes'; Lat. *favilla*, for **fovilla*, fr. **dhogʷh-*, 'glowing cinder'; *fovēre*, 'to warm'; fig., 'to cherish'; Scrt. *dáhati*, 'burns', *dāhaś*, 'heat, burning'; *ni-dāghá-ś*, 'simmer'; Lith. *dãgas*, 'harvest time', *degù*, 'I burn'; O. Slav. *žegą*, 'I burn'; Lett. *daglis*, 'tinder'; O. Prussian *dagis*, 'summer'; Alban. *djek*, 'I burn'; Czech *dahneti*, 'to burn'. See **fever, foment, tephrite. 1.** The period between sunrise and sunset, during which the sun gives light; opposed to *night*. Phr. *all day*, throughout the day; *clear as day*, as the light of day (lit. and fig.). **2. a** Twenty-four hours, the time taken by the earth to revolve once on its own axis, so as to bring a certain meridian once more into the same relative position to the sun (also *solar day*). *Lunar, sidereal, day*, taking the moon, a star, as point of reference. *Civil day*, from midnight to midnight. *Astronomical day*, from noon to noon. Phrs. *days of grace*, extra days allowed for payment after a bill falls due; *this day week*, corresponding day of following week; *every day, day by day*, (adv.) daily; hence, **b** the time taken by any heavenly body to revolve once on its own axis. **3. a** A particular day, on which some special event has taken, or will take, place: *Christmas Day, Armistice Day, the Last Day*; **b** by transference, an event happening on a certain day, specif., a contest &c.: *to win the day*; *the day is ours*. **4.** In wider sense: **a** a period of time, lifetime or portion of life-time, epoch: *the days of* *old*; *the days of Queen Elizabeth*; Phr. *to end one's days*, to die; **b** specif., time of flourishing, prosperity: *my day is done*; *feudalism has had its day*; Phr. *every dog has his day*, everyone has some chance of success; **c** an indefinite, unspecified, point of time, past or future: *the other day*; *some day*.

day-bed, n. A long couch, on which one can lie at full length; an early form of sofa.

day-blindness, n. A defect of sight which makes the sufferer unable to distinguish objects by daylight.

day-boarder, n. One who remains at school all day, and has at least one meal there, but returns home to sleep.

day-book, n. Book in which commercial or other transactions are recorded as soon as they take place.

day-boy, -girl, n. One who attends school daily, while living at home.

daybreak, n. [1. dā́brāk; 2. déibreik]. The dawn, first appearance of the sun at beginning of the day.

daydream, n. [1. dā́drēm; 2. déidrīm]. A reverie, musing; a visionary hope.

daydreamer, n. [1. dā́drēmer; 2. déidrīmə]. One who has daydreams.

day labour, n. Work paid for by the day.

day labourer, n. One who works and is paid by the day.

daylight, n. [1. dā́līt; 2. déilait]. The light of the sun; natural, as distinguished from artificial light; light, as distinguished from darkness or night. Phrs. (fig.) *to see daylight*, to understand, arrive at the solution of a problem; *let daylight into*, give publicity to.

daylight-saving, n. Scheme for taking full advantage of the hours of daylight in summer, adopted in England in 1916; it consists in advancing the clock one hour, thus beginning work an hour earlier at a certain day, and putting it back again at the end of the period, which is known as *Summer Time*.

day-lily, n. A garden flower, with long narrow leaves and trumpet-shaped, yellow or brownish-red flowers; the petals fall in a few hours.

daylong, adj. [1. dā́long; 2. déilɔŋ], fr. **day** & **long**. Lasting throughout the day.

day-owl, n. A kind of owl which sometimes hunts by day.

day-school, n. **a** One attended daily by children living at home; contrasted with *boarding-school*; **b** one where classes are held during the day; opposed to *night-school*, *evening-school*.

day-spring, n. The dawn, break of day; (also fig.) beginning.

day-star, n. The morning star, one rising before the sun.

daytaller, dataller, n. [1. dā́taler; 2. déitələ]. **day** & provinc. form of *teller*. See **tale**. One who works and is paid by the day, esp. of coal-miners.

daytime, n. [1. dā́tīm; 2. déitaim]. The period between sunrise and sunset, time of daylight.

daze (I.), vb. trans. [1. dāz; 2. deiz]. M.E. *dāsen*, 'to stupefy; grow dim, dizzy', fr. O.N. *dasa*, 'be sluggish'; cp. O.E. *dwǣsigean*, 'to become stupid', *dwǣs*, 'foolish, stupid'; perh. cogn. w. Lat. *furere*, 'to rage', if this be derived fr. base **dhwewes-*. See discussion under **fury**; cp. **dastard** & **dazzle**. To stupefy, stun, bewilder, as by a sudden blow or shock.

daze (II.), n., fr. prec. State of being confused; bewilderment.

dazedly, adv. [1. dā́zedli; 2. déizidli], fr. P.P. of **daze** (I.) & **-ly**. In a dazed, bewildered, stupefied manner.

dazzle (I.), vb. trans. & intrans. [1. dázl; 2. dǽzl], fr. **daze** (I.) & **-le**. **1. a** To render partially blind, deprive temporarily of capacity for clear sight, cloud the vision, by exposing the eyes to excess of very brilliant light: *to be dazzled by the sun, glare of headlights* &c.; **b** to confuse the sight of, prevent from distinguishing objects such as ships correctly, by painting them in a particular fashion, as in the Great War. **2.** (of moral effects) To overpower, to obscure the judgement of, with the sight of exceptional beauty, splendour, or with hopes of success, wealth &c.: *dazzled by the lady's beauty, by the prospect of fame*.

dazzle (II.), n., fr. prec. **a** Process of dazzling; **b** brilliance, that which dazzles.

dazzling, adj. [1. dázling; 2. dǽzliŋ], fr. Pres. Part. of **dazzle** (I.). Having the power to dazzle; of great brilliance or beauty.

dazzlingly, adv. Prec. & **-ly**. In a dazzling manner.

de-, pref., fr. Lat. prep. *dē*, 'from, away from' &c.; in composition it has in Lat. the force of **a** 'down, away', as in *descend, deduct* &c.; **b** 'deficiency', as in *detract*; **c** 'negation', as in *despair*; **d** 'deprivation', as in *decapitate*; **e** 'over', as in *dealbāre*, 'cover with white', see **daub**; **f** (intens.) expressing 'completeness', as in *defunct*; **g** giving bad sense, *deceive, delude*. *De-* in Engl. usage is sometimes fr. Fr. *dé-*, O. Fr. *des-*, wh. is fr. Lat. **dis-**, 'asunder, apart', as in *decompose*.

deacon, n. [1. dḗkun; 2. díkən]. M.E. *diacne*, O.E. *diacon*, fr. Lat. *diāconus*, fr. Gk. *diā́konos*, 'a servant; a minister of the church, deacon'; cp. Gk. *eg-koneîn*, 'to be quick, active, diligent', & *ag-koneîn*, 'to hasten'. The etymol. of the base *kon-* is unknown. See **dia-**. **a** (in the Anglican and Roman churches) A person ordained to an order of the ministry below that of priest; **b** (in the Presbyterian Church) a layman ordained and appointed to attend to the secular affairs of the church; **c** (in the Early Church) one of a special class of church-workers appointed to minister to the poor; **d** (in some dissenting bodies) an assistant to the regular minister.

deaconess, n. [1. dḗkunes; 2. díkənis], fr. prec. & **-ess**. (in the Early Church and some modern churches) **a** A woman with duties similar to those of a deacon; **b** a professed member of one of certain religious orders.

deaconhood, n. [1. dḗkunhòod; 2. díkənhùd]. **deacon** & **-hood**. The office of, state of being, a deacon.

deaconry, n. [1. dḗkunri; 2. díkənri]. **deacon** & **-ry**. Office of deacon; the body of deacons collectively.

deaconship, n. [1. dḗkunship; 2. díkənʃip], fr. **deacon** & **-ship**. The office of a deacon.

dead (I.), adj. [1. ded; 2. ded]. O.E. *dēad*, M.E. *dēde, deade*; O.H.G. *tōt*, O. Fris. *dād*, O.S. *dōd*, O.N. *dauþr*, Goth. *dauþs*. With this, fr. **dau-*, is associated by gradation Goth. *diwans*, 'mortal', fr. **deu-*. These represent an Aryan **dhow-*, **dhew-*, respectively, wh. may also be the base of Lat. *fūnus*, *fōnus*, 'burial', if this be for **fowenos*, fr. **dhow-*. See **funeral, die** (II.), & **death**. **1. a** (of plants and animals) No longer living; deprived of, having lost, life: *dead flowers*, faded, withered; Phr. *as dead as mutton, as a door-nail, as a nit*, quite dead; **b** (of inanimate objects) having never lived; not possessing, or having possessed, life and power of feeling, or of voluntary movement: *dead matter*. Hence, **2**, resembling death in any of its qualities, silence, immobility, coldness &c.: *a dead sleep*; *dead calm*; *dead weight* &c.; *dead finger*, numbed, made insensible by cold &c. **3. a** Absolute, complete: *dead certainty*; *dead level*; *dead failure*; *dead stop*; *dead heat* (in race), equality at finish; **b** sure, certain, unfailing: *a dead shot*, on the mark. **4. a** (of language) No longer spoken as ordinary medium of communication in a community; **b** (of customs &c.) no longer used or practised. **5.** Lacking vitality, liveliness, spirit, vigour; **a** (of human character) dull, lifeless, without animation; **b** (of sound) dull, heavy, not resonant, lacking a ring; **c** (of colour) dull, neutral, without brilliance or warmth; **d** (of surface of ground &c.) not fast, very slow: *a dead pitch*. **6.** (in various games, of the ball) Not in play.

dead (II.), adv., fr. prec. Thoroughly, completely, absolutely: *dead tired*; *the wind was dead against us, dead ahead*.

dead (III.), n., fr. adj. **1.** (coll.) *The dead*, those who are dead. **2.** *The dead of night*, middle of the night when all is dark and silent.

dead-alive, adj. Dispirited, monotonous; depressed, depressing.

dead-beat (I.), adj. (colloq.) Exhausted by fatigue.

dead-beat (II.), n. & adj. **a** n. Movement without recoil; watch-escapement working in this way; **b** adj., (in machinery, clockwork) moving without recoil, making a momentary stoppage without oscillation.

dead-centre, n. In crank-motion, that position in which the crank and the connecting rod are in a straight line, so that no force is exerted.

dead-drunk, n. So drunk as to be incapable of movement, speech &c.

deaden, vb. trans. [1. dédn; 2. dédn]. **dead** (I.) & **-en**. **1.** (of action on mind and feelings) To deprive of alertness, sensibility, feeling, render numb, insensible: *to deaden one's affections, taste* &c. **2.** (of action on senses) To diminish intensity, muffle: *deaden perception, a sound, pain*. **3.** (of bright surfaces) To remove, or cloud, lustre, diminish brilliance, or reflecting power: *to deaden the polish on a table* &c.

dead-eye, n. (naut.) A block with three holes, used for tightening the shrouds of a ship.

dead ground, n. Ground which is out of view or range of fire from guns &c.

deadhead, n. [1. déd-hed; 2. dédhed]. **1.** Person who attends a theatre, concert &c. with a complimentary ticket for which he pays nothing. **2.** A feeble person with no individuality, principles, courage, or energy, who contributes nothing to counsel or action.

dead heat, n. A race in which two or more competitors reach the winning-post together.

dead-house, n. A mortuary.

dead-letter, n. **1.** An undelivered, unclaimed, postal packet. **2.** A law, regulation, still unrepealed, but no longer enforced.

dead-letter office, n. Department of General Post Office to which undelivered letters are sent.

dead-lift, n. Lift, or pull, on a dead-weight; lift made with main strength.

dead-light, n. Strong metal cover or shutter over a port-hole or cabin window on board ship, to keep out water &c. in a storm.

deadliness, n. [1. dédlines; 2. dédlinis]. **deadly** & **-ness**. Quality of being deadly.

dead-lock, n. **dead** (I.) & **lock**. Complete stoppage (of negotiations &c.), standstill, state of affairs which makes progress in any direction impossible.

deadly (I.), adj. [1. dédli; 2. dédli]. **dead** (I.) & **-ly**. **1.** (lit. and fig.) Tending to cause death; fatal: *deadly poison, blow* &c.; specif., *deadly sin*, that which merits eternal damnation, unless repented of and pardoned. **2.** Implacable, virulent, inspired by hatred: *a deadly enemy, combat*. **3.** Excessive, insupportable: *deadly dullness*. Phr. (colloq.) *perfectly deadly*, highly objectionable, intolerable.

deadly (II.), adv., fr. prec. **1.** In a manner, to a degree, resembling death: *deadly pale, sick*. **2.** (colloq.) Excessively, to a high degree: *deadly dull*.

deadly nightshade, n. [1. dédli nī́tshād; 2. dédli náitʃeid]. Popular name of the belladonna plant, *Atropa Belladonna*.

dead march, n. A funeral march; solemn music for a funeral; specif. *the Dead March*, that in 'Saul', by Handel.

deadness, n. [1. dédnes; 2. dédnis]. See **dead** (I.) & **-ness**. **a** The state of being dead; **b** listlessness, lack of animation and vivacity.

dead-nettle, n. Variety of flowering herb, having leaves like those of the stinging-nettle, but devoid of a sting.

dead-point, n. Dead-centre.

dead-pull, n. Dead-lift.

dead-reckoning, n. (naut.) Calculation of a ship's position from distance run by log, and courses steered by compass, instead of by astronomical observations.

dead set, n. **1.** A dog's position in pointing to indicate the presence of game. **2. a** Direct and deliberate attack on particular person or body of persons; **b** determined attempt to carry out some action, or to achieve some desired object: *to make a dead set at a person*, (i.) to attack him directly with violence; (ii.) to attempt pertinaciously to win his confidence, become intimate with him, influence him.

dead wall, n. A blank wall with no openings of any kind.

dead-water, n. Still, motionless water; state of tide when there is least rise and fall.

dead-weight, n. Heavy, inert mass of anything.

dead-wind, n. A head wind directly against a ship's course.

deaf, adj. [1. def; 2. dɛf]. M.E. *deef, def*, O.E. *dēaf*; O.H.G. *toub*, O. Fris. *dāf*, O.S. *dōf*, O.N. *daufr*, Goth. *daubs*, 'deaf, dull, stupid'; cogn. w. Gk. *tuphlós* for **thuphlós*, 'blind; dim, obscure'; O. Ir. *dub*, 'black'; Aryan base **dhubh-*, **dhoubh-* &c. **dumb** is possibly fr. same base. **1. a** Wholly without the sense of hearing; **b** having an imperfect sense of hearing; Phrs. *deaf as a post, as an adder*, quite deaf; *to turn a deaf ear to*, refuse to listen. **2.** Inattentive to, heedless of: *deaf to all appeals, to advice* &c.

deaf-and-dumb, adj. Permanently unable either to hear or to speak, usually from birth.

deafen, vb. trans. [1. défn; 2. défn]. **deaf** & **-en.** **a** To deprive of the power of hearing, make deaf, esp. by loud noise; **b** to render a sound or musical note inaudible, or less audible; **c** to make walls, or floor, of a room impervious to sound.

deafening (I.), adj. [1. défning; 2. défniŋ], fr. Pres. Part. of prec. (of sounds) **a** Tending to deafen; **b** tending to make clear hearing difficult or impossible; hence, **c** very loud, producing great volume of sound: *deafening cheers, applause* &c.

deafening (II.), n. **deafen** & **-ing.** Material used in building to render walls and floors impervious to sound.

deafforest, vb. trans. [1. dèafórest; 2. dìæfɔ́rist], fr. **de-** & **afforest.** To disafforest.

deafly, adv. [1. défli; 2. défli]. See **deaf** & **-ly.** Without hearing, as though deaf.

deaf-mute, n. Deaf-and-dumb person.

deaf-mutism, n. Prec. & **-ism.** Condition of being a deaf-mute.

deafness, n. [1. défnes; 2. défnis]. **deaf** & **-ness.** Inability to hear.

deal (I.), vb. trans. & intrans. [1. dēl; 2. dīəl]. O.E. *dǣlan*, 'to divide, share', M.E. *dēlen*, 'deal, take part', fr. Gmc. **dail-jan*, fr. **dail-*, 'part'; cp. O.H.G. *teilan*, O. Fris. *dēla*, Goth. *dailjan*. See further under **dole** (I.). **A.** trans. **1.** To give, distribute, deliver: esp. *to deal a blow*, to strike a blow; *to deal a blow at*, a to strike, attempt to strike (a person); **b** to inflict a moral injury, wound, grieve; **c** to destroy (hopes &c.). **2.** Specif., *to deal cards*, to distribute proper number to each player. **B.** intrans. **1.** *To deal with* (*at*), patronize a tradesman, give one's custom to, buy from him: *to deal with, at, a particular shop.* **2.** *To deal in*, traffic; make a business of buying and selling certain goods: *to deal in diamonds, hay* &c. **3.** *To deal with*, **a** (of affairs) to take in hand, take measures regarding, act in a certain way; settle, arrange, manage: *to deal with a matter, with an emergency*; **b** (of persons) to conduct oneself, behave towards: *to deal fairly with*; *to deal effectively with a burglar*; **c** to discuss, argue about, treat: *to deal with a subject.* **4.** Specif., to distribute cards in a game: *it is your turn to deal.*

deal (II.), n. O.E. *dǣl*, 'part', fr. **dāli-*; M.E. *dēle*. See **dole** & **deal** (I.). A quantity, amount (only in certain phrases): *there's a deal of sense in what you say*; *a good deal, a great deal.*

deal (III.), n., fr. **deal** (I.). **1.** A business transaction, esp. one in which concessions are made on both sides; a bargain: *a fair, square deal.* Phr. *to do a deal with*, come to terms with, make a compromise. **2.** Act of distributing cards to players: *whose deal is it?*; *my deal* &c.

deal (IV.), n. & adj., fr. L.G. *dēle*, 'board'; cp. O.H.G. *tille*, Mod. Germ. *tille*; cogn. w. O.E. *þille*, 'structure of planks, flooring'. See **thill.** **1.** n. **a** A plank of fir wood; (technically) one at least 7 in. broad, and not more than 3 in. thick; hence, **b** fir or pine timber. **2.** adj. Made of deal or fir: *a deal table.*

dealer, n. [1. déler; 2. dílə]. See **deal** (I.) & **-er.** **a** One who deals, or traffics, in merchandise; **b** *the dealer*, player whose turn it is to distribute the cards.

dealing, n. [1. déling; 2. díliŋ]. See **deal** (I.) & **-ing.** **a** Conduct, behaviour, towards others: *honest, crooked, dealing*; **b** (often in pl.) intercourse, commerce, transactions with others: *to have (no) dealings with.*

dealt, vb. [1. delt; 2. dɛlt]. Pret. & P.P. of **deal** (I.).

deambulation, n. [1. dèambūláshun; 2. dìæmbjuléiʃən]. Lat. *deambulātiōn-(em)*, 'a walk'. See **de-** & **ambulatory, amble.** A walk, a strolling about.

deambulatory, adj. [1. deámbūlātori; 2. díæmbjuléitəri]. See prec. Wandering from place to place.

dean (I.), n. [1. dēn; 2. dīn]. M.E. *dēne*, fr. O. Fr. *deien*, fr. L. Lat. *decānus*, 'a superior set over ten (monks)', prob. fr. *decem*, 'ten'. See **decimal, ten,** & cp. **doyen.** **1.** (eccles.) The head of the chapter of a cathedral, who is also responsible for the upkeep of the fabric, for the services, and generally for the management of business connected with the cathedral. *Rural dean*, clergyman appointed by a bishop to act, under an archdeacon, as the officer responsible for the business of a division (group of parishes) of the diocese. **2.** (in most universities) The head of a faculty. **3.** (at Oxford) A fellow of a college with disciplinary duties over the undergraduates. **4.** *Dean of Arches*, chief judge of the Ecclesiastical Court of Arches, in province of Canterbury.

dean (II.), n. A valley. See **dene** (I.).

deanery, n. [1. déneri; 2. dínəri]. See **dean** (I.) & **-ery.** **a** The office of a dean; **b** the official residence of a dean; **c** that division of a diocese under the jurisdiction of a rural dean. Also *rural deanery.*

deanship, n. [1. dénship; 2. dínʃip], fr. **dean** (I.) & **-ship.** The office of a dean.

dear (I.), adj. [1. dēr; 2. diə]. O.E. *dēore, dȳre*, 'precious, beloved'; M.E. *dēre*, O.H.G. *tiuri*, O. Fris. *diore*, O.S. *diuri*, O.N. *dȳrr*. Kluge suggests connexion w. M.H.G. *dauern*, 'to last', fr. **dūrōn*, a Lat. loan-word, fr. *dūrāre*, 'to hold out, endure'. See this word under **durable.** **1. a** Precious, beloved, engaging the affections: *his dear mother*; *this dear land*; Phr. *for dear life*, as though one's life were in danger; **b** possessing engaging qualities, inspiring affection, charming, attractive: *he is a dear fellow*; *a dear little thing*; **c** as a polite form of address in letters: *Dear Sir, Dear Mrs. Tomkins* &c. **2. a** Costing much money, sold at a high price: *bread is dear this winter*; *too dear for me*, more than I can afford, or want to pay; **b** (of objects) sold at a price in excess of value: *furs are very dear in this shop*; **c** (of those demanding prices) *a dear shop*, one where excessive prices are charged; **d** (of prices) too high, excessive in relation to value of goods: *a pound is very dear for a pipe.*

dear (II.), n., fr. prec. **a** A dear, beloved person; sweetheart: *a shepherd and his dear*; **b** an affectionate mode of address; **c** a charming, delightful, amiable person: *isn't he a dear?*

dear (III.), adv., fr. **dear** (I.). At a high price, at too high a price: *to buy cheap and sell dear.* Phr. (fig.) *to pay dear for one's experience, sins, errors* &c.

dear (IV.), interj., fr. **dear** (I.). In the Phrs. *Oh, dear!, dear me!*, expressing sorrow, regret, impatience, wonder, contempt.

dearly, adv. [1. dérli; 2. díəli], fr. **dear** (I.) & **-ly.** **a** With much affection, fondly: *to love one's children dearly*; **b** at a high price, expensively; (esp. fig.) *experience has been dearly bought.*

dearness, n. [1. dérnes; 2. díənis], fr. **dear** (I.) & **-ness.** State of being dear, esp. in price.

dearth, n. [1. dërth; 2. dʌþ]. M.E. *derthe*; cp. O.H.G. *tiurida*, 'value, honour'; O.S. *diuritha*, 'value'; O.N. *dȳrð*. Not found in O.E., but formed later on anal. of *warm-th* &c. See **dear** (I.) & **-th.** *Dearth* orig. meant 'dearness in price'. Scarcity, want, lack; esp. *dearth of food*; *in time of dearth*, of famine.

deary, dearie, n. [1. déri; 2. díəri]. See **dear** (I.) & **-y.** (colloq., usually as vocative) Dear one, beloved.

death, n. [1. deth; 2. dɛþ]. O.E. *dēaþ*, M.E. *deað, dēth*, O.H.G. *tod*, O. Fris. *dāth*, O.N. *dauþi*, Goth. *dauþus*, fr. Gmc. stem **daw-*. See **dead** (I.) & **die** (II.). **1. a** The complete and permanent cessation of all vital functions in a living creature, the end of life; Phrs. *civil death*, deprivation of civil rights; *to put to death*, to kill, to have killed; *at death's door*, in danger of death; *in at the death* (of a fox or other hunted animal); (fig.) present at the last of a series of events; *tired, bored, sick* &c. *to death*, to extremity; **b** (fig., applied to non-material things) destruction, termination, sweeping away: *the death of one's hopes.* **2.** The state of being dead: *to lie still in death*; *united in death*; *in death they were not divided.* Phrs. *pale, silent, as death*; *worse than death*, very bad; *to hang on like grim death.* **3.** The cause of death: *rashness will be his death*; specif., a plague, pestilence; *Black Death*, a plague of 14th cent. Phrs. *will be the death of*, (i.) cause to die; (ii.) (fig.) afflict painfully, cause grief to; *to catch one's death* (*of cold*). **4.** Manner of dying: *to die a hero's death.* **5.** Period of date at which a person dies, taken as a chronological landmark: *the estates passed to the son on his father's death*; *most of Horace Walpole's letters were not published till long after his death.* **6.** Allegorical pictorial representation of a personification of death: *Dance of Death.*

death-adder, n. A very poisonous snake of Australia with a spined tail.

death-agony, n. The last agony or struggle before death takes place.

deathbed, n. [1. déthbed; 2. déþbed]. The bed in which a person dies; close of life: *on one's deathbed*, dying.

deathbell, n. [1. déthbel; 2. déþbɛl]. A bell rung or tolled to announce a death; the passing bell.

deathblow, n. [1. déthblō; 2. déþblou]. **a** Stroke, blow, which causes death; **b** moral shock having fatal results; **c** an action or event which destroys, sweeps away: *the deathblow to one's hopes.*

death-duty, n. Tax paid by a man's heirs on the property which he leaves at his death; a general term for the various duties so levied.

deathless, adj. [1. déthles; 2. déþlis]. See **death** & **-less.** (lit. and fig.) Not liable to die, immortal: *deathless fame.*

deathlessly, adv. Prec. & **-ly.** In an immortal manner.

deathlessness, n. See prec. & **-ness.** The quality of being immortal.

deathlike, adj. [1. déthlīk; 2. déþlaik]. **death** & **-like.** Resembling death.

deathly, adj. & adv. [1. déthli; 2. déþli], fr. **death** & **-ly.** **a** adj. Resembling death; **b** adv., in a manner resembling death.

death-mask, n. Cast in clay of a person's face taken immediately after death.

death-rate, n. The percentage of deaths among the population of a certain place during a stated period.

death-rattle, n. Sound heard in the throat of a dying person.

death's-head, n. **1. a** A human skull; **b** a model or picture of this. **2.** A large kind of hawk-moth, *Acherontia atropos*, with markings resembling a skull on its thorax.

death-trap, n. Something liable to cause death, a dangerous object or circumstance.

death-warrant, n. **a** Official document authorizing an execution; **b** (fig.) pronouncement, action, or event which destroys prospect of life or happiness.

death-watch, n. A small beetle, *Anobium*, which burrows into and destroys the timber of a house or room, and makes a ticking sound, popularly supposed to portend a death.

débâcle, n. [1. dābáhkl; 2. dēbákl]. Fr. n., fr. **de-** & *bâcler*, 'to bar, close up'; Low Lat. *baculāre*, fr. *baculum*, 'a stick, staff'; see **bacillus. 1. a** The breaking up of ice in a river; **b** (geol.) a violent flood, carrying with it masses of rock &c. **2.** (fig.) A sudden, overwhelming disaster; a reverse, downfall.

debar, vb. trans. [1. debár; 2. dibá]. **de-** & **bar (II.).** To prevent from enjoying; deprive of right, or privilege, to do something, or go somewhere: *to debar a person from voting, accepting an invitation, entering a house* &c.

debark, vb. intrans. & trans. [1. debárk; 2. dibák]. See **de-** & **bark (V.).** Cp. **disembark. a** intrans. To land from a ship, go ashore; **b** trans., to put (persons or things) ashore from a ship.

debarkation, n. [1. dèbarkáshun; 2. dìbākéiʃən], fr. prec. & **-ation.** Act or process of landing, or being landed, from a ship.

debarkment, n. [1. debárkment; 2. dibákmənt], fr. **debark** & **-ment.** Debarkation.

debase, vb. trans. [1. debás; 2. dibéis]. See **de-** & **abase. a** To lower the character of, detract from dignity or moral worth of, render base; **b** to lower the value of; specif., *to debase the coinage.*

debased, adj. [1. debást; 2. dibéist], fr. P.P. of prec. **a** Morally or physically base, degraded, degenerate; **b** lowered in value: *debased coinage*; **c** (her.) inverted, reversed.

debasement, n. [1. debásment; 2. dibéismənt], fr. **debase** & **-ment.** Act or process of debasing; the state of being debased.

debasing, adj. [1. debásing; 2. dibéisiŋ], fr. Pres. Part. of **debase.** Degrading, corrupting, esp. in moral sense.

debatable, adj. [1. debátabl; 2. dibéitəbl]. See next word & **-able. a** That can be debated, open to question; **b** (lit. and fig.) disputed, being contended for: *debatable ground.*

debate (I.), vb. trans. & intrans. [1. debát; 2. dibéit]. M.E. *debāten*, O. Fr. *debatre*, fr. **de-** & L. Lat. *batuere*, 'to strike, beat'. See **battle, batter (I.). A.** trans. **1.** To contest in words, argue, discuss thoroughly, thrash out: *to debate a question, a point.* **2.** To reflect on, consider, ponder: *to debate a matter in one's mind.* **B.** intrans. **a** To engage in discussion and argument, debate: *they were still debating when the house rose*; **b** to be engaged in, think over in, reflection: *I am just debating whether to go or stay.* Phr. *to debate with oneself.*

debate (II.), n., fr. prec. **1. a** Discussion of a measure, bill, subject raised in Parliament or other legislative assembly or at a public meeting: *rules of debate*: *to open the debate*; **b** (pl., *the debates*) printed official report of these in parliament. **2.** Controversy, discussion, argument: *to hold debate with oneself.*

debater, n. [1. debáter; 2. dibéitə]. **debate (I.)** & **-er.** One who debates; controversialist, disputant: *a skilful debater.*

debating society, n. [1. debáting sosíeti; 2. dibéitiŋ səsáiəti]. Society for holding debates on subjects of interest and controversy, conducted on parliamentary principles for practice in public speaking &c.

debauch (I.), vb. trans. [1. debáwch; 2. dibɔ́tʃ]. Earlier *debosch* &c., fr. O. Fr. *débaucher*, 'to entice from work'. The second element is doubtful, but cp. Fr. *ébauche*, 'rough sketch, something roughed out'; perh. fr. Gmc. *balk-*, 'block of timber' (see **balk (I.)**); O. Fr. *bauche*, 'workshop' (timber-yard ?). In this case *desbaucher* wd. mean orig. 'to dis-balk', or, as Skeat suggests, 'to take away framework of a building before it is finished'. An earlier suggestion was that the vb. meant orig. 'to entice away from the workshop'. Meyer-Lübke denies connexion between *bauche* & Gmc. *balko*. **a** To lead astray, seduce from right conduct or sound morals; to corrupt; **b** specif., to lead a woman astray, seduce her.

debauch (II.), n., fr. prec. (with indef. art.) Specific instance of licentious, immoral conduct; a gross example of sensual indulgence; a drinking bout.

debauched, adj. [1. debáwcht; 2. dibɔ́tʃt], fr. P.P. of **debauch (I.).** Dissipated, given to intemperance or sensual indulgence.

debauchee, n. [1. dèbawshḗ; 2. dèbɔʃí]. Fr. *débauché*, P.P. See **debauch** & **-ee.** Debauched, dissipated man.

debauchery, n. [1. debáwcheri; 2. dibɔ́tʃəri]. See **debauch** & **-ery.** Intemperance, sensual indulgence, dissipation.

debenture, n. [1. debénchur; 2. dibéntʃə]. Fr., fr. Lat. *debentur*, 'these (sums) are owing', the 3rd pers. pl. of *debēri*, 'to be owing', as first word of the certificate. See **debt. 1.** Certificate of stock held, money invested in a trading company &c., on condition of payment of interest at a guaranteed rate, such interest being a first charge on its property and assets. **2.** (orig. sense) Custom-house certificate entitling an importer of goods to the repayment of all or part of the import-duty when the goods are re-exported.

debentured, adj. [1. debénchurd; 2. dibéntʃəd], fr. prec. & **-ed.** (of duty-paid goods) Entitling the owner to repayment of import-duty on re-exportation.

debile, adj. [1. débīl; 2. díbail], fr. Lat. *dēbilis*, 'weak, without strength', fr. **de-**, 'from, decline from', & **bil-*, fr. Aryan base **bel-*; cogn. w. Scrt. *bálam*, 'strength, force'; *bālīyān*, compar. *báliṣṭhaš*, 'stronger, strongest'; Gk. compar. & superl. *beltiōn, béltistos*, 'better, best'; O. Slav. *boliš*, Russ. *bolshii*, 'greater'; see **Bolshevik.** (archaic) Weak, infirm.

debilitate, vb. trans. [1. debílitāt; 2. dibíliteit], fr. Lat. *dēbilitāt-(um)*, P.P. of *dēbilitāre*, 'to maim, weaken'. See prec. To render weak, feeble, infirm.

debilitating, adj. [1. debílitāting; 2. dibíliteitiŋ], fr. Pres. Part. of prec. Tending to debilitate, having a weakening, enervating effect: *a debilitating climate* &c.

debilitation, n. [1. debilitáshun; 2. dibìlitéiʃən]. See **debility** & **-ation.** The process of making feeble, weakening; the state of being enfeebled.

debility, n. [1. debíliti; 2. dibíliti]. See **debile** & **-ty.** Weakness, lack of power; feebleness of health.

debit (I.), n. [1. débit; 2. débit]. Lat. *debit-(um)*, fr. P.P. type of *debēre*. See **debt. a** Entry in an account recording a sum of money owing; contrasted with *credit*; **b** that side of an account on which such entries are made. Also *debit-side.*

debit (II.), vb. trans., fr. prec. To enter a sum as owed on a person's account: *to debit a person, debit his account, with five pounds*; to subtract such a sum from that standing to his credit.

debonair, adj. [1. dèbonár; 2. dèbənéə], fr. O. Fr. *de bonne aire*, 'of a gentle, pleasing disposition'. (of persons and manners) Genial, affable, easy, sprightly; (of moods) cheerful, happy, jocund, blithe.

debonairly, adv. Prec. & **-ly.** In a debonair manner.

debouch, vb. intrans. [1. debóuch, deboosh; 2. dibáutʃ, dibúʃ], fr. Fr. *déboucher*, 'open out, pour out', fr. **de-** & *bouche*, 'mouth', fr. Lat. *bucca*, 'the cheek, especially when puffed out in eating, speaking &c.'; see **buccal. a** (of rivers and streams) To flow out, emerge into an open or wider space (at the mouth): *a stream debouches into a larger river, and this into the sea*; **b** (of troops) to march out from narrow space, valley &c. into open ground.

debouchment, n. [1. debóuchment, debooshment; 2. dibáutʃmənt, dibúʃmənt]. Prec. & **-ment. a** Process of debouching; **b** mouth of a river; place where troops debouch.

débris, n. [1. dábrē; 2. déibrī]. Fr. (pl.), 'scattered, broken remains of something which has been destroyed', fr. O. Fr. *débriser*, 'to break down, shatter', possibly fr. a Celt. **bris-*; cp. O. Ir. *brissim*, 'I break', cogn. w. O.E. *berstan*, 'to burst, break'. See **burst. a** A collection of scattered, broken remains; fragments of something which has been destroyed; rubbish fallen from a ruined building &c.; **b** specif. (geol.) accumulation of broken fragments of rock &c. at the base of a mountain or cliff.

debruised, adj. [1. debróozd; 2. dibrúzd]. O. Fr. *débruisier*, 'to shatter'. **de-** & **bruise.** (her.) A charge crossed by an ordinary, usually by a bend.

debt, n. [1. det; 2. det]. M.E. *dette*, O. Fr. *dette*, fr. Lat. *dēbitum*, 'what is due, debt, obligation', fr. P.P. type of *dēbēre*, 'to owe, to be under obligations', fr. **dē-habēre*. See **de-** & **habit.** Something, material or non-material, owed, and bound to be paid, to another, or others; liability, obligation: *debt of ten pounds*; *debt of gratitude.* Phrs. *debt of honour*, one, as a sum lost in gambling, not recoverable by law; *debt of Nature*, death; *to pay one's debt to Nature*, to die; *to be in a person's debt*, owe him something; *a bad debt*, one which one will never recover.

debtor, n. [1. déter; 2. détə]. Prec. & **-or. 1.** One who is under material or moral obligations to another; specif., one who owes money. Contrasted with *creditor.* **2.** (book-keeping) Abbreviation *Dr.*, left or debit side of an account.

début, n. [1. dābū; 2. deby]. Fr., 'first stroke in certain games; first steps in a career, beginning', perh. fr. *but*, 'aim, goal' &c. See **butt (III.).** A person's first appearance in society, or as a performer in public: *to make one's début.*

débutant(e), n. [1. dābūtahn(t); 2. debytã(t)]. Fr., fr. prec. One, especially a woman, who makes a first appearance in society, or as a performer in public; specif., a girl about to be, or having recently been, presented at Court.

dec-, deca-, pref., fr. Gk. *déka*, 'ten'. Cogn. w. Scrt. *dáša*, Lat. *decem*, Lith. *dẽszimt*, O. Slav. *desętĭ*, Goth. *taihun*, O.E. *tīen* &c.; Aryan base **dekm̥*. See **ten, decimal.** (in compounds) Ten, tenfold.

decachord, n. [1. dékakord; 2. dékəkɔd]. Gk. *dekákhordos*, 'ten-stringed'. Prec. & **chord.** Ancient Greek harp with ten strings.

decadal, adj. [1. dékadl; 2. dékədl]. Next word & **-al.** Having to do with a decade; consisting of, arranged in, groups of ten.

decade, n. [1. dékad, dekád; 2. dékæd, dikéid], also **decad.** Fr., 'collection of ten', fr. Gk. *dékad-*, '10'. See **deca-** & **-ade. a** A group or series of ten things; **b** specif., period of ten years.

decadence, decadency, n. [1. dékadens(i); 2. dékədəns(i)]. Fr., fr. Low Lat. *decadentia*, 'falling down'. See **de-** & **cadence** & **-ency.** (only of non-material process) A falling to a lower level, deterioration; process of sinking to lower ideals of morality, art &c.; state of possessing such lower ideals.

decadent, adj. & n. [1. dékadent; 2. dékədənt]. See prec. & **-ent. 1.** adj. In a state or process of decadence; deteriorating. **2.** n. One belonging to, reflecting, the characteristics of a period of decadence.

decadently, adv. Prec. & **-ly.** In a decadent manner.

decagon, n. [1. dékagon; 2. dékəgən], fr. Med. Lat. *decagōnum*. See **deca-** & **-gon.** (geom.) A ten-sided plane figure.

decagonal, adj. [1. dekágonal; 2. dekǽgənl], fr. prec. & **-al.** Of a decagon; having ten sides.

decagram(me), n. [1. dékagràm; 2. dékəgræm]. **deca-** & **gramme.** A weight of ten grammes.

decalcification, n. [1. dèkalsifikā́shun; 2. dìkælsifikéiʃən]. **de- & calcification.** Process of removing lime from substances.

decalcify, vb. trans. [1. dēkálsifī; 2. dīkǽlsifai]. See **de- & calcify.** To remove lime from (esp. *bones*).

decalitre, n. [1. dékalēter; 2. dékəlītə]. **deca- & litre.** A measure of capacity, equal to ten litres.

decalogue, n. [1. dékalog; 2. dékəlɔg], fr. Gk. *dekálogos*, 'ten words, precepts'. See **deca- & logos.** The Ten Commandments.

Decameronic, adj. [1. dekàmerónik; 2. dəkæ̀mərɔ́nik], fr. Ital. *Decamerone*, title of work by Boccaccio, 1353, comprising 100 tales supposed to be told during 10 days of the plague in Florence, fr. Gk. *déka*, 'ten', see **deca-**, & *hḗmera*, 'day', see **ephemera.** Resembling, like the tales of, Boccaccio's 'Decameron'.

decametre, n. [1. dékamēter; 2. dékəmītə]. See **deca- & metre.** Measure of length, equal to 10 metres.

decamp, vb. intrans. [1. dekámp; 2. dikǽmp], fr. Fr. *décamper*, 'to raise camp; to run away'; **de- & camp. 1.** To break camp, leave a camping-ground. **2.** To depart with swiftness and secrecy; run away, clear out.

decampment, n. [1. dekámpment; 2. dikǽmpmənt]. Prec. & **-ment.** The act or process of decamping.

decanal, adj. [1. dekā́nal; 2. dikéinəl], fr. Lat. *decān-(us)*, 'dean', & **-al.** See **dean (I.).** Connected with, belonging to, a dean, or the office of dean.

decandrous, adj. [1. dekándrus; 2. dikǽndrəs], fr. **deca-,** & Gk. *andr-(ós)*, genit. of *anḗr*, 'a man', & **-ous.** See **androgynous.** (bot.) Having ten stamens.

decangular, adj. [1. dekánggūlar; 2. dekǽŋgjulə]. **deca- & angular.** (geom.) Having ten angles, as a decagon.

decani, n. [1. dekā́nī; 2. dikéinai]. Genit. of Lat. *decānus*, 'dean'; see **dean (I.). a** Lit., 'of the dean'; applied to south side of choir, where, in a cathedral, the dean sits; also to the singers who sit there; **b** (mus. direction) to be sung by the *decani*, in contrast to *cantoris*.

decant, vb. trans. [1. dekánt; 2. dikǽnt], fr. Fr. *décanter*, fr. **de-** & Lat. *cantharus*, 'a large drinking-vessel', fr. Gk. *kántharos*, 'a beetle', and, fr. some resemblance in shape, 'a two-handled cup'; etymol. dubious. To pour liquid gently from one vessel to another without disturbing the sediment; esp. wine from the bottle into a decanter.

decantation, n. [1. dèkantā́shun; 2. dìkæntéiʃən], fr. prec. & **-ation.** The process of decanting or being decanted.

decanter, n. [1. dekánter; 2. dikǽntə]. **decant & -er.** A vessel into which liquid is decanted; specif., an ornamented glass bottle or flagon, with a slender neck, into which wine is decanted for use at table.

decaphyllous, adj. [1. dèkafílus; 2. dèkəfíləs]. See **deca- & phyllo- & -ous.** (bot.) Having ten leaves; applied to the floral envelope, or perianth of flowers.

decapitate, vb. trans. [1. dekápitāt; 2. dikǽpiteit], fr. Low Lat. *dēcapitāt-(um)*, P.P. type of *dēcapitāre*, 'to cut off the head', fr. **de-** & *capit-*, stem of *caput*, 'head'. See **capital.** To cut off the head, to behead.

decapitation, n. [1. dekàpitā́shun; 2. dikæ̀pitéiʃən]. Prec. & **-ion.** The act or process of beheading or being beheaded.

decapod, n. & adj. [1. dékapod; 2. dékəpɔd], fr. **deca- & -pod.** (zool.) **1.** n. A member of an order (*Decapoda*) of crustaceans with five pairs of legs on the thorax, including the lobsters, shrimps &c. **2.** adj. Having five pairs of legs, belonging to the above order.

decapodal, decapodous, adj. [1. dekápodal, -us; 2. dikǽpədəl, -əs]. Prec. & **-al & -ous.** Having ten feet and five pairs of legs.

decarbonate, vb. trans. [1. dēkárbonāt; 2. dīkā́bəneit]. See **de- & carbonate.** To remove carbon dioxide from.

decarbonization, n. [1. dēkàrbonīzā́shun; 2. dīkā̀bənaizéiʃən], fr. next word & **-ation.** The process of decarbonizing, or of being decarbonized.

decarbonize, vb. trans. [1. dēkárbonīz; 2. dīkā́bənaiz]. See **de- & carbonize.** To deprive of carbon or carbonic acid.

decastich, n. [1. dékastik; 2. dékəstik]. See **deca- &** *stíkhos*, 'line of verse', see **stichic.** A poem of ten lines.

decastyle, n. [1. dékastīl; 2. dékəstail], fr. **deca- &** Gk. *stûlos*, 'a pillar'. See **style (II.).** (archit.) A portico or colonnade with ten columns.

decasyllabic, adj. & n. [1. dèkasilábik; 2. dèkəsilǽbik]. See **deca- & syllabic. 1.** adj. Having ten syllables; with lines of ten syllables. **2.** n. A verse-line of ten syllables.

decasyllable, n. [1. dèkasílabl; 2. dèkəsíləbl]. See **deca- & syllable.** A line of ten syllables.

decatholicize, vb. trans. [1. dèkathólisīz; 2. dìkəþɔ́lisaiz]. **de- & catholicize.** To deprive of its Catholic nature.

decay (I.), vb. intrans. [1. dekā́; 2. dikéi], fr. O. Fr. *decair*, 'to fall', fr. Low Lat. *dēcadere*, fr. **de-** & Lat. *cadere*, 'to fall'. See **cadence. 1.** intrans. **a** To become decomposed, rot; fall to pieces, disintegrate, through age &c.; **b** (of non-material things) to deteriorate, gradually lose good qualities, vigour, power &c. **2.** Often in P.P. as adj., rotten; declined, ruined: *decayed teeth*; *a decayed family.*

decay (II.), n., fr. prec. The state or process of decaying; **a** (of material process) decomposition, rot, disintegration: *the decay of the teeth*; **b** (of non-material things) decline, deterioration, loss of power, vigour, prosperity &c.: *decay of a state, family* &c.; *to be in, fall into, decay.*

decease (I.), n. [1. disḗs; 2. disís]. O. Fr. *deces*, fr. Lat. *dēcessus*, 'a departure, going away; retirement; death', fr. P.P. of *dēcēdere*, 'to depart'. See **de- & cease, cede.** (esp. legal) Death, departure from life.

decease (II.), vb. intrans., fr. prec. To die.

deceased, adj. & n. [1. desḗst; 2. disíst]. P.P. of prec. **a** adj. Dead, having ceased to live; **b** n., (esp. in legal use) *the deceased*, the dead person.

deceit, n. [1. desḗt; 2. disít]. O. Fr. *deceite*, P.P. of *deceveir*. See **deceive. a** The act of deceiving, causing a person to believe what is not true, misrepresentation of facts; **b** the quality of being deceitful.

deceitful, adj. [1. desḗtfool; 2. disítfəl], fr. prec. & **-ful. a** (of persons) Given to deceiving; treacherous; **b** (of actions, words &c.) uttered with the intention of deceiving, giving a false impression, deliberately misleading; **c** (of appearances) misleading, deceptive, giving false impression.

deceitfully, adv. Prec. & **-ly.** In a deceitful manner.

deceitfulness, n. See prec. & **-ness.** The quality of being deceitful; duplicity.

deceivable, adj. [1. desḗvabl; 2. disívəbl], fr. next word & **-able.** Able to be, liable to be, deceived.

deceive, vb. trans. & intrans. [1. desḗv; 2. disív]. O. Fr. *deceveir*, fr. Lat. *dēcipere*, 'to beguile, deceive, elude', fr. **de- &** *capere*, 'take'. See **de- & captive. 1.** trans. To cause to believe what is not true, by words, actions &c., to mislead wilfully; delude, give a false impression to: *to be deceived by appearances.* (also reflex.) To persuade oneself of something which is not true, to be under a delusion. **2.** intrans. To use or practise deceit: *words meant to deceive.*

decelerate, vb. trans. & intrans. [1. dēsélerāt; 2. dīséləreit]. See **de- & accelerate. 1.** trans. To decrease the speed or velocity of, as a machine, engine &c. **2.** intrans. To move at less speed, with less velocity.

deceleration, n. [1. dèselerā́shun; 2. dìseləréiʃən]. Prec. & **-ion. a** Act, process, of decelerating; **b** state of being decelerated.

December, n. [1. desémber; 2. disémbə]. **Lat.** *December*, 'the tenth month', of the old Roman year, fr. *decem* (see **deca- & ten**). The origin of the ending *-ber* is obscure. The twelfth and last month of the year.

decemvir, n. [1. desémvēr; 2. disémviə], fr. Lat. *decemviri*, 'a body or commission of ten men'. See **deca- & virile.** A member of a council, ruling body, of ten, esp. of that appointed in Rome in 451 B.C. to draw up a code of laws.

decemviral, adj. [1. desémviral; 2. disémvirəl]. Prec. & **-al.** Having to do with a decemvir.

decemvirate, n. [1. desémvirāt; 2. disémvireit]. **decemvir & -ate. a** Office of the decemvirs; **b** a body of ten in authority.

decency, n. [1. dḗsensi; 2. dísənsi]. **Fr.** *décence*, fr. Lat. *decentia*, 'decency'. **See decent & -cy. a** The quality of being decent, propriety, what is seemly and becoming: *things performed in decency and order*; **b** freedom from immodesty; decorum: *an offence against, breach of, decency*; **c** (colloq.) kindness, generosity, of nature, and in manner: *he had not the decency to say 'Thank you'.*

decennary, n. [1. dēsénari; 2. dīsénəri], fr. Lat. *decenn-(is)*, 'of ten years', fr. *decem*, 'ten', & *annus*, 'year'. See **deca-, ten, annual, & -ary.** A period of ten years.

decenniad, n. [1. dēséniad; 2. dīséniæd], as prec. & **-ad.** Period of ten years, decennium.

decennial, adj. [1. dēsénial; 2. dīséniəl]. Lat. *decenni-*, as prec., & **-al.** Consisting of, happening every, ten years.

decennially, adv. Prec. & **-ly.** Every ten years.

decennium, n. [1. dēsénium; 2. dīséniəm]. Lat. See prec. words. Decenniad.

decent, adj. [1. dḗsent; 2. dísənt], fr. Lat. *decent-(em)*, 'becoming, seemly' &c., Pres. Part. of impers. *dec-et*, 'it is seemly, is fitting'. Cp. Lat. *decus*, 'honour, ornament' (see **decorate, decorous**); Scrt. *daśasyáti*, 'he is gracious'; *dákšati*, 'is apt, proper, pleasing'; *dakšaš*, 'apt, clever'. The Aryan base is **dek̑-*, **dok̑-*, 'to seem good' &c. See **docile & dexter. 1.** Suitable, fitting, seemly, becoming; proper, well adapted to an occasion or situation: *to live in decent conditions, surroundings*; *to go to church in decent clothes.* **2.** Modest, delicate, chaste; exhibiting an exact propriety in speech, thought, conduct: *decent in conversation*; *stories which were not always decent.* **3.** (colloq.) Of very wide application and often vague significance; **a** (of persons) exhibiting kindness, good nature, generosity &c.; **b** (of things) satisfactory, pleasant, attractive; adequate, reaching a reasonable standard of excellence: *a very decent fellow*; *quite a decent house, cigar, sermon*; *to make a pretty decent headmaster.*

decently, adv. Prec. & **-ly. a** In a decent manner; becomingly, suitably: *decently housed, clothed*; *to behave decently*; **b** (colloq.) kindly, generously, handsomely: *to treat a man decently*; *to speak very decently about a man's services* &c.

decentralization, n. [1. dēsèntralīzā́shun; 2. dīsèntrəlaizéiʃən]. See next word & **-ation. a** Act of decentralizing; **b** state of being decentralized.

decentralize, vb. trans. [1. dēséntralīz; 2. dīséntrəlaiz]. **de- & centralize.** To remove (government, power, organization) from one centre, or point of concentration, to divide and distribute it among other or local centres of administration.

deception, n. [1. desépshun; 2. disépʃən], fr. Lat. *dēceptiōn-(em)*, fr. P.P. type *dēcept-(um)*, of *dēcipere*, 'to deceive'. See **deceive. 1. a** The act of deceiving: *to practise deception*; *an adept at the deception of the public*; **b** state of being deceived: *public deception was complete.* **2.** An action, process, or phenomenon which deceives the intelligence or the senses, whether designed to do so or not; either an illusion or a fraud: *a clever deception.*

deceptive, adj. [1. deséptiv; 2. diséptiv]. See prec. & **-ive**. Liable, designed to deceive, or mislead; creating a false impression.

deceptively, adv. Prec. & **-ly**. In a deceptive, misleading manner.

deceptiveness, n. See prec. & **-ness**. The quality of being deceptive.

dechristianization, n. [1. dēkrischanīzáshun; 2. dīkristʃənaizéiʃən]. See next word & **-ation**. Depriving, being deprived, of Christianity.

dechristianize, vb. trans. [1. dēkrischanīz; 2. dīkristʃənaiz]. **de-** & **Christianize**. To deprive of Christianity.

deci-, pref., fr. *deci-*, shortened fr. Lat. *decimus*, 'tenth', fr. Lat. *decem*, 'ten' (see **deca-**), used in the metric system to denote $\frac{1}{10}$ of the given unit, e.g. *decigramme, decimetre* &c.

decidable, adj. [1. desídabl; 2. disáidəbl]. Next word & **-able**. Capable of being decided.

decide, vb. trans. & intrans. [1. desíd; 2. disáid], fr. O. Fr. *decider*, fr. Lat. *dēcīdere*, 'to cut off'; fig., 'to decide, determine, settle'; fr. **dē-* (see **de-**) & *caedere*, 'to cut, hew; to strike, hit; to strike down, kill'. See this base under **cement**; the chain of meaning is 'to cut, to divide, to put on one side, compare one with another, distinguish, discriminate, pass a judgement'. Cp. Mod. Germ. *entscheiden*, 'to decide', & O.E. *ge-scād*, 'separation, distinction, discrimination', connected w. *scādan*, 'divide, separate' &c. See **shed (II.)**. **A.** trans. **1. a** To make up one's mind about, judge between possibilities: *to decide a point in one's own mind*; *decide what to do, how to do it*; **b** specif. (law) to come to a conclusion on a point of fact and give a verdict: *a question for the jury to decide*. **2. a** To bring a contest, dispute, to an end, by using influence, giving help to, supporting one side, and thus causing it to win: *to decide a battle by sending in fresh troops*; **b** to cause a discussion, argument, point at issue, to be settled in a particular way: *the case was decided in favour of the plaintiff*. **B.** intrans. **a** To make up one's mind, come to a conclusion: *to decide to sell one's house*; *to decide on a course of action*; **b** to form a judgement, determine, make a choice in favour of, express a preference for, one thing or course of action as against another: *to decide between two alternatives*; *to decide, to have decided, in favour of, against, the plaintiff*.

decided, adj. [1. desíded; 2. disáidid], fr. P.P. of prec. **1.** Unhesitating, expressing a definite opinion; determined, not vacillating: **a** (of things) *to give a decided answer*; *a man of decided opinions*; **b** (of persons &c.) *a decided and obstinate character*. **2.** Distinct, clearly marked, unambiguous, definite: *a decided difference*.

decidedly, adv. Prec. & **-ly**. **a** Firmly, definitely, without hesitation: *to speak, answer, decidedly*; **b** certainly, unquestionably: *decidedly better*.

deciduous, adj. [1. desídūus; 2. disídjuəs], fr. Lat. *dēciduus*, 'falling down, deciduous', fr. *dēcid-(ere)*, 'to fall off, down', fr. **dē-cadere*, & **-ous**. See **de-** & **cadence**. (of trees and shrubs) Shedding their leaves every year, not evergreen; (of deers' horns) shed each year.

decigramme, n. [1. désigràm; 2. désigræm]. **deci-** & **gramme**. (metric system) The tenth part of a gramme.

decilitre, n. [1. désilèter; 2. désilìtə]. See **deci-** & **litre**. (metric system) The tenth part of a litre.

decillion, n. [1. desílyun; 2. disíljən]. Formed fr. **deci-** w. the ending on anal. of *million, billion* &c. A million raised to the tenth power.

decimal (I.), adj. [1. désimal; 2. désiməl]. Low Lat. *decimāl-is*, 'connected with a tenth or tenths', fr. Lat. *decim-us*, 'tenth'; cp. Scrt. *daśamás*. See **deca-**, **ten**, & **-al**. **1.** (arith.) Based on the number 10 or $\frac{1}{10}$, proceeding by multiples of 10; **a** *decimal notation*, the system of notation based on the ten digits; **b** *decimal arithmetic*, that based on decimal notation; **c** *decimal fraction*, one whose denominator (not expressed) is ten or a power of ten; **d** *decimal point*, a dot used to indicate a decimal fraction. **2.** *Decimal classification*, a system of library classification and cataloguing, in which the field of knowledge is divided into ten classes, each divided and subdivided in tens. **3.** *Decimal system*, one in which weights and measures are reckoned in powers of ten; *decimal coinage*, the system of having all coins or monetary unit ten times, or one-tenth of, the value of the one above or below it in value.

decimal (II.), n., fr. prec. A decimal fraction. *Circulating decimal*, one in which a certain series of figures is repeated, in the same order, to infinity. *Recurring, repeating, decimal*, one in which one figure is repeated to infinity.

decimalism, n. [1. désimalizm; 2. désiməlizəm]. See **decimal** & **-ism**. **a** The use of a decimal system for reckoning weights, measures, coinage; **b** advocacy of use of this.

decimalist, n. [1. désimalist; 2. désiməlist]. See prec. & **-ist**. One who advocates the use of a decimal system.

decimalization, n. [1. désimalīzáshun; 2. désiməlaizéiʃən], fr. next word & **-ation**. The process of reducing, being reduced, to decimals.

decimalize, vb. trans. [1. désimalīz; 2. désiməlaiz]. See **decimal** & **-ize**. To reduce to a decimal fraction, to terms of a decimal system.

decimally, adv. [1. désimali; 2. désiməli], fr. **decimal (I.)** & **-ly**. By means of decimal fractions.

decimate, vb. trans. [1. désimāt; 2. désimeit], fr. Lat. *decimāt-(um)*, P.P. type of *decimāre*, 'to select by lot every tenth man for punishment'. See **decimal (I.)** & **-ate**. **a** To kill every tenth man, selected by lot (esp. in ancient Rome), as a punishment for a large body of troops, prisoners &c.; hence (in wider sense), **b** to reduce numbers of, kill; weed out, eliminate, by violent means a considerable proportion of a group of individuals: *the army was decimated by sickness*.

decimation, n. [1. dèsimáshun; 2. dèsiméiʃən], fr. prec. & **-ation**. The act or process of decimating, or of being decimated.

decipher, vb. trans. [1. desífer; 2. disáifə]. See **de-** & **cipher**. **a** To turn from a cipher into ordinary language or writing: '*Pepys's Diary*' *was easily deciphered*; **b** to make out, interpret, read, make sense of, what is indistinct, nearly illegible, or written in unfamiliar symbols: *to decipher a manuscript, an inscription in hieroglyphics, a badly written letter* &c.

decipherable, adj. [1. desíferabl; 2. disáifərəbl]. See prec. & **-able**. That can be deciphered.

decipherment, n. [1. desíferment; 2. disáifəmənt]. See **decipher** & **-ment**. **a** The act of deciphering; **b** solution of a cipher.

decision, n. [1. desízhun; 2. disížən], fr. Fr., fr. Lat. *dēcīsiōn-(em)*, 'decision, settlement', fr. *dēcīs-(um)*, P.P. type of *dēcīdere*. See **decide** & **-ion**. **1. a** Judgement, determination, choice, arrived at after comparing two things, the several claims of two or more parties, or several possible courses of action: *to arrive at a decision*; **b** specif. (law) the ruling, on points of law, given by a judge when sitting officially in a court of law: *the decision will be promulgated in due course*. **2.** Quality of being able to come to a decision; ability to decide, to make up one's mind, rapidly and finally; firmness, resolution: *to lack decision (of character)*; *a man of decision*.

decisive, adj. [1. desísiv; 2. disáisiv]. See prec. & **-ive**. **1. a** Tending to decide, or to terminate a contest, argument &c. one way or another: *the arrival of reinforcements was decisive in winning the battle*; **b** tending to influence the course of events: *this battle was decisive of the whole campaign*. **2. a** Tending to influence judgement · *decisive evidence*; **b** tending to enable a particular decision to be formed · *this fact is decisive for me*.

decisively, adv. Prec. & **-ly**. In a decisive manner: *the evidence of this witness weighed decisively*.

decisiveness, n. See prec. & **-ness**. The quality of being decisive.

decivilize, vb. trans. [1. dēsívilīz; 2. dīsívilaiz]. See **de-** & **civilize**. To render uncivilized, deprive of civilization.

deck (I.), vb. trans. [1. dek; 2. dek]. Not Engl. Prob. borrowed fr. M. Du. *decken*, 'to cover'. The Engl. equiv. is **thatch**. **1. a** To adorn, add some form of decoration, trimming, to (a house, dress &c.); **b** to give an appearance of gaiety to: *to deck a street with flags, a room with flowers* &c.; also *deck out*; *to deck oneself out with jewels*, dress up; (often used in poet.) *to deck (a lady's) head with flowers* &c. **2.** To construct a deck in, cover with a deck (a ship).

deck (II.), n. Same as prec. M. Du. *dek*, 'a cover, deck of a ship'. **1.** A wooden covering built across a ship, extending from side to side and over the whole or part of its length, often qualified as *main, upper, lower deck* &c., esp. *quarter-deck*. Phr. *clear the decks (for action)*, prepare for action (lit. and fig.). **2.** *Deck of cards*, a pack, so called because the cards cover one another.

deck-cabin, n. Cabin on the deck of a ship.

deck-cargo, n. Cargo carried on the deck of a ship instead of in the hold.

deck-chair, n. A light chair, easily portable, used on passenger-ships, in a garden &c.

-decker, n. [1. déker; 2. dékə]. **deck (II.)** & **-er**. Ship of so many decks: *three-decker* &c.

deck-hand, n. A man employed on deck of a vessel, for cleaning, handling cargo &c.

deck-house, n. A small building, or shelter &c., on deck of a ship.

deckle, n. [1. dékl; 2. dékl], fr. Mod. Germ. *deckel*, 'cover', dimin. of *decke*. See **thatch**. (in papermaking) A device for determining the size of the sheet in cutting the paper.

deckle-edge, n. The rough edge of hand-made paper.

deckle-edged, adj. Having rough, untrimmed edges.

declaim, vb. trans. & intrans. [1. deklám; 2. dikléim]. Lat. *dēclāmāre*, 'to practise speaking aloud; to bawl and bluster'. See **de-** & **claim**. **1.** trans. To utter, repeat (poetry &c.), as though to an audience, loudly and in a manner aiming at rhetorical effect: *to declaim verses*. **2.** intrans. To speak in a rhetorical manner, as though addressing an audience. *Declaim against*, protest against; attack violently in words.

declamation, n. [1. dèklamáshun; 2. dèkləméiʃən]. See prec. & **-ation**. **a** The act of declaiming, process of being declaimed; **b** the art of declaiming, of speaking in public in a clear, pointed, dramatic manner; **c** a speech uttered with dramatic or rhetorical effect.

declamatory, adj. [1. deklámatori; 2. diklǽmətəri]. See prec. & **-ory**. **a** Having to do with, of the nature of, resembling, declamation; **b** (in unfavourable sense) rhetorical, showily phrased and uttered, without being sound in argument.

declarable, adj. [1. deklárabl; 2. dikléərəbl]. See **declare** & **-able**. **a** That can be declared; **b** specif. (of contraband) dutiable, which ought to be declared as such.

declarant, n. [1. deklárant; 2. dikléərənt]. See **declare** & **-ant**. (legal) One who makes a formal declaration.

declaration, n. [1. dèklaráshun; 2. dèkləréiʃən]. Lat. *dēclārātiōn-(em)*, 'a making clear', fr. *dēclārāt-(um)*, P.P. of *dēclārāre*, 'to make known'. See **declare** & **-ation**. **1.** The act of declaring. **2.** That which is declared: **a** (law) solemn statement, affirmation (before a magistrate); **b** statement of a claim; **c** *declaration of war*, formal announcement by a government of its intention to engage in war with another power.

declarative, adj. [1. deklárativ; 2. diklǽrətiv], fr. Lat. *dēclārāt-*, as in prec. & **-ive.** Having nature of a declaration.

declaratory, adj. [1. dekláratori; 2. diklǽrətəri], fr. Lat. *dēclārāt-*, as in prec. & **-ory.** Declaring, explanatory, making a clear statement.

declare, vb. trans. & intrans. [1. deklā́r; 2. dikléə], fr. O. Fr. *declarer*, fr. Lat. *dēclārāre*, 'to make clear, manifest; to announce, proclaim', fr. **de-** & *clārus*. See **clear. A.** trans. **1.** To make known by words, signs &c., affirm, proclaim; to make a statement about, announce in words: *to declare the result of a contest, election* &c.; *he declared that he had eaten nothing all day*; *to declare oneself king*, proclaim by a formal, public announcement. Phr. *to declare (a bargain) off*, to announce it to be no longer binding; *to declare war (up)on*, announce formally the beginning of a state of hostility (against another country &c.); (also fig.) *to declare war on disease* &c. **2.** To make a formal statement about; specif. (of dutiable goods at a Custom-House) admit that one has such in one's possession: *she did not declare all the silk stockings she had bought in Paris.* **3.** Specif. (cards) to announce that one holds (certain cards); announce (a certain suit) as trumps. **4.** (reflex.) *Declare oneself*, show oneself in one's true colours, show what one really is or thinks. **B.** intrans. **1.** To make a declaration; to affirm positively. Phr. *well, I declare!*, exclamation of surprise. **2.** *Declare for, against*, to announce oneself in favour of, not in favour of. **3.** Specif. (cricket) to declare an innings closed.

declared, adj. [1. deklā́rd; 2. dikléəd], fr. P.P. of prec. Revealed, avowed, not secret: *a declared admirer.*

declaredly, adv. [1. deklā́redli; 2. dikléəridli]. Prec. & -ly. Avowedly, confessedly.

déclassé, adj. [1. dāklahsā; 2. dēklasē]. Fr. 'unclassed'. Having lost caste or class; having gone down in the world.

declension, n. [1. deklénshun; 2. diklénʃən], for *declination*, fr. Lat. *dēclīnātiōn-(em)*, 'falling away, bending aside', fr. *dēclīnāt-(um)*, P.P. type of *dēclīnāre*. See **decline** & **-ion. 1.** (lit.) The act or process of declining, falling away; (rare, chiefly fig. of non-material conditions and things) deterioration, falling away from, descent to something inferior, lapse: *declension from virtue.* **2.** (gram.) **a** The inflexion of nouns, pronouns, and adjectives; **b** a class of nouns &c. inflected in a particular way.

declensional, adj. [1. deklénshunal; 2. diklénʃənəl]. Prec. & **-al.** Belonging to, connected with, declensions: *declensional endings.*

declinable, adj. [1. deklī́nabl; 2. dikláinəbl]. See **decline** & **-able.** (gram.) Capable of being declined, or inflected.

declination, n. [1. dèklinā́shun; 2. dèklinéiʃən]. See **decline** & **-ation. a** (lit.) A sloping away from, deviation; **b** (astron.) angular distance of a heavenly body from celestial equator; **c** (of compass, magnetic needle) variation from the true meridian of a place.

declinator, n. [1. déklinātər; 2. déklineitə]. See prec. & **-or.** Instrument for measuring declination (in astron. &c.).

declinatory, adj. [1. deklī́natori; 2. dikláinətəri]. See prec. & **-ory. a** Pertaining to declination; **b** expressing refusal, declining.

decline (I.), vb. intrans. & trans. [1. deklī́n; 2. dikláin]. M.E. *declīnen*, 'avoid, eschew'; O. Fr. *décliner*, fr. Lat. *dēclīnāre*, 'to bend down, turn aside; to deviate from'; fig., 'to avoid, shun'; gram., 'to inflect (a part of speech)'; fr. **de-** & *clīnāre*, 'to bend'. The latter base is found in large groups of words, see **clinical, clement,** & cp. **declivity**; the Gmc. type is **hlain-*, **hlin-* &c., q.v. under **lean (II.)**; also, w. different formative element, **ladder, lid, link (I.)**. The fundamental meaning is 'to slope'. **A.** intrans. **1. a** To slope, bend downwards (rare in lit. sense); **b** to deteriorate, go back from a standard of excellence, stage of development, pitch of strength formerly existing: *the arts have declined among us*; *his health, intellect, courage* &c., *slowly declined*; **c** to diminish, be reduced in amount, severity: *the fever has sensibly declined*; *the birth-rate has been declining for some years.* **2.** To refuse to do something or go somewhere: *to decline to answer questions.* **B.** trans. **1.** (rare in lit. sense) To cause to slope, bend downwards: *to decline one's head on one's breast.* **2.** To refuse, reject, express one's non-acceptance of, by gesture, in writing, in uttered speech: *to decline an invitation, a proposal* &c.

decline (II.), n., fr. prec. **a** (fig.) Gradual falling away, weakening, deterioration: *the decline of faith, art, civilization* &c.; **b** diminution, approaching end, sinking to a close: *decline of*, or *in, strength, decline of life*; specif. **c** a wasting disease, phthisis, consumption: *to fall into a decline.*

declinometer, n. [1. dèklinómeter; 2. dèklinɔ́mitə]. See **decline** & **-meter.** An instrument for measuring declination of magnetic needle (phys.).

declivitous, adj. [1. deklívitus; 2. diklívitəs]. See next word & **-ous.** Having a downward slope; rather steep.

declivity, n. [1. deklíviti; 2. diklíviti], fr. Fr., fr. Lat. *dēclīvitāt-(em)*, fr. **de-** & *clīvus*, 'a slope, hill, height', fr. **klei-w*; cp. Goth. *hlaiw*, 'grave-mound', O.H.G. *hleo*, O.E. *hlāw, hlǣw*, 'tomb, mound, hill', fr. Aryan base **kloiw-, kleiw-* &c. For forms of the same stem w. different vowel-grades & different formative elements, see **decline, lid, lean (II.), ladder. a** Ground sloping downwards, a gentle hill, viewed from above; **b** the downward slope of ground.

declivous, adj. [1. deklívus; 2. dikláivəs]. See prec. & **-ous.** (esp. bot. and zool.) Having a downward slope.

declutch, vb. intrans. [1. dēklúch; 2. dīklátʃ]. See **de-** & **clutch.** (of a motor, engine &c.) To take out the clutch, remove connexion between engine and wheels &c.

decoct, vb. trans. [1. dekókt; 2. dikɔ́kt]. Lat. *decoct-(um)*, P.P. of *dēcoquere*, 'to boil down'. See **de-** & **cook**, also **concoct.** To boil down, extract essence from by boiling.

decoction, n. [1. dekókshun; 2. dikɔ́kʃən], fr. Lat. *dēcoctiōn-(em)*. See prec. & **-ion. a** The process of decocting; **b** essence extracted by decoction or boiling.

decode, vb. trans. [1. dēkṓd; 2. dīkóud]. See **de-** & **code.** To translate (a letter, telegram &c.) from a code into ordinary language.

decollate, vb. trans. [1. dekólāt; 2. dikɔ́leit], fr. Lat. *dēcollāt-(um)*, 'beheaded', P.P. of *dēcollāre*, fr. **de-** & *collum*, 'neck'. See **collar.** To behead, cut off the head of.

decollated, adj. [1. dēkólated; 2. dīkɔ́lətid]. P.P. of prec. (esp. of shells) With the point worn or broken off.

decollation, n. [1. dèkolā́shun; 2. dikəléiʃən]. See **decollate** & **-ion.** The act of beheading; process of being beheaded: (esp. of the putting to death of martyrs): *decollation of St. John.*

décolleté(e), adj. [1. dākoltā; 2. dekɔlte]. Fr. See prec. words. **a** (of dress &c.) Leaving neck and shoulders bare; **b** (of person) wearing such a dress.

decolour, vb. trans. [1. dēkúlur; 2. dikálə]. See **de-** & **colour.** To remove colour from, bleach.

decolourant, n. [1. dēkúlurant; 2. dīkálərənt]. See prec. & **-ant.** A substance that removes colour (from material &c.).

decolouration, n. [1. dèkulurā́shun; 2. dikaləréiʃən]. **decolour** & **-ation.** Removal, loss, of colour.

decolourization, n. [1. dēkùlurīzā́shun; 2. dīkàləraizéiʃən]. See next word & **-ation.** The act of decolourizing; process of being deprived of colour.

decolourize, vb. trans. [1. dēkúlurīz; 2. dīkáləraiz]. See **decolour** & **-ize.** To remove colour from.

decomplex, adj. [1. dèkómpleks, dḗkumplèks; 2. dīkɔ́mplɛks, dīkəmplèks]. See **de-** & **complex.** Composed of complex parts; doubly complex.

decompose, vb. trans. & intrans. [1. dèkumpṓz; 2. dìkəmpóuz]. **de-** & **compose. 1.** trans. **a** To cause to disintegrate; to resolve into constituent elements; **b** to cause to decay, rot. **2.** intrans. **a** To break up into constituent parts; **b** become rotten, decay.

decomposite, adj. & n. [1. dēkómpozit; 2. dikɔ́mpəzit]. See **de-** & **composite. a** adj. Made by compounding a substance, itself a compound, with another substance; **b** n., a substance so compounded.

decomposition, n. [1. dēkòmpozíshun; 2. dīkɔ̀mpəziʃən]. **de-** & **composition. a** The act or process of resolving, being resolved, into constituent parts; **b** the process of decaying; state of being decayed.

decompound (I.), adj. & n. [1. dèkómpound; 2. dikɔ́mpaund]. **de-** & **compound.** (esp. bot.) **a** adj. Formed of parts already compounded; **b** n., substance so compounded.

decompound (II.), vb. trans. [1. dèkumpóund; 2. dìkəmpáund], fr. prec. To make compound parts or substances into a further compound.

deconsecrate, vb. trans. [1. dēkónsekrāt; 2. dikɔ́nsikreit]. **de-** & **consecrate.** To remove character formerly imparted by consecration, devote (building, churchyard) to secular uses, secularize.

deconsecration, n. [1. dèkonsekrā́shun; 2. dìkɔnsikréiʃən]. Prec. & **-ation.** Act of deconsecrating; state of being deconsecrated.

decontrol, vb. trans. & n. [1. dḗkontrṓl; 2. dìkəntróul]. **de-** & **control. 1.** vb. To take out of control, to remove control from, esp. of Government control of certain trades, industries &c. **2.** n. Removal of control.

decorate, vb. trans. [1. dékorāt; 2. dékəreit], fr. Lat. *decorāt-(um)*, P.P. of *decorāre*, 'to decorate, adorn'; fig., 'to honour, distinguish', fr. *decor-*, stem of *decus*, 'ornament, embellishment; glory, dignity'. See **decent. 1. a** To adorn, add some special form of ornamentation to (esp. flags, flowers &c.) as a sign of rejoicing, or to celebrate some great event &c.: *to decorate a town for a royal visit*; *to decorate a house for Christmas*; **b** specif., *to decorate a room, house* &c., to paint, paper it; **c** to be, act as, an ornament to, adorn, make more gay, beautify &c.: *the skin of that tiger now decorates my hall.* **2.** (applied to persons) To show honour to, dignify, by bestowing an order of knighthood, and the badge of this, a medal &c.: *to decorate a person with the Order of the Bath.*

decorated, adj. [1. dékorāted; 2. dékəreitid]. P.P. of prec. **1. a** Adorned; **b** having an order or decoration. Specif. **2.** (archit.) belonging to a period of English Gothic, between Early English and Perpendicular.

decoration, n. [1. dèkorā́shun; 2. dèkəréiʃən]. See **decorate** & **-ion. 1.** The act of decorating; the state or process of being decorated. **2. a** Something used for purpose of decorating, that which beautifies; a particular style of ornamentation; **b** a medal, badge, or insignia of an order, or other honourable distinction conferred in recognition of services rendered to one's country. *Decoration Day*, Memorial Day.

decorative, adj. [1. dékorativ; 2. dékərətiv]. See **decorate** & **-ive.** Performing the function of decorating; giving an artistic effect, tending to beautify.

decoratively, adv. Prec. & **-ly.** In a decorative manner.

decorativeness, n. See prec. & **-ness.** Quality of being decorative.

decorator, n. [1. dékorātor; 2. dékəreitə]. **decorate** & **-or.** One who decorates; specif., one who makes a business of painting, papering, and generally doing up houses &c.

decorous, adj. [1. dekórus; 2. dikɔ́rəs], fr. Lat. *decōrus*, 'becoming, seemly, proper; adorned, elegant, fine', & **-ous**; fr. same base as **decent** & **decorate**. (of behaviour, appearance, dress &c.) In accordance with what is becoming, seemly; sober, appropriately dignified.

decorously, adv. Prec. & **-ly**. With propriety of manner, soberly, becomingly.

decorousness, n. See prec. & **-ness**. The quality of being decorous.

decorticate, vb. trans. [1. dēkórtikāt; 2. dīkɔ́tikeit]. **de-** & *cortic-*, stem of **cortex**, 'bark, rind', & **-ate**. To strip off the bark, outer covering, of.

decorum, n. [1. dekórum; 2. dikɔ́rəm]. Lat., neut. of adj. *decōr-us*. See **decorous**. Proper and seemly behaviour; the requirements of good taste, social conventions &c.

decoy (I.), n. [1. dekói; 2. dikɔ́i]. Used in 16th cent. Coined fr. **de-** & Du. *kooi*, 'a cage, lure', wh. itself is borrowed fr. Lat. *cavea*, 'excavated place, enclosure, den, cage'. See **cage** (I.). **1. a** A device for leading wild birds, esp. duck &c., into a snare; a lure; **b** (fig.) something or somebody used as an attraction for luring, enticing, a person into a dangerous or compromising position. **2.** An enclosed place, as a piece of water, into which birds can be lured to facilitate their capture.

decoy (II.), vb. trans., fr. prec. (lit. and fig.) To lead into a position of danger by means of some special allurement &c.

decoy-duck, n. A bird trained to lead others into such a place or position that they can be caught or shot easily (also fig., of persons).

decrease (I.), vb. intrans. & trans. [1. dekrḗs; 2. dikrīs], fr. O. Fr. *descreiss-*, P.P. type of *decroistre*, fr. Lat. *dēcrēscere*, 'to grow less, diminish'. See **de-** & **crescent**. **1.** intrans. (of material and non-material things) To become smaller, grow less, diminish in size, volume, amount, degree. **2.** trans. To cause to grow less, make smaller.

decrease (II.), n. [1. dḗkrēs; 2. díkrīs], fr. prec. A lessening, growing smaller; the act or process of decreasing, the state of being decreased: *decrease of a swelling*; *decrease in population*, *in* (or *of*) *income* &c.

decreasingly, adv. [1. dekrésingli; 2. dikrísiŋli], fr. Pres. Part. of **decrease** & **-ly**. In a manner showing gradual decrease.

decree (I.), n. [1. dekrḗ; 2. dikrí]. O. Fr. *decré*, fr. Lat. *dēcrētum*, 'a decision, decree', neut. of P.P. of *dēcernere*, 'to pronounce a decision, determine'. See **de-**, **certain**, **concern**, & **critic**. **1.** (law) **a** Decision, judgement, pronouncement, formal order, of a court of justice, tribunal, high authority: *to issue a decree*; *decree nisi* (divorce court), decree of divorce, becoming absolute after a fixed period, unless sufficient cause to the contrary is shown; **b** an order made by a legislative body. **2. a** (theol.) Fixed and eternal purpose of God which determines all events and conditions; **b** law made by a council of the church determining a point of doctrine or morals; **c** (fig.) anything fixed and unalterable: *a decree of nature, fate* &c.

decree (II.), vb. intrans. & trans., fr. prec. **a** intrans. To command, decide on, issue an ordinance, formal order, to the effect that: *to decree that . . .*; **b** trans., to order, enjoin: *to decree an annual observance*.

decrement, n. [1. dékriment; 2. dékrimənt], fr. Lat. *dēcrēment-(um)*, 'diminution, decrease'. See **decrease** & **-ment**. The process of decreasing; amount lost by gradual decrease, waste &c.; opposed to *increment*.

decremeter, n. [1. dekrémeter; 2. dikrémitə]. See prec. & **-meter**. Instrument for measuring dampening of oscillation in wireless telephony.

decrepit, adj. [1. dekrépit; 2. dikrépit], fr. Lat. *dēcrepitus*, orig. 'noiseless, moving noiselessly; worn out, very old, infirm', fr. **de-** & *crepitus*, 'a noise, creaking, crash', P.P. of *crepere*, 'to rattle, clatter, crash'; cp. Lat. *crepundia*, 'a child's rattle'; Scrt. *kṛpatē*, 'to chatter'. A probable cogn. is O.E. *hræfn*, 'a raven'. See **crepitate**, **raven** (I.). **a** (of persons) Worn out, enfeebled, by age or illness; tottery, moving about with difficulty, frail; **b** (of things) shaky, ramshackle, worn out by age and usage.

decrepitate, vb. trans. & intrans. [1. dekrépitāt; 2. dikrépiteit]. See **de-** & **crepitate**. **a** trans. To bring (salt, mineral &c.) to such a high degree of heat that it crackles; **b** intrans., (of salt and other minerals) to crackle when exposed to extreme heat.

decrepitation, n. [1. dekrèpitáshun; 2. dikrèpitéiʃən]. Prec. & **-ation**. Act of decrepitating; crackling through exposure to heat.

decrepitude, n. [1. dekrépitūd; 2. dikrépitjūd]. See **decrepit** & **-tude**. The state of being decrepit: *in the last stage of decrepitude*.

decrescendo, adv., adj., & n. [1. dåkreshéndō; 2. dèikrəʃéndou]. Ital. See **de-** & **crescent**. (direction in mus.) (To be played) with gradual reduction of loudness or resonance; a passage so played.

decrescent, adj. [1. dekrésent; 2. dikrésənt]. See **de-** & **crescent**. Growing smaller, diminishing, waning, esp. of moon.

decretal, n. [1. dekrḗtl; 2. dikrítl]. Fr. *décrétale*, fr. L. Lat. *dēcrētāle*, neut. adj., fr. *dēcrētālis*, 'pertaining to a decree', fr. *dēcrēt-(um)* & **-al**. See **decree**, **discern**. **a** A decree given by a high authority; esp. a decree made by the Pope on a point of ecclesiastical law; **b** (in pl.) a compilation of papal decrees, forming part of the canon law of the Roman Catholic Church.

decretalist, n. [1. dekrḗtalist; 2. dikrítəlist]. Prec. & **-ist**. One learned in *the decretals*.

decretist, n. [1. dekrḗtist; 2. dikrítist]. See prec. & **-ist**. Decretalist.

decretive, adj. [1. dekrḗtiv; 2. dikrítiv]. See **decretal** & **-ive**. Pertaining to, having force of, a decree.

decretory, adj. [1. dekrḗtori; 2. dikrítəri]. See **decretal** & **-ory**. **a** Having the character of a judicial decision or decree; **b** established by such pronouncement.

decrial, n. [1. dekríal; 2. dikráiəl]. **decry** & **-al**. The act of decrying.

decrustation, n. [1. dèkrustáshun; 2. dìkrastéiʃən]. See **de-** & **crust** & **-ation**. Act or process of removing a crust; opposed to *incrustation*.

decry, vb. trans. [1. dekrí; 2. dikrái]. See **de-** & **cry**. To cry down, to disparage, detract from credit or reputation of.

decuman, adj. [1. dékūman; 2. dékjumən], fr. Lat. *decumānus*, *decimānus*, 'pertaining to the tenth part', fr. *decima*, 'tenth part', fr. *decem*, 'ten'. See **deci-**, **deca-**, **decimal**. **1.** (of waves) Lit. the tenth; an extra large and powerful wave, from idea that every tenth wave was of such a character. **2.** (from Lat. *decumana porta*) Of the principal gate of a Roman legionary camp, by which were the quarters of the 10th cohort of the legion.

decumbence, n. [1. dekúmbens; 2. dikámbəns]. See next word & **-ce**. The state of being decumbent.

decumbent, adj. [1. dekúmbent; 2. dikámbənt], fr. Lat. *dēcumbent-(em)*, Pres. Part. of *dēcumbere*, 'to lie down'. See **de-** & base under **cubicle**. Lying, recumbent; specif. (bot., of stems and shoots) resting on, lying along, the ground.

decumbently, adv. Prec. & **-ly**. In a decumbent, prostrate, position.

decuple (I.), adj. & n. [1. dékūpl; 2. dékjupl], fr. Lat. *decuplus*, 'tenfold'. See **deca-** & **double**. **a** adj. Tenfold; **b** n., a number, amount, ten times as large as a given number or amount.

decuple (II.), vb. trans., fr. prec. To increase to an amount ten times as large.

decurion, n. [1. dekúrion; 2. dikjɔ́riən]. Lat. *decuriōn-(em)*, 'chief of a *decuria*, or company of ten', in Roman army, fr. *dec-*, (*decem*), 'ten', w. ending like that in *centuria*; see **centurion**, **century**. An officer in the Roman army, commanding ten men.

decurrency, n. [1. dekúrensi; 2. dikárənsi]. See next word & **-cy**. (bot.) The state of being decurrent.

decurrent, adj. [1. dekúrent; 2. dikárənt]. Lat., fr. Pres. Part. of *dēcurrere*, 'to run down'. See **de-** & **current** (I.). Running, extending, downward; specif. (bot., of a leaf) extending down the stem, whence it springs, and forming a projection along this.

decursive, adj. [1. dekérsiv; 2. dikásiv]. Lat. *dēcurs-(us)*, 'a running down, descent', & *-īvus*. See **de-** & **cursive**. Running, extending, downwards, decurrent.

decursively, adv. Prec. & **-ly**. In a decursive manner.

decussate (I.), vb. trans. & intrans. [1. dēkúsāt; 2. dikáseit], fr. Lat. *decussāt-(um)*, P.P. type of *decussāre*, 'to divide crosswise in form of X', fr. *decuss-is*, 'the number ten, the figure X', fr. *decem*, 'ten'. See **deca-**, **ten**. (of lines, rays of light &c.) To intersect at right angles, as in the form of X.

decussate (II.), **decussated**, adj. See prec. Crossing at right angles; specif. (bot., of a pair of leaves on a stem) growing at right angles to those below and above it.

dedicate, vb. trans. [1. dédikāt; 2. dédikeit], fr. Lat. *dēdicāt-(um)*, P.P. type of *dēdicāre*, 'to declare, announce, give out; to set apart, consecrate; to dedicate, inscribe (a book &c.)', fr. *de-* & *dīcere*, 'to show, tell'. **de-** & **diction** & **-ate**. **a** To devote, set apart, solemnly, often with prescribed forms and ceremonies, consecrate, to a sacred purpose: *to dedicate a building to God*; *dedicate one's life to God*; **b** to devote, give up, to a particular cause or purpose: *dedicate one's life to work, to pleasure*; *dedicate one's spare time to one's children*; (also reflex.) *to dedicate oneself to business* &c.; **c** to inscribe, address, in a complimentary paragraph, (a book &c.) to a person as a mark of admiration, gratitude, esteem &c.

dedicatee, n. [1. dèdikātḗ; 2. dèdikeitī]. Prec. & **-ee**. One to whom anything, as a book, is dedicated.

dedication, n. [1. dèdikáshun; 2. dèdikéiʃən]. See **dedicate** & **-ion**. **1. a** Act of dedicating; **b** state of being dedicated. **2.** Inscription, as at beginning of a book &c., dedicating it to a particular person.

dedicative, adj. [1. dédikātiv; 2. dédikeitiv]. See **dedicate** & **-ive**. Dedicatory.

dedicatory, adj. [1. dédikàtori; 2. dédikèitəri]. See **dedicate** & **-ory**. Connected with, implying, serving as, a dedication: *epistle dedicatory*.

deduce, vb. trans. [1. dedū́s; 2. didjū́s], fr. Lat. *dēdūcere*, 'to lead, bring, down; to lead forth, conduct; to deduct, divert; to derive, trace down', fr. **de-**, & *dūcere*, 'to lead'. See **duke**, & cp. **deduct**. **a** To trace down from, show succeeding stages of (a line of descent &c.); **b** to infer, arrive at a logical judgement, by process of deductive reasoning.

deducible, adj. [1. dedū́sibl; 2. didjū́sibl]. Prec. & **-ible**. That can be deduced, inferred.

deduct, vb. trans. [1. dedúkt; 2. didákt], fr. Lat. *dēduct-(um)*, P.P. type of *dēdūcere*. See **deduce**. To remove, take away, subtract, a part from a sum of money: *to deduct 5% from a year's salary for insurance*.

deduction, n. [1. dedúkshun; 2. didákʃən]. Lat. *dēductiōn-(em)*, 'leading away, drawing off'. Prec. & **-ion**. **1. a** The act or process of deducting; **b** that which is deducted, amount subtracted. **2. a** The act or process of deducing; **b** the conclusion, inference, reached by deducing. Cp. *induction*.

deductive, adj. [1. dedúktiv; 2. didáktiv]. See **deduct** & **-ive**. By deduction, based on deduction; *deductive reasoning*, method by which certain particular consequences or applications are deduced from general principles.

deductively, adv. Prec. & **-ly**. By methods of deduction, by deductive reasoning.

deed, n. [1. dēd; 2. dīd]. Common Gmc. O.E. *dǣd*, M.E. *dēde*, fr. W. Gmc. **dād-*, cp.

O.H.G. *tāt*, O.S. *dād*; also O.N. *dāð*; Goth. *(ga)dēþs*; Prim. Gmc. form **dǣd-*, fr. Aryan **dhē-t-*; for the base **dhē-*, **dhō-*, **dhə-*, 'put, place'. See **do, fact, thesis. 1.** Something done, performed, carried out; an action: *a good, evil, deed; the deeds of a hero; deeds done in this life will meet with due reward, or punishment, hereafter.* **2.** Actual fact, reality; esp. in Phrs. *in word and in deed, in very deed*; cp. *indeed.* **3. a** A legal document under seal, setting forth something that has been done, a grant, agreement &c.; **b** specif., document embodying a grant or conveyance of, and establishing a title to, land; *title deed.*

deed-poll, n. See **deed, poll (III.).** A deed as of gift &c., executed by one party only; so called because the paper on which it is written is *polled*, or cut straight and not indented; contrasted with *indenture.*

deem, vb. trans. [1. dēm; 2. dīm]. O.E. *dēman*, M.E. *dēme*, 'to judge, condemn; think, believe'; cp. O. Fris. *dēma*, O.N. *dǿma*, Goth. *dōmjan*; fr. Prim. Gmc. **dōm-*. See **doom.** The old meanings 'to pass a legal judgement upon, condemn', are now expressed by *to doom* (to death) and *condemn* respectively. **1.** To judge, consider, believe, hold a particular opinion: *to deem a proposal good.* **2.** To hold the opinion, believe (that): *I deem that this will never be proved; to deem it wise to . . .*

deemster, n. [1. dḗmster; 2. dímstə]. O.E. *dēmestre*, fem., 'she who deems, judges'; M.E. *dēmester*, 'judge'. **deem & -ster.** One of the two chief justices of the Isle of Man.

deep (I.), adj. [1. dēp; 2. dīp]. Common Gmc. **deup-*, O.E. *dēop*, M.E. *dēpe*; O.S. *diop*, O.H.G. *tiuf*, Goth. *diups.* Aryan **dheubh-*, **dhubh-* appears to be represented outside Gmc. only by Lith. *dúbs*, 'deep, hollow', *dúbe*, 'ditch, to nb'. **1. a** Reaching, extending, far downwards from surface, or from a given level: *a deep river; deep snow; deep bed of clay*; Phr. *in deep water*, in difficulties; **b** penetrating far below surface: *a deep wound; a deep hole in the ground; a deep mine*; **c** situated, placed, at a remote distance below the surface: *a deep spring of water; gold was found deep in the ground*; **d** of such a depth: *ten foot deep* &c. **2.** (of certain objects viewed only as surfaces) Broad, wide, having considerable vertical extension: *a deep fringe, border, hem*; extending laterally: *a deep ledge, shelf* &c. **3.** (transferred meanings) **a** (of the mind) Profound, capacious, possessing grasp; reverse of superficial: *a deep intellect*; **b** (of mental states and activities) thoroughly immersed in, penetrated with, absorbed by, having the mind occupied with: *deep in thought, meditation; deep in a book; deep in study*; **c** (fig., of persons) artful, cunning, concealing real feelings and motives: *he's a deep one.* **4.** Other special applications: **a** (of emotions) intense, strongly felt: *deep grief, gratitude, delight; a deep mystery, secret*, hard to understand, or find out; Phr. *deep Romany*, the purest form of Gipsy language, only intelligible to, or spoken by, those who have a profound knowledge of the tongue; **b** (of effects on senses, of sight or hearing): (of colours) intense, rich in pigment: *deep brown* &c.; (of sounds) resonant, low in tone: *a deep groan; a deep voice*, one capable of uttering deep sounds.

deep (II.), n., fr. prec. **1.** (poet.) **a** The sea: *in the cradle of the deep, the great deep, the mighty deep*; **b** the mysterious, unfathomable depths of being, of the universe: '*When that which drew from out the boundless deep, Turns again home*' (Tennyson). **2.** (naut.) The space between two fathom marks on a lead-line.

deep (III.), adv. O.E. *dēope.* See **deep (I.).** Deeply, far down; to, at, a great depth: *to dig deep; be buried deep; drink deep*, copiously.

deep-dyed, adj. [1. dḗp díd; 2. dīp dáid]. **deep (III.) & dye (II.).** (chiefly fig.) As it were stained with guilt, thoroughly bad: *a deep-dyed villain*; cp. **dye (I.).**

deepen, vb. trans. & intrans. [1. dḗpen; 2. dīpən]. See **deep (I.) & -en. A.** trans. **1. a** To make deeper, extend downwards, increase distance from surface: *deepen a ditch, a channel*; **b** to make broader: *to deepen a hem.* **2.** (of mental action, effect on emotions and senses) to make deeper, to intensify: *to deepen an impression; to deepen one's knowledge; depression was deepened by news of fresh disaster; to deepen a colour.* **B.** intrans. (lit.) **a** To become deeper: *the river channel is deepening*; **b** (fig., of material and non-material processes) to increase in intensity: *the darkness deepens; his voice has deepened; anxiety deepens with suspense.*

deep-felt, adj. **deep (III.) & felt (III.).** Felt with intensity.

deeping, n. [1. dḗping; 2. dípiŋ]. See **deep & -ing.** Section of a drift-net, a fathom deep.

deep-laid, adj. **deep (III.) & laid.** Cunningly and secretly devised, carefully planned, and capable of evading detection or suspicion: *deep-laid plot, schemes.*

deeply, adv. [1. dḗpli; 2. dípli]. **deep (I.) & -ly.** To a considerable depth; profoundly, intensely, strongly; with all senses of *deep*: *to dig deeply; to feel deeply* &c.

deep-mouthed, adj. **deep (I.) & mouthed.** (of dogs) Having a deep, resonant bark or bay.

deepness, n. [1. dḗpnes; 2. dípnis]. See **deep (I.) & -ness.** The quality of being deep; depth; degree of depth.

deep-rooted, adj. **deep (III.) & rooted. a** (lit.) Having deep roots; **b** (fig.) firmly established, not easily removed or eradicated: *deep-rooted objection, habit, prejudice.*

deep-sea, adj. Pertaining to the deeper parts of the sea, as distinct from the shallower water near land: *deep-sea fishing, dredging* &c.

deep-seated, adj. **deep (III.) & seated.** (of feelings, causes, diseases) Firmly established, penetrating far below the surface, not slight or superficial.

deer, n. [1. dēr; 2. diə]. O.E. *dēor*, 'beast, animal', M.E. *dēre*; cp. O.H.G. *tior*, O.S. *dier*, O.N. *diur*, O. Fris. *diar*, Goth. *dius*; Prim. Gmc. form **đeuz-*, fr. an Aryan base **dhēw-s-.* The orig. meaning of the base is 'smoke, steam, breath' &c. *Deer* is therefore the 'breathing, living, creature'; **beast**, for **dwēst-*, is also fr. a variant of this base, as also **dust** (Gmc.) & **fume** (Lat.). The name of several genera forming a family (*Cervidae*) of ruminants, characterized by having solid antlers, which are shed and renewed every year; cp. *fallow deer, red deer, reindeer* &c. The application of the word to animals of all kinds, as in O. and M.E. and in Shakespeare's '*Mice and rats and such small deer*', has long been obsolete.

deer-fence, n. Fence surrounding a deer-park, too high for the deer to leap.

deer-forest, n. Uncultivated land on which deer and other game are preserved.

deer-hound, n. One of a breed of large dogs used for hunting deer.

deer-lick, n. Salty spring or marsh, to which deer come to lick the ground.

deer-mouse, n. A small American rodent.

deer-neck, n. (of a horse) A thin, badly shaped neck.

deer-park, n. One in which deer are preserved.

deer-skin, n. **a** The hide of the deer; **b** leather made from this.

deer-stalker, n. **a** One who hunts deer by stalking; **b** old-fashioned kind of cap.

deer-stalking, n. The art or sport of hunting deer by stalking.

deface, vb. trans. [1. defás; 2. diféis], fr. Fr. *défacer.* See **de- & face. a** To spoil the appearance of, mar, disfigure; **b** specif. (of engraved inscriptions &c.) make indistinct, illegible, by injury to the surface of; to obliterate.

defaceable, adj. [1. defásabl; 2. diféisəbl]. Prec. & **-able.** Capable of being defaced.

defacement, n. [1. defásment; 2. diféismənt]. **deface & -ment. a** The act of defacing; state or process of being defaced; **b** something that defaces.

de facto, adv. [1. dḕ fáktō; 2. dī fǽktou]. Lat., 'in fact, in deed'. See **de- & fact.** In actual fact; contrasted with *de jure.*

defalcate, vb. intrans. [1. dḗfawlkāt; 2. dífɔ̄lkeit], fr. *dēfalcāt-(um)*, P.P. type of Med. Lat. *dēfalcāre*, 'to cut off, lop' (branches &c.); hence fig., 'to reduce, lessen, deduct'; fr. Lat. **de- &** *falc-(em)*, stem of *falx*, 'a sickle'. See **falchion.** (rare) To take for one's own use, to embezzle, money which one holds in trust for others; to show deficiency in funds entrusted to one, owing to one's misappropriation of them.

defalcation, n. [1. dḕfawlkáshun; 2. dīfɔ̄lkéiʃən]. See prec. & **-ion. a** The act of defalcating; misappropriation of property, embezzlement; **b** amount misappropriated, deficiency due to embezzlement.

defamation, n. [1. dḕfamáshun; 2. dīfəméiʃən]. See **defame & -ation.** Injury done to a person's reputation by or through slanderous statements: esp. *defamation of character.*

defamatorily, adv. [1. defámatorili; 2. difǽmətərili]. See next word & **-ly.** In a manner liable to defame, or injure a person's reputation.

defamatory, adj. [1. defámatori; 2. difǽmətəri], fr. Fr., fr. Lat. *diffāmāt-(um)*, P.P. type of *diffāmāre*, 'to defame'. See next word & **-ory.** Tending to defame, intended to injure a person's reputation: *defamatory libel, statement.*

defame, vb. trans. [1. defám; 2. diféim]. M.E. *defāme, diffāme*, fr. O. Fr. *diffamer*, fr. Lat. *diffāmāre*, 'to spread an evil report'. See **dis- & fame.** To injure, asperse, the character and reputation of, by evil speaking, by malicious statements &c.

defamingly, adv. [1. defámingli; 2. diféimiŋli]. Pres. Part. of prec. & **-ly.** In a defamatory manner.

default (I.), vb. intrans. & trans. [1. defáwlt; 2. difɔ̄lt]. M.E. *defauten*, fr. O. Fr. *default*, 3rd sing. pres. of *defaillir*, 'be wanting', fr. **de- &** Lat. *fallere*, 'to deceive'; see **false, fault, fail. 1.** intrans. **a** To fail in performance of a duty; **b** fail to carry out an obligation, esp. of financial nature; **c** fail to appear in a court of justice &c. when legally required to do so. **2.** trans. (law) To enter (a person) as a defaulter who fails to appear in a court of law to which he was summoned to appear.

default (II.), n. M.E., fr. O. Fr. *defaute*, see prec. **1. a** Failure to perform a certain duty or obligation, esp. of legal or financial nature; **b** failure to appear in a court of law when required. Phr. *judgement by default*, judgement given for plaintiff in a lawsuit when defendant fails to appear. **2.** Absence, lack, deficiency. Phr. *in default of*, in the absence of, for want of (thing required).

defaulter, n. [1. defáwlter; 2. difɔ̄ltə]. **default (I.) & -er.** One who defaults; specif. **a** one who fails to pay his debts; esp. on *stock exchange*, member who fails or is unable to pay claims and is therefore 'hammered'; **b** one who does not account for money in his charge, who defalcates; **c** one who fails to appear when summoned before a tribunal.

defeasance, n. [1. defḗzans; 2. difízəns], fr. O. Fr. *defesance*, 'undoing, defeat', fr. *defaire*, fr. **de- &** Lat. *facere*, 'to do'. See **defeat. 1.** (lit.) Defeat; still used by Spenser, but now obsolete in this sense. **2. a** The act of annulling, making null and void; **b** provision in a legal instrument, embodying a condition, which if carried out would invalidate the document.

defeasibility, n. [1. defḗzibíliti; 2. difízibíliti]. See next word & **-ity.** The state of being defeasible.

defeasible, adj. [1. defḗzibl; 2. difízibl]. See **defeasance & -ible.** Capable of annulment.

defeat (I.), vb. trans. [1. defḗt; 2. difít]. M.E. *defeiten*, fr. O. Fr. *de(s)feit*, P.P. of *de(s)faire*, fr. Lat. *dēficere*, 'forsake &c.; fail, be wanting', fr. *dē* & *facere*, 'make' &c. See **de- & defect, fact, feat. a** To vanquish, conquer, overthrow, get the better of, (an opponent) in a contest of any kind: *to defeat the enemy in a battle, another candidate in a parliamentary election* &c.; **b** (of effect on non-material things) to bring to nothing, frustrate: *to defeat one's plans, hopes* &c.

defeat (**II.**), n., fr. prec. **1.** **a** Act of defeating an opponent; conquest: *the general was decorated in recognition of his defeat of the enemy*; **b** process of being defeated; overthrow: *the enemy retired after his defeat by our general.* **2.** Frustration, destruction: *the defeat of one's hopes* &c.

defeatism, n. [1. defétizm; 2. difítizəm]. Prec. & **-ism**; fr. Fr. *défaitisme*. State of mind, principles, actions &c. of those who accepted the defeat of their own country, esp. in the Great War, as inevitable, and acted accordingly.

defeatist, n. [1. defétist; 2. difítist]. See prec. & **-ist**. Adherent of, believer in, defeatism.

defeature, vb. trans. [1 dēféchur; 2. difítʃə], fr. obs. n., O. Fr. *desfaiture*, 'unmaking, disfigurement', fr. O. Fr. P.P. *desfeit* &c. & **-ure**. See **defeat** (**I.**). To mar, spoil appearance of, make unrecognizable.

defecate, vb. trans. & intrans. [1. défēkāt; 2. dífikeit], fr. Lat. *dēfaecāt-(um)*, P.P. type of *dēfaecāre*, 'to strain, free from dregs'; fig., 'to purify, make clear'. See **de-** & **faeces**. **1.** trans. (lit. and fig.) To purify, clarify, by removing dregs, impurities &c. **2.** intrans. (lit. and fig.) **a** To give off, cast out, extraneous matter, impurities &c.; specif. **b** to void excrement from the bowels.

defecation, n. [1. dèfēkáshun; 2. dìfikéiʃən]. See prec. & **-ation**. **a** The removal of extraneous matter, purification; **b** specif., act of passing excrement from the bowels.

defect, n. [1. defékt; 2. difékt], fr. Lat. *dēfect-(um)*, P.P. type of *dēficere*, 'to fail, abandon, be wanting', fr. **de-** & *facere*, 'to do'. See **fact**. (of material or non-material things) Something wanting; a fault, imperfection; shortcoming: *a defect in one's character*; *a defect in the mechanism.*

defection, n. [1. deféksbun; 2. difékʃən], fr. Lat. *dēfectiōn-(em)*, 'a failure, deficiency, eclipse, desertion, revolt'. See prec. & **-ion**. The act of falling away from, deserting, a cause, leader &c.; failure in duty, abandonment of allegiance.

defective (**I.**), adj. [1. deféktiv; 2. diféktiv]. **defect** & **-ive**. **1.** Having defects; lacking something essential, not complete or perfect; faulty: **a** (of material things) *a defective machine, engine, boiler* &c.; **b** (of moral and intellectual states and qualities) *defective intelligence, memory*; *defective moral sense.* **2.** (gram., of verbs) Not having all the parts necessary to form a complete conjugation.

defective (**II.**), n., fr. prec. Specif., person who is mentally or morally wanting, or deficient; an imbecile.

defectively, adv. **defective** (**I.**) & **-ly**. In a defective manner, imperfectly.

defectiveness, n. See prec. & **-ness**. The state of being defective.

defence, n. [1. deféns; 2. diféns]. M.E. *defense*, fr. O. Fr., fr. Lat. *dēfens-(um)*, P.P. type of *dēfendere*, 'to ward off, repel'. See **defend**. **1.** **a** Act of defending, protecting, shielding, a person or thing against attack; Phr. *art of self-defence*, boxing; **b** (in moral sense) vindication, justification: *to make no defence against accusations*; *a defence of poetry.* **2.** That which defends, protects: *machine-guns are an excellent defence against attack*; (mil.) **a** *line of defence*, series of strongly held positions; **b** *defences* (of a town &c.), specif., fortifications, entanglements, guns &c. **3.** (law) Case stated in favour of person accused of crime, or of defendant in a trial in a court of justice: *the defence was weak*; *the case, counsel, for the defence.* *Defence of the Realm Acts*, various Acts of Parliament, passed during the Great War, giving the Government certain powers of control in various matters; usually abbreviated D.O.R.A.

defenceless, adj. [1. defénsles; 2. difénslis]. Prec. & **-less**. Without means of defence, unable to defend oneself, open to attack.

defencelessly, adv. Prec. & **-ly**. In a defenceless manner.

defencelessness, n. See prec. & **-ness**. The state of being defenceless.

defend, vb. trans. [1. defénd; 2. difénd]. M.E. *defenden*, fr. O. Fr. *defendre*, fr. Lat. *dēfendere*, 'to ward off, keep away; to watch over, protect'; fig., 'to support, maintain', fr. **de-** & **fendere*, 'to strike' (cp. **offend**), fr. **gʷhen-d-* or **gʷhen-dh-*. Cogn. w. Gk. *theínein*, 'to strike', for **khenjō*, fr. Aryan **gʷhen-jō*; cp. Scrt. *ghnánti*, 'they strike', *hanti*, 'he strikes'. Cp. also Gk. *phónos*, 'murder', fr. **gʷhon-*; Scrt. *ha-tás*, 'to kill', fr. **gʷhn-*. Cp. also Prim. Gmc. **ʒunþjō*, 'war' (fr. **gʷhn̥-tjā*), whence O.E. *gūþ*, fr. **gunþ-*, O.H.G. *gund-*; O.H.G. *gundfano*, 'banner' (see **gonfalon**); O. Ir. *gonim*, 'I strike'. See **fend**. **1.** (of material action) To shield against an attack, ward off an attack from, protect, keep from harm; prevent capture of: *to defend a person, one's country, a fortified post.* **2.** (of moral action) **a** To protect (oneself or others) against attack in word, to stand up for, argue in favour or support of, repel charges &c. against; **b** to justify, vindicate, plead reasonableness, justifiability of (actions, opinions, principles). **3.** (law) **a** (of counsel) To state a case for a person accused of a crime when he is tried in a court of law, endeavouring to establish his innocence by weakening or rebutting evidence brought against him, and adducing other evidence in his favour; **b** (of accused person, or defendant in civil action) *to defend the case*, to plead not guilty and endeavour through counsel to secure acquittal; to deny plaintiff's allegations, and fight the case.

defendant, n. [1. deféndant; 2. diféndənt]. Fr., fr. Pres. Part. of *défendre*. See prec. & **-ant**. The one defending a case; specif., person against whom an accusation is brought in a criminal trial; one who is prosecuted, or against whom a claim is made, the person sued, in a civil case.

defender, n. [1. defénder; 2. diféndə]. See **defend** & **-er**. One who defends; *Defender of the Faith*, hereditary title borne by British monarchs; originally bestowed on Henry VIII. by the Pope.

defensibility, n. [1. defènsibíliti; 2. difènsibíliti]. See next word & **-ity**. The quality of being defensible.

defensible, adj. [1. defénsibl; 2. difénsibl]. See **defence** & **-ible**. **a** (mil.) Capable of being defended against attack by armed forces; **b** (of conduct &c.) capable of being morally justified; justifiable on rational grounds.

defensibly, adv. Prec. & **-ly**. In a defensible manner, justifiably: *to act defensibly.*

defensive (**I.**), adj. [1. defénsiv; 2. difénsiv], fr. Fr., fr. Med. Lat. *dēfensīvus*. See **defence** & **-ive**. **a** Specif. (mil.) resisting attacks, protecting (contrasted with *offensive*): *defensive warfare*; **b** adapted to, prepared for, defence; expecting and prepared to repel attacks: *to take defensive measures*; *to assume a defensive attitude.*

defensive (**II.**), n., fr. prec. **a** Specif. (mil.) *the defensive*, the condition in which an army gives up attacking, and merely defends itself from, and holds its positions against, attack; **b** (of moral attitude) position of defence, state of being prepared to resist attack, and repel charges; esp. in Phr. *to be, act, on the defensive.*

defensively, adv. **defensive** (**I.**) & **-ly**. In a defensive manner, so as to secure defence.

defensory, adj. [1. defénsori; 2. difénsəri]. See **defence** & **-ory**. Adapted to defence, defensive.

defer (**I.**), vb. trans. & intrans. [1. defér; 2. difə́]. Shows confusion between prefixes **de-** & **dis-**; cp. next word. M.E. *differen*, fr. O. Fr. *differer*, fr. Lat. *differre*, 'to carry in different directions, disperse; to spread abroad, publish; to defer, put off'; intrans., 'to differ'; fr. **dis-** & *ferre*, 'to carry', see **-ferous**; cp. **differ**. **1.** trans. To put off, delay, postpone; set apart for performance &c. at a later date: *to defer action, payment, a visit* &c. Phrs. *deferred annuity*, one of the first payments of which is to be made after a specified interval, or after a specified event; *deferred pay*, part of a soldier's pay reserved for payment at a later date; *deferred shares*, the whole or part of the interest on which is reserved for payment, later than on prior shares. **2.** intrans. To delay, postpone action, procrastinate.

defer (**II.**), vb. intrans. [1. defér; 2. difə́], fr. Fr. *déférer*, fr. Lat. *dēferre*, 'to carry away'; fig., 'to hand over, refer, transfer', fr. **de-** & *ferre*, 'to carry', see **-ferous**. To yield, submit to, give the superior place to: *to defer to another's opinion, judgement*; *he defers to his wife in everything.*

deference, n. [1. déferens; 2. déførəns]. See prec. & **-ence**. The act of deferring to another; respect; recognition of superiority; submission to opinion, will, of a person: *to show deference to, treat with deference.* Phrs. *in deference to* (*your wishes* &c.), showing respect, consideration for, submitting to; *with all due deference to* (*you* &c.), polite formula when expressing difference of opinion.

deferent, adj. [1. déferent; 2. déførənt]. Lat. *dēferent-(em)*, Pres. Part. of *dēferre*, 'carry down, away'. See **defer** (**II.**). **1.** (anat.) Carrying fluids &c. away from a particular part or organ. **2.** (rare) Deferential.

deferential, adj. [1. dèferénshal; 2. dèførénʃəl], fr. Lat. *dēferent-(em)*, as in prec., & **-al**. Showing, expressing, deference; respectful.

deferentially, adv. Prec. & **-ly**. In a deferential manner.

deferment, n. [1. deférment; 2. difə́mənt]. See **defer** (**I.**) & **-ment**. The act of deferring, of putting off; state of being deferred.

defeudalize, vb. trans. [1. dēfū́dalīz; 2. difjū́dəlaiz]. **de-** & **feudal** & **-ize**. To deprive of feudal character.

defiance, n. [1. defíans; 2. difáiəns]. M.E. *deffia(u)nce*, O. Fr. *deffiance*. **defy** & **-ance**. The act of defying; state of being prepared to defy, or resist; a challenge to a contest. Phrs. *bid defiance to*; *set at defiance*, act in disobedience to, without regard for, set at nought; *in defiance of* (*orders* &c.), without regard for, going directly against, in spite of.

defiant, adj. [1. defíant; 2. difáiənt]. See **defy** & **-ant**. Expressing defiance, challenging, boldly disobedient.

defiantly, adv. Prec. & **-ly**. In a defiant manner.

deficiency, n. [1. defíshensi; 2. difíʃənsi], fr. Lat. *dēficientia*, 'lack, want', fr. *dēficient-(em)*, Pres. Part. of *dēficere*, 'to be wanting'. See **deficient** & **-cy**. **a** State of incompleteness, shortage, lack: *a deficiency of intellect, of food* &c.; **b** amount or sum by which something is deficient or falls short: *a deficiency of several tons, of ten pounds* &c.

deficient, adj. [1. defíshent; 2. difíʃənt], fr. Lat. *dēficient-(em)*, Pres. Part. of *dēficere*, 'to be wanting'. See **defect**. Wanting, lacking; incomplete, inadequate, in amount, quality, degree &c.; defective: *deficient in ammunition, faith* &c.; *mentally deficient*, imbecile.

deficiently, adv. Prec. & **-ly**. In an incomplete, insufficient, manner.

deficit, n. [1. défisit, défisit, defísit; 2. défisit, dífisit, difísit], fr. Fr., fr. Lat. *dēficit*, 'it is wanting', 3rd sing. pres. of *dēficere*, 'to fail, fall short, be wanting'. See **defect**. Shortage, amount by which credit side of an account falls short on balancing accounts; excess of expenditure over receipts, of liabilities over assets.

de fide, pred. adj. [1. dē fídē; 2. di fáidi]. Lat., 'according to faith'. See **fidelity**. Required to be held as an article of faith.

defilade, vb. trans. [1. dèfilád; 2. dèfiléid]. Fr., fr. *défiler*, 'to unthread', & **-ade**. See **de-** & **enfilade** & cp. **defile** (**II.**) (mil.) To protect (fortifications &c.) against enfilading fire.

defilading, n. [1. dèfiláding; 2. dèfiléidiŋ]. Pres. Part. of prec. (mil.) The science or act of constructing fortifications so as to withstand, give protection from, enfilading fire, or from fire from neighbouring heights.

defile (I.), vb. trans. [1. defíl; 2. difáil]. O.E. *fȳlan, ā-fȳlan,* 'to make foul, defile', fr. **fūljan*, cp. O.E. *fūl*, **foul**; M.E. *afulen, afīlen,* etc.; also *defoulen,* 'to pollute'. Mod. Eng. *defile,* is fr. M.E. *de-fīlen.* The Lat. or Fr. pref. **de-** to an Engl. word is due to a M.E. confusion between this & *defoulen,* O. Fr. *defouler,* 'trample under foot, insult'. There is no relation either in meaning or form, apart fr. the pref., between the Engl. & Fr. words. **a** (chiefly in moral sense) To render unclean, sully the purity of, to pollute: *to defile sacred things*; *to defile the mind, imagination*; **b** (in physical sense) chiefly in Phr. *to defile a river,* i.e. pour sewage &c. into it.

defile (II.), vb. intrans. [1. defíl; 2. difáil], fr. Fr. *défiler,* 'to unthread', fr. **de-** & **file** (III.). See **defilade, enfilade.** (esp. mil.) To march in files, in single file.

defile (III.), n. [1. défil; 2. dífail], fr. prec. A narrow valley, or outlet from a mountain, a pass (through which troops can march only in narrow files).

defilement, n. [1. defílment; 2. difáilmənt]. See **defile** (I.) & **-ment.** **a** The act of defiling; **b** state of being defiled; **c** that which defiles.

definable, adj. [1. defínabl; 2. difáinəbl]. **define** & **-able.** That can be defined, stated, explained, with precision.

definably, adv. Prec. & **-ly.** In a definable manner.

define, vb. trans. [1. defín; 2. difáin], fr. O. Fr. *definer,* fr. Lat. *dēfīnīre,* 'to limit, set bounds to'; fig., 'to mark out, determine; to explain or limit by definition', fr. **de-** & *fīnīre,* 'to enclose within boundaries, set a limit to; finish'. See **finish.** **1.** (of material things) To show clearly, mark distinctly the visible limits or outlines of: *a well-defined footprint*; *his profile was sharply defined against the light.* **2.** (of non-material things) To determine, and state precisely, the limits of; describe in exact terms: *to define one's meaning, duties, position* &c. **3.** Specif. (of words, terms &c.) to state precise meaning, describe manner of application, and explain various special uses; to limit and make clear the different significations and implications borne by a word.

definite, adj. [1. définit; 2. définit], fr. Lat. *dēfīnīt-(um),* P.P. of *dēfīnīre.* See prec. **1.** Clearly defined, precise, having exact, well-marked, limits; **a** exactly determined, finally appointed: *to make an appointment for a definite time and place*; **b** having a clear, precise meaning, unambiguous, unqualified, positive: *a definite answer, statement, opinion.* **2.** (gram.) *Definite article,* the word *the.*

definitely, adv. Prec. & **-ly.** In a definite manner; clearly, plainly, unambiguously.

definiteness, n. See prec. & **-ness.** The quality of being definite.

definition, n. [1. dèfiníshun; 2. dèfiníʃən]. See **definite** & **-ion.** **1.** The act of defining; state or process of being defined. Hence, **2.** A clear statement about a thing; account of its exact limits or nature; specif., a brief explanation of the precise meaning of a word. **3.** **a** Clearness of outline, distinctness; **b** power of a lens (telescopic, photographic &c.) to show an object clearly, with distinct outlines.

definitional, adj. [1. dèfiníshunal; 2. dèfiníʃənəl], fr. prec. & **-al.** Pertaining to a definition.

definitive, adj. [1. defínitiv; 2. difínitiv], fr. Lat. *dēfīnītīvus,* 'explanatory, definitive'. See **definite** & **-ive.** Making a precise statement; conclusive, obviating any further need for argument or inquiry; final.

definitively, adv. Prec. & **-ly.** In a definite manner.

deflagrate, vb. trans. & intrans. [1. déflagrāt; 2. dífləgreit], fr. Lat. *dēflāgrāt-(um),* P.P. type of *dēflāgrāre,* 'to be consumed, burnt up', fr. **de-** & *flāgrāre,* 'to blaze'. See **flagrant, flame.** **a** trans. To burn away, to blaze suddenly and fiercely; **b** intrans., to burn rapidly and fiercely, blaze up.

deflagration, n. [1. dèflagráshun; 2. dìfləgréiʃən]. Lat *dēflāgrātiōn-(em),* 'burning up, conflagration'. Prec. & **-ion.** The act or process of deflagrating.

deflagrator, n. [1. déflagrātor; 2. dífləgreitə]. See **deflagrate** & **-or.** (elect.) A device or instrument for causing combustion.

deflate, vb. trans. [1. dēflát; 2. dīfléit], fr. **de-** & Lat. *flāt-(um),* P.P. type of *flāre,* 'to blow'. See **flatus** & **blow** (I.). **a** To remove, let out, air or gas from anything such as a pneumatic tire, balloon &c. which is inflated, distended; **b** to reduce an inflated currency; opposite of *inflate.*

deflation, n. [1. dēfláshun; 2. dīfléiʃən]. See prec. & **-ion.** The act of deflating; state or process of being deflated.

deflect, vb. trans. & intrans. [1. deflékt; 2. diflékt], fr. Lat. *dēflectere,* 'to bend aside, downwards', fr. **de-** & *flectere,* 'to bend'. See **flex.** **a** trans. (lit. and fig.) To cause to turn aside, deviate; to change the course, direction of: *to deflect course of a bullet, rays of light, a person's thoughts*; **b** intrans., to deviate, turn aside, from a straight line, or from natural course.

deflective, adj. [1. defléktiv; 2. difléktiv]. See **deflect** & **-ive.** Able to deflect, tending to cause deflexion.

deflector, n. [1. defléktor; 2. difléktə]. See **deflect** & **-or.** That which causes deflexion; specif., a device for ensuring the proper mixing of air and gas for burning in a lamp &c.

deflexion, also **deflection**, n. [1. deflékshun; 2. diflékʃən]. Lat. *dēflexiōn-(em).* See prec. & **-ion.** The act of deflecting; state or process of being deflected.

deflorate, adj. [1. dēflórāt; 2. dīflɔ́reit], fr. L. Lat. *dēflōrāt-(um),* P.P. type of *dēflōrāre,* 'to deprive of flowers'. See **de-** & **flora.** (bot.) Having shed its flowers and pollen.

defloration, n. [1. dèfloráshun; 2. dìfləréiʃən]. Lat. *dēflōrātiōn-(em),* 'plucking of flowers; deprivation of virginity'. See prec. & **-ion.** The act of deflowering, depriving of virginity.

deflower, vb. trans. [1. deflóur; 2. difláuə], fr. O. Fr. *desflorer,* fr. L. Lat. *dēflōrāre,* 'to strip of flowers, spoil', fr. **de-** & Lat. *flōr-is,* genit. of *flōs,* 'a flower'. See **flora** & **flower.** To ravish, deprive of virginity.

defluent, adj. [1. déflooent; 2. dífluənt]. See **de-** & **fluent.** Flowing downward.

defoliate, vb. trans. & adj. [1. dēfóliāt; 2. dīfóulieit]. See **de-** & **foliate** (I.). (bot.) **a** vb. To remove leaves from; **b** adj., deprived of leaves.

defoliation, n. [1. dēfòliáshun; 2. dīfòuliéiʃən]. Prec. & **-ion.** The act of stripping of, shedding, leaves.

deforest, vb. trans. [1. dēfórest; 2. dīfɔ́rist]. See **de-** & **forest.** To disforest, to clear land of forest, or trees.

deform, vb. trans. [1. defórm; 2. difɔ́m], fr. Fr. *déformer,* fr. Lat. *dēformāre,* 'to deform, disfigure'; fig., 'to disgrace', fr. **de-** & *formāre,* 'to form, shape'. See **form** (II.). (lit. and fig.) To change shape or character of, for the worse, to spoil the shape of, make misshapen, spoil beauty of: *a deformed man, foot* &c.; *a deformed idea of poetry* &c.

deformation, n. [1. dèformáshun; 2. dīfɔméiʃən]. See prec. & **-ation.** (of material and non-material process) Act of altering for the worse, of deforming; state or process of being altered for the worse; opposite of *reformation.*

deformity, n. [1. defórmiti; 2. difɔ́miti], fr. O. Fr., fr. Lat. *dēformitāt-(em).* See **de-** & **form** (I.) & **-ity.** **1.** The state of being deformed. **2.** Something misshapen; specif. **a** some part, organ, limb, feature of the human or animal body, or some part of a plant, which is badly or abnormally shaped; **b** a moral defect, vice, of the character.

defraud, vb. trans. [1. defráwd; 2. difrɔ́d], fr. O. Fr. *defrauder,* fr. Lat. *dēfraudāre,* 'to cheat, defraud', fr. **de-** & *fraudāre,* 'to cheat', fr. *fraud-(em),* 'deceit, fraud'. See **fraud.** To deprive (a person or society) of due and lawful rights, to withhold from another anything to which he is lawfully entitled, by illegal, dishonest, unjust means; to cheat; specif., to swindle out of money. (Also used absol., esp. in legal phrase: *with intent to defraud.*)

defray, vb. trans. [1. defrá; 2. difréi]. O. Fr. *desfrayer,* 'to pay costs', cp. O. Fr. *frai-(ts),* 'cost', fr. Lat. *dis-* & Low Lat. *fredum,* 'fine, composition, cost'. This is a Gmc. loan-word, cp. O.H.G. *fridu,* 'peace; fine paid for breach of peace'. The O.E. cogn. is *frið(u),* 'peace, truce', wh. is cogn. either w. Lat. *prētium,* 'price' (see **precious** & **price**), or w. **free.** To pay, supply money for payment, bear cost of: *to defray the expenses, cost, of something.*

defrayal, n. [1. defráal; 2. difréiəl]. Prec. & **-al.** The act of defraying; payment.

defrayment, n. [1. defráment; 2. difréimənt]. **defray** & **-ment.** Defrayal.

defrock, vb. trans. [1. dēfrók; 2. dīfrɔ́k]. See **de-** & **frock.** To deprive of the status symbolized by a special dress; specif., to deprive of ecclesiastical status, unfrock.

deft, adj. [1. deft; 2. deft]. M.E. *deft,* O.E. *(ġe)dæfte,* 'meek, gentle' (see **daft**). Cp. O.E. *(ġe)dæftan,* 'to put in order, make smooth', *ġedæftliċe,* 'fitly, suitably', *ġedafen,* 'fitting, suitable'; O.N. *dafna,* 'to be capable, strong'; Goth. *gadaban,* 'to be suitable'. Cp. also O. Bulg. *dobrŭ,* 'beautiful, good', *doba,* 'suitability, fitness; opportunity', *(po)doba,* 'grace', *doblŭ,* 'strong'; Lith. *dabìnti,* 'to adorn', *dabnùs,* 'elegant'; Aryan base **dha-bh-*, **dhō-bh-*, 'to make fitting, make beautiful'; for lengthened grade cp. Goth. *ga-dōbs,* 'suitable'. The same base w. a different formative element, **dha-b-*, 'to make fitting, suitable, fit together', appears in Lat. *faber,* 'artificer' (see **fabric**); O.H.G. *taphar,* 'firm, strong, brave'; orig. 'well fitted together, firmly knit'. Cp. **dapper.** **a** (of persons) Skilful, neat, dexterous (esp. in the use of the hands); **b** (of hands, movements &c.); **c** (of work) showing skill, also requiring skill to accomplish, competent.

deftly, adv. Prec. & **-ly.** In a deft, skilful, manner.

deftness, n. See prec. & **-ness.** The quality of being deft.

defunct, adj. & n. [1. defúngkt; 2. difáŋkt], fr. Lat. *dēfunctus,* P.P. of *dēfungor,* 'I finish, have done with', hence, 'to die', fr. **de-** & *fung-i,* 'to perform'. See **function.** **a** adj. Dead, deceased; **b** n., a dead person, *the defunct.*

defy, vb. trans. [1. defí; 2. difái], fr. Fr. *défier,* fr. O. Fr. *desfier,* fr. assumed Low Lat. **disfidare,* 'to distrust', fr. **dis-** & Low Lat. *fīdāre,* 'to trust', fr. *fīdus,* 'trusty, faithful', cp. *fides,* 'trust, faith'; see **fidelity.** Cogn. w. Goth. *beidan,* 'await, expect'; O.E. *bīdan,* 'await, undergo'. See **bide.** **1.** To challenge; be prepared to resist, be ready to fight against. **2.** **a** (of persons) To resist, set at nought, be in open disobedience to: *to defy one's parents, the law* &c.; **b** (of things) to resist, defeat, offer great difficulties to: *the problem defies solution*; *the door defies all attempts to open it.*

degeneracy, n. [1. dejénerasi; 2. didžénərəsi]. See next word & **-cy.** The state of being degenerate.

degenerate (I.), vb. intrans. [1. dejénerāt; 2. didžénəreit], fr. Lat. *dēgenerāt-(um),* P.P. type of *dēgenerāre,* 'to become unlike one's race, degenerate', fr. **de-** & *gener-(is),* stem of *genus,* 'birth, descent; race'. See **genus.** To decline from a higher to a lower stage of development, inferior degree of excellence &c.

degenerate (II.), adj. & n. [1. dejénerat; 2. didžénərit], fr. Lat. *dēgenerātus.* See prec.

a adj. Having sunk below a former stage of development, degree of excellence &c. (physical or moral); having reverted to a lower type; **b** n., person or thing which is degenerate; specif., a person displaying physical, moral, or mental deficiency, abnormality, depravity &c.

degeneration, n. [1. dejènerā́shun; 2. didžènəréiʃən]. See **degenerate (I.)** & **-ation.** **a** The act or process of degenerating; state of being degenerate; **b** specif. (pathol.) change in the structure of a tissue through disease.

degenerative, adj. [1. dejénerativ; 2. didžénərətiv]. See **degenerate (I.)** & **-ive.** Causing degeneration.

deglutition, n. [1. dèglōōtíshun; 2. dìglūtíʃən], fr. Fr., fr. L. Lat. *dēglūtīt-(um)*, P.P. type of *dēglūtīre*, fr. **de-** & Lat. *glūtīre*, 'to swallow'. See **glut (I.)**. The act of swallowing.

degradation, n. [1. dègradā́shun; 2. dègrədéiʃən]. See **degrade** & **-ation.** **1. a** The act of degrading; state or process of being degraded; **b** state or condition of misery, squalor, involving loss of self-respect, moral character. **2. a** (biol.) Typical state which shows degraded forms of genera or species; **b** (chem.) splitting off of elements of a complex compound, reducing it to a more simple compound; **c** specif. (geol.) the wearing down of earth-surfaces, rocks &c. by natural agents (weather, water &c.).

degrade, vb. trans. & intrans. [1. degrā́d; 2. digréid], fr. O. Fr. *degrader*, fr. L. Lat. *dēgradāre*, fr. **de-** & *gradus*, 'a step'. See **gradus.** **1.** trans. **a** To bring down from a higher to a lower position, reduce rank of, esp. as punishment; **b** to reduce to a condition of physical or moral degradation; to debase, disgrace: *it degrades a man to have to act against his principles.* **2.** intrans. To sink to a lower position; lose rank; become degraded.

degraded, adj. [1. degrā́ded; 2. digréidid], fr. P.P. of prec. In, having sunk to, a low position; mean, base.

degrading, adj. [1. degrā́ding; 2. digréidiŋ], fr. Pres. Part. of **degrade.** Causing degradation; debasing.

degradingly, adv. Prec. & **-ly.** In a degrading manner.

degree, n. [1. degrḗ; 2. digrī́]. M.E. *degrē*, fr. O. Fr. *degre*, fr. Low Lat. *dēgradus*, fr. **de-** & Lat. *gradus*, 'a step, pace; position, station; rank'. See **gradus.** **1.** Amount, extent, of, stage reached, or exhibited; **a** of proficiency, progress: *degrees of goodness, skill; by degrees*, gradually; **b** intensity: *to a high degree*; Phr. *hot* &c. *to a degree*, very hot; **c** nearness to a common ancestor: *degrees of consanguinity.* **2.** Status, position, rank; **a** (in society) *a man of low degree*; **b** (in universities) rank, status, and title conferred, marking a stage of proficiency in studies: *the degree of master, doctor* &c.; **c** (in freemasonry) one of the various stages in the Craft, *master, entered apprentice* &c.; title conferred on those who have reached one of these stages. **3.** One of several units of measurement (of angles, arcs, temperature &c.): *degrees of latitude*, imaginary lines drawn round the globe parallel to the equator, at fixed intervals; *degrees of longitude*, imaginary lines drawn round the globe, passing through the poles, and intersecting the equator at right angles. **4.** Mark of measurement, division (esp. on mathematical or meteorological instruments), for measuring arcs, angles &c. **5.** (gram.) *Degree of comparison, positive, comparative, superlative degree*, modifications of forms of adjectives, either by addition of suffixes *-er*, *-est*, or by using *more, most*, in front of the adjective, to express increasing intensity in the quality denoted by this.

degression, n. [1. dēgréshun; 2. dīgréʃən]. Lat., fr. *dēgress-(um)*, P.P. type of *dēgredi*, 'to descend', fr. **de-** & *gradi*, 'to take steps, walk', fr. *gradus*, 'step'. See **gradus.** A going down; specif., a diminution in rate of taxation on sums below a certain amount.

degressive, adj. [1. dēgrésiv; 2. dīgrésiv]. Lat. *dēgress-*, as in prec., & **-ive.** Pertaining to degression; specif., of method of taxation.

degust, vb. trans. [1. dēgúst; 2. dīgást]. Lat. *dēgustāre*, 'to taste'. **de-** & *gustāre*, q.v. under **gust (II.)**. (rare) To taste, sample flavour of, thoughtfully, and with relish: *to degust a glass of wine, a cigar* &c.

degustation, n. [1. dḕgustā́shun; 2. dìgastéiʃən]. Prec. & **-ation.** Act of degusting or tasting.

dehisce, vb. intrans. [1. dēhís; 2. dīhís], fr. Lat. *dēhīscere*, 'to burst open', fr. **de-** & *hīscere*, 'to open slightly', inceptive of *hi-āre*, 'to open, gape'. See **hiatus.** (bot., of seed-vessels and anthers) To burst open.

dehiscence, n. [1. dēhísens; 2. dīhísəns]. Prec. & **-ence.** (bot.) **a** The process of dehiscing; **b** the manner in which a seed-vessel or anther opens to discharge seeds or pollen.

dehiscent, adj. [1. dēhísent; 2. dīhísənt]. See **dehisce** & **-ent.** (bot.) Having the habit of dehiscing.

dehortation, n. [1. dḕhortā́shun; 2. dìhōtéiʃən], fr. Lat. *dehortāt-(um)*, P.P. type of *dehortāri*, 'to dissuade', fr. **de-** & *hortāri*, 'to incite, urge'. See **hortation.** Dissuasion from, warning against.

dehortative, adj. [1. dēhórtativ; 2. dīhɔ́tətiv]. See **de-** & **hortative.** Serving for dissuasion, intended to dissuade.

dehumanize, vb. trans. [1. dēhū́manīz; 2. dīhjū́mənaiz]. See **de-** & **human** & **-ize.** To deprive wholly or partially of human qualities.

dehydrate, vb. trans. [1. dēhī́drāt; 2. dīháidreit]. See **de-** & **hydrate**, vb. (chem.) To remove water from.

dehydrogenize, vb. trans. [1. dēhī́drojenīz; 2. dīhàidrɔ́dʒənaiz]. See **de-** & **hydrogen** & **-ize.** (chem.) To deprive of hydrogen.

dehypnotize, vb. trans. [1. dēhípnotīz; 2. dīhípnətaiz]. See **de-** & **hypnotize.** To arouse from a hypnotic state, free from effects of hypnotism.

deicide, n. [1. dḗisīd; 2. dī́isaid], fr. Lat. *deus*, 'a god'. & **-cide.** See **deity.** **a** The act, crime, of killing a god; **b** one who kills a god.

deictic, adj. [1. dī́ktik; 2. dáiktik], fr. Gk. *deiktikós*, 'able to prove'; (of arguments) 'direct', fr. *deiktós*, 'capable of proof', fr. *deiknūmi*, 'I show'. See under **diction, digit,** & words there referred to, & **-ic.** (log.) Proving by direct demonstration.

deification, n. [1. dḕifikā́shun; 2. dìifikéiʃən]. See **deify** & **-ation.** **a** The act of deifying, of regarding, and venerating as a god; **b** state of being deified.

deiform, adj. [1. dḗiform; 2. dī́ifɔ̄m], fr. Med. Lat. *deiformis*, fr. Lat. *deus*, 'a god' (see **deity**), & **-form.** Having the form of a god.

deify, vb. trans. [1. dḗifī; 2. dī́ifai], fr. O. Fr. *déifier*, fr. L. Lat. *deificāre*, fr. *deus*, 'a god' (see **deity**), & **-fy.** To exalt to the rank of a divinity, make a god of; to look on, worship, as a god.

deign, vb. intrans. & trans. [1. dān; 2. dein]. M.E. *deinen*, fr. O. Fr. *deigner*, fr. Lat. *dignāri*, 'to deem worthy; to deign', fr. *dignus*, 'worthy'. See **dignity.** **1.** intrans. **a** To do something, behave in a way, which involves a gracious and voluntary descent from a position of recognized superiority; to condescend: *the king deigned to accept an address of welcome, to grant a private audience* &c.; **b** (ironic) *he is so important now that he doesn't deign to acknowledge his old friends*; **c** to stoop, lower oneself, sacrifice dignity by doing something: *I do not deign to reply to such impertinence.* **2.** trans. To condescend to do, or make: *to deign an answer.*

dei gratia, adv. [1. dḗī grā́shiā; 2. dī́ai gréiʃiei]. Lat. See **deity** & **grace.** By the Grace of God.

deinosauros &c. See **dinosaurus.**

de integro, adv. [1. dḗ, dā́ íntegrō; 2. dī́, déi íntigrou]. Lat. See **de-** & **integral.** Afresh.

deism, n. [1. dḗizm; 2. dī́izəm], fr. Fr. *déisme*, fr. Lat. type *dei-*, fr. *de-(us)*, 'god' (see **deity**), & **-ism.** Form of philosophical belief which accepts the existence of some form of Divine Being, but repudiates revelation, and religious dogma.

deist, n. [1. dḗist; 2. dī́ist], fr. Fr. See prec. & **-ist.** An adherent of deism.

deistic(al), adj. [1. dēístik(l); 2. dīístik(l)]. See prec. & **-ic.** Pertaining to deism.

deity, n. [1. dḗiti; 2. dī́iti], fr. Fr. *déité*, fr. Lat. *deitāt-(em)* (see **-ty**), fr. *deus*, 'a god', fr. **dēos*, fr. **deiwos*; cp. *dīv-us*, 'divine', fr. **dīw-*, fr. **dēw-*, fr. **deiw-ī* (see **divine**); cp. also Oscan *deivai*, 'goddesses'; Umbrian *deueia*, 'divine'; Scrt. *dēvá-š*, 'a god', *dēvī́*, 'goddess'; Lith. *dēvas*, Lett. *dēws*, O. Prussian *deiws*, 'a god'; O.H.G. *zio*, O.N. *Tȳr*, O.E. *Tīw* (see **Tuesday**). The orig. idea is 'the shining, glorious one'; other grades of the Aryan base **deiwo-s*, **diwo-s*, 'shining', are **dejewo-*, **djewo-*, **djēw-*, **diw-*, whence Lat. *diēs* (see **dies non**). Cp. further names **Jupiter** & **Diana**; Gk. *dîos*, 'divine' (fr. **diw-jos*), **Zeus**; Scrt. *div-iyaš*, 'celestial'. The base **deiw-* &c. is expanded fr. **dej-ā*, 'to shine', wh. appears in Gk. *daietai*, 'shines', *dêlos*, 'clear, evident' (fr. **dejə-los*) &c.; Scrt. *dī-*, 'to shine'. There is a possible remoter connexion w. Lat. *dīcere*, 'to say'; orig. 'to show, make clear'; Gk. *deiknūmi*, 'I show' (see **diction**); Goth. *taikns*, O.E. *tācen*, 'sign' (see **token, teach**). **1. a** The state of being a god, godhead, divinity; **b** a god: *pagan deities.* **2.** Specif., *the Deity*, God, the Supreme Being.

deject, vb. trans. [1. dejékt; 2. didžékt], fr. Lat. *dēject-(um)*, P.P. type of *dējicere*, 'to throw down, drive off'; fig., 'to deprive of, cause to relinquish', fr. **de-** & *jacere*, 'to throw'. See **jet (III.)**. (of effect on the mind) To cause to be gloomy, unhappy, to depress, cast down the spirits of.

dejecta, n. [1. dejékta; 2. didžéktə]. Lat., neut. pl. of P.P. of *dējicere.* See prec. Droppings, excrement.

dejected, adj. [1. dejékted; 2. didžéktid], fr. P.P. of **deject.** Cast down, depressed, in low spirits.

dejectedly, adv. Prec. & **-ly.** In a dejected manner.

dejection, n. [1. dejékshun; 2. didžékʃən]. See **deject** & **-ion.** **a** The state of being dejected, cast down, lowness of spirits; **b** (med.) excrement; evacuation of the bowels.

déjeuner, n. [1. dā́zhēnā; 2. dežøne]. Fr. See **dine.** Breakfast, as on the Continent, taken about midday, equivalent to English luncheon.

de jure, adv. [1. dē jōōri; 2. dī džúəri]. Lat. *dē jūre*, abl. of *jūs*, 'law, right'. See **de-** & **jus.** By right, rightfully; cp. *de facto.*

delaine, n. [1. delā́n; 2. diléin]. Fr. *de laine*, 'of wool', fr. Lat. *lāna*, 'wool'. See **lanate** & **wool.** A dress material made of a mixture of wool and cotton.

delate, vb. trans. [1. delā́t; 2. diléit], fr. Lat. *dēlāt-(um)*, P.P. type of *dēferre* (see **defer (II.)**), 'to bring down, carry away'; (law) 'to indict, inform against'. *Dēlātus* is fr. **de-** & *lātus* (P.P. of *ferre*, 'to carry'), fr. **tlātum.* See **tolerate** & **thole.** To inform, lodge information, against a person.

delation, n. [1. delā́shun; 2. diléiʃən], fr. Lat. *dēlātiōn-(em)*, 'denunciation, accusation'. See prec. & **-ion.** The act of informing against a person, accusation by an informer.

delator, n. [1. delā́ter; 2. diléitə]. Lat. See prec. & **-or.** An informer.

delay (I.), vb. trans. & intrans. [1. delā́; 2. diléi]. M.E. *delaien*, O. Fr. *delaier*, fr. Lat. *dīlātāre*, 'to expand, enlarge; extend, prolong', fr. *dīlāt-(um)*, P.P. type of *differre*, 'to scatter, disperse; to put off, defer'. See **defer (I.)**, & **dilate**, & cp. **delate.** **1.** trans. **a** To retard, make slow: *the train was delayed by frost*; **b** to postpone, put off, defer, cause to wait: *to delay action.* **2.** intrans. To linger, dawdle, postpone action, be slow.

delay (**II.**), n., fr. prec. The act of delaying; state of being delayed; postponement, tardiness.

del credere, adj. [1. del kráderi; 2. del krédəre]. Ital., lit. 'of trust'. See **de-** & **creed**. (law) Pertaining to an agent, *del credere agent*, who guarantees the solvency of a buyer.

dele, vb. trans. [1. délē; 2. dílī]. Imperat. of Lat. *dēlēre*, 'to wipe out, efface'. See **delete**. (typog. direction) Take, blot, out, omit (letter, word &c.) indicated; usually indicated by underlining word or passage and writing δ in margin of proof.

delectable, adj. [1. deléktabl; 2. diléktəbl], fr. O. Fr., fr. Lat. *dēlectābilis*, 'delightful, agreeable', fr. *dēlectāre*, 'to delight, attract'. See **delectation** & **-able**, & cp. **delight**. Causing delight, enjoyable, delightful.

delectably, adv. Prec. & **-ly**. In a delightful, agreeable, manner.

delectation, n. [1. dèlektáshun; 2. dìlɛktéiʃən], fr. Lat. *dēlectātiōn-(em)* (see **-ation**), fr. *dēlectāre*, 'to charm, delight, attract'; orig. 'to entice, allure', fr. *lacere*, 'to entice'; cogn. w. Lat. *laqueus*, 'noose'. See **lace** (**I.**). Act, process, of pleasing; pleasure, delight.

delectus, n. [1. deléktus; 2. diléktəs]. Lat., fr. *dēlectus*, P.P. of *dēligere*, 'to pick out, choose', fr. **de-** & *legere*, *lect-(um)*, 'to choose'. See **lecture**. A collection of passages from Latin authors, used as a school reading-book.

delegacy, n. [1. déligasi; 2. déligəsi]. See **delegate** & **-cy**. Body of delegates.

delegate (**I.**), vb. trans. [1. déligāt; 2. déligeit], fr. Lat. *dēlēgāt-(um)*, P.P. type of *dēlēgāre*, 'to send, remove, from one person to another, to transfer, commit to', fr. **de-** & *lēgāre*, 'to appoint as deputy'. See **legate**. **a** To appoint (a person) as representative, entrust with performance of duties, business &c.; **b** to entrust, commit (authority, duties &c.) to a deputy.

delegate (**II.**), n. [1. déligat; 2. déligit], fr. O. Fr. *delegat*, fr. Lat. *dēlēgāt-(us)*. See prec. One appointed as a deputy, representative.

delegation, n. [1. dèligáshun; 2. dèligéiʃən]. Lat. *dēlēgātiōn-(em)*. See **delegate** (**I.**) & **-ion**. **a** The act of delegating; appointment of deputies, representatives; entrusting (of authority &c.) to deputies; **b** body of delegates; esp. one deputed and sent by their own government to undertake diplomatic or commercial negotiations with a foreign power.

delete, vb. trans. [1. delét; 2. dilít], fr. Lat. *dēlēt-(um)*, P.P. type of *dēlēre*, 'to blot out, efface'; fig. 'to efface, obliterate'. The form *dēlē-re* &c. is apparently a new formation fr. *dēlē-vi*, perf. of *dē-linere*, fr. *linere*, 'to daub, smear' (esp. of smoothing down the wax on a writing-table); hence 'to erase'; cogn. w. *linīre*, 'to smear, anoint'. See **liniment**. (lit. and fig.) To erase, remove, obliterate: *to delete a clause, word, letter* &c.

deleterious, adj. [1. dèlitérius; 2. dèlitíəriəs]. L. Lat. *dēlētērius*, fr. Gk. *dēlētēri-os* (& **-ous**), fr. *dēléomai*, 'I harm, wound'; etymol. doubtful. Harmful, injurious (physically or morally).

deleteriously, adv. Prec. & **-ly**. In a harmful manner.

deleteriousness, n. See prec. & **-ness**. State of being deleterious or harmful.

deletion, n. [1. deléshun; 2. dilíʃən]. See **delete** & **-ion**. Act or process of deleting, blotting, or striking out; state of being deleted.

delf, delft, n. [1. delf(t); 2. dɛlf(t)]. A kind of glazed earthenware made at, or imitating that made at, Delft in Holland.

deliberate (**I.**), adj. [1. delíberat; 2. dilíbərit], fr. Lat. *dēlīberātus*. See next word. **a** Intentional, thought out beforehand, premeditated, not sudden and impulsive; **b** slow and careful in action, movements, speech &c.

deliberate (**II.**), vb. intrans. & trans. [1. delíberāt; 2. dilíbəreit], fr. Lat. *dēlīberāt-(um)*, P.P. type of *dēlīberāre*, 'to think over, weigh in one's mind, to take counsel about; to reflect; resolve, determine', orig. **dēlībrāre*, fr. **de-** & *lībra*, 'scales'; also 'something weighed; a pound'. See **libra**. **1.** intrans. To consider carefully, reflect, ponder; to think matter over thoroughly from all sides; take counsel (with oneself or others). **2.** trans. To consider, weigh in one's mind, reflect upon, discuss.

deliberately, adv. [1. delíbratli; 2. dilíbritli]. **deliberate** (**I.**) & **-ly**. In a deliberate manner.

deliberateness, n. [1. delíbratnes; 2. dilíbritnis]. See prec. & **-ness**. The quality of being deliberate in thought or action.

deliberation, n. [1. delìberáshun; 2. dilìbəréiʃən]. **deliberate** (**II.**) & **-ion**. **a** Act of deliberating; careful reflection, consideration of a question from all points of view; **b** slowness and carefulness in action, movement, speech &c.; deliberateness.

deliberative, adj. [1. delíberativ; 2. dilíbərətiv]. See **deliberate** (**II.**) & **-ive**. Connected with, displaying, deliberation; having the power and duty of deliberation: *a deliberative body, assembly.*

deliberatively, adv. Prec. & **-ly**. With deliberation.

delicacy, n. [1. délikasi; 2. délikəsi]. See **delicate** & **-acy**. **1. a** (of material objects) Having the qualities of slenderness and fineness, of shape and proportion: *delicacy of carving*; *delicacy of feature*; **b** (of the mind and emotions and their activities) refinement, sensitiveness, subtlety, fastidiousness: *delicacy of feeling, of thought, taste*; **c** (of colours) not crude, not intense or highly pigmented, easily faded or sullied: *delicacy of tint*; **d** (of situations involving human relations) difficulty, tendency to cause friction; ticklishness: *a position, negotiations, of extreme delicacy.* **2. a** Weakness, liability to disease, defectiveness in physical stamina, lack of robustness: *delicacy of health, constitution*; **b** specific form of bodily weakness, unhealthiness: *a delicacy of the lungs.* **3.** A choice, highly prized article of food, a luxury of diet: *all the delicacies of the season.*

delicate, adj. [1. délikat; 2. délikit]. Fr. *délicat*, fr. Lat. *dēlicātus*, 'delightful, charming, voluptuous; soft, tender'. Etymol. doubtful, but prob. connected w. Lat. *dēlicus*, 'weaned from the mother', fr. **de-**, 'from', & the base *lac*, 'milk'. See **lacteal** & **-ate**. The orig. sense according to this wd. be 'just weaned', therefore 'tender, easily destroyed'. **1. a** (of material objects) Highly, cunningly, wrought: *delicate tracery, workmanship*; well proportioned, well moulded; combining slenderness, shapeliness and frailty: *a delicate figure*; *delicate features*; **b** nicely adjusted, sensitive, easily put out of gear: *a delicate instrument*; **c** (of colour) not crude, not strongly pigmented; easily faded or injured: *a delicate shade of blue.* **2.** (of animate beings) **a** (their faculties and senses) Highly sensitive, responsive to stimuli, keenly perceptive, finely organized: *a delicate sense of hearing*; *a delicate touch*; **b** (of moral qualities and their expression) refined, chaste, free from coarseness, decent: *a delicate mind*; *conversation which is not over delicate*; Phr. *a delicate hint*, slight, unobtrusive. **3.** (of situations involving human relations) difficult to handle, ticklish, tending to friction and disagreement: *a delicate stage in the negotiations.* **4.** Frail in health, not robust, liable to become diseased, prone to illness: *he was very delicate as a child.*

delicious, adj. [1. delíshus; 2. dilíʃəs], fr. O. Fr. *delicieus*, fr. L. Lat. *dēliciōsus*, fr. Lat. *dēliciae*, 'charm, delight, pleasure', fr. **dēlaquiae*, fr. *laqueus*, 'a noose'. See **elicit** & **lace** (**I.**). Highly charming and delightful, very agreeable, affording intense pleasure and satisfaction to the senses or the mind: *a delicious perfume, taste, coolness* &c.; *a delicious book, story.*

deliciously, adv. Prec. & **-ly**. In a delicious manner.

deliciousness, n. See prec. & **-ness**. The quality of being delicious.

delict, n. [1. delíkt; 2. dilíkt], fr. Lat. *dēlictum*, 'a fault of omission'; hence 'a fault, crime generally', fr. P.P. type of *dēlinquere*, 'to fail, be wanting; commit a crime', fr. **de-** & *linquere*, 'to leave'. See **relinquish**. A crime, offence, against the law.

delight (**I.**), vb. trans. & intrans. [1. delít; 2. diláit]. M.E. *deliten*, fr. O. Fr. *deliter*, fr. Lat. *dēlectāre*, 'to charm, delight'. See **delectation**. The Mod. Engl. spelling is due to the anal. of **light** &c. **a** trans. To charm, please, give great pleasure to, be a source of enjoyment to: *to delight the ear*; *to delight the heart*; **b** intrans., to find great pleasure in, derive much enjoyment from, take delight in: *to delight in music.*

delight (**II.**), n., fr. prec. **a** Great pleasure; **b** a cause, source, of great pleasure.

delighted, adj. [1. delíted; 2. diláitid], fr. P.P. of **delight** (**I.**). Filled with delight, glad, joyous.

delightedly, adv. Prec. & **-ly**. With delight, very gladly.

delightful, adj. [1. delítfool; 2. diláitfəl]. **delight** (**II.**) & **-ful**. Productive of delight, very pleasing; (of persons) charming, winning, of fascinating manners.

delightfully, adv. Prec. & **-ly**. In a delightful manner, so as to cause delight.

delightsome, adj. [1. delítsum; 2. diláitsəm]. **delight** (**II.**) & **-some**. (archaic) Causing delight.

delimit, vb. trans. [1. delímit; 2. dilímit], fr. **de-** & **limit**. To define the limits of, fix boundaries of.

delimitate, vb. trans. [1. delímitāt; 2. dilímiteit], fr. Lat. *dēlīmitāt-(um)*, P.P. type of *dēlīmitāre*, 'to mark out'. See prec. & **-ate**. To fix the boundaries of.

delimitation, n. [1. delìmitáshun; 2. dilìmitéiʃən], fr. prec. & **-ation**. **a** Act of delimitating; **b** that which bounds and constitutes a limit.

delineate, vb. trans. [1. delíniāt; 2. dilínieit], fr. Lat. *dēlīneāt-(um)*, P.P. type of *dēlīneāre*, 'to sketch out'. See **de-** & **line** & **-ate**. **a** To trace in outline, to depict, draw; **b** (fig.) to describe in words.

delineation, n. [1. delìniáshun; 2. dilìniéiʃən]. Prec. & **-ation**. (lit. and fig.) **a** The act of delineating; **b** result of this, portrait, picture, whether in words or lines.

delinquency, n. [1. delíngkwensi; 2. dilíŋkwənsi], fr. Lat. *dēlinquentia*, 'a fault, crime' (rare), fr. *dēlinquere*, 'to fail, be wanting; commit a fault'. See **delict** & **-ency**. Fault, offence, omission of duty.

delinquent, n. [1. delíngkwent; 2. dilíŋkwənt]. See prec. & **-ent**. One who neglects a duty; one who commits a fault; a criminal.

deliquesce, vb. trans. [1. dèlikwés; 2. dìlikwés], fr. Lat. *dēliquescere*, 'to melt away, dissolve'; fig. 'disappear' (very rare), fr. **de-** & *liquescere*, 'to melt, become liquid'. See **liquescent**. To become liquid.

deliquescence, n. [1. dèlikwésens; 2. dìlikwésəns]. Prec. & **-ence**. The process of melting, becoming liquid; property of becoming liquid in air.

deliquescent, adj. [1. dèlikwéscent; 2. dìlikwésənt]. See prec. & **-ent**. In process of melting, becoming liquid.

delirious, adj. [1. delírius; 2. dilíriəs]. See **delirium** & **-ous**. **a** (of persons) In a state of delirium; with a mind disordered by illness, strong excitement &c.; **b** (of speech &c.) wild, incoherent, from illness &c.

deliriously, adv. Prec. & **-ly**. In a delirious manner, wildly, incoherently.

delirium, n. [1. delírium; 2. dilíriəm]. Lat. *dēlīrium*, 'madness, delirium', fr. *dēlīrāre*, orig. 'to turn aside from the furrow', hence 'to deviate, leave the straight line'; and fig. 'to become deranged, be delirious', fr. **de-** & *līra*, 'the earth thrown up between two furrows', hence 'a furrow'; *līra* is prob. fr. earlier **loisa*, fr. an Aryan base, **leis-*, **lois-*,

lis-*, 'a ridge of earth, rut, track'. In the Slav. languages the meaning is specialized as 'land turned up by the plough, cultivated ground'; O. Bulg. *lěcha*, O. Prussian *lyso*, 'tilled field'; Lith. *lýsė*, 'bed (in a garden)'. In Gmc. the sense 'trace, track', has become prominent; cp. O.H.G. *(wagan)leisa*, 'rut, track made by a cart'; M.H.G. *leis*, 'track'; Mod. Germ. *(ge)leise*, 'track'; cp. also Goth. *laists*, 'track'; O.H.G. *leist*, 'track, foot-print'; hence, 'shoemaker's last'; O.E. *lǣst*, 'footprint, last' (see **last (IV.)). From the idea of 'track, trace', came the sense 'to follow a track, trail'; hence, 'to hunt out, discover', & so 'to learn; teach'; cp. Goth. *lais*, 'I know', *laisjan*, 'teach'; O.H.G. *lēran*, 'teach', *lirnēn*, 'learn'; O.E. *leornian*, 'learn', q.v. under **learn**; cp. also Goth. *lists*, O.E., O.H.G. *list*, 'cunning'. Thus *delirium* is the state of being 'off the track'. Powerful disturbance of the mind, temporary madness, or mental disorder, produced by illness, or nervous shock &c., characterized by incoherent speech and illusions of the senses; specif., *delirium tremens* (colloq. abbreviation D.T.), violent delirium, caused by persistent and excessive drinking of alcoholic beverages, accompanied by tremblings of the hands &c. and terrifying visual hallucinations.

delitescence, n. [1. dèlitésens; 2. dìlitésəns], fr. Pres. Part. of Lat. *dēlitescere*, 'to hide, lie hid', fr. **de-** & *latescere*, 'to be concealed', fr. *latēre*, 'lie hidden'. See **latent**. The state of being delitescent.

delitescent, adj. [1. dèlitésent; 2. dìlitésənt]. See prec. & **-ent**. Not manifest, unrevealed, inactive, quiescent (specif., med. of symptoms of disease).

deliver, vb. trans. [1. delíver; 2. dilívə], fr. Fr. *délivrer*, fr. Low Lat. *dēliberāre*, fr. **de-** & Lat. *liberāre*, 'to set free'. See **liberate**. **1.** To set free, relieve, save (from danger, captivity, suffering, death, sin &c.). **2. a** To give up, hand over, distribute; esp. *to deliver letters* &c.; (law) to present formally (deeds &c.); **b** to pronounce, utter (a speech, sermon &c.); **c** (reflex.) *to deliver oneself of (an opinion* &c.); **d** to strike, aim (a blow &c.). **3. a** (of medical attendant) To help a woman in childbirth; **b** (pass., of woman) *to be delivered of a child*, to give birth to.

deliverance, n. [1. delíverans; 2. dilívərəns]. See prec. & **-ance**. **1.** The act of delivering; rescue, release, liberation. **2.** The formal pronouncement of an opinion.

delivery, n. [1. delíveri; 2. dilívəri], fr. O. Fr. *délivrée*, fem. P.P. of *délivrer*. See **deliver**. **1.** The act of delivering; specif. **a** the distribution of letters &c. by post-office officials; regular, periodic, performance of this act: *the early delivery*; **b** (law) the formal transfer of a deed &c.; **c** manner of uttering a speech, sermon &c.: *a good, poor, delivery*; **d** (in cricket &c.) mode of releasing ball from the hand in bowling. **2.** Process of being delivered of a child.

dell, n. [1. del; 2. dɛl]. O.E. *dell*, fr. Prim. Gmc. **dalj-*; cp. **dale**, fr. **dalo-*. A small wooded hollow, small nook or valley.

Della Cruscan, adj. & n. [1. dèla krúskan; 2. dèlə kráskən]. Ital. *crusca*, 'siftings, bran'. **1.** adj. Of, pertaining to, the Italian *Accademia della Crusca*, established in Florence in 16th cent., for 'sifting' the Italian language and purifying it. **2.** n. Member of this body.

Della Robbia, adj. [1. dèla róbya; 2. dèlə róbjə]. *Della Robbia ware*, a kind of enamelled glazed terra-cotta ware, moulded with reliefs, as made by Luca della Robbia, d. 1482, his family and pupils.

Delphic, adj. [1. délfik; 2. délfik], fr. Gk. *Delphikós*. Pertaining to Delphi, in ancient Greece, seat of Apollo and his oracle: *Delphic oracle*; *a Delphic utterance*, one like the ambiguous answers given by the oracle.

Delphinium, n. [1. delfínium; 2. dɛlfíniəm]. Latinized form of Gk. *delphinion*, 'larkspur', fr. shape of flowers, supposed to resemble a **dolphin**. A genus of herbaceous plants, including the larkspur.

delta, n. [1. délta; 2. déltə]. Gk. name for fourth letter of alphabet, formerly expressing sound of [d], fr. Heb. *dālet*. **a** The fourth letter of the Greek alphabet: Δ, δ; hence **b** the triangular tract of alluvial ground at the mouth of a river that enters the sea by two or more branches, specif., *the Delta*, that of the Nile.

deltaic, adj. [1. deltā́ik; 2. dɛltéiik]. See prec. & **-ic**. Forming a delta.

deltoid, adj. & n. [1. déltoid; 2. déltɔid]. See **delta** & **-oid**. **a** adj. Shaped like a delta, triangular; **b** n., the muscle that lifts the upper arm (from its shape).

delude, vb. trans. [1. delū́d; 2. diljū́d], fr. Lat. *dēlūdere*, 'to mock, deceive, play false', fr. **de-** & *lūdere*, 'to play, amuse oneself; to mock, ridicule'; cp. *lūdus*, 'a game, pastime', fr. O. Lat. *loidos*; prob. cogn. w. Gk. *loidoros*, 'harmful'; Aryan base **loid-*, **leid-*, **lid-*. See **ludicrous**. **a** To deceive, beguile; to mislead deliberately and intentionally; **b** *to delude oneself*, to deceive oneself, persuade oneself into believing what one wishes to believe, without sufficient evidence.

deluge (I.), n. [1. délūj; 2. déljūdž], fr. Fr., fr. Lat. *dīluvium*, 'a flood, inundation'; cp. Lat. *dīluere*, 'to wash away'. See **diluent**, **alluvion**, **lave**. **a** A great flood, torrential rush of water; specif., *the Deluge*, the great flood mentioned in Genesis; **b** (fig.) an overwhelming rush (of words, questions &c.).

deluge (II.), vb. trans., fr. prec. (lit. and fig.) To inundate, pour over, overwhelm with, or as with, a flood of water: *to deluge with rain*; *deluge with invitations* &c.

delundung, n. [1. delúndung; 2. dilándaŋ]. Native Malay name. A variety of civet of the Malay Archipelago.

delusion, n. [1. delū́zhun; 2. diljū́žən], fr. Lat. *dēlūsiōn-(em)*, 'a deceiving, deluding', fr. *dēlūs-(um)*, P.P. type of *dēlūdere*, & **-ion**. See **delude**. **a** The act of deluding, that which deludes; **b** mistaken belief, resulting from an error of judgement or of perceptive sense; **c** specif., persistent belief in something which has no existence in fact, a symptom of mental disorder or insanity.

delusive, adj. [1. delū́siv; 2. diljū́siv]. See prec. & **-ive**. Tending to delude or deceive, not real; illusionary.

delusively, adv. Prec. & **-ly**. In a delusive manner.

delusiveness, n. See prec. & **-ness**. The quality of being delusive.

delve (I.), vb. intrans. & trans. [1. delv; 2. dɛlv]. M.E. *delven*, O.E. *delfan*; cp. O. Fris. *delva*, O.S. *(be)delban*, O.H.G. *(pi)telfan*, Gmc. **đelƀ-*; Aryan base **dhel-bh*, 'to dig, penetrate downwards', perh., w. different formative elements, cogn. w. Gk. *thélumna*, 'the foundations, elements of things'. Archaic, now replaced by **dig**. Old strong vb. w. Pret. *d(e)alf*; now weak *delved*. **1.** intrans. **a** To perform act of digging, to dig assiduously, to burrow; often in Phr. *to dig and delve*; **b** (fig.) to immerse oneself in study of, make researches into a subject, or collection of objects, to look deeply into: *to delve into a language, into a set of documents*; *to delve among the relics of antiquity*. **2.** trans. To dig (the ground), penetrate by digging.

delve (II.), n. O.E. *(ge)delf*, 'hole, ditch', fr. prec. A depression, dip, hollow.

demagnetization, n. [1. dēmàgnitīzā́shun; 2. dīmæ̀gnitaizéiʃən]. Next word & **-ation**. **a** The act of demagnetizing; **b** state or process of being demagnetized.

demagnetize, vb. trans. [1. dēmágnitīz; 2. dīmǽgnitaiz]. See **de-** & **magnetize**. To remove magnetic property from.

demagogic, adj. [1. demagógik; 2. dɛməgɔ́gik]. See next word & **-ic**. Pertaining to a demagogue and his methods.

demagogue, n. [1. démagog; 2. déməgɔg], fr. Gk. *dēmagōgós*, 'a leader of the people; a factious orator, leader of the mob', fr. *dêmos*, 'people' (see **demos**), & *agōgós*, 'a guide, leader', redupl. form of base **āg-*, lengthened grade of Aryan base **ag-*, **og-*. The full grade appears in Lat. *ago*, 'to put in motion'. See **agent**, **act**, & words there referred to. One who stirs up by oratory and leads, or attempts to lead, the people; esp. one who appeals to popular emotion, rather than to reason; a political agitator.

demagogy, n. [1. démagogi; 2. déməgɔgi]. See prec. & **-y**. The principles and practices of a demagogue.

demand (I.), vb. trans. [1. demáhnd; 2. dimā́nd], fr. Fr., fr. Lat. *dēmandāre*, 'to give in charge, in trust'; 'hence to order, command', fr. **de-** & *mandāre*, 'to give in charge; enjoin, order'. See **mandamus**. **1.** trans. **a** (of persons) To ask in an emphatic, peremptory manner, ask for boldly, as a right; to require: *to demand an interview, an immediate answer, payment* &c.; **b** (of things) to need, require, call for, make essential: *an operation demanding great care*. **2.** (with dependent clause) To make a demand: *to demand to be told*.

demand (II.), n., fr. prec. **1. a** An urgent request; peremptory question; **b** a call, claim, that must be satisfied. **2.** (polit. econ.) The requirements of consumers; contrasted with *supply*. Phr. *to be in great demand*, much sought after.

demandable, adj. [1. demáhndabl; 2. dimā́ndəbl]. **demand (I.)** & **-able**. That can be demanded.

demandant, n. [1. demáhndant; 2. dimā́ndənt]. **demand (I.)** & **-ant**. (law) Plaintiff.

demarcate, vb. trans. [1. démarkàt; 2. dímākèit]. Formed fr. next word. (lit. and fig.) To mark, trace out, fix, the boundaries of.

demarcation, n. [1. dèmarkā́shun; 2. dìmākéiʃən]. Fr., fr. Span. *demarcacion*, fr. **de-** & *marcar*, 'to mark'. See **mark (II.)**. (lit. and fig.) Boundary line, limit, distinction; the act of setting or marking a boundary: *a line of demarcation*.

demarch, n. [1. démark; 2. dímāk]. Gk. *dḗmarkhos*. See **deme** & **arch-**. **1.** (in anct. Greece) Ruler, head-man of a deme. **2.** (in mod. Greece) Mayor.

démarche, n. [1. dāmarsh; 2. deimā́ʃ]. Fr., lit. 'movement aside', fr. **de-** & *marcher*, **march (IV.)**. Term used in diplomacy for a change or deviation from an existing policy in foreign relations; a fresh line of policy, esp. after one of strained relations.

dematerialize, vb. intrans. & trans. [1. dèmatḗrialīz; 2. dìmətíəriəlaiz]. See **de-** & **materialize**. **1.** intrans. To give up, abandon, material form; to become a spirit. **2.** trans. To deprive of, cause to give up, material form.

deme, n. [1. dēm; 2. dīm], fr. Gk. *dêmos*; see **demos**. A township in ancient Greece.

demean (I.), vb. reflex. [1. demḗn; 2. dimī́n]. M.E. *demeinen*, 'to manage', fr. O. Fr. *demener*, fr. **de-** & *mener*, 'to lead', fr. L. Lat. *mināre*, 'to drive (cattle), drive with blows and threatening cries', fr. Lat. *minārī*, 'to threaten'; orig. 'to jut out, overhang, project'. See **minatory**, **mount (I.)**. (reflex., archaic) To behave, conduct, comport oneself: *demean yourselves like men*.

demean (II.), vb. reflex. Prob. often associated w. prec. Formed fr. **de-** & **mean (III.)**, on anal. of **debase**. (reflex.) To lower, degrade, oneself, act in such a way as to lessen one's dignity: *to demean oneself by doing* &c.

demeanour, n. [1. demḗnur; 2. dimī́nə]. M.E. *demenure*. See **demean (I.)** & **-ure**. Mod. suff. on the anal. of *honour*, *flavour* &c. Behaviour, bearing, manner of conducting oneself, deportment.

dement, vb. trans. [1. demént; 2. dimént], fr. Lat. *dēmentāre*, 'to drive mad, craze, bewitch', fr. *dēment-(em)*, 'mad, raving', fr. **de-** & *mens*, 'mind'. See **mental**. To drive (a person) out of his senses, cause to become mad; usually in P.P. *demented*, used as adj.: *to be, to become, demented*, go mad;

(colloq.) in sense of crazy with worry, much wrought up: *it will drive me demented.*

dementedly, adv. [1. deméntedli; 2. diméntidli]. P.P. of prec. & **-ly**. In a wild, crazy manner.

démenti, n. [1. dāmontē; 2. demāti]. Fr., fr. *démentir*, 'to give the lie to, to contradict', fr. **de-** & Lat. *mentīri*, 'to lie', q.v. under **mendacious**. Term of diplomacy; an official contradiction, denial of some statement, rumour &c.

dementia, n. [1. demënsha; 2. dimënʃə]. Lat., fr. *dēment-(em)*. See **dement**. Insanity, characterized by gradual weakening of all the faculties; *senile dementia*, of extreme old age; *precocious dementia*, also *dementia praecox*, of adolescence.

demerit, n. [1. dēmérit; 2. dīmérit], fr. Lat. *dēmerit-(um)*, P.P. of *dēmerēre*, 'to deserve'. See **de-** & **merit**. Want of merit, fault, defect; a bad quality or feature.

demeritorious, adj. [1. dèmeritórius; 2. dìmeritɔ́riəs]. See prec. & **-ory** & **-ous**. (rare) Deserving ill, blameworthy, reverse of meritorious.

demersal, adj. [1. dēmérsl; 2. dīmə́sl], fr. obs. vb. *demerse*, 'to immerse, plunge in water', fr. **de-** & Lat. *mers-(um)*, P.P. type of *mergere*, see **merge**, & **-al**. Sunk, immersed; **a** of fish caught by trawl or line, not by drift-net; **b** of eggs of fish which develop below the surface.

demesne, n. [1. demán, demén; 2. diméin, dimín], fr. O. Fr. *demeine*. See **domain**. The *-s-* is due to confusion w. O. Fr. *mesnee* 'household', fr. Lat. *mansiōnem*. See **mansion**. Landed property kept in owners' hands for his own use, not let to tenants; specif., park and gardens surrounding the house. Phr. *royal demesne*, land held by the Crown; (law) *to hold in demesne*, have in one's possession (estates).

demi-, pref., fr. Fr., fr. Lat. *dīmidius*, 'half', *dīmidium*, 'a half', fr. **dis-** & *medius*, *-um*, 'middle'. See **medium**. Half, partial.

demigod, n. [1. démigòd; 2. démigɔ̀d]. **demi-** & **god**. **a** A hero who has been deified; **b** the son of a god and a mortal; **c** (fig.) person who is supposed to possess high heroic qualities, beauty, and virtue.

demijohn, n. [1. démijòn; 2. démidžɔ̀n]. Prob. fr. Fr. *dame-jeanne*, i.e. *Dame Jeanne*, as personification. A large narrow-necked bottle with a covering of wicker-work.

demi-lune, n. [1. démi lún; 2. démi ljún]. Fr. See **demi-** & **lune**. **a** A half-moon; **b** crescent-shaped fortification.

demi-monde, n. [1. dèmi mónd; 2. dèmi mɔ́nd]. Fr., 'half-world'. Class of females of dubious social standing and dingy or tarnished reputation; *demi-mondaine*, lady of this class.

demi-rep, n. [1. dèmi rép; 2. dèmi rép]. Abbr. for **demi-** & **repute**. Person, esp. woman, of doubtful character and suspected immorality.

demisable, adj. [1. demízabl; 2. dimáizəbl]. See **demise** (I.) & **able**. (of property &c.) That can be demised, conveyed, transferred.

demise (I.), vb. trans. [1. demíz; 2. dimáiz], fr. next word. **a** To leave as a legacy, convey, grant by a deed, lease &c.; **b** to give up, transfer (an estate &c.) to another by death.

demise (II.), n., fr. O. Fr. *demise*, P.P. of *desmettre*, 'to send away, dismiss'; reflex., 'to abdicate'. See **demit**. **1.** The act of demising, conveyance of property. **2. a** The laying aside, and transmission, of an estate, hereditary office &c., by death, esp. *demise of the Crown*, on death of the sovereign; hence, **b** (by transf.) death.

demisemiquaver, n. [1. dèmisémikwâver; 2. dèmisémikwèivə]. **demi-** & **semiquaver**. **a** A note in music, half the length of a semiquaver; **b** written or printed symbol representing this note.

demission, n. [1. demíshun; 2. dimíʃən], fr. Fr. *démission*, fr. L. Lat. *dismissiōn-(em)*, w. change of pref., fr. Lat. *dīmissiōnem*, 'a sending forth'. See **de-** & **mission**. The act of demitting; resignation, abdication, of an office.

demit, vb. trans. & intrans. [1. demít; 2. dimít], fr. O. Fr. *desmettre*, fr. **dis-** & Lat. *mittere*, 'to send'. See **mission**. **a** trans. To resign, give up (an office); **b** intrans., to resign office, abdicate; the word usually implies voluntary relinquishment.

demiurge, n. [1. démiërj; 2. dímiə̄dž], fr. Gk. *dēmiourgós*, 'a skilled workman; the maker of the world, creator', fr. *dḗmios*, 'belonging to the people' (see **demos**), & *érgon*, 'work', earlier **wergon*. See **energy** & **erg**, & cp. **work**. **a** In some ancient Greek states, a magistrate; **b** (in Gk. philos.) the creative spirit or agent who fashioned the world.

demiurgic, adj. [1. dèmiërjik; 2. dìmiə̄džik]. Prec. & **-ic**. Pertaining to the creative spirit.

demivolt, n. [1. démivolt; 2. démivɔlt], fr. Fr. *demi-volte*, fr. **demi-** & *volte*, 'a leap'. See **vault** (III.). (of a horse) A bound into the air with forelegs raised.

demobilization, n. [1. dēmòbilīzáshun; 2. dīmòubilaizéiʃən]. See next word & **-ation**. The act of demobilizing; state or process of being demobilized.

demobilize, vb. trans. [1. dēmóbilīz; 2. dīmóubilaiz]. See **de-** & **mobilize**. **a** To disband, break up, dismiss (forces &c.); **b** to discharge (an individual) from the army, at the end of a war, or campaign.

democracy, n. [1. demókrasi; 2. dimɔ́krəsi], fr. Fr. *démocratie*, fr. Lat., fr. Gk. *dēmokratía*, 'democracy, popular government'. See **demos** & **-cracy**. **a** A form of government in which all classes, including the lowest, have a voice in government, directly, or through their chosen representatives; hence, **b** a state having this form of government; **c** the lower classes, the people.

democrat, n. [1. démokrat; 2. déməkræt], fr. Fr. *démocrate*, fr. prec. **a** One who upholds the political rights of the people; one who supports, believes in, democracy; **b** (cap.) member of one of the two great political parties of the U.S.A.; contrasted with *Republican*.

democratic, adj. [1. dèmokrátik; 2. dèməkrǽtik]. See prec. & **-ic**. **a** Pertaining to, based on, democracy; believing in the rights of the people; **b** of, pertaining to, the political party, *Democratic Party*, in U.S.A.

democratically, adv. [1. dèmokrátikali; 2. dèməkrǽtikəli]. Prec. & **-al** & **-ly**. In a democratic manner.

democratism, n. [1. demókratizm; 2. dimɔ́krətizəm]. See **democrat** & **-ism**. The doctrines of democracy.

democratize, vb. trans. [1. demókratīz; 2. dimɔ́krətaiz]. See **democrat** & **-ize**. To make into a democracy; introduce democratic principles into.

demogorgon, n. [1. dḗmogórgon; 2. dímɔgɔ́gən]. Gk. *dêmos*, 'people' (see **demos**) & *gorgós*, 'terrible' (see **gorgon**); prob. fr. some Oriental name, assimilated to the Gk. by popular etymol. (Gk. mythol.) An unknown, terrible, and sinister deity.

demographic, adj. [1. dèmográfik; 2. dìmɔgrǽfik]. See next word & **-ic**. Pertaining to demography.

demography, n. [1. dēmógrafi; 2. dīmɔ́grəfi]. See **demos** & **-graphy**. Statistics of births, deaths, diseases &c., in a community.

demoiselle, n. [1. dèmwahzél; 2. dèmwazél]. Fr., 'young lady'. See **damsel**. **1.** (archaic) Young lady. **2. a** A kind of crane, the Numidian crane, of Northern Africa, with long feathers and white plumes above the eyes; **b** name of various kinds of dragon-fly.

demolish, vb. trans. [1. demólish; 2. dimɔ́liʃ], fr. Fr. *démolir* (see **-ish**), fr. Lat. *dēmōlīri*, 'to pull down, destroy', fr. **de-** & *mōlīri*, 'to construct', fr. *mōles*, 'mass'. See **mole** (II.). **a** (lit. and fig.) To overthrow, pull down, destroy, make an end of: *demolish a building, argument* &c.; **b** (colloq.) to consume, finish, eat up: *to demolish three eggs for breakfast.*

demolition, n. [1. dèmolíshun; 2. dèməlíʃən], fr. Fr., fr. Lat. *dēmōlitiōn-(em)*, 'a tearing down, demolishing', fr. *dēmōlīt-(um)*, P.P. type of *dēmōlīri*. See **demolish** & **-ion**. The act or process of demolishing; state of being demolished, esp. of the pulling down of buildings.

demon, **daemon**, n. [1. dḗmun; 2. dīmən], fr. L. Lat. *daemon*, 'a spirit, genius'; (eccles.) 'an evil spirit', fr. Gk. *daímōn*, lit. 'distributor, dispenser (of destiny)', hence 'a god; a god or goddess of inferior rank; a tutelary spirit, genius; an evil spirit', fr. Aryan base **dəi-*, **dāi-*, **dī-*; cp. Gk. *daiomai*, 'I distribute'. See **damn** & **time** & cp. **demos** & **deme**. **1.** (in anct. mythol.) **a** A spirit, supernatural being, ranking between gods and men; **b** a familiar, inspiring spirit, a genius: *the demon of Socrates*, usually spelt *daemon*. **2. a** A spirit of evil, devil; hence, **b** a wicked, malignant, and destructive person; personification of wickedness: *a regular demon.*

demonetization, n. [1. dēmónitīzáshun; 2. dīmɔ́nitaizéiʃən]. Next word & **-ation**. Act of demonetizing; state of being demonetized.

demonetize, vb. trans. [1. dēmónitīz, dēmúnitīz; 2. dīmɔ́nitaiz, dīmánitaiz], fr. **de-** & Lat. *monēta*, 'money' (see **money**), & **-ize**. To deprive currency of its standard value.

demoniac, adj. & n. [1. dēmṓniak; 2. dīmóuniæk], fr. L. Lat. *daemoniacus*, fr. Gk. *daimónios*, 'pertaining to a demon' (see **demon**), & **-ac**. **1.** adj. **a** Resembling, pertaining to, a demon; **b** under the power of a demon, possessed by an evil spirit. **2.** n. A person under the influence of a demon.

demoniacal, adj. [1. dèmoníakl; 2. dìmənáiəkl]. See **demoniac** & **-al**. **a** Pertaining to demons, of the nature of demons; **b** possessed by a demon, evil spirit; maddened.

demoniacally, adv. Prec. & **-ly**. In a demoniacal, frenzied, manner.

demonic, **daemonic**, adj. [1. dēmónik; 2. dīmɔ́nik], fr. Lat., fr. Gk. *daimonikós*, 'possessed by a demon'. See **demon** & **-ic**. Under the influence of a demon, inspired.

demonism, n. [1. dḗmonizm; 2. dímənizəm]. See **demon** & **-ism**. Belief in demons and in their power to influence human life.

demonist, n. [1. dḗmonist; 2. dímənist]. See **demon** & **-ist**. Adherent of demonism.

demonize, vb. trans. [1. dḗmonīz; 2. dímənaiz]. See **demon** & **-ize**. To convert into a demon; represent, conceive of, as a demon.

demonocracy, n. [1. dḗmonókrasi; 2. dímənɔ́krəsi]. See **demon** & **-cracy**. The rule of demons.

demonolatry, n. [1. dèmonólatri; 2. dìmənɔ́lətri]. See **demon** & **-latry**. The worship of ghosts, demons, and of malign spiritual powers.

demonologist, n. [1. dèmonólojist; 2. dìmənɔ́lədžist]. See next word & **-ist**. A student of demonology.

demonology, n. [1. dèmonóloji; 2. dìmənɔ́lədži]. See **demon** & **-logy**. The study of popular beliefs in demons and their influence.

demonstrability, n. [1. demónstrabíliti; 2. dimɔ́nstrəbíliti]. Next word & **-ity**. The quality of being demonstrable.

demonstrable, adj. [1. demónstrabl, démonstrabl; 2. dimɔ́nstrəbl, démənstrəbl], fr. Lat. *dēmonstrābilis*. See **demonstrate** & **-able**. Capable of being demonstrated, proved.

demonstrably, adv. [1. demónstrabli; 2. dimɔ́nstrəbli]. See prec. & **-ly**. In a manner that can be demonstrated.

demonstrate, vb. trans. & intrans. [1. démonstrāt; 2. démənstreit], fr. Lat. *dēmonstrāt-(um)*, P.P. type of *dēmonstrāre*, 'to point out, indicate'; fig. 'to show, prove', fr. **de-** & *monstrāre*, 'to show, point out'. See **monster**. **1.** trans. To show, prove by evidence and argument. **2.** intrans. **a** To make a manifestation or demonstration of feelings, sympathies, opinions; **b** specif. (mil.) to give evidence of, make a manifestation of force, readiness to fight &c.

demonstration, n. [1. dèmonstráshun; 2. dèmənstréiʃən]. See prec. & **-ation.** The act of demonstrating; specif. **a** a practical lesson, an exhibition of method; instruction by actual example; **b** clear and logical explanation or setting forth; **c** manifestation, open expression, of feelings by words or gestures; **d** expression of public feeling by acts, e.g. processions, mass-meetings &c.; **e** (mil.) exhibition of force, either to show readiness for war, or to deceive the enemy, as to one's real intentions.

demonstrationist, n. [1. dèmonstráshunist; 2. dèmənstréiʃənist]. See prec. & **-ist.** One who takes part in a public demonstration, as an expression of opinion on a political or social question.

demonstrative, adj. [1. demónstrativ; 2. dimɔ́nstrətiv]. See **demonstrate** & **-ive. 1. a** Showing clearly, pointing out: (esp. gram.) *demonstrative pronoun, adjective*; **b** proving logically, tending to prove. **2. a** (of persons, character &c.) Given to outward expression of feelings; expressing inward feeling; **b** (of feelings &c.) expressed openly, with complete lack of reserve.

demonstratively, adv. Prec. & **-ly.** In a demonstrative manner.

demonstrativeness, n. See prec. & **-ness.** The quality of being demonstrative.

demonstrator, n. [1. démonstrātor; 2. démənstreitə]. See **demonstrate** & **-or.** One who demonstrates; specif. **a** a teacher who does practical scientific work with pupils; esp. a junior teacher in a laboratory assisting a professor: *demonstrator in anatomy*; **b** one who takes part in a public demonstration.

demoralization, n. [1. demòralīzáshun; 2. dimɔ̀rəlaizéiʃən]. See next word & **-ation. a** Act or process of demoralizing; **b** state of being demoralized.

demoralize, vb. trans. [1. demóralīz; 2. dimɔ́rəlaiz], fr. Fr. *démoraliser.* See **de-** & **moral** & **-ize. a** To injure morally, weaken moral character of; **b** to undermine, weaken, self-control, discipline, courage of; to dishearten, disorganize.

demos, n. [1. dḗmos; 2. dímɔs]. Gk. *dêmos*, 'a division of a country, district, township'; hence 'the people of a country, inhabitants'; esp. 'the common people, lower classes'. Cogn. w. Scrt. *dā-ti*, 'to reap, gather in harvest, to share', & Gk. *daímōn*, lit. 'distributor'. See **demon.** The common people, lower classes; esp. in bad sense, considered as an irresponsible, uncontrollable rabble.

Demosthenic, adj. [1. dèmosthénik; 2. dìmɔsþénik]. Pertaining to or resembling the Athenian orator, Demosthenes; eloquent.

demotic, adj. [1. dēmótik; 2. dīmɔ́tik], fr. Gk. *dēmotikós*, 'for the people, in common use'. See **demos** & **-ic.** Popular, belonging to the people; specif., of the popular form of writing in Ancient Egypt, as distinct from *hieratic.*

demulcent, adj. & n. [1. dēmúlsent; 2. dīmálsənt], fr. Pres. Part. (see **-ent**) of Lat. *dēmulcēre*, 'to stroke down'; fig., 'to soften', fr. **de-** & *mulcēre*, 'to stroke'; fig. 'to soothe, soften, alleviate; caress, cajole'; prob. cogn. w. Lat. *mulcāre*, 'to treat roughly, to beat', & w. Lat. *multa*, orig. 'a punishment'; hence 'a pecuniary penalty, a fine'; see **mulct.** Cogn. also w. Gk. *bláp-tein*, 'to injure', *blábē* (by assimilation fr. **mlap-*), 'injury'; Scrt. *mṛktáś*, 'wounded'; Aryan base **mḷkʷ-*; the orig. meaning seems to have been 'to touch, stroke', subsequently differentiated into 'touch lightly, caress &c.', & 'touch, handle, roughly'; hence 'punish' &c. The same base **mḷ-*, **mel-*, w. a different suff., appears in Lat. *mulgēre*, 'to milk', Gk. *amélgein*, 'to milk'. See **milk. a** adj. Tending to soothe, softening; **b** n., a soothing substance (ointment or medicine).

demur (I.), vb. intrans. [1. demér; 2. dimə́], fr. O. Fr. *demeurer*, 'to tarry, linger', fr. Low Lat. *dēmorāre*, fr. Lat. *dēmorāri*, 'to linger, delay; to retard, detain', fr. **de-** & *morāri*, 'to delay, tarry; to detain, hinder'. See **moratory. a** To hesitate, object, have scruples about, raise objections to (a proposal): *demur to*; also absol.; **b** (law) to enter a demurrer.

demur (II.), n., fr. prec. Hesitation, expression of objections; esp. in Phr. *without demur.*

demure, adj. [1. demū́r; 2. dimjɔ́], fr. **de-** & O. Fr. *mure, meur*, fr. Lat. *mātūrus*, 'ripe, mature; fit, seasonable; powerful, vigorous'. See **mature. a** Modest, sober, staid; **b** affecting coyness and gravity of demeanour.

demurely, adv. Prec. & **-ly.** In a demure manner.

demureness, n. See prec. & **-ness.** The quality of being demure.

demurrable, adj. [1. demúrabl; 2. dimárəbl]. See **demur** (I.) & **-able.** (law) Of a character to warrant entering a demurrer.

demurrage, n. [1. demúrij; 2. dimáridž]. See **demur** (I.) & **-age. a** Undue delay, detention, of vessels in port, of railway trucks at junctions &c.; **b** compensation, allowance, for this; **c** fee charged by railway companies and others on account of property left on their premises by the owners.

demurrer, n. [1. demúrer; 2. dimárə], fr. O. Fr. *demorer* (infin.), used as n. See **demur** (I.). (law) A pleading by a party in a lawsuit that the case should be stopped, that the other (opposing) party should not be allowed to proceed, on the ground that the latter's case is insufficient in law to maintain his claim, or alleging some other legal flaw. Phr. *to put in a demurrer.*

demy, n. [1. demī́; 2. dimái]. See **demi-. 1.** A size of paper ($22\frac{1}{2} \times 17\frac{1}{2}$ ins.). **2.** The holder of a demyship, q.v., at Magdalen College, Oxford.

demyship, n. [1. demī́ship; 2. dimáiʃip]. Prec. & **-ship.** Peculiar type of scholarship at Magdalen College, Oxford, having originally half the value of a fellowship and held by graduates of the university who were unable through poverty to continue their studies without assistance.

den, n. [1. den; 2. den]. O.E. *denn*, 'a den, lair of wild beast'; cp. N.H.G. *tenne*, 'a threshing floor'; Du. *denne*, 'a floor'; O.H.G. *tan-(esil)*, 'a wild ass', *tanna*, 'fir'; M.L.G. *dan*, 'forest'; Prim. Gmc. **đan-jō*, **đan-wō.* The word is difficult to trace outside Gmc., & its orig. meaning is doubtful. It is perhaps cogn. w. Scrt. *dhan-vanaś*, 'fruit tree', & w. Gk. *thámnos*, 'thicket, copse' (? fr. **than-m-os*). **1. a** Retreat, lair, hiding-place of a wild animal; **b** cage for wild beasts in a menagerie or zoological garden. **2.** Dismal, small, squalid room. **3.** (colloq.) Small private room, such as a study or workshop.

denarius, n. [1. denā́rius; 2. dinéəriəs]. Lat. *dēnārius*, 'containing ten'; esp. 'a silver coin, containing orig. 10 asses', fr. *dēni*, 'ten each', fr. **dek-s-no-*, fr. *dec-em*, '10' (on anal. of *sēni* fr. **sex-ni*), see **deci-**, & **-ary.** Ancient Roman silver coin, worth about 9d. Hence English *d* as symbol for pence.

denary, adj. [1. dḗnari; 2. dínəri], fr. Lat. *dēnārius*, 'containing ten; a coin of the value of 10 asses'. See prec. Tenfold; increasing by tens.

denationalization, n. [1. dēnáshunalīzáshun; 2. dīnǽʃənəlaizéiʃən]. Next word & **-ation. a** The act or process of denationalizing; **b** state of being denationalized.

denationalize, vb. trans. [1. dēnáshunalīz; 2. dīnǽʃənəlaiz]. **de-** & **nationalize. 1. a** To deprive of national rights; **b** to overthrow from rank of an independent nation. **2.** To remove from possession of a nation.

denaturalization, n. [1. dēnachuralīzáshun; 2. dīnætʃərəlaizéiʃən]. Next word & **-ation.** The act or process of denaturalizing; state of being denaturalized.

denaturalize, vb. trans. [1. dēnáchuralīz; 2. dīnǽtʃərəlaiz]. See **de-** & **naturalize. a** To remove natural qualities of, alter characteristics of; **b** to deprive of naturalization, remove rights of citizenship.

denature, vb. trans. [1. dēnáchur; 2. dīnéitʃə], fr. Fr. *dénaturer.* See **dis-** & **nature.** To alter natural character of, make unfit for food, by adulteration &c.: *to denature alcohol*, render it unwholesome and unpleasing by addition of a substance which gives it a nasty taste.

dendr(i)-, dendro-, pref., fr. Gk. *déndron*, 'a tree', fr. **dendrewon*, perh. by haplology fr. **dendo-drewon*, fr. **dend-* for **gʷend-*, **gʷṇd-*, 'wood' (cp. Scrt. *gada*, 'club'), & **drew-on*, 'a tree'; cp. Goth. *triu*, O.E. *trēow-*, 'a tree', & see **tree, dryad.** Of a tree, of trees.

dendriform, adj. [1. déndriform; 2. déndrifɔ̄m]. See prec. & **form.** Having the appearance of, shaped like, a tree.

dendrite, n. [1. déndrīt; 2. déndrait], fr. Gk. *dendritēs*, 'of a tree'. See **dendri-** & **-ite.** Mineral with markings resembling trees or plants.

dendritic, adj. [1. dendrítik; 2. dendrítik]. See prec. & **-ic.** Having branched markings resembling trees or plants.

dendro-. See **dendri-.**

dendrodont, n. [1. déndrodònt; 2. déndrədɔ̀nt]. **dendro-** & Gk. *odónt-*, 'tooth', q.v. under **dent-.** A kind of fossil fish, the teeth of which show branching lines.

dendroid, adj. [1. déndroid; 2. déndrɔid]. **dendro-** & **-oid.** Resembling a tree.

dendrolite, n. [1. déndrolīt; 2. déndrəlait]. **dendro-** & **-lite.** A fossil plant.

dendrologist, n. [1. dendrólojist; 2. dendrɔ́lədžist]. See next word & **-ist.** A writer on, student of, dendrology.

dendrology, n. [1. dendróloji; 2. dendrɔ́lədži]. **dendro-** & **-logy.** The study of trees.

dendrometer, n. [1. dendrómeter; 2. dendrɔ́mitə]. **dendro-** & **-meter.** Instrument for measuring the height and diameter of trees.

dene (I.), also **dean**, n. [1. dēn; 2. dīn]. O.E. *denu*, M.E. *dēne*, 'a valley'; cogn. w. **den.** Small valley, hollow in a hill or down.

dene (II.), n. Perh. fr. Eastern form *dēne* of O.E. *-dȳne* (only in compounds), derivative of *dūn*, 'a hill, mound'. See **down** (II.). A low sandy tract of land near the sea.

denegation, n. [1. dènegáshun; 2. dìnigéiʃən], fr. Lat. *dēnegāt-(um)*, P.P. type of *dēnegāre*, 'to deny; to reject, refuse'. See **deny** & **-ation.** The act of denying; denial, refusal.

dene-hole, n. [1. dḗn hōl; 2. dín houl]. Etymol. uncertain; perh. fr. *Dane.* Ancient artificial cave found in the chalk hills of Kent and Essex.

dengue, n. [1. dénggā; 2. déŋgei]. Span., 'stiffness'; prob. corrupt. of African native name. Cp. Swahili *dinga.* An infectious, tropical and subtropical fever, accompanied by pains in the joints and eruption on the skin.

deniable, adj. [1. denī́abl; 2. dinájəbl]. See **deny** & **-able.** Capable of being denied.

denial, n. [1. denī́al; 2. dinájəl]. See **deny** & **-al. a** The act of denying; contradiction, refutation of statement: *to issue a strong, flat, denial*; **b** refusal, withholding: *denial of justice*; esp. *self-denial*, abstention from what gives one pleasure.

denier, n. [1. dénier; 2. déniə]. O. Fr. *denier*, fr. Lat. See **denarius.** (archaic) A copper coin of small value.

denigrate, vb. trans. [1. dénigrāt; 2. dénigreit], fr. Lat. *dēnigrāt-(um)*, P.P. type of *dēnigrāre*, 'to blacken thoroughly'; fig. 'to defame', fr. **de-** & *nigrāre*, 'to be black; to blacken'. See **negro.** To blacken; (in fig. sense) to cast aspersions on the character of, defame.

denigration, n. [1. dènigráshun; 2. dènigréiʃən]. See prec. & **-ation.** Defamation, blackening of character.

denim, n. [1. dénim; 2. dénim], fr. Fr. *serge de Nimes*, 'serge of Nimes', town in south of France. A coarse cotton drill, used for making overalls &c.

denitrate, vb. trans. [1. dēnī́trāt; 2. dīnáitreit]. **de-** & **nitrate.** To remove nitric acid from.

denitration, n. [1. dènītráshun; 2. dīnaitréiʃən]. Prec. & **-ion**. Process of removing nitric acid.

denitrify, vb. trans. [1. dēnítrifī; 2. dīnáitrifai]. See **de-** & **nitrify**. To denitrate.

denizen (I.), n. [1. dénizn; 2. dénizən], fr. O. Fr. *deinzein* (used in London Records to denote traders *within* the city franchise, contrasted w. *forein*, 'without'), fr. *deinz*, 'in', & *-ein*, see **-an**. *Deinz*, 'in' (Mod. Fr. *dans*), is fr. Lat. *dē* (see **de-**) & *intus*, 'within, from within', fr. *in* (see **in**), the suff.- *tus* expressing place whence. **a** An inhabitant; a person, animal &c. living in a particular place, country, region: *a denizen of the woods* &c.; **b** one admitted to the rights and privileges of an inhabitant; an alien admitted by naturalization to citizenship.

denizen (II.), vb. trans., fr. prec. **a** (usually pass.) To admit to the rights of an inhabitant, to settle, establish as inhabitant; **b** (of land, a country &c.) to supply with inhabitants, settle.

denominate, vb. trans. [1. denóminăt; 2. dinɔ́mineit], fr. Lat. *dēnōmināt-(um)*, P.P. type of *dēnōmināre*, 'to name specifically', fr. **de-** & *nōmināre*, 'to name, give a name to'. See **nominate**. To name, call, give a name to, designate.

denomination, n. [1. denòmináshun; 2. dinɔ̀minéiʃən]. See prec. & **-ation**. **1.** The act of naming; a name. Hence, **2**, the name of a particular class or kind. Specif., a particular religious body. **3.** (arith.) Units of measures of weight, length, money &c.: *to reduce feet and inches to the same denomination*.

denominational, adj. [1. denòmináshunal; 2. dinɔ̀minéiʃənəl]. Prec. & **-al**. Of, connected with, having character of, under the direction of, a particular religious body, or church: *denominational schools, religious teaching*.

denominationalize, vb. trans. [1. denòmináshunalīz; 2. dinɔ̀minéiʃənəlaiz]. Prec. & **-ize**. To make denominational, devote to the principles or interests of a particular class, or sect.

denominative, adj. [1. denóminativ; 2. dinɔ́minətiv]. See **denominate** & **-ive**. **a** Giving, having function of, a name; **b** (log.) possessing certain attributes which determine the name.

denominator, n. [1. denóminātor; 2. dinɔ́mineitə]. See **denominate** & **-or**. (arith.) That which names the class; the divisor, the lower number in a vulgar fraction.

denotation, n. [1. dènōtáshun; 2. dìnoutéiʃən], fr. Lat. *dēnotātiōn-(em)*, 'a marking or pointing out'. See **denote** & **-ation**. **1. a** The act, process, of denoting; **b** that by which anything is denoted, name, designation, graphic symbol &c. **2.** The meaning, exact force of a word. Specif. **3.** (log.) the number of objects to which a word or term refers, compared with *connotation*.

denotative, adj. [1. dēnótativ; 2. dīnóutətiv], fr. Lat. *dēnotāt-(um)*, P.P. type of *dēnotāre*, 'to mark out, specify', & **-ive**. See **denote**. Having the function of denoting, indicating, naming.

denotatively, adv. Prec. & **-ly**. In a denotative manner.

denote, vb. trans. [1. denṓt; 2. dinóut], fr. Fr. *dénoter*, fr. Lat. *dēnotāre*, 'to set a mark on; to point out, specify, designate; to stigmatize', fr. **de-** & *notāre*, 'to mark; to make a note of; to observe, note; to indicate, signify'. See **note (II.)**. **a** To mark, indicate, distinguish, by a sign or symbol; **b** (of a mark, sign, letter, word &c.) to be a symbol of, to express, mean.

dénouement, n. [1. dānóomon; 2. denūmã]. Fr., fr. *dénouer*, 'to untie, unravel', fr. **de-** & Lat. *nōdāre*, 'to furnish with knots; to tie in a knot', fr. *nōdus*, 'a knot; a knob, node'; fig. 'a knotty point, difficulty'. See **node**. The final situation, unravelling, last stage of development of a plot; final revelation, in play, book &c.; climax of a series of events.

denounce, vb. trans. [1. denóuns; 2. dináuns], fr. O. Fr. *denoncier*, fr. Lat. *dēnuntiāre*, (esp. legal) 'to make an official announcement of'; hence 'to announce, declare; to threaten, denounce'; fr. **de-** & *nuntiāre*, 'to declare, report, make known; to inform against, denounce', fr. *nuntius*, 'one who brings news, a messenger, reporter'. See **nuncio**. **1. a** (of action towards persons and their acts) To make a public accusation against, cry out against; to call down vengeance upon; **b** (archaic, of punishments &c.) to announce as being deserved: *to denounce judgement, vengeance, against*. **2.** To declare (a treaty &c.) at an end, repudiate it.

denouncement, n. [1. denóunsment; 2. dináunsmənt]. Prec. & **-ment**. Denunciation.

de novo, adv. [1. dē nṓvō; 2. dī nóuvou]. Lat., lit. 'from that which is new'. See **de-** & *novus*, 'new'. See **novel** & cp. **new**. All over again, afresh.

dense, adj. [1. dens; 2. dens], fr. Lat. *densus*, 'thick, with parts crowded closely together; set close, crowded'; (of speech) 'condensed, concise', fr. **dent-so*, or **dent-to*; Aryan base **den-t-*, **dn̥-t-* &c., 'close together, compact, thick'. Cp. Gk. *dasús*, 'thick' (see **dasy-**), fr. **dat-ús*, fr. **dn̥-t-us*. **a** Packed tightly together, compact, thick, with its parts crowded together; impenetrable: *a dense crowd; a dense forest; a dense fog*; **b** (fig.) thick in mind, difficult to penetrate with ideas; very stupid, slow of understanding.

densely, adv. Prec. & **-ly**. In a dense manner, thickly, closely.

denseness, n. See prec. & **-ness**. The quality of being dense.

densimeter, n. [1. densímeter; 2. densímitə], fr. Lat. *dens-(us)*. See **dense** & **-meter**. Instrument for measuring the density or specific gravity of a substance.

density, n. [1. dénsiti; 2. dénsiti], fr. Lat. *densitāt-(em)*, 'thickness, density'. See **dense** & **-ty**. **a** The quality of being dense; stupidity; **b** (specif., phys.) the proportion of mass to bulk or volume: specific gravity.

dent (I.), n. [1. dent; 2. dent]. M.E. *dent*, 'a blow', dialectal variant of **dint**; O.E. *dynt*, S. Eastern *dent*, 'a stroke, blow, bruise'. A slight irregularity, depression, in a hard surface made by a blow, or by pressure.

dent (II.), vb. trans., fr. prec. To impart a dent to.

dent-, denti-, pref., fr. Lat. *dent-is*, genit. of *dens*, 'a tooth'; hence 'a point, spike'; fig. 'envy, ill-will'; Aryan base **dn̥t-*, **dent-*, **dont-*. Cp. Gk. *odṓn, odónt-*, Scrt. *dant-am* (acc.), *datáś* (genit.), O. Ir. *dēt*, O.H.G. *zand*, Goth. *tunþ-us*, O.E. *tōþ* (see **tooth**), Lith. *dantis*. Cogn. also w. O.E. *tūsc* (see **tusk**). The full base was **edent-*, **edont-* &c., a participial formation fr. **ed-*, 'to eat'; cp. Lat. *edere*, 'to eat'. See **eat, edible**. Of a tooth, pertaining to teeth.

dental, adj. & n. [1. déntal; 2. déntəl]. See prec. & **-al**. **a** adj. Having to do with the teeth, or with dentistry: *dental surgeon*, a dentist; **b** adj. & n., (phon.) of certain consonantal sounds formed by placing point of tongue against, or near, the upper teeth; such sounds as [t, d, n, þ, ð].

dentate, adj. [1. déntāt; 2. dénteit]. See **dent-** & **-ate**. (of leaves) Having tooth-like projections and V-shaped indentations.

dentation, n. [1. dentáshun; 2. dentéiʃən]. See prec. & **-ion**. (bot.) **a** Quality of being dentate; **b** one of the projections on the edge of a leaf.

denticle, n. [1. déntikl; 2. déntikl], fr. Lat. *denticulus*, 'a small tooth'; hence (archit.) 'projecting bracket'. See **dent-** & **-cule**. **a** A small tooth; **b** a pointed projection; **c** (archit.) a dentil.

denticular, adj. [1. dentíkūlar; 2. dentíkjulə]. See prec. & **-ar**. Shaped like a small tooth.

denticulate(d), adj. [1. dentíkūlāt(ed); 2. dentíkjulèit(id)], fr. Lat. *denticulāt-(um)*, 'having small teeth'. See **denticle** & **-ate** & **-ed**. Furnished with small tooth-like projections.

denticulation, n. [1. dentìkūláshun; 2. dentìkjuléiʃən]. Prec. & **-ion**. The quality of being denticulate; indentation, notching.

dentiform, adj. [1. déntiform; 2. déntifɔ̄m]. See **denti-** & **form**. Tooth-shaped.

dentifrice, n. [1. déntifris; 2. déntifris], fr. Lat. *dentifricium*, 'powder for rubbing the teeth', fr. **denti-** & a formation fr. base *fric-*, 'rub', cp. *fricāre*, 'to rub'. See **friction**. Trade, or shop word for tooth-powder, or -paste.

dentigerous, adj. [1. dentíjerus; 2. dentídžərəs]. See **denti-** & **-gerous**. Having teeth, lit. tooth-bearing.

dentil, n. [1. déntil; 2. déntil], fr. O. Fr. *dentille*, dimin. of *dent*, 'tooth', fr. Lat. *dent-(em)*, 'tooth'. See **dent-**. (archit.) One of a series of small square projecting blocks in the moulding of a cornice.

dentil-cornice, n. A cornice ornamented with dentils.

dentilingual, adj. [1. déntilínggwal; 2. déntilíŋgwəl]. See **denti-** & **lingual**. (phon.) Of certain consonantal sounds formed by the point of the tongue against, or near, the upper teeth.

dentil-moulding, n. One consisting of dentils.

dentine, n. [1. déntin; 2. déntin]. See **dent-** & **-ine**. Hard substance, having the character of bone, of which the chief mass of the teeth is composed.

dentist, n. [1. déntist; 2. déntist]. See **dent-** & **-ist**. Medical man who devotes special attention to the care of the human teeth, who deals with diseases of the teeth, extracts and stops teeth, and fits artificial teeth when necessary.

dentistry, n. [1. déntistri; 2. déntistri]. Prec. & **-ry**. The art and practice of a dentist.

dentition, n. [1. dentíshun; 2. dentíʃən], fr. Lat. *dentītiōn-(em)*, 'teething', fr. *dentīt-(um)*, P.P. type of *dentīre*, (of children) 'to cut teeth', fr. *dent-(em)*, 'a tooth'. See **dent-** & **-ion**. **a** The process of development and cutting of teeth, teething; **b** the type, mode of arrangement, and number, of the teeth in man or in animal species; **c** the teeth of any individual collectively.

dentoid, adj. [1. déntoid; 2. déntɔid]. See **dent-** & **-oid**. Having the form of a tooth.

denture, n. [1. déntūr; 2. déntjə]. **dent-** & **-ure**. (dentist's word) A set of teeth, esp. of false teeth.

denudation, n. [1. dènūdáshun; 2. dìnjūdéiʃən]. Lat. *dēnūdātiōn-(em)*. See **denude** & **-ation**. **a** Act or process of denuding; **b** specif. (geol.) process of removing outer soil &c. from, of uncovering, rocks by action of natural forces, erosion.

denudative, adj. [1. denū́dativ; 2. dinjū́dətiv]. **denude** & **-ative**. Tending to denude.

denude, vb. trans. [1. denū́d; 2. dinjū́d], fr. Lat. *dēnūdāre*, 'to lay bare, strip'; fig. 'to reveal, disclose', fr. **de-** & *nūdāre*, 'to make naked'; fig. 'to disclose, expose', fr. *nūdus*, 'naked'. See **nude**. **a** To uncover, make bare; strip, deprive of natural covering: *a country denuded of vegetation*; **b** to deprive of a quality, possession &c.: *denuded of all decent feelings, of hope; denuded of every farthing he possessed*.

denunciation, n. [1. denùnsiáshun; 2. dinànsiéiʃən], fr. Lat. *dēnuntiātiōn-(em)*, 'an announcement, declaration'. See **denounce** & **-ation**. **a** The act of denouncing; **b** specific instance of this.

denunciative, adj. [1. denúnshiativ; 2. dinánʃiətiv], fr. Lat. *dēnuntiāt-(um)*, P.P. type of *dēnuntiāre*, 'to announce officially; to menace, threaten'. See **denounce** & **-ive**. Expressing, having character of, a denunciation; denunciatory.

denunciatory, adj. [1. denúnshiatori; 2. dinánʃiətəri]. See prec. & **-ory**. Denunciative.

deny, vb. trans. [1. dení; 2. dinái], fr. O. Fr. *denier*, fr. Lat. *dēnegāre*, 'to deny, gainsay; to reject, refuse'; fr. **de-** & *negāre*, 'to say no, deny, refuse'. See **negate**. **1.** To declare (a statement, implication &c.) to be false, to contradict, gainsay; challenge truth of: *to deny a statement, the truth of what is said; to deny that a statement is true.* **2. a** To refuse (a person his request), decline to grant (a request &c.): *he can deny his son nothing; I denied him what he asked*; **b** (reflex.) to withhold from, abstain from, practise abstinence: *to deny oneself every luxury, the pleasure of doing something* &c.; also absol. **3.** To disavow, disown, repudiate: *Peter denied his Master; to deny one's faith, country* &c.

deodand, n. [1. dḗodànd; 2. dîədæ̀nd], fr. Lat. *deo dandum*, 'to be given to God', fr. *deus* (see **deity**), & gerundive of *dare*, 'to give'. See **date (I.)**. (Engl. law) An object, animal &c., which had accidentally caused the death of a human being, and was on that account forfeited to the Crown, to be applied to pious purposes. This practice was abolished in 1846.

deodar, n. [1. dḗodar; 2. dîədā]. Hind. *de'odar*, fr. Scrt. *deva dara*, 'divine tree'; fr. *dēva-* 'divine' (see under **deity**), *dāru*, 'wood, tree'. See **tree**. A kind of cedar, native of the Himalayas, but growing readily in Europe.

deodorant, adj. & n. [1. dēṓdorant; 2. dîóudərənt]. See **deodorize** & **-ant. 1. adj.** Having the power of deodorizing or destroying bad smells. **2. n.** Substance which does this, deodorizer.

deodorization, n. [1. dēōdorīzā́shun; 2. dîóudəraizéiʃən]. Next word & **-ation.** The act or process of deodorizing.

deodorize, vb. trans. [1. dēṓdorīz; 2. dîóudəraiz], fr. **de-** & Lat. *odor*, 'a smell', see **odour**, & **-ize.** To remove odour from, specif. to destroy bad smells by applying some chemical substance as powder, liquid &c. with a stronger and more pleasant smell.

deodorizer, n. [1. dēṓdorīzer; 2. dîóudəraizə]. Prec. & **-er.** Substance which deodorizes, a deodorant.

deontological, adj. [1. dèontolójikl; 2. dìɔntəlɔ́dʒikl]. See **deontology** & **-ic** & **-al.** Pertaining to deontology.

deontologist, n. [1. dèontólojist; 2. dìɔntɔ́lədʒist]. Next word & **-ist.** A student of deontology.

deontology, n. [1. dèontóloji; 2. dìɔntɔ́lədʒi], fr. Gk. *deont-*, Pres. Part. stem of *deî*, 'one ought, it behoves one', impers., fr. *déō*, 'I need, have need of'; cp. Scrt. *dōṣaś*, 'want, need'. See **deutero-** & **-logy.** The theory of moral obligation.

deo volente, adv. [1. dḗō vōlénti; 2. dîou voulénti]. Abbr. D.V. [dí ví]. Lat., God willing, if God permit.

deoxidize, vb. trans. [1. dēóksidīz; 2. dîɔ́ksidaiz]. See **de-** & **oxidize. a** To remove oxygen from; **b** to reduce from the state of an oxide.

deoxygenate, vb. trans. [1. dēóksijenāt; 2. dîɔ́ksidʒineit]. See **de-** & **oxygen** & **-ate.** To deoxidise.

depart, vb. intrans. [1. depárt; 2. dipā́t], fr. O. Fr. *departir*, fr. **de-** & Lat. *partīre*, 'to share, divide, distribute, to separate'. **de-** & **part (II.). 1.** (archaic and poet., except in railway time-tables) To go away from, leave a place; (of person) take one's leave: *it is time to depart; to depart hence; the fever departed from him*; (also of trains): *departs 6.30*, leaves the station at. **2.** To take leave of life, to die; esp. in such a colloq. Phr. as *poor old Jones has departed at last*; set phrase on tombstones, otherwise archaic: *to depart this life.* **3.** *Depart from*: **a** to deviate from ordinary conduct, habit, custom; adopt different course: *to depart from tradition, from one's ordinary mode of life, usual behaviour* &c.; **b** to alter, make a change in: *to depart from one's previous intentions, plans* &c.; Phr. *to depart from one's word, promise* &c., to go back on, break, it.

departed (I.), adj. [1. depárted; 2. dipā́tid], fr. P.P. of prec. (archaic and poet.) Vanished, having passed away, no longer in existence: *departed joys.*

departed (II.), n., fr. prec. *The departed*, the dead (sing. and pl.).

department, n. [1. depártment; 2. dipā́tmənt], fr. Fr. *département*. See **depart** & **-ment.** Part of a whole, separated off, self-contained, and distinct from other parts in character and function. **1.** (of material things) **a** *Department of state*, special branch of administration or legislature &c.; **b** of a business concern, section dealing with particular aspects of the business: *shipping, export, retail department* &c.; **c** (in France) a principal administrative area: *the Department of Seine et Oise* &c. **2.** The office, or building in which the affairs of a department of the state, of business &c. are conducted, or where particular kinds of goods are sold: *This way to the accountant's department, the fancy goods department* &c.; *department store*, in American usage, a large, general retail shop, in which all sorts of goods are sold. **3.** (of non-material things) *A department of thought, speculation, learning* &c., branch, aspect, line, of philosophy or study.

departmental, adj. [1. dèpartméntl; 2. dìpātméntl]. Prec. & **-al.** Pertaining to a department, or to departments, not affecting the whole: *a question of departmental administration, orders* &c.

departmentalism, n. [1. dèpartméntalizm; 2. dìpātméntəlizəm]. Prec. & **-ism.** Strict adherence to departmental rules of administration; usually depreciatory; red-tape.

departmentally, adv. [1. dèpartméntali; 2. dìpātméntəli]. See prec. & **-ly.** According to, by, a department or departments.

departure, n. [1. depárchur; 2. dipā́tʃə]. See **depart** & **-ure. 1.** The act of departing, going away; starting, setting out: *she wept on his departure from home.* Phr. *to take one's departure*, go away. **2.** Deviation, turning aside, divergence, from habit, custom, established conditions &c.: *departure from ancient ways, from tradition* &c. Phr. *a new departure*, change of method, new course of action &c. **3.** (naut.) The distance travelled by a ship due east or west of starting-point.

depasturage, n. [1. depáhschurij; 2. dipā́stʃəridʒ]. Next word & **-age. a** Pasturing of cattle; **b** right to pasture cattle.

depasture, vb. trans. [1. depáhschur; 2. dipā́stʃə]. See **de-** & **pasture. a** (of cattle) To graze on (land); **b** (of persons) to use (land) for pasture; to put (cattle) to feed on land.

depauperate, vb. trans. [1. dēpáwperāt; 2. dîpɔ́pəreit], fr. Med. Lat. *dēpauperāt-(um)*, P.P. type of *dēpauperāre*, 'to make poor, impoverish'. **de-** & **pauper** & **-ate.** To impoverish, weaken, reduce strength of.

depauperation, n. [1. dēpàwperā́shun; 2. dîpɔ̀pəréiʃən]. See prec. & **-ation.** Impoverishment.

depauperize, vb. trans. [1. dēpáwperīz; 2. dîpɔ́pəraiz]. See **de-** & **pauper** & **-ize.** To get rid of, free from, paupers or poverty.

depend, vb. intrans. [1. depénd; 2. dipénd], fr. O. Fr. *dependre* (*-pendre* by anal. w. *pendre*, fr. *pendere*, 'to pay'), fr. Lat. *dēpendēre*, 'to hang from, hang down'; fig. 'to be dependent on, derived from, governed by', fr. **de-** & *pendēre*, 'to hang, be suspended; to float, hover'; fig. 'to rest, depend upon; to be in suspense, be doubtful'. See **pendant. 1.** (archaic and rare) To hang down, be suspended: *a picture depends from a hook.* **2.** (followed by *on* or *upon*) **a** To be supported by, rely on for support: *to depend on what one can earn*; **b** to put trust in, rely upon, be sure of: *a man to be depended on; you can't depend upon a cheap gun*; **c** to be contingent on, governed, conditioned, by, connected with; to vary in accordance with: *happiness depends partly on external circumstances, partly on one's own character; much depends upon the issue of the battle.* **3.** Law (of a suit) to be pending, awaiting final settlement.

dependable, adj. [1. depéndabl; 2. dipéndəbl]. See prec. & **-able.** Able to be depended on.

dependableness, n. Prec. & **-ness.** Quality of being dependable.

dependably, adv. **dependable** & **-ly.** In a dependable manner.

dependant, n. See **dependent (II.)**.

dependence, n. [1. depéndens; 2. dipéndəns]. **depend** & **-ence. 1.** The state of being dependent on, of being supported by, others, living at expense of others: *he refused to live in dependence on anyone.* **2. a** Trust, confidence, reliance: *to place dependence in (a person* &c.); **b** (rare) of that on which one can depend: *his brains were his only dependence.*

dependency, n. [1. depéndensi; 2. dipéndənsi]. See **depend** & **-ency. a** That which is dependent on, subject to, something else; **b** esp. a state subordinate to, governed in last resort by, another state.

dependent (I.), adj. [1. depéndent; 2. dipéndənt]. **depend** & **-ent. 1.** Depending, contingent on, governed by. **2. a** (of persons &c.) Relying for support: *dependent on one's parents, one's earnings* &c.; **b** (of financial position) not independent, subordinate, depending on other persons.

dependent (II.), dependant, n., fr. prec. One who is supported by another; a retainer, vassal, subordinate.

dephlogisticated, adj. [1. dèflojístikāted; 2. dìflɔdʒístikeitid]. See **de-** & **phlogistic** & **-ate** & **-ed.** (old chem.) Deprived of **phlogiston**; esp. *dephlogisticated air*, name first given to oxygen by its discoverer Priestley.

dephosphorization, n. [1. dēfósforīzā́shun; 2. dîfɔ́sfəraizéiʃən]. Next word & **-ation.** Process of removing phosphorus.

dephosphorize, vb. trans. [1. dēfósforīz; 2. dîfɔ́sfəraiz]. See **de-** & **phosphor(o)-** & **-ize.** To remove phosphorus from.

depict, vb. trans. [1. depíkt; 2. dipíkt], fr. Lat. *dēpict-(um)*, P.P. type of *dēpingere*, 'to portray, sketch, paint; to describe, represent; to embroider', fr. **de-** & *pingere*, 'to represent in a picture; to paint, colour; to adorn, decorate'. See **picture. a** To present a visual image of (an object or event); to draw, paint, sculpture; **b** to describe (an object or event) in words.

depiction, n. [1. depíkshun; 2. dipíkʃən]. Prec. & **-ion. a** The act, process, of depicting; **b** the drawn, painted, sculptured representation of something; verbal description of anything.

depicture, vb. trans. [1. depíkchur; 2. dipíktʃə]. **de-** & **picture (II.).** To represent, depict.

depilate, vb. trans. [1. dépilāt; 2. dípileit], fr. Lat. *dēpilāt-(um)*, P.P. type of *dēpilāre*, 'to pull out the hair, pluck feathers, of', fr. **de-** & *pilus*, 'a hair'. See **pile (VII.).** To remove hair from.

depilation, n. [1. dèpilā́shun; 2. dìpiléiʃən]. Prec. & **-ion.** The removal of hair.

depilatory, adj. & n. [1. depílatori; 2. dipílətəri]. **depilate** & **-ory. a** adj. Having effect of removing hair; **b** n., substance which does this.

deplenish, vb. trans. [1. deplénish; 2. dipléniʃ], fr. **de-** & O. Fr. *-plenir*, 'to fill', fr. Lat. *plēnus*, 'full'. See **plenum** & **-ish**, & cp. **replenish.** To remove contents from, reduce contents of, empty.

deplete, vb. trans. [1. deplḗt; 2. diplít], fr. Lat. *dēplēt-(um)*, P.P. type of *dēplēre*, 'to empty out, draw off, exhaust', fr. **de-** & *plēre*, 'to fill'; Aryan base **pelē-* 'to fill'. See **plenum**, cp. **complete, replete. a** To let out contents of, empty, reduce amount of, diminish, exhaust: *a depleted gas-bag; to deplete one's resources*; **b** specif. (med.) to relieve congestion.

depletion, n. [1. deplḗshun; 2. diplíʃən]. Prec. & **-ion. a** The act or process of depleting; **b** state of being depleted.

depletive, adj. [1. deplḗtiv; 2. diplítiv]. See **deplete** & **-ive.** Tending to deplete.

depletory, adj. [1. deplḗtori; 2. diplítəri]. See **deplete** & **-ory.** Depletive.

deplorable, adj. [1. deplórabl; 2. dìplɔ́rəbl]. **deplore** & **-able**. Of a nature to cause grief, or regret; lamentable, to be regretted; disastrous.

deplorably, adv. Prec. & **-ly**. In a deplorable manner, to a deplorable degree.

deplore, vb. trans. [1. deplór; 2. dìplɔ́]. Fr. *deplorer*, fr. Lat. *dēplōrāre*, 'to weep bitterly, wail; to bewail, lament'; fr. **de-** & *plōrāre*, 'to cry out, cry aloud; to wail, lament'; perh. imitative. See **implore**, **flow**. **a** To lament, regret, disapprove, condemn: *to deplore what has happened*; **b** to feel remorse for: *to deplore one's former sins and errors.*

deploy (**I.**), vb. trans. & intrans. [1. deplói; 2. dìplɔ́i], fr. Fr. *déployer*, fr. O. Fr. *despleier*, 'to spread out'. See **display**. (mil.) **a** trans. To extend, open out (troops &c.); **b** intrans., to spread out, extend from column into line.

deploy (**II.**), n., fr. prec. The act of deploying.

deployment, n. [1. deplóiment; 2. dìplɔ́imənt]. **deploy** (**I.**) & **-ment**. The act or process of deploying.

deplume, vb. trans. [1. deploóm; 2. dìplúm], fr. Fr. *déplumer*. See **de-** & **plume**. To pull the feathers out of, pluck.

depolarization, n. [1. dēpólarīzáshun; 2. dīpóulərəizéiʃən]. Next word & **-ation**. **a** The act or process of depolarizing; **b** state of being depolarized.

depolarize, vb. trans. [1. dēpólarīz; 2. dīpóulərəiz]. See **de-** & **polarize**. **1. a** (elect.) To destroy the polarity of; **b** (opt.) to deflect, change, the polarization of (rays &c.). **2.** (fig.) To disturb, destroy, upset (convictions &c.).

depone, vb. trans. & intrans. [1. depón; 2. dìpóun], fr. Lat. *dēpōnere*, 'to lay down, set down, put aside; to plant; to entrust, give up; to resign', fr. **de-** & *pōnere*, 'to put, place; to set up, erect; to appoint; to allege, maintain; to propose'. See **position**. (esp. in Scots law) To give evidence as a witness in court of law, make statement under oath, to depose.

deponent (**I.**), adj. [1. depónent; 2. dìpóunənt]. See prec. & **-ent**. (gram.) *Deponent verbs*, in Latin or Greek, originally reflexive, and having a passive form, but active meaning; so called from the idea that these verbs had laid aside their original passive force.

deponent (**II.**), n., fr. prec. **1.** (law) A person who makes a deposition under oath, in words or writing. **2.** A deponent verb.

depopulate, vb. trans. & intrans. [1. dēpópūlāt; 2. dīpɔ́pjuleit], fr. Lat. *dēpopulāt-(um)*, P.P. type of *dēpopulārī*, 'to lay waste, plunder'; fig. 'to waste, destroy, dissipate'. See **de-** & **populate**. **a** trans. To diminish, drive out, or destroy, population of (an area); **b** intrans. (rare), to become depopulated.

depopulation, n. [1. dēpopūláshun; 2. dīpɔpjuléiʃən]. Prec. & **-ation**. **a** Destruction of population; **b** decline in population.

deport (**I.**), vb. trans. [1. depórt; 2. dìpɔ́t], fr. Fr. *déporter*, fr. Lat. *dēportāre*, 'to carry off, take away', fr. **de-** & *portāre*, 'to carry'. See next word. To expel, cast out; to carry away; esp. to send (persons) out of the country as a punishment, or as undesirable aliens; to banish.

deport (**II.**), vb. reflex., fr. O. Fr. *deporter*, fr. **de-** & Lat. *portāre*, 'to bear, carry, bring; to import, imply; to endure'. See **port** (**IV.**). (obs.) *Deport oneself*, to behave, conduct, demean, oneself.

deportation, n. [1. dèportáshun; 2. dìpɔ̄téiʃən]. See **deport** (**I.**) & **-ation**. The act or process of deporting, state of being deported; expulsion from a country: *sentenced to deportation.*

deportment, n. [1. depórtment; 2. dìpɔ́tmənt]. See **deport** (**II.**) & **-ment**. **1.** (of persons) **a** Carriage of the body, mode of holding oneself in standing and walking; **b** manner of behaving; conduct, bearing, demeanour. **2.** (chem.) Manner in which a substance reacts to chemical treatment.

deposable, adj. [1. depózabl; 2. dìpóuzəbl]. See **depose** & **-able**. Capable of being, able to be, deposed.

depose, vb. trans. [1. depóz; 2. dìpóuz], fr. Fr. *déposer*, fr. **de-** & *poser*, 'to place, put, lay down'. This word & Ital. *posāre* &c. are fr. Lat. *pausāre*, 'to pause, halt, rest', wh. in the Romance languages acquired trans. force, & then came to mean 'to cause to rest, to lodge, to place'. This vb. thus took the place of Lat. *pōnere*, 'to place'; see **depone**, **position**, & **pose**. Thus **compose**, **depose**, **impose** &c. derive their second element fr. *paus-* (see **pause**), although the sense is exactly that of Lat. *pos-*, fr. *pōnere*. The influence of this vb. & its P.P. *positum* has contributed largely to the change of meaning of the old *pausāre*. **1.** To remove, oust (a person) from office; specif. to remove from position of king, to dethrone. **2.** To give evidence on oath, as a witness in a court of law, to depone.

deposit (**I.**), vb. trans. [1. depózit; 2. dìpɔ́zit], fr. Lat. *dēposit-(um)*, P.P. of *dēpōnere*, 'to lay down; to entrust, give up'. See **depone** & cp. prec. **1.** To place, lodge, bring and leave behind; specif. **a** (geol., of a stream &c.) to cover with, leave as, sediment: *to deposit soil*; **b** (of birds, insects, fish) to lay (eggs). **2.** To entrust for safe keeping, put in charge of; esp. to place money or valuables in a bank for security. **3.** To make a part-payment in advance, for goods, or on opening negotiations for a purchase, as a guarantee of future completion of purchase or bargain.

deposit (**II.**), n., fr. prec. Something deposited; specif. **1. a** (geol.) solid matter, sand, clay &c. held in solution in water and left behind as a coating, or stratum, when the water subsides or dries up; **b** any thin coating or sediment of solid matter contained in a liquid and deposited upon the sides, or at the bottom, of a vessel, e.g. of a winebottle. **2. a** Money paid into, entrusted to, a bank, upon which small rate of interest is received; Phr. *to have, place, money on deposit*; **b** sum of money paid in advance, in business transactions, as guarantee of good faith.

depositary, n. [1. depózitari; 2. dìpɔ́zitəri], fr. Lat. *dēpositārius*, 'one who receives a deposit, a trustee; a depositor'. See prec. & **-ary**. **a** Person receiving a deposit; **b** also used for *depository.*

deposition, n. [1. dèpozíshun; 2. dìpəzíʃən]. See **depose** (**I.**) & **-ition**. **1.** The act of deposing; state of being deposed; removal from power. **2.** (special use) **a** Taking down of the Saviour from the Cross; **b** painted or sculptured representation of this. **3.** Statement made under oath, sworn testimony; see **depone**.

depositor, n. [1. depózitor; 2. dìpɔ́zitə]. Lat. See **deposit** (**I.**) & **-or**. **a** Person who makes a deposit in a bank &c.; **b** person who, or apparatus which, spreads or deposits a substance, such as plaster.

depository, n. [1. depózitori; 2. dìpɔ́zitəri]. See **deposit** (**I.**) & **-ory**. **a** A place in which things are deposited, a storehouse; **b** (fig.) *he, his mind, is a depository of learning.*

depôt, n. [1. dépō; 2. dépou]. Fr. *dépôt*, fr. Lat. *dēpositum*. See **deposit**. **1.** A place in which goods are deposited, storehouse, headquarters for supply of goods &c. **2.** (mil.) **a** Regimental headquarters; **b** part of regiment (usually some of the officers and new recruits) stationed at headquarters while the remainder is on active service. **3.** (U.S.A.) Railway station.

depravation, n. [1. dèpraváshun; 2. dìprəvéiʃən], fr. Lat. *dēprāvātiōn-(em)*, 'a distorting; corrupting'. See **deprave** & **-ation**. **a** The act, process, of depraving; state of being depraved; moral corruption; **b** (without a moral significance) degeneration, deterioration of any kind.

deprave, vb. trans. [1. deprāv; 2. dìpréiv], fr. Lat. *dēprāvāre*, 'to distort, disfigure'; fig. 'to pervert, corrupt', fr. **de-** & *prāvus*, 'crooked, misshapen'; fig. 'perverse, vicious'. See **pravity**. To pervert, corrupt the morals or character of.

depraved, adj. [1. deprāvd; 2. dìpréivd], fr. P.P. of prec. Morally corrupt, perverted, vicious; degenerate.

depravity, n. [1. depráviti; 2. dìprǽviti]. See **deprave** & **-ity**. **a** Moral perversion, viciousness; **b** specif. (theol.) natural tendency of man to sin.

deprecate, vb. trans. [1. déprekāt; 2. déprikeit], fr. Lat. *dēprecāt-(um)*, P.P. type of *dēprecārī*, 'to avert by prayer; to pray for, intercede for', fr. **de-** & *precārī*, 'to pray, request, beseech'. See **pray**. **1.** (archaic) To pray, plead, against; seek to prevent, avert, by prayer or entreaty. **2.** To feel and express disapproval of, argue against: *the speaker strongly deprecated such rash assumptions*; *public alarm is much to be deprecated at the present moment.*

deprecatingly, adv. [1. déprekātingli; 2. déprikeitiŋli]. Pres. Part. of prec. & **-ly**. So as to express hope of averting by entreaty; disapprovingly.

deprecation, n. [1. dèprekáshun; 2. dèprikéiʃən], fr. Lat. *dēprecātiōn-(em)*, 'a warding off by prayer; a prayer for pardon'. See **deprecate** & **-ion**. The act of deprecating; pleading against; disapproval.

deprecative, adj. [1. déprekātiv; 2. déprikeitiv]. See **deprecate** & **-ive**. Expressing deprecation, deprecatory.

deprecatory, adj. [1. déprikātori, déprikatori; 2. déprikeitəri, déprikətəri]. See **deprecate** & **-ory**. Deprecative.

depreciate, vb. trans. & intrans. [1. depréshiāt; 2. dìpríʃieit], fr. Lat. *dēpretiāt-(um)*, P.P. type of *dēpretiāre*, 'to lower the price of'; fig. 'to make little of, to disparage', fr. **de-** & *pretium*, 'money, that for which something is bought; worth, value, price'. See **price**. **1.** trans. **a** To lower, diminish the value of, as by rough usage, hard wear; **b** (fig.) to undervalue, disparage, make little of. **2.** intrans. To decline in market value, or in price; to lose quality, or efficiency, as through hard wear.

depreciatingly, adv. [1. depréshiātingli; 2. dìpríʃieitiŋli]. Pres. Part. of prec. & **-ly**. In a manner expressing depreciation, disparagingly: *to speak depreciatingly of.*

depreciation, n. [1. deprèshiáshun; 2. dìprìʃiéiʃən]. See prec. & **-ion**. **1.** The process of depreciating, decline in value. Specif. **a** reduction in value of property &c. through ordinary wear and tear; **b** allowance made for this in valuations &c. **2.** (fig.) Disparagement, under-estimation.

depreciatory, adj. [1. depréshatori; 2. dìpríʃətəri]. See **depreciate** & **-ory**. (lit. and fig.) Tending to depreciate: **a** tending to reduce value (of objects); **b** tending to lessen the repute, credit &c. (of persons): *depreciatory remarks.*

depredation, n. [1. dèpredáshun; 2. dèpridéiʃən], fr. Fr., fr. Lat. *dēpraedātiōn-(em)*, 'a plundering', fr. *dēpraedāt-(um)*, P.P. type of *dēpraedārī*, 'to rob, plunder, pillage', fr. **de-** & *praedārī*, 'to plunder, spoil, rob', see **predatory**, & **-ion**. **a** Act of laying waste; incursion, plundering, robbery; **b** specific action of this kind, a theft; **c** encroachment, inroad, as of the sea on the coast.

depredator, n. [1. dépredātor; 2. déprideitə], fr. Lat. *dēpraedātor*, 'a robber, plunderer'. See prec. & **-or**. One who robs, plunders, despoils.

depress, vb. trans. [1. deprés; 2. diprés], fr. O. Fr. *depresser*, fr. Low Lat. **dēpressāre*, fr. *dēpress-(um)*, P.P. type of *dēprimere*, 'to press down, weigh down; to plant deep, sink deep'; fig. 'to depress, deject; to depreciate'. See **de-** & **press** (**I.**). **1. a** (of physical action) To press down, bring into a lower position by pulling or pressing; **b** (fig.) to reduce vigour of, weaken: *to depress the action of the heart.* **2.** (of action on mind or emotions) To discourage, damp the spirits or courage of, make dejected.

depressant, adj. & n. [1. deprésant; 2. dipréssant]. See prec. & **-ant.** (med.) **1.** adj. **a** Acting so as to depress or lower mental, nervous, or other physical activity; lowering; **b** sedative, quietening. **2.** n. Drug, such as various alkaloids, that acts in such a manner.

depressible, adj. [1. deprésibl; 2. diprésibl]. See **depress** & **-ible.** That can be, liable to be, depressed.

depressing, adj. [1. deprésing; 2. diprésiŋ], fr. Pres. Part. of **depress.** Specif. tending to depress, discourage, lower the spirits; dismal, gloomy.

depressingly, adv. Prec. & **-ly.** In a depressing manner, so as to cause depression.

depression, n. [1. depréshun; 2. dipréʃən]. See **depress** & **-ion. 1.** (of material things) A hollow, dip, concavity, in a surface: *a depression in the ground.* **2.** (of non-material things) **a** Lowness of spirits, gloom, dejection of mind: *to suffer from depression*; **b** slackness, inactivity, lack of vigour (in trade &c.). **3.** (nat. sc.) **a** (meteor.) Lowering of atmospheric pressure, indicated by fall of mercury in barometer; **b** (astron.) angular distance of a heavenly body below horizon.

depressor, n. [1. deprésor; 2. diprésə]. See **depress** & **-or.** (anat.) Muscle which draws down some part of the body. Also *depressor muscle.*

deprivable, adj. [1. deprívabl; 2. dipráivəbl]. See **deprive** & **-able.** Liable to suffer deprivation.

deprivation, n. [1. dèprivâshun; 2. dèprivéiʃən]. See next word & **-ation. 1.** Act of depriving, of dispossessing; specif. (eccles.) removal from a benefice, dismissal from office. **2.** Condition of being deprived of something; sense of loss; bereavement.

deprive, vb. trans. [1. deprív; 2. dipráiv], fr. O. Fr. *depriver*, fr. **de-** & Lat. *prīvāre*, 'to bereave, rob; to free, release'. See **private (I.). 1. a** To take something away from a person or thing, prevent use or enjoyment of: *to deprive a man of his books, of all hope, of the comforts of his home, of his reason, life* &c.; *to deprive a house of light and air*; **b** to shut off from, debar from, keep out of: *to deprive a person of his rights, of permission to enter the house, of the pleasure of one's society* &c. **2.** Specif. (eccles.) to remove, suspend, from enjoyment of a benefice, from possession of an office or dignity.

de profundis, adv. & n. [1. dé profúndis; 2. dí prəfándis]. Lat., 'from out of the depths', first words of Psalm 130, in Vulgate. See **de-** & **profound. 1.** adv. Out of the depths of sorrow or misery, of cry of despair &c. **2.** n. **a** (w. def. art.) The 130th Psalm; **b** (w. indef. art.) any cry of despair or misery, in speech or writing.

depth, n. [1. depth; 2. depþ]. Cp. O.E. *dīepe, dēpe, dēopness*, later *dēpþe*, formed fr. *dēpe*, 'deep', on anal. of *hēhþe*, 'height', fr. *hēah*, &c.; M.E. *dĕpþe*; cp. Goth. *diupiþa.* See **deep** & **-th. 1.** Condition of being deep, or at a great distance below surface. **2. a** The property of being intellectually or morally profound, abstruse, recondite, difficult of comprehension: *a mind, book, of no great depth*; **b** intensity, fervour: *depth of feeling, affection* &c.; **c** (of colour) strong tone, considerable amount of pigment; intensity, warmth, richness; **d** (of musical notes) low pitch. **3. a** Degree of distance below surface, measurement from the surface downwards: *the depth of the pond is ten feet*; *a foot in depth*; Phr. *out of one's depth*, in water too deep to touch bottom; (fig.) beyond one's knowledge, or mental abilities; **b** degree of distance from front to back, esp. of a shelf; **c** breadth, width, esp. of a border, hem, fringe &c. **4.** (gen. pl.) Something that is deep; specif. **a** a deep chasm, abyss; **b** (poet.) deep waters, the sea. Phr. *in the depth(s) of despair, woe, poverty* &c., lowest, most intense degree. **5. a** (of seasons) A central point, the middle of a continuous period: *in the depth of winter*; **b** *the depth of the country*, area remote from towns.

depth charge, n. Explosive charge, timed to explode at certain depth below surface of the water, for use against submarines.

depurate, vb. trans. [1. dépūrāt; 2. dépjureit], fr. **de-** & Lat. *pūrāt-(um)*, P.P. type of *pūrāre*, (very rare) 'to purify by religious rites', fr. *pūrus*, 'clean, pure; natural, unadorned; pure, chaste'. See **pure.** (rare) To free from impurities, purify.

depuration, n. [1. dèpūrâshun; 2. dèpjuréiʃən]. See prec. & **-ation.** The act or process of purifying.

depurative, adj. [1. depûrativ; 2. dipjɔ́rətiv]. See **depurate** & **-ive.** Tending, serving, to free from impurities, purifying.

deputation, n. [1. dèpūtâshun; 2. dèpjutéiʃən]. See **depute** & **-ation. 1.** The act of deputing. **2.** A group of persons appointed to act as deputies or representatives.

depute, vb. trans. [1. depût; 2. dipjût], fr. Lat. *dēputāre*, orig. a gardening term 'to prune, cut back, cut off; to think of, consider; to esteem, count as', fr. **de-** & *putāre*, 'to trim, prune; to cleanse; to put in order, settle, reckon up; to consider, reflect; to judge, think, believe'. See **putamen. a** To appoint one or more persons to act as representative of others, entrust them, as agents, with certain duties and functions; **b** (of duties, functions &c.) to transfer, delegate, performance of to others.

deputize, vb. intrans. [1. dépūtīz; 2. dépjutaiz]. See next word & **-ize.** To act as a deputy *for.*

deputy, n. [1. dépūti; 2. dépjuti], fr. Fr. *député*, P.P. of *députer.* See **depute** & **-y. 1.** One who acts for another and takes his place in performance of duties; one to whom another's functions and duties have been deputed; one who represents another by his presence on a special occasion. **2.** Parliamentary representative in France &c.; a member of the *Chamber of Deputies*, the lower house of the Legislature.

deracinate, vb. trans. [1. dērásināt; 2. dīrǽsineit], fr. Fr. *déraciner*, fr. **de-** & Low Lat. *rādīcīna*, dimin. of *rādix*, 'a root'; hence 'that on which something rests, a foundation, foot'; fig. 'basis, origin, source'. See **radix, radical,** & **-ate.** (lit. and fig.) To pull up, tear out, by the roots; extirpate entirely.

derail, vb. trans. [1. derâl; 2. diréil], fr. Fr. *dérailler.* See **de-** & **rail (IV.).** (railway and trams) To cause to leave the rails (usually in pass.): *the engine was derailed.*

derailment, n. [1. derâlment; 2. diréilmənt]. Prec. & **-ment.** The process of derailing, state of being derailed.

derange, vb. trans. [1. derânj; 2. diréindž], fr. Fr. *déranger*, 'put out of order, disturb', fr. **de-** & *ranger*, 'to put in order, put into position', see **range (I.). 1.** To put into disorder, upset, disturb, disorganize. **2.** (of action on the mind) To upset mental balance of, disturb mentally, cause to become insane; esp. *to be, become, (mentally) deranged.*

derangement, n. [1. derânjment; 2. diréindžmənt]. See prec. & **-ment. a** The act of deranging; specif. **b** the process of becoming, state of being, mentally deranged.

derate, vb. trans. [1. dērât; 2. díréit]. **de-** & **rate (I.).** To relieve (industries &c.) from the burden of local rates by an Act, known as the *Derating Act, 1929.*

Derby, n. [1. dárbi; 2. dấbi], fr. the name of the founder, the 12th Earl of Derby (1780). A horse-race for three-year-olds, held annually at Epsom, usually on the first Wednesday in June, known as *Derby Day.*

derelict, adj. & n. [1. dérelikt; 2. dérilikt], fr. Lat. *dērelict-(um)*, P.P. type of *dērelinquere*, 'to forsake, abandon; to bequeath', fr. **de-** & *relinquere*, 'to leave behind; to bequeath; to forsake, abandon; to resign, relinquish'. See **relinquish. a** adj. Abandoned as worthless; **b** n., something which has been abandoned as worthless and useless, esp. of ship at sea; also extended to things or persons that are old and worn out.

dereliction, n. [1. dèrelíkshun; 2. dèrilíkʃən], fr. Lat. *dērelictiōn-(em)*, 'an abandoning; neglect, disregarding'. See prec. & **-ion. 1. a** The act of abandoning; state or process of being abandoned; specif. **b** neglect, failure to carry out a task &c., remissness: *a dereliction of duty.* **2.** Land permanently exposed by retreat of the sea.

deride, vb. trans. [1. deríd; 2. diráid], fr. Lat. *dērīdēre*, 'to laugh to scorn, mock at', fr. **de-** & *rīdēre*, 'to laugh, smile'. See **risible. a** To mock, ridicule, laugh scornfully at; (more commonly) **b** to have, and express, contempt for; to hold of small account.

derision, n. [1. derízhun; 2. dirížən], fr. Lat. *dērīsiōn-(em)*, 'a mockery, derision', fr. *dērīs-(um)*, P.P. type of *dērīdēre*, 'to laugh to scorn'. See **deride. 1. a** The act of deriding, ridicule, contempt: *an object of derision*; **b** state or process of being derided: *to hold in derision*; *to be in derision.* **2.** (archaic) That which is derided, object of derision.

derisive, adj. [1. derísiv; 2. diráisiv]. See prec. & **-ive. a** Expressing ridicule; mocking, ironical: *derisive laughter*; **b** deserving derision, unavailing, futile, inadequate: *derisive attempts.*

derisively, adv. Prec. & **-ly.** In a manner expressing derision, mockingly.

derisory, adj. [1. derísori; 2. diráisəri]. See **derision** & **-ory.** Derisive, ironical: *derisory applause, laughter.*

derivable, adj. [1. derívabl; 2. diráivəbl]. **derive** & **-able.** Capable of being derived.

derivation, n. [1. dèrivâshun; 2. dèrivéiʃən]. See **derive** & **-ation. 1.** Process of deriving or being derived. **2. a** That from which something is derived; source, origin; esp. and specif. **b** the etymology, origin, of words; process of tracing back to earliest form and primary meaning.

derivative, adj. & n. [1. derívativ; 2. dirívətiv]. See next word & **-ative. a** adj. Not original, secondary, derived from something else; **b** n., that which is derived from, developed out of, capable of being traced back to, something else.

derive, vb. trans. & intrans. [1. derív; 2. diráiv], fr. Fr. *dériver*, fr. Lat. *dērīvāre*, 'to turn or draw off (liquid); to disperse'; fig. 'to divert', fr. **de-** & *rīvus*, 'a small stream'. See **river. A.** trans. **1.** To obtain, get, draw, from, as a source or origin: *to derive one's fortune from trade, one's character from one's father* &c. **2.** To trace source or origin back to: *to derive a family from the Conqueror*; *to derive a word from such-and-such a base*, to show the gradual path of development from a given starting-point. **B.** intrans. *Derive from*, to have as source, to spring, be derived, from: *English derives in the main from the common Germanic stock.*

derm(a), n. [1. dérm(a); 2. dấm(ə)], fr. Gk. *dérma*, 'skin', connected w. *dérō*, 'I flay', & **-m.** Cp. Gk. *dorá*, 'skin'; Scrt. *dr̥-tiš*, 'leather', related to *dr̥nāti*, Pret. *(da)dāra*, 'to split in pieces'; Lith. *(nu)dirtas*, 'flayed'; Goth. *(dis)tairan*, 'to tear to pieces'; O.H.G. *(fir)zeran*, O.E. *teran*, 'to tear' (see **tear (I.)**); O. Slav. *dera*, Lith. *dirti*, 'to flay'. The skin, esp. the true skin, or inner layer below epidermis.

-derm, suff., meaning 'skin, covering' &c., fr. prec. Cp. *ectoderm* &c.

dermal, adj. [1. dérmal; 2. dấməl]. **derm(a)** & **-al.** Pertaining to the skin.

dermatic, adj. [1. dermátik; 2. dāmǽtik], fr. Gk. *dermat-*, stem of *dérma*, 'skin' (see **derm(a)**), & **-ic.** Having to do with the skin; consisting of skin.

dermatitis, n. [1. dermatítis; 2. dāmətáitis]. Gk. *dermat-* (see prec.) & **-itis.** Inflammation of, eruption on, the true skin.

dermato-, pref., fr. Gk. *dérmato-s*, genit. of *dérma*, 'skin'. See **derm(a).** Pertaining to the skin.

dermatography, n. [1. dermatógrafi; 2. dāmətɔ́grəfi]. See **dermato-** & **-graphy.** Anatomical description of the skin.

dermatoid, adj. [1. dêrmatoid; 2. dǽmətɔid]. See **dermato-** & **-oid**. Resembling, made of, skin.

dermatologist, n. [1. dêrmatólojist; 2. dǽmətɔ́lədžist]. See next word & **-ist**. Skin specialist; student of the (human) skin and its diseases.

dermatology, n. [1. dêrmatóloji; 2. dǽmətɔ́lədži]. See **dermato-** & **-logy**. Special study of the skin, its diseases &c.

dermato-skeleton, n. [1. dêrmatō skéleton; 2. dǽmətouskélitən]. **dermato-** & **skeleton**. The hard outer covering of crustaceans and of many insects &c.

dermic, adj. [1. dêrmik; 2. dǽmik]. See **derm(a)** & **-ic**. Dermal.

dermo-, pref., fr. **derm(a)**. Same as **dermato-**.

dernier ressort, n. [1. dârniā resṓr; 2. déəniei resɔ́]. Fr., *dernier*, 'last', fr. O. Fr. *derreinnier*, see **darrein**, & *ressort*, see **resort (II.)**. Last expedient, resource.

derogate, vb. intrans. [1. dérogāt; 2. dérəgeit], fr. Lat. *dērogāt-(um)*, P.P. type of *dērogāre*, 'to repeal (part of a law), restrict; to remove, detract from; to disparage'. See **de-** & **rogation**. To take away, remove (a merit, good quality) from, to lessen, detract from: *to derogate from a man's reputation.*

derogation, n. [1. derogáshun; 2. derəgéiʃən]. Prec. & **-ion**. Injury to, lessening, harming (of dignity, authority &c.).

derogatory, adj. [1. derógatori; 2. dirɔ́gətəri]. See **derogate** & **-ory**. Tending to lessen, impair, disparage, discredit: *actions derogatory to one's dignity* &c.

derrick, n. [1. dérik; 2. dérik], fr. name of a hangman in early 18th cent. **a** (obs.) Gallows; **b** a kind of movable crane, apparatus for hoisting heavy weights, esp. on to or from a ship.

derring-do, n. [1. déring dōō; 2. dériŋ dú]. Used by Spenser as n., through a misunderstanding of Chaucer's '*In dorryng dōn that longyth to a knyght*', 'in daring to do that which &c.'. Revived by Scott. See **dare** & **do (I.)**. Reckless courage; valiant action.

derringer, n. [1. dérinjer; 2. dérindžə], fr. name of inventor. A small pocket-pistol with short barrel and large bore.

dervish, n. [1. dêrvish; 2. dǽviʃ]. Pers. *darvesh*, 'poor'. **1.** A member of a Mohammedan order of mendicant monks, vowed to a life of poverty: *dancing, howling, dervish.* **2.** One of the fanatical followers of the Sudanese Mahdi.

descant (I.), n. [1. déskant; 2. déskænt], fr. O. Fr. *deschant*, fr. Low Lat. *discantus*, fr. **dis-** & *cantus*, 'a melody, song'. See **chant**. (in anct. mus.) A song, melody; specif., a variation on the main air in plain song, sung or played as an accompaniment to it; an early form of counterpoint.

descant (II.), vb. intrans. [1. deskánt; 2. diskǽnt], fr. O. Fr. *deschanter*, fr. Low Lat. *discantāre*, fr. **dis-** & *cantāre*, 'to sing'. See prec. **a** (mus.) To sing, play, the descant to the main air; **b** to talk at length, hold forth, enlarge *upon* a topic in conversation.

descend, vb. intrans. & trans. [1. desénd; 2. disénd], fr. O. Fr. *descendre*, fr. Lat. *dēscendere*, intrans., 'to come down, sink'; fig. 'to lower oneself', fr. **de-** & *scandere*, 'to climb, go up'. See **scan**. **A.** intrans. **1. a** To take a downward course, move downwards, proceed, fall, to lower level, come down: *to descend from a hill-top*; *a balloon descended in our field*; **b** to incline, slope downwards: *the hill descends by a gradual slope to the plain.* **2. a** (of persons) *Descend from*, to derive descent from, have as ancestor: *he descends, is descended, from the Conqueror*; **b** (of property, and physical and mental qualities) to pass by inheritance, be transmitted: *the land descends to the eldest son*; *parental characters descend to offspring.* **3.** (only in Pres. Part.) *Descending scale*, diminishing in number, extent, pitch &c. **B.** trans. To traverse, pass along, or over, from higher to lower point in space, go down; go downwards into: *to descend a hill, a flight of stairs*; *to descend a mine.* **C.** Followed by prepositions. *Descend to*, (fig.) **a** to come down, stoop, lower oneself to something: *to descend to fraud*; **b** to come, pass on to: *descend to particulars. Descend upon*, **a** to attack suddenly, fall upon: *to descend upon an unprotected village, a sleeping enemy* &c.; **b** (fig.) (i.) to visit suddenly and unexpectedly: *to descend upon one's friends with a large party*; (ii.) to alight on, strike: *his master's anger descended upon him.*

descendable, adj. [1. deséndabl; 2. diséndəbl]. **descend** & **-able**. That can be conveyed as inheritance, passed on to an heir.

descendant, n. [1. deséndant; 2. diséndənt]. **descend** & **-ant**. A person, animal, or thing descended from another as ancestor or prototype.

descendible, adj. [1. deséndibl; 2. diséndibl]. **descend** & **-ible**. Descendable.

descent, n. [1. desént; 2. disént], fr. O. Fr. *descente*, fr. *descendre*. See **descend**. **1.** The act of descending; specif. **a** (physical) a going or coming down: *a descent with a parachute*; **b** a downward slope, gradual fall, incline: *the land slopes to the sea by a gradual descent*; **c** (fig.) *a descent from the sublime to the ridiculous.* **2.** A sudden attack, invasion: *a descent upon a village.* **3. a** Ancestry, lineage: *a distinguished, ancient, descent*; **b** inheritance: *to acquire a title by descent*; **c** transmission: *descent of property in female line*; *descent of ancestral characters.*

describable, adj. [1. deskríbabl; 2. diskráibəbl]. Next word & **-able**. That can be described.

describe, vb. trans. [1. deskríb; 2. diskráib], fr. Lat. *dēscrībere*, 'to write down, copy; to draw, sketch'; fig. 'to represent, describe', fr. **de-** & *scrībere*, 'to write'. See **scribe**. **1.** To state, depict, in speech or writing what a person, object &c., is like, give an account of, enumerate characteristic features of: *to describe a man, a landscape* &c. **2.** (geom.) To mark out, draw: *to describe a circle, a triangle.*

description, n. [1. deskrípshun; 2. diskrípʃən], fr. Lat. *dēscript-(um)*, P.P. type of *dēscrībere*. See **describe** & **-ion**. **1.** The act or process of describing. **2.** An account, enumeration, recital, report, of the characteristics, appearance, chief qualities, of a person, or thing: *a description of a landscape, a storm, a person's appearance* &c.; *no one answering to that description.* **3.** A group, class of things possessing well-marked features in common; sort, kind: *no clothes of any description*; *a man of that description*; *a speech of the poorest description.*

descriptive, adj. [1. deskríptiv; 2. diskríptiv], fr. Lat. *dēscript-(um)*. See prec. & **-ive**. **a** Serving to, intended to, describe: *descriptive writing* &c.; **b** given to, skilled in, describing: *a descriptive writer.*

descriptively, adv. Prec. & **-ly**. In a descriptive manner.

descry, vb. trans. [1. deskrí; 2. diskrái], fr. O. Fr. *descrier*, fr. Lat. *disquīrere*, 'to inquire carefully, investigate', fr. **dis-** & *quaerere*, 'to seek, inquire'. See **query**. To make out, be able to see, perceive distantly, discern; (poet.) to see.

desecrate, vb. trans. [1. désikrāt; 2. désikreit], fr. **de-** & Lat. *-secrāt-(um)*, formed on anal. of **consecrate**. To violate the sacredness of, profane; to deprive of sacred character.

desecration, n. [1. dèsikráshun; 2. dèsikréiʃən]. Prec. & **-ation**. **a** The act or process of desecrating; **b** state of being desecrated.

desert (I.), vb. trans. & intrans. [1. dezêrt; 2. dizǽt], fr. O. Fr. *deserter*, fr. Low Lat. *dēsertāre*, fr. *dēsert-(um)*, P.P. type of *dēserere*, 'to forsake, abandon', fr. **de-** & *serere*, 'to join'. See **series**. **1.** trans. **a** To give up, abandon, forsake, leave neglected (esp. that which has a claim on one): *to desert one's post, ship, family* &c.; **b** to fail, leave: *his self-assurance deserted him.* **2.** intrans. Specif. (mil. and nav.) to leave, abscond from service, in the army or navy, without permission.

desert (II.), adj. [1. dézert; 2. dézət], fr. O. Fr. *deserte*, P.P. of *deserter*. See prec. Uninhabited, waste, desolate: *a desert island, a desert place* &c.

desert (III.), n. [1. dézert; 2. dézət], fr. prec. **a** A wild, waste, uninhabited place or region, a wilderness; specif., tract of arid country covered with sand; **b** (poet., archaic) lonely, retired, quiet place; the country, as contrasted with the busy town: '*In vain to deserts thy retreat is made*' (Pope); **c** (fig.) arid, unfruitful, dull subject or mind.

desert (IV.), n. [1. dezêrt; 2. dizǽt], fr. O. Fr. *desert*, P.P. of *deservir*. See **deserve**. **1.** Merit, qualities deserving praise or reward: *to recognize real desert when one meets it*; *his desert is small.* **2.** What is deserved, earned, by qualities, character, conduct, whether reward for good, or punishment for evil; esp. *to meet with, obtain, one's deserts.*

deserter, n. [1. dezêrter; 2. dizǽtə], fr. **desert (I.)** & **-er**. **a** One who deserts, abandons, forsakes, a person or cause having a claim on him; specif. **b** one who deserts from the army or navy.

desertion, n. [1. dezêrshun; 2. dizǽʃən], fr. **desert (I.)** & **-ion**. **1.** The act of deserting, specif. **a** from army or navy; **b** of a wife and children by husband, as ground for judicial separation &c. **2.** State of being deserted.

deserve, vb. trans. & intrans. [1. dezêrv; 2. dizǽv], fr. O. Fr. *deservir*, fr. Lat. *dēservīre*, 'to serve diligently, be devoted to', fr. **de-** & *servīre*, 'to serve'. See **serve**. **1.** trans. **a** To earn, become entitled to, have a claim to, by reason of qualities, actions &c.: *to deserve a reward*; *deserve to be punished* &c.; **b** to claim, be of such a character as to justify, be worthy of, warrant &c.: *to deserve attention.* **2.** intrans. To be worthy of, to merit: *to deserve well, ill, of a person.*

deservedly, adv. [1. dezêrvedli; 2. dizǽvidli], fr. P.P. of prec. & **-ly**. In accordance with what one deserves, justly: *to be deservedly praised, punished.*

deserving, adj. [1. dezêrving; 2. dizǽviŋ]. Pres. Part. of **deserve**. Having merit, worthy of reward, help &c.: *a deserving case.*

déshabille. See **dishabille**.

desiccate, vb. trans. & intrans. [1. dē-, désikāt; 2. dī-, désikeit], fr. Lat. *dēsiccāt-(um)*, P.P. type of *dēsiccāre*, 'to dry up completely', fr. **de-** & *siccāre*, 'to make dry, drain', fr. *siccus*, 'dry', see **siccative**. **1.** trans. **a** To dry up, extract all moisture from; **b** specif., to reduce to powdered form by extraction of moisture: *desiccated milk.* **2.** intrans. To become completely dry.

desiccation, n. [1. dē-, dèsikáshun; 2. dī-, dèsikéiʃən]. See prec. & **-ation**. **a** Act or process of desiccating; **b** state of being desiccated.

desiccative, adj. [1. désikativ; 2. désikətiv]. See **desiccate** & **-ive**. Tending to dry up, remove moisture from a substance.

desiderate, vb. trans. [1. desíderāt; 2. disídəreit], fr. Lat. *dēsīderāt-(um)*, P.P. type of *dēsīderāre*, 'to feel the want of'. See **desire (I.)**. To recognize as missing, yet necessary; to feel lack of, and desire to acquire, or supply.

desiderative, adj. & n. [1. desíderativ; 2. disídərətiv]. See prec. & **-ive**. **a** adj. Expressing desire; (esp. gram., of verbs) expressing a desire to perform a particular action, as *ēsurio*, 'I desire to eat, am hungry'; **b** n., (gram.) a desiderative verb.

desideratum, pl. **desiderata**, n. [1. desìderā́tum, -a; 2. disìdəréitə(m)]. Lat. neut. P.P. of *dēsīderāre*. See **desire (I.)**. Something felt to be lacking, and therefore desired as necessary; an acknowledged want.

design (I.), vb. trans. & intrans. [1. dezín; 2. dizáin], fr. Fr. *désigner*, fr. Lat. *dēsignāre*, 'to mark out, define; to portray, depict'; fig. 'to indicate, point out, to appoint, elect'; fr. **de-** & *signāre*, 'to mark out, mark with a token'. See **sign**. **A.** trans. **1.** (of mental act) **a** To plan out, construct a plan or scheme for, conceive main outline of: *to* *design a book, musical composition* &c. **b** to select, destine, intend (a person or thing for a particular purpose): *to design one's son for, to be, a soldier*; *to design a room as a billiard-room.* **2.** (of physical act) To make, draw a plan of, to invent pattern for a material object: *to design a mode of decoration, a rock garden, dress* &c. **B.** intrans. To construct designs; to be a designer.

design (**II.**), n., fr. prec. **1.** (of non-material things) A scheme, plan, something planned out in one's mind; specif. **a** the general outline, construction, of a work of art or literature; **b** set, deliberate, purpose or intention: *by design and not by accident*; **c** nefarious, sinister, intention or purpose against, scheme for injuring: *to have designs on, against, a person.* **2.** (of material things) **a** Sketch, plan, pattern, or scheme drawn out, for some object to be constructed: *a design for a dress, building* &c.; **b** qualities of inventiveness, sense of proportion, suitable arrangement of parts &c., for beauty or use, exhibited by any constructed work: *a picture, building, lacking design*; *a machine of excellent design* &c.

designate (**I.**), vb. trans. [1. dézignāt; 2. dézigneit], fr. Lat. *dēsignāt-(um)*, P.P. type of *dēsignāre*, 'to mark out; to indicate, appoint, elect'. See **design** (**I.**). **a** To point out, indicate, mark out, show clearly; **b** to nominate for appointment to an office, select for special duty &c.

designate (**II.**), adj. [1. dézignat; 2. dézignit]. See prec. Appointed to an office, designated: *bishop designate.*

designation, n. [1. dèzignáshun; 2. dèzignéiʃən]. See **designate** (**I.**) & **-ion.** **a** The act of designating; state of being designated, nominated, appointed; **b** that which marks out, distinguishes, esp. particular, distinctive name.

designedly, adv. [1. dezínedli; 2. dizáinidli]. P.P. of **design** (**I.**) & **-ly.** According to plan, of set purpose, by design; contrasted with *accidentally.*

designer, n. [1. dezíner; 2. dizáinə]. **design** (**I.**) & **-er.** **a** One who designs, esp. one who invents plans from which things are constructed, decorated &c.; **b** (in bad sense) a schemer; sinister, underhand, plotter.

designing, adj. [1. dezíning; 2. dizáiniŋ], fr. Pres. Part. of **design** (**I.**). Artful, scheming; having sinister and interested motives for one's actions.

desilverize, vb. trans. [1. dēsílverīz; 2. dīsílvəraiz], fr. **de-** & **silver** & **-ize.** To remove silver from (esp. *lead*).

desinence, n. [1. désinens; 2. désinəns], fr. Lat. *dēsinere*, 'to cease, desist; to end, terminate', & **-ence**; *dēsinere* is fr. **de-** & *sinere*, 'to set down, leave; to allow, permit', cogn. w. Gk. *eáō* (fr. **sewājō*), 'I allow; let alone'; Aryan base **sēi-*, **si-*, 'to leave, leave off, cease'; other cognates are Scrt. *vi-syati*, 'stops, ceases, rests', *sātiš*, 'conclusion, close'; also Lat. *sē-rus*, 'late' (see **since**); *si-lēre*, 'to be silent' (see **silent**). See also **seed, sow** (**II.**). (rare) **a** End, discontinuance; **b** grammatical termination, suffix.

desipience, n. [1. desípiens; 2. disípiəns], fr. Lat. *dēsipientia*, fr. *dēsipere*, 'to act foolishly', fr. **de-** & *sapere*, 'to taste, have a sense of taste; to have sense, be wise', see **sapient**, & **-ence.** Foolish trifling, silliness.

desirability, n. [1. dezīrabíliti; 2. dizàiərəbíliti]. See next word & **-ity.** The quality of being desirable.

desirable, adj. [1. dezírabl; 2. dizáiərəbl]. See **desire** (**I.**) & **-able.** To be desired, provoking desire; worth having.

desirableness, n. Prec. & **-ness.** The quality of being desirable.

desirably, adv. See prec. & **-ly.** In a desirable manner.

desire (**I.**), vb. trans. [1. dezír; 2. dizáiə], fr. Fr. *désirer*, fr. Lat. *dēsīderāre*, 'to feel the want of'; etymol. doubtful; usually referred to **de-** & *sīder-(is)*, *sīdus*, 'star', cp. **consider.** **1.** To wish, long for ardently, hanker after, yearn for, feel strong craving for. **2.** To express a wish, to request; command that a person should do something: *I desire you to go at once*; *please desire Mr. Jones to come in.*

desire (**II.**), n., fr. prec. **1.** **a** Strong longing, craving, appetite, powerful wish to obtain, or enjoy something: *to have a desire for a glass of beer*; Phr. *to have no desire for, or to do*, not to want, to prefer not to; **b** specif., sexual appetence. **2.** Wish, hope, which has been expressed, request: *in accordance with your desire(s), I enclose a cheque* &c. **3.** That which is earnestly longed for; object of desire: *the World's Desire.*

desirous, adj. [1. dezírus; 2. dizáiərəs]. See prec. & **-ous.** Feeling a desire for, having a wish to obtain, or to do something: *desirous of success*; *desirous to succeed.*

desist, vb. intrans. [1. dezíst; 2. dizíst], fr. Fr., fr. Lat. *dēsistere*, orig. 'to stand aside; to abandon; stop, leave off', fr. **de-** & *sistere*, 'to cause to stand, place; to cause to appear (esp. in a law-court); to stop, arrest, fix in position; to stand fast', redupl. form of base **sta-*, wh. appears in Lat. *sta-re*, 'to stand'. See **state** (**I.**), **stand** (**I.**), **stance.** To stop, cease, discontinue action; constructions: **a** *to desist from doing, from attempts* &c.; **b** *it is no good, so you had better desist.*

desk, n. [1. desk; 2. desk]. M.E. *deske*, 'a desk, table, pulpit', fr. Low Lat. *desca*, 'a desk, table', fr. Lat. *discus*, 'a quoit'; hence (fr. the shape) 'a kind of dish'. See **disk.** **a** One of various kinds of pieces of furniture, in the form of a table to write at; sometimes made to shut with a movable flap: *knee-hole, roll-top, desk.* Phr. *to sit at the desk*, be engaged in writing; employed as a clerk; **b** portable box of wood, either polished and bound with brass, or covered with leather, and fitted with a lock, for holding writing materials, letters, and documents.

desman, n. [1. désman; 2. désmən]. Swed., 'musk'. A small mole-like aquatic mammal, of Russia and Pyrenees.

desolate (**I.**), vb. trans. [1. désolāt; 2. désəleit], fr. Lat. *dēsōlāt-(um)*, P.P. type of *dēsōlāre*, 'to make solitary, strip of inhabitants', fr. **de-** & *sōlus*, 'alone; lonely, forsaken, solitary; (of places) unfrequented'. See **sole** (**IV.**). **a** To lay waste, devastate: *to desolate a country* &c.; to make lonely (*a home, hearth* &c.); **b** to make lonely, sad, leave forlorn (*a person, a heart*).

desolate (**II.**), adj. [1. désolat; 2. désəlit]. See prec. **a** (of land &c.) Waste, uninhabited, desert, dismal; **b** (of buildings, home) neglected, forsaken, wretched; **c** (of persons) forlorn, lonely, abandoned.

desolately, adv. Prec. & **-ly.** In a desolate manner.

desolateness, n. See prec. & **-ness.** The state of being desolate.

desolation, n. [1. dèsoláshun; 2. dèsəléiʃən]. See **desolate** & **-ion.** **a** The act of desolating (a country &c.); **b** the state of being desolate; loneliness, misery.

despair (**I.**), vb. intrans. [1. despár; 2. dispéə]. M.E. *despeiren, desperen*, fr. O. Fr. *desperer*, fr. Lat. *dēspērāre*, 'to be hopeless, have no hope of', fr. **de-** & *spērāre*, 'to hope', fr. *spē-s*, 'hope'. The orig. meaning has been conjectured as 'to draw a breath of relief', or 'to hold one's breath from anticipation, excitement' &c., & that this word is cogn. w. Lat. *spīrāre*, 'to breathe, blow'. See **spirant, spirit.** To lose hope, be entirely without hope; to expect no improvement in circumstances: (with *of* and absol.) *to despair of success*; *his life was despaired of.*

despair (**II.**), n., fr. prec. **a** Entire absence of hope; hopelessness; Phr. *the depths of despair*; **b** that which causes despair: *to be the despair of one's friends.*

despairingly, adv. [1. despáringli; 2. dispéəriŋli]. Pres. Part. of **despair** (**I.**) & **-ly.** In a manner expressive of despair.

despatch. See **dispatch.**

desperado, n. [1. dèsperáhdō; 2. dèspərádou]. O. Span., adj., fr. Lat. *dēspērātus.* See **desperate.** A ruthless, reckless, villain; an unscrupulous ruffian.

desperate, adj. [1. désperit; 2. déspərit], fr. Lat. *dēspērātus*, 'hopeless, despaired of'. See **despair** (**I.**). **a** Beyond hope, extremely serious, with no prospect of amelioration: *a desperate state of affairs*; *his condition is desperate*; **b** wildly reckless, violent with the strength of despair, driven to extremity: *a desperate struggle*; *a desperate criminal.*

desperately, adv. Prec. & **-ly.** In a desperate manner.

desperateness, n. See prec. & **-ness.** The state of being desperate.

desperation, n. [1. dèsperáshun; 2. dèspəréiʃən], fr. Lat. *dēspērātiōn-(em)*, 'hopelessness, despair', fr. *dēspērāre*, 'to despair'. See **despair** (**I.**) & **-ation.** **a** The state of being desperate; **b** recklessness due to despair; **c** (colloq.) state of considerable excitement, irritation, violent rage: *to drive a person to desperation*, make him very angry.

despicable, adj. [1. déspikabl; 2. déspikəbl], fr. Fr., fr. L. Lat. *dēspicābilis*, 'despicable', fr. *dēspicere*, 'to look down on; to despise', fr. **de-** & *specere*, 'to look at', see **despise**, & **-able.** Worthy of being despised; mean, contemptible.

despicably, adv. Prec. & **-ly.** In a despicable manner.

despise, vb. trans. [1. despíz; 2. dispáiz]. M.E. *despisen*, fr. O. Fr. *despis-*, fr. *despire*, 'to despise', fr. *dēspicere*, 'to look down on'; fig. 'to despise'. See **de-** & **spy** (**I.**) & **species.** To look down upon, have a contempt for, contemn.

despite (**I.**), n. [1. despít; 2. dispáit], fr. O. Fr. *despit*, fr. Lat. *dēspectus*, 'a looking down, view from above'; fig. 'scorn, contempt', fr. P.P. type of *dēspicere*, 'to look down on; despise'. See **despise, spite.** **a** Malice, spite; scorn, contempt; Phr. *in despite of*, notwithstanding, in spite of; **b** (archaic) malicious act, injury: *to act in one's own despite.*

despite (**II.**), prep., fr. prec. Notwithstanding, in spite of: *despite our efforts* &c.

despiteful, adj. [1. despítfool; 2. dispáitfəl]. See **despite** (**I.**) & **-ful.** (archaic) Spiteful.

despitefully, adv. Prec. & **-ly.** (archaic) Spitefully, maliciously.

despoil, vb. trans. [1. despóil; 2. dispóil], fr. O. Fr. *despoiller*, fr. Lat. *dēspoliāre*, 'to rob, plunder', fr. **de-** & *spoliāre*, 'to strip of clothing'; hence in general, 'to rob, despoil'. See **spoil** (**II.**). To deprive by robbery, plunder, strip, bereave, take away by force.

despoliation, n. [1. despòliáshun; 2. dispòuliéiʃən], fr. O. Fr. *despoliation*, Lat. *dēspoliāt-(um)*, P.P. of *dēspoliāre*, 'to rob'. See **de-** & **spoliation.** The act or process of despoiling; the state of being despoiled.

despond (**I.**), vb. intrans. [1. despónd; 2. dispɔ́nd], fr. Lat. *dēspond-(ēre)*, 'to promise, pledge', esp. 'to promise in marriage; to give up, devote to, resign; to lose courage', fr. **de-** & *spondēre*, 'to promise, bind oneself, vow'. See **sponsion, respond.** To be depressed, dejected; to lose hope and courage.

despond (**II.**), n., fr. prec. (obs.) State of discouragement, dejection, despondency. Phr. *slough of Despond* (Bunyan, 'Pilgrim's Progress').

despondency, n. [1. despóndensi; 2. dispɔ́ndənsi]. **despond** (**I.**) & **-ency.** The state of being despondent, dejection of mind and spirits.

despondent, adj. [1. despóndent; 2. dispɔ́ndənt]. **despond** (**I.**) & **-ent.** Inclined to despond, lacking in hope and courage, dejected, gloomy, despairing.

despondently, adv. Prec. & **-ly.** In a despondent manner.

despondingly, adv. [1. despóndingli; 2. dispɔ́ndiŋli]. Pres. Part. of **despond** (**I.**) & **-ly.** Despondently.

despot, n. [1. déspot; 2. déspət]. O. Fr., fr. Gk. *despótēs*, orig. 'lord of a household', hence 'a master, owner, lord', esp. 'an absolute ruler'. The first element is prob. fr. **dems-*, 'a house'; cp. Lat. *domus*, house'. See **dome** & words there referred to. The second element is fr. same word as Gk. *pósis*, 'lord, husband', wh. stands for **potis*; cp. Lat. *potis*, 'capable, powerful' &c., also *potīri*, 'to be master', & *posse*, 'to be able'; cogn. w. Goth. *-faþs*, 'lord'. See **potent, power, possible. 1.** One who governs with absolute and uncontrolled authority. **2.** One who abuses his power as a ruler; a tyrant.

despotic, adj. [1. despótik; 2. dispɔ́tik], fr. Gk. *despotikós*, 'pertaining to a master; exercising despotic power; tyrannical'. See prec. & **-ic. a** Pertaining to a despot, having absolute power; hence, **b** tyrannical.

despotically, adv. [1. despótikali; 2. dispɔ́tikəli]. Prec. & **-al** & **-ly.** In a despotic manner, as a despot.

despotism, n. [1. déspotizm; 2. déspətizəm]. **despot** & **-ism. a** Government by a despot; **b** methods of despotic government, tyranny; **c** state governed by a despot.

despotist, n. [1. déspotist; 2. déspətist]. **despot** & **-ist.** One in favour of despotism.

desquamate, vb. trans. & intrans. [1. déskwamāt; 2. déskwəmeit], fr. Lat. *dēsquāmāt-(um)*, P.P. type of *dēsquāmāre*, 'to scale, peel off', fr. **de-** & *squāma*, 'scale'; etymol. doubtful. **A.** trans. To cause to peel, throw off, skin. **B.** intrans. (of skin) To peel off in scales.

desquamation, n. [1. dèskwamáshun; 2. dèskwəméiʃən]. Prec. & **-ion.** The process of desquamating.

desquamatory, adj. [1. deskwámatori; 2. diskwǽmətəri]. See prec. & **-ory.** Causing desquamation.

dessert, n. [1. dezért; 2. dizə́t], fr. O. Fr. *desserte*, fr. *desservir*, 'to clear the table', fr. Lat. **dis-** & *servīre*, 'to be a servant to, serve'. See **serve.** A course, consisting of fruit, sweets &c., served at the end of dinner.

dessert-spoon, n. A spoon of medium size, holding about twice as much as a teaspoon.

destination, n. [1. dèstinásh un; 2. dèstinéiʃən]. See next word & **-ation.** The place to which a person or thing is going, or being sent; place or spot which one aims at reaching.

destine, vb. trans. [1. déstin; 2. déstin], fr. O. Fr. *destiner*, fr. Lat. *dēstināre*, 'to fasten securely; to fix, determine, appoint; to aim at', fr. **de-** & **stanāre*, 'to place firmly', fr. Aryan base **stə-*, **stā-*, 'to stand'. See **stand (I.), state (I.)**, & words there referred to. See also **obstinate.** To determine the future of, decree, intend, fore-ordain (of decrees of God, Fate, and result of circumstances): *destined never to meet*; *destined for the Church.*

destiny, n. [1. déstini; 2. déstini], fr. O. Fr. *destinee*, fr. Lat. *dēstināt-(um)*, 'a mark, aim; a design, purpose', fr. P.P. of *dēstināre*, 'to fix securely; to appoint, destine'. See prec. **a** Pre-ordained fate, course of life, appointed lot: *a strange, a fortunate, destiny*; **b** personification of the force or power which determines fate; Providence.

destitute, adj. [1. déstitūt; 2. déstitjūt], fr. Lat. *dēstitūt-(um)*, P.P. type of *dēstituere*, 'to set down; to leave, desert, forsake; to disappoint, defraud', fr. **de-** & *statuere*, 'to cause to stand, put, place; to determine, decide'. See **statute. a** In want, in a state of poverty, deprived of means of support: *to be left destitute*; also as noun, *the destitute*; **b** (followed by *of*) without, lacking in, not possessing: *destitute of good feeling* &c.

destitution, n. [1. dèstitúshun; 2. dèstitjúʃən], fr. Lat. *dēstitūtiōn-(em)*, 'a forsaking'. See prec. & **-ion.** The state of being destitute, forsaken; unrelieved want, absolute poverty.

destrier, n. [1. déstrier; 2. déstriə]. O. Fr. *destrier*, 'a war-horse', fr. Low Lat. *dextrārius*, 'led by the hand'. See **dexter** & **-ary.** (archaic) A war-horse, charger.

destroy, vb. trans. [1. destrói; 2. distrɔ́i]. M.E. *destroien, destruien*, fr. O. Fr. *destruire*, fr. Low Lat. *dēstructere*, fr. *dēstruct-(um)*, P.P. type of *dēstruere*, 'to pull down, tear to pieces'; fig. 'to ruin, weaken', fr. **de-** & *struere*, 'to pile up; to build, construct'. See **structure, construct.** (of action on both material and non-material things) To bring to nothing, ruin; pull, crush, to pieces, sweep away, annihilate: *to destroy a town, a cobweb, a person's plans, hopes, dreams* &c.

destroyable, adj. [1. destróiabl; 2. distrɔ́iəbl]. Prec. & **-able.** Capable of being destroyed, destructible.

destroyer, n. [1. destróier; 2. distrɔ́iə]. **destroy** & **-er.** One who, that which, destroys. Specif. (nav., also *torpedo-boat destroyer*) a class of small fast warships carrying torpedoes, used for attacking torpedo-boats and submarines.

destructibility, n. [1. destrúktibíliti; 2. distráktibíliti]. See next word & **-ity.** The quality of being destructible.

destructible, adj. [1. destrúktibl; 2. distráktibl], fr. Lat. *dēstruct-(um)*, P.P. type of *dēstruere*, 'to pull down, pull to pieces'. See **destroy** & **-ible.** Capable of being destroyed, liable to destruction.

destruction, n. [1. destrúkshun; 2. distrákʃən], fr. Lat. *dēstructiōn-(em)*, 'a pulling down, destroying', fr. *dēstruct-(um)* (see prec.) & **-ion. a** The act or process of destroying; state of being destroyed; ruin; **b** that which destroys, causes ruin, downfall of: *over-confidence was his destruction.*

destructive, adj. [1. destrúktiv; 2. distráktiv]. See prec. & **-ive. a** Tending to destroy, harmful; **b** given to destroying, aiming at, liable to cause, destruction.

destructively, adv. Prec. & **-ly.** In a destructive manner.

destructiveness, n. See prec. & **-ness.** Quality of being destructive.

destructor, n. [1. destrúktor; 2. distráktə], fr. Lat. *dēstruct-(um)* (see **destruction**) & **-or.** That which, who, destroys; specif., a furnace for destroying rubbish.

desuetude, n. [1. déswetūd; 2. díswitjūd], fr. Fr., fr. Lat. *dēsuētūdo*, 'disuse, discontinuance', fr. *dēsuēt-(um)*, P.P. type of *dēsuēscere*, 'to discontinue, give up use of', fr. **de-** & *suēscere*, 'to become accustomed to', fr. *suēre*, 'to be accustomed'; lit. 'to make one's own', fr. Aryan base **swe-*, 'one's own, pertaining to oneself'. Cp. Gk. *éthos*, 'habit, custom', fr. **swedh-*; cp. Scrt. *swadhā*, 'custom'. See **ethic** & **sui**, & cp. **consuetude.** The state of being disused, of being no longer practised; discontinuance: *to fall into desuetude* (of a custom, practice &c.).

desulphurization, n. [1. désúlfurīzáshun; 2. dīsálfəraizéiʃən]. See next word & **-ation.** The act of desulphurizing.

desulphurize, vb. trans. [1. dēsúlfurīz; 2. dīsálfəraiz]. See **de-** & **sulphur** & **-ize.** To remove sulphur from.

desultorily, adv. [1. désultorili; 2. désəltərili]. **desultory** & **-ly.** In a desultory manner.

desultoriness, n. [1. désultorines; 2. désəltərinis]. See next word & **-ness.** Quality of being desultory.

desultory, adj. [1. désultori; 2. désəltəri], fr. Lat. *dēsultōrius*, 'pertaining to a circus-rider', fr. *dēsultor*, 'one who leaps, vaults'; esp. 'a circus-rider', fr. *dēsult-(um)*, P.P. type of *dēsilīre*, 'to leap down', fr. **de-** & *salīre*, 'to spring, leap, bound'. See **salient.** (of mental or physical activity) Passing abruptly from one activity to another; disconnected, not continuous; unmethodical, aimless.

desynonymize, vb. trans. [1. dèsinónimīz; 2. dīsinɔ́nimaiz]. See **de-** & **synonym** & **-ize.** To cause (words) to become differentiated in meaning.

detach, vb. trans. [1. detách; 2. ditǽtʃ], fr. Fr. *détacher*, fr. **de-** & Romance *tacca*, 'a nail', fr. Gmc. **tak-*. See **tack (I.). a** To unfasten, separate; **b** (mil. and nav.) to despatch (ship or body of troops) on special service.

detachable, adj. [1. detáchabl; 2. ditǽtʃəbl]. Prec. & **-able.** Capable of being detached, unfastened.

detached, adj. [1. detácht; 2. ditǽtʃt]. P.P. of **detach. a** (of concrete objects) Separate, distinct, standing alone, not directly connected with something else: *a detached house*; **b** (of mental states) unbiased, impartial, not swayed by exterior influences; impersonal: *a detached mind, view, opinion.*

detachedly, adv. [1. detáchedli; 2. ditǽtʃidli]. Prec. & **-ly.** In a detached manner.

detachment, n. [1. detáchment; 2. ditǽtʃmənt]. **detach** & **-ment. 1.** The act or process of detaching; state of being detached, esp. of mental states; mental isolation, aloofness; dissociation from surroundings: *an air of detachment.* **2.** That which is detached; specif. (mil. and nav.) a number of troops, ships &c. detached from main body for special service.

detail (I.), vb. trans. [1. detál; 2. ditéil], fr. Fr. *détailler*, fr. **de-** & *tailler*, 'to cut'. See **tally, tailor. 1.** To make a minute and particular report of, relate full details of: *to detail one's adventures.* **2.** (mil.) To select, appoint, for special service: *detail men for fatigue duty* &c.

detail (II.), n. [1. dḗtāl; 2. dīteil], fr. prec. **1. a** A section of a whole, particular fact, single subordinate part, item; Phrs. *in detail*, minutely, in all particulars; *to go into details*; **b** small, unimportant, insignificant circumstance: *a mere detail.* **2.** (art and archit.) Subordinate part, single section, in a scheme of decoration, construction &c.; manner of treatment of this.

detain, vb. trans. [1. detán; 2. ditéin], fr. O. Fr. *détenir*, fr. Lat. *dētinēre*, 'to keep back, restrain, detain', fr. **de-** & *tenēre*, 'to have, hold, keep; to maintain; to restrain'. See **tenable. a** To keep back, hinder, prevent (persons) from proceeding: *to be detained by business*; **b** to withhold, retain possession of, keep (things); **c** (law, specif.) to hold (a person) in custody, keep under arrest.

detainer, n. [1. detáner; 2. ditéinə]. Prec. & **-er.** (law) **a** Wrongful detention of goods; **b** writ authorizing the detention on another charge of a person already under arrest.

detect, vb. trans. [1. detékt; 2. ditékt], fr. Lat. *dētect-(um)*, P.P. type of *dētegere*, 'to uncover, expose'; fig. 'to discover; to reveal', fr. **de-** & *tegere*, 'to cover; to shelter; protect'; fig. 'to conceal'. See **tegument** & **thatch. 1.** To expose, bring to light, discover: *to detect a person in a dishonest act.* **2.** To receive a mental or sensuous impression of the presence of; discover, discern, perceive existence of: *I could detect no sign of disease.*

detectable, adj. [1. detéktabl; 2. ditéktəbl]. Prec. & **-able.** Capable of being detected.

detection, n. [1. detékshun; 2. ditékʃən]. **detect** & **-ion.** The act or process of detecting.

detective, adj. & n. [1. detéktiv; 2. ditéktiv]. **detect** & **-ive. 1.** adj. Aiding in, serving for, detection; dealing with detection: *a detective force. Detective story*, general term for a class of stories in which the interest is centred in a crime and the detection of the perpetrator. **2.** n. **a** A police-officer engaged in the special work of investigating criminal cases; esp. one who belongs to the Criminal Investigation Department (C.I.D.) at New Scotland Yard; **b** any person who undertakes to do such work: *private detective.*

detector, n. [1. detéktor; 2. ditéktə]. **detect** & **-or.** One who, that which, detects; specif., any of various devices or apparatus, as in wireless telephony, for converting the electric waves into a form that can be heard in the receiver, as: *a crystal, valve, detector.*

detent, n. [1. detént; 2. ditént], fr. Lat. *dētent-(um)*, P.P. type of *dētinēre*, 'to keep back, restrain, detain'. See **detain.** (mechan.) A catch which locks and unlocks wheels in machinery; esp. a catch for regulating the striking of a clock.

détente, n. [1. dātahnt; 2. detāt]. Fr. See prec. A term in diplomacy; a lessening in, relief from, a state of strained relations or diplomatic tension between two countries.

detention, n. [1. deténshun; 2. diténʃən], fr. Lat. *dētentiōn-(em)*, fr. *dētent-(um)*, P.P. type of *dētinēre*, 'to keep back, detain', see **detain**, & **-ion**. The act of detaining; state of being detained; specif. **a** keeping in after school hours as a punishment; **b** confinement, keeping in custody (of suspected or convicted person).

deter, vb. trans. [1. detér; 2. ditā́], fr. Lat. *dēterrēre*, 'to frighten, discourage from, prevent', fr. **de-** & *terrēre*, 'to frighten'. See **terrible**. To cause to hesitate, discourage from; prevent action of, by arousing doubt, fear, caution.

detergent, adj. & n. [1. detérjent; 2. ditā́dʒənt], fr. Lat. *dētergent-(em)*, Pres. Part. type of *dētergēre*, 'to wipe off, wipe away'; hence 'to cleanse by wiping, to clean out', fr. **de-** & *tergēre*, 'to wipe off, rub off; to cleanse, polish'; also fig. See **terse**. **1.** adj. Having the power of cleansing, purifying. **2.** n. A powerful cleansing substance.

deteriorate, vb. trans. & intrans. [1. detériorāt; 2. ditíəriəreit], fr. Lat. *dēteriōrāt-(um)*, P.P. type of *dēteriōrāre*, 'to make worse', fr. *dēterior*, 'lower, inferior'; fig., 'worse, meaner, degenerate' (& **-ate**), fr. obs. adv. **dē-tero*, 'down', compar. formed fr. **de-** 'down from'. For the suff. *-ter* see **inter (II.)** & **-ther**. **a** trans. To lessen the value of, cause to depreciate; **b** intrans., to become worse in quality, develop inferior characteristics.

deterioration, n. [1. detèrioráshun; 2. ditìəriəréiʃən]. See prec. & **-ion**. The process of deteriorating; the state of having deteriorated.

deteriorative, adj. [1. detériorātiv; 2. ditíəriəreitiv]. See **deteriorate** & **-ive**. Tending to deteriorate, having a destructive effect.

determent, n. [1. detérment; 2. ditā́mənt]. **deter** & **-ment**. **a** The act of deterring, discouraging; **b** that which deters.

determinable, adj. [1. detérminabl; 2. ditā́minəbl]. **determine** & **-able**. Capable of being determined.

determinant, adj. & n. [1. detérminant; 2. ditā́minənt]. **determine** & **-ant**. **1.** adj. Having the power of fixing, limiting, defining. **2.** n. That which determines, serves to determine; specif. (math.) a form of notation used for representing certain algebraic functions.

determinate, adj. [1. detérminat; 2. ditā́minit]. **determine** & **-ate**. Having the quality of being determined; fixed, definite.

determinately, adv. Prec. & **-ly**. In a determinate manner, exactly; resolutely.

determination, n. [1. detèrmináshun; 2. ditā̀minéiʃən]. **determine** & **-ation**. **1.** The act of determining, state or process of being determined (in all senses of the verb); specif. **a** (legal) decision, judicial sentence; **b** (med.) tendency (of blood &c.) to concentrate in a particular region, to go in a particular direction. **2.** (of mental quality) Firmness, fixity of purpose, resolution.

determinative, adj. & n. [1. detérminativ; 2. ditā́minətiv], fr. Lat. *dētermindruat-(um)*, P.P. type of *dētermindruare*, 'to bound, limit'. See **determine** & **-ive**. **a** adj. Having the power of directing, determining, serving to fix, limit, define; **b** n., that which is determinative, a determining factor.

determine, vb. trans. & intrans. [1. detérmin; 2. ditā́min], fr. O. Fr. *determiner*, fr. Lat. *dētermindruare*, 'to bound, limit, prescribe', fr. **de-** & *termināre*, 'to mark off by boundaries, to limit; to define; to close, terminate', fr. *terminus*, 'a limit'. See **terminate**. **A.** trans. **1.** **a** (archaic) To delimit, mark out, fix extent or scope of; **b** to fix, regulate, be the cause of, be the deciding factor in settling the form, quality, function of: *my course of action is determined by events; the size of boot is determined by the foot.* **2.** To cause a resolution, decision, to be formed in the mind: *this determines me to act at once.* **3.** To find out exactly, ascertain, fix precisely: *to determine the precise meaning of a word.* **B.** intrans. **1.** To make up one's mind, come to a decision, form fixed resolution: *to determine upon a course of action; to determine to succeed.* **2.** (law) To come to an end, close, terminate: e.g. *a lease determines on a given date.*

determined, adj. [1. detérmind; 2. ditā́mind]. Prec. & **-ed**. Firm, decided, resolute, unwavering: *a determined character; determined attack; I'm determined to succeed; more determined than ever to go.*

determinism, n. [1. detérminizm; 2. ditā́minizəm]. **determine** & **-ism**. The doctrine that man is not a free agent, but that his actions are determined by conditions independent of his will.

determinist, n. [1. detérminist; 2. ditā́minist]. See prec. & **-ist**. Believer in determinism.

deterministic, adj. [1. detèrminístik; 2. ditā̀minístik]. Prec. & **-ic**. Pertaining to determinism.

deterrence, n. [1. detérens; 2. ditérəns]. **deter** & **-ence**. **a** The act of deterring; **b** that which deters.

deterrent, adj. & n. [1. detérent; 2. ditérənt]. **deter** & **-ent**. **a** adj. Tending to deter, hindering, discouraging; **b** n., that which deters.

detersive, adj. & n. [1. detérsiv; 2. ditā́siv], fr. Lat. *dēters-(um)*, P.P. type of *dētergēre*, 'to wipe off; to clean by wiping'. See **detergent** & **-ive**. **a** adj. Having cleansing properties; **b** n., a cleansing substance.

detest, vb. trans. [1. detést; 2. ditést], fr. O. Fr. *detester*, fr. Lat. *dētestāri*, 'to curse by calling the gods to witness; to execrate, abominate; to avert, ward off', fr. **de-** & *testāri*, 'to be a witness, testify; to invoke as witness'. See **testament**. To hate, dislike strongly, to abhor, abominate.

detestable, adj. [1. detéstabl; 2. ditéstəbl], fr. Lat. *dētestābilis*, 'abominable, execrable'. See prec. & **-able**. Deserving detestation; abominable, hateful.

detestableness, n. Prec. & **-ness**. Quality of being detestable.

detestably, adv. See prec. & **-ly**. In a detestable manner.

detestation, n. [1. dètestáshun; 2. dītestéiʃən], fr. Lat. *dētestātiōn-(em)*, 'an execration, cursing; detestation'. See **detest** & **-ation**. **a** Hatred, extreme dislike; **b** object of dislike; something which is detested.

dethrone, vb. trans. [1. dethrón; 2. diþróun]. **de-** & **throne**. **a** To remove (a ruler) from the throne, depose; **b** (fig.) to oust, remove, a person from a position, from place he holds in popular estimation &c.

dethronement, n. [1. dethrónment; 2. diþróunmənt]. Prec. & **-ment**. Act of dethroning.

detinue, n. [1. détinū; 2. détinjū], fr. O. Fr. *detenue*, P.P. of *detenir*, 'to keep back, detain'. See **detain**. (law) Wrongful detention of personal property of another: *action of detinue*, one for the recovery of property wrongfully detained.

detonate, vb. trans. & intrans. [1. détonāt, dḗtonāt; 2. détəneit, dítəneit], fr. Lat. *dētonāt-(um)*, P.P. type of *dētonāre*, 'to thunder; to cease thundering', fr. **de-** & *tonāre*, 'to thunder; to roar, crash; to say with a voice of thunder'. See **thunder** & **tone**. **a** trans. To cause to explode; **b** intrans., to explode with a sudden loud noise; esp. of a fuse containing a charge which on explosion explodes another high explosive.

detonating, adj. [1. détonāting; 2. détəneitiŋ], fr. Pres. Part. of prec., as *detonating fuse*, one containing an explosive; *detonating powder*, as fulminate of mercury, which, on explosion, detonates another high explosive.

detonation, n. [1. detonáshun; 2. detənéiʃən]. **detonate** & **-ion**. The act or process of detonating; a violent explosion.

detonative, adj. [1. détonātiv; 2. détəneitiv]. **detonate** & **-ive**. Causing explosion.

detonator, n. [1. détonātor; 2. détəneitə]. **detonate** & **-or**. **a** Device for producing a loud report, e.g. a railway fog-signal; **b** a detonating fuse or powder.

détour, n. [1. dātóór; 2. deitúə]. Fr., fr. *détourner*. See **de-** & **tour**. A digression, going round; a departure from the straight or direct road.

detract, vb. trans. & intrans. [1. detrákt; 2. ditrǽkt], fr. Lat. *dētract-(um)*, P.P. type of *dētrahere*, 'to draw off, pull away; to take away, deduct; to disparage, lower in estimation', fr. **de-** & *trahere*, 'to draw, drag; to attract, influence'. See **tract (I.)**. **1.** trans. To take away from, diminish, the merit, credit, reputation of (a person); to lessen the usefulness, advantage, of (a thing): *her ugliness detracts something from her charm.* **2.** intrans. *To detract from*, to diminish; *that does not detract from his merit.*

detraction, n. [1. detrákshun; 2. ditrǽkʃən]. Prec. & **-ion**. **a** The act of detracting; **b** disparagement, depreciation.

detractive, adj. [1. detráktiv; 2. ditrǽktiv]. **detract** & **-ive**. Tending to detract.

detrain, vb. trans. & intrans. [1. detrā́n; 2. ditréin]. **de-** & **train (II.)**. (esp. of troops &c.) **a** trans. To set down from a train; **b** intrans., to alight from a train.

detriment, n. [1. détriment; 2. détrimənt], fr. Lat. *dētrīment-(um)*, 'a rubbing off; loss, damage; defeat, overthrow', fr. *dētrīt-(um)*, P.P. type of *dēterere*, 'to rub down, wear away', fr. *terere*, 'to rub, to lessen by rubbing, to polish'; fig., 'to wear away'; (of time) 'to pass'. See **de-**, **trite**, & **-ment**. Injury, harm, loss, disadvantage; esp. in Phrs. *to the detriment of (one's health); without detriment to (one's property).*

detrimental, adj. & n. [1. dètriméntl; 2. dètriméntl]. Prec. & **-al**. **1.** adj. Causing injury, harm, loss; likely to have a bad effect upon: *detrimental to health, to one's character, prospects* &c. **2.** n. (colloq.) An undesirable person, esp. an unwelcome, poor aspirant to a lady's hand.

detrimentally, adv. Prec. & **-ly**. In a manner likely to cause injury: *to affect a person detrimentally.*

detrital, adj. [1. dētrítl; 2. dītráitl]. See **detritus** & **-al**. Composed of detritus.

detrited, adj. [1. dētríted; 2. dītráitid]. See **detritus** & **-ed**. **a** Worn away; **b** formed by detrition.

detrition, n. [1. dētríshun; 2. dītríʃən], fr. Lat. *dētrīt-(um)*, see **detritus**, & **-ion**. (esp. geol.) Wearing down by constant friction.

detritus, n. [1. dētrítus; 2. dītráitəs]. Lat. *dētrītus*, 'rubbed away, worn down', P.P. of *dēterere*, 'to rub away, wear out'. See **detriment**. (geol.) A mass of fragments worn away by friction from rocks &c.

de trop, pred. adj. [1. de trṓ; 2. də tróu]. Fr. Too many; not wanted; in the way.

detruncate, vb. trans. [1. dētrúngkāt; 2. dītráŋkeit], fr. Lat. *dētruncāt-(um)*, P.P. type of *dētruncāre*, 'to lop; behead'. See **de-** & **truncate**. To cut off a portion of, shorten by cutting.

deuce, n. [1. dūs; 2. djūs], fr. Fr. *deux*, 'two', fr. Lat. *duos*, acc. of *duo*, 'two'. See **dual**. **1.** A card or die with two spots. **2.** The score of 40 all, at lawn tennis, after which one side has to win two consecutive points in order to win the game. **3.** (from idea of low point at cards or dice, see **1**) Bad luck, a nuisance; the devil: (colloq.) *the deuce of a row; go to the deuce*; as mild imprecation: *who, what, the deuce is that? why the deuce* &c.

deuced, adj. or adv. [1. dūst; 2. djūst]. Prec. & **-ed**. (colloq.) Confounded, extreme: *deuced bad.*

deucedly, adv. [1. dúsedli; 2. djúsidli]. Prec. & **-ly**. Extremely: *deucedly uncomfortable.*

deuteragonist, n. [1. dùterágonist; 2. djūtərǽgənist], fr. Gk. *deuteragōnistés*, 'an actor taking the second part in a drama'. See next word & **agonistic.** A character in a (esp. Greek) drama, next in importance to the protagonist.

deutero-, pref., fr. Gk. *deúteros*, 'second'; orig. 'at a distance; following (in time or space)'; cp. Scrt. *dūrâś*, 'distant', *dávīyān*, 'further off'; fr. base **deu-* 'to go away, become distant'; cp. base **deus*, 'need, want', whence Gk. *déō*, 'I want, need', fr. **deusō*; Scrt. *dōšaś*, 'absence, want'; unconnected w. Gk. *dúo*, 'two'. Second, secondary.

deuteronomic, adj. [1. dûteronómik; 2. djûtərənómik]. **Deuteronomy & -ic.** Of, pertaining to, the book of Deuteronomy.

deuteronomist, n. [1. dūteronomist; 2. djūtərónəmist]. Next word & **-ist.** Author or compiler of the book of Deuteronomy.

Deuteronomy, n. [1. dûterónomi; 2. djûtərónəmi], fr. Lat. *deuteronomia*, fr. Gk. *deúteros*, 'second', see **deutero-**, & *nómos*, 'custom, usage, law'. See **anomo-** & **nemesis.** The fifth book of the Pentateuch in the Old Testament, as containing the second book of the law of Moses.

deutoplasm, n. [1. dûtōplàzm; 2. djûtouplæzəm]. Invented word, as if shortened form of **deutero-** & **plasm**, on anal. of **protoplasm.** (biol.) The matter in an egg which supplies food for the embryo, as distinguished from the protoplasm.

deutzia, n. [1. dóitsia, dûtsia; 2. dóitsiə, djûtsiə], fr. Deutz, name of 18th-cent. Dutch botanist, & **-ia.** A shrub with small white flowers much cultivated in England; a native of China and Japan.

devastate, vb. trans. [1. dévastāt; 2. dévəsteit], fr. Lat. *dēvastā-(um)*, P.P. type of *dēvastāre*, 'to lay waste', fr. **de-** & *vastāre*, 'to make empty, desolate; to ravage, lay waste', fr. *vastus*, 'empty, unoccupied; huge'. See **vast.** (lit. and fig.) To lay waste, make desolate.

devastation, n. [1. dèvastáshun; 2. dèvəstéiʃən]. See prec. & **-ion.** a The act of devastating; b the state of being devastated.

develop, vb. trans. & intrans. [1. devélop; 2. divéləp], fr. Fr. *développer.* Etymol. of second element very doubtful. Apparently connected w. Lat. *volvere*, 'to roll' &c. (see **volute**), influenced by, & perh. amalgamated w., some other word. Cp. O. Fr. *enveloper* & O. Ital. *inviluppare.* **A.** trans. **1.** To cause to grow, unfold, expand, work more vigorously; **a** (of material things) *to develop one's business, resources, a mine* &c.; **b** *to develop the mind, memory, character* &c. **2. a** (of material processes) To cause to appear, to cause to become more clearly defined; specif., to make picture appear on photographic negative by treating chemically; **b** to enlarge upon, treat more fully, bring out, and explain meaning more clearly: *to develop an argument, a case, line of thought* &c. **B.** intrans. **1.** (of material things) To grow, unfold, take shape, become larger and more complex; evolve by natural process: *the oak develops from the acorn*; *the chicken develops in the egg* &c. **2.** (of non-material things) To become more clearly defined, assume definite shape, or character: *the plot* (of story or play) *develops on strange lines*; *the situation developed rapidly.*

developable, adj. [1. devélopabl; 2. divéləpəbl]. Prec. & **-able.** (rare) Capable of development.

developer, n. [1. devéloper; 2. divéləpə]. See **develop** & **-er.** One who, that which, causes something to develop; specif., a chemical for developing picture on photographic plates and films.

development, n. [1. devélopment; 2. divéləpmənt]. **develop** & **-ment. 1. a** The act or process of causing to develop: *engaged in the development of one's business*; **b** state or process of developing; growth, evolution, gradual progress, expansion: *the development of the human mind, of civilization*; *the development of animal life, of an animal, or plant.* **2.** A result of the process of development; something which shows itself as the product of prior causes and conditions: *class hatred is a new development in the social problem.*

developmental, adj. [1. devèlopméntl; 2. divèləpméntl]. Prec. & **-al.** Pertaining to development, belonging to a time of growth.

deviate, vb. intrans. & trans. [1. dévìāt; 2. dívieit], fr. Lat. **de-** & *via*, 'way, path', & **-ate**; cp. Lat. *dēvius*, 'off the road, out of the way, remote, unreasonable'. See **devious. 1.** intrans. (most commonly in fig. sense) To turn aside, swerve (from the right or direct course), diverge: *to deviate from truth*; *to deviate from syntactical rules.* **2.** trans. (rare, of material process) To cause to deviate.

deviation, n. [1. dèviáshun; 2. dìviéiʃən]. Prec. & **-ion.** **a** The act of deviating: *a deviation from the truth*; **b** amount of divergence (chiefly of physical process): *a slight deviation of the magnetic needle.*

device, n. [1. devís; 2. diváis]. M.E., fr. O. Fr. *devis*, fr. Lat. *dīvīs-(um)*, P.P. type of *dīvidere*, 'to separate; to distribute; to keep apart, distinguish'; see **divide.** The Lat. vb. seems to have acquired in Romance an additional meaning, 'to divide into parts, examine in detail'; hence 'examine carefully, reflect on; think out, imagine'. See **devise. 1. a** (in gen. sense) Something thought out, a plan, scheme, design; Phr. *to leave a person to his own devices*, leave him alone, give no help or advice; **b** (in bad sense) a crafty, malicious scheme or plan to do harm, a cunning plot: *the devices of the devil.* Cp. similar specialized meaning of *design.* **2.** (of material objects) The result of planning; an invention, mechanical contrivance to effect some particular purpose, a dodge: *a device for preventing babies falling out of bed*; *a device for catching flies* &c. **3.** An ornamental or symbolical design, consisting **a** of a pattern, figure &c., or **b** of an inscription in words.

devil (I.), n. [1. dévl; 2. dévl]. O.E. *dēofol*, M.E. *dēvel*; cp. O.H.G. *tiufal, tiubal*, Germ. *teufel*; a loan-word fr. Lat., fr. Gk. *diábolos*, 'a slanderer'; specif., 'the devil', fr. *diabállein*, 'to throw, carry, across; to set at variance; to attack, slander, accuse' (for meaning cp. **traduce**), fr. **dia-** & *bállein*, 'to throw'. See **ballistics. 1. a** The spirit of evil, Satan. Phrs. *devil's advocate* (Lat. *advocatus diaboli*), official appointed to oppose a proposed canonization; hence, depreciator; *between the devil and the deep sea*, in a perplexing situation; *give the devil his due*, be just, even to the least deserving; *to go to the devil*, be ruined, sink to a low state; *play the devil with*, ruin, injure; *devil's bones*, dice; *devil's books*, playing-cards; *Devil's Own*, the 88th Foot; the Inns of Court Rifle Corps; **b** various colloquial exclamatory phrases: *a devil of a time*; *the devil he did!*, it can hardly be possible; *devil a one*, none at all; *the very devil* (pred.), causing great difficulty, trouble; *the devil to pay, the devil and all to pay*, great trouble in store. **2. a** A wicked spirit, fiend, an evil power, demon; Phr. *a devil to work, to eat* &c.; **b** personification of some form of vice: *the devil of avarice*; **c** a wicked person; **d** a wretched and unfortunate person: *a poor devil*; **e** (zool.) the Tasmanian devil, q.v. **3.** Person holding subordinate position in various lines of business; specif. **a** (legal) junior counsel working (without fees) under a leader; *Attorney-General's devil*, junior Counsel to the Treasury; **b** a person, usually anonymous, employed by a writer for the more mechanical and laborious part of his work; **c** *printer's devil*, errand-boy in a printer's office. **4.** (cookery) Dish made with strong seasoning and hot condiments, esp. meat or fish of any kind grilled with mustard. **5.** Machine with sharp spikes, teeth &c. for breaking up or tearing some material, as raw cotton, wool &c.

devil (II.), vb. trans. & intrans., fr. prec. **1.** trans. To cook by grilling with mustard: *devilled bones* &c. **2.** intrans. To do subordinate work for another: *to devil for a barrister, for an author* &c.

devildom, n. [1. dévldom; 2. dévldəm]. **devil** & **-dom. a** The domain of devils; **b** the power, rank, condition of devils.

devil-fish, n. One of several kinds of large and hideous rays of the Atlantic; also applied to the cuttle-fish.

devilish, adj. & adv. [1. dévl-ish; 2. dévl-iʃ]. **devil (I.)** & **-ish. a** adj. Resembling the devil or his qualities, excessively evil; **b** adv. (colloq.) extremely, excessively, very: *devilish funny, nice, uncomfortable* &c.

devilishly, adv. Prec. & **-ly.** In a devilish manner: (often colloq. as intens.) *it hurt most devilishly*, very much.

devilishness, n. See prec. & **-ness.** Quality of being devilish.

devilism, n. [1. dévl-izm; 2. dévl-izəm]. **devil (I.)** & **-ism. a** Devilish nature or conduct; **b** worship of evil spirits, diabolism.

devil-may-care, adj. [1. dévl ma kår; 2. dévl mə kèə]. Heedless, reckless, happy-go-lucky.

devilment, n. [1. dévlment; 2. dévlmənt]. **devil (I.)** & **-ment. a** Devilish behaviour; **b** a mischievous, freakish prank.

devilry, n. [1. dévlri; 2. dévlri]. **devil (I.)** & **-ry. a** Devils collectively; **b** conduct worthy of a devil; cruel, abominable, behaviour.

devil's advocate. See **devil (I.), 1.**

devil's coach-horse, n. Popular name for a large black kind of beetle.

devil's darning-needle, n. Popular name of a dragon-fly.

devil-worship, n. The worship of devils and demons.

devious, adj. [1. dévius; 2. dívìəs], fr. Lat. *dēvius*, 'off the high-road, out of the way, devious; remote, sequestered; erroneous', fr. **de-** & *via*, 'a road, highway; a path, passage, channel; a method, manner'. See **via** & **-ous. a** (lit.) Not direct; roundabout; crooked, intricate: *devious paths*; **b** (fig., of thought and conduct) not straightforward; disingenuous, shifty.

deviously, adv. Prec. & **-ly.** In a devious manner.

deviousness, n. See prec. & **-ness.** Quality of being devious.

devisable, adj. [1. devízabl; 2. divaízəbl]. Next word & **-able.** Capable of being devised.

devise (I.), vb. trans. [1. devíz; 2. diváiz]. M.E. *devisen*, 'to divide; to tell of, describe; to contrive, plan', fr. O. Fr. *deviser*, fr. Lat. *dīvīs-(um)*, P.P. type of *dīvidere*, 'to separate, part asunder; to distribute; to distinguish'. For development of meaning see **device**, & cp. **divide**, wh. has kept the meaning of the Lat. vb. **1.** To invent, contrive, arrange a scheme for, think out: *to devise a plan of attack, means of escape* &c.; (also of material action) to plan out, invent, and produce a mechanical contrivance: *to devise a sanitary tobacco pipe.* **2.** (law) To transmit by will, leave as a legacy (real, as distinct from personal, estate).

devise (II.), n., fr. prec. (law) **a** The act of devising property; **b** clause in a will effecting this.

devisee, n. [1. devìzḗ; 2. dəvaizī]. See **devise (I.)** & **-ee.** A person to whom property is devised by will.

deviser (I.), n. [1. devízer; 2. diváizə]. **devise (I.)** & **-er.** One who devises anything.

deviser (II.), **devisor**, n. **devise (I.)** & **-er, -or.** (law) One who devises real property by will.

devitalization, n. [1. dēvìtalìzáshun; 2. dìvàitəlaizéiʃən]. Next word & **-ation.** The act or process of devitalizing; state of being devitalized.

devitalize, vb. trans. [1. dēvítalīz; 2. dīváitəlaiz]. See **de-** & **vitalize.** To deprive of animation; remove strength and vigour from.

devitrification, n. [1. dēvìtrifikáshun; 2. dìvìtrifikéiʃən]. See next word & **-fication.** The act or process of devitrifying; state of being made opaque.

devitrify, vb. trans. [1. dēvítrifì; 2. dīvítrifai]. See **de-** & **vitrify.** To remove, destroy, glassy character of; make opaque.

devoid, adj. [1. devóid; 2. divɔ́id]. Short form of P.P. of M.E. *devoiden*, 'to put away, get rid of', fr. O. Fr. *desvuidier*, fr. **dis-** & *vuide, voide*. See **void**. (followed by *of*) Lacking in, empty of, without: *a country devoid of inhabitants*; *devoid of sense, fear* &c.

devoir, n. [1. dévwar; 2. dévwā]. Fr., 'duty', fr. *devoir*, O. Fr. *deveir*, 'to owe', fr. Lat. *dēbēre*, 'to owe; to be under obligation, be indebted', fr. *dē-habēre*, 'to have something from another person'. See **de-, habit, debt, due**. **a** Duty, obligation, service; **b** (pl.) acts of civility, polite attentions: *to pay one's devoirs to*.

devolute, vb. trans. [1. dèvolū́t; 2. dìvəljū́t], fr. Lat. *dēvolūt-(um)*, P.P. type of *dēvolvere*, 'to roll down; to fall headlong'. See **devolve**. To transfer, delegate, (work &c.) to others.

devolution, n. [1. dèvolū́shun; 2. dìvəljū́ʃən], fr. Low Lat. *dēvolūtiōn-(em)*, fr. *dēvolūt-(um)*. See prec. & next word. **1.** Gradual descent through successive stages; esp. **a** transmission of property by direct descent; **b** (biol.) deterioration of species by gradual change; reverse of *evolution*. **2.** The act of devolving; delegation (of power or authority, duty, work &c.).

devolve, vb. trans. & intrans. [1. devólv; 2. divɔ́lv], fr. Lat. *dēvolvere*, 'to roll down; to fall headlong'; fig. 'to have recourse to, fall back on', fr. **de-** & *volvere*, 'to roll; roll along, turn about'; fig. 'to turn over in the mind, consider'. See **volute, volume**. **1.** trans. To transfer, delegate, depute: *devolve work, duty &c. on a representative*. **2.** intrans. (followed by *upon*) **a** (of functions, duties, responsibilities &c.) To pass to, fall to be performed by: *too much work devolves upon the second in command*; *after Nelson's death the supreme command devolved upon Collingwood*; **b** (of property) to pass by inheritance or succession.

Devonian, adj. & n. [1. devṓnian; 2. divóuniən]. **1.** adj. **a** Belonging to Devonshire; **b** (geol.) pertaining to strata lying between the Silurian and Carboniferous. **2.** n. Native or inhabitant of Devonshire.

devote, vb. trans. [1. devṓt; 2. divóut], fr. Lat. *dēvōt-(um)*, P.P. type of *dēvovēre*, 'to vow, devote (to a deity)'; hence (in general sense) 'to dedicate, give up; to devote to the gods of the infernal regions, to curse', fr. **de-** & *vovēre*, 'to vow, promise sacredly; to wish'. See **vote, vow**. **a** To give up, dedicate, set apart: *to devote one's life to art*; *devote time to study, one's money to charity*; **b** (reflex.) addict oneself to, give oneself to: *devote oneself to amusement*.

devoted, adj. [1. devṓted; 2. divóutid], P.P. of prec. (of persons) **a** Given up to, engrossed by: *devoted to sport*; hence, **b** fond of, deeply attached to, a person or thing: *a devoted husband, wife, mother* &c.; (also absol.) *she seems very devoted*, fond of son, husband &c.; Phr. *devoted head*, doomed, destined, to destruction.

devotedly, adv. Prec. & **-ly**. In a devoted manner, with devotion: *devotedly attached*.

devotee, n. [1. dèvotḗ; 2. dèvətī́]. **devote** & **-ee**. A person devoted to a service, pursuit, or cause, or person; a zealous upholder, votary: *a devotee of religion, music, learning* &c.

devotement, n. [1. devṓtment; 2. divóutmənt]. **devote** & **-ment**. (rare) The act of devoting; state of being devoted.

devotion, n. [1. devṓshun; 2. divóuʃən], fr. Lat. *dēvōtiōn-(em)*, 'a devoting, consecrating; execration; sorcery, enchantment', hence 'a spell'. See **devote** & **-ion**. **1. a** Condition of being devoted to a person or thing; strong affection, unselfish attachment and self-surrender: *the devotion of a mother for her child*; also, *passionate devotion to golf* &c.; **b** unswerving adherence, zealous, conscientious attachment to duty, moral obligations &c. **2.** Religious worship, adoration; pl., *devotions*, religious observances, prayers.

devotional, adj. [1. devṓshunal; 2. divóuʃənəl]. Prec. & **-al**. Connected with devotion; used in devotions: *devotional literature*.

devotionalism, n. [1. devṓshunalizm; 2. divóuʃənəlizəm]. See prec. & **-ism**. An addiction to excessive formal devotions.

devotionally, adv. [1. devṓshunali; 2. divóuʃənəli]. **devotional** & **-ly**. In a devotional manner.

devour, vb. trans. [1. devóur; 2. diváuə]. M.E. *devouren*, fr. O. Fr. *devorer*, fr. Lat. *dēvorāre*, 'to swallow, gulp down; to engulf, swallow up; to seize upon'; (of books) 'to read eagerly', fr. **de-** & *vorāre*, 'to swallow greedily; to overwhelm, swallow up; to pursue with eagerness'. See **voracious**. **1. a** (of men and animals) To eat, eat ravenously, hungrily, and greedily: *to devour one's dinner*; *the lion devours his prey*; **b** (of fire, pestilence &c.) to consume utterly, destroy. **2.** (fig.) **a** (of persons) To take in, absorb mentally, read with eagerness: *to devour a book*; **b** to gaze, look, at intently, keenly, eagerly: *his eyes devoured the well-known scene*; **c** (of powerful emotion) to overwhelm, possess utterly; move deeply: *devoured by curiosity, anxiety*.

devouringly, adv. [1. devóuringli; 2. diváuəriŋli], fr. Pres. Part. of prec. & **-ly**. (chiefly fig.) As though devouring; with ardent longing: *to gaze devouringly at*.

devout, adj. [1. devóut; 2. diváut]. M.E. *devōt, devout*, fr. O. Fr. *devōt*, fr. Lat. *dēvōt-(um)*. See **devote**. **1. a** (of persons) Reverently attentive to religious duties, devoted to religion; pious, good; **b** (of actions &c.) expressing reverent devotion. **2.** Devoted, intense, earnest: *a devout admirer* &c.

devoutly, adv. Prec. & **-ly**. In a devout manner.

devoutness, n. See prec. & **-ness**. Quality of being devout.

dew (I.), n. [1. dū; 2. djū]. O.E. *dēaw*, M.E. *dew, deu, deau*; O. Fris. *dau*, O.H.G. *tou*, fr. Gmc. **daʒwa* (whence also O.N. *dǫgg*); cogn. w. Lat. *favōnius* for **dhowōnios*, 'mild, west wind'; cp. Scrt. *dhávatē*, 'to run, flow', *dhāutiš*, 'a spring, stream'; Gk. *théō*, fr. **dhewō*, 'I run, flow; move quickly, whirl'. See **fume**. **1.** Moisture in the atmosphere, condensed on cold, exposed surfaces during the night, and appearing as small drops of water. **2.** (poet.) Anything resembling or suggestive of some quality of dew; **a** freshness, power of refreshing &c.: *the dew of youth*; **b** appearance, form, e.g. tears; *mountain dew*, whisky, esp. illicitly distilled whisky.

dew (II.), vb. trans., fr. prec. **a** To wet with, or as if with, dew; to bedew; **b** to condense, fall as dew.

dewan, n. [1. diwáhn; 2. diwā́n]. Arab. *diwan*. A finance minister in India; also the prime minister of one of the native, independent states of India.

dewberry, n. [1. dū́bèri; 2. djū́bèri]. A fruit resembling the blackberry, with slightly larger drupes, and more acid taste.

dew-claw, n. A rudimentary toe, or thumb, on the inside of a dog's leg, rather higher than the other toes, and not touching the ground.

dew-drop, n. A drop of moisture condensed in the form of dew.

dew-fall, n. Evening, the time when the dew is forming.

dewily, adv. [1. dū́ili; 2. djū́ili]. **dewy** & **-ly**. Like dew.

dewiness, n. [1. dū́ines; 2. djū́inis]. **dewy** & **-ness**. Condition of being dewy; wetness, moisture, from dew.

dewlap, n. [1. dū́lap; 2. djū́læp]. M.E. *dēulappe*. **dew** & **lap (I.)**. **a** A thick fold of skin hanging from the throat of cattle; **b** a similar formation in other animals; **c** (colloq. and vulg.) flesh below human chin when fat and puffy.

dewless, adj. [1. dū́les; 2. djū́lis]. **dew** & **-less**. Without dew, not dewy.

dew-point, n. The temperature to which exposed surfaces must be lowered before dew can condense upon them.

dew-pond, n. Ancient artificial pond, as often found on Sussex downs, which always contains water; probably fed by the dew from surrounding area draining into it, or by night mists.

dewy, adj. [1. dū́i; 2. djū́i]. **dew (I.)** & **-y**. **1. a** Covered with, moist with, dew; characterized by dew: *dewy eve* (poet.); *a dewy night*; **b** (poet., of eyes) wet with tears. **2.** (poet.) Resembling dew, in coming gently and refreshingly: *dewy slumbers* &c.

dexter, adj. [1. dékster; 2. dékstə]. Lat. *dexter*, 'on the right'; hence 'skilful, adroit; favourable, propitious'. Formed w. compar. suff. *-ter-os* fr. base **deks-*, 'on the right side'; cp. Umbrian *destrame*, 'on the right'; Gk. *dexiterós*, 'on the right'. Cp. also, w. different suff., Gk. *dexiós*, 'on the right; propitious; skilful'; Scrt. *dákšina-š*, 'on the right; southwards'; also 'skilful'; Lith. *deszinē̃*, 'the right hand'; O. Ir. *dess*, 'to the right, southwards'; Goth. *taihswa*, 'right'; O.H.G. *zeso*, 'right', *zesawa*, 'the right hand'. The base **dek̑-s-* is expanded fr. **dek̑-*, 'to seem good, be suitable' (see **decent**), the right hand or side being considered the stronger, more propitious. For the Lat. suff. *-ter-* see **-ther, other, either**. On the right-hand side; (her.) the dexter side of a shield is that on the left of a person looking at it; opposed to *sinister*.

dexterity, n. [1. dekstériti; 2. dekstériti], fr. Lat. *dexteritāt-(em)*, 'skilfulness, handiness'. See prec. & **-ity**. **1. a** Skill, deftness, adroitness in action and movement, specif. in manual acts; **b** intellectual adroitness, facility. **2.** Habitual use of the right hand in preference to the left.

dext(e)rous, adj. [1. dékst(e)rus; 2. dékst(ə)rəs]. **dexter** & **-ous**. **1. a** Skilful, neat, expert in movements and actions, esp. in the use of the hands; **b** ready, adroit, quick, in mental activities. **2.** Using the right hand in preference to the left.

dext(e)rously, adv. Prec. & **-ly**. In a dexterous manner.

dext(e)rousness, n. See prec. & **-ness**. Dexterity.

dextrin(e), n. [1. dékstrin; 2. dékstrin]. See next word & **-in(e)**. An adhesive substance, gum, made from starch, used on back of postage stamps &c., and for sizing paper, stiffening cotton fabrics &c.

dextro-, pref., fr. Lat. *dextrō*, dat. of **dexter**. Towards the right; esp. in chemical terms with reference to substances which cause the plane of a polarized ray of light to rotate from left to right.

dextrose, n. [1. dékstrōs; 2. dékstrous]. **dexter** & **-ose**. Starch sugar, obtained from starch or dried grapes or other fruits, the crystals of which rotate polarized light to the right; contrasted with *laevulose*.

dextrous, adj. See **dexterous**.

dey, n. [1. dā; 2. dei]. Fr., fr. Turkish *dāi*, lit. 'uncle on mother's side'; title used by the janissaries of a commander. **a** The title of the chief of the janissaries in Algiers, when a Turkish province; hence, **b** title used by the French of the Turkish Governor of Algiers until its conquest.

dhobi, n. [1. dṓbi; 2. dóubi]. Hind. A low-caste Hindu, employed as a laundry-man in India.

dhole, n. [1. dōl; 2. doul]. Hind. The wild dog of India and Central Asia, hunting in packs.

dhoti, n. [1. dṓti; 2. dóuti]. Hind. The narrow loin-cloth worn by Hindu men.

dhow, n. [1. dou; 2. dau]. Etymol. unknown. An Arabian coasting-vessel with a broad stern, one mast, and large lateen sail.

dhurrie, dhurry, n. [1. dúri; 2. dári], fr. Hind. *dari*. An Indian cotton fabric with fringed ends, used for curtains &c.

di- (I.), pref. Form of Lat. **dis-**, used in compounds, expressing idea of separation: occurring before the consonants: *b, v, m; d, l, n, s*; confused in O. Fr. & M.E. w. **de-**.

di- (II.), pref. used in chemical terms; Gk. *di-*, 'twice, double', used in composition. Cp. Gk. *dis*, 'twice', fr. Aryan **dwi-s*, 'twice, double'; cp. Lat. *bis* (O. Lat. *duis*), 'twice' (see **bi-**); Scrt. *dviś*; O.N. *tvis-var*, 'twice', M.H.G. *zwis*, 'twice'. Aryan base **dwei-*, **dwoi-*, **dwi-*, 'two'; cp. Scrt. *dvitīyaś*, 'the second'; Lat. *bi-(pēs)* (see **biped**); O.E. *twi-(fēte)*, 'two-footed'; fr. Aryan type **dwei-* comes Lat. *bī-(duum)*, 'two days'; Goth. *tweifls*, O.H.G. *zwīfal*, 'doubt', O.H.G. *zwīg*, 'branch' (see **twig**); fr. **dwoi-*, Gk. *doiós*, 'twofold' (fr. **dwoi-jos*); Scrt. *dvayáś*, 'double'; O. Bulg. *dvojĭ*, 'double'; Goth. *twaddjē* (fr. **dwoj-jē*), O.N. *tveggia*, O.H.G. *zweio*, 'of two'; O.S. *twēne*, 'two' (fr. Gmc. **twai-n-*, Aryan **dwoi-n-*). For other forms of the base see **two, dual.** Two, twice, double.

di- (III.) = **dia-**, before vowels.

dia-, pref. Gk. *diá*, prep., 'through, throughout (of place and time); through the agency of, by means of'; used in Gk., also, as pref. expressing **a** motion through; **b** separation; **c** pre-eminence. Gk. *diá* is prob. fr. **disa-*, fr. base **dis-*, parallel w. **dwi-s-*, **dwi-*, see **di-** (II.), the orig. sense having been that of parting asunder, separating; fr. this meaning was derived that of 'penetrating into', then 'through, throughout, across' (both of motion & of rest). Found as pref. in Gk. words, & in scientific terms formed fr. Gk.

diabase, n. [1. díabās; 2. dáiəbeis]. Fr., fr. Gk. *diábasis*, 'crossing over, passage through' (see **dia-** & **basis**), prob. fr. line of cleavage. Cp. **dolerite.** (mineral.) A crystalline granular rock, greenstone, whinstone, or trap.

diabetes, n. [1. dīabḗtēz; 2. dáiəbítīz]. Gk. *diabḗtēs*, 'diabetes', fr. **dia-** & *-bḗtēs*, 'a walking, moving, flowing', apparently same base as in *bētármōn*, 'a dancer', fr. **bēt-os*, 'a step', cogn. w. Gk. *bainein*, 'to go', see **base** (I.); cp. Scrt. *gātram*, 'foot'. A disease characterized by excessive production of sugar in the system and abnormal secretion of urine.

diabetic, adj. & n. [1. dīabḗtik; 2. dàiəbítik]. See prec. & **-ic.** **1.** adj. Pertaining to, suffering from, diabetes. **2.** n. A diabetic patient.

diablerie, n. [1. dēáhbleri; 2. diáblari]. Fr., fr. *diable*, fr. Lat., fr. Gk. *diábolos*, 'an accuser; the devil', see **devil** (I.), & **-ry.** **a** The work of devils, sorcery; **b** fascination, witchery.

diabolic(al), adj. [1. dīabólik(l); 2. dàiəbɔ́lik(l)], fr. Fr., fr. Gk. *diabolikós*, 'slanderous, devilish'. See **devil** (I.) & **-ic** & **-al.** **a** Pertaining to, resembling, the devil: *a diabolic grin*; **b** devilish, fiendish: *diabolical cruelty.*

diabolically, adv. Prec. & **-ly.** In a diabolical, devilish manner, fiendishly.

diabolism, n. [1. diábolizm; 2. daiǽbəlizəm]. See prec. words & **-ism.** **a** Worship of the devil, or of demons; **b** qualities, nature, resembling that of the devil.

diabolize, vb. trans. [1. dīábolīz; 2. daiǽbəlaiz]. See prec. & **-ize.** To make into, represent as, a devil.

diabolo, n. [1. dēábolō; 2. diǽbəlou]. Invented word; fr. Gk. **dia-** & *bolé*, 'a throw'; cogn. w. *bállein*, 'to throw'. See **ballistics.** Game which consists in balancing, and whirling, upon a string held by sticks attached to either end, a kind of wooden reel, and throwing it across to another player who catches and returns it, and so on, until one or other player misses his catch and drops the reel.

diacaustic, adj. & n. [1. dīakáwstik; 2. daiəkɔ́stik], fr. **dia-** & **caustic.** **a** adj. Of a kind of caustic curve formed by refraction; **b** n., a diacaustic curve.

diachylon, diachylum, n. [1. dīákilon, -um; 2. daiǽkilən, -əm]. Med. Lat. *diachylum*, 'a plaster made of the juices of herbs', fr. Gk. **dia-**, 'from, by means of', & *khulón*, 'juices'. See **chyle.** Sticking-plaster made up with olive-oil and oxide of lead on a linen backing.

diaconal, adj. [1. dīákonal; 2. daiǽkənəl], fr. L. Lat. *diaconāl-(is)*. See **deacon** & **-al.** Pertaining to a deacon.

diaconate, n. [1. dīákonat; 2. daiǽkənit], fr. L. Lat. *diaconāt-(us)*. See **deacon** & **-ate.** **a** The office of a deacon; **b** period of tenure of this office; **c** body of deacons; deacons collectively.

diacoustic, adj. [1. dīakóustik; 2. dàiəkáustik]. See **dia-** & **acoustic.** Of, pertaining to, the refraction of sound through various mediums.

diacoustics, n. pl., fr. prec. Branch of acoustics dealing with such refracted sounds.

diacritic, n. & adj. [1. dīakrítik; 2. dàiəkrítik], fr. Gk. *diakritik-(ós)*, 'marking separation, able to distinguish'. See **dia-** & **critic.** **a** n. (lit.) Distinguishing mark; specif. mark placed over or under a letter to express some special phonetic value, as ′ ¯ ¸; **b** adj., also *diacritical*, pertaining to, of nature of, a diacritic.

diactinic, adj. [1. dīaktínik; 2. dàiæktínik]. See **di-** (III.) & Gk. *aktís*, 'a ray'. See **actinic.** Capable of transmitting the actinic or chemical rays of the sun.

diadem, n. [1. díadem; 2. dáiədɛm], fr. O. Fr., fr. Lat. *diadēma*, 'a royal head-dress', fr. Gk. *diádēma*, 'a head-band, fillet; one emblematic of royalty', fr. **dia-** & **dēm-*, 'something bound on'; cf. Scrt. *dā́ma*, 'a bond'; & fr. reduced grade **dm̥-*, Lat. *re-dim-īre*, 'to crown'. **a** A fillet, crown, worn on the head as a sign of royal power; **b** crown, wreath of flowers &c. betokening distinction of some kind; **c** royal power, sovereignty.

diademed, adj. [1. díademd; 2. dáiədɛmd]. Prec. & **-ed.** Wearing a diadem, crowned.

diaeresis, n. [1. dīḗresis; 2. dai-íərəsis], fr. Lat., fr. Gk. *diairesis*, 'division into parts'; (rhet.) 'division of a subject into heads'; (gram.) 'separation of a diphthong into two syllables', fr. **di-** (III.) & *hairéō*, 'I take, seize upon'. Etymol. unknown. Cp. **aphaeresis.** (in print. and writing) A mark, generally two dots, placed on the second of two consecutive vowels, to indicate that it forms separate syllable from the first: e.g. *coöperate.*

diagnose, vb. trans. [1. dīagnṓz; 2. dàiəgnóuz], fr. next word. To ascertain the nature of a disease by observing the symptoms.

diagnosis, n. [1. dīagnṓsis; 2. daiəgnóusis]. Gk. *diágnōsis*, 'a distinguishing, discriminating' (esp. of medical diagnosis); 'a resolving, decision', fr. **dia-** & *gnôsis*, 'an inquiry, investigation; knowledge'. See **gnosis.** **a** Accurate investigation and discrimination by means of data; specif. **b** the identification of a disease from its symptoms; a summary of the symptoms of a disease.

diagnostic, adj. & n. [1. dīagnóstik; 2. dàiəgnɔ́stik], fr. Gk. *diagnōstikós*, 'able to distinguish'. See prec. & **-ic.** **1.** adj. Characteristic, distinguishing, forming basis of diagnosis. **2.** n. **a** Symptom of a disease; **b** pl., branch of medicine dealing with symptoms.

diagnostician, n. [1. dīagnostíshan; 2. dàiəgnɔstíʃən]. Prec. & **-ian.** A student of diagnostics.

diagonal (I.), adj. [1. díágonal; 2. daiǽgənəl], fr. Lat. *diagonāl-(is)*, fr. Gk. *diagṓnios*, 'from angle to angle', fr. **dia-** & *gōnía*, 'an angle; a joiner's square'. See **-gon.** **1.** Extending between two opposite angles of a rectilineal figure: *diagonal line.* **2.** Going from corner to corner, oblique. **3.** Crossed by oblique lines, or markings: esp. *diagonal cloth.*

diagonal (II.), n., fr. prec. A straight line drawn between opposite angles of a rectilineal figure: *the diagonals of a parallelogram.*

diagonally, adv. Prec. & **-ly.** In a diagonal manner, obliquely, from corner to corner.

diagram, n. [1. díagram; 2. dáiəgræm], fr. Fr. *diagramme*, fr. Gk. *diágramma*, 'something marked out by lines, a plan, geometrical figure; a written list; an edict, decree; the musical scale'. See **dia-** & **-gram.** **a** (geom.) A figure drawn to assist in demonstrating **a** theorem &c.; **b** a plan, figure, to illustrate a statement, explanation &c.; graphic representation of statistics, proportions &c. by means of lines, geometrical figures &c.: *a diagram showing the relative population of European countries, relations of the Aryan languages* &c.

diagrammatic, adj. [1. dīagramátik; 2. dàiəgrəmǽtik], fr. Gk. *diágrammat-*, stem of *diágramma*, see prec., & **-ic.** Pertaining to, in the form of, a diagram.

diagrammatically, adv. [1. dīagramátikali; 2. dàiəgrəmǽtikəli]. See prec. & **-al** & **-ly.** By means of a diagram.

diagrammatize, vb. trans. [1. dīagrámatīz; 2. dàiəgrǽmətaiz]. See **diagrammatic** & **-ize.** To put into the form of, represent by, a diagram.

diagraph, n. [1. díagrahf; 2. dáiəgrāf]. See **dia-** & **-graph.** Instrument for drawing enlarged copies of drawings, maps &c.

dial (I.), n. [1. díal; 2. dáiəl], fr. Low Lat. *diāl-(is)*, 'pertaining to the day, daily', fr. Lat. *dies*, 'a day', & **-al.** See **dies non.** **1.** The face of a sundial, clock, or watch, on which the hours are marked, and the time is indicated by the shadow of the style or gnomon, or by hands moved by spring and cog-wheels. **2.** Any flat, round plate, resembling a clock-face, showing, by means of moving pointers, the measurement of weight, consumption &c., e.g. on weighing machine, gas-meter &c. **3.** (slang) A human face.

dial (II.), vb. trans., fr. prec. (rare) To measure by means of a dial.

dialect, n. [1. díalekt; 2. dáiəlekt], fr. Lat. *dialect-(os)*, 'a manner of speaking, dialect', fr. Gk. *diálekt-(os)*, 'talk, discourse, discussion; language, articulate speech; the language of a district, local speech', fr. *dialégomai*, 'I talk with; discourse upon, discuss', fr. *dialégein*, 'to pick out, to distinguish', fr. **dia-** & *légein*, 'to collect; to pick out, select, enumerate; to say, speak'. See **legend, lecture, logos.** Type, form, variety, of speech spoken by a particular community, either in a definite region or area (*Regional Dialect*), or among a given class (*Class Dialect*), distinguished to a greater or less degree from other forms of speech by differences of pronunciation, grammatical forms, syntax, idioms, vocabulary. There is no essential distinction between a dialect and a language, but it is often convenient, and the usual practice, to apply the former term to subordinate varieties of speech, in use among comparatively small communities, and the latter, to the speech of whole peoples or nations, esp. to that type (itself a dialect in the stricter sense) which is the vehicle of the main body of the people's literature. No language constitutes an absolute unity in its spoken forms, but is differentiated into several sub-varieties or dialects.

dialectal, adj. [1. dīaléktal; 2. daiəléktəl]. See prec. & **-al.** **a** Pertaining to a dialect, of a dialect; **b** (less correctly) pertaining to dialectic.

dialectally, adv. Prec. & **-ly.** In dialect, in a dialectal manner.

dialectic (I.), adj. [1. dīaléktik; 2. daiəléktik]. **dialect** & **-ic.** **1.** Pertaining to dialectic. **2.** Confused with, and used for, *dialectal.*

dialectic (II.), n., fr. O. Fr. *dialectique*, fr. Lat. *dialectica*, 'dialectics', fr. Gk. *dialektiké*, 'the art of discussion by means of question and answer, of evolving truths by logical discussion'. See **dialect** & **-ic.** Also pl., *dialectics*, the critical analysis of mental processes; art of logical discussion and disputation.

dialectical, adj. [1. dīaléktikl; 2. daiəléktikl]. Prec. & **-al.** **1.** Pertaining to dialectics. **2.** Pertaining to dialect, dialectal.

dialectically, adv. Prec. & **-ly.** By dialectic.

dialectician, n. [1. dīalektíshan; 2. dàiəlektíʃən]. See **dialectic** (II.) & **-ician.** One who is proficient in dialectics.

dialectology, n. [1. dīalektóloji; 2. dàiəlektɔ́lədži]. See **dialect** & **-logy**. The study of dialects, or subordinate varieties of speech.

diallage, n. [1. dīalaj; 2. dáiəlidž], fr. Gk. *diallagé*, 'change', fr. **dia-** & *állos*, 'other'. See **allo-**. (mineral.) A dark-green laminated form of pyroxene, with irregular planes of fracture.

dialling, n. [1. dīaling; 2. dáiəliŋ]. **dial (I.)** & **-ing**. **a** Construction of dials; **b** measurement of time &c. by dials.

dialogic, adj. [1. dīalójik; 2. dàiəlɔ́džik], fr. Med. Lat. *dialogic-(us)*. See **dialogue** & **-ic**. Pertaining to, in the form of, dialogue.

dialogist, n. [1. diálojist; 2. daiǽlədžist]. See next word & **-ist**. (rare) **a** A writer of dialogue; **b** a speaker in a dialogue.

dialogue, n. [1. dīalog; dáiəlɔg], fr. Fr., fr. Lat. *dialogus*, 'a conversation', fr. Gk. *diálogos*, 'a conversation, dialogue'. See **dia-** & **logos**. **1.** Conversation, talking, intercourse by means of the spoken language. **2.** Representation of conversation in writing, in drama, novels &c.

dialyse, vb. trans. [1. dīalīz; 2. dáiəlaiz], fr. **dialysis**. (chem.) To separate crystalline from non-crystalline or colloid substances in a mixture by filtering through parchment in a dialyser.

dialyser, n. [1. dīalīzer; 2. dáiəlaizə]. Prec. & **-er**. (chem.) A drum with membranous or parchment bottom, in which substances can be subjected to dialysis by placing it in water, the colloid substances remaining, the crystalline filtering through into the water.

dialysis, n. [1. diálisis; 2. daiǽlisis]. Gk. *diálusis*, 'a separating, disbanding; dissolution'. See **dia-** & **-lysis**. (chem.) Separation of crystalline from non-crystalline or colloid substances in a mixture by a dialyser.

dialytic, adj. [1. dīalítik; 2. daiəlítik], fr. Gk. *dialutikós*. See **dia-** & **-lytic**. Of, pertaining to, dialysis.

diamagnetic, adj. & n. [1. dīamagnétik; 2. dàiəmægnétik]. See **dia-** & **magnetic**. **a** adj. Exhibiting diamagnetism; **b** n., substance, such as bismuth, which does this.

diamagnetically, adv. [1. dīamagnétikali; 2. dàiəmægnétikəli]. Prec. & **-al** & **-ly**. By diamagnetism.

diamagnetism, n. [1. dīamágnetizm; 2. dàiəmǽgnitizəm]. See **dia-** & **magnetism**. The property of certain substances to tend to take up a position at right angles to direction of the magnetic current.

diamantiferous, adj. [1. dīamantíferus; 2. dàiəməntífərəs], fr. Fr. *diamantifère*, w. Anglicized ending. See **diamond** & **-ferous**. Diamond-bearing.

diameter, n. [1. dīámeter; 2. daiǽmitə], fr. O. Fr. *diametre*, fr. Lat., fr. Gk. *diámetros*, 'the diagonal of a parallelogram; the diameter of a circle', fr. **dia-** & **-meter**. **1.** A straight line passing through the centre of a geometrical figure (esp. figure bounded by curves) and extending from side to side. **2.** Measurement through the centre of a solid; transverse measurement, thickness; *the diameter of a tree-trunk*. **3.** Unit of measurement of magnifying power of lenses.

diametral, adj. [1. dīámetral; 2. daiǽmitrəl]. See prec. & **-al**. Pertaining to a diameter.

diametrical, adj. [1. dīamétrikl; 2. dàiəmétrikl], fr. Gk. *diametrik-(ós)*, 'diametrical, diagonal', & **-al**. See **diameter** & **-ic**. **1.** Pertaining to a diameter; diametral. **2.** (lit. and fig.) Exactly opposite, as are the two ends of a diameter; directly contrary.

diametrically, adv. Prec. & **-ly**. (lit. and fig.) Exactly, directly, absolutely: *diametrically opposite, opposed.*

diamond (I.), n. [1. dīamond; 2. dáiəmənd]. M.E. *diamaund*, fr. O. Fr. *diamant*, fr. L. Lat. *diamant-(em)*, acc. of *diamas*, fr. Lat., fr. Gk. *adámas*, 'adamant, the hardest metal; the diamond'. See **adamant**. **1.** A precious stone composed of crystallized carbon, usually colourless and of great brilliance; the hardest substance known; Phrs. *a diamond of the first water*, of the most precious kind; *black diamond*, (i.) a dark-coloured diamond; (ii.) coal; *rough diamond*, (i.) an uncut diamond, (ii.) a worthy but uncultured person; *diamond cut diamond*, of persons who are a match for each other, esp. in cunning; *diamond wedding*, sixtieth anniversary of wedding. **2.** A tool with a small diamond fixed at the end, used for cutting glass. **3. a** A plane figure with four equal or nearly equal sides, and with two acute and two obtuse angles; **b** (at cards) a card marked with red figures of a diamond; (pl.) the suit; Phr. *a small diamond*, one of the cards of lowest value in the suit. **4.** (typog.) One of the smallest sizes of type.

diamond (II.), adj., fr. prec. **1. a** Made of, set with, diamonds: *diamond brooch* &c.; **b** rich in, producing, diamonds: *diamond clay, field, mine* &c. **2.** Shaped like a diamond: *a diamond window-pane.*

diamond (III.), vb. trans., fr. **diamond (I.)**. To set with, adorn with, diamonds, or with something resembling them in appearance.

diamond-back, n. A kind of moth.

diamond-drill, n. Species of rock drill set with diamonds.

diamond-field, n. Land in which diamonds are found.

diamondiferous, adj. [1. dīamondíferus; 2. dàiəməndífərəs]. See **diamond** & **-ferous**. Yielding diamonds.

diamond-point, n. **1.** A tool tipped with a diamond, used in engraving. **2.** (railway) Oblique intersection of two sets of rails.

diamond-snake, n. One with diamond-shaped markings, found in Australia.

diamond-wise, adv. Obliquely, in the shape of a diamond.

Diana, n. [1. dīána; 2. daiǽnə]. Lat., earlier *Diviana*; see **deity** for etymol. **1.** Roman goddess, equivalent of Greek Artemis, esp. of the moon, and the chase. **2.** A huntress; lady who hunts.

diana monkey, n. A West African species of monkey, with a white crescent-shaped mark on its forehead and white fringed cheeks.

Dianthus, n. [1. dīánthus; 2. daiǽnþəs]. Invented word, fr. Gk. *Diós*, genit. of **Zeus**, & *ánthos*, 'flower', see **anther**. (bot.) Genus of flowering plants which includes the pinks, carnations &c.

diapason, n. [1. dīapā́zn; 2. dàiəpéizn], fr. Gk. *diapāsôn*, 'the octave scale', fr. *dià pasôn*, 'through all (the strings)', fr. **dia-** & *pâs*, 'all'. See **pan-**. **1. a** (mus.) All the voices or parts combining in harmony; **b** a passage of music containing a splendid burst of harmony. **2.** The full range, compass, of a voice or instrument. **3.** One of two principal stops of an organ, extending through the whole scale of the instrument.

diaper (I.), n. [1. dīaper; 2. dáiəpə], fr. O. Fr. *diapre, diaspre*, fr. Byzantine Gk. *díaspros*, fr. Gk. **dia-** & *áspros*, 'white', also 'rough', Lat. *asper*, 'rough, uneven; harsh, bitter; rough, violent, fierce'. See **asperity**. **1. a** Linen material woven with diamond pattern; **b** napkin or towel made of this. **2.** Ornamental design consisting of a series of diamond-shaped figures: *diaper pattern.*

diaper (II.), vb. trans., fr. prec. To ornament with a design of diamond-shaped figures.

diaphanous, adj. [1. dīáfanus; 2. daiǽfənəs], fr. Med. Lat. *diaphanus*, fr. Gk. *diaphanés*, 'transparent'; fig., 'manifest, distinct', fr. **dia-** & *phaínein*, 'to show, make visible, cause to appear'. See **phantasm** & **-ous**. Allowing the light to pass through; transparent, translucent.

diaphoresis, n. [1. dīaforḗsis; 2. dàiəfɔrísis]. Gk., fr. **dia-** & *phoréein*, 'to carry'. See **-ferous** & **-phore**. (med.) Perspiration, esp. when profuse and artificially produced.

diaphoretic, adj. & n. [1. dīaforétik; 2. dàiəfɔrétik], fr. Gk. *diaphorētikós*. See prec. **1.** adj. Producing, inducing, profuse perspiration. **2.** n. Substance, drug &c. which does this.

diaphragm, n. [1. dīafràm; 2. dáiəfræm], fr. Gk. *diáphragma*, 'a barrier, partition', esp. 'the midriff muscle', fr. **dia-** & *phrágma*, 'a fence, paling'; cp. Gk. *phrássein*, fr. **phrak-j-*, 'to protect, fence round'; cogn. w. Lat. *farcīre*, 'to stuff', see **farce (II.)**, & *frequens*, 'thronged, thickly pressed together' &c. See **frequent**. **1.** (anat.) The muscular wall separating the thorax from the abdomen. **2.** A partition wall, barrier, **a** in certain kinds of shell-fish; **b** in some musical instruments. **3.** (opt.) A disk with a circular hole in the centre for cutting off part of a ray of light.

diaphragmatic, adj. [1. dīafragmátik; 2. dàiəfrægmǽtik], fr. Gk. *diaphrágmat-(os)*, genit. of *diáphragma*, 'diaphragm'. See prec. & **-ic**. Pertaining to the diaphragm.

diarchy, n. [1. dīarki; 2. dáiāki], fr. Gk. **di- (II.)**, 'double, dual', & *-archy*, on anal. of *monarchy*, see **arch-**; the irregularly formed *dyarchy* is common and should be avoided. Rule, government, shared by two powers, parties &c., specif., applied to the system of Government in British India in which certain powers are transferred to the elected legislatures and others reserved to the Governor-in-Council.

diarial, adj. [1. dīā́rial; 2. daiéəriəl]. **diary** & **-al**. Pertaining to, in the form of, a diary.

diarist, n. [1. dīarist; 2. dáiərist]. **diary** & **-ist**. One who keeps a diary.

diaristic, adj. [1. dīarístik; 2. daiərístik]. Prec. & **-ic**. Pertaining to a diarist.

diarize, vb. intrans. [1. dīarīz; 2. dáiəraiz]. **diary** & **-ize**. To record events &c. in a diary, keep a diary.

diarrhoea, n. [1. dīarḗa; 2. daiəríə], fr. Gk. *diárrhoia*, 'diarrhoea', fr. **dia-** & *rhóia*, 'a flow, flowing', q.v. under **rheo-**. Excessive, irritable laxity of the bowels.

diarrhoeal, adj. [1. dīarḗal; 2. daiəríəl]. Prec. & **-al**. Pertaining to diarrhoea.

diary, n. [1. dīari; 2. dáiəri], fr. Lat. *diārium*, 'a daily allowance (of food &c.)', fr. *dies*, 'a day' (see **dies non**), & **-ary**. **a** A daily record of events; **b** book in which this is written; **c** book, often in form of an almanac, with ruled and dated pages for making notes of engagements, and memoranda each day.

Diaspora, n. [1. diáspora; 2. daiǽspərə]. Gk. *diasporá*, 'a scattering, dispersion'. See **dia-** & **spore**. The Dispersion, i.e. of the Jews, after the Exile, among various nations of the Gentiles.

diastase, n. [1. dīastās; 2. dáiəsteis]. Fr., fr. Gk. *diástasis*, 'separation'. See **dia-** & **state (I.)**. (physiol. chem.) An enzyme or ferment, found in animals as in the saliva, and plants, as in malt, acting on carbohydrates, turning starch into sugar and playing an important part in metabolism.

diastatic, adj. [1. dīastátik; 2. daiəstǽtik]. See prec. Having the properties of diastase.

diastole, n. [1. dīástoli; 2. daiǽstəli], fr. Gk. *diastolḗ*, 'expansion, dilatation; a distinction, distinct statement'; gram., 'the lengthening of a syllable'; cogn. w. *diastéllein*, 'to separate, expand, dilate; to distinguish, define', fr. **dia-** & *stéllein*, 'to put into order, equip, arrange, make ready'; cp. Gk. *stolḗ*, 'equipment, dress, garment', Lat. *stola*, 'gown, robe'. See **stele**. (med.) The dilatation of the heart, opposed to, and alternating with, contraction or *systole*, q.v.

diastyle, n. [1. dīastīl; 2. dáiəstail], fr. Gk. *diástūlos*, 'diastyle', fr. **dia-** & *stûlos*, 'a pillar'. See **style (III.)**. (archit.) Grouping of a series of pillars in pairs, with an interval between each pair of columns equal to three times the diameter of one column.

diatessaron, n. [1. dīatésaron; 2. dàiətésərɔn]. Gk. *dià tessárōn*, 'by four'. See **tessera**. A harmony of the four gospels.

diathermancy, n. [1. dīathérmansi; 2. dàiəþə́mənsi], fr. Fr. *diathermansie*. See **diathermic** & **-ancy**. The property of transmitting radiant heat.

diathermanous, adj. [1. dīathérmanus; 2. daiəþə́mənəs]. See prec. & **-ous**. Capable of transmitting radiant heat; diathermic.

diathermic, adj. [1. dīathĕrmik; 2. daiəþə́mik], fr. Gk. *diátherm-(os)*, 'thoroughly warm', & **-ic**. See **dia-** & **therm**. Diathermanous.

diathesis, n. [1. dīáthesis; 2. daiǽþisis], Gk. *diáthesis*, 'an arrangement, putting in order; composition (of a work of art &c.); the act of disposing of, selling; physical condition, state'. See **dia-** & **thesis**. (med.) Bodily constitution which predisposes to certain diseases, or kinds of disease.

diatom, n. [1. dīatòm; 2. dáiətòm], fr. Gk. *diátom-(os)*, 'a cutting through, severance', fr. **dia-** & *tómos*, 'cutting; thing cut, section'. See **tome**. A microscopic marine or freshwater vegetable organism, consisting of one cell.

diatomaceous, adj. [1. dīatomáshus; 2. daiətəméiʃəs]. Prec. & **-aceous**. Abounding in diatoms.

diatomic, adj. [1. dīatómik; 2. daiətómik]. See **di- (II.)** & **atom** & **-ic**. (chem.) Consisting of two atoms.

diatonic, adj. [1. dīatónik; 2. daiətónik], fr. Fr. *diatonique*, fr. Gk. *diatonik-(ós)*, 'pertaining to the diatonic scale', fr. *diátonon*, 'the diatonic scale, with intervals of a tone'. See **dia-** & **tonic (I.)**. (mus.) **a** (of scales) The regular major or minor; **b** (of harmonics) Composed in the ordinary major or minor key without chromatic variations.

diatribe, n. [1. dīatrīb; 2. dáiətraib], fr. Fr. *diatribe*, fr. Lat., fr. Gk. *diatribḗ*, 'a wearing away' (esp. of time); 'a pastime, amusement; labour, occupation; delay, waste of time'; fr. *diatrībein*, 'to rub, to rub away, consume; to spend time; to delay, hinder, waste time', fr. **dia-** & *tríbein*, 'to rub, wear out by rubbing'; cp. *tríbos*, 'a beaten track; a rubbing, attrition; practice, use'; Lat. *trī-vī*, pret. of *terere*, 'to rub'. See **tribulation** & **trite**. Wordy attack; speech consisting of vituperation; invective uttered against a person, party, or policy.

diazo-compounds, n. [1. dīazō kòmpoundz; 2. daiǽzou kòmpaundz]. See **di- (II.)** & **azo-**. (chem.) Organic compounds derived from aromatic hydrocarbons with characteristic grouping of two nitrogen atoms.

dib, n. [1. dib; 2. dib]. Etymol. dubious; possibly variant of **dab (I.)**. **1.** A knucklebone, as used in an old child's game. **2.** (pl., *dibs*) **a** Bone counters, used in playing cards &c., hence, **b** (slang) coin, money: *he's after the dibs*, anxious to get money.

dibasic, adj. [1. dībásik; 2. daibéisik]. See **di- (II.)** & **basic**. (chem., of acids) Having two atoms of hydrogen replaced by bases.

dibble (I.), **dibber**, n. [1. díbl, díber; 2. dibl, díbə]. L.M.E. *debylle*; prob. connected w. **dab**. A pointed tool of wood or iron, for making small holes in the ground for planting seeds, potatoes &c.

dibble (II.), vb. trans., fr. prec. To plant with a dibble: *to dibble in (potatoes &c.)*.

dicast, n. [1. díkast; 2. díkæst], fr. Gk. *dikastḗs*, 'a judge; an Athenian juryman', fr. *dikázein*, 'to judge, give judgement on', fr. *díkē*, 'right, custom, usage, law; justice; lawsuit, trial', fr. reduced grade **dik*-, of Aryan base **deik*-, **doik*-, 'to show, point out'. See **diction**. (Gk. antiq.) A judge; a member of the highest Athenian court.

dicastery, n. [1. dikástri; 2. dikǽstri], fr. Gk. *dikastḗrion*, 'a court of justice; the court, judges'. See prec. (Gk. antiq.) Body of judges or *dicasts*.

dice (I.), n. [1. dīs; 2. dais], pl. of **die (I.)**.

dice (II.), vb. intrans. See **die (I.)**. To play with dice.

dice-box, n. Deep, narrow box of leather or thin wood, from which dice are thrown.

dicer, n. [1. díser; 2. dáisə]. See **dice (II.)** & **-er**. One who plays at dice; a gambler.

dichlamydeous, adj. [1. dīklamídeus; 2. daikləmídjəs], fr. **di- (II.)** & Gk. *khlamúd-os*, genit. of *khlamús*, 'a short mantle', esp. 'a military cloak', & **-ous**. Origin of *khlamús* is uncertain. (bot.) Having both calyx and corolla.

dichogamous, adj. [1. dikógamus; 2. dikógəməs]. See next word & **-ous**. (bot.) Characterized by dichogamy.

dichogamy, n. [1. dikógami; 2. dikógəmi], fr. Gk. *dikho*-, combining form of *díkha*, 'in two, apart, separate (fr. **di- (II.)** & adv. suff. **ghō*-, cp. Scrt. (*viśvà*)-*ha*, 'every time') & **-gamy**. (bot.) The maturing of the stamens and pistils in a plant at different times, preventing self-fertilization.

dichotomic, adj. [1. dikotómik; 2. dikətómik]. See **dichotomy** & **-ic**. Dichotomous.

dichotomous, adj. [1. dikótomus; 2. dikótəməs]. See **dichotomy** & **-ous**. (bot.) Branching regularly in pairs.

dichotomously, adv. Prec. & **-ly**. In a dichotomous manner; by dichotomy.

dichotomy, n. [1. dikótomi; 2. dikótəmi], fr. Gk. *dikho*-, 'in two, asunder', see **dichogamous**, & **-tomy**. **1.** (log.) Division into two classes, one positive, the other negative. **2.** (bot.) A mode of branching by repeated bifurcation.

dichroic, adj. [1. dīkrṓik; 2. daikróuik]. See **dichroism** & **-ic**. Characterized by dichroism.

dichroism, n. [1. díkrōizm; 2. dáikrouizəm], fr. Gk. *díkhro-(os)*, 'two coloured', fr. **di- (II.)** & *khrṓs*, 'the skin'; hence 'the colour of the skin, complexion'; hence 'colour'. See **chrome** & **-ism**. The property of certain crystals of exhibiting different colours when looked at from different angles.

dichromatic, adj. [1. dīkrōmátik; 2. daikroumǽtik]. See **di- (II.)** & **chromatic**. Having two colours, esp. (zool.) of certain species of birds and insects which exhibit two phases of colour.

dichromic, adj. [1. dīkrṓmik; 2. daikróumik], fr. Gk. *dikhrōm-(os)*, 'two-coloured', & **-ic**. See **di- (II.)** & **chrome**. (of colour-blind vision) Able to distinguish two of the three primary colours.

dickens, n. [1. díkenz; 2. díkinz], fr. 16th cent.; prob. variant of *Dickon*, short for Richard. (colloq.) The devil, as mild expletive, in Phr. *what the dickens* &c.

dicker (I.), n. [1. díker; 2. díkə], fr. L.G. *decker*, 'group of ten things', fr. Lat. *decuria*, 'a company, group, of ten; a division, class', fr. *decem*, 'ten'. See **deci-**. (commerc.) Ten, a group, set, of ten; esp. ten hides.

dicker (II.), vb. intrans., fr. prec. To haggle, bargain, chaffer.

dicky (I.), **dickey**, n. [1. díki; 2. díki]. Etymol. doubtful. (slang) **1.** A false shirt-front. **2.** Small seat for servant at back in old-fashioned horse-carriage, also *dickey-seat*; also a small extra folding seat at back of a two-seater motor car.

dicky (II.), adj. Origin doubtful. (slang) Shaky, unsteady, tottery; weak, uncertain in health &c.: *very dicky on his pins*; (of business concerns &c.) unsound, liable to fail.

dicky-bird, n. Child's word for a bird.

dicotyledon, n. [1. dīkotilḗdn; 2. daikətilídn]. See **di- (II.)** & **cotyledon**. (bot.) A plant with two cotyledons, or seed-leaves.

dicotyledonous, adj. [1. dīkotilḗdonus; 2. daikətilídənəs]. Prec. & **-ous**. (bot.) Having two cotyledons.

dicrotic, adj. [1. dīkrótik; 2. daikrótik], fr. Gk. *díkrotos*, 'a double beat', fr. **di- (II.)** & *krótein*, 'to beat, strike', & **-ic**. The base is **krot*-, **kret*-; cp. the nasalized form in O.E. *hrindan*, O.N. *hrinda*, 'to strike'. (med., of the pulse) Doubly pulsating with two beats of the artery to one of the pulse.

dicrotism, n. [1. díkrotizm; 2. dáikrətizəm]. See prec. & **-ism**. (med.) Condition in which there is a dicrotic pulse.

dictagraph, see **dictograph**.

dictaphone, n. [1. díktafōn; 2. díktəfoun], fr. **dictate** & **-phone**. Trade name for a kind of phonograph into which letters &c. are dictated; the receiving cylinder is transferred to a machine which reproduces the sound to a typist.

dictate (I.), n. [1. díktāt; 2. díkteit], fr. Lat. *dictāt-(um)*, 'something dictated', neut. P.P. of *dictāre*, 'to declare, repeat; to dictate'. See next word. An order, command, direction; a prompting that must be obeyed: esp. *the dictates of reason, conscience, fancy, prudence* &c.

dictate (II.), vb. trans. & intrans. [1. diktā́t; 2. diktéit], fr. Lat. *dictāt-(um)*, P.P. type of *dictāre*, 'to say often, to declare repeatedly; to say aloud (for writing); to make, compose', fr. *dict-(um)*, P.P. type of *dīcere*, 'to say'. See **diction**. **A.** trans. **1.** To read or utter aloud something intended to be written down by another: *to dictate a letter, a passage to be taken down* &c. **2.** To command with authority, give orders for, prescribe: *to dictate terms to a vanquished enemy*. **B.** intrans. **1.** To dictate letters &c.: *to dictate to one's typist, to a class* &c. **2.** To make authoritative suggestions which have almost the form and force of commands; direct; lay down the law: *to refuse to be dictated to*.

dictation, n. [1. diktā́shun; 2. diktéiʃən]. See prec. & **-ion**. **1.** The act of dictating, commanding: *to do something at another's dictation*. **2.** That which is dictated, read aloud; specif., passage dictated to be taken down as an exercise in spelling.

dictator, n. [1. diktā́tor; 2. diktéitə]. Lat., 'an extraordinary magistrate at Rome, granted temporarily absolute power'. See **dictate (II.)** & **-or**. One who dictates; specif., one who assumes or is granted absolute power as an absolute ruler.

dictatorial, adj. [1. diktatṓrial; 2. diktətṓriəl]. See **dictator** & **-al**. **1.** Pertaining to a dictator. **2.** Resembling the characteristics of a dictator, imperious; tending to give orders and insist on their being carried out; inclined to urge one's own opinions and to expect them to be accepted.

dictatorially, adv. Prec. & **-ly**. In a dictatorial manner.

dictatorship, n. [1. diktā́torship; 2. diktéitəʃip]. See **dictator** & **-ship**. The office, tenure of office, of dictator. Phr. *the dictatorship of the proletariat*, centralization of all political and economic power in the hands of the proletariat or working classes; one of the main tenets of Communism as practised, or supposed to be practised, in Russia.

diction, n. [1. díkshun; 2. díkʃən], fr. Lat. *dictiōn-(em)*, 'a saying, speaking; a speech; an oracular utterance', fr. *dict-(um)*, P.P. type of *dīcere*, 'show, tell', fr. **deik*-, & **-ion**; cp. Scrt. *diśtiś*, 'inscription, direction', fr. **dik t*-. The base *deik*-, **doik*-, **dik*-, 'to point out, indicate; tell, speak', is a very fruitful one. Cp. Gk. *deik-nūmi*, 'I show, point out', *deikēlon*, 'exhibition' &c.; Scrt. *diśáti*, 'he shows' &c.; O.E. *tēon*, 'to show', fr. **tīhan*; Goth. *gateihan*, O.H.G. *zīhan*, 'to show'; further, w. Aryan grade **doik*-(*ná*), Goth. *taikns*, 'sign'; O.E. *tācn* (see **token**), & Goth. *taiknjan*, 'to show', & O.E. *tǣcan*, fr. **tākjan*; see **teach**. The same base occurs unstressed in Lat. *-dex*, as in *index*, *judex*, 'judge' &c. See **index**, **judge**, **judicial**. Cp. also **deictic** & **digit**. **1.** Choice of vocabulary in speaking and writing; characteristic vocabulary used by a speaker or writer. **2.** Specif., *poetic diction*, characteristic choice of words for use in poetry; such words and phrases as are not normally used except in poetry.

dictionary, n. [1. díkshunari; 2. díkʃənəri], fr. Med. Lat. *dictiōnārium*. See **diction** & **-ary**. **1.** A book containing an alphabetical list of the words, or a selection of the words, of a language, with either, **a** an explanation and definition of each word in the same language; or **b** a list of words from another language, corresponding as nearly as possible to it in meaning: *a French-English dictionary*; **c** book giving a brief definition as a mere label for each word, and a full account of the history of each word, as far back as possible, with illustrative cognates from other languages: *an etymological dictionary*. Hence, **2.** A book containing a series of articles on some branch of knowledge, arranged alphabetically according to the word denoting the particular subject: *dictionary of the Bible, of the Prayer Book, of Biography*; *Medical dictionary* &c.

dictograph, n. [1. díktograhf; 2. díktəgrāf]. Invented word fr. **dictum** & **graph.** Trade name for a kind of a telephonic sound-recording instrument.

dictum, n., pl. **dicta** [1. díktum, -a; 2. díktəm, -ə]. Lat. *dictum*, 'something spoken, a word, saying; a maxim, proverb; an order, command', neut. form of *dict-(us)*, P.P. type of *dīcere*, 'to say, declare, narrate, tell; to assert, affirm; to pronounce, deliver; to nominate, appoint'. See **diction.** **a** A formal expression of opinion, authoritative pronouncement; **b** a maxim, proverb, saying; **c** (law) judge's opinion, not having the legal authority of a ruling on a point of law: *obiter dicta*, q.v. under **obiter.**

did, vb. [1. did; 2. did]. O.E. *dyde*, M.E. *dude, dide*, Pret. of **do.**

didactic, adj. [1. didáktik; 2. didǽktik], fr. Gk. *didaktikós*, 'skilled in teaching', fr. *didaktós*, 'taught, instructed', & **-ic**; cp. Gk. *didáskein*, 'to teach', fr. **di-dak-skō*; Aryan base **dək̑-*, reduced fr. **dēk̑-*, 'to make agreeable', wh. is apparently a parallel form to the base **dek̑-, dok̑,- *dk̑-*, 'to appear good, fitting'. See **decent, docile,** & cp. Lat. *disc-ere*, 'to learn', fr. **di-dk-sk-*. **a** (of writings and utterances) For the purpose of instruction, designed to give moral instruction: *didactic poetry*; **b** (of persons, nearly always in unfavourable sense) too much inclined to instruct, esp. those who do not wish to learn, and on unsuitable occasions; tending to hold forth and lay down the law.

didactically, adv. [1. didáktikali; 2. didǽktikəli]. See prec. & **-al** & **-ly.** In a didactic manner, in the manner of a (pedantic) teacher.

didacticism, n. [1. didáktisizm; 2. didǽktisizəm]. See **didactic** & **-ism.** The quality, mind, and manner natural to didactic persons.

didapper, n. [1. didàper; 2. dáidæpə]. L.M.E. *dydoppar* for *dive dapper*, wh. occurs in Shakespeare; cp. O.E. *dūfedoppa*, glossed as *pelicanus*. See **dive,** & **deep, dip.** A small diving-bird, the little grebe or dabchick.

diddle, vb. trans. [1. didl; 2. didl]. Origin uncertain. (slang) To cheat, swindle: *to diddle a person out of his money*; *we've been diddled.*

didymium, n. [1. didímium; 2. didímiəm], fr. Gk. *didumos*, 'twin', fr. **di- (II.)** & **du-mos*; perh. cogn. w. *dúo*, 'two'. See **dual, two.** A rare metal always found associated with lanthanum.

die (I.), n. [1. dī; 2. dai]. M.E. *dē*, O. Fr. *de, det*, fr. Lat. *datum*, P.P. type of *dare*, 'to give'. See **date (I.).** **1.** (pl. *dice*) A small ivory or bone cube, used in games of chance; each face is marked with black spots varying in number from one to six. Phr. *the die is cast*, one's lot, course &c. is irrevocably determined. (*N.B.*: The pl. *dice* is far oftener used than the sing., which is hardly ever heard *dice* being felt as collective. *Die* is generally avoided, and *one of the dice* substituted for it.) **2.** (pl. *dies*) **a** A piece of metal with a design or inscription deeply engraved on it for stamping upon other material, upon which the design appears in relief, as on a coin, medal &c., or on stiff paper; **b** (archit.) the cubical part of a pedestal, plinth, between base and cornice; **c** (mechan.) a metal perforated block, used in cutting screws; also similar object used in various mechanical operations, as in ore-crushing &c.

die (II.), vb. intrans. M.E. *dīen, dēyen, dēȝen*, fr. O.N. *deyja*; cp. O. Fris. *dēja*, O.L.G. *dōjan*, O.H.G. *touwan*, 'to die'; Goth. *(af-)daujan*, 'to exhaust'; Prim. Gmc. **đaw-j-*, fr. Aryan base **dhow-, *dhew-*, 'to die'. This is perh. cogn. w. Lat. *fūnus, fōnus*, 'a funeral, burial'; hence 'death', wh. may be fr. earlier **fowen-os*, fr. **dhow-*; see **funeral**; cp. Goth. *diw-ans*, 'mortal', fr. **đew-*, fr. Aryan **dhew-*; O. Ir. *duine*, 'man'. **death** & **dead** are fr. a form of **đaw-*, w. a participial suff. **A. 1.** To suffer complete and permanent cessation of all vital functions; to come to the end of one's life, cease to live: *to die of hunger, in battle, for a cause* &c.; *to die a violent death.* Phrs. *never say die*, persevere courageously; *to die game*, die fighting, not in a cowardly manner; *die hard*, with obstinate resistance; *die in harness*, while still at work; *die of laughing*, laugh till one is utterly worn out, exhausted, speechless; to laugh long and violently; *die in the last ditch*, making a desperate defence; *die in one's bed*, a natural death. Hence various fig. uses: **2.** (of non-material things) to be lost, become extinct, pass from human ken, perish: *his secret died with him*; *never-dying fame.* **3.** To break off association with, have nothing more to do with; disclaim allegiance to: *to die to the world* &c. **4.** (of sounds, light &c.) To become faint, lose strength, fade away gradually: *the dying day.* **5.** (slang), *am, is* &c., *dying to* &c. To wish very much, feel a strong desire, be very anxious to do or be something: *to be dying to know, see, something*; *dying to be a soldier.* **B.** Followed by adverbs or prepositions. *Die away* (of sound, light &c.), to fade gradually, become fainter, lose strength. *Die back* (of plants), **a** to wither down to the root, while this remains alive and shoots another year; **b** to begin to die from the extremities of the branches. *Die down*, **a** (of sound, light &c.) to fade, gradually disappear, decrease in strength, intensity: *the clamour died down*; **b** (of plants) to wither down to the ground. *Die off* (of a family, race, plants &c.), die one by one. *Die out* (lit. and fig., of race, custom &c.), become extinct.

die-away, adj. [1. dī awà; 2. dái əwèi]. Affectedly sentimental, languishing as though strongly affected by emotion: *a die-away look, glance* &c.

dielectric, adj. & n. [1. dìeléktrik; 2. dàiiléktrik]. **di- (III.)** & **electric.** **a** adj. Non-conductive, insulating; **b** n., an insulator or non-conductor used to separate conductors at different potentials.

Diesel engine, n. [1. dēzel énjin; 2. dízəl éndžin], fr. R. Diesel, d. 1913, the inventor. Form of internal combustion engine in which heavy, crude oil, as petroleum, is used as fuel, ignition being obtained by heat generated by compression of air, the propellant power being by expansion of gas.

die-sinker, n. **die (I.)** & **sinker.** Craftsman who engraves dies for stamping.

dies irae, n. [1. dīēz īrē; 2. dái-īz áiəri]. Lat., 'day of wrath'. **a** The day of judgement; the last day; **b** (caps.) the first words and title of a mediaeval Latin hymn.

dies non, n. [1. dīēz nón; 2. dái-īz nɔ́n]. Lat. *diēs nōn (jūridicus)*, 'day on which the law-courts do not sit'. Lat. *diēs* (nom.) is a new formation on the anal. of the acc. *diē-m*, in place of the nom. **diēus*, fr. **diēw-os*; Aryan base **dejew-, *djew-*, 'the bright, shining one'. For other forms of the same base see **deity** & words there referred to. Lat. *nōn* is fr. O. Lat. *noen(um)*, i.e. **n'oinom*, 'not one', fr. *nē-*, 'not' (see **no**), & O. Lat. *oinos*, 'one' (see **uni-**); cp. O.H.G. *nein*, O.S. *nēn*, 'no'. **a** (law) A day on which no legal business can be transacted; **b** day on which no business is done; one which has to be left out of the reckoning.

diet (I.), n. [1. díet; 2. dáiət], fr. Med. Lat. *dieta*, perh. fr. next word through confusion w. Lat. *diēs*, 'a day'; or perh. fr. Gk. *diaita*, 'arbiter, arbitration', prob. fr. **dia-** & **ait-*, 'share, divide'; cp. Gk. *aisa*, 'lot, fate', fr. **ait-ja*, 'to destine'. A third possibility is that **diet (I.)** is a specialized form of **diet (II.)**, fr. Gk. *diaita*, in the sense of 'dining-room, summer-house' &c.; hence 'hall, meeting-place'; hence 'assembly'. **a** An international assembly, conference; **b** a parliamentary, administrative, assembly, e.g. in Denmark, Sweden &c.

diet (II.), n., fr. O. Fr. *diete*, fr. Lat. *diaeta*, 'a mode of living, diet; a dining-room, summer-house' &c., fr. Gk. *díaita*, 'a way of life (referring esp. to food and dress); a dwelling; medically prescribed diet', fr. Aryan **gʷjəi-*, reduced grade of base **gʷejē(i)-*, 'to live'; for other forms of the base see **zoo-, bio-, quick**, also **vital.** **1.** What one habitually eats and drinks; usual fare, manner of feeding: *a frugal diet.* **2.** Course of food specially selected or prescribed: *a diet of nuts and hot water*; *to put a patient on a special diet.*

diet (III.), vb. trans., fr. prec. To prescribe for another, select for oneself, a special course of food: *his doctor dieted him rigorously*; *to be obliged to diet oneself.*

dietary, adj. & n. [1. díetari; 2. dáiətəri]. See **diet (II.)** & **-ary.** **1.** adj. Pertaining to diet. **2.** n. **a** Prescribed diet, course of feeding; **b** daily allowance of food.

dietetic, adj. [1. dīetétik; 2. daiətétik], fr. Lat., fr. Gk. *diaitētikós*, 'of, for diet', fr. *diaitēt-*, stem of *diaitáein*, 'to diet, feed in a certain way', fr. *díaita*, 'diet'. See **diet (II.).** Pertaining to diet.

dietetics, n., fr. prec. The study of food in its relation to human needs, health &c.

dif-, pref., = **dis-**, q.v., before *f* (by assimilation) in Lat. words. Sometimes confused in O. Fr. w. **de-.**

differ, vb. intrans. [1. dífer; 2. dífə], fr. Fr. *différer*, fr. Lat. *differre*, 'to carry in different directions, scatter; to disturb, distract; to publish, make known; to put off, defer; to differ, be distinguished from'. See **dif-** & **-ferous.** **1. a** To be unlike, be distinct from, something else, have distinguishing characteristics: *men differ in habits and appearance*; Phr. *tastes differ*; **b** *differ from*, be distinguished from, unlike: *French differs from English in having far more verbal inflexions.* **2.** To disagree with, be of another opinion: *to differ from, with, a person*; also absol., *we differed long ago, but have made it up* (meaning derived from *to differ in opinion*). Phr. *I beg to differ*, I disagree.

difference, n. [1. díferens; 2. dífərəns], fr. Fr. *différence*, fr. Lat. *differentia*, 'diversity, difference'. See **differ** & **-ence.** **1.** The state of being different; unlikeness: *a difference in quality, temperature, appearance* &c. Phr. *it makes no difference*, is of no importance. **2.** That which produces difference; distinguishing mark, characteristic: *the chief difference between the two brothers is that one is tall and fair, the other short and dark.* **3.** Amount by which one thing differs from another: *a difference of a yard, of five pounds.* Phr. *to split the difference*, to meet half way, make a compromise. **4.** The act of differing in opinion; condition of holding an opinion other than that of someone else; disagreement, dissension: *they have had differences and won't speak to each other now.* **5.** (her.) Addition to, or change in, a coat of arms.

different, adj. [1. diferent; 2. dífərənt]. Lat. *different-(em)*, Pres. Part. type of *differre.* See **differ** & **-ent.** **a** Not the same, distinct: *these are different people with the same name*; **b** unlike, not resembling; having other qualities, characteristics; various: *different kinds*; *the tastes are quite different*; *more different than one expected*; *a lot of different things.*

differentia, n. [1. diferénshia; 2. difərénʃiə]. Lat., 'difference, diversity'. See **difference.** A point of difference, distinguishing characteristic; specif., essential difference, (esp. log.) that which distinguishes one species from another of the same genus.

differential (I.), adj. [1. diferénshal; 2. difərénʃəl], fr. Med. Lat. *differentiālis.* See **difference** & **-al.** **1. a** Relating to, constituting, a difference; characteristic, distinguishing: *differential character*; **b** (math.) having infinitely small quantitative differences: *differential calculus.* **2.** (econ.) Depending on a difference of advantage which one party in an agreement has over others: *differential tariff* &c. **3.** (mechan.) Exhibiting, characterized by, producing, different motions, amounts of pressure &c.: *differential screw, motion* &c.; *differential gear*, system of gear wheels connecting two shafts or axles, permitting one to revolve at a different speed from that of the other.

differential (II.), n., fr. prec. **a** (math.) The infinitely small degree of difference between two consecutive values of a variable; **b** (mechan.) a differential gear.

differential calculus, n. [1. diferénshal kálkūlus; 2. dɪfərénʃəl kǽlkjuləs]. (math.) The method of analysis for ascertaining the value of the differential.

differentially, adv. [1. diferénshali; 2. dɪfərénʃəli]. **differential** (I.) & **-ly**. In a differential manner, by way of differentiation.

differentiate, vb. trans. & intrans. [1. diferénshiāt; 2. dɪfərénʃieit], fr. Med. Lat. *differentiāt-(um)*, P.P. type of *differentiāre*. See **differentia** & **-ate**. **A.** trans. **1.** To perceive a difference, be able to distinguish, discriminate, between: *I am unable to differentiate one from the other.* **2.** (of characteristic features) To constitute a difference, serve to distinguish between: *the characteristic treatment of certain original consonants differentiates clearly the O.H.G. from the other W. Gmc. dialects.* **3.** To produce differences in, cause to become unlike; to develop differently in some special way: *O.E. and O.S. had been differentiated in the Continental period.* **B.** intrans. (of several individuals) To become different, grow apart, unlike, acquire fresh characteristics: *languages tend to differentiate more and more from the ancestral type as time goes on.*

differentiation, n. [1. diferenshiáshun; 2. dɪfərenʃiéiʃən]. See prec. & **-ion**. **a** The act or process of differentiating; **b** process of becoming differentiated; **c** state of being differentiated.

differently, adv. [1. díferentli; 2. dífərəntli]. **different** & **-ly**. In a different manner.

difficile, adj. [1. dífisēl; 2. dífisīl]. Mod. Fr., 'difficult' (in various senses). (of persons) Difficult, **3**.

difficult, adj. [1. dífiklt; 2. dífiklt]. Lat. *difficilis*, 'difficult, hard to do, to understand'; (of character) 'morose, hard to manage, obstinate', fr. **dif-** & *facilis*, 'easy'; see **facile**. The ending *-ult* shows the word to be a new formation fr. **difficulty**. In M.E. the Fr. form *difficile* is used. **1.** (of physical action) Hard to do; **a** laborious, involving great effort, needing exercise of strength and force; **b** demanding great skill, delicacy of handling and touch, careful and minute adjustment &c. **2.** (of mental action) Hard to understand; demanding intellectual effort, requiring concentrated attention. **3.** **a** (of persons) Not easy to deal with or approach; exacting, hard to please; touchy, easily offended; **b** (of circumstances, situations) awkward, hard to contend with, oppressive, vexatious.

difficulty, n. [1. dífiklti; 2. dífiklti], fr. Fr., fr. Lat. *difficultāt-(em)*, 'difficulty, trouble, distress; obstinacy, moroseness'. See **dif-** & **faculty**. **1.** The quality of being difficult, of requiring effort, of being hard to do, or to understand &c.: *a task of difficulty*; *to walk with difficulty*; *to find difficulty in understanding.* **2.** **a** Something which is physically or intellectually difficult, hard to do or understand: *a task presenting many difficulties*; *to face, overcome, every difficulty*; **b** objection, demur, cavilling, obstruction: *to raise, make, difficulties*; *put difficulties in the way.* **3.** State of financial embarrassment: *to be in difficulties.*

diffidence, n. [1. dífidens; 2. dífidəns], fr. Lat. *diffīdentia*, 'want of confidence, distrust, diffidence'. See next word & **-ce**. The mental state of being diffident; want of self-confidence, or self-assertion; modesty, shyness.

diffident, adj. [1. dífident; 2. dífidənt], fr. *diffīdent-(em)*, Pres. Part. type of Lat. *diffīdere*, 'to distrust; be hopeless, despair', fr. **dif-** & *fīdere*, 'to trust, confide in', fr. *fīd-us*, 'to be depended on, reliable, trusty; certain, sure'. See **fidelity** & **-ent**. Lacking self-confidence; reluctant to assert oneself; shy, retiring.

diffidently, adv. Prec. & **-ly**. In a diffident manner, without self-assertion.

diffluence, n. [1. díflooens; 2. dífluəns]. See next word & **-ence**. The state of being diffluent; fluidity.

diffluent, adj. [1. díflooent; 2. dífluənt], fr. Lat. *diffluent-(em)*, Pres. Part. type of *diffluere*, 'to flow away; to melt away, disappear'; fig. 'to be lost in, given up to', fr. **dif-** & *fluere*, 'to flow, stream, pour; to proceed, move on; to pass away, vanish, to be diffuse'. See **fluent**. Fluid, flowing in different directions; melting, becoming liquid.

diffract, vb. trans. [1. difrákt; 2. difrǽkt], fr. Lat. *diffract-(um)*, P.P. type of *diffringere*, 'to break, shatter', fr. **dif-** & *frangere*, 'to break, shatter, shiver; to grind, crush'; fig. 'to weaken, diminish'. See **fraction**. **a** (opt.) To break up a ray of light into separate parts, deflect, modify by diffraction; **b** also to break up sound-waves &c.

diffraction, n. [1. difrákshun; 2. difrǽkʃən]. Prec. & **-ion**. **a** The deflexion, breaking up or modification, of a ray of light when passing by the edge of an opaque body or through a narrow slit, forming dark and light or differently coloured bands; **b** similar process or phenomenon in sound-waves and electricity.

diffractive, adj. [1. difráktiv; 2. difrǽktiv]. **diffract** & **-ive**. Causing diffraction.

diffractively, adv. Prec. & **-ly**. In such a manner as to cause diffraction.

diffuse (I.), adj. [1. difús; 2. difjús], fr. Lat. *diffūs-(um)*, P.P. type of *diffundere*, 'to pour forth, spread; to scatter, spread about'. See **dif-** & **fuse** (I.). **a** (of speech, style, verbal expression) Lacking conciseness, straying from the point, wordy; **b** (of persons) tending to ramble, lacking power of concise expression; verbose, long-winded.

diffuse (II.), vb. trans. & intrans. [1. difúz; 2. difjúz]. See prec. **1.** trans. **a** To shed out, spread abroad, send, give out, cause to spread in different directions: (i.) (of non-material things) *to diffuse learning, kindness, a sense of well-being* &c.; (ii.) (material things) *to diffuse light, heat, odours* &c.; **b** (phys.) to cause (gases &c.) to mix by diffusion. **2.** intrans. (of fluids) To mix by diffusion.

diffusely, adv. [1. difúsli; 2. difjúsli]. **diffuse** (I.) & **-ly**. In a diffuse manner.

diffuseness, n. [1. difúsnes; 2. difjúsnis]. **diffuse** (I.) & **-ness**. **a** Quality of being diffuse; **b** specific instance of this.

diffusibility, n. [1. difúzibíliti; 2. difjúzibíliti]. See next word & **-ity**. Property of being diffusible.

diffusible, adj. [1. difúzibl; 2. difjúzibl]. See **diffuse** (II.) & **-ible**. Capable of being diffused.

diffusion, n. [1. difúzhun; 2. difjúžn]. **diffuse** (II.) & **-ion**. **a** The act or process of diffusing; state of being diffused; circulation, dissemination; **b** specif. (phys.) the intermingling of two fluids (gases, liquids &c.) not caused by external force.

diffusive, adj. [1. difúsiv; 2. difjúsiv]. **diffuse** (I.) & **-ive**. Tending to spread, circulate, be diffused.

diffusively, adv. Prec. & **-ly**. In a diffusive manner.

diffusiveness, n. See prec. & **-ness**. Quality, or property, of being diffusive.

dig (I.), vb. trans. & intrans. [1. dig; 2. dig]. M.E. (14th cent.) *diggen*, perh. fr. O. Fr. *diguer*, 'to make a dike, build an embankment, to hollow out the ground', fr. *digue*, 'dike', wh. is prob. fr. a L.G. stem **dīk-*, as in **dike**. In spite of its comparatively late appearance & rather doubtful origin, the word has completely ousted the orig. Engl. **delve**. **A.** trans. **1.** To break up ground with a spade or trowel: *to dig the ground*; **a** to break up ground in a similar way with hands, claws &c.; **b** to make by digging: *dig a trench, hole, ditch, well* &c.; **c** to break through, force a way through, by digging: *to dig one's way out*; **d** to remove from ground by digging: *to dig potatoes.* **2.** (fig.) To make laborious search for, in, investigate carefully: *to dig (out) the facts from books*; *dig out the truth somehow.* **3.** (colloq.) To poke, push, thrust at, nudge: *to dig a person in the ribs.* **B.** intrans. **a** To perform the act of digging in the earth &c. with a spade: *to dig for gold*; **b** to perform a similar act with hands, claws &c. **C.** Followed by prepositions. *Dig in*, **a** to mix with, put below surface of soil by digging (of manure &c.); **b** to entrench, protect by digging a trench: *to dig oneself in*; **c** to thrust, push by a violent movement: *to dig one's spurs into a horse. Dig into*, to penetrate by digging. *Dig out*, **a** (a hole) make one by digging; **b** (of something which has gone, been put, below the ground) to reveal, expose, remove from ground by digging: *to dig out a fox, badger* &c. *Dig up*, **a** (in the ground) to remove by digging something (potatoes &c.) grown in the ground; **b** to break up fallow or uncultivated land: *to dig a field up.*

dig (II.), n., fr. prec. (colloq.) **a** A poke, nudge: *a dig in the ribs*; **b** (fig.) a sarcastic comment, taunt, levelled at a person: *a dig at one's opponents.*

digamist, n. [1. dígamist; 2. dígəmist]. See **digamy** & **-ist**. One who marries for the second time, as distinct from *bigamist.*

digamma, n. [1. dīgáma; 2. daigǽmə]. Gk. *digamma*, fr. **di-** (II.) & **gamma**, fr. its shape, wh. was that of double Γ or gamma. The symbol, or letter (F), expressing the original Aryan, and Primitive Greek sound [w]; still written in the oldest Greek inscriptions, but very early disused in all dialects, as the sound itself disappeared.

digamous, adj. [1. dígamus; 2. dígəməs], fr. Lat., fr. Gk. *digamos*, 'twice-married'. See next word & **-ous**. Pertaining to a second marriage.

digamy, n. [1. dígami; 2. dígəmi], fr. Lat., fr. Gk. *digamía*, 'second marriage'. See **di-** (II.) & **-gamy**. Second marriage; having a second husband or wife; contrast *bigamy.*

digastric, adj. & n. [1. dīgástrik; 2. daigǽstrik], fr. **di-** (II.) & Gk. *gastr-(ós)*, genit. of *gastḗr*, 'the belly; anything bulging or swollen', & **-ic**. See **gastric**. (anat.) **a** adj. (of a muscle) Having two swollen ends; **b** n., (also *digastric muscle*) the muscle that depresses the lower jaw.

digest (I.), vb. trans. & intrans. [1. dī-, dijést; 2. dai-, didžést], fr. Lat. *dīgest-(um)*, P.P. type of *dīgerere*, 'to carry in different directions, divide, spread about, sort'; hence 'to distribute food to the different parts of the body, to digest; to arrange, put in order'. **dis-** & **gerent**. **A.** trans. **1.** (of physiological process) To convert (food) by chemical action in the mouth, stomach, and bowels, into a substance which is capable of assimilation and absorption by the blood. **2.** (of psychological process) **a** To take in, absorb, assimilate in the mind, to make part of one's knowledge, part of one's stock of ideas, and general mental equipment: *to digest a mass of facts, series of books* &c.; **b** (fig.) to tolerate, put up with, bear without resentment or regret, (a slight, insult, loss &c.); to accept without incredulity (a statement &c.): *this conduct is more than I can digest.* **3.** (chem.) To render (a substance) soluble by exposure to heat or moisture, and cause it to be absorbed by a liquid. **B.** intrans. To undergo digestion, assimilation, absorption, physiological or chemical.

digest (II.), n. [1. díjest; 2. dáidžest], fr. Lat. *digesta*, neut. pl. of P.P. type of *dīgerere*. See prec. **a** A concise summary, condensed and abridged but exhaustive statement; esp. of a code of laws; **b** specif., *the Digest*, summary of Roman laws compiled by order of Justinian; also the *Pandects of Justinian.*

digester, n. [1. dijéster; 2. didžéstə]. **digest (I.)** & **-er.** One who, that which, digests; specif. (in cookery) a large vessel for long, slow process of cooking.

digestibility, n. [1. dijèstibíliti; 2. didžèstibíliti]. See next word & **-ity.** The property of being digestible.

digestible, adj. [1. dijéstibl; 2. didžéstibl]. **digest (I.)** & **-ible.** Capable of being digested.

digestibly, adv. Prec. & **-ly.** In a digestible form.

digestion, n. [1. dijéschun; 2. didžéstʃən], fr. Lat. *dīgestiōn-(em)*, 'digestion of food; division, classification'. **digest (I.)** & **-ion. 1.** (physiol.) **a** Process of digesting, state or process of being digested; **b** capacity for digesting food easily and thoroughly: *a good* or *bad digestion.* **2.** (mental) **a** Process of intellectual absorption; **b** capacity for this.

digestive, adj. & n. [1. dijéstiv; 2. didžéstiv]. **digest (I.)** & **-ive. 1.** adj. **a** Pertaining to digestion; **b** aiding in, promoting, digestion. **2.** n. Substance which aids or promotes digestion.

digestively, adv. Prec. & **-ly.** In a digestive manner or state.

digestiveness, n. See prec. & **-ness.** State, quality, of being digestive.

diggable, adj. [1. dígabl; 2. dígəbl]. See **dig (I.)** & **-able.** Capable of being dug.

digger, n. [1. díger; 2. dígə]. **dig (I.)** & **-er. 1. a** One who, that which, digs; specif. **b** one who digs for gold; also *gold-digger.* **2.** Burrowing wasp; also *digger-wasp.* **3.** (pl.) A tribe of Indians in western North America, who live mainly on roots.

diggings, n. [1. digingz; 2. díginz]. **dig (I.)** & **-ing. 1.** Area in which gold is dug, gold-field. **2.** (colloq.) Lodgings.

dight, vb. trans. [1. dīt; 2. dait]. O.E. *dihtan*, 'compose, write'; M.E. *dihten*, 'to prepare, set in order, guide, dispose'; cp. O.H.G. *dihtōn*, 'to make poetry'; fr. Lat. *dictāre*, 'to say, declare, repeat; to dictate; to make, compose'. See **dictate.** Obs. till revived by Scott. (archaic and poet., usually in P.P.) To prepare, array, adorn, dress: '*With blushing rose-buds gaily dight*'.

digit, n. [1. díjit; 2. dídžit], fr. Lat. *digit-(us)*, 'a finger, a toe, an inch'; prob. fr. earlier **dicitus*, fr. base **dik̑-*, reduced grade of base **deik̑-*, **doik̑-*, 'to show, point out'. See **diction.** See **toe** for similar development in meaning. **1. a** A finger; hence, **b** (zool.) a finger or toe; **c** the breadth of the finger, about three-quarters of an inch. **2.** (arith.) One of the numbers or figures from 0 to 9. **3.** (astron.) A twelfth part of the diameter of the sun or moon (term used to express amount obscured in an eclipse).

digital, adj. & n. [1. díjitl; 2. dídžitl]. See prec. & **-al. 1.** adj. Pertaining to the fingers. **2.** n. One of the keys of an instrument such as the organ or piano.

digitalin, n. [1. dìjitálin; 2. dìdžitéilin]. See next word & **-in.** A poison obtained from the leaves of the foxglove.

digitalis, n. [1. dìjitális; 2. dìdžitéilis]. Mod. Bot. Lat., fr. **digit** & **-al**; prob. suggested by the Germ. *finger(hut)*, 'thimble', popular name for the foxglove. **a** A genus of plants, including the common foxglove; **b** a poisonous, medicinal drug obtained from the purple foxglove, used to increase blood-pressure in diseases of the heart.

digitate(d), adj. [1. díjitat, -āted; 2. dídžitət, -eitid]. See **digit** & **-ate** & **-ed. a** (zool.) Having separate fingers or toes, not web-footed; **b** (bot.) having long finger-like divisions or lobes.

digitation, n. [1. dìjitáshun; 2. dìdžitéiʃən]. See prec. & **-ion.** State of being digitate(d).

digitigrade, adj. & n. [1. díjitigrād; 2. didžitigreid], fr. Lat. *digit-(us)* (see **digit**) & *gradus*, 'step'. See **gradus.** (zool.) **a** adj. Walking on the toes, without placing the whole of the foot on the ground; **b** n., a digitigrade animal.

diglyph, n. [1. díglif; 2. dáiglif], fr. Gk. *digluphos*, 'doubly indented', fr. **di- (II.)** & *gluphḗ*, 'carving'. See **dactylioglyph** (archit.) An ornamental double groove on a tablet &c.

dignified, adj. [1. dígnifīd; 2. dígnifaid]. P.P. of next word. Possessing and exhibiting stateliness, dignity, of bearing and character.

dignify, vb. trans. [1. dígnifī; 2. dígnifai], fr. O. Fr. *dignifier*, fr. L. Lat. *dignificāre.* See **dignity** & **-fy. a** To do honour to, make noble, show worthiness of, render illustrious, exalt: '*Rejudge his acts, and dignify disgrace*' (Pope); **b** to confer an appearance of honour upon, esp. by giving a high-sounding name: *he dignifies his few books by the name of library.*

dignitary, n. [1. dígnitari; 2. dígnitəri]. See next word & **-ary.** (esp. eccles.) A person holding a high and dignified office.

dignity, n. [1. dígniti; 2. dígniti], fr. O. Fr., *dignete*, fr. Lat. *dignitāt-(em)*, 'worth, merit; grandeur, rank, power', fr. *dignus*, 'suitable, becoming, proper', fr. **deknos* (w. *k* voiced by assimilation to foll. *n*), fr. Aryan base **dek̑-*, **dok̑-*, 'to seem good'. See **decent. 1. a** (of the mind and character) Serenity, loftiness, elevation; **b** (of manner, bearing &c.) calm stateliness; placid, unruffled grace. **2. a** An office or position which carries with it respect and deference; high repute, estimation: *a place of the highest dignity*; *to uphold the dignity of the Bench*; **b** a specific honour conveying exalted rank to the holder: *to confer the dignity of a peerage.*

digraph, n. [1. dígrahf; 2. dáigrāf], fr. **di- (II.)** & **-graph.** Combination of two letters representing a single sound; e.g. *sh* in *ship.*

digress, vb. intrans. [1. dīgrés, digrés; 2. daigrés, digrés], fr. Lat. *dīgress-(um)*, P.P. type of *dīgredi*, 'to step aside, depart; to deviate, digress'; fr. **di- (I.)** & *gradi*, 'to step, walk', fr. *gradus*, 'a step'; See **gradus.** (more rarely) **a** To leave the direct line or course, turn aside, stray; usually **b** (fig., of verbal expression) to depart from the main theme, turn aside temporarily to a different subject; to wander, be diffuse.

digression, n. [1. dīgréshun, digréshun; 2. daigréʃən, digréʃən], fr. Lat. *dīgressiōn-(em)*, 'a departing, separating'; fig. 'digression'. See **digress** & **-ion.** The act of digressing; temporary departure from chief subject in speech or writing.

digressive, adj. [1. dīgrésiv, digrésiv; 2. daigrésiv, digrésiv]. See **digress** & **-ive. a** (of mode of expression) Departing from, leading away from, the main subject; divagating; **b** (of persons) given to digression.

digressively, adv. Prec. & **-ly.** In a digressive manner; as a digression.

dihedral, adj. [1. dīhḗdral; 2. daihídrəl], fr. **di- (II.)** & Gk. *hédra*, 'a seat, chair, base'. See **-hedral.** Having two plane faces.

dikast. See **dicast.**

dik-dik, n. [1. dík dik; 2. dík dik]. Native name. A very small antelope, genus *Madoqua*, of N.E. Africa, with long hairy nose.

dike (I.), **dyke**, n. [1. dīk; 2. daik]. M.E. *dīk*, fr. O.N. *dīk*, 'a dike, ditch'. See **ditch. 1.** A ditch, watercourse. **2. a** An embankment, bank, esp. one built up to prevent low country from being flooded; **b** (fig.) a protective barrier: *the dikes have burst, revolution is overwhelming us.* **3.** (geol.) Igneous rock, forced, while in a melted state, into fissures of other rock.

dike (II.), vb. trans., fr. prec. To protect (land &c.) by constructing dikes, supply with dikes.

dike-reeve, n. See prec. & **reeve.** A superintendent of the dikes, drainage &c., of the fens.

dilapidate, vb. trans. & intrans. [1. dilápidāt; 2. dilǽpideit], fr. Lat. *dīlapidāt-(um)*, P.P. type of *dīlapidāre*, 'to demolish', lit. 'pull out the stones of a structure', fr. **di- (I.)** & *lapidāre*, 'to throw stones at', fr. *lapid-*, 'stone'. See **lapidary, lapis lazuli. a** trans. To bring into, cause to fall into, a state of disrepair; to ruin; **b** intrans., to fall into bad condition, become in need of repair; decay, deteriorate.

dilapidated, adj. [1. dilápidāted; 2. dilǽpideitid], fr. P.P. of prec. **a** (of buildings) Fallen into decay, tumbling down, ruinous, tottery; **b** of various ruinous things: *dilapidated fortune, furniture*; **c** (of human beings) untidy, dishevelled, shabby, down-at-heel.

dilapidation, n. [1. dilàpidáshun; 2. dilæ̀pidéiʃən]. **dilapidate** & **-ion. 1. a** Process of becoming, state of being, dilapidated; **b** specif., the decay, deterioration, wear and tear of ecclesiastical property (buildings &c.) while held by a particular incumbent; (pl.) particular objects thus dilapidated: *to pay for dilapidations.* **2.** The act of causing dilapidation.

dilatability, n. [1. dilàtabíliti; 2. dilèitəbíliti]. See next word & **-ity.** The property of being dilatable.

dilatable, adj. [1. dīlátabl; 2. dailéitəbl]. **dilate** & **-able.** Capable of dilation.

dilatation, n. [1. dīlatáshun; 2. dailətéiʃən], fr. Lat. *dīlātāt-(um)*, P.P. type of *dīlātāre*, 'to enlarge, widen, expand' (lit. and fig.), see next word & **-ion.** The act or process of dilating; state of being dilated; expansion.

dilate, vb. intrans. & trans. [1. dīlát, dilát; 2. dailéit, diléit], fr. Lat. *dīlātāre*, 'to widen, enlarge, extend'; fig. 'to expand'; fr. **di- (I.)** & *lāt-us*, 'broad, wide, extensive; copious, diffuse'. See **latitude. 1.** intrans. **a** To grow larger, swell out, expand in all directions; **b** (fig.) *dilate upon*, to speak or write at length, enlarge: *to dilate upon a subject.* **2.** trans. To cause to expand, make grow larger; enlarge, widen.

dilation, n. [1. diláshun, dīláshun; 2. diléiʃən, dailéiʃən]. See prec. & **-ion.** Dilatation.

dilator, n. [1. dīlátor; 2. dailéitə]. See **dilate** & **-or.** An agent causing dilation; specif. (anat.) a muscle that dilates an organ.

dilatorily, adv. [1. dílatorili; 2. dílətərili], fr. **dilatory** & **-ly.** In a dilatory manner.

dilatoriness, n. [1. dílatorines; 2. dílətərinis]. Next word & **-ness.** The quality of being dilatory; tardiness.

dilatory, adj. [1. dílatori; 2. dílətəri], fr. Lat. *dīlātōrius*, 'dilatory', fr. *dīlāt-(um)*, P.P. type of *differre*, 'to spread about, part asunder; to publish, divulge; to put off, delay'. See **defer. a** Slow in getting things done, loitering; inclined to inaction and delay; **b** (of action) belated.

dilemma, n. [1. diléma, dīléma; 2. dilémə, dailémə]. Lat., fr. Gk. *dilēmma*, 'a double proposition, dilemma', fr. **di- (II.)** & *lêmma*, 'something received, income, receipts', (in log.) 'an assumption'; fr. **lābh-ma*; cp. Gk. *lambánein*, 'to take, seize', fr. **labh-*, cp. Gk. *láphūron*, 'something seized, booty'. Aryan base **labh-*, **lābh-*, 'to take, seize'; cp. Scrt. *lábhatē*, *lambhatē*, 'seizes'; Lith. *lōbis*, 'possession'. Cp. **lemma. a** (log.) Choice, in argument, between two alternative difficulties: *to be put into a dilemma*; *on the horns of a dilemma*; **b** (in gen.) a difficult, perplexing situation, one surrounded by obstacles; choice of evils.

dilettante, pl. **dilettanti**, n. & adj. [1. dilitánti, -ē; 2. dilitǽnti, -i]. Ital., fr. *dilettare*, fr. Lat. *dēlectāre*, 'to delight, engage, attract'. See **delectation** & **-ant. 1.** n. An amateur lover of art and letters without deep knowledge of any subject. **2.** adj. Amateur, unprofessional, superficial.

dilettantish, adj. [1. dilitántish; 2. dilitǽntiʃ]. Prec. & **-ish.** Given to dilettantism, superficial.

dilettantism, n. [1. dilitántizm; 2. dilitǽntizəm]. **dilettante** & **-ism.** Amateur dabbling in art and letters; superficial knowledge of a subject.

diligence (I.), n. [1. dílijens; 2. dílidžəns], fr. Fr., fr. Lat. *dīligentia*, 'carefulness, scrupulous attention; economy, frugality'. See **diligent** & **-ce.** The quality of being diligent;

industry, careful application to work, constant, pertinacious effort.

diligence (II.), n. [1. dilizhahns; 2. dilizás]. Fr. Same as prec. Ironically so called fr. its habitual slowness. A public stage-coach conveying passengers and luggage (esp. in France and Switzerland); foreign public motor coach.

diligent, adj. [1. dílijent; 2. dílidžənt], fr. Fr., fr. Lat. *dīligent-(em)*, Pres. Part. type of *dīlig-ere*, 'to value highly, love'. Prob. fr. **dis-lego*, 'I trouble about a matter', fr. same base as in Gk. *alégein*, 'to concern oneself', *álgos*, 'pain, trouble'; see **-algia**, & cp. **religion** & **neglect**. **a** (of persons) Industrious, working with careful and persistent effort; **b** (of work, manner of work &c.) carried out with care and concentrated effort; painstaking, laborious.

diligently, adv. Prec. & **-ly**. In a diligent manner.

dill, n. [1. dil; 2. dil]. M.E. *dille, dile*, O.E. *dile*; cp. O.H.G. *tilli*. An annual herb, *Anethum*, belonging to the parsley family, having umbelliferous yellow flowers, the seeds of which yield a strongly smelling oil which is used as a carminative for colic and wind; *dill-water*, medicine obtained by steeping these seeds, or by diluting the oil; used as an infant's medicine to cure wind &c.

dilly-dally, vb. intrans. [1. díli dáli; 2. díli dæli]. Redupl. form of **dally**. To hesitate, waste time in vacillation.

diluent, adj. & n. [1. dílūent; 2. dáiljūənt], fr. Pres. Part. of Lat. *dīluere*, 'to wash away, dissolve; to temper, dilute; to weaken, remove'; fr. **di-** (I.) & *luere*, 'to wash'. See **alluvion** & **lave**. **1.** adj. Used for diluting, having the property of diluting. **2.** n. That which dilutes; specif. (med.) a remedy used to increase the fluidity of the blood.

dilute (I.), vb. trans. [1. dīlū́t; 2. dailjū́t], fr. Lat. *dīlūt-(um)*, P.P. type of *dīluere*, 'to wash away, dissolve, dilute'. See prec. **a** To make thinner, weaker, or more fluid, by the addition of another substance or fluid; **b** (fig.) to weaken force of, alter general character of, by mixture with something different.

dilute (II.), adj. [1. dílūt, dīlū́t; 2. dáiljūt, dailjū́t], fr. Lat. *dīlūt-(um)*, as prec. Weakened, thinned down (lit. and fig.).

dilution, n. [1. dilū́shun; 2. dailjū́ʃən]. See **dilute** (I.) & **-ion**. **1.** **a** The act, or process, of diluting; state of being diluted; **b** (lit. and fig.) weakening, watering down, by dilution. **2.** Something which has been diluted.

diluvial, adj. [1. dilóōvial; 2. dil(j)ū́viəl], fr. L. Lat. *dīluviālis*, fr. **diluvium**, see **alluvion, deluge**, & **-al**. **a** Pertaining to a flood, specif. that of Noah; **b** produced by an unusual deluge, esp. by the deluge caused by the melting of the great northern ice-sheet; *diluvial deposits, formations*, accumulations of débris carried down by the floods of the diluvian epoch.

diluvialist, n. [1. dilóōvialist; 2. dil(j)ū́viəlist]. Prec. & **-ist**. One who explains certain geological phenomena as due to the Deluge.

diluvian, adj. [1. dilóōvian; 2. dil(j)ū́viən]. See next word & **-an**. Pertaining to a flood; *diluvian epoch*, (geol.) a division of the Quaternary period, characterized by large deposits of débris from the floods from the great northern ice-sheet.

diluvium, n. [1. dilóōvium; 2. dil(j)ū́viəm]. Lat., 'a flood, deluge'; fig., 'destruction'; fr. **di-** (I.) & grade **lu-* of base **lou-* &c., 'to wash, wash away', whence Lat. *lavere*, 'to wash' (fr. **lowe-*). See **lave** & **deluge**. (geol.) A solid accumulation of débris, a deposit due to a powerful action of water.

dim (I.), adj. [1. dim; 2. dim]. O.E. *dimm*, 'dim, obscure'; M.E. *dim(m)*, O. Fris. *dim*, O.N. *dimmr*; O.H.G. *timbar*, 'gloomy, obscure'; cogn. w. O. Ir. *deim*, 'dark, obscure', & w. Gk. *themerós*, 'grave, serious'; Aryan base **dhemi-*, 'gloomy, obscure'. **1.** **a** (of light) Faint, lacking in brightness, partially obscured; **b** (by transf., of objects) not clearly seen, indistinct, shadowy; **c** (of sight, eyes) unable to see clearly, defective. **2.** (of sounds) Indistinct, faint, not clearly heard, esp. from being far away. **3.** (fig., of mental impressions and ideas) Faint, vague, not clearly defined: *a dim idea*; *the memory of it has grown dim.*

dim (II.), vb. trans. & intrans., fr. prec. **1.** trans. **a** To cause to grow, make, dim; **b** to outshine; cause to seem dim, render dull by comparison: *the light of a candle is dimmed by that of the sun.* **2.** intrans. To grow dim, fade, become indistinct.

dime, n. [1. dīm; 2. daim]. M.E. *dīme*, fr. Fr. *dīme*, fr. O. Fr. *disme*, 'a tenth part, tithe'. See **decimal**. (U.S.A.) **a** A silver coin of the United States, worth ten cents (one-tenth of a dollar). Phr. *not care a dime*, probable origin of that which now substitutes *damn* for last word; **b** used attributively, for something very cheap and inferior: *a dime museum, novel* &c.

dimension, n. [1. diménshun; 2. diménʃən], fr. Lat. *dīmensiōn-(em)*, 'a measuring', fr. *dīmens-(um)*, P.P. type of *dīmētīri*, 'to measure out'; fr. **di-** (I.) & *mētīri*, 'to measure; to go through, traverse; to judge, consider'. See **measure** (I.). **1.** Measurement of extent in any one of three single directions, as *length, depth, breadth* &c. **2.** (math.) Extension of above meaning to include any number of additional dimensions, e.g. *n dimensions, a fourth dimension* &c.; see also **space-time**. **3.** (pl.) **a** Extent of measurement in all three directions: *the dimensions of a room*; hence **b** size, capacity: *a house, a bowl* &c., *of considerable dimensions*; (of non-material things) importance, scope: *a scheme of vast dimensions.*

dimensional, adj. [1. diménshunal; 2. diménʃənəl]. Prec. & **-al**. Having measurement, capable of being measured. Used in compounds: *one-dimensional* (applied to a line), *two-dimensional*, with measurement in two directions; *three-dimensional space*, that of length, breadth, and depth &c.

dimensionless, adj. [1. diménshunles; 2. diménʃənlis]. **dimension** & **-less**. (of a point) Having no dimensions, without length, breadth, or height.

dimerous, adj. [1. dímerus; 2. dímərəs], fr. **di-** (II.) & Gk. *méros*, 'a part, lot', & **-ous**. Cp. Lat. *merēre*, 'obtain, acquire, deserve', lit. 'to receive one's share'. See **merit**. (bot. and entom.) Having, consisting of, two parts, joints, members.

dimeter, n. [1. dímeter; 2. dímitə], fr. Lat., fr. Gk. *dimetros*, 'having two measures', fr. **di-** & *métron*, 'a measure'. See **-meter**. A verse consisting of two measures.

dimidiate, adj. [1. dimídiāt; 2. daimídieit], fr. Lat. *dīmidiāt-(us)*, P.P. type of *dīmidiāre*, 'to halve, divide into halves', fr. Lat. *dīmidius*, 'through the middle, half', fr. **dis-medios*. See **dis-** & **medium**. Divided into halves, split into two equal parts.

diminish, vb. trans. & intrans. [1. dimínish; 2. diminiʃ]. Fr. *diminuer*, 'reduce'; not fr. Lat. *dēminuere*, 'to lessen' &c., but new formation fr. **di-** (I.), intens. & **minish**. **a** trans. To cause to grow smaller, lessen, reduce; **b** intrans., to become smaller, be reduced in quantity, grow less.

diminishable, adj. [1. dimínishabl; 2. dimíniʃəbl]. Prec. & **-able**. That can be diminished.

diminished, adj. [1. dimínisht; 2. dimíniʃt], P.P. of **diminish**. **a** Lessened, reduced, brought lower: Phr. *to hide one's diminished head*, to feel shamed or abashed; cp. Milton, '*at whose sight all the stars Hide their diminished heads*' (P.L. iv. 34, 5); **b** (mus., of intervals) lessened by one chromatic semitone.

diminishingly, adv. [1. dimínishingli; 2. diminiʃiŋli]. Pres. Part. of **diminish** & **-ly**. In a diminishing manner, growing gradually smaller.

diminuendo, n. & adv. [1. diminūéndō; 2. diminjuéndou]. Ital., fr. Pres. Part. of *diminuire*, fr. Lat. *dēminuere*, 'to lessen, make smaller', fr. **di-** (I.) & *minuere*, 'to make smaller; to chop in pieces; to detract from, impair; to alter, modify'. See **minute** (III.). (mus.) **1.** n. **a** A gradual decrease in the volume of sound, reduction of loudness; **b** a passage to be played or sung with such a gradual decrease. **2.** adv. Getting gradually softer; opposed to *crescendo.*

diminution, n. [1. diminū́shun; 2. diminjū́ʃən], fr. Lat. *dīminūtiōn-(em)*, also *dēminūtiōn-(em)*, 'a lessening, diminishing', fr. *dēminūt-(um)*, P.P. type of *dēminuere*, 'to lessen, take from'. See prec. & **-ion**. The act, or process, of diminishing; state of being diminished; gradual lessening in size, quality, amount &c.: *my resources show a considerable diminution.*

diminutival, adj. [1. diminūtívl; 2. diminjutáivl]. See next word & **-al**. Pertaining to a diminutive.

diminutive, adj. & n. [1. dimínūtiv; 2. diminjutiv]. See **diminution** & **-ive**. **1.** adj. **a** Very small, tiny, miniature; **b** (gram.) expressing diminution, smallness in size; often expressed by special suffix, e.g. *-let.* **2.** n. (gram.) A word thus formed, to express diminished size, minuteness.

diminutively, adv. Prec. & **-ly**. In a diminutive manner.

diminutiveness, n. See prec. & **-ness**. The state of being diminutive.

dimissory, adj. [1. dimísori; 2. daimísəri], fr. L. Lat. *dīmissōrius*. See **dismiss** & **-ory**. Giving leave to depart; (esp. eccles.) *letter dimissory* (from the bishop of a diocese).

dimity, n. [1. dímiti; 2. dímiti], fr. Ital. *dimito*, fr. Low Lat. *dimitum*, fr. Gk. *dímitos*, 'of double thread'; also as n., 'dimity'; fr. **di-** (II.) & *mitos*, 'a thread, warp-thread; string (of a lyre)'; etymol. unknown. A strong cotton material with raised patterns, usually white, used for curtains &c.

dimly, adv. [1. dímli; 2. dímli]. **dim** (I.) & **-ly**. In a dim manner; faintly, indistinctly.

dimmish, adj. [1. dímish; 2. dímiʃ]. **dim** (I.) & **-ish**. Fairly dim, partially obscured.

dimness, n. [1. dímnis; 2. dímnis]. **dim** (I.) & **-ness**. The state of being dim.

dimorphic, dimorphous, adj. [1. dīmórfik, -fus; 2. daimɔ́fik, -fəs], fr. Gk. *dimorph-(os)*, 'two-formed' (fr. **di-** (II.) & *morphḗ*, 'form, shape'), & **-ic, -ous**. See **morphology**. (bot., chem., zool.) Exhibiting dimorphism.

dimorphism, n. [1. dīmórfizm; 2. daimɔ́fizəm]. See prec. & **-ism**. (biol.) Difference of structure, colour &c. between members of same species.

dimple (I.), n. [1. dímpl; 2. dímpl]. Not found till 15th cent.; perh. cogn. w. O.H.G. *dumphilo*, Germ. *tümpel*, 'a pool'. **a** A rounded hollow, slight depression in surface of the flesh, esp. in cheek, chin, arms &c.; **b** a slight depression in the ground, surface of water &c.

dimple (II.), vb. trans. & intrans., fr. prec. **a** trans. To form, produce, show, dimples in: *the wind dimples the surface of the lake*; **b** intrans., to become dimpled, show, form, dimples: *to dimple with laughter.*

dimply, adj. [1. dímpli; 2. dímpli], fr. **dimple** (I.) & **-y**. Having dimples, full of dimples.

din (I.), n. [1. din; 2. din]. O.E. *dyne*, M.E. *dine*, O.N. *dynr*, fr. Prim. Gmc. **dun-i*; cp. O.S., M. Du. *done*, fr. Prim. Gmc. **dun-o*, perh. cogn. w. Gk. *thûnos*, 'attack'; Scrt. *dhūn-oti*, 'to shake violently', fr. Aryan base **dhūn-*, 'to be violent, attack fiercely', w. the meaning specialized in Gmc. to 'sound caused by violent blows'; cp. **dint**. The base is perh. extended fr. **dhew-a-*, **dhow-a*, **dhu-*, 'to move rapidly'. See **dew, dull, fury, fume**. Loud, continuous, clamour or clatter, confusing noise.

din (II.), vb. trans. & intrans. M.E. *dinien*, O.E. *dynian*; cp. O.N. *dynja*, O.S. *dunian*. See prec. **1.** trans. To express, repeat, with insistent clamour, or with persistence: *to* *din something into a person's ears, head.* **2.** intrans. To make a loud, persistent, confusing noise.

dinanderie, n. [1. dinónderē; 2. dīnā́dərī], fr. *Dinand*, now *Dinant*, in Belgium, where such articles were made. Collective term for decorated articles of brass and copper.

dinar, n. [1. dēnár; 2. dīná]. Arab., Pers., fr. Gk. *dēnárion*, fr. Lat. *dēnārius*. See **denier**. **1.** (hist.) An old Byzantine gold coin. **2. a** Persian money of account of small value; **b** the Serbian silver coin and monetary unit, equivalent to the 'franc' &c.

dine, vb. intrans. & trans. [1. dīn; 2. dain], fr. Fr. *dîner*, prob. fr. Low Lat. **disjejūnāre*, 'to break one's fast', fr. **dis-** & *jējūnus*, 'fasting; scanty, thin; poor, mean, powerless; barren, unproductive'. See **jejune** & cp. **déjeuner**. **1.** intrans. To take dinner, eat the chief meal of the day: *to dine late* &c.; *to dine out*, away from home; *to dine with Duke Humphrey*, old Elizabethan saying meaning to go without one's dinner, from Duke Humphrey's aisle in St. Paul's, much frequented at dinner-time by penniless people. **2.** trans. **a** (of persons) To entertain, give dinner to: *I dined him handsomely*; **b** (of a room, table &c.) to afford accommodation for dining for, be large enough for: *this table dines twelve comfortably.*

diner, n. [1. dīner; 2. dáinə]. Prec. & **-er**. **1.** One who dines: *a regular, great, diner-out*, one who dines away from home very often, as a guest of other people. **2.** (colloq.) A dining-car on a railway train.

ding, vb. trans. [1. ding; 2. diŋ]. M.E. *dingen, dengen*, Pret. *dang, dong*, P.P. *dungen*; cogn. w. O.N. *dengja*, 'to hammer'; Swed. *dänga*, 'to bang'. (archaic or dial.) To throw, hurl, beat.

ding-dong, n. & adj. [1. díng dóng; 2. díŋ dɔ́ŋ]. Imitative. **1.** n. **a** The continuously repeated stroke of a bell; **b** any loud, clanging sound resembling this. **2.** adj. Repeated in continuous succession or alternation, esp. of contests with varying change on one side or another, hence, vigorously fought: *a ding-dong fight, race* &c.

dinghy, n. [1. dínggi; 2. díŋgi], fr. Hind. *dengī*, 'a rowing-boat'. **a** A small boat carried on a ship; **b** a small pleasure-boat.

dingily, adv. [1. dínjili; 2. dínd̷žili]. See **dingy** & **-ly**. In a dingy manner, condition.

dinginess, n. [1. dínjines; 2. díndžinis]. See prec. & **-ness**. State, quality, of being dingy.

dingle, n. [1. dínggl; 2. díŋgl]. M.E. *dingel*, 'a deep hollow'. Origin uncertain. A wooded hollow; a dell, a small valley.

dingo, n. [1. dínggō; 2. díŋgou], fr. native name. Australian wild dog.

dingy, adj. [1. dínji; 2. dínd̷ži]. Perh. fr. **dung**; O.E. **dyngig*. **a** (of surfaces) Not fresh, bright, and clean; dull, tarnished, lustreless, discoloured; **b** (of character, reputation) doubtful, besmirched, disreputable; **c** (of places) dirty, dismal; **d** (of persons) shabby, ill-dressed, lacking freshness of appearance.

dining-car, n. [1. dīning kàr; 2. dáiniŋ kā]. Special coach on a railway train, in which meals are served, a restaurant car.

dining-room, n. [1. dīning ròom; 2. dáiniŋ rùm]. A room for having meals in (esp. dinner).

dinky, adj. [1. díngki; 2. díŋki]. Prob. fr. Scots & Nthn. dial. *dink, denk*, 'neat, trim'. (colloq.) Neat, dainty, smart.

dinner, n. [1. díner; 2. dínə], fr. Fr. *dîner*, n. fr. vb. See **dine**. **a** The principal meal of the day, whether taken in the evening or in the middle of the day; **b** a formal public dinner, in honour of some person, or to celebrate some event.

dinner-bell, n. A large bell rung to announce meals.

dinner-hour, n. The hour at which or during which one dines.

dinner-jacket, n. Black coat without tails, worn by men in the evening on informal occasions.

dinnerless, adj. [1. dínerles; 2. dínəlis]. Without having had dinner.

dinner-napkin, n. Table-napkin of large size.

dinner-party, n. Evening party to which guests are invited for dinner.

dinner-service, -set, n. Special set of plates, dishes &c. used at dinner.

dinner-table, n. Table used for dining.

dinner-time, n. The hour at which one dines.

dinner-waggon, n. Set of shelves on legs and castors to hold plates, dishes, spare silver &c.; sometimes used in a dining-room.

dinoceras, n. [1. dīnóseras; 2. dainɔ́sərəs], fr. Gk. *deinós*, see **dinosaur**, & *kéras*, 'horn', see **kerato-**. An extinct, gigantic, horned, herbivorous mammal.

dinornis, n. [1. dīnórnis; 2. dainɔ́nis], fr. Gk. *deinós*, see next word, & Gk. *órnis*, 'bird', see **ornithology**. A large, extinct bird, incapable of flight, resembling an ostrich, of which the New Zealand moa, q.v., was one.

dinosaur, n. [1. dínosòr; 2. dáinəsɔ̀], fr. Gk. *deinós*, 'terrible; mighty, powerful; clever, skilful', fr. **dwei-nos*; cp. Gk. *deídō*, 'I fear', fr. **de-dwei-a, déos*, 'fear', fr. **dwei-os, deilós*, 'weak, cowardly', fr. **dwei-el-os*; Aryan base **dwei-, *dwoi-* 'to fear'. Cp. Scrt. *dvḗṣ̌ti*, 'to hate', *dvḗšaš*, 'hatred', fr. **dwei-s-*, see **dire**; & Gk. *saúra, saûros*, 'lizard'. See **saurian**. A gigantic, extinct reptile of the Mesozoic age.

dinothere, dinotherium, n. [1. dínothēr, dīnothērium; 2. dáinəþiə, dainəþíəriəm], fr. Gk. *deinós*, 'terrible' (see prec.), & *thḗr*, 'wild beast'. Cp. Lith. *žvėris*, O. Slav. *zvěrĭ*, 'wild beast'; Lat. *ferus*, 'savage'; Aryan base **ghʷer-os*, 'wild beast'. See **ferocious**. A gigantic, extinct animal belonging to the same order as the elephant.

dint (I.), n. [1. dint; 2. dint]. M.E. *dint*, O.E. *dynt*, 'a blow, stroke'; see **dent** & cp. Swed. *dunt*, O.N. *dyntr*. **1.** A violent stroke, blow; force, violence; obsolescent except in Phr. *by dint of*, by means of. **2.** A depression in a hard surface made by a blow.

dint (II.), vb. trans. M.E. *dinten*, fr. O.E. *dyntan*, 'to strike'. See prec. To cause a dint on a surface by means of a blow.

diocesan, adj. & n. [1. dīósezn; 2. daiɔ́sizn]. See next word & **-an**. **a** adj. Of or concerning a diocese: *diocesan clergy, business*; **b** n., the ruler of a diocese, a bishop considered in relation to his diocese or to the clergy of the diocese: *the matter must be referred to your diocesan.*

diocese, n. [1. díosis; 2. dáiəsis], fr. O. Fr. *diocīse, diocēse*, fr. Med. Lat. *diocesis*, fr. Lat., fr. Gk. *dioikēsis*, 'administration, control'; (eccles.) 'a diocese', fr. **di-** (III.) & *oikéō*, 'I inhabit, have one's abode in; settle, colonize; direct, manage', fr. *oîkos*, 'house, dwelling'. See **economy**. The district under the jurisdiction of a bishop.

dioecious, adj. [1. dīḗshus; 2. daiī́ʃəs], fr. **di-** (II.) & Gk. *oîkos*, 'house, dwelling'. See **economy** & **-ous**. (bot. & zool.) Having the male and female reproductive organs respectively in different individuals.

Dionysiac, Dionysian, adj. [1. dīonísiak, -ian; 2. daiənáisiæk, -iən], fr. Lat. *Dionȳsiacus*, fr. name of the Gk. god, *Dionysus*, & **-ac, -an**. Of, pertaining to, Dionysus, or to the festivals held in his honour.

dioptric, adj. & n. [1. dīóptrik; 2. daiɔ́ptrik], fr. Gk. *dioptrikós*, fr. *dioptra*, 'an optical instrument for surveying', fr. **di-** (III.) & stem *op-*, 'eye'. See **optic**. **1.** adj. **a** Pertaining to refraction of light; **b** assisting the sight by means of refraction and not reflection. **2.** n. **a** Unit used to express the refractive power of a lens; **b** (pl.) that part of the science of optics which deals with refraction by lenses.

diorama, n. [1. dīoráhma; 2. daiərā́mə], fr. **di-** (III.) & Gk. *hórāma*, 'something seen, a spectacle', fr. *horáō*, 'I see, look at', fr. **worā*, 'attention'; cogn. w. O.H.G., O.S. *wara*, O.E. *waru*, 'attention'; O.E. *wær*, 'watchful, wise'. See **ware** (II.). **a** Exhibition of realistic scenic painting and natural effects produced by pictures variously coloured, lighted, and distanced; **b** building where such an exhibition is shown.

diorite, n. [1. díorīt; 2. dáiərait], fr. **di-** (II.) & *horizein*, 'to mark a boundary (*hóros*), to separate'. See **horizon** & **-ite**. (geol.) A group of granitic, igneous rocks, composed of felspar and hornblende.

dioxide, n. [1. dīóksīd; 2. daiɔ́ksaid]. See **di-** (II.) & **oxide**. (chem.) A compound of two parts of oxygen with one of metal.

dip (I.), vb. trans. & intrans. [1. dip; 2. dip]. O.E. *dyppan*, M.E. *dippen*, 'to dip, immerse'; cp. Dan. *dyppe*, Fris. *dippe*, Gmc. **đup-jan*, fr. Aryan base **dhu-b-, *dhou-b-*, 'a hole, hollow'. See **deep**. **A.** trans. **1.** To put or plunge momentarily into liquid; to lower into liquid and take out again: *to dip one's fingers in water.* Specific meanings: **a** to dye, by dipping material in liquid dye; **b** to wash (sheep) in disinfecting preparations; **c** to make (candles) by dipping wick in melted tallow. **2.** To lower and raise again quickly: *to dip a flag* &c. **B.** intrans. **1. a** To slope down, descend gradually (of land, a road &c.); **b** to go, sink, down, or appear to sink, below a certain level: *the sun dips below the sea, the horizon* &c.; **c** (geol., of strata) to slope down so as to make an angle with the horizontal. **2.** (fig.) *Dip into* (a book, branch of study &c.), glance at, examine, cursorily; investigate superficially or briefly.

dip (II.), n., fr. prec. **1.** The act or process of dipping or being dipped; immersion, plunging into liquid: *a dip in the sea.* **2.** (by transf.) **a** Liquid in which something is dipped; esp. preparation for washing sheep: *sheep-dip*; **b** a candle made by dipping a wick into melted tallow: *a farthing dip.* **3.** (of land, road &c.) The process of dipping; a slope, hollow, gradual descent: *a dip in the ground.* **4.** Scientific uses: **a** the inclination of strata to the horizontal; **b** the inclination of a magnetic needle to the horizontal; **c** the apparent depression of the horizon when looked at from a point above the ground.

diphtheria, n. [1. difthḗria; 2. difþíəriə], fr. Fr. *diphthérie*, fr. Gk. *diphthéra*, 'prepared hide, leather; a leathern garment; a bag, wallet'. Etymol. doubtful. The word is perh. cogn. w. Gk. *déphein, dépsein*, 'to soften by working with the hand'. Cp. O.H.G. *zispen*, 'to trample on'. A dangerous, infectious disease, affecting chiefly the mucous membrane of the throat and air-passages, which become highly inflamed and covered with a sloughing membrane.

diphtherial, adj. [1. difthḗrial; 2. difþíəriəl]. Prec. & **-al**. Pertaining to diphtheria.

diphtheric, adj. [1. difthérik; 2. difþérik]. See prec. & **-ic**. Pertaining to diphtheria.

diphtheritic, adj. [1. diftherítik; 2. difþərítik]. Fr. *diptheritique*. See **diphtheria** & **-ic**. Pertaining to, affected by, diphtheria: *diphtheritic membrane, throat* &c.

diphtheroid, adj. [1. diftheroid; 2. difþərɔid]. See **diphtheria** & **-oid**. Of the nature of diphtheria.

diphthong, n. [1. difthong; 2. difþɔŋ], fr. Fr. *diphthongue*, fr. Lat., fr. Gk. *diphthoggos*, 'having two sounds; a diphthong', fr. **di-** (II.) & *phthóggos*, 'a sound; a voice; a vowel'; cp. *phthégma*, 'voice, speech', *phthéggomai*, 'to speak'; cp. **apophthegm**. The orig. form of the word is doubtful. **1.** Combination of two distinct vowel-sounds, uttered in rapid succession, one of which is more strongly stressed than the other and is alone syllabic, so that they constitute together only a single syllable, e.g. *ái, éi, áu*, &c. **2.** (in popular usage). **a** Two successive letters; often erroneously so called where they do not express a true diphthong at all, as *au* in *cause*, &c.; **b** letter formed of two ligatured letters, as *œ*. Such usage is grossly inaccurate.

diphthongal, adj. [1. difthónggal; 2. difþɔ́ŋgəl]. See prec. & **-al**. Of the nature of a diphthong.

diphthongization, n. [1. dìfthonggīzáshun; 2. dìfþɔŋgaizéiʃən]. See next word & **-ation.** (philol.) Development of a diphthongal pronunciation from what was originally a single vowel, e.g. ī sound in O.E. *wīf* [ī] has become Mod. [*ai*].

diphthongize, vb. trans. [1. dífthonggīz; 2. dífþɔŋgaiz]. See **diphthong** & **-ize.** To develop a diphthong from a single vowel sound.

dipl(o)-, pref., fr. Gk. *diplóos*, 'double', fr. **di- (II.)** & **-pl-*, cp. Lat. *du-pl-us*, 'double' (see **double**), reduced form of base **pel-* &c., 'to bend'. See **pliant, fold (I.)** (in scientific terms) Double, in two separate parts.

diploblastic, adj. [1. dìplōblástik; 2. dìploublǽstik]. See prec. & first element in **blastoderm** & **-ic.** (biol.) Having two germ layers only, as a jelly-fish &c.

diplocardiac, adj. [1. dìplōkárdiak; 2. dìploukā́diæk]. **diplo-** & **cardiac.** (biol.) Having the heart double or divided, as in mammals and birds.

diplodocus, n. [1. dìplōdókus; 2. dìploudɔ́kəs], fr. **diplo-** & Gk. *dokós*, 'beam bar, shaft', fr. the double bony bars protecting the blood-vessels beneath the long tail. For the second element see **dogma.** A gigantic, North American extinct dinosaur, with enormous tail and neck and diminutive head.

diploma, n. [1. diplṓma; 2. diplóumə]. Lat. *diplōma*, 'a state letter; a document granting a privilege', fr. Gk. *diplōma*, 'a folded paper, a letter of recommendation; a letter of licence, privilege' &c., fr. Gk. *diplóos*, 'double'. See **dipl(o)-. 1.** An official document, a charter granted by the State. **2.** A certificate granted by an authority to confer an honour or privilege; esp. a certificate given by a university or other learned body attesting the holder's proficiency in a certain branch of study: *a diploma in architecture, in education* &c.

diplomacy, n. [1. diplṓmasi; 2. diplóuməsi], fr. Fr. *diplomatie.* See **diploma.** The specialized meaning has come from the idea of a state document. **1.** The art and business of conducting and managing affairs of state, esp. those concerned with international relations. **2. a** Skill in this science; hence, **b** tact and skill in dealing with people; adroitness in managing situations involving clash of human relations and interests.

diplomaed, adj. [1. diplṓmad; 2. diplóuməd]. **diploma** & **-ed.** Holding a diploma.

diplomat, n. [1. díplomat; 2. dípləmæt], fr. Fr. *diplomate*, back-formation fr. *diplomatique.* See next word. **a** A person professionally employed in the management of state business, esp. of international relations; **b** a person of tact and skill in dealing with affairs and people.

diplomatic, adj. [1. diplomátik; 2. dipləmǽtik], fr. Fr. *diplomatique*, fr. Mod. Lat. *diplomaticus*, fr. Gk. *diplōmat-*, stem of *diplōma* (see **diploma**), 'a folded state letter', & **-ic. 1. a** Pertaining to diplomacy: *diplomatic service*, that connected with embassies in foreign countries; **b** (of persons) skilled in conducting and managing human relations; adroit, tactful; **c** (of conduct, actions, words &c.) tactful, ingratiating; conducive to easy, pleasant, smooth running of business. **2. a** Relating to the minute study, and to the deciphering of documents; hence, **b** (of printed text) printed directly from the manuscript without emendations &c.

diplomatically, adv. [1. dìplomátikali; 2. dìpləmǽtikəli]. Prec. & **-al** & **-ly.** In a diplomatic manner.

diplomatics, n. [1. dìplomátiks; 2. dìpləmǽtiks]. See **diplomatic, 2.** The science of dealing with, and effectively using, manuscripts; of determining their age, authenticity, and place of origin from internal evidence.

diplomatist, n. [1. diplṓmatist; 2. diplóumətist]. **diplomat** & **-ist.** Diplomat.

diplomatize, vb. intrans. [1. diplṓmatīz; 2. diplóumətaiz]. **diplomat** & **-ize.** To carry on diplomatic negotiations.

dipnoi, n. pl. [1. dípnōi; 2. dípnoui], fr. Gk. *dipnoos*, 'doubly breathing'. See **di- (II.)** & **pneuma.** (zool.) A group of fishes, able to breathe water and air by means of lung-like organs, living in muddy pools &c. which dry during hot weather. Also called lung-fishes or mud-fishes.

dipolar, adj. [1. dīpólar; 2. daipóulə], fr. **di- (II.)** & **polar.** Having two poles, as a magnet.

dipolarize, vb. trans. [1. dīpólarīz; 2. daipóuləraiz]. Prec. & **-ize.** To magnetize a bar of iron.

dipper, n. [1. díper; 2. dípə]. See **dip (I.)** & **-er.** Something that dips, or is used for dipping; specif. **a** a kind of diving-bird; **b** a cup-shaped vessel with a long handle, used for ladling liquid; **c** a member of an American sect of Baptists; **d** popular name of the Great Bear or Charles's Wain.

dipsomania, n. [1. dìpsománia; 2. dìpsəméinjə], fr. Gk. *dipsos, dipsa*, 'thirst', & **mania.** The etymol. of the first element is unknown. A form of insanity, consisting of an irresistible craving for alcohol.

dipsomaniac, n. [1. dìpsomániak; 2. dìpsəméiniæk]. See prec. & **maniac.** A person afflicted with dipsomania.

Diptera, n. [1. díptera; 2. díptərə], fr. Lat., fr. Gk. *dipter-(os)*, 'with two wings'; (of a temple) 'with a double peristyle', fr. **di- (II.)** & *pterón*, 'a feather, wing'; hence 'anything resembling a wing'. See **ptero-.** An order of insects which have two wings only, popularly known as flies.

dipteral, adj. [1. dípteral; 2. díptərəl]. See prec. & **-al. 1.** (of insects) Dipterous. **2.** (archit.) Built with two peristyles.

dipterous, adj. [1. dípterus; 2. díptərəs]. See **Diptera** & **-ous. a** (entom.) Belonging to the order *Diptera*; **b** (bot., of seeds) two-winged.

diptych, n. [1. díptik; 2. díptik], fr. Gk. *díptukha*, 'a double tablet', fr. *díptukhos*, 'folded double', fr. **di- (II.)** & *ptukhé*, 'a fold, layer, plate; a cleft, gully; a writing-tablet'; perh. dissimilated fr. **phthukh-*, fr. Aryan **bh(th)ugh-*, **bheugh-*, 'to fold'; cp. Goth. *biugan*, 'to bend'. See **bow (I.) 1.** Ancient writing-tablet folded in the middle, made usually of wood coated with wax. **2.** A painting or carving on two tablets connected with hinges.

dire, adj. [1. dīr; 2. daiə], fr. Lat. *dīrus*, 'fearful, terrible; ill-omened; cruel'. Cp. Zend *dvaēthā*, 'menace'; Gk. *deinós*, 'terrible'. The Lat. form is fr. older **dei-rus*, w. dialectal (prob. Umbrian) *d* (instead of *b*) fr. Aryan *dw-*; Aryan base **dwei-*, **dwoi-*, 'to fear'. See **dinosaur.** Dreadful, terrible, disastrous; (also poet. *direful*).

direct (I.), vb. trans. & intrans. [1. dirékt; 2. dirékt], fr. Lat. *dīrect-(um)*, P.P. type of *dīrigere*, 'to put into a straight line, set straight, draw up; to aim, direct; to guide, arrange', fr. **di- (I.)** & *regere*, 'to put or lead in a straight line; to guide, lead; to control, correct'. See **rectum, regent, right. A.** trans. **1. a** To guide, control, manage; regulate affairs or progress of: *to direct a business, a campaign* &c.; **b** to take the lead in a piece of work and give instructions to those carrying it out: *to direct the building of a house.* **2.** To cause to turn in a particular direction, concentrate on a particular object: *to direct one's eyes, attention, efforts &c. towards an object.* **3. a** To address, make remarks &c. to a person, whether orally or in writing: *to direct one's remarks, observations (to)*; **b** to write, put a name and address on (a missive &c.): *to direct a letter, envelope, parcel.* **4.** To point out the way to a place, instruct which road &c. to take: *can you direct me to the butcher's?* **B.** intrans. To perform the act of directing.

direct (II.), adj., fr. Lat. *directus.* See prec. **1. a** Straight, undeviating, as short as possible: *the direct road, route*; hence, **b** not turned aside, deflected, intercepted, or interfered with on the way: *a direct hit*; *the direct rays of the sun*; **c** (geneal.) lineal, traced continuously from father to son: *direct descent, descendant*; **d** (fig.) immediate, without intermediate agent: *direct influence*; *direct tax*; *direct action*, that taken by a large group of workmen, by means of an immediate strike &c., without reference to ordinary trade union methods or parliamentary action &c.; **e** (in contrasting) exact, diametrical: *the direct opposite.* **2.** (fig.) Straightforward, unhesitating, going straight to the point: *a direct question.* **3.** (gram., of speech) In the words actually used by the speaker.

direct (III.), adv., fr. prec. In a straight line; without interrupting journey; not going round about: *to go direct to London*; *the train goes there direct.*

direction, n. [1. dirékshun; 2. dirékʃən], fr. Lat. *dīrectiōn-(em)*, 'a making straight, an aiming, guiding'. **direct (I.)** & **-ion. 1.** The course taken by a moving object; path along which movement proceeds; point towards which movement or progress tends, towards which one turns, looks &c.: *in the direction of London*; *from all directions*; (also fig.) *reforms in many directions.* **2. a** Management, control, guidance: *to work under the direction of another*; **b** body of persons who control, manage; board of directors, directorate. **3. a** An order, expression of wishes; instruction: *to give directions*; **b** information, description, instruction, how something should be done, used &c.: *full directions inside*, (of machine, medicine &c.). **4.** Address (on a letter &c.).

direction finder, n. Wireless aerial so constructed as to indicate direction from which wireless signals are coming.

directive, adj. [1. diréktiv; 2. diréktiv]. **direct (I.)** & **-ive.** Intended, tending, to direct; having the function of directing.

directly, adv. [1. diréktli; 2. diréktli]. **direct (II.)** & **-ly. 1.** (of space) In a direct manner, straight, undeviatingly: *to look directly at, go directly towards, a person.* **2.** (of manner) Immediately, without intervening conditions, circumstances: *to be directly affected.* **3.** (of time) **a** Immediately, now, at once; **b** in a short time, very soon. **4.** (colloq., as conj.) As soon as: *I will come directly I have finished.*

directness, n. [1. diréktnes; 2. diréktnis]. **direct (II.)** & **-ness.** The quality of being direct (in various senses); esp. **a** of going straight to the point; downrightness: *directness of manner, speech*; **b** act of concentrating the glance straight at: *directness of look*; **c** quality of being unimpeded, of coming straight from the source: *directness of information.*

directoire, n. & adj. [1. diréktwar; 2. diréktwā], fr. Lat. *dīrectōrium.* See **directory. a** n. French Revolutionary Government of 1795–99; **b** adj., belonging to this period; specif., applied to furniture and style of decoration of the period.

director, n. [1. diréktor; 2. diréktə]. **direct (I.)** & **-or.** One who, that which, directs; specif. **a** one who guides, instructs, governs, controls: *a director of studies*; **b** a member of the board of management of a commercial company.

directorate, n. [1. diréktorat; 2. diréktərit]. See prec. & **-ate. a** The office of director; **b** board of directors of a commercial company &c.

directorship, n. [1. diréktorship; 2. diréktəʃip]. **director** & **-ship. a** The office of director; **b** period of tenure of this office.

directory (I.), adj. [1. diréktori; 2. diréktəri]. **direct (I.)** & **-ory.** Guiding, giving instructions, advising.

directory (II.), n., fr. prec. **1.** That which directs; specif. **a** a book of instructions, a book of devotions; **b** a book containing lists of names and addresses of persons arranged alphabetically, or according to some other specific plan, of inhabitants of a county, town &c.; list of telephone subscribers,

members of trades &c., and their addresses. **2.** (hist.) French Revolutionary Government of 1795–99, the Directory, in French, *Directoire.*
directress, adj. [1. diréktres; 2. diréktris]. **director** & **-ess**. Fem. of director.
directrix, n. [1. diréktriks; 2. diréktriks]. Lat. See **director** & **-trix**. **1.** Directress. **2.** (geom.) A fixed line used as a guide in describing a circle or curved surface.
direful, adj. [1. dīrfool; 2. dáiəful]. **dire** & **-ful**. (poet. or rhet.) Terrible, dreadful; causing terror, fraught with, inspiring, horror: *direful tidings.*
direfully, adv. Prec. & **-ly**. In a direful manner.
direly, adv. [1. dírli; 2. dáiəli]. **dire** & **-ly**. Direfully.
dirge, n. [1. dĕrj; 2. dǝ̄dž], fr. Lat. *dīrige* (imperat. of *dīrigere*, see **direct** (I.)), the first word, fr. Ps. v. 8, in the Latin Office for the Burial of the Dead. A song of lament, sung in memory of, or at the burial of, the dead; a lament.
dirhem, n. [1. dĕrhém; 2. diəhém]. Arab.; corrupt. of Gk. *drakhmé*. See **drachma**. **1.** Moslem measure of troy weight, about 45 grains. **2.** Small silver coin, current in Morocco, value about 4d.
dirigible, adj. & n. [1. dírijibl; 2. díridžibl], fr. Lat. *dīrigere*, 'to put into a straight line; to send in a straight line, aim; to arrange, guide'. See **direct** (I.) & **-ible**. **1.** adj. (esp. of balloons) Capable of being steered. **2.** n. A dirigible balloon, one of the ancestors of the modern airship.
diriment, adj. [1. díriment; 2. dírimənt], fr. Lat. *dirimere*, 'to separate, part, divide; to interrupt, disturb; destroy, frustrate', fr. **dis-** & *emere*, orig. 'to take, receive; to buy; to win over, gain'. See **exempt** & **-ent**. Rendering null and void; esp. *diriment impediment*, one that invalidates a marriage from the start.
dirk (I.), n. [1. dĕrk; 2. dǝ̄k]. 17th cent. *dork*, prob. same as Swed. *dolk*, Germ. *dolch*, 'short sword, dagger'. Origin doubtful. A short dagger; esp. that formerly used by Scottish Highlanders; now worn as part of full Highland dress; also one worn as a side-arm by midshipmen in the Royal Navy.
dirk (II.), vb. trans., fr. prec. To stab with a dirk.
dirt, n. [1. dĕrt; 2. dǝ̄t]. M.E. *drit*, 'dirt, excrement', fr. O.N. *dritr*, M. Du. *drijt*. Etymol. doubtful; perh. cogn. w. Lat. *foria*, 'diarrhoea'; Mod. Bulg. *driskati*, Czech. *dřistati*, 'excrement'; Aryan base **dhṛ-i-*, **dhor-i-*, perh. extended fr. the base **dho-*, **dhe-*, 'to flow'. See **dew**. **1. a** Filth, unclean matter of any kind, filthy, wet mud: *hands covered with dirt; to roll in the dirt;* Phr. (fig.) *to eat dirt*, submit to insults &c.; **b** dust, accumulated fine particles of matter, rubbish in neglected rooms, houses &c.; **c** (fig.) anything valueless; Phrs. *as cheap as dirt; to treat a person like dirt.* **2.** Earth, ground, soil. Phr. *yellow dirt*, gold. **3.** Uncleanliness, condition of filth and squalor: *to live in a state of dirt.* **4.** (fig.) Abusive, insulting, or impure and obscene thought and expression.
dirt-bed, n. (geol.) A layer of mould containing the remains of plants, found in the Purbeck limestone.
dirt-cheap, adj. (colloq.) Cheap as dirt, very cheap.
dirtily, adv. [1. dĕrtili; 2. dǝ̄tili]. **dirty** (I.) & **-ly**. In a dirty manner.
dirtiness, n. [1. dĕrtines; 2. dǝ̄tinis]. **dirty** (I.) & **-ness**. The quality of being dirty.
dirt-track, n. A track, made of rolled earth or cinders, on which motor-cyclists race, hence *dirt-track racing.*
dirty (I.), adj. [1. dĕrti; 2. dǝ̄ti]. **dirt** & **-y**. **1. a** Smeared, covered, with dirt; foul, soiled; capable of soiling: *a dirty face, hands; a dirty room;* **b** specif., *a dirty wound*, one not surgically clean, containing impure matter; septic. **2.** (of weather) Rough, stormy, rainy, squally. **3.** (fig.) **a** Base, sordid, ungenerous, mean: *dirty conduct;* Phr. (colloq.) *to do the dirty on*, to treat shabbily; **b** unclean, impure, obscene: *a dirty mind, book* &c.
dirty (II.), vb. trans., fr. prec. To make dirty, soil.
dis-, pref., fr. Lat. pref. *dis-*, expressing separation, parting, dividing; also negation, difference. The pref. becomes *dī-* (see **di-** (I.)), **dif-**, before certain sounds; cogn. w. O.E. *te-*, O.S. *te-*, *ti-*, O.H.G. *ze-*, *zi-*, 'apart, asunder', Aryan **dis-*, 'apart, asunder, separate', cogn. w. Aryan base **dwi-s-*, 'two'; cp. Goth. *twis*, 'apart'; O.H.G. *zwis-ki*, 'double', *in zwiskēn*, 'between'. See **bis, two, double**. Expressing: **1.** Separation, severing, sundering. **2.** Negation, the reverse of the uncompounded form. **3.** Deprivation, taking away, removal.
disability, n. [1. disabíliti; 2. disəbíliti], fr. obs. adj. *disable*, fr. **dis-** & **able**. See **-ity**. **1. a** The state of being disabled; **b** the state of being legally unqualified to perform an action, incapacity. **2.** Something that disables; a disqualification, disadvantage.
disable, vb. trans. [1. disábl; 2. diséibl]. **dis-** & **able**. **1.** To make unfit (physically), incapacitate, deprive of power of action; to injure, cripple. **2.** (legal) To disqualify; make or pronounce incapable.
disablement, n. [1. disáblment; 2. diséiblmənt]. See prec. & **-ment**. **a** The act of disabling; **b** disability; esp. a physical disability.
disabuse, vb. trans. [1. disabúz; 2. disəbjúz]. **dis-** & **abuse**. To reveal the truth to, undeceive, free from error or illusion.
disaccord (I.), n. [1. disakórd; 2. disəkɔ́d]. **dis-** & **accord** (II.). Want of agreement; incongruity.
disaccord (II.), vb. intrans. **dis-** & **accord** (I.). To disagree; be inharmonious.
disaccustom, vb. trans. [1. disakústom; 2. disəkástəm]. **dis-** & **accustom**. To make unaccustomed, to wean from a habit.
disadvantage, n. [1. disadváhntij; 2. disədvántidž]. **dis-** & **advantage**. An unfavourable circumstance or condition, something that hinders progress, success; a drawback: *it is no disadvantage to be small; at a disadvantage*, in an inferior position for doing something.
disadvantageous, adj. [1. disadvantájus; 2. disædvæntéidžəs]. **dis-** & **advantageous**. Causing disadvantage, prejudicial, unfavourable.
disadvantageously, adv. Prec. & **-ly**. In a disadvantageous manner.
disaffected, adj. [1. disafékted; 2. disəféktid]. P.P. of obs. or rare vb. *disaffect*. **dis-** & **affect**. Discontented, estranged, unfriendly, disloyal.
disaffection, n. [1. disafékshun; 2. disəfékʃən]. See prec. & **-ion**. The state of being disaffected; estrangement, disloyalty, withdrawal of allegiance.
disaffirm, vb. trans. [1. disafĕrm; 2. disəfǝ́m]. See **dis-** & **affirm**. (legal) To set aside, reverse: *to disaffirm the decision of a lower court.*
disaffirmation, n. [1. disafermáshun; 2. disæfəméiʃən]. See prec. & **-ation**. The act of disaffirming.
disafforest, vb. trans. [1. disafórest; 2. disəfɔ́rist], fr. Med. Lat. *disafforestāre*. **dis-** & **afforest**. **a** To reduce from the status of a forest to that of ordinary land; **b** to cut down forest, deprive an area of forest.
disafforestation, n. [1. disaforestáshun; 2. disəfɔristéiʃən]. Prec. & **-ation**. The act or process of disafforesting; state of being disafforested.
disagree, vb. intrans. [1. disagré; 2. disəgrí]. **dis-** & **agree**. **1.** To be different, not to agree, to have points of difference: *the two reports of the affair disagree.* **2.** *Disagree with*: **a** To differ, hold different opinions; **b** to quarrel, to be at variance; also absol., *whenever we meet, we disagree.* **3.** *Disagree with*, (of physical effects) to have a bad effect upon the health, be injurious, not to suit: *something has disagreed with me; pork always disagrees with me;* also absol., *violent exercise after a meal is apt to disagree.*
disagreeable, adj. [1. disagréabl; 2. disəgríəbl]. **dis-** & **agreeable**. **a** (of persons, character &c.) Bad tempered, cross, not affable or kind; difficult to get on with; **b** (of things, events &c.) not giving pleasure, distasteful, unpleasant, repugnant.
disagreeableness, n. Prec. & **-ness**. The quality of being disagreeable.
disagreeably, adv. See prec. & **-ly**. In a disagreeable manner.
disagreement, n. [1. disagrément; 2. disəgrímənt]. **disagree** & **-ment**. **1. a** The act of disagreeing; **b** want of agreement; difference of opinion. **2.** Specific difference of opinion, dispute, quarrel.
disallow, vb. trans. [1. disalóu; 2. disəláu], fr. O. Fr. *desalouer*. **dis-** & **allow**. To refuse to permit or sanction; to reject as unfounded or illegal: *to disallow a claim* &c.
disannul, vb. trans. [1. disanúl; 2. disənál]. **dis-** & **annul**. To cancel, do away with, annul completely.
disappear, vb. intrans. [1. disapér; 2. disəpíə]. **dis-** & **appear**. **1.** To pass out of sight, vanish. **2.** To pass out of existence, become extinct, be lost.
disappearance, n. [1. disapérans; 2. disəpíərəns]. **dis-** & **appearance**. **a** State of being invisible or non-existent; **b** process of passing out of sight or existence.
disappoint, vb. trans. [1. disapóint; 2. disəpɔ́int], fr. Fr. *désappointer*. **dis-** & **appoint**. **1.** (of effect on persons) **a** To fail to realize hopes or expectations of; fail to perform promises: *his behaviour has disappointed me; to be disappointed in a person or thing;* **b** to baffle, balk, deprive of: *to be disappointed of one's prize, purpose.* **2.** (of effect on nonmaterial things) To thwart, frustrate, upset: *to disappoint a person's plans, designs* &c.
disappointed, adj. [1. disapóinted; 2. disəpɔ́intid], fr. P.P. of prec. Cheated of one's expectations, hopes &c.; balked in one's plans &c.
disappointedly, adv. Prec. & **-ly**. In a disappointed manner.
disappointing, adj. [1. disapóinting; 2. disəpɔ́intiŋ]. Pres. Part. of **disappoint**. Causing disappointment, not fulfilling hopes or expectations.
disappointingly, adv. Prec. & **-ly**. In a disappointing manner.
disappointment, n. [1. disapóintment; 2. disəpɔ́intmənt]. **disappoint** & **-ment**. **1.** State of being disappointed. **2.** That which causes disappointment, which disappoints.
disapprobation, n. [1. disaprōbáshun; 2. disæproubéiʃən]. **dis-** & **approbation**. The act of disapproving; disapproval, unfavourable opinion.
disapprobative, adj. [1. disaprṓbātiv; 2. disəpróubeitiv]. See prec. & **-ive**. Expressing, characterized by, disapproval.
disapprobatory, adj. [1. disaprṓbatori; 2. disəpróubətəri]. See **dis-** & **approbation** & **-ory**. Disapprobative.
disapproval, n. [1. disaprōōvl; 2. disəprúvl]. **dis-** & **approval**. The act of disapproving; unfavourable opinion.
disapprove, vb. trans. & intrans. [1. disaprōōv; 2. disəprúv]. **dis-** & **approve**. **1.** trans. To fail to approve, form unfavourable judgement upon: *I can but disapprove your action.* **2.** intrans. **a** To hold unfavourable opinions, be in hostile state of mind: *to disapprove of a person, an action;* **b** to express an unfavourable opinion: *I have heard everything, and entirely disapprove.*
disapprovingly, adv. [1. disaprōōvingli; 2. disəprúviŋli]. Pres. Part. of prec. & **-ly**. In a manner expressing disapproval.
disarm, vb. trans. & intrans. [1. disárm; 2. disám]. **dis-** & **arm** (III.). **A.** trans.

1. To remove weapons from, to deprive of weapons, or of means of attack. 2. (fig.) To conciliate, to allay suspicions of, appease anger or hostility, to render friendly by one's conduct, words &c.: *to disarm criticism*; *to be disarmed by a person's frankness and candour*. **B.** intrans. (of nations) To reduce or abolish military or naval equipment, reduce means of attack and defence.

disarmament, n. [1. disármament; 2. disáməmənt]. **dis-** & **armament**. **a** The action of reducing the scale of naval or military equipment of a nation, of diminishing its striking power; **b** act of removing offensive and defensive equipment from a ship &c.; **c** the state of being disarmed.

disarrange, vb. trans. [1. disaránj; 2. disəréindž]. **dis-** & **arrange**. To put out of order, put into confusion, disturb, upset arrangement of: *to disarrange a person's plans, hair, furniture* &c.

disarrangement, n. [1. disaránjment; 2. disəréindžmənt]. See prec. & **-ment**. The act of disarranging; state of being disarranged, disorder.

disarray (I.), vb. trans. [1. disará; 2. disəréi]. **dis-** & **array**. **a** To put into disorder, disturb, throw into confusion; **b** (archaic, poet.) to remove clothes of, undress.

disarray (II.), n., fr. prec. The state of being disarrayed; disorder, confusion.

disarticulate, vb. trans. [1. disartíkūlāt; 2. disātíkjuleit]. **dis-** & **articulate**. To take to pieces, separate at the joints.

disarticulation, n. [1. disartikūláshun; 2. disātikjuléiʃən]. Prec. & **-ation**. The act of disarticulating; state of being disarticulated.

disaster, n. [1. dizáhster; 2. dizástə]. M.E., fr. O. Fr. *désastre*, lit. 'hostile star, fate'; hence 'calamity', fr. **dis-** & Lat. *astrum*, fr. Gk. *ástron*, 'a star'. See **astral**. **a** Calamity, misfortune; **b** event causing severe distress or ruin; a blow, stroke of ill-fortune.

disastrous, adj. [1. dizáhstrus; 2. dizástrəs]. See prec. & **-ous**. Causing, fraught with, disaster, calamitous.

disastrously, adv. Prec. & **-ly**. In a disastrous manner.

disavow, vb. trans. [1. disavóu; 2. disəváu], fr. Fr. *désavouer*. **dis-** & **avow**. To reject, deny belief in or approval of, repudiate.

disavowal, n. [1. disavóual; 2. disəváuəl]. **dis-** & **avowal**. Refusal to acknowledge, repudiation.

disband, vb. trans. & intrans. [1. disbǽnd; 2. disbǽnd]. **dis-** & **band (I.)**. **a** trans. To bring to an end as an organized force, to break up (troops &c.); **b** intrans., (of troops &c.) to scatter, disperse.

disbar, vb. trans. [1. disbár; 2. disbá]. **dis-** & **bar (I.)**. To dismiss, expel from the bar, to deprive of status of barrister, by authority of the Benchers of an Inn of Court.

disbarment, n. [1. disbárment; 2. disbámənt]. See prec. & **-ment**. The act of disbarring; state of being disbarred.

disbelief, n. [1. disbeléf; 2. disbilíf]. **dis-** & **belief**. Absence of belief.

disbelieve, vb. trans. & intrans. [1. disbelév; 2. disbilív]. **dis-** & **believe**. 1. trans. **a** To be unable or unwilling to believe a statement, or doctrine; to hold that a statement or doctrine is untrue, to withhold credence from: *to disbelieve a story*; **b** to place no reliance in a person in respect of what he says, to refuse to believe him: *to disbelieve a witness*. 2. intrans. To have no belief in, refuse to place credit in: *to disbelieve in a person, in what he says*.

disbeliever, n. [1. disbeléver; 2. disbilívə]. Prec. & **-er**. One who disbelieves; specif., in religious doctrines.

disbench, vb. trans. [1. disbénch; 2. disbéntʃ]. **dis-** & **bench**. To deprive of the privilege of a *Bencher*, i.e. of membership of an Inn of Court.

disbranch, vb. trans. [1. disbráhnch; 2. disbrántʃ]. **dis-** & **branch**. To remove branches from.

disbud, vb. trans. [1. disbúd; 2. disbád]. **dis-** & **bud**. To remove buds from, in order to increase the growth of the buds and shoots left.

disburden, vb. trans. [1. disbérdn; 2. disbádn]. **dis-** & **burden**. To relieve of a load, esp. (fig.) *to disburden one's mind (of)*.

disburse, vb. trans. & intrans. [1. disbérs; 2. disbás], fr. O. Fr. *desbourser*. **dis-** & **bourse**. **a** trans. To give, pay out, spend (money); **b** intrans., to make payments of money.

disbursement, n. [1. disbérsment; 2. disbásmənt]. See prec. & **-ment**. Expenditure, payment of money.

disc. See **disk**.

discalceate, discalceated, discalced, adj. [1. diskálsiāt(ed), diskálst; 2. diskǽlsieit(id), diskǽlst], fr. Lat. *discalceātus*, 'barefooted', fr. **dis-** & P.P. type of *calceāre*, 'to furnish with shoes', fr. *calceus*, 'a shoe'. See **calceolaria**. (of members of religious orders) Unshod, barefooted, or wearing sandals.

discard (I.), vb. trans. [1. diskárd; 2. diskád]. **dis-** & **card (II.)**. (lit.) 1. To throw away cards as valueless in the game. Hence 2, to give up as being of no more use, abandon, throw aside; reject something one has formerly held, someone for whom one had affection &c.

discard (II.), n. Usually [1. dískard; 2. dískād], fr. prec. **a** The act of discarding at cards; **b** card so thrown out.

discern, vb. trans. [1. disérn; 2. disə́n], fr. Fr. *discerner*, fr. Lat. *discernere*, 'to divide, separate; to distinguish, discern; to determine, decide', fr. **dis-** & *cernere*, 'to sift; to distinguish, perceive; to understand; to judge, decide'. See **certain** & **concern**. **a** To perceive, make out clearly, distinguish, by means of the senses, esp. by the sight: *to discern a distant object*; **b** to distinguish with the mind, to make out: *to discern no difference*; *to discern the meaning of*.

discernible, adj. [1. disérnibl; 2. disə́nibl]. See prec. & **-ible**. That can be discerned.

discernibly, adv. Prec. & **-ly**. In a discernible manner, perceptibly.

discerning, adj. [1. disérning; 2. disə́niŋ]. Pres. Part. of **discern**. Having keen perception, discriminating; gifted with insight.

discernment, n. [1. disérnment; 2. disə́nmənt]. See **discern** & **-ment**. Keenness of mental perception, faculty of discrimination; insight, sagacity; penetration: *discernment of character*.

discerptibility, n. [1. disérptibíliti; 2. disə́ptibíliti]. See next word & **-ity**. (rare) The quality of being discerptible.

discerptible, adj. [1. disérptibl; 2. disə́ptibl], fr. Lat. *discerpt-(um)*, P.P. type of *discerpere*, 'to pluck in pieces; to scatter, disperse', fr. **dis-** & *carpere*, 'to pluck, gather; to graze on'; fig. 'to snatch, gather; to slander; to cut to pieces, divide; to pass over, sail through'. See **carpel**. (rare) That can be severed, pulled to pieces.

discerption, n. [1. disérpshun; 2. disə́pʃən], fr. Lat. *discerptiōn-(em)*, 'a tearing in pieces'. See **discerptible** & **-ion**. (rare) The action of tearing to pieces, disunion; the state or process of being pulled apart.

discharge (I.), vb. trans. [1. dischárj; 2. distʃádž], fr. O. Fr. *descharger*. See **dis-** & **charge**. 1. To take, or send, out contents of; specif. **a** to fire (a gun &c.); **b** to remove electricity from (substance charged with it). 2. To give or send out, emit, eject: *a sewer discharges its contents*; *chimney discharges smoke* &c.; specif. **a** (of a ship) to unload, remove (cargo &c.); **b** (of a wound, abscess &c.) to emit matter; 3. **a** To dismiss, release, allow to depart from service, regular attendance &c.: (i.) in good sense, *to discharge a soldier, a patient from hospital, a prisoner* &c.; (ii.) in bad sense, *to discharge a servant for misconduct*; **b** to relieve from the order of a court: *discharged bankrupt*. 4. (fig.) **a** To perform, carry out (duty &c.); **b** to pay, make payment for (a debt &c.).

discharge (II.), n., fr. prec. 1. The process of discharging: *the discharge of a gun* &c. 2. The act of giving or sending out; **a** (of cargo), unloading; **b** (of an abscess &c.) emission of matter, that which is discharged from an abscess &c. 3. **a** Dismissal; release from duty, service &c.; **b** testimonial to character and capacity given to discharged person; **c** order of release from order of a court: *to get, apply for, one's discharge in bankruptcy*. 4. Performance, carrying out: *discharge of one's duties*.

discharger, n. [1. dischárjer; 2. distʃádžə]. **discharge (I.)** & **-er**. One who, that which, discharges; specif. (elect.) a contrivance for removing electricity from a substance that has been charged with it.

discharging-arch, n. [1. dischárjing árch; 2. distʃádžiŋ átʃ], fr. Pres. Part. of **discharge (I.)** & **arch**. (archit.) Arch built over the lintel of a door to relieve the weight of masonry above it.

disciple, n. [1. disípl; 2. disáipl], fr. O.E. *discipul*, fr. Lat. *discipulus*, 'a learner, pupil, an apprentice'; (eccles.) 'a follower of Christ', fr. **dis-cipere*, 'to take in mentally, to learn', fr. **dis-** & *capere*, 'to take, receive'. See under **captive** & **-ule**. **a** A follower, adherent, of any particular school or leader of religion, thought, learning, art &c. Specif. **b** an early follower of Christ; esp. one of the twelve Apostles.

discipleship, n. [1. disíplship; 2. disáiplʃip]. Prec. & **-ship**. The office or position of a disciple; period of being a disciple.

disciplinable, adj. [1. disiplínabl; 2. disipláinəbl]. **discipline (II.)** & **-able**. (rare) Capable of being brought under discipline.

disciplinal, adj. [1. disiplínal; 2. disipláinəl]. **discipline (I.)** & **-al**. Pertaining to discipline.

disciplinarian, n. [1. disiplinárian; 2. disiplinέəriən]. See next word & **-an**. One who maintains and enforces discipline.

disciplinary, adj. [1. disiplínari; 2. disipláinəri]. See next word & **-ary**. Pertaining to discipline; involving mental and moral training.

discipline (I.), n. [1. dísiplin; 2. dísiplin], fr. Lat. *disciplīna*, 'instruction, teaching; knowledge, science'. See **disciple** & **-ine**. 1. **a** Systematic training, exercise, development and control, of the mental, moral, and physical faculties: *school discipline*; *the discipline of hard work, of adversity*; **b** system of instruction and control, inculcating submission to established authority; obedience to command of superiors, self-control, orderly behaviour: *military discipline*; *people nowadays need not more liberty but more discipline*; *to enforce discipline*. 2. Result of disciplinary control and training: **a** command of the mental, moral, and physical faculties; **b** orderliness of behaviour, submission to properly constituted authority. 3. Particular mode of imparting discipline, training, control; **a** (intellectual) a branch of learning, methods of a given study; **b** (moral) punishment, chastisement; **c** (eccles.) penance, mortification.

discipline (II.), vb. trans., fr. prec. To provide discipline in any sense, to control, train mentally, morally, and physically.

discipular, adj. [1. disípūlar; 2. disípjulə]. See **disciple** & **-ar**. Pertaining to a disciple.

disclaim, vb. trans. & intrans. [1. disklám; 2. diskléim], fr. O. Fr. *desclamer*. See **dis-** & **claim**. 1. trans. **a** To give up claim to, renounce right in; **b** to repudiate, disavow (responsibility &c.) 2. intrans. (rare) To make a disclaimer.

disclaimer, n. [1. disklámer; 2. diskléimə]. Prec. & **-er**. (law) Denial, disavowal, repudiation, renunciation, as of a claim, title, interest &c.

disclose, vb. trans. [1. disklóz; 2. disklóuz], fr. O. Fr. *desclos-*, P.P. type of *desclore*, fr. **dis-** & Lat. *claus-(um)*, *claudere*, 'to shut'. See **close (I.)** & **(III.)**. (of material and non-material things) To reveal, bring to light, show, by removing something that covers or conceals: *to disclose a hidden treasure, a secret* &c.

disclosure, n. [1. disklṓzhur; 2. disklóužə]. See prec. & **-ure**. **a** The act of disclosing; **b** the state of being disclosed; **c** something that is disclosed, a revelation.

discobolus, n. [1. diskóbolus; 2. diskɔ́bələs]. Lat. *discobolus*, 'a quoit-thrower', fr. Gk. *diskobólos*, 'a quoit-thrower', fr. *dískos*, 'a quoit' (see **disk**), & *-bólos*, 'a throwing'; cp. *bolḗ*, 'the stroke of a missile', *bállein*, 'to throw'. See **ballistics**. (archaeol.) **a** A quoit-thrower; **b** Greek statue of a quoit-thrower.

discoid, adj. [1. dískoid; 2. dískɔid]. **disk** & **-oid**. Having the form of a disk.

discolo(u)ration, n. [1. diskùlurā́shun; 2. diskàləréiʃən]. See next word & **-ation**. The act or process of discolouring; state of being discoloured.

discolour, vb. trans. & intrans. [1. diskúlur; 2. diskálə], fr. O. Fr. *descolorer*, fr. **dis-** & Lat. *colōrāre*, 'to colour'. See **colour (II.)**. **1.** trans. To alter, spoil, or destroy, the colour of. **2.** intrans. To become discoloured, to be stained, tarnished.

discomfit, vb. trans. [1. diskúmfit; 2. diskámfit], fr. O. Fr. *desconfit*, 'defeated', fr. L. Lat. *disconfect-(us)*, fr. Lat. **dis-** & *confect-(um)*, P.P. type of *conficere*, 'to prepare, execute; to produce, effect; to wear out, consume'. See **confection**. **a** (archaic) To defeat, get the better of; **b** to upset the plans of, disconcert, put out of countenance.

discomfiture, n. [1. diskúmfichur; 2. diskámfitʃə]. Prec. & **-ure**. The act of discomfiting; state of being discomfited.

discomfort (I.), n. [1. diskúmfurt; 2. diskámfət], fr. O.E. *desconfort*. See **dis-** & **comfort**. Want of comfort (mental or physical); absence of ease and well-being; inconvenience, hardship.

discomfort (II.), vb. trans., fr. prec. (rare) To cause discomfort to.

discommode, vb. trans. [1. diskumṓd; 2. diskəmóud], fr. **dis-** & obs. *commode*, fr. Lat. *commodāre*, 'to make fit or suitable, to accommodate; to bestow, lend', fr. *commodus*, 'fit, perfect, proper, convenient'. See **commode**. To trouble, disturb, cause inconvenience to.

discommon, vb. trans. [1. diskómon; 2. diskɔ́mən]. **dis-** & **common**. **1.** To enclose common land, thus depriving it of its character; cause it to cease to be common land. **2. a** (Oxford and Cambridge Universities, archaic) To deprive (a tradesman) of the right to the custom of undergraduates; **b** to withdraw the right of commons.

discompose, vb. trans. [1. diskumpṓz; 2. diskəmpóuz]. **dis-** & **compose**. To disturb the calmness or self-possession of.

discomposedly, adv. [1. diskumpṓzedli; 2. diskəmpóuzidli]. P.P. of prec. & **-ly**. In a discomposed manner.

discomposingly, adv. [1. diskumpṓzingli; 2. diskəmpóuziŋli]. Pres. Part. of **discompose** & **-ly**. In a manner causing discomposure.

discomposure, n. [1. diskumpṓzhur; 2. diskəmpóužə]. **discompose** & **-ure**. Ruffled state of mind, absence of calmness and composure, embarrassment.

disconcert, vb. trans. [1. diskunsḗrt; 2. diskənsə́t]. See **dis-** & **concert (II.)**. **a** (action on persons) To upset balance and self-possession of, discompose, embarrass; **b** (of plans &c.) to disturb, upset, throw into confusion.

disconcertment, n. [1. diskunsḗrtment; 2. diskənsə́tmənt]. Prec. & **-ment**. State of being disconcerted.

disconnect, vb. trans. [1. diskunékt; 2. diskənékt]. **dis-** & **connect**. To sever connexion between (two things); to separate.

disconnected, adj. [1. diskunékted; 2. diskənéktid]. P.P. of prec. **a** (esp. of thought and its expression) Separated, having connexion severed, not properly related or co-ordinated; **b** (of events) unrelated by cause and effect, not dependent one on the other.

disconnectedly, adv. Prec. & **-ly**. In a disconnected manner: *to speak, think, disconnectedly*.

disconnectedness, n. See prec. & **-ness**. Quality of being disconnected.

disconnexion, less correctly **disconnection**, n. [1. diskunékshun; 2. diskənékʃən]. **disconnect** & **-ion**. **a** Act of disconnecting; state of being disconnected; **b** disconnectedness.

disconsolate, adj. [1. diskónsolat; 2. diskɔ́nsəlit], fr. Med. Lat. *disconsōlāt-us*, fr. **dis-** & Lat. *consōlāt-(um)*, P.P. type of *consōlāri*, 'to console, comfort; to alleviate, soothe'. See **console (I.)**. Without comfort or consolation, refusing to be consoled, forlorn, sad.

disconsolately, adv. Prec. & **-ly**. In a disconsolate manner.

discontent (I.), n. [1. diskuntént; 2. diskəntént]. **dis-** & **content (III.)**. Want of content; dissatisfaction.

discontent (II.), vb. trans., fr. prec. To make dissatisfied, to cause to lose pleasure in, fail to please: (chiefly in P.P. as adj.) *to be discontented with one's lot*.

discontentedly, adv. [1. diskunténtedli; 2. diskənténtidli]. P.P. of prec. & **-ly**. In a discontented, dissatisfied, manner.

discontentedness, n. [1. diskunténtednes; 2. diskənténtidnis]. See prec. & **-ness**. Quality, state, of being discontented.

discontentment, n. [1. diskunténtment; 2. diskənténtmənt]. See **discontent (II.)** & **-ment**. The state of being discontented.

discontiguous, adj. [1. diskuntígūus; 2. diskəntígjuəs]. **dis-** & **contiguous**. Not lying side by side, not touching, with space intervening.

discontinuance, n. [1. diskuntínūans; 2. diskəntínjuəns]. See **discontinue** & **-ance**. The act of discontinuing; state of being discontinued, interrupted; cessation.

discontinuation, n. [1. dìskuntinūā́shun; 2. dìskəntinjuéiʃən]. See next word & **-ation**. Discontinuance.

discontinue, vb. trans. & intrans. [1. dìskuntínū; 2. dìskəntínjū], fr. Fr. *discontinuer*, fr. Med. Lat. *discontinuāre*, fr. **dis-** & Lat. *continuāre*, 'to join together, unite; to continue; to perform successively'. See **continue**. **a** trans. To stop, cease, break off, interrupt, intermit: *to discontinue a habit, one's visits, dining at the club* &c.; **b** intrans., to cease, come to an end: *publication will discontinue*.

discontinuity, n. [1. dìskontinū́iti; 2. dìskəntinjū́iti]. **dis-** & **continuity**. The quality of being discontinuous; lack of continuity, absence of logical or other sequence: *discontinuity of ideas*.

discontinuous, adj. [1. diskuntínūus; 2. diskəntínjuəs]. **dis-** & **continuous**. **a** (of events or actions) Not continuous, suffering interruption; intermittent; **b** (of extension in space) not unbroken, separated by intervening spaces.

discontinuously, adv. Prec. & **-ly**. Not continuously.

discord (I.), n. [1. dískord; 2. dískɔ̄d], fr. O. Fr. *descord*; see next word. **1.** Absence of friendly feelings, want of spiritual harmony; disagreement; opposite of *concord*. **2.** (in mus.) Combination, or simultaneous sounding, of notes which do not harmonize.

discord (II.), vb. intrans. [1. diskórd; 2. diskɔ́d], fr. O. Fr. *descorder*, fr. Lat. *discordāre*, 'to be at variance, differ; to be out of harmony', fr. *discord-(em)*, *discors*, 'at variance, disagreeing; inharmonious; distinct, different', fr. **dis-** & *cord-(em)*, 'heart'. See **cordate**. (rare) **a** To disagree, be at variance *with*; **b** (mus.) to be out of harmony, not to harmonize, to jar on the ear.

discordance, n. [1. diskórdans; 2. diskɔ́dəns]. See prec. & **-ance**. Want of harmony, disagreement; **a** in feelings; **b** in musical notes.

discordant, adj. [1. diskórdant; 2. diskɔ́dənt]. **discord (II.)** & **-ant**. **a** (of feelings) Not in agreement, jarring; **b** (of sounds) not harmonious, unmusical, unpleasing.

discordantly, adv. Prec. & **-ly**. In a discordant manner.

discount (I.), n. [1. dískount; 2. dískaunt], fr. 16th cent. Fr. *descompte*. See next word. Reduction made from a whole; specif. **a** sum deducted from price of goods when payment is made at, or shortly after, time of purchase; any deduction from price; **b** sum deducted from bill of exchange &c., by a person advancing money on it, to cover amount of interest payable on it until it is due. Phr. *at a discount*, below par, having gone down in value; hence, easy to obtain.

discount (II.), vb. trans. [1. diskóunt; 2. diskáunt], fr. O. Fr. *descompter, desconter*, fr. Med. Lat. *discomputāre*, fr. **dis-** & Lat. *computāre*, 'to sum up, reckon up'. See **compute**. **a** To advance money, or to receive money in advance, in payment for (a bill of exchange &c. not yet due); **b** to depreciate, lessen value of, put a lower value on: *my gains were largely discounted by my subsequent losses*; **c** (of mental process) to believe only part of a statement, allow for exaggeration, inaccuracy &c.: *I discount a great deal of what I hear*.

discountable, adj. [1. diskóuntabl; 2. diskáuntəbl]. **discount (II.)** & **-able**. That can be discounted.

discountenance, vb. trans. [1. diskóuntenans; 2. diskáuntinəns]. **dis-** & **countenance (II.)**. To refrain from sanctioning, refuse one's support to, approval of; to disapprove, discourage, attempt to prevent.

discourage, vb. trans. [1. diskúrij; 2. diskáridž], fr. O. Fr. *descoragier*. See **dis-** & **courage**. **1.** To deprive of spirit and confidence, dishearten, instil hesitation or doubt into. **2. a** (effect on persons) To attempt to dissuade from doing something: *to discourage a person from doing*; **b** (effect on action) to attempt to prevent, thwart, to put obstacles in the way of: *to discourage all attempts at study*.

discouragement, n. [1. diskúrijment; 2. diskáridžmənt]. Prec. & **-ment**. **a** The act of discouraging; state of being discouraged; **b** something that discourages.

discouragingly, adv. [1. diskúrijingli; 2. diskáridžiŋli]. Pres. Part. of **discourage** & **-ly**. In a manner tending to discourage.

discourse (I.), n. [1. diskórs; 2. diskɔ̄s], fr. Fr. *discours*, fr. Lat. *discursus*, 'a running to and fro'; (in L. Lat.) 'a conversation, discourse', fr. **dis-** & *cursus*, 'a course, journey, passage; progress, direction'. See **course**. **a** A formal speech or lecture to an audience; **b** (more rarely) a written treatise; **c** informal talk, conversation.

discourse (II.), vb. intrans. [1. diskórs; 2. diskɔ̄s], fr. prec. Followed by *upon*, or absolute. **a** To hold forth, lecture, preach, make a formal speech, harangue; **b** (more rarely) to treat in writing; **c** to converse: *to discourse together*.

discourteous, adj. [1. diskórtius, diskḗrtius; 2. diskɔ̄tjəs, diskə́tjəs], fr. **dis-** & **courteous**. Ill-mannered, ill-bred, lacking in courtesy.

discourteously, adv. Prec. & **-ly**. In a discourteous manner.

discourtesy, n. [1. diskórtesi, diskḗrtesi; 2. diskɔ̄tisi, diskə́tisi]. See **dis-** & **courtesy**. **a** Quality of being discourteous; bad manners, ill-breeding, offensive behaviour, rudeness; **b** specific example of this, a discourteous action, speech &c.

discover, vb. trans. [1. diskúver; 2. diskávə], fr. O. Fr. *descovrir*, fr. Med. Lat. *discooperire*. See **dis-** & **cover (I.)**. **1.** (archaic) To reveal, make known, expose, to show (something unknown to others): *to discover a secret to one's friends*. **2. a** To find out (esp. something previously unknown): *to discover radium*; **b** to realize, become aware of, the existence of: *to discover a plot, a new country* &c.

discoverable, adj. [1. diskúverabl; 2. diskávərəbl]. Prec. & **-able**. Capable of being discovered.

discovert, adj. [1. diskúvert; 2. dɪskávət], fr. O. Fr. *discoverte*, P.P. of *descovrir*. See **discover**. (law) Without a husband (of spinster or widow).

discovery, n. [1. diskúveri; 2. dɪskávəri], fr. **discover**, on the anal. of **recovery**. **1.** **a** The act of discovering; **b** something that is discovered: *to make a discovery*, i.e. find (out) something. **2.** (rare) Act of revealing, of making (a secret &c.) known. **3.** (law) Disclosure of documents, facts, in answer to interrogatories, affording evidence affecting the rights of a party in an action claiming them.

discredit (I.), n. [1. diskrédit; 2. dɪskrédɪt]. **dis-** & **credit** (I.). **1.** Loss of credit or reputation: *to bring discredit on oneself*. **2.** Something harmful to reputation, something involving loss of credit and renown. **3.** Lack of confidence or belief in; doubt: *to throw discredit on*.

discredit (II.), vb. trans. **dis-** & **credit** (II.). **1.** To refuse credit to, credence, confidence in: *to discredit all that is said*. **2.** To bring into discredit, disrepute; damage reputation of, destroy confidence in: *his behaviour discredits him hopelessly with the public*.

discreditable, adj. [1. diskréditabl; 2. dɪskrédɪtəbl]. Prec. & **-able**. Damaging, bringing discredit upon; harmful to reputation; causing loss of confidence or belief: *discreditable conduct, behaviour* &c.

discreditably, adv. Prec. & **-ly**. In a discreditable manner.

discreet, adj. [1. diskrḗt; 2. dɪskrít], fr. O. Fr. *discret*, fr. L. Lat. *discrētus*, 'discerning', fr. *discrētiōn-(em)*, 'discernment'. See **discretion**. **a** (of persons) Judicious in action, speech, manner; avoiding even the appearance of evil; **b** (of action or speech) judicious, careful, prudent, circumspect.

discreetly, adv. Prec. & **-ly**. In a discreet manner.

discrepancy, n. [1. diskrépansi; 2. dɪskrépənsi]. See next word & **-cy**. **a** The quality of being discrepant; inconsistency; **b** specific instance of inconsistency; contradiction, inconsequence, in speech or action.

discrepant, adj. [1. diskrépant; 2. dɪskrépənt], fr. Fr., fr. Lat. *discrepant-(em)*, Pres. Part. of *discrepāre*, 'to differ in sound; to vary, differ', fr. **dis-** & *crepāre*, 'to rattle, clash; to chatter'. See **crepitate**. (of several things) Contradictory, inconsistent, at variance, not agreeing or fitting one with another.

discrepantly, adv. Prec. & **-ly**. In a discrepant manner.

discrete, adj. [1. diskrḗt; 2. dɪskrít], fr. Lat. *discrēt-(um)*, P.P. type of Lat. *discernere*, 'to divide, separate; to distinguish; to determine, decide'. See **discern** & cp. **discreet**. Separate, disunited, discontinuous, unrelated.

discreteness, n. Prec. & **-ness**. Quality of being discrete.

discretion, n. [1. diskréshun; 2. dɪskréʃən], fr. Lat. *discrētiōn-(em)*, 'separation, distinction; judgement, discernment', fr. *discrēt-(us)*. See **discrete** & **-ion**. **a** Discernment in estimating a situation, and shaping one's behaviour to suit it; prudence, carefulness, circumspection in word and deed; fear of taking risks; Phr. *discretion is the better part of valour*, unnecessary risks should not be run; **b** freedom of choice, ability to make decisions, liberty to act according to one's own judgement: *to use one's own discretion*; Phrs. *within one's discretion*, left to one's judgement; *to surrender at discretion*, unconditionally, without making terms; *years of discretion*, age at which one is capable of choosing one's own course of action.

discretionary, adj. [1. diskréshunari; 2. dɪskréʃənəri]. See prec. & **-ary**. Determined, regulated, only by one's discretion: *discretionary powers to act*.

discriminate, vb. intrans. & trans. [1. diskríminăt; 2. dɪskrímɪneit], fr. Lat. *discrimināt-(um)*, P.P. type of *discrimināre*, 'to divide, separate'; fig. 'to distinguish; to distribute, apportion', fr. *discrimen*, 'an intervening space, interval; distinction, difference; critical moment, turning-point, crisis; danger, hazard', fr. **dis-** & **crī-men*, fr. Aryan base **(s)krēi-*, **(s)krī-*, 'to divide, separate'. Cp. Gk. *krīnō*, 'to separate, distinguish' (see **critic**); Lat. *cernere*, 'to divide, separate; to recognize, perceive' (see **concern, certain**); Lat. *crībrum*, 'sieve' (see **cribriform, riddle** (III.)). The base **(s)k(e)rēi-* &c. is an expansion of the base **(s)ker-*, 'to cut'. See **cortex, carnal, scribe**. **A.** intrans. **1.** To perceive differences, distinguish (between): *to discriminate between A and B*. **2.** To distinguish by different treatment; make mark out, select, for special treatment; make distinctions, treat differently: *to discriminate in favour of A, against B*. **B.** trans. **1.** To distinguish carefully, mark differences in: *to discriminate A from B*. **2.** To serve as a distinction, distinguish: *his great stature discriminated him from his followers*.

discriminating, adj. [1. diskrímināting; 2. dɪskrímɪneitɪŋ]. Pres. Part. of prec. **1.** (of persons and faculties) Able to make, perceive, minute distinctions, able to discern subtle differences; perceptive: *discriminating taste*; *a discriminating palate*. **2.** Same as **differential**: *discriminating tariff* &c.

discrimination, n. [1. diskrìmināshun; 2. dɪskrìmɪnéiʃən]. **discriminate** & **-ion**. **1.** The act of discriminating. **2.** Capacity for discriminating; ability to perceive subtle distinctions; perception.

discriminative, adj. [1. diskríminativ; 2. dɪskrímɪnətɪv]. **discriminate** & **-ive**. **a** (of persons &c.) Observing, able to perceive, distinctions, differences; **b** (of objects, qualities &c.) distinguishing, serving to distinguish; characteristic.

discrown, vb. trans. [1. diskróun; 2. dɪskráun]. **dis-** & **crown**. To take the crown from, deprive of kingship.

discursive, adj. [1. diskérsiv; 2. dɪskə́sɪv], fr. Lat. *discurs-(um)*, P.P. type of *discurrere*, 'to run to and fro, run about; to traverse, hasten through, to discourse of, speak at length on', fr. **dis-** & *currere*, 'to move quickly; to run, hasten, fly'. See **course** & **current** & **-ive**. (of persons and modes of expression) Dealing with wide range of subjects and ideas, rambling in various directions, wandering from one point to another.

discursively, adv. Prec. & **-ly**. In a discursive manner.

discursiveness, n. See prec. & **-ness**. The quality of being discursive.

discus, n. [1. dískus; 2. dɪ́skəs]. Lat. fr. Gk. *diskos*, 'quoit'. See **disk**. The quoit, of stone or metal, thrown in ancient Greek athletics, cp. *discobolus*, and revived as one of the contests in modern Olympic games.

discuss, vb. trans. [1. diskús; 2. dɪskás], fr. Lat. *discuss-(um)*, P.P. type of *discutere*, 'to shatter, dash to pieces; to scatter, disperse, dissipate'; fig. 'to dispel, disperse, frustrate', fr. **dis-** & *quatere*, 'to shake, agitate; to wield, brandish; to beat, strike, shake, shatter'; fig. 'to agitate, excite'. See **quash**. **1.** To debate, examine (a subject, problem &c.) critically, from various points of view, considering pros and cons; to elucidate, separate and appraise the various sides or aspects of a question in their relations and bearings; either **a** by disputation, and argument, between several persons in conversation or public debate; or **b** in written treatise or lecture. **2.** (journalistic use) To eat or drink with appreciation: *discuss a roast duck, bottle of wine* &c.

discussible, adj. [1. diskúsibl; 2. dɪskásɪbl]. Prec. & **-ible**. Capable of being discussed.

discussion, n. [1. diskúshun; 2. dɪskáʃən], fr. Lat. *discussiōn-(em)*, 'a shaking; examination, discussion'. See **discuss** & **-ion**. **a** The act or process of discussing; state of being discussed: *a question under discussion*; **b** debate on, critical examination of, a problem &c.

disdain (I.), vb. trans. [1. disdā́n; 2. dɪsdéin], fr. O. Fr. *desdeigner*, fr. Lat. *dēdignāre*, 'to scorn, refuse, reject', fr. **de-** & *dignus*, 'suitable, fitting, worthy'. See **deign, dignity**. **a** (of persons and things) To look down upon, treat with contempt, scorn: *to disdain flattery and flatterers*; **b** to be too proud to do something, to consider it beneath one's dignity: *to disdain to notice an insult*.

disdain (II.), n., fr. prec. **a** Feeling of scorn, contempt; attitude of personal superiority to a person, thing, or action; **b** expression of the feelings in manner, looks &c.; hauteur, lofty, contemptuous aloofness.

disdainful, adj. [1. disdā́nfool; 2. dɪsdéinfəl]. Prec. & **-ful**. (of persons, state of mind and expression of this) Haughty, scornful, contemptuous.

disdainfully, adv. Prec. & **-ly**. In a disdainful manner.

disease, n. [1. dizḗz; 2. dɪzíz]. O. Fr. *desaise*. See **dis-** & **ease** (I.). **1.** Abnormal condition constituting a deviation from a sound state of health, characterized by disturbance, derangement, or impairment of functions; **a** in the human body or mind; **b** in animals and plants; **c** (fig.) in social or other institutions; contrasted with *health*. **2.** A specific form of disturbance or derangement of physical, mental, social, functions, which exhibits characteristic symptoms; often, in the case of physical ailments, accompanied by the presence of specific parasitic organisms in the blood or tissues.

diseased, adj. [1. dizḗzd; 2. dɪzízd]. Prec. & **-ed**. Suffering from disease; impaired, stunted, blasted, by disease.

disembark, vb. intrans. & trans. [1. dìsembárk; 2. dìsɪmbák], fr. Fr. *désembarquer*. See **dis-** & **embark**. **a** intrans. To land, go ashore from vessel; **b** trans., to put (persons and goods) ashore from a vessel.

disembarkation, n. [1. dìsembarkā́shun; 2. dìsɪmbàkéiʃən]. Prec. & **-ation**. **a** Act of landing; **b** process of being landed, from a vessel.

disembarrass, vb. trans. [1. dìsembáras; 2. dìsɪmbǽrəs]. **dis-** & **embarrass**. To rid, free, oneself or others from a cause, or source, of annoyance, hindrance, trouble, burden.

disembarrassment, n. [1. dìsembárasment; 2. dìsɪmbǽrəsmənt]. Prec. & **-ment**. The act or process of disembarrassing; state of being disembarrassed.

disembodiment, n. [1. dìsembódiment; 2. dìsɪmbɔ́dɪmənt]. Next word & **-ment**. The act or process of disembodying; state of being disembodied.

disembody, vb. trans. [1. dìsembódi; 2. dìsɪmbɔ́di]. **dis-** & **embody**. **1.** To separate from the body; to set free from concrete form: *a disembodied spirit*. **2.** To disband, break up (body of troops).

disembogue, vb. trans. & intrans. [1. dìsembṓg; 2. dìsɪmbóug], fr. Span. *desembocar*, fr. **dis-** & *embocar*, 'to enter, put into, the mouth', fr. *en-*, 'in' (see **in-**), & *boca*, 'mouth', fr. Low Lat. *bucca*, 'mouth', fr. Lat. *bucca*, 'cheek'. See **buccal**. (of a river) **1.** trans. To discharge (its waters) at its mouth. **2.** intrans. To pour, empty itself into sea, lake &c.

disembosom, vb. trans. & refl. [1. dìsembóozm; 2. dìsɪmbúzəm]. **dis-** & **embosom**. **a** trans. To reveal, make known; **b** (reflex.) to unburden (oneself) of a secret.

disembowel, vb. trans. [1. dìsembóuel; 2. dìsɪmbáuɪl]. **dis-** & **embowel**. To remove the entrails of; to eviscerate, gut.

disembroil, vb. trans. [1. dìsembróil; 2. dìsɪmbrɔ́il]. **dis-** & **embroil**. To free from embroilment, disentangle.

disenchant, vb. trans. [1. dìsencháhnt; 2. dìsɪntʃánt], fr. O. Fr. *desenchanter*. See **dis-** & **enchant**. To set free from a spell; to disillusion, dispel glamour from.

disenchantment, n. [1. dìsencháhntment; 2. dìsɪntʃántmənt]. Prec. & **-ment**. The act of disenchanting, state of being disenchanted; disillusionment.

disencumber, vb. trans. [1. dìsenkúmber; 2. dìsinkámbə]. **dis-** & **encumber.** To free from a burden, from something that hinders.

disendow, vb. trans. [1. dìsendóu; 2. dìsindáu]. **dis-** & **endow.** To deprive of endowments; esp. to deprive a Church or other institution of its endowments and funds.

disendowment, n. [1. dìsendóument; 2. dìsindáumənt]. Prec. & **-ment.** **a** The act of disendowing; **b** state of being disendowed.

disenfranchise, vb. trans. [1. dìsenfránchīz; 2. dìsinfrǽntʃaiz]. **dis-** & **enfranchise.** To disfranchise.

disengage, vb. trans. [1. dìsengáj; 2. dìsingéidž]. **dis-** & **engage.** To unfasten, set free, release.

disengaged, adj. [1. dìsengájd; 2. dìsingéidžd]. P.P. of prec. (esp. of persons) At liberty, to receive visitors &c.

disengagement, n. [1. dìsengájment; 2. dìsingéidžmənt]. **disengage** & **-ment.** **a** Act of disengaging; **b** state of being disengaged.

disentail, vb. trans. [1. dìsentál; 2. dìsintéil]. **dis-** & **entail.** To cut off the entail of (property &c.).

disentangle, vb. trans. & intrans. [1. dìsentánggl; 2. dìsintǽŋgl]. **dis-** & **entangle.** **1.** trans. **a** To undo, unravel, untwist, extricate from confusion, set free; **b** (fig.) to free from confusion, perplexity, complications, set in order. **2.** intrans. (lit. and fig.) To become clear of entanglement, untwist.

disentanglement, n. [1. dìsentángglment; 2. dìsintǽŋglmənt]. Prec. & **-ment.** The act of disentangling, state of being disentangled.

disenthral(l), vb. trans. [1. dìsenthráwl; 2. dìsinþrɔ́l]. **dis-** & **enthral.** To set at liberty, free from slavery.

disenthralment, n. [1. dìsenthráwlment; 2. dìsinþrɔ́lmənt]. Prec. & **-ment.** Release from slavery.

disentomb, vb. trans. [1. dìsentóom; 2. dìsintúm]. **dis-** & **entomb.** To remove from a tomb, disinter.

disestablish, vb. trans. [1. dìsestáblish; 2. dìsistǽbliʃ]. **dis-** & **establish.** **a** To break up, upset an established state of things, displace a person from an established position; **b** specif., to alter constitutional position of an institution, esp. of a national Church, by abolishing its connexion with the State.

disestablishment, n. [1. dìsestáblishment; 2. dìsistǽbliʃmənt]. Prec. & **-ment.** The act or process of disestablishing; state of being disestablished; specif., *disestablishment of the Church.*

disfavour (I.), n. [1. disfávor; 2. disféivə]. **dis-** & **favour** (I.). **a** Dislike, disapproval: *to regard a person with disfavour*; **b** state of being out of favour, of being in disgrace, under a cloud: *to fall into disfavour.*

disfavour (II.), vb. trans. **dis-** & **favour** (II.) To regard with disapproval, consider unfavourably.

disfiguration, n. [1. disfigūráshun; 2. disfigjəréiʃən]. See next word & **-ation.** **a** The act of disfiguring; state of being disfigured; **b** something that disfigures, a blemish. See *disfigurement*, which is more used.

disfigure, vb. trans. [1. disfígur; 2. disfígə], fr. O. Fr. *desfigurer*, fr. **dis-** & Lat. *figūrāre*, 'to form, fashion; to imagine; to pronounce, utter'. See **figure.** To spoil the shape or appearance of; to mar, cau e a blemish in; to render unsightly; to detract from excellence or value of.

disfigured, adj. [1. disfígurd; 2. disfígəd], fr. P.P. of prec. **a** Rendered ugly, having lost comeliness, symmetry; destroyed, marred: *a face much disfigured by scars*; **b** impaired in quality, made inferior, spoilt: *a book gravely disfigured by the verbosity and inelegance of its style.*

disfigurement, n. [1. disfígurment; 2. disfígəmənt]. **disfigure** & **-ment.** **a** (rare) Act of disfiguring; **b** that which disfigures; a blemish, defect.

disforest, vb. trans. [1. disfórest; 2. disfɔ́rist]. **dis-** & **forest.** **a** To clear of trees; **b** to disafforest, q.v.

disfranchise, vb. trans. [1. disfránchīz; 2. disfrǽntʃaiz]. **dis-** & **franchise.** To deprive of rights of citizenship, specif., of right to vote at parliamentary or other elections.

disfranchisement, n. [1. disfránchizment; 2. disfrǽntʃizmənt]. Prec. & **-ment.** The act of disfranchising; state of being disfranchised.

disfrock, vb. trans. [1. disfrók; 2. disfrɔ́k]. **dis-** & **frock.** To deprive of clerical status, to unfrock.

disgorge, vb. trans. & intrans. [1. disgórj; 2. disgɔ́dž], fr. O. Fr. *desgorger.* See **dis-** & **gorge.** **A.** trans. **1. a** To throw out, eject, from, or as from, throat; **b** to pour forth, as a river its waters; **c** (fig.) to give up, surrender (something wrongfully seized): *to disgorge ill-gotten gains.* **B.** intrans. **a** To pour forth (of a river): *to disgorge into a lake*; **b** to perform the act of making restitution: *the law will soon make him disgorge.*

disgrace (I.), n. [1. disgrás; 2. disgréis], fr. Fr. *disgrâce*, fr. Ital. *disgrazia*, fr. Med. Lat. *disgratia*, fr. **dis-** & Lat. *grātia*, 'favour, esteem; mark of favour, kindness, courtesy; gratitude; charm, loveliness'. See **grace** (I.). **a** Loss of honour, favour, reputation; disrepute, discredit, shame: *to bring disgrace on one's family*; **b** state of being held in low esteem, disfavour, consequent upon worthlessness of character, discreditable conduct &c.: *to be in disgrace*; **c** person guilty of discreditable conduct; action or circumstance which is shameful; thing which is discreditable to those who made it or selected it, by being bad, shabby, ugly or useless; something which is all or any of these, considered as a source of discredit, shame, reproach, disrepute: *you are a disgrace to your country*; *such cruelty is a disgrace to humanity, to civilization*; *this carpet is a disgrace to the house.*

disgrace (II.), vb. trans., fr. prec. **1.** To bring shame, reproach, upon, cause loss of honour to: *to disgrace one's name.* **2.** To degrade, remove ignominiously from favour or status: *a cowardly officer must be publicly disgraced.*

disgraceful, adj. [1. disgrásfool; 2. disgréisfəl]. **disgrace** (I.) & **-ful.** Involving shame, reproach, dishonour; discreditable, shameful.

disgracefully, adv. Prec. & **-ly.** In a disgraceful manner.

disgracefulness, n. See prec. & **-ness.** The quality of being disgraceful.

disgruntled, adj. [1. disgrúntld; 2. disgrántld], fr. **dis-** & obs. *gruntle*, freq. form of **grunt,** & **-ed.** Discontented, disappointed, displeased; sulky.

disguise (I.), vb. trans. [1. disgíz; 2. disgáiz], fr. O. Fr. *desguisier.* See **dis-** & **guise.** **1.** To change appearance or outward character of, conceal identity by causing to appear different from accustomed form or character, and like someone, or something else: **a** *to disguise oneself*, to dress up, wear strange clothes, a wig, false beard, or other aids to concealment; **b** *to disguise oneself as* (*a policeman*), make oneself look like (a policeman); **c** (of things) *a door disguised as a bookcase.* **2.** To conceal, give impression of (mental states & activities) being other than they really are: *to disguise one's sorrow beneath a careless manner*; *to disguise one's intentions, feelings.*

disguise (II.), n., fr. prec. (lit. and fig.) Something assumed for the purpose of concealing identity; alteration of appearance; manner assumed to hide feelings &c. Phr. *a blessing in disguise*, good fortune that is not at first apparent.

disgust (I.), n. [1. disgúst; 2. disgast], fr. Fr., fr. **dis-** & Lat. *gustus*, 'a tasting; a relish, light dish; a taste, flavour; a foretaste, sample'. See **gust** (II.). (moral and physical) Strong feeling of aversion, repugnance; loathing, nausea.

disgust (II.), vb. trans., fr. Fr., fr. **dis-** & Lat. *gustāre*, 'to taste'. See prec. To cause, provoke, disgust in; to excite strong distaste, aversion, loathing (physical or moral).

disgusted, adj. [1. disgústed; 2. disgástid], fr. P.P. of prec. **a** Provoked to, filled with, loathing and aversion; **b** disappointed, angry.

disgustedly, adv. Prec. & **-ly.** In a manner expressing disgust.

disgustful, adj. [1. disgústfool; 2. disgástful]. **disgust** (I.) & **-ful.** Causing disgust; offensive, digusting.

disgusting, adj. [1. disgústing; 2. disgástiŋ], fr. Pres. Part. of **disgust** (II.). Liable to cause disgust; causing loathing and repugnance; nauseating, revolting, sickening.

disgustingly, adv. Prec. & **-ly.** In such a manner as to excite disgust; also (colloq.) as mere intensive: *disgustingly rich* &c.

dish (I.), n. [1. dish; 2. diʃ]. M.E. *disch, dish*, O.E. *disc*, cp. Germ. *tisch*, 'table', fr. Lat. *discus*, 'a quoit'; hence (from the shape) 'a dish; a dial'. See **disk.** **a** A flat-bottomed shallow vessel, of earthenware, porcelain, glass, or metal, with a rim round the edge, or with raised sides, for holding food: *vegetable dish, meat dish* &c.; hence **b** amount of food served in a dish: *a dish of fish, of beans* &c.; (archaic) *a dish of tea*, a cup of tea; **c** specific kind of food, or food prepared in a particular way: *a plain, elaborate, dainty, dish*; Phr. *standing dish*, one habitually served; *made dishes*, prepared from many ingredients.

dish (II.), vb. trans., fr. prec. **1. a** To put into a dish; usually *dish up*, serve up food for table; also **b** (fig.) to present to a person's attention: *to dish up an old story.* **2.** (colloq.) To upset, spoil, thwart, circumvent, bring to nought (plans, devices &c.); to check, disconcert, the author of such: *to dish one's opponents*; *the publication of the letter dished all his chances.*

dishabille, n. [1. disabḗl; 2. disəbíəl]. Fr. *déshabillé*, P.P. of *déshabiller*, 'to undress'. State of being partially undressed, or half-dressed; usually *in dishabille.*

dishabituate, vb. trans. [1. dis-habítūāt; 2. dishəbítjueit]. **dis-** & **habituate.** To disaccustom, cause one to give up, get out of a habit, usage, practice.

dishallucination, n. [1. dis-halūsináshun; 2. dishəljusinéiʃən]. **dis-** & **hallucination.** Act or process of destroying an hallucination; disillusionment.

disharmonious, adj. [1. dìs-harmónius; 2. dìshāmóunjəs]. **disharmony** & **-ous.** Not harmonizing, discordant.

disharmonize, vb. trans. [1. dis-hármunīz; 2. disháːmənaiz]. **dis-** & **harmonize.** To destroy the harmony of, make into a discord; make to disagree.

disharmony, n. [1. dis-hármuni; 2. disháːməni]. **dis-** & **harmony.** Want of harmony; discord.

dish-cloth, n. Cloth used for washing or drying dishes and crockery.

dish-cover, n. Cover of metal, china &c. fitting on to dish to keep contents hot.

dishearten, vb. trans. [1. dis-hártn; 2. disháːtn]. **dis-** & **hearten.** To deprive of confidence or courage; to render despondent and dissatisfied with oneself and one's work.

disheartenment, n. [1. dis-hártnment; 2. disháːtnmənt]. Prec. & **-ment.** The act of disheartening; state of being disheartened.

disherison, n. [1. dis-hérisn; 2. dishérisn], fr. O. Fr. *disheriteisun*, fr. **dis-** & Lat. *hērēditāt-(um)*, P.P. type of *hērēditāre*, 'to inherit', & **-son.** See **hereditary.** (archaic) **a** The act of disinheriting; **b** state of being disinherited.

dishevelled, adj. [1. dishévld; 2. diʃévld], fr. O. Fr. *deschevelé* (& **-ed**), fr. **dis-** & *chevel*, 'hair', fr. Lat. *capillus*, 'hair'. See **capillary.** **a** (of hair) In disorder, ruffled; **b** (of persons) untidy, with clothes, hair &c., in disorder; unkempt.

dishonest, adj. [1. disónest; 2. disɔ́nist], fr. O. Fr. *deshoneste*, fr. Lat. *dehonestus*, 'unbecoming, improper'. See **de-** & **honest.**

a (of persons) Lacking honesty, inclined to claim, or appropriate, more than one has a right to; not upright and straightforward in one's dealings with others; inclined, accustomed, to defraud others, or to steal their property; **b** (of actions and utterances) (i.) intended to deceive others, deliberately misleading; (ii.) designed to secure property or privileges unjustly; **c** (of work) hastily, carelessly, perfunctorily, carried out; done so as to deceive by specious appearance of being better than it really is; **d** (of thought) timid, not pushed to logical conclusion; shirking difficult facts, avoiding undesired conclusions.

dishonestly, adv. Prec. & **-ly.** By fraudulent means, in a dishonest manner.

dishonesty, n. [1. disónesti; 2. disɔ́nisti], fr. O. Fr. *deshonesté.* See **dis-** & **honesty.** **a** Quality of being dishonest; **b** act, word, thought, done, said, conceived, in a dishonest way, for purpose of deceiving or defrauding: *a piece of dishonesty.*

dishonour (**I.**), n. [1. disónor; 2. disɔ́nə], fr. O. Fr. *deshonor.* See **dis-** & **honour.** **1. a** The state of being disgraced; ignominy; **b** absence, loss of honour, shame; **c** feeling and expression of disrespect; insult, indignity: *offer him no dishonour.* **2.** That which brings dishonour and disgrace; discreditable, disgraceful, person or thing.

dishonour (**II.**), vb. trans., fr. O. Fr. *deshonorer*, fr. Lat. *dehonōrāre*, 'to dishonour'. See **dis-** & **honour** (**II.**). **1.** To treat in a disparaging manner, offer indignity to. **2. a** To bring shame upon, cause loss of credit or honour to; specif. **b** to violate the chastity of. **3.** To refuse to pay or perform; to repudiate: *to dishonour a cheque; to dishonour one's word, promise.*

dishonourable, adj. [1. disónorabl; 2. disɔ́nərəbl]. **dis-** & **honourable.** **a** (of persons) Lacking honour, uprightness, honesty; not honourable; **b** (of actions &c.) springing from discreditable, mean, base, motives; bringing dishonour, of a nature to sully the character and reputation.

dishonourableness, n. Prec. & **-ness.** State or quality of being dishonourable.

dishonourably, adv. See prec. & **-ly.** In a dishonourable manner.

dishorn, vb. trans. [1. dis-hórn; 2. dishɔ́n]. **dis-** & **horn.** To remove the horns of.

dish-water, n. Water in which plates, dishes &c. have been washed.

disillusion (**I.**), vb. trans. [1. disilúzhun; 2. disiljúžn]. **dis-** & **illusion.** To free from illusion, reveal truth and reality to.

disillusion (**II.**), n., fr. prec. The state or process of being disillusioned.

disillusionize, vb. trans. [1. disilúzhunīz; 2. disiljúžənaiz]. **dis-** & **illusion** & **-ize.** To disillusion.

disillusionment, n. [1. disilúzhunment; 2. disiljúžənmənt]. **disillusion** & **-ment.** **a** The act or process of disillusioning; **b** the state of being disillusioned.

disinclination, n. [1. disinklinā́shun; 2. disinklinéiʃən]. **dis-** & **inclination.** Absence of desire for, feeling against; unwillingness, reluctance, dislike: *to have a disinclination for work; a disinclination to meet people.*

disincline, vb. trans. [1. disinklín; 2. disinkláin]. **dis-** & **incline.** To make unwilling, render reluctant: *disinclined to accept.*

disincorporate, vb. trans. [1. disinkórporāt; 2. disinkɔ́pəreit]. **dis-** & **incorporate.** To break up, destroy corporateness of, cause to cease being corporate.

disinfect, vb. trans. [1. disinfékt; 2. disinfékt]. **dis-** & **infect.** To destroy infection, remove germs of disease from (a wound, room &c.).

disinfectant, adj. & n. [1. disinféktant; 2. disinféktənt]. Prec. & **-ant.** **a** adj. Able to destroy infectious disease germs; **b** n., substance used for disinfecting.

disinfection, n. [1. disinfékshun; 2. disinfékʃən]. **disinfect** & **-ion.** The destruction of disease germs; act of disinfecting, process of being disinfected.

disingenuous, adj. [1. disinjénūus; 2. disindžénjuəs]. **dis-** & **ingenuous.** Insincere, actuated by concealed motives, not candid or straightforward; dishonest.

disingenuously, adv. Prec. & **-ly.** In a disingenuous manner.

disingenuousness, n. See prec. & **-ness.** The quality of being disingenuous.

disinherit, vb. trans. [1. disinhérit; 2. disinhérit]. **dis-** & **inherit** (obs. sense, 'to make one's heir'). To deprive of right to inherit; to remove from position of heir.

disinheritance, n. [1. disinhéritans; 2. disinhéritəns]. Prec. & **-ance.** **a** The act of disinheriting; **b** state of being disinherited.

disintegrate, vb. trans. & intrans. [1. disíntegrāt; 2. disíntigreit]. **dis-** & **integrate.** **a** trans. To cause to divide, split up, resolve into parts or elements; **b** intrans., to break up, cease to be a unity, resolve into separate parts or elements; hence, to fall into decay, fall to pieces.

disintegration, n. [1. disintegrā́shun; 2. disintigréiʃən]. Prec. & **-ion.** The act or process of disintegrating.

disintegrator, n. [1. disíntegrātor; 2. disíntigreitə]. **disintegrate** & **-or.** Agent causing disintegration.

disinter, vb. trans. [1. disintér; 2. disintā́]. **dis-** & **inter.** (lit. and fig.) To dig up what is buried or hidden; unearth, bring to light.

disinterested, adj. [1. disíntrested; 2. disíntristid]. **dis-** & **interest** & **-ed.** (of person, action, speech &c.) Not influenced or actuated by, not expressing, personal interests; without selfish motives.

disinterestedly, adv. Prec. & **-ly.** In a disinterested manner.

disinterestedness, n. See prec. & **-ness.** Quality of being disinterested.

disinterment, n. [1. disintérment; 2. disintā́mənt]. **disinter** & **-ment.** The act of disinterring; exhumation; unearthing what is buried or hidden.

disject, vb. trans. [1. disjékt; 2. disdžékt]. Lat. *disject-(um)*, P.P. type of *dis(j)icere*, 'to throw asunder, scatter', fr. *jacere*, 'to hurl'. See **dis-** & **jactitation** & **jet.** To hurl asunder, fling apart, scatter, disperse.

disjecta membra, n. [1. disjékta mémbra; 2. disdžéktə mémbrə]. Lat., 'scattered limbs, portions'. See prec. & **member.** Scattered fragments.

disjoin, vb. trans. [1. disjóin; 2. disdžɔ́in], fr. O. Fr. *desjoindre*, fr. Lat. *disjungere*, 'to disunite, separate' (lit. and fig.). **dis-** & **join.** To disunite, sever connexion of.

disjoint, vb. trans. [1. disjóint; 2. disdžɔ́int], fr. O. Fr. *desjoint*, P.P. of *desjoindre.* See prec. To take to pieces, separate at the joints.

disjointed, adj. [1. disjóinted; 2. disdžɔ́intid], fr. P.P. of prec. **a** (of a body) (i.) Having the limbs separated at the joints; (ii.) loosely jointed, or seeming so; **b** (of thought and expression) lacking coherence, without logical connexion and sequence; broken, disconnected.

disjointedly, adv. Prec. & **-ly.** In a disjointed manner; without logical sequence: *to speak, think, disjointedly.*

disjointedness, n. See prec. & **-ness.** The quality of being disjointed.

disjunction, n. [1. disjúngkshun; 2. disdžáŋkʃən], fr. Lat. *disjunctiōn-(em)*, 'a separation'; (philos.) 'an opposition of two propositions'. **dis-** & **junction.** Separation into parts, disconnexion, severance.

disjunctive, adj. [1. disjúngktiv; 2. disdžáŋktiv], fr. Lat. *disjunctīv-(us)*, fr. *disjunct-(um)*, P.P. type of *disjungere*, 'to disunite, separate'. See **disjoin.** **a** Disuniting, causing or involving separation; **b** specif. (gram.) *disjunctive conjunction*, one expressing an opposition of ideas between those contained in the clauses or words it connects, as: *either . . . or . . .*

disk, disc, n. [1. disk; 2. disk], fr. Lat. *disc-(us)*, 'a quoit'; hence from the shape, 'a dish; disk of a sundial', fr. Gk. *diskos*, 'a quoit', fr. **dik-skos*; cp. *dikein*, 'to throw', *dik-tuon*, 'a thread, net'; etymol. uncertain. **a** Plane surface enclosed by a circle; **b** a round, apparently flat, figure: *the sun's, moon's, disk*; **c** a round, flat, thin sheet or portion of metal, wood &c.; **d** a discus or quoit.

dislike (**I.**), vb. trans. [1. dislík; 2. disláik]. See **dis-** & **like** (**III.**). Not to like; to feel aversion to; rather weaker than *detest.*

dislike (**II.**), n., fr. prec. Feeling of aversion, antipathy; weaker than *detestation.*

dislocate, vb. trans. [1. díslokāt; 2. dísləkeit], fr. Med. Lat. *dislocāt-(um)*, P.P. type of *dislocāre*, fr. **dis-** & Lat. *locāre*, 'to put, place, dispose'. See **locate.** **1.** To put out of place, specif. (med., of the two parts of a joint) to put out of joint: *to dislocate one's knee, shoulder* &c. **2.** (fig.) To disturb so as to interfere with smooth and normal working: *to dislocate traffic, business, trade* &c.

dislocation, n. [1. dislokā́shun; 2. disləkéiʃən]. Prec. & **-ion.** **a** The act or process of dislocating; **b** state of being dislocated.

dislodge, vb. trans. [1. dislój; 2. dislɔ́dž], fr. O. Fr. *desloger.* See **dis-** & **lodge** (**II.**). To remove from position, overthrow, upset from place; expresses idea **a** of upsetting, removing, a person or thing from his or its permanent and normal position: *to dislodge a stone from a building*; **b** to remove, drive out, person, animal, thing which occupies a position temporarily: *the enemy were easily dislodged from the hill.*

dislodgement, n. [1. dislójment; 2. dislɔ́džmənt]. Prec. & **-ment.** Removal from position; ejection.

disloyal, adj. [1. dislóial; 2. dislɔ́iəl], fr. O. Fr. *desloial.* See **dis-** & **loyal.** Unfaithful, untrue; not fulfilling the obligations of allegiance, friendship &c.; specif., not loyal to one's king.

disloyalist, n. [1. dislóialist; 2. dislɔ́iəlist]. Prec. & **-ist.** One who is on principle disloyal (to government &c.).

disloyally, adv. [1. dislóiali; 2. dislɔ́iəli], fr. **disloyal** & **-ly.** In a disloyal manner.

disloyalty, n. [1. dislóialti; 2. dislɔ́iəlti]. **disloyal** & **-ty.** The quality of being disloyal; faithlessness to allegiance.

dismal, adj. [1. dízmal; 2. dízməl], fr. O. Fr. n. *dis mal*, 'unlucky day', fr. Lat. *dies mali*, 'ill-omened days'. See **dies non** & **mal-.** **a** (of places, rooms &c.) Having depressing effect on the spirits by reason of being dark, bleak, bare, lonely &c.; **b** (of the mind and spirits) lacking vivacity; depressed, gloomy, sad; **c** (of persons, voice, expression of countenance &c.) evincing, exhibiting, a dismal state of mind &c.; **d** generally, expressing or promoting a dismal state of mind.

dismally, adv. Prec. & **-ly.** In a dismal manner.

dismalness, n. See prec. & **-ness.** The state or quality of being dismal.

dismantle, vb. trans. [1. dismántl; 2. dismǽntl], fr. O. Fr. *desmanteller.* **dis-** & **mantle** (**II.**). **a** To remove furnishings from, strip of appointments and equipment: *to dismantle a house, room* &c.; **b** specif., *to dismantle a ship, fort*, remove and destroy means of defence and offence.

dismask, vb. trans. [1. dismáhsk; 2. dismásk]. **dis-** & **mask.** To reveal, disclose.

dismast, vb. trans. [1. dismáhst; 2. dismást]. **dis-** & **mast.** To take away, throw down, tear out, the masts of a ship, as by storm, gun-fire, or by other deliberate act.

dismay (**I.**), vb. trans. [1. dismā́; 2. disméi]. Prob. fr. O. Fr., fr. **dis-** & Gmc. **magan*, 'to be strong'. See **may** (**I.**). To fill with apprehension, consternation; to alarm, discourage.

dismay (**II.**), n., fr. prec. Consternation, fright, apprehension.

dismember, vb. trans. [1. dismémber; 2. dismémbə], fr. O. Fr. *desmembrer.* See **dis-** & **member.** To take to pieces, tear asunder; divide up, separate into portions.

dismemberment, n. [1. dismémberment; 2. dismémbəmənt]. Prec. & **-ment.** Partition, taking to pieces.

dismiss, vb. trans. [1. dismís; 2. d*i*smís]. With change of pref. fr. Lat. *dīmiss-(um)*, P.P. type of *dīmittere*, 'to send away', fr. **di-** (**I.**) & *mittere*, 'to send'. See **mission.** **1. a** To release, allow to go, send away, from one's presence: *the king dismissed the general with gracious words after a long interview*; **b** to remove, expel, from an office, post, situation, esp. for misconduct or incompetence: *to dismiss an officer from the army, a servant from his place* &c.; special mil. Phr. *to be dismissed the service*; **c** specif. (mil.) to allow soldiers to fall out of ranks, and to go away, after parade; also, as command indicating that permission for this is given. **2. a** To banish, eliminate, from the mind, throw off, cease to think of: *to dismiss all thoughts of revenge*; **b** to get rid of, put aside, a subject of consideration and discussion, regard it as settled and done with: *he dismissed the alleged threats of revolution as the ravings of a few half-crazy cranks*; **c** (law) *to dismiss an appeal* &c., to refuse to hear, disallow it.

dismissal, n. [1. dismísal; 2. d*i*smísəl]. Prec. & **-al.** **a** The act of dismissing; **b** state of being dismissed.

dismissible, adj. [1. dismísibl; 2. d*i*smís*i*bl]. **dismiss** & **-ible.** Liable to be dismissed.

dismount, vb. intrans. & trans. [1. dismóunt; 2. d*i*smáunt]. **dis-** & **mount** (**II.**). **A.** intrans. To get off a horse &c., alight. **B.** trans. **1.** To cause to get off or alight from a horse &c.; to unhorse, throw. **2.** To take down, remove (a thing), from that on which it is mounted, special stand &c.: *to dismount a gun.*

disobedience, n. [1. disobḗdyens; 2. d*i*səbídjəns]. **dis-** & **obedience.** Refusal to obey orders, non-observance of lawful commands.

disobedient, adj. [1. disobḗdyent; 2. d*i*səbídjənt]. **dis-** & **obedient.** Guilty of disobedience.

disobediently, adv. Prec. & **-ly.** In a disobedient manner.

disobey, vb. trans. & intrans. [1. disobā́; 2. d*i*səbéi], fr. Fr. *désobéir.* See **dis-** & **obey.** **1.** trans. **a** To refuse to listen to a person who gives orders: *to disobey one's parents*; **b** to disregard orders, refuse to carry them out: *to disobey the commands of one's parents.* **2.** intrans. To be guilty of disobedience: *to disobey is an unpardonable crime in a soldier.*

disoblige, vb. trans. [1. disoblíj; 2. d*i*səbláidž]. **dis-** & **oblige.** To ignore the wishes of, fail in consideration for; to do something which another does not want done, or fail to do that which he desires to see done.

disobliging, adj. [1. disoblíjing; 2. d*i*səbláidžiŋ]. Pres. Part. of prec. Unwilling to consider, in habit of ignoring, the wishes, convenience, of others.

disobligingly, adv. Prec. & **-ly.** In a disobliging manner.

disobligingness, n. See prec. & **-ness.** Unwillingness to oblige.

disorder (**I.**), n. [1. disórder; 2. d*i*sɔ́də]. **dis-** & **order** (**I.**). **1.** Lack of order, confusion; muddle, untidiness. **2.** Civil or political unrest; lack of orderliness of conduct, absence of the restraint imposed by law. **3.** Lack of order, disturbance, in working of bodily functions; hence, illness, disease.

disorder (**II.**), vb. trans., fr. prec. **1.** To put into confusion, upset neat and due arrangement of. **2.** To upset the health of (mind or body).

disordered, adj. [1. disórderd; 2. d*i*sɔ́dəd], fr. P.P. of prec. Out of order, confused &c. (in various senses); specif., of mental and bodily derangement: *a disordered brain, stomach* &c.

disorderliness, n. [1. disórderlines; 2. d*i*sɔ́dəl*i*n*i*s]. See next word & **-ness.** Quality or state of being disorderly.

disorderly, adv. [1. disórderli; 2. d*i*sɔ́dəl*i*]. **disorder** (**I.**) & **-ly.** **a** Out of order, untidy, in confusion; **b** defying law and order; unruly, lawless: *disorderly conduct.* Phr. specif., *disorderly house*, a brothel.

disorganization, n. [1. disòrganīzā́shun; 2. d*i*sɔ̀gənaizéiʃən]. Next word & **-ation.** State of being disorganized; confusion, interruption.

disorganize, vb. trans. [1. disórganīz; 2. d*i*sɔ́gənaiz]. **dis-** & **organize.** To upset arrangement of, disturb, interrupt working of, an orderly system.

disorientate, vb. trans. [1. disṓrientāt; 2. d*i*sɔ́riənteit]. **dis-** & **orientate.** **1.** To turn something away from the east; specif., build a church in such a way that its chancel does not face east. **2. a** To cause to lose bearings, to confuse the sense of direction; **b** (fig.) to perplex, as by confronting with unfamiliar circumstances, placing in strange surroundings and conditions.

disorientation, n. [1. disṑrientā́shun; 2. d*i*sɔ̀riəntéiʃən]. Prec. & **-ation.** State of being disorientated.

disown, vb. trans. [1. disṓn; 2. d*i*sóun]. **dis-** & **own** (**II.**). To deny ownership or authorship of; repudiate association with, or relationship to.

disparage, vb. trans. [1. dispárij; 2. d*i*spǽridž], fr. O. Fr. *desparagier*, 'to marry a person of different rank', fr. **dis-** & *parage*, 'equality'. See **par** & **-age.** To throw doubt and discredit upon, to belittle, minimize importance of; to insinuate that someone is of doubtful character or ability, or that something is inferior in quality.

disparagement, n. [1. dispárijment; 2. d*i*spǽridžmənt]. Prec. & **-ment.** **a** The act of disparaging; **b** that which causes loss of credit.

disparagingly, adv. [1. dispárijingli; 2. d*i*spǽrədž*i*ŋl*i*], fr. Pres. Part. of **disparage** & **-ly.** In a disparaging manner, slightingly; in such a way as to cast a slur upon.

disparate, adj. [1. dísparāt; 2. díspəreit], fr. Lat. **dis-** & *parāt-(um)*, P.P. type of *parāre*, 'to prepare'. See **pare.** **a** Unequal, not comparable in kind, quality, amount; **b** dissimilar, essentially different, incongruous.

disparately, adv. Prec. & **-ly.** In a disparate manner.

disparateness, n. See prec. & **-ness.** Quality of being disparate.

disparity, n. [1. dispáriti; 2. d*i*spǽr*i*t*i*], fr. Fr. *disparité.* **dis-** & **parity.** Disparateness, inequality, unlikeness, incongruity: *disparity in age, position, attainments.*

dispart (**I.**), vb. trans. & intrans. [1. dispárt; 2. d*i*spát], fr. Lat. *dispartīre*, 'to divide, distribute', fr. **dis-** & *partīre*, 'to divide'. See **part** (**II.**). **a** trans. (rare or obs.) To divide up, separate; **b** intrans., to open, become separate.

dispart (**II.**), n. See prec. (in gunnery) That difference in the thickness of the metal of a gun, and therefore of semidiameter at the breech and at the muzzle, which is to be taken into account when aiming.

dispassionate, adj. [1. dispáshunat; 2. d*i*spǽʃən*i*t]. **dis-** & **passionate.** Calm, uninfluenced by passion or emotion; impartial, unbiassed.

dispassionately, adv. Prec. & **-ly.** Without passion or prejudice, calmly, impartially.

dispassionateness, n. See prec. & **-ness.** Condition or quality of being dispassionate.

dispatch, despatch (**I.**), vb. trans. [1. dispách; 2. d*i*spǽtʃ], fr. Ital. (16th cent.) *dispacciāre*, 'to hasten, speed'; prob. fr. **dis-** & Low Lat. **-pactāre*, fr. Lat. *pactus*, 'fixed, fastened', P.P. of *pangere*, 'to fasten, drive in'; fig., 'to settle, determine'. See **pact.** **1.** To send off, start on a journey to some particular destination: *to dispatch a messenger, a parcel.* **2. a** To transact quickly, execute, complete, with promptness: *to dispatch business* &c.; **b** to complete a meal, eat it up: *to dispatch one's dinner*; **c** to bring another's life to an end, finish him off: *the executioner soon dispatched the prisoners.*

dispatch (**II.**), n., fr. prec. **1. a** The act of dispatching; state of being dispatched; **b** something that is dispatched; esp. a written official message, report, description, of an event, transaction, or situation. **2.** Promptness, rapid transaction of business: *to do something with dispatch.* **3.** Act of killing. Phr. *happy dispatch*, hara-kiri; rapid execution.

dispatch-box, -case, n. Box, case, to hold dispatches or other documents.

dispel, vb. trans. [1. dispél; 2. d*i*spél], fr. Lat. *dispellere*, 'to drive away, scatter'; fig. 'to dispel', fr. **dis-** & *pellere*, 'to strike, beat; to push, drive; to banish, expel; to impress, affect'. See **pulse** (**I.**). (of non-material things, states &c.) To drive away, disperse, scatter, force to depart, cause to disappear: *the sun dispels the darkness*; *to dispel fears, dark thoughts, apprehensions.*

dispensable, adj. [1. dispénsabl; 2. d*i*spénsəbl]. **dispense** & **-able.** **a** That can be dispensed with, done without, not essential; **b** (eccles. law) admitting of dispensation.

dispensary, n. [1. dispénsari; 2. d*i*spénsər*i*]. **dispense** & **-ary.** Place where medicines are dispensed.

dispensation, n. [1. dispensā́shun; 2. d*i*spənséiʃən]. **dispense** & **-ation.** **1.** Act of dispensing or distributing; something dispensed or given out; **a** decree, ordering of Providence, or of Fate; **b** set of laws or ordinances promulgated under divine authority: *Mosaic, Christian, dispensation.* **2. a** (law) Relaxation, or suspension of a law in favour of a particular person; **b** specif. (R.C. Ch.) exemption from performance of duty customarily imposed, special permission to do something (e.g. to marry within certain degree of affinity) ordinarily forbidden.

dispense, vb. trans. & intrans. [1. dispéns; 2. d*i*spéns], fr. O. Fr. *dispenser*, fr. Lat. *dispensāre*, 'to pay out, distribute; to manage, regulate (expenses); to manage, control, distribute, impart', fr. *dispens-(um)*, P.P. type of *dispendere*, 'to weigh out', fr. **dis-** & *pendere*, 'to weigh, weigh out; to pay out; to weigh, consider, ponder'. See **pension, spend.** **1.** trans. **a** (of material and non-material things) To distribute, give out, administer: *to dispense food, charity*; *to dispense justice*; **b** specif., to make up and give out (medicines). **2.** intrans. **a** To grant dispensations in Roman Catholic sense, q.v. under *dispensation*; **b** to dispense medicines: *he practises medicine here, but does not dispense.* *Dispense with*, to do without, forgo: *to dispense with a person's services.*

dispenser, n. [1. dispénser; 2. d*i*spénsə]. Prec. & **-er.** One who dispenses medicines, person trained in chemistry to read prescriptions and make up medicines and act as assistant to a doctor or in a dispensary.

dispeople, vb. trans. [1. dispḗpl; 2. d*i*spípl], fr. O. Fr. *despeupler*, fr. Lat. *dēpopulāre*, 'to lay waste, make desolate', fr. **de-** & *populāre*, 'to ravage, lay waste, destroy', fr. *populus*, 'people; a crowd, throng; a region, district'. See **people.** To remove inhabitants from, diminish the population of.

dispersal, n. [1. dispérsl; 2. d*i*spǽsl]. **disperse** & **-al.** **a** The act of dispersing; **b** state of being dispersed.

disperse, vb. trans. & intrans. [1. dispérs; 2. d*i*spǽs], fr. Lat. *dispers-(um)*, P.P. type of *dispergere*, 'to scatter, disperse', fr. **di-** (**I.**) & *spargere*, 'to sprinkle; to scatter, strew; to disperse, divide; to spread abroad, circulate'. See **sparse.** **1.** trans. **a** (of material and non-material things) To scatter, drive away or asunder; to cause to go away in different directions: *to disperse a crowd*; *to disperse phantoms*; *the wind has dispersed the clouds*; **b** to station, place, in more or less widely separated positions: *the troops were dispersed along a wide front.* **2.** intrans. To go in different directions, scatter: *the crowd soon dispersed* &c.

dispersedly, adv. [1. dispérsedli; 2. d*i*spǽs*i*dl*i*], P.P. of prec. & **-ly.** From, or in, different directions, here and there.

dispersion, n. [1. dispérshun; 2. d*i*spǽʃən], fr. Lat. *dispersiōn-(em)*, 'a scattering'. See **disperse** & **-ion.** **1. a** The act of dispersing;

state of being dispersed; **b** those who are dispersed, esp. *the Dispersion*, the Jewish tribes which did not return to Jerusalem after the Babylonish Captivity; cp. *Diaspora*. **2.** Specif., the breaking up of light into its constituent rays by a prism.

dispersive, adj. [1. dispérsiv; 2. dispə́siv]. **disperse** & **-ive.** Tending to disperse, causing dispersion.

dispersively, adv. Prec. & **-ly.** So as to cause dispersion.

dispersiveness, n. See prec. & **-ness.** Quality of being dispersive.

dispirit, vb. trans. [1. dispírit; 2. dispírit]. **dis-** & **spirit.** To damp the spirits of, cast down, deject, discourage.

dispiritedly, adv. [1. dispíritedli; 2. dispíritidli], P.P. of prec. & **-ly.** In a dispirited, dejected, manner.

dispiteous, adj. [1. dispítius; 2. dispítiəs]. **dis-** & **piteous.** (pseudo-archaic) Without pity, ruthless.

displace, vb. trans. [1. displā́s; 2. displéis], fr. O. Fr. *desplacer*. See **dis-** & **place.** (of material and non-material things) **a** To put out of position, remove from ordinary or fitting place; **b** to take the place of, oust.

displacement, n. [1. displā́sment; 2. displéismənt]. **displace** & **-ment.** **1.** Removal from position, displacing. **2.** Amount by which something is displaced; specif., the amount of liquid moved from its original position by a foreign body floating on, or in, it: *a ship of 10,000 tons displacement.*

display (I.), vb. trans. [1. displā́; 2. displéi], fr. O. Fr. *despleier*, 'to unfold', fr. Lat. *displicāre*, fr. **dis-** & *plicāre*, 'to fold; to wind or coil up'. See **plicate.** **1. a** (of material things) To show, exhibit, allow to be seen, dispose, spread out so as to make clearly visible: *to display the royal arms over one's door*; *to display the national flag*; *to display all one's best plate* &c.; **b** (of feelings and mental qualities) to express outwardly, make manifest, evince, show signs of possessing: *to display great intelligence, bravery, resourcefulness*; *to display no fear*; *to display perfect confidence in oneself* &c. **2.** (typog.) To print conspicuously, in large, prominent type.

display (II.), n., fr. prec. **1.** Show, exhibition, manifestation; **a** (of material things) *a fine display of bunting, fat cattle* &c.; **b** (of non-material things) *a notable display of loyalty, courage, skill* &c. **2.** (in unfavourable sense) **a** Ostentatious exhibition showing off, exaggerated lavishness, arrogant splendour: *he likes to make a display*; *vulgar display*; *to be too fond of display*; **b** ostentatious expression or manifestation of feelings which are not sincere, or of qualities but slightly possessed: *to make great display of affection, sorrow, generosity* &c.

displayed, adj. [1. displā́d; 2. displéid], fr. P.P. of **display** (I.). (her.) Of bird, with expanded wings and legs spread out.

displease, vb. trans. [1. displḗz; 2. displíz], fr. O. Fr. *desplaisir*, fr. **dis-** & Lat. *placēre*, 'to please, satisfy'. See **please.** To cause displeasure, dissatisfaction to; to provoke, incur, the disapproval, anger, of.

displeasing, adj. [1. displḗzing; 2. displíziŋ]. Pres. Part. of prec. Not pleasing, disagreeable; causing annoyance, disgust, anger; (more commonly applied to things than to persons).

displeasingly, adv. Prec. & **-ly.** In a displeasing manner.

displeasure (I.), n. [1. displézhur; 2. displéžə]. **dis-** & **pleasure.** Dissatisfaction, indignation, anger.

displeasure (II.), vb. trans., fr. prec. (rare) To cause displeasure to, interfere with pleasure of.

displume, vb. trans. [1. displo͞om; 2. displúm]. **dis-** & **plume.** (poet.) To deprive of feathers.

disport (I.), vb. intrans. & reflex. [1. dispórt; 2. dispɔ́t], fr. O. Fr. (*se*) *desporter*, 'to detach oneself from one's work, amuse oneself', fr. **dis-** & Lat. *portāre*, 'to carry, bear, bring; to endure'. See **port** (II.), & cp. **sport.** To play, amuse, oneself; to gambol, frolic; (usually reflex.) *to disport oneself.*

disport (II.), n., fr. prec. (archaic) Act of disporting; sport, mirth, pastime, frolic.

disposable, adj. [1. dispṓzabl; 2. dispóuzəbl]. **dispose** & **-able.** **a** At disposal; **b** capable of being disposed of, made over, sold; **c** not assigned to any specific purpose, free to be used.

disposal, n. [1. dispṓzl; 2. dispóuzl]. Next word & **-al.** Act of disposing of (in various senses); **a** conveyance, transference, making over, by will &c.: *disposal of property*; **b** management, use, mode of employing: *the skilful disposal of troops*; **c** power to use, freedom to convert to any purpose: *at one's own disposal*; *to have entire disposal of an estate.*

dispose, vb. trans. & intrans. [1. dispṓz; 2. dispóuz], fr. O. Fr. *disposer*, perh. fr. Low Lat. **disposāre*, fr. P.P. type *dispos-(itus)*, of Lat. *dispōnere*, 'to place here and there, distribute at intervals; to arrange, set in order; to plan, settle, determine', fr. **dis-** & *pōnere*, 'to put, place; to build, erect; to lay aside; to reckon, consider; allege'. See **position.** **A.** trans. **1. a** (of material things) To put in position, arrange: *to dispose troops in a particular way*; **b** (of non-material things) to order, regulate, direct, settle course of: *God disposes all things according to His will.* **2.** To induce a particular state of mind, to turn, incline the wishes towards, persuade in favour of: *our passions often dispose us to folly*; *I am disposed to help you*; *to be disposed to think so-and-so*; *well disposed towards.* **B.** intrans. To determine, settle, the course of things: *man proposes, God disposes.* **C.** (followed by *of*) *Dispose of*, to get rid of, have done with, finish with, settle finally; **a** by consuming: *to dispose of food* &c.; **b** by selling, giving away &c.: *to dispose of property*; **c** by rendering innocuous: *to dispose of an enemy*; **d** by refuting: *to dispose of an argument*; **e** by performing (a task) once and for all: *to dispose of a piece of business.*

disposition, n. [1. dispozíshun; 2. dispəzíʃən], fr. Lat. *dispositiōn-(em)*, 'disposition, arrangement'. See **dis-** & **position** & prec. **1. a** Arrangement, specific use made of, mode of placing: *the disposition of troops*; **b** direction, ordering, guidance, disposal; power of ordering or disposing: *to have property in one's own disposition*; *God has the supreme disposition of all things.* **2.** Combination, sum, of moral and intellectual qualities peculiar to each human being; natural bent, inclination, or constitution of mind, character, nature: *a generous, cruel* &c., *disposition.*

dispossess, vb. trans. [1. dispozés; 2. dispəzés], fr. O. Fr. *despossesser*. **dis-** & **possess.** **a** To deprive of possession, remove property from; specif., deprive of possession of land; **b** to deprive of occupation of land &c.; to eject, oust.

dispossession, n. [1. dispozéshun; 2. dispəzéʃən]. Prec. & **-ion.** **a** The act of dispossessing; **b** state of being dispossessed.

dispraise (I.), vb. trans. [1. disprā́z; 2. dispréiz], fr. O. Fr. *despreisier*, fr. Lat. *dēpretiāre*, 'to lower the price of, undervalue; to disregard, make light of'. See **depreciate.** To speak slightingly of, depreciate, disparage.

dispraise (II.), n., fr. prec. Depreciation, disparagement: *to speak in dispraise of person or thing.*

disproof, n. [1. dispro͞of; 2. disprúf], fr. **dis-** & **proof.** **a** The act of disproving; fact of being disproved, refutation; **b** that which disproves.

disproportion, n. [1. dispropórshun; 2. disprəpɔ́ʃən]. **dis-** & **proportion.** The state of being out of proportion.

disproportionate, adj. [1. dispropórshunat; 2. disprəpɔ́ʃənit]. Prec. & **-ate.** Out of proportion; of the wrong size, or amount, in relation to something else.

disproportionately, adv. Prec. & **-ly.** In a manner showing lack of right proportion.

disprove, vb. trans. [1. dispro͞ov; 2. disprúv], fr. O. Fr. *desprover*. See **dis-** & **prove.** To refute, prove the contrary of, show to be false.

disputable, adj. [1. díspūtabl; 2. dispjutəbl]. **dispute** (I.) & **-able.** **a** Capable of being disputed, open to argument; **b** of doubtful truth, uncertain.

disputably, adv. Prec. & **-ly.** In a disputable manner.

disputant, n. [1. díspūtant; 2. díspjutənt]. **dispute** (I.) & **-ant.** One taking part in a dispute.

disputation, n. [1. dìspūtā́shun; 2. dìspjutéiʃən]. **dispute** (I.) & **-ation.** Controversial discussion, verbal argument.

disputatious, adj. [1. dìspūtā́shus; 2. dìspjutéiʃəs]. See prec. & **-ous.** Argumentative, inclined to dispute and controversy.

disputatiously, adv. Prec. & **-ly.** In a disputatious manner.

disputatiousness, n. See prec. & **-ness.** State or quality of mind of a disputatious person.

dispute (I.), vb. trans. & intrans. [1. dispū́t; 2. dispjút], fr. O. Fr. *desputer*, fr. Lat. *disputāre*, 'to reckon up, calculate, to examine, investigate; to discuss, argue', fr. **dis-** & *putāre*, 'to clean, cleanse; to reckon up, settle carefully; to reflect on, consider'. See **putative.** **A.** trans. **1. a** To discuss, debate, talk over, considering for and against, treat as subject for controversy: *to dispute a question, the rights and wrongs of*; **b** to question the truth, or validity of, call in question, challenge, argue against: *to dispute a statement, a claim, a right, an alleged fact* &c. **2.** To oppose, endeavour to prevent by force, offer opposition to: *to dispute the enemy's advance.* **B.** intrans. To engage in argument, enter into controversy, discuss a matter controversially; to wrangle, quarrel.

dispute (II.), n., fr. prec. Argument, controversy, wordy contest; a quarrel, wrangling. Phrs. *in dispute*, under discussion, being contended for; *beyond dispute*, not needing discussion, not doubtful, finally decided.

disqualification, n. [1. diskwòlifikā́shun; 2. diskwɔ̀lifikéiʃən]. See **dis-** & **qualification** & next word. **a** The act of disqualifying, state of being disqualified; **b** that which disqualifies.

disqualify, vb. trans. [1. diskwólifī; 2. diskwɔ́lifai]. **dis-** & **qualify.** **1. a** To render unfit for a particular purpose; make ineligible for special post or office: *his appearance alone would disqualify him for the position of headmaster*; **b** to incapacitate for performance of particular duties or functions: *I am disqualified by my weak heart for serving in the army.* **2.** To declare that a person is disqualified (for any office, function &c.), and order that he shall be held to be so.

disquiet (I.), n. [1. diskwī́et; 2. diskwáiət]. **dis-** & **quiet** (II.). Restlessness, uneasiness of mind, body, or in social and political affairs; disturbance, anxiety of mind, apprehension of evil.

disquiet (II.), vb. trans. **dis-** & **quiet** (III.) (of mental and moral processes) To make restless, trouble, disturb, render anxious, apprehensive; to fill with misgiving: *to be disquieted by the news*; *my heart is disquieted.*

disquiet (III.), adj. **dis-** & **quiet** (I.). (rare) Restless, uneasy, troubled.

disquietness, n. [1. diskwī́etnes; 2. diskwáiətnis]. Prec. & **-ness.** (rare) Disquietude.

disquietude, n. [1. diskwī́etūd; 2. diskwáiətjūd]. See **disquiet** (III.) & **-tude.** The state of disquiet, restlessness, anxiety, apprehension.

disquisition, n. [1. dìskwizíshun; 2. dìskwizíʃən], fr. Lat. *disquīsītiōn-(em)*, 'an inquiry (esp. judicial)', fr. *disquīsīt-(um)*, P.P. type of *disquīrere*, 'to inquire carefully', fr. **dis-** & *quaerere*, 'to seek, to get, obtain; to ask, inquire; examine, investigate'. See **query.** A systematic treatise, elaborate dissertation, on a particular subject.

disquisitional, adj. [1. dìskwizíshunal ; 2. dìskwizíʃənəl]. Prec. & **-al.** Pertaining to, of the nature of, a disquisition.

disrate, vb. trans. [1. disrā́t ; 2. disréit]. **dis-** & **rate (I.)**. (naut.) To reduce to a lower rating.

disregard (I.), vb. trans. [1. dìsregárd ; 2. dìsrigā́d]. **dis-** & **regard.** To ignore, pay no attention to, to give no heed, or consideration to; to take no account of: *to disregard a remark, sign, entreaty; we may disregard this item in estimating expenses.*

disregard (II.), n., fr. prec. Want of attention, ignoring, indifference.

disrelish (I.), n. [1. disrélish ; 2. disréliʃ]. **dis-** & **relish (I.)**. (rare) Disfavour, want of liking, aversion: *to regard a person with disrelish.*

disrelish (II.), vb. trans., fr. prec. (rare) To dislike, feel repugnance to, aversion for.

disrepair, n. [1. disrepā́r ; 2. dìsripéə]. **dis-** & **repair (II.)**. Condition of dilapidation, state of shabbiness, disorder, or partial ruin, into which buildings fall from neglect and lack of repair.

disreputable, adj. [1. disrépūtabl ; 2. disrépjutəbl]. **dis-** & **reputable.** Not of good repute, not respectable; degraded, dissipated, in appearance or character.

disreputableness, n. Prec. & **-ness.** Condition of being disreputable.

disreputably, adv. See prec. & **-ly.** In a disreputable manner.

disrepute, n. [1. disrepū́t ; 2. dìsripjū́t]. **dis-** & **repute.** Want of repute, disfavour; the state of having lost reputation, fame, vogue.

disrespect, n. [1. dìsrespékt ; 2. dìsrispékt]. See **dis-** & **respect.** Want of respect, lack of deference, impoliteness: *to show, treat with, disrespect.*

disrespectful, adj. [1. dìsrespéktfool ; 2. dìsrispéktfəl]. Prec. & **-ful.** Wanting in respect; not showing fitting deference or consideration for another's position or character: *disrespectful manner, remark* &c.

disrespectfully, adv. Prec. & **-ly.** Rudely, in a disrespectful manner.

disrespectfulness, n. See prec. & **-ness.** Want of respect.

disrobe, vb. trans. & intrans. [1. disrṓb ; 2. disróub]. **dis-** & **robe.** **a** trans. To remove clothes, covering of, undress; **b** intrans., to take off one's clothes, undress; specif., to take off official robes.

disroot, vb. trans. [1. disrōōt ; 2. disrū́t]. **dis-** & **root.** To dig up by the roots, remove.

disrupt, vb. trans. [1. disrúpt ; 2. disrápt]. Back-formation fr. next word. To break up, break to pieces, shatter; usually of act of destroying an institution or state.

disruption, n. [1. disrúpshun ; 2. disrápʃən], fr. Lat. *disrupt-(um)*, P.P. type of *disrumpere*, 'to break to pieces; to sever, sunder', fr. **dis-** & *rumpere*, 'to break, burst, tear; to annul, interrupt', see **rupture**, & **-ion.** Act or process of disrupting (a state, institution &c.): *the disruption of the Russian Empire by the Bolsheviks.* Specif., *the Disruption*, the schism which took place in the Scottish Church in 1843.

disruptive, adj. [1. disrúptiv ; 2. disráptiv], fr. Lat. *disrupt-(um)* (see prec.) & **-ive.** Causing disruption.

dissatisfaction, n. [1. dissàtisfákshun ; 2. dissæ̀tisfǽkʃən]. **dis-** & **satisfaction.** The state of being dissatisfied; displeasure, disapproval, discontent; feeling that one's expectations or requirements have not been fulfilled: *to express great dissatisfaction at the way the work had been done.*

dissatisfied, adj. [1. dissátisfīd ; 2. dissǽtisfaid], fr. P.P. of next word. **a** (followed by *with*) Not satisfied with, not pleased with, disappointed in; **b** esp. when used attributively, discontented, inclined to repine at one's circumstances: *a thoroughly dissatisfied person.*

dissatisfy, vb. trans. [1. dissátisfī ; 2. dissǽtisfai]. **dis-** & **satisfy.** To fail to please, not to fulfil expectations formed.

dissect, vb. trans. [1. disékt ; 2. disékt], fr. Lat. *dissect-(um)*, P.P. type of *dissecāre*, 'to cut in pieces', fr. **dis-** & *secāre*, 'to cut, cut off; to tear, wound; to divide, cleave'. See **section.** **1.** **a** To cut up, to cut in pieces, divide, carefully and minutely; specif. **b** (anat.) to cut, divide up, a dead body of man, or animal, or a plant for the purpose of studying its structure in detail. **2.** (fig.) To divide, analyse, a problem, statement, argument, theory &c. minutely and carefully, into various parts, and examine and study it thoroughly in all its aspects.

dissecting-room, n. [1. disékting ròom ; 2. diséktiŋ rùm]. Room (in school of medicine &c.) where bodies are dissected by students of anatomy.

dissection, n. [1. disékshun ; 2. disékʃən]. **dissect** & **-ion.** **a** The act of dissecting; state or process of being dissected; **b** a specimen, part of a body, which has been carefully dissected: *a beautiful dissection of a head and neck.*

dissector, n. [1. diséktur ; 2. diséktə]. **dissect** & **-or.** One who dissects; demonstrator of anatomy who instructs by dissection of dead body.

disseize, vb. trans. [1. dissḗz ; 2. dissíz], fr. O. Fr. *dessaisir.* See **dis-** & **seize.** (law) To deprive, dispossess, of estates, esp. wrongfully.

disseizin, disseisin, n. [1. dissḗzin ; 2. dissízin], fr. O. Fr. *dessaisine.* See **dis-** & **seizin.** (law) Act of disseizing; state of being disseized.

dissemble, vb. trans. & intrans. [1. disémbl ; 2. disémbl]. Through the influence of **resemble**, fr. obs. *dissimill, dissimule*, fr. O. Fr. *dissimuler*, fr. Lat. *dissimulāre*, 'to disguise, hide, conceal', fr. **dis-** & *simulāre*, 'to copy, imitate; to assume, pretend, counterfeit'. See **simulate.** **a** trans. To conceal, disguise; to make (a thing, feeling &c.) appear different from its real nature: *to dissemble one's emotion, anger* &c.; **b** intrans., to carry out the act of concealing one's feelings, motives; act in such a way as to do this, and to give wrong impression of one's feelings; to deceive: *we must dissemble.*

dissembler, n. [1. disémbler ; 2. disémblə]. Prec. & **-er.** One who deceives by concealing his real motives, emotions &c.; a hypocrite.

disseminate, vb. trans. [1. diséminā̆t ; 2. diséminеit], fr. Lat. *dissēmināt-(um)*, P.P. type of *dissēmināre*, 'to scatter seed'; hence 'to spread abroad, disseminate', fr. **dis-** & *sēmināre*, 'to sow; to beget; to plant, propagate'. See **semen.** To scatter, spread abroad, as seed; esp. (fig.) *to disseminate the teaching of the Gospel, sedition* &c.

dissemination, n. [1. disèminā́shun ; 2. disèminéiʃən], fr. Lat. *dissēminātiōn-(em)*, 'a scattering of seed, disseminating'. Prec. & **-ation.** Sowing, scattering abroad (esp. fig.).

disseminator, n. [1. diséminātor ; 2. diséminеitə]. **disseminate** & **-or.** One who disseminates.

dissension, n. [1. disénshun ; 2. disénʃən], fr. Lat. *dissensiōn-(em)*, 'dissension, disagreement, discord', fr. Lat. *dissens-(um)*, P.P. type of *dissentīre*, 'to disagree, differ in opinion; to be unlike'. See next word & **-ion.** Difference of opinion, disagreement, falling out, quarrelling, strife.

dissent (I.), vb. intrans. [1. disént ; 2. disént], fr. Lat. *dissentīre*, 'to disagree, differ in opinion, be unlike', fr. **dis-** & *sentīre*, 'to perceive by the senses; to feel, experience; to observe, notice, think, believe'. See **sentient.** **a** To disagree, hold a different opinion: *to dissent strongly from what has been said*; **b** specif., to hold views differing from those taught by the established church: *dissenting minister, chapel*, not belonging to the Church of England.

dissent (II.), n., fr. prec. **a** Disagreement, difference of opinion: *to express strong dissent*; **b** specif. (often with cap.) non-acceptance of the doctrines of the established church, **nonconformity**: *Dissent is strong in Wales.*

dissenter, n. [1. disénter ; 2. diséntə]. **dissent (I.)** & **-er.** **a** One who dissents; specif. **b** one who refuses to accept the doctrines and discipline of the Church of England; a nonconformist.

dissentient, adj. & n. [1. disénshent ; 2. disénʃənt], fr. Lat. *dissentient-(em)*, Pres. Part. type of *dissentīre.* See **dissent (I.)** & **-ent.** **a** adj. Disagreeing, expressing a different opinion: *without a dissentient voice*; **b** n., one who disagrees; one who expresses disagreement: *the motion was passed with only two dissentients.*

dissepiment, n. [1. disépiment ; 2. disépimənt], fr. Lat. *dissaepīment-(um)*, 'a partition', fr. **dis-** & *saepīmentum*, 'a hedge, enclosure', fr. *saepīre*, 'to hedge in, fence in; to enclose, surround; to impede'. See **septum** & **-ment.** (bot.) A partition, dividing-wall.

dissert, vb. trans. [1. disért ; 2. disə́t], fr. Lat. *dissert-(um)*, P.P. type of *disserere*, 'to discuss, examine, discourse on', fr. **dis-** & *serere*, 'to join, bind together; to plait, entwine; to connect, combine, compose'. See **series.** To write a treatise, pronounce a discourse on a particular subject, esp. *dissert upon.*

dissertate, vb. intrans. [1. dísertāt ; 2. dísəteit], fr. Lat. *dissertāt-(um)*, P.P. type of *dissertāre*, 'to discuss, argue, debate, a matter', fr. *dissert-(um).* See prec. To dissert.

dissertation, n. [1. disertā́shun ; 2. disətéiʃən], fr. Lat. *dissertātiōn-(em)*, 'a spoken discourse'. See prec. & **-ation.** A written or spoken formal discourse on a particular subject; esp. a treatise written as a prescribed exercise for a university degree.

disserve, vb. trans. [1. dissérv ; 2. dissə́v]. **dis-** & **serve.** To do harm to, injure interests of, treat badly.

disservice, n. [1. dissérvis ; 2. dissə́vis]. **dis-** & **service.** Disobliging or harmful action; an ill turn.

dissever, vb. trans. [1. disév er ; 2. disévə]. **dis-** & **sever.** To cut apart, separate.

disseverance, n. [1. diséverans ; 2. disévərəns]. Prec. & **-ance.** Separation, cutting apart.

dissidence, n. [1. dísidens ; 2. dísidəns], fr. Lat. *dissidentia*, 'difference, diversity'. See next word & **-ence.** Dissent, refusal to agree.

dissident, adj. & n. [1. dísident ; 2. dísidənt], fr. Lat. *dissident-(em)*, Pres. Part. type of *dissidēre*, 'to sit apart, be remote; to disagree, be at variance, to be unlike', fr. **dis-** & *sedēre*, 'to sit'. See **sedentary.** **a** adj. Disagreeing, of a different opinion; **b** n., one who disagrees, a dissentient.

dissight, n. [1. disī́t ; 2. disáit]. **dis-** & **sight.** (rare) Something which is unsightly; an eyesore.

dissimilar, adj. [1. disímilar ; 2. disímilə]. **dis-** & **similar.** Not resembling, unlike; having different qualities, properties, appearance &c. (followed by *to*).

dissimilarity, n. [1. disimiláriti ; 2. disimilǽriti]. **dis-** & **similarity.** Want of resemblance; unlikeness, difference.

dissimilarly, adv. [1. disímilarli ; 2. disímiləli]. **dis-** & **similarly.** In a dissimilar manner, in a different way.

dissimilate, vb. trans. [1. disímilāt ; 2. disímileit], fr. Lat. *dissimil-(is)*, 'unlike, different', see next word & **-ate**, on the anal. of **assimilate.** (philol.) To develop differences in two originally similar sounds, occurring in same word.

dissimilation, n. [1. disìmilā́shun ; 2. disìmiléiʃən]. See prec. & **-ation.** The process of dissimilating; difference caused by this.

dissimilitude, n. [1. dìsimílitūd ; 2. dìsimílitjūd], fr. Lat. *dissimilitūd-(inem)*, 'unlikeness', fr. *dissimilis*, 'unlike', fr. **dis-** & *similis*, 'like, resembling'. See **similar** & **-tude.** Want of resemblance, unlikeness.

dissimulate, vb. trans. & intrans. [1. disímūlāt ; 2. disímjuleit], fr. Lat. *dissimulāt-(um)*, P.P. type of Lat. *dissimulāre*, 'to disguise, conceal, keep secret'. See **dissemble.** **a** trans. To conceal, dissemble, by assumed feelings &c.; **b** intrans., to conceal one's feelings, motives &c., deceive, dissemble.

dissimulation, n. [1. disìmūlāshun; 2. dìsìmju-léiʃən], fr. Lat. *dissimulātiōn-(em)*, 'a concealing, disguising, dissimulation'. See prec. & **-ation.** **a** The act of dissimulating; **b** that which is dissimulated.

dissipate, vb. trans. & intrans. [1. dísipāt; 2. dísipeit], fr. Lat. *dissipāt-(um)*, P.P. type of *dissipāre*, 'to scatter, disperse; put to flight; to demolish, destroy; to squander', fr. **dis-** & *sipāre, supāre*, 'to throw'. The *i* of the compounds is perh. unrounded fr. [y], earlier [u], before foll. lip-consonant; prob. cogn. w. Lith. *sùpti*, 'to swing, rock'; O. Bulg. *svepiti sę*, 'to shake', *rasypati*, 'to dissipate'. The Aryan base is prob. **sup-*, **suep-*, 'throw'; cp. Scrt. *vápati*, 'throws'. **A.** trans. **1.** To scatter, drive away, dispel: **a** (lit.) *the wind dissipates the clouds* &c.; **b** (fig.) *to dissipate gloom, sorrows* &c. **2.** To waste by extravagance, in wantonness, debauchery, or frivolity &c.: *to dissipate one's fortune, time* &c. **B.** intrans. **1.** To pass away, vanish: *clouds dissipate before the wind.* **2.** To engage in frivolous or dissolute occupations: *so many temptations to dissipate and idle.*

dissipated, adj. [1. dísipāted; 2. dísipeitid], fr. P.P. of prec. (of persons) Given to dissipation; hence, debauched, wild, dissolute.

dissipation, n. [1. disipāshun; 2. disipéiʃən]. **dissipate & -ion. 1.** Dispersion, driving away, scattering: **a** *dissipation of darkness, clouds, grief, doubts* &c.; **b** extravagance, wasteful expenditure: *dissipation of time, fortune, property, money, energy.* **2.** Trivial and frivolous gaiety and amusement; intemperance, debauchery: *to waste one's energies in dissipation.*

dissociable, adj. [1. disṓshiabl; 2. disóuʃiəbl], fr. Lat. *dissociābilis*, 'dividing, separating; incompatible'. See **dissociate & -able.** Capable of being dissociated.

dissocialize, vb. trans. [1. disṓshializ; 2. disóuʃəlaiz]. **dis- & social & -ize.** To render unsociable, make averse to society.

dissociate, vb. trans. [1. disṓshiāt; 2. disóuʃieit], fr. Lat. *dissociāt-(um)*, P.P. type of *dissociāre*, 'to disunite; to set at variance', fr. **dis-** & *sociāre*, 'to associate, unite together', fr. *socius*, 'a companion'. See **social. 1.** To separate, break union between, think of as distinct: *it is difficult to dissociate the man from his office; one must dissociate these two ideas.* **2.** (reflex.) To repudiate connexion, disavow participation in or agreement with: *to dissociate oneself from others; from the opinions first expressed, from what has been said* &c.

dissociation, n. [1. disṑsiāshun; 2. disòusiéiʃən]. Prec. & **-ation.** Act of dissociating; state of being dissociated; severance of connexion, keeping distinct.

dissociative, adj. [1. disṓshiativ; 2. disóuʃiətiv]. See **dissociate & -ive.** Tending to cause dissociation.

dissolubility, n. [1. disòlūbíliti, dìsoloobíliti; 2. dìsɔ̀ljubíliti, dìsəlubíliti]. See next word & **-ity.** The property of being dissoluble.

dissoluble, adj. [1. disólūbl, dísoloobl; 2. disɔ́ljubl, dísəlubl], fr. Lat. *dissolūbilis*, 'that can be dissolved'. See **dis- & soluble. 1.** Capable of being dissolved, or disintegrated. **2.** (of non-material things) Capable of being annulled, made void: *in the eyes of the Church no marriage is dissoluble.*

dissolute, adj. [1. dísolūt; 2. dísəljūt], fr. Lat. *dissolūt-(um)*, P.P. type of *dissolvere*, 'to separate, disunite, dissolve; to abolish, annul'. See **dissolve.** Lax, unbalanced, in conduct and morals.

dissolutely, adv. Prec. & **-ly.** In a dissolute manner.

dissoluteness, n. See prec. & **-ness.** The quality of being dissolute; immoral conduct and mode of life.

dissolution, n. [1. disolū́shun; 2. dìsəljū́ʃən], fr. Lat. *dissolūtiōn-(em)*, 'dissolving, destroying; interruption, disconnexion', fr. *dissolūt-(um)*, P.P. type of *dissolvere*, 'to dissolve, loosen, break up'. See **dissolve. 1.** **a** The act or process of dissolving; **b** state of being dissolved. **2.** (fig.) **a** The undoing of a bond: *dissolution of marriage, partnership* &c.; **b** dismissal, breaking up, of an assembly; esp. *dissolution of Parliament*, before a General Election; cp. *prorogation*; **c** the final disintegration of vital functions and powers; death.

dissolvable, adj. [1. dizólvabl; 2. dizɔ́lvəbl]. Next word & **-able.** Capable of being dissolved.

dissolve, vb. trans. & intrans. [1. dizólv; 2. dizɔ́lv], fr. Lat. *dissolvere*, 'to loosen, disunite, separate; to abolish, annul'. **dis- & solve**; cp. **dissolution. A.** trans. **1.** To break up into parts, cause to disintegrate; cause to melt, cause to pass from a solid to a liquid state: *to dissolve salt in water; sun dissolves ice.* Phr. *dissolved in tears*, shedding floods of tears. **2.** **a** To dismiss, disperse, terminate, end: *to dissolve Parliament*; **b** to annul, cancel, declare null and void: *to dissolve a marriage, a business partnership.* **B.** intrans. **1.** To melt down, liquefy, decompose, disintegrate: *snow dissolves in the sun; sugar dissolves in water.* **2.** **a** To vanish gradually from sight, fade away, become faint: *the vision seemed to dissolve before our eyes*; **b** (of Parliament) to disperse, end, terminate.

dissolvent, adj. & n. [1. dizólvent; 2. dizɔ́lvənt]. Prec. & **-ent.** **a** adj. Having the property of dissolving substances; **b** n., substance which causes another to dissolve.

dissonance, n. [1. dísonans; 2. dísənəns]. See next word & **-ance. 1.** (mus.) **a** Combination of notes that do not harmonize; discord; **b** a chord requiring resolution. **2.** (fig.) Lack of moral harmony, disagreement, clash of wills or temperaments.

dissonant, adj. [1. dísonant; 2. dísənənt], fr. Lat. *dissonant-(em)*, Pres. Part. type of *dissonāre*, 'to disagree in sound; to differ, disagree'. See **dis- & sonant. 1.** (mus.) Not harmonizing; discordant, harsh, ill-sounding. **2.** (fig.) Exhibiting disagreement in desires, opinions, temperaments; incompatible in character, inharmonious.

dissonantly, adv. Prec. & **-ly.** In a dissonant, inharmonious manner.

dissuade, vb. trans. [1. diswā́d; 2. diswéid], fr. Lat. *dissuādēre*, 'to advise against, resist, oppose by argument', fr. **dis-** & *suādēre*, 'to recommend, urge, persuade'. See **suasion. 1.** To advise against, endeavour to persuade (a person) not to do something, to urge arguments against some proposed action with a view to inducing a person not to do it: *I should strongly dissuade you from leaving the university too soon.* **2.** To succeed in persuading against doing something; to induce a person to relinquish intended action, divert him from his purpose: *I am thankful that I was dissuaded from the attempt.*

dissuasion, n. [1. diswā́zhun; 2. diswéižən], fr. Lat. *dissuāsiōn-(em)*, 'advice against an action', fr. *dissuās-(um)*, P.P. type of *dissuādēre*, 'to advise against'. See **dissuade & -ion.** The act of dissuading, advice against.

dissuasive, adj. [1. diswā́siv; 2. diswéisiv]. See prec. & **-ive.** Tending to, intended to, dissuade.

dissuasively, adv. Prec. & **-ly.** So as to dissuade.

dissyllabic, also **disyllabic**, adj. [1. dìsilábik; 2. dìsilǽbik]. See **di- (II.) & syllabic.** (of words or metrical feet) Having, consisting of, two syllables.

dissyllabically, adv. [1. dìsilábikali; 2. dìsilǽbikəli]. See prec. & **-al & -ly.** As two syllables.

dissyllable, disyllable, n. [1. disílabl; 2. disíləbl], fr. Fr. See **di- (II.) & syllable.** A word of two syllables.

dissymmetrical, adj. [1. dìsimétrikl; 2. dìsimétrikl]. **dis- & symmetrical. a** Not symmetrical; **b** symmetrical in opposite directions, e.g. right and left hand gloves.

dissymmetry, n. [1. disímetri; 2. disímitri]. **dis- & symmetry. a** Lack of symmetry; **b** symmetry in opposite directions.

distaff, n. [1. dístahf; 2. dístāf]. O.E. *distæf*, M.E. *distaf, disestafe*. See **staff**, & cp. M.L.G. *dīse*, 'flax prepared for spinning'; cp. **dizen.** Stick on which wool, flax &c. is wound for spinning; portion of spinning-wheel used for this purpose. Phr. *the distaff side*, maternal side, female line.

distal, adj. [1. dístal; 2. dístəl], fr. **distant** w. suff. on anal. of *central* &c. (anat.) At the end remote from attachment to body: *distal end of a bone, limb.* Contrasted with *proximal.*

distance (I.), n. [1. dístans; 2. dístəns]. Fr., fr. Lat. *distantia*, 'distance, remoteness, difference'. See **distant & -ce.** (general sense) Remoteness; difference. Various shades of meaning: **1.** Remoteness in space; **a** the space, long or short, which intervenes between two points, or two distinct objects: *we usually reckon distance in miles*; **b** the amount of space between two objects, degree of remoteness one from the other: *what is the distance from here to London?; the distance must be very great*; Phr. *striking, hailing, distance*, that degree of distance at which one can strike or hail effectively; **c** a great or considerable amount of space between two objects: *to live at a distance; in the distance*, far away (from here); *a good distance off*, a long way; *it is quite a distance from here, no distance at all.* Phrs. *to keep one's distance*, keep away from, court no familiarity; *to keep a person at a distance*, treat him coldly, without cordiality, refuse to become intimate with. **2.** Pictorial representation of different degrees of distance **a** from the beholder; **b** between different objects represented in the same picture. **3.** Remoteness in time: A long period, considerable amount of time: *to look back over a distance of forty years; at this distance of time.* **4.** (of degree of similarity) Unlikeness, marked difference: *how great is the distance between the art of the Egyptians and of the Greeks; the distance between the culture of the lowest savages and that of primitive man is but slight.* **5.** Degree of remoteness in blood-relationship: *there is some distance between the two branches of the family.*

distance (II.), vb. trans., fr. prec. To put space between two objects; to get in advance of, outstrip, in physical or intellectual contest: *to distance one's pursuers, rivals* &c.

distant, adj. [1. dístant; 2. dístənt], fr. Lat. *distant-(em)*, Pres. Part. of *distāre*, 'to stand apart; to be remote, distant', fr. **di- (I.)** & *stāre*, 'to stand'. See **stand (I.), state (I.). 1.** (of space) **a** Far-off; remote (in space or time): *a distant view*; **b** at a distance of: *some miles distant.* **2.** (of degree of similarity) Faint, not easily perceived: *a distant likeness, resemblance.* **3.** (of manner) Without cordiality, cold, not inviting intimacy: *a distant politeness; to be rather distant.* **4.** (of blood-relationship) Not close, derived from remote ancestor: *a distant cousin, kinsman.*

distantly, adv. Prec. & **-ly.** In a distant manner (in all senses).

distaste, n. [1. distā́st; 2. distéist]. **dis- & taste (I.).** (followed by *for*) Dislike, aversion, repugnance: *a distaste for hard work.*

distasteful, adj. [1. distā́stfool; 2. distéistfəl]. Prec. & **-ful.** Provoking distaste, exciting aversion; repellent.

distastefulness, n. Prec. & **-ness.** The quality of being distasteful.

distemper (I.), vb. trans. [1. distémper; 2. distémpə], fr. O. Fr. *destemprer*, fr. Med. Lat. *distemperāre*, fr. **dis-** & *temperāre*, 'to combine in due proportion; qualify, temper', See **temper (I.).** (chiefly adjectivally in P.P.) To disturb, put out of order, upset balance of; esp. *a distempered mind.*

distemper (II.), n., fr. prec. **a** (archaic) Illness, abnormal condition of mind or body; **b** now, specifically and more commonly, an inflammatory disease in dogs; **c** (fig.) social discontent, disorder, unrest.

distemper (III.), n. Same as **distemper** (I.) Cp. O. Fr. *destrempror*, later *destremper*, 'to steep, soak, moisten with water' &c., & Mod. Fr. *tremper*, 'soak, dye'. A special preparation of colouring matter, size &c. applied to the interior walls of houses &c.; also, tempera.

distemper (IV.), vb. trans., fr. prec. To coat with distemper.

distend, vb. trans. & intrans. [1. disténd; 2. disténd], fr. Lat. *distendere*, 'to stretch out, extend; to swell out, extend', fr. **dis-** & *tendere*, 'stretch'. See **tend** (II.), **tendon**, & **tense** (II.). **1.** (obs.) To stretch out (trans. & intrans.). **2. a** trans. (of a hollow, elastic body, bladder &c.) To fill out, inflate, blow out, cause to swell; **b** intrans., to become unnaturally or excessively inflated, or blown out, as by pressure of air &c. from within.

distensibility, n. [1. distènsibíliti; 2. distènsibíliti]. See next word & **-ity**. The quality of being distensible.

distensible, adj. [1. disténsibl; 2. disténsibl], fr. Lat. *distens-(um)*, P.P. type of *distendere*, 'to extend; to distend'. See **distend** & **-ible**. Capable of being distended.

distension, n. [1. disténshun; 2. disténʃən]. See prec. & **-ion**. Act or process of distending; state of being distended; inflation.

distich, n. [1. dístik; 2. dístik], fr. Lat. *distichon*, fr. Gk. *dístikhon*, 'a distich', fr. **di-** (II.) & *stíkhos*, 'a line'. See **stichic**. (pros.) Group of two lines; a couplet.

distichous, adj. [1. dístikus; 2. dístikəs], fr. Lat., fr. Gk. *dístikhos*, 'of two lines'. See prec. & **-ous**. (bot.) Arranged in two rows.

distil, vb. trans. & intrans. [1. distíl; 2. distíl], fr. Lat. *distilläre*, *dëstilläre*, 'to drip, trickle down, to distil', fr. **di-** (I.) & *stilläre*, 'to drop, trickle'. See **still** (V.) **A.** trans. **1.** To give out in drops, to cause to trickle; to exhale. **2.** To evaporate liquid and condense it again. **3. a** To extract the essence or spirit of a substance by evaporation and condensation; **b** to manufacture by evaporation and condensation, as whisky, scent &c. **4.** (fig., of non-material things) To extract essence, capture spirit of: *to distil wisdom, poetry*. **B.** intrans. To fall in drops, to trickle, come forth slowly.

distillate, n. [1. dístilāt; 2. dístileit], fr. Lat. *distillāt-(um)*, P.P. type of *distilläre*, 'to trickle, drip; to distil'. See prec. & **-ate**. Essence or spirit procured by distilling.

distillation, n. [1. distiláshun; 2. distiléiʃən]. Prec. & **-ation**. Act or process of distilling.

distillatory, adj. [1. distílatori; 2. distílətəri]. **distillate** & **-ory**. For, used in, distilling.

distiller, n. [1. distíler; 2. distílə]. **distil** & **-er**. Person who distils, esp. alcoholic spirit: *whisky distillers*.

distillery, n. [1. distíleri; 2. distíləri]. **distil** & **-ery**. A place where distilling (esp. of whisky, gin &c.) is carried on.

distinct, adj. [1. distíngkt; 2. distíŋkt], fr. Lat. *distinct-(us)* 'separate, distinct, marked at different points, adorned, spangled', fr. P.P. of *distinguere*, 'to separate, divide; to distinguish, discriminate; to punctuate; to adorn'. See **distinguish**. **1.** Separate, not connected, not confused with something else, individual; independent, having separate existence; different, not the same: *Old English and Old Frisian, though closely related, are perfectly distinct dialects*; *these two ideas must be kept distinct one from the other*; '*to have a distinct line of one's own*. **2. a** Well marked, clear, easily seen, capable of being perceived: *distinct writing*; *the earth's shadow on the moon was quite distinct*; *the inscriptions on the rock are no longer very distinct*; **b** definite, well-defined, unmistakable: *a distinct improvement*. **3.** (poet. and archaic) Adorned, variegated.

distinction, n. [1. distíngkshun; 2. distíŋkʃən]. Prec. & **-ion**. **1.** The act of keeping distinct, of distinguishing: *to make, draw, a distinction between two things*; *a distinction without a difference*. **2.** That which distinguishes, characteristic feature, point of difference, individuality: *I can see no distinction between the two cases*. **3. a** (i.) Quality of mind, bearing, character, which raises its possessor above the ordinary, and singles him out as a superior and lofty spirit: *to possess innate distinction of manner, character* &c.; (ii.) expression of such qualities in literary or artistic style; **b** a mark of favour and approbation bestowed by public authority as a reward for, and recognition of, services rendered: *loaded with distinctions from king and countrymen*. **4.** Condition of being distinguished, of possessing distinction or distinctions; eminence, repute: *to have the distinction of being associated with such a great man*; *a writer of distinction*.

distinctive, adj. [1. distíngktiv; 2. distíŋktiv]. **distinct** & **-ive**. Serving to distinguish, marking a difference, making distinct.

distinctively, adv. Prec. & **-ly**. In a distinctive manner.

distinctiveness, n. See prec. & **-ness**. The quality of being distinctive.

distinctly, adv. [1. distíngktli; 2. distíŋktli]. **distinct** & **-ly**. In a distinct manner (in all senses); **a** clearly, unmistakably: *distinctly visible*; *to speak distinctly*; **b** unambiguously, definitely, beyond possibility of doubt: *it must be distinctly understood that*, &c.; *he was told distinctly to remain where he was*; (colloq.) *that is distinctly annoying*.

distinctness, n. [1. distíngktnes; 2. distíŋktnis]. See prec. & **-ness**. The property or quality of being distinct.

distingué, adj. [1. distánggā; 2. distǽŋgei]. Fr., P.P. & adj., 'distinguished'. Having an air of distinction.

distinguish, vb. trans. & intrans. [1. distínggwish; 2. distíŋgwiʃ], fr. Lat. *distinguere*, 'to separate; to distinguish, discriminate; to punctuate; to adorn', & **-ish**. The Lat. vb. is fr. a base **stĭg-*, 'to prick, mark', w. infixed nasal. Cp. **stigma**, **stick** (I.), **instigate**. **A.** trans. **1. a** To perceive, make out clearly, discern: *to distinguish a distant object*; **b** to perceive difference or distinction between: *I can hardly distinguish one from the other, they are so much alike*. **2.** To be a mark of difference, act as distinguishing feature, be a characteristic of, to give individuality to: *each rank in the army is distinguished by a special badge*. **3. a** To bring credit and distinction on, make famous, prominent: (i.) *to distinguish oneself in one's profession*; (ii.) (ironical) to make oneself notorious: *he distinguished himself by deeply offending everyone present*; **b** to mark out for peculiar favour, honour by commendation: *Milton from his youth was distinguished by many famous men*. **B.** intrans. To make distinctions, exercise discrimination: *you are confusing things, let us distinguish*.

distinguishable, adj. [1. distínggwishabl; 2. distíŋgwiʃəbl]. Prec. & **-able**. Capable of being distinguished.

distinguishably, adv. Prec. & **-ly**. In a distinguishable manner.

distinguished, adj. [1. distínggwisht; 2. distíŋgwiʃt], fr. P.P. of **distinguish**. In various senses; esp. **a** marked by, exhibiting, innate distinction: *a distinguished appearance, manner, style* &c.; **b** possessing, having acquired, distinctions; recognized as having performed meritorious service, as having remarkable attainments; hence, celebrated, famous: *a distinguished writer, career* &c. *Distinguished Service Order*, abbr. D.S.O., an order established in 1886 for officers in army and navy for distinguished service in presence of the enemy.

distort, vb. trans. [1. distórt; 2. distɔ́t], fr. Lat. *distort-(um)*, P.P. type of *distorquēre*, 'to turn different ways, to twist; to torture', fr. **dis-** & *torquēre*, 'to turn, twist, bend'. See **torque**. **1.** To twist out of normal shape, pull awry; to alter, spoil the shape of: *his face was distorted by fury*. **2.** (of non-material things) To pervert, give false impression of, mis-state, misrepresent: *to distort the truth*; *to distort facts to suit one's argument*; *a distorted version of the story*.

distortedly, adv. [1. distórtedli; 2. distɔ́tidli]. P.P. of prec. & **-ly**. In a distorted manner.

distortion, n. [1. distórshun; 2. distɔ́ʃən]. **distort** & **-ion**. **1.** Act or process of distorting, twisting, misrepresenting: *his countenance underwent a sudden horrible distortion*. **2.** Something distorted; **a** a twist, deformation: *a distortion of the face, limbs* &c.; **b** perversion, misrepresentation, travesty: *a distortion of the truth* &c.

distortionist, n. [1. distórshunist; 2. distɔ́ʃənist]. Prec. & **-ist**. An acrobat who twists his body into unnatural shapes; a contortionist.

distract, vb. trans. [1. distrákt; 2. distrǽkt], fr. Lat. *distract-(um)*, P.P. type of *distrahere*, 'to pull apart, separate by force; to distract, perplex', fr. **dis-** & *trahere*, 'to draw, pull'. See **tract** (I.). (lit.) To pull apart, draw aside (only of mental processes). **1. a** To take, divert, the mind, thoughts &c. away from some fixed object of contemplation: *reading distracts the mind from grief*; **b** to direct the mind, turn it aside from its proper, immediate, object: *I cannot work if my attention is being distracted by constant interruptions*. **2.** To attract the thoughts in various directions; **a** to perplex, puzzle, bewilder, confuse: *my thoughts are distracted by so many different duties and occupations*; **b** to perplex the mind, draw it from its normal balance to the point of madness: *her mind had been distracted by grief*. Phr. *to drive distracted*, (i.) render mentally unbalanced, make mad; (ii.) to bewilder, cause extreme perplexity to.

distracted, adj. [1. distrákted; 2. distrǽktid], fr. P.P. of prec. Extremely disturbed in mind, frantic through grief, worry &c.; mad.

distractedly, adv. Prec. & **-ly**. In a distracted manner.

distractingly, adv. [1. distráktingli; 2. distrǽktiŋli]. Pres. Part. of **distract** & **-ly**. In a manner calculated to distract.

distraction, n. [1. distrákshun; 2. distrǽkʃən], fr. Lat. *distractiōn-(em)*, 'pulling apart, dividing'. See **distract** & **-ion**. **1. a** The act or process of distracting; **b** state of being distracted. **2.** (in favourable sense) Something that attracts and holds the mind and attention pleasurably; amusement, diversion, recreation: *not to have enough distractions*. **3.** Bewilderment, confusion of mind, madness: *to be driven to distraction*. Phr. *to love to distraction*, love passionately.

distrain, vb. intrans. [1. distrán; 2. distréin], fr. O. Fr. *destraindre*, fr. Lat. *distringere*, 'to stretch out; to engage, detain', fr. **di-** (I.) & *stringere*, 'to draw tight, bind, squeeze; to touch lightly; to compress, abridge'. See **strain**, **stringent**, **strict**. To seize goods in payment for money due, or in order to force debtor to pay: *to distrain upon a person, his goods, for rent*.

distrainee, n. [1. distrānḗ; 2. distreiní]. Prec. & **-ee**. A person whose goods are seized in payment of a debt.

distrainment, n. [1. distránment; 2. distréinmənt]. **distrain** & **-ment**. The act of distraining.

distraint, n. [1. distránt; 2. distréint], fr. O. Fr. *destraint*, P.P. of *destraindre*. See **distrain**. The act or process of distraining.

distrait, adj. [1. distrá; 2. distréi]. Fr. (P.P. of *distraire*), fr. Lat. *distractum*, see **distract**. Absent-minded, preoccupied.

distraught, adj. [1. distráwt; 2. distrɔ́t]. M.E. *distrauhte*, *distract*, 'distracted', fr. Lat. *distractus*, 'divided; perplexed'. Variant of **distract**. Confused in mind, bewildered; perplexed by doubt and anxiety; mad.

distress (I.), n. [1. distrés; 2. distrés]. M.E. *destresse*, *distresse*, fr. O. Fr. *destrece*, fr. Low Lat. **districtia*, fr. Lat. *district-(um)*, P.P. type of *distringere*, 'to draw tight, bind, squeeze; distract, harass'. See **distrain**. **1.** (of mental state) **a** Sorrow, grief, affliction: *distress of mind*; **b** that which causes sorrow

&c.: *his conduct was a great distress to his father.* **2.** (of physical state) Extreme discomfort, malaise, pain, exhaustion: *the horse, runner, showed signs of distress.* **3.** (of external conditions) **a** Great poverty, misery, lack of means of support: *to relieve distress*; **b** danger, difficulty, imminent peril: *a ship in distress.* **4.** (law) **a** Right of landlord to distrain on goods of tenant for non-payment of rent; **b** distraint.

distress (II.), vb. trans., fr. O. Fr. *destresser*, fr. Low Lat. *districtiāre*. See prec. **a** To afflict, cause distress, sorrow, to: *most distressing news*; Phr. *to distress oneself*, to feel anxiety, become anxious, allow oneself to be worried: **b** to exhaust by physical exertion, cause bodily pain: *the horses were much distressed during the last few hours of the march.*

distressful, adj. [1. distrésfool; 2. dɪstrésfəl]. **distress** (I.) & **-ful**. **a** Suffering distress; **b** causing distress.

distressfully, adv. Prec. & **-ly**. In a distressful manner.

distress-gun, n. One fired by a ship in distress, as call for help.

distressingly, adv. [1. distrésingli; 2. dɪstrésiŋli]. Pres. Part. of **distress** (II.) & **-ly**. So as to cause distress.

distributable, adj. [1. distríbūtabl; 2. dɪstríbjutəbl]. Next word & **-able**. Capable of being distributed; available for distribution.

distribute, vb. trans. & intrans. [1. distríbūt; 2. dɪstríbjūt], fr. Lat. *distribūt-(um)*, P.P. type of *distribuere*, 'to divide, distribute'. See **dis-** & **tribute**. **A.** trans. **1.** To dispense, administer: *to distribute justice.* **2.** **a** To hand out, allot, (material objects) among a number of persons: *to distribute money, blankets, to the poor*; **b** to deposit at various places: *to distribute circulars, letters, at a number of houses.* **3.** To spread out, so as to cover a specified area: *to distribute manure over a field.* **4.** (typog.) To break up type that has been used for printing and put back each letter into its proper compartment in the cases. **5.** (log., chiefly in P.P.) To use a term in its fullest extent, so that it stands for everything to which it can be applied: *distributed middle term.* **B.** intrans. To perform the act of distribution: '*To do good and to distribute, forget not*'.

distribution, n. [1. distribū́shun; 2. dìstribjū́ʃən]. Prec. & **-ion**. **1.** The act or process of distributing; condition of being distributed. **2.** (log.) The use of a term in the widest sense, applying it to all objects denoted by it. **3.** (polit. econ.) **a** Process of distributing commodities from producers to consumers; **b** apportionment of profit from a commodity among the various interests, land, labour, capital, which co-operate in its production. **4.** Mode in which, and extent to which, anything is distributed; precise way in which things occur in particular places and areas: *certain types of animal and plant life have a very wide distribution in Europe*; *the distribution of dialect features*; *the distribution of a particular sound in a given type of English*, i.e. in what words it is used.

distributional, adj. [1. distribū́shunal; 2. dìstribjū́ʃənəl]. Prec. & **-al**. Pertaining to distribution.

distributive, adj. & n. [1. distríbūtiv; 2. dɪstríbjutiv]. **distribute** & **-ive**. **1.** adj. **a** Carrying out act or process of distribution; involving distribution; **b** implying reference to each member of a group or class, not to class as a whole. **2.** n. A distributive pronoun or adjective.

distributively, adv. Prec. & **-ly**. Severally, individually, separately.

district (I.), n. [1. dístrikt; 2. dístrikt], fr. Med. Lat. *districtus*, 'district', fr. Lat. *district-(um)*, P.P. type of *distringere*, 'to stretch out in different directions' &c. See **distrain, strict**. **1.** A defined tract of land, part of a country marked out for some specific purpose, usually administrative; territory over which a particular official, or official body, has jurisdiction; specif., administrative division of a province, county, city, parish; also attrib., as: *rural, urban, district council* &c. **2.** (in general sense) Region, area, part of a country.

district (II.), vb. trans., fr. prec. To divide up into districts.

district visitor, n. A person working as a clergyman's assistant in a particular part of a parish.

distrust (I.), n. [1. distrúst; 2. dɪstrást]. **dis-** & **trust** (I.). Want of confidence; doubt, suspicion.

distrust (II.), vb. trans. **dis-** & **trust** (II.). To feel distrust concerning, lack confidence in, be suspicious of.

distrustful, adj. [1. distrústfool; 2. dɪstrástfəl]. **distrust** (I.) & **-ful**. Animated by distrust, unwilling to place reliance on; doubtful, suspicious.

distrustfully, adv. Prec. & **-ly**. In a distrustful manner; with distrust and suspicion.

disturb, vb. trans. [1. distérb; 2. dɪstə́b], fr. O. Fr. *destorber*, fr. Lat. *disturbāre*, 'to drive asunder, throw into disorder; to frustrate', fr. **dis-** & *turbāre*, 'to agitate, confuse', fr. *turba*, 'an uproar, tumult; a crowd, multitude'. See **turbid**. **1.** (of material and non-material things) To interrupt, interfere with, alter, the normal condition; to break up state of order, calm and quiet: **a** *to disturb the surface of a lake*, ruffle it; *to disturb the good order of a house, of the furniture* &c., disarrange it; **b** *to disturb one's thoughts, reflexions, train of ideas, one's serenity of mind*, break in upon, interrupt; **c** *to disturb one's plans, one's work*; **d** *to disturb the peace*, cause uproar, social unrest &c. **2** (law) *To disturb the freehold*, to break up, dig, the ground, esp. for the purpose of removing a growing tree &c.

disturbance, n. [1. distérbans; 2. dɪstə́bəns]. Prec. & **-ance**. **1.** The act of disturbing. **2.** **a** Something that disturbs; **b** result of disturbing; confusion, interruption, uproar: specif., *to cause a disturbance*, provoke breach of the peace. **3.** (law) Act of hindering a person from enjoyment of his rights.

disunion, n. [1. disū́nion; 2. dɪsjū́njən]. **dis-** & **union**. (of non-material process) **a** Rupture of union, severance, breaking of connecting bond: *disunion of Church and State*; **b** disagreement, discord, dissension.

disunite, vb. trans. & intrans. [1. disūnít; 2. dìsjunáit]. **dis-** & **unite**. **a** trans. To sever connexion between, cause to separate, destroy union of; **b** intrans., to become separate.

disunited, adj. [1. disūníted; 2. dìsjunáitid]. fr. P.P. of prec. **a** (of physical condition) Not united, separate, disconnected; **b** specif. (of human relations) differing in opinions and purpose; at variance.

disuse (I.), vb. trans. [1. disū́z; 2. dɪsjū́z]. **dis-** & **use** (II.). To cease to use, to use no longer (esp. in P.P.).

disuse (II.), n. [1. disū́s; 2. dɪsjū́s]. **dis-** & **use** (I.). The state of not being used: *to fall into disuse*; *become rusty from disuse.*

disyllabic &c. See **dissyllabic** &c.

ditch (I.), n. [1. dich; 2. ditʃ]. O.E. *dīc*, M.E. *dīch*, O. Fris. *dīk*, M.H.G. *tīch*, O.N. *dīk*; prob. cogn. w. Gk. *thégein*, 'to sharpen'; Lat. *fīgere*, 'to fix, fasten, drive in'; Bret. *dag*, 'dagger'; Aryan base **dhāig-*, **dhīg-*, **dhəg-*, 'sharp, pointed'. The word seems to have been applied in Gmc. to the sloping mound formed by earth dug out of a hollow, then to the hollow itself. Cp. **dike**. **a** A narrow channel, dug in the ground, for conveying or draining off water; **b** a larger excavation, resembling this in shape, for defence &c.; Phr. *to die in the last ditch*, defend position (lit. or fig.) to the last; **c** natural watercourse resembling a ditch.

ditch (II.), vb. trans. & intrans., fr. prec. To make, mend, clear ditches.

ditcher, n. [1. dícher; 2. dítʃə]. Prec. & **-er**. Man who makes and mends ditches; usually *hedger and ditcher.*

ditching, n. [1. díching; 2. dítʃiŋ]. **ditch** (I.) & **-ing** (not Pres. Part.). Art, occupation, of making and mending ditches; esp. in Phr. *hedging and ditching.*

ditch-water, n. Stagnant water. Phr. *dull as ditch-water*, intensely dull.

ditheism, n. [1. díthēizm; 2. dáiþi-izəm]. See **di-** (II.) & **theism**. Dualism; belief in the existence of two gods or ruling principles.

dithyramb, n. [1. díthiram; 2. díþiræm], fr. Lat., fr. Gk. *dīthúrambos*, 'dithyramb; poem in honour of Bacchus'. Etymol. unknown. **a** In Ancient Greek sense; **b** any wild chant or song of a highly emotional character.

dithyrambic, adj. [1. dìthirámbik; 2. dìþiræ̀mbik]. Prec. & **-ic**. Of the nature of a dithyramb.

dittany, n. [1. dítani; 2. dítəni]. M.E. *detane, detany*, fr. O. Fr. *ditain*, fr. Lat. *dictamnum*, fr. Gk. *diktam(n)on*, named after Mount *Dicte* in Crete. A small perennial herb, producing a fragrant oil, once used as a tonic.

ditto, n. [1. dítō; 2. dítou]. Ital., fr. Lat. *dicto*, dat. of *dictus*, P.P. of Lat. *dīcere*, 'to say'. See **dictum**. **1.** Lit. (as has been) said; used in English in sense of 'the same', to avoid repetition of word: *paid to Messrs. Jones £10, ditto to Messrs. Brown.* Abbreviation *Do.* Phr. *to say ditto to*, say the same as, agree with. **2.** (slang, pl.) *Dittoes*, suit of clothes made all of the same pattern of cloth.

dittographic, adj. [1. ditográfik; 2. ditəgræ̀fik]. See next word & **-ic**. Pertaining to, caused by, dittography.

dittography, n. [1. ditógrafi; 2. ditɔ́grəfi], fr. Gk. *dittós*, 'double, twofold', fr. **dikh-jos*; cp. *dikha*, 'doubly, separately', fr. **di-*, 'two' (see **di-** (II.)) & a suff. **-gh-a*, as in Scrt. *(viśva)-ha*, 'every time'. For the suff. see **-graphy**. The mechanical and unintentional repetition of a letter or letters by a copyist.

ditty, n. [1. díti; 2. díti]. M.E. *dite*, fr. O. Fr. *dité*, fr. Lat. *dictāt-(um)*, P.P. type of *dictāre*, 'to say often; to prescribe, order; to compose'. See **dictate**. A short, simple song, or poem intended to be sung.

ditty-bag, -box, n. Etymol. unknown. Sailor's, soldier's receptacle for holding needles, cotton, and odds and ends.

diuretic, adj. & n. [1. dìūrétik; 2. dàijurétik], fr. Lat., fr. Gk. *di-ourētikós*, fr. **di-** (II.) & *ouréein*, 'to make water', & **-ic**. See **urine**. **a** adj. Promoting the secretion of urine; **b** n., anything, esp. a medicine, having this effect.

diurnal, adj. [1. dīérnal; 2. daiə́nəl], fr. Lat. *diurnālis*, 'daily', fr. *diurnus*, 'daily', formed fr. *di-(ēs)*, 'a day', on the anal. of *nocturnus*, 'nightly'. See **dies non, deity,** & cp. **journal**. **a** Of, or belonging to the day; opposed to *nocturnal*: '*this diurnal star*' (the sun) (Milton); **b** daily, taking place every day: '*earth's diurnal course*' (Wordsworth); **c** (bot. and zool.) lasting, living, for a day.

diurnally, adv. Prec. & **-ly**. By day; daily.

diva, n. [1. dḗva; 2. dívə]. Ital., fr. Lat. *dīva*, 'a goddess', fem. form of *dīvus*, 'a god', fr. **deiw-os*. See **deity, divine**. A principal woman singer, prima donna.

divagate, vb. intrans. [1. dívagāt; 2. dáivəgeit], fr. Lat. *dīvagāt-(um)*, P.P. type of *dīvagāri*, 'to wander about', fr. **di-** (I.) & *vagāri*, 'to wander, ramble; to spread, be diffused'. See **vagary**. **a** To wander about, stray; **b** to ramble, digress, in speech, become diffuse and wordy; stray from point.

divagation, n. [1. dìvagā́shun; 2. daivəgéiʃən]. Prec. & **-ation**. A wandering, straying; digression.

divalent, adj. [1. dìvā́lent; 2. dàivéilənt]. See **di-** & **valent**. (chem.) Having a valency of two, combining with two radicals, bivalent.

divan, n. [1. dìván; 2. daivǽn]. Pers. *diwān*, 'collection of books; a council'. **1.** **a** Oriental (esp. Turkish) court of justice or state council; **b** the room in which such councils are held. **2.** A long, low, cushioned seat against the wall of a room. **3. a** Saloon where coffee and cigars are consumed; **b** high-flown name for a tobacconist's shop, *cigar divan.*

divaricate (**I.**), vb. intrans. [1. dīvárikāt; 2. daivǽrikeit], fr. Lat. *dīvāricāt-(um)*, P.P. type of *dīvāricāre*, 'to spread asunder', fr. **di-** (**I.**) & *vāricāre*, 'to stand with legs apart', fr. *vāricus*, 'with feet apart, straddling', fr. *vārus*, 'crooked, bent outwards or inwards'. See **varus.** To divide into branches, fork out, diverge.

divaricate (**II.**), adj. See prec. (bot. and zool.) Spreading apart, branching, divergent.

divarication, n. [1. dīvàrikáshun; 2. daivæ̀rikéiʃən]. See prec. & **-ation.** Branching, forking.

dive (**I.**), vb. intrans. [1. dīv; 2. daiv]. O.E. *dȳfan*, 'to dip, plunge', M.E. *dīven*, 'to dive', w. added sense of O.E. *dūfan*, 'to sink, plunge'; cp. O.N. *dȳfa*; Gmc. **dūb(j)a-*, fr. Aryan **dhūbh-*, 'to go down into water'; prob. cogn. w. **deep, dip. 1.** Specif. **a** to plunge into water head foremost; **b** to go suddenly beneath surface of water when swimming. **2.** To go under water, often in specially made dress, for some specific purpose, e.g. for salvage work, to seek sponges, pearls &c. **3. a** To make a rapid, plunging movement on land, go headlong, hurl oneself, plunge suddenly into something: *to dive into the bushes; dive down an alley* &c.; **b** to thrust one's hand, suddenly and rapidly, into a bag, pocket, cupboard &c., in order to find or extract something. **4.** (fig.) To immerse oneself deeply, especially for a brief space, in the study of a subject, or in a book.

dive (**II.**), n., fr. prec. **a** A specific act of diving into water &c.; **b** an underground or basement room in a restaurant, inn &c., where some speciality is sold: *an oyster dive.*

diver, n. [1. dīver; 2. dáivə]. **dive** (**I.**) & **-er. 1.** One who dives; specif. **a** one who works under water for some special purpose, e.g. collecting pearls, sponges &c.; **b** one professionally engaged in diving in a specially contrived helmet, into which air is pumped through tubes, and a waterproof suit covering the rest of the body except the hands. **2.** One of several kinds of water birds.

diverge, vb. intrans. [1. dīvérj, divérj; 2. daivə́dž, divə́dž], fr. **di-** (**I.**) & Lat. *vergere*, 'to bend, turn, incline'. See **verge** (**II.**). **a** To divide, go in different directions, separate; **b** to become different, vary from an original form; **c** (of several sets of opinions &c.) to differ, tend in different directions.

divergence, -cy, n. [1. dīvérjens(i); 2. daivə́džəns(i)]. Prec. & **-ence** & **-cy.** The process of diverging; deviation, difference.

divergent, adj. [1. dīvérjent; 2. daivə́džənt]. See **diverge** & **-ent.** Going in a different direction, deviating, branching off.

divergently, adv. Prec. & **-ly.** In different directions.

divergingly, adv. [1. dīvérjingli; 2. daivə́džiŋli]. Pres. Part of **diverge** & **-ly.** So as to exhibit divergence.

divers, adj. [1. dīverz; 2. dáivəz], fr. O. Fr., fr. Lat. *dīvers-(um)*, P.P. type of *divertere*, 'to turn different ways, part, separate; to deviate, differ', fr. **di-** (**I.**) & *vertere*, 'to turn'. See **version.** (archaic) Several, different, various: *in divers manners and places.*

diverse, adj. [1. divérs, dīvérs; 2. divə́s, daivə́s]. Variant of prec. Dissimilar, of different kinds, varied.

diversely, adv. Prec. & **-ly.** In different ways, dissimilarly.

diversification, n. [1. divèrsifikáshun; 2. divə̀sifikéiʃən]. See **diversify** & **-fication.** Process of diversifying, state of being diversified.

diversified, adj. [1 divérsifīd; 2. divə́sifaid], fr. P.P. of **diversify.** Presenting variety of form, colour, features &c.; varied: *the country is diversified by undulations, woodland* &c.

diversiform, adj. [1. divérsiform; 2. divə́sifōm]. See **diverse** & **-form.** Of several shapes.

diversify, vb. trans. [1. divérsifī, dīvérsifī; 2. divə́sifai, daivə́sifai], fr. O. Fr. *diversifier.* See **diverse** & **-fy.** To produce variety in, vary the form and appearance of, to break monotony of.

diversion, n. [1. di-, dīvérshun; 2. di-, daivə́ʃən], fr. Med. Lat. *diversiōn-(em).* See **diverse** & **-ion. 1.** The act of diverting, turning aside, giving a different direction to something. **2. a** The distraction of attention, a turning of the mind to a different object; specif. (mil.) **b** the drawing of an enemy's attention from a particular point, by an attack, or demonstration, at another point. **3.** That which diverts the attention agreeably; recreation, amusement.

diversity, n. [1. dīvérsiti; 2. daivə́siti], fr. O. Fr. *diversité*, fr. Lat. *dīversitāt-(em)*, 'diversity, difference; disagreement'. See **diverse** & **-ity. 1.** State of being different, unlikeness; variety, difference; **a** in outward form, appearance, structure; **b** in mental and moral character, thoughts, opinions &c. **2.** (poet.) Variegation, difference in colour: '*Blushing in bright diversities of day*' (Pope).

divert, vb. trans. [1. dīvért; 2. daivə́t], fr. O. Fr. *divertir*, fr. Lat. *dīvertere*, 'to go in different ways, separate; to deviate, differ', fr. **di-** (**I.**) & *vertere*, 'to turn'. See **vertex, version. 1.** (of physical action) To turn aside, cause to proceed in another direction: *to divert the course of a stream* &c. **2.** (of action on the mind &c.) **a** To distract, turn aside, give another bent to, the thoughts, attention &c.; **b** specif., to occupy the mind agreeably, to amuse, entertain: *to be greatly diverted by a play* &c.

diverting, adj. [1. dīvérting; 2. daivə́tiŋ], fr. Pres. Part. of prec. Causing amusement; entertaining.

divertingly, adv. Prec. & **-ly.** In a diverting manner.

divest, vb. trans. [1. dīvést, divést; 2. daivést, divést], fr. O. Fr. *desvestir*, fr. **dis-** & Lat. *vestīre*, 'to clothe', fr. *vestis*, 'garment'. See **vest** (**I.**). **1.** To strip, take off, remove; **a** (reflex.) *to divest oneself of garments*, to undress; **b** *to divest a person of his coat* &c., to take it off him. **2.** (fig.) **a** (reflex.) To surrender: *to divest oneself of one's wealth* &c.; **b** to dispossess, deprive of, remove from possession of: *to divest a person of his office, rank, honours* &c.

divestiture, n. [1. dīvéstichur; 2. daivéstitʃə]. See prec. & cp. **investiture.** Divestment.

divestment, n. [1. dīvéstment; 2. daivéstment]. **divest** & **-ment. a** The act of divesting; **b** state of being divested.

divide (**I.**), vb. trans. & intrans. [1. divīd; 2. diváid], fr. Lat. *dīvidere*, 'to force apart, separate; to distribute, apportion; to separate, distinguish'; fr. **di-** (**I.**) & **-vid-ere*, 'to set apart, separate, divide'; cp. Lat. *vidua*, 'widow'; further Scrt. *vindhátē*, 'becomes empty, is wanting in', *viddhás*, 'pierced'; *vidhuras*, 'separated'. Cogn. w. O.H.G. *wis-an*, 'to avoid', Aryan **weidh-so-*, &, w. different grade, O.H.G. *weiso*, Mod. Germ. *waise*, 'orphan', Aryan **woidh-so-*. See further under **widow. A.** trans. **1.** To separate, split up into parts: *to divide a cake into several pieces.* **2.** (followed by *with, between*, or *among*) **a** To share out, cut up and apportion: *to divide something among*, or *between, several persons*; *to divide with another*, give him part and take part oneself. **b** (fig.) to spend, apportion time, energy &c., in several directions: *to divide one's time between work and play.* **3.** (followed by *from*) to set apart, arrange in separate groups: *to divide the sheep from the goats.* **4.** To intervene between two objects, or two parts of same thing; to part, separate, serve as a separating line, barrier, or boundary: *a road, a river, a paling, divides the two portions of the estate*; *to divide the hair in the middle.* **5.** (of non-material processes) **a** To set at variance, antagonize, cause disagreement: *no quarrels shall divide us*; *opinions are divided on the point*; Phr. *a house divided against itself*; **b** to cause one to hesitate in mind between two decisions, incline now to this course, now to that: '*This way and that dividing the swift mind*' (Tennyson); *my mind is divided on the point.* **6.** To cause members of a deliberative body to vote on a motion, thus dividing it into those for, and those against: *I shall divide the house on this point.* **7.** (math.) To find out how many times one number is contained in another. **B.** intrans. **1.** To separate, split up, cease to be one, and become several. **2.** (of Parliament and other deliberative bodies) To separate for voting, to vote for or against, a motion: *the house then divided*; *Divide! Divide!*, cry to indicate that enough has been said, and that the vote should now be taken.

divide (**II.**), n., fr. prec. Something that divides, esp. (in U.S.A.) a watershed. Phr. *the Great Divide*, death.

divided, adj. [1. divīded; 2. diváidid], fr. P.P. of **divide** (**I.**). (in vbl. senses) Specif. (phon.) *divided consonant*, one formed by contact of part of the tongue with upper teeth, gums, soft or hard palate, in such a way that the air-stream is allowed on either side, or one side, of the point of contact, thus producing different types of *l-* sound; popularly called *liquid consonant.*

dividend, n. [1. dividend; 2. dívidənd], fr. Fr. *dividende*, fr. Lat. *dīvidendum*, 'to be divided'. See **divide** (**I.**). **1. a** Interest payable on money invested; trading company's profits. Phr. *to declare a dividend*, to announce that one will be paid; **b** amount divided among creditors from the estate of a bankrupt; **c** amount of profit on purchases repaid to members of a co-operative society. **2.** (math.) Number to be divided by another.

dividend-warrant, n. Certificate entitling holder to receive payment of dividend.

divider, n. [1. divīder; 2. diváidə]. **divide** (**I.**) & **-er.** One who, that which, divides; specif., *dividers*, compasses for measuring or marking off distances.

divi-divi, n. [1. dívi dívi; 2. dívi dívi]. Native name. South American and West Indian plant whose seeds are used in tanning and leather dressing.

dividual, adj. [1. divídūal; 2. divídjuəl]. Lat. *dīvidu-(us)*, 'divided, separate', & **-al.** Separate; divisible.

divination, n. [1. dìvinā́shun; 2. dìvinéiʃən], fr. Fr., fr. Lat. *dīvīnātiōn-(em)*, 'the power of foreseeing'. **divine** (**III.**) & **-ation. a** The act of divining; faculty of discovering, or foretelling something still unknown, by supernatural means; **b** a prediction.

divine (**I.**), adj. [1. divīn; 2. diváin], fr. O. Fr. *devin*, fr. Lat. *dīvīnus*, 'belonging to a deity', fr. **deiw-in-*, fr. **deiw-os-*, 'a god'. See **deity. 1. a** Belonging to, like, having the nature of, God, or a god; devoted to God; **b** granted by God: *divine right (of kings).* **2.** (hyperbolical) Supremely excellent: *the divine Shakespeare*; often (vulg. colloq.) meaning no more than very good, pleasing, agreeable: *what divine weather, muffins* &c.!

divine (**II.**), n., fr. prec. **a** One learned in, a student of, theology; **b** (colloq.) a clergyman.

divine (**III.**), vb. trans., fr. O. Fr. *deviner*, fr. Lat. *dīvīnāre*, 'to foresee; to foretell', fr. *dīvīn-(us)*, 'divine'. See **divine** (**I.**). **a** To foretell the future, make a discovery, by supernatural means; **b** to discover by conjecture or intuition: *to divine a person's intention* &c.

divinely, adv. [1. divīnli; 2. diváinli]. **divine** (**I.**) & **-ly.** In a divine manner, in a manner supremely excellent.

diviner, n. [1. divīner; 2. diváinə]. **divine** (**III.**) & **-er.** One who divines; specif., a water-finder, one who professes to discover underground springs by means of a divining-rod; also *water-diviner* or *dowser.*

diving-bell, n. [1. díving bèl; 2. dáiviŋ bèl]. Apparatus lowered into the water, in which persons can remain under water, being kept dry, and supplied with air pumped through tubes from above.

diving-dress, n. Suit of special clothes, used by divers, with weighted boots and air-tight helmet through which air-pipes enter.

divining-rod, n. [1. divíning rod; 2. diváiniŋ rɔd]. Forked twig of green hazel or withy, with which some persons appear to be able to discover water or metals below the ground; the 'rod' is held by both hands, and twitches when held over water.

divinity, n. [1. divíniti; 2. divíniti], fr. O. Fr. *devinite*, fr. Lat. *dīvīnitāt-(em)*, 'divinity; divine quality'. See **divine** (**I.**) & **-ity**. **1.** The property of being divine, of being God: *the divinity of Christ*. **2.** A divine being: *the Divinity*, God; *a divinity*, a heathen deity. **3.** The scientific study of theology.

divinity calf, n. (book-binding) Dark-brown calf-leather, so called from being formerly used in binding theological books.

divinization, n. [1. dìvinīzā́shun; 2. dìvinaizéiʃən]. Next word & **-ation**. Deification.

divinize, vb. trans. [1 dívinīz; 2. dívinaiz]. See **divine** (**I.**) & **-ize**. (rare) To raise to the rank of a god, deify.

divisibility, n. [1. divizibíliti; 2. divìzibíliti]. See next word & **-ity**. The quality of being divisible.

divisible, adj. [1. divízibl; 2. divízibl], fr. Lat. *dīvīsibilis*, 'divisible'. See next word & **-ible**. **a** Capable of being divided into parts; **b** (math., of numbers) exactly containing another number a certain number of times, without leaving a remainder.

division, n. [1. divízhun; 2. divížən], fr. Lat. *dīvīsiōn-(em)*, 'the act of dividing, process of being divided', fr. *dī-vīs-(um)* (fr. **-weidh-to-*), P.P. type of *dīvidere*, 'to divide'. See **divide** (**I.**). **1.** The act, or process of dividing, state of being divided; **a** (of material things) separation, distribution &c.; **b** (of mental processes) disunion, difference of opinion, antagonism, opposing interests &c.; sections of a community so divided. **2.** (parl. &c.) Separation of members into two groups for voting; act of voting on a motion. **3.** (math.) Process of dividing one number by another. **4.** Something that divides; a partition, barrier. **5.** Something that is divided from a whole; **a** section of country distinguished for administrative or parliamentary purposes; **b** (mil.) three, or four, brigades, commanded by a major-general, forming a complete unit, with cavalry and artillery &c., three or four of which form an army corps; **c** (nav.) group of four war vessels, as unit of a squadron or fleet; **d** class, as in a school, government department, prison &c.

divisional, adj. [1. divízhunal; 2. divížənəl]. Prec. & **-al**. Pertaining to a division.

divisionally, adv. Prec. & **-ly**. By division, or divisions.

divisor, n. [1. divízor; 2. diváizə]. See **division** & **-or**. (math.) The number by which another is divided.

divorce (**I.**), n. [1. divórs; 2. divɔ̄́s], fr. Fr., fr. Lat. *dīvortium*, 'a separation; point of separation; dissolution of marriage', fr. *dīvortere*, *dīvertere*, 'to turn different ways, to separate; to turn aside'. See **divert**, **vortex**. **1.** Legal dissolution of marriage contract between husband and wife. **2.** (fig.) Separation, severance, of connexion and relation: *the divorce between religion and science*.

divorce (**II.**), vb. trans., fr. prec. **1.** To get rid of, separate oneself from (wife or husband) by obtaining a legal dissolution of marriage. **2.** (fig.) To separate, disunite, tear asunder, sever connexion between: *to divorce one's conduct from one's principles*.

divorceable, adj. [1. divórsabl; 2. divɔ̄́səbl]. Prec. & **-able**. Capable of being, liable to be, divorced.

divorcee, n. [1. dìvorsḗ; 2. dìvɔ̄sí]. **divorce** (**II.**) & **-ee**. A spouse who is divorced from the other.

divorcement, n. [1. divórsment; 2. divɔ̄́smənt]. **divorce** (**II.**) & **-ment**. The act, or process, of divorcing; state of being divorced.

divot, n. [1. dívot; 2. dívət]. Etymol. unknown. (Scots) **a** A piece of turf for burning; **b** (golf) piece of turf cut out by club of player when striking the ball.

divulgation, n. [1. dìvulgā́shun; 2. dàivəlgéiʃən]. Next word & **-ation**. The act, or process, of divulging; state of being divulged.

divulge, vb. trans. [1. divúlj; 2. diváldž], fr. Lat. *dīvulgāre*, 'to make known, publish', fr. **di-** (**I.**) & *vulgāre*, 'to make common or universal; to make known; spread abroad'. See **vulgus**. To make known, reveal, communicate, allow to transpire: *to divulge a secret, news* &c.

divulgement, n. [1. divúljment; 2. diváldžmənt]. Prec. & **-ment**. The act of divulging; state of being divulged.

divulgence, n. [1. divúljens; 2. diváldžəns]. **divulge** & **-ence**. Act of divulging, divulgement.

diwan. See **dewan**.

dixie, n. [1. díksi; 2. díksi]. Origin unknown. (mil. colloq.) A mess-tin or cooking-pot.

dizen, vb. trans. [1. dízen; 2. dáizən]. Cp. L.G. *dīse*, 'flax prepared for spinning'; Gmc. **dīs-* 'prepare, make ready or fit'; cp. **distaff**. To dress gaily, adorn, deck.

dizzily, adv. [1. dízili; 2. dízili], fr. **dizzy** & **-ly**. In a dizzy manner; in such a manner as to cause dizziness.

dizziness, n. [1. dízines; 2. dízinis], fr. next word & **-ness**. The state of being dizzy.

dizzy (**I.**), adj. [1. dízi; 2. dízi]. O.E. *dysiġ*, 'foolish'; M.E. *disi*, 'stupid, foolish'; cp. M. Du. *deusig*, O.H.G. *tusīg*; also Dan. *dōsig*, 'drowsy'; Gmc. **dus-*, 'to be foolish, irrational, out of one's mind'; Aryan base **dhewes-*, **dheus-*, **dhus-*, 'to be mad, to rage'; cp. Gk. *thuiás*, 'a Bacchante' (fr. **thus-ia-*, fr. **dhus-*). For the base **dhewā-*, &c. see **beast, fume** &c. **1.** **a** Suffering from vertigo, giddy; **b** perplexed in mind, bewildered. **2.** Causing dizziness, liable to make dizzy: *a dizzy height*; *a dizzy whirling*.

dizzy (**II.**), vb. trans., fr. prec. To make dizzy, confuse, bewilder.

do (**I.**), vb. trans., intrans., & auxil. [1. dōō; 2. dū]. M.E. *dōn*, O.E. *dōn*; cp. O.H.G. *tuon*, O.L.G. *dōn*, *duan*, O. Fris. *dua*, Gmc. **dō-*. The Aryan base **dhō-*, **dhē-*, **dhə-*, 'to place, put', has numerous derivatives in the Indo-Gmc. languages. Cp. Scrt. *(dá)dhāti*, 'place'; Gk. *títhēmi*, 'I put, place; make, cause to become; maintain'; Lat. *(ab)dere*, 'to place apart, remove', *(crē)dere*, 'to believe, trust' (see **creed**), *(per)dere*, 'to waste, lose' (see **perdition**); O. Slav. *děją*, Lith. *dḗmi*, 'place'; Gael. *dede*, 'placed'. With suff. *-k-*: **dhək-*, **dhēk-*, 'to make, construct'; Lat. *facere*, 'to make, do' (fr. **dhə-k-*), *fēci*, 'I made' (fr. **dhē-k-*); Gk. *thḗkē*, 'box'; Scrt. *dhākáš*, 'receptacle'. With participial suff. *-t-*, **dhət-*, **dhēt-*: Scrt. *dhitiš*, 'the act of placing'; Gk. *thésis*, 'the act of placing' (see **thesis**); Goth. *(ga)dēþs*, O.H.G. *tāt* (see **deed**). With suff. *-m-*: **dhēm-*, **dhōm-*, 'something that is placed, fixed'; Gk. *thémis* (>**dhəm-*), 'law' (see **theme, anathema**), *thém-ethla*, 'foundations'; Scrt. *dhā́man-* 'law'; Goth. *dōms*, O.H.G. *tuom*, 'judgement' (see **doom**). **A.** trans. **1.** Uses once common, now obsolete: **a** To put, to place, bring to a given position or state: *they did him in prison* &c.; now only in archaic and obsolescent phrase *to do to death*; **b** to procure the carrying out of a certain action, to get, have, it done (*do*, followed by infin., comparable to Fr. use of *faire*, and former Engl. use of *let*): *he did him kill*, had him killed. **2.** **a** To carry out action so as to affect something, bring action to bear on something; occupy oneself with, accomplish, to perform, execute: *get something to do*; *to do one's work, duty*; *what shall I do next?*; *to do a good deed*; *to do the best one can*; Phr. *to do things well, handsomely, on a grand scale, shabbily* &c.; **b** to perform, execute, carry on as one's regular occupation: *he ought to do something at his age*; *he can find nothing to do just now*; *to do reviewing, lecturing, charring* &c.; **c** (in P.P.) to complete, finish: *his work is done*; *some is still unfinished but most is already done*; Phr. *to have done with*, to give up, forsake; cease from doing; make an end of doing; see **done**, adj. **3.** **a** To bestow, confer: *to do homage, reverence, justice to*; Phrs. *to do one good*; *do a good turn to*; **b** to involve, be source of, bring about, procure for: *that does you great credit, honour* &c.; **c** to inflict upon, afflict with: *to do one harm, an injury*. **4.** To perform some specific act in regard to a thing or person arising naturally from one's particular relation to it or him, or from the actual circumstances of the moment; in many special senses, e.g.: *to do the flowers* (in a room), arrange them in vases, with water, &c.: *to do one's hair*, brush it, make it tidy; *to do one's correspondence*, answer one's letters &c.; *every one is being vaccinated here, hadn't you better be done too?* **5.** To cook food; cook food thoroughly: *mind you do the beef thoroughly*; *I like my meat very well done*; *take out the vegetables and do them a little longer*. Phr. *done to a turn*, perfectly cooked. **6.** To visit a place as a sightseer, go round it and inspect all the objects of interest: *you can't do Oxford properly in a day*; *to do the British Museum, National Gallery* &c. **7.** (colloq.) To cheat, deceive, swindle, get the better of: *I'm afraid you've been done*; *he did me over that bargain*; *I don't want you to feel that I'm doing you*. Phr. (vulg.) *to do in the eye, do brown*, cheat badly. **8.** To suit, be convenient to; be adequate for purpose: *if I might stay the night, that would do me very well*; *will this racquet do you?* **9.** To play the part of, act in capacity of: *I saw Irving do Hamlet many years ago*; *he does the host admirably*. **10.** (colloq.) **a** To treat, behave to, entertain: *to do a man well, handsomely*; **b** (reflex.) *to do oneself well, proud*, indulge oneself, live luxuriously. **11.** To perform, complete, a journey, traverse a certain distance: *to do twenty miles a day on foot*; *to do the distance, journey, in an hour* &c. **B.** intrans. **1.** To act, engage in some form of activity: *to do and die*; *let us be up and doing*. Phrs. *to have to do with*, be concerned with, associated with, have dealings with; *have nothing to do with him, or his schemes*; *that has nothing to do with the question*, is not related to it. **2.** **a** To suit, be fitting; to be tolerable, or tolerated: *this will never do*; *it doesn't do to be rude to strangers*; **b** to be good enough, adequate for a particular purpose; to suffice: *this sort of work won't do for me*; *these boots will hardly do for riding in*; *that will do*, enough of that, desist! **3.** **a** To thrive, flourish, prosper, succeed, in career, profession &c.: *he is doing very well at the Bar* &c.; **b** to maintain good health; improve in health, make progress towards recovery: *mother and child are both doing well*; *the patient is better, he will do now*; **c** (of plants) to thrive, flourish, grow well: *azaleas won't do where there is lime in the soil*. **C.** *Do* as auxiliary verb: **1.** In declaratory sentences such constructions as *I do think*, *I did hope* &c., for *I think*, *I hoped*, are now only used in poetry, unless when the idea is strongly emphasized and the chief stress is placed on *do*, *did*; e.g., *I dó think you ought to go*, I am strongly of the opinion &c.; *I did hope he would have behaved properly*, I hoped very much &c.; *he did eat a lot*; *dó come and stay*, as pressing invitation. Also absol. in earnest entreaty, referring to an action already mentioned: *surely you can stay the night*; *now dó*. **2.** In negative sentences such constructions as *I see not, he came not*, are now archaic, obsolete, or poetical; in ordinary speech the construction used is *I do not* (*don't*) *see*; *he did not* (*didn't*) *come.* The negative is only placed directly after a verbal form in the auxiliaries, and old irregular verbs such as *dare, can.* **3.** Interrogative sentences: *hear you?*; *told I you?* (now archaic and poet.); ordinary construction: *do you hear, did I tell you?* Auxiliaries, and *can, dare,* alone have the old construction: *can you?*; *are you?*; *dare you?* **4.** Rhetorical inversions after adverbial phrases, *well do I remember it*; *never did I see such a fool,* sometimes used, for sake of emphasis, for *I remember it well*; *I never saw such a fool.* **D.** Followed by prep. or adv. *Do away,* trans., to remove, obliterate; *do away with,* intrans., get rid of; to kill. *Do for,* intrans., **a** to finish off, ruin; to kill; **b** to perform service for, look after wants of, specif., to act as housekeeper. *Do in,* trans. (colloq.), to murder. *Do out,* trans., clean out, wash, sweep away dust &c.: *to do out a room, a stable* &c. *Do to,* intrans., to treat, deal with, behave to: *what have they done to you*; *do to others as you expect them to do to you. Do up,* trans., **a** repair, smarten up, renovate, decorate: *to do the house up*; **b** to arrange in order, place on, arrange round, head: *to do up one's hair*; **c** to button up, fasten with hooks and eyes &c.: *to do up a bodice, dress*; **d** (in P.P.) exhausted, worn out: *quite done up after the journey. Do with,* intrans., **a** to get on with, tolerate, endure: *I can't do with him or with his insolence*; **b** to be satisfied with: *can you do with cold boiled mutton for dinner?*; **c** (facetious) to be glad to have, be ready to take; to need: *you could do with a square meal, I dare say*; *I could do with a good night's rest. Do without,* intrans., to manage, carry on without, to dispense with, deny oneself: *can you do without tobacco for a week?*; *we must do without a holiday this year.*

do (II.), n., fr. prec. (colloq.) **1.** A swindle, fraud, deception: *he was a fool not to see that the scheme was a do from the start.* **2.** An elaborate entertainment, a festive gathering, party: *we've got a do on to-night.* **3.** (in pl.) Action, transaction, share; in Phr. *fair do's!,* play fair, share and share alike.

do (III.), n. [1. dō; 2. dou]. (mus.) First of the syllables used in *solmization,* q.v.; the first tone of the scale.

doable, adj. [1. dōōabl; 2. dúəbl]. **do** (I.) & **-able.** Able to be done.

doat. See **dote.**

dobbin, n. [1. dóbin; 2. dɔ́bin], fr. *Robin, Robert.* Name for a horse, usually for a patient, old farm-horse.

Docetism, n. [1. dōsétizm; 2. dousítizəm], fr. Med. Lat. *docetae* & **-ism,** fr. Gk. *dokētai,* fr. *dokeîn,* 'to seem; to have an appearance of; to adopt an opinion, to believe', fr. Aryan base **dok'*-, **dek'*- &c., 'to seem good'. See **dogma, docile, decent.** Heresy of the Docetae, prevalent in 2nd cent. A.D., which denied the reality of Christ's human body.

doch-an-doris, n. [1. dógh an dóris; 2. dɔ́χ ən dɔ́ris]. Gael. *deoch,* 'drink', *an,* 'the', *doruis,* genit. of *dorus,* 'door'. A parting drink, stirrup-cup.

docile, adj. [1. dōsil; 2. dóusail], fr. Fr., Lat. *docilis,* 'docile, easily taught', fr. *docēre,* 'to teach, inform, show', & **-il(e).** The stem **dok-*, 'to cause to appear', is a form of the Aryan base **dek'*-, **dok*- &c., 'to seem good, to appear'; cp. Lat. *decet,* 'it befits' &c. See **decent, decorous,** & words there referred to. (of men and animals) Capable of being taught, of learning; tractable, easy to manage, amenable to training and discipline.

docilely, adv. Prec. & **-ly.** In a docile manner.

docility, n. [1. dōsíliti; 2. dousíliti]. **docile** & **-ity.** Quality of being docile.

dock (I.), n. [1. dok; 2. dɔk]. O.E. *docce,* M.E. *docke.* A coarse weed, genus *Rumex,* with large leaves and small green flowers.

dock (II.), n. Cp. Du. *dokke.* Origin obscure. An enclosure (in sea or river) where ships are loaded, repaired &c., often with gates through which the water can be let in or out. *Dry-dock, graving-dock,* one with water excluded; *floating-dock,* enclosure with walls floating in the water, and with contrivances for pumping out the water; *wet-dock,* containing water about level with high tide.

dock (III.), n. Perh. same as prec. Enclosed space reserved for prisoner on trial in criminal court. Phr. *to be in the dock,* to be the person tried, the suspected criminal as distinct from others in court.

dock (IV.), vb. trans. & intrans., fr. **dock** (II.). **a** trans. To bring (a ship) into dock; **b** intrans. (of a ship), to come, go, into dock.

dock (V.), n. M.E. *dok,* fr. O.N. *dokkr,* 'tail'. The solid part of an animal's tail.

dock (VI.), vb. trans. M.E. *docken,* fr. prec. **1.** To clip off, cut short; esp. to shorten an animal's tail. **2.** To cut down, cut off supplies, lessen, diminish, **a** salary, wages, allowance of money &c.; also **b** of food; **c** honours, triumph, possessions, and attributes generally; **d** (law) *to dock the entail,* to break the entail.

dockage, n. [1. dókij; 2. dɔ́kidž]. **dock** (II.) & **-age.** **a** Accommodation given to a ship in a dock; **b** money payable for such accommodation.

dock-dues. Same as **dockage, b.**

docker, n. [1. dóker; 2. dɔ́kə]. **dock** (II.) & **-er.** Labourer who works in a dock.

docket (I.), n. [1. dóket; 2. dɔ́kit]. Late M.E. Etymol. unknown. **1.** (law) Brief abstract of a legal judgement. **2. a** A label attached to a bale of goods, with instructions where and to whom they are to be delivered; **b** memorandum attached to a document, containing abstract of its contents.

docket (II.), vb. trans., fr. prec. To enter on a docket.

dockize, vb. trans. [1. dókīz; 2. dɔ́kaiz]. **dock** (II.) & **-ize.** To build docks in (a river, harbour &c.); to transform (a river) into a series of docks.

dock-master, n. Superintendent of a dock or dockyard.

dockyard, n. [1. dókyard; 2. dɔ́kjād]. Series of docks with equipment for ship-building and repairing, store-houses &c.

doctor (I.), n. [1. dóktor; 2. dɔ́ktə], fr. Lat. *doctor,* 'a teacher', fr. *doct-(um),* P.P. type of *docēre,* 'to teach, show, tell', & **-or.** See **docile** & **decent.** **1.** Teacher, learned man; specif., one of the early fathers and teachers of the Christian Church. **2.** One who holds the highest degree in any faculty of a university: *Doctor of Divinity, of Civil Law, Medicine* &c. **3.** (popular) A medical practitioner, whether a Doctor of Medicine or not: *better send for the doctor*; *going to see a doctor.* **4.** A kind of artificial dark-green fly for fishing.

doctor (II.), vb. trans. & intrans., fr. prec. **A.** trans. **1. a** (rare) To confer the degree of doctor on; **b** to address as, by title of, doctor. **2. a** To give medical treatment to; **b** to mend, repair something (machinery &c.) which is out of order. **3. a** To adulterate (food, wine &c.); specif., to put drugs in a person's drink; also *doctor up*; **b** to make fraudulent alterations in, falsify: *to doctor accounts, evidence* &c. **B.** intrans. (rare) To practise medicine.

doctoral, adj. [1. dóktoral; 2. dɔ́ktərəl]. **doctor** (I.) & **-al.** Pertaining to, coming from, a doctor or teacher; authoritative.

doctorate, n. [1. dóktorit; 2. dɔ́ktərit]. **doctor** (I.) & **-ate.** The degree and status of a university doctor.

doctorial, adj. [1. doktṓrial; 2. dɔktɔ́riəl]. **doctor** (I.) & **-ial.** Doctoral.

Doctors' Commons, n., fr. the commons, or common table of the society. **a** Ancient Society or College of English Civil Lawyers, dissolved in 1857; **b** the original site of hall and buildings of the society, in which, later, certain courts were held.

doctrinaire, n. & adj. [1. dòktrinā́r; 2. dɔ̀ktrinɛ́ə], fr. Fr. See **doctrine** & **-ary.** **1.** n. A narrow-minded person who urges the application of doctrines to which he holds, with extreme obstinacy, without considering their practicability, or applicability to particular cases. **2.** adj. Resembling, belonging to the character of, a doctrinaire; aggressively obstinate in pressing impracticable doctrines.

doctrinal, adj. [1. doktrī́nal, dóktrinal; 2. dɔktráinəl, dɔ́ktrinəl]. **doctrine** & **-al.** Having to do with, based on, doctrine; specif., that of the Christian Church.

doctrinally, adv. Prec. & **-ly.** In accordance with, from the point of view of, doctrine.

doctrinarian, n. & adj. [1. doktrinā́rian; 2. dɔktrinɛ́əriən]. **doctrine** & **-arian.** Doctrinaire.

doctrinarianism, n. [1. dòktrinā́rianizm; 2. dɔ̀ktrinɛ́əriənizəm]. Prec. & **-ism.** The holding of doctrinarian principles.

doctrine, n. [1. dóktrin; 2. dɔ́ktrin], fr. Fr., fr. Lat. *doctrīna,* 'teaching, instruction; science, learning'. See **doctor** & **-ine.** **1.** Something that is taught, instruction. **2. a** Principle of belief; **b** body of religious, political, or scientific teaching and principles.

doctrinism, n. [1. dóktrinizm; 2. dɔ́ktrinizəm]. Prec. & **-ism.** Exaggerated, unreasoning belief in some particular doctrine.

doctrinist, n. [1. dóktrinist; 2. dɔ́ktrinist]. See prec. & **-ist.** Believer in some particular doctrine.

document (I.), n. [1. dókūment; 2. dɔ́kjumənt], fr. O. Fr., fr. Lat. *document-(um),* 'an example, pattern, warning; specimen', fr. base *doc-u-,* as in **docile,** & **-ment.** **a** Something written; **b** inscription, or other writing, which conveys information, and which is relied on as evidence for establishing facts; **c** *human document,* set of facts or incidents which throw light on human nature.

document (II.), vb. trans., fr. prec. **a** To bring written evidence in proof of; **b** to supply with documentary evidence.

documentary, adj. [1. dòkūméntari; 2. dɔkjuméntəri]. **document** (I.) & **-ary.** In the form of a document, written.

documentation, n. [1. dòkūmentā́shun; 2. dɔkjuməntéiʃən]. **document** & **-ation.** The use of documentary evidence; the supplying of such in a book or article.

documented, adj. [1. dókūmented; 2. dɔ́kjumentid], fr. P.P. of **document** (II.). Supported by, supplied with, documentary evidence.

dodder (I.), n. [1. dóder; 2. dɔ́də]. M.E. *doder.* Cp. M.H.G. *toter,* N.H.G. *dotter.* A parasitic, twining plant, with thread-like stem and fine scales in place of leaves.

dodder (II.), vb. intrans. See next word; meaning perh. first, to be lopped, like a tree, then to be old and feeble, like a tree that has lost its head from age; hence, to walk and behave like a feeble old man. **a** To walk or move shakily, from age or weakness; to tremble, shake, totter; also *to dodder along*; **b** to ramble on in speech in a feeble, foolish, confused manner; to talk nonsense; **c** to be in a state of intellectual decrepitude.

doddered, adj. [1. dóderd; 2. dɔ́dəd]. Cp. archaic & provinc. *dod,* 'clip, lop off'. (of trees) Pollarded, shrouded, with top lopped.

dodder-grass, n. Quaking-grass.

doddery, adj. [1. dóderi; 2. dɔ́dəri], fr. **dodder** (II.) & **-y.** **a** Tottery, shaky, infirm, in the gait; **b** foolish, weak-minded; foolishly loquacious.

dodeca-, pref., fr. Gk. *dṓdeka,* 'twelve', fr. *dō-,* 'two', fr. **dwō-*, see **dual,** & **deca-.** Twelve.

dodecagon, n. [1. dōdékagon; 2. doudékəgən]. Prec. & **-gon.** A plane figure with twelve sides.

dodecahedron, n. [1. dṑdekahḗdron; 2. dòudɛkəhídrən]. **dodeca-** & **-hedron.** Solid figure with twelve faces.

dodecasyllable, n. [1. dṑdekasílabl; 2. dòudɛkəsíləbl]. **dodeca-** & **syllable.** A verse-line of twelve syllables.

dodge (I.), vb. trans. & intrans. [1. doj; 2. dɔdž]. Origin unknown. Used in late 16th cent. in sense of 'to turn, wheel about'.

A. trans. 1. To avoid (a blow), escape from (pursuit), by twisting or turning quickly aside or in an unexpected direction. 2. (of moral activities) To evade (difficulties and problems) by finesse, cunning, ingenious intellectual juggling. B. intrans. To practise bodily or moral dodging; to twist aside; to shuffle, behave disingenuously, evade the truth.

dodge (II.), n. See prec. 1. a The act of bodily dodging; (colloq.) b trick, deception, quibble, evasion of the truth; c (in innocent sense) plan, method, device: *a good dodge for remembering names.* 2. (colloq.) An ingenious contrivance: *a dodge for catching flies.*

dodger, n. [1. dójer; 2. dɔ́dʒə]. **dodge** (I.) & **-er**. One who dodges; a dishonest, shuffling, dissembling rogue; a trickster.

dodgy, adj. [1. dóji; 2. dɔ́dʒi]. **dodge** (II.) & **-y**. a (of persons) Given to dodging; artful, dishonest; b (of things, colloq.) ingenious; tricky, intricate.

dodo, n. [1. dṓdō; 2. dóudou], fr. Port. *doudo*, 'stupid'. An extinct bird, rather larger than a swan, short-legged and clumsy, with rudimentary wings; formerly found in Mauritius.

doe, n. [1. dō; 2. dou]. O.E. *dā*, M.E. *dō*; possibly a loan-word fr. Lat. *dāma*, 'deer', apparently fr. Aryan **dăm-*, 'horned animal'; cp. O. Ir. *dam* (*allaid*), 'stag'; Corn. *da*, 'deer'; Bret. *dauat*, 'sheep'; Gk. *damálēs*, 'young bull'. Female of fallow-deer; also female of rabbit, rat, mouse, and ferret.

Doe, John, n. (legal hist.) The name of fictitious plaintiff in old action for ejectment, the defendant being a fictitious *Richard Roe*.

doer, n. [1. dōōer; 2. dúə]. **do** & **-er**. a One who does something; one who acts: *he is a doer, not a talker*; b one who acts or behaves in a specified way: *a doer of good, of evil*; *an evil doer*; c (of plants) *a good doer*, one which flourishes and thrives; *a bad doer*, one difficult to rear and make grow, which tends to die or dwindle.

doeskin, n. [1. dṓskin; 2. dóuskin]. **doe** & **skin**. 1. The skin of the doe. 2. a Fine leather made of this; b material made in imitation of this.

doff, vb. trans. [1. dof; 2. dɔf]. Contracted fr. **do** & **off**. a To take off, remove, esp. the hat; (less commonly) to remove other garments; b (of non-material things) lay aside, give up, abandon: *to doff one's grand airs, professorial manner* &c.

dog (I.), n. [1. dog; 2. dɔg]. M.E. *dogge*, O.E. *docga*. Cp. M. Du. *dogge*; etymol. unknown. 1. a A common, domesticated, carnivorous mammal, *Canis familiaris*, of which many varieties exist; Phrs. *to give, throw, to the dogs*, throw away, as something of no value; *to go to the dogs*, be ruined; *to rain cats and dogs*, rain very heavily; *to lead a dog's life*, be continually harassed; *to die a dog's death, the death of a dog*, die in shame and misery; *dog in the manger*, one who neither makes use of a thing himself, nor will permit others to do so; *to let sleeping dogs lie*, not to stimulate activities that may prove dangerous; *to treat a person like, worse than, a dog*; *give a dog a bad name and hang him*, a person who has once got a bad reputation gets no credit for anything he does; b one of several allied varieties of quadruped, belonging to family *Canidae*, living in a wild state, as the wolf, jackal &c.; c (i.) specif., the male of the domestic and other varieties of the species; (ii.) applied also to male ferret and other animals; (often attrib.) *dog-wolf, dog-fox, dog-ferret* &c. 2. Applied to human beings: a a worthless, abandoned, infamous person; a term of abuse; Phr. *a dirty dog*; b (slang, affectionate or facetious) a fellow, young spark: *lucky, gay, dog.* 3. (pl.) Metal supports on a hearth for holding logs. 4. (astron.) a Either of the two constellations, *Canis Major* or *Minor*, the Greater or Lesser Dog; b (pl.) also the *Hunting Dogs, Canes Venatici*, constellation near the Great Bear.

dog (II.), vb. trans., fr. prec. a To follow closely as a dog does; follow in tracks of, be at the heels of: *to dog a person's footsteps*; b (fig., of misfortune, disaster &c.) to attend closely, pursue relentlessly.

dogaressa, n. [1. dṓgarésa; 2. dòugərésə]. Ital., fem. of *doge*. See **doge**. Wife of the doge of Venice or Genoa.

dogate, n. [1. dṓgāt; 2. dóugeit], fr. Fr., fr. Ital. *dogato*. See **doge** & **-ate**. The office of doge.

dog-bane, n. A perennial herb, with a fibrous stem, producing a milky juice, used medicinally.

dog-berry, n. The fruit of the dogwood, q.v.

dog-biscuit, n. Special kind of thick, hard biscuit, composed of meal and small pieces of meat, for feeding dogs.

dog-box, n. Part of a railway van used for conveying dogs.

dog-brier, n. The dog-rose.

dog-cart, n. A high, two- or four-wheeled carriage with two seats back to back, and an enclosed space below in which sporting dogs could be carried.

dog-collar, n. a A collar worn by a dog; b a high, stiff collar, fastened behind, as often worn by the clergy.

dog-days, n. The hottest part of the year, during part of July and August; formerly specif., that time of the year when Sirius, the dog-star, rises and sets with the sun.

doge, n. [1. dōj; 2. doudʒ], fr. Fr., fr. Ital., fr. Lat. *duce*, abl. of *dux*, 'a leader'. See **duke**. The chief magistrate in the ancient republics of Venice and Genoa.

dog-eared, adj. (of a book) Having the corners of the leaves turned down and crumpled.

dog-faced, adj. Having a face like a dog; applied to a species of baboon.

dog-fish, n. The name of several small species of shark, notable for their voracity.

dogged, adj. [1. dóged; 2. dɔ́gid]. See **dog** & **-ed**. Obstinate, stubborn, persistent, not yielding to pressure. Phr. *it's dogged (that) does it*, resolution and concentration can overcome difficulties.

doggedly, adv. Prec. & **-ly**. In a dogged manner.

doggedness, n. See prec. & **-ness**. Quality of being dogged; tenacity, obstinacy.

dogger, n. [1. dóger; 2. dɔ́gə]. Etymol. doubtful. A kind of two-masted Dutch fishing-boat, used in the North Sea.

doggerel, n. & adj. [1. dógerel; 2. dɔ́gərəl]. Etymol. unknown. a n. Rough, inartistic, jingling verse; b adj. (of verse), careless, irregular, meaningless.

dogginess, n. [1. dógines; 2. dɔ́ginis]. See **doggy** & **-ness**. a Quality of being like, or devoted to, dogs; b odour of dogs.

doggish, adj. [1. dógish; 2. dɔ́giʃ]. **dog** & **-ish**. Like a dog; surly, with uncertain temper.

doggy, adj. [1. dógi; 2. dɔ́gi]. **dog** & **-y**. a Belonging to, resembling, a dog; b fond of dogs.

dog-latin, n. Incorrect, barbarous Latin.

dog-lead, n. A chain, or leather strap with a swivel, for leading or fastening a dog.

dogma, n. [1. dógma; 2. dɔ́gmə], pl. *dogmas*, occasionally, following Gk., *dogmata*. [1. dógmata; 2. dɔ́gmətə]. Gk. *dógma*, 'an opinion; an ordinance'; cp. Gk. *dokein*, 'to believe'; *dókimos*, 'acceptable', fr. Aryan base **dok̑-*, **dek̑-*, **dk̑-*, 'to seem good; to be acceptable; to accept', also in concrete sense, 'that which receives or holds'; cp. Gk. *dokánē*, 'box, fork', *dokós*, 'beam, shaft'; cp. **diplodocus**. See **decent, docile**. 1. a Something laid down by authority of the Church as true, and necessary to be believed; b such principles and essentials of doctrine collectively. 2. An opinion, body of opinions, enunciated as true, held with tenacity, and strongly insisted upon by those who believe them: *philosophic, scientific, dogma.*

dogmatic, adj. [1. dogmátik; 2. dɔgmǽtik], fr. Lat., fr. Gk. *dogmatikós*, fr. *dógmat-(os)*, genit. of *dógma* (see prec.), & **-ic**. 1. Pertaining to, concerned with, Christian dogma: *dogmatic theology.* 2. a (of persons) Arrogant, insistent, positive, and emphatic in expressing opinion; dictatorial; b (of expressions of opinion) authoritative, positive, as though precluding any possibility of doubt.

dogmatically, adv. [1. dogmátikali; 2. dɔgmǽtikəli]. Prec. & **-al** & **-ly**. In a dogmatic manner.

dogmatics, n. [1. dogmátiks; 2. dɔgmǽtiks]. Systematic study of essential dogmas of Christianity; branch of learning dealing with these.

dogmatism, n. [1. dógmatizm; 2. dɔ́gmətizəm]. See **dogmatic** & **-ism**. The practice of dogmatizing; dogmatic, positive, quality or state of mind.

dogmatist, n. [1. dógmatist; 2. dɔ́gmətist]. See next word & **-ist**. a A person who dogmatizes, one who attaches great weight to dogma; b a student of Christian dogma.

dogmatize, vb. trans. & intrans. [1. dógmatīz; 2. dɔ́gmətaiz]. See **dogmatic** & **-ize**. a trans. To formulate, express, as a dogma; b intrans., to assert an opinion positively and emphatically; to express an emphatic, unqualified opinion; to lay down the law.

dog-rose, n. The common wild rose.

dog's-eared, adj. Dog-eared.

dog-shore, n. Heavy piece of timber used as prop for a ship before launching.

dog-skin, n. Leather made of the skin of a dog.

dog's letter, n. Old name for R, on account of the trilled sound which it expressed; called in Latin *littera canina.*

dog's-mercury, n. A perennial, low-growing herb, with small green flowers.

dog-star, n. Popular name for Sirius, the principal star in the constellation *Canis Major.*

dog-tired, adj. Very tired, dead-beat, worn out by fatigue.

dog-tooth, adj. (archit.) A moulding, consisting of a series of pyramid-shaped projections, characteristic of the later Norman and Early English styles: *dog-tooth moulding, pattern.*

dog-violet, n. Scentless, wild violet.

dog-watch, n. (naut.) One of the two two-hour watches, from 4 to 6 or 6 to 8 P.M.

dogwood, n. [1. dógwood; 2. dɔ́gwud]. One of several varieties of cornel, a flowering shrub.

doily, n. [1. dóili; 2. dóili], fr. name of inventor of material. Small round or square piece of linen or cambric, often fringed and decorated, used for putting under a finger-bowl, or other vessel, on a table.

doing, n. [1. dōōing; 2. dúiŋ], fr. **do** & **-ing**. (in pl.) Actions, activities, deeds; behaviour, conduct: *he gave an interesting account of his doings in Africa*; *we shall one day receive the just reward of our doings on earth.*

doit, n. [1. doit; 2. dɔit], fr. Du. *duit*, a small coin worth about ⅛th of a penny. A coin of trifling value; only in Phr. *not worth a doit.*

doited, adj. [1. dóited; 2. dɔ́itid]. Origin unknown. Crazed, foolish.

dolce far niente, n. Engl. [1. dólchi fàr niénti; 2. dɔ́ltʃi fā̀ niénti]; Ital. [dōltʃɛ far njɛ̄ntɛ]. Ital., lit. 'sweet doing nothing'. Condition of agreeable inactivity.

doldrums, n. [1. dóldrumz; 2. dɔ́ldrəmz]. Etymol. dubious; perh. allied to **dull**. A provincial word. a Low spirits, depression; Phr. *to be in the doldrums*, depressed, glum; b (naut.) region of sea near the Equator, usually calm, with little wind.

dole (I.), n. [1. dōl; 2. doul]. O.E. *dāl*, 'part, division', M.E. *dōl*, Gmc. **dail-*; cp. **deal** (I.), O.E. *dǣl*, fr. Gmc. **dail-i*. Cp. also Goth. *dails*, O.H.G. *teil*, 'part'. 1. (archaic and obs.) That which is given out, apportioned; hence, fate. 2. Something given or paid out: a a charitable gift, form of assistance; b something distributed in small, limited shares; c specif., weekly payment received by an unemployed workman, under various Insurance Acts, from funds to which the State, the employers, and the workmen themselves have contributed, and also, when the contributions have been exhausted, from state funds: *to go, be, on the dole.*

dole (**II.**), vb. trans., fr. prec. Gen. *to dole out*, to give out, distribute, esp. reluctantly and in small portions.

dole (**III.**), n. M.E., fr. O. Fr. *doel* (cp. Fr. *deuil*, 'mourning'), fr. Low Lat. *dolium*, 'sorrow', fr. Lat. *dolēre*, 'to suffer; to grieve, lament', fr. Aryan base **del-*, **dol-*, 'to split, cut, carve'; cp. Scrt. *dálati*, 'splits', *dalam*, 'a piece', Lat. *dōlium*, 'vessel'. See **daedal.** The sense 'sorrow', wh. seems to be confined to Lat., developed through the stages 'wound, affliction' &c. (archaic and poet.) Grief, affliction; lamentation: *to make one's dole.*

doleful, adj. [1. dṓlfool; 2. dóulfəl]. See prec. & **-ful.** Woeful, sad, mournful, melancholy, dismal, lugubrious: *a doleful tale, look.*

dolefully, adv. Prec. & **-ly.** In a doleful manner.

dolefulness, n. See prec. & **-ness.** The state or quality of being doleful.

dolerite, n. [1. dólerīt; 2. dɔ́lərait], fr. Gk. *dolerós*, 'deceptive', fr. *dólos*, 'deceit', see **dolose**, & **-ite.** A coarse, crystalline form of basalt, so-called as easily confused with *diorite.*

dolichocephalic, adj. [1. dòlikōsefálik; 2. dɔ̀likousefǽlik], fr. Gk. *dolikhós*, 'long', & **-cephalic.** Cp. Scrt. *dīrghás*, O. Pers. *darga*, O. Slav. *dlŭgŭ*, 'long'. Aryan base **delāgh-*, 'long'; cp. the nasalized form of the base, **dlongh-*, in Lat. *longus*; this relationship is, however, questioned by some. See remarks under **long** (**I.**). **a** (of skull) Long in proportion to its breadth; **b** (of men and races) having skulls of this shape.

doll, n. [1. dol; 2. dɔl], fr. woman's name, familiar form of *Dorothy.* This word has taken the place of M.E. *popet.* See **puppet. a** Child's toy representing human being; **b** woman or girl with a delicate but rather insipid prettiness, and exquisitely turned out, esp. when slightly stupid and hare-brained.

dollar, n. [1. dólar; 2. dɔ́lə], fr. Germ. *taler*, short for *Joachimstaler*, the coin being first made at the Joachimstal silver-mines in Bohemia; N.H.G. *t(h)al*, 'valley'. See **dale. 1.** Originally the German taler (3 marks). **2. a** Unit of coinage in U.S.A., Canada &c., 100 cents, equal to about 4s. 2d. in English money; **b** a coin of this value. Phr. *the dollars*, money, wealth. **3.** (colloq.) 5s.; *half a dollar*, 2s. 6d.

dollish, adj. [1. dólish; 2. dɔ́liʃ]. **doll** & **-ish.** Simperingly, and insipidly pretty and neat; like a doll.

dollishness, n. Prec. & **-ness.** Neat, insipid prettiness, like that of a doll.

dollop, n. [1. dólop; 2. dɔ́ləp]. Etymol. unknown. A big, coarse, shapeless lump, esp. of pudding, cheese, butter &c.

dolly, n. & vb. [1. dóli; 2. dɔ́li]. **doll** & **-y. 1.** n. **a** Child's word for a doll; **b** wooden implement for beating clothes in laundry-work; **c** device for pile-driving in mining. **2.** vb. To use a dolly **1. b.**

dolly-shop, n. Marine store and pawnshop.

dolly-tub, n. Wash-tub.

Dolly Varden, n. [1. dòli várdn; 2. dɔ̀li vɑ́dn], fr. Dickens's character in 'Barnaby Rudge'. Woman's hat and dress of peculiar, fantastic style.

dolman, n. [1. dólman; 2. dɔ́lmən], fr. Turk. *dōlāmān.* **a** A long, loose, Turkish robe; **b** kind of coat or cloak, worn like a cape, with sleeves hanging loose, used by Hussar regiments; similar garment worn by women.

dolmen, n. [1. dólmen; 2. dɔ́lmən], fr. Fr., perh. fr. Corn. *doll*, 'hole', *men*, 'stone'. Prehistoric megalithic stone chamber formed by a large flat stone laid across, and supported by, others placed upright; a cromlech.

dolomite, n. [1. dólomīt; 2. dɔ́ləmait], fr. name of Fr. geologist, Dolomieu (1750–1801), & **-ite.** Crystalline rock composed of carbonate of lime, with a certain proportion of carbonate of magnesia, occurring in parts of England and Scotland and in S. Tyrol; *the Dolomites*, curiously shaped group of mountains of this rock, in Tyrol.

dolomitic, adj. [1. dolomítik; 2. dɔləmítik]. Prec. & **-ic.** Pertaining to, composed of, resembling, dolomite.

dolorous, adj. [1. dólorus; 2. dɔ́lərəs], fr. O. Fr. **dolour** & **-ous.** See **dole** (**III.**). Mournful, sad, doleful.

dolorously, adv. Prec. & **-ly.** In a dolorous manner.

dolose, adj. [1. dṓlōs; 2. dóulous], fr. Lat. *dolōsus*, 'crafty, deceitful', fr. *dol-(us)*, 'deceit, cunning', & **-ose**; cp. Gk. *dólos*, 'deceit'; O.N. *tāl*, 'deceit'; O.H.G. *zāla*, 'ambush, danger'. If the last is cogn. w. O.H.G. *zālōn*, 'to snatch away, rob', the stem of *dolus* is perh. fr. the Aryan base **dōl-*, **dĕl-*, 'to cut, split, separate'. See **dole** (**I.**). (legal and archaic) With criminal intent, with intent to defraud.

dolour, n. [1. dólur; 2. dɔ́lə], fr. O. Fr., fr. Lat. *dolōr-(em)*, 'pain; distress, sorrow', fr. *dolēre*, 'to suffer'. See **dole** (**III.**). (poet.) Grief, sorrow, trouble. *Dolours of Mary*, the seven sorrows of B.V.M.

dolphin, n. [1. dólfin; 2. dɔ́lfin], fr. O. Fr. *daulphin*, fr. Lat. *delphīnus*, fr. Gk. *delphînos*, genit. of *delphis*, 'a dolphin'. Etymol. unknown. Cp. **delphinium** & **dauphin. 1. a** The name given to several species of cetaceans with a beak or long snout; often called a 'porpoise', q.v., from which they are to be distinguished; **b** (her.) representation of this in form of a curved fish. **2.** Popular name of a brilliantly coloured fish, the dorado, q.v., which changes colour when dying.

dolt, n. [1. dōlt; 2. doult]. M.E. *dold*, 'dulled'. See **dull** (**II.**). A heavy, stupid, slow-witted, dull person.

doltish, adj. [1. dṓltish; 2. dóultiʃ]. Prec. & **-ish.** Dull, stupid, heavy.

doltishness, n. See prec. & **-ness.** The state of being a dolt.

Dom, n. [1. dom; 2. dɔm]. Abbr. of Lat. *dominus*, 'lord', orig. 'master of a house', w. adj. suff., fr. Aryan **dom-os*, 'house', see **dome** (**I.**); cp. Scrt. *dámūnaš*, 'belonging to a house'. **a** Title given, and used as form of address, to certain of the higher Roman Catholic dignitaries, and to the members of certain monastic orders, esp. Benedictine; **b** Portuguese equivalent of Don, as title.

-dom, suff., O.E. *-dōm*, expressing (i.) authority, jurisdiction, domain, as in *kingdom, earldom*, & (ii.) a vaguer idea of mere abstraction, as in *freedom* &c. From O.E. *dōm*, 'judgement, authority' &c. See **doom.**

domain, n. [1. dōmā́n; 2. douméin], fr. Fr. *domaine*, fr. Lat. *dominicum*, neut. adj., 'belonging to a lord'. See **Dom, dome. 1. a** Land owned or ruled over by one person; **b** (more gen.) lands, landed property, estates; territory, realm; *Eminent Domain*, in U.S.A., sovereign power inherent in a State, giving right over private property for public uses. **2.** (fig.) Realm, sphere of knowledge or thought &c.: *the domain of philosophy, natural science.*

domanial, adj. [1. dōmā́nial; 2. douméiniəl]. Prec. & **-ial.** Belonging or relating to the territory under a single jurisdiction or ownership.

dome (**I.**), n. [1. dōm; 2. doum], fr. Fr., fr. Lat. *domus*, 'a house, home, building'. Cogn. w. Gk. *dómos*, Scrt. *dámaš*, O. Bulg. *domŭ*, 'house', all fr. stem **domu-*, **domo-*; a cons. stem **dŏm-*, **dĕm-*, **dm̥-* appears in Gk. *dôma*, 'house', *des-(pótēs)*, 'despot', orig. 'lord of a house', fr. genit. **dems-*. see **despot**; Gk. *dápedon*, 'ground about a house', fr. **dm̥-*; Lith. *dim-stis*, 'estate, yard'. The Aryan base **demā-* &c., 'to build', appears also in Gk. *démein*, 'to build'; *démas*, 'shape, form'; Goth. *timrjan*, 'to build', O.H.G. *zimberen*, O.E. *timbrian*, 'to build of wood', O.H.G. *zimbar*, 'wood for building; house; room' (see **timber**). The orig. meaning of **demā* may have been 'to make suitable, adapt, fit together'; cp. Goth. *(ga)timan*; O.S. *teman*; O.H.G. *zeman*, 'to suit'. Lat. *domāre*, Gk. *damáein*, Goth. *tamjan*, 'to tame' &c., are prob. fr. the same base, in the sense of 'to make domestic, bring to the house'. See **tame. 1.** (poet. and obs.) A building; large house, a palace. **2. a** A rounded globe-shaped roof; a cupola; hence **b** something shaped like a dome: *the dome of his lofty brow* &c.

dome (**II.**), vb. trans. & intrans., fr. prec. **a** To roof with a dome; **b** to swell into the form of a dome.

domed, adj. [1. dōmd; 2. doumd], fr. P.P. of prec. **a** Covered, roofed, with a dome; **b** shaped like a dome.

Domesday (**Book**), n. [1. dṓōmzdā (book); 2. dúmzdei (buk)]. O.E. *dōmesdæġ*, 'day of judgement'. See **doom** & **day.** Once the popular, now the official name, for the record of the Great Inquisition of William the Conqueror, in 1086, in which all the lands in the greater part of England are enumerated, together with the names of their holders, and the extent and value of the properties. Abbreviation D.B.

domestic (**I.**), adj. [1. dō-, doméstik; 2. dou-, dəméstik], fr. Fr., fr. Lat. *domesticus*, 'belonging to the house; private', fr. *domus*, 'house, home'. See **dome. 1. a** Pertaining to the home or family: *domestic troubles*; *domestic servant*, one employed, and living, in a household. **b** remaining much at home, devoted to, interested in household affairs. **2.** Having to do with a particular country, community, corporation: *domestic and foreign policy.* **3.** (of animals) Tamed by, associating with, man; habitually living in or about one household, and having their wants supplied by man; contrasted with *wild.*

domestic (**II.**), n., fr. prec. A servant employed in a household.

domesticable, adj. [1. dōméstikabl; 2. douméstikəbl]. **domestic** & **-able.** Capable of being domesticated.

domestically, adv. [1. dōméstikali; 2. douméstikəli]. **domestic** & **-al** & **-ly.** In a domestic manner.

domesticate, vb. trans. [1. dōméstikāt; 2. douméstikeit], fr. Med. Lat. *domesticāt-(um)*, P.P. of *domesticāre*, fr. Lat. *domestic-(us)*, 'of the household; private'. See **domestic** & **-ate. 1.** To render attached to, fond of, domestic life, and household interests. **2.** To tame animals, bring them under human control, accustom them to live with human beings, fit them for man's service.

domestication, n. [1. dōmèstikā́shun; 2. doumèstikéiʃən]. Prec. & **-ation. a** The act or process of domesticating; **b** state of being domesticated.

domesticity, n. [1. dò-, dòmestísiti; 2. dòu-, dɔ̀mistísiti]. **domestic** & **-ity. a** Life in the home and family; **b** attachment to this.

domett, n. [1. dómet; 2. dɔ́mit]. Origin unknown. Cloth of wool and cotton used for making shrouds.

domic(al), adj. [1. dṓmik(l); 2. dóumik(l)]. See **dome** & **-ic** & **-al.** Resembling a dome.

domicile (**I.**), n. [1. dómisīl; 2. dɔ́misail], fr. Fr., fr. Lat. *domicilium*, 'dwelling, place of abode', prob. fr. **domicula*, dimin. of *domus*, 'house, home'. See **dome. 1. a** Permanent or usual dwelling-place; home, residence; **b** (legal) place regarded and accepted officially as a person's permanent residence; fact of being domiciled. **2.** The place at which a bill of exchange is payable.

domicile (**II.**), vb. trans., fr. prec. **1.** To establish, cause to reside permanently, in particular country or place. **2.** To make a bill of exchange payable at a given place.

domiciliary, adj. [1. dòmisílyari; 2. dɔ̀misíljəri]. See **domicile** (**I.**) & **-ary.** Connected with a dwelling-house, or with domicile. Phr. *domiciliary visit*, authorized official visit, to a private house.

dominance, n. [1. dóminans; 2. dɔ́minəns]. See **dominant, dominate,** & **-ance.** The fact of being dominant; authority; outstanding importance, prevailing influence.

dominant, adj. & n. [1. dóminant; 2. dómin-ənt], fr. Lat. *dominant-(em)*, 'prevailing', Pres. Part. type of *dominārī*, 'to have dominion'. See **dominate**. **1.** adj. **a** Ruling, having authority, prevailing; **b** having chief prominence and importance; **c** (mus.) having harmonic importance. **2.** n. (mus.) The fifth note in the scale.

dominantly, adv. Prec. & **-ly**. In a dominant manner.

dominate, vb. trans. & intrans. [1. dóminát; 2. dómineit], fr. Lat. *domināt-(um)*, P.P. type of *dominārī*, 'to rule, reign, govern', fr. *dominus*, 'lord'. See **Dom, dome**. **A.** trans. **1.** (of moral action) **a** (on persons) to exercise control over, to enforce one's will upon, to influence, sway: *to dominate others by force of character*; **b** (on the mind and mental processes) to direct, bring into subjection, restrain, discipline, regulate: *to dominate one's passions, emotions* &c.; **c** to affect, occupy the mind strongly, permeate; act as principal motive: *two rival passions, love and duty, dominated his mind.* **2.** (of material objects) To tower above, overhang, overlook: *the lighthouse dominates the sea for several miles*; *a foreground dominated by a single lofty elm.* **B.** intrans. **a** To exercise the power of dominating (**A. 1**); **b** to be higher than surrounding objects (**A. 2**). *Dominate over*, to dominate (**A. 1** and **2**); also, to domineer.

domination, n. [1. dòmináshun; 2. dòminéiʃən]. Prec. & **-ation**. **1.** The act of dominating; state of being dominated. **2.** (pl., eccles.) The fourth rank of angels: *dominations, principalities, and powers.*

domineer, vb. intrans. [1. dòminḗr; 2. dòminíə], fr. Du. *domineren*, fr. Fr. *dominer*, fr. Lat. *dominārī*, 'to rule, reign'. See **dominate**. **a** To exercise authority and influence, whether personal or derived from an official position, in a harsh and arrogant manner; **b** to assert one's own opinions and wishes too emphatically, and endeavour to impose them on others with too great vehemence and insistence. *Domineer over*, to impose a too rigorous authority or influence upon.

domineering, adj. [1. dòminḗring; 2. dòminíəriŋ], fr. Pres. Part. of prec. Inclined to domineer, arrogant, self-assertive, seeking to impose one's own views on others.

domineeringly, adv. Prec. & **-ly**. In a domineering way.

dominical, adj. [1. domínikl; 2. dəmínikl], fr. Low Lat. *dominicālis*, fr. Lat. *dominicus*, 'belonging to a master', fr. *dominus*, 'lord' (see **Dom**) & **-ic** & **-al**. **a** Belonging to our Lord: *dominical year*, of the Christian era; **b** having to do with Sunday, the Lord's day, esp. *dominical letter*, one of the seven letters, A-G, denoting Sunday in a Church Calendar.

Dominican, adj. & n. [1. domínikan; 2. dəmínikən], fr. Med. Lat. *Dominicānus*, fr. *Dominicus* (& **-an**), the Latinized name of Domingo de Guzman (St. Dominic, 1170–1221), a Spaniard, founder of the Dominican order of monks; fr. Lat. *dominus*, 'lord, master'. See **Dom**. **a** adj. Belonging to the order of monks founded by St. Dominic in 1215, called *Friars Preachers*, or *Black Friars*; **b** n., a monk of this order.

dominie, n. [1. dómini; 2. dómini], fr. Lat. *domine*, voc. of *dominus*, 'master, lord'. See **Dom**. (Scots) A schoolmaster.

dominion, n. [1. domínyun; 2. dəmínjən]. O. Fr., fr. Low Lat. *dominiōn-(em)*, fr. Lat. *dominium*, 'lordship', fr. *dominus*, 'lord'. See **Dom**. **1.** Authority, power to rule, supremacy, sovereignty. **2.** Formerly, territory under jurisdiction of any feudal lord, now only that under the supreme authority of the king. **3.** Specif. **a** general title for the self-governing territories and peoples of the British Empire: *the Dominions beyond the Seas*; **b** official title of Canada and New Zealand.

domino (I.), n. [1. dóminō; 2. dóminou]. Span., fr. Lat. *domino*, dat. of *dominus*, 'lord'. See **Dom, dome**. Formerly a robe or hood worn by a master or teacher; one worn by canons of a cathedral; hence, **a** long loose robe, with hood and mask to hide the face, worn at masquerades &c.; **b** person wearing a domino.

domino (II.), n. Origin doubtful. One of 28 oblong pieces, of bone or ivory, having one side black, the other white, the latter divided in two spaces, blank or marked with black spots, used for the game of *dominoes*.

dominoed, adj. [1. dóminōd; 2. dóminoud]. **domino** (I.) & **-ed**. Wearing, disguised by, a domino.

don (I.), n. [1. don; 2. dən]. Span., fr. Lat. *dominus*, 'lord'. See **Dom**. **1.** (cap.) **a** Spanish title, prefixed to name; formerly applied only to noblemen; **b** a Spaniard. **2.** **a** Fellow or tutor of a college at Oxford or Cambridge; **b** a master at Winchester. **3.** (slang) One specially skilled in something, an adept.

don (II.), vb. trans. Contracted fr. **do** & **on**; cp. **doff**. To put on, assume: *to don a cloak, hat* &c.

donah, n. [1. dṓna; 2. dóunə]. Corrupt. of Span. *doña* & Port. *dona*, 'lady', fr. Lat. *domina*, fem. of *dominus*. See **Dom**. (slang) Sweetheart, lover, mistress.

donate, vb. trans. [1. dōnát; 2. dounéit]. Back formation fr. next word. (an American usage) To make a donation of; to give, present: *to donate funds to a university* &c.

donation, n. [1. dōnáshun; 2. dounéiʃən]. Lat. *dōnātiōn-(em)*, 'a presenting, giving', fr. *dōnāt-(um)*, P.P. type of *dōnāre*, 'to present, bestow, grant', & **-ion**. Cp. *dōnum*, 'a gift, present, sacrifice'; cogn. w. Scrt. *dānám*, W. *dawn*, 'a gift'; O. Ir. *dān*, 'talent, gift'; O. Slav. *danĭ*, 'tribute'. Formed w. suff. *-n-* fr. Aryan **dō-*, 'to give'. See **date** (I.), **dose**, **dot** (III.). **a** The act of giving; **b** something given, gift; esp. money given for charity.

Donatist, adj. & n. [1. dṓnatist; 2. dóunətist], fr. Donatus, leader of the sect. **a** adj. Of, pertaining to, a schism and sect of the 4th cent. A.D. in Africa; **b** n., follower, adherent, of this schism and sect.

donative, n. & adj. [1. dṓnativ; 2. dóunətiv], fr. Lat. *dōnātīvum*, 'official gift, gratuity', fr. *dōnāt-(um)*, P.P. type of *dōnāre*, 'to give', & **-ive**. See **donation**. **1.** n. **a** A Church living which could be bestowed by the patron, without presentation to, or investment by, the ordinary, and which was also exempt from visitation by the latter. Diocesans had no jurisdiction over donatives; abolished in 1908; **b** an official gift. **2.** adj. Of the nature of a donative.

donatory, n. [1. dṓnatori; 2. dóunətəri], fr. Med. Lat. *dōnātōrius*, fr. Lat. *dōnāt-(um)*, P.P. of *dōnāre*, 'to give'; see prec. & **-ory**. One who receives a donation.

done, adj. [1. dun; 2. dan], fr. P.P. of **do**; M.E. *dōn*, O.E. *ġedōn*. **a** Tired out, exhausted; **b** (of food) properly, sufficiently, cooked; **c** (slang) swindled, tricked. Also *done brown.*

donee, n. [1. dōnḗ; 2. douní]. See **donor** & **-ee**. One who receives a gift.

donga, n. [1. dóngga; 2. dóŋgə]. Bantu word. A channel, gully, carved out by the action of water, esp. in S. Africa.

donjon, n. [1. dúnjun; 2. dándʒən]. M.E. alternative spelling of **dungeon**. A castle keep.

donkey, n. [1. dóngki; 2. dóŋki]. Etymol. dubious. Perh. fr. **dun** w. dimin. endings *-ick* & **-y**. **a** Word in common and ordinary use for the ass; **b** person who behaves in a foolish manner.

donkey-engine, n. A small steam-engine, esp. one in use on board ship for loading cargo &c.

donnish, adj. [1. dónish; 2. dóniʃ]. **don** (I.), **2**, & **-ish**. (of manner and appearance) Like a don; stiff, priggish, pedantic, old-maidish.

donor, n. [1. dṓnor; 2. dóunə, dóunō], fr. O. Fr. *doneur*, fr. Lat. *dōnātōr-(em)*, 'a giver'. See **donation** & **-or**. A person who makes a gift, a donation; giver.

doolie, n. [1. dṓōli; 2. dúli]. Hind. *doli*. An Indian litter, esp. one used for military ambulance.

doom (I.), n. [1. dōōm; 2. dūm]. O.E. & M.E. *dōm*; O.L.G., O. Fris. *dōm*; O.N. *dōmr*, Goth. *dōms*, O.H.G. *tuom*, 'judgement, decree'; Gmc. **dōm-a-* (cp. **deem**, fr. **dōm-ja-*), fr. Aryan **dhōm-*, 'something done, fixed, established' (cp. Scrt. *dhāman-*, 'law'; Gk. *thémis*, 'law' &c.), formed w. suff. *-m*, fr. the Aryan base **dhē-, dhō-*, 'to put, place, do'. See **do** & words there referred to. **1.** (archaic) Judgement, sentence. **2.** (hist.) Judicial decree. **3.** Fate, evil destiny, ruin, destruction. **4.** The Day of Judgement; esp. in Phr. *the day of doom, the crack of doom.*

doom (II.), vb. trans., fr. prec. **a** To sentence, pronounce judgement on: *to doom a man to death*; **b** (chiefly in P.P.), to destine, condemn, fate: *doomed to failure.*

doomsday, n. [1. dṓōmzdā; 2. dúmzdei]. O.E. *dōmesdæġ*, 'day of judgement', fr. genit. of *dōm*, 'doom' (see **doom**), & *dæġ*, **day**. The Last Judgement. Phr. *from now till doomsday*, for ever.

Doomsday Book. See **Domesday Book**.

door, n. [1. dōr; 2. dō]. M.E. *dōre, dŭre*, O.E. *duru*; cp. O. Fris. *dure*, O.H.G. *turi, tora*, Goth. *daurō*, O.N. *dyrr*, Gmc. **dur-*. Cognates are found in most of the Aryan languages. The Aryan base is **dhwĕr-(a)-*, **dhwōr-(a)-*, **dhur-*, 'door'. Cp. Gk. *thúrā*, 'door', *thurṓn*, 'entrance hall'; Lat. *foris*, 'door', *forās*, 'out', *forum*, 'court-yard; market-place' (fr. **dhwor-um*; see **forum**); Scrt. *dvār*, pl. *dvāraš*, 'doors' (fr. **dhwōr-*, cons. stem); Lith. *dvāras*, 'court', *dùrys*, 'door'; Lett. *duris*, O. Prussian *dauris*, 'door'; Gaul. *dor* (fr. **dhworā*), O. Ir. *dorus*, W. *drws*, 'door'. See **thyroid**. **1.** Wooden or metal structure for closing the opening of, or entrance to, building, room, cupboard, safe &c., moving on hinges or sliding in grooves: *to close, bang, knock at, a door.* Phrs. *next door*, (in) the next house; *next door to*, very nearly; *front door*, chief door into house; *out of doors*, in the open air; *to lay at a person's door*, impute to him; *at death's door*, near death; *don't darken my doors again*, I forbid you my house. **2.** Entrance to building, room &c. into which a door fits; doorway. Phr. *to show a person the door*, turn him out of the house. **3.** (fig.) A means of access, of attaining something: *a door to success.*

door-bell, n. Bell worked from outside, but ringing inside, a house, to announce arrival of one seeking admittance.

door-case, n. Wooden framework into which a door fits.

door-frame, n. Door-case.

door-keeper, n. **1.** One who guards a door; porter, janitor. **2.** One holding the lowest of the minor orders in Roman Church.

door-mat, n. Rough mat placed at outer door for wiping the boots or shoes of those entering house.

door-nail, n. Large-headed nail with which wooden doors were formerly studded. Phr. *dead as a door-nail*, quite dead.

door-plate, n. Brass plate outside house, office &c., upon which name of occupant is engraved.

door-post, n. Side piece of door-frame, jamb. Phr. *deaf as a door-post*, quite deaf.

door-step, n. Step up to front or other outer door of house.

door-stone, n. Stone slab in front of door of house.

door-way, n. The opening in a wall into which a door fits, entrance to house or oom.

dope (I.), n. [1. dōp; 2. doup], fr. Du. *doop*, 'liquid, sauce'; cp. Du. *doopen*, 'dip'. Connected w. **deep** & **dip**. **1.** Thick liquid, or semi-liquid, for lubricating &c.; specif., a varnish used for tautening and making air-tight the fabric of the wings of aeroplanes and envelope of airships. **2.** (colloq.) **a** Drug, such as opium, used to doctor a horse, or any stimulant given to a horse before a race; hence, any narcotic or other harmful drug; **b** (fig.) something which dulls or blunts or deceives the conscience.

dope (II.), vb. trans., fr. prec. **1.** To apply dope or varnish to. **2.** (colloq.) **a** To give dope or drug to: *to dope a horse*; *dope oneself with cocaine* &c.; **b** (fig.) to allay conscientious scruples by plausible lies; to hoodwink.

doper, n. [1. dōper; 2. dóupə]. Prec. & **-er.** One who dopes (a horse &c.).

doppel-gänger, n. [1. dópl génger; 2. dɔ́pl gέŋə]. Germ., lit. 'double walker'. See **double** & **gang.** The phantasm or wraith of a living person; apparition of oneself, as a warning of death or disaster.

dopper, n. [1. dóper; 2. dɔ́pə]. S. Afr. Du., = 'dipper'. Member of the Dutch Reformed Church of S. Africa.

dor, n. [1. dōr; 2. dō]. O.E. *dora*, 'humble-bee', M.E. *dore*; cp. also provinc. Engl. *dumble-dore*, fr. Gmc. **duran-*; cp. Lett. *(dun)duris*, 'drone'. *(den)deris*, 'a whimpering child'; Ir. *derdrethar*, 'he cries'. Cp. also Gk. *thórubos*, 'confused noise'; Aryan base **dher-*, **dhor-*, **dhr̥-*, 'to make a noise'. Perh. allied to **drone** & **dream.** A humming, droning insect, the dor-beetle.

dorado, n. [1. doráhdō; 2. dərádou]. Span., fr. Lat. *deaurātus*, P.P. of *deaurāre*, 'to gild', fr. **de-** & *aurum*, 'gold'. See **aurum.** Brilliantly coloured sea-fish, *Coryphaena*, often wrongly called a dolphin; its colours change and fade when dying.

dor-beetle, n. The cockchafer.

Dorcas (society), n. [1. dórkas sosíeti; 2. dɔ́kəs səsáiəti], fr. name of the woman whom St. Peter raised from the dead, and who made garments for the poor. Meeting, society, of charitable ladies who assemble at regular intervals and sew, knit, and otherwise make clothes for the poor.

dor-hawk, n. Provincial name for the night-jar or goat-sucker.

Dorian, adj. & n. [1. dṓrian; 2. dɔ́riən], fr. Lat., fr. Gk. *Dṓrios* (& **-an**), 'belonging to Doris'. **1.** adj. Belonging to, pertaining to, **a** Doris, one of the districts of ancient Greece, or **b** the race which about the 10th cent. B.C. invaded Greece from the north, conquering the earlier inhabitants of Laconia, Crete, and other regions. **2.** n. **a** An inhabitant of Doris; **b** member of the Dorian race.

Doric, adj. & n. [1. dórik; 2. dɔ́rik]. Gk. *Dōrikós*. See prec. & **-ic. 1.** adj. Pertaining to Doris or the Dorians; **a** (archit.) *Doric order*, the first of the three Greek orders of architecture, the columns of which are distinguished by being thick in proportion to the height, by having a plain capital, by the absence of mouldings at the foot, and by broad, shallow flutings; **b** (of dial.) unpolished, rough, rustic. **2.** n. **a** The Doric dialect; hence, **b** uncultivated provincial dialect: *to speak one's native Doric.*

Dorize, vb. trans. & intrans. [1. dṓrīz; 2. dɔ́raiz], fr. Gk. *dōrízein*. To make or become Doric or Dorian in language, customs &c.

Dorking, adj. & n. [1. dórking; 2. dɔ́kiŋ]. Name of town in Surrey. **a** adj. Of a breed of domestic fowl; **b** n., fowl of such breed.

dormancy, n. [1. dórmansi; 2. dɔ́mənsi]. See next word & **-ancy.** The state of being dormant, quiescence.

dormant, adj. [1. dórmant; 2. dɔ́mənt]. O. Fr. *dormant*, Pres. Part. of *dormir*, fr. Lat. *dormīre*, 'to sleep'. Cogn. w. O. Slav. *drěmati*, 'to sleep, doze'; Gk. *édrathon*, 'slept', fr. **e-dr̥m-dhom*; Aryan base **derĕm-*, **dorĕm-*, **dr̥m-* &c., 'to sleep'. **1. a** Remaining in a state of inactivity (of hibernating animals, and of seeds during winter); **b** (fig.) inactive, undeveloped, not used: *dormant faculties* &c.; **c** not used; not acting, quiescent: *to lie dormant*; **d** (of peerage and other dignities) not claimed, often used wrongly for one in abeyance. **2.** (her.) Figure of animal represented as lying asleep.

dormer, dormer-window, n. [1. dórmer; 2. dɔ́mə], fr. O. Fr. *dormeour*, fr. Lat. *dormitōrium*, 'sleeping-room', fr. *dormīt-(um)*, P.P. type of *dormīre*, 'to sleep'. See prec. & **-ory.** A vertical window in a sloping roof.

dormitory, n. [1. dórmitori; 2. dɔ́mitəri], fr. Lat. *dormitōrium*, 'sleeping-room'. See prec. A sleeping apartment for a number of persons, often divided into cubicles; esp. used of such rooms in schools and institutions.

dormouse, n. [1. dórmous; 2. dɔ́maus]. Possibly fr. O. Fr. *dorm-* (see **dormant**) & **mouse.** Small hibernating animal resembling a mouse, and intermediate between this and a squirrel.

dormy, adj. [1. dórmi; 2. dɔ́mi]. Origin unknown. (of a golf player) Leading by as many holes as still remain to be played.

dorsal, adj. & n. [1. dórsal; 2. dɔ́səl]. Lat. *dorsālis*, 'pertaining to the back', fr. *dorsum*, 'back'. See **dors(o)-. a** adj. Pertaining to, on, near, the back: *dorsal fins* &c.; **b** n., a dossal, q.v.

dorsally, adv. Prec. & **-ly.** By, along, the back.

dors(o)-, pref. Form of Lat. *dorsum*, 'back', used in compounds; prob. cogn. w. *deorsum*, 'turned away', fr. **dēvorsum*, fr. **de-** & *vors-(um)*, P.P. type of *vertere*, 'to turn'. See **vortex** & **version.** Of, or on, the back: chiefly in anatomical terminology, as: *dors-abdominal*, of back and abdominal region; *dorso-lateral*, of back and side; *dorso-ventral*, having upper and lower parts alike.

dorter, dortour, n. [1. dórter; 2. dɔ́tə]. O. Fr., fr. L. Lat. See **dormitory** & cp. **dormer.** The dormitory or sleeping quarters of a monastery.

dory (I.), n. [1. dṓri; 2. dɔ́ri], fr. Fr. *dorée*, fr. Lat. *deaurātus*, 'gilt'. See **dorado.** Sea-fish of a yellow colour, with delicate, edible flesh. Also *John Dory.*

dory (II.), n. Origin doubtful. Light, flat-bottomed ship's boat, used by the cod-fishers of Newfoundland and N. America.

dosage, n. [1. dósij; 2. dóusidž]. See next word & **-age. 1.** The act or practice of dosing. **2.** The amount of medicine to be taken at one time.

dose (I.), n. [1. dōs; 2. dous]. Fr., fr. Gk. *dósis*, 'a gift', fr. **dot-is* for **də-t-is*, fr. Aryan base **dō-*, **də-*, 'to give', w. P.P. suff. *-t*. See **date** (I.), **donation. a** Amount of medicine administered, or ordered to be taken, at one time; **b** (fig.) a portion, something administered: *a dose of flattery*. Phr. *to have a regular dose of anything*, too much.

dose (II.), vb. trans., fr. prec. To administer medicine to.

doss, n. & vb. intrans. [1. dos; 2. dɔs]. Origin unknown. (low slang) **a** n. A bed; **b** vb., to go to bed, to sleep.

dossal, n. [1. dósal; 2. dɔ́səl]. Fr., fr. Med. Lat. *dossale*, *dorsale*, fr. Lat. *dorsum*, 'back', & **-al.** Cp. **dorsal.** A cloth hung at the back of the chancel, behind the altar, varying in colour according to the Church's seasons.

doss-house, n. Place where a bed can be obtained for a night at a small cost; specif., a common lodging-house.

dossier, n. [1. dósiā; 2. dɔ́siei]. Fr., 'collection of documents', fr. *dos*, 'back', fr. Lat. *dorsum*, 'back'. See **dors(o)-.** A collection of documents and records containing information concerning some particular person, event, or incident.

dot (I.), n. [1. dot; 2. dɔt]. O.E. *dott*, 'speck, head of a boil'. **1. a** A very small rounded mark made with pen, pencil &c.; esp. point placed over *i* or *j*, or used as diacritical mark: *dot and dash*, short and long symbols &c., as in Morse telegraphy and signalling; **b** (mus.) point placed after a note or rest, indicating increase of length by one-half. **2.** Anything resembling a dot in size or appearance: *the ship became a mere dot on the horizon.*

dot (II.), vb. trans., fr. prec. **a** To mark with a dot: *to dot an i*; (mus.) *dotted note*, one marked with a dot, denoting that its length is increased by a half; Phrs. *to dot one's i's*, to behave with circumspection and punctiliousness; *dot-and-go-one*, noise made by a wooden leg, hence, man with a wooden leg, his walk; as adj., limping; *to dot a man one*, strike him; **b** to make, trace, by means of dots (esp. in P.P.): *a dotted line*; **c** to diversify as by dots, to scatter here and there on: *to dot houses over the countryside*; *a field dotted with sheep.*

dot (III.), n. [1. dot; 2. dɔt]. Fr., 'marriage portion', fr. Lat. *dōt-(em)* in same sense, fr. base **dō-*, 'to give'. See **donation** & **endow.** Woman's marriage portion, dowry.

dotage, n. [1. dótij; 2. dóutidž]. See **dote** & **-age.** Feebleness of mind and body due to old age; senility: *to be in one's dotage*, to be very old; to grow foolish.

dotard, n. [1. dṓtard; 2. dóutəd]. See next word & **-ard.** A foolish, doddering old person; one afflicted by senility.

dote, doat, vb. intrans. [1. dōt; 2. dout]. M.E. *dotien*; cp. M. Du. *doten*, O. Fr. *(re)doter*, fr. L.G. **1.** To be in one's dotage, be weak and unbalanced in mind; to show signs of senility. **2.** *Dote upon*, be deeply attached to, have extreme fondness for; to love blindly.

doting, adj. [1. dṓting; 2. dóutiŋ], fr. Pres. Part. of prec. Loving, devoted, filled with fond solicitude: *a doting husband.*

dotingly, adv. Prec. & **-ly.** In a doting manner.

dotterel, n. [1. dótrel; 2. dɔ́trəl]. See **dote** & **-rel.** A kind of plover, coloured fawn, brown, and black; supposed to be very stupid, and to allow itself to be caught easily.

dottle, n. [1. dótl; 2. dɔ́tl]. **dot** (I.) & **-le.** Wad of tobacco left in a pipe after smoking.

dotty, adj. [1. dóti; 2. dɔ́ti]. **dot** (I.) & **-y. 1.** Marked with dots; dotted about. **2.** (slang) Weak in the head, partially mad; queer in mind and behaviour.

douane, n. [1. dooáhn; 2. duán]. Fr., fr. Arab. *diwān*. See **divan.** A custom-house at a frontier between two countries.

double (I.), adj. [1. dúbl; 2. dábl]. M.E., fr. O. Fr., fr. Lat. *duplus*, 'double, twofold'; cp. also **duplex**; cogn. w. Gk. *(di)plóos*, 'double'. The first element is fr. Lat. *duo*, 'two' (see **dual**); the second fr. Aryan base **pel-*, **pl-*, 'fold', wh. appears in Goth. *twei-fl-s*, O.H.G. *zwei-fal*, 'doubt', & w. suff. in Goth. *(ain)-falþs*, 'single'; O.H.G. *einfalt* &c.; Gk. *(di)plásios*, 'double'. See **fold, -fold, diploma, plait, plexus, simple. 1.** (of amount) Twice as much, multiplied by two, as much again: *a double share, portion*; *my income is double what it was*; *to do double work*; *double width*. **2.** (of quality) Twice as good, valuable, strong, thick, powerful &c.; **a** (non-material) *the worth and beauty of this poem are double those of the author's earlier work*; **b** (material) *double ale, double Gloster (cheese)* &c. **3.** (of use and function) **a** Intended, serving, for two persons or things: *double bed, double harness*; **b** acting, performing a movement, twice: *double lock*; **c** intended for, serving, two different purposes: *to pay a double debt*; *to have a double advantage*; *to perform a double service*. **4.** (mode of arrangement, form) **a** Consisting of two, composed of a pair, having two identical parts: *double row*; *double doors*; *a knife with a double edge*; *ship, box, with a double bottom*; *gun with a double barrel*; *a double stem*; *a double flower, blossom*, one having greatly increased number of petals; **b** having, consisting of, two layers, thicknesses; folded in two: *a double coat of paint, a double lining, blanket*. **5.** (of moral & intellectual processes and their expression in word or action) Two-fold, having two, different, aspects or bearings; **a** (in bad sense) deliberately expressing one thing and meaning, or doing, another; insincere, deceitful, treacherous: *to wear a double face*; *a double character*; *double dealing, conduct*; **b** (in innocent sense) capable of two different interpretations, ambiguous: *a double meaning, significance.*

double (II.), adv., fr. prec. **a** Twice over; twice as much: *to pay double*; *to cost double what it did before*; **b** in a pair, in (a) couple(s); as two: *to ride double* (two on same horse); *to see double*, of a drunken man.

double (III.), n., fr. **double** (I.) & (IV.). **1.** (from **double** (I.)) **a** Twice the amount: *to take the double of what one has a right to*; **b** specif., a slow, level run of about twice the speed of ordinary walking or marching: *to advance at the double*. **2.** A duplicate, person or thing exactly resembling another: *to meet one's double*. **3.** (tennis) Game played with two a side: *mixed doubles*, played by two men and two women. **4.** A copper coin used in Guernsey, equal to $\frac{1}{8}$ of a penny. **5.** (from **double** (IV.)) A rapid twist, turn, dodging; act of doubling back on one's tracks.

double (IV.), vb. trans. & intrans., fr. O. Fr. *doubler*, fr. Lat. *duplāre*, 'to double', fr. *duplus*, 'double'. See **double** (I.). **A.** trans. **1.** To multiply by two, increase an amount to twice as much as it was: *to double one's fortune, stake, offer* &c. **2.** (of an actor) *To double the parts of*, act two characters in same play. **3.** To bend, fold over, superimpose one thickness of something on another: *to double a blanket, shawl* &c. Phr. *to double one's fists*, close, clench, as for fighting. **4.** (naut.) To sail round, turn the corner of: *to double Cape Horn*. **B.** intrans. **1.** To become double in amount or size (also reflex.). **2.** To move in double time, run. **3.** To turn back, dodge, sharply, in running to escape pursuit. **C.** Followed by preposition or adverb. *Double back*, **a** trans., to draw, fold back; **b** intrans., to run rapidly back on one's tracks in avoiding pursuit. *Double in*, trans., to fold, turn, tuck, something inwards. *Double up*, **1.** trans., **a** to fold, roll, up; **b** to cause (a person) to curl up, hunch himself together, with pain &c.; **c** (fig.) to cause (a person) to collapse with shock of grief &c.; **2.** intrans., **a** to be capable of being rolled, folded up: *the rug won't double up neatly*; **b** (of persons) to curl up, collapse.

double axe, n. Axe with two blades and edges.

double-barrelled, adj. **a** (of a gun) Having two barrels; **b** (fig.) having two bearings, capable of being taken in two ways, ambiguous: *a double-barrelled compliment*.

double-bass, n. [1. dúbl bás; 2. dábl béis]. Largest of the fiddles, much larger than a 'cello.

double-bedded, adj. [1. dùbl béded; 2. dàbl bédid]. Containing two beds; containing a double bed.

double-breasted, adj. [1. dùbl brésted; 2. dàbl bréstid]. Of a body garment, having two rows of buttons and button-holes, so that it can be folded across and fastened either side.

double cross, vb. trans. (slang, of thieves, swindlers &c.) To betray, cheat, swindle (one another).

double-dealer, n. One who speaks and behaves differently according to circumstances, who says one thing and means, or does, another; a dissembler.

double-dealing, n. & adj. **a** n. Deceit, duplicity; **b** adj., deceitful, insincere.

double-decker, n. Ship with two decks.

double Dutch, n. (colloq.) An unintelligible language; language one does not understand.

double-dyed, adj. [1. dùbl díd; 2. dàbl dáid]. **a** Having been twice immersed, steeped in dye to secure greater permanence of colour; **b** (fig.) (i.) steeped in iniquity: *double-dyed villain*; (ii.) thoroughly imbued with certain opinions, habits &c.; thorough-paced: *a double-dyed Tory*.

double eagle, n. **a** (her.) An eagle with two heads; **b** gold coin of the U.S.A., value 10 dollars.

double-edged, adj. [1. dùbl éjd; 2. dàbl édžd]. **a** Having two sharp edges; **b** (fig., of an argument &c.) cutting both ways, telling against, as well as for.

double entendre, n. [1. dōōbl ontondr; 2. dūbl ātādr]. Fr., 'twofold sense'. Statement, phrase, capable of a double interpretation; esp. of one innocent, and another malicious, or improper meaning.

double-entry, n. System of book-keeping, in which each transaction is entered on the debtor side of one account and on the credit side of another.

double-faced, adj. Hypocritical.

double-first, n. University degree with first-class honours: **a** in two parts of the examination; **b** in two different examinations; **c** in examinations in two different subjects or Honour Schools. In Oxford the phrase implies a first class, e.g. in both Classical Honour Moderations and in the Classical Final Honour examination or *Greats*.

double-lock, vb. trans. To turn the key twice, so as to shoot second bolt; to fasten with special security.

doubleness, n. [1. dúblnes; 2. dáblnis]. **double** (I.) & **-ness**. The quality or state of being double.

double-quick, adj. & adv. **a** Especially quick(ly); **b** in double time, at the double.

double-reef, vb. trans. To take two reefs in a sail.

double star, n. Two stars very near together, only distinguishable from one another by means of a telescope.

double-stop, vb. intrans. (violin-playing) To place fingers so as to form note on two strings and play on both at the same time.

doublet, n. [1. dúblet; 2. dáblit]. Fr. See **double** (I.) & **-et**. **1.** (archaic) Close-fitting garment covering the upper part of the body. **2.** One of several words derived ultimately from same source, but coming into a language through different channels, from different dialects, or at different periods, and differentiated in form and often in meaning, e.g. *frail* and *fragile*; *hospital, hostel, hotel* &c. (**3.** pl.) Two birds killed by shots, fired in rapid succession, from one double-barrelled gun.

double time, n. March step, fastest next to an actual run.

doubling, vbl. n. [1. dúbling; 2. dábliŋ], fr. **double** (IV.) & **-ing**. **1.** Action of one who doubles; **a** act of multiplying by two: *the doubling of one's income*; **b** act of darting back, dodging, in evading pursuit &c.: *he escaped his pursuers only by innumerable turnings and doublings*. **2.** (her., in pl.) Linings of robes of state &c. and of mantlings in coats of arms.

doubloon, n. [1. dublōōn; 2. dablūn], fr. Fr. *doublon*, fr. Span. *doblón*. See **double** (I.) & **-oon**. Obsolete Spanish gold coin, of varying value, properly a double pistole, worth about a guinea.

doublure, n. [1. dōōblūr; 2. dūbljuə]. Fr., 'lining'. Lining; specif., ornamental lining, esp. of leather, of binding of a book.

doubly, adv. [1. dúbli; 2. dábli]. **double** (I.) & **-ly**. To twice the extent, or amount.

doubt (I.), vb. intrans. & trans. [1. dout; 2. daut], fr. O. Fr. *douter*, fr. Lat. *dubitāre*, 'to hesitate in opinion, be uncertain; to reflect, deliberate', freq. formed fr. O. Lat. *dubat*, 'he is doubtful', fr. *dubius*, 'doubtful'. See **dubious**. **A.** intrans. **1. a** To hesitate, waver, be uncertain, in opinions or convictions; specif. **b** to have difficulty in believing religious doctrine, to feel uncertain about the truth of revealed religion: *I would like to believe, but my reason makes me doubt*. **2.** To have misgivings, hesitations, qualms, as to what to do; feel uncertain as to what has happened, or what will happen: *I doubt whether you ought to accept*; *I doubt very much whether I shall be able to come*; *I don't doubt that you are honest*; *I doubt if that was intended to mean what you think it means*. **B.** trans. **1. a** To hesitate, be unable to believe; to disbelieve; attach no credit to; call in question the existence of something, that something has happened, the truth of a statement: *to doubt the existence of God, one's own existence*; *to doubt the evidence of one's senses*; *to doubt a person's honesty*; **b** to entertain suspicions about a person's honesty, straightforwardness, loyalty: *I refuse to doubt so old a friend*; *you surely don't doubt me*. **2.** (archaic) To fear, be afraid, dread, have evil anticipations concerning: *to doubt the arrival of bad news at any moment*.

doubt (II.), n., fr. O. Fr. *doute*, fr. prec. **1.** (of mental attitude or condition) Lack of firm conviction, absence of certainty, inclination towards disbelief: '*There lives more faith in honest doubt, Believe me, than in half the creeds*' (Tennyson); *to be in doubt what one ought to do*. **2.** Condition of uncertainty in events and circumstances: *the issue of the fight was still in doubt*. **3.** Specific case in which proof is lacking; a misgiving; feeling of hesitation in the mind on which side truth lies: *to have grave doubts about something*; *my doubts are dispelled*. Phrs. (*there is*) *no doubt*; *without doubt*, it is certain, certainly; *to give a person the benefit of the doubt*, believe the best of him, until the reverse is proved.

doubtful, adj. [1. dóutfool; 2. dáutfəl]. Prec. & **-ful**. **1. a** (of persons) Feeling, filled with, doubt; not convinced, uncertain: *I am doubtful what I ought to do*; *to be doubtful of the wisdom of an action*; **b** (of statements &c.) expressing or provoking doubt, not dispelling uncertainty: *a doubtful reply*. Phr. *a doubtful blessing*, something which may or may not be such. **2.** (of events, circumstances, of things in relation to human action) **a** Unsettled, undecided, hanging in the balance: *the outcome of the struggle was long doubtful*; **b** fraught with fears, misgivings; obscure: *a doubtful future*; *to pursue a doubtful path* (fig.). **3. a** (of persons and actions) Giving rise to doubt as to integrity; suspicious, not definitely felt to be above suspicion; shady: *a doubtful character, reputation*; Phr. *in doubtful taste*, bad taste; **b** (of places) squalid, disreputable, sinister: *a doubtful neighbourhood*.

doubtfully, adv. Prec. & **-ly**. In a doubtful manner (in various senses).

doubtfulness, n. See prec. & **-ness**. The state of being doubtful.

doubting, adj. [1. dóuting; 2. dáutiŋ], fr. Pres. Part. of **doubt** (I.). Feeling doubt; especially feeling dread, hesitation, apprehension: *a doubting heart*.

doubtingly, adv. See prec. & **-ly**. In a doubting manner.

doubtless, adj. & adv. [1. dóutles; 2. dáutlis], fr. **doubt** (II.) & **-less**. **1.** adj. (rare) Feeling no hesitation, fear, apprehension. **2.** adv. **a** Without doubt, certainly; **b** probably: *I shall doubtless see you tomorrow*.

douce, adj. [1. dōōs; 2. dūs]. Fr., fem. of *doux*, 'sweet, gentle', fr. Lat. *dulcis*. See **dulcet**. Scots word, sometimes used in English; sedate, gentle.

douceur, n. [1. dōōsér; 2. dūsá]. Fr., 'sweetness; a favour'. See prec. Gratuity, tip; a bribe.

douche (I.), n. [1. dōōsh; 2. dūʃ]. Fr., fr. Ital. *doccia*, 'water-pipe', fr. Lat. *ductus*, 'a conduit' (cp. **aqueduct**), fr. P.P. type of *dūcere*, 'to lead, draw, conduct'. See **duct** & **duke**. **a** A jet or shower of water passing through perforated ducts of metal, and directed upon some part of the body; **b** bath, injection by this means. Phr. *to throw a cold douche upon*, (fig.) to damp, extinguish, enthusiasm for support of any scheme &c.

douche (II.), vb. trans., fr. prec. To apply a douche to.

dough, n. [1. dō; 2. dou]. O.E. *dāg*, M.E. *dōȝ, dōgh, dou*; cogn. w. O.H.G. *teig*, O.N. *deigr*, Goth. *daigs*; cp. Goth. *digrei*, 'strength, solidity, abundance'; O.N. *digr*, 'stout, large' Cogn. w. Gk. *teikhos*, 'wall', orig. 'clay wall' (see **paradise**). Scrt. *dēhaś*, 'body, figure', *dēhī*, 'earthwork', *déhmi*, 'smear over, stick together'; Goth. *deigan*, 'to smear'; Lat. *fingere* (w. infixed *n*), 'to form, model, fashion; to touch, stroke'; Aryan base **dheigh-*, **dhoigh-*, **dhigh-*, 'to form out of clay; to smear, cement'. Cp. also Lat. *figūra*, 'something formed, figure'.

See **figure, fiction, fictile, effigy, duff.** **1.** Thick mass of uncooked flour, or meal, moistened with water, milk &c., kneaded ready for making into bread. **2.** (slang, esp. U.S.A.) Money.

doughboy, n. [1. dṓboi; 2. dóubɔi]. **1.** Small, boiled suet dumpling. **2.** (slang, U.S.A.) American soldier.

doughiness, n. [1. dṓines; 2. dóuinis]. **doughy & -ness.** State or consistency resembling that of dough.

doughnut, n. [1. dṓnut; 2. dóunat]. Small cake made of dough mixed with eggs and sugar and fried in deep fat.

doughtily, adv. [1. dóutili; 2. dáutili]. **doughty & -ly.** In a valiant manner.

doughtiness, n. [1. dóutines; 2. dáutinis]. Next word & **-ness.** The quality of being doughty; valour, stoutness of heart.

doughty, adj. [1. dóuti; 2. dáuti]. O.E. *dohtiġ, dyhtiġ,* M.E. *duhtiȝ*; cp. M.H.G. *tühtic,* 'powerful, capable'; fr. base in O.E. *dugan,* 'be valiant', pret. *dēag*; O.H.G. *touc,* Goth. *daug,* 'it is suitable, useful'; cogn. w. Gk. *teúkhein,* 'to make, form, produce'; Aryan base **dheugh-, *dhough-,* 'to make suitable'. (archaic) Bold, valiant: *a doughty warrior; doughty deeds.*

doughy, adj. [1. dṓi; 2. dóui]. **dough & -y.** **a** Resembling dough in appearance or texture; **b** (fig.) dull, heavy, in the intellect.

Douglas spruce, n., also **fir, pine** [1. dúglas sprōōs; 2. dáglǝs sprūs], fr. David Douglas, a botanist, who introduced it to Great Britain in 1827. A tall, N. American conifer, with spreading branches and flat needle-like leaves and pendulous cones, producing a valuable hard timber.

Doukhobors, n. pl. [1. dōōkōborz; 2. dúkoubɔ̄z], fr. Russ., lit. 'spirit fighters'. The name given by the Orthodox Church to a nonconformist sect, styling themselves the 'Universal Brotherhood', having much in common with the Quakers.

doum, n. [1. dōōm, doum; 2. dūm, daum]. Arab. *dum, daum.* A palm tree of Upper Egypt, bearing fruit about the size of an apple.

dour, adj. [1. door; 2. duǝ]. Scots, perh. fr. Lat. *dūrus,* 'hard'. See **durable.** Cold, aloof, stern, forbidding, in manner and character.

dourly, adv. Prec. & **-ly.** In a dour, stern manner.

dourness, n. See prec. & **-ness.** State, quality, of being dour.

douse, dowse, vb. trans. [1. dous; 2. daus]. Etymol. unknown; not connected w. **dowse (II.).** **1.** To dip, plunge, in water; to throw water over. **2. a** (naut.) To lower suddenly (a sail); **b** (colloq.) to extinguish a light: *to douse the glim,* put out the light.

dove, n. [1. duv; 2. dav]. O.E. *dūfe-* (only in compound), M.E. *dūve,* O.H.G. *tūbo,* Goth. *dūbo,* perh. connected w. O.E. *dūfan, dȳfan,* 'to dive' (see **dive**), in allusion to the flight of the bird. **1.** One of many varieties of pigeon, all of which have characteristic murmuring cry: *ring-dove, rock-dove, turtle-dove* &c. **2. a** A symbol of peace; **b** a name of, and symbol for, the Holy Ghost. **3.** A term of endearment.

dove-colour(ed), n. & adj. Soft, pinkish grey.

dove-cot(e), n. [1. dúv kot; 2. dáv kǝt, kɔt]. A small house containing a series of nesting-boxes for pigeons; often set on a pole, or against the upper part of a building. Phr. *a flutter in the dove-cot,* excitement among quiet people.

dove-eyed, adj. Having innocent and gentle eyes like those of a dove.

dove-like, adj. Like a dove, gentle, tender.

dove's-foot, n. A kind of wild geranium.

dovetail (I.), n. [1. dúvtāl; 2. dávteil]. See **dove & tail,** named fr. shape of tenon. A method of joining planks, timbers &c. together, by fitting wedge-shaped projections ('tenon') in one piece into cavities of corresponding shape ('mortise') in another.

dovetail (II.), vb. trans. & intrans., fr. prec. **1.** trans. **a** To join together by means of dovetails; **b** (fig.) to fit (facts, points of information &c.) together. **2.** intrans. (lit. and fig.) *To dovetail in(to),* to fit together closely, be easily linked up.

dowager, n. [1. dóuajer; 2. dáuǝdžǝ], fr. O. Fr. *douagere,* fr. O. Fr. *douage,* 'dower'. See **dower, endow, & -age & -er.** A widow who has received a dower from her husband; esp. title given to the widow of a prince, nobleman &c. to distinguish her from the wife of her husband's heir: *dowager duchess; queen-dowager* &c.

dowdily, adv. [1. dóudili; 2. dáudili]. **dowdy & -ly.** In a dowdy, unfashionable manner.

dowdiness, n. [1. dóudines; 2. dáudinis]. Next word & **-ness.** Quality of being dowdy.

dowdy, adj. & n. [1. dóudi; 2. dáudi]. M.E. *doude* &c., 'slut'; cp. **duds.** **1.** adj. **a** (of woman) Ill-dressed, with no elegance or smartness; **b** (of dress) unfashionable, clumsy, badly made, lacking style. **2.** n. A dowdy woman.

dowdyish, adj. [1. dóudi-ish; 2. dáudi-iʃ]. Prec. & **-ish.** Inclined to be dowdy, somewhat dowdy.

dowel (I.), n. [1. dóuel; 2. dáuil]. Cp. L.G. *dovel,* Mod. Germ. *dōbel,* 'plug'. Pin or peg of wood, iron &c., without a head, for joining two pieces of wood &c. together.

dowel (II.), vb. trans., fr. prec. To fasten with dowels.

dower (I.), n. [1. dóuer; 2. dáuǝ]. M.E. *dowere, dowarie,* fr. O. Fr. *douaire,* fr. Low Lat. *dōtārium,* fr. Lat. *dōt-(em), dōs,* 'marriage portion; a property, talent', & **-ary.** The form *dōs* is fr. **dōts,* fr. Aryan base **dō-,* 'to give'; cp. **donation & dot (III.).** **1. a** Widow's share of husband's property, jointure; **b** property brought by wife to husband, dowry. **2.** Natural gift, talent, endowment.

dower (II.), vb. trans., fr. prec. **1.** To provide with a dower. **2.** To bestow upon, give talent to, endow with.

dowerless, adj. [1. dóuerles; 2. dáuǝlis]. **dower (I.) & -less.** Without a dower or portion.

dowlas, n. [1. dóulas; 2. dáulǝs], fr. the name of the town of Daoulas, near Brest, in Brittany. Kind of coarse calico.

down (I.), n. [1. doun; 2. daun]. Scand.; M.E. *doun,* fr. O.N. *dūnn*; further connexions obscure. **1. a** The fine, soft plumage under a bird's feathers; **b** a young bird's first coat of soft plumage; Phr. *as soft as down.* **2.** Any light, fine, soft, fluffy substance resembling down, e.g. the soft hair on new-born infants and young animals such as the rabbit; that first appearing on a boy's face; the hairy coat of some plants; fine fibre attached to some seeds, such as those of thistle, dandelion &c.

down (II.), n. O.E. *dūn,* 'hill', M.E. *dūne*; of Celt. origin, cp. Ir. *dūn,* 'fortified hill, fort, town'. Prob. cogn. w. O.E. *tūn,* 'enclosure, estate, village' &c. See **town.** **1.** Bare, open, uplands, esp. (in pl.) the chalky hills of Southern England: *South Downs, North Downs* &c. **2.** *The Downs,* part of the Straits of Dover, inside the Goodwin Sands.

down (III.), adv. O.E. *of dūne, ādūne,* lit. 'from the hill'. See prec. Engl. alone of the Gmc. languages uses this particular word to express the varied ideas now associated with it, and the noun from which the adv. &c. has been developed is an early loan-word fr. Celtic. Such a method of expressing the ideas of rest at, & motion to, a lower position may be paralleled fr. other languages: cp. Goth. *dalaþ,* 'down', lit. 'towards the valley', fr. *dal,* 'valley'; & Fr. *aval,* 'down stream', also lit. 'towards the valley', fr. Lat. *ad vallem.* Generally, *down* expresses lower position, whence, inferiority; decrease; nearness in time &c.; contrasted with *up.* **A.** Expressing relations in space: **1.** (with vbs. expressing motion) **a** descent from higher to lower position: *to go, come, glance (the eye) down, sink, run, fall, pull down*; Phrs. *down on (a man &c.),* severe with, hostile to; *to come down on,* censure, punish; *to put down,* stop, abolish, abuses &c.; **b** movement from upright to recumbent position: *to tumble, be knocked, lie, down*; Phrs. *down!,* order to dog, lie down!; *down with!,* let us abolish (lit. and fig.); **c** movement from inland towards sea: *to go down to the coast*; of a river, from source towards mouth: *to flow down*; **d** movement from place of more to one of less importance: *to go down from town, down to the country*; specif., *to go down from Oxford, from the University,* to leave, permanently or temporarily. **2.** (with vbs., expressing continuance in position) **a** In a low or lower position, lowered, recumbent on the ground: *to leave the blinds down; several trees are down; down on one's back; to hit a man when he's down,* also fig. Phr., to show severity, unkindness, to one already unfortunate; *to get, to have, something down (on paper),* written; *(will suit me) down to the ground,* thoroughly; **b** sloping, hanging, projecting, downwards: *down on the left side,* of anything which is supposed to stand at given height; Phr. *down at heel,* having worn-out boots, shabby generally. **B.** Expressing decrease of degree, intensity, amount, bulk &c. **1. a** Decrease of violence; abatement, subsidence &c.: *the gale, wind, storm, has died, gone, down*; **b** (of intensity) *the temperature is down,* less hot. **2. a** Deterioration of quality: *the excellence of many articles made in this country has gone down of late years*; **b** decline in social position, importance, standing, reputation &c.: *to come down in the world*; Phrs. *down and out,* ruined and helpless; *to put a man down,* snub him; *shout down,* refuse a hearing to, and drown what another says; **c** (of physical or moral state) (i.) exhausted, enfeebled, worn out: *she is thoroughly down (in health) and must be fed up*; (ii.) depressed, out of spirits; Phrs. *down on one's luck; down in the mouth.* **3.** Decrease in amount, number: *the birth-rate is very much down; the yield of corn is down compared with last year.* **4.** Decrease in bulk: *to boil down, wear down, grind down.* **C.** Expressing relation to completion of action: **1.** Nearer to the end, remoter from start: *to read from the beginning down to chapter v.* &c.; *I have done down to the end of letter D* &c. **2.** Implying successful accomplishment: *to track, run down at last,* to catch what one is seeking or pursuing. Phr. *to run down a person,* disparage him. **D.** (of relations in time) Expressing greater remoteness from past, nearness to present: *down to the time of Elizabeth; I now come down to the day before yesterday; to look down through the ages, from the past.*

down (IV.), prep., fr. prec. **A.** Relations in space: **1.** (of motion) **a** Along, from higher to lower position, in descending direction, along the course of: *down the hill* &c.; **b** *down the river, stream,* in the direction in which it flows; **c** *down wind,* in the direction it is blowing; **d** *to go down the road* &c., along, away from given point. **2.** (of rest) **a** At a lower position or point: *to live further down the river*; **b** at a remoter point: *a station down the line.* **B.** Relations in time: Passing through from remoter to nearer point: *down the ages, years.*

down (V.), adj., fr. **down (III.)** (of direction) Downward, descending; going down (in various senses): *on the down grade; the down train,* one from London; *down side,* that on which down trains pass.

down (VI.), vb. trans., fr. prec. (colloq.) **a** To bring, put down, to lower, knock down; to suppress, defeat, baffle: *to down one's opponents, down opposition*; **b** to place, lay down: *to down tools,* to strike.

down (VII.), n., fr. **down (V.)** **1.** Lower position, lack of prosperity. In Phr. *ups and downs of life, fate* &c. **2.** (colloq.) Dislike of, grudge

. against, a person. In Phr. *to have a down on someone.*

downcast (**I.**), adj. [1. dóunkahst; 2. dáunkāst]. **down** (**III.**) & **cast**. **a** (of eyes, look &c.) Looking downwards; **b** depressed, damped in spirits, discouraged.

down-cast (**II.**), n. (min.) A ventilation shaft.

down-draught, n. A downward current of air.

downfall, n. [1. dóunfawl; 2. dáunfōl]. **a** The act of falling, descending; something which falls; a heavy fall of rain, snow &c.; **b** (fig.) overthrow, ruin, destruction.

downhearted, adj. [1. dóunhárted; 2. dáunhātid]. In low spirits, dejected, despondent.

downhill (**I.**), adv. [1. dòunhíl; 2. dàunhíl]. In a downward direction, from a hill or slope, towards the foot. Phr. (fig.) *to go downhill*, to go from bad to worse, deteriorate in fortunes, character, health.

downhill (**II.**), adj. [1. dóunhil; 2. dáunhil]. Having or following a downward slope.

downiness, n. [1. dóunines; 2. dáuninis]. See **downy** (**II.**) & **-ness**. The quality of being downy.

Downing Street, n. [1. dóuning; 2. dáuniŋ]. Named after Sir George Downing, d. 1684. Street leading from Whitehall to St. James's Park, London, in which are the official residence of the Prime Minister, No. 10, and that of the Chancellor of the Exchequer, hence, as synonym of the Cabinet or Government of the day: *an unpleasant shock to Downing Street.*

downpour, n. [1. dóunpōr; 2. dáunpɔ]. Heavy fall of water, esp. of rain.

downright, adj. & adv. [1. dóunrīt; 2. dáunrait]. M.E. *dūn rihte.* See **down** (**III.**) & **right**. **1.** adj. **a** Straightforward, frank, bluff, honest, definite: *a downright sort of man*; **b** out-and-out, absolute, unqualified: *downright nonsense.* **2.** adv. Absolutely, really, thoroughly: *to be downright unpleasant* &c.

downrightness, n. [1. dounrítnes; 2. daunráitnis]. Prec. & **-ness**. The quality of being downright.

downstairs (**I.**), adv. [1. dòunstárz; 2. dàunstéəz]. Notion of *stairs* often lost. To, or at, a lower floor of a house: *he is waiting downstairs*; *to go downstairs by lift.*

downstair(s) (**II.**), adj. [1. dóunstār(z); 2. dáunstɛə(z)]. On a lower floor; esp. on the ground floor: *a downstairs room.*

down-trodden, adj. [1. dóun trodn; 2. dáun trɔdn]. Kept in subjection, tyrannized over, oppressed.

downward, adj. [1. dóunward; 2. dáunwəd]. O.E. *ādūnweard.* See **down** (**IV.**) & **-ward**. **1.** Passing from a higher to a lower level or position: *downward slope, movement.* **2.** Proceeding from an earlier to a later point of time. **3.** Tending, declining, passing towards a lower state of excellence; in state of deterioration: *downward career.*

downward(s), adv. In a downward direction.

downy (**I.**), adj. [1. dóuni; 2. dauni]. **down** (**I.**) & **-y**. **1.** Like down in texture and appearance. **2.** (slang) Astute, wideawake, beneath an appearance of innocence; knowing: *a downy old bird.*

downy (**II.**), adj. **down** (**II.**) & **-y**. (of country) Resembling, having character of, downs; undulating.

dowry, n. [1. dóuri; 2. dáuəri]. M.E. *dowerie*, fr. O. Fr. *douaire.* See **dower** (**I.**) & **-y**. **a** A woman's marriage-portion; **b** (fig., poet.) A natural gift, endowment.

dowse (**I.**). See **douse**.

dowse (**II.**), vb. intrans. [1. dous; 2. daus]. Apparently Corn.; etymol. unknown. To seek water by means of a divining-rod.

dowser, n. [1. dóuser; 2. dáusə]. Prec. & **-er**. One who dowses; water-finder.

dowsing-rod, n. [1. dóusing rod; 2. dáusiŋ rɔd]. Divining-rod.

doxology, n. [1. dòksóloji; 2. dɔ̀ksɔ́lədži], fr. Med. Lat., fr. Gk. *dóxa*, 'a notion; an opinion; honour, glory', & **-logy**. The form *dóxa* is fr. earlier **doktia*, fr. Gk. *dokéein*, 'to think, believe'. See **dogma**, **decent**. Hymn of praise; specif., liturgical formula beginning *Glory be to the Father* &c., sung at the end of canticles and psalms.

doxy (**I.**), n. [1. dóksi; 2. dɔ́ksi]. Final sylls. of **orthodoxy**. See prec. (colloq.) An opinion, doctrine, theory: *orthodoxy and every other doxy.*

doxy (**II.**), n. Origin unknown. Cant term for sweetheart; female tramp or beggar.

doyen, n. [1. dwáhyan; 2. dwajǣ]. Fr., 'dean, senior member of a body'; fr. Lat. *decānus.* See **decanal** & **dean**. Senior member of a body or profession.

doze (**I.**), vb. intrans. [1. dōz; 2. douz]. Cp. Dan. *döse*, 'to be drowsy', *dösig*, 'sleepy'; prob. cogn. w. O.E. *dysig.* See **dizzy**. To sleep lightly and intermittently, be half asleep.

doze (**II.**), n., fr. prec. A short, light sleep.

dozen, n. [1. dúzn; 2. dázn]. M.E. *dozaine*, fr. O. Fr. *dozeine*, fr. Lat. *duodecim*, 'twelve'. See **duodecimo**. **1. a** (used as numeral adj.) Twelve things of one kind: *one, three, twelve* &c., *dozen eggs, bottles of wine* &c.; after *several, many*, in pl. followed by *of*: *several dozens of port* &c.; **b** a collection or group of twelve things of the same kind: *I'll take a dozen of them.* Phr. *baker's dozen*, thirteen. **2.** (colloq.) An indefinite number: *dozens of people.*

dozily, adv. [1. dṓzili; 2. dóuzili]. **dozy** & **-ly**. In a dozy, drowsy manner.

doziness, n. [1. dṓzines; 2. dóuzinis]. See prec. & **-ness**. Condition of being dozy; drowsiness.

dozy, adj. [1. dṓzi; 2. dóuzi]. **doze** & **-y**. Inclined to doze; drowsy, sleepy.

drab (**I.**), adj. & n. [1. drab; 2. dræb]. Perh. fr. Fr. *drap*, 'cloth'. See **drape**. **1.** adj. **a** Of a dull, dingy fawn or brown, mud colour; (fig.) **b** gloomy, dingy; undiversified, monotonous, colourless: *a drab existence.* **2.** n. A pale, dull brown: *to paint the walls a useful drab.*

drab (**II.**), n. Celt.; cp. Ir. *drabog*, 'a slut'. **a** A low, slatternly, untidy woman; **b** (archaic) a prostitute.

drabbet, n. [1. drábit; 2. drǽbit]. Fr. *drap*, 'cloth', & **-et**. See **drape**. A coarse, unbleached linen material.

drabble, vb. intrans. & trans. [1. drábl; 2. drǽbl]. M.E. *drabelen*, L.G. loan-word. **a** intrans. To splash about in, flounder through, mud and water; **b** trans., to make wet and muddy by dragging through mire &c.

Dracaena, n. [1. drasḗna; 2. dræsínə], fr. Gk. *drákaina*, fem. of *drákōn.* See **dragon**. **a** Genus of flowering, liliaceous trees and shrubs, one of which, the dragon-tree of the Canary Islands, is of large size and yields dragon's-blood; **b** name given to an allied genus of cultivated shrubs with beautiful foliage.

drachm, n. [1. dram; 2. dræm]. See next word & **dram**. **a** Drachma; **b** a weight. See **dram**.

drachma, n. [1. drákma; 2. drǽkmə]. Lat., fr. Gk. *drakhmḗ*, 'an Attic weight, 66½ grains; a silver coin'; orig. 'a handful'; cp. *drágma*, 'a handful of corn, a sheaf', *dráx*, 'handful' (fr. **drakh-*), *drássomai* (fr. **drakh-so-*), 'clutch, grasp, seize'. Cp. also O. Slav. *(po)dragŭ*, 'border'; O.N. *targa*, O.E. *targe*, 'shield', orig. 'rim of shield' (see **targe**); O.H.G. *zarga*, 'enclosure'. **1. a** Ancient Greek silver coin, worth about 9¾d.; **b** the modern Greek monetary unit and coin, equivalent to the franc. **2.** Unit of weight in ancient Greece, about 2 dwt. 7 grains troy.

Draco, n. [1. drā́kō; 2. dréikou]. Lat. See **dragon**. **1.** (astron.) The Dragon, a northern constellation between the Great and Little Bear. **2.** (zool.) A genus of small flying lizards.

draconian, adj. [1. drakṓnian; 2. drækóuniən], fr. the name of the Athenian *Drakōn* (see **dragon**), who introduced a code of laws in 621 B.C. (of laws) Of extreme severity, harsh.

draconic, adj. [1. drakónik; 2. drækɔ́nik]. See prec. & **-ic**. Draconian, harsh.

draff, n. [1. draf; 2. dræf]. M.E. *draf*, 'dregs'; cp. M. Du., Swed. *draf*; N.H.G. *träber*, 'husks'. Cp. O.N. *drafli*, 'curdled milk'; Ir. *drabh*, 'dregs, yeast'; O.E. *drōf*, O.H.G. *truobi*, 'troubled, sad'; Goth. *drōbjan*, O.E. *drēfan*, 'to trouble'; Lith. *drimbù*, 'to fall in clots'; Gk. *tréphein*, 'to curdle (milk); to feed, nourish'; *thrómbos*, 'a clot'. Aryan base **dherebh-*, **dhrebh-*, 'to thicken', expanded fr. **dher-*, **dhr-*, 'firm'. See **fort**, **trophic**, **thrombosis**. Sediment, refuse, esp. from malt after brewing; wash for feeding pigs.

draft (**I.**), n. [1. drahft; 2. drāft]. Variant spelling of **draught**. See also **draw**. **1.** A body of men detached from a larger body for a special purpose. **2.** A roughly executed outline, plan, scheme, for book, document, picture, machinery &c. **3. a** An order for payment of money by a bank &c.; **b** the drawing of money in this way.

draft (**II.**), vb. trans., fr. prec. **1.** To select and send (men) from a larger body, to be dispatched on special duty. **2.** To prepare, draw up in outline, a rough plan, sketch, scheme for something to be constructed, written &c.; specif., to draw up outline, or finished plan, for a Bill to come before Parliament.

drafting, vbl. n. [1. dráhfting; 2. drā́ftiŋ]. Prec. & **-ing**. **a** Act of drawing up an outline or draft of a Bill &c.; **b** way in which a Bill &c. is drafted: *the drafting of this clause is very obscure.*

draftsman, **draughtsman**, n. [1. dráhftsman; 2. drā́ftsmən]. **1.** One who prepares drawings, plans &c., as in architecture or engineering. **2.** One who prepares, draws up a scheme for, a document, piece of writing; specif., one who drafts a Bill for Parliament &c.: *parliamentary draftsman.*

drag (**I.**), vb. trans. & intrans. [1. drag; 2. dræg]. Scand.; M.E. *draggen*; cp. Swed. *dragga*; cogn. w. O.E. *dragan.* See **draw**. **A.** trans. To pull roughly, to pull along (esp. something heavy, for which effort is required), pull with force. Various specific meanings: **a** To harrow (fields); **b** to trail along the ground: *to drag one's feet*; **c** to use grappling-irons, nets &c. to search for something under water: *to drag the pond*; **d** (colloq.) *to drag up* (*a child*), to bring up in a rough and careless manner; Phr. (of a ship) *to drag its anchor*, draw it from sea-bottom. **B.** intrans. **a** To trail, be pulled along, e.g. a ship's anchor when it has not taken hold; *to walk with dragging feet*; **b** (lit. and fig.) to produce sensation of dragging, tugging: *a dragging pain*; *anxiety dragging at one's heart-strings*; **c** to be tedious, hang heavy, pass slowly and tediously: *the performance dragged*; *time drags*; *one's life drags on*; **d** to go too slowly, not be up to time: *the choir dragged behind the organ in the last hymn.*

drag (**II.**), n., fr. prec. **1.** Something that is dragged; specif. **a** a four-wheeled private coach with seats on top; **b** an appliance for dredging, for bringing things up from under water; **c** a heavy harrow; **d** (i.) a strong-smelling object dragged along or across country for several miles, to make an artificial trail for hounds; (ii.) a hunt at which a drag is used. **2. a** Something that drags, or hinders progress; esp. iron shoe fixed on wheel to act as brake; **b** (fig.) something that hinders, cripples, impedes; a burden: *a drag on one's resources, career* &c.

draggle, vb. trans. & intrans. [1. drágl; 2. drǽgl]. **drag** (**I.**) & **-le**. **1.** trans. To trail (skirts &c.) through mud and mire. **2.** intrans. To be dragged, trail, in the mud.

draggled, adj. [1. drágld; 2. drǽgld], fr. P.P. of prec. Shabby and dirty, crumpled and stained, as from being dragged through mud &c.: *a draggled appearance.*

draggle-tail(ed), n. & adj. [1. drágl tâl(d); 2. drǽgl tèil(d)]. **a** n. A slovenly, ill-dressed woman, esp. one with drooping, muddy skirts; **b** adj., having skirts dragging untidily on the ground; slatternly.

drag hunt, n. Hunt in which no fox or hare is chased, but in which hounds follow a scent artificially made. See **drag (II.)**.

drag-net, n. A net dragged along the ground to catch small birds, or through the water to catch fish.

dragoman, n. [1. drágoman; 2. drǽgəmən]. Fr., fr. Arab. *targuman*, 'interpreter'. See **Targum.** An interpreter in Arabic, Turkish, Persian; also a guide, in the East.

dragon, n. [1. drágun; 2. drǽgən]. Fr., fr. Lat. *dracōn-(em)*, *draco*, fr. Gk. *drákōn*, 'a dragon; a large serpent', lit. 'the sharp-sighted one'; cp. Gk. *dérkomai*, 'look at'; Aryan base **derk-*, **dṛk-* &c., 'to see'. Other cognates are O. Ir. *derc*, 'eye'; Goth. *(ga)tarhjan*, 'make distinct'; O.E. *torht*, O.H.G. *zoraht*, 'bright, clear'. **1. a** A fabulous monster, represented as a winged reptile, with scales, four legs and claws, and breathing out fire and smoke: *St. George and the dragon*; **b** (her.) a representation of this monster (in various forms), cp. *Wyvern*: *the red dragon of Wales*; **c** (fig., from legend of dragons guarding treasures) a fierce, vigilant female companion or chaperon of a young girl. **2.** (Bib.) Term used in A.V. to translate various Hebrew words as: *the dragon, that old serpent, which is Satan* (Rev. xx. 2). **3.** (astron.) The constellation Draco, q.v. **4.** (zool.) **a** a giant lizard of Komodo, island in Malay Archipelago; **b** a small lizard, genus *Draco*, of the East Indies, which flies through the air by means of membranes along its sides; **c** a special breed of domestic pigeon. **5.** Name of an old short musket or carbine used by cavalry. See **dragoon.**

dragonet, n. [1. drágunet; 2. drǽgənɛt]. Fr., dimin. of **dragon**. Name of a small, very brightly coloured sea-fish, allied to the goby, with large, spined fins.

dragon-fly, n. A brightly coloured, iridescent insect, having a large head, long slender body, and two pairs of strong, filmy wings, capable of a very rapid, darting flight.

dragonnade, n. [1. dragunâd; 2. drægənéid]. Fr., 'attack by dragoons'. See **dragoon** & **-ade. 1.** (hist., usually pl.) Persecution of French Protestants by Louis XIV., who quartered regiments of dragoons on the Protestant villages, with orders to terrorize the inhabitants. **2.** Rapid incursion carried out by armed forces.

dragon's-blood, n. Red, resinous substance exuded by certain kinds of East Indian palm fruit, also obtained from the dragon-tree, used for colouring varnishes, lacquer &c.

dragon's head, -tail, n. (astron.) Ascending or descending node of the moon or planet, indicated by the symbols ☊, ☋.

dragon-tree, n. A very tall tree, genus *Dracaena*, of the Canary Islands, which yields dragon's-blood.

dragoon (I.), n. [1. dragōōn; 2. drəgū́n]. Fr. *dragon*, 'carbine', so called as breathing fire. See **dragon, 4. a** (orig.) A mounted infantry-man, armed with a carbine called a 'dragon'; **b** a soldier belonging to certain regiments of cavalry; **c** a rough, fierce, terrifying man.

dragoon (II.), vb. trans., fr. prec. To discipline by severe, harsh, measures; enforce rigid discipline upon.

drail, n. [1. drāl; 2. dreil]. Not found in O.E., though it might well have existed in the form **drægel*, or **dregel*, the first element being *drag-*, as in O.E. *dragan*, 'to draw' (see **draw**), & the second the common formative, dimin. suff. *-il*. The word *dræǵ(e)*, 'drag-net', actually does occur, formed fr. same base, see **dray.** A suggestion has been made that the Mod. *drail* is a compromise between *draw* & *trail*. **1.** A line and hook used in trolling, weighted to keep the latter at desired depth. **2.** Adjustable part of the beam of a plough.

drain (I.), vb. trans. & intrans. [1. drān; 2. drein]. O.E. *drēahnian*, 'to strain, strain out'; M.E. *drēnen, dreinen*. The O.E. base *drēah-* is in gradational relation to that in O.E. *drūgian*, 'to become dry', & *drȳge*, adj., 'dry'. See **dry. A.** trans. **1.** (of action on land &c.) **a** (of human action) To draw excess of water, or other moisture, away by cutting channels, or placing pipes &c. to carry it off: *a farmer must drain his land*; **b** (of action of river, watercourses, pipes &c.) to carry away water from land: *the river drains the whole countryside*; **c** (by extension) to carry off impure matter from a wound by tubes. **2.** (of action on water &c.) to carry it away; **a** to make channels &c. to carry it; **b** (of a river, pipes &c.) to receive water and carry it away, allow it to flow through and away: *the river drains the water from the whole countryside*; **c** (by extension) to cleanse, free, a wound from matter by allowing this to flow out through tubes. Also *drain away*, in above senses implying rather more complete action or process. **3.** (fig.) To drink up: **a** (of effect on liquid) to consume, swallow down: *to drain a pint of wine*; **b** (of effect on drinking vessel) to swallow the contents of: *to drain a pint-pot of wine.* Phrs. *to drain dry, to the dregs*, drink up completely; (fig.) *to drain the cup of sorrow to the dregs*, experience direst misfortune, grief &c. **4.** (fig.) **a** To deprive of resources, impoverish: *to be drained of one's wealth*; *to drain a country of men and treasure*; **b** to withdraw, carry away, exhaust (money, treasure, resources &c.). **5.** (recent, from **drain (II.)**) To supply (a city, house &c.) with drainage system: (esp. in P.P.) *well, badly, drained.* **B.** intrans. **1.** (of liquid) **a** (often *drain away*) To flow, trickle, slowly away; to drip away: *the water will soon drain away*; **b** (fig.) *his life was slowly draining away*, he was bleeding to death. **2.** (of land or other substances containing liquid) To allow this to escape, undergo process of being drained: *this field drains into the river.*

drain (II.), n., fr. prec. **1.** Artificial channel along which water flows; pipe, ditch &c. for conveying superfluous water away from land or from buildings. **2.** (in pl.) System of sewers and pipes leading through and from a house or town for carrying off sewage and water: *something wrong with the drains again.* **3.** A tube for drawing off inflammatory matter from a wound, abscess &c. **4.** (fig.) A cause of exhaustion, constant exhausting demand, strain, on strength, time, resources &c.: *a great drain on my purse, health.* **5.** (colloq.) A small quantity of liquid, esp. a small drink, a mouthful.

drainage, n. [1. drānij; 2. dréinidž]. **drain (I.)** & **-age. 1.** The act of draining; process of being drained; specif. **a** system of draining, carrying off of water from land; **b** system of sewers and pipes which carry away liquid impurities from a house or city; **c** process or system of draining off matter from a wound &c. **2.** Water, sewage &c. carried off by draining.

drainage-basin, n. The area drained by one river or river-system.

drainage-tube, n. A small piece of tubing, rendered aseptic, inserted in a wound for draining off pus.

drainer, n. [1. drāner; 2. dréinə]. **drain (I.)** & **-er.** A device for draining away liquid, esp. in domestic economy.

drain-pipe, n. A large pipe, usually of earthenware, used for draining buildings.

drake (I.), n. [1. drāk; 2. dreik]. Not in O.E. in present sense. O.E. *draca*, 'dragon', is fr. Lat. (see **dragon**), & *drake* may be same word w. transferred meaning. M.E. *drāke* wd. be normal development of *draca*, but it may have a continental origin; cp. L.G. *draak* & O.H.G. *entrache*, prob. fr. *ant-, enti-*, 'duck'. The male of the duck. Phr. *ducks and drakes*, see **duck (I.)**.

drake (II.), n. O.E. *draca*, M.E. *drāke*, 'dragon', fr. Lat. *draco*. See **dragon. 1.** A kind of may-fly, used as bait in river-fishing. **2. a** An obsolete form of cannon of small size; **b** a Norseman's beaked war galley.

dram, n. [1. dram; 2. dræm]. See **drachm. 1.** A unit of weight; **a** (avoirdupois) $\frac{1}{16}$ of an ounce; **b** (apoth.) $\frac{1}{8}$ of an ounce. **2.** (of liquids) **a** $\frac{1}{8}$ of a fluid ounce; hence, **b** a small quantity of spirit. Phrs. *fond of a dram*, addicted to drink; *dram-drinker*, one who drinks spirits frequently.

drama, n. [1. dráhma; 2. drā́mə]. L. Lat., fr. Gk. *drâma*, 'a deed; action represented on the stage, drama', fr. *drā́ō*, 'do, perform an action', & *-m*. Cp. Gk. *(a)dranḗs*, 'not strong, feeble', *drāstḗrios*, 'active'; Lith. *daraũ*, 'to do', *darbas*, 'work'; Aryan base, **derā-*, **drā-*, **drə-*, 'to do, to work, be active'. See **drastic, dromedary. 1.** A composition for performance on the stage. **2.** The composition or performance of stage-plays considered as an art. **3.** A series of striking and interesting events marked by an interplay of human passion.

dramatic, adj. [1. dramátik; 2. drəmǽtik], fr. Gk. *dramatikós*, fr. *drâmat-(os)*, genit. of *drâma*. See prec. & **-ic. 1.** Pertaining to, connected with, the drama: *dramatic performance.* **2. a** (of events &c.) Resembling a drama in being characterized by interesting and arresting human action, and the interplay of passions and characters; **b** (of manner, mode of speech &c.) sudden and striking; exhibiting unexpectedly some play of human passion, revealing some interesting aspect of character, creating an interesting situation.

dramatically, adv. [1. dramátikali; 2. drəmǽtikəli]. See prec. & **-al** & **-ly. a** In a dramatic manner; **b** in a manner deliberately adopted and not natural to oneself.

dramatis personae, n. pl. [1. drámatis persṓnē; 2. drǽmətis pȧsóunī]. Lat. The characters in a given play; list of these.

dramatist, n. [1. drámatist; 2. drǽmətist], fr. Gk. *drâmat-(os)*, genit. of *drâma* (see **drama**), & **-ist.** A writer of plays.

dramatization, n. [1. dràmatīzā́shun; 2. dræmətaizéiʃən]. Next word & **-ation.** The art or act of dramatizing; that which is dramatized.

dramatize, vb. trans. [1. drámatīz; 2. drǽmətaiz]. See **dramatist** & **-ize.** To put (a story, series of events &c.) into the form of a play.

dramaturge, n. [1. drámatērj; 2. drǽmətȧdž], fr. Fr., fr. Gk. *drāmatourgós*, 'a maker of plays', fr. *drāmat-* (see **drama**) & *érg-(on)*, 'work'. See **ergon** & **work.** A dramatist.

dramaturgic, adj. [1. dràmatḗrjik; 2. dræmətȧ́džik]. Prec. & **-ic.** Relating to the writing of plays.

dramaturgist, n. [1. drámatērjist; 2. drǽmətȧdžist]. **dramaturge** & **-ist.** Dramaturge.

dramaturgy, n. [1. drámatērji; 2. drǽmətȧdži]. **dramaturge** & **-y.** The art of composing dramas, and of producing them on the stage.

drank, vb. [1. drangk; 2. dræŋk]. O.E., M.E. *dranc*. Pret. of **drink.**

drape, vb. trans. [1. drāp; 2. dreip], fr. O. Fr. *draper*, fr. *drap*, 'cloth'; Low Lat. *drappum*, the origin of wh. is unknown. **a** To hang (a fabric, cloak &c.) over something and arrange it so that it falls in loose folds: *to drape a mantle round the shoulders*; **b** to cover (something) with piece of fabric, loose garment &c., so that the latter hangs in folds: *to drape the figure, oneself, wall* &c.

draper, n. [1. drā́per; 2. dréipə]. M.E. *draper*, fr. O. Fr. *drapier*. See prec. & **-er.** The old form still survives in the family name *Drapier*. Formerly a maker of, now a dealer in, cloth and other woven materials, and in articles made from these; esp. a person who has a shop where these things are sold: *to go to a draper's*, to his shop.

drapery, n. [1. drā́peri; 2. dréipəri], fr. O. Fr. *draperie*. See **drape** & **-ery. 1. a** The series, collection, of folds into which a soft material falls when thrown over, or gathered round, something; **b** the fabric, garment &c. which drapes, and forms folds round, something. Both also in pl. *draperies.* **2. a** The representation of drapery in painting or sculpture; **b** the technique of the artistic treatment of drapery by the painter or sculptor. **3. a** The trade of a draper; **b a** draper's wares collectively; **c** place where draper carries on business, a draper's shop. Also *drapery establishment*; *drapery stores.*

drastic, adj. [1. drástik; 2. drǽstik], fr. Gk. *drastik-(ós)*, 'violent, active'; cp. *drāstḗrios*, 'active', *drēstḗr*, 'a labourer', *drastéos*, 'to be done', & see **drama. a** Having a powerful effect, acting with force; esp. *to apply drastic remedies* (lit. and fig.); **b** thoroughgoing: *to make drastic alterations.*

drastically, adv. [1. drástikali; 2. drǽstikəli]. See prec. & **-al** & **-ly.** In a drastic manner.

drat, interj. [1. drat; 2. dræt], fr. *'od rot*, the first, unstressed, vowel being dropped, & that of second syll. being unrounded, as in *plat* (of ground) for *plot*, *Gad* for *God* &c. Low, but mild, expletive about equivalent to *bother, confound, dash*: *drat it, drat you,* bother it, confound you.

draught (I.), n. [1. drahft; 2. drāft]. O.E. *draht*, M.E. *drauht, draȝt*; cp. M.H.G. *dracht*, O.N. *drattr.* Gmc. **đraχ-t-*, fr. **đraȝ-an*, 'to draw'. See **draft, drag, draw. 1. a** The act of drawing; Phr. *beast of draught*, horse, ox &c. for drawing cart &c.; **b** the drawing of liquid from one vessel into another. Phr. *on draught*, (of beer &c.) from a cask that has been opened. **2.** Something that is drawn; specif. **a** amount of liquid drunk at one time: *a draught of water* &c.; Phrs. *to drink at a, one, draught*, drink right off without stopping; (also fig.) *a draught of happiness*; **b** dose of medicine mixed and prepared ready for drinking: *black draught*, a strong purgative medicine, a mixture of senna and magnesia; **c** amount of water a ship draws, the depth of water required to float her; **d** current of air passing through a confined space, e.g. a room, chimney &c. **3.** Same as **draft** (I.). **4.** (pl. *draughts*, from pieces being 'drawn' or moved) Game played by two people on a chess-board, with 24 flat, wooden disks (draughtsmen), 12 black and 12 white a side; known as checkers in U.S.A.

draught (II.), vb. trans., fr. prec. To draft.

draughtboard, n. [1. dráhftbord; 2. drāftbɔ̄d]. Board marked in alternate black and white squares for game of draughts.

draught-horse, n. Powerful, heavy type of cart-horse, capable of pulling heavy weights.

draughtiness, n. [1. dráhftines; 2. drāftinis]. **draughty** & **-ness.** The state of being draughty.

draughts, n. See **draught, 4.**

draughtsman, n. [1. dráhftsman; 2. drāftsmən]. **1.** Draftsman, q.v. **2.** One of the pieces used in the game of draughts.

draughtsmanship, n. [1. dráhftsmanship; 2. drāftsmənʃip]. Prec. & **-ship.** Skill in the work of drawing, preparing plans &c.

draughty, adj. [1. dráhfti; 2. drāfti]. **draught** (I.) & **-y.** Exposed to, letting in, currents of air.

Dravidian, adj. & n. [1. dravídian; 2. drəvídjən], fr. Scrt. *Drāvida*, a district of southern India. **a** adj. Pertaining to the non-Aryan races of southern India; **b** n., the language of the Dravidian races.

draw (I.), vb. trans. & intrans. [1. draw; 2. drɔ̄]. O.E. *dragan*, 'to draw'; M.E. *drawen, draȝen, drahen*; cogn. w. O.N. *draga*, 'to draw'; O. Fris. *draga*, 'to carry'; O.H.G. *tragan*, Goth. *dragan*, 'to carry'; Gmc. **đraȝ-*. Cp. O.N. *drōg*, 'grazing, scraping; inroad, excursion'; O. Swed. *drøgh*, 'sledge'. There are no certain cognates outside Gmc. See **drawl, drag, draught, dredge. A.** trans. To cause an object to move from one position to another by the exertion of force, usually towards, in the direction of, the agent exerting force if stationary, or after and with it if in motion; opposed to *push.* Various specific meanings: **1.** To pull towards one by a movement of hand or arm: *to draw a book towards one*; *to draw rein*, pull up a horse, stop; **a** to extract by pulling (cork, tooth, sword from sheath &c.); Phrs. *to draw the sword*, engage in hostilities, declare war: *at daggers drawn*, openly hostile; *to draw the teeth of*, make harmless; *to draw a knife*, take out and threaten to attack with it; *to draw stumps*, (at cricket) pull them up, as sign of end of game; **b** to pull a bow-string in order to shoot off an arrow; Phrs. *to draw the long bow*, to exaggerate, romance; *to draw a bow at a venture*, make a chance allusion or remark which hits the mark; **c** to take out by means of a bucket: *to draw water from a well*; **d** (i.) to attract, cause to be directed towards one: *to draw the enemy's fire*; *to draw attention to*; (ii.) to allure, excite affection, admiration, in: *to draw an audience*; *to feel drawn to someone*; '*Beauty draws us with a single hair*' (Pope); **e** to remove entrails of (chicken &c.); *hanged, drawn, and quartered*, mediaeval punishment of traitors. **2.** To drag along; **a** to pull along after one: *to draw a cart, train* &c.; **b** to cause to move along with one's hand: *to draw a curtain* (*over a window*); Phr. *to draw a veil over*, refrain from revealing; **c** to lead, induce to accompany one: *to draw a person aside.* **3.** To take, breathe (air) in; Phrs. *to draw breath*, pause for rest; *to draw one's first breath*, be born; *draw one's last breath*, die. **4.** To obtain, cause to appear; specif. **a** to procure, receive, derive: *to draw salary, money from a bank* &c.; (mil.) *to draw rations*; **b** (of non-material things) *to draw inspiration, information, from*; **c** to deduce, arrive at by logical process: *to draw an inference, a conclusion.* **5. a** To cause to flow: *to draw blood*; *draw beer from a cask* &c.; Phrs. *draw it mild!*, don't exaggerate, don't overdo it! &c.; *draw first blood*, make the first attack; **b** to elicit, compel: *to draw tears, applause* &c.; **c** to obtain by lot or chance: *to draw a blank, a prize* (lit. and fig.); **d** to provoke, excite, irritate; cause to express opinion, wish &c.: *to draw a person on a subject*; *not to be drawn.* **6. a** To draft, write in formal order: *draw a deed, bill of exchange, cheque* &c.; **b** to formulate: *to draw a distinction.* **7.** (of muscular action) To distort, pull awry, strain: *a face drawn with pain*; *a drawn look.* **8.** To search, (covert &c.) for game, a fox. Phr. *to draw blank*, fail to find fox &c. in covert; also fig. **9.** (of a vessel) To sink in the water to a certain depth: *a ship drawing 20 feet.* **10.** To finish a contest, match, game &c. without either side having won: *the game was (left) drawn.* **11.** To extract strength by infusion: *to draw tea.* **12.** To delineate, sketch out a design, or picture, with a pen, pencil, or brush: *to draw a line, picture, portrait* &c. Phrs. *to draw the line*, set limits; *to draw the line at*, not to tolerate; *draw a parallel (between)*, point out resemblance; *to draw it fine*, leave a narrow margin. **13.** (of wire) To manufacture by drawing metal rods through series of holes of graduated size. **B.** intrans. **1.** (of tea &c.) To become stronger by infusion: *leave the tea to draw.* **2.** To permit the passage of a current of air: *the chimney draws well.* **3.** To be in the habit, be capable, of producing pictures &c. with pen, pencil, or brush: *to draw very badly.* **4.** To cast lots: *we'd better draw for partners.* **5.** To end a game without deciding winner: *play to win, not draw.* **6.** To unsheathe a sword: *draw, and defend yourself!* **7.** To approach, come towards: *to draw near, nigh*; *to draw to a conclusion*; *to draw level*, to come up to, attain equal position. **C.** Followed by various prepositions and adverbs. *Draw away*, to get in advance of. *Draw back*, **a** trans., to cause to move backwards; **b** intrans., to retreat, go backwards; to hesitate, back out. *Draw down*, trans., **a** to cause to descend, pull down: *draw down the blind*; *draw down the curtain* (to end play; also fig.); **b** to bring upon one: *to draw down anger* &c. *Draw in*, trans., **a** to pull in; Phr. *to draw in one's horns*, become more cautious; **b** curtail, reduce: *to draw in one's expenditure*; intrans., **a** to become shorter: *the days are drawing in*; **b** to make curtailment in expenditure: *time to draw in.* *Draw off*, **a** trans., to cause to flow out or away (surplus water &c.); **b** intrans., to move away. *Draw on*, **a** trans., to pull on or over: *to draw on a pair of boots*; **b** intrans., to make demands on: *to draw on one's imagination, capital* &c.; **c** to approach: *winter is drawing on.* *Draw out*, trans., **a** to pull, stretch out, lengthen; **b** to remove something from somewhere: *to draw out a sovereign from one's purse*; **c** to elicit confidences from, induce to talk: *a little flattery will draw him out*; **d** to map out, plan, set out in writing: *to draw out a scheme*: intrans., to extend, last a long time: *the speech drew out interminably.* *Draw round*, intrans., to come, move, gather, round: *to draw round the fire, the table* &c. *Draw up*, **a** trans., to set in regular order: *troops, a document*, &c.; **b** *to draw oneself up*, assume an erect attitude; **c** intrans., to stop: *the carriage drew up before the door.*

draw (II.), n., fr. prec. **1.** The act of drawing; specif. a drawing of lots, lottery; **b** end of game with winner undecided. **2.** Something that draws; specif. a something that attracts, allures: *the new play proved a great draw*; **b** a remark intended to provoke retort.

drawback, n. [1. dráwbak; 2. drɔ́bæk], fr. **draw** (I.) & **back** (IV.). **1.** Something that interferes with comfort or progress; a disadvantage: *to succeed in spite of drawbacks.* **2.** Amount of duty paid on imported goods, remitted on their exportation.

drawbridge, n. [1. dráwbrij; 2. drɔ́bridž]. A light bridge made to be raised or lowered at will by chains and pulleys: **a** one thrown across a moat, before gate of castle or fortified town; **b** one spanning a small river, canal &c., and raised to permit passage of vessels.

Drawcansir, n. [1. drawkánser; 2. drɔkǽnsə], fr. character in Duke of Buckingham's play 'The Rehearsal' (1672). Blustering bully; a person who is a curse to his own side as much as to the other.

drawee, n. [1. draw-é; 2. drɔí]. **draw** (I.) & **-ee.** The person on whom a bill of exchange &c. is drawn.

drawer, n. [1. dráw-er; 2. drɔ́(ə)]. **draw** (I.) & **-er. 1.** A lidless box with a handle at one side, made to slide in and out of framework in table, cupboard &c. *Chest of drawers*, article of furniture consisting of a flat-topped framework, enclosing a set of drawers one below the other. **2.** (pl.) A two-legged undergarment fastening round the waist.

drawing, n. [1. dráw-ing; 2. drɔ́iŋ]. **draw** (I.) & **-ing. 1.** The art or process of tracing lines and curves of various forms to make a design, or picture, by means of a pen, pencil, brush, on paper or other material. Phr. *out of drawing*, incorrectly drawn, with wrong perspective &c. **2.** A picture thus produced: *a drawing of a head, a tree* &c.

drawing-board, n. A flat piece of wood on which paper, canvas &c. is stretched for drawing or painting.

drawing-pin, n. A small tack with a large flat head for holding paper &c. in position on a drawing-board, notice-board &c.

drawing-room, n. Contracted fr. *withdrawing-room.* See **withdraw. 1.** A room in which guests are received and entertained; the room to which people withdraw after dinner. **2.** A formal reception at court, at which ladies are presented; a Court, which is now the term used; contrasted with *levee.*

drawl (I.), vb. intrans. & trans. [1. drawl; 2. drɔ̄l]. Scand., cp. O.N. *dralla*, 'to loiter', fr. **drag-la.* Same base as **drag** & **draw. 1.** intrans. To speak with exaggerated slowness, with the sounds unduly prolonged. **2.** trans. To utter in this way: *to drawl a prayer.* Also *drawl out.*

drawl (II.), n., fr. prec. A manner of speech, characterized by an exaggerated slowness of utterance.

drawling, adj. [1. dráwling; 2. drɔ́liŋ], fr. Pres. Part. of **drawl** (I.). Dragging, slow: *a drawling way of speaking.*

drawlingly, adv. Prec. & **-ly**. In a drawling manner.

drawn, vb. [1. drawn; 2. drɔn]. O.E. *dragen*, M.E. *drāwen*. P.P. of **draw** (I.)

drawplate, n. [1. dráwplāt; 2. drɔ́pleit]. Plate with holes or dies, through which wire is drawn in course of manufacture.

draw-well, n. A well from which water is drawn with a bucket.

dray, n. [1. drā; 2. drei]. M.E. *dreye*, cp. O.E. *dræġ(e)*, 'drag-net', fr. **dragi-*, cp. *dragan*. See **drail** & **draw** (I.). A low, flat, heavy cart, usually with four wheels, used for the conveyance of heavy goods.

dray-horse, n. Strong horse for pulling a dray.

drayman, n. [1. dráman; 2. dréimən]. The driver of a dray.

dread (I.), vb. trans. & intrans. [1. dred; 2. dred]. M.E. *drēden*. The O.E. vb. *-drǣdan* only occurs in compounds, *on-drǣdan*, 'to dread', *of-drǣdd*, 'afraid'; no other Gmc. language has such a form as *drǣd-* &c. uncompounded. The most probable explanation is that the word is a very old W. Gmc. compound of *ond-*, *and-* (see **and**), & Gmc. *rǣd*, 'counsel, advice' &c. O.E. *on-drǣdan*, then, would be for *ond-rǣdan*; cp. O.S. *an-* & *and-drādan*, & O.H.G. *int-rāten*, 'to fear', orig. 'to set the mind against'; cp. Mod. Germ. *entraten*, 'to do without'. The final *-d* of the pref. was, as it were, detached, & prefixed to *-rǣd*, whence the later formation of *-drǣdan* & M.E. *drēden*. The uncompounded *drǣdan* occurs in the 11th cent. See **read** (I.). **a** trans. To fear, feel terror at, be afraid of; esp. to look forward to with misgiving; be apprehensive of: *to dread the coming of winter*; *to dread the damp for one's rheumatism*; '*Teach me to die, that I may dread The grave as little as my bed*' (Bishop Ken's Evening Hymn); **b** intrans., to feel fear and misgiving; to have fear and anxiety for the future: *be stout of heart and do not dread.*

dread (II.), n. M.E. *drēd(e)*, 'fear, doubt', fr. prec. Anxious terror, awe; timid, shrinking fear; anticipation of evil, apprehensiveness of something which may happen: *to have a dread of being asked to speak in public.* Phr. *to be, live, in dread of*, be constantly apprehensive of something which will or may come.

dread (III.), adj., fr. old P.P. of **dread** (I.). (archaic and poet.) Inspiring solemn terror; awesome: *the last dread moment*; *dread summons* (e.g. to execution).

dreaded, adj. [1. dréded; 2. drédid], fr. P.P. of **dread** (I.). Looked forward to, anticipated with terror: *the dreaded moment had at last arrived.*

dreadful, adj. [1. drédfool; 2. drédfəl], fr. **dread** (II.) & **-ful**. **1.** Inspiring fear, terror, horror; terrible: *a dreadful monster, dreadful pain, a dreadful face, story, voice* &c. **2.** (colloq., in much weakened sense) Unpleasant, tiresome: *a dreadful bore*; *penny dreadful*, cheap, sensational story of crime and bloodshed.

dreadfully, adv. Prec. & **-ly**. **a** In a manner exciting terror; **b** (colloq., in weakened sense, as mere intens.) *a dreadfully long lecture, bad pudding*, very, too, long; very bad.

dreadnought, n. [1. drédnawt; 2. drédnɔt]. **dread** (I.) & **nought**. **1.** A very thick cloth used for heavy coats. **2. a** (cap.) Name of the first of a type of 20th-cent. battleship, with high speed and main armament of heavy guns all of the same calibre; **b** any battleship of this type; *super-Dreadnought*, battleship larger and more heavily armed than the original 'Dreadnought' class.

dream (I.), n. [1. drēm; 2. drim]. O.E. *drēam*, 'joy, bliss, mirth, revelry: melody', never 'dream'; M.E. *drēm(e)*, 'joy, minstrelsy, sound; dream, vision'; O.H.G. *troum*, 'dream'; O.L.G. *drōm*, 'song, mirth'; O.N. *draumr*, 'dream'. Although in form the present-day word is normally descended fr. the O.E., the Later M.E. & present-day sense is derived fr. the O.N. The connexion of the two meanings is at first not clear, but, unless we dispute the orig. identity of the O.E. & O.L.G. on the one hand w. the O.N. & O.H.G. words on the other, both meanings are established in the old W. Gmc. languages, & since one is found in O.N. also, it is probable that both senses existed in Prim. Gmc. It is further probable that we may connect these words w. O.S. *bi-driogan*, 'to deceive', O.H.G. *triogan*, 'to lie', & w. the close cognates of these, O.N. *draugr*, O.S. *gi-drōg*, 'phantom'; see also **fraud**. In this case we have to assume an Aryan **dhrow-* &c. w. a formative element *-m* in one case (*drēam* &c.) & *-gh* in the other (*draugr* &c.). It is unnecessary to assume w. Kluge that Gmc. **draum-* (whence *drēam, trōm, traum* & *draumr* mentioned above) stands for **drauȝma-*. The ideas of 'deception, lying vision, phantom, dream', are closely connected, & this development of meaning presents no difficulty. Cp. further Scrt. *dhrútiš*, 'deception', & other Scrt. words therewith associated. From the base **dhrew-* &c. etymologists derive also Gk. *thréomai* (for **drewo*), 'to shout', & *thróos* (for **drowo-*), 'sound of voices, murmur', & *thrûlos*, 'murmur, sound, rumour'. (With this sense of the base we connect **dor** & **drone**.) If this be sound, we have an orig. base wh. has been specialized in two different ways, both developments of meaning being preserved in Gmc. The chain must have been something like this: (i.) Sound, shout, rumour, lying rumour, lie, deception, deception of the sight, a phantom, deceptive vision, a dream. (ii.) Sound, shout, shout of revelry, melody &c.; joy, mirth, bliss. Thus the double development of meaning appears to be harmonized. **1. a** Illusion of the senses, especially of the sight, and, less often, of the hearing, occurring in sleep, in which the mind imagines the sights and sounds are clearly perceptible by the senses; a vision of the night; **b** (poet., by extension) sleep in general: *to go to one's dreams*, go to bed, to sleep; Phr. *the land of dreams*, sleep; **c** an abstracted preoccupied state of mind, in which one is immersed in one's own thoughts, and scarcely alive to outward realities: *to be, to live, go about, in a dream.* **2. a** An unreal, imaginary, baseless impression, something that has never happened or existed, which one believes to be real; **b** a visionary hope or aspiration, upon which one has dwelt with longing for its fulfilment: *it has long been a dream of mine to retire and live by the sea*; *to realize all one's dreams, one's fondest dreams.* **3.** Some thing, or person, set of circumstances, so beautiful and enchanting as to seem only possible in the unreal world of dreams: *my life at sea was simply a dream of delight*; *she looked a perfect dream*; *one long dream of happiness.*

dream (II.), vb. intrans. & trans., fr. prec. **A.** intrans. **1.** To have dreams during sleep: *to dream that one was in France*; *to dream of home.* Phr. *I shouldn't dream of (doing) such a thing* &c., under no circumstances would I do, allow &c., such a thing. **2. a** To have aspirations, hopes, ideals, longings, for the future: *to dream that one will be happy and rich some day*; **b** to have an unfounded, baseless, impression, conviction of the existence, or occurrence of something: *I never said anything of the sort, you must be dreaming.* **B.** trans. **1.** (in very few constructions) To have the experience of dreaming: *to dream a dream, dreams*; *you must have dreamt it*; the usual construction is intrans.: *to dream of, about, something.* **2.** *Dream away one's time, life, the hours*, to spend in dreams.

dreamer, n. [1. drémer; 2. drímə]. Prec. & **-er**. **1.** One who dreams. **2.** One who forms visionary schemes; an unpractical person.

dream-hole, n. Perh. in old sense of 'mirth, revelry'. See **dream** (I.). A hole left in the fabric of a tower, or steeple, to admit light, and let sound, as of bells, issue.

dreamily, adv. [1. drémili; 2. drímili]. **dreamy** & **-ly**. Like one in a dream.

dreaminess, n. [1. drémines; 2. dríminis]. **dreamy** & **-ness**. The state of being dreamy.

dreamland, n. [1. drémland; 2. drímlænd]. **a** An imaginary country seen in dreams, flights of fancy or imagination; **b** sleep.

dreamless, adj. [1. drémles; 2. drímlis], fr. **dream** (I.) & **-less**. Without, unbroken by, dreams: *dreamless sleep, night*, &c.

dreamlessly, adv. Prec. & **-ly**. Without dreaming.

dreamlike, adj. [1. drémlīk; 2. drímlaik]. **dream** (I.) & **like** (I.). **a** Like a dream; **b** unreal, shadowy.

dream-world, n. A beautiful, unreal world of the imagination, or one seen in dreams.

dreamy, adj. [1. drémi; 2. drími]. **dream** (I.) & **-y**. **1.** (of persons) Given to, preoccupied with, immersed in, waking dreams, in fanciful visions; inattentive to ordinary external affairs. **2.** (of things) Resembling things seen or heard in dreams, vague, shadowy, elusive: *dreamy music, eyes* &c.

drear, adj. [1. drēr; 2. driə]. Shortened fr. **dreary**. (poet.) Inspiring gloom, melancholy, dismal thoughts, in the mind: *the landscape drear.*

drearily, adv. [1. drérili; 2. dríərili], fr. **dreary** & **-ly**. Sadly, dismally.

dreariness, n. [1. drérines; 2. dríərinis], fr. **dreary** & **-ness**. The state of being dreary; **a** (of persons and character) lack of spirits and animation; dullness; **b** (of things and circumstances) quality of causing dismalness of mind; inspiring melancholy.

dreary, adj. [1. dréri; 2. dríəri]. O.E. *drēoriġ*, 'blood-stained; weeping, sad', fr. *drēor*, 'blood'; M.E. *drēri*, 'sad'; O.H.G. *trūric*, 'sad'; orig. 'that which falls, drips'; cogn. w. O.E. *drēosan*, 'to fall', *dryre*, 'fall, ruin', Goth. *driusan*, O.L.G. *driosan*, 'to fall, drip'. This appears to be the orig. sense of the base; whence the meaning 'that which falls', whence 'dripping blood', 'falling dew, rain, tears'; hence 'sadness'; cp. also Goth. *drau(h)sna*, 'piece, mouthful'; M.H.G. *trōr*, 'dew, rain'; Lith. *druskà*, 'salt'; Lett. *druska*, 'piece, crumb'. Further cognates uncertain; cp. **dross, drowse, & drop**. **a** (of things) Inspiring melancholy, causing depression of spirits; gloomy; tedious; **b** (of persons) inspired by these feelings, dismal, lugubrious.

dredge (I.), n. [1. drej; 2. dredž]. Prob. connected w. **draw**; the O.E. form wd. be **drečġ*, fr. **draȝja-*. A device for scraping up material from bottom of river or sea, in order to clear a channel, or to collect oysters and other organisms.

dredge (II.), vb. trans. & intrans. **1.** trans. **a** (usually with *up*) To bring to the surface from under water by means of a dredge: *to dredge (up) mud, oysters* &c.; **b** to clear out, deepen (a channel &c.) by means of a dredge. **2.** intrans. To use a dredge: *to dredge for oysters.*

dredge (III.), vb. trans., fr. M.E. *draggē*, 'sweetmeat', fr. O. Fr. *dragee*, fr. Lat. *tragēmata*, 'dessert, confectionery', fr. Gk. *trágēma*, 'preserved fruits, sweetmeats', cogn. w. Gk. *trṓgein*, 'chew, gnaw, nibble'; *trōgália*, 'dessert'; *trṓglē*, 'a hole made by gnawing, a mouse hole; a hole'. Perh. allied to O.E. *þurh*, 'through', Goth. *þairh* &c. See **through**. Aryan base **trōg-*, **trəg-*, 'to gnaw, nibble, make a hole in'. To sprinkle: *to dredge flour over meat, sugar over cake* &c.; *meat with flour* &c.

dredger (I.), n. [1. dréjer; 2. drédžə]. **dredge** (I.) & **-er**. A boat carrying a dredge.

dredger (II.), n. **dredge** (III.) & **-er**. A sprinkler, metal box, case with perforated lid: *flour-dredger* &c.

dree, vb. trans. [1. drē; 2. drī]. O.E. *drēogan*, 'to endure, suffer; accomplish', M.E. *drēzen*, Goth. *driugan*, 'to endure military service'. See **drudge**. (archaic) To suffer, endure. Now only in Phr. *to dree one's weird*, suffer, work out one's fate.

dreg, n. [1. dreg; 2. dreg]. Scand.; M.E. *dreg*, fr. O.N. *dreggjar*, 'dregs'; cp. Swed. *drägg*, 'dregs'. Connected w. **trachea**. (usually in pl. *dregs*) Sediment left after liquid is poured off; worthless refuse: *to drink to the dregs*; (also fig.) *dregs of society*, lowest, most worthless class.

dreggy, adj. [1. drégi; 2. drégi]. Prec. & **-y**. Containing dregs or sediment.

drench (I.), n. [1. drench; 2. drentʃ]. O.E. *drenč*, 'drink, potion'; M.E. *drench*. See next word. A medicinal draught; now esp. one administered to a horse or cow.

drench (II.), vb. trans. O.E. *drenčan*, 'to give to drink; to drown', M.E. *drinchen*, 'to drown, plunge in water', fr. **drank-jan*, fr. the Pret. type of *drincan*, 'to drink'. See **drink** (I.). **1**. To administer a medicinal draught to, esp. to a horse or cow. **2**. To make thoroughly wet, to soak thoroughly, in water or other liquid: *drenched with rain* &c.

drencher, n. [1. dréncher; 2. dréntʃə]. Prec. & **-er**. That which drenches: **a** device for administering a drench to horse or cow: **b** (colloq.) a soaking shower of rain &c.

dress (I.), vb. trans. & intrans. [1. dres; 2. dres]. M.E. *dressen*, 'to direct, set in order; prepare, equip, dress', fr. O. Fr. *dresser*, fr. Med. Lat. **dīrectiāre*, fr. Lat. *dīrectus*, 'straight'. See **direct** (I.). **A**. trans. To put into order, arrange, dispose suitably, prepare. Various specific meanings: **1**. (mil.) To put into a straight line (troops &c.). **2**. To set in order, arrange, smooth, brush &c.: *to dress one's hair*. **3**. To give particular treatment to: **a** to wash, bandage &c., apply remedies to: *to dress a wound* &c.; **b** to prepare, make suitable for some special purpose: *to dress leather, stone, ground, food* &c. **4**. **a** To cover with, put, clothes upon: *to dress oneself, a child* &c.; **b** to provide with clothes: *to dress one's daughter on £100 a year*; **c** to adorn, decorate, make attractive: *to dress a shop-window* &c.; (also poet.) '*and all her silken flanks with garlands dressed*' (Keats). **B**. intrans. **1**. (mil.) To get into line, form a straight line with others: *to dress by the right*. **2**. **a** To put on clothes, array oneself: *get up and dress quickly*; specif., to put on evening dress; Phrs. *to dress for dinner*; *we don't dress (for dinner)*; **b** to choose, provide oneself with, clothes; to put on one's clothes, dress oneself in a particular way: *to dress well, badly* &c. **C**. Followed by preposition or adverb. *Dress down*, trans., **a** to rub (a horse) down; **b** (fig.) to administer a scolding, or a thrashing to. *Dress out*, to adorn, deck. *Dress up*, **a** trans., to adorn, clothe elaborately; **b** intrans., to put on a costume as a disguise, to appear in masquerade.

dress (II.), n., fr. prec. **1**. That which is worn as a covering for the body; attire, clothing, garments; esp. outer garments; *full dress*, most elaborate (uniform &c.) worn on special occasions; *evening dress*, that worn for dinner &c.; *morning dress*, ordinary clothes, as distinct from those worn in the evening. **2**. (preceded by article) Outer garment worn by woman, girl, or infant; a frock: *a nice dress*; *a new dress*. **3**. In extended sense: covering, outward adornment: *trees put on their spring dress*.

dress-circle, n. The lowest gallery in a theatre, in which it is customary to wear evening-dress.

dress-coat, n. Black swallow-tailed coat, worn by men in evening-dress.

dresser (I.), n. [1. dréser; 2. drésə]. **dress** (I.) & **-er**. One who dresses; specif. **a** one who dresses shop-windows; **b** one who dresses wounds in hospital; assistant to a surgeon at an operation; **c** one who dresses leather; **d** attendant in a theatre who assists in the dressing of actors and actresses, and looks after costumes &c.

dresser (II.), n. M.E. *dressour, dressure*, fr. O. Fr. *dresseur*, fr. *dresser*, 'to direct, dress'. See **dress** (I.). A kind of kitchen table or sideboard, fitted with a broad flat shelf, with drawers, cupboards, or other receptacles below, and narrower shelves above, for china &c.

dressiness, n. [1. drésines; 2. drésinis]. **dressy** & **-ness**. Condition, quality, of being dressy, smartness of clothes and appearance.

dressing, n. [1. drésing; 2. drésiŋ]. **dress** (I.) & **-ing**. **1**. Arrangement, preparation, adjusting, making fit or suitable for some special purpose; esp. in compounds: *hair-dressing, window-dressing* &c. **2**. Something used in dressing. Various specific meanings: **a** A sauce used as an additional relish for food, esp. for fish and salad; **b** remedies, bandages &c., applied to a wound; **c** manure, fertilizing agency, applied to ground: *a dressing of lime*; **d** substance used to stiffen silk, cotton &c., during process of manufacture. **3**. (colloq.) Usually *dressing down*, a thrashing, rating, scolding: *to give a person a good dressing down*.

dressing-bag, -case, n. A light, portable case or bag of leather &c., fitted with pockets, straps &c., for holding brushes, bottles &c.

dressing-bell, n. Bell rung to indicate the hour for dressing; esp. for putting on evening-dress, changing for dinner &c.

dressing-gown, n. A loose gown, long coat-like wrap, worn while one dresses, or in undress.

dressing-jacket, n. Loose, short, sleeved coat worn by women while dressing.

dressing-room, n. Room for dressing in; distinct from, and often opening out of, bedroom.

dressing-table, n. Table fitted with looking-glass, for use while dressing.

dressmaker, n. [1. drésmàker; 2. drésmèikə]. One who makes clothes for women and children.

dressmaking, n. [1. drésmàking; 2. drésmèikiŋ]. **a** The art or process of making clothes; **b** the business of a dressmaker.

dressy, adj. [1. drési; 2. drési]. **dress** (II.) & **-y**. (vulg.) **a** (of persons) Fond of, in the habit of wearing, actually wearing smart, fashionable, and showy clothes; **b** (of clothes) smart, elaborate, fashionable; suitable for smart or ceremonial occasions.

drew, vb. [1. droo; 2. drū]. O.E. *drēow*, M.E. *drēw*. Pret. of **draw**.

drey, n. [1. drā; 2. drei]. Origin doubtful. A squirrel's nest.

dribble, vb. intrans. & trans. [1. dríbl; 2. dríbl]. Freq. of obs. *drib*, a variant of **drip**. **1**. intrans. **a** To flow out, flow, drop by drop, trickle; specif. **b** to allow saliva to flow from the mouth (said of babies). **2**. trans. **a** To cause or allow to flow in drops; **b** (football) to take (ball) up the field by means of repeated short kicks, keeping the ball close to one and under control.

dribbler, n. [1. dríbler; 2. dríblə]. Prec. & **-er**. One who dribbles, esp. at football: *a neat dribbler*.

driblet, n. [1. dríblet; 2. dríblit]. See prec. & **-let**. A small portion, amount; esp. in Phr. *by driblets*, little by little, a small quantity at a time.

dried, vb. [1. drīd; 2. draid]. Pret. & P.P. of **dry** (II.).

drift (I.), n. [1. drift; 2. drift]. M.E. *drifte*, 'the act of driving; something that is driven, a herd'; cogn. w. M. Du. *drift*, O.H.G. *trift*, O.N. *tript*. See **drive** (I.). **1**. Act of driving, state or process of being driven; esp. **a** slow current in the sea, caused by the wind; **b** amount of deviation in a ship's course, caused by currents; **c** (of currents) rate of movement. **2**. (of mental process) Tendency or trend in a mode of thought, reasoning &c.; meaning, upshot of what is said &c.: *the drift of an argument, speech*; *I don't understand your drift*. **3**. Something that is driven; **a** a heap (of snow, leaves &c.) piled up by wind, sea &c.; **b** (geol.) deposit (of sand, gravel, shells &c.) transported by moving water, ice &c.; **c** (min.) horizontal boring; **d** ford in S. African river. **4**. (in non-material things and affairs) State of being driven, impelled, directed, determined, by circumstances, fate, chance, rather than by deliberate and volitional action: *my mind is in a state of drift*; *a policy of drift*.

drift (II.), vb. intrans. & trans., fr. prec. **A**. intrans. **1**. **a** To float along (upon water) with the tide, current, wind &c.: *to drift out to sea*; *to drift down the river*; Phr. *to drift apart*, (fig.) to become estranged; **b** to be driven, piled up by wind, to form a drift: *the snow, fallen leaves, have drifted*. **2**. (fig.) To be carried, to move, along gradually and unconsciously by force of circumstances, tendencies &c.: *to drift into war*; *the country is drifting towards bankruptcy*; *to be merely drifting*, not directing one's affairs by exertion of will. **B**. trans. **a** (of action of water currents) To cause to float, drive, in particular direction: *the tide has drifted the boat out to sea*; **b** (of action of wind or water) to cause to become heaped up: *the wind has drifted a mass of snow in front of the door*.

driftage, n. [1. dríftij; 2. dríftidž]. **drift** (II.) & **-age**. **a** Amount of drifting, esp. of a ship; **b** something that has drifted, esp. wreck, seaweed &c. thrown ashore by the tide.

drift-anchor, n. A wooden structure, resembling a raft, thrown out from a ship to keep her head to the wind during a storm.

drifter, n. [1. drífter; 2. dríftə]. **drift** (II.) & **-er**. **1**. One who, that which, drifts. **2**. Boat carrying drift-nets.

drift-ice, n. Broken ice carried along in masses by currents of wind and water.

drift-net, n. Large fishing-net suspended between two boats, or supported by corks or buoys, allowed to drift with the tide.

drift-wood, n. Wood cast ashore by the tide.

drill (I.), n. [1. dril; 2. dril]. Perh. fr. Du. *dril*, 'boring-tool', fr. *drillen*, 'to bore'; prob. cogn. w. O.E. *þȳrel*, 'hole'. See **thrill** & **nostril**. Instrument for boring through hard substances, wood, stone, metal &c., by means of a revolving point and cutting edge; worked by hand or mechanically.

drill (II.), vb. trans., fr. prec. To pierce, bore hole in; to bore (a hole) with a drill.

drill (III.), vb. trans. & intrans., fr. Du. *drillen*; prob. fr. prec., fr. the primitive idea of shaking, brandishing, a boring-tool, thence of flourishing a weapon. **1**. trans. **a** To train (persons) by causing them to carry out at repeated intervals a systematic series of bodily movements and to maintain certain bodily postures: *to drill troops* &c.; **b** to subject to a rigorous mental discipline: *to drill schoolboys in Latin grammar*. **2**. intrans. (esp. mil.) To undergo a training in, and carry out a systematic series of, physical exercises: *Gentlemen Cadets at Sandhurst drill for hours every day*.

drill (IV.), n., fr. prec. System of physical discipline consisting of certain bodily movements, postures &c.; esp. that used in the army in training bodies of troops to stand and march in line, to wheel in regular formation &c.

drill (V.), n. Perh. same as **drill** (I.), but origin obscure. **1**. Narrow furrow made in the ground to receive seeds. **2**. A machine for making furrows and sowing seed in them.

drill (VI.), vb. trans., fr. prec. **a** To sow (seed) in narrow trenches, or on ridges; **b** to sow seeds in rows, in trenches &c., on (land).

drill (VII.), n., fr. Germ. *drillich*, 'ticking', fr. Lat. *trilīc-(em)*, 'triply twilled', fr. **tri-** & *līcium*, 'a thread of the web'. See **oblique**. Coarsely woven, twilled material of linen or cotton.

drill (VIII.) or **dril**, n. Native name. A kind of baboon, found in Guinea, smaller than the mandrill, and without the coloured patches characteristic of that animal.

drill-sergeant, n. A sergeant in the army whose duty it is to drill and train soldiers.

drily, adv. See **dryly**.

drink (I.), vb. trans. & intrans. [1. dringk; 2. driŋk]. O.E. *drincan*, M.E. *drinken*; cogn. w. O.H.G. *trinkan*, O. Fris. *drinka*, O.L.G. *drincan*, O.N. *drekka*, Goth. *drigkan*. **A.** trans. **1.** (of a man or animal) **a** To take into the mouth and swallow liquid: *to drink nothing but water*; *will you drink claret or burgundy?*; Phrs. *to drink the health of, success to, drink the toast of*, to express wish for health &c. while drinking; *to drink oneself to death*, die from effects of strong drink; **b** to empty (a vessel) by swallowing its contents: *to drink a glass of milk* &c.; (also fig.) *to drink the cup of agony, joy* &c.; Phr. *I could drink the sea dry*, am very thirsty. **2.** **a** (of plants and porous substances) To absorb moisture; **b** (of persons, animals) to breathe in deeply: *to drink the air*. **3.** (fig.) *Drink in*, to absorb with eagerness, take in (through the senses), receive into one's mind: *to drink in impressions, sounds, wisdom*. **B.** intrans. **a** To perform the act of drinking: *to eat and drink*; specif. **b** to consume intoxicating liquor; **c** to consume habitually too much intoxicating liquor; Phrs. *to drink hard, drink like a fish*; *to drink to*, to drink while expressing good wishes to; *to drink deep (of)*, drink a large quantity (of); *to drink out of*, drink contents of.

drink (II.), n., fr. prec. **a** Liquid intended, provided, for drinking: *to keep food and drink in the house*; **b** portion of liquid consumed: *to take, have, a drink*; *a drink of water*; **c** specif., strong, intoxicating liquor: *to be too fond of drink*. Phr. *in drink*, intoxicated.

drinkable, adj. [1. dríngkabl; 2. dríŋkəbl]. **drink** (I.) & **-able**. Fit or suitable for drinking.

drinking, n. [1. dríngking; 2. dríŋkiŋ]. **drink** (I.) & **-ing**. **a** Act or process of consuming, absorbing, liquid; **b** habitual act of consuming strong drink in excess: *given to, too fond of, drinking*.

drinking-bout, n. Prolonged spell of drinking.

drinking-fountain, n. A device for providing a supply of drinking-water in public places.

drinking-horn, n. Cup or goblet made of, or resembling, an animal's horn.

drinking-song, n. One in celebration of delights of drinking, or to be sung at a convivial meeting.

drinking-water, n. Water intended for drinking.

drink-offering, n. A sacrifice of wine, oil &c., a libation.

drip (I.), vb. intrans. & trans. [1. drip; 2. drip]. M.E. *drippen*, O.E. *dryppan*; cp. M.H.G. *trupfen*, M.L.G. *druppen*, Dan. *dryppe*, Gmc. **drup-jan*, 'to fall in drops'. See **drop** (I.). **1.** intrans. **a** To trickle, ooze, fall, drop by drop: *rain dripping from the trees*; **b** to allow liquid to fall drop by drop: *the tap is dripping*; *to drip with wet*. **2.** trans. To cause to flow, let fall, drop by drop: *the comb drips honey*.

drip (II.), n., fr. prec. **1.** **a** The slow falling of liquid drop by drop; **b** liquid thus falling. **2.** The sound made by liquid falling in drops. **3.** (archit.) Drip-stone.

dripping (I.), adj. [1. dríping; 2. dripiŋ], fr. Pres. Part. of **drip** (I.). Thoroughly wet, so that liquid runs from it: *a dripping mackintosh*. Phr. *dripping wet*, very wet.

dripping (II.), n. **drip** (I.) & **-ing**. **1.** The falling of liquid in drops. **2.** Liquid which has dripped; specif., fat melted and drained from meat while roasting.

dripping-pan, n. Shallow pan in which meat is roasted; one into which the fat drips from roasting meat.

drip-stone, n. Projecting moulding placed along upper part of building, and over doors, windows &c., to prevent rain running down and injuring walls, mullions &c.; often highly ornamented and forming important architectural feature.

drive (I.), vb. trans. & intrans. [1. drīv; 2. draiv]. M.E. *drīven*, O.E. *drīfan*; cp. O.H.G. *trīban*, O. Fris. *drīva*, O.N. *drīfa*, Goth. *dreiban*. Gmc. **drīb-*, possibly fr. base **dher-ei-bh-*, **dhr-ei-bh-*, **dhroibh-* &c., 'to utter cries', hence 'to urge on with cries'. See **dream, dor, drone**. **A.** trans. **1.** To communicate motion to; **a** to urge on by blows, cries, gestures &c.: *to drive cattle, grouse, game* &c.; Phr. *to drive into a corner*, put into difficulties; **b** to cause to penetrate by repeated blows with a hammer: *to drive a nail*; **c** to hit a ball hard or far by a single blow with a bat, racket, club, at cricket, tennis, golf. **2.** To direct course, control speed &c. of horse or other animal attached to a vehicle: *to drive a pair, a donkey*; hence, **a** to direct course of (vehicle or agricultural implement attached to horse &c.): *to drive a carriage, a plough* &c.; Phr. *to drive one's own carriage*, keep a carriage for one's own use; **b** to convey in a vehicle: *to drive a person home, to the station* &c.; **c** to control, cause to work (engine, machine, whether stationary or moving from place to place): *to drive a motor-car, locomotive, crane* &c.; **d** (chiefly in P.P.) to cause to move or work by imparting stored energy: *engine driven by steam, oil, electricity* &c. **3.** To carry on, perform, effect: *to drive a trade, a bargain*. **4.** (fig.) To compel, exert strong pressure on: *driven to steal by hunger*; *drive to drink, to despair*; *drive mad*. **5.** To construct by engineering operations, usually on a large scale, involving cutting and levelling: *to drive a tunnel through a hill, a railroad through the desert*. **B.** intrans. **a** To rush, to press forward rapidly, be carried violently along: *the ship drove swiftly across the waves*; *driving rain*; Phr. *to let drive (at)*, to aim a blow, a missile, at; **b** to perform action of driving a horse, motor-car &c.: *can you drive?*; *to learn how to drive*; **c** to travel, go out in a vehicle which is driven: *will you walk or drive?*; *to drive through London*; **d** to perform action of driving a ball at cricket, golf &c.: *to drive to the boundary*; *knows how to drive but can't putt*. **C.** Followed by various prepositions and adverbs. *Drive at* (colloq., chiefly fig.), intrans., intend, aim at, mean: *I can't make out what he is driving at*. *Drive away*, trans., **a** to compel to depart, send off; **b** (fig.) to banish, dispel: *to drive away care, ill-temper* &c.; **c** intrans., to depart in a driven vehicle. *Drive home*, **a** *drive a nail home*, force in (wood &c.) up to the head; **b** *to drive an argument, a fact, home*, force into mind of hearer or reader by emphasis, repetition, convincing proof. *Drive in*, **a** intrans., to enter in a vehicle; **b** trans., to compel to enter: *to drive the cows in*; (also fig.) *to drive a lesson into a stupid boy's head*. *Drive up*, **a** intrans. to come up to, reach, by travelling in a driven vehicle: *to drive up the avenue, up to the door*; **b** trans. to cause horse &c. drawing a vehicle to come or go up: *to drive a carriage, a horse, up the lane*.

drive (II.), n., fr. prec. **1.** Act of driving in a vehicle; process of being driven in a vehicle, whether drawn by a horse or otherwise propelled: *to go for a drive in a dog-cart, in a motor-car*. **2.** Path or road along which one drives; specif. **a** an approach to a house through a park or garden; **b** a broad path cut through a wood. **3.** Act of driving game toward the guns. **4.** **a** Force, movement, imparted to an object by striking it, e.g. to a ball struck by a bat or golf club; **b** moral force, energy of character; capacity for doing and getting things done, and for stimulating activity in others.

drivel (I.), vb. intrans. [1. drívl; 2. drívl]. M.E. *drivelen, drevelen, dravelen*, O.E. *dreflian*, 'to snivel'. **a** (rare) To allow saliva to run from the mouth, as a child or idiot; **b** to talk in a foolish, irrational manner; to talk nonsense: *a drivelling idiot*, a perfect fool.

drivel (II.), n., fr. prec. Stupid, nonsensical talk; statements, expressions, devoid of sense.

driveller, n. [1. dríveler; 2. drívələ]. **drivel** (I.) & **-er**. One who talks nonsense.

driven, adj. [1. dríven; 2. drivən]. P.P. of **drive** (I.). O.E. *drifen*, M.E. *driven*. **1.** Usually qualified: *a hard-driven horse*; *a recklessly driven car*. **2.** Brought to a certain state by driving: *driven mad by worry, drink*. **3.** Drifted by wind: *as white as driven snow*, pure white.

driver, n. [1. dríver; 2. dráivə]. **drive** (I.) & **-er**. One who, that which, drives. Various specific meanings: **a** A person who drives a horse in a carriage; a coachman; **b** one who controls a mechanically driven vehicle, motor-car, steam locomotive &c. and causes it to move along; **c** one who controls a stationary engine; **d** one who drives cattle, a drover; **e** (golf) a wooden-headed club for long-distance driving from the tee.

driver-ant, n. A stinging African ant.

driving, vbl. n. [1. dríving; 2. dráiviŋ]. **drive** (I.) & **-ing**. Act performed by one who, or thing which, drives (in any sense); **a** *to be fond of driving*; *to admire a person's driving*; **b** (golf) power of making a ball travel a long distance in a particular direction: *his driving was very poor*; **c** *the driving of a wheel*.

driving-belt, n. Belt by which motion is communicated from an engine to machinery.

driving-iron, n. (golf) A heavy, iron-headed club.

driving-wheel, n. Wheel by means of which motion is communicated from one part of engine or machinery to another.

drizzle (I.), impers. vb. [1. drízl; 2. drízl]. cogn. w. O.E. *drēosan*, 'to fall' (see **dreary**), w. freq. suff. **-le**. To rain fine and thick.

drizzle (II.), n., fr. prec. Fine, thick rain.

drizzly, adj. [1. drízli; 2. drízli]. Prec. & **-y**. (of weather) Inclined to drizzle.

drogher, n. [1. dróger; 2. dróugə]. Du., lit. 'a drier', fr. *droogen*, orig. 'a small vessel in which herrings were dried'. See **dry**. A heavy, slow-sailing, West Indian coasting-vessel.

drogue, n. [1. drōg; 2. droug]. Origin doubtful. The suggestion of possible connexion with **drag** is an obvious one to make, but doesn't help much. Small buoy at the end of harpoon-line.

droit, n. [1. droit; 2. drɔit]. Fr., fr. Low Lat. *drictum*, fr. Lat. *dīrect-(um)*. See **direct**. Legal right. *Droits of Admiralty*, rights in enemy ships captured in port.

droll, adj. & n. & vb. intrans. [1. drōl; 2. droul]. Earlier Fr. *drole*, Mod. Fr. *drôle*, 'a merry companion, a wag' &c., fr. L.G. source; cp. M. Du. *droll*, 'a juggler'. Origin unknown. **1.** adj. Comical, grotesquely amusing, laughable, waggish: *a droll fellow, saying* &c. **2.** n. **a** A droll person, clown: *to play the droll*; **b** that which is droll: *he was a master of the droll*. **3.** vb. To play the droll; to be laughable, grotesquely amusing.

drollery, n. [1. dróleri; 2. dróuləri]. Prec. & **-ery**. Laughable talk or tricks, comicality, waggishness; whimsicality, pleasant absurdity.

drollness, n. [1. drṓlnes; 2. dróulnis]. **droll** & **-ness**. The quality of being droll.

drolly, adv. [1. drṓlli; 2. dróulli]. **droll** & **-ly**. In a quaint, laughable, comical manner.

-drome, suff. [1. drōm; 2. droum], fr. Gk. *drómos*, 'race-course' (see next word), used in Gk. compounds as *hippodrome* & in modern coined words as *aerodrome*.

dromedary, n. [1. drómedari, drúmedari; 2. drɔ́midəri, drámidəri], fr. O. Fr. *dromadaire*, fr. L. Lat. *dromedarius*, fr. Lat. *dromad-(is)*, *dromas*, 'a camel', & **-ary**, fr. Gk. *dromás*, genit. *dromádos*, 'running; a runner; a dromedary'; cp. Gk. *dromaîos kámēlos*, 'a dromedary'; cogn. w. Gk. *(dé)droma*, 'ran', *drómos*, 'course'. Cp. also Gk. *drāpétēs*, 'a fugitive', *apo-didrā́skein*, 'to run away, escape', *drāsmós*, 'flight'; Scrt. *drā́ti*, 'to run', *drámati*, 'to run', *drāpayati*, 'to cause to run'. Aryan base is **derā-*, **drā-*, **drŏ-*, 'to run'; perh. identical w. the base **derā-*, *drə-, 'to work, be active'. See **drama.** Arabian riding-camel, with one hump and a high speed of motion.

dromond, n. [1. drómund; 2. drɔ́mənd]. M.E. *dromoun(d)*, fr. O. Fr. *dromont*, fr. Byzantine Gk. *drómōn*, fr. *drómos*, 'running, race'. See prec. Large, fast-sailing mediaeval ship.

-dromous. See **-drome** & **-ous.** Suff. signifying 'running, going' (esp. of fish); as *anadromous* &c.

drone (I.), n. [1. drōn; 2. droun]. M.E. *drōne*, O.E. *drān*, *drǣn*, 'drone (bee)', as though fr. Gmc. **drain-*, **draini-*, but cogn. w. N.H.G. *drohne*, O.L.G. pl. *drani*, O.H.G. *treno*, 'drone'; O.S. *drān*, *dreno*; Gmc. **đrān-* **đran-*. The O.E. form is perh. borrowed fr. O.S. Aryan base **dhrĕn-* &c., 'to make a noise'; cp. Gk. dial. *thrōnax*, 'a drone', *thrênos*, 'a dirge', *(ten)thrēnē*, 'wasp', *anthrēne*, 'drone'; Scrt. *dhránati*, 'resounds'; Goth. *drunjus*, 'sound'; M. Ir. *drēsacht* (fr. **dhrens-*), 'a creaking sound', whence also Lat. *drensāre*, (of a swan) 'to cry'. The base **dhrĕn-* &c. is expanded fr. **dher-*, **dhr̥-*, 'to make a noise'. See **dor, dream. 1. a** The male of the honey-bee, which does no work; **b** (fig.) an idler, one who depends for existence on the work or bounty of others. **2.** A low, deep, humming sound, such as that produced by bees; any similar sound: *drone of a song, voice.* **3. a** One of the largest tubes of the bagpipes, producing a deep, vibrant, note; **b** sound, note of this pipe.

drone (II.), vb. trans. & intrans., fr. prec. **A.** trans. To utter in a dull, monotonous tone: *to drone (out) the psalms.* **B.** intrans. **1. a** To produce a deep, humming sound (of bees and other insects, of moving machines &c.); **b** to sing or speak in a dull, slow, spiritless, monotonous voice. **2.** To live idly.

droningly, adv. [1. drṓningli; 2. dróuniŋli]. Pres. Part. of prec. & **-ly.** In a droning voice.

droop (I.), vb. intrans. & trans. [1. drōōp; 2. drūp], fr. M.E. *droupen*, fr. O.N. *drūpa*, 'to droop, sink', cogn. w. **drop. 1.** intrans. **a** To sink, hang, down slightly, project forward and downwards: *her head drooped dejectedly*; *branches that droop over the water*; **b** to flag, pine, wilt, to show signs of weakness, lack of proper nourishment &c.: *plants droop from drought*; *children droop in great heat*; **c** (of the spirits &c.) *to droop with sorrow, loneliness* &c. **2.** trans. (rare) To lower, cause to hang down: *to droop the head.*

droop (II.), n., fr. prec. Process or condition of drooping: *a droop of the left eyelid.*

drooping, adj. [1. drōōping; 2. drūpiŋ], fr. Pres. Part. of **droop** (I.). Tending to flag or droop: *drooping boughs*; *drooping eyelids, spirits* &c.

droopingly, adv. Prec. & **-ly.** In a weak, drooping manner.

drop (I.), n. [1. drop; 2. drɔp]. O.E. *dropa*, 'drop'; M.E. *drope*; cogn. w. O.N. *dropi*, O.H.G. *tropfo*, O.L.G. *dropo*; also w. O.E. *drēopan*, 'to drop, drip', whence provinc. Engl. *dreep.* Cp., w. different formative element, Gk. *trúphos*, 'piece', & *truphḗ*, 'softness, luxury', fr. Aryan **dhrubh-*, **dhreubh-* &c. Cp. also Gk. *thrúptein*, 'to break', *thrúmma*, 'fragment'; Lett. *drubascha*, 'fragment'. See **drip**; & remoter cognates under **dreary. 1. a** A small globular mass of liquid, clinging to some point or edge, falling, or about to fall: *a drop of rain, dew* &c.; specif. **b** amount of liquid contained in a drop, considered as a measure: *two drops of quinine*; *the drops*, medicine to be measured out in drops; **c** a small quantity of liquid: *a drop of tea, water, brandy* &c. Phrs. *to take a drop too much*, get drunk; *a drop in the bucket, ocean* &c., trifling amount compared with the whole. **2.** Anything resembling a drop in form or size; **a** (of jewels) a diamond, pearl &c. set as a pendant, ear-ring &c.; (also attrib.) *a drop-pearl* &c.; **b** a small round sweetmeat: *acid, chocolate, drops.* The following senses are new formations from verb: **3. a** The distance between a higher and lower object, esp. considered as a space through which a person or thing is about to fall; fall, descent: *a drop of ten feet from the window to the ground*; **b** specif., length of rope allowed in hanging a man by the public executioner; **c** act of allowing oneself or something else, to fall; act of so falling: *an easy drop*; **d** (football) a drop-kick. **4.** Some mechanical device contrived to fall when required; e.g. **a** curtain made to fall in front of the stage at a theatre; **b** movable piece of pendent metal which covers keyhole of a door, drawer &c.; **c** part of a platform held in position by a bolt, and which falls downwards on hinges when this is withdrawn, used for hanging criminals. **5.** Decrease in amount, degree: *drop in prices, in temperature.*

drop (II.), vb. trans. & intrans. O.E. *dropian.* See prec. **A.** trans. **1.** To allow, cause (liquid) to fall drop by drop: *to drop honey.* Phr. *to drop a tear over*, lament, regret. **2.** To allow to fall down, esp. by releasing hold of; **a** to permit to slip from one's hands, whether by accident or design: *to drop a book, a baby*; *to drop a catch, ball (at cricket)*; Phr. *to drop a brick*, say or do something which causes offence, embarrassment &c.; **b** to release from jaws, beak, claws, and allow to fall, or escape: *the tiger, hawk &c. dropped his prey*; **c** to fail to pronounce or write: *to drop one's h's, a letter.* **3.** (of various actions implying release; causing, allowing, to descend) **a** *To drop anchor*, lower, allow to slide, into the sea; **b** *to drop a stitch* (in knitting), let it slip off the needle; **c** *to drop one's purse*, let fall and lose; Phr. *to drop money over a transaction*, to lose it; **d** to cause (a ball) to fall as if dropped from above: *to drop ball over a player's head, to the back of the court, on to the green*; **e** (Rugby football) to score (goal) by drop-kick. **4. a** To set down, permit to alight from a vehicle: *I'm driving your way, so I'll drop you at your door*; **b** to part company with one whom one is walking with: *we may as well walk as far as my house together, and you can drop me there.* **5.** To cause to fall by a blow, a shot &c.: *to drop a couple of birds.* **6.** To dispatch a written message, letter &c. (from idea of dropping it into the post): *to drop a line, a post card to.* **7. a** To give up, bring to an end, break off, relinquish, the acquaintance of: *to drop one's friends*; *to drop a person*; **b** to cease to pursue, or to practise: *to drop one's studies*; *to drop (the habit of) smoking.* Phr. *to drop the subject*, cease to consider, have no more to do with it. **8.** To utter casually, to let fall, make an observation: *to drop a hint, suggestion, a remark.* **9.** To reduce force, intensity, pitch, or sonority of: *to drop the voice at the end of a sentence.* **10.** (of mares, cows, ewes) *To drop their foals, calves, lambs*, to give birth to prematurely. **B.** intrans. **1.** (of water or other liquid) To fall in drops, fall drop by drop; drip: *rain drops from the clouds* &c. **2.** To fall down suddenly to the ground: *to drop as if one had been shot.* Phrs. *to work, go, till one drops*, work &c. to the utmost of one's capacity, to point of exhaustion; *ready to drop*, very exhausted, worn out. **3.** To lower oneself gradually with hands and arms, and allow oneself to fall gently to the ground at a lower level: *to drop from a window-sill into the garden.* **4. a** To droop, fall below a given level, sink below a given straight line, or desired position: *the hinges of the door have dropped slightly*; **b** to open, become lowered from a joint: *his jaw dropped.* **5.** To become reduced in amount, degree, intensity, tone: *prices, temperature, wind, storm, the voice &c. drop(s)*, become smaller, less hot, less violent, less loud. **6.** To cease to be considered or discussed, dealt with: *to let a subject, matter, drop.* **C.** Followed by various prepositions and adverbs. *Drop behind*, to come to a position in the rear (of). *Drop down (stream)*, to go with the current. *Drop in*, intrans., (colloq.) to make a casual visit; *drop in on*, pay sudden, casual visits to (person). *Drop on*, trans., (fig.) to single out for blame, to scold, rate soundly. *Drop off*, **a** to go away, become fewer: *my audience has dropped off latterly*; **b** to decline, diminish: *his practice has dropped off. Drop out*, intrans., to cease to take part in affairs and activities, cease to count: *to drop out of things.*

drop-curtain, n. Painted curtain lowered from a roller, in front of the stage of a theatre.

drop-hammer, n. Kind of mechanical hammer used in forging steel, consisting of heavy weight let drop upon the metal to be forged.

drop-kick, n. (Rugby football) One in which the ball is kicked as it touches the ground after being dropped from the hands held out in front of player; opposed to *punt.*

droplet, n. [1. dróplet; 2. drɔ́plit]. **drop** (I.) & **-let.** A small drop.

dropping fire, n. [1. dróping fīr; 2. drɔ́piŋ fáiə]. (mil.) Discharge of small arms at frequent, irregular intervals.

droppings, n. [1. drópingz; 2. drɔ́piŋz]. See **drop** (II.) & **-ing.** What is dropped; specif., dung of animals.

drop-scene, n. Drop-curtain.

dropsical, adj. [1. drópsikl; 2. drɔ́psikl]. See **dropsy** & **-ic** & **-al. a** Affected with dropsy; **b** resembling dropsy in appearance; unnaturally swollen.

dropsically, adv. Prec. & **-ly.** In a dropsical condition.

dropsy, n. [1. drópsi; 2. drɔ́psi]. M.E. *dropsie*, fr. O. Fr. *idropesie*, fr. Lat. *hydrōpisis*, fr. Gk. *húdrōps*, 'dropsy', fr. *húdōr*, 'water'. See **hydro-.** An unnatural collection of watery fluid in the cavities or tissues of the body.

dropwort, n. [1. drópwĕrt; 2. drɔ́pwʌt]. **drop** (II.) & **wort. a** A perennial plant, genus *Spiraea*, having small, pendulous, white flowers; it grows in meadows and resembles the meadowsweet; **b** the water dropwort, q.v.

Drosera, n. [1. drósera; 2. drɔ́sərə], fr. Gk. *droserós*, 'dewy', fr. *drósos*, 'dew'. Etymol. doubtful. (bot.) A genus of insectivorous plants, the sundew.

droshky, drosky, n. [1. dróshki; 2. drɔ́ʃki], fr. Russ. *drozhki*, dimin. of *drogi*, 'wagon', fr. *drogá*, 'wooden bar between front and back axles'; prob. cogn w. Lith. *diřžti*, 'to harden'; O. Slav. *drŭžati*, 'to hold'; Scrt. *dr̥ḍháš*, 'firm'; perh. cogn. w. Lat. *fortis*, O. Lat. *forctus.* See **firm, fort.** Light, low, four-wheeled open carriage used in Russia; also a light two-wheeled carriage resembling a victoria, formerly used in Germany, esp. as a cab plying for hire.

drosometer, n. [1. drosómeter; 2. drɔsɔ́mitə], fr. Gk. *drósos*, 'dew', see **Drosera,** & **-meter.** Instrument, apparatus, for measuring the fall of dew.

dross, n. [1. dros; 2. drɔs]. O.E. & M.E. *drōs*, 'dregs, dirt'; O.H.G. *(gi)tros*, M.L.G. *drōs*; cp. N.H.G. *drusen*, 'husks, dregs'; Du. *droesem*; origin uncertain; possibly cogn. w. **dreary. 1. a** Waste matter, refuse, rubbish; **b** specif., scum of foreign matter which rises to the surface of molten metal. **2.** (in spiritual sense) Something worthless, something possessing no real value; earthly joys contrasted with heavenly treasures.

drossiness, n. [1. drósines; 2. drɔ́sinis]. Next word & **-ness.** The state of being drossy.

drossy, adj. [1. drósi; 2. drɔ́si]. **dross** & **-y.** Worthless; containing or composed of rubbish; resembling dross.

drought, n. [1. drout; 2. draut]. O.E. *drūgoþ*; M.E. *drūhþe, droughte*; cp. L.G. *drūgde*, M. Du. *drooghte.* See **dry** (I.) **1. a** Excessive dryness, want of moisture, esp. in the atmosphere and soil; **b** dryness of body, desire for drink, thirst. **2.** Spell of dry weather lasting long enough for the land to become parched.

droughtiness, n. [1. dróutines; 2. dráutinis]. Next word & **-ness.** Condition of being droughty.

droughty, adj. [1. dróuti; 2. dráuti]. **drought** & **-y.** Affected by, suffering from, drought.

drove (I.), vb. [1. drōv; 2. drouv]. O.E. *drāf*, M.E. *drōf*. Pret. of **drive** (I.).

drove (II.), n. [1. drōv; 2. drouv]. O.E. *drāf*, *drǣf*, 'drove, herd; band'; M.E. *drōve*, *drōf*. Cp. M.H.G. *treip*, fr. that grade of *drīfan*, 'drive', wh. occurs also in Pret. sing. See prec. & **drive**. Herd or flock of sheep or cattle; considered as associated, or moving, together.

drover, n. [1. dróver; 2. dróuvə]. See prec. & **-er**. One who drives cattle, esp. to market.

drown, vb. intrans. & trans. [1. droun; 2. draun]. M.E. *drounen*, O.N. *drukkna*, Swed. *drunkna*, *drukna*. The O.E. word is *druncnian*. Related to **drink**; cp. **drunk**. **A.** intrans. To lose one's life by suffocation in water; usually *to be drowned*. **B.** trans. **1.** To suffocate to death in water: *to drown a kitten*. Phr. *eyes drowned in tears*, suffused in. **2.** To cause oneself to forget sorrows &c. by drinking: *to drown one's cares in wine*. **3.** To muffle sound, render inaudible: *his voice was drowned by the coughing of the audience.*

drowning, n. [1. dróuning; 2. dráuniŋ]. Prec. & **-ing**. Act, process, of being drowned: *death by drowning*; *save from drowning*.

drowse (I.), vb. intrans. & trans. [1. drouz; 2. drauz], fr. O.E. *drūsian*, 'to be languid'; prob. cogn. w. O.E. *drēosan*, 'to fall'. See **dreary**. **1.** intrans. To doze, sleep lightly, be half asleep. **2.** trans. **a** To make sleepy; **b** to pass (time) in drowsing, dozing: *to drowse away one's time*.

drowse (II.), n., fr. prec. A doze, half sleep; sleepiness, sluggishness.

drowsily, adv. [1. dróuzili; 2. dráuzili]. See **drowsy** & **-ly**. In a drowsy, sleepy manner.

drowsiness, n. [1. dróuzines; 2. dráuzinis]. Next word & **-ness**. The state of being drowsy, inclined to sleep.

drowsy, adj. [1. dróuzi; 2. dráuzi]. **drowse** & **-y**. **a** Inclined to sleep, sleepy; lethargic; **b** inducing sleep, soporific.

drub, vb. trans. & intrans. [1. drub; 2. drab]. Possibly of Scand. origin, cp. Swed. *drabba*, 'to hit'. **a** trans. To beat with a stick, belabour; **b** intrans., to give repeated blows, to stamp: *to drub with the heels.*

drubbing, n. [1. drúbing; 2. drábiŋ]. Prec. & **-ing**. A beating.

drudge (I.), n. [1. druj; 2. dradž], fr. O.E. **dryċġ* (unrecorded, but cp. the O.E. personal name *Dryċġhelm*), fr. the base **dreug-*, **drug-*, as in O.E. *drēogan*, 'carry out, perform, a duty, or service' &c. See **dree**. An overworked toiler, one compelled to perform laborious, monotonous tasks; a slavish menial, subject to the tyranny of a master.

drudge (II.), vb. intrans., fr. prec. To work like a drudge; to labour incessantly and slavishly *at*.

drudgery, n. [1. drújeri; 2. drádžəri]. **drudge** & **-ery**. Hard, dull, wearisome, mechanical, slavish toil.

drudgingly, adv. [1. drújingli; 2. drádžiŋli]. Pres. Part. of **drudge** (II.) & **-ly**. Laboriously, like a drudge.

drug (I.), n. [1. drug; 2. drag]. M.E. *drogge*, *drugge*, fr. Fr. *drogue*; origin uncertain; possibly fr. a Gmc. source (cp. Du. *droog*, 'dry'), in wh. case the orig. sense wd. be 'dried herbs'. **1.** **a** Any substance, whether vegetable or mineral, used for medicinal purposes: *Food and Drugs Acts*, against adulteration of such; **b** (in a sinister sense) a medicinal substance improperly used, and taken in excess so that it has a deleterious effect, esp. *narcotic drugs*. **2.** Unsalable goods, something no longer salable because too abundant. Phr. *a drug in the market*.

drug (II.), vb. trans. & intrans., fr. prec. **A.** trans. **1.** **a** To mix drugs with, add drugs to, something intended for consumption; specif. **b** to add a deleterious, esp. a narcotic drug to food or drink. **2.** **a** To administer a drug to (a person); **b** specif., to administer a dangerous amount of a drug, esp. of a narcotic drug to. **B.** intrans. To be in the habit of taking drugs; esp. to be in the habit of taking an excessive and harmful quantity of drugs, or of a drug.

drugget, n. [1. drúget; 2. drágit], fr. Fr. *droguet*. Origin doubtful. Coarse woollen material, used chiefly for floor-coverings.

druggist, n. [1. drúgist; 2. drágist]. **drug** (I.) & **-ist**. A tradesman who sells drugs and medical appliances; an apothecary, pharmaceutical chemist.

druid, n. [1. dro͞oid; 2. drúid], fr. Fr., fr. Lat. *Druidae*, 'Druids', fr. O. Celt. *druid*, fr. **dru-wid*, **dru-*, 'much; very; strong', & **wid-* 'know'. For the latter element see **wit**; for the former, see **dryad**, **tree**. **1.** **a** A member of the ancient Celtic priesthood which included prophets, priests, poets, judges, and magicians; **b** hence, official of the Welsh Eisteddfod. **2.** Member of a kind of mutual benefit society, founded in 18th cent.

druidess, n. [1. dro͞oides; 2. drúidis]. Prec. & **-ess**. A female druid.

druidic(al), adj. [1. dro͞oídik(l); 2. druídik(l)]. See **druid** & **-ic** & **-al**. Pertaining to the druids or to their rites.

druidism, n. [1. dro͞oidizm; 2. drúidizəm]. **druid** & **-ism**. The religious system of the ancient Celts of Gaul and Britain.

drum (I.), n. [1. drum; 2. dram]. Cp. Du. *trom*, N.H.G. *trommel*; prob. imitative. **1.** **a** A musical instrument, consisting of parchment stretched over the openings of a cylindrical or hemispherical framework, played by beating with a padded stick; of various types, as *side-drum*, *kettle drum* &c.; **b** (pl.) the drums and players of such in an orchestra or band: *drums and fifes*; **c** sound of or as of a beaten drum. **2.** One of various things resembling a drum in shape; a hollow cylinder on which cables are wound; **b** box for packing preserved fruit &c.; **c** the tympanum, or membrane dividing the inner and outer ear. **3.** (archit.) **a** The vertical wall which supports a dome or cupola; **b** one of the cylindrical blocks which form the shaft of a column; **c** the solid part of the capital of a Corinthian column. **4.** (archaic and obs.) Evening party, rout, cp. *kettle drum*.

drum (II.), vb. trans. & intrans., fr. prec. **A.** trans. **1.** **a** To play on a drum: *to drum a tune*; Phrs. *to drum out*, expel (from regiment) with accompaniment of beaten drums; *drum up*, summon by beating drum; **b** to make a sound by thumping, rapping, upon a resounding medium: *to drum the table with one's fingers* &c. **2.** To beat into a person's mind by constant repetition: *to drum Latin into a boy*; or *into a boy's head*. **B.** intrans. **a** To play the drum; **b** to thump, rap, continuously: *to drum with one's heels on the floor*; **c** (of birds &c.) to produce a sound like that of a drum, by beating of wings &c.

drum (III.). See **drumlin**.

drum-fire, n. Rapid, persistent, heavy gunfire, esp. as concentrated on a particular objective, as a line of trenches &c.

drum-fish, n. A large sea-fish which produces a loud drumming sound.

drum-head, n. **drum** (I.) & **head**. The parchment stretched over the opening of a drum. Phr. *drum-head court-martial*, one summoned hastily in an emergency, usually on a field of battle, or on the line of march.

drum(lin), n. [1. drúm(lin); 2. drám(lin)], fr. O. Ir. *druim*, 'back, ridge', & **-ling**. Cp. Gael. *trum*, 'back, ridge'; Bret. *adrén*, 'behind'. (geol.) Long ridge formed by glacial drift.

drum-major, n. Sergeant in command of regimental drummers.

drummer, n. [1. drúmer; 2. drámə]. **drum** (II.) & **-er**. **1.** One who plays the drum; esp. one who plays the drum in a military band. **2.** (U.S.A.) A commercial traveller, as going about drumming up custom or customers.

Drummond light, n. [1. drúmund līt; 2. drámənd lait], fr. name of inventor, Thomas Drummond, 1797–1840. Lime-light.

drumstick, n. [1. drúmstik; 2. drámstik]. **a** Stick with padded knob at one end for beating a drum; **b** (from its shape) the lower part of the leg of a cooked chicken.

drunk (I.), adj. [1. drungk; 2. draŋk]. O.E. *druncen*, M.E. *drunke(n)*. P.P. of **drink**. **a** Overcome by strong drink; inebriated; Phrs. *to get drunk*, to become inebriated; *as drunk as a lord*, *as a fish*, very drunk; *dead drunk*, unconscious from drink; **b** deeply affected, and slightly unbalanced, temporarily, in mind, by some powerful emotion: *drunk with success*, *happiness* &c.

drunk (II.), n., fr. prec. **1.** **a** Case of drunkenness brought before a magistrate; **b** the person there charged with drunkenness; **c** a drunken man. **2.** (slang) A drinking party.

drunkard, n. [1. drúngkard; 2. dráŋkəd]. See **drunk** (I.) & **-ard**. One habitually given to drunkenness.

drunken, adj. [1. drúngken; 2. dráŋkən]. See **drunk** (I.) & **-en**. Old P.P. of **drink**. Attrib. adj. **1.** **a** Intoxicated, in a state of inebriation: *a drunken man*; **b** given to getting drunk: *a drunken old ruffian*. **2.** Characterized by, arising from, drunkenness: *a drunken brawl*, *frolic* &c.

drunkenly, adv. Prec. & **-ly**. In a drunken, intoxicated manner.

drunkenness, n. See prec. & **-ness**. The state of being drunk; intoxication, inebriety.

drupaceous, adj. [1. dro͞opáshus; 2. drūpéiʃəs]. Next word & **-aceous**. (bot.) Pertaining to, producing, drupes.

drupe, n. [1. dro͞op; 2. drūp], fr. Lat. *drūpa* (*oliva*), 'an over-ripe olive', fr. Gk. *drúppā*, 'an over-ripe olive'. (bot.) A fruit, consisting of a hard kernel containing the seed, surrounded by a soft, fleshy pulp; e.g. plum, peach, cherry.

drupel, n. [1. dro͞opl; 2. drúpl]. See prec. & **-el**. A little drupe, such as one of the juicy grains of the raspberry, blackberry.

drupelet, n. [1. dro͞oplet; 2. drúplit]. **drupe** & **-let**. Drupel.

druse (I.), n. [1. dro͞oz; 2. drūz]. Germ. *druse*, fr. Czech *druza*, 'piece of crystallized ore'. A space or chink in rock, studded with small crystals.

Druse (II.), n., fr. the name of the founder of sect, Ismail al-Darazi, 11th cent. Member of a Mohammedan sect inhabiting the mountains of Lebanon in Syria.

dry (I.), adj. [1. drī; 2. drai], O.E. *drȳġe*, M.E. *drīȝe*, *drīe*; cp. L.G. *drūge*, M. Du. *droogh* O.H.G. *trucchen*, Mod. Germ. *trocken*, 'dry', O.N. *draugr*. Further cognates unknown. **1.** Lacking in, free from, moisture; opposed to *wet*. Phrs. *as dry as a bone*, *bone dry*, absolutely dry; *with dry eyes*, free from tears, unmoved. **2.** In special connexions: **a** *dry land*, contrasted with the sea; **b** *dry bread*, *toast*, without butter &c.; **c** *dry goods*, cloth, linen &c., as distinct from groceries, meat &c. **3.** Various specific meanings: **a** (of climate, weather) not rainy, showing a low rainfall; **b** (of a well) not yielding water; (of a cow) not yielding milk; **c** (of men) thirsty, in need of drink; *dry work*, a kind causing thirst; **d** (of wine) containing little sugar, unsweetened, astringent; **e** U.S.A., under a law prohibiting sale and consumption of alcoholic drink: *America has gone dry*; *a dry town*, *state*, *political party* &c. **4.** (of non-material things) **a** *A dry book*, *lecture* &c., unenlivened by emotional appeal, unimaginative; not exciting interest; arid; **b** *dry humour*, quiet, undemonstrative, keen, quaint; **c** *dry facts*, plain, unadorned, undisguised.

dry (II.), vb. intrans. & trans., fr. O.E. *drȳġan*, trans. 'to dry, to wipe off', fr. *drȳġe*, 'dry'. See prec. **A.** intrans. To become dry; to give up, lose, moisture by dripping or evaporation: *clothes hung up to dry*; *the lawn will soon dry in the wind*. *Dry up*, **a** (of a stream, well) to cease to yield water; **b** (of other wet objects generally) to become completely dry; **c** (fig.) to become barren of ideas, become intellectually or spiritually unproductive; **d** (colloq., slang) to stop speaking; Phr. *oh! dry up!*, stop talking, making a noise &c. **B.** trans. **1. a** To extract moisture from: *the sun dries the grass*; **b** to cause moisture to evaporate from, by exposing to heat, air &c.: *to dry herbs*; *to dry clothes by the fire* &c. **2.** To remove moisture from by wiping: specif., *to dry oneself, one's hands*, after washing; *to dry one's eyes*, wipe tears away; *to dry one's tears*, wipe away; (fig.) cease to mourn.

dry (III.), n., fr. **dry** (I.). Dry weather, drought; dryness: (*to arrive*) *in the dry*, without experiencing rain, without a wetting.

dryad, n. [1. dríad; 2. dráiæd], fr. Lat. *Dryades*, fr. Gk. *druádes*, 'dryads', sing. *druás*, fr. *drûs*, genit. *druós*, 'an oak; a tree'. Cp. Gk. *drūmós*, 'forest'; Scrt. *dhruváš*, 'firm, sure'; O. Pruss. *druvi*, 'faith'; Scrt. *druvayáš*, 'wooden vessel'; O. Slav. *drŭva*, 'wood'. Cp. also Scrt. *drumáš*, 'tree'; *dru-ṣád*, 'perched on a tree'; Celt. *dru-*, 'very' (as intens.); *Druides* (fr. **dru-wid*, 'very wise'), see **druid**; O.E. *trum*, 'firm' (see **trim**). For other forms of the base see **tree**, & words there referred to. A spirit of the trees; a forest nymph.

dryasdust, n. & adj. [1. dríazdust; 2. dráiəzdast]. **a** n. (with cap.) Intolerably pedantic, dull and uninteresting learned man; **b** adj., possessing the qualities of such a man.

dry battery, n. Electric battery composed of voltaic cells containing absorbent matter and sealed to prevent leakage.

dry bob, n. At Eton, one who plays cricket, as opposed to *wet bob*, one who rows.

dry dock, n. Dock, from which water can be entirely drawn leaving vessel on stocks for repair &c.; a graving dock. Phr. *to go into dry dock*, to be laid up for repairs &c.

dryer, drier, n. [1. dríer; 2. dráiə]. **dry** (II.) & **-er.** That which dries, esp. substance mixed with paints, varnishes &c., to hasten the process of drying.

dry-fly, n. Artificial fly used in fishing, which is not immersed in the water but thrown so as to appear to hover on surface, and which is dried by waving in the air before next cast.

dry-fly fishing, n. That practised with a dry fly.

dryish, adj. [1. dríish; 2. dráiiʃ]. **dry** (I.) & **-ish.** Partly, fairly, dry.

dryly, drily, adv. [1. dríli; 2. dráili]. **dry** (I.) & **-ly.** (esp. fig.) In a dry manner.

dry masonry, n. That built without use of mortar, or other adhesive matter, between the stones.

dry measure, n. Measure of bulk, used esp. for grain.

dryness, n. [1. drínes; 2. dráinis]. **dry** (I.) & **-ness.** The state of being dry.

dry-nurse (I.), n. **a** Nurse who looks after an infant without suckling it; **b** (fig.) one who teaches another with great care, helping him over every difficulty.

dry-nurse (II.), vb. trans. To look after, take charge of, instruct &c., as a nurse does an infant. See prec. **b.**

dry plate, n. Photographic sensitized plate coated with a film which does not require to be immersed in solution before exposure.

dry-point, adj., n., & vb. intrans. **a** adj. A needle for copper-plate engraving without the use of acid; **b** n., an engraving produced with this; **c** vb., to use a dry-point.

dry-rot, n. **a** Fungoidal disease attacking wood, and reducing it to powder; **b** hence, concealed degeneration, unsuspected decay of character, stability &c.

drysalter, n. [1. drísawlter; 2. dráisōltə]. **dry** (I.) & **salt** & **-er.** Dealer in dried and salted produce; also in pickles, tinned goods, oils &c.

drysaltery, n. [1. drísáwlteri; 2. draisóltəri]. Prec. & **-y.** The shop or trade of a drysalter.

dryshod, adj. [1. dríshod; 2. dráiʃɔd]. With dry feet; without getting one's feet wet.

dry wall, n. One constructed without use of mortar between the stones.

dry walling, n. Act and art of constructing dry walls; length of dry wall.

dual, adj. & n. [1. dūal; 2. djūəl], fr. Lat. *duālis*, 'containing two', fr. *duo*, 'two', & **-al.** Cp. Gk. *dúō, dúo*; Scrt. *dvā(u), duvā(u)*, m., *dvḗ, duvḗ*, f.; O. Ir. *dāu, dā*, m., *dī*, f.; W. *dau*, m., *dwy*, f.; Lith. *dù* (fr. **dvů*), m., *dvì* (fr. **dvḗ*), f.; O. Slav. *dŭva, dva*, m., *dŭvě, dvě*, f.; Goth. *twa*, neut.; O.N. *tvau*; O.E. *tū*. Aryan base **duwō-*, **dwō-*. For Gmc. forms see **two.** See further **bi-, di-, dis-, dubious, duple, duplex, twi-, twig, twin. 1.** adj. **a** Pertaining to, expressing the number, two; double, twofold, having two parts: *dual control, personality* &c. **b** (gram.) applied to a special form of a noun, pronoun, adjective, or verb, used to denote two persons or things only. **2.** n. (gram.) The dual number.

dualin, n. [1. dūalin; 2. djūəlin]. Prec. & **-in.** A kind of dynamite, an explosive made of sawdust, nitre, and nitro-glycerine.

dualism, n. [1. dūalizm; 2. djūəlizəm]. **dual** & **-ism. a** The state of being twofold, double; duality; **b** any religious or philosophical system based on the conception of the twofold nature of the universe, as consisting of two principles, e.g. mind and matter.

dualist, n. [1. dūalist; 2. djūəlist]. **dual** & **-ist.** A believer in some form of dualism.

dualistic, adj. [1. dūalístik; 2. djūəlístik]. Prec. & **-ic.** Having to do with, based on, dualism.

duality, n. [1. dūáliti; 2. djuǽliti]. **dual** & **-ity.** The state of being twofold, double, having a twofold nature.

dualize, vb. trans. [1. dūalīz; 2. djūəlaiz]. **dual** & **-ize.** To make into two, regard as two.

dually, adv. [1. dūali; 2. djūəli]. **dual** & **-ly.** In a dual form or manner.

dub (I.), n. [1. dub; 2. dab]. Provinc. Engl. Origin obscure. A small pool.

dub (II.), vb. trans. M.E. *dubben*, 'dub, adorn', Late O.E. *dubbian*, 'dub (knight)'. Perh. fr. O. Fr. *adober*, 'to adorn, equip with arms'. Origin unknown. **1.** To lay a sword on a man's shoulders in conferring knighthood, to make a knight: *to dub a man knight.* **2.** To designate as, confer a name, nickname, title, upon: *to dub a man a knave.*

dub (III.), vb. trans. Perh. same as prec. To dress, rub, with grease &c.: *to dub leather, boots, a dry-fly* &c.

dubbin, n. [1. dubin; 2. dábin]. Prec. & **-ing.** Specially prepared adhesive and penetrating grease for softening and waterproofing leather, esp. boots and gaiters.

dubiety, n. [1. dūbíeti; 2. djūbáiiti], fr. L. Lat. *dubietāt-(em)*, 'doubt, uncertainty'. See **doubt** & **dubious.** Hesitancy, uncertainty, doubtful feeling.

dubious, adj. [1. dūbius; 2. djūbiəs], fr. L. Lat. *dubiōsus*, 'doubtful', fr. *dubius*, 'doubtful, vacillating, fluctuating', fr. *du-*, 'two' (see **dual**); *-bius* is either fr. the stem **bhū-*, 'to be' (see **be-** & **future**), or fr. the stem **bhē-*, 'to seem, appear' (see **phantasm**). Orig. meaning wd. be 'double-seeming'. **1.** (of persons) **a** (chiefly predicatively) Feeling, doubt, hesitancy, uncertainty: *to be dubious what to do, of a man's honesty, about the weather*; **b** inspiring doubt, of doubtful antecedents and character; with implication of shadiness and disreputability; Phr. *a dubious character*, a shady individual; see **doubtful**; **c** unknown, whose identity can only be surmised: '*His death was destined to a foreign strand, A petty fortress, and a dubious hand*' (Dr. Johnson). **2.** (of non-material things and circumstances) **a** Bearing more than one interpretation, one at least, unfavourable: *a dubious compliment*; **b** liable to turn out either well or ill, of uncertain value or issue: *a dubious blessing*; *the result is still dubious.*

dubiously, adv. Prec. & **-ly.** In a dubious manner, doubtfully.

dubiousness, n. See prec. & **-ness.** The state of being dubious; uncertainty.

dubitation, n. [1. dūbitáshun; 2. djūbitéiʃən], fr. Fr., fr. Lat. *dubitātiōn-(em)*, 'doubt, uncertainty', fr. *dubitāt-(um)*, P.P. type of *dubitāre*, 'to waver, doubt, be uncertain', freq. fr. O. Lat. *dubat*, 'he doubts', fr. *dubius* 'doubtful'. See **dubious** & **-ation.** (rare) The act of doubting, state of being doubtful, hesitancy, uncertainty.

dubitative, adj. [1. dūbitativ; 2. djūbitətiv], fr. Lat. *dubitātīvus*, 'doubtful'. See prec. & **-ive. a** Doubting, hesitancy; **b** expressing doubt, hesitation.

dubitatively, adv. Prec. & **-ly.** Doubtingly, with hesitation.

ducal, adj. [1. dūkl; 2. djūkl], fr. Fr., fr. L. Lat. *ducālis*, 'belonging to a leader', fr. *duc-(em), dux*, 'a leader', & **-al.** See **duke.** Pertaining to, suitable for, a duke; resembling a duke in position, wealth &c.

ducally, adv. Prec. & **-ly.** In a ducal manner, as befits a duke.

ducat, n. [1. dúkat; 2. dákət], fr. Fr., fr. Ital. *ducato*, 'duchy', fr. Lat. *ducātus*, 'military command'. See **duchy.** The coin was first struck in the Duchy of Apulia in 1140. A coin of gold or silver worth about nine shillings, formerly issued in several European countries; esp. the coin as struck in Venice in 13th cent., and money of account, later known as sequin.

duce, n. [1. dōōchā; 2. dūtʃe]. Ital., 'leader, chief', fr. Lat. *dux*, see **duke.** A leader, chief, esp. in Phr. *il duce*, 'the chief', of Benito Mussolini.

duchess, n. [1. dúches; 2. dátʃis], fr. Fr. *duchesse*, fr. Low Lat. *ducissa*. See **duke** & **-ess. a** The wife, widow, of a duke; **b** a woman who holds, in her own right, the sovereignty of a duchy.

duchy, n. [1. dúchi; 2. dátʃi], fr. O. Fr. *duché*, fr. L. Lat. *ducātus*, 'military command', fr. *duc-(em), dux*, 'a leader', & **-ate.** See **duke.** The dominions ruled over by a duke who is a sovereign prince: *the Duchy* (or *Grand Duchy*) *of Luxemburg* &c. Duchy is not the same as **dukedom**; in Great Britain there are only the *Duchy of Lancaster* and that of *Cornwall*, which are appanages of the Crown of England, but which possess a certain administrative independence and courts; the latter is held by the Prince of Wales for the time being; *Lancaster*, held by the Crown, provides the *Chancellor of the Duchy*, who is a member of the Government of the day; *the delectable Duchy*, Cornwall.

duck (I.), n. [1. duk; 2. dak]. O.E. *dūce*, 'duck', lit. 'the diving-bird'; M.E. *duke*. See next word. **1. a** Generic name of a web-footed, short-legged, broad-beaked water-bird, both wild and domesticated; Phrs. *like a duck in a thunderstorm*, with eyes turned up and a languishing look; *like water off a duck's back*, without making any impression; (*to take to something*) *like a duck to water*, naturally, without any difficulty; *ducks and drakes*, a game, consisting of making a flat stone skip over the surface of water; *to play ducks and drakes with* (*money*), spend extravagantly; *a lame duck*, disabled person, ship &c.; **b** the female of the species; as distinguished from *drake*; **c** the flesh of the duck, as a food: *a slice of duck.* **2. a** A term of endearment; **b** an attractive, delightful person: *she's a perfect duck.* **3.** (cricket &c.) The score of zero; for *duck's-egg*.

duck (II.), vb. intrans. & trans. M.E. *douken*, 'to dip, duck'; cp. M.L.G. *dūken*, M. Du. *dūken, duiken*, M.H.G. *tauchen*, 'to dip, plunge, duck'. The vb. is not recorded in O.E., but *dūce* (see prec.) is fr. same source. **A.** intrans. **1.** To stoop, crouch down suddenly and rapidly, to lower the head, or the whole body, suddenly and rapidly as though to avoid a blow, or missile, or to escape observation. **2.** To dive suddenly below surface of water; to thrust one's head under water; this is doubtless the primary meaning, though now become secondary. **B.** trans. **a** To lower suddenly by a rapid movement: *to duck one's head*; **b** to thrust under water suddenly and rapidly, to immerse suddenly in water: *children have to be ducked in the sea in order to accustom them to the feel of the water.*

duck (III.), n., fr. prec. **a** A sudden downward jerk, swift lowering of the head or whole body; **b** a sudden dip under or into water.

duck (IV.), n. Prob. fr. Du. *doeck*, 'linen cloth'. Cp. also O.N. *dūkr*, 'cloth, towel', & Mod. Germ. *tuch*, 'cloth'. **a** A kind of coarse linen or cotton cloth, used for clothing by sailors and by others in the tropics; **b** (pl.) trousers made of this material.

duck-bill, n. **1.** Variety of red wheat. **2.** Duck-billed platypus.

duck-billed platypus, n. [1. dúk bild plátipus; 2. dák bild plǽtipəs]. Australian, oviparous mammal, the ornithorhynchus, with a broad, flat beak like a duck's, and webbed feet.

duck-boards, n. pl. Flat pieces of board or planking laid across swampy ground, in water-logged trenches &c., to afford a dry footing.

ducker, n. [1. dúker; 2. dákə]. **duck** (II.) & **-er.** A diving-bird, esp. the dabchick.

duck-hawk, n. The marsh-harrier.

ducking, n. [1. dúking; 2. dákiŋ]. **duck** (II.) & **-ing.** **a** An immersion in water; **b** a thorough wetting however received: *to fall into the sea and get a good ducking*; *the rain came down in sheets and gave us a regular ducking.*

ducking-stool, n. A seat at the end of long pole, which acted as a lever, used formerly for punishing scolds and other objectionable women, by plunging them suddenly into a pond &c. by its means.

duck-legged, adj. Having short legs, which impart a waddling gait like that of a duck.

duckling, n. [1. dúkling; 2. dákliŋ]. **duck** (I.) & **-ling.** A young duck.

duck-pond, n. A pond for, or used by, tame ducks.

duck's-egg, n., fr. the resemblance of the figure 0 to the shape of an egg. (cricket) Batsman's failure to score in an innings.

duck-shot, n. Shot of special size for shooting wild duck.

duckweed, n. [1. dúkwēd; 2. dákwīd]. One of several species of small plants growing on the surface of ponds; so called because they are eaten by water-birds.

ducky, adj. & n. [1. dúki; 2. dáki]. **duck** (I.) & **-y.** (colloq.) Term of endearment; equivalent to dear, darling &c.

duct, n. [1. dukt; 2. dakt], fr. Lat. *duct-(us)*, 'a leading, conducting', fr. P.P. type of *dūcere*, 'to lead, conduct, draw'. See **duke.** A tube or channel for conveying fluid; **a** (in animals) channel conveying secretions from glands &c.; **b** (in plant tissues) canal holding water, air &c.

-duct, suff. Same as prec. In compounds **aqueduct, viaduct.**

ductile, adj. [1. dúktīl; 2. dáktail]. Fr., fr. Lat. *ductilis*, fr. base *duct-* (see prec.) & **-ile.** **1. a** (of metals) Capable of being drawn out into a thread or wire; capable of being worked; malleable; **b** (of clay &c.) plastic, easily moulded. **2.** (of character) Capable of being influenced; easily moulded, tractable, docile.

ductility, n. [1. duktíliti; 2. daktíliti]. See prec. & **-ity.** The quality of being ductile.

ductless, adj. [1. dúktles; 2. dáktlis]. **duct** & **-less.** Not possessing ducts, without a duct; specif. (anat.) *ductless glands*, those which, as the thyroid, thymus, spleen &c., have internal secretions which drain direct into the veins and lymphatics; certain of these have endocrine secretions; see **endocrine.**

dud, n. [1. dud; 2. dad]. Origin doubtful; perh. connected w. **dodder** &c. (slang) **a** A shell which does not explode; **b** something which is not a success, which does not fulfil its purpose; a failure, disappointment; also of persons.

dude, n. [1. dūd; 2. djūd]. Origin unknown. (American slang; not used in English) A foppish, dandified fellow.

dudgeon (I.), n. [1. dújn; 2. dádžn]. Orig. sense 'boxwood'. A.-Fr. *digeon*, L.M.E. *dogeon*, Early Mod. *dudgin*. Origin doubtful. (archaic) The hilt of a dagger.

dudgeon (II.), n. Origin unknown. Offended feelings, anger, resentment; esp. in Phr. *in high dudgeon.*

dud(h)een, n. In England, where the word is only known from dictionaries, or books on Ireland, it is pronounced in any way suggested to the speaker by the spelling; in Ireland, where the word is known to most, though only used jocularly, the pronunciation is, or used to be [1. dōōdhĕn; 2. dūðīn]. Origin of first element doubtful; *-een* is a dimin. A short or small tobacco pipe; a tobacco pipe.

duds, n. pl. [1. dudz; 2. dadz]. Scand., L.M.E. *dudde*, 'cloth', fr. O.N. *duði*, 'swaddling-clothes'; cp. *duða*, 'to wrap up'. (slang) Old, shabby clothes; wearing apparel generally.

due (I.), adj. [1. dū; 2. djū]. M.E. *due*, fr. O. Fr. *deu(t)*, fr. L. Lat. *debutum*, Lat. *debitum*, 'owed', P.P. of *debēre*, 'to owe'. See **debt, debit.** **1.** (of debts, sums of money) Owing, (now) payable; (only pred.) *his wages are due*; *the debt is due.* **2.** (of non-material obligations) Fitting, proper, adequate; deserved, proper to be given, shown, observed: *the obedience due to parents*; *the respect due to learning*; *with due ceremony*; *with due regard to, for.* Phrs. *in due course*, in proper time; *it is due to him to say* &c., fair, just, required by justice; *with all due respect to you.* **3.** (pred. only) Appointed, timed, for a certain time, date: *the mail is due tomorrow*; *when is the train due?* **4.** Caused by, to be attributed to as cause &c.: *his death was due to negligence*; *the tendency to believe that all our social ills are due to the Government of the day*; *due to* is often incorrectly used as a preposition, 'owing to': *the shares fell rapidly, due to unfounded rumours*; correctly, *the fall of the shares was due to* &c.

due (II.), adv., fr. prec. (of direction, before names of points of the compass) Exactly, directly: *the wind is due east*; *to sail due south.*

due (III.), n., fr. **due** (I.). **a** (of monetary debts) That which has to be paid, toll, fee, esp. a charge levied by legal authority; (in pl.) *harbour dues*; **b** (of non-material debts) that which must be rendered according to custom, justice, desert: *respect and homage are a sovereign's due.* Phrs. *to give a man his due*; *to give the devil his due*, to do justice even to the undeserving.

duel (I.), n. [1. dúel; 2. djúil], fr. Fr., fr. Med. use of O. Lat. *duellum*, 'war, fight', fr. *duo*, 'two': Class. Lat. *bellum.* See **bellicose** & **dual.** Contest between two persons or parties; specif. **a** a formally conducted fight between two persons armed with lethal weapons, each of whom tries to kill or injure the other; **b** *the duel*, custom, system, which permits such fights; **c** an intellectual contest between two persons or parties: *a duel of wits.*

duel (II.), vb. intrans., fr. prec. To fight a duel.

duelling, n. [1. dúeling; 2. djúiliŋ]. Prec. & **-ing.** Act of fighting a duel; practice of fighting duels; (also attrib.) *duelling pistols.*

duellist, n. [1. dúelist; 2. djúilist]. See **duel** & **-ist.** One of the combatants in a duel; one skilled in fighting duels: *a famous duellist.*

duenna, n. [1. dūéna; 2. djūénə]. Span. *dueña*, fr. Lat. *domina*, 'mistress'. See **dame.** **a** An elderly woman in charge of young girls in a Spanish family; hence, **b** a chaperon.

duet, n. [1. dūét; 2. djūét], fr. Ital. *duetto*, dimin. of *duo*, 'duet', fr. Lat. *duo*, 'two'. See **dual.** **a** A musical composition for two performers, vocal or instrumental; **b** (facetiously) a conversation in which only two people take part.

duettist, n. [1. dūétist; 2. djūétist]. Prec. & **-ist.** Performer in a duet.

duff (I.), n. [1. duf; 2. daf]. Dial. form of **dough**; cp. **enough.** (sailor's word) Boiled suet pudding; usually *plum-duff.*

duff (II.), vb. trans. Perh. a back formation fr. **duffer.** (slang) **a** To make old goods look like new, to fake; **b** to steal cattle and change the branding mark. (Not a common word.)

duffel, duffle, n. [1. dúfl; 2. dáfl], fr. the town Duffel, near Antwerp. **a** A thick, woollen frieze cloth with soft thick nap; **b** change of clothes; collectively, kit, for camping out.

duffel grey, adj. Of the colour of duffel.

duffer, n. [1. dúfer; 2. dáfə]. Origin doubtful. **1.** (obs. or archaic) **a** A pedlar, a seller of cheap rubbish; **b** one who fakes sham valuables, jewels, pictures &c. **2.** Something that is useless, worthless, and spurious. **3.** (most usual sense) **a** A thick-witted, slow, dull fool; one who is too stupid to understand or to learn; **b** a clumsy person, one unskilled at any game.

dug (I.), vb. [1. dug; 2. dag]. Pret. & P.P. of **dig.**

dug (II.), n. Cp. Swed. *dægga*, Dan. *dægge*, 'to suckle'. A teat of female mammals; no longer applied to human female breast.

dugong, n. [1. dúgong; 2. djúgɔŋ], fr. Malay word. Herbivorous aquatic mammal, about 8 to 12 ft. long; known also as the *sea-cow*; it resembles a miniature whale.

dug-out, n. [1. dúg out; 2. dág aut]. P.P. of **dig** & **out.** **1.** Canoe made from a hollowed-out tree-trunk. **2.** A rough cavity or hole, dug in a hill-side or in the ground, roofed with logs, turf &c., for shelter against bombs and gun-fire. **3.** (slang) A person who has retired from his profession, but whose services are utilized on emergency; applied during Great War to military and naval officers who were brought out of retirement and entrusted with military and naval duties.

duiker, n. [1. díker; 2. dáikə]. S. Afr. Du., lit. 'diver'. See **duck** (II.). A small S. African horned antelope, so called from its habit of diving into and disappearing in thick scrub or bush.

duke, n. [1. dūk; 2. djūk], fr. O. Fr. *duc*, fr. Lat. *duc-(em)*, acc. of *dux*, 'leader, chief, commander', wh. shows the reduced grade of the base of Lat. *dūcere*, 'to draw, carry along; lead'; O. Lat. *doucere*, fr. **douk-, *deuk-*; cp. the cogn. O.E. *-toga* (in *heretoga*, 'army-leader'), fr. Gmc. **tuga-*, weak grade of **teuχ-*, wh. is seen in O.E. *tēon* (fr. **teoh-an*), 'to pull, tug, draw'; cp. Goth. *tiuhan*, O.H.G. *ziohan*, Mod. Germ. *ziehen*, 'to draw', *Herzog*, 'duke'. Thus the Lat. n. & vb. are respectively the exact cognates of the O.E. words. **1.** (obs. or liter.) A military leader, captain, commander. **2.** (in Germany before the Great War) Also grand duke, *Grossherzog*, an independent sovereign prince, not entitled 'king', as: *Grand Duke of Baden* &c. **3.** (in other countries, including British Isles) **a** Highest hereditary rank in the peerage; **b** person holding that rank. **4.** (low slang) *The dukes*, fists.

dukedom, n. [1. dúkdum; 2. djúkdəm]. Prec. & **-dom.** **a** (Great Britain) The rank and status of a duke: **b** dominions of a duke who is a sovereign prince; a duchy.

Dukeries, n. pl. [1. dúkeriz; 2. djúkəriz]. See **duke** & **-ery.** Area in Nottinghamshire in which are several large estates owned by dukes.

Dukhobors. See **Doukhobors.**

dulcet, adj. [1. dúlset; 2. dálsit], fr. O. Fr. *doucet*, dimin. of *doux*, 'sweet', influenced by Ital. *dolcetto*, fr. Lat. *dulcis*, 'sweet'; fig. 'charming, pleasant', fr. **doluc-is*; cogn. w. Gk. *glukús*, 'sweet', wh. is for **dluk-us.* The base is perhaps imitative in origin & suggestive of the sound made in sucking honey fr. the comb. Cp. **glycerine.** **a** (esp. of sounds) Sweet, melodious, pleasing: '*dulcet symphonies and voices sweet*' (Milton, P.L. i. 712); **b** sweet to the taste: '*She tempers dulcet creams*' (ib. v. 347).

dulcification, n. [1. dùlsifikā́shun; 2. dàlsifikéiʃən]. See next word & **-fication.** The act of dulcifying; state or process of being dulcified.

dulcify, vb. trans. [1. dúlsifī; 2. dálsifai], fr. Lat. *dulcificāre*, 'to sweeten', fr. *dulc-(is)*, 'sweet'. See **dulcet** & **-fy.** (lit. and fig.) To sweeten, free from acidity &c.

dulcimer, n. [1. dúlsimer; 2. dálsimə], fr. O. Fr. *doulcimer*, fr. Ital. *dolcemele*, fr. Lat. *dulcis*, 'sweet' (see **dulcet**), & Gk. *mélos*, 'song, melody'; see **melody.** **a** An old musical instrument, consisting of metal strings stretched over a hollow sounding-board, played by being struck with leather-covered hammers; **b** the ancient Jewish dulcimer, a kind of harp.

Dulcinea, n. [1. dulsínea; 2. dalsíniə]. Name of Don Quixote's mistress. A lady-love, endowed by her admirer with every virtue and charm of mind and person.

dull (I.), adj. [1. dul; 2. dal]. O.E. **dyll* is not found, but cp. the near cogn. O.E. *dol*, 'foolish, dull-witted'; M.E. *dulle*, 'dull, stupid'; O.L.G. *dol*, O.H.G. *tol*, 'mad'; connected w. Goth. *dwals*, 'foolish'; O.H.G. *gitwelan*, 'to be perplexed'. This word seems to have had primarily a mental application, and the various other senses appear to have been developed from this, contrary to the usual process. See further under **dwell.** **1. a** (of the mind) Obtuse, slow at understanding, dense, stupid; **b** (of persons) possessing this kind of mind. **2.** Making no appeal to the imagination, incapable of arousing interest, lacking liveliness of thought or fancy; tedious: *a dull sermon, book* &c. Phr. *as dull as ditch-water*, very dull. **3. a** (of the senses) Slow in perception, blunted, not keen, incapable of receiving clear or vivid impressions: *dull sight, hearing, sense of touch*; **b** (of things affecting the senses) incapable of producing clear and vivid impressions; dim, indistinct, cloudy, vague, not intense: *a dull light, colour, sound, clang*; *a dull pain* &c. **4.** In various senses implying absence of some quality desired or expected: **a** lack of keenness, sharpness: *a dull razor, edge*; **b** lack of clearness, brightness: *dull weather*; *a dull day*; *a dull mirror*; **c** lack of briskness, activity: *trade is dull.*

dull (II.), vb. trans. & intrans., fr. prec. **A.** trans. **1. a** (of action on the mind) To render obtuse, to make slow at receiving impressions, to clog, stupefy: *an intelligence dulled by mechanical labours*; **b** (of effect on mental activities and emotions) to render less intense, reduce force of: *sorrow is dulled by the passage of time.* **2. a** (of action on the senses) To blunt, to render inapt at perceiving, to impair efficiency of: *to dull the sight by over-strain*; **b** (effect on sensations) to calm down, mitigate, soothe: *to dull pain by narcotics*; to blunt, diminish in intensity, impair: *pleasure is dulled by anxiety of mind.* **3.** (of effect on inanimate objects) **a** To lessen, remove, keenness, render inapt for cutting: *to dull a razor's edge*; Phr. *to dull the edge of appetite, pleasure* &c., to reduce, spoil; **b** to make cloudy, diminish brightness of: *to dull the surface of a mirror.* **B.** intrans. (rare) **a** To become dull; **b** to produce, cause, dulling effect.

dullard, n. [1. dúlard; 2. dáləd]. **dull** (I.) & **-ard.** A dull, heavy, slow-witted person.

dullish, adj. [1. dúlish; 2. dáliʃ]. **dull** (I.) & **-ish.** Inclined to be, rather, dull.

dullness, n. [1. dúlnes; 2. dálnis]. **dull** (I.) & **-ness.** The state of being dull (in all senses).

dully, adv. [1. dúlli; 2. dálli]. **dull** (I.) & **-ly.** In a dull manner.

dulse, n. [1. duls; 2. dals]. Gael. *duileasg.* An edible seaweed, brownish-red in colour, found on the coasts of Ireland and Scotland.

duly, adv. [1. dū́li; 2. djū́li]. **due** (I.) & **-ly.** In a fit and proper manner; at the proper time.

duma, n. [1. dōōma; 2. dū́mə]. Russ., 'thought, care; deliberative assembly, council'; cp. Russ. *dumaí*, 'believe, think'; Bulg. *duma*, 'word', *dúman*, 'I speak' &c.; the word is a Gmc. loan-word, fr. **dōm-*, 'judgement' &c. See **doom.** Under the old régime, the Russian parliament or national legislative assembly; abolished by the Bolshevists.

dumb (I.), adj. [1. dum; 2. dam]. O.E. & M.E. *dumb*, O. Fris. *dumb*, O.N. *dumbr*, Goth. *dumbs*, O.H.G. *tumb*, Mod. Germ. *dumm*, 'stupid'. Origin & further connexions very doubtful. **1.** (of human beings) **a** Permanently incapable of speech; unable to utter articulate sounds: *dumb from birth*; *a dumb man*; Phrs. *deaf and dumb*, unable to speak because absolutely deaf; *dumb animals*, the lower creation; **b** silent at a given moment, not actually speaking: *to remain dumb*; Phrs. *to be dumb concerning something*, not to reveal, keep secret; *to be (struck) dumb with horror, surprise* &c.; *dumb despair*, such that he who feels it is for the time incapable of vocal expression; **c** incapable of, slow at, ineffectual in, expressing ideas and emotions: *he's rather dumb in society*; Phrs. *a dumb dog*, a silent, taciturn fellow; *dumb show*, expressive action, unaccompanied by words. **2.** (of lower animals) Silent, not uttering their natural, characteristic cries. **3.** (of inanimate objects) **a** (of parts of musical instruments &c.) Not producing the required musical sound: *this piano has several dumb notes*; **b** (of inanimate nature, chiefly poet.) giving vent to no noise or sound: *the forests, woods, rivers, hills* &c. *were dumb.*

dumb (II.), vb. trans., fr. prec. (rare) To make dumb, silence.

dumb-barge, n. A heavy barge, without sails, depending on towing as means of movement.

dumb-bell, n., fr. their shape & the movements of person using them; the exercise with these, formerly called 'ringing the dumb bells'. (usually spoken of in pl.) *Pair of dumb-bells*, two round masses of iron of varying weight, connected by short thick bar which serves as a handle; held in the hand during performance of series of movements with the arms, to develop the muscles of arms and shoulders: *dumb-bell exercise.*

dumb crambo, n. Game of dumb show; see **crambo.**

dumbfound, vb. trans. [1. dumfóund; 2. damfáund]. Blending of **dumb** & **confound.** To astound, dismay, strike dumb with amazement.

dumbly, adv. [1. dúmli; 2. dámli]. **dumb** & **-ly.** Without speaking.

dumbness, n. [1. dúmnes; 2. dámnis]. **dumb** & **-ness.** The state of being dumb.

dumb piano, n. Set of keys resembling those of a pianoforte, which move on being struck by the fingers, but which are not connected with levers, hammers, wires &c., and which therefore produce no sound, used for exercising the fingers of a player without annoying others.

dumb-waiter, n. A kind of table, with round top and lower shelf, fixed to, and revolving on a pedestal, for holding dishes &c., in a dining-room; also a kind of round tray supported by and revolving on a low short base, placed in centre of dining-table, to enable persons on both sides of table to reach articles of food standing on it.

dumdum, n. [1. dúmdum; 2. dámdam], fr. Dumdum, near Calcutta. A bullet with a soft, or flat nose, which expands on impact.

dummy (I.), adj. [1. dúmi; 2. dámi]. See **dumb** & **-y.** Sham, counterfeit, used in pretence: *dummy cartridge*, empty one used for practice.

dummy (II.), n., fr. prec. **1.** A sham object representing, taking the place of, a real one; specif., a figure resembling the human form, clothed and exhibited: *tailor's dummy*; *barber's dummy*, one placed in shop-window to show off wigs &c.; *baby's dummy*, rubber teat used by ignorant mothers to keep baby quiet; a comforter. **2.** A person who appears for show, but takes no real part. **3. a** (whist) A fourth hand without a player, exposed on the table and played by partner. *Dummy whist, dummy*, whist played by three people and a dummy; *double dummy*, whist played by two people, with the two dummy hands exposed; **b** (bridge) one of the four hands, exposed on the table and played by the partner.

dump (I.), n. [1. dump; 2. damp]. Found later than, & perh. formed fr. **dumpy.** Something small, solid, and stumpy; a thick, solid, shapeless lump; specif. **a** an obsolete Australian coin; **b** a small leaden counter; **c** a quoit made of twisted rope.

dump (II.), vb. trans. & intrans.; cp. Dan. *dumpe*, Norw. *dumpa*, 'to fall down with a bump'; prob. imitative. **A.** trans. **1.** To set down abruptly, clumsily, and with a bump; esp. to empty or tilt out things of no value; specif., to deposit rubbish from a town. **2.** (commerc.) To place a quantity of goods at a low price upon the market; specif., to export goods to a foreign country and sell at a price below cost or below price of the home market, in order to undersell or to get rid of surplus goods without reducing price at home. **B.** intrans. To drop down abruptly and heavily.

dump (III.), n., fr. prec. **a** Place for depositing rubbish; **b** (mil.) large concentration of stores, from which supplies are drawn as required, esp. *ammunition dump.*

dumpiness, n. [1. dúmpines; 2. dámpinis]. **dumpy** & **-ness.** The state of being dumpy.

dumping, n. [1. dúmping; 2. dámpiŋ]. **dump** (II.) & **-ing.** The export of goods to foreign market below cost.

dumpling, n. [1. dúmpling; 2. dámpliŋ]. **dump** (I.) & **-ling.** **a** A small lump of suet and dough boiled in water, stock &c.; **b** apple enclosed in pastry and baked; *apple-dumpling.*

dumps, n. [1. dumps; 2. damps]. Cp. Mod. Germ. *dumpf*, 'hollow, gloomy, musty'; perh. connected w. **damp.** A state of depression, low spirits. Phrs. *in the dumps*; *doleful dumps.*

dumpy, adj. & n. [1. dúmpi; 2. dámpi]. Origin unknown; earlier than **dump** (I.). **1.** adj. Short and solid, stumpy, squat. **2.** n. One of a short-legged breed of hens.

dumpy-level, n. A spirit-level with a short (dumpy) telescope attached; used in land-surveying.

dun (I.), adj. & n. [1. dun; 2. dan]. O.E. *dunn*, 'dun, dark brown', M.E. *dunn, donn.* Perh. fr. Celt.; cp. Ir. *dunn*, Gael. *donn.* **1.** adj. Of a dull, greyish-brown colour. **2.** n. **a** This colour; **b** variety of artificial fly for fishing.

dun (II.), vb. trans. Perh. fr. M.E. *dunien*, 'to resound, clamour', dial. form for **din.** To demand of (person) with insistence the payment of a debt; to importune, clamour for payment from (person).

dun (III.), n., fr. prec. A creditor who constantly, clamorously, and insistently demands payment of a debt.

dun (IV.), n. Celt., 'hill'. See **down** (I.) & cp. **dune.** A hill, esp. one with a stronghold or fort upon it, common in Scottish and Irish place-names, as *Dundee, Dundalk* &c.

dun-bird, n. **dun** (I.) & **bird.** The pochard.

dunce, n. [1. duns; 2. dans]. Orig. *a Dunsman*, contemptuous term applied in 14th cent. by the followers of St. Thomas Aquinas to those of John Duns Scotus. A stupid, ignorant person, incapable of learning or understanding; a child who is notably backward in his studies. *Dunce's cap*, tall cone of paper worn in class, as a punishment, by stupid, idle children who refuse to learn their lessons.

dunderhead, n. [1. dúnderhĕd; 2. dándəhĕd]. Origin unknown. A stupid, wrong-headed person, a dunce, a blockhead.

dunderheaded, adj. [1. dúnderhĕded; 2. dándəhĕdid]. Prec. & **-ed.** Stupid, thick-headed.

dune, n. [1. dūn; 2. djūn], fr. Fr., fr. O.D. *dûna*, 'a hill'; Celt. loan-word; same as O.E. *dūn*. See **down (I.)** & **dun (IV.)**. Stretch or mound of sand, usually heaped up by wind, near seashore.

dung (I.), n. [1. dung; 2. daŋ]. O.E. & O. Fris. *dung*, M.E. *dunge*, *donge*; M. Du. *dunge*; Swed. *dynga*, 'muck', Dan. *dynge*, 'heap, mass', O.N. *dyngja*, 'a heap'; perh. connected w. **ding**. Cp. **dingy**. The excrement of animals, manure.

dung (II.), vb. intrans. & trans., fr. prec. **a** intrans. To drop excrement; **b** trans., to manure (ground), to put manure on.

dungaree, n. [1. dùnggaré; 2. dàŋgərí]. Hind. *dungrī*. Coarse, cotton fabric, used for sail-cloth, or for sailor's trousers or overalls.

dung-beetle, n. One of several kinds of beetle, whose larva develops in dung.

dung-cart, n. Cart used for carrying manure.

dungeon (I.), n. [1. dúnjun; 2. dándžən]. M.E. *donjon*, *dongeon*, fr. O. Fr. *donjon*, fr. Low Lat. *domniōn-(em)*, fr. Lat. *dominus*, 'lord'. See **dom** & cp. **dominion**. **1.** Usually *donjon*, q.v.: the strongest, central tower of a castle, the keep. **2.** A dark, damp underground vault in a castle, used as a prison.

dungeon (II.), vb. trans., fr. prec. (rare) To shut up in a dungeon.

dung-fork, n. A fork or prong used for throwing and spreading manure.

dunghill, n. [1. dúng-hill; 2. dáŋhil]. A heap of manure. *Dunghill cock*, a barndoor cock, not pure bred.

duniwassal, n. [1. dôoniwósl; 2. d(j)ûniwɔ́sl]. Gael. *duine*, 'man', & *vasal*, 'nobly born'. A Highland gentleman; one who, though not himself a chief, is sprung from same ancestor as the chief.

dunlin, n. [1. dúnlin; 2. dánlin]. See **dun (I.)** & **-ling**. (ornith.) Kind of sandpiper, reddish and white in the summer, dull grey and white in the winter.

dunnage, n. [1. dúnij; 2. dánidž]. Etymol. unknown. Pieces of wood, branches, or other material, placed among cargo to prevent shifting, or in the bottom of the hold, under cargo, to prevent injury from water.

dunnock, n. [1. dúnok; 2. dánək]. See **dun (I.)** & **-ock**. (provinc.) The hedge-sparrow.

duodecimal (I.), adj. [1. dûodésiml; 2. djûədésiml]. Lat. *duodecimus*, 'twelfth', & **-al**. See **duodecimo**. Of twelve; belonging to a system of reckoning by twelves, or twelfths: *duodecimal notation*.

duodecimal (II.), n., fr. prec. **a** A twelfth part; **b** (pl.) system of numbers whose denominations rise in scale of twelves instead of tens.

duodecimo, n. [1. dûodésimou; 2. djûədésimou]. Lat., abl. of *duodecimus*, 'twelfth', fr. *duo*, 'two' (see **dual**), & *decimus*, 'tenth' (see **decimal**). Cp. Gk. *dṓdeka*, *duṓdeka*; Scrt. *dvādaĉa*. **a** (abbr. 12*mo*.) Form of book for which the printer's sheet is folded into twelve, each page being about 4½ × 7½ inches; **b** book of this size.

duodenal, adj. [1. dûodḗnal; 2. djûədínl]. See next word & **-al**. Pertaining to, situated in, the duodenum: *duodenal ulcer*.

duodenary, adj. [1. dûodḗnari; 2. djûədínəri], fr. Lat. *duodēnārius*, 'containing twelve'; fr. *duodēni* (distrib. num.), 'twelve each', fr. *duo-*, **dec-sni*. See **duodecimo** & **-ary**, **denarius**. In twelves, increasing by twelves.

duodenitis, n. [1. dûodēnītis; 2. djûədīnáitis]. See next word & **-itis**. Inflammation of the duodenum.

duodenum, n. [1. dûodḗnum; 2. djûədínəm]. Med. Lat. See **duodenary**. (anat.) The upper part of the small intestine, opening directly from the stomach; so called from its length, of about 12 inches.

duologue, n. [1. dûolog; 2. djûəlɔg]. Formed fr. Gk. *duō*, 'two', on the anal. of **monologue**. See **dual** & **-logue**. A conversation between two people, esp. for dramatic representation.

duomo, n. [1. dwṓmō; 2. dwóumō]. Ital., = **dome**. A cathedral in Italy.

dupability, n. [1. dûpabíliti; 2. djûpəbíliti]. See next word & **-ity**. The quality of being dupable.

dupable, adj. [1. dûpabl; 2. djûpəbl]. See **dupe (II.)** & **-able**. Capable of being duped.

dupe (I.), n. [1. dūp; 2. djūp], fr. Fr. Etymol. unknown. One who is misled, imposed upon, cheated.

dupe (II.), vb. trans. See prec. To cheat, deceive, mislead, trick.

dupery, n. [1. dûperi; 2. djûpəri]. See prec. & **-ery**. The art or practice of deceiving.

duple, adj. [1. dûpl; 2. djûpl], fr. Lat. *duplus*, 'double, twofold'. See **double (I.)**. Double; (only in) **a** *duple ratio*, in which the first term is double the second; **b** (mus.) *duple time*, with two beats in a bar.

duplex, adj. [1. dûpleks; 2. djûplɛks]. Lat., 'twofold, double'; cp. Umbr. *tu-plak*, Gk. *diplax*, 'double'. The first element is fr. *duo*, 'two'; see **dual** &c.; the second is cogn. w. Lat. *plāga*, Gk. *plāgá*, 'blow, stroke', in sense of 'time' (see **plague**). It is not connected w. Lat. *plicāre*, 'to fold', & *plectere*, 'to twist, interweave' &c., the former of wh. does occur in Lat. *explicāre*, 'to unfold' &c., see **explicit**, & wh. lurks also in Lat. *duplus*, 'double', see **double**. Double, twofold; largely used in respect of the structure of parts of machines. *Duplex lamp*, one having a double burner and two wicks.

duplicate (I.), adj. [1. dûplikit; 2. djûplikit], fr. Lat. *duplicāt-(um)*, P.P. type of *duplicāre*, 'to double; to enlarge'; fr. *duplic-*, stem of **duplex**. **a** Double; **b** exactly resembling, or reproducing something else; being a duplicate of something; **c** (math.) *duplicate proportion*, that of one square to another.

duplicate (II.), n., fr. prec. An exact copy, or reproduction of something, identical with it in every detail.

duplicate (III.), vb. trans. [1. dûplikāt; 2. djûplikeit]. See **duplicate (I.)**. **a** To make double, twofold; increase by the same amount: *to duplicate expenses*; **b** to make an exact copy of, reproduce.

duplication, n. [1. dûplikáshun; 2. djûplikéiʃən]. Prec. & **-ation**. The act or process of duplicating; state of being duplicated.

duplicator, n. [1. dûplikātor; 2. djûplikeitə]. **duplicate (III.)** & **-or**. Machine for making copies of written or typewritten documents.

duplicity, n. [1. dūplísiti; 2. djūplísiti], fr. Fr., fr. Lat. *duplicitāt-(em)*, 'the state of being double', fr. *duplic-*, stem of **duplex**, & **-ity**. Double dealing, deception, bad faith.

durability, n. [1. dūrabíliti; 2. djōrəbíliti]. See next word & **-ity**. The quality of being durable.

durable, adj. [1. dúrabl; 2. djṓrəbl], fr. Lat. *dūrābilis*, 'lasting', fr. *dūrāre*, 'to harden, to last', fr. *dūrus*, 'hard', w. dissimilation fr. **drūros*, 'as hard as wood', fr. **dreuros* (cp. Gk. *drûs*, 'oak tree'), & Scrt. *dārunáś*, 'hard, rough'. The same base, w. different grade & other formative elements, occurs in O.E. *trum*, 'strong'; Lith. *drútas*, 'strong'. See further under **druid, dryad, tree, trim.** (of material and non-material things) Lasting, not perishable, able to resist wear and strain &c.: *a durable cloth, pair of boots*; *a durable friendship, peace* &c.

durableness, n. Prec. & **-ness**. Durability.

durably, adv. See prec. & **-ly**. In a durable manner.

duralumin, n. [1. dūrálūmin; 2. djurǽljumin]. Invented word from Lat. *dūrus*, 'hard', see **durable**, & **aluminium**. Trade name for a light and strong aluminium alloy with admixtures of copper, manganese, and magnesium; except that it cannot be cast, the alloy serves many purposes of steel where lightness is important.

dura mater, n. [1. dúra máter; 2. djúərə méitə]. Lat., lit. 'hard mother', see **durable** & **maternal**, as being supposed to be the 'mother' or source of other membranes. (anat.) The tough outer membrane which surrounds the brain and spinal cord.

duramen, n. [1. dúramen; 2. djúərəmɛn]. Lat., 'hardness; branch of a vine'. See **durable**. (bot.) The hard, tough heart of wood surrounded by the sap wood or alburnum.

durance, n. [1. dúrans; 2. djṓrəns], fr. Fr., fr. *durer*, 'to endure', fr. Lat. *dūrant-(em)*, Pres. Part. type of *dūrāre*, 'to harden; to last; to endure, be patient'. See **durable** & **-ance**. Confinement, imprisonment; esp. in Phrs. *in durance*; *in durance vile*.

duration, n. [1. dūráshun; 2. djōréiʃən], fr. L. Lat. *dūrātiōn-(em)*, fr. *dūrāt-(um)*, P.P. type of *dūrāre*, 'to harden; to last; to endure'. See **durable** & **-ation**. **a** Continuance in time; durability; **b** length of existence; period of time during which a thing lasts: *the duration of the war*; *of short duration*.

durbar, n. [1. dérbar; 2. dábā]. Hind. *darbar*, 'the court of a ruler'. State levee or reception of native princes in India held by the king as Emperor of India, or by the viceroy, as his deputy &c.

dure, vb. intrans. [1. dūr; 2. djō, djuə]. M.E. *dūren*, O. Fr. *durer*, 'to last', fr. Lat. *dūrāre*, 'to last'. See **durable.** (obs. or poet.) To continue, last, endure.

duress(e), n. [1. dūres, dūrés; 2. djṓrɛs, djōrés]. M.E. *duresse*, 'harm, hardship', fr. O. Fr. *duresce*, fr. Lat. *dūritia*, 'hardness; harshness, austerity; insensibility', fr. *dūrus*, 'hard'. See **durable** & **-ess**. **1.** Imprisonment, restraint of liberty. **2.** (esp. legal) Constraint, compulsion, by threats of personal violence &c.: *to do something under duress*.

durian, n. [1. dúrian; 2. djúəriən]. Malay word. Fruit of the *durio*, a tree growing in the E. Indian islands; the fruit is round or oval, has a prickly rind and a soft juicy pulp, which, in spite of its offensive smell, has an agreeable flavour.

during, prep. [1. dúring; 2. djṓriŋ]. Pres. Part. of **dure**, used in imitation of Lat. abl. absolute construction. **1.** Throughout the duration, continuance of; all through: *the sun gives light during the day*. **2.** In the course of, at some point of time within: *a shower of rain fell during the evening*.

durio, n. [1. dūriō; 2. djúəriou], fr. Malay *dūrī*, 'thorn'. Tree growing in the E. Indian islands, which bears the *durian*, q.v.

durmast, n. [1. dérmahst; 2. dámāst]. First element of unknown origin; the second is **mast (II.)**, 'fruit of beech and oak trees'. A variety of oak, with the acorns growing in clusters, producing a hard, valuable wood.

durra, dhurra, n. [1. dóora; 2. dúrə], fr. Arab. *durah*. A food plant, a kind of millet; known also as *Indian millet*.

durst, vb. [1. dërst; 2. dāst]. O.E., M.E. *dorste*. Pret. of **dare**.

dusk (I.), adj. [1. dusk; 2. dask]. O.E. *dosc*, *dox*, 'dark-coloured'; M.E. *dusk*, *dosk*; cp. O.N. *dusk*, 'mist'; Swed. *duska*, 'to be misty, drizzle', fr. Aryan base **dhus-ko-*, whence also Lat. *fuscus*, 'dark, misty; dull brown', for **dhusko-*, & *furvus*, 'dark brown, swarthy', for **dhus-wo-*. Further connexions are doubtful; that suggested w. O.E. *deorc*, '**dark**', offers difficulty. Shadowy, obscure, dim, inclined to darkness; now only poet. and replaced by *dusky*.

dusk (II.), n., fr. prec. The dim light just before darkness sets in; late twilight.

dusk (III.), vb. trans. & intrans., fr. **dusk (I.)**. (poet.) To make, become, shadowy or dusky.

duskily, adv. [1. dúskili; 2. dáskili]. **dusky** & **-ly**. Darkly, dimly, in a shadowy manner.

duskiness, n. [1. dúskines; 2. dáskinis]. **dusky** & **-ness**. The state of being dusky; specif. (of complexion) swarthiness.

duskish, adj. [1. dúskish; 2. dáskiʃ]. **dusk (I.)** & **-ish**. Fairly dusky.

dusky, adj. [1. dúski; 2. dáski]. **dusk (I.)** & **-y**. **a** Shady, shadowy, dim, dark: *a dusky thicket*; **b** dark in colour; specif. (of the complexion) swarthy; betraying **black blood**: *a dusky bride*, a black lady.

dust (I.), n. [1. dust; 2. dast]. O.E. *dūst*, M.E. *dust, doust*; cp. M. Du. *donst*, O.H.G. *tunst*, Mod. Germ. *dunst*, 'steam, vapour'; O.N. *dust*, 'dust'. The base orig. meant 'breath, vapour', then, 'dust as fine as vapour'. See further derivatives of this base under **fume, beast, & deer. 1. a** Minute dry particles of mineral, or other matter, deposited on the earth or other surface, or suspended in the air; Phrs. *to bite the dust*, to roll on the ground; be killed, wounded; *to lick the dust*, to grovel, show abject humiliation; *to throw dust in a person's eyes*, mislead; *to shake the dust off one's feet*, to depart in contempt and indignation; *in the dust*, humbled; **b** minute particles of gold washed out of auriferous deposit: *gold dust*; hence (slang) *dust*, money. **2.** A cloud of dust: *the dust raised by a motor* &c. (colloq.) Phr. *to make, raise, kick up, a dust*, to make a disturbance, commotion. **3.** (poet. and elevated style) The decayed and mouldered remains of the dead human body: *to be buried with the dust of one's ancestors*. Phr. *honoured dust*, remains of the dead.

dust (II.), vb. trans. & intrans., fr. prec. **A.** trans. **1.** To sprinkle, cover with, a fine layer of some powdery substance: *to dust a cake with sugar* &c. **2.** To remove dust from: *to dust furniture, a room* &c. Phr. *to dust a person's jacket for him*, give him a thrashing. **B.** intrans. **1.** To perform the task of removing dust from furniture, floor &c. **2.** (of birds) To take a dust-bath.

dust-bin, n. Receptacle for ashes and other household rubbish.

dust-brand, n. Disease attacking corn; smut.

dust-cart, n. A cart which goes from house to house in towns and removes rubbish from dust-bins.

dust-coat, n. A light overcoat worn to keep dust off the clothes, when travelling by road or rail.

dust-colour, n. A pale, dull brown.

duster, n. [1. dúster; 2. dástə]. **dust (II.) & -er. 1.** A person who dusts. **2.** A cloth for wiping and removing dust from furniture &c. **3.** Device for sprinkling sugar, pepper &c.

dustily, adv. [1. dústili; 2. dástili]. **dusty & -ly.** With dust, accompanied by dust.

dustiness, n. [1. dústines; 2. dástinis]. **dusty & -ness.** The state of being dusty.

dusting, vbl. n. [1. dústing; 2. dástiŋ]. **dust (I.) & -ing. 1. a** Act of removing dust, by wiping, from exposed surfaces in a room; **b** (slang) a thrashing. **2.** Antiseptic powder used for wounds.

dustless, adj. [1. dústles; 2. dástlis]. **dust (I.) & less.** Without dust.

dustman, n. [1. dústman; 2. dástmən]. **1.** One whose employment is to remove rubbish from dust-bins &c. **2.** Sleepiness; genius of sleep in mythology of the nursery; cp. *sand-man*.

dust-pan, n. Broad, half-covered shovel, into which dust is swept from the floor.

dust-proof, adj. Impervious to, excluding, protecting from, dust.

dust-shot, n. The smallest size of shot.

dusty, adj. [1. dústi; 2. dásti]. **dust (I.) & -y. 1.** Full of, coated, covered, with, dust. Phr. *not so dusty*, (colloq.) not so bad; fairly good. **2.** Resembling dust in texture, powdery, crumbly. **3.** Of the colour of dust.

dusty miller, n. **1.** The auricula. **2.** A kind of artificial fly for fishing.

Dutch, adj. & n. [1. duch; 2. datʃ]. M. Du. *dutsch*, 'Dutch, German', identical w. Goth. *þiodiskō*, adv., 'in heathen-wise'; O.E. *þēodisc*, 'Gentile'; O.S. *thiudisc*, O.H.G. *diutisk*, 'belonging to the people'; Mod. Germ. *deutsch*, 'German'. The first element is fr. Gmc. **þeud-*, 'people, nation'; the second is Gmc. *-isk-*, q.v. under **-ish.** The first element is Common Gmc.; O.E. *þēod*, O. Fris. *thiade*, O.S. *thioda*, O.H.G. *diota*, O.N. *þioð*. Outside Gmc. the base appears in Lith. *tauta*, 'country'; Oscan *touto*, 'community'; O. Ir. *tuath*, 'people'. See further under **Teuton.** The term was used formerly of Germany and the Germans quite as much as of Holland and its language and people; and it was customary to distinguish between High and Low Dutch, meaning what we call respectively German and Dutch. **1.** adj. Pertaining to Holland or its inhabitants; made in, invented in, Holland; characteristic of the Dutch. Phr. *Dutch courage*, see **courage. 2.** n. **a** The people of Holland: *the Dutch*; **b** the language of Holland. Phr. *double Dutch*, unintelligible language.

Dutch auction, n. One at which the auctioneer gradually reduces the price named, until he obtains a bid.

Dutch barn, n. A large, roofed shed, with open sides, for storing hay and straw.

Dutch cheese, n. Hard, round cheese made in Holland, usually coloured red outside.

Dutch clover, n. The white clover.

Dutchman, n. [1. dúchman; 2. dátʃmən]. A native of Holland. Phr. *Flying Dutchman*, **a** a spectral ship appearing, according to legends, near the Cape of Good Hope; **b** opera on this legend by Wagner (1843); **c** name given formerly to an express train on the Great Western Railway, running from Paddington to Cornwall.

Dutch oven, n. Device for roasting meat or game in front of the fire, consisting of a metal box with one open side within which the joint or bird is placed.

duteous, adj. [1. dūtyus; 2. djūtjəs]. See **duty & -ous.** (of person or conduct) Animated by a sense of duty, showing proper obedience or respect; dutiful.

duteously, adv. Prec. & **-ly.** In a duteous manner.

duteousness, n. See prec. & **-ness.** Quality of being duteous.

dutiable, adj. [1. dūtiabl; 2. djūtiəbl]. **duty & -able.** (of imported goods &c.) Liable to duty at the Custom House.

dutiful, adj. [1. dūtifool; 2. djūtifəl]. **duty & -ful.** Rendering, showing, proper respect, obedience, service.

dutifully, adv. Prec. & **-ly.** In a dutiful manner.

dutifulness, n. See prec. & **-ness.** The quality of being dutiful.

duty, n. [1. dūti; 2. djūti]. M.E. *dutē, deutē*, fr. O. Fr. *duetē*. See **due & -ty. 1. a** Obligation, task, line of action or conduct, imposed by law, custom, morality, and conscience: *one's duty to God, to one's country, to one's parents* &c.; *it is a good man's duty to serve his king*; *he only did his duty*; **b** specific expression of respect, homage &c., esp. in Phr. *present my humble duty to his Grace* &c. **2. a** Task, work, attached to a particular post or office and bound to be performed by the holder: *the duties of an Archbishop are no light ones*; *a butler's duties are often exacting*; *to be on, off, duty*; Phr. *to do duty for*, serve instead of; **b** specif., the task of taking services in church: *as the rector is away the vicar of the next parish will take the duty in our church next Sunday*. **3.** Payment which has to be made to the government on the importation, exportation, purchase &c. of certain goods, or on certain legal transactions, transfer of property &c.: *customs, excise, death duties* &c. **4.** (mechan.) Amount of work done by an engine &c. in proportion to amount of fuel consumed. **5.** Amount of water required to irrigate an acre of land, known as *the duty of water*.

duty-free, adj. (of goods) Not liable to customs duty.

duumvir, n. [1. dūúmver; 2. djūámvə]. Lat. *duumvir*, 'a member of a Roman court or council of two people', fr. Lat. *duo*, 'two', *vir*, 'a man'. See **dual, virile.** One of two officials holding office jointly.

duumvirate, n. [1. dūúmvirat; 2. djūámvirit]. Lat. *duumvirātus*, 'the office of a duumvir'. See prec. & **-ate.** An office held jointly by two persons; council of two.

dwale, n. [1. dwāl; 2. dweil]. Of Scand. origin. (chiefly Nthn.) The deadly nightshade.

dwarf (I.), n. [1. dworf; 2. dwɔ̄f]. O.E. *dweorg*, M.E. *dwergh, dwerf*; cp. O.N. *dvergr*, O.H.G. *twerg, zwerg*, Du. *dwerg*. Etymol. unknown. **1.** A person, animal, or plant, considerably below the usual size of the species. **2.** One of several varieties of small mythological beings; esp. one of the small metal-workers of Scandinavian mythology.

dwarf (II.), adj., fr. prec. Of less than the usual size; belonging to a small variety, esp. in names of plants: *dwarf beans, oak* &c.

dwarf (III.), vb. trans., fr. **dwarf (I.). 1.** To hinder the growth of, stop mental or physical development of. **2.** To cause to look small by comparison: *a tiny church still further dwarfed by the large surrounding elms*.

dwarfish, adj. [1. dwórfish; 2. dwɔ̄fiʃ]. **dwarf (I.) & -ish.** Like a dwarf, undersized, stunted; (of intellect) undeveloped.

dwarfishness, n. Prec. & **-ness.** Quality of being dwarfish.

dwell (I.), vb. intrans. [1. dwel; 2. dwɛl]. Scand. Cp. O.N. *dvelja*, 'to dwell, delay, tarry, abide'; the corresponding native word is O.E. *dwellan*, 'to lead astray, deceive'; also *dwelian*, 'to lead astray, lead into error and wrong-doing; deceive, thwart, afflict; to lose right direction, go astray, wander'; M.E. *dwellen*, 'to delay, dwell'. Other close cognates in O.E. are: *dwolian*, 'to stray, err'; (*ġe*)*dwola*, 'error, heresy', also 'deceiver, heretic'; *dwolung*, 'insanity'. So far as the earliest Engl. meaning is concerned it is clear fr. above that it was 'to wander, to err; to go astray, go out of one's way', & thence 'to go astray intellectually or morally'. Cp. also the related O.E. *dol*, 'foolish' (see **dull**). The other Gmc. languages, apart fr. the Scand., appear to attach closely allied meanings to this base: Goth. *dwals*, 'foolish', *dwaliþa*, 'folly'; O.S. *dwelan*, 'to err'; O.H.G. *twaljan*, 'hinder, delay'. This last sense is the connecting link between that of 'wandering' & 'dwelling'; 'to wander, having lost one's way; to linger, delay, in doubt which way to go', & finally, 'to remain where one is'. It is possible to reach a yet more primitive meaning fr. the Gk. cognates *tholós*, 'mud, dirt'; *tholerós*, 'muddy, troubled' (of water &c.); hence, 'disturbed in mind, mad, passionate'. The ideas of folly, error &c., so anciently & widely expressed by the base, may have come straight fr. a primitive sense 'obscure, dark, lacking clearness'; or they may be a secondary development fr. the sense 'wander; stray'. These last must have been orig. 'to go astray in the dark'. **1.** (followed by *at, in, on*) To live, reside, make one's home: *to dwell at home, abroad, in the country* &c.; *to dwell on the top of a hill*. In sense **1** the word is now largely replaced by *live, reside*. **2. a** (followed by *on, upon*) To linger upon in thought, allow the mind to fix on; to brood over, ponder: *to dwell on old wrongs*; *to allow the mind to dwell on the pleasures of the past*; **b** to linger over in speaking; pause to treat of, deal with: *the Prime Minister dwelt, in his speech, upon the state of India*; **c** to linger over, pause while performing an act: *don't dwell so much on your stroke* (in rowing &c.). **3.** (of a singer or speaker) *To dwell on a note, on a word*, to linger over, spin out; pause over.

dwell (II.), n., fr. prec. **a** Short regular cessation of the motion of a machine; **b** hesitation, slight pause, of a horse before taking a jump.

dweller, n. [1. dwéler; 2. dwélə]. **dwell (I.) & -er. 1.** Inhabitant, permanent resident: *dwellers in cities*; *town dwellers* &c. **2.** A horse that hesitates at a fence.

dwelling, n. [1. dwéling; 2. dwéliŋ]. **dwell (I.) & -ing.** Place of human habitation; abode, residence, house.

dwelling-house, n. A house for living in, as distinct from shop, public building, &c.

dwelling-place, n. Place of residence, abode.

dwindle, vb. intrans. [1. dwíndl; 2. dwíndl], fr. stem *dwin-* as in O.E. *-dwīnan*, M.E. *dwīnen*, 'to become smaller, waste away, fade', & **-le**; cp. also O.N. *dvīna*, M. Du. *dwīnen*, Dan. *tvine*, 'to pine away'. To grow smaller, shrink, diminish; to shrink and waste away from sickness or old age: *his great fortune dwindled rapidly; a dwindling reputation.*

dwindler, n. [1. dwíndler; 2. dwíndlə], fr. prec. & **-er.** A small, stunted, ill-nourished, ill-developed person or animal.

dwine, vb. intrans. [1. dwīn; 2. dwain]. See **dwindle.** (provinc. or archaic) To pine, fail in health and strength.

dyad, n. [1. díad; 2. dáiəd]. Fr. *dyade*, fr. Lat., fr. Gk. *duád-*, stem of *duás*, 'the number two', fr. *dúō*, 'two'. See **dual. 1.** Two units considered as one, a pair. **2.** (chem.) Radical, element with combining power of two atoms of hydrogen.

dyadic, adj. [1. diádik; 2. daiǽdik]. See prec. & **-ic.** Pertaining to a dyad.

Dyak, n. [1. díak; 2. dáiæk]. Malay, 'savage'. One of the aboriginal races of Borneo.

dyarchy. See **diarchy.**

dye (**I.**), n. [1. dī; 2. dai]. O.E. *dēag*, 'dye, colour'; M.E. *dīe*, *dēh*, *deih*. Origin uncertain. **a** Substance, colouring-matter, used for imparting colours to fabrics, &c.; **b** colour obtained by dyeing. Phr. *of the deepest dye*, of the most atrocious character.

dye (**II.**), vb. trans. & intrans., fr. O.E. *dēagian*, 'to dye', fr. *dēag*, 'dye'. See prec. **A.** trans. **1. a** To impart a colour to, esp. by immersion in liquid colouring-matter; to stain, tinge. Phr. *to dye in grain, in the wool*, while the material is in a raw state; **b** (poet.) of natural process, to give colour to: *the sunset dyed the mountain-tops a rosy pink; deep blushes dyed her cheek.* **B.** intrans. To take on colour from the process of dyeing: *this material will not dye well.*

dye-house, n. A building in which process of dyeing is carried on.

dyeing, n. [1. díing; 2. dái-iŋ]. **dye** (**II.**) & **-ing. a** The act or process of imparting colours to fabrics &c.; **b** this considered as a trade; the business of a dyer.

dyer, n. [1. díer; 2. dáiə]. **dye** (**II.**) & **-er.** One who makes a trade of dyeing fabrics.

dyer's broom, n. A plant yielding a yellow dye.

dyer's weed, n. A plant resembling mignonette, yielding a yellow dye.

dye-stuff, n. Substance used for dyeing.

dye-wood, n. Wood from which a dye is extracted.

dye-works, n. A building or group of buildings where the trade of dyeing is carried on.

dying, adj. [1. díing; 2. dáiiŋ]. Pres. Part of **die** (**II.**). **1. a** At point of death; in process of passing away, of coming to an end; in process of ruin or decay: *a dying man, horse; the dying year; a dying cause, State;* **b** associated with death, with the hour of death, &c.: *one's dying words, wish* &c.; Phr. *till one's dying day*, all the re t of one's life. **2.** Languishing: *she gave him such a dying look.* **3.** vbl. n. Act, process, of leaving this life; death: *Taylor's 'Holy Dying'.*

dyingness, n. Prec., **2**, & **-ness.** State of languor or languishing (Congreve).

dyke. See **dike.**

dyna-, pref., fr. Gk. *dúnamis*, 'power, authority' &c.; cp. Gk. *dunatós*, 'strong, able'; perh. cogn. w. Lat. *bonus*, 'good' (fr. **dwenos*), see **bounty**; possibly also w. O.E. &c. *tūn*, 'enclosure, strong place', see **town**; & Celt. *dun*, 'hill', see **down** (**I.**).

dynamic (**I.**), adj. [1. dīnámik; 2. dainǽmik]. Fr. *dynamique*, fr. Gk. *dúnamis*, 'power, strength; faculty, capability; authority'. See prec. & **-ic. 1.** adj. **a** Pertaining to force in motion; opposed to *static*; **b** (med.) functional; **c** pertaining to dynamics. **2. a** Producing physical energy, force, action; **b** possessing energy of character; forceful. **3.** (philos.) Pertaining to dynamism.

dynamic (**II.**), n., fr. prec. (rare) Motive power.

dynamical, adj. [1. dīnámikl; 2. dainǽmikl]. **dynamic** (**I.**) & **-al.** Pertaining to dynamics; of force in operation.

dynamically, adv. Prec. & **-ly.** In a dynamical manner.

dynamics, n., pl. used as sing. [1. dīnámiks; 2. dainǽmiks]. See **dynamic. a** That branch of physics which treats of matter in motion and of the energy causing motion; **b** the energy, force, or forces producing and regulating activity in any form.

dynamism, n. [1. dínamizm; 2. dáinəmizəm]. See **dyna-** & **-ism.** (philos.) School of thought which regards all the phenomena of the universe as resulting entirely from the action of natural forces.

dynamist, n. [1. dínamist; 2. dáinəmist]. Gk. *dúnamis*, 'power' &c. See **dyna-** & **-ist. 1.** A student of dynamics. **2.** An adherent of dynamism.

dynamite (**I.**), n. [1. dínamīt; 2. dáinəmait]. Gk. *dúnamis*, 'power' &c. See **dyna-** & **-ite.** A high explosive composed of nitroglycerine mixed with some absorbent such as porous silica.

dynamite (**II.**), vb. trans., fr. prec. To blow up, destroy, with dynamite.

dynamiter, n. [1. dínamīter; 2. dáinəmaitə]. Prec. & **-er.** One who uses dynamite, esp. for criminal, revolutionary, purposes.

dynamitic, adj. [1. dīnamítik; 2. dainəmítik]. See **dynamite** & **-ic.** Pertaining to dynamite, highly explosive.

dynamitism, n. [1. dínamītizm; 2. dáinəmaitizəm]. See **dynamite** & **-ism.** School of political philosophy which advocates use of dynamite to effect its ideals.

dynamo-, pref. Form fr. Gk. *dúnamis* used in modern compound words expressing ideas connected with electricity. See **dyna-.**

dynamo, n. [1. dínamō; 2. dáinəmou]. Machine which converts mechanical energy into electrical energy. For *dynamo-electric.*

dynamometer, n. [1. dìnamómeter; 2. dàinəmɔ́mitə]. See **dynamo-** & **-meter. 1.** A machine for measuring amount of force exerted (by an engine &c.). **2.** An instrument for measuring the magnifying power of a telescope.

dynast, n. [1. dínast, dínast; 2. dáinæst, dínæst], fr. Gk. *dunástēs*, 'a ruler'. See **dyna-.** Hereditary ruler, prince, member of a dynasty.

dynastic, adj. [1. dīnástik; 2. dainǽstik]. See prec. & **-ic.** Pertaining to a dynasty.

dynastically, adv. [1. dīnástikali; 2. dainǽstikəli]. Prec. & **-al** & **-ly.** In accordance with dynastic descent, principles &c.

dynasty, n. [1. dínasti, dínasti; 2. dáinəsti, dínəsti]. Fr. *dynastie*, fr. L. Lat. *dynastia*, fr. Gk. *dunasteía*, 'lordship, sovereignty'. Cp. **dynast** & **dyna-.** Succession of rulers belonging to same family.

dyne, n. [1. dīn; 2. dain]. Fr., fr. Gk. *dúnamis*, 'power' &c. See **dyna-.** (phys.) Unit of force which, acting on a mass of one gramme, gives it in one second an acceleration of one centimetre per second.

dys-, pref., fr. Gk. *dus-*, w. pejorative force, 'bad'; cp. Scrt. *duš*, Goth. *tuz-*, O.H.G. *zur-*, O.E. *tor-*; prob. cogn. w. Scrt. *dōsaš*, 'lack, want'. Found chiefly in Greek words or prefixed to words borrowed from Greek; giving a pejorative or negative sense.

dysenteric, adj. [1. dìsentérik; 2. dìsintérik]. See next word & **-ic.** Pertaining to, of the nature of, dysentery.

dysentery, n. [1. dísnteri; 2. dísntəri], fr. O. Fr. *dissenterie*, fr. Lat., fr. Gk. *dusentería*, 'dysentery'; **dys-** & Gk. *éntera*, 'intestines'. See **entero-.** Severe inflammation of the mucous membrane of the large intestine, associated with diarrhoea and passage of blood.

dyslogistic, adj. [1. dìslojístik; 2. dìslədžístik]. Formed w. pref. **dys-** on the anal. of **eulogistic.** Unfavourable; contrasted with *eulogistic.*

dyslogistically, adv. [1. dìslojístikali; 2. dìslədžístikəli]. Prec. & **-al** & **-ly.** In a dyslogistic sense.

dyspepsia, n. [1. dispépsia; 2. dispépsiə], fr. med. Gk. *duspepsia*, fr. **dys-** & *péssō*, *péptein*, 'ripen; cook; digest'. See **pepsin** & **cook.** Difficulty in digesting food, indigestion.

dyspeptic, adj. & n. [1. dispéptik; 2. dispéptik]. See prec. & **-ic. 1.** adj. **a** Pertaining to, suffering from, dyspepsia; **b** arising from dyspepsia; gloomy, morbid. **2.** n. A person suffering from dyspepsia.

dyspnoea, n. [1. dispnḗa; 2. dispníə], fr. Lat., fr. Gk. *dúspnoia*, 'difficulty in breathing', fr. *dúspnoos*, 'short of breath', fr. **dys-** & *pnoḗ*, 'breath'. See **pneuma.** Difficulty in breathing.

E

E, e, [1. ē; 2. ī]. The fifth letter of the Phoenician, Latin, Greek alphabets, hence also in English and other languages; for its use in abbrevations see end of Dictionary. (mus.) The third tone in the modal major scale, and fifth in minor scale.

e-, pref. Lat. **ex-** before certain consonants.

each, pron. & adj. [1. ēch; 2. ītʃ]. O.E. *ǣlc*, *ǣghwylc*, M.E. *euch*, *ech*. Two forms existed already in Gmc.: **ai-galīk-*, **ai-gahwalīk*; cp. O.H.G. *eogilīh*, *eogihwelih*. The pref. in both cases is Gmc. **aiw-*, 'ever, always' (see **aye**). For Gmc. **-galīk* see **like** (**I.**); for Gmc. **-ga-hwalīk* see under **which.** Every one of a group of two or more considered separately and regarded as individual members: *each of us, each and all, each other.*

eager, adj. [1. ḗger; 2. ígə]. M.E. *eger*, fr. O. Fr. *aigre*, fr. Lat. *ācrem*, nom. *ācer*, 'sharp, pointed; dazzling, piercing'; fig. 'acute, penetrating; ardent, zealous'. See **acerbity, acrid. 1.** Filled with earnest desire, keenly anxious to do something, impatient: *eager to begin, to be off* &c. **2.** (obs., of physical conditions) Sharp, cutting: '*A nipping and an eager air*' (Shakespeare).

eagerly, adv. Prec. & **-ly.** In an eager manner.

eagerness, n. See prec. & **-ness.** The quality or state of being eager; keenness, zest, zeal.

eagle, n. [1. ḗgl; 2. ígl]. M.E. *egle*, fr. O. Fr. *aigle*, fr. Lat. *aquila*, 'an eagle', hence 'the standard of a Roman legion'. The Lat. word refers to the dark colour of the bird, & is fr. Lat. *aquilus*, 'dark-coloured'. Probable cognates are Lett. *akls*, Lith. *ãklas*, 'blind'; cp. **aquiline. 1.** Large bird of prey, belonging to the falcon family, genus *Aquila*, with hooked beak, powerful wings, and keen sight, of which the *golden eagle*, the *bald-headed eagle* of N. America, the *sea-eagle* are the best known. **2.** A military standard of the Roman or French Empires bearing the figure of an eagle: *the eagles of Rome* &c. **3.** A gold coin of U.S.A., worth ten dollars. **4. a** Figure of an eagle displayed as an heraldic or national emblem, esp. the single-headed eagle of Imperial France, Germany, and the U.S.A., or the double-headed eagle of the former Austrian and Russian Empires; **b** name of two former Prussian Orders of Knighthood, the *Black* and *Red Eagle.*

eagle-eyed, adj. Having keen sight, like an eagle.

eagle-owl, n. The large horned European owl.

eaglet, n. [1. églet; 2. íglit]. **eagle** & **-et.** A young eagle.

eagre, n. [1. éger; 2. ígə]. Etymol. unknown. The sudden rise of the flood in a tidal river; a tidal wave associated specially with the estuaries of Severn and Humber; a bore.

eam, n. See **eme**

ean, vb. trans. [1. ēn; 2. in]. Variant of **yean.** (of sheep and goats) To bring forth young.

-ean, -aean, -ian, suff. forming adjs. & ns., denoting 'belonging to; like'; [íən] when stressed, [iən] unstressed. From stem *ai-*, *ei-* of Gk. adjs. & ns., *ae-*, *i* of Lat. adjs. & ns., & **-an**: *Pompeian, Tyrrhenean, Aegean.* Also fr. Engl. words ending in *-ey*: *Bodleian.*

eanling, n. [1. énling; 2. ínliŋ]. See **yeanling.** Young lamb or kid.

ear (I.), n. [1. ēr; 2. iə]. O.E. *ēare*, M.E. *ēre*; cp. O. Fris. *āre*, O.L.G. *ōra*, O.N. *eyra*, Goth. *ausō*, 'ear'. The base **áus-*, *ŏus-*, 'ear', appears in most of the Aryan languages; cp. Lat. *auris*, 'ear'; Gk. *oûs* (fr.**ous-os*), O. Slav. *uši* (dual), Ir. *ō*, 'ear'. The word is cogn. w. Lat. *audīre*, 'to hear; to learn, understand', for **aus-d-*. See **audible.** 1. a The organ of hearing, most often with special reference to its external portion, the outer ear. (fig.) *To bring (something) about one's ears*, bring crashing down, involve in ruin; *set by the ears*, set at variance, cause quarrel; *in at one ear and out at the other*, making no impression; *over head and ears*, deeply involved in; b sense of hearing, attention; Phrs. *to be all ears*, attend eagerly; *prick up one's ears*, take notice of; *have a person's ear*, have his favourable attention; *give ear to*, listen; *a word in one's ear*, private word, whisper; *send a person off with a flea in his ear*, compel to listen to unpleasant truths about himself; to rebuff; (fig.) *an ear for music*, aptitude for music; c power of distinguishing different musical or speech sounds; sense of tune: *to have a poor, good, ear, no ear.* 2. (not common) Any ear-shaped object, as the small projecting handle of a jug or pot.

ear (II.), vb. trans. O.E. *erian*, M.E. *ēren.* Cp. O. Fris. *era*, O.H.G. *erren*, O.N. *erja*, Goth. *arjan*, 'to plough'; cogn. w. Lat. *arāre*, Gk. *aróō*, 'plough, till'. See further under **arable.** (archaic or obs.) To plough the land.

ear (III.), n. O.E. *ēar*, M.E. *ēre*, *ear*, 'ear of corn'. Cp. O.H.G. *ehir*, *ahir*, Mod. Germ. *ähre*, M.L.G. *ār*, Goth. *ahs*, 'ear of corn'; cogn. w. Lat. *acus*, 'chaff, husk', as 'something sharp, pointed'; cp. Lat. *acus*, 'a needle', *ăcer*, 'sharp', q.v. under **acrid, acerbity.** Spiked cluster of seeds, or grain of any cereal plant: *ear of corn*; *ear of barley* &c.

ear-ache, n. Pain in the internal ear.

ear-drum, n. Sensitive vibrating membrane in inner ear which receives the impression of sounds; the tympanum.

eared, adj. [1. ērd; 2. iəd]. **ear** (I.) or (III.) & **-ed.** Having ears: a of men and animals; b of cups or other vessels; c of cereals.

earing, n. [1. éring; 2. íəriŋ]. **ear** (I.) & **-ing.** (naut.) A small rope by which the upper corner of a sail is bent or reefed.

earl, n. [1. ērl; 2. ǝ̄l]. O.E. *eorl*, M.E. *erl*; cp. O.L.G. *erl*, O.N. *jarl*; the orig. sense is prob. 'one who is quick, active, keen', & the word is in this case cogn. w. Lat. *orīri*, 'to rise', see **origin**, & w. O.E. *irnan* &c., 'to run', see **run.** a Rank or degree, in British Peerage below that of marquess; b title borne by holder of this rank; c person holding this rank. *Earl Marshal*, president of the College of Heralds, the officer of State who directs great ceremonials, as at a Coronation &c.; the office is hereditary in the family of Howard, Dukes of Norfolk.

earldom, n. [1. érldum; 2. ǝ́ldəm]. Prec. & **-dom.** 1. The dignity or rank of earl with rights and privileges attached thereto: *to confer an earldom on.* 2. (obs.) a A Jurisdiction of an earl; b territory over which this extends.

earless, adj. [1. érles; 2. íəlis]. Lacking ears: a of men and animals (fr. **ear** (I.) & **-less**); b of plants (fr. **ear** (III.) & **-less**).

earliness, n. [1. érlines; 2. ǝ́linis]. **early** (II.) & **-ness.** State, quality, of being early.

early (I.), adv. [1. érli; 2. ǝ́li]. O.E. *ǣrlīce*, M.E. *erliche*, *erli*; fr. O.E. *ǣr*, 'before, early', see **ere**, & **-ly.** 1. (in time) Near the beginning of a given period, soon: *early in the year*; *early in the day*, in good time; *early in life*, while still young. 2. a Near the beginning of a series of events or actions: *early in the proceedings*; b among the first in a series or succession of individuals: *the name Henry occurs early in the list of English kings since the Conquest.*

early (II.), adj., fr. prec. 1. Near to the beginning of a given period of time—day, season, year &c., *early breakfast, an early riser, early tomatoes.* Phrs. *the early bird*, one who arrives in good time; *one's early days*, youth; *it is early days yet* (*to make up one's mind* &c.), too soon. *Early English Style*, the first pointed Gothic style of English architecture. 2. In advance of usual or expected time: *an early season, spring* &c., something which shows its characteristic features before usual date; *an early maturity of mind*; *an early death*, occurring in youth or middle age.

earmark (I.), vb. trans. [1. érmark; 2. íəmāk]. 1. To put mark, usually a notch, in ears of sheep or other animals whereby owners may recognize them. 2. (fig.) To mark the pages of a book by turning down the corners. See **dog-ear.** 3. (fig.) To set aside, assign, money or other property for a specific use or purpose: *a large part of the benefaction is definitely earmarked for scientific research.*

earmark (II.), n. a A distinctive mark; b corner of page of a book which has been turned down, dog-ear.

earn, vb. trans. [1. ērn; 2. ǝ̄n]. O.E. *earnian*, M.E. *ernien*, *ernen*; cp. O.H.G. *arnēn*, 'to earn', fr. **aznōjan*; cogn. w. Goth. *as-ans*, 'time of harvest'; O.H.G. *arn*, 'harvest'; O.N. *ǫnn*, 'work in the fields'; O. Prussian *assanis*, 'harvest'. The orig. meaning seems to have been 'harvest', thence, 'proceeds of the harvest', thence, more widely, 'gains, earnings'. Cp. O.S. *asna*, 'toll, tribute'; O. Fris. *esna*, 'reward'. 1. a To gain (esp. money, wages &c.) by work: *to earn wages, one's livelihood* &c.; Phr. *to earn one's daily bread*; b to gain by merit; *to earn fame.* 2. Specif., to deserve what is earned: *he received many and rich rewards, but he had earned them.*

earnest (I.), adj. [1. érnest; 2. ǝ́nist]. O.E. *eornost*, M.E. *ernest.* Cp. O.H.G. *ernust*, Mod. Germ. *ernst*, 'serious'. See next word. 1. (of persons) a (i.) Having serious, solemn cast of mind; (ii.) steadfast, determined of purpose: *an earnest worker*; b specif., possessing sincere and deep religious convictions: *an earnest Christian.* 2. (of states and activities of mind) Serious, determined, strenuous, intense: *an earnest mind*; *an earnest endeavour, desire* &c.

earnest (II.), n. O.E. *eornost*, 'zeal, earnestness'; O.H.G. *ernust*, 'a struggle'; firmness in word and deed'; cp. Goth. *arni-ba*, 'firmly, securely', cogn. w. Scrt. *árna-*, 'raging, agitated', & Gk. *órnūmi*, 'rouse, stir up'. Chiefly in Phr. *in earnest*, which is found already in O.E. *on eornost*, serious, determined, sincere, not jesting: *I am perfectly in earnest in what I say*; *I can't believe it, you are surely not in earnest.*

earnest (III.), n. Unconnected w. prec. M.E. *ernest, ernes, erles, erres*, 'earnest-money'; fr. Lat. *arrha*, (*arrabo*), 'a pledge', through Gk. *arrabṓn*, fr. Heb. *ērābōn*, 'a pledge'. Pledge, token; specif., money paid as instalment in token of bargain made: *an earnest of more to come*; (also in full) *earnest money.*

earnestly, adv. **earnest** (I.) & **-ly.** In an earnest manner.

earnestness, n. See prec. & **-ness.** State, quality, of being earnest.

earning(s), n. pl. [1. érningz; 2. ǝ́niŋz]. O.E. *earnung*, 'merit'. See **earn** & **-ing.** What is earned, any payment received for work done or services rendered.

earring, ear-ring, n. [1. éring; 2. íəriŋ]. Metal ring worn in lobe of the ear, either plain or jewelled, or with jewelled pendant attached.

ear-shot, n. **ear** (I.) & **shot.** The distance within which a sound can be heard: *within, out of, ear-shot.*

earth (I.), n. [1. ērth; 2. ǝ̄þ]. O.E. *eorþe*, M.E. *erþe*; cp. O.H.G. *erda*, O.S. *ertha*, O. Fris. *erthe*, O.N. *iörþ.* Goth. *airþa*; Mod. Germ. *erde*, Du. *aard*; prob. cogn. w. Gk. *éraze*, 'to earth'. Other cognates outside Gmc. are uncertain. 1. a The world we live on regarded as a separate planet; the terrestrial globe: *the earth revolves on its axis*; Phr. *how on earth* &c., in what possible way; b the inhabitants of the globe: '*The whole earth was of one language*' (Genesis). 2. a The dry land of the planet as opposed to the sea: '*The waters covered the face of the earth*'; b the material globe as contrasted with Heaven: '*In six days the Lord made heaven and earth*'; Phr. *to move heaven and earth*, make great efforts; c surface of the globe; the ground, as opposed to the air or sky: *the airship crashed to the earth*; Phr. (fig.) *to come back to earth*, to come back to practical realities from a state of dreamy speculation. 3. a The actual material composing the surface of the globe; soil, mould: *to fill a pit with earth*; b (fig.) the lower, material part of human nature: *of the earth earthy.* 4. The hole or lair of a badger, fox &c. Phr. *to take earth, run, go, to earth*, of fox, to go into its hole; (fig.) *run to earth* (trans.), (i.) pursue, trace something to its source; (ii.) to discover as a result of search: *to run a person, a reference, to earth*; *to stop an earth*, to block it, after fox has left it, so that it cannot run to earth during the hunt. 5. (elect.) Communication with the earth as by an electric wire carrying current to the ground to complete a circuit. 6. (chem.) a (hist.) One of the elements of the ancient philosophers and alchemists: *earth, air, fire, water*; b in modern chemistry, term used of certain oxides, as *alkaline earths*, such as lime, an oxide of calcium; *metallic* or *rare earths*, metallic oxides, such as cerium, ytterbium &c., some of which yield radium.

earth (II.), vb. trans., fr. prec. 1. (gen. *earth up*) Cover with earth: *to earth up the roots of a tree when planting*; *to earth up potatoes, celery*, bring earth some way up the stem of the growing plants. 2. (special use) To put electric wire into earth to complete circuit.

earth-board, n. That part of a plough which turns over the earth, the mould-board.

earth-born, adj. a Born, sprung, from the earth, or soil; autochthonous; b (mythol.) emerging at birth from the ground, of certain deities &c.; c human, mortal; concerned with earthly things.

earth-closet, n. A privy, in which dry earth is used to cover and deodorize the contents.

earthen, adj. [1. érthen; 2. ǝ́þən]. **earth** (I.) & **-en.** Cp. O.E. *ierðen*, *erðen* &c., 'of earth'. Made of earth or of baked clay.

earthenware, n. [1. érthenwār; 2. ǝ́þənwɛə]. Prec. & **-ware.** Utensils made of baked clay.

earthiness, n. [1. érthines; 2. ǝ́þinis]. **earthy** & **-ness.** State of being earthy.

earth-light. See **earth-shine.**

earthliness, n. [1. érthlines; 2. ǝ́þlinis]. See next word & **-ness.** State of being earthly.

earthly, adj. [1. érthli; 2. ǝ́þli]. **earth** (I.) & **-ly.** Belonging to the earth; esp. contrasted with *heavenly* or *spiritual*: *earthly joys are transitory*; (colloq. Phrs.) *no earthly use*, no use at all; (vulg. slang) *not an earthly*, not an (earthly) chance.

earth-nut, n. The edible, rather sweet tuber-like root of an umbelliferous plant, resembling a chestnut, also called pig-nut, ground-nut &c.

earth pillar, n. (geol.) A pillar or column of soft rock, clay &c., capped with a hard rock, left isolated by the wearing down by weather of the surrounding softer earth and rocks.

earthquake, n. [1. érthkwāk; 2. ʌ́þkweik]. **1.** A tremor or convulsion of the surface of the earth due to volcanic activity, faults in the earth's crust &c. **2.** (fig.) Any great social or political upheaval, disaster, or disturbance.

earth-shine, -light, n. Illumination of the moon by reflected light from the earth, seen just before or after the new moon.

earthward(s), adv. [1. érthwardz; 2. ʌ́þwədz]. Towards the earth.

earthwork, n. [1. érthwĕrk; 2. ʌ́þwʌk]. Rampart, fortification made by throwing up a bank of earth, leaving a ditch in front and trench behind it.

earthworm, n. [1. érthwĕrm; 2. ʌ́þwʌm]. Segmented worm living in the soil, with round body and tapering ends and moving by numerous bristles attached to the segments; the commonest is *Lumbricus terrestris.*

earthy, adj. [1. érthi; 2. ʌ́þi]. **earth (I.)** & **-y.** **a** Consisting of or resembling earth: *an earthy consistency*; **b** gross, connected with lower nature of man; (contrasted with *spiritual*): *of the earth earthy.*

ear-trumpet, n. Funnel-shaped instrument, the thin end of which is placed in the ear, while being held so that the broad end collects the utterance of speakers, to assist deaf persons to hear more readily.

ear-wax, n. Wax secreted by the glands of the ear; cerumen.

earwig, n. [1. érwig; 2. íəwig]. O.E. *ēar-wicga*, 'earwig', fr. O.E. *ēare*, 'ear', & *wicga*, 'an insect, beetle', fr. **weg-ja*; cp. O.E. *wegan*, 'to move, carry'. See **way, vehicle.** Small dark-coloured wriggling insect, of the family *Forficulidae*, once popularly supposed to creep into the brain through the ear.

ease (I.), n. [1. ēz; 2. īz]. M.E. *ese*, fr. O. Fr. *aise*; prob. fr. O. Fr. *aisance*, 'surroundings of a house', fr. Lat. *adjacentia.* See **adjacent.** **1.** (of physical states) **a** Comfort, freedom from constraint: *to take one's ease*; **b** relief from pain: '*For so to interpose a little ease*' (Milton); specif. **c** room, space, absence of tightness (in fit of clothes, boots &c.): *more ease across the chest*; (mil.) *stand at ease*, stand with legs apart and muscles relaxed in restful attitude—opposite of *at attention.* **2.** (of mental states) **a** Freedom from worry, trouble of mind, or anxiety: *be at ease*; **b** freedom from constraint of manner, from embarrassment, or awkwardness; well-bred elegance of manner: *to be at ease in society.* **3.** (of worldly circumstances) Financial well-being, wealth, affluence, freedom from penury: *live at ease.* **4.** Absence of physical or intellectual difficulty, arising either from ability and skill of the performer, or from the simplicity of the task: *to learn with ease*; *to walk twenty miles with ease*; *the ease with which the engine was started, or with which he started the engine, was remarkable.*

ease (II.), vb. trans., fr. prec. **1 a** To make looser, less tightly fitting: *to ease a coat under the arms*; *to ease a boot at the toe* &c.; **b** to loosen a door, drawer &c., which jams, make less tight, remove pressure from. **2. a** To mitigate, relieve (bodily pain), or (person) from this: *to ease the pain of a wound* &c.; **b** to give consolation; to relieve (mental pain, anxiety of mind); or (person) from these: *to ease one's anxiety*; *ease one's mind. Ease down*, trans. and intrans., to slacken, relax, lessen, speed, strain, effort. *Ease off*, **1.** intrans., **a** to draw away, withdraw, move away slightly; **b** to relax effort, strain. **2.** trans. To pull away gradually, to push off (a boat) from the shore, &c.

easeful, adj. [1. ézfool; 2. ízful]. **ease (I.)** & **-ful.** Providing, promoting, ease; characterized by ease.

easel, n. [1. ézl; 2. ízl], fr. Du. *ezel*, 'ass; easel'. Cp. similar use of *horse.* See **ass.** Upright framework, usually of wood, used to support picture during process of painting, or to display it when painted; *easel picture*, one of moderate size, suitable for display on an easel.

easeless, adj. [1. ézles; 2. ízlis]. **ease (I.)** & **-less.** **a** Devoid of ease; **b** incapable of being eased.

easement, n. [1. ézment; 2. ízmənt]. O. Fr. *aisement.* See **ease (I.)** & **-ment.** **1.** (archaic) That which affords relief from suffering. **2.** (law) Right acquired by grant or prescription by a landowner over another's land, *e.g.* light, support, right of way &c.

easily, adv. [1. ézili; 2. ízili]. **easy** & **-ly.** **a** Without difficulty or inconvenience; **b** smoothly: *the engine was running easily.*

easiness, n. [1. ézines; 2. ízinis]. **easy** & **-ness.** **1.** The quality of being accomplished with ease: *the easiness of a task.* **2.** Freedom, unembarrassment, ease, of manner.

east (I.), n. [1. ēst; 2. īst]. O.E. *ēast*, M.E. *east, est.* Cp. O. Fris. *āst*, M. Du. *oost*, Mod. Germ. *osten*; O.N. *aust-*; fr. Gmc. **austr(a)-*, 'eastwards', fr. **ausr-*, cogn. w. Lat. *aurōra* (fr. **ausōs-*), 'dawn, daybreak', hence, 'the East'; Gk. *héōs, ēṓs* (fr. **ausōs*), Scrt. *ušā́s*, 'dawn'; Lith. *auszrà*, 'dawn'. Cp. also Lat. *auster*, 'south wind', q.v. under **austral**, & cp. **aurora.** **1. a** That quarter of the sky in which the sun first rises; **b** one of the four cardinal points of the compass, 90 degrees to the right of North; **c** the east end of a church: *to turn to the east at the Creed.* **2.** Specif. (cap.) the countries which lie in the eastern part of the globe, the orient; *the Near East*, Turkey, Balkans &c.; *Far East*, China, Japan &c.; *Middle East*, Persia, Mesopotamia &c.

east (II.), adj., fr. prec. **1.** Lying in the direction of the rising of the sun, situated in the east; coming from the east: *east wind.* **2.** (of church) Toward that part of the chancel in which the altar stands, whether the church is correctly orientated or not: *the east end of a church.*

east (III.), adv., fr. **east (I.).** In easterly direction, towards the east: *to go east.*

East End, n. The poorer districts of London lying to the east; contrasted with *West End.*

East-Ender, n. [1. ēst énder; 2. īst éndə]. Inhabitant of the East End of London; one of the masses.

Easter, n. [1. éster; 2. ístə]. O.E. *Easter, Eastron* (pl.), M.E. *ester, estern*; prob. fr. *Eastre, Eostre*, name of goddess of light and spring. Connected w. Lat. **aurora,** 'dawn' &c., & **east.** Festival of the Christian Church, commemorating the Resurrection of Christ, held on the first Sunday after calendar full moon on or after March 21st. Also attrib.: *Easter Day*, Easter Sunday, the first day of Easter week; *Easter egg*, natural or artificial egg, often dyed in bright colours, given and exchanged at Easter time; *Easter-tide*, season of Easter, Easter week; *Easter week*, that commencing with Easter Sunday.

easterly, adj. [1. ésterli; 2. ístəli]. Next word & **-ly.** In, or coming from, direction of the east: *easterly gales.*

eastern, adj. & n. [1. éstern; 2. ístən]. O.E. *ēasterne*, M.E. *esterne.* **east** & adj. suff. *-ern.* **1.** adj. **a** Looking toward the east: *eastern window*; **b** connected with the east portion of the world: *the Eastern Church*, the Orthodox, Greek Church; *the Eastern Question*, political problem of eastern European countries, esp. of Turkey, in relation to Russia; expression has different significance since the political convulsions in both empires. **2.** n. Member of one of the Oriental races: *an Eastern.*

easternmost, adj. superl. [1. ésternmōst; 2. ístənmoust]. Prec. & **-most.** In most easterly quarter or direction.

easting, n. [1. ésting; 2. ístiŋ]. **east** & **-ing.** (naut.) **a** Distance covered or gained by sailing in an easterly direction; **b** easterly course or direction.

eastward, adv. & adj. [1. éstward; 2. ístwəd]. **east** & **-ward.** Towards the east.

easy (I.), adj. [1. ézi; 2. ízi], fr. O. Fr. *aisié*, Fr. *aisé*, P.P. of *aisier*, 'to ease', fr. *aise*, q.v. under **ease (I.).** **1. a** Simple, not difficult to do, capable of being accomplished with ease: *an easy task*; **b** not difficult to understand, or to learn: *an easy problem, an easy language.* **2.** (of physical conditions) **a** Characterized by, promoting, comfort, freedom from restraint; (of clothes &c.) loose-fitting, comfortable: *an easy coat*; **b** free from pain, comfortable: *to feel easier since taking one's medicine.* **3.** Specific uses: **a** (in commerc. jargon) *an easy market*, one in which there is little demand; *rubber, oils, are easy*, not sought after; **b** (in card games) *honours (are) easy*, evenly divided between both parties. **4.** (of worldly circumstances) Wealthy, affluent, not straitened: *in easy circumstances.* **5. a** (of mental states) Tranquil, calm, free from anxiety: *an easy mind*; *to feel easy about the future*; **b** (of moral states) not strict, over tolerant, pliant: *easy in one's morals*; *of easy virtue.* **6.** Unembarrassed, not stiff or awkward; frank, affable: *easy manners*; *easy to get on with*; *very easy in conversation.* Phr. *free and easy*, unrestrained in manners, casual.

easy (II.), adv., fr. prec. Often used for ***easily*** in colloquial speech; various Phrs.: *to go easy*, not to exert oneself; *I can do it easy*; *to take it, things, easy*, not to exert oneself unduly; (mil.) *to stand easy*, to stand with more freedom of movement than when 'at ease'.

easy (III.), n., fr. **easy (I.).** (colloq.) Brief period of cessation from strenuous physical or intellectual work; so also as command: *easy all!*, stop rowing.

easy-chair, n. Comfortable lounge chair, arm-chair.

easy-going, adj. Inclined to take things easily; not strenuous, severe, or censorious; placable; casual, careless.

eat (I.), vb. trans. & intrans. [1. ēt; 2. īt]. O.E. *etan*, M.E. *ēten*; cp. O.H.G. *ezzan*, O. Fris. *ita*, O.L.G. *etan*, O.N. *eta*, Goth. *itan*, 'to eat'. The word is found in this sense in most Aryan languages: Lat. *edere*, Gk. *édō*, Scrt. *ádmi*, Lith. *ēdu.* **A.** trans. To receive into the system as food through the mouth: *to eat a good breakfast, six eggs at a sitting* &c. Phrs. *to eat one's words*, take a statement back, recant; *to eat one's heart out*, brood over misfortune; *to eat its head off*, used of a horse which costs more to feed than it is worth, or than is proportionate to the work it does; *to eat one's terms or dinners*, qualify for the bar by eating the compulsory number of dinners in an Inn of Court; *good to eat*, wholesome, pleasant, as food. **B.** intrans. **1.** To partake of food: *to do nothing but eat and sleep*; *to be too ill to eat.* Phr. *to eat well*, have a good appetite. **2.** (of food, vulg. colloq. use) To have a (good or bad) taste when eaten: *this venison has hung a month, it ought to eat well.* **C.** Followed by prepositions or adverb. *Eat away*, trans., to gnaw into, consume gradually, as by eating: *the face of the corpse was eaten away by rats*; *frost and weather had eaten away the mortar* &c. *Eat in*, intrans., to penetrate by chemical action, to bite in. *Eat into*, intrans., **a** to penetrate by chemical action; **b** to consume, waste portion of, by extravagance: *he had seriously eaten into his fortune by careless habits. Eat up*, trans., to devour, consume completely: *to eat up one's dinner.* Phr. *eaten up with pride*, consumed with, overpowered by, pride.

eat (II.), vb. [1. et; 2. ɛt]. O.E. *ǣt*; M.E. *ēt, ett.* Pret. of prec. Cp. **ate.**

eatable, adj. [1. établ; 2. ítəbl]. **eat (I.)** & **-able.** In a fit condition, of a suitable character, to be eaten; pleasant, or tolerable, to eat: *this egg is barely eatable.*

eatables, n. [1. établz; 2. ítəblz], fr. prec. (coll. pl.) Food, things to eat.

eater, n. [1. éter; 2. ítə]. **eat (I.)** & **-er.** One who eats.

eating (I.), vbl. n. [1. éting; 2. ítiŋ]. **eat (I.)** & **-ing.** **a** The act of partaking of food: *fond of, given up to, eating and drinking*; **b** that which is, or can be, eaten; food: *quails are excellent eating.*

eating (II.), adj., fr. Pres. Part. of **eat (I.)**. Gnawing, corroding: *an eating sorrow at the heart.*

eating-house, n. Shop where food is sold ready cooked for consumption and served on the premises; restaurant.

Eau de Cologne, n. [1. ó de kolón; 2. óu də kəlóun]. Fr., fr. Lat. *aqua*, 'water', q.v. under **aquatic**, & Pl.-N. Strong scent in spirituous form, manufactured at Cologne in Germany.

eau de vie, n. [1. ò de vé; 2. òu də ví]. Fr., lit. 'water of life'. Name given to any strong spirit. See prec. & **vital.** Brandy.

eaves, n. pl. [1. ēvz; 2. īvz]. O.E. *yfese, efese* sing., M.E. *evese*, 'edge, border, eaves'. Cp. M.L.G. *ovese*, O. Fris. *ose*; prob. cogn. w. O.E. *ufan*, 'above', *ofer*, 'over'. See **over, above.** The edge of a roof which projects beyond the walls of the building. Now felt, and used, as a plural noun, though historically a singular.

eavesdrop, vb. intrans. [1. évzdrop; 2. ívzdrɔp]. To listen surreptitiously to private conversation, not intended for one to hear, in the hope of learning secrets; originally to stand under the eaves of a house near to the windows to listen to what is said within.

eavesdropper, n. [1. évzdroper; 2. ívzdrɔpə]. Prec. & **-er.** One who listens secretly, and dishonourably, to private conversation.

eavesdropping, n. [1. évzdroping; 2. ívzdrɔpiŋ]. See prec. & **-ing.** The act of deliberately listening to private conversation.

ebb (I.), vb. intrans. [1. eb; 2. ɛb]. O.E. *ebbian*, M.E. *ebben*, fr. O.E. *ebba*, 'ebb'. See next word. **a** (of the tide in sea or river) To flow back, retreat; **b** (fig., of blood, life, spirits, courage, light &c.) to ooze out, decline, grow faint: *daylight was ebbing fast*; often *to ebb away*: *his life was rapidly ebbing away.*

ebb (II.), n. O.E. *ebba*; cp. O. Fris. *ebbe*, 'ebb'. Etymol. doubtful. **a** The retreat, going down, or out, of the tide; contrasted with *flood*; **b** (fig.) decline (of life &c.).

ebb-tide, n. Retreating tide.

Eblis, n. [1. éblis; 2. éblis], fr. Arab. *Iblis.* The prince of the fallen angels, Satan.

ebon, adj. [1. ébun; 2. ébən]. M.E. *eban*, fr. Lat. *(h)ebenus*, fr. Gk. *ébenos*, an Egyptian loan-word. (poet.) **a** Made of ebony; **b** resembling ebony in colour, perfectly black: *ebon locks.*

ebonite, n. [1. ébunīt; 2. ébənait]. **ebony** & **-ite.** Hard, dark-coloured substance composed of rubber combined with sulphur by heat, commonly used for electrical insulation purposes. Also called *vulcanite.*

ebonize, vb. trans. [1. ébunīz; 2. ébənaiz]. See next word & **-ize.** To stain and polish light-coloured wood, to make it resemble ebony.

ebony (I.), n. [1. ébuni; 2. ébəni], fr. Lat. *(h)ebeninus*, 'of ebony', fr. *(h)ebenus*, 'ebony'. See **ebon.** **a** Heavy, hard, durable wood yielded by certain tropical trees, dark in colour, taking a fine polish and becoming jet black when treated; **b** this as symbolical of blackness.

ebony (II.), adj. **a** Like ebony, made of ebony: *an ebony wand*; **b** black as ebony.

ebriety, n. [1. ēbríeti; 2. ībráiiti], fr. Fr. *ébriété*, fr. Lat. *ēbrietāt-(em)*, 'drunkenness', fr. *ēbrius*, 'intoxicated'. See next word & **-ty.** State of intoxication, drunkenness.

ebrious, adj. [1. ébrius; 2. íbriəs], fr. Lat. *ēbrius*, 'intoxicated', fr. **e-**, 'out', used as intens.; the second element is obscure. Cp. **sober.** (rare) **a** Inclined to excessive drinking; **b** intoxicated.

ebullience, -cy, n. [1. ēbúliens(i); 2. ībáliəns(i)]. See next word & **-ence, -ency.** State of being ebullient; spontaneous overflow of high spirits.

ebullient, adj. [1. ēbúlient; 2. ībáliənt], fr. Lat. *ēbullient-(em)*, Pres. Part. type of *ēbullīre*, 'to boil, bubble up; to make a boisterous appearance', fr. **e-** & *bullīre*, 'to bubble, boil'; fig. 'to boil with rage', q.v. under **boil.** Bubbling over with high spirits; full of life and vigour; exuberant.

ebullition, n. [1. èbūlíshun; 2. èbjulíʃən], fr. Lat. *ēbullītiōn-(em)*, 'a bubbling up', fr. *ēbullīt-(um)*, P.P. type of *ēbullīre*, 'to boil or bubble up' (lit. and fig.). See **ebullient** & **-ion.** **a** Act of boiling up; **b** (fig.) sudden outburst of some emotion: *ebullition of rage* &c.

eburnine, adj. [1. éburnīn; 2. ébənain]. Formed w. suff. **-ine**, fr. Lat. *eburn-(us)*, 'of ivory', fr. *ebur*, 'ivory'; perh. borrowed fr. Egyptian *āb, ābu*, 'elephant; ivory'. Made of, or resembling, ivory.

ec-, pref., fr. Gk. *ek-*, see **ex- (II.)**.

ecarté, n. [1. ākártā; 2. eikátei]. Fr., P.P. of *écarter*, 'to discard', fr. **e-** & *carte*, 'a card', q.v. under **card (II.)**. French card-game for two persons played with thirty-two cards, down to the sevens, having as its characteristic feature the discarding of certain cards in play, the king being the highest card.

ecbolic, adj. [1. ekbólik; 2. ɛkbólik], fr. Gk. *ekbolé*, 'a throwing out, abortion', fr. *ek-*, see **ex-**, & *bállein*, 'to throw', see **ballistic.** (med., of drugs) Causing abortion, abortifacient.

ecce homo, n. [1. èkse hṓmō; 2. èksi hóumou]. Lat., 'behold the man'. See John xix. 5. A picture, sculpture, of Christ crowned with thorns.

eccentric (I.), adj. [1. ekséntrik; 2. iksɛ́ntrik], fr. L. Lat. *eccentricus*, fr. Gk. *ékkentros*, 'out of the centre, eccentric', fr. *ek-*, 'out of', see **ex-**, & *kéntron*, 'centre'. See **centre.** **1. a** (of circles) Not described from the same centre, not concentric; **b** (astron.) (i.) of orbit of planets, not circular; (ii.) of planet, moving in an eccentric orbit. **2.** (fig.) **a** Not conforming to the ordinary rules of action and conduct; out of the ordinary; odd, original, unconventional, whimsical; **b** (of persons) so odd, and different from others, as to be considered strange in the head; slightly crazy.

eccentric (II.), n., fr. prec. **1.** An eccentric person; an odd, quaint, unconventional fellow. **2.** A mechanical device for taking a back and forward motion from the revolving, driving shaft of an engine.

eccentrically, adv. [1. ekséntrikali; 2. iksɛ́ntrikəli]. **eccentric (I.)** & **-al** & **-ly.** In an eccentric manner.

eccentricity, n. [1. èksentrísiti; 2. èksentrísiti]. **eccentric** & **-ity.** State of being eccentric. **1.** (in physical senses) Deviation from the centre; specif., distance of the centre of the orbit of a planet from the centre of the body round which it revolves. **2.** (of persons &c.) Oddity, deviation from ordinary or normal conduct: *eccentricity in dress, appearance, manner* &c.; *we must overlook these little eccentricities.*

ecchymosis, n. [1. èkimṓsis; 2. èkimóusis], fr. Gk. *ekkhúmōsis*, 'extravasation, bruise', fr. *ekkhumoûsthai*, 'to pour out, extravasate', fr. *ek-*, see **ex-**, & *khéein*, 'to pour,' see **chyle.** (med.) A severe bruise, with black-and-blue discolouration of the skin.

ecclesia, n. [1. eklḗzia; 2. iklíziə]. Gk. *ekklēsia*, 'an assembly of citizens, legislative assembly'; in Late Gk., 'the church', fr. *ekkaléō*, 'call out, summon forth; to elicit, provoke', fr. *ek-*, 'out' (see **ex-**), & *kaléō*, 'I call, summon', q.v. under **calends.** **1.** Assembly of citizens for political purposes, in ancient Greek states. (later) **2.** A church; **a** the body of members; **b** the building.

ecclesiast, n. [1. eklḗziast; 2. iklíziæst], fr. Gk. *ekklēsiastḗs*, 'a member of the ecclesia', fr. prec. **1.** (rare) A priest. **2.** Member of an ecclesia.

ecclesiastic, n. & adj. [1. eklēziástik; 2. iklīziǽstik]. Prec. & **-ic.** **a** n. One in Holy Orders in the Christian Church; **b** adj., ecclesiastical.

ecclesiastical, adj. [1. iklèziástikl; 2. iklīziǽstikl]. Prec. & **-al.** Pertaining to the Christian Church, its organization, authority, and character; contrasted with *secular*: *ecclesiastical history, ceremonies, tradition* &c. *Ecclesiastical Court*, one having jurisdiction in purely ecclesiastical matters.

ecclesiastically, adv. Prec. & **-ly.** In an ecclesiastical manner.

ecclesiasticism, n. [1. eklèziástisizm; 2. iklīziǽstisizəm]. **ecclesiastic** & **-ism.** **a** The principles, customs, observances of the Christian Church; **b** exaggerated attachment to the external and formal side of ecclesiastical observances and discipline.

ecclesiological, adj. [1. eklèziolójikl; 2. iklīziəlɔ́džikl]. See **ecclesiology** & **-ical.** Of, pertaining to, ecclesiology.

ecclesiologist, n. [1. eklèziólojist; 2. iklīziɔ́lədžist]. See next word & **-ist.** Student of ecclesiology.

ecclesiology, n. [1. eklèzióloji; 2. iklīziɔ́lədži]. **ecclesia** & **-ology.** The science and study **a** of the history, nature, and constitution of the Church; **b** of the building and decoration of churches.

ecdysis, n. [1. ékdisis; 2. ékdisis], fr. Gk. *ékdusis*, 'a putting off, getting out of, shedding', fr. *ekdúein*, 'to put off, shed', fr. *ek-*, 'out' (see **ex-**), & *dúein*, 'to sink, plunge, into; to penetrate'. Perh. cogn. w. Scrt. *dōsaš*, 'night, darkness'. (zool.) The shedding, sloughing of skin by snakes, shells by crustaceans &c., at certain periods.

echelon, n. & vb. trans. [1. éshelon; 2. éʃəlɔ̃, éʃəlɔn]. Fr., fr. *échelle*, 'ladder', fr. Lat. *scāla*, 'a flight of steps, a ladder'. See **scale (V.)**. **1.** n. Arrangement of troops drawn up in step-like formation, consisting of a series of parallel bodies, no two of which are in the same line, and the front of each body being clear of those in advance: *to move forward in (en) echelon*; also used of similar formation of ships or position of fortification, gun emplacements &c. **2.** vb. To move, place (troops &c.), in echelon.

echidna, n. [1. ekídna; 2. ikídnə], fr. Gk. *ékhidna*, 'a viper', fr. an adj. *ekhidn-os*, fr. *ékhis*, 'a viper'; cogn. w. O.H.G. *egala*, Norw. *igle*, 'leech'; Aryan base **eghi-*. An Australian ant-eating, egg-laying mammal, somewhat resembling a hedgehog, having spines as well as hair upon its skin and snout-like toothless jaws; also called porcupine ant-eater. It forms with the duck-billed platypus the group of animals known as Monotremata.

echinate, adj. [1. ékināt; 2. ékineit]. See **echinus** & **-ate.** Set with bristles or prickles.

echinite, n. [1. ékinīt; 2. ékinait]. See **echinus** & **-ite.** A fossil echinus or sea-urchin.

echino-, pref., fr. **echinus**, used in forming compounds, signifying 'prickly, spiny' &c.

echinocactus, n. [1. ekínōkǽktus; 2. ikáinoukǽktəs]. Prec. & **cactus.** (bot.) A genus of S. American flowering cacti, cylindrical in shape with ridged divisions and covered with spines.

echinoderm, n. [1. ekínodĕrm; 2. ikáinədām]. See **echino-** & **derm.** (zool.) A member of the class *Echinodermata*, which includes the star-fishes, sea-urchins &c.

echinus, n., pl. **echini** [1. ekínus, -ī; 2. ikáinəs, -ai]. Lat., fr. Gk. *ekhînos*, 'hedgehog, sea-urchin'; cogn. w. O.H.G. *igel*, O. Slav. *ježĭ*, Lith. *ežỹs*, 'hedgehog'; Aryan base **eg hi-*. **a** (zool.) The sea-urchin; esp. the typical genus of sea-urchins; **b** (archit.) rounded moulding in the capital of a Doric and Ionic column.

echo (I.), n. [1. ékō; 2. ékou]. Lat. *ēchō*, fr. Gk. *ēkhṓ*, 'a sound, noise; echo'; cp. Gk. *ēkhḗ*, 'noise', *ēkhéō*, 'resound'. Cognates in other languages are doubtful. **1.** (cap.) In Greek mythology the nymph who personified the echo and whose voice this was supposed to reflect. **2. a** The repetition of a sound, reflected back when the sound-waves strike appropriately situated opposing surfaces; **b** an effect obtained in poetry by the repetition of the vowel of the last syllable of one line near the beginning of the next line; verse-echo. **3.** (fig.) **a** Repetition of the opinions, imitation of the expressions, of another person: *the diction of Wordsworth's early poems is an echo of Pope*; **b** person who slavishly copies another or repeats his words, opinions &c.

echo (II.), vb. trans. & intrans., fr. prec. **A.** trans. **a** (of reflecting surfaces) To repeat sounds: *the valleys echo the voices of the birds*; **b** to repeat the opinions of another: *he echoes his wife in everything.* **B.** intrans. **a** To resound with an echo, to reverberate: *he made the valleys echo as he sang*; **b** *echo through*, to ring out, fill with sound: *his voice echoed through the hall.*

echoic, adj. [1. ekóik; 2. ikóuik]. **echo (I.)** & **-ic.** Of the nature of, resembling, an echo; hence (philol.) imitative, onomatopoeic.

echoism, n. [1. ékōizm; 2. ékouizəm]. See prec. & **-ism.** The imitation of sounds, onomatopoeia.

éclair, n. [1. āklár; 2. eiklέə]. Fr. A small thin, long cake filled with cream flavoured with chocolate &c. and covered with icing.

eclampsia, n. [1. eklámpsia; 2. iklǽmpsiə]. New Lat. fr. Late Gk. *éklampsis*, 'a shining forth, brightness', fr. *eklámpein*, 'to shine forth', fr. *ek-*, see **ex-**, & *lámpein*, 'to shine'. See **lamp.** (med.) **a** A form of epileptic fit or premonitory fit, marked by visual hallucinations of flashes of light; specif. **b** a convulsive attack or series of fits, due to poisoning of the system, occurring during pregnancy or after childbirth.

éclat, n. [1. ākláh; 2. eklá]. Fr., 'noise, clap', fr. *éclater*, 'to burst, burst out'; of Gmc. origin, cp. Ital. *schiattare*, 'to burst', fr. a Gmc. **s(k)lait-*, 'split, burst, slit' &c., cp. O.S. *slītan*, O.E. *slītan*, Pret. *slāt* (fr. **slait*). See **slit.** Distinction, signal success or brilliance; applause: *he came out of the affair with éclat.*

eclectic, adj. & n. [1. ekléktik; 2. ikléktik], fr. Gk. *eklektikós*, 'picking out, selecting; eclectic', fr. *ek-*, see **ex-**, & *lekt-*, stem of *légein*, 'to pick out, choose, gather, to count, reckon; to enumerate'. Cogn. w. Lat. *legere*, 'to pick up, gather'; to choose, collect; read', see **lecture, legend. 1.** adj. **a** Belonging to ancient school of philosophers who selected the doctrines that suited them from various systems; **b** given to selecting, picking, and choosing, in matters of thought and taste, from various sources; not following exclusively a single school or authority. **2.** n. **a** One who belonged to the school of eclectic philosophers; **b** one who follows eclectic methods in thought and art.

eclectically, adv. [1. ekléktikali; 2. ikléktikəli]. Prec. & **-al** & **-ly.** In an eclectic manner.

eclecticism, n. [1. ekléktisizm; 2. ikléktisizəm]. **eclectic** & **-ism.** System, methods, of an eclectic.

eclipse (I.), n. [1. eklíps; 2. iklíps], fr. O. Fr., fr. Lat., fr. Gk. *ékleipsis*, 'abandonment, forsaking; eclipse; failure, cessation', fr. *ekleípein*, 'to leave out, pass over; to forsake; to cease; to be eclipsed', fr. *ek-*, see **ex-**, & *leípein*, 'to leave, to depart', q.v. under **relinquish. 1.** Total or partial obscuration of the light **a** of the sun, through the passing of the moon between it and the earth; **b** of the moon by the earth's shadow; **c** of a satellite by its primary's shadow. **2.** (fig.) Extinction, obscurement of the mind, reputation &c.: *his fame has suffered an eclipse.*

eclipse (II.), vb. trans., fr. prec. **1.** (of planets) To obscure the light of (another planet) by eclipse. **2.** (fig.) To deprive of splendour, pre-eminence; throw into shade, outvie, surpass: *the queen's beauty appeared to eclipse that of every other lady present.*

ecliptic, adj. & n. [1. eklíptik; 2. iklíptik], fr. Gk. *ekleiptikós*, see **eclipse**, which takes place on the line of an ecliptic. **1.** adj. Pertaining to an ecliptic or an eclipse. **2.** n. **a** The apparent orbit or great circle travelled by the sun from west to east through the heavens in the course of a year; **b** an apparent great circle on the globe corresponding to the sun's ecliptic.

eclogue, n. [1. éklog; 2. éklɔg], fr. Lat. *ecloga*, fr. Gk. *eklogḗ*, 'choice, selection; an extract from a book', fr. *eklégein*, 'to pick out, select', fr. *ek-*, 'out' (see **ex-**), & *légein*, 'to choose; collect; count, enumerate'. See **lecture, legend.** Short poem of a pastoral character, the model of which was given by Virgil's *Eclogues.*

ecology. See **oecology.**

economic, adj. [1. ēkonómik; 2. īkənɔ́mik]. **economy** & **-ic. 1.** Pertaining to the management of a household or estate. **2.** Pertaining to the management of the affairs of a community or state with reference to its sources of supply, and to its expenditure. **3.** Pertaining to the satisfaction of man's material needs, and to the practical application of science to this end: *economic botany, entomology* &c. **4.** (popular) Economical.

economical, adj. [1. ēkonómikl; 2. īkənɔ́mikl]. Prec. & **-al. a** (of persons) Careful and watchful of expenditure, tending to husband resources; thrifty; reverse of *extravagant*; also *economical of one's time*, not wasting it; **b** extended to material appliances, tending to save material resources: *an economical stove, engine* &c., consuming small quantity of fuel in proportion to work done; **c** (of methods &c.) promoting economy, preventing waste.

economically, adv. [1. ēkonómikali; 2. īkənɔ́mikəli]. Prec. & **-ly. a** In an economical, thrifty manner; **b** from an economic standpoint.

economics, n. [1. ēkonómiks; 2. īkənɔ́miks]. See **economic.** The science and study of the general principles which govern the production and distribution of wealth; also *political economy.*

economize, vb. intrans. [1. ēkónomīz; 2. īkɔ́nəmaiz]. **economy** & **-ize.** To manage resources well, avoid unprofitable expenditure; reduce expenditure, practise frugality.

economy, n. [1. ēkónomi; 2. īkɔ́nəmi], fr. Lat. *oeconomia*, fr. Gk. *oikonomía*, 'the management of a household; administration; thrift', fr. *oikonóm-(os)*, 'one who manages a household, a steward, housekeeper', fr. *oîkos*, 'house, dwelling, place to live in; household affairs; house-property'; for **woikos*, cogn. w. Lat. *vīcus*, 'village, hamlet, district', see **vicinage**; also w. Scrt. *vēśáś*, 'house', & *viś-*, 'habitation', cp. further Goth. *weihs*, 'village'; O.E. *wīc*, 'dwelling, village', see **wick (II.)**; the second element is *nomos*, 'managing', fr. *némein*, 'to deal out, dispense; to hold sway, manage; to inhabit; to graze, pasture'. See **nomad. 1.** The principles of the management of a household: *domestic economy.* **2. a** Judicious management of wealth in any form; esp. practice of thrift, frugality; avoidance of extravagance; **b** careful husbanding of time, labour &c., wise expenditure of these; **c** *political economy*, economics. **3.** (theol.) **a** Dispensation: *the Mosaic economy*; **b** specif., *economy of truth*, such doctrinal interpretation as is befitting or suitable for the individual learner; hence, by transference, frugality, sparing use of truth.

ecru, adj. [1. ākrōō; 2. eikrû]. Fr. *écru*, 'unbleached', **ex-** & Lat. *crūd-(um)*, 'raw'. See **crude.** The light brown colour or finish of unbleached linen.

ecstasy, n. [1. ékstasi; 2. ékstəsi]. O. Fr. *extasie*, fr. L. Lat. *ecstasis*, fr. Gk. *ékstasis*, 'removal from the proper place; distraction of mind; astonishment; trance', fr. *ek-*, 'from, out of' (see **ex-**), & *stásis*, 'a standing still; position; state, condition', fr. Aryan **sthə-ti-s*, whence Gmc. **stadi-*; O.E. *stede*, 'place' (see **stead**). The Aryan base is **sthā-*, **sthə-*, 'to stand'. See **stand (I.)**, **state (I.). a** State of extreme emotional exaltation; rapture; **b** strong feeling, esp. but not necessarily, pleasurable: *an ecstasy of delight, of grief*; Phr. *in ecstasies over something*, highly delighted, enthusiastic in praise of.

ecstatic, adj. [1. ekstátik; 2. ikstǽtik], fr. Gk. *ekstatikós*, 'unstable, out of one's senses', fr. *ékstasis*, 'removal from position; distraction, ecstasy'. See **ecstasy** & **-ic.** Of the nature of ecstasy; causing ecstasy.

ecstatically, adv. [1. ekstátikali; 2. ikstǽtikəli]. Prec. & **-al** & **-ly.** In an ecstatic, enraptured manner.

ecto-, pref., fr. Gk. *ektós*, 'outside'. See **ex-.** First element in many compound words made, and chiefly used, by biologists.

ectoblast, n. [1. éktōblahst; 2. éktoublāst]. Prec. & Gk. *blástos*, 'a sprout'. Etymol. uncertain. See **blastoderm.** (biol.) Outer membrane of a cell.

ectoderm, n. [1. éktōdĕrm; 2. éktoudʌm]. **ecto-** & **-derm.** (biol.) Outer membrane investing a cell.

ectoplasm, n. [1. éktōplazm; 2. éktouplæzəm]. **ecto-** & **plasm.** (biol.) **a** External layer of protoplasm in a cell; **b** a spiritualistic term for the supposed emanation of a psychic body from that of a medium.

écu, n. [1. ákū; 2. eky]. Fr., fr. O. Fr. *escu*, fr. Lat. *scūtum*, 'shield'. See **scutum.** An old French silver coin of the 17th and 18th cents., equivalent to about five francs.

ecumenic(al), **oecumenical**, adj. [1. ēkūménik(l); 2. īkjuménik(l)]. The O.E.D. adopts, & editors recommend, the latter spelling, wh. indeed follows the L. Lat. usage of *oe* for Gk. *oi*, though in Engl. the spelling *e-* appears to be more usual in this word. L. Lat. *oecūmenicus*, fr. Gk. *oikoumenikós*, 'universal', fr. *oikouménē gē*, 'the inhabited world'. First element is Gk. *oîkos*, 'house, dwelling', fr. **woik-*, cogn. w. Lat. *vīcus*, 'district, quarter, hamlet'. See **economy** & **vicinage.** General, universal; specif., embracing or representative of the whole Early Christian Church (now applied only to Roman Catholic Church): *an ecumenical council.*

eczema, n. [1. ékzima; 2. ékzimə], fr. Gk. *ékzema*, fr. *ek-*, 'out of' (see **ex-**), & *zéma*, 'that which is boiled', fr. *zéō*, 'boil'; cogn. w. Scrt. *yásati*, 'to boil', O.H.G. *iesan*, 'to ferment'. Another grade of the Aryan base **jes-*, **jos-*, 'to bubble up'; hence 'to boil' appears in Gk. *zóē*, 'foam'. See **yeast.** Inflammatory disease of the skin of various kinds.

eczematous, adj. [1. ekzḗmatus; 2. ɛkzímətəs]. Gr. *ekzémat-*. See prec. & Lat. suff. *-ōsus*, see **-ous.** Arising from, having character of, eczema.

-ed. P.P. suff. of weak vbs. O.E. *-ed, -ad, -od.* Used also to form adjs. fr. ns., *e.g. armoured*, 'covered, provided, with armour'.

edacious, adj. [1. ēdáshus; 2. īdéiʃəs], fr. Lat. *edāc-(em)*, *edax*, 'voracious; devouring, destroying', fr. Lat. *ed-(ere)*, 'to eat' (see under **eat**), & adj. suff. *-ac-* & **-ous. a** Pertaining to eating; voracious, devouring; **b** (fig.) consuming, tending to swallow up: *edacious time.*

Edam, n. [1. ḗdam; 2. ī́dæm]. Name of village in Holland. Also *Edam cheese*, a round rich Dutch cheese, of yellow colour, usually with a rind dyed dark red.

Edda, n. [1. éda; 2. édə]. O.N. The meaning & history of the word are quite clear. The nearest cognates in O.N. are *ōdr*, 'mad, frantic', & *ōðr*, 'spirit, mind', & further in sense of 'song, poetry'. *Edda* is fr. Prim. Norse **ōð-iþu*, whence w. *i*-mutation, *ēdda.* The Gmc. base is **wōþ-* wh. expresses the ideas of 'exaltation of spirits' on the one hand, & 'poetry, song' &c. on the other; O.N. loses initial *w-* before rounded vowel, *ō*, *ū* &c. Cp. Goth. *wōþs*, 'mad, possessed'; O.E. *wōþ*, 'sound, clamour, melody, song'; & further *wōd*, 'mad, frenzied', whence M.E.

wōde, 'mad, frantic', so common in Chaucer; O.H.G. *wuot*, 'madness', Mod. Germ. *wuth*, 'fury', *wüthen*, 'to be enraged'. Outside Gmc. we have Lat. *vātēs*, 'soothsayer, prophet', also 'bard, poet'. This is said to be borrowed fr. Celt., cp. O. Ir. *fāith*, 'poet', & W. *gwaird*, 'poem'. The same base occurs in Scrt. *api-vátati*, 'understands'. The word was originally applied only to the book written by Snorri Sturlason (c. 1241), containing mythological lore, and the rules of verse-making; the term was later extended to ancient artificial poetry generally.

eddy (**I.**), n. [1. édi; 2. édi]. M.E. *ydy*, fr. O.N. *iða*, 'whirlpool'. **a** Small circling wavelet, or series of these; miniature whirlpool in surface of water; **b** current of air, dust, mist &c. moving in a kind of spiral.

eddy (**II.**), vb. intrans., fr. prec. To move like an eddy, to move round in small circles; **a** of water, air, mist &c.; **b** (by extension) of bodies of people, to wander, drift about in circles.

edelweiss, n. [1. ádlvīs; 2. éidlvais]. Germ. *edel*, 'noble', & *weiss*, 'white'. Small Alpine rock plant growing only at the higher altitudes, bearing white, woolly, star-shaped flowers.

edema. See **oedema.**

Eden, n. [1. édn; 2. ídn]. Heb., 'delight'. **a** The garden in which Adam and Eve were placed at their creation; **b** (rare) any specially delightful place, or state of special happiness.

edentate, adj. [1. ēdéntāt; 2. īdénteit], fr. Lat. *ēdentāt-(us)*, 'toothless, with the teeth knocked out', fr. **e-** & *dent-*, stem of *dens*, 'tooth' (see **denti-**), & **-ate.** **a** Lacking teeth, toothless; **b** (specif., zool.) of, belonging to, the lowest order, *Edentata*, of placental mammals, without incisors and canine teeth, including the armadillo, sloth, ant-eater &c.

edge (**I.**), n. [1. ej; 2. edž]. O.E. *ecǵ*, M.E. *egge*. Cp. O. Fris. *eg*, O.L.G. *eggia*, O.H.G. *ekka*, O.N. *egg*, 'edge, point', *eggja*, 'to provoke', see **egg** (**II.**). Cogn. w. Lat. *aciēs*, 'sharp edge, point; keenness' (lit. and fig.); 'battle-array of an army'. Aryan base **ăk-*, **ŏk-*, 'sharp'. Cp. Lat. *ācer*, 'sharp'; Gk. *ákaina*, 'point, needle', *ákros*, 'sharp'. See further under **acrid, acute.** **1.** Sharp, narrow side or border of anything; **a** specif. (of a cutting instrument, sword, knife &c.) *a sharp, keen edge*; *to put an edge on, take the edge off, a knife*; *inside, outside edge*, (of a skate) of movement on either of these edges; Phrs. *to give the edge of one's tongue to*, speak sharply to, scold; *give an edge to, take edge off, one's appetite*, to stimulate or deaden the freshness of appetite; *take the edge off an argument*, deprive it of force; *set one's nerves on edge*, irritate, exasperate; *set the teeth on edge*, give physical sensation of discomfort, as by a shrill scraping sound; **b** projecting ledge, top, or side, of other objects: *edge of a roof, of a mountain*; *an edge of rock*; *the sharp edge of a table* &c. **2.** Boundary, extreme border, that part of surface of anything which is furthest from the centre; the part near to this border: *edge of a wood*, either the part just inside or that just outside; *edge of a lake*, either the water near shore, or part of shore near the water; *edge of a table*; *to sit on the edge of a chair*, on extreme outer portion of seat near the front legs; *edge of a page*, either, the blank margin of unprinted paper beyond the line of print, or, the outer section in thickness of paper: *gilt edges, uncut edges* &c.; *on the edge of a precipice*, on the brink.

edge (**II.**), vb. trans., fr. prec. **A.** trans. **1.** **a** To give cutting edge to, to sharpen; **b** to furnish with border: *to edge a path with box*; *hills edge the plain*; **c** to impart a clean edge to, trim, clip: *to edge the border of a lawn.* **2.** To form a border or edge, act as edging; to pass, run, along edge or border: *a road edged with grass*; *a river bank edged with flowers.* **B.** Followed by preposition or adverb. *Edge away*, sidle away, move away obliquely and cautiously. *Edge into*, **a** trans., to introduce cautiously or with difficulty, insinuate: *to edge oneself into the conversation*; **b** intrans., to advance, move, gradually and indirectly. *Edge off*, sidle away. *Edge out*, to move out gradually and cautiously.

edge-bone, corrupt. of **aitch-bone.**

edge(d)-tool, n. [1. èj(d) tōōl; 2. èdž(d) tûl]. One having a cutting edge. Phr. *to play with edge(d) tools*, to engage in a course of action, unthinkingly or carelessly, which may prove dangerous, or have unpleasant consequences.

edgeways, adv. [1. éjwāz; 2. édžweiz]. **edge** (**I.**) & **-ways.** By the edge; sideways; with edge outwards. Phr. *not to be able to get a word in edgeways*, be prevented from speaking by the volubility of others.

edgewise, adv. [1. éjwīz; 2. édžwaiz]. **edge** (**I.**) & **-wise.** Edgeways.

edging, n. [1. éjing; 2. édžiŋ]. **edge** (**I.**) & **-ing.** Something used to form, or forming naturally, an edge or border: *an edging of lace, of flowers, clipped box* &c.

edging-shears, n. Gardener's shears with long blades used for trimming the grass at the edges of a lawn round beds, or bordering a path.

edging-tool, n. Sharp crescent-shaped blade, with long handle like that of a spade, fixed on upper side, used for shaping exterior edges of turf in lawns.

edgy, adj. [1. éji; 2. édži]. **edge** (**I.**) & **-y.** **a** Having sharp edges; **b** (of drawings, paintings &c.) having unduly sharp outlines.

edibility, n. [1. èdibíliti; 2. èdibíliti]. Next word & **-ity.** Suitability for food, quality of being edible.

edible, adj. [1. édibl; 2. édibl], fr. L. Lat. *edibilis*, 'eatable'; Lat. *edere*, 'to eat', & **-ble.** See **eat.** Suitable for human food; wholesome to eat.

edict, n. [1. édikt; 2. ídikt], fr. Lat. *ēdictum*, 'proclamation, ordinance; order, command' **e-** & **diction.** Order formally issued by authority; a decree.

edification, n. [1. èdifikáshun; 2. èdifikéiʃən]. Lat. *aedificātiōn-(em)*, 'a structure', fr. *aedificāt-(um)*, P.P. type of *aedificāre*, 'to build', & **-ion.** See next word. **a** Act of edifying, state of being edified; **b** building up, formation, of moral or spiritual nature; moral improvement and instruction.

edifice, n. [1. édifis; 2. édifis], fr. Fr., fr. Lat. *aedificium*, 'a building', fr. *aedis*, 'temple; house' (see **aedile**) & *-fic-*, unstressed form of *fac-(ere)*, 'to make'. See **-fic.** **1.** A building, structure, especially **a** of a large public building, or a private mansion; also **b** of smaller erections: *an imposing, noble edifice* &c.; *a humble edifice of timber* &c. **2.** Something formed in the mind: *the whole edifice of his hopes and plans collapsed at once.*

edify, vb. trans. [1. édifī; 2. édifai], fr. Fr. *édifier*, fr. Lat. *aedificāre*, 'to build; to raise, erect; to instruct, edify'. See prec. **a** (archaic, poet.) To build, in material sense; **b** to build up, form, develop, moral, spiritual, and intellectual character of; to give moral instruction to, to improve.

edifying, adj. [1. édifī-ing; 2. édifai-iŋ]. Pres. Part. of prec. Promoting moral or spiritual improvement; instructive, uplifting.

edit, vb. trans. [1. édit; 2. édit], fr. Lat. *ēdit-(um)*, P.P. type of *ēdere*, 'to give, put, bring, forth; to publish; to relate; tell'; fr. **e-**, 'out', & *dare*, 'to give', q.v. under **date** (**I.**). **1.** **a** To prepare for publication the works of another author, or any documents, with care for exactness of text, critical annotation, revision &c.; **b** to pick out certain passages for publication, omitting what is unsuitable, undesirable, or badly written: *this book will require some severe editing before it can be published.* **2.** Specif., *to edit a newspaper, journal* &c., to direct, plan, and produce it, be responsible for what appears and generally supervise contents; to act as editor.

edition, n. [1. edíshun; 2. idíʃən], fr. Lat. *ēditiōn-(em).* See prec. & **-ion.** **1.** **a** The shape, size, style, in which a book is issued: *pocket edition, cheap edition, library edition*; *édition de luxe* (pron. as Fr.), sumptuous and expensive edition of a book; **b** (fig.) a repetition of something in slightly different form; person who resembles another in appearance, character &c.: *he's an inferior edition of his father.* **2.** The total number of copies of a book, newspaper &c., issued from the press at the same time: *limited edition, first edition* &c. **3.** The series in which, or press from which, a book is issued: *Aldine edition, Kelmscott edition.* **4.** The issue or reissue of a book, or literary work, with critical and scholarly attention by another to the state of the text, elucidation of obscurities &c.: *Chambers's edition of 'Beowulf'.*

editio princeps, n. [1. edíshiō prínseps; 2. idíʃiou prínseps]. Lat., 'first edition'. See **edition**, and **prince.** First printed edition.

editor, n. [1. éditor; 2. éditə]. Lat. **edit** & **-or.** **1.** One who edits, prepares a book for publication; one who makes a critical edition. **2.** One who directs and conducts the publication of a newspaper, journal &c.

editorial (**I.**), adj. [1. èditṓrial; 2. èditɔ́riəl]. Prec. & **-ial.** Pertaining to an editor or editing: *editorial chair, office, capacity* &c.

editorial (**II.**), n., fr. prec. A leading article in a newspaper; esp. one written by, or under direct supervision of, the editor, and assumed to express his views.

editorially, adv. **editorial** (**I.**) & **-ly.** In the manner of, as, an editor.

editorship, n. [1. éditorship; 2. éditəʃip]. **editor** & **-ship.** The position and authority of an editor.

editress, n. [1. éditres; 2. éditris]. **editor** & **-ess.** A female editor.

educable, adj. [1. édūkabl; 2. édjukəbl]. Lat. *ēduc-(āre)*, 'to educate' (see **educate**) & **-able.** Capable of being educated.

educate, vb. trans. [1. édūkāt; 2. édjukeit], fr. Lat. *ēducāt-(um)*, P.P. type of *ēducāre*, 'to bring up, rear, educate; to train, foster'; fr. *ēdūcere*, 'to lead out, bring out; to summon; to export; to bring up (a child); to raise, build up'. See **e-** & **duct.** **1.** To train, develop, cultivate, instruct the mind of; to form the moral character of; **a** oneself; **b** another; applied both to the person and his mind: *to educate a child*; *to educate the mind of a child* &c. **2.** To form and develop some particular faculty: *to educate a person's taste in literature*; *to educate the ear* &c. **3.** To bear the expenses of another's education: *he educated his brothers after their father's death.*

educated, adj. [1. édūkāted; 2. édjukeitid], fr. P.P. of prec. Highly trained, cultivated; intellectually and morally developed; specif., *an educated man*, one who has been systematically instructed and intellectually disciplined; contrasted with *illiterate, uneducated*: *an educated taste, mind* &c.

education, n. [1. èdūkáshun; 2. èdjukéiʃən], fr. Lat. *ēducātiōn-(em)*, 'bringing up, training, education'. See **educate** & **-ion.** **1.** Discipline, development, and training of the mind, character, and faculties. **2.** Specif. **a** instruction and training of the young; **b** organized system of instruction as existing in a given state.

educational, adj. [1. èdūkáshunal; 2. èdjukéiʃənəl]. Prec. & **-al.** **a** Connected with education; **b** having property of educating, instructing, developing the mind and character.

educationalist, n. [1. èdūkáshunalist; 2. èdjukéiʃənəlist]. Prec. & **-ist.** One concerned with the theory, practice, or organization of education.

educationally, adv. [1. èdūkáshunali; 2. èdjukéiʃənəli]. **educational** & **-ly.** By education, from the standpoint of education.

educationist, n. [1. èdūkáshunist; 2. èdjukéiʃənist]. **education** & **-ist.** Educationalist.

educative, adj. [1. édūkativ; 2. édjukətiv]. **educate** & **-ive.** (not of persons) Having the property of educating, developing; tending to promote mental or moral growth.

educe, vb. trans. [1. edū́s; 2. idjū́s], fr. Lat. *ēdūcere*, 'to draw, lead, bring, out; to summon; to send out, export; to draw up, raise, build up; to rear, bring up (a child)'. From **e-** & *dūcere*, 'to lead'. See **duct** & **duke.** **1.** To bring out, elicit, a latent quality of mind or character: *to educe all that is best in man.* **2.** To infer, deduce, draw (a conclusion) from data. **3.** (chem.) To separate, extract, from a compound substance.

educible, adj. [1. edū́sibl; 2. idjū́sibl]. Prec. & **-ible.** Capable of being educed.

educt, n. [1. ḗdukt; 2. ídakt], fr. Lat. *ēduct-(um)*, P.P. type of *ēdūcere*, 'to lead, draw out'. See **educe.** (chem.) Something separated out from a compound, by analysis.

eduction, n. [1. edúkshun; 2. idákʃən], fr. Lat. *ēductiōn-(em)*, 'a removal, going out'. Prec. & **-ion.** The act of educing; that which is educed.

eduction-pipe, n. Exhaust pipe of steam engine.

edulcorate, vb. trans. [1. edúlkorāt; 2. idálkəreit], fr. L. Lat. *ēdulcōrāt-(um)*, P.P. type of *ēdulcōrāre*, fr. Lat. *dulcor*, 'sweetness', fr. *dulcis*, 'sweet'; see **e-** & **dulcet** & **-ate.** To free from acid.

edulcoration, n. [1. edùlkoráshun; 2. idàlkəréiʃən]. Prec. & **-ation.** The act or process of edulcorating.

Edwardian, adj. [1. edwórdian; 2. ɛdwɔ́diən]. Edward & **-ian.** Of the time of any one of the Edwards, Kings of England: *an Edwardian castle*, built in reign of Edward I.; *the Edwardian Prayer Book*, of Edward VI.; specif., of reign of Edward VII., as contrasted with *Victorian* and *Georgian.*

-ee, suff. forming ns.; fr. O. Fr. *-é* (P.P. of vbs. in *-er*), fr. Lat. *-ātus*; see **-ate.** In old words the suff. expresses person who undergoes an action, or on whom some right is conferred: *lessee, grantee.* In modern words it is simply the Fr. P.P. as in *employee*; or has a very general sense of connexion, e.g. *bargee*, man on, or in charge of, a barge.

eel, n. [1. ēl; 2. īl]. M.E. *ēl*, O.E. *ǣl.* Cogn. w. O.H.G. *āl*, O.N. *āll*, Du. *aal.* One of a number of varieties of fresh water and sea fishes with a long, snake-like, very agile body, covered with extremely smooth skin, and when cooked, exhibiting greasy, gelatinous flesh. Phrs. *as slippery as an eel* (lit. and fig.); *to wriggle like an eel.*

eel-pout, n. See prec. & **pout (I.).** **a** The burbot; **b** name of certain kinds of blenny.

eel-spear, n. Instrument with barbed prongs for spearing eels.

e'en, n. & adv. [1. ēn; 2. īn]. Poetical variant of **even (I.)** & **(II.).**

-eer, suff., fr. Fr. *-ier*, fr. Lat. *-ārius.* See **-ary.** Expresses an agent; one who makes, is concerned with, manages, drives, produces: *muleteer, charioteer.* See also **-ier**; in recent formations often conveying derogatory sense: *profiteer.*

e'er, adv. [1. ār; 2. ɛə]. Poetical variant of **ever.**

eerie, eery, adj. [1. ḗri; 2. íəri]. M.E. *ēri*, 'timid', apparently fr. O.E. *earg, earh, ærg* &c., 'cowardly', wh. is cogn. w. O.H.G. *arg*, & O.N. *argr*, 'cowardly, wicked'. **a** Inspiring a feeling of mystery and dread; weird, uncanny; **b** (only provinc.) timidly restless, uneasy.

eerily, adv. [1. ḗrili; 2. íərili]. Prec. & **-ly.** In an eerie manner.

eeriness, n. [1. ḗrines; 2. íərinis]. See prec. & **-ness.** The quality of being eerie.

ef-, pref. Lat. *ef-*, by assimilation fr. **ex-** before *f.*

efface, vb. trans. [1. efás; 2. iféis], fr. Fr. *effacer*, 'wipe out, destroy', fr. **ef-** & Lat. *facies*, 'form, shape, appearance, look'. See **face.** **1.** (of material things) To erase, remove from a surface, rub out, blur: *time has effaced the youthful curves of her features and figure.* **2.** (of mental images) to blot out, render indistinct, obliterate: *to efface the memory of the past.* **3.** (reflex.) *To efface oneself*, render oneself inconspicuous, keep in the background, withdraw from observation.

effaceable, adj. [1. efásabl; 2. iféisəbl]. Prec. & **-able.** Capable of being effaced.

effacement, n. [1. efásment; 2. iféismənt]. **efface** & **-ment.** **a** The act of effacing; **b** state of being effaced.

effect (I.), n. [1. efékt; 2. ifékt], fr. O. Fr., fr. Lat. *effectus*, 'accomplishment, performance; effect, result'; fr. *effect-(um)*, P.P. type of *efficere*, 'to execute, accomplish, make, fashion; to produce, amount to'; fr. **ef-** & *facere*, 'to make, do'. See **fact.** **1.** State of things, conditions, arising from, caused by, an action or a process; a result, affecting mind or body, or external nature: *suffering from the effects of heat; the effects of light upon the eye, on plants; the sleeping-draught produced a rapid and profound effect; fear of punishment has a deterrent effect on criminals; cheerful companionship has a good effect on the spirits; argument had no effect upon his stubborn mind.* Phrs. *of no effect*, useless; *in effect*, in fact, for practical purposes; *to take effect*, to become operative; to result in what was intended. **2.** Impression produced upon the perceptive faculties: **a** by deliberately planned artistic design: *some painters get their effects by striking contrast of colours; Pope produces infinite variety of effect by his skilful handling of the couplet*; **b** by the phenomena of nature: *we get wonderful cloud effects in the English lake country.* **3.** Impression produced upon the mind, direction given to the thoughts and feelings by a deliberate action, or utterance calculated to cause such a result: *to talk, do something for effect.* **4.** Bearing, force, meaning: *the effect of this paragraph is to stultify what precedes.* **5.** (pl.) Goods and chattels, property: *they went leaving their personal effects behind; no effects*, N/E, as marked by bank on dishonoured cheque for which there are no funds.

effect (II.), vb. trans., fr. prec. To bring about, cause to happen, produce as result of an action or process.

effective, adj. & n. [1. eféktiv; 2. iféktiv], fr. Fr., fr. Lat. *effectīvus*, 'productive, effective'; **effect (I.)** & **-ive.** **1.** adj. **a** Producing a result, bringing about an intended result; productive of effect, competent: *to take effective measures; the treatment was effective*; specif. **b** (mil.) capable of being employed for active service. **2.** Producing a striking impression: *an effective scheme of decoration.* **3.** n. (pl.) *Effectives*, effective troops.

effectively, adv. Prec. & **-ly.** **a** In an effective manner; **b** in effect, as a matter of fact.

effectiveness, n. See prec. & **-ness.** The quality of being effective.

effectual, adj. [1. eféktūal; 2. iféktjuəl], fr. O. Fr., fr. L. Lat. *effectuālis*, fr. *effectus* (see **effect**) & **-al.** **1.** Producing the effect intended; adequate: *the punishment was effectual and the offence was not repeated.* **2.** Having legal force, taking effect, valid.

effectually, adv. Prec. & **-ly.** In an effectual manner.

effectualness, n. See prec. & **-ness.** The quality of being effectual.

effectuate, vb. trans. [1. eféktūāt; 2. iféktjueit], fr. **effectual** & **-ate.** To cause, accomplish, bring about.

effectuation, n. [1. efèktūáshun; 2. ifèktjuéiʃən]. Prec. & **-ion.** The act of effectuating; accomplishment.

effeminacy, n. [1. eféminasi; 2. iféminəsi]. See next word & **-acy.** The state of being effeminate.

effeminate, adj. [1. eféminat; 2. iféminit], fr. Lat. *effēmināt-(us)*, 'womanish, effeminate', P.P. of *effēmināre*, 'to make womanish, enervate'; fr. **ef-** & *fēmina*, 'a woman'. See **feminine.** (of men) Unmanly, possessing qualities usually found in a woman; weak, womanish; lacking courage, firmness, hardihood.

effeminately, adv. Prec. & **-ly.** In an effeminate manner.

effendi, n. [1. eféndi; 2. iféndi], fr. Turk. *efendi*, 'master', fr. Gk. *authéntēs*, 'a master, autocrat'. See **authentic.** Title given in Turkey, Egypt, &c., to an official or man of learning; or as polite mode of address to a gentleman.

efferent, adj. [1. éferent; 2. éfərənt], fr. Lat. *efferent-(em)*, Pres. Part. of *efferre*, 'to carry out or away, bring forth; to spread abroad, publish'; fr. **ef-** & *ferre*, 'to carry'. See **bear (I.).** (physiol.) Conveying, leading, outwards (from an organ &c.), as blood-vessels, nerves &c.; opposed to *afferent.*

effervesce, vb. intrans. [1. èfervés; 2. èfəvés], fr. Lat. *effervescere*, 'to boil up, bubble', fr. **ef-** & *fervēre*, 'to be hot'. See **fervent.** **1.** (of liquid) To give out bubbles, to liberate gas in the form of bubbles. **2.** (fig., of persons) To be in high spirits, be excited &c. **3.** (of gas) To come out in the form of bubbles, to rise in bubbles from a liquid.

effervescence, -cy, n. [1. èfervésens(i); 2. èfəvésəns(i)]. Prec. & **-ence** & **-cy.** Process of effervescing; state of being effervescent.

effervescent, adj. [1. èfervésent; 2. èfəvésənt]. Lat. *effervescent-(em)*, Pres. Part. type of *effervescere.* See **effervesce** & **-ent.** (lit. and fig.) Bubbling, sparkling, giving out gas in bubbles.

effete, adj. [1. efḗt; 2. ifít], fr. Lat. *effētus*, 'that has brought forth young; exhausted, worn out'; fr. **ef-**, & *fētus*, 'that has brought forth'. See **foetus.** (gen. in moral sense) Worn out, exhausted; incapable of producing anything, sterile: *an effete civilization, system of education* &c.

effeteness, n. Prec. & **-ness.** State of being effete.

efficacious, adj. [1. èfikáshus; 2. èfikéiʃəs], fr. Lat. *efficāci-*, fr. *efficax*, 'powerful, efficacious'; fr. *efficere*, 'to execute, accomplish', see **effect**, & **-ous.** Capable of producing a desired result; having the effect intended.

efficaciously, adv. Prec. & **-ly.** In an efficacious manner.

efficacy, n. [1. éfikasi; 2. éfikəsi]. Lat. *efficac-*, fr. *efficax*, 'powerful, efficacious'. See **efficacious** & **-y.** The quality of being efficacious; effectiveness.

efficiency, n. [1. efíshensi; 2. ifíʃənsi]. See next word & **-cy.** The state, quality, of being efficient; efficient power; specif. (phys. and mechan.) the proportion of energy or work produced to that put in.

efficient, adj. [1. efíshent; 2. ifíʃənt]. Lat. *efficient-(em)*, Pres. Part. type of *efficere*, 'accomplish, carry out'. See **effect.** **a** Producing a result; effective, adequate; Phr. *efficient cause*, the cause which actually or directly produces the effect; **b** (of persons) capable; able to perform an action and bring about the desired result; competent.

efficiently, adv. Prec. & **-ly.** In an efficient manner.

effigy, n. [1. éfiji; 2. éfidži], fr. Fr. *effigie*, fr. Lat. *effigies*, 'a likeness, portrait; a statue, image'. Cp. *effingere*, 'to form, fashion (artistically); to portray', & see **ef-**, & **figure.** A portrait, likeness; a figure representing a person; image: *to be burnt in effigy*, to have one's image burnt, in mockery, indignation &c.

effloresce, vb. intrans. [1. èflorés; 2. èflərés], fr. Lat. *efflōrescere*, 'to blossom'; fig., 'to spring up, flourish', fr. **ef-** & *flōrescere*, 'to begin to blossom'. See **florescence.** **a** (bot.) To come into flower, to blossom; (also fig.); **b** (chem.) to become covered with a crust due to chemical action.

efflorescence, n. [1. eflorésens; 2. ɛflərésəns]. **ef-** & **florescence.** The process of efflorescing.

efflorescent, adj. [1. eflorésent; 2. ɛflərésənt]. **ef-** & **florescent.** Efflorescing, tending to effloresce.

effluence, n. [1. éflooens; 2. éfluəns]. See **ef-** & **fluency**. **a** The process of flowing, pouring out; **b** that which flows out: '*Bright effluence of essence increate*' (Milton, P.L.).

effluent, adj. & n. [1. éflooent; 2. éfluənt]. **ef-** & **fluent**. **1.** adj. Proceeding outwards, flowing forth. **2.** n. **a** A river or stream flowing out of a larger river or of a lake; **b** body of water with its contents coming from a sewer, a factory &c., into a river or stream.

effluvium, n., pl. **effluvia** [1. eflóovium, -ia; 2. iflúviəm, -iə]. L. Lat. *effluvium*, 'a flowing out; outlet'; fr. *effluere*, 'to flow out'; cp. Lat. *fluvius*, 'a stream'; the base is **fluw*. See **fluent** & **flow**. Vapour, exhalation; tainted exhalation, odour.

efflux, n. [1. éfluks; 2. éflaks], fr. Lat. *efflux-(um)*, P.P. type of *effluere*, 'to flow out'. See **ef-** & **flux**. **a** (of material and non-material things) The process of flowing out; **b** that which flows out; **c** (of time) passage, lapse, expiry.

effluxion, n. [1. eflúkshun; 2. iflákʃən]. See prec. & **-ion**. (rare) Efflux.

effort, n. [1. éfort; 2. éfət]. O. Fr. *esfort, esforz*, formed fr. vb. *efforcier*, 'make an effort' &c., fr. Med. Lat. *exfortiāre*, fr. **ex-**, & Lat. *fortis*, 'strong', lit. 'a putting forth of strength'. See **fort**. **1.** Powerful mental or physical exertion, strenuous action; employment of strength in performing an action; a strain: *climbing hills is too great an effort for old people*. **2.** Deliberate exertion of physical or mental force or strength with the intention, for the purpose, of accomplishing something; an attempt, endeavour: *efforts too feeble to be successful*; *to make an effort to learn, to rise* &c. **3.** (colloq.) Result of an effort, something accomplished: *his performance was rather a good effort*.

effortless, adj. [1. éfortles; 2. éfətlis]. Prec. & **-less**. **a** (of persons) Making no effort, not exerting oneself; **b** (of actions) performed without effort.

effrontery, n. [1. efrúnteri; 2. ifrántəri], fr. Fr. *effronterie*, fr. *effronté*, 'bold, shameless' (& **-ery**), fr. Low Lat. **effrontāt-(us)*, fr. Lat. *effrontis*, 'shameless', fr. **ex-** & *frontis*, 'forehead, brow; front, outside'. See **front**. Impudence, audacity.

effulgence, n. [1. efúljens; 2. ifáldžəns]. See next word & **-ence**. Stream of brightness; radiance, splendour.

effulgent, adj. [1. efúljent; 2. ifáldžənt], fr. Lat. *effulgent-(em)*, Pres. Part. type of *effulgēre*, 'to shine forth', fr. **ef-**, & *fulgēre*, 'to shine, gleam, flash'. See **fulgent**. Sending out a beam of light; shining, radiant.

effulgently, adv. Prec. & **-ly**. Radiantly.

effuse (I.), vb. trans. & intrans. [1. efúz; 2. ifjúz], fr. Lat. *effūs-(um)*, P.P. type of Lat. *effundere*, 'to pour forth, spread abroad', fr. **ef-**, & *fundere*, 'to pour forth, shed; to overcome, destroy'. See **fuse** (I.). (lit. and fig.) **a** trans. To pour out, diffuse; **b** intrans., to issue, stream forth.

effuse (II.), adj. [1. efús; 2. ifjús], fr. Lat. *effūs-(us)*, 'poured or spread out'. See prec. (bot.) Spread out (of types of plant).

effusion, n. [1. efúzhun; 2. ifjúžən], fr. Lat. *effūsiōn-(em)*, 'a pouring forth; profusion, extravagance'. **effuse** (I.) & **-ion**. **1.** (of material things) **a** The act of pouring forth: *to be guilty of effusion of blood*, i.e. bloodshed; **b** shedding, loss: esp. *to suffer from an effusion of blood*. **2.** (of non-material things) Rapid, emotional, unrestrained expression in speech or writing: esp. *poetical effusions*.

effusive, adj. [1. efúsiv; 2. ifjúsiv]. **effuse** (I.) & **-ive**. (of persons and modes of expression) Expressing feeling without reserve; demonstrative; profuse: *effusive in one's gratitude*; *effusive compliments*.

effusively, adv. Prec. & **-ly**. In an effusive manner.

effusiveness, n. See prec. & **-ness**. The quality of being effusive, demonstrativeness; unreserved expression of cordiality of feeling.

eft, n. [1. eft; 2. eft]. O.E. *efeta*, 'newt', M.E. *evete, eute, efte* &c. Etymol. unknown. Variant of **newt**. (archaic and provinc.) A newt.

eftsoon(s), adv. [1. eftsóon(z); 2. eftsún(z)]. O.E. *eftsōna*, M.E. *eftsōne(s)*, 'immediately afterwards, very soon'. See **aft** & **soon**. (archaic) Immediately afterwards.

egad, interj. [1. egád; 2. igǽd]. Prob. for *ah God*. See **gad** (I.). (archaic and obsolesc.) Expletive equivalent to *by Jove* &c.

egg (I.), n. [1. eg; 2. eg]. Scand.; M.E., fr. O.N. *egg*, cogn. w. O.E. *ǣġ* (whence M.E. *ēi*), & w. O.H.G. *ei*; Gmc. **ajjom*, Aryan **o(w)j-om*, 'egg'; cp. Lat. *ōvum*, 'egg'. See **ovum**. **1. a** A rounded body, having a thin, brittle shell or an outer elastic coat, produced by birds, some reptiles, fish &c., containing the germ from which a new individual of the species is developed; ovum; hence, **b** the egg of a bird, esp. of domestic fowl, as an article of food: *eggs and bacon, a poached egg* &c. Phrs. *to put all one's eggs into one basket*, risk everything on one enterprise; *to teach one's grandmother to suck eggs*, instruct one who knows more than oneself; (colloq.) *a bad egg*, a worthless person; (fig.) *in the egg*, undeveloped, in the first stages; *egg and anchor, egg and dart* (archit.), form of moulding consisting of an egg-shaped ornament, alternating with one in form of spear-head. **2.** (biol.) Female reproductive cell in animals and plants.

egg (II.), vb. trans. M.E. *eggen*, fr. O.N. *eggja*, 'to provoke, incite'. Cogn. w. **edge** (II.). (usually) *To egg on*: to incite, urge: *to egg a person on to do something*.

egg-cup, n. Small cup for holding a boiled egg at table.

egger, n. [1. éger; 2. égə]. Etymol. unknown. Popular name of various moths, the larvae of which are destructive to foliage of trees &c.

egg-flip, egg-nog, n. Drink composed of eggs beaten up in milk, with sugar, and wine or spirits.

eggler, n. [1. égler; 2. églə]. (provinc.) Itinerant buyer of, and dealer in, eggs.

egg-nog. See **egg-flip**.

egg-plant, n. An East Indian plant, with egg-shaped, purple fruit, eaten as a vegetable; the aubergine.

egg-shaped, adj. Having somewhat the form of an egg; ovoid.

egg-shell, n. Thin, brittle shell forming outer covering of a bird's egg. *Egg-shell china*, a kind of thin, transparent china.

egg-spoon, n. Small spoon for eating a boiled egg out of its shell.

egg-tooth, n. Small projection on unhatched bird's beak, with which it chips its way out of the shell.

eglantine, n. [1. églantīn; 2. égləntain], fr. Fr., fr. O. Fr. *aiglent* & **-ine**; connected w. Lat. *acus*, 'needle'. See **acute**. The sweet-brier.

ego, n. [1. égō; 2. égo]. Lat. *ego*, 'I'; cogn. w. **I**. That part of the individual which thinks consciously; contrasted with *non-ego*.

egoism, n. [1. égōizm; 2. égouizəm]. Prec. & **-ism**. **1.** (philos.) Doctrine that self-interest is the spring and motive of human action. **2. a** State or habit of mind in which self is the main preoccupation; self-centredness; **b** selfishness, concentration of mind on one's own interests and advantage; reverse of *altruism*.

egoist, n. [1. égōist; 2. égouist]. **ego** & **-ist**. **1.** One who holds the philosophical doctrine of egoism. **2.** One whose mind is excessively centred in himself and his own interests.

egoistic(al), adj. [1. ègōístik(l); 2. ègouístik(l)]. Prec. & **-ic** & **-al**. Pertaining to an egoist, or to egoism.

egoistically, adv. Prec. & **-ly**. In an egoistic manner.

egotism, n. [1. égotizm; 2. égətizəm]. **ego** & **-ism** w. intrusive *t*. Habit of thinking and talking too much about oneself; self-conceit; egoism.

egotist, n. [1. égotist; 2. égətist]. See prec. & **-ist**. One given to egotism.

egotistic(al), adj. [1. ègotístik(l); 2. ègətístik(l)]. Prec. & **-ic** & **-al**. Inclined to exalt and dwell on oneself, and one's doings.

egotistically, adv. Prec. & **-ly**. In an egotistic manner.

egotize, vb. intrans. [1. égotīz; 2. égətaiz]. See **egotism** & **-ize**. (rare) To play the egotist.

egregious, adj. [1. egréjus; 2. igrídžəs], fr. Lat. *ēgregius*, 'distinguished, excellent, surpassing', orig. 'chosen from the herd', fr. **e-** & *gregi-*, stem of *grex*, 'a herd, flock'. See **gregarious** & **-ous**. (now only in unfavourable sense) Distinguished from the rest of a class or group by undesirable qualities; remarkable for possession of bad qualities; notorious, outstandingly bad: *an egregious fool, egregious folly, error* &c.

egregiously, adv. Prec. & **-ly**. In an egregious manner.

egregiousness, n. Prec. & **-ness**. The quality of being egregious.

egress, n. [1. égres; 2. ígres], fr. Lat. *ēgressus*, 'going away, departure; disembarking; digression', fr. P.P. type of *ēgredior*, 'come out; ascend; digress; to surpass, exceed'. See **e-** & **gradus**. **1.** The act of going or coming out. **2.** The power or right of going or coming out. **3.** Way out, exit.

egression, n. [1. ēgréshun; 2. īgréʃən], fr. Lat. *ēgressiōn-(em)*, 'a going or coming out; a digression'. Prec. & **-ion**. The act of going or coming out.

egret, n. [1. égret; 2. ígret], fr. O. Fr. *egrette, aigrette*, dimin. of O. Fr. *aigron*, a variant form of O. Fr. *hairon*. See **heron**. **1. a** Name of the lesser white heron or of other species of small herons which have long, delicate, white tail and back feathers during the breeding season; **b** a plume of these feathers, an aigrette, q.v. **2.** The soft, feathery seed crown of thistles, dandelions &c.

Egyptian, adj. & n. [1. ejípshun; 2. idžípʃən], fr. Egypt (& **-ian**), fr. Lat., fr. Gk. *Aiguptos*, 'the river Nile; Egypt'. **1.** adj. Pertaining to Egypt. **2.** n. **a** A native of Egypt; **b** (archaic) a gipsy; **c** (colloq.) an Egyptian cigarette.

Egyptologist, n. [1. èjiptólojist; 2. ìdžiptólədžist]. Next word & **-ist**. A student of Egyptology.

Egyptology, n. [1. èjiptóloji; 2. ìdžiptólədži]. Egypt & **-logy**. The study of Egyptian antiquities, architecture &c.

eh, interrog. interj. [1. ā; 2. ei]. **a** = What did you say? (not polite); **b** = don't you agree with me?

eider, n. [1. íder; 2. áidə]. Scand.; Swed. *eider*, O.N. *æðar*, genit. of *æðr*. A large, wild duck, genus *Somateria*, living on the sea coasts in northern Europe &c.; also *eider-duck*.

eider-down, n. **a** The fine, soft down of the eider-duck; **b** a bed-quilt stuffed with eider-down.

eidograph, n. [1. ídograhf; 2. áidəgrāf], fr. Gk. *eidos*, 'form, appearance', cogn. w. Gk. *idein*, 'to see', fr. the base **weid-* &c., 'to see, know', q.v. under **idea** & **wit**, & **-graph**. An instrument for reproducing drawings on larger or smaller scale.

eidolon, n. [1. īdólon; 2. aidóulən]. Gk. *eidōlon*, 'an image, phantom; idea'. See **idol**. A phantom, apparition.

eight, adj. & n. [1. āt; 2. eit]. M.E. *eihte*, O.E. *eahta*; cogn. w. O.H.G., O.L.G. *ahto*, O. Fris. *achta*, O.N. *ātta*, Goth. *ahtau*. Cp. Lat. *octo*, Gk. *oktṓ*, 'eight'; also O. Ir. *ocht-n*, Lith. *asztùnì*, Scrt. *aṣṭā, aṣṭāu*. **1.** adj. One more than seven, one less than nine. **2.** n. **a** The figure representing the number eight, 8, Roman viii.; **b** a group, set, team &c. of eight: *The Eights*, inter-collegiate boat-races at Oxford and Cambridge with eight oarsmen in each boat. Phrs. *figure of eight*, figure cut on the ice by a skater; *piece of eight*, a Spanish coin, dollar, of the value of 8 reals.

eighteen, adj. & n. [1. ātḗn; 2. eitín]. M.E. *eihtene, eiȝtetene*, O.E. *eahtatiene, eahtatēne*. **eight** & **-teen**. Eight plus ten.

eighteenth, adj. & n. [1. ātḗnth; 2. eitínþ]. Prec. & **-th**. Following seventeen others in a series.

eighth, adj. & n. [1. ātth; 2. eitþ]. O.E. *eahtuþe*, M.E. *eihteþe, eȝteþe*; cp. O.H.G. *ahtudo*, O.N. *āttundi*, Goth. *ahtuda*. **eight** & **-th**. **a** adj. Following seven others in a series. **b** n. eighth part.

eighthly, adv. Prec. & **-ly**. In the eighth place of a series.

eightieth, adj. & n. [1. átieth; 2. éitiiþ]. Next word & **-eth**. Following 79 of a series.

eighty, adj. & n. [1. áti; 2. éiti]. M.E. *eihti*, O.E. *eahtatiġ*. Cp. O.H.G. *ahtozug*. **eight** & **-ty** (II.). **a** adj. Ten times eight; **b** n., the number equal to eight times ten. Phr. *the eighties* (*of such and such a century*), the years eighty to eighty-nine inclusive.

eirenicon, n. [1. īrḗnikon; 2. airínikən], fr. Gk. *eirēnikós*, 'peaceful', fr. *eirḗnē*, 'peace'. Etymol. uncertain. Proposal, pronouncement, tending to, enjoining, peace; esp. one issued by ecclesiastical authority.

eisteddfod, n. [1. āstédhvod; 2. eistéðvɔd]. Welsh 'session', fr. *eistedd*, 'to sit'. Annual assembly of Welsh bards, held in various places, to preserve and encourage Welsh music, literature &c.

either, adj., pron., & adv. [1. ídher, édher; 2. áiðə, íðə]. M.E. *eiþer, eiȝþer*, O.E. *ǣġðer, ǣghwæþer*, fr. **ā-gihwæþer*, fr. Gmc. **aiw-*, 'ever, every' (see **aye**), & **gihwaþar-*, 'each'. See **whether**. **1.** adj. **a** One of two: *sit on either side of the table*; *either half of the cake*; **b** each of two things: *curtains hanging on either side of the window*. **2.** pron. One of two things: *either will do*. **3.** adv., conj. **a** Implying a choice of alternatives: *either one thing or the other*; **b** (with negative) also, together with another: *if he does not come I shall not either*.

ejaculate, vb. trans. [1. ejákūlāt; 2. idžǽkjuleit], fr. Lat. *ējaculāt-(um)*, P.P. type of Lat. *ējaculārī*, 'to shoot out, throw out', fr. **e-** & *jaculārī*, 'to throw, hurl, cast; to assail; to aim at, strive for', fr. *jaculum*, 'a dart, javelin', fr. *jacere*, 'to throw'. See **jactitation**. **1.** To pronounce suddenly; exclaim. **2.** To eject, discharge (liquids) suddenly.

ejaculation, n. [1. ejàkūlā́shun; 2. idžǽkjuléiʃən]. Prec. & **-ation**. **1.** The act of ejaculating. **2.** Something ejaculated; **a** a sudden exclamation, abrupt cry; **b** liquid &c. suddenly ejected.

ejaculatory, adj. [1. ejákūlatori; 2. idžǽkjulətəri]. **ejaculate** & **-ory**. **1.** Of the nature of an ejaculation; pronounced swiftly and abruptly. **2.** (of ducts) Fitted to the purpose of ejecting or throwing out.

eject (I.), vb. trans. [1. ejékt; 2. idžékt], fr. Lat. *ēject-(um)*, P.P. type of Lat. *ējicere*, 'to cast or drive out, expel; to rush out', fr. **e-** & *jacere*, 'to throw'. See **jet** & **jactitation**. **1. a** To turn, fling, out, dismiss, send off or away, cause removal of: *eject an agitator from a meeting*; **b** specif. (law) to dispossess, evict from property. **2.** To give or send out, discharge, emit: *to eject smoke* &c.

eject (II.), n. [1. ḗjekt; 2. ídžekt], fr. prec. Something inferred as existing in the consciousness of another.

ejection, n. [1. ejékshun; 2. idžékʃən]. **eject** (I.) & **-ion**. The act of ejecting; state or process of being ejected.

ejective, adj. [1. ejéktiv; 2. idžéktiv]. **eject** (I.) & **-ive**. **1.** Pertaining to ejection, causing ejection. **2.** Pertaining to an eject.

ejectment, n. [1. ejéktment; 2. idžéktmənt]. **eject** (I.) & **-ment**. **a** Ejection; **b** (legal) an action for the recovery, possession, of land.

ejector, n. [1. ejéktor; 2. idžéktə]. **eject** (I.) & **-or**. One who, that which, ejects; specif., device for ejecting objects, as that part of the mechanism of a breech-loading rifle or gun which throws out the cartridge after disharge.

eke (I.), adv. [1. ēk; 2. ík]. O.E. *ēac*, M.E. *ēke, ēc*; cogn. w. O.H.G. *ouh*, O.L.G. *ōc*, O. Fris. *āk*, O.N. *auk*, Goth. *auk*, 'also'; Gmc. **auk-*, cogn. w. **eke** (II.). (archaic) Also, moreover: '*A trainband captain eke was he, Of famous London town*' (Cowper).

eke (II.), vb. trans. M.E. *ēken*, fr. O.E. *ēac(i)an*, 'to increase'; cogn. w. O.H.G. *ouhhōn*, O.N. *auka*, Goth. *aukan*, 'to grow, increase'; also w. O.E. *īecan, ēcan*, 'to increase', fr. **aukjan*. Cp. Lat. *augēre*, Scrt. *ṓjaś*, 'power'; O. Ir. *ōg*, 'whole, entire'; Lith. *áugu*, 'grow'; Lett. *augsts*, 'high', *aukts*, 'high'. Aryan base **aug-, *aweg-, *awog-*, 'to increase', whence also Scrt. *vakṣ́ayati*, 'grows', Gk. *aéxō*, 'increase (fr. **aweks-*); Goth. *wahsjan*, 'to grow'. See **wax** (III.), **auction**, **augment**. *To eke out*, to increase, add to, supplement, spin out: *to eke out one's livelihood*.

-el. See **-le**.

elaborate (I.), adj. [1. eláborat; 2. ilǽbərit], fr. Lat. *ēlabōrāt-(um)*, P.P. type of *ēlabōrāre*, 'to exert oneself, endeavour; to labour on, work out', fr. **e-** & *labōrāre*, 'to work, labour, strive'. See **labour** (II.). Worked out in much detail; complicated: *an elaborate design*; *elaborate directions*; *an elaborate dinner*.

elaborate (II.), vb. trans. [1. eláborāt; 2. ilǽbəreit]. See prec. **a** To work out, produce by physical or mental work; **b** to design or execute in detail; to add detail, develop, make more elaborate: *just elaborate your proposals a little*.

elaborately, adv. [1. eláboratli; 2. ilǽbəritli]. **elaborate** (I.) & **-ly**. In an elaborate manner.

elaborateness, n. [1. eláboratnes; 2. ilǽbəritnis]. **elaborate** (I.) & **-ness**. The quality of being elaborate.

elaboration, n. [1. elàborā́shun; 2. ilǽbəréiʃən]. **elaborate** (II.) & **-ion**. The act or process of elaborating; of adding detail to, improving: *to spend time on the elaboration of a scheme*.

elaborative, adj. [1. eláborativ; 2. ilǽbərətiv]. **elaborate** (II.) & **-ive**. Tending to elaborate.

elaeo-, pref., fr. Gk. *élaion*, 'olive oil, oil', see **olive** & **oil**, used to form compounds, as: *elaeometer* [1. èlēómeter; 2. èliɔ́mitə], instrument for measuring the density and purity of oils.

élan, n. [1. ālón; 2. eilā́]. Fr., 'impetus; impetuosity', fr. vb. *élancer*, 'to throw', **e-** & *lancer*, orig. 'to throw a lance; to throw'. See **lance**, **launch** (I.). Dash, impetuosity, vigour, enthusiasm.

eland, n. [1. ḗland; 2. íland]. Du. *eland*, 'elk'. Cp. N.H.G. *elenthier*. The largest of South African antelopes, *Taurotragus oryx*, horned and of very heavy build.

elapse, vb. intrans. [1. eláps; 2. ilǽps], fr. Lat. *ēlaps-(um)*, P.P. type of Lat. *ēlābī*, 'to slip away, glide away, escape; to pass, disappear', fr. **e-** & *lābī*, 'to slide, slip; to glide, pass, away'. See **lapse**. (of time) To pass, slip past, glide away.

elastic (I.), adj. [1. elástik, eláhstik; 2. ilǽstik, ilā́stik], fr. Gk. *elastik-(ós)*, 'spontaneous, impulsive', fr. *elaúnein*, 'to drive, set in motion; to expel; strike, harass', fr. **ela-wn-ō*; cp. Gk. *eláein*, 'to drive'; Lat. *alacer*, 'active'; Goth. *aljan*, 'zeal'. See **alacrity**. **1. a** (of solids, gases, liquids) Having the property of resilience; tending to return to original shape, size, position, after being submitted to pressure or extension; capable of expansion; the typically elastic substance is rubber; **b** (of non-material things) capable of adaptation, not rigid and limited: *let us make our regulations as elastic as possible*. **2.** Flexible, yielding, pliant, springy: *an elastic cane, bones* &c. **3.** (in moral sense) **a** Adaptable, buoyant, recovering easily from depression: *elastic temperament*; **b** complaisant, easy, accommodating; not too scrupulous: *his sense of honour was rather elastic*; *he was blessed or cursed with an elastic conscience*.

elastic (II.), n., fr. prec. Cord or ribbon, manufactured from cotton, silk &c., with strands of rubber.

elastically, adv. [1. elástikali; 2. ilǽstikəli]. **elastic** (I.) & **-al** & **-ly**. In an elastic state or condition or manner.

elasticity, n. [1. èlastísiti; 2. ìlæstísiti]. **elastic** (I.) & **-ity**. The property of being elastic, resilience (in material and moral senses).

elate (I.), vb. trans. [1. elā́t; 2. iléit], fr. Lat. *ēlāt-(um)*, P.P. type of Lat. *efferre*, 'to bring or carry out; to utter, publish; to raise, lift up, elevate; to rise, advance, be haughty'; *lāt-*, is fr. **tlāt-*, fr. base **tel-*. See **tolerate**, **thole**. To put into high spirits, encourage, make proud: *elated by success* &c.

elate (II.), adj. See prec. Proud, uplifted in mind, elated.

elater, n. [1. élater; 2. élətə], fr. Gk. *elatḗr*, 'driver', fr. *elaúnein*, 'to drive'; cp. **elastic**. **1.** (bot.) A minute elastic filament in certain lowly organized plants, such as the liverworts &c., which disperses the ripe spores. **2.** (zool.) The typical genus of the family *Elateridae*, which includes the click beetles &c.

elaterium, n. [1. èlatḗrium; 2. èlətíəriəm]. Lat., fr. Gk. *elatḗrion*, neut. sing. of *elatḗrios*, 'driving'. See prec. (med.) A strongly purgative substance obtained from the squirting or wild cucumber, used in cases of dropsy &c.

elation, n. [1. elā́shun; 2. iléiʃən], fr. Lat. *ēlātiōn-(em)*, 'a carrying out; a lifting up'; fig. 'transport, passion; exaltation; pride, elation', fr. Lat. *ēlāt-(us)*, see **elate**, & **-ion**. The state of being elated; high spirits, exaltation; proud satisfaction.

elbow (I.), n. [1. élbō; 2. élbou]. M.E. *elbowe*, fr. O.E. *elnboga*, 'elbow'. Cp. N.H.G. *ellenbogen*, Du. *elleboog*, O.N. *ōl(n)bogi*, fr. Gmc. **alin-o*, 'the forearm', & **bogo-n*, 'a bow, curve'. See **ell**, **bow** (I.) **1. a** The joint between the forearm and upper arm; esp. the pointed exterior of this. Phrs. *at one's elbow*, close to; *more power to your elbow*, expression of good wishes; **b** corresponding part of a sleeve. Phr. *out at elbows*, shabby, poverty-stricken. **2.** Anything shaped, bent, like an elbow, as a sharp bend in a pipe &c.

elbow (II.), vb. trans., fr. prec. To push, shove, thrust, with, or as with, the elbows: *to elbow one's way through a crowd*; *to elbow a person out of the way*.

elbow-chair, n. A chair with raised arms on which the elbows of the person sitting in it may rest.

elbow-grease, n. Strenuous activity in rubbing and polishing.

elbow-room, n. Space enough to move in.

elchee, n. [1. élchē; 2. éltʃi]. Turk. *īlchi*, 'representative of an *īl*, a nomad tribe', hence 'an envoy'. An ambassador, envoy.

eld, n. [1. eld; 2. eld]. M.E. *elde*, O.E. *eldo*, 'age'; cp. O.H.G. *eltī, altī*, O.L.G. *eldī*, O.N. *elli*, fr. Gmc. **ald-ī*, 'age', fr. **ald-*, 'old'. See **old**. (archaic) **a** Old age; **b** antiquity, days of yore, former times.

elder (I.), adj. & n. [1. élder; 2. éldə]. O.E. *eldre*, 'older'; M.E. *eldre*. See **old** & **-er**, compar. suff. **1.** adj. (of two in same family &c.) Born earlier, older, senior: *the elder brother*; *the elder of the two*. **2.** n. **a** (pl.) Those of an earlier generation: *to obey one's elders*; **b** person with claims to respect and authority by reason of age and experience. **3. a** Person of dignity and authority, by reason of his age &c., among the Jews and in the early Christian Church; **b** one ordained to specific functions and authority in one of the modern Presbyterian Churches.

elder (II.), n. O.E. *ellern*, M.E. *elder, eller, ellerne*; cp. M.L.G. *alhorn, elhorn*. A genus, *Sambucus*, of trees and shrubs, with broad, flat clusters of white flowers which have a powerful, sickly odour. Also called *stinking elder*.

elder-berry, n. The dark-purple fruit of the elder.

elder-berry wine, n. Wine made from elder-berries.

elderliness, n. [1. élderlines; 2. éldəlinis]. Next word & **-ness**. The state of being elderly.

elderly, adj. [1. élderli; 2. éldəli]. **elder (I.)** & **-ly**. Oldish, fairly old, approaching old age.

eldership, n. [1. éldership; 2. éldəʃip]. **elder (I.)** & **-ship**. The office of elder in one of the Presbyterian Churches.

eldest, adj. [1. éldest; 2. éldist]. M.E. *eldest*, O.E. *eldesta, ieldesta*. See **old** & **-est**. Now only used of first-born, or oldest survivor, of a family of brothers and sisters: *eldest son, daughter, brother* &c.

El Dorado, n. [1. èl doráhdō; 2. èl dərádou]. Span., 'the golden (country)'. See **dorado**. An imaginary country or city of gold; hence, an ideal land of wealth and plenty.

eldritch, adj. [1. éldrich; 2. éldritʃ]. Origin doubtful. (Scots.)Uncanny, terrifying, hideous.

Eleatic, adj. [1. èleátik; 2. èliǽtik], fr. Elea (Velia), ancient Greek colony in Italy. Of, pertaining to, a school of Greek philosophy of the 6th cent. B.C., of which the principal doctrine was the unity of being, and its chief exponent Parmenides.

elecampane, n. [1. èlekámpān; 2. èlikǽmpein], fr. Med. Lat. *enula campana*, fr. Lat. *inula (campana)*, 'elecampane', w. metathesis fr. Gk. *helénion*, 'elecampane', fr. *hélos*, 'a marsh, marshy ground', perh. fr. **selos*, cogn. w. Scrt. *sáraš*, 'lake, pool', & w. O.E. *sol*, 'mud, muddy pool', see **sully**; the second element is prob. L. Lat. *campana*, 'a bell', see **campanile**, or fr. Lat. *campanea*, 'of the fields', see **champaign**. A perennial, herbaceous plant with rayed yellow flowers; its pungent, aromatic root was formerly much used as a tonic drug and as a sweetmeat.

elect (I.), vb. trans. & intrans. [1. elékt; 2. ilékt], fr. Lat. *ēlect-(um)*, P.P. type of *ēligere*, 'to choose, pick out; to pluck up, weed', fr. **e-** & *legere*, 'to gather, collect; to gather, pick; to extract, remove; to select; to behold, view, observe; to read'. See **legend, legible, lecture**. **1.** trans. To choose, select (a person for an office), by vote: *to elect a member of Parliament, a chairman* &c.; *to elect a person to the presidency*, or *to be president*. In this sense the word implies not merely *choosing*, but also *appointing*, a person to a post or office. **2.** intrans. To decide, make up one's mind, to do something: *he elected to remain at home.*

elect (II.), adj. See prec. Specially selected, chosen, marked out; elected to some office &c.; the word generally implies that the person elected has not yet entered upon the duties of his office; e.g. *bishop elect*, one not yet consecrated, and enthroned; *bride elect*, lady about to be, but not yet, married.

elect (III.), n., fr. prec. Chosen person, one selected for some particular position or privilege (esp. by God): *God's elect, the home of the elect.*

election, n. [1. elékshun; 2. ilékʃən], fr. Lat. *ēlectiōn-(em)*, 'choice, selection', fr. *ēlect-(us)*, 'chosen, selected'. **elect (I.)** & **-ion**. The act of electing; state of being elected; specif. **a** (theol.) the predestination of certain persons to salvation in accordance with the will of God: *by election and grace*; **b** (polit.) *general election*, election of members of Parliament by all parts of the country; *by-election*, election of member of Parliament to a single seat that has fallen vacant.

electioneer, vb. intrans. [1. elèkshunḗr; 2. ilèkʃəníə]. Prec. & **-eer**. (polit.) To work on behalf of a candidate's election for Parliament.

electioneering, n. [1. elèkshunḗring; 2. ilèkʃəníəriŋ]. Prec. & **-ing**. Act of canvassing for votes, speaking in public, and otherwise promoting the election of a particular candidate for Parliament.

elective, adj. [1. eléktiv; 2. iléktiv]. **elect (I.)** & **-ive**. **1. a** (of an office &c.) Bestowed, conferred, awarded by a process of election; **b** (of a body) constituted, chosen, by election. **2.** Having the power to elect; for the purpose of electing: *an elective body*, body of electors. **3.** (chem.) *Elective affinity*, tendency in substances to combine with others.

electively, adv. Prec. & **-ly**. In an elective manner.

elector, n. [1. eléktor; 2. iléktə]. **elect (I.)** & **-or**. **1.** One who elects, has the right to elect; specif. **a** one entitled to vote for a candidate for Parliament; **b** member of an electoral body, charged with selection of a candidate for a post or office. **2.** (hist., cap.) One of the princes of the ancient German or Holy Roman Empire who elected the Emperor (911 to 1803).

electoral, adj. [1. eléktoral; 2. iléktərəl]. Prec. & **-al**. **1.** Pertaining to an elector or to election. *Electoral college*, U.S.A., the body of Presidential electors of a State or of these bodies united. **2.** Pertaining to a German elector or electorate. *Electoral cap*, one of scarlet and ermine worn by the Electors; *Electoral Prince*, an Elector.

electorate, n. [1. eléktorat, -āt; 2. iléktərit, -eit]. **elector** & **-ate**. **1.** The whole body of those entitled to vote at Parliamentary elections. **2.** Office, jurisdiction, or territories of a German Elector.

electress, n. [1. eléktres; 2. iléktris]. **elector** & **-ess**. The wife or widow of a German Electoral Prince.

electric (I.), adj. [1. eléktrik; 2. iléktrik], fr. Lat. *electrica*, applied by William Gilbert (1544–1603) to substances which, like amber, attract other substances when rubbed, fr. Gk. *ēlektron*, 'amber'. See **electron**. **1.** Charged with, produced by, worked with, producing electricity: *electric lamp, iron, railway* &c., worked by electricity; *electric light*, produced by electricity; *electric shock*. Phrs. *electric blue*, a brilliant blue; *electric eel*, a freshwater, eel-like fish, *Gymnotus*, found in S. America, capable of giving an electric shock; *electric ray*, torpedo fish, with same power as the electric eel; *electric seal*, trade name for rabbit fur dyed and treated to imitate true sealskin. **2.** (fig.) Electrical, q.v., **b**.

electric (II.), n., fr. prec. (obsolesc.) A substance which can be electrified by friction, and which is a non-conductor of electricity.

electrical, adj. [1. eléktrikl; 2. iléktrikl]. **electric (I.)** & **-al**. **a** Pertaining to, having to do with, electricity; **b** (fig.) producing sudden and striking effect upon the mind.

electrically, adv. Prec. & **-ly**. By means of electricity.

electrician, n. [1. èlektríshan; 2. èliktríʃən]. **electric (I.)** & **-ian**. **a** A student of electricity; **b** a mechanic who makes, manages, repairs, electric machinery.

electricity, n. [1. èlektrísiti; 2. èliktrísiti]. **electric (I.)** & **-ity**. **a** A form of energy, the ultimate nature of which is unknown, exhibited in various phases as heat, light, chemical change, and mechanical power; **b** science which deals with these phenomena; **c** (colloq.) supply of electricity in form of current for lighting, power &c.

electrification, n. [1. elèktrifikáshun; 2. ilèktrifikéiʃən]. See next word & **-fication**. The act or process of electrifying; state of being electrified.

electrify, vb. trans. [1. eléktrifī; 2. iléktrifai]. **electric** & **-fy**. **1.** To charge with electricity. **2.** To introduce electricity as motive power: *to electrify a railway system.* **3.** (fig.) To startle, rouse, to cause sudden excitement in: *to electrify an audience.*

electrize, vb. trans. [1. eléktrīz; 2. iléktraiz]. **electro-** & **-ize**. Electrify.

electro-, pref. Form of Gk. *ēlektron*, 'amber', used in compounds. See **electron**. Pertaining to, produced by, electricity.

electro-biology, n. [1. eléktrō bīóloji; 2. iléktrou baiɔ́lədʒi]. The science of electricity in relation to living organisms.

electro-chemistry, n. [1. eléktrō kémistri; 2. iléktrou kémistri]. That branch of science which deals with the chemical changes produced by electricity.

electrocute, vb. trans. [1. eléktrōkūt; 2. iléktroukjūt], fr. **electro-**, on the anal. of *execute*. To put to death by means of electricity (specif. as capital punishment).

electrocution, n. [1. elèktrōkúshun; 2. ilèktroukjúʃən]. Formed on anal. of *execution*. Execution by electricity.

electrode, n. [1. eléktrōd; 2. iléktroud], fr. **electro-** & Gk. *hodós*, 'way, path, track; a voyaging; manner, method, system'; see **hodometer**. Either of the two terminating points of a conductor from which an electric current passes into another medium. See **anode** & **cathode**.

electro-dynamics, n. [1. eléktrō dīnámiks; 2. iléktrou dainǽmiks]. Branch of physics dealing with all the phenomena of electricity in action.

electro-kinetics, n. [1. eléktrō kīnétiks; 2. iléktrou kainétiks]. The branch of physics which deals with electricity in motion, cp. *electrostatics*.

electrolier, n. [1. elèktrōlḗr; 2. ilèktroulíə]. Formed fr. **electro-** on anal. of *chandelier*. Hanging support for electric lamps, resembling a chandelier in form.

electrolyse, vb. trans. [1. eléktrōlīz; 2. iléktroulaiz], fr. next word. To decompose a liquid by electricity.

electrolysis, n. [1. èlektrólisis; 2. èlektrɔ́lisis], fr. **electro-** & Gk. *lúsis*, 'a setting free, releasing; atonement; dissolution', fr. *lúein*, 'to loose, unfasten; dissolve'. See cognates under **loose (I.)**. Chemical decomposition by means of electric action.

electrolyte, n. [1. eléktrōlīt; 2. iléktroulait]. Substance decomposed by electric action; solution carrying an electric current.

electrolytic, adj. [1. elèktrōlítik; 2. ilèktroulítik]. Of, pertaining to, electrolysis.

electro-magnet, n. [1. eléktrō mágnet; 2. iléktrou mǽgnit]. Magnet which owes its power of attraction to an electric current passing through the wire wound round it.

electro-magnetism, n. [1. eléktrō mágnetìzm; 2. iléktrou mǽgnitìzəm]. Prec. & **-ism**. **a** Magnetic force produced by means of electricity; **b** the study of this.

electro-metallurgy, n. [1. eléktrō metálurji; 2. iléktrou metǽlədʒi]. Branch of metallurgy in which electricity is used in various processes, e.g. smelting, welding &c.

electrometer, n. [1. èlektrómeter; 2. èlektrɔ́mitə]. **electro-** & **meter**. An instrument for measuring minute differences of voltage.

electromotion, n. [1. elèktrōmóshun; 2. ilèktroumóuʃən]. **electro-** & **motion**. **a** Motion of the electric current; **b** motive power obtained from electricity.

electromotive, adj. [1. elèktrōmótiv; 2. ilèktroumóutiv]. **electro-** & **motive**. Of, pertaining to, electromotion; esp. *electromotive force*, abbr. E.M.F., force set up by difference of potential in electric circuit, producing electric current.

electron, n. [1. eléktron; 2. iléktrɔn]. Gk. *ēlektron*, 'amber; also, a compound of gold and silver'. Cp. Gk. *ēléktōr*, 'beaming; the sun'; *Ēlectrā* (pers. name). Etymol. doubtful. **1.** Alloy of gold and silver used by the ancients, also *electrum*. **2.** Unit of negative electricity, one of the two elementary constituents of all varieties of matter, the positive unit being proton; an electron is calculated as 1/50,000 of the diameter of an atom.

electro-negative, adj. [1. eléktrō négativ; 2. iléktrou négətiv]. (physical chem.) Charged with negative electricity.

electro-plate (I.), vb. trans. [1. elèktrō plā́t; 2. ilèktrou pléit]. To coat metal with silver by an electric process.

electro-plate (II.), n. [1. eléktrō plāt; 2. iléktrou pleit]. Metal articles, e.g. spoons, forks, dishes &c., coated with silver by means of an electric process.

electro-polar, adj. [1. eléktrō pólar; 2. iléktrou póulə]. **electro-** & **polar**. Having electrical polarity, charged positively at one end and negatively at the other.

electro-positive, adj. [1. eléktrō pózitiv; 2. *i*léktro*u* pɔ́zit*i*v]. (physical chem.) Charged with positive electricity.

electroscope, n. [1. eléktroskōp; 2. *i*léktrəsko*u*p]. **electro-** & **-scope**. Device which demonstrates visibly the presence or absence, and also sign, i.e. whether positive or negative, of electricity in a body.

electrostatics, n. [1. elèktrōstátiks; 2. *i*lèktro*u*stǽt*i*ks]. **electro-** & **statics.** That branch of physics which treats of the phenomena of electricity when at rest, that is, of bodies charged with electricity.

electro-therapeutics, -therapy, n. [1. eléktrō thèrapūtiks, -thérapi; 2. *i*léktro*u* þèrəpjū́t*i*ks, -þérəp*i*]. **electro-** & **therapeutics.** Electrical treatment, cure of diseases.

electro-thermal, adj. [1. eléktrō thērmal; 2. *i*léktrō þǽməl]. **electro-** & **thermal. a** Pertaining to the production of heat by electricity; **b** combining heat and electricity.

electrotype, n. [1. eléktrotīp; 2. *i*léktrət*ai*p]. Plate used in printing, upon which the desired impression is fixed by an electroplating process.

electrum, n. [1. eléktrum; 2. *i*léktrəm]. Lat., fr. Gk. *élektron*. See **electron. 1.** Amber. **2.** A pale yellow alloy of silver and gold, used in ancient Greece for coins.

electuary, n. [1. eléktūari; 2. *i*léktj*u*ər*i*], fr. Low Lat. *ēlectuārium, ēlectārium*, 'electuary', perh. fr. Gk. *ekleikt-*, fr. *ekleikhein*, 'to lick out', fr. *leikhein*, 'to lick'. See **lick (I.)**. Mixture of medicinal drugs with a sweet, sticky substance such as honey or syrup.

eleemosynary, adj. [1. èliēmózinari; 2. èl*ī*mɔ́z*i*nər*i*], fr. Med. Lat. *eleēmosynārius*, fr. Lat. *eleēmosyna*, 'alms', fr. Gk. *eleēmosúnē*, 'pity; charity, alms'. See **alms** & **-ary. 1.** Charitable, bestowing alms; given as alms. **2.** Depending on charity.

elegance, n. [1. élegans; 2. él*i*gəns]. **elegant** & **-ce.** The quality of being elegant.

elegancy, n. [1. éleganśi; 2. él*i*gəns*i*]. See prec. & **-cy. a** Elegance; **b** particular instance of this.

elegant, adj. [1. élegant; 2. él*i*gənt], fr. Lat. *ēligant-(em), ēlegant-(em)*, 'fine, neat; tasteful; fastidious, luxurious', fr. Pres. Part. type of *ēligere*, 'to choose, pick out, select'. See **elect (I.). 1.** (of persons, character, manners, bearing &c.) Refined, polished, well-bred, highly cultivated, displaying fastidious taste, grace, ease. **2.** (of material things) Displaying grace of form, justness of proportion, beauty and harmony of parts. **3.** (of non-material things, esp. artistic and literary compositions) Highly wrought, displaying taste, refinement, and propriety, in conception and execution.

elegantly, adv. Prec. & **-ly.** In an elegant manner.

elegiac, adj. & n. [1. èlejíak; 2. èl*i*dž*ái*ək], fr. Lat. *elegiac-us*, fr. Gk. *elegiakós*. **elegy** & **-ac. 1.** adj. **a** (of metre) Used for, suitable for, elegies: *elegiac couplets*, alternate hexameter and pentameter lines; hence, **b** sad, solemn, mournful. **2.** n. (pl.) *Elegiacs*, verse of this kind.

elegize, vb. trans. & intrans. [1. élejīz; 2. él*i*dž*ai*z]. See next word & **-ize. 1.** trans. To compose an elegy upon, celebrate in an elegy. **2.** intrans. To write elegies.

elegy, n. [1. éleji; 2. él*i*dž*i*], fr. Fr. *élégie*, fr. Lat., fr. Gk. *elegeía*, 'elegy'; cp. Gk. *élegos*, 'song of lament'; prob. of Eastern origin. **1.** A poem in elegiac verse. **2.** A song of mourning; a poem about, in celebration of, the dead, and expressing grief at the loss.

element, n. [1. élement; 2. él*i*mənt]. Lat. *elementum*, 'natural element'; usually in pl. *elementa*, 'first principles, rudiments of an art or science'. The etymol. is still a subject of speculation. One suggestion is that the word stands for *alimentum*, meaning 'something out of which something else has grown', cp. *alere*, 'to nourish, feed' &c., & see **aliment**; another that it is derived fr. *el, em, en, LMN*, equivalent to *ABC*. **1.** One of the essential constituent parts of anything, assumed to be irreducible by analysis to a simpler form; **a** one of the simple substances or principles, of which, according to ancient philosophers, the material universe is composed: *the four elements*, earth, air, fire, water; Phrs. *in, out of, one's element*, (fig.) in, not in, appropriate or congenial surroundings; *the devouring element*, fire; **b** forces of nature, esp. as exhibited in disturbances of the atmosphere: *the fury of, exposed to, the elements*. **2.** (chem. and phys.) A substance which cannot, by chemical processes, be broken up, or separated, into substances of different nature from itself; a substance which is not a compound, but homologous, and of uniform character in all its parts; e.g. gold, silver, radium, helium &c. **3.** An essential ingredient of anything; one of the constituents, components, characteristic features, of anything; **a** of material things: *silicates are an important element in glass*; **b** of non-material things: *physical sensations are elements of consciousness*; *justice is an important element of good government*; **c** minute portion, a trace: *there is an element of truth in what you say*; *an element of humour in the situation*. **4.** (in pl.) Beginnings, rudiments, outlines, fundamental principles of a study, philosophical system &c.: *to master the elements of grammar*. **5.** Specif. (theol., cap., pl.) the bread and wine used in the Eucharist.

elemental (I.), adj. [1. èleméntl; 2. èl*i*méntl]. Prec. & **-al. a** Pertaining to the four elements, or to natural forces; resembling natural forces or phenomena; simple, primal: *elemental forces*; **b** pertaining to the beginnings, the first principles of a study &c.: *elemental studies* &c.; more usually *elementary*; **c** forming a component part.

elemental (II.), n., fr. prec. A spirit of earth, air, fire, or water.

elementarily, adv. [1. èleméntarili; 2. èl*i*méntər*i*l*i*]. **elementary** & **-ly.** In an elementary manner.

elementariness, n. [1. èleméntarines; 2. èl*i*méntər*i*n*i*s]. See next word & **-ness.** The quality of being elementary.

elementary, adj. [1. èleméntari; 2. èl*i*méntər*i*], fr. Lat. *elementārius*, 'elementary'. **element** & **-ary. 1. a** Pertaining to the elements, rudiments, or first principles; at the beginning, in the first stages (of a branch of learning): *an elementary grammar, school*; *elementary education, knowledge*; hence, **b** undeveloped, incipient, slight: *his knowledge was of the most elementary kind*. **2.** (chem.) That cannot be resolved into simpler parts or analysed.

elemi, n. [1. élemi; 2. él*i*m*i*], in Fr., Ital., Span. Prob. an Oriental word. A pungent resinous substance, obtained from an East Indian tree, used in ointments and varnishes.

elenchus, n. [1. eléngkus; 2. *i*léŋkəs]. L. Lat. *elenchus*, fr. Gk. *élegkhos*, 'disproof, refutation; argument'; cp. *élegkhos*, 'blame, disgrace'; *elegkhḗs*, 'cowardly'; *elégkhein*, 'to disgrace; disprove; convict'. Etymol. doubtful. Disproof, refutation, by argument.

elenctic, adj. [1. eléngktik; 2. *i*léŋkt*i*k], fr. Gk. *elegktikós*, 'fond of cross-examining'. See prec. & **-ic.** Pertaining to, given to, argument, cross-examining, testing by argument.

elephant, n. [1. élefant; 2. él*i*fənt]. M.E. *elifaunt, olifaunt*, fr. O. Fr. *olifant*, fr. Lat. *elephant-us*, fr. Gk. *eléphant-(os)*, genit. of *eléphās*, 'an elephant; ivory'. The second element, *-ephās*, is borrowed fr. Egyptian; cp. Egyptian *āb(u)*, Coptic *eb(o)u*, 'elephant'. Etymol. of first element doubtful. **1. a** A very large pachydermatous quadruped, with large tusks and a long trunk; there are two surviving species, the Indian and the African, the latter being distinguished by a straighter back and very large ears; *white elephant*, an albino type, held sacred in Siam, hence, (fig.) a useless, costly encumbrance; **b** (obs.) ivory. **2.** A particular large size of drawing paper, 28 in. by 23 in.

elephantiasis, n. [1. èlefantíasis; 2. èl*i*fænt*ái*əsis], fr. Lat., fr. Gk. *eléphant-(os)*. See prec. & **-asis.** An endemic disease of the skin, characterized by very great thickening and inflammation.

elephantine, adj. [1. èlefántīn; 2. èl*i*fǽnt*ai*n]. **elephant** & **-ine. 1.** Pertaining to an elephant. **2. a** Resembling an elephant in size or movement; clumsy, ungainly, ponderous, slow: *elephantine proportions, gambols* &c.; **b** (fig.) *elephantine humour*.

elephantoid, adj. [1. èlefántoid; 2. èl*i*fǽntɔ*i*d]. **elephant** & **-oid.** Like an elephant.

elephant's ear, n. The begonia, from shape of its leaves.

elephant's foot, n. Popular name of an American plant of the aster family, and of an African plant with edible root.

elephant shrew, n. A small insectivorous quadruped, a native of Africa, having a long snout.

elephant thorn, n. The East Indian acacia.

Eleusinian, adj. [1. èlūsínian; 2. èlj*u*sínjən], fr. Lat., fr. Gk. *Eleusîn-(os)*, 'of Eleusis', a city of Attica. *Eleusinian mysteries*, rites celebrated yearly at Eleusis, in honour of Demeter.

eleuthero-, pref., fr. Gk. *eleútheros*, 'free'; cogn. w. Lat. *liber*, 'free', q.v. under **liberal.** Free; of freedom.

eleutheromania, n. [1. elūtherōmánia; 2. eljūþəro*u*méiniə]. Prec. & **mania.** Fanatical striving for an ideal state of freedom.

eleutheropetalous, adj. [1. elūtherōpétalus; 2. eljūþəro*u*pétələs]. See prec. & **petal** & **-ous.** (bot.) Having free, distinct petals.

elevate, vb. trans. [1. élevāt; 2. él*i*veit], fr. Lat. *ēlevāt-(um)*, P.P. type of *ēlevāre*, 'to raise, lift up; to lighten, alleviate; to make light of, disparage'; fr. **e-** & *levāre*, 'to raise, lift up; console, refresh; relieve, release'. See **lever, levant. 1.** (of action affecting material things) To lift up, raise from lower to higher position; except in specif. senses, *put up, lift, raise* are usually better words. Specif., to lift up the Elements in the Eucharist after consecration. **2.** Various uses: **a** To direct the eyes, looks, to a higher level; **b** *to elevate the voice*, to speak louder or in higher pitch; **c** to raise to higher social or official position: *to elevate an unknown man to the post of Prime Minister*; **d** to raise to higher moral level: *elevating thoughts, conversation* &c.

elevated, adj. [1. élevāted; 2. él*i*veit*i*d], fr. P.P. of prec. **1.** (in moral sense) Lofty, dignified, noble: *an elevated style*; of a high moral or intellectual quality, edifying: *elevated thoughts, conversation*. **2.** (colloq. euphemism) Drunk.

elevation, n. [1. èlevā́shun; 2. èl*i*véiʃən], fr. Lat. *ēlevātiōn-(em)*, 'a lifting, raising'. **elevate** & **-ion. 1. a** Act of lifting or raising something to a higher level or position; hardly used except in Phrs. *the Elevation, Elevation of the Host*, i.e. lifting up after the consecration; **b** raising in status: *elevation to the peerage* &c. Loftiness, dignity, eloquence: *elevation of thought, style* &c. **3.** Something elevated, raised up; specif., a portion of ground higher than the surrounding country; a hill. **4.** (archit.) A flat drawing or plan, made to scale, of one side of a building.

elevator, n. [1. élevātor; 2. él*i*veitə]. **elevate** & **-or.** That which elevates; specif. **a** (U.S.A.) a lift; **b** a machine for conveying straw, grain &c. to top of stack, into granary &c.; **c** a muscle raising arm, leg &c.

elevatory, adj. [1. élevātori; 2. él*i*veitər*i*]. **elevate** & **-ory.** Having the function of raising, tending to elevate.

eleven, adj. & n. [1. elévn; 2. *i*lévn]. M.E. *ellevene, enleven, endleve*; O.E. *endlufon, endlyfon, ellefne*; cp. O.H.G. *einlif*; O.L.G. *ellevan*; O. Fris. *andlova, elleva*; O.N. *ellifu*; Goth. *ainlif*; fr. Gmc. **ain-*, see **one,** & **-lif-*, 'left after ten', fr. Aryan **-lihʷ-*, 'left', fr. the same base as Lat. *linquere*, Gk. *leipein*, 'to leave, leave behind'. Cp. Lith. *vēnu-lika*, 'eleven'. See **twelve, relinquish. a** adj.

One more than ten ; **b** n., *an eleven*, a group of eleven persons or things ; esp. a cricket team.

eleventh, adj. [1. elévnth ; 2. ilévnþ]. **eleven** & **-th.** Following ten others in a series. Phr. *eleventh hour*, the last possible moment.

elf, n. [1. elf ; 2. ɛlf]. M.E. *elfe, alfe* ; O.E. *elf, ælf*. Cp. O.H.G. *alp* ; M.L.G. *alf* ; O.N. *alfr* ; possibly (w. the idea of 'bright, resplendent') cogn. w. Lat. *albus*, Gk. *alphós*, 'white'. See **alb. 1.** (Gmc. mythol.) A diminutive, supernatural being, whether malevolent or the reverse, supposed to haunt woods and caves. **2.** A small human creature, either **a** a mischievous child, or **b** a strange, dwarfish, weird person.

elf-bolt, n. Flint arrow-head, formerly supposed to have been made by elves.

elfin, adj. [1. élfin ; 2. élfin]. Perh. fr. M.E., genit. pl. *elvene*, 'of elves'. See **elf.** Of, pertaining to, an elf ; fairylike.

elfish, adj. [1. élfish ; 2. élfiʃ]. **elf** & **-ish. a** (archaic) Pertaining to the fairies, to fairyland ; **b** like an elf ; small, mischievous.

elf-land, n. The country of the elves.

elf-lock, n. Tangled lock of hair, supposed to be the work of elves.

elicit, vb. trans. [1. elísit ; 2. ilísit], fr. Lat. *ēlicit-(um)*, P.P. type of *ēlicere*, 'to draw forth', fr. **e-** & *lacere*, 'to entice, allure'. Cogn. w. *laqueus*, 'a noose', *dēliciae*, 'delight, charm'. Cogn. also w. O. Slav. *ląka*, 'malice', *ląkati*, 'deceive', *polęči*, 'noose' ; Lett. *lenza*, 'snare' ; Czech *lákati*, 'to allure'. Cp. **delicious** & **lace.** To draw forth, bring out ; provoke, cause to come forth : *to elicit a reply* ; *to elicit a fact, the truth from a reluctant witness.*

elide, vb. trans. [1. elíd ; 2. iláid], fr. Lat. *ēlīdere*, 'to strike out, force out ; to drive out ; to break to pieces, destroy ; to elide' ; fr. **e-** & *laedere*, 'to hurt, injure ; vex, offend'. See **lesion.** To leave out a vowel in pronunciation, as in Gray's '*Awaits alike th' inevitable hour*'.

eligibility, n. [1. èlijibíliti ; 2. èlidžibíliti]. See next word & **-ity.** The quality of being eligible.

eligible, adj. [1. élijibl ; 2. élidžibl], fr. Fr., fr. Lat. *ēligere*, 'to choose, pick out'. See **elect** & **-ible. 1.** Legally qualified for election to a post or office. **2. a** Having proper qualifications for : *eligible for membership, office* &c. ; **b** suitable for selection, fit, desirable, satisfactory : *an eligible young man.*

eligibly, adv. Prec. & **-ly.** In an eligible manner.

eliminable, adj. [1. elíminabl ; 2. ilíminəbl]. See next word & **-able.** That can be eliminated

eliminate, vb. trans. [1. elíminãt ; 2. ilímineit], fr. Lat. *ēlīmināt-(um)*, P.P. type of *ēlīmināre*, 'to turn out of doors, banish', fr. **e-** & *līmen*, 'threshold, entrance'. See **limen. 1.** (not used of physical action) To exclude, remove, blot out, get rid of : *to eliminate errors, all superfluous words* &c. **2.** (chemical process) To purge away, drive out : *to eliminate uric acid from the system.* **3.** To set aside, cut out, remove, from consideration by logical process : *to eliminate a possibility.*

elimination, n. [1. elimināshun ; 2. ilìminéiʃən]. Prec. & **-ion.** The act or process of eliminating ; state of being eliminated.

eliminator, n. [1. elíminãtor ; 2. ilímineitə]. See prec. & **-or.** A device, in wireless, for drawing high tension current from the electric supply mains instead of from batteries.

elision, n. [1. elízhun ; 2. ilížn], fr. Lat. *ēlīsiōn-(em)*, 'striking out ; elision', fr. *ēlīs-(um)*, P.P. type of *ēlīdere*, 'to press, strike out ; to omit, elide', & **-ion.** See **elide.** The act or process of eliding, state of being elided ; specif., the omission of a vowel in pronunciation, esp. before a following vowel.

élite, n. [1. ālḗt ; 2. eilít]. Fr., 'choice, select', P.P. of *élire.* See **elect.** A choice, select body of persons ; the flower : *the élite (of society)* ; *corps d'élite*, select, picked body of troops.

elixir, n. [1. elíkser ; 2. ilíksə]. Med. Lat. fr. Arab. *al-iksir*, fr. *al*, 'the', & *iksir*, 'elixir', prob. fr. Late Gk. *xḗrion*, 'a kind of medicinal substance', fr. *xērós*, 'dry ; harsh ; lean, haggard'. See **xero-. 1.** A liquid substance formerly supposed to have the power **a** of prolonging life (elixir of life) ; **b** of transmuting all metals into gold ; also *philosopher's stone.* **2.** A powerful, invigorating remedy.

Elizabethan, adj. & n. [1. elìzabḗthan ; 2. ilìzəbíþən]. Elizabeth & **-an. 1.** adj. Belonging to the age of Queen Elizabeth ; pertaining to Elizabeth : *Elizabethan literature, buildings* ; *the Elizabethan age.* **2.** n. One who lived in the time of Elizabeth ; esp. a writer of this age.

elk, n. [1. elk ; 2. ɛlk]. The O.E. form of the word is *eolh, elh*, cogn. w. O.N. *elgr*, Swed. *elg*, O.H.G. *elho, elaho.* Lat. *alcē(s)*, Gk. *álkē*, are prob. borrowed fr. a Gmc. stem **alχis.* The largest of the deer, of heavy build and having spreading palmated antlers ; found in Northern Europe, Asia, and North America ; in Canada and U.S.A. it is called *moose*, and 'elk' is used of the *wapiti.*

ell, n. [1. el ; 2. ɛl]. M.E. *elne, elle*, O.E. *eln* ; cp. O.H.G. *elna, elina*, O.N. *ǫln*, Goth. *aleina* ; cogn. w. Lat. *ulna* (fr. **ōlenā*), 'elbow, arm' ; Gk. *ōlénē*, 'elbow' ; W. *elin*, 'elbow' ; M. Ir. *uile*, 'elbow', fr. Aryan base **ōlenā-*, **ōlen-*, 'a bend, curve', w. *-n* suff. fr. **ōlē-*, 'to bend'. Cp. w. a different suff. Lith. *alkunė́*, 'elbow'. See **lizard, lacertian, leg.** A measure of length, 1¼ yds. ; originally taken from the length of the arm. Phr. *if you give him an inch, he'll take an ell*, will presume on kindness or concessions.

ellebore. See **hellebore.**

ellipse, n. [1. elíps ; 2. ilíps], fr. Lat. *ellipsis*, fr. Gk. *élleipsis*, 'a falling short, defect', fr. *elleípein*, 'to fall short, fail ; to leave undone, omit', fr. **en-** & *leípein*, 'to leave, forsake, abandon ; to be wanting, be left behind ; to fail'. See **relinquish, loan. 1.** A regular, symmetrical, curved figure with the length greater than the breadth ; an oval. **2.** (geom.) Section of a cone produced by a plane making an angle with the base of the cone.

ellipsis, n. [1. elípsis ; 2. ilípsis]. See prec. (syntax) Omission of word or words, usually such as will be inevitably supplied by the mind, or understood, in the construction of a sentence, e.g. *the food I like*, i.e. *which I like* ; *he was dark and his brother fair*, i.e. *was fair.*

ellipsoid, n. [1. elípsoid ; 2. ilípsɔid]. **ellipse** & **-oid.** (geom.) Solid figure corresponding to an ellipse.

elliptic(al), adj. [1. elíptik(l) ; 2. ilíptik(l)]. See **ellipse** & **-ic** & **-al. 1.** Pertaining to, having the shape of, an ellipse. **2.** Pertaining to an ellipsis, having some part omitted.

elliptically, adv. Prec. & **-ly.** In an elliptical manner.

ellipticity, n. [1. èliptísiti ; 2. èliptísiti]. **elliptic** & **-ity.** The state of being an ellipse.

elm, n. [1. elm ; 2. ɛlm]. M.E., O.E. *elm* ; cp. O.N. *almr* ; cogn. w. Lat. *ulmus*, 'elm' (fr. **olm-*), & w. Ir. *lem*, 'elm'. A genus, *Ulmus*, of deciduous trees, attaining great height and bulk and living as long as 300 years, with rough bark, serrated leaves ; common in most parts of England.

elmy, adj. [1. élmi ; 2. élmi]. Prec. & **-y.** Covered with, abounding in, elms.

elocution, n. [1. èlokū́shun ; 2. èləkjúʃən], fr. Lat. *ēlocūtiōn-(em)*, 'a speaking aloud, utterance ; oratorical delivery', fr. **e-** & *locūtio*, 'a speaking ; speech, discourse'. See **loquacious. 1.** Style, mode, of utterance : *to have a bad elocution.* **2.** The art of clear and effective utterance, esp. in public speaking ; including elegant pronunciation, proper management of the voice, & clear expression of meaning by means of uttered speech.

elocutionary, adj. [1. èlokū́shunari ; 2. èləkjúʃənəri]. Prec. & **-ary.** Pertaining to elocution.

elocutionist, n. [1. èlokū́shunist ; 2. èləkjúʃənist]. **elocution** & **-ist.** A teacher of, one skilled in, elocution.

elogium, n. [1. ēlṓjium ; 2. ilóudžiəm]. Lat., 'maxim ; inscription on tombstone' ; fr. Gk. *elegeîon* ; cp. Gk. *élegos*, 'dirge', & see **elegy.** Cp. Fr. *éloge.* (rare, archaic) An address, short written sketch, in praise of one dead.

elohist, n. [1. elṓhist ; 2. ilóuhist], fr. Heb. *Elohim*, n. pl., 'God', & **-ist.** One of the writers of the elohistic parts of the Old Testament.

elohistic, adj. [1. èlohístik ; 2. èlɔhístik]. Prec. & **-ic.** Applied to those parts of the Old Testament in which the word *Elohim* replaces the word *Yahveh* as the name for God.

elongate (I.), vb. trans. & intrans. [1. ḗlonggāt ; 2. ílɔŋgeit], fr. Lat. *ēlongāt-(um)*, P.P. type of *ēlongāre*, 'to prolong, protract ; to withdraw ; keep aloof', fr. **e-** & *longus*, 'long'. See **long. 1.** trans. To make long, draw out, lengthen. **2.** intrans. To extend, stretch out, be long and slender, taper.

elongate (II.), adj., fr. prec. (bot. and zool.) Long and thin, drawn-out.

elongation, n. [1. èlonggā́shun ; 2. ìlɔŋgéiʃən]. Prec. & **-ion.** The act of elongating, state of being elongated ; lengthening, prolongation.

elope, vb. intrans. [1. elṓp ; 2. ilóup]. O. Fr. *alouper*, of Gmc. origin ; cp. M.E. *lōpen*, 'to run', fr. O.N. *hlaupa.* The Engl. cogn. is **leap.** To run away, escape surreptitiously ; esp. with a person of opposite sex.

elopement, n. [1. elṓpment ; 2. ilóupmənt]. Prec. & **-ment.** The act of eloping.

eloquence, n. [1. élokwens ; 2. éləkwəns], fr. Lat. *ēloquentia*, 'eloquence', fr. *ēloquor*, 'I speak, utter, express, declare ; to speak in an oratorical manner', fr. **e-** & *loquor*, 'I speak'. See **loquacious** & **-ence.** The power of arousing emotion in one's hearers or readers by the persuasiveness, force, fluency, grace, expressiveness &c., of verbal expression.

eloquent, adj. [1. élokwent ; 2. éləkwənt], fr. Lat. *ēloquent-(em)*, Pres. Part. type of *ēloquor*, 'I speak, utter, pronounce ; I speak eloquently'. See prec. & **-ent. a** (of speaker or writer) Possessing eloquence ; ready in speech, capable of fluent, appropriate, expressive language ; persuasive ; **b** (of speech or writing) exhibiting copiousness and grace, fitness, of expression ; moving.

eloquently, adv. Prec. & **-ly.** In an eloquent manner.

else, adv. [1. els ; 2. ɛls]. O.E. & M.E. *elles* ; cp. O.H.G. *elles, alles*, Goth. *aljis* ; cp. O.E. *el-þēod*, 'foreign nation', *elelendisc*, 'foreign' ; O.H.G. *elilenti*, 'foreign, exiled' (N.H.G. *elend*, 'misery'). Cogn. w. Lat. *alius*, 'another' ; Gk. *állos* ; Umbrian *arsir*, 'another' ; O. Ir. *aile*, 'other' ; Bret. *eil*, 'second' ; Gall. *Allo(broges).* Aryan stem **al-jos*, 'other, another'. **1.** With negative, interrogative, and indefinite pronouns : **a** Besides, in addition, as well : *no one else to come* ; *did you see anyone else? what else shall I say?* ; **b** instead, as a substitute : *nothing, something, else to be done* ; *somebody else's hat.* **2.** (gen. preceded by *or*) If not, under other circumstances, otherwise : *come, or else stop away* ; *take care, or else you will fall.*

elsewhere, adv. [1. elswā́r ; 2. ɛlswéə]. O.E. *elleshwǣr*, M.E. *elleswhar.* See **else** & **where.** At, in, to, another place, somewhere different : *to live, go, elsewhere.*

elucidate, vb. trans. [1. ēlū́sidāt ; 2. ìljúsideit], fr. L. Lat. *ēlūcidāt-(um)*, P.P. type of *ēlūcidāre*, 'to enlighten', fr. **e-** & *lūcid-us*, 'clear, bright, shining ; distinct, lucid'. See **lucid** & **-ate.** To explain, make clear, bring out the meaning of : *to elucidate a statement* &c.

elucidation, n. [1. ēlūsidā́shun ; 2. ìljusidéiʃən]. Prec. & **-ion.** The act or process of elucidating.

elucidative, adj. [1. ēlū́sidātiv ; 2. ìljúsidèitiv]. **elucidate** & **-ive.** Tending to, intended to, elucidate ; explanatory.

elucidatory, adj. [1. elū́sidātori ; 2. iljúsidèitəri]. **elucidate** & **-ory.** Elucidative.

elude, vb. trans. [1. ēlūd; 2. iljūd], fr. Lat. *ēlūdere*, 'to cease playing; to escape or parry (a blow); to deceive, frustrate; to make sport of', fr. **e-** & *lūdere*, 'to play'. See **ludicrous. a** To escape from by strategy or guile, to dodge; avoid being caught by: *to elude pursuit, one's pursuers, payment*; **b** to escape the mind or perceptions: *to elude observation; the meaning eludes me.*

elusion, n. [1. ēlūzhun; 2. iljūžən], fr. Lat. *ēlūs-(um)*, P.P. type of *ēlūdere*, 'to stop playing; to escape; to deceive'. See **elude** & **-ion.** The act of eluding.

elusive, adj. [1. ēlūsiv; 2. iljūsiv]. See prec. & **-ive. 1. a** Inclined to evade, escape, elude: *an elusive person*; **b** tending to escape the memory, difficult to grasp or retain: *an elusive argument.* **2.** Tending to allow escape, not tenacious: *an elusive memory.*

elusively, adv. Prec. & **-ly.** In an elusive manner.

elusiveness, n. See prec. & **-ness.** The quality of being elusive.

elusory, adj. [1. ēlūsori; 2. iljūsəri]. See **elusion** & **-ory.** (of mental impressions) Tending to slip away, elusive.

elvan, n. [1. élvan; 2. élvən]. Origin unknown. A kind of crystalline rock, sometimes appearing as veins in granite.

elver, n. [1. élver; 2. élvə], fr. *eel fare.* See **eel** & **fare (III.).** A young eel.

elvish, adj. [1. élvish; 2. élviʃ]. Variant of **elfish.**

Elysian, adj. [1. elízian; 2. ilíziən]. See next word & **-an.** Pertaining to, in, Elysium.

Elysium, n. [1. elízium; 2. iliziəm]. Lat., fr. Gk. *ēlúsion (pédion)*, 'Elysian (plain)'. Etymol. doubtful. **1.** (Gk. mythol.) The home of the blessed after death. Hence, **2**, a place or state of complete happiness.

elytrum, elytron, n., pl. **elytra** [1. élitrum, -on, -a; 2. élitrəm, -ən, -ə]. Lat., fr. Gk. *élutron*, 'sheath, case', fr. *elúein*, 'to roll round, enfold', q.v. under **volute.** The hard, outer wing-case of coleopterous insects.

elzevir, adj. & n. [1. élzevēr; 2. élzivīə]. **1.** adj. **a** (of book) Printed by the 17th cent. Dutch printers of the name; **b** (typog.) of type used by, or similar to that used by, the Elzevirs. **2.** n. A book printed by the Elzevirs.

em-, pref. Form of **en-**, used before *p, b, m.*

em, n. [1. em; 2. ɛm]. (typog.) Unit of measurement of printed matter on page, line &c.; square of the body of a type, originally taken from space occupied by the letter *m* as printed.

emaciate, vb. trans. [1. ēmáshiāt; 2. iméiʃieit], fr. Lat. *ēmaciāt-(um)*, P.P. type of *ēmaciāre*, 'to waste away, make lean', fr. **e-** & *maciāre*, 'to make thin', fr. *maciēs*, 'thinness'; cp. *macer*, 'thin', which is cogn. w. Gk. *makrós*, 'long'; also w. O.E. *mæger*, O.H.G. *magar*, 'lean'. Possibly also connected w. Goth. *mag*, O.E. *mæg*, 'I can, may'. See **may, macerate, meagre.** (very rare as vb.) To reduce in weight, to cause to become excessively thin.

emaciated, adj. [1. ēmáshiāted; 2. iméiʃieitid], fr. P.P. of prec. (of persons) Very thin, wasted and reduced in flesh by starvation or disease.

emaciation, n. [1. ēmàsiáshun; 2. imèisiéiʃən]. **emaciate** & **-ion.** Condition of abnormal and unhealthy thinness, caused by disease or lack of nutrition.

emanate, vb. intrans. [1. émanāt; 2. émaneit], fr. Lat. *ēmānāt-(um)*, P.P. type of *ēmānāre*, 'to flow, spring from, proceed from', fr. **e-** & *mānāre*, 'to flow, run, distil; to spread, diffuse', fr. **mad-nāre*, cogn. w. *madēre*, 'to drip'. Cp. Gk. *madáō*, 'become moist, melt', & *madarós*, 'loose' &c. To flow, proceed from, issue forth, have origin in; chiefly **a** of non-material things: *a subtle influence emanated from him; ideas emanate from the brain; the suggestion, hint, emanated in the first instance from Government circles*; **b** of material things such as odours, fragrance, light, sounds, vapour, heat; **c** otherwise only in *books emanating from a well-known press* &c.

emanation, n. [1. èmanáshun; 2. èmənéiʃən], fr. L. Lat. *ēmānātiōn-(em)*, 'emanation'; prec. & **-ion.** Something which emanates; **a** (material things) odour, vapour, fragrance &c.: *unhealthy emanations from the river mud*; **b** (of moral qualities) influence, outpouring, effluence.

emanative, adj. [1. émanàtiv; 2. émənèitiv]. **emanate** & **-ive.** Of the nature of an emanation.

emancipate, vb. trans. [1. ēmánsipāt; 2. imǽnsipeit], fr. Lat. *ēmancipāt-(um)*, P.P. type of *ēmancipāre*, 'to declare (a person) free and independent; liberate a son from paternal authority, to transfer one's authority; to give up, surrender', fr. **e-** & *mancipāre*, 'to transfer property; to dispose of; to give up', fr. *mancip-(is)*, genit. of *manceps*, 'purchaser'; cp. *mancipium*, 'legal purchase', right of ownership'. See **manciple. 1.** (Rom. law) To release a child from parental control. **2. a** To give legal freedom to, set free from bondage or servitude: *to emancipate slaves*; **b** to release from legal or moral constraint or control: *to emancipate oneself from the power of sin, from debt, from tedious duties* &c

emancipated, adj. [1. emánsipāted; 2. imǽnsipeitid], fr. P.P. of prec. **a** Set free from legal compulsion; **b** set free from political and moral restraint; **c** (special use) freed from restraint of social convention and custom; hence, unconventional, being a law to oneself: *an emancipated young woman.*

emancipation, n. [1. ēmànsipáshun; 2. imǽnsipéiʃən]. Lat. *ēmancipātiōn-(em)*, 'the release (of a son) from parental authority; transfer of property or authority'. See prec. & **-ion.** The act or process of emancipating; state of being emancipated; setting free from restraint; removal of political or legal disqualifications: specif., *emancipation of the negro; Catholic emancipation.*

emancipationist, n. [1. ēmànsipáshunist; 2. imǽnsipéiʃənist]. See prec. & **-ist.** One who advocates emancipation from political or religious disabilities.

emancipatory, adj. [1. ēmánsipàtori; 2. imǽnsipèitəri]. **emancipate** & **-ory.** Serving to emancipate.

emancipist, n. [1. ēmánsipist; 2. imǽnsipist]. See **emancipate** & **-ist.** An ex-convict.

emasculate (I.), vb. trans. [1. ēmáskūlāt; 2. imǽskjuleit]. Lat. *ēmasculāt-(um)*, P.P. type of *ēmasculāre*, 'to emasculate'. **e-** & *masculus*, 'male; manly, bold'. See **masculine** & **-ate. 1.** To deprive of male properties, to castrate. **2.** (fig.) To weaken, deprive of vigour, lessen force of.

emasculate (II.), gen. **emasculated**, adj. [1. emáskūlat, -āted; 2. imǽskjulət, -eitid], fr. prec. Effeminate, lacking physical, moral, or intellectual vigour.

emasculation, n. [1. ēmàskūláshun; 2. imǽskjuléiʃən]. **emasculate** & **-ion.** The act of emasculating; state of being emasculated.

emasculative, adj. [1. ēmáskūlativ; 2. imǽskjulətiv]. **emasculate** & **-ive.** Tending to emasculate.

emasculatory, adj. [1. ēmáskūlatori; 2. imǽskjulətəri]. **emasculate** & **-ory.** Emasculative.

embalm, vb. trans. [1. embáhm; 2. imbám], fr. Fr. *embaumer.* **em-** & **balm. 1.** To preserve (a dead body) from decay by removing viscera and injecting with various preservative and disinfectant substances, originally with balm or other aromatic spices. **2.** (fig.) To preserve memory of, cherish: '*Tears eternal that embalm the dead*' (Pope), i.e. preserve their memory. **3.** To impart a perfume to, make fragrant: '*The circumambient air embalmed with flowers*'.

embalmment, n. [1. embáhmment; 2. imbámmənt]. Prec. & **-ment.** The act, or process, of embalming; state of being embalmed.

embank, vb. trans. [1. embángk; 2. imbǽŋk]. **em-** & **bank (II.).** To keep within limits (a river &c.) by construction of banks, walls &c.; to construct a bank for.

embankment, n. [1. embángkment; 2. imbǽŋkmənt]. Prec. & **-ment. 1.** The act of embanking; state of being embanked. **2. a** Structure of stone &c. designed to keep a river &c. from overflowing, or from washing away its natural banks; specif., *The Embankment*, particular stretch of road on the embankment of left bank of the Thames in London; **b** artificial bank, built up to carry a railway line or a road.

embargo (I.), n. [1. embárgō; 2. ɛmbágou], fr. Span. *embargar*, fr. **em-** & Low Lat. **barricāre*, fr. *barra*, 'a bar, barrier'. See **barricade. 1.** An order of the Admiralty to prevent foreign ships from entering a home port, or to prevent any ships from leaving port. **2.** Temporary stoppage of trade, or particular branch of trade, by authority of the government: *to be under an embargo.* **3.** Any prohibition: *to lay an embargo upon.*

embargo (II.), vb. trans., fr. prec. **1.** To lay (ships, trade) under an embargo. **2.** To seize by authority of the state, requisition.

embark, vb. trans. & intrans. [1. embárk; 2. imbák], fr. Fr. *embarquer*, fr. Low Lat. *imbarcāre*, fr. **em-** & *barca*, 'a small boat'. See **bark (V.). A.** intrans. **1. a** To go on board a ship; **b** to start on journey. **2.** (fig.) To start, to take part in, to engage in: *to embark upon a venture.* **B.** trans. To receive, take on board a ship: *to embark passengers and cargo.*

embarkation, n. [1. èmbarkáshun; 2. èmbākéiʃən]. See prec. & **-ation. a** The act of embarking, taking, or going, on board ship: *embarkation of passengers*; **b** that which is embarked.

embarras de richesse, n. [1. ombahráh de rēshés; 2. ãbara də riʃés]. Fr. See next word. Not now used in that language, the phrase in wh. is *embarras du choix.* Superfluity of good things.

embarrass, vb. trans. [1. embáras; 2. imbǽrəs], fr. Fr. *embarrasser*, fr. **em-** & Span. *barras*, 'bars'. See **bar (I.). 1. a** To hinder (movement); encumber, entangle, obstruct: *to embarrass one's movements*; **b** (fig.) specif., to cause financial stringency: *his affairs had become embarrassed through unfortunate speculations.* **2.** To throw into perplexity, cause confusion of mind; put out of countenance; cause feeling of constraint: *I was much embarrassed at meeting, at a dinner-party, the man whose book I had just reviewed.*

embarrassingly, adv. [1. embárasingli; 2. imbǽrəsiŋli]. Pres. Part. of prec. & **-ly.** In an embarrassing manner; so as to cause embarrassment.

embarrassment, n. [1. embárasment; 2. imbǽrəsmənt]. **embarrass** & **-ment. 1.** The act of embarrassing, state of being embarrassed; **a** in freedom of movement; **b** in financial affairs; **c** in mind; condition of being put out of countenance; awkwardness. **2.** That which embarrasses; **a** cause of difficulty in moving; **b** source of financial distress; **c** cause of awkwardness; disconcerting circumstance or situation.

embassy, n. [1. émbasi; 2. émbəsi], fr. O. Fr. *ambassée*, fr. Low Lat. **ambactiata*, fr. Lat. *ambactia*, 'service, duty'. See **ambassador. 1.** An ambassador's staff, or household; body of persons connected by their duties with him. **2. a** The official residence of an ambassador in a foreign capital; **b** the office where he transacts his business. **3. a** Particular duty or mission with which an ambassador is charged; **b** any mission, set of negotiations, with which an agent is charged; particular message which he has to deliver.

embattle (I.), vb. trans. [1. embátl; 2. imbǽtl], fr. O. Fr. *embataillier*, fr. **em-** & *bataille*, 'battle'. See **battle.** To prepare for conflict, put in order of, draw up for, battle (rare except in P.P.). See below.

embattle (**II.**), vb. trans., fr. **em-** & M.E. *bataile*, 'to embattle'. See **battlement**. To build battlements on: *to embattle a wall, tower* &c.

embattled, adj. [1. embátld; 2. *i*mbǽtld]. P.P. of prec. words. **a** Formed, drawn up, in battle array: *embattled line*; **b** (her.) line formed like the battlements on a tower.

embay, vb. trans. [1. embā́; 2. *i*mbéi]. See **em-** & **bay** (**I.**). **1.** To shelter (a fleet &c.) as though in a bay. **2.** To form into bays.

embayment, n. [1. embā́ment; 2. *i*mbéimənt], fr. prec. & **-ment**. Formation like that of a bay.

embed, imbed, vb. trans. [1. embéd; 2. *i*mbéd], fr. **em-** & **bed**. **1.** (of material things) To implant a thing deeply and firmly in some other substance, so that it remains wholly or partially surrounded by this: *to embed a stone in plaster*; *a thorn embedded in the finger* &c. **2.** (of non-material things) To fix deeply in the mind, memory, habits &c.: *the facts are embedded for ever in my recollection*.

embellish, vb. trans. [1. embélish; 2. *i*mbéli∫]. M.E. *embellischen*, fr. O. Fr. *embelliss-*, Pres. stem of *embellir*, 'beautify', fr. **em-** & *bel*, 'beautiful', fr. Lat. *bellus*, 'pretty'. See **beauty, belle**. **1.** To render more beautiful, improve appearance of; to adorn, add ornaments to. **2.** To touch up, improve (a story, narrative &c.) by adding striking incidents, touches of humour, pathos &c.; generally, to render more interesting, often at expense of strict veracity.

embellishment, n. [1. embélishment; 2. *i*mbéli∫mənt]. Prec. & **-ment**. **1.** The act of embellishing; state of being embellished. **2.** That which embellishes; adornment, artistic touch.

ember, n. [1. émber; 2. émbə]. O.E. *ǣmerġe*, 'embers, ashes'; M.E. *emmeres*; cp. O.N. *eimyria*; O.H.G. *eimuria*. Glowing fragments of wood, coal &c., in a dying fire; smouldering ashes; usually in pl.

ember days, n. O.E. *ymbrenu*, 'ember days', for *ymbryne*, 'motion round, lapse of time'; M.E. *embir-dayes* &c. (S.E. type); fr. *ymb*, 'round, about', see **ambi-**, & *ryne*, 'course, running', see **run**. Regularly occurring days of prayer and fasting at four seasons in the Church's year: Wed., Fri., Sat. after 1st Sunday in Lent; after Whitsun; after Sept. 14th (Holy Cross Day); after Dec. 13th (St. Lucy's Day).

ember (**goose**), n., fr. Norse *emmer*. Sea-bird found in the Orkneys; the loon.

ember-week, n. One in which ember days occur.

embezzle, vb. trans. [1. embézl; 2. *i*mbézl]. O. Fr. *embesilles*, O. Fr. *besil*, 'ill treatment'. Etymol. uncertain. To convert fraudulently to one's own use, money entrusted to one's charge.

embezzlement, n. [1. embézlment; 2. *i*mbézlmənt]. Prec. & **-ment**. The act of embezzling.

embezzler, n. [1. embézler; 2. *i*mbézlə]. See prec. & **-er**. One guilty of embezzlement.

embitter, vb. trans. [1. embíter; 2. *i*mbítə], fr. **em-** & **bitter**. (only fig.) To render bitter. **a** (of persons) To arouse ill feelings in, render morose, disappointed; **b** (of the mind, feelings, relations &c.) to fill with bitterness; to render worse what is already bad; to aggravate, make more intense.

embitterment, n. [1. embíterment; 2. *i*mbítəmənt]. Prec. & **-ment**. The act or process of embittering; state of being embittered.

emblazon, vb. trans. [1. emblā́zn; 2. *i*mbléizn]. **em-** & **blazon**. **1. a** To portray, esp. a coat of arms, on a shield; **b** to adorn a shield &c. with a coat of arms. **2.** (fig.) To proclaim fame of, extol.

emblazonment, n. [1. emblā́znment; 2. *i*mbléiznmənt]. Prec. & **-ment**. **1.** Act of emblazoning. **2.** That which is emblazoned; blazon.

emblazonry, n. [1. emblā́znri; 2. *i*mbléiznri]. **em-** & **blazonry**. Blazonry.

emblem (**I.**), n. [1. émblem; 2. émbləm], fr. Lat., fr. Gk. *émblēma*, 'something inserted or inlaid'; cogn. w. *embállein*, 'to throw in, put in; to make an inroad', fr. **em-** & *bállein*, 'to throw, hurl; to strike'; cp. *blêma*, 'a throw (of dice); a shot'; & see **ballistics**. Visible representation of an idea or quality, a symbol; a symbolic figure or device.

emblem (**II.**), vb. trans., fr. prec. (rare) To be an emblem of, be typical of.

emblematic, adj. [1. èmblemátik; 2. èmbl*i*mǽt*i*k], fr. Gk. *émblēmat-*, stem of *émblēma*. See prec. & **-ic**. Of the nature of an emblem; symbolical.

emblematically, adv. [1. èmblemátikali; 2. èmbl*i*mǽt*i*kəl*i*]. Prec. & **-al** & **-ly**. By means of an emblem.

emblematist, n. [1. emblématist; 2. *i*mblémətist]. See **emblematic** & **-ist**. One who devises emblems or symbols.

emblematize, vb. trans. [1. emblématīz; 2. *i*mblémətaiz]. See prec. & **-ize**. To represent something by means of an emblem.

emblement(s), n. [1. émblement(s); 2. émbləmənt(s)], fr. O. Fr. *emblaement*, fr. *emblaer*, 'to sow', fr. Low Lat. *imbladāre*, fr. **em-** & Low Lat. *blādum* for *ablātum*, 'carried away', that wh. was removed, or carried off the land, hence, by specializing process, 'wheat'. Cp. Fr. *blé*. Lat. *lātum*, used as P.P. of *ferre*, 'bear', is for **tlāt-*, fr. base **tol-*, q.v. under **tolerate**. (usually pl.) Crops sown on arable land; profits of such crops.

embodiment, n. [1. embódiment; 2. *i*mbɔ́d*i*mənt]. See next word & **-ment**. **a** The act of embodying; **b** that which embodies, or is embodied.

embody, vb. trans. [1. embódi; 2. *i*mbɔ́d*i*]. **em-** & **body**. **1.** To enclose in a body, to give a corporeal form to: *an embodied spirit*. **2.** To give concrete form to; express a thought, emotion, attitude of mind &c. in a concrete work of art: *to embody religious aspirations in a cathedral*; *in 'Paradise Lost' Milton embodied the ripe fruits of his genius*; *to embody one's views in a speech*. **3. a** To make part of an organized body: *in 1870 the various German states were all embodied in the Empire*; **b** to collect together, and include in a single instrument: *the book of statutes of a university embodies all the rules and ordinances under which it works*.

embog, vb. trans. [1. embóg; 2. *i*mbɔ́g]. **em-** & **bog**. **a** To cause to become stuck in a bog; **b** (fig.) to cause to become entangled in intellectual difficulties.

embolden, vb. trans. [1. embṓlden; 2. *i*mbóuldn]. **em-** & **bold** & **-en**. To give courage and confidence to.

embolism, n. [1. émbolizm; 2. émbəlizəm], fr. Gk. *émbol-(os)*, 'something put in, a wedge', & **-ism**, cogn. w. *embállein*, 'to throw, thrust in'; **em-** & *bállein*, 'throw'. See **ballistics**. (med.) Clot of blood obstructing a blood-vessel.

embonpoint, n. [1. ombonpwán; 2. ā̃bɔ̃pwǣ̃]. Fr. for *en bon point*, 'in good condition'; hence n., 'stoutness'. Cp. Chaucer's *in good point*. Stoutness, portliness of figure.

embosom, vb. trans. [1. embóozm; 2. *i*mbúzm]. **em-** & **bosom**. **a** To take into one's arms, press to one's breast; **b** (of hills, woods &c.) to surround, shut in.

emboss, vb. trans. [1. embós; 2. *i*mbɔ́s], fr. O. Fr. See **em-** & **boss**. **1.** To cover surface of, with designs in raised work; to adorn with figures, designs &c., in relief: *to emboss an object with a design*. **2.** To execute a design in raised work upon a surface: *to emboss a pattern on metal*.

embossment, n. [1. embósment; 2. *i*mbɔ́smənt]. Prec. & **-ment**. **a** Act of embossing, state of being embossed; **b** that which is embossed; design in relief.

embouchure, n. [1. ombo͞oshúr; 2. ā̃bū∫úə]. Fr., 'mouth of a river; mouthpiece of musical instrument' &c., fr. **em-** & *bouche*, 'mouth' (see **debouch**), & **-ure**. **1.** Mouth of a river, estuary. **2. a** Mouthpiece of musical instrument; **b** mode of placing lips in playing a wind instrument.

embow, vb. trans. [1. embṓ; 2. ɛmbóu]. **em-** & **bow** (**I.**). (archaic) To bend into form of an arch, or bow.

embowed, adj. [1. embṓd; 2. ɛmbóud], fr. P.P. of prec. **1.** Arched, curved, bent like a bow; vaulted. **2.** (her.) Curved or bent like a bow; e.g. *a dolphin embowed*.

embowel, vb. trans. [1. embóuel; 2. *i*mbáuil], fr. O. Fr. *enboueler*, perh. for *esboueler*. **em-** & **bowel**. Usually *disembowel*. **1.** To remove the entrails of, to eviscerate. **2.** To plunge into, embed in.

embower, vb. trans. [1. embóuer; 2. *i*mbáuə]. **em-** & **bower**. To enclose, lap round as in a bower: *a house embowered in trees*.

embrace (**I.**), vb. trans. [1. embrā́s; 2. *i*mbréis]. M.E. *embracen*, fr. O. Fr. *embracer*, 'to take into one's arms'; **em-** & O. Fr. *braz*, 'arm', fr. Lat. *brachium*. See **brace**. **1. a** (of one person) To take, fold, clasp another in one's arms: *to embrace one's children*; **b** used absol., of two persons: *they met and embraced*. **2.** (fig.) **a** To seize, avail oneself of: *to embrace an opportunity, offer* &c.; **b** to adopt: *to embrace Christianity*; **c** to engage in, set out on: *to embrace the career of a missionary*. **3. a** To include, comprehend, comprise: *his studies embraced many subjects*; *this book embraces the whole field of ancient Greek history*; **b** to take in by perception: *he embraced the whole scene with one rapid glance*.

embrace (**II.**), n., fr. prec. A clasp, a hug; close, intimate, folding in the arms.

embracement, n. [1. embrā́sment; 2. *i*mbréismənt]. **embrace** (**I.**) & **-ment**. An embrace.

embracer (**I.**), n. [1. embrā́ser; 2. *i*mbréisə]. **embrace** (**I.**) & **-er**. One who embraces.

embracer (**II.**), n., fr. O. Fr. *embraceur*, 'instigator, corrupter', fr. *embraser*, 'to set on fire, instigate'. See **em-** & **brase**. (law) One guilty of embracery.

embracery, n. [1. embrā́seri; 2. *i*mbréisəri]. Prec. & **-y**. (law) Attempt to corrupt, or influence by corrupt means, a court, jury &c.

embranchment, n. [1. embráhnchment; 2. *i*mbrántʃmənt]. **em-** & **branch** & **-ment**. A branching or forking out, ramification; esp. of a river.

embrangle, vb. trans. [1. embránggl; 2. ɛmbrǽŋgl]. Bogus word; apparently a blend of *embroil* & *entangle*. To mix up, entangle.

embrasure, n. [1. embrā́zhur; 2. *i*mbréiʒə]. O. Fr. *embraser*; of unknown origin. **a** (archit.) Recessed opening, or splay, in interior wall for window or doorway; esp. such an opening with sides bevelled so that the aperture is wider inside than outside; **b** (fort.) similar opening in a rampart or fortified wall &c., through which guns &c., can be fired.

embrocate, vb. trans. [1. émbrōkāt; 2. émbroukèit], fr. Med. Lat. *embrocāt-(um)*, P.P. type of *embrocāre*, fr. Gk. *émbrokhē*, 'fomentation', fr. *embrékhein*, 'to foment'; **em-** & *brékhein*, 'to water, wet, cause to rain', perh. for **mregh-*. Cp. Lett. *mergût*, 'to rain gently'; *merga*, 'rain'. To apply liquid remedies, lotions, externally in form of fomentation or by rubbing.

embrocation, n. [1. èmbrokā́shun; 2. èmbrəkéi∫ən]. Prec. & **-ation**. Medicinal lotion, applied as fomentation or by rubbing into an affected part as sprain &c.

embroider, vb. trans. & intrans. [1. embróider; 2. *i*mbrɔ́idə]. M.E., fr. **em-** & O. Fr. *broder*, *border*, 'to work the edge of', fr. *bord*, 'edge, margin'. See **border**. **A.** trans. **1.** To work designs with a needle, in silk, wool &c.: **a** *to embroider a pattern*; **b** *to embroider a handkerchief with a pattern*. **2.** To embellish, touch up, improve (a story &c.), by adding fanciful details. **B.** intrans. To carry out, perform, action of embroidery.

embroidery, n. [1. embróideri; 2. *i*mbrɔ́idəri], fr. prec. & **-y**. **a** Ornamentation of fabrics by needlework; **b** (fig.) adornment, diversification of colour in nature, by flowers &c.

embroil, vb. trans. [1. embróil; 2. *i*mbrói*l*], fr. Fr. *embrouiller*. See **em-** & **broil (II.)**. **1.** To draw into, entangle, cause to take part in (hostilities, disturbance &c.): *to become embroiled in a dispute* &c. **2.** To make confused, bring into disorder, to muddle (business affairs &c.).

embroilment, n. [1. embróilment; 2. *i*mbrói*l*mənt]. See prec. & **-ment**. The act of embroiling; state of being embroiled.

embrown, vb. trans. [1. embróun; 2. *i*mbráun], fr. **em-** & **brown**. To impart a brown colour to, to make brown.

embryo (I.), n. & adj. [1. émbriō; 2. émbri*ou*], fr. Med. Lat. *embryo*, fr. Gk. *émbruon*, 'a newborn lamb; an embryo'; cogn. w. *brúein*, 'to be full, to swell; to burst forth with'; *bruáktēs*, '(of Pan) the god of joviality'; *brúon*, 'moss; a cluster of flowers'; *bruóeis*, 'mossy, weedy; budding, flourishing'. Etymol. doubtful, but see **bryologist**. **1.** n. **a** An organism in the earliest stages of its development before birth; **b** (of material and non-material things) anything rudimentary, in an early stage of development; Phr. *in embryo*, in an incipient stage, not yet developed. **2.** adj. Rudimentary, not fully developed, embryonic.

embryo- (II.), pref., fr. prec. Pertaining to an embryo or foetus.

embryogeny, n. [1. èmbriójeni; 2. èmbri*ó*džəni]. Prec. & **-geny**. **a** The formation and development of the embryo; **b** the science treating of this.

embryology, n. [1. èmbriólogi; 2. èmbri*ó*lədži]. **embryo** & **-logy**. The science of the formation and growth of the embryo.

embryonic, adj. [1. èmbriónik; 2. èmbri*ó*ni*k*], fr. Med. Lat. *embryōn-(is)*, genit. of *embryo*. **embryo** & **-ic**. Pertaining to an embryo; resembling this; in an undeveloped state, rudimentary.

eme, n. [1. ēm; 2. īm]. O.E. *ēam*, cogn. w. Du. *oom*, Germ. *oheim*, Lat. *avunculus*. Cp. **atavism**. (Scots or provinc.) Uncle; also friend, gossip.

emend, vb. trans. [1. ē-, eménd; 2. ī-, *i*ménd], fr. Lat. *ēmendāre*, 'to correct, improve, emend', fr. **e-** & *menda*, 'a fault, defect, blemish; an error, mistake'; cp. Scrt. *mindā*, 'physical blemish'; O. Ir. *mennair*, 'blemish'. Etymol. doubtful; cp. **amend**, fr. Lat. through Fr. To correct a mistake in (a document, text &c.); to suggest a reading different from that in text, on the ground that it makes better sense, and is more likely to be the original.

emendation, n. [1. èmendáshun; 2. ìmendéiʃən], fr. Lat. *ēmendātiōn-(em)*, 'a correction, emendation'. Prec. & **-ation**. **a** The act of emending; **b** an alteration made in a text with a view to restoring what seems likely to have been the original reading.

emendatory, adj. [1. eméndatori; 2. *i*méndətəri], fr. Lat. *ēmendāt-(um)*, P.P. type of *ēmendāre*, 'to correct'. See prec. & **-ory**. Of the nature of an emendation; tending to improve and emend.

emerald (I.), n. [1. émerald; 2. ém(ə)rəld]. M.E. *emeraude*, fr. O. Fr. *esmeralde*, *esmeraude*, fr. Lat. *smaragdum*, (acc.) fr. Gk. *smáragdos*, *máragdos*, 'emerald'; of Heb. origin. **1.** A precious stone resembling the beryl, of a bright green colour; the *Oriental emerald* is a rare green variety of corundum, akin to the sapphire. **2.** The colour of the emerald, a vivid green. **3.** A variety of printing-type, intermediate in size between minion and nonpareil.

emerald (II.), adj., fr. prec. **a** Made of, set with, emeralds: *an emerald ring* &c.; **b** pertaining to, resembling, having the colour of, an emerald; Phr. *Emerald Isle*, Ireland, from the colour of its grass and foliage.

emeraldine, n. [1. émeraldēn; 2. émrəldīn]. **emerald** & **-ine**. A kind of dark green dye.

emerge, vb. trans. [1. ēmérj; 2. īmə́dž], fr. Lat. *ēmergere*, 'to come forth, rise up; to extricate oneself, get free'; fr. **e-** & *mergere*, 'to dip, immerse, sink; to drive or fix in; to overwhelm'. See **merge**. **1.** (of persons and material things) **a** To come into view from obscurity or concealment: *to emerge from hiding, from retirement* &c.; **b** to come out of some enfolding medium, esp. from water: *to emerge from the sea*; **c** (fig.) to pass from obscure, or humble circumstances to superior condition; come out of social obscurity: *many famous men have emerged from poverty and mean surroundings*. **2.** (of non-material things) To come to light, become apparent, become known; to be elicited by inquiry and investigation: *no new facts emerged as a result of these researches*; *several striking ideas emerged in the course of his remarks*.

emergence, n. [1. emérjens; 2. *i*mə́džəns]. Prec. & **-ence**. Process of emerging.

emergency, n. [1. emérjensi; 2. *i*mə́džənsi]. Prec. & **-y**. A sudden, unexpected event or happening; combination of circumstances calling for swift and decided action: *ready for all emergencies*; *a useful man in an emergency*.

emergency ration, n. Ration of concentrated food &c., issued to troops on active service, only to be used in emergency, also called 'iron ration'.

emergent, adj. [1. ēmérjent; 2. īmə́džənt]. Lat. *ēmergent-(em)*, Pres. Part. of *ēmergere*. See **emerge**. Arising, coming forth, from that which surrounds or conceals; in process of emerging.

emeritus, adj. [1. ēméritus; 2. īméritəs]. Lat. *ēmeritus*, 'a veteran; a soldier who has served his time'; fr. **e-** & *meritus*, P.P. of *merēri*, 'to earn, gain, acquire, to deserve, be entitled to'. See **merit**. Having retired or resigned after long and honourable service: *emeritus Professor*, title conferred by a university on one who has retired from his chair.

emerods, n. pl. [1. émerodz; 2. émərədz]. O. Fr. *emmeroides*. See **haemorrhoids**. (Bibl. and obs.).

emersion, n. [1. ēmérshun; 2. īmə́ʃən], fr. Lat. *ēmers-(um)*, P.P. type of *ēmergere*, 'to come forth, rise up; to raise oneself, get clear'. See **emerge** & **-ion**. Process of emerging; specif. (astron.) the reappearance of a heavenly body after eclipse.

emery, n. [1. émeri; 2. éməri], fr. O. Fr. *emeril*, fr. Low Lat. *smericulum*, fr. Gk. *smēris*, *smúris*, 'emery-powder'. Cp. Gk. *(s)murízein*, 'to anoint with perfumes'; *múron*, 'perfumed oil'; cogn. w. Goth. *smairþr*, 'fatness.' See **smear**. A very hard, granular variety of corundum, used in the form of powder for grinding and polishing metal.

emery-bag, n. Small bag of emery-powder, used for polishing and sharpening needles, by plunging them into it.

emery-cloth, -paper, n. Cloth or paper with coating of emery-powder, for rubbing and polishing metal.

emetic, adj. & n. [1. emétik; 2. *i*méti*k*], fr. Gk. *emetikós*, 'emetic', fr. *eméō* for **wem-jō*, 'vomit'. See **vomit**. **a** adj. Causing vomiting; **b** n., anything which, taken internally, causes vomiting; drug or other substance taken for this purpose.

émeute, n. [1. ēmūt; 2. īmjūt] or [1. āmét; 2. emøt]. Fr., fr. Lat. *ēmōtum*, *-a*, P.P. of *ēmovēre*, 'to move away, upheave'. See **emotion**, & **e-** & **motion**. A riot, serious disorderly rising of the inhabitants of a town or district.

emigrant, adj. & n. [1. émigrant; 2. émigrənt]. Lat. *ēmīgrant-(em)*, Pres. Part. of *ēmīgrāre*. See **emigrate**. **1.** adj. **a** In the act of emigrating, about to emigrate; **b** pertaining to emigrants. **2.** n. One who emigrates.

emigrate, vb. intrans. [1. émigrāt; 2. émigreit], fr. Lat. *ēmīgrāt-(um)*, P.P. type of *ēmīgrāre*, 'to move away, move out'; fr. **e-** & *mīgrāre*, 'to move; to change one's position or residence'. See **migrate**. **a** To leave one country or state in order to settle in another, esp. in a colony &c.; to change one's country of residence permanently: *many now are compelled to emigrate in order to make a livelihood*; **b** (colloq.) to move to a new place of residence (not necessarily in another country).

emigration, n. [1. èmigráshun; 2. èmigréiʃən]. Prec. & **-ion**. The act of emigrating.

emigratory, adj. [1. émigràtori; 2. émigrèitəri]. **emigrate** & **-ory**. (of birds) In the habit of emigrating; migratory.

émigré, n. [1. émigrā; 2. émigrei]. Fr. P.P. An emigrant; specif., a person compelled to leave France at the time of the Revolution.

eminence, n. [1. éminens; 2. éminəns]. See next word & **-ce**. **1.** Something eminent, lofty, high; something which rises above surrounding objects; a hill, cliff, high ground, rising to considerably higher level than that of country round it &c. **2. a** Loftiness, superiority, of position, station, rank, office: '*By merit raised to that bad eminence*' (Milton); *a position of eminence in the world*; **b** distinction of character, abilities, attainments; hence celebrity, fame: *a man of eminence in the world of learning* &c.; *his eminence was due to several important discoveries*; **c** (cap.) a title of honour given to cardinals in R.C. Church: *your, his, Eminence*.

eminent, adj. [1. éminent; 2. éminənt], fr. Lat. *ēminent-(em)*, Pres. Part. of *ēminēre*, 'to stand out, project; be eminent'; fr. **e-** & **minēre*, 'to project'. See **minatory** & **mount**. **1.** (of persons) Outstanding, distinguished, of high position, prominent; famous: *an eminent statesman, soldier*. **2.** (of qualities of mind &c.) Outstanding, conspicuous, clearly perceptible: *a man of eminent goodness, impartiality* &c.; for *eminent domain* see **domain**.

eminently, adv. Prec. & **-ly**. In an eminent manner; esp. in sense conspicuously: *eminently fair*.

emir, n. [1. emḗr; 2. *i*míə], fr. Arab. *amir*, 'commander'. See **ameer**. **a** Mohammedan title given to an independent prince, chief &c., in Arabia &c.; **b** a descendant of Mohammed, entitled to certain privileges.

emissary, n. [1. émisari; 2. émisəri], fr. L. Lat. *ēmissārius*, 'one sent out', fr. *ēmiss-(um)*, P.P. type of *ēmittere*, 'to send forth; to give out'. See **emit** & **-ary**. One entrusted with delivery of a message; one charged with conducting negotiations; often used with rather sinister implication: *an emissary of the Devil*.

emission, n. [1. emíshun; 2. *i*míʃən], fr. Lat. *ēmissiōn-(em)*, 'a giving or sending out', fr. *ēmiss-(um)*, P.P. type of *ēmittere*, 'to give or send out, emit'. See **emit** & **-ion**. **1.** The act or process of emitting: *the emission of light, heat, odour* &c. **2.** That which is emitted, in various senses; a flow, discharge.

emissive, adj. [1. emísiv; 2. *i*mísiv]. See prec. & **-ive**. Having the property of emitting.

emit, vb. trans. [1. emít; 2. *i*mít], fr. Lat. *ēmittere*, 'to give or send out, emit'; fr. **e-** & *mittere*, 'to send'. See **mission**, **mittimus**. **1. a** To give out, cause to issue forth, send forth: *the sun emits light and heat*; *to emit a sound*; **b** to give off: *to emit an odour*; **c** to discharge, eject: *a wound emits purulent matter*. **2.** To issue, put into circulation: *to emit paper money* &c.

emmet, n. [1. émet; 2. émit]. O.E. *ǣmete*; M.E. *emte*, *amete*. Variant of **ant**.

emollient, adj. & n. [1. emólient; 2. *i*móliənt]. Lat. *ēmollient-(em)*, Pres. Part. type of *ēmollīre*, 'to soften, sooth'; fr. **e-** & *moll-(is)*, 'soft'. See **mollify**. **1.** adj. **a** Having the property of softening and soothing; making soft and supple; **b** (fig.) tending to mollify, soothe the mind. **2.** n. Medicinal substance which soothes; one which softens hardened or inflamed tissues.

emolument, n. [1. emólūment; 2. *i*móljumənt], fr. Lat. *ēmolument-(um)* for *ēmolimentum*, 'what is got by exertion, gain, profit, advantage'; fr. *ēmolere*, 'to grind out'. **e-** & *molere*, 'to grind in a mill'. See **molar** & **mill**. Profits, salary, fees, derived from an office or occupation.

emotion, n. [1. emóshun; 2. imóuʃən], fr. Lat. *ēmōt-(um)*, P.P. type of *ēmovēre*, 'to remove, move away; shake, upheave', & **-ion. e- & motion. 1.** Stirring up, agitation, excitement of the feelings: *I cannot hear that song without emotion.* **2.** Any of the feelings, contrasted with the mental processes of reasoning; the feelings of joy, grief, hatred, love, fear &c. *Emotion*, in popular language, refers to feelings arising from the heart, not from a rational activity of the intellect: *to appeal to the emotions rather than to the reason; a man of strong, feeble, emotions.*

emotional, adj. [1. emóshunal; 2. imóuʃənəl]. Prec. & **-al. 1.** Pertaining to, connected with, seated in, addressed to, the feelings or emotions: *an emotional appeal.* **2.** (of persons) **a** Having strong emotions; having feelings easily aroused: *an emotional nature, woman* &c.; **b** capable of expressing emotions: *an emotional actor.* **3.** (of artistic expression) Deeply imbued with emotion; produced under stress of, and expressing, strong emotion: *emotional music, poetry* &c.

emotionalism, n. [1. emóshunalizm; 2. imóuʃənəlizəm]. Prec. & **-ism.** Habit of encouraging and cultivating a highly sensitive, excited state of the feelings.

emotionalist, n. [1. emóshunalist; 2. imóuʃənəlist]. **emotional & -ist.** One who is a prey to emotionalism.

emotionality, n. [1. emòshunáliti; 2. imòuʃənǽliti]. **emotional & -ity.** State of being emotional, emotional habit of mind.

emotionalize, vb. trans. [1. emóshunalīz; 2. imóuʃənəlaiz]. **emotional & -ize.** To consider in emotional aspect, to treat emotionally: *to emotionalize history.*

emotionally, adv. [1. emóshunali; 2. imóuʃənəli]. **emotional & -ly.** In an emotional manner.

emotionless, adj. [1. emóshunles; 2. imóuʃənlis]. **emotion & -less.** Lacking, free from, emotion; not expressing emotion: *an emotionless nature; an emotionless voice.*

emotive, adj. [1. ēmótiv; 2. īmóutiv], fr. Lat. *ēmōt-(um)*, P.P. type of *ēmovēre*, 'to remove' &c., & **-ive.** See **emotion. a** Causing, expressing, emotion: *the emotive side of human nature;* **b** based on, inspired by, consideration of emotion: *the emotive aspect of poetry.*

emotively, adv. Prec. & **-ly.** In an emotive manner.

emotivity, n. [1. èmōtíviti; 2. ìmoutíviti]. **emotive & -ity.** Capacity for emotion; emotional quality.

empanel, impanel, vb. trans. [1. empánl; 2. impǽnl], fr. O. Fr. *empaneller.* See **em- & panel.** To form, call together, enrol (a jury).

emperor, n. [1. émperor; 2. émpərə], fr. O. Fr. *empereor*, fr. Lat. *imperātor*, 'a ruler, commander, military commander; emperor', fr. *imperāre*, 'to hold supreme command', fr. **im-** & *parāre*, 'to prepare, make ready; to direct, command'. See **pare & -or. 1.** The ruler of an empire; one holding supreme authority over more than one kingdom; specif. **a** (hist.) the head of the Roman Empire, West or East, and of the later Holy Roman Empire; **b** the King of England as Emperor of India &c. **2.** One of various kinds of butterflies; e.g. *Purple Emperor, Grey Emperor* &c.

emphasis, n. [1. émfasis; 2. émfəsis]. Gk. *émphasis*, 'outward appearance; reflection; declaration; significance, emphasis', fr. **em-** & *phásis* (fr. *phn̥-t-is), 'accusation, information', fr. same base as *phainein*, 'to show, make visible; appear' (for *phn̥-jō). See **phantasm, phase. 1.** (of mental attitude) Special importance, significance, weight, meaning, moral or emotional value, attached to an idea, principle, feeling: *to lay special emphasis upon the study of languages in education; to place great emphasis upon sacraments in religious life.* **2.** (of the expression of sense of importance &c.) Any device or method used for calling special attention to importance of something expressed, or of one part of something compared with the rest; way of rendering specially significant, of calling attention to some particular thing; **a** (in speech) stress, accent; greater force, or higher pitch, with which a syllable of a word or part of a sentence is uttered: *to put too much emphasis on the last syllable;* **b** (in pictorial art) special distinctness of outline or vividness of colour: *the emphasis in Constable's pictures is often on the foreground.* **3.** An emphatic, categorical assertion: *I wish to say this with all the emphasis at my command.*

emphasize, vb. trans. [1. émfasīz; 2. émfəsaiz]. Prec. & **-ize. 1.** To indicate and assert importance of something; to call attention to special significance, value, weight &c. of something: *I must emphasize the necessity for immediate action; to emphasize the extent and variety of a man's work.* **2.** To give special prominence, significance to, render distinct, outstanding from rest by contrasts of various kinds; **a** (in speech) to accentuate, lay stress on, utter with greater force than the rest, a syllable, or a part of a sentence: *to emphasize all the wrong words; don't emphasize the personal pronouns so much;* **b** (in art) to render specially perceptible, or striking; to call attention to, enhance, by distinctness of line, vividness, and contrasts of colour in painting: *the painter has emphasized the right eye in a remarkable way;* by differences of loudness, time, and so on in music &c.

emphatic, adj. [1. emfátik; 2. imfǽtik], fr. Gk. *emphatikós*, 'expressive, vivid, forcible'. See **emphasis.** Expressing, characterized by, emphasis (in all senses). **1.** (of mental state or activity) Distinct, clear, positive: *an emphatic opinion.* **2.** (of expression of these in speech and writing) Clear, definite, incisive, unambiguous: *an emphatic pronouncement, statement.* **3.** (of mode of utterance) Characterized by marked contrasts, of strong and weak stress, of pitch &c., or by excessive care and clearness of articulation: *he is tedious to listen to, his pronunciation is far too emphatic.*

emphatically, adv. [1. emfátikali; 2. imfǽtikəli]. Prec. & **-al & -ly.** In an emphatic manner.

emphysema, n. [1. èmfisḗma; 2. èmfisíma], fr. Gk. *emphū́sēma*, 'inflation', fr. *emphūsáein*, fr. *en-* 'in', & *phūsáein*, 'to blow'; cp. *phūsa*, 'breath, blast'; cogn. w. Mod. Pers. *pūk*, 'act of blowing'; prob. imit. (med.) An abnormal inflation produced by air in the cellular tissues of the lungs or respiratory passages.

empire (I.), n. [1. émpīr; 2. émpaiə], fr. Fr., fr. O. Fr. *emperie*, fr. Lat. *imperium*, 'command, authority, power', esp. 'military command; dominion, sovereignty', fr. *imperāre*, 'to rule, govern, command, direct'. See **emperor, imperious. 1. a** Full and far-reaching sovereignty, supreme power over a wide domain; **b** (fig.) moral sway, influence. **2.** The dominion of an emperor; group of independent states, kingdoms, duchies &c. under the supreme rule of an emperor: *the Empire*, the British Empire, all lands under the British Crown; specif. (hist.) *Holy Roman Empire*, mediaeval empire formerly consisting of part of the Roman Empire of the West, together with the territory of Charlemagne; *Eastern and Western Empires*, the two portions into which the Roman Empire was divided in 395.

empire (II.), adj. Of, pertaining to, an empire; specif. (of style of dress, furniture &c.) of the first or second Napoleonic Empire of France.

Empire Day, n. May 24th, Queen Victoria's birthday, celebrated throughout the British Empire.

empiric (I.), n. [1. empírik; 2. empírik], fr. Lat., fr. Gk. *empeirikós*, 'experienced (applied to certain doctors who based their methods on experience and not on theory)', fr. **em-** & *peîra*, 'trial, attempt, experiment', & **-ic.** See **pirate. 1.** Member of an ancient sect of physicians who rejected all theory and relied upon experience alone. **2. a** One who is ignorant of scientific theory and principle and relies entirely upon practical experiment and experience; **b** unorthodox medical practitioner, a quack.

empiric (II.), **empirical**, adj. [1. empírik(l); 2. ɛmpírik(l)], fr. prec. (& **-al**). **1.** Based upon experiment. **2.** Based upon experiment and practical experience alone, without any regard to theory.

empirically, adv., fr. prec. & **-ly.** By experiment, according to experience: *to judge empirically.*

empiricism, n. [1. empírisizm; 2. ɛmpírisizəm]. **empiric & -ism.** Empirical method; quality of being empiric.

empiricist, n. [1. empírisist; 2. ɛmpírisist]. **empiric & -ist.** One who employs empirical methods; an empiric.

emplacement, n. [1. emplásment; 2. impléismənt]. **em- & place & -ment. a** A situation, site; **b** precise position in which something (esp. a building) is placed; **c** specif., platform for mounting heavy guns.

emplane, vb. trans. & intrans. [1. emplán; 2. empléin]. **em- & plane (V.). a** trans. To embark (passengers &c.) on an aeroplane; **b** intrans., to embark on an aeroplane.

employ (I.), vb. trans. [1. emplói; 2. implói], fr. Fr. *employer*, fr. Lat. *implicāre*, 'to enfold, fold up; include'. See **imply, implicate, plicate. 1. a** To make use of (a person's) services, to have working for one: *to employ a lawyer to draw up one's will;* **b** to provide occupation for, give work to: *the new road will employ thousands of men;* **c** (reflex.) occupy oneself, spend one's time, on; to engage in a pursuit: *how do you employ yourself of an evening?;* **d** to spend, take up, time: *your time, leisure, might be better employed learning something useful.* **2.** To make use of something as means or instrument, to use for a purpose, as a means of performing an action: *to employ a knife to cut up one's food, petrol to remove spots from clothes* &c.

employ (II.), n. See prec. **1.** (obs. or poet.) Occupation, business, work, employment. **2.** Position of working for another; service: *to have many persons in one's employ.*

employable, adj. [1. emplóiabl; 2. implóiəbl]. **employ (I.) & -able.** Capable of being utilized; capable of performing duties, work &c.; worth employing.

employee, employé, n. [1. emplóiyē, omplwáhyā; 2. ɛmplóiji, ɑ̃plwaje]. Fr. **employ & -ee.** One who is employed by another to perform certain work: *this firm treats its employees very well.*

employer, n. [1. emplóier; 2. implóiə]. **employ & -er.** One who employs; one who engages others to perform certain work for him: *an employer of labour; the miners and their employers.*

employment, n. [1. emplóiment; 2. implóimənt]. **employ & -ment. 1. a** Act of employing others, use of services of others: *the employment of labour, good workmen* &c.; **b** act of employing, or using a thing for a particular purpose: *the employment of steam-ploughs, employment of capital;* **c** use of, manner of spending: *the employment of one's time.* **2.** Work, occupation, provided for oneself or others: *out of employment; to lose one's employment.*

empoison, vb. trans. [1. empóizn; 2. impóizn]. **em- & poison. a** To make poisonous, to corrupt, taint; **b** (fig.) to instil feelings of anger into the mind, to poison.

emporium, n. [1. empórium; 2. ɛmpóriəm], fr. Lat., fr. Gk. *empórion*, 'a trading-place, market', fr. *émporos*, 'a traveller, voyager'; hence 'a trader, merchant', fr. **em-** & *póros*, 'a passage, way, road; a means, method'. Connected w. Gk. *peirein* (fr. *per-jō), 'to pierce; to cross, traverse, make a way through'. See **fare (III.), pirate. a** A place where trading is carried on; a centre of commercial activity: *London is the world's emporium;* **b** (tradesman's usage) a large shop.

empower, vb. trans. [1. empóuer; 2. impáuə]. **em-** & **power**. To give power to; **a** to give a person capacity, enable, to perform some physical or mental activity; **b** to delegate authority to, authorize, give legal right: *I empower you to sign the document on my behalf.*

empress, n. [1. émpres; 2. émpris], fr. O. Fr. *emperesse*, Lat. *imperātrix*. See **emperor** & **-ess**. **1. a** The wife of an emperor; **b** a woman ruling an empire in her own right. **2.** (fig.) Woman exercising great authority or influence: *the empress of my heart.*

empress cloth, n. Woollen fabric resembling merino cloth.

empressement, n. [1. omprésmon; 2. ãprésmã]. Fr. See **impress**. **a** Zeal, eagerness; **b** exhibition of desire to please, or to make much of, another; cordiality: *there was no empressement on either side when they met.*

emprise, n. [1. empríz; 2. impráiz], fr. O. Fr. *emprise*, fem. type of P.P. of *emprendre*, fr. Low Lat. **imprehendere*, 'to take, undertake', fr. **em-** & *prehendere*, 'to take, seize, grasp'. See **prize**. (archaic and poet.) Adventure, enterprise, undertaking.

emptiness, n. [1. émptines; 2. émptinis]. Next word & **-ness**. Condition of being empty.

empty (I.), adj. [1. émpti; 2. émpti]. M.E. *emti, amti*, O.E. *ǣm(e)tig*, 'vacant, at leisure, unoccupied', fr. O.E. *ǣmetta*, 'leisure', & adj. suff. (see **-y**); prob. fr. a Gmc. **ǣmōtja*, 'not occupied by business'; hence 'at leisure; vacant, unoccupied', fr. a deprivative pref. **ǣ-*, & **mōt-*, 'a meeting, assembly'. See **moot**. The modern use of the word, in its application to material things, is derived fr. the older, abstract meaning. **1.** (of material things) **a** Devoid of contents, containing nothing, having nothing inside it, holding or enclosing nothing: *an empty box, bottle, cupboard, envelope* &c.; Phrs. *on an empty stomach* (after fasting); *to feel empty*, hungry; **b** not containing something which it habitually or usually contains, which is generally associated with it: *an empty house*, without occupants, with no one in it; without furniture or occupants; *an empty street*, with no people or traffic in it; *an empty truck*, without a load. Phrs. *the town, London, is very empty*, a few hundreds (or thousands) of the fashionable world are away; *empty stomachs*, hungry people; *empty cupboards*, lack of food. **2.** (of non-material things) **a** (of the mind &c.) Not occupied by thoughts, ideas &c.; vacant; **b** (of vbl. expression) without sense, meaning, or sincerity: *empty words, promises* &c.; *words empty of meaning*, void; **c** unsubstantial, unsatisfying, devoid of worth or solidity: *empty pleasures, frivolity* &c.

empty (II.), n., fr. prec. Something that is empty, esp. a box, crate, truck &c., emptied of the goods it contained: *returned empties.*

empty (III.), vb. trans. & intrans., fr. **empty** (I.); cp. O.E. *ǣmtian*, 'to be vacant; to be at leisure'. **A.** trans. **1. a** To remove, take, or pour out, the contents of: *to empty one's cup, glass*, specif. to drink up contents; *to empty a box* (by unpacking it &c.); *to empty a bucket*; **b** of it to cause to come out of, leave, depart from: *the rain soon emptied the streets*; *the building was emptied in six minutes.* **2.** To remove, take, or pour out, (contents) from a vessel, receptacle &c.: *to empty water out of a glass, dust out of the dust-pan* &c. **B.** intrans. **a** To become empty, be deprived of contents: *the bath empties very slowly*; often reflex., **b** (of river) *to empty itself into the sea* &c., to flow, pour its water, discharge.

empty-handed, adj. Bringing, taking away, nothing with one.

empty-headed, adj. Shallow-minded, lacking ideas, ignorant.

empurple, vb. trans. [1. empérpl; 2. impə́pl]. See **em-** & **purple**. To make purple or red.

empyema, n. [1. èmpīéma; 2. èmpai-ímə]. Gk. *empúēma*, 'suppuration'; cp. Gk. *pûon* (for **pūson*), 'matter', & Lat. *pūs*, 'pus, matter'. See **em-** & **pus**. Accumulation of pus in a cavity of the body, esp. in or round the lungs.

empyemic, adj. [1. èmpīémik; 2. èmpai-ímik]. Prec. & **-ic**. Connected with, of nature of, empyema.

empyreal, adj. [1. èmpiréal; 2. èmpiríəl]. See next word & **-al**. Formed of pure fire; pertaining to the empyrean as the region of fire.

empyrean, adj. & n. [1. èmpiréan; 2. èmpiríən]. Med. Lat. *empyreus*, fr. Gk. *émpur-(os)*, 'of fire; in or on the fire; exposed to fire, heat; of or for a burnt-offering', fr. **em-** & *pûr*, 'fire', see **pyre**, & **-an**. **1.** adj. Pertaining to the empyrean, empyreal. **2.** n. **a** The highest heavens, originally as the region of pure fire, later as the abode of God; **b** the upper air, sky, the visible heaven.

emu, n. [1. émū; 2. ímjū]. Etymol. doubtful, prob. fr. Port. *ema*, 'ostrich'. One of a species of Australian birds, with rudimentary wings and long, powerful legs. The emu is second in size only to the ostrich, of existing birds, and is closely related to this.

emulate, vb. trans. [1. émūlāt; 2. émjuleit], fr. Lat. *aemulāt-(um)*, P.P. type of *aemulārī*, 'to strive to equal', fr. *aemulus*, 'imitating, rivalling', for older **aim-*, fr. different grade of base seen in Lat. *im-āgo*, 'likeness', & *imitārī*, 'imitate'. See **image, imitate**. To endeavour to equal, try to come up with, vie with, try to surpass, another in actions, character, or qualities: *to emulate the courage of one's ancestors.*

emulation, n. [1. èmūlā́shun; 2. èmjuléiʃən]. Prec. & **-ion**. **a** The act of emulating; **b** the desire to equal or surpass another's qualities or actions; rivalry: *a spirit of emulation.*

emulative, adj. [1. émūlātiv; 2. émjuleitiv]. **emulate** & **-ive**. Connected with, characterized by, arising from, emulation.

emulous, adj. [1. émūlus; 2. émjuləs], fr. Lat. *aemul-(us)*, 'rivalling', & **-ous**. See **emulate**. (of persons) **a** Anxious, striving, to equal or surpass another, in action, quality &c.: *emulous of another's valour*; **b** eager for, desirous of, seeking (without implying rivalry): *emulous of success, fame* &c.

emulously, adv. Prec. & **-ly**. In an emulous manner.

emulsify, vb. trans. [1. ēmúlsifī; 2. imálsifai], fr. Lat. *ēmuls-(um)*, P.P. type of *ēmulgēre*, 'to milk out, drain out', (& **-fy**), fr. **e-** & *mulgēre*, 'to milk', q.v. under **milk**. To convert into milky fluid.

emulsion, n. [1. emúlshun; 2. imálʃən], fr. Lat. *ēmuls-(um)* (see prec.) & **-ion**. **a** An oily liquid resembling milk in colour and consistency; **b** specif. (med.) preparation of this kind designed for curative purposes.

emulsionize, vb. trans. [1. emúlshunīz; 2. imálʃənaiz]. See prec. & **-ize**. To make into an emulsion.

emulsive, adj. [1. ēmúlsiv; 2. imálsiv]. Lat. *emuls-* (see **emulsion**) & **-ive**. **a** Of the nature of an emulsion; **b** capable of emulsifying.

emunctory, adj. & n. [1. ēmúngktori; 2. imáŋktəri], fr. Lat. *ēmunct-(um)*, P.P. type of *ēmungere*, 'to blow the nose', fr. **e-** & *mungere*, 'to blow the nose'. See **mucus**. **a** adj. Serving to carry off waste matter from the body; **b** n., a duct or organ which does this.

en- (I.), pref. (**em-** before lip-consonants *b, p, m*), fr. Fr., fr. Lat. *in-, im-*, q.v. under **in-**. Besides occurring in O. Fr. words, *en-, em-* are used to form vbs. fr. Engl. words: **a** fr. other vbs., w. sense 'in, into; within', e.g. *entwine, enfold, enshroud*; **b** fr. ns., w. sense 'to put into', e.g. *enshrine, embed, embay*; **c** fr. ns. & adjs., w. sense 'to make, cause to become', e.g. *embitter, endear, ennoble, enslave.*

en- (II.), pref. Gk. *en* (*em-* before lip-consonants, as prec.), 'on, in' &c.; in compounds has the force **a** w. vbs. 'near, at, in,' e.g. *enthusiasm*; **b** w. adj. expresses a modified degree, like Engl. *-ish*, or possession of a quality, e.g. *enharmonic.*

-en (I.), old dimin. suff. O.E. *-en*, fr. earlier *-in*, as in *chicken, kitten* &c.

-en (II.), old fem. suff. O.E. *-en*, fr. *-in*, O.E. *wylfen*, 'she-wolf', cp. O.E. *wulf*; *vixen*, O.E. *fyxen*, cp. *fox*.

-en (III.). Now a suff. used in pl. of weak ns., *oxen, brethren* &c. Formerly in all Aryan languages, in so-called weak or *n*-stems. The case endings were originally added to this stem; cp. Lat. *homo* (earlier *homon-*), acc. *homin-em* &c. In O.E. the base stem *-an* remains in the oblique cases, e.g. *ēage*, 'eye', genit. sing. &c., *ēagan*. In genit. pl., however, an ending is suffixed to this stem, *ēagen-a*, 'of the eyes'

-en (IV.). Suff. forming adjs. fr. ns., w. sense of 'made of, composed of'. It survives in many words, e.g. *oaken, woollen, golden* &c.

-en (V.). Suff. forming vbs. fr. adjs., w. sense 'to make, or become', e.g. *deepen, widen, soften*. Only a few of these vbs. existed in O.E., e.g. *fæstnian*, 'make fast' &c., *fasten*; some are of M.E. & more of modern origin.

enable, vb. trans. [1. enā́bl; 2. inéibl]. See **en** & **able**. To make able, render capable, give the power or means to; give legal power or right to: *money enables one to do many things which cannot be done without it*; *the law now enables a wife to divorce her husband without having to prove cruelty.*

enabling, adj. [1. enā́bling; 2. inéibliŋ], fr. Pres. Part. of prec. In the terms *enabling bill, enabling act*, one which renders legal a certain action on the part of an individual, or a body; an act which gives new legal powers to an individual or body.

enact, vb. trans. [1. enákt; 2. inǽkt]. See **en-** & **act** (I.) **1. a** To make into a law, to render a measure valid and legal by a legislative act; **b** to decree: *enacting clause*, that clause in a parliamentary bill which specifically gives legal sanction to the provisions. **2. a** To act, play, perform (a part): *to enact a play, a character in a play*; **b** (fig., chiefly in pass., of events &c.) to come to pass, take place: *the tragic scene where the murder was enacted.*

enaction, n. [1. enákshun; 2. inǽkʃən]. See prec. & **-ion**. The act or process of enacting a legislative measure.

enactive, adj. [1. enáktiv; 2. inǽktiv]. **enact** & **-ive**. Having the power to enact, the force of enacting.

enactment, n. [1. enáktment; 2. inǽktmənt]. **enact** & **-ment**. **a** Enaction; **b** that which is enacted; a measure having legal sanction and validity.

enamel (I.), n. [1. enáml; 2. inǽml]. M.E. *enamayl*, fr. **en-** & *amayle, ammel* &c., fr. O. Fr. *esmail*; cp. Ital. *smalto*. These are borrowed fr. Gmc.; cp. O.H.G. *smaltzjan*, 'to smelt', q.v. under **smelt** (I.). **1. a** Substance which being subjected to great heat melts, and on cooling forms a hard, smooth, glassy, brittle coating, applied in a thin layer to the surface of metals &c. for ornament or as protection; **b** a kind of paint or varnish, applied with a brush to wood &c., which, on drying, retains a high glaze and forms a very smooth surface. **2.** Hence, any smooth, hard surface-layer; the outer coating of a tooth &c.

enamel (II.), vb. trans., fr. prec. **1. a** To coat, cover, with enamel; to inlay with enamel; **b** to represent (a design &c.) in enamel. **2.** (poet.) To cover with bright and variegated pattern, to give variety of colour to the surface of; esp. *fields enamelled with flowers* &c.

enamour, vb. trans. [1. enámur; 2. inǽmə], fr. O. Fr. *enamourer*, fr. **en-** & *amour*, 'love', fr. Lat. *amōr-(em)*. See **amorous**. (chiefly in pass.) **a** *To be, become, enamoured of*, to be, fall, in love with a person of opposite sex; **b** (in more general sense) to be fond of, strongly attracted by: *to be enamoured of fame, of sport* &c.

enarthrosis, n. [1. ènarthrṓsis; 2. ènāpróusis], fr. **en-** (II.) & Gk. *árthr-(on)*, 'a joint', esp. 'the ankle-joint', & **-osis**. See **arthritis**. A ball-and-socket joint, e.g. the hip-joint.

en bloc, adv. [1. on blok ; 2. ã blɔk]. Fr. As a whole, in the mass.

encaenia, n. [1. ensḗnia ; 2. insínjə]. Lat., 'a dedication festival', fr. Gk. *egkainia*, 'a feast of reconsecration', fr. **en- (II.)** & *kainós*, 'new, fresh ; novel'. See **kainite.** Annual ceremony at Oxford, in commemoration of the founders and benefactors of the university, at which honorary degrees are conferred ; also *Commemoration*, popularly *Commem.*

encage, incage, vb. trans. [1. enkáj ; 2. inkéidž]. **en- & cage.** To shut up in, or as in, a cage.

encamp, vb. intrans. & trans. [1. enkámp ; 2. inkǽmp]. **en- & camp. 1.** intrans. To pitch a camp, to settle in a camp : *the troops encamped in a valley.* **2.** trans. To place in, cause to settle in, a camp : *to encamp troops.*

encampment, n. [1. enkámpment ; 2. inkǽmpmənt]. See prec. & **-ment. 1.** The act or process of encamping. **2. a** Place where a military camp is, or has been, pitched ; group of tents &c. forming a camp ; **b** any temporary shelter, whether of tents or covered waggons &c., for one person or for a party ; site of such a resting-place.

encase, vb. trans. [1. enkás ; 2. inkéis], fr. **en- & case.** To cover completely, enclose, as in a case : *encased in armour.*

encasement, n. [1. enkásment ; 2. inkéismənt]. See prec. & **-ment. a** The act of encasing ; **b** that which encases.

encash, vb. trans. [1. enkásh ; 2. inkǽʃ]. **en- & cash.** To turn into cash ; to receive in form of cash.

encaustic, adj. & n. [1. enkáwstik ; 2. inkɔ́stik], fr. Gk. *egkaustikós*, 'burnt in' ; cp. *égkaustos*, fr. *egkaiein*, 'to burn in'. See **en- (II.) & caustic. 1.** adj. Burnt in : *encaustic tile*, one with coloured design burnt into it. **2.** n. **a** Art of fixing colours and designs by burning them in ; **b** material thus made and ornamented.

-ence, suff. fr. O. Fr. *-ence*, or direct fr. Lat. *-entia*, forming abstract ns. fr. Pres. Part. stem *-ent.* See **-ent, -ance, -ency.**

enceinte, adj. & n. [1. onsánt ; 2. ãsǽt]. Fr., fr. Lat. *incincta*, P.P. of *incingere*, 'to gird, surround'. See **en-** (or **in-**) & **cincture. 1.** adj. (of women) With child, pregnant. **2.** n. **a** An enclosure of fortifications, the main lines of defence of a fortified place ; **b** space so enclosed.

encephalic, adj. [1. ènsefálik ; 2. ènsifǽlik], fr. Gk. *egképhal-(os)*, 'the brain' (& **-ic**), fr. **en-** & *kephalḗ*, 'the head'. See **cephalic.** Pertaining to the brain.

encephalitis, n. [1. ènsefalítis ; 2. ènsefəláitis]. See prec. & **-itis.** (med.) Inflammation of the brain; specif., *encephalitis lethargica*, sleepy sickness.

enchain, vb. trans. [1. enchán ; 2. intʃéin], fr. O. Fr. *enchainer.* See **en- & chain. a** To put into, fasten with, chains, to fetter ; **b** (fig., of the mind, thought, feelings) to rivet, hold fast, keep fixed.

enchainment, n. [1. enchánment ; 2. intʃéinmənt]. See prec. & **-ment.** The act of enchaining ; process of being enchained.

enchant, vb. trans. [1. enchahnt ; 2. intʃánt], fr. Fr. *enchanter*, fr. Lat. *incantāre*, 'to sing ; to say or chant a charm over ; to bewitch'. See **incantation.** To cast a spell over ; (chiefly in fig. sense) to delight, charm, entrance, captivate.

enchanter, n. [1. encháhnter ; 2. intʃántə]. Prec. & **-er.** One who enchants ; specif. **a** one who casts spells, a magician ; **b** one who charms and delights.

enchanting, adj. [1. encháhnting ; 2. intʃántiŋ]. Pres. Part. of **enchant.** Delightful, bewitching, charming.

enchantingly, adv. Prec. & **-ly.** In an enchanting manner.

enchantment, n. [1. encháhntment ; 2. intʃántmənt]. **enchant & -ment. 1.** The act of enchanting, state of being enchanted. **2.** That which enchants ; **a** magic, spell, incantation, charm ; **b** (fig.) delight ; influence exerted by some enchanting, bewitching person or thing : *the enchantment of her smile.*

enchantress, n. [1. encháhntres ; 2. intʃántris]. See **enchanter & -ess. a** A female magician ; **b** (fig.) a bewitching, enchanting, charming woman.

enchase, vb. trans. [1. enchás ; 2. intʃéis]. Fr. *enchâsser.* See **chase (III.), 1.** To set, frame in : *diamonds enchased in gold.* **2.** To ornament by embossing.

encheiridion, enchiridion, n. [1. ènkī-, ènkirídion ; 2. ènkai-, ènkirídiən]. Gk. *egkheirídion*, 'handbook', **en-** & *kheir*, 'hand'. See **cheiro-.** A handbook, manual.

enchorial, enchoric, adj. [1. enkórial, enkórik ; 2. enkɔ́riəl, enkɔ́rik], fr. Gk. *egkhṓrios*, 'of the country, native', fr. **en-** & *khṓra*, 'place, country', see **chorology.** Belonging to a country ; native, common, popular, esp. of the written characters of ancient Egypt, demotic.

encircle, vb. trans. [1. ensérkl ; 2. insə́kl]. **en- & circle. a** To surround, form circle, or part of a circle, round : *a lake encircled by the loveliest woods* ; **b** to go, pass, round : *a wireless message encircles the globe in a few moments.*

enclasp, vb. trans. [1. enkláhsp ; 2. inklásp]. **en- & clasp.** To take into one's clasp, to embrace, enfold in one's arms.

enclave, n. [1. enkláv, onklahv ; 2. enkléiv, ãklāv]. Fr., fr. *enclaver*, fr. Low Lat. *inclavāre*, fr. Lat. **in-** & *clāvāre*, 'to fasten with nails, nail up', fr. *clāvus*, 'a nail', q.v. under **clef.** A district, or territory, enclosed within, surrounded by, foreign territory.

enclitic, adj. & n. [1. enklítik ; 2. inklítik], fr. Lat., fr. Gk. *egklitikós*, 'throwing its accent back to the preceding word', fr. **en-** & *klínein*, 'to lean'. See **climate, climax, clinical, lean (II.), & -ic. a** adj. Applied to a word or particle completely without stress in the sentence, and forming a mere suffix to preceding word ; e.g. *'ll* in *I'll = I will*, [ail] ; **b** n., an enclitic pronoun, particle &c.

enclitically, adv. [1. enklítikali ; 2. inklítikəli]. See prec. & **-al & -ly.** As an enclitic.

enclose, vb. trans. [1. enklóz ; 2. inklóuz]. **en- & close. 1.** To surround completely, shut off from what lies around : *to enclose a garden with a fence, a dot with a circle* ; *the wall encloses the park.* **2.** To shut up, insert, in a closed receptacle ; **a** *to enclose a jewel in a casket* ; **b** to place inside a wrapper, cover, envelope, generally along with something else : *I enclose a cheque herewith* (i.e. in this envelope) ; *I'll enclose your letter* (*along*) *with mine* (i.e. put in same envelope).

enclosure, n. [1. enklózhur ; 2. inklóužə], fr. O. Fr. *enclos*, P.P. type of *enclore*, 'to enclose'. See prec. & **-ure. 1.** Act of enclosing, as by a fence &c. ; specif., enclosing of common land, and converting into private property, by statutes, *Enclosure Acts.* **2.** That which is enclosed, specif. **a** land surrounded by a fence, wall &c. ; **b** anything enclosed with a letter, in same envelope. **3.** That which encloses ; wall, fence &c.

enclothe, vb. trans. [1. enklódh ; 2. inklóuð]. **en- & clothe.** To clothe.

encloud, vb. trans. [1. enklóud ; 2. inkláud]. **en- & cloud.** To envelop with cloud.

encomiast, n. [1. enkómiast ; 2. inkóumiəst], fr. Gk. *egkōmiastḗs*, 'one who praises', fr. *egkōmiázein*, 'to praise, extol'. See **encomium.** One who writes, utters, composes, an encomium.

encomiastic, adj. [1. enkòmiástik ; 2. inkòumiǽstik]. Prec. & **-ic.** Pertaining to an encomiast, or an encomium ; of the nature of an encomium.

encomium, n. [1. enkómium ; 2. inkóumiəm]. Lat., fr. Gk. *egkṓmion*, 'a panegyric, eulogy', fr. **en-** & *kṓmos*, 'a feast, banquet ; revelry, merry-making ; an ode sung as part of festivities', q.v. under **comedy.** A formal expression of praise, high commendation, a panegyric.

encompass, vb. trans. [1. enkúmpas ; 2. inkámpəs]. **en- & compass.** To be, stand, or go, round, to surround, to form or describe a circle round ; **a** (lit.) *a castle encompassed with lofty walls* ; **b** (fig.) *encompassed with perils* ; *to encompass with care and attention.*

encompassment, n. [1. enkúmpasment ; 2. inkámpəsmənt]. Prec. & **-ment.** The act of encompassing, state of being encompassed.

encore (I.), interj. [1. ongkōr ; 2. ãkɔ̄(r)]. Fr., 'again, still, yet' (not used in Fr. in Engl. senses) ; Ital. *ancora* ; perh. fr. Lat. *in hanc hōram*, 'to this hour'. See **hour.** (do it, sing it, play it) Again ; as request from audience for repetition of performance.

encore (II.), n., fr. prec. **a** A call (of word '*encore*') from an audience at a concert &c. for repetition of some part of the performance : *to get an encore* ; **b** song, or other performance, repeated at request of audience ; also different song &c. sung in response to request : *to sing three encores.*

encore (III.), vb., fr. prec. **a** To make request (by shouting '*encore*') for repetition of part of a performance : *to encore a song* &c. ; **b** to express approbation of a performer by requesting him to repeat part of his performance : *to encore a singer.*

encounter (I.), vb. trans. & intrans. [1. enkóunter ; 2. inkáuntə], fr. O. Fr. *encontrer*, 'to meet', fr. Low Lat. *incontrāre*, fr. **in-** & *contra*, 'against'. See **contra-. A.** trans. **1.** To meet face to face, come across : *to encounter a friend on the road.* **2.** To meet in hostility : **a** *to encounter the enemy on the field* ; **b** (fig.) to oppose, be opposed by, in debate &c. **3.** To be beset, opposed by, find oneself confronted by : *to encounter difficulties and dangers.* **B.** intrans. To meet : *he and I have not encountered for years*, implying a casual, indifferent meeting ; **b** opposition.

encounter (II.), n., fr. O. Fr. *encontre.* See prec. A meeting, confrontation, **a** of an indifferent character : often *unexpected encounter* ; **b** hostile meeting of opposing individuals or parties ; conflict (lit. and fig.).

encourage, vb. trans. [1. enkúrj ; 2. inkáridž], fr. O. Fr. *encoragier.* **en- & courage. 1. a** (of human action) To put courage into a person, to inspire with confidence, give him fresh heart, to undertake something, or to continue a line of action, by expressing approval of him, his plans, his achievement : *your appreciation of my work encourages me greatly* ; **b** (of influence of circumstances) to incite, render confident and desirous to do, or to continue to do, something : *my success on a former occasion encourages me to repeat my experiment.* **2.** To help a person to do, render him assistance in doing, something ; to incite, try to induce, persuade, a person to pursue, or continue, a line of action ; **a** (in good sense) *to encourage a man in his efforts to improve* ; **b** (in bad sense) *to encourage a man in his idleness and dissipation* &c. **3.** To foster, promote, support, assist forward, further, a cause, an action, line of conduct &c. ; **a** (in good sense) *to encourage learning and piety* ; **b** (in bad sense) to foment, aggravate &c. : *indiscriminate charity is said to encourage thriftlessness and want.*

encouragement, n. [1. enkúrijment ; 2. inkáridžmənt]. Prec. & **-ment.** Act of encouraging ; source of moral or material aid ; inducement, persuasion, stimulus, support, help : *to give encouragement to deserving and struggling students* ; *praise judiciously bestowed acts as an encouragement to the young* ; *grants for the encouragement of research.*

encouraging, adj. [1. enkúrijing ; 2. inkáridžiŋ], fr. Pres. Part. of **encourage.** Tending to encourage (in various senses) ; inspiring confidence and hope for the future : *an encouraging report of progress made.*

encouragingly, adv. Prec. & **-ly.** So as to encourage.

encrimson, vb. trans. [1. enkrímzun ; 2. enkrímzən]. **en- & crimson.** To make crimson.

encroach, vb. intrans. [1. enkrṓch; 2. *in*krṓutʃ]. M.E. *encrochen*, fr. O. Fr. *encrochier*, 'seize upon', lit. 'catch with a hook', fr. *croche*, 'a hook'. See **en-** & **crochet**. Followed by *upon*, *on*, or absol. **1. a** (in moral sense) To go, force oneself, beyond one's own legitimate province, usurp (rights, privileges, duties, position belonging to another); **b** (in physical sense) to go upon, make use of, territory belonging to another: *you have encroached upon my land here*; **c** (of the sea) to advance upon, pass beyond original limits, increase space occupied: *the sea has encroached (on the land) at many points*. **2.** To trespass upon, take up time of another unduly; intrude: *to encroach upon one's leisure*.

encroachment, n. [1. enkrṓchment; 2. *in*krṓutʃmənt]. See prec. & **-ment**. **a** The act of encroaching; intrusion, infringement; **b** that which is gained by encroaching: *an encroachment of the sea*.

encrust, incrust, vb. trans. & intrans. [1. inkrúst; 2. *in*krást], fr. **en-** & **crust**. **1.** trans. **a** To cover as with a crust; **b** to stud thickly with: *a casket encrusted with jewels*. **2.** intrans. To form, develop into, a crust.

encrustment, n. [1. enkrustment; 2. *in*krástmənt]. See prec. & **-ment**. The act or process of encrusting.

encumber, vb. trans. [1. enkúmber; 2. *in*kámbə], fr. Fr. *encombrer*. See **en-** & **cumber**. **1.** (of physical action) **a** To get in the way of, embarrass, hinder, interfere with freedom of, be a burden to: *to be encumbered with a long cloak*; **b** to fill, choke up, to crowd: *a passage encumbered with furniture*. **2.** (in moral sense) To obstruct the mind or its operations: *encumbered with doubts*. **3.** To burden, embarrass financially: *encumbered with debts*; *an estate encumbered with mortgages* &c.

encumbrance, n. [1. enkúmbrans; 2. *in*kámbrəns]. See **encumber** & **-ance**. **1. a** Anything that prevents or impedes action or movement; a hindrance, burden: *a heavy coat is an encumbrance in walking*; **b** a mental or moral burden: *many of his old supporters he regarded as mere encumbrances*. **2. a** (law) A claim or charge upon property, mortgage, jointure &c.: *estate freed from all encumbrances*; **b** a person, esp. a child, dependent upon one for support: *wanted, man and wife without encumbrances for domestic service*.

encumbrancer, n. [1. enkúmbranser; 2. *in*kámbrənsə]. See prec. & **-er**. (law) A person who has a legal charge, mortgage &c. on an estate.

-ency, suff. denoting quality. See **-ence** & **-y**.

encyclic(al), n. & adj. [1. ensíklik(l); 2. ensík*l*ik(l)], fr. L. Lat. *encyclicus*, fr. Gk. *egkúklios*, 'in a circle'; fr. **en-** & *kúklos*, 'a circle'. See **cycle**. **1.** n. An authoritative letter or message, circulated by the Pope to the whole Roman Church. **2.** adj. Pertaining to such a document.

encyclop(a)edia, n. [1. ensīklōpḗdia; 2. *in*sàikloupídjə]. **en-** & **cyclopaedia**. **1.** A volume, or set of volumes, containing classified information **a** on all branches of learning; **b** on one specific subject; e.g. *encyclopedia of gardening, art* &c. The contents are usually arranged alphabetically. **2.** Specif., *The Encyclopedia*, a French general encyclopedia produced by Diderot and D'Alembert shortly before the French Revolution.

encyclop(a)edic(al), adj. [1. ensīklōpḗdik(l); 2. *in*sàikloupídik(l)]. See prec. & **-ic** & **-al**. Of the nature of an encyclopedia; containing information upon a wide range of topics; all-embracing, comprehensive: *an encyclopedic work, mind* &c.

encyclop(a)edist, n. [1. ensīklōpḗdist; 2. *in*sàikloupídist]. **encyclop(a)edia** & **-ist**. **a** One who writes, compiles, edits, an encyclopedia; **b** specif. (with cap.) one of the editors of the 18th cent. French Encyclopedia.

encyst, vb. trans. [1. ensíst; 2. ensíst]. **en-** & **cyst**. To enclose, envelop, in a cyst.

encystation, n. [1. ènsistā́shun; 2. ènsistéiʃən]. Prec. & **-ation**. (zool.) The process of becoming enclosed in a cyst.

encystment, n. [1. ensístment; 2. ensístmənt]. **encyst** & **-ment**. Encystation.

end (I.), n. [1. end; 2. end]. O.E. & M.E. *ende*, O.S. *endi*, O.H.G. *anti*, *enti*, Du. *einde*; Goth. *andeis*. The only cogn. outside Gmc. appears to be Scrt. *anta*, 'boundary, limit, end'. In reference to space: **1.** (of material things) Point beyond which a thing is not extended, prolonged, continued; the final extremity, limit, termination: *the end of a line, road, piece of string* &c.; *to sign one's name at the end of a letter*. Phrs. *at a loose end*, without settled occupation or fixed ties; *to make both ends meet*, to keep one's expenditure within the limits of one's income; *at the end of one's tether*, at the limit of one's patience, endurance, capacity &c. **2.** Referring to amount, mass, quantity &c.: **a** (of material things) shrinkage, dwindling, lessening, exhaustion: *end of supplies, stores, funds, resources*; **b** (of non-material things) *at the end of one's patience, endurance*; *at one's wits' end*, harassed, perplexed. **3.** By extension of meaning: **a** that part towards or near the final extremity: *the other end of the room*; *to live at the other end of the street*; *to step on the end of a cat's tail*; *at the end of the platform*; *to sit one at each end of the table*; Phrs. *odds and ends*, remnants; *candle-ends*, small pieces of candle left unburnt; *rope's-end*, short piece of rope used for flogging; *the end of the table*, the head of the table; *the east, west, end*, of a town; **b** remote, distant area, quarter: *the other end of the world*; *the ends of the earth*. **4.** Part, especially that towards one extremity, of an object, specially shaped, or designed for particular purpose: *to stand a barrel on its end*; *to stand on end*, stand upright; *to put two things end to end*; (colloq.) *the business end* (of a stick &c.). Phrs. *end on*, with the end facing one; *two hours on end* (fig., of time), consecutively: *the thin end of the wedge*, (fig.) first step leading to further developments; *to get hold of the wrong end of the stick*, to misapprehend, form wrong notion of something. In reference to time: **5. a** Period, point of time, in which something ceases to exist, when it disappears, decays, dies, passes out of human ken; conclusion, close: *the end of the year, of a day, of an hour*; *the end of the world*; *the end of a story*; '*of making many books there is no end*'; Phrs. *in the end*, finally, after all; *to put an end to, make an end of*, to cause to cease, to abolish, destroy; (colloq.) *no end (of a swell* &c.), very considerable; *no end (disappointed)* &c., immeasurably; **b** specif., the end of one's life; death: *to be near one's end*; *to hasten one's end*; hence, the cause of death, destruction, downfall: *his recklessness will be the end of him*; *you'll be the end of me*. Of actions, processes, series of events: **6.** Concluding stage, final phase **a** (of an action): *the end of a speech*; *the end of one's work*; *end of the piece, play*; **b** (of a process) *the end of oppression*; *end of litigation*; **c** (of a series of events) *the end of the festivities, end of a campaign*. **7. a** That at which one aims, that which one hopes, or intends, to accomplish; aim, object, purpose: *to gain one's ends*; *to that end we are and were created*; *the end justifies the means*; **b** that to which events &c., tend; the result, issue, consequence: *the end of it all was that a violent quarrel took place*; *it is difficult to foresee the end*.

end (II.), vb. intrans. & trans. O.E. *endian*. See prec. **A.** intrans. **1.** To come to an end, to stop; to reach a limit, termination; **a** (of material things) *the road ended in a field*; **b** (of non-material things) *when does the term end?*; *there the story ends*. **2.** To discontinue any action or process; to finish speaking &c.: *I end as I began, by thanking you*. **B.** trans. **1.** To bring to an end, cause to cease; to terminate, finish: *that ended the argument*. **2.** To spend the concluding part of: *to end one's days in the workhouse*. **C.** Followed by preposition or adverb. *End in*, intrans. **1.** To have as its concluding portion, termination, **a** (of material things) *a cow's tail ends in a tuft of hair*; **b** (of non-material things) *her sentence ended in a shriek*. **2.** To result in: *the enterprise ended in disaster*; *it ended in his going off in a rage*. Phr. *to end in smoke*, come to nothing, have no result. *End off*, **a** trans., to finish off, complete, bring to an end, discontinue: *to end off a speech, book* &c.; **b** intrans., to come to an end, terminate, break off: *the story ends off rather suddenly*. *End up*, same as prec. Phr. *to play 'God save the King' to end up with*. *End with*, **a** trans., bring to an end in a certain way: *to end a lecture with a quotation*; **b** intrans., to come to an end in a certain way: *the day ended with a storm*.

endamage, vb. trans. [1. endámij; 2. *in*dǽmidž]. **en-** & **damage**. To damage, cause damage to.

endanger, vb. trans. [1. endā́njer; 2. *in*déindžə]. **en-** & **danger**. To bring into danger, expose to risk, render precarious: *to endanger one's life, chance of success*.

endear, vb. trans. [1. endḗr; 2. endíə], fr. **en-** & **dear**. To render dear, inspire affection for, attach: *his kindness of heart endeared him to all*; *to endear oneself to one's friends*.

endearing, adj. [1. endḗring; 2. endíəriŋ], fr. Pres. Part. of prec. Tending to attach, to captivate affections; attractive: *an endearing manner, smile* &c.

endearingly, adv. Prec. & **-ly**. In an endearing manner.

endearment, n. [1. endḗrment; 2. *in*díəmənt]. **endear** & **-ment**. **1.** The act of endearing, state of being endeared; affection: *term of endearment*. **2.** Expression of affection in words or actions; caress, blandishment: *she got weary of his endearments*.

endeavour (I.), vb. intrans. [1. endéver; 2. *in*dévə]. In M.E. the phrase was *to put oneself in devoir*, i.e. 'do one's duty', cp. Fr. *se mettre en devoir*. In 15th cent. & later the vb. was reflex.: *he endevoired him to please God*, that is, 'regarded it as a duty, made it his business to' &c. Prayer Book has phrase *daily endeavour ourselves* &c. See **en-** & **devoir**. **a** (usually followed by infin.) To try, make an effort; esp. to try hard, to do one's best: *to endeavour to do one's duty, to learn one's lessons*; *I'll endeavour to help you*; **b** (more rarely absol.) *Is he improving at all? Well, he's endeavouring*.

endeavour (II.), n., fr. prec. An effort, attempt to accomplish something: *to do one's best endeavours*; *our endeavours are too weak*; *all his endeavours were (in) vain*.

endemic(al), adj. [1. endémik(l); 2. endémik(l)], fr. Gk. **en-** (II.) & *dêmos*, 'people', see **demos**, & **-ic**. **1.** adj. **a** (of disease &c.) Peculiar to, prevalent in, usually found in a particular country, or area, or among a special class; contrasted with *epidemic*; **b** (of plants or animals) indigenous, belonging to a specific country, area &c.; contrasted with *exotic*. **2.** n. An endemic disease.

endemically, adv. [1. endémikali; 2. endémikəli]. See prec. & **-al** & **-ly**. As an endemic.

endermic, adj. [1. endérmik; 2. endə́mik]. **en-** & **derm(a)** & **-ic**. (med.) Applied to, acting through, the skin.

ending, n. [1. énding; 2. éndiŋ]. See **end (I.)** & **-ing**. **1. a** Conclusion, final part: *a play with a tragic, happy, ending*; **b** specif., end of life; death: *his ending was peaceful*. **2.** Grammatical suffix: *case-ending*; *the endings of the verbs*.

endive, n. [1. éndiv; 2. éndiv]. Fr., fr. Lat. *intibus, -um* fr. Gk. *éntubon*, prob. of Semitic origin. A herb, a kind of chicory with curly, pale leaves, used as a salad during winter.

endless, adj. [1. éndles; 2. éndlis]. O.E. *endelēas*. See **end (I.)** & **-less**. **1. a** Lasting for ever: *the endless ages of eternity*; **b** extending to infinity, limitless, boundless: *the endless* *mercy of God.* 2. (mechan.) *Endless chain* &c., one with joined ends in form of a circle, running on pulleys &c. 3. a Very long, too long, lasting for an excessive length of time; interminable: *an endless sermon, lecture, argument* &c.; b frequently, constantly, repeated, making an unbroken series, innumerable, incessant: *endless attempts were made on his life; endless demands on one's time; this will save endless trouble.*

endlessly, adv. Prec. & **-ly**. Interminably; unceasingly, incessantly.

endlessness, n. See prec. & **-ness**. The quality of being endless.

end man, n. One at the end of a row; specif., one sitting at one end of a minstrel troupe, who leads the performance and makes facetious conversation with the performer at the other end.

endmost, adj. [1. éndmōst; 2. éndmoust]. **end** & **-most**. Farthest off, remotest.

endo-, pref. Form of Gk. *éndon*, 'within', used in compounds, fr. *en-*, 'in' (see **en- (II.)**), & locative **dom-*; perh. fr. base **dom-*, 'house'. See **dome**.

endocarditis, n. [1. èndōkardítis; 2. èndoukādáitis]. See next word & **-itis**. (med.) Inflammation of the endocardium.

endocardium, n. [1. èndōkárdium; 2. èndoukádiəm]. See **endo-** & **cardio-**. (anat.) Membranous lining of the heart.

endocarp, n. [1. éndōkarp; 2. éndoukāp]. See **endo-** & **carpel**. (bot.) The inner layer of the seed-vessel of a plant.

endocrine, adj. & n. [1. éndōkrīn; 2. éndoukrain], fr. **endo-** & Gk. *krínein*, 'to separate' &c. See **critic**. (physiol.) 1. adj. a (of certain glands) Secreting internally, such as certain ductless glands, as the thyroid, thymus gland &c., the secretion of which is absorbed directly by the vessels passing through them; b (of secretions) secreted internally. 2. n. A secretion from such gland; a hormone.

endoderm, n. [1. éndōdērm; 2. éndoudām]. **endo-** & **-derm**. a (anat. and biol.) The epithelial lining of the alimentary canal; the hypoblast of the embryo; b (bot.) the inner layer of the cortex.

endodermic, adj. [1. èndōdérmik; 2. èndoudámik]. Prec. & **-ic**. Of, pertaining to, derived from, the endoderm.

endogamous, adj. [1. endógamus; 2. endógəməs]. See next word & **-ous**. Pertaining to, practising, endogamy.

endogamy, n. [1. endógami; 2. endógəmi]. **endo-** & Gk. *gámos*, 'marriage'. See **gamo-**. (anthrop.) Marriage only within the tribe or clan; contrasted with *exogamy*.

endogen, n. [1. éndōjen; 2. éndoudžən]. **endo-** & **-gen**. (bot.) Name formerly given to a class of seed plants, such as palms &c., which were supposed to grow from within.

endogenous, adj. [1. endójenus; 2. endódžənəs]. Prec. & **-ous**. (biol.) Growing from within, developing internally, as spores or cells inside the original cell.

endolymph, n. [1. éndōlimf; 2. éndoulimf]. **endo-** & **lymph**. The fluid in the labyrinth of the internal ear.

endomorph, n. [1. éndōmorf; 2. éndoumōf]. **endo-** & Gk. *morphḗ*, 'form'. See **morphology**. (mineral.) A mineral, esp. crystal, enclosed in, or intrusive in, another, esp. crystalline mineral.

endoparasite, n. [1. èndōpárasīt; 2. èndoupǽrəsait]. **endo-** & **parasite**. An internal parasite, such as a tapeworm.

endoplasm, n. [1. éndōplazm; 2. éndouplæzəm]. **endo-** & **plasm**. The inner layer of protoplasm in a cell; also called *endosarc*.

endorse, indorse, vb. trans. [1. indórs; 2. indṓs], fr. **en-** & Lat. *dors-(um)*, 'back'; cp. M.E. *endosse*, fr. O. Fr. *endosser*, fr. Med. Lat. *indorsāre*, 'to endorse', fr. **in-** & Lat. *dorsum*. See **dorsal**. 1. To write on the back of (a document); esp. to sign one's name on the back of (a cheque, bill &c.), so as to assign or transfer it, or secure payment for it. 2. To write (a note, comment, indication of contents) on the back of a document. 3. (fig.) To corroborate, confirm; to sanction, approve, ratify: *to endorse everything that a speaker has said.*

endorsee, n. [1. èndorsḗ; 2. èndōsī]. Prec. & **-ee**. Person in whose favour a document, such as a bill &c. is endorsed.

endorsement, indorsement, n. [1. indórsment; 2. indṓsmənt]. See prec. & **-ment**. 1. a The act of endorsing; b something written on the back of a document, e.g. a note, or signature. 2. (fig.) Corroboration, approval, of a statement &c.

endorser, n. [1. endórser; 2. indṓsə]. **endorse** & **-er**. Person by whom cheque, bill &c. is endorsed.

endosarc, n. [1. éndōsark; 2. éndousāk]. **endo-** & Gk. *sark-(ós), sárx*, 'flesh'. See **sarco-**. Endoplasm.

endoskeleton, n. [1. èndōskéletun; 2. èndouskélitən]. **endo-** & **skeleton**. The internal supporting bony framework of vertebrates, the true skeleton, as contrasted with the *exoskeleton*, as of crustaceans &c.

endosmosis, n. [1. èndosmṓsis; 2. èndosmóusis]. **endo-** & **osmosis**. The more rapid mingling of the less dense of two fluids or gases with the more dense, through a membrane &c.; contrasted with *exosmosis*.

endosperm, n. [1. éndōspērm; 2. éndouspām]. **endo-** & **sperm**. (bot.) The nutritive matter stored up in the embryo of seed-plants, formerly known as albumen.

endow, vb. trans. [1. endóu; 2. endáu], fr. **en-** & Fr. *douer*, 'to bestow'. See **dower**. 1. To bestow property upon; give or leave money, so as to provide permanent financial support for an institution, office &c. 2. (esp. in P.P.) To furnish, supply (a person) with qualities, talents &c.: *endowed with genius.*

endowment, n. [1. endóument; 2. endáumənt]. Prec. & **-ment**. 1. a The act of endowing, state of being endowed; b property settled permanently on an institution, or person. 2. Mental qualities, regarded as having been bestowed by nature or derived from ancestors: *mental endowments.*

endowment policy, n. A policy of insurance by which a fixed sum is to be paid at a fixed date, or at death should that occur before that date.

end-paper, n. Blank leaf at the beginning and end of a book.

end rhyme, n. One at the end of verses.

endue, indue, vb. trans. [1. indū́; 2. indjū́], fr. O. Fr. *enduire*, fr. Lat. *indūcere*, 'to lead', see **induce**, with meaning confused with Lat. *induere*, 'to put on'. See **exuviae**. 1. (archaic and rare) a To put on, assume (a garment &c.); b to clothe, invest (a person); followed by *with*. 2. To bestow spiritual qualities and benefits upon; to furnish, endow with: '*Endue him plenteously with heavenly gifts*' (Prayer Book).

endurable, adj. [1. endū́rabl; 2. indjṓrəbl]. **endure** & **-able**. That can be endured.

endurance, n. [1. endū́rans; 2. indjṓrəns]. **endure** & **-ance**. a The act of enduring; b the power of enduring.

endure, vb. trans. & intrans. [1. endū́r; 2. indjṓ], fr. O. Fr. *endurer*, fr. Lat. *indūrāre*, 'to harden, make hard', fr. **in-** & *dūrāre*, 'to harden'. See **durable**. A. trans. 1. a To bear with fortitude, bear up against, sustain: *learn to endure suffering; to endure without flinching the rigours of an arctic winter;* b to sustain without breaking: *the frail structure could hardly endure the buffets of the storm.* 2. To tolerate, suffer, put up with, offer no resistance to: *she had to endure the horrid embraces of her captors.* Phrs. *not to be able to endure*, to dislike extremely, detest, be unable to stand or put up with: *I can't endure cold mutton; she will never marry him, she can't endure him.* B. intrans. 1. To remain undestroyed, persist, continue in existence; to last: *his fame will endure for ever; as long as life endures.* 2. To remain firm, staunch, unmoved, in face of trial, pain, strain &c.: *help cannot reach us, we must endure to the end.*

enduring, adj. [1. endū́ring; 2. indjṓriŋ], fr. Pres. Part. of prec. Lasting, permanent: *an enduring fame, glory* &c.

enduringly, adv. Prec. & **-ly**. In a lasting and permanent manner.

enduringness, n. See prec. & **-ness**. State, quality, of being enduring or lasting.

endways, adv. [1. éndwāz; 2. éndweiz]. **end** & **-ways**. With the end forward, facing the spectator; on end.

endwise, adv. [1. éndwīz; 2. éndwaiz]. **end** & **-wise**. Endways.

-ene, suff. [1. ēn; 2. īn]. Used by chemists to denominate certain hydrocarbons—*benzene* &c. Origin doubtful.

enema, n. [1. enḗma; 2. enímə]. Lat., fr. Gk. *énema*, fr. *eniénai*, 'throw, send, in' (see **en-**), *hiénai*, 'send, project, throw', cogn. w. Scrt. *vḗti*, 'strive after'; Lith. *vejù*, 'to pursue'. Injection of a fluid into the rectum; a clyster.

enemy, n. [1. énemi; 2. énimi], fr. O. Fr. *enemi*, fr. Lat. *inimīcus*, 'hostile, unfriendly; an enemy', fr. **in-** & *amīcus*, 'a friend'. See **amicable**. 1. One animated with hatred and malignity towards another; one who attempts to injure another in every way; a foe, opponent; specif., *the old Enemy*, the Devil. Phrs. *how goes the enemy?*, what time is it?; *to be one's own enemy*, to prejudice one's prospects by one's conduct &c. 2. a A nation, state, army, at war with another; b part of a hostile force: *our fleet attacked the enemy at once;* c attrib. *the enemy fleet*, &c. 3. a A person whose aims, interests, ideals, and efforts are opposed to a cause, principle, method &c.: *an enemy of freedom, of Free Trade, of progress* &c.; b a hostile force or factor, one force or influence that is injurious to another: *sunshine is the enemy of ill-health.*

energetic, adj. [1. ènerjétik; 2. ènədžétik], fr. Gk. *energētikós*, fr. *energeîn*, 'to work, to be strenuous, active'. See **energy**. (of person, action &c.) Displaying energy, forceful, vigorously active and efficient.

energetically, adv. [1. ènerjétikali; 2. ènədžétikəli]. See prec., **-al**, & **-ly**. In an energetic manner.

energetics, n. [1. ènerjétiks; 2. ènədžétiks]. The science of energy.

energic, adj. [1. enḗrjik; 2. inádžik]. **energy** & **-ic**. (rare) Energetic.

energize, vb. trans. & intrans. [1. énerjīz; 2. énədžaiz], fr. **energy** & **-ize**. 1. trans. To fill with energy, to stimulate to activity, to stir up. 2. intrans. To display energy, to act with force and vigour.

energumen, n. [1. ènergū́men; 2. ènəgjū́mən], fr. L. Lat. *energūmenos*, 'one possessed of the devil', fr. Gk. *energoúmenos*, fr. Pass. Part. of *energeîn*, 'to work'. See **energetic**. a A demoniac; b a fanatic.

energy, n. [1. énerji; 2. énədži], fr. L. Lat. *energīa*, fr. Gk. *enérgeia*, 'energy, efficiency', fr. **en-** & *érgon*, 'work', for **werg-*. See **ergon** & **work**. 1. a Power, force, whether exercised or latent, causing motion or action; inherent tendency to move or act: *mental, physical energy;* b (in persons) inherent tendency to be active, strenuous, and to get things done; capacity for action and activity: *full of energy; to apply one's energies to something;* c (in verbal or artistic expression) force, vigour, strength, effectiveness: *an excessive energy of phrase, line* &c. 2. a (mechan.) Capacity for doing work, latent or potential, operative or kinetic; b (phys.) one of the primary concepts of the material world, cp. *time, space.*

enervate (I.), vb. trans. [1. énervāt; 2. énəveit], fr. Lat. *ēnervāt-(um)*, P.P. type of *ēnervāre*, 'to weaken, enervate', fr. **e-** & *nervus*, 'a nerve, sinew'. See **nerve**. To reduce strength of, take the vitality out of, to weaken physically, mentally, or morally: *an enervating climate; an enervated style.*

enervate (II.), adj. See prec. Weakened, deprived of vigour.

enervation, n. [1. ènervā́shun; 2. ènəvéiʃən]. See prec. & **-ation.** The act or process of enervating; state of being enervated.

enface, vb. trans. [1. enfā́s; 2. inféis]. **en-** & **face.** To write or print something on the face of a document.

enfant terrible, n. [1. ónfon terḗbl; 2. ãfã teribl]. Fr., lit. 'terrible child'. Precocious child whose behaviour, questions, chatter &c. cause embarrassment to its elders; an indiscreet, irresponsible person.

enfeeble, vb. trans. [1. enfḗbl; 2. infíbl], fr. O. Fr. *enfeblir*. **en-** & **feeble.** To render feeble, to weaken.

enfeoff, vb. trans. [1. enféf, enfḗf; 2. ɛnféf, ɛnfíf], fr. O. Fr. *enfeffer*. See **en-** & **fief.** To grant lands in fee to; to invest with the fief or fee of an estate.

enfeoffment, n. [1. enféfment; 2. inféfmənt]. See prec. & **-ment. a** The act or process of enfeoffing; state of being enfeoffed; **b** deed or instrument conveying lands in fee; **c** that with which one is enfeoffed.

enfetter, vb. trans. [1. enféter; 2. ɛnfétə]. **en-** & **fetter.** To put fetters upon, bind with fetters; (in physical and moral senses).

enfilade (I.), vb. trans. [1. ènfilā́d; 2. ènfiléid], fr. Fr. *enfiler*, & **-ade.** See **file** (II.). To rake the whole of a line of troops, or length of a trench, with gunfire; to command, with guns, the position occupied by troops in such a way as to be able to enfilade them.

enfilade (II.), n., fr. prec. Enfilading fire.

enfold, infold, vb. trans. [1. infṓld; 2. infóuld]. **en-** & **fold. a** To fold or wrap up, to envelop; **b** to clasp in one's arms.

enforce, vb. trans. [1. enfórs; 2. infɔ́s], fr. O. Fr. *enforcer*, fr. Low Lat. *infortiāre*. See **en-** & **force. 1.** To make effective, to demand, insist on, observance of: *to enforce a law.* **2.** To secure observance of, compel action, by force; exact on pain of violent measures: *enforce obedience, where it is not given willingly.* **3.** To urge strongly, present in a forcible manner, impress on one's hearers &c.: *Dr. Johnson says that Watts did not see how corporeal action could enforce religious truth.*

enforceable, adj. [1. enfórsabl; 2. infɔ́səbl]. Prec. & **-able.** Capable of being enforced.

enforcement, n. [1. enfórsment; 2. infɔ́smənt]. **enforce** & **-ment.** The act of enforcing; state of being enforced.

enfranchise, vb. trans. [1. enfránchīz; 2. infrǽntʃaiz], fr. O. Fr. *enfranchir*. **en-** & **franchise. 1.** To grant political privileges to, to constitute one a parliamentary elector: *women were enfranchised in 1918.* **2.** To grant privileges to, to make into a parliamentary constituency: *to enfranchise a town* &c. **3.** To convert into freehold: *to enfranchise leaseholds.* **4.** To release, emancipate, set free: *to enfranchise slaves.*

enfranchisement, n. [1. enfránchizment; 2. infrǽntʃizmənt]. Prec. & **-ment.** The act of enfranchising, state of being enfranchised.

engage, vb. trans. & intrans. [1. engā́j; 2. ingéidž], fr. Fr. *engager*. **en-** & **gage. A.** trans. **1. a** (often reflex.) To bind oneself by a promise, pledge &c., to impose an obligation on, make an action obligatory for: *to engage oneself to do something*; **b** to bind oneself to marry a particular person: *he had engaged himself to a charming girl.* **2.** To obtain a claim on, gain a right to the use (of things) or services (of persons) by payment, agreement, contract, &c.: *to engage a servant* &c.; **b** to cause to be reserved for one's use: *to engage a seat, rooms, a cab* &c. **3. a** To occupy, fill up the time of; to employ (whether temporarily or as permanent occupation): *engaged in letter-writing*; *to have one's time fully engaged*; **b** to occupy, take hold of, retain, attract, secure: *to engage a person's attention, affections* &c.; **c** to draw into, cause to take part in: *to engage a person in conversation.* **4.** To provoke to conflict, compel to fight by beginning hostilities with: *to engage the enemy.* **5.** (mechan.) To take hold of, fasten, interlock with: *two cogwheels engage each other.* **B.** intrans. **1. a** To undertake, pledge oneself, promise, to do something: *I'll engage to find the money if you can find the right man*; **b** to assert the truth of, make oneself responsible for the truth of a statement: *I'll engage that what he says may be relied upon.* **2. a** To begin, provoke, hostilities by attacking: *the orders are, engage at once*; **b** (fencing) to keep one's own sword in touch with opponent's sword. **C.** *Engage in*, to take part in; **a** as permanent business or profession: *to engage in teaching, in the hardware trade*; **b** as temporary activity; to join in: *to engage in conversation, in a game of tennis.*

engaged, adj. [1. engā́jd; 2. ingéidžd], fr. P.P. of prec. Various senses: (of persons) **a** having one's time occupied, being oneself occupied or busy, through some fixed arrangement: *I can't dine with you to-morrow, I'm engaged already*; **b** betrothed: *an engaged pair*; **c** (of things) bespoke, promised, hired: *this seat is engaged*; *every place in the theatre is engaged.*

engagement, n. [1. engā́jment; 2. ingéidžmənt]. **engage** & **-ment. 1. a** A binding pledge or undertaking: *an honest man will not break his engagements to his friends*; **b** fixed arrangement to do something, go somewhere, meet someone, at particular time: *I have several engagements for tomorrow.* **2.** Arrangement between two persons to be married; betrothal: *her engagement has been broken off.* **3.** Encounter between military or naval forces; battle, combat: *an advance in force to bring about an engagement.*

engaging, adj. [1. engā́jing; 2. ingéidžiŋ], fr. Pres. Part. of **engage.** Of a character to provoke affection, attachment, liking; attractive, charming: *an engaging smile, manner.*

engagingly, adv. Prec. &**- ly.** In an engaging, charming manner.

engarland, vb. trans. [1. engárland; 2. ingā́lənd]. **en-** & **garland.** To adorn, deck, with garlands.

engender, vb. trans. [1. enjénder; 2. indžéndə], fr. Fr. *engendrer*, fr. Lat. *ingenerāre*, 'to implant, produce, engender; to create, generate'. See **in-** & **generate.** (fig.) **a** To bring into being, to cause, produce, be the source of: *pity often engenders love*; **b** to excite, arouse, stir up: *poverty engenders misery, and too often, crime as well.*

engine (I.), n. [1. énjin; 2. éndžin], fr. O. Fr. *engin*, fr. Lat. *ingenium*, 'nature, natural quality; character, disposition; capacity, talent, ability, cleverness'. See **en-** & **genius** & cp. **ingenious. 1.** (archaic) **a** A device; **b** an instrument of war, a machine used in warfare. **2. a** One of many types of machines for converting physical force or energy, as heat, into mechanical power; a prime mover; specif., as usually qualified by the power used: *steam-, oil-engine*, or method, construction &c.: *internal combustion engine*; **b** (specif.) a locomotive. **3.** Any particular mechanical device or appliance: *fire-, beer-engine.*

engine (II.), vb. trans., fr. prec. To furnish with an engine, or with an engine of a certain type or horse power, esp. in P.P. and qualified: *over-, under-engined.*

engine-driver, n. Specif., one who drives a locomotive.

engineer (I.), n. [1. ènjinḗr; 2. èndžiníə], fr. O. Fr. *engineor*, fr. Low Lat. *ingeniātōr-(em)*, fr. *ingeniāt-(um)*, P.P. type of *ingeniāre*, 'to be skilful'; fr. Lat. *ingenium*, 'nature; character; ability, skill'. **engine** & **-eer. 1.** A person engaged in one of the various branches of the engineering profession; one who is trained in the scientific principles of mathematics, physics, and mechanics, underlying the design, construction, and use, of all kinds of machines; or in the theory and practice involved in building roads, railways, bridges &c.: *electrical, mining, sanitary engineer*; *civil engineer*, general term for a member of any of the various branches of engineering other than military. **2. a** Member of a military corps, *Royal Engineers*, which constructs fortifications, field works, conducts siege operations, builds bridges, roads &c., and controls the communications by telegraph or telephone &c.; **b** member of that branch of the naval service which controls the driving engines and machines of a ship of war. **3.** A mechanic engaged in the practical management of engines and other machines.

engineer (II.), vb. trans. & intrans., fr. prec. **A.** trans. **1.** To design, construct, direct construction of anything in the capacity of engineer: *to engineer a road* &c. **2.** (fig.) To devise, construct, plan, and carry out, some intricate series of negotiations: *to engineer a scheme, a plot* &c. **B.** intrans. To be occupied in engineering work.

engineering, n. [1. ènjinḗring; 2. èndžiníəriŋ]. Prec. & **-ing. a** The science of the design, construction, and control, of engines, machinery &c.; of the construction of military or public works &c.; **b** the profession of an engineer.

enginery, n. [1. énjinri; 2. éndžinri]. See **engine** & **-ery.** (rare) Engines, machines, collectively.

engine-turning, n. Method of ornamenting metal &c. with lines engraved by machinery.

engirdle, vb. trans. [1. engẽrdl; 2. ingə́dl]. **en-** & **girdle.** To surround with, or as with, a girdle.

English (I.), adj. & n. [1. ínggish; 2. íŋgliʃ]. O.E. *englisc*, *ænglisc*, 'English', fr. *Engle*, *Angle*, Germanic tribe settled in Britain, & **-ish. 1.** adj. **a** Pertaining to, belonging to, England or the English; **b** in the English language. **2.** n. **a** The people of England: *the English are a great people*; **b** the English language. Phrs. *King's English*, standard, correct, English; *plain English*, intelligible style; *not English*, bad, unidiomatic style. **3.** A size of type.

English (II.), vb. trans., fr. prec. To translate into English.

Englishman, -woman, n. [1. ínggIishman, -wòoman; 2. íŋgliʃmən, -wùmən]. Person of English race and blood.

Englishry, n. [1. ínggIishri; 2. íngliʃri]. **English** (I.) & **-ry.** Collectively, a group of people of English descent; esp. the English population of Ireland.

engorge, vb. trans. [1. engórj; 2. ingɔ́dž], fr. Fr. *engorger*. **en-** & **gorge. a** To devour greedily and in large quantities; **b** (med.) *engorged*, congested.

engorgement, n. [1. engórjment; 2. ingɔ́džmənt]. Prec. & **-ment.** The act of engorging; state of being engorged.

engraft, ingraft, vb. trans. [1. engráhft; 2. ingrā́ft]. **en-** & **graft. a** To insert (a shoot) into the stem of another plant, to graft; **b** (fig.) to introduce, implant, establish: *to engraft principles, maxims, virtues &c. in the mind.*

engrailed, adj. [1. engrā́ld; 2. ingréild]. P.P. fr. M.E. *engrailen*, fr. O. Fr. *engresler*, fr. **en-** & *gresle*, 'hail', fr. O.H.G. *gresilon*, prob. connected w. **grit.** (her.) Edged with small semicircles having the points turned outward.

engrain, ingrain, vb. trans. [1. ingrā́n; 2. ingréin], fr. **en-** & **grain** (I.). **a** (usually fig.) To incorporate into the texture and fibre of a substance, to saturate with, so as to impart a lasting colour or tendency: *engrained habits, virtues, prejudices* &c.; **b** (in P.P., of person) thorough, complete, inveterate: *an engrained scoundrel.*

engrave, vb. trans. [1. engrā́v; 2. ingréiv]. **en-** & **grave** (I.). **1. a** To ornament, form a design or inscription on (metal, stone &c.) by lines cut into it: *to engrave a tablet with an inscription*; **b** to cut, carve, incise (lines, a design &c.) on a hard surface: *to engrave an inscription on a tablet*; **c** to reproduce a picture, by lines cut in a metal plate, for printing off impressions. **2.** (fig.) To make a deep impression, imprint ineffaceably, fix firmly: *to engrave a scene upon one's memory.*

engraver, n. [1. engrâver; 2. ingréivə]. Prec. & **-er**. One who engraves; specif., one engaged in the art of engraving designs upon metal, stone &c.

engraving, n. [1. engrâving; 2. ingréiviŋ]. **engrave** & **-ing**. **1.** The art of an engraver. **2.** A reproduction of a picture made from an engraved plate or block.

engross, vb. trans. [1. engrṓs; 2. ingróus], fr. A.-Fr. *engrosser*, fr. **en-** & L. Lat. *gross-(us)*, 'large, thick'. See **gross**. **1. a** To write, copy (a deed, document &c.), in a clear, large hand; to write out in legal form; transcribe in a formal, prescribed manner; **b** to draw up in formal order, express in legal, prescribed form. **2.** (archaic) To buy up large quantities, or whole available supply, of commodities, so as to control prices. (Cp. Fr. *acheter en gros*, 'to buy wholesale'.) Whence **3.** To take up, occupy exclusively, monopolize, absorb: *this business engrosses my whole time and attention.*

engrossing, adj. [1. engrṓsing; 2. ingróusiŋ]. Pres. Part. of prec. Tending to occupy one's time, having property of capturing and holding one's attention and interest; absorbing: *an engrossing task, novel,* &c.

engrossment, n. [1. engrṓsment; 2. ingróusmənt]. **engross** & **-ment**. **1.** The act of engrossing, of writing in large formal script. **2.** Something that is engrossed, a deed, document.

engulf, vb. trans. [1. engúlf; 2. ingálf]. **en-** & **gulf**. To plunge, absorb, as in a gulf, swallow up, overwhelm completely.

engulfment, n. [1. engúlfment; 2. ingálfmənt]. Prec. & **-ment**. The process of engulfing; state of being engulfed.

enhance, vb. trans. [1. enháhns; 2. inhā́ns]. M.E. *enhauncen, enhansen*, fr. A.-Fr. *enhauncer*, fr. O. Fr. *enhaucer*, fr. Low Lat. **inaltiāre*, 'to raise', fr. **in-** & *altus*, 'high'. See **altitude**. **1.** The old sense 'to raise' is obs. except in heraldry, *enhanced*. **2.** (of non-material things) To heighten, intensify, add to, the characteristic or inherent qualities of something: *to enhance the beauty, value, horror, difficulty, wickedness &c. of.*

enhanced, adj. [1. enháhnst; 2. inhā́nst], fr. P.P. of prec. (her.) Of bearings placed above their usual position on the shield.

enhancement, n. [1. enháhnsment; 2. inhā́nsmənt]. See prec. & **-ment**. The act or process of enhancing.

enharmonic, n. & adj. [1. ènharmónik; 2. ènhāmɔ́nik]. **en-** & **harmonic**. (mus.) **1.** n. An interval less than a semitone. **2.** adj. Having intervals of this sort.

enharmonically, adv. [1. ènharmónikali; 2. ènhāmɔ́nikəli]. Prec. & **-al** & **-ly**. In an enharmonic manner, by means of enharmonics.

enhydrous, adj. [1. enhídrus; 2. enháidrəs]. See **en-** & **hydro-** & **-ous**. Of crystals, containing water.

enigma, n. [1. enígma; 2. inígmə], fr. Lat., fr. Gk. *aínigma*, 'a mysterious saying, a riddle', fr. *ainissomai*, 'speak in riddles', fr. *ainos*, 'a tale, story, fable, allegory; a saying, proverb; praise'. Cp. w. different formative suff., Goth. *ai-þ-s*, 'oath', see **oath**. **1.** A riddle, puzzle. **2.** (fig.) **a** Situation or circumstance difficult to understand; **b** mysterious, baffling person.

enigmatic(al), adj. [1. ènigmátik(l); 2. ènigmǽtik(l)]. Through Lat. fr. Gk. *ainigmat-(os)*, genit. of *aínigma*, 'an ambiguous saying, a riddle', & **-ic** & **-al**. See prec. **a** Of the nature of an enigma, puzzling; ambiguous, obscure; **b** (of persons, character &c.) mysterious, baffling curiosity, difficult to understand.

enigmatically, adv. Prec. & **-ly**. In an enigmatic manner.

enigmatize, vb. trans. [1. enígmatīz; 2. inígmətaiz], fr. Lat., fr. Gk. *ainigmat-(os)*, genit. of *ainigma*, 'a riddle', & **-ize**. See **enigma**. To put into the form of an enigma, present as an enigma.

enisle, inisle, vb. trans. [1. inīl; 2. ináil]. **en-** & **isle**. **1. a** To make an island of; **b** to place on an island. **2.** (fig.) To isolate, set apart, render solitary.

enjambment, n. [1. enjámbment; 2. indžǽmbmənt], fr. Fr., fr. *enjamber*, fr. **en-** & *jambe*, 'leg', & **-ment**. See **jamb**. (pros.) The continuation of the sense and sentence beyond the end of the second line of a couplet.

enjoin, vb. trans. [1. enjóin; 2. indžɔ́in], fr. Fr. *enjoign-*, stem of *enjoindre*, fr. Lat. *injungere*, 'to join, fasten into; to attach'; fig., 'to occasion, inflict upon; to charge, impose upon'. See **injunction**, **join**. **1. a** To impose (action, line of conduct &c.) as an obligation; demand, insist on, give orders for: *to enjoin silence, obedience* &c.; *to enjoin diligence upon a person*; **b** also in construction: *to enjoin that* . . . **2.** To instruct, command, put under an obligation, give directions to (persons): *to enjoin a person to be obedient.*

enjoy, vb. trans. & reflex. [1. enjói; 2. indžɔ́i], fr. O. Fr. *enjoier*, 'to cause to enjoy'; **en-** & **joy**. **A.** trans. **1.** (of mental and physical experience) To derive pleasure from, take delight in, experience feelings of satisfaction: *to enjoy a visit, a book*; *to enjoy listening to music*; *to enjoy one's food, walking, a cold bath* &c. **2. a** To have, possess, have the use of: *to enjoy a modest income*; *to enjoy good health*; specif. **b** to possess sexually. **B.** *Enjoy oneself*, to experience feelings of pleasure, to have a pleasant experience, to have a good time.

enjoyable, adj. [1. enjóiabl; 2. indžɔ́iəbl]. Prec. & **-able**. **a** Capable of giving enjoyment; pleasant, agreeable; **b** capable of being enjoyed.

enjoyableness, n. Prec. & **-ness**. Quality of being enjoyable.

enjoyably, adv. See prec. & **-ly**. In an enjoyable manner.

enjoyment, n. [1. enjóiment; 2. indžɔ́imənt]. **enjoy** & **-ment**. **1. a** Act or state of enjoying (in all senses): *enjoyment of health, rights, property* &c.; **b** sense of pleasure, delight, satisfaction: *to take enjoyment in festivities.* **2.** That which affords, source of, pleasure, satisfaction &c.; *his visit was a great enjoyment to me.*

enkindle, vb. trans. [1. enkíndl; 2. inkíndl]. **en-** & **kindle**. **1.** (rare, of fire) To light, cause to blaze up, to flame. **2.** (in spiritual sense) To inflame, inspire, rouse, excite: *to enkindle a desire for liberty in the hearts of the people*; *to enkindle passion.*

enlace, vb. trans. [1. enlās; 2. inléis], fr. Fr. *enlacer*, fr. Low Lat. *inlaciāre*, fr. **in-** & *laciāre*, 'to entangle, entwine', fr. Lat. *laqueus*, 'a noose, snare'. See **lace (I.)**. To encircle, entwine, surround, enfold.

enlacement, n. [1. enlāsment; 2. inléismənt]. Prec. & **-ment**. The act of enlacing; state of being enlaced.

enlarge, vb. trans. & intrans. [1. enlárj; 2. inlā́dž]. **en-** & **large**. **A.** trans. **1.** (obs.) To set at large, release from captivity. **2.** To make larger, increase the size, capacity, of; **a** (of material things) *to enlarge one's house, a book, a coat*; **b** specif. (of photographs) to reproduce on larger scale. **3.** (of the mind and its capacities) To widen by instruction and experience, give greater breadth and range to: *to enlarge the mind, the heart, the sympathies, comprehension* &c. **B.** intrans. **a** To grow larger; **b** specif. (of photographs) to be capable of enlargement; **c** *enlarge upon*, to express oneself at length upon, expatiate, give details concerning: *I need not enlarge further upon this point.*

enlargement, n. [1. enlárjment; 2. inlā́džmənt]. Prec. & **-ment**. **1.** (physical and mental) Act or process of enlarging; state of being enlarged: *the enlargement of a house, of one's mind* &c. **2.** That which is added by enlarging, an addition: *to build an enlargement to a theatre* &c. **3.** (photog.) A reproduction on larger scale.

enlighten, vb. trans. [1. enlītn; 2. inláitn]. **en-** & **lighten**. **1.** (archaic and poet.) To shed light upon, illuminate, give light to. **2.** (in moral sense) **a** To impart knowledge, perception, discernment to, give mental or spiritual understanding to; to free from prejudice, narrow-mindedness, superstition &c.: *to enlighten the ignorant, the heathen* &c.; **b** to give information, make meaning clear to: *to enlighten a person as to one's intentions.*

enlightened, adj. [1. enlītnd; 2. inláitnd], fr. P.P. of prec. (only in spiritual sense) **a** Instructed, informed, having mental and emotional faculties developed and widened; not bound by ignorance, prejudice &c.: *an enlightened age, community* &c.; *an enlightened understanding, intelligence* &c.; **b** specif., in state of understanding and comprehension arising from possession of all facts and information bearing on particular point or situation: *thoroughly enlightened upon the question.*

enlightening, adj. [1. enlītening; 2. inláitəniŋ], fr. Pres. Part. of **enlighten**. Tending to enlighten; **a** giving an insight into a person's character, thought, intentions, feelings &c.: *his speech was not very enlightening as to his intentions*; **b** tending to impart intellectual or spiritual instruction or understanding: *an enlightening discourse* &c.

enlightenment, n. [1. enlītnment; 2. inláitnmənt]. **enlighten** & **-ment**. **a** Act or process of enlightening: *to labour for the enlightenment of mankind*; **b** state of being enlightened, of intellectual and moral advancement: *an age of enlightenment.*

enlink, vb. trans. [1. enlíngk; 2. inlíŋk]. **en-** & **link**. (lit. and fig.) To link together, join by links, connect, unite, link up.

enlist, vb. trans. & intrans. [1. enlíst; 2. inlíst]. **en-** & **list (III.)**. **A.** trans. **1.** To engage, enrol, for naval or military service. **2.** To secure, obtain, assistance, support, sympathy, participation &c., in a cause, project, work &c.: *to enlist a person, a person's sympathy, in an enterprise.* **B.** intrans. **a** To enter naval or military service voluntarily; to enrol one's name as a member of the army or navy; **b** (fig.) to give one's support to, co-operate, participate, in the work of, enter the service of: *to enlist under the banner of revolt.*

enlistment, n. [1. enlístment; 2. inlístmənt]. Prec. & **-ment**. The act of enlisting; state of being enlisted; specif., enrolment in the army or navy.

enliven, vb. trans. [1. enlīven; 2. inláivən]. **en-** & **life** & **-en**. To give life and liveliness to; **a** to add gaiety, humour, interest to: *enliven the conversation, the proceedings* &c.; **b** to make more active, brisker; *to enliven business, trade* &c.; **c** to cheer up, render less gloomy, remove dullness, depression of &c.: *to enliven the dreary routine of duty by occasional bursts of dissipation.*

en masse, n. [1. on máhs; 2. ã más]. Fr. See **in** & **mass (II.)**. All together, as a whole.

enmesh, emmesh, vb. trans. [1. enmésh, emésh; 2. inméʃ, iméʃ]. **en-** & **mesh**. (lit. and fig.) To entangle, as in meshes of a net: *enmeshed in difficulties.*

enmeshment, n. [1. enméshment; 2. inméʃmənt]. Prec. & **-ment**. The act of enmeshing; state of being enmeshed.

enmity, n. [1. énmiti; 2. énmiti]. M.E. *enmyte*, fr. O. Fr. *enemistie*, Lat. *inimīcitia*, 'hostility', fr. *inimīc-(us)*, 'an enemy'. See **inimical** & **enemy**. Hatred, hostile feelings, animosity, antagonism. Phr. *at enmity with*, opposed, antagonistic to.

ennead, n. [1. énēad; 2. éniæd], fr. Gk. *enneád-(os)*, genit. of *enne-ás*, 'a group of nine', fr. *enneá*, 'nine', & **-ad**. Gk. *enneá* (fr. **ennéwa*) is cogn. w. Lat. *novem*, Scrt. *náva*, 'nine', Goth. *niun*. Aryan base **enewn̥*, **newn̥*, **nown̥*, 'nine'. See **nine**. A group of nine things (books, treatises, poems, points &c.).

ennoble, vb. trans. [1. enṓbl; 2. inóubl]. **en-** & **noble**. **1.** To raise a person to the rank of a noble, create him a peer, make him a member of the nobility. **2.** (in moral sense) To make noble; to dignify, elevate: *a character ennobled by suffering.*

ennoblement, n. [1. enṓblment; 2. inóublmənt]. Prec. & **-ment.** The act of ennobling; state of being ennobled.

ennui, n. [1. ónwē; 2. ãnwī]. Fr., fr. O. Fr. *enoi*, fr. Lat. *in odio*, 'in dislike, enmity'. See **odium**, & cp. **annoy.** Weariness of mind, boredom, lack of interest.

enormity, n. [1. enórmiti; 2. inɔ́miti], fr. Fr. *énormité*, fr. Lat. *ēnormitāt-(em)*, 'hugeness, vastness', fr. *ēnormis*, 'unusual; immoderate, immense', see next word & **-ity. 1.** Outrageousness, extreme wickedness, inordinate iniquity: *the enormity of an offence.* **2.** An outrageous crime, a criminal action.

enormous, adj. [1. enórmus; 2. inɔ́məs], fr. Lat. *ēnorm-(is)*, 'unusual, irregular; immoderate, immense', fr. **e-** & *norma*, 'a rule, pattern', see **norm,** & **-ous.** Very great, huge, immense, of extreme size; **a** (of material things) *an enormous animal, building, meal*; **b** (of non-material things) *an enormous difference*; *the affair assumed enormous dimensions.* (The sense 'outrageous, wicked' &c. now obs.)

enormously, adv. Prec. & **-ly.** In an enormous manner, to a very great extent: *the place has changed enormously*; *enormously improved.*

enormousness, n. See prec. & **-ness.** The quality of being enormous.

enough (I.), adj. [1. enúf; 2. ináf]. O.E. *ġenōh*; M.E. *inogh, enouh*; cp. O.L.G. *ginōg*; O.H.G. *genuog*; O.N. *gnōgr*; Goth. *ganōhs*. Cogn. w. Goth. *ganah*; O.H.G. *ginah*, 'it suffices'; fr. Gmc. pref. **ga-* (see **y-**) & Aryan base **nōk̑-*, **enōk̑-*, **enek̑-*, 'to obtain, bring'. Cp. Gk. *enegkeîn*, 'to carry'; Scrt. *aśnṓti*, 'to reach, obtain'; *nā́śati*, 'to reach'; O. Slav. *nesti*, 'to carry'; Gk. *ógkos*, 'burden'. As much as is required, necessary, desirable; forming the requisite amount; adequately meeting a need, desire, expectation; sufficient; **a** (of material things) *to have enough bread*; *not enough heat to boil the kettle*; **b** (of non-material things) *he hasn't enough sense to realize his mistake*; *he does not take enough care of himself*; *time enough for the purpose.*

enough (II.), n., fr. prec. (of material and non-material things) **a** The required amount; as much as is necessary, advisable; **a** necessary quantity, plenty, a sufficiency: *enough to eat*; *enough and to spare*; *more than enough*; *enough of everything*; *I have quite enough*; **b** too much; the limit of what can be tolerated: *I've had quite, about, enough of your impudence.* Phr. *enough of that!*, say no more, be quiet; stop that, keep still!

enough (III.), adv., fr. **enough** (I.). To the requisite degree, sufficiently: *the meat is done enough, not enough cooked*; *he is not conscientious enough.* Phrs. *sure enough*, without any doubt; certainly, indeed; *well enough*, **a** passably, fairly well: *he plays well enough*; **b** quite well: *she could do it well enough if she liked.* Phr. *it's not good enough*, not worth while, not up to one's expectations.

enounce, vb. trans. [1. ēnóuns; 2. īnáuns], fr. Fr. *énoncer*, fr. Lat. *ēnuntiāre*, 'to disclose, publish, report; to say, declare', fr. **e-** & *nuntiāre*, 'to announce, declare, make known', fr. *nunti-(us)*, 'announcing, proclaiming, declaring'. See **nuncio, enunciate. a** To express in words, to declare, proclaim, announce (a proposition &c.); **b** to enunciate, pronounce, utter (words &c.).

enouncement, n. [1. enóunsment; 2. ináunsmənt]. Prec. & **-ment. a** Act of enouncing; **b** that which is enounced.

enow, adj., n., & adv. [1. enóu; 2. ináu]. Variant of **enough.** M.E. *inōwe.* (archaic and poet.) Same as **enough.**

en passant, adv. [1. on páhson; 2. ã pásã]. Fr. *en*, 'in', & Pres. Part. of *passer*, 'to pass'. In passing; by the way.

enquire, enquiry. See **inquire, inquiry.**

enrage, vb. trans. & intrans. [1. enrā́j; 2. inréidž], fr. O. Fr. *enrager.* **en-** & **rage. 1.** trans. To put into a rage, rouse to fury, infuriate. **2.** intrans. (rare) To get into a rage, become angry.

en rapport, adv. [1. on rapṓr; 2. ã rapɔ̄(r)]. Fr. In sympathetic relation with, or to; having communication with.

enrapture, vb. trans. [1. enrápchur; 2. inrǽptʃə]. **en-** & **rapture.** To delight, captivate, entrance, transport with joy or pleasure.

enravish, vb. trans. [1. enrávish; 2. inrǽviʃ]. **en-** & **ravish.** To give great delight to, enrapture.

enregiment, vb. trans. [1. enréjiment; 2. inrédžimənt]. **en-** & **regiment.** To form into a regiment, to organize.

enregister, vb. trans. [1. enréjister; 2. inrédžistə]. **en-** & **register.** To enter in a register; to enrol; to record.

en règle, adj. & adv. [1. on rágl; 2. ã rḗgl̥]. Fr. See **in** & **regular.** In order, according to rule, in due form; required by convention.

enrich, vb. trans. [1. enrích; 2. inrítʃ]. **en-** & **rich. 1.** To make rich; **a** add to material wealth and prosperity of: *enriched by commerce, by successful speculation* &c.; **b** to add to material value, or magnificence of: *an ornament &c., enriched with gems, with elaborate carving.* **2.** (of soil) To make more fertile and productive by addition of chemical substances: *poor land needs to be considerably enriched before it will bear good crops.* **3.** (of non-material things) **a** (of the mind &c.) to store with knowledge, develop capacities of by education and experience; **b** (of any aesthetic creation) to add beauty, ornament, variety to; improve, enhance: *a style enriched with a lofty diction.*

enrobe, vb. trans. [1. enrṓb; 2. enróub]. **en-** & **robe.** To invest, adorn, with, or as with, a robe.

enrol, vb. trans. [1. enrṓl; 2. inróul]. **en-** & **roll** (I.). **1. a** To enter, make record of (a name) in a roll, list, register; **b** specif., to enter person's name as member of a body or organization. **2.** (fig.) To record, preserve memory of, perpetuate: *their names are enrolled in the book of fame.*

enrolment, n. [1. enrṓlment; 2. inróulmənt]. Prec. & **-ment.** Act of enrolling; registration.

en route, adv. [1. on rōōt; 2. ã rū́t]. Fr. See **in**; *route* is fr. Lat. *rupta via*, 'a (road) broken, or cut through (obstacles)'. See **rupture.** On the way.

ensample, n. [1. ensáhmpl; 2. insā́mpl]. M.E. *ensample, asample*, O. Fr. *essample.* See **en-** & **sample.** (archaic) An example.

ensanguined, adj. [1. ensánggwind; 2. ɛnsǽŋgwind]. **en-** & Lat. *sanguin-(em)*, 'blood', see **sanguine,** & **-ed. a** Blood-stained; **b** red like blood.

ensconce, vb. trans. [1. enskóns; 2. inskɔ́ns]. **en-** & **sconce.** To establish, place, conceal, safely or comfortably.

ensemble, n. [1. onsómbl; 2. ãsā́bl]. Fr., 'together; total', fr. Lat. *insimul*, 'at the same time'. See **simultaneous, assemble. 1.** Also *tout ensemble*; something considered as a whole; the general effect, without reference to detail. **2.** (mus.) Passage of music in which soloists and chorus combine.

enshrine, vb. trans. [1. enshrín; 2. inʃráin]. **en-** & **shrine. a** To place, preserve in, or as in, a shrine; **b** (fig.) to preserve and cherish, as in a shrine: *a memory enshrined in one's heart.*

enshrinement, n. [1. enshrínment; 2. inʃráinmənt]. Prec. & **-ment.** The act of enshrining, state of being enshrined.

enshroud, vb. trans. [1. enshróud; 2. inʃráud]. **en-** & **shroud.** (lit. and fig.) To cover as with a shroud; to wrap, envelop, conceal: *enshrouded in mist.*

ensign, n. [1. énsīn; 2. ɛ́nsain], fr. O. Fr. *enseigne*, fr. Lat. *insignia*, pl. of *insigne*, 'mark, sign, signal; badge of office; standard', fr. **in-** & *signum*, 'a sign, mark, token', &c. See **insignia, sign. 1.** A symbol, emblem, token, badge, of office, authority &c. **2.** Banner, flag, standard; national flag; colours of regiment; esp. (British) red, white, or blue flag with Union Jack in corner: *red ensign*, flag of merchant service; *blue ensign*, of naval reserve; *white ensign*, of Royal Navy. **3. a** (mil.) Formerly, an infantry officer of the lowest commissioned rank, so called from his duty of carrying the regimental colours; now called *second lieutenant*; (U.S.A. navy) commissioned officer of the lowest rank.

ensigncy, n. [1. énsīnsi; 2. ɛ́nsainsi]. Prec. & **-cy.** Rank, commission, of an ensign.

ensilage (I.), n. [1. énsilij; 2. ɛ́nsilidž]. See **en-** & **silo** & **-age. a** The process of storing and preserving green fodder in a silo without previously drying; **b** fodder stored thus.

ensilage (II.), vb. trans., fr. prec. To preserve (fodder) by ensilage.

ensile, vb. trans. [1. ensíl; 2. ɛnsáil]. Fr. *ensiler*, fr. Span. *ensilar.* **en-** & **silo.** To store (clover &c.) in a silo.

enslave, vb. trans. [1. enslā́v; 2. insléiv]. **en-** & **slave. 1.** To make a slave or slaves of, reduce to condition of a slave, deprive of liberty. **2.** (fig.) To dominate completely the mind, desires, passions; to enthral, bring into subjection intellectually or morally: *enslaved by beauty, one's passions* &c.

enslavement, n. [1. enslā́vment; 2. insléivmənt]. Prec. & **-ment.** The act of enslaving; state of being enslaved.

enslaver, n. [1. enslā́ver; 2. insléivə]. **en-slave** & **-er.** One who enslaves; specif., woman who dominates a man by her allurements.

ensnare, vb. trans. [1. ensnā́r; 2. insnɛ́ə]. **en-** & **snare. a** To catch in a snare, take in a trap; **b** (fig.) to obtain power or influence over by cunning; to allure, entrap.

ensoul, insoul, vb. trans. [1. ensṓl; 2. insóul]. **en-** & **soul.** To bestow a soul upon.

ensphere, vb. trans. [1. ensfḗr; 2. insfíə]. **en-** & **sphere.** To enclose in a sphere, to surround, encircle.

ensue, vb. trans. & intrans. [1. ensū́; 2. insjū́], fr. O. Fr. *ensuivre*, fr. Low Lat. *insequere*, fr. Lat. *insequi*, 'to follow, pursue; to strive after; to follow, succeed', fr. **in-** & *sequi*, 'to follow'. See **sequela** & cp. **suit** (II.). **1.** trans. (obs. and Bib.) To follow, pursue, strive after: *seek peace and ensue it.* **2.** intrans. To follow, result; appear, happen, as consequence; be consequent on: *the evils that ensue from lack of stable government.*

ensuing, adj. [1. ensū́ing; 2. insjū́iŋ], fr. Pres. Part. of prec. **a** Following, succeeding, coming next in time: *during the ensuing months*; **b** following as a consequence: *the revolution and the ensuing economic collapse.*

ensure, vb. trans. [1. enshṓōr; 2. inʃɔ́], fr. A.-Fr. *enseurer*, fr. O. Fr. *seur*, 'sure, secure'. **en-** & **sure. 1.** To make safe, secure; guard, protect: *to ensure oneself against the cold, danger* &c. **2. a** To make certain of, secure the certainty of, guarantee: *I cannot ensure his being there in time*; **b** to secure as a certainty: *to ensure a post for a person.*

enswathe, vb. trans. [1. enswā́dh; 2. inswéið]. **en-** & **swathe.** (lit. and fig.) To wrap, bind up; to enfold, bind round.

enswathement, n. [1. enswā́dhment; 2. inswéiðmənt]. Prec. & **-ment. a** The act of enswathing; state of being enswathed; **b** something that enswathes; a wrapping, bandage.

-ent, suff. forming ns. and adjs.; fr. Lat. *-ent-*, Pres. Part. stem of vbs. of 2nd, 3rd, & 4th conjugations: e.g. *regent, solvent* &c.

entablature, n. [1. entáblachur; 2. entǽblətʃə], fr. Ital. *intavolatura*, fr. *intavolare*, fr. **in-** & *tavola*, 'a table, base', fr. Lat. *tabula*, 'a board, table'. See **table.** (archit.) Structure, consisting of cornice, frieze, and architrave, immediately above, and supported by, a column and capital.

entablement, n. [1. entā́blment; 2. intéiblmənt]. Fr. See **en-** & **table** & **-ment. 1.** Entablature. **2.** Flat platform on which a statue stands, above the base and dado.

entail (**I.**), vb. trans. [1. entā́l; 2. intéil]. **en-** & *tail*, 'limitation', fr. O. Fr. *tailler*, 'to cut', Low Lat. *taliāre*, 'to cut', cp. Ital. *tagliare*, & see **tailor**. **1.** (law) To settle succession of an estate inalienably in a particular line of descent. **2.** To carry with it as a necessary accompaniment or consequence: *this plan will entail enormous labour upon those who carry it out*; *his mode of life entailed great expense.*

entail (**II.**), n. [1. éntāl; 2. énteil], fr. prec. **a** Act of settling succession of an estate inalienably on descendants of a particular person in a special order; **b** estate the inheritance of which is so settled.

entailment, n. [1. entā́lment; 2. intéilmənt]. Prec. & **-ment**. The act of entailing; state of being entailed.

entangle, vb. trans. [1. entánggl; 2. intǽŋgl]. **en-** & **tangle**. **1.** To arrest progress of by laying hold of, winding round; to catch: *entangle one's feet in trailing creeper* &c.; *a fishing line gets entangled in bushes* &c. **2.** (fig.) **a** To involve in difficulties, put into difficult position, surround with a network of unfavourable circumstances: *to entangle oneself in debt*; **b** to entrap, obtain power and influence over: *easily entangled by blandishments and flattery.*

entanglement, n. [1. entánggIment; 2. intǽŋglmənt]. Prec. & **-ment**. **1. a** Act of entangling, state of being entangled; **b** (fig.) a situation from which it is difficult to extricate oneself. **2.** Specif. (mil.), wire twisted and interwoven so as to form an obstacle, in which the enemy may become entangled.

entasis, n. [1. éntasis; 2. éntəsis]. Gk., 'a stretching', fr. *enteínein*, 'to stretch', fr. **en-** & *teínein*, 'to stretch', q.v. under **tone**. (archit.) A slight convexity in the shaft of a column or in a tall spire introduced to correct the visual illusion of concavity in a straight, upright object.

entelechy, n. [1. entéleki; 2. entéləki], fr. Gk. *entelékheia*, a term formed by Aristotle, fr. *en télei ékhein*, 'to have in perfection', fr. **en**, 'in', *télos*, 'end, perfection', & *ékhein*, 'to have, hold'. See **teleology** & **epoch**. In Aristotelian and Scholastic philosophy, a term used to signify the perfect form attained by anything by reason of which it actually exists and realizes its true function, the actual as opposed to its potential cause.

entellus monkey, n. [1. entélus mùngki; 2. entéləs màŋki]. So called prob. fr. name of a mythical Sicilian boxer and hero. Scientific name of the langur or hanuman, the long-tailed sacred monkey of India.

entente, n. [1. ontónt; 2. ātā́t]. Fr., fr. P.P. of *entendre*, 'to understand' &c., Lat. *intendere*. See **intend**. An understanding between two governments; specif. (*entente cordiale*) friendly understanding and relations established between England and France in 1905, less formal and strictly defined than an alliance.

enter, vb. trans. & intrans. [1. énter; 2. éntə]. M.E. *entren*, fr. O. Fr. *entrer*, fr. Lat. *intrāre*, 'to go into', formed fr. Lat. *intrā*, 'within'. See **intra-**. **A.** trans. **1.** (of physical action or movement) **a** To come, go, pass, inside, or within, an enclosed or covered space: *to enter a room, house, cave, tunnel, tent, field* &c.; Phr. (fig.) *to enter the lists* (*against*), espouse a cause, engage in controversy, come forward as a champion for, or opponent of; **b** to penetrate, pierce and pass into or through (flesh &c.): *the bullet entered the skull behind the right ear.* **2.** (of mental process) To occur, come into the mind, be in the thoughts: *such an idea never entered my head.* **3.** To go into, join, become a member, of a body, society, profession &c.: *to enter a university, a club, the Army, the Church.* **4. a** To put down in writing, add (name) to a list; enrol as a member, or future member, of a society &c.: *to enter a boy's name, a boy, for a public school*; **b** to make record or note of, to register: *to enter an engagement, an event, in a diary*; *to enter a sum in a ledger* &c.; Phr. *to enter a protest*, lit., make official record of in books of deliberative body; (fig.) to make a protest in general. **B.** intrans. **a** To carry out action of entering, coming in: *at this moment the king entered*; Phr. (as stage direction) *enter first murderer* &c.; **b** to penetrate: *the mark where the bullet had entered was quite visible.* **C.** Followed by adverbs or prepositions. *Enter for*, **a** trans., to put down the name of, obtain admission for, register as taking part in: *to enter a yacht for a race*; **b** intrans., to enrol one's name, register, be admitted, as a competitor in: *to enter for a race. Enter into*, **1. a** to engage in, begin to take part in, occupy oneself with: *to enter into conversation, negotiations*; **b** to proceed to the discussion of, discuss, deal with: *to enter into particulars, details*; **c** to engage oneself, bind oneself by, take upon oneself as an obligation, become a party to: *to enter into a compact, engagement, treaty*; **2.** to form part of, be a factor in, be a component of; **a** (of material things) *water enters into the composition of all vegetables*; **b** (of non-material things) *that possibility did not enter into our calculations*; **3. a** to sympathize with, be able to realize, appreciate, comprehend: *to enter into a person's feelings, ideas* &c.; *to enter into the fun of the thing*; **b** to share, take part in, partake: *to enter into all the amusements and gaieties of the place. Enter up*, to complete entries in, insert all necessary items in: *to enter up a ledger, an account in a ledger. Enter upon*, **a** to take possession of, begin to enjoy: *to enter upon an inheritance*; **b** to begin, set out on, embark upon: *to enter upon one's duties, a career, a new life*; *to enter upon a new phase, stage.*

enterable, adj. [1. énterabl; 2. éntərəbl]. Prec. & **-able**. Capable of being entered.

enteric, adj. & n. [1. entérik; 2. entérik], fr. Gk. *enterikós*, fr. *énter-(on)*, 'intestine', fr. **en-** & compar. suff. *-t(e)ro*; cogn. w. Lat. *interus*, 'inside'; *intrā*, 'within'; Scrt. *ántaraś*, 'interior'; O. Slav. *ątro-ba*, 'entrails'. See **inter-**. **a** adj. Of, pertaining to, the intestines: *enteric fever*, typhoid; **b** n., enteric fever.

enteritis, n. [1. enterítis; 2. entəráitis]. See prec. & **-itis**. A general term for various inflammatory conditions of the intestines.

entero-, pref. Form of Gk. *énteron*, 'intestine', see **enteric**, used in composition, in formation of words used in medicine; e.g. *enterolith*, 'stone in the intestines'.

enterprise, n. [1. énterprīz; 2. éntəpraiz], fr. O. Fr. *entreprise*, fr. P.P. of *entreprendre*, 'to undertake', fr. *entre*, 'between' (see **inter-**) & Lat. *pre(he)ndere*, 'to take, lay hold of, seize; reach, attain'. See **prize** (**III.**). **1.** Something undertaken, attempted; a plan, undertaking, project, scheme; esp. a daring, difficult venture, a bold, adventurous scheme. **2.** Quality of mind which inclines to boldness and confidence in embarking upon new and difficult or risky ventures; capacity for initiating new lines of action: *a spirit of enterprise*; *to have no enterprise.* **3.** Act of initiating and embarking upon new ventures: *many national movements begin with private enterprise.*

enterprising, adj. [1. énterprīzing; 2. éntəpraiziŋ]. Prec. & **-ing**. **a** (of persons and their character) Inclined to adventurous activity, having capacity for starting new ventures; **b** (of action) proceeding from, exhibiting, a spirit of enterprise.

enterprisingly, adv. Prec. & **-ly**. In an enterprising manner.

entertain, vb. trans. & intrans. [1. èntertā́n; 2. èntətéin], fr. Fr. *entretenir*, fr. Lat. **inter-** & *tenēre*, 'to hold; to possess; to preserve, guard; to maintain, support; to have in the mind, know'. See **tenable** & **tend**. **A.** trans. **1.** (archaic) To keep up, carry on, maintain (a correspondence &c.). **2. a** To have in one's mind, cherish, foster: *to entertain a hope, idea*; **b** to reflect favourably on, consider, approve the possibility or desirability of: *I cannot entertain such a proposal.* **3.** To give, show, hospitality to; receive as guest(s): *to entertain a party at dinner.* Phr. *to entertain angels unawares.* **4.** To amuse, divert, interest, occupy the mind of agreeably: *the play entertained us very much*; *to entertain the company with tricks.* **B.** intrans. To make a practice, be in the habit, of showing hospitality: *these people entertain a great deal.*

entertained, adj. [1. èntertā́nd; 2. èntətéind], fr. P.P. of prec. Amused, diverted, agreeably interested: *I was more entertained by watching the audience than by the performers.*

entertaining, adj. [1. èntertā́ning; 2. èntətéiniŋ]. Prec. & **-ing**. Amusing, diverting, agreeable; affording amusement or pleasant diversion: *an entertaining conversation, story*; *an entertaining talker.*

entertainingly, adv. Prec. & **-ly**. In an entertaining manner.

entertainment, n. [1. èntertā́nment; 2. èntətéinmənt]. **entertain** & **-ment**. Act of entertaining; state of being entertained. In various senses: **1. a** bestowal of hospitality; a party, reception: *to give an entertainment to one's friends*; **b** hospitality in general: *a good house for entertainment.* Phr. *house of entertainment*, hostelry, inn, public-house. **2. a** Performance or exhibition designed to interest or amuse: *a theatrical, musical, entertainment*; **b** amused, interested, state of mind; amusement, interest: *his antics were a perpetual source of entertainment.*

enthral(**l**), vb. trans. [1. enthráwl; 2. inþrɔ́l]. **en-** & **thrall**. **1.** (rare and archaic) To hold in thrall, to bring into bondage, enslave. **2.** (fig., mental or moral effect) To obtain power over, captivate, charm, absorb, hold: *to be enthralled by a novel, by beauty* &c.

enthralling, adj. [1. enthráwling; 2. inþrɔ́liŋ], fr. Pres. Part. of prec. Of such a character as to absorb the attention and interest; possessing great and absorbing interest: *an enthralling occupation, story* &c.

enthralment, n. [1. enthráwlment; 2. inþrɔ́lmənt]. Prec. & **-ment**. The act of enthralling; state of being enthralled.

enthrone, vb. trans. [1. enthrṓn; 2. inþróun]. **en-** & **throne**. **1.** To place (a king or bishop) on a throne; specif., to invest with regal or ecclesiastical dignity by a formal ceremony. **2.** (fig.) To accord a position of importance and pre-eminence to, in one's judgement or affection: *the old Queen was enthroned in the hearts of her people.*

enthronement, n. [1. enthrṓnment; 2. inþróunmənt]. Prec. & **-ment**. The act of enthroning; state of being enthroned; the ceremony of enthroning.

enthronization, n. [1. enthrṑnīzā́shun; 2. inþròunaizéiʃən]. **enthrone** & **-ize** & **-ation**. (lit. and fig.) Enthronement.

enthuse, vb. intrans. [1. enthū́z; 2. inþjúz], fr. next word. (colloq.) To become enthusiastic, express enthusiasm.

enthusiasm, n. [1. enthū́ziazm; 2. inþjúziæzəm], fr. L. Lat., fr. Gk. *enthousiasmós*, 'inspiration, enthusiasm', fr. *enthousiázein*, 'to be inspired, in ecstasy, possessed by a god, divinely inspired', fr. *éntheos*, 'inspired, possessed, by a god', fr. **en-** & *théos*, 'a god'. See **theo-**. **1.** Intense admiration of, zeal for, an object or cause: *enthusiasm for the king, for the war, for sport.* **2.** Outward manifestations of zeal, approval, admiration: *his appearance was greeted with an outburst of enthusiasm.* **3.** Religious or spiritual exaltation; pietism, mysticism; used disparagingly in 17th cent. of the religious attitude of the Puritans, and in 18th of that of the Methodists.

enthusiast, n. [1. enthū́ziast; 2. inþjúziæst], fr. Gk. *enthousiastés*, 'an enthusiast', fr. *enthousiázein*, 'to be inspired'. See prec. **1.** One who is animated by intense, fiery zeal for an object or a cause. **2.** Formerly in disparaging sense of certain types of religious zealots. See prec. **3.**

enthusiastic, adj. [1. enthūziástik; 2. *in*þjūzi*æ*st*i*k]. Prec. & **-ic**. **1. a** (of persons) Full of enthusiasm, ardent, zealous: *an enthusiastic supporter*; **b** (of action, speech, conduct &c.) expressing, characterized by, enthusiasm; cordial, eager, ardent: *an enthusiastic welcome*; *to give enthusiastic support to a cause*. **2.** Formerly in disparaging sense; possessing religious enthusiasm, q.v.

enthusiastically, adv. [1. enthūziástikali; 2. *in*þjūzi*æ*st*i*kəli]. Prec. & **-al** & **-ly**. In an enthusiastic manner.

enthymeme, n. [1. énthimēm; 2. *é*nþ*i*mīm], fr. Lat., fr. Gk. *enthū́mēma*, 'a thought, argument', fr. *enthūmeîsthai*, 'consider, reflect on', fr. **en-** & *thūmós*, 'the mind, soul', q.v. under **fume**. (log.) A syllogism with one premise omitted, as 'we are beggars and therefore cannot be choosers'; the major premise, 'beggars cannot be choosers', being suppressed.

entice, vb. trans. [1. entís; 2. *intáis*]. M.E. *entisen*, fr. O. Fr. *enticier*, prob. orig. 'to set on fire', hence 'to cause to desire ardently'; cp. Mod. Fr. *attiser*, 'to stir a fire', fr. **en-** & Lat. *titio*, 'a burning brand'. Cogn. w. Gk. *tītṓ*, 'day', *Tītā́n*, 'the sun-god'. Cp. **Titan**. To allure, tempt, persuade, to go somewhere or do something, by holding out an attraction, offering a bait; often *entice away*.

enticement, n. [1. entísment; 2. *intáis*mənt]. Prec. & **-ment**. **1.** The act of enticing; state of being enticed. **2.** Something that entices; an allurement.

enticing, adj. [1. entísing; 2. *intáisiŋ*], fr. Pres. Part. of **entice**. Tending to entice; alluring, inviting, attractive: *an enticing prospect*.

enticingly, adv. Prec. & **-ly**. In an enticing manner.

entire, adj. & n. [1. entír; 2. *intáiə*], fr. O. Fr. *entier*, fr. Lat. *integrum*, nom. *integer*, 'undiminished, whole; unimpaired, uninjured; fresh, new; honest, virtuous'. See **integer**. **1.** adj. Whole, complete. In various senses: **a** (of a set or collection) not broken into, having full number: *our best china tea-service is not quite entire*; **b** not defective, unbroken, not cracked or flawed: *the plate is very nearly entire, merely having the edge slightly chipped*; **c** full, perfect: *entire love, entire ignorance* &c.; **d** (of male animals) ungelded. **2.** n. **a** Something unalloyed, unmixed; a substance having same quality and kind throughout: specif. (of beer &c.) *Droughty's entire*; **b** an uncastrated animal, a stallion.

entirely, adv. Prec. & **-ly**. **a** Completely, wholly; without qualification; not in part only: *entirely lost, forgotten* &c.; **b** solely, only, alone: *to be devoted entirely to money-making*.

entireness, n. See prec. & **-ness**. The state of being entire.

entirety, n. [1. entírti; 2. *intáiəti*], fr. O. Fr. *entiereté*, fr. Lat. *integritāt-(em)*, 'completeness, soundness; blamelessness, integrity'. See **integrity**. **1.** The state of being entire, completeness; esp. in Phr. *in its entirety*. **2.** (law) Property of the whole of which two persons are jointly seized.

entitle, vb. trans. [1. entítl; 2. *intáit*l], fr. O. Fr. *entiteler*, fr. L. Lat. *intitulāre*, 'to give a name to'. **in-** & **title**. **1.** To give a title, name, appellation, to persons or things; to designate. **2.** To give, carry, imply, a right or claim to: *this ticket entitles the holder to a seat in the stalls*; *his age and learning entitled him to respect*.

entity, n. [1. éntiti; 2. *é*nt*i*ti], fr. Fr. *entité*, L. Lat. *entitāt-(em)*, fr. *enti-* stem of L. Lat. *ens*, 'a thing', Pres. Part. of *esse*, 'to be', on the anal. of *praesens, absens* &c. See **esse**. A real thing in itself, distinct from its qualities and attributes; being, existence.

ento-, pref. meaning 'within', fr. Gk. *entó-(s)*, 'within, inside'. Cogn. w. Lat. *intus*, 'within, place whence', fr. **in-**; as *entophyte, entozoa* &c.

entomb, vb. trans. [1. entōōm; 2. *intúm*]. **en-** & **tomb**. (lit. and fig.) **a** To place, enclose, in a tomb; **b** to be a tomb for, enclose as in a tomb.

entombment, n. [1. entōōmment; 2. *intúm*mənt]. Prec. & **-ment**. The act of entombing; state of being entombed.

entomic, adj. [1. entómik; 2. ɛnt*ɔ́*m*i*k]. Next word & **-ic**. Of, pertaining to, insects.

entomo-, pref. meaning 'insect; of insects'; fr. Gk. *éntomo-(s)*, 'cut up, cut in pieces', so called from shape and structure; cp. **insect**; fr. **en-** & *tómos*, 'something cut off, a slice, section; a volume'. See **tome**.

entomological, adj. [èntomolójikl; 2. èntəməl*ɔ́*dž*i*kl]. **entomology** & **-ic** & **-al**. Pertaining to entomology.

entomologist, n. [1. èntomólojist; 2. èntəm*ɔ́*lədžist]. **entomology** & **-ist**. A student of entomology.

entomologize, vb. trans. [1. èntomólojīz; 2. èntəm*ɔ́*lədž*aiz*]. Next word & **-ize**. To study entomology.

entomology, n. [1. entomóloji; 2. ɛntəm*ɔ́*lədži]. **entomo-** & **-logy**. Scientific study of insects, also used to embrace the study of spiders &c., which scientifically are not insects at all; *economic entomology*, study of insect pests.

entomophilous, adj. [1. èntomófilus; 2. èntəm*ɔ́*f*i*ləs]. **entomo-** & **-philous**. (bot., of plants) Attracting insects for purpose of fertilization, fertilized by insects.

entophyte, n. [1. éntōfīt; 2. éntou*fait*]. **ento-** & Gk. *phutón*, 'plant', see **-phyte**. A vegetable parasite, such as a fungus or bacterium, living within the body of an animal or of another plant.

entourage, n. [1. ontōōrahzh; 2. ɑ̃tūrāž]. Fr. **a** Environment, surroundings, circumstances; **b** followers, retainers, circle of attendants.

entozoa, n. pl. [1. èntōzóa; 2. èntouzóuə]. **ento-** & Gk. *zôa*, 'animals'. See **zoo-**. Internal parasites, such as intestinal worms.

entr'acte, n. [1. ontrakt; 2. ɑ̃trakt]. Fr. **a** Interval between two acts of a play or opera; **b** an independent performance, interlude, performed during such an interval.

entrails, n. pl. [1. éntrālz; 2. éntreilz]. M.E. *entraille*, fr. O. Fr. *entraille*, fr. Low Lat. *intrālia*, fr. Lat. *inter*, 'within'. See **inter-**. Internal organs, viscera, guts; specif., intestines.

entrain, vb. trans. & intrans. [1. entrán; 2. *intréin*]. **en-** & **train**. **a** trans. To put into a train: *to entrain troops*; **b** intrans., to get into a train.

entrammel, vb. trans. [1. entráml; 2. *intræ*ml]. **en-** & **trammel**. To hamper, trammel.

entrance (I.), n. [1. éntrans; 2. éntrəns]. O. Fr. See **enter** & **-ance**. **1.** The act of entering; coming or going in; specif. **a** the coming of an actor on to the stage; **b** the act of beginning a career, a new occupation, act of becoming a member of some organized body: *entrance into life, a profession* &c. **2.** The right of entering, admission: *to force an entrance*; *to have (free) entrance to*. *Entrance examination*, one which those must pass who seek to enter a university, public school &c.; *entrance fee*, one payable **a** before entering a society, club, college &c.; **b** before being allowed to enter certain buildings, entertainments &c. **3.** Opening, passage, by which entrance is made; point of ingress; a door, portal &c.: *the entrance to a house*; *the entrance of a cave, tunnel* &c.; *at the entrance*, in the doorway, near the door &c.

entrance (II.), vb. trans. [1. entráhns; 2. *in*tr*ā́*ns]. **en-** & **trance**. **1.** To throw into a trance. **2.** (fig.) To transport, carry away, with joy, delight &c.; to put into a state of ecstasy, to enrapture.

entrancement, n. [1. entráhnsment; 2. *in*tr*ā́*nsmənt]. Prec. & **-ment**. **1.** The act of entrancing; state of being entranced. **2.** Something that entrances.

entrancing, adj. [1. entráhnsing; 2. *intrā́nsiŋ*], Pres. Part. of **entrance (II.)**. Having power to entrance; charming, enchanting.

entrancingly, adv. Prec. & **-ly**. In an entrancing manner.

entrant, n. [1. éntrant; 2. éntrənt]. Fr., Pres. Part. of *entrer*, 'to enter'. **enter** & **-ant**. One who enters; one who is entering a profession, a society &c.; one who enters for a contest, competition &c.

entrap, vb. trans. [1. entráp; 2. *intræ*p], fr. O. Fr. *entraper*. **en-** & **trap**. (rare in lit. sense) **a** To catch, take, in, or as in, a trap; ensnare; **b** (fig.) to get a person into one's power, to deceive by cunning, artifice; to ensnare, beguile, cozen: *to be entrapped into doing something*.

entreat, vb. trans. [1. entrḗt; 2. *intrī́t*], fr. O. Fr. *entraiter*. **en-** & **treat**. **1.** (archaic and Bib.) To treat, behave to: *evilly entreated*. **2.** To beg earnestly, express a fervent desire, beseech, implore.

entreating, adj. [1. entrḗting; 2. *intrī́tiŋ*]. Pres. Part. of prec. Conveying entreaty; imploring.

entreatingly, adv. Prec. & **-ly**. In an entreating manner.

entreaty, n. [1. entrḗti; 2. *intrī́ti*]. **entreat** & **-y**. Urgent request, insistent demand, earnest prayer.

entrée, n. [1. ontrā; 2. ɑ̃trei]. Fr. See **entry**. **1.** The privilege, right, of entering; right of admission: *to have the entrée of a house, social circle* &c. **2.** A course at a meal, served between the fish and the joint.

entremets, n. [1. ontrmā; 2. ɑ̃trmei]. Fr., lit. 'between the dishes'. Side-dish, extra dish served between two courses of a dinner.

entrench, intrench, vb. trans. [1. intrénch; 2. *intrénʃ*]. **en-** & **trench**. **1. a** To surround, protect (a town, camp, forces &c.) with entrenchments; **b** (fig.) *to entrench oneself*, to establish oneself firmly and securely in a position. **2.** (rare) *Entrench upon*, encroach.

entrenchment, n. [1. intrénchment; 2. *in*trénʃmənt]. Prec. & **-ment**. **1.** The act of entrenching; state of being entrenched. **2.** (mil.) A trench for defensive purposes, including parapet of earth.

entre nous, adv. [1. ontr nōō; 2. ɑ̃tr nū]. Fr. Between ourselves; speaking confidentially.

entrepôt, n. [1. ontrpō; 2. ɑ̃trpo(u)]. Fr., fr. Lat. *interpositum*, 'that which is placed between'. See **inter-** & **position**. A place where goods are stored until exported or distributed; a warehouse; distributing centre.

entrepreneur, n. [1. ontrprenḗr; 2. ɑ̃trprənœr]. Fr., cp. **enterprise**. One who promotes, organizes, manages, an undertaking; specif., one who organizes theatrical or musical performances.

entresol, n. [1. óntrsòl; 2. ɑ̃́trsɔl]. Fr. A storey between the ground floor and first floor of a building.

entropy, n. [1. éntropi; 2. éntrəpi], fr. **en-** & Gk. *tropḗ*, 'a turn; change', & **-y** on anal. of **energy**. See **trope**. (phys.) Measure of the waste thermal energy, not available for conversion into mechanical work; symbol ϕ, *phi*.

entrust, intrust, vb. trans. [1. intrúst; 2. *in*trást]. **en-** & **trust**. **1.** To put into the hands of, hand over to, give into care of: *to entrust (the care of) one's daughter to a faithful friend*. **2.** To assign as a task or duty to be performed: *to entrust the duty of doing something to (a person)*; or *to entrust a person with a duty* &c.

entry, n. [1. éntri; 2. éntri], fr. Fr. *entrée*, fr. Lat. *intrāta*, P.P. type of *intrāre*, 'to go in, enter, penetrate'. See **enter**. **1.** Act of entering, of coming or going into, entrance. **2.** Way, passage, alley &c., whereby entrance is made; an approach. **3.** (law) Act of taking possession of lands or tenements by setting foot on or in them. **4.** Note, minute, or record, entered in a ledger &c.

entry-clerk, n. One who makes entries of business transactions.

entwine, intwine, vb. trans. [1. intwín; 2. *intwáin*]. **en-** & **twine**. **1.** To twist, weave, twine, together; interlace. **2.** To twist round, wreathe, wind round: *a tree entwined with ivy*; *entwined by one another's arms*. **3.** To make by twining together: *to entwine a garland*.

entwist, intwist, vb. trans. [1. intwíst; 2. *i*ntwíst]. **en-** & **twist**. **a** To make into a twist; **b** to twist together.

enucleate, vb. trans. [1. ēnūkliāt; 2. īnjūkl*i*-e*i*t], fr. Lat. *ēnūcleāt-(um)*, P.P. type of *ēnūcleāre*, 'to take out the kernel, remove from the husk'; (fig.) 'to make clear, explain', fr. **e-** & *nūcle-(us)*, 'a nut, kernel'. See **nucleus**. **1.** To strip of ambiguity, make clear, bring to light. **2.** (surg.) To remove (a tumour &c.) from its covering sac.

enucleation, n. [1. ēnūkliáshun; 2. īnjū-kl*i*é*i*ʃən]. Prec. & **-ion**. The act of enucleating.

enumerate, vb. trans. [1. ē-, enumerāt; 2. ī-, *i*njūməre*i*t], fr. Lat. *ēnumerāt-(us)*, P.P. type of *ēnumerāre*, 'to count, count out; to recount, relate, enumerate', fr. **e-** & *numerāre*, 'to count, number'. See **number (II.)**. **1.** To compute number of, count up one after another. **2.** To rehearse in order, go through a list of.

enumeration, n. [1. enūmeráshun; 2. *i*njū-məré*i*ʃən]. Prec. & **-ion**. **a** The act of enumerating; state of being enumerated; **b** a list, detailed account; list of items mentioned singly.

enumerative, adj. [1. enūmerativ; 2. *i*njū-mərət*i*v]. **enumerate** & **-ive**. Enumerating, pertaining to enumeration.

enunciate, vb. trans. [1. enúnshiāt, -siāt; 2. *i*nánʃie*i*t, -sie*i*t], fr. Lat. *ēnuntiāt-(um)*, P.P. type of *ēnuntiāre*, 'to disclose, report, tell; to express, declare; to pronounce', fr. **e-** & *nuntiāre*, 'to announce, declare, make known', fr. *nunti-(us)*, 'a bearer of news, messenger'. See **nuncio**. **1.** To propound, declare, state formally and definitely: *enunciate a theory, doctrine* &c. **2.** To utter articulately, pronounce.

enunciation, n. [1. enùnsiáshun; 2. *i*nànsié*i*-ʃən]. Prec. & **-ion**. **1.** The act of enunciating; state of being enunciated. **2.** Manner of enunciating.

enunciative, adv. [1. enúnshativ; 2. *i*nán-ʃət*i*v]. **enunciate** & **-ive**. **a** Declaring, enunciating; declaratory; **b** pertaining to enunciation.

enure. See **inure**.

envelop, vb. trans. [1. envélop; 2. *i*nvéləp], fr. O. Fr. *enveloper*. See **en-** & **develop**. **a** (of material process) To wrap round, enfold, cover completely: *enveloped in flames, in mist*; *to envelop oneself in a blanket*; **b** (fig., of action on non-material things) to obscure, conceal, render difficult to know or understand: *the subject was enveloped in mystery*.

envelope, n. [1. énvelōp, ónvelop; 2. énvəloup, ónvəloup, ãvəloup], fr. Fr. *enveloppe*, n., fr. prec. That in which something is folded, enclosed, wrapped up; outer covering, wrapping; specif. **a** a case or cover of paper for enclosing letters &c., with gummed flap for closing; **b** the outer covering enclosing the gas bag, or bags, of a balloon or airship.

envelopment, n. [1. envélopment; 2. *i*nvéləp-mənt]. **envelop** & **-ment**. **1.** The act of enveloping; state of being enveloped. **2.** Something that envelops; a covering.

envenom, vb. trans. [1. envénum; 2. *i*nvénəm]. **en-** & **venom**. **a** To make poisonous; apply venom to; infuse poison into; **b** (fig.) to fill, imbue, with malice, bitterness, malignity: *envenomed words, feelings* &c.; *an envenomed tongue*.

enviable, adj. [1. énviabl; 2. énv*i*əbl]. **envy** & **-able**. **a** (of thing) So desirable as to arouse envy: *an enviable possession, position*; **b** (of possessor) provoking envy by possessing desirable thing: *these enviable young ladies*.

enviably, adv. Prec. & **-ly**. In an enviable manner.

envious, adj. [1. énvius; 2. énv*i*əs], fr. O. Fr. *envieus*, fr. Lat. *invidiōsus*, 'full of envy, envious; exciting envy'. See **invidious**. **1.** (of person or feeling) Animated by, experiencing, envy: *envious of another's luck*. **2.** (of words, looks &c.) Expressing envy, characterized by envy: *an envious glance*.

enviously, adv. Prec. & **-ly**. In an envious manner.

environ, vb. trans. [1. envírun; 2. *i*nváiərən], fr. Fr. *environner*, fr. O. Fr. *environ*. See **environs**. (lit. and fig.) To surround, encompass, form a circle round, encircle: *environed by hills*; *environed by perils*; (archaic) '*a damzel environed with a garland*' (Spenser).

environment, n. [1. envírunment; 2. *i*nváiərən-mənt]. Prec. & **-ment**. **1.** The act of environing; state of being environed. **2.** That which surrounds; specif. (biol.) surroundings and circumstances in which an organism lives; external conditions of life: *quick to adapt itself to its environment*; (also fig.) *social, moral, and religious environment*.

environs, n. [1. énvirunz, envírunz; 2. énv*i*rənz, *i*nváiərənz], fr. O. Fr. *environ*, fr. **en-** & *viron*, 'circuit, going round', fr. *virer*, 'to turn round'. See **veer**. District immediately surrounding, lying on the outskirts of, a place; outlying suburbs; surrounding country: *Oxford and its environs*.

envisage, vb. trans. [1. envízij; 2. *i*nvízidž], fr. O. Fr. *envisager*. **en-** & **visage**. **1.** To face, look in the face, confront: *envisage facts, realities, dangers* &c. **2.** To visualize, bring before the mind's eye, contemplate.

envoy (I.), n. [1. énvoi; 2. énvɔ*i*]. O. Fr., fr. *envoiier*, 'to send', fr. *en voie*, 'on the way'. See **voyage**. Concluding, valedictory, stanza of an archaic type of poem, esp. of the ballade; according to convention usually beginning—'*Prince . . .*'

envoy (II.), n., fr. Fr. *envoyé*, P.P. of O. Fr. *envoiier*, 'to send out'. See prec. **a** One entrusted with a mission; messenger, agent, representative; **b** specif., a diplomatic representative, of rank below that of ambassador; minister plenipotentiary.

envy (I.), n. [1. énvi; 2. énv*i*]. O. Fr. *envie*, fr. Lat. *invidia*, 'envy, jealousy', fr. *invidēre*, 'to look maliciously at, look askance at; to be prejudiced against; to envy, grudge'. See **invidious**. **1.** Feeling of grudging ill-will provoked by the superior talents, possessions, success, or other advantages enjoyed by another, combined with mortification at one's own deficiency in such qualities or advantages: *envy, hatred, and malice*. **2.** That which causes, the object of, envious feeling; **a** the person whose possessions, qualities, excite envy: *her beauty made her the envy of many less lavishly endowed*; **b** the possessions, qualities, themselves: *his hunters were the envy of the countryside*. (Often in innocent sense.)

envy (II.), vb. trans., fr. Fr. *envier*, fr. Low Lat. *invidiāre*, 'to envy', fr. *invidia*, 'envy'. See prec. To have feelings of envy, excited by a person enjoying superior advantages &c., or by the advantages themselves; constructions: **a** *you are a very lucky man, I must say I envy you*; **b** *I envy your good fortune*; **c** *I envy you your pleasant rooms*; Phr. (with neg.), *I don't envy him his ugly, ill-tempered wife*, I'm glad she's not my wife.

enwind, vb. trans. [1. enwínd; 2. *i*nwáind]. **en-** & **wind (IV.)**. (of a thing) To wind, twist, coil (itself), round something else.

enwomb, vb. trans. [1. enwóōm; 2. *i*nwúm]. **en-** & **womb**. To enclose, conceal, as in the womb.

enwrap, inwrap, vb. trans. [1. inráp; 2. *i*n-rǽp]. **en-** & **wrap**. (lit. and fig.) To wrap up, enfold, lap, surround, cover with wrapping.

enwreathe, vb. trans. [1. enrédh; 2. *i*nríð]. **en-** & **wreathe**. **1.** To wind round, surround, with, as with, a wreath. **2.** To twist together, intertwine.

enzoötic, adj. [1. ènzoōtik; 2. ènzouɔ́t*i*k], fr. **en-** & Gk. *zôon*, 'animal', see **zoo-**, & **-ic**. Of diseases, affecting animals over a certain area or at specific season, corresponding to *endemic* in man.

enzyme, n. [1. énzīm; 2. énza*i*m], fr. Late Gk. *énzumos*, 'leavened', fr. Gk. **en-**, 'in', & *zúmē*, 'leaven'. See **zymotic**. (biol.) A chemical ferment, contrasted with yeast and other organic ferments.

eo-, pref., fr. Gk. *ēṓs*, 'dawn', fr. **āusōs* (see **aurora**), used to form technical terms in palaeontology and geology with force of 'very early or earliest known in time'.

eoanthropus, n. [1. ēōanthrṓpus; 2. ìouæn-þróupəs]. **eo-** & Latinized form of Gk. *ánthrōpos*, 'man'. See **anthropo-**. One of the earliest and most primitive human types; definitely distinguished, however, from the highest type of anthropoid ape, typified by the skull found at Piltdown, Sussex, hence also known as *Piltdown man*.

eocene, adj. [1. ḗosēn; 2. íousīn]. **eo-** & Gk. *kainós*, 'new, recent'. See **kainite** & cp. **recent**. (geol.) Belonging to the earliest, lowest division of the Tertiary period.

eohippus, n. [1. ēōhípus; ìouhípəs]. **eo-** & Gk. *hippos*, 'horse'. See **hippo-**. An extinct animal, known by its fossilized remains, regarded as the earliest progenitor or congener of the horse.

eolith, n. [1. ḗolith; 2. íoul*i*þ]. See next word. The earliest, very rudely formed flint implement; a rough stone, but slightly adapted from natural state, having much less elaboration than a palaeolithic implement.

eolithic, adj. [1. ēōlíthik; 2. ìoulíþ*i*k]. **eo-** & Gk. *lithos*, 'a stone'. See **litho-**. (geol. and archaeol.) Pertaining to the earliest part of the Stone Age or to a period preceding the Palaeolithic Age.

eon. See **aeon**.

eosin(e), n. [1. ḗosin; 2. íous*i*n], fr. Gk. *ēṓs*, 'dawn'. See **eo-** & **-in(e)**. A pink, rose-coloured fluorescent dyestuff, used for staining microscopic objects.

-eous, adjectival suff. denoting 'of the nature of'; fr. Lat. *-e-(us)* & **-ous**. **a** Added directly to Lat. nouns: *igneous, aqueous*; **b** to Fr. nouns: *duteous, beauteous*.

ep-, pref. Gk. **epi-** before vowels.

epact, n. [1. ḗpakt; 2. ípækt], fr. Fr. *épacte*, fr. Lat., fr. Gk. *epactḗ*, 'epact', fr. *epaktai* (*hēmérai*), 'intercalary days', fr. *epágein*, 'to bring in, bring forward; to add, intercalate', fr. **ep-** & *ágein*, 'to do'. See under **agent**. **1.** The excess of the solar year over 12 lunar months. **2.** The age of the moon on the first day of the year.

eparch, n. [1. épark; 2. épāk], fr. Gk. *éparkh-(os)*, 'a commander, governor', fr. **ep-** & *arkhós*, 'a leader, chief'. See **arch-**. **a** Governor of an eparchy; **b** bishop of an eparchy.

eparchy, n. [1. éparki; 2. épāk*i*], fr. Gk. *eparkhía*, 'province'; prec. & **-y**. **1.** A subdivision of the modern kingdom of Greece. **2.** (Gk. Ch.) A Russian diocese.

epaulement, n. [1. āpōlmon; 2. epolmã]. Fr., fr. *épauler*, 'to support with the shoulder', fr. *épaule*, 'shoulder'. See next word & **-ment**. (fort.) A breastwork, thrown up to protect the side of a battery &c. from a flanking fire.

epaulette, n. [1. épolet; 2. épəlɛt], fr. Fr. *épaulette*, dimin. of *épaule*, 'shoulder', earlier *espaule*, fr. L. Lat. *spatula, spathula*, dimin. of *spatha*, 'a broad, flat wooden instrument; any broad, flat object'. See **spatula**. An ornamental piece on shoulder of military or naval uniform; worn only by officers in the British navy; army officers now wear a shoulder-strap with badge of rank.

epenthesis, n. [1. epénthesis; 2. ɛpénþəs*i*s]. Gk., 'insertion'. **epi-** & **en-** & **thesis**. (gram.) **a** A letter or syllable inserted in a syllable or word; **b** often misleadingly applied by extension from a mere graphic process, to describe a fact of pronunciation; specif., e.g. to the *i* which often arises in Greek from the diphthonging of a vowel before a fronted, or 'palatalized' consonant, as in *keírō*, 'I clip, cut', fr. **ker-jō*, where *j* first fronts the *r*, which in its turn diphthongizes the *e* by producing a glide sound between itself and the latter.

epergne, n. [1. āpērn, āpārn; 2. eipā́n, eipḗən]. Said to be fr. Fr. *épargne*, 'a saving', the origin of wh. is unknown. Large, branched, ornamental centre-piece of porcelain, silver, or gold, for table, for holding fruit &c., consisting of several divisions or receptacles combined, supported by a stand.

epexegesis, n. [1. èpeksejḗsis; 2. èpɛksidžī́sis]. **ep-** & **exegesis**. An added explanation, further elucidation.

epexegetical, adj. [1. èpeksejétikl; 2. èpɛksidžétikl]. **ep-** & **exegetical**. Of, pertaining to, epexegesis.

epexegetically, adv. Prec. & **-ly**. By means of epexegesis.

eph-, pref. Gk. **epi-** before *h*.

ephebe, ephebus, n. [1. eféb, -us; 2. ɛfī́b, -as], fr. Lat., fr. Gk. *éphēbos*, 'a youth', fr. **eph-** & *hḗbē*, 'youth, early manhood'. See **Hebe**. (in ancient Greece) A free-born citizen between the ages of 18 and 20.

ephemera, ephemeron, n. [1. efémera, efémera, -ron; 2. ifímərə, ifémərə, -rɔn], fr. Gk. *ephḗmeros*, 'living only for a day; short-lived; temporary', fr. **eph-** & *hēméra*, 'day'. By the side of the aspirated (Attic) form, other dialects have *h*-less forms, *ēmar, āméra* &c. The forms w. *h-* suggest a base **sēm-*, **sām-*, & a connexion w. Scrt. *sáma-*, 'year', & Gmc. *sumar*, 'summer' (see **summer**), but it is not certain that the *h-* is not secondarily developed through factors not at present understood, & that the Aryan form was not **āmer-* wh. appears to be the base of Armen. *awr*, 'day'. **a** Insect, genus of insects, such as the may-fly, living only for a day; **b** a short-lived thing.

ephemeral, adj. [1. efémeral, -emeral; 2. ifímərəl, -émərəl]. Prec. & **-al**. **1.** Living, lasting, only for a day (of insects, flowers &c.). **2.** (fig.) Fleeting, transitory, of short duration, soon passing away: *ephemeral pleasures, prosperity, beliefs* &c.

ephemerality, n. [1. efèmeráliti, efèmeráliti; 2. ifìmərǽliti, ifèmərǽliti]. Prec. & **-ity**. The quality of being ephemeral.

ephemerid, n. [1. efémerid; 2. ifémərid], fr. **ephemera** (a) and **-id**, fr. Lat. *-idae*, pl. suff., 'family of'. (zool.) One of a family, *Ephemeridae*, of slender, delicate flying insects, such as the may-flies, which live but a few hours.

ephemeris, n. [1. efémeris, efémeris; 2. ifíməris, ifémoris], fr. Gk. *ephēmeris*, 'a diary, journal; a calendar', fr. *ephḗmer-(os)*, 'lasting for a day'. See **ephemera**. An astronomical calendar or almanac; a table giving the positions of a celestial body on successive days.

ephod, n. [1. éfod; 2. ífɔd]. Heb., fr. *āphad*, 'to put on'. **a** Outer, coloured, embroidered vestment of Jewish high priest, with shoulder-pieces bearing the names of the twelve tribes engraved on onyx; **b** a priestly garment connected with divination by lots.

ephor, n. [1. éfōr; 2. éfɔ̄], fr. Gk. *éphor-(os)*, 'an overseer; ephor', fr. **eph-** & *horáein*, 'to see, look, perceive', fr. base **worā-*, 'attention', cogn. w. O.E. *waru*, O.S., O.H.G. *wara*, 'attention'; Lat. *vereor*, 'observe with fear'. See **ware (II.)**. **1.** (in ancient Greece) One of five magistrates holding supreme power, in Sparta &c. **2.** (in modern Greece) Name of various administrative officials, e.g. *Ephor of Antiquities* &c.

epi-, pref. Gk. *epí*, 'at, upon; over; up to; on account of; beyond, besides'; in composition, 'rest at; after, in time; addition, accompaniment; reciprocal action'. Cogn. w. Scrt. *ápi*, 'also, besides; on, at'; cp. also Goth. *if-tuma*, 'later'. By the side of *épi* there was also *ópi-*, Gk. *ópithen*, 'from behind', Scrt. *abhi*, for first element of wh. cp. **ob-**, & for the second **by**. *Epi* appears to have assumed in part the functions of **obhi-*, 'towards, on'.

epiblast, n. [1. épiblahst; 2. épiblāst]. **epi-** & first element of **blastoderm**. (biol.) The outer germ layer of the embryo.

epic, n. & adj. [1. épik; 2. épik], fr. Lat., fr. Gk. *epik-(ós)*, adj., 'epic', fr. *ép-(os)*, 'a word; a speech, tale; song, lay; epic poetry'. See **epos** & **-ic**. **1.** n. A narrative poem, in primitive times one which was recited, describing a series of deeds and adventures of a hero who is the central figure. **2.** adj. Pertaining to, connected with, of the nature of, an epic.

epical, adj. [1. épikl; 2. épikl]. Prec. & **-al**. Epic.

epically, adv. Prec. & **-ly**. In the manner of an epic.

epicedium, n. [1. èpisḗdium; 2. èpisídiəm], fr. Lat. *epicēdīum*, fr. Gk. *epikḗdeion*, 'a dirge, elegy', fr. **epi-** & *kēdeía*, 'care for the dead, funeral', fr. *kēdos*, 'care, concern for; trouble, sorrow; funeral rites'. Cp. Gk. *kḗdeios*, 'dear, precious', *akēdḗs*, 'unfeeling, indifferent'. Cogn. w. Zend *sādra*, 'evil, unhappiness'; Goth. *hatis*, O.E. *hate, hete*, 'hatred, anger'. The base **kād-*, **kəd-*, meant, apparently, 'strong feeling, disposition of mind'; this might be favourable, cp. the Gk. senses, or unfavourable, as in those of the other languages. See further under **hate (I.)**. A funeral hymn, dirge.

epicene, adj. & n. [1. épisēn; 2. épisīn], fr. Lat. *epicoenus*, fr. Gk. *epíkoin-(os)*, 'common, promiscuous'; (gram.) 'of both genders', fr. **epi-** & *koinós*, 'common'. See **coeno-**. **1.** adj. **a** (gram.) Of common gender, denoting either sex; **b** (of persons) having the characteristics of both sexes; **c** of indeterminate character, neither one thing nor the other. **2.** n. One who, thing which, is epicene.

epicentrum, epicentre, n. [1. èpiséntrum, -sénter; 2. èpiséntrəm, -séntə], fr. Gk. *epíkentros*, 'at the central point'. **epi-** & **centre**. Area of the earth's surface immediately above the centre of origin of an earthquake.

epicure, n. [1. épikūr; 2. épikjɔ̄], fr. Lat. *Epicurus*, fr. Gk. *Epíkouros*, Gk. philosopher who was regarded as teaching the doctrine that the pleasures of the senses are the highest good. One who enjoys luxury and pleasure inordinately, esp. one who understands, is fastidious regarding, and enjoys the pleasures of, delicate food and drink.

epicurean, adj. & n. [1. èpikūréan; 2. èpikjɔ̄ríən]. Prec. & **-ean**. **a** adj. Connected with an epicure and his tastes; **b** n., an epicure.

Epicureanism, n. [1. èpikūréanizm; 2. èpikjɔ̄ríənizəm]. Prec. & **-ism**. **a** The doctrines of Epicurus; **b** epicurism.

epicurism, n. [1. épikūrizm; 2. épikjɔ̄rizəm]. **epicure** & **-ism**. The state of being an epicure; the cultivation of a delicate and fastidious taste in eating and drinking.

epicycle, n. [1. épisīkl; 2. épisaikl], fr. Gk. *epíkuklos*. **epi-** & **cycle**. A circle whose centre moves round the circumference of another and larger circle.

epicyclic, adj. [1. èpisíklik; 2. èpisíklik]. Prec. & **-ic**. Pertaining to, of the nature of, an epicycle.

epicycloid, n. [1. èpisíkloid; 2. èpisáikloid]. **epicycle** & **-oid**. Curve traced by a point on the circumference of a circle rolling upon the outer circumference of another circle.

epicycloidal, adj. [1. èpisīklóidl; 2. èpisaiklóidl]. Prec. & **-al**. **a** Tracing an epicycloid; **b** having the form of an epicycloid.

epideictic, adj. [1. èpidíktik; 2. èpidáiktik], fr. Gk. *epideiktik-(ós)*, 'for displaying, showing off; ostentatious'. **epi-** & **deictic**. **a** Serving to display, exhibit, show off; **b** designed for display, intended to be impressive, ostentatious.

epidemic (I.), epidemical, adj. [1. èpidémik(l); 2. èpidémik(l)], fr. Fr. *épidémique*, fr. *épidémie*, fr. L. Lat., fr. Gk. *epidēmía*, 'staying at home; prevalence of an epidemic', fr. *epidēm-(os)*, 'at home; current; epidemic'. **epi-** & *dēmos*, 'people'. See **demos** & **-ic** & **-al**. **a** (of disease) Prevalent among, affecting, a large number of persons in a community at the same time for a limited period; contrasted with *endemic*; **b** (fig., of ideas, fashions &c.) generally prevailing, prevalent.

epidemic (II.), n., fr. prec. An epidemic disease; also fig.

epidemically, adv. [1. èpidémikali; 2. èpidémikəli]. **epidemical** & **-ly**. As an epidemic.

epidemiology, n. [1. èpidēmiólojī; 2. èpidimiɔ́lədži], fr. Gk. *epidḗmio-(s)*, 'prevalent among the people', & **-logy**. See **epidemic**. The study of epidemics.

epidermal, adj. [1. èpidérmal; 2. èpidámǝl], fr. Gk. *epiderm-(is)* (see **epidermis**) & **-al**. Pertaining to the skin.

epidermic, adj. [1. èpidérmik; 2. èpidámik], fr. Gk. *epiderm-(is)* (see next word) & **-ic**. Epidermal.

epidermis, n. [1. èpidérmis; 2. èpidámis]. Gk. *epidermis*, 'the outer skin'. **epi-** & **-derm**. The outer skin, cuticle, of animals; outer skin of the eggs of molluscs; external integument of seed plants.

epigastric, adj. [1. èpigástrik; 2. èpigǽstrik]. Gk. *epigástri-(os)*, 'over the belly', & **-ic**. See **epi-** & **gastric**. (anat.) Situated, lying on, or above, the stomach.

epigastrium, n. [1. èpigástrium; 2. èpigǽstriəm], fr. Gk. *epigástrion*. See prec. (anat.) Epigastric region of the body.

epigene, adj. [1. épijēn; 2. épidžīn], fr. Fr., fr. Gk. *epigenḗ-(s)*, 'growing upon or after'. See **epi-** & **-gen**. **a** (geol.) Formed upon the surface of the earth; **b** (crystal.) foreign, of forms not natural to the substances in which the crystals occur.

epigenesis, n. [1. èpigénesis; 2. èpidžénisis]. **epi-** & **genesis**. (biol.) Theory that each germ or embryo is a fresh creation, and not arising naturally from reproductive tendencies and processes.

epiglottic, adj. [1. èpiglótik; 2. èpiglɔ́tik], fr. Gk. *epiglōtt-(is)* (see next word) & **-ic**. Belonging to the epiglottis.

epiglottis, n. [1. èpiglótis; 2. èpiglɔ́tis], fr. Gk. *epiglōttis*, 'epiglottis'. **epi-** & **glottis**. The triangular cartilage situated at the base of the tongue, which closes the windpipe or larynx during the act of swallowing.

epigram, n. [1. épigram; 2. épigræm], fr. Fr., fr. Lat., fr. Gk. *epigramma*, 'an inscription; epigram'. **epi-** & **-gram**. Brief, pointed sentence, in prose or verse, expressing a witty, often a satirical, idea tersely and compactly.

epigrammatic, adj. [1. èpigramátik; 2. èpigrəmǽtik], fr. Gk. *epigrámmat-*, stem of *epigramma* (see prec.), & **-ic**. **a** Like, suitable to, an epigram; short, pointed, pithy; **b** characterized by epigrams; **c** (of persons) inclined to make epigrams.

epigrammatically, adv. [1. èpigramátikali; 2. èpigrəmǽtikəli]. Prec. & **-al** & **-ly**. In an epigrammatic manner; as an epigram.

epigrammatist, n. [1. èpigrámatist; 2. èpigrǽmətist]. See **epigrammatic** & **-ist**. One who frequently makes epigrams; one who makes a particular epigram.

epigrammatize, vb. trans. & intrans. [1. èpigrámatiz; 2. èpigrǽmətaiz]. See prec. & **-ize**. **1.** trans. To put into epigrammatic form. **2.** intrans. To write or speak epigrammatically.

epigraph, n. [1. épigrahf; 2. épigrāf], fr. Gk. *epigraphḗ*, 'an inscription'. **epi-** & **-graph**. **1.** An inscription carved on stone or other hard surface. **2.** Inscription, motto &c. prefixed to a book or chapter.

epigraphic, adj. [1. èpigráfik; 2. èpigrǽfik]. Prec. & **-ic**. Of an epigraph; of the nature of an epigraph.

epigraphist, n. [1. epígrafist; 2. ɛpígrəfist]. **epigraph** & **-ist**. A student of epigraphy.

epigraphy, n. [1. epígrafi; 2. ɛpígrəfi]. **epigraph** & **-y**. The study of (ancient) inscriptions on stone, metal &c.

epilepsy, n. [1. épilepsi; 2. épilɛpsi], fr. O. Fr. *epilepsie*, fr. Lat., fr. Gk. *epilēpsía*, 'epilepsy', fr. *epilambánein*, 'to take, get'; (of disease) 'to seize, attack', fr. **epi-** & *lambánein* (fr. **(s)lab-*), 'to get, take, grasp, seize; to receive; apprehend', fr. Aryan *(s)ləgʷ-, 'to seize, take'; cp. Gk. *lázomai*, 'I take'; fr. *lagʷ-jo-*. Cp. **catalepsy.** Nervous disease characterized by intermittent fits, during which the sufferer becomes unconscious and falls down, and is convulsed with muscular twitchings; called also the *falling sickness*; also in a milder form without convulsions, but with a temporary loss of consciousness and a feeling of giddiness, called *minor, masked, epilepsy* or *petit mal.*

epileptic, adj. & n. [1. èpiléptik; 2. èpiléptik], fr. Fr., fr. Gk. *epilēptik-(ós)*, 'epileptic', fr. *epilēpt-*, stem of *epilēpsia* (see prec.), & **-ic.** **1.** adj. **a** Connected with, resembling, arising from, epilepsy; **b** suffering from epilepsy. **2.** n. An epileptic person.

epilogist, n. [1. epílojist; 2. epíladžist]. Next word & **-ist.** Composer or speaker of an epilogue.

epilogue, n. [1. épilog; 2. épilɔg]. Fr., fr. Lat. *epilogus*, fr. Gk. *epílogos*, 'peroration; concluding part of a play'. **epi-** & **-logue.** **1.** The concluding part of a speech, book, or other literary composition; peroration. **2.** Concluding speech, generally in verse, at end of a play, addressed to the audience and spoken by one of the actors.

epiphany, n. [1. epífani; 2. ipífəni], fr. O. Fr. *epiphanie*, fr. L. Lat., fr. Late Gk. *epipháni̇a*, fr. Gk. *epiphán-(eia)*, 'manifestation', & **-y.** Gk. *epipháneia* is fr. *epiphan-ḗs*, 'appearing, coming to light; manifest, evident', fr. **epi-** & *phaínein*, 'to bring to light, disclose' (fr. **phan-jo-*). See **phantasm, phantom.** **1.** (cap.) **a** The manifestation of the Saviour to the Gentiles, symbolized by the visit of the Magi; **b** the festival of the Christian Church commemorating this, celebrated on January 6th; Twelfth Night. **2.** The bodily manifestation of a deity or superhuman being.

epiphyte, n. [1. épifit; 2. épifait]. **epi-** & **-phyte.** A non-parasitic plant growing on another plant, deriving moisture from the air; an air plant.

epiphytic, epiphytal, adj. [1. èpifítik, -fítl; 2. èpifítik, -fáitl]. See prec. & **-ic** & **-al.** Of the nature of an epiphyte.

episcopacy, n. [1. epískopasi; 2. ipískəpəsi], fr. Lat. *epīscop-(us)*, 'bishop', & **-acy.** See next word. **a** Principle and system of church government by bishops; **b** (with def. art.) the whole body of bishops, episcopate.

episcopal, adj. [1. epískopal; 2. ipískəpəl], fr. L. Lat. *epīscopāl-(is)*, 'episcopal', fr. *epīscop-(us)*, 'an overseer'; (eccles.) 'a bishop', & **-al.** A loan-word fr. Gk. *epískopos*, 'an overseer, guardian; a scout; a bishop', fr. **epi-** & *skopós*, 'one who watches'. See **scope** & **bishop.** Connected with, pertaining to, coming from, a bishop or bishops, or from episcopacy: *episcopal orders, ordination, functions, benediction* &c.

episcopalian, adj. & n. [1. episkopálian; 2. ipìskəpéiliən]. Prec. & **-ian.** **1.** adj. Pertaining to bishops and to episcopacy. **2.** n. **a** Member of an episcopal church; **b** one who believes in episcopacy.

episcopalianism, n. [1. episkopálianizm; 2. ipìskəpéiliənizəm]. Prec. & **-ism.** Doctrine that bishops are essential to the being of a church.

episcopalism, n. [1. epískopalizm; 2. ipískəpəlizəm]. **episcopal** & **-ism.** Doctrine that authority resides in the whole body of bishops and not in a single individual; contrasted with *papalism.*

episcopally, adv. [1. epískopali; 2. ipískəpəli]. **episcopal** & **-ly.** **a** As a bishop; **b** by bishops.

episcopate, n. [1. epískopāt; 2. ipískəp(e)it]. See **episcopal** & **-ate.** **1. a** The office or dignity of a bishop; **b** a bishop's see; **c** a bishop's term of office. **2.** The whole body of bishops.

episode, n. [1. épisōd; 2. épisoud], fr. Gk. *epeisód-(ion)*, 'episode', fr. **ep-** & *eisod-(os)*, 'entrance; place of entrance', fr. *eis*, 'into, to' (fr. **ens*, fr. *en*, 'in', q.v. under **en- (II.)**), & *hodós*, 'a way, road'. See **hodometer, sedate, sit, seat.** **1.** (Gk. drama) Part of a tragedy, corresponding to an act, introduced between two choric songs. **2.** A separate and independent narrative of events or actions, introduced into the body of a play or novel. **3.** One of a series of events, esp. an important incident or experience.

episodic(al), adj. [1. èpisódik(l); 2. èpisɔ́dik(l)]. Prec. & **-ic** & **-al.** Of the nature of an episode; occurring as an episode; incidental.

episodically, adv. Prec. & **-ly.** In the manner of an episode.

epispastic, adj. & n. [1. èpispástik; 2. èpispǽstik], fr. Gk. *epispastik-(ós)*, 'drawing out', fr. **epi-** & *spastikós*, 'drawing, absorbing', fr. *spáein*, 'to draw' (fr. **spasein*). See **spasm.** (med.) **1.** adj. Causing blistering of the skin. **2.** n. Medicinal substance that produces a blister; vesicatory.

epistaxis, n. [1. èpistáksis; 2. èpistǽksis]. Gk., 'dropping', fr. *epistázein*, 'to drop'. See **epi-** & **stacte.** (med.) Bleeding of the nose.

epistemology, n. [1. epìstēmóloji; 2. ipìstimɔ́lədži], fr. Gk. *epistḗmē*, 'knowledge, understanding, science', & **-logy.** The first element is fr. Gk. *epístamai*, 'I know how; understand, know', orig. 'put oneself in the position appropriate for', fr. **epi-** & **stha-*, reduced grade of **sthē-*, 'to stand'. See **stand, state.** The theory of the basis and methods of knowledge.

epistle, n. [1. episl; 2. ipísl], fr. O. Fr. *epistle*, fr. Lat. *epistola*, fr. Gk. *epistolḗ*, 'something sent by a messenger; a message; a letter', fr. *epistéllein*, 'to send to; to send a message; to order, command', fr. **epi-** & *stéllein*, 'to put in order, put in position; to make ready, prepare, equip; to send out; to fetch, bring'. See **stele.** **1.** A written communication, letter, addressed to a person or group of persons, esp. one of a formal and instructive character; one written with care and elegance. **2.** (eccles., cap.) **a** One of the letters, or collections of letters, of St. Paul, St. Peter &c., included in the New Testament; **b** portion of one of these appointed to be read on a particular day, and forming part of the service of the Eucharist. *Epistle side*, that side of the altar from which the Epistle is read, the south side.

epistolary, adj. [1. epístolari; 2. ipístələri], fr. Fr., fr. L. Lat. *epistolāris*, 'epistolary', fr. *epistola*, 'a letter'. See prec. & **-ary.** Pertaining to, connected with, epistles or letters; **a** carried on by means of letters: *epistolary communications* &c.; **b** adapted to, used in, letters: *epistolary style* &c.

epistoler, n. [1. epístoler; 2. ipístələ], fr. Fr. *epistolier*, see prec. Priest who reads the Epistle at the Eucharist; cp. *gospeller.*

epistrophe, n. [1. epístrofi; 2. ipístrəfi], fr. Gk. *epistrophḗ*, 'a turning or wheeling about'. **epi-** & **strophe.** (rhet.) The repetition of the same word at the end of several successive clauses or sentences.

epistyle, n. [1. épistīl; 2. épistail], fr. Lat., fr. Gk. *epistúlion*, 'architrave'. **epi-** & **style (II.).** (archit.) Architrave.

epitaph, n. [1. épitahf; 2. épitāf], fr. Lat. *epitaph-(ium)*, fr. Gk. *epitáphion*, 'a funeral oration', fr. **epi-** & *táph-(os)*, 'funeral, rites of burial; grave, tomb'. Cp. Gk. *táphros*, 'a ditch', *tháptein*, 'to bury'. Etymol. doubtful. **1.** An inscription, on a tomb or monument, in memory of the dead. **2.** A short poem or prose statement in memory of a dead person, written as if to be inscribed on a tombstone, usually containing a tribute to the deceased, or moral reflexions on the uncertainty of human life &c.

epithalamial, adj. [1. èpithalámial; 2. èpiþəléimiəl], fr. Gk. *epithalámi-(on)*, 'bridal song', & **-al.** See **epithalamium.** Of, of the character of, an epithalamium.

epithalamic, adj. [1. èpithalámik; 2. èpiþəlǽmik]. See next word & **-ic.** Epithalamial.

epithalamium, n. [1. èpithalámium; 2. èpiþəléimiəm], fr. Lat., fr. Gk. *epithalámion*, 'a bridal song', fr. **epi-** & *thálam-(os)*, 'bridal chamber'. See **thalamus.** A poem or song in honour of a wedding; bridal song.

epithelial, adj. [1. èpithélial; 2. èpiþíliəl]. See next word & **-al.** Pertaining to, of the nature of, the epithelium.

epithelium, n. [1. èpithélium; 2. èpiþíliəm], fr. **epi-** & Gk. *thēlḗ*, 'teat', & Lat. ending *-um*; cogn. w. Lat. *fēlāre*, 'to suck'; *fīlius*, 'son'; the same base **dhē-* also occurs in Lat. *fēmina*, 'woman'. See **filial, feminine.** **a** (biol.) Cellular tissue forming the superficial layer of the skin and mucous membrane; **b** (bot.) thin epidermis lining inner cavities of plants.

epithet, n. [1. épithet; 2. épiþet], fr. Lat., fr. Gk. *epithet-(on)*, 'something added; an adjunct, adjective', fr. *epitithēmi*, 'I add', fr. **epi-** & *tithēmi*, 'put, place'. See **theme, thesis.** **1.** An adjective denoting some quality or attribute of the person or thing to which it refers. **2.** A descriptive, significant name; an additional name or title expressing an attribute of the person or thing referred to.

epithetic(al), adj. [1. èpithétik(l); 2. èpiþétik(l)]. Prec. & **-ic** & **-al.** Pertaining to an epithet; serving for, used as, an epithet.

epithetically, adv. Prec. & **-ly.** As an epithet.

epitome, n. [1. epítomi; 2. ipítəmi], fr. Gk. *epitomḗ*, 'an abridgment', fr. *epitémnein*, 'to cut short, abridge'. See **epi-** & **tome.** **1. a** A concise statement of the leading points of a book or other literary composition; **a** summary, abstract, digest; **b** a concise, condensed statement, report, of the main features of a series of events, or of a detailed scheme, argument &c. **2.** (fig.) A representation in miniature; **a** something exhibiting, on a small scale, the chief characteristics of another object; **b** a person who combines in himself many different qualities and aptitudes: '*A man so various that he seemed to be Not one, but all mankind's epitome*' (Dryden).

epitomist, n. [1. epítomist; 2. ipítəmist]. Prec. & **-ist.** One who makes an epitome.

epitomize, vb. trans. [1. epítomīz; 2. ipítəmaiz]. **epitome** & **-ize.** To abridge, summarize.

epizoön, n., pl. **epizoa** [1. èpizóon, -zóa; 2. èpizóuən, -zóuə], fr. **epi-** & Gk. *zôon*, 'animal'. See **zoo-.** An external parasitic animal.

epizoötic, adj. [1. èpizōótik; 2. èpizouɔ́tik]. See prec. & **-ic.** **a** Parasitic on other animals; specif. **b** (of diseases) prevalent among animals, corresponding to *epidemic*, in man.

epoch, n. [1. épok; 2. ípɔk], fr. Low Lat. *epoche*, fr. Gk. *epokhḗ*, 'a check, cessation; a stoppage, pause'; fr. *epékhein*, 'to have hold of, hold on to; to keep back, withhold; to stop, pause', fr. **ep-** & *ékhein*, 'to hold, have, possess'. Cp. Gk. *okhéō*, 'hold, contain'; *okheé*, 'cavern'; cogn. w. Scrt. *sáhatē*, 'to obtain power over, master'; *sáhaš*, 'strength'; Goth. *sigis*; O.E. *sige*, 'victory' (fr. **seg-i-*). Cp. also Gk. *á-skhetos*, 'irresistible'; *iskhás*, 'anchor'. See also **schema.** **1.** Beginning of a new stage or period, **a** fresh departure, in history, life, knowledge &c.: *the publication of the 'Origin of Species' marks an epoch in biology.* **2.** Period of time, distinguished from others by a series of characteristic historical and political events, intellectual movements &c.: *an epoch of revolution, religious enthusiasm* &c. **3.** (geol.) Minor division of geological time.

epochal, adj. [1. épokl; 2. ípɔkl]. Prec. & **-al.** Belonging to, characteristic of, marking, an epoch.

epoch-making, adj. Constituting a new departure, marking a fresh epoch: *an epoch-making discovery.*

epode, n. [1. épōd; 2. époud], fr. O. Fr., fr. Lat. *epodus*, fr. Gk. *epōdós*, 'last portion of an ode; a refrain'. **ep-** & **ode.** Kind of ancient lyric poem; used by Horace.

eponym, n. [1. éponim; 2. épənim], fr. Lat., fr. Gk. *epṓnum-(os)*, 'given as a name; named, surnamed', fr. **ep-** & *ónoma*, 'a name'. See **onomatopoeia**. Real or mythical person from whom a clan, family, nation, or place derives its name.

eponymous, adj. [1. epónimus; 2. epɔ́niməs]. Prec. & **-ous**. Giving name to tribe, country &c.: *an eponymous hero, founder* &c.

epopee, n. [1. èpōpḗ; 2. èpoupí], fr. Fr. *épopée*, fr. Gk. *epopoiía*, 'an epic poem; epic poetry', fr. *epopoiós*, 'an epic poet', fr. *épo-(s)*, 'a word; poetry' (see foll.) & *poiéein*, 'to make, produce, create'. See **poem**. An epic poem; epic poetry.

epos, n. [1. épos; 2. épɔs]. Lat., fr. Gk. *épos*, 'a word; a speech, tale; a song, lay; heroic poetry; epic'; earlier **wop-*, fr. **wokʷ-*; cogn. w. Scrt. *vácaš*, 'word'; *vákti*, 'to say'; Lat. *vox*, 'voice'; *vocāre*, 'to call'. See further under **voice**, **vocal**. **1.** Succession of events of epic character and importance. **2.** Primitive epic poem, or poetry, not written, but handed down by verbal tradition.

Epsom salts, n. [1. épsum sáwlts; 2. épsəm sɔ́lts], fr. Epsom in Surrey. White crystals of sulphate of magnesia, having the same chemical constituents as Epsom water; used medicinally as a purgative.

equability, n. [1. èkwabíliti; 2. ìkwəbíliti]. **equable** & **-(i)ty**. Lat. *aequābilitāt-(em)*. Quality, condition, of being equable: *equability of heat, of temperament.*

equable, adj. [1. ékwabl, ḗkwabl; 2. ékwəbl, íkwəbl]. Lat. *aequābilis*, 'uniform, steady'; fr. *aequā-*, see next word, & *-bilis*, see **-ble**. Steady, uniform; not given to sudden or great variation; not verging towards extremes: *an equable climate, disposition, temper.*

equal (I.), adj. [1. ḗkwal; 2. íkwəl]. Lat. *aequālis*, 'even, level, smooth; steady; equal, like', fr. Lat. *aequ-(us)*, 'level, equal, like', & adj. suff. *-ālis*, see **-al**. Etymol. uncertain; perh. cogn. w. Lith. *aikszte*, 'flat surface'; cp. Lat. *aequor*, 'a plain; the sea'. **1.** (in physical sense) Of like amount, size, degree, quality &c.; identical in respect of these: *two equal parts; several things of equal height, weight, magnitude, value* &c.; *things which are equal to the same thing are equal to one another.* Phr. *to be equal to doing*, able, competent, strong enough to do; *to be equal to a dinner party three days running* &c. **2.** (of moral qualities, status &c.) Possessing same degree of force, capacity, scope: *two friends possessed of equal affection for each other; two officers of equal rank*; (absol.) *all men are equal in the sight of God*, neither higher nor lower than, superior nor inferior to, each other; Phr. *on equal terms* (of two persons or groups). **3.** (of the mind and its condition) Equable, tranquil, unruffled: *to preserve an equal mind amid dangers and anxieties.*

equal (II.), n., fr. prec. A person of, possessing, same standing, rank, intelligence, age, or other position and qualities as another; one neither superior nor inferior to another in any such respect: *one's equals in age and experience; in learning, intelligence* &c.; specif. sense, of the same rank, or social class: *some prefer to mix with their inferiors rather than with their equals.*

equal (III.), vb., fr. **equal (I.)**. **1.** To be equal to, come up to, be level with, in possession of, any quality, to be as good as: *to equal another in intelligence, vigilance* &c.; *this wine does not equal the first in flavour.* **2.** To be commensurate with, identical with, in quantity, number, magnitude.

equality, n. [1. ēkwóliti; 2. ìkwɔ́liti]. Lat. *aequālitāt-(em)*. See **equal (I.)** & **-ity**. State, condition, of being equal (in all senses). Phr. *on an equality with*, (of persons) on equal terms with; (of things) identical, to be judged by same standard.

equalization, n. [1. èkwalīzā́shun; 2. ìkwəlaizéiʃən]. Next word & **-ation**. Process of equalizing; state of being equalized.

equalize, vb. trans. [1. ḗkwalīz; 2. íkwəlaiz]. **equal (I.)** & **-ize**. To make (things) equal.

equally, adv. [1. ḗkwali; 2. íkwəli]. **equal** & **-ly**. In an equal manner; to an equal degree.

equanimity, n. [1. èkwanímiti; 2. ìkwənímiti]. Lat. *aequanimitāt-(em)*, 'evenness of mind, impartiality, patience, calmness'; fr. *aequus*, 'even, level', see **equal (I.)**, & *animus*, 'soul, thought'. See **animus**. Calmness, tranquillity of mind; composure, serenity, imperturbability: *to bear the buffetings of fate with equanimity.*

equate, vb. trans. & intrans. [1. ēkwā́t; 2. ìkwéit], fr. Lat. *aequāt-(um)*, P.P. type of *aequāre*, 'to make level' &c. See **equal (I.)**. **a** trans. To consider, represent, treat, as equivalent or equal: *I am unable to equate your statement with my own observation of the facts*; **b** intrans. (rare) to be equal, show equality with.

equation, n. [1. ēkwā́shun; 2. ìkwéiʃən]. Lat. *aequātiōn-(em)*, 'an equalizing'. Prec. & **-ion**. **1.** Act or process of equalizing, or equating; state of being equalized or equated; (in various senses, as in astronomy, chemistry &c.) Phr. *personal equation*, allowance for individual differences and variations in quickness and character of mental and physiological processes. **2.** (math.) The expression of equality between two quantities, usually as in algebra, involving known and unknown quantities, of various types, as *quadratic, simultaneous equations* &c.

equational, adj. [1. ēkwā́shunal; 2. ìkwéiʃənəl]. Prec. & **-al**. Pertaining to, of the nature of, an equation.

equationally, adv. Prec. & **-ly**. By means of an equation.

equator, n. [1. ēkwā́ter; 2. ìkwéitə], fr. L. Lat. *aequātor*, lit. 'one who, that which, equalizes'. See **equate** & **-or**. **a** Imaginary great circle round earth's surface, equidistant from the two poles, which divides the globe into two equal parts, the Northern and Southern Hemispheres; **b** (astron.) similar great circle of the celestial sphere, corresponding to the terrestrial equator.

equatorial, adj. & n. [1. ēkwatṓrial; 2. ìkwətɔ́riəl]. Lat. *aequātōr* & **-ial**. See prec. **1.** adj. At, near, pertaining to, the equator: *Equatorial Africa, climate* &c. **2.** n. A telescope, also *equatorial telescope*, so mounted that it can follow a heavenly body from its rising to its setting.

equerry, n., now usually [1. ékweri; 2. ékwəri], formerly, & still among some old-fashioned speakers [1. ekwéri; 2. ikwéri], fr. Fr. *écurie*, O. Fr. *escurie*, 'stable', fr. Low Lat. *scūria*, a Gmc. loan-word, cp. O.H.G. *scūr* & *sciura*, 'shed, shelter'. The word is cogn. w. Engl. **sky** & **shower**. *Equerry* has been associated w., & influenced by, the entirely different word Lat. *equus*, 'horse'. See **equestrian** & **esquire**. **1.** Originally an officer in charge of a prince's stables, a master of the horse. **2.** Officer of a Royal household, in personal attendance upon the King, Queen, or other member of the Royal family.

equestrian, adj. & n. [1. ekwéstrian; 2. ikwéstriən]. Lat. *equester*, stem *equestri-*, 'pertaining to a horseman', & **-an**. *Eques-ter* is derived fr. *eques*, 'a horseman', & the suff. *-ter* expressing an agent. *Eques* is connected w. *equus*, 'horse', see **equine**. **1.** adj. Belonging to, concerned with, horsemanship; mounted, horsed: *equestrian exercises*, exercises performed on horseback; *equestrian skill*, horsemanship; *an equestrian statue*, one depicting a person on horseback. **2.** n. A horseman.

equestrienne, n. [1. ākestrién; 2. èikestrién], bogus Fr., fr. prec. w. fem. suff. *-enne*. A horsewoman; specif., a professional female performer on horseback.

equi-, pref., fr. Lat. *aequus*, 'equal'. See **equal**, wh. sense it retains in compounds.

equiangular, adj. [1. ḗkwiánggūlar; 2. íkwiǽŋgjulə]. Having only equal angles, e.g. the figure of a square.

Equidae, n. pl. [1. ékwidē; 2. ékwidī]. Mod. Lat., fr. *equus*, 'horse'. See **equine**. (zool.) The horse family, including the horse, ass, zebra, and several extinct species.

equidistance, n. [1. èkwidístans; 2. ìkwidístəns]. Equal distance.

equidistant, adj. [1. èkwidístant; 2. ìkwidístənt]. (of several points in space) Separated by the same amount of distance.

equilateral, adj. & n. [1. èkwiláteral; 2. ìkwilǽtərəl]. **a** adj. Having all sides equal; **b** n., an equilateral figure.

equilibrate, vb. trans. & intrans. [1. èkwilíbrāt; 2. ìkwiláibreit]. Lat. *aequilībrāt-(um)*, P.P. type of *aequilībrāre*, 'to balance'. See **equilibrium**. **a** trans. To cause (two things) to balance; **b** intrans., (of two things) to balance.

equilibration, n. [1. èkwilībrā́shun; 2. ìkwilaibréiʃən]. Prec. & **-ion**. Act of keeping, state of being, balanced.

equilibrist, n. [1. ēkwílibrist; 2. ìkwílibrist]. Fr. *équilibriste*, 'balancer', specif., 'tight-rope walker'; see **equilibrium** & **-ist**. One who performs tricks of balancing himself, or other objects, in unnatural and difficult positions.

equilibrium, n. [1. èkwilíbrium; 2. ìkwilíbriəm]. Lat. *aequilībrium*, 'even balance', fr. *aequus*, see **equal**, & *lībra*, 'balance, pair of scales'. See **libra**. **a** State of perfect balance, adjustment between opposing forces whereby a given position of a body is maintained; **b** (fig.) even balance and adjustment of conflicting interests, policies, motives: *political equilibrium.*

equimultiple, n. [1. èkwimúltipl; 2. ìkwimáltipl]. **equi-** & **multiple**. One of the products arising from multiplication of two or more numbers or quantities by same number or quantity.

equine, n. [1. ḗkwīn; 2. íkwain]. Lat. *equīnus*, 'pertaining to horses', fr. *equus*, 'horse', also *equa*, 'mare', wh. are cogn. w. Gk. *hippos* for **ekwos*; see **hippo-**; Scrt. *aśvaš*; Lith. *aszvà*, Goth. *aihwa-*, O.E. *eoh*, fr. *ehw-*, O.H.G. *ehu-*, O. Ir. *ech*, W. *ep*. Further connexions are doubtful. Pertaining to, resembling, of the nature of, a horse.

equinoctial, adj. & n. [1. èkwi-, èkwinókshal; 2. ìkwi-, èkwinɔ́kʃəl]. Lat. *aequinoctiāl-(em)*. See next word. **1.** adj. **a** Pertaining to, connected with, an equinox: *equinoctial points*, the two points where the equator and the ecliptic intersect; **b** occurring, happening at or near the time of the equinox: *equinoctial gales.* **2.** n. An equinoctial gale.

equinox, n. [1. ḗkwi-, ékwinoks; 2. íkwi-, ékwinɔks]. Fr. *équinoxe*; Lat. *aequi-noctium*, 'equal night', fr. *aequus*, see **equal (I.)**, & *noct-*, stem of *nox*, 'night'. See **nocturnal** & **night**. **1.** Time at which the sun crosses the equator, and when its centre coincides with one of the equinoctial points (March 20 and Sept. 22 or 23); at these times, day and night are of equal length. **2.** (popular) An equinoctial gale or storm.

equip, vb. trans. [1. ekwíp; 2. ikwíp]. 16th cent. *esquippe*, fr. A.-Fr. *esquipper*, fr. **ex-** & O.N. *skipa*, 'set in order, arrange'; perh. fr. *skip*, 'ship', & meaning orig. 'to fit out a ship, arrange (things, stores &c.) on a ship'. See **ship**. **1.** **a** To fit out, provide, supply with what is necessary for particular purpose: *to equip a ship for a voyage, an army for the field, a person for a trip, expedition* &c.; **b** to dress, accoutre, with the clothes, ornaments &c. suitable for particular occasion: *fully equipped in his armour.* **2.** (of mental action) To supply with training, learning, knowledge, for intellectual tasks: *to equip one's son for life with a sound education* &c.

equipage, n. [1. ékwipij; 2. ékwipidž]. Prec. & **-age**. **1.** **a** Retinue, train, travelling accessories, band of attendants &c. collectively: *the Lord Mayor's equipage*; **b** (archaic) a carriage, horses, and servants, turn-out: *a splendid equipage drove up to my door.* **2.** Collection of various small, convenient objects, suitable and useful for particular purpose: e.g. *a dressing equipage*, collection of brushes, combs, mirrors, bottles, razors &c. esp. when fitted compactly into a receptacle with places for each article; *tea equipage*, tea table and appointments.

equipment, n. [1. ekwípment; 2. ikwípmənt]. **equip** & **-ment**. **1. a** Act of equipping; **b** state of being equipped. **2.** (often pl.) That which is used for equipping: *the necessary equipments for a voyage; a soldier's equipment.*

equipoise, n. [1. ékwipoiz; 2. íkwipɔiz]. **equi-** & **poise**. Balance, equilibrium; in physical and moral sense.

equipollence, n. [1. èkwipólens; 2. ìkwipɔ́ləns], fr. next word & **-ce**. **a** Equality of force, value, meaning; **b** something which is equipollent.

equipollent, adj. & n. [1. èkwipólent; 2. ìkwipɔ́lənt]. Fr., fr. Lat. *aequipollent-(em)*, 'of equal value or significance', fr. *aequus*, see **equi-**, & Pres. Part. of *pollēre*, 'to be powerful, able'; prob. cogn. w. Lat. *plēnum*, 'full', see **plenum**, w. Gk. *polús*, 'much', see **poly-**, & **full**. **a** adj. Equal in force, equivalent; **b** n., that which is equipollent.

equiponderant, adj. [1. èkwipónderant; 2. ìkwipɔ́ndərənt], fr. stem of next word, w. suff. **-ant**. Of equal weight.

equiponderate, vb. trans. [1. èkwipónderāt; 2. ìkwipɔ́ndəreit]. See **equi-**, **ponder** & **-ate**. To counterbalance.

equipotential, adj. [1. èkwipōténshal; 2. ìkwipoutén∫əl]. **equi-** & **potential**. (phys.) Having equal potential force at all points.

Equisetum, n. [1. èkwisḗtum; 2. èkwisítəm]. Lat., fr. *equus*, 'horse', see **equine**, & *sēta*, or *saeta*, 'stiff hair, bristle', cogn. w. O.E. *sāda*, 'string, noose', O.H.G. *seito*; cp. Mod. Germ. *saite*, 'a string', see **seta**. (bot.) Genus of plants with jointed stems; also called horse-tail.

equitable, adj. [1. ékwitabl; 2. ékwitəbl]. Fr. *équitable*. See **equity** & **-able**. Possessing, exhibiting, equity; just, fair, reasonable.

equitableness, n. Prec. & **-ness**. Quality, condition, of being equitable.

equitably, adv. See prec. & **-ly**. In an equitable manner; according to the rules of equity.

equitant, adj. [1. ékwitant; 2. ékwitənt]. Lat. *equitant-(em)*, Pres. Part. of *equitāre*, 'to ride', formed fr. *equit-*, stem of *eques*, 'horseman'. See **equine**. (bot., of leaves) Having bases which overlap each other.

equitation, n. [1. èkwitáshun; 2. èkwitéi∫en]. Fr., fr. Lat. *equitātiōn-(em)*, 'horsemanship', fr. *equitāt-*. See prec. & **-ion**. Art of riding, horsemanship.

equity, n. [1. ékwiti; 2. ékwiti]. Fr. *équité*, fr. Lat. *aequitāt-(em)*, 'conformity, symmetry; just conduct, fairness', fr. *aequus*, 'level' &c. See **equal** & **-ity**. **1.** Fairness, uprightness, of mind; impartiality, justice in conduct. **2.** (law) **a** System of justice, and body of rules, outside of, and supplementary to, Common Law, which grew out of the administration of justice by the King's chancellor; **b** an equitable claim or right: *equity of redemption*, right to redeem a mortgage by payment of capital sum and interest.

equivalence, n. [1. ekwívalens; 2. ikwívələns]. **equi-** & **valence**. Condition of being equal or equivalent; equality, identity of value, power, significance.

equivalent, adj. & n. [1. ekwívalent; 2. ikwívələnt]. Fr., fr. Lat. *aequus*, see **equal**, & *valent-(em)*, Pres. Part. of *valēre*, 'to be strong; to be worth'. See **valiant**. **1.** adj. Equal to, or identical with, in value, amount, meaning &c.: *the Anglo-Saxon word eorl, 'earl', seems often to be equivalent to our 'gentleman'.* **2.** n. Something which is equivalent: *I promised him five pounds, or its equivalent in books.*

equivocal (I.), adj. [1. ekwívokl; 2. ikwívəkl]. Lat. *aequivocus*, 'of equal voice, or significance; ambiguous'. See **equi-** & **vocal**. **1.** Capable of more than one interpretation, of doubtful significance; ambiguous: *an equivocal sentence, expression* &c. **2.** (of behaviour, actions &c.) Capable of being assigned to more than one kind of motive; giving rise to suspicion. **3.** Dubious, ambiguous, uncertain, not well assured: *an equivocal success; in an equivocal position.*

equivocal (II.), n. fr. prec. (rare) An equivocal, ambiguous word or expression.

equivocally, adv. **equivocal (I.)** & **-ly**. In an equivocal, dubious, uncertain manner.

equivocalness, n. **equivocal (I.)** & **-ness**. Quality of being equivocal; ambiguity.

equivocate, vb. intrans. [1. ekwívokāt; 2. ikwívəkeit], fr. L. Lat. *aequivocāt-(um)*, P.P. type of *aequivocāre*. See **equivocal**. To make use of ambiguous terms, express oneself in words capable of more than one interpretation, with the deliberate intention to mislead; to palter with the truth, to shuffle, to dodge.

equivocation, n. [1. ekwìvokáshun; 2. ikwìvəkéi∫ən]. Prec. & **-ion**. Act of equivocating; a quibble, an evasion of the truth.

equivocator, n. [1. ekwívokātor; 2. ikwívəkeitə]. **equivocate** & **-or**. One who equivocates.

equivoque, n. [1. èkwivók; 2. èkwivóuk]. Fr., 'word or phrase used in a double sense'. Lat. *aequivocus*. See prec. words. A verbal ambiguity, a pun.

-er, suff. **1.** Still a living and very productive suffix; fr. O.E. *-ere*, W. Gmc. **-arja-*; **a** used to form nouns denoting an agent, from verbs: O.E. *bæcere*, 'baker', fr. *bacan*; added later to verbal bases: *driver, hunter* &c.; **b** used to form nouns from other nouns, denoting persons who make, or are associated with certain objects: O.E. *bōcere*, 'writer, scribe', fr. *bōc*, 'book'; cp. also later *hatter, poulter* &c.; **c** used to denote an instrument, when added to verbal stems: *sweeper, roller, blotter, (gas-)burner, (pen)holder, poker, chopper* &c.; **d** indicating a resident in, or at: *Londoner, cottager, Westerner, villager* &c.; **e** in modern colloquial formations, used to denote things or actions connected with the idea of the basal word: *diner*, dining carriage on a train; *tenner*, ten-pound note; *breather*, time in which to breathe &c. **2.** fr. O. Fr. *-ier*, A.-Fr. *-er*, fr. Lat. *-ārius*, cogn. w. **1. b**, and often indistinguishable from it; denotes person who does the action, makes the thing, follows occupation, expressed by basal word: *carpenter, potter; fruiter-er, poulter-er* &c., have the suffix twice, the latter being perhaps English *-er* **1**. **3.** Comparative suffix, O.E. *-ra*, M.E. *-re*: *sooner* &c. **4.** Fr. infinitive; in law terms, expressing action denoted by the verb: *user, disclaimer, rejoinder* &c. **5.** O.E. verbal formative element *-rian*: *slumber*; and later verbs *glitter, shimmer, glimmer*. See also **-ier**, **-yer**.

era, n. [1. ḗra; 2. íərə]. Lat. *aera*, neut. pl. '(brass) counters; items of a calculation'; fr. *aes*, 'brass'. See this base under **ore**. **1.** Method of dating time from some particular point or event: *Christian era.* **2.** Historical period, epoch.

eradiation, n. [1. ērādiáshun; 2. īrèidiéi∫ən]. **e-** & **radiation**. Giving out, emission, **a** of light and heat; **b** of moral influence.

eradicable, adj. [1. ērádikabl; 2. īrǽdikəbl]. See next word & **-able**. Capable of being rooted out.

eradicate, vb. trans. [1. ērádikāt; 2. īrǽdikeit]. Lat. *ērādīcāt-(um)*, P.P. type of *ērādīcāre*, 'to root out'. **e-** & *rādic-*, 'root'. See **radical**, **radix**. To tear up by the roots, root out, esp. in fig. sense, to extirpate, abolish, get rid of, destroy.

eradication, n. [1. ērādikáshun; 2. īrǽdikéi∫ən]. Prec. & **-ion**. Act of eradicating; state of being eradicated.

eradicative, adj. [1. ērádikātiv; 2. īrǽdikeitiv]. **eradicate** & **-ive**. Tending, serving, to eradicate.

eradicator, n. [1. ērádikātor; 2. īrǽdikeitə]. **eradicate** & **-or**. Instrument for uprooting weeds.

erase, vb. trans. [1. eráz; 2. iréiz]. Lat. *ērās-(um)*, P.P. type of *ērādere*, 'to scratch, cut, scrape off'; **e-** & **rase**. **1.** To scratch out, wipe, rub out, or off, something written, drawn, painted, cut &c.: *to erase an inscription, a name from a list.* **2.** (fig., of non-material things) To blot out, expunge, dismiss from the mind &c.: *to erase a hope from one's mind.*

erased, adj. [1. erázd; 2. iréizd], fr. P.P. of prec. **1.** Effaced, blotted out (lit. and fig.). **2.** (her.) Represented with lower edge ragged, as though roughly torn.

eraser, n. [1. erázer; 2. iréizə]. **erase** & **-er**. One who, that which, erases; specif., an instrument, or a preparation of rubber, for rubbing out what has been written, drawn &c.

erasion, n. [1. erázhun; 2. iréiʒən]. **erase** & **-ion**. Process of erasing; specif. (surg.) removal of diseased tissue by scraping.

Erastian, adj. [1. ērástian; 2. īrǽstiən, irǽst∫ən], fr. Erastus, a German follower of Zwingli in 16th cent., & **-ian**. Belonging to, arising from, in accordance with, the principles of Erastus.

Erastianism, n. [1. ērástianizm; 2. īrǽstiənizəm]. Prec. & **-ism**. Theory that in Church government the ecclesiastical should be subordinated to the secular power, that the State should direct and determine the affairs of the Church.

erasure, n. [1. erázhur; 2. iréiʒə]. **erase** & **-ure**. **a** Process of erasing, rubbing, blotting out; **b** something, word &c., rubbed out; **c** place in text where erasure has been made.

erbium, n. [1. érbium; 2. ʌ́biəm], fr. Ytterby, in Sweden. (chem.) A rare metal, allied to yttrium and ytterbium.

ere, adv. & prep. [1. ār; 2. εə]. O.E. *ǣr*, 'soon; formerly; before (in time)'; M.E. *ēr*; old compar., cp. Goth. *airis*, 'earlier'. adv. & *airiza*, fr. *air*, 'early', O.H.G. *ēr*, *eiris*; O.E. has a new compar. *ǣrra*, adj. Cp. Gk. *ēri*, 'early in the morning'. (archaic and poet.) **1.** adv. (conj.) **a** (of time) Before: *come ere (it is) too late*; **b** expressing preference, sooner, rather, than: *I would die ere I would consent.* **2.** prep. (of time) Before: *he died ere daybreak; ere long*, before long, soon.

erect (I.), adj. [1. erékt; 2. irékt]. Lat. *ērect-(um)*, 'upright, lofty, elevate, noble', P.P. type of *ērigere*, 'to put up, put straight, raise', fr. **e-** & *regere*, 'to stretch, keep or lead straight; to guide, direct, rule'; cogn. w. Goth. *rikan*, 'to reach', & *uf-rakjan*, 'to stretch, reach'; also Goth. *raihts*, 'straight', O.E. *riht*, 'straight' &c. See **right (I.)**. Cp. also Scrt. *ṛjyati*, 'he stretches'; Gk. *orégein*, 'I reach out, extend', whence *orektós*, 'stretched out, presented'. See **rectum** & cp. **regal**. **1. a** Straight, upstanding, not lying down, curved, or stooping: *an erect figure*; **b** uplifted, raised: *with head, hand &c. erect.* **2.** Bristling, standing up: *with every hair erect.* **3.** (of the mind, spirits &c.) Not depressed; alert. **4.** (her., of a charge) Naturally horizontal, placed perpendicularly.

erect (II.) also **erectly**, adv., fr. prec. In an upright, horizontal position: *to stand erect.*

erect (III.), vb. trans., fr. **erect (I.)**. **1.** To put, raise, into an upright position: *to erect a flagstaff.* **2.** To construct, build, rear: *to erect a house, tomb, monument, a shed* &c. **3.** To establish, raise to more important status: *to erect a custom into a law.*

erectile, adj. [1. eréktīl; 2. iréktail]. Prec. & **-ile**. Capable of becoming erect; specif. (physiol.) *erectile tissue*, becoming rigid from dilatation of the blood-vessels it contains.

erection, n. [1. erékshun; 2. irék∫ən]. **erect (III.)** & **-ion**. **1. a** Act or process of erecting; **b** state of being erected. **2.** Something which is erected; a building: *the new bank was a handsome erection.*

erective, adj. [1. eréktiv; 2. iréktiv]. **erect (III.)** & **-ive**. Tending to make erect.

erector, n. [1. eréktor; 2. iréktə]. **erect (III.)** & **-or**. One who, that which, erects; specif. (anat.) a muscle which raises, and maintains, a part in an erect position.

eremite, n. [1. érimīt; 2. érimait], variant of **hermit**, M.E. *eremite*, fr. Lat. *herēmīta*. Religious recluse, hermit.

eremitic(al), adj. [1. èrimítik(l); 2. èrimítik-(əl)]. Prec. & **-ic** (& **-al**). Connected with an eremite.

erenow, adv. [1. ārnóu; 2. èənáu]. **ere** & **now**. Before this time, heretofore.

erethism, n. [1. érēthizm; 2. érīþizəm]. Fr. *éréthisme*, fr. Gk. *erethismós*, 'irritation'; fr. *eréthein*, *erethízein*, 'to rouse, stir'; formed by addition of *-dh-* (Gk. *-th-*), fr. base *er-*, *or-*, 'to rise', as in *órnūmi*, 'raise', Lat. *orior*, 'rise'. See **orient**. (physiol.) Abnormal irritability of an organ, tissue &c.

erewhile, adv. [1. ārwíl; 2. èəwáil]. **ere** & **while**. A short time ago; a little before.

erg, n. [1. ërg; 2. ʌ̄g]. New coinage fr. Gk. *érgon*, 'work'. See **ergon**. (phys.) The unit of energy; amount of work done by a force of one dyne acting for a distance of one centimetre.

ergo, adv. [1. ërgō; 2. ʌ́gou]. Lat., 'therefore', cp. *ergā*, prep., 'opposite, towards', said to be fr. *ē regō*, 'from the direction', fr. an obs. n. connected w. *regere*, 'to direct', q.v. under **regal**. Therefore; chiefly colloquial and facetious.

ergon, n. [1. ërgon; 2. ʌ́gən]. Gk., 'work, action', for **werg-*, cogn. w. Gmc. **werk-* &c. See **work (I.)**. **a** Work, in terms of heat; **b** erg.

ergot, n. [1. ërgot; 2. ʌ́gət]. Fr., 'spur of a cock; disease in cereals'. Origin unknown. **1.** Disease caused by a fungus in cereals, esp. in rye. **2. a** The fungoid growth which produces the disease; **b** drug made of this, used in midwifery to contract uterus after childbirth.

ergoted, adj. [1. ërgoted; 2. ʌ́gətid]. Prec. & **-ed**. Infected with the ergot fungus.

ergotic, adj. [1. ërgótik; 2. ʌgótik]. **ergot** & **-ic**. Connected with, made from, ergot: *ergotic acid*.

ergotin, n. [1. ërgotin; 2. ʌ́gətin]. **ergot** & **-in**. (pharmacol.) Extract of ergot.

ergotism, n. [1. ërgotizm; 2. ʌ́gətizəm]. **ergot** & **-ism**. Disease contracted from eating bread made from ergoted grain, or from overdoses of the drug.

ergotization, n. [1. ërgotizáshun; 2. ʌ̀gətai-zéiʃən]. Prec. & **-ation**. **a** Condition of being infected with ergot; **b** condition of suffering from ergotism.

ergotize, vb. trans. [1. ërgotīz; 2. ʌ́gətaiz]. **ergot** & **-ize**. To infect with ergot.

Erica, n. (in spite of Lat. *ī* pronounced by gardeners &c.) [1. érika; 2. érikə], fr. Lat. *erīce*, fr. Gk. *ereíkē*, 'heath', fr. **wereik-*, cogn. w. O. Ir. *froech*, Lith. *viržis*, 'heath'. (bot.) Heath, the typical genus of the family *Ericaceae* which includes also azaleas, rhododendrons &c.

Erin, n. [1. érin; 2. érin]. Ir. *Erinn*, oblique case of *Eire*, Ireland. Ancient native name of Ireland.

eristic, adj. & n. [1. erístik; 2. erístik]. Gk. *eristikós*, 'connected with strife', fr. *eristés*, 'wrangler', fr. *éris*, 'strife, debate'. Etymol. doubtful, possibly connected w. Scrt. *ári̇š*, 'hostile'. **1.** adj. Pertaining to, provoking, argument, controversial. **2.** n. **a** A controversialist; **b** controversial argument.

ermine, n. [1. ërmin; 2. ʌ́min]. M.E. *ermin* &c., fr. O. Fr. *(h)ermine*, A.-Fr. *hermine*; Low Lat. *armelīnus*, 'ermine fur'; the word is prob. of Gmc. origin; cp. O.E. *hearma*, 'fieldmouse, dormouse', also L.O.E. *hearmascinnen*, 'of ermine skins'; O.H.G. *harmo*, 'an ermine'; w. this is cogn. Lith. *szarmů*; Aryan **k̑arm-*, or **k̑orm-*. Another suggestion is that the O. Fr. &c., came fr. *(mūs) Arménius*, 'Armenian mouse'. If this be so then the O.E. & Lith. words have nothing to do w. our word. **1.** The common stoat, which in cold climates, as N. Europe and Canada, has a very fine thick fur, in winter a pure white, with a jet black tip to the tail. **2.** Fur made from the winter coat of this animal, made up with the black tips of the tails arranged at regular intervals, thus forming a series of black points. **3.** (fig.) The functions of a judge of the High Court, so called because the robes are trimmed with ermine: *to wear, assume, the ermine*. **4.** (her.) One of the recognized furs; depicted as a white field with black spots of peculiar shape.

ermines, n. pl., fr. prec. (her.) Fur represented by white spots on a black field, or field sable, powdering argent.

erminois, n. [1. ërminois; 2. ʌ́minəis]. O. Fr. See prec. (her.) Fur represented by black spots on yellow or dotted field, otherwise, field or, powdering sable.

-ern, adj. suff. representing O.E. *-erne*, Gmc. **-rōnj-*; cp. O.H.G. *-rōni*, in *nordarōni*, 'northern' &c.

erne, n. [1. ërn; 2. ʌn]. O.E. *earn*; cogn. w. O.H.G. *aro*, O.N. *örn*, Gk. *órnis*, 'bird'. See **ornithology**. The white-tailed sea-eagle.

erode, vb. [1. eród; 2. iróud]. Lat. *ērōdere*, 'to gnaw away, consume'. See **e-** & **rodent**. To eat into, wear away, corrode, destroy; specif. **a** of a disease which destroys tissues; **b** of the action of sea and weather upon land; **c** of action of acids.

erodent, adj. [1. erődent; 2. iróudənt], fr. Lat. *ērōdent-(em)*, Pres. Part. of *ērōdere*, 'to gnaw away'. See prec. Tending to cause, causing erosion.

erogenous, adj. [1. erójenus; 2. irɔ́džinəs], fr. Gk. *érōs*, 'love', see **erotic** & **-gen** & **-ous**. Productive of, tending to arouse, sexual desire.

erosion, n. [1. erőzhun; 2. iróužən]. Lat. *ērōs-(um)*, P.P. type of *ērōdere*, & **-ion**. See **erode**. Process of eroding, esp. the action of disease, weather, and currents, and of acids; the condition of being eroded.

erosive, adj. [1. erősiv; 2. iróusiv]. Lat. *ērōs-*, see prec., & **-ive**. Eroding, causing erosion, having the property of eating, wearing, away.

erotic(al), adj. [1. erótik(l); 2. irɔ́tik(l)]. Gk. *erōtikós*, 'connected with amatory desire', fr. *érōs*, stem *erōt-*, 'love, desire; god of love'; cp. *éramai*, 'I love, desire, long for'. Relationships doubtful; perh. connected w. Scrt. *ariš*, 'filled with desire, zealous' &c. **a** Pertaining to, dealing with, sexual love and desire: *erotic poetry*; **b** (of persons, temperaments &c.) amative, amorous, given to sexual passion.

eroticism, n. [1. erótisizm; 2. irɔ́tisizəm]. Prec. & **-ism**. Erotic temperament; erotic habit of mind.

erotomania, n. [1. eròtōmánia; 2. iròutou-méiniə]. See **erotic** & **mania**. Excessive preoccupation with amorous thoughts; insanity arising from erotic passion.

err, vb. intrans. [1. ër; 2. ʌ]. Fr. *errer*, 'to wander'; Lat. *errāre*, 'to wander, stray about; to wander from the subject; to wander from the truth, mistake, err'. Cogn. w. Goth. *airzeis*, 'astray, going astray', & *airzjan*, 'to lead astray, deceive'; O.H.G. *irri*, 'in error, wrong'; O.E. *ierre*, 'angry'; Scrt. *iraryáti*, 'he is enraged'. **1.** (obs.) To wander out of one's way, go astray. **2.** To miss, depart from, intellectual truth; to be mistaken, make a mistake; to judge wrongly from imperfect knowledge: *men erred greatly in believing that all languages were derived from Hebrew*. **3. a** To depart from moral truth; to commit sin, to be guilty of an offence against the divine law of conduct: '*To err is human, to forgive divine*' (Pope); **b** to depart from the truth in religious faith, to hold wrong doctrines: *Protestants and Roman Catholics each think the others err in some of the essentials of belief*.

errand, n. [1. érand; 2. érənd]. O.E. *ǣrende*, 'message, tidings'; M.E. *ērende*; cogn. w. O.S. *ārundi*, O.H.G. *ārunti*; fr. O.E. *ār*, 'messenger'; O.S. *ēru*, Goth. *airus*. **1.** Particular business entrusted to an agent or messenger: *to go on, run, errands*. **2.** A special business, mission with definite purpose: *I have come on an errand of mercy*. Phr. *a fool's errand*, mission without a real object; one which is bound to fail.

errand-boy, n. Youth employed by a shop or business firm, whose duty is to carry messages, letters, deliver goods to customers &c.

errant, adj. [1. érant; 2. érənt]. Fr., Pres. Part. fr. L. Lat. *iterant-(em)*, Pres. Part. of L. Lat. *iterāre*, 'to go on a journey', fr. *iter*, 'journey'; cp. O. Fr. *edrer*, later *errer*. See **iterate**. The word has been confused w. Fr. *errer*, fr. Lat. *errāre*, q.v. under **err**. **1.** Wandering, travelling about on the lookout for adventure and the opportunity to perform chivalric deeds; esp. *knight-errant*, q.v. **2.** Going astray; (of thoughts) wandering from the point; (of conduct) deviating from correctness and good behaviour.

errantry, n. [1. érantri; 2. érəntri]. Prec. & **-ry**. Principles and conduct of a knight-errant.

erratic (I.), adj. [1. erátik; 2. irǽtik]. Fr. *erratique*, fr. Lat. *errāticus*, 'wandering, roving', fr. *errāt-*, P.P. type of *errāre*, 'to wander' &c. See **err** & **-ic**. **1. a** (of conduct) Not governed by ordinary fixed standards; irresponsible, eccentric: *erratic behaviour*; **b** (of the mind and affections) wandering, lacking fixed purpose; incapable of concentration on single object. **2.** (geol.) Wandering, transported from original position to another, often remote, by natural forces, glaciers, currents &c.: *an erratic boulder*.

erratic (II.), n., fr. prec. A person of erratic mind or conduct.

erratum, n., pl. **errata** [1. erātum, -a; 2. er-éitə(m)]. Lat., P.P. neut. of *errāre*, 'go astray'. See **err**. Mistake in writing or printing.

erring, adj. [1. ëring; 2. ʌ́riŋ], fr. Pres. Part. of **err**. Guilty of bad conduct, sinful; having been led astray.

erroneous, adj. [1. erőneus; 2. eróuniəs]. Lat. *errōneus*, 'wandering, straying', & **-ous**. See **err**. **1.** Mistaken; based on, containing, error, wrong; esp. *erroneous belief, opinions* &c. **2.** Used partly in literal sense by Milton: '*On th' Aleian field I fall, Erroneous there to wander and forlorne*' ('P. L.').

erroneously, adv. Prec. & **-ly**. In a mistaken manner.

error, n. [1. éror; 2. érə]. O. Fr., fr. Lat. *errōr-(em)*, a wandering or straying about; wavering, uncertainty; a departing from the truth, delusions'. See **err**. **1. a** Mistaken belief; holding of what is spiritually or intellectually untrue; fault, mistake: *an error of judgement, of faith*; **b** erroneous, mistaken, state of mind; delusion: *to be in error*. **2.** Moral offence, something done amiss, wickedness: *errors of commission and omission*. **3. a** (math. and nat. sci.) Difference between observed or calculated position, movement, action, and the true one; **b** (law) mistake of law or fact in legal proceedings: *writ of error*, writ for reversal of judgement for error. **4.** Used literally in 17th cent. of a wandering, irregular course: *error by sea*.

Erse, n. [1. ërs; 2. ʌs]. Variant of **Irish**. The ancient Celtic language of the Highlands of Scotland or of Ireland.

erst, adv. [1. ërst; 2. ʌst]. O.E. *ǣrest*; superl. of **ere**. (archaic) Sooner, formerly.

erstwhile, adv. [1. ërstwīl; 2. ʌ́stwail]. Prec. & **while**. (archaic) At an earlier time, formerly.

erubescence, -cy, n. [1. èrūbésens(i); 2. èrju-bésəns(i)]. See next word & **-ce** & **-y**. Process of becoming red; blush.

erubescent, adj. [1. èrūbésent; 2. èrjubésənt]. Lat. *ērubescent-(em)*, Pres. Part. of *ērubescere*, 'to grow red', fr. **e-** & *rubescere*, fr. *rubeus*, or *ruber*, 'red', fr. **rubes-* (see **red** & **ruby**), & inchoate *-esc-*, see **-ish**. Turning red, blushing.

eruct, vb. trans. & intrans. [1. erúkt; 2. irákt]. Fr. *éructer*, fr. Lat. See next word. To belch, vomit out.

eructate, vb intrans. [1. ērúktāt; 2. irákteit], fr. Lat. *ēructāt-(um)*, P.P. of *ēructāre*, 'to belch forth', **e-** & *ructāre*, 'to belch', formed fr. *(ē)-ructum*, P.P. of *ērūgere*, w. same meaning; cp. Gk. *ereúgomai*, 'I vomit', *erugḗ*, 'eructation'; cp. also O.E. *ed-recan*, 'to chew the cud', *ed-roc*, 'rumination', in wh. *ed-* = 're-'. See also **ruminate**. To expel wind upwards from stomach.

eructation, n. [1. èruktáshun; 2. ìraktéiʃən]. Prec. & **-ion**. Act or process of eructating.

erudite, adj. [1. érūdīt; 2. érjudait]. Lat. *ērudītus*, fr. P.P. type of *ērudīre*, 'to bring out of the rough, to polish, instruct', fr. **e-** & *rudis*, 'rough, in natural state'. See **rude**. Highly cultivated in mind, well read, learned.

eruditely, adv. Prec. & **-ly**. In a learned, scholarly manner.

eruditeness, n. See prec. & **-ness**. Quality of being erudite; learning.

erudition, n. [1. èrūdíshun; 2. èrjudíʃən]. Fr., fr. Lat. *ērudītiōn-(em)*, 'instruction, education'; formed fr. *ērudīt-*, P.P. type. See **erudite** & **-ion**. State of mind reached by painstaking instruction and study; scholarship, learning.

eruginous. See **aeruginous**.

erupt, vb. intrans. [1. erúpt; 2. iràpt]. Lat. *ērupt-(um)*, P.P. type of *ērumpere*, 'to burst, break out'. See **e-** & **rupture**. **1.** To burst through, or out (of ashes from volcano, a crowd from a building &c.). **2.** (of volcano) To become active, break into eruption.

eruption, n. [1. erúpshun; 2. iràpʃən]. Prec. & **-ion**. **1.** A bursting forth of ashes and lava from a volcano; of water from a geyser. **2.** Outburst of passion or emotion: *an eruption of rage, laughter, merriment* &c. **3.** (med.) **a** A rash, outbreak of pustules &c. upon the skin; **b** also *eruption of the teeth*, breaking through, appearance.

eruptive (I.), adj. [1. erúptiv; 2. iràptiv]. **erupt** & **-ive**. **1.** Inclined to burst out, break forth &c.; produced by eruption: *eruptive rock*. **2.** (med.) Attended by, characterized by, a rash or eruption: *an eruptive complaint*.

eruptive (II.), n., fr. prec. (geol.) An eruptive rock, one thrown up by an eruption.

eruptively, adv. **eruptive** (I.) & **-ly**. As, in form of, an eruption.

-(e)ry, suff. M.E. & O. Fr. *-erie*, formed w. suff. (= Lat. *-ia*) fr. O. Fr. *-ier* (cogn. w. *-er*) or *-eur* (see **-or**). Forming nouns expressing: **1.** Group of qualities, system of conduct, habits &c.: *tomfoolery, pedantry*. **2.** Trade, occupation, pursuit: *pottery, carpentry, forgery*. **3.** Place where something is produced or made: *piggery, bakery*; place where an occupation is carried on: *drapery, grocery*. **4.** A collection: *jewellery, napery* &c.

eryngo, n. [1. eríngō; 2. iríngou], fr. Lat. *eryngion*, fr. Gk. *ērúggion*, dimin. of *ēruggos*, 'sea-holly'. Candied root of sea-holly, formerly used for coughs.

erysipelas, n. [1. èrisípilas; 2. èrisípəlis, -əs]. Gk. *erusípelas*, fr. *eruthrós*, 'red', see under **ruby, red**, & *pélas*, 'skin', only found in composition, but an authentic word & cogn. w. Lat. *pellis*, 'skin', see **pelt** (I.), & w. O.E. *fell*, 'skin', see **fell** (I.), & *filmen*, see **film**. Acute inflammatory disease of the skin, accompanied by great reddening.

erythema, n. [1. èrithḗma; 2. èriþímə]. Gk., 'reddening of the skin, flush', fr. *eruthrós*, 'red'. See prec. Abnormal redness of the skin due to congestion of the blood-vessels.

escalade (I.), n. [1. èskalā́d; 2. èskəléid]. Fr., fr. Span. *escalada*. See **scale** & **-ade**. A climbing, scaling, by means of ladders; specif., an attack on, with a view to penetrating and capturing, (a fortress or citadel) by this means.

escalade (II.), vb. trans., fr. prec. To scale a wall, penetrate into a fortress, by means of ladders.

escalator, n. [1. éskalātor; éskəleitə]. Modern invented word. See **escalade**. An endless, moving staircase, as used, instead of lifts, in underground railways.

Escallonia, n. [1. èskalṓnia; 2. èskəlóuniə], fr. a Span. traveller called Escallon. Genus of South American shrubs with white or red flowers growing in clusters.

escallop, n. [1. eskálup; 2. ɛskǽləp]. See **scallop**. Scallop shell.

escalloped, adj. [1. eskálupt; 2. ɛskǽləpt]. Prec. & **-ed**. (her.) Indenture on shield in shape of scallop shell.

escapade, n. [1. èskapā́d, -áhd; 2. èskəpéid, -ā́d]. Fr., fr. Span. *escapada*, 'escape'. See **escape** (II.) & **-ade**. **a** An adventurous, mischievous, merry prank; **b** daring achievement; **c** an action in defiance of the rules of conventional propriety.

escape (I.), vb. intrans. & trans. [1. eskā́p; 2. iskéip]. M.E. *escāpen*, fr. O. Fr. *escaper*, dialectal variant of *eschaper*, fr. Lat. **ex-** 'out', & *cappă*, lit. 'out of one's cape; free'. See **cape** (I.) **A.** intrans. **1. a** To set oneself at liberty, get free, get out of, break loose from, prison, a cage, or confinement of any kind: *the prisoner, the tiger, canary, has escaped*; **b** to avoid, elude, a danger, punishment, disease, pain, or other ill: *three members of this family were killed in the war, but one escaped*. **2.** To pass through, flow away or out; come through an opening or chink: *pull out the plug and allow the bath water to escape*; specif., *the gas is escaping*, is coming through the pipe when it is not lit. **B.** trans. **1. a** To avoid, evade, elude, not be affected by: *to escape death, danger, sickness, unhappiness* &c.; **b** (in neg. construction) to avoid forming an opinion, to resist, prevent oneself coming to, a logical conclusion: *I am unable to escape the conviction that he is lying*. **2. a** To be missed by, pass, get away unnoticed by, not to be perceived by, the senses: *that object escaped me in my search*; **b** to pass out of the mind of, be forgotten by: *his name escapes me, escapes my memory for the moment*; **c** not to be understood by: *I'm afraid your point escapes me*; not to be noted: *to escape notice in the papers*. **3.** (fig., of verbal utterances, groans &c.) To burst out suddenly, or with violence, from: *a dreadful oath escaped him*; *a groan escaped his lips*.

escape (II.), n., fr. prec. The act of escaping. In various senses: **1.** Evasion, getting out, getting free, from captivity or confinement of any kind: *the escape of a prisoner*. **2.** Fortunate avoidance of disaster, suffering, misfortune, or danger of any kind; avoidance of evil consequences which might have ensued from some act, by not committing it; avoidance of such results, in spite of having done the act: *I was prevented at the last moment from travelling by the ship I had fixed on, and it turned out that I had a lucky escape, as she was wrecked*; *as he sat next a boy with mumps for several hours, his escape from infection was providential*. **3.** An outward trickle, flow, leakage, of liquid, vapour, gas: *an escape of steam, gas* &c. **4.** (mechan.) An escape pipe or valve which carries off steam or vapour.

escapement, n. [1. eskā́pment; 2. iskéipmənt]. **escape** (I.) & **-ment**. (lit.) Mode of escape; specif., one of various kinds of mechanical device connecting the revolving wheels in a clock or watch with the pendulum or balance; so called because by its movements the escapement allows, at regular intervals, a tooth of the wheel to escape from a pallet.

escarbuncle, n. [1. eskárbungkl; 2. ɛskā́baŋkl]. O. Fr. Cp. Mod. Fr. *escarboucle*, precious stone called **carbuncle**. (her.) Charge consisting of a central circular ornament with eight rays, intended to represent precious stones; supposed to have originated from the iron strips used to strengthen the shield, which were often studded with jewels.

escarp (I.), n. [1. eskárp; 2. ɛskā́p]. Span. *escarpa*. See **scarp** & **sharp**. (fort.) Steep bank sloping up to base of a rampart; contrasted with *counterscarp*; similar natural formation of the ground.

escarp (II.), vb. trans., fr. prec. To make into, provide with, an escarp.

escarpment, n. [1. eskárpment; 2. ɛskā́pmənt]. Prec. & **-ment**. Wide area in form of an escarp; ground cut away, or naturally falling in a steep slope, from base of a fortification; similar natural formation.

-esce, vbl. suff., as in *effervesce* &c., fr. Lat. *-esc-(ere)*, inchoative suff.; also w. Pres. Part. suff. *-escent*, & as n. *-escence*. See also **-ish**.

eschalot, n. See **shallot**.

eschar, n. [1. éskar; 2. éskā], fr. Lat. *eschara*, fr. Gk. *eskhára*, 'hearth; a burn'. See **scar**. (med.) A dry crust, or scab, on a burn.

escharotic, adj. & n. [1. eskarótik; 2. ɛskərɔ́tik], fr. Gk. *eskharōtikós*. See prec. & **-ic**. (med.) **a** adj. Causing, tending to cause, an eschar; caustic; **b** n., a caustic substance.

eschatology, n. [1. èskatóloji; 2. èskətɔ́lədži]. Gk. *éskhatos*, 'furthest, remotest, last', & **-logy**, fr. Gk. *ex*, 'outside', see **ex-**, & adj. suff. *k^wo-, & superl. suff. *-to*. The doctrine of the last things; theological teaching regarding death and the last judgement.

escheat (I.), n. [1. eschḗt; 2. ɛstʃít]. M.E. *eschete*, fr. O. Fr. *escheoite*, P.P. of *escheir*, 'to fall', fr. Lat. **ex-** & *cadere*, 'to fall'. See **cadency, cheat**. (law) **1. a** Reversion of land to the king or other feudal lord owing to failure of heirs; **b** forfeiture of land through attainder. **2.** Land which thus reverts or is forfeited.

escheat (II.), vb. intrans. & trans., fr. prec. **1.** intrans. (of law) To revert by escheat. **2.** trans. To confiscate property.

eschew, vb. trans. [1. eschóō; 2. is-, ɛstʃú]. M.E. *eschewen, eschiwen*, fr. A.-Fr. *eschuer*, O. Fr. *eschiver*, 'to shun, avoid'; Gmc. loan-word, cp. O.H.G. *sciuhan*, 'to fear'. See **shy** (I.). To shun, avoid, keep away from, as something wicked or harmful.

eschewal, n. [1. eschóōal; 2. ɛstʃúəl]. Prec. & **-al**. Act of eschewing.

eschscholtzia, n. [1. eskóltsia; 2. ɛskɔ́ltsiə]. Derived fr. surname of Russian botanist & **-ia**. Garden plant with yellow flowers; also called *California poppy*.

esclandre, n. [1. esklóndr; 2. ɛsklā́dr]. Fr., earlier *escandle*, fr. Lat. *scandalum*. See **scandal** & **slander**. A scandalous, disreputable affair.

escort (I.), n. [1. éskort; 2. éskōt]. Fr. *escorte*, fr. Ital. *scorta*, formed fr. *scorgere*, 'to perceive, lead', fr. Lat. **ex-** & *corrigere*, 'to correct'. See **correct**. **1. a** Body of armed troops accompanying an unarmed body, or an individual, to afford protection, or as a guard of honour; **b** ship or ships of war accompanying an unarmed or less powerful vessel as a means of protection. **2.** A person, or number of persons, who accompany another on a journey, for company or as a matter of politeness.

escort (II.), vb. trans. [1. eskórt; 2. iskɔ́t], fr. prec. To act as an escort to; to accompany, attend upon, with a view to give protection, as a matter of ceremony, or from courtesy.

escritoire, n. [1. éskritwar; 2. éskritwā]. Fr., 'a writing-desk, writing-table', fr. Lat. *scriptōrium*, 'place for writing'. See **script** & **-ory**. A writing-table fitted with drawers and pigeon-holes, and often made to close with a flap on hinges.

escrow, n. [1. eskrṓ; 2. ɛskróu], fr. O. Fr. *escroe, escroue*, 'roll of papers, book'. See **scroll**. (law) An engagement in writing, as a bond or deed to do something, handed to a third party to keep until some condition has been performed, and only taking effect after this has been fulfilled.

escudo, n. [1. eskóōdō; 2. ɛskúdou]. Span. & Port., fr. Lat. *scūtum*, 'shield'. See **escutcheon**. **1.** (hist.) A gold and silver coin of Spain and Portugal and their former dependencies in S. America. **2.** The monetary unit of Portugal, of nominal value of 4s. 5d.; silver coin of this value.

esculent, adj. & n. [1. éskūlent; 2. éskjulənt]. Lat. *esculentus*, 'good to eat, eatable', fr. *esca*, 'food', fr. **eds-kʷa-*, fr. base **ed(e)s-*, fr. **ed-*, 'to eat'. See **edible, eat**. See also **-lent**. **1.** adj. Fit for food, edible. **2.** n. Something suitable for human food.

escutcheon, n. [1. eskúchun; 2. ɛs-, iskátʃən]. O. Fr. *escuchon*, dialectal variant of *escuçon*, whence Mod. Fr. *écusson*, 'coat-of-arms', fr.

Low Lat. *scūtiōn-(em)*, fr. *scūtum*, 'shield'. This word is prob. connected w. Lat. *cutis*, 'skin, hide', & meant orig. 'shield of leather'. See **cutis.** (her.) Figure in form of a shield upon which armorial bearings are depicted. Phr. *a blot on one's escutcheon*, a stain on one's honour or reputation.

-ese, suff. [1. ēz; 2. īz]. O. Fr. *-eis*, Lat. *-ensis*. Suffix used to form adjectives or, more commonly, nouns, expressing **a** names of nations—*Portuguese* (also adj.); **b** language, or other attributes of persons, inhabitants of particular places, and peoples—*Japanese, Londonese*; esp. used to denote literary style and diction characteristic of particular writers: *Johnsonese* &c.

eskar, esker, n. [1. ésker; 2. éskə]. Ir. *eascra*. (geol.) Deposit of gravel left by stream coming from glacier.

Eskimo, Esquimau, n. & adj. [1. éskimō; 2. éskimou], fr. N. American (Algonquin) Indian name *eskimantik*, 'eater of raw flesh'. **1.** n. **a** Member of N. American Indian race inhabiting Arctic America and Greenland; **b** their language; **c** an Eskimo dog. **2.** adj. Of, pertaining to, the Eskimos. *Eskimo dog*, variety of dog bred and trained by the Eskimos to draw their sledges.

esophagus. See **oesophagus.**

esoteric, adj. & n. [1. èsōtérik; 2. èsoutérik]. Gk. *esōterikós*, 'inner', fr. *esṓteros*, 'inner'; compar. of *ésō*, 'in, within', cp. Gk. *eis*, 'into', fr. **ens*. See **en-** (II.). **1.** adj. **a** (of doctrine &c.) Intended for, understood by, those only who are initiated into the inner mysteries and secrets; contrasted with *exoteric*; **b** secret, private, confidential. **2.** n. An initiate.

esoterical, adj. [1. èsōtérikl; 2. èsoutérikl]. Prec. & **-al.** Esoteric, adj.

esoterically, adv. Prec. & **-ly.** In an esoteric manner; secretly.

espagnolette, n. [1. espànyōlét; 2. espænjəlét]. Fr., fr. *espagnol*, 'Spanish', & **-ette.** Bolt for a French casement window, consisting of a long rod with fastenings top and bottom, worked by a handle.

espalier, n. [1. espálier; 2. espǽliə]. Fr., fr. Ital. *spalliera*, fr. *spalla*, 'shoulder'. Cp. Fr. *épaule*, 'shoulder', fr. Lat. *spatula*, 'shoulder' (of animal). See **spatula.** (hort.) **a** A railing, or framework, with uprights at intervals, and bars or wires placed across these one above another about a foot apart; **b** a fruit tree trained along such a framework, or grown as though to be so trained, with branches springing from either side of a central stem, and usually kept at right angles to this.

esparto (grass), n. [1. espártō; 2. espátou]. Span., fr. Lat. *spartum*, fr. Gk. *spártos*. Tough kind of Spanish rush from which cord, baskets, rough cloth, paper, and other articles are made.

especial, adj. [1. espéshal; 2. ispéʃəl]. M.E., fr. O. Fr. See **special.** Outstanding, remarkable; marked out from others; principal, particular: *my especial aversion*; *an especial favourite.*

especially, adv. Prec. & **-ly.** To a marked degree; in an especial manner; in particular.

Esperantist, n. [1. èsperántist; 2. èspərǽntist]. Next word & **-ist.** User of Esperanto.

Esperanto, n. [1. èsperántō; 2. èspərǽntou]. The pseudonym of the author, fr. Span. *esperanza*, 'hope'. Artificial language invented by Dr. Zamenhof, and first advocated and described in 1887. The simplicity of the grammar and the fact that the pronunciation and accentuation are regular, and easy to acquire, while the vocabulary is based upon the commonest words in the best-known European languages, are supposed to make this language suitable as a means of international communication.

espionage, n. [1. èspionáhzh; 2. èspiənáž]. Fr., 'spying', fr. *espion*, 'spy', fr. Ital. *spione*, & **-age.** See **espy, spy.** Practice of spying; system of employing spies to observe and report on what is being said and done by individuals or groups; esp. systematic use of this means by governments for discovering the political and military secrets of other nations.

esplanade, n. [1. èsplanád; 2. èsplənéid]. Fr., fr. Span. *esplanada*, 'levelled place', fr. P.P., Lat. *explānāre*, 'to flatten'. See **explain.** Levelled terrace or embankment, esp. one for public walking and driving; a promenade; often one along a sea front.

espousal, n. [1. espóuzal; 2. espáuz(ə)l]. O. Fr. *espousailles*, Lat. *sponsālia*. See **spouse.** **1.** **a** Act of plighting troths, whether in betrothal or in actual marriage; **b** (in pl.) a wedding. **2.** (fig.) Act of espousing a cause.

espouse, vb. trans. [1. espóuz; 2. espáuz]. O. Fr. *espouser*, Lat. *sponsāre*. See **spouse. sponsor. 1.** To take in marriage; usually said of a man. **2.** To take up, give adherence and support to, (a cause &c.)

espressivo, adv. [1. èspresévō; 2. èspresívou]. Ital. (mus.) With expression.

esprit, n. [1. espré; 2. esprí]. Fr. See **spirit.** Wit, lively intelligence.

esprit de corps, n. [1. espré de kór; 2. esprí də kɔ́]. See prec. & **corps.** The spirit of loyalty and devotion to the body to which one belongs, and to its honour and well-being.

espy, vb. trans. [1. espí; 2. espái]. M.E. *espīen*, fr. O. Fr. *espier*; Gmc. loan-word. See **spy.** To catch sight of, perceive (with the eyes), detect.

-esque, suff. [1. esk; 2. esk]. Fr., fr. Ital. *-esco*, borrowed fr. Gmc. *-isk-*. See **-ish.** Adjective suffix expressing style, manner, resemblance: *Miltonesque*; *arabesque* &c.

Esquimau. See **Eskimo.**

esquire, n. [1. eskwír; 2. iskwáiə]. Full form of **squire**; M.E. *squyer*, fr. O. Fr. *escuyer*, fr. L. Lat. *scūtārius*, 'shield-bearer', fr. *scūtum*, 'shield'. See **escutcheon.** Originally a gentleman entitled to bear arms; now chiefly used as polite or respectful addition after the name of a gentleman, esp. on a letter addressed to him, or in a description in a formal document. Abbreviated to *Esq.* or *Esqre*.

-ess, suff., fr. Fr. *-esse*, L. Lat. *-issa*, fr. Gk. Suffix used to form feminine from masculine nouns: *poetess, mayoress* &c.

ess, n. [1. es; 2. es]. Object shaped like an S; esp. *Collar of esses.* See **esses.**

essay (I.), n. [1. ésā; 2. ései]. Earlier *assay*; Fr. *essai*, fr. Lat. *exagium*, 'weighing, trial of weight', **ex-** & *agere*, 'to do, drive' &c. See **agent. 1.** An attempt. **2.** A short treatise or excursus upon a particular subject.

essay (II.), vb. trans. & intrans. [1. esá; 2. eséi]. See prec. & **assay. 1.** trans. To make trial of, test, prove: *I must essay the quality of the new poet.* **2.** intrans. To attempt, try, make an effort to do something: '*Thrice he essayed* (to speak)' (Milton).

essayist, n. [1. ésāist; 2. ései-ist]. **essay (I.)** & **-ist.** A writer of essays.

esse, n. [1. ési; 2. ési]. Lat., 'to be'. The base **as-*, 'being, existence', occurs in various forms in all Aryan languages, Scrt. *as-mi*, 'I am'; Gk. *eimi* for **es-mi*; further, in Lat. *es*, 'thou art', *est*, 'he is'; Goth. *im*, 'am'; O.E. *eom* &c. See **am, essence, sooth,** &c. Being; actual, very existence: *it is an old controversy whether bishops are of the esse, or merely of the bene esse of the Church.*

essence, n. [1. ésens; 2. ésəns]. Fr., fr. Lat. *essentia*, 'being or essence of a thing', fr. *essent-*, stem of Pres. Part. of *esse*, 'to be'. See prec. **1.** (scholastic philos.) **a** That by which a thing exists; **b** essential, fundamental, nature or character of a thing. Most other usages are derived from this. **2.** Existence, fact of being. **3.** The ultimate, intrinsic nature and character of anything: *content is the essence of happiness.* **4.** A substance considered to comprise all the fundamental ingredients and qualities of that from which it is prepared; **a** a concentrated solid substance extracted or decocted from a much larger mass, and supposed to contain all the chemical properties of this; an extract: *essence of beef*; **b** a highly volatile, spirituous liquid prepared by distillation; a scent or perfume of this character; a strong potable liquor.

Essene, n. [1. esén; 2. esín]. Gk. *Essēnós*. Origin doubtful. Member of ancient Jewish sect of mystics.

essential, adj. [1. esénshal; 2. isénʃəl]. Lat. *essenti-*, see **essence,** & **-al. 1.** Pertaining to, of the nature of, the essence, or ultimate character of anything; distinctive, fundamental, elemental: *love of fair play is an essential part of the English character.* **2.** Not to be suppressed or eliminated, indispensable, required: *honesty is essential in a good servant.* **3.** Pertaining to, derived from, having the character of, an essence: *an essential oil.* **4.** (mus.) *Essential notes*, those which constitute a chord.

essentiality, n. [1. esènshiáliti; 2. isènʃiǽliti]. **essential** & **-ity.** Quality of being essential.

essentially, adv. [1. esénshali; 2. isénʃəli]. **essential** & **-ly.** In an essential manner, in essence; characteristically.

esses, n. [1. ésiz; 2. ésiz], fr. the two interlinked letters S. *Collar of esses* or *SS.*, collar or chain formed of a series of two interlinked gold letters, S, usually with other devices, such as knots and roses, between them, worn by the Lord Chief Justice of England, the Lord Mayor of London, various officials of the College of Heralds &c.; the origin and meaning of the letters being obscure.

essonite, n. [1. ésonīt; 2. ésənait], fr. Gk. *hḗssōn*, 'inferior to', compar. of *hêka*, 'faintly'; cogn. w. Lat. *sēgnis*, 'slow, idle'; fr. base **sēk-*, 'slow, weak'. Cinnamon-stone.

-est, suff. O.E. *-est*, *-ost* (*-ast*), Gmc. & Aryan superl. suff. of adj. & adv.

establish, vb. trans. [1. estáblish; 2. istǽbliʃ]. M.E. *establissen*, fr. O. Fr. vb. stem *establis-*, fr. Lat. *stabilīre*, 'to make firm', fr. *stabilis*, 'firm' &c. See **stable (I.). 1. a** To found, create, and place (system, institution, household, business, belief) on firm and permanent basis, to settle: *to establish a government, a university, a religion* &c.; **b** specif. (of a church) to make national, connect intimately with the state; **c** (of animals and plants) to introduce from a different area and make permanent among the species which flourish and propagate. **2.** Applied to persons: **a** to settle, install, in a position, office, business, career &c.: *to establish one's son, oneself, in trade, in a new mode of life* &c.; *to establish a person as governor* &c.; **b** to place, settle, ensconce in a particular locality, dwelling, seat: *to establish oneself in the country, in a new house*; *comfortably established in a good seat.* **3.** Applied to non-material things: **a** (of doctrines, conclusions, arguments) to prove beyond doubt, demonstrate truth of, gain acceptance for: *the law of gravity was conclusively established by Newton*; *to establish a theory, a view* &c.; **b** (of claims) to make good, prove validity of, gain recognition of: *to establish a claim to an ancient peerage*; **c** (of personal character, renown &c.) to render unassailable, gain general confidence in, win undisputed acceptance of: *to establish one's reputation as a surgeon*; *an established repute*; *his honesty and integrity are well established.*

established, adj. [1. estáblisht; 2. istǽbliʃt]. Prec. & **-ed.** Firmly founded, permanent; specif. **a** *Established Church*, one that is national, recognized, protected, often supported by, and closely connected with, the civil government of a state; **b** (biol., of animals and plants) firmly and permanently fixed among the species in an area.

establishment, n. [1. estáblishment; 2. istǽbliʃmənt]. **establish** & **-ment. 1.** Act or process of establishing; state of being established. **2.** Something established; **a** a place where definite activities are carried on; a household, thought of as a particular house, and all the business of conducting it : *to keep a handsome, well-ordered establishment* ; Phr. *a second, separate, establishment*, one kept secretly, for an irregular, extra-matrimonial connexion ; **b** the Established, national, Church. **3.** A department of state, maintained for specific purposes ; the totality of persons belonging to such a department : *the Naval, Military, Civil Service, Establishment.*

establishmentarian, n. [1. estàblishmentárian ; 2. istæbliʃmənteəriən]. Prec. & **-arian.** Supporter of the principle of an established church.

estate, n. [1. estát ; 2. istéit]. M.E. *estāt*, fr. O. Fr. *estat*, fr. Lat. *statum*, P.P. of *stāre*, 'to stand'. See **state (I.)**. **1. a** Stage, condition, period of life ; in Phr. (*to reach*) *man's estate, estate of manhood* ; **b** (archaic) social, political, circumstances, status, mode of life : *the holy estate of matrimony.* **2.** Political or social group and class ; political division of inhabitants of a state : *the three estates of the realm, the Lords Spiritual, Lords Temporal, and the Commons* ; *the fourth estate*, the press, a humorous application. **3.** (law) Possessions, belongings, property owned, whether a interest in land and tenements, which are *real estate* ; or **b** money, valuables, securities, and all property other than land, which are known as *personal estate.* **4.** Condition, circumstances, of worldly prosperity : *mind, body, and estate* ; *to suffer in one's estate.* **5.** Specific piece of property in land : *to own an estate in the country.*

esteem (I.), vb. trans. [1. estém ; 2. istím]. M.E. *estēmen*, O. Fr. *estimer*, fr. Lat. *aestimāre*, earlier *aestumāre*, 'to value, appraise ; to assess damages ; to consider, value highly ; to honour' ; cp. Gk. *aidoîos* for **aisd-*, 'regarded with awe and reverence, venerable, august', whence *aidéomai*, 'I fear, respect, reverence' ; also cogn. w. Goth. *aistan*, 'to dread, reverence'. The base **aisd-* is perhaps an amplification of **ais-*, 'honour', whence O.E. *ār*, fr. **aiz*, O.H.G. *āra*, Mod. Germ. *ehre*, 'respect, honour', & *-d-*, fr. base **dō-* &c., 'to give', q.v. under **date (I.)**, **donation** &c. Cp. **hiero-**. **1.** To feel respect for, hold in respect, consider highly, regard as worthy of honour and respect ; to venerate : *I like, but cannot esteem him* ; or qualified, *to esteem highly.* **2.** To consider, regard, judge : *I esteem riches a worthy aim.*

esteem (II.), n., fr. prec. **1.** (archaic) Judgement, appraisement of merit, estimation : *a poor creature in my esteem.* **2.** Favourable judgement, respect : *to hold (a person or thing) in (high) esteem.*

ester, n. [1. éster ; 2. éstə]. Invented by German chemist Gmelin to distinguish such substances from *ethers.* (chem.) A compound ether formed by the union of alcohols and acids with elimination of water.

estimable, adj. [1. éstimabl ; 2. éstiməbl]. Fr., fr. Lat. *aestimābilis*, 'valuable'. See **esteem (I.)** & **-able.** Worthy of esteem and respect.

estimableness, n. Prec. & **-ness.** Quality of being estimable.

estimably, adv. See prec. & **-ly.** In an estimable manner.

estimate (I.), vb. trans. & intrans. [1. éstimāt ; 2. éstimeit], fr. Lat. *aestimāt-(um)*, P.P. type of *aestimāre.* See **esteem (I.)**. **1.** trans. To compute, form a judgement as to (money) value of something, appraise at a certain value, put a price upon ; **a** (lit.) *I cannot estimate the value of your property without further investigation* ; *I estimate my losses at a thousand pounds* ; **b** (of non-material things) *to estimate a man's character, intellect, very high(ly).* **2.** intrans. To make, form, draw up, an estimate, chiefly in trade usage : *a contractor estimates for repair of a house.*

estimate (II.), n. [1. éstimat ; 2. éstimit]. See prec. **1. a** Judgement, computation, of value, size, amount, quality ; **b** specif., computation, in advance, of approximate cost of doing, making, something in a certain way : *my builder has greatly exceeded his estimate* ; **c** *the Estimates*, forecast made each year by Chancellor of Exchequer of probable national revenue and expenditure for coming year. **2.** A considered and careful judgement of moral or aesthetic values, or of a man's character, a summing up of this : *an estimate of Pope's place as a poet* ; *an estimate of a man's qualities as a general.*

estimation, n. [1. èstimáshun ; 2. èstiméiʃən]. Lat. *aestimātiōn-(em)*, '(money) value, valuation of a thing ; respect'. See **estimate (I.)** & **-ion.** **1.** Judgement, opinion : *in my estimation.* **2.** Estimate, computation (of value, size, amount, distance &c.) : *a hasty estimation of one's available resources.* **3.** Favourable judgement ; esteem, respect : *to win a person's estimation* ; *held in high estimation.*

estival. See **aestival.**

estoile, n. [1. estóil ; 2. εstóil]. O. Fr., fr. Lat. *stella*, 'star'. See **stellar.** (her.) Star with six or eight points, alternately straight and wavy.

estop, vb. trans. [1. estóp ; 2. εstóp], fr. O. Fr. *estoper.* See **stop.** (law) To bar by estoppel.

estoppel, n. [1. estópel ; 2. εstópəl]. Prec. & **-el** ; O. Fr. *estoupail*, 'stopper, bung'. (law) Preclusion of a statement or denial on account of some previous action or statement of same party which denies what is now attempted to be alleged, or alleges what is attempted to be denied.

estovers, n. pl. [1. estóverz ; 2. εstóuvəz], fr. O. Fr. *estover, estovoir*, 'necessaries, provision', properly an infin., 'to be necessary', used as n. ; etymol. doubtful ; possibly connected w. Lat. *stūdēre*, 'to study, desire' ; the word occurs also in Engl. as *stovor*, 'fodder for cattle', now obs. (law) **a** Wood which a tenant or copyholder has the right to cut from his holding, for the specific purpose of the holding, as for firewood, repairs of house and hedges &c. ; **b** the right to cut such wood. The proper English word was *bote*, O.E. *bōt*, see **boot (III.)**, and the rights were distinguished as *firebote, housebote, hedgebote* &c.

estrange, vb. trans. [1. estránj ; 2. istréindž]. O. Fr. *estrangier*, 'to remove', Lat. *extrāneāre*, 'to treat as a stranger'. See **strange.** **a** To alienate, separate, divide, in feeling and sympathy : *the two brothers had lately become estranged* ; **b** to alienate, destroy, affections of ; to hurt feelings of, offend : *his behaviour had estranged all his best friends* ; **c** to alienate, divert, turn away : *to estrange a person's love, affections* &c.

estrangement, n. [1. estránjment ; 2. istréindžmənt]. Prec. & **-ment.** Cancellation, cooling off, of affection between two persons &c.

estray, n. [1. estrá ; 2. εstréi], fr. O. Fr. *estrayer.* See **stray.** (law) A strayed domestic animal.

estreat, vb. trans. [1. estrét ; 2. istrít]. O. Fr. *estraite*, fr. Lat. *extractum.* See **extract.** (law) **a** To make an extract from records of a Court of Law, and return to Court of Exchequer, for purposes of prosecution ; **b** to exact as a levy or fine, for Court of Exchequer.

estrepement, n. [1. estrépment ; 2. εstrípmənt], fr. O. Fr. *estreper*, 'to damage, commit waste' ; etymol. uncertain, possibly fr. Lat. *ex(s)tirpāre.* See **extirpate.** (law) Waste committed by a tenant for life on lands, woods, or houses, to the damage of the reversioner.

estuary, n. [1. éstūari ; 2. éstʃuəri]. Lat. *aestuārium*, 'tide-place, creek, estuary', fr. *aestus*, fr. **aidh(s)-tus*, 'ebb and flow of the tide, the tide'. The orig. meaning of the base **aidh-* is 'to burn' &c., whence 'to boil, that which boils'. Thus *aestus* is ultimately 'the boiling, foaming sea', hence 'movement of the tide'. See further under **aedile, aestivate, edifice, ether.** Broad mouth of a river (into which the tide flows) when it widens out before reaching the sea ; in many cases an estuary is practically the sea, esp. at high tide.

esurience, -cy, n. [1. esúriens(i) ; 2. εsjúriəns(i)]. **esurient** & **-ce, -cy.** Hunger ; greed, voracity.

esurient, adj. [1. esúrient ; 2. εsjúriənt]. Lat. *ēsurient-(em)*, Pres. Part. of *ēsurīre*, desid. vb., fr. *ēs-*, P.P. type of *edere*, 'to eat'. See **edible, eat.** Eager to eat, very hungry, voracious ; grasping.

-et, suff. Fr., O. Fr. *-et, -ette*, Ital. *-etto, -etta.* Formerly dimin. suff., & still felt as such in *islet*, & slightly perh. in *pullet*, but having no such force now in *hatchet, pocket, packet* &c. Origin of suff. unknown ; recent discoveries have traced it in Etruscan.

etacism, n. [1. átasizm ; 2. éitəsizəm], fr. name of Gk. letter *ē* (*ēta*). Pronunciation of Gk. *ē* as [éi] or [ē], instead of in usual English way [ī].

étagère, n. [1. ātahzhár ; 2. etažéə]. Fr., fr. *étage*, 'shelf'. A piece of furniture, a cabinet with unenclosed shelves, for exhibition of small articles of artistic value &c.

état, n. [1. átah ; 2. eta]. Fr. See **estate.** State, estate of the realm ; *tiers état*, third estate, that of the citizens or bourgeoisie.

état major, n. [1. átah mahzhór ; 2. éta mažɔ́(r)]. Fr. (mil.) Staff.

et cetera, etcetera [1. ètsétera ; 2. ètsétərə]. Lat., 'and the other, the rest', neut. pl. of *cēterum.* The etymol. of *cē-* is disputed, but, as Walde suggests, it is prob. cogn. w. Gk. *kaí*, 'and' ; the second element is apparently cogn. w. Gk. *héteros*, 'the other'. See **hetero-**. **1.** And the rest, and so forth, and so on ; abbr. *etc.* or *&c.* **2.** n. pl. *Etceteras*, additional things, sundries, odds and ends : *a dinner of five courses and etceteras.*

etch, vb. trans. & intrans. [1. ech ; 2. εtʃ]. 17th cent., fr. Du. *etsen*, 'etch', fr. Germ. *ätzen*, 'to feed, bait ; to eat into with corrosives'. The base is Gmc. **æt-*, a gradational variant of **et-*, **eat.** **1.** trans. **a** To trace designs and pictures upon a metal plate with acids, which eat into the surface and make a negative, whence copies can be printed ; **b** to produce designs &c. by this means. **2.** intrans. To practise the art of an etcher.

etcher, n. [1. écher ; 2. étʃə]. Prec. & **-er.** An artist who etches designs and pictures on copper.

etching, vbl. n. [1. éching ; 2. étʃiŋ]. **etch** & **-ing.** **1.** The art of the etcher. **2.** Design or picture produced by this art.

eternal (I.), adj. [1. etérnal ; 2. itə́nəl]. Lat. *aetern-(us)*, 'everlasting', & **-al.** The first element is fr. **aevitern-*, fr. *aevum*, 'space of time'. See **aeon, age, aye,** adv. **1.** Without beginning or end ; of infinite duration, everlasting : *eternal life.* Phr. *the Eternal City*, Rome. **2. a** Without intermission, unceasing ; **b** (colloq.) too often repeated, too frequent : *eternal chatter.* **3.** Enduring, based upon immutable principles : *the eternal principles of art, justice* &c.

Eternal (II.), n., fr. prec. (cap.) Appellation of the Divinity.

eternally, adv. **eternal (I.)** & **-ly.** **a** Lasting throughout eternity ; **b** immutably ; **c** (too) frequently.

eterne, adj. [1. etérn ; 2. itə́n]. Fr., fr. Lat. *aeternus.* See **eternal.** (poet.) Eternal.

eternity, n. [1. etérniti ; 2. itə́niti]. Fr. *éternité*, fr. Lat. *aeternitāt-(em).* See **eternal** & **-ity.** **1.** Duration without beginning or end. **2.** Condition which begins after earthly life, that state which will last for ever ; the next world : *to hover between this life and eternity.* **3.** A period of time which is so long that it appears endless : *the sermon seemed to last an eternity.*

eternize, vb. trans. [1. etérnīz ; 2. itə́naiz]. **eterne** & **-ize.** **1.** To make eternal ; cause to last for eternity. **2.** To give immortal fame to, to render (memory, name &c.) immortal.

etesian, adj. [1. ētézian, étézhan ; 2. itíziən, ītíʒən]. Lat. *etēsiae* & **-an** ; fr. Gk. *etēsiai*, n., 'winds that prevail annually in Aegean, at midsummer' ; Lat. adj. *etēsius*, pertaining to these, fr. Gk. *etḗsios*, 'annual', fr. Gk. *étos*, 'year', for earlier **wétos*, cogn. w. Lat. *vetus, veter-is* &c., 'aged, long-standing'. See **veteran, wether, veal.** Annual; applied to periodical winds from the north, prevailing in Aegean during the summer.

ethane, n. [1. éthān; 2. ḗþein], fr. **ether** & **-ane.** (chem.) A colourless, odourless gas, found in gases from oil wells &c., ethyl hydride.

ether, n. [1. ḗther; 2. ī́þə]. Lat. *aether*, fr. Gk. *aithḗr*, 'the upper, purer, air', fr. base **aidh-*, 'to burn' &c. See **aedile, estuary. 1.** The substance of which, according to the ancients, the heavenly bodies are composed; the upper air, higher regions of space: *'An ampler ether, a diviner air'* (Wordsw., 'Laod.' 105). **2.** (phys.) Hypothetical medium, supposed to fill space, by means of vibrations in which light and other forms of radiation are transmitted. **3.** (chem.) Highly volatile liquid got from alcohol, used as anaesthetic.

ethereal, adj. [1. ēthḗreal; 2. īþíəriəl]. Prec. & **-al. 1.** Of, connected with, pertaining to, the ether. **2. a** Very light, like air; **b** hence (fig.), suggesting something finer, lighter, more spiritual than things of earth; spirit-like: *ethereal beauty, purity* &c.

ethereality, n. [1. ēthèreáliti; 2. īþìəriǽliti]. Prec. & **-ity.** Quality of being ethereal.

etherialization, n. [1. ēthèrializā́shun; 2. īþìəriəlaizéiʃən]. Prec. & **-ation.** Act or process of etherealizing.

etherealize, vb. trans. [1. ēthḗrealīz; 2. īþíəriəlaiz]. **ethereal** & **-ize. 1.** To spiritualize, regard, treat, as being ethereal. **2.** To convert into ether **3.**

etheric, adj. [1. ēthérik; 2. īþérik]. **ether** & **-ic.** (phys.) Connected with, by means of, the ether: *etheric telegraphy.*

etherification, n. [1. ēthèrifikā́shun; 2. īþèrifikéiʃən]. **ether** & **-fication.** Process of converting alcohol into ether.

etherify, vb. trans. [1. ēthérifī; 2. īþérifai]. **ether** & **-fy.** To convert (alcohol) into ether.

etherism, n. [1. ḗtherizm; 2. ī́þərizəm]. **ether** & **-ism.** (med.) Condition produced by excessive administration of ether.

etherization, n. [1. ētherīzā́shun; 2. īþəraizéiʃən]. Next word & **-ation. a** Administration of ether as an anaesthetic; **b** condition of anaesthesia produced by ether.

etherize, vb. trans. [1. ḗtheriz; 2. ī́þəraiz]. **ether** & **-ize. 1.** (med.) To reduce to a state of anaesthesia by administering ether. **2.** (chem.) To convert into ether.

ethic(al), adj. & n. [1. éthik(l); 2. éþik(l)]. Lat. *ethicus*, Gk. *ēthikós*, 'pertaining to morals', fr. *éthos*, also *êthos*, 'custom, usage', wh. comes fr. **swedh-*, **swēdh-*, cogn. w. Scrt. *swadha-*, 'essential quality, habit, dwelling', & *swa*, 'self'; Lat. *suēscere*, fr. **swedh-sko-*, 'to accustom oneself'; Goth. *swēs*, 'one's own', & perh. Goth. *sidus*, O.E. *sidu*, 'custom' &c. See **consuetude** & **ethnic. 1.** adj. Generally *ethical*; connected with moral action; connected with duties, moral feelings, morality. **2.** n. *Ethic(s)*, system of morality; systematic study of moral action.

ethically, adv. [1. éthikali; 2. éþikəli]. Prec. & **-ly.** From a moral or ethical standpoint, according to ethics.

ethicize, vb. trans. [1. éthisīz; 2. éþisaiz]. See **ethic** & **-ize.** To make ethical; to treat in relation to ethics.

ethico-, pref. Form of **ethic** used as pref. Expresses relation to ethics.

ethics, n. [1. éthiks; 2. éþiks]. See **ethic** & **-ics.** Morality; science of morality.

ethmoid(al), adj. [1. éthmoid, ethmóidl; 2. éþmɔid, eþmɔ́idl], fr. Gk. *ēthmoeidḗs*, 'like a sieve', fr. *ēthmós*, 'sieve', fr. *ēthéein*, 'to sift' (fr. **sēth-*), & **-oid** & **-al.** Cp. M.I. *sithlad*, 'sifting'; O.N. *sald*, O. Slav. *sito*, 'sieve'. (anat.) Of, pertaining to, the bone of the nose through which pass the olfactory nerves.

ethnic (I.), **ethnical**, adj. [1. éthnik(l); 2. éþnik(l)]. Gk. *ethnikós*, adj., fr. *éthnos*, 'race', *tà éthnē*, 'the nations, heathens, gentiles'. *Éthnos* is fr. **swedh-nos*, & is ultimately fr. same base as that of **ethic**; cp. (w. different formative elements) Scrt. *sabhā́*, 'relationship, community', & Goth. *sibja*, 'relationship', the ultimate meaning is '(one's) own, what is connected'; this is the base in Lat. *suus*, 'his' &c. Cp. **sui-. 1.** Connected with, characteristic of, a race; related to the moral and physical characters destinctive of a particular race. **2.** Heathen, gentile, contrasted with Christian or Jewish.

ethnic (II.), n., fr. prec. (obs.) A heathen.

ethnically, adv. [1. éthnikali; 2. éþnikəli]. **ethnical** & **-ly.** According to race, or racial characteristics.

ethno-, pref. Form of Gk. *éthnos*, 'race', used in composition. See **ethnic (I.).**

ethnography, n. [1. ethnógrafi; 2. eþnɔ́grəfi]. **ethno-** & **-graphy.** Systematic, scientific, description of races, including physical, mental, and moral features.

ethnologist, n. [1. ethnólojist; 2. eþnɔ́lədžist]. Next word & **-ist.** Student of ethnology.

ethnology, n. [1. ethnóloji; 2. eþnɔ́lədži]. **ethno-** & **-logy.** Science of racial characteristics, and of the distribution and classification of races.

ethologist, n. [1. ēthólojist; 2. īþɔ́lədžist]. Next word & **-ist.** Student of ethology.

ethology, n. [1. ēthóloji; 2. īþɔ́lədži]. Next word & **-logy.** The study of ethos.

ethos, n. [1. ḗthos; 2. ī́þɔs]. Gk. *ēthos*, 'disposition, temper, character'. Same word as that discussed under **ethic.** Characteristic and prevailing temper and disposition of, moral atmosphere within, a community.

ethyl, n. [1. éthil; 2. éþil]. **ether** & **-yl. a** (chem.) Basis of alcohol, the organic hydrocarbon radical of alcohol compounds, *ethyl alcohol*, the active, intoxicating principle of all alcohols; **b** a name given, commercially, to a kind of petrol, containing a lead tetrahyde.

etiolate, vb. trans. [1. étiolāt; 2. ítiəleit], fr. Fr. *étioler*; O. Fr. *estieuler*; perh. formed fr. Lat. *stipula*, 'a stalk'. See **stipule. 1.** (bot.) To cause to wither and pine away by deprivation of light and air. **2.** (fig.) To render poor, withered, shrunken, discoloured, feeble, as though from lack of air, food &c.

etiolated, adj. [1. étiolāted; 2. ítiəleitid]. Prec. & **-ed.** Withered, faded.

etiolation, n. [1. ètiolā́shun; 2. ìtiəléiʃən]. **etiolate** & **-ion.** Process of etiolating; results of this.

etiology. See **aetiology.**

etiquette, n. [1. ètikét; 2. ètikét]. Fr., 'a label'; of Gmc. origin; cp. L.G. *stikke*, 'to stick on'. See **stick (I.)**, & cp. **ticket.** Procedure, manners, forms, ceremonies prescribed by convention and custom: *a breach of etiquette; not etiquette to do so-and-so.*

etna, n. [1. étna; 2. étnə], fr. name of the volcano in Sicily. Device for boiling water, consisting of a metal vessel the base of which is fixed in a kind of cup containing spirit which is lighted.

Eton clothes. See **Etons.**

Eton coat, n. [1. ḗtn kōt; 2. ítn kóut], fr. Eton College. Short black coat worn by boys, reaching to waist, not made to button, having broad lapels like those of a man's swallow-tail coat.

Eton collar, n. Broad white linen collar worn with, and outside, an Eton coat.

Eton crop, n. Very closely cropped hair as worn by women, resembling that of a boy.

Etonian, n. [1. ētónian; 2. ītóuniən]. Boy at Eton College; *Old Etonian*, former member of College.

Eton jacket, n. Eton coat.

Etons, n. pl. [1. ḗtnz; 2. ítnz]. Eton coat, black waistcoat, and suitable trousers. Phr. *to go into Etons*, wear them for the first time, start wearing them.

et seq(q). [1. et sek; 2. ɛt sɛk]. For *sequentes* or *sequentia.* Lat. See **sequence.** And the following (words, pages &c.).

-ette, suff. [1. et; 2. ɛt]. Fr. fem. suff.; also sometimes dimin. Used in more recent introductions fr. Fr. See **-et. 1.** Diminutive force preserved in *statuette*; lost in *wagonette* and almost in *cigarette.* **2.** Expressing a woman engaged in, interested in, something: *suffragette.* **3.** Expressing an imitation: *leatherette*, sham leather.

étui, n. [1. ātwḗ; 2. eitwī]. Fr., O. Fr. *estui*; etymol. unknown. Small case; needle-case.

etymologic(al), adj. [1. ètimolójikl; 2. ètiməlɔ́džikl]. **etymology** & **-ic** & **-al.** Connected with, according to principles of, etymology.

etymologically, adv. Prec. & **-ly. a** According to the principles of etymology: *to trace a word etymologically*; **b** by etymology, by having common origin: *words etymologically related.*

etymologicon, n. [1. ètimolójikon; 2. ètiməlɔ́džikɔn]. Gk. See **etymology.** Etymological dictionary.

etymologist, n. [1. ètimólojist; 2. ètimɔ́lədžist]. **etymology** & **-ist.** Student of etymology.

etymologize, vb. intrans. [1. ètimólojīz; 2. ètimɔ́lədžaiz]. Next word & **-ize.** To study etymology; to make etymologies.

etymology, n. [1. ètimóloji; 2. ètimɔ́lədži]. Gk. *etumologia*, 'analysis, derivation of a word', lit. 'true account'. See **etymon** & **-logy. 1.** Systematic tracing of a word back as near as possible to its original form and meaning, by the methods of comparative philology, and by applying what is known of the history of the particular language in which it occurs. **2.** Branch of philology concerned with this process.

etymon, n. [1. étimon; 2. étimən]. Gk. *étumon*, 'what is true', neut. of *étumos*, 'true'; connected w. *eteós*, 'true, real, genuine', fr. **setewos*, cp. Scrt. *satya*, 'true'. The base is **set*, connected w. Lat. *es-t*, 'is', Gk. *eimi* for **es-mi*, 'am' &c. The full base is **eset-*. See other forms under **am, is, esse, sooth.** Primitive word-form whence derivatives are formed; an etymological base.

eu-, pref. Gk., 'well'; neut. of *eús*, 'good, noble, brave'; in Gk. compounds has the sense of 'great, abundant, easy' &c. *eu-* is for earlier **esu-*, & is fr. base **es-*, 'existing', w. further developed sense, 'good, powerful' &c. See **esse.** In modern English coinages, the prefix means 'well', and expresses satisfactoriness, advantage, completeness &c. Contrasted with **dys-.**

eucalyptus, n. [1. ùkalíptus; 2. jùkəlíptəs]. Gk. **eu-** & *kaluptós*, 'covered', P.P. of *kalúptein*, 'to cover, conceal'; cp. also Gk. *kalúptrā*, 'woman's veil'. The Gk. *kal-* stands for Aryan **kḷl-*, a form of the base **kĕl-*. See second element of **conceal, occult**; also **hole. 1.** (bot.) Large genus of trees indigenous to Australia, often called *gum trees*, from some species of which pungent oils, gums, tars are obtained, while others yield excellent timber. **2.** Eucalyptus oil &c., used for medicinal purposes.

eucharis, n. [1. ū́karis; 2. jū́kəris]. Gk., 'pleasant, agreeable'. See next word. American plant with white flowers; Amazon lily.

Eucharist, n. [1. ū́karist; 2. jū́kərist], fr. Gk. *eukharistia*, 'thankfulness, gratitude', cp. *eukháristos*, 'agreeable, pleasant; thankful', fr. **eu-** & *kháris*, 'favour, grace'; fr. same base is Gk. *khaírein*, 'to rejoice', fr. **khar-jō.* With different formative element, fr. same base, is Goth. *gairnjan*, 'to desire', O.E. *ġeornian.* See further under **yearn.** Lit., thanksgiving; (with cap.) **a** the Sacrament of the Body and Blood of Christ; **b** the consecrated elements: *to receive the Eucharist.*

eucharistic(al), adj. [1. ùkarístik(l); 2. jùkərístik(l)]. Prec. & **-ic** & **-al.** Pertaining to, connected with, arising from, the Eucharist: *eucharistic vestments*, those worn by the officiating clergy at the Mass.

euchre, n. & vb. trans. [1. ū́ker; 2. jū́kə]. Etymol. unknown. **1.** n. Card game. **2.** vb.

a To defeat (opponent) at the game; **b** (fig., slang.) to defeat purpose of, foil.

Euclid, n. [1. úklid; 2. júklid]. Gk., personal name *Eukleídēs*, Gk. geometer, c. 300 B.C. System of geometry based on Euclid's treatise.

eud(a)emonic(al), adj. [1. ūdēmónik(l); 2. jūdīmónik(l)]. **eu-** & **demonic** & **-al**, & cp. **daemon**. Producing happiness.

eudemonics, n. pl. [1. ūdēmóniks; 2. jūdīmóniks], fr. prec. Eudemonism; means of attaining happiness.

eudemonism, n. [1. ūdḗmunizm; 2. jūdímənizəm]. Gk. *eudaimonismós*, 'act of regarding as happy'. **eu-** & **demonism**. Ethical system which judges moral value of actions by their tendency to produce happiness.

eudiometer, n. [1. ūdiómeter; 2. jūdaiómitə]. Gk. *eúdios*, 'fine, serene', **eu-** & *diós*, genit. of *Zeus*, 'God of the sky', & **-meter**. Instrument for measuring and determining the constituents of gases; originally, the amount of oxygen in the atmosphere.

eugenic, adj. [1. ūjénik; 2. jūdžénik]. Gk. *eugenés*, 'well born', & **-ic**. See **eu-** & **genesis**. Connected with improvement of stock or race; tending to promote eugenics, q.v.

eugenics, n. pl., fr. prec. Study of best means of improving the race by careful selection of the parents.

euhemerism, n. [1. ūhḗmerizm; 2. jūhímərizəm]. Gk. name *Euhḗmeros*, a philosopher of about 300 B.C., & **-ism**. Theory that myths arise from an enhancement of traditional account of human beings and their actions.

euhemerist, n. [1. ūhḗmerist; 2. jūhímərist]. See prec. & **-ist**. One who believes that myths originate in traditions of human actions.

euhemeristic, adj. [1. ūhēmerístik; 2. jūhīmərístik]. Prec. & **-ic**. Pertaining to, based on, euhemerism.

euhemerize, vb. trans. [1. ūhḗmerīz; 2. jūhíməraiz]. See prec. & **-ize**. To interpret (myths) according to the principles of euhemerism.

eulogist, n. [1. úlojist; 2. júlədžist]. **eulogy** & **-ist**. Person who praises, who pronounces a eulogy.

eulogistic(al), adj. [1. ūlojístik(l); 2. jūlədžístik(l)]. Prec. & **-ic**, & **-al**. Pertaining to, of the nature of, eulogy; laudatory.

eulogistically, adv. Prec. & **-ly**. In a eulogistic manner.

eulogium, n. [1. ūlójium; 2. jūlóudžiəm]. L. Lat., fr. Gk. See **eulogy**. Eulogy.

eulogize, vb. trans. [1. úlojīz; 2. júlədžaiz]. Next word & **-ize**. To praise highly, speak well of, utter a eulogy concerning.

eulogy, n. [1. úloji; 2. júlədži]. Gk. *eulogia*, 'fair speaking, praise'. **eu-** & **-logy**. **1.** An utterance, pronouncement, oration, statement, whether written or spoken, in praise of a person or action: *to pronounce a eulogy upon the dead*. **2.** Praise, expression of favourable opinion; high commendation.

eunuch, n. [1. únuk; 2. júnək], fr. Lat. *eunuchus*, fr. Gk. *eunoûkhos*, lit. 'guardian of the bed', thence 'chamberlain', fr. *eunḗ*, 'couch, bed'; & *-okh-*, grade of *ékhein*, 'to hold, keep'. The original meaning of *eunḗ* is, 'lair, sleeping-place, retreat for shelter', also 'a tomb' (see development of meaning in **bed**); the most primitive senses of the base are found in Zend *ūna*, 'hole, crevice, in the ground', & O. Slav. *jama*, 'ditch', fr. **ōmā*, fr. **ŏumā*; *ékhein*, 'have, possess' &c., is fr. Aryan **segh-*, 'to seize, master, be master of'; cp. Goth. *sigis*, 'victory', O.E. *sige* &c. See **epoch**. **1.** A male person who has been emasculated. **2.** Such a person, formerly employed as an officer of state by Eastern potentates. **3.** A timid, spiritless, feeble man, lacking courage and robustness of character.

euonymus, n. [1. ūónimus; 2. jūónimǝs]. Lat. form of Gk. *euṓnumos*, 'of good name, propitious', also name of the spindle tree, fr. **eu-** & *ónoma*, *ónuma*, 'name'. See **onomatopoeia**. Genus of evergreen shrubs, including the spindle tree.

eupepsia, n. [1. ūpépsia; 2. jūpépsiə]. Gk. *eupepsía*, 'good digestion'. See **eu-** & **pepsin**, **peptic**. Good digestion. Converse of *dyspepsia*.

eupeptic, adj. [1. ūpéptik; 2. jūpéptik]. **eu-** & **peptic**. **1.** Having a good digestion. **2.** Promoting digestion; easy to digest.

euphemism, n. [1. úfemizm; 2. júfimizəm]. Gk. *euphēmía*, 'use of words of good omen, and avoidance of bad ones', fr. *euphēmein*, 'to use good words', & **-ism**; fr. Gk. **eu-** & *phēmí*, 'I speak', cogn. w. Lat. *fāma*, 'talk, rumour, report'. See **fame**. An elegant, refined, often indirect, or veiled, expression or word, used in the place of one which is coarse, obscene, brutal, unrefined, or merely blunt: *Safeguarding is a mere euphemism for Protection*; cp. use of *adventurer*, as = swindler, one who lives by his wits.

euphemistic(al), adj. [1. ūfemístik(l); 2. jūfimístik(l)]. Prec. w. substitution of suff. **-ist**, & **-ic**. Characterized by euphemism.

euphemistically, adv. Prec. & **-ly**. In a euphemistic manner.

euphemize, vb. trans. & intrans. [1. úfemīz; 2. júfimaiz]. See **euphemism** & **-ize**. **a** To refine one's mode of expression by use of euphemisms; **b** to use euphemisms.

euphonic(al), adj. [1. ūfónik(l); 2. jūfónik(l)]. **euphony** & **-ic** & **-al**. Connected with, in accordance with euphony.

euphonically, adv. Prec. & **-ly**. In a euphonical manner.

euphonious, adj. [1. ūfṓnius; 2. jūfóuniəs]. **euphony** & **-ous**. Pleasant-, smooth-, sweet-sounding.

euphoniously, adv. Prec. & **-ly**. In a euphonious manner.

euphonium, n. [1. ūfṓnium; 2. jūfóuniəm]. Formed on Lat. pattern fr. Gk. *eúphōnos*, 'sweet-voiced'. See next word. Small brass bass instrument with loud tone, resembling a saxhorn.

euphony, n. [1. úfonī; 2. júfəni]. Gk. *euphōnía*, 'sweetness of sound, or voice', fr. **eu-**, 'well', & *phōnḗ*, 'sound, tone, voice'. See **phone**. **1.** Sweetness of sound, harmony; such character and combination of sound as produces a pleasant effect to the ear. **2.** In obsolete philological works, certain sound changes were said to be made, '*for the sake of euphony*', or sometimes '*for greater ease of utterance*'; the theory of the nature of language upon which the view expressed in such statements was based has completely passed away.

Euphorbia, n. [1. ūfórbia; 2. jūfɔ́biə], fr. Gk. *euphórbion*, an African plant, called after *Euphorbos*, a Greek physician. (bot.) A genus of shrubs and herbs, the type of the family *Euphorbiaceae*, which includes spurges, box, castor-oil plant &c.

euphrasy, n. [1. úfrazi; 2. júfrəzi]. Gk. *euphrasia*, 'well-mindedness, delight'. **eu-** & *phras-*, form of base of wh. better-known type is *phrḗn*, 'mind', q.v. under first element of **phrenology**. A herb, also called *eyebright*.

euphuism, n. [1. úfūizm; 2. júfjuizəm], fr. *Euphues*, title of a sort of novel by John Lyly (1580), the style of which was very artificial, with carefully balanced sentences, abounding in antithesis, and remarkable for a high-flown, often far-fetched diction, & **-ism**. **1.** Originally the style of writing and speech affected by the imitators of Lyly. **2.** Any high-flown, artificial, precious style of writing and speaking.

euphuist, n. [1. úfūist; 2. júfjuist]. See prec. & **-ist**. **a** Lyly and his imitators in style; **b** one who affects a style of speech and writing which is artificial, precious, and abounding in rare words, epithets, and phrases &c.

euphuistic(al), adj. [1. ūfūístik(l); 2. jūfjuístik(l)]. Prec. & **-ic** & **-al**. Pertaining to, characterized by, euphuism.

euphuistically, adv. Prec. & **-ly**. In a euphuistic(al) manner.

Eurasian, adj. [1. ūrázhan, -ázian; 2. juréižən, -éiziən]. *Euro-*, fr. *Europe*, & *Asian*. Person, esp. in India, of mixed European and Asiatic parentage or descent; those of British parentage prefer the name 'Anglo-Indian', which is now the recognized name for these people.

eureka, interj. [1. ūrḗka; 2. juríkə]. Gk., 'I have found'; perf. of *heurískō*, 'I find'. See **heuristic**. Exclamation of triumph, I've got it! the difficulty is solved &c.

eurhythmics, n. pl. [1. ūríthmiks; 2. jūríþmiks]. **eu-** & **rhythmic**. The art of expressing harmony by gesture in which physical movement is made to reflect musical notation.

eusol, n. [1. úsol; 2. júsɔl]. **eu-** & first syll. of *solution*. (med.) A solution of chlorinated lime, bleaching powder, and boracic acid, used as an antiseptic lotion for wounds, bruises &c.

Eustachian, adj. [1. ūstákian; 2. jūstéikiən], fr. Eustachio, Ital. physician, d. 1574, & **-an**. (anat.) Named after, discovered by Eustachio, specif., *Eustachian tube*, air-passage leading from the ear-drum cavity to the back part of the mouth.

euthanasia, n. [1. ūthanázia; 2. jūþənéiziə]. Gk., 'easy dying', fr. **eu-** & *thánatos*, 'death'; see **thanato-**. Ir. *duine*, 'mortal, man', W. *dyn*, are perh. cogn. **1.** Easy, desirable mode of death, one devoid of suffering. **2.** Practice (sometimes advocated) of putting to death, by painless methods, persons who are stricken with incurable disease, to avoid prolongation of suffering.

evacuant, adj. & n. [1. ēvákūant; 2. ivǽkjuənt]. Lat. *ēvacuant-(em)*, Pres. Part. type of *ēvacuāre*. See next word. **a** adj. Causing evacuation, esp. of stomach, bowels &c.; **b** n., that which promotes, causes, evacuation.

evacuate, vb. trans. [1. ēvákūāt; 2. ivǽkjueit], fr. Lat. *ēvacuāt-(um)*, P.P. of *ēvacuāre*, 'to empty out, purge'. See **e-** & **vacant**. **1.** To empty out, rid of contents; specif. (med.) *evacuate the bowels*. **2.** (mil.) To clear out, withdraw, troops from (a position, fortress).

evacuation, n. [1. ēvakūáshun; 2. ivækjuéiʃən]. Prec. & **-ion**. **a** Act or process of evacuating in either sense; **b** matter which is evacuated, esp. from bowels.

evade, vb. trans. [1. ēvā́d; 2. ivéid], fr. Lat. *ēvādere*, 'to go out; get away, escape'. **e-** & *vādere*, 'make one's way, rush'; cp. Lat. *vadum*, 'a shallow, ford'; fr. Aryan **wădh-*, whence also O.E. *wadan*, 'go' &c. See **wade**. **1. a** To escape, get away, from, elude, throw off, baffle: *to evade one's pursuers*; *to evade pursuit* &c.; **b** to avoid deliberately, go aside so as not to meet: *to evade a bore at a party*. **2.** To avoid answering, equivocate concerning, dodge: *to evade a straight question*. **3. a** To disregard, manage to shirk, avoid discharge of: *evade a duty, debt, obligation* &c.; **b** to get round, dodge, escape full intention of by trickery: *to evade the law, the rules* &c.

evaginate, vb. trans. [1. ēvájināt; 2. ivǽdžineit]. Lat. *ēvāgināt-(um)*, P.P. of *ēvāgināre*, 'to draw (sword) out of a sheath', fr. **e-** & *vāgīna*, 'sheath'. To turn a tube, or tubular organ, inside out; to evert.

evagination, n. [1. ēvajináshun; 2. ivædžinéiʃən]. Prec. & **-ion**. Act of evaginating.

evaluate, vb. trans. [1. ēválūāt; 2. ivǽljueit]. See **e-** & **valuation**. To ascertain value or amount of; to appraise.

evaluation, n. [1. ēvalūáshun; 2. ivæljuéiʃən]. Prec. & **-ion**. Act or process of evaluating; result of such act or process.

evanesce, vb. intrans. [1. evanés; 2. ɛvənés]. Lat. *ēvānescere*, 'to pass away, vanish'. See **e-** & **vanish**. To disappear, vanish, melt away.

evanescence, n. [1. ēvanésens; 2. ɛ̀vənésəns]. Next word & **-ce**. Disappearance, process or fact of vanishing away; transitoriness.

evanescent, adj. [1. èvanésent; 2. èvənésənt]. Lat. *ēvānescent-(em)*, Pres. Part. type of *ēvānescere*, 'to vanish away'. See **evanesce** & **-ent.** Liable to fade, or pass away; transitory, fleeting.

evangel, n. [1. ēvánjel; 2. īvǽndžel]. Lat. *evangelium*, 'gospel', fr. Gk. *euaggélion*, 'reward of good tidings; glad tidings, the gospel', fr. **eu-**, 'well, good', & *aggelía*, 'message, tidings'; cp. *ággelos*, 'messenger, angel'. See **angel.** a Good tidings; specif., the message of Christianity, the Gospel; b one of the four Gospels.

evangelic(al) (I.), adj. [1. èvanjélik(l); 2. ìvændžélik(l)]. Prec. & **-ic** & **-al.** 1. Pertaining to, based on, the Gospel and its teachings: *evangelical preaching.* 2. Connected with a school of thought in the Church of England which emphasizes the doctrine of the necessity of man's redemption by faith, rather than the sacramental aspect of Christianity; belonging to what is also known as the *Low Church* party; distinctively Protestant in attitude, as contrasted with the *High Church*, or Anglican, Anglo-Catholic party.

evangelical (II.), n. An adherent of the evangelical or Low Church party in the Church of England.

evangelicalism, n. [1. èvanjélikalizm; 2. ìvændžélikəlizəm]. Prec. & **-ism.** System of thought and doctrines held by evangelicals.

evangelist, n. [1. ēvánjelist; 2. īvǽndžəlist]. Gk. *euaggelistḗs*, 'messenger'. **evangel** & **-ist.** 1. The writer of one of the four Gospels. 2. Any preacher of the Gospel; a (in Early Church) one who first preached the Gospel to a nation; b (in mod. times) a travelling preacher, not usually a regular minister in any Church; one who holds religious meetings, often in the open air, and preaches to any who care to listen.

evangelistic, adj. [1. ēvànjelístik; 2. īvæ̀ndžəlístik]. Prec. & **-ic.** Belonging to, connected with, an evangelist, or evangelists.

evangelization, n. [1. ēvànjelīzā́shun; 2. īvæ̀ndžəlaizéiʃən]. Next word & **-ation.** Act, process of evangelizing; condition of being evangelized.

evangelize, vb. trans. & intrans. [1. ēvánjelīz; 2. īvǽndžəlaiz]. **evangel** & **-ize.** 1. trans. a To preach the Gospel to; spread the knowledge of the Gospel among: *St. Augustine and his monks evangelized the South of England in the 7th cent.*; b to imbue with the teachings and principles of the Gospels. 2. intrans. To practise preaching, to preach the Gospel.

evanish, vb. intrans. [1. ēvánish; 2. īvǽniʃ]. O. Fr. *esvanir.* **e-** & **vanish.** To disappear, fade away, vanish.

evanishment, n. [1. ēvánishment; 2. īvǽniʃmənt]. Prec. & **-ment.** Process of vanishing; disappearance.

evaporate, vb. intrans. & trans. [1. ēváporāt; 2. īvǽpəreit], fr. *evapōrāt-(um)*, P.P. type of Lat. *ēvapōrāre*, 'to disperse in vapour'. See **e-** & **vapour.** A. intrans. 1. (of liquid, moisture) To pass away in the form of vapour; to become vapour and disappear. 2. (fig., of non-material things) To disperse, disappear, fade: *his hopes evaporated at the touch of stern reality.* B. trans. To cause to disperse in form of vapour.

evaporation, n. [1. ēvàporā́shun; 2. īvæ̀pəréiʃən]. Prec. & **-ion.** Process of evaporating; act of evaporating.

evaporative, adj. [1. ēváporativ; 2. īvǽpərətiv]. **evaporate** & **-ive.** Connected with, tending to cause, evaporation.

evasion, n. [1. ēvā́shun; 2. īvéižən]. L. Lat. *ēvāsiōn-(em)*, 'a going out', fr. Lat. *ēvās-(um)*, P.P. type of Lat. *ēvādere*, & **-ion.** See **evade.** Act of evading. 1. Escape. 2. a Act of avoiding, eluding, shirking: *evasion of one's responsibilities, duties, &c.*; b act of dodging, paltering with, the truth &c.; equivocation, sophistry: *his answer was a mere evasion.*

evasive, adj. [1. ēvā́siv; 2. īvéisiv]. Lat. *ēvās-* (see prec.) & **-ive.** (chiefly of non-material things) 1. Tending to escape one, elusive, difficult to grasp or retain: *the precise meaning of philosophical writers is often evasive; human joys are too often evasive.* 2. Designedly ambiguous, equivocal, shuffling, disingenuous, shirking the real point: *an evasive answer* &c.

evasively, adv. Prec. & **-ly.** In an evasive manner; equivocally: *to answer evasively.*

evasiveness, n. See prec. & **-ness.** Quality of being evasive; a elusiveness; transitoriness: *the evasiveness of human happiness*; b ambiguity, disingenuousness, equivocation: *an evasiveness in answering questions.*

eve (I.), n. [1. ēv; 2. īv]. M.E. *ēve.* Variant of **even** (I.). 1. (poet.) Evening. 2. a Time just before an event or action: *the eve of great events; on the eve of happiness* &c.; b specif. (eccles.) the day before a festival: *Easter Eve; St. John's Eve* &c.

Eve (II.), n. Proper name of the first woman, Heb. *Havvah, Khawwah*, 'life, living'. Symbolically used for women generally, who are supposed to inherit the characteristics of curiosity and other frailties possessed by our ancestress. Phr. *daughters of Eve*, women.

evection, n. [1. ēvékshun; 2. īvékʃən]. L. Lat. *ēvectiōn-(em)*, 'a flying upwards', fr. *ēvect-(um)* P.P. type of *ēvehere*, 'to carry, convey out', fr. **e-** & *vehere*, 'to carry' &c. See **vehement, vehicle, weigh.** (astron.) Irregularity of the moon in its orbit, due to the action of the sun.

even (I.), n. [1. ḗven; 2. ívən]. O.E. *ǣfen*, M.E. *ēven*; cp. O.S. *āƀand*, O.H.G. *āband*, Mod. Germ. *ābend.* The Scand. type, wh. may not be related to the W. Gmc. forms, is O.N. *aptan*, Mod. Swed. *afton*, Dan. *aften.* No light has so far been shed upon the origin of the word. (poet.) Evening.

even (II.), adj. O.E. *efen*, 'level, even, equal; adv. 'equally', M.E. *ēven*, O.S. *ēƀan*, O.H.G. *eban*, O.N. *jafn.* There are no certain cognates outside Gmc.; relationship has been suggested w. Lat. *aemulāre*, 'to strive to equal' (see **emulate**), *imitāri*, 'to represent, copy' (see **imitate**), & *imāgo*, 'copy, likeness', see **image.** This relationship, however, at present seems improbable. 1. (in material sense) Without irregularities, uniform; a (of surfaces) smooth, not undulating, flat; b (of lines) straight, parallel, in same plane with: *even with the ground*; c (of amounts, distances, heights) equal, identical; Phr. *even date*, (commerc. vulgarism) the same date; *to get, be even with a person*, have one's revenge, requite him; *odds are even*, the same whether for or against; d (of motion) regular, rhythmical, not intermittent: *the even beat of the heart.* 2. (of non-material things) a (of the mind and temper) The same under varying circumstances, and at all times; placid, equable; b (of justice, moral judgement &c.) impartial, fair; c (of conditions of human life) undiversified, monotonous, uneventful. 3. (of numbers) Capable of division by two without remainder; contrasted with *odd.*

even (III.), adv. Same as prec. 1. Evenly: *the two horses ran even.* 2. Just as, precisely, to the extent, in the degree or way stated: *it has turned out even as I expected.* 3. Just at the moment, at the same time as: *even as he was speaking a shot rang out.* 4. With force of intensive particle in various phrases, expressing the extreme limit of what is possible, or expected: *I even lent him my own books; I will forgive you all, even your insults; even now it is not too late* &c. *Even if*, notwithstanding that, although.

even (IV.), vb. trans. To make even; also *even up.*

even-handed, adj. Impartial, fair, unbiassed; esp. in Phr. *even-handed justice.*

evening, n. [1. ḗvning; 2. ívniŋ]. O.E. *ǣfnung*, fr. *ǣfen*, see **even** (I.), M.E. *ēvening.* 1. That part of the day during, and shortly after, sundown; the early part of the night. 2. Part of the night spent in a particular way: *musical evening. Evening clothes*, those of the conventional cut and make to be worn at night; *evening coat*, one customarily worn in the evening; *evening dress*, evening clothes.

evening primrose. n. A biennial plant, *Oenothera*, with pale yellow flowers, which open towards evening.

evening star, n. The planet specially noticeable in the west after sunset, usually Venus.

evenly, adv. [1. ḗvnli; 2. ívnli]. **even** (II.) & **-ly.** In an even manner, equally &c.

even-minded, adj. With even mind; calm, equable.

evenness, n. [1. ḗvnnes; 2. ívənnis]. **even** (II.) & **-ness.** Quality of being even.

evensong, n. [1. ḗvnsong; 2. ívnsɔŋ]. O.E. *ǣfensang.* **even** (I.) & **song.** 1. Sixth of the seven hours in R.C. Church. 2. a Office of Evening Prayer in Church of England; b service at which this is said.

event, n. [1. evént; 2. ivént]. O. Fr., fr. Lat. *ēventus*, 'occurrence, event', fr. *ēvent-(um)*, P.P. type of *ēvenīre*, 'to come forth; happen'. **e-** & *venīre*, 'to come' (see **venue**), wh. is fr. Aryan base **gʷem-* & cogn. w. **come.** 1. Something which comes to pass, befalls, happens; an incident, occurrence: *the various events of a long and adventurous career.* 2. Result, consequences of actions, processes &c.; the way in which a series of occurrences turns out; issue: *his plan of action, though carefully designed and attended with high expectations, was unhappy in the event.* Phrs. *in the event of his death*, should he die, *in the event of my being unable to* &c., if I am unable; *at all events*, in any case. 3. (sporting) An item in a programme of races, athletic sports &c.; a particular race, or other contest.

eventful, adj. [1. evéntfool; 2. ivéntfəl]. Prec. & **-ful.** Packed with, diversified by, abounding in, events.

eventfully, adv. Prec. & **-ly.** In an eventful manner.

eventfulness, n. See prec. & **-ness.** Fact, property, of being eventful.

eventide, n. [1. ḗvntīd; 2. ív(ə)ntaid]. O.E. *ǣfentīd.* **even** (I.) & **tide.** Evening; the time of evening.

eventual, adj. [1. evénchooal; 2. ivéntʃuəl]. See **event** & **-al.** Happening as result of a series of events; ultimate.

eventuality, n. [1. evènchooáliti; 2. ivèntʃuǽliti]. Prec. & **-ity.** Event which may happen as a consequence or contingency.

eventually, adv. [1. evénchooali; 2. ivéntʃuəli]. **eventual** & **-ly.** Ultimately, finally.

eventuate, vb. intrans. [1. ēvénchooāt; 2. īvéntʃueit]. See **eventual** & **-ate.** To happen, come to pass as result; to result in.

ever, adv. [1. éver; 2. évə]. O.E. *ǣfre*, M.E. *euere* &c.; the etymol. is quite obscure; prob. related to O.E. *ā*, 'always, ever', cp. Goth. *aiws*, 'an age', stem *aiwi-.* See **aeon** & **age, aye,** adv. 1. (archaic or poet.) a Always, continuously: *I have ever kept my word*; b repeatedly, incessantly: *he repeated ever the same words.* 2. (in neg., conditional, or interrog. sentence) At any time, on any occasion: *did you ever hear such nonsense?; not that I ever met him; as if I should ever promise such a thing!* 3 Expressing degree: *as much, as little, as ever I can.* Idiomatic Phrs. *ever and anon*, repeatedly but intermittently; from time to time; *for ever (and ever), for ever and a day*, eternally; (colloq., as intens.) *ever so much*, a great deal; *ever such a nice man*, very nice; *what ever do you mean?; why ever don't you eat your dinner?* &c.

everglade, n. [1. éverglād; 2. évəgleid]. **ever** & **glade.** Large tract of marshy ground, with patches of tall grass; esp. *the Everglades*, in Florida.

evergreen, adj. & n. [1. évergrēn; 2. évəgrīn]. 1. adj. (of shrubs and trees) Not losing foliage in winter, remaining green all the year round; contrasted with *deciduous.* 2. n. Tree or shrub of this description; e.g. most conifers, ivy, yew &c.

everlasting, adj. & n. [1. èverláhsting ; 2. èvəlástiŋ]. **1.** adj. a Lasting for ever : *everlasting glory, fame* &c. ; **b** lasting for a long time, durable : *everlasting colours* ; **c** lasting too long ; repeated until one is sick of it : *I cannot stand his everlasting jokes and foolish laughter.* **2.** n. Everlasting flower.

everlasting flower, n. A flower which on drying retains its petals and the colour of these ; the immortelle, *Helichrysum.*

everlastingly, adv. **everlasting** & **-ly.** For ever ; for a very long time.

everlastingness, n. See prec. & **-ness.** Quality of being everlasting.

evermore, adv. [1. évermŏr ; 2. évəmɔ̄]. **ever** & **more.** Eternally, for ever, from now onwards for ever.

eversion, n. [1. ēvérshun ; 2. ĭvíʃən]. Lat. *ēversiōn-(em)*, 'overthrowing, subversion', fr. *ēvers-(um)*, P.P. type of *ēvertere*. **e-** & **version.** Act of everting ; state of being everted.

evert, vb. trans. [1. ēvért ; 2. ĭvÁt]. Lat. *ēvertere*, 'to thrust out, twist'. See prec. To turn outwards, turn inside out ; chiefly of eyelids, intestine &c.

every, adj. [1. éveri ; 2. évəri]. M.E. *euerich, eueri*, fr. O.E. *ǣfre*, 'ever', & *ǣlc*, 'each'. See **ever** & **each. 1.** Each one, not omitting any ; all ; **a** (of a group) : *every face was wreathed in smiles* ; *I tried every horse I saw, till I got one to suit* ; *every day*, each day in succession ; **b** (of an indefinite number) *I enjoyed every hour* ; *with every good wish.* **2.** With numbers : a cardinal numbers, *every four days*, on the fourth of every group of four ; **b** with ordinal numbers, *every second man (in line)*, each alternate man. Phr. *every now and then, and again*, at intervals, from time to time.

everybody, n. [1. évribodi ; 2. évribɔdi]. **every** & **-body.** Each person, all people (with sing. vb.).

everyday, adj. [1. évridā ; 2. évridèi]. Common, familiar, usual, habitual : *an everyday occurrence.*

everyone, n. [1. évriwun ; 2. évriwan]. **every** & **one (II.).** Everybody.

everything, n. [1. évrithing ; 2. évriþiŋ]. a All, each thing or circumstance, omitting nothing : *to know everything* ; *to tell one everything* ; *everything interests me* ; **b** what is of chief importance, the chief thing to be considered : *wealth is not everything* ; *leisure is everything to me.*

everywhen, adv. [1. évriwen ; 2. évriwen]. (rare) At all times, always.

everywhere, adv. [1. évriwār ; 2. évriweə]. In all places.

evict, vb. trans. [1. ēvíkt ; 2. ĭvíkt], fr. Lat. *ēvict-(um)*, P.P. type of *ēvincere*, 'to overcome completely, to prevail'. See **e-** & **victor. 1.** To turn a tenant out of property by virtue of legal powers. **2.** To recover property by virtue of superior legal title.

eviction, n. [1. ēvíkshun ; 2. ĭvíkʃən]. Prec. & **-ion.** Act or process of evicting.

evidence (I.), n. [1. évidens ; 2. évidəns]. Fr., fr. Lat. *ēvidentia*, 'clearness, distinctness', fr. *ēvidenti-*, fr. **e-** & Pres. Part. type of *vidēre*, 'to see'. See **vision** & **wit. 1.** State of being evident. **2.** (law) Testimony, statement made on oath by a witness in a Court of Justice, concerning what he has seen, heard, or otherwise knows of his own knowledge, tending to prove a fact : *to give evidence* ; *hear, call, evidence* ; cp. *circumstantial evidence* and *king's evidence.* **3.** Something which makes evident ; fact, occurrence, statement, which proves, or establishes strong probability, that something else happened, has existed, was done &c.

evidence (II.), vb. trans., fr. prec. To prove, establish by evidence.

evident, adj. [1. évident ; 2. évidənt]. See **evidence (I.).** Plain, visible to the eyes ; clear to the mind ; manifest, obvious.

evidential, adj. [1. èvidénshal ; 2. èvidénʃəl]. Lat. *ēvidenti-*, see **evident**, & **-al.** Connected with, affording, of nature of, evidence.

evidentially, adv. Prec. & **-ly.** By means of evidence.

evidentiary, adj. [1. èvidénshari ; 2. èvidénʃəri]. See **evidential** & **-ary.** Evidential.

evidently, adv. [1. évidentli ; 2. évidəntli]. **evident** & **-ly.** Plainly, manifestly ; in an evident manner, obviously.

evil (I.), adj. [1. ḗvl, ḗvil ; 2. ívl, ívil]. O.E. *yfel*, adj., M.E. *iuel, euel* &c. ; O.H.G. *upil*, Mod. Germ. *übel* ; Goth. *ubils.* The etymol. is entirely obscure, but a connexion has been suggested w. **over** & **up**, *evil* being thus something 'over', or 'exceeding the limits'. Now chiefly in moral sense. Such uses as *evil fruit, evil beast* &c. are obs. **1.** Bad, reverse of good ; esp. morally wicked, filled with malice ; depraved : *evil men, evil devices, an evil life, evil speaking, lying and slandering.* Phr. the *Evil One*, Satan. **2.** Unfortunate, ill-omened ; boding misfortune, inauspicious : *fallen on evil days.* Phr. *the evil eye*, one supposed to bring misfortune by its glance.

evil (II.), n. O.E. *yfelu* &c. **1.** The negation of good ; anything which is opposed to well-being, health of body or mind ; physical disease, moral depravity, intellectual blindness and ignorance, political unrest, are various types of evil ; *king's evil*, scrofula. **2.** Misfortune, ill-luck, disaster : *to wish one evil* ; *to bode evil.*

evil (III.), adv., fr. prec. Badly, ill. Now rare, *ill* being usual.

evil-doer, n. A wicked person, one who does evil.

evil-eyed, adj. Having the evil eye.

evilly, adv. [1. ḗvili ; 2. ívəli, ívili]. **evil (I.)** & **-ly.** In an evil manner.

evil-minded, adj. Wicked, malicious, ill-disposed.

evince, vb. trans. [1. ēvíns ; 2. ĭvíns]. Lat. *ēvincere*, 'to vanquish', wh. appears to have no connexion w. present meaning. Cp. **evict.** The word appears to derive its present sense from **evidence (II.). 1.** To show, give evidence of possessing, feeling, &c. : *to evince great sorrow at parting.* **2.** (rare and archaic) To prove, make manifest : *to evince the truth.*

evirate, vb. trans. [1. ḗvirāt ; 2. ívireit], fr. Lat. *ēvirāt-(um)*, P.P. type of *ēvirāre*, 'to castrate' ; **e-** & *vir*, 'man'. See **virile.** To deprive of manhood, to castrate.

eviration, n. [1. èvirā́shun ; 2. ìviréiʃən]. Prec. & **-ion.** Act or process of evirating ; state of being evirated ; specif. (med.) loss of male characteristics.

eviscerate, vb. trans. [1. ēvíserāt ; 2. ĭvísəreit]. Lat. *ēviscerāt-(um)*, P.P. type of *ēviscerāre*, 'to take the bowels out of'. See **e-** & **viscera.** a To disembowel ; **b** (fig.) to take the point, force, essential character, from anything.

evisceration, n. [1. ēviserā́shun ; 2. ĭvìsəréiʃən]. Prec. & **-ion.** Act or process of eviscerating ; state of being eviscerated.

evocation, n. [1. èvōkā́shun ; 2. ìvoukéiʃən]. Fr., fr. Lat. *ēvocātiōn-(em)*, fr. *ēvocāt-(um)*, P.P. type of *ēvocāre.* See **evoke.** Act of calling up ; a summons ; esp. *evocation of spirits* ; *evocation of emotion* &c.

evocative, adj. [1. ēvókativ ; 2. ĭvɔ́kətiv]. Lat. *ēvocāt-*, as in prec., & **-ive.** Tending to evoke.

evoke, vb. trans. [1. ēvṓk ; 2. ĭvóuk]. Fr. *évoquer*, fr. Lat. *ēvocāre*, 'to call out, call forth'. **e-** & *vocāre*, 'to call', q.v. under **vocal, vocation, voice. 1.** To call up, summon, cause to appear : *to evoke spirits from the other world.* **2.** To call up, produce : *to evoke an image, an emotion in the mind, memories* ; *to evoke admiration, applause* &c.

evolute, n. [1. évolūt ; 2. évəljūt]. Lat. *ēvolūt-(um)*, P.P. type of *ēvolvere*, 'to unroll'. See next word. (math.) Special form of curve.

evolution, n. [1. èvolū́shun ; 2. ìvəljúʃən]. Lat. *ēvolūtiōn-(em)*, 'an unrolling of a scroll, opening of a book', fr. *ēvolūt-(um)*, P.P. type of *ēvolvere*, 'to unroll, unfold', fr. **e-** & *volvere*, 'to roll, turn about' &c. See **volume, volute** ; also **helix, well (II.). 1.** An unrolling, unfolding, esp. by a gradual and natural process ; applied to the process of gradual development wherever exhibited ; esp. *the evolution of a drama*, the gradual unfolding of the plot as expressed in the action. **2.** (biol.) **a** The course of development by natural processes, as seen in the animate world of nature, whether it affects the growth of the individual organism or that of the species ; the doctrine of evolution is opposed to the creationist view ; the latter holds that each variety in the vegetable and animal kingdoms was produced by a special creative act, whereas the doctrine of evolution is that all the innumerable varieties, species, and genera were gradually developed, or evolved, from a few simple ancestral forms or types ; **b** the doctrine concerning this process. **3.** (often pl.) The movements of a part of a machine, revolutions. **4.** (mil. and nav.) Organized, concerted movements of a body of troops, or of a number of ships ; manœuvres.

evolutional, adj. [1. èvolū́shunal ; 2. ìvəljúʃənəl]. Prec. & **-al.** Connected with, produced by, evolution.

evolutionally, adv. Prec. & **-ly.** By means of, in accordance with, a process of evolution.

evolutionary, adj. [1. èvolū́shunari ; 2. ìvəljúʃənəri]. **evolution** & **-ary.** Evolutional.

evolutionism, n. [1. èvolū́shunizm ; 2. ìvəljúʃənizəm]. **evolution** & **-ism.** Theory and doctrines of evolution ; opposed to *creationism.*

evolutionist, n. & adj. [1. èvolū́shunist ; 2. ìvəljúʃənist]. **evolution** & **-ist. 1.** n. Adherent of doctrine of evolution in nature. **2.** adj. Connected with the doctrine of evolution.

evolutionistic, adj. [1. ḗvolūshunístik ; 2. ívəljūʃənístik]. Prec. & **-ic.** Evolutionist, adj.

evolutive, adj. [1. èvolū́tiv ; 2. ìvəljūtiv]. See **evolution** & **-ive.** Tending to evolve ; tending to promote process of evolution.

evolve, vb. intrans. & trans. [1. ēvólv ; 2. ĭvɔ́lv]. Lat. *ēvolvere*, 'to unfold' &c. See **evolution. 1.** intrans. To unfold, develop by natural and gradual process of growth. Various senses : **a** of plot of a story or drama ; **b** of a living organism, species &c. ; **c** of political institutions ; **d** of the mind and ideas &c. **2.** trans. To cause to evolve ; to produce by gradual process ; esp. of mental processes : *to evolve a plan, theory* &c.

evulsion, n. [1. ēvúlshun ; 2. ĭválʃən]. Lat. *ēvulsiōn-(em)*, 'a pulling out' (of teeth &c.), fr. *ēvuls-(um)*, P.P. type of *ēvellere*, 'to pluck, tear, out' ; **e-** & *vellere*, 'to pull, pluck, off'. For the base **wel-*, **wḷ-* &c. see **vellicate.** A plucking out ; rooting out.

ewe, n. [1. ū ; 2. jū]. O.E. *eowu*, M.E. *ēwe* ; cp. Goth. *awēþi*, 'flock of sheep' ; O.E. *eowestre*, Goth. *awistr*, 'sheep-fold' ; cogn. w. Lat. *ovis*, 'sheep' ; Gk. *óis*, 'sheep' ; Scrt. *avi* ; Lith. *avis.* See **ovine.** Female of the sheep.

ewe-necked, adj. [1. ū nekt ; 2. jū nekt]. (of horses) Having a thin, poorly arched neck.

ewer, n. [1. ūer ; 2. jūə, jɔ̄(ə)]. In M.E., fr. A.-Fr. *ewiere*, O. Fr. *aiguiere*, 'water-vessel', fr. Lat. *aquāria*, fem. adj., fr. *aqua*, 'water'. See **aquatic** & **aquarium.** A jug, pitcher ; specif., large water-jug used in bedrooms.

ex, prep. [1. eks ; 2. eks]. Lat. See next word. In various phrases : **1.** *Ex officio*, by virtue of one's office, not by election. **2.** (commerc.) *Ex dividend*, (of stocks) not giving holder a right to, excluding, next dividend ; *ex ship, store* &c., (of goods) not subject to payment until removed from ship, store &c.

ex- (I.), pref. Lat. pref. fr. prep. *ex* ; in composition *ex-* remains, as a rule, unaltered before words beginning w. vowels, & before the cons. *h, c, p, q, s, t* ; becomes *ef-* before *f-* ; *ē-* before other cons. *Ex* is cogn. w. Gk. *ex-, ek-* (see **ex- (II.)** & **ec-**). The Lat. prep. has the following main senses : **a** (space) in downward direction, from, off, down from ; **b** (of time) from, since, after ; **c** (other relations) taking and receiving, physically and mentally ; from, out of, away from; through, on account of, in conformity with. In composition *ex-* has the force: **a** out of, forth, *excēdere*, 'to go away'; **b** change from one state to another, *effemināre*, 'to change (from man's disposition) to the disposition of a woman'; **c** deprivation, *effrēnātus*, 'unbridled'; **d** completion, termination, *efficere*, 'to bring to pass, effect'; **e** as intens., *ēlaborāre*, 'to work out, take pains with'. The above senses continue in, or underlie, the force of the pref. in Lat. loan-words in Engl. *Ex-* in *Ex-Viceroy* &c. means 'former'. See also **e-** & **ef-**.

ex- (II.), pref., fr. Gk. *ex-*, *ek-*, the former occurring before vowels, as in *éxarkhos*, 'leader' &c., the latter form before cons. The force of the prep. in Gk. is very similar to that of *ex-* in Lat. In composition *ek-*, *ex-*, signifies 'out, away, off'. See **ec-**.

exacerbate, vb. trans. [1. èksáserbāt; 2. èksǽsəbeit], fr. Lat. *exacerbāt-(um)*, P.P. type of *exacerbāre*, 'to exasperate, provoke; to grieve, afflict', fr. **ex-** & *acerbus*, 'bitter, sour; harsh, rigorous; grievous, sad'. See **acerbity.** To render worse, intensify, exaggerate (disease, ill-feeling &c.); to exasperate, provoke, irritate, embitter (persons and human relations).

exacerbation, n. [1. èksaserbáshun; 2. èksæsəbéiʃən]. Prec. & **-ion.** The act or process of exacerbating; state of being exacerbated.

exact (I.), adj. [1. egzákt; 2. igzǽkt], fr. Lat. *exact-(us)*, 'precise, accurate', fr. P.P. type of *exigere*, 'to demand, require'. See next word. **1.** (of material things) Conforming closely to a required standard of accuracy; absolutely correct, accurate: *an exact copy.* **2. a** (of mental processes and faculties) Capable of absolute accuracy: *an exact memory; exact ear for music* &c.; **b** (of verbal expression) leaving no room for error, doubt, or ambiguity &c.; precise: *exact directions; an exact account; exact meaning of a word.* **3.** (of persons) Possessing an exact mind; rigorously accurate in mind and method: *an exact scholar.*

exact (II.), vb. trans., fr. Lat. *exact-(um)*, P.P. type of Lat. *exigere*, 'to thrust out, expel; to thrust, drive; to demand, require, enforce', fr. **ex-** & *agere*, 'to drive, lead; conduct, impel; to do, perform'. See **act, agent. 1.** (of persons) To compel, insist on, demand and obtain, require peremptorily: *to exact obedience, respect* &c. **2.** (of work, circumstances &c.) To make necessary, render indispensable; demand: *this work exacts the closest attention* &c.

exactable, adj. [1. egzáktabl; 2. igzǽktəbl]. **exact (II.)** & **-able.** Capable of being exacted.

exacting, adj. [1. egzákting; 2. igzǽktiŋ], fr. Pres. Part. of **exact (II.)**. **a** (of persons and their characters) Making great or excessive demands, having many requirements; severe, tyrannical: *an exacting master; an exacting disposition*; **b** (of human activities) making great demands on one's physical or mental strength; on the attention, skill, care of the performer; arduous, exhausting: *exacting labour; exacting piece of work* &c.

exaction, n. [1. egzákshun; 2. igzǽkʃən], fr. Lat. *exactiōn-(em)*, 'a demanding, requisition; tax, tribute'. **exact (II.)** & **-ion. 1.** Excessive, extortionate, exorbitant, demand on strength, time, and resources &c.; severe requirements: *the exactions of life in society, of the teaching profession.* **2.** Something exacted; a tax, fee, esp. when considered arbitrary: *the exactions of the tax-collector.*

exactitude, n. [1. egzáktitūd; 2. igzǽktitjūd]. **exact (I.)** & **-tude.** The quality of being exact; preciseness, correctness, accuracy.

exactly, adv. [1. egzáktli; 2. igzǽktli]. **exact (I.)** & **-ly.** In an exact manner; precisely, just, quite, strictly.

exactness, n. [1. egzáktnes; 2. igzǽktnis]. **exact (I.)** & **-ness.** The quality of being exact; exactitude.

exaggerate, vb. trans. & intrans. [1. egzájerāt; 2. igzǽdžəreit], fr. Lat. *exaggerāt-(um)*, P.P. type of *exaggerāre*, 'to raise a mound, to heap up; to enlarge, increase; to amplify, heighten, magnify', fr. **ex-** & *aggerāre*, 'to heap up, pile up; to augment, increase', fr. *agger*, 'a mound, earthwork, rampart; a pile'; prob. fr. *aggerere*, 'to bring together; bring towards a place', fr. **ad-** & *gerere*, 'to bring, carry'. See **gerent. A.** trans. **1. a** To conceive of disproportionately; think of, dwell on, (some quality) as more important, intenser, more marked, than it really is: *you exaggerate your own importance; to exaggerate in one's mind the difficulties of the situation, the charms of a place, one's chances of success* &c.; **b** to give a disproportionate account of something; to represent, describe, something as greater, more important, better, worse &c. than it is in reality; to overstate the degree to which some quality exists: *to exaggerate the size of one's house, the amount of work one does; now, don't exaggerate the lady's beauty and attractions.* **2.** (in artistic representation) To over-emphasize, lay undue stress upon; to describe or depict some quality, feature, circumstance, so as to give a false impression of its relation to the whole: *Russian novels tend to exaggerate the gloomy and squalid aspects of life; some painters exaggerate their foregrounds.* **3.** (chiefly in P.P. as adj.) **a** To intensify, render more severe; to aggravate (disease &c.); **b** to enlarge abnormally: *the size of the heart was found to be greatly exaggerated by disease.* **B.** intrans. To practise exaggeration in statement: *don't trust what he says too implicitly, he always exaggerates.*

exaggerated, adj. [1. egzájerāted; 2. igzǽdžəreitid], fr. P.P. of prec. **1.** (of mental conceptions) Lacking proportion and perspective in some direction: *an exaggerated sense of one's own importance.* **2.** (of statements) Overgrown, over-enhanced, heightened beyond the limits of fact; extravagant: *an exaggerated account of sufferings.*

exaggeratedly, adv. Prec. & **-ly.** In an exaggerated manner.

exaggeration, n. [1. egzàjeráshun; 2. igzæ̀džəréiʃən]. **exaggerate** & **-ion.** Act of exaggerating; an exaggerated statement; hyperbole; over-emphasis.

exaggerative, adj. [1. egzájerātiv; 2. igzǽdžəreitiv]. **exaggerate** & **-ive.** Tending to exaggerate; characterized by exaggeration.

exaggeratively, adv. Prec. & **-ly.** In an exaggerative manner.

exalt, vb. trans. [1. egzáwlt; 2. igzɔ́lt]. Fr. *exalter*, fr. Lat. *exaltāre*, 'to raise, elevate, exalt; to deepen', fr. **ex-** & *altus*, 'high, deep'. See **alt, altitude. 1.** (rare or archaic in physical sense) To raise, lift up. **2.** To raise to superior, or to a high, rank or position: *exalted to the position of Prime Minister.* **3.** To praise, extol, proclaim greatness and merits of. **4.** To intensify effect of.

exaltation, n. [1. èksawltáshun; 2. èksɔltéiʃən]. Prec. & **-ation. 1.** The act of exalting; state of being exalted (in all senses of vb.). Specif., *the Exaltation of the Cross*, festival of the Roman Catholic Church commemorating the finding of the True Cross by the Empress Helena. **2. a** State of abnormal mental excitement, elation; condition of spiritual rapture; **b** condition of self-satisfaction, sense of well-being, arising from intoxication. **3.** (astrol.) That position of a planet in which its influence is most strongly exerted.

exalted, adj. [1. egzáwlted; 2. igzɔ́ltid], fr. P.P. of **exalt. 1. a** Highly placed, enjoying great and dignified position; noble: *an exalted personage; a person of exalted rank*; **b** (in moral or intellectual sense) noble, elevated, on a high level of perfection and refinement: *an exalted mind; an exalted style.* **2.** In a condition of exaltation; abnormally excited, wrought up.

exam, n. [1. egzám; 2. igzǽm]. Colloq. for **examination.**

examinant, n. [1. egzáminant; 2. igzǽminənt]. **examine** & **-ant.** An examiner.

examination, n. [1. egzàmináshun; 2. igzæ̀minéiʃən]. **examine** & **-ation. 1.** Act of examining; state of being examined. **2.** (of physical processes) **a** Scrutiny, inspection, by visual observation: *to make an examination of a museum specimen*; **b** specif., testing of, inquiry into, physical condition, state of health, degree of strength &c. by a medical man: *to undergo a medical examination.* **3.** (of mental process) Consideration, pondering, thinking over; weighing in the mind, analysis and balancing from various aspects: *to submit a question, problem, to an impartial examination.* **4.** Strict and formal testing, by written and oral question and answer, of a person's knowledge of, and proficiency in, a subject, or of his progress in studies; of his skill, experience, or other qualifications to undertake certain duties. **5.** (law) Questioning, by counsel, of a witness on oath, in a law-suit, in order to elicit his evidence: *examination in chief*, by his own counsel, *cross-examination*, by opposing counsel.

examinational, adj. [1. egzàmináshunal; 2. igzæ̀minéiʃənəl]. Prec. & **-al.** Connected with an examination; of the nature of examinations.

examination-paper, n. **a** A series of printed questions to be answered in writing by candidates in an examination &c.; **b** the written answers of a candidate to such questions.

examinatorial, adj. [1. egzàminatórial; 2. igzæ̀minətɔ́riəl], fr. Lat. *exāmināt-(um)*, P.P. type of *exāmināre*. See **examine** & **-ory** & **-al.** Pertaining to an examiner or examiners.

examine, vb. trans. [1. egzámin; 2. igzǽmin], fr. Fr., fr. Lat. *exāmināre*, 'to weigh'; fig. 'to consider, ponder; to examine, try, test', fr. *exāmen*, 'the tongue of a balance', hence 'a weighing, examination', fr. **ex-** & **agsmen*, fr. *ag-ere*, 'to drive, lead, bring'. See **act, agent. 1. a** (of physical process) To look at, inspect carefully, critically, and methodically; to scrutinize: *to examine a picture; to examine the records*; **b** (of mental process) to inquire into, investigate, to consider carefully, ponder over: *to examine a theory, statement, proposal*; **c** to probe, test, by introspection: *to examine one's own heart, conscience* &c. **2.** To test a person's knowledge, proficiency, qualifications, by means of oral or written questions. **3.** (law) To question (a witness) on oath, in a court of law, in order to establish a fact by his evidence. *Examine into*, to inquire into, investigate.

examinee, n. [1. egzàminḗ; 2. igzæminī]. **examine** & **-ee.** Candidate for examination; person being examined.

examiner, n. [1. egzáminer; 2. igzǽminə]. **examine** & **-er.** One who examines, esp. one who sets, and corrects or marks, an examination-paper for students: *to satisfy the examiners*, to pass an examination, but without honours or distinction.

example, n. [1. egzáhmpl; 2. igzámpl], fr. O. Fr., fr. Lat. *exemplum*, 'a sample; an imitation, copy; a pattern, model; precedent', fr. earlier **ex-em-lom*, fr. *exim-ere*, 'to take out, take away, remove'; *ex-* & *emere*, 'to take, receive'. See **exempt, sample. 1. a** Something which illustrates a statement or rule; an instance serving to confirm a statement: *an example of what is meant; examples of a grammatical usage* &c.; Phr. *for example*, by way of illustration; **b** a specimen, sample: *an example of Holbein's best work.* **2. a** A pattern, precedent, parallel: *the action is without example in the history of the country*; **b** (of conduct) something to be imitated, a precedent: *to give, set, a good example*; **c** an instance of something to be avoided; a warning, deterrent: *let this be an example to you*; Phrs. *to make an example of*, punish as a warning to others; *to follow his father's example*, imitate, whether for good or ill.

exanimate, adj. [1. eksánimat; 2. eksǽnimit], fr. Lat. *exanimāt-(um)*, P.P. type of *exani-*

māre, 'to deprive of air; to deprive of life; to put out of one's senses, agitate, terrify', fr. **ex-** & *anima*, 'air, breath, life'. See **animus**. **a** Deprived of life; dead; **b** lacking spirit, or animation; inert, lifeless.

exanthema, n., pl. **exanthemata** [1. èksanthḗma, -mata; 2. èksænþímə, -mətə], fr. Gk. *exánthēma*, 'bursting into flower; eruption', fr. *exánthein*, 'to burst into flower', fr. **ex-** (II.) & *ánthos*, 'flower'. See **anthology**. (med.) An eruption accompanied by fever, as in small-pox, scarlet fever &c.

exanthematous, adj. [1. èksanthḗmatus; 2. èksænþímətəs], fr. Gk. *exanthēmat-(os)*. See prec. & **-ous**. Of, pertaining to, displaying, attended by, exanthema.

exarch, n. [1. éksark; 2. éksāk], fr. Lat., fr. Gk. *éxarkhos*, 'a superintendent, governor', fr. **ex-** (II.) & *arkhós*, 'a guide, leader'. See **arch-**. **1.** (in Byzantine Empire) Governor of a province. **2.** (Gk. Ch.) **a** A patriarch; **b** a patriarchal legate; specif. **c** the supreme head of the Bulgarian Church, not under the authority of the Greek patriarch.

exarchate, n. [1. éksarkāt; 2. éksākeit]. Prec. & **-ate**. The office or jurisdiction of an exarch.

exasperate, vb. trans. [1. egzásperāt; 2. igzǽspəreit], fr. Lat. *exasperāt-(um)*, P.P. type of *exasperāre*, 'to roughen; to provoke, irritate', fr. **ex-** & *asperāre*, 'to make rough, uneven; to rouse up, excite', fr. *asper*, 'rough, uneven; harsh, sour'; fig. 'hard, harsh; fierce, savage'. See **asperity**. **1.** (of persons) To rouse the anger of, excite the wrath of; to provoke, irritate, infuriate. **2. a** (of disease, pain &c.) To intensify, increase the violence of, make worse; **b** (of anger, ill-feeling &c.) to inflame, provoke, heighten, aggravate.

exasperating, adj. [1. egzásperāting; 2. igzǽspəreitiŋ], fr. Pres. Part. of prec. Tending to exasperate, provoking, irritating.

exasperatingly, adv. Prec. & **-ly**. In an exasperating manner.

exasperation, n. [1. egzàsperā́shun; 2. igzæ̀spəréiʃən]. **exasperate** & **-ion**. The act of exasperating; state of being exasperated; great irritation of mind, anger.

excambion, n. [1. ekskámbion; 2. ɛkskǽmbiən], fr. Low Lat. *excambium*, fr. **ex-** & **cambium**. See **change**. (Scots law) Exchange, barter, of a piece of land for another; allowed in the case of settled property.

ex cathedra, adv. & adj. [1. èks káthedra, -ā; 2. èks kǽþidrə, -ei]. Lat., 'from the teacher's chair'. See **cathedral**. **1.** adv. Authoritatively, as from a seat of authority which cannot be questioned; specif. (of the Pope) *to speak ex cathedra*, to pronounce an infallible judgement on questions of faith or morals. **2.** adj. Authoritative and final: *an ex cathedra pronouncement.*

excavate, vb. trans. [1. ékskavāt; 2. ékskəveit], fr. *excavāt-(um)*, P.P. type of *excavāre*, 'to hollow out', fr. **ex-** & *cav-(us)*, 'a hole, hollow, cavity'. See **cave** (I.). **1. a** To hollow out, make a cavity in a rock; **b** to dig out, remove, soil by digging; **c** to form or shape by digging, hollowing: *to excavate a cave, trench.* **2.** To dig up, bring to light, unearth by digging: *to excavate a buried town.*

excavation, n. [1. èkskavā́shun; 2. èkskəvéiʃən]. Prec. & **-ion**. **1.** The act of excavating; state of being excavated. **2.** A hollow, cutting, channel &c., formed by excavating. **3.** (archaeol.) Something dug up, brought to light, by excavation; e.g. tomb, building &c. which had been buried.

excavator, n. [1. ékskavātor; 2. ékskəveitə]. **excavate** & **-or**. **a** Person engaged in excavation; **b** machine used in excavation.

exceed, vb. trans. & intrans. [1. eksḗd; 2. ɛksíd], fr. Fr., fr. Lat. *excēdere*, 'to go away, depart; to go beyond, rise above; to surpass, excel', fr. **ex-** & *cēdere*, 'to go, move; depart, withdraw; to submit, yield'. See **cede**. **A.** trans. **1.** To go beyond a limit, do more than is permitted by law or regulations: *to exceed one's instructions, authority* &c.; *to exceed the speed-limit* &c. **2.** To do more, be better, or worse than, reveal some quality to greater extent than was expected: *to exceed one's wildest dreams, anything one could have hoped, all anticipations.* **3.** To surpass, be greater than, superior to; **a** (in physical attributes) *to exceed another in height, beauty, strength* &c.; **b** (in moral qualities) *to exceed another in courage, in villainy* &c. **B.** intrans. **1.** To pass beyond recognized limits, be guilty of excess; specif., to eat or drink immoderately. **2.** To have superabundance of some quality: '*This one in beauty, that in strength exceeds*'.

exceeding, adj. & adv. [1. eksḗding; 2. ɛksídiŋ], fr. Pres. Part. of prec. **1.** adj. Great, surpassing, extreme, extraordinary: *a scene of exceeding beauty.* **2.** adv. (archaic) Exceedingly: *exceeding great.*

exceedingly, adv. Prec. & **-ly**. Extremely, extraordinarily, to a very high degree.

excel, vb. trans. & intrans. [1. eksél; 2. ɛksél], fr. Fr., fr. Lat. *excellere*, 'to rise, raise oneself; to be eminent, excel'. Cp. Lat. *collis*, 'hill', *columen*, 'summit; gable; pillar'. See **column**. **A.** trans. To rise above, surpass, be superior to: *to excel another in courage, virtue* &c., *in commanding men* &c.; *not to be excelled, he made a great effort and won the race.* **B.** intrans. To be superior, surpass others in, be distinguished for; to be pre-eminent in possessing or doing; to shine: *to excel in strength*; *in reading aloud*; *as an orator.*

excellence, n. [1. ékselens; 2. éksələns], fr. Fr., fr. Lat. *excellentia*, 'excellence, superiority'. **excellent** & **-ce**. **1.** The quality of being excellent; superiority, surpassing merit; extreme goodness. **2.** That in which a person excels; some surpassing quality: *his excellence as a rider and shot.*

excellency, n. [1. ékselensi; 2. éksələnsi], fr. Fr., fr. Lat. *excell-(ere)*, 'to excel', & **-ency**. See **excel**. **1.** (archaic) Excellence. **2.** Title given to ambassadors, viceroys, governors of colonies, and their wives: *Your, His, Her Excellency, their Excellencies.*

excellent, adj. [1. ékselent; 2. éksələnt]. Fr., fr. Lat. *excellent-(em)*, Pres. Part. of *excellere*. See **excel**. Having quality of excelling; very good, of great merit, value &c.

excellently, adv. Prec. & **-ly**. In an excellent manner.

excelsior, interj. [1. eksélsiōr; 2. ɛksélsiɔ̄]. Lat., compar. of *excels-(us)*, 'lofty, high; noble, sublime', P.P. of *excellere*, 'to excel'. See **excel**. (lit.) Higher; as motto, or watchword, implying aspiration towards progress and improvement.

except (I.), vb. trans. & intrans. [1. eksépt; 2. ɛksépt], fr. Fr., fr. Lat. *except-(um)*, P.P. of *excipere*, 'to take or draw out; to except, make an exception of'. **ex-** & *capere*, 'to take'. See **captive**. **A.** trans. To make an exception of, exclude; leave, keep, out (of a specified number, group &c.); to set apart from a general statement; leave out of account, omit: *to except certain names from a list*; *to except some persons from a general censure* &c. **B.** intrans. (followed by *against*) To make an objection, protest: *to except against a witness, statement* &c.

except (II.), prep., fr. Lat. *except-(o)*, fr. P.P. *exceptum* (see prec.) used in abl. absol. construction. Omitting, apart from, not including, with the exception of: *everyone is ready except you.* Phr. *except for*, but for, allowance being made for: *a charming book except for a few blunders.*

except (III.), conj., fr. prec. (archaic and Bib.) Unless: '*except the Lord keep the city, the watchman waketh but in vain*' (Psalms).

excepting, prep. [1. eksépting; 2. ikséptiŋ], fr. Pres. Part. of **except** (I.). With the exception of, except, excluding.

exception, n. [1. eksépshun; 2. iksépʃən], fr. O. Fr., fr. Lat. *exceptiōn-(em)*, 'exception, restriction, limitation'. **except** (I.) & **-ion**. **1.** Someone, something, excepted or excluded from a number of things or persons under consideration: *I make no exceptions*; *without exception*, everyone. Phr. *to take exception to*, to make objection to, demur to, protest against. **2.** Something which does not conform in behaviour or character to a series of observed phenomena; something different from others of the same class; something which shows a deviation from the ordinary and expected course of events: *an exception to a grammatical rule, to the ordinary run* &c. Phr. *the exception proves the rule* (a rather meaningless formula).

exceptionable, adj. [1. eksépshunabl; 2. iksépʃənəbl]. Prec. & **-able**. Open to objection.

exceptional, adj. [1. eksépshunal; 2. iksépʃənəl]. **exception** & **-al**. Of the nature of an exception; **a** out of the ordinary; hence, remarkable, rare; better or worse than ordinary: *exceptional advantages*; *exceptional misfortunes* &c.; **b** constituting a deviation from usual course, usage &c.; not conforming to, contravening, ordinary experience: *an exceptional occurrence*; *an exceptional use of a word* &c.

exceptionality, n. [1. eksèpshunáliti; 2. iksèpʃənǽliti]. Prec. & **-ity**. Quality of being exceptional.

exceptionally, adv. [1. eksépshunali; 2. iksépʃənəli]. **exceptional** & **-ly**. **a** As an exception, in an exceptional manner: *it happened quite exceptionally*; **b** to an exceptional degree; unusually, uncommonly: *an exceptionally handsome man*; *exceptionally bad harvest.*

exceptive, adj. [1. ekséptiv; 2. ikséptiv]. **except** (I.) & **-ive**. **a** Of the nature of an exception; **b** expressing, indicating, an exception.

excerpt (I.), vb. trans. [1. eksērpt; 2. iksɔ̄pt], fr. Lat. *excerpt-(um)*, P.P. type of Lat. *excerpere*, 'to pick out; to choose, select, gather, extract', fr. **ex-** & *carpere*, 'to pick, pluck, gather'. See **carpel**. To pick out, select, extract, a passage &c. for quotation from a book &c.

excerpt (II.), n. [1. éksērpt, eksērpt; 2. éksɔ̄pt, iksɔ̄pt], fr. Lat. *excerpt-(um)*, 'an extract, selection, from a book or other writing', fr. P.P. of *excerpere*, 'to pick; select, extract'. See prec. Something excerpted, an extract, passage quoted, from a book, speech &c.

excerptible, adj. [1. eksērptibl; 2. iksɔ̄ptibl]. **excerpt** (I.) & **-ible**. Capable of being excerpted.

excerption, n. [1. eksērpshun; 2. iksɔ̄pʃən]. **excerpt** (I.) & **-ion**. **a** Act of excerpting; **b** something excerpted, an excerpt.

excess, n. [1. eksés; 2. iksés]. Fr. *excès*, fr. Lat. *excess-(um)*, P.P. type of *excēdere*. See **exceed**. **1. a** Superabundance, redundancy; more than normal, more than is expected or required; too much: *an excess of animal strength and spirits*; *excess of blood to the head*; *an excess of kindness, zeal, harshness* &c.; **b** specif., immoderation, blameworthy lack of measure or circumspection in action or behaviour; intemperance, too great indulgence, esp. in eating and drinking; often in pl. *excesses*, course of intemperance &c.; Phrs. *to excess*, to too great an extent, or degree; *in excess of*, more than, beyond a certain limit. **2.** Amount over and above a certain fixed quantity; sum or amount by which one sum or amount exceeds another: *an excess of income over expenditure*; *an excess of industry over intelligence. Excess baggage*, that which is over and above what is allowed free by a railway, steamer &c. *Excess fare*, additional sum due on a ticket beyond what has been paid, on account of some advantage enjoyed by traveller (on railway). *Excess profits duty*, tax levied on business profits made in excess of the average profit during three years before outbreak of the Great War.

excessive, adj. [1. eksésiv; 2. iksésiv]. Prec. & **-ive**. Characterized by, showing, excess of any kind.

excessively, adv. Prec. & **-ly**. To an excessive degree, inordinately; (colloq. as mere intens.) *excessively fond of mutton* &c., very fond.

exchange (I.), vb. trans. & intrans. [1. ekschánj; 2. ikstʃéindž], fr. O. Fr. *eschangier*, fr. **ex-** & L. Lat. *cambiāre*, 'to exchange, barter'. See **change**. **A.** trans. **1. a** To give one thing and receive another in place of it: *to exchange English money for French*; **b** to give up, leave, quit (one place, possession, condition &c.) for another: *to exchange the bad weather of England for that of foreign countries.* **2.** To give and receive, give in return for something similar, interchange: *to exchange greetings, blows, hats, seats* &c. **B.** intrans. **1.** To carry out process of exchanging; make an exchange. **2.** *Exchange into*, leave a position, post &c. and go into another; specif. (mil.) *exchange into another regiment.*

exchange (II.), n., fr. O. Fr. *eschange*, fr. L. Lat. **ex-** & *cambium*, 'an exchange'. See **change** (II.). **1.** The act of exchanging; that which is exchanged: **a** *the exchange of money for goods*; *a good exchange*; **b** a give and take: *exchange of prisoners*; *exchange of civilities.* **2.** (financ.) **a** Method of settling debts between individuals in different countries by exchanging drafts or *bills of exchange*; **b** relation in value between the currencies of different countries: *rate of exchange.* **3.** (commerc.) Building, set of offices, market, in which certain kinds of business are transacted: *Cotton Exchange, Stock Exchange.* **4.** Central telephone office of a specific district, at which connexion is made between subscribers and between various areas or districts.

exchangeability, n. [1. ekschánjabíliti; 2. ikstʃéindžəbíliti]. See next word & **-ity**. The state of being exchangeable; exchangeable value.

exchangeable, adj. [1. ekschánjabl; 2. ikstʃéindžəbl]. **exchange** (I.) & **-able**. Capable of being exchanged.

exchequer, n. [1. ekschéker; 2. ikstʃékə], fr. O. Fr. *eschequier*, fr. Med. Lat. *scaccarium*, 'chess-board'. See **cheque, chequer, chess**; accounts were orig. made by counters arranged on a chequered board. **1.** The State administrative department controlling all matters connected with public revenue and finance; *Chancellor of the Exchequer*, the finance minister of the Cabinet, see also **treasury**; *Exchequer Bill*, an interest-bearing promissory note or bill issued by the Treasury under authority of Parliament for the payment of current expenditure of the State. **2. a** Treasury of a state; **b** (by extension) finances, funds, resources, of a person, group of persons, commercial firm &c. **3.** (legal hist.) An old judicial court, now merged in the King's Bench Division of the Supreme Court of Judicature.

excisable, adj. [1. eksízabl; 2. iksáizəbl]. **excise** (III.) & **-able**. Subject to excise, dutiable.

excise (I.), vb. trans. [1. eksíz; 2. iksáiz], fr. Lat. *excīs-(um)*, P.P. type of *excīdere*, 'to cut out, cut off; to lay waste, demolish', fr. **ex-** & *caedere*, 'to cut'. See **cement**. To cut out, remove, cut away.

excise (II.), n. [1. eksíz; 2. ɛksáiz]. Prob. fr. M. Du. *excijs*, fr. Low Lat. **accens-us*, fr. *accensāre*, 'to tax', fr. **ac-** & *census*, 'a register, census'. See **census**. **a** Duty, also *Excise duty*, payable to the revenue of a state, on articles manufactured within the country, also on licences; specif., duty paid on beer and spirits, licences for sale, manufacture &c.; **b** *the Excise*, branch of Inland Revenue dealing with the collection of excise.

excise (III.), vb. trans., fr. prec. To levy a tax on, put an excise duty on a home product.

exciseman, n. [1. eksízman; 2. iksáizmən]. **excise** (II.) & **man**. Government official who collects excise duties.

excision, n. [1. eksízhun; 2. ɛksížən]. **excise** (I.) & **-ion**. The act of excising or cutting out; removal of objects by cutting.

excitability, n. [1. eksítabíliti; 2. iksaitəbíliti]. See next word & **-ity**. The quality of being excitable.

excitable, adj. [1. eksítabl; 2. iksáitəbl]. **excite** & **-able**. Capable of being easily excited, susceptible to stimulation.

excitant, adj. & n. [1. eksítant; 2. ɛksáitənt]. **excite** & **-ant**. **1.** adj. Tending to excite. **2.** n. Substance having the property of stimulating the function of an organ, the nervous system &c.

excitation, n. [1. èksitáshun; 2. èksitéiʃən]. **excite** & **-ation**. The act or process of exciting; state of being excited.

excitative, adj. [1. eksítativ; 2. iksáitətiv]. **excite** & **-ative**. Tending to excite; of an exciting nature.

excitatory, adj. [1. eksítatori; 2. iksáitətəri]. **excite** & **-ory**. Excitative.

excite, vb. trans. [1. eksít; 2. iksáit], fr. Fr. *exciter*, fr. Lat. *excitāre*, 'to call out, bring out, wake, rouse up; to arouse, excite, stimulate', fr. **ex-** & *cit-(um)*, P.P. type of *ciēre*, 'to put in motion; to rouse up, summon; to call by name; to produce, effect'. See **cite**. To cause activity, stimulate, stir, disturb, arouse, provoke. In various applications: **1.** (as affecting human beings, mental processes, faculties &c.) **a** To cause excitement to, or in, rouse, call out of quiescence: *the patient must not be excited*; *excite affection, jealousy, hatred* &c.; **b** to cause, attract, awaken: *to excite attention, interest*; **c** to provoke, call into existence: *to excite rebellion, riot* &c. **2.** (of various physical processes) **a** *To excite a nerve*, to stimulate it, cause it to react, induce it to respond; **b** *to excite a dynamo*, energize it.

excited, adj. [1. eksíted; 2. iksáitid], fr. P.P. of prec. **a** (of persons) Strongly moved or disturbed emotionally; **b** (of feelings) wrought up, disturbed, agitated.

excitedly, adv. Prec. & **-ly**. In an excited manner.

excitement, n. [1. eksítment; 2. iksáitmənt]. **excite** & **-ment**. **1.** State of being mentally excited; agitation, disturbance; **a** pleasurable animation: *his good fortune caused great excitement in the family*; **b** unhealthy stimulation, exaltation, agitation, of mind: *the bad news threw her into a state of great excitement.* **2.** Something which causes excitement: *a life full of excitement*; *the excitements of town life.*

exciting, adj. [1. eksíting; 2. iksáitiŋ], fr. Pres. Part. of **excite**. Tending to cause excitement, arousing intense interest; agitating: *an exciting book, scene*; *exciting news.*

exclaim, vb. intrans. & trans. [1. eksklám; 2. ikskléim], fr. O. Fr. *exclaime*, pres. sing. stem of *exclamer*, fr. Lat. *exclāmāre*, 'to call out; to say aloud, exclaim'. **ex-** & **claim** (I.). **1.** intrans. To cry out suddenly, vehemently, esp. under stress of emotion or passion; utter a word or words on a sudden impulse. *Exclaim against*, speak, protest, vehemently against. **2.** trans. To utter (words) as an exclamation.

exclamation, n. [1. eksklamáshun; 2. ɛkskləméiʃən], fr. Lat. *exclāmātiōn-(em)*, 'a calling or crying out', fr. *exclāmāt-(um)*, P.P. type of *exclāmāre*, 'to cry out, exclaim', & **-ion**. See **exclaim**. **1.** Act of exclaiming. **2.** Sudden, emphatic, vehement, passionate utterance, whether of words, or of a mere cry, expressing emotion: *an exclamation of pain, sympathy* &c.; *note of exclamation*, mark of punctuation (!) put after a written or printed exclamation.

exclamatory, adj. [1. eksklámatori; 2. ɛksklǽmətəri]. See prec. & **-ory**. **a** (of persons) Given to frequent use of exclamations; **b** (of style, speech) characterized by, filled with, exclamations. *Exclamatory sentence*, one consisting of an exclamation; e.g. '*Would I had died for thee!*'

exclude, vb. trans. [1. eksklóod; 2. ɛksklúd], fr. Lat. *exclūd-(ere)*, 'to shut out; to remove, separate; to except, hinder, prevent', fr. **ex-** & **clūdere, claudere*, 'to shut up, close'. See **clause, close** (I.). **1.** To shut (a person) out, keep out from, refuse to admit to prevent from entering, **a** *from a place, house, room* &c.; **b** *from a post, position, rank, status, membership of a society* &c. **2.** (of action on non-material things) **a** To reject, refuse to admit, disallow, bar (evidence &c.); **b** to prevent, make impossible, forbid, cut out: *to exclude the possibility of.*

exclusion, n. [1. eksklóozhun; 2. ikskl úžən], fr. Lat. *exclūsiōn-(em)*, 'a shutting out, exclusion', fr. *exclūs-(um)*, P.P. type of *exclūdere*, 'to shut out', & **-ion**. See **exclude**. The act or process of excluding; state of being excluded. Phr. *to the exclusion of*, so as to exclude.

exclusive, adj. [1. ekskóosiv; 2. ikskl úsiv], fr. Lat. *exclūs-(um)* & **-ive**. See **exclude**. Tending to exclude; specif. **a** reserved for particular group or class, not accessible to others: *exclusive privileges*; **b** (i.) (of persons) keeping themselves remote from, unapproachable by, others who are judged to be inferior in birth, social standing, wealth, or talents: *somewhat exclusive in manner*; (ii.) (of societies) not to be easily entered: *the most exclusive circles*; *an exclusive club*; **c** tending to exclude other tastes, occupations, predilections: *exclusive hobbies, employment.*

exclusively, adv. Prec. & **-ly**. In an exclusive manner; by exclusion of all others; only, solely.

exclusiveness, n. See prec. & **-ness**. The quality of being exclusive.

exclusivism, n. [1. eksklóosivizm; 2. iksklúsivizəm]. **exclusive** & **-ism**. The quality of being exclusive.

excogitate, vb. trans. [1. ekskójitāt; 2. ɛkskɔ́džiteit], fr. Lat. *excōgitāt-(um)*, P.P. type of *excōgitāre*, 'to find out by thinking; to contrive, devise'. **ex-** & **cogitate**. To think out, invent, devise.

excogitation, n. [1. ekskòjitáshun; 2. ɛkskɔ̀džitéiʃən]. Prec. & **-ion**. The act of excogitating; something excogitated.

excogitative, adj. [1. ekskójitativ; 2. ɛkskɔ́džitətiv]. **excogitate** & **-ive**. Of the nature of, pertaining to, excogitation.

excommunicate (I.), vb. trans. [1. èkskomúnikāt; 2. èkskəmjúnikeit], fr. L. Lat. (eccles.) *excommūnicāt-(um)*, P.P. type of *excommūnicāre*, 'to excommunicate'. **ex-** & **communicate**. To place under a ban or anathema the effect of which is to deprive of right to participate in the sacraments, or in any privileges enjoyed as a member of the Christian Church.

excommunicate (II.), adj. [1. èkskomúnikat; 2. èkskəmjúnikət]. See prec. Excommunicated.

excommunication, n. [1. èkskomūnikáshun; 2. èkskəmjūnikéiʃən]. **excommunicate** (I.) & **-ion**. Act of excommunication; state of being excommunicated. *Major excommunication*, total deprivation of all privileges pertaining to a member of Christian Church, exclusion from all sacraments, and from social intercourse with other Christians; *Minor excommunication*, exclusion from participation in the sacraments.

excommunicative, adj. [1. èkskomúnikativ; 2. èkskəmjúnikətiv]. **excommunicate** & **-ive**. Pertaining to excommunication; pronouncing a decree of excommunication.

excoriate, vb. trans. [1. ekskóriāt; 2. ɛkskɔ́rieit]. Lat. *excoriāt-(um)*, P.P. type of *excoriāre*, 'to strip off'. **ex-** & *corium*, 'skin, hide, leather'. See **corium** & **cortex**. **a** To flay; **b** to graze, abrade, the skin.

excoriation, n. [1. ekskòriáshun; 2. ɛkskɔ̀riéiʃən]. Prec. & **-ion**. (i.) Act or process of excoriating; (ii.) state of being excoriated; (iii.) a graze, abrasion of the skin.

excorticate, vb. trans. [1. èkskórtikāt; 2. èkskɔ́tikeit], fr. Lat. *excorticāre*, fr. **ex-** & *cortic-*, 'rind, bark'. See **cortex** & **-ate**. To strip off the rind, bark, skin.

excortication, n. [1. èkskortikáshun; 2. èkskɔ̄tikéiʃən]. Prec. & **-ion**. Process or act of excorticating.

excrement, n. [1. ékskrement; 2. ékskrimənt]. Lat. *excrēmentum*, 'what is sifted out, refuse'; fr. **ex-** & *crē-*, as in *crē-tum*, 'sifted', P.P. of *cernere*, see **discern**, & **-ment**, base **krei-*, **kri-* &c. See **certain, critic, riddle.** Waste matter excreted by bowels; dung.

excremental, adj. [1. èkskreméntal; 2. èkskriméntəl]. Prec. & **-al.** Connected with, having nature of, excrement.

excrementitious, adj. [1. èkskrēmentíshus; 2. èkskrimentíʃəs]. **excrement & -ous.** Excremental.

excrescence, n. [1. ekskrésens; 2. ɛkskrésəns]. **excrescent & -ce.** **1.** Something growing out from something else; **a** natural, normal growth: *hair is an excrescence from the scalp*; **b** pathological growth: *a wen or excrescence on the head.* **2. a** A projection: *his nose formed a slight excrescence in a large face*; **b** (fig.) *the house seemed a mere unsightly excrescence in the landscape.* **3.** Outgrowth, secondary development or outcome: *this standing committee was an excrescence from the main body.*

excrescency, n. [1. ekskrésensi; 2. ɛkskrésənsi]. Prec. & **-cy.** Excrescence; specif. **a** an abnormal pathological growth; **b** an unsightly, redundant projection.

excrescent, adj. [1. ekskrésent; 2. ɛkskrésənt], fr. Lat. *excrescent-(em)*, Pres. Part. of *excrescere*, 'to grow out, rise up'. See **ex- & crescent.** Forming an excrescence, growing out; forming an abnormal addition. In unscientific and inaccurate phonetic terminology a sound which has developed from, and (only apparently) as an addition to another, is said to be *excrescent*, e.g. *d* in *gownd*, from *gown.* The expression is meaningless and quite misleading.

excreta, n. pl. [1. ekskrḗta; 2. ɛkskrítə]. Lat., neut. pl., fr. *excrēt-(us)*, P.P. of *excernere*, 'to sift, separate out'. See **excrement.** (physiol.) **a** Waste products eliminated from body; specif. **b** faecal matter, excrement.

excrete, vb. trans. [1. ekskrḗt; 2. ɛkskrít], fr. Lat. *excrēt-(um)*, P.P. type of *excernere*, 'to sift out' &c. See prec. (physiol.) To separate out, and eliminate by discharge, waste, deleterious products from bodily tissues, cp. *secrete.*

excretion, n. [1. ekskrḗshun; 2. ɛkskríʃən]. Prec. & **-ion.** **a** Process of excreting; **b** that which is excreted, waste product excreted, cp. *secretion.*

excretive, adj. [1. ekskrḗtiv; 2. ɛkskrítiv]. **excrete & -ive.** **a** Having function of excreting; **b** tending to encourage excretion.

excretory, adj. & n. [1. ekskrḗtori; 2. ɛkskrítəri]. **excrete & -ory.** **1.** adj. Serving to excrete: *an excretory organ.* **2.** n. Excretory organ.

excruciate, vb. trans. [1. ekskrṓōshiāt; 2. ɛkskrúʃieit], fr. Lat. *excruciāt-(um)*, P.P. type of *excruciāre*, 'to torture severely, distress'; fr. *cruc-(em)*, *crux*, 'cross'. See **crucify.** **a** To torture, cause bodily suffering to; **b** to distress, cause anguish of spirit to.

excruciating, adj. [1. ekskrṓōshiāting; 2. ɛkskrúʃieitiŋ]. Prec. & **-ing.** Causing severe bodily or mental pain; agonizing, torturing.

excruciatingly, adv. Prec. & **-ly.** In an excruciating, agonizing manner.

excruciation, n. [1. ekskrōōshiáshun; 2. ɛkskrùʃiéiʃən]. **excruciate & -ion.** **a** Act or process of excruciating; **b** result of such act or process; torture.

exculpate, vb. trans. [1. ékskulpāt; 2. ékskalpeit]. Lat., fr. **ex-** & *culpāt-(um)*, P.P. type of *culpāre*, 'to reproach, blame', fr. *culpa*, 'fault, blame'. See **culpable.** To free from blame, acquit of fault, hold and pronounce guiltless.

exculpation, n. [1. èkskulpáshun; 2. èkskalpéiʃən]. Prec. & **-ion.** Act of exculpating; state of being exculpated.

exculpatory, adj. [1. èkskulpátori; 2. èkskalpéitəri]. See prec. & **-ory.** Tending to, of a nature to, exculpate from imputed fault; tending to establish innocence.

excurrent, adj. [1. ekskúrent; 2. ɛkskárənt], fr. Lat. *excurrent-(em)*, Pres. Part. of *excurrere*, 'to flow, run, out'. See **ex- & current (I.)**; & cp. **excursus.** Running, flowing, out; specif. (bot.) radiating, ramifying from central axis or stem.

excurse, vb. intrans. [1. ekskérs; 2. ɛkskə́s]. Lat. See **excursus.** (rare) **a** To make an excursion; **b** (fig.) to wander from the point, digress.

excursion, n. [1. ekskérshun; 2. ɛkskə́ʃən]. Lat. *excursiōn-(em)*, 'running forth, sally, inroad'. See **excursus & -ion.** **1.** A going out, a journey; specif., a pleasure trip: *an excursion into the mountains, to the seaside.* **2.** (fig.) A deviation, a wandering from the point, a digression: *alarms and excursions.*

excursional, adj. [1. ekskérshunal; 2. ɛkskə́ʃənəl]. Prec. & **-al.** Connected with, of the nature of, an excursion.

excursionist, n. [1. ekskérshunist; 2. ɛkskə́ʃənist]. **excursion & -ist.** One making an excursion; specif., one out on a party of pleasure, esp. for a brief period; a tripper.

excursive, adj. [1. ekskérsiv; 2. ɛkskə́siv]. Lat. *excurs-*, as in **excursus**, & **-ive.** Given to digression; digressive; going far afield (lit. and fig.).

excursiveness, n. Prec. & **-ness.** Quality, habit, of being excursive, tendency to digression; long-windedness.

excursus, n. [1. ekskérsus; 2. ɛkskə́səs]. Lat., 'a running out', fr. *excurs-(um)*, P.P. type of *excurrere.* See **ex- & course.** A treatise, esp. a detailed essay on, or investigation of, some aspect of a subject dealt with more generally in a larger work, to which it is added as an appendix.

excusable, adj. [1. ekskúzabl; 2. ɛkskjúzəbl]. Next word & **-able.** Deserving to be excused; pardonable, justifiable: *an excusable error, oversight* &c.

excuse (I.), vb. trans. & intrans. [1. ekskúz; 2. ɛkskjúz]. M.E. *ex-*, *escūsen*, fr. O. Fr. *excuser*, fr. Lat. *excūsāre*, 'to release a person from a charge, free from blame; to apologize, plead excuse, for a fault committed'; fr. **ex-** & *causa*, 'charge' &c. See **cause (I.).** **A.** trans. **1. a** To attempt to exonerate (a person), allege extenuating circumstances for; to pardon, free (a person) from penalty for a fault: *I excuse him by assuming his conduct to be due to a lapse of memory*; *I will excuse you this time, next time you will be punished*; **b** release, absolve, exempt, from obligation: *to excuse a person from attendance at a meeting.* Phrs. (various polite formulas) *excuse me*, form for breaking into a speech or conversation with disagreement, protest &c., at what has been said; *if you'll kindly excuse me, I'm afraid I must go now.* **2. a** To find, allege, extenuating circumstances for (another's fault); to minimize (a fault); to pardon, overlook (a fault, injury &c.): *I find it hard to excuse his conduct*; *I can understand, but cannot excuse, his idleness, bad temper, unkindness* &c.; *pray excuse my interruption, apparent rudeness* &c.; **b** to cancel, remit (an obligation): *your attendance today is excused.* **3.** *To excuse oneself*, **a** to make excuses for, attempt to extenuate, allege justification for (one's conduct); **b** to apologize for omitting to do something, beg to be let off or excused: *to excuse oneself from being present, coming* &c. **B.** intrans. (rare) To practise forgiveness: *I can't forget, and I won't excuse.*

excuse (II.), n. [1. ekskús; 2. ɛkskjús], fr. prec. **a** Plea in justification; explanation given in defence of conduct; apology: *to make a poor excuse*; *to stammer out an excuse*; *please make my best excuses to Mrs. Jones*; **b** reason, ground alleged in extenuation of, motive assigned for, conduct; pretext: *my excuse must be that I did not know*; *have you no better excuse to give?*

exeat, n. [1. ékziat; 2. ékziæt]. Lat., 3rd pers. pres. subj. of *exīre*, 'to go out, away', 'let him go, he may go'. See **ex- (I.)** & **itinerant.** Short holiday of a few days granted to boys at public schools during term-time.

execrable, adj. [1. éksekrabl; 2. éksikrəbl]. Fr., fr. Lat. *execrābilis*, *execrā-*, as in **execrate**, & **-able.** Worthy of execration; detestable, abominable.

execrableness, n. Prec. & **-ness.** Quality of being execrable.

execrably, adv. See prec. & **-ly.** **a** In an execrable, detestable manner; **b** (colloq.) very badly: *she sang execrably.*

execrate, vb. trans. & intrans. [1. éksekrāt; 2. éksikreit], fr. Lat. *exsecrāt-(um)*, or *execrāt-(um)*, fr. *exsecrāri*, 'to curse', fr. **ex-** & *sacrāre*, 'to consecrate, set apart as holy', see **sacred**; *exsecrāri* was to reverse this process. **1.** trans. To regard, and denounce, as abominable, detestable; to detest, loathe. **2.** intrans. To utter imprecations, to curse and swear.

execration, n. [1. èksekráshun; 2. èksikréiʃən]. Prec. & **-ion.** **a** Act of execrating; **b** an imprecation, curse; **c** (rare) that which is execrated, cause of execration.

execrative, adj. [1. éksekrātiv; 2. éksikreitiv]. **execrate & -ive.** Of the nature of an execration.

execratory, adj. [1. éksekrātori; 2. éksikreitəri]. **execrate & -ory.** Execrative.

executant, n. [1. ekzékūtant; 2. ɛkzékjutənt]. **execute & -ant.** One who executes, carries out, performs; specif., one who performs on a musical instrument.

execute, vb. trans. [1. éksekūt; 2. éksikjūt], fr. Lat. *exsecūt-(um)*, P.P. type of *exsequi*, 'to follow to the end, pursue, carry out', fr. **ex-** & *sequi*, 'to follow'. See **sequela.** **1. a** To perform, carry out, bring to completion: *to execute a piece of work, a task &c., a purpose*; **b** (law) to complete a legal instrument, fulfil all conditions necessary to its validity: *to execute a deed, will* &c. **2.** To perform an action in conformity with, in obedience to, instructions: *to execute a person's orders, commands* &c. **3. a** To carry out, give concrete shape to (plans, designs), in production of artistic work, or works of craftsmanship: *this picture, statue, cabinet &c. was admirably designed, but the work is poorly executed*; **b** specif. (mus. and drama) to perform by singing, playing, acting: *the song, part in a play &c., was admirably executed.* **4.** To carry out a death sentence upon, deprive of life in accordance with a judicial sentence: *to execute a murderer.*

execution, n. [1. èksekúshun; 2. èksikjúʃən]. Lat. *exsecūtiōn-(em)*, 'performance'. See prec. & **-ion.** Act of executing (in any sense). Specif. **1. a** the carrying out, accomplishment, completion, of a piece of work, a task, scheme &c.; **b** completion of a legal instrument; **c** production of something from a design: *engaged in the execution of a statue, picture* &c. **2. a** Way in which a piece of work is carried out: *the execution leaves much to be desired, though the idea is good*; **b** specif., degree of skill, dexterity in performing a musical composition, vocally or instrumentally: *a great deal of execution*; *marvellous execution.* **3.** Fruitful result of work; effective action, esp. in Phr. *to do great execution*; often used with implication of destructive action: *the guns did great execution*; *he did great execution among the sandwiches*, eat a good number. **4.** Carrying out of death penalty upon a person; act of killing a person in obedience to legal sentence.

execution dock, n. Place in the London Docks where sailors, guilty of piracy or other capital offences, were hanged.

executioner, n. [1. èksekúshuner; 2. èksikjúʃənə]. **execution & -er.** Official who carries out judicial executions; a hangman.

executive, adj. & n. [1. ekzékūtiv; 2. ɛkzékjutiv]. **execute & -ive.** **1.** adj. Concerned with, having the authority, power, and capacity for, executing, carrying out certain duties and functions; specif., having function of carrying on the duties of the government and the management of states or other directing bodies: *an executive officer, duties; the executive branch of the legislature* &c. 2. n. Executive body in, branch of, a government.

executor, n. [1. ekzékūtor; 2. ɛkzékjutə, -jətə]. Lat. *ex(s)ecutor*, 'performer'. **execute** & **-or.** Person appointed by another to enforce, and carry out, the provisions of his will.

executorial, adj. [1. ekzèkūtórial; 2. ɛkzèkjutórial]. Prec. & **-ial.** Pertaining to an executor.

executorship, n. [1. ekzékūtorship; 2. ɛkzékjutəʃip]. **executor** & **-ship.** Office and duties of an executor.

executrix, n. [1. ekzékūtriks; 2. ɛkzékjutriks]. **executor** & **-ix.** Woman executor.

exegesis, n. [1. èksejḗsis; 2. èksidzísis]. Gk. *exḗgēsis*, 'statement, narrative; explanation', fr. *exēgéomai*, 'I lead, show the way; explain'; **ex-** (II.) & *hēgéomai*, 'I lead, guide, direct'. See **hegemony.** Explanation; specif., interpretation of the Holy Scriptures.

exegetic(al), adj. [1. èksejétik(l); 2. èksidžétik(l)]. Prec. & **-ic** & **-al.** Connected with, of the nature of, an interpretation; explanatory, expository.

exegetically, adv. Prec. & **-ly.** By way of, in the manner of, an exposition or interpretation.

exegetics, n. pl. [1. èksejétiks; 2. èksidžétiks], See **exegetic(al).** Science of Biblical or other criticism and interpretation.

exemplar, n. [1. egzémplar; 2. igzémplə]. Lat., 'pattern, model', fr. *exempl-*, as in *exemplum*, & **-ar.** See **example.** One who, that which, serves as a model and example, esp. in spiritual sense.

exemplary, adj. [1. egzémplari; 2. igzémpləri]. Prec. & **-y.** Serving as a model, deserving to be followed; hence, worthy, commendable.

exemplification, n. [1. egzèmplifikā́shun; 2. igzèmplifikéiʃən]. See **exemplify** & **-fic** & **-ation.** a Act or process of illustrating by example; b something which illustrates, exemplifies.

exemplify, vb. trans. [1. egzémplifī; 2. igzémplifai]. Lat. *exemplum*, see **example**, & **-fy.** 1. To serve as, furnish, an example; to illustrate by example. 2. To make an official copy of a document.

exempt (I.), vb. trans. [1. egzémpt; 2. igzémpt]. Lat. *exempt-(um)*, P.P. type of *eximere*, fr. **ex-** & *emere*, 'to take, receive, buy'; cp. Scrt. *yámati*, 'holds, keeps together'. Further connexions very doubtful. To release, excuse a person, from a duty or obligation: *to exempt a man from military service.*

exempt (II.), adj. Same as prec. Free, excused, released, quit of.

exemption, n. [1. egzémpshun; 2. igzémpʃən]. Lat. *exemptiōn-(em)*. See **exempt** & **-ion.** Act of exempting; state of being exempted, immunity: *exemption from taxation.*

exenterate, vb. trans. [1. eksénterāt; 2. ekséntəreit]. Lat. *exenterāt-(um)*, P.P. of *exenterāre*, 'to disembowel'; Gk. loan-word, **ex-** (II.) & *énteron*, 'intestine'. See **enteric.** (rare) To disembowel.

exequatur, n. [1. èksekwā́tur; 2. èksekwéitə]. Lat., 'he may perform (his duties)', 3rd pers. pres. subj. of *exsequi.* See **execute.** Official document of recognition issued to a consul in a foreign country by the government of the country to which he is accredited.

exequy, n. Usually in pl. **exequies** [1. éksikwi(z); 2. éksikwi(z)]. Lat. *exequiae*, or *exsequiae*, 'funeral procession', fr. *exsequi*, 'to follow out' &c. See **execute.** Funeral rites, ceremonies; funeral procession.

exercisable, adj. [1. éksersīzabl; 2. éksəsaizəbl]. **exercise** (II.) & **-able.** Capable of being exercised, esp. in sense 1, below.

exercise (I.), n. [1. éksersīz; 2. éksəsaiz]. Fr., fr. Lat. *exercitium*, fr. *exercit-(um)*, P.P. type of *exercēre*, 'to drill, train; to practise, follow an employment' &c. See **exercise** (II.). 1. a Series of bodily movements involving natural activity in use of body and limbs; healthy activity of body: *to take exercise; suffering from lack of exercise; riding, walking, digging, rowing are all healthy forms of exercise;* Phr. *carriage exercise*, driving out in a carriage; b any regular series of bodily movements designed to strengthen, develop, or train some particular muscle or organ, to render it supple, or to make some special use of it easy and habitual: *a gymnastic exercise; dumb-bell exercises; vocal exercises;* c series of repeated movements designed to give facility, dexterity, skill in handling and using some particular instrument: *five-finger exercises (for the piano); exercises on the harp, flute* &c.; d collection of written instructions, describing, illustrating, setting forth exercises designed for developing some particular function or form of dexterity: *book of exercises for the piano* &c. 2. Series of concerted movements executed by bodies of troops, or groups of ships. 3. a Mental exertion or series of exertions which train, discipline, develop, the mental faculties; any effort or activity of mind which does this: *exercises in logic, mathematics* &c.; *an exercise in clear thinking, of the memory;* b systematic practice in, attention to, attempt to solve, a set of problems in order to gain, increase, or test proficiency in some particular branch of knowledge: *exercise in French grammar; a Latin exercise;* c collection of written examples, passages for translation &c., designed to form basis for such practice. 4. (of mental faculties or qualities) The use, employment, calling into activity, or being: *the exercise of imagination, of will-power, patience* &c. 5. Religious practice and observance. 6. Series of acts, duties, obligations, esp. attendance at courses of instruction and passing of examinations or presentation of a thesis, imposed by a university as qualifications for attainment of a particular university status: *to perform the exercises required for the degree of D.D.* &c.

exercise (II.), vb. trans. & intrans., fr. prec. Cp. Lat. *exercēre*, 'to train, drill; to practise, employ oneself in', fr. **ex-** & *arcēre*, 'to enclose, hold; to keep in order' &c., fr. *arca*, 'a box, chest' &c. See **arcanum** & **ark.** A. trans. 1. To employ, make use of, exert; a (of bodily functions) *to exercise one's strength, sight;* b (of mental and spiritual faculties) *to exercise patience, judgement, prudence, intelligence* &c.; c to make use of powers, privileges &c.: *to exercise one's rights as a rate-payer* &c. 2. (of physical activities) a To move actively, cause to take exercise: *to exercise one's arms and legs; to exercise a horse, dog* &c.; b to execute, or cause to execute, movements; train, for purpose of gaining, or imparting, skill in, or familiarity with, some particular form of activity; to practise: *to exercise boys in swimming; to exercise oneself in fencing.* 3. To occupy the mind or mental faculties painfully; to tax, concern, perplex, afflict: *I am greatly exercised (in (my) mind) by his strange behaviour; I'm exercised about his future* &c. B. intrans. To give, take, exercise, engage in bodily activity: *my horse is out exercising for the race.*

exerciser, n. [1. éksersīzer; 2. éksəsaizə]. Prec. & **-er.** Mechanical device, apparatus, for taking certain forms of exercise.

exercitation, n. [1. ekzèrsitā́shun; 2. ɛkzàsitéiʃən]. Lat. *exercitātiōn-(em)*, 'exercise, practice', fr. *exercitāt-(um)*, P.P. type of *exercitāre*, freq. of *exercēre*, q.v. under **exercise** (II.), & **-ion.** Exercise, practice.

exergue, n. [1. ekzḗrg; 2. ɛkzə́g], fr. Gk. **ex-** & *érgon*, 'work'. See **ergon.** a Space between the bottom of the design on a medal or coin and the rim, often containing a date, designer's initials &c.; b that which is engraved in this space.

exert, vb. trans. [1. egzḗrt; 2. igzə́t]. Lat. *ex(s)ert-(um)*, P.P. type of *ex(s)erere*, 'put out, put forth, thrust out', fr. **ex-** & *serere*, 'to put in a row, connect, join, entwine' &c. See **series.** 1. To put forth, use, bring to bear, any mental or physical faculty: *to exert intelligence, influence, pressure, strength* &c. 2. (reflex.) *To exert oneself*, to make an effort, endeavour to accomplish something: *he doesn't exert himself much*, is slack; *to exert oneself in a matter.*

exertion, n. [1. egzḗrshun; 2. igzə́ʃən]. Prec. & **-ion.** 1. Act or process of exerting: *a wonderful exertion of will-power.* 2. Effort, output of force, esp. one which involves mental or physical strain: *mountain climbing entails serious exertion; it was no exertion to him to speak for three hours on end.*

exeunt, vb. intrans. [1. ékseunt; 2. éksiənt]. Lat., 3rd pers. pl. pres. indic. of *exīre*, 'to go out'. See **exeat.** (stage direction to actors) They go out, or off (the stage).

exfoliate, vb. intrans. & trans. [1. eksfṓliāt; 2. ɛksfóulieit]. Lat. *exfoliāt-(um)*, P.P. type of *exfoliāre*, 'to strip off leaves'; **ex-** (I.) & *folium*, 'a leaf'. See **folio.** 1. intrans. (of bodily tissues) To flake off, come off in strips or scales. 2. trans. (rare) To strip off.

exfoliation, n. [1. èksfōliā́shun; 2. èksfouliéiʃən]. Prec. & **-ion.** Process of exfoliating; state of being exfoliated.

exhalation, n. [1. èksalā́shun; 2. èksəléiʃən]. Lat. *exhālātiōn-(em)*, 'vapour'. **exhale** & **-ation.** 1. Act, process, of exhaling; breathing out, expiration; evaporation. 2. That which is exhaled; mist, vapour, fume, emanation, effluvium.

exhale, vb. trans. & intrans. [1. ekzā́l; 2. ɛkzéil]. Lat. *exhālāre*, 'to breathe out', fr. **ex-** & *hālāre*, 'to breathe, breathe out'; the *h-* is not orig., & the word is fr. *ālium*, *(allium)*, 'garlic', wh. stands for **an-slo-*, **an-* meaning 'breath' &c. See **alliaceous, animus, animate.** A. trans. 1. To breathe out, expel (air) from the lungs. 2. To give off vapour, emanation, effluvium. B. intrans. To evaporate, pass off, away, in vapour; to vanish away.

exhaust (I.), vb. trans. & intrans. [1. egzáwst; 2. igzɔ́st]. Lat. *exhaust-(um)*, P.P. type of *exhaurīre*, 'to draw out, empty', fr. **ex-** & *haurīre*, 'to draw out (water); to breathe, drink in'. This word is fr. base **(h)auz-*; cp. Gk. *aúō*, fr. **auzō*, 'I dry, wither'; perh. also cogn. w. Scrt. *ghásati*, 'injures', for wh. see **host** (I.); cp. also O.N. *ausa*, 'to draw off water &c.'. A. trans. 1. To drain off, use up, consume: *to exhaust the water in a vessel.* 2. (of non-material things) a To use up, consume &c.: *to exhaust one's health, strength, forbearance, patience;* b to treat fully, leave no part undealt with: *to exhaust a subject.* B. intrans. To empty, discharge: *the cistern exhausts into the drain.*

exhaust (II.), n. See prec. Contrivance in machines for discharging waste or superfluous steam, gas, water &c.; (also **attrib.**) *exhaust pipe, valve, steam* &c.

exhausted, adj. [1. egzáwsted; 2. igzɔ́stid]. **exhaust** (I.) & **-ed.** a Emptied, used up, consumed: *our provisions are exhausted;* b (of persons and animals) tired, fatigued, wearied, to excess; worn out: *to feel quite exhausted;* c (of non-material things) *my patience, power of endurance &c., is exhausted.*

exhaustedly, adv. Prec. & **-ly.** As though tired out.

exhaustedness, n. See prec. & **-ness.** State of being exhausted, tired out.

exhaustibility, n. [1. egzàwstibíliti; 2. igzɔ̀stibíliti]. Next word & **-ity.** Capacity for being exhausted.

exhaustible, adj. [1. egzáwstibl; 2. igzɔ́stibl]. **exhaust** (I.) & **-ible.** Capable of being exhausted.

exhaustibleness, n. See prec. & **-ness.** Property of being exhaustible.

exhausting, adj. [1. egzáwsting; 2. igzɔ́stiŋ], fr. Pres. Part. of **exhaust** (I.). Tending to exhaust; tiring, fatiguing.

exhaustingly, adv. Prec. & **-ly.** In an exhausting manner, so as to exhaust.

exhaustion, n. [1. egzáwschun; 2. igzɔ́stʃən]. **exhaust** (I.) & **-ion.** 1. Act or process of exhausting. 2. State of being exhausted;

specif. **a** complete consumption: *exhaustion of wealth, supplies, resources* &c.; **b** (of bodily or mental powers and faculties) intense fatigue, great weariness, draining away of vigour &c.: *exhaustion of brain; a state of exhaustion.*

exhaustive, adj. [1. egzáwstiv; 2. igzɔ́stiv]. **exhaust** (I.) & **-ive**. Having property of exhausting; specif. (of mental activity and its results) thoroughgoing, leaving nothing more to be done: *an exhaustive inquiry, investigation, treatment of a subject* &c.

exhaustively, adv. Prec. & **-ly**. In an exhaustive manner.

exhaustiveness, n. See prec. & **-ness**. Quality of being exhaustive.

exhibit (I.), vb. trans. & intrans. [1. egzíbit; 2. igzíbit]. Lat., fr. *exhibit-(um)*, P.P. type of *exhibēre*, 'to hold out, present; to display; to show oneself in a certain light, or character', fr. **ex-** & *habēre*, 'to have, hold, possess'. See **habit** (I.). **A.** trans. **1.** To show, display, set out, expose, for public inspection (pictures and other works of art, museum specimens, live-stock, articles for sale &c.). **2.** To make manifest, give evidence of, **a** (of physical process): *the building exhibited signs of dilapidation; the body exhibited traces of decay;* **b** (of action respecting mental and moral qualities) to show signs of possessing, reveal, make use of: *to exhibit courage, patience, acuteness of mind* &c. **B.** intrans. To show, offer objects &c. for public inspection: *he exhibits in all the galleries, in most of the agricultural shows* &c.

exhibit (II.), n., fr. prec. **a** Something exhibited at a show, gallery, museum &c.; **b** an object, document, put in as part of the evidence in a law case.

exhibition, n. [1. èksibíshun; 2. èksibíʃən]. **exhibit** (I.) & **-ion**. **1.** Act of exhibiting: *to have an opportunity for the exhibition of one's best qualities.* **2. a** Collection of goods exposed and offered for sale, of pictures, curiosities &c. exposed for inspection, of animals, plants &c. shown in competition for prizes &c.; **b** some thing or quality shown or manifested, which is absurd, grotesque, objectionable, contemptible: *to make an (a regular) exhibition of oneself.* **3.** Annual grant made to meritorious student by a school or college, in aid of his support.

exhibitioner, n. [1. èksibíshuner; 2. èksibíʃənə]. Prec. & **-er**. One holding an exhibition at a school or college.

exhibitor, n. [1. ekzíbitor; 2. ɛkzíbitə]. **exhibit** (I.) & **-or**. One who exhibits; esp. one exhibiting at an exhibition of pictures &c., or at show of live-stock &c.

exhilarant, adj. [1. egzílarant; 2. igzílərənt]. Lat. *exhilarant-(em)*, Pres. Part. of *exhilarāre*, 'to gladden, make merry'. See next word. Tending to cause mirth; exhilarating.

exhilarate, vb. trans. [1. egzílerāt; 2. igzíləreit]. Lat., fr. *exhilarāt-(um)*, P.P. type of *exhilarāre*, 'to gladden, cause to be merry &c.'. **ex-** & **hilarity, hilarious**. To cheer, raise spirits of, enliven, cause to become merry and cheerful.

exhilarated, adj. [1. egzílerāted; 2. igzíləreitid]. Prec. & **-ed**. Lively, cheerful; slightly intoxicated.

exhilarating, adj. [1. egzílerāting; 2. igzíləreitiŋ], fr. Pres. Part. of **exhilarate**. Tending to exhilarate, cheering.

exhilaratingly, adv. Prec. & **-ly**. In an exhilarating manner.

exhilaration, n. [1. egzìleráshun; 2. igzìləréiʃən]. **exhilarate** & **-ion**. Process of enlivening, exhilarating; state of being exhilarated.

exhilarative, adj. [1. egzílerativ; 2. igzílərətiv]. **exhilarate** & **-ive**. Having property of causing exhilaration.

exhort, vb. trans. & intrans. [1. egzórt; 2. igzɔ́t]. Fr. *exhorter*, fr. Lat. *exhortāre*, 'to incite, encourage'. See **ex-** & **hortative**. **1.** trans. To entreat, beg earnestly; encourage to do; to warn, admonish. **2.** intrans. To practise exhortation.

exhortation, n. [1. èksortáshun; 2. èksɔ̄téiʃən]. Lat. *exhortātiōn-(em)*. See prec. & **-ation**. **a** Act of exhorting; **b** earnest entreaty; admonition, warning.

exhortative, adj. [1. egzórtativ; 2. igzɔ́tətiv]. **ex-** & **hortative**. Of the nature of an exhortation.

exhortatory, adj. [1. egzórtatori; 2. igzɔ́tətəri]. **ex-** & **hortatory**. Exhortative.

exhumation, n. [1. èksūmáshun; 2. èksjuméiʃən]. Low Lat., 'unearthing'. **exhume** & **-ation**. Process of exhuming; act of digging up what has been put into the earth.

exhume, vb. trans. [1. ekzúm; 2. ikzjúm]. Fr. *exhumer*, fr. Low Lat. *exhumāre*, fr. **ex-** & *humus*, 'ground, soil'. See **humus**. To dig up, unearth; esp. to dig up a body that has been buried.

exigeant, adj. [1. éksijent; 2. éksidžənt]; also [1. ekzézhon; 2. ɛkzížã]. Fr., fr. Pres. Part. of *exiger*, fr. Lat. *exigere*, 'to drive out; search out', fr. **ex-** & *agere*, see **agent**. (of persons) Exacting, making great and severe demands. See **exigent**.

exigence, -cy, n. [1. éksijens(i); 2. éksidžəns(i)]. Lat. *exigent-(em)*, Pres. Part. of *exigere*. See prec. State of being exigent; state of urgency demanding instant attention and action.

exigent, adj. [1. éksijent; 2. éksidžənt]. Lat. *exigent-*. See prec. (of conditions and circumstances) Requiring immediate action, pressing, critical, urgent.

exigible, adj. [1. éksijibl; 2. éksidžibl]. Lat. *exig-(ere)*, see prec., & **-ible**. Capable of being exacted or demanded.

exiguity, n. [1. èksigúiti; 2. èksigjúiti]. Fr. *exiguïté*, fr. Lat. *exiguitāt-em*, 'scantiness, smallness'. See **exiguous** & **-ity**. State of being exiguous; smallness, scantiness.

exiguous, adj. [1. ekzígūus; 2. ɛkzígjuəs]. Lat. *exigu-(us)*, 'scanty, small, petty', fr. *exigere*, 'to weigh'. See **exigent** & **-ous**. Small, trifling, scanty, esp. in amount.

exiguousness, n. Prec. & **-ness**. Condition of being exiguous; scanty.

exile (I.), n. [1. éksīl; 2. éksail]. M.E., fr. Fr. *exil*, fr. Lat. *exilium, exsilium*, 'banishment'; cp. *exsul*, 'banished person'; first element **ex-**. The origin of second element is doubtful. In *exsul*, *-sul* is prob. fr. *solum*, 'soil', see **soil**; but the form *-silium* seems to suggest a connexion either orig. or by association of ideas, w. *ex(s)ilīre*, 'to spring forth', in wh. the second element is fr. *salīre*, 'to leap'. See **salient**. **a** Banishment from one's own country: *to go into exile;* **b** place of banishment.

exile (II.), n. Lat. *exsul*. See prec. Person banished, driven away, from his own country.

exile (III.), vb. trans. [1. éksīl, egzíl; 2. éksail, ɛgzáil]. See **exile** (I.). To make an exile of; to banish, keep (a person) out of his own country; esp. as a punishment.

exilian, exilic, adj. [1. egzílian, egzílik; 2. ɛgzáiliən, ɛgzáilik]. **exile** & **-an**, or **-ic**. Relating to the exile of the Jews in Babylon.

exility, n. [1. ekzíliti; 2. ɛkzíliti]. Lat. *exīlitāt-(em)*, 'meagreness, thinness', fr. *exīlis*, 'small, meagre, feeble'. Origin doubtful; perh. fr. **exagilis* & connected w. *exiguus*. See **exiguous**. Slenderness, meagreness.

exist, vb. intrans. [1. egzíst; 2. igzíst]. Fr. *exister*, fr. Lat. *ex(s)istere*, 'to stand forth, emerge, appear', fr. **ex-** & *sistere*, 'to set, place' &c., freq. of *stāre*, 'to stand'. See **state** (I.) & **stand** (I.). **1.** To have actual being, in the material universe, as spirit, or in the human mind: *God exists; good and evil exist; such things do not exist.* **2.** To be, occur, under specified conditions, or in certain places: *lime exists in many soils; certain revolutionary tendencies often exist in youthful minds.* **3.** To live, have vital functions: *men cannot exist without food and warmth.*

existence, n. [1. egzístens; 2. igzístəns]. Fr. See prec. & **-ence**. Fact or act of existing; being; life.

existential, adj. [1. èksisténshal; 2. èksisténʃəl]. Prec. & **-ial**. Involving, connected with, existence.

existing, adj. [1. egzísting; 2. igzístiŋ], fr. Pres. Part. of **exist**. Having existence, in existence: *existing forms of life.*

exit (I.), vb. [1. éksit; 2. éksit]. Lat., 3rd pers. sing. pres. indic. of *exīre*, 'to go out, away'. **ex-** & *īre*, 'to go'. See **itinerant**. (stage direction) He goes out, or off.

exit (II.), n. Lat. *exitium*, 'a going out; a way out', fr. *exit-(um)*, P.P. type of *exīre*. See prec. **1.** Mode of egress, way out. **2.** A going out, departure: *to make one's exit.*

ex-libris, n. [1. èks líbris; 2. èks láibris]. Lat., 'from the books of'. See **ex-** (I.) & **library**. A book-plate, consisting of the owner's name, and some device, armorial bearings &c., stamped on a sheet of paper which is pasted inside the cover of a book.

exo-, pref. Gk. *éxō*, 'outside'. See **ex-** (II.).

exoderm(is), n. [1. éksodërm, èksodérmis; 2. éksoudʌ̄m, èksoudʌ́mis]. Prec. & **-derm**. (bot.) External layer in roots.

exodus, n. [1. éksodus; 2. éksədəs]. Gk., fr. **ex-**, 'out', & *hodós*, 'way, road, journey', cogn. w. O. Slav. *choditi*, 'to go'; also w. Lat. *sed-*, 'sit', see **sedentary**, & *cēdere*, 'go', see **cede** & **hodometer**. Orig. sense of **sed-* is 'to place, place the foot down'. **1. a** An outward march, going out, flocking out: *an exodus takes place from London in summer;* **b** specif., the departure of the Israelites from Egypt. **2.** (cap.) The second book of the Old Testament, which records the going out from Egypt.

ex officio, adv. & adj. [1. èks ofísiō; 2. èks ɔfísiou]. Lat., 'by virtue of office'. **a** adv. *To be present at a committee ex officio;* **b** adj., *ex officio member.*

exogamic, exogamous, adj. [1. èksōgámik, ekzógamus; 2. èksougǽmik, ɛkzɔ́gəməs]. **exogamy** & **-ic** & **-ous**. Exhibiting, connected with, exogamy.

exogamy, n. [1. ekzógami; 2. ɛkzɔ́gəmi]. Gk. **exo-** & *gámos*, 'marriage'. See **gamo-**. Custom prevailing among some primitive peoples of marrying only outside the tribe, opposite of *endogamy.*

exogen, n. [1. éksojen; 2. éksədžən]. **exo-** & **-gen**. (bot.) A seed plant which grows by additional layers or rings on the outside; contrasted with *endogen.*

exon, n. [1. ékson; 2. éksɔn], fr. Fr. *exempt*. One of four officers commanding the Yeomen of the Guard, one of whom is always in attendance at Royal functions, state processions &c.

exonerate, vb. trans. [1. ekzónerāt; 2. ɛkzɔ́nəreit]. Lat. *exonerāt-(um)*, P.P. type of *exonerāre*, 'to free from a burden'; **ex-** & *onerāre*, 'to load', fr. *oner-*, stem of *onus*, 'load, burden'. See **onerous**. To clear from imputation of guilt, to free from a charge, free from blame.

exoneration, n. [1. ekzòneráshun; 2. ɛkzɔ̀nəréiʃən]. Prec. & **-ion**. Act of exonerating.

exonerative, adj. [1. ekzónerativ; 2. ɛkzɔ́nərətiv]. **exonerate** & **-ive**. Tending to exonerate.

exophthalmia, n. [1. èksofthálmia; 2. èksɔfþǽlmiə]. Gk. **ex-**, 'out', & *ophthalmós*, 'eye'. See **ophthalmia**. Abnormal protrusion of the eye-balls, due to disease.

exophthalmic, adj. [1. èksofthálmik; 2. èksɔfþǽlmik]. Prec. & **-ic**. Connected with, of the nature of, exophthalmia, esp. *exophthalmic goitre*, Graves' disease, q.v.

exophthalmos, -us, n. [1. èksofthálmus; 2. èksɔfþǽlmɔs, -əs]. Gk. See **exophthalmia**. Exophthalmia.

exorbitance, -cy, n. [1. ekzórbitans(i); 2. ɛkzɔ́bitəns(i)]. Next word & **-cy**. Excess, extravagance, esp. in claims, demands &c. The sense of moral extravagance, abnormality &c. is now obsolete.

exorbitant, adj. [1. ekzórbitant; 2. ɛkzɔ́bitənt]. Lat. *exorbitant-(em)*, Pres. Part. of *exorbitāre*, 'to go out of the track, deviate', fr. **ex-** & *orbita*, 'wheel-track, rut'. See **orbit**. **1.** (formerly, of conduct, ideas &c.) Passing ordinary bounds, eccentric, extravagant, immoderate &c. (obs.). **2.** (now chiefly of desires, claims, demands) Immoderate, extravagant.

exorbitantly, adv. Prec. & **-ly**. In an extravagant, exorbitant manner.

exorcism, n. [1. éksorsizm; 2. éksōsizəm]. See next word & **-ism**. **a** Act or process of exorcizing; **b** spell, ritual, used for this purpose.

exorcist, n. [1. éksorsist; 2. éksōsist]. Next word & **-ist**. One who exorcizes.

exorcize, -ise, vb. trans. [1. éksorsīz; 2. éksōsaiz]. Fr. *exorciser*, fr. Gk. *exorkizein*, 'to bind by an oath; to banish an evil spirit', fr. **ex-** (**II.**) & *horkizein*, 'to make to swear', fr. *hórkos*, 'an oath', for **sorkos*; cogn. w. Gk. *hérkos*, 'hedge, enclosure, fence', for **serk-*. The orig. sense is 'something woven, plaited, a hurdle', cp. Lat. *sarcina*, 'bundle, package', & *sarcīre*, 'to patch, restore, mend', cp. also Lat. *sartor* for **sarc-tor*, 'tailor'. See further under **sartorial**. **1. a** To drive out an evil spirit by performance of magic rites, utterance of charms &c.; to expel evil spirit, or quiet a troubled spirit by religious ceremonies, esp. by utterance of the Holy Name; **b** to lay a ghost. **2.** To summon, conjure up, a spirit.

exordial, adj. [1. egzórdial; 2. egzṓdiəl], fr. Lat. *exord-*. See next word & **-ial**. Connected with, having character of, an exordium.

exordium, n. [1. egzórdium; 2. egzṓdiəm]. Lat., 'beginning of a web, warp; beginning, generally, esp. of a speech', fr. *exordior*, 'begin a web, lay the warp; begin, esp. a speech'. **ex-** & *ordior*, 'lay a warp, begin'; same base as *orior*, 'rise, become visible, appear'. See **orient, origin, order**. Beginning, introductory part of a speech, sermon &c.

exoskeleton, n. [1. éksōskèleton; 2. éksouskèlitən]. **exo-** & **skeleton**. (zool.) **a** The bony external skeleton or covering of invertebrate animals, as shell of crustacea &c.; **b** the horny plates, nails, hoofs &c. of vertebrates.

exosmosis, n. [1. èksozmṓsis; 2. èksozmóusis]. **ex-** & **osmosis**. The outward slow flow, or osmosis, of a denser liquid or gas into a less dense liquid through a membrane, contrasted with *endosmosis*.

exoteric, adj. [1. èksotérik; 2. èksətérik]. Fr. *exotérique*, fr. Lat., fr. Gk. *exōterikós*, 'external'. **exo-**, w. comp. suff. Cp. **inter-**. (of religious or philosophical doctrine) External, capable of being understood by, suitable for, the public. Contrasted with *esoteric*.

exoterical, adj. [1. èksotérikl; 2. èksətérikl]. Prec. & **-al**. Exoteric.

exoterically, adv. Prec. & **-ly**. In an exoteric manner.

exotic, adj. [1. egzótik; 2. igzótik]. Fr. *exotique*, Lat. *exōticus*, fr. Gk. *exōtikós*, 'foreign, alien'; Eccles. Gk., 'heathen'. **exo-**, 'outside'. Not native; imported from abroad, foreign: *exotic fruits and flowers*; *an exotic cast of features*.

exotical, adj. [1. egzótikl; 2. igzótikl]. Prec. & **-al**. Exotic.

exotically, adv. Prec. & **-ly**. In a strange manner, like a foreigner.

exoticness, n. [1. egzótiknes; 2. igzótiknis]. See prec. & **-ness**. Quality of being exotic.

expand, vb. trans. & intrans. [1. ekspánd; 2. ikspǽnd]. Lat. *expandere*, 'to spread out, unfold', fr. **ex-** & *pandere*, 'spread out, extend' &c.; prob. fr. form of base in *patēre*, 'to lie open'. See **patent**. **A.** trans. **1.** To spread out, unfold and stretch out: *to expand the wings*; *a plant expands its leaves, a flower its petals* &c. **2.** To stretch, cause to occupy more space by distension; to cause to puff, swell, out: *to expand the chest*. **3. a** To amplify, extend, increase bulk and scope of: *to expand a pamphlet into a book*; **b** to increase in breadth and range: *to expand a child's mind by education*. **B.** intrans. To become expanded; specif. **1.** (of material objects) **a** to dilate, increase in volume: *water expands with heat* &c.; **b** to become spread out, widely opened: *the flower buds have not yet expanded*; **c** (fig.) to be extended, increased in size; to cover more space: *the building can only expand to the north*. **2.** (fig., of non-material things) To grow wider, more comprehensive: *the mind expands with knowledge and experience*; *one's interests expand with opportunity*.

expanse, n. [1. ekspáns; 2. ikspǽns]. Lat. *expansum*, P.P. of *expandere*. See prec. **1.** Broad, extended area in space; wide, open tract of the earth's surface: *an expanse of sky, of field, lake* &c. **2.** Expansion.

expansibility, n. [1. ekspànsibíliti; 2. ikspæ̀nsibíliti]. See next word & **-ity**. Capacity for expansion.

expansible, adj. [1. ekspánsibl; 2. ikspǽnsibl]. **expanse** & **-ible**. Capable of expanding or of being expanded.

expansile, adj. [1. ekspánsīl; 2. ikspǽnsail]. **expanse** & **-ile**. **a** Expansible; **b** tending to expand, characterized by expansibility.

expansion, n. [1. ekspánshun; 2. ikspǽnʃən]. Lat. *expans-(um)*, P.P. type of *expandere*. See **expand** & **-ion**. Process of expanding; state of being expanded (in various senses).

expansive, adj. [1. ekspánsiv; 2. ikspǽnsiv]. Lat., fr. *expans-*. See prec. & **-ive**. **a** Tending to expand, capable of expansion; **b** (of persons, character, expression) unreserved, frank, communicative, free, open.

expansively, adv. Prec. & **-ly**. In an expansive, frank, manner.

expansiveness, n. See prec. & **-ness**. Property, quality, of being expansive.

ex parte, adv. & adj. [1. èks párte; 2. èks pā́ti], Lat. **ex-**, 'from' &c., & abl. sing. of *pars*, 'part, side, party' &c., see **part**. **a** adv. As from, in interests of, one side only (in a dispute &c.); **b** adj., one-sided, biassed, interested, esp. *an ex parte statement*.

expatiate, vb. intrans. [1. ekspā́shiāt; 2. ekspéiʃieit]. Lat. *exspatiāt-(um)*, P.P. of *exspatiāri*, 'to spread out, extend; digress', fr. **ex-** & *spatiāri*, 'to walk about, go along; to spread out, expand', fr. *spatium*, 'space, room, dimension'. See **space**. **1.** To range, roam at large (now rare). **2.** *Expatiate upon*, to dwell at length upon, speak at length upon, treat at length; dilate, enlarge upon.

expatiation, n. [1. èkspāshiáshun; 2. èkspeiʃiéiʃən]. Prec. & **-ion**. Act of expatiating.

expatiatory, adj. [1. ekspā́shiatori; 2. ekspéiʃiətəri]. **expatiate** & **-ory**. Characterized by expatiation; diffuse.

expatriate, vb. trans. [1. ekspā́triāt; 2. ekspéitrieit]. L. Lat. *expatriāt-(um)*, P.P. of *expatriāre*, 'to expel from one's native land', formed fr. **ex-**, 'out', & *patria*, 'father-land, native land', fr. *pater*, 'father'. See **paternal, patriot**. **1.** To drive out, banish, expel (a person) from his native land. **2.** (reflex.) *Expatriate oneself*: **a** voluntarily to quit one's own country; **b** specif., to divest oneself of the status and privileges of a citizen of one's native country, give up one's nationality.

expatriation, n. [1. ekspàtriáshun; 2. ekspèitriéiʃən]. Prec. & **-ion**. Act of expatriating; state of being expatriated.

expect, vb. trans. & intrans. [1. ekspékt; 2. ikspékt]. Fr. *expecter*, Lat. *exspectāre*, 'to look out for, await; to desire, hope; to fear', fr. **ex-** & *spectāre*, 'to look at, behold' &c., fr. *specere*, 'to see'. See this base under **spectacle** & **species**. This word never expresses now the physical action of looking; it always refers to an attitude of mind. To look out for, await, look forward to, anticipate; generally implying belief that an event will happen, that a person will do something, that person or thing will appear. **A.** trans. **1.** (applied to persons) To await coming, appearance, of, be on the look out for; believe that a person is coming: *I expected you yesterday*; *I've been expecting you all the morning*; *don't expect me till you see me*. **2.** (applied to events) To believe that they will happen, to await the anticipated occurrence of: *I expected the war for years*; *I was expecting a thunderstorm at any moment*. **3.** (applied to material and non-material things and events) **a** To foresee, look forward to with hope and confidence; to desire and feel certain of securing: *your kindness is only what I expected from you*; *you expect too much from him*; *I expect nothing from such people*; *I never expected such treatment*; **b** (implying preparedness, or, in neg. sentences, unpreparedness) *when we attacked we found the enemy were expecting us*; *I was unable to answer, as I never expected that question*. **B.** intrans. To believe, think likely, to be prepared to find &c.: *will he come today? I don't expect so.*

expectance, -cy, n. [1. ekspéktans(i); 2. ikspéktəns(i)]. **expectant** & **-ce, -cy**. State of mind in which one expects; specif. **a** anxious, eager anticipation; condition of waiting for something to happen; generally implying hope that it will happen; **b** confident anticipation of receiving something in the future.

expectant, adj. & n. [1. ekspéktant; 2. ikspéktənt], fr. Lat. *exspectant-(em)*, Pres. Part. of *exspectāre*, 'to look out for'. See **expect**. **1.** adj. **a** In a state of expecting, in expectation; **b** pregnant: *expectant mother*; **c** in position of an onlooker, waiting on events but doing nothing. **2.** n. One who expects; specif., one waiting for, and expecting to receive, something.

expectantly, adv. Prec. & **-ly**. In an expectant manner.

expectation, n. [1. èkspektáshun; 2. èkspektéiʃən]. Lat., fr. *exspectāt-(um)*, P.P. type of *exspectāre* & **-ion**. See **expect**. **1. a** Act of expecting; **b** expectant state of mind; an awaiting, looking forward to: *contrary to, according to, expectation*. **2.** Something which is expected; **a** a probability based on certain grounds; contingency: *expectation of life*; **b** future prospects: *to have brilliant expectations*.

expectative, adj. [1. ekspéktativ; 2. ikspéktətiv]. See prec. & **-ive**. Connected with, constituting, an object of expectation.

expectorant, n. [1. ekspéktorant; 2. ekspéktərənt]. Lat., fr. *expectorant-(em)*, Pres. Part. of *expectorāre*, 'to drive from the breast'. See next word. Medicine which promotes, or facilitates, expectoration.

expectorate, vb. trans. & intrans. [1. ekspéktorāt; 2. ikspéktəreit]. Lat. *expectorāt-(um)*, P.P. type of *expectorāre*, 'to drive from the breast, or mind', formed fr. **ex-** & *pector-*, stem of *pectus*, 'breast, chest'. See **pectoral**. **1.** trans. To cough up, spit up, clear chest and throat of: *to expectorate phlegm* &c. **2.** intrans. **a** To cough up, blood, phlegm &c. from the lungs; **b** to eject saliva from the mouth, to spit.

expectoration, n. [1. ekspèktoráshun; 2. ekspèktəréiʃən]. Prec. & **-ion**. **a** Act of expectorating; **b** that which is expectorated.

expedience, -cy, n. [1. ekspḗdiens(i); 2. ekspídiəns(i)]. **expedient** & **-ce, -cy**. **1.** What is expedient; fitness, suitability; convenience. **2.** Interested motives, sense of self-interest, policy: *a matter of expediency*.

expedient (**I.**), adj. [1. ekspḗdient; 2. ekspídiənt], fr. Lat. *expedient-(em)*, Pres. Part. of *expedīre*, lit. 'to free one caught by the feet, to extricate, disengage', fr. **ex-** & *ped-*, stem of *pēs*, 'foot'. See **pedal**. (chiefly pred.) **1.** Suitable, convenient, adapted to the circumstances: *such action is hardly expedient at the present moment*. **2.** Advantageous, adapted to actual situation; based on hope of advantage rather than on principle; politic: *the execution of Queen Mary of Scotland was rather expedient than just*.

expedient (**II.**), n., fr. prec. A means to an end, mode of accomplishing something; shift, device.

expediential, adj. [1. ekspèdiénshal; 2. ɛkspìdiénʃəl]. **expedient** & **-ial**. Based on, directed by, expediency.

expediently, adv. [1. expédientli; 2. ɛkspídiəntli]. **expedient (I.)** & **-ly**. In a suitable, convenient, manner.

expedite (I.), vb. trans. [1. ékspedīt; 2. ékspidait]. Lat. *expedīt-(um)*, P.P. type of *expedīre*, q.v. under **expedient**. **1.** To hasten, speed up, render progress of easy, facilitate rapid progress of: *to expedite a negotiation; to expedite matters.* **2.** (not genuine Engl.) To send off, dispatch: *to expedite one's luggage*; cp. Fr. *expédier.*

expedite (II.), adj., fr. prec. Unhampered; rapid, prompt.

expeditely, adv. Prec. & **-ly**. Promptly, rapidly.

expedition, n. [1. èkspedíshun; 2. èkspidíʃən]. Lat. *expedītiōn-(em)*, 'a warlike enterprise', fr. *expedīt-(um)*, P.P. type of *expedīre*, & **-ion**. See **expedient**. **1. a** A setting forth, a journey, an outward march, esp. of armed men; a warlike undertaking; **b** a journey undertaken for some particular purpose, such as exploration, or pleasure: *an expedition to the North Pole; a hunting expedition.* **2.** The company of those who go on an expedition. **3.** Activity, promptness: *this must be done with expedition.*

expeditionary, adj. [1. èkspedíshunari; 2. èkspidíʃənəri]. Prec. & **-ary**. Connected with, of the nature of, an expedition.

expeditious, adj. [1. èkspedíshus; 2. èkspidíʃəs]. **expedite** & **-ous**. Cp. Lat. adv. *expedītē*, 'promptly', formed fr. *expedītum*. Swift and effective in movement or action; rapid, prompt.

expeditiously, adv. Prec. & **-ly**. Promptly, rapidly.

expel, vb. trans. [1. ekspél; 2. ikspél]. Lat. *expellere*, 'to thrust out, drive away', fr. **ex-**, 'out', & *pellere*, 'to push, strike'. The base, another form of wh. is *pul-* as in *pulsum*, P.P. of *pellere*, & *pulsus*, 'stroke', is discussed under **pulse (I.)**; cp. **compel, impel** & **anvil.** **1.** To drive out by violent means, cause to leave by exerting force: **a** *to expel an enemy from a trench*; **b** *to expel a disease by medical treatment.* **2. a** To dismiss, eject, (a person) from an office; **b** to turn (a person) out, deprive of membership, of a community or institution: *to expel a member from a club*; specif., to dismiss (a boy) from school for grave misconduct.

expellent, adj. & n. [1. ekspélent; 2. ikspélənt], fr. Pres. Part. of *expellere*. See prec. **1.** adj. Serving to expel. **2.** n. An expellent medicine.

expend, vb. trans. & intrans. [1. ekspénd; 2. ikspénd]. Lat. *expendere*, 'to weigh out; weigh out money, pay down', fr. **ex-** & *pendere*, 'to suspend, hang down; weigh; weigh mentally, ponder'. See **spend** & **pendent, ponder.** **A.** trans. **1.** To give out, pay out, spend (money or wealth). *Spend* is more commonly used in this sense. **2.** (of non-material things) To give out, make a call upon, use: *to expend time, trouble, thought, care* &c. *on something.* **B.** intrans. (rare) To spend money: *to prefer to expend rather than to save.*

expenditure, n. [1. ekspéndichur; 2. ikspénditʃə]. **expend** & **-ure**. **a** Act of expending; **b** that which is expended; (of money, time, care &c.).

expense, n. [1. ekspéns; 2. ikspéns]. Lat. *expens-(um)*, P.P. of *expendere*. See **expend**. **a** Act of expending; **b** (chiefly in pl.) that which is expended: *to cut down one's expenses; my expenses are heavy just now*; Phrs. *at my expense*, I having to pay (lit. and fig.); *at the expense of one's self-respect* &c., with loss of; **c** source of expense: *the education of a large family is a great expense.*

expensive, adj. [1. ekspénsiv; 2. ikspénsiv]. Prec. & **-ive**. **a** Causing expense, demanding, involving, outlay of money &c.; costing much money, dear: *expensive clothes, mode of living*; **b** making demands on time, labour &c.

expensively, adv. Prec. & **-ly**. In an expensive manner.

expensiveness, n. See prec. & **-ness**. Quality of being expensive.

experience (I.), n. [1. ekspériens; 2. ikspíəriəns]. In M.E., fr. Fr. *expérience*, fr. Lat. *experientia*, 'trial, proof, experiment', formed fr. *experient-(em)*, Pres. Part. type of *experīri*, 'to try, prove, put to the test', fr. **ex-** & base *perī(t)-* as in *perītus*, 'experienced, practised, skilful'. See this base under **peril.** **1.** (archaic or obs.) Trial, test: *to make experience of.* **2.** Process of acquiring knowledge of, familiarity with, insight into, expertness and skill in, some subject, mode of life, form of occupation &c., by actually living through certain events, or under certain conditions, or by actually doing, or observing, certain things: *to have, undergo, practical experience of life in the Colonies; experience of teaching, of fighting, farming* &c.; *nothing but actual experience can make a good soldier; to learn by experience.* **3.** Knowledge and familiarity, insight, skill, practice acquired by actually living in a certain way, dealing with certain facts, circumstances &c., by personal observation, by doing certain things, and engaging in certain pursuits: *to gain experience in commanding men, in managing an estate; to have the necessary experience for a post, for doing a piece of work* &c. **4.** The sum total of what has been observed, perceived, thought, felt, by the individual or by the race: *these things are entirely outside human experience; religious experience.* **5.** Something experienced; some event actually witnessed or lived through; an adventure; particular phase of mental or emotional activity: *to have a strange, interesting, experience; conversion is a peculiar spiritual experience.* **6.** *Experiences*, an account, narrative, description, of a series of experiences, adventures &c.

experience (II.), vb. trans., fr. prec. To have experience of; to undergo, endure, meet with: *to experience great hardships, difficulties, kindness, cruelty* &c.

experienced, adj. [1. ekspériенst; 2. ikspíəriənst]. **experience (I.)** & **-ed.** Having experience; specif., instructed, made skilful, judicious, competent, by personal observation, and by practice in particular kind of action &c.: *an experienced general, teacher, speaker, writer* &c.

experience table, n. Table showing probable mortality, or chance of life, at particular age, arrived at from the experience of insurance companies.

experiential, adj. [1. ekspèriénshal; 2. ikspìəriénʃəl]. See **experience** & **-al**. Pertaining to, based on, experience; empirical.

experientialism, n. [1. ekspèriénshalizm; 2. ikspìəriénʃəlizəm]. Prec. & **-ism**. Doctrine that all knowledge is derived from experience.

experientialist, n. [1. ekspèriénshalist; 2. ikspìəriénʃəlist]. **experiential** & **-ist**. Adherent of experientialism.

experiment (I.), n. [1. ekspériment; 2. ikspérimənt]. Lat. *experimentum*, fr. *experi-*, as in **experience**, & **-ment**. **1. a** (nat. sci.) A test, trial, carried out under certain strict conditions, in order to discover the result of combining certain substances under these conditions, or the behaviour of certain organisms under certain conditions: *a chemical experiment; an experiment in biology*; **b** any test or trial to establish, one way or another, something the issue of which is unknown or doubtful, esp. to the experimenter; a testing of alleged truths or facts: *to appoint so young a man was a bold experiment; a new experiment in education.* **2.** Act of making experiments, or an experiment; act of testing.

experiment (II.), vb. intrans., fr. prec. To make, try, experiments.

experimental, adj. [1. ekspèriméntal; 2. ikspèriméntəl]. Prec. & **-al**. **1.** Connected with, based on, of the nature of, an experiment. **2.** Relating to, based on, experience.

experimentalism, n. [1. ekspèriméntalizm; 2. ikspèriméntəlizəm]. Prec. & **-ism.** Doctrine, practice, of relying upon experiment; empiricism.

experimentalist, n. [1. ekspèriméntalist; 2. ikspèriméntəlist]. **experimental** & **-ist.** Believer in experimentalism.

experimentalize, vb. intrans. [1. ekspèriméntalīz; 2. ikspèriméntəlaiz]. **experimental** & **-ize.** To make experiments.

experimentally, adv. [1. ekspèriméntali; 2. ikspèriméntəli]. **experimental** & **-ly.** By means of experiment.

experimentation, n. [1. ekspèrimentáshun; 2. ikspèrimɛntéiʃən]. **experiment** & **-ation.** Practice of experimenting.

experimentize, vb. trans. & intrans. [1. ekspérimentīz; 2. ikspérimәntaiz]. **experiment** & **-ize.** **a** trans. To submit to experiment, try experiments upon; **b** intrans., to experiment.

expert (I.), adj. [1. ekspért; 2. ikspʌ́t]. Lat. *expert-(us)*, 'tried, proved; experienced in', P.P. of *experīri*, 'to test' &c. See **experience (I.)**. **1.** (of persons) **a** Possessing physical agility, skill, dexterity; deft, skilled in some handicraft, or manual work: *an expert fisherman, rider* &c.; *an expert glass-blower, carpenter* &c.; *to be expert in, at, carving, driving a motor* &c.; **b** possessing special knowledge or experience; learned in, well acquainted with, some particular branch of knowledge: *an expert palaeographer, botanist, writer of verses.* **2.** (of work) Performed by an expert craftsman; deftly, skilfully done.

expert (II.), n. [1. ékspërt; 2. ékspʌt], fr. prec. Person specially trained and practised in some branch of work or knowledge; one possessing special experience, knowledge, information; a specialist: *a linguistic expert, chemical expert, mining expert.*

expertly, adv. [1. ekspértli; 2. ikspʌ́tli]. **expert (I.)** & **-ly**. In a deft, skilful manner.

expertness, n. [1. ekspértnes; 2. ikspʌ́tnis]. **expert (I.)** & **-ness**. Quality of being expert; dexterity, skill.

expiable, adj. [1. ékspiabl; 2. ékspiəbl]. Fr. *expiable*, see next word & **-able**. Capable of expiation, of being expiated.

expiate, vb. trans. [1. ékspiāt; 2. ékspieit], fr. Lat. *expiāt-(um)*, P.P. of *expiāre*, 'to make satisfaction for, atone for; to make amends for', fr. **ex-** & *piāre*, 'to appease by sacrifice, to atone for', fr. *pius*, 'devout, righteous'. See **pious**. To make amends for, make complete satisfaction for, by undergoing punishment; pay the penalty of: *expiate sin, guilt, crime.*

expiation, n. [1. èkspiáshun; 2. èkspiéiʃən]. Prec. & **-ion**. Act of expiating; atonement made, satisfaction given, amends, for guilt, sin &c., by suffering penalty.

expiatory, adj. [1. ékspiàtori; 2. ékspièitəri]. **expiate** & **-ory**. Of the nature of expiation, tending to expiate, having property of expiating.

expiration, n. [1. èkspīráshun; 2. èkspairéiʃən]. Lat. *exspīrātiōn-(em)*, 'a breathing out, exhalation', fr. *exspīrāt-(um)*, P.P. type of *exspīrāre*, 'to breathe out, give out; lose; emit'. See **expire**. **1.** Act of breathing out. **2.** Completion, termination, expiry, of a period of time, of a truce, lease &c.

expiratory, adj. [1. ekspírator; 2. ɛkspáiərətəri], fr. Lat. *exspīrāt-*, as in prec., & **-ory.** Connected with, producing, the emission of air from the lungs: *an expiratory movement.*

expire, vb. intrans. & trans. [1. ekspír; 2. ikspáiə], fr. Fr. *expirer*, Lat. *exspīrāre*, 'to breathe out, to breathe one's last, die', fr. **ex-** & *spīrāre*, 'to breathe'. See **spirit.** **A.** intrans. **1.** To breathe out air, exhale. **2.** To breathe one's last, to die. **3.** (fig.) To die down, die out (of fire, light); to come to an end, terminate (of time, or anything measured in periods of time): *my lease, term of office* &c. *has expired.* **B.** trans. (rare) To breathe out: *to expire air, breath, from the lungs.*

expiry, n. [1. ekspíri; 2. *ikspáiəri*]. Prec. & **-y.** Termination, conclusion, of a period of time: *expiry of a lease, appointment, truce* &c.

explain, vb. trans. & intrans. [1. eksplán; 2. *ikspléin*]. Lat. *explānāre*, 'to spread out, flatten; to make clear', fr. **ex-** & *plānus*, 'level, flat, even; clear, distinct, intelligible'. See **plain (I.)**. **A.** trans. **1. a** To make clear, intelligible: *to explain obscurities*; **b** to clear away difficulties from, make meaning of clear; interpret, expound: *to explain a passage in a book, a statement*; *to explain the meaning of*; *to explain a situation.* **2. a** To justify by explanation: *to explain one's conduct*; **b** (reflex.) *to explain oneself*, to give an explanation in justification of one's apparent misconduct. **3.** *Explain away*, to give such reasons, explanations, in justification of (a fault, error, difficulty) &c., as to cause the fault &c. to seem less, and the difficulty to disappear. **B.** intrans. To give an explanation: *when you are wrong, never explain.*

explainable, adj. [1. eksplánabl; 2. *ikspléinəbl*]. Prec. & **-able.** Capable of being explained.

explanation, n. [1. èksplanáshun; 2. èksplənéiʃən]. Lat. *explānātiōn-(em)*, 'a making plain', fr. *explānāt-(um)*, P.P. type of *explānāre.* See **explain** & **-ation. 1. a** Act or process of explaining; **b** statement made to make (meaning, difficulties &c.) clear, plain, intelligible; an exposition, manifestation of what is obscure. **2.** Interpretation given in explaining; sense, meaning, interpretation, attributed to that which is explained: *to find a complete explanation of a mystery.*

explanative, adj. [1. eksplánativ; 2. *iksplǽnətiv*]. Lat. stem *explānāt-*, see prec., & **-ive.** Explanatory.

explanatorily, adv. [1. eksplánat(o)rili; 2. *iksplǽnət(ə)rili*]. Next word & **-ly.** By way of, as an, explanation.

explanatory, adj. [1. eksplánat(o)ri; 2. *iksplǽnət(ə)ri*]. Lat. *explānāt-*, see prec., & **-ory.** Tending to explain, providing an explanation.

expletive, adj. & n. [1. ekspl**ē**tiv; 2. *ikspl**í**tiv*]. Lat., fr. *explēt-(um)*, P.P. type of *explēre*, 'to fill up' &c., & **-ive**, fr. **ex-** & *plēre*, 'to fill', fr. base *plē-*, 'full', as in Lat. *plēnus.* See **plenum**; also second element in **complete. 1.** adj. Helping to fill up; used merely to fill up; superfluous. **2.** n. Word used with no specific meaning in sentence; specif., a meaningless profanity, an oath.

explicate, vb. trans. [1. éksplikāt; 2. ékspl*i*keit]. Lat. *explicāt-(um)*, P.P. type of *explicāre*, 'to unfold', fr. **ex-** & *plicāre*, 'to fold'; see **plicate** & **ply (I.).** Cp. **explicit.** To unfold, unravel, esp. to develop, unfold, an argument, make clearer what is implied in it.

explication, n. [1. èksplikáshun; 2. èkspl*i*kéiʃən]. Prec. & **-ion. 1.** Natural unfolding, e.g. of flowers. **2.** Explanation, exposition, interpretation. **3.** Detailed, analytical account of what is implied in a statement.

explicative, adj. [1. eksplíkativ; 2. ekspl*í*kətiv]. **explicate** & **-ive.** Tending, serving, to explicate.

explicatively, adv. Prec. & **-ly.** In an explicative, explanatory manner.

explicatory, adj. [1. eksplíkatori; 2. *ikspl**í**kətəri*]. **explicate** & **-ory.** Explicative.

explicit (I.), vb. [1. eksplisit; 2. *ikspl**í**sit*]. Lat., treated as 3rd pers. sing. pres.; orig. shortened form fr. P.P. *explicitum*, 'stated, fully set forth' &c., variant of *explicātum*, see **explicate.** At end of a book—'Here ends . . .'

explicit (II.), adj. Fr. *explicite*, fr. Lat. *explicāt-(um).* See **explicate.** Clearly stated, detailed, having whole meaning fully expressed; having nothing merely implied; opposite of *implicit*: *an explicit statement*; *to be quite explicit on a point.*

explicitly, adv. Prec. & **-ly.** In an explicit manner.

explode, vb. intrans. & trans. [1. ekspl**ṓ**d; 2. *ikspl**óu**d*], fr. Lat. *explōdere*, 'to drive out, or off (the stage) by clapping or hissing, to hoot off'; variant of *explaudere*; **ex-** & *plaudere*, 'clap, strike, beat'. See **plaudit, applaud. A.** intrans. **1.** To burst, expand, suddenly and violently with loud report; **a** of gunpowder and certain chemical combinations; **b** of receptacles containing vapour &c. at high pressure. **2. a** (of strong emotion) To burst forth, express itself suddenly and noisily (of laughter, anger); **b** (of persons) to give vent suddenly to violent and noisy emotion: *to explode with rage, laughter* &c. **B.** trans. **1.** To cause to explode, cause to expand suddenly and violently: *to explode a charge of gunpowder.* **2.** To destroy, shatter, dissipate, by showing baselessness or futility of: *to explode cherished beliefs*; (often in P.P. as attrib. adj.) *an exploded superstition, custom* &c.

exploit (I.), n. [1. éksploit; 2. éksploit]. M.E., 'success', fr. O. Fr.; also *expleit*; fr. *explicitum*, P.P. of *explicāre*, 'to unfold, display' &c. See **explicate.** A bold, adventurous, famous, deed.

exploit (II.), vb. trans. [1. eksplóit; 2. *iksplóit*]. O. Fr. *expleitier, exploitier*, Mod. Fr. *exploiter*, fr. prec. **1.** To make full use of, get value out of; utilize profitably: *to exploit a firm, a business* &c. **2.** (applied to persons) **a** To make an illegitimate use of, to turn a person's services, skill, knowledge &c. to one's own advantage by employing them to further one's own ends; to use (a person) so as to make a profit at his expense: *to exploit one's subordinates*; **b** specif. as term applied by socialists to all employment of labour under a capitalist system.

exploitable, adj. [1. eksplóitabl; 2. *iksplóitəbl*]. Prec. & **-able.** Capable of being used, worked, with profit.

exploitage, n. [1. eksplóitij; 2. *iksplóitidž*]. **exploit (II.)** & **-age.** Use for profit whether legitimate or the reverse.

exploitation, n. [1. èksploitáshun; 2. èksploitéiʃən]. Fr., fr. Lat. **exploit (II.)** & **-ation.** Act of exploiting; state of being exploited; exploitage.

exploiter, n. [1. eksplóiter; 2. *iksplóitə*]. **exploit (II.)** & **-er.** One who exploits in a bad sense.

exploration, n. [1. èksplōráshun; 2. èksplōréiʃən]. Lat. *explōrātiōn-(em)*, 'examination', fr. *explōrāt-(um)*, P.P. type of *explōrāre*, 'to search out, examine, investigate; to try, test', fr. **ex-** & *plōrāre*, 'to weep, lament'; the connexion in meaning of the compound w. the simple vb. is not obvious. It is said that *explōrāre* means orig. 'to cause to flow', hence 'to bring out, elicit'. The base **plō(u)-* means 'to flow'. For cognates see **flow.** See also **implore.** Act of exploring. Specif. **1.** act of travelling into an unknown region and investigating it from point of view of geology, fauna and flora, geography, ethnology &c. **2.** Examination of, inquiry into, a question, problem &c.

explore, vb. trans. & intrans. [1. eksplṓr; 2. *ikspl**ɔ̄***], fr. Fr. *explorer*, fr. Lat. *explōrāre.* See prec. **A.** trans. To investigate, search into, examine thoroughly. Specif. **1. a** to travel into, through, a strange region and investigate its geology, geography, fauna, peoples &c.: *to explore new countries* &c.; **b** to test, try: *to explore a channel, passage* &c. **2.** To investigate, examine, (a question, possibility &c.) **3.** (med. and surg.) To probe, investigate, depth, condition &c. of a wound. **B.** intrans. To carry out exploration.

explorer, n. [1. eksplṓrer; 2. *ikspl**ɔ̄**rə*]. Prec. & **-er.** One who explores; specif., one who visits unknown parts of the world for purposes of exploration.

explosion, n. [1. ekspl**ṓ**zhun; 2. *ikspl**óu**žən*]. Lat. *explōsiōn-(em)*, 'a driving away with clapping or hisses', *explōs-(um)*, P.P. type of *explōdere*, & **-ion.** See **explode. 1.** Act or process of exploding; a loud violent noise or report: **a** *an explosion of gunpowder*; **b** *an explosion of anger, laughter* &c. **2.** (antiquated phonetics) The off-glide, or puff of air made on opening a stop consonant. **3.** Outburst of gas or compressed air.

explosive, adj. & n. [1. ekspl**ṓ**siv; 2. *iksplóusiv*]. Lat. *explōs-(um)*, P.P. type of *explōdere*, & **-ive.** See prec. & **explode. 1.** adj. **a** Tending to go off, or explode, with noise and violence; **b** (fig.) tending to explode with anger or other strong emotion; hot-tempered, fiery. **2.** n. **a** Substance which has the property of exploding; **b** (phon.) rather antiquated term for one of a class of consonantal sounds better called *stops*, or *stop consonants.*

explosively, adv. Prec. **1,** & **-ly.** In an explosive manner.

explosiveness, n. See prec. & **-ness.** Quality of being explosive.

exponent, adj. & n. [1. eksp**ṓ**nent; 2. *ikspóunənt*], fr. Lat. *expōnent-(em)*, Pres. Part. of *expōnere*, 'to set out, expose, display, exhibit; to explain'; **ex-** & *pōnere*, 'to place'. See **depone** & **position. 1.** adj. Serving to set forth, to explain, expound, meaning of. **2.** n. **a** One who expounds, explains, interprets: *Huxley was a great popular exponent of evolution*; **b** (alg.) a symbol written above and to the right of another to indicate to what power the latter is to be taken; e.g. in b^2 the small figure is the exponent.

exponential, adj. [1. èkspōnénshal; 2. èkspounén(t)ʃəl]. Prec. & **-ial.** (math.) Relating to exponents.

export (I.), vb. trans. [1. ekspórt; 2. *iksp**ɔ̄**t*]. Lat. *exportāre*, 'to carry out, away', fr. **ex-** & *portāre*, 'to carry, bear, convey'. See **port (IV.).** To carry out; specif., to send (goods, merchandise) out of a country in the course of trade.

export (II.), n. [1. éksport; 2. ékspɔ̄t], fr. prec. **1.** Act, operation, of exporting goods: *to be engaged in export.* **2.** Something exported; article of merchandise sent from country of production into a foreign country: *balance of imports and exports*; *invisible exports*, such services as shipping, insurances, capital invested abroad &c., which are not included in the trade returns of a country.

exportation, n. [1. èksportáshun; 2. èkspɔ̄téiʃən]. Lat. *exportātiōn-(em)*, 'act of exporting; banishment', fr. *exportāt-(um)*, P.P. type of *exportāre.* See **export (I.)** & **-ion.** Act or process of exporting.

exporter, n. [1. eksp**ó**rter; 2. *iksp**ɔ̄**tə*]. **export (I.)** & **-er.** Trader who sends out articles of merchandise to foreign countries.

exposal, n. [1. ekspṓzal; 2. *ikspóuzəl*]. Next word & **-al.** Act, process, of exposing; state of being exposed; exposure.

expose, vb. trans. [1. ekspṓz; 2. *ikspóuz*]. Fr. *exposer*, fr. Lat. **ex-** & *pos-*, P.P. or Perf. type of *pōnere*, 'place'. See **position. 1.** To leave unprotected; to deprive of protection, shelter, or guard; to lay open to attack, injury, danger &c.; to allow to play upon: **a** *to expose troops to gun-fire*; *to expose the eyes to sunlight*; *to expose one's head to the rain*; *a situation exposed to every wind*; *to expose oneself to risk, danger*; also **b** (of non-material things) *to expose one's character to attack*; *to expose oneself to unfavourable comments.* **2.** Specif., to turn out and abandon to hunger and death; leave at the mercy of the elements: *to expose a child* (as is regularly done by certain tribes). **3.** Specif. (in photog.) to allow sunlight to fall upon for particular purpose: *to expose a film, a sensitive plate.* **4. a** To display for inspection, set out as an exhibit: *to expose articles for sale*; **b** (card games) to allow to be seen, turn up: *to expose a card.* **5.** To make manifest (villainy &c. of); to unmask, reveal guilt of: *to expose a plot, rascality* &c.; *to expose a rogue.*

exposé, n. [1. ekspṓzā; 2. ekspóuzei]. Fr., P.P. of *exposer.* See prec. An unmasking, revelation; making public of a scandal, discreditable conduct &c. hitherto kept secret.

exposed, adj. [1. ekspṓzd; 2. ikspóuzd], fr. P.P. of **expose**. **a** Unprotected, open, liable, to attack, danger &c.; specif. **b** open to the wind and weather &c.: *a house in an exposed position.*

exposedness, n. Prec. & **-ness.** Condition of being exposed.

exposition, n. [1. èkspozíshun; 2. èkspəzíʃən]. Lat. *expositiōn-(em)*, 'a showing forth' &c., fr. *exposit-(um)*, P.P. type of *expōnere*, & **-ion.** See **expose. 1.** A showing forth, elucidation, explanation of, commentary upon, as of meaning, theory, plan &c. **2.** Exhibition, show, public display, of objects of art &c. (Not strictly English sense; borrowed from French.)

expositive, adj. [1. ekspózitiv; 2. ikspɔ́zitiv]. Lat. *exposit-*, as in prec., & **-ive.** Of the nature of an exposition or explanation; tending to explain or expound.

expositor, n. [1. ekspózitor; 2. ikspɔ́zitə]. Lat. *exposit-* as in prec. & **-or.** One who expounds.

expository, adj. [1. ekspózitori; 2. ikspɔ́zitəri]. Lat. *exposit-* as in prec. & **-ory.** Expositive.

ex post facto, adv. & adj. [1. éks pōst fáktō; 2. éks poust fǽktou]. Lat., 'from what is done afterwards'. Retrospectively; retrospective.

expostulate, vb. intrans. [1. ekspóschoolāt; 2. ikspɔ́stʃuleit]. Lat. *expostulāt-(um)*, P.P. type of *expostulāre*, 'to demand urgently, vehemently'. See **ex-** & **postulate. a** (followed by *with*) To reason seriously with a person, pointing out, and protesting against, the impropriety of something which he has said or done; to remonstrate; **b** (absol.) to utter a protest against something said or done: *to expostulate in vain.*

expostulation, n. [1. ekspòschooláshun; 2. ikspɔ̀stʃuléiʃən]. Prec. & **-ion. a** Act of expostulating, remonstrating; **b** speech, words, uttered by way of expostulating with a person: *my expostulations were vain; he persisted in his conduct.*

expostulative, adj. [1. ekspóschoolātiv; 2. ikspɔ́stʃuleitiv]. **expostulate** & **-ive.** Of the nature of an expostulation.

expostulatory, adj. [1. ekspóschoolātori; 2. ikspɔ́stʃuleitəri]. **expostulate** & **-ory.** Expostulative.

exposure, n. [1. ekspṓzhur; 2. ikspóužə]. **expose** & **-ure. 1. a** Act of exposing, of laying bare, leaving unprotected &c.: *exposure of the bare head to the sun is very dangerous for Europeans in hot climates; the exposure of children is practised among some savage tribes;* **b** (in moral sense) act of unmasking, showing up, revealing, guilt, rascality, folly &c.: *those fearing exposure on account of some past indiscretion often fall a prey to blackmailers.* **2.** State of being exposed (in various senses): *exposure to the air, rain, sun; to die of exposure; exposure to risk, danger, anxiety* &c. **3.** Manifestation, act of showing, of allowing to be seen: **a** (eccles.) *exposure of the Host;* **b** *exposure of a card;* **c** (photog.) act of allowing sunlight to fall upon a sensitive plate &c. **4.** Aspect, direction in respect of the points of the compass, to which a house &c., looks, or from which the sun shines upon a given spot: *a north(erly), east(erly), exposure* &c.

expound, vb. trans. & intrans. [1. ekspóund; 2. ikspáund]. M.E. *expoun(d)en*, fr. Lat. *expōnere*, 'to set forth, explain' &c. See **exponent** & **expose. 1.** trans. To state, explain, set forth, make exposition of: *to expound one's views, a theory, the Scriptures* &c. **2.** intrans. To make an exposition.

expounder, n. [1. ekspóunder; 2. ikspáundə]. Prec. & **-er.** Person who expounds.

express (I.), adj. [1. eksprés; 2. iksprés]. Fr. *exprès*, fr. Lat. *expressum*, 'prominent, distinct; clear, plain', P.P. of *exprimere*, 'to squeeze out; to form by pressure; model, portray; to imitate, copy; describe in words', &c., fr. **ex-** & *premere*, 'to press'. See **press (I.). 1. a** (of statements &c.) Clear, definite, precise, explicit, unequivocal, not merely implied, but specifically stated: *an express command, utterance* &c.; **b** (of purpose &c.) of particular kind, clearly and specifically defined in the mind: *with the express intention, desire, purpose* &c. **2.** Designed for specific and particular function and purpose; hence, **a** sent on particular errand: *an express letter, messenger;* **b** dispatched, travelling, with increased speed: *an express train;* speed is also implied in **a. 3.** Exactly like, reproducing perfectly: '*the express image of his person*' (N.T.).

express (II.), adv., fr. prec. **1.** On purpose, expressly. **2.** By express (train): *to travel express.*

express (III.), n. See **express (I.). 1. a** A special messenger, or mode of conveyance; **b** message sent by either of these means. **2. a** Method of rapid transit of goods; **b** business company carrying on such a system. **3.** An express train.

express (IV.), vb. trans. See **express (I.). 1.** To press out (archaic or obs.) **2. a** To reveal, make manifest, declare, meaning, emotion, mental impression &c., by means of symbols, whether by words, as in speech, by visual images drawn or painted, by plastic form, or any other method; to depict, represent, signify, body forth; **b** (reflex.) *to express oneself*, make one's meaning, thoughts, feelings, known; say what one means: *unable to express oneself.* **3.** To send by express messenger, post &c.: *to express a letter.*

expressible, adj. [1. eksprésibl; 2. iksprésibl]. Prec. & **-ible.** Capable of being expressed.

expression, n. [1. ekspréshun; 2. ikspréʃən]. **express (IV)**. & **-ion. 1.** Act of expressing in all senses; specif. **a** representation of what is in the mind by language, or in artistic form of any kind: *to have the gift of verbal, pictorial, expression;* **b** mode of symbolizing, representing, something: *writing is the expression of sounds by graphic symbols.* **2. a** A particular mode of verbal expression, a combination of words; sentence, phrase, idiom: *he made use of a strange expression in conversation; a vulgar, clumsy, expression* &c.; **b** inflexion of voice, various modes of using voice expressive of emotion, in singing, reading &c.; **c** mode of expressing varying emotion in playing musical instrument; suggestion, manifestation, of feeling by this means. **3.** Cast of countenance, aspect of features, esp. considered as indicating a mood, a passion, an emotion, the character &c.

expressional, adj. [1. ekspréshunal; 2. ikspréʃənəl]. Prec. & **-al.** Relating to, connected with, expression.

expressionless, adj. [1. ekspréshunles; 2. ikspréʃənlis]. **expression** & **-less.** Devoid of, lacking, expression, **a** of the face; **b** of singing, reading, playing.

expressive, adj. [1. eksprésiv; 2. iksprésiv]. **express (IV.)** & **-ive. 1.** Expressing, indicating, making manifest: *a countenance expressive of the deepest misery.* **2.** Full of expression; betokening, revealing intelligence, feeling, hidden meaning &c.: *an expressive face, smile, glance, voice* &c.

expressively, adv. Prec. & **-ly.** In a manner expressing feeling &c., in an expressive manner.

expressiveness, n. See prec. & **-ness.** Quality of being expressive.

exprobration, n. [1. èksprōbráshun; 2. èksproubréiʃən]. Lat. *exprobrātiōn-(em)*, 'a reproaching', fr. *exprobrāt-(um)*, P.P. of *exprobrāre*, 'to accuse of something disgraceful, to upbraid', fr. **ex-** & *probrum*, 'shameful act; shame, disgrace'. See **opprobrium.** Censure, reproach.

expropriate, vb. trans. [1. eksprṓpriāt; 2. ɛkspróuprieit]. Low Lat. *expropriāt-(um)*, P.P. *expropriāre*, fr. **ex-** & *proprius*, 'one's own'. See **proper. a** To deprive of possession of; **b** to transfer (property) from one owner to another.

expropriation, n. [1. èksprōpriáshun; 2. èksproupriéiʃən]. Prec. & **-ion.** Act of expropriating; state of being expropriated.

expugn, vb. trans. [1. ekspū́n; 2. ɛkspjū́n]. Lat. *expugnāre*, 'to take by storm', fr. **ex-** & *pugnāre*, 'to fight, give battle', fr. *pugna*, 'a fight'. See **pugnacious.** To take by storm, to vanquish.

expugnable, adj. [1. ekspúgnabl; 2. ɛkspágnəbl]. Prec. & **-able.** Capable of being taken by storm.

expulsion, n. [1. ekspúlshun; 2. ikspálʃən]. Lat. *expulsiōn-(em)*, 'a driving out', fr. *expuls-(um)*, P.P. type of *expellere*, & **-ion.** See **expel. 1.** Act or process of driving out, expelling, forcing out; **a** the *expulsion of a cork from a bottle* &c.; *of the enemy from a trench* &c.; **b** dismissal, turning out from, deprivation of membership of: *the expulsion of a boy from a school, of a member from a club* &c. **2.** State of being expelled.

expulsive, adj. [1. ekspúlsiv; 2. ikspálsiv]. Lat. *expuls-*, as in prec. & **-ive.** Tending to expel; having property of expelling: *an expulsive force.*

expunction, n. [1. ekspúngkshun; 2. ikspáŋkʃən], fr. Lat. *expunct-(um)*, P.P. type of *expungere*, 'to prick out, erase', & **-ion.** See next word. Act of expunging; state of being expunged.

expunge, vb. trans. [1. ekspúnj; 2. ikspándž], fr. Lat. *expungere*, 'to prick out, put dots above or below to indicate erasure, to erase', fr. **ex-** & *pungere*, 'to prick, puncture' &c., fr. base **pung-*. See **pungent.** To wipe out, erase, delete: *to expunge a word from a sentence; a name, an entry, from a list* &c.

expurgate, vb. trans. [1. ékspergāt; 2. ékspəgeit], fr. Lat. *expurgāt-(um)*, P.P. type of *expurgāre*, 'to purge out, cleanse, purify', fr. **ex-** & *purgāre*, 'to clean, purify'. See **purge.** To clear, purify (a book) of what is offensive, obscene, improper, erroneous &c.

expurgation, n. [1. èkspergáshun; 2. èkspəgéiʃən]. Prec. & **-ion.** Act of expurgating; state of being expurgated.

expurgator, n. [1. ékspergātor; 2. ékspəgeitə]. **expurgate** & **-or.** One who expurgates.

expurgatory, adj. [1. eksp̃ergatori; 2. ikspə́gətəri]. See prec. & **-ory.** Of the nature of, pertaining to, expurgation; serving to purify.

exquisite, adj. & n. [1. ékskwizit; 2. ékskwizit]. Lat. *exquīsīt-(um)*, P.P. type of *exquīrere*, 'to seek out thoroughly'; the P.P. used as an adj. has sense of 'carefully sought out, ripely considered; choice, excellent'; fr. **ex-** & *quaerere*, 'to search for'. See **query, quest. 1.** adj. Select, choice; highly refined, delicate; brought to a high pitch of perfection. **2.** n. A man who possesses, or affects to possess, a hypersensitive taste and sensibilities; one who is fastidious to absurdity about his dress and habits, or who professes great delicacy and refinement of taste in art and literature; term usually applied to a mincing, finical, affected coxcomb.

exquisitely, adv. Prec. **1** & **-ly.** In an exquisite, refined, manner; delicately, beautifully, to perfection.

exquisiteness, n. See prec. & **-ness.** Quality of being exquisite.

exsanguinate, vb. trans. [1. eksánggwināt; 2. ɛksǽŋgwineit]. Lat. *exsanguināt-(us)*, 'bloodless', fr. **ex-** & *sanguin-(em)*, 'blood' (nom. *sanguis*). See **sanguine.** (rare) To render bloodless, deprive of blood, drain blood away from.

exsanguination, n. [1. èksanggwináshun; 2. èksæŋgwinéiʃən]. Prec. & **-ion.** Act or process of exsanguinating; state of being exsanguinated.

exsanguine, adj. [1. eksánggwin; 2. ɛksǽŋgwin]. See **ex-** & **sanguine.** Bloodless.

exscind, vb. trans. [1. eksínd; 2. ɛksínd]. Lat. *exscindere*, 'to tear down, extirpate', fr. **ex-** & *scindere*, 'to split, tear, cut asunder'; other forms of this base, without *n*, appear in the perf. *scid-* & the P.P. *scissum*, for **scid-tom*. See further discussion under the Gk. cognates **schism** & **schist**, & the Engl. cogn. **shed (I.).** To cut out, extirpate.

exsert, vb. trans. [1. eksêrt; 2. ɛksʌ́t]. New formation fr. Lat. *exsertum*, q.v. under **exert.** (bot.) To thrust out; put forth.

exserted, adj. [1. eksêrted; 2. ɛksʌ́tid]. Prec. & **-ed.** (bot. and zool.) Projecting, sticking out.

exsertion, n. [1. eksêrshun; 2. ɛksʌ́ʃən]. **exsert** & -ion. Protrusion.

ex-service, adj. Having served formerly in the army, navy, or air force, especially during the Great War.

exsiccate, vb. trans. [1. éksikāt; 2. éksikeit]. Lat. **ex-** & *siccāt-(um)*, P.P. type of *siccāre*, 'to dry up, make dry, drain', fr. *siccus*, 'dry', wh. is fr. **sisk*ʷ*os*; prob. cogn. w. O.E. *sēar*, cp. **sear (I.).** See **desiccate.** To dry up, render dry, drain moisture out of.

extant, adj. [1. ékstant, ekstánt; 2. ékstənt, ɛkstǽnt]. Lat. *ex(s)tant-(em)*, Pres. Part. of *exstāre*, fr. **ex-** & *stāre*, 'to stand'. See **ecstasy & stand (I.).** Still in existence; still surviving.

extasy, n. See **ecstasy.**

extemporaneous, adj. [1. ekstèmporáneus; 2. ɛkstèmpəréinjəs]. **extempore & -aneous.** Extempore.

extemporaneously, adv. Prec. & **-ly.** Extempore.

extemporaneousness, n. See prec. & **-ness.** Quality of being extemporaneous.

extemporarily, adv. [1. ekstémporarili; 2. ɛkstémpərərili]. Next word & **-ly.** Extempore.

extemporary, adj. [1. ekstémporari; 2. ɛkstémpərəri]. Next word & **-ary.** Extempore.

extempore, adv. & adj. [1. ekstémpori; 2. ɛkstémpəri]. Lat. *ex tempore*, 'out of the time'. See **temporal. 1.** adv. (of speaking, preaching &c.) Without notes, without preparation, or apparently so: *to preach extempore.* **2.** adj. *An extempore sermon* &c.

extemporization, n. [1. ekstèmporīzáshun; 2. ikstèmpəraizéiʃən]. Next word & **-ation. a** Act of extemporizing; **b** something done, said, played, without premeditation, on the spur of the moment.

extemporize, vb. trans. & intrans. [1. ekstémporīz; 2. ɛkstémpəraiz]. **extempore & -ize.** To do something without preparation or premeditation; to make up a speech, song, piece of music, on the spur of the moment.

extend, vb. trans. & intrans. [1. eksténd; 2. iksténd]. Lat. *extendere*, 'stretch out'. See **ex- & tend (II.). A.** trans. **1.** To stretch out, reach out, straighten outwards from the body: *to extend the hand.* **2.** To stretch between two points: *to extend a wire from post to post.* **3.** To prolong, continue, carry further; **a** (in space) *to extend a railway line, road &c. to the next town* &c.; **b** (in time) *to extend one's visit for a few days longer.* **4. a** (as affecting material things) To amplify, make larger, increase size of, cause to cover or enclose more space: *to extend the boundaries of a park; to extend a building*; **b** (affecting non-material things) to enlarge the field of, to give more scope to, to diffuse more widely, cause effects to be more widely felt: *to extend one's influence, power*; **c** to diffuse so as to reach: *to extend one's operations to wider circles*; **d** to give fuller or further meaning to: *to extend the force of a word or phrase.* **5.** To offer, bestow, confer: *to extend sympathy and kindness to one's neighbours.* **B.** intrans. To stretch, continue, to run, **a** (in space) *the road extends for miles*; **b** (in time) to last, persist &c.: *the tourist season extends from May till October.*

extended, adj. [1. eksténded; 2. iksténdid], fr. P.P. of prec. Stretched out, spread out, amplified; covering wide ground; lasting considerable time: *an extended inquiry, argument, discussion.*

extensibility, n. [1. ekstènsibíliti; 2. ikstènsibíliti]. Next word & **-ity.** Capacity for being extended.

extensible, adj. [1. eksténsibl; 2. iksténsibl]. Lat. *extens-(um)*, P.P. type of *extendere.* See **extend & -ible.** Capable of being extended; chiefly in material sense.

extensibleness, n. Prec. & **-ness.** Property of being extensible; extensibility.

extension, n. [1. eksténshun; 2. iksténʃən], fr. Lat. *extens-(um)*, P.P. type of *extendere*, 'to stretch out'. See **extend & -ion.** Act of extending; state of being extended (in many senses). **1.** A stretching out; broadening, amplification; continuation, diffusion: *the extension of a limb*, the opposite of *flexion*; *busy with the extension of one's premises*; also fig., *the extension of knowledge*; *the extension of influence.* **2.** Something extended **a** (of material things) enlargement, increase: *to build an extension to one's house*; continuation, lengthening: *to put an extension to riding-breeches*; **b** (of non-material things) continuation in time for further period: *an extension of leave of absence*; *university extension*, system which provides instruction of a university character for persons who are not members of a university; widening of significance: *extension of meaning of a word.* **3.** Amount, degree, by which a body can be stretched, extensile capacity. **4.** (logic) All the objects to which a term applies; cp. *intension.*

extensional, adj. [1. eksténshunal; 2. iksténʃənəl]. Prec. & **-al.** Relating to, connected with, extension.

extensive, adj. [1. eksténsiv; 2. iksténsiv]. Lat. *extens-(um)*, P.P. type of *extendere.* See **extend & extension & -ive. a** (in material sense) Broad, widespread, spacious, covering wide area: *extensive domains*; *extensive fields of crops*; **b** (of non-material things) far-reaching, comprehensive, thorough; made in, drawn from, many quarters: *extensive information*; *extensive inquiries, operations* &c.

extensively, adv. Prec. & **-ly.** In an extensive manner.

extensiveness, n. See prec. & **-ness.** Quality of being extensive.

extensor, n. [1. eksténsor; 2. iksténsō, -ə]. Lat. *extens-*, as in **extension & -or.** One who, that which, extends. Specif. (anat.) a muscle which serves to stretch, straighten out, a limb &c. Contrasted with *flexor.*

extent, n. [1. ekstént; 2. ikstént]. O. Fr. *estente*, Low Lat. *extenta*, fr. *extendere.* See **extend. 1. a** Area over which anything extends; size, length, height, bulk: *the extent of a park*; *the vast extent of St. Peter's at Rome*; **b** (also of non-material things) scope, limits: *the extent of one's patience*; *I learnt too late the full extent of his goodness.* **2.** Degree, measure: *to exert oneself to the utmost extent*; *I hardly know to what extent he can be trusted.* **3.** (law) A valuation of lands for purposes of taxation. **4.** (law) *Writ of extent*, writ under which the person and goods of a debtor can be seized.

extenuate, vb. trans. & intrans. [1. eksténūāt; 2. iksténjueit]. Lat. *extenuāt-(um)*, P.P. type of *extenuāre*, 'to make thin, to weaken; to make light of', fr. **ex-** & *tenuis*, 'thin'. See **tenuis & thin. A.** trans. **1.** To weaken, diminish, reduce in magnitude; esp. to lessen magnitude of (guilt), to take off from heinousness of (a crime or offence). **2.** To offer explanation in reduction of apparent culpability; to palliate, represent as less than appears or is alleged; to minimize: *I am not trying to extenuate a crime* &c. **B.** intrans. To attempt, practise, extenuation.

extenuating, adj. [1. eksténūāting; 2. iksténjueitiŋ], fr. Pres. Part. of prec. Tending to extenuate, serving to reduce heinousness of an offence; esp. *extenuating circumstances.*

extenuation, n. [1. ekstènūáshun; 2. ikstènjuéiʃən]. **extenuate & -ion. a** Act of extenuating; act of palliating, of attempting to lessen guilt; **b** state of being extenuated, palliation, reduction of culpability: *to plead poverty in extenuation of a theft.*

extenuatory, adj. [1. eksténūatori; 2. iksténjuətəri]. **extenuate & -ory.** Serving to extenuate; of the nature of an extenuation.

exterior (I.), adj. [1. ekstḗrior; 2. ikstíəriə]. Lat., comp. of *exter, exterus*, 'on the outside, external'. See **extra. 1. a** External, belonging to the outside; outermost: *an exterior wall, coat of paint* &c.; **b** (fig.) remote from, outside of: *exterior to one's real character.* **2.** Pertaining to the physical side of nature, as contrasted with the inner mind or spirit: *the exterior man*, the visible body. **3.** (polit.) Connected with matters external to the country, relating to foreign affairs: *exterior policy.*

exterior (II.), n., fr. prec. **1. a** (material) The outer surface, outside, of anything: *the exterior of a house, box* &c.; **b** (non-material) outer form, ceremony: *the exteriors of royalty, religion* &c. **2.** Outward appearance; physical, visible semblance: *a good man with a rough exterior.* **3.** Representation in a picture, or theatrical scenery, of a scene out of doors.

exteriority, n. [1. ekstèrióriti; 2. ikstìəriɔ́riti]. **exterior (I.) & -ity.** Condition, property, of being exterior.

exteriorize, vb. trans. [1. ekstḗriorīz; 2. ikstíəriəraiz]. **exterior & -ize.** To make exterior; to conceive of, and represent as a material reality.

exterminate, vb. trans. [1. ekstêrmināt; 2. ikstʌ́mineit]. Lat. *extermināt-(um)*, P.P. type of *extermināre*, 'to drive beyond the boundaries; to put away, remove', fr. **ex-** & *termināre*, 'to set bounds to, limit'. See **terminate.** To destroy, bring to an end, close existence of, to wipe out, extirpate: *to exterminate blackmailers*; *to exterminate garden pests, rats* &c.

extermination, n. [1. ekstêrmináshun; 2. ikstʌ̀minéiʃən]. Prec. & **-ion.** Act of exterminating; state of being exterminated.

exterminative, adj. [1. ekstêrminativ; 2. ikstʌ́minətiv]. **exterminate & -ive.** Tending to exterminate; exterminatory.

exterminator, n. [1. ekstêrminātor; 2. ikstʌ́mineitə]. **exterminate & -or.** One who, that which exterminates.

exterminatory, adj. [1. ekstêrminātori; 2. ikstʌ́mineitəri]. **exterminate & -ory.** Tending, serving, to exterminate.

external (I.), adj. [1. ekstêrnal; 2. ikstʌ́nəl]. Lat. *extern-(us)*, 'outward, external', & **-al.** See **ex- & exterior. 1.** Outward, being on the outside: *the external husk of a fruit.* **2. a** Outward and visible; material, as distinct from what is inward, spiritual, or mental: *to have every external grace and accomplishment*; **b** specif., relating to the outside of the body: *lotion for external application only.* **3. a** Existing apart from one's actual perception: *external nature, the external world*; **b** *external evidence*, that obtained from independent sources. **4.** (theol.) Consisting of corporeal acts, of outward forms and ceremonies, contrasted with inner, spiritual acts or conditions: *external religion, external observances.* **5.** (polit.) Connected with international, foreign, affairs: *external relations, politics.*

external (II.), n., fr. prec. Something external; something visible; (esp. pl.) outward show, appearance; deportment, manner &c., as distinct from that which is of the heart, intellect, character: *to attach too much importance to, judge by, externals.*

externalism, n. [1. ekstêrnalizm; 2. ɛkstʌ́nəlizəm]. Prec. & **-ism.** Quality of being external, of appealing to the senses; external forms.

externalist, n. [1. ekstêrnalist; 2. ɛkstʌ́nəlist]. **external & -ist.** One attached to externalism; one paying great regard to externals.

externality, n. [1. èkstërnáliti; 2. èkstʌ̄nǽliti]. **external & -ity.** State of being external.

externalization, n. [1. ekstêrnalīzáshun; 2. ɛkstʌ̀nəlaizéiʃən]. Next word & **-ation.** Act or process of externalizing.

externalize, vb. trans. [1. ekstêrnalīz; 2. ɛkstʌ́nəlaiz]. **external & -ize.** To conceive of as having external existence.

externally, adv. [1. ekstêrnali; 2. ɛkstʌ́nəli]. **external & -ly.** On, from, the outside.

exterritorial, adj. [1. èksteritórial; 2. èkstɛritɔ́riəl]. **ex-** & **territorial**. **a** Outside limits of a given territory; **b** not reckoned as belonging to, not subject to, the jurisdiction of a country; esp. of diplomatic personnel &c., in a foreign country.

exterritoriality, n. [1. èksteritōriáliti; 2. èkstɛritɔriǽliti]. Prec. & **-ity**. State of being exterritorial; freedom from jurisdiction, of diplomatic personnel.

exterritorially, adv. [1. èksteritóriali; 2. èkstɛritɔ́riəli]. **exterritorial** & **-ly**. In an exterritorial manner.

extinct, adj. [1. ekstíngkt; 2. ikstíŋkt]. Lat. *ex(s)tinct-(um)*, P.P. type fr. *ex(s)tinguere*, 'to put out, quench', fr. **ex-** & *stinguere*, 'to quench'. Etymol. uncertain. **1. a** (of light, fire) Having died down; quenched, extinguished, no longer bright or burning; **b** (of a volcano) no longer active, not given to eruption; Phr. (fig.) *an extinct volcano*, a person who has ceased to take an active part in life and affairs; **c** (fig., of passions and emotions) dead, no longer felt. **2. a** (of life) Having ceased; **b** (of species of animals and plants, races &c.) having died out, no longer living and propagating; **c** (of families) having no living descendant or representative. **3.** (of hereditary titles) Having ceased to exist through failure of heirs.

extinction, n. [1. ekstíngkshun; 2. ikstíŋkʃən]. Prec. & **-ion**. **1.** Act of extinguishing; state of being extinct (in all senses). **2.** Specif. (law) wiping out, paying off, satisfaction, or other suppression of a debt or claim.

extinctive, adj. [1. ekstíngktiv; 2. ikstíŋktiv]. **extinct** & **-ive**. Tending to extinguish.

extinguish, vb. trans. [1. ekstínggwish; 2. ikstíŋgwiʃ]. Lat. *extingu(ere)*, 'to quench'. See **extinct** & **-ish**. **1.** To put out, quench, stifle, put an end to: *to extinguish* **a** *fire, light*; **b** *life*; **c** *passions, emotions* (*love, hope* &c.); Phr. (fig.) *he was quite extinguished by* (*the side of*) *his brother* &c., his merits, brilliancy &c., were thrown into the shade in comparison. **2.** (law) *To extinguish a debt, claim, mortgage* &c., to wipe out, pay off.

extinguishable, adj. [1. ekstínggwishabl; 2. ikstíŋgwiʃəbl]. Prec. & **-able**. Capable of being extinguished.

extinguisher, n. [1. ekstínggwisher; 2. ikstíŋgwiʃə]. **extinguish** & **-er**. That which extinguishes. Specif. **a** conical, hollow object of metal or china placed over wick of lighted candle to put it out; **b** device for putting out flame of lighted lamp; **c** (fig.) dreary, lugubrious, gloomy person, who acts as a deterrent to others' mirth or happiness.

extinguishment, n. [1. ekstínggwishment; 2. ikstíŋgwiʃmənt]. **extinguish** & **-ment**. Act of extinguishing; state of being extinguished.

extirpate, vb. trans. [1. éksterpāt; 2. ékstəpeit]. Lat. *ex(s)tirpāt-(um)*, P.P. type of *ex(s)tirpāre*, 'to pluck out by the root', fr. **ex-** & *stirps*, 'stock, stem, root, scion'. Etymol. unknown. To tear up by the roots, root out, destroy, abolish. In various applications: **a** *to extirpate weeds, noxious plants* &c.; **b** *to extirpate a family, race*; **c** *to extirpate a nuisance, a social evil, a heresy* &c.; **d** (med.) *to extirpate an organ, a tumour* &c., remove it wholly.

extirpation, n. [1. èkstërpáshun; 2. èkstʌpéiʃən]. Prec. & **-ion**. Act or process of extirpating; state of being extirpated.

extirpator, n. [1. éksterpātor; 2. ékstəpeitə]. **extirpate** & **-or**. One who extirpates.

extol, vb. trans. [1. ekstól; 2. ikstɔ́l]. Lat. *extollere*, 'to lift up, raise, exalt' (lit. and fig.), fr. **ex-** & *tollere*, 'to lift, raise', fr. base **tḷ-* &c., as in *tolerāre*, 'to bear'. See **tolerate**, **thole (I.)**. To proclaim the merits and virtues of; to praise highly, to laud.

extort, vb. trans. [1. ekstórt; 2. ikstɔ́t]. Lat. *extort-(um)*, P.P. type of *extorquēre*, 'to twist out, wrench out', fr. **ex-** & *torquēre*, 'to twist, turn, wind'. The base **tṛkʷ-*, **terekʷ-*, **terkʷ-* &c., is found also in Lat. *torcular*, 'wine-press', *tormentum*, fr. **torkmentum*, 'instrument for turning, windlass' &c. (see **torment**), *torquis*, 'twisted neck-chain' (see **torque**), *tortus*, 'twisted' (see **tort**, **tortuous**.) See further details under these words, esp. **torque**. *Extort from*, to wring, twist out of (a person), exact, obtain from, force out of, by physical compulsion, threats, fraud, or other means, legal or illegal: *to extort money from*; *to extort a confession, promise, from*.

extortion, n. [1. ekstórshun; 2. ikstɔ́ʃən]. Prec. & **-ion**. Act or process of extorting; **a** process of exacting money &c., by force, threats, or other illegal means; **b** act of demanding an exorbitant price for an article offered for sale; overcharge; rapacity.

extortionate, adj. [1. ekstórshunat; 2. ikstɔ́ʃənit]. Prec. & **-ate**. In the nature of, characterized by, extortion; rapacious, exorbitant: *an extortionate charge, demand* &c.

extortioner, n. [1. ekstórshuner; 2. ikstɔ́ʃənə]. **extortion** & **-er**. One given to, practising, extortion.

extortive, adj. [1. ekstórtiv; 2. ikstɔ́tiv]. **extort** & **-ive**. Connected with extortion.

extra (I.), adj. [1. ékstra; 2. ékstrə]. Lat. *extrā*, adv., 'on the outside, without; except'; prep. 'outside of, beyond'. Connected w. Lat. *exterus, exterior* &c., fr. **ektero-*, influenced by **ex-**, see **exterior**. Additional to; over and above what is normal, or was originally expected, arranged, provided for: *extra work demands extra pay*; *extra food*; *extra charge* &c.; *dinner 5s., and wine extra*.

extra (II.), adv. Same as prec. Additionally; exceptionally; specially: *to work extra*; *try extra hard*; *extra good wine*.

extra (III.), n. Same as prec. Something additional, something extra, beyond what is customary, expected, bargained for; esp. something for which an extra, additional, charge is made: *the lodgings are five guineas a week, service, fire, light, and use of piano being extras*.

extra-, pref. See **extra (I.)**. Prefixed to adjectives, implying **a** outside of, situated outside of something: *extra-mural*, outside the walls; **b** not within, outside, beyond, the scope of: *extra-judicial*, outside the scope of the law, outside the functions of a judge, &c.

extra-canonical, adj. Outside, not included in, the canon, or canonical books.

extract (I.), vb. trans. [1. ekstrákt; 2. ikstrǽkt]. Lat. *extract-(um)*, P.P. type of *extrahere*, 'to draw out', fr. **ex-** & *trahere*, 'to draw'. See under **tract (I.)**, **traction**. **1.** To draw, pull, out, cause to come forth (of material action): *to extract a cork from a bottle*; *to extract a tooth*. **2.** To distil out, decoct, the essential principle from, by a chemical or other process: *to extract poisons from plants*; *to extract the nutritive properties of beef* &c. **3. a** To excerpt, to select, pick out, special words, passages &c., from, a book or document: *to extract forms, examples, rules &c., from a book*; **b** to submit (a document) to the process of excerption or extraction. **4. a** To derive, obtain, elicit (from persons): *I could extract nothing, no information, from him*; **b** to pick up, collect, get hold of (from books, systems &c.): *I have extracted several important principles from this sermon*; *to manage to extract some moral lessons from religious formularies*.

extract (II.), n. [1. ékstrakt; 2. ékstrækt], fr. prec. **a** Something extracted by chemical or mechanical process: *extract of roses, of beef* &c.; **b** something taken out, culled, selected, quoted, from a document: *a critical treatise on poetry with illustrative extracts*.

extractable, adj. [1. ekstráktabl; 2. ikstrǽktəbl]. **extract (I.)** & **-able**. Capable of being extracted.

extraction, n. [1. ekstrákshun; 2. ikstrǽkʃən]. **extract (I.)** & **-ion**. **1.** Act or process of extracting. In various senses: **a** pulling out: *the extraction of teeth, corks* &c.; **b** (chem.) *the extraction of the essence of substances*; **c** eliciting: *the extraction of information*. **2.** Something extracted; an extract. **3.** Place, source, of origin; lineage, descent: *a man of humble extraction, of foreign extraction*.

extractive, adj. & n. [1. ekstráktiv; 2. ikstrǽktiv]. **extract (I.)** & **-ive**. **1.** adj. **a** Tending to extract; **b** capable of being extracted. **2.** n. **a** An extractive substance; **b** an extract.

extractor, n. [1. ekstráktor; 2. ikstrǽktə]. **extract** (I.) & **-or**. **a** Person who extracts; **b** mechanical device for extracting anything.

extraditable, adj. [1. èkstradítabl; 2. èkstrədáitəbl]. Next word & **-able**. **a** (of persons) Liable to extradition; **b** (of an offence) rendering liable to extradition.

extradite, vb. trans. [1. ékstradīt; 2. ékstrədait]. Derivative fr. **extradition.** To hand over a foreign fugitive criminal, or foreigner suspected of a crime, to the authorities of justice of his own country.

extradition, n. [1. èkstradíshun; 2. èkstrədíʃən]. Lat., fr. **ex-** & *trāditiōn-(em)*, 'a delivering up, surrender'. See **tradition.** Surrender of a criminal who has taken refuge in a foreign country, to the justice of his own country, in accordance with the terms of *an extradition treaty* between the countries.

extrados, n. [1. ekstrádos; 2. ekstréidəs]. **Fr.** fr. **extra-** & *dos*, 'back', fr. Lat. *dorsum*. See **dorsal**. The exterior curved surface of an arch.

extra-mural, adj. Lat. See **extra-** & **mural.** Lit., outside the walls, e.g. **a** *extra-mural burial*; specif. **b** relating to teachers and teaching, connected with, but not actually under the direct jurisdiction of, a university.

extraneous, adj. [1. ekstrā́neus; 2. ekstréinjəs]. Lat. *extrāneus*, 'external, strange'; see **extra (I.)** & **-ous**. See also **strange**. **a** Not related to, unconnected with, external to, different from, strange, foreign: *to wash extraneous matter away from gold*; **b** (of non-material things) not germane to, unrelated to: *that question is extraneous to the matter in hand*.

extraneously, adv. Prec. & **-ly**. In an extraneous manner.

extraneousness, n. See prec. & **-ness**. Quality of being extraneous.

extraordinarily, adv. [1. ekstrórdinarili; 2. ikstrɔ́d(i)nərili]. **extraordinary** & **-ly**. In an extraordinary manner; to an extraordinary degree.

extraordinariness, n. [1. ekstrórdinarines; 2. ikstrɔ́dinərinis]. **extraordinary** & **-ness**. Quality of being extraordinary; a remarkable, rare, eccentric, feature or quality.

extraordinary, adj. [1. ekstrórdinari; 2. ikstrɔ́dn-(ə)ri]. Lat. *extra-ordinārius*, 'out of the common order'. See **extra-** & **ordinary**. **1.** Out of the common run or order, remarkable, noteworthy, so strange as to arrest attention, and to call for remark; **a** (in favourable sense) outstanding, beyond the ordinary in excellence &c.: *extraordinary genius, beauty, piety, goodness*; **b** (in unfavourable sense) unexpected, strange and causing misgiving; incomprehensible: *it is most extraordinary that he has not written*; **c** peculiar, eccentric: *an extraordinary mode of dress*; *an extraordinary appearance*; **d** surprising, uncalled-for, calling for excuse or explanation: *that is an extraordinary thing to say!* **2.** (special usage) pron. [1. èkstraórdinari; 2. èkstrəɔ́dinəri] *Ambassador, envoy, extraordinary*; *extraordinary ambassador*, one employed on special mission, or under exceptional circumstances.

extra-parochial, adj. Outside the boundaries of a parish.

extra-territorial, adj. Outside territorial jurisdiction; exterritorial.

extra-territoriality, n. Exterritoriality.

extravagance, **-cy**, n. [1. ekstrávagans(i); 2. ikstrǽvəgəns(i)]. **extravagant** & **-ce**, **-cy**. Quality of being extravagant. In various senses: **1.** Profusion in spending; lavish wastefulness in expending money and substance; thoughtless, excessive, prodigal, expenditure of money. 2. Lack of moderation and propriety in conduct or expression, undisciplined excess in behaviour and speech. 3. Specific instance of prodigality or excess in expenditure, conduct &c.: *it is a sheer extravagance to ride such expensive horses*; *your expression is a mere colloquial extravagance.*

extravagant, adj. [1. ekstrávagant; 2. ikstrǽvəgənt]. Fr., fr. Lat. **extra-** & *vagant-(em)*, Pres. Part. of *vagāri*, 'to wander, ramble, roam about'. See **vagary** & **vague**. Exceeding normal and reasonable bounds and limits, lacking moderation. 1. (in conduct and expression) Immoderate, unrestrained, wild, excessive: *extravagant behaviour*; *extravagant laughter*; *to load a person with extravagant praise, extravagant abuse.* 2. a (of expenditure) Profuse, excessively lavish, prodigal, wasteful, thriftless, reckless; b (of persons) given to prodigal, wasteful, reckless expenditure. 3. a (of demands, claims &c.) Unreasonably exacting, wild, passing the limits of what is just and reasonable; b (of price asked) excessively high, out of proportion to value, exorbitant.

extravagantly, adv. Prec. & **-ly**. In an extravagant manner (in all senses).

extravaganza, n. [1. ekstràvagánza; 2. ikstræ̀vəgǽnzə]. Ital. *stravaganza*, influenced by *extravagance*. A musical or non-musical burlesque or farce characterized by wildly irregular and improbable action.

extravagate, vb. intrans. [1. ekstrávagāt; 2. ikstrǽvəgeit]. Lat.; **extra-** & *vagāt-(um)*, P.P. of *vagāri*, 'to wander about'. See **extravagant**. Not common. a To wander aimlessly or widely; b to be extravagant.

extravasate, vb. trans. & intrans. [1. ekstrávasāt; 2. ekstrǽvəseit]. Lat.; **extra-** & *vās*, 'vessel', see **vase**, & **-ate**. (of action on blood, lymph &c.) 1. trans. To force out otherwise than through the normal channels. 2. intrans. To ooze, filter out (from a vein or artery), into surrounding tissues of the body, as result of bruise.

extravasation, n. [1. èkstravasáshun; 2. èkstrævəséiʃən]. Prec. & **-ion**. Process of extravasating; result of this, as seen in a bruise.

extreme (I.), adj. [1. ekstrḗm; 2. ikstrím]. Fr., fr. Lat. *extrēmus*, superl. of *exterus*, 'outside, outward, external'. See **exterior** & **extra (I.)**. 1. (relating to space) Furthest off, most remote; a at or near the edge of a flat surface: *the extreme border of a field*; *extreme limit of an area of land*; b nearest to either end of a line: *the extreme end of a line, of a rope* &c. 2. (relating to time) Earliest, or (more commonly) latest, most remote from middle point of a period: *extreme youth, extreme old age*; *in one's extreme moments*, just before death; *extreme unction*, sacrament of anointing shortly before death. 3. (of quality or degree) Very highest, most intense, greatest degree obtainable: *extreme good sense*; *extreme kindness, cleverness, patience, clearness* &c. 4. a (of opinions, temper &c.) Very advanced along a particular line; immoderate in any direction: *to hold extreme views in politics, on Baptism, the Eucharist* &c.; b (of persons) holding extreme views, going beyond what the majority consider reasonable: *the extreme men of one generation are often considered the moderates in the next.* 5. (of action and expression) Very severe, going to the last limit of severity; very drastic, uncompromising: *what he did was rather extreme, but circumstances required it*; *extreme measures*; *extreme punishment*; *an extreme thing to say.* Phr. *the extreme penalty (of the law)*, capital punishment.

extreme (II.), adv., fr. prec. Now obs. For *extremely*. Such phrases as *an extreme fine woman* &c. were common in 17th and 18th centuries.

extreme (III.), n., fr. **extreme (I.)**. 1. The extreme limit, utmost verge, extremity; now used almost entirely in non-material sense, except in *the extremes of north and south* and a few such phrases. 2. Utmost possible, tolerable, or conceivable degree: *extremes of heat and cold*; *an extreme of fashion.* Phr. *extremes meet*, used in various, often vague, senses. 3. a An extreme condition; specif., danger, misery, disaster &c.: *to be constantly in extremes*; b action demanded by extreme, stringent conditions: *to go to extremes.*

extremely, adv. **extreme (I.)** & **-ly**. 1. In an extreme manner; to an extreme degree: *it pains me extremely to have to say this.* 2. (colloq., used as mere intens.) Very: *an extremely nice young man.*

extremism, n. [1. ekstrḗmizm; 2. ikstrímizəm]. **extreme (I.)** & **-ism**. The state of being extreme in opinions; the holding of extreme views.

extremist, n. [1. ekstrḗmist; 2. ikstrímist]. **extreme (I.)** & **-ist**. One who favours extreme views, esp. in politics, religion &c.

extremity, n. [1. ekstrémiti; 2. ikstrémiti]. Fr. *extrémité*, fr. Lat. *extrēmitāt-(em)*. See **extreme (I.)** & **-ity**. (of material things) 1. Remotest part, furthest confines of an area: *the furthest extremity of Africa.* 2. a The hands or feet: *his extremities grew cold as death approached*; b the end, or point, of some other part of the body: *a pimple at the very extremity of the nose.* (of non-material things) 3. a Very highly developed condition; greatest, most intense degree: *an extremity of pain and misery*; b last, most severe and aggravated, degree of discomfort, suffering, poverty, embarrassment, misfortune &c.: *to be in a dire extremity*; *I turn to you for help in my extremity.* 4. An extreme measure; drastic, severe course of action: *as all else has failed I must now proceed to extremities.*

extricable, adj. [1. ékstrikabl; 2. ékstrikəbl]. See next word & **-able**. Capable of being extricated.

extricate, vb. trans. [1. ékstrikāt; 2. ékstrikeit]. Lat. *extrīcāt-(um)*, P.P. type of *extrīcāre*, 'to disentangle', fr. **ex-** & *trīcae* (pl.), 'trifles, nonsense; hindrances, perplexities'; prob. fr. Aryan *treik- & connected w. base *trek^w-, *terek^w- &c., 'to twist, wind', q.v. under **torque**, & cp. *torquēre*, 'twist' &c., fr. form *tr̥k^w- of this base, q.v. also under **tort**, **extort**. 1. To disentangle, release from restraining meshes, hindrances &c.: *the lion managed to extricate itself from the net.* 2. (fig.) To free (a person) from perplexities, difficulties, embarrassments, dangers &c.

extrication, n. [1. èkstrikáshun; 2. èkstrikéiʃən]. Prec. & **-ion**. Act of freeing from difficulties &c.; disentanglement.

extrinsic(al), adj. [1. ekstrínsik(l); 2. ikstrínsik(l)] or, when contrasted w. *intrinsic* [1. ékstrinsik; 2. ékstrinsik]. Fr. *extrinsèque*, fr. Lat. *extrinsecus*, 'from without, from abroad', fr. *exter-*, 'outward' &c., see **exterior**, & *secus*, 'by, beside, along', orig. 'following', & fr. Lat. base *seq-*, as in *sequor*, 'I follow', q.v. under **second** & **sequela**. Cp. also **intrinsic**. External, lying outside; not belonging to the real character or essence; not inherent: *good manners are not wholly extrinsic to a refined nature and noble character.*

extrinsically, adv. Prec. & **-ly**. In an extrinsic manner; as something extrinsic.

extrorse, adj. [1. ekstrórs; 2. ikstrɔ́s]. Lat. *extrorsus*, 'in an outward direction', fr. **extra-** & *versus*, 'turned', P.P. of *vertere*. See **version**, **verse**, **versus**. (bot., of anthers) Turned outwards, facing away from axis.

extroversion, n. [1. èkstrovérshun; 2. èkstrəvə́ʃən]. See prec. **extra-** & **version**. Act of turning outwards; condition of being so turned; specif. (surg.) *extroversion of the bladder* &c., state of being turned inside out.

extrovert, n. [1. ékstrōvërt; 2. ékstrouvə̄t]. See prec. Person psychologically averse from or not accustomed to introspection, as distinguished from *introvert.*

extrude, vb. trans. & intrans. [1. ekstrṓōd; 2. ikstrúd]. Lat. *extrūdere*, 'to thrust out, drive away', fr. **ex-** & *trūdere*, 'to push, shove', fr. Aryan base *treud-, *troud-, whence also O.E. *þrēotan*, 'to weary', & *þrēatan*, 'to urge on, press, afflict; threaten' &c. See further **threat** & **thrust**. 1. trans. To thrust out, push away; to drive out, expel. 2. intrans. To be extruded.

extrusion, n. [1. ekstrṓōzhun; 2. ikstrúžən], fr. Lat. *extrūs-(um)*, P.P. type of *extrūdere*. See prec. & **-ion**. Act of extruding; state of being extruded; expulsion.

extrusive, adj. [1. ekstrṓōsiv; 2. ikstrúsiv]. Lat. *extrūs-*, as in prec., & **-ive**. 1. Tending to extrude. 2. (geol.) Appearing on surface of the ground, as though thrust out: *extrusive rock.*

exuberance, -cy, n. [1. ekzúberans(i); 2. ikzjúbərəns(i)]. Fr. *exubérance*, Lat. *exūberantia*. See **exuberant** & **-ce**. Quality of being exuberant; abundance, copiousness, state of overflowing: (of material things) *an exuberance of vegetable growth*; (in non-material sense) *an exuberance of feeling, delight, mirth* &c.

exuberant, adj. [1. ekzúberant; 2. ikzjúbərənt]. Lat. *exūberant-(em)*, Pres. Part. of *exūberāre*, 'to come forth in abundance, grow luxuriantly, to abound', fr. **ex-** & *ūber*, 'udder; fertility'. See **uberous** & **udder**. 1. (of material things) a Growing copiously, abundantly; existing, occurring, in great abundance; excessively fertile, luxuriant: *exuberant growth, foliage*; b (of persons) overflowing with life and spirits; (of conditions) suggestive of life and vigour: *exuberant health.* 2. (of non-material things) a Full of life; brimming over with, expressing, gaiety and good humour: *exuberant spirits*; b (of manner) effusive, flamboyant; c (of speech and style) immoderately copious, flowery, unrestrained, too rich in ornament; d (of the mind and its processes) productive, fertile: *exuberant genius, imagination* &c.

exuberantly, adv. Prec. & **-ly**. In an exuberant manner; lavishly, abundantly, copiously.

exuberate, vb. intrans. [1. ekzúberāt; 2. ikzjúbəreit]. Lat. *exūberāt-(um)*, P.P. type of *exūberāre*. See **exuberant**. (rare) To abound, be exuberant.

exudation, n. [1. èksūdáshun; 2. èksjudéiʃən], fr. Lat. *exsūdāt-(um)*, P.P. type of *exsūdāre*, 'to come out by sweating', & **-ion**. See **exude**. Act or process of exuding; that which exudes; sweat or other humours.

exudative, adj. [1. ekzúdativ; 2. ikzjúdətiv]. Lat. *exsūdāt-*, as in prec., & **-ive**. Connected with exudation.

exude, vb. intrans. & trans. [1. ekzúd; 2. ikzjúd], fr. Lat. *exsūdāre*, 'to come out by sweating', fr. **ex-** & *sūdāre*, 'to sweat', fr. *sūdor*, 'sweat'; this is fr. Aryan *swoid-, & is precisely cogn. w. Gmc. *swait-, O.E. *swāt*, 'sweat', n., whence *swǣtan*, 'to sweat', fr. *swātjan. See **sudorific** & **sweat**. 1. intrans. To come out as sweat, or like sweat; to ooze, flow out, through the pores of an animal, or through corresponding organs of a plant: *sweat exudes from the pores*; *matter from a wound*; *sap, moisture from leaves.* 2. trans. To pass out through the pores &c.: *to exude sweat, moisture* &c.

exult, vb. intrans. [1. ekzúlt; 2. ikzʌ́lt], fr. Lat. *ex(s)ultāre*, 'to leap about; to leap for joy; to rejoice, triumph', fr. **ex-** & *saltāre*, 'to leap', freq. of *salīre*, 'to bound, jump'. See **salient**. To rejoice greatly; to be in high spirits, to be jubilant; to triumph gleefully: *to exult at, over, one's success.*

exultancy, n. [1. ekzúltansi; 2. ikzʌ́ltənsi]. **exultant** & **-cy**. State of exulting; jubilation, triumph.

exultant, adj. [1. ekzúltant; 2. ikzʌ́ltənt]. Lat. *ex(s)ultant-(em)*, Pres. Part. of *ex(s)ultāre*. See **exult**. Jubilant, gleefully triumphant.

exultantly, adv. Prec. & **-ly**. In an exultant manner; triumphantly.

exultation, n. [1. èksultáshun; 2. èksəltéiʃən]. Lat. *exultāt-(um)*, P.P. type of *exultāre*. See **exult** & **-ion**. Act of exulting; jubilation, triumphant mirth.

exuviae, n. pl. [1. ekzûviē; 2. ɛkzjûvii]. Lat., 'what is stripped off, clothing; cast-, or stripped-off skin of an animal; slough', fr. same base as *exuere*, 'to pull, strip, off', fr. **ex-** & **-ewō-*, wh. occurs also in Lat. *induere*, 'to pull on, put on (clothes &c.)'. Walde suggests that a form of the same base, reduced to *-w-* & w. amplification, occurs also in Lat. *vestis*, 'garment', wh. wd. represent **west-* fr. a full grade **ew-es-t-*. But the etymol. is obscure. See **vest.** Outer coverings of animals which have been cast, such as skins of snakes, shells of crustaceans &c.

exuvial, adj. [1. ekzûvial; 2. ɛkzjûviəl]. Prec. & **-al.** Pertaining to, consisting of, exuviae.

exuviate, vb. intrans. [1. ekzûviāt; 2. ɛkzjûvieit]. **exuviae** & **-ate.** To cast the skin, as does a snake.

exuviation, n. [1. ekzûviáshun; 2. ɛkzjûviéiʃən]. Prec. & **-ion.** Act or process of exuviating; cast-off skin or shell.

ex voto, adv. & n. [1. éks vṓtō; 2. éks vóutou]. Lat., 'as, in fulfilment of, a vow'. See **vote (I.).** **a** adv. In pursuance of a vow; **b** n., something offered on account of a vow, esp. thank-offering placed in a church after safe return from a voyage, recovery from illness &c.

eyas, n. [1. ías; 2. áiəs], for *a niais*, fr. Fr., 'nestling', fr. Low Lat. **nīdāc-em* fr. Lat. *nīdus*, 'nest'. See **nidus.** A nestling; specif., a young hawk taken from the nest.

eye (I.), n. [1. ī; 2. ai]. O.E. *ēage*, M.E. *ēye*, *īʒe*, *ȳe*. The Gmc. type was **augōn-*, as is shown by the O.E., & further by O.S. *ōga*, O.H.G. *ouga*, Mod. Germ. *auge*, Goth. *augō*, stem *augōn-*. The cognates outside Gmc. show that the diphthong is peculiar to Gmc., e.g. Lat. *oc-ulus*, Gk. *ókkos*, 'eye'; Scrt. *akši*, O. Slav. *oko*, O. Prussian *ackis* &c. The *au* in the Gmc. type of this word may be best accounted for by assuming that it has been influenced by the word for *ear*; Goth. *ausō*, O.E. *ēare* &c., where the *au* is orig.; see **ear (I.).** The close association in mind & speech between *eye* & *ear* is quite sufficient to explain the influence of the old form of the latter upon the former. See **ocular, oculist, optic.** **1. a** The organ of sight: *to lose an eye*; **b** (by transf.) the eyesight itself: *to injure one's eyes*; *to have sharp, weak, eyes*; **c** that part of the head or face around, or near the eye: *to hit a man, give him one, in the eye*; *a black eye*; Phrs., *to keep one's, an, eye on*, to observe, look after; *to keep one's, both, eyes wide open*, to be on the alert; (colloq.) *to do in the eye*, to cheat; *all my eye*, all nonsense; *up to the eyes in (business &c.)*, much occupied, overwhelmed with; *mind your eye!*, look out, be careful; *in the eye of the law*, as the law regards it; *oh my eye!*, exclamation of surprise &c.; *the mind's eye*, memory; *in the eye of the wind*, dead against the wind; *to see something with half an eye*, see it easily because it is obvious; *to clap eyes on*, to look at, see; *to make a person open his eyes*, surprise him; *to open a person's eyes to something*, make him aware of it, bring it to his notice; *to feast one's eyes on*, to look at with delight; *to run one's eye over*, glance at, survey, hastily; *to be unable to take one's eyes off*, be fascinated by, view with admiration; *one in the eye* (fig.), a snub, rebuff; *with the naked eye*, without the help of glasses. **2.** The external, visible portion of the eye, considered as a feature; specif., the iris: *to have lovely eyes, blue eyes* &c. Phr. *to make eyes at*, to look meaningly at, to ogle; *sheep's eyes*, amorous glances. **3.** Power of observation by eye, keenness of visual perception: *to have an eye for colour, for a pretty girl*; *where are your eyes?* Phrs. *to have an eye in one's head*; *an eye for business, for the main chance*; *the eye of a painter* &c. **4.** One of various objects resembling, or supposed to resemble, an eye; **a** bud, shoot on a plant; spot in a potato tuber whence new plants arise; **b** small metal loop for fastening clothes &c.: *hook and eye*; **c** loop, often having metal lining, at the end of a rope; **d** hole drilled in a needle, for holding thread; **e** the glass of a pair of spectacles.

eye (II.), vb. trans., fr. prec. To look at, survey, carefully and narrowly; to stare at; to glance at frequently.

eyeball, n. [1. íbawl; 2. áibɔ̄l]. The globular body comprising the eye and all the structures enclosed in the cornea.

eyebright, n. [1. íbrīt; 2. áibrait]. Small white flower, the euphrasy.

eyebrow, n. [1. íbrou; 2. áibrau]. **a** Bony ridge over the eye; **b** the arched row of hairs growing thereon.

eyed, adj. [1. īd; 2. aid]. **eye (I.)** & **-ed.** Having eyes; furnished with spots like eyes.

eyeglass, n. [1. íglahs; 2. áigl*ā*s]. Any of various contrivances with lenses for assisting the sight; **a** a single glass for fixing in the eye orbit, monocle; **b** usually *eyeglasses*, pair of lenses connected by bar which passes across or rests upon the top of the bridge of the nose; pince-nez, spectacles; **c** the eye-piece of telescope, field-glass, or microscope.

eye-hole, n. **1.** The eye orbit. **2.** Hole in anything through which the eye looks.

eyelash, n. [1. ílash; 2. áilæʃ]. One of the hairs which fringe the eyelids; *eyelashes*, the whole of these collectively.

eyeless, adj. [1. íles; 2. áilis]. **eye (I.)** & **-less.** Lacking eyes; blind: '*Eyeless in Gaza, at the mill with slaves*' (Milton, 'Samson').

eyelet, n. [1. ílet; 2. áilit]. M.E. *oilet*, O. Fr. *oillet*, 'little eye', fr. *œil*, 'eye'. The spelling influenced by **eye.** **a** Small hole worked in the material of a garment, through which a cord or hook is passed for fastening garment; **b** hole strengthened with metal ring, in a sail, rick-sheet &c., through which a rope is passed; **c** metal ring which lines this hole.

eyelid, n. [1. ílid; 2. áilid]. Movable flap of tissue which protects the eye.

eyemark, n. [1. ímark; 2. áimāk]. Mark for the eye; a spectacle.

eye-opener, n. (colloq.) **a** A surprising event, action, or narrative of such, which startles and disconcerts; **b** something, an action or event, which reveals some fact, circumstances, or state of mind hitherto unknown; something which opens one's eyes to facts &c.

eye-piece, n. The lens or combination of lenses in a telescope, microscope &c., through which the eye looks directly.

eye-service, n. That performed only while the master is watching.

eyeshot, n. [1. íshot; 2. áiʃɔt]. Reach of eye, range of vision: *within eyeshot.* Cp. *earshot.*

eye-sore, n. Something unpleasing or offensive to the eye.

eye-splice, n. One made in forming a loop with the end of a rope.

eye-tooth, n. One of the so-called canine teeth in upper jaw.

eyewash, n. [1. íwosh; 2. áiwɔʃ]. **a** Lotion for the eyes; **b** (slang) something done to impress an observer, which is either not done at all except under inspection, or which is of no practical utility.

eye witness, n. Person who actually sees **an** action performed, or an event happening.

eyot, n. [1. āt; 2. eit]; also **ait.** O.E. *īgeoð*, spelt *eyt* in early M.E., 'little island', dimin. of O.E. *ēġ*, *īġ*, 'island'. The suff. is apparently influenced by O. Fr. dimin. **-ot.** Small island, esp. in the Thames.

eyre, n. [1. ār; 2. ɛə]. M.E., fr. O. Fr. *eire*, 'journey, circuit, way'; cp. O. Fr. *eirer*, 'to journey', fr. L. Lat. *iterāre*, for *itinerāre*, fr. *iter*, 'a journey'. See **iterate.** Journey, circuit; used chiefly in connexion with the itinerant justices of Henry II., known **as** *Justices in Eyre.*

eyrie, eyry, n. See **aerie.**

F

F, f [1. ef; 2. ɛf]. The sixth letter of the alphabet; for use in abbreviation, symbols &c. see end of Dictionary; (mus.) fourth note in scale of C major.

fa, n. [1. fah; 2. fā]. Fourth of the syllables used in solmization, q.v.; the fourth note of the scale.

fabaceous, adj. [1. fabáshus; 2. fəbéiʃəs], fr. Lat. *fabāceus*, fr. *faba*, 'bean'; cogn. w. O. Slav. *bobŭ*, O. Prussian *babo*, 'bean'; relation w. **bean** doubtful. (bot.) Of, pertaining to, a plant family, *Fabaceae*, more or less identical with *Leguminosae*, of which the typical species is *Faba vulgaris*, the broad bean.

Fabian, n. & adj. [1. fábian; 2. féibiən], fr. Lat. *Fabiānus*, fr. the name of the Roman general Quintus Fabius, styled *Cunctator*, the delayer, one of the commanders against Hannibal. **1.** n. Member of socialist society founded in England in 1884, which advocates the gradual spreading of socialist principles by peaceful means. **2.** adj. **a** Employing, characterized by, cautious and dilatory methods to attain desired object (of military tactics and also of methods generally); **b** connected with, pertaining to, Fabians and their society: *Fabian Society.*

fable (I.), n. [1. fábl; 2. féibl], fr. Lat. *fābula*, 'narrative, account, story'; fr. base of *fāri*, 'to speak', & *fāma*, 'a report'; Aryan **bhā-*, 'to speak'. See **fame, fate.** **1.** A short tale intended to convey a moral, usually with animals or inanimate objects as actors: *Æsop's Fables.* **2.** A historical legend or myth. **3.** A statement having no basis in fact; a fiction, fantastic report, trumped-up story. **4.** (rare, archaic) The plot of a drama, epic &c.

fable (II.), vb. intrans., fr. O. Fr. *fabler*, fr. Lat. *fābulāri*, 'to speak', fr. *fābula*, 'a speech, tale'. See prec. To invent fictions; relate, and spread fictitious tales; to romance.

fabled, adj. [1. fábld; 2. féibld], fr. P.P. of prec. Invented, fictitious, mythical, legendary.

fabliau, n. [1. fábliō; 2. fæbliou], fr. Low Lat. **fābulellus*, dimin. of *fābula*, 'story' &c. See **fable.** Mediaeval French tale in verse, of a humorous and often of a coarse character.

fabric, n. [1. fábrik; 2. fæbrik], fr. Fr., fr. Lat. *fabrica*, 'a workshop; something constructed by a skilled workman; a building'; fr. *faber*, 'a worker in wood, stone &c.; an artificer'. Lat. *fab-* is fr. Aryan base **dhabh-*, **dhōbh-*, 'to make suitable; fit together; make beautiful' &c.; fr. same base comes Gmc. **dab-*, as in Goth. *gadaban*, 'to suit', & O.E. *ġe-dafnian*, 'to be fitting, becoming', also *ġe-dafen*, 'suitable, fitting, right', & *ġe-dæfte*, 'gentle, meek'. See further under **daft** & **deft.** The general meaning is something put together, from originally separate elements, with plan and design, so as to form a unity; something having construction. **1. a** A building, structure: '*From the earth a fabric huge Rose like an exhalation*' (Milton); **b** the actual construction, framework, walls &c. of a building as distinct from its decoration. **2.** (of non-material things) Mode of construction, framework, essential character of an institution, system &c.: *the fabric of society.* **3. a** Woven material of silk, wool, cotton &c.: *silk and woollen fabrics*; **b** the manner in which material is woven; quality, texture: *a cloth of exquisite fabric*; (also attrib.) *fabric gloves*, gloves made of textile, woven material, as cotton &c.

fabricate, vb. trans. [1. fábrikāt; 2. fǽbrikeit], fr. Lat. *fabricāt-(um)*, P.P. type of Lat. *fabricāre*, 'to make, construct', fr. *fabrica*, 'construction'. See prec. **1. a** To construct, make, manufacture; to put parts together to form a complete object; **b** to imitate with intent to deceive, fake, forge: *to fabricate a false will; to fabricate sham flint arrow-heads* &c. **2.** To invent falsely, trump up, concoct: *to fabricate a charge.*

fabrication, n. [1. fàbrikáshun; 2. fæbrikéiʃən]. Prec. & **-ion. 1.** The act of fabricating; state of being fabricated. **2.** Something fabricated; **a** (of material things) a forgery, sham, counterfeit; **b** an invention, fictitious statement: *his story was an entire fabrication.*

fabulist, n. [1. fábūlist; 2. fǽbjulist], fr. Fr. *fabuliste*, fr. Lat. *fābula*, 'a speech, tale', see **fable (I.)**, & **-ist. 1.** A composer, inventor, of fables. **2.** (rarely) One who invents false tales and reports; a liar.

fabulosity, n. [1. fàbūlósiti; 2. fæbjulɔ́siti], fr. Lat. *fābulōs-(us)*, 'fabulous' (& **-ity**), fr. *fābul-(a)*, 'a speech, fable', see **fable (I.)**, & **-ous.** The quality of being fabulous.

fabulous, adj. [1. fábūlus; 2. fǽbjūləs], fr. Lat. *fābul-(a)*, 'a speech, story'. See **fable** & **-ous. 1.** Belonging to, resembling, a fable; unhistorical, legendary, mythical: *a fabulous story; the unicorn, griffin, and other fabulous beasts.* **2.** Beyond the limit of belief; incredible, exaggerated; hence, very large, extensive: *fabulous wealth; a house of fabulous size.* **3.** Given to the composition of fables: *a fabulous writer* &c.

fabulously, adv. Prec. & **-ly.** In a fabulous manner; as a fable.

fabulousness, n. See prec. & **-ness.** The quality of being fabulous.

façade, n. [1. fasáhd; 2. fæsɑ́d]. Fr., fr. **face (I.)** & **-ade.** The front, principal face, of a building.

face (I.), n. [1. fās; 2. feis], fr. Fr., fr. Low Lat. *facia*, 'face, appearance', fr. Lat. *faciēs*, 'form, figure, shape; face, visage; outward appearance, look, aspect'. The word is fr. same base as Lat. *fax*, 'torch', stem *fac-*, 'to shine'. See also **facet** & **facetious. 1. a** Front of head, esp. of human head, from top of forehead to point of chin, including cheeks and features; countenance; Phrs. *to fly in the face of*, defy rashly; *to look a person in the face*, look steadily at; (fig.) *to be unable to look one in the face*, to feel shame in presence of; *to save (one's) face*, escape shame, disgrace, or humiliation; *to show one's face*, appear; *face to face with*, in the presence of, confronting; *in the face of*, in the presence of, confronting; in spite of; *to one's face*, openly, in one's presence; *to set one's face against*, disapprove of, oppose; **b** expression, look, cast of countenance: *a sad face, a face of anger*; Phrs. *to make, pull, a face*, to grimace; *to pull a long face*, to look dismal, disapproving &c.; *to put a bold face on (a situation* &c.), carry off boldly and with a confident manner. **2** (fig.) Audacity, impudence, impertinence; chiefly in such Phr. as, *to have the face to say, do* &c., to be impudent enough to. **3.** (of circumstances, situations) Outward appearance, first impression gained by superficial examination. Phrs. *on the face of it*, judging by appearances, at the first blush; *to put a new face on a matter*, cause to appear different, cause to produce different impression. **4. a** Surface, outer part: *on the face of the earth; face of a door, of cloth* &c.; **b** specif., hard, smooth outer surface cut on dressed stone. **5. a** The right side, most important side or surface, of anything; that side of an object which is designed for some special purpose: *the face of a building, house; face of a card*, the side on which the marks of value are; Phr. *to lie on its face*, wrong side up; **b** specif. (printing) that surface of type with which the impression is made. **6.** Dial of a clock or watch.

face (II.), vb. trans. & intrans., fr. prec. **A.** trans. **1. a** (of persons and other living beings) To be turned towards, have one's face and gaze directed towards, be opposite to: *the man now facing me is the one I mean; to face the enemy*; Phr. *to face the music*, be ready to undergo examination, trial &c.; **b** (of inanimate objects) to be oriented, turned towards, to look in particular direction: *the house faces the south; the window faces the street, sea* &c.; *the illustration should face p. 30 of the book.* **2. a** To dare, have courage, to come face to face with; to confront, oppose: *to face an opponent boldly, and refute him*; also *face up to; to face a lion and put him to flight*; **b** (fig.) to undergo with courage, to brave, stand up to; not to be afraid of, or disconcerted by: *he had faced risks, dangers, and death a hundred times; I can't face the disgrace of failure.* **3.** To recognize existence of, and be prepared to meet: *we've got to face facts; the new circumstances must be faced*; also *face up to.* **4.** To put a facing on to; **a** to apply, fasten, a layer of a different material on to outer surface of: *to face a building with marble, a cabinet with a veneer of rose-wood* &c.; **b** to attach facings, trimmings, ornaments to: *to face a coat with gold braid.* **5.** To put a hard, smooth outer surface on (stone); to dress: *this stone has not been properly faced.* **B.** intrans. **1.** To be oriented, look, be turned: *How does your house face? It faces (to the) north.* **2.** (mil.) To turn the body in given direction, using heels as a pivot, without shifting one's ground: *right face!*, word of command.

-faced, adj. [1. fāst; 2. feist]. **face (I.)** & **-ed.** Having a face of specified character, shape &c.: *double-faced.*

facer, n. [1. fáser; 2. féisə]. **face (I.)** & **-er. a** A severe blow in the face; **b** hence, anything that disconcerts; a sudden difficulty, problem.

facet, n. [1. fáset; 2. fǽsit], fr. Fr. *facette.* **face (I.)** & **-ette. a** One of many small plane surfaces into which precious stones are cut, and which many crystals have naturally; **b** similar surface in compound eye of insect.

faceted, adj. [1. fáseted; 2. fǽsitid]. Prec. & **-ed.** Having facets.

facetiae, n. [1. faséshiē; 2. fəsíʃii]. Lat., plur. of *facētia*, 'jest, witticism', fr. *facētus*, 'elegant, courteous, polite; witty, humorous'. See **facetious. 1.** Pleasantries, witticisms. **2.** Booksellers' term for books of a coarse or obscene character.

facetious, adj. [1. faséshus; 2. fəsíʃəs], fr. Fr., fr. Lat. *facēt-(us)*, 'elegant, polite; witty', see prec. & **-ous.** From same base as Lat. *fax*, 'torch', & *faciēs*, 'countenance'. Cp. **face (I.).** The orig. meaning of the base is 'shining, brilliant'. Jocose, waggish, slyly humorous.

facetiously, adv. Prec. & **-ly.** In a facetious manner.

facetiousness, n. See prec. & **-ness.** The quality of being facetious.

facia, n. [1. fásha; 2. fǽʃə]. See **fascia.** Flat plate or board on shop-front, exhibiting owner's name &c.

facial, adj. [1. fáshal; 2. féiʃəl], fr. Med. Lat. *faciāl-(is)*, fr. Lat. *faci-(ēs)*, 'face, appearance'. See **face (I.)** & **-al.** Of, pertaining to, the face: *facial expression, contour* &c.

facial angle, n. (anthrop.) That formed by intersection of a line drawn from base of skull outwards to base of nostril, with another drawn so as to pass from outside most prominent part of forehead to base of nostril.

-facient, suff. representing Lat. *-facient-(em)*, Pres. Part. of *-facere*, 'to make', added to intrans. vbs. in *-ē(re)*, to give trans. meaning, 'to cause to become'; forms adjs.: *liquefacient* &c. See **fact.**

facile, adj. [1. fásil, -il; 2. fǽsail, -il], fr. Fr., fr. Lat. *facilis*, 'easy; yielding, compliant', ultimately the word means 'do-able' & is fr. base *fac-*, as in *facere*, 'to make, do' &c. See **fact. 1.** Easily done; easily gained: *a facile victory.* **2.** (of work, expression &c.) Not requiring strenuous effort; showing signs of easy, rapid performance; hence, **a** fluent, easy, ready: *a facile style; facile verse* &c.; **b** (in unfavourable sense) hasty, superficial, glib; **c** (of persons) capable of producing facile work (in both senses). **3.** (of persons) Pliant, easily swayed, easy-going.

facile princeps, adj. [1. fásili prínseps; 2. fǽsili prínsεps]. Lat. Easily first, or pre-eminent.

facilitate, vb. trans. [1. fasílitāt; 2. fəsíliteit], fr. Lat. *facilit-(as)*, 'easiness, facility'. See **facility** & **-ate.** To make easy, lessen difficulty of, further, promote.

facilitation, n. [1. fasìlitáshun; 2. fəsìlitéiʃən]. Prec. & **-ion.** The act or process of facilitating.

facility, n. [1. fasíliti; 2. fəsíliti], fr. Fr. *facilité*, fr. Lat. *facilitāt-(em)*, 'easiness; fluency; willingness, affability'; fr. *facil-(is)*, 'easy'. See **facile** & **-ity. 1.** (somewhat rare) Absence of difficulty, ease. **2. a** Quality of mind which makes understanding and learning easy; aptitude, special talent: *to have great facility in learning languages*; **b** physical dexterity, deftness: *he showed marvellous facility in playing difficult music.* **3.** Circumstance conducive to the easy accomplishment of an object; opportunity, assistance: *my way of life offers no facilities for study; the accused was accorded every facility for producing evidence in his favour.*

facing, n. [1. fásing; 2. féisiŋ]. **face (II.)** & **-ing. 1.** Outer layer, coating, of different material: *a brick wall with a facing of stone.* **2.** (pl.). **a** Trimmings, ornamentation &c., fastened on to a garment, made of different colour or material from this: *a black coat with red silk facings*; specif. **b** *regimental facings*, distinctively coloured cuffs, collar &c. **3.** (pl., mil.) Turning movements carried out by soldier in drilling. Phr. *to put soldiers through their facings*, to test their knowledge of, and smartness in, drill; (fig.) *to put a person through his facings*, test his readiness in, knowledge of, anything.

facinorous, adj. [1. fasínorus; 2. fæsínərəs], fr. Lat. *facinorōsus*, fr. *facinus*, 'a deed', esp. 'a wicked deed, crime', fr. *facere*, 'to do'. See **fact** & **-ous.** (archaic or rare) Wicked, criminal, atrocious.

facsimile (I.), n. [1. faksímili; 2. fæksímili]. Lat. *fac*, imperat. sing. of *facere*, 'to make', see **fact**, & *simile*, neut. of *similis*, 'like', see **similar.** An exact copy, absolutely accurate reproduction: *a facsimile of a manuscript, picture, seal* &c.; *a facsimile edition of a manuscript, book* &c. Phr. *in facsimile*, exactly, accurately.

facsimile (II.), vb. trans., fr. prec. To reproduce in facsimile.

fact, n. [1. fakt; 2. fækt], fr. Lat. *fact-(um)*, 'something done, a deed, act', fr. P.P. type of *facere*, 'to do, make'; fr. Aryan base **dhē-*, **dhə-* &c., 'to place, put'. From this base comes also Gk. *ti-thē-mi*, 'I put, place'; Scrt. *á-dhām*, 'I put'; O.E. *dōn*, 'to do' &c. See **do, deed, thesis.** The base is extended by the formative element *-k-* in Lat. *facere* &c., cp. also perf. *fēc-i*, w. wh. cp. Gk. *thḗkē*, 'case to put something in'; Scrt. *dhākaś*, 'place where something is kept', all fr. type **dhēk-*. **1.** Something done, a deed, act; something that has happened, an event; now only in Phr. *before, after, the fact; to confess the fact.* **2.** Something, some object or condition that actually exists in space; an event, mental or physical, that has actually occurred; something which has been experienced: *poverty and crime are solid facts which have to be reckoned with.* **3. a** An event asserted to have happened; action alleged to have been done; something adduced as a truth: *the facts are as follows; it is not a fact that Scotsmen cannot see a joke*; **b** the statement of such assumed events: *I dispute all your facts.* **4.** The quality of being actual; reality, actuality; quality of being established by actual experience, as distinguished from theory, speculation, or the creation of fancy: *a story founded on fact; to distinguish fact from fiction.* Phrs. *as a* *matter of fact, in point of fact, in fact,* really, actually; *the fact of the matter is,* the truth about the matter is. **5.** (law) A circumstance presented as part of a case in a court of law as having actually occurred, and proved by evidence, as distinguished from the legal effect or bearing of such occurrence: *questions of fact are for the jury, questions of law for the judge to decide.*

faction, n. [1. fákshun; 2. fǽkʃən], fr. Fr., fr. Lat. *factiōn-(em),* 'a making, preparing; a company, class, set; a political party', fr. *fact-(um),* P.P. type of *facere,* 'to make'. See **fact** & **-ion.** **1.** A group of persons within a larger community, who dissociate themselves from the opinions and ideals commonly held; especially a discontented section, clique, cabal, within a political party: *the petty factions into which a once great party has split.* **2.** Spirit, principle, of dissension; party or sectional strife: *serious political controversy degenerated into mere faction.*

-faction, suff. forming ns., fr. Lat. vbs. in *-facere*; fr. P.P. type *-fact-(um)* & **-ion**: *satisfaction, stupefaction* &c. Occasionally forming ns. fr. Lat. vbs. in *-ficāre,* e.g. *petrifaction,* instead of **-fication.**

factional, adj. [1. fákshunl; 2. fǽkʃənəl]. **faction** & **-al.** Pertaining to faction, or to a faction.

factious, adj. [1. fákshus; 2. fǽkʃəs], fr. Lat. *factiōs-(us),* 'factious, seditious', fr. *factiō-(nem),* see **faction,** & **-ous.** Addicted to faction; tending to promote dissension; seditious.

factiously, adv. Prec. & **-ly.** In a factious manner.

factiousness, n. See prec. & **-ness.** The quality of being factious.

factitious, adj. [1. faktíshus; 2. fæktíʃəs], fr. Lat. *factīci-(us),* 'made by art, artificial', fr. *fact-(um),* P.P. type of *facere,* 'to make'. See **fact** & **-ous.** **1.** Artificial, as contrasted with natural; sham, unreal, spurious: *factitious enthusiasm.* **2.** Arising from, adapted to, a conventional, artificial standard: *factitious taste.*

factitiously, adv. Prec. & **-ly.** In a factitious manner.

factitiousness, n. See prec. & **-ness.** The quality of being factitious.

factitive, adj. [1. fáktitiv; 2. fǽktitiv], fr. Lat. *factit-(āre),* 'to do frequently, practise; to make, declare, a person something', freq. vb. fr. *fact-(um),* P.P. type of Lat. *facere,* 'to make'. See **fact** & **-ive.** (gram.) Causal; *factitive verbs* are those expressing the ideas of calling, making, thinking; speaking generally, these verbs express result of an action which produces a new condition, whether in reality or in thought: *he made his brother king*; *to call a man a fool*; *to think one's wife an angel.*

factitively, adv. Prec. & **-ly.** As a factitive verb.

factor, n. [1. fáktor; 2. fǽktə], fr. Fr., fr. Lat. *factor,* 'a maker, doer, performer', fr. *fact-(um),* P.P. type of *facere,* 'to make, do'. See **fact** & **-or.** **1. a** An agent, deputy, representative; **b** one who transacts business for others, on commission; **c** (Scots) a land-agent, steward of estate. **2.** (math.) Any of the numbers or quantities which, when multiplied together, form a product. **3. a** An element, constituent, ingredient which enters into the composition of anything, especially something non-material: *wealth may be a factor of happiness*; **b** something which helps to bring about a particular result; an element, influence; contributing force, determining cause, in a process: *evolutionary factors.*

factorage, n. [1. fáktorij; 2. fǽktəridž]. Prec. & **-age.** Commission payable to a factor (**1, b**).

factorial, n. & adj. [1. faktórial; 2. fæktóriəl]. **factor** & **-ial.** **1.** n. The product of a given series of consecutive integers from 1 upwards. **2.** adj. Pertaining to a factorial.

factory, n. [1. fáktori; 2. fǽktəri]. **factor** & **-y.** **1.** (orig. sense) Merchant's or factor's trading-station in a foreign country. **2.** A building or group of buildings where articles of commerce are manufactured; a manufactory, workshop; *Factory Acts,* statutes dealing with and regulating conditions of work, such as ventilation, safety of machinery, fire protection, working hours &c., in the interests of those employed.

factotum, n. [1. faktótum; 2. fæktóutəm]. Med. Lat., fr. Lat. *fac,* imper. sing. of *facere,* 'to do', see **fact,** & *tōtum,* neut. sing. of *tōtus,* 'all', see **total.** A servant who performs duties of the most varied kind for his master; a man of all work, handy man.

factual, adj. [1. fáktūal; 2. fǽktjuəl]. **fact** & **-al** on anal. of **actual.** Pertaining to facts; of the nature of a fact.

factum, n. [1. fáktum; 2. fǽktəm]. Lat. See **fact.** Statement of facts; memorandum summarizing the chief points in a case. (French legal term.)

facula, n. [1. fákūla; 2. fǽkjulə], fr. Lat. *facula,* 'a little torch', dimin. fr. *fac-,* the base of *fax,* 'a torch'. See **face (I.)** & **-ule.** One of the brilliant streaks on the sun's disk.

facular, adj. [1. fákūlar; 2. fǽkjulə]. Lat. *facul-a,* 'a torch', see prec., & **-ar.** Pertaining to a facula.

faculous, adj. [1. fákūlus; 2. fǽkjuləs]. See prec. & **-ous.** Facular.

facultative, adj. [1. fákultātiv; 2. fǽkəlteitiv]. Fr., fr. Lat. *facultāt-(em),* 'power'. See next word & **-ive.** Optional, permissive; contingent. (A French usage.)

faculty, n. [1. fákulti; 2. fǽkəlti], fr. Fr., fr. Lat. *facultāt-(em),* 'capability, power; abundance, plenty', fr. Lat. *facil-(is),* 'easy'. See **facile** & **-ty.** **1.** (archaic) Capacity, aptitude, for any form of action or performance. **2.** Special inherent gift, proficiency, aptitude, of mind or character: *to have a,* or *the faculty of making friends, of making oneself agreeable, for doing and saying the right thing*; intelligence: *the mental faculties.* **3. a** Natural function of a particular organ of the body: *the faculty of vision, touch* &c.; **b** one of the powers or special functions of the mind: *the faculty of speech.* **4. a** One of the great, main divisions of knowledge (formerly Divinity, Law, Medicine, Arts) which make up the studies of a university; **b** the organized body of recognized teachers, of all ranks, who represent each of these, and similar divisions or branches of knowledge, in a university; **c** (popular) *the faculty,* the medical profession. **5.** (law) Dispensation, license, authorization to do something; specif. (eccles.) such authorization granted by the Chancellor of a Diocese.

fad, n. [1. fad; 2. fæd]. Etymol. unknown. A whim, craze; a fanciful, unreasoning enthusiasm for something; a queer notion strongly held for a short time; a fussy insistence on some habit or custom; a crotchet: *to have a fad for keeping pigs*; *the present taste in poetry among the young is a mere passing fad*; *to be full of fads and fancies.*

faddiness, n. [1. fádines; 2. fǽdinis]. **faddy** & **-ness.** The quality of being faddy.

faddish, adj. [1. fádish; 2. fǽdiʃ]. **fad** & **-ish.** Inclined to be faddy.

faddishness, n. Prec. & **-ness.** The quality of being faddy.

faddism, n. [1. fádizm; 2. fǽdizəm]. **fad** & **-ism.** Faddiness.

faddist, n. [1. fádist; 2. fǽdist]. **fad** & **-ist.** One who is given to fads.

faddy, adj. [1. fádi; 2. fǽdi]. **fad** & **-y.** Given to fads; exaggeratedly insistent upon one's whims and fancies.

fade, vb. intrans. & trans. [1. fād; 2. feid], fr. O. Fr. *fader,* fr. *fade,* 'dull'; prob. fr. Lat. *vapidum,* lit. 'that which has emitted steam, which has lost its spirit; flat, insipid', connected w. *vapor,* 'exhalation, steam'. See **vapid** & **vapour.** **A.** intrans. **1.** (of living things) To lose strength, vigour, freshness; droop, wither; to wane: *the flowers have faded*; *beauty fades*; *faded youth.* **2.** (of sensuous impressions) To become weaker, fainter, less distinct, disappear gradually; **a** (of visual impressions) to become dim, less visible, less bright: *the vision, light, glow, outline, has faded*; *the colours fade into one another,* pass by imperceptible gradations one into another, become blended; **b** (of sounds) to grow less loud or clear, become inaudible, die away: *the music, tones of the voices, faded in the distance.* **3.** (of colour and coloured things) To lose intensity, become paler and less vivid; to lose colour. **4.** (of mental and emotional impressions) To become faint, to be eliminated, pass away from the consciousness: *love had faded from his heart*; *the idea has faded from my mind*; *all memory of the past has faded.* **B.** trans. To cause to lose intensity of colour; to take the colour out of: *the sun has faded the (colour of the) curtains.*

fadeless, adj. [1. fādles; 2. féidlis]. Prec. & **-less.** **a** Unfading; not liable to fade; **b** incapable of being faded.

fadelessly, adv. Prec. & **-ly.** So as not to fade or become faded.

faecal, adj. [1. fékal; 2. fíkəl], fr. Lat. *faec-,* stem of *faex,* 'grounds, sediment, dregs'. See next word & **-al.** Pertaining to faeces; chiefly in expression *faecal matter.*

faeces, n. [1. fésēz; 2. físiz]. Lat., pl. of *faex,* 'grounds, sediment, dregs'. Origin unknown. Waste matter, excrement, from the bowels.

faerie, faery, n. & adj. [1. fári; 2. féəri]. Old spelling of **fairy.** M.E. *faerie* means 'enchantment'. See **fay.** **1.** n. Fairyland; enchantment. **2.** adj. **a** Of the fairies, fairylike; **b** imaginary, visionary.

fag (I.), vb. trans. & intrans. [1. fag; 2. fæg]. Origin unknown. Skeat suggests that the word is a variant of **flag (I.),** 'to droop' &c. **A.** trans. **1.** To weary, fatigue, exhaust: *to be fagged out.* **2.** (at public schools) To employ (boy) as a fag. **B.** intrans. **1.** To work laboriously, toil, slave: *to fag (away) at accounts.* **2.** (at school) To act as a fag.

fag (II.), n. See prec. **1. a** Laborious work, toil; tedious or exhausting occupation: *what a fag!*; *it's too much (of a) fag*; **b** fatigue, weariness, exhaustion. **2.** (at public school) Lower-form boy who performs certain tasks for a senior. **3.** (slang) Cigarette. In this sense back-formation from *fag-end.*

fagaceous, adj. [1. fagáshus; 2. fægéiʃəs], fr. Lat. *fāgus,* 'beech', & **-aceous**; for etymol. & cognates see **beech.** (bot.) Of, pertaining to, the *Fagaceae,* the order of plants which includes the beech, typical genus *Fagus,* the oak and chestnut.

fag-end, n. Last and inferior part of anything; remnant.

faggot (I.), fagot, n. [1. fágot; 2. fǽgət], fr. Fr. *fagot*; Ital. *fagotto.* The base is *fag-,* the ending being a dimin. suff. Meyer-Lübke suggests that *fag-* is a back-formation fr. Gk. *phákelos,* 'bundle', the etymol. of wh. is uncertain. **a** A bundle of sticks for use as fuel; **b** a bundle of iron or steel rods; **c** kind of savoury rissole sold at pork butcher's.

faggot (II.), vb. trans. & intrans., fr. prec. **1.** trans. To bind up into faggots. **2.** intrans. To make faggots.

faggot-vote, n. One obtained by a person who not having the necessary property qualification, had sufficient property conveyed to him temporarily to enable him to vote.

faggot-voter, n. Person using a faggot-vote.

Fahrenheit, n. [1. fárenhīt; 2. fǽrən(h)ait], fr. name of inventor. Type of thermometer principally used in England, in which freezing-point is reckoned at 32°, and the boiling-point 212°.

faience, n. [1. fahyóns; 2. faiɑ̃s]. Fr., fr. name of Italian town, Faenza. A kind of glazed and painted porcelain.

fail (I.), n. [1. fāl; 2. feil], fr. O. Fr. *faile,* n., fr. *faillir,* 'to fail, deceive'. See next word. Failure; only in Phr. *without fail,* for certain.

fail (**II.**), vb. intrans. & trans., fr. O. Fr. *faillir*, fr. Low Lat. *fallīre*, fr. Lat. *fallere*, 'to deceive, cheat; disappoint, fail'. Prob. cogn. w. Gk. *phēlós*, 'deceitful', *phēlós*, 'I deceive'; other cognates are doubtful, but see **false**. **A.** intrans. **1.** To be insufficient, inadequate, in amount, to come short of normal or expected supply: *the potato crop has failed this year*; *our water supply has failed.* Phrs. (with indirect object) *time would fail me*, would be too short; *my heart failed me*, I grew frightened; *words fail me*, I don't know what to say or how to say it. **2. a** To grow weak, lose vigour, deteriorate, diminish in strength: *his health, sight, has failed sadly of late*; **b** (of persons) to grow feeble, become languid and weak in health, lose vitality: *he is very old and failing rapidly.* **3.** To come short of, be wanting, defective **a** in performance of an obligation: *he fails greatly in the respect due to his elders*; **b** in possession of some mental or moral quality: *he has plenty of ability, but fails in truthfulness.* Phr. *don't fail to let me know when you return* &c., don't omit to . . . **4. a** To be unable to do something which one has attempted, to be unsuccessful in doing something or attaining some object: *in spite of our efforts we failed to reach the top of the mountain*; *he failed to obtain the post he sought*; Phr. *I fail to see*, am unable to understand; **b** specif., to be unsuccessful in passing, be ploughed in, a test or examination: *to fail in the degree examination.* **5.** To be unable to meet one's financial obligations, to become bankrupt. **B.** trans. **1.** To disappoint person's hopes, not to render a person services expected; be lacking in one's support of, desert: *as usual he failed me at the last minute.* **2.** (colloq., of examiners) To cause to fail in an examination; to decide and declare a candidate that is unsuccessful in an examination: *the examiners have failed half the candidates.*

failing (**I.**), n. [1. fāling; 2. féiliŋ]. Prec. & **-ing**. Weakness, defect, imperfection, fault, shortcoming: *we all have our little failings.*

failing (**II.**), prep., fr. Pres. Part. of **fail** (**II.**). Used in absolute construction. Without, in default of: *failing an answer to my letter by tomorrow I shall telegraph.*

failure, n. [1. fālūr; 2. féiljə]. **fail** (**II.**) & **-ure**. **1. a** Shortage, a running short, inadequacy, insufficiency: *failure of crops, of supplies*; **b** a dwindling, diminution, falling off in vigour and vitality: *a failure in health.* **2.** Lack of success; fact of not attaining one's object, of not succeeding in an attempt: *all his efforts met with, ended in, failure.* **3. a** Action which does not attain its object; an unsuccessful effort: *the attack was a failure*; **b** thing which does not fulfil expectations, which does not answer its purpose: *my new electric pump has turned out a failure*; **c** person who fails, is unsuccessful in what he attempts: *Gray was a failure as a professor at Cambridge.* **4. a** Non-performance of action which was necessary, expected, incumbent upon one: *a failure to do what one has promised*; **b** neglect, omission, dereliction: *a failure in duty.* **5.** Financial inadequacy, inability to meet liability; bankruptcy.

fain (**I.**), adj. [1. fān; 2. fein]. O.E. *fæġen*, 'glad, rejoicing'; M.E. *fain*, 'joyful', fr. Gmc. **fag-*, **faχ-*; cp. Goth. *fah-eþs*, 'joy', & Goth. *fag-inōn*, 'to rejoice', related to O.E. (*ġe*)-*fēon*, fr. **feh-an*, 'to rejoice'; cp. O.H.G. (*gi-*)*fehan*, 'to rejoice'; this group of words is related more or less closely to a very large group in Lat. somewhat differentiated in meaning. See further on the Gmc. type under **fair** (**II.**), **fang**, & on the Lat. &c. under **pax** & **pact**. **1.** (pred., chiefly poet.) Inclined, disposed, ready, willing, glad: *our hearts were fain.* **2.** (pred. followed by *to*) Compelled, forced, under the necessity of: *he was fain to comply with their demands.*

fain (**II.**), adv., fr. prec. Gladly, with joy; only with *would* in such Phr. as: *he would fain depart*, would be glad to.

fain (**III.**), **fains**, vb. Etymol. unknown. In schoolboy formula, *fain I.!* Supposed to secure exemption from some undesired task or duty for those who utter it soon enough; e.g. *fain I keeping goal* &c.

fainéant, adj. & n. [1. fānāón; 2. feineiā], fr. Fr. *fainéant*, as though fr. *fai(re)*, 'to do', & O. Fr. *neant*, 'nothing'; in reality by popular etymol. fr. O. Fr. *faignant*, 'idler', fr. *faindre*. See **feign**. **1.** adj. Idle, inactive, inefficient. **2.** n. An inactive, inefficient person.

faint (**I.**), adj. [1. fānt; 2. feint]. M.E. *faint*, *feint*, O. Fr. *feint*, P.P. of *feindre*, 'to feign'. See **feign**. **1. a** (of actions) Feeble, impotent, weak, ineffectual: *to make a faint struggle, effort, attempt*; **b** (of character) timid, lacking in vigour, courage; unenterprising. Phr. *faint heart never won fair lady*, nothing valuable can be secured without courage and confidence. **2.** (of movement and bodily powers) a Weak, exhausted, faltering, failing: *his strength ebbed and grew faint*; *the beating of the heart, the breathing, became fainter*; **b** specif., dizzy, on the point of fainting: *to feel faint.* **3. a** (of anything affecting the bodily senses) Lacking in distinctness, not making a vivid impression; dull, dim, indistinct: *a faint tinge of pink*; *a faint sound*; *a faint resemblance*; Phr. *ruled faint* (also *feint*), of paper with fine faint rulings to guide the writing; **b** (of mental processes) vague, dim, slight: *to have a faint, not the faintest, idea of*; *faint praise*; *not the faintest hope.*

faint (**II.**), vb. intrans., fr. prec. **1.** (archaic) To lose heart, be discouraged, grow weak. **2. a** To languish and droop, grow weak and nerveless from overstraining, fatigue, hunger &c.; **b** specif., to be seized with temporary failure of heart's action; to experience vertigo, nausea; to become temporarily unconscious, to swoon.

faint (**III.**), n., fr. prec. The act of fainting; fainting fit, swoon. Phr. *a dead faint*, complete unconsciousness from fainting.

faint-heart, n. A faint-hearted person.

faint-hearted, adj. **faint** (**I.**) & **hearted**. Timid, timorous, cowardly; feeble, poor-spirited.

faint-heartedly, adv. Prec. & **-ly**. In a faint-hearted manner.

faint-heartedness, n. See prec. & **-ness**. The quality of being faint-hearted.

faintish, adj. [1. fāntish; 2. féintiʃ]. **faint** (**I.**) & **-ish**. Somewhat faint.

faintly, adv. [1. fāntli; 2. féintli]. **faint** (**I.**) & **-ly**. In a faint manner.

faintness, n. [1. fāntnes; 2. féintnis]. **faint** (**I.**) & **-ness**. The state of being faint.

faints, n. [1. fānts; 2. feints], fr. **faint** (**I.**). Impure spirit appearing at beginning and end of distillation.

fair (**I.**), n. [1. fār; 2. fɛə], fr. O. Fr. *feire*, Mod. Fr. *foire*, fr. Lat. *fēriae*, 'holidays, festivals'; prob. fr. earlier **fēs-*, wh. occurs also in Lat. *fēstum*, 'holiday, festival', q.v. under **feast**. See also **fane**. **a** Gathering, accompanied by entertainments and merry-making, which takes place at fixed periods and in fixed places, authorized and determined by statute, for sale of cattle, agricultural produce, and articles of various kinds which are generally specially brought together for the purpose by farmers and traders from different parts; Phr. *a day too late for the fair*, too late for some important event or occasion; **b** sale of small fancy articles in aid of some charitable or religious purpose.

fair (**II.**), adj. O.E. *fæġer*, 'beautiful, pleasant, sweet'; M.E. *feire* &c.; cogn. w. O.H.G. *fagar*, Goth. *fagars*, 'fair, beautiful'. The orig. sense seems to be 'well put together, well fitted, justly proportioned'. The above forms are all fr. Gmc. type **fag-*, related to wh., w. different vowel grade, is Gmc. **fōg-*, whence O.E. (*ġe-*)*fēgan*, 'to join together, put together, unite, fix', fr. **fōg-jan*, O.H.G. *fuogen*, 'join, unite'. Gmc. **fag-*, **fōg-*, represent respectively Aryan **pak̑-*, **pāk̑-*, meaning perh. orig. 'to twine, weave, bind', whence Lat. *pāc-(em)*, 'peace, union, agreement, concord', fr. *pāx*, q.v. under **pax**, also *pactum*, 'agreement, covenant'; see **pact**. Side by side w. the bases ending in *-k̑*, there seem also to have existed types **paĝ-*, **pōĝ-* &c., as in Lat. *pāgus*, 'country district, village', orig. 'a limited space', w. the idea of 'containing, grouping together'; see further under **pagan**. Another related word is Lat. *pāgina*, 'page of a book', lit. 'something bound, put, together, with others'; see **page** (**II.**); cp. Gk. *pég-nūmi*, 'I fasten together, make firm, build'. Cp. also **fain** (**I.**). **1. a** (chiefly poet.) Beautiful, lovely: *would that all men were brave, and all women fair*; *how fair the scene on which we gaze*; Phrs. *the fair sex*; *fair one*, a beautiful and beloved woman; (poet., archaic) *the fair*, (i.) womankind; (ii.) some specific woman; **b** clear, clean, fresh, unsullied; free from blemish: *fair water*; *a fair copy*, a clean and perfect one; (also fig.) *fair name, fame*; **c** (of the weather) fine, bright, dry, as distinct from wet, rainy, cloudy; **d** favourable, propitious, promising, advantageous; Phr. *to be in a fair way to*, be likely to, have a reasonable chance of; **e** specious, persuasive, plausible: *he gives us fair words, but does little.* **2. a** (of the mind, judgement, character) Impartial, just, imbued with justice; **b** (of action and conduct) inspired by, proceeding from, a just and impartial mind; equitable: *fair play*, straightforward honest conduct; **c** (of human beings) having an impartial, just mind; acting in just, equitable, honourable manner: *strict but fair.* **3.** Moderate, pretty good, tolerable, passable: *a fair chance of success*; *his knowledge is fair, but by no means perfect.* **4. a** Light-coloured, blond; contrasted with *dark*: *fair hair, complexion* &c.; **b** (of persons) having fair hair &c.

fair (**III.**), adv., fr. prec. **1.** Honestly, in accordance with what is just and equitable; according to the rules of the game &c.: *to play, fight, fair.* Phr. *to bid fair to*, show likelihood of. **2.** Politely, courteously, persuasively: *to speak a person fair.* **3.** Straight, directly: *to strike a man fair on the chin.*

fair-haired, adj. **fair** (**II.**) & **haired**. Having fair, light-coloured hair.

fairily, adv. [1. fārili; 2. féərili]. **fairy** & **-ly**. In a fairy-like manner.

fairing, n. [1. fāring; 2. féəriŋ]. **fair** (**I.**) & **-ing**. Gift bought at a fair.

fairish, adj. [1. fārish; 2. féəriʃ]. **fair** (**II.**) & **-ish**. Moderate, tolerable.

fairly, adv. [1. fārli; 2. féəli]. **fair** (**II.**) & **-ly**. **1.** Justly, impartially: *to act fairly by all men.* **2.** Moderately, tolerably: *fairly good*; *to hear fairly well.* **3.** Completely; thoroughly: *once the boat was fairly under way, they made good progress.*

fairness, n. [1. fārnes; 2. féənis]. **fair** (**II.**) & **-ness**. The quality of being fair (in all senses).

fair-spoken, adj. [1. fār spōken; 2. féə spòukən]. Polite, civil, urbane, persuasive.

fairway, n. [1. fārwā; 2. féəwei]. **a** Navigable channel in river, roadstead &c.; **b** (in golf) the stretch of trimmed turf, between tee and green, free from hazards and distinguished from the rough or natural ground on either side.

fair-weather, adj. (fig.) Only of service in pleasant, easy circumstances, not in time of danger or stress: *fair-weather friends.*

fairy (**I.**), n. [1. fāri; 2. féəri], fr. O. Fr. *faerie*, 'fairyland, enchantment', fr. *fae*, 'fairy'. See **fay**. Small supernatural being in human form.

fairy (**II.**), adj., fr. prec. **1.** Of, pertaining to, belonging to, fairies: *fairy wand*; *fairy voices* &c. **2.** Fairy-like, airy, dainty, delicate: *a fairy shape.*

fairydom, n. [1. fāridum; 2. féəridəm]. **fairy** (**I.**) & **-dom**. The country, domain, of the fairies.

fairyhood, n. [1. fárihood; 2. féərihud]. **fairy** (I.) & **-hood.** (rare) The condition of being a fairy.

fairyism, n. [1. fáriizm; 2. féəriizəm]. **fairy** (I.) & **-ism.** (rare) Belief in fairies.

fairyland, n. [1. fáriland; 2. féərilænd]. **a** The country of the fairies; an imaginary land of dreams; **b** a lovely, pleasant place or scene; **c** region of marvels: '*fairylands of science*' (Tennyson).

fairy-like, adj. Like a fairy.

fairy-ring, n. Circle of darker green on grassland, formed by fungoid growths, but popularly attributed to fairy dancers.

fairy-tale, n. **a** Story about fairies; **b** a marvellous, fictitious, incredible tale.

fait accompli, n. [1. fát akómplē; 2. féit akɔ̃plī]. Fr. See **fact** & **accomplish.** Something already done and settled.

faith, n. [1. fāth; 2. feiþ]. M.E. *feith*, fr. O. Fr. *fei*, 'faith', fr. Lat. *fides*, 'trust, belief'. See **fidelity** & **-th.** **1.** Trust, confidence, belief, reliance: *to have faith in.* **2. a** Personal realization of the truth of divine revelation: *to have faith in God*; Phr. *faith can remove mountains*; **b** system of belief, religious doctrine: *the Christian, Catholic, faith*; Phr. *Defender of the Faith* (Lat. *Fidei Defensor*), title granted to Henry VIII. in 1521 by Pope Leo X., and since borne by kings of England. **3.** Honesty, sincerity: *I ask you to believe what I say on the faith of an honest man.* Phrs. *in good faith*, with sincerity; *bad faith*, deceit, treachery; *Punic faith*, treachery. **4.** Promise, pledged word, undertaking: *to plight one's faith*; *to keep, break, faith with.*

faithful, adj. & n. [1. fāthfool; 2. féiþfəl]. Prec. & **-ful.** **1.** adj. Keeping faith, loyal, true; retaining allegiance to, trust in: *faithful friends, supporters* &c.; *faithful to one's promise, principles* &c. **2.** adj. **a** Reliable, trustworthy, veracious, accurate: *to give a faithful account of the course of events*; **b** accurate, exact: *a copy faithful in every detail.* **3.** n. *The faithful*, true believers; esp. Mohammedans.

faithfully, adv. Prec. & **-ly.** In a faithful manner; in good faith. Phr. *yours faithfully*, formula concluding letter.

faithfulness, n. See prec. & **-ness.** The quality of being faithful.

faith-healing, n. Alleged curing of disease by belief in efficacy of prayers offered with that intention, without assistance from a physician.

faithless, adj. [1. fāthles; 2. féiþlis]. **faith** & **-less.** **1.** (rare) Without faith, unbelieving. **2.** Not keeping faith, not adhering to allegiance, promises, duty; false, treacherous.

faithlessly, adv. Prec. & **-ly.** In a faithless manner.

faithlessness, n. See prec. & **-ness.** **a** The quality of being faithless; **b** an act of treachery, a breach of faith.

fake (I.), vb. trans. [1. fāk; 2. feik]. Etymol. doubtful. **a** To fabricate (a thing) in imitation of something else; esp. to counterfeit a rare, valuable, costly article with intent to pass it off as the genuine thing; **b** to alter (an object, document &c.), tamper with, touch up: *the picture is a genuine Corot, but parts have been faked.*

fake (II.), n., fr. prec. An imitation, a sham, a fabrication, a forgery.

fakir, n. [1. fakḗr; 2. fəkíə], fr. Arab. *faqīr*, 'a poor man'. Hindu or Mohammedan ascetic beggar, regarded in the East as a holy man.

falbala, n. [1. fálbalah; 2. fǽlbəlā]. Etymol. doubtful. Flounce, frill.

falcate, adj. [1. fálkāt; 2. fǽlkeit], fr. Lat. *falcāt-(us)*, 'sickle-shaped, hooked, curved', fr. *falc-(em)*, *falx*, 'a sickle, scythe', & **-ate.** Prob. cogn. w. Gk. *phálkēs*, 'rib of a ship'; Lat. *flectere*, 'to bend, curve'. See **flex.** (bot., zool.) Curved like a sickle; hooked.

falcated, adj. [1. fálkāted; 2. fǽlkeitid]. Prec. & **-ed.** (astron.) Sickle-shaped.

falchion, n. [1. fáwlchun; 2. fɔ̄ltʃən]. M.E. *fauchoun*, fr. O. Fr. *fauchon*, fr. Low Lat. **falciōn-(em)*, fr. Lat. *falc-(em)*, 'a sickle'. See **falcate** & **-ion.** A short, broad, curved sword.

falciform, adj. [1. fálsiform; 2. fǽlsifɔ̄m], fr. Lat. *falci-(s)*, genit. of *falx*, 'a sickle'. See **falcate** & **-form.** (anat.) Sickle-shaped.

falcon, n. [1. fáw(l)kn; 2. fɔ̄(l)kən]. M.E. *faucoun*, fr. O. Fr. *faucōn*, fr. L. Lat. *falcōn-(em)*, 'a falcon'; according to Walde a loan-word fr. Gmc.; cp. O.H.G. *falcho*, 'falcon'; but there was surely an association w. *falx*, 'sickle' (see **falcate**), fr. shape of beak. The Gmc. word itself may ultimately come fr. Lat. **1.** (ornith.) A sub-family of diurnal birds of prey, allied to the hawks, kites, and eagles, characterized by short, strong, curved beak, long talons, pointed wings, and the dark iris of the eye; it includes the peregrine falcon, gerfalcon, merlin, hobby, kestrel, and, sometimes, the goshawk. **2.** Specif., one of these birds, esp. female, trained to hunt game in the ancient sport of hawking or falconry. **3.** (by transf.) Form of light cannon of the 15th and 16th cents.

falconer, n. [1. fáw(l)kuner; 2. fɔ̄(l)kənə]. Prec. & **-er.** **1.** One who trains falcons for hunting. **2.** One who hunts with falcons.

falconet, n. [1. fáwlkunet; 2. fɔ̄lkənet], fr. Ital. *falconetto*, dimin. of *falcone*, 'falcon', q.v. **1.** A small Asiatic falcon. **2.** (hist.) A type of very small cannon of the 15th and 16th cents.

falconry, n. [1. fáw(l)kunri; 2. fɔ̄l(l)kənri]. **falcon** & **-ry.** **a** The sport of hunting with falcons; **b** the art of training and flying falcons in pursuit of game.

falderal, folderol, n. [1. fàlderál, fòlderól; 2. fæ̀ldərǽl, fɔ̀ldərɔ́l]. **a** A refrain, common in old songs; **b** a useless trifle, rubbish.

faldstool, n. [1. fáwldstōōl; 2. fɔ̄ldstūl], fr. Med. Lat. *faldistolium*, fr. O.H.G. *faldstuol*, fr. *fald-(an)*, 'to fold' (see **fold**), & *stuol*, 'chair' (see **stool**). **1.** Chair without arms, properly a portable one, made to fold up, and used by a bishop in a cathedral other than his own, or when visiting a church in his diocese. **2.** Desk with stool attached for kneeling on; esp. litany-desk.

Falernian, n. [1. falérnian; 2. fælə́niən], fr. Lat. (*vīnum*) *Falern-(um)* & **-ian**; fr. name of mountain in Campania. Wine made at Falerno in Italy, very celebrated in ancient times.

fall (I.), vb. intrans. [1. fawl; 2. fɔ̄l]. O.E. *f(e)allan*, M.E. *fallen*; cp. O.H.G., O.S. *fallan*, O. Fris., O.N. *falla*; cogn. w. Lith. *pùlti*, 'to fall', & in spite of the *s-* pref., also, apparently, w. Gk. *sphállein*, 'cause to fall, throw down; to stumble, fall; to be baffled'. **A. 1. a** To pass through space, unimpeded, from higher to lower level, to drop: *the apple falls from the tree*; *the meteorite falls from the sky*; *rain falls*; Phrs. *his eyes fell*, were directed lower; *his face fell*, expressed embarrassment, disconcertment &c.; *the curtain falls*, is lowered before stage to mark a break in, or conclusion of, the action of a play &c.; **b** (of mercury in thermometer or barometer) to occupy a lower position, reach lower point in the tube; hence, Phr. *the glass has fallen*, i.e. registers lower position of the mercury; also extended to temperature indicated by this: *the temperature has fallen*, it has grown colder. **2.** (of tall objects) To pass to horizontal position from vertical, bend from upright position to one in which the object lies flat; to collapse: *many trees fell in the storm*; *steeples and houses fell in the earthquake.* Phrs. *to fall in battle*, be killed; *to fall flat*, to fail to produce desired effect: *the joke fell flat*; *the fortress fell*, was taken. **3.** (of men and animals) To stumble, trip, lose footing, so that part of the body strikes the ground &c. with force; to come down: *to fall up-, downstairs*; *to fall over a chair in the dark*; *my horse fell going downhill.* **4. a** To flow, roll, rapidly to lower level: *the river falls into the sea, over the cliff*; **b** (of drapery, hair &c.) to hang down: *her golden hair fell in masses over her shoulders*; *drapery falling to the feet.* **5.** To abate, grow milder and less violent; (gen. expressing diminution of intensity) **a** *the wind has fallen during the night*; **b** (of states of mind) become sadder, quieter, less buoyant: *my spirits fell at the news of the disaster*; **c** to diminish in value or amount: *prices have fallen.* **6.** To succumb to temptation, yield to persuasion; be guilty of a moral lapse: *the serpent tempted Eve and she fell*; specif., *a fallen woman*, one guilty of unchastity. **7.** To come upon, as though descending upon: **a** *sleep, fear, fell suddenly upon them*; **b** of certain processes of nature: *darkness fell*; *evening, night, is falling fast.* **8.** To alight, strike, impinge upon: *the sunlight fell upon the highest mountain peaks.* **9.** To pass into a particular condition: **a** *to fall asleep*; **b** implying change to a worse condition of health, fortunes &c.: *to fall into a decline*; '*fallen on evil days*' (Milton, 'P. L.'). Phrs. *to fall foul of*: **a** (naut.) to come into collision with; **b** to quarrel with, arouse hostility in; *to fall short*: **a** to prove insufficient: *provisions fell short*; **b** fail to reach required point: *the arrow fell short*; **c** fail to reach required standard: *the result fell short of his expectations.* **10. a** To come by natural process; to lapse, revert: *in the absence of his superior the duty fell to him*; *the estate falls to the Crown*; **b** (of times and seasons) to come, occur, be: *Christmas falls on Tuesday this year.* **11.** (of speech) To be uttered: *not a word fell from his lips*; *I agree with what has fallen from the last speaker*, with what he has said. **B.** Followed by adverbs and prepositions. *Fall a-* (followed by vbl. n.), to begin: *to fall a-crying.* *Fall among*, to come by chance, happen to come into the midst of: *to fall among thieves.* *Fall astern*, to drop behind, pass to the rear. *Fall away*, **a** to draw back from friendship, allegiance &c.: *one's supporters fall away*; **b** to grow thin, emaciated. *Fall back*, to withdraw, retreat, give way. *Fall back upon*, **a** (mil.) to retreat to (a position, support &c.); **b** to have recourse to. *Fall behind*, to drop to the rear, lose ground. *Fall in*, **a** to tumble inwards, give way: *the roof, house* &c., *fell in*; **b** (esp. mil.) to take up appointed positions, in rank &c.; **c** to lapse; to terminate: *the lease falls in.* *Fall in with*, **a** to come by chance among; to come across; to light upon; **b** to comply with, agree to, yield to. *Fall off*, **a** to decrease in number or amount, withdraw, diminish: *his supporters are falling off*; **b** (naut. of ship) to fail to answer the helm. *Fall on*, **a** to begin operations (e.g. fighting, feeding &c.); **b** to attack, set upon; Phr. *to fall on one's feet*, be fortunate, happily circumstanced; have good luck &c. *Fall out*, **a** (mil.) to abandon position in ranks &c.; **b** to happen, turn out, result; **c** to quarrel. *Fall through*, to come to nothing: *the scheme fell through.* *Fall to*, **a** to begin, set to; **b** to begin an attack (esp. on enemy or food: *they fell to with good appetite*). *Fall upon*, trans., to attack.

fall (II.), n., fr. prec. **1.** The act of falling, a drop, unimpeded descent: *the fall of an apple*; *a fall from one's horse.* **2.** The act of passing from vertical to horizontal position, collapse, prostration: *the fall of a tower, building, tree* &c. **3.** (of persons and animals) The act of falling, tripping, a stumble: *to be injured by a fall.* **4.** (of fortified town &c.) Surrender, capitulation, submission: *the fall of Troy.* **5.** A reduction, diminution, in value, amount: *a fall in prices.* **6. a** A wrestling-bout; **b** a method of throwing one's opponent in wrestling; Phr. *to try a fall with*, engage in a wrestling-match (lit. and fig.). pit oneself against an opponent. **7.** (in moral sense) A moral lapse, yielding to temptation; specif., *the Fall of Man*, the sin of Adam and Eve. **8.** (U.S.A.) Autumn. **9.** Amount of something that falls at one time, as a single process: *a heavy fall of snow.* **10.** (usually pl.) Body of water falling over cliff &c.; cataract, cascade: *the Victoria Falls.*

fallacious, adj. [1. faláshus; 2. fəléiʃəs], fr. Lat. *fallāci-(s)*, nom. *fallax*, 'deceitful', & **-ous**. See **fallacy**. Based on error or false argument; misleading, deceptive.

fallaciously, adv. Prec. & **-ly**. In a fallacious manner.

fallaciousness, n. See prec. & **-ness**. The quality of being fallacious.

fallacy, n. [1. fálasi; 2. fǽləsi], fr. Lat. *fallācia*, 'deceit, artifice', fr. *fallāc-*, stem of *fallax*, 'deceptive', fr. *fall-(ere)*, 'to deceive', & **-y**. See **false**. **1. a** A false, mistaken, belief or opinion; error, delusion: *popular fallacies*; *the pathetic fallacy*, appeal to false sentiment, as by attributing human feelings to inanimate nature; **b** false reasoning, sophistry: *based on fallacy*. **2.** (log.) A breach of the rules of logical proof; argument, conclusion drawn, which breaks the laws of the syllogism; an example, type of such reasoning, e.g. *petitio principii*, undistributed middle, arguing in a circle &c.

fallal, n. [1. falál; 2. fælǽl]. Invented word. Trifling adornment, useless finery.

fallalery, n. [1. faláleri; 2. fælǽləri]. Prec. & **-ery**. Use of fallals.

fallen, vb. [1. fáwlen; 2. fɔ́lən] O.E. *f(e)allen*, M.E. *fallen*; P.P. of **fall (I.)**.

fallibility, n. [1. fàlibíliti; 2. fæ̀libíliti], fr. Low Lat. *fallibil-(is)*, 'capable of being deceived'. See next word & **-ity**. The quality of being fallible.

fallible, adj. [1. fálibl; 2. fǽlibl], fr. Low Lat. *fallibilis*, 'capable of being deceived', fr. Lat. *fall-(ere)*, 'to deceive'. See **fail (II.)** & **false**. Liable to error.

falling sickness, n. [1. fáwling sìknes; 2. fɔ́liŋ sìknis]. Old name of epilepsy, q.v., from liability of sufferer to fall over suddenly in a fit.

Fallopian, adj. [1. falópian; 2. fælóupiən], fr. Fallopio & **-an**. Of, discovered by, G. Fallopio, Italian physician, d. 1562; specif., *Fallopian tubes*, the oviducts of mammals.

fallow (I.), n. [1. fálō; 2. fǽlou]. M.E. *fal(o)we*; cp. O.E *fealg, fealh*, 'harrow'; cp. E. Fris. *falgen*, 'to fallow land', O.H.G. *felga*, 'harrow'. Land ploughed up but left unsown for a season.

fallow (II.), adj., fr. prec. **a** (of land) Ploughed up but left unsown: *to lie fallow*; also **b** (fig., of the mind) untrained, uncultivated.

fallow (III.), vb. trans., fr. **fallow (I.)**. To plough up, break up (land) without sowing it.

fallow (IV.), adj. O.E. *falo, fealo*, genit. *fealwes*, 'brown, dun, yellow'; M.E. *fāle*, fr. uninflected, also *falwe*, fr. inflected type, the latter being ancestor of Mod. Engl. form; cp. also O.H.G. *falo*, O.L.G. *falu*, O.N. *fǫlr*, cogn. w. Lat. *pallidus*, 'pale', *pallēre*, 'to be pale' (see **pale (II.)**, **pallor**); cp. also Gk. *peliós*, 'livid, ashen', *poliós*, 'grey'; Scrt. *palitáś*, 'grey, hoary'; O. Slav. *pelesŭ*, 'grey'. Of a brownish-yellow colour.

fallow-deer, n. **fallow (IV.)**. A species of deer of yellowish colour, spotted with white, genus *Dama*, smaller than the red deer, and often domesticated.

false (I.), adj. [1. fawls; 2. fɔls]. *Fals*, already in O.E., adj. & n., fr. O. Fr. *fals*, or direct fr. Lat. *fals-(um)*, P.P. of Lat. *fall-(ere)*, 'to deceive'. The etymol. of the Lat. word is doubtful, but it is prob. cogn. w. Gk. *phēlos, phēlós*, 'deceitful'. Perh. ultimately connected w. Aryan **bhā-* &c., 'to speak', as in Lat. *fābula*, q.v. under **fable**, w. sense of 'speak too much, deceive with speech' &c. **1.** Wrong, incorrect, inaccurate, mistaken: *false weights*; *a false note in music*; *a false alarm*; *to take a false step*; *to make a false start*; *false quantity*, wrong vowel-length; *false pride*, based on a mistaken idea. Phr. *(to sail) under false colours*, (i.) under a flag to which one has no right; (ii.) give oneself out as being other than one is. **2. a** Misleading, deceptive: *false doctrine*; *under false pretences*; *a false scent*; *to give a false impression*; Phr. *in a false position*, one which causes misunderstanding; **b** disloyal, untrue, unfaithful, treacherous: *to be false to one's trust*. **3. a** Not genuine; sham, counterfeit: *false coin*; **b** artificial, as distinct from natural: *false hair, teeth* &c.

false (II.), adv., fr. prec. Only in Phr. *to play one false*, to disappoint, betray, deceive.

false-hearted, adj. Treacherous, disloyal, deceitful.

falsehood, n. [1. fáwls-hood; 2. fɔ́lshud]. **false (I.)** & **-hood**. **1.** An uttered untruth, a lie: *to tell a falsehood*; *to utter falsehoods*. **2.** (rather rare) The state or quality of being false; falseness.

falsely, adv. [1. fáwlsli; 2. fɔ́lsli]. **false (I.)** & **-ly**. In a false manner.

falseness, n. [1. fáwlsnes; 2. fɔ́lsnis]. See prec. & **-ness**. The quality of being false (esp. in moral sense); deceitfulness; treachery, disloyalty: *falseness of heart*.

falsetto, n. & adj. [1. fawlsétō; 2. fɔlsétou]. Ital. dimin. of *falso*, 'false'. See **false (I.)**. **1.** n. **a** Male voice lacking virile quality and resembling a woman's voice in timbre; **b** notes of normal male voice produced so as to imitate effect of a woman's treble. **2.** adj. (of voice, or tones produced by voice) Having the quality of falsetto.

falsification, n. [1. fàwlsifikáshun; 2. fɔ̀lsifikéiʃən], fr. Low Lat. *falsific-(āre)*, 'to falsify', & **-ation**. See next word. The act of falsifying; state of being falsified.

falsify, vb. trans. [1. fáwlsifī; 2. fɔ́lsifai], fr. Fr. *falsifier*, fr. Low Lat. *falsificāre*, 'to falsify'. **false (I.)** & **-fy**. **1.** To misrepresent, give false impression of: *to falsify evidence*. **2.** To disappoint; prove to be baseless or erroneous: *my hopes have been falsified*. **3.** To alter (documents, statements &c.) so as to cause to convey different meaning, or one opposed to original sense; to tamper with, fake, with intent to deceive.

falsity, n. [1. fáwlsiti; 2. fɔ́lsiti]. **false (I.)** & **-ity**. The quality of being false; **a** (of statements) untruth, of nature of a lie; **b** (of character) deceitfulness, dishonesty, unfaithfulness; **c** (of conduct) treachery, disloyalty, double-dealing.

falter, vb. intrans. [1. fáwlter; 2. fɔ́ltə]. M.E. *falteren*; origin obscure; perh. Scand.; cp. O.N. *faltra(sk)*, 'to be encumbered, embarrassed'. **1. a** (of bodily movement) To move uncertainly and hesitatingly; to stumble, totter, be unsteady; **b** (of speech) to utter words with tremulous, broken voice; to hesitate, stammer, in speaking, as though under influence of strong emotion; *falter out*, trans., to utter with broken, hesitating voice. **2.** (of action) To hesitate, draw back, be daunted; to act half-heartedly.

faltering, adj. [1. fáwltering; 2. fɔ́ltəriŋ], fr. Pres. Part. of prec. Hesitating, unsteady, stumbling: *faltering steps*; *faltering voice, tongue*.

falteringly, adv. Prec. & **-ly**. In a faltering manner.

fame, n. [1. fām; 2. feim], fr. Fr., fr. Lat. *fāma*, 'report, rumour; public opinion, reputation'; cogn. w. Gk. *phḗmē*, 'a voice; a report, rumour; reputation'; w. suff. *-m*, fr. Aryan base **bhā-*, **bhō-*, **bhə-*, 'to speak, say'. Cp. Gk. *phē-mí*, 'I say, declare', *phōnḗ*, 'voice' (see **phone (I.)**), *phátis*, 'speech, saying'; Lat. *fāri*, 'to speak', *fateor*, 'I confess', *fābula*, 'speech, saying' (see **fable**), *fātum*, 'an utterance; a prediction, oracle; fate, destiny' (see **fate**); O.N. *bōn*, 'request, prayer' (see **boon**). **1.** Rumour; common estimation, opinion generally held: *the fame of these things was widely spread*; *to enjoy an ill fame*; specif. uses: *house of ill fame*, brothel; *woman of ill fame*, prostitute. **2.** Good repute, high reputation; glory, renown: *Gray's fame as a poet was at once established by the Elegy*; *some men are greedy for fame, others are indifferent*.

famed, adj. [1. fāmd; 2. feimd]. Prec. & **-ed**. **a** Reputed, reported, commonly believed: '*the fancy cannot cheat so well As she is famed to do*' (Keats); **b** celebrated, made famous: *a hero famed by poets*; **c** *famed for*, famous, renowned: *Liverpool is famed for its docks*.

familiar (I.), adj. [1. famílyar; 2. fəmíljə], fr. O. Fr. *familier*, fr. Lat. *familiāris*, 'pertaining to a household, domestic; friendly, intimate'. **family** & **-ar**. **1.** (archaic) Pertaining to one's family; domestic, private. **2.** Having close acquaintance, intimate: *on familiar terms*; *a familiar friend*; Phr. *familiar spirit*, demon supposed to attend on magician &c. **3.** (of persons, manners, modes of expression) Exhibiting, expressing, a vulgar heartiness or cordiality towards others; esp. evincing, and appearing to claim, greater degree of intimacy than is warranted by length of acquaintance with, or by one's standing relative to, another; forward, impudent, presuming: *his manner was ill-bred and familiar*. **4. a** Well known, accustomed, recognized: *to hear a familiar voice*; **b** ordinary, common, usual, commonplace: *a man who has lost a leg is a familiar sight since the Great War*. **5.** (of relations of persons to things) Acquainted with, well versed in, conversant with: *to be familiar with the facts, with a subject, with a name, a language* &c.

familiar (II.), n., fr. prec. **1.** Particular official in household of Pope or Roman Catholic bishop. **2. a** Intimate friend, close acquaintance; **b** familiar spirit.

familiarity, n. [1. famìliáriti; 2. fəmìliǽriti]. **familiar (I.)** & **-ity**. (of relations between persons) **1. a** Intimacy, closeness of friendship or acquaintance: *on terms of familiarity with*; **b** expression of intimacy by speech or manner; affability, cordiality: *he treated his friends with a kind and gentle familiarity*; **c** undue, forward, impertinent, presuming unceremoniousness in speech or manner: *he behaved with a familiarity which disgusted everyone*. **2.** Specific act, gesture, caress, expressing intimacy of relations: *to indulge in harmless familiarities with*. **3.** (of relations of persons to facts and things) Knowledge, acquaintance; state of being aware of, conversant with, well instructed in; experience of: *to show thorough familiarity with a subject, a language* &c.; *his familiarity with conditions of life among the poor was remarkable*. Phr. *familiarity breeds contempt*.

familiarization, n. [1. famìlyarīzáshun; 2. fəmìljəraizéiʃən]. Next word & **-ation**. The act of familiarizing, state of being familiarized.

familiarize, vb. trans. [1. famílyarīz; 2. fəmíljəraiz]. **familiar (I.)** & **-ize**. **a** To render something familiar, well known, habitual, to a person; to accustom a person to something, to make person familiarly acquainted with something: *to familiarize a boy with the use of the rod and gun*; *to familiarize a person with the manners of society*; **b** (reflex.) to accustom oneself to, to grow familiar, acquainted, with; become habitually conversant with: *to familiarize oneself with a foreign language, with the use of the axe, with the views of one's opponents*.

familiarly, adv. [1. famílyarli; 2. fəmíljəli]. **familiar (I.)** & **-ly**. In a familiar manner.

family (I.), n. [1. fámili; 2. fǽmili], fr. Lat. *familia*, 'household, domestic servants; estate, property', fr. *famul-(us)*, 'a servant', & **-y**. The etymol. of *famulus* is very doubtful. The word may have meant orig. 'dweller in a household', & be cogn. w. Scrt. *dhāman-*, 'dwelling', wh. is prob. fr. an Aryan base **dhō-*, **dhē-*, **dhə-* &c., 'to place, do, make, construct'. See **do, fact**, & words there referred to. **1.** (archaic) Group of persons living under same roof including both those actually related by blood, and all the others, dependents, friends &c., forming the household. **2. a** Group of persons consisting of two parents and all their children; **b** all the children of the same parents: *to have a large family*; *the eldest of the family*. Phr. *in the family way*, pregnant. **3. a** All that group of persons, living or dead, descended from a common ancestor: *my family has been in Devonshire since the Conquest*;

b group of persons related by blood or marriage. 4. High, ancient, illustrious, lineage: *a man of family*; *of no particular family*. 5. Group of living things having a common origin; a (bot., zool.) group of animals or plants descended from a common stock; a division of an order; b group of languages developed from a common parent language.

family (II.), n. used attrib., fr. prec. 1. Connected with, pertaining to, characteristic of, a family: *the family pride, features*; *a family likeness, family failing*. 2. Belonging to, in possession of, held by, a family: *family estate, pictures, jewels* &c. 3. a Domestic, dealing with, providing for, private families: *family butcher, lawyer, doctor*; b suitable for private families: *family hotel*. 4. Concerned with, related to, a particular family or household: *a purely family affair*; *family relations*. *Family Bible*, large Bible containing a record of the names, dates of birth, and of marriage of a man and his wife, and of those of their children. *Family circle*, group of closely related persons, and their intimate and constant associates. *Family friend*, friend of all members of a family; esp. one who is a friend of more than one generation. *Family living*, ecclesiastical benefice the patron of which is the head for the time being of a particular family. *Family man*, a a man who has a family; b man of domestic habits. *Family name*, a hereditary surname of a particular family; b Christian name, current, or frequently bestowed in a particular family. *Family tree*, a descent, series of steps in descent from an ancestor, or from several ancestors; b plan, diagram, table, exhibiting such descent; pedigree.

famine, n. [1. fámin; 2. fǽmin], fr. Fr., Low Lat. *_famina_, fr. Lat. *fam-(es)*, 'hunger', & **-ine**. The element *fa-* is prob. identical w. that in Lat. *fa-tīgāre*, 'to exhaust, tire' &c. See **fatigue**. 1. a Serious, acute, shortage of foodstuffs in a given area, at a particular time; b (by extension) shortage, lack, of particular article: *water famine*. 2. Lack of bodily nourishment; starvation.

famish, vb. trans. & intrans. [1. fámish; 2. fǽmiʃ], fr. obs. *fame*, 'to starve', fr. Lat. *fam-(es)*, 'hunger'. See prec. & **-ish**. **A.** trans. To cause to suffer hunger, starve. **B.** intrans. 1. To starve, suffer extreme hunger; colloq. Phr. *to be famishing*, be hungry. 2. To suffer great pain and exhaustion from cold.

famishing, adj. [1. fámishing; 2. fǽmiʃiŋ], fr. Pres. Part. of prec. a Causing hunger and starvation; b causing suffering and exhaustion from cold: *a famishing wind, winter* &c.

famous, adj. [1. fámus; 2. féiməs], fr. O. Fr. *fameus*, fr. Lat. *fāmōsus*, 'much talked of; renowned: notorious'. **fame** & **-ous**. 1. Possessing fame; well known, celebrated, noted, renowned. 2. (colloq.) Very good, excellent, satisfactory, capital: *to make a famous dinner*; *to have a famous appetite*.

famously, adv. **famous 2**, & **-ly**. (colloq.) Excellently, very well: *to get on famously with one's work*.

famulus, n. [1. fámūlus; 2. fǽmjuləs]. Lat. *famulus*, 'a servant'. See **family**. An attendant on a magician.

fan (I.), n. [1. fan; 2. fæn]. O.E. *fann*, M.E. *fan*, fr. Lat. *vannus*, 'winnowing-fan'; cp. Lat. *ventus*, 'wind'; Aryan base *_wan-_, *_wn̥-_, 'blowing, wind'. See **wind** (I.), **ventilate**. 1. An instrument or implement for agitating the air, or driving an air-current in a particular direction; specif. a winnowing-fan; b instrument rotated by electricity &c., for ventilating a room &c. by stirring up the air. 2. Specif., object of silk, feathers, paper &c., usually a sector of a circle, and made to fold up, held in the hand, by part forming apex of sector, and used by women, for agitating, stirring, the air, by backward and forward motions of wrist, so as to cool the face. 3. (archit.) A fan-shaped ornamental vaulting with lines diverging from a point. 4. Small sail on windmill, the function of which is to keep the large sails at right angles to the wind.

fan (II.), vb. trans. & intrans., fr. prec. 1. To separate grain from chaff by driving air upon, to winnow. 2. To cause an air-current in given direction, upon particular object by means of a fan held in the hand: *to fan oneself*; Phr. *to fan the flame*, cause excitement, emotion &c., to become more intense. 3. (poet., of air) To play, blow gently, upon, breathe on: '*cool gales shall fan the glade*' (Pope).

fan (III.), n. Origin doubtful, either shortened form of **fanatic**, or fr. **fan** (II.), as one who 'fans the flames', rouses enthusiasm &c. (U.S.A. slang) An enthusiastic supporter of some sport, form of entertainment &c.: *a baseball fan, film-fan* &c.

fanatic, n. & adj. [1. fanátik, fánatik; 2. fənǽtik, fǽnətik], fr. Lat. *fānātic-(us)*, 'pertaining to a temple; inspired, enthusiastic', fr. *fān-(um)*, 'a temple'. See **fane** & **-atic**. 1. n. A person having a stubborn, unshakable, violent, and unreasoning belief in, or enthusiasm for, some opinion, cause, or doctrine. 2. adj. Of, resembling, a fanatic.

fanatical, adj. [1. fanátikl; 2. fənǽtikl]. Prec. & **-al**. Of, pertaining to, resembling, a fanatic; imbued with fanaticism.

fanatically, adv. Prec. & **-ly**. In a fanatical manner.

fanaticism, n. [1. fanátisizm; 2. fənǽtisizəm]. **fanatic** & **-ism**. Violent and excessive enthusiasm; the unreasoning, stubborn opinion, or belief, of a fanatic.

fanaticize, vb. trans. & intrans. [1. fanátisīz; 2. fənǽtisaiz]. **fanatic** & **-ize**. 1. trans. To make into a fanatic. 2. intrans. To become a fanatic.

fancier, n. [1. fánsier; 2. fǽnsiə]. **fancy** (II.) & **-er**. One who has special knowledge, esp. of some class of animals; a judge, connoisseur: *a dog-fancier, pigeon-fancier* &c.

fanciful, adj. [1. fánsifool; 2. fǽnsiful]. **fancy** (I.) & **-ful**. 1. (of persons) a full of fancies, capricious, whimsical, faddy; b imaginative. 2. (of mental processes and conceptions) Springing from, directed by, fancy and whim, rather than by reason and experience; visionary, unreal, unsubstantial. 3. Fantastic, quaint: *fanciful drawings*.

fancifully, adv. Prec. & **-ly**. In a fanciful manner.

fancifulness, n. See prec. & **-ness**. The quality of being fanciful.

fancy (I.), n. [1. fánsi; 2. fǽnsi]. Contracted fr. **fantasy**. 1. Faculty of forming mental pictures of things not present; power of combining these into more complex pictures, and of relating such images to each other, or of perceiving relations and resemblances between them and other objects real or imaginary; imagination. *Fancy* is, however, sometimes used for a more or less passive process of mental vision, *imagination* being used for a more definitely creative mental act. 2. An image, or idea produced by the process of fancy: *the fancies of a poet*. 3. An opinion or belief formed without rational foundation, one which results from emotion or caprice, rather than from thoughtful reflection; a whim, vagary: *these are mere fancies, not convictions based upon reason*; *to have a fancy that . . .* 4. a Liking, fondness, partiality for: *to take a fancy to* (*a person or thing*); Phr. *to take, catch* (*my, his &c.*) *fancy*, attract, please; b inclination, desire for: *a passing fancy*; *I have a fancy for some hock with my dinner*. 5. *The fancy*, used collectively of those addicted to, or interested in, some particular sport, pursuit, or hobby, esp. of those connected with pugilism.

fancy (II.), adj., fr. prec. (only attrib.) 1. Based on, formed by, the fancy, not based upon facts and reality; fanciful, imaginary: *a fancy portrait*. 2. Elaborate, ornamental, decorated; not plain or ordinary: *fancy cakes*; *fancy goods*. 3. Fantastic, extravagant. Phr. *at a fancy price*, unreasonably dear. 4. (of animals &c.) Bred to a special type: *fancy dogs*.

fancy (III.), vb. trans., fr. **fancy** (I.). 1. To call up a mental image of, present to one's mind, imagine, conceive of: *somehow I can't fancy him as a soldier*; *fancy his doing a thing like that!* 2. a To have a fancy for, to feel inclined for, have an inclination for: *I don't fancy this place at all*; *I could fancy a devilled kidney*; b to take a fancy, or liking to, be favourably impressed by: *he's not at all the kind of man I fancy*; *I looked at the lodgings but didn't fancy them*; Phr. *to fancy oneself*, to have a high opinion of oneself, to be conceited. 3. To believe, be inclined to believe, be under the impression that; implying something short of absolute certainty: *I rather fancy that he is a widower*. 4. To believe without adequate grounds; be under the delusion that: *he fancies he can rise in his profession without hard work*.

fancy-dress, n. Fantastic, or picturesque, clothes worn at a masquerade &c.: *fancy-dress ball*, one at which fancy-dress is worn.

fancy fair, n. Sale of work &c., combined with various entertainments, usually for some charitable object, at which the sellers are picturesquely dressed up, or disguised.

fancy-work, n. Embroidery.

fandangle, n. [1. fandángl; 2. fændǽŋgl]. Sham word fr. following. Fantastic, fanciful ornament.

fandango, n. [1. fandánggō; 2. fændǽŋgou]. Span. a A Spanish dance, with movements varying from stateliness to extreme liveliness; b tune for such a dance.

fane, n. [1. fān; 2. fein]. Lat. *fānum*, 'a temple'. Prob. for earlier *_fas-nom_, 'consecrated place', fr. an O. Lat. stem *_fēs-_, *_fās-_, 'holy, consecrated'; cp. Lat. *fēriae*, 'holy day; festival' (see **fair** (I.)), *fēstus*, 'festive' (see **feast**); & further Scrt. *dhiš-nyaš*, 'gods'. The word is prob. connected w. the Aryan base *_dhē-_, *_dhə-_, 'to place, make, do', hence 'that which is ordained, decreed, established'; cp. Scrt. *dhāman-*, 'law'. See **do, fact, thesis**. (poet.) A temple: '*fanes of fruitless prayer*' (Tennyson).

fanfare, n. [1. fánfār, fonfar; 2. fǽnfɛə, fāfā(r)]. Fr., prob. imitative. See **flam**. A flourish, of trumpets, bugles &c.

fanfaronade, n. [1 fànfaronād; 2 fæ̀nfærənéid], fr. Fr. *fanfaronnade*, fr. *fanfaron* (fr. prec. & **-oon**) & **-ade**. 1. Fanfare. 2. Boasting talk, bluster, arrogance.

fang (I.), n. [1. fang; 2. fæŋ]. O.E. *fang*, 'a catching, seizing'; cp. O. Fris., O.N., M.H.G. *fang*; O.H.G. *fangōn*, O.N. *fanga*, O.E. *fōn* (fr. Gmc. *_fanχan-_), 'to seize', w. infixed *-n-* fr. Aryan base *_pāk̑-_, *_pək̑-_; *_pāĝ-_, *_pəĝ-_, 'to make firm, fasten together, fix'. Cp. Lat. *pangere*, 'to fix'; *pāx*, 'peace' (see **pax**); Gk. *pḗgnūmi*, 'I strengthen'; *pēgós*, 'firm'; Goth. *fagrs*, O.E. *fæġer*, 'beautiful', see **fair** (II.); Scrt. *pajráš*, 'strong, fine'; *pāčaš*, 'noose'. See further **page** (II.), **pale** (I.), **pagan**. 1. Long pointed tooth for seizing or holding; specif. a canine tooth of carnivorous animal; b long hollow or grooved tooth of poisonous snake, for injecting venom. 2. a The spike or tang of a tool &c., which is fixed into the handle; b the root of a tooth.

fang (II.), vb. trans. fr. prec. To pour water into a pump to make it start working; to prime (a pump).

fanged, adj. [1. fangd; 2. fæŋd]. **fang** (I.) & **-ed**. Provided, furnished with fangs.

fangless, adj. [1. fángles; 2. fǽŋlis]. **fang** (I.) & **-less**. Without fangs.

fan-light, n. **fan** (I.) & **light**. Fan-shaped window, esp. one over a door.

fanner, n. [1. fáner; 2. fǽnə]. **fan** (II.) & **-er**. A machine for winnowing grain.

fanon, n. [1. fánun; 2. fǽnən]. Fr., fr. Med. Lat. *fano*, fr. O.H.G. *fano*, Mod. Germ. *fahne*, 'flag'; cp. **gonfalon** & see **vane**. An ornamental scarf worn over the left arm by the Pope when celebrating Mass.

fan-tail, n. A variety of pigeon, with fan-shaped tail.

fan-tan, n. [1. fántán; 2. fǽntǽn]. Chinese. **a** A gambling game played by guessing number of coins hidden under a bowl; **b** a gambling game played with cards.

fantasia, n. [1. fantazḗa, fantáhzia, -ázia; 2. fantazía, fæntázia, -éizia]. Ital. See **fantasy**. **1.** A musical composition of irregular form, which follows no fixed plan but includes variety of airs and movements. **2.** An Arab or Moorish exhibition of riding with much firing of guns.

fantast, phantast, n. [1. fántast; 2. fǽntæst], fr. Med. Lat., fr. Gk. *phantastḗs*, 'a boaster', fr. *phantázein*, 'to make visible; to present to the mind, imagine; to make a show'. See under **phantasm**. A visionary; a person with fantastic ideas.

fantastic(al), adj. [1. fantástik(l); 2. fæntǽstik(l)], fr. Med. Lat. *fantastic-(us)*, fr. Gk. *phantastikós*, 'able to present to the mind, imagine; showing, presenting; making a show', fr. *phantast-(ḗs)*, 'one who makes a show' (see prec.), & **-ic** & **-al**. **a** (of objects) Odd, quaint, grotesque, eccentric: *fantastic shapes*; **b** (of ideas &c.) extravagant, fanciful, capricious; unreal, imaginary, visionary.

fantasticality, n. [1. fantàstikáliti; 2. fæntæ̀stikǽliti]. Prec. & **-ity**. The quality of being fantastic.

fantastically, adv. [1. fantástikali; 2. fæntǽstikəli]. See prec. & **-ly**. In a fantastic manner.

fantasticalness, n. [1. fantástiklnes; 2. fæntǽstikəlnis]. See prec. & **-ness**. The quality of being fantastic.

fantasy, phantasy, n. [1. fántazi; 2. fǽntəzi], fr. O. Fr. *fantasie*, fr. Lat., fr. Gk. *phantasía*, 'look, appearance; imagination; vision, image'. See under **phantasm**. **1.** Fancy, imagination. **2.** Product of the imagination; **a** an illusion; delusion, hallucination; **b** an artistic imaginative creation.

fantoccini, n. pl. [1. fàntochḗnē; 2. fæ̀ntətʃíni]. Ital., dimin. of *fante*, 'child'. See **infant**. **a** Marionettes, puppets; **b** a puppet-show.

fan-tracery, n. **fan (I.)** & **tracery**. Fan-vaulting.

fan-vaulting, n. See prec. & **vaulting**. (archit.) System of vaulting in which the ribs spread out like a fan; typical of late period of Perpendicular Gothic.

faquir. See **fakir**.

far (I.), adv. [1. far; 2. fā]. O.E. *feorr*, M.E. *fer*; cp. O.L.G. *ferr*, O. Fris. *fir*, O.H.G. *ferro*, O.N. *fiarri*, *fiarr*, Goth. *fairra*, Gmc. **ferr-*; cogn. w. Gk. *pérā*, 'beyond'; Scrt. *párā*, *paráś*, 'away, behind'; Lat. *porro*, 'further; forward; henceforth'; Gk. *pórrō*, *pórsō*, 'before; henceforth'; Aryan base **per-*, **por-*. Cp. further Aryan **peri-*, Lat. *per*, 'through, over, about' (see **per**); Scrt. *pári*, 'around'; Gk. *peri*, 'around' (see **peri-**). **1.** (expressing rest, usually followed by adv. or advbl. phrase) At a distance, remote, removed by a considerable interval; **a** (of space) *far beyond the sea*; *far above the trees*; *far ahead*; *far off*; *far from the town*; **b** (of time) *far back in the past*; **c** remote in fact: *far from a solution*; *far from completion*; Phr. *far be it from me to*, I have not the audacity to, no desire to. **2.** (expressing motion) To a distance, to a remote point; **a** (of space) *to travel far and wide*; *to swim far out*; *how far can you walk?*; *that is too far for me*; *to throw a ball far into the air*; **b** (of time) *to look far into the future*, *far back into the past*; **c** (of degree) *so far*, to that extent, up to that point; *how far*, to what extent; *so far as*, *in so far as*, to the extent that; *to go far*, reach an advanced stage, accomplish much, have success in undertakings. **3.** To a great degree, very much, considerably: *far better*; *far the best*; *far beyond my powers*. Phr. *far and away*, very much, considerably.

far (II.), adj., fr. prec. **a** Distant, remote, not near: *from a far country*; Phr. *a far cry*, a long way; **b** more distant, farther: *at the far side of the room*; Phr. *few and far between*, rare, occurring at infrequent intervals.

far (III.), n., fr. prec. In certain phrases: **a** a distant place: *to come from far*; **b** a great degree: *by far the best*.

farad, n. [1. fárad; 2. fǽrəd], fr. name of Michael Faraday, electrician (1791–1867). Unit of electric capacity.

faradaic, faradic, adj. [1. fàradáik, farádik; 2. fæ̀rədéiik, fərǽdik]. See prec. & **-ic**. Of, pertaining to, induced electrical currents, produced by inductive apparatus.

far-away, adj. **a** Distant, remote; **b** absent, abstracted: *a far-away look*.

farce (I.), n. [1. fars; 2. fās], fr. Fr. *farce*, fr. O. Fr. *farce*, 'stuffing', fr. Lat. *farcīre*, 'to stuff, cram'; *fartim*, 'closely, densely'; cp. *frequens*, 'pressed full, crowded, crammed; numerous; recurring often'; Gk. *phrássein*, 'to press'; Lith. *brukù*, 'to press into, cram'; O. Ir. *barc*, 'superfluity'; Aryan base **bhr-*, **bhṝ-*, 'to press, cram'. See **frequent**. The term *farce* was applied first to dramatic interludes. **1.** **a** A style of drama characterized by extravagant, boisterous humour; **b** a play of this character; a ludicrous comedy. **2.** **a** An absurd and ludicrous proceeding or situation; **b** something unreal; a sham, a fiction: *his pretence at work was a mere farce*.

farce (II.), vb. trans., fr. O. Fr. *farsir*, fr. Lat. *farcīre*, 'to stuff, cram'. See prec. (archaic, in cookery) To stuff, season (also fig.).

farceur, n. [1. farsḗr; 1. fāsā́]. Fr. **farce** & **-eur**. A joker, humorist.

farcical, adj. [1. fársikl; 2. fásikl]. **farce (I.)** & **-ic** & **-al**. **a** Resembling a farce, extravagantly comic; **b** absurd, unreal, sham.

farcicality, n. [1. fàrsikáliti; 2. fāsikǽliti]. Prec. & **-ity**. The quality of being farcical.

farcically, adv. [1. fársikali; 2. fásikəli]. See prec. & **-ly**. In a farcical manner.

farcy, n. [1. fársi; 2. fási], fr. Fr. *farcin*, fr. Lat. *farcīminum*, 'a disease in horses', fr. *farc-(īre)*, 'to stuff, cram'. See **farce (I.)**. A disease of the horse affecting the skin and blood-vessels; a kind of glanders.

farcy-bud, -button, n. A small swelling, symptomatic of farcy.

fardel, n. [1. fárdl; 2. fádl], fr. O. Fr. *fardel*, dimin. of *farde*, 'burden', possibly fr. Arab. *farde*, 'package'. (archaic) Cumbersome burden.

fare (I.), n. [1. fār; 2. fɛə]. O.E. *fær*, 'journey; road', fr. Gmc. stem. **far-*, 'to go'. See **fare (III.)**. **a** Sum charged for conveyance of passenger; **b** one who pays a fare for being carried in a hired vehicle.

fare (II.), n. O.E. *faru*, 'journey, expedition; troop, companions; baggage', fr. Gmc. **far-*, 'to go'. See next word. Diet, food and drink: *simple, homely fare*.

fare (III.), vb. intrans. O.E. *faran*; M.E. *faren*, 'to go, travel'; cp. O.H.G., O.L.G., Goth. *faran*; O.N., O. Fris. *fara*, 'go, travel'; also O.E. *fēran* (fr. **fōrjan*), O.H.G. *fuoren*, O.S. *fōrian*, 'to go; to carry'; cogn. w. Gk. *póros*, 'passage, way, track' (see **pore**); *peráein*, 'press through'; *peírein* (fr. **per-jō-*), 'to penetrate'; O. Bulg. *(na-)perja*, 'penetrate'; Scrt. *píparti*, 'leads'; *pārayati*, 'transports'. Aryan base **pĕr-*, **pŏr-*, **pr̥-*, 'completion of a forward movement'. See further **port (IV.)**, **porter**, **ford**, **per**, & words there referred to. **1.** (poet.) To go, travel, make one's way: *to fare forth on one's journey*. **2.** To get on; to achieve certain results as the consequence of action; prosper: *how did you fare in London?*; *it has fared ill with him*; *the undertaking has fared ill*; Phr. *you may go farther and fare worse*, be content with what you have.

fare (IV.), vb. intrans., fr. **fare (II.)**. To be supplied with, enjoy, food and drink; to feed: *to fare sumptuously every day*.

farewell (I.), interj. [1. fārwél; 2. fɛəwél]. Imperat. of **fare (III.)** & **well (III.)**. (as parting wish) May you prosper; good-bye. Phr. *farewell to*, enough of, no more of.

farewell (II.), n., fr. prec. **a** The act of taking leave, parting; departure; **b** parting salutation, last words spoken &c., on departure, final salute: *to make one's farewells*.

farewell (III.), adj. [1. fárwel; 2. féəwel], fr. prec. Pertaining to, spoken in, farewell: *a farewell speech*.

far-famed, adj. Widely celebrated, well known, world-famous.

far-fetched, adj. [1. fár fécht; 2. fá fétʃt]. Not occurring naturally; forced, strained: *a far-fetched analogy*; *his jokes were rather far-fetched*.

far-flung, adj. Widely spread or extended: *the far-flung British Empire*.

farina, n. [1. farína, farḗna; 2. fəráinə, fəríːnə]. Lat. *farīna*, 'ground corn, meal, flour; dust, powder', earlier **farrīna*, **farsīna*; cp. O. Slav. *brašŭno* (fr. **boršŭno-*), 'food, meal'; Goth. *barizeins*, 'of barley'; cp. also Lat. *far*, *farr-*, 'corn'; O.N. *barr*, O.E. *bere*, 'barley'; Russ. *borí*, 'barley'. See also **barley**. **1.** **a** Meal, flour, ground from corn, roots &c.; hence, **b** powdery substance; specif. (bot.) pollen. **2.** (chem) Starch.

farinaceous, adj. [1. fàrināshus; 2. fæ̀rinéiʃəs]. Prec. & **-aceous**. Resembling, containing, flour or meal; from cereals.

farinose, adj. [1. fárinōs; 2. fǽrinous]. **farina** & **-ose**. **a** Yielding, composed of, farina; **b** sprinkled with meal, powder &c.

farl, n. [1. farl; 2. fāl], fr. obs. *fardel*, 'quarter', fr. O.E. *feorðan dǣl*, 'fourth part'. See **fourth** & **deal (II.)**. (provinc.) Thin oatmeal cake; quarter section of round cake.

farm (I.), n. [1. farm; 2. fām]. M.E. *ferme*, 'farm, rent', fr. O. Fr. *ferme*, fr. Med. Lat. *firma*, 'fixed payment', fr. Lat. *firmāre*, 'to strengthen, fortify; to fix, establish', fr. *firm-(us)*, 'strong, stable, fixed, immovable'. See **firm (I.)**. **1.** Portion of land forming a single complete property, owned or rented by one person or group of persons, and worked as a unity for agricultural purposes: *home-farm*, single farm worked for owner of estate for household supplies, in distinction to farms which are let to tenants, or worked by owner as a commercial undertaking. **2.** House on farm in which the farmer lives, farm-house.

farm (II.), vb. trans. & intrans., fr. prec. **A.** trans. **1.** To devote (land, etc.) to agricultural uses, dairying, cultivation of crops, raising of stock &c.: *to farm 500 acres*. **2.** **a** To obtain control of and profits from (tax &c.) by making a fixed payment; **b** also *farm out*, to grant control of and profits derived from (land, revenue, tax &c.) on payment of a fixed sum; **c** to undertake care of (children &c.) for a fixed sum. **B.** intrans. To cultivate land; use land for raising crops, stock &c., and for dairying; be a farmer: *I farmed in Australia for many years*.

farm-bailiff, n. One managing a farm for the owner.

farmer, n. [1. fármer; 2. fámə]. **farm (II.)** & **-er**. One who farms; specif. **a** one who cultivates land that he owns or rents; **b** one who farms taxes &c.

farm-house, n. House designed as residence of the occupant of the farm on which it stands.

farming, n. [1. fárming; 2. fámiŋ]. **farm (II.)** & **-ing**. The business of a farmer; agricultural pursuits, agriculture.

farmstead, n. [1. fármsted; 2. fámstɛd]. **farm (I.)** & **stead**. Farm-house, together with barns and other buildings associated with it.

farm-yard, n. Enclosure formed by farm-buildings.

faro, n. [1. fārō; 2. féərou], fr. name Pharaoh. A gambling card-game played against a 'bank'.

far off, adj. [1. fár awf; 2. fár ōf]. Remote, distant (in space or time).

farouche, adj. [1. fahrōōsh; 2. fārúʃ]. Fr., fr. Lat. *ferōc-(em)*, *ferox*, 'wild, daring, fierce'. See **ferocious**. Shy, wild; awkward and repellent in manner, as though unused to, and unwilling to adapt oneself to, social conventions.

farraginous, adj. [1. farắjinus; 2. fəréidžinəs], fr. Lat. *farrāgin-(is)*, genit. of *farrāgo*, 'mixed fodder'. See next word & **-ous**. Miscellaneous, jumbled, forming a confused medley.

farrago, n. [1. faráhgō; 2. fərágou]. Lat. *farrāgo*, 'mixed fodder, mash for cattle', fr. Lat. *far*, 'grain, corn, meal'. See **farina**. Medley, jumble, confused mixture: *a farrago of nonsense.*

far-reaching, adj. [1. fár réching; 2. fá rītʃiŋ]. Exerting a wide influence; felt in many ways; causing important results: *a far-reaching effect*; *the might of the empire is far-reaching.*

farrier, n. [1. fárier; 2. fǽriə], fr. O. Fr. *ferrier*, fr. Lat. *ferrārius*, 'a blacksmith', fr. Lat. *ferr-(um)*, 'iron'. See **ferro-** & **-ier**. **1.** One who shoes horses; a blacksmith. **2.** (archaic) A veterinary surgeon, horse-doctor. **3.** Non-commissioned officer responsible for shoeing of horses of cavalry regiment.

farriery, n. [1. fárieri; 2. fǽriəri]. Prec. & **-y**. **1.** The art of shoeing horses. **2.** (archaic) Veterinary surgery.

farrow (I.), n. [1. fárō; 2. fǽrou]. O.E. *fearh*; M.E. *farh*, 'young pig'; cp. O.H.G. *farch*; cogn. w. Lat. *porcus*, 'pig' (see **pork**); M. Ir. *orc*, O. Bulg. *prase*, 'pig'; Lith. *parszēlis*, O.H.G. *farheli*, 'sucking-pig'. The act of farrowing; a litter of pigs.

farrow (II.), vb. trans. & intrans., fr. prec. **1.** trans. To give birth to (pigs). **2.** intrans. (of a sow) To bring forth young.

far-seeing, adj. [1. fár sēing; 2. fá sīiŋ]. Prudent, wise, having foresight.

far-sighted, adj. [1. fár sīted; 2. fá sáitid]. **a** Able to see distant objects; **b** (fig.) having mental penetration and foresight.

farther (I.), adv. [1. fárdher; 2. fáðə]. Variant of **further**, on anal. of **far**. **1.** To a more advanced, more remote, point of time or space; to a greater distance: *I can go no farther*; *he lives farther on*; *to see farther than another*. Phrs. *I'll see you farther first*, as emphatic refusal; *to go farther and fare worse*. **2.** (more commonly *further*) Besides, moreover.

farther (II.), adj. See prec. **1. a** More distant, remoter: *the farther shore*; **b** (more commonly *further*) more advanced, later: *a farther stage of development*; Phr. *until farther notice*, pending fresh, additional, different, information or instructions. **2.** (more commonly *further*) Additional, more: *have you anything farther to say?*; *to make no farther objection.*

farthermost, adj. [1. fárdhermōst; 2. fáðəmoust]. Prec. & **-most**. Most distant, remotest.

farthest (I.), adv. [1. fárdhest; 2. fáðist]. New formation fr. **furthest**, through influence of **far**. To, at, the greatest distance; to, at, the most remote point.

farthest (II.), adj. See prec. Most distant, remotest. Phr. *at farthest, at the farthest*, at most, latest.

farthing, n. [1. fárdhing; 2. fáðiŋ]. O.E. *feorðing*, M.E. *ferthing*; fr. O.E. *feorð-(a)*, 'fourth'. See **fourth** & **-ing**. **a** A quarter of a penny; **b** a copper coin worth this amount; Phr. *not worth, not to have, a brass farthing*, of no value; penniless.

farthingale, n. [1. fárdhinggāl; 2. fáðiŋgeil]. M.E. *vardingale*, fr. O. Fr. *verdugale*, fr. Span. *verdugado*, 'hooped', fr. *verdugo*, 'rod'. Framework of whalebone, hooped petticoat, for extending woman's skirts, an early form of crinoline, of the 16th and 17th cents.

fasces, n. [1. fásēz; 2. fǽsīz]. Lat. *fasces*, 'bundles', pl. of *fascis*, 'a bundle, faggot; packet'; cp. *fascia*, 'band, fillet, bandage'; M. Ir. *basc*, 'neckband'. Aryan **bhask-*, fr. **bhadhsk-*, 'to bind together'; prob. cogn. w. **bast**, fr. Aryan base **bhadh-sko-*. Bundle of rods surrounding an axe, carried by the lictors before chief magistrates in ancient Rome, as a symbol of authority.

fascia, n. [1. fáshia; 2. fǽʃiə]. Lat. *fascia*, 'a band, fillet'. See prec. **1.** (archit.) Flat band or strip of stone &c. between two mouldings. **2.** (anat.) Thin layer of connective tissue. **3.** Plate, band of metal or wood, over a shop front, bearing name &c. of the proprietor; also *facia.*

fasciated, adj. [1. fáshiāted; 2. fǽʃieitid], fr. Lat. *fasciāt-(um)*, P.P. type of *fasciāre*, 'to swathe', fr. *fascia*, 'a band'. See prec. & **-ed**. **1.** (bot.) United by connective tissue, grown together. **2.** Having transverse stripes.

fasciation, n. [1. fàshiáshun; 2. fæ̀ʃiéiʃən]. See prec. & **-ion**. The state of being fasciated.

fascicle, fascicule, n. [1. fásikl, -kūl; 2. fǽsikl, fǽsikjūl], fr. Lat. *fascicul-(us)*, 'a small bundle, bunch', fr. *fasci-(s)*, 'a bundle'. See **fasces** & **-cule**. **1.** (bot.) A small bunch, cluster. **2.** A single number of a book published in parts.

fascicular, adj. [1. fasíkūlar; 2. fæsíkjulə]. Prec. & **-ar**. (bot.) Pertaining to, forming, a fascicle; clustered together.

fasciculate, adj. [1. fasíkūlāt; 2. fæsíkjuleit]. **fascicule** & **-ate**. Fascicular.

fasciculation, n. [1. fasìkūláshun; 2. fæsìkjuléiʃən]. Prec. & **-ion**. The state of being fasciculate.

fascinate, vb. trans. [1. fásināt; 2. fǽsineit], fr. Lat. *fascināt-(um)*, P.P. of *fascināre*, 'to enchant, bewitch, charm', fr. *fascin-(um)*, 'a charm; witchcraft'; cp. Gk. *báskanos*, 'sorcerer'; *baskainein*, 'to use ill words to another; to bewitch'; prob. fr. Aryan **bhā-*, **bhə-*, 'to speak'. See **fable**. **a** To exercise an irresistible influence over; to subdue, deprive of power of movement, by fixed gaze: *the snake fascinates its victim*; **b** to enchant, bewitch, captivate.

fascinating, adj. [1. fásināting; 2. fǽsineitiŋ], fr. Pres. Part. of prec. Exercising fascination; strongly attractive, charming, bewitching, enchanting.

fascinatingly, adv. Prec. & **-ly**. In a fascinating manner.

fascination, n. [1. fàsináshun; 2. fæ̀sinéiʃən]. **fascinate** & **-ion**. **1.** Act of fascinating; state of being fascinated. **2.** Power to fascinate; powerful attraction, witchery, charm.

fascinator, n. [1. fásinātor; 2. fǽsineitə]. **fascinate** & **-or**. **1.** One who, that which, fascinates. **2.** (archaic) A kind of light shawl or wrap.

fascine, n. [1. fásēn; 2. fǽsīn], fr. Fr., fr. Lat. *fascīna*, 'faggot', fr. *fasc-(is)*, 'a bundle' (see **fasces**), & **-ine**. Faggot of brushwood used in military engineering for filling ditches, supporting the sides of trenches &c.

fascine dwelling, n. Prehistoric hut built near the shore of a lake upon a kind of platform rising to surface of the water, formed by faggots piled on the bottom and kept in place by upright wooden piles.

Fascism, n. [1. fásizm; 2. fǽsizəm], fr. Ital. *Fascismo*. See next word & **-ism**. The principles of the Fascists; theory and practice of state government adopted by the Fascists.

Fascist, n. & adj. [1. fásist; 2. fǽsist], fr. Ital. *Fascista*, pl. *Fascisti* [1. fashéstē; 2. fāʃístī], member of a *fascio*, political group of persons bound together by an oath & pledged to certain principles, fr. Lat. *fascis*, 'bundle'. See **fasces**. **1.** n. A member of an Italian political party, organized on military lines, by Benito Mussolini, in 1919, to combat Bolshevism and Communism and establish a strongly centralized government not based on parliamentary elections and principles. This succeeded in its aims in 1922. **2.** adj. Of, pertaining to, the Fascists or Fascism.

fash, vb. reflex. & trans. [1. fash; 2. fæʃ], fr. O. Fr. *fascher*, 'to trouble', fr. Provenç. *fastigar*, 'to become annoyed, wearied', fr. Lat. *fastīdium*, 'distaste, disgust, aversion', wh. is prob. for **farst-*, fr. Aryan **gharst-*, whence also O.H.G. *garst*, 'rancid, spoilt'; cp. Mod. Germ. *garstig*, 'foul, unclean'. Cp. **fastidious**. (Scots) **a** Generally *fash oneself*, to worry, be anxious; become excited and angry; also **b** trans., to worry, cause annoyance to, render angry and excited.

fashion (I.), n. [1. fáshun; 2. fǽʃən], fr. A.-Fr. *fachon*, O. Fr. *façon*, fr. Lat. *factiōn-(em)*, 'the act of making; a faction'. See **faction**. **1.** The manner, way, mode in which a thing is made or done; manner, make, shape, style, cut, external appearance: *to behave in a strange fashion*; *I don't like the fashion of his speech*; *to do a thing in one's own fashion*; *two things made after the same fashion*; Phrs. *after a fashion, in a fashion*, in a way, not particularly well; *after the fashion of*, like, in imitation of. **2.** That style, mode, habit, custom, generally prevailing, most in repute, and by convention regarded as the best and most admirable at a given period, or in given place; vogue; specif. **a** (of dress) *the latest Paris fashions*; *wide trousers were all the fashion then*, i.e. reputed, considered, smartest; *to set, follow, the fashion in dress*; **b** (in manners, conduct, thought, speech &c.) *it is no longer the fashion to get drunk after dinner*; *there are fashions in pronunciation as in dress*; Phr. *to be in the fashion*, behave &c., in accordance with this; **c** (of persons &c.) *to be the fashion*, be admired, regarded as a model, be popular and sought after; *a man of fashion*, one moving in high social circles, and following in all respects the conventions there recognized as polite.

fashion (II.), vb. trans., fr. prec. To form, shape, mould, contrive, make; **a** (of material things) *some savages fashion boats out of tree-trunks*; *to fashion a vase from clay*; **b** (of non-material things) *to fashion a tribal song.*

fashionable, adj. [1. fáshunabl; 2. fǽʃənəbl]. **fashion** (I.) & **-able**. **a** (of objects) In accordance with, conforming to, following, the fashion, in form, size, colour &c.: *fashionable clothes, furniture* &c.; **b** (of persons) following, guided by, conforming to, the fashion of upper classes; **c** (of habits, customs, pursuits) prevailing in, characteristic of, much in vogue in, a specific period and place: *a fashionable amusement*; **d** resorted to, patronized by, people of fashion: *a fashionable dressmaker, watering-place* &c.; Phr. (facetious) *a fashionable complaint*, one rife at given period; one from which several well-known and fashionable persons have suffered.

fashionableness, n. Prec. & **-ness**. The quality of being fashionable.

fashionably, adv. See prec. & **-ly**. In a fashionable manner; in accordance with the prevailing fashion.

fashion-plate, n. Engraved, often coloured picture, of human beings wearing clothes of latest designs, intended to show the fashions of the moment in dress.

fast (I.), adj. & adv. [1. fahst; 2. fāst]. O.E. *fæst*, M.E. *fast*; cp. O.L.G. *fast*, O.N. *fastr*, O.H.G. *festi*, O. Fris. *fest*; cp. Goth. *fastan*, 'to hold fast; to keep, observe'; prob. cogn. w. Scrt. *pastyà*, 'house, established dwelling-place.' The etymol. is obscure, but it is possible that the *-st-* is a reduced form of the base of **stand**, or of the base **sed-*, 'sit' &c. See **sit** & **nest**. **1.** adj. **a** Firmly fixed, established, not easily moved: *to take a fast hold of something*; *to make a boat fast*, fasten firmly; **b** (fig.) firm, devoted, loyal, sure: *a fast friend*; **c** (of colours) not easily faded. **2.** adv. (O.E. *fæste*, fr. prec.) In a firm, sure manner; in such a way as to ensure immovability, firmness, fixity; firmly, securely, fixedly: *to be fast bound by the feet*; *to hold fast by a rail*; Phrs. *fast asleep*, in profound sleep, sound asleep; *to stand fast*, not to move, esp. not to retreat, stand firm; *fast shut*, completely, firmly closed; *to play fast and loose*, behave inconsistently, with no fixed method; to be unreliable and inconstant.

fast (II.), adj. & adv. Same word as prec. The sense of 'rapid' is fr. Scand; cp. O.N. *fylja fast*, 'follow fast'. The adv. *faste*, 'rapidly', is found in Chaucer. The new sense must have arisen in such phrases as above wh. first meant 'to follow firmly, with determination, intently', & so on. Cp. the now archaic *to follow fast upon a person's tracks.* **1. adj.**

a Rapid, swift in movement, moving with speed, quick: *a fast horse, fast trot*; Phr. *a fast train*, one which does a given journey in a short time and stops at but few stations; **b** acting, doing something, rapidly; prompt; hurried: *a fast worker*; *a fast reader, speaker*; *fast bowler*, one who sends down fast balls; **c** in such a condition as to cause, promote, rapid movement; brisk: *a fast billiard table, tennis-court* &c., in which the balls rebound from cushion or ground with great swiftness. **2.** (of persons) Given to seeking amusement and pleasure, leading a feverish life, rushing from one form of excitement to another; restless; hence, dissipated, profligate, immoral; Phrs. *a fast woman*, one of loose morals; *to lead a fast life*, one of dissipation and immorality. **3.** adv. **a** Rapidly, swiftly; hurriedly: *to run, speak, fast*; **b** in rapid succession, thickly, frequently: *her tears fell fast.*

fast (III.), vb. intrans., fr. O.E. *fæstan*, 'to abstain from food'; M.E. *fasten*; cp. O.H.G. *fastēn*, Goth. *fastan*, 'to keep; to fast'; O.N. *fasta*, O. Fris. *festia*, 'to fast'. This word has same origin as **fast (I.)**. The orig. meaning of the vb. was 'to hold firmly', then to 'hold, restrain' &c., hence, 'restrain oneself, keep oneself from, abstain', finally, specifically, 'abstain from food'. **a** Specif., to go without all, or certain kinds of, food as a religious discipline, form of self-denial &c.; **b** (in gen. sense) to refrain from food, not to eat: *I have been fasting from breakfast till late at night.*

fast (IV.), n., fr. prec. **1.** The act of fasting; abstinence from food; Phr. *to break one's fast*, to take food after interval of fasting. **2.** Period or day appointed for fasting.

fast-day, n. Day appointed for fasting.

fasten, vb. trans. & intrans. [1. fáhsn; 2. fάsn]. O.E. *fæstnian*, 'to fasten, fix; conclude (peace); ratify (treaty &c.)'; M.E. *fastnen, festnen*; cp. O. Fris. *festna*, O.L.G. *fastnōn*. O.H.G. *festinōn*. **fast (I.)** & **-en**. **1.** trans. To make fast, firm, secure; to tie, attach, fix in position: *to fasten a door, a glove*; *to fasten a rope*; *to fasten a boat to a tree by a rope*; *to fasten two things together.* **2.** intrans. To become fastened, catch: *the lock, door, window* &c. *will not fasten.* **3.** Followed by various adverbs and prepositions. *Fasten off*, trans., (of stitch, thread &c.) to make firm, secure, prevent from slipping. *Fasten on, upon*, **a** trans., (fig.) to cause to be imputed to, assigned to; to fix; cause to cling to: *to fasten a crime, a nickname, on a person*; Phr. *to fasten one's eyes on*, gaze fixedly at; **b** intrans., (lit. and fig.) to clutch at, seize upon, take firm hold of: (i.) *to fasten upon one's prey*; (ii.) *to fasten upon an idea, suggestion, pretext* &c. *Fasten up*, trans., to close and make secure, make fast by a bond, catch &c.; tie up, nail up: *to fasten up a parcel, box* &c.

fastener, n. [1. fáhsener; 2. fάsn-ə]. Prec. & **-er**. **a** Person who fastens; **b** object, device, contrivance, for fastening things together: *paper-fastener.*

fastening, n. [1. fáhsening; 2. fάsn-iŋ]. **fasten** & **-ing**. **1.** The act or manner of making fast. **2.** That by which anything is fastened; a clasp, catch, bolt, latch, band &c.

fasti, n. pl. [1. fástī; 2. fǽstai]. Lat. *fasti*, 'a day on which courts could be held and judgements pronounced; a calendar of festivals and events'; fr. *fās*, 'divine law'; hence, 'that which is permitted, lawful', fr. Aryan base **bhā-*, 'to speak'. See **fable, fate, fame.** Record of events in chronological order, with date upon which each occurred.

fastidious, adj. [1. fastídyus; 2. fæstídjəs], fr. Lat. *fastīdiōs-(us)*, 'full of disgust; scornful, disdainful, squeamish', fr. *fastīdi-(um)*, 'loathing, disgust; contempt, pride', & **-ous**. Possibly fr. earlier **farstīdium*, cogn. w. M.H.G. *garst*, 'spoilt, sour', Mod. Germ. *garstig*, O.N. *gersta*, 'to spoil'; Lith. *grasùs*, 'repulsive'. See **fash.** **a** Given to picking and choosing, full of likes and dislikes; difficult, particular, hard to please; **b** sensitive, refined, highly cultivated; critical, discriminating: *a fastidious taste in art.*

fastidiously, adv. Prec. & **-ly**. In a fastidious manner.

fastidiousness, n. See prec. & **-ness**. The quality of being fastidious.

fastigiate, adj. [1. fastíjiāt; 2. fæstídžieit], fr. Lat. *fastīgi-(um)*, 'gable end, top of a gable; top, summit; slope, descent; highest degree, rank', & **-ate**. Earlier **farsti-*, cogn. w. Scrt. *bhṛ́ṣṭiṣ*, 'point, peak, angle'; O.H.G., O.N. *burst*, O.E. *byrst*, 'bristle' (see **bristle**); O.N. *barr*, 'needle'; O.E. *brord*, 'point'. Aryan base **bher-s-*, **bhṛ-s*, 'something pointed'. Sloping towards a point or ridge, inclining inwards.

fasting, n. [1. fáhsting; 2. fάstiŋ]. **fast (III.)** & **-ing**. Abstinence, self-denial in food, esp. as a religious observance.

fastish, adj. [1. fáhstish; 2. fάstiʃ]. **fast (I.)** & **(II.)** & **-ish**. Fairly fast.

fastness (I.), n. [1. fáhstnes; 2. fάstnis]. **fast (I.)** & **(II.)** & **-ness**. The quality of being fast.

fastness (II.), n. O.E. *fæsten*, 'fortress, castle'; M.E. *fastnes*, formed, w. addition of **-ness**, fr. **fast (I.)**. Stronghold, fortress; secure and remote retreat.

fastuous, adj. [1. fástūus; 2. fǽstjuəs]. Fr. *fastueux*, fr. Lat. *fastus*, 'pride, arrogance', & **-ous**, fr. Lat. *-ōsus*. Etymol. doubtful. (rare) Proud, ostentatious.

fastuously, adv. Prec. & **-ly**. Arrogantly, ostentatiously.

fastuousness, n. See prec. & **-ness**. Arrogance, ostentation, pomp.

fat (I.), adj. [1. fat; 2. fæt]. O.E. *fǣtt*, 'fat, obese; greasy; fertile, productive, rich'; M.E. *fātt*; cp. O.N. *feitr*, M. Du. *vet*, O.H.G. *feizit*; fr. P.P. of Gmc. **faitjan-*, 'to fatten', fr. **faito-*, 'fat'. Cogn. w. Gk. *pīdúein*, 'to gush forth'; O. Slav. *pitěti*, 'to nourish, feed'; further, Lat. *(o)pīmus*, 'fat, well-nourished; fertile, rich'; *pinguis*, 'fat' (see **pinguid**); Gk. *pīmelḗ*, 'fat'; *pī́ōn*, 'fat'; Scrt. *pīvān-*, 'swelling'; *pīvarā́ś*, 'fat'; *pīvaś*, 'fat'. Aryan base **pēi-*, **pōi-*, **pi-*, 'to swell out, gush out (of liquids, grease &c.)'. See **pine (II.), pituitary.** **1.** **a** Covered with fat, corpulent, obese, plump, stout, full-bodied: *you are getting too fat*; *fat cheeks*; Phrs. *fat woman*, one of excessive corpulence, exhibited as a show; *laugh and grow fat*; **b** specif., fattened, fatted by special feeding for exhibition, or for food: *a fat ox, sow* &c.; **c** (of meat) having considerable quantity of fat attached in proportion to lean: *this mutton is too fat for me.* **2.** (of food) Abounding in fat, oily, greasy, unctuous: *fat soup*; *a fat diet.* **3.** **a** Thick in proportion to length and breadth; stumpy, lumpy: *fat fingers*; *a fat slice*; **b** swelled out, plump, full: *the pods of the peas are getting fat*; Phr. (vulg.) *a fat lot you care*, (ironical) you don't care at all. **4.** Rich, prolific, fertile, productive: *fat pasture*; *fat soil.* **5.** Yielding a good income; profitable: *a fat job*; *a fat benefice.*

fat (II.), n. O.E. *fǣtt*. See prec. **1.** A greasy, soluble substance found in many parts of animal body; adipose tissue; also similar substance found in certain seeds, cp. *oil*; Phrs. *the fat is in the fire*, a step has been taken, something done, which commits to further action, or will produce excitement, indignation &c.; *to live on one's own fat*, consume one's capital, financial or intellectual. **2.** **a** The richest, best part of anything; Phr. *to live on the fat of the land*, to enjoy every luxury; **b** (theatr. slang) an important part in a play; **c** striking, attractive, impressive, pregnant, passage in a literary composition.

fat (III.), vb. trans. & intrans. O.E. *fǣttian*, 'to grow fat'. **1.** trans. Also *fat up*, to cause to become fat, fatten: *to fat (up) a beast for market*; Phr. *to kill the fatted calf*, hold joyful celebration, prepare a hospitable welcome; from Parable of Prodigal Son. **2.** intrans. To respond to the process of fatting: *these beasts are fatting up well.*

fat (IV.), n. Variant of **vat.** (archaic and obs. except in Authorized Version of Bible) A receptacle, vessel: '*digged a place for the winefat*' (Mark xii. 1).

fatal, adj. [1. fátl; 2. féitl], fr. Lat. *fātāl-(is)*, 'ordained by fate; destructive, deadly'; fr. Lat. *fāt-(um)*, 'fate' (see **fate**), & **-al**. **1.** (rare or obs.) Connected with, arising from, due to, decreed by, fate or destiny: *the fatal hour has struck.* Phr. *the fatal sisters*, the Fates. **2.** Causing death; inimical to, destructive of, life; mortal: *his wound proved fatal*; *a fatal explosion*; *the great heat was fatal to many persons.* **3.** Destructive, causing calamity; decisively disastrous; involving loss and ruin: *the event was fatal to my hopes*; *a fatal blunder*; *the hesitation and weakness of the general were fatal to the success of the attack.*

fatalism, n. [1. fátalizm; 2. féitəlizəm]. Prec. & **-ism**. **1.** The doctrine that all events are pre-ordained by fate, and inevitable. **2.** Belief in fatalism; acceptance of every event as inevitably determined by destiny.

fatalist, n. [1. fátalist; 2. féitəlist]. **fatal** & **-ist**. A believer in fatalism.

fatalistic, adj. [1. fâtalístik; 2. fèitəlístik]. Prec. & **-ic**. Pertaining to, founded on, fatalism; inclined to fatalism.

fatalistically, adv. [1. fâtalístikali; 2. fèitəlístikəli]. Prec. & **-al** & **-ly**. In a fatalistic manner.

fatality, n. [1. fatáliti; 2. fətǽliti], fr. Fr. *fatalité*, fr. L. Lat. *fātālitāt-(em)*, 'fatal necessity'; **fatal** & **-ity**. **1.** The state of being fatal. **2.** Something, especially of an unfortunate, unfavourable character which is destined by fate to happen; some inevitable (undesired) event, occurrence, circumstance: *there seems to be a fatality connected with my undertakings.* **3.** A calamity, disaster, esp. one which results in death.

fatalize, vb. intrans. & trans. [1. fátalīz; 2. féitəlaiz]. **fatal** & **-ize**. **1.** intrans. (rare) To be inclined to fatalism. **2.** trans. (rare) To cause to become a fatalist.

fatally, adv. [1. fátali; 2. féitəli]. **fatal** & **-ly**. In a fatal manner; **a** inevitably, as though decreed by fate; **b** so as to cause, or result in, death.

fata morgana, n. [1. fáhta morgáhna; 2. fάtə mōgάnə]. Ital., 'Morgan the Fairy', an enchantress who figures in Romances of the Round Table. A mirage, regarded as the work of fairies, visible in the Straits of Messina.

fate, n. [1. fāt; 2. feit], fr. Lat. *fāt-(um)*, 'that which is spoken; prediction, oracle; that which is ordained, fate, destiny; ill fate, calamity', fr. P.P. of *fāri*, 'to speak; to foretell, predict'. Cp. Lat. *fābula*, 'speech, saying', see **fable**; *fateor*, 'I confess'; *fāma*, 'report'. See **fame.** **1.** A supposed irresistible power controlling the course of all events: *fate had decided otherwise*; Phr. *as sure as fate*, quite certain. **2.** One through whom the power of fate is exercised; specif., *the Fates*, three Greek goddesses controlling human destiny. **3.** That which is decreed, ordained by fate; **a** one's lot, condition, destiny, state: *my fate has been a happy one*; **b** evil fate, doom, destruction: *to go to one's fate*; *the murderer met his fate with fortitude.* Phrs. *to seal, decide, a person's fate*, determine what is to happen to him; *to meet one's fate*, meet a lady with whom one falls in love and to whom one subsequently becomes engaged.

fated, adj. [1. fáted; 2. féitid]. Prec. & **-ed**. **1.** Appointed, decreed, ordained by fate: *one's fated lot.* **2.** Doomed, pre-ordained, destined: *to be fated to be hanged*; *a scheme fated to fail.*

fateful, adj. [1. fátfool; 2. féitfəl]. **fate** & **-ful**. Determining, fraught with fate, involving future destiny; decisive, irrevocable.

fatefully, adv. Prec. & **-ly**. In a fateful manner.

fathead, n. [1. fát-hed; 2. fǽthed]. **fat (I.)** & **head.** Dull, stupid, slow-witted person.

father (I.), n. [1. fáhdher; 2. fā́ðə]. O.E. *fæder*, 'father'; M.E. *fader*, O. Fris. *feder*, O.H.G. *fatar*, Goth. *fadar*, O.N. *faðir*; cogn. w. Lat. *pater*, Gk. *patḗr*, Scrt. *pitár*, O. Ir. *athir*; Aryan base **pətēr-*, 'father'. See **pater. 1.** Male parent; hence (by extension) **a** stepfather; **b** adoptive father; **c** father-in-law. Phrs. *the wish is father to the thought*, one tends to believe that which one wishes to be true or to happen; *to be a father to*, behave like a father, be kind to, protect and support. **2.** One who stands in the position of a parent and protector, one who is regarded as a father: *the king is the father of his people, the father of his country*; specif., *the Father*, God the Creator. **3. a** Ancestor, progenitor, forefather; Phrs. *to be gathered to one's fathers*, to die; *to sleep with one's fathers*, be dead; **b** the founder, originator, of anything; leader, author: *Boyle was described as the father of chemistry and brother of the Earl of Cork. The Early Fathers, Fathers of the Church*, early Christian teachers and writers; *Father of lies*, the devil; *Father of the Faithful*, the caliph; *Pilgrim Fathers*, one of those who sailed in the *Mayflower* from England and settled at Plymouth, in America, in 1620. **4.** One to whom reverence is due on account of position, age, seniority &c.; specif. **a** *the Holy Father*, the Pope; **b** *Right Reverend Father in God*, title of bishop; **c** *Most Reverend Father in God*, title of archbishop; **d** Roman Catholic priest who is a member of a religious community; **e** title of secular priest; *father confessor*, one to whom confession is made; **f** oldest member of a class, body &c.; *Father of the House*, member who has sat the longest without interruption; **g** as title, expressing veneration; Phrs. *Father Time, Father Thames, Father Christmas* &c., personification of these; **h** *Conscript Fathers*, members of ancient Roman senate.

father (II.), vb. trans., fr. prec. **1. a** To be the father of, beget; **b** (fig.) to be the author, originator, of. **2. a** To acknowledge oneself as the father of; **b** (fig.) to assume responsibility for (a book, a parliamentary Bill &c.). **3.** (*father on, upon*) **a** To charge with the paternity of; **b** (fig.) to saddle with responsibility for. **4.** To be a father to, care for, provide for, as a father.

fatherhood, n. [1. fáhdherhood; 2. fā́ðəhud]. **father** & **-hood.** The state of being a father.

father-in-law, n. [1. fáhdher in law; 2. fā́ðər *i*n lɔ]. Wife's or husband's father.

fatherland, n. [1. fáhdherland; 2. fā́ðəlænd]. Not a native word; translation of Germ. *Vaterland*, as this is of Lat. *patria*, 'native country'. Native country.

fatherless, adj. [1. fáhdherles; 2. fā́ðəl*i*s]. **father (I.)** & **-less.** Without a father living.

fatherlike, adj. [1. fáhdherlīk; 2. fā́ðəlaik]. **father (I.)** & **-like.** Like a father.

fatherliness, n. [1. fáhdherlines; 2. fā́ðəlin*i*s]. Next word & **-ness.** The quality of being fatherly.

fatherly, adv. [1. fáhdherli; 2. fā́ðəl*i*]. **father (I.)** & **-ly. a** Belonging to a father: *fatherly responsibility*; **b** like that of a father, kindly, protective, benevolent: *a fatherly smile.*

fathom (I.), n. [1. fádhm; 2. fǽðm]. O.E. *fæðm*, 'embrace; the outstretched arms; fathom measure'; M.E. *faðme*, 'fathom; embrace'; cp. O.S. *fathmōs*, pl., 'the outstretched arms, embrace'; O.H.G. *fadam*, 'length of thread'; O.N. *faðmr*, 'embrace; thread'; Goth. *faþa*, 'something that surrounds; a hedge, enclosure'; cp. further, Gk. *petánnūmi*, 'I spread out', *pétalon*, 'leaf; metal plate' (see **petal**); Lat. *patēre*, 'to be open' (see **patent**); Aryan base **petē-*, **potē-*, 'to spread'. **1.** A measure of length or depth, six feet, used principally of depth of water. **2.** A quantity of timber whose cross-section is six feet square.

fathom (II.), vb. trans. O.E. *fæðmian*, 'to embrace'; see prec. To plumb, sound, measure depth of; (chiefly of mental action) to understand; get to the bottom of, penetrate: *I cannot fathom his thoughts, intentions, meaning* &c.

fathomless, adj. [1. fádhumles; 2. fǽðml*i*s]. **fathom (I.)** & **-less.** (lit. and fig.) Impossible to fathom; very deep, unplumbed: *the fathomless depths of the sea.*

fathomlessly, adv. Prec. & **-ly.** In a manner, to an extent, impossible to fathom.

fathom-line, n. Sailor's line marked in fathoms, for taking soundings.

fatidical, adj. [1. fātídikl; 2. feitíd*i*kl]. Lat. *fātidic-(us)*, 'predicting future events, prophesying', & **-al**, fr. Lat. *fāt-(um)*, 'prophetic saying; prophesy; destiny' (see **fate**), & *dīc-(ere)*, 'to say' (see **diction**). (rare) Able to foretell the future; prophetic.

fatigue (I.), n. [1. fatḗg; 2. fətíg], fr. Fr. *fatigue*, fr. vb. *fatiguer*, 'to weary'. See next word. **1.** Weariness, exhaustion, of body or mind. **2.** (mechan.) Weakness in metal or wood caused by long-continued strain. **3. a** That which causes fatigue; wearisome toil, tiring occupation, exertion; **b** (mil.) non-military work performed by soldiers. Also *fatigue duty.*

fatigue (II.), vb. trans., fr. Fr. *fatiguer*, fr. Lat. *fatīgāre*, 'to weary; to vex, hinder', fr. earlier **fati-ago*; cp. *(af)fatim*, 'abundantly, exhaustively', *fatiscere*, 'to gape open, fall apart; be weary', fr. **fatis*, 'exhaustion'; cogn. w. Lat. *famēs*, 'hunger'; Gk. *khaínō* (fr. **khan-jō*), 'I yawn, gape open', *khános*, 'the open mouth; gulf, chasm', *khásma*, 'yawning gulf' (see **chasm**), *khḗmē*, 'a yawning'; Aryan base **ĝhē-*, **ĝhə-*, 'hunger; the open mouth' (see **famine** & **faucal**). To tire out, cause exhaustion to; to weary by bodily or mental work or strain.

fatigueless, adj. [1. fatḗgles; 2. fətígl*i*s]. **fatigue (I.)** & **-less.** Incapable of being fatigued; unwearied, unwearying.

fatigue-party, n. Military party told off for fatigue duty.

fatiguing, adj. [1. fatḗging; 2. fətígiŋ], fr. Pres. Part. of **fatigue (II.).** Causing fatigue, exhausting, tiring: *fatiguing work*; *a fatiguing day*; *hard work in great heat is very fatiguing.*

fatiguingly, adv. Prec. & **-ly.** In a fatiguing manner.

fatless, adj. [1. fátles; 2. fǽtl*i*s]. **fat (I.)** & **-less.** Without fat.

fatling, n. [1. fátling; 2. fǽtliŋ]. **fat (I.)** & **-ling.** Young animal that has been fattened.

fatness, n. [1. fátnes; 2. fǽtn*i*s]. **fat (I.)** & **-ness.** The quality, state, of being fat.

fatten, vb. trans. & intrans. [1. fátn; 2. fǽtn]. **fat (I.)** & **-en. 1.** trans. **a** To make fat, esp. animals for slaughter; **b** to make fertile, enrich (land). **2.** intrans. To become fat.

fattish, adj. [1. fátish; 2. fǽtiʃ]. **fat (I.)** & **-ish.** Fairly fat.

fatty (I.), adj. [1. fáti; 2. fǽt*i*]. **fat (I.)** & **-y. a** Like, or containing, fat: *fatty tissue*; **b** characterized by excessive fat: *fatty degeneration.*

fatty (II.), n., fr. prec. Fat child or person; esp. as familiar form of address.

fatuity, n. [1. fatū́iti; 2. fətjū́*i*t*i*], fr. Lat. *fatu-(us)*, 'foolish, silly', see **fatuous** & **-ity.** The quality of being fatuous; foolishness, inanity.

fatuous, adj. [1. fátūus; 2. fǽtjuəs], fr. Lat. *fatu-(us)*, 'foolish, silly; awkward', & **-ous.** The orig. meaning seems to have been 'abject, depressed; debased by stupidity'; in this case the word is fr. the Aryan base **bhāu-*, 'to beat down'; cp. Goth. *bauþs*, 'deaf, stupid'. See **beat**; also second element of **confute** &c. **a** (of persons) Silly, foolish; self-satisfied and inane; **b** expressing folly, imbecility, stupidity: *a fatuous smile*; **c** (of action) arising from, inspired by, folly &c.; futile: *a fatuous attempt.*

fatuously, adv. Prec. & **-ly.** In a fatuous manner.

fatuousness, n. See prec. & **-ness.** The quality of being fatuous.

fat-witted, adj. [1. fát wíted; 2. fǽt wít*i*d]. Stupid, dull.

faubourg, n. [1. fóboor; 2. fóubuə]. Fr., earlier *forbourg*, fr. *forsbourg*. The first element fr. Lat. *foris*, 'out of doors, outside', fr. *foris*, 'a door'; cp. **forum** & **door.** The second element is Gmc., 'town' &c.; see **borough.** Quarter, district, outside a town; suburb; often surviving as a name in the town itself.

faucal, adj. [1. fáwkl; 2. fɔ́kl], fr. Lat. *fauc-(ēs)*, 'throat; narrow passage'. Perh. cogn. w. O.H.G. *guomo*, O.N. *gōmr*, O.E. *gōma*, 'palate' (see **gum (I.)**); Lett. *gāmurs*, 'windpipe'; Lith. *gomurỹs*, 'palate'; Aryan base **ghē(u)-*, **ghō(u)-*, **ghəu-*, 'to gape open'; cp. the base **ghē-*, **ghə-*, in Lat. *famēs*, 'hunger' (see **famine**); Gk. *khános*, 'the open mouth', *khḗmē*, 'yawning'. Cp. **fatigue.** Pertaining to, produced in, the back of the throat.

faucet, n. [1. fáwset; 2. fɔ́s*i*t], fr. Fr. *fausset*, 'vent-peg'. Perh. fr. Lat. *falsāre*, 'to falsify'. See **false.** Tap for drawing liquid from barrel or vessel.

faugh, interj. Combination of letters used by writers, in representing conversation, as an exclamation expressive of disgust or contempt, but not corresponding apparently to any reality of utterance.

fault (I.), n. [1. fawlt; 2. fɔlt]. M.E. *faute*, fr. O. Fr., fr. Low Lat. **fallita*, P.P. of *fallere*, 'to deceive; to fail'. See **fail (II.). 1.** Something that destroys perfection; flaw, defect, failure, imperfection: **a** (of character) *over-generosity is his greatest fault*; *one cannot help liking him in spite of his many faults*; **b** (of conduct) *to acknowledge one's faults.* Phrs. *to find fault with*, (i.) complain of; (ii.) to rebuke, scold; *to a fault*, excessively, so as to amount to a defect. **2.** Responsibility, culpability, liability to blame, for something wrong or undesired: *the fault is his own*; *it was my fault that they were late.* **3.** Various specific uses: **a** a flaw in metal; **b** (geol.) displacement of part of strata causing loss of continuity of the strata; **c** (elect.) leakage in a circuit; **d** (hunting) loss of the scent. Phr. *to be at fault*, (i.) to lose the scent; (ii.) (fig.) to be at a loss. **4. a** A mistake, error; something done wrongly: *this exercise has many faults of grammar*; **b** specif. (lawn-tennis) ball wrongly placed by server; also *foot-fault*, error in position of the feet of server.

fault (II.), vb. intrans., fr. prec. (geol., of strata of rock) To become displaced.

faultfinder, n. [1. fáwltfīnder; 2. fɔ́ltfaində]. One given to finding fault.

faultfinding, adj. & n. [1. fáwltfīnding; 2. fɔ́ltfaindiŋ]. **1.** adj. Given to finding fault, critical. **2.** n. Complaint, harsh criticism.

faultily, adv. [1. fáwltili; 2. fɔ́ltil*i*]. **faulty** & **-ly.** In a faulty manner.

faultiness, n. [1. fáwltines; 2. fɔ́ltin*i*s]. **faulty** & **-ness.** The quality of being faulty.

faultless, adj. [1. fáwltles; 2. fɔ́ltl*i*s]. **fault** & **-less.** Without a fault, absolutely perfect.

faultlessly, adv. Prec. & **-ly.** In a faultless manner; perfectly, to perfection.

faultlessness, n. See prec. & **-ness.** The quality of being faultless; perfection.

faulty, adj. [1. fáwlti; 2. fɔ́lt*i*]. **fault (I.)** & **-y. a** Guilty of a fault, blameworthy, wrong, culpable; **b** defective, imperfect.

faun, n. [1. fawn; 2. fɔn], fr. Lat. *Faunus*, a god of agriculture, later identified w. Pan; fr. earlier **faweno-*, 'favourable, propitious'; cp. *favēre*, 'to be favourable'. See **favour.** (Roman mythol.) One of a class of deities of the woods and fields, represented with horns, goat's feet, and pointed ears.

fauna, n. [1. fáwna; 2. fɔ́nə], fr. Lat. *Fauna*, a goddess in Roman mythology, sister of Faunus. See prec. **1.** The whole group of animals existing within a certain area, or during a specific geological period: *the fauna of Britain, of the Ice Age.* **2.** A treatise on the fauna of a specific region or period.

faunal, adj. [1. fáwnal; 2. fṓnəl]. Prec. & **-al.** Pertaining to fauna.

faunist, n. [1. fáwnist; 2. fṓnist]. **fauna** & **-ist.** A student of fauna.

faunistic(al), adj. [1. fawnístik(l); 2. fōnístik(l)]. Prec. & **-ic** & **-al.** Pertaining to fauna or to faunists.

fauteuil, n. [1. fōtḗi; 2. foutā́i]. Anglicized pronunciation of Fr.; O. Fr. *faldestoel*, fr. O.H.G. *faltstuol*. See **faldstool.** **a** An armchair; **b** a stall in a theatre.

faux pas, n. [1. fṓ páh; 2. fóu pā́]. Fr., 'false step'. **a** A blunder, indiscretion, in speech or behaviour; an ill-judged, untimely utterance or action, esp. one which causes embarrassment to others; **b** breach of social usage and etiquette: *to make, commit, a faux pas*; **c** a moral lapse, fall from virtue; indiscreet, reprehensible conduct.

favour (**I.**), n. [1. fā́vur; 2. féivə], fr. Fr., fr. Lat. *favōr-(em)*, 'good-will, partiality; expression of favour, acclamation, applause', fr. *fav-(ēre)*, 'to be well disposed towards, to be favourable to, befriend'. Prob. ultimately connected w. the base **bhewā-*, **bhū-* &c., 'to exist'. See **be, future,** & **physio-.** **1. a** An inclination, desire, disposition, readiness, to aid, protect, show kindness to; good graces, countenance, support, good-will, approval: *to win a person's favour*; *to look with favour on a person, a project* &c.; Phrs. *to find favour in one's eyes*, please; *to stand high in a person's favour*; **b** excessive, unfair partiality: *I must decline to show favour to any of the candidates.* **2. a** A kindly, gracious, obliging act; esp. one done from kindness, and without any obligation: *may I ask a favour of you?*; *to do something as a favour*; *I regard this as a very great favour*; *may I ask for the favour of a reply?*; Phrs. *your favour of yesterday*, your letter (vulg. or commerc.); *by your favour*, with your permission; **b** undue advantage granted or obtained through partiality: *he gained his position more by favour than merit*; **c** (a woman's) consent to sexual intimacy (pl.): *she granted her favours to all and sundry*; *many besides the king enjoyed the favours of Barbara Villiers*; Phr. *the last favour*, possession (of a woman). **3.** Kindness, benefit, evidence of generosity, token of favour or esteem: *to receive, be grateful for, favours*; *to heap favours upon.* **4.** Advantageous circumstances, or conditions, something favourable: *the evidence is in his favour.* Phrs. *in favour of*, (of persons) favourable to, in sympathy with, desirous of: *I am quite in favour of a change*; (of things and actions) on behalf of, to the advantage of: *to withdraw in favour of another*; *to draw a cheque in a person's favour*; *under favour of the darkness*, under cover of. **5.** An ornament, decoration, generally in form of ribbons, rosette, or badge, worn in honour of some event: *wedding favours*; or as sign of membership of a society or party: *the Tory candidate and his supporters wore blue favours.*

favour (**II.**), vb. trans., fr. O. Fr. *favorer*, fr. Med. Lat. *favōrāre*. See prec. **1.** To show favour to, support, approve of: *to favour a proposal.* **2.** To show undue and unfair partiality to, give advantages to, to detriment of others: *he could never have risen to his present post had he not been favoured by the powers that be.* **3.** (of circumstances) To be advantageous for, tend to promote, encourage: *revolution always favours the rise of unscrupulous scoundrels to power.* **4.** (archaic) To resemble, be like, have similar features to: *the child favours his father.*

favourable, adj. [1. fā́vurabl; 2. féivərəbl]. **favour** (**I.**) & **-able.** **1.** (of persons) Well disposed towards, inclined to, in favour of: *to be favourable to a scheme.* **2.** (of material things and conditions, times &c.) Suitable, propitious; advantageous: *the tide, wind, is favourable for a start*; *the moment is not favourable for speculations*; *a favourable opportunity now presents itself*; *favourable answer*, the one desired, consent to request &c.; *favourable report*, satisfactory report, one in favour, in commendation of person, thing, action.

favourableness, n. Prec. & **-ness.** Condition, quality, of being favourable.

favourably, adv. See prec. & **-ly.** In a favourable manner.

favoured, adj. [1. fā́vurd; 2. féivəd], fr. P.P. of **favour** (**II.**). Fortunate, enjoying favour, specially happy: *this favoured clime*; *a favoured mortal.*

-favoured, suff. Of specific type or cast of countenance or features: *well-, ill-favoured.*

favouring, adj. [1. fā́vuring; 2. féivəriŋ], fr. Pres. Part. of **favour** (**II.**). Favourable, propitious: *favouring winds.*

favourite (**I.**), adj. [1. fā́vurit; 2. féivərit], fr. O. Fr. *favorit*, P.P. of *favorir*, 'to favour', variant of *favorer*. See **favour** (**II.**). Regarded with special favour, preferred, most liked: *my favourite novelist is Scott.*

favourite (**II.**), n., fr. prec. **1. a** (i.) Person who is preferred above another or others: *the elder of the two brothers is my favourite*; (ii.) person who is much and widely liked: *a general favourite*; **b** (in bad sense) (i.) person who is unduly favoured; (ii.) one who is beloved and pampered from base motives, esp. by a highly placed individual; a minion; (iii.) one who is specially, and unfairly favoured to the detriment of others. **2. a** Thing which is preferred to others: *that book is a great favourite of mine*; **b** specif., *the favourite*, horse considered most likely to win a race.

favouritism, n. [1. fā́vuritizm; 2. féivəritizem]. Prec. & **-ism.** **a** Practice of showing excessive and unfair partiality to favourites; **b** system under which rewards, promotion, and other advantages are gained by favourites.

favus, n. [1. fā́vus; 2. féivəs]. Lat., 'honeycomb', prob. orig. 'a building', fr. base **bhū-*, **bhewā-* &c., 'to be; to dwell; to build'. See **be, build.** A skin-disease, chiefly affecting the scalp, due to a parasitic fungus; the name is due to the small pits or depressions left on the scalp.

fawn (**I.**), n. [1. fawn; 2. fōn], fr. O. Fr. *faon*, fr. Med. Lat. *fētōn-(em)*, *fēto*, fr. Lat. *fētus*, *foetus* (see **foetus**), 'birth, bringing forth; offspring; a fawn'. **1.** A young deer; fallow deer of first year. Phr. *in fawn*, pregnant (of does). **2.** The colour of a fawn.

fawn (**II.**), adj., fr. prec. Pale greyish brown.

fawn (**III.**), vb. trans. & intrans., fr. **fawn** (**I.**). (of deer) **1.** trans. To give birth to (a fawn). **2.** intrans. To bring forth young.

fawn (**IV.**), vb. intrans. O.E. *fagenian*, *fahnian*; M.E. *faunen*, 'to rejoice, to flatter'. Cp. O.H.G. *faginōn*, Goth. *faginōn*. See **fain** (**I.**). **1.** (of dogs &c.) To show affection by leaping upon, licking hands of, pressing against, grovelling at feet of, a person. **2.** *Fawn upon, on*, to cringe to, flatter, act servilely towards, with a view to gain favour.

fawn-coloured, adj. **fawn** (**II.**). Of a pale greyish brown.

fawning, adj. [1. fáwning; 2. fṓniŋ], fr. Pres. Part. of **fawn** (**IV.**). **a** (of dogs) Demonstrative, expressing affection by wagging tail, licking master's hands &c.; **b** (of persons) servile, flattering: *a fawning courtier.*

fawningly, adv. Prec. & **-ly.** In a fawning manner.

fay, n. [1. fā; 2. fei], fr. O. Fr. *fae*, fr. Lat. *Fāta*, 'the Fates'. See **fate.** A fairy; a fragile, graceful, delicately beautiful child or girl.

fealty, n. [1. fḗalti; 2. fíəlti], fr. O. Fr. *feaulte*, fr. Lat. *fidēlitāt-(em)*, 'fidelity'. See **fidelity.** **1.** Specif., fidelity owed by a vassal to his feudal lord; obligations implied thereby: *to swear, do fealty (to, for).* **2.** (poet. or archaic) Faith, fidelity, loyalty in general.

fear (**I.**), n. [1. fēr; 2. fíə]. O.E. *fǣr*, 'danger; fear', M.E. *fēre*; cp. O.N. *fār*, O.H.G. *fāra*, 'danger'; Goth. *fērja*, 'pursuer'; cogn. w. Lat. *perīculum*, 'trial, experience; danger', q.v. under **peril.** **1. a** Emotion, state of mind, caused by a sense of impending danger, misfortune, pain &c.; terror, dread: *to be overcome by fear*; *to feel no fear in the midst of battle*; *I daren't enter for fear of the dog*; Phr. *to go in fear of one's life*; **b** a specific access of terror, grave anxiety, sinister anticipation: *grave fears are entertained for his safety*; *the fear of death was upon him.* **2.** Slight feeling of anxiety, solicitude, foreboding, in anticipation of some comparatively trivial risk, annoyance, disappointment: *I had a fear that you had lost the train*; *I have no fear that trout will be scarce this year.* **3.** Likelihood, probability, risk, chance, of some undesired event happening: *there is not the slightest fear of rain today*; *is there any fear of dinner being late?* Phrs. *for fear of* (*accident* &c.), in case of; (vulg.) *no fear!*, certainly not. **4.** Awe, veneration, respectful dread and reverence: *the fear of God*; Phr. *to put the fear of God into* (*a person*), to bring him to his senses, render him respectful and humble; to overawe.

fear (**II.**), vb. trans. & intrans. O.E. *fǣran*, M.E. *fēren*, fr. O.E. *fǣr*, 'danger, fear'. See prec. **A.** trans. **1.** To feel fear for, be frightened, terrified of, or by: *to fear death*; *I do not fear his threats.* **2.** To look forward to, anticipate, expect (some disaster): *to fear the worst.* **3.** To regard with awe, venerate, revere: *fear God, honour the king.* **4.** (archaic & poet.) To cause fear to; to frighten, terrify: '*bugs to fearen babes*' (Spenser); '*he feared the antelope*' (Keats). **B.** intrans. **1.** To be afraid, feel fear, be oppressed by terror. **2.** To be nervous, anxious, solicitous, be uneasy lest: *I fear it's too late*; *you are ill, I fear*; Phr. *never fear*, don't be anxious; *they will help you, never fear.*

fearful, adj. [1. fḗrfool; 2. fíəful]. **fear** (**I.**) & **-ful.** **1.** (archaic) **a** Feeling fear, timid, timorous, shrinking, frightened; **b** anticipating with fear, apprehensive, filled with misgiving, afraid: *to be fearful of falling, lest one fall*; **c** feeling awe, dread, reverence; '*Ye fearful saints, fresh courage take*' (Cowper). **2. a** Causing, inspiring, fear; awful, terrible; **b** (colloq.) very great, extraordinary, extreme: *a fearful bore.*

fearfully, adv. Prec. & **-ly.** In a fearful manner; to a fearful extent; often colloq. as mere intens.: *fearfully pleased* &c.

fearfulness, n. See prec. & **-ness.** The quality of being fearful.

fearless, adj. [1. fḗrles; 2. fíəlis]. **fear** (**I.**) & **-less.** Without fear; dauntless, courageous.

fearlessly, adv. Prec. & **-ly.** In a fearless manner, courageously.

fearlessness, n. See prec. & **-ness.** The quality of being fearless; courage, bravery.

fearnought, n. [1. fḗrnawt; 2. fíənōt]. **fear** (**II.**) & **nought.** A thick, tough woollen cloth; coat made from this.

fearsome, adj. [1. fḗrsum; 2. fíəsəm]. **fear** (**I.**) & **-some.** Inspiring fear; terrible, grisly.

fearsomely, adv. Prec. & **-ly.** In a fearsome manner.

fearsomeness, n. See prec. & **-ness.** The quality of being fearsome.

feasibility, n. [1. fēzibíliti; 2. fīzibíliti]. Next word & **-ity.** The quality of being feasible; practicability.

feasible, adj. [1. fḗzibl; 2. fízibl], fr. O. Fr. *fais-*, imperfect stem of *faire*, 'to do', fr. Lat. *facere* (see **fact**), & **-ible.** Capable of being done or carried out; possible, practicable.

feast (**I.**), n. [1. fēst; 2. fīst], fr. O. Fr. *feste*, fr. Lat. *fēsta*, 'festival'; holiday; festal banquet', fr. *fēstus*, 'solemn, festive; joyous, festal'; cp. Lat. *fēriae*, 'festival' (O. Lat. *fēsiae*; see **fair** (**I.**)); *fānum*, 'holy place' (fr. *fas-nom*; see **fane**); fr. O. Lat. stem **fēs-*, **fas-*, 'sacred', prob. fr. Aryan base **dhē-*, **dhə-*, 'to make, do'; cp. Gk. *thémis*, Scrt. *dhāman*, 'that which is appointed, fixed; law'. See **do,** & words there referred to. **1. a** Day of rejoicing, day or period of annual religious commemoration of some important event: *the Feast of the Epiphany*; *Feast of Pentecost*; Phrs. *movable feast*, varying in date, within certain limits; *immovable feast*, occurring on the same date each year; **b** day or period of secular rejoicing, festivity; annual festival. **2. a** Splendid, abundant, sumptuous, repast; esp. a public banquet; Phr. *a feast of fat things* (lit. and fig.); **b** (fig.) abundant, copious supply of delightful and enjoyable things: *an intellectual feast.*

feast (**II.**), vb. intrans. & trans., fr. prec. **1.** intrans. To partake of a feast; to fare sumptuously, abundantly. **2.** trans. **a** To give a feast to, feed sumptuously; **b** to give pleasure to, regale, delight: *to feast one's eyes on a landscape* &c.

feat (**I.**), n. [1. fēt; 2. fīt]. M.E. *feet, fait*, fr. O. Fr. *feet, feit*, fr. Lat. *fact-(um)*, 'deed'. Variant of **fact**. An action exhibiting unusual courage, endurance, strength, skill &c.; an exceptional deed, exploit: *a feat of strength, agility* &c.; *feats of arms*; *his performance was a regular feat.*

feat (**II.**), adj., fr. O. Fr. *feit, fait*, 'made', fr. Lat. *fact-(us)*, P.P. of Lat. *facere*, 'to make'. See prec. (archaic) Neat, deft, dexterous.

feather (**I.**), n. [1. fédher; 2. féðə]. O.E. *feðer*, M.E. *feðer*, O.H.G. *federa*, O.L.G. *fethera*, O.N. *fjoðr*, 'feather'. Cogn. w. Scrt. *pátra-m*, 'wing, feather'; Lat. *petere*, 'to go, travel, fly'; also *(acci)piter*, 'hawk'; Gk. *pterón*, 'wing' (see **ptero-**). Aryan base **pet(e)-r-, *pte-r-*, w. suff. *-r*, fr. base **pet-*, 'to fly'; cp. Gk. *pétomai*, 'I fly', *poté*, 'flight'; *pṓtēma*, 'flight'; Scrt. *pátati*, 'to fly'. See also **pen** (**III.**), **impetus**, **petition**. **1. a** One of the external growths covering body of, and forming plumage of a bird; Phrs. *as light as a feather*, very light; *to show the white feather*, turn tail, show cowardice; *birds of a feather*, persons of similar character; *in high feather*, in good spirits; *you might have knocked me down with a feather*, implying I was so much amazed, agitated &c. **b** part of feather fastened to arrow to guide its flight; **c** a plume, tuft, bunch &c. of feathers, worn as ornament; Phr. *a feather in one's cap*, achievement to be proud of; source of credit, kudos. **2.** Something resembling a feather in appearance; e.g. flaw in a gem, glass &c. **3.** Action of feathering an oar in rowing; position of blade of oar when this is done.

feather (**II.**), vb. trans. & intrans. O.E. *(ge)fiðerian*, 'to supply with feathers', fr. O.E. *feðer, fiðer*, 'feather'. See prec. **A.** trans. **1.** To cover with feathers; to fasten feathers to; adorn with, supply with, feathers: *to feather an arrow.* Phr. *to feather one's nest*, to make provision for the future, fill one's pocket, enrich oneself. **2.** To form a feathery fringe or covering for: *boughs feathered with frost.* **3.** (various specific uses) **a** (rowing) To turn an oar in a stroke so as to allow the water to slide off in a thin feather-like sheet; **b** (shooting) to hit (a bird) without killing it, but so as to cause feathers to fly from it. **B.** intrans. To perform act of feathering an oar.

feather-bed, n. Mattress filled with feathers.

feather-brain, n. A frivolous, shallow, foolish person.

feather-brained, adj. [1. fédher brȧnd; 2. féðə breind]. Silly, foolish, inane.

feather-brush, n. Brush consisting of a tuft of feathers on a long handle; a Turk's head.

feathered, adj. [1. fédherd; 2. féðəd]. **feather** (**I.**) & **-ed**. Having feathers: *the feathered tribes*, birds provided with feathers; in form of a feather: *feathered spray.*

feather-edge, n. Edge (of a board &c.) shaped like a fine wedge.

feather-head, n. Feather-brain.

featheriness, n. [1. fédherines; 2. féðərinis]. **feathery** & **-ness**. The quality of being feathery.

feathering, n. [1. fédhering; 2. féðəriŋ]. **feather** (**II.**) & **-ing**. **1. a** A bird's feathers, plumage; **b** the feathers of an arrow. **2.** Anything resembling a feather, feathers; **a** feather-like fringe &c., on animal's coat, tail &c.; **b** (archit.) cusp in tracery of a window &c.

featherless, adj. [1. fédherles; 2. féðəlis]. **feather** & **-less**. Without feathers.

featherlet, n. [1. fédherlet; 2. féðəlit]. **feather** (**I.**) & **-let**. A small feather.

feather-stitch, n. & vb. trans. Embroidery stitch forming a central line with short branches on either side.

feather weight, n. A very light person or thing; specif., boxer weighing less than 9 stone.

feathery, adj. [1. fédheri; 2. féðəri]. **feather** (**I.**) & **-y**. **a** Covered with, adorned with feathers; **b** resembling feathers, soft and light: *feathery snow.*

featly, adv. **feat** (**II.**) & **-ly**. (archaic) Deftly, dexterously.

feature (**I.**), n. [1. fécher; 2. fítʃə], fr. O. Fr. *faiture*, fr. Lat. *factūra*, 'something made', fr. *fact-(us)*, P.P. type of *fac-(ere)*, 'to make' (see **fact**) & **-ure**. **1.** One of the individual parts of the face; the eyes, nose, mouth, ears: *handsome, poor, striking, features.* **2. a** (of material things) Part, element, of something, esp. a striking, distinguishing characteristic: *a lake is an important feature in a landscape*; **b** (of non-material things) outstanding characteristic, typical, striking point: *the speech contained some excellent features.* **3.** The word is used by Milton in the sense of 'creature' or 'monster', referring to Death: '*the grim feature*' (P.L. x. 279).

feature (**II.**), vb. trans., fr. prec. **1.** To be a prominent feature of, be distinctive of. **2.** To portray, represent features of; esp. in recent usage referring to cinema actors and actresses.

featureless, adj. [1. fécherles; 2. fítʃəlis]. **feature** (**I.**) & **-less**. Without features, without anything distinctive or striking: *a featureless landscape.*

febrifugal, adj. [1. fèbrifúgal; 2. fèbrifjúgl]. Next word & **-al**. Pertaining to, of the nature of, a febrifuge.

febrifuge, n. [1. fébri-, fébrifūj; 2. fébri-, fíbrifjūdž], fr. Fr. *fébrifuge*, fr. Lat. *febris*, 'fever' (see **febrile**), & *fug-(āre)*, 'to put to flight' (see **-fuge**). A remedy for fever.

febrile, adj. [1. fébrīl; 2. fíbrail], fr. Fr., fr. Lat. *febrilis*, 'feverish', fr. *febr-(is)*, 'fever', & **-ile**; *febris* is prob. related to Lat. *favilla*, 'glowing ash', fr. **fovilla*, where *f-* is fr. Aryan **dh-*; cp. Scrt. *dáhati*, 'it burns'; fr. **dhagha-*; cp. also Scrt. *dāhaš*, 'ember, heat'; Lith. *dãgas*, 'harvest'; Goth. *dags*, 'day'. See further under **day**. Connected with, arising from, of the nature of, fever; feverish.

February, n. [1. fébrŭari; 2. fébruəri], fr. Lat. *Februārius*, 'the month of expiation (in which the feast of purification was held)', fr. *febru-(um)*, 'means of purification', cp. Lat. *februāre*, 'to purify'; fr. base **dhewe-* &c., 'breath, steam, smoke' &c. See further under **fume, dust, beast**. The second month of the year.

fecal, feces. See **faecal, faeces**.

fecit, vb. [1. fésit; 2. físit]. Lat. *fēcit*, 'made', perf. (3rd sing.) of *facere*, 'to make, do'. See **fact**. Mode of signing a work of art: *John Jones fecit* = did, made, this.

feckless, adj. [1. fékles; 2. féklis]. Etymol. doubtful; Scots & Nthn. *feck*, 'worth, value', possibly for *effect*, & **-less**. (provinc.) Thoughtless, careless, irresponsible.

fecklessly, adv. Prec. & **-ly**. In a feckless manner.

fecklessness, n. See prec. & **-ness**. The quality of being feckless.

feculence, n. [1. fékūlens; 2. fékjuləns], fr. Lat. *faeculentia*, 'dregs', fr. *faecul-(entus)*, 'abounding in dregs'. See **faeces** & **-ence**. **1.** The state or quality of being feculent. **2.** Dregs, sediment.

feculent, adj. [1. fékūlent; 2. fíkjulənt], fr. Lat. *faeculent-(us)*, 'abounding in dregs', fr. *faec-*, stem of *faex*, 'dregs, sediment'. See prec. & **-ent**. Muddy, turbid; foul.

fecund, adj. [1. fékund; 2. fíkənd], fr. Fr. *fécond*, fr. Lat. *fēcund-(us)*, 'fruitful, fertile'; cp. *fē-nus*, 'proceeds, increase'; connected w. *fēlāre*, 'to suckle'; also w. Gk. *thēlé*, 'mother's breast', also Lat. *fēmina*, 'woman'. See **feminine**. The base **dhēi-*, 'to suckle', is used to express 'plenty, fruitfulness, prosperity', as in Lat. *fēlix*, 'fruitful; auspicious; lucky, successful, happy'. See **felicity**. Fruitful, fertile, prolific (lit. and fig.): *fecund beasts, soil, mind* &c.

fecundate, vb. trans. [1. fíkundāt; 2. fíkəndeit]. Prec. & **-ate**. **a** To make fertile, fruitful; **b** to impregnate.

fecundation, n. [1. fèkundáshun; 2. fìkəndéiʃən]. Prec. & **-ion**. The act of fecundating; state of being fecundated.

fecundity, n. [1. fēkúnditi; 2. fikánditi]. **fecund** & **-ity**. The quality of being fecund, prolific; fertility, productiveness.

fed, vb. [1. fed; 2. fed]. O.E. *fēdde, (ge)fēdd*, M.E. *fedd(e)*. Pret. & P.P. of **feed**.

federal (**I.**), adj. [1. féderal; 2. fédərəl], fr. Fr. *fédéral*, fr. Lat. *foeder-*, stem of *foedus*, 'compact, treaty'; fr. **foid-*; connected w. Lat. *fīdāre*, 'to trust, put confidence in'; *fīdus*, 'trusty, faithful', fr. **feid-*. The Aryan forms are **bhoidh-, *bheidh-, *bhidh-*, 'to persuade; be persuaded, to trust', whence Gk. *peíthein*, 'to persuade', in pass. sense, 'to be won over; to believe, trust'. Further cognates are Goth. *bidjan*, 'to beg, pray'; O.E. *biddan*, q.v. under **bid** (**I.**), & perh. Goth. *baidjan*, 'to compel', O.E. *bǣdan*. **1.** (polit. and hist.) Connected with, based upon federation: *federal government*; *a federal state.* **2.** (theol.) *Federal theology*, a system based upon the doctrine of certain covenants between God and man.

federal (**II.**), n., fr. prec. **a** A federalist; member of a federal state; **b** one of the states of a federation.

federalism, n. [1. féderalizm; 2. fédərəlizəm]. Prec. & **-ism**. The doctrine of federal union.

federalist, n. [1. féderalist; 2. fédərəlist]. **federal** & **-ist**. A supporter of federalism, esp. a member of the Northern or Federal States during the American Civil War.

federalization, n. [1. fèderalīzáshun; 2. fèdərəlaizéiʃən]. Next word & **-ation**. The act of federalizing; state of being federalized.

federalize, vb. trans. [1. féderalīz; 2. fédərəlaiz]. **federal** & **-ize**. To form (states &c.) into a unity under a federal government.

federally, adv. [1. féderali; 2. fédərəli]. **federal** & **-ly**. In a federal manner; by means of federalization.

federate (**I.**), vb. trans. & intrans. [1. féderāt; 2. fédəreit], fr. Lat. *foederāt-(um)*, P.P. type of *foederāre*, 'to establish by treaty', fr. *foeder-*, stem of *foedus*, 'a treaty'. See **federal**. To unite independent states into a league under a central, federal government.

federate (**II.**), adj. [1. féderat; 2. fédərət], fr. Lat. *foederāt-(us)*, 'leagued together, allied'. See prec. United under a common federal government.

federation, n. [1. fèderáshun; 2. fèdəréiʃən]. Prec. & **-ion**. **1.** The act of federating; state of being federated; that form of government in which several states, each keeping an internal independence, are joined into a union for foreign affairs and certain other common objects. **2. a** A group of states forming a federal union; **b** federated body; league, association, society.

federationist, n. [1. federáshunist; 2. fedəréiʃənist]. Prec. & **-ist**. An advocate of federation.

federative, adj. [1. féderativ; 2. fédərətiv]. **federate** & **-ive**. Pertaining to federation; federal.

federatively, adv. Prec. & **-ly**. In a federative manner; federally.

fee (**I.**), n. [1. fē; 2. fī]. M.E. *fee*, 'payment', fr. O. Fr. *fé, fiu, feu*, fr. Med. Lat. *feudum*, 'fief' (see **feudal**); prob. of Gmc. origin, cp. O.H.G. *fihu*, 'cattle, property, payment', cogn. w. O.E. *feoh*, 'cattle, money, property'. No. **3** below may be either fr. the O. Fr., or may be direct fr., or at least influenced by, O.E. *feoh*. This word, fr. Gmc. **feχ(u)-*, fr.

Aryan *peku-, is cogn. w. Lat. *pecus*, 'flock (of sheep)' &c., & *pecūnia*, 'money'. See further under **fight** & **pecuniary**. **1.** (feudal law) Land held from a superior lord on consideration of service; feudal benefice, fief; *fee-farm*, land held in fee, at an annual rent, a form of fee-simple subject to a perpetual rent; *fee-simple*, estate inheritable without limitation, equivalent to freehold; *fee-tail*, estate inheritable only by direct, or specific class of, heirs. **2.** Homage due from a vassal to a superior lord: '*once did she hold the gorgeous East in fee*' (Wordsworth, of Venice). **3.** Payment made, sum charged for services rendered, or privileges granted, **a** by professional men: *lawyer's, doctor's, fee*; **b** by a public body: *officials' fees*; **c** by school, college, university: *entrance fee*; *terminal, school, degree, fees* &c.

fee (II.), vb. trans., fr. prec. **3.** To pay a fee to: *to fee a doctor*.

feeble, adj. [1. fēbl; 2. fíbl]. M.E. *fēble*, fr. O. Fr. *feble*, Mod. Fr. *faible*, fr. Lat. *flēbilis*, 'to be wept over, lamentable; weeping, tearful', fr. Lat. *flē-(re)*, 'to weep', & *-bilis* (see **-ble**). The base of Lat. *flē-* is Aryan *bhlē-, imitative word; cp. O. Slav. *blěja*, 'I bleat', & O.E. *blǣtan* (see **bleat**). **1.** (of living things and their bodily functions) Weak, lacking physical strength or health; devoid of vigour: *a feeble creature*; *a feeble body*; *a feeble grasp*; *a feeble pulse*. **2.** (of persons and mental powers) Intellectually weak, not mentally vigorous; deficient, imbecile: *a feeble mind, brain*. **3.** (of actions) Lacking energy and vigour; hesitating; weakly and ineffectively carried out; futile: *a feeble attempt, effort, attack, speech* &c. **4.** (of material objects) Frail, incapable of resistance to weight or strain; easily broken down, or upset: *a feeble barrier*; *a feeble fortress*.

feebleness, n. Prec. & **-ness**. The quality of being feeble; weakness, inefficiency.

feeblish, adj. [1. fēblish; 2. fíbliʃ]. **feeble** & **-ish**. Rather feeble.

feebly, adv. [1. fēbli; 2. fíbli]. **feeble** & **-ly**. In a feeble manner.

feed (I.), vb. trans. & intrans. [1. fēd; 2. fīd]. O.E. *fēdan*, M.E. *fēde*; cp. Goth. *fōdjan*, Gmc. *fōd-jan, fr. *fōd, 'food'. See **food**. **A.** trans. **1.** **a** To give, administer, food to, place food before, within reach of: *to feed the pigs, horses* &c.; *to feed a baby*; **b** (reflex.) *to feed oneself*, to put food into one's mouth with one's own hand: *the invalid is too weak to feed himself*. **2.** To nourish; to supply, provide, with bodily sustenance: *to be well, poorly, fed*; *feed one's family*; *God feeds the beasts of the field*. **3.** To supply with material; keep supplied, or filled: *to feed a machine*; *a river fed by tributaries*; *to feed the flames*. (fig.) Phr. *to feed the flame* (*of jealousy* &c.), to excite, stimulate, promote, render more acute. **4.** To give as food: *to feed turnips to cattle*. **B.** intrans. **a** (chiefly of animals) To consume food, to eat: *the cows are feeding in the pasture*; **b** (of persons; vulgar or facetious) to take a meal, consume food: *we feed at 8 o'clock*. **C.** Followed by adverbs and prepositions. *Feed on*, **a** to consume, take as food, use habitually as nourishment: *cattle feed chiefly on grass*; **b** to give to as food: *I feed my dogs on biscuits and broth*. *Feed up*, to give extra nourishment to, bring to high pitch of health by giving plentiful food to; to fatten: *this child needs feeding up*. Phr. (colloq.) *fed up*, having had enough of something, bored, wearied, satiated.

feed (II.), n., fr. prec. **1.** The act of feeding: *let the horse have a feed*; (vulg.) *to have a good feed*. Phr. (colloq.) *off one's feed*, suffering from loss of appetite. **2.** **a** Material given or taken as food, esp. of domestic animals; fodder; **b** amount of food given at one time: *to give a horse a feed of oats*. **3.** **a** Means, channel, by which material is conveyed to a machine &c.; **b** material supplied to a machine, to be operated on.

feeder, n. [1. fēder; 2. fídə]. **feed** (I.) & **-er**. **1.** (of animals and plants) One that feeds, esp. one that feeds in a specified manner: *a large feeder*; *a gross feeder*. **2.** A tributary stream. **3.** Device for supplying material to a machine. **4.** Napkin tied round child's neck to keep its clothes clean at meal times; bib.

feeding, adj. [1. fēding; 2. fídiŋ], fr. Pres. Part. of **feed** (I.). *Feeding storm*, one gradually increasing in violence.

feeding-bottle, n. Glass vessel from which liquid food is sucked by infants.

feed-tank, n. Tank supplying water to an engine.

fee-farm, n. See **fee** (I.).

fee-faw-fum, interj. & n. [1. fé fáw fúm; 2. fí fɔ̄ fám]. Utterance expressing rage and fury, attributed to ogres in fairy tales; hence, meaningless words of anger and threatening uttered by an arrogant person with intent to overawe his hearers.

feel (I.), vb. trans. & intrans. [1. fēl; 2. fīl]. O.E. *fēlan*, M.E. *fēlen*. Cp. O. Fris. *fēla*, O.H.G. *fuolan*, O.L.G. (*gi*)*fōlian*. Cogn. w. Scrt. *ā-sphālayati*, 'strikes'; Gk. *psēlaphān*, 'to grope', *psállein*, 'to pluck, pull, twitch; to strike (the strings of a musical instrument)', *psalmós*, 'harp-playing' (see **psalm**); Lat. *palpāre*, 'to touch, caress', *palpitāre*, 'to agitate, beat' (see **palpitate**); O. Slav. *palĭcĭ*, 'thumb'. Aryan base *(*s*)*phĕl-*, *(*s*)*p*(*h*)*ăl-*, 'to strike gently'. See further **palpable, palpebral, psalter**. **A.** trans. **1.** **a** To have physical sensation of; to experience, be conscious of, any kind of sensuous stimulus: *to feel heat and cold*; *to feel pain*; **b** to experience emotion, to have a moral, emotional, intellectual, sense of; to be animated by: *to feel sorrow, compunction, fear, delight*. **2.** To touch with the hand so as to test, or try, by tactile experience; to explore, test by touching with the fingers: *just feel how cold my hand is*; *to feel the edge of a knife*. Phr. *to feel one's way*, (i.) advance cautiously, and by groping, as a blind man, or one in the dark; (ii.) (fig.) to act with caution, tact, deliberation. **3.** **a** To have an acute sense of, be very sensitive to, suffer from, be oppressed by, physical facts or processes: *I don't feel the heat at all, I like it*; *infants feel the cold very much*; **b** to have acute emotional and moral sensitiveness to; to experience sorrow at, to resent, be grieved by: *I felt the insult deeply*; *to feel a friend's death*. **4.** **a** To discriminate exactly between various qualities of, to have a just and delicate sense of; to be emotionally stirred by: *to feel poetry, music*; *to feel the beauty of a landscape*; **b** to appreciate intellectually, to be alive to rational appeal of: *to feel the force of an argument, the truth of what is said* &c. **5.** **a** To entertain a notion that, to be of the opinion that; to hold, consider, be persuaded that: *I feel that I ought to say no more at present*; **b** to have a premonition, an intuition that; be persuaded that it is likely that: *to feel that some disaster is impending*. **B.** intrans. **1.** To be sentient; to be capable of sensation: *the dead cannot feel*. **2.** **a** To have a specific sensation, to experience within oneself: *to feel cold, ill, comfortable, hungry* &c.; **b** to be in a certain moral or emotional state: *to feel sad, depressed, happy* &c.; Phr. *to feel strongly about*, hold strong, definite opinions; *to feel for*, have sympathy with (a person); **c** to be in a specific intellectual state, or frame of mind: *to feel doubtful, certain*. Phr. *to feel like* (eating &c.), to be inclined for. **3.** To impart, give rise to, a specific sensation when touched, to produce a specific physical impression: *how cold your hand feels*. Phr. *it feels like rain* &c., gives the impression that there will be rain.

feel (II.), n., fr. prec. **1.** Sensation imparted by touch; sensation experienced by one who touches; feeling: *this handle has a sticky feel*; *I know this is silk by the feel*; *the cool feel of dewy grass*. **2.** Sense of touch: *rough and coarse to the feel*. **3.** Tact, instinctive feeling, flair: *to have a feel for good poetry*.

feeler, n. [1. fēler; 2. fílə]. **feel** (I.) & **-er**. **1.** One who, that which, feels; specif. (zool.) an organ of touch in certain animals. **2.** An action, or utterance, of a cautious, tentative character; an experimental act, or speech, carried out or made in order to elicit fuller information, to test the state of affairs, or of opinion, before defining one's views, outlining a policy &c.; a ballon d'essai.

feeling (I.), n. [1. fēling; 2. fíliŋ]. **feel** (I.) & **-ing**. **1.** Physical sensation, sentience; power of, and capacity for, experiencing sensation: *to lose all feeling from a sudden blow*. **2.** **a** A specific bodily sensation: *a feeling of discomfort, of well-being* &c.; **b** a specific emotion or sentiment: *a feeling of joy and gratitude*; **c** a premonition, intuition: *to have a feeling that something is going to happen*. **3.** (often in pl.) **a** The emotions, the emotional side of human character: *to appeal to the feelings rather than to the reason*; *to rouse the feelings*; Phrs. *to speak with feeling*, so as to express emotion; *a man of feeling*, sentimental person; *good feeling*, friendliness; *ill feeling*, animosity; *to hurt the feelings of*, to offend, wound; **b** specif., kindly, generous, sentiment; affections; sensitive, emotional, nature: *a man without any feeling(s)*. **4.** Excitement of mind, esp. angry, offended, ruffled, sentiment; hostile frame of mind: *the speech aroused strong feeling on all sides*; *I have really no feeling about his attack on me*; *feeling ran high at the time*. **5.** Intuitive aesthetic appreciation, delicate and just sensibility; discriminating taste: *to have a feeling for beauty in nature and in art*.

feeling (II.), adj., fr. Pres. Part. of **feel** (I.). Having, animated by, expressing, strong feeling and emotion: *a feeling heart, speech, remark* &c.

feelingly, adv. Prec. & **-ly**. So as to express emotion, as though animated by strong feeling: *to speak feelingly*.

fee-simple, fee-tail, n. See **fee** (I.).

feet, n. See **foot**.

fehmgericht, fehmic. See **vehmgericht** &c.

feign, vb. trans. & intrans. [1. fān; 2. fein]. M.E. *feinen*, fr. O. Fr. *feindre*, fr. Lat. *fingere*, 'to form, shape; to invent'; w. infixed *-n-*, fr. Aryan base *dheigh-, *dhigh-, 'to put together; form, shape'. See **figure, fictile, dough**. **A.** trans. **1.** **a** (archaic and poet.) To imagine, invent, fable: *tales such as poets feign*; **b** to invent, make up, fabricate: *to feign an excuse*. **2.** To pretend, assume, simulate: *to feign indifference*. **B.** intrans. To dissemble, make false representations.

feint (I.), n. [1. fānt; 2. feint], fr. O. Fr. *feinte*, fr. P.P. of *feindre*, 'to feign'. See prec. Lit. 'something feigned, or simulated'. **a** A misleading appearance, pretence, semblance: *to make a feint of doing something*; **b** an action intended to mislead; esp. a pretended attack in fencing, or in military operations, made to distract attention of opponent from real point of attack.

feint (II.), vb. intrans., fr. prec. To make a feint.

feint (III.), adj. & adv. See **faint**. **1.** adj. Indistinct, only in *feint* (also *faint*) *lines* (ruled on paper). **2.** adv. Indistinctly: *ruled feint* (of paper).

fel(d)spar, n. [1. fél(d)spar; 2. fél(d)spā]. Imitated fr. Germ. *feldspath*, fr. *feld*, 'field', q.v., & *spath*, 'spar'. See **spar**. One of several kinds of crystalline mineral, of various elements and colourings.

fel(d)spathic, adj. [1. fèl(d)spáthik; 2. fèl(d)spǽþik], fr. Germ. *feldspath* (see prec.) & **-ic**. Consisting of, containing, feldspar.

felicide, n. [1. félisid; 2. fílisaid], fr. Lat. *fēli-*, stem of *fēlēs*, 'a cat'. See **felid** & **-cide**. The killing of a cat.

felicific, adj. [1. fèlisífik; 2. fìlisífik], fr. Lat. *fēlīcific-(us)*, 'making happy', fr. *fēlīc-*, stem of *fēlix*, 'happy'. See **felicity** & **-fic**. (rare) Producing, tending to, happiness.

felicitate, vb. trans. [1. felísitāt; 2. filísiteit], fr. Lat. *fēlīcit-(as)*, 'happiness'. See **felicity** & **-ate**. **1.** (rare) To make happy. **2.** To wish happiness to, congratulate.

felicitation, n. [1. felìsitā́shun ; 2. filìsitéiʃən]. Prec. & **-ion.** Expression of good wishes.

felicitous, adj. [1. felísitus ; 2. filísitəs], fr. Lat. *fēlīcit-(as).* See **felicity** & **-ous. 1.** (rare) Happy ; causing happiness. **2.** Happy, apt, opportune, suitable and pleasing in a particular connexion : *a felicitous remark, phrase, allusion* &c.

felicitously, adv. Prec. & **-ly.** In a felicitous manner.

felicity, n. [1. felísiti ; 2. filísiti], fr. O. Fr. *felicité*, fr. Lat. *fēlīcitāt-(em)*, 'fruitfulness ; happiness ; good fortune ', fr. *fēlīc-*, stem of *fēlix*, 'fruitful, productive ; favourable, propitious ; lucky, fortunate, happy ', & **-ity.** *Fē-lix* is prob. to be connected w. *fē-cundus*, 'fruitful ', *fē-nus*, ' proceeds, interest ', *fē-tus*, 'a bringing forth ; offspring '. Cp. also Scrt. *dhānāš*, ' crops ' ; Aryan base **dhē-*, ' fruitful '. See **fecund** & **foetus.** A state of happiness ; contentment, blissfulness, prosperity.

felid, n. [1. félid ; 2. fílid], fr. Lat. *fēl-(ēs)*, 'cat ; marten ; pole-cat', & **-id.** The etymol. of the word is very doubtful. It is possibly cogn. w. W. *bele*, ' marten '. An animal of the cat-family, *Felidae*, which includes the lion, tiger, leopard &c.

feline, adj. & n. [1. félīn ; 2. fílain], fr. Lat. *fēlīnus*, ' of a cat ; cat-like ', fr. *fēl-(ēs)*, ' a cat ', & **-ine.** See prec. **1.** adj. **a** Connected with a cat, or with cats ; resembling, having the characteristics of, a cat ; **b** (fig.) cat-like, spiteful, treacherous. **2.** n. An animal belonging to the cat-tribe, felid.

felinity, n. [1. fēlíniti ; 2. filíniti]. Prec. & **-ity.** The quality of being feline.

fell (I.), n. [1. fel ; 2. fel]. O.E., M.E. *fel(l)*, O.L.G., O. Fris., O.H.G. *fel*, O.N. *-fell*, Goth. *-fill*, ' hide, skin '. Cogn. w. Lat. *pellis*, ' hide, skin ; leather ' ; Gk. *pélas*, ' skin ', *pélma*, 'sole ' ; Lith. *plėnė*, ' thin skin '. Aryan base **pel-*, **pḷ-*, ' skin '. See further **film, pellicle, erysipelas. 1. a** Animal's hide and hair ; hence, **b** human skin. **2.** Rough, thick mass of hair.

fell (II.), n. M.E. *fell*, fr. O.N. *fiall* ; prob. cogn. w. O.H.G. *felis*, ' rock ' (Mod. Germ. *fels*) ; Gk. *pélla*, Scrt. *pāsāṇáš*, ' stone, rock ' ; Aryan base **pels-*, ' rock '. Rocky upland ; lofty, bare, mountain slope ; mountain.

fell (III.), adj. O.E., M.E. *fel*, ' fierce, cruel ' ; cp. O. Fris., M. Du. *fel*, fr. Low Lat. *fello*, 'felon '. See **felon.** (archaic and poet.) Cruel, fierce, dire, ruthless.

fell (IV.), vb. trans. O.E. (non-W.-S.) *fellan*, M.E. *fellen* ; cp. O.L.G. *fellian*, O.H.G. *fellen* ; causative vb., fr. **fall-jan*, 'to fall'. See **fall. 1. a** To cause to fall ; to cut, strike, hurl, down : *to fell an ox* ; *to fell a man with a single blow* ; specif. **b** to cut down trees, timber. **2.** To turn and stitch down material left projecting beyond a seam : *to fell a seam.*

fell (V.), vb. O.E. *fēoll*, M.E. *fell.* Pret. of **fall.**

fellah, n., pl. **fellahin** [1. féla, felahḗn ; 2. féla, felahín]. Arab., ' ploughman '. Egyptian peasant, labourer.

felloe, felly, n. [1. féli ; 2. féli]. O.E. *felg, felge* ; M.E. *feli, felwe, felowe* ; cp. O.H.G. *felga*, M. Du. *velge.* **a** The rim of a wheel, in which the spokes are inserted ; **b** a segment of the rim of a wheel between the spokes.

fellow, n. [1. félō ; 2. félou]. O.E. *fēolaga*, M.E. *felawe* ; translated fr. O.N. *fēlagi*, ' one who lays down money ', hence ' partner ; fellow, companion ' ; cp. also O.N. *fēlag*, 'companionship ', lit. ' laying together of property '. See **fee (I.)** & **lay. 1.** Partner, sharer, participator in an action ; commonly in unfavourable sense, an accomplice : *fellows in crime* &c. (generally of men, rarely used of women). Phr. *to be hail fellow well met with*, on friendly, cordial terms with. **2. a** Companion, associate ; one sharing the same conditions, undergoing same experiences, as another : *fellows in misery, good fortune* &c. ; (also attrib.) *fellow-citizen, fellow-creature* &c. ; **b** a contemporary, equal ; a member of the same corporation : *we were fellows at school.* **3. a** Person of inferior rank ; formerly used as mode of address to such ; (obs.) **b** a rough, coarse, uncultivated man ; a boorish lout : '*lewd fellows of the baser sort*' ; '*Worth makes the man, the want of it the fellow*' (Pope) ; **c** general, colourless term for a male person, equivalent to man, chap : *a very pleasant fellow* ; *an able, a stupid, fellow.* Phrs. *a good fellow*, an honourable, sociable, agreeable man ; *my dear fellow*, intimate and friendly mode of address. **4.** (cap.) **a** Member of the governing body of a college at Oxford or Cambridge, or of Trinity College, Dublin, who receives certain emoluments and allowances ; **b** graduate elected as member of the governing body of University of London ; **c** associate, member, of one of several learned societies (elected in recognition of services to science or learning), or professional bodies (appointed by examination) : *Fellow of the Royal Society* (F.R.S.), *of the British Academy* (F.B.A.), *of the Royal College of Surgeons* (F.R.C.S.) &c. **5.** One of a pair of similar or identical objects, which match in design, colour, size &c. : *I've found one of my gloves, but the fellow is missing.*

fellow-feeling, n. A feeling in common, a sentiment or emotion shared by two persons ; sympathy.

fellowship, n. [1. félōship ; 2. félouʃip]. **fellow** & **-ship. 1. a** The state of being fellows, sharing participation, joint experience : *a fellowship in sorrow* ; **b** companionship, association, friendly intercourse : *to enjoy a cordial fellowship with one's friends.* **2.** A group of persons united by a common ideal, cause, belief, or interest ; a band, company, brotherhood, guild : '*the goodly fellowship of the prophets praise Thee*'. **3. a** Status, rank, dignity, of a College Fellow ; **b** status of a Fellow of a learned or professional body &c.

felly, n. See **felloe.**

felo de se, n. [1. félō di sḗ ; 2. félou di sí]. Low Lat., lit. ' murderer of himself ', see next word. **1.** One who is guilty of his own death. **2.** Suicide, self-murder.

felon (I.), n. & adj. [1. félun ; 2. félən]. M.E. *felun*, O. Fr. *felon*, ' wicked man, traitor ' ; Low Lat. *fellōn-(em)*, ' a criminal ' ; connected w. **fell (III.)** Origin unknown. **1.** n. **a** (law) A criminal, one who has committed a felony ; **b** a degraded ruffian. **2.** adj. (archaic and poet.) Criminal, wicked, treacherous : *a felon deed, blow* &c.

felon (II.), n. Perh. same word as prec. Painful swelling and inflammation of the finger ; an abscess on the finger ; whitlow.

felonious, adj. [1. felṓnius ; 2. filóunjəs]. **felony** & **-ous. a** (law) Pertaining to, involving, felony ; **b** criminal, wicked.

feloniously, adv. Prec. & **-ly.** In a felonious manner.

felonry, n. [1. félunri ; 2. félənri]. **felon (I.)** & **-ry.** Felons considered as a class ; a body of felons.

felony, n. [1. féluni ; 2. féləni]. **felon (I.)** & **-y.** (law) Any of the gravest kind of offences, formerly involving total forfeiture of all property, such as murder, rape, arson &c., now, such crime so designated by statute or regarded in common law as more heinous than a *misdemeanour.*

felsite, n. See **felstone.**

felspar, n. See **fel(d)spar.**

felstone, n. [1. félstun ; 2. félstən]. Imitated fr. Germ. *felsstein*, fr. *fels*, ' rock ' (see **fell (II.)**), & *stein*, ' stone '. See **stone.** A kind of rock containing a mixture of quartz and feldspar, felsite.

felt (I.), n. [1. felt ; 2. felt]. O.E., M.E. *felt* ; cp. M. Du. *vilt*, O.H.G. *filz*, ' felt '. The orig. meaning seems to have been ' something beaten, pressed, together '. In this case the word is prob. connected w. O.E. *anfilte*, O.H.G. *anevalz*, ' anvil ' (see **anvil**) ; Lat. *pellere*, ' to beat, strike, drive '. See **expel, pulse,** & cp. **filter. a** A fabric made by pressing wool, hair &c., mixed with glue, into a compact, tough mass ; **b** (attrib.) made of felt : *a felt hat.*

felt (II.), vb. trans. & intrans., fr. prec. **A.** trans. **1.** To make into felt, to mat. **2.** To cover with felt. **B.** intrans. To become matted.

felt (III.), vb. Pret. & P.P. of **feel.**

felucca, n. [1. felúka ; 2. filákə]. Ital., fr. Arab. A small Mediterranean coasting-vessel, with lateen sails, usually three-masted.

female (I.), adj. [1. fémāl ; 2. fímeil], fr. M.E. *femelle.* O. Fr. *femelle*, fr. Lat. *fēmella*, dimin. of *fēmina*, ' a woman ; female animal ' ; the second syll. influenced by *male.* See **feminine. 1.** Characterized by the capacity of bringing forth young : *the female sex.* **2.** Belonging to the female sex : *a female child, mammal, insect* &c. **3.** Pertaining to females or women : *female character, dress, education.* **4.** (bot.) Having a pistil and no stamens ; capable of being fertilized and bearing fruit. **5.** (mechan.) Having a part constructed to receive a corresponding part : *female thread, screw* (in a nut).

female (II.), n., fr. prec. **a** A female person or animal ; **b** (depreciatory) a woman.

feme covert, n. [1. fém kúvert ; 2. fém kávət]. A.-Fr., see **covert (II.).** (law) A married woman.

feme sole, n. [1. fém sṓl ; 2. fém sóul]. A.-Fr., ' woman alone '. (law) **a** An unmarried woman, widow, spinster ; **b** a married woman who has property-rights independent of her husband.

feminality, n. [1. fèminā́liti ; 2. fèminǽliti], fr. O. Fr. *feminal*, fr. Lat. *fēmina*, ' a woman ', see **feminine** & **-al** & **-ity.** The quality of being female ; feminine character.

femineity, n. [1. feminḗiti ; 2. fèminíiti], fr. Lat. *fēmine-(us)*, ' feminine ; effeminate ', & **-ity**, fr. *fēmina*, ' a woman '. See **feminine. 1.** The quality of being feminine, womanliness. **2.** Womanishness, effeminacy.

feminine, adj. [1. féminin ; 2. féminin], fr. O. Fr., fr. Lat. *fēminīn-(us)*, ' feminine ', fr. *fēmin-(a)*, ' a woman ', & **-ine.** The word apparently meant orig. ' she who suckles ', & comes fr. an Aryan base **dhē(i)-*, **dhī-*, **dhə(i)-*, ' to suck ', whence also Lat. *fēlāre*, ' to suck ', *filius* (fr. **fēlios*), ' son ' (see **filial**). Cp. also Gk. *thēlḗ*, ' female breast ', & see **fecund. 1. a** Pertaining to women ; **b** characteristic of a woman : *a feminine nature, voice* &c. ; **c** (of males) resembling a woman ; womanish, effeminate : *his feminine airs and graces.* **2.** (gram.) Having the form used in referring to females. **3.** (pros.) **a** *Feminine caesura*, following an unstressed syllable ; **b** *feminine ending*, having the accent on the last syllable but one ; **c** *feminine rhyme*, a double rhyme consisting of a stressed followed by an unstressed syllable.

femininely, adv. Prec. & **-ly.** In a feminine manner.

feminineness, n. See prec. & **-ness.** The quality of being feminine.

femininism, n. [1. fémininizm ; 2. femininizəm]. See prec. & **-ism. a** Tendency to be feminine or effeminate ; **b** a feminine idiom or expression.

femininity, n. [1. fèmininiti ; 2. fèmininiti]. **feminine** & **-ity.** The quality or state of being feminine ; womanliness.

feminism, n. [1. féminizm ; 2. féminizəm], fr. Lat. *fēmin-(a)*, ' woman ', see **feminine,** & **-ism.** The advocacy of women's rights ; movement for complete equality between the sexes in all respects.

feminist, n. [1. féminist ; 2. féminist]. See prec. & **-ist.** Advocate and supporter of feminism.

feminity, n. [1. feminiti ; 2. feminiti], fr. O. Fr. *feminité*, fr. Lat. *fēmin-(a)*, ' a woman ' ; see **feminine,** & **-ity.** Femininity.

feminization, n. [1. fèminīzā́shun ; 2. fèminaizéiʃən]. See next word & **-ation.** The act or process of making womanly, or womanish.

feminize, vb. trans. & intrans. [1. féminīz ; 2. féminaiz], fr. Lat. *fēmin-(a)*, ' a woman ', see **feminine,** & **-ize. 1.** trans. To render feminine ; endow with womanly character. **2.** intrans. To become womanly.

femme de chambre, n. [1. fam d' shombr; 2. fam də ʃɑ̃br]. Fr. **a** A lady's maid; **b** a chambermaid.

femoral, adj. [1. fémural; 2. féməral], fr. Lat. *femor-*, stem of *femur*, 'thigh', see next word, & **-al**. Pertaining to the thigh or femur: *femoral artery*.

femur, n. [1. fḗmur; 2. fímə]. Lat. *femur*, 'thigh'. Etymol. doubtful. The thigh-bone; the thigh.

fen, n. [1. fen; 2. fɛn]. O.E. *fenn*, M.E. *fen*; cp. O.N. *fen*, O. Fris. *fenne*, O.H.G. *fenni*, 'fen'; Goth. *fani*, 'mud, clay'. Cp. further M. Ir. *an*, 'water'; Gaul. *anam*, 'marsh' (fr. **pan-*); O. Prussian *pannean*, 'ditch'; also, w. suff. *-k-*, Scrt. *paṅkaś*, 'slime'. Cp. also O.H.G., O.E. *fūht*, 'damp' (fr. **fuŋχt-*). Low, flat, marshy land, partly flooded; specif., *the fens*, fen country in Lincolnshire, Cambridge &c.

fen-berry, n. Cranberry.

fence (I.), n. [1. fens; 2. fɛns]. Contracted fr. **defence**. **1. a** (archaic) A means of protection, shelter, defence; **b** a barrier erected round enclosed land; a hedge, railing &c.; *sunk fence*, ditch protecting field &c., usually with steeper side supported by a wall. Phr. *to sit on the fence*, hesitate between two opinions or lines of action. **2.** The art of using the sword in self-defence. Phr. *master of fence*, fine swordsman; (fig.) one who is skilled in argument, quick at repartee. **3.** (slang) **a** A receiver of stolen goods; **b** place where stolen goods are purchased. **4.** (mechan.) A guard or guide to limit the action of part of a machine.

fence (II.), vb. intrans. & trans., fr. prec. **A.** intrans. **1. a** To practise the art of sword-play; **b** (fig.) to evade, parry, a direct challenge or attack by questioner, opponent in argument &c.; to quibble, equivocate. **2.** (of a horse) To jump fences. **3.** (slang) To receive stolen goods. **B.** trans. (lit. and fig.) To enclose, secure, protect with, or as with, a fence, barrier &c.: *to fence land* &c. **C.** With various prepositions and adverbs. *Fence about, in, round*, trans., (lit. and fig.) to surround, protect, enclose; *to be fenced about with penalties*. *Fence off, out*, trans., (lit. and fig.) to turn aside, parry, repel, keep off: *to fence off the consequences of an action*. *Fence with*, intrans., to evade a direct reply to; quibble, avoid answering explicitly: *to fence with a question, an inquirer*.

fenceless, adj. [1. fénsles; 2. fénslis]. **fence** (I.) & **-less**. **a** Without a fence, unenclosed; **b** (poet.) without defence, unprotected.

fence-month, -season, -time, n. Close-time for game.

fencible, n. [1. fénsibl; 2. fénsibl]. Contracted fr. **defensible**. (hist.) Soldier employed only on home service.

fencing, n. [1. fénsing; 2. fénsiŋ]. **fence** (II.) & **-ing**. **1.** The art of sword-play. **2. a** Material for fences; **b** railing, fence, palisade; **c** collection, group, of fences.

fend, vb. trans. & intrans. [1. fend; 2. fɛnd]. Contracted fr. **defend**. **A.** trans. (lit. and fig.) *Fend off*, to keep off, ward off, defend oneself from: *to fend off a blow*; *to fend off the inevitable disclosure*. **B.** intrans. *Fend for*, to provide for, take care of: *to fend for oneself and one's children*.

fender, n. [1. fénder; 2. féndə]. Prec. & **-er**. **1.** Something used to prevent shock or injury due to collision, esp. a pad, band, piece of timber, or other device, attached to ship, boat &c. **2.** A metal contrivance placed round three sides of a hearth-stone to prevent burning fuel falling beyond the hearth.

fenderless, adj. [1. fénderles; 2. féndəlis]. Prec. & **-less**. Not provided with a fender.

fender-stool, n. Long, low stool placed outside a fender before a fire.

fenestella, n. [1. fènestéla; 2. fènistélə]. Lat. dimin. of *fenestra*, 'a window; a loophole'; prob. fr. a form **fenos*, 'light', cogn. w. Gk. *phanerós*, 'bright', *phainein* (fr. **phanjō-*), 'to shine' (see **phantasm**), fr. Aryan base **bhē̆-*, **bhə-*, 'to shine'. **a** A small window; **b** an opening in an altar front allowing relics to be seen; **c** niche on south side of altar containing the piscina.

fenestrate, adj. [1. fénestrāt; 2. fénɛstreit], fr. Lat. *fenestra*, 'an opening, window' (see prec.), & **-ate**. (bot., zool.) Having small window-like holes; perforated.

fenestration, n. [1. fènestrā́shun; 2. fènistréiʃən]. Prec. & **-ion**. **1.** (archit.) Arrangement of the windows in a building. **2.** (bot., zool.) State of being fenestrate or perforated.

fen fire, n. Will-o'-the-wisp.

Fenian, n. & adj. [1. fḗnyan; 2. fínjən], fr. O. Ir. *fēne*, 'inhabitant of Ireland'; a coined word w. some reference to or confusion w. *fiann féinne*, the mythical bodyguard of Finn MacCool. **1.** n. A member of a secret society, of a violent revolutionary character, founded in America, in the late 'forties of 19th cent., for the purpose of destroying English domination in Ireland. **2.** adj. Connected with Fenians.

fenianism, n. [1. fḗnyanizm; 2. fínjənizəm]. Prec. & **-ism**. The doctrines and policy of Fenians.

fenks, n. [1. fengks; 2. fɛŋks]. Etymol. unknown. Refuse from melted whale's blubber.

fenman, n. [1. fénman; 2. fénmən]. One who lives in the fens.

fennec, n. [1. fének; 2. fénɛk], fr. Arab. *fanek*. A small fawn-coloured African fox, with very large ears.

fennel, n. [1. fénl; 2. fénl]. O.E. *finul, finugl*, M.E. *fenil*, fr. Lat. *faeni-, fēniculum*, 'fennel', dimin. of *faenum, fēnum*, 'hay'; prob. fr. earlier **fend-snom*, 'something mowed, cut down', fr. **fendere*, 'to cut, strike'. See **defend**. A tall, umbelliferous, yellow-flowered perennial herb, used as a salad, also in sauces; the seeds are carminative.

fenny, adj. [1. féni; 2. féni]. **fen** & **-y**. **a** Containing, abounding in, of the nature of, a fen or fens; marshy, boggy; **b** found in fens.

fen-pole, n. Pole used in the fen-country for jumping ditches &c.

fen-reeve, n. Official having supervision over part of fens.

fen-runners, n. A kind of skates.

fenugreek, n. [1. fénūgrēk; 2. fénjugrīk], fr. Lat. *faenugraecum*, fr. *fēnum*, 'hay', see **fennel**, & *Graecus*, 'Greek'. A herb of the bean family, with aromatic leaves and edible seeds.

feoff, n. See next word & **fief**.

feoffee, n. [1. fefḗ; 2. fɛfī], fr. A.-Fr. *feoffé*, P.P. of *feoffer, fieffer*, 'endow', fr. *feoff, fief*, 'fief'. See **fee**. Person to whom freehold land is granted in fee; a public trustee.

feoffment, n. [1. féfment; 2. féfmənt]. **feoff** & **-ment**. The act of enfeoffing, or of granting freehold land in fee.

feoffor, feoffer, n. [1. féfer; 2. féfə]. **feoff** & **-or, -er**. One who grants a feoffment.

ferae naturae, adj. [1. fḗrē natū́rē; 2. fíərī nætjúərī]. Lat., 'of a wild nature', Lat. *ferus*, 'wild, untamed; savage'. See **ferocious**. Wild, not domesticated; living in a wild state: (law) *animals ferae naturae*, not in the possession, and therefore, by common law, not the property of anyone.

feral, adj. [1. fḗral; 2. fíərəl]. Lat. *fer-(a)*, 'a wild beast', fr. *ferus*, 'wild'. See **ferocious** & **-al**. **a** (of animals) Wild, savage, undomesticated; **b** (of plants) wild, uncultivated; **c** (of human beings and their behaviour &c.) uncivilized, barbarous, brutal.

fer de lance, n. [1. fār de lahns; 2. fɛ́r də lɑ̃s]. Fr., lit. 'iron of a lance; lance head'. See **ferro-**. A large, very poisonous snake of the West Indies and C. and S. America, *Lachesis lanceolata*.

feretory, n. [1. féretori; 2. féritəri]. M.E. *fertre*, 'shrine, tomb, bier', fr. O. Fr. *fiertre*, fr. Lat. *feretrum*, fr. Gk. *phéretron*, 'a bier, litter', fr. *phérein*, 'to carry'; cogn. w. O.E. *bǣr*, 'bier'. See **bear** (I.) & words there referred to. **1. a** Shrine in which the relics of saints are kept, reliquary; **b** that part of a church which contains a shrine. **2.** A bier.

ferial, adj. [1. fḗrial; 2. fíəriəl], fr. Fr., fr. Lat. *fēria*, 'holiday, festival; leisure, peace'; Eccles. Lat. 'week-day'. See **feast, fane**. **a** Denoting day on which no special observance is appointed by the Church; contrasted with *Feast Day*; **b** pertaining to, connected with, such days.

ferine, adj. [1. fḗrīn; 2. fíərain], fr. Lat. *ferīn-(us)*, 'pertaining to wild animals, savage, brutal', fr. *fer-(a)*, 'a wild animal', & **-ine**. See **feral**. Feral.

Feringhee, n. [1. feringgē; 2. fəríŋgi]. Pers. *Faranji*, fr. **Frank**. A name in India for a foreigner; specif. **a** a European; **b** a Eurasian, esp. a person half Indian, half Portuguese.

ferment (I.), n. [1. fĕrment; 2. fə́mɛnt], fr. Fr., fr. Lat. *fermentum*, 'substance causing fermentation'; fig. 'anger, passion'; cogn. w. O.E. *beorma*, 'yeast' (see **barm**); L.G. *barme*; Aryan base **bher-m-, *bhr̥-m-, *bhere-m-*, 'to boil'. See further **fervent, brew**. **1.** Substance causing fermentation, cp. *yeast* & *enzyme*. **2. a** Fermentation; **b** (fig.) agitation, tumult; state of mental, social, or political excitement, commotion: *the country was in a ferment*.

ferment (II.), vb. trans. & intrans. [1. fermént; 2. fəmént], fr. Fr., fr. Lat. *fermentāre*, 'to ferment; to break up, loosen; to sour, spoil', fr. *ferment-(um)*, 'substance causing fermentation'. See prec. **A.** trans. **a** To cause, produce, fermentation in; **b** (fig.) to stir up, excite, arouse, inflame, emotions, passions, unrest, turmoil &c. **B.** intrans. **a** To undergo the process of fermentation; **b** (fig.) to become mentally or politically agitated; get into a state of excitement or tumult.

fermentable, adj. [1. ferméntabl; 2. fəméntəbl]. Prec. & **-able**. Capable of being fermented.

fermentation, n. [1. fĕrmentā́shun; 2. fə̄mentéiʃən]. Lat. *fermentātiōn-(em)*. See **ferment** (II.) & **-ation**. **1.** Chemical process characterized by effervescence, caused by the presence of organic bodies, exhibited most typically by the action of yeast, and also, chemically, by enzymes. **2.** (fig.) Mental excitement and activity; political or social excitement, unrest, turmoil.

fermentative, adj. [1. fĕrméntativ; 2. fə̄méntətiv], fr. Lat. *fermentāt-(us)*, P.P. of *fermentāre*, 'to ferment', see **ferment** (II.), & **-ive**. **a** Causing, tending to produce, fermentation; **b** produced by fermentation.

fermentitious, adj. [1. fĕrmentíshus; 2. fə̄mentíʃəs]. **ferment** & **-itious**. Resembling, characterized by, fermentation.

fern, n. [1. fĕrn; 2. fə̄n]. O.E. *fearn*, M.E. *fern*; cp. O.H.G. *farn*, 'fern'; cogn. w. Scrt. *parṇám*, 'feather'; Lith. *spar̃nas*, 'wing'. **a** The popular name of a large phylum, *Pteridophyta*, of flowerless and cryptogamous plants, usually herbaceous, and having variously shaped fronds, each with a central stalk; it includes the true ferns, *Filicales*, as well as the horse-tails &c.; **b** a plant of this kind.

fernery, n. [1. fĕrneri; 2. fə̄nəri]. Prec. & **-ery**. Collection of growing ferns; specially prepared place for growing ferns in.

fernlike, adj. [1. fĕrnlīk; 2. fə̄nlaik]. **fern** & **-like**. Resembling a fern in appearance, mode of growth &c.

fern-owl, n. The nightjar.

fern-seed, n. The spores of ferns, formerly supposed to be seeds, and to have the property of making him who carried them invisible.

ferny, adj. [1. fĕrni; 2. fə̄ni]. **fern** & **-y**. **a** Resembling fern; **b** abounding in ferns.

ferocious, adj. [1. ferṓshus; 2. firóuʃəs], fr. Lat. *ferōc-*, stem of *ferox*, 'wild, bold; fierce, savage', fr. *ferus*, 'wild', & **-ous**. The Aryan base was **gʷeros*, whence w. lengthened grade, Gk. *thēr*, 'wild beast'; Lesbian *phēr*; see **theriac**. Fierce, savage; cruel, violent.

ferociously, adv. Prec. & **-ly.** In a ferocious manner.

ferociousness, n. See prec. & **-ness.** Quality of being ferocious; ferocity.

ferocity, n. [1. ferósiti; 2. firɔ́siti], fr. Fr. *férocité*, fr. Lat. *ferōcitāt-(em)*, 'fierceness', fr. *ferōci-(s)*, 'fierce'. See **ferocious** & **-ty.** The quality of being ferocious; fierceness, savagery.

-ferous, adjectival suff., fr. Lat. *-fer-*, 'producing, bearing', & **-ous.** The Lat. suff. *-fer-* is fr. *ferre*, 'to carry, bring, bear'; cogn. w. Gk. *phérein*, 'to carry'; Scrt. *bhárati*, 'carries'; O.E., O.H.G. *beran*, 'to carry'. See **bear (I.).** The force of the suff. is 'having, containing, producing'; it is used to form adjs. fr. ns. Some adjs. survive fr. Lat., e.g. *odorifer, aurifer*, & take in Engl. the additional adj. suff. *-ous*; but *-ferous* is a living suff., & new adjs. are formed on anal. of above, e.g. *argentiferous* (of earth &c.), 'silver bearing'.

ferox, n. [1. féroks; 2. férɔks], fr. Lat. name *Salmo ferox*. See **salmon, ferocious.** The great lake trout.

ferrate, n. [1. férāt; 2. féreit], fr. Lat. *ferr-(um)*, 'iron'. See **ferro-** & **-ate.** (chem.) A salt of ferric acid.

ferreous, adj. [1. féreus; 2. fériəs], fr. Lat. *ferre-(us)*, 'of iron', fr. *ferr-(um)*, 'iron'. See **ferro-** & **-ous.** Pertaining to, resembling, made of, containing, iron.

ferret (I.), n. [1. féret; 2. férit]. M.E. *feret, foret*, fr. O. Fr. *furet*, dimin. of *furon*, fr. Low Lat. *fūrōn-(em)*, 'a robber', fr. Lat. *fūr*, 'a thief, robber, rascal'. Cogn. w. Gk. *phṓr*, 'a thief', fr. base **bher-*, 'carry off'; cp. Gk. *phérein*, Lat. *ferre*, 'to carry'. See **furtive**, also **bear (I.), -ferous.** A small, yellowish-white, partially domesticated animal of weasel family, a variety of pole-cat, used for driving rabbits and rats out of their burrows and holes.

ferret (II.), vb. trans. & intrans., fr. prec. **A.** trans. To hunt (rats, rabbits) with ferrets. **B.** intrans. **a** To hunt with ferrets: *to go ferreting*; **b** (lit. and fig.) to make a minute and persevering search: *to ferret about in dark corners, among ancient records* &c. *Ferret out*, to discover with difficulty, as a result of minute and persevering search: *to ferret out a secret, a fugitive* &c.

ferret (III.), n., fr. Ital. *fioretti*, 'floss-silk', pl. of *fioretto*, dimin. of *fiore*, fr. Lat. *flōr-(is)*, 'a flower'. See **flora.** Narrow cotton or silk ribbon.

ferret (IV.), n. Fr., dimin. of *fer*, 'iron'. See **ferro-.** Iron rod used in glass-blowing to test the molten metal &c.

ferret-eyed, adj. Having blinking, beady eyes with red rims, suggesting those of a ferret in appearance.

ferrety, adj. [1. féreti; 2. fériti]. **ferret (I.)** & **-y.** Like a ferret.

ferri-, pref., fr. Lat. *ferr-(um)*, 'iron'. See **ferro-.** Containing iron in the ferric state.

ferriage, n. [1. fériij; 2. fériidž]. **ferry** & **-age. 1.** Conveyance by ferry. **2.** Charge made for this.

ferric, adj. [1 férik; 2. férik], fr. Lat. *ferr-(um)*, 'iron'. See **ferro-** & **-ic. 1.** Of, pertaining to, iron. **2.** (chem.) Containing iron in its highest combining power: *ferric acid*.

ferriferous, adj. [1. feríferus; 2. ferífərəs]. **ferri-** & **-ferous.** Yielding iron (of soil &c.).

ferro-, pref., fr. Lat. *ferr-(um)*, 'iron', fr. earlier **ferzom*, prob. a Semitic loan-word; cp. Sumerian *barzal*, Assyr. *parzilla*, Heb. *bar(ĕ)zel*. **1.** Containing, made of, iron. **2.** Containing iron in the ferrous state.

ferro-concrete, n. [1. férō kónkrēt; 2. férou kɔ́nkrīt]. Prec. & **concrete.** Concrete with an iron or steel framework embedded in it; reinforced concrete.

ferrotype, n. [1. férōtīp; 2. féroutaip]. **ferro-** & **type.** Photograph taken on a film spread on a thin iron plate.

ferrous, adj. [1. férus; 2. férəs], fr. Lat. *ferr-(um)*, 'iron'. See **ferro-** & **-ous. 1.** Of, pertaining to, obtained from, iron. **2.** (chem.) Containing iron in its lowest combining power: *ferrous sulphate*, copperas.

ferruginous, adj. [1. ferōōjinus; 2. ferúdžinəs], fr. Lat. *ferrūgin-*, stem of *ferrūgo*, 'rust; rust-colour', fr. Lat. *ferr-(um)*, 'iron', see **ferro-**, & **-ous. 1.** Containing iron. **2.** Rust-coloured, resembling iron-rust.

ferrule, n. [1. férūl; 2. férjūl]. Earlier *verrel*, fr. O. Fr. *virelle*, fr. Lat. *viriola*, dimin. of *viriae*, 'armlets, bracelets'; Celtic loan-word; cp. O. Ir. *fiar*, 'crooked'; W. *gwyr*, 'bent'. See **wire, withy, vine. a** Metal cap on the end of a stick, handle &c. to protect or strengthen it; **b** metal ring to strengthen a joint.

ferruled, adj. [1. férūld; 2. férjūld]. Prec. & **-ed.** Furnished with a ferrule.

ferry (I.), vb. trans. or intrans. [1. féri; 2. féri]. O.E. *ferian*, M.E. *ferien*, 'to carry, transport'. Cp. O.N. *ferja*, O.H.G. *ferren*, Goth. *farjan*, 'to carry'; causative vb. formed fr. Gmc. stem **far-*, 'to go'. See **fare (III.). A.** trans. To convey in a boat, on a raft &c. across a stream or other narrow piece of water. **B.** intrans. To cross a stream &c. in a boat, raft &c.

ferry (II.), n., fr. prec. **1. a** An organized system of transport, usually by means of a small boat, for passengers and goods across a stream &c.; applied to conveyance by small steamer across large river, e.g. the Mersey; **b** (law) the right of maintaining a ferry and charging fees for transportation by this means. **2.** A boat for transporting passengers and goods across a river &c.; ferry-boat. **3.** The place where ferry-boats cross a river &c.

ferry-boat, n. Boat used for ferrying passengers or goods across a stream &c.

ferry-bridge, n. Ferry-boat for transporting railway coaches.

ferryman, n. [1. fériman; 2. fériman]. Man in charge of a ferry.

fertile, adj. [1. fĕrtīl; 2. fə́tail], fr. O. Fr. *fertil*, fr. Lat. *fertilis*, 'fruitful, fertile', fr. a stem **fert-*, fr. *fer-re*, 'to carry, bear', & **-ile.** See **-ferous** & **bear (I.). a** Fruitful, productive, prolific, producing abundantly: *fertile soil*; **b** (fig.) productive (of thoughts and ideas): *a fertile imagination, brain* &c.; *fertile in excuses*.

fertility, n. [1. fĕrtíliti; 2. fətíliti]. Prec. & **-ity.** The quality, state, of being fertile.

fertilizable, adj. [1. fĕrtilīzabl; 2. fə́tilaizəbl]. **fertilize** & **-able.** Capable of being fertilized.

fertilization, n. [1. fĕrtilīzáshun; 2. fətilaizéiʃən]. Next word & **-ation.** The act of fertilizing; state of being fertilized. **1.** (of soils &c.) Enrichment by cultivation, addition of manures &c. **2.** (physiol. and biol.) Act or process by which the reproductive cell is impregnated by the male cell, both in animals and plants.

fertilize, vb. trans. [1. fĕrtilīz; 2. fə́tilaiz]. **fertile** & **-ize. 1.** To render fertile; cause to become fruitful and productive: *to fertilize the soil*. **2.** (physiol. and biol.) To fecundate, impregnate by action of the male element upon the female reproductive cell.

fertilizer, n. [1. fĕrtilīzer; 2. fə́tilaizə]. Prec. & **-er.** Substance for fertilizing land; manure, esp. chemical manures, as nitrates &c.

ferula, n. [1. féroola; 2. férulə]. Lat. *ferula*, 'the giant fennel; a branch, staff, rod', fr. stem **fer-* of Lat. *ferīre*, 'to strike, smite, cut, thrust', fr. Aryan base **bher-, *bhor-, *bherēi-, *bherā-*, 'to cut, strike, split'. Cp. Lat. *forāre*, 'to pierce'; O.H.G. *borōn*, O.E. *borian*, 'to pierce' (see **bore**); Gk. *pháreín*, 'to split'; O.H.G. *berjan*, 'to strike'; O. Ir. *bare*, 'anger, enmity'. See further **form, brim.** The giant fennel.

ferule (I.), n. [1. férūl; 2. férjūl], fr. Lat. *ferula*, 'the giant fennel; a slender branch, staff, rod'. See prec. **a** A flat rod or ruler used for punishing children; **b** this as symbol of parents', teachers', schoolmasters' authority: *to be under the ferule*, in charge of a teacher, in the condition of undergoing education.

ferule (II.), vb. trans., fr. prec. To strike, punish, with a ferule.

fervency, n. [1. fĕrvensi; 2. fə́vənsi], fr. Lat. *ferv-(ēre)*, 'to boil'. See next word & **-cy.** The quality of being fervent.

fervent, adj. [1. fĕrvent; 2. fə́vənt], fr. Lat. *fervent-(em)*, Pres. Part. of *fervēre*, 'to boil, glow; to foam, rage; to swarm'; fig. 'to be heated, agitated'. Aryan base **bh(e)rw-, *bh(e)rew-*, 'to boil', expanded fr. **bhere-*, 'to boil, bubble', q.v. under **bread, brew,** & cp. **ferment (I.). a** Burning, boiling, glowing; **b** (fig., of the mind, emotions, character &c.) ardent, intense: *fervent affection*; *fervent desire, hope* &c.

fervently, adv. Prec. & **-ly.** In a fervent manner.

fervid, adj. [1. fĕrvid; 2. fə́vid], fr. Lat. *fervid-(us)*, 'glowing, fiery'; fig. 'vehement, impetuous', fr. *ferv-(ēre)*, 'to boil, glow; to rage, be agitated'. See **fervent** & **-id.** Ardent, glowing, intense (chiefly of mind, emotions &c.; rare in material sense).

fervidly, adv. Prec. & **-ly.** In a fervid manner.

fervour, n. [1. fĕrvur; 2. fə́və], fr. O. Fr. *fervor*, fr. Lat. *fervōr-(em)*, 'raging, violent heat; passion, vehemence, ardour', fr. *ferv-(ēre)*, 'to boil'. See **fervent** & **-or. a** (rare) Violent, intense heat; chiefly **b** intensity of feeling; ardour, passion.

Fescennine, adj. [1. fésinīn; 2. fésinain], fr. Lat. *Fescennin-(us)*, fr. *Fescenn-(ia)*, 'a city on the Tiber', & **-ine.** Resembling the Fescennines; scurrilous, obscene, esp. *Fescennine verse*, cp. *satire*.

fescue, n. [1. féskū; 2. féskjū]. M.E. *festu*, 'bit of straw', fr. O. Fr. *festu*, fr. Lat. *festūca*, 'stalk, stem; a rod'; prob. fr. **ferstūca*; cogn. w. O.E. *byrst*, O.N. *burst*, 'a bristle', see **bristle**; Scrt. *bhṛṣṭiš*, 'point, spike, corner'; Lat. *fastīgium*, 'top of a gable; height, summit'. See **beard. 1.** (obs. or rare) A small pointer for indicating letters &c. to children. **2.** A kind of tough, slender meadow grass, genus *Festuca*, a valuable pasture grass for sheep &c.

fesse, n. [1. fes; 2. fes], fr. O. Fr. *fesse*, fr. Lat. *fascia*, 'a band, bandage'. See **fascia.** (her.) One of the ordinaries, consisting of a band placed horizontally across shield, in breadth one-third of the shield.

fess-point, n. (her.) Centre of shield.

fess-wise, -ways, fesse-, adv. In the manner of a fesse.

festal, adj. [1. féstal; 2. féstl], fr. O. Fr. *festal*, fr. *feste*, 'feast, festivity', see **feast,** & **-al. a** Of, pertaining to, a feast, festival: *festal music*; **b** joyous, gay.

festally, adv. Prec. & **-ly.** In a festal manner; joyously.

fester (I.), vb. intrans. & trans. [1. féster; 2. féstə], fr. M.E. *fester*, 'a sore, ulcer', fr. O. Fr. *festre*, fr. Lat. *fistula*, 'a pipe, tube; shepherd's pipe'. See **fistula. A.** intrans. **1. a** To generate morbid matter, suppurate; **b** to decay, rot, putrefy. **2.** (fig., of the feelings &c.) To become embittered, rankle. **B.** trans. To cause to fester, ulcerate.

fester (II.), n., fr. prec. An ulcer, festering wound.

festival (I.), adj. [1. féstival; 2. féstivəl], fr. O. Fr., fr. Med. Lat. *festival-(is)*, fr. Lat. *fēstīv-(us)*, 'lively, joyous, merry'. See **festive** & **-al.** Pertaining to a feast, festal.

festival (II.), n., fr. prec. **a** Joyful celebration, merry-making; **b** day or period appointed for celebration, commemoration: *a festival of the Church*; **c** periodic gathering for important musical performances: *the Three Choirs Festival*.

festive, adj. [1. féstiv; 2. féstiv], fr. Lat. *fēstīv-(us)*, 'gay, lively; agreeable, pleasant', fr. Lat. *fēst-(um)*, 'holiday, festival, feast, banquet'. See **feast** & **-ive. 1. a** Pertaining to a feast; **b** joyous, jovial, merry; **c** given to feasting and merrymaking; jovial, convivial. **2.** (Charterhouse slang) Presumptuous, impertinent, cheeky; applied esp. to conduct, utterances &c., which are out of keeping with, and unsuitable to, a boy's position in the school, or the length of time he has been there.

festively, adv. Prec. & **-ly**. In a festive manner.

festivity, n. [1. festíviti; 2. fɛstíviti], fr. O. Fr. *festivité*, fr. Lat. *fēstīvitāt-(em)*, 'gaiety, pleasantness, kindness; feast, festival'. **festive** & **-ity**. **1.** The quality of being festive; gaiety, merriment, joyousness. **2.** Festive action, cheerful proceeding; merrymaking to celebrate an event &c. (often pl.).

festoon (**I.**), n. [1. festóon; 2. fɛstún], fr. O. Fr. *feston*, fr. Ital. *festone*, prob. fr. *festa*, 'feast', fr. Lat. *fēst-(um)*. See **feast** & **-oon**. **a** Strip of material, or a garland, wreath, of flowers &c., suspended from either end, and hanging in a curve; **b** carved, sculptured, representation of this; a swag.

festoon (**II.**), vb. trans., fr. prec. **a** To cause to hang in a festoon, form into festoons; **b** to hang with, decorate with, festoons.

festoonery, n. [1. festóoneri; 2. fɛstúnəri]. **festoon** & **-ery**. Collection of festoons, drapery &c., forming a decoration for a person, building, or other object.

fetal. See **foetal**.

fetch (**I.**), vb. trans. [1. fech; 2. fɛtʃ]. O.E. *feččan*, earlier *fetian*, 'to fetch, summon, bring'. Etymol. quite uncertain. **1.** To go to another place from that in which one is before starting the action, and bring something back with one, or summon a person and conduct, or accompany him back: *to fetch a book from another room*; *to fetch the doctor from the next village* &c. Phr. *to fetch and carry*, **a** trans., *news, a report* &c., to retail, disseminate; **b** intrans., to bustle about, be occupied with trivial, petty duties. **2.** To bring out, produce from, procure, evoke: *to fetch water from a rock*; *to fetch tears from a person's eyes*. **3.** To produce by a physical act: *to fetch a sigh*. **4.** To strike a blow, execute a violent bodily movement: *to fetch a man a blow, one, on the nose*. **5.** To captivate, charm, fascinate: *the girl's beauty fetched him completely*. **6.** To yield a price, be sold for, bring in: *the pictures fetched excellent prices*; *this won't fetch much*.

fetch (**II.**), n., fr. prec. An artifice, trick, dodge.

fetch (**III.**), n. Etymol. unknown. An apparition, wraith, spectre; a person's double.

fetching, adj. [1. féching; 2. fɛ́tʃiŋ], fr. Pres. Part. of **fetch** (**I.**). (colloq.) Attractive, fascinating.

fête (**I.**), n. [1. fāt; 2. feit]. Fr. *fête*, fr. O. Fr. *feste*, 'feast, festival'. See **feast**. A festival, a cheerful entertainment: *a fête and gala*.

fête (**II.**), vb. trans., fr. prec. To honour (person) with celebrations; arrange festivities in honour of; to entertain splendidly.

fête-champêtre, n. [1. fāt shompâtr; 2. feit ʃãpeitr]. Fr. Entertainment out of doors; a kind of elaborate picnic.

fête day, n. Day on which a fête is held.

fetial (**I.**), adj. [1. féshl; 2. fíʃl], fr. Lat. *fētiāl-(is)*, 'belonging to the fetials'. See next word. *Fetial Law*, relating to international affairs, treaties of peace, and declarations of war.

fetial (**II.**), n., fr. Lat. *fētiāl-(es)*, 'a Roman college of priests', fr. **fēti-(s)*; cogn. w. Scrt. *dāta-*, 'law'; Aryan **dhē-ti-s*, 'edict, pronouncement', fr. base **dhē-*, **dhə-*, 'to make, do'. See **do**, **fact**. (Rom. antiq.) One of a body of twenty priests who acted as heralds, and conducted the ceremonies at the beginning and end of a war.

fetid, **fœtid**, adj. [1. fétid; 2. fítid], fr. Lat. *foet-*, *fēt-id-(us)*, 'stinking, disgusting', fr. *fēt-*, *foet-(ēre)*, 'to stink'. Possibly fr. earlier **dhū-it-*, P.P. type of Aryan **dhw-ijō-*, 'to smell', whence Lat. *(suf)fīre*, 'to fumigate', *fi-mus*, 'dung'. See also **fetor**. Having an offensive smell, stinking.

fetidly, adv. Prec. & **-ly**. In a fetid manner.

fetidness, n. See prec. & **-ness**. The quality of being fetid.

fetish, **fetich**(e), n. [1. fétish, fétish; 2. fítiʃ, fétiʃ], fr. Fr. *fétiche*, fr. Port. *feitiço*, 'charm, magic', fr. Lat. *factītius*, 'made by art'. See **factitious**. **a** A material object believed to be inhabited by a subservient spirit; **b** hence, anything regarded with exaggerated devotion, and exaggerated veneration: *he makes a perfect fetish of cricket*.

fetishism, n. [1. fétishizm; 2. fítiʃizəm]. Prec. & **-ism**. Belief that the services of a spirit may be appropriated by its material embodiment.

fetishist, n. [1. fétishist; 2. fítiʃist]. **fetish** & **-ist**. One attached to fetishism.

fetishistic, adj. [1. fètishístik; 2. fìtiʃístik]. Prec. & **-ic**. Pertaining to a fetish.

fetlock, n. [1. fétlok; 2. fétlɔk]. M.E. *fetlak*, *fitlok*; cp. Germ. *fiszloch*. Etymol. doubtful. Projecting cushion-like structure, bearing tuft of hair, on hinder side of a horse's leg just above the hoof; the joint of the leg nearest this.

fetor, **foetor**, n. [1. fétur; 2. fítə], fr. Lat. *fētor*, *foetor*, 'stench', fr. *foet-(ēre)*, 'to stink', & **-or**. Cp. Lat. *fimus*, 'dung, excrement'. Perh. ultimately related to Lat. *fūmus*, 'smoke, vapour' &c. See **fetid**, **fume** & words there referred to. Powerful, oppressive, offensive stench.

fetter (**I.**), n. [1. féter; 2. fétə]. O.E. *fetor*, M.E. *feter*; cp. O.L.G. *feter*, O.H.G. *fezera*, O.N. *fiöturr*; cp. also Lat. *pedica*, 'shackle, fetter, snare'; *(ex)pedīre*, 'to extricate, disentangle; to make ready, prepare' (see **expedite**); *(im)pedīre*, 'to tangle, ensnare, hamper; hinder, detain' (see **impede**); Gk. *pédē*, 'fetter'; Aryan **ped-*, 'fetter, snare; hindrance', fr. the base **ped-*, **pod-*, 'foot'. See **foot**, **pedal**. **a** Chain, shackle, for the feet, intended to prevent, or hinder, movement; **b** (fig., usually pl.) anything that hinders action or progress; a restraint, restriction; bonds, captivity.

fetter (**II.**), vb. trans., fr. prec. **a** To fasten, bind, with fetters; put in irons; to hinder, hamper; **b** (fig.) to check, impede, restrain: *fettered by convention*.

fetterless, adj. [1. féterles; 2. fétəlis]. **fetter** (**I.**) & **-less**. Without fetters, free.

fetterlock, n. [1. féterlok; 2. fétəlɔk]. **fetter** (**I.**) & **lock** (**I.**). (her.) Figure of a shackle for a horse, used as a charge.

fettle, n. [1. fétl; 2. fétl]. M.E. *fetlen*, vb., formed fr. O.E. *fetel*, 'girdle, belt'. Orig. sense prob. to gird up, prepare for action. Physical, or, more rarely, mental, condition, state, trim: *to be in good fettle*; *in fine fettle*.

fetus, n. See **foetus**.

fetwa, **futwa**, n. [1. fétwa, fútwa; 2. fétwə, fátwə]. Arab. *fatwā*. Judicial pronouncement of Mohammedan legal authority.

feu (**I.**), n. [1. fū; 2. fjū]. O. Fr. *fiu*, *fé*. See **fee**. (Scots law) **1.** **a** Tenure of land according to which the holder pays rent instead of performing military service; **b** a perpetual lease granted in return for fixed annual rent. **2.** Land held on condition of payment of rent.

feu (**II.**), vb. trans., fr. prec. (Scots law) To grant lease of (land) on feu.

feuar, n. [1. fūar; 2. fjúə]. **feu** (**I.**) & **-ar**. (Scots law) Person holding a feu.

feud (**I.**), n. [1. fūd; 2. fjūd]. M.E. *feide*, *fede*, fr. O. Fr. *fede*, fr. O.H.G. *fêhida*, 'enmity'; Mod. Germ. *fehde*; cogn. w. O.E. *fǣhþu*, 'enmity'; Gmc. **faihiþō*, 'enmity'; cp. O.E. *fāh*, 'enemy', q.v. under **foe**. **a** Enduring, hereditary, invincible enmity between two families, parties, clans &c. inspired by desire for revenge for previous injuries; **b** enmity, quarrel which is kept up over long period between individuals.

feud (**II.**), n., fr. O. Fr. *feud*, fr. Med. Lat. *feudum*, *feodum*. Prob. of same origin as **fee** & **fief**. (legal hist.) A feudal benefice; a right which was heritable although held at the will of a superior lord.

feudal, adj. [1. fúdl; 2. fjúdl], fr. O. Fr., fr. Med. Lat. *feudal-(is)*, fr. *feud-(um)*, 'fee, fief'. See **feud** (**II.**) & **-al**. **1.** Pertaining to, of the nature of, relating to, a feud (see prec.): *feudal tenure*; *feudal service*. **2.** Pertaining to the tenure by which feuds and fiefs were held: *feudal system*, feudalism, q.v. **3.** Connected with the *feudal system*: *feudal law*; *feudal barons*.

feudalism, n. [1. fúdalizm; 2. fjúdəlizəm]. **feudal** & **-ism**. System prevailing in the Middle Ages over the greater part of Europe, which determined the relations, relative rights, and duties &c., of lord and vassal, the basis of which was the tenure of land in exchange for certain military services performed by the latter for the former.

feudalist, n. [1. fúdalist; 2. fjúdəlist]. **feudal** & **-ist**. A student of feudalism.

feudalistic, adj. [1. fūdalístik; 2. fjūdəlístik]. Prec. & **-ic**. Pertaining to, of the nature of, feudalism.

feudality, n. [1. fūdáliti; 2. fjūdǽliti]. **feudal** & **-ity**. **1.** The state or quality of being feudal. **2.** Land held in fee; fief.

feudalization, n. [1. fùdalīzāshun; 2. fjùdəlaizéiʃən]. Next word & **-ation**. Act or process of imposing or establishing the feudal system, or one resembling it in character; act of introducing the principles and ideals of feudalism.

feudalize, vb. trans. [1. fúdalīz; 2. fjúdəlaiz]. **feudal** & **-ize**. To make feudal; establish feudal system in.

feudally, adv. [1. fúdali; 2. fjúdəli]. **feudal** & **-ly**. According to the feudal system, by feudal tenure.

feudatory, adj. & n. [1. fúdatori; 2. fjúdətəri], fr. Med. Lat. *feudāt-(us)*, P.P. of *feudāre*, 'to enfeoff', fr. *feud-(um)*, 'fief'. See **feud** (**II.**) & **-ory**. **1.** adj. **a** (of persons) Holding land by feudal tenure; **b** (of land) held in fee. **2.** n. Vassal holding land in fee.

feu de joie, n. [1. fē d' zhwah; 2. fø də žwā]. Fr., 'fire of joy'. Public bonfire kindled in token of rejoicing; guns fired in salute for same purpose.

feuilleton, n. [1. fëiton; 2. føitɔ̃]. Fr., fr. *feuille*, 'leaf'. See **folio**. Serial story, or literary article, published in a newspaper.

fever, n. [1. féver; 2. fívə]. O.E. *fefor*, *fefre*, M.E. *fev(e)re*, fr. Lat. *febris*, 'fever'. See **febrile**. Prob. cogn. w. Lat. *favilla*, 'embers' (fr. **fovilla*), fr. Aryan base **dhōgʷh-*, **dhegʷh-*, 'to burn', whence also Scrt. *dáhati*, 'burns'; O. Prussian *dagis*, 'summer', &c. The same base occurs in **day**. **1.** **a** A disordered condition of the system, characterized by abnormal rise of temperature; **b** one of several diseases characterized by fever: *scarlet fever*; *rheumatic, yellow, fever* &c. **2.** **a** Highly excited mental state, extreme nervous agitation: *to be in a fever of impatience*; **b** excessive interest in, devotion to, an object or occupation; craze.

fevered, adj. [1. féverd; 2. fívəd]. Prec. & **-ed**. **1.** Affected by fever, feverish. **2.** Disordered by fever; affected by extreme mental excitement and agitation: *fevered imagination*.

feverfew, n. [1. féverfū; 2. fívəfjū]. O.E. *feferfuge*, fr. Lat. *febrifugia*, 'a kind of herb', fr. *febri-(s)*, 'fever', see **fever**, & *fug-(āre)*, 'to put to flight'. See **fugitive**. A white-flowered herb of the aster family, *Pyrethrum*, possessing medicinal properties, allied to the camomile.

fever-heat, n. **a** Abnormally high bodily temperature; **b** extreme intensity: *the excitement rose to fever-heat*.

feverish, adj. [1. féverish; 2. fívəriʃ]. **fever** & **-ish**. **1.** **a** With abnormally high temperature, affected by fever: *feverish condition, hands* &c.; **b** caused by fever: *feverish dreams*. **2.** (fig.) Excited, agitated, restless: *a feverish desire for pleasure*. **3.** (of climate &c.) Liable to cause fever.

feverishly, adv. Prec. & **-ly**. In a feverish manner.

feverishness, n. See prec. & **-ness**. The state of being feverish.

feverous, adj. [1. féverus; 2. fívərəs]. **fever** & **-ous**. (rare) **a** Liable to cause fever, infested with fever; **b** excited, agitated.

fever tree, n. The eucalyptus.

few (**I.**), adj. [1. fū; 2. fjū]. O.E. *fēawe*, M.E. *fēwe*; cp. O. Fris. *fē*, O.L.G. *fāh*, O.H.G. *fō*, *fōh*, Goth. *fawai* (pl.); cogn. w. Lat. *paucus*, 'few, little' see (**paucity**); *pauper*, 'poor' (see **pauper**); Gk. *paûros*, 'few; little, small'. Aryan base **pauk-*(*w*)-, 'few, little'. **1.** Not many; of a restricted number; (contrasted with *many*; cp. *a few*): *few people are able to understand him*; *his friends are few*; *he has but few chances of success*; *to speak in few words*. Phrs. *every few hours, days, years* &c., once in a group of a few hours &c.; *some few*, a fair number of. **2.** A small number of; (contrasted with *none*): *a few people were present*; *the chairman said a few words*; *to buy something for a few pence*.

few (**II.**), pron. & n., fr. prec. **1.** Not many, a small number: *few are capable of such an achievement*; *few of the inhabitants were to be seen*. Phr. *the few*, the minority. **2.** A small number: *I saw a few of my friends*; *only a few grasped his meaning*. Phr. (colloq.) *a good few*, a considerable number.

fewness, n. **few** (**I.**) & **-ness**. The state of being few.

fey, adj. [1. fā; 2. fei]. O.E. *fǣge*, M.E. *feie*, 'doomed to death'; O.L.G. *fēgi*, O.N. *feigr*, O.H.G. *feigi*, M.H.G. *feige*, 'doomed to death'; Mod. Germ. *feige*, 'cowardly'; Gmc. **faig-*, 'injury, death'; cp. Gmc. **faiχ-*, 'enemy' (see **foe**); cogn. w. Lat. *piget*, 'it irks one, is troublesome'; Scrt. *píśunaš*, 'evil-minded, treacherous'; Lith. *peĩkti*, 'to blame'; O. Prussian *paikēmai*, 'to deceive'; M. Ir. *ōech*, 'enemy'. Aryan base **pei-k̑-*, **pei-g-*, **pi-k̑-*, **pi-g-*, 'evil, enmity, treachery'. Cp. further O.E. *fācen*, O.H.G. *feihhan*, 'cunning'; O.E. *ficol*, 'inconstant'. See **fickle**. Fated, doomed, to die; about to die; esp. in an abnormally gay and confident state of mind, supposed to precede sudden death.

fez, n. [1. fez; 2. fez], fr. Turk. *fes*; prob. fr. Fez, town in Morocco, as made there. Moslem low, tapering cap of red felt, flat topped, with a tassel.

fiacre, n. [1. féahkr; 2. fiākr]. Fr., fr. *Hôtel St. Fiacre*, inn in Paris, where carriages were first kept for hire; *Fiacre* (Fiachra) was a Celtic saint of the 7th cent. A French hackney cab.

fiancé(**e**), n. [1. fēáhnsā; 2. fiãsei]. Fr. *fiancé*(*e*), 'affianced, betrothed'. See **affiance**. Person to whom one is betrothed (*é* masc., *ée* fem.).

fiars, n. pl. [1. féarz; 2. fiāz], fr. O. Fr. *fuar*, 'price', fr. Low Lat. *forum*, 'price'. See **forum**. (Scots) Usually *fiars prices*, average prices for grain, fixed each February, governing rents, payments to clergy &c., based on the value of or originally paid in grain.

fiasco, n. [1. féaskō; 2. fiæskou]. Ital. *fiasco*, 'bottle'. See **flask**; origin of meaning obscure. Complete failure, a break-down; attempt that comes to nothing; course of action which has to be discontinued from lack of means or ability to carry it to a conclusion.

fiat, n. [1. fíat; 2. fáiæt]. Lat. *fiat*, 'let it be done', 3rd pers. sing. of subj. of *fieri*, 'to be done, to be, become', fr. Pres. stem *fi-o* &c., fr. Aryan **bhw-ijō*, fr. base **bhū-*, **bhewā-*, 'to be, become'; cp. Lat. *fui*, 'I was' (see under **future**); Scrt. *bhávati*, 'is, becomes, happens'; Gk. *phúsis*, 'nature' (see **physio-**). See also **build, favour**. A command, decree, authoritative order.

fib (**I.**), n. [1. fib; 2. fib]. Etymol. dubious. A mild tampering with the truth; a statement which is untrue but not important enough, nor constituting a sufficient deviation from the truth, to be called a lie.

fib (**II.**), vb. trans., fr. prec. To tell a fib, to lie.

fibber, n. [1. fíber; 2. fíbə]. Prec. & **-er**. One who tells fibs, a petty liar.

fibre, n. [1. fíber; 2. fáibə], fr. Fr., fr. Lat. *fibra*, 'fibre, filament; entrails'. Etymol. doubtful. **1. a** A single slender thread or filament combining with others to form animal or vegetable tissue; **b** anything of a thread-like character, resembling a fibre. **2.** A substance, structure, composed of fibres; esp. one that can be separated into threads or fibres for spinning &c. **3.** (fig.) Character, nature, inherent quality: *a man of fine, coarse, fibre*.

fibreless, adj. [1. fíberles; 2. fáibəlis]. Prec. & **-less**. **a** Without, free from, fibre; **b** lacking fibre (in fig. sense); devoid of strength of character.

fibriform, adj. [1. fíbriform; 2. fáibrifɔ̄m]. **fibre** & **-form**. Resembling, of the nature and structure of, fibre.

fibril, n. [1. fíbril; 2. fáibril]. Dimin. of **fibre**. **1.** A minute filament, a component part of a fibre. **2.** A minute rootlet.

fibrillar(**y**), adj. [1. fibrílar(i); 2. faibrílə(ri)]. Prec. & **-ar, -ary**. Pertaining to, composed of, fibrils.

fibrillate(**d**), adj. [1. fíbrilāt(ed); 2. fáibrileit(id)]. **fibril** & **-ate** (& **-ed**). Composed of fibrils, fibrous.

fibrillation, n. [1. fibrilā́shun; 2. fàibriléiʃən]. Prec. & **-ion**. The state of being fibrillate.

fibrilliform, adj. [1. fibríliform; 2. faibrílifɔ̄m]. **fibril** & **-form**. Having the form of fibrils.

fibrillose, adj. [1. fíbrilōs; 2. fáibrilous]. **fibril** & **-ose**. Composed of, resembling, fibres.

fibrin, n. [1. fíbrin; 2. fáibrin]. **fibre** & **-in**. **1.** A coagulable protein found in blood. **2.** A nitrogenous substance found in vegetable tissue.

fibrinous, adj. [1. fíbrinus; 2. fáibrinəs]. Prec. & **-ous**. Composed of, resembling, of the nature of fibrin.

fibro-, pref. fr. **fibre**. In compound words denoting 'fibrous, of fibre'.

fibroid, adj. & n. [1. fíbroid; 2. fáibrɔid]. **fibre** & **-oid**. **1.** adj. Of, pertaining to, or resembling, fibre. **2.** n. A fibrous tumour.

fibroin, n. [1. fíbrōin; 2. fáibrouin]. **fibro-** & **-in**. The substance of which raw silk and spiders' webs are chiefly composed.

fibroma, n. [1. fībrṓma; 2. faibróumə]. Mod. scientific Latin. A fibrous tumour.

fibrous, adj. [1. fíbrus; 2. fáibrəs]. **fibre** & **-ous**. Composed of, resembling, fibre.

fibrously, adv. Prec. & **-ly**. In a fibrous manner, as fibre.

fibrousness, n. See prec. & **-ness**. The quality of being fibrous.

fibula, n. [1. fíbūla; 2. fíbjulə]. Lat., 'a brooch, clasp, buckle'; cp. *fī-gere*, 'to stick, fasten, fix'. See **fix**. **1.** (archaeol.) A brooch. **2.** The thin outer bone of the leg.

fibular, adj. [1. fíbūlar; 2. fíbjulə]. Prec. & **-ar**. Of, pertaining to, near, the fibula.

-fic, (**-ific**), suff. representing Lat. *-fic-*(*us*), or Fr. *-fique*, adj. suff. consisting of the unstressed form of the vbl. stem *fac-*(*ere*), 'to make, do'. See **fact**. The suff. denotes 'making, causing to become', & forms adjs. **a** fr. ns.: *pacific, specific*; **b** fr. adjs.: *beatific, scientific*; **c** fr. vbs.: *terrific*. Many of these adjs. are derived fr. Lat. direct or through Fr.; others are modern formations.

-fication, suff. representing Lat. *-ficātiōn-*(*em*), forming ns. denoting action fr. vbs. in *-ficāre*; see **-fy**. The suff. in Engl. forms ns. fr. vbs. in *-ify* corresponding to Lat. vbs. in *-ficāre*: *pacification, glorification* &c. Cp. **faction**.

ficelle, adj. [1. fisél; 2. fisél]. Fr., 'string, thread, cord'. String-coloured (recent, shopkeeper's word).

fichu, n. [1. físhōō; 2. fíʃū]. Fr. A small, light, triangular garment, often like a folded handkerchief, worn by women round the neck and partly covering the shoulders.

fickle, adj. [1. fíkl; 2. fíkl]. O.E. *ficol*, M.E. *fikel*; cp. O.H.G. *feihhan*, O.E. *fācen* (Gmc. **faik-*), 'cunning', fr. Aryan base **pei-g-*, **pig-*, 'evil, enmity'. Cp. Lat. *piget*, 'it is irksome'; fr. same base are **fey, foe**. See **-le**. Changeable in the affections, inclinations, purpose; capricious, inconstant, unstable.

fickleness, n. Prec. & **-ness**. The quality of being fickle.

fictile, adj. [1. fíktīl, fíktil; 2. fíktail, fíktil], fr. Lat. *fictil-*(*is*), 'made of clay, earthen', fr. *fict-*(*us*), P.P. type of *fingere*, 'to touch, handle; to form, shape; to mould, model; to form mentally, conceive, imagine'. Aryan base **dheigh-*, **dhoigh-*, **dhigh-*, 'to form, mould'. See **feign, figure, dough, effigy, paradise**. **a** Capable of being moulded; plastic; **b** made of clay, moulded; **c** pertaining to pottery.

fiction, n. [1. fíkshun; 2. fíkʃən], fr. Lat. *fictiōn-*(*em*), 'a making, formation; a supposition, fiction; a fictitious assumption', fr. *fict-*(*um*), P.P. type of *fingere*, 'to fashion, form, mould; to imagine, conceive', & **-ion**. See prec. & words there referred to. **1. a** Something imagined, feigned, invented, as distinct from fact or truth: *fact is stranger than fiction*; **b** an imaginary, fictitious statement, account &c. **2. a** Literary compositions consisting of fictitious narrative of events; the representation of imaginary persons, their characters and actions, and the interplay of these, especially in novels, romances, dramas; **b** the art and practice of such creations. **3.** (law) *A legal fiction*, something assumed to be a fact, irrespective of whether it is so or not, in order to avoid some technical difficulty.

fictional, adj. [1. fíkshunal; 2. fíkʃənəl]. Prec. & **-al**. Pertaining to, belonging to, of the character of, fiction.

fictionist, n. [1. fíkshunist; 2. fíkʃənist]. **fiction** & **-ist**. A writer of fiction.

fictitious, adj. [1. fiktíshus; 2. fiktíʃəs], fr. Lat. *fictīci-*(*us*), 'not genuine; feigned'; Lat. *fict-*(*us*), P.P. type of *fingere*, 'to make, fashion; to imagine'. **fictile** & **-itious**. **a** Created by the fancy, imaginary, invented; not based on fact, not actually existing: *a fictitious narrative*; *fictitious characters, qualities* &c.; **b** not genuine; false, counterfeit; assumed: *a fictitious name*; **c** assumed as true by a legal fiction.

fictitiously, adv. Prec. & **-ly**. In a fictitious manner.

fictitiousness, n. See prec. & **-ness**. The quality of being fictitious.

fictive, adj. [1. fíktiv; 2. fíktiv], fr. Fr., fr. Lat. *fict-*(*um*), P.P. type of *fingere*, 'to form, shape; to imagine', & **-ive**. See **fictile**. Imaginary, invented; pertaining to fiction.

fid, n. [1. fid; 2. fid]. Etymol. doubtful. **1.** Bar of wood or metal used as support; (naut.) cross-piece for supporting topmast. **2.** Thick lump or slice of food &c.

fiddle (**I.**), n. [1. fídl; 2. fídl]. M.E. *fiðele*, 'fiddle'; cp. O.H.G. *fidula*, fr. Low Lat. *vītula*, fr. Lat. *vītulāri*, 'to celebrate a festival, be joyful'. Cp. *Vītula*, name of goddess of victory. The meaning of the vb. is 'to shout *vī*', that is a cry of joy or excitement; cp. Gk. *euoî*. The second element is fr. *tulere*, 'to bear, raise'; cp. *tuli*, used as perf. of *ferre*, 'bear'. See this base under **tolerate** & **thole**. **1. a** Instrument with hollow body, a neck with screws to which the four strings are attached, played with a bow, the notes being formed by the fingers pressing on that part of the strings close to the screws; violin; Phrs. *fit as a fiddle*, in perfect health; *to play second fiddle*, occupy a subordinate position; *a face as long as a fiddle*, having an anxious, gloomy expression; *fiddle pattern*, with handles shaped like a fiddle (of spoons and forks); **b** any instrument of the fiddle family, viola, violoncello, double bass. **2.** (naut.) Wooden framework fixed on tables on board ship in rough weather, to keep plates &c. from sliding off. **3.** Short flat piece of wood with a hole at either end, used for holding guy-ropes taut.

fiddle (**II.**), vb. trans. & intrans., fr. prec. **A.** trans. To play (an air &c.) upon the fiddle: *to fiddle a tune*. **B.** intrans. **1.** To play the fiddle. 2. a To waste time, spend one's time over trifles; esp. *to fiddle about doing nothing* &c.; b to fidget, play aimlessly: *to fiddle with a book, piece of string* &c.

fiddle-bow, n. Bow for playing the fiddle.

fiddle-case, n. Leather or wooden case for holding fiddle.

fiddlededee, interj. & n. [1. fídldedḗ; 2. fídldidī]. Nonsense, rubbish.

fiddle-faddle, vb. intrans., adj., & n. [1. fídl fadl; 2. fídlfædl]. 1. vb. intrans. To trifle; talk or spend time aimlessly. 2. adj. Unimportant, trifling, petty. 3. n. Triviality, nonsense, unimportant trifle.

fiddle-head, n. Carved scroll-work above bows of ship.

fiddler, n. [1. fídler; 2. fídlə]. **fiddle (II.)** & **-er**. 1. One who plays the fiddle. 2. A kind of crab.

fiddlestick, n. [1. fídlstik; 2. fídlstik]. Bow for playing the fiddle.

fiddlesticks, interj. Rubbish, nonsense.

fiddley, n. [1. fídli; 2. fídli]. Etymol. doubtful. (naut.) Iron framework round hatch leading to the stokehole.

fiddling, adj. [1. fídling; 2. fídliŋ]. **fiddle (II.)** & **-ing**. Useless, trifling, futile.

fidelity, n. [1. fidéliti; 2. fidéliti], fr. Fr. *fidélité*, fr. Lat. *fidēlitāt-(em)*, 'faithfulness, fidelity', fr. *fidēl-(is)*, 'true, faithful, sincere', fr. *fid-ēs*, 'faith, confidence, belief'; cp. Lat. *fīdūcia*, 'trust' (see **fiducial** & **faith**), *fīdere*, 'to trust, confide in', *fīdus*, 'faithful', *foedus* (earlier **foid-*), 'treaty, compact'; Aryan base **bheidh-*, **bhoidh-*, **bhidh-*, 'persuade, win confidence of, win over', whence also Gk. *peithein*, 'persuade' (perf. *pépoitha*), *pístis*, 'faith'; Goth. *bidjan*, O.E. *biddan*, 'to beg, pray; to command' (see **bid**). 1. Faithfulness, loyalty, devotion; firmness in allegiance: *fidelity to a cause, person, leader, principle* &c. 2. Strict adherence to fact; accuracy, exactitude: *to report a debate with fidelity*; *the facsimile reproduces the MS. with complete fidelity.*

fidget (I.), n. [1. fíjet; 2. fídžit], fr. obs. *fidge*, 'to jump, twitch'. Cp. O. Swed. *fikja*, 'to hurry about; to move restlessly, fidget'. 1. a Bodily restlessness causing frequent nervous movements: *to be in a fidget*; Phr. *the fidgets*, fit of restlessness; b restless, anxious, mental state; state of worry and restlessness; fussiness. 2. A person who fidgets physically, or mentally.

fidget (II.), vb. intrans. & trans., fr. prec. 1. intrans. a To move frequently, restlessly, nervously, and spasmodically; make idle, purposeless movements: *sit still and don't fidget!*; *to fidget with a pencil*; b to be in a restless, nervous, anxious state of mind; to worry, be anxious; to fuss; to be unable to concentrate attention. 2. trans. To make (a person) restless, nervous; disturb, worry: *it fidgets me not to know where he is.*

fidgetiness, n. [1. fíjetines; 2. fídžitinis]. Next word & **-ness**. State of being fidgety.

fidgety, adj. [1. fíjeti; 2. fídžiti]. **fidget (I.)** & **-y**. a Having the fidgets, inclined to fidget; physically restless, uneasy; b inclined to worry; anxious, nervous; crotchety, faddy; pernickety, fastidious.

fidibus, n. [1. fídibus; 2. fídibəs]. Etymol. unknown. A paper spill for lighting pipes &c.

fiducial, adj. [1. fidūshal; 2. faidjúʃəl], fr. Lat. *fīdūciāl-(is)*, 'reliable', fr. *fīdūcia*, 'trust, faith; reliability', & **-al**. Cp. Lat. *fīdere*, 'to trust' (see **confide**), *fidēs*, 'faith', & see other cognates under **fidelity**. 1. (astron., surveying &c.) *Fiducial line, point*, one from which measurements are made, or which is taken as the basis of calculation, comparison &c. 2. (rare) Of the nature of a trust, fiduciary.

fiduciary, adj. & n. [1. fidūshari; 2. faidjúʃəri], fr. Lat. *fīdūciāri-(us)*, 'relating to a thing held in trust; holding a thing in trust', fr. *fīdūcia*, 'trust, reliance' (see prec.), & **-ary**. 1. adj. a Of, pertaining to, one who holds a thing in trust; of a trustee; b held in trust; c (of paper currency) deriving its value from the confidence of the public. 2. n. One who holds a thing in trust; a trustee.

fidus Achates, n. [1. fīdus akā́tēz; 2. fáidəs əkéitīz]. Lat. *fīdus*, 'faithful' (see under **fidelity**), *Achātes*, a companion of Aeneas. A devoted follower, companion.

fie, interj. [1. fī; 2. fai]. Expressing disapproval, disgust, impatience (often ironical). Phr. *fie upon you*, shame on you!; *fie, for shame!*

fief, feoff, n. [1. fēf, fef; 2. fīf, fef]. O. Fr. *feof, fief, fiu, fé*, fr. Med. Lat. *feudum, feodum*, 'fief'. See **fee**. Land held by feudal tenure; fee, feud.

field (I.), n. [1. fēld; 2. fīəld]. O.E., M.E. *fēld*; cp. O. Fris. *field, feld*, O.L.G. *feld*, O.H.G. *felt*, 'field, plain'. Cp. further O.E. *folde*, O.S. *folde*, 'earth, land'; O.N. *fold*, 'meadow'; O. Bulg. *polje*, 'expense, field'; Russ. *polyj*, 'open'; Lat. *palam*, 'openly', *plānus*, 'flat, level'; Aryan base **pelā-*, **pelē-*, **plā-* &c., 'to spread out'. See **plain (I.)**. 1. a Open country: *flowers, beasts, of the field*; hence, b any wide expanse: '*The realms of ocean, or the fields of air*' (Dryden); c (esp. in compounds) a wide stretch, broad tract: *ice-field, snow-field.* 2. a Ground-work, background, of a flag, coin &c.; b (her.) whole surface, background, of a shield, or of single section of a quartered shield. 3. a A specific piece of meadow or arable land enclosed by a boundary, such as a hedge, ditch, bank &c.; b crop grown in a field: *a field of wheat.* 4. Tract of land yielding specified product: *gold-fields, coal-fields* &c. 5. a Scene of battle, locality where battle takes place, battle-field: *the field of Agincourt*; b a battle: *a hard-fought field*; c a campaign; Phrs. *in the field*, on campaign, on active service; *to take the field*, begin a campaign; *to keep the field*, continue operations; *hold the field*, hold one's ground. 6. Area of observation: *field of vision*; *field of a microscope, telescope* &c. 7. Area of operation, area over which a force is exerted: *magnetic field.* 8. Scope of study, research; province, department, region, realm, of knowledge or of action: *pre-eminent in one's own field*; *to cover a wide field of inquiry*; *a field of effort* &c. 9. A specific group of persons &c.; a all competitors in a contest; b all competitors in a horse race excepting the favourite; c (hunting) persons taking part, those following hounds on a given occasion; d (cricket) the side not batting; a member of this side, a fielder.

field (II.), vb. trans. & intrans., fr. prec. 1. trans. (in cricket, baseball &c.) To stop (ball) and return it. 2. intrans. To act as fielder.

field-allowance, n. (mil.) Officers' extra pay while on active service.

field-artillery, n. Light, movable artillery for use on campaign.

field-day, n. a (mil.) Day on which operations in the field are practised; b (fig.) day on which some noteworthy event takes place, or some interesting and notable action is performed.

fielder, n. [1. félder; 2. fīəldə]. (cricket &c.) One who fields.

fieldfare, n. [1. féldfār; 2. fīəldfɛə]. O.E., M.E. *feldefare*, fr. O.E. *feld*, 'field', q.v. It is doubtful whether second element is connected w. **fare (III.)**, 'to go'. A species of thrush of Northern Europe, visiting England in flocks in the winter.

field-glass, n. a Small portable binocular telescope; b the inner lens of a telescope or microscope.

field-grey, n. Germ. *feldgrau.* A greyish-green colour, as of the uniform of the German army in the Great War, corresponding to British khaki.

field-gun, n. Easily-moved cannon for use in the field, as distinct from siege guns and light horse artillery.

field-hospital, n. Temporary hospital on or near field of battle; dressing station.

field-ice, n. Large expanse of flat floating ice, as distinct from icebergs.

field-marshal, n. Highest rank in the British and some other armies.

field-mouse, n. Small variety of mouse living in the open; harvest-mouse.

field-officer, n. Commissioned army officer of the rank of major, lieutenant-colonel, or colonel.

field-piece, n. A field-gun.

field-preacher, n. Irregular evangelist who holds services in the open air.

fieldsman, n. [1. féldzman; 2. fīəldzmən]. One who fields, in cricket, baseball &c.

field-sports, n. a Those carried on in the open, esp. hunting, shooting, and fishing; b athletic sports, such as the high and broad jump, putting the weight &c., which are not held on the track as are the various races.

field-telegraph, -telephone, n. Portable telegraph, telephone, for use in the battle-field.

field-ward(s), adv. [1. féldward(z); 2. fīəldwəd(z)]. **field** & **-ward(s)**. Towards the fields.

fieldwork, n. [1. féldwĕrk; 2. fīəldwāk]. Temporary earthwork.

fiend, n. [1. fēnd; 2. fīnd]. O.E. *fēond*, 'enemy', lit. 'the hater'; M.E. *fēnd.* Cp. O.L.G. *fiond*, O. Fris. *fiand*, O.H.G. *fīant*, O.N. *fiandi*, Goth. *fijands*, fr. *fijan*, 'to hate'. The ending is that of Pres. Part.; fr. Gmc. **fī-*, 'to hate'; cp. O.E. *fēon*, Goth. *fijan*, O.N. *fia*, fr. Aryan base **pē(i)-*, **pī-*, 'to hate, harm', cogn. w. Goth. *faian*, 'to blame'; Gk. *pêma*, 'suffering', *pērós*, 'disabled'; Scrt. *pāpáś*, 'bad', *pīyati*, 'injures'. a An evil spirit, demon; specif., the Devil, as the Arch Enemy; b a person of intense wickedness, malice; c (journalese) one excessively devoted to some particular thing or habit &c.: *a fresh-air fiend*; *a drug-fiend.*

fiendish, adj. [1. féndish; 2. fíndiʃ]. Prec. & **-ish**. Like a fiend; intensely evil; cruel, malevolent.

fiendishly, adv. Prec. & **-ly**. In a fiendish manner.

fiendishness, n. See prec. & **-ness**. The quality of being fiendish.

fiendlike, adj. [1. féndlīk; 2. fíndlaik]. **fiend** & **-like**. Like a fiend.

fierce, adj. [1. fērs; 2. fiəs]. M.E. *fers, fiers*, fr. O. Fr. *fier(s)*, fr. Lat. *ferus*, 'wild, untamed; barbarous'. See **ferocious, feral.** 1. a (of living beings) Savage, wild, untamed; cruel; having or expressing a violent and fiery temper: *a fierce fighter, fierce dog, fierce expression of countenance*; b (of the elements &c.) wild, unrestrained, raging, violent: *a fierce tempest.* 2. Eager, intense, ardent, vehement: *fierce hatred*; *a fierce desire.*

fiercely, adv. Prec. & **-ly**. In a fierce manner.

fierceness, n. See prec. & **-ness**. The quality of being fierce.

fieri facias, n. [1. fíerī fásias; 2. fáiərai fǽsiæs]. Lat., 'cause it to be done'. abbr. *fi. fa.* Name of writ issued to a sheriff commanding him to see that satisfaction is made to one who has obtained judgement for a debt.

fierily, adv. [1. fíerili; 2. fáiərili]. **fiery** & **-ly**. In a fiery manner.

fieriness, n. [1. fíerines; 2. fáiərinis]. Next word & **-ness**. The quality of being fiery.

fiery, adj. [1. fíeri; 2. fáiəri]. **fire** & **-y**. 1. Made of, containing, fire; burning, flaming: *a fiery furnace.* 2. Resembling fire; a (to the sight) glowing, flaming, glaring: *a fiery sky*; *fiery eyes*; *fiery-red*; b (to the touch, taste) hot, burning, scorching: *fiery heat*; *fiery spirit*; *fiery taste.* 3. (fig.) a (of person or character) Eager, impetuous, hasty, passionate; easily roused, irritable, hasty, choleric: *a fiery disposition*; b (of expression of feeling) vehement, passionate, expressing keenness of emotion, enthusiastic, fervent: *a fiery speech*; c (of horses) spirited, mettlesome. Phr. *fiery steed*, spirited horse. 4. (min., of gas &c.) Inflammable, liable to explode.

fiery cross, n. Wooden cross with arms charred or dipped in blood, formerly sent among the members of a Highland clan as a call to arms.

fife (I.), n. [1. fīf; 2. faif], fr. Fr. *fifre*, 'piper, pipe', fr. O.H.G. *pfīfāri*, 'piper', fr. *pfīfa*, fr. Lat. *pīpa*, q.v. under **pipe**. **1.** A small, shrill, flute-like wind instrument used in military bands: *a drum and fife band*. **2.** A fife-player, fifer: *watch the drums and fifes march by*.

fife (II.), vb. trans. & intrans., fr. prec. Rare. **1.** trans. To play (a tune &c.) on the fife. **2.** intrans. To play the fife.

fifer, n. [1. fífer; 2. fáifə]. Prec. & **-er**. One who plays the fife.

fife-rail, n. Supposed to be so called as seat for a fifer who played while anchor was weighed. (naut.) Rail round the mainmast for holding belaying-pins &c.

fifteen, adj. & n. [1. fiftḗn; 2. fiftín]. O.E. *fīftēne*, M.E. *fīftēne*. **five** & **-teen**. **1.** adj. Cardinal number; five and ten, one more than fourteen. **2.** n. **a** A group of fifteen persons; esp. a Rugby football team; **b** *the Fifteen*, Jacobite insurrection in 1715.

fifteenth, adj. & n. [1. fiftḗnth; 2. fiftínþ]. Prec. & **-th**. **1.** adj. Following fourteen others in a series. **2.** n. **a** Fifteenth object &c. in a series; **b** one of fifteen equal parts.

fifth, adj. & n. [1. fifth; 2. fifþ]. O.E. *fīfta*, M.E. & Tudor Engl. *fifte* (later *fifþe*, by anal. w. **fourth** &c.). Cp. O. Fris. *fīfta*, O.H.G. *fimfto*, O.N. *fimte*; cogn. w. Gk. *pémptos*, 'fifth' (fr. **peŋkʷtos*); Lat. *quintus* (see **quint**); Lith. *peñktas*, O. Slav. *pętŭ*, Scrt. *pancathā́ś*, O. Ir. *cōiced*, fr. Aryan **peŋkʷ-*, 'five'. See **five**. **1.** adj. **a** Following four others in a series; Phrs. *fifth wheel*, extra wheel of vehicle, for support or emergency; hence, anything superfluous or rarely used; *fifth-monarchy men*, sect of fanatics in the middle of the 17th cent., who expected the immediate coming of Christ to establish a fifth universal empire; **b** forming one of five equal parts into which a thing is, or is considered as being, divided: *a fifth part*. **2.** n. **a** Fifth object &c. in a series; **b** one of five equal parts; **c** (mus.) an interval of five semitones; concord of two notes at this interval.

fifthly, adv. Prec. & **-ly**. In the fifth place.

fiftieth, adj. & n. [1. fíftieth; 2. fíftiiþ]. **fifty** & **-eth**. **1.** adj. **a** Following forty-nine others in a series; **b** forming one of fifty equal parts. **2.** n. **a** Fiftieth object, person &c. in a series; **b** a fiftieth part.

fifty, adj. & n. [1. fífti; 2. fífti]. O.E. *fīftiġ*, M.E. *fifti*. **five** & **-ty**. **1.** numeral adj. Five times ten. **2.** n. **a** The number equal to five times ten; symbol representing this number; **b** a group or set of fifty persons or things. Phrs. *the fifties*, the years fifty to fifty-nine inclusive in a century; *fifty-fifty* (colloq.), equal shares; *to go fifty-fifty with a person*, to share equally with, in losses &c.

fiftyfold, adj. & adv. [1. fíftifōld; 2. fíftifould]. Prec. & **-fold**. Multiplied by fifty.

fig (I.), n. [1. fig; 2. fig], fr. Fr. *figue*, fr. Low Lat. **fīca*, fr. Lat. *fīcus*, 'fig-tree, fig', wh., together w. Gk. *sûkon*, is prob. borrowed fr. some Mediterranean dialect. **a** A fruit shaped somewhat like a pear, with thick, juicy, green rind, sweet pulpy flesh full of seeds, eaten fresh or dried: *green figs*, fresh, ripe figs; *pulled figs*, dried Turkey figs; Phr. *I don't care a fig for . . .* (contemptuous) nothing at all; **b** tree bearing this fruit.

fig (II.), n., fr. **figure**. **a** Array, dress; Phr. *in full fig*, full dress; **b** condition, spirits: *to be in good fig*.

fig (III.), vb. trans., fr. prec. To dress up; give a fine appearance to, make handsome or elegant: *to fig out a horse, a person*.

fight (I.), vb. trans. & intrans. [1. fīt; 2. fait]. O.E. *feohtan*, M.E. *fehten*; cp. O. Fris. *fiuchta*, O.H.G. *fehtan*, 'fight'. The word is prob. cogn. w. Lat. *pecten*, 'comb', *pectere*, 'to comb'; Gk. *kteis*, genit. *ktenós* (fr. **pkten-*), 'a comb'; hence 'anything pointed, a rake, harrow' &c.; Aryan base **pektēn*, **pktēn*, 'a comb'; see **ctenoid**. The meaning seems to be generalized in Gmc. to 'anything pointed', & subsequently specialized to 'a weapon'; hence, the vb. **feχtan-*, 'to use weapons, to fight'. The Aryan base **pekten-* &c. is expanded fr. the base **pek̂-*, 'wool, hair'; fr. same base are Gk. *pékos*, 'fleece, wool', *pókos*, 'wool, lock or tuft of wool'; Scrt. *pakšman*, 'eyebrows, hair'; O.H.G. *fahs*, O.E. *feax*, 'hair'; O.N. *fax*, 'mane'. Cp. further Aryan base **peku-*, 'animal valued for its wool'; hence 'any domestic animal'; Lat. *pecus*, 'cattle'; Scrt. *páśu*, O.H.G. *fihu*, O.E. *feoh*, 'cattle', hence 'property, money'. See **pecuniary, peculiar**. **A.** trans. **1. a** To contend against bodily, with violence, by means of weapons; to attempt to kill, or render incapable of further resistance: *to fight the Germans*; *to fight a battle*, take part as a combatant in a battle; **b** to oppose by action or argument, contend hotly with, otherwise than by personal violence: *to fight the opposition candidate in an election*. Phr. *to fight it out*, fight (with weapons or arguments) until decision is reached. **2.** To defend, uphold, maintain, by fighting: *to fight a case*. Phrs. *fight one's way*, make advance possible by fighting those who oppose it; (fig.) *fight one's way in life, in the world* &c., contend with, and overcome, difficulties. **3.** To manage, guide, control, manœuvre, in battle: *to fight a ship*; *fight a gun*, fire it, or direct its fire, in battle. **4.** To cause to fight, set on to fight (cocks &c.). **B.** intrans. **1. a** To enter into a physical combat or contest; to engage in bodily struggle, contend in battle: *too proud to fight*; *the dogs are fighting*; Phrs. *to fight shy of*, to avoid, keep away, hold aloof from; *fight to a finish*, until a decision is reached; **b** to engage in wordy combat; offer opposition by argument &c.; to enter into dispute. **C.** Followed by adverbs and prepositions. *Fight against, with*, to strive, struggle, contend, against; strive to overcome: *to fight with an opponent*; *fight against overwhelming odds*; *to fight against temptation*; *fight with the temptation to* &c. *Fight off*, to drive off, repel, expel, by fighting.

fight (II.), n. O.E. *ġefeoht*, M.E. *fiht* &c. See prec. **1.** The act of fighting; specif. **a** contest, physical struggle, combat, with weapons or fists, between two persons or parties or between two or more armed ships; a battle; a struggle with teeth, claws, hoofs &c. between animals: *fights by land and sea*; *a dog fight*; *prize fight*, pugilistic contest; Phrs. *a free fight*, confused struggle with no well-defined sides; *to put up a good fight*, to fight with spirit and courage; **b** a contest of argument; a vigorous attempt to carry one's point, realize one's aims &c. against opposition: *the bill was passed after a stubborn fight in the House*. **2.** Capacity, spirit, inclination, to fight; pugnacity, fighting spirit: *to have plenty of fight left in one*. Phr. *to show fight*, give proof of readiness to fight.

fighter, n. [1. fíter; 2. fáitə]. **fight** (I.) & **-er**. One who fights; one who is able, inclined, eager, to fight.

fighting, adj. [1. fíting; 2. fáitiŋ], fr. Pres. Part. of **fight** (I.). **a** Able, ready, to fight; accustomed, inclined, to fight: *to come of a fighting family*; **b** pertaining to, suitable for, fight: *fighting qualities*. Phr. *a fighting chance*, an opportunity for, possibility of, success after, a struggle.

fighting-cock, n. A game-cock trained to fight. Phrs. *to live like a fighting-cock*, live on luxurious food; *feel like a fighting-cock*, feel fit, in good condition.

fighting-men, n. Soldiers.

fig-leaf, n. **1.** The leaf of the fig tree. **2.** (fig.) Device for hiding what is indecorous; from use in classical statues, also with allusion to Adam and Eve.

figment, n. [1. fígment; 2. fígmənt], fr. L. Lat. *figment-(um)*, 'formation; a figure, image; a fiction'. Cp. Lat. *figūra*, 'something made; figure, shape'. See **figure** & **-ment**. **1.** Something invented, feigned; fictitious statement. **2.** Something imaginary, lacking reality and substance; a creation of the imagination: *a figment of the mind*.

fig tree, n. A tree that bears figs.

figurant(e) (I.), n. [1. fígūrant; 2. fígjurənt], fr. Fr. *figurant(e)*. A ballet-dancer, male or female.

figurante (II.), n., pl. **-i** [1. figūránte, -ē; 2. figjurǽnti, -ī], fr. Ital. *figurante*. Figurant.

figuration, n. [1. figūráshun; 2. figjuréiʃən], fr. Fr., fr. Lat. *figūrātiōn-(em)*, 'shape, form; imagination, fancy; figurative mode of speaking'. See **figure** (I.) & **-ation**. **1. a** The act of forming, shaping, fashioning, giving shape to; **b** the act of marking or ornamenting with figures. **2.** Appearance given by shaping; form, fashion, conformation.

figurative, adj. [1. fígūrativ; 2. fígjurətiv], fr. L. Lat. *figūrātīv-(us)*, 'pertaining to the figurative mode of speaking', fr. *figūrāt-(um)*, P.P. of *figūrāre*, 'to fashion, shape; to imagine, picture; to adorn with figurative language', fr. *figūra*, 'form, shape; quality, kind; figure of speech'. See **figure** (I.) & **-ive**. **1. a** Not literal; having a symbolical meaning; metaphorical: *the figurative use of a word*; *in a figurative sense*; **b** (of speech, writing &c.) adorned by, abounding in, figures of speech: *a figurative style*; **c** (of person) given to using figures of speech: *a figurative writer*. **2.** Representing an idea by means of a symbol; emblematic, symbolic, typical: *a figurative design, object* &c. **3.** Pertaining to pictorial or plastic representation of form or figure: *figurative art*.

figuratively, adv. Prec. & **-ly**. In a figurative manner; metaphorically.

figurativeness, n. See prec. & **-ness**. The quality of being figurative.

figure (I.), n. [1. fíger; 2. fígə], fr. Lat. *figūra*, 'form, shape; nature, kind, species; figure of speech'; cp. Lat. *fingere*, 'to shape, form' (see **feign, fictile, fiction**), *figulus*, 'a potter', *fīlum* (fr. **figslom*), 'form, outward shape'; Aryan base **dheigh-*, **dhoigh-*, **dhigh-*, 'to form out of clay, to model, mould; to shape, form'. See further derivatives fr. this under **dough**. **1.** Human form; specif. **a** considered with regard to shape, outline, proportions: *a bad, good, handsome, figure*; Phr. *a fine figure of a man*, a man of well-developed figure; **b** a person having a fine, stately form and bearing: *he made an imposing figure in the procession*. **2. a** Person's appearance on a particular occasion; Phr. *to cut a poor figure*, make an undistinguished, ignominious appearance, impression; **b** a person considered in the light of the effect produced by his actions and career, personality, influence: *one of the great figures of his age*. **3.** Representation, esp. of human figure; **a** carved or moulded representation of human or animal form: *a figure of an apostle in a niche*; the *figure of fun*, person of ludicrous appearance; **b** pictorial representation, image, of human or other figure &c.: *a wall decorated with figures of cupids, birds, flowers*. **4. a** Device, artistic decoration, design, tracery &c.; carved ornamentation; **b** representation, illustration, of some object, esp. in a book; diagram. **5. a** (rhet.) Imaginative, metaphorical, phrase or expression; also *figure of speech*; **b** (gram.) deviation from ordinary usage for the sake of ornament, e.g. *pleonasm, zeugma*. **6. a** Graphic symbol, esp. one representing a number; **b** specif., figure cut on ice by skater. **7.** Number, amount, thought of as represented in figures: *to buy at a high, low, figure*. **8.** (pl.) The art of dealing with numbers; arithmetic: *to be a poor hand at figures*. **9.** Specif. uses: **a** (astrol.) a horoscope; **b** (dancing) part of a square or country-dance, distinguished by a specific series of steps and movements; **c** (log.) form of the syllogism; **d** (mus.) short series of notes or chords which produce the effect of a unity.

figure (II.), vb. trans. & intrans., fr. prec. **A.** trans. **a** To represent in concrete form, as a picture, model, image &c.; to depict, give form to, delineate, portray; **b** to represent mentally, imagine, fancy, form in the mind: *to figure something to oneself*; **c** (mus.) to indicate the accompanying chords, by writing the figures, under or over the bars: *figured bass*. **B.** intrans. **1.** To play part, be prominent, appear: *to figure largely in an account, a narrative* &c.; *to figure as a king in a pageant*. **2.** To make calculations, compute, reckon; do arithmetic. **C.** Followed by adverbs. *Figure out*, **a** to calculate arithmetically, to arrive at a result by arithmetical calculation; **b** think out, excogitate. *Figure up* (rare), to calculate, compute, add, reckon up.

figured, adj. [1. fígerd; 2. fígəd]. **figure (I.)** & **-ed.** **1.** Marked, engraved, printed, adorned, with a pattern, design: *figured silk*. **2.** Figurative. **3.** (her.) Of bearings, depicted with a human face.

figure-dance, n. A dance with complicated figures and evolutions.

figure-head, n. **1. a** Carved representation of human or other figure or of a head alone, placed so as to project as ornament from bow of ship, below bowsprit, generally symbolizing name of this; **b** hence (facet.), a person's face. **2.** (fig.) Nominal head or leader with no real authority or influence; one chosen to fill a position on account of his name, rank, appearance, or some quality other than intellectual ability.

figurine, n. [1. fígūrēn; 2. fígjurīn], fr. Fr., fr. Ital. *figurina*, dimin. of *figūra*, 'a figure'. See **figure (I.)**. A small figure or group modelled in terra-cotta &c.; statuette.

filament, n. [1. fílament; 2. fíləmənt], fr. L. Lat. *fīlā-(re)*, 'to spin', fr. *fīl-(um)*, 'thread'. See **file (III.)** & **-ment.** A fine, slender thread or thread-like structure, fibre; specif. **a** (bot.) the thread-like part of the stamen of a flower; **b** fine, metallic thread of high electric resistance used to produce light in electric lamp bulbs and to give off electrons in wireless valves.

filamentary, adj. [1. filaméntari; 2. filəméntəri]. Prec. & **-ary.** Made of, resembling, a filament; furnished with filaments.

filamented, adj. [1. fílamented; 2. fíləmentid]. **filament** & **-ed.** Supplied with filaments.

filamentous, adj. [1. filaméntus; 2. filəméntəs]. **filament** & **-ous.** Thread-like.

Filaria, n., pl. **Filariae** [1. filária, -ē; 2. filéəriə, -ī]. Neo-Lat., fr. Lat. *fīl-(um)*, 'thread'. See prec. words & **file (III.)**. (zool.) The name of a genus or group of thread-like parasitic worms, injected into the blood of animals or men by the agency of mosquitoes and causing such diseases as elephantiasis &c.

filariasis, n. [1. filaríasis; 2. filəráiəsis]. Prec. & **-asis.** (pathol.) Name of diseases caused by Filaria.

filature, n. [1. fílachur; 2. fílətʃə], fr. Fr., fr. L. Lat. *fīlāt-(um)*, P.P. type of *fīlāre*, 'to spin', see **filament** & **-ure.** **1.** The process of reeling off raw silk from cocoons. **2.** A machine or establishment for this process.

filbert, n. [1. fílbert; 2. fílbət], fr. Fr. *noix de Filbert*, 'nut of St. Philibert'. **a** The edible nut of the cultivated hazel; **b** the hazel tree.

filch, vb. trans. [1. filch; 2. filtʃ]. Etymol. unknown. To steal, pilfer.

file (I.), n. [1. fīl; 2. fail]. O.E. *fēol, fīl*, M.E. *file*. Cp. O.H.G. *fīla, fīhala*, Du. *vijl*. Prob. cogn. w. Gk. *poikílos*, 'variegated, embroidered, inlaid'; Scrt. *piṣā́ti*, 'to adorn; to cut'; Lith. *pëiszù*, 'to engrave, write'; O.E. *fāh*, 'variegated'. Aryan base **peik̑-, *poik̑-, *pik̑-*, 'to adorn, whether by painting or carving'; hence, on the one hand, 'to colour', on the other, 'to cut, carve, chisel'. Cp. the similar base **peig-* (with the same meaning as **peik̑-*), whence Lat. *pingere*, 'to paint, embroider'. See **picture**, also **pigment, finch, picric.** **1.** Tool of hard steel with rough, serrated, grating surface, used for smoothing roughness on metal surface, and for cutting through metal bands, rings &c. by grating. **2.** (fig.) That which smooths, polishes, or perfects, esp. of literary work: *it needs the file*. **3.** (vulg.) A person, esp. one who is shrewd, cunning, artful.

file (II.), vb. trans., fr. prec. **1.** To use a file upon; to smooth or cut through with a file. Hence, **2.** (fig.) To polish, remove defects from (literary style, compositions &c.).

file (III.), n., fr. Fr. *fil*, fr. Lat. *fīlum*, 'thread'. Prob. fr. Aryan **ghinslo-*, whence also Lith. *gìsla*, O. Prussian *gislo*, O. Slav. *žila*, 'vein'. It is possible that Lat. *fūnis*, 'rope, line, cord', is fr. another form of same base, w. different suff. See **funicular.** **1. a** Device for threading or transfixing papers, so as to keep them together; **b** also, generally, any method of keeping documents in classified order for convenient and easy reference. **2.** Collection of papers, cards for reference, and other documents kept in or on a file.

file (IV.), vb. trans., fr. prec. **a** To arrange letters, papers &c. systematically in a file; **b** specif., to place documents among others in a public record office.

file (V.), n., fr. next word. **1.** (mil.) A front-rank man and the corresponding rear-rank man. Phrs. *blank file*, with no rear-rank; *a file of men*, a file detached for some special purpose; *to march in file*, in double columns; *half a file*, one man; *single, Indian, file*, one behind the other in single line; *rank and file*, **a** privates and corporals; **b** (fig.) ordinary people, as distinct from those of distinction or importance. **2. a** A row of persons or objects one behind another; **b** (chess) single row of squares forming a vertical line across the board.

file (VI.), vb. intrans. & trans., fr. Fr. *filer*, fr. L. Lat. *fīlāre*, fr. Lat. *fīl-(um)*, 'thread'. See **file (III.)**. **1.** intrans. To march, move, in file; esp. *to file in, file out*, (of several persons) to enter or quit a building, assembly &c. one after another; *to file away, off*, march off in file. **2.** trans. To cause, order, to move in files.

file-fish, n. A tropical sea-fish, with rough prickles instead of scales and a file-like dorsal fin; one kind is known as the trigger fish.

filemot, adj. & n. [1. fílemot; 2. fílimət], fr. Fr. *feuille morte*, 'dead leaf'. **1.** adj. Of the colour of a faded leaf, yellowish-brown. **2.** n. Dead-leaf colour.

filial, adj. [1. fílyal; 2. filjəl], fr. L. Lat. *fīliāl-(is)*, 'filial', fr. Lat. *fīli-(us)*, 'a son', & **-al.** *Fīlius* (fr. **fēlios*), orig. 'a suckling', is cogn. w. *fēlāre*, 'to suck'; cp. Gk. *thēlḗ*, 'breast'; Scrt. *dhārú-š*, 'sucking'; Lith. *dėlė̃*, 'leech'; Lett. *dīlit*, 'to suck'. Aryan base **dhēi-l-, *dhi-l-*, expanded fr. the base **dhēi-, *dhi-, *dhəi-*, 'to suck'. See **feminine.** Pertaining to a son or daughter; becoming, suitable to, due from, a son or daughter: *filial obedience*.

filially, adv. Prec. & **-ly.** In a filial manner.

filiate. See **affiliate.**

filiation, n. [1. filiáshun; 2. filiéiʃən], fr. Fr., fr. Med. Lat. *fīliātiōn-(em)*, fr. *fīliāre*, 'to give birth to'. See **filial.** **1. a** The state of being a child; filial relation; **b** the state of being a descendant; descent from. **2.** The formation, adoption, of new branch of a society &c.; affiliation.

filibeg, philibeg, n. [1. fílibeg; 2. fílibɛg], fr. Gael. *feileadh beag*, 'small fold'. The kilt.

filibuster (I.), n. [1. fílibuster; 2. fílibastə], fr. Span. *filibustero*, form of Du. *vrijbuiter*. See **freebooter.** **1.** An irregular combatant against a foreign state; a pirate, freebooter. **2.** (polit. slang, U.S.A.) **a** A member of a legislative chamber who deliberately obstructs business by talking &c. in order to defeat a bill; **b** instance of such political obstruction.

filibuster (II.), vb. intrans., fr. prec. To act as a filibuster, in both meanings of the word.

Filicales, n. pl. [1. filikálēz; 2. filikéiliz]. Neo-Lat., fr. Lat. *filic-(em), filix*, 'fern', etymol. doubtful, & **-al.** (bot.) The order of Pteridophyta which includes the true ferns, as distinguished from the horsetails and lycopods.

filigree, n. [1. fíligrē; 2. filigrī], fr. Fr. *filigrane*, fr. Ital. *filigrana*, fr. Lat. *fīl-(um)*, 'thread', see **file (III.)**, & *grān-(um)*, 'grain', see **grain.** **1. a** Ornamental, lace-like tracery of gold or silver wire; **b** any fine metal openwork; anything resembling this in form or device. **2.** A frail, delicate, creation of the mind.

filigreed, adj. [1. filigrēd; 2. filigrīd]. Prec. & **-ed.** Adorned with filigree.

filing, n. [1. fíling; 2. fáiliŋ]. **file (II.)** & **-ing.** Particle of metal removed with a file.

fill (I.), vb. trans. & intrans. [1. fil; 2. fil]. O.E. *fyllan*, M.E. *fillen*. Cp. O.N. *fylla*, O. Fris. *fella*, Goth. *fulljan*, fr. Gmc. **full-*, 'full'. See **full (I.)**. **A.** trans. **1. a** To put into (a vessel or enclosed space) as much of something as it will conveniently contain or is intended to hold; to put in a considerable amount, supply, of something: *to fill a cup*; *to fill a room with books*; *to fill a church with people*; *pockets filled with money*; **b** to put, pour, into, (something) as much as it can contain; to pack, stuff, cram, to utmost capacity; to cause whole space of to be occupied: *to fill a glass with water, a box with books* &c. **2.** In various figurative uses: **a** (mental) To acquire or impart, information, knowledge: *to fill one's mind*; **b** to cause to become full; to instil into; imbue: *to fill one's heart with hope*; *to fill one with dismay*. **3.** To occupy, be in, a space; pervade; **a** (of material substances) *smoke filled the room*; *the rail exactly filled the gap in the fence*; **b** (of non-material things) *an idea fills one's mind to the exclusion of everything else*; *sorrow fills one's heart*. **4. a** To occupy a place, position: *he fills the office satisfactorily*; **b** to put a person into, appoint him to, a position, post, office &c.: *to fill an office*; *his place will not be easily filled*. **B.** intrans. To become full; **a** (of material things) *the church filled rapidly*; *the cistern is empty but will soon fill again*; *the sails filled with wind*; **b** (of non-material process) *my heart fills with pleasure*. **C.** Followed by various adverbs. *Fill in*, trans., **a** to add, insert, something lacking in a document &c.: *to fill in one's name, a date* &c.; **b** to fill up, fill completely (a hollow, excavation &c.). *Fill out*, trans., **a** to become enlarged to normal or required limit, expand, be distended: *the balloon filled out as the gas was pumped into it*; **b** to become fat, put on flesh: *his cheeks have filled out since I last saw him*. *Fill up*, **1.** trans., **a** to fill completely, make full: *to fill up one's cup*; **b** to make too full, encumber, crowd: *to fill up one's room with furniture*. Phr. *to fill up an official form*, to complete by making necessary additions, by inserting particulars in spaces left for the purpose. **2.** intrans. To become full: *the theatre filled up rapidly*.

fill (II.), n., fr. O.E. *fyllo*, M.E. *fille*; cp. O.H.G. *fullī*, Goth. *fullei*, fr. Gmc. **ful-*, 'full'. See **full (I.)**. **1. a** (of material things) That which fills, satisfies; a full supply; as much as is required: *to eat, drink, one's fill*; **b** (of non-material things) a considerable amount, abundant supply, full allowance: *to weep one's fill*; *to have one's fill of sorrow*. **2.** That which fills a given space: *a fill of tobacco*, as much as fills a pipe.

fille de chambre, n. [1. féi' d' shómbr; 2. fīj də ʃɑ̃br]. Fr. Chambermaid.

fille de joie, n. [1. féi' d' zhwah; 2. fīj də žwā]. Fr., lit. 'daughter of joy'. Disreputable woman; prostitute.

fillet (I.), n. [1. filet; 2. filit], fr. Fr. *filet*, fr. Lat. *fīl-(um)*, 'thread', see **file (III.)** & **-et.** A narrow band, strip; esp. narrow band for encircling the head, or binding the hair. Various specific uses: **a** Thick slice of meat, esp. cut from under part of sirloin of beef, or from thick part of leg of veal or mutton; **b** flat slice of fish, cut lengthwise and without bone; **c** (archit.) narrow band between two mouldings; narrow flat strip separating two flutes of a column; **d** (her.) narrow horizontal band across base of the chief and occupying a fourth of its width.

fillet (II.), vb. trans., fr. prec. **1.** To bind with a fillet. **2.** To remove bones of a fish and cut it into slices before cooking.

filling, n. [1. fíling; 2. fíliŋ]. **fill (I.)** & **-ing.** That which is used to fill something; specif. (dentist's word) gold &c. used to stop a tooth.

fillip (I.), n. [1. fílip; 2. fílip]. Prob. imitative. **1. a** Sharp jerk, or flip, made by a finger when released suddenly from being tightly pressed by the thumb; **b** light blow given by finger thus released. **2.** Slight mental or physical stimulus; spur, incentive, tonic: *a fillip to the memory; champagne gives a useful fillip on occasion.* **3.** Trifle, thing of no importance.

fillip (II.), vb. trans. & intrans., fr. prec. **1.** trans. **a** To give a fillip to, strike as by a fillip; **b** to drive along, cause to move, by a fillip; **c** to stimulate, rouse, urge to action. **2.** intrans. To make a fillip.

fillister, n. [1. fílister; 2. fílistə]. Etymol. unknown. **a** A kind of plane for grooving; **b** a groove on outer edge of window-sash.

filly, n. [1. fíli; 2. fíli]. Prob. fr. O.N. *fylja*, fr. Gmc. **ful-jō*, fem. of **ful-*, 'foal'. See **foal.** **1.** Female foal, young mare, corresponding to male *colt.* **2.** A lively young girl.

film (I.), n. [1. film; 2. film], fr. O.E. *filmen*, 'membrane'; M.E. *filme*; cogn. w. Gk. *pélma*, 'sole of foot or shoe'; Aryan base **pel-m-*, 'skin'; cp. (fr. **pel-n-*) Lat. *pellis*, 'skin, hide'; see **pellicle**; O.H.G. *fel*, O.E. *fell*, 'skin', see **fell (I.).** **1.** A fine, thin, delicate layer, skin, coating: *a film of oil, glaze, dust.* Phr. *eyes covered with the film of death*, having lost natural brightness and appearing to be covered with a film. **2.** Fine, delicate filament: *a film of gossamer.* **3.** (photog.) Flexible sheet of gelatine or similar material made to roll, with sensitized surface upon which the photograph is taken; the film thus becomes the negative; esp. used in cinematography; hence, *the films*, a cinema show, the pictures &c.; also attrib.: *a film play, film actor* &c.

film (II.), vb. intrans. & trans., fr. prec. **A.** intrans. *film over*, to become covered with a film. **B.** trans. **1.** To cover with a film. **2.** (photog.) To reproduce on a film; take a photograph of; esp. to take series of instantaneous photographs of, for cinematograph.

filminess, n. [1. fílmines; 2. fílminis]. Next word & **-ness.** The quality of being filmy.

filmy, adj. [1. fílmi; 2. fílmi]. **film (I.)** & **-y.** Like a film in structure or appearance; thin, gauzy, delicate: *filmy clouds; a filmy veil.*

filoselle, n. [1. filosél; 2. filɔsél]. Fr., fr. Ital. *filosello*; cp. Lat. *fīlum*, 'thread', q.v. under **file (III.).** A kind of floss-silk.

fils, n. [1. fēs; 2. fis]. Fr., fr. Lat. *fīlius*, 'a son'. See **filial.** Son (used after name to distinguish father from son): *Dumas fils.*

filter (I.), n. [1. fílter; 2. fíltə], fr. O. Fr. *filtre*, fr. Med. Lat. *filtrum, feltrum*, 'a strainer'. Same word as **felt (I.)**, this substance being used for straining liquids. **1. a** A device, machine, for straining impurities out of liquids; **b** specif., device for straining, purifying, clarifying, water. **2.** Porous substance, such as charcoal, gravel &c., which acts as a filter.

filter (II.), vb. trans. & intrans., fr. prec. **1.** trans. **a** To strain liquid, pass it through a filter; **b** (of filter itself) to eliminate impurities from. **2.** intrans. **a** Often, *filter through*, to pass through, flow as through a filter; to percolate: *to filter through the sand*; **b** (fig., of news, rumours &c.) to become known, leak out.

filterable, adj. [1. fílterabl; 2. fíltərəbl]. Prec. & **-able.** Capable of being filtered; able to pass or percolate through a filter.

filter-bed, n. Reservoir with artificially constructed bottom of sand, gravel, or other porous substance for filtering water, sewage &c.

filter-paper, n. Porous kind of paper used as a filter, esp. in chemistry.

filth, n. [1. filth; 2. filþ]. O.E. *fȳlð*, M.E. *filþe* &c.; O.H.G. *fūlida*, fr. Gmc. **fūl-*, 'foul' (see **foul**) & suff. *-iþa.* See **-th. a** Anything filthy; substance that defiles in a disgusting manner; nasty and revolting dirt; **b** (fig.) moral impurity or defilement; obscenity, corruption.

filthily, adv. [1. fílthili; 2. fílþili]. **filthy** & **-ly.** In a filthy manner.

filthiness, n. [1. fílthines; 2. fílþinis]. Next word & **-ness.** The state or quality of being filthy; something physically or morally filthy; defilement, filth.

filthy, adj. [1. fílthi; 2. fílþi]. **filth** & **-y. a** Of the nature of, full of, covered with, filth; foul, unclean, loathsome; **b** (in moral sense) impure, obscene, corrupt.

filtrate (I.), vb. trans. & intrans. [1. fíltrāt; 2. fíltreit]. **filter (I.)** & **-ate.** To filter.

filtrate (II.), n. See prec. Liquid obtained by filtering.

filtration, n. [1. filtráshun; 2. filtréiʃən]. **filtrate (I.)** & **-ion.** The act or process of filtering; percolation.

fimbriate(d), adj. [1. fímbriāt(ed); 2. fímbrieit(id)], fr. Lat. *fimbria*, 'thread, fibre, fringe', & **-ate** & **-ed.** Possibly fr. **find-sriā*, 'something split up', fr. *findere*, 'to split'. See **fissile** & cp. **fringe. 1.** (bot., zool.) With a border or fringe of fibre, hairs &c. **2.** (her.) An ordinary having a narrow border of a different tincture (colour) is said to be fimbriated.

fin, n. [1. fin; 2. fin]. O.E. *finn*, M.E. *finne.* Cp. M. Du. *vinne.* Prob. fr. Aryan **pid-na*, 'something pointed'; cp. Lat. *pinna* (fr. **pid-(s)nā*), 'a pinnacle; fin'; Aryan base **(s)pid-, *(s)pit-*, 'a point, spike'. See **spica** & words there referred to. **1. a** One of several flat membranous projections from the body of a fish, used for balancing, steering, and propelling; **b** similar organ in cetaceans; **c** a small, vertical device resembling the fin of a fish attached to parts of aircraft to secure stability. **2.** (slang) Hand. Phr. *tip, give, us your fin*, shake hands.

finable, adj. [1. fínabl; 2. fáinəbl]. **fine (II.)** & **-able.** Capable of being fined; liable to a fine.

final (I.), adj. [1. fínl; 2. fáinl], fr. Fr., fr. Lat. *fīnāl-(is)*, 'final', fr. Lat. *fīn-(is)*, 'limit, boundary; end, extremity'. See **finis** & **-al. 1.** Pertaining to the end, at the end; last, concluding: *the final chapter of a book.* **2.** Conclusive, decisive, determining; admitting of no further argument: *my decision is quite final; a final issue, judgement* &c. **3.** *Final cause*, the ultimate cause, starting-point, agency which initiates.

final (II.), n., fr. prec. Something that is final; concluding act or event of a series: **a** university examination for degree: *the law final*; **b** (also pl.) *to run, play, in the finals*, last heat of a race, decisive set or game in a match &c.

finale, n. [1. fináhle; 2. fināli], fr. Ital., fr. Lat., dat. sing. of *fīnālis*, 'last, concluding'. See prec. **1.** (mus.) Last movement of a symphony, sonata &c.; concluding number of an act of an opera. **2.** That which concludes, winds up, a work, series of acts &c.

finalist, n. [1. fínalist; 2. fáinəlist]. **final (II.)** & **-ist.** Competitor who is in the finals of a race, game &c.

finality, n. [1. fínáliti; 2. fainǽliti], fr. Fr., fr. L. Lat. *fīnālitāt-(em)*, 'the state of being final'. **final (I.)** & **-ity. 1.** The state or quality of being final, settled, complete; conclusiveness, completeness: *to speak with finality; to claim finality for a statement, conclusion, theory.* Phr. *an air of finality*, one which gives the impression that everything is settled, that there is nothing more to be said, no further appeal. **2.** Something that is final; a final, conclusive, finishing, action, statement, arrangement &c.

finally, adv. [1. fínali; 2. fáinəli]. **final (I.)** & **-ly. 1.** Lastly, in conclusion; in, at, the end: *finally, I have to say a few words on . . .* **2.** Completely, irrevocably: *the matter is finally settled.*

finance (I.), n. [1. fínáns, fináns; 2. fainǽns, finǽns], fr. O. Fr. *fin-(er)*, 'to settle a debt, dispute', fr. *fin*, 'end, settlement'. See **fine (I.)** & **-ance. 1.** The science and methods of the raising and control of public revenue and expenditure; the management of money affairs: *a student of finance; a system of finance*; (also attrib.) *Finance Act*, the act putting in force the budget of the year. **2.** (pl.) Revenue, pecuniary resources, funds: *the finances of the country, of a person* &c.

finance (II.), vb. trans. & intrans., fr. prec. **1.** trans. To furnish, supply, funds for; provide capital for: *to finance a commercial undertaking, an exploring expedition; to finance a young man at the university.* **2.** intrans. (rare) To engage in financial affairs, deal in finance.

financial, adj. [1. fínánshal, finánshal; 2. fainǽnʃəl, finǽnʃəl]. **finance (I.)** & **-ial.** Pertaining to finance, money matters, revenue: *financial year*, period of one year at the end of which the public accounts are balanced.

financially, adv. Prec. & **-ly.** In a financial manner; as regards finance.

financier (I.), n. [1. fínánsier, finánsier; 2. fainǽnsiə, finǽnsiə]. **finance** & **-ier. 1.** One who is skilled in the raising and control of public money, or in the theory of revenue. **2.** One who engages in important operations involving finance.

financier (II.), vb. intrans. [1. fínansḗr, finansḗr; 2. fàinænsíə, finænsíə], fr. prec. (rare) To engage in financial operations, act as a financier.

finback, n. [1. fínbak; 2. fínbæk]. A species of whale, the rorqual.

finch, n. [1. finch; 2. fin(t)ʃ]. O.E. *finc*, M.E. *finch.* Cp. O.H.G. *finco.* Prob. (w. the meaning 'brightly coloured') cogn. w. Lat. *pingere*, 'to paint' (see **picture**); Gk. *piggalos*, 'a lizard'; Scrt. *pinjáraš*, 'reddish-yellow', *piŋgaš*, 'reddish-brown'; w. infixed *-n-* fr. Aryan base **peig-, *pig-*; also **peiǩ-, *piǩ-*, 'to adorn by painting or engraving' (see **pigment, file (I.)**). One of various species of small passerine seed-eating birds, family *Fringillidae.* See **goldfinch, chaffinch, greenfinch, bullfinch** &c.

find (I.), vb. trans. & intrans. [1. fīnd; 2. faind]. O.E. *findan*, M.E. *finden.* Cp. O.L.G., O.H.G. *findan*, O.N. *finna*, Goth. *finþan.* The orig. meaning was 'to come upon, come up to'; Aryan base **pent-, *pn̥t-*, 'to come, go'. Cp. Scrt. *pánthāš*, 'path, way'; Gk. *patéō*, 'I step', *pátos* (fr. **pn̥t-*), 'path, step'; O. Prussian *pintis*, 'road'; Lat. *pontem*, 'bridge' (see **pons**); Gk. *póntos*, 'open sea'; O.H.G. *funden*, 'to hasten', *fendo*, 'pedestrian'. **A.** trans. **1.** To discover as result of deliberate search; **a** to discover for the first time: *after months of digging they found very little gold*; **b** to come upon, recover, regain possession of, something which has been lost: *I can't find my knife anywhere.* Phrs. *to find one's way*, discover which way to go; *to find one's way home in time for dinner*, to go, reach, home; *rivers find their way to the sea* &c., go, get to; *to find one's place*, (in a book) turn to the required page &c.; *to find Christ*, become convinced by spiritual experience of the truth of Christianity; *to find oneself*, discover one's real ideals, bent, walk in life &c.; *I could find it in my heart to . . .*, I am inclined to. **2.** To learn, discover, become informed of, a fact by experience: *to find reading tedious; to find lobster indigestible; to find the night air pleasant; I hope you found your bed comfortable; to find a house in a filthy state; to find that one was mistaken.* **3.** To discover, invent, produce, as result of mental activity: *to find nothing new to say.* **4. a** To provide: *to find the money for a commercial undertaking; forty pounds a year and all found*; **b** to provide, furnish, equip with: *to find one's son with everything requisite for farming abroad; the house was well found in plate and linen*; **c** to equip mentally, instruct in: *to be well found in classical learning.* **5.** (law) To judge, consider as a result of deliberation: *to find a prisoner guilty, that the deceased had been murdered by a person unknown.* **B.** intrans.

1. (law) To come to a certain legal decision, return a verdict: *the jury found for the plaintiff.* **2.** (hunting) To discover game.

find (**II.**), n., fr. prec. Something found; a discovery, esp. a valuable or gratifying discovery: *I had made a great find in an old book shop yesterday; this hotel is a regular find.*

findable, adj. [1. findabl; 2. fáindəbl]. **find** (**I.**) & **-able.** Capable of being found.

finder, n. [1. finder; 2. fáində]. **find** (**I.**) & **-er.** One who, that which, finds; specif. **a** a lens on the outside of a camera for finding position of object to be photographed; **b** small telescope attached to larger one for finding position of object of observation.

fin de siècle, adj. [1. fán d' syékl; 2. fæ̃ də sjɛkḷ]. Fr., 'end of the century'. (of persons, ideas, conduct, works of art &c.) Belonging to, typical of, the end of the 19th cent.; said in reference to anything considered especially advanced, or progressive, at that date; hence often, cynical; devoid of the old-fashioned ideals and principles, lacking belief in traditional codes of morality &c.

finding, n. [1. finding; 2. fáindiŋ]. **find** (**I.**) & **-ing.** (law) Conclusion arrived at by court of justice, by a judge or jury.

fine (**I.**), n. [1. fin; 2. fain]. M.E. *fīn(e)*, fr. O. Fr. *fin*, 'end; settlement', fr. Lat. *fīnis*, 'limit, boundary; end; extremity'. See **finis.** End, conclusion; only in Phr. *in fine*, finally, in conclusion, in short.

fine (**II.**), n. Same word as prec. **1.** Sum of money demanded by legal authority as a penalty for an offence which, when paid, settles the matter. **2. a** Sum paid to the king or other feudal lord by holder of land; an alienation; **b** payment made to lessor on renewal of a lease; *fine and recovery*, old fictitious action for conveyance of land.

fine (**III.**), vb. trans. & intrans., fr. prec. To exact a fine from, punish by a fine: *to fine a person half a crown.*

fine (**IV.**), adj., fr. Fr. *fin*, fr. Romance *fino*; etymol. doubtful; perh. a back-formation fr. Lat. *fīnīre*, 'to finish' (see **finish**); Germ. *fein* is fr. Romance. **1. a** Slender, thin, delicate: *fine thread, wire* &c.; **b** of slender proportions: *a fine ankle.* **2. a** Sharp, keen, thin: *a fine edge; a fine point*; **b** having a fine point or edge: *a fine pen.* **3.** Minute, consisting of very small particles: *fine rain, dust, flour, powder* &c. **4.** (of gas &c.) Rare, not dense. **5.** Of delicate texture: *fine linen, lace* &c.; *a fine skin.* **6.** Free from impurities, refined: *fine gold* &c.; (also of coinage) having a stated proportion of pure gold &c. in it. **7.** Healthy, bracing, salubrious: *fine climate, air* &c. **8.** (of weather) **a** Bright, clear, pleasant; **b** free from rain, temporarily not raining. Phrs. *one, some, fine day; one of these fine days*, at some indefinite date. **9.** Large, extensive, striking, imposing: *a fine view; a fine expanse of ocean.* **10. a** (of persons, or the human form) Well-developed, large, of striking proportions: *a fine woman; a fine child for his age; a fine head and shoulders*; **b** (of animals and animal products) well-grown, in good condition, perfect: *a fine bullock, goose,* &c.; *a fine tiger-skin; a fine ham; a fine pair of horns*; **c** (of plants and vegetable products) large, well-grown; without blemish; well-proportioned: *a fine cedar, sweet-pea* &c.; *fine tomatoes.* **11. a** Good of its kind, excellent, desirable, above the average: *a fine specimen; a fine example of early printing*; **b** (colloq.) thoroughly satisfactory: *to have a fine time; a poker makes a fine weapon against a burglar; it will be a fine thing for him*; (often ironically) *to lead a person a fine dance; that's a fine excuse!*, a very poor one. **12.** Perfect, finished, well-trained, artistic; **a** (of person): *a fine performer*; **b** (of mode of expression): *fine singing.* **13.** Elegant, ornate; handsome: *fine clothes.* Phr. *fine feathers*, elegant attire. **14.** Ostentatious, showy, over-refined, pretentious: *she is too much of a fine lady for me.* **15.** *Fine arts*, those appealing to one's sense of beauty, not merely utilitarian. **16. a** (of intellectual qualities) Keen, subtle, acute: *a fine mind rather than a powerful one*; **b** (of moral qualities) noble, elevated, exhibiting probity: *a fine character.* **17.** Eminent, excelling, distinguished, highly accomplished: *a fine singer, poet* &c. **18. a** Discriminating, delicate in perception, subtle: *a fine sense of humour*; **b** requiring discrimination, delicate, subtle: *a fine distinction.* **19.** (of products of intellect) **a** Polished, finished, elaborated: *a fine piece of writing; fine compliments*; **b** over-elaborate, pretentious, ostentatious, showy; distinguished by meretricious ornament: in Phr. *fine writing.* **20.** Delicate, of careful, detailed, and intricate workmanship: *a fine design, fine tracery.*

fine (**V.**), adv., fr. prec. Finely (in various senses), esp. in Phr. *to run, cut, it* (*rather*) *fine*, leave oneself, provide oneself with, barely enough of anything (esp. of time); *that will suit me fine*, very well.

fine (**VI.**), n., fr. **fine** (**IV.**). Fine weather: *to get home in the fine.*

fine (**VII.**), vb. intrans. & trans., fr. **fine** (**IV.**). **1.** intrans. **a** (of liquid; also *fine down*) To become clear, be purified; **b** to become slenderer, more delicate, in form &c. **2.** trans. (also *fine down*) To clarify, refine (liquid &c.).

fine-draw, vb. trans. **1.** To join the edges of two pieces of material, or two edges of a tear in woven material, in such a way that the stitches of the join are invisible. **2.** To draw out (wire &c.) to a very high degree of fineness.

fine-drawn, adj. **1.** (of a rent in cloth &c.) Having the edges drawn together and sewn in such a way that the stitches are invisible. **2. a** (of wire) Drawn out very thin; **b** (of arguments) invented, stated, with ingenuity and subtlety.

finely, adv. [1. finli; 2. fáinli]. **fine** (**IV.**) & **-ly.** In a fine manner.

fineness, n. [1. finnes; 2. fáinnis]. **fine** (**IV.**) & **-ness.** **1.** The quality of being fine (in various senses); **a** thinness, slenderness: *fineness of thread* &c.; **b** delicacy, softness, suppleness: *fineness of a fabric*; **c** (of gold, silver) purity, high proportion of pure gold or silver in a coinage. **2.** (of form) Slenderness, elegance, shapeliness, delicacy. **3.** (of quality in material things) Excellence, perfection. **4.** (of the quality of the mind and its activities) Acuteness, subtlety; justness, exactitude, accuracy: *fineness of intellect; fineness of observation.* **5.** (of the senses) Acuteness, keenness, sensibility.

finery (**I.**), n. [1. fineri; 2. fáinəri]. **fine** (**IV.**) & **-ery.** Something that is fine; esp. elaborate personal adornment; gay clothes, ornaments, and other additions to the dress, designed to give a gay, elegant appearance. Also: *the garden in its summer finery.*

finery (**II.**), n., fr. Fr., fr. *finer*, 'to refine', fr. Romance *fīnāre*, fr. Lat. *fīn-(is)*, 'end'. See **finis.** Charcoal hearth for making cast-iron malleable, or for making steel from pig-iron.

fine-spun, adj. **a** Drawn out to extreme fineness, thinness; fragile, delicate; **b** (fig.) over-subtle, over-elaborated.

finesse (**I.**), n. [1. finés; 2. finés], fr. Fr. **fine** (**IV.**) & **-ess.** **1.** Careful, subtle, delicate action; skilful, adroit handling of a situation, so that a purpose is gained without arousing hostility and opposition. **2.** (in unfavourable sense) Artfulness, cunning; action intended to mislead as to one's real intentions and aims. **3.** (whist &c.) Attempt to take trick with, or by playing, a low card, while holding a higher card of the same suit.

finesse (**II.**), vb. intrans. & trans., fr. prec. **A.** intrans. **1.** To make use of finesse. **2.** (whist &c.) To attempt to take a trick by means of finesse. **B.** trans. **1.** To overcome by finesse. **2.** (whist &c.) To play (a card) as a finesse.

finger (**I.**), n. [1. fingger; 2. fíŋgə]. O.E., M.E. *finger*, O.H.G. *finger*, O.N. *fingr*, Goth. *figgrs.* Gmc. **fiŋgʷra-*, Aryan **penkʷró*, 'group of five', fr. base **penkʷ-e-*, 'five'. See **five** & **fist.** **1. a** One of the five separate members forming the extremity of the hand; **b** any one of these members excluding the thumb. Phrs. *by a finger's breadth*, by a very narrow margin; *the finger of God*, the direct intervention of Providence; *to have* (*knowledge* &c.) *at one's fingers' ends*, to know thoroughly, be familiar with; *to one's finger-tips*, completely, thoroughly; *to have a finger in the pie*, to be concerned with, take part in, an affair; *his fingers are all thumbs*, he is clumsy in using his hands; *to lay a finger on*, to touch, with hostile intent; *to put one's finger on*, indicate precisely; *to let slip through one's fingers*, to allow to escape; *my fingers itch to do so and so*, I am eager, impatient, to do it; *not to lift, stir, a finger to help*, to make not the slightest effort to help; *to be able to twist* (*a person*) *round one's* (*little*) *finger*, to have great influence over, dominate unduly. **2.** Part of glove covering a finger. **3.** Anything shaped like a finger; **a** a small, narrow piece: *a finger of cake* &c.; **b** a small, projecting piece (in a machine &c.) resembling a finger. **4.** The breadth of a finger, as a measure of depth (of liquid &c.). **5.** One of the pointers or hands of a clock or watch.

finger (**II.**), vb. trans., fr. prec. **1. a** To touch, handle, with the fingers; **b** to touch, take, accept wrongfully: *to finger a bribe.* **2.** (mus.) **a** To play (an instrument) with the fingers; **b** to play (a passage &c.), using specified fingers; **c** to indicate on (written or printed music) a specific order of using the fingers.

finger-alphabet, n. Series of positions of the hands and fingers used as symbols for letters in communicating with the deaf and dumb.

finger and toe, n. A disease of various roots, esp. turnips; dactylorhiza.

finger-board, n. **a** That part of a violin or other similar musical instrument upon which the fingers press the strings in forming the notes; **b** keyboard, manual, of a piano.

finger-bowl, n. Small bowl containing water placed by each person at luncheon or dinner, for cleansing the fingers after dessert.

-fingered, adj. [1. finggerd; 2. fíŋgəd]. **finger** (**I.**) & **-ed.** Having fingers of a specified kind: *light-fingered*, having light, nimble fingers, esp. *light-fingered gentry*, pick-pockets.

finger-fish, n. A star-fish.

finger-glass, n. Finger-bowl.

fingering (**I.**), n. [1. fingggering; 2. fíŋgəriŋ]. **finger** (**II.**) & **-ing.** **a** Order of using the fingers in playing a musical instrument; **b** signs on written or printed music indicating this order.

fingering (**II.**), n. Earlier *fingram*, prob. fr. Fr. *fin grain.* See **fine** (**III.**) & **grain.** Fine kind of wool for stockings &c.

finger-language, n. Finger-alphabet.

fingerless, adj. [1. finggerles; 2. fíŋgəlis]. **finger** (**I.**) & **-less.** Without fingers.

finger-mark, n. Imprint, stain, left by finger on a surface.

finger-nail, n. Nail at end of finger.

finger-plate, n. Flat plate fixed on door near handle to protect it from finger-marks.

finger-post, n. Post erected at cross-road &c. to indicate direction; sign-post.

finger-print, n. Impression made by, or taken from, the pad or cushion of the finger-tips, used as a means of identifying criminals.

finger-stall, n. Small cover, like the finger of a glove, worn to protect injured finger.

finial, n. [1. finial; 2. fíniəl], fr. Lat. *fīn-(is)*, 'end'. See **finis** & **-ial.** (archit.) Projecting ornament at the apex of a gable, pinnacle &c.

finical, adj. [1. finikl; 2. fínikl]. Etymol. doubtful. Cp. **finicking.** **a** (of persons) Over-fastidious, trivial, fussy; full of petty whims and crotchets; **b** (of things) excessively elaborated, with much unimportant detail.

finicality, n. [1. finikáliti; 2. finikǽliti]. Prec. & **-ity.** The quality of being finical.

finically, adv. [1. fínikali; 2. fínikəli]. **finical** & **-ly**. In a finical manner.

finicalness, n. [1. fíniklnes; 2. fíniklnis]. **finical** & **-ness**. The quality of being finical.

finicking, **finikin**, adj. [1. fíniking, -in; 2. fínikiŋ, -in]. Etymol. doubtful. Du. has *fijnkens*, 'accurately, neatly'. Finical.

finicky, adj. [1. fíniki; 2. fíniki]. Finicking.

fining, n. [1. fíning; 2. fáiniŋ]. **fine** (**VI.**) & **-ing**. **a** Act of fining, refining, or clarifying; **b** (pl.) substance used in clarifying wine &c.

finis, n. [1. fínis; 2. fáinis]. Lat. *fīnis*, 'boundary, limit, border; end, conclusion; final point, extremity; aim, object'. Prob. earlier **fīgsnis*, 'something firmly fixed'; cp. *figere*, 'to fix, fasten'. See **fix**, **ditch**, & cp. **define**, **final**. **a** (at end of book) The end, conclusion; **b** close (of life &c.).

finish (**I.**), vb. trans. & intrans. [1. fínish; 2. fíniʃ]. M.E. *finishen*, fr. O. Fr. *fin-(ir)*, 'to finish', & **-ish**, fr. Lat. *fīnīre*, 'to fix, determine; set limits to; end, finish'. Cp. Lat. *fīn-(is)*, 'end', *dēfīn-(īre)*, 'to limit, define', & see prec. **A.** trans. **1. a** To bring to an end, complete (an action or series of actions): *to finish one's work*; *to finish an investigation*; *to finish doing something*; **b** to complete something under construction, something that one is making &c.: *my house will soon be finished.* **2.** To go, work, through completely, come to the end of: *to finish a book.* **3.** To consume entirely, eat or drink up: *to finish a goose at one meal.* **4.** To put an end to; exhaust; to kill, destroy: *I finished him with a single blow*; *the long march has quite finished the troops.* **5.** To give final touches to, complete, make perfect down to last detail: *to finish a picture properly*; *old French furniture is often not so beautifully finished as English.* **B.** intrans. **1.** To bring any action to an end, to complete it: *I can't come till I have finished.* **2.** To come to a conclusion, to end, conclude: *I thought the sermon would never finish.* **C.** Followed by adverbs. *Finish off*, trans., **a** to bring a piece of work to a state of completion: *I have a few jobs I must finish off*; **b** to destroy, kill: *I had a fever in India which nearly finished me off. Finish up*, trans., **a** to finish off; **b** to consume entirely, eat up: *he finished up the remains of the mutton for dinner.*

finish (**II.**), n., fr. prec. **1.** Concluding stage, last part: *the finish of a race, a hunt* &c. Phr. *to be in at the finish* (lit. and fig.), take part in final stages of a series of actions; *to fight to a finish*, until one of the combatants is completely overcome. **2.** The state of being finished; state of completeness, final elaboration and perfection: *his style, manners, lack(s) finish.* **3. a** Something which completes the appearance, which gives the final touch of perfection: *the picture gives just the right finish to the room*; **b** mode of finishing anything: *a smooth, delicate, dull, finish.*

finish (**III.**), adj. [1. fínish; 2. fáiniʃ]. **fine** (**III.**) & **-ish**. Fairly fine; fairly slender, thin &c.

finisher, n. [1. fínisher; 2. fíniʃə]. **finish** (**I.**) & **-er**. One who, that which, finishes; specif. **a** person or machine that gives the final touches to an article in process of manufacture; **b** (colloq.) a final, decisive blow.

finite, adj. [1. fínīt; 2. fáinait], fr. Lat. *fīnīt-(um)*, P.P. type of *fīnīre*, 'to fix, determine; set limits to; end, finish'. See **finish** (**I.**). **1.** Bounded, limited; subject to limitations; contrasted with *infinite*: *our finite intelligence.* **2.** (gram.) *Finite verb*, any part that can be used as predicate; so called because it is limited as to number and person.

finitely, adv. Prec. & **-ly**. In a finite manner.

finiteness, n. See prec. & **-ness**. The quality of being finite.

finless, adj. [1. fínles; 2. fínlis]. **fin** & **-less**. Without fins.

Finn, n. [1. fin; 2. fin]. O.E. *Finnas*, 'Finns'. A member of the race, who call themselves Suomi, inhabiting Finland.

finnan-haddock, n. [1. fínan hádok; 2. fínən hǽdək]. Said to be fr. Findhorn, fishing port in Scotland. Haddock cut open, salted, and cured with peat-smoke.

finner, n. [1. fíner; 2. fínə]. **fin** & **-er**. The fin-back or rorqual.

Finnic, adj. [1. fínik; 2. fínik]. **Finn** & **-ic**. Pertaining to the Finns, to their language, or to the family of languages to which this belongs.

Finnish, adj. & n. [1. fínish; 2. fíniʃ]. **Finn** & **-ish**. **1** adj. Pertaining to the Finns or their language. **2.** n. The language of the Finns.

Finno-Ugrian, n. & adj. [1. finō úgrian; 2. finou jū́grian]. See **Ugrian**.

finny, adj. [1. fíni; 2. fíni]. **fin** & **-y**. **1.** Having fins. Phr. *finny tribes*, (poet.) fish. **2.** (poet.) Abounding in fish.

Finsen light, n. [1. fínsen līt; 2. fínsən lait]. After Niels Finsen, Danish doctor. A special form of electric light, enabling ultra-violet rays to be concentrated on surface exposed to it; used in treatment of lupus &c.

fiord, **fjord**, n. [1. fyord; 2. fjōd]. Norw. Cogn. w. O.E. *ford*. See **ford**, **firth**, & **frith**. A long narrow arm of the sea, between high, rocky cliffs, esp. in Norway.

fiorin, n. [1. fíorin; 2. fáiərin]. Ir. *fiothran*. A kind of meadow grass.

fir, n. [1. fĕr; 2. fā]. O.E. **fyrh* (not recorded), mutated form corresponding to *furh-(wudu)*, 'fir-wood'; M.E. *firre*. Cp. O.N. *fura*, O.H.G. *foraha*, 'fir'; also O.H.G. *fereh-(eih)*, 'mountain oak'. The Aryan type was **pérkʷo-*, whence also Lat. *quercus*, 'oak' (cp. **Quercus**), fr. **perkʷos*. **1.** One of numerous varieties of pinaceous trees (*Abies* or *Picea*); they are mostly evergreen, resinous, and coniferous, and have the needles arranged singly on the shoots, cp. *pine.* **2.** The wood of the fir. *Fir-cone*, fruit of the fir, more rarely *fir-apple.*

fire (**I.**), n. [1. fīr; 2. faiə]. O.E. *fȳr*, M.E. *fīr*; O.H.G. *fūir*, *fiur*; O.N. (poet.) *furr*, 'fire'; Gk. *pũr*, 'fire'; Aryan base **pū̆*, 'bright, shining; clear, pure'; the meaning has, on the one hand, been specialized to 'fire'; on the other hand, to 'clean, pure'; cp. Lat. *pūrus*, 'clean', *purgāre*, 'to purify' (see **pure**, **purge**); Scrt. *pūtaś*, 'pure', *punā́ti*, 'purifies' (see **pyre**). **1.** (anct. phys. and popular usage) One of the four elements which compose the universe. **2.** The principle present in combustion, producing heat and light; flame. Phrs. *to set fire to, set on fire*, to cause to burn, to ignite, kindle; *to set the Thames on fire*, to achieve something remarkable; *to catch, take, fire*, be ignited, begin to burn; *on fire*, (i.) burning, ignited; (ii.) (fig.) eager, excited, roused; *to strike fire*, to produce a spark or fire by concussion; *to play with fire*, trifle with something likely to prove dangerous. **3. a** Conflagration, destructive burning: *to insure against fire*; Phr. *to go through fire and water*, endure perils of all kinds; **b** a specific conflagration, burning: *the fire spread rapidly from house to house.* **4.** Small portion, collection, of glowing, smouldering, or blazing material, wood, coal &c., used to produce heat, for warming and cooking: *to have a fire in one's room*; *it is too warm for fires.* Phrs. *to lay a fire*, arrange fuel in position for lighting; *out of the frying-pan into the fire*, from one predicament to another, from bad to worse. **5.** (of mental quality) Animation, strong feeling, spiritual energy; fervour, ardour: '*His was the bard's immortal name, His was the hero's soul of fire*' (Scott, 'Last Minstrel', vi. xiii.); *eyes full of fire*, fierce, flashing, strong, bright glance. **6.** Firing, shooting; discharge of fire-arms: *exposed to enemy's fire.* Phrs. *under fire*, being shot at; *to open fire*, begin shooting; *cease fire*, stop shooting; *between two fires*, shot at, attacked, from two directions; *running fire*, rapid succession of shots; (fig.) swift succession of criticisms &c.

fire (**II.**), vb. trans. & intrans., fr. prec. **A.** trans. **1.** To set fire to, ignite, cause to begin burning: *to fire a house*; *to fire the grass* &c. **2.** To submit, subject, to heat; specif., **a** to bake (bricks &c.); **b** to dry, cure (tea &c.); **c** (veter. surg.) to cauterize. **3.** To tend, feed, supply (a furnace &c.) with fuel. **4. a** To discharge, cause to go off, explode (fire-arms): *to fire a pistol*; (also slang) to discharge from service, to sack; **b** to discharge fire-arms in a specific manner, for a specific purpose: *to fire a volley, a salute, a broadside* &c.; **c** (fig.) to address, direct at, suddenly: *to fire questions at a person.* **5.** (of action on the mind) To animate, excite, arouse, stimulate, inflame: *to fire the imagination, blood* &c. **B.** intrans. **1.** (of explosives) To catch fire, be ignited. **2.** To discharge fire-arms: *to give the order to fire*; *to fire at, on, upon, the enemy.* **C.** Followed by adverbs and prepositions. *Fire away*, **a** intrans., (colloq.) to begin, start off, go ahead; **b** trans., to expend, use up, by firing: *to fire away ammunition. Fire off*, trans., to discharge (lit. and fig.): *to fire off a gun, questions* &c. *Fire out*, trans., (slang) to dismiss, send off, eject, expel. *Fire up*, intrans., to become suddenly excited, indignant: *when he sneered at her son, she fired up at once.*

fire-alarm, n. Apparatus for announcing an outbreak of fire.

fire-arm, n. A weapon from which a missile is propelled by an explosive.

fireback, n. [1. fírbak; 2. fáiəbæk]. **1.** A kind of East Indian pheasant, part of the back of which is fiery red. **2.** Plate of iron, fire-clay, or brick at the back of a grate, the purpose of which is to reflect heat into the room.

fireball, n. [1. fírbawl; 2. fáiəbōl]. **1.** A meteor. **2.** (mil.) A bag filled with combustibles and used for lighting or causing conflagration.

fire-balloon, n. Balloon filled with hot air, supplied by fire burning at its mouth.

fire-blight, n. A disease of hops.

fire-box, n. That part of an engine in which the fuel is burnt.

fire-brand, n. **a** A piece of burning wood; **b** (fig.) person who excites the minds of others, one who stirs up strife, revolt, discontent &c.

fire-brick, n. Fireproof brick used in fire-places.

fire-brigade, n. Organized body of men for extinguishing conflagrations.

fire-bug, n. U.S.A. **a** Firefly; **b** (slang) an incendiary.

fire-clay, n. A special kind of clay, capable of sustaining great heat, used in making fire-bricks.

fire-control, n. Control from a central position by various systems, mechanical or otherwise, of the fire of the guns of a warship.

fire-damp, n. An explosive gas generated in coal-mines.

fire-dog, n. Metal support for logs of burning wood on an open hearth; andiron.

fire-drill, n. **a** Fire-brigade practice; **b** organized practice and instruction for school-children &c. in proper action in case of fire.

fire-eater, n. **a** Juggler who claims to eat fire; **b** person who is always eager for a fight; **a** hot-tempered, quarrelsome person.

fire-engine, n. Combination of vehicle and machine, in former capacity carrying firemen, ladders, hose pipes &c. to the scene of a fire; the machine is a powerful pump for throwing a stream of water with considerable force and for some distance through the hose upon the flames.

fire-escape, n. **a** Device consisting of ladders, and a long canvas tube fixed to a tall portable frame, down which people escape from a burning building; **b** iron staircase on exterior of building, esp. for use in emergency.

fire-extinguisher, n. A portable metal container, from which a chemical liquid can be readily discharged at early stages of a fire.

firefly, n. [1. fírflī; 2. fáiəflai]. An insect emitting a phosphorescent light from some part of its body, esp. one of several varieties of American and W. Indian beetles, esp. the click-beetle, family *Elateridae.*

fire-guard, n. Metal framework or grating round a fireplace.

fire-hose, n. Hose for conveying water and discharging it upon the flames of a conflagration.
fire-insurance, n. Insurance against loss by fire.
fire-irons, n. Instruments for tending fire, poker, tongs, and shovel.
fireless, adj. [1. fírles; 2. fáiəlis]. **fire** (**I.**) & **-less.** Without a fire.
fire-light, n. Light cast by a fire, esp. by one burning in a grate.
fire-lighter, n. Small object made of highly inflammable material, used to facilitate the kindling of a fire in a grate.
firelock, n. [1. fírlok; 2. fáiəlɔk]. Obsolete kind of musket fired by sparks produced by a steel hammer striking a piece of flint.
fireman, n. [1. fírman; 2. fáiəmən]. **1.** Member of a fire-brigade. **2.** Man who feeds the fire of a steam-engine &c. with fuel; stoker.
fire-office, n. Office of a fire-insurance company.
fire-pan, n. Pan for holding burning fuel.
fireplace, n. [1. fírplās; 2. fáiəpleis]. Specially constructed part of a room, in which a fire may be lighted, generally including the grate, the cavity in the wall in which this is fixed, and the ornamented structure surrounding the opening.
fire-plug, n. Metal pipe connected with a water-main, provided with a movable cap screwed down on to it when not in use, and made so that a fire-hose can be attached.
fire-policy, n. Document setting forth the terms of a fire-insurance contract.
fireproof, adj. [1. fírproof; 2. fáiəprūf]. Proof against fire; not liable to be destroyed or affected by fire; non-inflammable.
fire-screen, n. One intended to give protection against the heat of the fire in a room.
fire-ship, n. Ship filled with combustibles, ignited, and allowed to drift so as to set fire to enemy shipping.
fireside, n. [1. fírsíd; 2. fáiəsáid]. **a** Part of room near fireplace; (fig.) **b** home; family life.
fire-step, n. Step in a trench allowing soldier to fire over the parapet.
fire-stick, n. One of two pieces of wood used by primitive races to make fire by friction.
fire-stone, n. Kind of fireproof stone.
fire-trap, n. Building dangerous in case of fire by reason of its inflammability or its lack of proper exits.
fire-warden, n. Forest official whose chief duty is to prevent or check fires.
fire-water, n. Name supposed to be used by American Indians for ardent spirits.
firewood, n. [1. fírwood; 2. fáiəwud]. Wood for fuel.
firework, n. [1. fírwěrk; 2. fáiəwǝ̄k]. Device for producing various effects of lighting by means of combustibles, explosives &c. used for display, as signal &c.
fire-worship, n. Worship of fire as a deity, or as the symbol of a deity.
firing, n. [1. fíring; 2. fáiəriŋ]. **fire** (**II.**) & **-ing.** **1.** The discharge of fire-arms. **2.** Material for feeding a fire; fuel.
firing-line, n. That area of a zone of military operations within effective range of the enemy; the troops within such an area.
firing-party, -squad, n. Small party or squad of soldiers detailed for duty, **a** for shooting soldier condemned by court-martial; **b** for firing a volley over the grave of soldier buried with military honours.
firkin, n. [1. fěrkin; 2. fǝ́kin]. Earlier *ferdekin*; prob. fr. M. Du. *vierde*, 'fourth', cogn. w. **fourth**, & **-kin.** A small barrel, for holding liquid, butter &c., having a capacity of 8 to 9 gallons.
firm (**I.**), adj. [1. fěrm; 2. fǝ̄m], (influenced by Latin spelling), fr. O. Fr. *ferme*, fr. Lat. *firmus*, 'steadfast, stable, strong; constant, faithful'. Cp. Lat. *ferē*, *fermē*, 'nearly'; *frētus*, 'relying on'; Scrt. *dhārāyati*, 'holds, supports', *dhármaš*, 'custom, law'; Lith. *dernie*, 'treaty'; Gk. *thrónos*, 'seat' (see **throne**), *thrânos*, 'stool'; Aryan base **dherē-* **dher(ə)-*, **dhrē-*, 'to hold, support'. Cp. **fort** & words there referred to. **1.** (referring to material consistency) Solid, compact, not yielding to pressure; closely knit: *firm flesh.* Phrs. *firm ground*, the land as opposed to the sea; (fig.) *to be on firm ground*, sure of one's facts. **2.** (of degree of material stability) Not easily shaken, upset or moved; fixed, rigid, stable, fast: *roots firm in the earth*; *firm on one's legs.* Phr. *as firm as a rock.* **3. a** (of the mind and character) Resolute, steadfast, determined, inflexible; **b** (of thoughts, beliefs, aspirations) unshakable, strongly fixed: *a firm faith, hope, conviction.* **4.** (of behaviour and conduct) Resolute; showing decision of character and purpose; not easily swayed; stern, unyielding: *firm government, management*; *firm treatment of children*; *firm measures.* **5. a** (of effort) Strongly, steadily, and consistently continued and exerted or applied: *firm pressure*; **b** (of bodily action) vigorous, steady, unwavering: *a firm step, tread, voice, glance* &c. Phr. *a firm offer*, one that one is prepared to stick to. **6.** (of markets and prices) Not fluctuating, steady at one rate or value.
firm (**II.**), adv., fr. prec. Firmly, fast: *to stand firm.*
firm (**III.**), vb. trans. & intrans., fr. **firm** (**I.**). (rare) **1.** trans. **a** To make firm, solid: *to firm the ground after planting*; **b** to fix firmly. **2.** intrans. To become firm, solidify.
firm (**IV.**), n., fr. Ital. *firma*, 'confirmation, signature'; cp. L. Lat. *firmāre*, 'to sign, confirm', fr. Lat. *firmus.* See **firm** (**I.**). Group of persons associated as partners for the conduct of a business undertaking &c.
firmament, n. [1. fěrmament; 2. fǝ́məmənt], fr. Lat. *firmāmentum*, 'a support; the sky fixed above the earth'. **firm** (**I.**) & **-ment.** The whole expanse of the sky.
firmamental, adj. [1. fěrmaméntl; 2. fǝ̄məméntl]. Prec. & **-al.** Of, pertaining to, the firmament.
firman, n. [1. fěrman; 2. fǝ́mən], fr. Pers. *ferman.* Decree, sanction, licence, authority to travel &c. given by Oriental sovereign.
firmly, adv. [1. fěrmli; 2. fǝ́mli]. **firm** (**I.**) & **-ly.** **1.** In a firm manner; solidly, immovably, fixedly: *to fix a post firmly in the ground.* **2.** With decision, resolutely, unwaveringly: *to speak firmly.*
firmness, n. [1. fěrmnes; 2. fǝ́mnis]. **firm** (**I.**) & **-ness.** The quality of being firm (in various senses); **a** solidity of consistency; **b** stability; **c** resolution, determination of character, conduct &c.
firry, adj. [1. fěri; 2. fǝ́ri]. **fir** & **-y.** Abounding in firs.
first (**I.**), adj. [1. fěrst; 2. fǝ̄st]. O.E. *fyrst*, M.E. *first(e)*, superl. fr. Gmc. stem **fur* (see **fore, former**); O.H.G. *furisto*, 'first', cogn. w. Lat. *prīmus*, 'first' (see **prime, primary**). **1.** Ordinal number of *one*; expressing, denoting, that which begins a series; occurring, doing something, before others: *the first month of the year, the first man to cross the Atlantic, the first guests to arrive*; *Edward the First*; *a first coat* (of paint &c.); *First Day*, Quaker's term for Sunday; *the first Empire*, that of France under Napoleon I.; *first floor, storey*, that over the ground floor (U.S.A., ground floor); *first night*, earliest performance of play. Phrs. *first blood*, first wound given in duel or other combat; *in the first place*, before one does anything else; *at first sight*, at the first superficial or hasty inspection or consideration; *first thing*, at the earliest possible moment: *I will do it (the) first thing tomorrow.* **2.** Earliest in time; most forward: *the first son to be born to him*; precocious: *the first flowers of spring.* **3.** Foremost in position; occupying position in advance of all others; earliest met with, seen &c. in advancing from, or towards, a given direction: *the first house you come to*; *the first land sighted on the return voyage*; *the first man I saw on arrival.* **4.** (of persons) Occupying the chief rank; principal; **a** (in social position) *the first subject of the king*; *the first gentleman in Europe*; **b** (often caps., in a hierarchy, in an organized body of persons): *the first officer of a ship*; *First Lord of the Admiralty, of Treasury*; *First Secretary of Legation*; *first violin*, leading violinist in an orchestra; **c** (in attainments, achievements, reputation): *the first scholar of his day*; *the first general in Europe.* **5.** (of things) **a** Primary, of most importance: *the First Cause*, the primordial cause of all causes; *first cost*, original cost apart from incidental expenses, such as carriage &c.; **b** of first quality: *a diamond of the first water.*
first (**II.**), n., fr. prec. **1.** Beginning: *at (the) first*; *from the first*; *from first to last*, from beginning to end. **2.** In various elliptical Phrs.: *the first of August*, first day; *the first of Victoria*, first regnal year; *to take a first*, place in the first class in examination; *he got a first at Oxford*, took a first class in an Honour School; *first of exchange*, first copy of bill of exchange. **3.** (mus.) Highest voice in part singing; leading instrument of its kind in orchestra. **4.** *Firsts*, commodity, such as butter, of best quality.
first (**III.**), adv. O.E. *fyrst*, M.E. *first.* See **first** (**I.**). **1.** Before everything else, at the beginning or head; first in time, place, or degree: *he first asked my name*; *to stand, rank, first.* Phrs. *first and foremost*, emphatic for first; *first and last*, altogether, all included; *first or last* (archaic or rare) sooner or later. **2.** (referring to time) **a** Before the occurrence, performance &c. of something specified or implied: *I can't go out yet, I have many things to do first*; **b** for the first time: *I first met him ten years ago.* **3.** Sooner, rather, preferably: *when called upon to reveal the names of his accomplices he said he would die first*; (colloq.) *I'll see him hanged first.*
first-aid, n. Preliminary, esp. skilled, help given to injured person before arrival of doctor: *a first-aid class.*
first-begotten, adj. [1. fěrst begótn; 2. fǝ̄st bigɔ́tn]. Begotten before any other children.
first-born, adj. & n. **a** adj. Born before any other children in a family; eldest: *my first-born child*; **b** n., first-born son or daughter.
first-chop, adj. See **chop** (**IV.**) in sense of trade-mark, seal. Of the finest brand, the best.
first-class, adj. & adv. [1. fěrst kláhs; 2. fǝ́st klā́s] when predicative; [1. fěrst klahs; 2. fǝ́st klās] when before n. **1.** adj. **a** Belonging to the first, highest, or best class; having the best qualities of the kind; superior: *a first-class hotel, tailor, cricket match*; *the weather was first-class*; **b** of best accommodation in train, steamer &c.: *first-class carriage, berth* &c. **2.** adv. **a** (colloq., rather vulg.) Excellently, splendidly, very well: *he plays first-class*; *to feel first-class*, in the best health; **b** by the first-class on a train, ship &c.: *to travel first-class.*
first-foot, n. (Scots usage) Person who first crosses threshold of a house at the New Year.
first-fruits, n., pl. **1. a** Earliest produce of the season, esp. when dedicated to God by ancient religious custom; **b** (fig.) earliest product of labours: *this book is the first-fruits of many years' study.* **2.** (hist.) First year's revenue from tenant-in-chief or holder of ecclesiastical benefice; annates.
first-hand, adj. & adv. [1. fěrst hand, fěrst hánd; 2. fǝ́st hænd, fǝ́st hǽnd]. **1.** adj. Obtained directly from the source: *first-hand information.* Phr. *at first-hand.* **2.** adv. Directly from the source, maker &c.: *to learn something first-hand.*
firstling, n. [1. fěrstling; 2. fǝ́stliŋ]. **first** (**I.**) & **-ling.** (archaic, bib.) First-born domestic animal.
firstly, adv. [1. fěrstli; 2. fǝ́stli]. **first** (**I.**) & **-ly.** In the first place; coming into common use instead of *first*, but often objected to; it occurs especially in enumeration, through influence of *secondly* &c.
first-nighter, n. [1. fěrst níter; 2. fǝ̄st náitə]. (colloq.) Person who habitually attends first performances of plays.

first-rate, adj., n., & adv. [1. fĕrst rāt, fĕrst rāt; 2. fāst réit, fāst reit]. **1.** adj. **a** (naval hist.) Belonging to the class of largest and most powerful ships; hence, **b** belonging to the first class or order; of superior kind, excellent: *a first-rate dinner*; *his acting was first-rate.* **2.** n. (naval) First-rate ship. **3.** adv. (colloq.) In a first-rate manner, extremely well: *he is getting on first-rate.*

firth, n. [1. fĕrth; 2. fāþ]. M. Scots, fr. O.N. *firð-*, stem of *fjörðr*, 'fiord', cogn. w. Lat. *portus*, 'harbour', fr. Aryan base **per-*, 'to proceed'. Variant of **frith.** (in Scotland) Estuary or long narrow inlet of the sea.

fisc, n. [1. fisk; 2. fisk]. Fr., fr. Lat. *fiscus*, 'woven basket, purse, treasury'; cp. Lat. *fiscina*, 'basket'; etymol. doubtful. State treasury; rare, except **a** (Rom. hist.) treasury of the Republic; later, Emperor's privy purse; **b** (Scots, usually *fisk*) Crown treasury: *the estate escheated to the fisk.*

fiscal, adj. & n. [1. fískal; 2. fískəl]. Fr., fr. Lat. *fiscāl-(is)*. Prec. & **-al.** **1.** adj. Pertaining to the public revenue: *Procurator-fiscal*, public prosecutor for minor criminal offences in Scotland. **2.** n. (in various foreign countries) A high legal official; (in Scotland) Procurator-fiscal.

fiscally, adv. Prec. & **-ly.** In a fiscal relation.

fish (I.), n. [1. fish; 2. fiʃ]. O.E. *fisċ*, M.E. *fisch*, O.S., O.H.G. *fisc*, Mod. Germ. *fisch*, Goth. *fisks*, O.N. *fiskr*; Common Gmc. cogn. w. Lat. *piscis*, O. Ir. *iasc* for **pisc-*. W. *pysg* &c. is a fresh borrowing fr. Lat. Further connexions are doubtful, but two suggestions have been put forward: (i.) relationship w. Lat. *pinna*, 'fin'; O.E. *finn*, see **fin**; (ii.) w. Scrt. *piččhā*, 'slime', *piččhalaš*, 'slimy'. Pl. *fishes*, often *fish*, esp. as food, fr. collective use. **1. a** Cold-blooded vertebrate animal, living entirely in water and breathing by gills, having no limbs except in the modified form of fins; Phrs. *to drink like a fish*, drink to excess; *as drunk as a fish*, very drunk; *to feed the fishes*, to be sea-sick; to be drowned; *to land one's fish*, to secure what one has worked or intrigued for; *a fish out of water*, person in strange, unfamiliar surroundings; **b** (loosely) animal living in the water, esp. those sold for food, as crabs or oysters &c.; (also in compounds) *shellfish*, *starfish*; **c** the flesh of fishes as an article of food or commerce: *to eat fish on Fridays*; *fish is cheap*; **d** fishes in the mass, esp. as living in particular body of water: *to catch fish*; *there are lots of fish of many kinds in the lake*; Phrs. *all is fish that comes to his net*, he takes everything without discrimination; *to have other fish to fry* (colloq.), something else to do, more urgent business to attend to; *there are* (or *is*) *as good fish in the sea as ever came out of it*, what is lost or missed can be replaced; *neither fish, flesh, nor fowl* (*nor good red herring*), (colloq.) thing unsatisfactory because indeterminate, nondescript; *a pretty kettle of fish*, (colloq.) a fine mess, complication &c.; *to cry stinking fish*, to disparage one's self or one's own work; **e** (fig., slightly contempt.), person, with qualifying adjective: *a cool, dull, loose, odd, queer, poor fish.* **2.** (attrib.) Consisting of, concerned with, fish: *a fish dinner, market.* Phr. *a fish story*, lying, boastful tale, properly of one's angling prowess. **3.** Counter shaped like a fish, used in card games &c. Probably originally from French; see **fish** (III.).

fish (II.), vb. intrans. & trans. O.E. *fiscian*, 'to catch fish'. See prec. **A.** intrans. **1.** To catch, or attempt to catch, fish with a net, baited hook, or artificial fly &c.; to practice the occupation of fishing as a business or for sport: *to fish in the sea*; *to fish for a livelihood*; *to go out fishing.* Phr. *to fish in troubled waters*, to make a profit out of a disturbed situation. **2.** (fig., often followed by *for*) To throw out covert hints, feelers, in order to obtain a compliment, an advantage, to extract information, get knowledge of secrets &c.: *he came round fishing for an invitation*; *I could see that he was merely fishing for information.* **3.** *Fish for*, to seek for certain things (coral, pearls, oysters &c.) which are found in the sea, lakes &c. **B.** trans. **1.** To attempt to catch fish in; to use means for catching fish in: *you must come and fish my lake*; *this stream has been over fished*; *to fish the mouth of a river.* **2.** To attempt to catch by fishing: *I think it's better sport to fish trout than salmon.* **C.** Followed by preposition or adverb. *Fish out*, trans., **a** to exhaust supply of fish in (a piece of water) by excessive fishing: *the stream is quite fished out*; **b** to bring up, produce, pull something up or out, from an obscure place: *to fish half a crown out of one's pocket*; *he fished out an old coat from the wardrobe. Fish up*, trans., **a** same as preceding **b**; **b** to pull up out of the water: *to fish up a dead dog from the pond.*

fish (III.), n. & vb. trans. Fr. *fiche*, 'a fixing, stake, pin, peg, counter in games', fr. *ficher*, 'to fix, fasten, drive in', fr. Romance type **ficcāre*, for Lat. *fīgere*, q.v. under **fix** (I.). The n. has prob. been associated w. **fish** (I.) fr. supposed resemblance in shape. **1.** n. **a** Piece of wood or iron used as longitudinal clamp to strengthen another, or to join two pieces together; fishplate on railway line; **b** counter, often shaped like a fish, in certain games; see **fish** (I.). **2.** vb. trans. To strengthen or join together by means of a fish.

fishable, adj. [1. físhabl; 2. fíʃəbl]. **fish** (II.) & **-able.** Capable of being fished: *a fishable stream.*

fishball, n. [1. físhbáwl; 2. fíʃbɔ̄l]. Fried cake of shredded fish and potato.

fishbolt, n. [1. físhbōlt; 2. fíʃboult]. **fish** (III.) & **bolt** (I.). Bolt fastening two fish-plates to rail, or fish to mast &c.

fishbone, n. [1. físhbōn; 2. fíʃboun]. Bone of a fish, esp. one of the small, slender bones found in herrings &c., liable to lodge in the throat.

fish-carver, n. Fish slice.

fisher, n. [1. físher; 2. fíʃə]. O.E. *fisċere*, M.E. *fischere.* **fish** (II.) & **-er.** **a** Person who fishes; **b** fishing vessel; **c** animal that catches fish; specif., kind of N. American weasel.

fisherman, n. [1. físherman; 2. fíʃəmən]. **a** Man whose occupation is to catch fish; **b** one who fishes for sport; angler: *a keen fisherman*; **c** one skilful in the angler's art: *I fear he will never make a fisherman.*

fishery, n. [1. físheri; 2. fíʃəri]. **fish** (I.) & **-ery.** **a** Action, business, or industry of fishing; **b** legal right of fishing in particular waters; **c** region, part of the sea &c. where fishing is carried on.

fish-globe, n. More or less globular glass bowl in which live fishes are kept.

fish-glue, n. Powerful adhesive substance made from the bones of fish boiled down.

fish-hawk, n. Osprey.

fish-hook, n. Barbed hook attached to line, used to catch fish.

fishily, adv. [1. físhili; 2. fíʃili]. **fishy** & **-ly.** In a fishy manner.

fishiness, n. [1. físhines; 2. fíʃinis]. **fishy** & **-ness.** Quality of being fishy.

fishing, n. [1. físhing; 2. fíʃiŋ]. **fish** (II.) & **-ing.** **1.** Action or process of catching fish, whether as a business or as a sport: *to earn one's livelihood by fishing*; *to be fond of fishing*; also attributive as *fishing rod, net, tackle* &c. **2.** Legal rights to fish in certain waters: *to own, let, the fishing in a lake, or river.* **3.** That piece of water, stretch of river &c., over which rights of fishing are enjoyed: *to take a fishing in Scotland.*

fish-kettle, n. Large kettle or pot, in which fish can be boiled whole.

fish-knife, n. Knife with silver or plated blade, for eating fish.

fish-ladder, n. Flight of steps enabling salmon &c. to ascend falls of a river.

fishlike, adj. [1. físhlīk; 2. fíʃlaik]. Resembling, suggesting, fish or a fish: '*A very ancient and fish-like smell*' (Shakespeare); said also of a cold, unemotional, listless person.

fishmonger, n. [1. físhmungger; 2. fíʃmaŋgə]. **fish** (I.) & **-monger.** Dealer in fish, and other edible products of the water.

fishplate, n. [1. físhplāt; 2. fíʃpleit]. **fish** (III.) & **plate** (I.). One of pair of steel plates or fishes by which two rails on railway are bolted together.

fishpond, n. [1. físhpond; 2. fíʃpɔnd]. Pond in which fish are bred, and kept for food.

fishpot, n. [1. físhpot; 2. fíʃpɔt]. Wicker trap for catching lobsters, crabs, eels &c.

fish sauce, n. [1. físh saws, físh sáws; 2. fíʃ sɔ̄s, fíʃ sɔ̄s]. **a** Sauce used to flavour fish; **b** sauce made of fish.

fishskin, n. [1. físhskin; 2. fíʃskin]. **1.** Skin of a fish; specif., prepared rough skin of some kinds of shark, used for polishing wood. **2.** (med.) Rough, scaly condition of skin.

fish-slice, n. [1. físh slīs; 2. fíʃ slais]. Broad-bladed knife of silver, or plated metal, for carving and serving fish; utensil for handling fish when cooking.

fishtail, adj. [1. físhtāl; 2. fíʃteil]. Shaped like the tail of a fish: *fishtail burner*, gas burner with flat jet; *fishtail wind*, shifting wind blowing down rifle-range.

fishwife, n. [1. físhwīf; 2. fíʃwaif]. Woman who sells fish retail; female hawker of fish.

fishy, adj. [1. físhi; 2. fíʃi]. **fish** (I.) & **-y.** **1.** Consisting of, abounding in, fish: *a fishy diet.* **2.** Pertaining to, resembling or suggesting, fish; **a** in smell; **b** like a fish's eye, dull, lustreless, expressionless, vacant: *a fishy diamond, eye, stare.* **3.** (colloq.) Questionable, dubious, suspicious: *a fishy transaction, tale.*

fisk, n. Variant spelling of **fisc.**

fissi-, pref. Lat. See next word. Form used in compounds of Latin origin, denoting **a** cleft, divided, as *fissidactyl*, having separate digits; **b** by fission, as *fissiparous*, reproducing by fission.

fissile, adj. [1. físīl; 2. físail]. Lat. *fissil-(is)*, 'that may be cleft or split', fr. *fiss-(um)*, P.P. type of *findere*, 'to cleave', cogn. w. Scrt. *bhidyatē*, 'to cleave, disjoin'; see further under **bite** (I.) & **-ile.** Capable of being cleft or split; easily splitting.

fissility, n. [1. fisíliti; 2. fisíliti]. Prec. & **-ity.** Quality of being fissile.

fission, n. [1. físhun; 2. fíʃən]. Lat. *fissiōn-(em)*, 'a cleaving', fr. base *fiss-(um).* See **fissile** & **-ion.** Process of cleaving, splitting off; specif. (biol.) *reproduction by fission*, by division.

fissure, n. [1. físhur; 2. fíʃə]. Fr., fr. Lat. *fissūra*, 'a cleft, chink', fr. base *fiss-*, see **fissile**, & **-ure.** **a** Cleft, crack, chink, in ground, rock &c.; specif. **b** (anat. &c.) narrow opening between lobes, or parts, of an organ, e.g. in brain or liver; **c** split or crack in bodily tissue.

fissured, adj. [1. físhurd; 2. fíʃəd]. Prec. & **-ed.** Cracked, cleft, split open; having a fissure or fissures: *a fissured rock.*

fist, n. & vb. trans. [1. fist; 2. fist]. O.E. *fȳst*, M.E. *fust*, *fist*; cp. O.H.G. *fūst*, Mod. Germ. *faust* &c.; Gmc. type **fūhstiz*, fr. **fuŋχ-st-iz*, 'collection of five (fingers)', cogn. w. O. Slav. *pęsti*, Russ. *piasti*, 'fist', fr. Aryan base **peŋqʷe*, q.v. under **five** & **finger.** Cp. further Gk. *púx*, 'with the fist', *pug-mḗ*, Lat. *pug-nus*, 'fist', wh. may be cogn. See **pugnacious.** **A.** n. **1. a** Hand clenched or tightly closed, with fingers bent, as for striking; **b** (colloq.) hand: *give us your fist*, shake hands. **2.** Handwriting: *to write an ugly fist.* **B.** vb. trans. **a** To strike with the fist; **b** (chiefly naut.) to grasp, handle.

-fisted, adj. [1. fisted; 2. fístid]. Prec. & **-ed.** Form used in compounds, denoting having a (particular kind of) fist, as *close-fisted, hard-fisted.*

fistic(al), adj. [1. fístik(l); 2. fístik(l)]. **fist** & **-ic** (& **-al**). Popular colloquialism, used in reference to boxing, relating to, fought with, fists: *fistic skill, contest* &c.

fisticuff, n. [1. fístikuf; 2. fístikaf]. *Fisty*, 'pertaining to a fist', & **cuff**. Cuff or blow with the fist; (usually pl.) a fight with the fists; a brawl: *to come to fisticuffs.*

fist-law, n. After Germ. *faustrecht.* Such law or justice as is merely the expression of superiority in brute force; right of the stronger.

fistula, n. [1. físchoola; 2. fístʃulə]. Lat., 'pipe, tube, fistula', dimin. form, prob. fr. stem of *findere*, 'to cleave'. See **fissile**; cp. **fester**. **1.** Pipe-like organ in various insects and other animals. **2.** An opening or channel the result of disease, such as an ulcer, formed by collection of pus, into some normal duct or passage of the body, or forming a new external vent in the bodily tissues.

fistular, adj. [1. físchoolar; 2. fístʃulə]. Lat. *fistulār-(is).* Prec. & **-ar**. Pertaining to a fistula.

fistulous, adj. [1. físchoolus; 2. fístʃuləs]. Lat. *fistulōs-(us)*, 'pipe-shaped'. **fistula** & **-ous**. Fistular.

fit (I.), n. [1. fit; 2. fit]. O.E. (found only once), M.E. *fitt*, 'strife, contest', cp. O.E. *fettian* (once), 'to contend', *fitung*, 'a fighting'; M.E. *fiten*, 'to quarrel with'; of unknown origin, connexion w. **fit (II.)** is doubtful. **1. a** Sudden, sharp attack of some illness, often with unconsciousness and convulsions; seizure; spasm, paroxysm: *a fainting fit*; *an hysterical fit*; *a fit of epilepsy, apoplexy*; (colloq., fig.) Phr. *to give one a fit* (or *fits*), to shock, surprise, or enrage one; to outrage one's feelings; *to beat, knock, one into fits*, to beat or defeat one completely; **b** uncontrollable, sudden, acute attack or access of any bodily affection: *a fit of coughing, weeping, laughter.* **2.** (fig.) **a** Passing whim or impulse: *in a fit of generosity he gave half a crown to a beggar*; *he writes verses when the fit is on him*, when in the mood; *a fit of anger, rage*; **b** spasmodic, impulsive effort. Phr. *by fits (and starts)*, in sudden, transient bursts of energy.

fit (II.), n. O.E. *fitt*, fem. 'a song', M.E. *fitte*, 'stanza'; of uncertain origin; perh. related to O.H.G. *fiza*, 'list of cloth'; Mod. Germ. *fitze*, Dan. *fid*, 'skein'; O.N. *fit*, 'hem, web of bird's foot'. For the supposed connexion, cp. **hymn, rhapsody.** (archaic) Section of ballad or song; canto.

fit (III.), vb. trans. & intrans. M.E. *fitten*; of doubtful origin; cp. M. Du. *vitten*, 'to fit, suit, square', & perh. O.N. *fitja*, 'to knit'. **A.** trans. **1.** To be fit for, to suit, be adjusted or adapted to; **a** in shape, size, contour &c.: *this coat doesn't fit me*; *the nut won't fit the bolt*; *the key fits the lock*; **b** (of non-material things) to be suitable to, consonant, in harmony, in agreement, with: *the tune exactly fits the words*; *the punishment fits the crime.* Phr. *to fit the case*, be adapted to the particular circumstances. **2.** To make to fit, to suit, to adjust, adapt; **a** (of material things) to fashion, adjust, to the proper shape or size for the intended purpose: *to fit a plank in the floor*; *to fit a coat on a person*; also non-material: *to fit one's plans to suit others*; to prepare, qualify, make suitable, ready, for a position, action &c.: *hard training fitted him to march*, or *for long marches*; *to fit oneself for new duties.* **3. a** To furnish with what is fit or suitable: *to fit a library with shelves*; **b** to supply (person) with article of dress that fits: *to fit a man with a coat*; **c** to adjust garment to fit him: *to go to the tailor's to be fitted.* **B.** intrans. **a** (of material things) To be adapted to, agree with, the shape, size, of something else: *the coat fits perfectly*; *the broken pieces won't fit*; Phr. *to fit like a glove* (also fig.); **b** (rare) to be suitable, seemly; to befit. **C.** In phrases with prepositions or adverbs. *Fit in*, **a** trans., to insert neatly or suitably; to find a suitable place or time for, in a scheme, series, or arrangement: *to fit in a day for you*; *an awkward fact for the historian to fit in*; **b** intrans., to occupy a suitable position in space, time, or rank, in relation to something else: *it fits in well with my arrangements*; **c** to adapt oneself to company or surroundings: *he doesn't fit in well with a party of fox-hunting squires. Fit on*, **a** trans., to put on (garment) for purpose of fitting; **b** intrans., to go well, be adapted easily, to be placed in given position: *I can't make the cover of the tin fit on. Fit out*, trans., **a** to equip, furnish, prepare for use: *to fit out a ship for a voyage*; *to fit out an expedition*; **b** to supply with: *to fit a man out with travelling kit. Fit up*, trans., to get ready, prepare; furnish with fittings, supply with things, adjuncts, necessary or suitable: *to fit up a suite of rooms*; *fitted up with electric light.*

fit (IV.), adj. M.E. *fitte*, n., 'equal, peer', Late M.E., adj.; related to prec., & perh. affected in meaning by M.E. *fet*, 'skilful, handsome', fr. O. Fr. *fait.* See **feat**. **1. a** Suitable, adapted, adjusted, appropriate, to a purpose, function, requirement, standard &c.: *a land fit for heroes*; *fit time and place*; Phrs. *fit for a king*, of the best quality; *the survival of the fittest*, of the types best adapted to the environment; **b** qualified, in a suitable state, properly prepared; competent, worthy: *I am not fit to be seen*; *not fit to live*; *not fit to hold a candle to him*; **c** in such a condition or mood (of distress &c.) as to be ready: *I walked till I was fit to drop*; (also vulg., quasi-adverbial after vb.) *she cried fit to break her heart*; *he laughed fit to burst.* **2.** Fitting, becoming, seemly, proper: *it is fit that we should rejoice.* Phrs. *to think fit to*, to decide, prefer, choose to; often slightly sarcastic: *he didn't think fit to recognize me.* **3.** Prepared by bodily training &c. for a race, campaign, or any severe effort; hence (colloq.), strong and well, in good health or condition, vigorous: *to feel, keep, fit.* Phr. *as fit as a fiddle, as a flea*, in the best possible health or condition.

fit (V.), n., fr. **fit (III.)**. **a** Thing that fits or is adjusted: *the jacket is a bad, an easy, fit*; **b** adjustment, fitting: *it will be a tight, awkward, fit to get it all in.*

fitch (I.), n. [1. fich; 2. fitʃ]. Obsolete variant of **vetch**.

fitch (II.) n. M. Du. *fisse*, 'polecat', cp. Du. *vies*, 'stinking, nasty'. See **fizz**. **a** (obs. or provinc.) Polecat; **b** polecat's hair or fur; brush made of it.

fitché, fitchy, adj. [1. fíchi; 2. fítʃi]. Fr. *fiché*, P.P. of *ficher*, 'to fix'. See **fish (III.)**. (her., of cross) Pointed at lower end, as though for fixing in the ground.

fitchet, n. [1. fíchet; 2. fítʃit]. **fitch (II.)** & dimin. **-et**. Polecat.

fitchew, n. [1. fíchōō; 2. fítʃū]. M.E., fr. O. Fr. *fissel, fichau*; ending fr. dimin. suff. **-el**, fr. a Gmc. source. See **fitch (II.)**. Polecat.

fitful, adj. [1. fítfool; 2. fítfəl, -ful]. **fit (I.)** & **-ful**. Characterized by, recurring in, alternate periods of activity and quiescence; intermittent; spasmodic; capricious: *a fitful breeze*; '*Life's fitful fever*' (Shakespeare); *a fitful worker.*

fitfully, adv. Prec. & **-ly**. In a fitful manner; by fits and starts, intermittently.

fitfulness, n. See prec. & **-ness**. Quality of being fitful.

fitly, adv. [1. fítli; 2. fítli]. **fit (IV.)** & **-ly**. In a fit manner, suitably, appropriately.

fitment, n. [1. fitment; 2. fítmənt]. **fit (III.)** & **-ment**. Equipment; detail of furnishing; (often pl.) fittings.

fitness, n. [1. fítnes; 2. fítnis]. **fit (IV.)** & **-ness**. State or quality of being fit; **a** suitability, congruity, appropriateness; **b** good bodily health and condition.

fit-out, n. [1. fít out; 2. fít aut]. **fit (III.)** & **out**. (colloq.) Equipment, outfit.

fitter, n. [1. fíter; 2. fítə]. **fit (III.)** & **-er**. Person who fits; specif. **a** tailor who fits clothes to the person; **b** mechanic who adjusts metal fittings.

fitting (I.), adj. [1. fíting; 2. fítiŋ], fr. Pres. Part. of **fit (III.)**. Suitable, appropriate, proper, meet.

fitting (II.), n. **fit (III.)** & **-ing**. **1.** Action of person or thing that fits. **2.** Thing that is fitted to another thing; (often pl.) fixture in building &c.; detachable part of machine &c., accessory.

fittingly, adv. **fitting (I.)** & **-ly**. In a fitting manner, suitably, appropriately.

fittingness, n. See prec. & **-ness**. Suitability, appropriateness.

fitting-shop, n. Workshop in which parts of machine are fitted together.

fitz-, pref. [1. fits; 2. fits]. A.-Fr., fr. Fr. *fils*, 'son' (see **filial**); used in proper names meaning 'son of', *Fitzgerald* &c.; often of illegitimate descendants of a king, or princes of the blood royal, *Fitzwilliam, Fitz James* &c.

five (I.), adj. [1. fīv; 2. faiv]. O.E., M.E. *fīf* for **finf*, cogn. w. O.S. *fīf*, Du. *vijf*, O.H.G., Goth. *fimf*, Germ. *fünf*, O.N. *fimm* &c.; Common Gmc. type **pemp-*, fr. **peŋkʷ-*, w. assimilation of final *kʷ* to initial *p*; cp. Scrt. *pañca*, Lith. *penkì*, Gk. *pémpe, pénte*, Lat. *quinque*, O. Ir. *coic*, O.W. *pimp* &c. Four and one. Phrs. *the five senses*, sight, hearing, taste, smell, and touch; *the five wits* (archaic): **a** the five senses; **b** the five supposed mental faculties; *five-finger exercise*, piano exercise for all the fingers.

five (II.), n. fr. prec. **1. a** The sum of four and one (of number or amount); **b** symbol for this number. **2.** Playing-card, domino &c. with five pips: *the five of spades.* **3.** (cricket) *Hit for five* (runs). **4.** The hour of five. Phr. *five o'clock tea.* **5.** Finger, in Phr. (vulgar) *bunch of fives*, hand. **6.** (colloq., pl.) The 5 per cents. **7.** (pl.) Size in gloves, boots &c.

fivefold, adj. & adv. [1. fívfōld; 2. fáivfould]. O.E. *fīff(e)ald.* Prec. & **-fold**. **1.** adj. **a** Repeated, multiplied, five times, quintuple; **b** having five divisions: *a fivefold leaf.* **2.** adv. Five times, to a fivefold degree.

five-line(d), adj. [1. fív līn(d); 2. fáiv lain(d)]. Formerly in Phr. *five-line(d) whip*, urgent call by party whip to members of Parliament to attend sitting, underlined five times.

fivepenny (bit), n. [1. fívpeni, fípeni (bit); 2. fáivpəni, fípəni (bit)]. Silver coin, now obsolete, worth fivepence.

five-per-cents, n. [1. fív per sents; 2. fáiv pə sɛnts, fáiv pə sénts]. Stock paying 5 per cent interest.

fiver, n. [1. fíver; 2. fáivə]. **five** & **-er**. (colloq.) **a** Five-pound note; **b** a hit in cricket on which five runs are gained.

fives, n. [1. fīvz; 2. faivz]. Pl. of **five**. Origin of name uncertain. Ball-game for two or four persons, played in walled court, with hand in a padded glove or with small bat.

fives-ball, n. Small hard ball used in fives.

fivescore, adj. & n. [1. fívskōr; 2. fáivskɔ̄]. (archaic or provinc.) A hundred.

fives-court, n. Walled court in which fives is played.

fix (I.), vb. trans. & intrans. [1. fiks; 2. fiks]. M.E. *fixen* (apparently older than Fr. *fixer*), fr. M.E. *fix*, 'fixed', fr. Lat. *fix-(um)*, P.P. type of *figere*, 'to fix', or directly fr. L. Lat. freq. *fixāre*, fr. same stem. The base is prob. identical w. that in Lith. *dýgstu*, 'to fix, cement'; see also **ditch**. **A.** trans. **1.** (of material actions) **a** To make firm, fast, stable, or immovable; to attach firmly, fasten, secure: *to fix a loose plank*; *to fix a feather in one's hat, a lid on a box*; Phr. *to fix the blame on a person*, to attribute, bring home to, convict of; **b** to arrange, put right, put in order: *to fix a machine so that it will work* (American slang). **2.** (of intellectual action) **a** To form and retain a clear, firm, lasting mental impression of: *to fix something in one's mind*; **b** to determine upon, arrange, appoint: *to fix a date for meeting* &c.; **c** to come to a decision concerning, settle in one's mind: *to fix a price, rent, amount to be paid for anything* &c.; **d** to ascertain beyond doubt, discover with certainty: *the exact spot where the ark rested has never been definitely fixed*; *what you say fixes it*; **e** to render permanent and unchangeable, make unalterable: *to fix*

English spelling; *to fix Easter*, to keep it on the same date every year. **3.** To direct steadily and unwaveringly, keep unmoved, rivet; **a** (in physical sense) *to fix one's eyes, gaze, upon*; **b** (of non-material things) *to fix one's thoughts, hopes, on a thing.* **4.** To attract, draw, and retain, keep directed towards: *the sight fixed my attention.* **5.** To direct steady gaze at, keep one's eyes fixed upon: *he fixed me with a stony stare.* **6.** (scient. and techn.). **a** To make stable, non-volatile, or solid by a chemical process: *to fix nitrogen, mercury*; **b** (photog.) to render permanent, prevent from fading by chemical treatment: *to fix a photograph*; **c** (of colours, dyes) to prevent from fading or altering, make fast; **d** to kill and preserve from decay by use of a chemical agent: *to fix a microscopic specimen*; **e** (entom.) to arrange in desired position and render this permanent: *to fix a butterfly*; **f** (biol.) to render permanent, and perpetuate, characteristic features of: *to fix the breed, type, strain of a species.* **B.** intrans. To become fixed; specif., to lose instability, volatility, or fluidity. **C.** Phrases with adverbs. *Fix on* or *upon*, intrans., to decide on, pitch on, choose, select: *to fix on a date for a journey. Fix up*, trans., (colloq.) **a** to provide, make, suitable arrangements for: *I can easily fix you up for the night*; **b** to settle, arrange, decide on: *we have fixed up a date for the dance*; **c** to organize, superintend: *to fix up a tennis tournament*; **d** to make up, settle amicably, come to friendly understanding concerning: *we have fixed up our little differences satisfactorily.*

fix (II.), n., fr. prec. (colloq.) Awkward, difficult situation, dilemma.

fixable, adj. [1. fíksabl; 2. fíksəbl]. **fix** (I.) & **-able.** Capable of being fixed.

fixation, n. [1. fiksáshun; 2. fikséiʃən], fr. Fr., fr. L. Lat. *fixātiōn-(em)*; base *fix-*, see **fix**, & **-ation.** (chiefly scient.) Act or process of fixing.

fixative, adj. & n. [1. fíksativ; 2. fíksətiv]. **fix**, **-ate** & **-ive.** **1.** adj. Capable of fixing, used for fixing or rendering fast or permanent. **2.** n. Fixing agent; mordant &c.

fixature, n. [1. fíksachur; 2. fíksətʃə]. **fix**, **-ate** & **-ure.** (trade word) Sticky substance used for keeping the hair in desired position.

fixed, adj. [1. fikst; 2. fikst]. P.P. of **fix** (I.). **1.** (of material objects) **a** In established invariable position; immovable, stationary: *fixed star*; **b** not moving, kept motionless: *fixed gaze.* **2.** (of ideas, opinions &c.) Invariable, rigid, unchanging; firmly held and adhered to; inflexible, unalterable, immutable. **3.** (of material conditions) Definitely determined; settled, decided upon; hence, not liable to variation: *fixed price.*

fixedly, adv. [1. fíksedli; 2. fíksidli]. Prec. & **-ly.** (in physical and non-material senses) In a fixed manner; **a** not moving, unwaveringly: *to look fixedly at*; **b** determinedly, with resolution: *to have one's ideal fixedly set before one.*

fixedness, n. [1. fíksednes; 2. fíksidnis]. See prec. & **-ness.** State of being fixed, fixity.

fixer, n. [1. fíkser; 2. fíksə]. **fix** (I.) & **-er.** Person or thing that fixes; specif., chemical agent that fixes photograph, dye &c.

fixings, n., pl. [1. fíksingz; 2. fíksiŋz]. **fix** (I.) & **-ing.** (Amer. colloq.) Equipment, outfit, accessories, trimmings.

fixity, n. [1. fíksiti; 2. fíksiti]. Lat. *fix-(us)*, 'fixed' (see **fix** (I.)), & **-ity**; cp. Fr. *fixité.* State of being fixed; permanence; immobility; invariability: *fixity of tenure*; *fixity of look*; *fixity of habits.*

fixture, n. [1. fíkschur; 2. fíkstʃə]. Corrupt. of obs. *fixure*, fr. L. Lat. *fixūra*; **fix** (I.) & **-ure**, prob. on anal. of *mixture.* **1.** (rare) Action of fixing; state of being fixed. **2. a** Thing fixed or fastened in position, especially as part of apparatus: *electric light fixtures*; **b** (law, pl.) furniture or fittings attached to a building or land which usually have to be purchased with it; **c** (colloq.) person who remains long, or too long, in a place: *I'm a fixture now at Oxford*; *our guest seems to be a fixture.* **3.** Sporting event of which the date has been determined in advance: *racing, cricket, fixtures for the season*; dates of such events.

fizgig, n. [1. fízgig; 2. fízgig]. **1.** Flirtatious, noisy girl. **2.** Kind of noisy firework which makes frequent explosions.

fizz (I.), vb. intrans. [1. fiz; 2. fiz]. Imitative; cp. O.N. *fīsa*, 'to break wind', whence M.E. *fīs*, n. Cp. **fitch** (II.). **a** To make a spluttering, hissing noise, like a firework; **b** (of liquid) to effervesce, to sparkle.

fizz (II.), n., fr. prec. **a** Fizzing noise; **b** effervescence; **c** (slang) champagne; (rarely) effervescent wine in general.

fizzle (I.), vb. intrans. [1. fízl; 2. fízl]. **fizz** (I.) & **-le.** To make a slight fizzing. Phr. *fizzle out*, **a** to go out after spluttering, as a damp fuse or firework; **b** (fig.) to end in a fiasco; come to an end lamely, prematurely, or feebly.

fizzle (II.), n., fr. prec. **a** Act or process of fizzling; **b** (colloq.) fiasco.

fizzy, adj. [1. fízi; 2. fízi]. **fizz** (II.) & **-y.** (colloq.) Effervescent, sparkling.

fjord. Variant of **fiord.**

flabbergast, vb. trans. [1. flábergahst; 2. flǽbəgāst]. Of doubtful origin; second element prob. associated w. **ghastly, aghast.** (colloq.) To astound, fill with amazement, confound with astonishment; to disconcert by sudden and unexpected speech or action.

flabbily, adv. [1. flábili; 2. flǽbili]. **flabby** & **-ly.** In a flabby manner.

flabbiness, n. [1. flábines; 2. flǽbinis]. Next word & **-ness.** **a** (of substances) Condition of being flabby; flaccidity; **b** (fig., of mind and character) lack of moral fibre.

flabby, adj. [1. flábi; 2. flǽbi]. Perh. variant of obsolesc. or dialectal *flappy*, 'inclined to flap', as loose flesh; cp. L.G. *flabbe*, 'hanging lip,' Dan. *flab*, 'chops'; prob. imitative. Cp. **flap.** **a** Hanging loosely, limp, soft, yielding, flaccid: *flabby cheeks, muscles*; **b** (fig., of intellect, character, and expressions of these) weak, feeble, lacking in moral force or stamina: *a flabby character, speech.*

flabellate, adj. [1. flabélāt; 2. flæbéleit]. Lat. *flābell-*, stem of **flabellum**, & **-ate.** Fan-shaped, flabelliform.

flabelliform, adj. [1. flabéliform; 2. flæbélifōm]. Lat. *flābelli-*, form of **flabellum** used in compounds, & **-form.** Shaped like a fan, or like sector of a circle.

flabellum, n. [1. flabélum; 2. flæbéləm]. Lat. *flābellum*, 'fan, fly-whisk', dimin. (see **-el**) fr. *flābrum*, 'breeze', fr. *flāre*, 'to blow'. See **flatulent**; also **blast, blow** (I.). **1.** Fan of white feathers borne before the Pope on ceremonial occasions. **2.** (zool.) Fan-shaped organ or part of animal.

flaccid, adj. [1. fláksid; 2. flǽksid]. Lat. *flaccid-(us)*, fr. *flaccus*, 'flabby'. **a** (of muscle &c.) Yielding to pressure, soft, flabby; also **b** (fig., of mind &c.) weak, nerveless.

flaccidity, n. [1. flaksíditi; 2. flæksíditi]. Prec. & **-ity.** Condition of being flaccid.

flag (I.), vb. intrans. & trans. [1. flag; 2. flæg]. Apparently a form of obsolesc. *flack*, 'to flap, flutter', M.E. *flacken*; cp. O.E. *flacor*, 'flickering'; M. Du. *vlacken*, Swed. *flacka*, 'to flutter'; Icel. *flakka*, 'to rove', *flaka*, 'to flap, be loose'. The sense is affected by O. Fr. *flaquir*, 'to flag, be weary', fr. *flac*, 'feeble, faint', fr. Lat. *flacc-(us)*, 'flabby'. See **flaccid.** **1.** intrans. **a** (of physical process) To droop, hang loosely or slackly, become limp and weak: *plants flagging from drought*; **b** (of non-material things) to languish, become faint, feeble; to die out, diminish: *my interest in the subject is flagging more and more.* **2.** trans. (rare) To cause to flag.

flag (II.), n. M.E. *flagge, flegge*, related to prec. fr. the waving of the blades in the wind; cp. Du. *vlag*, Dan. *flæg*, 'iris'. **1.** One of several plants with long sword-shaped leaves or blades; specif. **a** yellow British iris growing in water, the common purple iris grown in gardens, also other species; **b** *sweet flag*, reed-like British water-plant of arum family; **c** pl., *flags*, or *flag*, kind of coarse grass. **2.** Blade of plant.

flag (III.), n. Prob. same as prec. The word, though in other Gmc. languages (cp. Du. *vlag*, Germ. *flagge*), appears first in Engl. in 15th cent. **1. a** Sheet of bunting or other light cloth, usually oblong in shape, and bearing a definite device and colour, attached by one side to staff or halyard, as signal, or as symbol, ensign, or distinguishing mark of nation, regiment, company, or other association, or of individual; a banner; Phrs. *black flag*, pirate's ensign; piracy; signal that no quarter will be given; signal (on gaol) that prisoner has been executed; *red flag*, symbol of defiance, of revolution, of Socialism or Communism; *white flag*, signal for parley, or of truce or surrender; *to hang out, show, the white flag*, (fig.) to surrender, yield; *yellow flag*, signal of quarantine, infectious disease &c.; *to dip the flag*, lower it and then hoist it, as salute; *to strike the (one's) flag*, to surrender; *under the flag of*, ranged on the side of; **b** (nav.) ensign flown by admiral on his ship when in command. Phr. *the admiral has hoisted, struck, his flag*, has assumed, relinquished, command. **2.** Bushy tail of certain dogs, such as setters.

flag (IV.), vb. trans., fr. prec. **1.** To put a flag or flags on; to adorn or mark out with flags: *to flag the streets for a festival*; *to flag a course* (for a race). **2.** To signal a message, order &c. with flags &c.

flag (V.), n. Prob. fr. **flag** (I.); cp. **flag** (II., III.). (coll.) **a** Quill-feathers on bird's wing; **b** feathers on leg of hawk, owl &c.

flag (VI.), n. Obs., 'slice of turf'. M.E. *flagge*; cp. Icel. *flag*, 'spot where a turf has been cut', *flaga*, 'flagstone'; Dan. *iis-flage*, 'ice-floe'. See **flake** (I.), **flaw, floe** & perh. **flay.** **a** Paving-stone, flagstone; **b** stone pavement; **c** hard stone that splits into flakes, suitable for paving.

flag (VII.), vb. trans., fr. prec. To pave with flagstones.

flag-captain, n. Captain of flagship.

flag-day, n. Day on which money is collected in the streets for some charitable or public purpose, miniature flags being worn by those who have contributed.

flagellant, adj. & n. [1. flájelant; 2. flǽdžilənt]. Lat. *flagellant-(em)*, Pres. Part. type of *flagellāre*, 'to scourge', fr. **flagellum.** **1.** adj. Practising flagellation. **2.** n. Ascetic who scourges himself; specif. (cap.) member of any body of religious zealots, chiefly mediaeval, who scourge themselves publicly.

flagellate (I.), vb. trans. [1. flájelāt; 2. flǽdžileit]. Lat. *flagellāt-(um)*, P.P. type of *flagellāre.* See prec. To scourge, flog, whip.

flagellate (II.), adj. See prec. (biol.) **a** Furnished with a flagellum or flagella; **b** shaped like a flagellum.

flagellation, n. [1. flàjeláshun; 2. flæ̀džiléiʃən]. Lat. *flagellātiōn-(em).* See **flagellate** (II.) & **-ion.** Act of scourging or whipping.

flagellatory, adj. [1. flájelātori; 2. flǽdžileitəri]. **flagellate** (II.) & **-ory.** Pertaining to flagellation.

flagelliform, adj. [1. flajéliform; 2. flædžélifōm]. Lat. *flagelli-*, combining form of **flagellum**, & **-form.** Shaped like the lash of a whip or a flagellum.

flagellum, n. [1. flajélum; 2. flædžéləm]. Lat., 'whip', dimin. (see **-el**) of *flagrum*, 'scourge'. Gmc. cognates are found in O.N. *blaka*, 'to strike, beat the wings', *blak*, 'a blow'. **a** (biol.) Long flexible whip-like process of a cell, capable of rapid motion; **b** (bot.) runner.

flageolet (I.), n. [1. flàjōlét; 2. flæ̀džoulét]. Fr., dimin. (see **-et**) of O. Fr. *flajol, flageol*, fr. O. Provenç. *flaujol-s*, 'flageolet', prob. fr. unrecorded Low Lat. type **flaviolus*, perh. fr. *flāre*, 'to blow'. Small pipe-shaped wind instrument with mouthpiece at end and six holes.

flageolet (II.), n. [1. flajolét, flazholá; 2. flædžəlét, flažəléi]. Fr., fr. O. Fr. *fageolet*, dimin. of *fageol*, fr. Lat. *faseŏlus*, dimin. of *fas-*, *phasēlus*, fr. Gk. *phásēlos*, 'a kind of bean'. A kind of kidney-bean.

flagging, n. [1. flǽging; 2. flǽgiŋ]. **flag** (**VII.**) & **-ing. a** Process of laying flagstones; **b** pavement of flagstones.

flaggy (**I.**), adj. [1. flági; 2. flǽgi]. M.E. *flaggi*. **flag** (II.) & **-y**. Abounding in the plants called flags.

flaggy (II.), adj. **flag** (**VI.**) & **-y**. Pertaining to, resembling, flagstone.

flagitious, adj. [1. flajíshus; 2. flədžíʃəs], fr. Lat. *flāgitiōs-(us)*, 'disgraceful', fr. *flāgiti-(um)*, 'passionate or furious demand', hence 'shameful deed', fr. *flāgitāre*, 'to demand passionately', cp. *flagrāre*, 'to flame, blaze'. See **flagrant**. (of person or action) Atrociously wicked, criminal; disgraceful, shameful.

flagitiously, adv. Prec. & **-ly**. In a flagitious manner.

flagitiousness, n. See prec. & **-ness**. Quality of being flagitious; atrocious wickedness.

flag-lieutenant, n. Flag officer's aide-de-camp.

flag-list, n. Roll of flag-officers.

flagman, n. [1. flágman; 2. flǽgmən]. Man who signals with a flag, esp. in horse-racing.

flag-officer, n. Naval officer (admiral, vice-admiral, rear-admiral) commanding fleet or squadron and flying his own flag.

flagon, n. [1. flágun; 2. flǽgən]. O. Fr. *flascon*, *flagon*, Mod. Fr. *flacon*, fr. Low Lat. *flascōn-(em)*, augmentative (see **-oon**) of *flascus*, *flasca*, **flask. a** Vessel for serving wine at table, with narrow neck, a handle, and spout; specif., that used for the Eucharist; **b** (trade word) large vessel with flattened sides, holding about one or two quarts.

flagrancy, n. [1. flágransi; 2. fléigrənsi]. See next word & **-cy**. Cp. Lat. *flagrantia*, 'a burning, ardour'. Quality of being flagrant; notoriety; glaring, scandalous character (of an action).

flagrant, adj. [1. flágrant; 2. fléigrənt]. Fr., fr. Lat. *flagrant-(em)*, Pres. Part. type of *flagrāre*, 'to blaze, burn, be inflamed with passion', fr. Lat. base *flag-*, 'blaze', in grade relation to *fulg-ēre*, 'to shine' (see **refulgent**, **fulminate**); cogn. w. Scrt. *bhrāj*, 'to shine'; Gk. *phlégein*, 'to burn', *phlóx*, 'flame' (see **phlox**), also w. **bleach**, **blank**, **bright. a** (of action) Notoriously, obtrusively, evil; glaring, scandalous: *a flagrant offence, crime*; **b** (of persons) guilty of such crime, or offence: *a flagrant sinner*.

flagrante delicto, adv. [1. flagránte delíktō; 2. flægrǽnti dilíktou]. Lat. In open act of committing a crime or offence.

flagrantly, adv. [1. flágrantli; 2. fléigrəntli]. In a flagrant manner.

flagship, n. [1. flágship; 2. flǽgʃip]. Ship flying the flag of the admiral commanding fleet or squadron.

flagstaff, n. [1. flágstahf; 2. flǽgstāf]. Staff from which a flag is flown.

flagstone, n. [1. flágstōn; 2. flǽgstoun]. Large flat stone used as flag for paving.

flagwagging, n. [1. flágwàging; 2. flǽgwæ̀giŋ]. **a** (mil., colloq.) Action of signalling with flags; **b** (fig.) bellicose, provocative, bragging talk.

flail, n. [1. flāl; 2. fleil]. O.E. *fligel*, O.H.G. *flegil*; but M.E. *fleȝl*, *fleil*, whence present form, is more directly due to O. Fr. *fla(i)el* (cp. Mod. Fr. *fléau*); all fr. Lat. *flagellum*, 'scourge'. See **flagellum**. Implement, now rarely used, for threshing grain by hand, consisting of stout stick attached to end of handle so as to swing freely.

flair, n. [1. flār; 2. flɛə]. Fr., 'power of scenting out, right instinct for', fr. vb. *flairer*, 'scent out', fr. Low Lat. *flagrāre*, 'scent (out)', by dissimilation fr. Lat. *fragrāre*, 'to have a smell'. See **flagrant** & **fragrant**. Instinctive discernment: *a flair for good poetry*.

flake (**I.**), n. [1. flāk; 2. fleik]. M.E., prob. of Scand. origin, cp. O.N. *flaki*, 'flake'; Swed. *flake*, 'plate' (*isflake*, 'icefloe'); Norw. *flak*, 'slice'; Du. *flage*, 'snowflake'; Icel. *flakna*, *flagna*, 'to flake off'; cogn. w. **flag** (**VI.**) **floe**, **flaw**, & perh. **flay**. Prob. fr. Aryan base **plag-*, 'to beat'. See **plague**. **1. a** Thin, flat piece that splits, or scales off, or is chipped or peeled from anything: *a flake of stone, flint, fish, orange-peel*; **b** (perhaps confused with **flock**) small light mass of: *flake of snow*, (more rarely) *of burning material*. **2.** Kind of carnation with striped flowers.

flake (**II.**), vb. trans. & intrans., fr. prec. **A.** trans. **1.** To form or gather into flakes; to split off into flakes: *the frost flakes the stone*. **2.** To cover, sprinkle, with flakes, to fleck. **B.** intrans. **1.** To split or fall away in flakes, to scale; also, *flake off* or *away*. **2.** To fall in flakes (of snow &c.).

flake (**III.**), n. Cp. O.N. *flake*, Du. *vlaak*, 'paling, hurdle'. **a** Rack or stage on which goods are stored or dried; **b** light platform hung over ship's side for workman.

flake-white, n. White pigment made of scales of white lead.

flakiness, n. [1. flákines; 2. fléikinis]. **flaky** & **-ness**. Quality of being flaky; tendency to flake.

flaky, adj. [1. fláki; 2. fléiki]. **flake** (**I.**) & **-y**. Having the nature of a flake or flakes; in form of a flake.

flam, n. & vb. trans. [1. flam; 2. flæm]. Shortened fr. obs. & provinc. *flamfew*, 'gewgaw, trifle', fr. obs. Fr. *fanfelue* (Mod. Fr. *fanfreluche*) in same sense, fr. Low Lat. type **fanfalūca*, fr. Gk. *pomphólux*, 'air-bladder'; cp. Span. *fanfarria*, 'idle boasting'. See **fanfare**, **flimflam**. **1.** n. **a** Sham, deceitful trick, lie; nonsense; **b** kind of flourish on drum. **2.** vb. To trick, deceive, cheat: *to flam one off with lies*.

flambé, adj. [1. flómbā; 2. flā̃bē]. Fr., P.P. of *flamber*, 'to blaze, singe'. See **flame**. (of porcelain &c.) Decorated with irregular splashes of coloured glaze.

flambeau, n. [1. flámbō; 2. flǽmbou]. Fr., fr. Low Lat. *flambellum*, dimin. of *flamma*, **flame**. Large torch with several waxed wicks, used on ceremonial occasions.

flamboyance, **-cy**, n. [1. flambóians(i); 2. flæmbóiəns(i)]. See next word & **-ce** or **-cy**. Quality of being flamboyant in sense **2**.

flamboyant, adj. [1. flambóiant; 2. flæmbóiənt]. Fr., Pres. Part. of *flamboyer*, 'to flame', fr. O. Fr. *flambe*, 'flame', fr. Lat. *flamma*, q.v. under **flame** (**I.**). **1.** Specif. (archit.) pertaining to the latest phase of continental, esp. French, Gothic; characterized by flowing, flame-like tracery, and florid ornament. **2.** (of taste, style, personal adornment &c.) Excessively ornate; highly coloured; florid; too conspicuous.

flame (**I.**), n. [1. flām; 2. fleim]. M.E. *flamme*, *flaume*, fr. O. Fr. *flam(m)e*, fr. Lat. *flamma*, prob. for **flag-ma*, fr. base **flag-*, 'to blaze, burn', & substant. formative *-m-*. See under **flagrant**, **phlegm**, **phlox**, & cp. etymol. of **black**. **1.** Luminous, incandescent heat; mass of burning gas or vapour, rising from burning matter &c.; such masses collectively. Phrs. *to commit to the flames*, to burn; *in flames*, flaming, blazing; *to burst into flame(s)*, to blaze up suddenly. **2.** Lurid brightness resembling flame; fiery glow, blaze of light or colour: *the flames of sunset*. **3.** (fig.) **a** Burning, ardent passion, or emotion: *flames of wrath, love, zeal*; *to fan the flame*, to intensify passion or emotion; **b** intense, powerful, mental activity: *the flame of his intellect, imagination* &c. **4.** (familiar and colloq.) Beloved person, sweetheart: esp. *an old flame (of his)*.

flame (**II.**), vb. intrans. M.E. *flam(m)en*, fr. O. Fr. *flam(m)er*, fr. Lat. *flammāre*. See prec. **1.** To emit a flame or flames; to burn as a flame; to blaze. **2. a** To produce effect resembling flame; to glow brightly, with luminosity or colour; to flare, glare; to have a fiery red or yellow colour: *the western sky flames*; *the garden flames with tulips*; **b** (of human beings) to blush deeply or suddenly: *her face flamed with excitement*; **c** to become violently excited, show vehement passion or fervour: *to flame with indignation*. *Flame out*, intrans., **a** to burst out with flames; **b** (of temper &c.) to be suddenly and forcibly expressed. *Flame up*, intrans., **a** to rise up in flame; blaze up; **b** to become suddenly and violently angry or excited; **c** (of passion &c.) to become roused.

flame-coloured, adj. Having the colour of flame, bright scarlet.

flame-flower, n. Flower popularly called red-hot poker, *Kniphofia* or *Tritoma*.

flameless, adj. [1. flāmles; 2. fléimlis]. **flame** (**I.**) & **-less**. Devoid of flame.

flamen, n. [1. flāmen; 2. fléimɛn]. Lat. *flāmen*, perh. orig. 'blower' (of the sacrificial fire), fr. *flāre*, 'to blow', & formative *-men*, denoting agent, or for **flag-men*, 'burner'. See **flagrant**, **flame**. Ancient Roman priest of a particular deity.

flame-projector or **-thrower**, n. Cp. Germ. *flammenwerfer*, 'flame-thrower'. War-engine which pumps blazing liquid or flame into enemy trenches &c.

flaming, adj. [1. flāming; 2. fléimiŋ]. **flame** (**II.**) & **-ing**. **1.** In a condition of burning with flame; throwing out flames, blazing. **2.** Very bright and hot: *a flaming August*. **3.** Glaring, very gaudy or bright in colour: *flaming colours*. **4.** (of feelings) Intensely ardent, fervent: *flaming patriotism*.

flamingly, adv. Prec. & **-ly**. So as to emit flames; so as to glow with colour.

flamingo, n. [1. flamínggō; 2. fləmíŋgou]. Formerly *flamengo*, fr. Port.; cp. Span. *flamenco*, fr. Provenç. *flamenc*, fr. *flama*, 'flame', & *-enc*, fr. Gmc. *-ing*. See **-ing**. Member of a widely distributed family of aquatic birds with very long legs and necks and webbed feet; so called from the scarlet colour in the wings.

flamy, adj. [1. flāmi; 2. fléimi]. **flame** (**I.**) & **-y**. Pertaining to, resembling, flame.

flan, n. [1. flan; 2. flæn], or as Fr. M.E. *fla(u)n*, *flawn*, fr. O. Fr. *flaon*, fr. Med. Lat. *fladōnem*, fr. O.H.G. *flado*, 'flat cake'. Shell of pastry filled with fruit &c.

flanch, n. [1. flansh; 2. flænʃ]. O. Fr. *flanche*. See **flange** & **flank**. (her.) One of two segments of a circle, curving towards the centre of the shield and placed opposite each other at either side of this.

flânerie, n. [1. fláhnerē; 2. flā́nərī]. Fr. See next word. Idling, loafing.

flâneur, n. [1. flahnēr; 2. flānā́], Fr., fr. *flâner*, 'to idle'. See **flaunt**. Gentle, dreamy loafer, esp. one who idles about the streets.

flange (**I.**), n. [1. flanj; 2. flæn(d)ž]. Provincial E. *flanch*, 'projection', fr. O. Fr. *flanche*, fem. variant of *flanc*, 'side'. See **flank** (**I.**). **1. a** Projecting rim, edge, or rib on wheel, rail, girder, pipe &c.; **b** attrib., as *flange coupling, joint, rail*. **2.** Founder's tool for making flanges.

flange (**II.**), vb. trans., fr. prec. To furnish with a flange: *a flanged wheel*.

flank (**I.**), n. [1. flangk; 2. flæŋk]. M.E. *flanke*, fr. O. Fr. *flanc*, of Gmc. origin; cp. O.H.G. *hlanca*, 'loin, side'. See **lank**. **1.** Fleshy part of the side of human or animal body between ribs and hip, esp. as butcher's term: *flank of beef*. **2. a** Side of a mountain or hill, of a fortification or other building; **b** (mil., nav.) right or left side of an armed force: *to cover, expose, the flanks*. Phr. *in flank*, at the side. **3.** attrib. adj. (mil., nav., from prec.) Pertaining to a flank. Phr. *flank attack*, one made on the enemy's flank; *flank march*, one parallel to that of the enemy; *flank movement*, one made with the object of turning the enemy's flank.

flank (**II.**), vb. trans. & intrans. Fr. *flanquer*. See prec. **A.** trans. **1. a** To be situated on the side or flank of; **b** to place on the flank, at the side of. **2.** (mil., nav.) **a** To protect the flank of; **b** to pass along the flank of; **c** to attack or threaten in flank; to enfilade. **B.** intrans. To be situated at the side of, border on.

flanker, n. [1. flángker; 2. flǽŋkə]. Prec. & **-er**. (mil.) a Fortification protecting or threatening flank; b (pl.) skirmishers on flank of marching column.

flannel, n., adj., & vb. trans. [1. flánel; 2. flǽnəl]. Earlier *flannen*, perh. fr. O. Fr. *flaine*, 'blanket', & **-en**, or fr. W. *gwlanen*, 'woollen', fr. *gwlân*, 'wool', cogn. w. Lat. *lāna*. See **lanate** & **wool**. 1. n. a Soft, loosely woven woollen fabric, with or without nap; b piece of such stuff used for cleansing and rubbing; c *flannels*, clothes made of flannel, esp. for games; d (old-fashioned colloq.) flannel underclothes. 2. adj. Made of flannel: *flannel trousers*. 3. vb. To rub with flannel.

flannelette, n. [1. flànelét; 2. flæ̀nəlét]. Prec. & **-ette**. Cotton fabric imitating flannel.

flannelled, adj. [1. fláneld; 2. flǽnəld]. **flannel** & **-ed**. Dressed in flannel clothes.

flannelly, adj. [1. fláneli; 2. flǽnəli]. **flannel** & **-y**. Resembling flannel.

flap (I.), vb. trans. & intrans. [1. flap; 2. flæp]. M.E. *flappen*, prob. imitative; cp. Du. *flappen*, also **flabby**, **flip**, **flop**, **slap** &c. A. trans. 1. To administer light blow, to slap with anything soft and yielding and having a broad, flat surface, such as a piece of fabric, a fan, or the palm of the hand: *to flap one's face*; *to flap flies away*. 2. To impart a rapid, upward and downward movement or series of such; to move rapidly downwards; only used of flat objects: *to flap one's hand*; *a bird flaps its wings*. 3. To cause to flap, flutter, wave: *the wind flaps the sails*. 4. To cause to hang, turn down, like a flap: *to flap one's hat at one side*. B. intrans. 1. To move lightly up and down, or to and fro; to flutter loosely: *a bird's wings flap*; *a flag flaps in the wind*; *broad trousers flapping about the feet*. 2. To hang down as a flap: *the brim of his hat flapped over one eye*.

flap (II.), n. M.E., 'blow, fly-flap'; as prec.; cp. Du. *flap*, 'stroke, blow'. 1. Action, motion, or sound of flapping; light stroke with broad surface, strap: *a flap in the face*. 2. Thing that flaps or is flapped; specif. a piece of flexible material attached at one side or end, often covering opening &c.: *the bag has a leather flap over the keyhole*; *a flap over the pocket*; *the flap of a purse*; b the broad, soft brim of a hat; c kind of fan or whisk for driving away or killing flies; flapper: *fly-flap*; d flat piece, part of anything, made to hang down, or move, when required, e.g. hinged leaf of table, desk &c.; e (surg.) piece of skin, or skin and flesh, left attached at one side only and wrapped over wound after amputation, so as to grow to it. 3. Long, flexible, pendant ears of certain animals, e.g. of spaniels &c.

flapdoodle, n. [1. flápdōōdl; 2. flǽpdūdl]. Fanciful concoction. (colloq.) Humbug, nonsense.

flap-eared, adj. Having broad, hanging ears.

flapjack, n. [1. flápjak; 2. flǽpdžæk]. **flap** (I.) & **Jack** (I.). Kind of large pancake.

flapper, n. [1. fláper; 2. flǽpə]. **flap** (I.) & **-er**. Person or thing that flaps; specif. a fly-flap; clapper for scaring birds; swingle of flail; b flipper of seal or other animal; tail of crustacean; c (slang) the hand; d kind of skate (fish); e young wild duck, partridge &c. that cannot yet fly; hence, f (colloq.) young, inexperienced, undeveloped girl, not quite grown up.

flare (I.), vb. intrans. [1. flār; 2. flɛə]. Recorded first in sense 'to spread out', but perh. cogn. w. Norw. *flara*, 'to blaze, flame', a form of *fladra*, 'to blaze, make a show'. 1. (of fire and light; also *flare up*) a To blaze up with large or unsteady flames; b to emit a glaring, dazzling, or fitful light; to display glaring colours; c (of a lamp) to burn up too high; to shoot a thin flame some way up the chimney; to smoke. 2. (fig.) Often *flare up, out*, to burst out into a rage, fly into a passion. 3. a To spread outwards, as a bowl or skirt; b (naut.) to spread out upwards, as bows of a ship; also trans.

flare (II.), n., fr. prec. 1. Bright, unsteady blaze, as of leaping flames: *the flare of torches*. 2. Flaming light burnt for a few seconds as signal, usually at sea or on coast. 3. Kind of fogging of photographic negative. 4. (fig.) a (rare, colloq.) Ostentation, swagger; b sudden outburst of anger. 5. Outward curvature, swelling, bulge.

flare-up, n. [1. flār úp; 2. flɛ̀ər ʌ́p]. 1. Sudden burst of flame; flare as signal. 2. (fig., colloq.) Any sudden burst, outbreak, of strong feeling or its expression; a sudden outburst of anger; tumultuous quarrel; b sudden, noisy, ostentatious display of social gaiety &c.

flaring, adj. [1. flāring; 2. flɛ́əriŋ]. Pres. Part. of **flare** (I.). 1. Blazing brightly and unsteadily. 2. (fig.) Glaring, gaudily or garishly obtrusive: *a flaring advertisement*. 3. Spreading outwards.

flaringly, adv. Prec. & **-ly**. In a flaring manner.

flash (I.), vb. intrans. & trans. [1. flash; 2. flæʃ]. M.E., 'to splash'. Origin uncertain. Partly imitative of rapid movement &c., & perh. influenced in form & meaning by a variety of words, e.g. *flare, flush, ash* &c. A. intrans. 1. a To emit a sudden and momentary bright ray of light, whether by combustion or explosion or reflexion; to shine suddenly, gleam out, and die away: *the lightning flashed out from the clouds*; *armour flashed in the sun*; b (of the eyes) to light up, sparkle, become momentarily brilliant: *his eyes flashed with anger, excitement* &c. 2. To move with great rapidity across the field of vision: *a few swallows flashed past*; *the express flashed through the station*. 3. (fig.) a (of the wit, humour, spirit) To be brilliant, scintillate; become suddenly and momentarily apparent: *his old spirit, art, flashed out occasionally*; b (of thoughts, ideas &c.) to occur suddenly to, pass through, the mind; esp. *flash across, flash into, flash through, the mind*. 4. (of molten glass) To expand into a sheet. B. trans. 1. a To emit or reflect light &c. in flashes: *the fires flashed their light through the forest glades*; b to direct light suddenly, to cause to flash: *to flash a lantern in a man's eyes*; c (fig.) *to flash a look, glance, smile* &c., to direct momentarily and rapidly. 2. To cause to flare up suddenly: *to flash powder*. 3. To transmit messages, signals &c. rapidly, suddenly, by instantaneous action; a by heliograph; b by electricity, wireless &c.: *to flash the news across the Atlantic*; c (fig.) to convey by sudden conviction &c. to the mind: *a sense of peace was flashed into his soul*. 4. To protect (roof &c.) against rain and wet by covering with lead, slates &c.

flash (II.), n., fr. prec. 1. Sudden, brief, momentary, blaze or gleam of light: *a flash of lightning, of a gun*. 2. (fig.) Sudden, brief outburst of emotion, or mental illumination or brilliance: *a flash of hope, gaiety, inspiration, wit, humour*. 3. Space of time occupied by a flash; a very brief period, a moment, instant, twinkling: *gone in a flash*; *to grasp the situation in a flash*. Phr. *a flash in the pan*, effort that makes a stir, but soon fails, from the flashing of old-fashioned flintlock musket. 4. Vulgar, flashy display. 5. Thieves' slang. 6. a Rapid stream of water released from a weir, flushing a channel; b device for releasing flash of water. 7. Obsolete slang for a wig; now surviving as name of piece of black material with long ends, worn at the back of the collar by the Royal Welch Fusiliers.

flash (III.), adj., fr. prec. a Showy, meretricious; hence, b counterfeit, spurious: *flash jewellery, coin, notes*; c dressed in a showy, vulgarly ostentatious way, as sharpers and others of the criminal or vicious classes; d pertaining to such persons: *a flash term, flash language*.

flash-board, n. **flash** (I.) & **board** (I.). Hatch for retaining water in mill-stream and letting it flow when required into the leat.

flasher, n. [1. flásher; 2. flǽʃə]. **flash** (I.) & **-er**. Person or thing that flashes; specif., boiler in which water is flashed, or turned rapidly into steam, also called *flash boiler*.

flash-house, n. House frequented by flash people; house of ill-fame.

flashily, adv. [1. fláshili; 2. flǽʃili]. **flashy** & **-ly**. In a flashy manner.

flashiness, n. [1. fláshines; 2. flǽʃinis]. **flashy** & **-ness**. Quality of being flashy.

flashing, n. [1. fláshing; 2. flǽʃiŋ]. **flash** (I.) & **-ing**. 1. Action of person or thing that flashes. 2. Heating of globe of crown-glass to cause it to flash. 3. Material used to flash a roof.

flashlight, n. [1. fláshlīt; 2. flǽʃlait]. Light that flashes, specif. a one in a lighthouse that shines intermittently at definite brief periods; b lamp used for signalling by flashes; c bright momentary light used in taking photographs: (attrib.) *a flashlight photograph*.

flashpoint, n. [1. fláshpoint; 2. flǽʃpɔint]. Lowest degree of temperature at which the vapour from an oil or spirit will ignite.

flashy, adj. [1. fláshi; 2. flǽʃi]. **flash** (II.) & **-y**. Superficially brilliant but worthless; gaudy, showy, tawdry, meretricious.

flask (I.), n. [1. flahsk; 2. flāsk]. O.E. *flasce*, *flaxe*, 'bottle', fr. Low Lat. *flasca*, the origin of wh. is uncertain. Also borrowed in other Gmc. languages; cp. O.H.G. *flasca*, Mod. Germ. *flasche*, 'bottle'. Perh. ultimately fr. Lat. *vasculum*, dimin. of *vās*, 'vessel'. See **vas**. A bottle; usually confined to one of several specific uses: 1. Small flattened bottle for wine or oil (rare or archaic). 2. Small flattened glass or metal bottle, often partly covered with leather, for carrying wine or spirits in the pocket: *spirit, brandy, flask*; *hunting flask*. 3. Metal or horn receptacle for carrying gunpowder about the person: *powder-flask*.

flask (II.), n. Fr. *flasque*, 'cheek', (in technical senses) 'top or bottom of bellows'; of Gmc. origin. Cp. Germ. *flach*, 'flat'. See **flay**. 1. Frame, in two or more parts, holding sand used as mould in founding. 2. Either of the two plates forming the sides of the trail of gun-carriage.

flasket, n. [1. fláhsket; 2. flāskit]. O. Fr. *flasquet*, dimin. of *flasque*, 'bottle'. See **flask** (I.) & **-et**. 1. Small flask. 2. (archaic) Long shallow basket with two handles.

flat (I.), adj. [1. flat; 2. flæt]. Scand., M.E., fr. O.N. *flat-r*, cp. O.H.G. *flaz*, & the O.E. *flet*, 'floor'. See **flat** (V.). 1. (of surfaces) a Level, even and horizontal, without elevations or depressions: *a flat roof*; *flat ground*; Phrs. *flat race*, one without obstacles to be jumped; *to knock a person flat*, so that he is prostrate; b extended on the ground; inclined, bent over towards the ground: *the storm left the wheat flat*; *an earthquake laid the city flat*; c projecting but slightly from surrounding surface: *a flat arch*; *flat candlestick*, short broad one for carrying. 2. a Lying in one plane; having a plane surface; extended mainly in one plane, broad and relatively thin: *the flat hand*, palm with fingers extended; b even, with a plane surface: *the picture is (hangs) flat against the wall*; c deviating only slightly from one plane: *a flat face, nose*; *flat relief*; *a flat golf club*, one with the head at a very obtuse angle to the shaft. 3. (paint.) a Lacking in relief; not suggesting depth; b uniform: *a flat wash, tint*. 4. a (of mental condition) Depressed in spirits, dull, listless; lacking animation, alertness, interest &c.: *we all feel very flat now he has gone away*; b (of external surroundings as affecting the mind) depressing, uninteresting, monotonous, undiversified: *life is very flat in a small village*; c (of forms of expression) dull, not arousing interest, lacking brilliance: *a flat speech*. 5. a (commerc.) Inactive, lacking in demand or competition: *tea closed flat*; *flat prices*, uniformly low; b (of liquor) lacking, or having lost, sparkle or effervescence. 6. (fig.) a Admitting no exceptions; b uniform, not graded: *a flat rate* *of 3 per cent*; **c** unqualified, absolute, plain, downright: *to give a flat denial*; *flat lunacy, blasphemy*. Phr. *that's flat*, that is my last word. **7.** (mus.) Lower than the 'natural' note, opposed to *sharp*: *his singing is flat*; *the piano is flat*; *A flat*, note or semitone lower than A natural, denoted by symbol ♭. **8.** (phon.) *Flat vowel*, one in the articulation of which the tongue is kept relatively level, so that neither the back nor the front has a greater elevation, e.g. [ǎ] in *bird* &c.

flat (**II.**), adv., fr. prec. **1.** So as to be flat; prone, recumbently: *to fall, lie, flat, on one's face*, on the ground. Phr. (fig., of remarks &c.) *to fall flat*, to fail to win applause; **2.** Entirely, directly, altogether: *to go flat against orders*. **3.** (colloq.) Bluntly, positively, absolutely: *I told him flat*. **4.** (mus.) In a flat manner: *to sing flat*, below the proper pitch. **5.** (finance) Without interest: *the bonds are sold flat*.

flat (**III.**), n., fr. **flat** (**I.**). **1. a** Flat surface: *to represent an object in the flat*, in two dimensions, as by drawing, distinguished from *in the round*; *to draw from the flat*, from a pictorial copy; **b** flat part of a thing: *the flat of one's sword, of the hand*. **2. a** Tract of flat land, esp. low-lying marsh; broad, level foreshore: *mud-flat*; **b** shoal, shallow. **3.** Flat object (in many technical senses); flat-bottomed boat; flat, shallow basket; American platform car; theatrical scenery on flat frame, pushed on from wings, &c. **4.** (mus.) **a** Note a semitone below natural; **b** symbol (♭) for this; **c** black key in piano by which flat note is produced. **5.** (colloq.) Stupid person easily tricked or gulled; dupe.

flat (**IV.**), vb. trans. & intrans., fr. **flat** (**I.**). **1.** trans. (rare) To render flat, flatten. **2.** intrans. (rare) To become flat, insipid, or dull.

flat (**V.**), n. Cp. O.E., M.E. *flet*, 'ground, floor', M.E., 'apartment'; O.S., O.N. *flet*, O.H.G. *flazzi*, 'floor', Germ. *flötz*, 'stratum'. This Gmc. base is doubtless cogn., though w. quite different formative elements, w. Lat. *plānus*, 'flat', q.v. under **plain** (**I.**). **a** Storey or floor in a house or other building; **b** floor of a house, or part of it, arranged as separate, self-contained dwelling; (pl.) house divided into a number of such independent dwellings.

flat-boat, n. Flat-bottomed boat used for transporting bulky objects.

flatfish, n. [1. flátfish; 2. flǽtfiʃ]. One of a number of fish, such as the turbot &c., having both eyes on the same side of the skull, and a superficial area of considerable size relative to the thickness of the body

flatfoot, n. [1. flátfoot; 2. flǽtfut]. Condition of being flatfooted.

flatfooted, adj. [1. flátfóoted; 2. flǽtfútid]. Having feet with flat soles and lacking an arched instep.

flathead, adj. & n. [1. flát-hed; 2. flǽt-hed]. **1.** adj. Having a flat head, either naturally so or from artificial deformation. **2.** n. **a** A North American snake; **b** one of several Australian fishes.

flat-iron, n. Iron implement used when heated for smoothing clothes &c., consisting of a flat, heavy, smooth plate with a handle above.

flatling, adv. & adj. [1. flátling; 2. flǽtliŋ]. **flat** (**I.**) & **-ling** (**II.**). (archaic) **a** adv. (i.) In a flat position; (ii.) with the flat part (of sword &c.); **b** adj., lying, falling flat; struck with the flat: *a flatling blow*.

flatly, adv. [1. flátli; 2. flǽtli]. **flat** (**I.**) & **-ly**. In a flat manner (in various senses).

flatness, n. [1. flátnes; 2. flǽtnis]. M.E. *flatnesse*. **flat** (**I.**) & **-ness**. Condition or quality of being flat.

flatten, vb. trans. & intrans. [1. flátn; 2. flǽtn]. **flat** (**I.**) & **-en**. **1.** trans. To make, render, flat (lit. or fig.); to render dull or vapid; to lower the musical pitch of; *flatten out*, **a** to flatten by spreading out, as by rolling or hammering; **b** (fig.) to strike with dismay, to disconcert. **2.** intrans. To become flat (lit. or fig.).

flatter (**I.**), n. [1. fláter; 2. flǽtə]. **flat** (**IV.**) & **-er**. Implement for flatting or flattening, used in metal working.

flatter (**II.**), vb. trans. [1. fláter; 2. flǽtə]. M.E. *flateren*; prob. formed fr. O. Fr. *flaterie*, q.v. under **flattery**. Ultimately fr. Gmc. source, in sense of 'to smooth down'. See **flat** (**I.**). **1.** To praise insincerely, adulate, fawn upon; to pay insincere and unmerited compliments to, esp. with a view to ingratiating oneself. **2.** To represent in too favourable a light (not necessarily from insincerity) **a** by attributing moral or intellectual qualities in excess of those actually existing; **b** by depicting as possessing beauty of face and form greater than the reality: *the painter has flattered his model*; *this portrait certainly does not flatter you*; **c** polite formula of self-disparagement in reply to a compliment: *oh, you flatter me*. **3.** (reflex.) *To flatter oneself that*, to congratulate oneself on, be glad to know, be convinced that, and acknowledge some self-satisfaction in the fact: *I rather flatter myself I can tell a genuine piece of Chippendale when I see it*. **4.** To please, soothe, gratify: *everything that can flatter and delight the senses*.

flatterer, n. [1. fláterer; 2. flǽtərə]. Prec. & **-er**. Person who flatters; **a** a sycophant, toady; **b** (in unobjectionable sense) one who pays compliments, who says pleasant things.

flattering, adj. [1. flátering; 2. flǽtəriŋ], fr. Pres. Part. of **flatter** (**II.**). **a** Ingratiating, wheedling, adulatory: *a flattering tongue*; **b** conveying an exaggerated impression of merit, beauty &c.: *a flattering likeness*; *a flattering review, biography*; **c** pleasing, delightful.

flatteringly, adv. Prec. & **-ly**. In a flattering manner, so as to flatter.

flattery, n. [1. fláteri; 2. flǽtəri]. M.E., O. Fr. *flaterie*, Mod. Fr. *flatterie*, fr. O. Fr. *flater*, 'to smooth, flatter', fr. a Gmc. source (see **flat** (**I.**)) & **-ery**. Cp. **flatter** (**II.**). Excessive, insincere praise; adulation.

flatting, n. [1. fláting; 2. flǽtiŋ]. **flat** (**IV.**) & **-ing**. Process of making flat (in various technical senses); specif. **a** process of rolling out metal into thin sheets; attrib., *flatting mill*; **b** process of applying paint or gilding without gloss, or of removing gloss.

flattish, adj. [1. flátish; 2. flǽtiʃ]. **flat** (**I.**) & **-ish**. Rather flat.

flatulence, flatulency, n. [1. flátū-, fláchoolens(i); 2. flǽtju-, flǽtʃuləns(i)]. See next word and **-ence, -ency**. **1.** Wind, gas, in the stomach or bowels. **2.** Quality of being flatulent (in non-material sense).

flatulent, adj. [1. flátu-, fláchoolent; 2. flǽtju-, flǽtʃulənt]. Fr., fr. Low Lat. *flātulent-*(*us*), fr. Lat. *flāt-*(*us*), 'a blowing'. See **flatus**. **1.** Pertaining to, affected with, flatus or wind in the stomach or bowels. **2.** (fig., of speech) Windy, empty, vapid: *a flatulent harangue, speaker*.

flatulently, adv. Prec. & **-ly**. In a flatulent manner.

flatus, n. [1. flātus; 2. fléitəs]. Lat. *flātus* (*ventris*), 'blowing (of the stomach)', vbl. n., fr. *flāre*, 'to blow', fr. Aryan base **bhlē-* &c., 'to blow' (as wind). Cp. **blow** (**I.**), **bladder, blast**. Accumulation of wind or gas in the stomach or bowels.

flatways, flatwise, adv. [1. flátwāz, -wīz; 2. flǽtweiz, *-waiz*]. **flat** (**I.**) & **-ways, -wise**. So as to lie flat.

flaunt (**I.**), vb. intrans. & trans. [1. flawnt; 2. flɔ̄nt]. Provinc. Engl. *flant*, 'to gad about, esp. in finery', prob. preserves the orig. sense; of Scand. origin; cp. Norw. *flanta*, 'to gad about', extended fr. *flana*, 'to climb, rove about'; Dan. *flane*, 'to flirt', *flane*, 'a giddy girl'; also Fr. (fr. Scand.) *flâner*, 'to loaf, stroll, idle'; cogn. w. Gk. *plánē*, 'wandering'. See **planet**. **1.** intrans. To move about, wave, flutter, proudly, ostentatiously, or impudently; to make a display or parade, esp. in fine clothes or gaudy colours: *banners flaunt in the breeze*; *overdressed women flaunt through the streets*. **2.** trans. **a** To flourish, wave proudly or insolently: *to flaunt a flag*; **b** to parade, make a display of: *to flaunt one's vices*.

flaunt (**II.**), n., fr. prec. **a** Action of flaunting, parade; **b** (obs. or rare) thing displayed or paraded (Shakespeare).

flaunting, adj. [1. fláwnting; 2. flɔ́ntiŋ]. Pres. Part. of **flaunt** (**I.**). Ostentatious, showy.

flauntingly, adv. Prec. & **-ly**. In a flaunting manner, ostentatiously.

flaunty, adj. [1. fláwnti; 2. flɔ́nti]. **flaunt** (**II.**) & **-y**. (rare) Flaunting, showy.

flautist, n. [1. fláwtist; 2. flɔ́tist]. It. *flautista*, fr. Low Lat. *flauta*, 'flute', see **flute**, & **-ist**. Flute-player.

flavescent, adj. [1. flāvésent; 2. fleivésənt]. Lat. *flāvescent-*(*em*), Pres. Part. of *flāvescere*, 'to become yellow', inceptive vb. fr. *flāv-*(*us*), 'yellow'. Aryan base **ghel-*, 'yellowish, greenish', whence also O.E. *ġeolu*. See further under **gold** & **yellow**. Turning yellow; tending to acquire a slightly yellow tint.

flavine, n. [1. flāvēn; 2. fléivīn], fr. Lat. *flāvus*, 'yellow'. See prec. & **-ive**. A yellow, artificial dyestuff.

flavorous, adj. [1. flāvorus; 2. fléivərəs]. Next word & **-ous**. Having an agreeable flavour.

flavour (**I.**), n. [1. flāvor; 2. fléivə]. In early use often, if not always, 'odour, scent'; M.E. *flavor*, fr. O. Fr. *flaveur*, prob. altered on the anal. of *saveur*, 'savour', fr. *flaor, flaur, fleur* (two sylls.), 'odour', perh. fr. a Low Lat. type **flātōr-em*, lit. 'blower', agent-n. fr. *flāre*, 'to blow' (see **flatus**); cp. It. *fiatore*, 'bad smell'. **1.** (archaic or obs.) Fragrance, aroma. **2.** Taste; quality which gives a distinctive taste to a thing, savour; mixed sensation of taste and smell; relish, smack. **3.** (of non-material quality) Distinctive quality affecting the aesthetic taste or feeling; savour, spice: *a flavour of adventure, of romance, about the affair*.

flavour (**II.**), vb. trans., fr. prec. **a** To give a flavour or relish to (dish &c.), to season: *to flavour soup with onions*; **b** (fig.) to add savour or zest to; to furnish with a distinctive quality.

flavouring, n. [1. flāvuring; 2. fléivəriŋ]. Prec. & **-ing**. **a** Substance with a distinct, characteristic flavour; essence, spice, or herb, used to give relish to food; **b** feature giving characteristic aesthetic or moral quality.

flavourless, adj. [1. flāvorles; 2. fléivəlis]. **flavour** (**I.**) & **-less**. Lacking distinctive flavour or character.

flavoursome, adj. [1. flāvorsum; 2. fléivəsəm]. **flavour** (**I.**) & **-some**. (rare) Having a flavour.

flaw (**I.**), n. [1. flaw; 2. flɔ̄]. M.E. *flawe, flai*, 'flake of snow or fire'; cp. Swed. *flage*, 'flaw, crack, breach, flake', O.N. *flaga*, 'slab', also **flag** (**VI.**), **flake**, & perh. **flay**. **1.** Defect, blemish, usually in form of a slight fissure or rift, in material, esp. in the texture of metal that has been cast, which renders the material liable to break. **2. a** Visible, natural defect, blemish, disfigurement, spot, fleck, in an object, specif. in precious stones; **b** defect, fault, in a manufactured article, due to error or carelessness of workmanship. **3.** (in non-material sense) **a** Moral, or logical defect, error; lapse from correctness; blemish in character, weak point in reasoning &c.: *a flaw in an argument, in an otherwise perfect character* &c.; **b** an error in conduct or action. **4.** (law) Something omitted, or incorrectly stated, which invalidates a legal instrument.

flaw (**II.**), vb. trans., fr. prec. (rare) **a** To make a flaw or rift in; **b** to invalidate.

flaw (**III.**), n. Cp. Du. *vlaag*, Norw., Dan. *flage*, 'gust of wind', perh. fr. Gmc. base **flaχ-*, 'to strike'. See **flay**. Sudden gust of wind, squall; brief storm of wind with snow, hail, or rain.

flawless, adj. [1. flawles; 2. flɔ́lis]. **flaw** (**I.**) & **-less**. (in material and non-material senses)

Free from defect or blemish; perfect; irreproachable: *a flawless diamond*; *his work was flawless*; *flawless manners and behaviour.*

flawlessly, adv. Prec. & **-ly**. In a flawless manner.

flawlessness, n. See prec. & **-ness**. Quality or state of being flawless; perfection.

flax, n. [1. flaks; 2. flæks]. O.E. *fleax*, M.E. *flax*; O.H.G. *flahs*, Mod. Germ. *flachs*; Gmc. base **fleχ-*, 'to plait, weave'; cp. Goth. *flah-ta*, 'plaiting of hair'; Germ. *flechten*, 'to plait', cogn. w. Gk. *plékein*, Lat. *plectere*, 'to plait, weave'; Lat. *plicāre*, 'to fold'. See **fold (I.)**, **plait**, **ply (I.)**. **a** Slender herb, *Linum*, with blue flowers, narrow leaves, and tough stalk, cultivated for its fibre from which linen is made, and for its seeds which produce linseed oil; **b** fibre of this prepared for spinning.

flax-brake, n. Machine for separating the fibrous part of flax.

flax-comb, n. Heckle for dressing flax.

flax-dresser, n. Person who prepares flax for spinning.

flaxen, adj. [1. fláksen; 2. flǽks(ə)n]. O.E. *fleaxen*. **flax** & **-en**. **a** Made of, pertaining to, flax; **b** having the colour of unbleached flax; pale yellowish, straw coloured.

flaxen-haired, adj. Having flaxen hair.

flax lily, n. New Zealand plant of lily family, producing tough fibre used for weaving.

flax-seed, n. Seed of the flax plant; linseed.

flaxy, adj. [1. fláksi; 2. flǽksi]. **flax** & **-y**. Pertaining to, like, flax.

flay, vb. trans. [1. flā; 2. flei]. O.E. *flēan* fr. **flah-an*, cp. P.P. *flag-en*, *flægen*, O.N. *flā* (P.P. *fleg-inn*); cogn. w. Germ. *flach*, 'flat', **fluke (I.)**; cp. Lith. *plak-ù*, 'I strike'; Lat. *plāga*, 'a stroke'; Lat. *plangere*, 'to beat the breast' &c. See **flag (VI.)**, **plague**. **1.** To strip off the skin or hide from; to skin. **2.** (fig.) **a** To extort money or goods from, to reduce to penury by unjust exactions; to pillage, plunder, fleece; **b** to criticise savagely or pitilessly.

flayflint, n. [1. fláflint; 2. fléiflint]. (rare) Miser, skinflint.

flea, n. [1. flē; 2. flī]. O.E. *flēah*, fr. Gmc. **flauχ-*, M.E. *flee*; cp. Du. *vloo*, Germ. *floh*, O.N. *flō*; prob. related to **flee**. **a** Small wingless, leaping, blood-sucking insect, *Pulex*, infesting the coats of animals, and biting human beings on occasion; Phr. *a flea in one's ear*, a sharp rebuff, snub; **b** small flea-like animal, esp. *flea-beetle* &c.; in compounds *sand-flea*, *water-flea*, minute crustaceans.

fleabane, n. [1. flḗbān; 2. flībein]. Strong-smelling composite British plant, said to drive away fleas.

flea-beetle, n. One of several small leaping beetles infesting plants.

flea-bite, n. **1. a** Small red spot on human skin, caused by bite of a flea; **b** (fig.) trifling pain or inconvenience; trifle: *the cost is a mere flea-bite.* **2.** Small patch of reddish hair on white horse.

flea-bitten, adj. **a** Bitten by a flea or fleas; **b** (of horse) having light coat sprinkled with small patches of reddish hair.

flea-hopper, n. Garden pest infesting beans.

flea-louse, n. Garden pest infesting pear trees.

fleam, n. [1. flēm; 2. flīm]. O. Fr. *flieme* (Mod. Fr. *flamme*), fr. Low Lat. *fledomum*, *fletoma*, fr. Lat. *phlebotomus*, fr. Gk. *phlebotómos*, 'lancet'. See **phlebotomy**. Lancet for bleeding cattle or horses.

fleawort, n. [1. flḗwěrt; 2. flīwāt]. Kind of plantain, the seeds of which are used medicinally; one of various plants which are supposed to destroy fleas.

flèche, n. [1. flāsh; 2. fleiʃ]. Fr., lit. 'arrow', perh. of Celt. origin, cp. O. Ir. *flesc*, 'rod, wand'. (archit.) Slender spire over intersection of nave and transept of Gothic church.

fleck, n. & vb. trans. [1. flek; 2. flek]. M.E. *flekked*, P.P.; cp. Du. *vlek*, Germ. *fleck*, O.N. *flekk-r*, 'spot', O.N. *flekka*, 'to spot', *flikki*, 'a patch,' Germ. *flicken*, 'to patch', &c. Perh. cogn. w. **flake**. **1.** n. **a** Spot, small patch: *flecks of sunlight*; **b** freckle; **c** speck, particle: *a fleck of dust.* **2.** vb. To spot, sprinkle with flecks; dapple.

flecker, vb. trans. [1. fléker; 2. flékə]. **fleck**, vb., & freq. **-er**. To fleck, scatter spots or specks over.

fleckless, adj. [1. flékles; 2. fléklis]. **fleck**, n., & **-less**. Having no fleck; spotless.

flection. See **flexion**.

fled, vb. [1. fled; 2. fled]. M.E. *fledde*; Pret. & P.P. of **flee**.

fledge, vb. trans. & intrans. [1. flej; 2. fledž], fr. obs. adj. *fledge*, 'fledged' (Milton), fr. M.E. *flegge*, orig. a Kentish or Essex form of *fligge*, fr. O.E. (*un*)*flyċġe*, '(un)fledged'; cp. M. Du. *vlugge*, O.H.G. *flucchi*, Mod. Germ. (fr. L.G.) *flügge*, fr. Gmc. type **flug-ja*, fr. **flug-*, another grade of **fleug-*, 'to fly'. See **fly (II.)**. **1.** trans. **a** (of young bird) To grow feathers on (itself); **b** to rear (young bird) until it is fledged; **c** (fig.) to grow hair on (chin &c.); **d** to furnish with feathers: *to fledge an arrow, a nest.* **2.** intrans. To acquire full plumage; to become able to fly.

fledged, adj. [1. flejd; 2. fledžd], fr. P.P. of prec. (of young bird) Having the wing-feathers developed; able to fly.

fledgeless, adj. [1. fléjles; 2. flédžlis]. **fledge** & **-less**. Unfledged.

fledgeling, n. [1. fléjling; 2. flédžliŋ]. **fledge** & **-ling**. **a** Young bird just fledged; **b** (fig.) a child; young, tender, inexperienced person.

fledgy, adj. [1. fléji; 2. flédži]. **fledge** & **-y**. (rare) Feathered, downy (Keats).

flee, vb. intrans. & trans. [1. flē; 2. flī]. O.E. *flēon*, *flīon* (strong), for **flēohan*, M.E. *fleen*, O.S., O.H.G. *fliohan*, O.N. *flȳja*, 'to fly from pursuit; put to flight'; Goth. *þliuhan*, if the same word (wh. is unproved in spite of identity of meaning), is an unexplained eccentricity, & in any case affords no proof that *þ* was the orig. Gmc. initial cons., or that the Aryan began w. *t*. No cognates exist outside Gmc. apparently, unless we may connect w. Lat. *plūma*, 'feather', q.v. under **plume (I.)**. See **fly (II.)**. The pres. is now archaic or only in liter. use, being replaced in common speech by **fly (I.)**. **A.** intrans. **1. a** To fly from pursuit, run or hasten away, depart hurriedly, retreat as from an enemy: *the troops fled in disorder*; **b** to avoid by departure: *to flee from the plague*; **c** (in moral sense) to eschew, avoid: *to flee from temptation.* **2.** (only in Past and P.P.) To vanish, pass away: *life had fled* or *was fled*; (archaic in pres. or infin.) '*sorrow and sighing shall flee away*', Psalm, 35, 10. **B.** trans. To hasten away from; to avoid, shun; to forsake: *to flee the haunts of men.*

fleece (I.), n. [1. flēs; 2. flīs]. O.E. *flēos*, *flīes* &c., M.E. *flees*; cp. Du. *vlies*, M.H.G. *vlius*, Mod. Germ. *fliess*; Gmc. type **fliusi*, the first part of wh. is prob. cogn. w. Lat. *plū-ma*, 'soft feather, down', q.v. under **plume**. **a** Mass of wool growing over body of sheep or other animal, or shorn from it; *the Golden Fleece*, Austrian and Spanish order of knighthood (from the Greek myth of Jason); **b** (fig.) soft mass resembling wool, covering anything, as woolly or curly head of hair, sheet of soft snow &c.

fleece (II.), vb. trans., fr. prec. **a** (archaic and rare) To shear fleece from (sheep); **b** (fig.) to despoil, beggar, plunder, by extortion, or trickery; to swindle: *to fleece a person of all he possesses*; *fleeced by card-sharpers*; cp. such expressions as *to flay* (in fig. sense).

fleeceable, adj. [1. flḗsabl; 2. flīsəbl]. Prec. & **-able**. Capable of being fleeced; gullible.

fleecy, adj. [1. flḗsi; 2. flīsi]. **fleece (I.)** & **-y**. **a** Bearing a fleece or fleeces: *fleecy flocks*; **b** like a fleece, in appearance or texture; soft, flocculent: *fleecy hair*; *a fleecy cloud*, *snow-drift.*

fleer, vb. intrans. & n. [1. flēr; 2. fliə]. M.E. *flerien*, *fliren*, Scots dial. *fleyr*, fr. Scand.; cp. Norw. *flira*, *flisa*, 'to titter, giggle, grin', of unknown origin. (provinc.) **1.** vb. intrans. To grin, leer, grimace or laugh contemptuously; to jeer, sneer: *to fleer at one.* **2.** n. Contemptuous or mocking grimace, laugh, or speech.

fleet (I.), vb. intrans. & trans. [1. flēt; 2. flīt]. O.E. *flēotan*, 'to float, swim', M.E. *flēten*, 'to flow, swim, float'; O.S. *fliotan*, O.H.G. *fliozan*, Germ. *fliessen*, O.N. *fljōta*; connected w. **flit**, **flutter**, & also **flow**. (rare except in Pres. Part. as adj.) **1.** intrans. **a** To glide away, pass swiftly and silently: *the years fleet by*; **b** to fly or move swiftly, flit; **c** (naut.) to shift. **2.** trans. **a** (obs.) To while away: '*fleet the time carelessly*' (Shakespeare); **b** (naut.) to move, shift.

fleet (II.), adj. First recorded in early Mod. E., fr. or closely related to prec., cp. O.N. *fljōt-r*, 'swift'. Rapid in movement; swift: *a fleet horse*; *fleet of foot.*

fleet (III.), n. O.E. *flēot*, M.E. *fleet*; as **fleet (I.)**, cp. M. Du. *vliet*, L.G. *fleet*, Germ. *fliess*. (obs. or provinc. except in Place-Names) **a** Creek, inlet, small stream, esp. *the Fleet*, stream flowing through part of the City of London, now covered over; also abbr. for *the Fleet Prison*, formerly used for debtors, situated near this stream; **b** (attrib.) *Fleet chaplain*, clergyman who used to celebrate clandestine marriages in the Fleet Prison; *Fleet marriage*, such a marriage; *Fleet Street*, street near the Fleet famous as centre of journalism; hence, journalists collectively.

fleet (IV.), n. O.E. *flēot*, 'ship, vessel', M.E. *flēte*, 'fleet', fr. **fleet (I.)**. **1.** Number of vessels sailing or acting together: *the Yarmouth fishing fleet*; *a fleet of whalers.* **2.** Specif. (nav.) **a** organized force of warships, larger than squadron, under one chief command: *the Channel Fleet*; Phr. *a fleet in being*, fleet able to hold the sea, though generally too weak to attack; **b** entire naval force of a nation; navy; Phr. *Admiral of the Fleet*, highest British naval rank. **3.** (fig.) collection of vehicles, esp. when used together: *a fleet of motor-cars, of tanks.*

fleeting, adj. [1. flḗting; 2. flītiŋ], fr. Pres. Part. of **fleet (I.)**. (liter.) Gliding away, passing swiftly and silently; transient, transitory.

fleetly, adv. [1. flḗtli; 2. flītli]. **fleet (II.)** & **-ly**. In a fleet manner, swiftly.

fleetness, n. [1. flḗtnes; 2. flītnis]. **fleet (II.)** & **-ness**. Swiftness, rapidity of movement.

Flemish, adj. [1. flémish; 2. flémiʃ]. M. Du. *Vlaemisch*, Mod. Du. *Vlaamsch*, fr. base *Vlām-*, as in *Fleming* & *Flanders*. Pertaining to Flanders or the Flemings; *Flemish brick*, kind of hard yellow brick for paving; *Flemish horse*, draught horse of large heavy breed.

flench, **flense**, **flinch**, vb. trans. [1. flinsh; 2. flinʃ], fr. Du. *vlenzen*, or Dan. *flense*. To strip blubber from (whale), skin from (seal &c.).

flesh (I.), n. [1. flesh; 2. fleʃ]. O.E. *flǣsċ*, M.E. *flēsch*; cp. O.S. *flēsc*, O.H.G. *fleisc*, Mod. Germ. *fleisch*, 'flesh'; O.N., Dan., *flesk*, 'pork, bacon'; Gmc. base **flaisk-* is of uncertain origin & has no authenticated cognates. **1. a** Soft parts of animal body, chiefly muscular tissue, between skin and bones: *the flesh of the cheeks, of the back* &c.; Phrs. *flesh and blood*, body, living person; *one's own flesh and blood*, kindred, near relation; *to make one's flesh creep*, to make one shudder with fright or apprehension; (*to have one's*) *pound of flesh*, demand stipulated, and ruthlessly or inhumanly pressed (after the story of Shylock in Shakespeare, 'Merchant of Venice'); *proud flesh*, granulated growth over wound; *to make, put on, flesh*, to grow fatter; *to lose flesh*, to become thinner; *in flesh*, fat; *in the flesh*, alive; as a reality; **b** muscular tissue and fat of animal, regarded as food, now generally replaced by *meat*: *wolves live on flesh*; often excluding fish, and sometimes birds: *neither fish, flesh, nor fowl*, neither one thing nor another, of indeterminate character; **c** (paint.) surface of human body: *masterly treatment of flesh*; **d** solid, pulpy part of fruit or vegetables. **2.** The human body and its attributes as distinguished from the intellectual and spiritual faculties: *the ills of the* *flesh*; *the spirit is willing but the flesh is weak*; Phrs. *arm of flesh*, material force; *to be made, become, one flesh*, intimately united, as husband and wife; *to be made flesh*, to become incarnate. 3. a Animal nature of man, bodily appetites, propensities, and lusts: *sins of the flesh*; hence, b addiction to bodily appetites; sensuality: *the World, the Flesh, and the Devil.* 4. (fig., Bib.) Chiefly *all flesh*, mankind, human nature: *has gone the way of all flesh*, has shared the common lot of mankind.

flesh (II.), vb. trans., fr. prec. 1. a To incite, stimulate (hawk or hound), to hunt by feeding on flesh of game it has killed; (fig.) b to incite, inure (person), to bloodshed &c. by foretaste. 2. To thrust a weapon into, embed in, flesh: *to flesh one's sword.* 3. To cause to put on flesh, fatten. 4. To scrape off particles of flesh adhering to newly stripped hide.

flesh-brush, n. Brush used on skin to stimulate circulation.

flesh-coloured, adj. Having the natural colour of the surface of the human body; (only in reference to that of a person of a white race), pale, yellowish pink.

flesh-eater, n. Person or animal that habitually eats flesh; a carnivore.

flesh-eating, adj. Habitually eating flesh; carnivorous.

flesher, n. [1. flésher; 2. fléʃə]. **flesh** (I.) & **-er.** A butcher (chiefly Scots).

flesh-feeding, adj. Flesh-eating.

flesh-fly, n. M.E. *fleschflīe.* Any fly which lays its eggs in dead or living animal flesh, and whose larvæ feed on this.

flesh-glove, n. Glove used for rubbing the flesh to stimulate circulation.

flesh-hook, n. M.E. *flesch-hook.* a Hook used for hanging flesh, as in butcher's shop; b (Bib.) hook used for lifting flesh from pot.

fleshiness, n. [1. fléshines; 2. fléʃinis]. **fleshy** & **-ness.** Condition of being fleshy; corpulence.

fleshings, n. pl. [1. fléshingz; 2. fléʃiŋz]. **flesh** & **-ing.** Skin-coloured tights worn by acrobats, actors &c.

fleshless, adj. [1. fléshles; 2. fléʃlis]. **flesh** & **-less.** Destitute of flesh: *fleshless bones.*

fleshliness, n. [1. fléshlines; 2. fléʃlinis]. O.E. *flǣsclīcness*, M.E. *fleschlinesse.* Next word & **-ness.** Quality of being fleshly; sensuality.

fleshly, adj. [1. fléshli; 2. fléʃli]. O.E. *flǣsclīc*, M.E. *fleschlīch.* **flesh** (I.) & **-ly.** 1. (archaic) Made of, pertaining to, flesh: *the fleshly envelope*, the body. 2. Pertaining to the body and its character; corporeal: *the fleshly nature of man.* 3. Addicted to, prone to indulge, the bodily appetites; carnal, sensual.

fleshmeat, n. [1. fléshmēt; 2. fléʃmīt]. O.E. *flǣscmete.* (archaic) Food that consists of animal flesh.

fleshment, n. [1. fléshment; 2. fléʃmənt]. **flesh** (I.) & **-ment.** Action of fleshing (hound, person &c.) (Shakespeare).

fleshpot, n. [1. fléshpot; 2. fléʃpɔt]. a Vessel in which flesh is cooked; hence, b (fig.) luxury after which one hankers: *the fleshpots of Egypt.*

flesh tint, n. (paint.) Colour representing that of surface of human body.

flesh-wound, n. Wound which penetrates or tears the muscular tissue below the skin, but which does not reach any internal organ, or break a bone.

fleshy, adj. [1. fléshi; 2. fléʃi]. M.E. *flēschi.* **flesh** (I.) & **-y.** 1. Pertaining to, consisting of, flesh. 2. Having much flesh, corpulent, fat.

fletch, vb. trans. [1. flech; 2. fletʃ], fr. Fr. *flèche*, 'arrow'. See **flèche.** (archaic) To feather, put feather on (arrow).

fletcher, n. [1. flécher; 2. flétʃə]. O. Fr. *flechier.* See prec. & **-er.** (archaic) Maker of arrows.

fleur-de-lis, also **fleur-de-luce**, n. [1. flêr de lē, -lūs; 2. flʌ̄ də lī, -ljūs]. Fr., 'flower of lily', see **flower** & **lily.** (her.). Representation of garden lily or iris; the armorial bearing of the Kings of France from 1147; also borne by some British families.

fleuret, n. [1. flōōret; 2. flúərɛt]. Fr. *fleurette*, dimin. of *fleur.* See **flower** & **-et.** Conventionalized representation of a small flower, used as an ornament.

fleuron, n. [1. flêron; 2. flʌ̄rɔn]. Fr., augment. of *fleur*, 'flower'. See **-oon.** Flower-like ornament, used in various arts.

fleury, fleurée, flory, adj. [1. flōōri; 2. flúəri]. Fr. *fleuri*, 'covered with flowers', P.P. of *fleurir*, q.v. under **flourish** (I.). (her.) Sprinkled, adorned, with fleurs-de-lis.

flew, vb. [1. flōō; 2. flū]. O.E. *flēah*, M.E. *flew.* Pret. of **fly** (II.).

flewed, adj. [1. flōōd; 2. flūd]. *Flew*, sing. of next word, & **-ed.** (rare) Having flews (Shakespeare).

flews, n. pl. [1. flōōz; 2. flūz]. Origin unknown. Loose, hanging chaps of bloodhound or other dog.

flex (I.), vb. trans. & intrans. [1. fleks; 2. flɛks]. Lat. *flex-(um)*, P.P. type of *flectere*, 'to bend'. Prob. connected w. Lat. *falc-em*, 'sickle', see **falcon**; the base is obscure, but Walde suggests that it is a modified form of that in Lat. *plectere*, 'to bend, interweave', q.v. under **plexus, plash** (IV.), **fold** (I.). 1. trans. To bend; chiefly a (med., anat., of joints) to bend in the natural manner; b (geol., of strata) to fold. 2. intrans. (of joints) To be bent, allow of bending.

flex (II.), n. Abbr. fr. **flexible.** Flexible insulated wire for conveying electric current to lamp &c.

flexibility, n. [1. flèksibíliti; 2. flèksibíliti]. Fr. *flexibilité*, fr. Lat. *flexibilitāt-em.* See next word & **-ity.** Quality of being flexible.

flexible, adj. [1. fléksibl; 2. fléksibl]. Fr., fr. Lat. *flexibilis*, 'pliant'. See **flex** (I.) & **-ible.** 1. a Capable of being bent; pliant: *flexible wire*; b (of the voice) capable of modulation. 2. a (of the mind and character) Pliable, compliant, tractable; open and adaptable to new ideas and circumstances; (in bad sense) complaisant; b (of style, language) adaptable, plastic; expressing, capable of expressing, variety of ideas and emotions; c (of persons) versatile; capable of easily adapting themselves to circumstances.

flexibly, adv. Prec. & **-ly.** In a flexible manner.

flexile, adj. [1. fléksil; 2. fléksail]. Lat. *flexil-(is)*, 'pliant, supple; curved'. **flex** (I.) & **-ile.** Flexible (in lit. and fig. senses).

flexility, n. [1. fleksíliti; 2. flɛksíliti]. Prec. & **-ity.** Quality of being flexible.

flexion, incorrectly **flection**, n. [1. flékshun; 2. flékʃən]. Fr., fr. Lat. *flexiōn-(em)*, 'a bending, turning; curve; modulation, change'. **flex** (I.) & **-ion.** 1. a Action of bending; b thing bent, fold. 2. (anat.) Inward bending of a joint, action of flexor; contrasted with *extension.* 3. (gram.) Inflexion.

flexional, adj. [1. flékshunal; 2. flékʃənəl]. Prec. & **-al.** Pertaining to, capable of, flexion, or inflexion.

flexionless, adj. [1. flékshunles; 2. flékʃənlis]. **flexion** & **-less.** (gram.) Incapable of, lacking, flexion.

flexor, n. [1. fléksor; 2. fléksə]. Mod. Lat. **flex** (I.) & **-or.** (anat.) Muscle that bends a joint inwards; contrasted w. *extensor.*

flexuose, adj. [1. fléksūōs; 2. fléksjuous]. Lat. *flexuōs-(us)*, 'full of turns, tortuous', fr. *flexu-s*, 'a bending'. See **flex** & **-ose.** Flexuous.

flexuosity, n. [1. flèksūósiti; 2. flèksjuósiti]. Prec. & **-ity**; cp. Fr. *flexuosité.* Quality or state of being flexuous.

flexuous, adj. [1. fléksūus; 2. fléksjuəs]. Lat. *flexuōs-(us).* See **flexuose**; cp. Fr. *flexueux.* a Bending, curving; full of curves; sinuous, tortuous, winding; b (fig.) yielding, wavering.

flexuously, adv. Prec. & **-ly.** In a flexuous manner.

flexure, n. [1. flékshur; 2. flékʃə]. Lat. *flexūra.* See **flex** & **-ure.** Act or process of flexing, bending, curving, or bowing; also a bend, curve, or fold; specif., curvature or sagging of heavy body due to its weight, or of stratum under pressure.

flibbertigibbet, n. [1. flíbertijìbit; 2. flíbitidžìbit]. Invented word. Irresponsible, unreliable, wavering person with no concentration of mind or character, and no fixity of purpose.

flick, vb. trans. & n. [1. flik; 2. flik]. Perh. a weakened form of obs. or provinc. *flack*, vb., 'to flap, flutter', n., 'stroke, blow'; cogn. w. Gk. *plēgé*, 'stroke', Lat. *plangere*, 'to beat the breast' &c. See **plague.** 1. vb. trans. a To strike, tap, or flip very lightly with a rapid jerky movement, as of a whip, handkerchief, or finger-nail: *to flick a lazy horse*; *to flick away a crumb*; b to jerk (whip &c.) rapidly at anything. 2. n. Smart, light, jerky stroke or blow, as of a whip, lash, or of the finger.

flicker (I.), vb. intrans. & n. [1. flíker; 2. flíkə]. O.E. *flicorian, -erian*, M.E. *flikeren, flekeren*, 'to flutter, waver'; cp. Du. *flikkeren*, 'to sparkle', fr. base **flik-*, as prec. & freq. **-er.** 1. vb. intrans. a To flutter, quiver, waver: *flags, leaves, flicker in the wind*; *flickering shadows*; b to burn unsteadily, burn up and die down with quick alternations: *the candle flickers*; c (fig.) *a last faint hope flickered up and died.* 2. n. a Fluttering, quivering motion, as of fluttering bird, or agitated leaves; b brief leaping or dart of flame; (also fig.) *a feeble flicker of animation.*

flicker (II.), n. Perh. fr. **flick** & **-er**, or imitat. of note. Golden-winged woodpecker of N. America.

flier, also **flyer**, n. [1. flíer; 2. fláiə]. **fly** (I.) & **-er.** Person or thing that flies.

flight (I.), n. [1. flīt; 2. flait]. O.E. *flyht*, M.E. *fliȝt.* See **fly** (I.) & subst. suff. **-t.** 1. a Action or process of flying, as by winged creature: *a bird takes its flight*; b free movement through the air: *flight of a bullet, spear, aeroplane, balloon*; c manner of flying: *a steady, heavy, dipping, flight*; d pursuit of prey by flying hawk; e migration of birds or insects: *the spring and autumn flights of swallows.* 2. Distance traversed by flying, by bird, airship, aeroplane &c.: *a long flight.* 3. (in non-material sense) a Process of passing away, passage, lapse: *the flight of time*; departure: *the spirit takes, wings, its flight.* 4. Action of mental aspiration; bold or sustained mental effort; excursion, or sally: *a flight of imagination, wit, fancy, ambition.* 5. a Number of creatures or things flying together; flock (of birds, esp. migrating); volley (of missiles): *a flight of starlings, arrows*; Phr. *in the first flight*, of the highest class or rank; b (coll.) young birds produced in the same season; c a formation, a unit, of aeroplanes, under a flight-lieutenant. 6. a Continuous set or series of stairs or steps; b series of hurdles across racing track; c series of locks on canal, of terraces &c. 7. (archery) a Contest in long-distance shooting; b arrow used for such shooting.

flight (II.), n. M.E. *fluht, fliȝt*, fr. *flēoh-*, stem of O.E. *flēon*, see **flee**, & subst. suff. **-t**; cp. Germ. *flucht* &c. Confused w. prec. Act of fleeing; hurried retreat, running away: *the Flight into Egypt*; *Mahomet's Flight from Mecca.* Phrs. *to take flight, take to flight*, to flee; *to put to flight*, to rout.

flight (III.), vb. trans. & intrans. **flight** (I.). 1. trans. a To shoot (birds) flying in a flight or flock; b to put feather in: *to flight an arrow.* 2. intrans. (of birds) To fly or migrate in a flight or flock.

flight-arrow, n. One used for long-distance shooting.

flight-feather, n. One of the quill-feathers of a bird's wing.

flightily, adv. [1. flítili; 2. fláitili]. **flighty** & **-ly.** In a flighty manner.

flightiness, n. [1. flítines; 2. fláitinis]. **flighty** & **-ness.** Quality of being flighty; levity, of character or conduct.

flight lieutenant, n. Rank in Royal Air Force, equivalent to captain in the army.

flight-muscle, n. Bird's muscle used in flying.

flight-shooting, n. (archery) Long-distance shooting.

flighty, adj. [1. flíti; 2. fláiti]. **flight (I.)** & **-y**. **1.** (of character and conduct) Volatile, capricious, giddy, fickle; ill-balanced. **2.** (obs.) Fleeting, transient (Shakespeare).

flimflam, n. [1. flímflam; 2. flímflæm]. Redupl. fr. **flam**. Nonsense, humbug; a trick, flam.

flimsily, adv. [1. flímzili; 2. flímzili]. **flimsy** & **-ly**. In a flimsy manner.

flimsiness, n. [1. flímzines; 2. flímzinis]. Next word & **-ness**. Quality of being flimsy; instability, lack of solidity; (in material and non-material sense) *flimsiness of structure* (in a house &c.); *flimsiness of an argument.*

flimsy, adj. & n. [1. flímzi; 2. flímzi]. Of uncertain origin, perh. fr. **film** & **-y**, w. insertion of *s* as in *clumsy, tipsy, tricksy*; cp. Dan. dial. *flims*, 'film'. **1.** adj. **a** (of material things) Thin and fragile, slight, unsubstantial; lacking durability and solidity; poorly constructed, easily torn or damaged: *flimsy paper, muslin*; *a flimsy structure of lath and plaster*; **b** (of non-material things) weak, inadequate, shallow, paltry; ill-knit, not thought out; ill-founded: *a flimsy pretext, argument, pretension.* **2.** n. (colloq.) A flimsy object; specif. **a** thin sheet of paper; transfer paper; **b** reporter's paper, hence newspaper copy; **c** (slang) banknote; **d** (slang) telegram.

flinch (I.), vb. intrans. [1. flinsh; 2. flinʃ]. O. Fr. *flenchir, flainchir*, 'to turn aside, bend', perh. fr. O.H.G. **hlencan* (M.H.G. & Mod. Germ. *lenken*), 'to turn aside', fr. *hlanca*, 'side' (see **flank**); prob. influenced by Fr. *fléchir*, 'to bend'. To draw, start, back, as in fear or pain; to shrink (from anything painful or hard); wince: *to bear pain without flinching*; *to flinch from an unpleasant duty.*

flinch (II.). Variant of **flense**.

flinders, n. pl. [1. flínderz; 2. flíndəz]. M. Scots *flendris*; cp. Du. *flenter*, 'rags', & see **flounder (I.)** Fragments, shreds, splinters (rare, chiefly in Phr. *to break, fly, in flinders*).

fling (I.), vb. trans. & intrans. [1. fling; 2. fliŋ]. M.E. *flingen*, 'to rush', intrans.; prob. Scand., cp. Swed. *flänga*, 'to use violent action, romp'. Origin obscure. The general sense is to cast, throw, usually with the implication of a certain degree of vehemence, violence, impatience, haste, attending the action. **A.** trans. **1. a** To propel forcibly through the air, to hurl, throw: *to fling a stone, a spear*; *fling a dead cat on a dust heap*; *fling one's hat in the air* &c.; *to fling a coil of rope*; Phr. *to fling one's clothes on*, dress rapidly; **b** to move arms or men rapidly to a given point: *to fling three divisions, many guns, into a battle.* **2.** To move some part of the body rapidly, violently, or impulsively: *to fling one's arms round a person's neck*; *the horse flung his head about, his heels up.* **3.** (reflex.) **a** To cast oneself, move with haste or violence, into a given position: *to fling oneself into the saddle, into a chair*; *to fling oneself into one's clothes*, dress hastily; **b** (fig.) to enter into, embark upon, take up, esp. with spirit and determination: *to fling oneself whole-heartedly into an undertaking, pursuit* &c. Phr. *to fling oneself upon a person's mercy, generosity* &c., to surrender onself, trust to. **4. a** In various other phrases as equivalent of *throw* or *cast*: *to fling caution to the winds*; *to fling off pursuers*, outdistance, escape from; *to fling something in a person's teeth, face*, reproach him with it; **b** to scatter broadcast: *to fling money to the crowd*; **c** (poet.) to diffuse, shed abroad: *the flowers fling their fragrance all around.* **B.** intrans. Generally followed by preposition or adverb. **1.** To rush impetuously and vehemently, to go, turn abruptly, as under stress of strong feeling; to flounce: *to fling out of doors in a rage*; *to fling away, off, without a word.* **2.** *Fling out*, **a** (of horse) kick, lash out; **b** (of persons) to launch, burst out, into passionate, reckless protest, abuse &c.

fling (II.), n., fr. prec. **1. a** Act of flinging, throwing, or hurling an object; throw, cast; **b** (fig.) sharp, sudden, or brief invective, sarcastic hit; taunt, flout, sally, gibe: *to have a fling at one's old enemy.* **2. a** Vehement and sudden movement, as of restive horse; fit of kicking and plunging; Phr. *in full fling*, in full course, active progress; **b** specif., *a fling of the dice*, cast; **c** (fig.) fit of abandonment to rage or other passion, or to dissipation or pleasure of any kind: *to have one's fling.* **3.** *Highland fling*, **a** Scottish dance with rapid steps, and movements of arms in time to the tune; **b** air to which this is danced.

flint (I.), n. [1. flint; 2. flint]. In O.E. & M.E.; cogn. w. Gk. *plinth-(os)*, 'brick'. See **plinth**. **1. a** Very hard dark grey or brown form of quartz, occurring in irregular nodules or lumps in chalk &c.; **b** (fig.) anything very hard, obdurate, or unyielding: *a heart of flint.* **2.** A nodule or piece of flint. Phr. *to skin a flint*, be very stingy or miserly; *to wring water from a flint*, to perform the impossible or miraculous; *as hard as a flint*; specif. **a** a piece of flint shaped for producing fire on being struck with steel, esp. in tinderbox or musket; **b** ancient prehistoric implement made from chipped flint.

flint (II.), adj., fr. prec. Consisting, made of, flint: *flint arrow, flint axe*; *flint implements*, prehistoric tools or weapons made of chipped or flaked flint.

flint-glass, n. Dense, lustrous kind of glass, originally made from calcined flint; crystal glass.

flintiness, n. [1. flíntines; 2. flíntinis]. **flinty** & **-ness**. Quality of being flinty; extreme hardness; chiefly in fig. sense.

flint-knapper, n. Man who breaks flints for road-making; formerly one who chipped flints for flint-locks &c.

flint-lock, n. **a** Ancient type of gun-lock with piece of flint fixed in hammer or cock, for igniting the priming; **b** gun with this type of lock.

flinty, adj. [1. flínti; 2. flínti]. **flint** & **-y**. **a** Consisting of, abounding in, flint: *a flinty soil*; **b** (lit. and fig.) resembling flint; hard, obdurate.

flip (I.), vb. trans. & intrans. [1. flip; 2. flip]. Perh. a variant of **flap (I.)**; cp. M.E. *flipen*, 'to pull' (off a fleece). Cp. **fillip, flippant**. **1.** trans. **a** To propel or tap smartly as with the nail of finger or thumb; to fillip, flick, jerk; **b** to move about rapidly or jerkily. **2.** intrans. To make smart, light stroke, as with finger or whip.

flip (II.), n., fr. prec. Act of flipping, fillip, flick.

flip (III.), n. Prob. fr. **flip (I.)**, in sense, 'beat up, whip'. Drink composed of hot milk, egg, sugar, and sherry, or spirits.

flip-flap, flip-flop, n. Jingle fr. **flip (I.)** & **flap, flop**. **1. a** Flapping noise; **b** a kind of firework. **2.** A somersault.

flippancy, n. [1. flípansi; 2. flípənsi]. Next word & **-cy**, on anal. of words of Fr. origin. Quality of being flippant; levity of speech or mind.

flippant, adj. [1. flípant; 2. flípənt]. Origin doubtful. Lacking seriousness, weight, gravity in feeling and expression; characterized by levity; pert, frivolous.

flippantly, adv. Prec. & **-ly**. In a flippant manner.

flipper, n. [1. flíper; 2. flípə]. **flip (I.)** & **-er**. **a** Limb of mammal, bird, or reptile adapted for swimming, as of whale, penguin, turtle; **b** (slang and facetious) the human hand.

flirt (I.), vb. trans. & intrans. [1. flërt; 2. flʌt]. Of obscure origin; perh. connected w. O.E. *fleardian* (rare), 'to play the fool', fr. *fleard* (rare), 'a trifle, deception', derived fr. or cogn. w. O.N. *flærð*, 'deceit'. Cp. also E. Fris. *flirtje*, 'a giddy girl'. **A.** trans. To jerk, flick, shake, or wave quickly: *a bird flirts its tail*; *to flirt a fan*, to make play with it, open and shut it quickly. **B.** intrans. **1.** To move fitfully or jerkily. **2. a** To play at love-making, to court triflingly or without serious intentions; to coquet; **b** to cultivate superficially friendly relations; to toy, dally: *some Socialists flirted with Imperialism.*

flirt (II.), n., fr. prec. **1.** Sudden brisk movement, jerk, flick, as with tail or fan. **2.** Man or woman who flirts; a philanderer, coquette.

flirtation, n. [1. flërtáshun; 2. flʌtéiʃən]. **flirt (I.)** & **-ation**. Action or practice of flirting, making love for amusement, coquetry.

flirtatious, adj. [1. flërtáshus; 2. flʌtéiʃəs]. As prec. & **-atious**. Addicted to flirtation; inclined to flirt; light, frivolous, in behaviour, esp. in dealings with the opposite sex.

flirty, adj. [1. flérti; 2. flʌti]. **flirt** & **-y**. Inclined to flirt, coquettish.

flit (I.), vb. intrans. [1. flit; 2. flit]. M.E. *flitten, flutten*, 'to carry away, go away, migrate', fr. O.N. *flytja*, 'to cause to flit', weak grade of *fljōta*, 'to float, flow', cogn. w. O.E. *flēotan*, q.v. under **fleet (I.)**. **1.** (of flying creatures) **a** To fly lightly and quietly from place to place; to rove about in flight: *bats and moths flit hither and thither in the dusk*; *to flit from tree to tree*; **b** to pass with silent, steady flight: *to flit past.* **2. a** (of persons) To move about lightly and quietly: *nurses flit through the hospital ward*; **b** (fig.) (of thoughts, dreams &c.) to come and go unobtrusively: *fancies flit through one's mind.* **3. a** (Scot. or North. Engl.) To remove from one house to another, change one's place of abode; **b** to leave one's quarters secretly, by stealth, esp. to escape creditors.

flit (II.), n., fr. prec. Act of flitting, esp. sudden or secret change of abode.

flitch, n. [1. flich; 2. flitʃ]. O.E. *flicce*, 'flitch of bacon', M.E. *flicche*; cp. O.N. *flikki*, 'a patch', fr. Gmc. base **flaik-*, 'broad, flat'. See **fleck**. **1. a** Side of a pig salted and cured; *the Dunmow Flitch*, a flitch of bacon given yearly to the happiest married couple claiming it; **b** steak of halibut; **c** square of blubber. **2.** Outside slice sawn from tree trunk.

flite, flyte, vb. intrans. & trans. [1. flīt; 2. flait]. O.E. *flītan*, M.E. *flīten*; cp. O.H.G. *flīzan*, Mod. Germ. *fleiss*, 'diligence'. (archaic and Scots) **a** intrans. To quarrel, wrangle; **b** trans., to quarrel with, scold, abuse.

fliting, flyting, n. [1. flíting; 2. fláitiŋ]. M.E. *fliting*. Prec. & **-ing**. (archaic or Scots) Scolding, wrangling; specif. (hist.) contest in mutual metrical abuse between two poets.

flitter, vb. intrans. [1. fliter; 2. flitə]. Apparently a variant of **flutter (I.)**. To flutter, flit about as a bird.

flittermouse, n. [1. flítermous; 2. flítəmaus]. Dial. word; apparently an old compound; cp. O.H.G. cogn. *flēdarmūs*, 'bat'. Prec. & **mouse**. Bat.

flivver, n. [1. fliver; 2. flívə]. Invented word. (slang, U.S.A.) A cheap motor-car.

flix, n. [1. fliks; 2. fliks]. Origin unknown. Down, fur, from breast, esp. of rabbit or beaver.

float (I.), vb. intrans. & trans. [1. flōt; 2. flout]. Late O.E. *flotian*, M.E. *flotien* (rare), fr. stem *flot-* (cp. next word), fr. Gmc. **flut-ōjan*, weak grade of *flēotan*, 'to float', q.v. under **fleet (I.)**. This vb. has ousted **fleet (I.)** through influence of O. Fr. *floter*, Mod. Fr. *flotter*, 'to float', fr. Gmc. source. **A.** intrans. **1. a** To rest or drift on, buoyed up on, or near, the surface of water or other liquid; to be suspended in water &c.; opposite of *to sink*: *a cork floats in water*; **b** specif., to remain balanced and buoyed up in water without swimming, and neither sinking nor moving along. **2.** To be suspended in, hover in, drift, or glide through, the air, as in water: *clouds float in the sky*; *dust floats in the air*; *gossamer floats on the breeze.* **3.** (fig.) **a** To move with a stately, gliding gait; **b** to drift about, wander or move aimlessly or vaguely: *ideas floating in the mind.* **B.** trans. **1.** To set afloat, cause to float, bring to surface of water and cause to stay there : *to float a ship*. **2.** (of a liquid) To bear up, buoy up, retain suspended on the surface : *enough water to float a ship* ; *the tide floated us into the harbour*. **3.** To cause to float or hover in the air : *coal gas will float a balloon*. **4.** To flood, drench, cover, a surface with water. **5.** (commerc.) To start, launch, set going, set on foot, put in circulation : *to float a loan, company, scheme*.

float (**II.**), n. O.E. *flota*, 'that which floats; a ship'. See prec. **1.** Thing that floats on surface of, or in a liquid (in many senses); specif. **a** raft; floating stage; **b** cork or quill on fishing line, used to prevent bait from sinking below a certain depth ; **c** one of series of masses of cork attached to edge of fishing net to keep it afloat; **d** hollow ball at end of lever attached to valve in cistern to regulate depth of water; **e** air-bladder of fish or other water animal. **2. a** Kind of cart with low floor, for conveying heavy goods, as cans of milk, coal &c.; **b** low wheeled platform drawn in procession with group of persons in costume &c. **3. a** Wooden implement used for spreading plaster on wall &c.; **b** kind of file for smoothing. **4.** Float-board. **5.** (sing. or pl.) Footlights in theatre.

floatable, adj. [1. flṓtabl; 2. flóutəbl]. **float** (**I.**) & **-able**. Cp. Fr. *flottable*. **a** Capable of floating or being floated ; **b** (of stream) deep enough for floating a raft.

flo(a)tage, flotage, n. [1. flṓtij; 2. flóutidž]. **float** (**I.**) & **-age**. Cp. Fr. *flottage*. **1.** State of floating; ability to float, buoyancy. **2. a** (coll.) Things that float, floating matter, flotsam; **b** right to take flotsam. **3.** The part of a ship above the water-line.

floatation, n. [1. flōtā́shun; 2. floutéiʃən]. **float** (**I.**) & **-ation**, or Fr. *flotation*. **1.** State of floating. **2.** *Centre of floatation*, centre of gravity in floating body. **3.** The launching of a commercial or other undertaking.

float-board, n. One of the boards fixed at intervals round the wheel of an undershot water-mill or of a paddle-steamer.

float-bridge, n. Bridge built on rafts.

floater, n. [1. flṓter; 2. flóutə]. **a** Person or thing that floats ; **b** (finance, colloq.) security payable to bearer.

float-grass, n. One of several kinds of marsh grass.

floating (**I.**), vbl. n. [1. flṓting; 2. flóutiŋ]. **float** (**I.**) & **-ing**. Act or process of floating (in various senses).

floating (**II.**), adj., fr. Pres. Part. of **float** (**I.**). **1. a** Borne up by a liquid, buoyant, resting or drifting on the surface of water : *floating wreckage*. Various specific uses: *floating anchor*, drag-anchor, sea-anchor ; *floating battery*, raft or other vessel used as platform for guns in coast defence or attack on fortifications ; *floating dock*, dry dock floating on the sea, capable of being partly submerged to admit vessel, and then raised to lift vessel out of water ; *floating harbour*, one formed by floating anchored breakwater of timber ; *floating island*, mass of floating decayed vegetation &c., supporting fresh vegetation ; also artificial raft anchored in river, lake &c., for raising crops &c. ; *floating light*, lightship or other floating structure bearing beacon for navigation ; life-buoy with light for use at night ; **b** suspended or drifting in air or other gaseous medium : *floating thistledown* ; **c** pertaining to cargoes at sea : *floating rate, trade*. **2.** Not attached to, or fixed in, one place, loose, shifting, movable. Specific uses: *floating kidney, liver*, one abnormally capable of displacement ; *floating rib*, one of the lower ribs not attached to the breastbone; *floating capital*, movable capital, such as money, goods, distinguished from *fixed capital* ; *floating charge, debt*, one fluctuating or varying according to circumstances ; *floating policy*, insurance policy of which the application is not in the first instance specified ; *floating population*, shifting, variable part of the population of a place, as of a seaport.

floating bridge, n. **a** Bridge of boats, pontoons, or rafts ; also floating part of a bridge, made to swing open ; **b** kind of large ferry-boat hauled across water by chain attached to both banks ; **c** kind of military bridge for crossing moats &c.

float-stone, n. Sense **1.** fr. **float** (**I.**) ; **2.** fr. **float** (**II.**). **1.** One of several kinds of light stone that float in water. **2.** Stone used for smoothing brickwork.

floccillation, n. [1. flòksilā́shun ; 2. flɔ̀ksiléiʃən], fr. Lat. *floccus*, 'flock of wool', see **flock** (**I.**), & Lat. dimin. *-ill-us*, & **-ation**. (med.) Plucking at bedclothes by patient in delirium.

floccose, adj. [1. flókōs ; 2. flɔ́kous]. L. Lat. *floccōs-(us)*. See **flock** (**I.**) & **-ose**. Woolly, tufty ; specif. (bot.) bearing woolly tufts.

floccule, n. [1. flókūl; 2. flɔ́kjūl]. See **flocculus**. **a** Detached mass of wool or of substance of similar structure ; **b** flaky substance in a precipitate.

flocculence, n. [1. flókūlens ; 2. flɔ́kjuləns]. See next word & **-ence**. Quality or state of being flocculent.

flocculent, adj. [1. flókūlent ; 2. flɔ́kjulənt]. *Floccul-*, as in **flocculus**, & **-ent**. Resembling wool or flock ; having consistency, or consisting, of flaky, fibrous matter.

flocculose, adj. [1. flókūlōs ; 2. flɔ́kjulous]. *Floccul-*, stem of **flocculus**, & **-ose**. Flocculent.

flocculous, adj. [1. flókūlus ; 2. flɔ́kjuləs]. As prec. & **-ous**. Flocculent.

flocculus, n. [1. flókūlus ; 2. flɔ́kjuləs]. Mod. Lat. dimin. of **floccus**. **1.** Small tuft of woolly or curling hairs. **2.** (anat.) Small lobe on lower side of cerebellum. **3.** (astron.) Cloud-like mass of vapours in sun's atmosphere.

floccus, n. [1. flókus ; 2. flɔ́kəs]. Lat., 'lock, flock of wool', fr. Aryan **bhlod-kos* ; cogn. w. Gk. *phládein*, 'to tear'. Other cognates doubtful. **a** Tuft of wool or hair ; tuft at end of animal's tail ; **b** first down of young birds.

flock (**I.**), n. [1. flok ; 2. flɔk]. M.E. *flocke*, fr. O. Fr. *floc*, fr. Lat. See **floccus**. **1. a** Small lock, bunch, or tuft of wool ; **b** (pl.) shredded woollen or cotton waste used to stuff mattresses &c.; **c** (coll., sing. or pl.) minute fragments of wool used to make flockpaper. **2.** (pl.) Flocculent precipitate floating in solution.

flock (**II.**), vb. trans., fr. **flock** (**I.**). **a** To attach flocks to paper (see **flockpaper**); **b** to roughen surface of glass so as to give it a flocky appearance.

flock (**III.**), n. O.E. *flocc*, M.E. *floc* ; cp. O.N. *flokk-r*, 'troop, band' ; cognates outside Gmc. appear to be lacking. Assemblage, company, crowd. Specif. **1. a** collection of certain animals ; used esp. of sheep, goats, geese, ducks, or other of the smaller gregarious domestic animals ; a number of these which belong to one owner and live and feed together ; (often, esp. in pl.) sheep : *master of many flocks* ; *flocks and herds*, sheep and cattle ; **b** natural assemblage of gregarious birds : *a flock of gulls, chaffinches* ; or of wild sheep or goats, or sometimes of other animals, as seals. Phr. *the flower of the flock* (fig.), handsomest, cleverest, most satisfactory, member of a family. **2.** (of human beings) **a** Crowd, bevy, of persons (often pl.) : *people came in flocks* ; *a whole flock of visitors* ; **b** company under one guide or guardian, esp. the children of one family or school : *the mother, teacher, with her little flock* ; **c** the Christian Church in relation to Christ as the Good Shepherd : *the flock of Christ* ; **d** a Christian congregation in relation to its pastor. **3.** (of inanimate things, rare) Large collection or number, heap : *a flock of pamphlets*.

flock (**IV.**), vb. intrans. & trans., fr. prec. **A.** intrans. **1. a** (of human beings) To crowd, come, together, form a flock : *to flock together* ; **b** to move all together in a single body or crowd : *the crowd flocked into the church* ; *to flock to hear a famous preacher*. **2.** (of birds) To assemble in large numbers, esp. preparatory to a flight. **B.** trans. (rare) To bring together, form, into a flock.

flockbed, n. [1. flókbéd ; 2. flɔ́kbéd]. **flock** (**I.**) Bed stuffed with flocks.

flockmaster, n. [1. flókmàhster ; 2. flɔ́kmàstə]. **flock** (**III.**). Owner or keeper of flocks of sheep.

flockpaper, n. [1. flókpāper; 2. flɔ́kpeipə]. Wall-paper coated all over or in patterns with **flock** ((**I.**), **1, c**).

floe, n. [1. flō ; 2. flou]. Icel. *flō*, 'layer', or Dan. *(iis)flage*, '(ice) floe'. See **flag** (**VI.**), **flake, flaw.** Large sheet or field of floating ice on sea.

flog, vb. trans. & intrans. [1. flog ; 2. flɔg]. First in 17th cent. as cant word, perh. school slang, fr. Lat. *flagellare*, 'to scourge'. See **flagellate**. **A.** trans. **1.** To beat hard, thrash, scourge, with whip, stick, or the like ; to lash ; to punish by thrashing ; specif., to inflict severest form of corporal punishment on a schoolboy, usually with a birch rod. Phrs. *to flog a dead horse*, to try to revive interest in a stale or worn-out controversy ; to waste one's efforts ; *to flog the water*, to keep throwing a fly over it in fishing ; *to flog (a donkey &c.) along*, compel to go, drive, by flogging ; *to flog (laziness) out of, (Latin) into, a boy*, to induce to abandon, to learn, by use of corporal punishment. **2.** To hit very hard : *to flog the bowling*, at cricket. **B.** intrans. (of sails) To flap noisily and violently in the wind.

flogging, vbl. n. [1. flóging ; 2. flɔ́giŋ]. Prec. & **-ing**. Punishment by beating, corporal punishment : *flogging is an excellent thing if administered judiciously*.

flood (**I.**), n. [1. flud ; 2. flad]. O.E., M.E. *flōd*, 'a flowing, flow, stream' &c. ; Common Gmc., O.S., *flōd*, O.H.G. *fluot*, Goth. *flōdus* &c. Closely related is Gk. *plōtós*, adj., 'floating, navigable' ; & fr. same Aryan base **plōu-* &c., also Lat. *plōrare*, 'to weep, lament', orig. 'to stream at the eyes' ; cp. **deplore** ; & see also under **flow** (**I.**). **1. a** Large body of water collected in an unusual place ; generally due to a river &c. overflowing its banks, or abnormal rainfall ; inundation, deluge : *the floods are out all along the railway line* ; specif. **b** *the Flood*, that described in the story of Noah in Genesis, the Deluge. **2.** (archaic or poet.) The sea ; a river, any large body of water ; a lake. **3.** Flow or rising of the tide : *the tide is at the flood*. Phr. *at the flood*, at the favourable moment. **4. a** Copious discharge, or torrent, of water or other liquid : *a flood of water poured from the roof* ; *floods of rain* ; Phr. *floods of ink*, copious writing, esp. in controversy ; **b** violent and copious weeping : *a flood of tears*. **5.** (fig.) Great flow, torrent, gust, outpouring, outburst : **a** (of emotion) *a flood of anger* ; **b** (of utterance or expression) *a flood of calumny* ; *floods of words*.

flood (**II.**), vb. trans. & intrans., fr. prec. **A.** trans. **1. a** (of water) To cover with a flood, inundate, deluge ; to discharge a large volume of water over or into, to drench : *the river has flooded the meadows* ; *to flood the drains* ; **b** (of human agency) to cause to become covered with water, let water in upon : *to flood a meadow by opening the sluices*. **2.** To cause to become swollen with excessive addition of water : *the river is flooded by the rains*. **3.** (fig.) To crowd into, throng ; overwhelm : *applicants flooded the offices* ; *to be flooded with inquirers*. **B.** intrans. **1. a** (of river) To overflow, brim over ; **b** (of tide) to rise, be at the flood. **2.** (med.) To have uterine haemorrhage.

floodgate, n. [1. flúdgāt ; 2. fládgeit]. M.E. *flōdȝat*. **a** Gate in river or stream, opened to release flood water, and closed to retain water in channel ; sluice ; lower gate of lock ; **b** (fig.) thing that restrains a flood or outburst : '*The floodgates of her eyes*' (Shakespeare) ; *to open the floodgates of wrath, passion* &c.

flooding, n. [1. flúding ; 2. fládiŋ]. Emission of a flood, torrent, or stream ; specif., uterine haemorrhage.

floodmark, n. [1. flúdmark; 2. fládmāk]. Mark or line indicating level of a flood or of high water.

floodometer, n. [1. fludómeter; 2. fladɔ́mitə]. Hybrid. **flood** (I.) & **-meter.** Instrument for recording height of floods.

floodtide, n. [1. flúdtīd; 2. fládtaid]. Rising tide; also fig.: *floodtide of success.*

floor (I.), n. [1. flōr; 2. flɔ̄]. O.E., M.E. *flōr*; cp. Du. *vloer*, Germ. *flur* &c.; fr. Aryan base **plā-*, 'to spread out', which occurs also in Lat. *plānus*, 'level, flat'. See **plain** (I.). **1. a** Horizontal surface, made of timber or stone, forming bottom of room or passage; that part upon which one stands in a room &c.; **b** horizontal part of ship's bottom; **c** surface of bridge or pier on which one treads; **d** structure of wood or other material dividing storeys of a building. **2.** Main area of hall used for assemblies, as distinguished from platform and gallery. Phrs. *floor of the House*, part of House of Parliament where members sit; *to take the floor* (chiefly American), to address a meeting. **3.** Horizontal division of a building, separated from that above it and below it by beams, girders, rafters &c. which support the floor (in sense **1**) and the ceiling; storey. **4.** Lowest ground surface; bottom: *floor of the sea, of a cave* &c.

floor (II.), vb. trans., fr. prec. **1.** To furnish (a building, room) with a floor or floors. **2. a** To strike down to the floor or ground: *to floor a man with one's fist*; **b** (in fig. sense, colloq.) to confound, defeat, or perplex thoroughly; to silence, pose: *to be floored*; *this argument, question, floored him completely.* Phr. (slang) *to floor a question, a paper* (in an examination), to answer it satisfactorily.

floorcloth, n. [1. flórklawth; 2. flɔ́klɔþ]. Strong, woven material, with hard, shiny, damp-proof surface, used for covering floors.

floorer, n. [1. flórer; 2. flɔ́rə]. (slang) A puzzling question that one cannot answer, a poser; situation, event, which baffles or defeats one.

flooring, n. [1. flóring; 2. flɔ́riŋ]. **floor** & **-ing. a** Material of which floors are made; **b** floor, floor structure.

floor-walker, n. (Am. usage) Shop-walker.

flop (I.), vb. intrans. & trans. [1. flop; 2. flɔp]. Originally a provinc. variant of **flap.** (colloq.) **1.** intrans. **a** To flap about; throw oneself, move, tumble, clumsily about; to fall in a helpless, heavy, clumsy or noisy manner; to fall in a heap: *to flop into an arm-chair, down on one's knees*; *a seal flops in a pool*; **b** to descend with a sudden, heavy or hollow flapping sound: *a water-rat flopped into the water.* **2.** trans. **a** To flap, strike, throw, or set down heavily, clumsily, and noisily: *to flop down a sack of corn*; **b** to let down (broad brim of hat).

flop (II.), n. **a** Act or motion of flopping; **b** noise of flopping; **c** (slang) fiasco, failure.

flop (III.), adv. With a flop: *to fall flop into the water.*

floppily, adv. [1. flópili; 2. flɔ́pili]. **floppy** & **-ly.** (colloq.) In a floppy manner.

floppiness, n. [1. flópines; 2. flɔ́pinis]. **floppy** & **-ness.** (colloq.) State of being floppy; slackness in bearing or character.

floppy, adj. [1. flópi; 2. flɔ́pi]. **flop** & **-y. a** Flopping, inclined to flop; slack, inactive; reverse of tense or alert in mind and body; **b** (of style) loose, inaccurate, careless; showing lack of control.

flora, n. [1. flóra; 2. flɔ́rə]. Lat. *Flōra*, 'goddess of flowers', fr. **flōza*, cp. Lat. *flōs*, genit. *flōris*, fr. **flōzis*, 'flower'. See **floral, flower, blossom, blow. a** Aggregate of vegetable species native to, and characteristic of, a region or a geological epoch; **b** (cap.) systematic treatise, or classified list, of such aggregate.

floral, adj. [1. flóral; 2. flɔ́rəl]. Lat. *flōrāl-(is)*, 'pertaining to Flora'. Prec. & **-al. 1.** Pertaining to a flora or floras: *floral zone*, area with characteristic vegetation. **2.** Pertaining to a flower or flowers: *floral envelope*, perianth; *floral decorations.*

florally, adv. Prec. & **-ly.** In regard to flora or to flowers.

Floréal, n. [1. flórāal; 2. flɔ̄reiǣl], fr. Lat. *flōreālis*, fr. *flōs, flōris*, 'flower'. See **flower.** Eighth month of the French Revolutionary calendar, April 20th to May 19th.

florence flask, n. [1. flórens fláhsk; 2. flɔ́rəns flȧsk]. Roundish, long-necked flask, often protected with basket-work.

Florentine, adj. & n. [1. flórentīn; 2. flɔ́rəntain]. Lat. *Flōrentīn-(us)*, 'pertaining to *Florentia* or Florence'. See **-ine. 1.** adj. Pertaining to the city of Florence in Tuscany; *Florentine iris*, large white or pale blue species of iris. **2.** n. (l.c.) **a** Kind of twilled silk fabric; **b** kind of meat pie.

florescence, n. [1. florésens; 2. flɔrésəns]. See next word & **-ce. a** Bursting into flower, beginning of blossoming; **b** season when plant is in flower; **c** (fig.) period of success.

florescent, adj. [1. florésent; 2. flɔrésənt]. Lat. *flōrescent-(em)*, Pres. Part. type of *flōrescere*, 'to begin to flower', fr. *flōrēre*, 'to flower, flourish', fr. *flōr-*, form of *flōs*, 'flower'. See **flower** (I.). Bursting into flower.

floret, n. [1. flóret; 2. flɔ́rɛt]. M.E. *flourette*, fr. O. Fr. *florete* (Mod. Fr. *fleurette*), dimin. of *flor, flur*, **flower** (I.). **1.** Small flower, floweret. **2.** (bot.) One of the small, separate flowers which together make up the disk and ray of a composite flower, or the compact flower-head in some other families.

floriate(d), adj. [1. flóriāt(ed); 2. flɔ́rieit(id)]. Lat. *flōri-*, form of *flōs*, **flower** (I.), used in compounds, & **-ate** (& **-ed**). Decorated with a floral motive or motives.

floriation, n. [1. flòriáshun; 2. flɔ̀riéiʃən]. Prec. & **-ation.** Floriated decoration.

floricultural, adj. [1. flòrikúlchural; 2. flɔ̀rikáltʃərəl]. See next word & **-al.** Pertaining to floriculture.

floriculture, n. [1. flórikulchur; 2. flɔ́rikaltʃə]. *Flōri-*, as in **floriate,** & **culture.** Art of cultivating flowers.

floriculturist, n. [1. flòrikúlchurist; 2. flɔ̀rikáltʃərist]. Prec. & **-ist.** One who practises floriculture.

florid, adj. [1. flórid; 2. flɔ́rid]. Lat. *flōridum*, 'abounding in flowers', fr. *flōr-(ēre)*, 'to flower', fr. *flōr-(em)*, **flower** (I.). **1.** (archaic or rare) full of flowers, flowery; decorated with floral designs. **2. a** Elaborately or profusely decorated or embellished, excessively ornate: *florid rhetoric, music, carving*; *a florid prose style*; **b** (cap., archit.) pertaining to the last phase of Gothic; Flamboyant or Perpendicular; **c** (of complexion) having a high colour; ruddy; **d** (of dress, personal appearance &c.) over-elaborate, too rich in colour and quality; loud, vulgar.

Florida, adj. [1. flórida; 2. flɔ́ridə]. Attrib. use of the name Florida, a state of the N. American Union, fr. Span. *Pascua Florida*, 'flowery Easter'. Pertaining to Florida: *Florida boxwood* or *wood*, hard wood used for inlaying; *Florida water*, perfume like eau-de-Cologne.

floridity, n. [1. floríditi; 2. flɔríditi]. **florid** & **-ity.** Quality of being florid.

floridly, adv. [1. flóridli; 2. flɔ́ridli]. **florid** & **-ly.** In a florid manner.

floridness, n. [1. flóridnes; 2. flɔ́ridnis]. **florid** & **-ness.** Floridity.

floriferous, adj. [1. flōríferus; 2. flɔ̄rífərəs]. Lat. *flōrifer*, 'bearing flowers', & **-ous**; fr. *flōri-*, form of *flōs*, 'flower', used in composition. See **flower** & **-ferous.** Bearing or producing flowers; blossoming abundantly.

florilegium, n. [1. flòriléjium; 2. flɔ̀rilídžiəm]. Lat., fr. *flōrilegus*, 'culling, picking flowers', fr. *flōri-*, as in prec. words, & *leg-*, cp. *legere*, 'to pick, choose; pick out; read', q.v. under **lecture.** A Lat. equiv. of Gk. *anthologia.* See **anthology. 1. a** Collection of flowers; **b** descriptive list of such. **2.** An anthology.

florin, n. [1. flórin; 2. flɔ́rin]. M.E., O. Fr., influenced by Lat., fr. Ital. *fiorino*, 'little flower, florin', dimin. of *fiore*, fr. Lat. *flōrem*, **flower** (I.). **1.** (hist.) **a** Mediaeval gold coin of Florence, so called from the device it bore, a lily, the badge of that city; **b** gold coin of Edward III. of England, equivalent to a noble, or 6s. 8d. **2. a** Current British silver coin of 2s.; **b** name applied to the Dutch guilder and the former Austrian gulden.

florist, n. [1. flórist; 2. flɔ́rist]. Lat. *flōr-(em)*. See **flower** (I.) & **-ist.** Person who sells, and sometimes himself grows, flowers, or ornamental plants.

-florous, suff. Lat *-flōrus*, 'flowered'. See **flower** & **-ous.** Having some, many, flowers: *uniflorous*, having a single flower &c.

floruit, n. [1. flórūit; 2. flɔ́rjuit]. Lat., 'he flourished', Pret. of *flōrēre*, lit. 'to flower, flourish'. See **flower** (I.). Period at which a person was alive or active (used when years of birth and death are unknown).

flory, adj. [1. flóri; 2. flɔ́ri]. Variant of **fleury.**

floscular, adj. [1. flóskūlar; 2. flɔ́skjulə]. Next word & **-ar.** Having composite flowers.

floscule, n. [1. flóskūl; 2. flɔ́skjūl]. Lat. *flōscul-(us)*, 'little flower', dimin. of *flōs*, 'flower.' See **flower.** A floret.

flosculous, adj. [1. flóskūlus; 2. flɔ́skjuləs]. **floscule** & **-ous.** Floscular.

flosh, n. [1. flosh; 2. flɔʃ]. Variant of next word. (Rare; archaic or provinc.)

floss, n. [1. flos; 2. flɔs]. Orig. in phrase *floss silk* (see below), ad. fr. Fr. *soie floche*, or Ital. *seta floscia*, or in Venet. dial. *flossa*; Fr. *floche*, perh. fr. Ital. *floscia*, fem. of *floscio*, 'soft, flaccid,' fr. Lat. *fluxum*, 'loose', P.P. of *fluere*, 'to flow' (see **fluent, flux**). But cp. O. Fr. *flocher*, 'to form into flocks', fr. *floc*, **flock** (I.), also O. Fr. *flosche*, 'down'. **1.** (coll.) **a** The short, loose fibres forming outer envelope of silkworm's cocoon; **b** silk spun from this, *floss silk.* **2.** Soft silky substance resembling floss silk; specif. **a** tassel of hanging styles in flower of maize; down on husk of bean; **b** body feather of ostrich.

floss silk, n. Soft fluffy silk fibre, composed of floss, spun, but not twisted, used in embroidery and cheap silk goods.

flossy, adj. [1. flósi; 2. flɔ́si]. **floss** & **-y.** Composed of, or resembling, floss.

flotage, n. See **floatage.**

flotant, adj. [1. flótant; 2. flóutənt]. O. Fr., Pres. Part. of *floter*. See **float** (I.). (her.) Floating in water; flying, streaming in air.

flotation, n. See **floatation.**

flotilla, n. [1. flotíla; 2. flə-, floutílə]. Span., dimin. of *flota*, 'fleet', like O. Fr. *flote*, Mod. Fr. *flotte*, fr. Gmc. base as in **float.** Fleet of small ships or boats, as for service in war.

flotsam, n. [1. flótsam; 2. flɔ́tsəm]. Earlier *flotson*, fr. A.-Fr. *floteson*, 'flotsam', fr. O. Fr. *flotaison*, 'a floating, flooding', vbl. n., fr. *floter*. See **float.** (law) Wreckage or goods found floating on the sea: *flotsam and jetsam.*

flounce (I.), vb. intrans. & n. [1. flouns; 2. flauns]. Prob. of Scand. origin; cp. M. Swed. *flunsa*, 'to dip, plunge', Norw. 'to hurry', perh. an extended form related to Norw. *funa*, 'to sprawl, struggle'. See **flounder** (II.). **1.** vb. To throw oneself about violently or spasmodically; to plunge, flounder, fling about impatiently or excitedly: *to flounce out of the room in a rage.* **2.** n. Action of flouncing.

flounce (II.), n. & vb. trans. Variant of **frounce. 1.** n. Strip of woven material, cloth, silk, lace &c., gathered or pleated and sewn by upper edge round woman's skirt as ornament. **2.** vb. To furnish with flounce or flounces.

flouncing, n. [1. flóunsing; 2. fláunsiŋ]. Prec. & **-ing.** Material used for flounces.

flounder (I.), n. [1. flóunder; 2. fláundə]. M.E. *flondire*, prob. fr. O. Fr. *flondre*, of Scand. origin, cp. Swed., Norw. *flundra*, O.N. *flyðra*; cogn. w. Norw. *flindra*, 'slice'. See **flinders.** Perhaps cogn. w. Lat. *planta*, 'sole of the foot', see **plant** (I.). One of several of the smaller edible flat-fishes.

flounder (II.), vb. intrans. & n. Origin unknown. **1.** vb. **a** To make vehement but awkward and helpless efforts to rise or advance, as through water or mire; to stagger, roll, or wallow helplessly: *to flounder through, into, a morass*; *a porpoise floundering in a shoal*; **b** (fig.) to speak, act, as though confused in mind; to blunder, stumble, hesitate, become involved in speech and expression. **2.** n. Action of floundering.

flour, n. & vb. trans. [1. flour; 2. fláuə]. M.E. *flour (of whete)*, cp. Fr. *fleur de farine*, 'flower or finest part of meal'. Merely a variant of **flower** (I.). **1.** n. **a** Finely ground, or ground and bolted, meal, esp. of wheat; **b** any very fine, soft powder. **2.** (rare) vb. **a** To reduce to flour; **b** to sprinkle or cover with flour.

flour-beetle, n. Beetle breeding in flour.

flour-box, n. Flour-dredger.

flour-dredge, -dredger, n. Perforated tin box used for dredging or sprinkling flour.

flourish (I.), vb. intrans. & trans. [1. flúrish; 2. fláriʃ]. M.E. *florisshen, flurisshen*, fr. O. Fr. *flurir, florir* (Pres. Part. *flurissant*; Mod. Fr. *fleurir, fleurissant*), fr. Lat. *flōrēre*, 'to blossom, flourish', & its inceptive *flōrescere*. See **florid, flower** (I.), also **-ish**. **A.** intrans. **1. a** (of plant) To grow vigorously or luxuriantly, to thrive, be in a healthy condition; **b** generally, to thrive, prosper, succeed, be in a vigorous state; **c** (of eminent person, chiefly Pret., cp. **floruit**), to be active, productive, pursuing one's calling (at such a time): *The philosopher Socrates flourished 400 B.C.* **2.** To make or perform a flourish of any kind; specif. **a** to make fanciful, waving movements, as of the arms; **b** to write in an affectedly ornate hand; to make fanciful strokes with the pen; **c** to use flowery or florid language; to talk boastfully; **d** to make musical flourishes; to sound a fanfare. **B.** trans. **1.** (rare) To decorate with flowery or fanciful ornament. **2.** To move, wave, swing, brandish; shake in a fantastic or ostentatious manner; to flaunt: *to flourish a sword, a handkerchief, one's arms.*

flourish (II.), n., fr. prec. **1.** (rare) Flourishing state, prosperity: *in full flourish.* **2.** The movement of flourishing, brandishing, anything; wave, rapid swing: *a flourish of swords, of one's hat* &c. **3.** Decorative or fanciful curved line or lines in handwriting, engraving, or printing, appended to signature, initial letter &c. **4.** Flowery or florid expression or passage in speech or writing; rhetorical ornament or display. **5.** (mus.) Florid or showy passage, often improvised as prelude or addition to a piece. **6.** Fanfare, esp. to welcome distinguished visitor: *a flourish of trumpets*; (this phrase also fig.) an ostentatious introduction or advertisement, e.g. in the press.

flourishing, adj. [1. flúrishing; 2. fláriʃiŋ]. Pres. Part. of **flourish** (I.). Vigorous, thriving, in good health; prosperous, successful; happy.

flourishy, adj. [1. flúrishi; 2. fláriʃi]. **flourish** (II.) & **-y.** Having, abounding in, flourishes.

flourmill, n. [1. flóurmil; 2. fláuəmil]. Mill in which grain is ground into flour.

flour-moth, n. Moth whose larva infests flour.

floury, adj. [1. flóuri; 2. fláuəri]. **flour** & **-y.** **a** Pertaining to, consisting of, sprinkled with, flour; **b** resembling flour.

flout (I.), vb. trans. & intrans. [1. flout; 2. flaut], fr. 16th cent., prob. a special sense of M.E. *floutin* (see **flute**); cp. M. Du. *fluyten*, 'to play the flute; to jeer; to impose on'. **1.** trans. To mock at, show scorn of, treat with contempt; disregard contemptuously: *to flout one's advice.* **2.** intrans. To utter contemptuous speech, to jeer, scoff, behave with contempt: *to flout at one.*

flout (II.), n., fr. prec. Expression of contempt, insulting speech or act; gibe, jeer, mockery, scoffing.

flow (I.), vb. intrans. [1. flō; 2. flou]. O.E. *flōwan*, O.N. *flōa*, fr. same base as **flood.** Outside Gmc., Aryan **plōw-* has given rise to Gk. *plóein*, for **plōw-*, 'to float, swim' &c.; O. Slav. *plova*, 'I swim'; Lat. *pluere*, 'to rain'. See **pluvial. 1. a** (of water and other liquids) To move along, stream, glide, run; to gush: *rivers flow down to the sea*; *tears flow from the eyes*; Phrs. *to flow like water* (esp. of wine), to be forthcoming in lavish abundance; *to flow with milk and honey*, abound in good things; **b** specif. (of the blood) to circulate: *royal blood flows in his veins*; Phr. *blood will flow*, (before things are settled &c.) there will be bloodshed; **c** (of air, fine sand, molten metal, lava &c.) to move along, run as though flowing: *hot air flows up the chimney*; *sand flows through an hour-glass.* **2.** (of the tide) To rise, come in; reverse of *to ebb.* **3.** (of a number, series, of moving objects) To pass, move along in continuous sequence like a stream: *the crowd, traffic, flows past the Marble Arch all day.* **4.** (of various non-material things) To come forth, run easily and continuously; glide along, pass (said of eloquence, conversation, verse &c.): '*There the last numbers flowed from Cowley's tongue*' (Pope); also of life, time. **5.** (in fig. sense) To proceed from, be due to, as a cause; to spring, be derived from, as a source: *many excellent results flowed from his action*; '*Praise God from Whom all blessings flow*'. **6.** (of drapery, long hair &c.) To fall in loose folds or masses, stream down, descend in waves: *robes that flowed from his shoulders*; *hair flowing down her back.*

flow (II.), n., fr. prec. **1. a** Process of flowing in various senses; manner of flowing; current: *to proceed with steady flow*; **b** specif., the rise, coming in, of the tide; opposite of *ebb.* **2.** Something which flows; stream, gush, outburst; **a** of water, blood, oil &c.; also of air; **b** (in non-material sense) *flow of conversation, wit, words* &c.; Phr. *flow of spirits*, unflagging cheerfulness. **3.** Amount of substance that flows; quantity, output: *a daily flow of 1000 gallons*; *a good flow of milk.*

flower (I.), n. [1. flóuer; 2. fláuə]. M.E., O.Fr. *flour, flūr, flōr* (Mod. Fr. *fleur*), fr. Lat. *flōr-(em)*, acc. of *flōs*, w. change of *s*, through *z*, to *r* between vowels; Aryan base **bhlō-*, 'to swell, blow'. See Gmc. derivations fr. this base under **blade, blood, bloom, blossom, blow** (I.). Lat. *folium*, 'leaf', q.v. under **folio**, is prob. also cogn. **1. a** (bot.) That part of seed plant comprising the reproductive organs, esp. when furnished with a perianth, between opening of bud and development of seed-vessel; **b** popularly, any of the variously coloured heads of plants, composed of floral leaves or petals; blossom; **c** flowering herb or plant smaller than a shrub, whether actually in flower or not; **d** state of blooming: *in flower.* **2.** Carven or other representation of a flower; conventional ornament suggested by form of a flower; Phr. *flowers of speech*, rhetorical, picturesque, decorative expression. **3.** The finest, choicest, part, or result, of anything; **a** height of strength, vigour, activity: *the flower of one's age, life, strength*; **b** finest, ripest, intellectual product: *flower of scholarship, of poetry*; **c** (of human beings) noblest, bravest, most beautiful, most distinguished part of a population, or group of men, at a given time; the cream, finest type, embodiment of the best qualities: *the flower of the youth of the country, of the army, of chivalry*; *the flower of the countryside.* **4.** (old chem.) **a** Fine powder left after sublimation: *flowers of sulphur*; **b** scum from fermentation.

flower (II.), vb. intrans. & trans., fr. prec. **1.** intrans. **a** To produce, bear, a flower or flowers; to bloom, blossom; **b** (fig.) to be in, come into, prime, or state of highest vigour: *the Italian genius flowered at the Renaissance.* **2.** trans. (rare) **a** To cause, or allow, to flower: *to flower hyacinths in a greenhouse*; **b** to decorate with a floral pattern.

flowerage, n. [1. flóuerij; 2. fláuəridž]. **flower** (I.) & **-age.** (rare) **a** State of flowering; **b** flowers collectively.

flower-bearing, adj. Producing flowers: *a flower-bearing stem.*

flowerbed, n. [1. flóuerbed; 2. fláuəbed]. Garden bed in which flowers are grown.

flowerbud, n. [1. flóuerbud; 2. fláuəbad]. Bud which develops into a flower.

flower-de-luce, n. [1. flóuer de lūs; 2. fláuə də ljūs]. Variant of **fleur-de-lis. a** Fleur-de-lis; **b** iris.

flowered, adj. [1. flóuerd; 2. fláuəd]. **flower** (I.) & **-ed.** Decorated with floral pattern: *flowered silk, chintz, gown* &c.

flowerer, n. [1. flóuerer; 2. fláuərə]. **flower** (II.) & **-er.** Plant that flowers: *an early flowerer.*

floweret, n. [1. flóueret; 2. fláuərit]. **flower** (I.) & **-et.** Cp. **floret.** (poet.) Little flower.

flower-garden, n. Garden devoted to the cultivation and display of flowers; contrasted with *kitchen-garden.*

flower girl, n. Girl or woman who retails flowers in the street or market.

floweriness, n. [1. flóuerines; 2. fláuərinis]. **flowery** & **-ness.** Quality of being flowery (lit. and fig.).

flowering, adj. [1. flóuering; 2. fláuəriŋ], fr. Pres. Part. of **flower** (II.). Bearing flowers, blooming; having conspicuous flowers; grown on account of its flowers: *flowering shrub, tree*; specif., *flowering currant*, ribes; *flowering fern*, king fern; *flowering rush*, British water plant unrelated to the rush, with pink flower.

flowerless, adj. [1. flóuerles; 2. fláuəlis]. M.E. *flourelēs.* **flower** (I.) & **-less.** Bearing no flowers; having lost or shed its flowers.

flower-piece, n. Picture of flowers.

flowerpot, n. [1. flóuerpot; 2. fláuəpɔt]. Pot of coarse ware, in which plants are grown.

flower service, n. Church service at which offerings of flowers are made for the sick.

flower show, n. Exhibition at which flowers and ornamental plants are shown, and prizes given for the best specimens of each class.

flowerstalk, n. [1. flóuerstawk; 2. fláuəstōk]. Stem supporting flower; peduncle.

flowery, adj. [1. flóueri; 2. fláuəri]. M.E. *flouri.* **flower** (I.) & **-y. 1. a** Abounding in, covered with, flowers: *a flowery meadow*; **b** resembling flowers: *a flowery pattern*; *the Flowery Land* or *Kingdom*, China (rendering of Chinese designation meaning 'polished nation'). **2.** (of language and style) Highly ornate, abounding in fanciful or rhetorical figures; florid: *a flowery address, style.*

flowing, adj. [1. flṓing; 2. flóuiŋ]. Pres. Part. of **flow** (I.). That flows (in any sense); specif. **a** steadily and smoothly moving, as a fluid; running: *flowing water*; **b** rising, advancing: *the flowing tide*; (fig.) steady progressive movement, as of public opinion; **c** (of language) fluent, moving easily and smoothly: *flowing periods*; **d** (of graphic lines or contours) smoothly curving without breaks or abrupt changes of direction; **e** descending in loose folds: *flowing draperies.*

flowingly, adv. Prec. & **-ly.** In a flowing manner.

flow-line, n. (geol.) Line in igneous rock caused by its flow when molten.

flown (I.), vb. [1. flōn; 2. floun]. O.E. *flogen*, M.E. *flōwen.* P.P. of **fly** (II.).

flown (II.), adj. Obs. P.P. of **flow** (I.). **1.** (obs. or archaic) Flushed, exalted: '*Flown with insolence and wine*' (Milton). **2.** Having colours which flow into one another: *flown porcelain.*

flu, flue, n. [1. flōō; 2. flū]. Abbr. fr. **influenza.** (colloq. or slang) Influenza.

fluctuant, adj. [1. flúktūant; 2. fláktjuənt]. Lat. *fluctuant-(em).* Pres. Part. of *fluctuāre.* See next word. (rare) Undulating, moving like a wave.

fluctuate, vb. intrans. & trans. [1. flúktūāt; 2. fláktjueit], fr. Lat. *fluctuāt-(um)*, P.P. type of *fluctuāre*, 'to move as a wave', fr. *fluctu-s*, 'wave', fr. *fluct-*, early P.P. stem of *fluere*, 'to flow'. See **fluent** & **-ate. 1.** intrans. **a** To move alternately up and down or backwards and forwards; waver; **b** (fig.) to vary irregularly in quantity or degree; be unstable: *the patient's temperature, the price, opinion, fluctuates.* **2.** trans. To cause to fluctuate: '*And fluctuates all the still perfume*' (Tennyson, 'In Mem.', xcv.).

fluctuation, n. [1. flùktūā́shun; 2. flaktjuéiʃən]. Fr., fr. Lat. *fluctuātiōn-(em)*, fr. *fluctuāre*. See prec. & **-ion.** **a** Alternate motion in different directions as of a wave; **b** irregular variation in quantity or degree; instability; vacillation, wavering.

flue (**I.**), n. [1. flōō; 2. flū]. Of uncertain origin, perh. fr. O. Fr. *flue*, 'a flowing', fr. *fluer*, 'to flow', fr. Lat. *fluere*. See **fluent.** Perh. confused w. Du. *vloei-pijp*, 'ventilating-shaft', lit. 'flow-pipe'. Tube, pipe, or shaft for the conveyance of air, smoke, flame, or gas; specif. **a** small chimney, separate passage in chimney; **b** hot air pipe for heating a room &c.; **c** tube conveying flames and hot air through boiler; **d** mouthpiece of flue-pipe in organ.

flue (**II.**), vb. intrans. & trans., fr. obs. or provinc. adj. *flue*, 'shallow, open, flaring or expanding', of uncertain origin, perh. cogn. w. **flow** (**I.**), or fr. Fr. *fluer*, 'to flow', see prec.; cp. Fr. dimin. adj. *fluet*, 'lean, thin, slender'. **1.** intrans. To be splayed, as opening or jamb in thick walls. **2.** trans. To splay (windows &c.).

flue (**III.**), n. M.E. *fluwe*, *flowe*; cp. Flem. *vluwe*, L.G. *flog*, E. Fris. *flüg*, Norw. *flu*, perh. fr. Gmc. base **flug-*, weak grade of **fleug-*, **fly** (**I.**). See **fluff.** Loose, light, flocculent, fluffy mass of small filaments or fragments of wool, cotton &c.; esp. as a form of dust that collects under furniture &c.

flue (**IV.**), n. Cp. M. Du., Flem. *vluwe*, Du. *flouw*, 'fishing net', Fr. *flue*, 'part of net'. One of several kinds of fishing net.

fluency, n. [1. flōōensi; 2. flúənsi]. **fluent** & **-cy.** Cp. Lat. *fluentia*. Quality of being fluent; readiness, copiousness of speech; easy smoothness of, and movement in, style.

fluent (**I.**), adj. [1. flōōent; 2. flúənt]. Fr., fr. Lat. *fluent-(em)*, Pres. Part. type of *fluere* 'to flow', cogn. w. Gk. *phlúein*, 'to boil over, bubble up, spout, babble'. Prob. fr. Aryan base **bhleu-g-*, 'to gush, stream out', an expansion of **bh(e)l-* &c., 'to swell', q.v. under **blade, flower** &c. Cp. **flux.** **1.** (rare) Flowing; capable of flowing, fluid, mobile. **2.** Proceeding smoothly, easily, or gracefully: *fluent curves, contours*; **a** (of speech) uttered readily, easily, or rapidly: *to speak fluent French*; **b** (of speaker) able to speak readily: *a fluent orator*; (often slightly ironical) glib, voluble but shallow: *fluent phrases.* **3.** (math.) Flowing, fluential.

fluent (**II.**), n., fr. prec. (math.) Flowing quantity or function in fluxions.

fluential, adj. [1. flooénshal; 2. fluénʃəl]. Prec. & **-ial.** (math.) Pertaining to a fluent.

fluently, adv. [1. flōōentli; 2. flúəntli]. **fluent** & **-ly.** In a fluent, easy, ready, copious manner.

flue-pipe, n. Pipe of organ or other musical instrument, in which sound is produced by current of air striking edge of mouthpiece.

flue-work, n. In organ, flue-pipes collectively.

fluey, adj. [1. flōōi; 2. flúi]. **flue** (**III.**) & **-y.** Like flue, fluffy.

fluff (**I.**), n. [1. fluf; 2. flaf]. Perh. a variant of **flue** (**III.**). **a** Very soft light mass of down, hair, wool, or other filaments, flue; first soft growth of beard; **b** (theatr. slang) imperfectly learnt part.

fluff (**II.**), vb. trans. & intrans., fr. prec. **1.** trans. To make fluffy, give a fluffy appearance to. **2.** intrans. **a** To become fluffy; **b** to speak one's part incorrectly on the stage.

fluffiness, n. [1. flúfines; 2. fláfinis]. **fluffy** & **-ness** Quality of being fluffy.

fluffy, adj. [1. flúfi; 2. fláfi]. **fluff** & **-y.** **1.** Pertaining to, having, or resembling, fluff; covered with or consisting of very soft wool or hair; downy; furry. **2.** (slang) **a** Forgetful of acting part; **b** drunk, unsteady.

flugelman, n. Variant of **fugleman.**

fluid, adj. & n. [1. flōōid; 2. flúid]. Fr. *fluide*, fr. Lat. *fluid-(us)*, fr. *fluere*, 'to flow'. See **fluent.** **1.** adj. **a** Capable of flowing, not solid; liquid, viscid, or gaseous; **b** (fig.) not rigid or fixed, capable of change, mobile, plastic: *the opinions of the young are fluid.* **2.** n. **a** (phys.) Liquid, viscid, or gaseous substance; (in popular speech) liquid; **b** (obs. phys. and popular) *electric fluid*, hypothetical substance formerly supposed to cause electric, magnetic, or mesmeric phenomena.

fluidal, adj. [1. flōōidal; 2. flúidəl]. Prec. & **-al.** Pertaining to a fluid.

fluidify, vb. trans. [1. flōōídifī; 2. fluídifai]. **fluid** & **-fy.** To make or render fluid.

fluidity, n. [1. flōōíditi; 2. fluíditi]. Fr. *fluidité.* **fluid** & **-ity.** **1.** **a** Quality of being fluid; liquid, viscid, or gaseous state; **b** (fig.) lack of fixed or definite form, liability to alteration. **2.** Fluid substance, condition.

fluidize, vb. trans. [1. flōōidīz; 2. flúidaiz]. **fluid** & **-ize.** To render fluid, fluidify.

fluke (**I.**), n. [1. flōōk; 2. flūk]. Scots & provinc. *flook* is etymologically more correct; O.E. *flōc*, M.E. *flōke*, *flūke*, 'kind of flat-fish', cp. O.N. *flōki*; prob. fr. a different grade of Gmc. base **flak-*, 'flat'. See **flake.** **1.** Flounder or other flat-fish. **2.** Flat parasitic worm, shaped rather like flat-fish, infesting liver of sheep &c. and causing liver-rot. **3.** Kind of kidney potato.

fluke (**II.**), n. Perh. special sense of prec. fr. its shape & flatness. **1.** **a** Broad, flattened, barbed extremity of the arm of an anchor, by which it attaches itself to the ground; **b** barbed head or barb of harpoon, lance, arrow &c. **2.** Either lobe of a whale's tail.

fluke (**III.**), n., & vb. intrans. & trans.; first in connexion w. billiards; origin unknown. **1.** n. **a** Lucky accidental stroke or shot in billiards or other game; **b** (colloq.) piece of good luck, accidental success, happy chance. **2.** vb. **a** intrans. To make a fluke; **b** trans., to hit, gain, by a fluke.

fluke-worm, n. Parasitic worm in liver of sheep; fluke.

flukily, adv. [1. flōōkili; 2. flúkili]. **fluky** & **-ly.** (colloq.) In a fluky, chancy manner, by luck.

flukiness, n. [1. flōōkines; 2. flúkinis]. **fluky** & **-ness.** (colloq.) Quality of being fluky.

fluky, adj. [1. flōōki; 2. flúki]. **fluke** (**I.** & **III.**) & **-y.** **1.** (colloq.) **a** Having the nature of a fluke (**III.**); lucky, chance: *a fluky shot*; **b** uncertain, shifting, incalculable: *a fluky breeze.* **2.** Suffering from, infested by, flukes (**I.**), **2.**

flume, n., & vb. intrans. & trans. [1. flōōm; 2. flūm]. M.E., fr. O. Fr. *flum*, 'river', fr. Lat. *flūmen* for **fleugs-men*, 'river, flowing water'; fr. same base as *fluere*, 'to flow' (see **fluent**), & subst. suff. *-men.* **1.** n. **a** (chiefly Am.) Artificial channel, generally in form of wooden troughs, for conveying water down incline, for power, transport &c.; chute; **b** (Am.) narrow ravine containing stream. **2.** vb. (chiefly Am.) **a** intrans. To make a flume or flumes; **b** trans., to convey, transport, by flume.

flummery, n. [1. flúmeri; 2. flámәri]. Origin unknown. **1.** **a** Sour jelly made of oatmeal boiled with the husks; sowens; **b** sweet blancmange made of flour, eggs, cream, fruit &c. **2.** (fig.) Insipid, shallow talk; humbug, nonsense.

flummox, vb. trans. [1. flúmuks; 2. flámәks]. Also *flummix*, of unknown origin. (slang) To confound, abash; disconcert.

flump, vb. intrans. & trans., & n. [1. flump; 2. flamp]. Perh. a 'portmanteau-word', concocted fr. *fall* & *plump.* (colloq.) **1.** vb. **a** intrans. To fall with a thud or dull, heavy noise, to flop, plump; **b** trans., to throw or put down with a dull, heavy noise. **2.** n. Act or noise of flumping.

flung, vb. [1. flung; 2. flaŋ]. O.E., M.E. *flungen*, P.P.; cp. O.E. Pret. sing. *flang.* Pret. & P.P. of **fling.**

flunkey, n. [1. flúngki; 2. fláŋki]. Orig. Scots, cp. Fr. *flanquer*, 'to run at the side of, to stand by, to assist', fr. *flanc*, **flank.** (contemptuous) **a** Liveried man-servant, lackey; **b** (fig.) an obsequious, servile, cringing person; toady, snob.

flunkeydom, n. [1. flúngkidum; 2. fláŋkidәm]. Prec. & **-dom.** Flunkeys collectively; obsequious persons or toadies as a class.

flunkeyish, adj. [1. flúngki-ish; 2. fláŋkiiʃ]. **flunkey** & **-ish.** Like a flunkey, obsequious, servile.

flunkeyism, n. [1. flúngki-izm; 2. fláŋkiizәm]. **flunkey** & **-ism.** Quality of being a flunkey.

fluo-, fluor-, pref. Abbr. fr. **fluorine,** or fr. Fr. *fluor*, 'fluorine'. (chem.) Forms used in combination, denoting fluorine, as *fluosilicate, fluorspatite.*

fluor, n. [1. flōōor; 2. flúɔ]. Lat., 'a flowing, flux', fr. *fluere*, 'to flow' (see **fluent** & **-or**); orig. applied to minerals (1546) as a rendering of Germ. *fluss*, 'a flowing, flux'. One of several varieties of mineral containing fluorine; fluorite, fluor-spar.

fluoresce, vb. intrans. [1. flōōorés; 2. fluərés]. Back-formation fr. **fluorescence, fluorescent.** To exhibit fluorescence.

fluorescence, n. [1. flōōorésens; 2. fluərésəns]. Fr., fr. *fluorine*, 'fluor-spar', wh. exhibits this property, & *-escence*, on anal. of *opalescence, phosphorescence.* Property possessed by certain transparent substances of emitting light rays of a different colour from those reflected or transmitted, esp. of producing light from invisible rays, as Röntgen rays.

fluorescent, adj. [1. flōōorésent; 2. fluərésənt]. As prec. & **-ent.** Exhibiting fluorescence.

fluoric, adj. [1. flōōórik; 2. fluɔ́rik]. Fr. *fluor*, 'fluorine', q.v., & **-ic**; cp. Fr. *fluorique.* (chem.) Pertaining to fluorine.

fluoride, n. [1. flōōorīd; 2. flúəraid]. **fluor** & **-ide.** (chem.) Compound of fluorine.

fluorine, n. [1. flōōorēn, -īn; 2. flúərīn, -ain]. Fr. *fluor*, 'fluorine', fr. Lat. *fluor* (see **fluor**) & **-ine,** on anal. of the related *chlorine, iodine* &c. Non-metallic, very active element, at ordinary temperatures a pungent yellow gas.

fluorite, n. [1. flōōorīt; 2. flúərait]. **fluor** & **-ite.** Fluor-spar.

fluoro-, pref. Fr. *fluor*, 'fluorine'. See **fluor.** Form used in combination denoting: **a** fluorine, as *fluoroform*, gas resembling chloroform; **b** fluorescence, as *fluoroscope*, q.v.

fluoroscope, n. [1. flōōoroskōp; 2. flúərəskoup]. Prec. & **-scope.** Instrument for observing fluorescence, consisting of box with fluorescent screen at end opposite the eyes.

fluoroscopy, n. [1. flōōoróskopi; 2. fluərɔ́skəpi]. Prec. & **-y.** Examination of object with Röntgen rays and fluorescent screen.

fluor-spar, n. **fluor,** because used as a flux, & **spar** (**II.**); cp. Germ. *flussspat*, lit. 'flux-spar'. Calcium fluoride or fluorite, a transparent crystalline mineral of various colours, oftenest purple or blue, popularly called Derbyshire spar or Blue John.

flurry (**I.**), n. [1. flúri; 2. flári]. Orig. of wind, prob. extended fr. *flurr*, obs. provinc. 'to whir', provinc. 'to ruffle, disarrange'; cp. Norw. *flura*, 'to be in disorder'; perh. associated w. **hurry.** **1.** Sudden, brief gust of wind, often with rain, hail, or snow; a squall. **2.** State of hurry and confusion of mind; fussiness; commotion, nervous agitation. Specif. **3.** Death-throes of harpooned whale.

flurry (**II.**), vb. trans., fr. prec. To make nervous, bewilder, fluster, by haste or bustle.

flush (**I.**), vb. intrans. & trans., & n. [1. flush; 2. flaʃ]. M.E. *flūsen*, *flussh*, 'to fly, fly about quickly' (of a bird); of obscure origin, but perh., as Skeat suggests, fr. O. Fr. *fluiss-*, Pres. Part. type of *fluir*, 'to flow', & orig. used in sense of 'murmur', as flowing water, & 'to rustle', as wind. *Flusch* is used in M. Scots for 'pool'. Skeat cites M. Du. *fluysen*, 'to gush', prob. fr. O. Fr., wh. may itself be of Gmc. origin; cp. O.H.G. *fliossan*, 'to flow', cogn. w. O.E. *flēotan* q.v. under fleet (I.). But the word may be imitative of the sound of whirring wings. 1. vb. a intrans. To fly, start, up, rise suddenly, from concealment, as bird when startled; b trans., to cause (bird) to flush; to put up. 2. n. a Act of flushing; b flock of birds put up together.

flush (II.), vb. intrans. & trans. Of uncertain origin, perh. same as prec. Sense A, 3 prob. affected by **blush**. A. intrans. 1. To rush in a flood, flow copiously; (of blood) to rush into the face. 2. To be flooded, suddenly overspread or filled with a liquid. 3. a To be suffused with blood, turn red, blush; also *flush up*; b (fig.) to glow suddenly, become ruddy. 4. (rare, of plant) To throw out sprouts or shoots. B. trans. 1. To flood with water or other liquid; to wash out, cleanse with a copious stream: *to flush a meadow, a drain*; *blood flushes the veins.* 2. To redden, cause to blush or glow: *running, excitement, shame, flushes the cheeks.* 3. (with hint of 2) To exhilarate, elate, animate, inflame the spirits or passions of: *flushed with pride, victory, wine.*

flush (III.), n., fr. prec. 1. a Sudden rush, outpouring, or flood of water or other liquid; specif., flushing of drain; race or stream from mill-wheel; b sudden rapid growth of vegetation, bursting into leaf: *the first flush of spring*; c fresh glow of health and vigour: *in the flush of youth*; d sudden abundancy, cp. **flush** (IV.). 2. a Sudden rush of blood to the face, blush; b (poet., fig.) reddening, ruddy glow: *flush of dawn*; c hot fit of fever; d rush of joyous excitement, pride, or other uplifting feeling, exhilaration: *the flush of triumph, hope.*

flush (IV.), adj. & adv., fr. **flush** (II.). A. adj. 1. (of a stream) In full flow, brimming, in flood. 2. In the same plane, forming one continuous surface; even, level: *the windows are flush with the wall.* 3. (colloq.) a Having an abundant supply, amply furnished with: *flush of money*; b abundant: *money is flush*; c lavish, prodigal: *he is very flush with his money.* B. adv. In a flush manner, in one plane, on a level.

flush (V.), vb. trans., fr. prec. To level, make even with a surface, fill up.

flush (VI.), n. & adj. Fr. & Span. *flux*, fr. Lat. *flux-(us)*, 'a flowing'. See **flux**. (card-playing, esp. poker) 1. n. Run of the same suit; hand of the same suit. 2. adj. Consisting of cards of the same suit: *flush sequence*, in poker, five cards in sequence all of the same suit.

flusher, n. [1. flúsher; 2. fláʃə]. **flush** (II.) & **-er**. a Man employed to flush sewers; b appliance for flushing sewers.

flushing box (cistern, tank), n. [1. flúshing boks; 2. fláʃiŋ bɔks]. Small cistern supplied with water for flushing latrine &c.

flushness, n. [1. flúshnes; 2. fláʃnis]. **flush** (IV.) & **-ness**. (colloq.) State of being flush, esp. of money.

fluster (I.), vb. trans. & intrans. [1. flúster; 2. flástə]. Cp. Icel. *flaustra*, 'to be flustered', fr. *flaust-r*, 'a fluster, hurry'; also Mod. Germ. *flüstern*, 'to whisper', & E. Fris. *flöstern, flustern*, 'to rustle as wind'. 1. trans. To make nervously agitated; to muddle, fuss, flurry; *fluster oneself*, worry, fuss. 2. intrans. a To be confused with drink; b to be nervously agitated, flurried.

fluster (II.), n., fr. prec. State or condition of being flustered: *all in a fluster.*

Flustra, n. [1. flústra; 2. flástrə]. Mod. Lat. generic name invented by Linnæus, perh. fr. Lat. *flustra*, neut. pl., 'calm at sea', connected w. *fluere*, 'to flow', see **fluent**. (zool.) Colony of marine Polyzoa resembling seaweed.

flute (I.), n. [1. flōōt; 2. flūt]. M.E. *floute*, n., *floutin*, vb., later assimilated to Mod. Fr. *flûte, flûter*, fr. O. Fr. *fleute, flaute, flahute*, n., *flauter*, vb.; cp. Low Lat. *flauta*, Ital. *flauto*, Mod. Provenç. *flahuto, flavuto, flaguto*. Perh. imitative, extended fr. Lat. *flāre*, 'to blow'. See **flatus**, also **flageolet, flout**. 1. a Musical wind instrument, consisting of wooden pipe with blow-hole formerly at one end, now at side, and a series of holes stopped by fingers or keys; b man who plays the flute in an orchestra; c organ-stop sounding like a flute. 2. (archit. &c.) Fluting; vertical groove cut as ornamentation on surface of column. 3. Object more or less resembling a flute in shape; specif. a tall narrow wine-glass; b long, thin French roll of bread.

flute (II.), vb. intrans. & trans., fr. prec. 1. intrans. a To play the flute; b to sing or speak in flute-like tones. 2. trans. a To play (air) on the flute; b to utter in flute-like tones. 3. To make flutes in (column &c.).

fluted, adj. [1. flōōted; 2. flūtid]. P.P. of **flute** (II.). 1. (of sound) Produced as by flute; fluty. 2. Furnished with flutings, channelled, grooved: *a fluted column.*

fluter, n. [1. flōōter; 2. flūtə]. **flute** (II.) & **-er**. 1. Flutist. 2. Tool for making flutes or grooves.

fluting, n. [1. flōōting; 2. flūtiŋ]. **flute** (II.) & **-ing**. 1. Action of playing the flute. 2. a Decoration on surface of column &c., consisting of carved vertical grooves; b groove made in ruffle or other article of dress; c such flutes collectively.

flutist, n. [1. flōōtist; 2. flūtist]. Fr. *flûtiste*. **flute** & **-ist**. Player on the flute; flautist.

flutter (I.), vb. intrans. & trans. [1. flúter; 2. flátə]. O.E. *flotorian, floterian*, M.E. *floteren*, 'to be tossed by waves, flutter as bird', freq. fr. O.E. **flot-* (fr. **flut-*), weak grade of *flēotan*, **fleet** (I.). Cp. L.G. *fluttern*, 'to flutter', Norw. *flotra*, 'to swim with difficulty'. A. intrans. 1. (of birds) To move the wings rapidly and tremulously; to fly with such motion of wings; to fly in a fitful, aimless, or helpless way; to flit. 2. (of loose, light material) To flap in the wind, vibrate or wave irregularly or fitfully; to quiver: *flags flutter*; *a curtain flutters in the draught*; *a petal flutters to the ground.* 3. (of heart or pulse) To beat rapidly, irregularly, and feebly. 4. (of persons) To tremble with excitement or fear; to move about tremulously; act in an agitated, confused way. B. trans. 1. To cause to flutter or flap; to agitate, wave irregularly: *a bird flutters its wings*; *to flutter a handkerchief.* 2. To throw into a state of mental agitation, tremor, alarm, confusion. Phr. *to flutter the dovecotes*, to alarm or excite quiet, timid people.

flutter (II.), n., fr. prec. 1. Action or process of fluttering. 2. a State of mental agitation or nervous excitement: *to put one in a flutter*; b sensation, stir: *to cause a flutter.* 3. (colloq. or slang) Mild gamble or speculation: *to have a flutter at bridge, in mining shares.*

fluty, adj. [1. flōōti; 2. flūti]. **flute** (I.) & **-y**. Having tones of a clear mellow quality, like those of a flute.

fluvial, adj. [1. flōōvial; 2. flūviəl]. Fr., fr. Lat. *fluviāl-(is)*, fr. *fluvi-(us)*, earlier **flowi-os*, 'river', connected w. *fluere*, 'to flow' (see **fluent** & **-al**). See also **flux**. Pertaining to a river or rivers; living in rivers.

fluviatic, adj. [1. flōōviátik; 2. flūviǽtik]. Lat. *fluviātic-(us)*, as prec., & **-atic**. Fluvial.

fluviatile, adj. [1. flōōviatīl; 2. flūvíətail]. Fr., fr. Lat. *fluviātil-(is)*. Pertaining to a river or rivers, fluvial.

fluvio-, pref. [1. flōōviō; 2. flūviou]. Lat. *fluvius*, 'river'. See **fluvial**. Form used in combination, denoting river, as *fluvioglacial*, pertaining to streams flowing from glaciers; *fluviograph, fluviometer*, instrument for recording level of a river; *fluviomarine*, formed by a river and the sea together: *a fluviomarine deposit.*

flux (I.), n. [1. fluks; 2. flaks]. M.E., Fr., fr. Lat. *fluxus*, 'a flowing', fr. *flux-(um)* for **flugsom* (fr. **bhlu-g-*), P.P. type of *fluere*, 'to flow'. See **fluent, flume, fluvial**. 1. Flow, state of flowing, motion of fluid; fluidity; specif. a inflow of the tide; b excessive or morbid discharge of liquid from the body: *bloody flux* (Bib.), dysentery; liquid thus discharged; c (fig.) copious flow of talk, garrulity: *a perfect flux of words.* 2. (fig.) Continuous process; passing away and on; process of change, succession: *everything is in a state of flux and reflux.* 3. (phys.) a Rate of flow of current, as of water, electricity, heat; b quantity flowing across given area in unit of time. 4. (math.) Continuous motion: *a line is the flux of a point.* 5. a Substance mixed with a mineral to facilitate fusion; b fusion.

flux (II.), vb. intrans. & trans., fr. prec. 1. intrans. a (rare) To flow; to rise as tide; b to be discharged from the body in a flux; c to fuse, melt. 2. trans. a (med.) To produce a flux in; to purge; b to fuse, as with a flux.

fluxation, n. [1. fluksáshun; 2. flakséiʃən]. **flux** (I.) & **-ation**. Act or process of fluxing.

fluxibility, n. [1. flùksibíliti; 2. flàksibíliti]. See next word & **-ity**. Quality of being fluxible.

fluxible, adj. [1. flúksibl; 2. fláksibl]. Fr., fr. L. Lat. *fluxibil-(is)*, 'fluid'. **flux** & **-ible**. Capable of fusion.

fluxion, n. [1. flúkshun; 2. flákʃən]. Fr., fr. Lat. type **fluxiōn-em*, fr. **flux** & **-ion**. 1. a (archaic or rare) Flow of a liquid; discharge; b (med.) morbid flow of liquid to an organ of the body, determination of blood &c. 2. a (rare) Continuous variation; b (math.) rate of the continuous variation of a quantity; (pl.) Newtonian calculus.

fluxional, adj. [1. flúkshunal; 2. flákʃənəl]. Prec. & **-al**. Pertaining to fluxions.

fluxionary, adj. [1. flúkshunari; 2. flákʃənəri]. **fluxion** & **-ary**. Fluxional.

fly (I.), n. [1. flī; 2. flai]. O.E. *flēoge, flȳge*, M.E. *flēȝe, flīe*, O.H.G. *flioga*, Mod. Germ. *fliege*, Icel., Swed. *fluga*. From same base as next word. 1. (popular usage) One of numerous species of small flying insects having two transparent wings. Phrs. *a fly in amber*, a well-preserved relic; *a fly in the ointment*, trifle that spoils or diminishes enjoyment or value of a thing; *a fly on the wheel*, person who overrates his own influence or importance in some action or event. 2. (zool.) Member of the order of *Diptera* or two-winged insects, including flies and gnats. 3. Object representing some form of fly or gnat, made of silk, feathers &c., attached to a fish-hook, and cast lightly by means of a rod and line upon the surface of river or lake to induce fish to rise. 4. Disease caused in vegetables and other plants by flies or other small insects: *there is a good deal of fly on the beans this year.* 5. Person or mechanical appliance that removes sheets, when printed, from the press.

fly (II.), vb. intrans. & trans. O.E. *flēogan*, M.E. *flēgen, flīen*, O.H.G. *fliogan* (Mod. Germ. *fliegen*), O.N. *fljūga*; cp. also, w. different grade, Goth. *(us-)flaugjan*, 'to cause to fly up, away' &c. Gmc. types **fleug-, *flaug-, *flug-* &c., fr. Aryan **pleugh-, *plough-, *plugh-* &c., whence also Lat. *plūma*, 'feather, wing', q.v. under **plume**. Connexion w. **flee** is probable, though disputed by those who, on account of Goth. form, assume *t* as the orig. Aryan initial of this word. A. intrans. 1. To move in and through the air by means of wings, as birds, bats, insects. Phrs. *as the crow flies*, in a straight line across country; *the bird has flown*, the person sought has left, disappeared; *to fly high, to fly at high game*, to have lofty aims, ambitions &c. 2. a To move in and through the air by mechanical means; used of any kind of aeroplane, airship &c., and of the persons in them: *the airship flew to Paris*; *to fly to Paris in an aeroplane*; b to be borne up by the air or wind in a manner resembling that of a bird in the air: *a paper kite flies.* 3. To pass rapidly through the air, in a manner resembling flight; a of things propelled, bullets, arrows &c.: Phr. *to let fly (at)*, to shoot (at); (fig.) to utter violent abuse (at); b (of light objects, particles driven by the wind) to be blown: *sparks fly upward*; *dust flies in* *clouds*; *loose pieces of paper fly about* &c.; Phr. *to make the feathers, dust, fly,* cause a turmoil, engender strife; **c** (of animate things) to leap lightly and swiftly for some distance through the air: *he flew over the hedge at a bound.* **4.** To be borne up, spread out, agitated, by the wind; to stream out, flutter, wave in the air or wind: *with garments, hair, flying behind him*; *flags flew from every mast.* Phr. *with flags flying,* as a conqueror, in triumph. **5. a** (of persons) To go with great speed, move in given direction with haste and impetuosity; to hasten, rush: *I flew to meet him*; *to fly to a person's arms*; *he simply flew down the road*; *it is getting late, I must fly,* must hurry off; Phrs. *time flies,* passes rapidly; *to fly in the face of Providence,* to take a course which is clearly dangerous; **b** (of inanimate things) to be moved suddenly, rapidly, and violently; to be hurled: *the window flew up*; *the door flew open*; *the wheel flew round*; Phrs. *to fly to arms,* prepare hastily for war; *to send things flying,* scatter them by hasty, sudden movement; *to send a person flying,* dismiss him abruptly, drive him away; *to fly in pieces* (of brittle substance), smash to atoms; *to make the money fly,* squander it. **6.** (Pret. *fled*) To retreat hastily, run away, take to flight, flee (gen. used now instead of *flee*). **B.** trans. **1.** To cause, allow, to fly: *to fly a hawk, pigeons* &c. **2.** To bring into position, condition &c. for flight, direct flight of, control while flying: *to fly an airship* &c.; *to fly* (also *sail*) *a kite.* **3.** To display from mast or flag-pole, allow to stream in the wind: *to fly a flag.* Phr. (nav.) *to fly one's flag,* to assume, exercise, admiral's functions. **4.** Specif. (athletics) to jump (an obstacle) by springing from one foot and alighting on the other: *to fly a hurdle.* **5.** (Pres. only) To run away, flee from: *to fly the approach of danger.* **C.** Followed by preposition or adverb. *Fly at,* intrans., **a** to rush violently upon with intent to assault; to attack: *the dog flew at the tramp*; **b** (fig.) to attack with words, vituperate. *Fly into,* intrans., to be carried away, transported; esp. *to fly into a temper, rage, fit* &c. *Fly off,* intrans., to hurry, rush, dart, away. Phr. *to fly off at a tangent,* to start a topic quite irrelevant to the matter in hand. *Fly out at,* intrans., to burst out suddenly into anger with, assail with abuse.

fly (**III.**), n., fr. prec. The relation in sense between this n., in some of its senses, & the vb. is not always apparent. **1.** Act of flying, flight; distance flown: *to have a fly in an aeroplane.* **2.** In various senses, derived perhaps from idea of rapid movement, e.g. four-wheeled covered one-horse carriage working for hire (probably abbreviated from *fly-by-night*). **3.** Flap of cloth (variously applied); **a** part of flag at side opposite staff; width of flag from staff to outer edge; **b** flap of canvas covering entrance to tent; **c** flap of cloth, on garment, covering buttons. **4.** Contrivance for regulating speed of clockwork or accumulating power; fly-wheel &c. **5.** (pl.) Space with gallery or galleries over proscenium of theatre, where scenes &c. are shifted.

fly (**IV.**), adj. Perh. fr. **fly** (**I.**). (colloq. or slang) **a** Quick, agile, nimble; **b** knowing, sharp, wideawake.

fly agaric, n. Poisonous fungus resembling mushroom.

fly-away, adj. & n. **1.** adj. **a** (of dress, hair &c.) Flying loose, streaming; **b** (of person) flighty, volatile. **2.** n. Fly-away person or thing; a fugitive.

flybane, n. [1. flíbān; 2. fláibein]. Plant or substance that kills flies.

fly-bitten, adj. Marked with spots as from bites of flies.

fly-blister, n. (med.) One produced by cantharides or Spanish fly.

fly-blow, n. & vb. trans. **1.** n. **a** Egg or larva of flesh-fly, deposited in living or dead flesh; **b** condition of being fly-blown. **2.** vb. (of flesh-fly) To deposit eggs in; also fig.

fly-blown, adj. **a** Infested or tainted with fly-blows, maggoty; **b** (fig.) discredited, tarnished: *a fly-blown reputation.*

fly-boat, n. Du. *vlieboot,* 'flat-bottomed coasting vessel', fr. *vliegen,* 'to fly', & *boot,* 'boat'. See **fly** (**II.**) & **boat**. Long, narrow canal boat for passenger traffic.

fly-book, n. Kind of pocket-book or case specially adapted for keeping artificial flies for fishing.

fly-by-night, n. [1. flí bī nīt; 2. flái bai nait]. **1. a** Person who gads about by night; **b** debtor who decamps by night. **2.** (obs.) Kind of wheeled sedan-chair.

fly-catcher, n. **1.** One of several small European birds that feed on flies; one of several American birds unrelated to these. **2.** Device for catching flies. **3.** Plant which entraps flies in a kind of cup-shaped receptacle and assimilates them.

fly-fish, vb. intrans. To catch, or attempt to catch, fish with artificial, more rarely with real, flies.

fly-fisher, n. Person who fly-fishes.

fly-fishing, n. Act, art, of catching fish by means of flies fastened to a hook.

fly-flap, n. Implement with long handle and one broad pliant end, for driving away or killing flies.

flying (**I.**), adj. [1. flíing; 2. fláiiŋ], fr. Pres. Part of **fly** (**II.**). **1. a** Capable of flight, habitually practising flight in, or through, the air: *flying insect, dragon* &c.; *flying fox*; **b** adapted, prepared, for flight: *flying machine*; **c** hurried, hasty, as though occurring during brief suspension of flight: *flying visit.* **2.** Streaming loose, flowing, in the air: *flying hair*; *flying colours,* waving regimental standards. Phr. *with flying colours,* in triumph, with great success. **3.** Resembling flight through the air: *flying leap, bound.* **4.** Speedy, very fast: *flying squad,* special detachment of police provided with fast motor-cars or motor-cycles.

flying (**II.**), n. **fly** (**II.**) & **-ing**. Action, motion, of person or thing that flies (in any sense); (attrib.) *flying country,* country in which horsemen can ride fast; *flying shot,* shot at a flying or rapidly moving object.

flying-bridge, n. **1. a** Ferry-boat attached by rope to fixed object, and swinging across river, usually by action of current; **b** pontoon bridge or other floating bridge. **2.** Highest of several bridges on ship.

flying-buttress, n. Buttress built into an outer wall so as to give extra support and carry part of the weight, with the top sloping to an inner wall, or, if the buttress is in the form of a detached column, bearing one end of a half-arch, the other end of which is connected with the wall.

flying-column, n. Military force equipped for rapid movement, and supplied so as to be practically independent of main base.

flying-fish, n. One of several allied fishes found in warm seas, that when pursued leap out of the water, and make a short flight, resembling that of a bird, by means of pectoral fins.

flying-fox, n. A large fruit-eating bat.

flying-frog, n. A large East Indian tree-frog with large webbed feet, enabling it to spring from tree to tree.

flying-officer, n. Commissioned officer in Royal Air Force, next in rank below flight-lieutenant.

flying-phalanger, n. Small Australian marsupial, resembling the flying-squirrel.

flying-squirrel, n. **a** Kind of squirrel with expansible fold of skin, joining front and back limbs, enabling it to take flying leaps; **b** flying-phalanger.

fly-leaf, n. **a** Blank leaf at beginning or end of book; **b** circular printed on single sheet.

flyman, n. [1. flíman; 2. fláimən]. **1.** Man who drives the carriage called a fly. **2.** Man stationed in the flies of a theatre to shift scenes &c.

fly-net, n. **fly** (**II.**) & **net** (**I.**); cp. O.E. *fleohnet.* Net for protecting horse from flies.

fly-paper, n. Paper treated with adhesive or poisonous substance, used hung up, or spread out, for catching or killing flies.

fly-rail, n. Hinged bracket at side of table, which can be pulled out to support hinged leaf.

fly-rod, n. Rod for fly-fishing.

fly-sheet, n. Loose printed sheet; handbill.

flyte. Variant of **flite**.

flyting. Variant of **fliting**.

fly-trap, n. **1.** Trap for catching flies. **2.** One of several plants which entrap and digest small insects; the pitcher plant; *Venus's fly-trap,* American plant of sundew family.

fly-wheel, n. Heavy, rapidly revolving wheel attached to machine for regulating speed.

fly-whisk, n. Light whisk for driving off flies.

foal (**I.**), n. [1. fōl; 2. foul]. O.E. *fola,* M.E. *fōle*; Common Gmc., cp. O.H.G. *folo,* Mod. Germ. *fohlen,* Goth. *fula,* O.N. *foli*; cogn. w. Gk. *pôlos,* 'foal', Lat. *pullus,* 'young animal'. See **filly, pullet**. Young of horse, ass, or other member of the horse family, whether colt or filly. Phr. *in foal, with foal,* (of mare &c.) pregnant.

foal (**II.**), vb. intrans. & trans. fr. prec. **a** intrans. To bear a foal; **b** trans., (of mare) give birth to: *a colt foaled by a thoroughbred mare.*

foalfoot, n. [1. fṓlfoot; 2. fóulfut]. (bot.) Coltsfoot.

foam (**I.**), n. [1. fōm; 2. foum]. O.E. *fām,* M.E. *fōm,* O.H.G., Mod. Germ. *feim*; cogn. w. Scrt. *phēna-,* O. Slav. *pěna,* 'foam'; also Lat. *pūmex,* 'pumice', & perh. *spūma* for **(s)poima,* 'foam'. See **pumice, spume**. **1.** White, fleecy mass of small bubbles, froth, on surface of agitated or effervescing liquid, e.g. on waves of the sea; newly drawn ale &c. **2.** (poet.) The sea itself: *to sail the foam.* **3.** Anything resembling foam; thick sweat or saliva from horse; profuse saliva in human beings.

foam (**II.**), vb. intrans. O.E. *fāmigan,* M.E. *fāmien, fōmen,* fr. prec. **1.** intrans. (of water or other liquid) To boil, be agitated, effervesce, so as to produce foam; to have foam on the surface; to froth: *foaming ale* &c. **2.** (of horses and human beings) To produce, exude, emit, saliva or sweat resembling foam, whether from exertion, disease, or fury: *foaming steeds.* Phr. *to foam at the mouth,* as in a fit, or (fig.) to be furiously angry. **3.** To issue in foam: *milk foaming into the pails.*

foamless, adj. [1. fṓmles; 2. fóumlis]. **foam** (**I.**) & **-less**. Devoid of foam.

foamy, adj. [1. fṓmi; 2. fóumi]. O.E. *fāmiġ,* M.E. *fōmi.* **foam** (**I.**) & **-y**. Consisting of, resembling, covered with, foam.

fob (**I.**), n. [1. fob; 2. fɔb]. Of L.G. origin; cp. the L.G. dimin. *fob-ke,* 'little pocket', & H.G. provinc. *fuppe,* 'pocket'. Small pocket for watch &c., opening from waistband of breeches.

fob (**II.**), vb. trans. Back-formation fr. M.E. *fobbere,* 'cheater', fr. *fobbe,* variant of *foppe,* 'fool'. See **fop**. (obs.) To cheat, deceive. Survives only in *fob off*: **a** to impose (something worthless or undesirable) upon a person by fraud or trickery: *to fob off a spurious antique on one*; **b** to delude (a person) into accepting something worthless: *to fob one off with empty promises.*

focal, adj. [1. fṓkal; 2. fóukəl]. Fr., fr. **focus** & **-al**. Pertaining to a focus: *focal distance* or *length,* distance from focus to centre of the lens or mirror; *focal plane,* plane parallel to that of lens or mirror, passing through its focus.

focalization, n. [1. fòkalīzā́shun; 2. fòukəlaizéiʃən]. Next word & **-ation**. Action of focalizing; state of being focalized.

focalize, vb. trans. [1. fṓkaliz; 2. fóukəlaiz]. **focal** & **-ize**. To focus (lit. and fig.).

focimeter, n. [1. fōsímeter; 2. fousímitə]. *Foci-,* combining form of **focus**, & **-meter**. Instrument for measuring focal distances.

focimetry, n. [1. fōsímetri; 2. fousímətri]. As prec. & **-meter**. Measurement of focal distances.

fo'c's'le, n. [1. fóksl; 2. fóuk(ə)sl]. Phonetic spelling of **forecastle**.

focus (I.), n. [1. fókus; 2. fóukəs]. Lat. *focus*, 'fireplace, hearth; fireside, home'. Prob. not related to O.E. *bacan*, q.v. under **bake**; more likely connected w. Lat. *facies*, 'appearance, aspect, shape, beauty; face'. See **face**. The orig. sense wd. thus be 'shining, glowing, place'. **1. a** Point at which converging rays of light, heat, or waves of sound meet after refraction or reflection; **b** also *virtual focus*, point at which rays appear to meet, or would meet if prolonged in a straight line; **c** adjustment of instrument or distance so as to produce sharp definition of image; Phrs. *in focus*, (of optical instruments) adjusted so as to give clear and sharp outlines in image; (fig., of description &c.) clearly and definitely presented; *out of focus*, not adjusted, distorted (also fig.); **d** focal length. **2.** (geom.) One of two points having a definite relation to a curve. **3.** (fig.) Point or area of greatest intensity or activity; centre of radiation or dispersion: *a focus of sedition*; *focus of a disease*, part of the body where it originates or is most active; *focus of an earthquake*, subterranean centre, below epicentre.

focus (II.), vb. trans. & intrans., fr. prec. **1.** trans. **a** To cause to converge: *to focus the sun's rays with a burning-glass*; **b** to adjust (instrument or eye) to object, so as to produce a clear image, to focalize; **c** to obtain a clear image of (object) by adjusting instrument; **d** (of mental action) To concentrate: *to focus one's attention, thoughts, on a subject*. **2.** intrans. (of rays &c.) To converge.

fodder, n. & vb. trans. [1. fóder; 2. fɔ́də]. O.E. *fōdor*, later *foddor*, M.E. *foder*, fr. O.E. *fōda*, 'food'; O.H.G. *fuotar*, Mod. Germ. *futter*, Icel. *fōðr*. See **food**. **1.** n. Food, other than growing grass, supplied to horses, cattle, sheep, and other large domestic animals. **2.** vb. To feed with fodder.

fodderer, n. [1. fóderer; 2. fɔ́dərə]. Prec. & **-er**. Person who fodders animals.

fodderless, adj. [1. fóderles; 2. fɔ́dəlis]. **fodder** & **-less**. Having no fodder.

foe, n. [1. fō; 2. fou]. O.E. *fāh*, 'proscribed, hostile', fr. **faih-*; cp. also O.E. *fǣhþ(o)*, 'enmity', corresponding to O.H.G. *fēhida*, both fr. **faih-iþā* (cp. **feud (I.)**); cp. also O.E. *fǣge*, O.H.G. *feigi*, 'fated to die', Mod. Germ. *feige*, 'cowardly' (see **fey**). The base, Aryan **pei-k̑-*, **poik̑-*, **pik̑-* &c., 'to be hostile, evil-minded' &c., is further seen in Lat. *piget*, 'it irks' &c.; Lith. *piktas*, 'wicked, angry', *paikas*, 'bad, stupid'; Scrt. *piśačáś*, 'demon'. See also **fickle**. **1.** (chiefly poet. or liter.) **a** Enemy, opponent, adversary (in war); **b** person who is unfriendly to one, ill-wisher: '*No Frenchman is my foe*' (Macaulay). **2.** One opposed to some particular principle, system, condition &c.: *a foe to Nonconformity, to Jewish influence* &c. **3.** Something prejudicial, destructive, incompatible: *idleness is a foe to virtue*; *cleanliness is a foe to disease*.

Foehn, Föhn, n. [1. fēn; 2. fān]. Swiss Germ., perh. fr. Lat. *Favōnius*, 'west wind', connected w. *favēre*. See **favour**. Hot dry wind which blows down Alpine valleys.

foe-like, adj. **foe** & **-like**. Resembling a foe.

foeman, n. [1. fōman; 2. fóumən]. O.E. *fāhman*, M.E. *fōmon*. **foe** & **man**. (archaic or poet.) Enemy in war. Phr. *a foeman worthy of one's steel*, a brave enemy; (fig.) a stout, fair, competent opponent of any kind.

foetal, fetal, adj. [1. fētl; 2. fítl]. Lat. *fēt-*, stem of **foetus**, & **-al**. Pertaining to a foetus.

foetation, fetation, n. [1. fētáshun; 2. fītéiʃən]. Lat. *fētāt-*, P.P. stem of *fētāre*, 'to bring forth', fr. *fētus*. See **foetus** & **-ion**. Formation and growth of a foetus; pregnancy.

foeticide, feticide, n. [1. fētisīd; 2. fítisaid]. Lat. *fēti-*, combining form of *fētus*. **foetus** & **-cide**. Act of killing a foetus, or causing abortion.

foetus, fetus, n. [1. fētus; 2. fítəs]. Lat. *fētus*, incorrectly *foetus*, 'a bringing forth, offspring', fr. *fēt-*, P.P. stem of O. Lat. *fēre*, 'to impregnate'; fr. Aryan base **dhē-*, 'to produce'. See **fecundity, felicity, feline, feminine**. Young of an animal in the womb or egg in advanced stage of development.

fog (I.), n. [1. fog; 2. fɔg]. M.E. *fogge*, 'rank grass', of Scand. origin; cp. Norw. *fogg*, 'long straggling grass in a moist hollow', Dan. *fugtig*, Germ. *feucht*, 'damp'. Coarse, long grass which has not been grazed; new growth after mowing; aftergrass, aftermath.

fog (II.), vb. trans. & intrans., fr. prec. **1.** trans. **a** To leave (grass) standing until winter; **b** to feed (animals) on fog. **2.** intrans. *Fog off* (of plant), to die off from damp.

fog (III.), n. Of Scand. origin; cp. Dan. (*sene-*) *fog*, 'driving, thickly falling snow', Icel. *fok*, 'spray, snowdrift', *fjūk*, 'snowstorm'. Perh. back-formation fr. **foggy** in sense 'covered with rank grass, mossy, marshy, damp'. **1. a** Thick mist; water vapour or cloud resting on land or water; **b** cloud of smoke, dust, spray &c., obscuring the air. **2.** Blurred or cloudy condition of a photographic negative or print. **3.** (fig.) State of obscurity, bewilderment; lack of clarity or intelligibility; mental confusion or ignorance: *the fog of war*; *to have one's mind in a fog*.

fog (IV.), vb. trans. & intrans. fr. prec. **1.** trans. **a** To envelop in fog, befog; **b** to produce foggy effect in photograph; **c** (fig.) to render obscure to the understanding; to confuse, perplex, bewilder the mind. **2.** intrans. **a** To become foggy; **b** to become fogged, as a photograph; **c** to place fog-signals on railway.

fogbank, n. [1. fógbangk; 2. fɔ́gbæŋk]. Mass or belt of fog on the sea.

fogbound, adj. [1. fógbound; 2. fɔ́gbaund]. Detained by fog, esp. of ship at sea.

fogbow, n. [1. fógbō; 2. fɔ́gbou]. Arch of whitish light, caused by the sun's rays striking the particles of vapour in a fog.

fogey, fogy, n. [1. fōgi; 2. fóugi]. Origin unknown. Old or middle-aged man who is out of touch with the ideas and habits of the time; a fussy, dull, slow, old-fashioned person; often *old fogey*.

fogeydom, n. [1. fōgidum; 2. fóugidəm]. **fogey** & **-dom**. Fogeys collectively; character, manners, or ideas of fogeys.

fogeyish, adj. [1. fōgiish: 2. fóugiiʃ]. See prec. & **-ish**. Pertaining to, resembling, a fogey.

fogeyism, n. [1. fōgiizm; 2. fóugiizəm]. See prec. & **-ism**. Quality of being a fogey.

foggage, n. [1. fógij; 2. fɔ́gidž]. **fog** (I.) & **-age**. **a** (chiefly Scots) Fog (I.); **b** (Scots law) right of pasturing cattle on fog.

fogger, n. [1. fóger; 2. fɔ́gə]. **fog** (II.) & **-er**. Man who places fog-signals on railway.

foggily, adv. [1. fógili; 2. fɔ́gili]. **foggy** (II.) & **-ly**. In a foggy manner; with fog in the atmosphere &c.

fogginess, n. [1. fógines; 2. fɔ́ginis]. Next word & **-ness**. Condition of being enveloped in fog, of being pervaded with fog (lit. and fig.).

foggy (I.), adj. [1. fógi; 2. fɔ́gi]. **fog** (I.) & **-y**. Pertaining to, abounding in, resembling, the kind of grass called fog.

foggy (II.), adj., fr. **fog** (II.) & **-y**. **1. a** Pertaining to; full of, enveloped in, resembling, fog; misty, murky: *a foggy atmosphere, day*; **b** (of photograph) blurred, indistinct. **2.** (fig.) **a** (of ideas &c.) Obscure, not clear to the mind; **b** (of the mind) confused, perplexed.

foghorn, n. [1. fóg-horn; 2. fɔ́ghōn]. Powerful horn, often blown by steam, to give warning of a ship's whereabouts in a fog.

fog-signal, n. Warning signal in fog; specif., detonating cap placed on rail and exploded by train.

fogy. See **fogey**.

foh, interj. Variant of **faugh**.

Föhn. See **Foehn**.

foible, n. [1. fóibl; 2. fóibl]. Obs. Fr. form of *faible* (see **feeble**); cp. Fr. *faible* in sense of 'weakness'. **1.** Weak point in one's character; little frailty, failing; esp. inclination to be unwarrantably vain about some imagined quality or accomplishment: *one of his foibles is to think he can sing*. **2.** (fencing) Pliant part of sword-blade from middle to point.

foil (I.), n. [1. foil; 2. fɔil]. M.E. 'leaf', fr. O. Fr. *foil, fuil*, fr. Lat. *folium*, 'leaf'; cp. Fr. *feuille*, fr. Lat. pl., *folia*. See **folio, counterfoil, trefoil**. **1.** Leaf-shaped space between two cusps in Gothic tracery (cp. *trefoil, quatrefoil, cinquefoil*). **2. a** Sheet of metal beaten very thin: *lead, silver, foil*; **b** thin coat of quicksilver amalgam as used behind glass of mirror and for other purposes. **3.** (fig.) Thing or person enhancing or setting off qualities of another by contrast.

foil (II.), vb. trans., fr. prec. **1.** (archit.) To furnish with foils: *a foiled arch*. **2. a** To cover or back with foil or a foil; **b** (fig., rare) to set off as a foil.

foil (III.), vb. trans. & intrans. M.E. *foilen*, 'to trample', prob. fr. O. Fr., *fuler, fouler, foler* (Mod. Fr. *fouler*), 'to trample on', fr. L. Lat. *fullāre*, 'to full' (cloth), fr. *fullo*, 'a fuller'. See **full** (I.) The diphthong in Engl. may be due to confusion w. Fr. *fouiller*, 'to dig for, ransack'; fr. Romance type **fodiculāre*, dimin. fr. Lat. *fodicāre*, 'to dig'. **1.** trans. **a** (hunt.) To spoil or confuse (the scent, trail), by retracing or crossing track; **b** to baffle, baulk, frustrate (a person, attempt, action); to parry, repel (an attack). **2.** intrans. (hunt.) To foil the scent or trail.

foil (IV.), n., fr. prec. **1.** Trail of hunted animal. Phr. *to run (upon) the foil*, to foil the scent or trail. **2.** (archaic) Check, frustration, repulse: *to put to the foil*.

foil (V.), n. Of uncertain origin; perh. a special sense of **foil** (IV.), because the sword is only used to check or baffle the antagonist; cp. the obs. pl. *at foils*, 'parrying'; otherwise a corrupt. of **foin**. Light sword only used in fencing, with button on point to prevent injury in thrusting.

foilable, adj. [1. fóilabl; 2. fóiləbl]. **foil** (III.) & **-able**. Liable to be foiled or frustrated.

foiling (I.), n. [1. fóiling; 2. fóiliŋ]. **foil** (I.) & **-ing**. (archit.) Decoration consisting of foils.

foiling (II.), n. **foil** (II.) & **-ing**. (hunt.) Trail of deer.

foin, vb. intrans. [1. foin; 2. fɔin]. M.E. *foinen*, fr. O.F. *foi(s)ne*, 'fish-spear', fr. Lat. *fuscina*, origin unexplained; cp. Fr. provinc. *fouiner*, 'to spear eels'. (archaic) To lunge, thrust with sword, spear, or other weapon.

foison, n. [1. fóizon; 2. fóizən]. O. Fr., fr. Lat. *fūsiōn-(em)*, 'a pouring'. See **fusion**. (archaic) Plenty, abundance; a bountiful harvest.

foist, vb. trans. [1. foist; 2. fɔist]. Orig. a gambling term, 'to palm' (false die), fr. Du. *vuisten*, 'to take in the fist', fr. *vuist*, **fist**. To palm off, pass, impose, introduce or interpolate fraudulently or unwarrantably: *to foist a forged bank-note upon one*; *to foist a clause into an Act of Parliament*.

fold (I.), vb. trans. & intrans. [1. fōld; 2. fould]. O.E. (Merc.) *faldan* (W.S. *fealdan*), M.E. *fōlden*; Common Gmc., cp. O.H.G. *faltan*, Mod. Germ. *falten*, Goth. *falþan*, O.N. *falda*; Gmc. type **falþan-*, cogn. w. Gk. *plássein* for **plat-jein*, 'to form, mould' (see **plastic, plaster**), (*di*)*plásios*, '(two)fold', & perh. Scrt. *puṭa-*, 'a fold'. Cogn. also w. Lat. *-pl-us* in *duplus* (see **double**), & prob. w. Lat. *plicāre*, 'to fold' (see **ply (I.)**). **A.** trans. **1.** To lay or press one part of (flexible thing) against another; to bend over or back on itself; to double up: *to fold clothes, a sheet*; *to fold down the corner of a page*; Phrs. *to fold one's arms*, to twine them together on one's chest; (fig.) to abstain from action; *to fold one's hands*, to clasp them together; *fold up*, to double, wrap together, tidily and symmetrically, by folding; to reduce to a more compact shape by folding: *to fold up a newspaper.* **2.** To wrap, wind, round a thing: *to fold one's cloak about one.* **3. a** To enclose in folds, enfold, wrap up in sheet &c., swathe, envelop: *to fold an object in paper*; *clouds fold the hills*; **b** to clasp, embrace: *to fold a person in one's arms, to one's breast.* **B.** intrans. To be folded; to be capable of folding: *the shutters fold back.*

fold (II.), n. M.E. *feald, fold.* See prec. **1. a** Part of flexible material that is folded, bent over, or doubled; plait, layer; coil of rope, snake, &c.; **b** depression or hollow in material made by folding: *to carry something in a fold of one's robe*; **c** crease or wrinkle made by folding. **2. a** Hollow in undulating ground: *a fold of the hills*; specif. **b** (geol.) dip in strata.

fold (III.), n. O.E. *falod, falud,* later *fāld,* 'cowshed, shelter made with boards, fold', fr. *fala,* 'board, plank', M.E. *fōld,* cp. Dan. *fold,* 'sheep-pen', Du. *vaalt,* 'dung-pit'. **1. a** Enclosure for sheep, usually made of wattle hurdles or rough stone; pen; **b** the sheep in a fold, flock. **2.** (fig.) The Church; a church or religious congregation; *the true Fold,* name used of itself by each branch of the Church.

fold (IV.), vb. trans., fr. prec. **a** To enclose in a fold; **b** to manure (land) by keeping sheep in a fold on it.

-fold, suff. O.E. *-feald,* M.E. *-fāld, -fōld*; Common Gmc., cp. O.S. *-fald,* O.H.G., Mod. Germ. *-falt,* Goth. *-falþ-s,* O.N. *-fald-r,* fr. base of **fold** (I.); Lat. *-plus* (*duplus* &c.), Gk. *ha-plós,* 'single'; also *-plásios,* '-fold', cp. **haplo-.** Suff. added to cardinal number denoting multiplication, increase: *twofold,* double; *threefold,* triple &c. These forms now largely replaced by Lat. words in *-ble, -ple.*

folder, n. [1. fṓlder; 2. fóuldə]. **fold** (I.) & **-er.** **1. a** Person or thing that folds; specif. **b** instrument for folding paper. **2.** Thing that can be folded up; specif. **a** printed paper thus made; **b** (pl.) pair of folding eyeglasses.

folderol, n. Variant of **falderal.**

folding (I.), adj. [1. fṓlding; 2. fóuldiŋ]. Pres. Part. of **fold** (I.). Capable of folding or being folded: *folding boat, chair*; *folding bed,* one that can be shut up and stood by the wall of the room; *folding door* (usually pl.), one consisting of two or more leaves with hinges.

folding (II.), n. **fold** (II.) & **-ing.** **a** Keeping or enclosing of sheep in a fold; **b** manure from a fold.

foliaceous, adj. [1. fòliā́shus; 2. fòuliéiʃəs]. Lat. *foliāce-(us),* fr. *folium,* 'leaf'. See **folio** & **-aceous.** Pertaining to, resembling, the leaf or leaves of a plant, or foliage.

foliage, n. [1. fṓliij; 2. fóuliidʒ]. O. Fr. *foillage, fueillage* (Mod. Fr. *feuillage*), fr. *feuille,* 'leaf'; fr. Lat. *foli-(a),* 'leaves'. See **folio** & **-age.** **a** Leaves of plant collectively, esp. as growing; leafage; (attrib.) *foliage leaf,* leaf in strict sense, as distinguished from petal, sepal, bract &c.; *foliage plant,* one cultivated for its handsome foliage rather than its flowers; **b** (art) decoration resembling leaves.

foliaged, adj. [1. fṓliijd; 2. fóuliidʒd]. Prec. & **-ed.** Having foliage, generally in composition, as *dark-, heavy-foliaged.*

foliar, adj. [1. fṓliar; 2. fóuliə]. Lat. *foli-(um),* 'leaf', see **folio,** & **-ar.** (bot.) Pertaining to a leaf or leaves.

foliate (I.), vb. trans. & intrans. [1. fṓliāt; 2. fóulieit], fr. Lat. *foliāt-(um).* See **folio** & **-ate.** **1.** trans. **a** (archit.) To decorate with foils or foliage; **b** to beat (gold &c.) into leaf or foil; **c** to furnish (mirror) with foil; **d** to number leaves of (book) instead of pages. **2.** intrans. To split into laminae.

foliate (II.), adj. See prec. **a** Furnished with, bearing, a leaf or leaves; **b** resembling a leaf.

foliated, adj. [1. fṓliāted; 2. fóulieitid]. Prec. & **-ed.** **a** Having leaves or leaf-like ornaments, marks, or forms; **b** capable of splitting into laminae.

foliation, n. [1. fòliā́shun; 2. fòuliéiʃən], fr. **foliate** & **-ion.** **1.** Action or process of foliating; state of being foliated. **2.** Production of leaves, leafing of plant.

foliature, n. [1. fṓliachur; 2. fóuliətʃə]. Lat. *foliātūra,* 'foliage'. See **foliate** & **-ure.** The leaves of a tree collectively; foliage.

folio (I.), n. [1. fṓliō; 2. fóuliou]. Abbr. fr. Lat. *in foliō,* 'on leaf . . .', in references; abl. of *folium,* 'leaf'. The Aryan base is **bhlē-, *bhlō-* &c., 'to swell'; whence also Lat. *flōs* (see **flower**), O.E. *blǣd,* 'leaf' &c. (see **blade**); O.E. *bȳle,* 'swelling' (see **boil** (I.)); Gk. *phúllon,* 'leaf'. See also **blow** (IV.), **bloom, blossom.** **1. a** Sheet of paper folded once to make two leaves of a book or manuscript; hence, **b** large size of paper used for this purpose. **2. a** Volume made of such sheets folded once; **b** size of such volume; largest ordinary class of volume: *two volumes (in) folio.* **3.** (book-keeping) Page, or two opposite pages, of ledger used for both sides of an account. **4. a** Leaf of manuscript or printed book numbered only in front; **b** (print.) page number of book. **5.** (law) Unit for estimating length of document, in Britain 72 words, or 90 for an Act of Parliament. **6.** (attrib.) Of the size of a folded folio: *a folio volume.*

folio (II.), vb. trans., fr. prec. To number the leaves of (book) on one side only.

foliole, n. [1. fṓliōl; 2. fóulioul]. Fr., fr. L. Lat. *foliolum,* dimin. of *folium,* 'leaf'. See **folio.** **a** (bot.) Separate part of compound leaf; leaflet; **b** (zool.) small organ resembling a leaf.

foliose, adj. [1. fṓliōs; 2. fóulious]. Lat. *foliōs-(us).* See **folio** & **-ose.** (bot.) Leafy.

folk, n. [1. fōk; 2. fouk]. O.E. *folc,* M.E. *fōlk,* cp. O.S., O.H.G. *folk,* Mod. Germ. *volk,* O.N. *fōlk,* fr. Germ. **fulk-a,* 'people, crowd, nation, army'. This Gmc. word is prob. connected w. the equally widespread **full** (I.). Cp. Lat. *populus,* 'people, nation', fr. **po-pel-os,* w. reduplication of base **pel-,* 'fill' (see **popular**), & Lat. *plēb-s,* 'common people' (see **plebs, plebeian**), both connected w. Lat. *plēre,* 'to fill', *plēnus,* 'full' (see **plenum**); O. Slav. *plŭkŭ,* 'army', Russ. *polk,* are borrowed fr. Gmc. **1.** Large community, nation; (in this sense, a revival of O.E. usage, perhaps influenced by Mod. Germ.). **2.** (with pl. vb.) People in general, the public: *folk will believe anything they are told.* **3.** Class of people specified: *rich, poor, old, young, folk*; (colloq., pl.) *my folks,* my relations; *the old folks at home.*

folk-dance, n. **a** One of the old traditional dances of the country; **b** music for this.

folk-etymology, n. Ad. fr. Germ. *volksetymologie.* Popular, non-scientific etymology.

folkland, n. [1. fōkland; 2. fóuklænd]. Mod. adaptation of O.E. *folcland.* **folk** & **land** (I.). (hist.) In Anglo-Saxon law, land held by customary right, and not, as bookland, by written title.

folklore, n. [1. fṓklōr; 2. fóuklɔ̄]. **folk** & **lore** (I.). Mod. concoction. Aggregate of traditional popular beliefs, tales, sayings, and customs; the scientific study of these.

folklorist, n. [1. fṓklòrist; 2. fóuklɔ̀rist]. Prec. & **-ist.** Person versed in the study of folklore.

folkmote, folkmoot, n. [1. fṓkmōt, -mōōt; 2. fóukmout, -mūt]. Mod. adaptation of O.E. *folcmōt, -ġemōt.* **folk** & **moot** (I.). (hist.) General assembly of the men of a town or district in Anglo-Saxon England.

folksong, n. [1. fṓksong; 2. fóuksɔŋ]. **folk** & **song,** after Germ. *volkslied.* Traditional song and melody, current among the common people and usually of unknown origin.

folktale, n. [1. fṓktāl; 2. fóukteil]. Mod. concoction on Germ. model. Traditional tale, usually with mythical elements, current among the common people.

follicle, n. [1. fólikl; 2. fɔ́likl]. Fr., fr. Lat. *follicul-(us),* 'little bag, pod', dimin. of *follis,* 'bellows'; fr. base **bhlē-* &c., 'swell, blow'. See **bellows, belly, blow** (II.), **flower** &c. **a** (bot.) Seed vessel from single carpel, opening on one side only; **b** (zool.) cocoon; **c** (anat.) small deep or narrow-mouthed sac or gland: *a hair follicle.*

follicular, adj. [1. folíkūlar; 2. fəlíkjulə]. Lat. *folliculār-(is).* See prec. & **-ar.** Pertaining to a follicle.

folliculate(d), adj. [1. folíkūlāt(ed); 2. fəlíkjuleit(id)]. See prec. & **-ate.** Having, consisting of, a follicle or follicles.

follow (I.), vb. trans. & intrans. [1. fólō; 2. fɔ́lou]. O.E. *folgian,* fr. **fulgōjan,* M.E. *folewen* &c., Common Gmc., O.S. *folgōn,* O.H.G. *folgen,* O.N. *fylgja*; only found in Gmc. & supposed by some to be an old compound of the base of **full** (I.), & that of **go,** & to have had primary sense of 'accompany'. **A.** trans. **1. a** To come or go after; Phrs. *to follow one's nose,* go straight ahead; *to follow hounds,* to hunt; *follow the plough,* guide it, to plough; **b** to pursue, chase, hunt: *to follow a retreating enemy*; *to follow the fox.* **2. a** (in physical sense) To go, walk, along, or by: *to follow a road*; **b** (fig.) adopt, pursue (line of conduct &c.): *to follow a course, plan of action.* **3. a** To come after in time, be later than: *night follows day*; *Monday follows Sunday*; **b** to occur, take place, after: *a sermon followed the service.* **4. a** To succeed (person) in an office, a position &c.: *to follow one's father in his estates*; *to follow one's senior in command of a regiment* &c.; **b** to come after or next to, in order of rank or precedence: *earls follow marquises.* **5.** To engage in, pursue, a particular profession, occupation: *to follow the trade of a hatter.* Phr. *to follow the law, the sea,* to be a lawyer, sailor. **6. a** To be an adherent, disciple, of a person in his moral or intellectual teaching; to adopt a person's ideals, views, precepts &c., imitate his conduct, regard as a leader: *to follow a blind guide*; *to follow the best authorities*; to agree with: *I am unable to follow you in all your views*; **b** to abide by, obey, act in accordance with: *to follow directions, instructions, precepts* &c.; Phrs. *to follow a lead*: (i.) (cards) play after and in accordance with another player; (ii.) (fig.) to act in accordance with a hint received; *to follow suit*: (i.) (cards) play card of suit which has been led; (ii.) to imitate what has already been done. **7.** To understand clearly and in detail, to grasp thoroughly with the mind; to keep pace mentally with exposition, or gradual unfolding of; to take in: *to follow an argument*; *to follow an explanation*; *to follow a teacher in his demonstration.* **8. a** To keep the sight or hearing concentrated on moving or changing objects, so that one perceives each movement or change: *to follow a procession, review, cricket match &c. with a field-glass*; *to follow a conversation through a closed door*; **b** to keep in touch with, keep attention fixed upon, a series of events, changing state of affairs &c.: *I don't follow French politics very carefully*; **c** to think out, concentrate the mind upon, pursue a certain series of ideas: *to follow a train of thought.* **B.** intrans. **1.** To come after, and later: *go on ahead and I will follow with the dog.* **2.** To occur later: *after what has already happened no one knows what may follow.* **3.** To occur as a natural or logical consequence; (gen. impers.): *from what you say it follows that he must be dismissed.* **C.** Followed by preposition or adverb. *Follow on,* intrans., **a** (colloq.) to follow after an interval; **b** to keep up a pursuit, press on; **c** (cricket) to have a second innings following the first, when other side leads by certain number of runs; **d** (billiards) to cause ball to continue travelling in straight line after striking another ball; (of ball itself) to do this. *Follow out,* trans., to pursue, carry out, to a conclusion: *to follow out a plan, a design, instructions.* *Follow through,* intrans., **a** to continue a stroke, as in golf, tennis &c., to the fullest extent of arms and body, weight, after striking the ball, so as to give it the greatest amount of carry; **b** (of ball, as at billiards) to follow on. *Follow up*, trans., **a** to pursue with persistence; to continue the act of pursuing: *to follow up a wounded deer*; **b** (fig.) to prosecute to a conclusion a clue, a suggestion &c.; **c** to enhance the effect of by further action: *to follow up a blow, a victory*; **d** (football &c.) to keep near player on own side who has ball, so as to support him.

follow (II.), n., fr. prec. **1.** Act or process of following; specif., billiard stroke in which the player's ball follows another ball after striking it; also *follow through*, continuation of stroke, as at golf &c. **2.** (colloq.) Small portion of food served as second helping in restaurant &c.

follower, n. [1. fólōer; 2. fɔ́louə]. O.E. *folgere*, M.E. *folwere*. **follow** (I.) & **-er**. **1.** Person who follows; specif. **a** disciple, adherent: *a follower of Cobden*; **b** a retainer; **c** one who follows an army as a hanger-on. **2.** Man who courts a girl, esp. a maid-servant: *no followers allowed*. **3.** Part of machine actuated by another part.

following (I.), adj. [1. fólōing; 2. fɔ́louiŋ], fr. Pres. Part. of **follow** (I.). That follows (in any sense); specif. **a** next after, subsequent: *following day*; **b** *the following*, that, those, to be mentioned immediately: *the following have received honorary degrees*; **c** (of wind or tide) moving in the same direction as the vessel.

following (II.), n. **follow** (I.) & **-ing**. Body of followers or adherents.

follow-my-leader, n. [1. fólō mi léder; 2. fɔ́lou mi lídə]. Children's game in which the players imitate every movement of the leader.

follow-on, n. [1. fòlō ón; 2. fɔ̀lou ɔ́n]. (cricket) Second innings immediately following the first by the side behind by a certain number of runs.

folly, n. [1. fóli; 2. fɔ́li]. M.E., O.F., Mod. Fr. *folie*, fr. O. Fr. *fol* (Mod. Fr. *fou*), 'fool, madman'. See **fool** & **-y**. Sense **3** perh. fr. special sense of Fr. *folie*, 'favourite abode, pleasure pavilion'. **1.** Foolish state or quality of mind; stupidity, imbecility, irrationality: *an action due to folly*. **2.** Foolish action, behaviour, utterance: *it is folly to yield to threats*; *what you propose is mere folly*. **3.** A useless, fantastic structure, built from foolish caprice.

foment, vb. trans. [1. fōmént; 2. foumént]. Fr. *fomenter*, fr. L. Lat. *fōmentāre*, fr. Lat. *fōmentum*, 'poultice' &c., for **fovimentum*, fr. *fovēre*, 'to warm'; the etymol. of the base is not clear. See **-ment**. **1. a** To apply a hot or medicated lotion, or poultice to; to bathe with warm water &c. **2.** (fig.) To cherish, stimulate, instigate; encourage, promote: *to foment disorder, rebellion, hatred.*

fomentation, n. [1. fòmentáshun; 2. fòumentéiʃən]. Fr., fr. Lat. *fōmentātiōn-(em)*. Prec. & **-ation**. **1. a** Action of fomenting or warming; **b** lotion, poultice, hot compress, or other means used for fomenting. **2.** Instigation, encouragement (of discontent &c.).

fomenter, n. [1. fōménter; 2. fouméntə]. **foment** & **-er**. One who foments, esp. strife, disorder &c.

fond, adj. [1. fond; 2. fɔnd]. M.E. *fonned*, 'infatuated', P.P. of *fonnen*, 'to dote, to befool', whence Mod. Provinc. Engl. *fun*, 'to hoax' (see **fun**), fr. M.E. *fon, fonne*, 'fool', also 'foolish'; of Scand. origin, cp. Icel. *fāni*, 'foolish', *fāna*, 'to act foolishly', Swed. *fåne*, 'fool'. **1. a** (obs. or archaic) Foolish, vain, inept: '*A very foolish fond old man*' ('King Lear'); **b** credulous, foolishly sanguine: *to nourish a fond hope, fond imaginings.* **2. a** Foolishly doting, infatuated; over-indulgent; esp. *fond and foolish*; **b** loving, affectionate: *a fond father.* **3. a** *Fond of*, attached to, having affection for: *fond of one's mother*; **b** deriving enjoyment from, taking pleasure in; addicted to: *fond of smoking*; *fond of drink.*

fondant, n. [1. fóndant; 2. fɔ́ndənt]. Fr., 'a sweetmeat', fr. Pres. Part. of *fondre*, 'to melt', fr. Lat. *fundere*, 'to pour'. See **found** (II.). Kind of soft sweetmeat, made of flavoured sugar, which melts easily in the mouth.

fondle, vb. trans. & intrans. [1. fóndl; 2. fɔ́ndl]. Obs. *fond*, 'to be fond', fr. **fond** & freq. **-le**. **a** trans. To caress, stroke, or toy with lovingly; dandle; **b** intrans., (rare) indulge in caresses: *to fondle with one.*

fondling, n. [1. fóndling; 2. fɔ́ndliŋ]. **fond** & **-ling**. Person who is fondled or doted on; object of foolish affection; darling, pet.

fondly, adv. [1. fóndli; 2. fɔ́ndli]. **fond** & **-ly**. In a fond manner; **a** vainly, in ignorance, being misled: *as I fondly imagined*; **b** with affection, lovingly: *to gaze fondly at.*

fondness, n. [1. fóndnes; 2. fɔ́ndnis]. M.E. *fonnednesse*, 'foolishness'. **fond** & **-ness**. Quality of being fond; doting affection, love, liking.

fondue, n. [1. fóndū; 2. fɔ́ndjū]. Fr., fr. fem. P.P. of *fondre*, 'to melt', as **fondant**. Dish of scrambled eggs with melted cheese.

font (I.), n. [1. font; 2. fɔnt]. O.E., M.E., & also O. Fr. *font*, 'baptismal font', fr. Lat. *font-(em)*, 'fountain, source', in Eccles. Lat., 'font'. The etymol. is quite uncertain. **1. a** Receptacle for baptismal water, usually of carved stone, fixed in church or baptistery; **b** (rare) holy water stoup. **2.** (poet.) Fountain, spring, well. **3.** (modern) Oil reservoir of lamp.

font (II.). See **fount** (typog.).

fontal, adj. [1. fóntal; 2. fɔ́ntəl]. Low Lat. *fontāl-(is)*. **font** (I.) & **-al**. **1.** Pertaining to a fountain-head, original. **2.** Baptismal.

fontanel, fontanelle, n. [1. fòntanél; 2. fɔ̀ntənél]. Fr. *fontanelle*, dimin. fr. Low Lat. *fontāna*. See **fountain** & **-el**. (anat.) Space covered with membrane at angles between bones of skull of young mammals.

food, n. [1. fōōd; 2. fūd]. O.E. *fōda*, M.E. *fōde*; cp. Goth. *fōd-eins*, 'food', *fōdjan*, 'to feed', also w. different gradation O.N. *fæða*, 'food'; cogn. w. Gk. *paté-esthai*, 'to feed', Lat. *pā-bulum*, 'food' (see **pabulum**); *pā-nes*, 'bread', *pā-scere*, 'to feed'; *pāstor* (see **pastor** & **pasture**). Cogn. w. **feed** & **foster**. **1. a** Matter which can be eaten or absorbed, and assimilated, by animal or plant; nutriment, aliment, victuals; specif. **b** solid nourishment, contrasted with drink; Phrs. (*to become*) *food for fishes*, (be) drowned; *food for worms*, dead; *food for the flames*; *food for powder*, soldiers. **2.** Particular kind of solid nourishment, esp. a patent preparation: *an infant's food*; *a breakfast food.* **3.** (fig.) Something that provides mental stimulus, which develops and sustains spiritual nature of man: *mental, spiritual food*; *food for thought, reflection.*

food controller, n. Person who determines amount of food to be supplied per head of population in times of scarcity, and who organizes the storing and distribution of supplies.

foodless, adj. [1. fōōdles; 2. fūdlis]. **food** & **-less**. Destitute of food.

foodstuff, n. [1. fōōdstuf; 2. fūdstaf]. (commerc.) Material for food, article of food in bulk: *the importation of foodstuffs.*

fool (I.), n. [1. fōōl; 2. fūl]. M.E. *fōl*, fr. O. Fr. *fol* (Mod. Fr. *fou*), 'fool, madman', fr. Lat. *follis*, 'bellows, ball filled with air', in Low Lat. 'empty-headed person'. See **follicle** & **bellows**. **1. a** (archaic) An imbecile, idiot, person mentally deficient; hence **b** silly or stupid person, one devoid of wisdom, judgement, sense, or prudence (commonly applied in contempt or scorn, often with a suggestion of moral weakness): *what a fool the man is!* Phrs. *to be no fool*, be very shrewd; *fool's mate*, (chess) checkmate with one's second move; *fools' paradise*, (i.) limbo on confines of hell, formerly supposed to be the destination of fools; (ii.) (often *fool's paradise*) state of happiness based on illusion; imaginary good fortune; **c** dupe, butt, victim of jest: *the fool of fate*; *All Fools' Day*, popular name for the 1st of April, when hoaxes are played off; *April fool*, person then hoaxed; *to be a fool for one's pains*, to gain no result or reward from one's efforts; *fool's errand*, undertaking which proves abortive; *to make a fool of*, to befool, mislead, dupe; **d** (Bib.) wicked, immoral, or impious person (*Proverbs, passim*). **2.** Man, often eccentric or half-witted, or feigning madness, formerly kept in household of prince or noble to make jests; jester, buffoon, clown. Phr. *to play the fool*, to indulge in buffoonery or clownish jests; also (see **1. a**) to behave with levity or folly: *to play the fool with*, (i.) to deceive, seduce; (ii.) to spoil, destroy.

fool (II.), vb. intrans. & trans., fr. prec. **1.** intrans. To behave as a fool, act with levity. **2.** trans. To make a fool of, befool; make (person) appear silly or ridiculous; to dupe, hoax, trifle with. **3.** Followed by adverb or preposition. *Fool about* (Am. *fool around*), intrans., to idle, loiter or hang about, foolishly, and with no set purpose. *Fool away*, trans., to waste in folly, fritter away: *to fool away one's time, health, money*. *Fool out of*, trans., to deprive of by resorting to deceit, trick out of: *to fool one out of one's fortune*. *Fool with*, intrans., to trifle, meddle, play foolishly with: *to fool with a loaded gun.*

fool (III.), n. Of uncertain origin, perh. fr. **fool** (I.) (cp. **trifle**) or fr. Fr. *fouler*, 'to trample, crush' (grapes). See **full** (V.). Dish consisting of fruit, cooked and whipped up with cream or milk: *gooseberry fool.*

foolery, n. [1. fōōleri; 2. fúləri]. **fool** (I.) & **-ery**. **a** Behaviour, actions, of a fool; **b** foolish act or notion.

foolhardily, adv. [1. fōōlhárdili; 2. fùlhádili]. M.E. *foolhardilī*. **foolhardy** & **-ly**. In a foolhardy manner.

foolhardiness, n. [1. fōōlhárdines; 2. fùlhádinis]. M.E. *foolhardinesse*. Next word & **-ness**. Quality of being foolhardy.

foolhardy, adj. [1. fōōlhardi; 2. fúlhādi]. M.E. *folherdi*, fr. O. Fr. *fol hardi*. **fool** (I.) & **hardy**. Foolishly daring; venturesome, rash; fond of taking risks.

fooling, n. [1. fōōling; 2. fúliŋ]. **fool** (II.) & **-ing**. Action of playing the fool; jesting, buffoonery; humorous nonsense.

foolish, adj. [1. fōōlish; 2. fúliʃ]. **fool** (I.) & **-ish**. **1.** (of persons) **a** Silly, unwise, imprudent; **b** weak-minded, imbecile. **2.** (of actions and conduct) Exhibiting, resulting from, folly; ill-considered, unwise.

foolishly, adv. Prec. & **-ly**. In a foolish manner.

foolishness, n. See prec. & **-ness**. Quality or state of being foolish.

foolproof, adj. [1. fōōlprōōf; 2. fúlprūf]. (colloq.) Proof against fools; not liable to be spoilt or to do harm when misused or tampered with; so contrived that even a fool cannot misunderstand it.

foolscap, n. [1. fōōlskap; 2. fúlskæp]. **1.** Usually *fool's cap* or *fool's-cap*. **a** Close-fitting hood, adorned with bells and crest like cock's comb, formerly worn by jester; **b** dunce's cap. **2.** Size of writing paper, usually long folio, 17 × 13 in. unfolded (formerly bearing watermark of fool's cap and bells).

fool's parsley, n. [1. fōōlz pársli; 2. fúlz pásli]. Poisonous umbelliferous British plant, resembling parsley and liable to be mistaken for it.

foot (I.), n., pl. **feet**, [1. foot, fēt; 2. fut, fīt]. O.E., M.E. *fōt*, Common Gmc.; cp. O.H.G. *fuoz*, Mod. Germ. *fuss*, Goth. *fōtus*, O.N. *fōtr*; cogn. w. Scrt. *pād-aś*, 'foot', *pad*, 'to go'; Russ. *pod-oshva*, 'sole of foot'; Lith. *pad-as*, 'sole', *ped-a*, 'footprint'; Gk. *poús*, stem *pod-*, 'foot', *pédē*, 'fetter'; Lat. *pēs*, stem *ped-*, 'foot'. See **pedal**. **1.** Terminal part of leg of man and other animals, upon which they stand and walk, in man the part below the ankle-joint, considered as a single, separate limb or member; Phrs. *at one's feet*, absolutely at one's disposal, to pick and choose from; *to have the ball at one's feet*, to have an opportunity of succeeding or distinguishing oneself; *to carry one off one's feet,* (i.) to lift one off the ground, knock one down, as a wave or strong wind; (ii.) (fig.) to overpower one with emotion and enthusiasm; *to change foot* or *feet,* to keep the time with the other foot in marching; *to fall on one's feet,* to have good luck, find oneself in agreeable circumstances; *to find one's feet,* gain experience, skill &c., in new surroundings; *to take the length of a person's foot,* (slang) to discover his weak points, size him up; *to be carried out, leave, feet foremost,* (colloq.) in one's coffin; *light, heavy, foot,* light tread &c.; *fleet, swift, of foot,* able to run fast; *to have one foot in the grave,* to be very old, ill, or decrepit; to be near death; *to keep one's feet,* save oneself from falling; *on foot,* (i.) standing or walking; contrasted with riding &c.; (ii.) (fig.) in progress, started, proceeding; *to set on foot,* to start, set going; *on one's feet,* (i.) standing up, esp. to speak; (ii.) (fig.) well again after illness; (iii.) financially independent; *to set a person, thing, on his, its, feet,* render self-supporting; *a foot's pace,* a walk; *to put one's foot down,* to act with decision; *to put one's foot in it,* (colloq.) to make an awkward blunder, to make a faux pas, cause embarrassment; *to put one's best foot foremost,* (colloq.) (i.) to walk one's best; (ii.) do one's best; *wet, damp, under foot,* on the surface of the ground, for walking; *to tread, trample, under foot,* (fig.) to crush, oppress, tyrannize over. **2.** Organ of one of the lower forms of creatures, by means of which it creeps or attaches itself: *the foot of a snail; of a caterpillar.* **3.** (bot.) Part by which a petal or hair is attached. **4.** That part of a stocking which covers the foot. **5. a** That part of thing on which it stands, esp. when shaped so as to form a base: *the foot of a wine-glass;* **b** distinct terminal part of leg of table, chair, &c. **6.** Generally, lowest part, bottom, base: *the foot of a mountain, pillar, wall, page, list.* **7.** End of bed, couch, grave &c., where occupant's feet are, contrasted with the *head.* **8.** (mil.) Foot soldiers, infantry: *a regiment of foot; the 42nd foot; horse and foot.* **9.** Lineal measure of 12 inches, or a third of a yard; hence, *square foot* and *cubic foot,* both called simply *foot* where there is no ambiguity. Pl. *feet* and *foot,* latter chiefly in measurements: *two foot* (or *feet*) *six;* and attrib.: *a two-foot rule.* **10.** Unit in scansion of verse; containing in English and most modern poetry one strong stress or accent. **11.** (pl. *foots*) Sediment, dregs; coarse sugar, etc.

foot (II.), vb. trans. & intrans., fr. prec. **A.** trans. **1. a** To tread, step, pace, walk or dance over: *to foot the road, the floor;* **b** to perform (a dance), dance (a figure &c.): *to foot a measure;* **c** *to foot it,* (i.) to dance; (ii.) (colloq.) to go on foot. **2.** Also *foot up,* add up (account); Phr. (colloq.) *to foot the bill,* pay expenses. **3.** To supply a new foot to (a stocking &c.). **B.** intrans. (colloq.) *Foot up* (*to*), mount up: *the items foot up to £100.*

foot-and-mouth disease, n. Contagious disease of cattle and other animals, resembling eczema, with eruptions in mouth and feet, communicated to animals feeding in contaminated pasture; aphthous fever.

football, n. [1. fóotbawl; 2. fútbōl]. **1. a** Large round or egg-shaped leather ball, inflated with air, used in games. **2.** Game played with such a ball, by two teams in field with goal at each end; of two main types, *Association* and *Rugby,* qq.v.

footballer, n. [fóotbawler; 2. fútbōlə]. Player of football.

footbath, n. [1. fóotbahth; 2. fútbāþ]. Portable bath for the feet.

footboard, n. [1. fóotbord; 2. fútbōd]. **1.** Board on which one can stand or step; specif. **a** board running along side of railway carriage, lower than floor; step below door of motor-car; **b** footplate; **c** platform for footman at back of carriage. **2.** Sloping board on which coachman places his feet when driving.

footboy, n. [1. fóotboi; 2. fútbɔi]. Young manservant.

footbridge, n. [1. fóotbrij; 2. fútbridž]. Narrow, light, bridge confined to the use of pedestrians.

footdrill, n. [1. fóotdril; 2. fútdril]. (mil.) Most elementary form of military exercises, designed to train soldiers in proper carriage of the body, and in the various turns and movements carried out, in combination, by dismounted men.

foot drop, n. Paralytic affection of flexor muscles of the foot.

footed, adj. [1. fóoted; 2. fútid]. Having feet or a foot: *footed like a cat;* chiefly in composition, as *four-footed.*

footer, n. [1. fóoter; 2. fútə]. (slang) The game of football.

footfall, n. [1. fóotfawl; 2. fútfōl]. **a** Footstep, tread; **b** sound of footsteps.

footgear, n. [1. fóotgēr; 2. fútgiə]. (coll.) Coverings for the feet, boots, shoes, stockings &c.

Foot Guards, n. pl. (mil.) Infantry regiments of the Household Brigade of Guards, comprising the Grenadier, Coldstream, Scots, Irish, and Welsh Guards.

foothill, n. [1. fóot-hil; 2. fúthil]. Hill at the foot of mountain or higher hill; usually pl.

foothold, n. [1. fóot-hōld; 2. fúthould]. **a** Surface affording support for the foot; **b** (fig.) stable or secure position.

footing, n. [1. fóoting; 2. fútiŋ]. **foot (I.)** & **-ing. 1. a** Action of placing the feet; position of the feet when standing: *mind your footing when you climb;* **b** (archaic or rare) stepping, walking, tread; movement of the feet in dancing &c.; **c** foothold, place in which one can stand. **2.** (fig.) Basis, position that supports one; hence, established or recognized standing, status; position in relation to another person: *to obtain a footing in society; to be on a friendly footing with one.* Phr. *to pay* (*for*) *one's footing,* to make a customary gift or entertainment on admission to a society, trade &c. **3. a** Making of a foot or feet; material of which they are made: *the footing of a stocking; footing for lace,* plain edge or strip attached to pattern lace; **b** projecting course or courses at the foot of a wall. **4.** Adding up of a column of figures; sum total of figures.

footle, vb. intrans. & n. [1. fōōtl; 2. fūtl]. Perh. formed, w. freq. suff. **-le,** fr. provinc. *footy* [fūti], 'musty, paltry, contemptible', fr. Early Mod. Engl. *foughtie;* cp. Du. *vochtig,* Dan. *fugtig,* Germ. *feucht,* 'damp', also O.E. *fūht,* 'moisture'. See **fog (I.).** (colloq. or slang) **a** vb. To trifle, behave or talk in a silly way; **b** n., nonsense, twaddle; foolishness.

footless, adj. [1. fóotles; 2. fútlis]. **foot (I.)** & **-less. a** Having no feet; **b** (poet.) untrodden.

footlight, n. [1. fóotlīt; 2. fútlait]. **a** One of row of lamps, screened from auditorium, along front of the stage in a theatre; **b** (fig., pl.) the stage, the profession of acting.

footling, adj. [1. fōōtling; 2. fūtliŋ], fr. Pres. Part. of **footle.** (colloq. or slang) Trifling, paltry, silly.

footman, n. [1. fóotman; 2. fútmən]. M.E. *fōtman.* **foot (I.)** & **man. 1. a** Domestic man-servant, generally in livery, who admits visitors, waits at table, attends master when driving &c.; **b** (archaic) foot soldier. **2.** Kind of moth.

footmark, n. [1. fóotmark; 2. fútmāk]. Footprint.

footmuff, n. [1. fóotmuf; 2. fútmaf]. Thick bag or muff in which the feet are placed to keep them warm.

footnote, n. & vb. trans. [1. fóotnōt; 2. fútnout]. **a** n. Note at the foot of a printed or written page; **b** vb., to supply with footnotes.

footpace, n. [1. fóotpās; 2. fútpeis]. **1.** Walking pace. **2.** Dais, altar platform.

footpad, n. [1. fóotpad; 2. fútpæd]. See **pad (II.).** Highway robber who goes on foot.

footpage, n. [1. fóotpāj; 2. fútpeidž]. Page; boy who delivers messages &c.

footpath, n. [1. fóotpahth; 2. fútpāþ]. Narrow path only to be used by persons walking; esp. one across fields; raised path for persons on foot, along country road.

footplate, n. [1. fóotplāt; 2. fútpleit]. Platform at back of locomotive for driver and fireman.

foot-pound, n. Unit of energy, being the amount of energy expended in raising one pound avoirdupois one foot.

footprint, n. [1. fóotprint; 2. fútprint]. Print or impression of a foot.

foot-pump, n. Pump for inflating tyres &c., worked, or held in position, by the foot.

footrace, n. [1. fóotrās; 2. fútreis]. Contest of speed in running or walking.

footrail, n. [1. fóotrāl; 2. fútreil]. (naut.) Rope fixed horizontally, below yard, on which men stand to reef sail.

footrot, n. [1. fóotrot; 2. fútrɔt]. Contagious bacterial disease in feet of sheep and cattle.

foot-rule, n. Rigid measure or ruler one foot long.

footscald, n. [1. fóotskawld; 2. fútskōld]. Inflamed or bruised condition of sole of horse's foot.

foot-soldier, n. An infantry soldier.

footsore, adj. [1. fóotsōr; 2. fútsō]. Affected with soreness or tenderness in the feet, generally from excessive walking.

footstalk, n. [1. fóotstawk; 2. fútstōk]. **a** (bot.) Stalk of a leaf, petiole; stalk of a flower, pedicel or peduncle; **b** (zool.) stalk of sedentary animal, as barnacle.

footstep, n. [1. fóotstep; 2. fútstɛp]. **1. a** Action of stepping; distance stepped; **b** noise made by stepping: *I hear footsteps.* **2. a** Footprint; **b** (fig.) trace or mark, vestige, of past action: *to follow in one's footsteps,* imitate his actions.

footstone, n. [1. fóotstōn; 2. fútstoun]. **a** Stone set at the foot of a grave; **b** foundation stone.

footstool, n. [1. fóotstōōl; 2. fútstūl]. Low stool on which the feet are placed when sitting.

foot-ton, n. Unit of energy, being that expended in raising one ton one foot.

footwarmer, n. [1. fóotwawmer; 2. fútwōmə]. Apparatus for warming the feet; formerly used in railway carriages, consisting of a receptacle filled with hot water.

footwear, n. [1. fóotwār; 2. fútwɛə]. Trade term for boots and shoes collectively.

footworn, adj. [1. fóotworn; 2. fútwōn]. **1.** Worn or abraded by the feet: *a footworn pavement.* **2.** Having weary feet, footsore: *a footworn wanderer.*

foozle (I.), vb. trans. & intrans. [1. fōōzl; 2. fūzl]. Etymol. uncertain. (colloq.) **1.** trans. **a** To bungle, do clumsily or ineffectively; **b** (golf) to spoil (stroke in golf). **2.** intrans. To act clumsily and inexpertly.

foozle (II.), n., fr. prec. Clumsy, ineffective action; bad stroke or shot in golf.

fop, n. [1. fop; 2. fɔp]. M.E. *foppe, fobbe,* 'fool', cp. Du., Germ. *foppen,* 'to befool, hoax, chaff', also **fob (II.).** Finicky, fatuous fellow who is vain of, and fastidious about, his appearance, dress, or manners &c.; conceited puppy, coxcomb; dandy, exquisite.

fopling, n. [1. fópling; 2. fɔ́pliŋ]. Prec. & **-ling.** Trifling, insignificant fellow who apes the affectations of a fop.

foppery, n. [1. fóperi; 2. fɔ́pəri]. See prec. & **-ery.** Trivial affectation, sham refinement, in manners, bearing, speech, dress, and taste generally, unsupported by real good breeding or sincerity of feeling; coxcombry.

foppish, adj. [1. fópish; 2. fɔ́piʃ]. **fop** & **-ish.** Pertaining to, resembling, having the character of a fop.

foppishly, adv. Prec. & **-ly.** In a foppish manner.

foppishness, n. See prec. & **-ness.** Manners, affectation, of a fop; foppery.

for (I.), prep. Stressed form [1. fōr; 2. fō(r)], unstressed form [1. fer; 2. fə(r)]. O.E. *for,* w. very much the same force as in Mod. Engl.;

O.S. *fur*, O.H.G. *furi*, Mod. Germ. *für*, 'for'; Goth. *faur*. The word is closely related in origin, in the old Gmc. languages, & associated in meaning, w. O.E. *fore*, 'before; on account of' &c., q.v. under **fore**; of same origin also as Goth. *fair-*, *fra-*, inseparable pref. (see **for-**). These words, fr. Aryan **pr̥-*, **per-* &c., have numerous cognates, w. various meanings, in the other branches of Aryan speech. Cp. Lat. *prae*, 'before, in front; by the side of, in comparison with; for, because of, on account of' &c. (see **pre-**); Gk. *pará*, 'from beside; by the side of, by; to, towards; beyond, except; compared with; during' (see **para-**); see further cognates under **per-** & **pro-**. **1.** Expressing benefit, advantage, favour, suitability, or the reverse: *a present for you*; *for my sake*; *a great pleasure for me*; *very good for you*; *too good for him*; *a rebuff, disappointment, for him*; *a great pity for some things*; *not good for gout*. **2. a** Expressing end, purpose, aim, intention: *to go to Scotland for grouse shooting*; *to come for dinner*; *to send for a doctor*; *to work for one's living*; *to go out for a walk*; *just for fun*; Phr. (vulg.) *to go for a soldier*; (archaic or provinc. when followed by infin.) '*What went ye out for to see?*'; *I should like for to go with you*; **b** expressing wish, desire, expectation: *to wait for an answer*; *to long for fine weather*; *to hope for better things*; *anxious for peace*; '*O for a draught of vintage*' (Keats). **3.** Expressing cause, reason; on account, because of: *for many reasons*; *for fear of*; *for the love of God*; *tremble for his safety*; *I can't see anything for the fog*. **4.** Expressing **a** duration of time: *to stay for a week*; *for the present*; *to last for an hour*; Phr. *for good*, permanently; **b** length, extension, distance: *to run for a mile*; *the forest stretches for a long way*; **c** sum, price; to such an amount: *to sell a horse for twenty pounds*; *all out for forty runs*. **5. a** Direction, tendency towards: '*Fair stood the wind for France*' (Drayton); **b** destination to which person, ship, train &c. is bound or thing being sent: *to start for India*; *the train for London*; *letters for home*; **c** point of time at which something is fixed to happen: *the ceremony was arranged for two o'clock*. **6. a** Equivalence, exchange, substitution, requital: *to plant three trees for every one that is cut down*; *I give you a horse for your gun*; Phr. *to give one a Roland for his Oliver*, to return an equivalent for injuries inflicted; to reply in similar terms to caustic remark &c.; **b** penalty, reward: *beaten for stealing*; *to suffer for one's sins*; *to get a medal for saving life*; **c** representation: *no one would think that this picture was drawn for a portrait*; '*The picture that thou see'st here cut, It was for gentle Shakespeare put*'. **7.** Considering certain conditions and circumstances: *a good piece of work for so young a man*; *rather cold for August*. **8.** Followed by *all*, expressing opposition, obstacle; in spite of: *for all that*; *for all his professions, I do not believe him*. **9.** In Phrs. *as for me*, *as for that* &c., in respect of, regarding, so far as concerns.

for (II.), conj. M.E., 'because', abbr. fr. earlier *for þon*, *þī*, *þat*, representing O.E. *for-þām-þē*, *for-þȳ*, 'for this thing, that'. See prec. **a** (introducing co-ordinate explanatory sentence) Seeing that, since, as, because: *I am thirsty, for the sun is hot*; **b** (introducing separate sentence) the explanation of the foregoing is or was that . . .: *he felt no fear for he was very brave*.

for-, pref. Early O.E. *fær-*, *fer-*, later replaced by *for-*, the orig. stressed form used w. ns., M.E. *for-*; cp. O.H.G. *fir-*, *far-*, Mod. Germ. *ver-*, Goth. *fair-* (for **fer-*); Aryan types **peri*, **per*, whence Scrt. *pári*, O. Slav. *prě-*, Russ. *pere-*, Lith. *per̃*, *per-*, Gk. *peri-*, Lat. *per-*. A form of the base found in **fore** (cp. **para-**, **per-**, **peri-**, **pre-**, **pro-**), w. the senses 'forward, through, or across, out beyond, past'; hence 'thoroughly, in excess, to a wrong end, ruinously', cp. **perdition**, **perish**, **pervert**, corresponding to Germ. pref. *ver-*, as in *ver-kommen*, 'to come to grief, perish'; Goth *fra-*, as in *fra-kunnan*, 'to despise', fr. *kunnan*, 'to know'. See **fret** (I.). Prefix used with verbs and their derivatives, all except in *forfend* of English origin, **a** as intensive: *forgather*, *forlorn*, *forpine*, *forspent*, *forwearied*, *forworn*; **b** expressing destruction, detriment: *fordo*, *forswear*; **c** expressing omission, exclusion; refusal, neglect: *forbear*, *forbid*, *forfend*, *forgo*, *forsake*, *forswear* (**1. a**). The full original force of the prefix is, however, lost in some of these words.

forage (I.), n. [1. fórij; 2. fɔ́ridž]. M.E., fr. O. Fr. *fourage*, *forrage* (Mod. Fr. *fourrage*), fr. O. Fr. *forrer*, 'to forage', fr. *forre*, *fuerre* (Mod. Fr. *feurre*) 'fodder', fr. Low Lat. *fōdrum*, fr. a Gmc. source. See **fodder** & **-age**. **a** Fodder, provender for horses or other beasts, esp. those of a camp or military force; **b** action of obtaining forage or provisions of any kind.

forage (II.), vb. trans. & intrans. Prec., cp. O. & Mod. Fr. *fourrager*. **1.** trans. **a** To supply (horses, camp) with forage; **b** to obtain forage from; to plunder, pillage, ransack, ravage (place); **c** to obtain by foraging. **2.** intrans. **a** To go about in search of forage; **b** to search for supplies or something one needs: *to forage (about) for a meal*; *to forage about to find a book*.

forage cap, n. (mil.) Undress cap of infantry.

forager, n. [1. fórijer; 2. fɔ́ridžə]. M.E., fr. O. Fr. *fourrageur*; see **forage** (I.) & **-er**. Person who forages.

foramen, n. [1. forámen; 2. fɔréimen]. Lat. *forāmen*, 'hole, opening', fr. *forāre*, 'to bore', cogn. w. Gk. *pharáein*, 'to plough'; also w. O.E. *borian*, 'to bore', & n. suff. *-men*. See **bore** (I.), & cp. **perforate**, **pharynx**. (anat., bot., zool.) Natural perforation or small orifice in bone &c.

foraminate(d), adj. [1. foráminãt(ed); 2. fɔréimineit(id)]. L. Lat. *forāmināt-(um)*, fr. *forāmin-*, stem of *forāmen* (see prec.) & **-ate**. Having a foramen or foramina; perforated.

Foraminifera, n. pl. [1. fòràminífera; 2. fɔ̀reiminífərə]. Mod. Lat., fr. *forāmini-*, combining form fr. *forāmin-*, stem of *forāmen* (see **foramen**) & *-fer-re*, 'to bear'. See **-ferous**. (zool.) Order of minute, mostly marine animals, having calcareous shell with orifices through which filaments are protruded.

foraminiferal, **foraminiferous**, adj. [1. fòràminíferal, -us; 2. fɔ̀reiminífərəl, -əs]. Prec. & **-al**, **-ous** Containing foraminifera.

foraminous, adj. [1. foráminus; 2. fɔréiminəs]. Lat. *forāminōs-(us)*, see **foraminate**, & **-ous**. Perforated, having foramina.

forasmuch, conj. [1. fórazmúch; 2. fɔ́rəzmátʃ, fərəzmátʃ]. **for** (I.) & **as** & **much**. (liter. and in legal formulae) *Forasmuch as*: seeing that, considering that, since.

foray (I.), n. [1. fórã; 2. fɔ́rei]. M.E. *forrai*, *ferrai*. See next word. (orig. Scots and Nthn.) A raid, plundering or ravaging incursion.

foray (II.), vb. trans. & intrans. M.E. *forraien*, perh. a back-formation fr. *forreyer*. See next word. (orig. Scots and Nthn.) **a** trans. To raid, ravage, make an incursion into; **b** intrans., to go out foraging or pillaging, make a predatory raid.

forayer, n. [1. fóraer; 2. fɔ́reiə]. M.E. *forreier*, 'forager, harbinger', perh. fr. O.F. *forrier*, fr. *forrer*. See **forage** (I.) & **-er**. Person who forays.

forbad, **forbade**, vb. [1. forbád, forbā́d; 2. fɔ̄bǽd, fɔ̄béid]. Pret. of **forbid**.

forbear (I.), vb. trans. & intrans. [1. forbā́r; 2. fɔ̄béə]. O.E. *forberan*, 'to restrain, endure'; M.E. *forbēren* (**for-** & **bear** (I.)); cp. O.H.G. *furiberan*. **1.** trans. **a** To restrain oneself from, refrain or abstain from, avoid; to desist from: *to forbear angry feelings*; *to forbear gluttony*; *to forbear to strike*; **b** (obs. or archaic) to bear with, be patient or tolerant towards: '*Forbearing one another in love*' (Ephes. iv. 2). **2.** intrans. To refrain, abstain, desist, check oneself: *I longed to punch his head, but I forbore*; *forbear from complaining*.

forbear (II.), n. [1. fórbãr; 2. fɔ̄bɛə]. M.E. (orig. Scots), fr. **fore-** & **be** &**-er**. Ancestor, forefather; predecessor: *a forbear of mine*; *one of my forbears*.

forbearance, n. [1. forbárans; 2. fɔ̄béərəns]. **forbear** (I.) & **-ance**. **a** Act or quality of forbearing; self-restraint, patience or indulgence toward one who provokes or annoys; unwillingness to retaliate or exact penalty; leniency: *to treat an offender with excessive forbearance*; **b** (law) omission to exact performance of obligation.

forbearing, adj. [1. forbáring; 2. fɔ̄béəriŋ], fr. Pres. Part. of **forbear** (I.). Disposed to forbear; patient, long-suffering, lenient.

forbearingly, adv. Prec. & **-ly**. In a forbearing manner.

forbid, vb. trans. [1. forbíd; 2. fəbíd]. O.E. *forbēodan*, M.E. *forbēden*, w. meaning of Mod. vb. The old vb. *bēodan*, 'to command', is completely lost, though its sense is transferred to *biddan* (see **bid**), an unrelated vb. w., formerly, quite a different meaning. See **for-** & **bid**. **a** To refuse to allow; to command or order not to be or do; to prohibit, interdict: *duelling is forbidden*; *to forbid one to speak*; *we are forbidden to steal*; *I am forbidden tobacco*, to smoke it; Phr. *to forbid the banns*, to declare publicly that they are invalid; **b** (ellipt.): *to forbid one (to enter) the house, the country*; **c** to make logically or physically impossible, exclude, prevent: *this fact forbids the assumption of his guilt*; *high walls forbid all approach*. Phr. *God forbid!*, solemn assertion of desire that a thing may not happen: *God forbid that you should ever regret your marriage, that I should injure you*.

forbiddance, n. [1. forbídans; 2. fəbídəns]. Prec. & **-ance**. (obs. or rare) Prohibition.

forbidden, adj. [1. forbídn; 2. fəbídn]. P.P. of **forbid**. Not allowed, prohibited, interdicted. Phrs. *forbidden city*, city or part of city from which all but privileged persons are excluded; *the forbidden degrees*, prohibited degrees of marriage; *forbidden fruit*, **a** the fruit which Adam and Eve were forbidden to eat; **b** (fig.) an unlawful or prohibited pleasure, thing coveted because forbidden; **c** kind of shaddock or other citron.

forbidder, n. [1. forbíder; 2. fəbídə]. **forbid** & **-er**. Person that forbids.

forbidding, adj. [1. forbíding; 2. fəbídiŋ]. Pres. Part. of **forbid**. **a** Repellent, dangerous-looking, threatening: *forbidding cliffs fringe the coast*; *forbidding thunder-clouds*; **b** unattractive, repulsive; sinister: *forbidding countenance, features, manner*.

forbiddingly, adv. Prec. & **-ly**. In a forbidding manner.

forbiddingness, n. See prec. & **-ness**. Quality, state, of being forbidding.

forbore, vb. [1. forbór; 2. fɔ̄bɔ́]. Pret. of **forbear** (I.).

forby, **forbye**, prep. & adv. [1. forbí; 2. fəbái]. M.E. *forbī*. **fore-** & **by**. Cp. Germ. *vorbei*. (Scots, archaic or provinc.) **a** prep. Beside, not to mention; **b** adv., besides, in addition.

force (I.), n. [1. fors; 2. fɔ̄s]. M.E., fr. O. Fr., 'strength', fr. Low Lat. *fortia*, formed fr. Lat. *fortis*, 'strong'. See **fort**. Orig. only of muscular & moral strength. **1.** (phys.) Defined by Newton as that which changes, or tends to produce change of, motion in a body on which it acts; more recently defined as the rate per unit of length at which energy is transferred or transformed. The term is applied to the phenomena of gravitation, to those of electricity and magnetism, and to the power engendered by steam &c. **2. a** Muscular strength, vigour; Phr. *brute force*, sheer strength or violence, unassisted by intelligence; **b** exhibition, exertion, of physical strength, esp. vehement and violent use of this: *the police had to employ force to induce the prisoner to accompany them*; *they held him firmly but used no force*; **c** (law) compulsion, constraint illegally exerted, including not only the application of physical violence, but also threats and intimidation. **3. a** Violent motion of an inanimate body in falling, sliding &c.; momentum, impetus: *a mass of rock fell with considerable force*; **b** violent disruptive action of an explosive &c.: *killed by the force of an explosion*. **4. a** Intellectual, emotional, or moral vigour: *force of mind, force of character*; *overcome by the force of his emotions*; **b** intangible spiritual influence which affects men's minds, opinions, and conduct; something which modifies these, and predisposes in a given direction; moral stimulus, persuasion: *a force for good*; *religion and politics are powerful forces in society*; also of persons exerting such influence: *he soon became a force in the country*; **c** effect, result, of exercise of such influence: *the force of example, of public opinion*; **d** power of convincing, persuading; cogency: *the force of an argument, of an objection*; *by force of contrast*. **5.** External conditions which affect and modify behaviour, habits, mode of life; stress, compulsion: *by force of circumstances*. **6.** Legal power of binding; validity: *the force of an agreement*; *a rule no longer in force*; *to come into force*, become operative. **7.** Precise function, meaning, significance, bearing: *force of a word, phrase, clause* &c. **8.** Military, naval, air, power; organized and armed strength; **a** *the forces of the Crown*, army and navy; **b** specif., organized body of armed men: *a small force of infantry, cavalry* &c.; **c** body of men organized to preserve civil order: *police force*; *the Force*, the police.

force (**II.**), vb. trans. M.E. *forcen*, O. Fr. *forcier*, Low Lat. *fortiāre*. See prec. **1.** To apply physical force to, use bodily strength in order to execute one's purpose, obtain one's wish &c.; specif. **a** to rape, violate; **b** to break through, or into, by use of violence: *to force one's way*; *to force an entry*; *to force the pass*; **c** (mil.) *to force a position*, capture by force. **2. a** To use an effort in order to produce; to strain after in an unnatural manner: *to force a smile, a jest* &c.; **b** to use undue effort upon, exert beyond limits of capacity; to overstrain: *to force the voice*; *to force a child's intelligence*. **3. a** To compel, constrain, by physical or moral means: *to force a man to confess*; *I am forced by necessity to yield*; *if he won't act voluntarily, he must be forced*; **b** to extort, wring from, elicit by force of any kind: *to force a surrender, confession*; (mil.) *to force an action*, compel enemy to fight. **4.** (hort.) To cause plants to grow, to flower, fruit &c., before the natural season by subjecting to extra heat, giving careful protection to, manuring heavily &c.: *to force strawberries, asparagus* &c. **5.** (cards) **a** To compel an opponent to play a trump by leading a suit of which he has no cards; **b** to manœuvre a person into selecting a particular card from a pack while preserving the illusion that he is choosing freely.

force (**III.**), n. North., also *foss*, fr. O.N. *fors*, later *foss*; cp. Swed. *forsa, frusa*, 'to gush'. (chiefly provinc.) Waterfall.

force (**IV.**), vb. trans. Variant of **farce** (**II.**); Fr. *farcir*, 'to stuff'; Engl. word prob. influenced by **force** (**II.**). (rare) To stuff, season (meat); cp. *forcemeat*.

forced, adj. [1. forst; 2. fɔ̄st]. P.P. of **force** (**II.**). **1.** Made, performed, by means of external force, by necessity, under compulsion: *forced labour, service*; *a forced landing from an aeroplane*; *a forced loan*, one extorted. **2.** Effected, produced, only through the exertion of unusual or special effort; not spontaneous or natural: *a forced laugh*; *a forced style*. Phr. *forced march*, very rapid march in military emergency; *forced draught*, one produced by mechanical means to increase heat of furnace.

forcedly, adv. [1. fórsedli; 2. fɔ̄sidli]. Prec. & **-ly**. In a forced manner; by compulsion.

forceful, adj. [1. fórsfool; 2. fɔ̄sfəl]. **force** (**I.**) & **-ful**. Full of force, forcible; (esp. in moral sense) having vigorous, energetic personality or character.

forcefully, adv. Prec. & **-ly**. In a forceful manner.

forcefulness, n. See prec. & **-ness**. Quality of being forceful.

forceless, adj. [1. fórsles; 2. fɔ̄slis]. **force** (**I.**) & **-less**. Devoid of force.

force majeure, n. [1. fòrs mahzhẽr; 2. fɔ̀s mažə̃]. Fr., 'superior strength'. See **force** (**I.**) & **major** (**II.**). (law) Irresistible force or coercion; that exerted by a powerful state on a weak one.

forcemeat, n. [1. fórsmēt; 2. fɔ̄smīt]. **force** (**IV.**) & **meat**. Minced and seasoned meat, usually for stuffing.

forceps, n. [1. fórseps; 2. fɔ̄sεps]. Lat., 'pair of tongs, pincers', fr. **formi-ceps*, fr. *form-(us)*, 'hot', cogn. w. **therm**, **warm**, & stem of *capere*, 'to hold, take'. See **captive**. **a** Pair of pincers or tweezers used in surgery or in delicate mechanical work; **b** (zool.) grasping organ of insect or other animal, resembling forceps.

force-pump, n. Kind of pump which forces water or other liquid through a pipe by action of a plunger or piston without valve; contrasted with a *lift pump*.

forcer, n. [1. fórser; 2. fɔ̄sə]. **force** (**II.**) & **-er**. Person or thing that forces; specif., piston of force-pump.

forcible, adj. [1. fórsibl; 2. fɔ̄sibl]. O. Fr. **force** (**II.**) & **-ible**. **1.** Done, effected, by or with force or compulsion. Phr. *forcible entry and detainer*, illegal occupation of property by violence or display of force. **2.** Having, displaying, force; convincing, compelling, persuasive: *a forcible speaker, word, expression*. Phr. *forcible-feeble*, displaying show of vigour and force with nothing behind it.

forcibly, adv. Prec. & **-ly**. In a forcible manner.

forcing, n. [1. fórsing; 2. fɔ̄siŋ]. **force** (**II.**) & **-ing**. **1.** Action of person or thing that forces; process of bringing force to bear on a thing, of hastening growth of plant &c.: *plants for forcing*. **2.** (attrib.) *Forcing bed*, hotbed for plants; *forcing house*, greenhouse in which growth of plants is accelerated; *forcing pump*, force-pump.

forcipate(**d**), adj. [1. fórsipāt(ed); 2. fɔ̄sipeit(id)]. Lat. *forcip-*, stem of **forceps**, & **-ate**. Having the form of a forceps.

forcite, n. [1. fórsīt; 2. fɔ̄sait]. **force** (**I.**) & **-ite**. Kind of dynamite.

forclose, forclosure, n. See **foreclose, foreclosure**.

ford (**I.**), n. [1. ford; 2. fɔ̄d]. O.E., M.E., cp. O.H.G. *furt*; cogn. w. Lat. *portus*, 'harbour' (orig. 'entrance, house-door, passage'). See **port** (**I.**). Extended fr. a different grade of the base seen in O.E. *faran*, 'to go' &c. See **fare** (**III.**). Shallow place in river or body of water, where passage is practicable by wading or on stepping-stones.

ford (**II.**), vb. trans., fr. prec. **a** To cross (a river &c.) by a ford; **b** to wade across, ford or no ford.

fordable, adj. [1. fórdabl; 2. fɔ̄dəbl]. Prec. & **-able**. Capable of being forded.

fordless, adj. [1. fórdles; 2. fɔ̄dlis]. **ford** (**I.**) & **-less**. Having no ford.

fordo, vb. trans. [1. fordóō; 2. fɔ̄dú]. O.E., M.E. *fordōn*. **for-** & **do**. (archaic or obs.) **a** To undo, destroy, ruin; **b** to weary out.

fordone, adj. [1. fordún; 2. fɔ̄dán]. P.P. of prec. (archaic or obs., chiefly pred.) Wearied out, exhausted with fatigue.

fore (**I.**), prep. & adv. [1. fōr; 2. fɔ̄]. O.E. *fore*, 'before, in the sight of'; M.E. *fōre*, Common Gmc., cp. O.H.G. *fora, furi*, Mod. Germ. *vor*, 'before', *für*, 'for'; Goth. *faura* for **fura*, 'before'; Aryan **per-*, **pr̥-* &c. See **for** (**I.**), **for-**, **before**, **first**, **former**, **forth**, **per-**, **primary**, **primus**, **pre-**, **pro-**. **1.** prep. (archaic or rare, chiefly in oaths) Before, in the sight of: *fore Heaven, I am innocent*; *fore George*, by George (prob. altered from *fore God*). **2.** adv. (naut.) In front; only in Phr. *fore and aft*, in the fore part and hinder part of the ship. See **fore-and-aft**.

fore (**II.**), adj. & n., fr. prec. **1.** adj. Situated in front or in the forward part: *the fore files came under fire*; *the fore part of the train*. **2.** n. Front, forward part; only naut. or in Phr. *to the fore*, to or at the front, to or in a prominent position; notably active.

fore (**III.**), interj. Prob. abbr. fr. **before**. (golf) Warning call by player to person in the way.

fore-, fr. **fore** (**I.**). Pref. used in forming vbs., participial adjs., & ns., denoting: **a** before, in front, in place or degree, as *forelock*, *foreman*; **b** front part of, as *forearm* (I.), *forequarter*; **c** before in time, in advance; preceding, as *foresee*, *forenoon*; **d** for *for-* (O. Fr. *fors*, 'without'), in *foreclose*.

fore-and-aft, adj. [1. fŏr and áhft; 2. fɔ̆r ənd ắft]. (chiefly naut.) Having the direction of the ship's length; longitudinal: *a fore-and-aft rig*.

fore-and-after, n. [1. fŏr and áhfter; 2. fɔ̆r ənd ắftə]. Prec. & **-er**. (colloq.) Vessel with fore-and-aft rig.

forearm (**I.**), n. [1. fórarm; 2. fɔ̄rām]. **fore-** & **arm** (**I.**). Part of the arm between the elbow and hand; corresponding part in animal.

forearm (**II.**), vb. trans. [1. fŏrárm; 2. fɔ̆rā́m]. **fore-** & **arm** (**III.**) To arm, take defensive measures beforehand, in advance: '*Forewarned is forearmed*' (proverb).

forebode, vb. trans. [1. forbṓd; 2. fɔ̄bóud]. O.E. *forebodian*. See **fore-** & **bode**. **1. a** To foretell, predict; to portend, be an omen of; **b** to indicate beforehand: *the sky forebodes a storm*. **2.** To have a gloomy presentiment of, to augur misfortune concerning: *I forebode disaster for the enterprise*.

foreboding, vbl. n. [1. forbṓding; 2. fɔ̄bóudiŋ]. Prec. & **-ing**. **a** Evil omen or presage; **b** presentiment or apprehension of evil.

forebodingly, adv. Prec. & **-ly**. In a foreboding manner.

forecabin, n. [1. fórkàbin; 2. fɔ̄kæbin]. **fore-** & **cabin** (**I.**). Quarters in forepart of ship, accommodating second-class passengers.

forecarriage, n. [1. fórkarij; 2. fɔ̄kæridž]. Front part of a four-wheeled horse vehicle including the two front wheels constructed to turn on a pivot.

forecast (**I.**), vb. trans. [1. forkáhst; 2. fɔ̄kā́st]. M.E. *forncast* (P.P.); **fore-** & **cast** (**I.**). To calculate, estimate, conjecture (event, result) beforehand, to estimate the probable course or outcome of: *to forecast tomorrow's weather, the winners in a race*.

forecast (**II.**), n. [1. fórkahst; 2. fɔ̄kāst]. Prec. **a** Calculation, estimate, or conjecture regarding future event or development: *a weather forecast*; **b** (rare) faculty of foresight or forethought.

forecaster, n. [1. forkáhster; 2. fɔ̄kā́stə]. See prec. & **-er**. Person who forecasts.

forecastle, n. [1. fóksl; 2. fóuksl]. **fore-** & **castle**. (naut.) **a** (hist.) Short, elevated deck in bows of ship, formerly used to command deck of enemy ship; **b** forepart of deck of warship; **c** crew's quarters in forepart of merchant ship.

foreclose, vb. trans. [1. forklṓz; 2. fɔ̄klóuz]. M.E. *forclōsen*, fr. O. Fr. *forclos*, P.P. of *forclore*, 'to exclude', fr. O. Fr. (Mod. Fr. *hors*) *fors*, fr. Lat. *foris*, 'outside, out of doors', orig. abl. pl. of O. Lat. *fora*, 'door', cp. Lat. *foris*, 'door' (see **forum, forensic**), & O. Fr. *clorre*, fr. Lat. *claudere*, 'to shut'. See **close** (**III.**). **1.** (law) **a** To shut out, bar, preclude; exclude (person) from enjoyment: *to foreclose a person of a property*; **b** to deprive (mortgagor) of the right of redemption on failure to pay; **c** to prevent the redemption of (mortgage); **d** to take away (right or equity of redemption) from mortgagor. **2.** To close or settle (issue, question) beforehand; to anticipate the conclusion of: *to attempt to foreclose discussion*.

foreclosure, n. [1. forklṓzhur ; 2. fɔ̄klóužə]. Prec. & **-ure.** Act or process of foreclosing; annihilation of right to redeem a mortgage.

forecourt, n. [1. fórkort ; 2. fɔ́kɔ̄t]. **fore-** & **court (I.).** Court in front of building.

foredeck, n. [1. fórdek ; 2. fɔ́dɛk]. **fore-** & **deck (II.).** Front part of ship's deck.

foredoom, vb. trans. [1. fordṓōm ; 2. fɔ̄dū́m]. **fore-** & **doom.** To condemn in advance; to doom to penalty from the outset; (usually fig.) to predestine to evil: *the attempt was foredoomed to failure.*

forefather, n. [1. fórfahdher ; 2. fɔ́fāðə]. M.E. *forefader*; cp. O.N. *forfaðir*; **fore-** & **father.** a Remote male ancestor; b (pl.) past generations, predecessors.

forefinger, n. [1. fórfingger ; 2. fɔ́fiŋgə]. M.E. **fore-** & **finger.** Finger next the thumb; first finger.

forefoot, n. [1. fórfoot ; 2. fɔ́fut]. M.E. *forefōt.* **fore-** & **foot.** 1. One of animal's front pair of feet. 2. (naut.) Foremost timber of keel, curving upward to stem.

forefront, n. [1. fórfrunt ; 2. fɔ́frant]. Emphatic for front: a extreme front; in Phr. *in the forefront of the battle*; b (fig.) position of chief importance; centre of greatest activity and interest.

foregather. See **forgather.**

foregift, n. [1. fórgift ; 2. fɔ́gift]. (law) Premium paid by tenant for lease or its renewal.

forego, vb. trans. [1. forgṓ ; 2. fɔ̄góu]. **fore-** & **go.** 1. (rare) To go before, precede, in time, place, or degree. 2. Forgo, q.v.

foregoer, n. [1. forgṓer ; 2. fɔ̄góuə]. M.E. *foregōere.* Prec. & **-er.** One who precedes.

foregoing, adj. [1. fórgōing ; 2. fɔ́gouiŋ]. Pres. Part. of **forego.** Preceding; already mentioned: *the foregoing are only a few of the instances.*

foregone, adj. [1. fórgon ; 2. fɔ́gɔn]. P.P. of **forego.** Anticipated. Phr. *foregone conclusion,* a a premature conclusion, one that anticipates the evidence; b issue that never was in doubt, that may be confidently foretold; inevitable result.

foreground, n. [1. fórground ; 2. fɔ́graund]. **fore-** & **ground**; prob. as a term in painting after Du. *voorgrond.* a That part of a scene which lies nearest to the spectator; b that part of a picture representing this; c (fig.) the most conspicuous, prominent, position: *to be, keep oneself, in the foreground.*

forehammer, n. [1. fórhamer ; 2. fɔ́hæmə]. **fore-** & **hammer (I.).** Sledge-hammer used in conjunction with hand-hammer.

forehand, n. & adj. [1. fórhand ; 2. fɔ́hænd]. **fore-** & **hand (I.)**; cp. **beforehand.** 1. n. Part of horse in front of the rider. 2. adj. (lawn tennis &c.) Pertaining to a normal stroke made with palm of hand holding the racket turned in direction of the stroke, contrasted with *backhand.*

forehanded, adj. [1. fórhánded ; 2. fɔ́hǽndid]. (chiefly Am.) Acting, done in good time, timely; (Am.) thrifty.

forehead, n. [1. fórid, -ed ; 2. fɔ́rid, -ɛd], vulg. or mod. [1. fórhed ; 2. fɔ́hɛd]. O.E. *forhēafod,* M.E. *forhēved.* **fore-** & **head (I.).** a Brow, upper part of face and skull between eyebrows and beginning of the hair; b (fig., obs. or archaic) effrontery, impudence.

foreign, adj. [1. fórin ; 2. fɔ́rin]. M.E. *forein, foreyne,* fr. O. Fr. *forain,* fr. Low Lat. type **forānus* for *forāneus,* 'residing outside', fr. Lat. *forās* (of motion), 'out of doors, outside', orig. acc. pl. of O. Lat. *fora,* 'door'. See **forum.** 1. a Not belonging to, or originating in that which is specified; introduced from without; extraneous, alien, strange: *deceit is foreign to his nature*; b unconnected, irrelevant, impertinent: *the question is foreign to the matter in hand.* 2. (med. &c.) Not organically related to, not forming a structural part of, an organism: *a foreign substance, body, in the eye.* 3. a Pertaining to, characteristic of, derived, coming, from, country, state, nation or nationality other than the speaker's; not native; exotic, alien: *a foreign accent, manners*; *foreign goods*; Phrs. *foreign affairs,* policy, business connected with foreign countries, contrasted with *home affairs*; *Foreign Secretary,* q.v. under *Foreign Office*; *foreign note-paper,* thin paper for letters to be sent abroad; *foreign parts,* countries outside the British Isles; *foreign policy,* policy in relation to foreign states; b (law) having, subject to, laws or jurisdiction different from those of the country specified: *a foreign bill of exchange.*

foreigner, n. [1. fóriner ; 2. fɔ́rinə]. Prec. & **-er.** a Person of foreign nationality, one owing allegiance to another state; (popularly) person of another, alien, race or speech; b (colloq.) animal, plant, ship, security, of foreign origin.

foreignism, n. [1. fórinizm ; 2. fɔ́rinizəm]. **foreign** & **-ism.** Idiom, peculiarity, of foreign origin.

foreignize, vb. trans. [1. fórinīz ; 2. fɔ́rinaiz]. **foreign** & **-ize.** (rare) To make foreign; cause to resemble a foreigner.

Foreign Legion, n. A volunteer force recruited by France from foreigners, for service abroad.

foreignness, n. [1. fórinnes ; 2. fɔ́rinnis]. **foreign** & **-ness.** Quality of being foreign.

Foreign Office, n. Department of state dealing with foreign affairs, with relations with foreign states, at the head of which is the *Foreign Secretary,* in full Secretary of State for Foreign Affairs.

forejudge, vb. trans. [1. forjúj ; 2. fɔ̄džádž]. **fore-** & **judge (II.).** To judge, decide about, before knowing the relevant facts; to prejudge.

forejudgement, n. [1. forjújment ; 2. fɔ̄džádžmənt]. See prec. & **-ment.** Act of forejudging; premature or anticipatory decision.

foreknow, vb. trans. [1. fornṓ ; 2. fɔ̄nóu]. **fore-** & **know.** To know beforehand, have prescience of.

foreknowable, adj. [1. fornṓabl ; 2. fɔ̄nóuəbl]. Prec. & **-able.** Capable of being known in advance.

foreknowledge, n. [1. fornólej ; 2. fɔ̄nɔ́lidž]. **fore-** & **knowledge.** Knowledge of that which will be; prescience.

forel, forrel, n. [1. fórel ; 2. fɔ́rəl]. M.E. *forel,* fr. O.F. *forrel* (Mod. Fr. *fourreau*), 'sheath'; dimin. (see **-el**) of O.F. *fuerre* (Mod. Fr. *feurre,* 'straw for thatch'), fr. Low Lat. *fōdrus,* 'case', of Gmc. origin; cp. O.H.G. *fuotar,* Mod. Germ. *futter,* Goth. *fōdr,* 'case, covering', cogn. w. Scrt. *pātra-m,* 'receptacle'. See **fur.** Kind of parchment or vellum of which book covers are made.

foreland, n. [1. fórland ; 2. fɔ́lənd]. M.E. *forlond,* **fore-** & **land**; in sense 3 fr. Germ. *vorland.* 1. Tract of land jutting into the sea, headland, cape: *the North Foreland.* 2. Strip of land in front of an embankment or wall of fortress. 3. Coast land in relation to region behind it; distinguished from *hinterland.*

foreleg, n. [1. fórleg ; 2. fɔ́lɛg]. **fore-** & **leg.** Front leg of an animal.

forelock (I.), n. [1. fórlok ; 2. fɔ́lɔk]. **fore-** & **lock (I.).** Lock of hair above the forehead. Phrs. *take time by the forelock,* to seize the first opportunity, act with promptness; *to pull (his) forelock,* rustic mode of saluting superiors.

forelock (II.), n. & vb. trans. **fore-** & **lock (II.).** 1. n. Linchpin; pin passed through hole in bolt to fasten it. 2. vb. To fasten with a forelock.

foreman, n. [1. fórman ; 2. fɔ́mən]. **fore-** & **man**; cp. Germ. *vormann,* 'leader of a file' &c. a President of jury; b chief workman who acts as overseer and superintendent of a body of workmen.

foremast, n. [1. fórmahst ; 2. fɔ́māst]. **fore-** & **mast (I.).** 1. The mast, properly lower section of it, nearest the bow of a ship. 2. (attrib.) *Foremast hand, seaman* &c., sailor below rank of petty officer.

foremost, adj. & adv. [1. fórmōst ; 2. fɔ́moust]. O.E., M.E. *formest,* double superlative, fr. O.E. *for-ma,* superl. of *fore* (see **fore**), cp. Lat. *prī-m-us,* 'first', & **-est,** altered, like **utmost** &c., by assimilation to **most.** 1. adj. a First in position, situated in front: *head foremost,* headlong; b (rare) first in time; c first in degree, rank, dignity; most remarkable or distinguished, chief: *the foremost statesman of his age.* 2. adv. Firstly; chiefly in Phr. *first and foremost,* emphatic for first, before all else.

forename, n. [1. fórnām ; 2. fɔ́neim]. Formed on model of Germ. *vorname.* (rare.) Name preceding surname; Christian name.

forenoon, n. [1. fórnōōn ; 2. fɔ́nūn]. **fore-** & **noon.** (Chiefly Scots. Not commonly current in Engl. usage.) Part of the day before noon; morning.

forensic, adj. [1. forénsik ; 2. fɔrénsik]. Lat. *forensis,* 'pertaining to the forum or to public speaking'. **forum,** & adj. suff. *-ensis* & **-ic.** Pertaining to law-courts, having the qualities of a lawyer: *forensic eloquence, ability*; *forensic medicine,* medical jurisprudence.

forensically, adv. [1. forénsikali ; 2. fɔrénsikəli]. Prec. & **-al** & **-ly.** In a forensic manner.

foreordain, vb. trans. [1. fȯrordā́n ; 2. fɔ̄rɔdéin]. **fore-** & **ordain.** (chiefly theol.) To ordain, determine, beforehand; preordain, predestine.

foreordainment, n. [1. fȯrordā́nment ; 2. fɔ̄rɔdéinmənt]. Prec. & **-ment.** (rare) Foreordination.

foreordinate, vb. trans. [1. fȯrórdināt ; 2. fɔ̄rɔ́dineit]. **foreordain** & **-ate.** To foreordain.

foreordination, n. [1. fȯrordinā́shun ; 2. fɔ̄rɔdinéiʃən]. Prec. & **-ion.** Act of foreordaining; predestination.

forepart, n. [1. fórpart ; 2. fɔ́pāt]. **fore-** & **part.** First part; part in front.

forepeak, n. [1. fórpēk ; 2. fɔ́pīk]. **fore-** & **peak.** Pointed part of hold of ship, in bows.

forereach, vb. trans. & intrans. [1. fōrrḗch ; 2. fɔ̄rī́tʃ]. **fore-** & **reach.** To overtake and pass, in sailing, (also fig.).

forerun, vb. trans. [1. fōrrún ; 2. fɔ̄rán]. **fore-** & **run.** (archaic or rare) a To go before, precede, be in advance of; b to be the precursor of, to herald, foreshadow.

forerunner, n. [1. fórrùner ; 2. fɔ́rànə]. Prec. & **-er.** 1. a Person who goes in advance of another to prepare for, or announce, him, precursor, harbinger; b person who precedes another in time, and begins, or lays foundations of, work completed, or brought to a higher stage of perfection by his successors: *Chaucer and Spenser were forerunners of Milton in English poetry.* 2. Sign that something is to follow, prognostic of disease.

foresail, n. [1. fórsal ; 2. fɔ́səl]. **fore-** & **sail.** Principal sail on foremast.

foresay, vb. trans. [1. forsā́ ; 2. fɔ̄séi]. **fore-** & **say.** (rare) To foretell, predict.

foresee, vb. trans. [1. forsḗ ; 2. fɔ̄sī́]. **fore-** & **see (I.)**; cp. O.E. *foresēon,* Germ. *vorsehen* &c. 1. To see beforehand (in vision &c.); to have foreknowledge of. 2. To be aware, to infer, in advance.

foreseeing, adj. [1. forsḗing ; 2. fɔ̄sī́iŋ], fr. Pres. Part. of prec. a Seeing or knowing beforehand, prescient; b having foresight, provident, prudent.

foreseeingly, adv. Prec. & **-ly.** In a foreseeing manner.

foreseer, n. [1. forsḗr ; 2. fɔ̄sī́ə]. **foresee** & **-er.** Person who foresees.

foreshadow, vb. trans. [1. forshádō ; 2. fɔ̄ʃǽdou]. **fore-** & **shadow.** (theol.) To typify beforehand, prefigure; hence generally, to suggest, indicate in advance; to presage, adumbrate.

foresheet, n. [1. fórshēt ; 2. fɔ́ʃīt]. **fore-** & **sheet.** 1. Sheet or rope attached to foresail. 2. (pl.) Space at bow end of open boat.

foreship, n. [1. fórship ; 2. fɔ́ʃip]. O.E. *forscip,* M.E. *foreschip.* **fore-** & **ship (I.)**; cp. Du. *voorschip.* (obs.) Front part, bows, of ship.

foreshore, n. [1. fórshor; 2. fɔ́ʃɔ]. **fore- & shore.** Part of the shore between high and low water marks; (loosely) strip of waste land along the coast.

foreshorten, vb. trans. [1. forshórten; 2. fɔʃɔ́tn]. **fore- & shorten.** In the graphic arts, or sculpture in relief, to represent (object) in accordance with laws of visual perspective, thereby shortening the lines projecting towards the spectator.

foreshortening, n. [1. forshórtning; 2. fɔʃɔ́tniŋ]. Prec. & **-ing.** Effect of visual perspective whereby projecting lines are apparently shortened; representation of this.

foreshow, foreshew, vb. trans. [1. forshṓ; 2. fɔʃóu]. O.E. *foresċēawian*, 'to foresee'; **fore- & show (I.).** To show, indicate, beforehand; to prefigure, foretell.

foreshower, foreshewer, n. [1. forshṓer; 2. fɔʃóuə]. Prec. & **-er.** One who foreshows.

foreshowing, foreshewing, n. [1. forshṓing; 2. fɔʃóuiŋ]. O.E. *foresċēawung*, 'prudence, providence', M.E. *forschēwing*. **foreshow & -ing.** Action of person or thing that foreshows; revelation of what is to come in the future; prefiguration.

foreside, n. [1. fórsīd; 2. fɔ́said]. **fore- & side.** (archaic) Front.

foresight, n. [1. fórsīt; 2. fɔ́sait]. M.E. *foresiht*. **fore- & sight**; cp. Germ. *vorsicht*. **1. a** Act of foreseeing; prevision; foreknowledge; **b** forethought, prudent regard for the future. **2.** Sight on muzzle of gun.

foresighted, adj. [1. fòrsíted; 2. fɔ̀sáitid]. Prec. & **-ed.** Having foresight; prudently regardful of the future.

foresignify, vb. trans. [1. forsígnifī; 2. fɔsígnifai]. **fore- & signify.** (rare) To signify beforehand, prefigure.

foreskin, n. [1. fórskin; 2. fɔ́skin]. **fore- & skin.** Skin covering the glans of the penis; prepuce.

foresleeve, n. [1. fórslēv; 2. fɔ́slīv]. M.E. *foresleve*. **fore- & sleeve.** (obs.) **a** Detachable sleeve covering forearm; **b** part of sleeve from elbow to wrist.

forespeak, vb. trans. [1. forspḗk; 2. fɔspík]. **fore- & speak.** (rare) To predict.

forest (I.), n. [1. fórest; 2. fɔ́rist]. M.E., fr. O. Fr. (Mod. Fr. *forêt*), fr. Low Lat. *forestis (silva)*, 'unenclosed woodland or hunting ground', orig. adj., 'lying open'; cp. Low Lat. *foresta*, 'a wood'; fr. Lat. *foris*, 'outside'. See **forum. 1. a** (hist.) Royal demesne, consisting of unenclosed land, mostly wooded, formerly strictly preserved for hunting; **b** large tract of land, wholly or partially covered with timber trees, whether growing naturally or specially planted; **c** large unenclosed tract of waste land, heath &c., now often almost denuded of trees; often carefully preserved for game: *deer forest*; **d** (fig.) something resembling a forest of trees: *a forest of masts*, large collection of shipping; *a forest of chimneys*; *forest of spears*. **2.** (attrib.) Pertaining to a forest or forests: *forest ponies*, ponies bred, and running wild in a forest; *forest fly*, large kind attacking horses; *forest laws*, (hist.) laws regulating royal forests; *forest marble*, oolitic marble of Wychwood Forest, Oxon.; *forest oak*, she-oak; *forest ranger*, keeper of a royal forest; *forest tree*, any large kind of timber tree such as are grown in forests; contrasted with *fruit tree*.

forest (II.), vb. trans., fr. prec. To afforest.

forestage, n. [1. fórestij; 2. fɔ́ristidž]. O. Fr. **forest (I.) & -age.** (hist.) **1.** Duty paid to royal foresters. **2.** Service paid by forester. **3.** Right to take wood from forest.

forestal, adj. [1. fórestal; 2. fɔ́ristəl]. **forest & -al.** Pertaining to a forest.

forestall (I.), n. [1. forstáwl; 2. fɔstɔ́l]. O.E. *foresteall, forsteall*, 'assault; ambush; interference', M.E. *forstal*; **fore & O.E. *steall***, 'act of standing, place'. See **stall (I.).** (hist. and obs.) **a** The crime of waylaying on a highway; **b** feudal lord's jurisdiction over this.

forestall (II.), vb. trans. M.E. *forstallen*, 'to obstruct a man's trade, by buying up his goods on the way to market,' fr. prec. **1.** (obs.) To interfere with normal trading; to obstruct, intercept on the highway, esp. goods on their way to market, to buy up these with the object of running up and controlling the price; formerly a legal offence, cp. *regrate*. **2.** To be beforehand, get ahead of, another by anticipating his thought or action, and preventing him from performing the latter; to upset a person's plans by acting before the normal time.

forestaller, n. [1. fòrstáwler; 2. fɔ̀stɔ́lə]. Prec. & **-er. a** One who forestalls; **b** one guilty of the legal offence of forestalling.

forestation, n. [1. fòrestáshun; 2. fɔ̀ristéiʃən]. **forest (II.) & -ation.** Planting of forests; afforestation.

forestay, n. [1. fórstā; 2. fɔ́stei]. **fore- & stay (III.).** (naut.) Stay from head of foremast to bowsprit.

forester, n. [1. fórester; 2. fɔ́ristə]. M.E., fr. O. Fr. *forestier*, fr. Low Lat. *forestārius*. **forest (I.) & -er. 1. a** Official charged with the care of a forest, and of the trees and game in it; **b** man who works in a forest, cutting trees, clearing undergrowth &c.; **c** forest dweller, human or animal. **2.** One of several species of moth.

forestry, n. [1. fórestri; 2. fɔ́ristri]. O. Fr. *foresterie*. **forest (I.) & -ry. 1.** Art of planting, improving, and managing forests. **2.** Forests collectively; forest land.

foretaste (I.), n. [1. fórtāst; 2. fɔ́teist]. **fore- & taste (II.).** First or preliminary taste, slight experience of something which one is afterwards to enjoy or suffer; anticipation.

foretaste (II.), vb. trans. [1. fortā́st; 2. fɔtéist]. **fore- & taste (I.).** (rare) To taste beforehand, have a slight anticipatory experience of.

foretell, vb. trans. [1. fortél; 2. fɔtél]. M.E. *foretellen*. **fore- & tell.** To tell or announce beforehand; to predict, prophesy.

foreteller, n. [1. fortéler; 2. fɔtélə]. Prec. & **-er.** One who foretells.

forethink, vb. trans. [1. forthíngk; 2. fɔþíŋk]. **fore- & think.** Cp. O.E. *foreþencan*. (rare or obs.) To think of beforehand, to realize mentally before occurrence.

forethought (I.), n. [1. fórthawt; 2. fɔ́þɔt]. M.E. *foreþouht*. **fore- & thought.** Careful, prudent thought for the future; consideration of future possibilities; foresight.

forethought (II.), adj. [1. forthá́wt; 2. fɔþɔ́t], fr. P.P. of **forethink.** (obs. or rare) Thought of, planned, beforehand.

foretime, n. [1. fórtīm; 2. fɔ́taim]. **fore- & time.** Early times; old time, former days.

foretoken (I.), n. [1. fórtōken; 2. fɔ́toukən]. O.E. *foretācn*, M.E. *foretōkne*; **fore- & token**; cp. Germ. *vorzeichen* &c. Premonitory sign; premonitory omen.

foretoken (II.), vb. trans. [1. fortṓken; 2. fɔtóukən], fr. prec. Cp. O.E. *foretācnian*. To give a foretoken of; to signify beforehand, foreshadow.

foretooth, n. [1. fórtōōth; 2. fɔ́tūþ]. O.E. *foretōð*, M.E. *foretōð*. Front tooth, incisor.

foretop, n. [1. fórtop; 2. fɔ́tɔp]. M.E. **fore- & top.** (naut.) Platform at top of foremast.

fore-topgallant, adj. [1. fór topgálant; 2. fɔ̀ tɔpgǽlənt]. **fore- & topgallant.** Belonging to the mast, sail &c., above the foretopmast.

fore-topman, n. [1. fòr tópman; 2. fɔ̀ tɔ́pmən]. **fore-top & man.** (naut.) Man stationed on top of foremast.

fore-topmast, n. [1. fòr tópmahst; 2. fɔ̀ tɔ́pmāst]. **fore- & topmast.** Mast above the foremast.

fore-topsail, n. [1. fòr tópsal; 2. fɔ̀ tɔ́psəl]. **fore- & topsail.** Sail on fore-topmast.

foretype, n. [1. fórtīp; 2. fɔ́taip]. **fore- & type.** Type, symbol, foreshadowing of something to come.

forever, adv. & n. [1. forév̈er; 2. fərévə]. **for & ever. a** adv. For ever; **b** n., eternity.

forewarn, vb. trans. [1. forwórn; 2. fɔwɔ́n]. **fore- & warn.** To warn beforehand.

forewoman, n. [1. fórwooman; 2. fɔ́wumən]. **fore- & woman. a** President of jury of matrons; **b** woman who is overseer and superintendent of a body of workwomen.

foreword, n. [1. fórwërd; 2. fɔ́wɜ̄d]. **fore- & word**, after model of Germ. *vorwort*. Preface, prefatory note, to a book.

foreyard, n. [1. fóryard; 2. fɔ́jād]. **fore- & yard.** Lowest yard on foremast.

forfars, n. pl. [1. fórfarz; 2. fɔ́fəz], fr. Forfar, town in Scotland. Kind of coarse unbleached linen cloth.

forfeit (I.), n. [1. fórfit; 2. fɔ́fit]. M.E., fr. O. Fr., 'crime punishable by fine; the fine itself', P.P. of *forfaire*, 'to transgress', fr. Low Lat. *forisfactum*, P.P. of *forisfacere*, lit., 'to act outside, beyond, the limits of the law', fr. Lat. *foris*, 'outside'. See **forum & fact. 1.** (obs.) A crime, offence. **2.** That of which one is deprived or mulcted as a punishment for an offence; the fine paid for an offence: *his life was the forfeit of his crime.* **3.** A stake deposited in game of *forfeits*, lost under certain conditions. **4.** Act or process of deprivation as a forfeit for an offence; forfeiture.

forfeit (II.), adj. See prec. (of property &c.) Confiscated by law, taken away, as punishment for an offence: *the lands and titles of the Jacobite lords were forfeit.*

forfeit (III.), vb. trans. M.E. *forfeten*, 'to transgress, forfeit'. See **forfeit (I.). 1. a** To lose, be deprived, mulcted of, suffer confiscation of, as punishment for a crime: *to forfeit one's property for rebellion*; **b** to be fined, deprived of legally, for irregularity of any sort: *to forfeit a motor licence.* **2.** To lose in consequence of an act or of conduct of any kind: *to forfeit one's life on the battlefield, the esteem of one's friends by one's bad manners.*

forfeitable, adj. [1. fórfitabl; 2. fɔ́fitəbl]. **forfeit (II.) & -able.** Liable to be forfeited.

forfeiter, n. [1. fórfiter; 2. fɔ́fitə]. M.E. *forfetour*, Low Lat. *forefactor*; **forfeit (II.) & -er.** Person who forfeits.

forfeiture, n. [1. fórfichur; 2. fɔ́fitʃə]. M.E. *forfeture*. See **forfeit (II.) & -ure.** Act or process of forfeiting something as a penalty for an offence, or as a result of an action: *the forfeiture of property, of one's good name.*

forfend, vb. trans. [1. forfénd; 2. fɔfénd]. M.E. *forfenden*, 'to keep, protect, prohibit'; hybrid fr. **for- & fend.** (archaic) To ward off, avert; chiefly in *Heaven, God, forfend.*

forfex, n. [1. fórfeks; 2. fɔ́feks]. Lat., 'pair of shears or scissors, claw of crab or insect'. Etymol. uncertain. The first element may be *forf-*, fr. **bhorbh-*, cp. Scrt. *bardhakaš*, 'shearing, cutting'. The base is perh. an extension of that seen in *for-* as in Lat. *forāre*, 'pierce'. See **foramen. 1.** (rare) Used by Pope for pair of scissors in *Rape of the Lock.* **2.** (zool.) Scissor-like organ at tail of certain insects, as earwig.

forficate, adj. [1. fórfikāt; 2. fɔ́fikeit]. Lat. *forfic-*, stem of prec., & **-ate.** (zool.) Shaped like shears or scissors.

forgather, vb. intrans. [1. forgádher; 2. fɔgǽðə]. **for- & gather.** (orig. Scots) To assemble, come together, in intimate, friendly, way; to meet socially, associate: *to forgather with friends; he and I forgathered abroad.*

forgave, vb. [1. forgā́v; 2. fɔgéiv]. O.E. *forġeaf*. Pret. of **forgive.**

forge (I.), n. [1. forj; 2. fɔdž]. M.E., O. & Mod. Fr., fr. Lat. *fabrica*, 'workshop of one who works in hard materials'. See **fabric. 1. a** Blacksmith's workshop, smithy; **b** furnace or hearth for smith's work; **c** establishment or plant for hammering, working, shaping, red-hot metal. **2.** (fig.) Workshop, place where plans, ideas &c. are shaped.

forge (II.), vb. trans. & intrans. M.E. *forgen*, fr. O. Fr. *forgier* (Mod. Fr. *forger*), fr. Lat. *fabricāri, -āre*, 'to make of hard materials, forge', fr. *fabrica*. See prec. **A.** trans. **1. a** To soften (iron or other metal) by heat and shape by hammering; to work (iron); **b** to make by this process: *to forge an anchor.*

2. (of non-material things) To fashion, frame, fabricate by effort or art; to invent, hammer out: *to forge a design, scheme, rhymes.* 3. a To make, fabricate, with fraudulent or deceitful intent: *to forge an inscription, an antique*; b to imitate, counterfeit deceitfully; to falsify: *to forge a person's signature*; *to forge a cheque.* B. intrans. 1. To work metal, as a smith. 2. To commit forgery; to counterfeit fraudulently.

forge (**III.**), vb. trans. & intrans. Of uncertain origin, perh. a special sense of prec. a trans. (rare) To impel or haul (ship) forward slowly and laboriously; b intrans., gen. *forge ahead* (of ship), to move forward slowly and steadily; (of horse, or runner in a race &c.) to advance gradually to the foremost place.

forgeable, adj. [1. fórjabl; 2. fɔ́džəbl]. M.E.; **forge (II.) & -able.** Capable of being forged.

forger, n. [1. fórjer; 2. fɔ́džə]. **forge (II.) & -er**; cp. Fr. *forgeur*, fr. Lat. *fabricātor.* Person who imitates (esp. signatures and documents) fraudulently; one who commits forgery.

forgery, n. [1. fórjeri; 2. fɔ́džəri]. Fr. *forgerie*, 'forging of metal'; **forge (II.) & -ry.** 1. (law) Felony or misdemeanour of making or altering a written instrument or document with intent to defraud. 2. Action of counterfeiting or falsifying. 3. Document, signature or other thing forged or fraudulently counterfeited.

forget, vb. trans. & intrans. [1. forgét; 2. fəgét] O.E. *forġietan, -ġetan*, M.E. *forȝēten, -gēten* &c. See **for- & get (I.)**. A. trans. 1. a To lose recollection of something previously known, to have no longer in the memory, allow to escape from the mind, to cease to remember: *I quite forget your name*; *you've forgotten all your French*; b to lack the power of retaining in the memory: *I always forget dates.* 2. To omit by inadvertence; to fail to mention; disregard unintentionally; to fail to do something that one intended from absent-mindedness or the like: *the following names were forgotten in drawing up the list*; *I forgot to say that I shall be away tomorrow*; *to forget to shave, to put on one's collar* &c. 3. To treat with inattention, to neglect, ignore, take no thought for: *don't forget the poor crossing-sweeper*; *to forget one's duties*; *his inestimable services were forgotten by the authorities.* Phr. *to forget oneself*, a to think only of others, act unselfishly; b to behave in an unseemly manner, in a way inconsistent with one's position, and unsuitable to one's surroundings. B. intrans. To cease to exercise the memory; not to remember. Phr. *forget and forgive*, to banish all ill-will for past injuries from the mind.

forgetful, adj. [1. forgétfool; 2. fəgétfəl]. M.E. *forȝetful*; **forget & -ful.** a Inclined or prone to forget, having a bad memory; b *forgetful of*, not remembering some specific thing.

forgetfully, adv. Prec. & **-ly.** In a forgetful manner.

forgetfulness, n. See prec. & **-ness.** Quality of being forgetful; disposition to forget.

forget-me-not, n. [1. forgét me nòt; 2. fəgét mi nɔ̀t]. Adapted in 16th cent. fr. obs. Fr. *ne m'oubliez mye*, lit. 'forget me not'. Perennial marsh plant of borage family with small blue flowers in clusters; any other species of the genus *Myosotis*; scorpion-grass.

forgettable, adj. [1. forgétabl; 2. fəgétəbl]. **forget & -able.** Liable to be forgotten.

forgivable, adj. [1. forgívabl; 2. fəgívəbl]. Next word & **-able.** Capable of being forgiven; pardonable.

forgive, vb. trans. & intrans. [1. forgív; 2. fəgív]. O.E. *forġiefan, forġifan*, 'to give up, forgive', M.E. *forȝeven, forȝiven*, fr. **for- & give.** A. trans. 1. (of action affecting relations of one person with another) a To give up or waive claim to, remit, cancel, excuse: *to forgive a debt*; b to renounce exaction of penalty for; overlook, pardon: *to forgive an insult, a sin* &c. 2. (of action affecting persons) To cease to bear anger or resentment towards; to forgo the desire to be avenged on or to punish; to absolve, pardon, show clemency to: *to forgive one's enemies* &c. 3. With double object: *to forgive a person his debt*; *his offences were forgiven him*, or *he was forgiven his offences.* B. intrans. To exercise forgiveness; to be inclined to pardon: *he is not a man who easily forgives.*

forgiveness, n. [1. forgívnes; 2. fəgívnis]. O.E. *forġifenness, forġifeness*, M.E. *forȝivenesse*; fr. *forġifen*, P.P. of **forgive, & -ness.** 1. a Act of forgiving; b state of being forgiven, pardon. 2. State, attitude, of mind of one who pardons; disposition to forgive.

forgiving, adj. [1. forgíving; 2. fəgíviŋ]. Pres. Part. of **forgive.** Exercising forgiveness; ready, inclined, to forgive: *a forgiving spirit, nature.*

forgivingly, adv. Prec. & **-ly.** In a forgiving manner or spirit.

forgivingness, n. See prec. & **-ness.** Quality of being ready to forgive.

forgo, vb. trans. [1. forgṓ; 2. fɔgóu]. O.E. *forgān*, 'to go over, forgo, neglect', M.E. *forgōn*; **for- & go.** The common spelling *forego* is historically erroneous. To go without, dispense with, relinquish, abstain from.

forgot, forgotten, vb. [1. forgót(n); 2. fəgɔ́t(n)]. Pret. & P.P. of **forget.**

forisfamiliate, vb. trans. & intrans. [1. fòrisfamíliāt; 2. fɔ̀risfəmílieit]. Low Lat. *forisfamiliāt-*, P.P. stem of *forisfamiliāre*, fr. *forīs*, 'outside', see **forum**, & *familia*, **family.** (Scots law) a trans. To put (a son) with his consent in possession of property as his share of the estate; to portion off; to free from parental authority and dependence; b intrans., to renounce legal title to further share of property on acceptance of share, as in a.

forisfamiliation, n. [1. fórisfamìliáshun; 2. fɔ́risfəmìliéiʃən]. See prec. & **-ion.** (Scots law) Action of forisfamiliating.

forjudge, vb. trans. [1. forjúj; 2. fɔdžádž]. M.E. *forjugen*, fr. O. Fr. *forjuger*, fr. *for(s)-*, 'wrongly', fr. Lat. *foris*, 'outside', see **forum, & judge (II.).** a (law) To dispossess by judgement of a court; b (rare) to prejudge.

forjudgement, n. [1. forjújment; 2. fɔdžádžmənt]. Prec. & **-ment.** (law) Judgement of a court by which a person is dispossessed.

fork (**I.**), n. [1. fork; 2. fɔ̄k]. O.E. *forca*, M.E. *forke* (cp. O.N. *fork-r*, O. Fr. *furke*), fr. Lat. *furca.* No satisfactory etymol. of the Lat. word has been proposed. Name of any of several implements the primitive shape of which was Y, that is, it consisted of a handle, one end of which was divided into two diverging points. Upon this conception the use of the word to express the idea of bifurcation is evidently based. A fork may now be generally defined as an implement with a handle at the end of which are two or more prongs or spikes. 1. a Implement with a long wooden handle, surmounted by an iron head with two long, sharpish prongs (shaped U), used for lifting, carrying, pitching hay, dung &c.; b smaller, lighter implement for tossing and moving hay and straw, esp. in a stable &c.; also called *stable fork, stable prong*; c implement with shorter handle and an iron head and three or more stout, flat prongs with points, used for breaking up ground: *garden fork.* 2. Small implement of silver or other metal, with a handle, and two, three, or four prongs, used a at table for conveying food to the mouth: *table fork*; b for cooking &c. Phr. *to play a good knife and fork*, to have a good appetite. 3. Instrument shaped like a fork, made of metal, and so contrived as to give forth a particular musical note when the prongs are struck, and the end placed upon some resonant object or material: *tuning-fork.* 4. One of various objects having approximately the shape of the primitive fork; forking, bifurcation; a stake, piece of wood, with bifurcated end; b *the fork of a road, river, bough*; c part of the human body where the legs branch from the trunk; d shape, as it appears to the eye, of a flash of lightning. 5. Attack by knight &c. on two chessmen.

fork (**II.**), vb. trans. & intrans. fr. prec. A. trans. 1. To use a fork upon; specif. a to lift, carry, throw (hay, dung &c.); b to break (ground) with a fork; c to lift, or move (food) with a table fork. 2. To make into a fork; to cause to bifurcate. 3. To attack two men simultaneously with a knight &c. in chess. B. intrans. (of river, road, bough &c.) To divide into two branches, to bifurcate. C. Followed by adverb. *Fork in*, trans., a to throw in with a fork; b to put into with a fork: *to fork in manure to a flower-bed* &c. *Fork out*, 1. trans., a to extract by means of a fork; b (slang) to pay out: *to fork out money*; 2. intrans., *to fork out*, to pay out, esp. readily and handsomely.

forked, adj. [1. forkt; 2. fɔ̄kt]. **fork (I.) & -ed.** Having a fork; shaped like a fork; divided into branches, cleft: *a forked beard*; *forked lightning*; *a bird with a forked tail.*

fork-tailed, adj. Having a forked tail.

forky, adj. [1. fórki; 2. fɔ́ki]. **fork (I.) & -y.** Forked, fork-shaped.

forlorn, adj. [1. forlórn; 2. fəlɔ́n]. O.E., M.E. *forloren*, P.P. of O.E. *forlēosan*, 'to lose', **for- & lorn.** See **lose.** a (archaic or poet.) Bereft, forsaken, deserted: *forlorn of hope*; b desolate, desperate; neglected, wretched.

forlorn hope, n. Adaptation, wrongly interpreted, of Du. *verloren hoop*, lit. 'lost troop'. See prec. & **heap (I.).** 1. a (mil.) Body of picked men engaged in specially dangerous operation; such operation; b (fig.) enterprise of any kind offering faint prospect of success. 2. Very faint hope: *to cherish a forlorn hope* (through confusion with *hope*).

forlornly, adv. **forlorn & -ly.** In a forlorn manner.

forlornness, n. **forlorn & -ness.** State, condition, of being forlorn.

form (**I.**), n. [1. form; 2. fɔ̄m]. M.E., O. & Mod. Fr. *forme*, fr. Lat. *forma*, 'shape, figure, beauty, plan, pattern' &c.; prob. fr. same base as *ferīre*, 'to beat, cut', in wh. case the root meaning is 'something cut, struck, out'; for similar transference of meaning cp. Gk. *túpos*, 'blow; impression made by a blow; stamp, impress, type' &c. (see **type**), & *túptein*, 'to strike'. The Aryan base in this case is **bhṛm-, *bhrem-* &c., whence also possibly O.E. *brim*, 'edge, border, point of division' &c. See **brim.** 1. Relative grouping of the parts of a thing; configuration, outline, contour, shape, figure, conformation, esp. as distinguished from material or colour; specif. a (archaic) shapeliness, beauty; b concrete image, shape, visible appearance, whether of animate or inanimate things: *the dark forms of the trees and rocks*; c the human body: *fair of form and face*; *a well-proportioned form* &c.; d characteristic shape, appearance, guise: *to appear in the form of a man.* 2. a (of concrete things) Method of arrangement, mode of organization, way in which parts of a whole are grouped and interrelated: *the ideas embodied in the document are sound, but the general form is confused and obscure*; *in the form of a drama*; b (of expression of ideas and emotions) style, mode of expression, manner of presentation, artistic shape: *literary form*; *a sense of form in painting*; senses a & b are both used in distinction to *subject-matter, content.* 3. a Particular mode of existence, or manifestation of action: *a form of government, of religion*; *of activity* &c.; hence, b modification, aspect: *English 'tooth', and Latin 'dens' are different forms of the same original word*; *coal is a form of carbon*; c (biol.) type of life, or structure: *forms of animal and vegetable life.* 4. (philos.) The intrinsic, essential, ideal character of a thing; the collection of qualities, internal constitution, which make a thing what it is. 5. An established method of action and behaviour, prescribed by rule or custom; a (of behaviour in society) manners, etiquette, convention; esp. the recognized kind: *good form is an affair of the feelings as well as an outward observance*; **b** (of public observance) ceremonial, series of prescribed actions, movements, utterances &c.: *the coronation of a British sovereign is accompanied by many ancient forms*; *to attach importance to forms*; *a matter of form*; **c** embodiment in documentary shape of a fixed, prescribed, order of words &c.; formula, formulary: *the form of Morning Prayer*; *form of prayer used at sea*; *a form of words*. **6.** A model, pattern (in several senses); specif., printed official document in which various items are to be filled in in writing under several heads: *income tax form*; *form of application (for a licence &c.)*. **7.** Physical and mental condition as fitting a person for some kind of bodily or intellectual action: *in good form for running, for lecturing &c.*; specif., *to be in good form*, to be in good health and spirits, lively in body and mind. **8.** **a** Wooden bench, usually without a back, on which a number of persons can sit, as used in schools; **b** class in a public school, grammar school, or preparatory school. **9.** Place in which a hare couches; lair. **10.** (print.; usually *forme*) Collection of type ready set up and locked into chase ready for printing.

form (II.), vb. trans. & intrans. M.E. *formen*, O. Fr. *former*, fr. Lat. *formāre*. See prec. **A.** trans. **1.** (of material action) **a** To give form to; to shape, fashion by manual acts: *to form a vessel out of clay*; **b** to utter, pronounce, frame: *the baby was beginning to form short words*; *his lips could hardly form a sentence*. **2.** To put together, build up, constitute, create, out of separate elements. In various senses: **a** to plan out and construct: *to form a garden in an open field*; **b** (gram. and rhet.) *to form words*, create them by putting together base, stem, suffix; *to form sentences*, build them up by arranging words in requisite order; **c** to be the source of, cause to develop: *the rain soon formed large pools on the lawn*. **3.** To constitute, act as, become, make up; be used as, afford: *the clouds formed a veil over the mountain-tops*; *his small capital formed a useful basis on which to build a fortune*; *chocolate forms a wholesome substitute for more solid food*. **4.** **a** (of mental action) To call up in the mind; excogitate, conceive: *to form an idea, a concept, a plan*; **b** to train, develop, educate, build up: *to form the mind, character &c.* **5.** To organize, construct, bring together: *to form a regiment, an army*; *to form a class for beginners in Italian, a society &c.* **6.** (mil.) To draw up, arrange, cause to assume a particular order: *to form a regiment into columns*; *to form fours*. **B.** intrans. **1.** **a** (of material objects) To take shape, assume a form: *clouds are forming on the hills*; *crystals form in the retort*; **b** (of non-material things) to arise in the mind; come into existence, develop: *the idea, hope, belief &c., slowly formed in my mind*; *a spirit of discontent is rapidly forming among the people*. **2.** (nav. and mil.) To assume a formation, move into a particular order: *to form into line*.

form-, for **formic**. Used in composition.

-form. Fr. *-forme*, fr. Lat. *-formis*, fr. *forma*. See **form (I.)**. Suffix denoting: **a** having (so many) forms, as *multiform*, *uniform*; **b** having the form of, as *cruciform*.

formal, adj. [1. fórmal; 2. fɔ̄məl]. Lat. *formālis*. See **form (I.)** & **-al**. **1.** Pertaining to the external form; apparent: *a formal resemblance*. **2.** Pertaining to the inner form or reality; essential. **3.** **a** Performed according to, characterized by attention to, prescribed and recognized forms; ceremonious; stiff: *formal manners*; *a formal bow, bearing &c.*; **b** devoted to, observant of, forms; punctilious, precise: *a formal man*. **4.** **a** Done in proper form, characterized by due observance of custom, order, rule; orderly, regular: *a formal receipt, agreement, permission*; **b** (of concrete objects) made according to rule; symmetrical, trim: *formal dress*; *a beard of formal cut*; *formal garden*, one exhibiting symmetrical shapes and geometrical lines, in which everything is rigidly balanced and artificially ordered. **5.** Being purely a matter of form and outward appearance, but lacking reality: *his politeness is merely formal*; *formal religion, acquiescence &c.*

formaldehyde, n. [1. formáldihīd; 2. fɔ̄mǽldihaid]. **form-** & **aldehyde**. Chemical compound used as deodorant and antiseptic &c.

formalin, n. [1. fórmalin; 2. fɔ̄məlin]. Prec. shortened & **-in**. Aqueous solution of formaldehyde.

formalise, vb. See **formalize**.

formalism, n. [1. fórmalizm; 2. fɔ̄məlizəm]. Fr. *formalisme*. **formal** & **-ism**. Quality of being, tendency to become, formal; excessive or exclusive insistence on, or preoccupation with, formalities, esp. in religion or the arts.

formalist, n. [1. fórmalist; 2. fɔ̄məlist]. Fr. *formaliste*. **formal** & **-ist**. Person addicted to formalism, esp. in religion; one who adheres rigidly to rules and set forms, to the neglect of inner spiritual reality; a precisian, pedant.

formalistic, adj. [1. fòrmalístik; 2. fɔ̄məlístik]. Prec. & **-ic**. Pertaining to formalism or a formalist.

formality, n. [1. formáliti; 2. fɔ̄mǽliti]. Fr. *formalité*. **formal** & **-ity**. **1.** Quality of being formal; specif. **a** observance of, conformity to, established forms, rules, or order; propriety, orderliness; **b** excessive regularity, precision, or conventionality, as in manners, conduct, reasoning; **c** stiffness and lifelessness of design in art. **2.** Formal or conventional act, customary proceeding or requirement; ceremony, esp. one devoid of practical significance or use: *to comply with all legal formalities*; *a mere formality*.

formalization, n. [1. fòrmalīzáshun; 2. fɔ̄məlaizéiʃən]. Next word & **-ation**. Action of formalizing.

formalize, vb. trans. & intrans. [1. fórmalīz; 2. fɔ̄məlaiz]. **formal** & **-ize**. **1.** trans. **a** To give form to; **b** to render formal. **2.** intrans. To behave in a formal manner.

formally, adv. [1. fórmali; 2. fɔ̄məli]. **formal** & **-ly**. In a formal manner.

formant, n. [1. fórmant; 2. fɔ̄mənt]. Fr., Pres. Part. of *former*, 'to form'. Inherent tone or pitch of a vowel sound, determined by the position and condition of tongue and position of lips, and independent of the tone of the voice.

format, n. [1. fórmah; 2. fɔ̄mā]. Fr., fr. Lat. *formāt-*, P.P. stem of *formāre*. See **form (II.)**. Shape and size of a book as published; style, get-up.

formation, n. [1. formáshun; 2. fɔ̄méiʃən]. Fr., fr. Lat. *formātiōn-(em)*, 'a shaping'. **form (II.)** & **-ation**. **1.** Action or process of forming (in any sense). **2.** Manner in which a thing is formed, arrangement of parts; structure, conformation. **3.** (mil. and nav.) Arrangement or disposition of troops or vessels. **4.** Thing in relation to its forming or structure; specif. (geol.) small group, usually less than series, of stratified rocks of similar character.

formational, adj. [1. fòrmáshunal; 2. fɔ̄méiʃənəl]. Prec. & **-al**. Pertaining to formation or a formation.

formative (I.), adj. [1. fórmativ; 2. fɔ̄mətiv]. Fr. *formatif*. **form (II.)** & **-ative**. **1.** **a** Giving form, capable of forming; tending to develop and shape; plastic, creative: *the formative energy of a plant*; **b** pertaining to formation. **2.** (gram.) *Formative element*, one used in combination with another or others to form a word, e.g. a prefix, suffix, or other, internal, part, the identity and origin of which are often indiscoverable.

formative (II.), n., fr. prec. A formative element.

forme, n. Variant of **form (I.) 10.**

former (I.), n. [1. fórmer; 2. fɔ̄mə]. M.E. *formeour*, *former*, fr. O. Fr. type **formeor*, fr. Lat. *formātor*. **form (II.)** & **-er**. **a** Person who forms; **b** thing used in forming or shaping articles, mould, gauge, pattern &c.

former (II.), adj. M.E. *formere*, compar., back-formation fr. *formest*. See **foremost**. **a** Preceding in time, earlier, prior, previous: *in former times*; **b** *the former*; quasi-pronoun, opposed to *the latter*, of two persons, things, or groups; the one, those, mentioned first and immediately before: *they keep horses and cattle, the former for riding, the latter for food.*

formerly, adv. Prec. & **-ly**. In the past, at a former time, once.

formic, adj. [1. fórmik; 2. fɔ̄mik]. Abbr. for **formicic*, fr. Lat. *formīca*, 'ant', & **-ic**. This Lat. word is a puzzle; it has been suggested that it stands for **vormica*, fr. **morvica*, but the form is irregular. If the explanation be right, the word is perh. cogn. w. Gk. *múrmēk-s*, 'ant'. See also second element of **pismire**. Pertaining to, found in, ants: *formic acid*, irritant, volatile organic substance, occurring in ants, stinging nettles &c., and produced artificially.

formicary, n. [1. fórmikari; 2. fɔ̄mikəri]. Low Lat. *formīcāri-(um)*, fr. Lat. *formīca*, 'ant'. See prec. & **-ary**. Ants' nest, ant-hill.

formicate, vb. intrans. [1. fórmikāt; 2. fɔ̄mikeit]. Lat. *formīcāt-(um)*, P.P. of *formīcāre*, 'to creep like ants, feel like the creeping of ants'. See prec. To creep, swarm, with ants.

formication, n. [1. fòrmikáshun; 2. fɔ̄mikéiʃən]. Prec. & **-ion**. (med.) Morbid sensation of tingling, as if ants were creeping over the skin.

formidability, n. [1. fòrmidabíliti; 2. fɔ̄midəbíliti]. Lat. *formīdābil-(is)* (see next word) & **-ity**. Quality of being formidable.

formidable, adj. [1. fórmidabl; 2. fɔ̄midəbl]. Fr., fr. Lat. *formīdābil-(is)*, fr. *formīdāre*, 'to fear, dread', fr. *form-īdo*, 'terror'; perh. cogn. w. Gk. *mormṓ*, 'monster, bogey, hobgoblin'. **1.** Causing, inspiring, fear, dread, awe; terrifying, awe-inspiring: *a formidable appearance*. **2.** Difficult to accomplish, presenting obstacles; requiring effort to overcome: *a formidable task*; *a formidable army*. **3.** Considerable in bulk, amount, number: *a formidable pile of letters, helping of pudding.*

formidableness, n. Prec. & **-ness**. Quality of being formidable; formidability.

formidably, adv. [1. fórmidabli; 2. fɔ̄midəbli]. **formidable** & **-ly**. In a formidable manner.

formless, adj. [1. fórmles; 2. fɔ̄mlis]. **form (I.)** & **-less**. Having no form; shapeless; indefinite; having no definite plan or design, amorphous.

formlessly, adv. Prec. & **-ly**. In a formless manner.

formlessness, n. See prec. & **-ness**. Quality of being formless; absence, lack, of form, shape, design.

formula, n. [1. fórmūla; 2. fɔ̄mjulə], pl. *formulas* or *formulae* [1. fórmūlē; 2. fɔ̄mjulī]. Lat., 'small pattern, rule, formula &c.', fr. *forma*, **form (I.)**, & dimin. suff. *-ula*. See **-ule**. **1.** **a** Set form of words, prescribed for use, or habitual, on certain occasions: *a legal formula*; *the baptismal formula*; **b** (contempt.) conventional phrase, rule, custom, belief &c.: *to swallow formulas*; *to repeat the hackneyed formulas of condolence*. Specif. **2.** **a** definition of a theological doctrine or doctrines, confession of faith, creed: *the Chalcedonian formula*; **b** pharmaceutical recipe. **3.** **a** (math.) Concise statement, usually in algebraic symbols, of a general principle, law, truth, or theory, for application to particular instances; **b** (chem.) symbolic representation of the composition or atomic structure of a substance.

formular, adj. [1. fórmūlar; 2. fɔ̄mjulə]. Prec. & **-ar**. (rare) Pertaining to a formula or formulas.

formularization, n. [1. fòrmūlarīzáshun; 2. fɔ̄mjuləraizéiʃən]. Next word & **-ation**. Act of formularizing.

formularize, vb. trans. [1. fórmūlarīz ; 2. fɔ̄mjuləraiz]. **formular & -ize.** To express in a formula, formulate.

formulary, adj. & n. [1. fórmūlari ; 2. fɔ̄mjuləri]. Lat. *formulāri-(us)*, 'lawyer who composes writs', properly adj. **formula & -ary.** Cp. Fr. *formulaire.* **1.** adj. Pertaining to a formula or formulas ; prescribed ; ritual. **2.** n. Collection of formulas ; book containing liturgical or other formulas.

formulate, vb. trans. [1. fórmūlāt ; 2. fɔ̄mjuleit]. **formula & -ate.** To reduce to, express in, a formula or formulas ; to express in a precise form : *to formulate a scientific theory, proposals for reform.*

formulation, n. [1. fòrmūlā́shun ; 2. fɔ̄mjuléiʃən]. Prec. & **-ion.** Act of formulating.

formulism, n. [1. fórmūlizm ; 2. fɔ̄mjulizəm]. **formula & -ism.** Addiction to, excessive belief in or reliance on, formulas.

formulist, n. [1. fórmūlist ; 2. fɔ̄mjulist]. **formula & -ist.** Person addicted to formulas or formulism, and inclined to decide questions and regulate his conduct by their means instead of by principle and judgement.

formulistic, adj. [1. fòrmūlístik ; 2. fɔ̄mjulístik]. Prec. & **-ic.** Pertaining to formulism or formulists.

formulization, n. [1. fòrmūlīzā́shun ; 2. fɔ̄mjulaizéiʃən]. Next word & **-ation.** (rare) Act of formulizing.

formulize, vb. trans. [1. fórmūlīz ; 2. fɔ̄mjulaiz]. **formula & -ize.** (rare) To formulate.

fornent, prep. [1. fornént ; 2. fɔ̄nént]. See **fore** (I.), adv., & **anent.** Scots & Nthn. **1. a** Opposite to ; **b** near, alongside of. **2.** Respecting, in connexion with.

fornicate (I.), vb. intrans. [1. fórnikāt ; 2. fɔ̄nikeit]. Eccles. Lat. *fornicāt-(um)*, P.P. type of *fornicāri*, 'to visit a brothel', fr. Lat. *fornic-*, stem of *fornix*, 'arch, vault, brothel', prob. cogn. w. O. Lat. *forn-us*, later *furnus*, 'oven', & w. Lat. *fornax*, 'furnace'. See **furnace.** To commit fornication.

fornicate(d) (II.), adj. [1. fórnikāt(ed) ; 2. fɔ̄nikeit(id)]. Lat. *fornicāt-(um)*, 'vaulted, arched', fr. *fornix*, 'arch' (see prec.), & **-ate.** (bot.) Arching over ; having arch-shaped appendages.

fornication, n. [1. fòrnikā́shun ; 2. fɔ̄nikéiʃən]. M.E. *fornicatioun*, fr. O. & Mod. Fr. *fornication*, fr. eccles. Lat. *fornicātiōn-(em)*, fr. *fornicāt-* (see **fornicate** (I.)) & **-ion.** Sexual intercourse between unmarried persons ; or between a married and an unmarried person.

fornicator, n. [1. fórnikāter ; 2. fɔ̄nikeitə]. M.E. *fornicatour*, fr. O. & Mod. Fr. *fornicateur*, fr. eccles. Lat. *fornicātōr-(em)* ; as prec. & **-or.** Person who fornicates.

fornicatress, n. [1. fórnikātres ; 2. fɔ̄nikeitris]. Prec. & **-ess.** Female guilty of fornication.

forpine, vb. intrans. [1. forpín ; 2. fɔ̄páin]. M.E. *forpīnen*, 'to torture, pine, famish'. **for- & pine** (I.). (archaic, chiefly P.P.) To pine away, waste away, through pain, hunger &c.

forrader, adv. [1. fórader ; 2. fɔ́rədə]. Phonetic spelling of old pronunciation of compar. of **forward.** In Phr. *to get no forrader*, to make no progress.

forrel, n. Alternative spelling of **forel.**

forsake, vb. trans. [1. forsā́k ; 2. fəséik]. O.E. *forsacan*, 'to refuse, relinquish, deny', prob. orig. 'to oppose strongly', M.E. *forsāken*, 'to forsake' ; O.H.G. *forsahhan*, Sw. *försaka* ; fr. **for-** & O.E. *sacan*, 'to disagree, contend, quarrel', fr. *sacu*, 'dispute, quarrel, strife' ; cf. Goth. *sakan*, 'to strive, dispute'. See **sake. 1.** To abandon, desert ; to break off social relations with (a person) : *to forsake one's old friends, one's children.* **2.** To give up, relinquish, renounce (a habit, practice, former way of life &c.)

forsaken, adj. [1. forsā́ken ; 2. fəséik(ə)n], fr. P.P. of prec. O.E. *forsacen.* Abandoned, deserted.

forsaker, n. [1. forsā́ker ; 2. fəséikə]. **forsake & -er.** One who forsakes.

forsook, vb. [1. forsóok ; 2. fəsúk]. O.E. *forsōc*, M.E. *forsōk.* Pret. of **forsake.**

forsooth, adv. [1. forsōōth ; 2. fəsúþ]. O.E., M.E. *for sōðe*, 'for a truth'. **for** (I.) & **sooth.** (now always ironical) Truly, indeed, no doubt : *and he forsooth expecting to be well paid for doing nothing !*

forspent, adj. [1. forspént ; 2. fɔ̄spént]. P.P. of obs. *forspend*, 'to spend entirely' ; O.E. *forspendan*, 'to squander' ; M.E. *forspenden.* **for- & spend.** (archaic) Exhausted, wearied out.

forswear, vb. trans. & intrans. [1. forswā́r ; 2. fɔ̄swéə]. O.E. *forswerian*, 'to renounce', also 'swear falsely' ; M.E. *forswērien* ; cp. Germ. *verschwören*, 'to conspire'. **for- & swear. A.** trans. **1. a** To renounce, refuse, or deny on oath or by solemn protestation ; to abjure ; **b** to give up, abandon, use or practice of. **2.** *To forswear oneself*, to perjure oneself. **B.** intrans. To swear falsely.

forsworn, adj. [1. forswórn ; 2. fɔ̄swɔ́n]. P.P. of prec. O.E., M.E. *forsworen.* Having sworn falsely ; perjured.

forsythia, n. [1. forsíthia ; 2. fɔ̄sáiþiə]. Mod. Lat., generic name fr. William Forsyth (1737–1804), gardener. Shrub, originally from Asia Minor, growing freely in English gardens; cultivated for its profuse yellow blossoms, which it bears in the spring.

fort, n. [1. fort ; 2. fɔ̄t]. O. & Mod. Fr., fr. Low Lat. *fortis* (*domus*), 'a strong house, fortress', fr. Lat. *fortis*, 'strong, bold', O. Lat. *forctis*, 'strong', cp. O. Lat. *forctus* (& *horctus*), 'good'. It has been suggested that the Lat. forms represent Aryan **bhergh-* & are cogn. w. O.E. *beorgan*, 'to hide, protect', & *burg*, 'fortified place' &c., see **borough** ; other authorities derive the Lat. forms fr. Aryan **dherg̑h-*, whence also Lat. *firmus*, see **firm** (I.), & Scrt. *dṛdhás*, 'firm, strong'. **a** Building or group of buildings and earthworks, strengthened as far as possible to withstand artillery fire, and armed and equipped for military defence ; now usually detached part of system of defences ; **b** fortified trading post, esp. on confines of civilization.

fortalice, n. [1. fórtalis ; 2. fɔ̄təlis]. O. Fr. *fortelesce*, cp. Span. *fortaleza*, fr. Low Lat. *fortalitia, -itium*, 'fortress', fr. *fortis*, 'strong'. See prec. **a** Small fort or outwork ; **b** (archaic or poet.) Fortress.

forte (I.), n. [1. fort ; 2. fɔ̄t]. Fr. *fort*, 'strong ; strength' ; *-e* has been erroneously added, as in *locale, morale.* See **fort. 1.** Quality or accomplishment in which one excels ; strong point. **2.** Part of sword blade between the hilt and middle.

forte (II.), adj., adv., & n. [1. fórte ; 2. fɔ̄ti]. Ital., fr. Lat. *fortis*, 'strong'. See **fort.** (mus.) **1.** adj. Loud. **2.** adv. Loudly. **3.** n. Loud passage. (Symbol *f.*)

forte-piano, adj., adv., & n. [1. fórte piáhnō ; 2. fɔ̄ti piánou]. Ital., 'loud-soft'. See prec. & **piano.** (mus.) **1.** adj. First loud and then soft. **2.** adv. In this manner. **3.** n. Passage played or sung thus.

forth, adv. & prep. [1. forth ; 2. fɔ̄þ]. O.E., M.E. *forð*, cp. Du. *voort*, Germ. *fort* &c. ; fr. **fore** & suff. *-þ-*, Aryan *-*to-*. **1.** adv. **a** Forwards, onwards, in place, time, or degree : *to go forth to battle* ; *from this day forth* ; archaic except in Phr. *and so forth*, and so on, and the like, &c. ; *so far forth*, to that extent ; *so far forth as*, to whatever extent ; *back and forth*, (Am.) backwards and forwards, to and fro ; **b** into general view or notice (chiefly with vbs.) : *to bring forth young* ; *to put forth leaves* ; *to come, set, stand, look, show, hold, forth* &c., see each of these. **2.** prep. (obs. or archaic) Forth from ; from out of : *to go forth the house.*

forthcome, vb. intrans. [1. forthkúm ; 2. fɔ̄þkám]. **forth & come.** Cp. O.E. *forðcuman.* (rare) To be forthcoming.

forthcoming (I.), adj. [1. forthkúming ; 2. fɔ̄þkámiŋ]. Pres. Part. of prec. **1.** About to appear, approaching : *a list of forthcoming works.* **2.** Ready, at hand, available, when required : *the promised help was not forthcoming.* **3.** (of persons, their manners, and characters) Easy of access, gracious, affable, courteous ; communicative.

forthcoming (II.), n. **forthcome & -ing.** Process of coming forth, appearing.

forthright (I.), adv. [1. fórthrīt ; 2. fɔ̄þrait]. O.E. *forð rihte*, 'at once, instantly'. **forth & right** (II.). (archaic) **a** Straightforward ; **b** at once, straightway.

forthright (II.), adj. & n. O.E., M.E. *forð riht* ; **forth & right** (I.). (archaic) **1.** adj. **a** Going straight on, direct ; **b** (fig.) straightforward, outspoken, downright, candid. **2.** n. Straight course : '*Forthrights and meanders*' (Shakespeare).

forthwith, adv. [1. forthwídh, -wíth ; 2. fɔ̄þwíð, -wíþ]. M.E. *forð wið* ; **forth & with** used absol. ; cp. M.E. *forthwithall* ; representing O.E. *forð mid*, 'forward with'. Immediately, at once.

fortieth, adj. & n. [1. fórtieth ; 2. fɔ̄ti-iþ]. O.E. *fēowertigoða*, M.E. *fēowertiȝðe.* **forty & -th** (II.). **a** adj. Ordinal of *forty* ; **b** n., fortieth part.

fortifiable, adj. [1. fórtifīabl ; 2. fɔ̄tifaiəbl]. **fortify & -able.** Capable of being fortified.

fortification, n. [1. fòrtifikā́shun ; 2. fɔ̄tifikéiʃən]. Fr., fr. Lat. *fortificātiōn-(em)*, 'act of strengthening', fr. *fortificāre.* **fortify & -ation. 1.** Action of fortifying or strengthening ; specif., strengthening of wine or other liquor by adding alcohol. **2.** Act, process, art, of making a town or other place militarily strong by the erection of defensive works. **3.** *Fortifications*, complex or aggregate of defensive works ; town walls, towers &c., earthworks, fortified lines.

fortifier, n. [1. fórtifīer ; 2. fɔ̄tifaiə]. Next word & **-er.** Person or thing that fortifies ; specif. (facet.) alcoholic drink taken nominally as a tonic, or pick-me-up.

fortify, vb. trans. [1. fórtifī ; 2. fɔ̄tifai]. Fr. *fortifier*, fr. Lat. *fortificāre.* See **fort & -fy. 1.** To make strong or stronger, to strengthen ; specif. **a** to make (structure) more enduring ; **b** to strengthen liquor by adding alcohol ; **c** to make a person physically, mentally, or morally stronger : *to fortify oneself against the cold* ; *fortified with the last rites of the Church* ; **d** to corroborate, confirm : *to fortify one's case with statistics, a statement with facts.* **2.** (mil.) To protect a place against attack, by building defensive works ; to convert into a fortress.

fortissimo, adv. [1. fortísimō ; 2. fɔ̄tísimou]. Ital., fr. dat. of Lat. *fortissimus*, superl. of *fortis*, 'strong'. See **fort.** (mus.) Very loud. (Abbreviation, *ff.*)

fortitude, n. [1. fórtitūd ; 2. fɔ̄titjūd]. Fr., fr. Lat. *fortitūdo*, 'strength, courage', fr. *fortis*, 'strong'. See **fort & -tude.** Calm, sustained courage, resolute endurance, in the face of pain, danger, or trouble.

fortnight, n. [1. fórtnīt ; 2. fɔ̄tnait]. O.E. *fēowertȳne niht*, 'fourteen nights' (night being unit in reckoning time), M.E. *fourte(n) niȝt.* See **fourteen, night, & cp. sennight.** Period of fourteen days or two weeks : *yesterday, today, Monday, fortnight*, at a date a fortnight after yesterday &c.

fortnightly, adj. & adv. [1. fórtnītli ; 2. fɔ̄tnaitli]. Prec. & **-ly. a** adj. Happening, performed, produced &c., at intervals of a fortnight ; **b** adv., at intervals of a fortnight.

fortress, n. & vb. trans. [1. fórtres ; 2. fɔ̄tris]. M.E. *fortresse*, fr. O. Fr. *fort(e)rece, forteresse*, variant of *fortelesce.* See **fortalice. 1.** n. Fortified place, stronghold ; town or permanent camp protected by strong fortified lines, forts, or defensive works. **2.** vb. (rare) To furnish with a fortress.

fortuitism, n. [1. fortū́itizm ; 2. fɔ̄tjúitizəm]. Lat. *fortuit-(us)*, see **fortuitous, & -ism.** Doctrine that evolutionary changes are the result, not of design, but of the fortuitous operation of natural laws.

fortuitist, n. [1. fortū́itist ; 2. fɔ̄tjúitist]. See prec. & **-ist.** Adherent of fortuitism.

fortuitous, adj. [1. fortúitus; 2. fɔtjúitəs]. Lat. *fortuit-(us)*, 'casual, accidental', fr. *fort-*, stem of *fors*, 'chance', see **fortune**, & **-ous**. Due to, happening by, chance or accident; casual.

fortuitously, adv. Prec. & **-ly**. In a fortuitous manner; casually, accidentally.

fortuitousness, n. See prec. & **-ness**. Quality of being fortuitous.

fortuity, n. [1. fortúiti; 2. fɔtjúiti]. Fr. *fortuité* for **fortuit-ité*. See **fortuitous** & **-ity**. **a** Fortuitousness, accidental character; **b** accidental occurrence.

fortunate (I.), adj. [1. fórchunit, fórtūnat; 2. fɔ́tʃənit, fɔ́tjunət]. Lat. *fortūnāt-(us)*, P.P. of *fortūnāre*, 'to make prosperous'. See **fortune** (II.) & **-ate**. **1.** Enjoying good fortune; having some unexpected or unearned good; lucky, happy: *the fortunate possessor of building land.* **2.** Bringing or heralding good fortune, auspicious: *born under a fortunate star*; *a fortunate speculation.*

fortunate (II.), n., fr. prec. (rare) Fortunate person.

fortunately, adv. [1. fórchunatli, fórtūnatli; 2. fɔ́tʃənətli, -junətli]. **fortunate** (I.) & **-ly**. **a** In a fortunate manner; **b** by good fortune, happily: *fortunately I remembered the address.*

fortune (I.), n. [1. fórchun, fórtūn; 2. fɔ́tʃən, fɔ́tjūn]. M.E., O. & Mod. Fr. *fortūne*, fr. Lat. *fortūna*, 'chance, good luck, fate; goddess of fate', fr. *fort-*, stem of *fors*, 'chance, luck,' fr. base *fer-*, 'to bear', see **-ferous** & **bear** (I.). **1. a** Chance, luck, hazard; the apparently accidental or incalculable element in affairs: *by good fortune*; Phrs. *a soldier of fortune*, one who offers his services to any employer or cause he chooses; *to try one's fortune*, to take a risk, make a venture; *the fortune of war.* **b** This personified as a goddess. **2.** Fate, destiny, lot in life, esp. one's future lot; Phr. *to tell fortunes*, to profess to foretell person's future fate or destiny. **3. a** (i.) Good fortune, good luck; (ii.) prosperity, success, wealth: *to seek one's fortune*; *a man of fortune*; **b** large possessions, wealth: *to make, inherit, have, a fortune*; Phrs. *to marry a fortune*, to marry a wealthy woman; *a small fortune* (colloq.), a considerable sum.

fortune (II.), vb. intrans. & trans. M.E. *fortūnen*, fr. O. Fr. *fortuner*, fr. Lat. *fortūnāre*, 'to make prosperous', fr. *fortūna*. See prec. (archaic) **a** intrans. To chance, happen: *it fortuned that he was passing*; Phr. *to fortune upon*, happen to find; **b** trans., (rare) to furnish with a fortune or estate.

fortune-hunter, n. Person who makes unscrupulous efforts to obtain wealth, esp. by marriage.

fortune-hunting, n. Action, occupation, of a fortune-hunter.

fortuneless, adj. [1. fórchunles; 2. fɔ́tʃənlis]. **fortune** (I.) & **-less**. **a** Having no good fortune; **b** having no wealth.

fortune-teller, n. One who professes to predict person's destinies, as by palmistry &c.

fortune-telling, n. Action, practice of predicting people's destinies.

forty, adj. & n. [1. fórti; 2. fɔ́ti]. O.E. *fēowertiġ*, M.E. *fowerti, fourti*; **four** & **-ty**. **1.** adj. Four times ten. Phr. *forty winks*, (colloq.) a short sleep or nap, esp. by day. **2.** n. Sum of four tens: *a man of forty*; *he is under forty*; *in the forties*, between the ages of 39 and 50. Phr. *the Forty*, body of 40 persons, as the French Academy; *the forties*, the years 1840–49, 1740–49 &c.; *the (roaring) forties*, stormy zone of N. Atlantic between 39° and 50° N. lat.; *the Forty-five*, Jacobite rising of 1745: *out in (the) Forty-five.*

forum, n. [1. fórum; 2. fɔ́rəm]. Lat., 'market place, place for public business'. Orig. the forecourt of a house where business was transacted; from same base as Lat. *fori-*, 'door', whence *foris*, 'outside'. *Forum* prob. derives its orig. sense fr. being outside the house. See further under **door**, wh. is cogn. **1.** Market-place of ancient Rome or of Roman town, used for legal, political, and other public business. **2.** (fig.) The law-courts, esp. as contrasted with parliament: *the forum and the senate.* **3.** (fig.) Tribunal, organ of judgement or decision: *the forum of public opinion, of conscience.*

forward (I.), adv. [1. fórward; 2. fɔ́wəd]. The old received pron. [1. fórad; 2. fɔ́rəd] is now obs., provinc., or vulg., except in naut. use. Cp. **forrader**. O.E. *foreweard, forweard*, adj., rarely adv., M.E. *foreward*, adv. & adj., the adv. being derived fr. O.E. *on foreweardan*, 'in a forward (position)'; **fore-** & **-ward**. Mod. adj. & n. fr. adv. See also **forwards**. **1. a** Towards the front, forepart, or place before one; onward, in the direction in which one is facing: *to go, hurry, look forward*; Phr. *to play forward*, (cricket) to reach or step forward to play the ball; *forward!*, (mil.) command to advance; **b** in advance, ahead, of another or the main body: *scouts were sent forward*; **c** (fig.) in a progressive manner, so as to advance or make progress: *to help a movement forward by work or money*; **d** into notice or prominence: *to bring, put, set forward*; *to come forward*; Phr. *to put oneself forward*, assume undue importance. **2.** (naut.) In the forepart of the ship, contrasted with *aft.* **3.** Towards the future, onwards in time: *from this time forward.* Phr. *carriage forward*, (of goods) to be paid for at destination; *to date forward*, to post-date; *to look forward*, to consider the future; *to look forward to*, await, expect, with pleasurable anticipations.

forward (II.), adj. **1. a** Situated in front of, before, one; in the forepart of a thing, specif. (naut.) of a ship; **b** moving forward, advancing: *a forward march*; cricket, *forward play* (see prec. **1. a**). **2.** (fig.) Progressive, advanced, endeavouring to make progress in ideas, policy &c.: *a forward movement in a party, the Church* &c. **3.** (fig.) **a** In the habit of putting oneself unduly forward; officious, presumptuous, impudent, pert: *a forward minx*; **b** prompt, quick, eager: *the crew were forward to assist.* **4.** (commerc.) Pertaining to, concerned with, the future, esp. with produce that is not yet ready: *forward buying, prices*; *a forward contract.* **5.** Well advanced, hastening to maturity; early, precocious; **a** of physical condition: *a forward spring*; **b** of mental condition: *a forward pupil*; *to be forward with one's work.*

forward (III.), n., fr. prec. **a** (in football, polo, and hockey) One of the players in the front line; **b** (fig., pl.) group of persons working in advance of main body; pioneers: *the Liberal Forwards.*

forward (IV.), vb. trans., fr. **forward** (I.). **1.** To help to advance, to further, promote; to hasten progress and development of: *to forward a plan, scheme.* **2. a** To send forward, post on farther (letter, parcel &c.) to person for whom it is intended: *to forward letters to a new address*; **b** to dispatch, send: *the goods shall be forwarded to your house.*

forwarder, n. [1. fórwarder; 2. fɔ́wədə]. Prec. & **-er**. Person who forwards; specif., one who undertakes delivery of goods to carrier.

forwarding, n. [1. fórwarding; 2. fɔ́wədiŋ]. **forward** (II.) & **-ing**. Action of one who forwards; business of a forwarder.

forwardness, n. [1. fórwardnes; 2. fɔ́wədnis]. **forward** (II.) & **-ness**. **1.** State or quality of being forward; specif., state of being advanced, or early mature or ripe (of physical and mental condition): *the forwardness of the season, of the crops, of a pupil.* **2. a** Undue readiness to push oneself forward; officiousness, pertness, presumption; **b** readiness, willingness, promptness.

forwards, adv. [1. fórwardz; 2. fɔ́wədz]. M.E. *forewardes*; **forward** (I.) & genit. suff. *-s*, wh. was often used adverbially. See **-wards**. Used indifferently with *forward* in many adverbial phrases: (*to walk &c.*) *backwards and forwards*; *to look forwards*, to look ahead, to the future; *to move a thing forwards* &c.

forwearied, adj. [1. forwḗrid; 2. fɔ̄wíərid]. M.E. *forwērīed*, P.P. of *forwērien*, 'to weary out'; **for-** & **weary** (II.). (archaic or poet.) Utterly wearied, tired out.

forwhy, adv. & conj. [1. forwī́; 2. fɔ̄wái]. O.E. *for hwȳ*, 'because', instrumental of *hwæt*, 'what'. See **what**. (archaic and obs.) **a** adv. Why, wherefore; **b** conj., because.

forworn, adj. [1. forwórn; 2. fɔ̄wɔ́n]. P.P. of obs. *forwear*, O.E. *forwerian*, M.E. *forwērien*, 'to wear out'; **for-** & **wear** (I.), perh. confused w. O.E. *forworen*, 'decayed, worn out', fr. **for-** & *woren*, P.P. of *wesan*, 'to be'. See **was**. (archaic or poet.) Worn out, exhausted.

fossa, n., pl. **fossae** [1. fósa, -ē; 2. fɔ́sə, -ī]. Lat. See next word. (anat.) Groove, pit, depression, small cavity, as *nasal, cranial fossae* &c.

fosse, n. [1. fos; 2. fɔs]. M.E., O. & Mod. Fr., fr. Lat. *fossa*, 'ditch' (for *fossa terra*, 'dug earth'), fem. P.P. of *fodere*, 'to dig'; cp. O. Slav. *bodā*, 'I prick, pierce'; Lith. *bedeti*, 'to dig, hollow out'; fr. the same base is Goth. *badi*, 'bed'. See **bed**. **1.** Dry or wet ditch, moat, or trench; esp. in fortification; ditch running parallel with rampart made of materials dug from it. **2.** (anat.) Groove or depression as in a bone.

fossette, n. [1. fosét; 2. fɔsét]. Fr., 'small hollow, dimple'. Prec. & **-ette**. Little depression, a dimple.

fossick, vb. intrans. & trans. [1. fósik; 2. fɔ́sik]. Prob. eastern dial. *fussock, fussick*, 'to bustle about, make a fuss'. See **fuss** & **-ock**. **1.** intrans. **a** (Austral. min.) To search for gold in old workings, crevices &c.; **b** (fig., colloq.) to search, rummage, for pickings. **2.** trans. To dig (gold &c.).

fossicker, n. [1. fósiker; 2. fɔ́sikə]. Prec. & **-er**. Gold miner who fossicks.

fossil, n. & adj. [1. fósl, fósil; 2. fɔ́sl, -il]. Fr. *fossile*, fr. Lat. *fossil-(is)*, 'that may be dug up', fr. *foss-*, P.P. stem of *fodere*, 'to dig'. See **fosse** & **-ile**. **1.** n. **a** Remains of animal or vegetable organism, or cast or trace of such, as footprint, found petrified, and naturally imbedded in stratified rock; **b** (fig.) old person who retains unchanged the habits or ideas of a past age; institution or thing that has survived its use, without adaptation to changed conditions. **2.** adj. Having the nature and character of a fossil, connected with, resembling, a fossil: *a fossil fish*; *fossil remains* &c.; *a fossil bone, shell, tree, footprint.*

fossiliferous, adj. [1. fòsilíferus; 2. fɔ̀silífərəs]. Lat. *fossili-*, stem of *fossilis* (see prec.), & **-ferous**. Bearing, containing, fossils: *fossiliferous rocks.*

fossilization, n. [1. fòsilīzā́shun; 2. fɔ̀silaizéiʃən]. Next word & **-ation**; cp. Fr. *fossilisation.* **a** Process of becoming fossilized; **b** something which is fossilized.

fossilize, vb. trans. & intrans. [1. fósilīz; 2. fɔ́silaiz]. **fossil** & **-ize**. **1.** trans. **a** To convert into a fossil, to petrify; **b** (fig.) to render antiquated or incapable of progress or adaptation to circumstances. **2.** intrans. **a** To become fossilized or petrified; **b** (fig.) to grow antiquated; **c** (rare) to search for fossils.

fossorial, adj. [1. fosórial; 2. fɔsɔ́riəl]. Lat. *fossōri-(us)*, 'adapted for digging', fr. *fossor*, agent-n. fr. *foss-*, P.P. stem of *fodere*, 'to dig'. See **fosse** & **-or** & **-al**. (zool.) **a** Digging, burrowing: *fossorial wasp*; **b** adapted for burrowing: *the fossorial feet of the mole.*

foster (I.), adj. [1. fóster; 2. fɔ́stə]. O.E. *fōstor, fōster*, M.E. *foster*, 'nursing, nourishment'; cp. O.N. *fōstr*; connected w. O.E. *fōda* (see **food**); Gmc. type **fōstr-*, fr. **fōsr-*, fr. Aryan **pāssr-*, fr. **pāt-tr-*, fr. base **pā-*, 'to feed', whence Lat. *pāscere*, 'to feed', *pābulum*, 'food', *pāstor*, 'shepherd' (see **pabulum, pastor, pasture**). (rare, except in composition) Pertaining to fostering; connected, not by birth, but by nursing or rearing: *foster-parents* &c.

foster (II.), vb. trans. O.E. *fōstrian*, M.E. *fostren*, fr. prec.; cp. O.N. *fōstra*. **1. a** To nurse, nourish, rear, bring up; to cherish, tend: *to foster a child, the sick* &c.; **b** (fig.) to encourage, promote, stimulate: *schools to foster artistic talent*; *to foster social evils.* **2.** To cherish, harbour in one's heart: *to foster a desire for revenge, an idea, hope* &c.

fosterage, n. [1. fósterij; 2. fɔ́stəridž]. Prec. & **-age**. **a** Act of fostering; **b** custom or practice of employing foster-mothers.

foster-brother, n. O.E. *fōsterbrōðor*. **foster** (I.) & **brother**. One of two male persons, not actual brothers by blood, who are being, or have been, nursed, suckled, and brought up by the same woman, the mother of one of them.

foster-child, n. Child nursed or brought up by foster-parent.

fosterer, n. [1. fósterer; 2. fɔ́stərə]. **foster** (II.) & **-er**. Person who fosters.

foster-father, n. O.E. *fōsterfæder*, M.E. *fosterfader*. Man who takes, or has taken, the place of father to one in one's childhood; the husband of foster-mother.

fosterling, n. [1. fósterling; 2. fɔ́stəliŋ]. O.E. *fōstorling*, M.E. *fosterling*. **foster** (I.) & **-ling**. Foster-child, nursling.

foster-mother, n. O.E. *fōstormōdor*, M.E. *vostermōder*. **1.** Woman who suckles the child of another, or brings it up; woman standing in such a relation to one. **2.** Device, furnished with a means of heating, for protecting and keeping warm young chicks hatched by an incubator, or taken from the hen as soon as hatched.

foster-parent, n. Foster-father or foster-mother.

foster-sister, n. O.E. *fōstersweostor*. Female person, not actual sister, who is, or has been, nursed, or brought up, with another, by a woman who is the mother of one of them.

fostress, n. [1. fóstres; 2. fɔ́stris]. **foster** (II.) & **-ess**. Woman who fosters.

foudroyant, adj. [1. fōōdróiant; 2. fūdrɔ́iənt, -rwaiā]. Fr., Pres. Part. of *foudroyer*, 'to strike with lightning', fr. *foudre*, 'lightning', fr. Lat. *fulgur*. See **fulgurite, fulgent.** (med.) Attacking one suddenly and overwhelmingly; fulminant: *foudroyant paralysis.*

fought, vb. [1. fawt; 2. fōt]. O.E. Pret. *feaht*, M.E. *fauht*. Pret. & P.P. of **fight**.

foughten, adj. [1. fáwtn; 2. fɔ́t(ə)n]. O.E. *fohten*, M.E. *foughten*; old P.P. of **fight** (I.). (archaic, poet.) Fought; esp. *the foughten field.*

foul (I.), adj. [1. foul; 2. faul]. O.E. *fūl*, M.E. *fūl, foul*, O.H.G. *fūl*, Goth. *fūl-s*, O.N. *fūll*, fr. Aryan base **pū-*; cp. Lat. *pūs*, 'foul matter produced by inflammation' &c. (see **pus**), *pūtēre*, 'to stink', *pūtridus*, 'rotten' (see **putrid**); further Gk. *pŭthein*, 'to rot' &c.; Scrt. *pūyati*, 'stinks'. See **filth** & **filthy**. **1. a** Filthy, covered with filth, extremely dirty, unclean; the word expresses a degree of filth so great as to cause disgust and loathing: *a foul hovel*; *the floor was foul with the dirt of weeks*; **b** putrescent, septic: *wounds foul for lack of dressing*; **c** offensive, revolting to the senses; suggestive of filth: *a foul smell*; Phr. *foul linen*, such as requires to be washed, soiled linen; **d** (of disease) very severe, disgusting, infectious. **2. a** Clogged up with dirt and impurities, not clear: *a foul pipe, gun-barrel* &c.; **b** specif. (of a ship) having hull covered with barnacles and other accretions; **c** (of fish) in poor condition, esp. after spawning. **3.** (naut., of ropes and cordage &c.) Tending to jam; jammed, caught in other ropes, pulleys, chains &c. Phr. *a foul berth*, one in which a ship is in danger of collision. **4. a** (of weather) Stormy, squally; **b** (of wind) contrary, adverse. **5.** (print. and writing) Full of erasures and corrections: *a foul proof*; *foul copy.* **6.** Ugly; only in Phr. *be she fair or foul* &c. **7.** (in moral sense) **a** Vile, wicked, abominable: *a foul crime, wrong* &c.; **b** stained, polluted, with vice or crime: *a foul rogue*; Phr. *the foul fiend*, the devil; **c** impure, obscene, unclean: *foul language*; *a foul term, expression.* **8. a** Underhand, treacherous, unfair: *foul play*, cheating; *a foul blow*; Phr. *foul play*, specif., crime; **b** not in accordance with the rules or laws of sport; sometimes implying only error, and not deliberate unfairness: *a foul stroke*; *foul riding* (in a race) generally implies unfair riding. Phr. *by fair means or foul*, without scruple, somehow or other. **9.** (in colloq. use) Often employed of material objects, circumstances, behaviour &c., to express merely strong disapproval or dislike, having sense of very bad, unpleasant, unsatisfactory &c.: *my cold is perfectly foul*; *he is a foul dancer*, dances badly; *a foul journey*, inconvenient, uncomfortable; and so on.

foul (II.), adv., fr. prec. Foully. Phrs. *to fall (run) foul of*, (naut.) to become entangled with, collide with; (fig.) to come into conflict with, be involved in difficulties or a quarrel with; *to hit foul*, (boxing) to hit in contravention of the rules, esp. to hit below the belt; (fig.) to treat unfairly: *to play one foul*, to deal deceitfully with one in a game, or (fig.) in earnest.

foul (III.), n., fr. **foul** (I.) **1.** (rare) Foul weather; ill-fortune; chiefly in Phr. *through fair and through foul.* **2.** (naut.) Entanglement, as of ropes; slight collision, as of oars or boats. **3.** (sport) Deliberate obstruction of opponent when contrary to rules of the game; wilful or accidental breach of rules which affects result of game. Phr. *to claim a foul*, to demand annulment of opponent's victory, or a penalty, for breach of rules.

foul (IV.), vb. intrans. & trans. O.E. *fūlian*, 'to become foul, rot'; M.E. *fūlen*, 'to befoul'; fr. **foul** (I.) **A.** intrans. **1.** (rare) To become foul, dirty, or offensive. **2.** To become clogged or choked with waste matter, as the products of combustion: *a gun-barrel fouls.* **3.** To become entangled, as a rope. **4.** To come into collision: *our boat fouled on leaving harbour.* **B.** trans. **1. a** To make foul or dirty; to defile, soil, befoul; Phrs. *to foul one's hands with*, lower oneself by having to do with; '*It's an ill bird that fouls its own nest*' (proverb), it is unseemly to defame one's self, one's own family or belongings; **b** (fig.) to render vile or loathsome: *to foul one's reputation*; to dishonour, asperse, slander: *to foul a person's name.* **2.** To impede, obstruct; specif. **a** to clog, choke: *to foul a gun (gun-barrel)*; **b** to cover (ship's bottom) with growths that impair speed; **c** to block (railway line, traffic); **d** to entangle (rope, &c.); to become entangled, collide, with: *the yacht fouled a buoy*; **e** (sport) to get in the way of, collide with, try to hinder or thwart (competitor) in irregular or unfair way.

foulard, n. [1. fōōlard; 2. fūlād]. Fr., of uncertain origin. **a** Thin, soft textile of silk, or silk and cotton; **b** handkerchief made of this.

foully, adv. [1. fóulli; 2. fáulli]. O.E. *fūllīce*, M.E. *fūllīche*. **foul** (I.) & **-ly**. In a foul, dirty manner; **a** in a physically offensive or disgusting manner; **b** in a morally loathsome or abominable manner; vilely, obscenely.

foul-mouthed, adj. Speaking foully, vilely, or obscenely; addicted to foul language.

foulness, n. [1. fóulnes; 2. fáulnis]. O.E. *fūlness*, M.E. *fūlnesse*. **foul** (I.) & **-ness**. **a** Quality of being foul; **b** something physically or morally foul.

foul-spoken, adj. **a** Foully spoken; **b** speaking foully, foul-mouthed.

foul-tongued, adj. [1. fóul tŭngd; 2. fául tăŋd]. Foul-mouthed.

foumart, n. [1. fōōmart; 2. fūmăt]. M.E. *fulmart, fulmard*, fr. **foul** (I.) & O.E. *mearð* (see **marten**); cp. Fr. *marte*. Polecat.

found (I.), vb. trans. & intrans. [1. found; 2. faund]. M.E. *founden*, fr. O. Fr. *funder, fonder* (Mod. Fr. *fonder*), fr. Lat. *fundāre*, fr. *fundus*, bottom. See **fund**. **A.** trans. **1. a** To lay the foundation of; to begin the building or construction of: *Romulus founded Rome*; *this church was founded in the 12th century*; **b** to establish, set up, institute, originate: *to found a dynasty*; Phr. *to found a family*, to be the first of a family to acquire for it a recognized and influential social status; **c** to create as permanent institution, to settle the original rules of and provide endowment for: *to found a college, hospital, association*; **d** to initiate, invent, set going, by intellectual activity: *to found a theory, system of philosophy* &c.; **e** to start, lay basis of; to be the originator of: *to found a fortune.* **2.** To construct out of, adapt from, elements already in existence, using these as a basis: *a novel founded on old legends*; *founded on fact*, not entirely an invention. **3.** To base, rely on as a sound foundation: *I found my hopes of success on my own hard work, to found an argument on well-known facts.* **B.** intrans. (rare) To be based; to depend.

found (II.), vb. trans. Fr. *fondre*, 'to melt', fr. Lat. *fundere*, 'to pour, cast, melt (metal)'; Lat. base extended fr. Aryan **ĝheu-*, **ĝhu-* &c., whence also Goth. *giutan*, O.E. *gēotan*, O.S. *geotan*, O.H.G. *giozan*, 'to pour'; also Gk. *khé(w)-ein*, 'to pour'; O.N. *gjō-sa*, 'to gush' &c. See **chyle, fuse** (I.), **futile, geyser, gush, gut.** **a** To melt (metal or materials for making glass) and pour into a mould; **b** to make by pouring molten metal or glass into a mould: *to found a bell.*

found (III.), vb. Pret. & P.P. of **find.** O.E., M.E. *funden.* (special sense) Provided, equipped with: *well found in plate and linen* &c. Phr. *all found* (of servants' wages), with everything provided.

foundation, n. [1. foundáshun; 2. faundéiʃən]. M.E. *foundacioun*, fr. O. & Mod. Fr. *fondation*, fr. Lat. *fundātiōn-(em)*, 'a founding', vbl. n. fr. *fundāre*. See **found** (I.) & **-ation**. **1.** Action of founding, placing on a basis, or establishing; settlement, institution: *the foundation of London took place at an unknown date.* Phr. *Old Foundation*, (of cathedrals) secular cathedrals founded before the Reformation; *New Foundation*, old monastic cathedrals refounded by Henry VIII., and new cathedrals founded at the time of, and since, the Reformation. **2.** That on which a thing rests or is sustained; part of a thing which underlies and supports the rest; base, basis; specif. **a** (often pl.) substructure of building, usually underground; solid mass of masonry or of natural rock on which walls are built; **b** piece of strong or stiff material on which the rest of a garment is built up, usually interlining; **c** first row of stitches in knitting or crochet. **3.** Principle, ground, basis on which an idea, belief, or system of ideas is based, or which supplies motive for course of action; underlying reason: *the foundations of belief*; *the rumour is without foundation.* **4.** Underlying circumstances, basis, starting-point: *the foundation(s) of one's career, of one's fortune.* **5. a** Thing which is founded or maintained by a fund; endowed institution or society, as a college, monastery, library &c.; **b** fund for the endowment of an institution, society &c.; endowment. Phr. *on the foundation* (of an institution), a beneficiary of such an endowment.

foundationer, n. [1. foundáshuner; 2. faundéiʃənə]. Prec. & **-er**. Member of a college or school who is on the foundation.

foundationless, adj. [1. foundáshunles; 2. faundéiʃənlis]. **foundation** & **-less**. Lacking foundation.

foundation school, n. School with a permanent endowment.

foundation stone, n. **1. a** Stone forming part of the foundation of a building; **b** stone laid with ceremony and inscribed to commemorate the foundation of a building, usually a public building. **2.** (fig.) Fundamental fact or principle.

founded, adj. [1. fóunded; 2. fáundid], fr. P.P. of **found** (I.). Usually *well-, ill-founded*, having a good, a bad, foundation; in non-material sense: *ill-founded hopes, reports* &c.

founder (**I.**), n. [1. fóunder; 2. fáundə]. M.E. *foundeōr*, fr. O. Fr. *fondeor*, fr. Lat. *fundātor*, agent-n. fr. *fundāre*. See **found** (**I.**) & **-er**. Person who founds, sets up, or establishes something, esp. a society or institution. Phrs. *founder's kin*, persons related to founder of college, school &c., thereby eligible for election &c.; *founder's day*, that on which an institution specially honours the memory of the founder; *founder's prayers*, religious service at which names of founders and benefactors are rehearsed, and thanks given for benefactions; *founders' shares*, those allotted to original promoters of a company.

founder (**II.**), n. **found** (**II.**) & **-er**; cp. Fr. *fondeur*. Person who founds or casts metal or glass. Generally in compounds: *ironfounder* &c.

founder (**III.**), vb. intrans. & trans. M.E. *foundren*, fr. O. Fr. *fondrer*, 'to submerge, sink in, collapse'; irreg. formed fr. *fond*, 'bottom'. See **fund** (**I.**). **1.** intrans. **a** (of ship) To fill with water and go down; **b** (of horse) to fall, to break down, esp. through lameness or fatigue; to sink or stick fast in soft ground; also of rider; **c** (of building, bank of earth; gen.) to give way, sink, collapse. **2.** trans. **a** (esp. of ship or horse) To cause to founder; **b** (golf) to drive (ball) into soft ground.

founder (**IV.**), n., fr. prec. Inflammation of horse's foot; also, rheumatic affection of horse's chest-muscles.

foundership, n. [1. fóundership; 2. fáundəʃip]. **founder** (**I.**) & **-ship**. Quality or state of a founder or establisher.

foundling, n. [1. fóundling; 2. fáundliŋ]. M.E. *fundeling*, fr. O.E. *fund-*, weak grade of *findan* (**find**), cp. **found** (**III.**), & **-ling**; cp. Du. *vondeling*, M.H.G. *vundelinc*. Child found abandoned by, or destitute of, parent or guardian.

foundling hospital, n. Institution or building for the maintenance of foundlings.

foundress, n. [1. fóundres; 2. fáundris]. **founder** (**I.**) & **-ess**. Female founder or establisher.

foundry, foundery, n. [1. fóundri; 2. fáundri]. **found** (**II.**) & **-(e)ry**. **a** Act, process, of founding or casting metal &c.; **b** place, works, where this process is carried out.

fount (**I.**), n. [1. fount; 2. faunt]. M.E., fr. O. Fr. *funt*, fr. Lat. *font-(em)*, 'fountain' &c.; differentiated in early Mod. Engl. fr. **font**. (liter. or poet.) **a** Fountain, spring of water; (fig.) source; **b** font.

fount (**II.**), n. Fr. *fonte*, 'casting (of metal)', fr. *fondre*, **found** (**II.**). Set of printers' type of one size and design; also *font*.

fountain, n. [1. fóuntin; 2. fáuntin]. O. Fr. *funtaine*; cp. Mod. Fr. *fontaine*, fr. L. Lat. *fontāna*, 'spring, fountain', prop. fem. of Lat. adj. *fontānus*, 'pertaining to a spring', fr. *font-(em)*. See **font** & **-an**. **1.** (archaic or poet.) Spring of water naturally issuing from the earth; source of stream. **2.** Artificial jet of water rising or spouting from pipe; group of such jets; structure, generally ornamental, containing one or more streams of water flowing or falling into basin or basins; structure supplying drinking water in public place. **3.** Reservoir, as for oil in lamp, or ink in a *fountain pen*. **4.** (fig.) Source, origin: *the Crown is the fountain of honour*.

fountain head, n. **a** Source, spring, from which stream or river flows; **b** (fig.) source, origin; *the fountain head of knowledge*, person or place whence knowledge comes.

fountain pen, n. Pen containing reservoir from which ink flows to the nib.

four, adj. & n. [1. fōr; 2. fɔ̄]. O.E. *fēower*, M.E. *fower, fowre*, cp. O.S. *fiuwar*, O.H.G. *fior*, Mod. Germ. *vier*, O.N. *fior-ir*, representing an Aryan variant type **petwər*, due perh. to influence of **penkʷe*, 'five', for orig. type **kʷetwər*; cp. also O.E. *fiđer-fōte*, 'four-footed' &c.; Goth. *fidwōr*; fr. same type also Gk. (Aeolian) *pisures*, (Boeotian) *péttares*, & W. *pedwar*; fr. the other type come Lat. *quatuor*, see **quadri-**, Scrt. *čatvắr-aš*, O. Slav. *četyre*, Lith. *keturi*, Gk. *téttares* &c., for **kʷetwar-*, O. Ir. *cethir*. **1.** adj. Three and one; Phr. *to be four*, four years old; *the four corners of the earth* (Bib.), the furthest regions; *within the four corners* (*of an act*), within its range or scope; *within the four seas*, in Great Britain; *to the four winds* (archaic or Bib.), in all directions. **2.** n. **a** Sum of three and one; **b** symbol for this; **c** playing card, domino, face of die &c., marked with four pips: *the four of clubs*; **d** four years: *a child of four*; **e** four o'clock: *come at four*; **f** four horses: *coach and four*; **g** (cricket) hit for four runs; **h** (colloq.) four-oared boat or crew; *fours*, race rowed with such boats; **i** (mil.) *fours*, marching formation four deep: *fours right*; *form fours*; **j** *fours*, 4% stock; **k** Phr. *on all fours*, on hands and knees or feet.

four-ale, n. Ale sold at fourpence a quart.

four-cornered, adj. [1. fōr kórnerd; 2. fɔ̄ kɔ̄nəd]. M.E. *fowre-cornered*. Having four corners.

four-course, adj. **a** (agric.) Having four crops in rotation; **b** (of meal) having four courses.

four-dimensional, adj. Pertaining to, existing in, four dimensions: *four-dimensional space*.

four-flusher, n. (slang, U.S.A.) One who bluffs, at poker, playing and betting as if he held a flush or five cards of the same suit, when he only holds four.

fourfold, adj. & adv. [1. fórfōld; 2. fɔ̄fould]. O.E. *fēowerfeald*, M.E. *fourvald*. **four** & **-fold**. **1.** adj. **a** Repeated, multiplied, four times, quadruple: *a fourfold profit*; **b** having four folds or divisions: *a fourfold leaf*. **2.** adv. Four times, to a fourfold degree.

four-footed, adj. pred. [1. fōr fóoted; 2. fɔ̄ fútid]; attrib. [1. fórfuted; 2. fɔ̄futid]. M.E. *fourfōted*. Having four feet, quadruped.

four-foot way, n. (railways) Space 4 ft. 8½ in. wide, between pair of rails.

fourgon, n. [1. fōōrgon; 2. fūrgɔ̄]. Fr. Baggage wagon.

four-handed, adj. [1. fōr hánded, fór hànded; 2. fɔ̄ hǽndid, fɔ̄ hæ̀ndid]. See note on **four-footed**. **1.** Having four hands, as monkey, quadrumanous. **2.** **a** Played, as game, by four persons; **b** played, as piece of music for piano, by two persons.

four-horse, four-horsed, adj. [1. fōr hōrs(t); 2. fɔ̄ hɔ̄s(t)]. Drawn by four horses.

Fourierism, n. [1. fóorierizm; 2. fúəriərizəm], fr. Fourier, French Socialist (1772–1837). System for reorganizing society.

four-in-hand, adv., adj., & n. **a** Team of four horses harnessed together for drawing coach or carriage; **b** vehicle drawn by four horses, and horses drawing it.

four-legged, adj. Having four legs; pertaining to a quadruped.

four oar, n. Boat with four oars.

four o'clock, n. [1. fōr oklók; 2. fɔ̄r əklɔ́k]. **1.** (of time) Four hours after mid-day or midnight. **2.** Plant, *Mirabilis jalapa*, also called marvel of Peru.

four-part, adj. (mus.) **a** Arranged for four voices: *a four-part song*; **b** quadruple: *four-part time*.

fourpence, n. [1. fórpens; 2. fɔ̄pəns]. **a** Sum of four pennies; **b** British silver coin of this value formerly current, fourpenny piece.

fourpenny, adj. & n. [1. fórpeni; 2. fɔ̄pəni]. **1.** adj. Having the price or value of fourpence: *a fourpenny loaf*; *fourpenny bit, piece* (obs.), British silver coin worth fourpence. **2.** n. **a** Fourpenny piece; **b** ale costing fourpence a quart.

fourpost, adj. [1. fórpōst; 2. fɔ̄poust]. (of a bed) Having four posts at the corners, supporting frame for hanging curtains.

fourposter, n. [1. fōrpóster; 2. fɔ̄póustə]. Fourpost bedstead.

four-pounder, n. [1. fōr póunder; 2. fɔ̄ páundə]. Gun throwing shot weighing 4 lbs.

fourscore, adj. & n. [1. fórskór; 2. fɔ̄skɔ̄]. (archaic) Eighty.

foursome, n. [1. fórsum; 2. fɔ̄səm]. Orig. Scots adj. **four** & **-some**. (golf) Game between two pairs of players, each side using one ball: *mixed foursome*, one with man and woman on each side.

foursquare, adj., adv., & n. [1. fòrskwắr; 2. fɔ̀skwέə]. (archaic) Square.

fourteen, adj. & n. [1. fórtḗn; 2. fɔ̄tín]. O.E. *fēowertȳne, -tēne*, M.E. *fowertēne*. **four** & **-teen**. **a** adj. Four more than ten; **b** n., sum of ten and four; symbol for this.

fourteenth, adj. & n. [1. fórtḗnth; 2. fɔ̄tínþ]. **fourteen** & **-th**, replacing O.E. *fēowertēođa*, M.E. *fourtēođe*. **1.** adj. Ordinal of *fourteen*; **a** next after thirteenth; **b** consisting of a fourteenth. **2.** n. One of fourteen equal parts.

fourth, adj., adv., & n. [1. forth; 2. fɔ̄þ]. O.E. *fēorđa*, M.E. *fēorđe, ferđe*. **four** & **-th**. **1.** adj. Ordinal of *four*; **a** next after third; Phr. *the fourth estate* (colloq.), journalism, the public press; *fourth dimension* (see **dimension, 2**); **b** consisting of a quarter. **2.** adv. In the fourth place. **3.** n. **a** Fourth part, quarter; **b** fourth day of the month; Phr. *the Fourth* (*of July*), (U.S.A.) Independence Day; **c** (mus.) interval of four diatonic degrees; tone separated by this interval from another; harmonic combination of the two; **d** (pl., commerc.) goods of class inferior to thirds.

fourthly, adv. [1. fórthli; 2. fɔ̄þli]. Prec. & **-ly**. In the fourth place (only in enumeration).

four-wheeled, adj. Having four wheels.

four-wheeler, n. (colloq., now rare) Four-wheeled hackney carriage or cab.

fowl (**I.**), n. [1. foul; 2. faul]. O.E. *fugol*, M.E. *fuȝel, fowel*; Common Gmc., cp. O.H.G. *fugal, fogal*, Mod. Germ., Du. *vogel*, Goth. *fugl-s*, O.N. *fugl, fogl*; Gmc. type **fugl-az*, **fogl-az*, perh. for **flug-l-*, fr. **flug-*, weak grade of **fleugan-*, 'to fly', & suff. *-l-*. See **fly** (**I.**). **1.** **a** (archaic or poet.) Bird, generally: *the fowls of the air*; **b** (with qualifying adj.) bird of one of the larger kinds: *sea fowl, water fowl, wild fowl*; (also coll.) *a flock of water fowl*. **2.** Specif. **a** a cock or hen, esp. when full grown, of domestic breeds or their wild congeners: *a barndoor fowl*; *to keep fowls*; *a pair of roast fowls*; *game fowl, jungle fowl*; **b** flesh of mature cock or hen; of any edible bird; in Phr. *neither fish, flesh, nor fowl*.

fowl (**II.**), vb. intrans. O.E. *fuglian*, M.E. *foulen*; fr. prec. (obs.) To shoot, snare, catch, or pursue birds, esp. large or edible birds.

fowler, n. [1. fóuler; 2. fáulə]. O.E. *fugelere*, M.E. *fuȝelere*. **fowl** (**I.**) & **-er**. Person who shoots or traps wild-fowl.

fowling, n. [1. fóuling; 2. fáuliŋ]. M.E. *foulinge*. **fowl** (**II.**) & **-ing**. Act, sport, of killing or trapping wild-fowl.

fowling-piece, n. Light shot-gun for shooting birds.

fowl-run, n. Enclosed piece of ground in which poultry are kept.

fox (**I.**), n. [1. foks; 2. fɔks]. O.E., M.E.; O.H.G. *fuhs*, Gmc. type* *fuχ-sa-*, extended fr. **fuχ-*, cp. O.H.G. *foha*, Goth. *fauhō*, O.N. *fōa*, 'vixen'; possibly cogn. w. Scrt. *puččha*, 'tail, brush'. See also **vixen**. **1.** **a** Animal of dog family, genus *Vulpes*, smaller than wolf, of reddish colour with large bushy tail, preserved in the British Isles in wild state for hunting; one of several related species: *silver fox*; **b** fur of fox. **2.** (fig.) Cunning, crafty, or sly person.

fox (**II.**), vb. trans. & intrans., fr. prec. **A.** trans. **1.** **a** (chiefly P.P.) To discolour (paper) with brown or reddish spots: *the engraving is badly foxed*; **b** to make (beer &c.) sour in the process of fermenting. **2.** To deceive. **B.** intrans. **1.** To behave craftily, as a fox. **2.** To become foxed, as paper. **3.** To become foxed, as beer.

fox and geese, n. Game played on board by two players, one with sixteen pieces, called geese, the other with one, called the fox.

fox-brush, n. Fox's tail.

fox-earth, n. Burrow of fox.

foxglove, n. [1. fóksgluv; 2. fɔ́ksglav.] O.E. *foxes glōfa*, M.E. *foxes glōve*. British wild plant, *Digitalis*, also cultivated in gardens, with tall raceme of purplish red, or white, tubular flowers.

foxhound, n. [1. fóks-hound; 2. fɔ́kshaund]. Parti-coloured hound of powerful breed, used for hunting the fox.

fox-hunt, n. Pursuit of fox on horses with hounds.

fox-hunter, n. Person who hunts the fox.

fox-hunting, n. Act, sport, of hunting the fox.

foxiness, n. [1. fóksines; 2. fɔ́ksinis]. **foxy** & **-ness**. Quality of being foxy.

foxtail, n. [1. fókstāl; 2. fɔ́ksteil]. **1.** Fox's tail or brush. **2.** One of several kinds of grass with bushy spike.

fox terrier, n. Terrier of breed originally used for driving fox from cover; either smooth-coated or wire-haired, and white with yellowish-brown, or black spots.

foxtrot, n. [1. fókstrot; 2. fɔ́kstrɔt]. **a** Kind of easy short-stepping trot of horse; **b** dance of American origin.

foxy, adj. [1. fóksi; 2. fɔ́ksi]. **fox (I.)** & **-y**. **1.** Like a fox; specif. **a** cunning, crafty; **b** of the colour of a fox, reddish or yellowish brown; *foxy hair*, red hair; **c** having a strong, rank smell. **2.** (of paper &c.) Marked with brown spots from damp. **3.** (of alcoholic drink) Sour through bad fermentation.

foyer, n. [1. fwáhyā; 2. fwájei]. Fr., fr. Lat. *focāri-(um)*, adj. neut., 'pertaining to a hearth or fireplace'. See **focus** & **-ary**. Part of theatre for use of public, esp. during intervals.

Fra, n. [1. frah; 2. frā]. Ital. Abbreviated form of **frate**, as form of address of a friar: *Fra Lippo Lippi*.

fracas, n. [1. frákah; 2. frǽkā]. Fr., fr. Ital. *fracasso*, 'a crash', fr. *fracassare*, 'to break in pieces', fr. *fra*, 'among', fr. Lat. *infrā*, 'below' (see **infra**), & *cassāre*, 'to break', fr. Lat. *quassāre*, 'to shake, shatter' (see **quash**). Noisy dispute, brawl; uproar.

fractile, adj. [1. fráktīl; 2. frǽktail], fr. Lat. *fract-(um)*, P.P. type of *frangere*, 'to break' (see next word), & **-ile**. (geol.) Indicating fracture of rocks.

fraction, n. [1. frákshun; 2. frǽkʃən]. M.E. *fraccion*, fr. O. & Mod. Fr. *fraction*, fr. L. Lat. *fractiōn-(em)*, 'a breaking', fr. *frac-(tum)*, fr. **frag-(tom)*, P.P. type of *frangere*, 'to break'; the Lat. base is fr. Aryan **bhreg-* &c., represented in Gmc. by O.E. *brecan* &c., q.v. under **break (I.)**, & **brook (I.)**. **1.** Action of breaking or dividing; specif. (eccles.) ritual breaking of the bread at the consecration of the Eucharist. **2.** Something broken, or broken off; a small detached portion; a very small part, amount, degree; **a** rarely of material objects and usually in neg. sentences: *he did not swerve from his principles by a fraction*; **b** (chem.) substance separated by precipitation or crystallization. **3.** (arith.) Quantity less or more than an integer; *decimal fraction*, one expressed decimally; *vulgar fraction*, one with numerator above, and denominator below a line; *compound fraction*, fraction of a fraction.

fractional, adj. [1. frákshunal; 2. frǽkʃənəl]. Prec. & **-al**. **a** Pertaining to a fraction or fractions: *fractional crystallization, distillation, precipitation*, one producing fractions; *fractional currency*, one consisting of coins or notes which are fractions of the monetary unit; **b** forming a fraction, esp. on the Stock Exchange, less than the accepted unit of 100 shares &c.; **c** (colloq.) consisting of a very small part, insignificant.

fractionally, adv. Prec. & **-ly**. In a fractional manner; by fractions.

fractionary, adj. [1. frákshunari; 2. frǽkʃənəri]. **fraction** & **-ary**; cp. Fr. *fractionnaire*. Fractional, pertaining to fractions; fragmentary.

fractionate, vb. trans. [1. frákshunāt; 2. frǽkʃəneit]. **fraction** & **-ate**. (chem.) To separate into fractions.

fractionation, n. [1. fràkshunā́shun; 2. frækʃənéiʃən]. Prec. & **-ion**. (chem.) Process of fractionating.

fractionize, vb. trans. [1. frákshunīz; 2. frǽkʃənaiz]. **fraction** & **-ize**. To divide or separate into fractions.

fractious, adj. [1. frákshus; 2. frǽkʃəs]. Prob. formed fr. **fraction** in obs. sense, 'brawling, dissension', on anal. of *captious* &c. Peevish, irritable, cross.

fractiously, adv. Prec. & **-ly**. In a fractious manner.

fractiousness, n. See prec. & **-ness**. Quality of being fractious.

fracture (I.), n. [1. frákchur; 2. frǽktʃə]. Fr. *fracture*, n., *fracturer*, vb. trans., fr. Lat. *fractūra*, vbl. n. fr. *fract-*, as in **fraction**, & **-ure**. **1.** Breaking, breach, break, state of being broken; specif. **a** (surg.) breaking of a bone or cartilage: *compound fracture*, one producing rupture of the skin; *simple fracture*, one without this; **b** (phon.) diphthongization of certain O.E. vowels before certain groups of consonants; sometimes called *breaking*. **2.** (min.) Surface of mineral when broken across the plane of cleavage: *flint has a conchoidal fracture*.

fracture (II.), vb. trans. & intrans. See prec. **1.** trans. To break, esp. something hard: *to fracture one's thigh, arm* &c.; *to fracture a pane of glass*. **2.** intrans. To become fractured, be liable to break: *a child's bones fracture easily*.

fraenum, frenum, n. [1. frḗnum; 2. frínəm]. Lat. *frēnum, fraenum*, 'bridle, curb, bit, ligament'. Origin & connexions very doubtful. See second syll. of **refrain (I.)**. Possibly related to Lat. *frendere*, 'to gnash the teeth', in wh. case 'bit' wd. be the earlier sense. The base of *frendere* is Aryan **ghren(dh)-*, whence also **grind**. (anat. and zool.) Small ligament supporting organ or keeping it in place, as under the tongue.

fragile, adj. [1. frájīl; 2. frǽdžail]. Fr., fr. Lat. *fragilis*, fr. *frag-*. See **fraction** & **-ile**; cp. **frail (II.)**. **a** Easily broken, shattered, or damaged; brittle: *a fragile substance*; **b** having a delicate structure or constitution; frail: *fragile health*; **c** not durable or lasting; easily destroyed: *fragile happiness*.

fragility, n. [1. frajíliti; 2. frədžíliti]. M.E., fr. O. Fr. *fragilitē*, fr. Lat. *fragilitāt-(em)*. Prec. & **-ity**. Quality of being fragile; brittleness, delicacy.

fragment, n. [1. frágment; 2. frǽgmənt]. Fr., fr. Lat. *fragment-(um)*; fr. *frag-*. See **fraction** & **-ment**. **a** (of material and non-material things) Piece broken off, detached portion of a thing: *the vase lay in fragments*; *only fragments of the speech could be heard*; *a few fragments of Sappho's poetry survive*; **b** unfinished, incomplete, portion of a literary or artistic work: '*Edwin Drood*' *unfortunately is only a fragment*.

fragmental, adj. [1. fragméntal; 2. frægméntəl]. Prec. & **-al**. (geol.) Consisting wholly or mainly of fragments of older rock.

fragmentarily, adv. [1. frágmentarili; 2. frǽgməntərili]. **fragmentary** & **-ly**. In a fragmentary manner.

fragmentariness, n. [1. frágmentarines; 2. frǽgməntərinis]. See next word & **-ness**. Quality of being fragmentary.

fragmentary, adj. [1. frágmentari; 2. frǽgməntəri]. **fragment** & **-ary**; cp. Fr. *fragmentaire*. Consisting of fragments or detached portions; incomplete: *a fragmentary manuscript*; (geol.) fragmental.

fragrance, n. [1. frā́grans; 2. fréigrəns]. Fr., fr. Lat. *frāgrantia*. See next word & **-ce**. **a** Quality of being fragrant; **b** pleasant, sweet smell; perfume.

fragrant, adj. [1. frā́grant; 2. fréigrənt]. Fr., or Lat. *frāgrant-(em)*, Pres. Part. of *frāgrāre*, 'to emit a smell, be fragrant'; prob. cogn. w. O.H.G. *bracko*, 'a hound that follows scent'. See **brach**. Having a pleasant or sweet smell or odour; sweet-scented; (also fig.) delightful, full of charm: *fragrant memories*.

fragrantly, adv. Prec. & **-ly**. In a fragrant manner; with fragrance.

frail (I.), n. [1. frāl; 2. freil]. M.E. *fraiel*, fr. O. Fr. *frael, freel, fleel*, 'rush basket for fruit,' fr. Lat. *flagellum*, 'vine-shoot, scourge'; in L. Lat. 'basket for fruit'. See **flagellum**, **flail**. **a** Rush basket in which figs, raisins, or other fruit are packed; **b** quantity of raisins, commonly 75 lb., packed in a frail.

frail (II.), adj. M.E. *frēle*, fr. O. Fr. *frele, fraile*, the vernacular form fr. Lat. *fragilis*. Cp. **fragile**. **a** Fragile, not robust or vigorous, weak; having delicate health, prone to illness; **b** (i) easily crushed and broken: *a frail structure*; (ii) easily ruined or destroyed; precarious: *man's life, happiness, is frail*; **c** morally weak, easily tempted or seduced from virtue; (euphemism) unchaste: *fair and frail ladies of the Restoration*.

frailty, n. [1. frā́lti; 2. fréiəlti]. M.E. *frēletē*, fr. O. Fr. *fraileté*, fr. Lat. *fragilitāt-(em)*. See **fragility**. **a** Quality of being frail; **b** a moral weakness, fault, failing.

fraise (I.), n. [1. frāz; 2. freiz]. Fr., orig. 'ruff', of uncertain origin; in sense **2** through Fr. *fraiser*, 'to enlarge (a hole)'. **1.** (fort.) Palisade of pointed stakes in a horizontal or sloping position. **2.** Kind of reamer or instrument for enlarging holes in stone.

fraise (II.), vb. trans., fr. Fr. *fraiser*, fr. prec. To ream or enlarge (hole in stone).

framboesia, n. [1. frambḗzia; 2. fræmbíziə]. Mod. Lat., fr. Fr. *framboise*, 'raspberry', perh. fr. Du. *braam-bezie*, 'blackberry'. See **bramble**, **berry**. The yaws, a tropical skin disease of negroes, producing small tumours resembling raspberries in appearance.

frame (I.), vb. trans. & intrans. [1. frām; 2. freim]. O.E. *framian*, 'to avail, be profitable'; M.E. *frāmien*, 'to be profitable; frame, construct', fr. O.E. *fram*, 'vigorous, bold, excellent', orig. 'pushing forward', fr. *fram* (see **from**); cp. O.N. *frama*, 'to be profitable'. Sense **A, 3**, fr. **frame (II.)**. **A.** trans. **1. a** (now chiefly of intellectual action) To contrive, devise, make, put together, elaborate: *to frame a plan, a theory, a petition, a system of philosophy, a lie* &c.; also **b** (of physical action) *to frame a shelter out of brushwood*; **c** to express in words; construct, put together, build up: *to frame a sentence*; **d** to articulate, pronounce, utter: *his lips could hardly frame the words*. **2. a** To design, adapt, fit for some special purpose (in physical and moral sense): *a structure framed to resist the fiercest storms*; *a man not framed for trials and hardships*; **b** to dispose, arrange, bring into position: *to frame one's lips to flattery*. **3. a** To provide with a frame: *to frame a picture*; **b** to serve as a frame, enclose like a frame: *a lake framed in woods*. **B.** intrans. To progress, develop, take shape: *our plans, preparations, are framing well*.

frame (II.), n., fr. prec. **1.** Something framed and fitted together, a completed, well-knit structure; fabric: '*This universal frame*' (Milton); *the whole frame of the universe*. **2.** The skeleton of a building or structure, the essential structural elements which support the rest, and to which these are fixed or stretched; framework; *the frame of a building, ship, umbrella, airship* &c. **3.** The structure of the human or animal body; used both of the skeleton and of the body as a whole: *a man of iron frame*; *a horse with a good strong frame*. **4.** Construction consisting of a kind of box with solid sides, higher at the back than in front, with a sliding or hinged glazed top, used for forcing or rearing plants which require regular heat: *cucumber frame* &c. **5.** Border of wood, leather, silk, or other material, often carved and gilded when of large size, used to surround a picture: *picture, photograph frame*. **6.** Applied to various objects and appliances, in form of a framework, used for technical purposes: *embroidery frame* &c. **7.** Particular state of mind; mood, mental attitude: *a happy, discontented* &c., *frame of mind*. **8. a** (of non-material things)

Characteristic structure, constitution, mode of organization: *the frame of our legal system*; **b** (rare or obs.) mental or moral complexion, disposition: *a character of noble frame.*

frame-house, n. One that is half timbered; a house with a wooden framework covered with boards.

frameless, adj. [1. frâmles; 2. fréimlis]. **frame (II.)** & **-less.** Having no frame (in any sense).

framer, n. [1. frâmer; 2. fréimə]. **frame (I.)** & **-er.** One who frames (in various senses); **a** *the framers of British liberty*; **b** specif., man who makes and fits frames to pictures: *picture framer.*

frame-saw, n. Narrow saw kept tight by means of a light wooden frame which forms three sides of an oblong of which the saw itself is the fourth.

frame-up, n., fr. **frame (I.)**, to form a plan, scheme. (colloq., U.S.A.) A plot, underhand arranged scheme, swindle.

framework, n. [1. frâmwĕrk; 2. fréimwāk]. **frame (II.)** & **work.** Aggregate of fundamental parts of a structure, or of those which hold the rest together; substructure, skeleton; (also fig.) *the framework of society.*

framing, n. [1. frâming; 2. fréimiŋ]. M.E. *frāminge*, fr. **frame (I.)** & **-ing.** **1.** Action of person or thing that frames. **2.** Thing or material serving as a frame.

franc, n. [1. frangk; 2. fræŋk]. O. & Mod. Fr., prob. fr. Lat. legend *Francorum Rex*, 'King of the French', on gold coin of 1360. See **Frank (I.).** French silver coin, the monetary unit of France of 100 centimes, worth formerly 9½d. at par; corresponding coin or unit of Belgium or Switzerland, and under various names of the Latin monetary union; cp. *lira, peseta* &c.

franchise, n. [1. frânchīz; 2. fræntʃaiz]. M.E., O. & Mod. Fr., fr. Low Lat. type **franc-icia.* **frank (II.)** & **-ise.** **1. a** (law) Immunity, exemption or privilege, granted by the Crown or Government to an individual or corporation; **b** (rare) area to which such privilege applies. **2. a** Full membership of a corporation; **b** full rights of citizenship, esp. the right of voting in parliamentary, municipal, or other public elections; qualification for such right, suffrage: *the parliamentary, municipal, franchise.* Phr. *fancy franchise*, any arbitrary qualification for a vote.

Franciscan, adj. & n. [1. fransískan; 2. frænsískən]. Low Lat. *Franciscān-(us)*, fr. *Francisc-us*, 'Francis', orig. '**French**', & **-an.** **1.** adj. Pertaining to St. Francis of Assisi (1182-1226), or to the Order of St. Francis founded by him in 1209. **2.** n. Friar of the Franciscan Order, Minorite, Grey Friar; member of one of the affiliated orders.

Franco-, pref. [1. frángkō; 2. frǽŋkou]. L. Lat. *Franc-(us)*, **Frank (I.).** Form used in combination, chiefly with national or geographical names, denoting: **a** Frankish: *Franco-Gallic civilization*, that of Gaul under the Franks; **b** French: *the Franco-German*, or *Franco-Prussian War*, that waged (1870–71) between the French and Germans (Prussians).

francolin, n. [1. frángkolin; 2. frǽŋkəlin]. Fr., fr. Ital. *francolino.* One of several Asiatic and African partridges, esp. a species formerly inhabiting S. Europe.

Francophile, -phil, adj. & n. [1. frángkōfīl; 2. frǽŋkoufail]. **Franco-** & **-phile.** **a** adj. Friendly or favourable to the French; **b** n., Francophile person.

Francophobe, adj. & n. [1. frángkōfōb; 2. frǽŋkoufoub]. **Franco-** & **-phobe.** **a** adj. Dreading, or hostile to, the French; **b** n., Francophobe person.

franc-tireur, n. [1. fròn tērĕr; 2. frā tīrʌ́]. Fr., lit. 'free sharpshooter'. Irregular light infantryman.

frangibility, n. [1. frànjibíliti; 2. frændžibíliti]. Next word & **-ity.** Quality of being frangible.

frangible, adj. [1. frânjibl; 2. frǽndžibl]. M.E. *frangebill*, fr. O. Fr. *frangible*, fr. Low Lat. *frangibil-(is)*, fr. Lat. *frangere*, 'to break' (see **fraction**), & **-ible.** Capable of being broken; fragile.

frangipani, n. [1. frànjipáni, -páhni; 2. frændžipǽni, -pāni]; or more rarely **frangipane**, [1. frânjipān; 2. frǽndžipein]. Fr., fr. name of Roman family *Frangipani.* **1.** Kind of pastry made with almonds, sugar, and cream (said to have been invented by the French general, the Marquis Frangipani). **2.** Perfume made from red jasmine.

Frank (I.), n. [1. frangk; 2. fræŋk]. O.E. *Franca*, M.E. *Franke*, 'Frank, Frenchman', fr. L. Lat. *Francus*, O. Fr. *Franc*; cp. O.H.G. *Franko*; the people were named fr. the javelin, O.E. *franca*, O.N. *frakka.* **a** Person belonging to a West Germanic confederation on the Rhine, a branch of which founded the Kingdom of France; **b** (poet.) Frenchman; **c** Greek and Mohammedan generic name for a West European.

frank (II.), adj. Fr. *franc*, 'free' (same as prec.), fr. the Franks having been the only free class in Gaul. Freely revealing one's thoughts or feelings; sincere, candid, ingenuous: *a frank look in one's eyes*; outspoken: *a frank avowal of guilt*; *to be frank with one.*

frank (III.), vb. trans., fr. prec., in sense of 'free of charge'. To render free; in specific sense to free from expense; **a** *to frank a letter*, i.e. by putting one's signature on cover to enable it to be delivered free of postal charges; privilege formerly of Peers of the Realm and members of Parliament; **b** (in gen. use) to pass (a person) in to a meeting &c. free of charge; **c** to pay, be responsible for, a person's expenses for particular purpose.

frank (IV.), n., fr. prec. **a** Signature on cover of letter &c. authorizing free postal delivery; **b** letter or parcel thus sent; **c** right to use post free of charge.

frankalmoigne, -almoign, -almoin, n. [1. fràngkálmoin; 2. fræŋkǽlmɔin]. **frank (II.)** & A.-Fr. *almoine*, variant of O. Fr. *almosne*, Mod. Fr. *aumône*, 'alms' (see **almoner**). (law) Perpetual tenure of land by religious corporation, free of all payment except the duty of praying for the soul of the donor.

Frankenstein, n. [1. frángkenstīn; 2. frǽŋkənstain]. Name of central figure in a novel by Mary Wollstonecraft Shelley, 1818, who created a monster which became his curse; hence, *a Frankenstein's monster*, something which proves disastrous to the producer.

Frankfort black, n. [1. frángkfort blák; 2. frǽŋkfət blǽk], fr. name of German town. Pigment made of carbonized wine-lees &c., used in engraving.

frankincense, n. [1. frángkinsens; 2. frǽŋkinsens]. M.E., fr. O. Fr. *frank encens.* **frank (II.)**, in sense 'luxuriant', otherwise 'pure', & **incense.** Gum resin burning with sweet pungent odour, used in incense, produced by S. Asiatic trees of balsam family.

franklin, n. [1. frángklin; 2. frǽŋklin]. M.E. *frankelein, franklen*, fr. A.-Fr. *fraunkelayn* (cp. Low Lat. *francalānus*), fr. O. Fr. *franc*, 'free' (see **frank (II.)**), & *-lein, -lain*, fr. Gmc. source, corresponding to **-ling** (cp. *chamberlain*). Rather vague term indicating a smaller landowner in the Middle Ages; one below the rank of knight and above that of yeoman, corresponding to a country squire of moderate estate at the present time.

frankly, adv. [1. frángkli; 2. frǽŋkli]. **frank (II.)** & **-ly.** In a frank manner; to be frank: *frankly, I don't like him.*

frankness, n. [1. frángknes; 2. frǽŋknis]. **frank (II.)** & **-ness.** Quality of being frank; candour, ingenuousness; outspokenness.

frankpledge, n. [1. frángkplej; 2. frǽŋkpledž]. A.-Fr. *franc plege*, 'free pledge' (**frank (II.)** & **pledge (I.)**); perh. meaning 'pledge given by free men', or a mistranslation of O.E. *friðborh*, 'peace-pledge'. (hist., law) System by which all free men of a tithing were responsible for the general good behaviour of the members; the system died out under the early Tudors.

frantic, adj. [1. frántik; 2. frǽntik]. M.E. *frenetike, frantik*, fr. O. Fr. *frenetike*, fr. Gk. *phrēn*, 'mind' &c. See **phrenetic.** **1.** (archaic) Violently insane. **2. a** (of persons) Violently excited, esp. with rage, grief, or pain; frenzied, raving; **b** (of actions and behaviour) indicating or caused by frenzy: *frantic appeals for help*; **c** (of circumstances) of a character to render frantic: *frantic muddle.*

frantically, adv. [1. frántikali; 2. frǽntikəli]. Prec. & **-al** & **-ly.** In a frantic manner.

franticly, adv. [1. frántikli; 2. frǽntikli]. Hardly distinguished fr. prec. in rapid speech. (rare) Frantically.

frap, vb. trans. [1. frap; 2. fræp]. Fr. *frapper*, 'to strike, bind', of uncertain origin. (naut.) To bind firmly, to strengthen (ship &c.), by girding with cables.

frappé, adj. [1. frápā; 2. frǽpei]. Fr., P.P. of *frapper.* See prec. (of wine &c.) Iced.

frass, n. [1. fras; 2. fræs]. Germ., 'a devouring', vbl. n. fr. *fressen*, corresponding to O.E. *fretan*, 'to devour'. See **fret (I.).** Refuse or excrement left by insect larvae that bore into and eat wood.

frate, n. [1. fráhtā; 2. frátē]. Ital., 'brother'. See **fraternal.** A friar.

frater, n. See **fratery.**

fraternal, adj. [1. fratĕrnal; 2. frətʌ́n(ə)l]. O. & Mod. Fr. *fraternel*, fr. Low Lat. *frāternāl-(em)*, fr. Lat. *frātern-(us)*, 'brotherly', fr. *frāter*, q.v. under **brother**, & suff. *-n-us*, & **-al.** Brotherly, specif., pertaining to, designating, an association for mutual benefit; much used by Free Masons.

fraternity, n. [1. fratĕrniti; 2. frətʌ́niti]. M.E. *fraternitē*, fr. O. & Mod. Fr. *fraternité*, fr. Lat. *frāternitāt-(em)*, fr. *frātern-(us)*, as in prec. & **-ity.** **1. a** State or condition of being a brother or brothers; **b** quality or character of being brotherly or fraternal. **2.** Association of men united for common harmonious action; specif. **a** religious society, confraternity; **b** fraternal association or benefit society; **c** (Am.) society of students, usually secret, with branches in various colleges &c.: *a Greek-letter fraternity*; **d** (fig., and loosely) class of men with common pursuit or interest: *the angling fraternity*; *the fraternity of the Press.*

fraternization, n. [1. fràternīzáshun; 2. fræ̀tənaizéiʃən]. Next word & **-ation.** Act of fraternizing.

fraternize, vb. intrans. & trans. [1. fráternīz; 2. frǽtənaiz]. Fr. *fraterniser*, fr. Lat. *frātern-(us)*, see **fraternal**, & **-ize.** **a** intrans. To behave as a brother or brothers; hence, to associate with in a spirit of friendly equality; **b** trans., (rare) to cause to behave in a brotherly manner.

fraternizer, n. [1. fráternīzer; 2. frǽtənaizə]. Prec. & **-er.** Person who fraternizes.

fratery, fratry, frater, n. [1. frâtri, frâter; 2. fréitri, fréitə]. M.E. *freitour*, fr. O. Fr. *fraitur*, abbr. fr. *refreitor*, fr. Low Lat. *refectōrium*, **refectory.** (hist.) Refectory of a monastery.

fratricidal, adj. [1. fràtrisídal; 2. frèitrisáid(ə)l]. Next word & **-al.** Pertaining to fratricide (**I.** or **II.**); (fig.) pertaining to, involving, the slaughter of persons by their own kinsmen or fellow-countrymen; internecine: *a fratricidal struggle*, civil war.

fratricide (I.), n. [1. frâtrisīd; 2. fréitrisaid]. Fr., fr. Lat. *frātricīda*, fr. *frātri-*, combining form of *frāter*, **brother**, & **-cide.** Person who wilfully slays his own brother or sister.

fratricide (II.), n. Fr., fr. Lat. *frātricīdium*, see prec. Act of wilfully slaying one's own brother or sister.

frau, n. [1. frou; 2. frau]. Germ., fr. O.H.G. *vrouwa*, fem. of *vrō*; cp. Goth. *frauja*, 'lord'; fr. same base as Lat. *primus*, 'first' (see **primary**), & Engl. **fore** &c. German married woman or widow; title, corresponding to *Mrs.*, prefixed to her name.

fraud, n. [1. frawd; 2. frōd]. M.E., O. & Mod. Fr. *fraude*, fr. Lat. *fraud-(em)*, fr. a base *dhreu-(gh)- &c., 'to deceive'; cp. O.S. *bidriogan*, 'to deceive'; O.H.G. *triogan*; cp. also Mod. Germ. *trügen*, O.S. *gidrog*, 'a phantom, apparition'. O.H.G. *troum*, O.N. *draumr*, 'illusory vision, dream', are prob. related (see **dream (I.)**). **1.** Quality of being deliberately deceptive; trickery, wilful deceit, dishonesty: *his heart is full of fraud.* **2.** An act of wilful deception and dishonesty, carried out with a view to securing some advantage, profit &c. to which one is not entitled, at the expense of another; (law) some statement or suppression of fact in word or deed with intent to deceive. Law Phr. *in fraud of, to the fraud of*, with the result of defrauding; *constructive fraud*, fraud indirectly resulting from an action or omission, virtual fraud; *fraud in fact*, fraud which is the direct or immediate object of an action; *Statute of Frauds*, of 1677, setting out what transactions must be in writing to render them valid in law. Phr. *pious fraud*, act by which a person is deceived with a view to his spiritual or other good. **3.** (colloq.) Person, or thing, that deceives, imposes upon one; that falls short of professions, disappoints reasonable expectation; impostor, cheat, swindler; imposture, imposition: *the phrenologist turned out a pure fraud; much advertised nostrums are often frauds.*

fraudulence, -cy, n. [1. fráwdūlens (i); 2. frṓdjuləns(i)]. O. Fr., fr. Lat. *fraudulentia*, fr. *fraudulent-(us)*. See next word & **-ce** & **-cy**. Quality of being fraudulent.

fraudulent, adj. [1. fráwdūlent; 2. frṓdjulənt]. M.E., fr. Lat. *fraudulent-(us)*, fr. *fraud-(em)*. **fraud**. **a** Acting with fraud, deceitful: *a fraudulent trustee*; **b** having the nature of fraud; done or effected by fraud: *a fraudulent representation, conveyance.*

fraudulently, adv. Prec. & **-ly**. In a fraudulent manner.

fraught, adj. [1. frawt; 2. frōt]. P.P. of obs. vb. M.E. *fraghten*, fr. a L.G. or Flem. source; cp. L.G. *vrachten*, Du. *(be-)vrachten*, fr. L.G., Du. *vracht*, Germ. (fr. L.G.) *fracht*, 'load, cargo', whence M.E. *fraght*. See **freight**. Now only pred. **1.** (in lit. sense only, archaic or poet.) Laden, freighted: *an argosy fraught with precious wares.* **2.** (fig.) Charged, teeming, full of: *a policy fraught with danger; a heart fraught with sorrow.*

fräulein, n. [1. fróilīn; 2. frɔ́ilain]. Germ., fr. M.H.G. *vrouwelīn*, dimin. of *vrouwe*. See **frau**. **1.** German unmarried woman; originally a title of nobility. **2. a** German governess or teacher of German in England; **b** mode of address corresponding to *Miss*, prefixed to name or used alone.

Fraunhofer lines, n. [1. fróunhōfer līnz; 2. fráunhoufə lainz], fr. name of German physicist, d. 1826. The dark lines in the spectrum.

fraxinella, n. [1. fràksinéla; 2. frǽksinélə]. Lat. dimin. of *fraxinus*, 'ash tree'. Cp. Lat. *farnus*, 'ash tree' (fr. *farcsnos); cogn. w. Lith. *biržas*, Scrt. *bhurjaš*, O.E. *birce, beorc*, 'birch', q.v. under **birch**. Perennial plant with white flowers, and leaves somewhat resembling those of the ash.

fray (I.), n. [1. frā; 2. frei]. M.E. *frai*, abbr. fr. *affrai*, see **affray**. **a** Noisy or irregular fight, brawl; **b** (fig.) conflict of any kind: *eager for the fray.*

fray (II.), vb. trans. Abbr. fr. *affray*, vb. See **afraid**. (archaic) To frighten, scare: *to fray birds away.*

fray (III.), vb. trans. & intrans. Fr. *frayer*, fr. O. Fr. *freier*, 'to rub, grate on', fr. Lat. *fricāre*. See **fricative**. **1.** trans. **a** Also *fray out*, to render (cloth &c.) ragged or shabby by much use; especially to ravel the edges: *a frayed collar, shirt*; Phr. *to fray head* (of deer), to rub velvet off new antlers; **b** (fig.) of nerves. **2.** intrans. **a** To become frayed, as cloth; **b** to fray head, as deer.

fraying, n. [1. fráing; 2. fréi-iŋ]. Prec. & **-ing**. **a** Action of wearing or rubbing away; **b** thing frayed off.

frazil, n. [1. frázil; 2. frǽzil]. Canadian Fr. *frasil*, 'snow floating in water', perh. a special sense of Fr. *fraisil*, 'waste charcoal, coal cinders', fr. Low Lat. type *facīle, 'thing pertaining to a torch', fr. Lat. *fac-em, fax*, 'torch, firebrand'. See **facula** & **-ile**. (Canada and America) Ice formed at the bottom of a river &c.; anchor-ice.

frazzle, vb. trans. & intrans. & n. [1. frázl; 2. frǽzl]. Origin unknown (colloq., chiefly Am.) **1.** vb. **a** trans. To fray out, reduce to tatters; **b** intrans., to become frayed or tattered. **2.** n. Action of frazzling; rags and tatters. Phr. (slang) *to beat to a frazzle*, to beat thoroughly.

freak (I.), n. [1. frēk; 2. frīk]. First in Early Mod. Engl.; of doubtful origin, very improbably fr. the O.E. adj. *frec*, 'greedy, bold'; M.E. *frek(e)*, 'daring, insolent'; Common Gmc., cp. O.H.G. *freh*, 'greedy'; Mod. Germ. *frech*, 'insolent'; Goth. *(faihu-)frik-s*, 'greedy of money'; O.N. *frek-r*, 'greedy'. **1.** Absurd or ludicrous prank or whim; eccentric or capricious behaviour. **2. a** Abbreviation from *freak of nature*, rendering Lat. *lusus naturae*, abnormal natural product; monster, monstrosity, sport; **b** (colloq.) grotesque person.

freak (II.), vb. trans. Prob. introduced into literature by Milton, '*The pansy freak'd with jet*' ('Lycidas'), perh. a variant of provinc. Engl. *freck*, 'to dapple', See **freckle**. (poet. or lit.) To fleck, dapple, streak.

freakish, adj. [1. frékish; 2. fríkiʃ]. **freak (I.)** & **-ish**. **a** Given to freaks; whimsical, capricious; **b** resembling a freak; queer, odd.

freakishly, adv. Prec. & **-ly**. In a freakish manner.

freakishness, n. See prec. & **-ness**. Quality of being freakish; whimsicality, quaintness.

freckle, n. & vb. trans. & intrans. [1. frékl; 2. frékl]. Dimin. fr. base *frak-, 'spot', whence M.E. *frakin*, 'a freckle'; cp. O.N. pl. *freknur* &c. Vb. fr. n. **1.** n. Small yellowish spot on exposed surface of human skin, produced by effect of sunburn. **2.** vb. **a** trans. To cover with freckles, produce freckles on; **b** intrans., to become freckled.

freckled, adj. [1. frékld; 2. frékld]. Prec. & **-ed**. Having, covered with, freckles.

freckly, adv. [1. frékli; 2. frékli]. **freckle** & **-y**. Having many freckles.

free (I.), adj. [1. frē; 2. frī]. O.E. *frēo*, M.E. *frē*; O.H.G. *frī*; Goth. *freis*. The word is usually connected w. O.E. *frēon*, 'to love', & *frēond*, 'friend, lover'; Goth. *frijōn*, 'to love', & *frijōnds*, q.v. under **friend**. The connexion in meaning is not very clear, in spite of the meanings expressed by the base in Scrt. *prītá*, 'satisfied' &c., & O. Slav. *prijati, 'to be favourable.' Connexion w. Lat. *prīvus*, 'for oneself, peculiar, particular', has also been suggested, but the phonology is not clear. **1.** Enjoying political liberty; not enslaved, not in bondage or serfdom; not living, or acting, under compulsion: *England is a free country; all men are now free in America*; *free labour*, that of persons not slaves; *free speech*, right to express opinions openly. **2.** Not suffering imprisonment, out of prison, not confined or detained by justice: *the accused left the court a free man.* Phr. *to set, make free*, liberate; *to have, give one, a free hand*, power to act at one's own discretion. **3.** (of the intellect) Devoid of, unhampered by, prejudices, bias, preconceptions; unfettered by convention, tradition, authority; independent: *a free spirit; free play of mind, imagination* &c. **4.** (of action, manners, bearing &c.) **a** Easy, gracious, unconstrained, not stiff or stilted; **b** (in bad sense) not sufficiently restrained; not showing proper sense of decency and decorum; exhibiting undue licence: *his manners and speech were too free for perfect good breeding*; *free love*, cohabitation without marriage. Phr. *free and easy*, casual, unconventional, unceremonious. **5.** (of action and thought) Not compelled by necessity, independent; under one's own control, subject to one's own volition: *you are free to go or stay as you please; the human will is free.* Phr. *to have a free hand*, liberty to act at one's own discretion. **6. a** (of persons) Not occupied or busy; at leisure: *I am busy till six o'clock but free any time after*; **b** (of things) not in use, disengaged, available for use: *have you any rooms, seats &c., free?; to have one's hands free*, empty or disengaged (also fig.). **7. a** (of bodily movements) Not constrained, stiff, or halting; easy, graceful; marked by suppleness: *his gestures were free and unembarrassed; a free action*, esp. of a horse; *free in one's gait* &c.; **b** (fig., of liter. style) flowing, smooth; **c** (of lines or curves in drawing &c.) made with an unhesitating sweep; graceful, elegant. **8. a** Unrestricted, profuse, lavish: *this rose is a very free bloomer; to be free with one's money*; Phr. *(to spend, give &c.) with a free hand*, lavishly; **b** unconditioned, unlimited, absolute: *a free pardon; to make free use of*; **c** ready, spontaneous: *a free offer.* **9. a** Not bound by rules, irregular; not reducible to a hard and fast system: *free verse*; Phr. *a free fight*, confused, general mêlée; **b** not adhering with exactness to an original or model, not strictly literal or exact: *a free translation; a free copy, likeness* &c. **10. a** Not costing anything, obtainable without payment or price: *the beauties of Nature are free to all; all the seats in this church are free; to have free drinks all round*; Phr. *(to make a person) free of one's house* &c., give full permission to use; **b** not liable to be charged for, exempt from: *free of duty*, not taxable by customs; *free imports*, those on which no duty is payable; *free of income tax*, not liable to tax, having the tax already paid. **11. a** Unobstructed, clear of obstacles and encumbrances: *the way is free for an advance*; also (fig.) *to leave the way free for progress*; **b** unattached, not fastened, loose: *to leave one end of a rope free*; **c** (chem.) separate, uncombined: *free hydrogen.* **12.** (philol.) *Free accent*, one which is not placed always upon the same syllable of the same word, but whose position may vary in inflexion &c. **13.** *Free from*, **a** exempt from, lacking: *a day free from wind*; **b** delivered from, quit of, protected from: *free from unwelcome attentions; I want a seat free from draught; free from pain; free from encumbrances.* **14.** *Free of* **a** having passed beyond, outside of: *we're not free of the harbour, the suburbs, the station, yet*; **b** delivered, safe, from; clear of: *to be free of debt; we shall be free of infection in a week.*

free (II.), adv., fr. prec. Freely, in various senses: **1.** *To run free*, without obstruction. **2.** Without charge, gratis: *all members admitted free.*

free (III.), vb. trans. O.E. *frēon*. See **free (I.)**. **1.** To set free, set at liberty; to liberate. In various senses: **a** *to free a person from restraint*; **b** to deliver from: *to free the land from oppression*; **c** *to free a person from a charge, accusation* &c., to exonerate, acquit. **2.** To relieve from embarrassment, hindrances, obstacles: **a** (in physical sense) *to free one's hands from fetters* &c.; **b** (in fig. or moral sense) *to free a person from debt; to free the mind from anxiety* &c.

free and easy, adj. & n. **1.** adj. Informal, easy-going, unconstrained, unceremonious. **2.** n. (colloq.) Informal gathering or entertainment, esp. smoking concert.

freebench, n. [1. frébénsh; 2. fríbénʃ]. (law) Widow's dower derived from her husband's copyholds.

freeboard, n. [1. frébord; 2. fríbɔ̄d]. Part of side of ship between water-line and gunwale or deck.

freeboot, vb. intrans. [1. frébōōt; 2. fríbūt]. Back-formation, fr. **freebooter**. (rare) To be a freebooter.

freebooter, n. [1. frébōōter; 2. fríbūtə]. Prob. through Flem., fr. Du. *vrijbuiter*, agent-n., fr. *vrijbuiten*, 'to rob, plunder', fr.

vrijbuit, 'plunder'. See **free** (I.) & **booty.** Cp. **filibuster.** Person who plunders, or wages war for plunder, by sea or land, without authority from the state.

freebooting, n. [1. frḗbōōting; 2. fríbūtiŋ]. Action of a freebooter.

freeborn, adj. [1. frḗborn; 2. fríbɔ̄n]. Born free; not born in slavery or serfdom.

Free Church, n. & adj. **a** n. Church which is not established, or officially connected with the State: *the Free Churches*, the Nonconformist bodies in England; *the Free Church (of Scotland)*, part of the Presbyterian Church which seceded from the Scottish Establishment (reunited 1929); **b** adj., pertaining to a Free Church or Churches.

free city, n. **a** (hist.) City of the Holy Roman Empire, exempt from feudal obligations to any but the Emperor; **b** one of the three German cities of this class, Hamburg, Lübeck, and Bremen, which have maintained their liberties since the Middle Ages.

free company, n. One of the bands or armies of mercenary soldiers of the Middle Ages, hired by various states for their wars.

freedman, n. [1. frḗdman; 2. frídmæn]. Former slave who has been manumitted, or liberated from servitude.

freedom, n. [1. frḗdum; 2. frídəm]. O.E. *frēodōm*, M.E. *frēdōm*, used by Chaucer, 'C.T. Prologue', 46, in sense of 'politeness, good breeding'. **free** (I.) & **-dom. 1.** State of being free in any sense. **2.** Special senses: **a** frankness; unceremonious behaviour; excessive familiarity; act of this nature: *to use freedoms with one*; **b** easy, unconstrained action; boldness, unconventionality: *to paint, speak, with freedom.* **3. a** Rights and privileges of a corporate body, as a city or company; honorary grant of these: *the freedom of a city*; **b** (fig.) free permission to use something belonging to another: *the freedom of the house*; *Freedom of the Seas*, (international law) doctrine of the immunity of neutral shipping from interference by a belligerent navy in time of war.

free-hand, adj. & n. (art) **a** adj. Drawn, traced by the hand, with easy, sweeping movements: *free-hand drawing*; **b** n., free-hand drawing.

free-handed, adj. Generous, liberal, lavish.

free-hearted, adj. M.E. *frēhertid.* Frank, open, generous, unreserved in character.

free-heartedly, adv. Prec. & **-ly.** In a free-hearted manner.

freehold, n. [1. frḗhōld; 2. fríhould]. **free** (I.) & **hold** (I.). **a** Tenure of estate as absolute property, in fee-simple, fee-tail, or for life; similar tenure of office; **b** estate or office thus held.

freeholder, n. [1. frḗhōlder; 2. fríhouldə]. Prec. & **-er.** Possessor of a freehold.

free house, n. A public-house not 'tied' to a particular brewery for its beer &c.

free kick, n. (football) Kick allowed without interference, as penalty for breach of rules by other side.

freelance, n. [1. frḗláhns; 2. frílā́ns]. **a** (hist.) Soldier who fought as mercenary for any one who would pay him for his service; **b** (fig.) one who acts as his principles or inclinations prompt; one not controlled by a particular party, or body of authority; **c** journalist, writer on miscellaneous subjects, not attached to a particular paper &c.

free liver, n. Person who indulges his appetites freely; person addicted to the pleasures of the table.

free living, n. Gratification of one's appetites, unrestricted indulgence in pleasure.

freely, adv. [1. frḗli; 2. fríli]. O.E. *frēolīce.* **free** (I.) & **-ly.** In a free manner (in all senses).

freeman, n. [1. frḗmən; 2. frímən]. O.E.; M.E. *frēoman.* **free** (I.) & **man. 1.** Man who is not a slave, serf, or vassal; one legally independent. **2.** Person enjoying the full privileges of membership of a corporate body: *a freeman of the City of Oxford.*

freemartin, n. [1. frḗmartin; 2. frímātin]. Origin doubtful. Imperfectly developed cow-calf, usually twin of a bull.

freemason, n. [1. frḗmāsn; 2. fríméisn]. Prob. called *free* because allowed to move from town to town. **1.** (hist.) Member of association of skilled masons and builders. **2.** Member of an ancient fraternity, Free and Accepted Masons, practising benevolence and brotherliness, which possesses certain distinguishing signs and words, and carries out certain symbolic acts at its meetings.

freemasonry, n. [1. frḗmāsnri; 2. fríméisnri]. Prec. & **-ry. 1. a** System, organization of freemasons; **b** doctrines inculcated by and symbolical observances of freemasons. **2.** (fig.) Instinctive understanding between persons, based on like experience &c.

free on board, adj. Of goods, abbr. F.O.B. With all charges paid for delivery when put on board ship, train, or other means of conveyance.

freesia, n. [1. frḗzia; 2. fríziə]. Mod. Lat. generic name, after E. M. Fries, Swedish botanist (1794–1878). S. African bulbous plant of iris family, cultivated in greenhouses, with racemes of white or pale yellow flowers.

free-spoken, adj. Habitually speaking frankly and without reserve; outspoken.

free-spokenness, n. Prec. & **-ness.** Quality of being free-spoken.

freestone, n. [1. frḗstōn; 2. frístoun]. M.E. *freestōn*, transl. of Fr. *pierre franche.* Any kind of stone that can be worked or sawn freely without breaking; usually sandstone or limestone.

free-stone, n. Kind of peach in which the flesh is readily detached from the stone.

freethinker, n. [1. frḗthíngker; 2. fríþíŋkə]. Person who rejects all authority in religious matters; one who professes to form conclusions on such matters without the bias of preconceptions or traditions.

freethinking, n. [1. frḗthíngking; 2. fríþíŋkiŋ]. Habits of thought of a freethinker.

free thought, n. Thought on religious matters which is independent of authority or tradition.

free-tongued, adj. Free-spoken.

free trade, n. **1.** Trade carried on without any artificial encouragement, restriction, or regulation by Government; specif., international trade unrestricted by protective or preferential duties, bounties, or monopolies. **2.** (obs. or archaic) Smuggling.

free trader, n. **a** Adherent of the policy of free trade; **b** (obs.) smuggler.

free-wheel, n. & vb. intrans. **a** n. Driving wheel of bicycle, so constructed that it will rotate when the pedals are at rest; similar device in other machines; **b** vb. to move forward on a free-wheel bicycle with the pedals at rest.

free will, n. & adj. **1.** n. **a** Human will acting spontaneously, or without external compulsion, pressure, or influence. Phr. *of one's own free will*, voluntarily; **b** power of the human will (denied by determinists and predestinarians) to choose, either without any motive, or from motives created by the will itself. **2.** adj. **a** Spontaneous: *a free-will offering*; **b** pertaining to, holding, the doctrine of free will: *the Free Will Baptists.*

freewoman, n. [1. frḗwooman; 2. fríwumən]. **a** Woman who is not a slave or serf; **b** woman who possesses the freedom of a city.

freeze (I.), vb. intrans. & trans. [1. frēz; 2. friz]. O.E. *frēosan*, M.E. *frēsen*; Gmc. type **freusan-*, whence also O.H.G. *freosan*, Mod. Germ. *frieren*, O.N. *frjōsa*; cp. Goth. *frius*, 'frost'; fr. Aryan base **preus-*, 'to burn', whence also Scrt. *pluš*, 'to burn', Lat. *prūrīre*, 'to itch', *pruīna*, 'hoar-frost', *prūna*, 'live coal'. See **prurient. A.** intrans. **1. a** (impers.) to be cold enough to turn water into ice, to be frosty: *it froze hard last night*; **b** (of water) to become ice, wholly or partially: *a pond freezes over*, is covered with ice; (of substance which is ordinarily fluid) to be congealed or solidified by cold: *the mercury froze in the bulb*; **c** (of a solid thing containing or surrounded by moisture) to become rigid, stiff, or fixed by frost: *birds froze to their perches*; *hair freezes together*; *to freeze to death.* **2.** (fig.) **a** To feel very cold: *I am freezing*; **b** to be chilled or made momentarily rigid by some powerful emotion, terror: *the sight made my blood freeze*; **c** to become rigid or impassive: *his face froze into a sullen stare.* **B.** trans. **1. a** To convert (water or other substance ordinarily fluid) into a solid by lowering temperature; to congeal with cold; **b** to stiffen, harden, fix: *the road is frozen hard*; *ships were frozen in*; Phrs. *to be frozen to death*: (i.) to die from frost, (ii.) feel very cold; *to be frozen up*, to be rendered immovable or inactive by frost; **c** to preserve (meat &c.) by refrigeration. **2.** (fig.) To chill with terror; to unnerve, damp the ardour of, paralyse: *to freeze one with a frown.* Phr. *to freeze one's blood*, strike one with terror or horror. **C.** In phrases with adverb or preposition. *Freeze on to*, trans., (slang) to cling tightly to. *Freeze out*, trans., (slang) (of obnoxious person, business rival &c.), to get rid of, shake off, cause to give in.

freeze (II.), n., fr. prec. State of freezing; frost.

freezer, n. [1. frḗzer; 2. frízə]. **freeze** (I.) & **-er.** Person or thing that freezes; specif. **a** refrigerator; **b** (Austral. colloq.) one who breeds or deals in sheep for freezing.

freezing, adj. [1. frḗzing; 2. fríziŋ], fr. Pres. Part. of **freeze. a** That freezes, frosty; very cold; **b** (fig., of manners &c.) extremely chilling, icy; distant, repellent.

freezingly, adv. Prec. & **-ly.** (chiefly fig.) In a freezing manner.

freezing machine, n. Apparatus for making ice-cream, by use of a freezing mixture.

freezing mixture, n. Mixture, as of ice or snow with common salt, used to produce a low temperature.

freezing-point, n. Temperature at which a liquid congeals and solidifies; specif., that at which water freezes, 32° Fahrenheit.

freight (I.), n. [1. frāt; 2. freit]. M.E. *freyght, freit, freyte*, prob. fr. M. Du. *vrecht*, variant of M. & Mod. Du. *vracht.* See **fraught.** Gmc. type prob. **fra-aihtiz*, **fra-*, being related to **for-**, & **aihtiz*= O.E. *ǣht*, 'possession, property', vbl. n. fr. *agan*, **owe.** *Freight* may be influenced by O. & Mod. Fr. *fret*, 'hire of ship, cargo', fr. the corresponding O.H.G. *frēht*, 'earnings, hire'. **1. a** Hire, or charge for hire, of ship or other vessel for conveyance of goods; **b** conveyance, transport, of goods by water; **c** cargo, lading of vessel. **2.** (Am.) Charge for transport; transport, load, carried by land or water, esp. by railway; (attrib.) *freight train*, goods train; *freight car*, goods truck. **3.** (fig.) Load, burden.

freight (II.), vb. trans., fr. prec. **a** To hire, let out vessel (Am. also vehicle) for transport; **b** to load (vessel &c.).

freightage, n. [1. frātij; 2. fréitidž]. **freight** (I.) & **-age. a** Hire of vessel for transporting goods by water; **b** charge for transport of goods by water (Am. also by land); **c** action of freighting.

freighter, n. [1. frāter; 2. fréitə]. **freight** (II.) & **-er. 1. a** Person who charters and loads a vessel, or for whom a cargo or load is conveyed; **b** agent who transports goods by sea (Am. also by land). **2.** Cargo vessel.

French, adj. & n. [1. frensh; 2. frenʃ]. O.E. *Frenčisč*, M.E. *Frenkisch, Frensch*, fr. O.E. *Franca* (**Frank** (I.)) & **-ish**; cp. Low Lat. *Francisc-us.* **1.** adj. Pertaining to France or its people; having some quality of these. Phr. *to take French leave*, to depart without notice or permission. *French marigold*, garden variety like African marigold with red centre; *French partridge*, red-legged partridge; *French roll* or *bread*, kind of fancy bread; *French sash*, casement opening on hinges. **2.** n. **a** The French language; attrib., as *French master*; **b** (pl.) *the French*, the French people.

French bean, n. (Cook's and greengrocer's term.) Haricot, kidney bean; runner bean.
French chalk, n. Kind of steatite used for marking cloth, removing grease &c.
French grey, n. Purplish grey pigment.
French horn, n. Wind instrument derived from hunting horn, consisting of coiled metal tube with wide trumpet-like end.
Frenchification, n. [1. frènshifikáshun; 2. frènʃifikéiʃən]. **French** & link *-i-* & **-fication**. (colloq.) Action or process of Frenchifying.
Frenchify, vb. trans. [1. frénshifī; 2. frénʃifai]. See prec. & **-fy**. (colloq.) To render French; give French character to; to Gallicize.
Frenchman, n. [1. frénshman; 2. frénʃmən]. **a** Male person of French nationality or origin; **b** French ship.
Frenchness, n. [1. frénshnes; 2. frénʃnis]. Condition or quality of being French or like the French.
French polish, n. & vb. trans. **a** n. (cap.) Polish for wood, containing shellac in solution; **b** vb., usually *french-polish*, to treat with French polish.
french-polisher, n. Prec. & **-er**. Person whose trade it is to french-polish.
French window, n. A door, glazed wholly or in part, reaching to the floor and opening from a room on to a garden, balcony &c.
Frenchwoman, n. [1. frénshwooman; 2. frénʃwumən]. Female person of French nationality or origin.
frenetic, adj. [1. frenétik; 2. frenétik]. Earlier form of **frantic**. See **phrenetic**.
frenum, n. See **fraenum**.
frenzied, adj. [1. frénzid; 2. frénzid]. **frenzy** & **-ed**. Filled with, arising from, frenzy; frantic, infuriated, wildly excited: *frenzied efforts*.
frenziedly, adv. Prec. & **-ly**. In a frenzied manner.
frenzy, n. & vb. trans. [1. frénzi; 2. frénzi]. M.E., O. Fr. *frenesie* (Mod. Fr. *frénésie*), fr. Low Lat. *phrenesia*, fr. Lat. *phrenēsis*, fr. Late Gk. *phrénēsis*, for class. *phrenîtis*, 'inflammation of the brain, delirium', fr. *phren-*, stem of *phrén*, 'midriff, heart; senses, mind'. See **phrenetic**. **1.** n. **a** Wild or violent excitement; frantic or maddened condition; loss of mental balance or control, esp. through rage, grief, or pain; **b** paroxysm of madness. **2.** vb. (rare, except P.P.) To render frantic, fill with frenzy.
frequence, n. [1. frḗkwens; 2. fríkwəns]. Fr. *fréquence*, fr. Lat. *frequentia*. See **frequent**. Frequency.
frequency, n. [1. frḗkwensi; 2. fríkwənsi]. Lat. *frequentia*, 'a crowding, crowd'. **frequent (I.)** & **-cy**. **1.** State of being frequent; repeated occurrence; constant repetition, recurrence of action or process. **2.** (phys.) Rate of recurrence, with time unit expressed or understood; specif., of cycles of alternation of electric current: *a frequency of 25 (per second)*; (attrib.) *a high, low, frequency current*, qq.v. under **high, low frequency**.
frequent (I.), adj. [1. frḗkwent; 2. fríkwənt]. Fr. *fréquent*, fr. Lat. *frequent-(em)*, 'constant, repeated, crowded, numerous', properly Pres. Part. of a lost vb. **frequēre*, 'to cram', connected w. *farcīre*, 'to cram, stuff full'. See **farce (I.)** **1.** (of action) Often, constantly, repeated; carried out often and at short intervals: *a frequent laugh, jest; frequent teaching*. **2.** (of events, occurrences, phenomena generally) Constantly recurring: *frequent visits, thunderstorms; frequent pain*. **3.** (of persons) Constantly performing some action, doing something with frequency: *a frequent visitor; a frequent theatre-goer* &c. **4.** (of objects) Constantly, frequently found, seen &c.; hence, existing in large numbers; numerous, plentiful: *fossils are frequent in limestone; holes are frequent in old socks*.
frequent (II.), vb. trans. [1. frekwént; 2. frikwént]. Fr. *fréquenter*, fr. Lat. *frequentāre*, 'to resort to or do frequently, to crowd, celebrate', fr. *frequent-*, q.v. under prec. **1. a** To resort to, visit, often or habitually: *to frequent a library, a house, a preacher, concerts, the society of a person*; **b** to visit, inhabit, or haunt in large numbers, crowds, or flocks: *the ruins are frequented by jackdaws; tourists frequent the district*. **2.** (Gallicism) To associate constantly with, be often in company of: *to frequent learned men; I know him but I don't frequent him much*.
frequentation, n. [1. frèkwentáshun; 2. frìkwentéiʃən]. Fr. *fréquentation*, fr. Lat. *frequentātiōn-(em)*. Prec. & **-ation**. Action or practice of frequenting.
frequentative, adj. & n. [1. frekwéntativ; 2. frikwéntətiv]. L. Lat. *frequentātīv-(us)*, fr. *frequentāt-*, P.P. stem of *frequentāre* (see **frequent (II.)**) & **-ive**; cp. Fr. *fréquentatif*, fem. *-ive*. (gram.) **a** adj. Expressing or denoting frequent repetition, hence often intensity, of an action: *a frequentative verb*; **b** n., word (usually vb.) having a frequentative sense: *wrestle is a frequentative of wrest*.
frequenter, n. [1. frekwénter; 2. frikwéntə]. **frequent (II.)** & **-er**. Person who frequents.
frequently, adv. [1. frḗkwentli; 2. fríkwəntli]. **frequent (I.)** & **-ly**. Often, constantly.
fresco, n. & vb. trans. [1. fréskō; 2. fréskou]. Ital., lit. 'fresh', fr. O.H.G. *frisc*. See next word. **1.** n. **a** Method of painting in water colour on fresh plaster, used in mural decoration: *a painting in fresco*; **b** picture thus painted. **2.** vb. **a** To decorate (wall) with painting in fresco; **b** to paint (picture, subject) in fresco.
fresh (I.), adj. [1. fresh; 2. freʃ]. O.E. *fersc*, M.E. *fersch, fresch*, O.H.G. *frisc*; perh. fr. an old compound, Gmc. **fra-* & **i-*, 'going, coming forth', & *-sk*, adj. suff.; Aryan **pro-*, **i-* as in Lat. *īre*, 'to go'. See **pro-** & **iterate**. The word wd. then be cogn., apart fr. the suff., w. Goth. *fraiw*, 'seed, race, offspring'. **1. a** Newly grown, sprung; young, full of life, vigorous: *the fresh shoots of a plant*; **b** newly produced; just made: *fresh eggs, milk, flowers; bring some fresh tea, toast*; contrasted with *stale*. **2.** Preserving original soundness, vigour, beauty, health &c. unimpaired: (of food) **a** free from taint, odour, putrescence: *this meat is not very fresh*; specif. **b** not preserved, pickled, salted: *fresh meat is essential to health*; **c** (of bodily strength) not exhausted, vigorous: *to feel quite fresh after a long march*; (of a horse) lively, frisky; Phr. *as fresh as paint*, very fresh and strong; **d** (of colours, appearance of objects &c.) not worn by usage; unfaded, untarnished, unspoilt; clean, not soiled; vivid: *the colours in the paintings at Pompeii are still fresh; the binding, tapestry, chintz &c. doesn't look very fresh*; Phr. *fresh paint*, newly put on, not dry; (of meat) *too fresh*, not sufficiently hung; tough; **e** (of the complexion) high-coloured, blooming, suggestive of health. **3.** (of wind, weather, atmosphere, air &c.) **a** Cool, invigorating, brisk; **b** (of wind, breeze) strong, blowing with force; **c** specif., of air, pure, untainted, not exhausted; Phr. *in the fresh air*, out in the open, out of doors. **4.** Not salt: **a** *fresh water*, as distinct from *sea water*; **b** *fresh butter*, unsalted. **5.** Novel, not known, seen, experienced, before: *there is nothing fresh to tell; to see something fresh; no fresh news; to throw fresh light on a subject; to make a fresh start*. **6.** (of mental qualities and activities) **a** Vigorous, alert, original, spontaneous; not jaded or stale: *to preserve one's mind fresh in spite of one's numerous preoccupations*; **b** exhibiting qualities of originality, spontaneity &c.: *his remarks were always fresh and stimulating*. **7.** (slang) **a** Too lively from effects of strong drink; slightly tipsy; **b** (Am.) impudent, inclined to take liberties. **8.** Inexperienced, untrained, new; unaccustomed to one's work; green: *a fresh hand*, inexperienced person.
fresh (II.), n., fr. prec. **1.** An increased rush of water, freshet. **2.** Stream of fresh water flowing into salt water. **3.** Fresh time or period: *the fresh of the morning*.
fresh-blown, adj. (of flower) Newly blown.
fresh-coloured, adj. Having a fresh, bright and clear colour or complexion.
freshen, vb. trans. & intrans. [1. fréshen; 2. fréʃən]. **fresh (I.)** & **-en**. **1.** trans. **a** To make fresh, refresh, revivify (in various senses); also *freshen up*; **b** to remove salt from. **2.** intrans. To become fresh or fresher: *flowers freshen after rain; the wind is freshening*; also *freshen up*.
fresher, n. [1. frésher; 2. fréʃə]. **fresh (I.)** & **-er**. (univ. slang) Freshman.
freshet, n. [1. fréshet; 2. fréʃit]. **fresh (II.)** & **-et**. **1.** Sudden flood descending bed of river. **2.** Freshwater stream flowing into the sea.
freshly, adv. [1. fréshli; 2. fréʃli]. M.E. *freschlī*. **fresh (I.)** & **-ly**. **a** In a fresh manner (in various senses); **b** (followed by P.P.) newly, recently: *freshly painted, washed*.
freshman, n. [1. fréshman; 2. fréʃmən]. Student in his first year at a university or college; first-year man.
freshness, n. [1. fréshnes; 2. fréʃnis]. M.E. *freshnesse*. **fresh** & **-ness**. Quality of being fresh (in various senses): *freshness of the morning, of colour, of imagination* &c.
fresh-run, adj. (of a salmon, grilse) Newly come from the sea.
freshwater, adj. [1. fréshwawter; 2. fréʃwōtə]. Pertaining to, inhabiting, fresh water, water that is not salt: *freshwater fish, mussel; a freshwater fisherman*. Phr. *freshwater sailor*, one who only navigates rivers or lakes; (contemptuous) incompetent sailor.
fret (I.), vb. trans. & intrans. [1. fret; 2. fret]. O.E. *fretan*, M.E. *freten*, 'to devour, consume', fr. **for-** & **eat**; cp. Du. *freten*, Germ. *fressen*, Sw. *fräta*, also Goth. *fra-itan*. **A.** trans. (in physical sense mainly). **1. a** (archaic or poet.) To eat away, keep on gnawing or biting at: '*Like a moth fretting a garment*'; (of horse) to champ: *to fret the bit* (also *fret at*); **b** to erode, corrode, consume: *a knife fretted with rust*; **c** (fig.) to wear out, fray: '*Fretted fortunes*' (Shakespeare); **d** to make (passage) by eating or wearing away. **2.** (of wind &c.) To agitate, ruffle (surface of water). **3.** (usual sense, of action on the mind) **a** To cause grief, anxiety, to; to harass, chafe, vex, irritate, worry: *it frets me to know that he is unhappy; to fret one's life (out) with vain regrets; a heart fretted by care and anxiety*; **b** (reflex.) *to fret oneself to death*. **B.** intrans. (now only used of mental process) To grieve, feel anxiety, or mental distress generally; to be fretted, to repine, be filled with sadness; to worry, be in a state of grief, anxiety, unhappiness; to complain, be querulous: *since her husband's death she frets continually; you have nothing to fret about*.
fret (II.), n., fr. prec. **1.** The mental state or action of fretting: *in a constant state of fret*. **2.** That which causes one to fret; worry, anxiety, harassment: '*The weariness, the fever and the fret*' (Keats).
fret (III.), n. M.E. *fret, frette*, 'ornament, esp. of interlacing wire'; cp. O. Fr. *frete*, 'interlaced work, saltire' (Mod. Fr. *frette*, 'ferrule, hoop, saltire'); of uncertain origin, perh. fr. Low Lat. type **ferretta*, dimin. fr. Lat. *ferrum*, 'iron' (see **ferro-** & **-ette**). It seems highly probable that the M.E. word was at least influenced by, if not directly derived from, O.E. *frætwa*, 'ornament, trappings'. See also **fret (IV.)**. **1. a** Decorative pattern, usually forming border, in textiles, inlaid work, architecture &c., consisting of continuous series of short straight lines or bars joining one another or interlacing, usually at right angles; **b** (loosely) complicated, net-like carved work, esp. in Gothic architecture. **2.** (her.) Interlacing bands in saltire. **3.** (perh. a different word) Ridge or bar, often of wire, crossing finger-board of stringed instrument, to assist fingering.

fret (IV.), vb. trans. M.E. *fretten, fretien*, 'to adorn with interlaced work', fr. O. Fr. *freter*, 'to interlace, adorn', fr. *frete*, q.v. under prec. The M.E. vb. was almost certainly also associated w. the M.E. *(ȝe)fratewen*, 'to adorn', fr. O.E. *(ġe)frætewian, fretwian*; cp. O.S. *fratahōn*, 'to adorn'; Goth. *(us-)fratwjan*, 'to fit out'. The origin of this is doubtful. See prec. **a** To decorate with interlacing or net-like pattern, to variegate; **b** specif. (archit.) to decorate (ceiling, vault &c.) with pattern carved in relief: '*The long drawn aisle and fretted vault*' (Gray's 'Elegy').

fretful, adj. [1. frétfool; 2. frétfəl]. **fret (II.)** & **-ful**. Inclined to fret; irritable, querulous, complaining.

fretfully, adv. Prec. & **-ly**. In a fretful manner.

fretfulness, n. See prec. & **-ness**. Quality of being fretful.

fretsaw, n. [1. frétsaw; 2. frétsɔ̄]. **fret (IV.)** & **saw (I.)**. Fine narrow saw, fixed in rectangular frame, used for cutting out patterns in thin boards of wood or plates of metal &c.

fretted, adj. [1. frétid; 2. frétid], fr. P.P. of **fret (IV.)**. Adorned with fretwork, carving, or tracery.

fretty, adj. [1. fréti; 2. fréti], fr. P.P. of O. Fr. *freter*, 'to interlace'. See **fret (III. & IV.)**. (her.) Covered with a device representing narrow laths interlaced.

fretwork, n. [1. frétwërk; 2. frétwɅ̄k]. **fret (IV.)** & **work**. Ornamental carving in wood, cut out with a fretsaw.

Freudian, adj. [1. fróidian; 2. fróidiən]. Of, relating to, agreeing with, the theories and practice of Sigmund Freud, Austrian doctor, b. 1856, deviser of the method of psychoanalysis in treatment of nervous diseases &c.

friability, n. [1. frìabíliti; 2. fràiəbíliti]. Next word & **-ity**. State, quality, of being friable.

friable, adj. [1. fríabl; 2. fráiəbl]. Lat. *friābilis*, 'crumbling', fr. *friāre*, 'to crumble, rub, away'; fr. **mri-*, cp. Scrt. *mriyati*, 'dissolves'. Liable to crumble to powder, easily crumbled or pulverized.

friableness, n. [1. fríablnes; 2. fráiəblnis]. Prec. & **-ness**. Friability.

friar, n. [1. fríar; 2. fráiə]. M.E. *frēre*, fr. O. Fr. *freire, frere*, 'brother', fr. Lat. *frātr-(em), frāter*, 'brother'. See **fraternal** & **brother**. **1.** Member of one of several religious orders living under rule and bound by vows of chastity and poverty: *Black Friars, White Friars* &c. **2.** (print.) Patch of pale print on a page.

friar's balsam, n. Preparation applied to wounds; compound tincture of benzoin.

friar's cowl, n. Common plant or weed; also called *cuckoo pint*.

friary, n. [1. fríari; 2. fráiəri]. **friar** & **-ry**. Convent of friars.

fribble, vb. intrans. & n. [1. fríbl; 2. fríbl]. Perh. orig. imitative of stammering, in wh. sense it was formerly used; also influenced by Fr. *frivole*. See **frivolous**. **1.** vb. To fool away time; spend life in a futile, aimless, trivial manner. **2.** n. A futile, frivolous, ineffective person.

fricandeau, n. [1. fríkondō; 2. fríkãdou]. Fr. Stew of turkey or veal.

fricassee, n. & vb. trans. [1. frìkasḗ; 2. frìkəsī́]. Fr., origin uncertain; perh. connected w. Lat. *frīgere*, 'to fry' (see **fry (II.)**), influenced by *fricāre*, 'to rub' (see next word). **1.** n. Dish made of meat cut up into pieces and stewed with gravy and seasoning. **2.** vb. To convert (meat) into a fricassee.

fricative, adj. & n. [1. fríkativ; 2. fríkətiv]. Lat. *fricāt-*, P.P. stem of *fricāre*, 'to rub', & **-ive**; formed fr. *friāre*, 'to rub', q.v. under **friable**. **1.** adj. Having to do with, produced by, rubbing; specif. (phon., of sounds) produced by expelling the air-stream through a very narrow passage formed in the mouth with the tongue or lips: *fricative consonants*; also called *open consonants*, or *continuants*. **2.** n. A fricative consonant.

friction, n. [1. fríkshun; 2. fríkʃən]. Lat. *frictiōn-(em)*, fr. *frict-*, P.P. stem of *fricere*, 'to rub', variant of *fricāre*, q.v. under prec., & **-ion**. **1. a** Act of rubbing one thing against another; **b** (phys.) resistance encountered when the surface of one body moves upon or across that of another; similar resistance of the particles of which a substance is composed. **2.** (fig.) Clash, opposition, of two different temperaments, characters, sets of opinions &c.; antagonism, collision, difference of opinion: *considerable friction existed between the colonel and his second in command*.

frictional, adj. [1. fríkshunal; 2. fríkʃənəl]. Prec. & **-al**. Connected with, caused by, friction.

frictionally, adv. Prec. & **-ly**. By means of friction.

friction brake, n. One operating by means of friction.

frictionize, vb. trans. [1. fríkshunīz; 2. fríkʃənaiz]. **friction** & **-ize**. To bring friction to bear upon; to rub.

frictionless, adj. [1. fríkshunles; 2. fríkʃənlis]. **friction** & **-less**. Devoid of, not causing, friction.

friction-tight, adj. Having sufficient tightness to cause friction.

friction-wheel, n. One moved by friction.

Friday, n. [1. frídi; 2. fráidi]. O.E. *frīgedæġ*, O.H.G. *friatag*, O.N. *frījadagr*, fr. name of a goddess, *Frīg*, wife of Odin (O.E. *Wōdan*), & **day**; cogn. w. Scrt. *prijā*, 'wife', lit. 'beloved one', fr. same base as O.E. *frēon*, 'to love'. See **friend**. Sixth day of the week among Christians and Europeans. *Good Friday*, the Friday in Passion Week, commemorating the Crucifixion.

friend (I.), n. [1. frend; 2. frɛnd]. O.E. *frēond*, 'friend, lover'; M.E. *frĕnd*, O.S. *friund*, O.H.G. *friunt*, Goth. *frijōnds*. All formed fr. Pres. Part. of a vb. meaning 'to love'; cp. O.E. *frēon* &c. This is for earlier **frijōn* & survives as such in Goth. The Aryan base is **pri-*, 'to love', whence O. Slav. *prijati*, 'to be favourable', & *prijateli*, 'friend'. **free** may be fr. same base. See also **Friday**. **1.** Person for whom one entertains feelings of affection, esteem, respect, and with whom one associates frequently and intimately. Phrs. *to make friends*, become friendly again after a quarrel; *to make friends with*, become the friend of, become intimate with; *to be friends with*, be in relation of a friend to. **2.** Term used in addressing, or referring to, a person, **a** without any implication of friendly feeling: *look, my friend*; *my good friend*; *I was just telling our friend here that ...* &c.; **b** as formal mode of referring to a fellow-member of Parliament or of the Bar: *my honourable, my learned, friend*. **3. a** One favourable to a person, principle, or cause; a supporter, well-wisher: *he has been a good friend to me, no friend to me* &c.; *the friend of liberty*; *the poor man's friend*; **b** associate, companion, acquaintance; attendant: *the prisoner left the court with his friends*; *who was your friend in the brown wig?*; **c** animal or object closely associated with, and serviceable to, human beings: *the dog is naturally the friend of man*; *these pills are the dyspeptic's friend*. **4.** (cap.) Member of the sect known as *Quakers*, or *Society of Friends*.

friend (II.), vb. trans., fr. prec. (very rare) To be a friend to, to befriend.

friendless, adj. [1. fréndles; 2. fréndlis]. **friend (I.)** & **-less**. Devoid of, having no, friends.

friendlessness, n. [1. fréndlesnes; 2. fréndlisnis]. Prec. & **-ness**. State of being friendless.

friendliness, n. [1. fréndlines; 2. fréndlinis]. Next word & **-ness**. Friendly feeling and behaviour; kind, conciliatory attitude of mind.

friendly (I.), adj. [1. fréndli; 2. fréndli]. O.E. *frēondlić*, M.E. *frĕndlich, -li*. Prec. & **-ly**. **1.** Like a friend, having character and behaviour of a friend; amiable, amicable, kindly: *my new acquaintances were all very friendly*. **2.** Befitting, characteristic of, friends and friendship: *to have friendly relations with*. **3. a** Favourable to, supporting, approving: *I am not friendly to revolution*; **b** (of things) propitious, favourable, promoting good and well-being of: *friendly showers*.

friendly (II.), adv. O.E. *frēondlīće*, M.E. *frĕnd-*, adv. See prec. (rare and archaic) In a friendly manner: *to greet a man friendly*.

Friendly Society, n. A voluntary association for the mutual benefit and assistance of members, as in sickness, old age &c.

friendship, n. [1. fréndship; 2. frén(d)ʃip]. O.E. *frēondscipe*. **friend (I.)** & **-ship**. State of feeling existing between friends; kindly feeling, affection based on mutual respect; amity.

Friesic, adj. & n. [1. frḗzik; 2. frízik]. Du. *Vries* & **-ic**. See also **Frisian**. **a** adj. Pertaining to Friesland (Du. *Vriesland*) or the Frisians; pertaining to the language of the Frisians; **b** n., the language of the Frisians; Frisian.

frieze (I.), n. Always [1. frīz; 2. fraiz] in Ireland; in England generally [1. frēz; 2. frīz]. Connected w. Fr. *friser*, 'to curl'. See **frizz**. Kind of coarse, shaggy woollen cloth made in Ireland.

frieze (II.), vb. intrans. [1. frēz; 2. frīz], fr. Fr. *friser*. See **frizz**. To curl, to trim up.

frieze (III.), n. [1. frēz; 2. frīz]. Fr.; Ital. *freggio*, prob. fr. Lat. *Phrygius*, fr. Gk. *Phrúgios*, 'Phrygian'. **1.** (archit.) Part of the entablature between architrave and cornice. **2. a** Any ornamented horizontal band in a building; **b** strip of wall-paper or other decorative element, of different pattern or colour from the main paper, placed below the ceiling or cornice of a room.

frigate, n. [1. frígat; 2. frígit]. Fr., fr. Ital. *fregata*, of unknown origin. Large type of fast sailing-ship used in war before introduction of steam; next in size to ships of the line, carrying about 25 to 50 guns; corresponding in type and function to modern cruiser.

frigate bird, n. Large, strong-flying, rapacious sea-bird, found in the tropics; also known as the 'man-o'-war bird'.

fright (I.), n. [1. frīt; 2. frait]. O.E. *fyrhto*, M.E. *fyrhte, frighte* &c., O.S. & O.H.G. *forhta*, Goth. *faurhtei*, 'fear'. The base appears to be confined to Gmc. The suggestion of Bezzenberger &c. that it was cogn. w. Lat. *querquerus*, 'trembling', fr. an assumed **peskweros*, is now considered improbable by Walde. **1. a** State of great fear, terror, inspired by sudden danger: *to die of fright*; **b** specific access of extreme terror: *to have, get, a fright*; *to give a person a fright*. **2. a** (rare) Something causing extreme terror; **b** (colloq.) very ugly person or thing: *you look a perfect fright*.

fright (II.), vb. trans., fr. prec. or for **affright**. (rare or poet.) To inspire terror; to alarm.

frighten, vb. trans. [1. fríten; 2. fráit(ə)n]. **fright (I.)** & **-en**. To inspire with fear, to alarm, terrify, scare; esp. to alarm suddenly; *frighten into*, to drive into a specified condition, compel to do something, by fear: *to frighten a child into fits*; *to frighten a man into submission* &c.; *frighten out of*, to cause to abandon through fear: *to frighten a man out of drinking too much*.

frightened, adj. [1. frítend; 2. fráit(ə)nd], fr. P.P. of prec. Strongly affected by fear; terrified, afraid: *a frightened child*.

frightful, adj. [1. frítfool; 2. fráitf(ə)l]. **fright (I.)** & **-ful**. **1. a** Inspiring horror and terror; shocking, horrible: *a frightful sight*; *frightful atrocity*; **b** (colloq.) unpleasant, inspiring strong disapproval: *we had a frightful time in the train*. **2.** Hideous, shockingly ugly: *Oxford is being rapidly disfigured by frightful new houses, shops* &c.

frightfully, adv. Prec. & **-ly**. In a frightful manner; to a frightful extent; (colloq., as intens.) very.

frightfulness, n. See prec. & **-ness**. **a** Quality of being frightful; **b** specif. (transl. of Germ. *schrecklichkeit*) the system of terrorization practised by the Germans in the Great War upon the inhabitants of territories temporarily occupied by them.

frigid, adj. [1. fríjid; 2. frídžid]. Lat. *frīgidus*, 'cold', fr. *frīgus*, n., 'state of cold', *frīgēre*, 'to be cold'; fr. base **srīg-*, cp. Gk. *hrīgos*, 'frost', for **srīgos*; perh. connected w. Lat. *rigidus*, 'stiff, hard' (with frost). See **rigid**. **1.** Very cold (of climate and atmosphere): *frigid zone*, region within the circle of either pole. **2. a** (of temperament, character) Lacking warmth, fire, enthusiasm, strong passion; **b** (of manner) lacking animation and geniality; chilling, distant, forbidding, repellent; also **c** (of any mode of expression) passionless, devoid of feeling: *a frigid style, utterance, tone* &c.

frigidity, n. [1. frijíditi; 2. fridžíditi]. Fr. *frigidité*, fr. Lat. *frīgiditāt-(em)*. Prec. & **-ity**. (chiefly of non-material qualities) Condition of being frigid; coldness, indifference; absence of warmth and animation.

frigidly, adv. [1. fríjidli; 2. frídžidli]. **frigid** & **-ly**. In a frigid manner.

frigidness, n. [1. fríjidnes; 2. frídžidnis]. **frigid** & **-ness**. Frigidity.

frill (I.), n. [1. fril; 2. fril]. Origin uncertain. **1.** Narrow, crimped border or flounce, used as a trimming; **a** one of lace, muslin &c. worn round the neck or wrists; **b** one of paper used as an ornament round the narrow end of a ham &c. Phr. (fig.) *to put on (one's) frills*, give oneself, affect, airs of superiority &c. **2.** Useless, excessive, meretricious adornment: *a style with too many frills*. **3.** (photog.) Frill-like crinkling at the edge of a film.

frill (II.), vb. trans. & intrans., fr. prec. **1.** trans. To adorn with a frill. **2.** intrans. To form into something resembling a frill; specif. (of photographic film) to crinkle at the edges.

frilled, adj. [1. frild; 2. frild]. **frill** (I.) & **-ed**. Provided, adorned, with frills.

frillery, n. [1. fríleri; 2. frílәri]. **frill** (I.) & **-ery**. Collection of frills.

frilling, n. [1. fríling; 2. fríliŋ]. **frill** (I.) & **-ing**. Strips of material used for frills.

frilly, adj. [1. fríli; 2. fríli]. **frill** (I.) & **-y**. Covered with frills; resembling a frill or frills.

Frimaire, n. [1. frēmár; 2. frimέr], fr. Fr. *frimas*, 'hoar-frost'. See **rime**. Third month of the French Revolutionary calendar, November 21st to December 20th.

fringe (I.), n. [1. frinj; 2. frindž]. O. Fr. *frenge, fringe*, fr. Lat. *fimbria*, 'border, edge, fringe'; see **fimbriated**. **1.** Ornamented border or edging, often of loose threads, as at the end of a sash, an oriental rug &c., or on an outer edge of some portion of a garment, shawl &c. **2.** Something resembling a fringe; **a** border, margin of something, objects situated on this: *a common with a fringe of houses round it; a fringe of beard on the chin*; Phr. *Newgate fringe*, beard worn on throat and projecting below the chin, the chin itself and the lips being shaved; **b** specif., border of hair growing above woman's forehead, cut and left just long enough partially to cover the forehead. **3. a** Extreme outer edge: *on the fringe of the forest, crowd* &c.; **b** (fig.) elementary part, external aspects, initial stages of a subject of study: *the mere fringes of philosophy*.

fringe (II.), vb. trans., fr. prec. **1.** To put a fringe on to, provide with a fringe. **2.** (fig.) To serve as a fringe for: *houses fringed the road on either side*.

Fringillidae, n. pl. [1. frinjílidē; 2. frindžílidī], fr. Lat. *fringilla*, 'chaffinch'; cp. Scrt. *bhŕŋgaš*, 'a black bee', &, without the nasal, Lat. *frigere*, 'to squeak, squeal', Gk. *phrugilos*, a kind of bird. (ornith.) The family of birds which includes the finches &c.

fringy, adj. [1. frínji; 2. fríndži]. **fringe** (I.) & **-y**. **a** Having a fringe; **b** resembling, serving as, a fringe.

frippery, n. [1. fríperi; 2. frípәri]. Fr. *fripperie*, 'old clothes', fr. *frippe(s)*, 'old clothes'. Origin uncertain. **1.** (obs.) **a** Old, second-hand clothes; **b** place where these are sold; **c** business of buying and selling cast-off clothes. **2. a** Tawdry finery; **b** (fig.) sham elegance and refinement; trifling, contemptible adornment.

frisette, n. [1. frizét; 2. frizét]. **frizz** & **-ette**. Row of artificial curls worn on the forehead.

friseur, n. [1. frēzḗr; 2. frizə́]. Fr. See **frizz** & **-eur**. Hairdresser.

Frisian, adj. & n. [1. frízian; 2. fríziәn], fr. Low Lat. *Frisia* & **-an**. **1.** adj. Of, belonging to, Friesland, province of Holland, and district of Germany, or of the Frisian Islands, off the west coast of Denmark, Germany, and Holland; Friesic; *Frisian cattle*, special breed of cattle renowned as milkers. **2.** n. Friesic.

frisk (I.), n. [1. frisk; 2. frisk]. O. Fr. *frisque*, 'lively', prob. of Gmc. origin, cp. O.H.G. *frisk*. See **fresh**. **a** A frolic, a light-hearted sporting; **b** a light, agile leap or bound; a gambol.

frisk (II.), vb. intrans. & trans., fr. prec. **A.** intrans. **1.** To leap lightly and playfully; to bound, skip, gambol, about, as children and young animals. **2.** To indulge in light-hearted frolic; to disport oneself. **B.** trans. To move, flick, rapidly in a playful, sportive manner: *to frisk a fan; a lamb frisks its tail*.

frisket, n. [1. frísket; 2. fŕiskit]. Fr. *frisquette* Etymol. unknown. Iron frame for holding sheet of paper in position during printing.

friskiness, n. [1. fŕiskines; 2. fŕiskinis]. Next word & **-ness**. **a** State of being frisky; liveliness, sportiveness, playfulness; **b** behaviour of person or animal that is frisky; liveliness, playfulness of movement.

frisky, adj. [1. fríski; 2. fríski]. **frisk** (I.) & **-y**. Inclined to frisk (in both senses); **a** lively, frolicsome; indulging in playful gambols; specif. (of a horse) fresh, skittish, inclined to leap about, to kick up its legs &c.; **b** fond of amusement and gaiety; prone to levity of conduct.

frit, n. & vb. trans. [1. frit; 2. frit]. Ital. *fritta*, 'fried', P.P. fem. of *friggere*, 'to fry'. See **fry** (I.). **1.** n. Material from which glass is made, after being calcined in furnace, but before being vitrified. **2.** vb. To calcine materials for glass-making; to make into frit.

frit fly, n. Origin unknown. Small European fly which destroys grain.

frith (I.), n. [1. frith; 2. friþ]. Variant of **firth**.

frith (II.), n. M.E. w. metathesis fr. O.E. *fyrhþ(o)*, 'a wood', fr. Gmc. **furh-iþ-*, lit. 'a collection of fir trees'. See **fir**. The suff. *-iþ* is cogn. w. Lat. *-ētum*, as in *quercētum*, 'plantation of oaks', *pōmētum*, 'orchard' &c. **1.** (obs., or rare, except in Pl.-Ns.) Tract of wooded, or forest land; tract where there was formerly a forest, esp. a region much covered with brushwood: *Chapel-en-le-Frith*, Derbyshire. **2.** (provinc.) Small brushwood; the smaller boughs and twigs from the top of a tree.

fritillary, n. [1. fritílari; 2. fritílәri], more rarely [1. frítilari; 2. frítilәri]. Fr. *fritillaire*, Med. Lat. *fritillāria*, name of genus; fr. Lat. *fritillus*, 'dice-box'. Applied to flowers & butterflies on account of the markings on petals & wings respectively. The word is perh. connected w. Lat. *fritinnīre*, 'to twitter', & may refer to the rattle of dice. **1.** One of several varieties of purple or white bell-shaped flowers growing from bulbs, with slender springy stems, and petals which are often freaked or mottled. **2.** One of a genus of butterflies having usually brown wings spotted with black and pearly markings.

fritter (I.), n. [1. fríter; 2. fritә]. Fr. *friture*, 'something fried', fr. P.P. *frit* & **-ure**. See **fry** (I.). Slice of apple, orange &c., fried in batter.

fritter (II.), vb. trans. Origin doubtful, perh. fr. O. Fr. *freture*, fr. Lat. *fractūra*. See **fracture**. Generally, *fritter away*; to waste, dissipate, money, time, strength &c., in petty, trifling, futile pursuits and objects.

frivol, vb. intrans. & trans. [1. frívol; 2. frívәl]. New formation fr. **frivolous**. **1.** intrans. To engage in trifling, futile pursuits; to lead a frivolous life, spend one's time idly and unproductively. **2.** trans. (uncommon) *Frivol away*, same as *fritter away*.

frivolity, n. [1. frivóliti; 2. frivóliti]. **frivol-**, as in next word, & **-ity**. **1.** Lightness, superficiality of character, lack of seriousness and depth. **2.** A foolish, frivolous action.

frivolous, adj. [1. frívolus; 2. frívәlәs]. Lat. *frīvolus*, 'brittle, crumbling; silly, empty, paltry'; fr. same base as *friāre*, 'to crumble, rub', q.v. under **friable**, & **-ous**. **a** (of persons) Silly, futile, inclined to levity, unstable; not serious, paltry; having no depth of character, or power of concentration; **b** (of action, thought, character &c.) lacking importance, weight; superficial, trifling, petty.

frivolously, adv. Prec. & **-ly**. In a frivolous manner.

frivolousness, n. See prec. & **-ness**. Frivolity.

friz(z) (I.), vb. trans. & intrans. [1. friz; 2. friz]. Cp. Fr. *friser*, 'to curl'. **1.** trans. To curl, render curly, esp. of the hair. **2.** intrans. To become curly, become crisped into curls.

friz(z) (II.), n., fr. prec. Something curled; **a** mass or row of curls.

frizz (III.), vb. intrans. Imitative of sound, but perh. also associated w. **fry** (II.). To hiss and sputter, sizzle, as bacon when being fried.

frizzle (I.), vb. trans. & intrans. [1. frízl; 2. frízl]. **frizz** (I.) & **-le**. **1.** trans. To curl the hair into small tight curls; also *frizzle up*. **2.** intrans. (of the hair) To be crisped into small tight curls.

frizzle (II.), vb. trans. & intrans. **frizz** (III.) & **-le**. Doubtless associated w. prec. & referring not only to the sound, but to the curling up of what is fried. **1.** trans. **a** To fry thoroughly (bacon &c.), so that it hisses and becomes crisp; **b** to burn. **2.** intrans. **a** To be fried thoroughly, to become crisp from being fried; **b** to be exposed to great heat: *I was frizzling in Baghdad for months*.

frizzly, adj. [1. frízli; 2. frízli]. **frizz** (I.) & **-ly**. Curled; having masses of curls.

frizzy, adj. [1. frízi; 2. frízi]. **frizz** (I.) & **-y**. Curly.

fro, adv. [1. frō; 2. frou]. Scand., M.E., fr. O.N. *frā*; cogn. w. **from**. Only in Phr. *to and fro*; **a** backwards and forwards, up and down: *walking to and fro in the room*; **b** from one place to another: *my business takes me constantly to and fro*.

frock (I.), n. [1. frok; 2. frɔk]. Fr. *froc*, Low Lat. *froccus*, perh. fr. Lat. *floccus*, 'lock of wool', referring to a rough woolly garment. See **flock** (I.). Long outer garment, in various specific senses. **1.** Monk's coarse robe. **2. a** A woman's dress, including skirt and upper part; **b** a child's outer garment; **c** a long military coat, cut something like a frock-coat.

frock (II.), vb. trans., fr. prec. **1.** To clothe, cover, with a frock. **2.** (fig.) To make a monk of.

frock-coat, n. Long coat for men, shaped to the figure, with large lapels and long square tails or skirts; now nearly obsolete.

frog, n. [1. frog; 2. frɔg]. O.E. *frogga*, M.E. *frogge*; also another O.E. type *frosc, frox* &c., whence M.E. & Mod. Engl. dial. *frosk, frosh* &c.; cp. Mod. Germ. *frosch*. Etymol. at present unsettled. **1.** Amphibious, tailless animal, family *Ranidae*, developed from a tadpole, having a smooth shiny skin, webbed feet, short fore-, and long powerful hind-legs, with which it swims rapidly and, when on land, is able to make considerable leaps. **2.** (vulg., obsolesc.) A Frenchman, from the popular idea that the French lived largely on frogs. **3.** Elastic, horny pad in middle of lower surface of hoof of the horse, ass &c.; perhaps so called from its shape. **4.** (railways) Junction of several rails and tracks, which converge to, and branch out from a point of union; so called from resemblance to hind-leg of a frog with its branching toes. **5.** Ornament, often consisting of a loop and button of silk or wool, or sometimes merely of a kind of tuft, upon military cloaks, tunics, or academic robes; either from shape, or perhaps variant of Port. *froco*, fr. Lat. *floccus*, 'tuft of wool'.

frogbit, n. [1. frógbit; 2. frɔ́gb*i*t]. **frog** & **bit (I.)**. Popular name of a floating water plant, *Hydrocharis*, with white flowers.

frogged, adj. [1. frogd; 2. frɔgd]. **frog** & **-ed.** Adorned with frogs, in sense **5.**

froggy, n. [1. frógi; 2. frɔ́g*i*]. **frog** & **-y.** Diminutive of *frog*; child's word.

frog-hopper, n. Popular name of certain hopping or leaping insects, esp. of those whose larvae, covered with white froth, are attached to plants and known as 'cuckoo spit'.

frolic (I.), adj. [1. frólik; 2. frɔ́l*i*k], fr. Du. *vroolijk*, 'merry', cp. Mod. Germ. *fröhlich*, fr. *froh*, 'happy, glad', O.S. *frao*. (archaic) Merry, gamesome, jovial.

frolic (II.), n. & vb. intrans., fr. prec. **1.** n. A merrymaking, a jovial prank, bout of gaiety; an hilarious, roistering party; merriment, gaiety. **2.** vb. To engage in a frolic; to make merry; to play gay, lively pranks.

frolicsome, adj. [1. fróliksum; 2. frɔ́l*i*ksəm]. Prec. & **-some.** Inclined to frolic, full of high spirits; sportive, gamesome.

frolicsomely, adv. Prec. & **-ly.** In a frolicsome way.

frolicsomeness, n. See prec. & **-ness.** Quality, state, of being frolicsome.

from, prep. [1. from; 2. frɔm]; unstressed [frəm]. O.E. & M.E. *from*, earlier *fram*; O.S., O.H.G., Goth. *fram*, 'from, away, farther'; cp. also for sense, Goth. *framis*, 'farther'; cogn. also w. Goth. *fruma*, 'the first'; O.E. *forma*, 'first'. See **first** & **former.** The elementary sense appears to be 'far, away from'. Outside Gmc. cp. Gk. *prómos*, 'the foremost man; chief'. See also **primary, pro-.** *From* in a general way, expresses the ideas of separation, departure, removal, subtraction, exclusion, deprivation; it also indicates place whence motion takes place, person or place from whom or whence something comes, the starting-point, place of origin, and kindred notions. It occurs after vbs. expressing these. **1.** Indicating place or point *whence* a movement is made: **a** motion away: *to rise from a chair, jump from a window, fall from the sky; he went from me; gone from home*; **b** removal, subtraction: *a brand snatched from the burning; to brush a crumb from one's coat; take 6 from 10; to blot out a word from a page*; **c** deprivation: *to steal money from the till; to take his sword from a prisoner*; **d** prevention: *to save oneself from falling.* **2.** **a** Indicating place or position apart and separate, at or in which a thing is and remains: *to hang from a bough; to stay away from home*; **b** exclusion, prohibition: *prevented from coming in; cut off from civilization; shut out from light and warmth*; **c** degree of remoteness (in space or time): *a mile from home; five years from now.* **3.** **a** Indicating point of departure; source, place of origin: *to set out from London*; Phr. *(he is) from Berkshire*, a native, or resident of Berkshire; *gold from the mine; water from the well; from the counter; the train from Swindon; to speak from memory*; **b** indicating person who gives or sends, or place whence a thing is sent: *a present from his father; a letter from a friend; a parcel from the draper's; a message from America*; **c** indicating ground of an inference: *I judge from his conduct that he is insane*; **d** indicating model to which an action conforms: *to paint from nature, from the life.* **4.** Expressing difference, distinction: *not to know chalk from cheese; to distinguish good from bad.* **5.** Indicating point from which a process occurs, or an action is performed: *to look from a window; to hear from the next room; to jump from a wall.* **6.** Indicating reason, cause, motive: *to die from exhaustion; to suffer from indigestion; to act from the highest motives.* **7.** *from—to* expresses continuous, or repeated action, movement, process, or recurrence of these: *to go from house to house; from place to place; from one thing to another; from time to time.* **8.** Used before adverbs and adverbial phrases to express direction or position in space or time: *to come from beyond the mountains; to speak from under the bedclothes; to enter from outside; to send a message from over the sea; that dates from before the war.*

frond, n. [1. frond; 2. frɔnd]. Lat. *frond-(em)*, stem of *frons*, 'leafy branch, foliage'; perh. cogn. w. Gk. *thróna* (pl.), 'flowers embroidered on cloth; flowers used as charms'. Organ in ferns or other flowerless plants, resembling a leaf, but differing from this in bearing reproductive cells.

frondage, n. [1. fróndij; 2. frɔ́nd*i*dž]. Prec. & **-age.** Fronds collectively; foliage.

Fronde, n. [1. frawnd; 2. frɔ̄nd]. Fr., lit. 'sling'. **1.** (hist.) **a** Political party in France during minority of Louis XIV., 1648-1653, opposed to Cardinal Mazarin and the Court; **b** period of civil war &c. fomented thereby. **2.** A violent, political opposition.

frondescence, n. [1. frondésens; 2. frɔndésəns]. Lat. See next word & **-ce.** **a** Period, state, of putting forth leaves; **b** foliage.

frondescent, adj. [1. frondésent; 2. frɔndésənt]. Lat. *frondescent-(em)*, Pres. Part. of *frondescere*, 'to put forth leaves'. See **frond.** Putting forth fronds or leaves.

frondose, adj. [1. fróndōs; 2. frɔ́ndous]. **frond** & **-ose.** **a** (obs. or poet.) Bearing leaves; **b** bearing fronds.

front (I.), n. [1. frunt; 2. frant]. Lat. *front-(em), frons*, 'forehead, human brow, countenance; forepart of anything'. Origin doubtful. All the etymols. hitherto proposed are rejected as improbable by Walde. The most plausible of these 'improbabilities' is perhaps the derivation fr. **bhrēu-went*, 'having brows', wh. connects the word w. Gk. *ophrûs*, 'eye-brow', & Engl. **brow.** **1.** **a** (obs. or poet.) The human forehead, the face; **b** this as symbolical of character; esp. in bad sense, impudence, effrontery; Phr. *to have the front to . . .*, be impudent enough to; *to put a bold front on the situation*, to confront boldly. **2.** **a** The fore, or forward part of anything; **b** position before one; Phrs. *in front (of)*, to the fore, before, before the face of; *to come to the front*, become well known, important; *look to your front*, before you; **c** the most forward line held by a combatant in the sphere of military operations; firing-line; **d** the whole area of military activity. **3.** **a** Face of a building: *the north, east, front*; specif. **b** principal side with main entrance: *the front of the house*; contrasted with the *back.* **4.** **a** That region of land abutting, esp. on the sea, but also on a lake or large river; frontage; **b** promenade, parade, constructed along a sea-front, above the beach. **5.** Something fastened to the front of another thing; specif. **a** false border of hair worn upon front part of a woman's head; **b** breast of a shirt, esp. a stiffened front part of a white linen shirt; **c** altar frontal. **6.** (phon.) **a** Middle part of the tongue, that part with which are formed what are sometimes misleadingly called 'palatal' sounds; **b** the forward part of the mouth; **c** a sound uttered by the front of the tongue; a so-called 'palatal'.

front (II.), adj., fr. prec. **1.** Of, at, pertaining to, the front of anything; to the fore, forward: *front row, front door; front page*, that at beginning of a book, title-page. **2.** (phon., of sounds) Articulated with the front (i.e. middle) of the tongue; also called by some 'palatal': *front consonants, vowels.*

front (III.) adv. To the front: *eyes front.*

front (IV.), vb. trans. & intrans. **front (I.).** **A.** trans. **1.** (archaic) To confront. **2.** To face towards; turn front, or face, towards: *the castle fronts the sea.* **3.** (phon.) **a** To shift area of articulation further forwards in the mouth; **b** specif., to convert into a front sound. **B.** intrans. To face, look, towards.

frontage, n. [1. frúntij; 2. fránt*i*dž]. **front (I.)** & **-age.** **a** Front part of a building: **b** line of land, esp. of property fronting, bordering, a road, street, river &c.

frontager, n. [1. frúntijer; 2. fránt*i*džə]. Prec. & **-er.** Owner of property fronting or bordering a road &c.

frontal (I.), adj. [1. frúntl; 2. fránt(ə)l]. See **front (I.)** & **-al.** **a** Connected with the front; situated in front; Phr. (mil.) *frontal attack*, one delivered from direction towards which the enemy are facing, without any attempt at outflanking; **b** specif. (anat.) connected with the forehead or brow: *frontal bones* &c.

frontal (II.), n., fr. prec. **1.** Ornament, part of armour, worn on the forehead. **2.** (eccles.) Movable, often highly decorated covering, generally of embroidered fabric, hung in front of that part of the altar facing west.

frontier, n. [1. frúntier; 2. frántiə]. Fr. *frontière*, Low Lat. *frontaria.* See **front (I.)** & **-ier.** **1.** **a** The extreme limit, boundary, march, border-line, of a state where its territory abuts upon that of another state; **b** (attrib.) belonging to, situated on, a frontier: *a frontier station, fortress* &c. **2.** (fig., in non-material sense, often pl.) Extreme limits, limitations, confines, outposts: *frontiers of knowledge, of civilization.*

frontiersman, n. [1. frúntierzman; 2. frántiəzmən]. Dweller on a frontier.

Frontignac, n. [1. fróntinyak; 2. frɔ́ntinjæk]. Fr. adj. fr. Frontignan in France; influenced by Cognac, Armagnac &c. **a** Kind of **muscat** grape; **b** wine made from this.

fronting, vbl. n. [1. frúnting; 2. fránt*i*ŋ]. **front (IV.)** & **-ing.** **a** Process or action of putting nearer the front; specif. **b** (phon.) process of shifting articulation nearer forepart of the mouth; process of shifting articulation to front of the tongue; also called *palatalization.*

frontispiece, n. [1. frúntispēs; 2. frántispīs]. Fr. *frontispice*, fr. Low Lat. *frontispicium*, 'countenance; front of a church'; fr. *fronti-*, stem of *frons* (see **front (I.)**), & *spicere, specere*, 'to look' (see **species**). The last syll. has been assimilated to Engl. **piece.** The part which is first seen. Specif. **1.** The principal façade of a building. **2.** **a** Illustration or ornamental design at the beginning of a book; (more rarely) **b** front page of a book.

frontless, adj. [1. frúntles; 2. frántlis]. **front (I.)** & **-less.** **1.** Lacking a front. **2.** (archaic and rare) Having no modesty, impudent; unblushing.

frontlessly, adv. Prec. & **-ly.** Impudently.

frontlessness, n. See prec. & **-ness.** Impudence.

frontlet, n. [1. frúntlet; 2. frántl*i*t]. **front (I.)** & **-let.** **1.** **a** A band for, worn on, the forehead; a fillet; **b** front part of animal's head, esp. when of a different colour from the rest. **2.** Narrow strip added as a finish, hanging over upper part of an altar frontal.

fronto-, pref. [1. fróntō; 2. frɔ́ntou]. Form of Lat. *frons*, 'forehead' (see **front (I.)**), used in compounds, meaning 'connected with, on, the forehead; frontal'. *Fronto-parietal*, connected with the frontal and the parietal bones &c.

fronton, n. [1. frúnton; 2. frántən]. Ital. *frontone.* See **front (I.)** & **-oon.** (archit.) Pediment.

frore, adj. [1. frōr; 2. frɔ̄], fr. obs. P.P. of **freeze.** O.E. *froren*, M.E. *frōren.* Frosty, frozen, very cold: '*The parching air burns frore*' (Milton, 'P.L.').

frost (I.), n. [1. frawst, frost; 2. frɔ̄st, frɔst]. O.E. *forst, frost*, M.E. *forst, frost*; in most old Gmc. languages; fr. Gmc. **frus-ta*, fr. **fruz-ta*, formed fr. type **fruz-* of **freus-*, 'to freeze'; as in O.E. P.P. *froren*, fr. **fruz-an.* See prec. & **freeze.** **1.** **a** That condition of the atmosphere when ice forms, which begins to occur at a temperature of 32° Fahrenheit and under; **b** frozen state of the ground &c.; **c** effects of frost; ice; frozen, or partially frozen dew or vapour: *frost on the grass, on the window-panes* &c. **2.** (fig.) **a** Chilly moral atmosphere, depression of spirits, coolness, lack of animation at a social gathering; **b** (colloq.) result of such low spirits, failure of a social entertainment; failure generally, esp. lack of success of efforts to amuse: *the dance, play, book, turned out a frost.*

frost (II.), vb. trans. & intrans., fr. prec. **A.** trans. **1. a** To injure, wither, nip (plants), with frost; **b** (fig.) to affect with low spirits, chill. **2.** To give the appearance of frost to, to make frosted: *to frost a cake*, with icing or sprinkling of sugar; *to frost glass*, by giving it a roughened or granulated surface. **B.** intrans. To freeze slightly, produce slight degree of frost.

frostbite, n. [1. fráwstbīt; 2. frɔ́stbait]. Injury, resulting in a kind of gangrene, to the tissues of the body, caused by prolonged exposure to extreme cold.

frosted, adj. [1. fráwsted; 2. frɔ́stid]. **frost** (I.) & **-ed**. **1. a** Covered with, whitened by, frost; **b** (fig., of hair) whitened. **2. a** Affected, nipped, by frost; **b** (fig., of character, temperament &c.) repressed, chilled, frigid; not cheerful and genial. **3. a** (of glass) Having surface roughened, granulated, so as to produce effect resembling that of frost which destroys transparency but preserves some degree of translucency; **b** coated with white sugar, as a wedding-cake.

frostily, adv. [1. fráwstili; 2. frɔ́stili]. **frosty** & **-ly**. In a frosty manner: (chiefly fig.) *to smile frostily.*

frostiness, n. [1. fráwstines; 2. frɔ́stinis]. **frosty** & **-ness**. Condition of being frosty.

frosting, n. [1. fráwsting; 2. frɔ́stiŋ]. **frost** (I.) & **-ing**. **a** Coating of frost on windows &c.; **b** granulation on glass; **c** coating of sugar on cakes &c.

frostwork, n. [1. fráwstwërk; 2. frɔ́stwʌ̄k]. Pattern resembling tracery produced by frost on glass and other smooth surfaces.

frosty, adj. [1. fráwsti; 2. frɔ́sti]. **frost** (I.) & **-y**. **1. a** Characterized by presence of frost: *a frosty day, sky*; **b** covered with frost: *frosty ground, pavements, trees* &c.; **c** (fig.) white from age &c.: *a frosty head.* **2.** (of moral qualities) Cold, frigid, in feeling, repellent in manner; lacking animation and geniality: *a frosty nature*; *a frosty smile* &c.

froth (I.), n. [1. frawth, froth; 2. frɔþ, frɔþ]. M.E. *frothe*, fr. O.N. *froða*; not in O.E., wh., however, has the related vb. (*ā-*)*frēoðan*, 'to froth up'. Origin uncertain. **1.** Light mass of minute cohering bubbles formed on the surface of liquids by fermentation or agitation; spume, foam; similar collection of bubbles produced from saliva by disease or extreme mental excitement. **2.** (fig., of non-material things) Light, trifling, superficial thought and ideas; shallow, excited feelings; the expression of these; futile, worthless talk.

froth (II.), vb. intrans. & trans., fr. prec. **1.** intrans. **a** To produce, emit froth, to foam, bubble thickly: *the sea frothed on the rocks*; *beer froths in the glass*; *to froth at the mouth*; **b** (fig.) to utter shallow thoughts. **2.** trans. To cause to froth: *to froth eggs*, by beating them &c.

frothily, adv. [1. fráwthili; 2. frɔ́þili]. **frothy** & **-ly**. In a frothy manner.

frothiness, n. [1. fráwthines; 2. frɔ́þinis]. Next word & **-ness**. Quality, condition, of being frothy.

frothy, adj. [1. fráwthi; 2. frɔ́þi]. **froth** (I.) & **-y**. **1.** Consisting of froth; having consistency of froth. **2.** (fig.) Light, trifling, superficial; lacking substance, weight, depth, of thought and feeling: *a frothy preacher*; *frothy oratory* &c.

frou-frou, n. [1. froo froo; 2. frū frū]. Fr., imitative. Sound made by a soft, silky fabric when moved, crumpled, rubbed &c.; a rustle.

frounce (I.), vb. trans. & intrans. [1. frouns; 2. frauns]. M.E. *frouncen*, 'to wrinkle', O. Fr. *froncier*, Mod. Fr. *froncer*, 'to cause to wrinkle'; fr. Low Lat. **frontiare*, fr. *front-*. See **front** (I.). (archaic) **1.** trans. To make plaits, folds, wrinkles, in; adorn with plaits or flounces. **2.** intrans. To gather, form into folds or wrinkles.

frounce (II.), n., fr. prec. (archaic) **1.** A plait, fold, wrinkle; a curl. **2.** (fig.) Empty show, affectation.

frow, n. [1. frou; 2. frau]. Du. *vrouw*, 'woman'. See **frau**. Dutchwoman of humbler classes.

froward, adj. [1. fróard; 2. fróuəd]. **fro** & **-ward**. (archaic) Literally, turned away; hence, perverse in character and behaviour; disobedient, obstinate, refractory.

frowardly, adv. Prec. & **-ly**. Perversely.

frowardness, n. See prec. & **-ness**. Disobedience, perversity &c.

frown (I.), vb. intrans. & trans. [1. froun; 2. fraun]. M.E. *frounen*, fr. O. Fr. *froignier* &c., 'to frown, look sullenly'; prob. fr. Gmc. source; cp. Norw. *frōyna*, 'to make a wry face'. Origin uncertain. **A.** intrans. **1. a** To wrinkle the forehead; **b** to look sternly, gloomily, sullenly. **2.** (fig.) To be sullen; to disapprove; *frown at, on, upon*, to view with disfavour, disapprove of; be unfavourable to. **B.** trans. (rare) To express by frowning: *to frown disgust, disapproval* &c.; *frown down*, subdue by means of frowns.

frown (II.), n., fr. prec. **1.** A wrinkling of the brows; stern face, look, esp. one expressing sullenness, disapproval. **2.** State of being unfavourable, of disapproving; expression, manifestation, of disfavour and disapproval.

frowning, adj. [1. frouning; 2. fráuniŋ], fr. Pres. Part. of **frown** (I.). **1. a** Having, bearing, frowns: *a frowning face*; **b** disapproving, stern. **2.** (of inanimate objects) Inspiring awe, terror, dread; having dreadful, terrifying, appearance; menacing, lowering: *a frowning cliff, tower* &c.

frowningly, adv. Prec. & **-ly**. With a frown, or frowns.

frowsily, adv. [1. fróuzili; 2. fráuzili]. **frowsy** & **-ly**. In a frowsy manner, state &c.

frowsiness, n. [1. fróuzines; 2. fráuzinis]. See prec. & **-ness**. State, quality, of being frowsy.

frowst, n. [1. froust; 2. fraust], fr. next word. Frowsiness; stuffy atmosphere of a room.

frowsy, -zy, adj. [1. fróuzi; 2. fráuzi]. Origin unknown. **a** Stuffy, musty, ill-smelling, as of crowded or badly ventilated room; **b** dirty, draggled, unkempt, slatternly.

froze, vb. [1. frōz; 2. frouz]. Pret. of **freeze**, fr. P.P.; cp. M.E. Pret. *frēas*.

frozen, adj. [1. frózen; 2. fróuz(ə)n], fr. P.P. of **freeze**, fr. M.E. *frōren* (see **frore**), w. *z* introduced fr. infin. **1.** Congealed, turned to ice with extreme cold. **2.** Characterized by, subject to, extreme frost and cold: *the frozen regions of the pole.* **3.** (fig.) **a** Cold in feelings; extremely reticent, frigid in character and bearing; **b** (of feelings) pent-up, under severe constraint, suppressed. **4.** (of a ball in billiards) Touching, lying against, the cushion, or another ball.

Fructidor, n. [1. frúktidor; 2. fráktidɔ], fr. Lat. *fructus*, 'fruit', & Gk. *dôron*, 'gift'; 'the month of fruit'. See **fruit** & **date** (I.), **donor**. Name invented in France during the French Revolution for the last month of the new calendar; it began Aug. 18th and lasted till Sept. 16th.

fructiferous, adj. [1. fruktíferus; 2. fraktífərəs]. Lat. *fructifer*, 'fruit-bearing'. See **fruit** & **-ferous**. Bearing, yielding, fruit.

fructification, n. [1. frùktifikáshun; 2. fràktifikéiʃən]. Lat. *fructificātiōn-(em)*. See **fruit**, & **-fication**. **1.** Process of becoming fruitful, of forming fruit. **2.** Act or process of rendering fruitful; fertilization (esp. bot.).

fructify, vb. intrans. & trans. [1. frúktifī; 2. fráktifai]. Fr. *fructifier*, fr. Lat. *fructificāre*. See **fruit** & **-fy**. **1.** intrans. **a** (of plants &c.) To become fertile, to yield fruit; **b** (fig.) to yield results, come to maturity (of efforts, measures &c.). **2.** trans. To render fertile, fertilize, make productive.

fructose, n. [1. frúktōs; 2. fráktous]. Lat. *fructus*, see **fruit**, & **-ose**. Sugar derived from fruit.

fructuous, adj. [1. frúktūus; 2. fráktjuəs]. O. Fr., fr. Lat. *fructuōsus*, 'productive, fruitful'. See **fruit** & **-ous**. **a** (of trees &c.) Fruitful, productive; **b** (fig.) fruitful in results.

fructuously, adv. Prec. & **-ly**. Fruitfully.

fructuousness, n. See prec. & **-ness**. Quality, state, of being fruitful.

frugal, adj. [1. froogal; 2. frūg(ə)l]. Lat. *frūgālis*, 'pertaining to produce; thrifty, temperate'; fr. *frūg-*, stem of *frux*, 'fruits, produce, of the earth', & **-al**. See base *frūg-* under **fruit**. **1.** Economical, sparing, thrifty; not wasteful, lavish, or inclined to squander: *a frugal housekeeper.* **2.** Marked by thrift; used, enjoyed, with moderation; inexpensive: *a frugal dinner*; *frugal house-keeping.*

frugality, n. [1. froogáliti; 2. frūgǽliti]. Lat. *frūgālitāt-(em)*. See **frugal** & **-ity**. Frugalness, carefulness in using and spending; thrift.

frugally, adv. **frugal** & **-ly**. In a frugal, careful, thrifty manner.

frugalness, n. See prec. & **-ness**. Quality of being frugal; thrift, economy.

frugivorous, adj. [1. froojívérus; 2. frūdžívərəs]. Mod. Lat. formed on anal. of *carnivorous*, q.v. See base *frūg(i)-* under **frugal**, & **-vorous**. (zool., of classes of animals, as bats &c.) Feeding on fruit.

fruit (I.), n. [1. froot; 2. frūt]. M.E., fr. O. Fr. *frui(c)t*, fr. Lat. *fructus*, 'enjoyment; that which is enjoyed, proceeds, profit; produce, fruit; consequence, effect'. The base is *frūg-*, as seen in Lat. *frūgis*, genit. of *frūx*, 'fruits of the earth'; it is further found in Lat. *fruor*, 'feed oneself; enjoy, make use of', wh. is fr. **frugʷ-or*. This base appears also in Gmc. in the form **brūk-*; cp. O.E. *brūcan*, 'to make use of, enjoy'. See **brook** (II.). **1.** (gen. sense) Any product of a plant used by man for food or other purposes, including grain, cotton &c.: '*the kindly fruits of the earth*' (Prayer Book). **2.** Specif. **a** the edible, pulpy product of a plant, whether tree or shrub; not distinguished with any precision from a 'vegetable' in popular usage. Roughly speaking, a fruit is more often eaten raw, and is often sweetened with sugar, esp. when cooked; *fruit* is used collectively for the whole product, or fruitage, of a plant or tree: *some trees have lost all their fruit in the drought*; also **b** of the product in general: *to grow fruit*; *to like fruit.* **3.** (bot.) That part of a plant which contains the seed, including, besides what are popularly called fruits, all pods, nuts, berries, and grains. **4.** (archaic) Offspring of human beings or animals; children, young: *the fruit of the womb.* **5.** (gen. pl.) Product of any action, circumstance, process; result, effect; profit, reward: *to live to see the fruits of one's labours*; *the fruits of early training*; *the fruits of virtue and good living* &c.

fruit (II.), vb. intrans., fr. prec. To produce fruit: *in many soils the Ribston Pippin does not fruit well.*

fruitage, n. [1. frootij; 2. frūtidž]. **fruit** (I.) & **-age**. Fruits collectively, esp. the growing crop as a whole.

fruitarian, n. [1. frootárian; 2. frūtéəriən]. **fruit** & **-arian**; modern formation modelled on *vegetarian.* One who lives, or professes to live, almost entirely upon fruit.

fruit bud, n. Bud that produces blossom, whence later, fruit, as distinct from one producing foliage.

fruit-cake, n. Cake containing raisins, currants, or other dried fruit.

fruiter, n. [1. frooter; 2. frūtə]. **fruit** (II.) & **-er**. Tree that produces fruit: *a prolific fruiter.*

fruiterer, n. [1. frōōterer; 2. frútərə], fr. obs. *fruiter*, Fr. *fruitier*, 'seller of fruit', & (redundant) **-er.** Person who sells fruit retail, but, as a rule, does not grow it.

fruit-fly, n. One of various kinds of fly which lay their eggs in young growing fruit, and whose larvae when hatched feed on, and destroy the fruit.

fruitful, adj. [1. frōōtfool; 2. frútf(ə)l]. **fruit (I.)** & **-ful. 1.** Producing fruit; productive, prolific: *a fruitful tree, soil* &c. Phr. *a fruitful vine*, a woman who bears a large family. **2.** Productive of, yielding, results; successful in producing effects: *fruitful labours; a fruitful career.*

fruitfully, adv. Prec. & **-ful. a** So as to produce fruit; **b** in an effective manner.

fruitfulness, n. See prec. & **-ness.** Quality of being fruitful, in all senses.

fruition, n. [1. frōōíshun; 2. fruíʃən]. Lat. *frūitiōn-(em)*, 'enjoyment', fr. *fruit-*, P.P. stem of *frūor*. See **fruit (I.)** & **-ion.** Use possession of anything; pleasure derived from possession; enjoyment.

fruitless, adj. [1. frōōtles; 2. frútlis]. **fruit (I.)** & **-less. 1.** Bearing no fruit. **2.** Having no result; vain, without effect, profitless: *fruitless efforts.*

fruitlessly, adv. Prec. & **-ly.** Vainly, ineffectually.

fruitlessness, n. See prec. & **-ness.** Uselessness, ineffectiveness.

fruit tree, n. One specially cultivated for its edible fruit.

fruity, adj. [1. frōōti; 2. fruti]. **fruit (I.)** & **-y.** Connected with, of the nature of, fruit; specif., resembling and suggesting fruit in taste and smell; pungent, aromatic: *a fruity wine.* Phr. *a fruity voice*, rich, sonorous, mellow voice.

frumentaceous, adj. [1. frōōmentáshus; 2. frūmentéiʃəs], fr. Lat. *frūmentum*, 'corn, grain', for **frūgmentum*, fr. *frūg-*, q.v. under **fruit (I.)** & **-aceous.** Made of, connected with, resembling, wheat or other grain.

frumenty, n., also **furmety** [1. frōōmenti, férmeti; 2. frúminti, fə́miti]. Fr. *fromentée*, fr. Lat. *frūmentum*, 'grain'. See prec. Dish made of wheat boiled in milk, sweetened, and spiced.

frump, n. [1. frump; 2. framp]. Origin doubtful. Plain, badly dressed, dowdy woman.

frumpish, adj. [1. frúmpish; 2. frámpiʃ]. Prec. & **-ish.** Like a frump; dowdy.

frumpy, adj. [1. frúmpi; 2. frámpi]. **frump** & **-y.** Frumpish.

frustrate (I.), adj. [1. frústrāt; 2. frástreit], fr. Lat. *frustrāt-(um)*, P.P. type of *frustrāri*, 'to deceive, disappoint'; formed fr. *frustrā*, 'uselessly, in vain'. This word is fr. same base as Lat. *fraus*, q.v. under **fraud.** (archaic) Frustrated.

frustrate (II.), vb. trans. [1. frùstrát; 2. fràstréit]. See prec. **1.** To baffle, circumvent; bring efforts of to nought, to balk: *to frustrate one's opponents.* **2.** To bring to nought, foil, render of no effect: *to frustrate the designs of one's enemies.*

frustration, n. [1. frustráshun; 2. frastréiʃən]. Prec. & **-ion.** Act, or process, of frustrating; nullification, overthrow.

frustule, n. [1. frústūl; 2. frástjūl]. Lat. *frustulum*, dimin. of *frustum*, 'piece'. See next word. Shell of a diatom.

frustum, n. [1. frústum; 2. frástəm]. Lat., 'piece, bit'. Several etymols. have been suggested. Perh. the most plausible is that wh. derives the word fr. earlier **fruds-tom*, fr. Aryan base **bhrud-* &c., & connects it w. O.E. *brēotan*, 'to break', & *brytta*, for **bruttja*, 'distributor' &c. See further under **brittle.** (geom.) Lower part of a solid figure when the top has been cut off parallel to base.

frutescent, adj. [1. frōōtésent; 2. frūtésənt]. Shortened fr. *fruticescent*. See next word & **-escent.** Resembling, of the nature of, a frutex.

frutex, n. [1. frōōteks; 2. frúteks]. Lat., 'a shrub, a bush'. Perh. orig., 'budding, sprouting plant', cp. Lat. *Frutis*, name for Venus. Cp. further O. Slav. *brŭstĭ*, 'bud'; & perh. Goth. *-brūps*, 'bride', q.v. under **bride.** Shrub with woody stem, smaller than a tree.

fruticose, adj. [1. frōōtikōs; 2. frútikous], fr. stem *frutic-*, of prec., & **-ose.** Resembling a shrub, bushy, shrubby.

fry (I.), n. [1. frī; 2. frai]. L.M.E. *frī*, 'seed, offspring'; cp. A.-Fr. *frie, fry*, 'spawn', variant of O. Fr. *froi*, 'spawn'. The word is perh. of Gmc. origin; cp. O.N. *frio*, Goth. **fraiw*, 'seed, descendants'. See the last under **fresh (I.).** Young fishes just hatched: *salmon fry* &c. Phr. *small fry*, (contemptuous) unimportant, insignificant persons; (facet.) young children.

fry (II.), vb. trans. & intrans. M.E. *frīen*, Fr. *frire*, fr. Lat. *frīgere*, 'to roast, parch, fry'; cp. Scrt. *bhṛjjáti*, 'he roasts'; Gk. *phrūgein*, 'to roast, bake'. **A.** trans. **1.** To cook in boiling fat. **2.** (fig., obs.) To torment, torture mentally. **B.** intrans. **1.** To be cooked in hot fat; undergo process of frying: *the sausages are frying briskly.* **2.** (archaic or obs.) **a** To undergo mental anguish, to be strongly agitated; **b** (of the sea) to boil, foam.

fry (III.), n., fr. prec. **1.** Dish of fried food. **2.** Certain internal organs of animals, usually cooked by frying: *pig's fry.* **3.** (colloq.) State of mental excitement.

fryer, frier, n. [1. frier; 2. fráiə]. **fry (II.)** & **-er. 1.** Person who fries. **2.** Article of food intended for frying.

frying-pan, n. [1. fríing pàn; 2. frái-iŋ pæ̀n]. Flat, shallow utensil of metal with a long handle, used for frying. Phr. *out of the frying-pan into the fire*, to escape one danger or difficulty and get involved in a worse.

fubsy, adj. [1. fúbzi; 2. fábzi]. Origin doubtful. (rare) Fat, plump, squat.

fuchsia, n. [1. fúsha; 2. fjúʃə]. Named after Fuchs, a German botanist. One of many varieties of plants with graceful, drooping flowers, red or pink, pink and white, or pink and purple in colour.

fuchsine, n. [1. fōōksēn; 2. fúksīn]. Prec. & **-ine.** Named fr. its colour. Chemical dye-stuff, dark red in colour.

fucus, n. [1. fúkus; 2. fjúkəs]. Lat., 'rock lichen', fr. Gk. *phûkos*, 'red paint, rouge; kind of seaweed from which this is obtained', fr. Heb. *pūk*. Kind of flat tough seaweed.

fuddle, vb. trans. & intrans. & n. [1. fúdl; 2. fádl]. Origin uncertain. **1.** vb. **a** trans. To render confused, and muddled in mind; render stupid and confused by intoxication, also *to fuddle oneself*; **b** intrans., to tipple (rare). **2.** n. Confusion of mind, hebetude.

fuddlement, n. [1. fúdlment; 2. fádlmənt]. Prec. & **-ment.** State of being fuddled.

fudge, n., interj. & vb. trans. [1. fuj; 2. fadž]. Origin uncertain. **1.** n. **a** Concocted story, nonsense, empty talk; **b** kind of soft, granulated toffee. **2.** interj. Nonsense! **3.** vb. trans. To fake, vamp, put together in a careless, dishonest manner; also *fudge up.*

fuel, n. & vb. trans. & intrans. [1. fúel; 2. fjúil, fjúəl]. O. Fr. *fouaille, fuaille*, fr. Low Lat. *focalia*, neut. pl., fr. Lat. *focus*, 'hearth; fire'. See **focus. 1.** n. Material used for fires; coal, wood, oil &c.; also fig., in Phr. *to add fuel to the flames*, to inflame, aggravate, already existing anger, passion &c. **2.** vb. **a** trans. To provide with fuel: *to fuel a ship*; **b** intrans. to procure, take in, provide oneself with fuel: *the ship put into port to fuel.*

fuelling, n. [1. fúeling; 2. fjúiliŋ]. Prec. & **-ing. a** Act or process of collecting or providing with fuel; **b** material used for fuel.

fug, n. & vb. intrans. [1. fug; 2. fag]. Origin unknown. (schoolboy word, colloq.). **1.** n. **a** Stuffiness, fustiness, closeness of air, as in an ill-ventilated room &c.; **b** dust, fluff, flue &c., such as collects under furniture, or in the seams of pockets. **2.** vb. To remain in a close warm room: *to sit fugging in the house*; (fig.) to lead a sedentary as contrasted with an active life in the open air.

fugacious, adj. [1. fūgáshus; 2. fjūgéiʃəs]. Lat. *fugāc-*, stem of *fugax*, 'apt to fly; transitory' & **-ous**; cp. *fugere*, 'to flee, take flight', & *fuga*, 'flight'; fr. Aryan base **bheugh-*, **bhugh-*, orig. 'to bend, curve', hence, 'to swerve aside in flight'; cp. Gk. *pheugein*, 'to flee', & *phugé*, 'flight'; Scrt. *bhujáti*, 'he bends, thrusts aside'; further O.E. *būgan*, 'to bend, stoop, bow down; swerve' &c.; & *boga*, 'bow (for arrows)'. See **bow (III.), bow (I.),** & **bight. 1.** Flying, disposed to flee, or pass away; hard to capture or keep; transitory, transient. **2.** (biol.) Lasting but a short time (of flowers and parts of these).

fugaciously, adv. Prec. & **-ly.** Transitorily, fleetingly.

fugaciousness, n. See prec. & **-ness.** Transience.

fugacity, n. [1. fūgásiti; 2. fjūgǽsiti]. Lat. *fugac-*, as in **fugacious**, & **-ity.** Fugaciousness.

fugal, adj. [1. fúgal; 2. fjúgəl]. **fugue** & **-al.** (mus.) Of the nature of, pertaining to a fugue.

fugally, adv. Prec. & **-ly.** In the manner of, by means of a fugue.

-fuge, suff. [1. fūj; 2. fjūdž]. Lat. *-fugus*, 'fleeing from', as in *lucifugus*, 'fleeing from light' &c.; in mod. compounds the suff. has sense of 'putting to flight'; cp. *febrifuge* &c. See base **fug-*, 'flight' &c., under **fugacious.**

fugginess, n. [1. fúgines; 2. fáginis]. Next word & **-ness.** State of being fuggy.

fuggy, adj. [1. fúgi; 2. fági]. **fug** & **-y. 1.** (of rooms, atmosphere &c.) Stuffy, close, ill-ventilated. **2.** (of persons) **a** Fond of warm rooms; afraid of fresh air and heedless of stuffiness; **b** fond of sedentary pursuits at home, rather than of sport &c., in the open.

fugient, adj. [1. fújient; 2. fjúdžiənt]. Lat. *fugient-(em)*, Pres. Part. of *fugere*, 'to flee'. See **fugacious.** Apt to flee; retiring.

fugitive (I.), adj. [1. fújitiv; 2. fjúdžitiv]. Lat. *fugitīvus*, 'running away', fr. stem *fugit-*, as in P.P. of *fugere*, 'to flee', q.v. under **fugacious,** & **-ive. 1.** Fleeing, running away; engaged in, having taken to, flight; esp. from danger, justice, compulsion &c.: *a fugitive prisoner, slave* &c. **2.** Liable to pass, to fade away; evanescent: *fugitive thoughts, colours* &c. **3.** Dealing with matters of passing, ephemeral interest; transient: *fugitive essays, verse* &c.

fugitive (II.), n. See prec. **1.** One who flees, or has fled, from pursuit, danger, constraint, justice; refugee; deserter &c.: *fugitives from the battle, from the invaded areas, from justice, from the army.* **2.** Something hard to catch: '*the swallow, light-winged fugitive*'.

fugle, vb. intrans. [1. fúgl; 2. fjúgl]. Back-formation fr. next word. To act as a fugleman.

fugleman, n. [1. fúglman; 2. fjúglmən], fr. Germ. *flügelmann*, man who acted as guide or model, on the 'wing' of a military formation, fr. *flügel*, 'a wing', fr. the same base as **flown (I.)** & **fly (II.). 1.** (rare) Soldier who is expert in drill, stationed as guide and leader, on wing of a company, to direct, or serve as model in movements &c. **2.** Leader, guide, spokesman.

fugue, n. [1. fūg; 2. fjūg]. Fr., fr. Ital. *fuga*, fr. Lat., 'flight'. See **fugacious.** (mus.) Contrapuntal composition with a 'subject' or chief theme, and subordinate themes which recur, together with their 'answers'.

fuguist, n. [1. fúgist; 2. fjúgist]. Prec. & **-ist.** Composer of fugues.

-ful, suff. [1. fool, fl; 2. -ful, -fəl, -fl]. Reduced form of **full (I.)**, used as suff. **1.** Used to form adjectives from nouns expressing a possession of qualities; full of, abounding in, characterized by: *plentiful, shameful, beautiful*; **b** forming adjectives from verbs, expressing 'tending to, able to': *wakeful.* **2.** Forming nouns from other nouns, and then denoting 'as much as will fill': *glassful, plateful, mouthful, handful.* These nouns are inflected finally, as completely welded unities: *cupfuls, spoonfuls* &c., not *cupsful* and so on.

fulcrum, n., learned pl. *fulcra* [1. fúlkrum; 2. fálkrəm]. Lat., 'bed-post', prob. for **fulc-clom*; connected w. Lat. *fulcīre*, 'to prop'; the base is perh. **bhelk-*, **bholk-* &c., whence O.E. *bealca*, 'beam', q.v. under **balk** (I.). **a** Object which supports a lever; precise point on which a lever rests when in action; **b** (fig.) anything used to attain an end, influence others &c.

fulfil(1), vb. trans. [1. foolfíl; 2. fulfíl]. M.E. *fulfillen* &c. See **full** (I.) & **fill** (I.). To carry out, perform, bring to completion; specif. **a** to discharge, perform adequately: *to fulfil one's duties*; **b** to satisfy, come up to, in performance: *to fulfil one's hopes, expectations*; *to fulfil desires*; **c** to comply with, observe, be faithful to: *to fulfil one's obligations*; *to fulfil conditions, a command, one's promises.*

fulfilment, n. [1. foolfílment; 2. fulfílmənt]. Prec. & **-ment**. **a** Completion, due performance of (duties); **b** compliance with, observance of (promises, the law, conditions, obligations &c.); **c** satisfaction, contentment, gratification of (desires, expectations, hopes).

fulgent, adj. [1. fúljent; 2. fáldžənt]. Lat., fr. *fulgent-(em)*, Pres. Part. of *fulgēre*, 'to shine'; fr. same base as *flagrāre*, 'to blaze, flame', q.v. under **flagrant.** (poet.) Shining, radiant, blazing.

fulgurant, adj. [1. fúlgūrant; 2. fálgjərənt]. Lat. *fulgurant-(em)*, Pres. Part. of *fulgurāre*, 'to lighten', fr. Lat. *fulgur*, 'lightning', fr. base **fulg-*, 'blaze' &c. as in prec. Flashing, like lightning.

fulgurite, n. [1. fúlgūrīt; 2. fálgjərait]. Lat. *fulgur*, 'lightning'. See prec. & **-ite**. Tubes of vitrified substance found in sand, formed by the passage of lightning.

fuliginous, adj. [1. fūlíjinus; 2. fjūlídžinəs]. Lat. *fūligin-*, stem of *fūlīgo*, 'soot', & **-ous**; fr. Aryan base **dhūlī-*, as in Scrt. *dhūli*, 'dust'; the same base with other formative elements occurs in Lat. *fūmus*, 'smoke, vapour'. See **fume** (I.) & **dust.** Connected with, resembling, soot; sooty, smoky.

full (I.), adj. [1. fool; 2. ful]. O.E. & M.E. *full*, also O.S.; O.H.G. *foll*, Goth. *fulls*; fr. Aryan **plnó-*; cp. w. different grade, Lat. *plēnus*, 'full', see **plenum, plenitude, plenty**; also Lat. *-plēre*, 'to fill', P.P. *-plētum*, whence the second syll. of **complete** &c. Exactly cogn. w. *full* are, Lith. *pilnas*, O. Slav. *plŭnŭ*, 'full'. See further **fill & folk.** **1. a** (of receptacle) Containing as much as it will hold, filled to utmost capacity; overflowing: *to pump till the cistern is full*; *a box full to overflowing*; *to have one's mouth full*; **b** (of buildings) crowded, packed: *a room full of furniture, of people*; *the room was full before the lecture began*; *a full house*, a crowded theatre; **c** (fig.) overflowing with, strongly affected by, emotion: *my heart is too full for words*; *a mind full of jealousy, bitterness* &c. **2.** Filled with food, satisfied, replete: *to eat till one is full*; *as full as one can hold.* **3.** Serving to fill, occupying completely a given space: *a full audience.* **4. a** Furnished, well provided, plentifully stored with, rich, abounding in: *rivers full of fish*; *woods full of game*; *a cake full of plums*; *pockets full of money*; *a house full of mice*; also **b** (of non-material things) *full of ideas*; *a book full of good things*; *his head is full of nonsense*; **c** much concerned with, engrossed by, having one's thoughts running on, occupied with; intent upon: *to be full of one's own affairs*; *full of one's subject.* **5. a** (of garments, drapery &c.) Ample, roomy, hanging in folds, flowing; loose, easy-fitting: *I like a coat made full across the chest*; **b** bulky, plump, swelling: *rather full in the face*; *a full throat and bosom*; *a full figure*; **c** (of supply, amount) copious, plentiful: *a full meal, full measure, a very full harvest.* **6. a** Complete; having attained to the expected or maximum degree of height, amount, volume, growth, development, intensity, perfection: *a full tide*; *full moon*; *in full bloom, a full crop of apples* &c.; *in full career of happiness, full vigour, strength*; *in full gallop*; *full speed*; *at full length*, stretched out, completely extended; *to spend one's full time*; *a full hour, a full orchestra*; **b** (of sounds) resonant, penetrating, possessing volume: *a full voice, full notes*; **c** (of wines) possessing rich, strong consistency, body and flavour. Phrs. *of full age*, having attained majority; *of full blood*, not mixed in race; *full brother, sister*, born of same father and mother; *in full cry*, of hounds following hot on scent; *full dress*, most elaborate dress, worn on ceremonial occasions; *in full fig*, in best, most splendid clothes; *in full feather*, same as *full fig*; also, in best possible physical and intellectual condition.

full (II.), n., fr. prec. Utmost extent, highest degree; chiefly in Phrs. *to the full*, completely; *in full*, fully, at full length, in the whole extent.

full (III.), adv., fr. **full** (I.). **1.** (as intens., archaic, or poet.) Entirely, completely, very: *full well*, very well, fully; '*Full many a flower is born to blush unseen*' (Gray's 'Elegy'); *full soon.* **2.** (joined by hyphen to adj. or P.P.) Fully, to the fullest extent, completely: *full-blown, full-grown.*

full (IV.), vb. trans. & intrans., fr. **full** (I.). **1.** trans. To make a garment, or part of it, full: *to full a sleeve* &c. **2.** intrans. To have fullness: *the folds don't full enough* (rare).

full (V.), vb. trans. O.E. *fullian*, 'to whiten cloth', borrowed fr. Lat. *fullō*, 'cloth-fuller'. See **fuller** (I.). To cleanse, formerly to whiten cloth; now chiefly to shrink and thicken cloth after weaving.

full-blooded, adj. [1. fóol blúded; 2. fúl bládid]. **1. a** Having copious supply of blood; (fig.) **b** (of persons, modes of expression &c.) lusty, vigorous, virile; passionate. **2.** Of unmixed race, pure: *a full-blooded negro, Jew, Englishman* &c.

full-blown, adj. **a** (of flowers) Completely expanded; **b** (of persons) stout, exuberant, expansive.

full-bodied, adj. Stout, inclined to corpulence.

full-bottomed, adj. [1. fóol bótumd; 2. fúl bɔ́təmd]. **1.** *Full-bottomed wig*, having large, broad bottom, like those still worn by K.C.'s in full dress. **2.** (of ships) Having great capacity below the water line.

fuller (I.), n. [1. fóoler; 2. fúlə]. O.E. *fullere*, fr. Lat. *fullō*, 'one who fulls, one who cleanses & whitens cloth'; cogn w. Gk. *phalós*, 'shining', *phaliós*, 'white'; Lith. *baltas*, 'white'; O. Slav. *belŭ*, 'white'; Scrt. *bhálam*, 'brightness'; O.E. *bǣl*, 'fire, blaze, funeral pile'. See this base further under **bald & balefire.** One whose trade is to full, cleanse, and dress freshly woven cloth.

fuller (II.), n. & vb. trans. Etymol. unknown. **1.** n. Tool used for grooving iron. **2.** vb. To groove with a fuller.

fuller's earth, n., fr. **fuller** (I.). Variety of soft yellowish clay, used by fullers to remove grease from newly woven cloth; also used in manufacture of some soaps.

full-eyed, adj. Having large, well opened, rather prominent eyes.

full-face, n. & adv. [1. fóol fās; 2. fúl feis] & adv. [1. fóol fás; 2. fúl féis]. **1.** n. Bold-faced type. **2.** adv. Having face turned full towards speaker or spectator.

full-faced, adj. Having broad or plump cheeks.

full-fledged, adj. [1. fóol fléjd; 2. fúl flédžd]. Having all the feathers grown; (fig.) fully established, developed: *a full-fledged barrister*, one who has been called to the bar, having completed his training.

full-grown, adj. Having reached limit of growth and development; fully grown.

full hand, n. (poker) A hand containing three of a kind, as three kings, fives &c., and a pair; also called 'full house'.

fulling, n. [1. fóoling; 2. fúliŋ]. **full** (V.) & **-ing.** Process of soaking, cleansing, twisting, shrinking newly made cloth, carried out by a fuller.

fulling-mill, n. Works in which process of fulling is carried out.

full-length, adj., n., & adv. **1.** adj. (of portrait) Showing, depicting, person's whole figure. **2.** n. A portrait depicting the whole figure. **3.** adv. In one whole length, at full length.

full-mouthed, adj. **1.** Having complete number of teeth. **2.** Uttered with full force of voice; loud.

fullness, n. [1. fóolnes; 2. fúlnis]. **full** (I.) & **-ness.** Condition, quality of being full (in various senses). **1.** (non-material) **a** Abundance, sufficiency, copiousness: *fullness of detail*; **b** completeness: *to write with great fullness of all that one sees*; **c** completion, fulfilment: *the fullness of joy*; *in the fullness of time.* **2.** (in material sense) **a** Amplitude, roominess: *a fullness of the skirts, sleeves* &c.; **b** stoutness, plumpness, corpulence: *a great fullness of bust, face*; **c** swelling, puffiness: *a fullness under the eyes*; **d** satiety, repletion: *to have a sense of fullness after meals.*

full-orbed, adj. [1. fóol órbd; 2. fúl ɔ̄bd]. (of the moon) Having the whole disk illuminated.

full-rigged, adj. Having full, maximum, number of masts and sails.

fully, adv. [1. fóoli; 2. fúli]. **full** (I.) & **-ly.** To the full; completely, entirely.

fulmar, n. [1. fóolmar; 2. fúlmā]. Scand. O.N. *fūll*, 'foul', & *mār*, 'sea mew'. See **foul & mew** (I.). Arctic sea-bird of the petrel family resembling a gull.

fulminant, adj. [1. fúlminant; 2. fálminənt]. Lat. *fulminant-(em)*, Pres. Part. of *fulmināre*, 'to lighten, to hurl lightnings', fr. *fulmen*, 'lightning', fr. **fulg-men*, wh. base see under **fulgent & flagrant.** (med.) Developing with lightning rapidity and suddenness: *a fulminant disease.*

fulminate (I.), vb. intrans. & trans. [1. fúlminăt; 2. fálmineit], fr. Lat. *fulmināt-(um)*, P.P. type of *fulmināre*, 'to lighten'. See prec. **A.** intrans. **1. a** To flash; **b** to explode violently, detonate. **2.** To issue commands, utter denunciations, in a vigorous, masterful manner: *fulminate against*, denounce forcibly and with an air of authority. **B.** trans. **1.** To cause to explode. **2.** To send forth, issue, with vehemence and authority: *to fulminate orders, decrees* &c.

fulminate (II.), n., fr. prec. (chem.) Highly sensitive explosive compound, *fulminate of mercury*, used for detonation of high explosives.

fulminating, adj. [1. fúlmināting; 2. fálmineitiŋ], fr. Pres. Part. of **fulminate** (I.). **1.** Thundering; exploding with great violence: *fulminating powder*, fulminate of mercury. **2.** (fig.) Expressing denunciations or threats with great violence. **3.** (med.) Developing suddenly and with great rapidity; fulminant.

fulmination, n. [1. fùlmināshun; 2. fàlminéiʃən]. Lat. *fulminātiōn-(em).* **fulminate** (I.) & **-ion.** **1.** Act of fulminating. **2.** Something fulminated; violent denunciation.

fulminator, n. [1. fúlminàtor; 2. fálminèitə]. Lat. **fulminate** (I.) & **-or.** One who fulminates; title applied to Jupiter.

fulminatory, adj. [1. fúlminàtori; 2. fálminèitəri]. **fulminate** (I.) & **-ory.** **a** Of the nature of a fulmination; **b** given to fulminating.

fulmine, vb. intrans. & trans. [1. fúlmin; 2. fálmin]. Fr. *fulminer*, fr. Lat. *fulmināre.* See **fulminant.** (rare) To fulminate.

fulminic, adj. [1. fulmínik; 2. falmínik]. Coined in 1800, fr. Lat. *fulmen*, 'lightning', see **fulminate**, & **-ic.** Explosive: *fulminic acid*, acid which combined with mercury forms highly explosive salts.

fulminous, adj. [1. fúlminus; 2. fálminəs]. Lat. *fulmen*, 'lightning'. See **fulminate** & **-ous.** Connected with, resembling, lightning.

fulsome, adj. [1. fóolsum; 2. fúlsəm]. **full** (I.) & **-some.** **1.** (obs. senses) Copious, excessive; fat, overgrown; nauseating, disgusting. **2.** Excessive and insincere; servile from base motive; chiefly *fulsome flattery, praise, admiration* &c.

fulsomely, adv. Prec. & **-ly**. In a fulsome manner.

fulsomeness, n. See prec. & **-ness**. Quality of being fulsome.

fulvescent, adj. [1. fulvésent; 2. falvésənt]. Lat. *fulvescent-(em)*, Pres. Part. of *fulvescere*, 'to become yellow', fr. *fulvus*, 'tawny', &c. See next word. Tending to become fulvous.

fulvous, adj. [1. fúlvus; 2. fálvəs]. Lat. *fulvus*, 'reddish-yellow, tawny', fr. same base as *flāvus*, 'gold-coloured'. See **flavescent**. Dull, reddish-yellow, tawny.

fumade, n. [1. fūmád; 2. fjūméid]. Span. *fumado*, fr. Lat. *fūmātum*, 'smoked'. See **fume (I. & II.)**. Smoked and salted fish, esp. pilchard.

fumarole, n. [1. fúmarōl; 2. fjúməroul]. Fr. *fumerolle*, Ital. *fumaruola*, fr. Lat. *fūmāriolum*, dimin. of *fūmārium*, 'smoke chamber'. See **fume** & **-ary**. Place in cone of a volcano whence fumes and vapour escape.

fumatorium, n. [1. fūmatórium; 2. fjūmətóriəm]. New formation fr. Lat. *fūmāt-(um)*, P.P. type of *fūmāre*, 'to smoke' (see **fume**), & *-ōrium* (see **-ory**). Place where things are smoked, fumigated &c.

fumatory, adj. & n. [1. fúmatori; 2. fjúmətəri]. See prec. **1.** adj. Connected with smoke or smoking. **2.** n. Fumatorium.

fumble (I.), vb. intrans. & trans. [1. fúmbl; 2. fámbl]. Cp. Swed. *fumla*, 'to grope', cogn. w. O.N. *fālma* & O.E. *folm*, 'hand'; further connexions under **feel** & **palm** (of hand). **1.** intrans. To grope with the hands clumsily, or uncertainly; to make a clumsy, hesitating, unskilful attempt to do something with the hands: *to fumble with a lock*; *to fumble about*, grope about, bungle. **2.** trans. To handle hesitatingly, clumsily, unskilfully; to bungle, make failure of some attempted action: *to fumble a ball* (in games), *a stroke* &c.

fumble (II.), n., fr. prec. Unskilful, hesitating, action or use of the hands; bungle.

fumbler, n. [1. fúmbler; 2. fámblə]. **fumble (I.)** & **-er**. One who fumbles; one who is awkward, clumsy, unskilful with his hands.

fumbling, adj. & n. [1. fúmbling; 2. fámbliŋ], fr. Pres. Part. of **fumble (I.)**; also vbl. n. **a** adj. Awkward, groping, uncertain; **b** n., action of a fumbler.

fume (I.), n. [1. fūm; 2. fjūm]. Fr., fr. Lat. *fūmus*, 'smoke, steam, vapour', cogn. w. Gk. *thūmós*, 'soul, life, breath'; Scrt. *dhūnōti*, 'shakes, whirls'; O. Slav. *dymŭ*, 'smoke, vapour'; O.E. *dūst*, 'dust' &c. See further under **theo-**, **dew**, **dust**, & **beast**. **1.** Smoke, pungent vapour; especially of an irritating, offensive kind; strong odour: cp. '*fishy fume*' (Milton, 'P. L.'); hot blast: *fumes of burning coal, of wine* &c.; *fumes of heat*. **2.** Excited, agitated, state of mind: *to be in a fume of anxiety*.

fume (II.), vb. intrans. & trans., fr. prec. **A.** intrans. **1. a** (obs. or poet.) To smoke, to steam; **b** to emit, give off, fumes or strong, pungent vapour; **c** *fume away*, to pass off in fume or vapour. **2.** (of mental action) To fret, chafe, fidget, worry; to be in an irritable, fussy state of mind; to be ruffled: *to fuss and fume*. **B.** trans. **1.** (rare) To fill with fumes. **2.** Specif., to darken the surface of wood for cabinet-making by exposure to fumes or smoke: *fumed oak*.

fumigate, vb. trans. [1. fūmigāt; 2. fjúmigeit], fr. Lat. *fūmigāt-(um)*, P.P. type of *fūmigāre*. See **fume (I.)**. To saturate with fumes or smoke, esp. for purposes of disinfection.

fumigation, n. [1. fūmigáshun; 2. fjūmigéiʃən]. Prec. & **-ion**. Act or process of fumigating.

fumigator, n. [1. fúmigātor; 2. fjúmigeitə]. **fumigate** & **-or**. **a** One who fumigates; **b** apparatus for fumigating.

fumigatory, adj. [1. fúmigātori; 2. fjúmigeitəri]. **fumigate** & **-ory**. Having the property of fumigating and disinfecting.

fuming box, n. [1. fúming bòks; 2. fjúmiŋ bɔ̀ks]. (photog.) Chamber where sensitized paper is subjected to the action of ammonia to hasten printing.

fumitory, n. [1. fúmitori; 2. fjúmitəri]. M.E., fr. O. Fr. *fumiterre*, 'smoke of the earth', fr. Lat. *fūmus*, 'smoke' (see **fume (I.)**), & *terra*, 'earth' (see **terra**). Herb of many varieties with flowers of various colours, formerly used as an antiscorbutic.

fumous, adj. [1. fúmus; 2. fjúməs]. Lat. *fūmōsus*, 'smoky, full of smoke'. See **fume (I.)** & **-ous**. Full of smoke; smoky.

fumy, adj. [1. fúmi; 2. fjúmi]. **fume (I.)** & **-y**. Full of fumes; giving off fumes; vaporous.

fun (I.), n. [1. fun; 2. fan]. Cp. M.E. *fonnen*, 'to be foolish'. See **fond**. Never preceded by indef. art. **1.** Merriment, mirth, gaiety, hilarity, frolic: *to be fond of fun*; *full of fun*; *full of his fun*. **2.** Source, cause, of merriment and amusement; an amusing person, thing, circumstance, occupation: *Mr. Jones is great fun*; *camping out is rather fun*; *I don't see the fun of practical joking*.

fun (II.), vb. intrans., fr. prec. (rare) To cause fun, jest; to play the fool; to hoodwink, bamboozle: chiefly in Pres. Part. *he is always funning*.

funambulist, n. [1. fūnámbūlist; 2. fjūnǽmbjulist], fr. Lat. *fūnis*, 'rope' (see **funicular**), & *ambulāre*, 'to walk', see **amble**, & **-ist**. Tight-rope walker.

function (I.), n. [1. fúngkshun; 2. fáŋkʃən]. Lat. *functiōn-(em)*, 'performance, execution', formed fr. *funct-*, P.P. stem of *fungi*, 'to discharge, perform, do', & **-ion**; the etymol. of the base is not clear. **1.** (general sense) Natural, normal action which a person or thing is appointed or designed to perform; special activity, operation, utility, purpose &c.: *the function of education is to develop the mind*. **2.** (physiol., biol.) Characteristic action or activity of an organ in the economy of an organism: *the functions of the nerves, leaves* &c. **3.** Allotted task, special duty; activity which it is incumbent upon a person to carry out; that series of actions imposed by moral or legal obligations: *the functions of an officer of state, of a schoolmaster*; *the functions of one's office* &c. **4.** Something which is performed; **a** a ceremony, celebration &c.: *the installation and enthronement of a bishop is an imposing function*; **b** (colloq.) a social gathering on an elaborate scale: *to go to a function at the palace* &c. **5.** (math.) A quantity is said to be the function of another, when for any particular value of one there is a corresponding value or set of values of the other.

function (II.), vb. intrans., fr. prec. To work, act, in performance of functions; to fulfil allotted task, duty, purpose.

functional, adj. [1. fúngkshunal; 2. fáŋkʃənəl]. **function (I.)** & **-al**. **a** Concerned with, pertaining to, based on, functions; **b** designed for, performing, a regular function; *functional organ*, contrasted with *rudimentary*; *functional disease*, one affecting, or arising from, the function of an organ.

functionally, adv. Prec. & **-ly**. In connexion with the functions; as regards the functions.

functionary, n. & adj. [1. fúngkshunari; 2. fáŋkʃənəri]. **function (I.)** & **-ary**. **1.** n. Person entrusted with certain functions; an official. **2.** adj. Functional.

functionate, vb. intrans. [1. fúngkshunāt; 2. fáŋkʃəneit]. **function (I.)** & **-ate**. To fulfil, perform, a function.

fund (I.), n. [1. fund; 2. fand]. Lat. *fundus*, 'bottom, basis, foundation', fr. Aryan base **bhudnó*; cp. Gk. *puthmēn*, 'bottom, base; root of a tree'; O.E. *botm*. See **bottom**. **1.** Permanent supply, accumulated store, stock (now only of non-material things): *a fund of good nature, humour, wit*; *fund of anecdote* &c. **2.** Accumulation, sum of money, set apart for some particular purpose, the principal and interest of which are available for that alone: *a fund for missionary purposes*; *a scholarship fund* &c.; *sinking fund*, q.v. **3.** (pl.) *Funds*, pecuniary resources; specif., those of a state; government securities: *to have money in the funds*.

fund (II.), vb. trans., fr. prec. To constitute, convert into, a fund; to provide a fund for payment of interest.

fundament, n. [1. fúndament; 2. fándəmənt]. Lat. *fundāmentum*, 'foundation, groundwork'. See **fund (I.)**. That part of the person upon which one sits; the buttocks.

fundamental, adj. & n. [1. fùndaméntal; 2. fàndəméntəl]. Prec. & **-al**. **1.** adj. (chiefly in non-material sense) **a** Basal, serving as a foundation; connected with the foundations, going to the root of things; hence, **b** essential, of primary importance, serving as necessary starting-point. **2.** n. **a** Essential, basal principle, rule: *the fundamentals of religion* &c.; **b** (mus.) lowest note of a chord.

fundamentalism, n. [1. fùndaméntalizm; 2. fàndəméntəlizəm]. Prec. & **-ism**. **a** Strict adherence to what are regarded as fundamental principles, esp. in religion; specif. **b** a firm belief in the Biblical account of the Creation and total rejection of evolution, and of the Darwinian theory of the origin of species.

fundamentalist, n. [1. fùndaméntalist; 2. fàndəméntəlist]. See prec. & **-ist**. Adherent of fundamentalism.

fundamentally, adv. [1. fùndaméntali; 2. fàndəméntəli]. Prec. & **-ly**. At, to, from, the bottom, from the foundations; essentially; completely: *fundamentally wrong*.

funded, adj. [1. fúnded; 2. fándid], fr. P.P. of **fund (II.)**. **1. a** Converted into a debt secured by state credit, repayable after fixed period, and bearing interest at regular intervals; **b** (rare) accumulated, stored in a fund. **2.** Invested in the funds, or state securities.

funding, vbl. n. [1. fúnding; 2. fándiŋ]. **fund (I.)** & **-ing**. Act or process of creating a funded debt.

funebrial, adj. [1. fūnébrial; 2. fjūníbriəl]. Lat. *fūnebri-*, 'pertaining to a funeral', & **-al**. See **funeral**. Connected with a funeral, or funereal ceremonies &c.

funeral, n. & adj. [1. fúneral; 2. fjúnərəl]. Fr. *funérailles*, Lat. *fūnerālia*, 'funeral rites', neut. pl. of *fūnerālis*, fr. *fūner-*, stem of *fūnus*, 'burial, funeral', & **-al**. *Fūnus* is perh. fr. **gheun-*, cogn. w. Goth. *gaunōn*, 'to lament', & *gaunōþs*, 'mourning, sorrow', O.N. *gaula-*, 'to howl'; others connect it w. Goth. *dauþs*, 'death', deriving it fr. **dhowenos*, cp. Goth. *diwans*, 'mortal'. See **death**, **die (II.)**. **1.** n. **a** A burial, interment of the dead, including all the rites and ceremonies connected with this; obsequies; **b** procession accompanying the corpse. **2.** adj. Connected with, pertaining to, a funeral or funerals: *funeral ceremonies, procession* &c.; *funeral urn*, one for holding the ashes of the dead after cremation; *funeral pile, pyre*, heap of wood &c., upon which a corpse was burnt.

funerary, adj. [1. fúnerari; 2. fjúnərəri]. Lat. *fūnerārius*, fr. *fūner-*, as in prec., & **-ary**. Of, pertaining to, a funeral.

funereal, adj. [1. fūnéreal; 2. fjūníəriəl]. Lat. *fūnere-(us)*. See prec. & **-al**. Adapted to, suitable for, a funeral; expressing gloom, dark; hence, mournful, dismal, lugubrious: *funereal garments, expression of face, voice* &c.

funereally, adv. Prec. & **-ly**. In a funereal manner; dismally, lugubriously.

fungible, adj. [1. fúnjibl; 2. fándžibl]. Med. Lat. *(res) fungibilis*, fr. *fungi*, 'to perform, discharge'. See **function (I.)** & **-ible**. (law, of goods) Capable of being used in place of another; mutually interchangeable; capable of being replaced by another specimen in discharge of a contract.

fungicide, n. [1. fúnjisīd; 2. fándžisaid]. See **fungus** & **-cide**. Substance that kills fungi.

fungiform, adj. [1. fúnjiform; 2. fándžifōm]. **fungus** & **-form**. Having the shape of a fungus.

fungin, n. [1. fúnjin; 2. fándžin]. **fungus** & **-in**. Substance composing the solid parts of a fungus.

fungoid, adj. [1. fúnggoid; 2. fáŋgɔid]. **fungus** & **-oid**. Like, characteristic of, a fungus.

fungosity, n. [1. funggósiti; 2. faŋgɔ́siti]. Lat. *fungōs-*, as in next word, & **-ity**. Fungoid excrescence, growth.

fungous, adj. [1. fúnggus; 2. fáŋgəs]. Lat. *fungōs-(us)*, 'spongy'. Next word & **-ous**. Spongy, having the structure of a fungus.

fungus, n., pl. **fungi** [1. fúnggus; 2. fáŋgəs]. Lat., 'mushroom', fr. Gk. *sphóggos*, 'sponge'. See **sponge**. One of a large group of vegetable growths ranging from the largest toadstools to microscopic organisms, and including mushrooms, puffballs, rusts, mildews &c.

fungusy, adj. [1. fúnggusi; 2. fáŋgəsi]. Prec. & **-y**. Affected by fungous growth.

funicular, adj. & n. [1. fūníkūlar; 2. fjūníkjulə], fr. Lat. *fūniculus*, 'a slender cord', dimin. of *fūnis*, 'rope, line, cord', & **-ar**; fr. Aryan **gʷhoin-is*, fr. wh. w. another grade & different formative element also Lat. *fīlum*, 'thread', for **gʷhin-slo-*. See this base under **file (III.)**, **filament**. **1.** adj. Connected with, worked by, a rope, cord &c.; esp. *funicular railway*, one in which a vehicle, running on a line, is drawn up a mountain by means of a metal cord passing over small easily running wheels, the other end of which is fastened to another car, specially weighted, at the top of the mountain, which runs down and pulls the lower car up. **2.** n. A funicular railway.

funk (I.), n. [1. fungk; 2. faŋk]. A slang word, first in 1743; origin unknown. (slang) **1.** Fear, cowardice, physical or moral; unworthy, unnecessary terror: *to be in a funk.* Phrs. *a blue funk*, state of great fear; *in a funk of*, afraid of. **2.** Person who feels funk; a coward.

funk (II.), vb. trans. & intrans., fr. prec. **1.** trans. **a** To fear, feel fear of, be afraid of, frightened by or at: *to funk pain, the rain, a scolding, a whipping*; **b** to shrink, flinch from, try to avoid: *to funk a difficult stroke, a difficulty, hard words.* **2.** intrans. To experience fear, play the coward: *he always funks when the pinch comes.*

funkiness, n. [1. fúngkines; 2. fáŋkinis]. Next word & **-ness**. State of being funky.

funky, adj. [1. fúngki; 2. fáŋki]. **funk (I.)** & **-y**. Feeling funk, frightened; given to funking, cowardly.

funnel, n. [1. fúnl; 2. fánəl]. M.E. *fonel*, fr. Fr., fr. Lat. *(in)fundibulum*, 'instrument for pouring into', fr. *fundere*, 'to pour'. See **found (II.)**. **1.** Instrument with a wide mouth leading into a tapering tube, used for pouring or transferring liquid from one vessel to another when the one into which the transference takes place has a narrow inlet. **2.** Cylindrical metal chimney or smoke-stack of a locomotive or steamship.

funnelled, adj. [1. fúneld; 2. fánəld]. Prec. & **-ed**. Provided with, shaped like, a funnel.

funnily, adv. [1. fúnili; 2. fánili]. **funny** & **-ly**. In a funny manner. Phr. *funnily enough*, strange to tell.

funniment, n. [1. fúniment; 2. fánimənt]. **funny** & **-ment**. Jest, comicality, piece of waggishness.

funniness, n. [1. fúnines; 2. fáninis]. **funny** & **-ness**. Quality of being funny.

funny (I.), adj. [1. fúni; 2. fáni]. **fun** & **-y**. **1.** Giving rise to fun; causing amusement; amusing, comical, laughable: *jokes are not always as funny as they are meant to be.* **2.** Strange, queer, unexpected, exceptional, out of the ordinary, difficult to explain: *a good man spoiled by a funny temper; a funny way to behave.* Phrs. *a funny thing*, a remarkable, puzzling circumstance; *a funny business*, affair, conduct, which appears to be touched with dishonesty, or to show a lack of straightforwardness; *there's something funny about it*, something underhand, not straightforward; *to feel funny, to go all funny*, to feel queer, ill; to become unwell; to present a strange appearance.

funny (II.), n. Small clinker-built rowing-boat.

funny-bone, n. Sensitive, pointed bone at elbow joint.

fur (I.), n. [1. fĕr; 2. fā̆]. M.E. *forre, furre*, 'fur', orig. 'case, covering; lining'; fr. O. Fr. *forre, fuerre*, 'scabbard'; cp. Span. *forro*, 'lining'; Ital. *fodero*, 'lining; sheath, scabbard'; fr. a Gmc. source, cp. Goth. *fōdr*, 'sheath for a sword, scabbard', & O.N. *fōðr*, 'lining', fr. Aryan base **pōi-*, 'to guard, protect', cp. Scrt. *pātra-*, 'receptacle'; *pāmi*, 'I protect'; Gk. *pōma*, 'cover', & *poimḗn*, 'shepherd'. **1. a** Short, soft hair forming the coats of certain species of animals; **b** animals with coats of this kind collectively; Phr. *fur and feather*, rabbits, hares &c. and birds; *to make the fur fly*, (fig.) to cause trouble, disturbance, quarrelling, to stir up dissension. **2. a** Coat of an animal when stripped off, cured and prepared, and fashioned into coats, linings &c.; **b** (pl.) such skins collectively; peltry: *a fine collection of furs.* **3.** Coating, deposit, of various kinds; **a** that on the human tongue in illness; **b** limy deposit left from water when boiled: *fur on inside of a boiler, saucepan* &c. **4.** (her.) One of certain tinctures, represented on the escutcheon by spots of varying size, shape, arrangement.

fur (II.), vb. trans. & intrans. Prob. fr. prec., q.v., but cp. O. Fr. *fourrer*, 'to line' &c. **A.** trans. **1.** To trim, line, cover, with fur (only in P.P. as adj.): *a furred gown* &c. **2.** To coat, cover, with a deposit; **a** *hard water furs kettles and boilers* &c.; **b** *the tongue becomes furred in influenza.* **3.** To level a floor &c., with furring, q.v.: *fur up, down.* **B.** intrans. To become furred; **a** of boilers &c.; **b** of the tongue.

furbelow, n. [1. fĕrbelō; 2. fā̆bilou]. By popular etymol. for **falbala**. Flounce on a woman's garment. Phr. *flounces and furbelows*, collection of pleats, flounces, trimmings.

furbelowed, adj. Prec. & **-ed**. Covered with furbelows.

furbish, vb. trans. [1. fĕrbish; 2. fā̆biʃ]. M.E. *forbischen*, fr. O. Fr. *fourbiss-*, Pres. Part. type of *fourbir*, 'to clean, polish'; fr. M.H.G. *furben*, 'polish, rub bright'; cognates are doubtful. To scour, clean, polish, burnish: *to furbish armour, a sword* &c.; *furbish up* **a** to revive, clean, polish up, smarten up, esp. after disuse or neglect: *to furbish up a room, old furniture, clothes* &c.; **b** (fig., of non-material things) to touch up, adapt for use: *to furbish up an old sermon.*

furcate, adj. & vb. intrans. [1. fĕrkāt; 2. fā̆keit]. Lat. *furca*, 'fork'. See **fork** & **-ate**. **1.** adj. Forked, dividing into two branches. **2.** vb. To divide, branch into a fork.

furcation, n. [1. fĕrkáshun; 2. fā̆kéiʃən]. Prec. & **-ion**. Process, act, of furcating.

furfuraceous, adj. [1. fùrfūráshus; 2. fā̆fjuréiʃəs], fr. Lat. *furfurāceus*, fr. *furfur*, 'bran, scurf', fr. **far-far*. See **farina** & cp. **barley**. **a** Covered with dandruff or scurf; scurfy; **b** (bot.) covered with bran-like scales.

furfurol, n. [1. fĕrfūrol; 2. fā̆fjurɔl]. Lat. *furfur*, 'bran', see prec., & **-ol**. (chem.) Colourless volatile oil, produced in distillation of bran, wood, and other carbohydrates.

furibund, adj. [1. fūribund; 2. fjɔ́riband]. Lat. *furibundus*, 'raging, furious'; fr. *furia*. See **fury**. (rare) Mad with rage, furious.

furious, adj. [1. fūrius; 2. fjɔ́riəs]. Lat. *furiōsus*, 'full of rage and madness'. See **fury** & **-ous**. **1. a** (of the mind and feelings) Greatly excited, frenzied, incensed; roused to the point of fury; **b** (of the passions and their effects) raging, violent, uncontrollable: *furious love, hate, resentment* &c.; evincing such feelings: *a furious quarrel, struggle* &c.; *furious glances.* **2.** (of persons) **a** Inspired with fury, mad with rage, violently angry, enraged: *he was simply furious*; **b** savage, fierce, vehement. **3.** (of the elements) In a state of violent agitation; raging, boisterous: *a furious storm, sea* &c.

furiously, adv. Prec. & **-ly**. In a furious manner; with great violence; boisterously.

furiousness, n. See prec. & **-ness**. Condition of being furious; fury.

furl, vb. trans. & n. [1. fĕrl; 2. fā̆l]. Perh. fr. O. Fr. *fardeler*, 'to make into a bundle'. Cp. **fardel**. **1.** vb. **a** trans. To fold, roll up, and make secure: *to furl sails, a flag*; (poet.) to close, fold: (of a bird) *furl its wings*; **b** intrans., to become rolled up. **2.** n. **a** Act of furling; **b** something furled, coiled.

furlong, n. [1. fĕrlong; 2. fā̆lɔŋ]. O.E. *furlang*, M.E. *furlong, -lang, -lung*, 'length of a furrow'. See **furrow** & **long**. Measure of distance, the eighth part of a mile, 220 yards.

furlough, n. & vb. trans. [1. fĕrlō; 2. fā̆lou]. Du. *verlop*, 'permission', cp. Mod. Germ. *verlaub*; the pref. is cogn. w. **for-**, & the second element w. **leave**, 'permission'. **1.** n. Leave of absence from duty granted to a soldier, sailor, or government official. **2.** vb. (rare) To grant leave of absence to.

furmety, n. See **frumenty** &c.

furnace, n. & vb. trans. [1. fĕrnis; 2. fā̆nis]. M.E. *forneis, fornais*, fr. O. Fr. *fornais*, fr. Lat. *fornācem*, acc. of *fornax*, 'an oven', fr. *fornus*, 'oven', fr. Aryan **ghr̥n-*, cp. also O. Slav. *grunilo*, 'stove, oven', & Scrt. *ghr̥nṓti*, 'glows, shines'. The base is a variant of that fr. wh. comes Lat. *formus*, 'warm', fr. **gʷhr̥m-*, whence also Gk. *thermós*, 'warm'. See **therm**, & further under **warm**. **1.** n. An enclosed chamber of brick &c. or vessel of iron in which great heat is generated for purposes of warming houses, water &c., or for smelting metal and other purposes. **2.** vb. (rare except in P.P.) To supply with a furnace, or furnaces.

furnish, vb. trans. & intrans. [1. fĕrnish; 2. fā̆niʃ]. O. Fr. *fornir, furnir, fournir* for **fourmir*, cp. A.-Fr. *furmir*; borrowed fr. O.H.G. *frumjan*, 'to perform, provide' &c.; fr. another form of same base comes O.E. *fremman*, 'to further, advance' &c., fr. **framm-jan*, fr. *fram*, 'from'. See this base further under **frame, from.** See **-ish (II.)**. **A.** trans. **1.** To provide, supply, fit out, equip; **a** of material action: *to furnish a garden with flowers, a library with books*; **b** of intellectual action: *to furnish a person with information; I can explain, but I can't furnish you with intelligence to understand.* **2.** Specif., to stock, fit out, equip (house, room, office &c.) for use with furniture (in various senses) and all necessary appointments. Phr. *furnished house*, one that is let or hired with furniture in it. **B.** intrans. To engage in the occupation of furnishing, of supplying furniture for, a house: *I shan't be in any hurry to furnish.*

furnisher, n. [1. fĕrnisher; 2. fā̆niʃə]. Prec. & **-er**. One who furnishes; specif., a tradesman who sells furniture for houses.

furnishing, n. [1. fĕrnishing; 2. fā̆niʃiŋ]. **furnish** & **-ing**. **1.** The act of equipping a house with furniture: *furnishing is an expensive business.* **2.** (pl.) **a** Ornaments, adornments; **b** apparatus, furniture &c. for a house.

furniture, n. [1. fĕrnichur; 2. fā̆nitʃə]. Stem of **furnish** & **-ure**. **1.** That with which anything is furnished, equipped, fitted out; in material and non-material senses: *the furniture of a bookshelf, of one's mind.* **2.** (specif. collectively) Movable articles of household requirement in a house, esp. the larger pieces, chairs, tables, sofas, mirrors, bookcases, sideboards &c.: *a piece of furniture; full of fine old furniture.* **3.** (archaic) All the articles necessary for the equipment of a man and horse; armour and harness. **4.** Articles necessary for full equipment of a ship, machine &c.

furore, n. [1. fūrōre; 2. fjurɔ̄ri]. Ital., fr. Lat. *furor*, 'rage, madness'. See **fury**. Widespread, enthusiastic, excited, admiration; craze, 'rage': *the play created a regular furore.*

furred, adj. [1. fērd; 2. fʌ̄d]. **fur (I.)** & **-ed**, or P.P. of **fur (II.)**. **a** Trimmed, covered, with fur; **b** overlaid with unhealthy covering (of sick man's tongue); **c** coated with lining deposit (of kettles &c.).

furrier, n. [1. fúrier; 2. fáriə]. **fur (I.)** & **-ier**. Tradesman who sells furs, and supplies coats &c. made of fur.

furriery, n. [1. fúrieri; 2. fáriəri]. Prec. & **-ry**. **1.** The business of a furrier; the fur trade. **2.** Furs collectively.

furring, vbl. n. [1. fēring; 2. fʌ̄riŋ]. **fur (I.)** & **-ing**. **1.** Collection of fur for lining or trimming. **2 a** Process of depositing lime from water on the inside of kettles &c.; **b** the deposit itself. **3.** Process of levelling the surface of a wall, beam &c., in building, by covering with thin casing of wood or other material, preparatory to plastering &c.

furring tile, n. One, usually of fire-proof material, affixed to walls by means of spikes.

furrow (I.), n. [1. fúrō; 2. fárou]. O.E. *furh*, M.E. *forou* &c.; O.H.G. *furuh*; cogn. w. Lat. *porca*, 'ridge between furrows'; the further etymol. is very uncertain. **1. a** Groove, channel, made in land, esp. by a plough; **b** (poet.) (i.) plough land; (ii.) act of ploughing: '*their furrow oft the stubborn glebe hath broke*' (Gray's 'Elegy'); also **c** any prolonged groove in land, e.g. a cart-rut &c. **2.** A deep wrinkle on the face or forehead.

furrow (II.), vb. trans., fr. prec. To make furrows; **a** to plough; **b** (poet.) to cross the sea in a ship: *to furrow the ocean with keels* &c.; **c** to cause wrinkles on the face &c.: *a brow furrowed with sorrows.*

furrowing, n. [1. fúrōing; 2. fárouiŋ]. Prec. & **-ing**. Corrosion of metal by action of acids &c.

furry, adj. [1. fēri; 2. fʌ̄ri]. **fur (I.)** & **-y**. Covered with fur; having appearance and texture of fur.

further (I.), compar. adv. having no positive [1. fērdher; 2. fʌ̄ðə]. O.E. *furðor*, formed fr. *forð*, 'forwards' (see **forth**), but used as compar. of *fore*, 'before, above'; cp. Gk. *próteros*, 'before, former'. For the old compar. ending *-ter-*, Gmc. *-þer-* &c., see **-ther** & **other**. **1.** Used as compar. of *far*; see also **farther**. On the whole, although *further* and *farther* are often used indifferently, the latter tends to be chiefly used in literal sense, the former in derived, secondary senses; to a greater distance, degree of remoteness: *to go further* (or *farther*) *away*; *not further* (or *farther*) *than a mile from here*; *as far as this but no further* (or *farther*). Phr. *I'll see him further first*, expressing strong withholding of consent or agreement. **2.** Besides, in addition, also, moreover: *we have seen further that . . .*; *let me further tell you. . . .* Phrs. *to inquire further*, make additional inquiries; *to be further continued*, for an additional period, to an additional occasion.

further (II.), adj. O.E. *furthra*. See prec. **1.** More remote, more distant: *the further end of the village*; *the further side of the road, river* &c. **2.** Additional, going beyond that already existing, seen, known, or referred to &c.: *to obtain further information*; *let us have no further talk and delay*; *there is this further advantage.*

further (III.), vb. trans. O.E. *fyrðrian*, 'to advance, promote', fr. **furþr-jan*. See **further (I.)**. To bring to a further, superior, stage of progress; to forward, promote: *to further one's plans, hopes* &c.

furtherance, n. [1. fērdherans; 2. fʌ̄ðərəns]. Prec. & **-ance**. Act or process of furthering, advancing; promotion: *the furtherance of one's schemes.*

furthermore, adv. [1. fērdhermōr; 2. fʌ̄ðəmɔ̄]. **further (I.)** & **-more**. Moreover, in addition to something already referred to.

furthermost, adj. [1. fērdhermōst; 2. fʌ̄ðəmoust]. **further (I.)** & **-most**. Farthermost.

furthest, adj. & adv. [1. fērdhest; 2. fʌ̄ðist]. Superl. formed on anal. of *further*; *furth-* & **-est**. Used as superl. of *far*; most remote, farthest.

furtive, adj. [1. fērtiv; 2. fʌ̄tiv]. Lat. *furtīvus*, 'stolen; secret, concealed', fr. *furt-*, as in *furtum*, 'theft', fr. *fūr*, 'a thief', fr. **fōr*; cp. the cogn. Gk. *phṓr*, 'thief'; fr. Aryan base **bher-* &c., 'to carry, bear (away)'; Lat. *fer-* (see **fertile, -ferous**). See further under **bear (I.)**. **a** (of actions) Done secretly and surreptitiously; clandestine, stealthy, covert, hole-and-corner: *a furtive blow, gesture, movement, glance, smile, measure* &c.; **b** (of persons) given to behaving in a furtive manner; secretive, behaving as though anxious to escape observation: *furtive in one's movements, actions* &c.

furtively, adv. Prec. & **-ly**. In a furtive manner; covertly, stealthily.

furtiveness, n. See prec. & **-ness**. Quality of being furtive.

furuncle, n. [1. fúrungkl; 2. fjúraŋkl]. Lat. *fūrunculus*, 'petty thief', dimin. of *fūr*, 'thief'. See **furtive**. (med.) Small suppurating, inflammatory tumour; a boil.

furuncular, adj. [1. fūrúngkūlar; 2. fjuráŋkjulə]. Prec. & **-ar**. Of the nature of, resembling, a furuncle.

furunculous, adj. [1. fūrúngkūlus; 2. fjuráŋkjuləs]. **furuncle** & **-ous**. **a** Afflicted with boils; **b** apt to cause boils.

fury, n. [1. fūri; 2. fjɔ̄ri]. M.E., fr. O. Fr. *furie*, fr. Lat. *furia*, 'rage' &c., fr. *furere*, 'to rage, rave, be distracted, mad'. Prob. fr. Aryan base **bhur-*, of wh. a fuller form is **bhereu-*, 'to be in violent movement, to be agitated', cp. Lat. *fervēre*, 'to b̶r̶ ' (see **fervent**); more closely connected w. *furia, furĕre*, are Gk. *phúrein*, 'to mix, mingle; confound, confuse'; Gmc. *phurmós*, 'confusion'. The root meaning of *fury* wd. seem to be 'confusion, perplexity, agitation of mind'. **1.** Violent excitement, agitation of mind; rage; **a** extreme anger, tempestuous wrath; **b** violence, vehemence, of the passions: *the fury of desire* &c.; **c** (of actions) violence inspired by such passions and feelings: *the fury of battle, of an attack* &c. **2. a** Violence, boisterousness, raging, of the elements: *the fury of the storm, waves* &c.; **b** intensity: *the full fury of the sun's blaze.* **3.** (class. mythol., cap.) **a** An avenging spirit; **b** one of the Fates: *the blind Fury with the abhorred shears*, Milton, 'Lyc.' **4.** A violent, unrestrainable person, esp. a violent, ungovernable woman; a virago.

furze, n. [1. fērz; 2. fʌ̄z]. O.E. *fyrs*; possibly cogn. w. Lat. *porrum* for **pors-om*, 'leek', though this is denied by Walde, & certainly the connexion between the two plants is not obvious. Thick-growing, wild, evergreen shrub, with spikes instead of leaves, bearing yellow flowers; also called *gorse* and *whin.*

furzy, adj. [1. fērzi; 2. fʌ̄zi]. Prec. & **-y**. Covered with, abounding in, furze.

fuscous, adj. [1. fúskus; 2. fáskəs]. Lat. *fuscus*, 'dark, swarthy', & **-ous**. *Fuscus* is fr. Aryan **dhus-ko*; cp. also Lat. *furvus*, 'dark, dusky, gloomy', fr. **dhus-wos*; a close cogn. is O.E. *dox, dosc*, 'dark-coloured', fr. Germ. **duska-*. See **dusk**. Dark in colour, brown or greyish black.

fuse (I.), vb. trans. & intrans. [1. fūz; 2. fjūz], fr. Lat. *fūsum*, P.P. of Lat. *fundere*, 'to pour, to melt' (see **found (II.)**); *fūs-um* is fr. **ǵheud-tom*; this base appears in Gmc. as **geut-*, **gut-*; cp. Goth. *giutan*, O.E. *ġēotan*, 'to pour' (see second syll. of **ingot**, & **gut (I.)**). **A.** trans. **1.** To melt (metal) by heat, liquefy, dissolve. **2.** To cause to mingle together, to blend. **B.** intrans. **1.** To become liquid, be melted. **2.** To intermingle, become blended. (For use of term in electricity see next word.)

fuse (II.), n. Ital. *fuso*, fr. Lat. *fūsus*, 'spindle'. Etymol. doubtful. Walde tentatively suggests connexion w. prec., assuming that possibly the name was first given to stones used as spindles wh. had been shaped by the action of water. This is perh. far-fetched. Name given to various mechanical devices: **1.** A tube filled with combustible or explosive material, used to start explosion in blasting operations, explosive shells &c. **2.** (elect.) Bar of metal inserted as a precaution in electric circuit, which melts, 'fuses', and interrupts the circuit when current exceeds a given strength. In this sense the meaning is probably associated with **fuse (I.)**.

fusee, n. [1. fūzḗ; 2. fjuzī]. Fr. *fusée*, 'spindleful', fr. Med. Lat. *fūsāta*, fr. Lat. *fūs-(us)*, see **fuse (II.)**. **1.** Conical wheel with a spiral groove in old-fashioned clock, from which a cord is unwound by the turning of a barrel containing the spring. **2.** Bony growth on horse's leg. **3.** Kind of match used formerly for lighting a pipe in a wind, having a large head, which on being struck flames and glows for some time, and is attached to the shank by thin threads; also called a *braided light.*

fuselage, n. [1. fūzelij; 2. fjūzilidž], or as Fr. Fr., fr. *fusil*, O. Fr. *fusel*, 'spindle', see **fusil (I.)**, & **-age**. The body of an aeroplane, containing the pilot's seat &c., of long, narrow, spindle-shaped form.

fusel oil, n. [1. fūzl óil; 2. fjúzl ɔ́il]. Germ., 'bad spirit', fr. *fuseln*. See **foozle**. Oily liquid of unpleasant taste, associated with whisky or other spirit insufficiently distilled or matured.

fusibility, n. [1. fūzibíliti; 2. fjūzibíliti]. Next word & **-ity**. Capacity for being fused; degree to which this exists.

fusible, adj. [1. fūzibl; 2. fjūzibl]. **fuse (I.)** & **-ible**. Capable of being fused.

fusiform, adj. [1. fūziform; 2. fjūzifɔ̄m]. **fuse (II.)** & **-form**. Shaped like a spindle; broadest in the middle and tapering towards either end.

fusil (I.), n. [1. fūzil; 2. fjūzil]. O. Fr. *fusel*, fr. Lat. *fūsellum*, little spindle', dimin. of *fūsus*, 'spindle'. See **fuse (II.)**. (her.) Figure resembling the *lozenge*, but longer and narrower, and sharper at upper and lower ends.

fusil (II.), n. Fr., fr. Ital. *focile*, fr. Lat. *focus*, 'hearth', w. dimin. suff. See **focus**. Old-fashioned light musket, now obsolete.

fusile, adj. [1. fūsil, -il; 2. fjūsail, -il]. Lat. *fūsilis*. See **fuse (I.)** & **-ile**. Molten, fluid.

fusilier, n. [1. fūzilḗr; 2. fjūzilíə]. **fusil (II.)** & **-ier**. **1.** (obs.) Soldier armed with a fusil. **2.** Soldier belonging to one of those British regiments who were formerly armed with fusils: *Royal Fusiliers* &c.

fusillade, n. & vb. trans. [1. fūzilád; 2. fjūziléid]. Fr. See **fusil (II.)** & **-ade**. **1.** n. Rapid and continuous fire from a number of firearms. **2.** vb. To shoot down with such a discharge.

fusilly, adj. [1. fūzili; 2. fjūzili]. **fusil (I.)** & **-y**. (her., of shield) Covered with fusils.

fusing, n. [1. fūzing; 2. fjūziŋ]. **fuse (I.)** & **-ing**. Process of melting; fusion.

fusion, n. [1. fūzhun; 2. fjūžən]. Lat. *fūsiōn-(em)*, 'a pouring out', fr. *fūs-*, P.P. type of *fundere*, 'to pour, melt' (see **fuse (I.)**). See also **foison**, & second element in **confusion, profusion** &c. **1. a** Action or process of melting, liquefying metals by subjecting them to intense heat; **b** condition of being melted. **2.** (in material and non-material sense) **a** Act or process of blending, mixing things, as though melting them together; **b** result of such act or process; things blended, mingled, mixed, together; a blend, intimate mixture, coalition: *fusion of race, speech, creeds* &c.; *fusion of political parties.*

fusionism, n. [1. fūzhunizm; 2. fjūžənizəm]. Prec. & **-ism**. Theory in favour of fusion, of races, creeds, parties &c.

fusionist, n. [1. fūzhunist; 2. fjūžənist]. **fusion** & **-ist**. Advocate of fusionism.

fuss (I.), n. [1. fus; 2. fas]. No history or cognates; prob. imitative of hissing, or puffing sound. **1.** A nervous, highly excited, irascible state of mind, in which unnecessary anxiety is felt and expressed regarding unimportant things: *to get into a fuss*; *in a state of fuss.* **2.** Nervous, rapid, excited activity; a bustle, commotion, tumultuous state of affairs: *there was a terrible fuss on the platform when the king arrived.* Phrs. *to make a fuss*, cause trouble, make angry complaints; *make a fuss of (a person)*, treat with marked consideration, be attentive to; *make a fuss about*, **a** complain angrily about; **b** be ostentatious, make a parade of.

fuss (II.), vb. intrans. & trans., fr. prec. **1.** intrans. To get nervously excited, to worry, chafe; *fuss about*, to bustle about in an excited, agitated way. **2.** trans. To worry, bother, put into state of commotion and agitation; make nervous or anxious.

fussily, adv. [1. fúsili; 2. fásili]. **fussy** & **-ly.** In a fussy manner.

fussiness, n. [1. fúsines; 2. fásinis]. See prec. & **-ness.** State of being fussy.

fussy, adj. [1. fúsi; 2. fási]. **fuss** (I.) & **-y.** **1. a** (of persons) Tending to fuss or to make a fuss; insisting strongly on trivial details; fidgety, full of fads and crotchets; **b** (of behaviour) nervous, jumpy; lacking restraint, calm, dignity. **2.** Exhibiting unnecessary and trivial detail; finicky; reverse of simple or restrained: *a fussy literary style*; *fussy ornamentation* &c.

fust, n. [1. fust; 2. fast]. O. Fr. *fust*, 'staff; cask (made of staves)', Mod. Fr. *fût*; Lat. *fustis*, 'cudgel, staff'; fr. Aryan **bhudstis*; cp. O.N. *beysta*, 'to knock, strike'; cp. second element in **confute**; cogn. w. O.E. *bēatan*, 'to beat' (see **beat** (I.)). **1.** The shaft of a column. **2.** Stale, musty smell; originally the smell of a cask (see meanings of O. Fr. *fust* above).

fustanella, n. [1. fùstanéla; 2. fàstənélə]. Fr. *fustanelle*, dimin. of Ital. *fustagno*, fr. Mod. Gk. *phoústani*, 'fustian'. See next word. Short skirt of stiffened linen, somewhat resembling a highland kilt in shape, worn by men in Albania and some parts of modern Greece.

fustian, n. & adj. [1. fústian; 2. fástiən]. M.E. *fustane, fustyane*, fr. O. Fr. *fustaigne*; cp. Ital. *fustagno*, fr. Mod. Gk. *phoústani*, named after Fustāt, near Cairo, where the material was made. **1.** n. **a** Coarse, twilled cloth with a nap resembling velveteen; corduroy; **b** (fig.) pretentious, high-sounding, but empty talk or style; bombast, claptrap. **2.** adj. **a** Made of fustian; **b** (fig.) pretentious, empty, bombastic.

fustic, n. [1. fústik; 2. fástik]. Arab. *fustuq*, fr. Pers. *pistah.* See **pistachio.** **a** The wood of a tree that grows in Mexico, yielding a yellow dye; **b** the dye itself.

fustigate, vb. trans. [1. fústigāt; 2. fástigeit]. Lat. *fustīgāt-(um)*, P.P. type of *fustīgāre*, 'to cudgel', fr. *fustis*, 'stick, cudgel'. See **fust.** To thrash with a stick.

fustigation, n. [1. fùstigā́shun; 2. fàstigéiʃən]. Prec. & **-ion.** A thrashing.

fustiness, n. [1. fústines; 2. fástinis]. **fusty** & **-ness.** Condition of being fusty; stale, mouldy, musty smell.

fusty, adj. [1. fústi; 2. fásti]. **fust** & **-y.** **1.** Smelling stale and mouldy; stuffy. **2.** (fig.) Lacking freshness, stale; old-fashioned; out of touch with life and realities: *a fusty pedant*; *a fusty book*; Phr. *musty fusty.*

futchel(l), n. [1. fúchel; 2. fátʃəl]. Origin unknown. A timber supporting the shafts or the axle-bar of a vehicle.

futharc, futhorc, n. [1. fóōdhark, -ork; 2. fúðāk, -ōk]. Runic alphabet; so called from the first six letters; *th* is written þ.

futile, adj. [1. fū́tīl; 2. fjū́tail]. Lat. *fūtilis*, 'easily poured, brittle; worthless'; prob. fr. **fud-*, Aryan **ghu-d-*, 'pour' (see **fuse** (I.)), the series of changes in meaning being 'flowing, tending to flow, not easily contained, mobile, restless, volatile, unreliable, worthless'. **a** (of persons) Frivolous, ineffective, inane, superficial, inept; **b** (of action) accomplishing nothing; ineffectual, vain, useless, fruitless: *a futile attempt.*

futilely, adv. Prec. & **-ly.** In a futile manner.

futileness, n. See prec. & **-ness.** State or quality of being futile; inanity, ineptitude; uselessness, fruitlessness, ineffectualness.

futility, n. [1. fūtíliti; 2. fjūtíliti]. Lat. *fūtilitāt-(em)*, 'worthlessness'. See **futile** & **-ity.** **1. a** Emptiness, frivolousness, ineffectiveness, of mind and character; **b** uselessness, fruitlessness, worthlessness. **2. a** A foolish, futile action; piece of folly; **b** futile person.

futtock, n. [1. fútok; 2. fátək]. Origin uncertain; several writers suggest derivation fr. *foot hook.* **1.** A crooked lower timber of a ship below the deck, esp. one passing across and over keel. **2.** (attrib.) *Futtock plates*, iron plates in a ship's top, to which the dead-eyes are fastened; *futtock-shrouds*, small shrouds beneath a ship's top.

future (I.), adj. [1. fū́chur; 2. fjū́tʃə]. Fr. *futur*, fr. Lat. *futūrum*, 'about to be', used as fut. part. of *esse*, 'to be'; cp. Lat. *fui*; fr. Aryan base **bhū-*, **bheu-* &c., 'to become, exist, generate' &c.; whence also O.E. *bēon* &c. (see **be**); Gk. *phúein*, 'to produce, bring forth, make to grow' &c., *phûma*, 'growth', *phúsis*, 'nature' (see **physio-** & **phylo-**); Scrt. *bhávati*, 'is, exists, happens', *bhūmiš*, 'earth'; O. Slav. *byti*, 'to be, become, grow'. See also **boor, bower, build.** **1. a** Happening hereafter; going, about, to happen in a time later than, after, this present: *future events*; **b** that will exist, that will appear, be born, come into existence, at a time subsequent to, later than, the present: *future ages*; *future generations of men*; *the Future Life*, that which will follow mortal, earthly, existence; the Hereafter. **2.** Of, connected with, expressing, time that is to come: *future tense.*

future (II.), n., fr. prec. **1.** Time to come, the time which will follow this present: *no one can predict what will happen in the future*; *to prepare for the future.* **2.** What will happen to a person, country &c. in the time to come; career, life, fate; esp. with an idea of favourable conditions, developments: *to provide for the future of one's family*; *to have a great future*; *to have no future.* **3.** *The Future*, the Future Life, life beyond mortal existence. **4.** (commerc.) *Futures*, goods, esp. grain, cotton, wool &c., bought at prices ruling when bargain is made, and paid for and delivered, subsequently.

futureless, adj. [1. fū́churles; 2. fjū́tʃəlis]. Prec. & **-less.** Without hope or expectation of a future.

futurist, n. [1. fū́churist; 2. fjū́tʃərist]. **future** (II.) & **-ist.** **1.** Person who looks forward to future fulfilment of Biblical prophecies. **2.** One of a school of modern painters &c. whose work few persons can appreciate in the present, and who, supposing themselves to be ahead of their age, are presumed to be working for the applause of the future.

futurity, n. [1. fūtū́riti; 2. fjūtjṓriti]. **future** (II.) & **-ity.** **1. a** Time to come; the future; **b** specif., the time after this mortal life. **2.** *Futurities*, future events.

futurity race, n. One for futurity stakes.

futurity stakes, n. Stakes competed for, in racing, a considerable time after the competitors are entered.

fuzz, n. [1. fuz; 2. faz]. Light, tangled mass of fibres, threads, hair &c., of stiffer or wirier consistency than *fluff.*

fuzziness, n. [1. fúzines; 2. fázinis]. Next word & **-ness.** Quality of being fuzzy.

fuzzy, adj. [1. fúzi; 2. fázi]. **fuzz** & **-y.** Fluffy, consisting of, having consistency of, fuzz.

Fuzzy-wuzzy, n. [1. fúzi wúzi; 2. fázi wázi]. (slang) Soudanese fighting man in his natural, wild state.

-fy, suff. [1. fī; 2. fai], fr. Fr. *-fier*, fr. Lat. *-ficāre*; see **-fic** & **-fication**; fr. Lat. *fac-*, 'to make, cause' &c. The suff. means 'make, cause to become', & is added freely to adjs. & ns.: *beatify, deify, Frenchify* &c. In jocular formations fr. Engl. words the suff. often has an intens. or freq. force; e.g. *speechify*, 'to keep on making speeches'. For base see **fact.**

fylfot, n. [1. fílfot; 2. fílfət]. Said to mean 'fill the foot', of a window, in reference to device in lower half of a stained-glass window. The swastika, the symbol 卍.

fytte. See **fit** (II.).

G

G, g [1. jē; 2. džī]. The seventh letter of the English & other alphabets, as in Latin &c.; for abbreviations &c. see end of Dictionary; (mus.) the fifth note of the major scale of C.

gab, n. [1. gab; 2. gæb]. Du. *gabberen*, 'to joke, to chatter', Fr. *gaber*, 'to deceive', akin to 'gabble, gape' (colloq.). Loquacity, talkativeness; chatter. Phr. *the gift of the gab*, readiness, fluency, of speech.

gabardine. See **gaberdine.**

gabble (I.), vb. intrans. & trans. [1. gábl; 2. gǽbl]. Freq. of *gab*, akin to *gobble*; imitative in origin. **1.** intrans. To chatter, jabber, talk, speak rapidly and indistinctly: *speak more slowly, don't gabble.* **2.** trans. To utter rapidly and indistinctly: *to gabble one's prayers*; *gabble out an apology* &c.

gabble (II.), n., fr. prec. **a** Rapid, indistinct talk or utterance; **b** foolish, meaningless talk.

gabbler, n. [1. gábler; 2. gǽblə]. **gabble** (I.) & **-er.** One who gabbles; chatterer.

gabbro, n. [1. gábrō; 2. gǽbrou]. Ital. name for certain kinds of rock in N. Italy, including serpentine. (geol.) A basic, igneous rock, resembling granite, having a mottled appearance, composed of feldspar, augite &c.

gabelle, n. [1. gabél; 2. gæbél]. Fr., 'tax on salt', fr. Span. *gabela*, O. Ital. *cabella, caballa*, Arab. *qabala*, 'tax, tribute'; apparently confused w. *gavel* (see **gavelkind**). **1.** A tax, or impost, levied in certain continental countries. **2.** Specif., an indirect tax on salt levied by the State in France under the Old Régime.

gaberdine, gabardine, n. [1. gáberdēn; 2. gǽbədīn], fr. O. Fr. *gauvardine*; prob. fr. M.H.G. *wallevart*, 'pilgrimage, journey', fr. O.H.G. *wall-ōn*, 'to roam, wander', & O.H.G. *fart*, 'journey', fr. *faran*, 'to go'. See under **walk** & **fare.** **1.** A long, loose gown; specif., garment prescribed for Jews in the Middle Ages. **2.** A kind of thin cloth.

gabion, n. [1. gā́biun; 2. géibiən]. Fr., fr. Ital. *gabbione*, augm. of *gabbia*, Low Lat. *gabia*, Lat. *cavea*, 'a cage'. See **cage.** **1.** (fort.) A bottomless basket or cylinder of wicker-work or the like, filled with earth, used to form temporary defences, parapets &c. against the enemy's fire or as a revetment. **2.** A similar contrivance filled with stones and sunk at a harbour mouth or elsewhere in order to form a bar.

gabionade, n. [1. gā̀biunā́d; 2. gèibiənéid].

See prec. & **-ade.** Any work composed of gabions; **a** protective traverse sheltering guns; **b** lines of sunken gabions forming the nucleus for a sand-bar in harbour-works.

gable, n. [1. gābl; 2. géibl]. M.E., fr. O. Fr. *gable*, fr. O.N. *gafl*; cp. O.H.G. *gebal*, 'skull, head', *gabala*, 'fork'; Goth. *gibla*, 'gable, pinnacle'. Cogn. w. Gk. *kephalḗ*, 'head'. See **cephalic. 1.** Angular upper part of wall of building, enclosed by sloping sides of roof. **2.** End wall of a building, the upper part of which consists of a gable. **3.** Architectural ornament shaped like a gable.

gabled, adj. [1. gābld; 2. géibld]. Prec. & **-ed.** Finished with, in form of, a gable.

gable-end, n. End wall finished with a gable.

gablet, n. [1. gāblet; 2. géiblit]. **gable & -et.** Small gable-shaped canopy over window &c., as ornament.

gable-window, n. Window opening from a gable.

gaby, n. [1. gābi; 2. géibi]. Etymol. uncertain. Foolish person, simpleton, ninny.

gad (I.), interj. [1. gad; 2. gæd]. Variant of **God**, showing the un-rounding of the vowel, which is fairly frequent in 16th- & 17th-cent. English. A meaningless exclamatory utterance.

gad (II.), vb. intrans. Prob. back-formation fr. obs. *gadling*; O.E. *gædeling*, M.E. *gadeling*; cp. O.H.G. *gateling*, O.S. *gaduling*; Goth. *gadiliggs*; dimin. of Gmc. **gad-*, 'companion' (O.E. *ġe-gada*; M.H.G. *gate*). See **gather. 1.** To run about from one place to another, esp. in search of amusement and excitement; to waste time in aimless wandering; usually *gad about*. **2.** (of plants) To straggle: '*With wild thyme and the gadding vine o'ergrown*' (Milton, 'Lyc.').

gad (III.), n. Apparently variant of **goad**; cp. **gad-fly. a** The point of a spear or arrow; **b** a goad; **c** bar or wedge of steel used in quarrying.

gadabout, n. [1. gádabout; 2. gǽdəbaut]. **gad (II.) & about.** Person given to gadding.

gad-fly, n. First element, prob. O.E. *gād*, 'goad', w. shortening of vowel before following two consonants in combination. See **goad. 1.** Fly attacking cattle. **2.** An irritating person.

gadget, n. [1. gájet; 2. gǽdžit]. Origin unknown; first a naval term. (colloq.) **a** Any ingenious fitting, contrivance, or accessory, to a motor-car &c.; **b** (contemptuous) a small, trifling, complicated, fussy, rather useless object.

Gadhelic, adj. & n. [1. gadélik, -ēlik; 2. gædélik, gædílik]. Ir. *Gaedheal*, 'Gael', & **-ic. 1.** adj. Pertaining to the Gaels of Scotland, Ireland, and the Isle of Man. **2.** n. The dialects of the Gadhelic tribes, Irish Gaelic, Scottish Gaelic, and Manx.

Gadidae, n. pl. [1. gádidē; 2. gǽdidī], fr. Neo-Lat. *gadus*, fr. Late Gk. *gádos*, 'a kind of fish'. (zool.) The family of sea-fishes which includes the cod-fish, genus *Gadus*, the haddock, pollack &c.

gadoid, adj. [1. gádoid; 2. gǽdɔid]. See prec. & **-oid.** Resembling, belonging to, the cod fishes, the family Gadidae.

gadroon, n. [1. gadrōōn; 2. gədrún], fr. Fr. *godron*. Etymol. doubtful. One of a series of raised bosses used as an ornament on the border of a cup &c., or in architecture.

Gaekwar, Gaikwar, n. [1. gíkwar; 2. gáikwā]. Hind., properly a family name of the dynasty. Title of the ruler of Baroda, in India.

Gael, n. [1. gāl; 2. geil], fr. Scottish Gaelic, *Gaidheal*. Scottish or (more rarely) Irish Celt.

Gaelic, adj. & n. [1. gālik; 2. géilik]. Prec. & **-ic. 1.** adj. Pertaining to the Gaels, or to their language. **2.** n. **a** Celtic speech of Scotland, Ireland, and the Isle of Man; Gadhelic; this as distinguished from Brythonic or Cymric, i.e. Welsh, Cornish, and Breton; **b** one of these dialects, esp. Scottish Gaelic.

gaff (I.), n. [1. gaf; 2. gæf], fr. Fr. *gaffe*, 'boat-hook, gaff'. **1.** Iron hook set on short handle for landing salmon &c. **2.** A kind of fish-spear. **3.** (naut.) Spar for extending upper edge of fore-and-aft sail. Phr. (vulg. slang) *to blow the guff*, give away, divulge, a secret.

gaff (II.), vb. trans., fr. prec. To spear, or land (fish) with a gaff.

gaff (III.), n. Cp. Fr. *faire une gaffe*, 'commit an error of tact or manners'; perh. same as **gaff (I.).** (slang) Low-class theatre or other place of amusement.

gaffer, n. [1. gáfer; 2. gǽfə]. Contracted fr. **grandfather** through intermediate *granfer*, or fr. **godfather. 1.** A queer, talkative, old fellow, esp. an aged rustic; used as mode of address, sometimes prefixed to name. **2.** Foreman of a gang of labourers.

gag (I.), n. [1. gag; 2. gæg], fr. next word. **1.** Anything thrust into, or covering, person's mouth to silence him; specif. (surg.) a device for holding patient's mouth open during operation. **2.** (fig.) **a** Anything acting as check or restraint on speech; **b** (parl.) closure. **3.** (slang) Deceit, imposture, hoax. **4.** (theatr. slang) Words, not in the book, interpolated by actor into his part.

gag (II.), vb. trans. & intrans. M.E. *gaggen*, 'to gag, suffocate'. Prob. imitative of sound of choking. **A.** trans. **1.** To silence, prevent from speaking, by filling or covering the mouth. **2.** (fig.) To restrain from, deprive of power of, free speech, deny expression to; to silence by authority. **3.** (slang, rare) To deceive, impose upon, hoax. **B.** intrans. (theatr. slang) To interpolate one's own words into a part.

gage (I.), n. [1. gāj; 2. geidž]. M.E. *gage*, fr. O. Fr. *guage*; of Gmc. origin. See **wage, wed. 1.** A pledge, guarantee, security. **2. a** Symbol of challenge to fight; glove &c., proffered as challenge; Phr. *to throw down a gage*, to challenge; **b** a challenge.

gage (II.), vb. trans., fr. prec. To offer as pledge or security; to engage, stake.

gage (III.), n. See **gauge.**

gaggle (I.), n. [1. gágl; 2. gǽgl]. Cp. O.N. *gaggl*, 'flock of geese'. Prob. imitative of the birds' cries. (archaic) *Gaggle of geese*, all those feeding, or being driven, together; a flock.

gaggle (II.), vb. intrans. To cackle.

gaiety, n. [1. gāiti; 2. géiiti], fr. Fr. *gaieté*. **gay & -ty. 1.** The state or quality of being gay; mirth, light-heartedness. **2.** (of inanimate things) Brightness, gay appearance, cheerfulness. **3.** (often pl.) Festivity, merry-making, light, gay entertainment: *the gaieties of the London season*.

gaily, adv. [1. gāli; 2. géili]. **gay & -ly.** In a gay manner; so as to express, suggest, or induce gaiety; a light-heartedly, cheerfully; **b** brightly, in bright, strong colours: *gaily lighted windows*; *gaily painted walls* &c.

gain (I.), vb. trans. & intrans. [1. gān; 2. gein]. This word appears to represent two quite distinct orig. words; the form might result fr. either, the meanings include those of both; (1) M.E. *gain*, 'advantage, profit', & *gainen*, 'to be of use, to profit'. This is of Scand. origin & is not found in O.E. or O.H.G., but is fr. O.N. *gagn*, 'advantage, use, avail'. The cognates *geigan*, 'strive', & *ga-geigan*, 'to obtain, win', occur in Goth. (2) O. Fr. *gaagnier*, Mod. Fr. *gagner*, 'to gain' &c., wh. orig. meant 'to derive profit from cultivating the soil', also 'to obtain pasture, feed'. Cp. M.E., fr. O. Fr. *gainage*, 'profit from cultivation of soil'. This = Ital. *guadagnare*, & is derived fr. Gmc., cp. O.H.G. *weidanjan*, 'to pasture, feed, cattle', wh. comes fr. O.H.G. *weida*, 'food, fodder, pasture'; also 'hunting, hunting-ground', cp. Mod. Germ. *weide*, 'meadow, pasturage'. With this are cogn., O.E. *wāþ*, 'wandering, travelling; hunting', & O.N. *veiðr*, 'catch of fish; hunting'. A remoter cogn. is Lat. *vēnāri*, 'to hunt', q.v. under **venery (I.) & venison. A.** trans. **1.** To obtain, secure, by labour and industry; to earn: *to gain one's living, livelihood* &c. **2.** To obtain by effort or merit, esp. in competition; to win: *to gain a victory*; *to gain a prize*; *to gain the chief applause*; *to gain an advantage over another*; *to gain the upper hand*, obtain predominating position, influence. **3.** To acquire as an increase of, secure as an addition to, one's possessions; obtain as a profit (opposed to *lose*); **a** (of material things): *to gain wealth*; *to gain the whole world and lose one's soul*; *to gain five pounds over a transaction*; *to gain a faithful servant*; **b** (of non-material advantage): *to gain fresh honours*; *to gain kudos*; *gain experience*; Phrs. *to gain strength*, improve in health and vigour; *to gain ground* (fig.), to make progress; *to gain time*, (i.) to save time, get something done more quickly; (ii.) to secure extra allowance of time; cause delay deliberately. **4.** To reach, attain to, arrive at (esp. as a result of effort): *to gain the summit of a mountain*; *to gain the harbour*; *to gain shelter*. **B.** intrans. **1.** To derive benefit, to profit: *you may suffer at first, but you will gain in the end by your unselfishness.* **2.** To improve, become enhanced in value, merit &c.: *his writing gained by continued practice.* Phr. *to gain by comparison*, to create more favourable impression, appear to be all the better, in contrast with something else. **C.** Followed by preposition or adv. *Gain on, upon*, **1. a** to get nearer to, decrease distance between, overtake: *to gain on one's prey*; **b** to move faster than, make more progress than, outstrip: *to gain on one's pursuers.* **2.** (of sea) To encroach upon (the land). **3.** (fig.) To make progress in the favour of, grow upon. *Gain over*, to bring to one's side, prevail upon, win over.

gain (II.), n. See prec. **1.** Increase, addition; **a** (of material possessions, wealth &c.) profit, earnings, winnings; opposite of *loss*: *the gain(s) from scientific work is (are) small, compared with the profits from commerce*; **b** (of non-material advantage) *increase of wealth is not always a gain to one's happiness*; *a gain to knowledge*; *intellectual gain.* **2.** Process of gaining, of acquiring, and accumulating, material wealth: *blinded by the love of gain.* **3.** Increase, enhancement, **a** in value; **b** in magnitude, bulk, strength &c.

gainable, adj. [1. gānabl; 2. géinəbl]. Prec. & **-able.** Capable of being gained.

gainful, adj. [1. gānfool; 2. géinful]. **gain (II.) & -ful. 1.** Yielding gain; profitable. **2.** Eager for gain.

gainings, n. [1. gāningz; 2. géiniŋz]. **gain (II.) & -ing (I.).** What is gained: **a** earnings; **b** profits, emoluments; **c** something acquired by victory; winnings.

gainless, adj. [1. gānles; 2. géinlis]. **gain (II.) & -less.** Yielding no gain; profitless; unavailing.

gainly, adj. [1. gānli; 2. géinli]. M.E. *geinliche, -ly*, 'gracious', cp. M.E. *gein*, 'convenient, ready; direct', fr. O.N. *gegn*; ultimately same word as in **again.** (obs. or provinc.) Comely; graceful, alert, in movements, cp. *ungainly*.

gainsay, vb. trans. [1. gānsá; 2. geinséi]. M.E. *gainseie*, fr. O.N. *gegn*, 'against', cogn. w. **again, & say.** To contradict, dispute, deny.

gainst, prep. [1. gānst; 2. geinst]. Contracted fr. **against.** (poet.) Against.

gait, n. [1. gāt; 2. geit]. Variant of **gate (II.).** Manner of walking; carriage of the body in walking or running: *an awkward, slouching gait.*

gaiter, n. [1. gāter; 2. géitə], fr. Fr. *guêtre*, 'gaiter'. Origin doubtful. Cloth or leather covering for leg from knee to ankle, or for ankle only.

gaitered, adj. [1. gāterd; 2. géitəd]. Prec. & **-ed. a** Wearing gaiters; **b** covered by gaiter(s).

gala, n. [1. gāla; 2. géilə]. Fr., fr. Ital. *gala*. Prob. of Gmc. origin; cp. O. Fr. *galer*, 'to rejoice, make merry', & see **gallant.** Time of rejoicing and merry-making; festivity, fête.

galactic, adj. [1. galáktik; 2. gəlǽktik], fr. Gk. *galáktik-(os)*, 'milky', fr. *gálakt-(os)*, genit. of *gála*, 'milk'. See next word & **-ic**. (astron.) Pertaining to the Milky Way or Galaxy.

galacto-, pref. representing Gk. *gálakto-(s)*, genit. of *gála*, 'milk', cogn. w. Lat. *lac*, genit. *lactis*, 'milk' (see **lacteal**), fr. **glag-t-*. (in scientific terms) Milk; e.g. *galactometer*, instrument for testing quality of milk; *galactophorous*, (of ducts) conveying milk.

gala-day, n. Day of festivity and merry-making.

gala-dress, n. Dress suitable for festive occasion; full-dress.

galago, n. [1. galágō; 2. gəléigou]. Native name. A genus of small tropical African lemurs, with large ears and long tail.

galangale, n. See **galingale**.

galantine, n. [1. gàlantḗn; 2. gǽləntīn]. Fr. Dish made of chicken, veal &c., boned, cut small, and seasoned; usually rolled, boiled, and eaten cold.

galanty show, n. [1. galánti shō; 2. gəlǽnti ʃou]. Prob. fr. Ital. *galanti*, pl. of *galante*, 'fine gentleman'. See **gallant**. **a** Shadow pantomime thrown on screen by moving puppets; **b** popularly, any spectacular theatrical performance; or (contempt.) ceremonial proceedings supposed to resemble this.

galaxy, n. [1. gálaksi; 2. gǽləksi], fr. Fr. *galaxie*, fr. L. Lat., fr. Gk. *galaxías*, 'the Milky Way', fr. *gálakt-*, stem of *gála*, 'milk'. See **galacto-**. **1.** The Milky Way, an irregular luminous band extending across the heavens, consisting of innumerable stars, too distant to be seen separately by the naked eye. **2.** A splendid or illustrious assembly; brilliant group: *a galaxy of beauty*.

galbanum, n. [1. gálbanum; 2. gǽlbənəm]. Lat., fr. Gk. *khalbánē*, prob. a Semitic loan-word. An aromatic, resinous juice obtained from a variety of the plant *ferula*.

gale (I.), n. [1. gāl; 2. geil]. O.E. *gagel*, M.E. *gawel*, M.H.G. *gagel*, 'sweet-gale'. An aromatic shrub; bog-myrtle; generally *sweet-gale*.

gale (II.), n. Etymol. doubtful. Connexion w. O.E. &c., *galan*, 'to sing'; or on the other hand, w. Dan. *gal*, 'furious', appears to be merely speculative & fanciful. **1. a** (popular) A strong, violent, boisterous wind; **b** specif., a wind with any velocity between 25 and 75 miles per hour: *a gale of wind*; *it is blowing a gale*. **2.** (poet.) A breeze, a light air.

gale (III.), n. Perh. fr. a Late M.E. form **gāl-*, contracted fr. *-gavel*, 'tribute, rent, tax'. See **gavelkind**. (rare) Rent paid at fixed intervals.

galea, n. [1. gālea; 2. géiliə]. Lat. *galea*, 'leather helmet; guinea-fowl's crest'. Prob. a loan-word fr. Gk. *galéē*, 'weasel, polecat, marten', w. the name transferred first to 'skin or hide, leather', & then to 'something made of leather'. Gk. *galéē* is cogn. w. Scrt. *giriš*, 'mouse'; Lat. *glīs*, 'dormouse'. (bot., zool.) Helmet-shaped structure, covering, or process.

galeate(d), adj. [1. gāliāt(ed); 2. géilieit(id)]. Prec. & **-ate** (& **-ed**). Covered with, furnished with, a helmet-shaped structure or process.

galeeny, n. [1. galḗni; 2. gəlīni], fr. Span. *gallina* (*morisca*), 'Moorish hen', fr. Lat. *gallīna*, 'hen'. See **gallinaceous**. A guinea-fowl.

Galen, n. [1. gālen; 2. géilen], fr. Lat., fr. *Galēnos*, a Greek physician & medical writer who died c. A.D. 200. (facet.) A physician.

galena, n. [1. galḗna; 2. gəlīnə]. Lat., 'lead ore', fr. Gk. *galḗnē*, 'calmness as of the sea; lead sulphide'; connected w. Gk. *geláein*, 'to smile', wh. is prob. cogn. w. O.H.G. *kleini*, 'bright, elegant', O.E. *clǣne*, see **clean**. Native lead sulphide; ore from which lead is extracted, also called 'lead glance'.

galenic(al), adj. [1. gālḗnik(l); 2. geilínik(l)]. See **Galen** & **-ic** (& **-al**). **1.** Of, pertaining to, resembling the methods of, Galen. **2.** (of remedies) Compounded of vegetable substances without chemical process.

Galilee, n. [1. gálilē; 2. gǽlilī], fr. district in Palestine; prob. fr. 'Galilee of the Gentiles' (Matt. iv. 15), therefore of something less sacred. Porch or chapel at west end of certain cathedral churches.

galimatias, n. [1. gàlimátias; 2. gæ̀limǽtiæs]. Fr., 'nonsense, gibberish'. Etymol. uncertain, but Meyer-Lübke suggests derivation fr. *garrimantia*, humorously concocted by Albertus Magnus fr. *garrīre*, 'to prate, chatter', on anal. of *necromantia*, *geomantia* &c. Confused jumble of words, nonsensical medley; confused jargon with words from different languages.

galingale, n. [1. gálinggāl; 2. gǽliŋgeil], fr. O. Fr. *galingal*, fr. Arab. *khalanjān*, perh. fr. Chinese. **1.** Aromatic root of certain East Indian herbs of the ginger family. **2.** A kind of sedge of the south of England, the sweet sedge.

galiot, n. See **galliot**.

galipot, n. [1. gálipot; 2. gǽlipɔt]. Fr. Etymol. unknown. Resinous substance which oozes from fir trees, and becomes hard when dried by the air.

gall (I.), n. [1. gawl; 2. gɔ̄l]. Prob. fr. O.N. *gall*; cp. also O.E. *ġ(e)alla*, 'gall, bile'; M.E. *galle*, 'gall, bile; bitter substance; anger'; O.S., O.H.G. *galla*; cogn. w. Gk. *kholḗ*, *khólos*, 'bile'; (fig.) 'anger, hatred' (see **choler**), cogn. w. Lat. *fel*, 'gall'. See further under **yellow**. **1. a** Bitter, greenish or yellowish fluid secreted by the liver into the gall-bladder (of lower animals); bile; **b** gall-bladder. **2.** (fig.) **a** Bitterness, rancour, malignity; Phrs. *gall and wormwood*, something causing intense bitterness of feeling; *a pen dipped in gall*, expressing bitterness, malevolence; **b** (Am. slang) effrontery, audacity, impudence: *to have the gall to do* &c.

gall (II.), n. O.E. *ġ(e)alla*, M.E. *galle*, 'gall, sore place'; cp. O.N. *galli*, M.H.G. *galle*; perh. fr. Lat. *galla*, 'gall-nut'. (See **gall (IV.)**). **1.** Swelling, blister, on horse. **2.** Sore (esp. on horse) produced by friction or pressure; abrasion.

gall (III.), vb. trans., fr. prec. **1.** To injure, break, the surface of, make sore, by rubbing; to abrade. **2.** (fig.) To irritate, chafe, provoke, mortify; also absol.: *that remark galls*.

gall (IV.), n., fr. Fr. *galle*, fr. Lat. *galla*, 'gall-nut'. Walde suggests an earlier form **galnā*, fr. Aryan base **gel-*, **gḷ-* &c., 'to form into a ball'. See **globe**, **gland**, & further **clot**, **cleat**. Small excrescence produced on tree (esp. oak) by insect: *oak-gall*, used in dyeing, medicine &c.

gallant (I.), adj. [1. gálant; 2. gǽlənt], fr. Fr. *galant*, Pres. Part. of O. Fr. *galer*, 'to make merry'; prob. of Gmc. origin; cp. O.H.G. *wallōn*, 'to wander, rove', q.v. under **walk**. **1.** (archaic, of appearance) **a** Gaily attired, fine, showy, decorative: *to make a gallant show*; **b** (specif. of ship or horse), making a fine, imposing show; noble, stately, imposing. **2.** Brave, daring, chivalrous, noble: *a gallant knight, soldier* &c.; (parl.) *the honourable and gallant member*, in referring to member of Army or Navy sitting as M.P. **3.** (also [1. galánt; 2. gəlǽnt]) Showing especial courtesy and deference to women. **4.** (also [1. galánt; 2. gəlǽnt]) Pertaining to love; amorous: *gallant adventures*.

gallant (II.), n. [1. gálant, galánt; 2. gǽlənt, gəlǽnt], fr. prec. **1.** Young man of fashion; one of gay and dashing manners. **2. a** Man courteous and attentive to women; **b** (in good and bad sense) lover.

gallant (III.), vb. trans. & intrans., fr. prec. (rare) **1.** trans. **a** To escort, accompany, attend (lady); **b** to act as lover to, flirt with. **2.** intrans. To play the gallant.

gallantly, adv. [1. gálantli; 2. gǽləntli]. **gallant** (I.) & **-ly**. **1.** Bravely, nobly, chivalrously. **2.** Deferentially, devotedly; after the manner of a lover or admirer.

gallantry, n. [1. gálantri; 2. gǽləntri], fr. Fr. *galanterie*. **gallant** (I.) & **-ery**. **1. a** Spirit of courage and chivalry; bravery, daring, intrepidity; **b** specific exhibition of these qualities; gallant conduct, deed. **2. a** Chivalrous and courteous attention to women; **b** specif., amorous affairs, intrigue.

gall-bladder, n. Small membranous sac or duct below liver, containing gall.

galleass, n. [1. gálias; 2. gǽliæs], fr. O. Fr. *galeasse*, fr. Ital. *galeazza*, fr. Med. Lat. *galea*, 'galley'. See **galley**. Large, heavy, three-masted galley, formerly used on the Mediterranean.

galleon, n. [1. gáliun; 2. gǽliən], fr. Span. *galeon*, fr. Med. Lat. *galeōn-(em)*, fr. Med. Lat. *galea*, 'galley'. See **galley** & **-on**, **-oon**. Old Spanish sailing ship, usually with three or four decks, used for war and commerce.

galleried, adj. [1. gálerid; 2. gǽlərid]. Next word & **-ed**. Furnished with a gallery; pierced with galleries.

gallery, n. [1. gáleri; 2 gǽləri], fr. Fr. *galerie*. Etymol. doubtful. **1.** Long, narrow passage in thickness of wall, or projecting from wall and supported by corbels, at side or end of room &c. above floor level, and open to interior. **2.** Long, narrow, covered court or passage, open at one side; loggia, cloister. **3.** Raised platform in church, hall &c., projecting from wall and supported by pillars, to give extra accommodation. **4.** (theatr.) **a** Uppermost tier, where cheapest seats are usually placed; **b** audience using these seats, regarded as least intellectual or refined section of audience; hence, **c** popular, uncultivated taste. Phr. *to play to the gallery*, make a bid for popularity by appealing to the tastes, passions, or prejudices of the mob. **5.** Long, narrow room; broad corridor. **6.** Room or building for exhibition of works of art. **7.** (min., mil. engin.) Underground communicating passage.

gallery-hit, n. (cricket, theatre &c.) Spectacular stroke or performance designed to please the crowd.

galley, n. [1. gáli; 2. gǽli]. M.E. *galeie*, fr. O. Fr. *galie*, *galee*, fr. Med. Lat. *galea*. Etymol. doubtful. **1.** Ancient war-ship fitted with benches for rowers. **2.** Low, single-decked ship with masts and oars, in former times rowed chiefly by slaves or criminals, hence, pl., a form of penal servitude of France, Spain, and other Mediterranean countries: *to be sent to the galleys*, undergo punishment of such form. **3.** Large rowing-boat, especially of the type used by captain of man-of-war. **4.** Kitchen on board ship. **5.** (print.) **a** Shallow tray with adjustable sides, to which type is transferred from the composing-stick, before being divided into pages; **b** galley-proof.

galley-proof, n. (print.) Impression from type in galley, before division into pages.

galley-slave, n. **a** Slave or criminal condemned to work in galley; hence, **b** person forced to work unreasonably hard; drudge.

galley-worm, n. A millipede, so called from number of its legs, supposed to move like oars of a galley.

gall-fly, n. Insect causing galls on plants.

galliambic, adj. & n. [1. gàliámbik; 2. gæ̀liǽmbik], fr. Lat. *galliambus*, 'song of the priests of Cybele', fr. *Gall-(i)*, 'the priests of Cybele' (named fr. their raving, fr. *Gallus*, a river whose water caused insanity), & **iambus**. **1.** adj. **a** (class. pros.) Written in feet of four syllables, consisting of a pyrrhic (⏑ ⏑) and a spondee (– –) or 'Ionic *a minore*'; as Catullus's *Attis* and Tennyson's *Boadicea*. **2.** n. Galliambic verse.

galliard, n. [1. gáliard; 2. gǽljād], fr. O. Fr. *gaillard*, 'gay, merry'. Animated dance of 16th and 17th cent. for two persons.

Gallic (I.), adj. [1. gálik; 2. gǽlik], fr. Lat. *Gallic-(us)*, 'of the Gauls', fr. *Gall-(us)*, 'a Gaul', & **-ic**. **a** Of, relating to, Gaul or the Gauls; **b** French.

gallic (II.), adj., fr. **gall** (IV.) & **-ic**. Pertaining to, obtained from, galls; as *gallic acid*.

Gallican, adj. & n. [1. gálikan ; 2. gǽlikən], fr. Lat. *Gallicān-(us)*, 'of Gaul'. See **Gallic** (I.) & **-an. 1.** adj. **a** Of, pertaining to, the Roman Catholic Church in France ; **b** belonging to a former body of French Roman Catholics claiming a certain amount of independence of Papal authority. **2.** n. **a** Member of the Roman Catholic Church in France ; **b** a supporter of Gallicanism.

Gallicanism, n. [1. gálikanizm ; 2. gǽlikənizəm]. Prec. & **-ism.** Principles of a body of French Roman Catholics enunciated in 1682, claiming partial autonomy for the national Church of France.

Gallicanist, n. [1. gálikanist ; 2. gǽlikənist]. **Gallican** & **-ist.** Supporter of Gallicanism.

gallice, adv. [1. gálise ; 2. gǽlisi]. Lat. *gallicē*, 'in Gaulish', fr. *Gallic-(us)*, 'gallic'. See **Gallic (I.).** In French (in giving French form of name, or translation of phrase &c.).

gallicism, n. [1. gálisizm ; 2. gǽlisizəm]. **Gallic (I.)** & **-ism.** French word, idiom, or mode of expression, introduced in speaking or writing another language.

Gallicize, vb. trans. [1. gálisīz ; 2. gǽlisaiz]. **Gallic (I.)** & **-ize.** To make French, in feeling, opinion, language &c. ; to Frenchify.

galligaskins, n. pl. [1. gàligáskinz ; 2. gæ̀ligǽskinz], fr. Fr. *garguesque*, fr. Ital. *grechesca*, fem. of *grechesco*, fr. *Grec-(o)*, 'Greek' (see **Greek**), & **-esque.** (chiefly facetious, rather vaguely used) Gaiters, coverings for the legs ; wide breeches.

gallimaufry, n. [1. gàlimáwfri ; 2. gæ̀limɔ́fri], fr. Fr. *galimafrée*, 'hash, ragout' ; etymol. doubtful. Heterogeneous collection, confused medley.

gallinacean, adj. [1. gàlináshun ; 2. gæ̀linéiʃən], fr. Lat. *gallīnāce-(us)*, 'gallinaceous' (see next word), & **-an.** Gallinaceous.

gallinaceous, adj. [1. gàlináshus ; 2. gæ̀linéiʃəs], fr. Lat. *gallīnāceus*, 'of domestic poultry', fr. *gallīn-(a)*, 'hen' (fr. *gall-(us)*, 'cock', & **-ina (I.)**), & **-aceous.** The etymol. of *gallus* is doubtful ; it is prob. cogn. w. O.N. *kalla*, 'to cry out ; to name' (see **call** & **glory**) ; O. Slav. *glasŭ*, 'voice', *glagolati*, 'to speak'. Of that order of birds which includes domestic poultry, pheasants, grouse &c.

gallinazo, n. [1. gàlinázō ; 2. gæ̀linéizou], fr. Span. *gallinaza*, fr. Lat. *gallīna*, 'hen'. See prec. An American vulture.

galling, adj. [1. gáwling ; 2. gɔ́liŋ], fr. Pres. Part. of **gall (III.).** (chiefly fig.) Causing soreness of feeling ; humiliating, wounding, irritating.

gallinule, n. [1. gálinūl ; 2. gǽlinjūl]. L. Lat. *gallīnula*, dimin. of *gallīna*, 'hen'. See **gallinaceous.** A water-fowl, moor-hen.

Gallio, n. [1. gáliō ; 2. gǽliou], fr. name of a Roman proconsul (Acts xviii. 17). Official who shirks responsibility of dealing with any matters outside his immediate department or concerns ; an indifferent, easy-going person.

galliot, n. [1. gáliot ; 2. gǽliət]. M.E., fr. O. Fr. *galiote.* **galley** & dimin. suff. **-ot.** Fast ship moved by both sails and oars, formerly used on the Mediterranean.

gallipot, n. [1. gálipòt ; 2. gǽlipɔ̀t]. Prob. **galley** & **pot**, as being shipped in galleys fr. Mediterranean coasts. Glazed jar or pot of coarse earthenware &c., chiefly used for holding preserves ; jam-pot.

gallium, n. [1. gálium ; 2. gǽliəm], fr. Lat. *gall-(us)*, 'cock' (see **gallinaceous**), as translation of Christian name of discoverer, Lecoq de Boisbaudran, & **-ium.** A rare metallic element, soft and greyish white in colour.

gallivant, vb. intrans. [1. gàlivánt ; 2. gæ̀livǽnt]. Prob. connected w. **gallant. a** To run after, go about with, members of opposite sex ; **b** to gad about, esp. in pleasure-seeking.

gall-nut, n. **gall (IV.).** Oak-apple.

Gallo-, pref. [1. gálō ; 2. gǽlou], representing Lat. *gall-(us)*, 'a Gaul'. French ; e.g. *Gallomania*, craze for imitating French fashions &c. ; *Gallophobia*, hatred of anything French.

gallon, n. [1. gálun ; 2. gǽlən]. M.E. *galoun*, fr. A.-Fr. *galon* ; etymol. obscure ; cp. Fr. *jale*, 'bowl'. **a** A measure of liquid or dry capacity, equal to 4 quarts ; **b** this amount of liquid or of corn.

galloon, n. [1. galóon ; 2. gəlún], fr. Fr. *galon*, 'lace', fr. O. Fr. *galonner*, 'to bind the hair, deck with bands', prob. fr. *galer*, 'to make merry', q.v. under **gallant.** Strong narrow braid for trimming, binding &c., of cotton or silk, sometimes interwoven with gold or silver.

gallop (I.), n. [1. gálup ; 2. gǽləp]. See next word. **1.** The fastest pace of quadrupeds, all four feet being in the air together at one stage of each stride ; Phrs. *at full gallop, at a gallop*, at this pace. **2.** A ride on a galloping horse ; quick ride : *to go for a gallop.*

gallop (II.), vb. intrans. & trans., fr. Fr. *galoper* ; prob. of Gmc. origin ; perh. same as **wallop. A.** intrans. **1. a** (of quadruped) To move at a gallop ; **b** (of rider) to ride at a gallop. **2.** (of person speaking or reading) To hurry, go excessively fast : *to gallop through a book* &c. **3.** To progress, develop, rapidly : *galloping consumption.* **B.** trans. To cause to gallop, send along at a gallop : *to gallop a horse.*

gallopade, n. [1. gàlopád ; 2. gæ̀ləpéid]. Fr. fr. **galop** & **-ade. a** A quick, lively dance ; **b** music for such a dance.

galloper, n. [1. gáluper ; 2. gǽləpə]. **gallop (II.)** & **-er. 1.** One who, that which, gallops. **2.** (mil.) **a** An aide-de-camp ; **b** a small field-gun.

Gallovidian, n. [1. gàlōvídian ; 2. gæ̀louvídiən], fr. Med. Lat. *Gallovidia*, Latinized form of *Galloway*, & **-an.** A native of Galloway.

Galloway, n. [1. gálowā ; 2. gǽləwei], fr. place-name, Scotland. **1.** A small, strong horse, of type originally bred in Galloway. **2.** A breed of cattle.

gallows, n. [1. gálōz ; 2. gǽlouz]. O.E. *galga*, M.E. *gal(o)we* ; cp. O.N. *galgi* ; O.H.G. *galgo* ; Goth. *galga* ; etymol. obscure. **1.** Framework of post(s) with cross-beam, on which criminals are hanged. Phrs. *to come to the gallows*, be hanged ; *a gallows look*, look of a criminal who ought to be hanged. **2.** Any structure or framework resembling gallows.

gallows-bird, n. Criminal who deserves hanging.

gallows-ripe, adj. Deserving to be hanged.

gallows-tree, n. Gallows.

gall-stone, n. Calculus formed in the gall-bladder or gall-ducts.

galop, n. & vb. intrans. [1. gálup ; 2. gǽləp]. Fr., fr. *galoper*, q.v. under **gallop (II.). 1.** n. **a** A quick dance in 2/4 time ; **b** music for this dance. **2.** vb. intrans. To dance a galop.

galore, adv. & n. [1. galór ; 2. gəlɔ́]. Ir. *go leór*, 'enough', fr. advbl. particle *go* & adj. *leór*, 'sufficient' ; O. Ir. *lour*, M. Ir. *lōr*, 'enough', perh. cogn. w. Gk. *ploûtos*, 'riches', q.v. under **plutocracy. 1.** adv. Plentifully, in abundance : *flowers and fruit galore.* **2.** n. (rare or obs.) Plenty, abundance.

galosh, n. See **golosh.**

galumph, vb. intrans. [1. galúmf ; 2. gəlʌ́mf]. Invented by Lewis Carroll ; combination of *gallop* & *triumph.* To prance about, or along, expressing self-satisfaction and triumph.

galvanic, adj. [1. galvánik ; 2. gælvǽnik]. See **galvanism** & **-ic. 1.** (elect.) Relating to, produced by, galvanism ; producing electricity by chemical voltaic action. **2.** (fig., of movement &c.) Caused, worked, by sudden stimulus ; spasmodic, unnatural.

galvanically, adv. [1. galvánikali ; 2. gælvǽnikəli]. Prec. & **-al** & **-ly.** By galvanism ; in a galvanic manner.

galvanism, n. [1. gálvanizm ; 2. gǽlvənizəm], fr. name of discoverer, Galvani (d. 1798), & **-ism. 1.** Electricity produced by chemical action. **2. a** Branch of electrical science treating of this ; **b** treatment of diseases &c. by use of galvanic battery.

galvanist, n. [1. gálvanist ; 2. gǽlvənist], fr. name *Galvan-(i)* (see prec.) & **-ist.** A student of galvanism.

galvanization, n. [1. gàlvanīzáshun ; 2. gæ̀lvənaizéiʃən]. Next word & **-ation.** Act or process of galvanizing ; state of being galvanized.

galvanize, vb. trans. [1. gálvanīz ; 2. gǽlvənaiz]. See **galvanism** & **-ize. 1. a** To subject to galvanic action, electrify by galvanism ; **b** (fig.) startle, stimulate, into sudden activity. **2.** To coat with metal, originally by use of galvanic battery ; *galvanized iron*, corrugated sheet iron coated with zinc, to prevent rust, usually without any galvanic process.

galvano-, pref. Form, used in combination, fr. name Galvani. See **galvanism.** Galvanism ; galvanic : *galvanometer*, instrument for measuring strength of galvanic current.

Galwegian, adj. & n. [1. gàlwéjian ; 2. gæ̀lwídžiən], fr. Galloway, on anal. of *Norwegian.* **1.** adj. Of Galloway. **2.** n. Native of Galloway.

gamba, n. [1. gámba ; 2. gǽmbə]. Ital., fr. L. Lat., 'leg', orig. an abbr. for *viol da gamba* (see **viol**) ; Lat. *gamba*, also written *camba*, is prob. borrowed fr. Gk. *kampḗ*, 'wind, twist, turn'. See **gambit.** Organ-stop producing a note with a tone like that of a viol.

gambade, n. [1. gambád ; 2. gæmbéid]. Fr. *gambade.* See next word. Gambado.

gambado, n. [1. gambádō ; 2. gæmbéidou], fr. Span. *gambada*, fr. Ital. *gambata*, 'gambol' (see **gambol**). **1.** Horse's spring into the air, curvet. **2.** A caper, gambol, prank.

gambeson, n. [1. gámbisun ; 2. gǽmbisən], fr. O. Fr. *gambaison, gambeson*, fr. O. Fr. *gambais, wambais*, fr. O.H.G. *wamba*, 'stomach'. See **womb.** (hist.) Doublet of leather or quilted cloth worn for defence.

gambier, n. [1. gámbier ; 2. gǽmbiə]. Malay *gambir*, 'plant yielding gambier'. Astringent substance prepared from East Indian plant, and used in tanning, dyeing &c.

gambit, n. [1. gámbit ; 2. gǽmbit], fr. Ital. *gambetto*, 'a tripping up', fr. *gamba*, 'a leg', fr. L. Lat. *gamba*, 'fetlock ; hoof ; leg' (cp. **gamba**), prob. a loan-word, fr. Gk. *kampḗ*, 'a turn, bend ; joint' ; cogn. w. Lat. *campus*, 'level place, plain, field', orig. 'depression, subsidence' (see **camp**) ; Lith. *kampas*, 'corner, angle ; region' ; *kumpti*, 'to bend, bow' ; Scrt. *kumpaś*, 'having the hand useless' ; Goth. *hamfs*, 'maimed', orig. 'deformed' ; O.S. *hōf*, O.H.G. *hamf*, 'crippled'. **a** One of several opening moves in chess, in which a pawn is risked for the purpose of gaining an advantage later ; **b** (fig.) initial move in an action or transaction.

gamble (I.), vb. intrans. & trans. [1. gámbl ; 2. gǽmbl]. Prob. fr. *gamel, fr. M.E. *gamenen*, 'to play, joke ; to amuse', fr. *gamen*, 'a game'. See **game (I.). A.** intrans. **1.** To play games of chance with money staked on result ; to play for high stakes ; to speculate in financial transactions : *to gamble in railway shares, in sugar* &c. **2.** (fig.) To take great risks in order to secure possible profit or advantage : *to gamble with one's future.* **B.** trans. *gamble away.* To waste, squander (fortune, estate) in gambling.

gamble (II.), n., fr. prec. **a** The act of gambling ; **b** any risky undertaking, venture, speculation.

gambler, n. [1. gámbler ; 2. gǽmblə]. **gamble (I.)** & **-er.** Person given to gambling ; a gamester.

gamblesome, adj. [1. gámblsum ; 2. gǽmblsəm]. **gamble (I.)** & **-some.** Given to gambling.

gambling, n. [1. gámbling ; 2. gǽmbliŋ]. **gamble (I.)** & vbl. n. suff. **-ing.** Playing games for money, gaming.

gamboge, n. [1. gàmbóozh ; 2. gæ̀mbúž], fr. Mod. Lat. *gambogium*, fr. Cambodia, in Indo-China. A brownish gum-resin obtained from trees of Siam, Cambodia, and Ceylon, used in medicine, and to produce a yellow pigment.

gambol, n. & vb. intrans. [1. gámbl; 2. gǽmbl]. Earlier *gambolde*, fr. O. Fr. *gambade*, 'a leap, caper', fr. Ital. *gambata*, 'a caper, kick', fr. *gamba*, 'a leg', q.v. under **gambit**. **1.** n. A skip, playful caper, frolicsome movement or series of movements; used especially of young lambs and of children. **2.** vb. To skip, caper, frolic, frisk.

game (I.), n. [1. gām; 2. geim]. O.E. *gamen*, 'amusement, game, sport; joy, merriment; joke'; M.E. *gāme(n)*, 'sport, game, jest'. Cp. O.H.G., O.S., O.N. *gaman*, O. Fris. *game*. It has been suggested that these stand for **ga-am-*, the second element being cogn. w. that in Lat. *amāre*, 'to love' (see **amative**); this is, however, quite uncertain. **1.** Sport, amusement, frolic, play: **2.** One of many particular kinds of contest conducted according to fixed rules, and entered into for exercise, amusement, recreation &c.: *the game of cricket, tennis* &c. Phr. *to play the game*, play according to rules of game; (fig.) to behave in a straightforward, honourable manner; *to have the game in one's hands*, be sure of success. **3.** Single round of some contests, e.g. tennis &c. **4.** Success in a game: *this game is yours.* **5.** (pl.) Athletic, dramatic, musical, literary, or other contests, esp. in ancient Greece or Rome as public diversion or celebration: *Olympic games.* **6.** Jest, joke, fun; opposed to *earnest*: *to speak in game.* Phrs. *to make game of*, ridicule, laugh at; *to have a game with*, to hoodwink, befool. **7. a** Scheme, project, undertaking, esp. one whose object is to defeat another person or plan: *the game of war, politics* &c.; *to play a losing, double, game* &c.; Phr. *the game is up*, the scheme is a failure; *game not worth the candle*, unprofitable enterprise; **b** (i) artful scheme, trick, dodge: *don't try any of your games; we saw through your game; he's been up to his old games again*; (ii) scheme intention, proposed plan: *I wish I knew what his game is.* **8. a** Wild animal or bird hunted for food, for sport, or as harmful animal that must be destroyed; **b** animals and birds that may be hunted, considered collectively: *big game*, the larger kinds of hunted animals, elephants, tigers, lions &c.; **c** flesh of game: *to eat game; game pie*; **d** (fig.) any object of pursuit, material or non-material; quarry: *fair game*, legitimate, natural, object of pursuit; one open to attack &c.: *forbidden game*, prohibited object of pursuit; *to fly at higher game*, have more ambitious end or objective.

game (II.), adj., fr. **game-cock**. **1.** Spirited, courageous, plucky; ready to begin or continue fighting; refusing to give in without a struggle. Phr. *to die game*, valiantly fighting to the last. **2.** Ready, spirited enough for, willing: *to be game for anything, to do something.*

game (III.), vb. intrans. & trans., fr. **game (I.)**. **1.** intrans. To gamble, play game of chance for money. **2.** trans. (followed by *away*) *game away* (*property* &c.): to waste, lose, in gaming.

game (IV.), adj. Origin doubtful. Injured, useless, crippled: *a game leg.*

Game Act, n. (usually pl.) Laws controlling preserving, killing, selling &c. of game.

game-bag, n. Bag to hold game when killed.

game-chicken, -cock, n. Chicken, cock, of kind bred for fighting.

gamekeeper, n. [1. gámkēper; 2. géimkīpə]. Man employed to look after game-preserve, rear game &c.

game-law(s), n. Game Act.

game-licence, n. Licence obtained on payment, entitling holder to kill or sell game.

gamely, adv. [1. gámli; 2. géimli]. **game (II.)** & **-ly**. In a game manner; pluckily.

gameness, n. [1. gámnes; 2. géimnis]. **game (II.)** & **-ness**. The quality of being game; pluck.

gamesome, adj. [1. gámsum; 2. géimsəm]. **game (I.)** & **-some**. Playful, merry, sportive, frolicsome.

gamesomely, adv. Prec. & **-ly**. In a gamesome manner.

gamesomeness, n. See prec. & **-ness**. The quality of being gamesome.

gamester, n. [1. gámster; 2. géimstə]. **game (III.)** & **-ster**. Person given to gaming; a gambler.

gamete, n. [1. gamḗt; 2. gæmít], fr. Gk. *gametḗ*, 'wife', fr. *gamé-(ein)*, 'to marry', fr. *gám-(os)*, 'marriage'. See **gamo-**. Reproductive cell which unites with another to form germ of new individual.

game-tenant, n. Person renting shooting or fishing rights.

gamey, adj. See **gamy**.

gamin, n. [1. gáman; 2. gǽmæ̃]. Fr. Etymol. unknown. Street arab; mischievous, neglected, or homeless boy.

gaming, n. [1. gáming; 2. géimiŋ]. **game (III.)** & vbl. n. suff. **-ing**. Playing for money, gambling.

gaming-house, n. House in which gambling is carried on as a source of profit to the proprietor.

gaming-table, n. **a** Table used, or having apparatus for, gambling; **b** (fig.) gambling.

gamma, n. [1. gáma; 2. gǽmə]. Gk. *gámma*, fr. Hebrew *gimel*. **1.** Third letter of Greek alphabet: $\gamma, \Gamma = g$. **2.** Symbol for the third of a series, as *gamma-rays*. **3.** A kind of European moth, with γ-shaped mark on wing.

gammer, n. [1. gámer; 2. gǽmə]. Contracted fr. *grandmother*, through intermediate *granmer*, or fr. *godmother*. Cp. **gaffer**. Old countrywoman.

gammon (I.), n. & vb. trans. [1. gámun; 2. gǽmən], fr. A.-Fr. *gambon*, fr. O. Fr. *gambe*, 'leg', fr. L. Lat. *gamba*, 'leg', see **gambit**, & **-oon**. **1.** n. **a** Part of flitch of bacon including ham; **b** a cured ham. **2.** vb. To cure (bacon).

gammon (II.), vb. trans. & n. Etymol. unknown. (naut.) **1.** vb. To make fast (bowsprit) to stem of vessel. **2.** n. (also *gammoning*) Lashing of rope, chain &c., securing bowsprit to stem.

gammon (III.), n. & interj. Perh. fr. M.E. *gamen*, 'game'. See **game (I.)**. **1.** n. Nonsense, humbug; a hoax, deception. **2.** interj. Nonsense!

gammon (IV.), vb. trans. & intrans. Prob. fr. **gammon (V.)**. **1.** trans. To hoax, hoodwink, deceive, impose upon. **2.** intrans. To speak or act so as to deceive; to dissemble.

gammon (V.), n. & vb. trans. Perh. fr. M.E. *gamen*, 'game'. See **backgammon** & **game (I.)**. **1.** n. Victory (at backgammon) won in specific way. **2.** vb. To defeat (opponent) in this way.

gamo-, pref. [1. gámō; 2. gǽmou], representing Gk. *gám-(s)*, 'marriage' prob. cogn. w. Lat. *geminus*, 'twin'; M. Ir. *gemel*, 'fetter'; O.N. *kimbell*, 'bundle'; Gk. *gambrós*, 'relation by marriage; son-in-law, brother-in-law'; Lat. *gener* (fr. **gemer*), 'son-in-law'; Aryan base **gem-*, **gm̥-*, 'to join, unite'. (esp. bot.) United, coalescing, e.g. *gamopetalous*, with petals joined together; *gamosepalous* &c.

-gamous, suff., forming adjs., w. sense 'marrying', fr. Gk. *gám-(os)*, 'marriage'. See prec. & **-ous**; e.g. *polygamous, bigamous* &c.

gamp, n. [1. gamp; 2. gæmp], fr. the umbrella of Mrs. Gamp in Dickens's *Martin Chuzzlewit*. **a** A large, bulging, untidily rolled umbrella; **b** (facet. and colloq.) any kind of umbrella.

gamut, n. [1. gámut; 2. gǽmət], fr. Med. Lat. *gamma ut*, fr. **gamma**, name given by Guido d'Arezzo (11th cent.) to lowest note of mediaeval scale (see **1** below), & *ut*, name of first note of hexachord, the names of these notes being taken fr. the italicized sylls. of an old Latin hymn to St. John. **1.** Lowest note of mediaeval scale, i.e. G below middle C, two semitones below lowest note of classical scale; note written on lowest line of bass stave. **2.** Mediaeval scale, including all notes from G on lowest line of bass stave to E in top space of treble stave. **3.** Type of musical scale used in specific period. **4.** Whole range or compass of voice or instrument. **5.** (fig.) Whole extent, scope, range: *to experience the whole gamut of suffering.*

gamy, gamey, adj. [1. gámi; 2. géimi]. **game (I.)** & **-y**. **a** Having the flavour or smell of game; **b** high, strong, to the smell or taste; verging towards putrescence.

-gamy, suff., forming ns., w. sense 'marrying, uniting', fr. Gk. *gám-(os)*, 'marriage', see **gamo-**, & **-y**; e.g. *bigamy, exogamy* &c.

gander, n. [1. gánder; 2. gǽndə]. O.E. *ganra, gandra*, M.E. *gandre*; cp. Du. *gander*, prob. fr. **ganza-*, variant of **gans-*. See **goose**. **1.** A male goose. **2.** Fool, dullard, simpleton.

gang, (I.), n. [1. gang; 2. gæŋ]. M.E. *gang*, 'the act of going, walking; a passage; a band, troop', fr. O.E. *gang*, 'the act of going, progression; passage, channel, course'; cogn. w. O.H.G. *gang*, O.N. *gangr*, Goth. *gaggs*, fr. Gmc. **gang-*, 'to go'; O.E. *gangan*, O.N. *ganga*, Goth. *gaggan*. Cogn. w. Scrt. *jangha*, 'lower leg'; Lith. *žengiù*, 'step, walk'; prob. ultimately related to **go**. **1.** A band, group, squad; **a** of labourers working together; **b** of slaves, prisoners &c. **2.** (in bad sense) **a** A group of persons organized for evil or criminal purpose: *a gang of burglars* &c.; **b** (colloq., in disparagement) a body, party, group, of persons: *I am sick of the whole gang of university wire-pullers.* **3.** Set of tools designed, arranged, to work together.

gang (II.), vb. See prec. (Scots) To go: *gang one's own gait*, go one's own way, adopt one's own course of action.

gang-board, n. M.E. *gang*, 'a going; passage'. See **gang (I.)** & **board**. Plank, usually provided with cleats, laid across from vessel to wharf &c. or to another vessel, as means of egress or ingress; gangway.

gange, vb. trans. [1. ganj; 2. gændž]. Origin unknown. To bind part of fishing-line or cast, next hook, with fine thread, so as to strengthen or protect it.

ganger, n. [1. gánger; 2. gǽŋə]. **gang (I.)** & **-er**. Foreman of gang of labourers or workmen.

ganging, n. [1. gánjing; 2. gǽndžiŋ]. **gange** & **-ing**. The act or process of twisting wire round fishing-line.

gangliated, adj. [1. gánggliāted; 2. gǽŋglieitid], fr. Gk. *gágglí-(on)*, 'swelling', see **ganglion**, & **-ate** & **-ed**. Having ganglia.

gangliform, adj. [1. gánggliform; 2. gǽŋglifōm], fr. Gk. *gágglí-(on)*, 'swelling' (see next word), & **-form**. Shaped like a ganglion.

ganglion, n. [1. gánggliun; 2. gǽŋgliən], fr. Gk. *gágglion*, 'a swelling, excrescence; gland'. Etymol. doubtful. **1. a** Nerve-centre; mass or group of nerve-cells; **b** (fig.) centre of activity; centre from which several forms of intellectual or industrial activity radiate. **2.** Small tumour, or sac, containing fluid, usually on a sinew.

ganglionated, adj. [1. gánggliunāted; 2. gǽŋgliəneitid]. Prec. & **-ate** & **-ed**. Having ganglia.

ganglion-cell, n. Nucleated cell forming part of ganglion.

ganglionic, adj. [1. gàngglíónik; 2. gæ̀ŋgliɔ́nik]. **ganglion** & **-ic**. Of, pertaining to, resembling, a ganglion.

gang-plank, n. Gang-board.

gangrene (I.), n. [1. gánggrēn; 2. gǽŋgrīn], fr. Lat. *gangraena*, fr. Gk. *gággraina*, 'gangrene'; perh. cogn. w. Gk. *góggros*, 'excrescence on trees'; O.N. *kǫkkr*, 'mass of earth'; Lett. *gungis*, 'swelling, growth'. **1.** Mortification in some part of a living body, due to imperfect nutrition of the part; necrosis. **2.** (fig.) Source of corruption, decay.

gangrene (II.), vb. trans. & intrans., fr. prec. **1.** trans. To cause gangrene, set up mortification in. **2.** intrans. To become gangrenous.

gangrenous, adj. [1. gánggrenus; 2. gǽŋgrinəs]. **gangrene (I.)** & **-ous**. Of the nature of, affected by, gangrene.

gangster, n. [1. gángster; 2. gǽŋstə]. **gang**

(**I.**) & **-ster.** (Am. usage) Member of a gang of toughs or criminals.

gangue, n. [1. gang; 2. gæŋ], fr. Fr. *gangue*, fr. Germ. *gang*, 'a going, walking; step, gait; a passage, channel, course; vein, lode', fr. O.H.G. *gang*, q.v. under **gang** (**I.**). (min.) Rock &c. in which metallic ore is embedded; matrix.

gangway, n. [1. gángwā; 2. gǽŋwei], fr. O.E. *gangweġ*, 'road', fr. *gang*, 'a going, walking; passage, way; course, channel'. See **gang** (**I.**) & **way**. Passage, way of approach, of ingress and egress. Specif. **1.** **a** Passage between rows of seats, as in theatre, lecture-hall &c.; **b** esp. the passage across the floor of the House of Commons, below the front benches of the Ministry and Opposition. **2.** **a** Bridge giving communication between the land and a ship lying alongside wharf; gang-plank; **b** opening in ship's bulwarks in which this is placed.

ganister, gannister, n. [1. gánister; 2. gǽnistə]. Origin unknown; apparently a local name in Yorkshire. A hard siliceous rock mixed with clay found in the Yorkshire coal measures; it is made into fire-resisting bricks and used for lining metallurgical furnaces.

gannet, n. [1. gánet; 2. gǽnit]. O.E. *ganot*; cp. O.H.G. *ganazzo*, 'gander'; Du. *gent*, 'gander'. Same base as **gander, goose.** The solan-goose.

ganoid, adj. & n. [1. gánoid; 2. gǽnɔid], fr. Fr. *ganoïde*, fr. Gk. *gán-(os)*, 'brilliance, splendour, joy', & **-oid**; cp. Gk. *gánumai*, 'rejoice' (fr. **gaw-new-mi*), *gēthéō* (fr. **gāw-etheō*), Lat. *gaudēre* (fr. **gaw-idēre*), 'to be joyful'; Aryan base **gāu-*, 'to rejoice'. See **gaud.** **1.** adj. **a** (of fish-scales) Smooth, hard, and polished; having the appearance of enamel; **b** (of fish) having such scales, as the sturgeon &c. **2.** n. A ganoid fish.

gantlet, gantlope, n. See **gauntlet** (**II.**).

gantry, n. [1. gántri; 2. gǽntri]. O. Fr. dial. *gantier*, Mod. Fr. *chantier*, 'framework', & in various other senses, fr. Lat. *cantērius*, 'beast of burden, pack-mule; framework, trellis' &c. (cp. our use of *horse* in similar sense); loan-word fr. Gk. *kanthélios*, 'pack-ass', fr. *kánthōn*, in same sense, the origin of wh. is unknown. **1.** A frame-like structure supported at each end, made to span a distance; **a** one built across several lines of rails, supporting signals; **b** bridge or platform carrying a travelling crane. **2.** Wooden frame to support barrels in a cellar &c.

gantry-crane, n. Travelling crane mounted on platform.

Ganymede, n. [1. gánimēd; 2. gǽnimīd], fr. Lat., fr. Gk. *Ganumḗdēs*, cupbearer to Zeus. **1.** (facet.) A young waiter. **2.** (astron.) One of the satellites of Jupiter.

gaol (**I.**), **jail**, n. [1. jāl; 2. džeil]. M.E. *jaiole, gaile*, fr. A.-Fr. *gaiole, gaole*, fr. O. Fr. *jaiole*, fr. Low Lat. **gabiola*, dimin. of Lat. *cavea*, 'a cage'. See **cage.** **1.** Building for confinement of persons arrested or sentenced by law; prison. **2.** Confinement in a gaol: *to suffer the workhouse or the gaol.*

gaol (**II.**), vb. trans., fr. prec. To put in gaol, imprison.

gaol-bird, n. Habitual criminal; convict.

gaol-delivery, n. A criminal assize for the trial of prisoners committed to gaol.

gaoler, jailer, jailor, n. [1. jáler; 2. džéilə]. **gaol** & **-er, -or.** **a** Man in charge of gaol, or of prisoners in gaol; **b** person responsible for keeping another in custody.

gaoleress, jaileress, jailoress, n. [1. jáleres; 2. džéiləris]. Prec. & **-ess.** Woman in charge of female prisoners.

gaol-fever, n. Typhus fever, formerly prevalent in prisons.

gap, n. [1. gap; 2. gæp]. O.N. *gap*, 'chasm, abyss, deep sea'; M.E. *gappe*, 'space, gap, interval'; cp. O.N. *gapa*, 'to yawn, split open'; Mod. Germ. *gaffen*, 'to stand open-mouthed'; Aryan base **ghə-(p)*, 'opening'; cp., w. different formative suff., Gk. *kháskō*, 'yawn', *khainō*, 'open' (fr. **khan-jō*), *khásma*, 'chasm, gulf' (see **chasm**); & w. a different grade of vowel, Gk. *khêtos*, 'a chest, coffer', *khēramós*, 'a hole, cavity'. See **gasp, chaos, hiatus,** & cp. **gape.** **1.** Hole in hedge, fence, wall &c.; cleft, opening, breach. **2.** Deep ravine, gully, gorge. **3.** (in non-material sense) Interval, vacant period, blank; interruption of continuity; lacuna: *a gap in historical records*; *gaps in one's knowledge.* Phr. *to fill, stop, a gap*, supply something lacking.

gape (**I.**), vb. intrans. [1. gāp; 2. geip]. M.E. *gappen*, fr. O.N. See prec. **1.** **a** (of human beings) To yawn; **b** to have and keep the mouth open, especially when staring, in a foolish, vacant manner, as from surprise, wonder &c.: *to stand gaping*; *to gape at*, to exhibit signs of foolish, ignorant wonder. **2.** (of the earth, or other solid substance) **a** To be opened, to open; to cleave or burst open; **b** to be, remain, stand open.

gape (**II.**), n., fr. prec. **1.** The act of gaping; a yawn. **2.** *The gapes*, **a** a disease of birds, characterized by constant gaping; **b** a fit of yawning. **3.** (zool.) Extent of extremest possible opening of mouth. **4.** An opening, gap, fissure, empty space.

gaper, n. [1. gáper; 2. géipə]. **gape** (**I.**) & **-er.** One who, that which, gapes; specif. **a** kind of shell-fish; **b** a kind of bird.

gappy, adj. [1. gápi; 2. gǽpi]. **gap** & **-y.** Having many gaps; not continuous or unbroken.

garage, n. & vb. trans. [1. gárahzh, gárij; 2. gǽrāž, gǽridž]. Fr., lit. 'protection, guardianship', fr. (*se*) *gar-(er)*, 'to be on one's guard, protect oneself', & **-age.** Of Gmc. origin. See **ware** (**II.**) & **wary.** **1.** n. **a** Building, shed, or part of one, in which vehicles are housed; specif., one set apart for housing motor-cars; **b** commercial establishment where motor-cars are stored, repaired, cleaned &c., and at which fittings and petrol for cars can be obtained. **2.** vb. To put (a motor-car) into a garage.

garb (**I.**), n. [1. garb; 2. gāb], fr. Ital. *garbo*, 'elegance, grace'. Of Gmc. origin. Cp. O.H.G. *gar(a)wi*, 'preparation'. See **gear** (**I.**) Style of dress, costume, attire; esp. style characteristic of occupation, period, country &c.: *in the garb of a sailor*; *clerical garb*; *fantastic garb.*

garb (**II.**), vb. trans., fr. prec. To dress, attire, array, clothe: *to garb oneself, be garbed, in motley.*

garb (**III.**), n. O. Fr. *garbe* (Mod. Fr. *gerbe*), fr. O.H.G. *garba*, 'sheaf, handful', wh. is fr. same base as **grip** & **gripe.** (her.) Representation of a sheaf of corn.

garbage, n. [1. gárbij; 2. gā́bidž]. Perh. fr. O. Fr. *garbe*, 'a sheaf'. See prec. **a** Offal, refuse; waste matter removed from animal carcase intended for food; hence, **b** (fig.) anything worthless, offensive: *literary garbage* &c.

garble, vb. trans. [1. gárbl; 2. gā́bl], fr. Ital. *garbell-(are)*, fr. Arab. *gharbala*, 'to sift'. **1.** (rare) To sort, sift, pick out what is good in, take best of. **2.** (in bad sense) To select, over-emphasize, parts of, make suppressions in, so as to misrepresent facts; to falsify, pervert, distort: *a garbled text, account, statement* &c.

garboard, n. [1. gárbord; 2. gā́bəd], fr. Du. *gaarboord*, fr. *gaar*, 'to gather', & *boord*, 'board'. *Garboard strake*, a row of planks above keel on outside of ship's bottom; **b** similar row of plates in ship built of iron.

garçon, n. [1. gárson; 2. garsɔ̃]. Fr., 'boy; waiter', fr. *gars, garce*, 'girl'; Meyer-Lübke regards this as a Gmc. loan-word & connects w. O.H.G. *warza*, 'wart'. The relation in meaning is obscure! Waiter in a French hotel.

gardant, also **guardant**, adj. [1. gárdant; 2. gā́dənt]. Fr., Pres. Part. of O. Fr. *garder* 'to guard, watch, look at; to keep, preserve'. See **guard, ward.** (her., of animals) Depicted with head and face turned towards the spectator, looking straight forward, full-face.

garden (**I.**), n. [1. gárdn; 2. gā́dn]. M.E. *gardin*, fr. A.-Fr. *gardin*, fr. Gmc. Cp. Mod. Germ. *garten*, O.H.G. *garto*, 'garden'; O.H.G. *gart*, cogn. w. O.E. *ġeard*, 'enclosure, court; dwelling'. See **yard**, & words there referred to; also **garth.** **1.** Piece of cultivated ground, often surrounding or adjoining house, for growing flowers, vegetables, fruit, trees &c., and including lawns, paths, and sometimes water &c.; *kitchen garden*, for growing vegetables for domestic use; *hanging garden*, laid out in terraces; *market garden*, for growing flowers, vegetables, fruit &c. for sale; *rock garden*, with mounds or slopes of pieces of rock built into soil between, for growing rock plants, ferns &c. **2.** (often in pl.) Piece of enclosed ground for public enjoyment, planted with specimen flowers, trees, often with lawns and walks and glades &c., open to the public, and controlled and kept up by a public authority: *Botanic Garden(s)*; *Kensington Gardens* (London). **3.** Specially fertile or highly cultivated region. Phr. *the garden of England*, Kent, Isle of Wight. **4.** (pl.) Applied to rows of houses in towns, built round, or looking into a planted open space: *Sussex Gardens, Queen's Gardens* &c. **5.** (attrib.) **a** Cultivated, as distinct from wild: *garden plants*; *garden hyacinths*; **b** found in, frequenting, gardens: *garden snail*; **c** of, pertaining to, used in, a garden: *garden wall, gate, roller* &c. **6.** *The Garden*, the school of Epicurus.

garden (**II.**), vb. intrans., fr. prec. To cultivate, work in, a garden.

garden city, n. An industrial town laid out with wide tree-planted roads, and plenty of garden space for houses and generally on the lines of a 'garden suburb', q.v.

gardened, adj. [1. gárdnd; 2. gā́dnd]. **garden** (**I.**) & **-ed.** Cultivated, laid out as a garden; having a garden.

gardener, n. [1. gárdner; 2. gā́dn-ə]. **garden** (**II.**) & **-er.** **a** Person whose trade and occupation is to look after, cultivate, lay out, and plant gardens; **b** person who gardens for pleasure; one skilled in management of gardens and plants.

gardenesque, adj. [1. gàrdn-ésk; 2. gàdn-ésk]. **garden** (**I.**) & **-esque.** Like a garden.

garden-frame, n. Frame for forcing plants.

garden-glass, n. Bell-glass for covering plants.

gardenia, n. [1. gardénia; 2. gādínjə], fr. name of an American botanist, Alex. Garden (d. 1791), & **-ia.** Genus of trees and shrubs, mainly tropical, with large, scented, yellow or white flowers.

gardening, n. [1. gárdning; 2. gā́d(ə)niŋ]. **garden** (**II.**) & **-ing** (**I.**). The art or occupation of cultivating a garden.

garden-party, n. Social gathering held out of doors in a garden, or park.

garden-plot, n. Piece of ground cultivated as a garden.

garden-seat, n. Seat used in, suitable for, a garden.

garden-stuff, n. Garden produce, flowers, vegetables &c.

garden-suburb, n. Tract of land adjoining a town, laid out for building, but so designed as to avoid appearance of a town, by leaving as much open space as possible round the houses, and by judicious planting of trees and shrubs &c.

garden-white, n. A kind of cabbage-butterfly.

garefowl, n. [1. gárfoul; 2. géəfaul], fr. O.N. *geir-fugl.* See first element of next word, & **fowl.** **a** The great auk; **b** the razor-billed auk.

garfish, n. [1. gárfish; 2. gā́fiʃ]. M.E. *garfisch*, fr. O.E. *ġār*, 'spear, javelin', cogn. w. O.N. *geirr*; cp. prec. & see **gore** & **fish.** A long, slender fish, with jaws prolonged and tapering to a point.

gargantuan, adj. [1. gargántūan; 2. gāgǽntjuən], fr. *Gargantua*, hero of Rabelais' work of same name, described as a giant w. a huge appetite,

& **-an.** Resembling, suitable to, characteristic of, Gargantua; very large; esp. *gargantuan meal, banquet* &c.; *gargantuan appetite.*

garget, n. [1. gárget; 2. gágit]. M.E. *gargate,* 'throat', fr. O. Fr. *gargate.* Etymol. doubtful. **1.** A swelling of the throat in pigs and cattle. **2.** Inflammation of the udder in cows or sheep.

gargle (I.), vb. intrans. & trans. [1. gárgl; 2. gágl], fr. Fr. *gargouiller,* 'to gargle', fr. *gargouille,* 'throat'. See **gargoyle. 1.** intrans. To rinse, wash, the throat with liquid, agitated and prevented from entering the windpipe by a continuous stream of air which is allowed to pass from the lungs. **2.** trans. In Phr. *to gargle the throat,* treat it by gargling.

gargle (II.), n., fr. prec. Medicated liquid used for gargling.

gargoyle, gurgoyle, n. [1. gárgoil, gérgoil; 2. gágɔil, gə́gɔil], fr. O. Fr. *gargouille,* 'throat; water-spout, gargoyle', fr. Lat. *gurgulio,* 'gullet, windpipe', w. dissimilation fr. **gurgurio,* redupl. form; cp. Lat. *gurges,* 'whirlpool'; Scrt. *gárgaras,* 'abyss, whirlpool'; O. Slav. *grŭlo,* Russ. *górlo,* 'throat'. See **gurgle.** Form of projecting waterspout used in Gothic architecture, often carved into grotesque representation of a human or animal figure; so devised that the water from the roof is conveyed through the mouth and is delivered clear of the walls of the building.

garibaldi, n. [1. gàribáldi; 2. gæribǽldi]. Name of Italian patriot (died 1882). Kind of loose blouse worn by women in imitation of the red shirts of Garibaldi's followers.

garish, adj. [1. gárish; 2. gέəriʃ]. Perh. connected w. M.E. *gaure,* 'to stare', & **-ish.** Gaudy, showy, ostentatious; too bright or highly coloured.

garishly, adv. Prec. & **-ly.** In a garish manner.

garishness, n. See prec. & **-ness.** The quality of being garish.

garland (I.), n. [1. gárland; 2. gáland]. M.E., fr. O. Fr. *gerlonde, garlande* &c., prob. of Gmc. origin; cp. Frankish *waron,* 'to bind'. **1.** Wreath of flowers, or leaves, worn on head or round neck; also one used to adorn buildings &c., as decoration, token of rejoicing, victory &c. **2.** (fig.) Token of victory, success; prize won in a contest; token of admiration and homage accorded to victor or successful contestant. **3.** Representation of a garland, painted, carved, cast in metal &c. **4.** (archaic) Anthology, collection of poems or literary excerpts.

garland (II.), vb. trans., fr. prec. To hang, adorn, with garlands; to wreathe.

garlic, n. [1. gárlik; 2. gálik]. O.E. *gārlēac,* M.E. *gārlěk;* fr. O.E. *gār,* 'spear', see **gore** (II.), & *lēac,* 'leek', see **leek.** Perennial plant of onion kind, with long tapering leaves, and very pungent bulbous root with characteristic flavour, used for seasoning.

garlicky, adj. [1. gárliki; 2. gáliki]. Prec. & **-y.** Like garlic; having the smell or taste of garlic.

garment (I.), n. [1. gárment; 2. gámənt]. M.E. *gar(ne)ment,* fr. O. Fr. *garniment,* fr. *garni-(r),* 'to fortify; to furnish, provide; to adorn' (see **garnish**) & **-ment. 1. a** An article of clothing; **b** (pl.) dress, costume, clothes. **2.** (fig.) Outer covering, outward appearance, of anything: *the earth's garment of green.*

garment (II.), vb. trans., fr. prec. (poet., but rare, and chiefly in P.P.) To array, robe, clothe.

garner (I.), n. [1. gárner; 2. gánə], fr. O. Fr. *gerner,* fr. Lat. *grānārium,* 'granary'. See **granary.** (usually poet. or fig.) **a** Storehouse, place for storing corn &c.; hence, **b** store, accumulation; e.g. **a** collection of literary pieces.

garner (II.), vb. trans., fr. prec. (usually fig. or poet.) To store up, accumulate.

garnet, n. [1. gárnet; 2. gánit]. M.E. *gernet, garnet,* fr. O. Fr. *grenat,* fr. Med. Lat. *granat-(um),* see **pomegranate,** fr. resemblance of stone to pomegranate seeds. **1.** A vitreous mineral of various colours, red, brown, green &c. **2.** Deep-red variety of garnet, semi-precious stone, cut as a gem.

garnish (I.), vb. trans. [1. gárnish; 2. gániʃ], fr. O. Fr. *garn-(ir),* 'to fortify; to provide, furnish; to adorn', & **-ish.** Of Gmc. origin; cp. O.H.G. *warnōn,* 'provide, equip'. See **warn. 1. a** To decorate, adorn, improve appearance of. Phr. *swept and garnished,* thoroughly cleansed and brightened up; **b** specif., of food for table: *to garnish a dish with parsley, slices of lemon* &c. **2.** (legal) To warn (a person) by serving him with a 'garnishee' order. **3.** (her.) *Garnished,* ornamented with devices of specified tincture.

garnish (II.), n., fr. prec. **1. a** Anything used as decoration; **b** specif., articles used as embellishment, or as a relish, placed round a dish for the table. **2.** Literary ornament, embellishment.

garnishee (I.), n. & adj. [1. gàrnishḗ; 2. gàniʃí]. **garnish** (I.) & **-ee.** (law) **1.** n. **a** Person holding money or property of, or owing money to, another, on whom notice is served by a creditor of the latter under order of the court not to pay or hand over such money &c.; **b** procedure of attachment by this means. **2.** adj. *Garnishee order,* order obtained from a court by a creditor attaching funds of a debt or in hands of a third party.

garnishee (II.), vb. trans., fr. prec. **1.** To serve garnishee order on (party holding funds &c., of another). **2.** To attach (funds) in hands of a third party by a garnishee order.

garnishing, n. [1. gárnishing; 2. gániʃiŋ]. **garnish** (I.) & **-ing** (I.). Thing used as garnish.

garnishment, n. [1. gárnishment; 2. gániʃmənt]. **garnish** (I.) & **-ment. 1.** Ornament, embellishment. **2.** (law) Notice given to a person that he will be summoned to a court.

garniture, n. [1. gárnichur; 2. gánitʃə], fr. Fr., fr. *garn-(ir),* 'to furnish, provide; to adorn', see **garnish** (II.), & P.P. ending *-it,* & **-ure.** That which serves to adorn or embellish; ornament, furniture.

garotte. See **garrotte.**

garret (I.), n. [1. gáret; 2. gǽrət], fr. O. Fr. *garite,* 'watch-tower', Mod. Fr. *guérite,* 'sentinel's box', fr. P.P. stem of *garir,* 'to guard, defend', fr. Gmc.; cp. O.H.G. *werien,* Goth. *warjan,* 'to defend'. Cp. **garage** & see **ware** (II.) & **wary. a** Room immediately below the roof of house, with ceiling and sometimes walls formed by slope of roof; attic; (loosely) **b** room on top storey of a house, attic; esp. a poor small wretched room.

garret (II.), vb. trans. Etymol. unknown. (archit.) To fill up interstices in coarse masonry by inserting small pieces of stone after the work of building is done.

garreteer, n. [1. garetḗr; 2. gærətíə]. **garret** (I.) & **-eer.** Person living in garret; esp. poor writer, literary hack.

garreting, n. [1. gáreting; 2. gǽritiŋ]. See **garret** (II.) & **-ing. a** Process of filling up interstices between joints of coarse masonry with small splinters of stone; **b** result of this process; **c** material used.

garrison (I.), n. [1. gárisun; 2. gǽrisən], fr. O. Fr. *garison,* 'defence', fr. *gari(r),* 'to defend', see **garret,** & **-son,** confused in meaning w. obsolete *garnison,* 'supply, provision', fr. Fr. *garni-(r),* 'to furnish'. See **garnish.** Military force stationed in town, fortress &c., to defend it.

garrison (II.), vb. trans., fr. prec. **a** To furnish (town, fortress &c.) with garrison; **b** to act as a garrison for, to occupy (town &c.) for defence; **c** to detail, send (troops &c.) as garrison.

garrison artillery, n. **a** Heavy artillery used for defence of fortifications, as distinguished from *field artillery;* **b** a corps, trained for the use of such artillery.

garrison town, n. Town in which a garrison is stationed.

garron, n. [1. gárun; 2. gǽrən], fr. Gael. *gearran.* (Scots) Small, common breed of horse.

garrot, n. [1. gárut; 2. gǽrət], fr. Fr. *garrot.* Etymol. unknown. A kind of sea-duck.

garrotte, garotte (I.), n. [1. garót; 2. gərɔ́t]. Span. *garrote,* 'stick'; specif., 'stick twisted in rope &c., to tighten it'; etymol. uncertain. **1.** Instrument used for capital punishment in Spain and Portugal, originally with apparatus for strangling, now with brass collar fitted with a point which enters the spinal cord. **2.** Execution by means of the garrotte. **3.** Highway robber's method of strangling victim by approaching him from behind and putting cord, strap &c., across his throat.

garrotte (II.), vb. trans., fr. prec. **1.** To execute by strangling, with a garrotte. **2.** To strangle and rob.

garrotter, n. [1. garóter; 2. gərɔ́tə]. Prec. & **-er.** Highway robber who strangles his victims.

garrulity, n. [1. garōōliti; 2. gərū́liti], fr. Lat. *garrulitāt-(em),* 'chattering, loquacity', fr. *garrul-(us),* 'talkative'. See next word & **-ity.** Talkativeness, loquacity; tendency to chatter or talk constantly.

garrulous, adj. [1. gároolus; 2. gǽruləs], fr. Lat. *garrul-(us),* 'chattering, babbling, talkative', fr. *garr-īre,* 'to talk, chatter', & **-ous;** cp. Gk. *gêrus,* 'voice'; O. Ir. *gairm,* 'call, cry'; O.H.G. *kara,* 'lament'. See **charm** (I.). **a** Given to constant talking on trivial matters; talkative, loquacious; **b** (of stream &c.) producing a constant ripple of sound; babbling, chattering.

garrulously, adv. Prec. & **-ly.** In a garrulous manner.

garrulousness, n. See prec. & **-ness.** The quality of being garrulous; garrulity.

garter (I.), n. [1. gárter; 2. gátə], fr. O. Fr. *gartier,* fr. *garet,* 'bend of the knee'; prob. Celt.; cp. Bret. *gar,* W. *gār,* 'bone of leg'. **1.** Band worn round leg above or below knee to keep stocking in place. **2.** (cap.) **a** Highest order of knighthood in Great Britain, founded c. 1344; **b** badge of this order of knighthood; **c** Garter King of Arms; **d** membership of the order.

garter (II.), vb. trans., fr. prec. **1. a** To support (stocking) with garter; **b** to bind (leg) with garter. **2.** To invest (person) with the Order of the Garter.

Garter King of Arms, n. One of three chief heralds of the College of Arms of England.

garter-snake, n. One of several species of harmless American snake, named from its markings.

garth, n. [1. garth; 2. gāþ], fr. O.N. *garþr,* 'enclosed court, yard; dwelling'. Cogn. w. O.H.G. *gart;* O.E. *ġeard.* See **yard** (II.). (archaic and dialectal) Enclosed space; yard, court, garden.

gas (I.), n. [1. gas; 2. gæs]. Word invented by Belgian chemist, van Helmont (d. 1644), & suggested by Gk. *kháos,* see **chaos. 1.** One of variously composed vaporous substances, having the property of, and tendency to, indefinite expansion; in popular usage, gas made from coal, used for heating and lighting. Phrs. *to light the gas, turn down the gas* &c. **2.** Specif. (mil.) one of various kinds of poisonous gases used in warfare. **3.** Kind of gas (nitrous oxide) used as anaesthetic (also *laughing-gas*). **4.** (min.) Mixture of air and fire-damp. **5.** (fig., colloq.) Empty talk; eloquence devoid of substance. **6.** (Am.) Gasolene, petrol. Phr. *to step on the gas,* accelerate (in motor-car).

gas (II.), vb. trans. & intrans., fr. prec. **1.** trans. (mil.) To poison by gas fumes. **2.** intrans. (colloq.) To talk nonsense at great length.

gas-bag, n. **1.** Bag for containing gas, as of a balloon, or airship. **2.** (colloq.) Person who talks nonsense at great length; loquacious twaddler.

gas-bracket, n. Pipe projecting from wall of room &c., fitted with burner for lighting by gas.

gas-buoy, n. A buoy containing a small tank or reservoir of illuminating gas, used for lighting a fairway, marking a shoal &c. at night.

gas-burner, n. Pierced jet through which illuminating gas passes from pipe to the air.

gas-coal, n. Kind of coal from which gas for lighting is obtained.

Gascon, n. [1. gáskon; 2. gǽskən]. Fr. **a** A native of Gascony; **b** a boaster, blusterer.

gasconade, n. & vb. intrans. [1. gaskonā́d; 2. gæskənéid], fr. Fr., fr. prec. & **-ade**. **1.** n. Boastful talk, bluster, brag. **2.** vb. To boast.

gaseity, n. [1. gasḗiti; 2. gæsíiti]. See **gaseous** & **-ity**. The quality of being gaseous.

gaselier, n. [1. gàselḗr; 2. gæ̀silíə], fr. **gas**, w. ending formed on anal. of *chandelier*. Hanging and branching structure consisting of tubes supplying several gas-burners.

gas-engine, n. Engine driven by regularly recurring explosions of gas in cylinder.

gaseous, adj. [1. gā́seus; 2. géisiəs]. **gas** & **-eous**. Of the nature of, in the form of, gas.

gas-fire, n. Fire in which the heat is supplied by gas.

gas-fitter, n. **a** Workman who instals gas-pipes, brackets &c.; **b** tradesman supplying these.

gas-fittings, n. Pipes, lamps &c. for heating or lighting by gas.

gas gangrene, n. A form of spreading gangrene occurring in wounds infected by a special bacillus, which forms bubbles of gas.

gash (I.), n. [1. gash; 2. gæʃ]. M.E. *garse*, n., fr. O. Fr. *garser*, prob. fr. L. Lat. *caraxāre*, fr. Gk. *kharássein*, 'to sharpen; to cut, scratch, incise; inscribe'; cp. Gk. *khárax*, 'pointed stake'; whence Gk. *kharaktḗr*, 'engraved mark'. See **character**. Long, deep cut; slash; fissure, cleft (in land).

gash (II.), vb. trans., fr. prec. To cut deeply, slash.

gas-helmet, n. Covering for the head and face, used as a protection against poison gas in warfare, for rescue work in mines, or in cases of fire &c.; a gas-mask; the impregnated air before being breathed is passed through or over chemicals able to absorb and extract the poison gas.

gasifiable, adj. [1. gásifīabl; 2. gǽsifàiəbl]. **gasify** & **-able**. Capable of being converted into gas.

gasification, n. [1. gàsifikā́shun; 2. gæ̀sifikéiʃən]. **gas** & **-fication**. Process of gasifying; state of being gasified.

gasiform, adj. [1. gásiform; 2. gǽsifɔ̄m]. **gas** & **-form**. In the form of gas; gaseous.

gasify, vb. trans. [1. gásifī; 2. gǽsifai]. **gas** & **-fy**. To convert into gas, obtain gas from.

gasket, n. [1. gásket; 2. gǽskit]. Ital. *gaschetta*, 'rope end', cp. Fr. *garcette*. **1.** (naut.) Piece of rope or strip of canvas used to tie furled sail to yard. **2.** Piece of tow &c. packed round piston &c., or in joint to make it water-tight.

gas-light, n. **a** Light produced by gas; **b** lamp or burner lit by gas.

gas-main, n. Chief pipe conveying gas from gas-works which supplies smaller pipes in houses &c.

gas-man, n. **a** Man employed in the manufacture of gas; **b** man who collects money payable for supply of gas.

gas-mantle, n. Device for increasing the illuminating power of gas, consisting of a net of cotton fabric chemically treated with thorium &c., which becomes incandescent when it is heated by the gas flame enclosed by it.

gas-mask, n. A form of gas-helmet, q.v.

gas-meter, n. Instrument registering quantity of gas consumed.

gasogene, n. See **gazogene**.

gasolene, -ine, n. [1. gásolēn; 2. gǽsəlīn]. **gas** & **-ol** & **-ene**. **a** Inflammable liquid produced in distilling petroleum; used for lighting and heating; **b** (Am.) petrol used for internal combustion engine.

gasometer, n. [1. gasómeter; 2. gæsɔ́mitə]. **gas** & **-o-** & **-meter**. **1.** Large tank at gas-works for storing gas. **2.** (chem.) Apparatus for collecting, containing, or measuring gas.

gasp (I.), vb. intrans. & trans. [1. gahsp; 2. gāsp]. M.E. *gaspen*, fr. O.N. *geispa*, 'to yawn'; cp. w. different formative elements, O.E. *ģiscian*, 'to sob'; O.N. *gjā*, 'cleft, split'; *gīna*, 'to gape open'; O.E. *gīnan*, 'to gape, split'; *ģinian*, 'to yawn'; O. Slav. *zěvati*; Lith. *žióju*, 'to yawn'; Lat. *hiāre*, 'to split, yawn, gape'. Aryan base **ghē(i)-*, **ghī-*, **ghə-*, 'to gape open; to be empty'. See further **chaos, gape, hiatus, yawn.** **1.** intrans. **a** To struggle for breath; breathe through the mouth with difficulty, and in a rapid, spasmodic manner; to pant; **b** to catch the breath in astonishment &c. **2.** trans. *Gasp out*, **a** to utter with gasps: *to gasp out a few words*; **b** *to gasp out one's life*, to die.

gasp (II.), n., fr. prec. Sudden catching of the breath through fear, astonishment, exhaustion &c. Phr. *at the, one's, last gasp*, in extremity, at the point of death.

gasper, n. [1. gáhsper; 2. gā́spə]. **gasp (I.)** & **-er**. (slang) A cheap cigarette; a fag.

gasping, adj. [1. gáhsping; 2. gā́spiŋ], fr. Pres. Part. of **gasp (I.)**. Convulsive, spasmodic.

gaspingly, adv. Prec. & **-ly**. In a gasping manner; with gasps.

gas-pipe, n. Pipe for conveying gas.

gas-ring, n. Tubular ring attached to gas-pipe, pierced with holes for gas-jets to supply heat for cooking.

gas-shell, n. Explosive shell filled with poisonous or blistering gas or chemical, fired from a gun or dropped by aeroplane in war.

gas-stove, n. Cooking stove heated by gas.

gassy, adj. [1. gási; 2. gǽsi]. **gas** & **-y**. **1.** **a** Gaseous; **b** full of gas. **2.** (of talk &c.) Boastful, empty, pretentious.

gas-tar, n. Coal-tar.

gast(e)ropod, n. [1. gást(e)ropòd; 2. gǽst(ə)rəpɔ̀d]. **gastr(o)-** & Gk. *pod-*, stem of *poús*, 'foot', q.v. under **pedal** & **-pod**. Member of a class of molluscs which move by means of a muscular disk on the surface of the stomach; e.g. snails, limpets, slugs &c.

gasteropodous, adj. [1. gàsterópodus; 2. gæ̀stərɔ́pədəs]. Prec. & **-ous**. Of the nature of a gasteropod.

gastraea, n. [1. gastrḗa; 2. gæstríə]. Scientific coinage fr. Gk. *gastḗr*, 'belly'. See **gastr(o)-**. Hypothetical primitive ancestral form of animal life.

gastric, adj. [1. gástrik; 2. gǽstrik]. See **gastr(o)-** & **-ic**. Of, connected with, the stomach: *gastric juice*, thin acid fluid secreted by glands of stomach and acting as digestive; *gastric ulcer*, one in the stomach.

gastritis, n. [1. gastrītis; 2. gæstráitis]. **gastr(o)-** & **-itis**. Inflammation of the stomach.

gastr(o)-, pref. representing Gk. *gast(e)r-*, stem of *gastḗr*, 'stomach', prob. fr. **gms-*, w. orig. sense 'receptacle'; cp. Gk. *gémein*, 'to be full', orig. 'to contain'; *gómos*, 'cargo, load'; no cognates apparently outside Gk. Connected with the stomach.

gastrologer, n. [1. gastrólojer; 2. gæstrɔ́lədžə]. **gastr(o)-** & **-loger**. Gastrologist.

gastrologist, n. [1. gastrólojist; 2. gæstrɔ́lədžist]. **gastr(o)-** & **-logist**. A student of gastrology; lover of good food well cooked.

gastrology, n. [1. gastróloji; 2. gæstrɔ́lədži]. **gastr(o)-** & **-logy**. The science of cookery.

gastronome, n. [1. gástronōm; 2. gǽstrənoum], fr. Fr., back-formation fr. **gastronomy**. Gastronomer.

gastronomer, n. [1. gastrónomer; 2. gæstrɔ́nəmə]. See **gastronomy** & **-er**. A connoisseur of cookery and good eating; an epicure.

gastronomic(al), adj. [1. gastronómik(l); 2. gæstrənɔ́mik(l)], fr. Gk. *gastronom-(ía)*, 'gastronomy'. See **gastronomy** & **-ic** & **-al**. Pertaining to gastronomy.

gastronomically, adv. Prec. & **-ly**. In a gastronomical manner.

gastronomist, n. [1. gastrónomist; 2. gæstrɔ́nəmist]. See next word & **-ist**. Gastronomer.

gastronomy, n. [1. gastrónomi; 2. gæstrɔ́nəmi], fr. Fr. *gastronomie*, fr. Gk. *gastronomía*, 'gastronomy', fr. **gastr(o)-**, on anal. of *astronomy*. The science or art of cookery and diet.

gas-works, n. Establishment for the manufacture of gas for heating and lighting.

gate (I.), n. [1. gāt; 2. geit], fr. M.E. *gāte*, derived fr. such an O.E. type as *gatu*, n. pl. of *ģeat*. Etymol. doubtful, but prob. connected w. **gate (III.)** & possibly w. **gait** & **gut**. A gate may be generally defined as one of various movable structures used for giving or denying ingress and egress through an opening in a wall, fence, hedge &c. It differs from a *door* in that while the latter word is primarily used of a structure closing an entrance to a closed and roofed building, a *gate* closes the entrance to an open space within an enclosure of walls &c., such as a field or court. A gate may consist of an open framework, or a solid structure, of wood or iron; it is hung from hinges and swings so as to close, or leave open, the space in the wall, fence &c. into which it fits, and it is capable of being fastened with a catch or lock. Specific uses: **1.** **a** Structure of kind described used to close the entrance into a courtyard or quadrangle of a large building such as a castle, college &c.; **b** one giving entrance through the wall surrounding a city; **c** one giving entrance to a stable, or other yard; **d** one leading through a wall, fence, or hedge into a park, garden, field; **e** one constructed and placed so as to close a roadway; *turnpike gate*. **2.** (loosely) The structure immediately surrounding a gate of any of the above kinds, including not only the gate itself, but also the posts from which the gate is hung, and the opening in the wall, fence &c. which the gate fills; i.e. the gateway; hence Phr. *to go through the gate*. **3.** **a** Number of persons entering the gate of a field in which sports or games are being held on a given day; those entering any form of public, open-air entertainment, exhibition &c.; **b** money taken at the gate on given occasion from those paying to see a match, exhibition &c.; gate-money. **4.** Wooden or iron structure in a canal, dock &c., used to control the in-rush or out-flow of water.

gate (II.), vb. trans., fr. prec. (Universities of Oxford and Cambridge) To confine to college after certain hours.

gate (III.), n. M.E. *gāte*, fr. O.N. *gata*, 'road, street'; cp. Mod. Germ. *gasse*, 'lane'; prob. connected w. **gate (I.)**. (Nthn.) Street, lane, passage; generally distinguished by special name prefixed.

gate-bill, n. (Universities of Oxford and Cambridge) **a** Record of undergraduate's absences from college after prescribed hours; **b** fines imposed for such absences.

gate-crasher, n. (slang) Person who intrudes at a private party, reception &c. to which he has not been invited; one who obtains admission to a public entertainment without a ticket.

gate-house, n. House at side of, or built over, a gate leading into a courtyard or quadrangle, park &c., used as porter's lodge, or as defensive structure with guard-rooms &c.

gate-keeper, n. Person in charge of gate and of its opening and shutting.

gate-legged table, n. Table with legs having bars resembling a wooden gate, made to swing back, so as to allow part of table-top to fold downwards.

gateless, adj. [1. gā́tles; 2. géitlis]. **gate (I.)** & **-less**. Without a gate.

gate-money, n. Money taken at entrance gate giving access to a match or open-air exhibition.

gate-post, n. One of two posts between which gate is swung. Phr. *between you and me and the gate-post*, in strict confidence.

gateway, n. [1. gā́twā; 2. géitwei]. **1.** Opening in wall, hedge, fence, filled by a gate. **2.** (fig.) Means of approach: *gateway to knowledge, success* &c.

gather, vb. trans. & intrans. [1. gádher; 2. gǽðə]. O.E. *gaderian*, M.E. *gadere(n)*; cp. O. Fris. *gadria*, M.H.G. *gatern*. Cp. further O.E. *geador*, 'together', *tōgæd(e)re*, 'together' (see **together**), (*ġe*)*gada*, 'companion'; Goth. *gadiliggs*, O.H.G. *gadulinc*, 'relative'; O.E. *gædeling*, 'companion'; O. Slav. *goditi*, 'to be pleasant, precious', *godinŭ*, 'acceptable'; Lett. *gāds*, 'property, provision'; Scrt. *gádhyaš*, 'to possess, retain, hold fast'. Aryan base **ghădh-*, **ghōdh-*, 'to possess; hence, to value'. See also **good**. **A.** trans. **1.** To bring together, cause to assemble; to draw: *he succeeded in gathering a crowd about him*. Phr. *to be gathered to one's fathers*, to die. **2.** To amass, acquire, obtain, collect gradually: *to gather wealth, a collection of valuables* &c. Phrs. *to gather strength, volume*, become stronger, larger; *gather way, speed*, (of moving body) increase in momentum, speed; *to gather one's energies*, make great effort of strength; *gather oneself together*, brace oneself for an effort. **3. a** To pick up, collect (inanimate objects or substances): *to gather shells, pebbles* &c.; *the bee gathers honey*; **b** to pick, pluck (growing things): *to gather flowers, blackberries* &c. **4. a** To take into, and store in, the mind; to acquire gradually: *to gather impressions, experience* &c.; **b** to derive a mental impression, acquire information: *I could gather nothing from his statement*. **5.** To form into folds, pleats; specif. in sewing, to draw (material) into small pleats by means of a thread drawn through it. Phr. *to gather the brows*, pucker, wrinkle, them. **B.** intrans. **1. a** To assemble, come together, congregate, form into masses: *a crowd had gathered*; *gathering clouds*; (also fig., of non-material things) *troubles and anxieties gathered round his later years*; **b** (chiefly fig.) to increase in volume, accumulate: *suspicion was gathering rapidly in his mind*. **2.** To form a suppurating swelling, fester. **C.** Followed by adverb. *Gather up*: **1. a** to pick up and place together: *to gather up the crumbs, one's work, books* &c.; also **b** (of mental action) *to gather up the threads (of a story* &c.); **2.** to draw up, contract (one's limbs &c.).

gathering, n. [1. gádhering; 2. gǽðəriŋ]. Prec. & **-ing**. Esp. **1.** an assembly, meeting, coming together: *a social, political, gathering* &c. **2.** A swelling, abscess. **3.** (bookbinding) Single folded sheet.

gathering-coal, n. Large lump placed on fire to keep it alight all night.

gathers, n. [1. gádherz; 2. gǽðəz], fr. **gather**. Small folds or pleats in material, garment &c. drawn together by a thread.

Gatling, n. [1. gátling; 2. gǽtliŋ], fr. name of American inventor (died 1903). Also *Gatling-gun*: a kind of quick-firing machine-gun.

gauche, adj. [1. gōsh; 2. gouʃ]. Fr., lit. 'left hand'; of Gmc. origin; cp. O.H.G. *welh*, 'soft, damp', Germ. *welk*, 'withered, faded', q.v. under **welk**. Tactless, awkward, lacking in social ease and grace.

gaucherie, n. [1. gṓsherē; 2. góuʃərī]. Fr. Prec. & **-ery**. Tactlessness; awkward, clumsy, action or manner.

gaucho, n. [1. góuchō; 2. gáutʃou]. Span., prob. fr. native Indian name. A cowboy, rider, of Argentine or Uruguay, of mixed European and Indian blood.

gaud, n. [1. gawd; 2. gɔ̄d], fr. O. Fr. *gaudir*, 'to make merry', fr. Lat. *gaudēre*, 'to rejoice, be pleased, delight in', fr. earlier **gāwid-*, fr. **gāwedh-*; cp. Gk. *gēthéō* (fr. **gāweth-éō*), 'to rejoice'; *gaû-ros*, 'proud'. See **joy**. **1.** Piece of showy finery; tasteless ornament. **2.** (pl.) Gaieties, pretentious ceremony.

gaudily, adv. [1. gáwdili; 2. gɔ̄dili]. **gaudy (II.)** & **-ly**. In a gaudy manner.

gaudiness, n. [1. gáwdines; 2. gɔ̄dinis]. **gaudy (II.)** & **-ness**. The quality of being gaudy.

gaudy (I.), n. [1. gáwdi; 2. gɔ̄di], fr. Lat. *gaudium*, 'joy, delight, gladness; expression or occasion of joy', fr. *gaud-(ēre)*, 'to rejoice'. See **gaud**. A feast, entertainment; esp. an annual or periodic college dinner given to former members.

gaudy (II.), adj. Prob. fr. prec. **1.** Gay, brilliant, showy: *gaudy plumage*; esp. garish, over-brilliant, vulgarly fine: *gaudy dress, decorations* &c. **2.** (of liter. style &c.) Over-elaborate, showy, ornate.

gauffer. See **goffer**.

gauge (I.), n. [1. gāj; 2. geidž], fr. A.-Fr. *gauge*. Origin doubtful. **1.** Standard measure; specif. **a** diameter of bore of gun; **b** thickness of sheet-metal; **c** distance between rails; *broad, narrow, gauge*, greater, less, than standard gauge of 56½ in. **2.** Instrument for determining, indicating, regulating, the measure, quantity, amount, capacity &c.; specif. **a** instruments recording amount of rainfall, height of tide, speed of wind, force of current &c.; **b** instrument for testing size of tools, wire &c.; **c** (print.) metal strip for regulating width of margin. **3.** (naut.) usually *gage*: position in relation to wind and to another vessel. Phr. *to have the weather gage of*, be to windward of; (fig.) to have the advantage of. **4.** (fig.) Extent, scope, compass. Phr. *to take the gauge of*, measure, estimate. **5.** (fig.) Means of estimating, reckoning, testing.

gauge (II.), vb. trans., fr. A.-Fr. *gauger*. **1.** To measure accurately, determine exact dimensions, quantity, force &c. of, **a** thing made in standard size(s), e.g. wire; **b** things varying in quantity &c., e.g. rainfall. **2.** To ascertain capacity of (vessel holding liquid, cask &c.). **3.** (referring to mental action) To estimate, measure, appraise; draw conclusion as to capacity or quality of; size up: *to gauge a person, a person's character* &c.

gaugeable, adj. [1. gā́jabl; 2. géidžəbl]. Prec. & **-able**. Capable of being gauged.

gauger, n. [1. gā́jer; 2. géidžə]. **gauge (II.)** & **-er**. (obs. Scots) One who gauges and measures the capacity of casks of excisable liquor; an exciseman.

gauging-rod, n. [1. gā́jing rŏd; 2. géidžiŋ rɔ̀d]. Instrument for ascertaining capacity of cask, esp. of excisable liquor.

Gaul, n. [1. gawl; 2. gɔ̄l], fr. name of country, *Gaul*, fr. Fr. *Gaule*, fr. Lat. *Gallia*, fr. *Gall-(us)*, 'a Gaul'. See **Gallic**. **1.** Native of ancient Gaul. **2.** (facetious) Frenchman.

Gaulish, adj. & n. [1. gáwlish; 2. gɔ̄liʃ]. Prec. & **-ish**. **1.** adj. **a** Of, pertaining to, the Gauls; **b** (facetious) French. **2.** n. The language of ancient Gaul.

gault, n. [1. gawlt; 2. gɔ̄lt]. Etymol. unknown. (geol.) Beds of clay between upper and lower greensand.

gaunt, adj. [1. gawnt; 2. gɔ̄nt]. Perh. Scand. Cp. Norw. *gand*, 'thin person'. **a** (of person, figure, face &c.) Thin, lean, haggard, emaciated; **b** (of trees, shadows &c.) long, lanky, uncannily attenuated; grim, forbidding.

gauntlet (I.), n. [1. gáwntlet; 2. gɔ̄ntlit], fr. Fr. *gantelet*, fr. *gant*, 'glove', fr. O. Swed. *wante*. **1.** (hist.) Leather glove covered with metal plates, forming part of armour; Phr. (lit. and fig.) *to throw down, fling down, the gauntlet*, to issue a challenge; *to take up the gauntlet*, accept a challenge. **2.** Strong glove with long, wide extension covering wrist, esp. for driving &c.

gauntlet, gantlet (II.), n. Earlier *gantlope*, fr. Swed. *gatlopp*, fr. *gata*, 'lane', cp. O.N. *gata*, 'road', q.v. under **gate (III.)**, & *lopp*, 'course', cogn. w. **leap**. *To run the gauntlet*, **a** as punishment, to pass between two rows of persons who strike the victim as he passes; **b** (fig.) to be exposed to hostile attacks, criticism &c.

gauntleted, adj. [1. gáwntleted; 2. gɔ̄ntlitid]. **gauntlet (I.)** & **-ed**. Having, wearing, a gauntlet.

gauntness, n. [1. gáwntnes; 2. gɔ̄ntnis]. **gaunt** & **-ness**. The quality or condition of being gaunt.

gauntry, n. See **gantry**.

gaur, n. [1. gour; 2. gauə]. Hind. The wild ox, *Bos gaurus*, of the Indian hill-forests and jungles.

gauze, n. [1. gawz; 2. gɔ̄z], fr. Fr. *gaze*. Etymol. uncertain. **1.** Very fine transparent fabric of silk or other thin substance. **2.** Thin mist, light fog, haze.

gauziness, n. [1. gáwzines; 2. gɔ̄zinis]. Next word & **-ness**. The quality of being gauzy.

gauzy, adj. [1. gáwzi; 2. gɔ̄zi]. **gauze** & **-y**. Like gauze; thin, fine, diaphanous.

gave, vb. [1. gāv; 2. geiv]. O.E. *ġeaf*, M.E. *ȝaf*, *gāve*. Pret. of **give**.

gavel, n. [1. gávl; 2. gǽvl]. Etymol. uncertain. Hammer, small mallet, used **a** by the chairman or presiding officer at a meeting, in calling for silence or for speakers to resume their seats &c.; **b** by auctioneers.

gavelkind, n. [1. gávlkīnd; 2. gǽvlkaind], fr. obs. *gavel*, O.E. *gafol*, 'tribute', fr. type *ġæf* (W.S. *ġeaf*), as in Pret. sing. of O.E. *ġ(i)efan*, 'to give'. See **gave**, **give**. Mode of land-tenure, now esp. in Kent and Wales, whereby property of man dying intestate is divided equally between all his sons.

gavial, n. [1. gā́vial; 2. géiviəl]. Fr., apparently erroneous form, fr. Hind. *ghariyāl*. A kind of crocodile with long, slender snout, found in the Ganges, Indus, and other rivers of India.

gavotte, n. [1. gavót; 2. gəvɔ́t]. Fr., fr. Provenç. *gavoto*, fr. *Gavot*, inhabitant of country round Gap in the Alps. **1.** A lively, dignified dance, resembling the minuet but in common time. **2. a** Music for the gavotte; **b** musical composition in common time, with two parts, each repeated, as part of a suite.

gawk, n. [1. gawk; 2. gɔ̄k]. Origin uncertain. An awkward, shy, and clumsy person.

gawkiness, n. [1. gáwkines; 2. gɔ̄kinis]. Next word & **-ness**. The quality of being gawky.

gawky, adj. & n. [1. gáwki; 2. gɔ̄ki]. **gawk** & **-y**. **1.** adj. Clumsy, awkward, ungainly. Applied to a tall, overgrown person. **2.** n. Gawky person.

gay, adj. [1. gā; 2. gei], fr. Fr. *gai*, perh. fr. O.H.G. *wāhi*, 'pretty'. **1. a** (of persons and their character, behaviour &c.) Filled with, expressing, inclined to, joy, and lively feeling; merry, light-hearted, cheerful: *gay voices*; *a gay dance, company, laugh* &c.; **b** (in bad sense) immoral, dissipated: *to lead a gay life*. Phr. (colloq.) *gay lady*, (i.) a light woman; (ii.) the queen in cards. **2.** (of sensuous impressions) Conveying sense of gaiety and liveliness, suggesting, conducing to this; hence, bright, showy, of brilliant appearance: *gay colours*; *gay garments, plumage* &c.; *a gay tune*.

gayal, n. [1. gī́al; 2. gáiəl]. Hind. A kind of ox domesticated in India, probably a form of the wild ox, the gaur.

gaze (I.), vb. intrans. [1. gāz; 2. geiz]. M.E. *gāsen*; Scand., cp. Swed. *gasa*. Origin doubtful. To fix one's eyes, look intently, fixedly, and wistfully: *to gaze into the sky, a person's face*; *to gaze at, on, upon, a thing* &c.

gaze (II.), n., fr. prec. Prolonged, steady look, fixed regard. Phr. *at gaze*, in the attitude of gazing.

gazebo, n. [1. gazḗbō; 2. gəzíbou]. Prob. facetious formation fr. **gaze (I.)**. Balcony, turret, summer-house, in a garden &c., commanding a wide view.

gazelle, n. [1. gazél; 2. gəzél]. Fr., fr. Arab. *ghazāl*. Small, delicately formed antelope of North Africa and Asia with large, gentle eyes.

gazette (I.), n. [1. gazét; 2. gəzét], fr. Fr., fr. Ital. *gazzetta*; origin doubtful; usually connected w. small Venetian coin of this name worth less than a penny. **1.** (hist.) **a** Record of current events, published periodically; news-sheet, journal; **b** used as title of various newspapers. **2. a** (cap.) One of four official journals, published in London, Edinburgh,

Belfast, and Dublin, giving lists of public, government, military, and naval appointments, and other public notices; **b** official publication of University of Oxford &c., containing university notices of all kinds.

gazette (II.), vb. trans., fr. prec. To publish in the Gazette (appointment, name of person appointed &c.).

gazetteer, n. [1. gàzetḗr; 2. gæzitíə]. **gazette** (I.) & **-eer** (from early use of gazetteer by gazette writers). Geographical dictionary.

gazogene, gasogene, n. [1. gáz-, gásojēn; 2. gǽz-, gǽsədžīn], fr. Fr. *gazogène*. **gas** & **-gen**. Apparatus for making aerated water.

gear (I.), n. [1. gēr; 2. gíə]. M.E. *gēre*, 'equipment, clothes, armour', prob. fr. O.N. *gervi*, 'equipment', cogn. w. O.E. *ġearwe*, O.H.G. *garawi*, fr. Gmc. **garw-*, 'ready, prepared'. Cp. **yare**. **1. a** (archaic) Apparel, clothes, equipment, accoutrements; **b** animal's harness, esp. that for draught animals. **2.** Apparatus, implements, tackle, for work &c. **3.** Piece of mechanism in machines consisting of a system of toothed wheels, which communicate motion to, or receive it from, each other; the gear controls the number and speed of the revolutions of the ultimate moving part (driven part) of the machinery relatively to those of the part from which the motive power of the machine is primarily derived (driving part); *high gear*, adjustment by which the driven part of the machinery moves relatively fast; *low gear*, adjustment whereby the driven part moves relatively slow. Phr. *out of gear*, not adjusted by, or connected with, the gearing mechanism; (fig., gen. of material and non-material conditions) not working smoothly, out of relation, inharmonious.

gear (II.), vb. trans. & intrans., fr. prec. **A.** trans. **1.** (also *gear up*) To harness. **2.** To put parts of machinery in relation, connect with, the gear. Phr. *to gear up, down*, to put into high, low, gear (see prec. **3**). **B.** intrans. To work in relation to the gear: *to gear with*.

gear-box, n. Case enclosing and protecting gear-wheels &c., of bicycle &c.

gear-case, n. Gear-box.

gearing, n. [1. gḗring; 2. gíəriŋ]. **gear** (I.) & **-ing**. System of cog-wheels forming gear of a machine.

gearless, adj. [1. gḗrles; 2. gíəlis]. **gear** (I.) & **-less**. Without a gear.

gear-wheel, n. Cog-wheel forming part of the gear mechanism.

gecko, n. [1. gékō; 2. gékou], fr. Malay. *gekoq*; imitative. Kind of house lizard, found in warm countries, having adhesive disks on its toes which facilitate climbing.

gee (I.), **gee-gee**, n. [1. jē-(jē); 2. džī-(džī)], fr. next word. (childish or colloq.) Horse.

gee (II.), **gee-up** &c., interj. Exclamation used to urge on a horse.

geese, pl. of **goose**.

geeser, geezer, n. [1. gḗzer; 2. gízə]. Variant of **guiser**. (colloq. slang) Old person, fellow, bloke.

gegenschein, n. [1. gágenshīn; 2. géigənʃain]. Germ. Counter-glow; a faint, luminous patch seen opposite the sun's place in the sky, while it is still below the horizon.

gehenna, n. [1. gehéna; 2. gihénə]. Eccles. Lat. *gehenna*, fr. Gk. *géenna*, fr. Heb. *Ge-Hinnom*, valley in which children were sacrificed to Moloch, hence, hell. **a** Hell; hence, **b** place of misery or torment.

geisha, n. [1. gásha; 2. géiʃə]. Jap. Japanese singing and dancing-girl.

gelatin(e), n. [1. jélatin, -ēn; 2. džélətin, -īn], fr. Fr. *gélatine*, fr. Ital. *gelatina*, fr. *gelata*, 'jelly', fr. Lat. *gelāta*, fem. P.P. of *gelāre*, 'to freeze; to stiffen'. See **gelid, jelly** & **-in**. Hard, brittle, transparent, brownish-yellow substance, having an unpleasant smell when dissolved in hot water; obtained, by long simmering, from animal tissue, bones, hoofs, horns &c.; *gelatine-paper*, covered with sensitized gelatine, for photography; *explosive, blasting, gelatine*, highly explosive compound of nitro-glycerine; *vegetable gelatine*, gelatinous substance contained in gluten.

gelatiniform, adj. [1. jèlatíniform, jelátiniform; 2. džèlətínifɔ̄m, džəlǽtinifɔ̄m]. Prec. & *-i-* & **-form**. In the form of gelatine.

gelatinize, vb. trans. & intrans. [1. jelátinīz; 2. dželǽtinaiz]. **gelatine** & **-ize**. **1.** trans. To convert into a jelly-like substance. **2.** intrans. To become gelatinous.

gelatinoid, adj. [1. jelátinoid; 2. dželǽtinɔid]. **gelatine** & **-oid**. Like gelatine in consistency.

gelatinous, adj. [1. jelátinus; 2. dželǽtinəs]. **gelatine** & **-ous**. Having consistency of gelatine or jelly.

gelation, n. [1. jeláshun; 2. dželéiʃən], fr. Lat. *gelātiōn-(em)*, 'freezing', fr. *gelāt-(um)*, P.P. type of *gelāre*, 'to freeze', & **-ion**. See **gelid**. See further **glacial**. Solidification by freezing.

geld, vb. trans. [1. geld; 2. geld], fr. O.N. *gelda*, 'to cut, geld'; cogn. w. Goth. *gilþa*, 'sickle', lit. 'cutting implement'. This represents an Aryan **ghelt-*, fr. wh. also Lith. *žirkles*, 'shears', w. dissimilation, fr. **ghlt-lo*, &, by a similar process Lat. *furcula*, 'forked prop'. See **fork**. To deprive of testicles; to castrate.

gelding, n. [1. gélding; 2. géldiŋ], fr. O.N. *geldingr*. Prec. & **-ing**. A gelded animal; specif., a castrated horse &c.

gelid, adj. [1. jélid; 2. džélid], fr. Lat. *gelid-(us)*, 'icy, frosty', fr. *gel-(us)*, 'frost, cold', cogn. w. *gelāre*, 'to freeze'; cp. also Lat. *glacies*, 'ice', see **glacial**; fr. base **gelā-*, 'to freeze cold', fr. forms of wh. come also **chill, cold, cool**. **1.** Icy, freezing, frosty, ice-cold. **2.** (fig., of temperament, manner &c.) Frigid, not cordial.

gelignite, n. [1. jélignīt; 2. džélignait]. Invented word fr. **gelatin** & Lat. *ign-(is)*, 'fire', see **ignite**, & **-ite**. A high-explosive used for blasting purposes.

gem (I.), n. [1. jem; 2. džem]. M.E. *gemme*, fr. Lat. *gemma*, 'a bud, gem'. See **gemma**. **1.** A precious stone, esp. when cut and polished. **2.** Carved or engraved precious or semi-precious stone. **3.** Anything of great beauty or value, or of exquisite finish; *the gem of the whole collection*, finest thing in it.

gem (II.), vb. trans., fr. prec. To set, stud, with, or as with, gems.

Gemara, n. [1. gemáhra; 2. gemā́rə]. Aramaic, 'completion'. Second part of Talmud, a commentary on the first part, the Mishna.

gemels, n. [1. jémelz; 2. džémelz]. O. Fr. 'twin', fr. base **gem-*, q.v. under **Gemini**, & **-el**. **1.** (her.) *bars-gemels*, or *gemels*, bars or barrulets borne in pairs on the shield. **2.** Gimbal.

geminate (I.), adj. [1. jéminat; 2. džéminət], fr. Lat. *gemināt-(um)*, P.P. type of *gemināre*, 'to double, repeat; to unite', fr. *gemin-(us)*, 'twin, double'. See **Gemini**. (bot., zool.) Occurring in pairs.

geminate (II.), vb. trans. [1. jéminàt; 2. džémineit]. See prec. **1.** To double, repeat. **2.** To place, arrange, in pairs.

gemination, n. [1. jèmináshun; 2. džèminéiʃən]. Prec. & **-ion**. The act of geminating, state of being geminated.

Gemini (I.), n. [1. jéminī; 2. džéminai]. Lat., 'twins'; specif., the constellation, Castor & Pollux, fr. pl. of *gemin-us*, 'twin; double, twofold', prob. cogn. w. Gk. *gaméō*, 'I marry' (see **gamo-**); Lat. *gener* (fr. **gem-*), 'son-in-law'; M. Ir. *gemel*, 'fetter'; O.N. *kimbell*, 'bundle'; Aryan base **gem-*, 'to join, unite, fasten'. (cap.) **a** The constellation of Castor and Pollux; **b** the third sign of the Zodiac.

gemini (II.), interj. [1. jémini; 2. džémini], fr. prec. (obs.) Exclamation expressing surprise &c.

gemma, n. [1. jéma; 2. džémə]. Lat. *gemma*, 'a bud; a precious stone, gem', fr. **gemb-mā*, cogn. w. Lith. *žémbu*, O. Slav. *zębati*, 'to bud, sprout'. The orig. meaning may have been 'small projection'; the nearest cognates appear to be Scrt. *jambhas*, O. Slav. *ząbŭ*, 'tooth'; Gk. *gómphos*, 'nail'. Aryan base **ĝembh-*, **gombh-*, **ĝmbh-* &c., 'pointed projection, peg, tooth &c.' See also **comb**. **1.** (bot.) **a** A leaf-bud; **b** (in mosses) small mass of cells separating from mother-plant to form a new plant. **2.** (zool.) Bud-like outgrowth in some organisms, developing into new individual.

gemmate (I.), adj. [1. jémàt; 2. džémeit], fr. Lat. *gemmāt-(us)*, P.P. of *gemmāre*, 'to bud', fr. *gemma*, 'a bud'. See prec. **a** Having buds; **b** reproducing by gemmation.

gemmate (II.), vb. intrans. [1. jemát; 2. džeméit], fr. Lat. *gemmāt-(um)*, P.P. type of *gemmāre*, 'to bud'. See **gemma**. **a** To bud, produce buds; **b** to be reproduced by gemmation.

gemmation, n. [1. jemáshun; 2. džeméiʃən]. Prec. & **-ion**. **1. a** The act or process of budding; **b** arrangement of buds on stem. **2.** Development of new individual from bud-like outgrowth which separates from parent organism.

gemmiferous, adj. [1. jemíferus; 2. džemífərəs], fr. Lat. *gemmifer*, 'bearing gems'. **gemma** & *-i-* & **-ferous**. **1.** Yielding gems. **2.** (bot. and zool.) Producing buds.

gemmiparous, adj. [1. jemíparus; 2. džemípərəs]. **gemma** & *-i-* & **-parous**. Propagating by means of buds.

gemmule, n. [1. jémūl; 2. džémjūl], fr. Fr., fr. Lat. *gemmula*, 'a little bud; small gem'. **gemma** & **-ule**. (zool. and bot.) A small, rudimentary gemma or bud.

gemmy, adj. [1. jémi; 2. džémi]. **gem** (I.) & **-y**. Containing, set with, gems; like a gem.

gemsbok, n. [1. gémzbok; 2. gémzbɔk]. Du.; cp. Germ. *gemsbock*, the buck or male of the chamois. A kind of South African antelope, with very long, straight, slender horns.

-gen, suff., representing Fr. *-gène*, fr. Gk. *-genēs*, 'born of, produced by, of the nature of', fr. stem **genē-*, fr. Aryan base **ĝ(e)nē-*, **ĝ(e)nō*, **ĝn-* &c., 'to produce, beget'. See **genus**, & words there referred to. The suff. forms scientific names, in the senses of **a** 'producing': *oxygen, nitrogen* &c.; **b** 'produced': *endogen*.

genappe, n. [1. zhenáp; 2. žənǽp], fr. town in Belgium. A smooth worsted yarn used in making braid &c.

gendarme, n. [1. zhondárm; 2. žā̃dā́m]. Fr., fr. *gens d'armes*, 'men at (of) arms'. **1.** Member of a military force in France used to preserve public order, and performing many of the functions of police. **2.** Projecting peak or tower of rock.

gendarmerie, n. [1. zhondármerē; 2. žā̃dā́məri]. Fr. Prec. & **-ery**. Military force consisting of gendarmes; these collectively.

gender (I.), n. [1. jénder; 2. džéndə]. M.E. *gendre*, 'kind, gender', fr. O. Fr. *genre, gendre*, fr. Lat. *gener-*, stem of *genus*, 'sort, kind, class'. See **genus**. **1.** Grammatical conception, corresponding to sex, or the absence of it, in nature, but, in many languages, not entirely coincident with it. Gender concerns primarily nouns, and thence pronouns, and adjectives which refer to, or are applied to these. The distinction is made between (i.) *natural gender* which corresponds exactly to sex or the absence of it, the names of male persons and animals being *masculine*, those of females *feminine*, those of inanimate objects *neuter* (or *common*); this holds in Modern English; (ii.) *grammatical gender*, which does not correspond to sex, as in many Aryan languages. Gender of nouns and adjectives is expressed in inflexional languages by the endings where these have not been lost, in personal pronouns usually by the general form as well. **2.** (colloq.) Sex.

gender (II.), vb. trans., fr. O. Fr. *gendrer*, fr. Lat. *generāre*, 'to engender, produce', fr. *gener-*, stem of **genus**. (poet.) To engender, generate.

genderless, adj. [1. jénderles; 2. džéndəlis]. **gender** (I.) & **-less**. Without gender.

gene, n. [1. jēn; 2. džīn]. See **-gen**, & cp. **genus**. (biol.) An assumed factor or causative agent of any distinctive character transmitted from parent to offspring.

genealogical, adj. [1. jèneal ójikl; 2. džīniəlódžikl], fr. Gk. *geneālogik-(ós)*, 'of genealogy', see **genealogy** & **-ic** & **-al**. **1.** Of, pertaining to, genealogy. **2.** Tracing, showing, genealogy or descent: *a genealogical table*; *genealogical tree*, diagram in form of branching tree, showing descent of person or animal.

genealogically, adv. Prec. & **-ly**. In a genealogical manner; according to descent.

genealogist, n. [1. jèneálojist; 2. džīniǽlədžist]. **genealogy** & **-ist**. A student of genealogy.

genealogize, vb. trans. & intrans. [1. jèneálojīz; 2. džīniǽlədžaiz]. Next word & **-ize**. **1.** trans. To trace descent of. **2.** intrans. To investigate genealogies.

genealogy, n. [1. jèneáloji; 2. džīniǽlədži], fr. L. Lat. *geneālogia*, fr. Gk. *geneālogía*, 'the making of a pedigree', fr. *geneá*, 'race, family'; see **genus**, & **-logy**. **1. a** Line of descent of persons and families from ancestors; pedigree; path of development of animals, plants, languages, from earlier ancestral types; **b** statement, account, table, diagram, setting forth a genealogy. **2.** Study, investigation, of the facts of descent; making of pedigrees.

general (I.), adj. [1. jéneral; 2. džén(ə)rəl]. M.E., fr. O. Fr., fr. Lat. *generāl-(is)*, 'of a specific kind, species; relating to all, general', fr. *gener-*, stem of **genus**, & **-al**. **1.** Not limited in application, entirely, or approximately; universal, extending widely; affecting all or many persons, all persons of a group &c., all parts or classes of anything; not particular, special, or local; widespread: *a matter of general interest, experience &c.*; *a general favourite*; *to issue a general pardon*; *the general idea is that . . .*; *the rain seems to have been general*; *there was a general panic, uproar &c.*; *General Confession*, one made aloud by whole congregation; *general meeting (of society &c.)*, of all members; *general election*, of parliamentary representatives throughout the country; *General Post Office*, head post office in London; *general strike*, strike of workmen belonging to all, or the greater number of, the trade unions of a country. **2.** Not limited in scope, not confined to specific subject, ranging over many subjects; not specialized: *general education, knowledge*; *a general examination, discussion &c.* **3.** Relating to a whole class; involving, referring to, the common attributes of a class or group: *a general term, name.* Phrs. *as a general rule*, in most cases, usually; *in general*, for the most part, apart from specific exceptions. **4.** Not restricted to one branch or department of occupation &c.; not specializing: *general practitioner*, doctor treating cases of all kinds, not a specialist; *general reader*, one not keeping to one branch of literature; *general servant*, doing all kinds of housework. **5. a** Existing only in outline; lacking details: *a general idea, impression &c.*; *a general resemblance*; **b** not specific; not going into detail, not minutely defined: *to speak in general terms*; *the statement is too general.* **6.** (mil.) *General Officer*, one above the rank of Colonel. **7.** (used after official title) Chief, leading, principal: *postmaster-general, attorney-general, chaplain-general &c.*

general (II.), n., fr. prec. **1.** *The general*, that which comprehends the whole of a class or group, and includes all the individuals, persons, things, ideas which compose it; contrasted with *the particular*. **2.** (archaic) The general public: '*caviar to the general*'. **3.** (mil.) Specif. **a** officer next in rank above a lieutenant-general and below a field-marshal; **b** officer above rank of colonel; a brigadier-general (now abolished), major-general, lieutenant-general, full general; **c** *general at sea*, title, under the Commonwealth, of three of the principal officers of the Navy. **4.** (mil.) A commander regarded from point of view of his strategical and tactical skill: *Marlborough was a great general.* **5.** Name given to head of certain religious orders, esp. of the Jesuits and of the Salvation Army. **6.** (colloq.) General servant.

General Assembly, n. Deliberative and legislative council of the whole of the Church of Scotland, represented by its ministers, which meets annually, presided over by a Moderator in the presence of the Lord High Commissioner representing the Sovereign.

general average, n. See **average** (I.).

General Council, n. (eccles.) One formerly summoned by the Emperor at the request of the Pope, consisting of all the Bishops of the Christian Church throughout the world.

generalissimo, n. [1. jèneralísimō; 2. dženərəlísimou]. Ital., superl. of *generale*, 'general'. See **general** (II.). Supreme commander of a great military force in the field, or of several such forces of allied states acting in conjunction.

generality, n. [1. jeneráliti; 2. dženərǽliti], fr. Fr., fr. Lat. *generālitāt-(em)*, 'generality'. **general** (I.) & **-ity**. **1.** The quality of being general, applicable to a whole class or group. **2.** General, undetailed, statement; a general law &c., without specific application: *to confine oneself to vague generalities.* **3.** The majority, bulk, greater proportion: *the generality of people are indifferent to the highest art.*

generalization, n. [1. jèneralīzáshun; 2. dženərəlaizéiʃən]. See next word & **-ation**. **1.** Mental process of generalizing. **2.** A notion, rule, law &c. resulting from such a process, derived, evolved, formulated, by observation of specific instances; an induction.

generalize, vb. intrans. & trans. [1. jéneralīz; 2. dženərəlaiz]. **general** (I.) & **-ize**. **A.** intrans. **1.** To draw a conclusion as to the whole from the observation of particular and special facts and instances; to formulate general principles covering or designed to cover an entire group or class of phenomena, from facts known, or supposed to be known, concerning a number of individual phenomena falling within the class. **2.** (in artistic expression) To emphasize general character, rather than special traits, features, and points of detail. **B.** trans. **1.** To reduce to generalization; formulate, state, in terms of general principles. **2.** (artistic expression) To describe, represent, with reference to general character, rather than to special features and details. **3.** To make general and widespread; give wide currency and vogue to.

generally, adv. [1. jénerali; 2. džén(ə)rəli]. **general** (I.) & **-ly**. **1.** Widely, including or applying to all; to or by most people: *an opinion generally held.* **2.** Without going into detail, not referring to individual cases; in a general sense: *speaking quite generally, I dislike actors.* **3.** As a rule, usually, in most cases: *dogs generally love their masters*; *we generally dine at eight.*

generalship, n. [1. jéneralship; 2. džén(ə)rəlʃip]. **general** (II.) & **-ship**. **1.** The office or rank of a general. **2. a** Military skill, strategy, tactics; hence **b** (in general sense) management, direction, skilful organization, leadership.

generate, vb. trans. [1. jénerāt; 2. džénəreit], fr. Lat. *generāt-(um)*, P.P. type of *generāre*, 'to produce, engender', fr. *gener-*, stem of *genus*, 'race, family, offspring'. See **genus**. **1.** (of physiological process) To produce new individual of a species, reproduce one's kind; procreate, beget. **2.** (of physical and chemical processes) To cause to occur, produce, result in: *friction generates heat*; *to generate gas, electricity.* **3.** (fig., of material and non-material processes) To give rise to, originate, be cause of: *misery often generates crime*; *dirt generates disease*; *difference of religious opinion often generates hatred.* **4.** (math.) To trace out, produce (a line, surface, solid).

generation, n. [1. jèneráshun; 2. dženəréiʃən], fr. Lat. *generātiōn-(em)*, 'generation'. Prec. & **-ion**. **1.** The act or process of generating; in reference **a** to physiological process, reproduction, procreation: *generation of bacteria &c.*; **b** to physical process, production, origination: *generation of heat, energy*; **c** (fig., rare) the process of causing, giving rise to; development: *generation of ill-feeling.* **2.** That which is generated; **a** single stage in natural descent: *Queen Victoria, King Edward VII., and the present King George represent three generations*; **b** all the individuals in the same degree of descent from a common ancestor; i.e. an individual and all his brothers and sisters form one generation; all the children of each of these form another, and so on: '*A link among the years to knit The generations each to each*' (Tennyson). **3.** Group of related persons, kindred, progeny: *the Bolsheviks murdered the Czar and all his generation.* **4.** All persons of approximately the same age, more loosely, those living at same time, whether related or not; the time in which they live, period, age: *few of the present generation can remember the excitement caused by the Tichborne case*; *the last generation*; Phr. *rising generation*, the younger persons living at a particular period. **5.** Period of time, roughly thirty years, which on an average separates each natural generation: *a generation ago women began to ride bicycles.*

generative, adj. [1. jénerativ; 2. džénərətiv]. **generate** & **-ive**. **1.** Of, pertaining to, generation; reproductive, procreative. **2.** Having the power of producing, originating: *generative force.*

generator, n. [1. jénerātor; 2. džénəreitə]. **generate** & **-or**. One who, that which, generates; specif., apparatus for generating gas, steam &c., or for converting mechanical into electrical energy; dynamo.

generatrix, n. [1. jènerátriks; 2. dženəréitriks]. Lat. (fem.) form of prec. (math.) The moving point, line or surface, which generates or traces out a line, surface, or solid.

generic, adj. [1. jenérik; 2. dženérik], fr. Lat. *gener-*, stem of **genus**, & **-ic**. **1.** Pertaining to, characteristic of, a whole genus or class. **2.** Applicable to every member of class or genus; not specific and individual: *a generic name.* **3.** Having a wide application, general, comprehensive.

generically, adv. [1. jenérikali; 2. dženérikəli]. Prec. & **-al** & **-ly**. In a generic manner.

generosity, n. [1. jènerósiti; 2. dženərɔ́siti], fr. Lat. *generōsitāt-(em)*, 'nobility; goodness, excellence'. See next word & **-ity**. **1.** The quality of being generous. **2.** Generous conduct or action; **a** chivalrous, noble, conduct; magnanimity; **b** liberality.

generous, adj. [1. jénerus; 2. džénərəs], fr. Lat. *generōs-(us)*, 'of noble birth; superior, excellent; noble-minded, magnanimous', fr. *gener-*, stem of **genus**. **1.** Noble-minded, free from meanness; gracious, magnanimous: *a generous spirit, nature*; *generous praise.* **2. a** (of person, character &c.) Bountiful, munificent, open-handed, ready to give; **b** (of gift &c.) showing generosity of mind, given readily and freely. **3. a** Abundant, plentiful, copious: *generous fare*; **b** large, ample: *of generous size, amount.* **4. a** (of soil) Rich, fertile; **b** (of colour) rich, deep, intense; **c** (of wine) rich, strong, full-bodied.

generously, adv. Prec. & **-ly**. In a generous manner.

genesis, n. [1. jénesis; 2. dženisis]. Lat., fr. Gk. *génesis*, 'origin, source; birth, descent'; fr. **genet-*, w. *-s-* for *-t-* before *-i-*; cp. *geneté*, 'birth', *genetḗr*, 'father' &c.; cp. further Gk. *génos*, 'birth' &c.; fr. Aryan base **gen-* &c., 'to produce, bring into being'. See **genus**, & words there referred to. **1.** Origin, birth, beginning; mode of formation or production. 2. (cap.) The first book of the Old Testament, giving the story of the Creation.

genet, n. [1. jénet; 2. džénit], fr. O. Fr. *genete*, fr. Arab. *jarnait*. a A kind of small civet-cat; b the fur of this animal, usually grey with dark blotches.

genetic(al), adj. [1. jenétik(l); 2. dženétik(l)]. Modern formation fr. stem *genet-*, as in **genesis**, & **-ic**, on anal. of **antithetic** &c. Of, pertaining to, determined by, the genesis, mode of production of anything: *genetic affinity*, one arising from a common origin.

-genetic, adj. suff. (see prec.) signifying 'pertaining to generation or genesis'; see **genesis**. a Producing, yielding; b produced, yielded by.

genetically, adv. [1. jenétikali; 2. dženétikəli]. See **genetic(al)** & **-ly**. According to the principles of genetics.

genetics, n. [1. jenétiks; 2. dženétiks]. Pl. of **genetic**, used as n. Branch of biology which deals with principles of heredity.

geneva (I.), n. [1. jenéva; 2. dženívə], fr. Du. *genever*, fr. O. Fr. *genevre*, fr. Lat. *jūniperus*, 'juniper' (see **juniper**), w. assimilation to name of town. See next word. Spirit distilled from grain and flavoured with juniper-berries; Hollands, gin.

Geneva (II.), n. Name of town in Switzerland. (used attrib.) Of, belonging to, originating in, Geneva: *Geneva bands*, strips of lawn suspended from front of neck; *Geneva gown*, black robe as worn by Calvinist ministers; *Geneva Convention*, international agreement (1864) providing for neutrality of hospitals &c. in war; *Geneva Cross*, red cross distinguishing hospitals &c. in time of war.

Genevan, adj. & n. [1. jenévan; 2. dženívən]. Prec. & **-an**. 1. adj. Of, pertaining to, Geneva. 2. n. a Native of Geneva; b adherent of Calvinism.

Genevese, adj. & n. [1. jènevéz; 2. dženivíz]. **Geneva** & **-ese**. Genevan.

genial (I.), adj. [1. jénial; 2. džíniəl], fr. Lat. *geniāl-(is)*, 'pertaining to generation or birth; nuptial; festive, jovial, pleasant', fr. *geni-(us)*, 'tutelary spirit'. See **genius** & **-al**. 1. (poet. and archaic) a Of, pertaining to, generation; fertile, productive; b connected with marriage, nuptial. 2. (of climate, air &c.) Mild, warm, benign. 3. a (of human character &c.) Kindly, benignant, affable; cheerfully amiable, cordial; b (of persons) exhibiting these qualities. 4. (rare) Relating to, exhibiting, genius.

genial (II.), adj. [1. jenial; 2. dženáiəl], fr. Gk. *génei-(on)*, 'chin', & **-al**. Cp. Gk. *génus*, 'the lower jaw'; cogn. w. Scrt. *hánuš*, 'jaw'; Lat. *gena*, 'cheek'; Goth. *kinnus*, 'jaw, cheek'; O.E. *ċinn*, 'chin' (see **chin**); cp. further, w. a different grade of vowel, Gk. *gnáthos* (see **gnathic**), Lith. *žándas*, 'jaw'. Aryan base **ĝen-*, **ĝn̥-* &c., 'lower part of face; jaw'. (zool.) Of, pertaining to, the chin: *genial plate, muscle* &c.

geniality, n. [1. jèniáliti; 2. džìniǽliti]. **genial** (I.) & **-ity**. Kindness, affability, cheerful benevolence of character, manner, or expression.

genialize, vb. trans. [1. jénialīz; 2. džínjəlaiz]. **genial** (I.) & **-ize**. To make pleasant, friendly, kindly.

genially, adv. [1. jéniali; 2. džínjəli]. **genial** (I.) & **-ly**. In a genial manner.

geniculate(d), adj. [1. jeníkūlàt(ed); 2. dženíkjulèit(id)], fr. Lat. *geniculāt-(us)*, (of plants) 'having knots or nodes; jointed', & **-ed**, fr. *genicul-(um)*, 'a knee; knot on stalk of plant', fr. *genu*, 'knee' (see **genual**), & **-cule**. (bot., zool. &c.) a Having a jointed stem; having joints or nodes; b bent like a knee.

genie, n. [1. jéni; 2. džíni], fr. Fr. *génie*, fr. Lat. *genius*, 'tutelary deity', see **genius**, but confused w. **jinnee**. Sprite, goblin, of a kind common in Arabian fairy-tales.

genio-, pref., representing Gk. *géneio-(n)*, 'chin'. See **genial** (II.). Connected with the chin; e.g. *genioglossal* [1. jeniōglósl; 2. dženàiouglɔ́səl] 'of the chin and tongue'.

genista, n. [1. jenísta; 2. dženístə]. Lat. *genista, genesta*, 'broom'. Etymol. unknown. A genus of shrub-like, leguminous plants, with yellow, more rarely white, flowers; (rare or obs.) the common broom.

genital, adj. & n. [1. jénitl; 2. dženítl], fr. Lat. *genitāl-(is)*, 'of generation or birth', fr. *genit-(um)*, P.P. type of *gignere*, 'to bear, bring forth, beget'; cp. also **genesis**, fr. base **ĝen-*, 'to bring into being', q.v. under **genus**. 1. adj. Pertaining to generation or to animal reproductive organs. 2. n. (pl.) External organs of generation.

genitival, adj. [1. jènitívl; 2. dženitáivl]. See next word & **-al**. Of, pertaining to, having form of, the genitive case.

genitive, adj. & n. [1. jénitiv; 2. dženítiv]. Lat. *genitīvus, genetīvus*, 'belonging to birth, generation'; also *genitīvus casus*, 'genitive case', lit. 'case expressing origin'; fr. *genit-*, as in **genital**, & **-ive**. (gram.) *Genitive case*, form of nouns, pronouns, or adjectives indicating source, origin, possession, kind, class &c.; partly corresponding to possessive case in English.

genito-, pref. representing Lat. *genit-(um)*, P.P. type of *gignere*, 'to beget, bear'. See **genital**. Of, pertaining to, the genital organs or their region; e.g. *genito-urinary* &c.

genius, n. [1. jénius; 2. džínjəs]. Lat. *genius*, 'tutelary deity: inclination, natural taste'; (rare) 'wit, talents'; orig. the personification of reproductive power; cogn. w. **genus**. 1. Tutelary deity, spirit, presiding over, guarding, a person, place, &c.; Phr. *good, evil, genius*: (i.) two opposed spirits, forces, directing human action; (ii.) person having great influence on another for good or evil. 2. Mood, feeling evoked by, spiritual atmosphere, association of ideas, inseparable from, a place. 3. a Inherent character, essential spirit, nature, principles, of a race, language, law, institution &c.; b prevailing tendency, dominant influence, guiding principle, of age, nation, community &c. 4. Natural endowments, capacity, inherent ability, aptitude: *the study of books is repugnant to the genius of many people*. 5. a Extraordinary and exceptional intellectual and imaginative endowment, power, faculty; specifically of a creative, inventive, originative kind; b person possessing such a faculty.

genius loci, n. [1. jénius lṓkī; 2. džínjəs lóukai]. Lat., '(tutelary) genius of the place'. See prec. & **locus**. Often used for atmosphere, associations, character &c. of a place.

Genoa, n. [1. jénōa; 2. dženouə]. Name of town in North Italy. *Genoa cake*, rich fruit cake with almonds on the top.

Genoese, adj. & n. [1. jènōéz; 2. dženouíz]. Prec. & **-ese**. 1. adj. Of, belonging to, Genoa. 2. n. Inhabitant of Genoa.

-genous, suffix forming adjs. meaning 'producing, generating', see **-gen** & **-ous**, as *autogenous* &c.

genre, n. [1. zhonr; 2. žãnr]. Variant of **gender**, fr. Fr. *genre*, 'kind, species', fr. Lat. *gener-*, stem of **genus**. 1. Kind, style, species. 2. *Genre painting*, style of painting portraying scenes from ordinary or rustic life; often used attributively, *genre pictures*.

genro, n. pl. [1. génrō; 2. génrou]. Jap. The 'elder' statesmen of Japan.

gens, n. [1. jenz; 2. dženz]. Lat. *gens*, stem *genti-*, 'race, clan; nation, people', fr. earlier **ĝn̥ti-s* or **ĝénti-(s)*. See **genus**, cogn. w. **kind** (I.). In ancient Rome and Greece, tribe, clan; group of families united by descent from a common ancestor, and by a common name.

gent, n. [1. jent; 2. džent]. Abbreviated form of **gentleman**. (colloq. and vulg.) Gentleman.

genteel, adj. [1. jentél; 2. džentíl]. Variant of **gentle**; derived afresh in 16th cent. fr. Fr. *gentil*, 'well-bred; nice'. See also **gentile**. 1. Formerly, well-bred, polite, having distinguished manners and appearance; expressing good breeding and usage with polite world. 2. Now either a (vulg.) used seriously in approximately above sense; or b (ironical) mincing, affected in manner; affecting a refinement which is not natural; exhibiting sham good manners; aping and assuming manners of a superior class.

genteelly, adv. Prec. & **-ly**. In a genteel manner.

gentian, n. [1. génshan; 2. dženʃən], fr. Lat. *gentiāna*, fr. name of Illyrian king, *Genti-(us)*, & **-an**. a Member of a large genus of herbs with bitter roots and bright, usually blue or yellow flowers; widely distributed and found esp. in mountainous country; b gentian-bitter.

gentian-bitter, n. Medicinal tonic substance extracted from roots of gentian.

gentile, adj. & n. [1. jéntīl; 2. džéntail]. Variant of **gentle**, fr. M.E. type *gentīl*, w. Fr. accentuation. See **gens** & **genus**. 1. adj. Not belonging to the Jewish race. 2. n. A person who is not a Jew.

gentiledom, n. [1. jéntīldum; 2. džéntaildəm]. Prec. & **-dom**. Whole of human race other than Jews.

gentilitial, adj. [1. jèntilíshal; 2. džentilíʃl], fr. Lat. *gentilīti-(us)*, 'belonging to a particular gens', fr. *gentīl-(is)*, 'of the same clan' (see **gentile**), & **-al**. Of, pertaining to, distinctive of, a gens or nation.

gentility, n. [1. jentíliti; 2. džentíliti], fr. O. Fr. *gentilité*, fr. Lat. *gentīlitāt-(em)*, 'relationship of members of a gens', fr. *gentīl-(is)*, 'of a gens'. Regarded as abstract n. associated w. **gentle** in sense 1, & w. **genteel** in sense 2. 1. (archaic) Gentle birth; status of a gentleman. 2. (usu. iron.) Second-rate politeness, genteel manners; sham, affected refinement; respectability. Phr. *shabby gentility*, attempt to maintain genteel appearance in face of poverty.

gentle (I.), adj. [1. jéntl; 2. džéntl], fr. M.E. type *géntil*, fr. O. Fr., 'well-bred', fr. Lat. *gentīlis*, 'belonging to same family or stock'. See **gens** & **genus**. 1. a Of good birth and breeding; well-born: *of gentle blood, birth*; Phr. *gentle and simple*, the well-born contrasted with those of humble rank; b (her.) entitled to bear arms; c (archaic) exhibiting the qualities natural to those of good birth; courteous, generous: *a gentle knight, gentle lady*; conventional Phr. *gentle reader*, formerly used by authors in their books. 2. a (of human disposition, character) Mild, kindly, sweet; serene, patient: *a gentle spirit, heart, nature* &c.; b (of conduct, behaviour) proceeding from these qualities; courteous, considerate, tolerant: *gentle bearing, manners, glance*; c (of human beings) possessing and exhibiting these qualities of nature and conduct; sweet-natured, amicable, peaceable; reverse of violent, self-assertive, harsh. 3. When applied to human actions, or to corporeal movements, the word nearly always implies certain moral qualities (as referred to in 2) as guiding and determining the character of the actions and movements; a (of actions) not severe, harsh; lenient, merciful, indulgent, clement, moderate: *a gentle reproof, rebuke, admonition, punishment*; *gentle rule, sway*; b (of bodily acts and movements) carefully, skilfully, controlled; kindly, benevolent; slow and deliberate, quiet; so carried out as not to wound or startle; not abrupt; caressing, soothing: *a gentle glance, smile*; *a gentle blow, tap, touch, push*; *a gentle voice, call* &c. 4. a (of movements of inanimate nature) Moderate, not violent or boisterous; slow, gradual: *a gentle breeze, a gentle swell, ripple*; *a gentle rustle in the grass or trees*, not loud &c.; b (of natural processes, conditions, and phenomena) *a gentle heat*, not excessive; *a gentle glow*, not too bright, not intense; *a gentle slope, declivity*; *a medicine gentle in its action*, mild, not drastic. 5. (of animals) Docile, easily managed; not fierce or restive.

gentle (II.), n., fr. prec. 1. (archaic) In Phr. *gentles all*, gentlemen. 2. Larva, maggot, of the bluebottle fly, used for fishing as bait; the name originated from the softness of the body.

gentlefolk(s), n. [1. jéntlfōk(s); 2. džéntlfouk(s)]. **gentle (I.)** & **folk**. People of gentle birth.

gentlehood, n. [1. jéntlhood; 2. džéntlhud]. **gentle (I.)** & **-hood**. (obs.) **a** Status or character of gentlefolk; **b** gentle, courteous behaviour.

gentleman, n. [1. jéntlman; 2. džéntlmən]. **gentle (I.)** & **man**. **1.** (hist.) Man entitled to bear arms, but not belonging to the nobility. **2.** (hist. and archaic) Man of good birth attached to court or large private establishment: *gentleman in waiting*. Phr. (ironical) *a gentleman's gentleman*, manservant. **3.** (legal) Man of independent income, without occupation. **4.** (various implications) **a** Man of gentle birth and good social position; one of the landed gentry, or a member of one of the honourable professions; **b** man of wealth or leisure; one who is not obliged to work for his living; **c** (in common usage) applied to any male human being, often to one of no social position, breeding, education, manners, or wealth. **5.** Man of keen sense of honour and chivalry, of refined feelings and instincts; man who shows courtesy and consideration for feelings of others. **6.** Polite form of address to members of audience: *gentlemen*; *ladies and gentlemen*. **7.** (facetious) *The old gentleman*, the devil.

gentleman-at-arms, n. Member of royal bodyguard on state occasions.

gentleman-commoner, n. One of a class of members of the university of Oxford who, by virtue of birth and age, ranked between graduates and undergraduates, wore special academic dress, and enjoyed certain privileges. They have now been abolished in all colleges except Worcester.

gentleman-farmer, n. Gentleman who owns and manages a farm.

gentlemanhood, n. [1. jéntlmanhòod; 2. džéntlmənhùd]. **gentleman** & **-hood**. (rare) The position or character of a gentleman.

gentlemanlike, adj. **gentleman** & **-like**. **a** (of persons) Having the manners and bearing of a gentleman; well-bred; **b** (of manners &c.) becoming, characteristic of, a gentleman.

gentlemanliness, n. [1. jéntlmanlines; 2. džéntlmənlinis]. See next word & **-ness**. The quality of being gentlemanlike.

gentlemanly, adj. [1. jéntlmanli; 2. džéntlmənli]. **gentleman** & **-ly**. Formerly regarded as a vulgarism; now has largely displaced *gentlemanlike*.

gentlemanship, n. [1. jéntlmanship; 2. džéntlmənʃip]. **gentleman** & **-ship**. (rare) The status or character of a gentleman.

gentleness, n. [1. jéntlnes; 2. džéntlnis]. **gentle (I.)** & **-ness**. The quality of being gentle; (in moral and physical sense) kindness, kindliness, mildness; absence of harshness, roughness, severity.

gentlewoman, n. [1. jéntlwòoman; 2. džéntlwùmən]. **gentle (I.)** & **woman**. **a** Woman of gentle birth; refined, well-bred, educated woman; lady; **b** formerly applied to a female attendant upon a woman of rank.

gentlewomanhood, n. [1. jéntlwòomanhood; 2. džéntlwùmənhud]. Prec. & **-hood**. The position or character of a gentlewoman.

gentlewomanlike, adj. [1. jéntlwòomanlīk; 2. džéntlwùmənlaik]. **gentlewoman** & **-like**. Like, befitting, a gentlewoman.

gentlewomanliness, n. [1. jéntlwoomanlines; 2. džéntlwumənlinis]. See next word & **-ness**. The quality of being gentlewomanly.

gentlewomanly, adj. [1. jéntlwoomanli; 2. džéntlwumənli]. **gentlewoman** & **-ly**. Like, befitting, a gentlewoman.

gently, adv. [1. jéntli; 2. džéntli]. **gentle (I.)** & **-ly**. **1.** After the manner of gentlefolk; only in such phrases as *gently born and bred*, *gently nurtured*. **2.** In a gentle manner; **a** kindly, mildly, without harshness or severity; **b** quietly, moderately, without roughness, violence, or boisterousness.

gentry, n. [1. jéntri; 2. džéntri]. Prob. fr. M.E. *gentris(e)*, fr. O. Fr. *genterise*, variant of *gentelise*, fr. *gentil*, 'gentle, well-bred'. See **gentle (I.)**. **1.** (archaic and obsolesc.) **a** Lineage, birth; **b** good birth. **2.** People of good birth and recognized social standing, below nobility. **3.** (in disparagement) People, class of people: *the less you have to do with these gentry the better*.

genual, adj. [1. jénūal; 2. džénjuəl], fr. Lat. *genu*, 'knee', & **-al**; cp. Gk. *gónu*, 'knee'; Scrt. *jānu*, 'knee'; Goth. *kniu*, 'knee'; Aryan base **ĝ ĕneu-*, **ĝ ŏneu-*, **ĝ nu-*, **ĝ neu-* &c., 'knee'. See **geniculate, kex, knee**. Of, pertaining to, the knee.

genuflect, vb. intrans. [1. jènūflékt; 2. džènjuflékt], fr. Med. Lat. *genuflect-(ere)*, fr. *genu*, 'knee' (see prec.), & *flectere*, 'to bend'. See **flex**. To bend the knee, specif. as act of reverence and humility in divine worship.

genuflectory, adj. [1. jènūfléktori; 2. džènjuflèktəri]. Prec. & **-ory**. Pertaining to the bending of the knees.

genuflexion, n. [1. jènūflékshun; 2. džènjuflékʃən], fr. Med. Lat. *genuflex-(um)*, P.P. type of *genuflectere*, 'to bend the knee'. See **genuflect** & **-ion**. The act of genuflecting, of bending the knee; salutation thus made, implying reverence and adoration.

genuine, adj. [1. jénūin; 2. džénjuin], fr. Lat. *genuīn-(us)*, 'innate, native, natural', fr. an *u*-stem **ĝ enu-*, fr. Aryan base **ĝ en-* &c., 'to bring into being'. See **genus** & **-ine**. **1.** Pure-bred; from the real, original, stock. **2.** **a** (of material objects) True, authentic, real; not false, fictitious, spurious: *a genuine Rubens*; *a genuine example of 15th-century binding*; **b** (of feelings) to be trusted, relied upon; sincere, not assumed; real: *genuine respect, regard, sorrow, repentance* &c.

genuinely, adv. Prec. & **-ly**. In a genuine manner.

genuineness, n. See prec. & **-ness**. The quality of being genuine.

genus, n., pl. **genera** [1. jénus, jénera; 2. džínəs, džénərə]. Lat. *genus*, 'descent, origin; race, stock; descendant, child; class, sort'; cogn. w. Gk. *génos*, Scrt. *jánaš*, 'race'. The Aryan base **ĝ (e)nē-*, **ĝ (e)nō-*, **ĝ n̥-* &c., 'to beget, to bear, to bring forth', is very widespread; cp. Scrt. *jánati*, 'begets', *janiman-*, 'birth'; Scrt. *jñātiš*, 'relative', *jātiš* (fr. **ĝ n̥-*), 'born'; Goth. *knōþs*, O.H.G. *chnuot*, 'race'; cp. further, w. reduplication, Lat. *gignere*, 'to beget, bear'; Gk. *gignomai*, 'to become, to be born'; also w. loss of initial *g-* in group *gn-*, Lat. *nāscor*, 'to be born', *nātus*, 'born' &c. See further **gens, genius, nation, nature, kind, kin, knave** &c. **1.** (biol.) Group of animals or plants, within a *family*, consisting of one or more *species*, with common characteristics distinguishing them from other groups; *the genus Homo*, man, mankind. **2.** (log.) A class of things or objects divided into subordinate groups or species, distinguished from each other by differentia. **3.** (in general sense) Kind, sort, class, species.

-geny, suff. representing Fr. *-génie*, fr. Gk. *-genēs*, 'born, born of' (see **-gen**), denoting mode of origin, production, evolution: *progeny*.

geo-, pref. representing Gk. *geō-*, fr. *gê*, 'the earth'. Etymol. unknown. Of the earth.

geocentric, adj. [1. jèoséntrik; 2. džìouséntrik]. **geo-** & **centre** & **-ic**. **1.** Having the earth as centre. **2.** Regarded as seen or measured from the centre of the earth.

geode, n. [1. jéōd; 2. džíoud], fr. Fr. *géode*, fr. L. Lat. *geōdes*, 'a precious stone', fr. Gk. *geṓdēs*, 'earth-like, earthy', fr. *gê*, 'the earth', & **-ode**. **a** Rounded concretionary stone with hollow centre lined with crystals; **b** the cavity in such a stone.

geodesic, adj. [1. jèodésik; 2. džìoudísik]. **geodesy** & **-ic**. Of, pertaining to, effected or determined by, geodesy.

geodesist, n. [1. jēódesist; 2. džiɔ́disist]. See next word & **-ist**. A student of geodesy.

geodesy, n. [1. jēódesi; 2. džiɔ́disi], fr. Fr. *géodésie*, fr. **geo-** & Gk. *daisia*, fr. *daiomai*, 'to divide'; cp. Scrt. *dáyatē*, 'to share'; *ditiš*, 'distribution'. The base is seen also in O.E. *tīd*, 'period of time' (see **tide**, & words there referred to); Aryan base **dāi-*, **dəi-*, **dī-*, 'to distribute, divide'. The science of measuring the earth and its surface; surveying on a large scale.

geodetic(al), adj. [1. jèōdétik(l); 2. džìoudétik(l)], fr. Fr., fr. **geo-** & Gk. *dait-*, stem cogn. w. *daíomai*, 'to divide'. See prec. & **-ic** & **-al**. Geodesic.

geodetically, adv. Prec. & **-ly**. In a geodetic manner; by geodesy.

geodic, adj. [1. jēódik; 2. džióudik]. **geode** & **-ic**. Of, pertaining to, a geode.

geognostic(al), adj. [1. jèognóstik(l); 2. džìəgnɔ́stik(l)]. **geo-** & Gk. *gnōst-(ós)*, later form of *gnōt-(ós)*, Perfect stem of *gignṓskein*, 'to know', redupl. form of Aryan base **ĝ (e)nō-* &c., 'to know'. See **know, gnosis**, & words there referred to. Of, pertaining to, geognosy.

geognosy, n. [1. jēógnosi; 2. džiɔ́gnəsi], fr. Fr. *géognosie*. See prec. **1.** Geology, esp. study of geology of a particular district. **2.** Study of the character and composition of the earth, and of the distribution of various kinds of rocks.

geographic(al), adj. [1. jēográfik(l); 2. džiəgrǽfik(l)]. See **geography** & **-ic** & **-al**. Of, relating to, geography. Phr. *geographical mile*, about 2000 yds., one degree of longitude on Equator.

geographically, adv. Prec. & **-ly**. In a geographical manner; from a geographical point of view.

geography, n. [1. jēógrafi; 2. džiɔ́grəfi], fr. Fr., fr. Lat., fr. Gk. *geōgraphia*, 'geography'. **geo-** & **-graphy**. **1.** A descriptive science, based on the study of the surface of the earth, its physical features, divisions, natural products, races, climate, and their distribution; *physical geography*, that branch treating of physical features, natural products &c.; *political, human, geography*, that treating of the political divisions of the earth's surface, its peoples, social organization &c. in relation to the physical features. Geography as such does not deal with the development of the physical features which it describes, and in this is in contrast with Geology. **2.** Arrangement, plan; relationship, situation, of different parts or sections of a place, building &c. **3.** A book on geography.

geoid, n. [1. jéoid; 2. džíɔid], fr. Gk. *geoeidḗs*, 'earthlike'. See **geo-** & **-oid**. The figure of the earth, an irregular sphere.

geologic(al), adj. [1. jēolójik(l); 2. džiəlɔ́džik(l)]. **geology** & **-ic** & **-al**. Of, pertaining to, geology.

geologically, adv. Prec. & **-ly**. In a geological manner; from a geological point of view.

geologist, n. [1. jēólojist; 2. džiɔ́lədžist]. **geology** & **-ist**. A student of geology.

geologize, vb. intrans. & trans. [1. jēolojīz; 2. džiɔ́lədžaiz]. See next word & **-ize**. **1.** intrans. To study geology, investigate geology of a district; to collect geological specimens. **2.** trans. To investigate (a district &c.) from a geological point of view.

geology, n. [1. jēóloji; 2. džiɔ́lədži]. **geo-** & **-logy**. **1.** Branch of science which deals with the structure and shape of the crust of the earth, and attempts to trace the evolution and mode of formation of these through the play of natural forces, from the records preserved in the rocks. **2.** The geological features found in a given area, or an account of these: *the geology of the Grampians*. **3.** A book on geology.

geomancy, n. [1. jéōmansi; 2. džíoumænsi], fr. Gk. *geōmanteia*. **geo-** & **-mancy**. Divination by means of figures formed by handfuls of earth or gravel thrown on the ground, or of points dotted at random upon paper &c.

geomantic, adj. [1. jèomántik; 2. džìəmǽntik]. See prec. & **-ic**. Pertaining to geomancy.

geometer, n. [1. jēómeter; 2. džiɔ́mitə], fr. Lat., fr. Gk. *geōmétrēs*, 'a measurer of the land', fr. **geo-** & *metr-(éō)*, 'I measure', q.v. under **-meter**. **1.** A student of geometry. **2.** Kind of moth, the caterpillars of which appear to measure out the ground as they move by drawing up and extending the body in loops.

geometric(al), adj. [1. jēométrik(l); 2. džiəmétrik(l)], fr. Gk. *geōmetrik-(ós)*, 'of geometry; geometrical', fr. **geometry** & **-ic** & **-al**. **1.** Of, pertaining to, according to the laws of, geometry. **2.** Resembling the figures of geometry; regular, symmetrical: *geometrical markings, patterns* &c.; *geometric spider*, one spinning a circular web; *geometrical tracery*, consisting of regular, geometrical figures, lines, curves &c.

geometrically, adv. Prec. & **-ly**. By geometry; according to the principles of geometry.

geometrician, n. [1. jēometríshan; 2. džiəmitríʃən]. **geometry** & **-ician**. A student of geometry.

geometrize, vb. intrans. & trans. [1. jēómetrīz; 2. džiɔ́mitraiz]. Next word & **-ize**. **1.** intrans. To study geometry; to follow geometric principles and methods. **2.** trans. To work out by geometric methods.

geometry, n. [1. jēómetri; 2. džiɔ́mitri], fr. Fr., fr. Lat. *geōmetria*, fr. Gk. *geōmetria*, 'measurement of the earth, geometry'. **geo-** & **-metry**. **1.** Branch of mathematical science treating of the properties of points, lines, surfaces, and solids, and their mutual relations in space. **2.** A book on geometry.

geophagist, n. [1. jēófagist; 2. džiɔ́fəgist]. See next word & **-ist**. Person given to geophagy.

geophagy, n. [1. jēófagi; 2. džiɔ́fəgi]. **geo-** & Gk. *phag-(ein)*, 'to eat', q.v. under **-phagous**, & **-y**. Tendency to eat earth; a symptom of mental disease.

geophone, n. [1. jēofōn; 2. džíəfoun]. **geo-** & **-phone**. Instrument for the detection of sounds passing through the earth, as in underground mining and tunnelling &c.

geophysical, adj. [1. jēofízikl; 2. džiəfízikl]. **geo-** & **physical**. Of, pertaining to, the physics of the earth's structure: *a geophysical survey*.

geophysics, n. [1. jēofíziks; 2. džiəfíziks]. **geo-** & **physics**. That branch of science which deals with the physics of the earth, the forces which modify its structure, and cause geological changes &c.

geoponic, adj. [1. jēopónik; 2. džiəpɔ́nik], fr. Gk. *geōpón-(os)*, 'husbandman', fr. **geo-** & *pónos*, 'toil, labour', & **-ic**. Cp. Gk. *pénomai*, 'toil, suffer hardship'; possibly cogn. w. Lith. *pinù*, 'to weave, plait', *pántis*, 'cord'; O. Slav. *pinq*, 'to stretch out'; O.E. *spannan*, 'to stretch, strain'; *spinnan*, 'to spin' (see **spin**); Aryan base *(s)pen-, 'to stretch; to strain'; hence, 'to strive, make an effort'. (rare) Concerned with, pertaining to, agriculture.

George, n. [1. jorj; 2. džɔdž], fr. Lat., fr. Gk. *Geōrgios*, name of a Cappadocian prince who was supposed to have been martyred in the time of Diocletian, & who later became a legendary hero. **1.** *St. George*, patron saint of England, and patron of the Order of the Garter; *St. George's Cross*, two red bars crossing in the centre at right angles. **2.** *George*, jewelled figure of St. George and the dragon, forming part of the Garter insignia. **3.** *By George*, exclamation, mild oath. **4.** A large brown earthenware jug for water, usually *brown george*.

georgette, n. [1. jorjét; 2. džɔdžét], fr. name of Fr. dressmaker. A thin, transparent, silk crêpe.

Georgian (I.), adj. [1. jórjian; 2. džɔ́džiən]. **George** & **-ian**. Of the time of any one of the Georges, kings of England: *a Georgian building; Georgian literature* &c.; specif. **a** of the 18th cent., of George I., II., and III., from 1715 on; **b** of the time of George V., contrasted with *Victorian* or *Edwardian*.

Georgian (II.), adj. & n. *Georgia* & **-an**. **1.** adj. **a** Of the country of Georgia, in the Caucasus; **b** of Georgia, one of the United States of America. **2.** n. **a** Inhabitant, language, of Georgia, Caucasus; **b** native of Georgia, U.S.A.

georgic, n. [1. jórjik; 2. džɔ́džik], fr. Lat. *geōrgic-(us)*, fr. Gk. *geōrgikós*, 'of husbandry, agricultural', fr. *geōrg-(ós)*, 'husbandman', & **-ic**; fr. *gāworgós, fr. *gā-, later *gê-*, 'earth' (see **geo-**), & base *worg-, *werg-, 'work', Gk. *érgon*, 'work'. See **ergon**. Single book of Virgil's poem on husbandry, *the Georgics*.

geotropic, adj. [1. jēotrópik; 2. džiətrɔ́pik]. See **geotropism** & **-ic**. Pertaining to geotropism

geotropically, adv. [1. jēotrópikali; 2. džiətrɔ́pikəli]. Prec. & **-al** & **-ly**. In a geotropical manner.

geotropism, n. [1. jēótropizm; 2. džiɔ́trəpizəm]. **geo-** & Gk. *trop-(é)*, 'a turning'. See **trope** & **-ism**. Tendency of the growing parts of plants to point, extend, towards (*positive geotropism*), or away from (*negative geotropism*), the centre of the earth.

geranium, n. [1. jerānium; 2. džiréinjəm]. Lat. *geranium*, fr. Gk. *geránion*, 'the plant crane's-bill', fr. Gk. *géran-(os)*, 'crane'; cp. Lith. *garnỹs*, 'heron'; O.H.G. *chranuch*, O.E. *cran*, 'crane'. See **crane**. **1.** One of a large genus of plants with white, red, or blue flowers, and lobed leaves, growing wild, or cultivated for ornament in gardens. **2.** Pelargonium.

gerb, n. [1. jërb; 2. džʌ̄b]. Variant of **garb (III.)**, 'sheaf'.

gerent, n. [1. jḗrent; 2. džíərənt], fr. Pres. Part. *gerent-(em)*, of Lat. *gerere*, 'to bear; to carry oneself; to comport oneself, behave; to have charge of, manage, govern'; fr. *ges-; cp. P.P. type *gestum*, see **gesture**; perh. cogn. w. O.N. *kasta*, 'to cast'. See **cast (I.)**. Person who governs, rules, directs; one holding power; rare, except as compound, *vicegerent*.

gerfalcon, n., also **gyrfalcon** [1. jḗrfaw(l)kn; 2. džʌ́fɔ(l)kən], fr. O. Fr. *gerfaucon*, prob. fr. O.H.G. *gîr*, Germ. *geier*, 'vulture', & **falcon**. Large falcon of the northern regions.

germ (I.), n. [1. jërm; 2. džʌ̄m], fr. Fr. *germe*, fr. Lat. *germen*, 'bud, sprout; embryo, germ'; dissimilated fr. *gen-men; cp. Scrt. *janman-*, 'birth, origin', fr. Aryan base *g̑enē- &c., 'to bring forth'. See **genus**. **1.** Rudimentary form capable of developing into a new individual. **2.** Microbe, bacillus, esp. one capable of causing disease. **3.** (fig.) That form or seed out of which something develops; elementary form, beginning, rudimentary stage; Phr. *in germ*, in elementary stage, undeveloped.

germ (II.), vb. intrans., fr. prec. (fig.) To originate, sprout, develop.

german (I.), adj. [1. jërman; 2. džʌ́mən], fr. O. Fr. *germain*, fr. Lat. *germān-(us)*, '(of brothers, sisters) having the same parents; closely allied; genuine, true'; cogn. w. *germen*, 'bud, offshoot; germ'. See **germ (I.)** & cp. **germane**. *Brother, sister, german*, having the same parents; *cousin german*, having the same grandparents.

German (II.), adj., fr. Lat. *Germān-(us)*, 'German'. Of, pertaining to, Germany, the Germans, their language &c.; *German measles*, a mild contagious disease resembling measles; *German sausage*, large sausage made of cooked and seasoned meat; *German text*, black letter; *German silver*, an alloy of nickel, zinc, and copper.

German (III.), n., fr. Lat. *Germān-(us)*, 'a German'. See prec. **1.** A native of Germany. **2.** The language of Germany; *High German*, group of dialects spoken originally in South and part of Central Germany, now standard language of the whole of Germany; *Low German*, local dialects of North Germany.

germander, n. [1. jërmánder; 2. džʌmǽndə], fr. Med. Lat. *germandra*, fr. Late Gk. *khamandra*, fr. *khamaidrūs*, fr. *khamai*, 'on the ground', q.v. under **chameleon**, & *drûs*, 'oak-tree'. See **dryad**. Member of a genus of aromatic, bitter, herbs, esp. the speedwell, with small bright blue flowers.

germane, adj. [1. jërmān; 2. džʌméin]. Variant of **german (I.)**. (only pred.) Relevant, appropriate, pertinent, to the **point**: *a remark hardly germane to the question*.

Germanic (I.), adj. [1. jërmánik; 2. džʌmǽnik], fr. Lat. *Germānic-(us)*, 'of the Germans'. **German (II.)** & **-ic**. **1.** Of, pertaining to, the Germans. **2.** Of the Teutonic race.

Germanic (II.), n., fr. prec. The language of the Teutons, esp. in its earliest form; *Primitive Germanic*, earliest form of Germanic speech; branch of Aryan family subsequently differentiated into West Germanic, North Germanic, East Germanic.

Germanism, n. [1. jërmanizm; 2. džʌ́mənizəm]. **German (II.)** & **-ism**. **1.** German spirit or characteristic; tendency towards, love for, Germany. **2.** German idiom, turn of phrase.

Germanity, n. [1. jërmániti; 2. džʌmǽniti]. **German (II.)** & **-ity**. German qualities, characteristics.

germanium, n. [1. jërmānium; 2. džʌméiniəm], fr. Lat. *Germānia*, 'Germany'. A rare metallic element, of greyish-white appearance, resembling tin and silicon and found in combination with argyrodite.

Germanization, n. [1. jërmanīzāshun; 2. džʌ̀mənaizéiʃən]. Next word & **-ation**. The act or process of Germanizing; state of being Germanized.

Germanize, vb. trans. & intrans. [1. jërmanīz; 2. džʌ́mənaiz]. **German (II.)** & **-ize**. **1.** trans. To make German, assimilate to German methods, thought &c. **2.** intrans. **a** To develop German qualities; **b** to use German methods &c.

Germano-, pref. **German** & *-o-*. Of Germany or the Germans.

Germanomania, n. [1. jërmanōmānia; 2. džʌ̀mænouméiniə]. Prec. & **mania**. Over-fondness for, imitation of, German ways.

Germanophil, n. [1. jërmánōfil; 2. džʌmǽnoufil]. **Germano-** & **-phil**. Person loving the Germans, and addicted to German ways.

Germanophobia, n. [1. jërmanōfóbia; 2. džʌ̀mænoufóubiə]. **Germano-** & **-phobia**. Hatred of anything German.

germ-cell, n. Cell in the body of an organism which is specialized for purpose of reproduction, and which when united to one of opposite sex, forms a new individual of the species.

germen, n. [1. jërmen; 2. džʌ́men]. Lat., 'bud, sprout, embryo; germ'. See **germ**. (bot.) Ovary, seed-vessel.

germicidal, adj. [1. jërmisídl; 2. džʌmisáidl]. Next word & **-al**. Tending to, having the power to, destroy germs.

germicide, adj. & n. [1. jërmisīd; 2. džʌ́misaid]. **germ** & *-i-* & **-cide**. **1.** adj. Capable of destroying germs, esp. disease-germs. **2.** n. Substance which does this.

germinal (I.), adj. [1. jërminal; 2. džʌ́minəl], fr. Lat. *germin-*, stem of *germen*, 'bud, shoot, germ'. See **germen** & **-al**. **1.** Of, pertaining to, of the nature of, a germ. **2.** (fig.) Rudimentary, in initial stage.

Germinal (II.), n. [1. jërminal; 2. džʌ́minəl], or as Fr. Fr. See prec. The seed month, that from March 21 to April 19 in the French Revolutionary Calendar.

germinally, adv. **germinal (I.)** & **-ly**. In a germinal manner, as a germ.

germinant, adj. [1. jërminant; 2. džʌ́minənt]. Lat. *germinant-(em)*, Pres. Part. of *germināre*, 'to germinate'. See next word. Germinating, beginning to develop, incipient.

germinate, vb. intrans. & trans. [1. jërminät; 2. džʌ́mineit], fr. Lat. *germināt-(um)*, P.P. type of *germināre*, 'to sprout, bud', fr. *germin-*, stem of *germen*, 'bud, shoot'. See **germ**. **1.** intrans. (lit. and fig.) To begin to sprout, shoot (as a seed does), to develop. **2.** trans. To cause to sprout or develop.

germination, n. [1. jĕrmináshun; 2. džə̀minéiʃən]. Prec. & **-ion**. The process of germinating; state of germinating.

germinative, adj. [1. jĕrminativ; 2. džə́minətiv]. **germinate & -ive**. Pertaining to, tending to cause, germination.

germon, n. [1. jĕrmun; 2. džə́mən]. Fr. A kind of tunny fish.

germ-plasm, n. (biol.) That nuclear part of the germ-cell, which, according to Weismann, continues from generation to generation and forms the basis of heredity.

gerontocracy, n. [1. jèrontókrasi; 2. džèrəntɔ́krəsi], fr. Gk. *geronto-*, stem of *gérōn*, 'old man', & **-cracy**; cp. Gk. *géras*, 'prerogative', orig. 'age, privilege of old age'; *geraiós*, 'old'; *gêras*, 'old age'; *graûs*, 'old woman; wrinkled skin'. Cogn. w. Scrt. *járan*, 'old, infirm'; *jarimā́*, 'age'; O. Slav. *zĭreti*, 'to ripen, mature'. Aryan base **g erē-*, 'to grow old'. See **corn (I.)**. **1.** Government by old men. **2.** Governing body of old men.

-gerous, suff. representing Lat. *-ger*, fr. *gerere*, 'to bear, produce; to carry; to do, perform, happen', see **gerent**, & **-ous**; forming adjs. w. sense 'producing; carrying'. Some of these adjs. represent Lat. words in *-ger*, e.g. *lanigerous*, others are modern formations fr. Lat. stems, e.g. *frondigerous*.

gerrymander (I.), vb. trans. [1. jèrimánder; 2. džèrimǽndə], fr. Elbridge Gerry, a governor of Massachusetts, who in 1812 is said to have divided a county into electoral divisions to benefit his own political party, & **(sala)-mander**. To manipulate, falsify, pervert, facts, so as to give untrue impression; to practise trickery; formerly used of political trickery, but now in more general sense.

gerrymander (II.), n. Same as prec. The act of gerrymandering.

gerund, n. [1. jérund; 2. džérənd], fr. Lat. *gerund-(ium)*, 'gerund', prob. fr. *gerund-(um)*, gerund of *gerere*, 'to do'. See **gerent**. **1.** (Lat. gram.) Verbal noun used for oblique cases of infinitive and governing the same cases as the verb from which it is derived. **2.** The so-called inflected infinitive in O.E., *to witanne* &c. **3.** English verbal noun in *-ing*, esp. when followed by a noun or pronoun as object.

gerund-grinder, n. Teacher of the elements of Latin grammar; schoolmaster.

gerundial, adj. [1. jerúndial; 2. džirándiəl]. **gerund & -ial**. Of, pertaining to, a gerund; like a gerund.

gerundival, adj. [1. jèrundívl; 2. džèrəndáivl]. Next word & **-al**. Of, pertaining to, gerundive.

gerundive, adj. & n. [1. jerúndiv; 2. džirándiv], fr. L. Lat. *gerundīv-(us)*. **gerund & -ive**. **1.** adj. Of, pertaining to, a gerund. **2.** n. Verbal adjective formed from stem of gerund, and expressing necessity, fitness &c.

gerundively, adv. Prec. & **-ly**. As a gerund or gerundive.

gesso, n. [1. jésō; 2. džésou]. Ital., fr. Lat. *gypsum*, 'plaster'. See **gypsum**. **a** Plaster of Paris prepared for use in sculpture &c.; **b** coat of this on surface prepared for painting.

gest, n. [1. jest; 2. džest], fr. Lat. *gesta*, 'deeds, acts', fr. Lat. *gest-(um)*, P.P. type of *gerere*, 'to bear, carry; to do, perform'. See **gerent**. (archaic) **a** Exploit, valiant deed; **b** tale of adventure.

gestation, n. [1. jestáshun; 2. džestéiʃən], fr. Lat. *gestātiōn-(em)*, 'a bearing, carrying', fr. *gestāre*, 'to carry about', fr. *gest-(um)*, P.P. type of *gerere*, 'to carry', see **gerent**, & **-ation**. **a** The act of carrying, state of being carried, in the womb, between times of conception and birth; **b** period of gestation.

gestatorial, adj. [1. jèstatórial; 2. džèstətɔ́riəl], fr. Lat. *gestātōri-(us)*, 'for carrying', fr. *gestāt-(um)*, P.P. type of *gestāre*, 'to carry about'. See prec. & **-ory** & **-al**. *Gestatorial chair*, ceremonial chair in which Pope is carried on certain occasions.

gesticulate, vb. intrans. & trans. [1. jestíkūlāt; 2. džestíkjuleit], fr. Lat. *gesticulāt-(um)*, P.P. type of *gesticulāri*, 'to make pantomimic gestures', fr. *gesticul-(us)*, 'gesticulation', dimin. of *gest-(us)*, 'gesture', fr. *gest-(um)*, P.P. type of *gerere*, 'to carry; to do'. See **gerent**. **1.** intrans. **a** To use motions of hands and arms to assist, illustrate, or express one's meaning; **b** to make frequent use of gesture; to move, wave, the hands excessively in speaking **2.** trans. To express by means of gesticulation.

gesticulation, n. [1. jèstikūláshun; 2. džèstikjuléiʃən]. Prec. & **-ion**. **a** The act of gesticulating; **b** emphatic gesture.

gesticulative, adj. [1. jestíkūlativ; 2. džestíkjulətiv]. **gesticulate & -ive**. Characterized by, accompanied by, gesticulation.

gesticulatory, adj. [1. jestíkūlatori; 2. džestíkjulətəri]. **gesticulate & -ory**. Of, pertaining to, expressing meaning by, gesticulation.

gesture (I.), n. [1. jéschur; 2. džéstʃə], fr. Med. Lat. *gestūra*, fr. Lat. *gest-(um)*, P.P. type of *gerere*, 'to carry; to wield, brandish'. See **gerent & -ure**. **1. a** Motion of hand or arm, expressing an emotion, idea, intention; one made to illustrate and emphasize what is being said; also **b** expressive movements of facial features; rapidly changing expressions of countenance: *facial gesture*. **2.** The practice and art of making expressive movements of body, limb &c., esp. for dramatic or rhetorical purposes. **3.** An action, or statement, intended to express, and to convey to others, a particular attitude of mind, or state of feeling: *a warlike gesture on the part of Russia*; *a gesture of friendship*.

gesture (II.), vb. intrans. & trans., fr. prec. To gesticulate.

get (I.), vb. trans. & intrans. [1. get; 2. get], fr. O.N. *geta*, 'to reach, obtain' &c. The word in O.E. occurs only compounded, *and-ġietan*, 'to understand', *be-ġietan*, 'to get, obtain; to beget' (see **beget**); *for-ġietan*, 'to forget' &c. (see **forget**). The initial *g-* in Mod. Engl. shows that the word is fr. O.N., as the O.E. form wd. have produced **yet*. Cp. O.S. *far-getan* &c., O.H.G. *fir-gezzan*, also *ir-gezzan*, 'forget'; Goth. *bi-gitan*, 'to find'. The base is fr. Aryan **ghe(n)d-an*, 'to seize, take', as in Lat. *pre-hendere*, 'to grasp, understand' (see **prehensile**); Gk. *khandánein*, 'to hold, take in, comprise'; O. Ir. *gataim*, 'I take'. **A.** trans. **1. a** To obtain possession of, acquire as one's own property: *I should prefer to get the smaller house*; *you may want it, but you'll never get it*; **b** to procure, purchase: *you had better get a new coat*; *I went and got some singing lessons in town*; **c** to receive something sent to one: *I get a letter every day*; *I never got your telegram*; **d** to gain, win, obtain as result of effort; to hit: *to get glory and wealth*; *to get several brace of pheasants*; *I got him first shot*; **e** to succeed in bringing to a certain place; to put into particular state or condition: *I got him to bed at last*; *to get a woman with child*; **f** (Scots) to be called, to be given the name of, be addressed as: *she always gets My Lady*; *he doesn't get Professor in his own town*; Phrs. *to get (a) hold of*, succeed in grasping (lit. and fig.); *I don't get you, it*, understand, catch meaning; *to get (a) cold*, catch cold; *to get it in the neck* (colloq.), (i.) be severely punished; (ii.) to suffer severely; *to get one's own way*, obtain what one wants, do what one likes &c. **2.** To engender, procreate, beget: *he seems unable to get children.* **3. a** To influence a person to do something; to induce, persuade: *to get a man to speak, come to dinner, do as one wants*; **b** to manage, contrive, that an animal, plant, or inanimate object shall behave, move &c. in a particular way: *to get the pig into the cart*; *get a horse into a loose-box*; *get a tree to grow in a bad soil*; *get a door to shut.* **4.** With *have* and P.P. To own, have as one's own, be in possession of: *I've got very little money*; *what an ugly face she's got*; *he'll lose all he's got if he isn't careful.* **5.** With *have* and P.P., followed by infinitive. To be under an obligation or compulsion to do (common colloq. usage): *I've got to go for the doctor at once*; *you've got to listen to what I say.* **6.** Followed by noun and P.P. To cause the performance of an action, bring it about that something is done, or put into a specified condition: *to get one's coat mended*; *to get one's hair cut.* **B.** intrans. **1.** Expressing idea of passing by a gradual process from one state to another; to become, grow: *she gets uglier every day*; *he got quarrelsome in his cups*; *to get old*; *to get better, worse*; *get angry*; *to get into a rage*; *to get silly.* **2.** To attain to, arrive at, reach: *to get home early*; *to get here, there, nowhere.* Phr. *to get there* (fig.), (i.) to achieve, accomplish something; (ii.) to understand what is said, grasp an idea; *to get nowhere* (fig.), to be futile, accomplish nothing; *to get on one's nerves*, irritate extremely. **3.** Followed by P.P. or adjective. To be put, put oneself, into certain condition; suffer, undergo, certain experience: *to get drunk*; *get hurt*; *get torn to bits*; *get wet*; *get cool*; *to get one's face scratched*; *to get one's feet wet.* Phr. *to get left*, be put in awkward position; be duped. **4.** To earn money, make a profit, gain: '*Getting and spending, we lay waste our powers*' (Wordsworth). **C.** In special senses when followed by an adverb or preposition. *Get about*, intrans., to walk about, attend to one's avocations. *Get along*, intrans., **a** to get on, fare, manage, contrive: *they can only just get along on their small income*; **b** (chiefly imperative, colloq.) to depart, begone: *get along with you!* *Get at*, intrans., **a** to obtain access to: *the books are locked up and we cannot get at them*; *just let me get at him!*; **b** (of non-material things) to grasp, ascertain: *to get at a meaning, result* &c. *Get away*, intrans., to leave (a place), go away. *Get away with*, **a** (colloq.) escape, carrying off booty; **b** Phr. *get away with you* (colloq., facetious), be off!; don't talk nonsense! *Get down*, descend, be able to come down; *get down to*, settle down to study or consider something. *Get home* (fig.), hit the mark, excite attention; *get home on (a person)*, make successful attack on; wound in sensitive spot. *Get in, (to)* enter (room, carriage &c.); trans., *to get a word in (edgeways)*, be able, with difficulty, to make a remark; *get a blow in*, place it judiciously and effectively. *Get off*, trans., **a** to dismount, alight, from (a horse); **b** to enable a person to escape punishment: *his counsel got him off*; **c** intrans., to escape punishment or misfortune. *Get on*, **a** intrans., to make progress, be successful; **b** *get on to one's feet*, stand up, esp. when about to speak; **c** trans., to put something on: *to get a coat on.* *Get on with* (persons), agree, have friendly social relations with. *Get over*, trans., **a** to cross, climb over (river, stile &c.); **b** to recover from (an illness); **c** to excuse, tolerate, recover from disgust: *I can't get over his abominable manners*; **d** to surmount (difficulties &c.); **e** to feel no longer, cease to lament: *she has quite got over the loss of her husband.* *Get out (of)*, intrans., **a** to come out from inside (of a carriage &c.); trans., **b** to remove, from storage &c., take out, produce: *to get out a good bottle of wine*; **c** to contrive to extract: *to get a cork out of a bottle*; **d** to extract information, confidences &c.: *I could get nothing out of him.* *Get round*, trans., **a** to cajole, have one's way with (persons); **b** to surmount, overcome (difficulties &c.). *Get together*, trans., to bring together, collect; intrans., to come, meet, together. *Get up*, trans., **a** to study, acquire some knowledge of (a subject); **b** *get oneself up*, dress up with care and elaboration; intrans., **c** to rise from bed: *to get up early of a morning*; rise from the ground; from one's seat to standing position: *we all got up when the King came in.*

get (II.), n., fr. prec. Offspring, progeny (of animals).

get-at-able, adj. [1. gètátabl; 2. gètǽtəbl]. Capable of being reached, easy of access, accessible (of places).

get-up, n. [1. get úp; 2. gɛt áp]. **a** Mode of dress, general appearance, so far as this is deliberately produced: *a queer get-up*; **b** specif. (of a book) ensemble of external characteristics, size, style of printing, binding &c.

geum, n. [1. jḗum; 2. dʒíəm]. Lat., 'herb-bennet'. **a** Garden plant cultivated for its white, red, or yellow flowers; **b** (bot., cap.) genus of plants including the herb-bennet.

gewgaw, n. [1. gū́gaw; 2. gjū́gɔ]. M.E. *giuegoue*; later *gugau*, *gewgaude* &c., 'toy'. Etymol. doubtful. An object of trifling value designed for external show; a frivolous, trifling thing; piece of vanity.

geyser, n. [1. gḗzer, gízer; 2. géizə, gáizə], fr. Geysir, name of particular geyser in Iceland, fr. Icel. *geisa*, 'to rage; to gush', cogn. w. Goth. *us-gaisjan*, 'to terrify'. See **ghost**. **1.** Natural spout of hot water rising from the earth to a considerable height, esp. common in Iceland and New Zealand. **2.** (often [1. gḗzer; 2. gízə]) Device for heating water for baths &c. by passing it over plates heated by gas.

ghastliness, n. [1. gáhstlines; 2. gástlinis]. **ghastly** & **-ness**. Condition or quality of being ghastly.

ghastly, adj. [1. gáhstli; 2. gástli]. Variant of **ghostly**, w. differentiated meaning. Normal development fr. O.E. *gāstlić*, M.E. *gāstli*; but the latter & the Mod. form might equally well come fr. O.E. *gǣstlić*, a by-form w. mutation, wh. occurs once w. the specific meaning, 'terrible, dreary'. *Gāstlić* in O.E. meant orig. simply, 'spiritual'. In Goth. the closely related vbs. *geisnan* & *(us-)gaisjan*, mean 'terrify', and in O.E. itself *gǣstan* means 'afflict, torment,' & Chaucer uses *gastly* very much in our sense. It may therefore, perh., be concluded that if *gǣstlić* & *gāstlić* were kept apart in O.E., they were confused later in sense as they were in form. **1.** Having the property of horrifying, terrifying; causing both repugnance and disgust: *a ghastly murder, story* &c. **2.** (of a person's appearance) Inspiring horror and pity, esp. implying that he is ill, miserable, pale, cadaverous: *to look perfectly ghastly*. **3.** In colloquial and slang usage may mean either very bad, shocking &c., or merely rather troublesome, unpleasant &c.: *a ghastly bore*; *the dinner was ghastly*; *a ghastly mess*, and so on.

ghât, ghaut, n. [1. gawt; 2. gɔt]. Hind., 'landing-place; path of descent to a river; mountain-pass'. **1.** A mountain-pass; erroneously applied by Europeans to certain mountain ranges: *the Western Ghâts*. **2.** An Indian riverside landing stairway.

Ghazi, n. [1. gáhzē; 2. gázī]. Arab., fr. *ghaza*, 'to fight'. **a** A Moslem fanatic, pledged to war against and kill the infidel; **b** title, meaning 'the victorious fighter', given to victorious Turkish generals.

ghee, n. [1. gē; 2. gī]. Hind. *ghi*, 'clarified butter'. Boiled clarified butter used in cookery in India.

gherkin, n. [1. gérkin; 2. gákin], fr. Du. *gurkje*, 'small cucumber'; cp. Mod. Germ. *gurke*, earlier *a(n)gurke*, cp. Dan. *agurk*; borrowed fr. Pol. *ogurek*, cp. Slovak *okurka*, wh. come ultimately fr. Late Gk. *aggoúrion*, 'water melon'; Anct. Gk. *áōros*, 'out of season, unripe', wh. is fr. *a-*, 'not', and *hṓrā*, 'season', cogn. w. Gmc. **jǣr*, 'year'. See **year**, also **hour**. Small variety of cucumber, used chiefly for pickling.

ghetto, n. [1. gétō; 2. gétou]. Ital. Orig. quarter in Venice & other Italian cities assigned to Jews; perh. fr. Lat. *Aegyptius*, 'Egyptian'; cp. Span. *gitano*, 'gipsy'. **a** Quarter of a town or district to which Jews were formerly confined, and which they were not allowed to leave after certain hours; **b** (colloq.) part of town where Jews abound: *Park Lane became a regular ghetto*.

Ghibelline, n. & adj. [1. gibelēn; 2. gíbəlīn, -in], fr. Ital. *Ghibellino*, possibly fr. Germ. *Waiblingen*, one of the imperial estates. **1.** n. Italian adherent of the Imperial party in the mediaeval Holy Roman Empire, opposed to the Papal party (see **Guelph**). **2.** adj. Pertaining to, adhering to, the Ghibellines.

ghost, n. [1. gōst; 2. goust]. O.E. *gāst*, 'life, spirit, soul; angel', M.E. *gōst*. The *h* in our present spelling was introduced by the early printers, prob. through the influence of Du. *gheest*. The word in above senses is confined to Gmc., &, more strictly, to West Gmc.; O.H.G. & Mod. Germ. *geist*, O.S. *gēst*. The Gmc. base **gais-*, however, is found in O.N. *geisa*, 'to rage', of fire, passion &c. (cp. **geyser**), & in Goth. *us-gais-jan*, & **geisan* (w. different gradation), 'to terrify, make aghast'. The Aryan base is **gheis-*, **ghois-* &c., & this is represented in Scrt. *hḗdaś*, 'wrath', fr. **gheizdas*, wh. wd. correspond to a Gmc. **gīst-*, a pretty close & exact cogn. of Gmc. **gaist-*, differing only in having a different vowel grade. Cp. **ghastly**. The fundamental meaning appears to be 'something raging, strong passion; spirit'. **1.** Spirit, principle of life, life itself, soul: *to give up the ghost* (archaic), to die. **2.** Human or Divine spirit: *to vex a person's ghost*; specif., *Holy Ghost*, third Person of the Trinity. **3. a** Apparition, wraith, disembodied spirit of the dead, manifesting itself to the senses of the living; spectre, phantom: *to be afraid of ghosts*; *to see, hear, a ghost*; *the ghost of Hamlet's father*; Phr. *as white as a ghost*, very white; *to look like a ghost*, white and thin; *to look as if one had seen a ghost*, look horrified, or frightened; *the ghost walks* (theatr.), salaries are paid; **b** (fig.) haunting, saddening recollection of earlier life: *ghosts of the past, of former days*. **4.** Anything shadowy, vague, filmy, slight, attenuated; a person who has grown thin and pale from sickness, or old age: *a mere ghost of his former self*. Phrs. *not to have the ghost of a chance*, no chance; *not the ghost of a notion, idea* &c. **5.** One who executes literary or artistic work for another who passes as the author.

ghost-dance, n. Religious dance of North American Indians.

ghostliness, n. [1. gṓstlines; 2. góustlinis]. Next word & **-ness**. **a** Quality of being ghostly, as distinct from bodily; **b** quality of being like a spectre; **c** quality of suggesting the presence of ghosts.

ghostly, adj. [1. gṓstli; 2. góustli]. **ghost** & **-ly**. **1.** Spiritual as opposed to bodily: *ghostly father*; *ghostly comfort* &c. **2.** Pertaining to or having the nature of a ghost or apparition: *ghostly visitant*. **3.** Like a ghost; vaporous, faint, shadowy: *trees loomed ghostly in the twilight*.

ghost moth, n. A night moth, so called from the white colour of the male and the peculiar flight.

ghost-word, n. An historically bogus word whose form is due to a misconception, or to popular etymology; e.g. *slughorn* for *slogan* (Browning), as though from 'horn'.

ghoul, n. [1. goul, gōōl; 2. gaul, gūl], fr. Arab. *ghūl*. **1.** Evil spirit supposed in the East to haunt burial-places and to feed on the dead; hence, **2.** (fig.) **a** person of horrible, revolting, inhuman tastes and habits; **b** person delighting in horrors.

ghoulish, adj. [1. góulish, gṓōlish; 2. gáuliʃ, gūliʃ]. Prec. & **-ish**. Like a ghoul; cruel, delighting in horrors; morbid.

ghoulishly, adv. Prec. & **-ly**. In a ghoulish manner.

ghyll, n. [1. gil; 2. gil]. Variant of **gill (III.)**. (Nthn.) A ravine, gully, chasm.

giant (I.), n. [1. jíant; 2. dʒáiənt]. M.E. *giant*, *geant* &c., fr. O. Fr. *geant*, fr. Lat. *gigant-(em)*, Gk. *gigant-*, stem of *gígas*, 'giant', possibly fr. a vb. **gigaínein*, fr. **gi-gan-jō*, redupl. form fr. Aryan base **ĝen-* &c., 'to bear, produce'. See **genus**. **1.** (class. mythol., cap.) **a** Fabulous monster, intermediate in nature between gods and men, and conceived of as possessing superhuman stature and strength, and warring continually with the gods; **b** somewhat analogous monster in mediaeval romance and folk-lore, generally described as hostile to men. **2. a** Man far above the average in height and size, specif., person of 7 ft. and upwards; **b** animal or plant of great size. **3.** (fig.) One surpassing the common run of men in mental qualities, genius, character &c.: *a giant among statesmen, poets* &c.

giant (II.), adj., fr. prec. Of extraordinary size and strength; very large; gigantic: *a giant potato*; *of giant strength, power* &c.; also in names of species of animals or plants of large size: *giant crab, giant nettle* &c.

giantess, n. [1. jíantes; 2. dʒáiəntis]. **giant (I.)** & **-ess**. Female giant.

giantism, n. [1. jíantizm; 2. dʒáiəntizəm]. **giant (I.)** & **-ism**. Pathological bodily condition in men or animals characterized by abnormal and disproportionate growth, esp. of the bones, which often become misshapen; the disease is usually accompanied by weakness and ill-health.

giantlike, adj. [1. jíantlīk; 2. dʒáiəntlaik]. **giant (I.)** & **-like**. Like a giant; immense.

giant powder, n. A kind of dynamite or high explosive.

giant('s)-stride, n. Gymnastic apparatus consisting of a tall, stout pole, having a revolving wheel on the top, from which ropes are suspended; a person grips one of these, and after running a few paces, takes off from the ground, flying out at the end of the rope as the wheel revolves.

giaour, n. [1. jour; 2. dʒáuə], fr. Pers. *gaur*. Term applied by the Turks to all who are not adherents of Islam; infidel; specif., a Christian.

gib (I.), n. [1. jib, gib; 2. dʒib, gib]. Etymol. doubtful. **a** The hook which appears on the lower jaw of male salmon after the breeding season; **b** a slip of wood or metal used for keeping parts of a machine tight.

gib (II.), n. Short for *Gilbert*. A tom-cat, esp. castrated cat; also *gib-cat*.

gibber, vb. intrans. [1. jíber; 2. dʒíbə]. Imitative. **a** To speak in a broken manner, as when the teeth are chattering with cold or fear; **b** to talk rapidly in an unintelligible language; **c** to talk unintelligibly; to talk nonsense.

gibberish, n. [1. jíberish; 2. dʒíbəriʃ]. Prec. & **-ish**. **a** Unintelligible chatter; indistinct speech; **b** unfamiliar language: *foreign gibberish*.

gibbet (I.), n. [1. jíbet; 2. dʒíbit]. M.E. *gebet*, *gibet*, fr. O. Fr. *gibet*, also meaning 'club'. Origin doubtful. Apparatus specially designed for execution by hanging; a gallows. Phr. *to die on the gibbet*, be hanged.

gibbet (II.), vb. trans., fr. prec. **1.** To hang upon a gibbet. **2.** (fig.) To expose, denounce publicly; hold up to contempt, ridicule, derision: *gibbeted in the press*.

gibbon, n. [1. gíbun; 2. gíbən]. Fr. Etymol. dubious, prob. fr. native name. One of several species of a genus of small anthropoid, tailless apes, arboreal in their habits, of the Malay archipelago.

gibbose. See **gibbous**.

gibbosity, n. [1. gibósiti; 2. gibɔ́siti]. Prec. & **-ity**. **1.** Quality of being gibbous. **2.** Lump, swelling, tumour, projection.

gibbous, gibbose, adj. [1. gíbus, gíbōs; 2. gíbəs, gíbous]. Lat. *gibbōsus*, fr. *gibb-(us)*, 'humped', cp. *gibba*, 'hump', & **-ous**. Etymol. uncertain. **a** Swollen, bulging, protuberant, convex; hunched, hump-backed; **b** (of the moon) between half and full.

gibe, jibe (I.), vb. intrans. [1. jīb; 2. dʒaib]. Cp. O.N. *geipa*, 'to talk nonsense'. To carp, utter biting, insolent, contemptuous remarks; to turn things into derision; sneer. *Gibe at*, make (person or thing) the subject of gibes; to deride, treat with expressed contempt.

gibe, jibe (II.), n., fr. prec. An expression of derision and contempt; mocking taunt, sneer.

gibingly, adv. [1. jíbingli; 2. dʒáibiŋli], fr. Pres. Part. of **gibe (I.)** & **-ly**. Mockingly, derisively.

giblets, n. pl. [1. jíblets; 2. džíblits]. M.E. *gibelet*, Fr. *gibelet*, O. Fr. *gibelotte*, 'ragout, stew'. Edible, but inferior parts of poultry, such as heart and gizzard: *giblet pie, giblet soup.*

gibus, n. [1. jíbus; 2. džáibəs]. Fr., fr. name of inventor. Opera hat, crush hat; a top hat covered with black silk which can be folded flat and carried under the arm when not in use.

giddily, adv. [1. gídili; 2. gídili]. **giddy** & **-ly**. In a giddy manner (in various senses).

giddiness, n. [1. gídines; 2. gídinis]. Next word & **-ness**. Condition of being giddy; **a** in physical; **b** in moral senses.

giddy, adj. [1. gídi; 2. gídi]. O.E. *gydig*, 'insane', perh. orig. 'divinely inspired, in a state of ecstasy', & fr. Gmc. **gud-*, 'god, deity'. See **god**. **1. a** (in physical sense, only pred.) Having feeling of vertigo, the sensation, often accompanied by nausea, of instability when trying to stand; sensation as though surrounding objects were revolving: *to feel, turn, giddy*; **b** (in moral sense, pred. and attrib.) exhibiting levity, or lack of stability, in mind and conduct; flighty, unbalanced in principles: *a giddy girl, giddy young thing; her conduct was rather giddy.* Phr. (vulg. colloq.) *a giddy goat*, feather-headed, irresponsible, foolish person. **2. a** Tending to cause, or suggesting likelihood of, physical giddiness, as from steepness, peril, or rapidity of movement, esp. of rotatory kind: *a giddy path, climb; giddy dance*; **b** tending to fatigue and dissipate one's energies and divert them from serious pursuits: *giddy whirl, round, of pleasure* &c. **3.** (fig.) Inspiring sense of transitoriness and insecurity: *giddy heights of fame, ambition* &c.

gidya, n. [1. gídya; 2. gídjə]. Native word. **a** Australian tree of mimosa tribe with very hard wood (*Acacia homalophylla*); **b** a long thin spear, made from wood of this, in use among the Australian aborigines.

gift (I.), n. [1. gift; 2. gift], fr. O.N. *gift*; the corresponding O.E. *ġift*, perh. also fr. O.N., means 'price of a wife': the O.E. word for 'gift, donation', is *ġiefu*. See base under **give**. **1.** That which is given; something transferred to another's possession, without price or any equivalent value being received in exchange; present, donation: *birthday, Christmas, gifts.* Phr. *I wouldn't take, have, it as a gift*, would not have it at any price. **2.** Right of bestowal, vested in patrons of church livings &c.: *in the gift of So-and-so.* **3.** Intellectual quality or endowment born with one and coming by nature; capacity, talent, aptitude: *a person of many gifts.* Phr. *gift of tongues*, facility in learning languages; *gift of the gab*, power of fluent speech.

gift (II.), vb. trans., fr. prec. To bestow (gifts) upon, endow with; (chiefly of non-material endowments) *we are all gifted with a conscience.*

gifted, adj. [1. gífted; 2. gíftid], fr. P.P. of prec. Possessing natural aptitudes, talents, qualities; accomplished, talented, naturally able: *a gifted man, composer, poet* &c.

gig, n. [1. gig; 2. gig]. Orig. meaning 'spinning or whipping top'. Etymol. dubious. **1.** A light, high, two-wheeled carriage, drawn by one horse. Phr. (archaic) *to drive a gig*, be a prosperous, respectable person. **2.** A ship's boat, long, light, and fast, for oars and sail, usually appropriated for the commanding officer: *the crew of the captain's gig.* **3.** A modified adaptation of a ship's gig, employed mainly in racing. **4.** A revolving toothed cylinder for teaseling woollen fabrics. **5. a** A kind of harpoon; **b** a hooked drag used for sweeping the surface-waters over a school of fish that refuse to bite. **6.** *Gig-lamps*, (facetious) spectacles.

gigantean, adj. [1. jigántean; 2. džaigǽntiən]. Lat. *gigantēus*, fr. Gk. *gigánteios*, w. substitution or addition of adj. suff. *-ānus*. See **giant** & **-an**. Like a giant in size; colossal.

gigantic, adj. [1. jigántik; 2. džaigǽntik], fr. Lat. *gigant(em)*, 'giant', fr. Gk. *gigant-*, stem of *gigās*, 'giant'. See **giant** & **-ic**. **1.** Of or pertaining to a giant (obs.). **2.** Specif., having the size and proportions of a giant; very large, enormous, huge, immense; very extensive, on very large scale.

gigantically, adv. [1. jigántikali; 2. džaigǽntikəli]. Prec. & **-al** & **-ly**. On a gigantic scale.

gigantomachy, n. [1. jìgantómaki; 2. džàigæntɔ́məki], fr. Gk. *gigantomakhia*, fr. *gigant-*, *gigās*, 'giant', & *mákhē*, 'battle'. See **giant** & **-machy**. **a** (class. mythol.) War between the Giants and the Gods; **b** a war between giant powers.

giggle, vb. intrans. & n. [1. gígl; 2. gígl]. Imitative. Cp. Germ. *gichelen*. **1.** vb. To laugh in a nervous, foolish manner; to utter repeatedly a continuous, high-pitched, convulsive peal of half-suppressed laughter. **2.** n. A laugh of this kind.

gigot, n. [1. jígot; 2. džígət]. Fr. *gigot*, fr. O. Fr. *gigue*. Leg of mutton.

gigue, n. [1. zhēg; 2. žīg]. O. Fr. *gigue*, a kind of fiddle, lively dance; Ital. *giga*, 'a fiddle', Span. & Port. *giga*. Cf. Germ. *geige*, M.H.G. *gige*; also Engl. **jig**. **1.** Ancient stringed instrument of violin family. **2. a** Species of lively old-time dance; **b** music to which this was danced.

Gilbertian, adj. [1. gilbérshan; 2. gilbʌ́ʃən], fr. W. S. Gilbert, collaborator w. Arthur Sullivan in the comic operas. Of, resembling, the main features of Gilbert's plots, dialogues &c.; topsy-turvy.

Gilbertine, n. & adj. [1. gilbértīn; 2. gilbʌ́tain], fr. St. Gilbert of Sempringham. **1.** n. A member of a religious order founded by St. Gilbert in 12th cent. **2.** adj. Of, pertaining to, St. Gilbert, or to the order founded by him.

gild (I.), n. See **guild**.

gild (II.), vb. trans. [1. gild; 2. gild]. O.E. *gyldan*, M.E. *gilde*, fr. Gmc. **guldjan*, fr. **guld-*, 'gold'. See **gold**. **1. a** To overlay, coat with gold or gold-leaf; **b** to paint with pigment mixed with gold, or a substance resembling it; Phr. *to gild the pill*, make unpleasant thing appear attractive. **2.** (poet.) **a** To light up, brighten, with a radiance as of gold: *sunset gilds the sky*; **b** to render beautiful, adorn, brighten. '*Whether old age with faint but cheerful ray, Attend to gild the evening of thy day*' (Pope).

gilded, adj. [1. gílded; 2. gíldid]. P.P. of prec., mostly used idiomatically. Overlaid, adorned, with gold leaf, gold dust, or pigment: *Gilded Chamber* (from its decoration), House of Lords; Phr. *gilded youth*, gay, fashionable, well-dressed, exquisite young man (or men) of wealth and position.

gilder, n. [1. gílder; 2. gíldə]. **gild (II.)** & **-er**. One who gilds; specif., one whose trade it is to put gold on to frames &c.: *carver and gilder*, usually associated with carving and picture-frame-making.

gilding, n. [1. gílding; 2. gíldiŋ]. **gild** & **-ing**. **a** Gold, or gold-coloured material put on to something in order to gild it; **b** act or process of covering with gold &c.; **c** (fig.) adornment; covering, concealment, of unpleasant facts, esp. in Phr. *gilding of the pill.*

gill (I.), n. [1. gil; 2. gil]. Scand.; M.E. *gylle*, O. Dan. *gælle*, O. Swed. *gel*. Cogn. w. Gk. *khelúnē*, 'lip, jaw', *kheilos*, 'lip, lip of vessel', for **kheljo-*, Aryan **ghel-*. **1.** One of a pair of organs with which a fish breathes under water, corresponding to the lungs of mammals. Phr. *green about the gills* (of human beings), sick-looking; disconcerted. **2.** Wattle of certain fowls. **3.** Radiating plates or ridges composing the under surface of mushroom or fungus.

gill (II.), n. [1. jil; 2. džil]. M.E. *gille, gylle*, O. Fr. *gelle*, Lat. *gillo, gello*, 'a cooling-vessel', cogn. w. *gelidus*, 'cold, frozen'. See **gelid**. **a** One quarter pint liquid measure; **b** vessel capable of containing this amount.

gill (III.), n. [1. gil; 2. gil], fr. O.N. *gil*, 'glen'; cp. O.N. *geil*, 'narrow pass'. Ravine, chasm; a woody glen traversed by a stream.

Gill, Jill (IV.), n. [1. jil; 2. džil]. Abbr. of *Gillian* or *Jillian*, corrupt. fr. *Juliana*. A girl, sweetheart: *every Jack has his Gill.*

gillie, n. [1. gíli; 2. gíli], fr. Gael. *gille*, 'servant, boy'. Name given in the Highlands of Scotland to an outdoor attendant; esp. a gamekeeper, or attendant on deerstalkers and fishermen.

gillyflower, n. [1. jíliflòur; 2. džíliflàuə]. M.E. *gilofre, gelofer*, fr. O. Fr. *girofle*, fr. L. Lat., fr. Gk. *karuóphullon*, fr. *káruo-(n)*, 'nut', cogn. w. **carinate**, & *phúllon*, 'leaf'. See **phyllo-**. **1.** Name applied to the clove pink, the wallflower, and the common stock. **2.** A species of apple.

gilt, n. [1. gilt; 2. gilt], fr. P.P. of **gild (II.)**. **1.** Gilding, gold laid on in plate, leaf, or dust; gold paint. **2.** (fig.) Superficial charm, beauty, attractiveness. Phr. *take the gilt off the gingerbread*, destroy illusion, spoil.

gilt-edged, adj. [1. gílt ejd; 2. gílt edžd]. **a** Having the edges gilt, e.g. the page of a book; **b** (fig.) of finest quality, esp. *gilt-edged security*, originally Government stock (from being printed on gilt-edged paper), hence, any very safe, sound investment, such as trustees are allowed to invest in.

gilt-head, n. Name of two varieties of sea fish.

gimbal, n. [1. jímbl; 2. džímbl]. O. Fr. *gemel*, Fr. *jumeau*, 'a twin', Lat. *gemellus*, dimin. of *geminus*, 'a twin'. See **Gemini** & **gemels**. **1. a** (in pl.) Device of combined rings for suspending a body (e.g. mariners' compass, barometer &c.), so that it retains its level, however its support be inclined, by the rolling of the ship; **b** usually *gimbal-*, or *gemel-ring*, a finger-ring consisting of two rings interlaced. **2.** Obsolete name for kind of pastry. See **jumble (III.)**.

gimcrack, n. & adj. [1. jímkrak; 2. džímkræk]. Prob. M.E. *gibecrake*, denoting apparently some kind of inlaid woodwork, perh. fr. O. Fr. *giber*, 'to handle roughly, shake', & **crack (I.)**. **a** n. A trumpery, frail, or tawdry object; a showy trifle; **b** adj., flimsy, trifling, tawdry, badly made.

gimcrackery, n. [1. jìmkrákeri; 2. džìmkrǽkəri]. Prec. & **-ery**. Collection of gimcracks.

gimlet, gimblet, n. [1. gímlet; 2. gímlit]. M.E. *gymlot*, fr. O. Fr. *gimbelet, guimbelet*, Mod. Fr. *gibelet*, dimin. of Gmc. origin. Boring tool with spiral cutting edge, and handle at right angles to shaft. Phr. *eyes like gimlets*, penetrating eyes; prying eyes.

gimp, n. [1. gimp; 2. gimp]. Cp. O. Fr. *guimpeure*, nasalized form of **guipure**, also Du. *gimp*, Germ. *gimpe*. Plaited or twisted cord of silk or other material used for trimming women's dresses, some academic gowns, and naval and military uniforms.

gin (I.), n. [1. jin; 2. džin], fr. Fr. *genièvre*, fr. Lat. *jūniperum*, q.v. under **juniper**; confused w. *Geneva* by popular etymol. **1.** A sweetish spirituous liquor distilled from grain or malt and flavoured with juniper berries. Phr. (vulg. and colloq.) *gin-and-water voice*, hoarse and raucous as from too much drinking. **2.** (attrib.) *Gin palace*, large, flamboyant public-house; *gin-sling*, an iced drink of gin, sugar, and various flavourings.

gin (II.), n. & vb. trans. M.E. Contraction of **engine**. **1.** n. **a** Machine, mechanical contrivance (obs. except in some techn. senses); kind of crane; appliance for extracting cotton seeds; **b** snare, trap; **c** (fig., obs.) crafty trick. **2.** vb. **a** To snare; **b** to extract seeds from (cotton).

gin (III.), vb. intrans. & trans. [1. gin; 2. gin]. M.E. *ginnen*; cp. O.E. *on-ginnan, be-ginnan.* See **begin**. (obs. or poet.) To begin.

gingall, jingal, n. [1. jínggawl; 2. džíŋgōl]. Hind. *janjal*. A fire-arm of China, India &c., either a light cannon mounted on a swivel or a heavy musket fired from a rest.

ginger (I.), n. [1. jínjer; 2. džíndžə]. O.E. *gingifer(e)*, M.E. *gingevir, gingivere*, cp. O.E. *gengibre, gengivre*, Mod. Fr. *gingembre*, fr. L. Lat. *zingiber*, fr. Gk. *ziggíber(is)*, fr. Sert.

śr̥ṅgavēra, lit. 'horn-body'. See **horn.** **1. a** Aromatic tropical plant; **b** prepared root of this used in medicine, as a condiment, and, boiled in sugar, as a sweetmeat. **2.** (colloq. and slang) **a** Energy, spirit, liveliness, go; **b** (of hair) a lively red (also used as adj.).

ginger (II.), vb. trans., fr. prec. **a** To flavour with ginger; **b** to stimulate (racehorse) with ginger; hence (colloq.) to enliven, stimulate, give more life and vigour to: (gen.) *ginger up* (a person, a performance &c.).

ginger-ale, n. Sweet aerated drink flavoured with ginger, citric acid, caramel &c., usually of a pale, yellowish-brown colour resembling that of ale.

ginger-beer, n. Sweet, straw-coloured, effervescent drink flavoured with ginger.

gingerbread, n. [1. jínjerbred; 2. džíndžəbred]. Kind of cake compounded with treacle or honey and ginger or other spices.

gingerbread nut, n. A round, sweet biscuit flavoured with ginger.

ginger cordial, n. A liqueur made from ginger.

gingerly, adj. & adv. [1. jínjerli; 2. džíndžəli]. Prob. fr. O. Fr. *genzor*, 'pretty, delicate', fr. Low Lat. type **gentiōr-*, compar. of **gent-*, for Lat. *genit-us*, 'born', whence O. Fr. *gent*, 'gentle'. See **gentle & -ly.** **a** adj. Cautious, acting with extreme care; dainty, finicking: *in a gingerly manner*; **b** adv., cautiously, delicately, shrinkingly: *to walk gingerly.*

ginger nut, n. Gingerbread nut.

ginger snap, n. Variety of gingerbread nut.

ginger wine, n. Fermented liquor made from ginger, lemons, raisins, and sugar.

gingery, adj. [1. jínjeri; 2. džíndžəri]. **ginger** (I.) **& -y.** **a** Of or pertaining to ginger; tasting of, or like, ginger; pungent, hot; (fig., of temperament) fiery, irascible, testy; **b** (of hair) reddish, or red in colour.

gingham, n. [1. gíngam; 2. gíŋəm]. Fr. *guingan*, fr. Malay *ginggang*, 'striped cotton'. **1.** A kind of cheap cotton or linen cloth striped or chequered and dyed in the yarn. **2.** (colloq.) An umbrella, esp. a large, clumsy one; so called because common sorts were formerly made of this material.

gingival, adj. [1. jinjíval; 2. džindžáivəl]. Lat. *gingīva*, 'the gums'. See **chin & gnathic & -al.** **1.** Of or pertaining to the gums. **2.** (phon.) Pronounced with the point of tongue-tip against the upper gums; also used substantively for *gingival sound.* Not much used; sounds thus made are better called *point alveolar.*

gingivitis, n. [1. jinjivítis; 2. džindživáitis]. See prec. & **-itis.** (med.) Inflammation of the gums.

ginglymoid(al), adj. [1. jingglimóid(l); 2. džiŋglimɔ́id(əl)]. See next word & **-oid & -al.** Connected with, resembling, a hinge joint; of the nature of a hinge-joint.

ginglymus, n. [1. jíngglimus; 2. džíŋgliməs]. Lat., fr. Gk. *gigglumos*, 'hinge joint'; cogn. w. **claw.** (anat.) Hinge joint, one which permits of no rotatory movement, e.g. the knee-joint.

ginkgo, n. [1. gíngkgō, jíngkgō; 2. gíŋkgou, džíŋkgou]. Jap. A tree of Japan and China with yellow fruit and handsome fan-shaped leaves.

ginseng, n. [1. jínséng; 2. džínséŋ]. Chin. *jênshên*, fr. *jên*, 'man', & *shên*, perh. 'image'; fr. form of root. **a** Genus of Chinese and N. American plants of ivy family; **b** Chinese drug prepared from aromatic root of this.

gipsy, gypsy (I.), n. & adj. [1. jípsi; 2. džípsi], fr. obs. *Gipsen, Giptian*, fr. M.E. *Egypcien*, 'Egyptian', fr. O. Fr. *Egyptien*, fr. L. Lat. *Aegyptiān-(us)*, fr. Lat. *Aegypti-(us)*, fr. Gk. *Aigúptios*, adj., fr. *Aigupt-(os)*, 'Egypt', & **-an.** The gipsies were wrongly supposed to have come from Egypt. **1.** n. **a** (cap. or l.c.) Member of a nomadic race of Indian origin, inhabiting many parts of Europe, Asia &c., living as horse-dealers, metal-workers, musicians, and fortune-tellers; **b** (l.c., fig.) person resembling a Gipsy in appearance, esp. in having a swarthy complexion, black sparkling eyes &c., or in roving or erratic habits. **2.** (cap.) The Gipsy language, Romany. **3.** adj. Pertaining to, resembling, a gipsy or gipsies: *a gipsy camp. Gipsy bonnet*, broad-brimmed hat tied under chin; *gipsy caravan, van*, covered wagon used to live and travel in; *gipsy flower, rose*, scabious; *gipsy moth*, European species of tussock moth; *gipsy table*, light, round table on three legs.

gipsy (II.), vb. intrans., fr. prec. To live temporarily like a gipsy, to camp out; to picnic.

gipsydom, n. [1. jípsidum; 2. džípsidəm]. **gipsy (I.) & -dom.** State of being a gipsy; the gipsies collectively.

gipsyfied, adj. [1. jípsifīd; 2. džípsifaid]. **gipsy & -fy & -ed.** Having become like a gipsy; addicted to gipsy life or habits.

gipsyhood, n. [1. jípsihood; 2. džípsihud]. **gipsy & -hood.** Condition, state, of a gipsy.

gipsyish, adj. [1. jípsiish; 2. džípsiiʃ]. **gipsy & -ish.** Like, rather like, a gipsy.

gipsyism, n. [1. jípsiizm; 2. džípsiizəm]. **gipsy & -ism.** Expression, habit, borrowed from gipsies.

giraffe, n. [1. jiráhf; 2. dživáf]. Fr., fr. Span. *girafa*, fr. Arab. *zarāfa, zorāfa.* Large African hoofed ruminant mammal with an enormously long neck, a back sloping downwards from shoulder to tail, a tawny skin crossed by a network of paler lines, and a narrow head surmounted by two short horns; the camelopard.

girandole, n. [1. jírandōl; 2. džírəndoul]. Fr., fr. Ital. *girandola*, dimin. of *giranda*, 'revolving jet', fr. Lat. *gȳrand-*, gerundial stem of *gȳrāre*, 'to turn, rotate'. See **gyrate.** Name given to a variety of ornamental objects of a more or less circular or radiating design; specif. **a** branching chandelier or candelabrum; **b** a kind of revolving firework; **c** rotating water-jet; **d** a kind of pendant, such as an earring, having smaller pendants attached.

girasole, n. [1. jírasōl; 2. džírəsoul]. Fr. *girasol*, Ital. *girasole*, fr. Lat. *gȳrāre*, 'to turn, rotate', & *sōl-*, 'the sun'. Cp. Fr. *tournesol.* See **gyrate, solar.** **1.** The sunflower (obs.). **2.** The fire opal.

gird (I.), vb. trans. [1. gërd; 2. gə̄d]. O.E. *gyrdan*, M.E. *girden*; cp. O.S. *gurdian*, Germ. *gürten* &c.; Gmc. weak vb. formed on base **gurđ-*. See further under **court, garden, girth, horticulture, yard** (II.). (chiefly liter.) **1. a** To encircle, esp. at waist, or oneself at waist, with belt, sash &c.: *he was girt about with a rope*; fig. in Phr. *to gird oneself (for a fight* &c.); (Bib.) *gird up one's loins*, brace oneself, prepare for strenuous action; **b** to attach to (person) by belt, girdle &c.: *to gird one with a sword*; **c** (fig.) to invest, equip: *girt with supreme power and authority*; **d** (gen.) to encircle, surround: *to gird a tree with iron bands*; *an island girded by the sea.* **2. a** To put on (girdle, belt &c.); **b** to confine (clothing) with girdle: *to gird one's robe about one*; to attach to one's body by belt, straps &c.: *to gird on one's armour, sword* &c.

gird (II.), vb. intrans. M.E. *girden*, 'to strike, pierce, cut through'; of doubtful origin. See **gride.** *Gird at*, to gibe, taunt, nag, carp at (a person); to chafe, complain, at (a thing).

gird (III.), n., fr. prec. A taunt, gibe, sneer.

girder (I.), n. [1. gërder; 2. gə́də], fr. **gird** (II.) **& -er.** One who girds or taunts.

girder (II.), n. **gird** (I.) **& -er.** Powerful support of timber, iron, or steel used in building and engineering to carry and distribute weights and thrusts; **a** a large wooden beam, or piece of steel, supporting upper floor of a house &c.; **b** one bearing superstructure of a bridge &c.

girderage, n. [1. gërderij; 2. gə́dəridž]. **girder (II.) & -age.** System of girders.

girdle (I.), n. [1. gërdl; 2. gə́dl]. O.E. *gyrdel*, fr. same base as **gird** (I.). **1.** Belt, cord, or strip of any material used to gird the waist and hold clothing in position. **2.** Thing which surrounds, encloses, or encompasses like a girdle: *within the girdle of the sea*; **a** zone, e.g. the zodiac, the equator; **b** ring-like structure: *the pelvic girdle*; **c** ring round tree made by removing bark; Phr. (fig.) *to put a girdle round*, travel round (Shakespeare); also to surround as with a girdle, e.g. by railway lines, telegraphic cables &c.

girdle (II.), vb. trans., fr. prec. **a** To gird, to equip with a girdle, a belt; **b** to bind about, to bandage around; **c** (fig.) to surround: *the town is girdled with railways.*

girdle (III.), n. Nthn. variant of **griddle.** Flat sheet of iron placed over fire for cooking certain types of cakes, scones &c.

girdle-cake, n. One cooked on a girdle.

girl, n. [1. gërl, gārl; 2. gə̄l, gɛəl]. O.E. *gyrl(e)*, 'virgin', M.E. *gerl, gurl*, 'young person of either sex', dimin., O.E. type **gyr-el*, fr. Gmc. **gur-*, 'child', cp. L.G. *gör*, Norw. *gorre* &c., 'child', possibly cogn. w. Gk. *kóros*, 'child', & dimin. *-il.* **1. a** A female child (as distinct from a boy): *his first child was a girl*; **b** female not yet adult; (by extension) **c** one still in the first flush of womanhood, below middle age: *she was married as a mere girl.* **2.** Specif. uses: **a** a maidservant; **b** one of a number of women engaged collectively as members of a business staff, theatrical company &c.: *shop girl.* **3.** (colloq., rather vulg.) **a** Sweetheart, fiancée: *Jones and his girl came to lunch*; **b** (familiar form of address) of woman of any age: *old girl.*

Girl Guide, n. Member of an organization for young girls based on the principles and practice of the Boy Scouts.

girlhood, n. [1. gërlhood; 2. gə́lhud]. **girl & -hood.** The period of life between childhood and womanhood.

girlish, adj. [1. gërlish; 2. gə́liʃ]. **girl & -ish.** **1.** Of or pertaining to a girl, or girlhood: *girlish pursuits, games* &c. **2.** Like a girl; fresh, youthful: *girlish appearance.* **3.** Applied to boys, unmanly, effeminate.

girlishly, adv. Prec. & **-ly.** In a girlish manner.

girlishness, n. See prec. & **-ness.** Quality of being girlish, in all senses.

giron, n. See **gyron.**

Girondin, Girondist, n. & adj. [1. jiróndin, -ist; 2. džirɔ́ndin, -ist]. Fr. *Girondin*, fr. *Gironde*, the chief members of the party being deputies of that department. A member of the moderate Republican party under the French Revolutionary government.

girt, n. & vb. trans. & intrans. [1. gërt; 2. gə̄t]. Variant of **girth.** **1.** n. Measurement round an object. **2.** vb. **a** trans. To measure girt of; **b** intrans., to be of such a girt.

girth (I.), n. [1. gërth; 2. gə̄þ]. M.E. *gerð*, fr. O.N. *gjörð*; cp. Goth. *gairda*, 'girdle'; fr. Gmc. base **gerđ-*, 'to enclose'. See **gird** (I.). **1. a** A strap or band passed round the belly of a horse, mule, or other beast of burden to secure a saddle, pack, rug &c.; **b** part of harness in draught animals which secures the saddle; belly-band. **2. a** Dimension round the waist or body of a person; hence, **b** large dimension, corpulence; obesity; **c** (of other objects) circumferential measure; circumference: *girth of a tree, of the earth.*

girth (II.), vb. trans., fr. prec. To put on, or tighten up, girths of a horse; also *girth up.*

gist, n. [1. jist; 2. džist]. O. Fr. *giste*, Mod. Fr. *gîte*, 'lying-place, lodgement', fr. O. Fr. *gésir*, Lat. *jacēre*, 'to lie'. See **adjacent.** **1.** (law) The essential grounds of an action at law, that which gives it force. **2.** Essence, pith, main points, of a subject, relevant to particular discussion: *the gist of the matter is . . .*

gith, n. [1. gith; 2. giþ]. O.E. *gip-corn.* Corncockle.

gittern, n. [1. gítërn; 2. gítə̄n]. See **cither(n).** Obsolete stringed musical instrument of the lute or guitar class.

give (I.), vb. trans. & intrans. [1. giv ; 2. giv]. The initial sound shows the influence of O.N. *gefa*, as it cannot be derived fr. O.E. *ġefan*, *ġi(e)fan*; M.E. has both *ȝive(n)*, *ȝēve(n)* &c. & *give(n)*, *gēve(n)* &c. ; the word is Common Gmc. ; cp. O.H.G. *geban*, Mod. Germ. *geben*, Goth. *giban*, O.N. *gefa* ; Gmc. type **geb-an-*, perh. cogn. w. Lith. *gabénti*, 'to bring', O. Ir. *gab-im*, 'I give, take'. **A.** trans. The basal meaning of this verb, from which all the others spring, seems to be the transference or passing of something, good or bad, material or non-material, whether for nothing or in exchange for something else from one person to another. From this general sense others arise — of conceding, dedicating, imparting something to another, in a literal or figurative sense, in fact of performing almost any overt act which affects some other person or thing ; then a general sense of producing something, acting as author, as the source or cause of something discernible by the senses or by the mental faculties. **1.** To transfer from one's own possession or control to that of another without any implication of exchange ; bestow freely and without price ; present, hand over to another as his own property ; (of material things) **a** *to give a handsome present* ; *to give half-a-crown* ; *to give money to the poor* ; **b** to pass on to, impart, communicate to, infect with (as a contagious malady) : *you've given me your cold* ; *one boy can give measles to a whole school* ; **c** (i.) (of non-material things ; spiritual benefits) to confer, endow with : *to give one's blessing* ; *to give one's good wishes* ; *to give encouragement to* ; (ii.) (of honours, posts, appointments &c.) to allot, assign to, confer on : *to give a man the place of honour* ; *to give the command of a regiment to* ; *to give a part in a play* (*to an actor*) ; *to give a title* ; Phrs. (the following fall under several of above categories) : *to give a dinner-party, a ball* ; *give a toast*, propose someone's health ; *I give you the King*, i.e. the toast of his health ; *I give you joy*, wish you happiness &c. ; *to give one's word*, promise faithfully ; *give my love, kind regards, to So-and-so*, express to him these sentiments from me ; *to give thanks*, to be thankful ; *give us a song !*, sing something ; *to give it*, as *I'll give it to you when I catch you*, *he gave it him hot* &c., punish, reprimand severely ; *to give a person a piece of one's mind*, say exactly what one thinks without reticence, hence, to censure ; *to give a dog a bad name*, (fig.) blacken person's character by insinuations ; *to give* (*a horse*) *his head*, loosen strain on bit, let him go his own pace ; (fig.) *to give a man his head*, let him have his own way ; *give me* (*Beethoven, cricket* &c.), I prefer (rather than other alternative). **2.** To transfer something to another in exchange for, or in consideration of, something else ; to pay ; **a** (for value received) *I gave a guinea for this hat* ; *how much did you give for that horse ?* ; **b** (in return for services rendered) *I'll give you five pounds for a week's work* ; *to give a fair day's wage for a fair day's work* ; **c** (as compensation for injury or loss &c.) *to give a man a hundred a year for the loss of his foot* ; **d** to inflict, impose, something as punishment or retribution : *to give a man six months' hard labour* ; *give a boy a good flogging* ; Phrs. *to give as good as one gets*, return chaff, insult, injury, in kind ; *to give tit for tat* ; (i.) repay an injury with another ; (ii.) make suitable reply ; *to give one a Roland for his Oliver*, same as prec. ; also, provide suitable opponent in any contest. **3.** To cause to occur, be a source of, supply ; **a** (as result of natural process or function) *cows give milk* ; *trees give fruit* ; *land gives crops* ; **b** to produce an effect as result of physical or mechanical action or process : *the sun gives light* ; *the gun gave a loud report* ; **c** (of effects on the mind or emotions) to evoke, provoke, excite, induce : *to give pleasure, sorrow, offence* ; **d** to occur as the outcome of mental process : *the most careful research on these lines has given no result.* **4.** To hand over to, entrust to, cause to pass temporarily into keeping of, another : *to give a porter one's bag to carry* ; *to give a groom one's horse to hold.* **5.** To concede, grant, allow : *I give you that point in the argument.* Phrs. *to give way*, be unable to resist ; to yield (lit. and fig.) ; *give way to*, (i.) to retreat before, (ii.) abandon, surrender, oneself to (temptation, despair &c.) ; *give ground* (esp. of troops), to retire ; *to give points to*, (i.) (of superior player) to give opponent initial advantage ; hence, (fig.) (ii.) to be superior to. **6.** (of mental or moral action) To devote, dedicate : *to give one's mind, attention, to* ; *to give one's life to study.* Phr. *to give one's life*, sacrifice it, die. **7.** To communicate, impart (knowledge, information &c.) to mind of another ; to state : *to give evidence* ; *give an account of* ; *give instructions, orders* &c. Phr. *to give lessons, instruction, in* (*mathematics* &c.), to teach, be a teacher of. **8. a** To carry out, execute, perform such muscular activities as are required to produce bodily movements : *to give a start of surprise, a leap, a shrug of the shoulders, a blow* &c. ; **b** to execute muscular movements of vocal organs which result in emission of sound : *to give a cry, a shout, loud laugh* &c. Phr. *to give tongue*, (i.) (of hounds) to cry, as when they pick up the scent ; (ii.) (fig., of persons) to chatter, cry out, esp. noisily and complainingly. **9.** To produce, represent, on the stage : *to give a concert, a performance of a play* &c. **10.** To exhibit (human character, passion), in art or literature ; to describe, express, (spirit of an age) ; portray (human form and feature, or features of external nature) in painting, or describe these in words : *Shakespeare gives us human nature in every degree, and under the stress of every emotion* ; *Sir Walter Scott gives the scenery of the Highlands with such fidelity that we feel as though we knew the places he describes* ; *Sir Joshua has given us the principal people of his day as they lived and went about their daily business.* **B.** intrans. **1.** To practise giving ; be in habit of bestowing ; exhibit generosity : *to give generously to charity.* **2.** To yield, relax, give way, break down, under violence or strain : *the foundations are giving.* **3.** To be springy, resilient, elastic, not rigid ; to yield, bend (of materials, wood, steel &c.) : *to give but not to break* ; *this chair gives comfortably.* **C.** In special senses when followed by adverb or preposition. *Give away*, trans., **a** to alienate, transfer absolutely ; **b** to sacrifice, surrender : *to give away an opportunity* ; **c** (colloq.) to betray, expose, show up, voluntarily or accidentally : *his accent gave him away* ; **d** to transfer to another's charge ; specif., *to give away the bride*, place her hand in that of bridegroom at marriage ceremony. *Give back*, trans., **a** to return, restore ; **b** to retort, repay, retaliate with : *give back insult for insult* ; **c** intrans., to fall back, retire. *Give forth*, trans., to publish, announce broadcast (often with suggestion of falsehood). *Give in*, **a** trans., to hand in, register, record in an appointed quarter ; **b** intrans., to surrender, yield. *Give out*, trans., **a** to distribute, apportion, allocate &c. ; **b** to publish, make known (notices, news &c.) ; **c** to allege, asseverate, bruit about : *to give it out that* &c. ; **d** to emit ; **e** intrans., to run short, come to an end, be exhausted, worn out, e.g. of supplies, strength. *Give over*, trans., **a** to deliver up, transfer ; **b** to cease, desist from ; intrans., **c** to stop, cease, come to a halt. *Give up*, trans., **a** to surrender, cede, sacrifice : *to give up one's place* ; **b** to renounce, abjure, abandon, forsake ; to abstain from : *to give up one's faith, smoking* ; **c** to despair of, declare to be beyond hope : *given up by the doctors* ; **d** admit that one cannot solve or guess, and cease trying to do so : *to give up a riddle, problem.* *Give upon*, intrans., (a vicious Gallicism) to overlook, command view of, look out on ; afford direct access to : *this window gives upon the street.*

give (II.), n., fr. prec., in intrans. sense **3.** Elasticity, resilience, pliancy, adaptability (of material substances), and fig. (of human mind and character). Phr. *give and take*, concessions on both sides in argument, negotiations &c.

given, adj. [1. givn ; 2. givn]. P.P. of **give** (I.). **1.** Specified ; agreed upon, stipulated : *within a given period.* **2.** (math. and log.) Laid down as an antecedent condition ; postulated, assumed, premised.

gizzard, n. [1. gizard ; 2. gizəd]. O. Fr. *guisier*, Fr. *gésier*, fr. Lat. *gīgēria* (pl.), 'cooked entrails of poultry'. Etymol. doubtful. **1.** One of the digestive organs of birds, forming a second stomach in which the food is ground. **2.** (colloq.) Throat. Phr. (fig.) *it, that, sticks in my gizzard*, I am reluctant to accept or agree to it ; I dislike it.

glabrous, adj. [1. glábrus ; 2. gléibrəs]. Lat. *glabr-(um)*, *glaber*, 'smooth, bald', Aryan type **ghladh-ro-*, cogn. w. Lith. *glodas*, 'smooth' &c., see **glad**, & **-ous**. (biol.) Hairless, bald ; hence, smooth.

glacé, adj. [1. glásā ; 2. glǽsei]. Fr., P.P. of *glacer*, 'to freeze, to glaze'. See next word. Having a smooth, shining surface ; **a** (of leather, fabrics &c.) : *glacé kid* ; **b** (of confectionery) coated with sugar : *glacé cherries, marrons glacés.*

glacial, adj. [1. glásial ; 2. gléisiəl]. Fr., fr. Lat. *glaciāl-(is)*, 'icy', fr. *glaci-(ēs)*, 'ice', for **gel-aci-*, cp. *gelu*, 'frost' ; & **-al**. See **chill, cold, cool, gelid.** **1.** Of or pertaining to ice, to the ice-age, or to glaciers : *glacial period* ; *glacial theory*, that relating to the action of glaciers. **2.** Of the nature of, like, ice ; icy, very cold : *glacial deposit* ; *glacial weather.* **3.** (fig. of manner, bearing, speech &c.) Unfriendly, distant, frigid.

glacialist, n. [1. glásialist ; 2. gléisiəlist]. Prec. & **-ist.** **a** One who supports the glacial theory ; **b** special student of glaciers, and their action.

glaciate, vb. trans. [1. glásiāt ; 2. gléisieit]. Lat. *glaciāt-(um)*, P.P. type of *glaciāre*, 'to turn to ice'. See **glacial, -ate.** **1. a** To freeze, turn to ice ; **b** (geol.) to affect by glacial action. **2.** To give a frosted surface to (metal &c.).

glacier, n. [1. glásier ; 2. glǽsiə]. Fr., fr. *glace*, fr. Lat. *glaciēs*, 'ice'. See **glacial** & **-ier.** Agglomerated ice and snow gradually moving down from a mountain slope into the valleys along a definite path.

glacier table, n. Block of stone left resting on a column of ice by retreating glacier.

glaciological, adj. [1. glàsiolójikl ; 2. glèisiəlɔ́dʒikl]. See **glaciology** & **-ic** & **-al.** Of or pertaining to glaciology.

glaciologist, n. [1. glàsiólojist ; 2. glèisiɔ́lədʒist]. See prec. & **-ist.** Student of glaciology.

glaciology, n. [1. glàsióloji ; 2. glèisiɔ́lədʒi]. See **glacier** & **-logy.** The study of glaciers.

glacis, n. [1. glásē, glásis ; 2. glǽsī, gléisis]. Fr., fr. O. Fr. *glacier*, 'to slip', fr. *glace*, 'ice', hence, 'smooth, level as ice'. See **glacial.** Smooth, gentle, slope or declivity ; esp. (fort.) external slope without cover from gunfire.

glad (I.), adj. [1. glad ; 2. glæd]. O.E. *glæd*, 'glad, bright, cheerful, kind, gracious' ; M.E. *glad* ; cp. O.H.G. *glat*, 'clear, bright' ; Mod. Germ. *glatt*, 'smooth' ; cogn. w. Lith. *glodas*, smooth' ; Russ. *gladkij*, 'even, smooth, polished' ; Lat. *glaber*, 'hairless', q.v. under **glabrous.** **1.** (of persons) **a** (attrib., archaic, or poet.) Happy, joyous ; **b** (pred.) pleased, filled with satisfaction : *I'm very glad to see you, glad I wasn't there* ; **c** (pred.) willing, well-disposed : *I shall be glad to do what I can, glad to help* &c. **2.** (of things) Full of, causing, gladness ; joyful : *a glad New Year* ; *glad tidings* ; '*glad evening and glad morn*' (Milton). Phrs. (vulg. slang) (*to give one*) *the glad eye*, give an alluring, inviting glance, ogle ; *glad rags*, best, smartest, clothes, specif. evening clothes.

glad (II.), vb. trans. O.E. *gladian*, M.E. *gladien* ; fr. prec. (archaic) To make glad, gladden.

gladden, vb. trans. & intrans. [1. gládn; 2. glǽdn]. **glad (I.)** & **-en**. **a** trans. To make glad; render happy; to cheer, exhilarate: *to be gladdened by the sight of home*; **b** intrans., to become glad.

glade, n. [1. glād; 2. gleid]. Prob. fr. base of **glad (I.)**, perh. through Scand., the sense being 'a place made smooth', or perh. 'bright, light'. Opening, clearing, in a wood, or forest &c.

gladiate, adj. [1. gládiāt; 2. glǽdieit], fr. Lat. *gladius*, 'sword', & **-ate**. According to Walde this Lat. word is related to Lat. *clādēs*, 'disaster, loss' &c., by an early change (dialectal ?) of *cl-* to *gl-*; cp. W. *cleddyf*, 'sword'. See further on this base under **clavicle, clause, cloister, glaive** & words there referred to. Sword-shaped.

gladiator, n. [1. gládiātor; 2. glǽdieitə]. Lat. *gladiātor*, lit. 'swordsman'. See prec. & **-or**. **1.** One who fought with a weapon against other men, or against wild beasts as a public spectacle in the ancient Roman games. **2.** (fig.) Polemical debater.

gladiatorial, adj. [1. glàdiatórial; 2. glæ̀diətɔ́riəl]. Lat. *gladiātōri-(us)*, fr. prec. & **-al**. Of or pertaining to gladiators, or to their fights.

gladiolus, n. [1. glàdiólus; 2. glæ̀dióuləs] or [1. gládiolus; 2. glǽdiələs]. Lat., 'little sword', dimin. of *gladius*. See **gladiate**. Plant of iris family, with erect sword-shaped leaves, and spike of brilliant flowers, cultivated in gardens.

gladly, adv. [1. gládli; 2. glǽdli]. O.E. *glædlīce*, M.E. *gladliche*; fr. **glad (I.)** & **-ly**. With gladness; cheerfully, willingly.

gladness, n. [1. gládnes; 2. glǽdnis]. O.E. *glædnes*, M.E. *gladnesse*; **glad (I.)** & **-ness**. State or condition of being glad; cheerfulness.

gladsome, adj. [1. gládsum; 2. glǽdsəm]. M.E. *gladsum*. **glad** & **-some**. (chiefly poet.) Cheering, exhilarating; also cheerful, joyous, happy; esp. *gladsome mind*.

Gladstone, n. [1. gládstun; 2. glǽdstən]. After W. E. Gladstone, Engl. statesman (1809–98). **1.** Kind of light leather portmanteau (also *Gladstone bag*). **2.** Kind of four-wheeled carriage with two inside seats.

glair (I.), n. [1. glār; 2. glɛə]. M.E. *gleyre*, fr. Fr. *glaire*, fr. L. Lat. *clāra (ōvi)*, 'clear, white (part of an egg)', fem. of Lat. *clārus*, q.v. under **clear**. **a** White of egg, used as varnish or size; **b** any white, viscous substance resembling white of egg.

glair (II.), vb. trans., fr. prec. To coat with glair.

glaireous, also **glairy**, adj. [1. glárius, glári; 2. glɛ́əriəs, glɛ́əri]. **glair** & **-eous, -y**; cp. Fr. *glaireux*. Like, of the nature of, glair; coated with glair.

glaive, n. [1. glāv; 2. gleiv]. M.E., Fr., fr. Lat. *gladium*, 'sword', modified prob. by Celt. **cladevo*; cp. O. Ir. *claideb*, W. *cleddyf*, 'sword', cogn. w. Lat. *clādēs*, 'slaughter'. See **claymore** & **gladiate**. (archaic) **a** Sword; **b** spear; specif. **c** variety of hafted weapon of halberd class.

glamo(u)rous, adj. [1. glámorus; 2. glǽmərəs]. Next word & **-ous**. Full of glamour, exercising fascination.

glamour, n. [1. glámur; 2. glǽmə]. Orig. Scots, corrupt form of **grammar** in sense, 'profound or occult learning', cp. **gramary(e)**, also Fr. *grimoire*, 'boo of magic'. Popularized by Scott. **a** E .chantment, spell, sorcery, magical illusion: *to cast a glamour over*; **b** feeling of mystical pleasure, delight, associated with some object or scene, or with memory of it; mysterious charm, elusive magic, esp. in poetry.

glamoury, adj. [1. glámori; 2. glǽməri]. See prec. & **-y**. Possessing glamour.

glance (I.), vb. intrans. & trans. [1. glahns; 2. glāns]. Of obscure origin, perh. due to blending of several words; cp. M.E. *glacen*, 'to glance aside, to flash', fr. O. Fr. *glacier*, 'to slip, slide', fr. Lat. *glaci-(ēs)*, 'ice', see **glacial**; cp. M.E. *glenten*, 'to shine, move quickly, glance', Swed. *glänta* (see **glint**); Du., Swed. *glans*, 'brightness'; Mod. Germ. *glanz*. **A.** intrans. **1. a** To strike obliquely, in such a way as to be deflected: *to glance aside, glance off (from)*, of an arrow or other missile, or a blow; **b** (of light) to be reflected from; flash, gleam fitfully; **c** (of bright object) to reflect light from surface, flash: *armour glancing in the sun*. **2.** *Glance at*, **a** to look at hurriedly, cursorily, momentarily; to read rapidly: *I just want to glance at the paper*; **b** (fig.) to refer to briefly and pass on to another subject. **B.** trans. (colloq.) In Phr. *to glance one's eye over, down*, to examine hastily, look through hurriedly and superficially.

glance (II.), n., fr. prec. **1. a** Oblique impact, causing deflection of the moving object; **b** (cricket) stroke with the bat held obliquely to the direction of the ball. **2.** Sudden transient gleam, flash of light, as from reflecting surface. **3. a** Swift, hasty look; a rapid view: *one glance was enough*; *to perceive at a glance*; **b** a meaning look, a directing of the eyes towards those of another: *a roguish glance*.

glance (III.), n. Prob. Germ. *glanz*, 'brightness, lustre'. See **glint**. (min. and metal.) A lustrous metallic sulphide: *lead glance*, galena &c.

glance (IV.), vb. trans. Perh. Du. *glanzen*, 'to polish', associated w. **glance (I.)**. To burnish, polish, metal.

glancing, adj. [1. gláhnsing; 2. glā́nsiŋ], fr. Pres. Part. of **glance (I.)**. **1.** Reflecting light in flashes, gleaming intermittently. **2.** (of a blow, shot &c.) Striking obliquely so as to be diverted.

gland, n. [1. gland; 2. glænd]. Fr. *glande*, fr. O. Fr. *glandre*, fr. Lat. *glandula*, 'gland of the throat', dimin. of *gland-(em)*, *glans*, 'acorn, pellet'. Cogn. w. Gk. *bálanos*, O. Slav. *želądĭ*, 'acorn', Lith. *gìlė*, 'gland'; cp. **balaniferous**. **1. a** Organ of an animal body, which secretes substances from the blood, and excretes them, or transforms them into fluids which perform many chemical functions essential to health or nutrition; **b** secreting organ of plant: *the poison glands of a nettle*. **2.** Specif. (in popular speech) the glands of the neck.

glandered, adj. [1. gláhnderd; 2. glā́ndəd]. **glanders** & **-ed**. Affected with glanders.

glanderous, adj. [1. gláhnderus; 2. glā́ndərəs]. **glanders** & **-ous**. Pertaining to glanders.

glanders, n. [1. gláhnderz; 2. glā́ndəz]. O. Fr. *glandres*, pl., fr. Lat. *glandulae*, 'glands of the throat'. See **gland** & **-ule**. Contagious disease of horses and other domestic animals, more rarely affecting human beings, accompanied by inflammation of mucous membrane and glands of lower jaw, and discharge of pus; farcy.

glandiferous, adj. [1. glandíferus; 2. glændífərəs]. **gland** & **-ferous**. Acorn-bearing.

glandiform, adj. [1. glándiform; 2. glǽndifɔ̄m]. **gland** & **-form**. Shaped like an acorn.

glandular, adj. [1. glándūlar; 2. glǽndjulə]. Lat. *glandula*, 'gland', see **gland**, & **-ar**. Pertaining to a gland or glands: *glandular extract*, extract from certain glands, as the thyroid &c., taken from animals, and used in the treatment of diseases due to deficiency of corresponding gland in human body; *glandular fever*, an infective fever of the lymphatic glands of the neck.

glandule, n. [1. glǽndūl; 2. glǽndjūl]. Fr., fr. Lat. *glandula*. See **gland** & **-ule**. **a** A small gland; **b** a small tumour.

glandulous, adj. [1. glándūlus; 2. glǽndjuləs]. **gland** & **-ule** & **-ous**. Glandular.

glare (I.), vb. intrans. [1. glār; 2. glɛə]. M.E. *glāren*, 'to shine'; cp. L.G. *glaren*, 'to glow', prob. for **glaz-*, fr. **glass**; cp. O.E. *glær*, 'amber'. Sense 2. is prob. affected by M.E. *glōren*, 'to stare', cp. Swed. *glōra*. **1.** To emit a dazzling, blinding light; to be intolerably bright. **2.** (of beast or person) To stare, fiercely or threateningly; also *glare at*.

glare (II.), n., fr. prec. **1. a** Dazzling light, blinding radiance, annoying brightness; Phr. *the glare of the footlights*, lure, publicity, of the stage; **b** (fig.) position of marked prominence; conspicuousness: *in the full glare of publicity*. **2.** Angry, arrogant stare; fierce, steady gaze.

glaring, vbl. adj. [1. glāring; 2. glɛ́əriŋ]. Pres. Part. of **glare (I.)**. **a** (of light) Dazzling, blinding, excessively and unpleasantly bright; **b** (of colour) gaudy, loud, too bright, garish, conspicuous; **c** (of non-material things) attracting attention by excess of bad qualities; obtrusive, flagrant: *glaring faults, errors*; *mistakes too glaring to be overlooked*.

glaringly, adv. Prec. & **-ly**. In a glaring manner.

glass (I.), n. [1. glahs; 2. glās]. O.E. *glæs*, M.E. *glas, gles*; cp. Du., Germ., O.N., Swed. *glas*, also Lat. *glǣs-um*, 'amber', fr. Gmc.; perh. fr. base of **glow**. **1. a** A transparent or translucent hard and brittle substance, made by fusing some form of silicate with other materials; used for window-panes, vessels, optical instruments &c.; Phr. *under glass*, in a frame or hothouse; **b** substance resembling true glass: *glass of antimony, arsenic glass*. **2.** (coll.) Objects, esp. vessels, made of glass; glassware: *glass and china*. **3.** Utensil, instrument, or part of object, made wholly or partly of glass; specif. **a** (i.) drinking-vessel, tumbler, wine-glass &c.; (ii.) the contents of a glass drinking-vessel: *glass of wine*; Phr. *to enjoy, be fond of, one's*, or *a glass now and then*, to be moderately fond of wine &c.; **b** mirror: *to look in the glass*; **c** optical instrument, as telescope, eyeglass; (in pl.) binoculars; spectacles: *to read without glasses*; **d** barometer: *the glass is falling*; **e** hour-glass, sand-glass.

glass (II.), vb. trans., fr. prec. **1.** To furnish, cover, or protect with glass, to glaze: *to glass a window, a picture, peaches*. **2.** To make glassy. **3.** To reflect, mirror: *the mountains glass themselves in the lake*.

glass-blower, n. [1. gláhs blōer; 2. glā́s blòuə]. One who blows and shapes glass.

glass-blowing, n. [1. gláhs blōing; 2. glā́s blòuiŋ]. Art, practice, of blowing glass.

glass-cloth, n. Cloth for drying and polishing glassware.

glass-culture, n. Rearing of fruit or plants under glass.

glasscutter, n. [1. gláhskùter; 2. glā́skàtə]. **1. a** One whose trade is to cut sheets of glass into suitable sizes for window-panes; **b** one whose trade is to ornament and polish the surface of glass. **2.** Tool for cutting glass.

glass eye, n. Imitation eye, made of glass.

glassful, n. [1. gláhsfòol; 2. glā́sfùl]. **glass** & **-ful**. **a** Contents of drinking-glass; **b** amount which drinking-glass will hold.

glass-gall, n. Scum which rises from materials of which glass is made, when in state of fusion.

glass glaze, n. Thick vitreous glaze.

glasshouse, n. [1. gláhs-hòus; 2. glā́shàus]. **a** Glass factory; **b** place for sale of glass; **c** conservatory, greenhouse; **d** photographer's studio.

Glassite, n. [1. gláhsīt; 2. glā́sait], fr. John Glas(s) (1695–1773), founder of Scottish sect. An adherent, follower, of Glass's doctrines; Sandemanian.

glassman, n. [1. gláhsman; 2. glā́smən]. **a** Vendor of glassware; **b** glazier.

glass oven, n. One for slowly cooling and tempering molten glass.

glass paper, n. Paper coated with powdered glass for scouring, or for smoothing woodwork.

glass snake, n. Kind of limbless lizard found in America; so called from its brittleness.

glassware, n. [1. gláhswār; 2. glā́swɛə]. (coll.) Small articles, such as tumblers, dishes &c., made of glass (trade word).

glasswork, n. [1. gláhswërk; 2. glā́swə̀k]. **1.** Trade, occupation of making glass. **2.** Glass factory. **3.** Articles made of glass.

glasswort, n. [1. gláhswêrt; 2. gláswʌt]. A maritime plant growing in salt marshes, from the ashes of which soda is obtained, used in glass-making; also known as *marsh samphire*.

glassy, adj. [1. gláhsi; 2. glási]. M.E. *glasi*. **glass & -y.** **1.** Resembling glass in appearance or texture. **2.** (fig.) **a** (of the sea, or lake &c.) Having a smooth, even, unruffled surface; **b** (of the eye) lacking appearance of life or fire, hence, expressionless, lifeless.

glauberite, n. [1. glóuberīt, gláwberīt; 2. gláubərait, glɔ́bərait], fr. J. R. Glauber, Germ. chemist (1604–1668), & **-ite.** (min.) Sulphate of sodium and calcium.

Glauber's salts, n. [1. gláwberz sáwlts; 2. glɔ́bəz sɔ́lts]. Sulphate of sodium, used medicinally as a saline aperient.

glaucescent, adj. [1. glawkésent; 2. glɔkésənt]. Lat. *glauc-(us,)* fr. Gk. *glaukós*, 'gleaming; bluish-green'. See **glaucous & -escent.** (bot.) Growing glaucous; somewhat glaucous.

glaucoma, n. [1. glawkṓma; 2. glɔkóumə]. See **glaucous & -oma.** (med.) A disease of the eye leading to blindness, characterized by bluish tinge of the pupil, and tension and hardness of the eyeball.

glaucomatous, adj. [1. glawkómatus; 2. glɔkóumətəs]. Prec. & **-ous**, *-t-*, being part of stem. Pertaining to, resembling, affected by, glaucoma.

glauconia, n. [1. glawkṓnia; 2. glɔkóuniə], fr. its colour. See **glaucous.** Burrowing snake, bluish-green or grey in colour.

glauconite, n. [1. gláwkonīt; 2. glɔ́kənait]. See next word & **-ite.** (min.) A dull green silicate found in greensand.

glaucous, adj. [1. gláwkus; 2. glɔ́kəs]. Lat. *glaucus*, fr. Gk. *glaukós*, 'gleaming, bright; bluish or greyish green', applied to the olive, & the willow; also to the eye. Cp. *glaúx*, 'the owl', fr. its glaring eyes. Prob. fr. same base as Gk. *geláō*, 'laugh', & *glḗnē*, 'pupil of the eye, eye-ball' (cp. **clean (I.)**); Lith. *žìlas*, 'grey', is fr. same base. The suff. is fr. Lat. *-ōsus*. See **-ous. a** Bluish green, or greenish blue; **b** (bot.) having a whitish bloom, such as that on a plum &c.

Glaucus, n. [1. gláwkus; 2. glɔ́kəs]. See prec. Genus of mollusc found in southern seas, blue and silvery white in colour.

glaze (I.), vb. trans. & intrans. [1. glāz; 2. gleiz]. O.E. *glæs*, 'glass', & adj. *glæsen*, 'of glass'. From these was formed a M.E. vb. *glāsen*. The lengthening of the vowel in the open syll., & the voicing of *s* between vowels, accounts for the difference in form fr. the n. See **glass. A.** trans. **1.** To put glass into: *to glaze a window*. **2. a** To coat with a glassy layer; **b** specif. (in cooking) cover with transparent, shiny film which dries hard; **c** to give a shiny, polished, glossy surface to leather, paper &c. **B.** intrans. To become glazed, or glassy in appearance; to lose life and fire, grow dim, esp. of the eyes with approach of death, or in illness.

glaze (II.), n., fr. prec. **1.** Act or process of glazing. **2.** Substance applied or process used in glazing; specif. **a** transparent coating on pottery; **b** (in paint.) thin wash, or superposed layer of varnish pigment; **c** (in cookery) jelly-like covering added to, or forming on, cold meats, e.g. galantines, tongues &c. **3.** (by extension) Pottery &c., which is glazed.

glazer, n. [1. glāzer; 2. gléizə]. **glaze (I.) & -er. 1.** Person whose trade is to put a glaze on anything. **2.** Tool for glazing, polishing &c.

glaze-wheel, n. A wooden wheel faced with emery &c., for polishing cutlery &c.

glazier, n. [1. glāzier; 2. gléiziə]. **glaze & -ier. 1.** One who cuts, supplies, and puts in glass panes to windows &c. **2.** A glazer of pottery &c.

glazing, n. [1. glāzing; 2. gléiziŋ]. **glaze (I.) & -ing. 1.** The act or process **a** of putting glass into windows &c.; **b** of coating with a glaze. **2.** Material used as a glaze for pottery, paper &c.

glazy, adj. [1. glāzi; 2. gléizi]. **glaze (II.) & -y. a** Resembling or akin to glaze; lustrous; **b** (of the eye) glazed, lacking fire, lifeless.

gleam (I.), n. [1. glēm; 2. glīm]. O.E. *glǣm*, M.E. *glēm*, 'splendour, radiance'; cp. O.H.G. *gleimo*; Gmc. **glaim-*, 'to shine'; see **glimmer. 1. a** Beam, ray, transient flash of light; **b** reflected brightness, light reflected from some polished substance; **c** suddenly perceived patch of colour: *gleam of gold and scarlet*. **2.** (fig.) **a** Sudden, faint flash of emotion or perception: *gleam of hope, intelligence*; **b** something suggesting spiritual radiance, vigour, freshness: '*Youth's golden gleam*' (Wordsworth).

gleam (II.), vb. intrans. M.E. *glēmen*, fr. prec. **1. a** (of sun, or other luminous body) To emit beams of light, flash, shine; **b** (of polished surfaces) to reflect light, glitter, sparkle: *gleaming armour, jewellery* &c. **2.** (fig., of qualities of mind and character) To be manifest, reveal itself: *courage gleamed in his eye*; *wit gleamed out in his talk.*

glean, vb. trans. & intrans. [1. glēn; 2. glīn]. M.E. *glēnen*, O. Fr. *glener*, *glaner*, fr. Low Lat. *glanāre*, prob. Celt., cp. W. *glan*, 'clean, tidy'. **A.** trans. **1. a** To pick up, gather, stray ears of corn left by reapers, or grapes omitted by vintagers: *to glean the corn that is left*; **b** to clean up, clear, a field or vineyard in this way: *glean a field*. **2.** To collect any trifling leavings. **3.** (fig., of non-material things) To collect, pick up, obtain, by diligent search: *to glean information*. **B.** intrans. **a** To go gleaning, gather stray leavings of reapers or vintagers; **b** (fig.) to acquire, pick up, odds and ends.

gleaner, n. [1. glḗner; 2. glínə]. One who gleans.

gleaning, n. [1. glḗning; 2. glíniŋ]. Prec. & **-ing. a** Act of gleaning after reapers &c.; **b** that which is collected in this process; **c** (fig., of non-material things; usually pl.) something collected, brought together from various sources; slight, stray fragments of knowledge &c.: *gleanings of science, from the poets* &c.

glebe, n. [1. glēb; 2. glīb]. Fr. *glèbe*, fr. Lat. *glēba*, earlier *glaeba*, 'lump of earth; land, soil'; connected w. Lat. *globus*, 'round, solid body', see **globe**, fr. base **gel-*, 'to roll up into a ball, stick together', & related to a large number of words: Lat. *glūten*, 'glue' (see **glue**); Gk. *gloiós*, 'sticky' &c. See further the numerous Gmc. cognates under **clay, claw, cleave**, 'stick to', **climb, clod, clog, clot, clue**; & others, fr. Lat., under **agglomerate** (fr. *glomus*, 'ball'). **1.** (archaic and poet.) Soil, earth, land: '*Their furrow oft the stubborn glebe hath broke*' (Gray's 'Elegy'). **2.** Land attached to an ecclesiastical benefice, and held by incumbent during his tenure.

Glecoma, n. [1. glēkṓma; 2. glīkóumə]. Gk. *glḗkhōn*, or *blḗkhōn*, 'pennyroyal'. Etymol. doubtful. Creeping plant of the mint family; ground-ivy.

glede, n. [1. glēd; 2. glīd]. O.E. *glīda*, 'kite', M.E. *glēde*; different gradation form fr. O.E. *glīdan*, 'to glide'. See **glide.** (ornith.) The common kite, *Milvus regalis*.

glee, n. [1. glē; 2. glī]. Cp. O.E. *glīw*, & *glēo(w)*, 'music, minstrelsy; mirth, jest'. Cp. Gk. *khleúē*, 'joke, jest', & Lith. *glaudas*, 'recreation, pastime'; O.N. *glaumr*, 'sprightliness', & O.E. *glēam*, 'merriment', are cognate. **1.** Merry, exultant happiness; gay, light-hearted mirth. **2.** (mus.) Part-song, often sung without accompaniment. *Glee club*, association formed for glee singing.

gleeful, adj. [1. glḗfool; 2. glífəl]. Prec. & **-ful. a** (of persons) Happy and exultant; gay, merry, hilarious; **b** (of non-material things) exciting, promoting, touched by, glee: *gleeful news*; *in gleeful mood.*

gleefully, adv. Prec. & **-ly.** In a gleeful manner; gaily, merrily.

gleek, n. [1. glēk; 2. glīk]. Obs. Fr. *ghelicque*, *glic*, fr. M. Du. *gelijck*, 'alike', cogn. w. Engl. **like (I.).** Obsolete card-game in which players scored by getting three cards alike, i.e. of the same rank in different suits.

gleemaiden, n. [1. glḗmāden; 2. glímèidən]. O.E. *glēo-mægden*, 'female minstrel'. (archaic) Wandering female singer, as in Scott's *Fair Maid of Perth*.

gleeman, n. [1. glḗman; 2. glímən]. O.E. *glēo-mann*, 'minstrel, jester'. See **glee & man.** (archaic) Strolling minstrel, the English equivalent of troubadour.

gleesome, adj. [1. glḗsum; 2. glísəm]. **glee & -some.** Gleeful.

gleet, n. [1. glēt; 2. glīt]. M.E. *glēte*, fr. O. Fr. *glete*, 'pus, filth'. Morbid, watery discharge from urethra.

gleg, adj. [1. gleg; 2. gleg]. Scand. Cp. O.N. *glöggr*. (Scots) Sharp, quick of perception, alert, keen.

glen, n. [1. glen; 2. glen]. M.E.; Gael. & Ir. *gleann*, fr. O. Ir. *glenn*. Narrow, lonely valley in the Scottish or Irish hills.

glengarry, n. [1. glèngári; 2. glèngǽri]. Name of district in Scotland. Tight-fitting Scots Highland cap, with narrow, sloping sides which open at the top, the crown being below this, and having long strings or ribbons at the back.

glenoid, adj. [1. glénoid; 2. glénɔid]. Gk. *glēnoeidḗs*, fr. *glḗnē*, 'socket of joint', & **-oid.** (anat.) Type of joint presenting a slight concave depression.

glib (I.), adj. [1. glib; 2. glib]. Orig. 'slippery'; cp. obs. *glibbery*; Du. *glibberig*, 'slippery', *glippen*, 'to slip away'. **a** (of persons) Superficially fluent, ready in speech; talkative, plausible, voluble without being convincing; **b** (of speech, utterance &c.) ready, pat, facile; copious and rapid, without expressing depth or thought.

glib (II.), n. Ir. *clib*, *glib*. (archaic) Kind of forelock peculiar to ancient Irish.

glibly, adv. **glib (I.) & -ly.** In a glib, fluent, plausible manner.

glibness, n. **glib (I.) & -ness.** Readiness in speech; fluency, volubility.

glide (I.), vb. intrans. [1. glīd; 2. glaid]. O.E. *glīdan*; cp. Du. *glijden*, Germ. *gleiten* &c. Perh. fr. **ga-līdan*; for pref. see **com-**, & for second element see **lead (IV.) & lode. 1. a** (of persons) To move along with a smooth, easy, noiseless walk, as though sliding along, with very slight apparent effort, or motion of the limbs; esp. of women: *to glide quietly out of the room*; **b** (of inanimate objects, e.g., a ship taking the water) to slip, slide easily and smoothly down an inclined plane; **c** (of flowing water) to flow smoothly and silently along its channel; **d** (of a boat on water) to float easily over the surface. **2. a** To slide smoothly through the air; **b** specif. (aeron., of a flying machine) to plane down, or with alternate downward and upward movements, without using engine.

glide (II.), n., fr. prec. **1.** Any kind of gliding movement. **2.** Arrangement, inclined plane &c., upon which a gliding movement can be executed; a slide.

glider, n. [1. glīder; 2. gláidə]. **glide & -er.** Any thing, or person that glides; specif., kind of air-craft specially designed for gliding in the air without aid of engines.

glim, n. [1. glim; 2. glim]. Variant of or cogn. w. **gleam.** (slang) Lamp or other artificial light; *dowse the glim*, put out the light.

glimmer (I.), vb. intrans. [1. glímer; 2. glímə]. M.E. *glimere(n)*, 'to shine'; O.E. *gleomu*, 'splendour'; cp. Germ. *glimmern*, Du. *glimre*, fr. Gmc. base **glim-*, another grade of **glaim-*, 'to shine', as in O.E. *glǣm*. See **gleam. a** (lit. and fig.) To shine intermittently, flicker; **b** to glow faintly.

glimmer (II.), n., fr. prec. **1. a** Fitful gleam, flicker, intermittent glow; **b** faint, feeble light. **2.** (fig., of mental processes) Slight, occasional, fitful, manifestation.

glimmering, n. [1. glímering; 2. glíməriŋ]. Prec. & **-ing.** A glimmer.

glimpse (I.), vb. trans. [1. glimps; 2. glimps]. M.E. *glimsen*, 'to shine', also 'to see imperfectly', fr. base **glim-** as **glimmer &**

formative *-s-*; cp. M. Du. *glinsen.* (rare) To see by glimpses, catch a brief sight of.

glimpse (II.), n., fr. prec. **1.** (obs.) Fugitive gleam, glimmer, glint: '*the glimpses of the moon*' (Shakespeare). **2.** Passing sight, fleeting impression of. Phr. *to catch a glimpse of,* see for a moment.

glint (I.), vb. intrans. [1. glint; 2. glint]. M.E. *glenten,* 'to shine, look, move quickly'; cp. Swed. *glänta,* M. Dan. *glinte,* M.H.G. *glinzen* &c., 'to shine'; perh. nasalized form of base **glit-*. See **glitter** & cp. **glance.** **a** (of luminous bodies) To shine with a fitful subdued gleam: *the sun glinted through the boughs*; **b** (of polished surfaces) To reflect light faintly at intervals: *to glint in the sun.*

glint (II.), n., fr. prec.; cp. M.E. *glent,* 'glimpse'. Sudden, faint gleam sparkle, flash.

glioma, n., pl. **gliomata** [1. glīóma, -mata; 2. glaióumə, -mətə]. Gk. *gliā,* 'glue', & **-oma.** See **glue.** Tumour affecting some part of the brain, spinal chord, or nervous system.

gliomatosis, n. [1. glìōmatósis; 2. glàioumətóusis]. Prec. & **-osis.** Disease characterized by gliomata.

gliomatous, adj. [1. glīṓmatus; 2. glaióumətəs]. *gliomat-,* see prec., & **-ous.** Of or pertaining to gliomata; akin to, resembling, affected by gliomata.

glissade (I.), n. [1. glisáhd, -ád; 2. glisád, -éid]. Fr., 'a slide', fr. *glisser,* 'to slip, glide, slide', of Gmc. origin, cp. Germ. *glitschen,* 'to slide', fr. base of **glide.** See **-ade.** **1.** Deliberate downhill glide over snow or ice, with alpenstock used as a check; practised by mountain-climbers. **2.** Sideward gliding step in dancing.

glissade (II.), vb. intrans., fr. prec. To make a glissade, either in mountain-climbing, or dancing.

glisten, vb. intrans. & n. [1. glísn; 2. glísn]. O.E. *glisnian,* M.E. *glisnien,* fr. **glis-,* base of O.E. *glisian,* O. Fris. *glisa,* 'to shine'. See **glitter.** **1.** vb. To reflect light; glitter, shine, sparkle: *to glisten with dew*; *his eyes glistened with excitement.* **2.** n. A reflection of light, a glitter, gleam.

glister, vb. intrans. & n. [1. glíster; 2. glístə]. M.E. *glisteren, glistren,* formed as prec. w. freq. *-er-*; cp. M. Du. *glisteren.* **1.** vb. To shine, gleam, twinkle. **2.** n. A twinkle, sparkle.

glitter (I.), vb. intrans. [1. glíter; 2. glítə]. M.E. *glit(e)ren,* w. formative *-er* (cp. M.H.G. *glitzern,* O.N. *glitra*), fr. **glit-,* as in O.E. *glitenian,* Goth. *glit-munjan,* 'to shine', another gradation form of Gmc. base **gleit-*; cp. O.S. *glītan,* O.H.G. *glīzzen,* Mod. Germ. *gleissen,* 'to glitter'; extended, like **gleim-,* **glis-* (see **gleam, glisten**), fr. **gli-, *glai-,* 'to shine' &c. This Gmc. base is prob. cogn. w. Lat. *laetus,* 'joyful, cheerful, sprightly', wh. may stand for **ghlai-tos.* **a** To shine, sparkle, blaze with light; **b** (fig.) to make a brave, splendid show; Phr. *all is not gold that glitters,* appearances may deceive.

glitter (II.), n., fr. prec. **a** Sparkle, shine, brightness; **b** (fig.) pomp, splendour, something that attracts the eye or imagination.

glittering, adj. [1. glítering; 2. glítəriŋ], fr. Pres. Part. of **glitter** (I.). **a** Sparkling, shining, brilliant; (fig.) **b** sumptuous, splendid: *glittering retinue*; **c** attractive but specious: *glittering promises*; *glittering prizes.*

gloaming, n. [1. glṓming; 2. glóumiŋ]. Lowland Scots. Origin doubtful. The vowel makes connexion w. **gloom** improbable. (provinc. or poet.) Twilight.

gloat, vb. intrans. [1. glōt; 2. glout]. Cp. O.N. *glotta,* 'to smile scornfully', Germ. *glotzen,* 'to stare'. **a** (gen.) *Gloat over,* dwell upon, contemplate with pleasure, enjoy sight, or thought of, exult in; (lit. and fig.) *to gloat over one's treasures*; *gloat over another's misfortunes*; **b** (without object) to exult silently, feel a subdued, but intense, satisfaction at something: *to sit gloating by oneself.*

gloating, adj. [1. glṓting; 2. glóutiŋ], fr. Pres. Part. of prec. Arising from, expressing, intense, but quiet, delight and exultation: *a gloating smile.*

globate, adj. [1. glṓbāt; 2. glóubeit]. See next word & **-ate.** Shaped like a globe; spherical.

globe, n. [1. glōb; 2. gloub]. Fr., fr. Lat. *glob-(us,)* 'round solid body, ball, sphere'. See **glebe, agglomerate.** **1. a** A round body whose surface is throughout equidistant from its centre; sphere, ball; **b** specif., the earth: *the terrestrial globe*; **c** any heavenly body. **2.** Spherical model of earth (*terrestrial globe*) or of the heavens (*celestial globe*) showing a map of principal continents, countries, mountain ranges &c., or of the constellations &c. Phr. *the use of the globes,* obsolete method of teaching geography and astronomy. **3.** Various globe-like objects, specif. **a** orb, one of the insignia of royalty, a small golden ball symbolizing sovereignty; **b** spherical glass vessel for holding water for gold-fish &c.; **c** glass cover for gas lamp, or electric light.

globe-amaranth, n. Indian garden plant.

globe-artichoke, n. The cardoon.

globe-dollar, n. Spanish coin (18th cent.).

globe-fish, n. Tropical variety of fish, which can assume a globular form.

globe-flower, n. Trollius, q.v.

globe-trotter, n. [1. glṓb tròter; 2. glóub trɔ̀tə]. One who travels continually and widely, esp. one who travels from restlessness or for amusement.

globose, adj. [1. glōbṓs; 2. gloubóus]. Lat. *globōs-(us).* **globe** & **-ous.** **a** Globular, spherical; **b** rounded, convex.

globosity, n. [1. glōbósiti; 2. gloubɔ́siti]. Prec. & **-ity.** Quality of being globose.

globular, adj. [1. glóbūlar; 2. glɔ́bjulə]. Next word & **-ar.** Globe-shaped, spherical.

globule, n. [1. glóbūl; 2. glɔ́bjūl]. Fr., fr. Lat. *globul-(us),* dimin. of *globus,* 'ball, sphere'. See **globe.** Minute spherical body, esp. of liquid; a drop.

globulin, n. [1. glóbūlin; 2. glɔ́bjulin]. Prec. & **-in.** Protein substance of albuminous character, insoluble in water; a constituent of haemoglobin.

globulous, adj. [1. glóbūlus; 2. glɔ́bjuləs]. **globule** & **-ous.** Of or pertaining to a globule; like a globule.

glochidiate, adj. [1. glōkídiāt; 2. gloukídieit], fr. Gk. *glōkhis,* 'point of an arrow', & **-ate.** See **gloss** (III.). (bot.) Barbed.

glochidium, n. [1. glōkídium; 2. gloukídiəm]. Mod. Lat. dimin. fr. Gk., *glōkhis.* See prec. Larva of fresh-water mussel.

glockenspiel, n. [1. glókenspēl; 2. glɔ́kənspīl]. Germ., 'play of bells', fr. *glocke,* 'bell' (see **clock**), & *spiel,* 'play' (see **spell** (IV.)). Musical instrument, originally a set of small bells, now a set of tuned steel bars, played with a hammer.

glomerate, vb. trans. & adj. [1. glómerāt; 2. glɔ́məreit]. Lat. *glomerāt-,* P.P. stem of *glomerāre,* fr. *glomer-,* stem of *glomus,* 'ball, sphere'. See **agglomerate** & **globe.** **a** vb. To roll up, collect into a ball or rounded mass; **b** adj., closely gathered together, accumulated.

glomeration, n. [1. glòmeráshun; 2. glɔ̀məréiʃən]. Prec. & **-ion.** **a** Process of glomerating; **b** that which is glomerated, a dense round mass; accumulation.

gloom (I.), n. [1. glōōm; 2. glūm]. O.E. *glōm,* 'twilight' (see **glow**), might well be the ancestor of this word, as regards both form & meaning, but there is a break in the recorded usage; it is suggested that the n. is formed fr. the now obsolesc. **gloom** (II.) See also **glum.** **1. a** Darkness, dimness of light, obscurity; **b** a dark place (poet.). **2.** (fig., of state of mind) Depression of spirits; sullenness, melancholy. **3.** Combination of conditions and circumstances of a kind to produce depression of spirits, cheerlessness &c.: *the gloom of poverty, solitude* &c.

gloom (II.), vb. intrans. M.E. *glom(m)en, glomben, gloumen,* 'to frown, be **gloomy, lour** (of weather)'; cp. Swed. *glomma,* L.G. *glummen,* 'to scowl' &c. See **glum.** (rare) **1. a** To grow dark, overcast; **b** to appear dimly, loom. **2.** (fig., of persons) To look, or behave, gloomily, show sullen discontent; to lour.

gloomily, adv. [1. glṓōmili; 2. glūmili]. Next word & **-ly.** In a gloomy manner (in all senses).

gloomy, adj. [1. glṓōmi; 2. glūmi]. **gloom** (I.) & **-y.** **a** Pervaded by gloom; dark, dismal: *a gloomy house*; **b** of a sombre temper; morose; moody, depressed: *a gloomy companion*; **c** not hopeful, cheerless, dismal: *gloomy prospects.*

gloria, n. [1. glória; 2. glɔ́riə]. Lat. See **glory.** The name of certain doxologies in the Liturgy, from the first word in each: *Gloria Patri,* Glory be to the Father &c.; *Gloria tibi . . .,* Glory be to thee . . .; *Gloria in excelsis,* Glory be (to God) on high.

glorification, n. [1. glòrifikáshun; 2. glɔ̀rifikéiʃən]. Lat. *glōri-,* fr. *glōria* (see **glory**) & **-fication.** **1. a** Act of glorifying, exalting, praising, worshipping God; **b** act of extolling, making much of: *the glorification of physical force.* **2.** State of being glorified.

glorify, vb. trans. [1. glórifī; 2. glɔ́rifai]. M.E. *glorifien,* fr. Fr. *glorifier,* fr. Lat. *glōrificāre.* See prec. & **-fy.** **1. a** To worship, exalt, praise (God, the Saints &c.); **b** to belaud, eulogize, extravagantly (persons, their actions or qualities). **2. a** To add glory to, make illustrious: *the names which glorify this age*; **b** to invest with glory: *glorified spirits in heaven.* **3.** (colloq., chiefly as attrib. P.P. *glorified*) Enriched, adorned, made larger or finer than usual: *the church is a sort of glorified barn.*

gloriole, n. [1. glóriōl; 2. glɔ́rioul]. Fr., fr. Lat. *glōriola,* dimin. of *glōria.* See **glory.** Circle or disk round the head in representations of saints &c.; a nimbus, halo, aureole.

glorious, adj. [1. glórius; 2. glɔ́riəs]. M.E., O. Fr. *glorius* (Mod. Fr. *glorieux*), fr. Lat. *glōriōs-(us).* **glory** & **-ous.** **1. a** Having heavenly or supernatural splendour and majesty: *a glorious vision*; **b** radiantly beautiful; sublime, majestic: *a glorious sunset*; *glorious music.* **2.** Having, or worthy to have, high renown; very illustrious, august, splendid, triumphant: *a glorious achievement, reign, victory.* **3.** (colloq.) **a** Thoroughly enjoyable, delightful: *to have a glorious time, holiday*; *glorious fun*; **b** accompanied, or caused, by reckless high spirits: *a glorious rag, row*; *a glorious mess,* complete, extravagant disorder and confusion.

glory (I.), n. [1. glóri; 2. glɔ́ri]. M.E., O. Fr. *glorie,* fr. Lat. *glōria,* 'fame, renown; ambition; boasting'; perh. for **glōsia*; connected w. Lat. *gloris* (in a gloss.) = Gk. *mutholόgos,* 'teller of legends'; fr. a base meaning 'cry out, sing' &c.; cp. O. Slav. *glasiki,* 'famous', & *glasŭ,* 'voice', Russ. *gólos,* 'voice'. From same base come prob. Lat. *gallus,* 'a cock', lit. 'the singer', & the Gmc. **kal-* as in O.N. *kalla,* 'call'. See **call** & **gallinaceous.** **1.** Splendour, magnificence, radiance; specif. **a** state in which Divine and celestial beings dwell; heavenly splendour and bliss: *to dwell with the saints in glory*; Phr. *gone to glory,* dead; **b** earthly pomp, splendour, triumph, pageantry: '*Solomon in all his glory*'; *the king reigned many years in great glory*; '*the glory that was Greece*' (Poe). **2. a** Worship, honour, adoration accorded to God: '*Glory to God in the highest*'; **b** honour and respect, triumph, accorded to, fame, high renown won by, human being through great services and achievements: *to win glory on the field of battle*; '*We left him alone in his glory*' (Wolfe); *to return with glory,* in triumph. **3.** Any splendid, brilliant, and impressive sight, esp. the radiancy of nature: *the glory of the morning*; *the glory of the woods in autumn*; *Old Glory,* the Stars and Stripes, national flag of U.S.A. **4. a** Highest point of success, prosperity &c.: *under George II. the Whig party was at its glory*; **b** high degree of pleasure, pride, satisfaction: *the poet was in his glory, surrounded by a crowd of admirers.* **5. a** Halo, nimbus, aureole, supposed to emanate from, and surround the head of, Divine or saintly beings; **b** pictorial representation of this by golden ring or disk.

glory (II.), vb. intrans., fr. prec. Followed by *in*): **1.** To take delight in, have keen feeling of exultation or triumph because of; take a pride in: *to glory in one's country's victory*; *to glory in one's health and strength.* **2.** To exult to excess, hence, to exhibit boastful arrogance, to boast of: *he glories in his own disgrace.*

glory hole, n. **a** (naut.) Steward's storeroom on board ship; **b** small lumber-room or cupboard in a house.

gloss (I.), n. [1. glos; 2. glɔs]. Provinc. & Scots in sense 'glow'; prob. fr. O.N. *glossi*, 'a blaze'; cp. Norw. *glosa*, M.H.G. *glosen*, 'to glow'. See **glow**. **1.** Sheen, polish; smooth bright surface which reflects light. **2.** (fig.) Superficial veneer of virtue &c.; specious show: *gloss of respectability.*

gloss (II.), vb. trans. & intrans., fr. prec. **A.** trans. **1.** To put a gloss upon, polish, make shiny the surface of. **2.** (fig., usually *gloss over*). To explain away, minimize by plausible arguments: *to gloss over one's faults.* (Probably influenced by **gloss (III.)**.) **B.** intrans. To take on a gloss, grow shiny: *serge is apt to gloss.*

gloss (III.), n. Lat. *glossa*, 'antiquated or foreign word needing elucidation', fr. Gk. *glôssa*, 'the tongue; speech'. This word is for **glōkhja*, cogn. w. Gk. *glōkhís*, 'a projecting point'; orig., in Gk., the tongue is 'the pointed thing'. **1.** In ancient MSS., explanation or interpretation of unfamiliar words or phrases, often written above the line, usually in a more familiar (or the native) language; hence, any succinct comment or elucidation. **2.** (extended fig. use) Favourable explanation offered for reprehensible speech or conduct.

gloss (IV.), vb. trans., fr. prec. **1.** To supply with glosses, write glosses to. **2.** *Gloss over*, extenuate, explain away (a fault). See however **gloss (II.) 2.**

glossarial, adj. [1. glosárial; 2. glɔséəriəl]. **glossary** & **-al**. Pertaining to, of nature of, a glossary: *glossarial index.*

glossarist, n. [1. glósarist; 2. glɔ́sərist]. **glossary** & **-ist**. Compiler of a glossary or glossaries.

glossary, n. [1. glósari; 2. glɔ́səri], fr. Lat. *glossāri-(um)*, 'collection, vocabulary of antiquated or foreign words', fr. *glossa*, q.v. under **gloss (III.)**, & **-ary**. Miniature dictionary; alphabetical list of unfamiliar words &c. of any kind, whether foreign or native.

glossator, n. [1. glosátor; 2. glɔséitə]. Low Lat. See **gloss (III.)**. Writer of glosses to texts.

glossic, n. [1. glósik; 2. glɔ́sik]. Coined fr. Gk. *glôssa*, 'tongue'. See **gloss (III.)** & **-ic**. System of phonetic notation invented by A. J. Ellis, and hardly used except by himself, and, in the 'seventies, by Henry Sweet; this alphabet was abandoned on account of its cumbrousness.

glossitis, n. [1. glosítis; 2. glɔsáitis]. Gk. *glôssa*, 'tongue'. See **gloss (III.)** & **-itis**, 'inflammation'. Inflammation of the tongue.

glosso-, pref. Form of Gk. *glôssa*, *glôtta*, tongue, 'language', used in compounds. See **gloss (III.)** for etymol.

glossograph, n. [1. glósōgrahf; 2. glɔ́sougrāf]. Prec. & **-graph**. Device for recording movements of tongue in speech.

glossographer, n. [1. glosógrafer; 2. glɔsɔ́grəfə]. **glosso-**, & **-graph** & **-er**. A writer of glosses; annotator.

glossological, adj. [1. glòsōlójikl; 2. glɔ̀soulɔ́džikl]. **glosso-** & **-logical**. (obs. term) Connected with the science of language.

glossologist, n. [1. glosólojist; 2. glɔsɔ́lədžist]. Next word & **-ist**. (obs. term) Student of the science of language.

glossology, n. [1. glosóloji; 2. glɔsɔ́lədži]. **glosso-** & **-logy**. Obsolete term for the science of language or comparative philology.

glossotomy, n. [1. glosótomi; 2. glɔsɔ́təmi]. **glosso-** & **-tomy**. (surg.) Cutting out, extirpation, of the tongue.

glottis, n. [1. glótis; 2. glɔ́tis]. Gk. *glôttis*, 'mouth of windpipe', fr. *glôtta*, variant in Attic dial. of *glôssa*, 'tongue'. See **gloss (III.)**. Opening between the vocal cords, which are situated in the larynx or upper part of the windpipe.

glottological, adj. [1. glòtolójikl; 2. glɔ̀təlɔ́džikl]. See **glottology** & **-ic** & **-al**. Pertaining to glottology.

glottologist, n. [1. glotólojist; 2. glɔtɔ́lədžist]. See next word & **-ist**. Student of glottology.

glottology, n. [1. glotóloji; 2. glɔtɔ́lədži]. See **glosso-** & **-logy**. Obsolete name for science of language or comparative philology.

glove (I.), n. [1. gluv; 2. glav]. O.E. *glōf*, 'glove, paw', perh. fr. **ga-lōf*; for pref. see **com-**, the second element being cogn. w. Goth. *lōfa*, 'palm of the hand'. The suggestion that the latter is cogn. w. Lat. *alapa*, 'box on the ear', & Gk. *kólaphos* is to be rejected; these are early borrowings fr. Heb. *khelaphōt*, pl. of *khelaph*, 'hammer'. **a** Covering for the hand and fingers, of leather, wool, or silk &c., and provided with separate compartments for each finger and for the thumb; **b** similar article made of leather, padded, and with separate compartment only for thumb, the fingers being all together; also *boxing-glove*; (fig.) *take off the gloves (to)*, from prize-ring, to fight in earnest, oppose strongly; *to fit like a glove*, fit exactly; *to be hand in glove with*, very intimate; in collusion with.

glove (II.), vb. trans., fr. prec. **a** To cover (the hand) with a glove; **b** to supply with gloves.

glove-fight, n. Boxing match in which gloves are worn.

glover, n. [1. glúver; 2. glávə]. **glove (I.)** & **-er**. **a** Person whose trade is to make gloves; **b** a retailer of gloves.

glow (I.), vb. intrans. [1. glō; 2. glou]. O.E. *glōwan*; O.S. *glōian*, O.H.G. *gluoen*, Mod. Germ. *glühen*, 'to glow'; base also in O.H.G. *gluot*, O.E. *glēd* (fr. **glōdi-*), 'hot coal, fire' &c. The base is widespread in the Aryan languages, the essential meaning being 'bright, shining'. Cp. Gk. *khlōrós*, 'light green, pale' (see **chloro-**); O.E. *glōm*, 'twilight, half-light' (see **gloom**), & O.N. *glāmer*, 'moon ('yellow-faced')', belong to same group. More remote fr. these, but doubtless fr. same base w. special suff., are the group of words **gold**, & its nearer cognates. **1.** To be luminous from intense heat; to be incandescent, red-hot, as metals, glass &c. in fusion. **2. a** To burn steadily with little or no flame (of partially burnt wood, coal &c., as opposed to *blaze*); **b** to emit a steady, even light (of lamps, fireflies). **3.** (fig., of persons) **a** To feel comfortably warm, as from robust health, after exercise &c.: *glow with health* &c.; **b** to swell, feel elated, be hot with emotion: *to glow with enthusiasm, pride, anger* &c. **4. a** (of colours, or coloured things) To be bright; to flame, show great intensity of colour: *the reds in this picture seem to glow*; *the picture glowed upon the wall*; *lilacs and laburnums glow in the parks*; **b** (of the cheeks) to flush, show red, from strong feeling or robust health: *cheeks that glow with shame, with pride, happiness, with health* &c.; **c** (of the eyes) to light up, flash: *his eyes glowed with anger, indignation* &c.

glow (II.), n., fr. prec. **1.** In first, material, sense the word implies, **a** a certain phase of combustion accompanied by both light and heat, but without flame or smoke: *the fire is in a glow*, red-hot; **b** light alone, generally diffused, regarded merely as visual sensation; a reddish luminosity: *glow of distant fires*; *glow of sunset in the sky.* **2. a** Sense of bodily warmth, comfort, and well-being: *all in a glow*; *a pleasant glow after a bath*; hence, (fig.) **b** sense of moral satisfaction: *glow of happiness*; **c** moral fervour, ardour: *in the first glow of enthusiasm.* **3. a** (of visual impression produced by bright and coloured objects) Vividness, penetrating intensity: *glow of colours, of the flowers*; **b** (of colour in cheeks) *a pink glow mounted to his cheeks.*

glower (I.), vb. intrans. [1. glour; 2. gláuə]. Orig. Scots & North. M.E. *glōren*, 'to glare, stare'; cp. M. Du. *gloeren*, 'to leer'; L.G. *gluren*, 'to be overcast'; Swed. *glōra*, 'to glare'; apparently related to **lour**, M. Du. *loeren*, L.G. *luren*, perh. w. pref. *ge-*, (see **com-**), or affected by **glare**. To lour; to stare gloomily, sullenly, threateningly; to scowl.

glower (II.), n., fr. prec. Grim, gloomy stare expressing disapproval, or ill-temper; a lowering look, scowl.

glowing, adj. [1. glōing; 2. glóuiŋ], fr. Pres. Part. of **glow (I.)**. **1.** In a glow, red-hot: *glowing embers.* **2. a** (of persons) Roused to moral or emotional fervour: *glowing patriot, evangelist, enthusiast* &c.; **b** (of the mind and emotions) intense, vivid, fervid, enthusiastic, deeply moved: *a glowing imagination*; *glowing admiration for.* Phr. *to give a glowing account of*, represent as highly admirable, exhibit enthusiasm in favour of. **3. a** (of colours &c.) Intense, vivid, bright, reverse of sombre, dull &c. Phr. *to paint in glowing colours*, describe in most favourable manner; **b** (of the cheeks) suffused with a blush, red from excitement, exertion, good health &c.

glowingly, adv. Prec. & **-ly**. **a** In a glowing manner; **b** (fig.) warmly, enthusiastically.

glow-worm, n. Wingless female of small European beetle, *Lampyris*, which emits a phosphorescent light.

gloxinia, n. [1. gloksínia; 2. glɔksíniə], fr. name of B. Gloxin, a German botanist. A tropical plant, genus *Sinningia*, cultivated in hot-houses for its beautiful bell-shaped flowers.

gloze, vb. intrans. [1. glōz; 2. glouz], fr. Fr. *gloser*. See **gloss (III.)**. *Gloze over*, to explain away, put favourable interpretation on, to gloss (over).

glucinum, n. [1. gloosínum; 2. glūsáinəm]. Fr. *-inium*, fr. Gk. *glukús*, sweet'. See **glyco-**. Beryllium, a white alkaline metal extracted from the beryl.

glucose, n. [1. glóokōs; 2. glúkous]. Concocted fr. Gk. *gleûkos*, 'must, sweet wine', connected with *glukús*, 'sweet'. See **glyco-** & **-ose**. (chem.) A form of sugar, dextrose, or grape sugar, made by treating starch with acids and used in brewing &c.

glucoside, n. [1. glóokōsid; 2. glúkousaid]. See prec. & **-ide**. (chem.) A compound substance which yields glucose by treatment with acids or ferments.

glucosuria. n. See **glycosuria**.

glue (I.), n. [1. gloo; 2. glū]. O. Fr. *glu*, 'birdlime', fr. L. Lat. *glūt-(em)*, *glūs*, fr. Lat. *glūten*, 'glue', cogn. w. Gk. *glóia*, 'glue', *gloiós*, 'sticky', fr. Aryan **gloi-*, wh. becomes **klai-* in Gmc.; cp. O.E. *clǣg*, fr. **klai-gi* (see **clay**). An enormous number of words are derived fr. the various forms of this base, wh. meant 'stick together, form a mass, roll up, gather into a ball' &c. See the native Engl. words **cleave (II.)**, 'stick to'; **clod**, **clot**, **clew**, **clue**, & others referred to under these, & further such words of Lat. origin as **glebe**, **globe**, **agglomerate**. Gelatinous, viscous, soluble, sticky substance obtained by boiling animal hides, hoofs, membranes, or bones; **a** powerful adhesive. Phr. (fig.) *to stick like glue to*, to accompany, shadow, attend, (a person) persistently.

glue (II.), vb. trans., fr. prec. **1. a** To coat with glue; **b** to stick, fasten, together with glue. **2.** (fig.) **a** (esp. in pass.) To be inseparable from, refuse to leave, be constantly in company of: *she remained glued to her mother the whole evening*; **b** to direct fixedly towards, concentrate upon: *to have one's eye glued to the keyhole.*

glue-pot, n. A double pot, with glue in inner,

and water in outer part, placed on fire to liquefy glue for use.

gluey, adj. [1. glo͞oi; 2. glúi]. **glue (I.)** & **-y.** Covered with glue; like glue in character and consistency; sticky and thick.

glum, adj. [1. glum; 2. glam]. Closely related to **gloom (II.)**. Morose, silent, depressed, sullenly despondent, moody.

glumaceous, adj. [1. glo͞omâshus; 2. glūméiʃəs]. See **glume** & **-aceous.** Having glumes, akin to glumes.

glumal, adj. [1. glo͞omal; 2. glúməl]. Next word & **-al.** Having a glume, distinguished by a glume.

glume, n. [1. glo͞om; 2. glūm]. Lat. *glūma*, 'husk, hull'. The Lat. word is fr. earlier **glub-ma* & related to *glūbere* 'to peel, shell'. Cp. Gk. *glúphō*, 'hollow out, engrave, cave', & *gluphis*, 'notch in an arrow' (see **glyph**). In Gmc. there are various cognates, e.g. O.E. *clēofan*, 'to split' (see **cleave (I.)** & **cleft (I.)**, & O.H.G. & Mod. Germ. *kluft*, 'cleft, split'. Bract, husk, or shell of flowering grasses.

glumly, adv. [1. glúmli; 2. glámli]. **glum** & **-ly.** In a glum, surly manner.

glumness, n. [1. glúmnes; 2. glámnis]. See prec. & **-ness.** The quality or state of being glum.

glumous, adj. [1. glo͞omus; 2. glúməs]. **glume** & **-ous.** Bearing glumes.

glut (I.), vb. trans. [1. glut; 2. glat]. M.E. *gluten*, fr. O. Fr. *glotir, gloutir*, 'to swallow, gulp down', fr. Lat. *glūtīre, glūttīre*, in same sense. Cp. also Lat. *in-gluviēs*, 'maw, crop; greed'. This word is fr. base **gel-* &c., 'to swallow', & is connected w. Lat. *gula*, 'throat, gullet', wh. has a near cousin in O.E. *ċeole*, 'throat' (fr. **ċela*), & O.H.G. *kela*, Mod. Germ. *kehle*, 'throat, neck'. Cp. **glutton** & **gullet.** **1.** (obs.) To swallow eagerly, guzzle. **2.** To regale to excess, feed to satiety; to surfeit, satiate: *to glut one's appetite.* **3.** (fig.) **a** To cloy, surfeit, sicken; esp. to indulge evil passions inordinately: *glut one's revenge*; hence, **b** to furnish superfluously, redundantly: *glut the market.*

glut (II.), n., fr. prec. Plentiful supply, superabundant quantity of anything; specif., of any marketable commodity, supply exceeding demand: *glut of eggs, plums, poultry* &c.

gluteal, adj. [1. glo͞otéal; 2. glūtíəl]. Formed fr. Gk. *gloutós*, 'rump', & **-al.** Cogn. w. Scrt. *glāúś*, 'ball', & ultimately related to the base seen in **glue** &c. Of, or pertaining to, the muscles of the buttocks.

gluten, n. [1. glo͞oten; 2. glūtən]. Lat., 'glue'. See **glue.** A tough, viscid albuminous nutritive substance, plentiful in wheat flour.

gluteus, n. [1. glo͞oteus; 2. glūtiəs]. Mod. Lat., fr. Gk. *gloutós*, 'rump'. See **gluteal.** Muscles of the buttocks.

glutinous, adj. [1. glo͞otenus; 2. glūtinəs]. Lat. *glūtin-(is)*, see **gluten**, & **-ous.** Of the nature of glue; adhesive, sticky.

glutton, n. [1. glútun; 2. glátən]. M.E. *glutūn*, fr. Fr. *glouton*, fr. Lat. *glūtōn-(em), gluttōn-(em), glūt(t)o*, 'a gormandizer', fr. *glūtīre*, 'to gulp down, swallow'. See **glut.** **1. a** Greedy, inordinate feeder, gormandizer, guzzler; **b** (fig., colloq.) one who is zealous, diligent, assiduous, unremitting; Phr. (fig.) *a glutton for work*, one who cannot have too much work; a good worker; *a glutton for punishment*, boxer who takes blows with indifference. **2.** (zool.) A carnivorous mammal, *Gulo luscus*, with long shaggy fur, found in Asia and North America, allied to the badger, weasel &c.; known also as *wolverine.*

gluttonous, adj. [1. glútunus; 2. glátənəs]. M.E. *glotonous.* Prec. & **-ous.** Fond of eating; inclined to think too much about food, and to eat to excess.

gluttony, n. [1. glútuni; 2. glátəni]. M.E. *glotonie*, fr. O. Fr. *gloutonie.* **glutton** & **-y.** The vice of the glutton; habit of intemperate eating.

glycerine, n. [1. glíserin; 2. glísərin]. Fr. *glycérine*, fr. Gk. *glukerós*, 'sweet', & **-ine**; cp. Gk. *glukús*, 'sweet'; these are for **dlukeros* &c., & are cogn. w. Lat. *dulcis*, 'sweet to the taste' &c., wh. is for **dolucis*, earlier **doleuk-is.* See **dulcet.** A sweet, colourless, viscous liquid extracted from various animal and plant fats, and as by-product in soap and candle-making; used in medicine, the manufacture of explosives, also to sweeten wines &c., and as a toilet preparation &c.

glyco-, pref. used in a number of newly invented scientific terms, fr. Gk. *glukús*, 'sweet'. See etymol. under **glycerine.**

glycogen, n. [1. glíkōjen; 2. gláikoudžen]. Prec. & **-gen.** (chem.) A carbohydrate, similar to starch, found in the liver and tissues of animals, also in certain fungi, producing glucose.

glycol, n. [1. glíkol; 2. gláikəl]. **glyco-** & **-ol.** (chem.) A class of substances, midway between glycerine and ethyl-alcohol.

glyconic, glyconian, adj. & n. [1. glīkónik, -kōnian; 2. glaikɔ́nik, -kóuniən], fr. *glukōneiós*, fr. *Glúkōn*, Greek poet. **a** adj. A form of Greek and Roman verse of four feet; **b** n., a verse in this metre.

glycosuria, n. [1. glìkōsúria; 2. glàikousjɔ́riə], fr. **glyco-**, w. *-s-* fr. **glucose**, & *-uria*, 'diseased condition of urine'. See **urine.** Disease in which glucose is excreted in the urine; form of diabetes.

glyph, n. [1. glif; 2. glif]. Fr. *glyphe*, fr. Gk. *gluphḗ*, cp. Gk. *glúphein*, 'to carve', &c.; fr. base **ghlubh-* &c.; cp. Lat. *glūbere*, 'peel bark off, strip' (see **glume**), & O.E. *clēofan*, 'split' &c. (see **cleave (I.)**). **a** (archit.) Vertical channel or groove; **b** (archaeol.) figure cut in relief.

glyphograph, n. [1. glífograhf; 2. glífəgrāf]. Prec. & **-graph.** Etched plate, or etching produced by glyphography.

glyphographic, adj. [1. glìfográfik; 2. glìfəgrǽfik]. Prec. & **-ic.** Of, or pertaining to, glyphography; produced by this process.

glyphography, n. [1. glifógrafi; 2. glifɔ́grəfi]. Gk. *glúphein*, 'cut, engrave'. See **glyph** & **-graphy.** Process by which a raised plate for printing is made from an etching by electrotypy.

glyptic, adj. [1. glíptik; 2. glíptik]. Gk. *gluptikós*, 'carving'. See **glyph.** Of, or pertaining to, carving or engraving; hence, *glyptics*, n. pl., the art or study of engraved gems, ivory &c.

glyptodon, n. [1. glíptodon; 2. glíptədɔn]. Gk. *glupt-(ós)*, fr. *glúphein*, 'engrave', see **glyph**, & *odónt-(a)*, 'tooth', wh. base see under **dental** & **tooth.** Cp. also **eat.** Extinct giant mammal with fluted teeth, whose remains are found in S. America, related to the armadillos.

glyptograph, n. [1. glíptograhf; 2. glíptəgrāf]. Gk. *gluptós*, 'carved', & **-graph.** See **glyph.** Engraved precious stone, seal &c.; the engraved design thereon.

glyptography, n. [1. gliptógrafi; 2. gliptɔ́grəfi]. Prec. & **-y.** Process, art, or study of gem-engraving.

gnarled, adj. [1. narld; 2. nāld]. O.N. *gnerr*, 'knot in wood'; cogn. w. M.E. *knarre*, 'knot in wood'; cp. *knar.* **a** (of trees) Having trunk or branches covered with knobs; rugged; **b** (of human beings) having rugged, knobby, weather-beaten appearance; **c** (fig., of character) cross-grained, cantankerous.

gnash, vb. trans. [1. nash; 2. næʃ]. Prob. imitative of sound; various Fris. & Scand. words, the origin of wh. is unknown, are quoted by Skeat & others, having some resemblance in form & meaning. Cp. O.E. *gnīdan*, 'to pulverize', wh. may be connected, & M.E. *gna(i)sten*, 'gnash the teeth'. Only in Phr. *to gnash the teeth*, to grind the teeth, champ, but chiefly fig., to exhibit rage by facial contortion; or simply, to show strong displeasure, to be in a rage.

gnashing, n. [1. náshing; 2. nǽʃiŋ]. Prec. & **-ing.** Act of grinding the teeth. Phr. (fig.) *gnashing of teeth*, rage, despair.

gnat, n. [1. nat; 2. næt]. O.E. *gnæt*; perh. connected w. O.N. *gnata*, 'to clash', fr. the noise of its wings. Any of various small two-winged insects or flies which bite and suck the blood. Phr. *to strain at a gnat*, stick at trifles.

gnathic, adj. [1. (g)náthik; 2. (g)nǽþik]. Gk. *gnáthos*, 'jaw, mouth', & **-ic**; fr. same base as Gk. *génus*, 'lower jaw', *géneion*, 'chin' (see **genial (II.)**); Lat. *gena*, 'cheek', & *genuīnus*, 'molar tooth', *gingīvae*, 'gums of the mouth'. See **gingival**; further, Goth. *kinnus*, O.E. *ċinn.* See **chin.** Of, or pertaining to, the jaw.

gnathism, n. [1. (g)náthizm; 2. (g)nǽþizəm]. See prec. & **-ism.** Relatively great projection of lower jaw; term as used in craniometry.

-gnathous, suff., fr. Gk. *gnáthos*, 'jaw'. See **gnathic** & **-ous.** Indicating the relative projection of lower jaw in craniometry, e.g. *prognathous.*

gnaw, vb. trans. & intrans. [1. naw; 2. nō]. O.E. *gnagan*, Engl. form, corresponding to Scand. **nag (II.)**. **1.** trans. & intrans. **a** To cut, wear, away by action of upper front teeth, as rats and mice &c.; **b** to scrape, chew, mumble, with the teeth generally: *like a dog gnawing (at) a bone.* **2.** trans. & intrans. (fig.) **a** (of physical pain and sickness) To harass continually, torment unceasingly; wear down, sap: *constantly gnawed by pain*; *fever gnawing at his life*; **b** (of mental grief and worry) to oppress, afflict, sharply and continually: *anxiety and distress gnawed at his heart.*

gnawing, n. & adj. [1. náwing; 2. nɔ́iŋ], n., prec. & **-ing**; adj., fr. Pres. Part. of prec. **1.** n. **a** Action or process of that which gnaws; **b** (fig.) dull, wearing, continuous pain of body or suffering of mind: *gnawings of hunger, conscience* &c. **2.** adj. That which gnaws (lit. and fig.): *a gnawing animal*, rodent; *gnawing pain, hunger, grief.*

gneiss, n. [1. nīs; 2. nais]. Germ. *gneis*, fr. O.H.G. *gneistan*, 'to sparkle'. Composite rock consisting of quartz, felspar, and mica.

gnome (I.), n. [1. nōm; 2. noum]. Fr., fr. a Neo-Lat. word *gnomus*, invented by Paracelsus; prob. fr. Gk. *gnṓmē*, 'intelligence'. See next word. **a** Fabulous, grotesque, dwarfish, misshapen sprite; kind of earth-goblin, believed to guard hidden treasure; **b** a grotesque, dwarfish person.

gnome (II.), n. Gk. *gnṓmē*, 'mind, thought, opinion', fr. base **gnō-.* See **gnomon.** Didactic, sententious, moral maxim; an aphorism.

gnomic(al), adj. [1. nómik(l); 2. nóumik(l)]. Gk. *gnōmik-(ós)*; prec. & **-ic** & **-al.** Connected with, based on, consisting of, gnomes; aphoristic, sententious; specif., *gnomic poetry*, type consisting chiefly in the expression of aphorisms and sententious platitudes and truisms.

gnomish, adj. [1. nómish; 2. nóumiʃ]. **gnome (I.)** & **-ish.** Like a sprite or gnome; freakish.

gnomon, n. [1. nómon; 2. nóumən]. Gk. *gnōmōn*, 'judge, interpreter', also 'a T-square', fr. base **ǵnō*, as in *gnṓmē*, 'intelligence', *gi-gnṓskein*, 'to learn' &c.; cogn. w. Lat. *(g)nōtus*, 'known' &c., see **notion**, & w. Engl. **know.** Index on a sundial, consisting of a rod which shows time by position of its shadow.

gnomonic, adj. [1. nōmónik; 2. noumɔ́nik]. Gk. *gnōmonik-(ós).* Prec. & **-ic.** Of, or pertaining to, gnomons, sundials; hence, *gnomonics*, n. pl., principles of constructing dials.

gnosis, n. [1. nósis; 2. nóusis]. Gk. *gnôsis*, 'knowledge, wisdom'; fr. base **ǵnō-*, 'to know', see **gnomon.** The higher, spiritual wisdom or knowledge, claimed by the Gnostics.

Gnostic, n. & adj. [1. nóstik; 2. nɔ́stik]. Gk. *gnōstikós*, 'knowing', fr. base in **gnomon.** **a** n. Member of the heretical Christian sect of *Gnostics* (mystics), of 2nd cent.; **b** adj., of, or pertaining to, gnosticism; characteristic of this heresy.

gnosticism, n. [1. nóstisizm; 2. nɔ́stisizəm]. Prec. & **-ism.** The heresy of the Gnostics.

gnu, n. [1. nū; 2. njū]. Hottentot name. (zool.) Large South African antelope with head, horns, and mane like those of an ox.

go (I.), vb. intrans. [1. gō; 2. gou]. O.E. *gān*, M.E. *gō(n)*; O.H.G. *gēn, gān*; Swed. *gå*. Orig. a vb. in *-mi*, as appears fr. O.H.G. *gām*, 'I go'. Of the various suggested etymols. the most probable is perh. that wh. derives the word fr. an Aryan base **g hēi-*, 'to move, leap', & connects it w. Scrt. *jihītē*, 'he goes away, goes forward; leaps up', & further w. Lat. *hēres*, q.v. under its Engl. derivative **heir**; & w. Lat. *haedus*, 'he-goat'. See further under **goat**; for Pret. *went*, see **wend**. **A.** intrans. **1.** **a** (archaic) To walk; **b** to move voluntarily, to proceed, from one place to another; to travel: *I shall go to France*; *let us go by train*; *to go on foot, by road* &c.; **c** (of inanimate things) to be moved, driven, propelled, from one place to another: *this train goes to London.* **2.** Specif. **a** to depart from, leave, place where speaker is; reverse of *come*: *it is really time for us to go*; *don't go yet*; **b** (of inanimate things; of conditions) to pass away from a given point in space, be moved off; disappear, cease to affect particular person or thing: *the clouds have gone and the sun has come out*; *I wish my pain would go*; *the train has just gone*; *a rifle bullet goes from the barrel with tremendous velocity*; *his life is going fast*; *all hope is gone*; **c** to be eliminated, got rid of, abolished: *drink must go!*; *this clause of the bill will have to go*; *that sentence goes altogether, as the passage now runs*; **d** to give way; be carried away, broken off, torn away &c.: *I thought every minute that the big elm would go*; *first the sail and then the mast went.* **3.** To move, execute movements, without departing from a given place: *I want to see the wheels go round.* **4.** **a** (of machinery) To move in the intended way, to perform the series of desired movements; work properly: *my watch won't go*; *the engine went beautifully all day*; *I hear the bells going*; Phr. *it has just gone six*, the clock has struck; **b** (i.) (of the heart) to act: *I could feel my heart going at a tremendous rate*; (ii.) of bodily organisms &c.: *he is going strong*, is full of health and vigour. **5.** **a** To engage in a particular line of action, conduct or thought; to follow a lead, be guided, directed, by: *I shall go entirely by what the doctor says*; **b** to behave in a particular way, carry out certain movements, gestures &c.: *all the time he was speaking he went like this*; *as he passed me, he went so*; (such phrases are accompanied by appropriate gesture, grimace &c.). **6.** To be current, be commonly stated: *the story goes that . . .* **7.** To be, live, exist, continually and habitually in particular condition: *to go hungry, empty*; *to go in rags*; *to go in fear of one's life*; *to go armed.* **8.** (only in Pres. Part.) To be available, to be in progress, on hand: *we have a prime leg of mutton going*; *there is sure to be some sort of dinner going.* **9.** **a** (with, following, adv. or adv. phr.) To proceed, pursue course, run, turn out: *things have gone badly with me of late*; *how did the play go?*; *everything went better than I expected*; **b** (unqualified by adv.) to turn out well, succeed, follow a prosperous course: *just the man to make things go.* **10.** To have a particular sequence, have a specified form, be expressed in way indicated: *this is how the tune goes*; *I forget exactly how the words go.* **11.** To pass into a particular state or condition; to become, turn; **a** (of physical states) *to go cold all over*; *to go to sleep*; *to go into a faint, swoon*; *to go black in the face*; *go green with envy, red with anger* &c.; Phr. *to go bad*, become putrid, sour, decayed; **b** (of mental conditions, phases of opinions &c.) become afflicted in particular way; adopt certain views: *to go mad*; *to go queer in the head*; *to go Conservative, Bolshevik*; Phr. *to go to pieces*, break up physically, mentally, or morally, or in all three ways. **12.** To be sold for, fetch a certain price: *eggs went for 3s. a dozen*; *don't let your house go too cheap.* **13.** To come to an issue, be decided: *the case went against him*; *how did the voting go?* **14.** To pass into possession of; come under control of; be allotted to; **a** (specif., by inheritance) *I have decided to whom my money is to go at my death*; *the estates went to the eldest son*; **b** (by natural course of events) *victory always goes to the strong*; *honours do not invariably go to the most deserving.* **15.** **a** To extend, be continued, run: *how far does this road go?*; *where does the path go to?*; *the boundary goes along the river and then northwards at right angles*; **b** to be capable of extension between two given points; to reach a given length or distance: *that sash will never go round her waist*; *the plank just goes across the brook.* **16.** **a** To have an allotted and habitual place or position; to be habitually kept in such a place: *that book goes on the top shelf*; *the silver goes in the safe every night*; **b** to be placed: *I want the large table to go in my room*; *where is this carpet to go?* **17.** (Pres. Part. *going*, followed by infin.) **a** expressing action or event in near or immediate future: *do you think it's going to rain?*; *your dog is going to kill that cat in a minute*; *there are* (colloq. *there's*) *going to be apple dumplings for dinner*; **b** expressing intention of future action: *I'm going to flog you*; *I'm not going to tell*; *I'm going to ask you a favour*; *are you going to behave like a gentleman or not?* **18.** **a** Phr. such as *go hunting* &c. Earlier (M.E.) *to go on hunting*; then *to go a hunting* &c., which is now archaic or provincial. The ending was formerly *-ung, -ing*, suffix forming verbal noun (which took the place of *-oþ, huntoþ*, 'act of hunting'). The construction is now felt as a Pres. Part. There is a certain restriction in the verbs with which the construction is used: *to go shooting, fishing, skating, skiing, blackberrying* &c.; **b** a different, but closely associated construction is *to go out fishing, shooting* &c.; and **c** more different still *to go (out) duck shooting*; **d** note Phr. *don't go picking the pears*; *don't go telling me lies*; also, *don't go and make a fool of yourself* (emphatic imperatives); also *he goes frightening people with his stories* &c., implying he makes a practice of ... Idiomatic Phrs.: *go it!*, (colloq.) play up, do your best! &c.; *you have been going it!* (*have* strongly stressed), you have apparently been indulging in excessive dissipation, or in extremely vigorous activity; *to go the whole hog*, think, speak, act, without any reservations or compromise; *to go all lengths*, show excess of zeal; act uncompromisingly and without restrictions; *to go to the bar*, become a barrister; *go to sea*, become a sailor; *to go the pace*, live a fast, dissipated life; *to go bang*, to explode; *to go bust*, (colloq.) to be ruined; *to go one better*, to outdo; (*all very well*) *so, as, far as it goes*, implying that further knowledge, information, experience are required before accepting, or acting on, a statement &c.; *to go for nothing, very little*, amount to, count as. **B.** Followed by adverbs and prepositions. *Go about*, **a** to circulate: *a story is going about*; **b** (naut., of a vessel) to tack. *Go against*, to oppose, run counter to: *it goes against my principles.* *Go ahead*, to make progress, push forward, pass competitors; Phr. *go ahead!*, **a** start, continue your journey, move forward!; **b** proceed with what you are saying or doing. *Go along*, to proceed, progress; (colloq., interj.) *go along (with you)!*, (i.) be off (away from here)!; (ii.) don't be absurd! *Go at*, (colloq.) to assail, rush at, attack: *he went at him with his fists*; Phr. *to go at it hammer and tongs*, undertake, tackle, energetically. *Go back*, **a** to return to place from which one has come; **b** (fig.) to pass acme, deteriorate: *these old trees are going back.* *Go back on*, (i.) to revoke, break, withdraw from (promise, bargain &c.); (ii.) to betray, play false (a person). *Go behind*, to search for, investigate, facts underlying: *to go behind the evidence*; *to go behind what has been said*, seek further information before accepting statement. *Go between*, to mediate, act as agent, between (cp. **go-between**). *Go beyond*, to exceed: *to go beyond one's orders.* *Go by*, to pass, elapse: *years have gone by* (cp. **bygone**). *Go down*, **a** to sink, be submerged; (of a heavenly body) to set; **b** (Oxford and Cambridge colloq.) to leave the University; **c** (colloq.) (i.) to be swallowed, slip down the throat; hence, (ii.) (fig.) be credited or approved: *that won't go down with me*; **d** to be remembered: *he will go down to posterity as a traitor.* *Go for*, **a** (colloq.) To attack vehemently by act or word: *the speaker went for the profiteers*; **b** to snatch at, aim at, try to get: *I should go for the cash.* *Go forth*, to be published: *an order went forth.* *Go in*, to enter: *to go in for an examination*; *to go in for golf, collecting, dissipation* &c., devote, addict oneself to; Phr. *go in and win!*, show enterprise and confidence. *Go into*, (i.) to occupy oneself with: *to go into details*; (ii.) to investigate, examine carefully: *to go into the evidence.* *Go near*, almost attain or succeed in: *he went near success, breaking the record.* *Go off*, **a** (i.) (of a firearm or explosive) to explode, be discharged; (ii.) (fig.) to burst out in word or act; **b** (colloq.) to deteriorate: *her voice is going off*; **c** to pursue a certain course, be carried out: *the performance went off well*; **d** to go away, run away, depart unexpectedly, abandoning one's responsibilities: *Jones has gone off with a friend's wife.* *Go on*, **a** to continue: *the battle went on all day*; **b** (colloq.) to persist in particular line of behaviour (usually in unfavourable sense): *don't go on like that*; (colloq. Phr.) *go on!*: (i.) continue; (ii.) (often ironical) nonsense!; **c** (cricket) to take turn at bowling. *Go on for*, to approach, as in *going on for fifty, for five o'clock.* *Go out*, **a** to attend social functions, cultivate society: *she goes out a great deal*; **b** to vacate an office, retire: *the minister who has gone out*; **c** to cease to be popular or in fashion: *whist has quite gone out*; **d** (i.) (of a fire, light) be extinguished; (ii.) (slang) to die; Phr. *my heart goes out to*, my sympathy, love, is drawn to, is aroused by. *Go over*, **a** to study, con, repeat, methodically, from beginning to end: *go over your lesson, your part*; *he went over the whole story*; **b** to examine carefully in every part: *the engineers went over the machine*; *go over the accounts.* *Go round*, to be sufficient in number or amount to allow of complete and equal distribution or apportionment: *there's not enough wine to go round.* *Go through* = *go over*, to examine with care, look into in detail: *to go through the arguments on the other side.* *Go through with*, to persist to the end of: *I am resolved to go through with it.* *Go to!* (obs. Bib. interj.), expressing exhortation, remonstrance &c.; come! *Go under*, **a** to sink, be submerged, hence, **b** (fig.) to succumb, fail, be ruined: *the firm has gone under.* *Go up*, to be blown up, explode: *to go up in flames, fire, smoke*; (of buildings) to be consumed by fire. *Go with*, **a** to accompany; Phrs. *I can't go with you in everything you say*, I can't agree; *to go with one's party*, act, vote, in accordance with their principles or opportunism; **b** (i.) (of material things) to match, be suitable to, to harmonize with: *the colour of her dress doesn't go at all with her hair*; *fish doesn't go well with tea*; *the old furniture goes very well with the house*; (ii.) (of non-material things) to be fitting with, be adapted to, agree, be in accordance with: *vulgar manners do not go with a noble nature.*

go (II.), n., fr. prec. (colloq. only) That which goes (in various senses of the vb.) **1.** That which runs its course, a performance, achievement; (in colloq. or slang phrases) *a rum go*, strange occurrence &c.: *here's a pretty go*, awkward situation; *all the go*, much in vogue; *no go*, not to be done, impracticable; *near go*, a narrow margin of safety, time &c.; a near thing, a narrow squeak. **2.** **a** Spell of action, turn: *let's have a go at it*; **b** quantity (of drink &c.) taken at one time. **3.** Action agreed upon, bargain: *Is it a go?* **4.** Activity, energy, spirit: *full of go*; Phr. *on the go*, (i.) restlessly active: *I've been on the go ever since daybreak*; (ii.) on the point of departure, just off.

goad (I.), n. [1. gōd; 2. goud]. O.E. *gād*, 'point of weapon, sting, goad' (see **gadfly**); cogn. w. Lombardic *gaida*, 'point of an arrow'. The base is prob. Aryan **g̑hai-*, as in Gk. *khaîos*, 'shepherd's staff', & this & the Engl. word are apparently related to O.E. *gār*, 'spear' &c. See further under **gore (II.)**. Scrt. *hētiš*, 'missile', fr. **g̑hait-*, appears to be the nearest cogn. outside Gmc. Cp. also Lat. *gaesum*, 'heavy javelin', fr. Gall. *gaiso-*, fr. the same base. **a** Sharp stick or other pointed implement used for prodding and driving cattle, elephants &c.; **b** (fig.) a moral irritant or stimulus, an incentive.

goad (II.), vb. trans., fr. prec. **1.** To prick, drive, urge forward with a goad. **2.** (fig.) To stimulate, incite, provoke, by continued moral irritation: *goad to madness, to rebellion, into fury; goaded by incessant pain.* **3.** To urge painfully, persuade with difficulty and by active measures into action: *he had to be goaded by threats into doing anything.*

goaf, n. [1. gōf; 2. gouf]. O.N. *gōlf*, 'floor, apartment', whence M.E. *golf*, mod. provinc. Engl. *goaf*, 'heap of sheaves &c. stored in barn'. (in coal mining) **a** The open space or stall left between the pillars when coal has been extracted; **b** waste matter left to fill up such space, more usually called 'gob'.

go-ahead, adj. [1. gō ahèd; 2. góu əhèd]. **go (I.)** & **ahead**. Enterprising, progressive, pushing.

goal, n. [1. gōl; 2. goul]. Perh. fr. unrecorded O.E. n. **gāl*, implied by *gǣlan*, 'to hinder'; cp. O.H.G. *ingeiltist*, 'thou didst hinder'; the word appears as *gōl* in M.E., meaning 'boundary', & in its present sense in 16th cent. **1. a** Post or other object set up to mark end of a race, winning-post; **b** specif., posts between which the ball has to pass in order to score at football and other games; **c** score made by the side which gets the ball through the posts at football &c.: *to, get, kick, a goal.* **2. a** Place which one wishes to reach on a journey; destination: *Naples is my goal on this tour*; also, **b** (in non-material sense) something set before one as an aim or ideal to be attained: *the goal of one's ambition, desires* &c.

goal-keeper, n. Player (in association football &c.) whose object is to prevent the ball from passing through the goal.

goal-line, n. Transverse line at end of playing-ground, level with the goal-posts.

goal-post, n. One of the upright posts between which the ball must pass in order for the attacking side to score a goal.

go-as-you-please, adj. [1. gó az ū plḗz; 2. góu əz ju plíz]. (of persons and things) **a** Unmethodical, casual, without plan; **b** not restricted by conditions.

goat, n. [1. gōt; 2. gout]. O.E. *gāt*, 'she-goat'; M.E. *goot*, Common Gmc., cp. Du. *gait*, O.H.G. *geiz*, Mod. Germ. *geiss*, Goth. *gaits*; O.N. *geit*, 'she-goat'; cogn. w. Lat. *haedus*, 'kid', prob. fr. Aryan base **ghai(d)-*, 'to leap', fr. another grade of wh. comes also Scrt. *jihītē*, 'he leaps, springs'. See **go. 1.** Member of a genus, *Capra*, of hollow-horned ruminants, wild or domesticated, allied to the sheep but covered with hair instead of wool and differentiated by the presence of a beard, horns in both sexes, and strong odour in the male. **2.** (astron.) *The Goat*, the zodiacal sign Capricorn. **3. a** The type of the wicked: *separate the sheep from the goats*; **b** a lustful, lecherous man: *an old goat*; **c** (colloq.) a giddy, foolish person: *to act, play, the (giddy) goat*, behave foolishly, frivolously &c.; *to get one's goat*, to annoy, irritate, make angry.

goatee, n. [1. gōtḗ; 2. goutí]. Prec. & **-ee.** Long, straggly beard worn on the chin, the upper lip and the cheeks being shaved; tuft of hair resembling a goat's beard.

goat-herd, n. O.E. *gāthyrde*, M.E. *gootherde*. **goat** & **herd.** Person whose business it is to look after a flock of goats.

goatish, adj. [1. gṓtish; 2. góutiʃ]. **goat** & **-ish.** Resembling a goat, **a** in certain physical habits and tendencies; lecherous; **b** in having a rank odour.

goatishly, adv. Prec. & **-ly.** In a goatish manner.

goatishness, n. See prec. & **-ness.** Quality of being goatish.

goat-moth, n. Large grey British moth with a goat-like odour.

goat-pepper, n. Variety of cayenne.

goat's-beard, n. Popular name of several plants: **a** salsify and others of the genus, the seeds being furnished with a pappus; **b** meadow-sweet; **c** a kind of fungus.

goat's-rue, n. Leguminous plant with mauve or white flowers, cultivated in gardens.

goatsucker, n. [1. gṓtsùker; 2. góutsàkə]. So called from erroneous notion of this bird's habits. Nightjar.

gob, n. [1. gob; 2. gɔb], fr. O. Fr. *gobe*, 'mouthful'. See **gobbet. 1.** (vulg.) Mouthful of saliva. **2.** (coal-mining) The waste material left to fill up a stall or 'goaf', often the source of dangerous fires, called *gobfires.*

gobang, goban, n. [1. gṓbang; 2. góubæŋ]. Popular etymol. fr. Jap. *goban*, fr. Chin. *k'i pan*, 'chessboard'. Japanese game resembling noughts and crosses, played on a chequered board of 256 squares, on which the two players alternately place counters, each endeavouring to place 5 in a row.

gobbet, n. [1. góbit; 2. gɔ́bit]. M.E. *gobet*, 'small piece', fr. Fr. *gobet*, 'mouthful, gobbling', dimin. of O. Fr. *gobe*, 'mouthful', of Celt. origin, cp. Ir. *gob*, 'beak, mouth'. See **gobble. 1.** A lump or morsel of food, esp. when in the mouth or just ejected from it. **2.** Portion of a text selected for translation or comment in an examination paper.

gobble (I.), vb. trans. & intrans. [1. góbl; 2. gɔ́bl]. Fr. *gober*, 'to swallow, bolt', fr. O. Fr. *gobe*. See prec. & freq. **-le. 1.** trans. Also, *gobble up*, to eat voraciously, noisily, greedily: *to gobble (up) everything that is put before one.* **2.** intrans. To eat fast, noisily, and greedily: *he doesn't eat, he simply gobbles.*

gobble (II.), vb. & n. Variant of **gabble. a** vb. To make the characteristic noise of a turkey-cock; **b** n. (also *gobble-gobble*) The noise made by a turkey.

gobble (III.), n. Origin doubtful. Possibly fr. **gobble (I.).** In golf, a quick putt into the hole.

gobbler (I.), n. [1. góbler; 2. gɔ́blə], fr. **gobble (I.).** One who gobbles food &c.

gobbler (II.), n., fr. **gobble (II.).** (colloq.) The turkey-cock; esp.: *a young gobbler.*

Gobelin, adj. & n. [1. góbelin, góbelan; 2. gɔ́bəlin, -lǣ]. Fr. *Gobelin*, name of a family of dyers, members of which founded the old royal French tapestry-works. **1.** adj. Of or pertaining to the work of the Gobelin looms; resembling Gobelin work: *Gobelin blue*, dull blue-green; *Gobelin stitch*, tapestry stitch; *Gobelin tapestry*, rich kind of tapestry, such as was made in the Gobelin factory. **2.** n. Gobelin tapestry, a specimen of it or of the same kind.

go-between, n. [1. gṓ betwḗn; 2. góu bitwín]. **go (I.)** & **between. a** Intermediary, middleman; spokesman; **b** agent, esp. in unfavourable sense, match-maker, pander; agent in a shady transaction.

goblet, n. [1. góblet; 2. gɔ́blit]. M.E., fr. Fr. *gobelet*, dimin. (see **-et**), of O. Fr. *gobel*, 'drinking-cup', fr. L. Lat. *cūpell-(us)*, dimin. of *cūpa*, 'tub, cask'. See **coop** & **cup. a** Drinking-vessel without handles, of metal or glass and provided with a foot; **b** (poet.) any kind of drinking-vessel.

goblin, n. [1. góblin; 2. gɔ́blin], fr. obs. Fr. *gobelin*, perh. fr. Low Lat. *cobālus*, 'kind of demon', fr. Gk. *kóbālos*, 'an impudent rogue; an evil spirit invoked by rogues', prob. of Phrygian origin. A malicious hideous sprite; bogey, demon.

goblin fish, n. A small spiny Australian fish of fantastic appearance.

goblinry, n. [1. góblinri; 2. gɔ́blinri]. **goblin** & **-ry.** Goblins collectively.

goby, n. [1. gṓbi; 2. góubi]. Lat. *gōbi-(us)*, fr. Gk. *kōbiós*. See **gudgeon.** Member of a group of small marine fishes, in which the ventral fins form an adhesive disk or sucker.

go-by, n. [1. gṓ bī; 2. góu bai]. Only in Phr. *to give the go-by*, **a** to avoid purposely, pass (person) without noticing (him); **b** to refrain from using, or doing; to avoid, pass over.

go-cart, n. **a** Frame on wheels, in which an infant can learn to walk; **b** one of several kinds of small vehicles propelled by hand; small, light perambulator.

god, n. [1. god; 2. gɔd]. O.E., M.E. *god*; Common Gmc., cp. O.S., Du. *god*, O.H.G. *got*, Mod. Germ. *gott* &c.; orig. neut. as Goth. *guþ*, O.N. *guð*. No certain cognates outside Gmc., but it prob. represents an Aryan neut. P.P. type **ghu-tóm*; cp. Scrt. *huta*, 'that to which sacrifice is made', fr. *hu*, 'to sacrifice' (cp. Gk. *khutón*, 'poured out', *khéein*, 'to pour'), or perh. Scrt. *hūta*, 'that which is invoked', fr. *hū*, 'to call upon'; cp. cognates given under **found (II.). 1. a** One of a class of powerful spirits, regarded as controlling a department of nature or of human activity, and as such generally worshipped; deity, divinity; Phrs. *god of love*, Cupid; *god of this world*, Satan; *a feast for the gods*, delicious food (also ironical); *a sight for the gods*, surprising or delightful spectacle; *ye gods!*, facetious exclamation of wonder; **b** male deity, as distinguished from goddess. **2.** (fig.) Object of excessive devotion: '*their god is their belly*'; (*little*) *tin god*, petty despot or official to whom extreme deference is paid; *the gods*, occupants of the gallery in a theatre (from their elevated position). **3.** (cap.) The Creator of all things; the Eternal Lord and Father of all; the Almighty; Phr. *God's acre* (translation of Germ. *Gottes-acker*), churchyard; *act of God*, (law) calamity beyond human control, as lightning stroke; *house of God*, temple, church, or other consecrated place of worship; (*nowhere on*) *God's earth*, the whole world; *God's truth*, the absolute truth; *under God*, recognizing the ruling of Providence, humanly speaking; *God willing*, if Providence permits; *he thinks himself God Almighty*, has an overweening conceit of himself, of his own importance; *God knows when, where, why* &c., no one else knows. In many exclamations, imprecations &c.; expressing vehement emotion: *My God!, good God!, O God!*; surprise: *God bless me!*; pity: *God help him!*; deprecation: *God forbid!*; pious gratitude: *thank God!*; often merely relief: *we've seen the last of him, thank God!* To avoid profanity the word *God* in exclamations is often omitted (see **gracious**), or altered (see **goodness, heaven**).

godchild, n. [1. gódchīld; 2. gɔ́dtʃaild]. M.E. **god** & **child.** Person for whom one acts as sponsor at his baptism.

goddaughter, n. [1. góddawter; 2. gɔ́ddɔ̀tə]. O.E. *goddohtor*, M.E. *goddoȝter*. **god** & **daughter.** Female godchild.

goddess, n. [1. gódes; 2. gɔ́dis]. Hybrid compound, fr. **god** & **-ess. a** Female deity; **b** (fig.) woman of notable attractions, adored woman.

godetia, n. [1. gōdḗsha; 2. goudíʃə]. Mod. Lat., fr. Godet, name of a Swiss botanist, & **-ia.** Garden flower, native of America, closely related to the evening primrose, with abundant crimson, purple, and white blossoms.

godfather, n. & vb. trans. [1. gódfàhdher; 2. gɔ́dfàðə]. O.E. *godfæder*, M.E. *godfader*. **god** & **father**, translating Lat. *pater in Deo.* **1.** n. Male sponsor at baptism. **2.** vb. trans. To act as godfather to, stand sponsor to.

godfearing, adj. [1. gódfēring; 2. gɔ́dfiəriŋ]. Having a devout fear or awe of God; reverent, pious.

godforsaken, adj. [1. gódforsàken; 2. gɔ́dfəsèikən]. (colloq.) **a** (of person) Abandoned, utterly depraved; **b** (of place) desolate, remote; devoid of resources or comforts; inspiring aversion.

godgiven, adj. [1. gódgiven; 2. gɔ́dgiv(ə)n]. Sent, given, by God; hence, welcome, opportune; eminently suitable for purpose.

Godhead, n. [1. gód-hed; 2. gɔ́dhed]. M.E. *godhed*. **God** & **-head**. **1.** Deity, Divine character; God's essence, nature. **2.** That of a god or goddess.

godless, adj. [1. gódles; 2. gɔ́dlis]. **god** & **-less**. **1. a** (of persons) Without God or a god; ignoring or denying God or the gods; hence, ungodly, irreligious; hence, impious. **2.** (rare) Deprived of the presence or of the care and protection of God: *a godless universe*.

godlessly, adv. Prec. & **-ly**. In a godless manner.

godlessness, n. See prec. & **-ness**. Condition of being godless.

godlike, adj. [1. gódlīk; 2. gɔ́dlaik]. **god** & **-like**. Like a god or God; of divine quality; majestic, august: *his godlike presence, brow*.

godliness, n. [1. gódlines; 2. gɔ́dlinis]. **godly** & **-ness**. Devotion to God, piety, devout conduct; holiness of character and life.

godly, adj. [1. gódli; 2. gɔ́dli]. **god** & **-ly**. Devoted to God, pious; *the godly*, pious, religious people (often ironical).

godmother, n. [1. gódmùdher; 2. gɔ́dmàðə]. O.E. *godmōdor*. **god** & **mother**. Woman who acts as sponsor to a child in baptism.

go-down, n. [1. gó doun; 2. góu daun]. Corruption of Malay. *godong*. Storehouse, warehouse in China or the East Indies.

godparent, n. [1. gódpârent; 2. gɔ́dpɛ̀ərənt]. Person of either sex who acts as sponsor to another in baptism.

godsend, n. [1. gódsend; 2. gɔ́dsend], fr. *God's*, & M.E. *sonde, sande*, 'what is sent, a message'; influenced by *send*. See **send**. Something that comes as a blessing; a useful, valued object; a fortunate, welcome occurrence; piece of good luck.

godship, n. [1. gódship; 2. gɔ́dʃip]. **god** & **-ship**. Character, nature, rank, of God, or a god.

godson, n. [1. gódsun; 2. gɔ́dsan]. **god** & **son**. Male person for whom one has stood sponsor in baptism.

godspeed, n. [1. gódspēd; 2. gɔ́dspíd]. Contracted fr. *God speed you*. Success, good luck; the blessing of God; in such Phr. as: *to wish, bid, a person godspeed*.

godward, adj. [1. gódward; 2. gɔ́dwəd]. **god** & **-ward**. Directed towards God; divine, concerned with God.

godwit, n. [1. gódwit; 2. gɔ́dwit]. Etymol. dubious. Smallish edible bird of snipe family, found on sea-shore.

goer, n. [1. góer; 2. góuə]. **go** (I.) & **-er**. Person or thing that goes; used esp. in describing pace and speed: *a good goer, poor goer* &c.

goffer, n. & vb. trans. [1. gófer; 2. góufə]. Fr. *gaufre*, 'tuck, pleat'; of Gmc. origin. See **wafer**. **1.** n. Pleat, gather, ornamental puckered border in garments &c. **2.** vb. To set (cloth, linen &c.) in pleats or gathers.

goffering, n. [1. gófering; 2. góufəriŋ]. Prec. & **-ing**. Act or process of setting in pleats, puckering, fluting; collection, series, of pleats, gathers, frills.

go-getter, n. [1. gó geter; 2. góu getə], fr. **go** & **get**. (slang, U.S.A.) A pushing, successful person, esp. in business.

goggle (I.), vb. intrans. [1. gógl; 2. gɔ́gl]. Origin suggested fr. Ir. *gog*, 'nod, slight motion', & **-le**. **1.** To stare with protruding, or widely opened eyes, as in amazement, terror &c. **2.** (of the eyes) To protrude, bulge, be wide open and staring.

goggle (II.), n., fr. prec. **1.** Wide-eyed stare expressing amazement or horror. **2. a** *Goggles*, spectacles with guards for protection against dust or glare (worn by motorists &c.); **b** (slang) spectacles generally.

goggle-eyed, adj. Having bulging, protruding eyes.

goggle-eyes, n. Staring, protruding eyes.

goglet, gugglet, n. [1. góglet; 2. gɔ́glit]. Corrupt. by Anglo-Indians of Port. *gorgoleta*. A porous earthenware jar in which water is kept cool.

Goidelic, adj. [1. goidélik; 2. gɔidélik]. O. Ir. *Goídel* (cp. **Gael**), & **-ic**. Pertaining to the race, language, &c. of the Gaels.

going, n. [1. góing; 2. góuiŋ]. **go** (I.) & **-ing**. **1. a** Act of one who goes; journey; movement in pursuance of one's ordinary occupations: '*Order my goings in thy paths*'; **b** specif., departure: *let me know the day of your going*. **2.** Mode of travelling, pace at which one travels: *40 miles an hour is pretty good going*. **3.** That upon which one travels, road, track &c., considered from the point of view of the ease, or the reverse, of travelling: *the going was very hard and difficult over the mountain roads*.

goitre, n. [1. góiter; 2. gɔ́itə]. Fr., fr. Lat. *guttur*, 'throat, throttle'. See **guttural**. Pathological enlargement of the thyroid gland, characterized by swellings round neck and throat, often reaching great size, associated with cretinism and myxoedema; *exophthalmic goitre*, also called Graves' disease, disease of thyroid gland, marked by heart affections, protruding eyeballs &c.

goitrous, adj. [1. góitrus; 2. gɔ́itrəs]. Fr. *goitreux*. See prec. & **-ous**. **a** Of or pertaining to goitre; of the nature of a goitre; **b** afflicted with goitre.

Golconda, n. [1. golkónda; 2. gɔlkɔ́ndə]. Name of a fortress near Hyderabad, India, once the treasure-house of the Nizam. (fig.) Any reputed source of unlimited wealth.

gold (I.), n. [1. gōld; 2. gould]. O.E. & M.E. *gōld*, also O.S., O. Fris. & O.H.G.; Goth. *gulþ*; cogn. w. O. Slav. *zlato*; cp. also O. Slav. *zlŭtŭ*, 'yellow'. There seem to have been two closely related Aryan bases **ghel-* & **ghel-*, both meaning 'yellow, yellowish'. See also **yellow** & **glow** (I.). **1.** A precious metal, yellow in colour, untarnishable, heavy in proportion to its bulk, and very ductile. **2.** (collect.) Objects made of gold; specif., minted gold, golden coinage: *to keep one's gold in a purse*. **3.** (fig.) Wealth, money, treasure: *greed of gold*. Phr. *all is not gold that glitters*, appearances may deceive; *heart of gold*, noble, generous nature; *cloth of gold*, rich fabric woven of, or shot with, gold thread. **4.** Gilding, lace, embroidery &c., of, or simulating, gold. **5.** A bright yellow colour resembling that of gold: *hair of gold*; *the red and gold of autumn*. **6.** (archery) Bull's eye, centre of target (usually gilt).

gold (II.), adj., fr. prec. Made of gold: *gold coins, ornaments*; *a gold watch, brooch* &c. Used commonly instead of *golden*.

gold-beater, n. One whose trade is to hammer out gold into very thin sheets for gilding.

gold-beater's skin, n. Very thin substance made from outer membrane of the intestine of an ox; used to separate the sheets of gold-leaf, and also for covering wounds, and sometimes for lining gas-bags of airships.

gold brick, n. Mass of gold, or what appears to be such, used as a lure by a swindler, who sells it to a dupe, and transfers to the latter a worthless substitute; hence, any worthless thing used to extract money fraudulently.

gold-digger, n. One who digs and searches for gold, especially an adventurer seeking his fortune by this means in an area where gold has been found, or where its presence is suspected.

gold dust, n. Fine particles of gold washed out in placer mining.

golden, adj. [1. gólden; 2. góuld(ə)n]. **gold** (I.) & **-en**. **1.** (rare and archaic) Made of gold: *a golden guinea*; otherwise *gold* is used in this sense except in fig. Phrs. *golden age* (fr. mythol.) primeval era of innocence and happiness; period of greatest glory or prosperity, zenith, apogee; *golden balls*, trade-sign of a pawnbroker, hence, pawnshop; *golden hours*, happy time; *golden calf*, wealth regarded as supreme object in life; *golden mean*, principle of avoiding extremes; moderation; *golden opportunity*, favourable opening, auspicious chance. **2.** Having the colour of gold; of a bright, shining, yellow colour suggesting that of gold: *golden hair*; *golden sunset, golden tinge* &c.

Golden Bull, n. Name of a mediaeval charter sealed with a gold bull or seal, esp. that issued by the Emperor Charles IV. in 1356, settling precedence among the Electoral princes &c.

golden-crested wren, n. A warbler, *Regulus cristatus*, with a crest of yellow feathers, also called *knight* or *gold-crest*.

golden eagle, n. Large eagle, now almost extinct in Great Britain, the plumage of whose head and neck is of a golden yellow colour.

golden eye, n. A diving duck of Northern hemispheres, genus *Clangula*, with black and white plumage and gold iris to the eye.

Golden Fleece, n. So called fr. its badge representing the golden fleece sought by the Argonauts. Order founded by Philip Duke of Burgundy in 1429; the order formerly existed both in Austria and Spain.

Golden Horde, n. So called fr. the magnificence of the leader's camp (Turk. *ordu*). Name given to a body of Tartars, under a grandson of Genghis Khan, who invaded Europe in 1237.

Golden Horn, n. Narrow inlet of Bosporus at Constantinople.

Golden Legend, n. English name of a collection of lives of Saints, compiled by Jacobus de Voragine, Archbishop of Genoa, in the late 13th cent.; it was translated into English from the French, and printed by Caxton in 1483.

golden-mouthed, adj. Eloquent; used of, and as translating the name of, St. Chrysostom.

golden number, n. The number used in calculating the date of Easter.

golden pheasant, n. Chinese variety of pheasant with brilliant plumage and bright yellow crest.

golden rod, n. Perennial herb with long stalks terminating in branching clusters of small, yellow flower-heads, genus *Solidago*.

golden rose, n. Rose of wrought gold with jewelled petals, blessed by the Pope, and sometimes presented by him to some great and highly favoured personage, or merely treasured up in the Vatican.

golden rule, n. Precept of the Saviour (Matt. vii. 12); in popular contracted form: *do as you would be done by*.

golden syrup, n. Sweet, pale yellow-coloured sticky substance used for food, made by refining treacle, or synthetically by a chemical process.

golden wedding, n. Fiftieth anniversary of wedding-day.

gold fever, n. Craze, eager desire, to explore for gold.

gold-field, n. Area in which deposits of gold are found.

goldfinch, n. [1. góldfinch; 2. góuldfinʃ]. Common British song-bird with black, white, and yellow plumage.

goldfish, n. [1. góldfish; 2. góuldfiʃ]. Small fish of the carp family, having deep gold-coloured scales, a native of China and Japan, though often kept in ponds and aquaria in this country.

gold lace, n. Braid or cord made of gold thread, much used as ornament, and in various arrangements as indication of rank in naval and military uniforms.

gold leaf, n. Very thin sheet beaten out of pure gold, used in gilding.

gold-mine, n. Place, area, where gold is mined; hence, source of great wealth (lit. and fig.).

gold plate, n. Table furniture, spoons, forks, dishes &c. made of gold.

gold size, n. Thin, very adhesive glue with which objects are coated before being covered with gold leaf.

goldsmith, n. [1. góldsmith; 2. góuldsmiþ]. Worker in gold; one who sells the work of goldsmiths.

Goldstick, n. [1. góldstik; 2. góuldstik]. Usually *Goldstick-in-waiting*; British Court official whose office is held in turns by the officers commanding the regiments of household cavalry; so called from a gilded wand which he bears before the sovereign on state occasions.

gold-thread, n. Plant of ranunculus class, *Coptis trifolia*, having white flowers and fibrous yellow roots; used medicinally and in dyeing.

golf, n. & vb. intrans. [1. go(l)f; 2. gɔ(l)f]. Scots word mentioned in 1457 in reference to the game. Origin uncertain; perh. connected w. Du. *kolf*, 'club for striking balls'; cp. also Swed. *kolf*, 'butt-end'. **1.** n. A game of Scottish origin, which consists in placing a small ball successively into each of a series of (9 or 18) holes in an open course or 'links', by striking with one of several clubs with wooden or iron heads. **2.** vb. To play golf.

golf-club, n. **1.** Implement used for striking the ball in golf. **2. a** Association for promoting play of the game, by laying out and keeping up a suitable course with bunkers, greens, holes &c.; **b** premises occupied by such an association.

golfer, n. [1. gólfer; 2. gɔ́(l)fə]. **golf & -er.** One who plays golf.

Golgotha, n. [1. gólgotha; 2. gɔ́lgəþə]. Lat., fr. Gk., fr. Heb. *gulgōleth*, 'skull'. A calvary.

Goliath, n. [1. gōlīath; 2. gouláiəþ]. Name of a giant mentioned in the Bible, who was slain by David. A man of great size and strength.

goliath beetle, n. Large black and white African beetle.

golliwog, n. [1. góliwog; 2. gɔ́liwɔg]. Concocted word with no history. **a** Hideous doll with black face, staring eyes, and thick black hair standing on end; **b** grotesque-looking, ugly person supposed to resemble such a doll.

golly, interj. [1. góli; 2. gɔ́li]. Negro modification of *God*. (familiar and colloq.; vulg. or facetious) Mild exclamatory expletive, expressing surprise &c., equivalent to *O Lord!*

goloptious, adj. [1. golópshus; 2. gəlɔ́pʃəs]. Comic word partly suggested by *voluptuous*. Delicious to the taste, luscious.

golosh, galosh, n. [1. golósh; 2. gəlɔ́ʃ]. Fr. *galoche*, prob. modified fr. Lat. *calopodium*, 'wooden shoe', fr. Gk. *kalopódion*, 'shoemaker's last', fr. *kâlon*, 'wood', & *pod-*, stem of *poús*, 'foot'. The origin of former appears to be unknown; for the latter word see **foot, pedal, & -pod.** Shoe made of thin india-rubber, with thick sole of same material, pulled on over other shoes or boots to protect them from wet.

gombeen man, n. [1. gòmbḗn man; 2. gɔ̀mbín mæn]. Ir.-Engl., fr. Mod. Ir. *gaimbin*, 'rent, interest', fr. Med. Lat. *cambium*, fr. *cambiāre*, 'to exchange', q.v. under **change (I.)**. Money-lender, usurer; often used in Ireland of a man who keeps a shop or public-house and lends money at exorbitant interest.

gombroon, n. [1. gòmbrōōn; 2. gɔ̀mbrún]. Name of town in Persia. Kind of white porcelain formerly made in Persia.

gomeral, n. [1. gómeral; 2. gɔ́mərəl]. Origin unknown. A stupid, staring, mannerless, loutish fellow; a stupid fool, idiot.

gomphosis, n. [1. gomfósis; 2. gɔmfóusis]. Gk. *gómphōsis*, 'a nailing together', fr. *gómphos*, 'nail, bolt'; cogn. w. Engl. *gum* (in the mouth). See **gum (I.) & -osis.** (anat.) An immovable union of bony parts of the body, e.g. the setting of teeth in the gums.

gomuti, n. [1. gōmōōti; 2. goumúti], fr. Malay. *gumuti*. A Malay palm with large feathery leaves, the fibres of the stalks of which are used for ropes &c., and the sap for making sugar and palm wine.

-gon, suff., fr. Gk. *-gōnos*, 'angled', fr. *gōnía*, 'angle, corner'; fr. same base as Gk. *gónu*, 'knee', Lat. *genu*, Goth. *kniu*, 'knee'. See **knee & geniculated.** In compounds denoting figures containing angles: *hexagon*, six-angled figure &c.

gonad, n. [1. gónad; 2. gɔ́næd], fr. Gk. *gonḗ*, 'generation, generating thing', fr. **g̑en-*, 'to produce, beget'. See **genus.** (biol.) A reproductive gland; the ovary of the female, testis of the male.

góndola, n. [1. góndola; 2. gɔ́ndələ]. Ital. Origin doubtful. **1.** Long, low, narrow, flat-bottomed boat used on the lagoons of Venice. **2.** The boat-shaped car attached to an air-ship.

gondolier, n. [1. gòndolḗr; 2. gɔ̀ndəlíə]. Prec. & **-ier.** Man who rows a gondola.

gone, adj. [1. gawn, gon; 2. gɔ̄n, gɔn]. O.E. *gān*, M.E. *gōn*. P.P. of **go.** Lost, ruined: *a gone case*; fated to die: *a gone man*. Phr. *a gone sensation, feeling*, one of faintness and weakness; *a gone coon*, ruined man; a dying man; dead man.

goneness, n. Prec. & **-ness.** State of exhaustion, esp. from lack of nourishment.

goner, n. [1. gáwner; 2. gɔ́nə], fr. **gone & -er.** (colloq. slang) **a** One socially, financially, ruined; **b** person who is threatened with death, imminent danger &c.

gonfalon, gonfanon, n. [1. gónfalon; 2. gɔ́nfələn]. O. Fr., fr. Ital. *gonfalone*, 'banner', fr. Gmc. source; cp. O.H.G. *gundfano*, 'banner', O.E. *gūþfana*, fr. *gund*, 'war', fr. Gmc. **gunþ-*, Aryan **gʷhn̥(t)-*, 'to kill', whence also Gk. *phónos*, 'slaughter' (fr. **gʷhon-*); *theínō*, 'I kill' (fr. **gʷhenjō*), Scrt. *hatáš*, 'kill', & Lat. *-fend-* in *dēfendere* (see **defend**); the second element is Gmc. **fano*, 'banner', q.v. under **vane.** A flag which hangs from a cross-piece, instead of being attached to a flagstaff, esp. as the banner in the Middle Ages of an Italian city state or of the Papacy.

gonfalonier, n. [1. gònfalonḗr; 2. gɔ̀nfələníə]. Prec. & **-ier.** One who carries a gonfalon; the standard-bearer, a high official of an Italian city state in the Middle Ages.

gong, n. [1. gong; 2. gɔŋ]. Malay.; imitative. Sheet of metal, or vessel of metal shaped like a pan or kettle &c., open at one side, suspended from a frame, and giving forth a powerful note on being struck with a kind of drumstick; used as mode of summons.

gonidium, n., pl. **gonidia** [1. gonídium, -ia; 2. gɔnídiəm, -iə]. Neo-Lat. dimin. formed fr. **gonad.** (biol.) The reproductive spore without distinctive sex, of such plants as lichens, algae &c.

goniometer, n. [1. gòniómeter; 2. gɔ̀niɔ́mitə], fr. Gk. *gōnía*, 'angle', & *métron*, 'measure'. See **-gon & -meter.** Instrument for measuring angles in solids, such as crystals &c.; also for measuring angle of rotation of aerial in wireless direction finder.

goniometric, adj. [1. gòniōmétrik; 2. gɔ̀nioumétrik]. Prec. & **-ic.** Connected with goniometry.

goniometry, n. [1. gòniómetri; 2. gɔ̀niɔ́mitri]. **goniometer & -y.** Theory and practice of measuring angles.

gonococcus, n., pl. **gonococci** [1. gònōkókus, -kī; 2. gɔ̀noukɔ́kəs, -kai], fr. first element in next word & Gk. *kókkos*, 'grain, seed', etymol. unknown. The micro-organism which causes gonorrhoea.

gonorrhoea, n. [1. gònorḗa; 2. gɔ̀nəríə]. Gk., fr. *gonḗ*, 'seed, that which produces, begets', fr. same base as **genus**, 'race' &c., & *hréein*, 'to flow', for **srewein*, see base **srew-*, 'to flow' &c., under **stream.** Contagious venereal disease attended with painful inflammation of urinary passage, and a morbid discharge from urethra &c.

gonorrhoeal, adj. [1. gònorḗal; 2. gɔ̀nəríəl]. Prec. & **-al.** Connected with, caused by, gonorrhoea.

good (I.), adj. [1. good; 2. gud]. O.E. *gōd*, M.E. *good* &c.; O.S. *gōd*, O.H.G. *guot*, O.N. *gōðr*, Goth. *gōþs*, 'good' &c. The word is in gradational relation to Goth. *gadiliggs*, 'relation, cousin', corresponding to O.E. *gædeling*, 'companion, kinsman'; further w. O.E. *(ġe)gada*, 'companion, associate', & *gadrian*, 'to gather, bring together' (see **gather**). The underlying idea of *good* was orig. 'joined, combined; well put together, fitting'. Cp. further O. Slav. *goditi*, 'to be agreeable', *godu*, 'time, occasion, suitable time', & Scrt. *gadhya-*, 'to hold fast' &c., for **ghadh-*. **1. a** (in physical sense) Of superior quality, excellent of its kind, satisfactory; possessing the qualities useful and necessary for its purpose: *a good road, house, knife*; *really good cloth*; *a good view* &c.; *good looks*, handsomeness; *a good family*, an ancient or aristocratic one; *good features*, well-shaped; **b** (in non-material sense) possessing qualities which appeal to the mind, gratify the taste and artistic sense &c.: *a good dictionary, textbook, sermon, argument, play*; *good literature*; *a good picture, colour*; *good manners, breeding*, polite, courteous, behaviour; **c** happy, agreeable, enjoyable, fortunate: *it is good to be rich and one's own master*; *to have a good time*. **2.** Suitable, serviceable for some specific purpose; producing favourable results in given case; beneficial, salutary, wholesome: **a** (physically) *good for the gout, for toothache*; *milk is good for children*; **b** (morally and mentally) *discipline is good for everybody*; *it is not good for a man to live alone*. Phrs. *all in good time*, at a suitable moment; *to come in good time*, punctually; *it is a good thing (that ...)*, it is fortunate. **3. a** Well and completely performed; thorough, satisfying: *to have a good meal*; *a good drink*; *what you want is a good thrashing*; *I gave him a good scolding*; *a good deal*, considerable amount; *a good while*, long time; **b** (often as intens. followed by another adj.) *good hard work*; *a good long walk*; *a good strong dose of salts*. **4.** (of persons and conduct) **a** Morally excellent, virtuous, observant of moral obligations; pious: *a good, holy, man*; *it is difficult to be good amid the temptations of the world*; *to lead a good life*; Phr. *good works*, pious acts, deeds of charity; **b** fulfilling adequately the obligations of some particular position or relation; dutiful, conscientious: *a good father and husband*; *a good king*; *a good boy*, well-behaved; *as good as gold* (esp. of children) well-behaved; **c** benevolent, kind, obliging, indulgent: *he is very good to his poorer neighbours*; *it is extremely good of you to take so much trouble*; Phrs. *be good enough to sign your name here*, form of polite request; *be good enough to hold your tongue*, peremptory command; *a good fellow*, kind-hearted, honest man; jolly companion; *my good man*, ironical or patronizing mode of address. **5.** (of persons) **a** Competent, skilled, efficient in some specified way: *good at figures, at languages, at Latin prose, at golf*; **b** (before ns. expressing an agent) capable of performing well some particular action; expert, clever: *a good rider, dancer, football-player, farmer, carpenter* &c.; **c** possessing some special form of knowledge, or intellectual quality: *a good lawyer, a good scholar, botanist* &c.; **d** suitable, qualified in some particular way for some specified functions: *a good man for the post*. **6.** (of things) **a** Sound, in perfect condition; fresh, unspoilt: *this egg is not quite good*; *meat won't remain good long in thundery weather*; **b** valid, genuine: *it is sometimes difficult to tell false money from good*; Phrs. *his word is as good as his bond*; *he as good as said so*, what he said was equivalent to; **c** strong, healthy, vigorous: *my sight is still good*; *to have good lungs*; **d** (of persons) capable of given amount of endurance; possessing requisite amount of strength and vigour; ready to undertake: *I'm good for another 10 miles if you like*; *he is good for some years more*, he will live that time; Phrs. *to be good for a hundred pounds*, to be willing and able to pay it; *a good life*, one it is safe to insure as likely to last long.

good (II.), n. O.E. *gōd*, n., 'a good thing; good action, goodness; benefit; property'. See prec. That which is good (in various senses): **1.** Moral virtue, integrity, merit; opposed to *evil, harm*: *I knew him well and could find no good in him*; *an influence for good*. Phr. *to do* *good*, perform virtuous, meritorious actions. **2.** Moral, intellectual, physical advantage; happiness, profit; cause, source, of improvement or welfare: *I am saying this for your good*; *the greatest good of the greatest number.* Phr. *what is the good of ...?*, of what use or profit?; *much good may it do you* (ironical), it won't profit you much; *to do one good*, (i.) improve him morally; (ii.) benefit his health: *the medicine has done me* (*my complaint*) *a lot of good*; *it is no good*, is useless; *to come to no good*, to land in disaster; (*gone* &c.) *for good*, permanently, for ever; *for good and all*, finally and irrevocably. **3.** (adj. as pl. n.) *The good*, good, virtuous persons; opposed to *the wicked*. **4.** (pl.) *Goods*: **a** property, possessions, esp. movables: *to steal a man's goods*; Phr. *goods and chattels*, personal belongings; **b** wares, merchandise; objects exhibited for sale: *the latest spring goods*; *leather goods* &c.; Phrs. *a lively piece of goods*, (facetious) of young woman; *to deliver the goods*, to do what you undertake or promise to do; **c** articles sent by railway other than livestock.

good-bye, interj. & n. [1. góod bí; 2. gúd bái] & [1. good bí; 2. gud bái], n. always latter. Contraction of *God be with ye.* **1.** interj. Form of salutation at parting; farewell. Phr. *to say good-bye*, to take one's farewell and depart: *I must say good-bye*, must go. **2.** n. A farewell: *the last good-byes have been spoken.*

good day, interj. & n. Form of salutation at meeting or parting.

good-for-nothing, adj. & n. [1. góod for nùthing; 2. gúd fə nàþiŋ]. **a** adj. Worthless, useless, chiefly of moral character: *a good-for-nothing rascal*; **b** n., a worthless person.

Good Friday, n. The Friday in Passion Week, observed as a fast in memory of the Crucifixion.

goodliness, n. [1. góodlines; 2. gúdlinis]. Next word & **-ness**. **a** Beauty; **b** excellence of quality.

goodly, adj. [1. góodli; 2. gúdli]. **good (I.)** & **-ly**. **a** Handsome, comely, well-favoured; **b** of large size, ample.

goodman, n. **1.** [1. góodman; 2. gúdmæn]. Master of the house, householder. **2.** [1. goodmán; 2. gudmǽn]. Husband.

good nature, n. Kindness of heart, affability; mildness and placability of temper.

good-natured, adj. [1. góod nàchurd; 2. gúd nèitʃəd], attributively; [1. good náchurd; 2. gud néitʃəd] as pred. Kind, obliging; ready to help others; not easily angered or offended.

good-naturedly, adv. Prec. & **-ly**. In a kind, obliging manner.

goodness, n. [1. góodnes; 2. gúdnis]. O.E. *gōdnes*. **good (I.)** & **-ness**. The quality of being good (in various senses). **1. a** Excellence of character; virtue, worth, piety, kindness: *goodness of heart* &c.; **b** excellence of quality: *goodness of workmanship, material* &c. **2.** Essence, strength, substance; best part of anything; esp. nourishing part of food stuffs: *to boil all the goodness out of meat.*

goods-train, n. Train which carries goods or freight only and no passengers.

good-tempered, adj. Having an amiable temper; not easily ruffled or provoked to anger.

good-temperedly, adv. In a good-tempered manner.

goodwill, n. [1. gòodwíl; 2. gùdwíl]. **1.** Kindly feeling, benevolence, amicability; kindly wishes for another's well-being. **2.** Cheerful, willing acquiescence; readiness. **3.** (law) *Goodwill of a business*, a salable if intangible commodity, consisting of the advantage which the business has acquired, and the probability of continued custom, owing to the skill with which it has been conducted, obligingness, and punctuality of those conducting it, and general reputation for competence and fair dealing.

goody (I.), n. [1. góodi; 2. gúdi]. **good (I.)** & **-y**. (obsolesc.) A sweetmeat.

goody (II.), n. Elderly female in a humble rank of life.

goody (III.) or **goody-goody**, adj. & n. [1. góodi(gòodi); 2. gúdi(gùdi)]. **1.** adj. Obtrusively and cantingly pious; weakly sanctimonious. **2.** n. Person exhibiting these qualities.

googly, n. [1. gōōgli; 2. gúgli]. Origin unknown. (cricket) Deceptive ball which breaks in from the off while delivered with a leg-break action.

gooroo, n. See **guru.**

goosander, n. [1. goosánder; 2. gūsǽndə]. Origin unknown. Large diving bird closely allied to the duck; called also *merganser.*

goose, n., pl. **geese** [1. gōōs, gēs; 2. gūs, gīs]. O.E. *gōs*, fr. **gans-*, cp. O.H.G. *gans*; cogn. w. Lat. *anser* for **hanser*; Gk. *khēn*; Scrt. *hãsaš*, 'water-bird'; all fr. Aryan base **ghans-* &c. Prob. connected w. Gk. *khás-kein*, 'to yawn', & perh. w. Lat. *hiāre*, q.v. under **hiatus. 1. a** A large web-footed bird, genus *Anser*, of the family *Anatidae*, which includes the ducks and swans, with longer neck than the duck, and habit of opening its bill wide and hissing when irritated; **b** (i.) common domestic bird of this genus; (ii.) specif., the female bird as distinguished from the *gander*. Phrs. *what is sauce for the goose is sauce for the gander*, what is fair for one is fair for the other; *all his geese are swans*, he exaggerates the advantages and merits of his belongings, or of his relations and friends; *he can't say bo to a goose*, is a timid person, lacking self-confidence; *to cook a person's goose*, to settle him. **2.** (fig.) A silly, flighty, empty-headed person. **3.** Iron used by tailors for smoothing and pressing.

gooseberry, n. [1. góozberi; 2. gúzbəri]. Prob. fr. **goose** & **berry**; Germ. name is *krausbeere*, Fr. *groseille*. **a** Large, sweet, juicy, green, golden, or red edible berry, with hard seeds and a hairy skin, growing on a thorny bush; **b** the plant or shrub producing gooseberries, *Ribes grossularia.* Phrs. *play gooseberry*, act as chaperon; *play old gooseberry with*, ruin; **c** fermented effervescing wine made from gooseberries, hence applied to various imitation champagnes made from various fruits &c.

gooseberry fool, n. Sweet dish composed of gooseberries boiled to a pulp, and mixed with cream and sugar.

goose club, n. Association formed in villages, the members of which contribute small sums periodically during several months, to provide geese for Christmas.

goose-flesh, n. Rough condition of surface of skin, arising suddenly from cold, fear &c.

goose grass, n. Trailing weed with slightly prickly adhesive leaves and stems, and seed vessels in the form of burrs, which stick to the clothes, or to animals' coats.

goose-skin, n. Goose-flesh.

goose-step, n. Balance step, *Paradeschritt*, practised in the German Army in marching, on ceremonial parades, in which the legs are alternately advanced without bending the knees; an exaggerated form of the slow march.

goosey, n. [1. gōōsi; 2. gûsi], dimin. of **goose.** Child's name for a goose; also applied playfully in mild censure, to a child.

gopher, n. [1. gōfer; 2. góufə]. Fr. *gaufre*, 'honeycomb', fr. the burrows of this animal. See **goffer.** Small American burrowing rodent somewhat resembling a large rat.

gopher-wood, n. Heb. *gōpher*. The wood of which Noah's ark was made, supposed to be cypress.

goral, n. [1. gōral; 2. gɔ̄rəl]. Native name. A horned ruminant of the Himalayas, with rough hair, allied to the goats and antelopes, resembling the European chamois.

gor-cock, n. [1. gōr kok; 2. gɔ̄ kɔk]. Etymol. of first element unknown. Male of red grouse.

Gordian, adj. [1. górdian; 2. gɔ̄diən], fr. Gordius, King of Phrygia, who tied a knot of wh. the oracle declared that he who untied it should be master of Asia; Alexander the Great, unable to undo it, severed it with his sword. Only in Phr. *Gordian knot*, baffling difficulty; *to cut the Gordian knot*, settle a difficult problem in the shortest way and by drastic means.

gore (I.), n. [1. gōr; 2. gɔ̄]. O.E. *gor*, 'dung, dirt'; also in O.H.G. & O.N., fr. Aryan **gʷhr̥-*, & perh. cogn. w. Lat. *foria*, 'excrement'. (archaic and poet.) **a** Blood that has flowed and become thickened and clotted; **b** blood generally, esp. blood shed from wounds.

gore (II.), n. & vb. trans. O.E. *gār*, 'spear', *gara*, 'triangular piece of land'; O.S., O.H.G. *gēr*; O.N. *geirr*; fr. Gmc. **gaiz-*, & cogn. w. O.E. *gād* for **gaizd-*, q.v. under **goad (I.).** Cp. also O.H.G. *geisala*, 'whip', Mod. Germ. *geissel*. The Aryan base was **ghais-* &c.; cp. Lat. *gaesum*, 'long, heavy javelin', fr. Gaul. *gaison*, 'spear', cp. O. Ir. *gae*. See also first element of **garlic. 1.** n. **a** Triangular piece of stuff let into a garment &c., to widen it, insertion, gusset; **b** (in Place-Names) spear-shaped piece of land. **2.** vb. **a** To insert a gore in (clothes &c.).

gore (III.), vb. trans. See prec. **a** (of cattle, boars &c.) To pierce, injure by piercing, with a horn, or tusk: *to be gored* (*to death*) *by a bull* &c.; **b** (of rocks) to pierce, tear (ships' side &c.), with jagged edges.

gorge (I.), n. [1. gorj; 2. gɔ̄dž]. Fr., 'throat', fr. Lat. *gurges*, 'whirlpool, abyss'; cp. also Lat. *gurgulio*, 'gullet, weasand'. The underlying idea is 'swallowing up'. The base shows partial reduplication, & is ultimately that in **gʷer-*, 'to swallow'. See **voracious** & second element of **devour.** See also **gargle** & **gurgle. 1.** Throat, obsolete except in Phr. *my gorge rises, rose*, I am (was) revolted, nauseated, filled with disgust and loathing. **2. a** Narrow valley, defile between high hills; **b** narrow entrance through the outer works of a fortified place.

gorge (II.), vb. intrans. & trans. & n. See prec. **1.** vb. **a** intrans. To eat greedily and ravenously; cram oneself with food: *to sit gorging for hours*; **b** trans., *to gorge a heavy meal* &c.; **c** (reflex.) *to gorge oneself* (*with*), to stuff oneself with food. **2.** n. Act of gorging; a copious, heavy meal, esp. one of excessive size.

gorged, adj. [1. gorjd; 2. gɔ̄džd], fr. P.P. of prec. **1.** Stuffed with food, filled to repletion and satiety. **2.** Distended, filled to bursting point: *arteries gorged with blood.* **3.** (her., of figures of animals) Depicted with a collar round the neck.

gorgeous, adj. [1. górjus; 2. gɔ̄džəs]. O. Fr. *gorgias*, n., 'a ruff for the throat'; hence, adj., 'decked out in finery; luxurious, magnificent' &c. See **gorge (I.)** & **-ous. a** Making a striking impression upon the eye; splendid, imposing, magnificent, resplendent; **b** (slang, expressing great delight and approval) capital, admirable, delectable: *gorgeous time*; *he is perfectly gorgeous as Romeo.*

gorgeously, adv. Prec. & **-ly.** In a gorgeous manner, splendidly, so as to make a fine show.

gorgeousness, n. See prec. & **-ness.** Quality of being gorgeous; splendour, magnificence.

gorget, n. [1. górjet; 2. gɔ̄džit]. Fr. *gorgete*, dimin. of **gorge. 1.** Piece of armour defending the throat; generally crescent-shaped. **2. a** Covering for the neck; collar; necklace; **b** crescent-shaped ornamental plate hung round the neck, in some armies, by officers in full-dress; **c** patch of colour different from rest of body, on the neck of a bird.

gorgio, n. [1. górjiō; 2. gɔ̄džiou]. Romany word. Gipsy name for a person not of gipsy blood.

Gorgon, n. [1. górgon; 2. gɔ̄gən]. Gk. *górgō*, 'a gorgon', fr. Gk. *gorgós*, 'terrible, fearful'; cogn. w. O. Ir. *garg*, 'savage'; & O. Slav. *groza*, 'horror, fear'. **a** (Gk. myth.) One of three females with snakes for hair, whose glance turned beholders to stone, esp. Medusa, slain by Perseus; hence, **b** (fig.) hideous, horrifying person or sight.

gorgonian, adj. [1. gorgónian ; 2. gōgóuniən]. Prec. & **-ian**. Pertaining to a Gorgon; having the property of turning men to stone.

Gorgonzola, n. [1. gòrgonzṓla ; 2. gōgənzóulə]. Name of town in Lombardy, near Milan. Kind of strong-flavoured Italian cheese, with blue mould running through it; somewhat similar to Stilton in taste and appearance.

gorilla, n. [1. goríla ; 2. gəríla]. Afr. word, 'wild man', recorded in Hanno's 'Periplus'. Largest of anthropoid apes, untamable and abnormally powerful, found in Central Africa.

gorily, adv. [1. gōrili ; 2. gōrili]. **gory & -ly.** In a gory manner.

gormandize, vb. intrans. [1. górmandīz ; 2. gōməndaiz]. **gourmand & -ize.** To eat to excess, to gorge, to feed like a glutton.

gormandizer, n. [1. górmandīzer ; 2. gōmənd-aizə]. Prec. & **-er.** A glutton, a greedy, voracious person ; one who eats to excess.

gorse, n. [1. gors ; 2. gōs]. O.E. *gorst* ; cogn. w. O.H.G. *gersta*, 'barley'. The ultimate meaning is 'prickly, spiky', fr. Aryan **gherzda-*, **ghrzd-* &c., whence also Lat. *hordeum*, fr. **horzd-*, 'barley' ; prob. connected w. Lat. *horrēre*, 'stand on end, bristle' (see **horror**); O.E. *grātan*, w. different gradational form, is prob. related. See **groats.** **1.** A spiny plant growing in form of a bush, with sweet-smelling yellow flowers ; furze. **2.** Collection of gorse bushes ; tract of land covered with these.

gory, adj. [1. gōri ; 2. gōri]. **gore (I.) & -y.** **a** Covered with gore, bloody, blood-stained ; **b** characterized by much bloodshed ; murderous : *a gory battle.*

gosh, n. [1. gosh; 2. gɔʃ]. Corrupt. of *God*. Only in *by gosh.* Vulgar, but not profane, expletive.

goshawk, n. [1. gós-hawk ; 2. gɔ́shōk]. O.E. *gōshafoc.* See **goose & hawk (I.).** Kind of large hawk, with very powerful flight.

gosling, n. [1. gózling ; 2. gɔ́zliŋ]. **goose & -ling.** The vowel of O.E. *gōs*, was shortened in M.E. before *-sl-*. Young goose.

gospel, n. [1. góspel ; 2. gɔ́spəl]. O.E. *gōdspell*, M.E. *gōdspel, gŏspel*, fr. *gōd*, see **good**, & *spell*, 'narrative, tidings' &c., see **spell (I.).** The compound is a translation of Lat. *evangelium.* See **evangel.** **1. a** One of the first four books of the New Testament, containing a narrative of the life and teaching of the Saviour : *the Gospel according to St. Luke* &c. ; Phr. *gospel oath*, one sworn upon a copy of the Gospels, and therefore inviolable ; *gospel truth*, something absolutely true ; *to take everything one hears as, for, gospel*, believe it true ; **b** specif. a part of one of the four Gospels read at the Eucharist ; hence, *gospel side*, of altar, the north side. **2.** The doctrines and principles set forth in the teaching of Jesus Christ as recorded in the Gospels ; hence, Christianity : *to preach the Gospel.* **3.** A principle, or rule of conduct &c. strongly held and proclaimed : *the gospel of health, temperance* &c.

gospelize, vb. trans. [1. góspelīz ; 2. gɔ́spəlaiz]. Prec. & **-ize.** To preach the Gospel to, instruct in principles and doctrines of Christianity ; to evangelize.

gospeller, n. [1. góspeler ; 2. gɔ́spələ]. O.E. *gōdspellere*, 'evangelist'. See prec. & **-er.** **1.** One of the four Evangelists. **2.** The priest who reads the Gospel at the celebration of the Eucharist. **3.** One who preaches the Gospel ; specif., an itinerant preacher. Phr. *hot gospeller*, ardent travelling preacher ; one who advocates any cause with enthusiasm.

gospodar, n. See **hospodar.**

gossamer, n. [1. gósamer ; 2. gɔ́səmə]. M.E. *gossomer*, fr. **goose & summer**, referring to the time of year, early November, St. Martin's summer, when geese were customarily eaten, and when the material thus named is abundant. **1.** Light, filmy, gauze-like material of fine threads of cobweb, seen floating in the air, or attached to bushes &c. **2.** Anything light and filmy ; applied by tradesmen to various light, thin substances, or to articles made of these.

gossamery, adj. [1. gósameri ; 2. gɔ́səməri]. Prec. & **-y.** Resembling, as light and thin as, gossamer.

gossip (I.), n. [1. gósip ; 2. gɔ́sip, -əp]. O.E. *godsibb*, 'sponsor', fr. **god** & *sibb*, 'relationship'. See **sib.** **1.** (obs.) **a** God-parent ; **b** intimate friend, crony, familiar. **2. a** Person given to chattering, esp. about the affairs of others ; tattler ; **b** one who spreads rumours or reports about others and their doings, without a scrupulous attention to veracity ; a chattering busybody. **3. a** Friendly, intimate conversation ; a chat : *to have a good gossip* ; **b** (esp. in unfavourable sense), talk about the business of others ; ill-natured, ill-founded, reports and rumours ; **c** personal, usually trivial, tittle-tattle in the daily press, about society people and notabilities of the hour ; also attrib. *gossip-column, gossip-writer.*

gossip (II.), vb. intrans., fr. prec. **a** To talk, hold conversation, of a casual, friendly kind ; **b** to spread ill-natured reports about other people ; to discuss the private affairs of others, indiscreetly, and maliciously.

gossipy, adj. [1. gósipi ; 2. gɔ́sipi]. Prec. & **-y.** **1.** (of persons) **a** Fond of familiar conversation and chat ; **b** inclined to discuss other people and their affairs in an unscrupulous, unfriendly manner. **2.** (of conversation) Of the nature of gossip ; trivial ; having no weight or authority ; based on, consisting of, idle rumours &c.

gossoon, n. [1. gòsṓōn ; 2. gɔsū́n]. Ir.-Engl., fr. Fr. *garçon*, 'boy', see **garçon.** (famil. and friendly) A young boy, ungrown lad, stripling.

Gossypium, n. [1. gosípium ; 2. gəsípiəm], fr. Lat. *gossypion*, 'the cotton-tree'. (bot.) Genus of malvaceous plants which includes the cotton plant.

got, vb. [1. got ; 2. gɔt]. M.E. Pret. *gat*, P.P. *geten, goten.* Pret. & P.P. of **get.**

Goth, n. [1. goth ; 2. gɔþ]. Lat. *Gothus*, Gk. *Góthos*, 'Goth'. **a** Member of ancient Germanic tribe who overran greater part of the Roman Empire ; **b** (fig.) a barbarous, uncouth person without cultivation of mind or taste.

Gothic (I.), adj. [1. góthik ; 2. gɔ́þik]. Prec. & **-ic.** **1. a** Of or pertaining to the Goths ; **b** like a Goth, hence (fig.), uncultivated, barbarous, lacking refinement of taste. **2. a** (archit.) In the Western European style of the later Middle Ages, characterized by pointed arches, clustered pillars &c. ; **b** (of script and print) having angular heavy characters like modern German type (contrasted with Roman or Italian type).

Gothic (II.), n., fr. prec. **1.** The language of the ancient Goths. **2.** Gothic architecture.

gouache, n. [1. gooáhsh ; 2. guáʃ]. Fr., fr. Ital. *guazzo.* **a** Mode of painting with water-colours mixed with gum ; **b** picture painted with such pigments.

Gouda, n. [1. góuda ; 2. gáudə]. Name of Dutch town. Small Dutch cheese.

gouge (I.), n. [1. gouj, gūj ; 2. gaudž, gūdž]. Fr., fr. L. Lat. *gubia*, wh. form occurs in Span. Origin uncertain. Tool used for making grooves, in form of a concave chisel, having cutting edges at the end, and on either side of, the hollowed blade.

gouge (II.), vb. trans., fr. prec. **1.** To cut grooves with a gouge. **2.** *Gouge out*, to prise out, dig, scoop, out ; esp. *to gouge out an eye.*

Goulard water, n. [1. gōōlárd wàwter ; 2. gūlád wɔ̄tə], fr. name of French doctor. Solution of acetate of lead ; lead lotion.

goulash, n. [1. gōōlahsh ; 2. gúlāʃ]. Germ. *gulasch*, fr. Hung. *gulyās-hus*, 'meat of a herdsman'. A rich stew of beefsteak and vegetables, flavoured with paprika &c.

gourd, n. [1. gōōrd ; 2. guəd]. Fr. *gourde*, O. Fr. *gouorde, gougorde*, fr. Lat. *cucurbita*, 'gourd'. See **cucumber.** **a** Hard-shelled, bulbous fruit of plants of the class of the melon, pumpkin, vegetable marrow &c. ; **b** vessel made from a gourd hollowed out and dried.

gourmand, n. [1. gōōrmand ; 2. gúəmənd], or as Fr. Perh. of Gmc. (Scand.) origin ; cp. O.N. *gormr*, 'ooze, mud, grounds'. Cp. O.E. *gor*, 'dung, filth'. See **gore (I.).** **a** One excessively fond of eating, and inclined to eat to excess ; a glutton ; **b** one who is fastidious about his food, one who has knowledge and discrimination in food ; more properly *gourmet.*

gourmet, n. [1. gōōrmā ; 2. gúəmei]. Fr., connected w. prec. Person who is fastidious and discriminating in what he eats and drinks ; a connoisseur in food and wine ; one who studies the fit and proper sequence of foods and drinks from the point of view at once of what pleases the palate and benefits the health.

gout n. [1. gout ; 2. gaut]. Fr. *goutte*, 'drop', fr. Lat. *gutta*, the origin of wh. is unexplained. **1.** (archaic and poet.) A drop, clot, esp. of blood. **2.** Disease due to excess of uric acid in the blood, characterized by deposits in the joints and fibres, causing swellings, tenderness, and paroxysms of pain.

gouty, adj. [1. góuti ; 2. gáuti]. Prec. & **-y.** **a** Of the nature of, caused by, gout : *gouty pains* ; **b** liable to, affected by, gout : *a gouty constitution* &c.

govern, vb. trans. & intrans. [1. gúvern ; 2. gávən]. Fr. *gouverner*, fr. Lat. *gubernāre*, 'to steer, pilot a ship ; to manage, conduct, govern', fr. Gk. *kubernân*, 'to steer ; to govern' ; cogn. w. Scrt. *kūbara-*, 'rudder, tiller'. Further relationships uncertain. **A.** trans. **1.** To direct, control, exercise authority over ; specif., to direct the public affairs of a state, nation &c., and the actions of the citizens ; to rule, whether by the administration of established laws, or by imposing an individual will. **2. a** To sway, determine actions and conduct of : *I shall be governed by the exigencies of the moment, by circumstances* &c. ; **b** to persuade, influence by appeal to reason &c. : *I will be governed by you in what I do* ; **c** to be determining motive, esp. to dominate, deprive of independence of will or judgement in action : *never let your passions govern you.* **3.** To determine, direct nature of (a process, series of events &c.) ; *similar principles govern the early history of all primitive peoples* ; *the state of weather in a given area is governed by what has happened thousands of miles away.* **4.** To control, curb, restrain, hold in subjection : *to govern one's passions* ; *one cannot completely govern one's thoughts at all times.* **5.** (gram., esp. of vbs. and preps.) To require a certain case in nouns : *to govern the dative* &c. ; to stand in a dependent relation to another word : *the object of a sentence is governed by a transitive verb.* **6.** To determine meaning of, modify bearing and force of : *the sense of the whole document is governed by the introductory clause.* **B.** intrans. To exercise the function, perform act of governing : *in Great Britain the Prime Minister is the man who really governs.*

governable, adj. [1. gúvernabl ; 2. gávənəbl]. Prec. & **-able.** Capable of being governed.

governance, n. [1. gúvernans ; 2. gávənəns]. **govern & -ance.** (archaic) Rule, dominion, control, government : '*the hearts of kings are in Thy rule and governance*'.

governess, n. [1. gúvernes ; 2. gávənis]. **govern & -ess.** **1.** (obs.) Female governor. **2.** Lady who conducts and directs the education of the young ; **a** esp. one who teaches in a private family : *my little girl does not go to school, she has a governess* ; **b** lady teacher in a school.

governing, adj. [1. gúverning ; 2. gávəniŋ], fr. Pres. Part. of **govern.** **1. a** Exercising political rule and influence in a state : *the governing classes* ; **b** exercising the functions of ruling, directing, guiding the affairs of an institution : *the governing body of a college consists of the Head and Fellows.* **2.** Having function or property of determining, predisposing &c. (in various senses) : *a governing principle* ; *a governing motive* &c.

government, n. [1. gúvernment; 2. gávənmənt]. Fr. *gouvernement*. See **govern** & **-ment**. **1. a** Act of governing, power to govern, a state: *the government of this country is in the hands of a few Ministers having the authority of the King and Parliament*; **b** act of governing an institution: *the school throve under the wise government of the headmaster.* **2.** (coll., cap.) Body of persons responsible for, and carrying on, the government of a country; the Ministers, Cabinet: *the early fall of the Government was confidently expected.* Phr. *against*, (facet.) *agin the Government*, apt to resist authority of any kind. **3. a** State; whole territory ruled by independent sovereign, or other authority; **b** a subdivision, province, of a state governed by an administrator under the supreme authority.

governmental, adj. [1. gùvernméntal; 2. gàvənméntəl]. Prec. & **-al**. Connected with government, or with a particular Government.

governor, n. [1. gúvernor; 2. gávənə]. M.E. *governour*, fr. O. Fr. *governeor*, Lat. *gubernātor*, 'steersman; ruler', fr. Lat. *guberna-*. See **govern** & **-or**. **1.** One who governs; a ruler; specif. **a** the ruler of a province or dependency of a state; **b** a member of the governing body of a hospital, public school &c. **2.** (slang) **a** One's father; **b** one's chief or employer: *the governor* [gávnə] (in both senses); **c** respectful and friendly mode of address to supposed superior (used esp. by workmen): *Look here, Governor!* = Sir. **3.** One of various devices for regulating movements and speed of machines.

governor-general, n. Governor of a colony or dominion; viceroy.

governor-generalship, n. Office, status, of a governor-general.

governorship, n. [1. gúvernorship; 2. gávənəʃip]. **governor** & **-ship**. Office, status, of a governor.

gowan, n. [1. góuan; 2. gáuən]. Origin doubtful; Skeat suggests connexion w. O.N. *gulr*, 'yellow', orig. applied on account of the colour to the marigold and buttercup. (Scots) The daisy.

gowk, n. [1. gouk; 2. gauk], fr. O.N. *gaukr*, 'cuckoo'; cogn. w. O.E. *ġēac*, 'cuckoo'. (north. provinc.) **a** Cuckoo; **b** a stupid, feckless person.

gown, n. & vb. trans. [1. goun; 2. gaun]. M.E., fr. O. Fr. *goune*, fr. L. Lat. *gunna*, 'a skin, fur; fur garment'; a Celt. word, cp. W. *gwn*. Prob. fr. **vosna*, the first syll. of wh. is cogn. w. Lat. *vestis*, 'robe' &c. See **vest** (I.). **1.** n. **a** A loose flowing garment; **b** a woman's dress; **c** a robe worn by members of a university, indicating the wearer's academic status. Phr. *town and gown*, city and university; **d** official robe worn by mayors, aldermen &c.; **e** robe of barrister worn in court: *in wig and gown*; *silk gown*, that of King's Counsel. **2.** vb. To clothe with a gown.

gownsman, n. [1. góunzman; 2. gáunzmən]. A member of a university, esp. one in residence; contrasted with *townsman*.

goyim, n. pl. [1. góiyim; 2. gɔ́ijim]. Heb., 'the nations'. The Gentiles; all non-Jewish peoples; in Yiddish abbreviated as *goy*, a non-Jew, Christian.

Graafian follicle or **vesicle**, n. [1. gráhfian; 2. gráfiən]. Named after de Graaf (d. 1673), Dutch anatomist. One of two small sacs which contain the eggs in the ovary of mammals.

graal, n. See **grail**.

grab (I.), vb. trans. [1. grab; 2. græb]. Cp. Swed. *grabba*, 'seize'; related to **grasp**, **grip** &c. **1.** (familiar and rather vulg.) To snatch, clutch, seize suddenly and rudely; to lay hold of: *he grabbed the purse and bolted*; (also absol.) *don't grab.* **2.** (fig.) To take possession of unscrupulously and avariciously: *A did the work and B grabbed the credit.*

grab (II.), n., fr. prec. **1.** A sudden snatch, hasty clutch: *to make a grab at a rope* &c. **2.** Mechanical device for seizing and lifting heavy weights.

grabber, n. [1. gráber; 2. grǽbə]. **grab** (I.) & **-er**. **a** One who grabs; **b** a greedy, avaricious person.

grace (I.), n. [1. grās; 2. greis]. M.E., fr. O. Fr. *grace*, fr. Lat. *grātia*, 'favour experienced by oneself, love &c.; charm, beauty, loveliness; favour, kindness shown to another; thanks, gratitude'; cogn. w. Scrt. *gūrtiš*, 'praise', *gṛṇāti*, 'he sings, praises, announces'; Lith. *girti*, 'to praise, celebrate'. Further connexions are doubtful & much disputed. **1.** (material sense) Pleasing, attractive quality; elegance; **a** (of form) refinement, symmetry, just proportion, harmony; **b** (of movement) ease, smoothness, delicacy, and dignity: *grace of bearing, carriage, action, deportment.* **2.** (of liter. and other style, and modes of expression) Elegance, polish, felicity, refinement; skilful, suitable, and congruous arrangement of parts; charm arising from what are felt to be the most suitable words &c. arranged in most agreeable order. **3. a** Air, manner, degree of willingness or obligingness, with which something is done; Phrs. *with a good grace*, pleasantly, readily; *with a bad, ill, grace*, ungraciously, churlishly, reluctantly; *to have the grace to do something*, the good manners, decent feeling necessary; **b** (in pl.) *graces*, collection, combination, of charming, delightful qualities of body, mind, manner; pleasant ways, attractive qualities of appearance, behaviour, movement &c.: *every lover sees a thousand graces in the beloved object*; Phr. *airs and graces*, affected habits of speech and manner; mannerisms, foppery; false refinements. **4. a** Favour, goodwill, willingness to grant something: *to sue for grace*; Phr. *to be in a person's good graces*, to be favourably regarded by him; **b** kindness, clemency, mercy; respite; esp. in Phrs. *an act of grace*, one done out of pure kindness, without any obligation existing; *to grant a week's grace*, to allow an extra week for the performance of some obligation after its performance has legally become due; *days of grace*, days allowed beyond appointed time in which a bill of exchange &c. must be met. **5.** (theol.) **a** Divine clemency, favour, and mercy towards mankind; Phr. *by the Grace of God, of Great Britain &c., King &c.*, part of the style of a sovereign of Great Britain; **b** state of acceptance and reconciliation with God: *a state of grace*; **c** a virtue, excellence of nature coming from God: *the grace of charity, humility &c.*; Phr. *the, this, year of grace*, (followed by date) the year of Our Lord. **6.** Form of thanksgiving said or sung before and after meals. **7.** A decree, act &c., by a government, or governing body of an institution; specif., one granting a privilege of some kind, e.g. those enacted by the Universities of Oxford and Cambridge. **8.** Form in addressing, or referring to, a duke or duchess, or an archbishop: *His, Her, Your, Grace.* **9.** (mus.) An added embellishment consisting of a flourish or trill &c. not forming essential part of the air. **10.** (class. mythol.) *The (three) Graces*, sister goddesses, represented as lovely maidens, closely associated with the Muses; Aglaia, Euphrosyne, Thalia.

grace (II.), vb. trans., fr. prec. To lend grace, give a charm to, make worthier; to adorn: *her presence graced the occasion*; *cheerfulness and goodwill graced the board, banquet*; *a character graced by every virtue.*

grace-cup, n. **1.** Cup used for drinking a toast at end of a banquet. **2.** Final drink, usually accompanied by a health or toast, immediately before departure.

graceful, adj. [1. grásfool; 2. gréisf(ə)l]. **grace** (I.) & **-ful**. Possessing, exhibiting, grace (in various senses); **a** of bodily and material form, outline, movement; **b** of thought and expression.

gracefully, adv. Prec. & **-ly**. In a graceful manner.

graceless, adj. [1. gråsles; 2. gréislis]. **grace** (I.) & **-less**. **a** Lacking spiritual grace; reprobate, depraved; **b** wanting grace or decency: *a graceless rogue.*

gracelessly, adv. Prec. & **-ly**. In a graceless manner.

grace-note, n. (mus.) A flourish or trill upon a note, given as an additional embellishment but not essential to the air.

gracile, adj. [1. grásil; 2. grǽsail]. Lat. *gracilis*, 'slender; meagre, scanty'; for earlier **cracilis*, cp. Lat. *cracens*, 'slender'; cogn. w. Scrt. *kṛśáš*, 'thin, weak'; Lith. *kárszati*, 'to be very old, to age'. Further connexions doubtful. (rare) **a** Slender, thin; **b** (by association with *grace*) elegantly slim and slender.

gracility, n. [1. grasíliti; 2. græsíliti]. Prec. & **-ity**. (rare) Quality of being gracile.

gracious, adj. [1. gráshus; 2. gréiʃəs]. O. Fr. *gracios* &c., fr. Lat. *grātiōsus*, 'enjoying favour; obliging'. See **grace** (I.) & **-ous**. **1.** (archaic in physical sense) Doing good: '*A gracious rain*'. **2. a** (archaic) Full of blessings: '*So hallow'd and so gracious is the time*' (of Christmas) (Shakespeare); **b** specif. of God, clement, merciful. **3.** (of persons, manner) Urbane, affable, conciliatory, winning; specif., conventionally of the King or Queen: *his gracious Majesty* &c. **4.** In exclamatory Phrs. *Gracious*, (orig. *Gracious God!*), *Gracious me!*, *Gracious Heaven!*, *Good Gracious!*

graciously, adv. Prec. & **-ly**. **a** In a gracious, winning, affable manner; **b** as an act of grace; benevolently, favourably.

graciousness, n. See prec. & **-ness**. Quality of being gracious; benignity, affability, amiability.

grackle, n. [1. grákl; 2. grǽkl]. Lat. *graculus*, 'jackdaw', of imitative origin. Indian bird of the starling family; the mynah.

gradate, vb. intrans. & trans. [1. gradát; 2. grədéit], fr. *grad-*, as in **grade** (I.), & **-ate**. Prob. back-formation fr. **gradation**. **1.** intrans. (of colours &c., or fig. of other things) To shade off, pass by insensible degrees, one into the other. **2.** trans. To cause to shade one into the other; arrange colours so that they do this.

gradation, n. [1. gradáshun; 2. grədéiʃən]. Lat. *gradātiōn-(em)*, 'that which goes up or down by regular intervals; a staircase'. See **grade** (I.) & **-ation**. **1.** Act, process, of grading; condition of being graded. **2.** A gradual and imperceptible shading off of one colour into another; gradual passage from one condition, quality, degree &c. into another. **3.** (philol.) Name given to the interchange of vowels observed in words from the same original base, caused by difference in the position of accent, or in the tone, in Primitive Aryan, and preserved in all the derived languages. Gradation, called *ablaut* by German philologists, affects both the quality of vowels, as in English *write, wrote*, and the quantity, as in Latin *sĕd-ēre*, 'to sit', compared with *sēd-i*, 'I sat'.

gradational, adj. [1. gradáshunal; 2. grədéiʃənəl]. Prec. & **-al**. Connected with, of the nature of, gradation (in various senses).

grade (I.), n. [1. grād; 2. greid]. Fr., fr. Lat. *gradus*, 'step, degree'. See **gradus**. **1.** Step, stage, degree; **a** (in rank) *a major in the army is one grade higher than a captain*; **b** (in quality, value) *a poor grade of oats* &c.; *a high grade of intelligence*; **c** (in proficiency, mental acquirements) specif., *higher grade schools.* **2.** Variety in animals, produced by cross-breeding. **3.** (philol.) One of the various possible forms in which the vowel of a base in an Aryan language may appear in a given word; thus O.E. *wrīt-(an)*, 'to write', is called the Strong, or Full Grade, because the *ī* (earlier *ei*) occurred in Aryan only when the chief stress fell upon the syllable containing it; *wrĭt-(en)*, *(-on)*, P.P. & Pret. pl., is known as the Weak, or Reduced Grade, because the old diphthong was 'reduced' to *ĭ* when it was unstressed, or weakly stressed. **4.** Gradient.

grade (**II.**), vb. trans., fr. prec. **1.** To classify, arrange in groups, or in successive order, according to varying rank, quality, character &c. **2.** To improve stock, in cattle breeding, by crossing with a better breed; also *grade up*. **3.** To reduce gradient, in a road &c.

-grade, suff., fr. Lat. *gradi*, 'to walk'. See **gradus.** (zool.) Suffix denoting mode of walking; e.g. *plantigrade*, an animal that walks flat on the soles of its feet.

gradient (**I.**), adj. [1. grádient; 2. gréidiənt]. Fr., Lat. *gradient-(em)*, Pres. Part. of *gradīri*, 'to go, walk'. See **gradus.** **1. a** Walking, moving along; **b** capable of walking. **2.** (her.) Shown as walking.

gradient (**II.**), n., fr. prec. **1.** Degree of slope, upwards or downwards, in a road, railway track &c. **2.** Amount of rise or fall in thermometer in varying temperature.

gradin(e), n. [1. grádin; 2. gréidin]. Fr. *gradin*, fr. Ital. *gradino*, dimin. of Lat. *gradus*, 'step'. See **gradus.** **1.** One of a series of low steps rising one above another, as in an amphitheatre. **2.** Shelf or ledge at the back of an altar on which candlesticks &c. are placed.

gradual (**I.**), adj. [1. grájooal, grádūal; 2. grǽdžuəl, grǽdjuəl]. Fr. *graduel*, fr. Lat. *gradu-*, stem of *gradus*, 'step, stage'. See **gradus** & **-al.** **a** Coming on, developing, slowly and by degrees; not sudden and instantaneous in manifestation; **b** sloping upwards or downward in a gentle, progressive, rise or fall: *a gradual ascent, fall, curve* &c.

gradual (**II.**), n. L. Lat. *graduale*, adj. neut. See prec. **1.** Antiphon sung, formerly from the altar steps, after the Epistle. **2.** Book for use of the choir, containing musical portions of the Mass.

gradually, adv. **gradual** (**I.**) & **-ly.** By degrees; in slow, steady progression.

graduate (**I.**), n. [1. grájooat, grádūat; 2. grǽdžuit, grǽdjuit], fr. Med. Lat. *graduātus* formed fr. *gradu-*, as in **gradual** (**I.**), & **-ate. a** One who has taken a degree in a university; **b** one who has passed all examinations after a course of training in one of a certain kind of college; esp. the Staff College at Camberley.

graduate (**II.**), vb. trans. & intrans. [1. grájooāt; grádūāt; 2. grǽdžueit, grǽdjueit]. See prec. **1.** trans. **a** To classify in order of degree; **b** to mark off a vessel, dial &c., so as to record relative degrees or measures: *graduated cup* (for measuring medicine). **2.** intrans. To take a degree, esp. the first, or Bachelor's degree at a university; to pass the examination at the end of a course at the Staff College.

graduation, n. [1. gràjooáshun, gràdūáshun; 2. grǽdžuéiʃən, grǽdjuéiʃən]. Med. Lat. *graduātiōn-(em)*. See prec. & **-ion. 1.** Act of taking an academic degree. **2.** Act or process of graduating, state of being graduated; **a** marking off of degrees of colour, intensity, measure &c.; **b** act of arranging, classifying, according to quality, character &c. **3.** Indication of measure, amount &c.: *the graduations on a medicine glass* &c.

gradus, n. [1. grádus; 2. gréidəs]. Lat., for *gradus ad Parnassum*, 'step to Parnassus'. The Lat. word means 'step, pace; stage, position; that on which one steps, a stair; a degree, rank' &c.; cogn. w. Goth. *griþs*, 'step, stage'; O. Slav. *gredą*, 'I come'; cp. further Scrt. *gṛdhyati*, 'he seeks, desires', orig. 'makes for'; the sense 'steps out towards' is once found. This fig. use of the base occurs also in Goth. *grēdus*, 'greed, hunger'; O.E. *grǣd*. See further under **greedy.** Book used by schoolboys to help in writing Latin verses, consisting of lists of Latin synonyms with all the quantities marked.

Graecism, Grecism, n. [1. grḗsizm; 2. grísizəm], fr. Fr. *grécisme*. See **Greek** & **-ism. a** A Greek idiom, form of expression, as used in another language; **b** spirit, influence of Greek art, and culture; imitation of this, Hellenism.

Graecize, Grecize, vb. trans. [1. grḗsīz; 2. grísaiz]. See prec. & **-ize.** To give a Greek form to; to Hellenize.

Graeco-, Greco-, pref. Form used in compounds, fr. Lat. *Graecus*, see **Greek**, as *Graeco-Roman* &c.

graffito, n. [1. grafḗtō; 2. grǽfítou]. Ital., dimin. of *graffio*, 'a scratching', fr. Gk. *gráphein*, 'to scratch; to write'. See **graph.** Ancient Roman inscription or design, rudely scratched on the walls of tombs, buildings &c.

graft (**I.**), n. [1. grahft; 2. grāft]. M.E., fr. O. Fr. *graffe*, 'a pencil', fr. Lat. *graphium*, Gk. *grapheîon*, 'writing stylus'. See **graph.** Named from resemblance of the slip or scion of plant used to a pointed pencil. The final *-t* is developed in 16th or 17th cent. Such 'parasitic' consonants are not infrequent in writings fr. 15th cent. onwards. **1. a** Living shoot, scion, or bud, from a tree, inserted into another stock to form a new growth; **b** process of making a graft. **2.** (surg.) A piece of living tissue, as skin, bone, or portion of gland, taken from a person or animal, and inserted to replace injured tissue or deficient gland (see vb., sense **1, b**). **3.** (Am. slang, origin doubtful, but probably the same word in extended use) **a** Dishonest dealing with a view to profit, esp. in political and municipal affairs; jobbery and corruption; **b** a swindle.

graft (**II.**), vb. trans. & intrans., fr. prec. **A.** trans. **1. a** To insert a living shoot, or bud, from a plant into another stock by a slit in the bark, or in the wood itself; to make a graft in; **b** (surg.) to introduce piece of sound skin or other tissue, taken from the same or another individual, into an injured part, where under favourable conditions it becomes incorporated in its new surroundings. **2.** (fig.) To attach one thing to another, so that they become inseparable: *to graft pagan rites upon Christian usage*. **B.** intrans. **1.** To practise grafting. **2.** (slang) To practise graft; engage in jobbery and corruption.

grafter, n. [1. gráhfter; 2. grā́ftə]. Prec. & **-er. a** One who grafts, a swindler; **b** (Am. slang) corrupt official &c.

grafting, n. [1. gráhfting; 2. grā́ftiŋ]. **graft** (**II.**) & **-ing. a** (hort.) Process of making grafts; method of propagating plants by this means; **b** (surg.) similar process in tissues of the body.

grail, graal, n. [1. grāl; 2. greil]. O. Fr. *graal*, *greal*; perh. fr. Low Lat. *gradalis*, *gradale*, orig. prob. a vessel divided into compartments for different kinds of food; usually *san greal* &c., 'holy dish'. The etymol. is very dubious. The supposed vessel in which Joseph of Arimathea collected the Saviour's blood; an object of quest for the Knights of the Round Table, according to Arthurian Legend.

grain (**I.**), n. [1. grān; 2. grein]. Fr., fr. Lat. *grānum*, 'grain, seed, small kernel', cogn. w. O. Slav. *zrŭno*, 'corn', & w. Goth. *kaurn*, O.E. *corn*. See **corn** (**I.**). The word is further connected by etymologists w. Scrt. *gīrṇáš*, 'crumbled up, decayed, rotten, old'; the Aryan base **ĝerā-* seems to have meant 'liable to crumble, brittle; worn, old' &c. Gk. *gérōn*, 'an old man' (see **gerontocracy**), is fr. same base, & the more primitive sense of 'rubbing, breaking down, pulverizing' &c., is seen in Goth. *(ga)-krōtōn*, 'to grind, pound, shatter'. **1. a** Small, hard seed of plant; hence, **b** (coll.) cereal produce, e.g. corn, rye, maize &c.; **c** small, round body: *grain of shot*; esp. tiny particle of sand, sugar, dust, ground coffee &c.; Phr. *to receive with a grain of salt*, make a mental reservation, show caution in accepting; **d** (in non-material sense) infinitesimal amount, scintilla, trace: *grain of sense, comfort, courage*. **2.** Smallest unit of apothecaries' ($\frac{1}{20}$ scruple) and troy ($\frac{1}{24}$ dwt.) weights. **3. a** Direction, characteristic distribution, of fibres or particles in wood, leather, stone &c.; texture: *fine, coarse, grain*; Phrs. (fig.) *against the grain*, repugnant, distasteful, contrary to tastes and feelings; *in grain*, by nature, fundamentally; **b** rough, granular surface: *grain side of leather*. **4.** (obs.) **a** Cochineal dye; **b** crimson or purple dye; **c** any fast, permanent dye: *to dye in grain*, dye a fast colour.

grain (**II.**), vb. trans., fr. prec. **a** To reduce to fine particles; **b** to give a granular surface to (leather &c.); **c** to paint (wood, marble &c.) in imitation of fibres, or veining.

grains, n., pl. used as sing. [1. grānz; 2. greinz], fr. O.N. *grein*, 'division, branch, fork'; cp. Swed. *gren*, 'branch'. Fish-spear, or harpoon, with barbed prongs.

Grallatores, n. pl. [1. gràlatṓrēz; 2. grǽlətṓrīz]. Lat. *grallātor*, 'stilt walker', fr. *grallae*, 'stilts', for **gradlae*, & derived fr. *gradus* &c., 'a step'. See **gradus.** Wading-birds, with long legs, necks, and bills, such as cranes, snipe, herons &c.

grallatorial, adj. [1. gràlatṓrial; 2. grǽlətṓriəl]. Prec. & **-al.** Belonging to the class of wading-birds.

gralloch, n. & vb. trans. [1. grálok; 2. grǽlək]. Gael. *grealach*, 'intestines'. **1.** n. Entrails, offal, of a deer. **2.** vb. To remove the entrails &c. from a dead deer.

gram (**I.**), n. [1. gram; 2. græm]. Port. *grão*, fr. Lat. *grānum*, q.v. under **grain** (**I.**). Chick-pea, used as fodder.

gram (**II.**), n. See **gramme.**

-gram, suff., fr. Gk. *grámma*, 'something written, a letter', fr. base of *gráphein*, 'to write', q.v. under **graph.** Suff. used in compounds derived fr. Gk., such as *epigram*; in new formations fr. Gk. elements, *telegram*; & modern formations of mixed origin, *cablegram* &c.

grama (**grass**), n. [1. gráhma; 2. grā́mə]. Span., 'a kind of grass', fr. Lat. *grāmen*, 'grass'. See **gramin-.** Pasture grass in Western U.S.

gramary(e), n. [1. grámari; 2. grǽməri]. M.E. *gramery*, 'skill in grammar, learning'; hence 'skill in magic'. See **grammar**, & **glamour.** (archaic, restored by Scott) Magic.

gramercy, interj. [1. gramérsi; 2. grəmə́si]. Fr. *grand-merci*, 'great thanks'. (obs.) **a** Thanks; **b** as exclamation of surprise.

gramin(i)-, pref. Lat. stem of *grāmen*, 'grass'; the etymol. is doubtful; perh. fr. **gras-men*, the first element being possibly cogn. w. Gk. *gráein* for **grasein*, 'to gnaw, nibble', cp. Gk. *grástis*, 'green fodder'; Scrt. *grásati*, 'he swallows, devours'; not connected w. **grass** & **grow.** Occurring in various compounds.

graminaceous, adj. [1. gràmináshus; 2. grèimınéiʃəs]. Prec. & **-aceous.** Like grass; grassy.

gramineous, adj. [1. grāmíneus; 2. greimíniəs]. **gramin-** & **-eous.** Pertaining to grass; grass-like; belonging to the botanical family of the grasses.

graminiferous, adj. [1. gràminíferus; 2. grèimınífərəs]. **gramin-** & **-ferous.** Yielding, bearing, grass.

graminivorous, adj. [1. gràminívorus; 2. grèimınívərəs]. **gramin-** & **-vorous.** Grass-eating, feeding on grass.

grammalogue, n. [1. grámalog; 2. grǽməlɔg]. See **-gram** & **-logue.** Word represented by a logogram, q.v.

grammar, n. [1. grámar; 2. grǽmə]. M.E. *gramer*, O. Fr. *gramaire*; cp. L. Lat. *grammatica*, Gk. *grammatikḗ* (*tékhnē*) 'grammar', wh. wd. not account for our form. This must have been formed, perh. in Fr. itself, fr. the base *gram-* (see **-gram**), & suff. *-aire*, fr. Lat. *-ārius*, q.v. under **-ary. 1.** Branch of learning dealing with language and its analysis, from several points of view; the term includes the study of the pronunciation of a language, its inflexions, or other means used to express the relations of words to each other in sentences; syntax, and the principles of word-formation; it is also applied **a** to the purely descriptive study of the phenomena presented by a given language at a given moment; **b** to the historical treatment of these, which exhibits the changes which take place in a language from age to age; **c** to a study based on a comparison of the phenomena existing in several languages sprung from a common ancestor. **2.** A treatise dealing with any of the above aspects of language, or of a language. **3. a** The elements of a subject of learning; **b** (more rarely) a treatise of an elementary character on one of these.

grammarian, n. [1. gramárian; 2. grəméəriən]. Prec. & **-ian.** Student of grammar; one well versed in the study; writer upon any of the various aspects and kinds of grammar.

grammarless, adj. [1. grámarles; 2. grǽməlis]. **grammar** & **-less.** Devoid of grammar; lacking a knowledge, exhibiting ignorance, of grammar; illiterate.

grammar school, n. Formerly a school where Latin was taught; (at present) a middle-class endowed school ranking below one of the great Public Schools in popular estimation and standing, at which all subjects are taught up to the university stage.

grammatical, adj. [1. gramátikl; 2. grəmǽtikl], fr. Gk. *grammatik-(ós)*, 'skilled in letters, in grammar', fr. *grammat-*, stem of *grámma*, 'letter' &c., see **-gram**, & **-ic** & **-al. 1.** Of or pertaining to grammar. **2.** (of speech and style) In accordance with the rules of grammar; correct.

grammatically, adv. Prec. & **-ly. 1.** From the point of view of the science of grammar. **2.** In accordance with the rules of grammar; correctly.

grammaticalness, n. See prec. & **-ness.** Quality of being in accordance with the rules of grammar.

grammaticaster, n. [1. gramátikaster; 2. grəmǽtikæstə]. *Grammatic-*, as in **grammatical**, & **-aster.** A pettifogging grammarian; a pedant.

grammaticize, vb. trans. & intrans. [1. gramátisīz; 2. grəmǽtisaiz]. *Grammatic-*, see prec., & **-ize. 1.** trans. **a** To make grammatical; **b** to reduce to the rules of grammar. **2.** intrans. To treat of, discuss, points of grammar.

gramme, n. [1. gram; 2. græm]. Fr., fr. Gk. *grámma*, 'writing, written character, small weight', same word as the suff. **-gram.** Metric unit of weight (=1 cubic centimetre of water, or 15·43 grains troy).

gramophone, n. [1. grámofōn; 2. grǽməfōun]. Gk. *grámma*, 'letter, record', see prec., & *phōnḗ*, 'sound', q.v. under **phone (I.).** Machine, based on the phonograph, which records and reproduces musical and other sounds by means of a needle attached to a vibrating metal plate, the point of which touches a revolving disc.

grampus, n. [1. grámpus; 2. grǽmpəs]. O. Fr. *graspeis*, 'fat fish', fr. Lat. *crassus piscis* (see **crass**); cp. also Span. *gran pez*, 'large fish', fr. Lat. *grandis piscis*, 'large fish' (see **grand (I.) & piscary).** Spouting cetacean, *Orca gladiator* or the killer, belonging to the dolphin family. Phr. (colloq.) *to blow, snore, like a grampus*, snore loudly.

granadilla, n. [1. grànadíla; 2. grænədílə]. Span., dimin. of *granada*, 'pomegranate'. Fruit of kinds of passion-flower.

granary, n. [1. gránari; 2. grǽnəri]. Lat. *grānārium*, 'granary'. See **grain (I.)** & **-ary. 1.** Storehouse for grain. **2.** (by transf.) Country, region, rich in grain, supplying it to other countries: *Canada, the granary of the Empire* &c.

grand (I.), adj. [1. grand; 2. grænd]. M.E., fr. O. Fr., fr. Lat. *grandis*, 'full grown, large, tall; important, powerful', fr. **gʷrendh-* &c.; cp. Gk. *bréntʰos*, 'proud', *brenthúomai*, 'bear oneself proudly'. The orig. meaning of the base seems to be 'breast', cp. O. Slav. *grădĭ*, 'breast', & O. Ir. *bruinne*, O.W. *bronn* in same sense. The derived meanings have perh. sprung, on the one hand, fr. the idea of having the breasts developed, hence, 'full grown', &, on the other, fr. that of bearing the chest swelled out, as though with pride and self-importance. The essential meaning in English is magnificent, splendid, impressive, whence various shades of meaning are derived. **1.** (in material sense) **a** Magnificent, splendid, imposing: *the Lord Mayor's show was a grand spectacle*; *the view from here is grand*; **b** (colloq.) magnificent in appearance; esp. richly, finely, smartly, gaily dressed: *the General was very grand in full review order*; *where are you off to in those grand clothes?*; **c** large, and splendid; luxurious, handsome; on a scale of magnificence: *he lives in a grand house, and in grand style.* **2.** (of persons and their manners) **a** Important, distinguished: *the place was full of peers and ambassadors, and other grand people*; *he has the grand air, manner*; *a grand lady*; **b** expressing a consciousness of importance; self-important, lofty, haughty; pretentious: *he was much too grand to speak to his old friends*; *you're very grand no doubt, but you might answer a civil question.* **3.** (in moral sense) Impressive; possessing and expressing moral or intellectual greatness; august, majestic: *a grand character*; *a grand conception, achievement*; Phrs. *the grand style, in the grand manner*, (of literary and artistic productions) lofty, majestic style, suited to imposing themes. **4.** Most important, predominant, principal; (variously used) **a** *the grand question we have to decide is . . .*; *a grand mistake*; **b** main, largest among several; serving chief purposes; used on important occasions: *grand staircase, saloon*; **c** full, complete: *grand opera, grand orchestra.* **5.** (colloq.) Delightful, highly satisfactory and enjoyable: *to have a grand time*; *we had grand weather for our trip*; *it will be grand if you can come.*

grand (II.), n. Short for *grand piano.*

grandad, n. See **gran(d)-dad.**

grandam, n. [1. grándam; 2. grǽndæm]. **grand** & **dam.** Grandmother; old woman.

Grand Assize, n. (hist.) Species of extraordinary trial by jury, instituted by Henry II., in which, at the choice of the defendant, an action was decided by twelve knights instead of by battle.

grand-aunt, n. Aunt of either of one's parents; great-aunt.

grandchild, n. [1. grán(d)chīld; 2. grǽn(d)tʃaild]. Child of son or daughter.

Grand Cross, n. Highest rank in various orders of knighthood.

gran(d)-dad, n. [1. grándad; 2. grǽndæd]. Childish word, used affectionately by older persons, for grandfather.

granddaughter, n. [1. grándàwter; 2. grǽndɔ̀tə]. Daughter of one's child.

Grand Duchess, n. **a** Consort of a Grand Duke; **b** lady who is the ruler of a Grand Duchy in her own right; **c** the daughter of a Czar of Russia.

Grand Duchy, n. Independent state whose sovereign is a Grand Duke or Duchess.

Grand Duke, n. **a** Sovereign of a Grand Duchy; **b** son of a Czar of Russia.

grandee, n. [1. grandḗ; 2. grændí]. Sp. *grande*, 'great'. See **grand. a** Nobleman of the highest rank in Spain or Portugal; **b** an important personage.

grandeur, n. [1. gránjur, grándūr; 2. grǽndʒə; grǽndjuə]. Fr. See **grand. 1. a** Material splendour, brilliance; visible magnificence; **b** power, greatness of position; **c** solemn, impressive, external beauty: *grandeur of mountain scenery.* **2. a** (of persons) Moral greatness and impressiveness, augustness: *grandeur of character, nature*; **b** (of ideas &c.) greatness, magnitude, breadth; impressive range: *grandeur of conception, design* &c.

grandfather, n. [1. grándfàhdher; 2. grǽndfàðə]. **a** Father of either of one's parents; **b** a venerable old man.

grandfatherly, adj. Like, characteristic of, a grandfather; kind and solicitous in manner, benignant.

grandfather's clock, n. Large, standing clock in a tall narrow case, worked with weights and a pendulum.

grandiloquence, n. [1. grandílokwens; 2. grændíləkwəns]. Lat. See next word. **a** Act or habit of using big words and an imposing, pompous style; **b** pomposity of expression; bombast, boasting.

grandiloquent, adj. [1. grandílokwent; 2. grændíləkwənt]. The Lat. word is *grandiloquus*, 'lofty in speech; bombastic'; fr. *grandi-*, 'great' &c., see **grand (I.)**, & the base of *loqui*, 'to speak', q.v. under **locution.** The Engl. word has been formed w. the suff. of Pres. Part. *-ent-(em)*. **1.** (of persons) **a** Using high-flown language, fond of long words and pompous sentences; **b** boastful, bombastic, in speech. **2.** (of style) Exhibiting and expressing these qualities.

grandiloquently, adv. Prec. & **-ly.** In a grandiloquent manner.

grandiose, adj. [1. grándiōs; 2. grǽndious]. Fr. See **grand** & **-ose. a** Lofty, sublime, imposing; **b** (in bad sense) pretentious, affecting sham grandeur; bombastic, high-flown.

grandiosely, adv. Prec. & **-ly.** In a grandiose manner.

Grandisonian, adj. [1. gràndisṓnian; 2. grændisóuniən], fr. *Sir Charles Grandison*, hero of Richardson's novel of that name. Resembling this character, that is, possessing a chivalrous spirit, courtly manners, and irreproachable moral character.

grand juror, n. Member of a grand jury.

grand jury, n. Jury of persons returned by the High Sheriff, whose business is to hear a brief summary of the evidence to be presented against persons charged with crime, and to decide whether it is sufficient to justify the accused being brought to trial at the Assizes.

Grand Lodge, n. Principal and governing body of certain associations, such as the Freemasons, Orangemen &c.

grandly, adv. [1. grándli; 2. grǽndli]. **grand** & **-ly.** In a grand way.

grandmam(m)a, n. [1. grán(d)mamàh; 2. grǽn(d)məmā̀]. Familiarly abbreviated to *grandma* [1. gránmah; 2. grǽnmā]. Used by children in addressing, and referring to, a grandmother; the longer form was also often used formerly by grown-up persons.

Grand Master, n. **1.** (hist.) The chief, head of a military order of knighthood. **2.** Supreme head of all Freemasons in a country under the jurisdiction of a Grand Lodge; also Head of the Orangemen.

grandmother, n. [1. grán(d)mudher; 2. grǽn(d)maðə]. Mother of either of one's parents. Phr. *to teach one's grandmother*, proffer superfluous advice and help to one more experienced and skilled than oneself.

grandmotherly, adj. Prec. & **-ly. a** Like a grandmother, characteristic of a grandmother; chiefly **b** (fig., and contemptuous) inclined to be fussily interfering and insistent upon petty, trivial details: *grandmotherly legislation.*

grand-nephew, n. Son of one's nephew or niece.

grandness, n. [1. grándnes; 2. grǽndnis]. **grand (I.)** & **-ness.** Quality of being grand.

grand-niece, n. Daughter of one's nephew or niece.

grandpapa, n. [1. grán(d)papàh; 2. grǽn(d)pəpā̀]. Familiarly abbreviated to *grandpa* [1. gránpah; 2. grǽnpā]. Used familiarly but respectfully for grandfather.

grandparent, n. [1. grán(d)pàrent; 2. grǽn(d)pèərənt]. Parent's parent; grandfather or grandmother.

grandparentage, n. [1. grán(d)pàrentij; 2. grǽn(d)pèərəntidʒ]. Prec. & **-age. a** Condition of a grandparent; **b** that part of one's ancestry represented by one's grandparents.

grand piano, n. Large harp-shaped piano, in which the strings are parallel to the ground.

grand quarter, n. (her.) One of the primary quarters of shield when quartered, or divided into four equal parts.

grand quartering, n. (her.) Quarterings on the grand quarter.

grandsire, n. [1. grán(d)sīr; 2. grǽn(d)saiə]. **1.** (archaic) **a** Grandfather; **b** ancestor, forbear. **2.** Form of peal, rung with an odd number of bells.

grandson, n. [1. grán(d)sun; 2. grǽn(d)san]. Son of one's son, or of one's daughter.

grand-stand, n. Principal covered erection, with rising tiers of seats, for spectators at a race-meeting, or other out-of-doors spectacle.

grand-uncle, n. Uncle of either of one's parents; brother of a grandparent.

grange, n. [1. grānj; 2. grein(d)ž]. M.E., fr. A.-Fr. *gra(u)nge*, fr. Med. Lat. *granca*, *graniea*, 'barn'. See **grain (I.)**. **1.** (archaic) **a** Storehouse for grain; granary; **b** collection of buildings connected with storage of the grain from an estate, together with a dwelling-house. **2. a** Small country house with farm buildings in close proximity to it; **b** (gen.) a country gentleman's house of modest size and pretensions.

grangerism, n. [1. grānjerizm; 2. gréindžərizəm]. See **grangerize & -ism.** Practice of grangerizing.

grangerization, n. [1. grànjerīzáshun; 2. greindžəraizéiʃən]. Next word & **-ation. a** Act or process of grangerizing a book; **b** a grangerized book.

grangerize, vb. trans. [1. grānjerīz; 2. gréindžəraiz], fr. the name of Rev. James Granger (1723–76) who collected 14,000 engraved portraits to illustrate his 'Biographical History of England, 1769', & **-ize.** To illustrate a copy of a book, after publication, by inserting into it portraits, and other pictures of persons, places, buildings &c., mentioned in its pages.

grangerizer, n. [1. grānjerīzer; 2. gréindžəraizə]. Prec. & **-er.** One who grangerizes a book.

graniferous, adj. [1. graniferus; 2. grəníferəs], fr. Lat. *grānifer*. See **grain & -ferous.** Producing grain.

granite, n. [1. gránit; 2. grǽnit]. Fr. *granit*, fr. Ital. *granito*, 'granular stone'; fr. Lat. *grānum*, 'grain'. See **grain (I.)**. Very hard, granular rock of igneous origin, usually of a shade of grey or pink in colour, and capable of receiving a high polish. Phr. *as hard as granite*, very hard; (fig.) stubborn, obdurate.

granitic, adj. [1. granítik; 2. grænítik]. Prec. & **-ic.** Of the nature of granite, resembling granite in texture &c.

granitiform, adj. [1. granítiform; 2. grænítifōm]. **granite & -form.** Like granite in structure.

granivorous, adj. [1. granívorus; 2. grənívərəs]. See **grain & -vorous.** Feeding on grain.

grannie, n. See **granny.**

grannom, granam, n. [1. gránom; 2. grǽnəm]. Origin unknown. Species of reddish-brown waterfly; artificial form of this used in fishing.

granny, grannie, n. [1. gráni; 2. grǽni], fr. first syll. of **grandmother** & dimin. **-y, -ie. a** Affectionate, familiar form of *grandmother*, used as mode of address, and in speaking of a grandmother; **b** an old woman.

granny('s) knot, n. [1. gráni(z) nòt; 2. grǽni(z) nòt]. Incompetently tied knot which does not hold.

grant (I.), vb. trans. [1. grahnt; 2. grānt]. M.E. *granten*, fr. O. Fr. *graänter*, *graunter*, *creanter*, *craänter*, fr. L. Lat. *crēdentāre*, 'to promise'; formed fr. Lat. *crēdent-*, Pres. Part. stem of *crēdere*, 'to believe'. See **credo, credit, creed. 1.** To assent to, allow, permit to be realized; allow concession of; esp. in answer to supplication: *to grant a request, favour*; *to grant a pardon, a respite* &c.; '*Grant us Thy peace*'. **2. a** To bestow, allot, confer: *to grant a pension*; *God has granted us the blessings of health*; **b** to make over, assign, in a legal and formal manner: *to grant the lease of property*; *to grant rights of pasture*. **3. a** To concede, admit, acknowledge cogency of, make allowance of: *to grant the truth of what is said*; *I grant you the force of that argument*; Phr. *to take for granted*, to assume as a fact, as admitted, or as certain to happen; **b** to concede, assume, for the sake of argument: *granting for a moment that it really happened*; *granted that he did say so* . . .

grant (II.), n., fr. prec. **1.** Something granted, bestowed, allotted (gen. of material things): *a grant of money, lands* &c.; *a Government grant to universities*; *grant in aid*, one made to further some specific object. **2.** (law) Assignment, transfer, of property by deed.

grantable, adj. [1. gráhntabl; 2. grántəbl]. Prec. & **-able.** Capable of being granted, conceded, admitted.

grantee, n. [1. gràhntḗ; 2. grɑntí]. **grant (I.)** & **-ee.** One to whom a grant or conveyance is made.

grantor, n. [1. gràhntór; 2. grɑntɔ́]. **grant (I.)** & **-or.** (law) Person by whom a grant or conveyance is made.

granular, adj. [1. gránūlar; 2. grǽnjulə]. **granule & -ar.** Of or pertaining to a granule; having a grain-like texture or surface.

granulate, vb. trans. & intrans. [1. gránulāt; 2. grǽnjuleit]. **granule & -ate. 1.** trans. **a** To reduce to grains, particles; **b** to roughen on the surface (leather &c.). **2.** intrans. To become granular, assume a surface like goose-flesh.

granulated, adj. [1. gránūlāted; 2. grǽnjuleitid], fr. P.P. of prec. **1.** Consisting of, having consistency of, small grains: *granulated sugar*. **2.** Having a roughened, granular surface.

granulation, n. [1. grànūláshun; 2. grænjuléiʃən]. Prec. & **-ion. a** Formation of grains or granules; **b** (med.) curative formation of small, grain-like bodies on a wound.

granule, n. [1. gránūl; 2. grǽnjūl]. Fr., fr. L. Lat. *grānulum*, 'small grain', dimin. of *grānum*, 'grain'. See **grain (I.)**. Small, grain-like particle.

granuliform, adj. [1. gránūliform; 2. grǽnjulifōm]. **granule & -form.** Having the form or structure of a granule.

granulose, n. [1. gránūlōs; 2. grǽnjulous]. **granule & -ose.** Element of starch convertible by fermentation into sugar.

granulous, adj. [1. gránūlus; 2. grǽnjuləs]. **granule & -ous.** Resembling, consisting of, granules.

grape, n. [1. grāp; 2. greip]. O. Fr. *grāpe*, *crape*, 'bunch of grapes'; fr. O.H.G. *chrapfo*, 'hook'; allied to **cramp.** Cp. **grapnel. 1. a** Fruit of the vine; **b** plant on which the fruit grows; Phr. *sour grapes*, affected indifference to what one cannot obtain. **2.** (mil.) Grape-shot. **3.** (pl.) A disease attacking horse's fetlocks, characterized by clusters of warty excrescences.

grape-fruit, n. Large, round, pale yellow, tropical fruit having the shape of a large orange, but the colour and acid taste of a lemon; called also pomelo, and shaddock.

grape-hyacinth, n. Dark-blue hyacinth, *Muscari*, whose florets form dense rounded clusters.

grape-shot, n. Cluster of small iron balls, held together in a frame, fired, formerly, from a smooth-bore cannon; now superseded by shrapnel.

grape-stone, n. Seed of the grape.

grape-sugar, n. Form of sugar found in ripe grapes; and otherwise made from starch; glucose, or dextrose.

grape-vine, n. Vine proper, i.e. that which bears grapes, distinguished from other climbing plants so called.

graph, n. [1. graf, grahf; 2. græf, grāf]. Abbr. fr. *graphic formula*. Diagram which expresses statements, statistics, mathematical formulae &c., by means of lines and curves.

-graph, suff. [1. grahf; 2. grāf], fr. Gk. base meaning 'to scratch', hence, 'engrave, draw, write'; cp. *gráphein*, 'to draw, write' &c. Cogn. w. Gmc. **kerf-*, 'to cut' &c. See **carve.** Used to form new words, expressing chiefly modern scientific ideas and inventions, chiefly in compounds where first element is also from Greek. Forming ns. denoting **a** instrument for writing, drawing, or recording: *phonograph, telegraph*; **b** writing, picture or other representation specified in first element: *autograph, monograph, photograph.*

graphic, adj. [1. gráfik; 2. grǽfik]. Lat. *graphicus*, fr. Gk. *graphikós*, 'belonging to drawing or writing, picturesque'. See prec. & **-ic. 1.** Pertaining to writing, expressed in writing: *graphic symbols, error.* **2. a** Pertaining to, resembling, drawing, engraving or painting: *the graphic arts*; **b** (fig., of verbal and literary expression) calling up a picture in the mind; vivid: *a graphic description* &c. **3.** (science) Expressing, or elucidating by means of diagram; diagrammatic: *graphic algebra, formula, method.*

graphical, adj. [1. gráfikl; 2. grǽfikl]. Prec. & **-al.** Graphic. Rare, except in phrases: *graphical formula, method* &c. Phr. *graphical statics*, branch of statics in which results are obtained by empirical measurement of diagrams of forces.

graphically, adv. Prec. & **-ly.** In a graphic manner.

graphics, n. pl. [1. gráfiks; 2. grǽfiks], fr. **graphic. a** Art of making drawings, as projections, by geometrical rules, esp. in engineering and architecture; **b** calculation of stresses &c., by means of such drawings.

graphite, n. [1. gráfīt; 2. grǽfait]. See **-graph & -ite.** (mineral.) Form of carbon, otherwise called black-lead or plumbago, used in making lead-pencils.

graphitic, adj. [1. grafítik; 2. græfítik]. Prec. & **-ic.** Pertaining to, resembling, graphite.

grapho-, pref. used in compounds; fr. Gk. base *graph-*, 'to write, draw' &c. See **-graph.** Pertaining to, used for, writing, drawing, or recording.

grapholite, n. [1. gráfōlīt; 2. grǽfoulait]. Fr., fr. Gk., lit. 'writing stone'. Prec. & **-lite.** Kind of slate from which thin slabs are cut for making writing-slates.

graphologic(al), adj. [1. gràfolójik(l); 2. græfəlɔ́džik(l)]. **grapho- & -logic (& -al).** Pertaining to graphology.

graphologist, n. [1. grafólojist; 2. græfɔ́lədžist]. **graphology & -ist.** One versed in graphology.

graphology, n. [1. grafóloji; 2. græfɔ́lədži]. Next word & **-logy. 1.** Study of handwriting, esp. as expression of character. **2.** Art of using graphs; notation used in graphs.

graphomania, n. [1. gràfōmánia; 2. græfouméinia]. **grapho- & -mania.** Morbid desire to write.

graphomaniac, n. [1. gràfōmániak; 2. græfouméiniæk]. **grapho- & maniac.** One afflicted with graphomania.

graphometer, n. [1. grafómeter; 2. græfɔ́mitə]. **grapho- & meter.** Surveyor's instrument for measuring angles.

-graphy, suff. Fr. *-graphie*, fr. Lat. *-graphia*, fr. Gk. *-graphia*. See **-graph.** Form in compounds of Greek origin, denoting, **a** kind of pictorial representation: *lithography*; kind of writing or recording: *stenography, telegraphy*; **b** descriptive science: *geography, topography*; or literary form: *biography*; **c** treatise of such a class.

grapnel, n. [1. grápnel; 2. grǽpnəl]. M.E. *grapenel*, dimin. of O. Fr. *grapin*, 'kind of hook'; Mod. Fr. *grappin*, 'grapnel', fr. O. Fr. *grape*, Mod. Fr. *grappe*, 'hook'; of Gmc. origin (cp. **grip**). See **grape, -ine, -al.** Small anchor with several flukes for grappling enemy ship or for mooring boat, balloon &c.; grappling-iron.

grapple (I.), n. [1. grápl; 2. grǽpl]. O. Fr. *grappil*, 'ship's grapnel', dimin. of *grape*, 'hook'. See prec. (naut.) Grapnel, grappling-iron.

grapple (II.), vb. trans. & intrans., fr. prec. **A.** trans. **1.** (naut.) To lay hold of as with a grapple, esp. for boarding or close combat.

2. To grip, clutch, grasp, as with a wrestler's hold. 3. (fig.) To attach firmly and closely: '*grapple them (friends) to thy soul*' (Shakespeare). **B.** intrans. 1. (naut.) To use a grapple, engage in close combat. 2. a *Grapple with*, to close with antagonist, wrestle, engage in hand-to-hand struggle; b (fig.) to apply the mind with vigour and concentration: *to grapple with a problem.*

grapple (III.), n., fr. prec. (rare) a Firm, tenacious grip, clutch, hold, as of wrestler; b a fight, struggle, at close quarters.

grappling, n. [1. grápling; 2. grǽpliŋ]. **grapple** (II.) & **-ing**. a Act of using a grapple; b act of fighting at close quarters; c act of applying the mind to problem.

grappling-iron, n. Grapnel.

graptolite, n. [1. gráptolīt; 2. grǽptəlait]. Mod. Lat. *graptolithus*, fr. Gk. *graptós*, 'engraved, written', fr. *gráphein* (see **-graph**), & **-lite**. a Stone bearing natural markings resembling drawing or writing; b fossil remains of extinct marine zoophytes.

graptolitic, adj. [1. gràptolítik; 2. grӕptəlítik]. Prec. & **-ic**. Pertaining to graptolite.

grapy, adj. [1. grápi; 2. gréipi]. **grape** & **-y**. 1. Pertaining to, resembling, grapes or a grape in shape, taste &c. 2. (veter., of a horse) Suffering from grapes.

grasp (I.), vb. trans. & intrans. [1. grahsp; 2. grāsp]. M.E. *grapsen, graspen*, 'to grope', formed fr. stem of O.E. *grāpian* (fr. **graip-*), 'to grope'; cp. E. Fris., L.G. *grapsen*, 'to seize'. See **gripe** & **grip**. **A.** trans. 1. To take firm hold of, grip, seize with the hand, clutch; clasp in the arms. Phrs. *to grasp a nettle*, to take unpleasant task in hand resolutely; *to grasp the shadow and let go the substance*, surrender something real for some imaginary advantage. 2. (fig.) To seize with the mind; to apprehend, comprehend, understand: *to grasp an argument, meaning* &c. **B.** intrans. 1. To perform act of grasping. 2. (lit. and fig.) *Grasp at*, snatch at, clutch; seek eagerly to seize or secure. Phr. *to grasp at a straw*, (i.) to avail oneself of the slightest help in an emergency; (ii.) to seize on the faintest ray of hope.

grasp (II.), n., fr. prec. 1. a Firm hold, grip, clutch, embrace; b power over, control; secure possession: *in the tyrant's grasp.* c mental capacity, power of understanding or getting hold of; comprehension, intellectual range: *a grasp of details; a problem beyond one's grasp; a mind of wide grasp.* 2. Power or possibility of seizing; reach (usually fig.): *within one's grasp.*

grasping, adj. [1. gráhsping; 2. grǻspiŋ], fr. Pres. Part. of **grasp** (I.). (only fig.) Eager for gain; exacting, covetous, rapacious; anxious to secure the utmost to which one is entitled and a little more.

graspingly, adv. Prec. & **-ly**. In a grasping manner.

graspingness, n. See prec. & **-ness**. Quality of being grasping.

grass (I.), n. [1. grahs; 2. grās]. O.E. *gærs, græs*, 'grass, young corn', M.E. *gras* &c.; Common Gmc.; prob. related to **grow**, & **green**. Not related to Lat. *grāmen*, in spite of resemblance in form & meaning. See this under **gramin-**. 1. (coll.) a Wild, green, low-growing herbage, such as cattle feed on; Phrs. *out at grass*, (of horse &c.) turned out to graze; at pasture; (fig., of person) unemployed, taking a holiday; *to put out to grass*, send to graze; *to go to grass*, (of animal) to go to pasture; (fig., colloq., of person) to cease work, take a holiday; *not to let the grass grow under one's feet*, to set to work without wasting time; *to cut the grass*, mow the lawn; *to lay down in grass*, to plant (land) with grass; b specif., plants of a monocotyledonous group, with leaves in form of blades sheathing jointed stem, bearing small seeds in spikelets, used for pasture and hay, excluding some true grasses (see 2), but including some plants which are not, as sedges; c land covered with grass, meadows, pasture, lawns: *twenty acres of grass*; d (min.) surface of ground, pit-head. 2. (bot., pl. *grasses*) Any member of the Order *Gramineae* or *Poaceae*, including, as well as most grasses popularly so called, cereals, bamboos, and reeds.

grass (II.), vb. trans., fr. prec. 1. To plant grass seed on (land), so as to produce crop; cause to be covered with grass: *to grass a field*; to lay turf, for lawns: *to grass a quadrangle* &c. 2. a To graze, pasture, put to grass. 3. To place on the grass or ground; to spread on grass; to knock down (person), shoot down (bird); land (fish).

grass-blade, n. Blade of grass.

grass cloth, n. Cloth made of fibres of grass, or of ramie.

grass-cutter, n. 1. One who cuts grass; specif., servant in India whose business it is to obtain fodder. 2. Machine for cutting grass; a lawn-mower.

grassed, adj. [1. grahst; 2. grāst]. **grass** & **-ed**. a Of piece of land laid down in grass; with grass growing on it: *a grassed walk, court* &c.; b (golf, of a club) having the face slightly bevelled.

grass-finch, n. a One of several American finches; b one of several Australian weaver-birds.

grass-green, adj. & n. M.E. *grasgrēne*. a adj. Of a vivid shade of green, like that of young grass; b n., this shade of colour.

grass-grown, adj. Overgrown with grass, bearing grass.

grass hand, n. 1. Cursive Chinese or Japanese script. 2. (printer's slang) A casual worker in a printing office.

grasshopper, n. [1. gráhs-hoper; 2. grǻshɔpə]. O.E. *gærshoppa*, M.E. *greshoppe*, Early Mod. Engl. *grasshop*, & **-er**. See **grass** & **hop** (I.) Type of small insect allied to the locust, but with short antennae, having very powerful hind-legs enabling it to leap, and producing shrill chirping noise by rubbing the fore-wings with the hind-legs.

grassiness, n. [1. gráhsines; 2. grǻsinis]. **grassy** & **-ness**. Quality of being grassy.

grass lamb, n. Lamb fed by a dam that grazes.

grass-land, n. a (agric.) Land kept permanently under grass; b (geog.) region where grass predominates.

grassless, adj. [1. gráhsles; 2. grǻslis]. **grass** (I.) & **-less**. Devoid of grass.

grasslike, adj. [1. gráhslīk; 2. grǻslaik]. **grass** (I.) & **-like**. Resembling grass.

grass of Parnassus, n. [1. gráhs uv parnásus; 2. grǻs əv pānǽsəs]. British marsh plant with white flowers, related to saxifrage.

grass oil, n. Fragrant volatile oil extracted from Indian grasses.

grass parakeet, n. One of several Australian parakeets, including the budgerigar.

grass-plot, (archaic **-plat**), n. **grass** (I.) & **plot**. Plot of ground covered with grass; small lawn.

grass-snake, n. Common British harmless snake.

grass-tree, n. One of several Australasian trees with grass-like foliage.

grass widow, n. Of uncertain origin, perh. '*widow at grass*', i.e. on holiday. Wife whose husband is temporarily absent from her.

grass widower, n. Husband whose wife is temporarily absent from him.

grasswork, n. [1. gráhswẽrk; 2. grǻswǝ̄k]. (min.) Work done above ground.

grassworker, n. [1. gráhswẽrker; 2. grǻswǝ̄kə]. (min.) Man employed above ground.

grassy, adj. [1. gráhsi; 2. grǻsi]. **grass** & **-y**. a Pertaining to, resembling, grass; b covered with grass.

grate (I.), vb. trans. & intrans. [1. grāt; 2. greit]. M.E. *graten*, fr. O. Fr. *grater*, Mod. Fr. *gratter*, 'to scratch, scrape', Low Lat. *cratāre, gratāre* (whence Ital. *grattare*), of Gmc. origin, fr. type **krattōjan-*; cp. O.H.G. *chrazzōn, kratzōn*, Mod. Germ. *kratzen*, 'to scratch', Swed. *kratta*, Dan. *kratte*, 'scrape'. See **scratch** (I.). **A.** trans. 1. a To scrape, scratch, rub harshly or noisily, as with a hard, rough surface: *to grate the teeth*, gnash them; b to reduce to small shreds or grains by scraping: *to grate a nutmeg.* 2. To produce (harsh noise) by friction. **B.** intrans. 1. To produce friction, rub together roughly; esp. make harsh, discordant noise as of two pieces of metal rubbing together; jar: *wheels grate on an axle.* 2. *Grate on, upon*: a (of sounds) to produce a painful, unpleasant, effect upon the ear: *his voice grated upon my ear*; b (of moral effect) to shock, cause unpleasant impression upon; to jar: *such expressions rather grate upon me.*

grate (II.), n. M.E. *grate*, fr. Low Lat. *grāta*, earlier *crāta* (whence Ital. *grata*, 'grate, gridiron'), fr. Lat. *crātis*, 'hurdle, harrow'. Cp. **crate**, **hurdle**. Frame of metal bars; specif. a frame with iron bars in fireplace, for holding fuel; b (more commonly *grating*) iron bars placed outside a window or opening in wall &c.

grate (III.), vb. trans., fr. prec. To provide with a grate or grating.

grateful, adj. [1. grātfool; 2. gréitf(u)l]. Obs. Engl. *grate*, 'pleasing', fr. O. Fr. *grat* (fem. *grate*), fr. Lat. *grātus*, 'beloved, pleasing, thankful' (see **grace**), & **-ful**. 1. a Thankful; full of, feeling, gratitude; b expressing, exhibiting, gratitude: *grateful letter.* 2. Pleasing, acceptable, agreeable, gratifying, comforting, refreshing: *a grateful shade, warmth* &c.

gratefully, adv. Prec. & **-ly**. In a grateful manner; agreeably; thankfully.

gratefulness, n. See prec. & **-ness**. Quality of being grateful; a gratitude; b agreeableness.

grater, n. [1. grāter; 2. gréitə]. **grate** (I.) & **-er**. Person or thing that grates; specif., device with roughened metal surface for scraping: *nutmeg grater.*

gratification, n. [1. gràtifikáshun; 2. grӕtifikéiʃən]. Fr., fr. Lat. *grātificātiōn-(em)*, vbl. n. fr. *grātificāri*. See next word & **-ation**. 1. Act or process of gratifying; condition of being gratified; specif., satisfaction, indulgence, giving of pleasure; a to the physical senses and desires: *the gratification of sight and hearing; of a craving for drink; of one's passions* &c.; b of intellectual or spiritual needs and aspirations: *the gratification of one's love for art; gratification of one's desire for learning.* 2. a Pleasure, sense of satisfaction (chiefly in non-material sense): *your approval gives me much gratification*; *to have succeeded in one's aims is a source of gratification to one*; b that which gratifies: *it must be a gratification to know that one is liked.* 3. (obs. or archaic) A gratuity, reward.

gratify, vb. trans. [1. grátifī; 2. grǽtifai]. Fr. *gratifier*, fr. Lat. *grātificāre*, late form of deponent *grātificāri*, 'to do favour to, do as a favour', fr. *grātum*, neut. of *grātus*, 'pleasing', & *facere*, 'to do'. See **grace** & **-fy**. To please, give pleasure to, satisfy, be source of pleasure to, content; a (in material sense) *to gratify one's physical desires, passions* &c.; b (in non-material, spiritual sense, (i.) of persons) *I am much gratified by my son's success; your kindness and appreciation have gratified me highly*; (ii.) (of spiritual aspirations &c.) *to gratify one's taste for pictures, one's thirst for knowledge.*

gratifying, adj. [1. grátifiing; 2. grǽtifaiiŋ], fr. Pres. Part. of prec. Causing gratification; agreeable, satisfactory: *the success of the undertaking is most gratifying.*

gratin, n. [1. grátan; 2. grӕtǣ]. Fr., fr. O. Fr. *grater*, 'to scrape'. See **grate** (I.). Light crust covering a dish, consisting of bread-crumbs or grated cheese; dish prepared thus. Phr. *au gratin*, by the method of cooking with such crust.

grating (I.), n. [1. grāting; 2. gréitiŋ]. **grate** (III.) & **-ing**. 1. a Frame of parallel or cross bars, such as a window grating; b lattice covering ship's hatch or floor of boat; c horizontal timber frame supporting foundations of building. 2. (opt.) Series of very close, fine parallel lines, engraved on glass or other polished surface, or formed by wires, to produce spectra by diffraction.

grating (II.), adj. Pres. Part of **grate** (I.). Causing, consisting of, harsh, jarring, sound, as of friction between two objects: *a grating noise*; discordant, rasping: *a grating voice.*

gratingly, adv. Prec. & **-ly**. In a grating manner.

gratis, adv. & adj. [1. grâtis; 2. gréitis]. Lat. *grātis*, contr. fr. *grātiis*, 'by favour or kindness', abl. pl. of *grātia*, 'thanks, favour' &c. See **grace**. **a** adv. Without payment or charge; gratuitously: *to be admitted to a performance gratis*; **b** adj. (chiefly pred.), not charged for; free, gratuitous: *entrance is gratis*; also (colloq. & facet.) *free gratis for nothing.*

gratitude, n. [1. grátitūd; 2. grǽtitjūd]. Fr., fr. L. Lat. *grātitūdo*, fr. *grātus*. See **grateful** & **-tude**. Feeling of thankfulness for benefits received, for kindness rendered, or good fortune of any kind experienced.

gratuitous, adj. [1. gratûitus; 2. grətjûitəs], fr. Lat. *grātuitus*, 'done without reward or profit, spontaneous', fr. *grātus* (see **grateful**) & formative *-it-* & **-ous**. **1. a** Given or done without advantage or recompense, freely bestowed; obtained without payment, earning, or claim: *a gratuitous distribution of tickets*; *gratuitous blessings*; (econ.) naturally obtained without effort or outlay; **b** (law) benefiting one party only, opposed to *onerous*: *a gratuitous contract, conveyance, trust.* **2. a** (of actions) Uncalled-for, unnecessary, unwarranted; *a gratuitous blunder, lie, insult, assumption*; **b** (of persons) acting without apparent motive: *a gratuitous liar.*

gratuitously, adv. Prec. & **-ly**. In a gratuitous manner.

gratuitousness, n. See prec. & **-ness**. Quality of being gratuitous (esp. in sense **2, a**).

gratuity, n. [1. gratûiti; 2. grətjûiti], fr. Fr. *gratuité*, fr. L. Lat. *grātuitas*, 'free gift'. Cp. **gratuitous**. **a** Gift, esp. of money, usually in return for services rendered, bestowed on inferior at discretion of giver without stipulation; a tip; specif. **b** (mil.) money gift, bounty, given to soldier, esp. at end of service.

gratulate, vb. trans. [1. grátūlāt, gráchoolāt; 2. grǽtjuleit, grǽtʃuleit]. Lat. *grātulāt-(um)*, P.P. type of *grātulāri*, 'to evince joy, congratulate', w. formative *-ul-*, fr. *grātāri*, 'to manifest joy, congratulate', fr. *grātus*, 'pleasing'. See **grateful** &c. (archaic or obs.) **a** To show joy at sight of; **b** to congratulate.

gratulation, n. [1. gràtūlâshun; 2. grætjuléiʃən]. Lat. *grātulātiōn-(em)*. Prec. & **-ation**. (archaic) Rejoicing; congratulation.

gratulatory, adj. [1. grátūlātori; 2. grǽtjulèitəri]. **gratulate** & **-ory**. Expressing pleasure at another's good fortune; congratulatory.

gravamen, n. [1. grāvâmen; 2. greivéimen]. L. Lat. *gravāmen*, 'trouble, physical inconvenience', fr. *gravāre*, 'to burden, incommode, aggravate', fr. *gravis*, 'heavy' (see **grave** (IV.)), & *-men*, suff. forming vbl. n. w. pass. signification. **1.** Grievance, formal complaint; specif. (eccles.) one laid before Upper House of Convocation by Lower House. **2.** The really weighty, essential, important, part of a charge, accusation, or grievance &c.

grave (I.), vb. trans. & intrans. [1. grāv; 2. greiv]. O.E. *grafan*, 'to dig, carve', M.E. *graven*, O.S., O.H.G., Goth. &c. *graban*. See **graven** & **groove**. **A.** trans. **1.** (obs.) To dig: '*He hath graven and digged up a pit*' (Prayer Book, Ps. vii. 16). **2.** (archaic) **a** To hew out, carve; to incise, engrave, sculpture: *to grave marble with an inscription*; *to grave an inscription upon marble*; **b** to impress, implant, deeply or indelibly: *to grave words, counsel, in the heart.* **B.** intrans. To engrave, carve.

grave (II.), n. O.E. *græf*, 'cave, trench, grave', fr. prec.; cp. O.S. *graf*, O.H.G., Mod. Germ. *grab*, Goth. *graba*. **1. a** Excavation in earth for burial of corpse; **b** mound or other monument marking a place of burial; tomb, sepulchre. Phrs. *to find one's grave* (*in a place*), to meet one's death there; *to have one foot in the grave*, to be nearing death, be very old and infirm, or grievously ill; *silent, secret, as the grave*, absolutely silent, secret; *to sink into the grave*, to die; *enough to make* (person) *turn in his grave*, something that he would have strongly disapproved while living; *in one's grave*, dead. **2.** (fig.) **a** Death, state of being dead: *to dread the grave*; **b** place that proves fatal to life: *Sierra Leone was the white man's grave.* Phr. *grave of reputation*, place, conditions, in which reputations are lost.

grave (III.), vb. trans. Origin obscure; possibly fr. O. Fr. *grave*, Mod. Fr. *grève*, 'strand of sea or river'. Cp. **gravel**. (naut.) To renovate (wooden hull of ship) by burning off growths, and tarring or pitching, while on shore or in graving-dock.

grave (IV.), adj. & n. Fr., fr. Lat. *gravis*, 'heavy, grievous; important, grave'; fr. Aryan base *g^wer-, *$g^wr̥$- &c., whence also Scrt. *gurú-*, 'heavy; important; honourable' (see **guru**); Gk. *barús*, 'heavy' (see **baro-**, pref.); Goth. *kaúrus*, 'heavy'. Another dialectal variant in Lat. is *brūtus*, 'heavy, stupid' (see **brute**). **A.** adj. **1. a** Weighty, important, momentous, serious, demanding earnest attention: *to debate grave matters*; *grave responsibility*; **b** fraught with danger; ominous: *a grave question, international situation*; **c** (obs., of persons, writings &c.) deserving deference; authoritative: *a grave author.* **2.** (of persons) **a** Earnest, sedate: *a grave, quiet man*; **b** serious, solemn, apprehensive: *to look grave.* **3. a** (of the mind and character) Serious, austere, sober; reverse of frivolous or gay; **b** (of cast of features, voice &c.) expressive of a grave mind, mood, &c.; expressing apprehension. **4.** (phon.) **a** (of tonic accent) Low-pitched, falling; **b** *grave accent*, graphic symbol (\`) for this; in French this diacritic placed over *è* indicating special quality of vowel. **B.** n. Grave accent.

grave-clothes, n. pl. Clothes in which a corpse is buried; cerements, winding-sheet, shroud.

grave-digger, n. **1.** Person employed to dig graves. **2.** Burying beetle.

gravel (I.), n. [1. grávl; 2. grǽvl]. M.E. *gravelle, gravel*, fr. O. Fr. *gravele*, Mod. Fr. *gravelle*, 'gravel', prob. dimin. of O. Fr. *grave*, 'coarse sand with stones, sandy beach, strand', Mod. Fr. *grève*, fr. Celt. base **gravo-*. Cp. Bret. *grouan*, Corn. *grow*, 'gravel', W. *gro*, 'pebbles'. **1.** (coll.) Mixture of small pebbles and sand, clay &c. deposited on shore or in river-bed; used for spreading on or rolling into paths and drives; (min. phr.) *pay gravel*, auriferous gravel worth working. **2.** (med.) **a** Collection of small calculi, resembling gravel, in kidney or bladder; **b** disease characterized by gravel.

gravel (II.), vb. trans., fr. prec. **1.** To cover or repair with gravel: *to gravel a path, walk* &c. **2. a** (obs.) To run, drive (ship) on to a gravelly beach; to cause to stick fast in loose soil; hence **b** (fig.) to disconcert, embarrass, check, bring to a non-plus; to floor, esp. a speaker or writer: *to be gravelled for lack of matter.* **3.** To lame (horse) with gravel in shoe.

graveless, adj. [1. grávles; 2. gréivlis]. **grave** (II.) & **-less**. Without a grave, unburied.

gravelly, adj. [1. gráveli; 2. grǽv(ə)li]. **gravel** & **-ly**. **a** Of the nature of, consisting of, containing, gravel; **b** (med.) pertaining to gravel in kidneys or bladder.

gravel-pit, n. Pit from which gravel is dug.

gravel-stone, n. **a** Pebble contained in gravel; **b** renal calculus.

gravely, adv. [1. grávli; 2. gréivli]. **grave** (IV.) & **-ly**. In a grave manner; seriously.

graven, adj. [1. grávn; 2. gréivn]. Old P.P. of **grave** (I.). O.E. *grafen*, M.E. *grāven*. (archaic, Bib.) Carved, sculptured: *a graven image.*

graver, n. [1. gráver; 2. gréivə]. **grave** (I.) & **-er**. **1.** Person who carves or engraves, esp. one who incises letters &c. in stone. **2.** Instrument for carving or engraving; specif. **a** burin; **b** diamond-point used in metal-turning.

graves (I.), n. pl. Variant of **greaves**.

Graves (II.), n. [1. grahv; 2. grāv]. Fr. See **gravel**; so called fr. the gravelly soil on wh. the vines grow. A white wine from Bordeaux district.

Graves' disease, n. [1. grávz dizēz; 2. gréivz dizīz]. After R. J. Graves, Irish physician (1796–1853). (med.) Exophthalmic goitre, disease marked by enlargement of the thyroid gland, heart palpitation, and protrusion of the eyeballs; also called Basedow's disease.

gravestone, n. [1. grávstōn; 2. gréivstoun]. **grave** (II.) & **stone** (I.). Slab of stone placed either flat or perpendicularly over a grave, inscribed with names, age &c. of deceased; tombstone.

graveward, adv. & adj. [1. grávward; 2. gréivwəd]. **grave** (II.) & **-ward(s)**. **1.** adv. (also *gravewards*) Towards the grave, towards death. **2.** adj. Advancing towards the grave or death.

graveyard, n. [1. grávyard; 2. gréivjād]. **grave** (II.) & **yard** (II.). Enclosed area containing graves; cemetery; churchyard.

gravid, adj. [1. grávid; 2. grǽvid]. Lat. *gravidus*, 'loaded; pregnant', fr. *gravis*, 'heavy'. See **grave** (IV.). Pregnant, esp. med., of the uterus.

gravidity, n. [1. gravíditi; 2. grævíditi]. Lat. *graviditāt-(em)*. Prec. & **-ity**. Pregnancy.

graving-dock, n. [1. gráving dòk; 2. gréiviŋ dɔ̀k]. **grave** (III.) & **dock** (II.). Dry dock in which ships are laid up for cleaning and repairs.

graving tool, n. Tool for engraving; burin.

gravitate, vb. intrans. [1. grávitāt; 2. grǽviteit]. **gravity** & **-ate**. Cp. Fr. *graviter*. **1. a** (phys.) To move, tend to move, in direction of another body in accordance with law of gravitation; **b** to sink in liquid: *to gravitate to the bottom.* **2.** (fig.) To be drawn by natural impulse, to tend to go, in particular direction: *sons of soldiers naturally gravitate to the army*; *in the summer many gravitate to the seaside.*

gravitation, n. [1. gràvitâshun; 2. grævitéiʃən]. Prec. & **-ion**. **a** Act or process of gravitating; **b** process exhibiting law of gravity.

gravitational, adj. [1. gràvitâshunal; 2. grævitéiʃənəl]. Prec. & **-al**. Pertaining to gravitation.

gravitationally, adv. Prec. & **-ly**. In accordance with, by means of, gravitation.

gravitative, adj. [1. grávitativ; 2. grǽvitətiv]. **gravitate** & **-ive**. Tending to gravitate.

gravity, n. [1. gráviti; 2. grǽviti]. Fr. *gravité*, fr. Lat. *gravitāt-(em)*, 'weight, seriousness', fr. *gravis*, 'heavy' (see **grave** (IV.)), & **-ity**. **1.** (in moral sense) **a** Seriousness, sedateness, solemnity of character and bearing: *the gravity of his mind and appearance inspired confidence*; **b** seriousness, danger, menace: *the gravity of the situation cannot be disregarded*; **c** seriousness of guilt; enormity: *the gravity of his offence was such that it could not be overlooked.* **2.** (phys.) **a** *Law of gravity*, natural tendency of bodies to attract, and be attracted by, each other; **b** *specific gravity*, relative proportion of the weight of the volume of a substance to that of an equal volume of another taken as a standard unit, that of water for solids and liquids, of air for gases.

gravure, n. [1. gravûr; 2. grævjúə]. Abbr. fr. **photogravure**.

gravy, n. [1. grávi; 2. gréivi]. M.E. *grave*, *gravey*, written *graue, grauey*, 'dressing for meats made of broth, spices, wine' &c.

Origin unknown. **a** Juice that flows from meat while it is being cooked; **b** sauce for meat chiefly made of such juices.

gravy-boat, n. Boat-shaped vessel, or small tureen, in which gravy is served at table.

gray, adj. [1. grā; 2. grei]. Variant spelling of **grey**.

gray-fly, n. Prec. & **fly (I.)**. (obs.) Unknown droning fly, perhaps botfly or gadfly: '*What time the gray-fly winds her sultry horn*' (Milton, 'Lycidas', 28).

grayling, n. [1. grāling; 2. gréiliŋ]. **gray** & **-ling**. **1.** Grey freshwater fish, European or N. American, with high and long dorsal fins; related to trout. **2.** British or American butterfly with wings brown and yellow on upper side, grey on under side.

graze (I.), vb. intrans. & trans. [1. grāz; 2. greiz]. O.E. *grasian*, fr. *græs*. See **grass**. **1.** intrans. (of cattle &c.) To eat growing grass, feed in pasture. **2.** trans. **a** (of animals) To eat, feed on: *to graze the herbage*; (of persons) **b** to use grass-land as pasture, put cattle to feed on it: *to graze a field before haying it*; **c** to put out to graze: *to graze cattle all the winter.*

graze (II.), n., fr. prec. Grazing, pasturage.

graze (III.), vb. trans. Formed apparently fr. *grass* in sense, orig., of 'to touch, shave, brush the grass'; said first of a shot just *grazing* the ground. Cp. *to wool, to skin*, 'take off the wool, or the skin'. **a** To touch, rub, or scrape slightly, just to touch, during passage, or by a glancing blow: *a bullet grazed his cheek*; hence **b** to cause slight scrape to a surface: *to graze the skin.*

graze (IV.), n., fr. prec. Slight contact in passing; slight injury, abrasion, caused by grazing; spot where thing grazes.

grazier, n. [1. grāzier; 2. gréiziə]. **graze (I.)** & **-ier**. Person who grazes live stock; stock-breeder.

grease (I.), n. [1. grēs; 2. grīs]. M.E. *gresse*, *grēse*, fr. O. Fr. *gresse*, *graisse*, earlier *craisse*, Mod. Fr. *graisse*, fr. unrecorded Low Lat. **crassia*, 'fatness', fr. Lat. *crassus*, 'thick, fat'. See **crass**. **1.** Fat, in animal's body (obs., except of stag in hunting phr.): *in (pride, prime, of) grease*, fat, in good condition for killing. **2. a** Soft animal fat, obtained by melting; **b** semi-solid oily or fatty matter, esp. (i.) for lubrication, as *axle grease*; or (ii.) for making *grease paint*, used by actors &c. in making up; **c** oil exuding from a fleece; hence, uncleansed wool. **3.** (veter.) Inflammation of horse's fetlock, producing cracks and ulceration.

grease (II.), vb. trans. [1. grēz; 2. grīz], fr. prec. **a** To apply grease to, anoint, lubricate, with grease; make greasy stain on; **b** (fig., colloq. phr.) *to grease the palm, hand, of*, to give bribe or 'tip' to (cp. Fr. *graisser la patte à quelqu'un*); *to grease the wheels*, to make things run smoothly, esp. by aid of money.

grease-box, n. **grease (I.)** & **box (II.)**. Box containing lubricant attached to axle of railway carriage.

grease-paint, n. **grease (I.)** & **paint (II.)**. Mixture of grease and paint, used for the face by actors.

greaser, n. [1. grēzer; 2. grīzə]. **grease (II.)** & **-er**. **1.** Person who greases axles of railway train, or parts of machine. **2.** (Am. slang) Greasy person, esp. (contemptuously) Mexican or other Spanish-speaking American.

grease-trap, n. **grease (I.)** & **trap (I.)**. Trap at entrance to drain to catch grease from a sink and prevent it entering and blocking drain.

greasily, adv. [1. grēzili; 2. grīzili]. **greasy** & **-ly**. In a greasy manner.

greasiness, n. [1. grēzines; 2. grīzinis]. Next word & **-ness**. Quality of being greasy; (fig., of manner) oiliness, cringing attempt to ingratiate.

greasy, adj. [1. grēzi; 2. grīzi]. **grease (I.)** & **-y**. **1.** Pertaining to grease; **a** coated with grease: *my hands are greasy*; **b** containing, impregnated with, having consistency of, grease: *a greasy substance*; *greasy food, wool.* **2.** Special uses: **a** slimy, slippery with wet mud, as surface of road, mountain-slope; **b** extremely smooth and slippery to the touch, as soapstone, graphite; **c** (naut., of weather) thick, dirty, damp. **3.** (fig., of manners, speech &c.) Unpleasantly unctuous, oily, fawning.

greasy pole, n. One specially greased for climbing or walking on in rustic sports.

great (I.), adj. [1. grāt; 2. greit]. O.E. *grēat*, M.E. *grēte*; Common W. Gmc., cp. O. Fris. *grāt*, O.S. *grōt*, Du. *groot*, O.H.G. *grōz*, Mod. Germ. *gross*. No cognates outside Gmc. have yet been traced. **1.** Much exceeding average or ordinary example of its kind in volume, area, length, or any dimension; large, big; contrasted with *small, little*. General in elevated style, but in ordinary language tending in this literal sense to be restricted to following uses: **a** impressive or imposing as well as large (less emphatic than *huge, vast*): *a great mountain, river, city, building*; **b** large, with slight suggestion of dislike, annoyance, fear, or contempt: *take your great nose out of the way*; *he put his great foot on the flower-bed*; (emphasizing second epithet) *a great hulking fellow*; *a great big man, fish* &c. (*big* weakly stressed); **c** distinguishing individual from smaller ones of same kind (usually with defin. art. and cap.): *the Great Bear, Pyramid, Lakes, auk, mullein* &c.; (of letters of alphabet) capital: *great A*; also, *Great Britain*; *the great cats*, lions, tigers, leopards &c.; *great cattle*, (law) all cattle except sheep and yearlings; *great chair*, armchair; *great horse*, shire horse; *the great house*, chief house in village; *great organ*, chief manual in large organ; *great toe*, big toe, largest toe; *great wheel*, wheel in clock or watch driving rest; (cap.) large vertical wheel, driven by machinery, carrying seats for persons; worked for amusement; (so compar.) *the Greater Antilles*; *the greater spotted woodpecker*; Phrs. *Greater Britain*, parts of British Empire inhabited by British; *Greater London*, Metropolitan police area; **d** (with ns. of quantity or number) large in number, numerous, abundant: *a great deal, company, pile*; (with pl. vb.) *a great many (people* &c.), very many; **e** (of time) long, protracted: *a great age*; *a great while ago*; **f** (modifying and intensifying sense of n.) *great gross*, 12 gross; *great hundred*, 120; *great year*, period of precessional revolution of equinoxes, Platonic year. **2.** (archaic) Pregnant: *great with child.* **3. a** Surpassing in some quality, good or bad; eminent, egregious; existing in a high degree; intense, important: *a great light, noise, friend, rogue, fool*; *great patience, weakness*; (with agent-n.) acting much or often as specified: *a great talker, builder, novel-reader, lover, sinner, farmer*; vaguely intensive in colloq. Phrs. *no great matter to*, not important; *to have a great mind to*, feel very much inclined to; *to have a great notion that*, be inclined to think; **b** eminent in genius, ability, or power; excellent, superior: *a great soldier, composer, book, picture*; Phr. *a great little man*, one great in mind though small in body; **c** lofty, profound; sublime: *a great soul, thought, deed, truth*; **d** of high rank, birth or station: *a great noble, great lady*; *the great families*; (absol. pl.) *the great*, great people; **e** (colloq.) grand, splendid, delightful, highly amusing: *that's a great story*; *he was great when he spoke after dinner*; **f** (in pred.) *great in*, excelling in: *a nation great in arms*; (colloq.) *great at*, versed in, clever at: *great at golf*; (colloq.) *great on*, much interested in, keen on: *great on heraldry, discipline* &c. **4.** As title, quasi-title, or designation, *the great*, (and cap.); **a** (before common n., designating person) highest of class, supreme in power, dignity, or authority: *the Great Chamberlain, Khan, Mogul*; (designating event, action &c.) most important or notable of its kind: *the Great Charter, Plague, Rebellion, War*; **b** after proper name, title, or designation of eminent ruler, hero or saint: *Alexander, Charles &c., the Great*; (iron.) *Tom Thumb the Great.*

great (II.), n., fr. prec. **1.** Whole, gross, in Phr. *in the great*, including everything: *to build a ship in the great.* **2.** (pl.) *Greats.* (Oxford University colloq.) Final Honour School of Literae Humaniores (cp. *great go*).

great-, pref., fr. **great (I.)**. Form prefixed to words of relationship: *great-uncle, aunt, great-grandfather* &c., and, by analogy, to *nephew, grandson*, &c., to denote a further degree in ascending or descending scale. Repeated indefinitely, once for each additional degree, e.g. *great-great-great-aunt*, aunt of great-grandparent &c.

great circle, n. & adj. **great (I.)** & **circle (I.)**, abbr. fr. *great circle of a sphere.* **1.** n. Circle described on surface of sphere, such that its plane passes through centre; specif. (navig.) circle, arc of which forms shortest distance between two places. **2.** adj. Pertaining to great circle: *great circle chart, sailing, track.*

greatcoat, n. [1. grātkōt; 2. gréitkout]. **great (I.)** & **coat (I.)**. Coat worn outside ordinary coat and other clothes; overcoat.

Great Council, n. (Engl. hist.) King's council of tenants-in-chief, bishops, and abbots.

great custom, n. (Engl. hist.) Custom or duty formerly levied on exports and imports.

Great Dane, n. Very large smooth-haired dog, allied to the mastiff.

greaten, vb. trans. & intrans. [1. grātn; 2. gréitən]. M.E. *grētnen*, 'become great (pregnant)'. **great (I.)** & **-en**. (archaic and rare) **a** trans. To make great; **b** intrans., to become great.

great fee, n. (Eng. hist.) Feudal estate held directly from Crown.

great go, n. (Cambridge University colloq.) Final examination for B.A. degree.

great-grandchild, n. Child of grandchild.

great-granddaughter, n. Daughter of grandchild.

great-grandfather, n. Father of grandparent.

great-grandmam(m)a, -grandma, n. (Childish and colloq.) Great-grandmother.

great-grandmother, n. Mother of grandparent.

great-grandpa(pa), n. (Childish and colloq.) Great-grandfather.

great-grandparent, n. Parent of grandparent.

great-grandson, n. Son of grandchild.

great-great-, pref. See **great-**.

great-hearted, adj. **a** Brave, courageous, high-spirited; **b** noble-hearted, magnanimous, generous.

great line, n. & adj. **a** n. Long line for fishing at great depth; **b** adj., pertaining to, employing, a great line: *a great-line boat, great-line fishing.*

great-niece, n. Daughter of nephew or niece.

Great Power, n. (polit.) One of the states, exerting through their armaments and political power the chief influence in international relations.

great-primer, n. (typog.) Large size of type, between English and canon.

great-uncle, n. Uncle of parent; grand-uncle.

greave, n. [1. grēv; 2. grīv]. M.E. *grēve*, fr. O. Fr. *greve*, 'shank, shin, boot, greave'; cp. Sp. *greba, greva*, 'greave'. Plate armour for the shins.

greaved, adj. [1. grēvd; 2. grīvd]. Prec. & **-ed**. Protected with greaves.

greaves, graves, n. pl. [1. grēvz, grāvz; 2. grīvz, greivz]. O.E. *greofa*, perh. means 'melting-pot'. Origin of this unknown. Fibrous sediment in melted tallow, used as dogs' food and bait for fish.

grebe, n. [1. grēb; 2. grīb]. Fr. *grèbe*, fr. Lyons dial. *grēpe*; cp. Savoy dial. *griaibe*, 'sea-mew' (Cotgrave); perh. of Celt. origin, cp. Bret. *krib*, 'comb', W. *crib*, 'crest'; or more prob. fr. Lat. (*avis*) *crispa*, 'curly, frizzled', fr. tufts of feathers on the head & neck. One of several British diving birds, haunting fresh water, with imperfectly webbed feet, and no tail, including *great crested grebe* and *dabchick* or 'little grebe'.

Grecian, adj. & n. [1. grḗshn; 2. grīʃn]. Lat. *Graecia*, 'Greece', fr. *Graecus*, **Greek**, & *-ia*, suff. denoting country, & **-an. A.** adj. Greek, Hellenic. Obsolescent, though still used in a few locutions, as *Grecian architecture, profile*, and in phrases: *Grecian bend*, stooping attitude, supposed to imitate that of the Venus de Milo, affected by some women in the seventies of 19th cent.; *Grecian knot*, ancient Greek form of woman's coiffure, with coil at back of head; *Grecian slippers*, slippers of kind worn in Levant. **B.** n. (obsolesc. or archaic, except **2. b**) **1. a** Greek, Hellene; **b** Hellenized or Greek-speaking Jew (N.T., A.V.) **2. a** Greek scholar; **b** at Christ's Hospital, boy in highest form, *deputy Grecian*, one in the next form.

Grecism, Grecize, Greco-. Variants of **Graecism, Graecize, Graeco-.**

greed, n. [1. grēd; 2. grīd]. Back-formation fr. **greedy.** Excessive desire to acquire and possess; greediness, esp. **a** cupidity, covetousness, rapacity, avarice; **b** (more rarely) greediness in respect of food; voracity, gluttony: *it is sheer greed that makes him eat so much, he cannot be hungry.*

greedily, adv. [1. grḗdili; 2. grídili]. O.E. *grǣdiglīce.* **greedy** & **-ly.** In a greedy manner. Phr. *to eat greedily*, ravenously, as though hungry.

greediness, n. [1. grḗdines; 2. grídinis]. O.E. *grǣdignes.* Next word & **-ness.** Quality of being greedy, tendency to be greedy; **a** for food; voracity; **b** of gain &c.; cupidity, rapacity.

greedy, adj. [1. grḗdi; 2. grídi]. O.E. *grǣdig*, M.E. *grēdi* &c.; O.S. *grādag*, O.H.G. *grātag*, Goth. *grēdag-s*, O.N. *grāðug-r*; cp. Goth. *grēdus*, 'hunger', O.N. *grāðr*, 'hunger, greed'; O.E. **grǣd*, 'hunger' &c., is not recorded. Cogn. w. Scrt. *gṛdhra-*, 'greedy', *gardhaš*, 'greed', *gṛdhyati*, 'he seeks, desires', see **gradus**; & **-y. 1.** Excessively inclined to eat, esp. from gluttony, rather than from hunger; indulging appetite for food without restraint; insatiate, voracious, ravenous: *a greedy boy; he is not hungry, merely greedy.* **2.** (fig., often followed by *of, for*) **a** Excessively or viciously inclined to take good things for oneself; covetous, avaricious: *greedy for, of, gold, gain* &c.; expressing greed: *to cast greedy eyes upon*; **b** *greedy of, greedy for*, excessively or intensely eager to gain; longing for, desirous of: *greedy of praise, for love, admiration.*

Greek (I.), n. [1. grēk; 2. grīk]. O.E. *Grēc*, (also, pl.) *Crēc-as, Crēc-e* (this form apparently borrowed fr. O.H.G.), M.E. *Grēc*, Fr. *grec*, fr. Lat. *Graec-us*, fr. Gk. *Graïkós*, extended form (see **-ic**), fr. name, found in Lat. *Grai-us*, of small Hellenic tribe in Epirus, early known to Romans, & hence extended to Hellenes generally. **1. a** Member of the Hellenic race or nation, inhabitant of Hellas or Greece; **b** Hellenized Jew; **c** member of Greek Church. **2.** (fig.) **a** Person whose mind, temperament, or outlook is akin to that of an ancient Greek: *if Keats was a Greek he was much besides*; **b** (obs.) boon companion, often *merry Greek* (Shakespeare); cp. *grig.* **3.** The Greek language: Phr. *Greek to me*, unintelligible.

Greek (II.), adj., fr. prec. Pertaining to, resembling, Greece or the Greeks; Hellenic. Phrs. *on the Greek Calends*, never (because Greeks had none); *Greek Church*, **a** Orthodox Eastern Church; **b** established Church of republic of Greece; *Greek cross*, cross with equal limbs; *Greek fire*, combustible used by mediaeval Byzantines for firing enemy ships, or other structures.

Greekless, adj. [1. grḗkles; 2. gríklis]. **Greek** (I.) & **-less.** Ignorant of Greek. Phr. (Oxford) *Greekless Greek*, study of Greek literature in translations only.

Greek-letter fraternity, n. Students' society at American university, college, or school, designated by combination of Greek letters of alphabet, e.g. Phi, Beta, Kappa.

Greekling, n. [1. grḗkling; 2. gríkliŋ]. **Greek** (I.) & **-ling**, transl. of Lat. *Graeculus.* Puny or contemptible Greek.

green (I.), adj. [1. grēn; 2. grīn]. O.E., M.E. *grēne*, O.S. *grōni*, Du. *groen*, O.H.G. *gruoni*, Mod. Germ. *grün*, O.N. *grœnn* for **grœn-r*, Swed., Dan. *grön*, fr. Gmc. type **grōnjoz* for **grō-n-iz*, fr. base **grō-*, **gra-*, q.v. under **grow**; & cp. **grass. 1. a** Of colour between, or compounded of, yellow and blue, that of the leaves of most plants; the exact shade is often defined by prefixing noun, as *apple-green, grass-green, olive-green* &c., with or without hyphen; Phrs. *green book*, Government publication, issued in green cover; *green briar*, smilax; *green drake*, mayfly; *green earth*, glauconite; celadonite; *green fire*, firework composition containing barium nitrate, burning green; *green glass*, common bottle glass, green or of any other colour; *green man* (hist.), figure in masque, representing savage, dressed in green leaves; *green plover*, lapwing; *green soap*, curative soap made with potash and linseed oil; *green table*, gaming table, covered with baize; *green tea*, tea retaining green colour by being dried while fresh; **b** consisting of fresh vegetable matter: *green food, meat; a green crop, feed*; **c** verdant, with ground not covered with snow, mild: *a green Christmas, January, winter*; **d** having, producing, sickly greenish complexion; jaundiced, wan: *green jaundice*; Phr. *green with envy, jealousy*, pale or livid with such passion; (fig.) vehemently envious, jealous; *a green eye*, envious or jealous look. **2. a** (fig.) Immature, unripe: *green fruit*; not seasoned, matured, or dried: *green clay, fish, ginger, hides, pelts, starch, sugar, timber, wood*; not fired: *green bricks*; Phrs. *green duck*, one about 9 weeks old; *green goose*, one under 4 months old; *green charge*, imperfectly mixed gunpowder; *green manure*, green crop grown to be ploughed in; unrotted stable manure; *green wound*, unhealed wound; **b** (colloq.) (i.) immature, callow, raw; *a green youth*; (ii.) credulous; (iii.) (of a horse) untrained, not thoroughly broken: *this horse is still a bit green (in harness* &c.). **3.** (fig.) Fresh, flourishing, undecayed, verdant: *a green old age; to keep a memory green*; Phr. *in the green wood, tree* (Bib.), in time of vigour or prosperity.

green (II.), n., fr. prec. **1.** Greenness, green colour; a green element or part in a thing. **2.** (pl.) **a** (obs.) Vegetation, verdure: '*With sudden greens and herbage crowned*' (Addison, *Past. Hymn.*); **b** leaves and stalks of plants, of kinds that are cooked for human food, as of cabbage, spinach, sorrel. **3.** Grassy place, lawn, specif. **a** common land in village or town, used for public resort, for grazing geese &c.; **b** grass plot for special purpose, as bowling, bleaching; **c** (golf) smoothed and mown part of course, level space of fine turf surrounding hole: *putting green.* **4.** Green paint, dye, or other colouring matter; *Brunswick green*, pigment made of oxychloride of copper; *Paris green*, bright emerald green pigment and insecticide. **5. a** Green badge, as of Irish nationalism; bunch of shamrock or green ribbon: *the wearing of the green*; **b** (pl.) party or faction distinguished by green colours. **6.** Prime of life, full vigour: *in the green.* **7.** (colloq., fig.) Sign of inexperience, in Phr. *is there any green in my eye?*, do I look gullible?

green (III.), vb. trans. & intrans. O.E. *grēnian*, 'become green', fr. **green** (I.). **A.** trans. **1.** To make, colour, paint, green. **2.** To impose on, hoax, swindle. **3.** (bowls) To put (bowl) on the green. **B.** intrans. (rare) To become, turn, green.

greenback, n. [1. grḗnbak; 2. grínbæk]. **green** (I.) & **back** (I.). **1.** (colloq.) Legal tender note issued by U.S.A. government, printed in green on back. **2.** Popular name of several animals, as green plover, green frog &c.

Greenback Party, n. (colloq.) Former Independent Party in U.S.A., advocating Government paper money as sole currency.

green-blind, adj. Suffering from green-blindness.

green-blindness, n. Prec. & **-ness.** Form of colour-blindness in which red and green appear grey, and the yellow part of the spectrum is brightest.

green cheese, n. **1. a** Unripened cheese; **b** cheese coloured green with sage; **c** whey cheese. **2.** Cheese which is green from age, well-matured cheese.

green cloth, n. Green material, such as baize, used as covering for table; hence, **a** (fig.) gaming table; **b** esp. in Phr. *Board of Green Cloth* or *Green-cloth*, board of the Lord Steward in Royal Household, for examining and passing accounts; formerly court of justice with cognizance of offences committed within verge of royal court.

greenery, n. [1. grḗneri; 2. grínəri]. **green** (I.) & **-ery. 1.** (collect.) Green foliage, verdure. **2.** (rare) Greenhouse.

green-eyed, adj. **green** (I.) & **eyed.** Having green eyes; (fig.) in Phr. *green-eyed monster* (Shakespeare, 'Othello'), jealousy; hence, jealous.

greenfinch, n. [1. grḗnfinsh; 2. grínfinʃ]. British finch with stout beak and green plumage; green grosbeak, green linnet.

greenfly, n. [1. grḗnflī; 2. grínflai]. Green aphis, plant-louse.

greengage, n. [1. grḗngāj; 2. gríngéidž]. Named after Sir Wm. Gage, who introduced it into England from France, c. 1725. Cultivated variety of plum, with golden green skin and flesh.

greengill, n. [1. grḗngil; 2. gríngil]. **green** (I.) & **gill** (I.). Oyster with gills coloured green by feeding on minute green algae.

greengrocer, n. [1. grḗngrōser; 2. gríngrousə]. **green** (II.) & **grocer.** Retail dealer in fresh vegetables and fruit.

greengrocery, n. [1. grḗngrōseri; 2. gríngrousəri]. Prec. & **-y. a** Business, **b** shop, **c** goods, of greengrocer.

greenheart, n. [1. grḗnhart; 2. grínhāt]. **a** West Indian and South American tree, producing very hard timber; **b** wood of this.

greenhorn, n. [1. grḗnhorn; 2. grínhōn]. **green** (I.) & **horn** (I.). Lit. 'green beak, callow bird'. **a** Inexperienced or untrained person, novice; **b** one easily duped, a simpleton.

greenhouse, n. [1. grḗnhous; 2. grínhaus]. Building, largely of glass, and often artificially heated, used to protect delicate plants from cold, or to ripen fruit: *greenhouse plant* &c., one that will only thrive in greenhouse.

greening (I.), n. [1. grḗning; 2. gríniŋ]. **green** (I.) & **-ing** (I.). **1.** (rare) Verdure (Keats). **2.** Turning green of oysters, production of greengills.

greening (II.), n. **green** (II.) & **-ing** (III.). Green variety of apple.

greenish, adj. [1. grḗnish; 2. gríniʃ]. **green** (I.) & **-ish.** Somewhat green, tending towards the colour of green.

greenishness, n. Prec. & **-ness.** Quality of being greenish.

greenling, n. [1. grḗnling; 2. grínliŋ]. **green** (II.) & **-ling.** Variety of fish found in N. Pacific; also called *rock trout.*

greenly, adv. [1. grḗnli; 2. grínli]. **green** (I.) & **-ly. a** With green; **b** (fig.) in a fresh or immature manner; foolishly (Shakespeare).

greenness, n. [1. grḗnnes; 2. grínnis]. **green** (I.) & **-ness.** Quality of being green (lit. or fig.).

greenroom, n. [1. grḗnroom; 2. grínrum]. **green** (I.) & **room. 1.** Room in theatre, formerly decorated in green, for actors and actresses when off stage. **2.** Room in factory or warehouse for unfinished or unseasoned wares, as unfired pottery.

greensand, n. [1. grḗnsand; 2. grínsænd]. **green** (I.) & **sand** (I.). **a** (mineral.) Glauconite, green earth; **b** (geol.) marine formation between Wealden clay and chalk, often containing large proportion of glauconite.

greenshank, n. [1. grḗnshangk; 2. grínʃæŋk]. **green (I.)** & **shank.** (ornith.) Large British sandpiper, with greenish legs.

greensick, adj. [1. grḗnsik; 2. grínsik]. Back-formation fr. next word. (rare) Suffering from greensickness.

greensickness, n. **green (I.)** & **sickness.** **a** A form of anaemia; chlorosis; **b** (fig.) emotional malaise of adolescence.

greenstick, n. [1. grḗnstik; 2. grínstik]. **green (I.)** & **stick (II.).** Partial fracture of bone, esp. in child, when one side of the bone bends without breaking; *greenstick fracture.*

greenstone, n. [1. grḗnstōn; 2. grínstoun]. **green** & **stone.** New Zealand nephrite or jade.

greenstuff, n. [1. grḗnstuf; 2. grínstaf]. **green (I.)** & **stuff (I.).** Green vegetables.

greensward, n. [1. grḗnsword; 2. grínswɔ̄d]. **green (I.)** & **sward.** Green turf.

greenth, n. [1. grēnth; 2. grinþ]. **green (I.)** & **-th.** Mod. formation on anal. of **warmth** &c. Cp. **coolth.** (rare) Greenness; herbage, green foliage.

greenwax, n. [1. grḗnwaks; 2. grínwæks]. **green (I.)** & **wax (I.).** (hist.) **a** Seal of green wax, formerly attached to document issued by Exchequer to sheriff; hence, **b** such document; **c** fine levied by virtue of it.

greenweed, n. [1. grḗnwēd; 2. grínwīd]. **green (I.)** & **weed (I.).** Dyer's weed, genista.

Greenwich time, n. [1. grínij tím; 2. grínidž táim]. Solar time of meridian of Greenwich, adopted as standard time.

greenwood, n. [1. grḗnwood; 2. grínwud]. **green (I.)** & **wood.** (chiefly liter. and poet.) Woodland in leaf, esp. as haunt of outlaws.

greeny, adj. [1. grḗni; 2. gríni]. **green (I.)** & **-y.** (colloq.) Greenish: *greeny yellow.*

greenyard, n. [1. grḗnyard; 2. grínjād]. **green (I.)** & **yard.** Pound for stray beasts.

greet (I.), vb. trans. [1. grēt; 2. grīt]. O.E. *grētan*, 'to approach, visit; attack; greet', M.E. *grēten*, O. Fris. *grēta*, O.S. *grōtian*, Du. *groeten*, O.H.G. *gruoz(z)an*, Mod. Germ. *grüssen*, fr. W. Gmc. type **grōtjan-*; cognates outside Gmc. not traced. **1. a** To hail, address, salute, with expression of friendliness, respect, or pleasure, by word or gesture, on meeting, or by message, as in letter: *to greet with a cheery word, an embrace*; **b** to express pleasure at (event): *many greeted the return of Charles with relief.* **2.** To receive (person, utterance, or event) with expression of suspicion or displeasure: *to greet with a scowl, a volley of arrows*; *the remark was greeted with hisses.* **3.** (of sensuous impression) To manifest itself to, obtrude upon, strike (organ of sense): *music greets the ear.*

greet (II.), vb. intrans. & trans. O.E. *grǣtan*, *grētan*, 'to bewail, weep'; M.E. *grēten*, *grāten*; Goth. *grētan*, O.N. *grāta*, 'weep'; perh. cogn. w. Scrt. *hrād-*, 'to resound, roar'; perh. affected by cogn. O.E. *grēotan*, 'to weep', cp. O.S. *griotan.* (archaic or Scots and Nthn. dial.) **a** intrans. To weep, lament; **b** trans., to bewail, lament.

greeting, n. [1. grḗting; 2. grítiŋ]. **greet (I.)** & **-ing.** **a** Action of one who greets; salutation; welcome; **b** friendly or complimentary message.

greffier, n. [1. gréfiā; 2. gréfiei]. Fr., fr. Low Lat. *grafārius, graphiārius*, fr. Lat. *graphium*, 'writing stylus', whence Fr. *greffe*, 'record office'. See **graft** & **-ier.** (in Channel Islands) Registrar, notary.

gregarious, adj. [1. gregárius; 2. grigéəriəs]. Lat. *gregāri-(us)*, 'belonging to flock', fr. *greg-*, stem of *grex*, 'flock'; cogn. w. O. Ir. *graig*, 'herd of horses', W. *gre*, 'flock'; perh. w. Gk. *ageirein*, 'to gather together', *gárgara*, 'heaps, plenty', *agorá*, 'crowd'; prob. a partial reduplication of base **ger-*, 'gather together', whence, without reduplication, O.E. *cor-ðor*, 'troop, assemblage', & **-ary** & **-ous.** Cp. **agoraphobia** & **panegyric.** **1. a** Pertaining to flock or community; **b** living in flocks, herds, or communities; **c** (bot.) growing in clusters. **2.** (of persons) Fond of the society of fellow-men; sociable.

gregariously, adv. Prec. & **-ly.** In a gregarious manner.

gregariousness, n. See prec. & **-ness.** Quality of being gregarious.

grego, n. [1. grḗgō; 2. grígou]. Romanic form of Lat. *Graecus*, 'Greek'. Short, hooded Levantine cloak.

Gregorian, adj. & n. [1. gregórian; 2. grigɔ́riən]. Low Lat. *Grēgoriānus* (see **-an**), fr. *Grēgorius*, fr. Gk. *Grēgórios*, personal name. **1.** adj. Pertaining to, invented by, Gregorius or Gregory; specif. **a** Pope Gregory I. (590–604): *Gregorian chant, music, tones*, plain-song, introduced by him; **b** Pope Gregory XIII. (1572–85); Phr. *Gregorian calendar*, reformed calendar established by him, 1582, year of *Gregorian epoch*; **c** James Gregory (1638–75), Scottish astronomer. Phr. *Gregorian telescope*, earliest type of reflecting telescope. **2.** n. **a** Gregorian chant, plain-song; **b** Gregorian telescope.

Gregory powder, n. [1. grégori pòuder; 2. grégəri pàudə], fr. J. Gregory, Scottish physician (1753–1821). (pharm.) Nauseous aperient powder containing rhubarb and magnesia.

gremial, adj. & n. [1. grḗmial; 2. grímiəl]. Low Lat. *gremiālis*, adj., fr. Lat. *gremium*, 'bosom, lap'; prob. cogn. w. O.E. *crammian*, 'to stuff'. See **cram (I.)** & **germ** & **-al.** **1.** adj. **a** Pertaining to lap or bosom; **b** pertaining to vestment called gremial. **2.** n. Ecclesiastical vestment, in form of silk apron, placed on bishop's lap at mass or ordination.

grenade, n. [1. grenád; 2. grənéid]. O. Fr., Fr., fr. Span. *granada*, 'pomegranate, grenade'. See **pomegranate** & cp. **garnet.** **1.** (mil.) Small bomb or shell, thrown by hand into enemy trench &c. Now usually *hand-grenade.* **2.** Globular bottle containing chemicals, breaking on impact, used for extinguishing fire, also for testing drains.

grenadier, n. [1. grènadḗr; 2. grènədíə]. Fr. See prec. & **-ier.** **1.** (mil.) **a** (hist.) Soldier employed to throw grenades; esp. one of a right flank company of a regiment trained in use of grenades; **b** (now) in British Army, member of regiment known as *Grenadier Guards* or *Grenadiers*, first regiment of household infantry. **2.** (zool.) **a** Weaver-bird or grosbeak of South Africa, with red and black plumage; **b** one of a family of marine fishes, *Macrouridae.*

grenadine (I.), n. [1. grénadèn; 2. grénədìn]. Fr. *grenadin*; most prob. fr. *grenade.* See **pomegranate.** **1.** (hort.) Middle-sized, strongly scented carnation. **2.** (cookery) Fricandeau of veal or poultry, filleted and glazed.

grenadine (II.), n. Fr. (1) Perh. fr. *Granada* in Spain; (2) and (3) fr. *grenade*, 'pomegranate', as in prec.; cp. **grenade** & **-ine.** **1.** Fine, thin silk or woollen fabric for dresses. **2.** Cordial from pomegranate. **3.** Red dye.

Gresham's law, n. [1. gréshamz láw; 2. gréʃəmz lɔ̄], fr. Sir Thomas Gresham, founder of the Royal Exchange, d. 1579. (econ.) The tendency for bad money to drive good money out of circulation.

gressorial, adj. [1. gresórial; 2. grεsɔ́riəl]. Lat. *gressor*, 'walker', agent-n. fr. type *gress-*, as in P.P. of *gradi*, 'to walk' (see **gradus**), & **-or** & **-ial.** (zool.) Adapted for walking, of birds with feet having three toes in front and one behind; also of certain long-legged insects.

grew, vb. [1. grōō; 2. grū]. O.E. *grēow*, M.E. *greu*; Pret. of **grow.**

grey (I.), **gray**, adj. [1. grā; 2. grei]. O.E. *grǣg*, M.E. *grai, grei*; O. Fris. *grē*, O.H.G. *grāw, grāu*, O.N. *grā-r*; Engl. form fr. Gmc. type **grǣw-ja-*, Aryan **ĝhrē-wos*, fr. wh. base many authorities agree in deriving Lat. *rāvus*, 'greyish or tawny', for **gravus*, though the consonants offer some difficulty, also, fr. different grade, Gk. *khar-opós*, 'bright-eyed'. The base is supposed to have meant orig. 'to gleam, shine'. **1.** (in a physical sense) **a** Of a colour between white and black, or bluish: *a friar of orders grey*, one habited in grey; *grey hair, grey eyes, grey clothes* &c.; Phrs. *grey hairs*, (fig.) old age; *the grey mare is the better horse*, the wife rules husband; **b** (of complexion) pale, colourless, livid as with illness, or from mental pain &c.; **c** (of weather &c.) dull, cloudy, overcast, not sunny: *a grey day, sky*; half dark, dim: *the grey dawn.* **2.** (in non-material sense) Dreary, dull, colourless, sombre, dismal: *grey thoughts, future, surroundings*; *life had been rather grey for him of late.*

grey (II.), **gray**, n., fr. prec. **1. a** Grey colour, a grey shade or tint; grey clothing: *to dress in grey*; **b** grey pigment or dye. **2.** Grey horse: *the Greys, the Scots Greys*, designation of Second Dragoons in British Army, from their grey horses.

grey (III.), **gray**, vb. trans. & intrans., fr. **grey (I.).** **a** trans. To make grey; **b** intrans., to become grey.

greyback, n. [1. grábak; 2. gréibæk]. **a** (Am. hist., colloq.) Confederate soldier in Civil War, wearing grey uniform; **b** fungus infesting peach; **c** one of various animals, as grey whale, hooded crow, scaup duck.

greybeard (I.), n. [1. grábērd; 2. gréibiəd]. **1.** Grey-bearded man, old man. **2.** Stone-ware jug for liquor, with face of bearded man on neck. **3.** Kind of lichen with long straggling tufts.

greybeard (II.), adj. (archaic) Grey-bearded.

grey-bearded, adj. Having a grey beard.

greycoat, n. [1. grákōt; 2. gréikout]. Person wearing a grey coat; specif., a soldier with a grey uniform.

grey-drake, n. May fly, ephemera; artificial fly for fishing in imitation of this.

grey-eyed, adj. **grey (I.)** & **eyed.** Having grey eyes.

Grey Friar, n. A Franciscan, from the colour of the habit.

grey goose, n. Common British wild goose; greylag.

grey-haired, adj. Having grey hair; middle-aged, old.

grey head, n. **1.** Old, grey-haired person. **2.** Old, male sperm-whale.

grey-headed, adj. Grey-haired, old.

grey hen, n. **1.** Female black grouse. **2.** Kind of stone-ware bottle.

greyhound, n. [1. gráhound; 2. gréihaund]. O.E. *grīghund* for **grieĝhund*, M.E. *grihond, greuhond, greihound* &c., = O.N. *greyhund-r*, fr. *grey*, 'dog' (etymol. doubtful), & *hund-r*, hound; not connected w. **grey.** **a** Slender, extremely swift breed of dog, with long, pointed muzzle, used for coursing hares; Phrs. *as swift, lithe, as a greyhound*; *greyhound racing*, racing of greyhounds on track in chase of an electrically moved artificial hare; **b** (fig., liter.) swift steamship: *ocean greyhound.*

grey iron, n. Kind of cast iron containing much graphite.

greyish, adj. [1. gráish; 2. gréiiʃ]. **grey (I.)** & **-ish.** Somewhat grey; **a** specif., of a white which has become dulled, clouded, darkened; **b** of a bright colour which has lost its intensity.

greylag, n. [1. grálag; 2. gréilæg]. **grey (I.)**, & perh. **lag (IV.)**, in obs. sense, 'last to leave', because it leaves England after other migrants. Grey goose.

greyling, n. See **grayling.**

greyly, adv. [1. gráli; 2. gréili]. **grey (I.)** & **-ly.** In a grey manner, with a grey colour: *dawn rose greyly.*

grey matter, n. **a** (physiol., obs.) Brownish-grey mass of nerve-cells forming active centres of brain and spinal column; **b** (fig., colloq.) brains, intelligence.

grey mullet, n. Species so coloured; distinguished fr. *red mullet.*

greyness, n. [1. grā́nes; 2. gréinis]. **grey (I.)** & **-ness**. Quality of being grey; grey colour.

grey squirrel, n. Large N. American squirrel, now naturalized in Britain.

greystone, n. [1. grā́stōn; 2. gréistoun]. (mineral.) Volcanic rock, consisting of feldspar and augite.

greywacke, n. [1. grā́wak; 2. gréiwæk]. **grey (I.)** & **wacke**, after Germ. *grauwacke*. (geol., mineral.) Kind of conglomerate sandstone, containing nodules of quartz, feldspar, slate &c.

greywether, n. [1. grā́wédher; 2. gréiwéðə]. **grey (I.)** & **wether**, fr. its appearance. Erratic block of sandstone, occurring on chalk downs; sarsen stone.

grey whale, n. Large species of N. Pacific whale.

grey wolf, n. N. American species; also *timber wolf*.

gribble, n. [1. gríbl; 2. gríbl]. Prob. fr. **grub (I.)**, & **-le**, dimin. or agent-suff. Small marine crustacean that burrows into timber.

grid, n. [1. grid; 2. grid]. Contraction or back-formation fr. **gridiron**. Grating, gridiron, griddle; specif. **a** in wireless apparatus, network of wire between filament and plate of valve; for *grid-leak* see **leak (II.), 3, b**; **b** gridiron **2, b**.

griddle (I.), n. [1. grídl; 2. grídl]. M.E. *gredil, gredel*, fr. A.-Fr. *gridil*, cp. O. Fr. *greïl*, Norm. dial. *grédil*, fr. Low Lat. type **crātīculum* for *crātīcula*, dimin. of *crātis*, 'hurdle'; cp. **crate, grate (II.), grill**. See also **girdle (III.)**. **1.** Iron plate, with handle in form of a half-hoop, placed over fire for cooking scones &c. **2.** (min.) Wire sieve for screening ore.

griddle (II.), vb. trans., fr. prec. **1.** To cook on griddle. **2.** (min.) To screen with griddle.

griddle-cake, n. **griddle (I.)** & **cake (I.)**. Flat cake cooked on a griddle over the fire.

gride (I.), vb. trans. & intrans. [1. grīd; 2. graid]. Prob. by metathesis of *r*, fr. **gird (II.)**. Present meaning **2.** appar. developed through suggestion of sound. Cp. **grate (I.)**. **1.** trans. (obs.) To cut, pierce (lit. and fig.) (Spenser, Milton). **2.** intrans. (lit., of weapon, door-bolt &c.) To be thrust, pushed, with harsh, grating noise; (of two objects rubbing against each other) to grate, jar, scrape.

gride (II.), n., fr. prec. Harsh, rasping or grating noise.

gridelin, n. [1. grídelin; 2. grídəlin]. Fr. *gris de lin*, 'grey of flax'. Cp. **grisette**. Violet-grey colour.

gridiron, n. [1. grídīern; 2. grídaiən]. M.E. *gredire, gridire, gredirne, gredīren*, 'griddle', perh. orig. a mere variant of **griddle**, assimilated to **iron**, a M.E. form of wh. was *ire*. Cp. similar change in **andiron**. **1. a** Object consisting of metal bars running parallel, held together in square or oblong frame, and usually provided with longish handle, for broiling or grilling meat or fish over clear fire; **b** (hist.) similar grating of great size, used as instrument of torture by fire. **2.** One of several objects, resembling gridiron in shape; **a** (naut.) frame in dry dock to support ship &c.; **b** (theatr.) frame above stage holding appliances for drop-scenes; **c** (rlys.) series of parallel rails for shunting; **d** network of high-pressure cables for supply of electrical power.

gridiron pendulum, n. Pendulum containing series of parallel rods of two different metals so arranged as to compensate for alterations in length caused by temperature.

grief, n. [1. grēf; 2. grīf]. In M.E., fr. Fr., 'sad, heavy', also n., 'sadness' &c., fr. Lat. *grave*, neut. of *gravis*, 'heavy'. See **grave (IV.)**. **1.** (obs. or archaic) Hurt, bodily or mental pain, sorrow; injury, wrong; Phrs. *to come to grief*, (i.) sustain bodily injury; (ii.) to fail, land in disaster; *bring to grief*, cause to miscarry, ruin. **2.** (of inward feeling) Deep, protracted, mental suffering; sorrow, distress, woe: *to suffer grief at the loss of a son* &c.; *to die of grief*. **3.** Cause, source, of grief, sorrow, distress, or regret: *his conduct was a grief to his friends*.

griefless, adj. [1. grḗfles; 2. grīflis]. Prec. & **-less**. Without grief.

grievance, n. [1. grḗvans; 2. grívəns]. M.E., O. Fr. *grevance*, fr. *grever*, 'to grieve'. See **grieve** & **-ance**. **a** Real or imaginary ground for complaint; act or conduct rightly or wrongly alleged to be cause of harm or inconvenience: *to nurse a grievance*; **b** (obs.) act of grieving; grief (Milton).

grieve (I.), vb. trans. & intrans. [1. grēv; 2. grīv]. M.E. *greven*, fr. O. Fr. *grever* (in Mod. Fr., 'to burden, encumber'), fr. Lat. *gravāre*, 'to burden', fr. *gravis*, 'heavy'. **grave (IV.)**. **1.** trans. To cause grief to; to distress, pain. **2.** intrans. **a** (absol.) To feel grief: *do not grieve—look on the bright side*; **b** *grieve at*, feel grief on account of; *grieve for*, to lament, regret, sorrow after; *grieve over*, dwell on and feel grief concerning.

grieve (II.), n. Perh. a Nthn. Engl. form of O.E. *ġerēfa*, 'steward' &c. See **reeve (II.)**. **a** (hist.) Legal officer in a town or shire; a prefect; **b** (Scots) bailiff, overseer of farm.

grievingly, adv. [1. grḗvingli; 2. grívinli]. Pres. Part. of **grieve (I.)** & **-ly**. With feelings of grief.

grievous, adj. [1. grḗvus; 2. grívəs]. M.E. *grevous*, fr. O. Fr. *grevous*. **grief** & **-ous**. **1.** (archaic) Physically heavy, burdensome: *burthens too grievous to be borne*. **2. a** Causing grief, distress, pain, or sorrow of any kind; distressing; oppressive: *grievous pain, tyranny, cruelty*; *grievous bodily harm*; **b** of a kind to grieve over; lamentable, deplorable; deserving censure: *grievous mistake, accident, sin*. **3.** (archaic) Expressing grief: *a grievous cry*.

grievously, adv. Prec. & **-ly**. In a grievous manner.

grievousness, n. See prec. & **-ness**. Quality of being grievous.

griffin (I.), griffon, gryphon, n. [1. grífin, grífun; 2. grífin, grífən]. M.E. *griffōn, griffyn*, fr. O. Fr. *grifoun* (Mod. Fr. *griffon*), fr. Lat. *grȳphus*, fr. Gk. *grūp-s*, fr. *grūp-ós*, 'curved, hook-beaked', perh. cogn. w. **creep** & **cripple**; cp. also **crumb**; *gryphon* is a pseudo-classical form. **a** Mythical animal, with head, beak, wings, and talons of eagle, erect ears, and body of lion; **b** (her.) figure of this creature as charge, crest &c.; **c** (fig.) vigilant guardian, esp. duenna, chaperon.

griffin (II.), n. Origin doubtful. (Anglo-Ind. colloq.) European newly arrived in India or the East; inexperienced new-comer.

griffon (I.). Variant of **griffin (I.)**.

griffon (II.), n. [1. grífon; 2. grífɔ̃]. Fr.; prob. same word as in **griffin (I.)**. Sporting dog of continental breed, with coarse hair; *Brussels griffon*, toy variety of this.

griffon (III.), gryphon vulture, n. **griffon (I.)** & **vulture**. Large species of Old World vulture.

grig, n. [1. grig; 2. grig]. Perh. Scand.; cp. Swed. dial. *kräk, krik*, Norw. *krek*, 'little, crawling creature'. **1. a** Small or young eel; sand eel: *as merry as a grig* (perh. for *Greek*), very lively, gay; **b** a cricket; grasshopper. **2.** Small, short-legged breed of poultry.

grill (I.), n. [1. gril; 2. gril]. Fr. *gril*, O. Fr. *grail, greïl*. See **griddle**. In **1 b** fr. **grille**; in **2**, perh. fr. **grill (II.)**. **1. a** Gridiron; **b** grating; **c** pattern composed of cross-bars, esp. for defacing postage stamp. **2. a** Act or process of grilling; **b** grilled food: *mixed grill*, dish composed of various grilled meats &c.; **c** grill-room.

grill (II.), vb. trans. & intrans. Fr. *griller*, fr. *gril*. **grill (I.)**; sense **2** fr. prec., **1, c**. **A.** trans. **1. a** To broil on grill or gridiron; **b** to cook (oysters &c.) in scallop; **c** (fig.) to roast, scorch, torture by extreme heat, as of tropical sun. **2.** To deface (stamp) with grill. **B.** intrans. **a** To be broiled on grill; **b** (fig.) to be exposed to extreme heat: *to grill in the sun*.

grillage, n. [1. grílij; 2. grílidž]. Fr. See **grill (I.)** & **-age**. **1.** (engin.) Heavy frame of cross-bars to support foundation of structure. **2.** Ground-work of lace design, resembling grating.

grille, grill, n. [1. gril; 2. gril]. Fr., fr. Lat. *crātīcula*. See **grill (I.)**. Screen or lattice of open work, usually of parallel or cross-bars, closing space in building, as window or hole in door, or surrounding private place; specif., the screen or lattice formerly in front of the ladies' gallery in the House of Commons.

grill-room, n. Room in restaurant where meat and fish are grilled and served.

grilse, n. [1. grils; 2. grils]. Of doubtful origin, prob. false sing. fr. pl. *grilles*, A.-Fr. (15th cent.) *grillez*; perh. fr. O. Fr. *grisle, grille*, 'greyish', dimin. of *gris*, 'grey'; cp. **grisette, grizzle**. Young salmon on its first return to river from sea; or, according to some, a distinct species closely allied to salmon.

grim, adj. [1. grim; 2. grim]. O.E. *grim*, 'fierce, cruel, angry, severe'; also in O.S., O. Fris., O.H.G.; O.N. *grimm-r*. Another grade is seen in O.E., O.S., O.H.G. *gram*, O.N. *gram-r*, 'angry, hostile'; fr. Aryan **gʷrem-*, **gʷrom-*, whence also Gk. *brémein*, 'to roar' (of wind, sea &c.), & *brontḗ*, 'thunder', cp. **brontosaurus**. **1. a** Fierce, cruel: '*the grim wolf*' (Milton); **b** severe, stern, forbidding: *a grim smile*; **c** inflexible; fiercely or sternly determined: *grim courage*; Phr. *hold on like grim death*, with a firm, determined, relentless grip; **d** sinister, ghastly, frightful: *a grim truth, joke, task*; *rather a grim business*.

grimace (I.), n. [1. grimā́s; 2. griméis]. Fr. *grimace*, 'wrinkle, wry face', prob. fr. O. Fr. *grimache*, 'embarrassment' (causing wrinkling of brows ?), fr. Romanic stem found in Ital. *grimo*, 'wrinkled', fr. Gmc., either fr. base of **grim** in sense of 'frowning', or connected w. O.E. &c. *grīma*, 'mask, visor'. Contortion, distortion, of face; ugly facial expression; **a** deliberate, expressing ridicule, disgust, contempt &c., or with intent to amuse; **b** involuntary, caused by pain &c. **2.** Habit of grimacing.

grimace (II.), vb. intrans., fr. prec., cp. Fr. *grimacer*. To make grimaces.

grimacer, n. [1. grimā́ser; 2. griméisə]. **grimace (I.)** & **-er**. One who makes grimaces.

grimalkin, n. [1. grimálkin; 2. grimǽlkin]. Earlier *Graymalkin*, in Shakespeare (Macbeth, I. i. 8), proper name of familiar spirit in form of she-cat, fr. **grey (I.)** & M.E. *Malkyn*, woman's name, also 'drab, slut', dimin. (cp. **-kin**) of M.E. *Malt, Mault*, 'Maud', fr. O. Fr. *Mahou(l)te, Malde* &c., of Gmc. origin, cp. O.E. *Mǣðhild*, O.H.G. *Māthilt*, of wh. Mathilda is Latinized form. Generic name for a cat, the cat tribe, like *Bruin* for a bear &c.

grime (I.), n. [1. grīm; 2. graim]. M.E. *grīm*, fr. continental L.G.; cp. W. Flem. *grijm*, Du. *grim, griim* &c., 'lamp-black, soot, grime', Swed. dial. *grima*, 'smut on face'; prob. orig. 'thing smeared'; cp. O.E. *be-grīwan*, 'to steep, smear', cogn. w. Gk. *khríein*, 'to smear, anoint'. See **chrism**. **a** Dirt, soot, deposited upon a surface; **b** general condition of dirt and dinginess; squalor; **c** moral degradation & defilement.

grime (II.), vb. trans., fr. prec. To soil, blacken, with grime; begrime.

grimily, adv. [1. grī́mili; 2. gráimili]. **grimy** & **-ly**. In a grimy manner.

griminess, n. [1. grī́mines; 2. gráiminis]. **grimy** & **-ness**. Quality of being grimy.

grimly, adv. [1. grímli; 2. grímli]. O.E. *grimlīċe*, fr. **grim** & **-ly**. In a grim manner.

grimness, n. [1. grímnes; 2. grímnis]. O.E. *grimnes*, M.E. *grymnesse*, fr. **grim** & **-ness**. Quality of being grim.

grim-visaged, adj. [1. grím-vízijd; 2. grím-vizidžd]. **grim** & **visage** & **-ed**. Having a grim, stern, forbidding face.

grimy, adj. [1. grími; 2. gráimi]. **grime (I.)** & **-y.** Covered with, consisting of, grime; sooty, dirty, dingy.

grin (I.), vb. intrans. & trans. [1. grin; 2. grin]. O.E. *grennian*, 'to bare the teeth, as with pain', M.E. *grennien, grünnien*; O.H.G. *grennan*, 'to mutter', O.N. *grenja*, 'to howl', may have been influenced in meaning by the Gmc. base **grain-*, 'howl' &c., as in O.E. *grānian*. See **groan. 1.** intrans. **a** (obs. or rare) To draw the lips back and show the teeth in pain or anger, like a snarling dog: '*to grin like a dog*' (Bib.); **b** to smile silently, and broadly, so that the lips are drawn back, and upwards at corners, and the teeth exposed; the action is supposed to express vulgar mirth, malevolence, or vacuity of mind. Phrs. (colloq.) *to grin and bear it*, to suffer pain or trouble with forced cheerfulness; (colloq.) *to grin like a Cheshire cat*; *to grin through a horse-collar*. competition in rustic sports. **2.** trans. (rare) To express by grinning.

grin (II.), n., fr. prec. Distortion of the mouth and exposure of teeth caused by grinning. Phr. (colloq.) *a broad grin*; *always on the grin*, perpetually in act of grinning.

grind (I.), vb. trans. & intrans. [1. grīnd; 2. graind]. O.E. *grindan* (strong), M.E. *grīnden*, fr. W. Gmc. type **grend-*, Aryan **ghrendh-*, **gherendh-* &c., 'to rub, grind' &c., whence also Lat. *frendere*, 'to grind; to gnash the teeth', w. *fr-* instead of *(h)r-*, fr. **ghr-* through influence of *fricāre*, 'to rub' &c.; also Lith. *grendu*, 'I rub', & Gk. *khraínō*, 'I smear', fr. **ghrn̥-jō*, & *khérados*, 'gravel', fr. **gherndh-*. Cp. further perh. **ground (I.). A.** trans. **1. a** To reduce to fragments or powder, by rubbing or crushing between two hard surfaces of which one usually revolves; to pulverize, triturate: *to grind something to powder*; *grind corn, coffee* &c.; **b** to break up, wear away, by friction, as the waves on rocks &c. **2.** (of moral action or process) To wear out, fatigue, reduce, by subjecting to cruelty, hardship, misery &c.; to afflict, oppress, esp. by extortion; to crush: *ground by tyranny, poverty, misery*. **3. a** To wear down, polish, surface of by friction: *to grind a lens*; **b** to sharpen edge of with revolving stone; to whet: *to grind a knife, axe, scythe, sword*; Phr. *to have an axe to grind*, have a personal interest to promote; **c** to roughen surface of by friction: *to grind glass*; (fig., Bib.) *to grind the faces of (the poor)*, to oppress by extortion &c. **4. a** To work, actuate, (grinding instrument), by turning handle round: *to grind a hand-mill, barrel-organ*; **b** to press upon with a turning, grinding motion: *to grind something into the ground with one's heel*; Phr. *to grind the teeth*. **5.** To produce by grinding: *to grind meal, flour*. **6.** (fig., colloq.) To teach assiduously or laboriously; to cram, coach: *to grind a person in Latin*; *to grind Latin into his head*. **B.** intrans. **1. a** To perform the act or function of grinding in any sense: Phr. *the mills of God grind slowly*, Divine purpose slowly revealed; **b** (fig.) to work laboriously, drudge, toil, esp. to study hard; gen. *grind (away) at*: *to grind away at one's duties, at examination subjects*. **2.** To be capable of being ground: *this wheat grinds well*. **C.** Followed by preposition or adverb. *Grind down*, trans. & intrans.: **1.** trans., **a** to reduce to powder &c. by grinding; **b** to wear away, reduce in bulk, by grinding: *to grind down a knife*; **c** (fig.) to oppress, subject to hardship, cruelty &c.: *ground down by poverty*; **2.** intrans., to be capable of being ground down: *this corn will grind down into a nice white flour*. *Grind out*, trans.: **a** to produce, cause to appear, by grinding: *to grind out a tune on an organ*; **b** (of intellectual action) to produce something with effort and difficulty: *to grind out a few verses each year*. *Grind up*, trans., to reduce to small particles or fragments by grinding.

grind (II.), n., fr. prec. **1.** Act of grinding. **2.** (fig., colloq.) **a** A hard, protracted, laborious, or monotonous piece of physical or intellectual work: *sawing hard oak is a considerable grind*; *he finds it a hard grind to learn a language*; **b** strenuous walk for exercise: *a Sunday grind*; **c** steeplechase: *the 'Varsity grind*.

grinder, n. [1. grínder; 2. gráində]. O.E. *grindere*, M.E. *grīndere*. **grind (I.)** & **-er. 1.** One that grinds; as *knife-grinder, organ-grinder*; (med.) *grinder's asthma, phthisis, rot*, lung disease caused by inhaling fine particles while grinding; (slang) **a** private tutor, crammer; **b** hard student. **2.** Thing that grinds; specif. **a** upper mill-stone; **b** molar tooth; (pl., colloq.) teeth.

grinding (I.), adj. [1. grínding; 2. gráindiŋ], fr. Pres. Part. of **grind (I.)**. **a** Exacting, tedious: *grinding toil*; **b** oppressive: *grinding tyranny*; **c** causing wearing, unceasing pain: *a grinding toothache*.

grinding (II.), n. **grind (I.)** & **-ing.** Action of person or thing that grinds.

grindingly, adv. **grinding (I.)** & **-ly.** In a grinding manner.

grindstone, n. [1. grín(d)stōn; 2. gráin(d)stoun, -stən]. **grind (I.)** & **stone (I.). 1.** Disk of hard sandstone revolving on axle, for grinding tools or polishing. Phr. *to hold, keep, put, one's nose to the grindstone*, to compel one to work hard and continuously. **2.** Kind of stone of which grindstones are made.

Gringo, n. [1. gríngɡō; 2. gríŋgou]. Origin doubtful. Mexican contemptuous name for an American of U.S.; equivalent to Yankee.

grinner, n. [1. gríner; 2. grínə]. **grin (I.)** & **-er.** One that grins.

grinning, adj. [1. gríning; 2. gríniŋ], fr. Pres. Part. of **grin (I.)**. Having a grin on the face: *a grinning urchin*.

grinningly, adv. Prec. & **-ly.** With a grin, as though grinning.

grip (I.), vb. trans. [1. grip; 2. grip]. O.E. *grippan*, 'to seize', cogn. w. *grīpan*, 'seize, clutch', q.v. under **gripe (I.)**. The word has superseded the cogn. *gripe* in most senses. **1.** (of living things) **a** To seize firmly, grasp, clutch; **b** to maintain a tight hold of. **2.** (of inanimate things) **a** To hold, catch, so as to retard motion, e.g. of machinery: *the brake doesn't grip the wheel properly*; **b** to encumber, enfold, hold fast: *the boat was gripped by the ice*. **3.** (fig., of action on, or of, the mind or emotions) **a** To awake interest; arrest, rivet, appeal powerfully to, the mind or attention, of: *to grip one's attention*; *to grip an audience*; **b** to occupy fully, affect strongly, the emotions of: *fear gripped his heart*; **c** to comprehend, grasp, obtain or maintain intellectual mastery of: *I cannot grip his argument*.

grip (II.), n. O.E. *gripe*, 'grasp, clutch' (cp. *gripa*, 'handful'), cogn. w. *grīpan*, 'gripe'; cp. O.H.G. *grif*, Mod. Germ. *griff*, 'that which seizes; claw; that which is seized; a handle'. Gmc. **grip-* is the reduced grade of **grīp-*, q.v. under **gripe. 1.** Act of gripping or seizing; grasp, clutch. Phr. *come to grips*, (of wrestlers) lay hold of each other; (fig.) engage in a close and serious struggle. **2.** Manner of gripping: *the eagle has a strong grip*; (of shaking hands) *a freemason is recognized by his grip*. **3.** (techn.) **a** Handle of a weapon; **b** appliance for gripping, clutch. **4.** (fig.) **a** Power of grasping with the mind, of understanding: *his mind has lost its grip*; hence, **b** faculty of understanding a situation and of coping with it in a practical way; control: *to have a good grip on a situation, of the state of affairs* &c.; **c** ability to hold attention or maintain keen interest: *to have a grip on an audience*. **5.** (American usage) Gripsack.

grip (III.), n. O.E. *grēp(e)*, *grype*, 'trench, ditch, drain'; cp. L.G. *grüppe*, Du. *grep*. (provinc.) Small ditch, open drain.

grip-brake, n. One which acts by gripping axle and delaying the revolutions of this.

gripe (I.), vb. trans. [1. grīp; 2. graip]. O.E. & O.S. *grīpan*, 'seize, grasp'; Mod. Germ. *greifen*, 'seize'; O.H.G. *grīfan*, Goth. *greipan*, O.N. *grīpa*. The Gmc. types are **grīp-*, **graip-*, **grīp-*, wh. wd. correspond to Aryan **ghreib-*, **ghroib-*, but relations outside Gmc. are very doubtful. The original use in general sense of to clutch, grasp &c. is practically obsolete, and the word has been specialized to express a specific kind of griping, pinching &c., that of pain in the bowels: *to be badly griped*; *to be griped by colic*. Used esp. of a horse which gets colic from eating too much green food.

gripe (II.), n., fr. prec. **1.** (rare) Act of griping; clutch, grasp; (fig.) *in the gripe of winter*. **2.** (pl., vulg.) *The gripes*, colic. **3.** (rare) Handle of a weapon or implement. **4.** (pl., naut.) Set of ropes, dead-eyes, and hooks for hanging a boat to the davits.

grippe, n. [1. grip; 2. grip]. Fr., 'influenza', fr. *gripper*, 'to seize'. See **grip (I.)**. (colloq.) Influenza.

gripper, n. [1. gríper; 2. grípə]. **grip (I.)** & **-er.** Person or thing that grips.

gripsack, n. [1. grípsak; 2. grípsæk]. **grip (I.)** & **sack (I.)**. (adopted from America) Hand-bag, suit-case &c. used by travellers.

grisaille, n. Engl. pronunc. [1. grizā́l; 2. grizéil]. Fr., fr. *gris*, 'grey', & *-aille*, forming coll. ns., fr. Lat. *-ālia*, neut. pl. of adjectival suff. *-ālis*. Fr. *gris* is of Gmc. origin; cp. O.S., M.H.G., *grīs*, 'grey-haired', Germ. *greis*, 'an old man'. Kind of painting in grey monochrome, imitating sculpture in relief, applied to mural decoration, illumination, stained glass &c.

grisamber, n. [1. grizámber; 2. grizǽmbə]. (obs.) Ambergris. Used by Milton, 'P.R.' ii. 341-4: '*Meats . . . grisamber-steamed*'.

grisette, n. [1. grizét; 2. grizét]. Fr., orig. a grey dress worn by working-class women, fem. dimin. of *gris*, 'grey'; of Gmc. origin. Cp. M.H.G. *grīse*, 'grey', & **-ette.** A young French woman or girl of the artisan class.

griskin, n. [1. grískin; 2. gŕiskin]. Dimin. of M.E. *grīs*, 'pig', fr. O.N. *grīss*, 'young pig'. (lit.) A little pig; joint of bacon-pig cut from the backbone or loin.

grisly, adj. [1. grízli; 2. grízli]. O.E. *grislīc*, 'horrible', fr. *gris-*, cogn. w. *grīsan*, 'to shudder, be terrified', & *-līc* (see **-ly**); cp. O. Fris. *grīslīk, gryslīk*, O.H.G. *grisenlich*. Etymol. doubtful, & relationship w. Germ. *grässlich* unexplained. **a** Tending to make one shudder; inspiring terror; loathsome and horrifying; **b** (in colloq. use with weakened meaning) unpleasant, nasty, very bad, dismal.

grison, n. [1. grízun, grízun; 2. gráizən, grízən]. Fr. *grison*, properly 'greyish', fr. *gris*, 'grey'. See **grisette.** (zool.) **a** South American mammal, of the weasel family, greyish above and black below; **b** greyish South American monkey.

grist (I.), n. [1. grist; 2. grist]. O.E. *grīst*, *gyrst*, 'grinding, corn to be ground'; perh. fr. Gmc. **grin(d)st*, fr. Gmc. base **grind-*, q.v. under **grind. a** Corn for grinding; Phrs. *to bring grist to the mill*, to be a source of gain; *all is grist that comes to his mill*, he turns everything to account; **b** grain that has been ground, esp. malt.

grist (II.), n. Etymol. obscure; perh. connected w. **gird (I.)**, **girdle.** Size of rope.

gristle, n. [1. grísl; 2. grísl]. O.E. & O. Fris. *gristel*; etymol. unknown. O.H.G. *krustila*, wh. has same meaning, is difficult to relate on account of vowel. This word, however, is connected w. the rare O.E. *grost*, 'gristle'. Cartilage; esp. in cooked meat. Phr. *in the gristle*, immature (Burke, alluding to the cartilaginous bones of very young animals).

gristly, adv. [1. grísli; 2. grísli]. Prec. & **-ly.** Of the nature of, resembling, containing, gristle.

grit (I.), n. [1. grit; 2. grit]. O.E. *grēot*, 'grit, sand, dust, earth, gravel'; M.E. *grēt*, O.S. *griot*, O.H.G. *grioz*, Germ. *gries*, O. Fris.

grēt, O.N. *grjōt*. The present Engl. form is due to an early shortening of Early Mod. [grīt]. The Gmc. base **greut-*, **grut-* &c. corresponds to Aryan **ghreud-* &c. wh. appears in Lat. as *rūdus* (for **greudos*), 'stones broken small and mixed with lime, for plastering walls'. Another form of the base appears in O.E. *grȳt* (fr. **grūti-*), *grūt*, 'coarse meal' (wh. see under **grout**), *grytta*, exactly cogn. w. O.H.G. *gruzze*, Mod. Germ. *grütze*, 'grain of sand, or of corn'; cp. further, Lith. *grúdas*, 'grain of corn'. See also **groats**. **1. a** (coll.) Small fragments of stone, coarse sand or dust, gravel; Phr. (fig.) *to put (a little) grit in the machine*, do, say, something which hampers action, or prevents business from running smoothly; **b** (geol.) one of several kinds of hard, esp. siliceous or calcareous, sandstone: *millstone grit*, *grindstone grit*; cp. *gritstone*. **2.** (fig.) Moral firmness, endurance, strength of character.

grit (II.), vb. intrans. & trans., fr. prec. **1.** intrans. To grate; to produce, or give evidence of occurrence of, friction, as through the presence of grit in a machine; emit a noise such as arises from grit in a machine. **2.** trans. In Phr. *to grit the teeth*, gnash, grind, make a grating sound by rubbing the edges of the teeth together.

grits, n. pl. [1. grits; 2. grits], fr. O.E. *grytt(a)*, 'coarse meal'; closely related to **grit** (I.), as also **groat** & **grout**. Coarsely ground grain, esp. oats or wheat.

gritstone, n. [1. grítstōn; 2. grítstoun]. **grit** (I.) & **stone**. Hard gritty sandstone.

grittiness, n. [1. grítines; 2. grítinis]. **gritty** & **-ness**. The quality of being gritty.

gritty, adj. [1. gríti; 2. gríti]. **grit** (I.) & **-y**. Containing, resembling, grit.

grivet, n. [1. grívet; 2. grívit]. Fr. Origin unknown. Monkey, of N. East Africa, with a greyish-green back.

grizzle (I.), n. [1. grízl; 2. grízl]. M.E., fr. O. Fr. *grisel*, 'grey-haired man', fr. dimin. of *gris*, 'grey'. Cp. **grisette**. (rare and obsolesc.) **a** A grey thing, esp. a horse, a wig, a partly burnt brick; **b** grey colour.

grizzle (II.), vb. intrans. Perh. freq. or dimin. vb. fr. **grouse** (II.). (colloq., esp. of young children) To keep on grumbling or whimpering; to fret.

grizzled, adj. [1. grízld; 2. grízld]. **grizzle** (I.) & **-ed**. **a** (chiefly of human hair, beard &c.) Grey, turning grey, shot or streaked with grey; **b** speckled with a light or dark shade so that the effect is greyish, as *grizzled skipper*, a butterfly.

grizzly, adj. & n. [1. grízli; 2. grízli]. **grizzle** (I.) & **-y**. **a** adj. Greyish, grizzled; only in *grizzly bear*, a large, fierce bear of the Rocky Mountains. The application of the word here is possibly influenced by *grisly*; indeed it is sometimes so spelt when applied to the bear; **b** n., the grizzly bear.

groan (I.), vb. intrans. & trans. [1. grōn; 2. groun]. O.E. *grānian*, 'groan, murmur'; cp. Du. *grijnen*, 'weep, grumble', O.H.G. *grīnan*, 'mutter', Mod. Germ. *greinen*, 'weep'; (obs.) 'grin, growl'. Not found outside Gmc. Cp. **grin**. **1.** intrans. **a** To utter a deep sound expressing bodily or mental distress; more violent, or impatient, than *moan*; to indicate disapproval by groans; **b** to show deep distress, suffer profoundly; *groan under*, suffer deeply from cruelty, severity, oppression &c.; **c** (by transf.) (of inanimate things) to make a deep harsh noise like a groan; creak, e.g. as a ship's timbers in a storm &c.; Phr. *the table literally groaned with food*, was loaded with; **d** to speak in a voice like a groan: *'I'm ruined,' he groaned.* **2.** trans. **a** *Groan (out)*, to utter, express, relate, in a dismal voice, as with a groan: *to groan out the tale of one's woes*; **b** *groan down (a speaker)*, silence, interrupt, with sounds of disapproval resembling groans.

groan (II.), n., fr. prec. **a** Sound made in groaning; deep, inarticulate, often involuntary, voiced sound, uttered by those suffering mental or bodily distress or pain; **b** (fig.) loudly uttered complaint; **c** noise made to indicate disapproval, esp. of a public speaker; **d** deep, harsh, creaking sound resembling a groan, made by heavy timber &c. when subjected to strain and twisting.

groaning, vbl. n. & adj. [1. gróning; 2. gróuniŋ], n. fr. **groan** (I.) & **-ing**; adj., Pres. Part. of same vb. **1.** vbl. n. Act of making a groan. **2.** adj. Making groans. Phr. *groaning board*, abundantly laden table.

groat, n. [1. grōt; 2. grout]. M.E. *grōte*, fr. M. Du. *groot* or M.L.G. *grote*, 'groat', lit. 'great', because thicker than the small coins in earlier use. See **great**. **a** Small coin current at Bremen and in the Low Countries in the Middle Ages; **b** silver English coin nominally worth 4d., first issued by Edward III., and current until 1662.

groats, n. pl. [1. grōts; 2. grouts]. O.E. *grot*, 'coarse meal'; M.E. *grōtes*. The O.E. word is fr. Gmc. **gruta-*, the reduced grade of **greut-*, O.E. *grēot*, wh. see under **grit** (I.). See also **grout**. Hulled oats or other grain; grits.

grocer, n. [1. gróser; 2. gróusə]. M.E. *grosser*, 'dealer in spices', fr. O. Fr. *(marchant) grossier*, 'wholesale merchant', fr. *gros*, 'gross', & **-ier**. See **gross**. Dealer in dry and preserved foods, spices, condiments, sugar, tea &c., and in various household requisites, such as soap, candles &c.

grocer's itch, n. Kind of eczema produced by the sugar mite.

grocery, n. [1. gróseri; 2. gróusəri]. O. Fr. *grosserie*, 'wholesale sale of goods, goods thus sold'. See **grocer** & **-ery**. **a** The trade of a grocer: *a grocery business*; **b** (coll., usually pl.) goods sold by a grocer.

grog, n. [1. grog; 2. grɔg]. Said to be named from 'Grogram' or 'Old Grog', nicknames of Admiral Edward Vernon (1684–1757), who wore a cloak (or breeches) of **grogram**, and was the first to issue this drink to his men. Any kind of spirit (orig. rum) diluted with water and used as a drink. A sailor's word; comparatively rarely used except in nautical circles, or in allusion to sailors' drink.

grog-blossom, n. (colloq. and vulg) Pimple or other eruption on the face, supposed to be caused by excessive drinking of spirits.

grogginess, n. [1. grógines; 2. grɔ́ginis]. Next word & **-ness**. (colloq.) State of being groggy.

groggy, adj. [1. grógi; 2. grɔ́gi]. **grog** & **-y**. (colloq.) **1.** (rare now in this, the orig. sense) Affected, intoxicated, by grog or other alcoholic drink; addicted to drink. **2.** (of persons and horses &c.) **a** Inclined to stagger, as though from drinking; weak on the legs, tottery, having an uncertain, unsteady gait; **b** shaky, in poor, weak, health; weak and unsteady, esp. from illness or nervous shock; **c** (of objects which should normally stand firmly and steadily) shaky, unsteady, likely to collapse, e.g. of pillars, walls, houses &c.; weak, badly fastened together; liable to break off or give way; loose, as legs of chairs and tables &c. (Very widely applied.)

grogram, n. [1. grógram; 2. gróugrəm]. Fr. *gros grain*, 'coarse grain'. See **gross**, **grain**. **a** Coarse kind of cloth, generally containing silk and mohair, sometimes stiffened with gum; **b** article of clothing made of this.

grog-shop, n. Small shop where grog is sold, low public-house.

groin (I.), n. [1. groin; 2. grɔin]. M.E. *grynde* (c. 1400), Early Mod. Engl. *grynde*, *grīne*, *groyne*. (For the change of vowel cp. *boil*, 'ulcer', fr. M.E. *bīle*.) Origin obscure; perh. O.E. *grynde* (once recorded), 'abyss', a lost meaning of wh. word may have been 'depression, hollow', fr. *grund*, 'bottom, deep, ground'; cp. O.E. *gryndan*, 'descend'. See **ground**. **1.** Depression in the body between thigh and abdomen. **2. a** (archit.) Curved line, arris, formed by the intersection of two vaults; rib covering the line; **b** (math.) volume contained by intersection of two cylinders; surface of the same. **3.** Groyne, q.v.

groin (II.), vb. trans. & intrans., fr. prec. (archit.) **a** trans. To make in form of groins: *'The hand that . . . groined the aisles'* (Emerson); **b** intrans., to form a groin.

groined, adj. [1. groind; 2. grɔind], fr. P.P. of **groin** (II.). (archit.) Made with groins: *a groined vault.*

groining, vbl. n. [1. gróining; 2. grɔ́iniŋ]. **groin** (II.) & **-ing**. (archit.) **a** Making of groins; **b** (coll.) groins, groined work.

grommet, n. See **grummet**.

gromwell, n. [1. grómwel; 2. grɔ́mwəl]. M.E. *grummel*, *gromelle*, *gromali*, fr. O. Fr. *gromil* (Mod. Fr. *grémil*), perh. a form of O. Fr. *grumel*, 'pellet, grain', Fr. *grumeau*, 'clot, lump', Lat. *grūmulus*, 'hillock', dimin. of *grūmus*, 'little heap, hillock'. See **grume**. A low-growing plant, allied to borage, with blue flowers and hard stony seeds, whence its botanical name *Lithospermum*.

groom (I.), n. [1. grōōm, groom; 2. grūm, grum]. M.E. *grōm(e)*, 'boy, groom'; cp. M. Du. *grom*, O.N. *gromr*, 'boy'; perh. shortened fr. O. Fr. *gromet*, 'man-servant' (whence obs. E. *grummet*, 'cabin-boy'), apparently dimin. of a lost O. Fr. **grome*, wh. may, however, be immediate source. There has prob. been confusion w. O.E. *guma*, 'man'. Cp. **bridegroom**. **1. a** (archaic) Boy or man, esp. one employed as a servant; **b** officer in royal household: *groom of the Great Chamber*, in charge of king's bedroom; *groom of the stole*, (formerly) in charge of wardrobe; *groom in waiting*, in attendance on king. **2.** Man-servant in charge of horses. **3.** Bridegroom.

groom (II.), vb. trans. [1. grōōm; 2. grūm], fr. prec. **a** To rub down, brush, clean, (a horse); **b** (of human beings, chiefly in P.P. & as adj.) to smarten up, bestow care upon one's person or dress: *to be, look, well, badly groomed*, well, badly, dressed or got up.

groom-porter, n. **groom** (I.) & **porter** (II.). (hist.) Officer of the royal household formerly in charge of the gaming tables and other furniture.

groomsman, n. [1. grōōmzman; 2. grumzmən]. **groom** (I.) & **man**. Friend in attendance on bridegroom at wedding; best man.

groove (I.), n. [1. grōōv; 2. grūv], fr. Du. *groef*, *groeve*, 'trench, groove', also 'pit, mine'. This word is not found in O.E. as a n., though the precise cogn. form *grōf* occurs as the normal Pret. of the strong vb. *grafan*, 'to dig, carve'. The W. Gmc. type **grǣf-*, besides appearing in infin. & pres. of this vb., occurs also as O.E. *græf*, 'cave, grave'. See **grave** (I.) & (II.). **1.** Long narrow hollow trench, or channel, made in surface of wood, stone, metal, or other material. Phrs. (fig.) *to get into a groove*, to acquire fixed habits of thought or conduct; *his mind works in a narrow groove*, within narrow limits. **2.** Various specific and technical uses, e.g.: **a** rabbet in edge of board; **b** hollow at bottom of printer's type; **c** spiral hollow in bore of rifle or gun &c. **3.** (by transf.) Long narrow hollow generally: *the river has cut a deep groove through the plain.*

groove (II.), vb. trans., fr. prec. To cut a groove in, furnish with grooves.

grooved, adj. [1. grōōvd; 2. grūvd], fr. P.P. of prec. Furnished with a groove or grooves; furrowed.

groover, n. [1. grōōver; 2. grūvə]. **groove** (II.) & **-er**. **a** Person who makes grooves; **b** specif., grooving tool.

grooviness, n. [1. grōōvines; 2. grūvinis]. **groovy** & **-ness**. Quality of being groovy; fixity of habits.

grooving, n. [1. grōōving; 2. grūviŋ]. **groove** (II.) & **-ing**. Act or process of making grooves. (in compounds) *Grooving plane, saw.*

groovy, adj. [1. grōōvi; 2. grūvi]. **groove** (I.) & **-y**. (only in fig. sense) Inclined to get into a groove, tending to fixity and narrowness of mental habit; one-sided, narrow-minded.

grope, vb. intrans. & trans. [1. grōp; 2. group]. O.E. *grāpian*, 'feel with the hand', fr. *grāp*, 'grasp, clutch'; cogn. w. O.E. *grīpan*, 'to clutch' &c. See **gripe**. **1.** intrans. Also *grope about*. **a** To search tentatively with the hands, feel round, as a blind person or one in the dark; fumble: *to grope in the dark, grope for the door-handle, for one's hat under the seat* &c.; **b** (fig.) to search, or otherwise act, in a tentative, uncertain, or hesitating manner: *to grope for a clue; grope about for information.* **2.** trans. Chiefly in Phr. *to grope one's way*; **a** to feel one's way, hesitatingly and doubtfully, as in the dark; **b** (fig., of spiritual and intellectual process) to attempt to settle or overcome difficulties, doubts, obscurities &c. by patient, cautious thought and inquiry: *to grope one's way towards clear understanding, towards religious convictions* &c.

groper, n. [1. grṓper; 2. gróupə]. Variant of **grouper**. **a** (zool.) Variant form of *grouper* (fish), esp. applied in Australia to several kinds of fish; **b** (Australian slang) an inhabitant of Western Australia.

gropingly, adv. [1. grṓpingli; 2. gróupiŋli]. **grope** & **-ing** & **-ly**. In the manner of one that gropes; (lit. and fig.) in a hesitating, uncertain, fumbling manner.

grosbeak, also **grossbeak**, n. [1. grṓsbēk; 2. gróusbīk]. Fr. *grosbec*, 'grosbeak'. See **gross** & **beak**. (zool.) One of several kinds of finch having broad, conical beaks. *Common grosbeak*, hawfinch; *green grosbeak*, greenfinch; *pine grosbeak*, pine bullfinch.

groschen, n. [1. grṓshen; 2. gróuʃən]. Mod. Germ., fr. M.H.G. *grosse*, 'groschen', fr. L. Lat. *grossus*, 'groschen', fr. Lat. *grossus*, 'thick' (see **gross**), & *-chen*, dimin. suff. (see **-kin**). **1.** (hist.) Small silver coin, and money of account, formerly current in Germany, sometimes a 30th of a thaler, but of varying value. **2.** A German ten-pfennig piece.

gross (I.), adj. [1. grōs; 2. grous]. M.E. *grōs*, 'large', fr. Fr. *gros*, 'big, thick, stout', fr. L. Lat. (4th cent.) *grossus*, 'thick', the origin of wh. is obscure; it may be cogn. w. M. Ir. *bras*, 'big', Corn. *bras*, 'thick'. **1. a** Big, bulky, thick, burly; usually in depreciatory sense, excessively fat, coarse: *a gross body; gross features*; **b** coarse grained: *a gross powder*; **c** (of air, liquids &c.) dense: *gross vapours, humours.* **2.** Coarse, unrefined, not delicate; crass, rank: *gross vegetation, food; a gross feeder*, one who enjoys coarse and plentiful food. **3.** (of the senses) Dull, blunt, insensitive: *a gross ear.* **4.** (obs.) Palpable: '*To all sense 'tis gross*' (Shakespeare). **5.** (fig.) Indelicate, coarse, unrefined, vulgar, obscene: *gross language, manners; a gross story, jest.* **6. a** Excessively clumsy or inept; extravagantly wrong, flagrant: *a gross blunder; gross carelessness; a gross overcharge, insult, injustice*; **b** (law) *gross negligence*, negligence involving wanton disregard of consequences of an act; *gross dereliction of duty*, wanton abandonment of one's duty. **7. a** Comprehensive; without deductions, including everything; total: *gross income, amount; gross weight*, including tare &c.; (math.) *gross error*, sum of all errors; **b** (law) Phrs. *gross adventure*, loan on bottomry, including partial liability for gross average; *gross average*, charge or loss involving ship as well as cargo, general average.

gross (II.), n., fr. prec. **1. a** Bulk, mass. Now chiefly in Phrs. *in (the) gross, by the gross*, in, by bulk, in the mass, taken as a whole, wholesale; **b** (law) *in gross*, absolute, entire in itself, not as an appendage to something else, annexed, not to the land, but to a person: *advowson, common, servitude, villain, in gross.* **2.** (commerc.) Twelve dozen, 144; *great gross*, twelve gross, 1728.

grossly, adv. **gross** (I.) & **-ly**. In a gross manner; coarsely, flagrantly.

grossness, n. **gross** (I.) & **-ness**. The quality of being gross; **a** (of size) excessive bulkiness, fatness, thickness; **b** (of non-material things) coarseness; indelicacy, vulgarity, obscenity; **c** high degree of some bad quality; enormity: *the grossness of one's misstatement, error* &c.

grossulaceous, adj. [1. gròsūlā́shus; 2. gròsjuléiʃəs]. Contracted fr. *grossulariaceous*, fr. Mod. Lat. *grossularia*, fr. Fr. *groseille*, 'gooseberry', & Lat. *-aria*, **-ary**, & **-aceous**. (bot.) Belonging to the order of *Grossulariaceae*, which includes the gooseberry and currants.

grossular, adj. & n. [1. grósūlar; 2. grɔ́sjulə]. Mod. Lat. *grossularis*, adj., fr. *grossularia*. See prec. **1.** adj. Belonging to, resembling, the gooseberry, esp. (mineral.) *grossular garnet.* **2.** n. (mineral.) Pale green, yellow, brown, or red variety of garnet, found in Siberia, also called *grossularite.*

grot, n. [1. grot; 2. grɔt]. Fr. *grotte*, fr. Ital. *grotta*, fr. Lat. *crupta, crypta*, 'subterranean passage, vault, cavern', fr. Gk. *krúptē*, or *kruptḗ*, 'vault', orig. fem. of vbl. adj. *kruptós*, 'concealed', fr. *krúptein*, 'to hide, conceal'. See **crypt**. (poet.) Grotto, cave.

grotesque, adj. & n. [1. grōtésk; 2. groutésk]. Fr., n. & adj., fr. Ital. *grottesca* (sc. *pittura*), 'grotesque painting', i.e. one of the kind found in a *grotta* (see **grot**), or ancient Roman crypt or other excavated chamber, & *-esco*, **-esque**. **1.** adj. **a** (art) In or belonging to a decorative style, esp. of painting and sculpture in relief, characterized by fantastic combinations of human, animal, and vegetable forms; (properly applied to Roman and Renaissance ornament, but extended to Gothic, Oriental, and other art); hence, **b** quaint, bizarre, fantastic; humorously extravagant or incongruous: *grotesque gestures of a baboon*; **c** ridiculous, ludicrous, absurd: *grotesque manners, appearance; a grotesque mistake.* **2.** n. **a** (art) Fantastic style in painting, sculpture, literature &c.: *the grotesque in art and literature*; **b** a quaint, bizarre, figure, face, or person: *a grotesque.*

grotesquely, adv. Prec. & **-ly**. In a grotesque manner.

grotesqueness, n. See prec. & **-ness**. Quality of being grotesque.

grotto, n. [1. grótō; 2. grɔ́tou]. pl. *grottoes, grottos.* Corrupt form of earlier *grotta*, fr. Ital. *grotta*. See **grot**. **a** Chamber, formed in, or imitating, a cave, usually lined with rough rocks and fancifully decorated with shells &c., forming a cool retreat or summer-house; **b** shrine formed in a similar manner; miniature cave built of shells on St. James's day in honour of that saint; **c** small natural cave or grot.

grouch, n. [1. grouch; 2. grautʃ]. Variant of **grouse** (II.), cp. **grudge**. (colloq.) Sulkiness, ill-temper.

ground (I.), n. [1. ground; 2. graund]. O.E. *grūnd*, 'bottom, ground, earth, depth'; M.E. *ground*, 'soil; foundation, reason'; O.S., Mod. Germ. *grund*, O.H.G. *grunt*, Goth. *grundu-* (in compos. *grundu-waddjus*, 'ground-wall, foundation'); O.N. *grunnr*, 'bottom'. Perh. orig. 'fine sand, grit' &c., & cogn. w. **grind**. **1.** Bottom, base, lowest part; depth: (obs. except fig.) *from the ground of the heart.* **2.** Bottom of sea or other body of water; shallow area of sea fished by fishing-fleet. Phrs. *to take ground*, (of a vessel) to strike the bottom, be stranded; *to touch ground*, (i.) come lightly into contact with the bottom; (ii.) (fig.) to reach definite facts, get to realities, in discussion. Cp. *aground*; *ground-bait.* **3. a** Soil, earth, land: *fruits of the ground; to till the ground; poor, fertile, ground*; Phrs. *to break fresh ground*, (i.) bring virgin soil under cultivation; (ii.) (fig.) to do something hitherto untried, do pioneer-work; *forbidden ground*, (fig.) topic excluded from discussion or reference; *common ground*, (fig.) point of contact, one on which agreement exists, between two persons or parties; **b** surface of the earth: *to fall to, lie on, spring from, the ground; she seemed hardly to touch the ground as she walked*; Phrs. *above ground*, alive; *below ground*, dead and buried; *to cover ground*, traverse space, travel; *to cut the ground from under one's feet*, to embarrass one by anticipating arguments, defence &c.; *to hold, stand, one's ground*, maintain one's position or claim, hold one's own against assailant; *to gain ground*, (i.) advance, progress; (ii.) (fig.) gain real advantage; *to give, lose, ground*, be forced back, fail to maintain one's position or claim, or one's full advantage in a contest; (colloq.) *down to the ground*, entirely, absolutely: *that suits me down to the ground*; **c** (min.) strata containing a lode or seam. **4. a** Area, piece of land; esp. one set apart for some particular purpose or pursuit: *a football, cricket, ground; recreation ground; parade ground*; **b** region devoted to some particular occupation, or where some process habitually occurs: *hunting-, fishing-ground; breeding-ground.* **5.** (pl.) Large garden, small park &c., usually immediately surrounding a dwelling-house or other building, including lawns, shrubberies, walks, &c., but not orchards or kitchen-garden. **6.** *Grounds* (perhaps from P.P. of **grind**): small particles which settle at the bottom of a vessel containing liquid; lees, dregs, sediment; esp. *coffee-grounds.* **7.** Underlying surface, background, on which decoration is placed; first coat of paint; in relief sculpture, plane from which figures stand out; in textiles &c., prevailing colour, relieved by decorative design: *roses on a black ground.* **8.** Composition spread over plate in etching to resist acid where not cut through. **9.** (mus.) **a** Composition in which a series of notes is continually repeated in the bass, with varying melody; **b** (obs.) plain-song as basis for descants. **10. a** Foundation or basis; underlying or originating force, substance, or idea: *God is the ultimate ground of all reality*; **b** in philosophy, sum of conditions, as distinguished from cause. **11. a** (often pl.) Intellectual starting-point, or basis; rational sanction, reason: *to have good ground(s) for thinking; grounds of complaint; to have no ground(s) for believing . . .*; **b** inducement, motive, cause, pretext: *to furnish grounds for suspicion; I see no ground for his action.*

ground (II.), vb. intrans. & trans., fr. prec. **A.** intrans. (naut.) Of a vessel, to strike the ground or bottom, esp. so as to be stopped in her course, be stranded, run aground. **B.** trans. **1.** To bring to ground; specif. (mil.) *ground arms*, to lay (arms) on the ground. **2.** (naut.) To cause to run aground. **3.** (elect.) To connect (an electric wire or other conductor) with the ground; to earth. **4.** (in non-material sense) To base, found upon, use as a rational basis: *to ground one's arguments on experience.* **5.** To teach elements of a subject to, provide with a knowledge of: *to ground a child in arithmetic; well-grounded in Latin.*

ground (III.), adj. P.P. of **grind** (I.). **1.** Reduced to grains or powder by grinding: *ground rice.* **2.** Prepared, treated, by grinding the surface; **a** smoothed, polished by grinding: *ground cock*, cock of which the plug is made to fit closely, by grinding; *ground joint*, joint in which the two surfaces are ground; **b** roughened by grinding: *ground glass*, glass rendered non-transparent by grinding one surface.

groundage, n. [1. gróundij; 2. gráundidʒ]. **ground** (I.) & **-age**. Due charged for letting a ship lie on shore or in a harbour.

ground-angling, n. Angling with a weight at the end of the line, and the hook a little above it.

ground-annual, n. (Scots law) Ground-rent charged annually before the land is built on.

ground-ash, n. Ash sapling; walking-stick or switch consisting of young ash-plant with the root for a handle, contrasted with one cut from a bough of a larger tree.

ground-bait, n. Bait scattered at bottom of water by angler to attract fish.

ground-bass, n. (mus.) Bass which continually repeats a short independent movement.

ground-box, n. Dwarf variety of box-plant used for edging.

ground-colour, n. **a** First coat of paint; **b** colour of background in decoration.

grounded, adj. [1. gróunded; 2. gráundid]. P.P. of **ground (II.)**. Based, founded, established, usually with adv.: *a well-grounded suspicion.*

groundedly, adv. Prec. & **-ly**. **a** With good ground, reasonably; **b** firmly (Browning).

ground elder, n. Common British creeping weed with leaves like those of the elder.

grounder, n. [1. gróunder; 2. gráundə]. (cricket) Ball that keeps close to ground when struck by the bat.

ground-fish, n. Fish of any kind that lives near the bottom.

ground-floor, n. That floor of a house which is nearest to the level of the ground. Phr. (colloq.) *to get in, be let in, on the ground-floor*, to obtain shares in a company or other concern on same terms as original promoters.

ground game, n. (coll.) Game that cannot fly; hares and rabbits.

ground-ice, n. Ice which forms at bottom of river or other body of water.

grounding, n. [1. gróunding; 2. gráundiŋ]. **1.** Act of bringing to, placing on, the ground. **2.** Act or process of laying, preparing, a ground, surface or base, in various arts. **3.** Thorough instruction in the essential elements of a branch of knowledge: *a good grounding in French.*

ground-ivy, n. **a** Variety of ivy which grows and creeps along the ground; **b** small creeping labiate British plant, with purplish flowers.

ground-landlord, n. Owner of site on which building stands or is to stand, to whom lessee pays rent for the land.

groundless, adj. [1. gróundles; 2. gráundlis]. O.E. *grundlēas*, 'bottomless, boundless'. **ground (I.)** & **-less**. Devoid of foundation, cause, reason; unfounded, baseless: *groundless fears, rumours* &c.

groundlessly, adv. Prec. & **-ly**. Without cause or reason.

groundlessness, n. See prec. & **-ness**. Lack of foundation, cause, or reason; baselessness.

groundling, n. [1. gróundling; 2. gráundliŋ]. **ground (I.)** & **-ling**. **1.** (hist.) Low-class spectator in Elizabethan theatre, who stood on the ground, or in what is now the pit: '*To split the ears of the groundlings*' (Shakespeare, 'Hamlet', III. ii. 12). **2.** (fig.) Person of low taste, Philistine. **3.** One of several ground fishes, esp. spined loach and black goby. **4.** (attrib. as adj.) Vulgar, low (Lamb).

ground(s)man, n. [1. gróundzman; 2. gráundzmæn]. One, usually a professional player, employed to attend to a cricket field or other ground kept for games or sports.

ground nut, n. The pea nut or earth nut, a leguminous plant of S. America and W. Indies, the stalks of which bend down to the ground in which the pods develop; the seeds are used as food and yield a valuable oil.

ground-pearl, n. Female of a W. Indian scale-insect, forming a kind of hard shell over itself.

ground-pig, n. African rodent, related to porcupines, living in burrow.

ground-pine, n. **a** British labiate plant, with odour of resin; **b** one of two species of club-moss.

ground-plan, n. **a** (archit.) Plan of building on the ground level or ground-floor; **b** (fig.) general scheme or design: *ground-plan of a scientific theory.*

ground-plane, n. In perspective drawing, horizontal plane of projection, on which objects stand.

ground-rent, n. Rent paid by lessee to owner of land upon which buildings are constructed, for right to occupy and improve it.

ground-sea, n. Ground swell.

groundsel (I.), n. [1. gróun(d)sel; 2. gráun(d)səl]. O.E. *grundeswelge*, lit. 'ground swallower', perh. because it spreads rapidly, & occupies much ground; or by popular etymol., fr. earlier *gundeswelge*, fr. *gund*, 'pus', & *swelgan* (see **swallow (I.)**), 'absorb', fr. its use in making poultices for wounds. **a** Small plant of the Composite order, with yellow flowers and flying seed-vessels; a very common English weed; used for feeding caged birds; **b** small maritime American tree of the same order.

groundsel (II.), n. **ground (I.)** & **sill**. (archaic) Horizontal timber serving as foundation for wooden frame, as sill of a door.

ground-swell, n. Condition of the sea in which a slow swell continues after the wind has dropped.

ground-water, n. Water that collects underground, as in mines.

groundwork, n. [1. gróundwěrk; 2. gráundwāk]. **1.** **a** (in material sense) Basis, underlying support, or framework of a structure; **b** (non-material sense) foundation, essential and fundamental part of intellectual or artistic work. **2.** Underlying, fundamental principle.

group (I.), n. [1. gro͞op; 2. grūp]. Fr. *groupe*, fr. Ital. *gruppo*, also *groppo*; prob. of Gmc. origin, cp. O.H.G. *chropp*, 'lump, swelling (on human neck); bird's crop'. See **crop (I.)**. **1.** Assemblage, aggregation, collection of objects, animate or inanimate, standing, or occurring at a given moment, in such close proximity to each other, and so far separated from others, as to strike the eye, or be thought of, as a loosely connected unity; **a** a band, knot, cluster: *a group of persons, cows*; *a group of trees, rocks, stars* &c.; **b** (painting and sculpture &c.) representation in art of several figures, placed together as part of a deliberate design. **2.** (science) Assemblage, aggregation, of living organisms, or of inorganic objects conceived of as having (i.) a natural affinity, relationship, association; as possessing (ii.) a genealogical or historical connexion; (iii.) resemblance or common features: *a group of fish, plants*; *a geological group (of rocks)*; *a group of languages.* **3.** (mus.) Series of notes having their stems connected by a line in notation. **4.** Aggregation of persons sharing the same special views, theories, aspirations, beliefs, in politics, religion, art, philosophy &c.; generally used of smaller parties within the main society, party, church &c.; *the free-trade group in the Conservative party*; *the Romanizing group.*

group (II.), vb. trans. & intrans., fr. prec. **A.** trans. **1.** **a** To form into, arrange in, groups with a view to artistic effect: *to group a wedding-party for a photograph*; **b** to classify according to some specific plan or system based on community of origin, external resemblance, or the possession of some common characteristic or trait: *roses are best grouped together in the garden by colours*; *languages are grouped in accordance with their genealogical relation.* **2.** (reflex.) To constitute a group or groups; to cluster, gather, come together: *the party grouped themselves round the fire.* **B.** intrans. To allow of grouping; to occur in, fall into, a group or groups: *the outlying farm-buildings group splendidly in the landscape.*

group captain, n. Rank in Royal Air Force, equivalent to a colonel in the army.

grouped, adj. [1. gro͞opt; 2. grūpt]. P.P. of prec. (specif. archit.) *Grouped columns*, three or more having the same pedestal.

grouper, n. [1. gro͞oper; 2. grūpə]. Port. *garupa*; perh. a native S. Am. word. **a** One of many allied marine fishes, related to sea bass, of warmer American coasts of Atlantic and Pacific; **b** one of various Australian kinds, also known as *groper.*

grouping, n. [1. gro͞oping; 2. grūpiŋ]. **group (II.)** & **-ing**. **a** Act of arranging in, putting into, a group or groups; **b** mode of arrangement in a group or groups.

grouse (I.), n., pl. **grouse** [1. grous; 2. graus]. Found in 17th cent. Of unknown origin. One of several kinds of wild gallinaceous game-birds with feathered feet, esp., in British Isles, the *red grouse* (*Lagopus scoticus*), the reddish-brown, speckled bird of the heather moors of Scotland and Yorkshire &c.; also *black grouse*, black game (black cock and grey hen); *white*, or *willow grouse*, the ptarmigan; *wood*, or *great grouse*, capercailzie.

grouse (II.), vb. intrans. Prob. fr. O. Fr. *grousser* (whence Med. Lat. *groussāre*), form of *groucier*, 'to murmur'. See **grudge**, & cp. **grizzle (II.)**. (colloq.) To grumble, murmur.

grouse disease, n. Disease of the red grouse, caused by a parasitic worm infesting young heather.

grouse-moor, n. Stretch of heather moor where grouse breed and over which they are shot.

grouser, n. [1. gróuser; 2. gráusə]. **grouse (II.)** & **-er**. One who grouses.

grouse-shooting, n. Sport of shooting the red grouse, usually driven over *grouse-butts*, which begins annually on Aug. 12th.

grout (I.), vb. intrans. & trans. [1. grout; 2. graut]. Origin uncertain; perh. fr. O.E. *grūt*, 'grains of meal', also 'fright, terror', a gradational variant of base of O.E. *grēot*, 'earth, dust' &c. See **grit, groats, grout (II.)**. This Gmc. word is cogn. w. Lat. *rūdus*, 'stones broken small and mixed with lime', fr. base **ghreud-*, 'to rub, pulverize'. See also **gruesome**. (of swine, not in frequent use) **a** intrans. To root or rout about in the earth with the snout; **b** trans., to turn up by rooting.

grout (II.), n. O.E. *grūt*, 'coarse meal, malt grains'. See prec. Coarse meal, pollard (usually in pl. *grouts*).

grout (III.), vb. intrans. & trans. & n. 16th cent. Fr. *grouter*, of Gmc. origin. See prec. **a** vb. To fill up interstices of loose or decayed masonry with cement in liquid form which hardens and forms a solid mass; the process is often carried out by injecting the liquid under pressure; **b** n., material used in the process.

grouting, n. [1. gróuting; 2. gráutiŋ]. Prec. & **-ing**. **a** Action or process of filling up defective masonry by injection of liquid cement &c.; **b** materials employed for this.

grove, n. [1. grōv; 2. grouv]. O.E. *grāf*, 'grove, copse', connected w. wh. is O.E. *grǣfa*, 'grove, thicket, brushwood'. No other cognates known. **1.** (chiefly liter.) Small wood, esp. one planted for ornament or pleasure. **2.** **a** A group of trees, as a centre of worship in various pagan religions; **b** used erroneously in A.V. to translate Hebrew *asherah*, 'sacred pillar', & *ēshel*, 'tamarisk'.

grovel, vb. intrans. [1. gróvl; 2. grɔ́vl]. Formed fr. M.E. adv. *grufelinge, grovelinge*, 'on the face', wh. is fr. Phr. *o grūfe*, O.N. *ā grūfu*, 'on the face', & advbl. suff. *-linge*, q.v. under **-long** (as in *headlong*), of wh. it is a variant. The old adv. was taken for a Pres. Part., & the suff. supposed to be *-ing*; the first element is obscure. **1.** To lie flat, wriggling, squirming on the ground. **2.** (fig.) **a** To debase one's self, behave abjectly, before another: *to grovel before*, or *to, authority*; **b** to occupy one's self with base or mean things.

groveller, n. [1. gróv(e)ler; 2. grɔ́v(ə)lə]. Prec. & **-er**. One who grovels; **a** a sycophant; **b** one of low mean tastes.

grovelling, adv. & adj. [1. gróv(e)ling; 2. grɔ́v(ə)liŋ]. M.E. adv. *grufelinge*, 'on the face'. See **grovel**. Now felt as a Pres. Part., & formed afresh fr. the new vb. **1.** adv. (archaic or obs.) On the face, prone, esp. in an abject manner: '*Upon thy belly grovelling thou shalt go*' (Milton, 'P.L.'). **2.** adj. (chiefly in fig. sense) **a** Abject, servile, obsequious, cringing; **b** base, mean, sordid: *a grovelling nature, grovelling ideals.*

grovellingly, adv. Prec. & **-ly**. In a grovelling manner.

grovy, adj. [1. grōvi; 2. gróuvi]. **grove** & **-y**. Covered with, abounding in, groves.

grow, vb. intrans. & trans. [1. grō; 2. grou]. O.E. *grōwan*, 'grow' (of plants); O.H.G. *gruoan*, 'grow, grow green'; prob. connected w. **green**, but not w. Lat. *grāmen*, 'grass'. See **gramin-**. **A.** intrans. **1.** (of organic process) **a** To develop, increase in size by formation of new tissue. Originally of plants, but extended to animals and persons in place of archaic *wax*; **b** (of plants) to live, flourish, occur, be produced: *the olive grows in Italy*; *rhododendrons won't grow in a limy soil.* **2. a** (of material things) To increase in volume, size, amount, length &c.: *you have grown since I saw you last*; *his hair has grown*; *the National Debt has grown enormously since the war*; Phr. *to grow in (experience, wisdom* &c.), to attain to greater degree of; **b** (of non-material things) to increase in degree, attain greater intensity: '*still the wonder grew*'; *my difficulties are growing.* **3.** (followed by pred. adj., adv., n., or phr.; expressing change, passage from one state to another) To become, turn: *to grow grey, old, rich, pale, silly*; *growing quite a handsome fellow*; *to grow less*, diminish. **B.** trans. To cultivate, cause to grow: *to grow roses, apples* &c. Phr. *to grow a beard* &c., to allow to grow. **C.** Followed by preposition and adverb. *Grow down*, intrans., to diminish in height, become shorter. *Grow on*, intrans., **a** to establish ascendancy over: *a habit that rapidly grows on one*; **b** to become endeared to, win the affection or admiration of, captivate taste of: *a wine, picture, place &c., that grows on one.* *Grow out*, intrans., **a** to sprout, chit, e.g. as corn after it has been reaped; **b** (of potatoes) to produce fresh crop from the new tubers before being lifted. *Grow out of*, intrans., **a** to divest oneself of, cease to practise, abandon: *to grow out of a bad habit*; **b** to become too big for, outgrow: *to grow out of one's clothes.* *Grow up*, intrans., (chiefly of persons) to attain full development of body and mind, pass into stage of an adult, reach maturity.

growable, adj. [1. grṓabl; 2. gróuəbl]. Prec. & **-able.** Capable of being cultivated with success, of being raised, made to grow.

grower, n. [1. gróer; 2. gróuə]. **grow** & **-er.** **1.** (with epith. adj.) Plant that grows in specific way: *a free, shy, rank, grower.* **2.** Person who cultivates flowers or vegetable produce, esp. for the market: *a well-known grower of roses.*

growing (I.), n. [1. grṓing; 2. gróuiŋ]. **grow** & **-ing.** State or condition of increasing organically; growth.

growing (II.), adj., fr. Pres. Part. of **grow.** **1.** Associated with growth: *growing pains*, neuralgic pains in the young, formerly associated with growth, now attributed to a disposition to rheumatism; *growing point*, (bot.) extremity of axis, consisting of undifferentiated tissue, from which growth proceeds. **2.** Suitable for, encouraging, growth: *growing weather*, weather that promotes growth of crops &c.; *growing season*, that at which growth of plants takes place. **3. a** In process of growth and organic development: *a growing child*; **b** increasing, rising, in size, extent, volume, intensity &c.: *growing discontent, anxiety, prosperity* &c.

growingly, adv. Prec. & **-ly.** Increasingly.

growl (I.), vb. intrans. & trans. [1. groul; 2. graul]. M.E. *groule*, fr. A.-Fr. *grouler*, 'make noise like a crane', Picard *grouler*, 'murmur, grumble'; of Gmc. origin. Cp. E. Fris. *grullen*, W. Flem., Du., Germ. *grollen* &c. **A.** intrans. **a** (of animals) To utter a deep rumbling noise in the throat, expressing irritation or menace, as an angry dog; **b** (of human beings) to speak, or utter sounds, with a deep, harsh, surly voice, resembling the sound made by an angry animal; **c** (of inanimate things) rumble threateningly: *thunder growled in the distance.* **B.** trans. Also *growl out*, express, utter, with growls, say in a surly, gruff voice: *he growled (out) his disapproval.*

growl (II.), n., fr. prec. Sound made by person, animal &c., that growls.

growler, n. [1. gróuler; 2. gráulə]. **growl** (I.) & **-er.** **a** Person or thing that growls; **b** one of several kinds of fishes that grunt when removed from the water, as the grunt and gurnard; **c** (slang) old-fashioned four-wheeled horse-cab, chiefly applied to the type formerly used in London; so called from the rattling or creaking sounds which it emitted when in motion.

grown, adj. [1. grōn; 2. groun]. P.P. of **grow.** **a** Fully developed, having reached full height; mature: *a grown man*; **b** (with qualifying adv.) *well-, ill-grown tree* &c.

growth, n. [1. grōth; 2. grouþ]. Cp. O.N. *grōði*, 'growth'. Not in early use in Engl.; prob. a new formation on anal. of *length, breadth* &c. See **grow** & **-th.** **1. a** Organic process of growing; increase by formation of new organic tissue: *growth is rapid in infancy*; **b** development, natural progress: *growth of institutions, of national spirit* &c. **2.** Increase in size, length, quantity, or numbers: *the alarming growth of the population, of intemperance, armaments* &c. **3.** Act of causing to grow; cultivation: *apples of foreign growth*; *the farm is devoted to the growth of fruit.* **4. a** That which grows, esp. vegetation and hair: *the luxuriant growths of the tropics*; *a week's growth on the chin*; **b** (pathol.) a morbid formation of tissue, esp. internally: *a malignant, cancerous growth*; also an external excrescence.

groyne, n. [1. groin; 2. grɔin]. Variant spelling, w. differentiated meaning, of **groin.** Breakwater, usually of timber, crossing foreshore and projecting into sea, to prevent shifting of beach and erosion of coast.

grub (I.), vb. trans. & intrans. [1. grub; 2. grab]. M.E. *grubben, grobben*, 'dig'. Origin uncertain; perh. connected w. O.N. *gryfja*, 'a pit'. **A.** trans. (usually with *up, out*). **1. a** To dig up: *to grub up nettles, the roots of a tree, bushes*; **b** (fig., colloq.) to search out arduously, extract, from archives, books &c.: *he grubbed up the family history*; *grub up facts for a speech, examination* &c. **2.** To clear (ground) by digging up roots. **B.** intrans. **a** To dig up roots, clear ground; **b** toil, drudge; **c** (fig., colloq.) to search arduously, pursue tedious researches: *to grub about among records.*

grub (II.), n. M.E. *grubbe*, prob. fr. prec. **1.** Larva of insect, esp. one of various kinds of beetle, or larva that lives in soil, on plants, or in bodies of animals. **2.** (perhaps from idea of getting dirty from digging (**grub** (I.)) A dirty, slovenly person. **3.** (cricket) Ball that rolls along or keeps near the ground when bowled or batted.

grub (III.), n. & vb. intrans. & trans., perh. fr. prec. (slang) **1.** n. Food, specif. (among schoolboys) extra food from home, sweets, delicacies &c. **2.** vb. **a** intrans. To consume food; **b** trans. (rare) supply with food (Dickens).

grub-axe, also **grubbing-axe**, n. [1. grúb(ing) àks; 2. gráb(iŋ) æks]. Implement in form of a kind of pick, with a cutting edge, used for cutting and extracting roots.

grubber, n. [1. grúber; 2. grábə]. M.E. *grubbare.* **grub** (I.) & **-er.** **a** Person who grubs up roots &c.; **b** implement for grubbing.

grubbiness, n. [1. grúbines; 2. grábinis]. Next word & **-ness.** Dirtiness (esp. of the person or dress); slovenliness, squalor.

grubby, adj. [1. grúbi; 2. grábi]. **grub** (II.) & **-y.** **1.** Infested with grubs. **2.** Dirty, grimy, unwashed, uncared-for.

grub-hoe, n. Kind of hoe for clearing the ground.

grubstake, n. & vb. trans. [1. grúbstāk; 2. grábsteik], fr. **grub** (III.) & **stake.** (Am. min. slang) **1.** n. **a** Provisions, stores &c. supplied to a prospector on condition of getting some share in what he finds; **b** share in mine obtained in this way. **2.** vb. **a** To supply provisions on such terms; **b** to obtain share in mine by such means.

Grub-street, n. *Grub Street*, near Moorfields (now Milton Street), was in 17th and 18th cents. a haunt of booksellers' hacks and mean writers. **1.** (coll.) **a** Literary hacks; **b** mean, catchpenny publications. **2.** (attrib.) Connected with, typical of, resembling, mean scribblers or their writings.

grudge (I.), vb. intrans. & trans. [1. gruj; 2. gradž]. M.E. *grucchen, grugge*, 'murmur, grudge', Scots dial. *grutch*, fr. O. Fr. *groucier, groucher*, also *grousser* (see **grouse** (II.)), Mod. Fr. *gruger*, 'murmur, repine', of doubtful origin. **1.** intrans. (now rare or obs.) To murmur, complain, show discontent, ill-will, or envy: '*They will grudge if they be not satisfied*' (Ps. lix., Coverdale); '*Grudge not one against another*' (N.T., A.V.). **2.** trans. (with indirect object of person) **a** To show ill-will or envy on account of, resent, be reluctant, through ill-will, stinginess &c., to give or allow: *to grudge a person the very food he eats*; **b** to envy a person some possession or enjoyment, and feel annoyance at it: *I grudge such a stupid fellow his fine house and pictures*; also followed by *to*: *one can grudge no success to such a worthy man.*

grudge (II.), n., fr. prec. Occasion, cause, pretext, for ill-will, resentment or envy; real or imagined grievance; feeling of ill-will, envy, spite. Phrs. *to bear a grudge against*, to cherish, harbour, a grievance or angry feeling against; *to owe a person a grudge*, to feel that one has adequate reason to be annoyed with a person.

grudging, adj. [1. grújing; 2. grádžiŋ], fr. Pres. Part. of **grudge** (I.). **a** (of persons) (i.) Niggardly, stingy; (ii.) ungenerous; **b** (of feelings, actions, conduct) arising from, betokening, envious ill-nature; evincing reluctance and lack of generosity; ungracious: *a grudging acknowledgement, praise, expression of gratitude* &c.

grudgingly, adv. Prec. & **-ly.** In a grudging manner, without generosity, stingily.

gruel (I.), n. [1. grōōel; 2. grúil]. O.F. (cp. Mod. Fr. *gruau*), fr. L. Lat. *grūtellum*, dimin. of L. Lat. *grūtum*, 'meal', fr. a Gmc. word cogn. w. O.E. *grūt*, 'meal'. See **grout** (II.). Thin, watery porridge made of oatmeal or other meal, boiled in water or milk; slang Phrs.: *have, get, take, one's gruel*, (i.) be severely punished; (ii.) be killed; *to give a man his gruel*, punish severely; kill. (Probably from use of gruel by invalids.)

gruel (II.), vb. trans., fr. prec. (slang) **a** To punish severely, submit to harsh, rigorous treatment; **b** (rarely) kill.

gruelling (I.), adj. [1. grōōeling; 2. grúiliŋ], fr. Pres. Part. of prec. (slang) Severe, exhausting: *a gruelling race.*

gruelling (II.), vbl. n. (slang) Punishment, severe handling.

gruesome, adj. [1. grōōsum; 2. grúsəm], fr. M.E. *grūwen*, cp. obs. or dial. Engl. *grue*, 'to shudder, shiver', & **-some.** Cp. M.L.G., M.H.G. *grūwen*, Germ. *grauen*, O. Swed. *grūa*, Dan. *grūe*, 'shudder, dread'. The identical cogn. appears in Du. *gruwzaam*, 'terrible', Germ. *grausam*, 'cruel', Dan. *grusom*, 'cruel', Norw. *gruvsam*, 'frightful'. The Gmc. base *grū- is prob. the same as that wh. occurs w. an additional *-t* in O.E. *grēot, grūt*, 'fright', also 'grains of meal', q.v. under **grout** (I.) & **grit**; fr. Aryan *ghreu-(d-), meaning 'to rub, wear down, pulverize', & in non-material sense, 'to terrify'. Cp. further O.H.G. *grūsōn*, 'to feel terror'; M.H.G. *griul*, 'horror', Mod. Germ. *gräuel.* Inspiring horror and repugnance; grisly, macabre.

gruesomely, adv. Prec. & **-ly.** In a gruesome manner.

gruesomeness, n. See prec. & **-ness.** Quality of being gruesome.

gruff, adj. [1. gruf; 2. graf]. Early Mod. Lowland Scots *grof*, 'coarse, rough' (of stones), perh. borrowed fr. a L.G. or Scand. source; cp. Du., L.G., E. Fris. *grof*, O.H.G. *gerob, grop*, Germ. *grob*, 'coarse, rough' (lit. & fig.), Swed. *grof*, Dan. *grov.* The O.H.G. *gerob* shows that *g-* represents the pref. O.E. *ġe-*, Goth. *ga-*, (see **y-**), & the stem is perh. that of O.E. *hrēof*, 'rough'. **a** (of the voice) Rough, harsh, loud and unmusical; deep and hoarse; **b** (of manner) abrupt, displaying angry impatience, or ill-nature.

gruffish, adj. [1. grúfish; 2. gráfiʃ]. Prec. & **-ish.** Somewhat gruff.

gruffly, adv. [1. grúfli; 2. gráfli]. **gruff** & **-ly.** In a gruff manner; sternly, roughly.

gruffness, n. [1. grúfnes; 2. gráfnis]. **gruff** & **-ness.** Quality of being gruff.

grumble (I.), vb. intrans. & trans. [1. grúmbl; 2. grámbl]. Picard *grumeler, groumeler*, Fr. *grommeler*, 'grumble, mutter', fr. a Gmc. source, cp. O.H.G. *grummeln*, L.G. *grummelen*, M. Du. *grommelen*, frequentatives (see **-le**) of a Gmc. vb. found in M. Du. *grommen*, 'to grumble, growl', grade of stem **gremm-*, 'to be angry', found in **grim. A.** intrans. **1.** To mutter or murmur angrily, make a low growling, sullen noise; of distant thunder &c., to rumble. **2. a** (followed by *at, over, about*) To complain, murmur, express dissatisfaction or discontent, sullenly or peevishly: *to grumble at, about, one's food*; **b** (absolutely) *don't grumble!*; *to be always grumbling.* **B.** trans. (often with *out*). To utter, say, in tone of peevish dissatisfaction.

grumble (II.), n., fr. prec. **a** Process of, sound made by, grumbling, rumbling &c. as of thunder; **b** act of complaining; uttered complaint.

grumbler, n. [1. grúmbler; 2. grámblə]. **grumble** (I.) & **-er.** One who grumbles.

grumbling, adj. [1. grúmbling; 2. grámbliŋ]. Pres. Part. of **grumble** (I.). **a** Inclined to grumble and complain; fault-finding, dissatisfied; **b** (of pain &c.) gnawing, dull, and incessant.

grumblingly, adv. Prec. & **-ly.** In a grumbling manner.

grume, n. [1. grōōm; 2. grūm]. Obs. Fr. *grume*, 'knot, bunch, cluster', fr. L. Lat. *grūmus*, 'little heap of earth'; orig. perh. a pile scraped, or scratched, together w. the bent fingers; cogn. w. Gk. *grupós*, 'curved, hook-nosed', & *grūps*, 'griffin' (see **griffin**); cp. further O.H.G. *krouwon*, 'to scratch'. All these words express the idea of something bent, or curved, & are connected w. W. *crwm*, 'bent'. (med.) Clot of blood; viscous fluid.

grummet, grommet, n. [1. grúmet; 2. grámit]. O. Fr. *gromette* (15th cent.), Mod. Fr. *gourmette*, 'curb, curb-chain of bridle', fr. or influenced by Fr. *gourmer*, 'to curb', prob. fr. **grum-*, 'something curved or bent', see prec., & dimin. suff. (naut.) **a** Ring at end of rope made by looping and splicing one or more strands, used as rowlock &c.; **b** metal ring in eyelet, as at edge of sail; **c** wad of twisted hemp &c., used for stopping steam leak.

grumous, grumose, adj. [1. grōōmus, -ōs; 2. grúməs, -ous]. **grume** & **-ous, -ose. 1.** (med.) Containing, resembling, grume; clotted. **2.** (bot.) Clubbed, knotted.

grumpily, adv. [1. grúmpili; 2. grámpili]. **grumpy** & **-ly.** (colloq.) In a grumpy manner.

grumpiness, n. [1. grúmpines; 2. grámpinis]. Next word & **-ness.** (colloq.) Quality of being grumpy; surliness.

grumpy, adj. [1. grúmpi; 2. grámpi]. Obs. *grump*, 'offence, snub', & **-y**; cp. Scots *grumph*, n. & vb.; prob. connected w. **grunt, grumble** (I.). (colloq.) Irritable, surly, peevish, bad-tempered, ill-conditioned.

Grundyism, n. [1. grúndi-izm: 2. grándi-izəm], fr. *Mrs. Grundy*, a character referred to in the phr. '*What will Mrs. Grundy say?*' which often recurs in comedy 'Speed the Plough' (1798), by Thos. Morton (d. 1838). **a** Excessively conventional or prudish standard of propriety and morals; ultra-respectability; **b** example of this.

grunt (I.), vb. intrans. & trans. [1. grunt; 2. grant]. O.E. *grunnettan* (once in a gloss.), M.E. *grunten*, fr. O.E. *grunian*, 'grunt', & *-ettan*, O.E. intens. or freq. suff. = Goth. *-atjan*, O.H.G. *-azzan*; cp. O.H.G., Mod. Germ. *grunzen*, Dan. *grynte*, Swed. *grymta*, 'grunt'; of imitative origin; cp. Lat. *grunnīre*, 'grunt', also **grumble** (I.), **grumpy. 1.** intrans. **a** (of animals, specif. of pigs) To utter a deep, rough, nasal sound; **b** (of persons) to utter an inarticulate sound, resembling this, expressing irritation, annoyance, contempt, or boredom. **2.** trans. To utter, with a grunt.

grunt (II.), n., fr. prec. **1.** Deep, nasal, snorting sound, made by a pig; similar noise uttered by other animal or person. **2.** One of a family of W. Indian marine fishes that grunt, related to snappers.

grunter, n. [1. grúnter; 2. grántə]. M.E. *gruntare*, fr. **grunt** (I.) & **-er. a** Animal or person that grunts, esp. pig; **b** one of several grunting fishes.

grunting, adj. [1. grúnting; 2. grántiŋ], fr. Pres. Part. of **grunt** (I.). Uttering grunts habitually: *grunting cow, ox*, the yak.

gruntingly, adv. Prec. & **-ly.** In a grunting manner.

Gruyère, n. [1. grōōyār; 2. grújɛə]. For *Gruyère cheese*, fr. *La Gruyère*, pastoral district in canton Fribourg, Switzerland, where it was orig. made. Kind of whole-milk cheese, made in Switzerland and E. France, having a distinctive flavour and a peculiar porous texture.

gryphon, n. Variant spelling of **griffin** (I.).

grysbok, n. [1. grísbok; 2. gráisbək]. Du., fr. *grijs*, 'grey', see **grisette**, & *bok*, see **buck.** Small greyish antelope of S. Africa.

guacharo, n. [1. gwahcháhrō; 2. gwátʃárou]. Span., fr. native name. A S. American night bird, allied to the night-jars; the young yield an oil, used as butter, whence the variant name *oil-bird.*

guaco, n. [1. gwáhkō; 2. gwákou]. Span. A S. American climbing plant, the dried leaves of which are eaten by the natives as an antidote to snake-bite.

guaiacol, n. [1. gwíakol; 2. gwáiəkɔl]. See next word & **-ol.** A strong-smelling colourless oil, obtained from creosote or wood tar by distillation, used medicinally in cases of tuberculosis of the lungs.

guaiacum, n. [1. gwíakum; 2. gwáiəkəm]. Mod. Lat. *guaiacum*, fr. Span. *guayaco*, fr. Haïtian name. **a** Wood of tropical American trees of genus *Guaiacum*, used as timber, *lignum vitae*; **b** resin from one of these trees, still used in medicine, in cases of rheumatism and in tuberculosis.

guan, n. [1. gwahn; 2. gwān]. Native name. Large game bird of S. America, allied to the curassow.

guanaco, n. [1. gwanáhkō; 2. gwənákou]. Span., fr. Peruv. *huanacu.* Large wild llama of the Andes.

guano, n. & vb. trans. [1. gwáhnō; 2. gwánou]. Span., fr. Peruv. *huanu*, 'dung'. **1.** n. **a** Manure, rich in phosphates and ammonia, consisting of dung of sea-birds; found in deposits on west coast of S. America and in Pacific; **b** artificial or natural manure with similar properties. **2.** vb. To manure with guano.

guarana, n. [1. gwaráhna; 2. gwəránə]. Native name. A Brazilian climbing plant, from the dried seeds of which a tonic, astringent drink is made.

guarantee (I.), n. [1. gàrantḗ; 2. gæ̀rəntí]. Formed on anal. of other law terms in **-ee** fr. **guarantor, guaranty.** (law) **1.** Person who receives a guaranty or surety. **2.** One who gives a guaranty; guarantor; surety. **3.** Act of one who acts as guarantor; pledge, promise that certain conditions covenanted for in a transaction will be fulfilled. **4.** Something given as security for this.

guarantee (II.), vb. trans., fr. prec. **1. a** To act as guarantor, agree formally to be answerable for; protect with one's credit, give security for: *to guarantee a loan, a dividend of 10%*; **b** to make oneself responsible for another's liabilities, for faithful performance of legal obligations by another: *to guarantee a man's debts, overdraft*; *to guarantee that a contract shall be faithfully performed*; *to guarantee that a debt shall be paid*; **c** to undertake to protect, insure, indemnify, a person against certain contingencies: *to be guaranteed against loss.* **2. a** To undertake something to be as stated: *good quality and durability are specially guaranteed*; **b** to engage, undertake to do something, or to secure that something shall be done: *I will guarantee the reconstruction of your house within a year*; *to guarantee one's success*; *the company is unable to guarantee the punctual arrival of trains.* **3.** (popular usage) To promise, undertake; to state with certainty and conviction; affirm, as certain, or extremely likely, the existence of something, occurrence of some event, performance of some action: *perfect satisfaction is guaranteed to our customers*; *to guarantee that a person will be pleased*; *I will guarantee that he will refuse to come after all.*

guarantor, n. [1. gàrantṓr; 2. gæ̀rəntɔ́]. Med. Lat. See next word & **-or.** (law) Person giving a guaranty.

guaranty, n. [1. gáranti; 2. gǽrənti]. Older form of **guarantee**; A.-Fr. *guarantie*, O. Fr. *garantie*, 'thing warranted', fem. of *garanti*, P.P. of *garantir*, fr. O. Fr. *garant*; of Gmc. origin. See **warrant, warranty.** (law) **1. a** Written promise or contract to be responsible for failure of another to perform undertaking, as to pay debt; **b** promise to maintain or secure possession by, or other right of, another; **c** in international law, obligation undertaken by state or states to maintain specified right of another state, or to enforce terms of agreement between two parties. **2.** Something offered as security or pledge by a guarantor to enforce obligation.

guard (I.), n. [1. gard; 2. gād]. O. Fr. *guarde, garde*, 'watching', fr. Gmc. source; the same word as **ward** (I.). **1. a** Action of watching against danger or surprise; watchfulness, wariness, vigilance, caution; Phr. *to keep guard*, maintain watch against danger, be alert, vigilant; **b** in fencing, use of bayonet; in boxing &c., specific posture, or attitude of defence: *to learn all the guards*; Phrs. *on (one's) guard*, watchful against attack, alert, vigilant: *off one's guard*, unprepared for, against, danger; **c** (cricket) position in which bat is held to defend wicket; Phrs. *to give guard*, indicate such position to batsman; *to take guard*, place bat in such position. **2.** Person or body of persons that keeps watch against danger; protector, defender, guardian; specif. **a** (mil. and nav.) sentry, sentinel; Phrs. *to mount guard*, assume duty of sentry; *to relieve guard*, take place of sentry going off duty; *to stand guard*, act as sentry; **b** (mil.) escort, armed man or body of men accompanying traveller &c.; *guard of honour*, escort appointed as compliment to distinguished visitor &c.; **c** (mil. and nav.) armed man or men in charge of prisoner or prisoners; **d** (mil.) body of men, regiment, whose duty is to protect person of the Sovereign; (pl.) *the Guards*, regiments of household troops, as *Life Guards, Royal Horse Guards, Grenadier Guards* &c., extended also to *Dragoon Guards*; **e** part of army on march in van or rear, thus having main duty of repelling attack: *advanced guard, rear-guard.* **3.** Official in charge of train or stage-coach. **4.** Any one of various objects designed to afford protection from different kinds of accidents or to prevent loss; **a** part of sword-hilt protecting hand; **b** hinged bar on carving-fork to prevent the left hand from being cut if the knife should slip; **c** plate over trigger of fire-arm; **d** framework of wire, or iron bars, placed in front of fire-grate to prevent burning cinders &c. from flying out; **e** chain or cord attaching watch to dress; **f** cord attaching man's hat to some part of dress; **g** ring worn above wedding-ring to prevent this from slipping off.

guard (II.), vb. trans. & intrans. O. Fr. *guarder*, Mod. Fr. *garder*, fr. a Gmc. source; cp. O.S. *wardōn.* See **ward** (II.). In some senses fr. prec. **A.** trans. **1.** To keep watch over, take care of, keep safe, protect, defend: *to guard life and property*; *to guard one's reputation.* **2.** In games such as chess &c., *to guard a man, piece &c.*, prevent from being taken by placing another by it. **3.** To watch over (prisoner, lunatic &c.), so as to prevent escape or mischief; to restrain, hold in check by watching. **B.** intrans. **1.** (often followed by *against*) To prevent by vigilance, and precautions: *to guard against temptation, suspicion, misunderstanding, risk of infection* &c. **2.** (fencing) To use a guard, assume defensive posture.

guardant, gardant, adj. [1. gárdant; 2. gā́dənt]. Fr., Pres. Part., 'looking'. See prec. (her.) Looking out from the field.

guard boat, n. Boat employed as guard; esp. **a** naval boat used to go rounds of fleet in harbour; **b** boat sent round by harbour authorities to enforce regulations.

guard-chain, n. Small chain attaching watch, brooch, or other object to dress.

guarded, adj. [1. gárded; 2. gā́did]. P.P. of **guard (I.)**. (of mode of expression) Cautious, discreet, reticent; non-committal: *guarded remarks*; *be very guarded in what you say.*

guardedly, adv. Prec. & **-ly**. In a guarded, cautious manner, esp. of speech or writing.

guardedness, n. See prec. & **-ness**. Caution, discretion, careful reticence; esp. in expression of ideas, promises, hopes &c.

guard-house, n. **a** Building occupied by guard; **b** one in which prisoners are guarded.

guardian, n. [1. gárdian; 2. gā́diən]. O. Fr. *guardene, guarden, garden*, Mod. Fr. *gardien*; variant of **warden**. **1.** Protector, defender, custodian; person or other agent who has charge of and protects a person or thing: specif., member of board recently abolished, administering poor law in union of parishes; also *guardian of the poor.* **2.** (law) One who has legal custody of the person or estate of an infant or of a person declared incapable of conducting his own affairs, esp. custodian (jointly with mother, if living) of person or estate of an orphan, or infant whose parents are incapable of exercising guardianship. *Guardian by nature, natural guardian*, father or mother in capacity of guardian; *guardian by statute, testamentary guardian*, one appointed by deed or will. *Guardian in socage*, person, being the next in blood who cannot inherit, who is guardian for an infant of lands in socage. *Guardian ad litem* (Lat., 'for the suit'), person appointed to act for infant in law-suit. *Guardian of the spiritualities, temporalities*, person to whom is committed spiritual jurisdiction, temporal jurisdiction and profits, of a diocese, during vacancy. **3.** Superior of Franciscan convent.

guardian angel, n. Angel whose office is to watch over and protect a person, community, or place; good genius.

guardianship, n. [1. gárdianship; 2. gā́diənʃip]. **guardian** & **-ship.** Office, function, of guardian.

guard-rail, n. **a** Rail for the hand, on staircase &c., to save those going up and down from falling; **b** any rail which affords protection, e.g. from moving machinery &c.

guard-ring, n. One worn above wedding-ring, to prevent this from slipping off; keeper.

guard-room, n. **a** Room occupied by guard; **b** room where prisoners, esp. soldiers under arrest, are kept.

guardship, n. [1. gárdship; 2. gā́dʃip]. Warship stationed in harbour or river for defence against surprise attack, for direction of naval affairs, and for reception of seamen until they join their ships.

guardsman, n. [1. gárdzman; 2. gā́dzmən]. Officer or man of a regiment of Guards.

guard-wire, n. (elect.) Wire fixed transversely above live wire to prevent broken telegraph or telephone wires from falling on to it.

guava, n. [1. gwáhva; 2. gwā́və], fr. Span. *guayaba*, 'guava fruit', prob. fr. native Am. name. **a** Small tree of myrtle order, native of tropical America; **b** fruit of this, which has a very pungent characteristic taste; used for making jelly and preserve.

gubernatorial, adj. [1. gûbernatórial; 2. gjûbənətɔ́riəl], fr. Lat. *gubernātōri-*, stem of *gubernātor*, 'steersman; ruler', & **-al.** See **governor** & **govern.** Belonging to, connected with, a governor.

gudgeon (I.), n. [1. gújun; 2. gádžən]. M.E. *gojon*, fr. Fr. *goujon*, 'gudgeon', fr. Lat. *gōbiōn-(em)*, extended form of *gōbius*, 'gudgeon', fr. Gk. *kōbiós*. See **goby. 1.** Small British freshwater fish of carp family. **2.** (fig.) Person who can be easily duped.

gudgeon (II.), n. M.E. *gojone*, fr. O. Fr. *gojon*, Mod. Fr. *goujon*, 'sculptor's chisel, gudgeon, dowel'. See **gouge** & **-on, -oon. 1.** Pivot or journal at end of moving shaft or axle; *gudgeon block*, bearing on which gudgeon turns; *gudgeon pin*, pin joining piston-rod to connecting-rod. **2.** Socket or eye in which hinge turns; socket of rudder. **3.** Pin fixed in two stone blocks to hold them together.

guelder rose, n. [1. gélder rṓz; 2. géldə róuz]. Fr. *rose de Gueldre*, 'rose of Guelders', former duchy of Gelderland, a province of Holland. Small tree of honeysuckle family, *Viburnum*, bearing globular clusters of white flowers; snowball tree, one of several foreign species grown in gardens.

Guelph, Guelf, n. [1. gwelf; 2. gwɛlf], fr. Ital. *Guelfo*, fr. Gmc. *Welf* (a form of *wolf*), ancestor of the royal stock whence the English Georges were descended; family name of British sovereigns fr. George I. to Queen Victoria. Member of mediaeval Italian political faction, from 12th to 15th cent., which supported the authority of the Popes as against that of the German Emperors; the opposed faction were the *Ghibellines.*

Guelphic, adj. [1. gwélfik; 2. gwélfik]. Prec. & **-ic.** Belonging to, connected with, the Guelphs.

guenon, n. [1. genón; 2. gənɔ̃]. Fr. *guenon*, 'she-monkey', of unknown origin. One of a genus of long-tailed African monkeys, resembling the macaque.

guerdon (I.), n. [1. gĕrdun; 2. gǽd(ə)n]. M.E. *guerdon*, fr. O. Fr. *guerdon*, of hybrid origin, fr. Med. Lat. *widerdōnum* (9th cent.), 'recompense' (whence also Ital. *guiderdone*), the first element of wh. is fr. O.H.G. *widar*, 'against, back', see **withers**, & the second is Lat. *dōnum*, 'gift', see **donation**; the O.H.G. word was *widarlōn* (cp. O.E. *wiðerlēan*), 'return gift, recompense', fr. *widar* as above & *lōn*, 'reward, gift', Common Gmc., cp. O.E. *lēan*, Goth. *laun.* (liter.) Recompense, reward.

guerdon (II.), vb. trans. M.E. *guerdonen*, fr. O. Fr. *guerredoner*, fr. prec. (liter.) To recompense, reward.

guereza, n. [1. geréza; 2. gerízə]. Native name. A large African monkey of Abyssinia and Zanzibar, genus *Colobus*, with long, silky black and white hair.

guerilla, n. See **guerrilla.**

Guernsey, n. [1. gĕrnzi; 2. gǽnzi], fr. name of one of Channel Islands. **1.** One of a breed of cattle reared in the island. Also attrib.: *Guernsey cattle, cow* &c. **2.** Kind of blue, knitted woollen tunic, jersey, or sweater, with hole for neck, worn by seamen and children.

guerrilla, also **guerilla**, n. [1. gerĭla; 2. gərílə]. Span. *guerrilla*, 'little war', dimin. of *guerra*, 'war', fr. O.H.G. *werra*, 'strife', see **war**, & dimin. suff. **1.** Irregular war or campaign, waged by armed bands, usually of insurgents or volunteers. **2.** Person conducting, or fighting in, such warfare. **3.** Attrib., in *guerrilla band, chief, war* &c.

guess (I.), vb. trans. & intrans. [1. ges; 2. gɛs]. M.E. *gessen*, in sense of 'think, suppose, believe'; prob. fr. a L.G. or Scand. source; cp. M.L.G. *gissen*, M. Du. *ghissen*, N. Fris. *gezze, gedze*; M. Dan. *gidze, gitse, getse*; Mod. Dan. *gisse*; Swed. *gissa*, 'guess'; prob. derived by addition of suff. w. *-s-*, fr. Gmc. base seen in **get.** Cp. Icel. *geta*, 'get; guess'; Dan. *gjette*, 'guess'. The spelling *gu-* is a survival of the Fr. mode of expressing the sound [g], as distinct fr. [dž], before *e.* **A.** trans. **1.** To come to a conclusion, make deduction, form a judgement concerning, in a tentative way, from data, or for reasons, which seem to establish a strong probability although not sufficient to give certainty: *from his appearance I should guess his age at 40*; *I guess your weight at 10 stone.* **2.** To judge, form and express an opinion concerning, at a venture, without having any materials upon which to base a judgement: *I can only guess the reasons for his conduct, as I have no certain knowledge.* **3.** To hit upon, or attempt to hit upon, correct solution of by a happy conjecture, without any real data: *to guess a riddle*; *I can't guess your thoughts*; *he guessed the right answer at once*; cp. Chaucer, *Of twenty yeer of age he was I gesse*, Prol. 'C.T.' 82. **4.** (archaic or Am.) To suppose, believe, feel certain of or that: *I guess we shall lose the train.* **B.** intrans. **a** To hazard a conjecture, make a shot, without having any knowledge upon which to base a genuine opinion: *if you don't know the meaning of a word say so, don't guess*; *you evidently know nothing about the subject and are merely guessing*; **b** also, *guess at*: *I can't even guess at what you mean*, can form no opinion concerning.

guess (II.), n., fr. prec. Conjecture, opinion formed intuitively or without adequate evidence; surmise, shot: *a lucky guess.*

guess-rope, guess-warp, n. See **guest-rope, -warp.**

guess-work, n. Process of guessing, without adequate data; theory, view, arrived at thus.

guest (I.), n. [1. gest; 2. gest]. O.E. (non-W. Sax.), *ġest*, 'stranger, visitor, friendly or hostile', fr. *gasti-* w. *i-* mutation, (W.S. *ġiest*). The initial sound of *g* is due to influence of O.N. *gestr.* The normal mod. form of O.E. *ġ* is *y* as in O.E. *ġiest*, 'yeast', q.v.; for spelling *gue-*, cp. remarks under **guess.** O.S., L.G., O.H.G., Mod. Germ. *gast*, Goth. *gast-s*; cogn. w. O. Slav. *gosti*, 'guest', & Lat. *hostis*, 'stranger, foreigner, enemy'. See further under **host** & **hostile. 1. a** (i.) Person enjoying another's hospitality, at the latter's own house, or elsewhere, whether during prolonged stay, at a single meal, or at a party &c.: *I was his guest for three weeks*; *a few guests to dinner*; *lunch with me at the hotel as my guest*, i.e. I paying; (ii.) also *the guest of the city, of the University* &c.; **b** fig. of birds &c.: *the swallow is a summer guest in Britain.* **2.** Person staying in an inn, or other house of entertainment, and paying for his accommodation. Phr. *paying guest*, boarder in a private house. **3.** Animal, esp. insect, inhabiting nest, or other abode, of one of another kind whose food it shares: *guest ant* &c.

guest (II.), vb. trans. & intrans., fr. prec. (rare or obs.) **a** trans. To entertain as a guest; **b** intrans., to be a guest.

guest-chamber, n. Room set apart for use of guests; used esp. in an institution; corresponding to *spare-room* in private house.

guestling, n. [1. géstling; 2. géstliŋ]. Prob. fr. **guest (I.)** & **-ling**, because the representatives of the subordinate ports may have been at first invited to sit in this court as guests of the Cinque Ports. (law) Term used in, and as contraction for, Phr. *Brotherhood and Guestling*, second court of the Cinque Ports, consisting of the members of the Court of Brotherhood, together with representatives of the corporate members.

guest-night, n. Evening when guests are entertained at dinner by a society.

guest-rite, n. Ceremonial observance, custom, connected with entertainment of a guest.

guest-room, n. Guest-chamber.

guest-rope, also **guess-rope**, n. [1. gés(t) rōp; 2. gés(t) roup]. Origin of first element unknown; possibly the word means 'rope to aid guest coming aboard'. See **guest-warp.** (naut.) **a** Rope attached to ship's side for boatmen coming alongside to hold; **b** rope to steady boat in tow in addition to tow-rope; **c** rope or hawser for warping ship, carried by boat to object to which it can be attached.

guestship, n. [1. géstship; 2. géstʃip]. **guest** & **-ship.** Fact of being a guest; status of guest.

guest-warp, also **guess-warp**, n. [1. gés(t) worp; 2. gés(t) wɔ̄p]. See **guest-rope** & **warp (II.)**; *guess-warp* seems to be the more usual form. (naut.) Guest-rope, **a** and **c**; *guess-warp boom*, spar projecting from ship's side with rope to secure boat.

guffaw, n. & vb. [1. gufáw; 2. gafɔ́]. Imitative; orig. Scots. **1.** n. Sudden outburst of loud, rude laughter; noisy, coarse, vulgar laugh, horse laugh. **2.** vb. To utter such a laugh.

guggle, vb. intrans. [1. gúgl; 2. gágl]. Imitative; cp. **gurgle** & **gargle**. To make a noise like that of water flowing from a bottle; to gurgle.

guhr, n. [1. gōor; 2. guə]. Germ., lit. 'fermentation', different grade fr. stem of *garen*, O.H.G. *jesan*, 'to ferment'; cp. **yeast.** **(miner.)** Earthy deposit, white, red, or yellow, produced in crevices by action of water.

guidable, adj. [1. gídabl; 2. gáidəbl]. **guide (I.)** & **-able**. Amenable to guidance, capable of being guided.

guidage, n. [1. gídij; 2. gáididž]. Fr., 'guiding'. See **guide** & **-age**. (law, obs. or hist.) Fee paid for safe-conduct.

guidance, n. [1. gídans; 2. gáidəns]. **guide (I.)** & **-ance.** **a** Act of guiding, directing, conducting; **b** process of being guided; direction, instruction.

guide (I.), vb. trans. [1. gīd; 2. gaid]. M.E. *gīden*, fr. O. Fr. *guider*, for older *guier* (M.E. *gien*), assimilated to corresponding O. Provenç. *guidar*, 'to guide'; cp. Ital. *guidare*; fr. a W. Gmc. source; cp. O.S., O.E. *wītan*, 'take heed to, guard; impute', O.H.G., *wīzan*, 'impute, determine', Mod. Germ. *weisen*, 'show, point out'; Goth. *-weitan*, 'see'; cp. also O.E. *wīsian*, 'guide, show the way to', fr. same base; fr. Gmc. base **wīt-*, strong grade of **wit-*, 'know'. See **wise, write, wit, guy** (rope). **1.** (action of persons or animate creatures) **a** To accompany (a person) and show way to a place: *the blind man was guided by his dog*; *he guided me across the fields, through the forest, to the house*; **b** to assist, direct, by bodily movements and support: *to guide the steps of*; *to guide a person's hand*; **c** to give intellectual or spiritual instruction and help to; direct studies of: *to guide a person through the intricacies of the Greek syntax.* **2.** To control, direct, rule, lead, act as governor of: *to guide the state.* **3.** (action of thought, feelings, and other non-material things) To control, influence, actuate, a person or his conduct; act as motive or inducement to: *to be guided by one's sense of duty, by one's passions, by one's love for truth.* **4.** (action of inanimate things) To direct; to indicate, point out, serve as an indication of, direction; show the road: *the lights in the harbour guided the ship to port.*

guide (II.), n. M.E. *gīde*, fr. O. Fr. *guide*, orig. fem., fr. older *guie*, assimilated to O.Provenç. & Ital. *guida*, fr. prec. **1.** **a** Person accompanying another to show way to, or position of, a place or thing; specif., one hired, to show way to and assist a traveller, on mountains, through strange country &c., or to conduct visitors round a town, museum &c.; **b** (mil., pl.) body of troops trained for reconnoitring: *Corps of Guides*, mobile force in Indian army, for frontier service; **c** Girl Guide, q.v. **2.** **a** Person who guides, directs, helps, (another) in intellectual and spiritual matters: '*Thou wert my guide, philosopher, and friend*' (Pope); *one's guide in religion* &c.; **b** one whose example is followed as a model of conduct &c.: *I early took my father as my exemplar and guide through life.* **3.** A thing which guides; **a** something which indicates the way to, direction, position of, a thing, place &c., by an impression made on the senses: *the lights of the camp and the distant shouts of men were my guides*; **b** book giving instructions, explanations, practical directions: *a guide to English studies*; *guide to poultry keeping*; **c** a guide-book; **d** a principle, belief, ideal, feeling &c. which influences conduct, action, or thought: *instinct is not always a safe guide*; *whim and prejudice are poor guides.* **4.** One of various objects of technical utility, specif., e.g. **a** (surg.) device for guiding a probe; **b** one of several small rings on a fishing-rod through which the line passes &c.

guide-book, n. Book containing directions for visiting a country, town, district &c., with information regarding hotels, routes, objects of note &c.; similar book for visitors to a museum, building &c.

guideless, adj. [1. gídles; 2. gáidlis]. **guide (II.)** & **-less**. Without a guide or guidance.

guide-post, n. **guide (I.)** & **post (I.)**. Post, generally at cross-roads, bearing board indicating direction to places.

guide-rail, n. (rlys.) Additional rail to prevent wheels from leaving main rails.

guide-rope, n. Small rope to steady and direct swinging load; guy.

guideway, n. [1. gídwā; 2. gáidwei]. (mechan.) Groove or other track in which a moving part travels.

guiding, adj. & n. [1. gíding; 2. gáidiŋ]. **a** adj., fr. Pres. Part. of **guide (I.)**, acting as a guide: *a guiding star, light, principle* &c.; **b** n., fr. **guide (I.)** & **-ing**. Guidance.

guidon, n. [1. gédon; 2. gídɔ̄]. Fr., perh. fr. Ital. *guidone*, augmentative of *guida*. See **guide** & **-oon.** (mil.) **a** Pennant or small flag carried by cavalry regiments; **b** bearer of such pennant.

guild, also **gild**, n. [1. gild; 2. gild]. O.E. *ġ(i)eld*, M.E. *ȝilde, gilde*, 'payment', also 'guild, fraternity' (from contributions of members), (*ġe*)*ġield*, 'guild', fr. *ġieldan*, 'pay'. See **yield**. The present form of the word, esp. the initial *g-*, is prob. due to Scand. influence; cp. O.N. *gildi*, 'payment', & Mod. Dan. *gilde* w. Engl. sense; A.-Fr. *guilde*, fr. Low Lat. *gilda*, a loan-word fr. Gmc., may have helped. **Yield** preserves the orig. Engl. sound initially. The spelling *guild* first occurs about 1600. An association with a common fund and aim; chiefly, a mediaeval, religious, charitable, technical, commercial, or administrative association; **b** by a revival of the word, a modern association with specific aim: *a guild of bank clerks.*

guilder, n. [1. gílder; 2. gíldə]. Corrupt. of Du. *gulden*, pronounced without the *-n*. See **gulden.** Dutch or German coin.

guildhall, n. [1. gíldháwl; 2. gíldhɔ̄l]. **a** Hall used for meetings of mediaeval guild; **b** town-hall, city-hall, esp. where the corporation was a guild; specif. (cap.) the hall of the Corporation of the City of London.

guild merchant, n. The second word is here used adjectivally, following the Fr. order, A.-Fr. *guilde merchante*, Low Lat. *gilda mercatoria.* (hist.) **a** General association of merchants in a borough, possessing trade monopoly; **b** liberty or privilege granted to such merchants.

guildry, n. [1. gíldri; 2. gíldri]. **guild** & **-ry.** (hist.) In Scotland, association of merchants who were freemen of a royal burgh.

guild socialism, n. Form of socialism aiming at modified revival of guild system with national guild council.

guild socialist, n. Adherent of guild socialism.

guile, n. [1. gīl; 2. gail]. M.E. *gīle*, fr. O. Fr. *guile*, fr. a Gmc. source. See **wile.** Wiliness, deceit, craftiness.

guileful, adj. [1. gílfool; 2. gáilfəl]. **guile** & **-ful.** Full of guile.

guilefully, adv. Prec. & **-ly.** In a guileful manner; with guile.

guilefulness, n. See prec. & **-ness.** Quality of being guileful.

guileless, adj. [1. gílles; 2. gáillis]. **guile** & **-less.** Without guile.

guilelessly, adv. Prec. & **-ly.** In a guileless manner; innocently.

guilelessness, n. See prec. & **-ness.** Quality of being guileless; innocency.

guillemot, n. [1. gílimot; 2. gílimɔt]. Fr., dimin. of the name *Guillaume*, 'William'; cp. the Engl. surname *Wilmot*, also *willock*, Sussex name of guillemot. The Fr. name was possibly suggested by Bret. *gwelan*, **gull (I.)**. One of several web-footed sea-birds of the auk family, but with narrow bills.

guilloche, n. [1. gilósh; 2. gilóuʃ]. Fr. *guilloche*, earlier *guillochis*, name of a tool; perh. fr. name of early designer, Guillot. (archit.) Decorative pattern, used as border, consisting of two or more interlaced waving bands with circular spaces between them.

guillotine (I.), n. [1. gilotén; 2. gilətín]. Fr., after the physician J. I. Guillotin (1738–1814), who advocated its adoption in France, 1789. **1.** Machine for beheading persons, consisting of a weighted axe-head falling between two grooved posts connected by cross-bar at top; esp. improved form adopted in France in 1792. **2.** **a** Machine for slicing off edges of sheets of book; **b** surgical instrument for excision of uvula &c. **3.** (colloq.) Resolution of House of Commons fixing times for votes on bill: *the guillotine fell at 11 P.M. and the House divided.*

guillotine (II.), vb. trans. Fr. *guillotiner*, fr. prec. **a** To behead with guillotine; **b** to cut or cut off with guillotine **(I.)**, **2**; **c** (colloq.) to expedite passage of (bill) by guillotine **(I.)**, **3.**

guilt, n. [1. gilt; 2. gilt]. Found nowhere but in Engl.; O.E. *gylt*, 'guilt, sin, crime, debt, fine, forfeiture', M.E. *gult, gilt*, 'guilt, debt', fr. Gmc. type **gultiz*, the origin of wh. is quite uncertain. Possibly connected w. O.E. *ġieldan*, 'to pay', q.v. under **yield** & **guild.** **1.** **a** Fact of having offended; state of responsible person who has knowingly and wilfully committed an offence, crime, sin, against moral, human, or divine law; culpability; **b** (theol.) sin; opposed to *innocence.* **2.** (law) Wilful violation by responsible person of criminal law; criminality.

guiltily, adv. [1. gíltili; 2. gíltili]. **guilty** & **-ly.** In a guilty manner; as though guilty.

guiltiness, n. [1. gíltines; 2. gíltinis]. **guilty** & **-ness.** State of being guilty; guilt.

guiltless, adj. [1. gíltles; 2. gíltlis]. **guilt** & **-less.** **a** Without guilt; innocent; **b** (colloq.) not responsible for, incapable, innocent, of: *guiltless of writing poems, of reading Greek.*

guiltlessly, adv. Prec. & **-ly.** In a guiltless manner; innocently.

guiltlessness, n. See prec. & **-ness.** State of being guiltless; innocence.

guilty, adj. [1. gílti; 2. gílti]. O.E. *gyltiġ*, 'guilty, liable', M.E. *gulti, gilti*, fr. **guilt** & **-y.** **1.** **a** Having incurred guilt, having committed a crime or sin: *guilty of murder*; **b** (of lesser faults than are implied by *guilt*), culpable, deserving blame, offending: *guilty of a blunder, of bad taste, of a breach of good manners.* **2.** **a** Pertaining to, involving, guilt: *guilty knowledge, a guilty secret*; **b** declaring, betraying guilt: *a guilty conscience, look, blush.* **3.** (obs.) Liable (to), deserving (of penalty): *guilty of death.*

guimp, n. See **gimp.**

guinea, n. [1. gíni; 2. gíni], fr. Port. *Guiné*, country in W. Africa. **a** Former English gold coin, at first made of gold from Guinea, nominally worth 20s. to 21s.; **b** monetary unit of 21s. used in reckoning professional fees, prices of goods &c.

guinea-corn, n. *Guinea* (country) & **corn.** **a** Durra, Indian millet; **b** pearl millet.

guinea-fowl, n. *Guinea* (country) & **fowl.** Gallinaceous African bird, also called '*galeeny*', of grey colour speckled with white, also all white; domesticated in Europe &c. for its flesh and eggs; also any of several related birds.

guinea grains, n. pl. Seeds of *Amomum*, guinea pepper, grains of Paradise, used in veterinary medicine.

guinea grass, n. A tall grass of W. Africa and the W. Indies used for fodder.

guinea-hen, n. Female guinea-fowl.

guinea pepper, n. *Guinea* (country), in error for *Guiana*. a Aromatic fruit of *Xylopicrum*, an African tree; the tree; b guinea grains; c cayenne pepper.

guinea-pig, n. Of uncertain origin, perh. for *Guiana* **pig**, or **cony** & **pig** (formerly called *pig cony*). **1.** Small particoloured domesticated rodent, variety of S. American cavy, somewhat like pig in shape. **2.** (colloq., contempt.) Person who receives guinea fees for small services, esp. (i.) company director for attending board meetings, or (ii.) a clergyman taking temporary duty in another parish than his own who receives a guinea for each service he conducts.

guinea-worm, n. Worm, of tropical Africa &c., parasitic in tissues of man and horse, esp. in legs and feet, causing sores.

guipure, n. [1. gépūr; 2. gípjuə]. Fr., fr. *guiper*, 'to cover (cord) with silk'. See **whip** & **-ure**. One of several kinds of lace, esp. with large pattern and no mesh ground; lace made with gimp; gimp.

guise, n. [1. gīz; 2. gaiz]. M.E., fr. Fr., fr. O.H.G. *wīsa*, Mod. Germ. *weise*, 'manner, way, mode'. See **wise (II.)** & cp. **disguise**. **1.** a (archaic) Manner, customary behaviour, fashion: *he behaved after the natural guise of such people*; b style of dress or equipment, garb, get-up: *a foreigner in strange guise appeared before us*. **2.** Assumed dress or appearance, as in masquerade; disguise; also fig.: *under the guise of friendship* &c., under pretence of.

guiser, n. [1. gízer; 2. gáizə]. **guise (I.)** & **-er**. a (provinc.) Mummer, actor in a mummery; b (colloq.) *an old guiser*, old person, bloke &c.; also *geezer*.

guitar, n. [1. gitár; 2. gitā́]. Span. *guitarra* (whence also Fr. *guitare*), fr. Lat. *cithara*. See **cithern**. Six-stringed lute with fretted finger-board.

guitarist, n. [1. gitáhrist; 2. gitā́rist]. Prec. & **-ist**. Player on guitar.

gulch, n. [1. gulsh; 2. galʃ]. Prob. fr. obs. or dial. Engl. *gulch*, 'to swallow greedily', M.E. *gulchen*; borrowed fr. some continental Gmc. tongue, cp. Germ. dial. *gulken*, *glucken*, Swed. dial. *gōlka*, prob. imitative. Cp. **gulp**. (Am., esp. in gold-mining districts) Deep ravine or torrent-bed.

gulden, n. [1. gōōlden; 2. gûldən]. Du., Germ. *gulden*, fr. M.H.G. *guldīn*, 'made of gold'. See **golden** & cp. **guilder**. a (hist.) Silver coin (orig. gold) and money of account, formerly issued by Austria and other German states; florin; hence, b silver coin and money of account of Netherlands; guilder; worth about 1s. 8d.

gules, n. & adj. [1. gūlz; 2. gjūlz]. M.E. *goules*, fr. O. Fr. *goles, goules, geules* (Mod. Fr. *gueules*), cp. L. Lat. *gulae*, 'gules'; of uncertain origin, perh. fr. Lat. *gulae*, 'jaws'. Cp. **gullet**. (her.) a n. The colour red; b adj., red.

gulf (I.), n. [1. gulf; 2. galf]. M.E. *goulf*, fr. O. Fr. *goulfe*, fr. Provenç. *golfo*, fr. Late Gk. *kólph-os* for Gk. *kólp-os*, 'bosom, hollow, bay'. If this is fr. Aryan **kʷolp-*, then cp. O.E. *hwealf*, 'a vault, hollow'; if fr. **kʷolkʷ-*, then cp. O.E. *healh*, 'nook, corner, retired place, bay', & see **haugh**. **1.** Large inlet of sea or lake into land, usually larger than bay, or running more deeply into land in proportion to width. **2.** Deep hollow, gap, or breach; (esp. poet.) abyss, ocean depth; (fig.) impassable boundary or barrier, in allusion to Luke xvi. 26: '*Between us and you there is a great gulf fixed*'. **3.** a Whirlpool, eddy that sucks things down: '*It may be that the gulfs will wash us down*' (Tennyson, 'Ulysses'); also b (fig.) specif. (univ. colloq.) at Oxford and Cambridge, place in list, hence position, of candidates for honours who fail to attain them, but receive a pass degree; the lowest distinction conferred by the University: *to get a gulf*.

gulf (II.), vb. trans., fr. prec. **1.** To suck down into abyss or deep water, swallow up, engulf. **2.** (univ. colloq.) To place (candidate for honours) in a gulf, award ordinary degree to.

Gulf Stream, n. Warm ocean current flowing N.E. from Gulf of Mexico to European coasts.

Gulf-weed, n. Sea-weed bearing air-bladders, found in Gulf Stream &c.; sargasso.

gulfy, adj. [1. gúlfi; 2. gálfi]. **gulf (I.)** & **-y**. Full of whirlpools.

gull (I.), n. [1. gul; 2. gal]. Corn. *gwilan, gullan*, W. *gwylan* (i.e. *gūylan*), Bret. *gwelan*, (whence Fr. *goéland*), O. Ir. *foilenn*, Gael., Ir. *faoileann*, fr. Celt. type **woilenno-*, prob. 'wailer'. Member of group of web-footed, gregarious, fish-eating sea-birds, powerful fliers, usually white, but grey or black in parts; sea-mew.

gull (II.), n. In sense **1**, prob. O.N. *gul-r*, **yellow**, whence perh. sense **2** (cp. *pigeon*); cp. also M. Du. *gulle*, 'great wench without wit' (Hexham), L.G. *gull*, E. Fris. *gul*, 'soft, mild, good-natured'. Possibly, however, source of **2** is obs. vb. *gull*, 'to stuff, cram with food', fr. O. Fr. *goule*, **gullet**, in wh. case **2** is fr. **gull (III.)**. **1.** (obs. or dial.) Unfledged bird, nestling: '*that ungentle gull, the cuckoo's bird*' (Shakespeare, '1 Henry IV.'). **2.** Person easily tricked or befooled; dupe.

gull (III.), vb. trans. See prec. To dupe, trick, swindle.

gull-catcher, n. (obs.) Person who makes dupes of others (Shakespeare, 'Twelfth Night').

gullet, n. [1. gúlet; 2. gálit]. M.E. *golet*, fr. O. Fr. *goulet*, dimin. of *gole, goule* (Mod. Fr. *gueule*), 'throat', fr. Lat. *gula*; cogn. w. O.E. *ċeole*, 'throat'; O.H.G. *kela*, Mod. Germ. *kehle*, 'throat'; fr. same base comes Lat. *glūtīre*, 'to swallow' (see **glutton**). See also **gully**. **1.** Passage from mouth to stomach; oesophagus, throat. **2.** (fig.) Water-channel, gully.

gullibility, n. [1. gùlibíliti; 2. gàlibíliti]. **gullible** & **-ity**. (colloq.) Capacity for being gulled.

gullible, adj. [1. gúlibl; 2. gálibl]. **gull (III.)** & **-ible**. (colloq.) Capable of being gulled; easily fooled, or duped; credulous.

gully (I.), n. [1. gúli; 2. gáli]. Either directly fr. Fr. *goulet*, 'bottle-neck, funnel-like opening', see **gullet**, or corrupt. of that word. **1.** a Small ravine or hollow water-course, esp. one ordinarily dry; b artificial channel for water; gutter, drain. **2.** Hollow rail for trams; tram-plate.

gully (II.), vb. trans., fr. prec. To form gully or gullies in, to furrow by running water.

gully-drain, n. Drain conveying water from gully or gutter to sewer.

gully-hole, n. Shaft in street gutter covered with grating, to carry off surface drainage.

gully-trap, n. Trap in gully-hole.

gulosity, n. [1. gūlósiti; 2. gjūlɔ́siti], fr. L. Lat. *gulōsitāt-(em)*, fr. *gulōsus*, 'gluttonous', fr. *gula*, 'throat'. See **gullet**. (rare) Gluttony, voracity.

gulp (I.), vb. trans. & intrans. [1. gulp; 2. galp]. M.E. *gulpen, gloppen, glubben*, of continental Gmc. origin, cp. M. Du. *golpen*, Du., E. Fris. *gulpen*, 'swallow eagerly', also Swed. dial. *gliopa*, Norw. *glupa* (both strong vbs.), 'swallow', prob. of imitative origin. **1.** trans. (usually *gulp down*) a To swallow hastily, noisily, or by mouthfuls, esp. liquid; b to repress, choke back, as if by action of swallowing: *to gulp down sobs, emotion*; c (fig.) to listen to, accept (a statement) with eagerness or credulity: *a public always eager to gulp down a sensational story*. **2.** intrans. To swallow with a convulsive movement or spasm.

gulp (II.), n., fr. prec. a Action of gulping or swallowing hastily; Phr. (*to swallow*) *at one gulp*, with a single act of swallowing; b convulsive movement or noise made while swallowing; c large mouthful, esp. of drink.

gulpingly, adv. [1. gúlpingli; 2. gálpiŋli], fr. Pres. Part. of **gulp (II.)** & **-ly**. In a gulping manner, with gulps.

gulpy, adj. [1. gúlpi; 2. gálpi]. **gulp (II.)** & **-y**. Pertaining to, resembling, a gulp: *gulpy sobs*.

gum (I.), n. [1. gum; 2. gam]. O.E. *gōma*, 'palate', pl. *gōman*, 'jaws'; M.E. *gōme*, *gūme*; O.H.G. *guomo, gaumo* &c.; Mod. Germ. *gaumen*; O.N. *gōmr*; all fr. Aryan base **gʰēw-* &c., 'to gape, yawn', whence also Gk. *khaûnos*, 'gaping', *khḗmē*, 'a gaping', & *kháos*, 'empty space', fr. **gʰəwos*. See **chaos**. (usually pl.) Firm tissues in upper and lower jaws in which the teeth are set.

gum (II.), n. M.E. *gumme, gomme*, fr. Fr. *gomme*, fr. Lat. *gummi*, fr. Gk. *kómmi*, prob. fr. Egypt. *kamī*. **1.** a One of several sticky, viscid substances, usually exuding from trees or shrubs, solidifying in air, but soluble in water; b preparation of such substance for use as adhesive &c. **2.** (in wider sense) Viscid, vegetable substance, including mucilages, resins &c.: *chewing-gum*, made from chicle and flavoured. **3.** A gum tree, esp. eucalyptus: *a plantation of blue gums*.

gum (III.), vb. trans. & intrans., fr. prec. Cp. Fr. *gommer*. **1.** trans. To apply gum to surface of; to stick, fasten, or stiffen with gum: *to gum down, in, together, up*. **2.** intrans. (of trees) To exude gum; specif., of fruit trees of plum species, to produce gum in excess, a sign of unhealthy condition.

gum arabic, n. **gum (II.)** & **Arabic**, after Lat. *gummi Arābicum*. Fine kind of gum produced by acacia.

gumbo, gombo, n. [1. gúmbō; 2. gámbou], fr. *kingombo*, native name. a A malvaceous tropical herb, also known as *okra*, of Africa and the W. Indies, but cultivated elsewhere for its mucilaginous pods used for thickening soups &c.; b soup thickened with these pods.

gumboil, n. [1. gúmboil; 2. gámbɔil]. **gum (I.)** & **-boil (I.)**. Boil or small abscess on the gums.

gumdigger, n. [1. gúmdiger; 2. gámdigə]. **gum (III.)** & **digger**. (in New Zealand) Person who digs for fossil kauri gum.

gum-dragon, n. Corrupt. of **gum tragacanth**. Gum obtained from Asiatic conifers, used medicinally; also called tragacanth.

gum-drop, n. **gum (III.)** & **drop (II.)**. Sweetmeat in form of drop, with gummy basis.

gum-elastic, n. After Mod. Lat. *gummi elasticum*. Indiarubber, caoutchouc.

gum-juniper, n. The sandarac tree.

gumma, n. [1. gúma; 2. gámə], pl. *gummas, gummata* [1. gúmata; 2. gámətə]. Mod. Lat., fr. Lat. *gummi*, **gum (II.)**, fr. nature of contents. (pathol.) Soft, syphilitic tumour.

gummatous, adj. [1. gúmatus; 2. gámətəs]. *Gummat-*, stem of Mod. Lat. *gumma*, see prec., & **-ous**. Pertaining to, resembling, a gumma.

gummiferous, adj. [1. gumíferus; 2. gamífərəs]. Lat. *gummi*, **gum (II.)**, & **-ferous**. Producing gum.

gumminess, n. [1. gúmines; 2. gáminis]. **gummy** & **-ness**. State of being gummy.

gumming, n. [1. gúming; 2. gámiŋ]. **gum (III.)** & **-ing**. **1.** Production of gum; specif., as morbid exudation from cherry and plum trees. **2.** Application of gum to surface, as in lithography.

gummous, adj. [1. gúmus; 2. gáməs]. Lat. *gummōs-(us)*, whence also Fr. *gommeux*. **gum (II.)** & **-ous**. **1.** Pertaining to, consisting of, resembling, gum; gummy. **2.** (pathol.) Pertaining to a gumma.

gummy, adj. [1. gúmi; 2. gámi]. **gum (II.)** & **-y**. **1.** Pertaining to gum, of viscid or sticky consistency, like gum. **2.** Covered or smeared with gum.

gumption, n. [1. gúmpshun; 2. gámpʃən]. Orig. Scots, of uncertain origin, possibly fr. O.N. *gaum-r, gaum*, 'care, heed', M.E. *gōme*, cogn. w. O.E. *ġēme*, W.S. *ġīeme*, 'care, heed', & *ġīeman* &c., 'to take care', O.S. *gōma*, O.H.G. *gauma, gouma*, Goth. *gaumjan* &c., 'to care for, heed', fr. **ga-um-jan*, the second syll. of wh. is perh. cogn. w. Lat. *ōmen* (see **omen**). Suff. *-tion* prob. by facetious assimilation to words of Lat. origin. (colloq.) Practical ability making for success; shrewdness in conduct of affairs; common sense, intelligence.

gum-rash, n. **gum (I.)** & **rash (II.)**. Rash on gums of teething child; red gum.

gum-resin, n. **gum (II.)** & **resin.** Natural mixture of a gum and a resin, often exuding together.

gum tragacanth, n. **gum (II.)** & **tragacanth.** Tragacanth.

gum tree, n. One of several gum-producing trees of N. America and Australia, esp. the eucalyptus, called also the *blue gum.* Phr. (colloq.): (*a 'possum) up a gum tree,* driven to bay, cornered, in a fix.

gumwood, n. [1. gúmwood; 2. gámwud]. Wood of the gum tree or eucalyptus.

gun (I.), n. [1. gun; 2. gan]. M.E. *gonnylde* (*gonnylde gnoste,* 'spark of gun', before 1327), later *gonne* (Chaucer), prob. respectively the woman's name *Gunnild* & its shortened form *Gunne,* the former (*Domina Gunilda*) being applied to a war-engine in 1330–31. Cp. such names as *Mons Meg, Long Tom, Big Bertha* &c. *Gunnild,* fr. O.N. *Gunnhildr,* fr. *gunn-r,* 'war', & *hild-r,* 'battle', but the orig. meaning of the name has nothing to do w. the above use. **1. a** (i.) Metal tube from which missiles are propelled, usually by discharge of explosive in closed end; any kind of fire-arm, often defined by word prefixed, as *machine gun, Lewis gun, elephant gun, sporting gun*; also (ii.) similar instrument acting without combustion as *air-gun, spring-gun, pop-gun*; Phrs. *great gun,* (i.) (obs.) cannon; (ii.) (fig., colloq.) eminent person; *to blow great guns,* (naut.) to blow a gale; **b** (mil. and nav.) cannon, piece of ordnance, often excluding howitzers and mortars; Phrs. *gun of position,* heavy field gun; *to stand, stick, to one's guns,* (fig.) maintain one's point of view, opinions, against attack; *son of a gun,* (naut., colloq.) worthless, despicable fellow; *as sure as a gun,* without doubt, certainly; **c** (in popular use) any fire-arm carried in the hand, except, though colloquially often including, pistol or revolver; specif., a sporting gun, as dist. from *rifle.* **2.** Discharge of cannon as salute or signal: *a salute of seven guns*; *the evening gun.* **3.** Person using a gun, esp. considered as a member of a shooting party.

gun (II.), vb. intrans., fr. prec. To use a gun; to go shooting.

gun-barrel, n. **gun (I.)** & **barrel.** Barrel or tube of gun.

gunboat, n. [1. gúnbōt; 2. gánbout]. **gun (I.)** & **boat (I.).** Small warship, **a** carrying one or more heavy guns; **b** of shallow draught, adapted for service on rivers.

gun captain, n. (nav.) Petty officer commanding crew of gun.

gun-carriage, n. Apparatus with wheels upon which a cannon is mounted and on which it is transported.

gun-case, n. Case to contain sporting gun.

gun-cotton, n. **gun (I.)** & **cotton (I.).** High explosive made by soaking cotton or cellulose in nitric and sulphuric acids.

gun deck, n. (nav.) Deck carrying guns; specif., deck next below main deck; formerly, any of several decks below spar deck.

gun-fire, n. **1.** Discharge of gun or guns; specif. (mil. and nav.) use of fire-arms as distinct from other tactics. **2.** Time when morning or evening gun is fired.

gun-flint, n. Shaped flint striking spark to ignite charge in old flintlock guns.

gun-harpoon, n. Harpoon fired from gun, in whale-fishing.

gun-house, n. Structure covering gun and gunners to protect them from enemy fire.

gun-lock, n. **gun (I.)** & **lock (II.).** Mechanical appliance, consisting of trigger, hammer &c., by which gun is fired.

gunman, n. [1. gúnman; 2. gánmən]. **1.** Man employed in making guns. **2.** Man armed with gun or revolver, esp. armed supporter of a faction; armed bandit.

gun metal, n. **a** Alloy of copper and tin or zinc, formerly used for making cannon; **b** metal used for fancy goods, treated to resemble true gun metal.

gunnage, n. [1. gúnij; 2. gánidž]. **gun (I.)** & **-age.** Number of guns carried by warship.

gunned, adj. [1. gund; 2. gand]. **gun (I.)** & **-ed.** Provided with cannon: *a ship heavily gunned*; usually in combination, as *over-, under-gunned.*

gunnel (I.), n. [1. gúnl; 2. gánl]. Origin uncertain. Kind of blenny inhabiting N. Atlantic.

gunnel (II.), n. See **gunwale.**

gunner, n. [1. gúner; 2. gánə]. **gun (I.)** & **-er. 1.** Man who works a gun; specif. **a** (mil.) artilleryman, officer or private; **b** (nav.) warrant-officer in charge of ordnance; Phr. *to kiss, marry, the gunner's daughter,* (naut., obs.) to be tied to a gun and flogged. **2.** Person carrying sporting gun to shoot animals. **3.** Horse trained in the artillery.

gunner's mate, n. Petty officer assisting gunner.

gunnery, n. [1. gúneri; 2. gánəri]. **gun (I.)** & **-ery.** Theory and practice of using cannon; art of artillery.

gunnery-ship, n. **gunnery** & **ship (I.).** Naval vessel on which gunnery is taught.

gunning, n. [1. gúning; 2. gániŋ]. **gun (II.)** & **-ing.** Use of a gun; shooting.

gunny, n. [1. gúni; 2. gáni]. Hind. & Marathi *gōni,* 'sack, sacking', fr. Scrt. *gōni,* 'sack'. Kind of coarse sacking of jute; often attrib., as *gunny bag, cloth, sack.*

gun-pit, n. **1.** (mil.) Excavation to contain gun and crew as protection against enemy fire. **2.** Pit in which cannon is cast or welded together.

gun-port, n. Port-hole in ship's side through which the muzzle of a cannon protrudes.

gunpowder, n. [1. gúnpouder; 2. gánpaudə]. **gun (I.)** & **powder (I.).** Granulated mechanical mixture of pulverized saltpetre, charcoal, and sulphur, forming explosive used for fire-arms, blasting &c. *Gunpowder Plot,* Papist plot to blow up James I. and his Parliament on Nov. 5th, 1605.

gunpowder tea, n. So called from its appearance. Superior kind of green tea, consisting of leaves separately rolled into pellets.

gun-room, n. **gun (I.)** & **room. a** Room in private house in which guns and sporting tackle are kept; **b** (nav.) room on lower deck of warship; formerly for use of gunner, now junior officers' mess-room.

gun-runner, n. Person engaged in gun-running.

gun-running, n. **gun (I.)** & **running.** Illicit introduction of fire-arms into a district, esp. for use of disaffected inhabitants.

gunshot, n. [1. gúnshot; 2. gánʃɔt]. **gun (I.)** & **shot (III.). 1. a** Firing of gun; **b** (attrib.) caused by gunshot: *gunshot wounds.* **2.** Range of gun: *out of gunshot.*

gunshy, adj. [1. gúnshī; 2. gánʃai]. **gun (I.)** & **shy (I.).** Liable to fright at firing of gun, esp. of a sporting dog or a horse.

gunsmith, n. [1. gúnsmith; 2. gánsmiþ]. Person who makes and repairs small arms.

gun-stock, n. **gun (I.)** & **stock (I.).** Wooden shaped block or support into which barrel of gun is fitted.

gun-stone, n. (obs.) Round stone formerly used as cannon-ball.

gun-tackle, n. **gun (I.)** & **tackle (I.).** (obs.) Tackle by which ship's guns were formerly attached to ports.

gunter, n. [1. gúnter; 2. gántə]. After Edmund Gunter, English mathematician (1581–1626), inventor of the scale. **1.** Two-foot rule marked with scales of chords, logarithms &c., used in navigation and surveying, also called *Gunter's scale*; Phr. *according to Gunter* (Am.), precisely, correctly. **2.** (naut.) Topmast sliding up and down lower mast in rings (from resemblance to **1**); sail carried by such topmast; (also attrib.) *gunter rig* &c.

gunwale, n. [1. gúnl; 2. gánl]. **gun (I.)** & **wale,** 'strake'. (naut.) **a** In decked ship, uppermost wale or strake, below bulwarks; **b** in open boat, course of timber running round sides on top of uppermost strake; Phrs. *gunwale down, gunwale to,* of vessel, listing, so that gunwale is nearly on level with water; *gunwale under,* with gunwale submerged.

gurge, n. [1. gĕrj; 2. gʌdž]. Lat. *gurges,* q.v. under **gurgle.** (obs. or rare) Whirlpool (Milton).

gurgitation, n. [1. gĕrjitáshun; 2. gʌdžitéiʃən]. Lat. *gurgitāt-,* P.P. stem of *gurgitāre,* 'to surge', fr. *gurgit-,* stem of *gurges,* 'whirlpool', cp. O.H.G. *kwerka,* 'neck, throat, crop', Scrt. *gargara-,* see **gorge,** & **-ion.** Surging, whirling, or eddying of liquid, as when boiling.

gurgle (I.), vb. intrans. [1. gĕrgl; 2. gʌgl]. Prob. fr. O. Fr. *gorguler* or obs. Ital. *gorgolare,* Mod. Ital. *gorgogliare,* fr. Lat. *gurgulio,* 'gullet', connected w. Lat. *gurges,* 'whirlpool', cogn. w. O.H.G. *querechela,* Lith. *gurklys,* Russ. *górlo,* 'throat'. Cp. also Germ. *gurgeln,* 'to gargle, warble, gurgle' (= Du. *gorgelen*), fr. O.H.G. *gurgula,* 'throat', fr. Lat. *gurgulio.* Cp. **gorge, gargle, gargoyle. a** (of liquids &c.) To make a bubbling, purling, or rippling sound, as of water flowing from bottle or over stones; **b** (of persons) to make bubbling sound in throat, as infant, when pleased.

gurgle (II.), n., fr. prec. Gurgling sound.

Gurkha, Goorkha, n. [1. gōōrka; 2. gúəkə]. Name of province in Nepal. A military race, of mixed Aryan-Mongol blood, settled in Nepal, enlisted in specific (*Gurkha*) regiments in the British Indian Army.

gurnard, n. [1. gĕrnard; 2. gʌnəd]. O. Fr. *gornard, gornart* (cp. Mod. Fr. *grognard,* 'grumbler'), prob. fr. Provenç. *gourgna,* 'to grunt' (whence *gournau,* 'gurnard'), metathetic form of *grougna* = Fr. *grogner,* fr. Lat. *grunn-īre,* 'to grunt', & **-ard.** The fish grunts when taken from water. Cp. **grunt.** One of a family, *Triglidae,* of small marine fishes with large head, plates on face, and six pectoral feelers.

gurnet, n. [1. gĕrnet; 2. gʌnit]. As prec., w. suff. **-et.** Variant of *gurnard.*

gurry, n. [1. gúri; 2. gári]. Hind. *gaṛhī.* (Anglo-Ind.) Small fort.

guru, n. [1. gōōrōō; 2. gûrū]. Hind. *gurū,* fr. Scrt. *gurú-,* 'heavy, venerable; a teacher'. See **grave (IV.).** Indian religious teacher.

gush (I.), vb. intrans. [1. gush; 2. gaʃ]. M.E. *guschen, gosshe,* of uncertain origin, either imitative, or perh. related to E. Fris., L.G. *gūsen,* M. Du. *guysen,* O.N. *gusa,* fr. strong vb. *gjosa,* 'to gush'; perh. fr. Gmc. base **gut-sk-,* cp. Du. *gudsen,* 'to gush', extended fr. **gut-,* weak grade of **geut-,* 'pour'. Cp. **geyser, gut. 1. a** To stream, burst, spring, forth; flow, abundantly and vehemently, as from an orifice; esp. of water, blood, and other liquids; **b** (fig., of words or other sounds) to be uttered in quick succession, copiously or impulsively. **2. a** *Gush with,* to emit an abundant stream of liquid, to spout: *fountains gushed with wine*; **b** (fig., of persons) to talk effusively or with sentimental extravagance; to exhibit enthusiasm in a silly, extravagant, or affected manner; also *gush over,* to talk effusively about.

gush (II.), n., fr. prec. **1.** Action of gushing; **a** vehement flow or jet of liquid from orifice; sudden outburst, as from well or pipe; **b** (fig.) torrent of words or other sounds. **2.** (fig., abstract) Unrestrained, effusive sentimentality, esp. in language; affected display of emotion.

gusher, n. [1. gúsher; 2. gáʃə]. **gush (I.)** & **-er.** Thing or person that gushes; specif. **a** petroleum well that emits jet of oil; **b** silly, effusive, emotional person.

gushing, adj. [1. gúshing; 2. gáʃiŋ], fr. Pres. Part. of **gush (I.) a** Pouring out in violent, profuse flow; **b** emitting a vehement flow of liquid; **c** (fig.) exhibiting extravagant or affected emotion, addicted to gush: *a gushing person, letter, style.*

gushingly, adv. Prec. & **-ly.** In a gushing manner.

gushy, adj. [1. gúshi; 2. gáʃi]. **gush (II.)** & **-y.** Gushing; (fig.) addicted to gush.

gusset (I.), n. [1. gúset; 2. gásit]. M.E.

guschet, fr. O. Fr. *gousset*, 'gusset', dimin. (see **-et**) of *gousse*, 'pod, husk, nut-shell', Ital. *guscio*, of unknown origin. **1.** (hist.) Piece of chain-mail inserted in joint of armour, at arm-pit. **2. a** Piece of cloth of triangular, diamond, or other shape inserted in garment to enlarge or strengthen part; **b** piece of leather similarly inserted in glove; **c** triangular elastic piece in side of shoe or boot. **3.** Iron brace for strengthening corner of structure. **4.** (her.) Triangular abatement on escutcheon; modification of a pall.

gusset (II.), vb. trans., fr. prec. To furnish with a gusset or gussets.

gust (I.), n. [1. gust; 2. gast]. O.N. *gust-r*, 'gust, blast', fr. stem *gus-*, wk. grade of *gjosa*, 'to **gush**', & *-t*. **a** Sudden, brief blast of wind; flaw; (fig.) of other physical things, as fire, sound; **b** (fig.) brief outburst of intense anger or other passion: *a gust of rage, desire* &c.

gust (II.), n. Lat. *gustus*, 'tasting, taste', cp. *gustāre*, 'to taste, enjoy'; cogn. w. Scrt. *júṣtiš*, 'love token, favour', *juṣátē*, 'enjoy', Goth. *kustus*; 'taste', Germ. *kosten*, 'to taste, try'; fr. Aryan base **g̑eus-*, 'to taste, pick out, choose', whence also Goth. *kiusan*, O.E. *čēosan*. See **choose**. **a** Relish, gusto; **b** (obs. or archaic) taste, flavour; aesthetic taste.

gustation, n. [1. gustā́shun; 2. gastéiʃən]. Lat. *gustātiōn-(em)*, vbl. n. fr. *gustāre*, 'to taste', & **-ion**. See **gust (II.)** & **-ation**. Action, faculty, of tasting.

gustative, adj. [1. gústativ; 2. gástətiv]. Lat. *gustāt-*, as in prec., & **-ive**. Pertaining to sense of taste; gustatory.

gustatory, adj. [1. gústatori; 2. gástətri]. Lat. *gustāt-* as prec. & **-ory**. (anat., physiol.) Pertaining to the sense, or to an organ of taste: *gustatory cell, hair, nerve*.

gustful, adj. [1. gústfool; 2. gástfəl]. **gust** (I.) & **-ful**. Full of gusts of wind, squally, gusty.

gustily, adv. [1. gústili; 2. gástili]. **gusty** & **-ly**. In a gusty manner; in gusts.

gusto, n. [1. gústō; 2. gástou]. Ital., fr. Lat. *gust-(us)*. See **gust** (II.). **a** (archaic) Flavour; **b** relish, zest, delicate enjoyment.

gusty, adj. [1. gústi; 2. gásti]. **gust** (I.) & **-y**. Abounding in gusts of wind, blustery.

gut (I.), n. [1. gut; 2. gat]. O.E. **gutt*, recorded in pl. *guttas*, 'entrails', M.E. *gut*, *gutte*; cp. Germ. *gosse*, 'gutter, drain, water-pipe, sink'; prob. connected w. M.E. *gōte*, 'channel, stream', Mod. Engl. dial. *goit, gut*, 'water-course, drain'; fr. Gmc. **gut-*, wk. grade of **geut-*, 'to pour', O.E. *gēotan*, Mod. Germ. *giessen*, Goth. *giutan*, O.N. *gjōta*, cogn. w. Lat. *fud-*, stem of *fundere*, 'to pour'. Cp. **found** (II.) & **chyle**. **1. a** Alimentary canal; specif., that part below the stomach; bowel; **b** (in pl. colloq., not delicate) bowels, intestines, entrails: *a pain in the guts*; *to run a man through the guts*. **2.** (fig.; pl.; colloq.) **a** Content, esp. valuable, essential part; Phr. *to have no guts*, to be hollow, lacking substance; **b** (of persons; familiar and vulg.) stamina, spirit, courage, vigour of character, determination: *a man with plenty of guts*. **3. a** Fine cord made from intestine of sheep &c., for strings of musical instruments and surgical stitching; the so-called catgut; **b** tough material drawn from silkworm, used in making casts for fishing lines. **4.** Narrow passage; **a** in watercourse; in bend of a river; **b** in street; narrow lane.

gut (II.), vb. trans. & intrans., fr. prec. **1.** trans. esp. **a** (of preparing fish, game, poultry &c., for cooking) To disembowel, remove guts, and internal organs of; eviscerate, clean out (fish); **b** (fig.) to remove entire contents of; plunder thoroughly; destroy whole interior of (building), esp. by fire; to burn out: *a house completely gutted by fire*; **c** to extract the gist of (a book, treatise &c.), by rapid reading. **2.** intrans. (vulgar) To eat gluttonously.

gutta (I.), n., pl. **guttae** [1. gúta, gútē; 2. gátə, gátī]. Lat., 'drop'; initial *g-* is dialectal for *f-*; the word is fr. base **fut-*, 'pour', q.v. under **found** (II.). (archit.) In Doric entablature, one of a number of small rounded ornaments, probably representing heads of wooden pegs or tree-nails, studding lower surface of mutules and triglyphs.

gutta (II.), n. See next word. **a** (chem.) Principal constituent of gutta-percha; **b** gutta-percha.

gutta-percha, n. [1. gúta pe̊rcha, -ka; 2. gátə-pə̂tʃə, -kə]. Malay. *gatah*, 'gum', doubtless associated w. Lat. *gutta*, 'drop', & Malay. *percha*, 'gutta-percha tree'. Elastic substance, formed by dried juice of several Malaysian trees, used for electric insulators, golf balls &c.

guttate, adj. [1. gútāt; 2. gáteit]. Lat. *guttāt-(um)*, P.P. of *guttāre*, 'to drop', fr. *gutta*, 'drop'. See **gutta** (I.). (zool., bot.) Speckled as with drops.

gutté(e), **guttee**, **gutty**, adj. [1. gúti; 2. gáti]. O. Fr. *goté*, fr. Lat. *guttāt-(um)*. See prec. (her., of the field, or shield) Sprinkled with drops (of gold, silver, or tears &c.).

gutter (I.), n. [1. gúter; 2. gátə]. M.E. *gotere*, fr. O. Fr. *gutiere, goutiere*, Mod. Fr. *gouttière*, 'gutter under eaves; channel, groove', fr. O. Fr. *gote, goute*, 'drop', fr. Lat. *gutta*, see **gutta** (I.), & adjectival fem. suff. *-ière*, fr. Lat. *-āria*. See **-er** & cp. **gout**. **1.** Open channel made to carry away water, specif. **a** narrow metal trough fixed under eaves to carry away rain water; **b** channel along a street, between road and path, to drain away surface water. **2. a** Channel worn by running water, melted wax &c.; **b** groove, such as that worn in vent of gun by firing. **3.** (print.) Grooved strip of wood or metal for separating pages of type in forme. **4.** (fig., of **1, b**) Lowest, most degraded, social environment; the slums: *language, manners, of the gutter*; *to rise from the gutter*.

gutter (II.), vb. trans. & intrans., fr. prec. **1.** trans. **a** To furnish with gutter or gutters; **b** to form channels in, furrow (as running water). **2.** intrans. **a** To trickle down, form gutter or channel; **b** specif. (of burning candle) to let melted wax drip down sides.

guttering, n. [1. gútering; 2. gátəriŋ]. **gutter** (II.) & **-ing**. **1. a** Action of making gutters; **b** set of gutters; **c** length of spouting to be cut into gutters. **2.** Process of dripping or flowing, as melting wax.

gutter-man, n. Man who stands in street gutter to hawk goods.

guttersnipe, n. [1. gútersnīp; 2. gátəsnaip]. **gutter** (I.) & **snipe** (I.). **a** Child or young person born, and living, in slums; street urchin or arab; **b** (Am. slang) stockbroker who is not member of Stock Exchange; kerb-stone broker.

guttiferous, adj. [1. gutíferus; 2. gatífərəs]. Lat. See **gutta** (I.) & **-ferous**. (bot.) Producing or exuding drops, as of gum or resin.

guttiform, adj. [1. gútiform; 2. gátifōm]. See first element of prec. & **-form**. Drop-shaped.

guttle, vb. intrans. & trans. [1. gútl; 2. gátl]. **gut** (II.) & **-le**. Prob. suggested by **guzzle**. To eat gluttonously, to gormandize.

guttler, n. [1. gútler; 2. gátlə]. Prec. & **-er**. One who guttles, glutton.

guttural (I.), adj. & n. [1. gútural; 2. gátərəl]. Fr., fr. Lat. *guttur*, 'throat', prob. connected w. **gutta** (I.), & **-al**. **1.** adj. Pertaining to the throat, specif. **a** (phon., of cons. and vowels) strictly, produced in the throat, but loosely and inaccurately applied to those formed by back of tongue and soft palate or velum; velar, back; **b** (popularly) having a deep, harsh, rasping, throaty quality, or uttering 'guttural' sounds: *the guttural speech of a Dutchman or Arab*. **2.** n. (phon.) Guttural consonant or vowel; velar, back sound.

gutturalism, n. [1. gúturalizm; 2. gátərəlizəm]. **guttural** (I.) & **-ism**. Guttural quality, tendency to gutturalize.

gutturalization, n. [1. gùturalīzā́shun; 2. gàtərəlaizéiʃən]. Next word & **-ation**. Process of sound change whereby the place of articulation is gradually shifted to back of tongue (a bad term).

gutturalize, vb. trans. [1. gúturalīz; 2. gátərəlaiz]. **guttural** (I.) & **-ize**. **a** To pronounce gutturally, give guttural quality to; **b** to shift area of articulation from front to back.

gutturally, adv. [1. gúturali; 2. gátərəli]. **guttural** (I.) & **-ly**. In a guttural manner.

gutturo-, combining form [1. gúturō; 2. gátərou]. Lat. *guttur*, 'throat'. **a** Pertaining to throat, as *gutturo-maxillary*; **b** (phon.) partaking of guttural character, as *gutturo-nasal, gutturo-palatal*.

gutty (I.), adj. See **gutté(e)**.

gutty (II.), n. [1. gúti; 2. gáti]. Abbr. for *gutta-percha ball* & **-y**. Gutta-percha golf-ball.

guy (I.), n. [1. gī; 2. gai]. O. Fr. *guie*, older form of *guide*. See **guide** (I.). **a** Rope used to guide and steady load while hoisting; **b** rope, wire, chain, or rod used as stay, as for spar in ship, derrick, suspension bridge; also *guy rope*.

guy (II.), vb. trans. O. Fr. *guier*. See prec. To guide or steady with a guy.

guy (III.), n. After Guy Fawkes, conspirator, appointed to blow up Houses of Parliament; name fr. Fr. *Guy*, Ital. *Guido*, fr. Gmc. *Wido*. **1.** Grotesque effigy of Guy Fawkes, carried about, and finally burnt on Nov. 5th, to commemorate discovery of Gunpowder Plot, 1605; hence, any ridiculous effigy. **2. a** Person who is guyed, or made a butt for ridicule; **b** a ridiculously or badly dressed person, one presenting a grotesque appearance; a dowdy, fright, scarecrow: *to look a regular guy*; **c** (Am. colloq.) chap, fellow.

guy (IV.), vb. trans., fr. prec. **a** To represent by a grotesque effigy, display in effigy; **b** to treat with ridicule; to chaff, banter, make a fool of.

guy (V.), n. & vb. intrans. Origin unknown. (slang) **1.** n. Action of decamping or escaping; Phr. *to do a guy*, disappear: *to give the guy to*, run away from, escape from. **2.** vb. To decamp, escape, run away.

guy rope, n. **guy** (I.) & **rope** (I.). Rope used as guy.

guzzle, vb. intrans. & trans. & n. [1. gúzl; 2. gázl]. Prob. of Fr. origin, cp. O. Fr. *gosillier*, Fr. *gosier*, 'gullet', O. Fr. *desgosiller*, *desgouziller*, 'to gulp, swallow down,' also 'to vomit'; perh. of Gmc. origin, cp. Fr. Lorraine dial. *gosse*, 'throat, stomach of fatted animal', Germ. dial. *guschel, gosche*, 'chaps, mouth', Germ. *gosse*, 'gutter, drain'. See **gut** (I.). **1.** vb. **a** intrans. To drink or eat greedily or copiously: *he guzzles all day*; **b** trans., (i.) to eat or drink greedily: *to sit guzzling beer*; (ii.) to squander by guzzling: *to guzzle one's money away*. **2.** n. Bout of excessive drinking or eating.

guzzler, n. [1. gúzler; 2. gázlə]. Prec. & **-er**. One who guzzles.

gwyniad, n. [1. gwíniad; 2. gwíniæd]. W., fr. *gwyn*, 'white'. Small fish of salmon family, inhabiting Welsh and English lakes; the powan.

gybe (I.), vb. intrans. & trans. & n. [1. jīb; 2. džaib]. Cp. obs. Du. *gijben*, Mod. *gijpen*. See **jib** (II.), of wh. it appears to be a variant. (naut.) **1.** vb. **a** intrans. (of boom or sail) To swing with the wind from one side to the other; to take the wind on the other quarter, to jib; **b** trans., to cause to gybe. **2.** n. Process of gybing or jibbing.

gyle, n. [1. gīl; 2. gail]. Du. *gaijl*, 'unfermented beer', *gijlen*, 'to ferment'. (brewing) **a** Fermenting wort; **b** amount of beer or ale brewed at once; **c** fermenting-tun or vat.

gymkhana, n. [1. jimkáhna; 2. džimkā́nə]. Hind. *gendkhana*, 'racket-court', fr. *gend*, 'ball', & *khana*, 'house', assimil. to **gymnastic, gymnasium**. Fête, with athletic displays or sports.

gymnasial, adj. [1. jimnā́zial; 2. džimnéiziəl]. **gymnasium** & **-al**. (rare) Pertaining to a gymnasium.

gymnasiarch, n. [1. jimnáziark; 2. džimnéiziǣk]. Lat. *gymnasiarchus*, fr. Gk. *gumnasiarkhos*. See **gymnasium** & **-arch**. At ancient Athens, public officer supervising training and contests of athletes.

gymnasium, n. [1. jimnázium; 2. džimnéiziəm]. Lat., fr. Gk. *gumnásion*, fr. *gumnázein*, 'to exercise the body', fr. *gumn-ós*, 'naked', because athletes trained naked. See **gymno-**. **1. a** School for gymnastics, as in ancient Greece; **b** hall or area provided with appliances, where gymnastics are taught and practised. **2.** In Germany and some other countries, a boys' school of highest class, providing humanistic education, as contrasted with a *realschule* or technical school.

gymnast, n. [1. jímnast; 2. džímnæst]. Fr. *gymnaste*, fr. Gk. *gumnastés*, 'trainer of athletes', fr. *gumnázein*. See prec. & **-ast**. One who practises, or is skilled in, gymnastics.

gymnastic, adj. & n. [1. jimnástik; 2. džimnǽstik]. Prec. & **-ic**. **1. adj. a** Pertaining to gymnastics or bodily exercises, promoting muscular strength or agility; **b** (fig.) providing mental discipline or training, promoting mental agility. **2. n. a** (usually pl.) Art and practice of training the body to be healthy, strong, and agile; distinct from athletics, in which competition is an essential element; exercises designed to promote strength and agility; **b** exercise or discipline, designed to train the intellect: *the study of logic is a mental gymnastic*.

gymnastically, adv. [1. jimnástikali; 2. džimnǽstikəli]. Prec. & **-al** & **-ly**. In a gymnastic manner.

gymno-, pref. Gk. *gumnós*, 'naked', wh. stands for **ngum-no-*, showing in first syll. the 'vanishing' grade of a base **nogʷ-*, cp. Lat. *nūdus* for **nogʷedos* (see **nude**); fr. same base is Gmc. **nakʷəda-*, whence O.E. *nacod*, q.v. under **naked**. Form in compounds of Greek origin, denoting naked, uncovered; esp. in bot., as *gymnocarpous*, having exposed fruit; *gymnogynous*, having the ovary exposed; *gymnospore*, naked spore &c.

gymnorhinal, adj. [1. jìmnorínal; 2. džìmnəráinəl]. **gymno-** & Gk. *rhin-*, stem of *rhís*, 'nostril', see **rhino-**, & **-al**. (zool). Having naked nostrils, as certain crows.

gymnosophist, n. [1. jìmnósofist; 2. džìmnósəfist]. Lat. *gymnosophista*, fr. Gk. *gumnosophistés*. See **gymno-** & **sophist**. Name applied by Greeks to members of an Indian ascetic sect, who lived naked.

gymnosophy, n. [1. jìmnósofi; 2. džìmnósəfi]. As prec. & **-sophy**. Discipline or doctrine of gymnosophists.

gymnosperm, n. [1. jímnospërm; 2. džímnəspām]. **gymno-** & Gk. *spérma*, 'seed'. See **sperm** (I.). (bot.) Plant of class of which the seeds are not contained in receptacle, including conifers and cycads.

gymnospermous, adj. [1. jìmnospërmus; 2. džìmnəspámǝs]. Prec. & **-ous**. (bot.) Having seeds not enclosed in receptacle.

gymnotus, n. [1. jimnótus; 2. džimnóutəs]. Mod. Lat., fr. **gymno-** & Gk. *nōtos*, 'back', prob. cogn. w. Lat. *nates*, 'buttocks', see **noto-**. (zool.) S. American freshwater fish, capable of discharging electric current; electric eel.

gymp, n. Variant of **gimp**.

gynaeceum, n. [1. gìnesēum; 2. gàinəsíəm]. Lat. *gynaecēum*, fr. Gk. *gunaikeîon*, prob. neut. adj., 'belonging to woman or women', fr. *gunaik-*. See **gynaeco-**. **1.** (Gk. antiq.) Apartments in house reserved for women. **2.** (bot.) Aggregate of female organs in plant.

gynaeco-, gyneco-, pref. Gk. *gunaik-*, stem of *guné*, 'woman, female', for **gʷənē*, fr. Aryan base **gʷenā*; cogn. w. O.E. *cwene*, 'woman', & *cwēn*, 'queen'. See **quean, queen**. Form in compounds of Greek origin, denoting, pertaining to woman or women, female.

gynaecocracy, n. [1. gìnēkókrasi; 2. gàinikókrəsi]. Gk. *gunaikokratia*. Prec. & **-cracy**. Government by women, or by a woman.

gynaecocrat, n. [1. gìnēkokrat; 2. gainíkəkræt]. As prec. & **-crat**. Supporter of gynaecocracy.

gynaecocratic, adj. [1. gìnēkokrátik; 2. gàinīkəkrǽtik]. Prec. & **-ic**. Pertaining to gynaecocracy.

gynaecological, adj. [1. gìnekolójikl; 2. gàinikəlódzikl]. **gynaecology** & **-ic** & **-al**. Pertaining to gynaecology.

gynaecologist, n. [1. gìnekólojist; 2. gàinikólədžist]. Next word & **-ist**. One skilled in gynaecology.

gynaecology, n. [1. gìnekóloji; 2. gàinikólədži]. **gynaeco-** & **-logy**. (med.) Science dealing with diseases peculiar to women.

gyno-, pref. Abbreviated form of **gynaeco-**.

gynocracy, n. [1. ginókrasi; 2. gainókrəsi]. **gyno-** & **-cracy**. Gynaecocracy.

gynoecium, gynecium, n. [1. gìnésium; 2. gainísiəm]. Incorrect forms of **gynaeceum** (bot.), due to confusion with *-oecium* as in *androecium*, fr. Gk. *oikíon*, 'house', q.v. under **economy**. Same as *gynaeceum* in botanical sense.

-gynous, suff. [1. jinus, ginus; 2. džinəs, ginəs]. Gk. *guné*, 'woman, female'. See **gynaeco-** & **-ous**. Combining form in adjs. of Gk. origin, denoting, pertaining to the female, esp. in botany, as **androgynous**.

gyp, n. [1. jip; 2. džip]. Origin uncertain, perh. abbr. fr. obs. *gippo*, 'man's short tunic', also 'scullion', fr. obs. Fr. *jupeau*, dimin. of *jupe*, 'skirt', cp. Span. *(al-)juba*, fr. Arab. *jubbah*. (univ., colloq.) Male servant in a college at Cambridge or Durham.

gypseous, adj. [1. jípsius; 2. džípsiəs]. Lat. *gypse-(us)*, fr. **gypsum**, & **-ous**. Pertaining to, resembling, gypsum.

gypsiferous, adj. [1. jipsíferus; 2. džipsífərəs]. **gypsum** & **-ferous**. Producing or containing gypsum.

gypsophila, n. [1. jipsófila; 2. džipsófilə]. Mod. Lat., fr. Gk. *gúpsos*, 'chalk, gypsum', & *phil-ein*, 'to love'. See **gypsum** & **-philo-**. Plant related to the pinks, bearing sprays of small pink or white flowers.

gypsous, adj. [1. jípsus; 2. džípsəs]. Next word & **-ous**. Gypseous.

gypsum, n. [1. jípsum; 2. džípsəm]. Lat., fr. Gk. *gúps-(os)*, prob. fr. an oriental language; cp. Pers. *jabsīn*, 'lime', Arab. *jibs*, 'plaster, mortar'. Hydrous sulphate of calcium, found in various forms, including alabaster; used for making plaster of Paris, and as dressing for soil.

gypsy, n. See **gipsy**.

gyral, adj. [1. jíral; 2. džáiərəl]. **gyre** & **-al**. **a** Moving in a circle, gyratory; **b** (anat.) pertaining to a gyrus.

gyrally, adv. Prec. & **-ly**. In a gyral manner.

gyrate (I.), vb. intrans. [1. jīrát; 2. džaiəréit], fr. Lat. *gȳrāt-(um)*, P.P. type of *gȳrāre*, 'to turn round, revolve', fr. *gȳrus*, **gyre**. To revolve round central point, whirl round.

gyrate (II.), adj. [1. jírāt; 2. džáiəreit]. Lat. *gȳrāt-(um)*. See prec. Coiled, convolute, esp. in botany.

gyration, n. [1. jīráshun; 2. džaiəréiʃən]. Prec. & **-ion**. **a** Action of gyrating or revolving; revolution; **b** (zool.) single whorl of spiral shell.

gyrational, adj. [1. jīráshunal; 2. džaiəréiʃənəl]. Prec. & **-al**. Pertaining to gyration.

gyratory, adj. [1. jíratori; 2. džáiərətəri]. Lat. *gȳrāt-*, as **gyrate** (I.), & **-ory**. Pertaining to gyration; turning, revolving in a circle.

gyre, n. & vb. intrans. [1. jír; 2. džáiə]. Lat. *gȳrus*, 'circle', *gȳrāre*, 'to revolve', fr. Gk. *gûr-os*, 'ring'; cogn. w. Norw. *kūra*, 'to bend, twist', Lith. *gaurai*, 'hair'; Ir. *keuru*, 'curved'. **1.** n. **a** Circular or spiral motion, gyration; **b** form described by gyrating body; vortex. **2.** vb. To gyrate.

gyrfalcon, n. Variant of **gerfalcon**.

gyro-, pref. See **gyre**. Combining form denoting, pertaining to gyration.

gyro-compass, n. [1. jíro kùmpas; 2. džáiərou kàmpəs]. **gyro-** & **compass**. A gyroscope with compass card attached, used esp. on naval vessels, where the ordinary magnetic compass tends to become disturbed and unreliable.

gyrograph, n. [1. jírograhf; 2. džáiərəgrāf]. **gyro-** & **graph**. Instrument for recording revolutions of wheel &c.

gyromancy, n. [1. jírōmànsi; 2. džáiəroumǣnsi]. Fr. *gyromancie*, fr. **gyro-** & **mancy**. Divination by walking in a circle till one becomes giddy and falls, place or direction of fall being considered significant.

gyron, giron, n. [1. jíron; 2. džáiərən]. Fr. *giron*, 'triangular piece', fr. O.H.G. *gēro*, 'gusset', cogn. w. O.E. *gār*, 'spear'. See **gore** (I.), **garlic**. (her.) Wedge-shaped subordinary, in form of triangle, equal to one-eighth of escutcheon, enclosed by two lines from fesse-point or centre and part of edge.

gyronny, adj. [1. jíruni; 2. džáiərəni]. Fr. *gironné*. Prec. & **-y**. (her., of escutcheon) Divided into gyrons.

gyroplane, n. [1. jíroplān; 2. džáiərəplein]. **gyro-** & **-plane**. Aeroplane furnished with one or more horizontal or nearly horizontal propellers, enabling it to hover or move vertically.

gyroscope, n. [1. jíroskōp; 2. džáiərəskoup]. **gyro-** & **-scope**. Heavy fly-wheel, which when rotating tends to remain in same place, used to illustrate laws of rotation, also to stabilize mono-rail car, aeroplane, steamer &c., and in the gyro-compass.

gyroscopic, adj. [1. jìroskópik; 2. džàiərəskópik]. Prec. & **-ic**. Pertaining to a gyroscope or its action: *gyroscopic compass*, gyro-compass.

gyrostat, n. [1. jírostat; 2. džáiərəstæt]. **gyro-** & Gk. *statós*, 'standing'. Cp. **static**. Modified form of gyroscope, in which wheel is fixed in rigid case with flange.

gyrostatic, adj. & n. [1. jìrostátik; 2. džàiərəstǽtik]. Prec. & **-ic**. **a** adj. Pertaining to gyrostat or gyrostatics; **b** n., pl. *gyrostatics*, branch of dynamics dealing with gyrating bodies.

gyve, n. [1. jīv; 2. džaiv]. M.E. pl. *gives*, *gyves*, fr. A.-Fr. *guives*, perh. fr. O.E. *wiððe*, '**withy**, thong, bond'. (usually pl.) Shackles, fetters, handcuffs.

H

H, h, [1. āch; 2. eitʃ]. The eighth letter of the English alphabet. **1.** Expressing an aspirate or rough breathing, or, more accurately, a stressed breath on-glide, before vowels; Phr. *to drop one's aitches*, omit an aspirate where it should be pronounced. **2.** Written after *t*, & *p*, to express respectively the simple consonantal sounds [þ, ð; f], and after *c* to express [tʃ]. For use in abbreviations see end of Dictionary.

ha, interj. [1. hah; 2. hā]. Exclamation of surprise &c. See also **hum** & **haw**.

habeas corpus, n. [1. hábeas kórpus; 2. héibiəs kɔ̄pəs]. Lat., 'thou must have the body'. (law) Writ ordering production of prisoner in court or before judge, esp. in order to determine justice of his arrest and detention.

habendum, n. [1. habéndum; 2. hæbéndəm]. Lat., 'to be had', neut. sing. gerundive of *habēre*, 'to have', because Lat. formula begins thus. (law) Part of deed following premises, defining estate which the grantee is 'to have and to hold'.

haberdasher, n. [1. háberdasher; 2. hǽbədæʃə]. M.E. *haberdashere*, fr. obs. Engl. *haberdash*, 'small wares', prob. fr. A.-Fr. *hapertas*, 'kind of stuff'. Of unknown origin. **a** Dealer in small articles, such as tapes, pins, needles &c., usually as part of a drapery business; **b** dealer in men's shirts, ties, collars &c.

haberdashery, n. [1. háberdasheri; 2. hǽbədæʃəri]. Prec. & **-y.** Goods sold by haberdasher.

habergeon, n. [1. háberjun; 2. hǽbədžən]. M.E. & O. Fr. *haubergeoun*, dimin. of O. Fr. *hauberc*, **hauberk.** Short coat of mail, reaching from neck to waist, usually without sleeves.

habiliment, n. [1. habíliment; 2. hæbílimənt]. Fr. *habillement*, 'clothing', fr. *habiller*, 'to dress', orig. 'to fit out, make ready', fr. *habile*, 'able', fr. Lat. *habilis* (see **ability**) & **-ment**; cp. **habit.** Dress, clothing (chiefly in pl.).

habit (**I.**), n. [1. hábit; 2. hǽbit]. M.E., fr. Fr., fr. Lat. *habit-(us)*, 'condition, habit, dress', fr. *habit-(um)*, P.P. type of *habēre*, 'to have'; reflex. w. *se* ('self'), 'to be constituted, be in a condition'. The etymol. of this very common Lat. word is doubtful; it has prob. no connexion w. O.E. *habban*, q.v. under **have. 1. a** Ordinary or settled condition, constitution, or disposition, of mind or body, esp. (med.) temperament, physiological constitution: *habit of body*; *a man of a gouty habit*; **b** (biol.) characteristic, normal mode of growth or life: *the arboreal habit*; *a plant of trailing habit.* **2. a** Usual behaviour or course of action; **b** act of an individual frequently repeated; acquired tendency; practice which has become customary or automatic: *to fall into, break off, a habit*; *a habit of instant obedience*; *a nasty habit of swearing*; *to get into bad habits.* **3.** Dress, garment; esp. **a** one worn by member of a society or class: *a monk's habit*; **b** one worn on particular occasions: *a doctor's convocation habit*; **c** also *riding habit*, a wide skirt worn by women when riding.

habit (**II.**), vb. trans. M.E. *habiten*, 'inhabit', fr. Fr. *habiter*, fr. Lat. *habitāre*, fr. stem *habit-*, as prec. **1.** (obs.) To inhabit, dwell in. **2.** To dress, clothe, esp. in dress of an order: *the bishop habited in his rochet.*

habitability, n. [1. hàbitabíliti; 2. hæbitəbíliti]. **habitable** & **-ity.** State of being habitable.

habitable, adj. [1. hábitabl; 2. hǽbitəbl]. M.E., fr. O. Fr., fr. Lat. *habitābilis.* See **habit** (**II.**) & **-able.** Capable of being inhabited; suitable and fit for habitation: *the habitable earth*; *a habitable house.*

habitableness, n. Prec. & **-ness.** Quality of being habitable.

habitably, adv. [1. hábitabli; 2. hǽbitəbli]. **habitable** & **-ly.** In a habitable manner.

habitant, n. [1. hábitant; 2. hǽbitənt]. Fr., fr. Pres. Part. of *habiter.* See **habit** (**II.**). Inhabitant; specif., French inhabitant of Canada or Louisiana.

habitat, n. [1. hábitat; 2. hǽbitæt]. Lat., 'it inhabits', fr. *habitāre*, 'to inhabit'. See **habit** (**II.**). **a** (biol.) Kind of region naturally inhabited by animal or plant; natural environment; **b** region or locality where anything commonly occurs.

habitation, n. [1. hàbitáshun; 2. hæbitéiʃən]. M.E., fr. O. Fr., *habitacion*, fr. Lat. *habitātiōn(em).* See **habit** (**II.**) & **-ation. 1.** Act or state of inhabiting; occupancy: *house no longer fit for habitation.* **2. a** Dwelling-place, abode, residence; **b** name assumed by a local branch or 'lodge' of Primrose League.

habitual, adj. [1. habíchooal; 2. həbítʃuəl], fr. L. Lat. *habituāl-(is)*, whence also Fr. *habituel.* See **habit** (**I.**) & **-al. 1.** (of things) Usual, frequent, customary, of the nature of a habit: *an habitual smile, joke, seat.* **2.** (of persons) Acting by habit, addicted to a specified practice: *an habitual liar, drunkard, criminal.*

habitually, adv. Prec. & **-ly.** As a habit, by force of habit, commonly, as a usual practice.

habitualness, n. See prec. & **-ness.** Quality of being habitual.

habituate, vb. trans. [1. habíchooāt; 2. habítʃueit], fr. Lat. *habituāt-(um)*, P.P. of *habituāre*, fr. *habitu-s.* See **habit** (**I.**). Followed by *to*: **a** (reflex.) To accustom oneself, become used to: *to habituate oneself to hard work*; **b** to make accustomed to, render familiar with: *to habituate a horse to harness.*

habituation, n. [1. habìchooáshun; 2. həbìtʃuéiʃən]. Prec. & **-ion.** Process of habituating; condition of being habituated.

habitude, n. [1. hábitūd; 2. hǽbitjūd]. Fr., fr. Lat. *habitūdo*, 'condition'. See **habit** (**I.**) & **-tude.** (rare) **a** Usual custom; habit, wont; **b** customary state of mind, disposition; **c** habit of body.

habitué, n. [1. habítūā; 2. həbítjuei]. Fr. P.P. of *habituer.* See **habituate.** One who frequents, haunts, or habitually visits: *an habitué of the opera, of the turf* &c.

hachures, n. pl. No recognized pronunc. in Engl.; best as Fr. [1. ahshūr; 2. āʃýr]. Fr., fr. *hacher*, 'to cut'. See **hatchet, hash** & **-ure.** Lines used in shading in an engraving or drawing, esp. to indicate variation of slope or height in maps.

hacienda, n. [1. (h)àsiénda; 2. (h)æ̀siéndə]. Span., fr. O. Span. *facienda*, 'employment, estate', fr. Lat. *facienda*, 'things to be done', neut. pl. gerundive of *facere*, 'to do'. See **fact.** (in Spanish America &c.) **a** Estate for stock-raising, ranch; plantation; **b** establishment employing labour; factory.

hack (**I.**), vb. trans. & intrans. [1. hak; 2. hæk]. O.E. *haccian*, M.E. *hacken*; O. Fris. *(to-)hak(k)ia*, M. Du., M.H.G., Mod. Germ. *hacken*, Swed. *hacka*, Dan. *hakke.* Origin obscure. **A.** trans. **1. a** To chop, cut, as with axe, esp. roughly, clumsily, or carelessly; to slash, gash; **b** to roughen (stone) with hack-hammer; **c** to trim (hedge &c.) as with bill. **2.** To break up (soil) as with mattock or hoe. Phr. *to hack in wheat*, to sow it while breaking up soil. **3.** To kick (leg) with boot: *to hack a man's shin at football.* **B.** intrans. **1.** To practise hacking in any sense. **2.** To cough in harsh, dry manner. (See **hawk** (**III.**).)

hack (**II.**), n., fr. prec. **1.** Action of hacking; specif. **a** stroke or chop as of axe; **b** hacking cough. **2. a** Cut, notch, gash, or wound made by hacking; **b** bruise or abrasion made by kick, as on shin.

hack (**III.**), n. Cp. Germ. *hacke*, 'axe, hoe, mattock, pickaxe', Dan. *hakke*, 'mattock'. Cp. **hack** (**I.**). (not common) Name given to various cutting tools of the pickaxe type.

hack (**IV.**), n. & vb. trans. O.E. *hæc*, **hatch** (**I.**). **1.** n. **a** (obs., falconry) Board to hold hawk's meat; Phr. *to be at hack*, of eyas hawk, to be kept in partial restraint; **b** grating or rack, as for drying fish or cheese, holding food for cattle &c.; **c** pile or stack of unburnt bricks, arranged for drying. **2.** vb. **a** (obs., falconry) To keep at hack; **b** to put (cheese, fish &c.) on hack or rack for drying.

hack (**V.**), n. Perh. abbr. fr. **hackney** (**I.**), but cp. O. Fr. *haque*, perh. fr. Span. *haca*, fr. O. Span. *faca*, 'nag'. **1. a** (i.) Horse let out on hire, esp. for riding; (ii.) saddle-horse of medium quality; **b** (i.) horse employed for all sorts of work; (ii.) overworked horse, jade. **2.** (fig., contempt.) Person employed to do dull, tedious work, such as dictionary-making, the writing of inferior newspaper articles, or other forms of drudgery. **3.** (attrib.) **a** Done by, fit only for, a hack: *hack work*; **b** occupied in such work: *hack writers.*

hack (**VI.**), vb. trans. & intrans., fr. prec. **1.** trans. **a** To let out (horse &c.) for hire; **b** to use (a horse) as a hack; **c** (fig.) to employ as a hack writer or drudge. **2.** intrans. To jog along on a horse: *to hack along.*

hackberry, n. Variant of **hagberry.**

hackbut, n. [1. hákbut; 2. hǽkbət]. O. Fr. *haquebute*, fr. Du. *haakbus.* See **arquebus.**

hackery, n. [1. hákeri; 2. hǽkəri]. Hind. *chhakṛā*, 'cart', cp. Scrt. *čakra*, 'wheel'; cp. **cycle** & **wheel.** Indian bullock-cart.

hack-hammer, n. Mason's tool, resembling adze with hammer head.

hacking, adj. [1. háking; 2. hǽkiŋ]. Pres. Part. of **hack** (**I.**). Chiefly *hacking cough*, dry, hard cough.

hackle (**I.**), n. & vb. [1. hákl; 2. hǽkl], fr. O.E. *hacele*, 'cloak', M.E. *hakele.* Etymol. unknown. **1.** n. **a** Long feathers on neck of domestic cock; **b** tuft made from these, to imitate the legs, on an artificial fly for fishing. **2.** vb. To put hackles on to (rare).

hackle (**II.**), vb. trans., fr. **hack** (**I.**) & **-le.** (rare or provinc.) To hack roughly.

hackle (**III.**), n. M.E. *hakell, hekele*, fr. O.E. **hacul, *hecele*, both cogn. w. **hook.** Comb for dressing raw silk or flax.

hackney (**I.**), n. [1. hákni; 2. hǽkni]. M.E. *hakenē, hakenei*; cp. Med. Lat. *hackeneius*, A.-Fr. *hakenai*, O. Fr. *haquenée*, 'pad-horse'; cp. **hack** (**V.**); etymol. uncertain. **1.** Medium-sized horse of about 15 hands used for ordinary hacking and driving. **2.** (obs.) Hackney carriage.

hackney (**II.**), vb. trans., fr. prec. To render trite, commonplace, unimpressive by familiarity. Rare except in P.P. as adj.: *a hackneyed phrase* &c.

hackney carriage, n. Horsed vehicle plying for hire.

hackney coach, n. One plying for hire.

hackneyed, adj. [1. háknid; 2. hǽknid], fr. P.P. of **hackney** (**II.**). Vulgarized, commonplace, trite.

hacksaw, n. [1. háksaw; 2. hǽksɔ̄]. **hack** (**I.**) & **saw** (**I.**). Saw, with narrow blade set in a bow, used for cutting metal.

hackwork, n. [1. hákwĕrk; 2. hǽkwə̄k]. **hack** (**V.**) & **work.** Work of inferior, more or less mechanical, kind not requiring much effort or originality of mind.

had, vb. [1. had; 2. hæd]. O.E. *hæfde*, M.E. *hadde, had.* Pret. & P.P. of **have.**

haddock, n. [1. hádok; 2. hǽdək]. M.E. *hadok.* Origin unknown. Edible sea fish, *Gadus aeglefinus*, allied to the cod.

hade, n. & vb. intrans. [1. hād; 2. heid]. Of uncertain origin; perh. fr. Norw. dial. *hadd*, 'slope'. (min. and geol.) **1.** n. Inclination from the vertical of fault or vein. **2.** vb. To incline from the vertical.

Hades, n. [1. hādēz; 2. héidīz]. Gk. *Hā́dēs*, 'god of the nether world, Pluto', derived, perh. wrongly, by the ancients fr. *a-*, 'not', & *id-eîn*, 'to see' (q.v. under **idea**), thus 'the unseen'. **1.** Lower world, hell. **2.** Intermediate state or abode of the departed.

hadj, also **hajj**, n. [1. haj; 2. hædž]. Arab. *ḥajj*, fr. *ḥajja*, 'to walk, go on pilgrimage'. Moslem pilgrimage to Mecca.

hadji, also **hajji**, n. [1. hájē; 2. hǽdžī]. Arab. *ḥajji.* See prec. Moslem pilgrim to Mecca, used as title of respect and honour.

haecceity, n. [1. heksḗiti; 2. heksī́iti]. Med. Lat. *haecceitas*, fr. *haecce* (*res*), 'this (thing)', fem. sing. of *hicce*, intens. form of *hic*, 'this', & *-itas*, **-ity.** (scholast. philos.) 'Thisness', individuality.

haemal, adj. [1. hḗmal; 2. hī́məl]. Gk. *haîma*, 'blood' & **-al**; *haîma* is for **saima*, & prob. cogn. w. O.H.G. *seim*, 'virgin honey'. Cp. **anaemia.** It has been further suggested that the Aryan base was **saisma-*, & some scholars think that the word contains the base *-is-* wh. in Scrt. means 'juice, drink', also 'refreshment'. Pertaining to the blood.

haemat-, pref. Variant of **haemato-**, used before words beginning with a vowel.

haematic, adj. & n. [1. hēmátik; 2. hīmǽtik]. Gk. *haimatikós*, fr. Gk. *haimat-*, stem of *haîma*, see **haemal**, & adj. suff., see **-ic. a** adj. Pertaining to, containing, like, blood; blood-red; **b** n., medicine acting on the blood.

haematin, n. [1. hḗmatin; 2. hī́mætin]. Modern concoction fr. *haemat-.* See prec. & **-in.** (chem.) Substance found in the blood, the pigment or colouring matter of haemoglobin.

haematite, hematite, n. [1. hḗmatīt; 2. hímətait]. Lat. *haematītēs*, fr. Gk. *haimatī́tēs*, lit. 'bloodlike'; **haemat-** & **-ite**. A red iron ore, ferric oxide; in earthy state it is known as *red ochre*; in crystallized state it is steel grey in colour and is known as *specular iron*.

haematitic, adj. [1. hēmatítik; 2. hīmətáitik]. Prec. & **-ic**. Pertaining to, like, haematite.

haemato-, pref. Gk. *haimat-*, stem of *haîma*, 'blood', see **haemal**. Pertaining to or containing blood.

haematocele, n. [1. hḗmatōsēl; 2. hímətousīl]. Prec. & Gk. *kḗlē*, 'tumour'. See **-cele**. Tumour containing blood.

haematocyte, n. [1. hḗmatōsīt; 2. hímətousait]. **haemato-** & **-cyte**. Blood cell.

haematuria, n. [1. hēmatū́ria; 2. hīmətjúəriə]. Mod. Lat., fr. **haemat-** & **-uria**. Discharge of blood in the urine.

haemo-, pref. Same as **haemato-**.

haemoglobin, n. [1. hèmōglṓbin; 2. hìmouglóubin]. **haemo-** & **globe** & **-in**. (physiol.) The complex protein substance of the red corpuscles in the blood of vertebrate animals, which absorbs oxygen from the air and transports it to every part of the body, acting as chlorophyll in plants.

haemophilia, n. [1. hèmōfília; 2. hìmoufíliə]. **haemo-** & Gk. *philia*, 'friendship, affection', here in sense of 'tendency towards', q.v. under **philo-**. (med.) Hereditary disease characterized by tendency to frequent, and excessive haemorrhage; popularly called 'bleeding'.

haemoptysis, n. [1. hèmōptísis; 2. hìmouptáisis]. **haemo-** & Gk. *ptúsis*, 'spitting', fr. *ptúein*, 'to spit'. See **spit (III.)**. (med.) Spitting of blood.

haemorrhage, hemorrhage, n. [1. hémorij; 2. héməridž]. Lat. *haemorrhagia*, fr. Gk. *haimorrhagia*, 'violent bleeding', **haemo-** & *rhag-*, 'bursting out', another grade of wh. base is seen in Gk. *rhēg-nūmai* (for *wrēg), 'to break, burst', cogn. w. **wreck, wreak**. (med.) Bleeding.

haemorrhagic, hemorrhagic, adj. [1. hèmorájik; 2. hèmərǽdžik]. Prec. & **-ic**. Pertaining to haemorrhage.

haemorrhoidal, hemorrhoidal, adj. [1. hèmoróidal; 2. hèmərɔ́idəl]. Fr. *hémorroïdal*. See next word & **-al**. Pertaining to, having character of, haemorrhoids.

haemorrhoids, hemorrhoids, n. pl. [1. hémoroidz; 2. héməroidz]. Fr. *hémorroïde*, fr. Lat. *haemorrhoïda*, fr. Gk. *haimorrhoïd-*, stem of *haimorrhoïs*, fr. *haimórrhoos*, 'flowing with blood', **haemo-** & *rhé-ein* for *srew-ein, 'to flow'; cogn. w. **stream**. Cp. **emerods**. Medical name for disease popularly called piles.

haemostasis, n. [1. hèmōstásis; 2. hìmoustéisis]. **haemo-** & Gk. *stásis*, 'standing still, stoppage', see **static**. Stoppage of bleeding, as by tying of a blood-vessel or by use of a haemostatic.

haemostatic, n. [1. hèmōstátik; 2. hìmoustǽtik]. See prec. & **static**. Something which stops bleeding; a styptic.

hafiz, n. [1. háhfiz; 2. hā́fiz]. Pers. Mohammedan who knows Koran by heart.

hafnium, n. [1. háfnium; 2. hǽfniəm], fr. Hafnia, Lat. name of Copenhagen. One of the group of rare-earth chemical elements, found with zirconium.

haft, n. & vb. trans. [1. hahft; 2. hāft]. O.E. *hæft*, M.E. *haft* &c. Connected w. O.E. *habban*, 'to have, hold'. See **have**. **1.** n. **a** Handle, or part grasped by the hand, of a knife, dagger &c.; **b** part of a spindle. **2.** vb. To supply with a haft, esp. in P.P. *hafted*.

hag (I.), n. [1. hag; 2. hæg]. M.E. *hagge*, the origin of wh. is unknown. O.E. & the other Gmc. languages have words somewhat resembling this in form w. approximately the same meaning; none of these, however, throws any light on the M.E. form. A hideous, malevolent, disgusting old woman.

hag (II.), n. Scand. Cp. O.N. *hǫgg*, 'ravine, cut, gap', fr. *hǫggva*, 'to cut, hack', cogn. w. **hew**. (Nthn. provincialism) **a** Projecting edge of peat-cutting in bog, hillock of firmer ground in bog or moss; **b** break or soft place in bog.

hagberry, hackberry, n. [1. hág-, hakberi; 2. hǽg-, hækbəri]. Scand., cp. Icel. *hegg-r*, Swed. *hägg*, Dan. *haeggebaer*. See **berry**. **a** (Scots) Bird cherry; **b** (Am.) a tree, genus *Celtis*, with small, reddish, edible drupes, usually called *hackberry*.

hagfish, n. [1. hágfish; 2. hǽgfiʃ]. Origin doubtful. Parasitic marine creature allied to the lamprey, which burrows into the bodies of fish and preys upon their vitals.

haggadah, n. [1. hagáhdah; 2. həgā́dā]. Heb., 'tale, story'. The legendary or narrative part of the Talmud.

haggard (I.), adj. [1. hágard; 2. hǽgəd]. Prob. fr. next word, meaning orig. 'wild-looking' as Mod. Fr. *hagard*. Origin unknown. (of the face) Having a worn, wasted look, as if harassed by want of sleep, hunger, fever, or anxiety; gaunt, drawn, pinched.

haggard (II.), adj. & n. (falconry) **a** adj. Hard to tame; **b** n., untamed hawk.

haggardness, n. **haggard (I.)** & **-ness**. State of being haggard.

haggis, n. [1. hágis; 2. hǽgis]. M.E. *hageys*, *hag(g)as*, *hakkys*, cp. Scots. dial. *hag*, 'to hack, cut, chop', Scand., connected w. O.N. *hǫggva*, 'to strike, hack &c.'. Cp. **hag (II.)**. Native Scottish dish made of various parts from the inside of a sheep, minced fine, mixed with suet, oatmeal, onions, and pepper, and boiled in a sheep's stomach.

haggish, adj. [1. hágish; 2. hǽgiʃ]. **hag (I.)** & **-ish**. (of women) Resembling a hag; worn-looking, ugly, gaunt, and scraggy.

haggishly, adv. Prec. & **-ly**. In the manner of a hag.

haggishness, n. See prec. & **-ness**. Quality of being haggish.

haggle, vb. intrans. & n. [1. hágl; 2. hǽgl]. Perh. orig. a Scots word; freq. of *hag*, 'to hack, chop'. See **hag (II.), haggis**, & **-le**. Cp. **higgle**. **1.** vb. To wrangle, dispute, over anything in a petty, mean way; esp. over the price of an article; to attempt to cut down price asked. **2.** n. Wrangle over terms; act of haggling.

hagiarchy, n. [1. hágiarki; 2. hǽgiāki]. **hagio-** & **-archy**. **1.** Rule, government by saints, or by men in holy orders. **2.** Order, hierarchy, of saints.

hagio-, pref. Gk. *hági-os*, 'holy, sacred', fr. *hágos*, 'awe', cogn. w. Scrt. *yájyaś*, 'venerable', *yája*, 'venerate'. Pertaining to that which is holy, or to saints.

hagiocracy, n. [1. hàgiókrasi; 2. hæ̀giɔ́krəsi]. Prec. & **-cracy**. Government, dominion, exercised by saints, or by persons considered holy.

Hagiographa, n. pl. [1. hàgiógrafa; 2. hæ̀giɔ́grəfə]. Lat., fr. Gk. *hagiógrapha* (*biblia*), '(books) sacredly written', neut. pl. of *hagiógraphos*. See **hagio-** & **-graph**. One of the three Jewish divisions of O.T.; all the books which are not the Law or the Prophets.

hagiographer, n. [1. hàgiógrafer; 2. hæ̀giɔ́grəfə]. **1.** (fr. prec. & **-er**) Writer of any of the Hagiographa. **2.** (fr. **hagio-** & **-grapher**) Writer of life of a saint.

hagiographic(al), adj. [1. hàgiōgráfik(l); 2. hæ̀giougrǽfik(l)]. See prec. & **-ic** & **-al**. **a** Pertaining to the Hagiographa; **b** pertaining to hagiography.

hagiography, n. [1. hàgiógrafi; 2. hæ̀giɔ́grəfi]. **hagio-** & **-graphy**. **a** Study of saints and saints' lives; **b** collection of such lives.

hagiolater, n. [1. hàgiólater; 2. hæ̀giɔ́lətə]. See **hagiolatry**. One addicted to hagiolatry.

hagiolatrous, adj. [1. hàgiólatrus; 2. hæ̀giɔ́lətrəs]. **hagiolatry** & **-ous**. **a** Of the nature of, pertaining to, hagiolatry; **b** (of persons) addicted to hagiolatry.

hagiolatry, n. [1. hàgiólatri; 2. hæ̀giɔ́lətri]. **hagio-** & Gk. *latreia*, 'service, worship'; formed on anal. of **idolatry**. Excessive worship and veneration paid to saints.

hagiologic(al), adj. [1. hàgiōlójik(l); 2. hæ̀giolɔ́džik(l)]. **hagiology** & **-ic** (& **-al**). Pertaining to hagiology.

hagiologist, n. [1. hàgiólojist; 2. hæ̀giɔ́lədžist]. Next word & **-ist**. One skilled in hagiology.

hagiology, n. [1. hàgióloji; 2. hæ̀giɔ́lədži]. **hagio-** & **-logy**. **a** Study of saints or of lives of saints; **b** treatise on these; collection of such lives.

hagioscope, n. [1. hágiōskōp; 2. hǽgiouskòup]. **hagio-** & **-scope**. (archit.) Narrow passage or opening cut through a wall in a church near chancel end, to enable those in the side aisle to see the altar at the Elevation of the Host; also called a *squint*.

hag-ridden, adj. [1. hágridn; 2. hǽgridn]. **hag (I.)** & *ridden*, P.P. of **ride (I.)**. Obsessed or harassed by a witch or female bogey.

ha ha (I.), interj., n., vb. intrans., & adj. [1. hah háh; 2. hā hā́]. **1.** interj. & n. **a** Conventional representation of laughter; **b** exclamation of scorn or triumph. **2.** vb. To exclaim or laugh thus. **3.** adj. Foppish, supercilious: *rather a ha ha manner*.

ha-ha (II.), haha, haw-haw, n. [1. háh hah, háw haw; 2. hā́ hā, hɔ́ hɔ̄], fr. prec. Sunk fence, in ditch, not visible until one is close to it, usually as boundary to garden.

haik, haick, n. [1. hīk; 2. haik]. Arab. *ḥaïk*, fr. *ḥāka*, 'to weave'. Woollen or cotton sheet worn by Arabs as mantle wrapping head and body.

hail (I.), n. [1. hāl; 2. heil]. O.E. *hagol*, *hæġel*, *hæġl*; M.E. *haȝel*, *hawel*; O.H.G. *hagal*; Common Gmc.; cogn. w. Gk. *kákhlēx*, 'round pebble'. (coll.) **1.** **a** Small lumps of ice falling like rain from the sky; **b** shower, storm of hail. **2.** (fig.) Said of anything which falls rapidly, or repeatedly and with violence: *a hail of blows, bullets* &c.

hail (II.), vb. intrans. & trans. O.E. *hagalian*, M.E. *haȝelen*, fr. prec. **1.** intrans. **a** (impers.) To precipitate, drop, shower down, hail; **b** (fig.) to fall in showers, like hail. **2.** trans. (fig.) To hurl, deliver, violently and rapidly: *to hail stones, curses, on one*.

hail (III.), interj., fr. O.N. *heill*, adj. & n., 'whole, prosperous' &c., see **hale (I.)**. The O.E. cogn. is *hāl*, 'whole, healthy' (see **whole**); also *hǣl(u)*, 'health, prosperity'. See **heal, health**. *Hail* as a greeting is elliptical for 'be thou hail', i.e. healthy, prosperous &c. (obs., except poet. and liter.) Mode of greeting, see above; Phr. (adjectival or adv.) *to be hail fellow well met with everybody*, to be on easy cordial terms, or to make show of being so.

hail (IV.), vb. trans. & intrans. M.E. *heilin*, fr. O.N. *heilla*, 'to greet', fr. *heill*, see prec. **A.** trans. **1.** **a** To say 'hail' to, greet, salute, welcome, congratulate; **b** (with complementary obj.) to call, address as, in salutation: *'All men hailed me happy'* (Milton); *to hail him king*. **2.** (naut.) To shout to, accost, signal to (a passing vessel); hence generally, to call out to, address in passing, attract attention of: *I was hailed by a stranger in the street*; *to hail a cab*. **B.** intrans. **1.** (naut.) **a** To shout, signal, to a vessel; **b** to announce one's home port or port from which one comes; hence, Phr. (naut. and colloq.) *to hail from*, to come from, esp. as one's home: *where do you hail from?*

hail (V.), n., fr. prec. **1.** Action of hailing, salutation. **2.** Distance within which shout can be heard at sea: *within hail*.

Hail Mary, n. [1. hāl mā́ri; 2. héil mɛ́əri]. First words of the angelic salutation to B.V.M., see Luke i. 28. Name of prayer of invocation to B.V.M., from opening words, *Ave Maria*: *to say three Hail Marys*.

hailstone, n. [1. hā́lstōn; 2. héilstoun]. O.E. *hagolstān*; cp. M.H.G. *hagelsten*, O.N. *haglsteinn* &c.; fr. **hail (I.)** & **stone (I.)**. Pellet of hail.

hailstorm, n. [1. hā́lstorm; 2. héilstɔ̄m]. **hail (I.)** & **storm (I.)**. Storm of hail.

haily, adj. [1. hā́li; 2. héili]. **hail (I.)** & **-y.** Pertaining to, accompanied by, hail (I.).

hair, n. [1. hār; 2. hɛə]. O.E. *hǣr*, M.E. *hēr* &c., O. Fris. *hēr*, O.S., O.H.G., O.N. *hār* &c.; the Mod. Engl. form is due to confusion w. M.E. *heire, haire*, 'hair-shirt', fr. O. Fr. *haire*, itself a loan-word fr. O.H.G. *hārra*, a derivative fr. *hār*; cp. also O.E. *hǣre*, O.N. *hǣra*, 'hair-shirt'. Outside Gmc. there are many derivatives fr. the Aryan base **kʷer-*, **kʷor-*, *kʷēr-* &c.; Lat. *corium*, 'hide, leather'. See **corium, coriaceous.** The orig. sense of the base is 'to tear', then 'something which is peeled, or torn off', whence 'skin, something growing on the skin'. For similar development of meaning see **derma.** (coll.) **1.** (physiol. and biol.) Fine, threadlike outgrowth from the skin of mammals, including fur on animals; the corresponding growth on human head and other parts of the body; the bristles of a pig, spines of a porcupine, and the whiskers of a cat. **2.** Specif., the growth covering the human head; also called *the hair of the head*: *to lose one's hair*, (i.) become bald; (ii.) (colloq.) to get angry or excited; *to cut, brush, one's hair* &c. Phrs. *to wear one's own hair*, not a wig; *to comb a person's hair for him* (fig.), give him a severe scolding; *to make one's hair stand on end* (fig.), to amaze, terrify one, make one shudder with horror; *keep your hair on* (slang), don't get excited; (of a girl) *to put up her hair, put her hair up*, to start wearing it rolled up on the head, as a grown-up woman; *to put down, let down, her hair*, remove hair-pins and allow the hair to hang down over shoulders &c. **3. a** Single thread or filament of hair: *to find a hair in one's soup*; Phrs. *to a hair, to the turn of a hair*, exactly; *not to turn a hair*, to show no nervousness or fear in trying situation; show no fatigue; *to split hairs*, to draw over-subtle distinctions; (colloq.) *a hair of the dog that bit one* (fig.), the same conduct, method, substance used remedially, which has already been prejudicial; specif., alcoholic liquor for a person suffering from effects of drink; **b** pl. *hairs* used collectively in archaic phr.: *to bring down one's grey hairs in sorrow to the grave.* **4. a** Fine filament resembling a hair, growing from surface of leaf or stalk &c., of a plant; **b** hair-like fibre, as seen in composition of paper when this is roughened or torn. **5.** A very fine wire, or spring resembling a hair.

hairball, n. [1. hā́rbawl; 2. héəbɔ̄l]. Roundish object composed of felt-like substance, found in stomachs of some animals, e.g. cows and cats, composed of hairs licked off and swallowed; also called *bezoar.*

hairbell, n. Variant spelling of **harebell.**

hairbreadth, n. & adj. [1. hā́rbredth; 2. héəbrɛdþ]. **1.** n. Also *hair's breadth*, breadth of a hair; very short space: *missed by a hairbreadth, (hair's breadth).* **2.** adj. Extremely narrow; barely or narrowly attained: *a hairbreadth escape.*

hairbrush, n. [1. hā́rbrush; 2. héəbraʃ]. Brush used for the hair.

haircloth, n. [1. hā́rklawth; 2. héəklɔ̄þ]. Cloth woven wholly or partially with horsehair.

hair-compasses, n. pl. Form of draughtsman's compasses adjusted by fine screw.

hairdresser, n. [1. hā́rdrèser; 2. héədrèsə]. Tradesman whose occupation is to dress and cut the hair.

hairdressing, n. [1. hā́rdrèsing; 2. héədrèsiŋ]. **a** Trade of a hairdresser; **b** action of dressing hair.

haired, adj. [1. hārd; 2. hɛəd]. **hair** & **-ed.** Furnished with hair.

hair-grass, n. One of several kinds of grass with very slender culms or leaves.

hairiness, n. [1. hā́rines; 2. héərinis]. **hairy** & **-ness.** State of being hairy.

hair-lace, n. Lace or fillet for binding or securing woman's hair.

hairless, adj. [1. hā́rles; 2. héəlis]. **hair** & **-less.** Without hair; bald.

hairlike, adj. [1. hā́rlīk; 2. héəlaik]. **hair** & **-like.** Resembling hair or a hair.

hair-line, n. **1.** Very thin line, like hair; specif., upstroke of letter. **2.** Line or cord made of hair; specif., fishing-line of horsehair.

hair-net, n. Fine net, made of hair or silk, for confining woman's hair and keeping it neat.

hair-oil, n. Oil used for greasing the hair.

hair-pencil, n. Camel's-hair brush, esp. fine one used in water-colour drawing.

hairpin, n. [1. hā́rpin; 2. héəpin]. **a** Device for fastening woman's hair, consisting of piece of metal, ivory, tortoiseshell, with two prongs; also **b** (attrib.) in Phr. *hairpin bend*, sharp bend in road, nearly reversing direction, esp. on steep gradient.

hair-powder, n. Scented white powder, formerly sprinkled over hair or wig; still occasionally used by liveried men-servants on their own hair.

hair's breadth, n. Same as **hairbreadth.**

hair seal, n. An eared seal or sea-bear, which is not covered with fur or seal-skin.

hair-shirt, n. Shirt, or strip of cloth round loins, made of horse-hair, worn by ascetics as a penance.

hair-space, n. (typog.) **a** Narrowest space between words in printing; **b** narrow type used for it.

hair-splitter, n. [1. hā́r spliter; 2. héə splitə]. **hair** & **split** & **-er.** Person addicted to hair-splitting; quibbler.

hair-splitting, n. & adj. [1. hā́r spliting; 2. héə splitiŋ]. **hair** & **split** & **-ing.** **a** n. Drawing of distinctions with excessive or pedantic subtlety, esp. in argument; quibbling; **b** adj., tending to quibble; characterized by quibbling.

hair-spring, n. Very fine recoil spring in watch.

hairstreak, n. [1. hā́rstrēk; 2. héəstrīk]. One of group of small British butterflies, related to blues, having fine streak across under-side of wings.

hair-stroke, n. Any very fine line in writing or printing; specif., fine horizontal line at top or bottom of letter; serif.

hair-trigger, n. One which fires revolver &c. on the slightest pressure.

hairy, adj. [1. hā́ri; 2. héəri]. **hair** & **-y.** **a** Pertaining to, of the nature of, hair; **b** furnished or covered with hair.

hake (I.), n. [1. hāk; 2. heik]. M.E. *hāke*, perh. fr. Gmc. base **hak-*, 'to pierce, bite'; cp. O.E. *haca*, 'hook', see **hook (I.)**. One of several coarse edible sea fishes, *Merluccius*, allied to cod.

hake (II.), n. Etymol. doubtful. Cp. **hack (IV.)**. Wooden frame on which unburnt bricks are dried.

hakim (I.), n. [1. háhkim; 2. hā́kim]. Arab. *ḥākim.* A Moslem judge or Governor in India and the East.

hakim (II.), n. [1. hakḗm; 2. hækím]. Arab. *ḥakīm*, 'wise'. A Moslem physician in India and the East.

halation, n. [1. halā́shun; 2. hæléiʃən], fr. **halo** & **-ation.** (photog.) A bright patch or ring of light, like a halo, on a developed plate.

halberd, halbert, n. [1. hál-, háwberd, hál-, háwbert; 2. hǽl-, hɔ́bəd, hǽl-, hɔ́bət]. O. Fr. *halebarde*, fr. M.H.G. *halmbarte*, earlier *helmbarte.* The origin of this word is a matter of pure speculation. It is said to be possibly fr. *helm*, 'helmet', & *barta*, 'axe', meaning one used for cleaving helmets; O.H.G. *barta* is apparently closely related to *bart*, 'beard', & was perh. so called fr. the shape of the blade. See **helm (II.)** & **beard.** Battle-axe with long handle and a spike projecting above the blade; really an axe-blade fastened to a spear.

halberdier, n. [1. hàlberdḗr; 2. hælbədíə]. Fr., fr. prec. & **-ier.** Soldier armed with a halberd; later, a person bearing a similarly shaped instrument for show at civic functions.

halcyon, n. & adj. [1. hálsiun; 2. hǽlsiən]. Lat. *(h)alcyōn*, fr. Gk. *alkuṓn*, less correctly *halkuṓn*, 'kingfisher', cogn. w. O.H.G. *alacra*, 'a kind of diving-bird', & w. Lat. *alcēdo*, stem *alcēdōn-*, but explained by popular etymol. as fr. Gk. *hál-s*, 'sea', & *kúōn*, 'conceiving'. Some philologists suggest that Lat. *alcēdo* is a loan fr. Gk., & that the Gk. word is related to **swallow (III.)**. **1.** n. **a** Kingfisher, esp. in connexion with ancient belief that it built floating nest on sea, which remained calm about winter solstice while the eggs were being hatched; **b** member of genus of Australian and Asiatic kingfishers. **2.** adj. Pertaining to the halcyon; tranquil, peaceful. Phr. *halcyon days*, period of calm weather about winter solstice; hence, (fig.) time of tranquillity and happiness.

hale (I.), adj. [1. hāl; 2. heil]. North. dial. type fr. O.E. *hāl.* See **whole.** (only of persons) Sound, healthy, robust, vigorous. Phr. *hale and hearty*; esp. of elderly persons, or those who have been ailing.

hale (II.), vb. trans. M.E. *halien, halen*, Mod. Engl. **haul (I.)**, either (1) directly fr. a L.G. source, cp. O. Fris. *halia*, O.S. *halōn*, 'to pull'; also O.E. *(ġe-)holian*, 'to acquire, get', & O.H.G. *halōn, holōn*, Germ. *holen*, 'to summon, fetch'; or (2) through Fr. *haler*, 'to haul, tow', fr. above; cogn. w. Lat. *calāre*, Gk. *kaléein*, 'to summon'. See **calends.** (archaic; now usually *haul*) To haul, drag along, pull; constrain to go: *to hale a man before a magistrate.*

haleness, n. [1. hā́lnes; 2. héilnis]. **hale (I.)** & **-ness.** Health, sound condition of body, esp. in an old person.

half (I.), n. [1. hahf; 2. hāf]. O.E. (Angl.) & M.E. *half*, 'side, half'; cp. O.S., O.H.G. *halpa*, Goth. *halba.* Outside Gmc., cognates are Scrt. *kalp-ayati*, 'arrange, distribute', & the variant Lat. *scalpere*, 'to carve, scratch' &c., & a number of words beginning w. *sk-*. The orig. sense of the base seem to have been 'divide, split up'. See further under **scale** (of fish), **shelf, shell.** **1.** One of two precisely equal parts into which a thing is or can be divided; **a** (of numbers) *the half of six is three*; **b** (of amounts, measures) *eighteen inches is half a yard*; *a pint is the half of a quart*; **c** (of material objects) *to saw a plank into two exact halves*; Phrs. *to go halves in*, to share alike; *to see with half an eye*, easily, immediately; *half a loaf is better than no bread*, be content with what one can get. (*N.B.*—In many phrases *of* is omitted; e.g. *half a mile*; *half a pint*; *half an inch*; *half a cup.*) **2. a** One of two portions of a thing which are of approximately the same size, amount &c.; **b** (still more loosely) either of two portions or divisions of a thing, amount &c., without regard to their equality in size: *he ate by far the larger half of the meal himself*; *to waste half (of) one's time*; *I couldn't hear half of what he said*; Phrs. *one's better half*, wife; *to cut a stick in half*, into two pieces; *to do something by halves*, incompletely, not thoroughly; *too good, clever, by half*, (ironic) much too good, better than was expected; unnecessarily good, clever &c. **3.** A specific portion or period of time, esp. at some schools, a school term: *he entered the school in the summer half, and only stayed three halves.* **4.** Side, party in a transaction; chiefly in legal agreements &c.: *John Brown of the one half, and George Grey of the other half.*

half (II.), adj. See prec. **1.** Consisting of, equivalent to, one of two precisely equal parts, amounts, degrees &c.: *to own a half share in a business.* **2. a** Consisting of, equivalent to, one of two approximately equal parts, amounts &c.; possessing in the same degree two distinct qualities or characters; **b** not complete, imperfect, partial: *a half conviction*; *a half light*; *half truth* &c.

half (III.), adv. See **half (I.)**. **1.** To the extent of a half: *my work is half done*; '*half angel and half bird*'; *half a fool, half a knave.* **2. a** To a considerable extent: *I am half inclined to agree with you*; **b** very nearly: *half dead*; *half asleep*; *half raw*; Phrs. *not half good enough for you*, quite inadequate; *I don't* *half like it*, I don't like it at all; *not half bad*, very good; **c** to a slight extent, imperfectly, inadequately, insufficiently: *half-educated*; *half-cooked*; Phr. (vulg. slang) *not half*: *Do you like beer? Oh, not half!* = 'don't I just, I should think I did' &c.

half-and-half, adj. & n. **1.** adj. **a** Composed of two things in equal quantities; **b** (in unfavourable sense) neither one thing nor the other: *he's not a sound Tory, rather half-and-half.* **2.** n. Mixture of beer and stout in equal quantities.

half-back, n. **a** Position in football or hockey between forwards and backs; **b** player in such position.

half-baked, adj. [1. háhf bắkt; 2. hắf béikt]. **1.** Partially or incompletely baked. **2.** (fig.) **a** Imperfectly developed, mentally immature, raw; **b** socially inexperienced: *a half-baked youth*; **c** (of ideas &c.) crude, undigested: *half-baked theories, views.*

halfbeak, n. [1. háhfbēk; 2. hắfbīk]. One of several marine fishes, resembling the garfish, with lower jaw rather like a bird's beak.

half-binding, n. Style of binding in which only back, corners, and strips adjoining back of a book are of leather.

half-blood, n. & adj. [1. háhf blud; 2. hắf blad]. **half (II.)** & **blood (I.)**. **A.** n. **1.** **a** Blood relationship through one parent only: *brothers of the half-blood* [1. háhf blúd; 2. hắf blắd]; **b** person thus related to another. **2.** Person born of parents of two different races; half-breed. **B.** adj. Half-blooded.

half-blooded, adj. **a** Having only one common parent; **b** born of parents belonging to two different races or species.

half-boot, n. Boot reaching about half-way up calf of leg.

half-bound, adj. (bookbinding) Bound in half-binding.

half-bred, adj. **1.** Of mixed breed, mongrel. **2.** Possessing imperfect breeding.

half-breed, n. **a** Person whose parents are of different races; specif., mixture of white man and American Indian; **b** hybrid animal or plant.

half-brother, n. Brother of the half-blood, brother by one parent.

half-butt, n. Billiard butt or cue intermediate between longest cue and one of ordinary length.

half-caste, n. & adj. **half (II.)** & **caste**. **1.** n. Child of a European and an Oriental, or member of a coloured race, esp. of non-European mother. **2.** adj. Pertaining to a half-caste; born of mixed European and Asiatic parentage.

half-cloth, n. & adj. **1.** n. Bookbinding with cloth sides and leather back. **2.** adj. Bound in half-cloth.

half-cock, n. & vb. trans. **1.** n. Half-raised position of trigger of gun when held by sear, or first notch. **2.** vb. To fix trigger of (gun) at half-cock.

half-crown, n. **half (II.)** & **crown (I.)**. **a** British silver coin, of value of two shillings and sixpence; **b** sum of money represented by this coin.

half-deck, n. Deck extending over half or a part of vessel.

half-decked, adj. [1. háhf dekt; 2. hắf dɛkt]. Prec. & **-ed**. Furnished with half-deck.

half-diphthong, n. Vague, unscientific term, used to denote some vowel combination which the user cannot describe accurately.

half-done, adj. **half (III.)** & **done**. Half-completed; specif., half-cooked.

half-hardy, adj. **half (III.)** & **hardy (I.)**. (hort.) Of garden plants, resisting ordinary changes of weather, but not severe frost.

half-hearted, adj. **half (II.)** & **hearted**. **a** Lacking resolution or zeal, not enthusiastic; faintly interested, lukewarm; **b** having conflicting aims or feelings, divided in sympathy.

half-heartedly, adv. In a half-hearted manner.

half-heartedness, n. Quality of being half-hearted.

half-hitch, n. Kind of hitch made by bending rope or thread and pulling end through bight.

half-holiday, n. Holiday lasting for the afternoon, or afternoon and evening.

half-hourly, adj. & adv. **a** adj. Occurring every half-hour, at intervals of half an hour; **b** adv., at intervals of half an hour.

half-length, adj. & n. **a** adj. Of half the full length; specif. (of portraits) depicting upper half of the person; **b** n., half-length portrait.

half-line, n. **half (II.)** & **line (I.)**. (geom.) Straight line extended from a point indefinitely in one direction.

half-mast, n., adv., & vb. trans. **1.** n. Position of flag when flown near middle of mast or gaff, as sign of mourning or signal of distress. **2.** adv. At half-mast: *half-mast high.* **3.** vb. To fly (flag) at half-mast: *to half-mast a flag.*

half-measure, n. Inadequate means taken to secure end.

half-moon, n. **1.** Moon at quarter, showing half of its disk. **2.** Half-disk, object of this shape. **3.** Edible fish of ovate form inhabiting Pacific.

half-mourning, n. **a** Costume of black relieved with white, grey, or lavender, often worn as transition from full mourning to ordinary dress; **b** period during which half-mourning is worn.

half-nelson, n. [1. hahf nélsun; 2. hāf nélsən]. Wrestling hold by which wrestler, facing opponent's back, hooks one arm under corresponding armpit of latter, and presses both hands on back of neck.

half-note, n. (mus.) Minim.

half-one, n. (golf) Handicap by which player owes one at every second hole.

halfpace, n. [1. háhfpās; 2. hắfpeis]. Corrupt. of earlier *halpace*, prob. fr. O. Fr. *halt* (Mod. *haut*), 'high' (see **haughty**), & *pas*, 'step' (see **pace**). **a** Platform approached by steps, as for throne or altar; dais; **b** landing or broad step on staircase, esp. at turn of stairs.

halfpaced, adj. [1. háhfpāst; 2. hắfpeist]. Prec. &- **ed**. (of staircase) Furnished with a halfpace.

half-pay, n. & adj. **a** n. Reduced pay, approximately half, given to officer of navy or army when not employed, or when retired; **b** adj., receiving half-pay: *a half-pay colonel* &c.

halfpenny, n. & adj. [1. hắpni; 2. héipni]. **1.** n. **a** British bronze coin worth half a penny; **b** pl. *halfpence*, (colloq.) any small coins, coppers; Phr. *to receive more kicks than halfpence*, more blame than praise or reward. **2.** adj. Worth a halfpenny, hence trumpery, worthless.

halfpennyworth, n. [1. hắpniwërth, hắporth; 2. héipniwāþ, héipəþ]. Prec. & **worth**. Quantity of commodity worth, or sold for, a halfpenny.

half-price, adv. At half the usual price or charge: *children (are admitted) half-price.*

half-rater, n. [1. háhf rắter; 2. hắf réitə]. Small racing yacht, of which maximum size is variously prescribed, often 20 ft. length at water-line.

half-round, adj. **a** Semicircular; **b** of semicircular section, of the form of half a cylinder: *a half-round file.*

half-royal, n. Kind of millboard or pasteboard.

half-seas-over, adj. Only pred. **a** (naut.) half across the sea; **b** (fig., colloq.) half-drunk.

half-shift, n. (mus.) Second position of hand in playing violin or similar instrument; shift in which first finger occupies original place of second.

half-sister, n. Sister by one parent.

half-sovereign, n. British gold coin of value of ten shillings.

half-timbered, adj. **half (III.)** & **timbered**. (archit.) Having walls made of timber frame with spaces filled with other material: *a half-timbered house-front.*

half-time, n. **a** Work and pay for half the day only: *to go on half time*; **b** (football &c.) interval between the two halves of play.

half-timer, n. [1. háhf tímer; 2. hắf táimə]. Prec. & **-er**. Child of school age excused attendance for about half-time in order to work for wages.

half-tint, n. **a** (in painting, engraving &c.) Tint intermediate between high light and deep shade; **b** (in water-colour) faint wash.

half-title, n. Title of book or of section of book printed at head of first page of text, or on otherwise blank page.

half-tone, n. & adj. **A.** n. **1.** **a** Half tint in painting, engraving, or photograph; **b** photo-engraving made by half-tone process. **2.** (mus.) Semitone. **B.** adj. Pertaining to half-tone; specif., pertaining to process of photo-engraving in which half-tones are reproduced by transmission of photographic image through glass screen ruled with fine cross lines.

half-truth, n. Statement which omits many relevant and significant facts.

half-uncial, adj. & n. **a** adj. Written partly in uncial, partly in cursive characters; **b** n., half-uncial script.

half-volley, n. & vb. trans. & intrans. **1.** n. (in cricket, lawn-tennis and similar games) Return of ball as soon as it touches ground. **2.** vb. To deliver or play (ball) in half-volley.

half-way, adj. & adv. **1.** adj. Equally distant from the two ends or extremes. Phr. *half-way house*, inn or other house about midway between the starting-point and termination of a journey. **2.** adv. In the middle; Phr. *to meet one half-way*, to be ready for compromise or mutual concessions.

half-witted, adj. Imbecile, mentally deficient.

half-year, n. **a** Period of six months; **b** term at school or university where there are only two in year; semester.

half-yearly, adj. & adv. Prec. & **-ly**. **a** adj. Occurring every half-year; **b** adv., at intervals of half a year.

halibut, n. [1. hálibut; 2. hǽlibat]. M.E. *hāli*, **holy**, & **butt**, prob. because eaten on holidays, cp. Du. *heilbot*, Germ. *heilbutt*. Largest kind of flatfish, *Hippoglossus vulgaris*, with edible but coarse flesh, inhabiting northern seas.

halidom, n. [1. hálidom; 2. hǽlidəm]. O.E. *hāligdōm*, 'holiness, relic, sacrament, sanctuary', M.E. *hălidŏm*, 'sanctuary, relic'. See **holy** & **-dom**. (obs. or archaic) A holy thing or object; relic &c. Phr. (obs.) *by my halidom*, form of oath.

halieutic, adj. & n. [1. hàliútik; 2. hæliútik]. Lat. *halieutic-(us)*, fr. Gk. *halieutik-ós*, 'pertaining to fishing', fr. *halieúein*, 'to fish', fr. *hál-s*, 'salt sea', for **sal-*, cp. Lat. *sāl*, 'salt'. See **sal (I.)** & **salt**. **a** adj. Pertaining to fishing; **b** n. (pl.), art of fishing, treatise on same.

haliotis, n. [1. hàliṓtis; 2. hæliόutis]. Mod. Lat., fr. Gk. *hál-s*, 'salt, sea', see prec., & *ōt-*, stem of *oûs*, **ear (I.)**. Abalone, ear-shell.

halitosis, n. [1. hàlitṓsis; 2. hèilitóusis]. Invented word fr. Lat. *hālitus*, 'breath', fr. *hālāre*, 'to breathe'. See **exhale** & **-osis**. Medical term for foul breath.

hall, n. [1. hawl; 2. hɔl]. O.E. *heall*, *hall*, M.E. *halle*, 'hall'; O.S., O.H.G. *halla*. This Common Gmc. word is cogn. w. Lat. *cella* (see **cell**); Gk. *kaliá*, 'hut, cabin' &c. The orig. sense of Aryan base **k'el-* &c. is 'hide, protect'; cp. Gk. *kalúptein*, 'to cover'; Lat. *cēlare*, 'hide' (see **conceal**); & further O.E. *helan*, 'to hide', *heolstor*, 'hiding-place, darkness' &c.; *helm*, 'helmet, protection'. See **helm (II.)** & **holster**. **1.** Originally a hall was **a** the great apartment, constituting the principal part of the dwelling of a king, chief, baron &c., in which most of the social occupations of life were carried on, esp. eating and merry-making; **b** the whole dwelling where such an apartment existed, including the various other rooms and dwellings which clustered round it; **c** now applied to the large room in a castle, palace, mansion, chiefly used for dining: *banqueting hall*; **d** large dining-room in a college, school &c.; Phr. *a hall*, dinner eaten in hall; **e** *servants' hall*, sitting- and dining-room for servants in a private house.

2. Principal house in a place, esp. the large residence belonging to the owner of a country estate. **3.** Large building, generally with some architectural pretensions, used for public purposes; **a** one where county and municipal business, or the administration of justice, is carried on: *Town Hall, County Hall; Hall of Justice* &c.; **b** place of meeting of philanthropic, religious, and other organizations and societies: *Masonic Hall, Mission Hall* &c.; **c** building used for public instruction, entertainments, and social functions; **d** building in which certain members of a university reside; in Oxford and Cambridge the term covers colleges, but refers specifically to smaller teaching institutions and their buildings: *hall of residence* &c.; **e** headquarters of learned, or professional society, trade guild &c.: *Surgeons' Hall, Fishmongers' Hall* &c. **4.** Portion of a public building or private house, situated near the entrance; **a** in large public building or private house, a spacious apartment communicating with outer air by means of principal door, and opening into other rooms; **b** in small houses, space, passage, or lobby immediately inside front door.

hallelujah, -iah, interj. & n. [1. hàlilōōya; 2. hæ̀lilūjə]. Heb. *hallēlū-yah*, 'praise ye Jehovah'. Cp. **alleluia**. Pious ejaculation in praise and adoration of God, used in Jewish and Christian worship. Phr. (colloq.) *Hallelujah lass*, female member of Salvation Army.

halliard, n. See **halyard**.

hallmark (I.), n. [1. háwlmark; 2. hɔ́lmāk]. **a** Official mark stamped on gold or silver plate at Goldsmiths' Hall or by assay officers to guarantee quality; **b** (fig.) token, criterion, of quality or distinction: *the hallmark of gentility*.

hallmark (II.), vb. trans., fr. prec. **a** To stamp (plate) with hallmark; **b** (fig.) to furnish with criterion of quality.

hallmoot, n. [1. háwlmōōt; 2. hɔ́lmūt]. O.E. **hall-ġemōt*, 'hall-meeting', M.E. *halimōt*. See **hall, moot**. (hist.) Court of lord of manor, held in his hall; court-baron.

hallo, halloa, interj., n., & vb. intrans. [1. huló, haló; 2. halóu, hælóu]. Imit. See also **hollo**. **a** interj. Cry to attract attention; also cry of surprise; **b** n., this cry; **c** vb., to utter this cry.

halloo (I.), interj. & n. [1. halōō; 2. həlū]. Perh. variant of prec., or M.E. *halow*, 'call, shout'. See **hallow** (III.). **a** A call to hounds during chase; **b** shout given to attract attention.

halloo (II.), vb. trans. & intrans., fr. prec. Cp. **hallow** (III.). **1.** trans. **a** To incite hounds by shouting 'halloo!'; **b** to chase with shouts; **c** to shout 'halloo!' to attract attention of; to shout to or at a person. **2.** intrans. To shout 'halloo!' **a** to hounds; **b** in order to attract attention; Phr. *don't halloo till you are out of the wood*, don't triumph until all difficulties are surmounted.

hallow (I.), n. [1. hálō; 2. hǽlou]. O.E. *hālga*, 'holy person, saint', M.E. *hālwe*, fr. wk. form of adj. *hāliġ*, 'holy'. See **holy**. Obsolete except in *All Hallows*.

hallow (II.), vb. trans. O.E. *hālgian*, 'to consecrate'; M.E. *hālȝien, hālewen*, cp. O.S. *hēlagōn*, O.H.G. *heilagōn*. See prec. & **holy**. **a** To regard as holy, to reverence: '*hallowed be thy name*'; **b** to make holy: *a place hallowed by sacred memories*; **c** devote to sacred use, to dedicate to God, or to some cause: *a life hallowed by piety and goodness*.

hallow (III.). Variant of **hallo, halloo, hollo**.

Hallowe'en, n. [1. hàlōwḗn; 2. hæ̀louín]. **hallow** (I.) & Scots or North. *e'en*, contr. fr. **even** (I.). (chiefly Scots) The eve or vigil of Hallowmas or All Saints, Oct. 31st, esp. its evening.

Hallowmas, n. [1. hálōmas; 2. hǽloumæs]. **hallow** (I.) & **mass** (I.). (archaic) The Church festival of All Saints, Nov. 1st.

Hallstatt, adj. [1. hálstat; 2. hǽlstæt], fr. name of town in Austria near wh. first discovery was made. Of, pertaining to, a period of prehistoric civilization in Europe during which iron began to take the place of bronze.

hallucinate, vb. trans. [1. halū́sināt; 2. həljū́sineit]. Lat. *hallūcināt-(um)*, P.P. type of *hallūcinārī*, correctly *ālūcinārī*, deponent vb., 'to wander in mind, dream, rave', cogn. w. Gk. *aliéein, halúein*, 'to wander in mind', & *ēleós*, 'distracted, crazed'. Origin of these unknown. (rare) To affect with hallucination, produce hallucination in mind of.

hallucination, n. [1. halūsinā́shun; 2. həljūsinéiʃən]. See prec. & **-ion**. **a** Fancied perception by the senses of something which has no external, objective existence; **b** that which is supposed to be perceived.

hallucinative, adj. [1. halū́sinativ; 2. həljū́sinətiv]. **hallucinate** & **-ive**. Pertaining to hallucination; hallucinatory.

hallucinatory, adj. [1. halū́sinatori; 2. həljū́sinətəri]. **hallucinate** & **-ory**. Pertaining to, of the nature of, an hallucination.

hallux, n., pl. **halluces**, [1. háluks, hálūsēz; 2. hǽlaks, hǽljūsīz]. Mistaken form of Lat. *(h)allex, -icis*, 'great toe'. (anat.) First digit on hindleg of mammal; great toe of man; hind toe of bird.

halm, n. See **haulm**.

halma, n. [1. hálma; 2. hǽlmə]. Gk. *hálma*, 'a leaping', fr. *hal-ésthai*, 'to leap'. Cp. **salient**. Game played on board of 256 squares by two or four players, in which pieces proceed by moves or jumps from one corner to that opposite.

halo, n. [1. hā́lō; 2. héilou]. Fr., fr. Lat. *halō*, acc. of *halōs*, 'halo', fr. Gk. *hálōs*, 'threshing-floor, in which oxen walked in circle'; hence, 'disk of sun or moon, halo', fr. *aleîn*, 'to grind, pound', cogn. w. Scrt. *lāvaš*, 'cutting'. **1.** Ring of light surrounding sun or moon. **2. a** Aureole in form of ring, or disk, shown in pictorial representations round or above head of the Saviour and of saints; **b** (fig.) glory, glamour, investing idealized person, institution, or thing: *Arthur wears a halo of romance*. **3.** (anat., pathol.) Areola or coloured ring round nipple, vesicle, or pustule.

haloed, adj. [1. hā́lōd; 2. héiloud]. Prec. & **-ed**. Provided, represented, with a halo.

halogen, n. [1. hálōjen; 2. hǽloudžen]. Gk. *hál-s*, see **salt**, & **-gen**. (chem.) Element, or other radical, forming a salt in combination with a metal.

halogenous, adj. [1. halójenus; 2. hælɔ́džənəs]. Prec. & **-ous**. Pertaining to, of the nature of, halogen.

haloid, adj. & n. [1. háloid; 2. hǽlɔid]. Gk. *hál-s*, 'salt'. See **saline** & **-oid**. (chem.) **a** adj. Resembling common salt; **b** n., substance of this kind.

halt (I.), adj. [1. hawlt; 2. hɔlt]. O.E. *halt, healt*, M.E. *halt*, Common Gmc.; cp. O.H.G. *halz*, Goth. *-halt-s* &c. Etymol. doubtful; not cogn. w. Lat. *claudus*, 'lame'. (archaic) Lame, halting in gait.

halt (II.), vb. intrans. O.E. *haltian, healtian*, M.E. *halten*, fr. prec. **1.** (archaic) To be lame, walk lamely, limp: *to halt in one's gait*. **2.** (fig.) **a** To hesitate, vacillate, stand in doubt: '*How long halt ye between two opinions?*' (1 Kings xviii. 21); **b** to speak with a hesitation, in a stumbling, disconnected manner; **c** (of verse) to run lamely, be metrically faulty; **d** (of argument) to be defective; to proceed illogically or inconclusively.

halt (III.), n., fr. prec. (archaic) Lameness, limp: *a halt in one's walk*.

halt (IV.), n., fr. Fr. *halte*, fr. Germ. *halt (machen)*, 'stopping, halt', fr. *halten*, 'to hold, stop, check'. Cogn. w. **hold** (I.). **1. a** (mil.) Temporary stoppage of moving troops: *to make, call, a halt*; **b** (gen.) cessation, stoppage, of walking or other movement; **c** pause in any form of activity. **2. a** Place on railway line at which a halt is made; place where trains stop for brief space of time to take up and let down passengers; **b** stopping-place of trams &c.

halt (V.), vb. intrans. & trans. Prec., orig., *make halt*, fr. Germ. *halt machen*. **1.** intrans. **a** (mil.) To cease marching, come to a halt; **b** to pause during walk, or other form of movement; to cease activity and to remain at rest for a time. **2.** trans. (mil.) To make (troops) halt.

halter, n. & vb. trans. [1. háwlter; 2. hɔ́ltə]. O.E. *hælfter, hælftre*, M.E. *halfter, halter*; cp. O.S. *haliftra*, M.L.G. *halter*, O.H.G. *halftra*. Etymol. obscure; possibly allied to **helve**. **1.** n. **a** Short rope, usually attached to a head-stall for leading a horse; **b** rope with noose for hanging person; Phr. *to come to the halter*, be hanged as a criminal. **2.** vb. (rare) To put a halter on to.

halter break, vb. trans. To break, accustom (colt &c.) to a halter.

halting, adj. [1. háwlting; 2. hɔ́ltiŋ], fr. Pres. Part. of **halt** (I.). **1.** (of gait) Stumbling, uncertain, limping. **2.** (fig., of speech, verse, argument) Uncertain, hesitating, stumbling, jerky; (of persons) speaking or arguing thus.

haltingly, adv. Prec. & **-ly**. In a halting manner, with hesitation.

halting-place, n. Place where a halt is made.

halve, vb. trans. [1. hahv; 2. hāv]. M.E. *halven*, fr. **half** (I.). **1.** To divide into halves. **2.** To share equally (with another): *to halve expenses with*. Phr. (golf) *to halve a hole with*, to reach it in as many strokes as, to tie with (opponent); so *to halve a match*. **3.** To diminish by a half: *this will halve the profits*. **4.** (carpent.) To fit two pieces of wood together by cutting each at place where they are to cross to half its thickness.

halyard, halliard, haulyard, n. [1. hályard; 2. hǽljəd]. Cp. M.E. *halier*, 'carrier, porter, halyard', fr. *halien*, **hale** (II.). The second element is **yard** (I.). (naut.) Rope &c., for hoisting or lowering flag, sails &c.

ham (I.), n. [1. ham; 2. hæm]. O.E. *ham(m), homm*, M.E. *hamme*; cp. O.H.G. *hamma*, Du. *ham*, O.N. *hōm*; prob. cogn. w. Celt. base **kamb-os*, 'bent, crooked' (W. *cam*), whence L. Lat. *camba*, 'bend of leg'. See **gambol, jamb**. **1. a** (obs.) Inner or hinder part of knee, hock; cp. Shakespeare, '*Old men have most weak hams*'; **b** back of thigh with buttock: *to squat on one's hams*. **2. a** Thigh of animal; specif., a pig's leg salted, smoked, and seasoned for eating; **b** portion, slices, of this; meat of this considered as an article of diet: *to have ham for breakfast*.

ham (II.), n. (i.) In some Pl.-Ns. this is fr. prec. & means 'bend of a river', e.g. *Fulham*, O.E. *Fullanhamm*; (ii.) in the majority of Pl.-Ns. the suff. is shortened in the unstressed position, fr. O.E. *hām*, 'dwelling' &c. See **hamlet** & **home**.

hamadryad, n. [1. hàmadríad; 2. hæ̀mədráiæd]. Lat. *hamadryad-(is)*, fr. stem of Gk. *hamadruás*, nymph whose life began and ended with that of a tree, fr. *háma*, 'together with' (cp. **same**), & *druás*, 'wood nymph'. See **dryad**. **1.** (Gk. mythol.) Tree-nymph. **2. a** King cobra of India; **b** sacred baboon of ancient Egypt, now found in Abyssinia and Arabia.

hamartiology, n. [1. hàmartiólọji; 2. hæ̀mātiɔ́lədži]. Gk. *hamartía*, 'sin', fr. *hamartánein*, 'to miss the mark, fail, sin', the etymol. of wh. is uncertain, & **-logy**. Branch of theology dealing with sin; treatise on this.

Hamburgh, n. [1. hámbro; 2. hǽmbrə]. Earlier spelling of Hamburg, a town in Germany. **1.** Kind of black grape; also *Black Hamburghs*. **2.** Breed of domestic fowl.

hames, n. pl. [1. hāmz; 2. heimz]. M.E. *hāme* (fr. O.E. *hama*, 'dress, covering'?); cp. M. Du. *hamme*, Du. *haam*, 'hame'; also M.H.G. *hame*, Germ. *hamen*, 'hoop-net, fish-hook'. Outside Gmc. cp. perh. Lat. *camus*, 'bent inwards', & *camera*, 'a vault &c.' borrowed fr. the cogn. Gk. *kamára*, 'vaulted chamber' &c. (see **camera, chamber**); further Scrt. *šamyā*, 'pin of yoke'. For other probable Gmc. cognates see **hem** (I.). Pair of curved pieces of metal, rarely of wood, passing on either side of the collar in draught harness, kept in place by a strap and buckle above and below the collar, and having each a metal loop to which the traces are attached.

hamesucken, n. [1. hàmsúken; 2. hèimsákən]. O.E. *hāmsōcn*, 'attacking enemy in his house, house-breaking', M.E. *hāmsōcne*, cp. O.N. *heimsōkn* (cp. O. Fris. *hamsekenge*, 'attack on one's house', Germ. *heimsuchung*, 'visitation, affliction'); fr. O.E. *hām*, 'home, house' (see **home**), & *sōcn*, 'attack' (cp. **seek**). The above form is Nthn. in type. (Scots law) Offence of assaulting person in his own dwelling-house.

hamite (I.), n. [1. hā́mīt; 2. héimait]. Lat. *hām-(us)*, 'hook' (etymol. doubtful), & **-ite**. (paleont.) Fossil cephalopod with shell bent back like hook.

Hamite (II.), n. [1. hámīt; 2. hǽmait], fr. name of *Ham*, son of Noah, supposed ancestor, & **-ite**. Member of race with S. European and Semitic affinities, predominant in N. and N.E. Africa, including many Egyptians, Somalis &c., and possibly Berbers and Tuaregs.

Hamitic, adj. [1. hamítik; 2. hæmítik]. Prec. & **-ic**. Pertaining to Hamites or their languages.

hamlet, n. [1. hámlet; 2. hǽmlit]. M.E., A.-Fr. *hamelet*, 'small village', fr. O. Fr. *hamel* & dimin. suff. **-et** (Mod. Fr. *hameau*), itself fr. L.G. *hām* & the further dimin. suff. *-il-* (see **-le**); cp. O.E. *hām*. See **home**. A small village.

hammam, hummum, n. [1. hámam, húmum; 2. hǽmæm, hámam]. Arab. *ḥammām*. Turkish bath or bath-house.

hammer (I.), n. [1. hámer; 2. hǽmə]. O.E. *hamor, hamer*, M.E. *hamur, hamer*, cp. O.S. *hamur*, O.H.G. *hamar*, O.N. *hamar-r*, fr. Gmc. type **ham-r-az*, w. suff. *-r*, as in *thunder* &c.; the orig. sense was 'stone', cp. O.N. *hamarr*, wh. still retains the meaning 'rock, crag'. Cognates outside Gmc. are Scrt. *aśman*, '(meteoric) stone', O. Slav. *kaméni*, Lith. *akmú*, 'stone', Gk. *ákmōn* for **k̑m̥ōn-*, '(stone) anvil'. The word therefore, in the sense existing in all Gmc. languages, goes back to the Stone Age. **1.** Tool for striking, consisting of a relatively long handle, with heavy metal head set at right angles to it, used to drive nails, chisels &c.; to work metal; to break stones &c. by repeated blows. Phr. *throwing the hammer*, hurling heavy hammer with long, pliant handle as a trial of strength; *to go, be at, it hammer and tongs*, with great animation, noise, and violence, or (fig.) with energy. **2.** Applied to various objects and appliances for striking; **a** device somewhat resembling hammer in shape, which strikes the bell in a clock, or the dial of electric bell; **b** device worked by levers which strikes string of piano &c.; **c** wooden mallet used by auctioneer to announce that lot is sold: *auctioneer's hammer*; Phr. *to bring, send to, come under, the hammer*, sell, be sold, by auction; **d** striking part of gun-lock, which ignites priming, moved by the trigger; **e** heavy, striking part of large machine, raised and lowered by steam, used in metal working on a large scale: *steam hammer*.

hammer (II.), vb. trans. & intrans., fr. prec. **A.** trans. **1. a** To strike, drive, with a hammer: *to hammer a nail into a plank*; **b** to use a hammer for making: *to hammer a rough box together*; **c** to work and shape (metal) by striking repeated blows with a hammer (cp. **hammered**, adj.). **2. a** To strike violently and repeatedly, esp. with the fists: *Carpentier was badly hammered in several rounds*; **b** to attack (enemy) violently in war, esp. by heavy artillery. **3.** To defeat in any contest by vigorous effort and attack: *the visiting cricket team were badly hammered.* **4.** (Stock Exchange) To declare (a member) a defaulter (attention being drawn to declaration by hammering three times). **B.** intrans. **1.** To ply a hammer. **2.** *Hammer away*, **a** to engage in continuous action: *to hammer away at a task*; **b** to make noise like hammer-blows: *the guns are hammering away.* **C.** Followed by prepositions & adverbs. *Hammer at*, intrans., **1.** to strike repeated blows upon: *to hammer at the door*; **2.** (fig.) **a** to approach, plead with (a person) repeatedly and insistently: *he was always hammering at me to let him ride*; **b** to pursue a course of action with determination and persistence, work hard at: *I've been hammering (away) at the dictionary all day. Hammer down*, trans., to fasten down by hammering nails into: *to hammer down the lid of a packing-case. Hammer in, into*, trans., **a** to drive in by hammering: *to hammer in a nail*, or *a nail in*; **b** (fig.) to instil knowledge, ideas &c. into a person's mind by repeated instruction, explanation &c.: *I want to hammer in a few facts if I can*; *I can't hammer anything into his thick head. Hammer out*, trans., **1. a** to flatten, cause a substance to become thinner, and to be extended over wider surface by hammering: *to hammer out metal very thin* &c.; **b** to smooth out, remove, by hammering: *to hammer out the dints in a silver teapot*; **2.** (fig.) **a** to elucidate a problem &c. by repeated thought or discussion: *to hammer out the question in friendly debate* &c.; **b** to shape, devise, plan out, construct, scheme, &c., by assiduous thought: *I've had some trouble over my book, report, lecture &c., but I shall hammer out something at last.*

hammer-beam, n. **hammer** (I.) & **beam**. (archit.) One of pair of short horizontal beams, projecting inwards from base of roof, supported by hammer-braces, and supporting collar-braces.

hammer-blow, n. Heavy, severe, repeated blows, as from a hammer.

hammer-brace, n. **hammer** (I.) & **brace** (I.). (archit.) One of pair of braces or ribs rising from corbels to support hammer-beams in roof.

hammer-cloth, n. Early Mod. E. *hamerclothe* (1465), of uncertain origin, but prob. so called because it covered the box in which, formerly, were carried hammers and other tools for repairing the carriage on a journey. Ornamental cloth covering driver's seat on coach or horse-carriage.

hammered, adj. [1. hámerd; 2. hǽməd]. P.P. of **hammer** (II.). Wrought, shaped, by hammer: *a gate of hammered iron*; specif. **a** (of thin metal ware) shaped with light hand hammer, retaining marks of its blows: *hammered work*; **b** (of glass) irregularly indented on one side.

hammer-head, n. **1.** Head of hammer. **2.** One of various animals with head somewhat resembling that of hammer, as the hammer-headed shark.

hammer-headed, adj. As prec. & **-ed**. Having head like that of hammer: *hammer-headed shark.*

hammering, adj. & n. [1. hámering; 2. hǽməriŋ]. Fr. Pres. Part. of **hammer** (III.) & vbl. n. **hammer** (II.) & **-ing**. **1.** adj. Loud, or heavy, and repeated, as though delivered by a hammer: *hammering blows.* **2.** vbl. n. **a** Sound of hammers striking; **b** the striking of hammers; **c** (fig.) defeat by repeated attacks or blows: *to give a man a good hammering.*

hammerless, adj. [1. hámerles; 2. hǽməlis]. **hammer** (I.) & **-less**. Specif. **a** without a hammer; **b** (of small arms) having hammer or equivalent appliance within lock.

hammer-lock, n. Hold by which wrestler bends and presses opponent's arm behind latter's back.

hammer-man, n. **hammer** (I.) & **man** (I.). Man who plies a hammer, as in forge.

hammer-smith, n. **hammer** (I.) & **smith**. One who uses hammer.

hammer-toe, n. (med.) Toe permanently deformed by being bent inwards.

hammock, n. [1. hámuk; 2. hǽmək]. Span. *hamaca*, of W. Indian, prob. Carib., origin. Bed or couch made from a long, narrow piece of canvas or netting, loosely stretched, and swung with cords from beams in ships, or from trees in gardens.

hammock-chair, n. Prec. & **chair** (I.). Folding easy-chair with seat and back formed by strip of canvas hanging freely from both ends.

hammy, adj. [1. hámi; 2. hǽmi]. **ham** (I.) & **-y**. Having the smell or flavour of ham.

hamose, hamous, adj. [1. hā́mōs, hā́mus; 2. héimous, héiməs]. Lat. *hām-(us)*, 'hook', the origin of wh. is uncertain, & **-ose, -ous**. (bot.) Terminating in a hook.

hamper (I.), vb. trans. [1. hámper; 2. hǽmpə]. M.E. *hampren*, of uncertain origin. **a** To impede, hinder, trammel, obstruct, prevent free movement of: *the swimmer was hampered by his clothes*; *a hampered lock*; **b** (also of effect on non-material things) *his mind is hampered by prejudice.*

hamper (II.), n., fr. prec. **1.** (naut.) Things that are useful in their place, but occasionally a nuisance; esp. *top hamper*. **2.** *Top hamper*, the smaller boughs and thinner stem forming the uppermost part, about one-third of entire length, of a tree; useless as timber and suitable only as firewood.

hamper (III.), n. Variant of **hanaper**. **a** Strong basket with lid, used for carriage of articles; esp. of vegetables, poultry &c.; **b** specif., hamper packed with eatables sent to a schoolboy: *to get a fine hamper from home.*

hamshackle, vb. trans. [1. hámshakl; 2. hǽmʃækl]. Prob. fr. **ham** (I.) & **shackle**, 'tie by the hams or legs'. (provinc.) To hinder (horse &c.) from straying by means of rope connecting head with foreleg.

hamster, n. [1. hámster; 2. hǽmstə]. Germ., fr. O.H.G. *hāmistro, hāmastro* (see **-ster**); cp. Russ. *chomiak*, 'hamster'. Kind of large rat, found in E. Europe &c., having a short tail and large cheek-pouches; German marmot.

hamstring (I.), n. [1. hámstring; 2. hǽmstriŋ]. **ham** (I.) & **string** (I.). **a** (in man) Tendon at back of knee; **b** (in horse &c.) great tendon behind hock, Achilles tendon.

hamstring (II.), vb. trans., fr. prec. **a** To lame by cutting a hamstring; to **hough**; **b** (fig.) to cripple, disable.

hamulus, n. [1. hámūlus; 2. hǽmjuləs]. **Lat.** *hāmulus*, 'little hook', dimin. of *hāmus*, 'hook', the etymol. of wh. is uncertain. (anat.) Small hook-like process, as on barbicel of a feather.

hanap, n. [1. hánap; 2. hǽnæp]. Fr., of Gmc. origin. See next word. Mediaeval drinking-cup or goblet with stem and foot.

hanaper, n. [1. hánaper; 2. hǽnəpə]. M.E. *hanypere*, fr. O. Fr. *hanapier* (L. Lat. *hanapērium*), 'large vessel to keep cups in', fr. *hanap*, fr. L.G., cp. O.E. *hnæpp*, 'cup, bowl'; cp. O.H.G. *hnapf*, Germ. *napf*. (hist.) **1.** Basket or hamper in which writs were deposited in Court of Chancery. **2.** Former office (abolished 1832) in Court of Chancery, into which fees were paid for sealing and enrolling documents; also called *Hanaper Office.*

hance, n. [1. hans, hahns; 2. hæns, hāns]. Of uncertain origin, associated w. **haunch** (I.), if not a form of it; cp. obs. Engl. *hance*, 'to raise'. See **enhance**. (archit.) **a** Part where curve is greatest in arch with three or more centres; also *haunch*: *hance arch*, arch with three or more centres; **b** half arch supporting straight lintel.

hand (I.), n. [1. hand; 2. hænd]. O.E. & M.E. *hand*; in all Gmc. languages. Cogn., in different grade, w. Goth. *hinþan*, 'to seize', & O.E. *hȳþ*, 'that which is seized, booty', fr. **hunþi-*. The orig. sense of *hand* is apparently 'that which seizes, the grasper' &c. It has been suggested that the Gmc. forms of the base are fr. Aryan **k̑emt-*, **k̑omt-* &c., & that fr. the latter comes also Lat. *com-, cum*, 'together with' &c. See **com-**. **1. a** Part of human body, forming extremity of the fore-arm, below wrist-joint, and consisting of the palm, knuckles, fingers, and thumb; **b** corresponding member on foreleg of animals, esp. of apes, frogs &c.; Phrs. *at hand*, close, near; in near future; *by hand*, through instrumentality of hand, as *done, made, by hand*, not by machinery; *delivered by hand*, not through post; *to bring up by hand*, rear child &c. by bottle, not with mother's milk; *from hand to hand*, from one person to another; *from hand to mouth*, precariously, without provision for future; *to fight hand to hand*, at close quarters, exchanging actual blows; *hand in hand*, holding each other's hands; *in hand*, (of work) in process of execution; *to put in hand*, start doing, begin, work &c.; *to have in hand*, to have (a stock of) something in one's possession, to have under (one's) control; *to take in hand*, deal with, get into order; bring under discipline, control &c.; *to do something out of hand*, at once, without preparation or delay; *to feed out of one's hand*, (fig.) to be docile, amenable to control; *to come to hand*, be found, turn up; *ready to one's hand, under one's hand*, convenient, available for use; *your letter*, or *yours, to hand*, (commerc.) received; *to win hands down*, easily, without effort; *hands off!*, don't touch; (fig.) don't interfere (with); *hands up!*, put your hands up in token of surrender; *to wait on hand and foot*, assiduously; *hand in* (or *and*) *glove with*, in confidence of, intimate with; *to lend, bear, a hand*, give assistance; *not to lift a hand*, to make no effort, do nothing; *to lift one's hand to, against*, threaten to attack; to attack, strike; *to put, set, one's hand to*, undertake, begin work at; *to lay* (*violent*) *hands on* (a person), to attack, strike; *to lay hands on* (a thing), get hold of, seize; *to keep one's hand in*, keep in practice, retain one's skill; *to have one's hands full*, to be busy; *to keep one's hand on, a firm hand on*, retain control of, exercise control over; *a bird in the hand*, something gained, acquired, possessed; an assured gain or possession; *on hand*, available; *on one's hands*, under one's charge, responsibility; (*to get something*) *off one's hands*, out of one's charge, get rid of; *time hangs heavy on my hands*, passes slowly and tediously; *heavy on hand*, (of persons) dull, poor company; *to give one's hand on a bargain*, promise to stick to it; *to ask for, win, a lady's hand*, propose marriage, gain consent to marriage. **2.** Symbolical of some activity, function, influence; **a** guardianship, keeping, care, charge &c.: *we are all in the hands of God*; *to leave a child in very good hands*; **b** possession, custody: *the documents are in my solicitor's hands*; **c** authority, jurisdiction, power, control: *to fall into the hands of one's enemies*; Phr. *to keep a person, one's desires, well in hand*, under discipline, in control; *the situation is well in hand*, being effectively dealt with; *to get, be, out of hand*, out of control; *to have a person's fate, life, in one's hands*, at one's disposal; *I am entirely in your hands*, subject to your wishes; *in the hands of money-lenders*, their victim; *the upper hand* (*of*), advantage over; *a high hand*, arrogance; dictatorial, arbitrary, manner or conduct; *an iron hand, a heavy hand*, great severity; **d** agency, instrumentality; influence: *we see the hand of God in Nature*; *the hand of Napoleon was seen and felt in every department of national life*; **e** source of, authority for, information: *to hear something at first hand*. **3.** **a** Mode of using the hand, degree of manual skill, dexterity, control, in some particular operation; touch: *to have a light hand at pastry*; *to have good hands in riding or driving*; **b** artistic, executive skill; artistic quality, style, touch: *the picture, poem &c., showed the hand of a master*. **4.** **a** Person who uses, works with, his hands; specif., one of a band of workers in a factory, at docks, member of ship's crew &c.: *Government shipyards employ several thousand hands*; *the ship was lost with all hands*; Phrs. *an old hand*, person of experience; *a poor hand at* (golf, rowing &c.) not good at, poor performer; **b** person considered as producer of some artistic or literary work: *the book was the work of several hands*; *the picture is clearly by some skilled hand*. **5.** Direction, position, side, thought of primarily as indicated by the left or right hand: *he was escorted by a policeman on either hand*; Phr. *on one hand . . . on the other* (*hand*), from one point of view . . . from another . . .; *on all hands*, from every direction, on all sides. **6.** **a** Handwriting, type of script: *to write a good hand*; *it is possible to distinguish several hands in the MS. of the Laud Chronicle*; **b** signature: *given under my hand*; *to set one's hand to a document*. **7.** (card games) **a** The whole number of cards dealt out to a player for one game: *to have a wretched hand*; Phrs. *to play a good hand*, play well; *to take a hand at bridge*, to play; *to take a hand at, have a hand in*, (fig.) take part in, be concerned with; *to play for one's own hand*, (fig.) to act from motives of self-interest; *to play into one another's hands*, (fig.) to help each other by concerted action, (in good and bad sense); **b** one of the players at game of cards; Phr. *a cool hand*, impudent person; **c** a round in a game of cards: *to play another hand*. **8.** (measurement) The approximate breadth of the hand, four inches; only used in measuring horses; the number of hands being counted from the ground to top of shoulder. **9.** Indicator on dial of clock or watch. **10.** *Bloody Hand*, armorial device of Ulster; borne also by baronets on their coats of arms.

hand (II.), vb. trans., fr. prec. **A.** trans. **1.** **a** To pass, transmit, put, into another's hands: *please hand the key to my agent*; specif. **b** to put into another's hands as a gift or reward, to give: *I have pleasure in handing you the prize for reading*; *to hand a person five pounds*; **c** to pass (a dish &c.) to another at table: *would you kindly hand me the muffins?* **2.** To transmit, convey to another's keeping or possession by any means, to send, by letter &c.: *I have pleasure in handing you the enclosed cheque*. **B.** Followed by preposition or adverb. *Hand down*. **1.** to take from a higher place and deliver to another: *to hand down plates from a shelf*; **2.** to conduct, accompany, from higher to lower level: *shall I hand her ladyship down to her carriage?*; **3.** to transmit **a** as an inheritance or heirloom: *to hand down one's property, a picture, to one's descendants*; **b** to transmit through the ages (a tradition, privilege, custom &c.): *our freedom has been handed down to us by our ancestors*; *to hand down a legend* &c.; **c** to transmit (a physical or mental trait) by biological inheritance: *it is said that acquired characters are not handed down to offspring*. *Hand in*, trans., **1.** **a** to deliver by hand, give into keeping (from outside a house &c.): *to hand in a note at the door*; **b** to send, transmit, to an official authority, esp.: *to hand in one's resignation*; Phr. *to hand in one's checks*, to die; **2.** (archaic) to conduct, lead, give an arm to, accompany, from one place, or room, to another: *the squire handed in the vicar's lady*, i.e. took her in (to dinner). *Hand on*, trans., **1.** to pass by hand, or send, from one person to another: *when you've read this, kindly hand it on to your friends*; **2.** same as *hand down* **3.** *Hand out*, **1.** trans., **a** to give out, distribute: *to hand out blankets to the poor at Christmas*; **b** to assist to get out, by giving hand to; to conduct: *to hand a lady out of her carriage*; **2.** intrans., (colloq.) to spend, give out money: *he is quite rich, but he doesn't like handing out*. *Hand over*, **1.** trans., to deliver into another's keeping, transfer from one's own to another's possession: *to hand over all one's property to one's son*; *hand over one's affairs to a lawyer*; **2.** intrans., (mil.) to transfer one's duties, command, stores, position, headquarters &c., to another: *we handed over to the French*. *Hand round*, trans., to distribute, carry round, to a series of persons: *to hand round tea*. *Hand up*, trans., to pass something by hand, from a lower to a higher position: *to hand up luggage from the hold of a ship*.

handbag, n. [1. hándbag; 2. hǽndbæg]. Light bag that can be carried by handle in one hand.

handball, n. [1. hándbawl; 2. hǽndbōl]. In M.E. **1.** Small ball which can be thrown or struck by hand. **2.** Game in which this is used.

handbarrow, n. [1. hándbàrō; 2. hǽndbæ̀rou]. M.E. *hand-barow*(*e*). Small light cart or barrow with two wheels, and handles by which it is pushed along.

handbell, n. [1. hándbel; 2. hǽndbɛl]. Portable bell with a handle at the top, rung by being shaken by the hand.

handbill, n. [1. hándbil; 2. hǽndbil]. Printed notice, advertisement &c., on small sheet, distributed by hand.

handbook, n. [1. hándbook; 2. hǽndbuk]. Mod. formation on model of Germ. *handbuch*; but *handbōc* existed in O.E. **a** Systematic treatise on special subject, manual, compendium: *handbook of anatomy*; guide-book: *handbook to a collection of coins, to Holland*; **b** betting book carried by bookmaker.

handbreadth, n. [1. hándbredth; 2. hǽndbrɛdþ]. Width of palm of hand, esp. as linear measure.

hand-canter, n. Easy canter, speed of which is checked by hand on bridle.

handcart, n. [1. hándkart; 2. hǽndkāt]. Small cart pushed or pulled by hand.

handcuff, n. & vb. trans. [1. hándkuf; 2. hǽndkaf]. Apparently fr. O.E., M.E. *hondcops* (sing.), 'pair of handcuffs, manacle', w. second element influenced by *cuffs*, fr. **hand** (I.) & O.E. *cops*, 'fetter', fr. Lat. *compēs*, fr. **con-**, 'together', & *pēs* (stem *ped-*). See **foot** & **pedal**. **1.** n. One of pair of iron rings made to open and lock, connected by short chain or bar, used to manacle the wrists of a prisoner (usually pl.) **2.** vb. To put handcuffs on to.

hand-drill, n. Small drill worked by hand, by means of cog-wheel and crank.

handed, adj. [1. hánded; 2. hǽndid]. **hand** (I.) & **-ed**. **1.** Having a hand or hands; chiefly in compounds *neat-handed, heavy-handed* &c. **2.** Played by so many hands or players: *four-handed game at tennis* &c.

handfast (I.), vb. trans. [1. hándfast; 2. hǽndfāst]. O.E. *handfæstan*, M.E. *handfæsten*; fr. **hand** (I.) & *fæstan*, 'to make firm' (see **fast** (I.)); cp. O.N. *handfesta*, 'to pledge, betroth'. **a** (archaic) To pledge, contract with, by holding hand; to betroth; **b** (hist., chiefly Scots) to give verbal pledge with handgrasp, formerly constituting, by custom, an irregular, probationary, marital union, binding for a year and a day.

handfast (II.), adj. & n. M.E. *handfest*, P.P. of prec. (archaic) **1.** adj. Betrothed, contracted, by handfasting. **2.** n. Confirmation of contract by handgrasp; betrothal; handfasting.

handfasting, n. [1. hándfahsting; 2. hǽndfāstiŋ] O.E. *handfæstung*, fr. **handfast** (I.) & **-ing**. (archaic or hist.) Act of one who handfasts; betrothal; probationary marital union.

handful, n. [1. hán(d)fool; 2. hǽn(d)ful]. O.E. *handfull*, M.E. *handful*, fr. **hand** (I.) & **-ful**. **1.** **a** Quantity of anything that fills the hand or can be grasped by the hand: *a handful of sand, straw*; specif. **b** eighth of a pound of flax. **2.** (fig.) Very small number: *the fort was held by a handful of men*. **3.** (colloq.) Person or animal only to be managed or controlled by exerting all one's energy; undisciplined boy or girl.

hand-gallop, n. Easy gallop, speed of which is controlled by one hand on bridle.

hand-gear, n. **a** Part of machine worked by hand, as starting or regulating gear; specif. **b** (in steamship) emergency steering gear.

hand-glass, n. Glass that can be held in or lifted by the hand; specif. **a** bell-glass or small glazed frame for protecting plants from frost; **b** magnifying glass with handle; **c** small mirror with handle; **d** (naut.) small sand-glass for timing log-line.

hand-grenade, n. Small bomb or grenade thrown by hand.

handgrip, n. [1. hándgrip; 2. hǽndgrip]. O.E. *handgripe*. **1.** Grasp of the hand; **a** as salutation, sign of friendship &c.; **b** a close, hand-to-hand conflict: *to come to handgrips*. **2.** Handle, hilt.

hand-hammer, n. Hammer wielded by (one) hand; specif. **a** blacksmith's hammer for one hand, distinguished from sledge-hammer; **b** mason's hammer with two smooth faces.

handhold, n. [1. hánd-hōld; 2. hǽndhould]. **a** Action of holding with hand; **b** object such as a projection of rock, that climber can grasp, cp. *foothold*.

handicap (I.), n. [1. hándikap; 2. hǽndikæp], fr. *hand in cap*, the precise origin of wh. is conjectural; the phrase prob. referred to a game. **1.** **a** Some form of obstacle, disadvantage, in time, weight, score &c., hindrance, difficulty, imposed upon a competitor as player, runner, horse &c., of superior strength, skill &c., in a contest, the object of which is to put him approximately on a level with inferior opponents; **b** a contest of any kind in which handicaps are imposed. **2.** (fig.) Disability of any kind which puts a person at a disadvantage compared with his fellows, in any form of action, intellectual or physical; any circumstance or set of conditions which render a person's life, career, position in society &c. difficult or embarrassed.

handicap (II.), vb. trans., fr. prec. **a** To impose a handicap upon; **b** (fig.) to place at a disadvantage, encumber, embarrass: *to be handicapped by poverty* &c.

handicapper, n. [1. hándikaper; 2. hǽndikæpə]. Prec. & **-er**. Person who decides on handicaps to be imposed upon competitors in a contest of any kind.

handicraft, n. [1. hándikràhft; 2. hǽndikrâft]. O.E. *handcræft*, 'power or skill of hand, handicraft', fr. **hand** (I.) & **craft**; altered in Early Mod. Engl. to *handicraft* on anal. of **handiwork**. **a** Skilled work performed by hand, as weaving, joinery, pottery; **b** skill in working with the hand, manual dexterity.

handicraftsman, n. [1. hándikràhftsman; 2. hǽndikrâftsmən]. Prec. & **man** (I.). One occupied with a handicraft.

handily, adv. [1. hándili; 2. hǽndili]. **handy** & **-ly**. In a handy manner; dexterously; conveniently.

handiness, n. [1. hándines; 2. hǽndinis]. **handy** & **-ness**. Quality of being handy.

hand-in-hand, adv. With one hand holding that of another person.

handiwork, n. [1. hándiwěrk; 2. hǽndiwʌ̄k]. O.E. *handġeweorc*, M.E. *handȝewerc*, fr. **hand** (I.) & O.E. *ġeweorc*, coll. derivative fr. *weorc*. See **work**. **a** (i.) Work done by hand, labour of one's hands; (ii.) performance, operation; **b** thing made by hand; something a particular person has made: *I suppose this box is your handiwork*.

handkerchief, n. [1. hángkerchif; 2. hǽŋkətʃif], vulgarly [1. -chēf; 2. -tʃīf]. **hand** (I.) & **kerchief** (I.). **a** Square piece of linen, cotton, silk &c., carried in pocket (*pocket-handkerchief*), or otherwise on the person, used for wiping nose, face, or eyes; Phr. *to throw the handkerchief to*: (i.) (lit.) in games, signifying to call upon (player) to take his turn, esp. to chase thrower; (ii.) (fig.) to single out for special favour, by some sign of invitation; **b** piece of silk or other material worn round neck; a small shawl of silk, lawn &c.

handle (I.), n. [1. hándl; 2. hǽndl]. O.E. *handle*, M.E. *handele* (cp. Dan. *handel*), fr. **hand** (I.) & **-le**. Part of utensil, tool, vessel &c., made to be held by the hand, for lifting, pulling, turning &c. Phr. (fig.) *to give a handle to (one's enemies)*, provide them a means of attacking one; also more generally, provide a pretext; *a handle to one's name*, a title.

handle (II.). vb. trans. O.E. *handlian*, M.E. *handl(i)en*. See **hand** (I.) & **-le**. **1.** **a** To use the hands upon, to touch, feel with, take into, move with, the hand: *heavy timber is awkward stuff to handle*; **b** to deal with, treat, behave to (in material and non-material senses): *to be roughly handled by the mob*; *he was rather severely handled in the witness box*. **2.** (commerce) To deal in, pass through one's hands as a commodity: *to handle thousands of pigs in the course of the year*. **3.** **a** To manipulate, manage with the hand: *to handle the reins, a gun* &c.; **b** to control, use for a particular purpose; direct movements or action of: *to handle troops, a fleet* &c.; **c** to manage, cope, deal, with: *the police handle the traffic very efficiently*; **d** (of intellectual activity) to treat of, elucidate, expound: *to handle a subject, theme, problem* &c.

handle-bar, n. Cross-bar with handle at each end for steering bicycle.

handless, adj. [1. hándles; 2. hǽndlis]. M.E. *handlēs*, fr. **hand** (I.) & **-less**. **a** Without hands; **b** (fig.) clumsy, incapable of using hands well.

hand-line, n. Fishing line without rod.

handling, n. [1. hándling; 2. hǽndliŋ]. O.E. *handlung*, M.E. *handlinge*, fr. **handle** (II.) & **-ing**. Action of one who handles; specif., treatment of subject by speaker, writer, or artist.

hand-loom, n. Loom worked by hand.

hand-made, adj. Made by hand, as distinct from machine-made.

handmaid, n. [1. hán(d)mād; 2. hǽn(d)meid]. **hand** (I.) & **maid**. **a** Female attendant; **b** (fig.) virtue, quality, branch of knowledge, closely associated with, and complemental to another; **c** kind of moth, larva of which feeds on apple tree; also *handmaid moth*.

handmaiden, n. [1. hándmādn; 2. hǽndmeidn]. **hand** (I.) & **maiden**. Same as prec. **a**.

hand-mill, n. Small mill worked by hand, e.g. for grinding coffee &c.

hand of glory, n. Transl. of Fr. *main de gloire*, popular corrupt. of *mandragore*. See **mandrake**. Charm formerly used by thieves and others, consisting of **a** mandrake root; **b** preserved hand of an executed murderer holding a candle.

hand-organ, n. Barrel-organ played by crank-handle turned by hand.

hand-post, n. Sign-post; originally one with representation of a hand pointing in a given direction &c.

hand-rail, n. Rail that may be held for support by hand, as on staircase.

handsaw, n. [1. hándsaw; 2. hǽndsɔ̄]. Saw worked with one hand.

hand's breadth, n. Same as **handbreadth**.

handscreen, n. [1. hán(d)skrēn; 2. hǽn(d)-skrīn]. Screen held in hand to protect face from fire or sun.

handsel (I.), **hansel**, n. [1. hán(d)sel; 2. hǽn(d)-səl]. M.E. *handsale*, *hansel*; fr. O.N. *handsale*, fr. **hand** (I.) & **sale**, 'bargain'; cp. O.E. *handselen* (rare), 'delivery into hand'. **1.** (legal hist.) Transaction confirmed by shaking hands. **2.** (archaic or obs.) Earnest, first instalment of payment; hence (fig.) earnest, foretaste. **3.** Gift, payment, or feast made at beginning of new enterprise &c., regarded as bringing good luck.

handsel (II.), **hansel**, vb. trans. See prec. **1.** (archaic) To pledge oneself to, conclude handsel with, give handsel or earnest to. **2.** To inaugurate by handsel, bring good luck to, by initial gift, payment, feast &c.

handshake, n. [1. hándshāk; 2. hǽn(d)ʃeik]. Shaking or grasping of another's hand, in accosting or bidding farewell &c.

handsome, adj. [1. hánsum; 2. hǽnsəm]. M.E. *handsom*, 'easy to handle, convenient,' fr. **hand** & **-some**. **1.** **a** (obs.) Convenient, suitable, handy; **b** (archaic) becoming, decorous, well-bred: *handsome manners, style*; **c** generous, liberal, magnanimous: *to make handsome amends, a handsome apology, compliment, present*; *very handsome of you to say so*; *handsome is that handsome does* (proverb); Phr. (colloq.) *to come down handsome*, behave generously, esp. in money matters; **d** ample, considerable: *a handsome sum, margin, fortune*. **2.** **a** Well-proportioned, pleasing to the eye, comely, fine; generally implying in addition, imposing size, stateliness, dignity &c.: *a handsome pile of buildings, tree, flower, dog, design, dress*; **b** (of persons) good-looking; well-proportioned and comely; having well-shaped features and dignified bearing; possessing robust or virile beauty: *a handsome girl, old man, boy* &c.; *handsome features*.

handsomely, adv. Prec. & **-ly**. In a handsome manner; (in various senses) *to behave handsomely*; *to be handsomely rewarded*; *the house was handsomely furnished*.

handsomeness, n. See prec. & **-ness**. Quality of being handsome.

handspike, n. [1. hán(d)spīk; 2. hǽn(d)spaik]. **hand** (I.) & **spike** (I.). **a** Lever for shifting heavy objects, as guns, by hand; **b** spoke of capstan or windlass.

handspring, n. [1. hándspring; 2. hǽndspriŋ]. Kind of somersault in which hand or hands are placed on ground.

handstaff, n. [1. hán(d)stahf; 2. hǽn(d)stâf]. M.E. *handestaffe*, fr. **hand** (I.) & **staff**. Handle of flail.

hand-taut, adj. Hand-tight.

hand-tight, adj. (naut.) Of rope &c. as tight as hand alone can make it; fairly tight.

hand-to-hand, adj. & adv. **a** adj. Waged at close quarters: *a hand-to-hand struggle*; **b** adv., at close quarters, in close conflict: *to fight hand-to-hand*.

hand-to-mouth, adj. & adv. **a** adj. Uncertain, precarious; **b** adv., precariously.

handwheel, n. [1. hándwēl; 2. hǽndwīl]. Wheel turned by hand, as for actuating brake &c.

handwork, n. [1. hándwěrk; 2. hǽndwʌ̄k]. O.E. *handweorc*, M.E. *hondwerke*. Work done by hand, not by machine.

handworked, adj. [1. hándwěrkt; 2. hǽndwʌ̄kt]. Wrought by hand, not machine-made.

handwriting, n. [1. hándrīting; 2. hǽndraitiŋ]. **a** Writing by hand; manner or style of writing, script, characteristic of individual; **b** something written by hand; manuscript.

handy (I.), adj. [1. hándi; 2. hǽndi]. **hand** (I.) & **-y**; cp. Du. *handig*, 'handy, expert'; perh. altered through influence of **hand** (I.), fr. M.E. *hendi*, 'handy, apt, courteous', fr. O.E. *-hendiġ* (as in *listhendiġ*, 'having skilful hands'), formed as above; Swed. *händig*, Dan. *handig*, 'dexterous'. **1.** (of persons) Skilled with hands, dexterous, adroit: *handy with the needle*. **2.** (of things) **a** Suitable for handling, easily managed, well adapted for use, convenient: *a handy tool, ship, reference book*; **b** within reach of, ready to, the hand, close at hand, easily available: *you'd better have the whip handy*; **c** easily reached, not distant: *the post-office is handy*.

handy (II.), adv., fr. prec. (colloq., of persons) Near by, in an easily accessible spot: *the doctor lives quite handy*.

handy-dandy, n. M.E. *handi-dandi*, 'juggling trick with hands, bribe'; jingle formed fr. **hand** (I.). Children's game.

handy-man, n. **handy** & **man** (I.). Man employed in, and (supposed to be) clever at, various kinds of manual work; hence (colloq.) man-of-war's man, bluejacket.

hang (I.), vb. trans. & intrans. [1. hang; 2. hæŋ]. In O.E. there were two vbs. fr. same orig. base: *-hōn* strong trans. (only in compounds), fr. Gmc. **haŋχ-an*, whence also Goth. *hāhan*, wh. has disappeared altogether; & *hangian*, wk. trans., fr. Gmc. **haŋȝ-ōjan*. The present Engl. vb. is, so far as its form goes, descended fr. this, no doubt also supported by O.N. *hanga*, intrans. The Aryan base was *k̑enk-, *k̑onk- &c., whence also Lat. *cunctāri*, 'to tarry, linger, hesitate', Scrt. *śankatē*, 'hesitates, doubts', & *śanka*, 'fear, suspicion, doubt'. The senses 'delay, impend' &c. still exist in the Engl. vb., but they are prob. secondary. 'Hang' is now always strong, w. Pret. & P.P. *hung*, except in trans. sense of 'execute', (see **A 2**), in wh. Pret. & P.P. are usually *hanged*, though *hung* is also common colloquially. **A.** trans. **1.** To support from above, as by attaching to a cord &c., or to a hook &c., so as to allow to swing unsupported from below; to suspend: *to hang one's hat on a peg*; *to hang a flitch of bacon from a rafter*. Phr. *to hang the head*, (i.) allow it to fall forward on the breast; (ii.) (fig.) to exhibit signs of shame. **2. a** To execute, deprive of life, by hanging by the neck, thus either strangling or dislocating neck: *to be hanged* (*hung*) *for murder*; Phrs. *a hanging judge*, a stern, severe one, who likes to hang a criminal when he deserves it; *oh, hang it!*, mild expletive, expressing annoyance; *oh, hang it all!*, expressive of mild remonstrance; *I'm hanged if I know* &c., I don't know; formula of judicial sentence: *to be hanged by the neck*; **b** (reflex.) *to hang oneself*, to commit suicide by hanging. **3.** (special senses) **a** To hang up, suspend (meat, game &c.), after it is killed, until it is in proper condition for eating: *this mutton hasn't been hung long enough*; *venison requires to be well hung* &c.; **b** *to hang a door*, place upon its hinges, and fix these to door-post, so that the door will open and shut; *to hang wall-paper*, fix it to the wall; **c** *to hang a scythe-blade*, attach to handle; **d** *to hang pictures*, suspend by cords, chains &c., from a rail, or hooks fastened into wall; specif., to hang in a gallery for exhibition; **e** *to hang curtains*, to suspend them over window, door &c., from rings running on a rod. **4.** To bedrape, bedeck, cover with hangings, or articles that hang: *the fronts of the houses in the main streets were all hung with flags and bunting*; *the trees are thickly hung with fruit*. **5.** To delay, only in Phr. *to hang fire*: **a** (of firearm) not to go off at once; **b** (fig., of events, action &c.) to be delayed, be slow in coming to a head; *to hang a leg* (obs. or rare), to hesitate to move. **B.** intrans. **1.** To be hung, be in state of suspension, to depend, dangle: *his hat was hanging on a peg*; *hanging by a rope in mid-air*; *her portrait hangs over the mantelpiece*. Phr. *to hang by a thread, by a* (*single*) *hair*, (fig.) to depend on very little, to be very precarious, in great danger &c. **2.** To be executed by hanging: *he deserves to hang for his crime*. Phr. *to let* (*something*) *go hang*, to be indifferent, take no care of, or for. **3.** (of drapery, clothes &c.) To fall, flow, over the person; be adapted to height, shape &c., of wearer: *I don't like the way his coat hangs*; *the mantle hung gracefully over her stately form*. Phr. *to hang together*, (i.) (of persons) to be intimately associated, support, back, each other; (ii.) (of material things) to fit in together, be properly related as parts of a whole; have parts properly fitted and adjusted; (iii.) (of non-material things) to be consistent, logical, well arranged: *his story doesn't hang together well*. **C.** Followed by preposition or adverb. *Hang about*, intrans., **1.** (with prep.) **a** To cluster round, press against: *the children hung about their mother*; **b** to haunt, frequent, infest: *I saw a tramp hanging about the garden*; **2.** (with adv.) **a** to prowl round, idle, loiter, loaf about: *hanging about all day doing nothing*; **b** to be in the neighbourhood, imminent: *there is thunder, rain &c. hanging about*. *Hang around*, intrans., same as prec.; with adv. more American than English. *Hang back*, intrans., **a** to start backwards, hesitate to move; **b** (fig.) to hesitate to act, shirk action. *Hang down*, intrans., to descend; pass, go, in downward direction, the higher portion being fixed: *a rope hanging down from a window*; *her hair hung down her back*. *Hang on*, intrans., **1.** to cling tight, continue to hold on, support oneself by clinging: *help! I can't hang on much longer*; Phrs. *to hang on like grim death*, very tight; *to hang on by one's eyelids*, precariously, with great effort; **2.** (fig.) to persevere, persist, in a course of action, line of conduct &c., exhibit tenacity of purpose &c.: *your task is tedious and difficult, but you must hang on till it is done*; **3.** see *hang upon*. *Hang out*, **1.** trans., to exhibit by suspending outside building, window &c.: *to hang out flags*: **2.** intrans., **a** to lean, thrust oneself, out: *to hang out of window*; **b** (colloq. slang) to live, take up one's quarters, reside, lodge: *where do you hang out?* *Hang over*, intrans., **a** to keep close to: *to hang over the fire*; **b** to hover, brood, above, rest upon: *clouds hanging over the mountain peaks*; **c** to project over, overhang, overarch: *trees hanging over a lake*; *the cliff hangs over the road here*; **d** (fig.) to be imminent, threaten, oppress, loom ahead: *I can't settle down to work with this examination hanging over me*; *I feel that some great disaster is hanging over you*. *Hang round*, intrans., same as *hang about*. *Hang up*, trans., **1.** to hang in suitable or accustomed place; often implying placing a thing where it will not be in the way when not in immediate use: *come in and hang up your hat*; *hang up the scythe in the tree when you've done with it*; Phr. *to hang up one's hat* (*in another's house*), stay there a long time; **2.** (fig.) to delay, retard; interrupt, suspend, progress of; postpone: *the whole business was hung up owing to his dilatoriness*; *the measure was hung up for a whole session*. *Hang upon*, intrans., to lean, support oneself, upon: *to hang upon a person's arm*; Phr. *to hang upon a person's lips, words*, to listen attentively, attach great importance, to what he says.

hang (**II.**), n. **1.** (of material objects) **a** The way a thing hangs: *the hang of a coat, dress* &c.; **b** the way a thing is put together, the way it works, the mode of using: *the hang of a machine*; **c** (of intellectual matters) meaning, drift, significance: *the hang of an argument, subject of study* &c. Phr. *to get, see, the hang of*, to understand. **2.** (rare) Slowing down, delay in forward movement: *the hang of a boat between strokes of the oars*. **3.** Gentle expletive, *I don't care a hang*, I care nothing at all; milder than *a damn*.

hangar, n. [1. hánggar; 2. hǽŋgā]. Fr., 'shed'; etymol. doubtful. A shed for aeroplanes or airships.

hanger (**I.**), n. [1. hánger; 2. hǽŋə]. **hang** (**I.**) & **-er**. **1.** Person who hangs. Chiefly in compounds, as *billhanger*, *paperhanger* &c. **2.** Any of various objects **a** which hang, as a small, naval sword, hung from a belt, or **b** which are for hanging other things from; specif., an iron hook in shape of S used for hanging a pot over a fire; **c** character shaped like S turned backwards, found in old-fashioned copy-books to teach children to write: *pot-hooks and hangers*.

hanger (**II.**), n. O.E. *hangra*, fr. *hangian*, **hang** (**I.**). Wood on steep slope, hanging wood.

hanger-on, n., pl. *hangers-on*. **1.** (colloq.) Person who hangs or depends on, or persistently attaches himself to, another person or to a society; parasite, toady; place-hunter. **2.** (min.) Man who places a coal corf in position for raising to surface.

hangfire, n. [1. hángfīr; 2. hǽŋfaiə]. **hang** (**I.**) & **fire** (**I.**). Delay in explosion of charge of gun.

hanging (**I.**), n. [1. hánging; 2. hǽŋiŋ]. **hang** (**I.**) & **-ing**. **1.** Action of one who hangs; state of being hung or hanged; suspension; specif., putting person to death, execution, by hanging. **2.** Thing which hangs or is hung; specif. (often pl.) cloth, drapery, which hangs as part of furniture of room; wall-paper. **3.** (used attrib. as an adj.) Connected with execution by hanging; deserving, likely to lead to, the death penalty: *a hanging matter* &c. **4.** (attrib.) Used for hanging: *a hanging cupboard*.

hanging (**II.**), adj. Pres. Part. of **hang** (**I.**). Which hangs (in all senses): *hanging lamp*; *hanging garden, wood* &c.

hangman, n. [1. hángman; 2. hǽŋmən]. Public executioner.

hangnail, n. [1. hángnāl; 2. hǽŋneil]. Popular form of **agnail**. Fragment of torn skin attached to root of finger-nail.

hank, n. [1. hangk; 2. hæŋk]. In M.E., cp. M.E. *hanken*, 'to tie up, fetter', Swed. *hanka*, 'to tie up', fr. O.N. *hanki*, 'hasp, clasp', *hōnk*, 'hank, coil'. **1.** Coil, skein, of yarn, string &c., generally of specific length. **2.** (naut.) Ring sliding on stay, to attach stay-sail.

hanker, vb. intrans. [1. hángker; 2. hǽŋkə]. Prob. a L.G. loan, cp. Flem. *hankeren*, 'long for'. Origin unknown. **a** *Hanker after*, to long for something which is out of one's reach, which is forbidden: *to hanker after the pleasures of one's youth, after forbidden fruit* &c.; **b** *hanker for*, to desire intensely, be eager for, crave: *to hanker for affection, for food when one is hungry* &c.

hankering, n. [1. hángkering; 2. hǽŋkəriŋ]. Prec. & **-ing**. A longing, yearning.

hankeringly, adv. Pres. Part. of **hanker** & **-ly**. In the manner of one who hankers.

hanky-panky, n. [1. hángki pángki; 2. hǽŋki pǽŋki]. (colloq.) Underhand dealing, trickery; action, conduct, intended to baffle and deceive; immoral conduct. Phr. *to be up to some hanky-panky*.

Hansard, n. [1. hánsard; 2. hǽnsəd], fr. name of Luke Hansard (1752–1828) and descendants who printed these reports until 1889. Official report of proceedings in British Parliament.

Hansardize, vb. trans. [1. hánsardīz; 2. hǽnsədaiz]. Prec. & **-ize**. To confront (a member of Parliament) with former utterance recorded in Hansard.

Hanse, n. [1. hans; 2. hæns]. O. Fr., fr. O.H.G. *hansa*, Mod. Germ. *hanse*; cp. Goth. *hansa*, O.E. *hōs*, 'band of men'. The etymol. of this Gmc. word is uncertain, but **cosmos** may be a cogn. (hist.) **1. a** Mediaeval guild of merchants, esp. in N. Europe; **b** (cap.) great league of N. European commercial towns, flourishing in 14th and 15th cents. **2.** Fee exacted by a merchant guild as entrance fee or tribute.

Hanseatic, adj. [1. hànseátik; 2. hæ̀nsiǽtik]. Low Lat. *hanseātic-(us)*. See prec., **-ate**, & **-ic**. Pertaining to the Hanse: *the Hanseatic League, towns*.

hansom (**cab**), n. [1. hánsum (káb); 2. hǽnsəm (kǽb)]. After J. A. Hansom (1803–82), inventor. Light two-wheeled covered hackney carriage for two passengers, with raised seat for driver at back, now obsolete.

hap (**I.**), n. [1. hap; 2. hæp]. M.E. *hap*, fr. O.N. *happ*; cp. O.E. (*ge-*)*hæp*, 'fit, convenient'; cogn. w. O. Ir. *cob*, Ir. *cobh*, 'victory, triumph'. Other cognates not identified. (archaic or liter.) **a** Chance, fortune, lot: *it was my good hap to meet him*; **b** accidental occurrence, happening.

hap (**II.**), vb. intrans., impers. & personal. M.E. *happen*, fr. prec.; cp. Swed. *happa*. (archaic or liter.) To happen, chance, befall.

hap (**III.**), vb. intrans. L. Germ., cp. N. Fris. *happe*, 'snatch, clutch'. (of a dog) *Hap at*, to make a sudden, rapid snap at.

hapax legomenon, n. [1. hápaks legómenon; 2. hǽpæks lɛgɔ́minɔn]. Gk. *hápax*, 'once', & *legómenon*, 'said'. A rare word, form, or phrase; more strictly, one only once recorded.

haphazard, n. & adj. [1. hápházard; 2. hǽphǽzəd]. **hap** (**I.**) & **hazard** (**I.**). **1.** n. Chance, accident; in Phr. *at haphazard*, at random, fortuitously. **2.** adj. Random, fortuitous: *a haphazard collection*.

hapless, adj. [1. háples; 2. hǽplis]. **hap** (**I.**) in obs. sense, 'good luck', & **-less**. Unlucky, unfortunate.

haplessly, adv. Prec. & **-ly**. In a hapless manner, unfortunately.

haplessness, n. See prec. & **-ness**. Quality, state, of being hapless.

haplo-, pref. Gk. *haplóos*, 'simple, single', fr. *ha-* for Aryan *sm-, 'together, one' (see **henotheism**, **simple**, **single**), & *-pló-os*, 'fold'. Form in compounds of Gk. origin, denoting 'simple, single; simply, singly, once'.

haplography, n. [1. haplógrafi; 2. hæplɔ́grəfi]. **haplo- & -graphy.** a Copyist's error consisting of writing only once letter or letters which should be written twice, as *petion* for *petition*; **b** reading arising from such error.

haplology, n. [1. haplóloji; 2. hæplɔ́lədži]. **haplo- & -logy.** Elimination of a syllable which is identical, at least in its initial consonant, with the next syllable in the same word.

haply, adv. [1. hápli; 2. hǽpli]. **hap (I.)** & **-ly.** (archaic) By hap, by chance; perhaps.

ha'p'orth, n. [1. hā́porth; 2. héipəþ]. Colloquial form of *halfpennyworth*.

happen, vb. intrans. [1. hápen; 2. hǽpən]. M.E. *hapenen*. See **hap (II.)** & **-en.** **1.** **a** (of events &c.) To befall, come to pass, take place: *much has happened since we met*; *these things will happen*; Phr. *something must have happened*, some striking event, esp. misfortune, has occurred; **b** (colloq., of persons) to appear, come into one's life, as one in a natural sequence of events: *he did not seek out a wife deliberately, she just happened*; **c** (impers. construction, archaic) *it happened that the King died that year*. **2.** **a** To chance; to be, casually, by accident, chance, and without deliberate design, intention, or arrangement, in a particular situation, state &c.: *I happen to know all about it*; *I happened to be at home when he called*; *this happens to be my birthday*; *do you happen to remember his name?*; **b** (impers. constructions) *it so happens that I am free today*; *it happens to be a fine hot day*; *as it happens I have left my money at home*. **3.** Followed by preposition. *Happen on*, to come upon, find, by chance, light upon, stumble across: *to happen upon the very thing one wants*; *to happen upon an old friend* &c. *Happen to*, to befall, overtake, come upon, occur to, overwhelm: *something dreadful has happened to me*; euphemistic Phr. *if anything happens to* (person), if he dies, or is killed.

happening, n. [1. hápening; 2. hǽpəniŋ]. Prec. & **-ing.** Something that happens; an event, occurrence: *a fortunate, strange, happening*.

happily, adv. [1. hápili; 2. hǽpili]. M.E. *happiliche*, fr. **happy** & **-ly.** **1.** In a happy manner; in the enjoyment of happiness: *to live happily ever after*. **2.** For *haply*; **a** by chance; **b** by fortunate chance, luckily: *happily the father died before the son's disgrace*.

happiness, n. [1. hápines; 2. hǽpinis]. Next word & **-ness.** State, condition, of being happy; felicity.

happy, adj. [1. hápi; 2. hǽpi]. M.E. *happi*, fr. **hap (I.)** & **-y.** **1.** **a** Lucky, fortunate: *a happy guess, shot*; *happy man!*; Phr. *the happy dispatch*, hara-kiri; **b** apt, well-adjusted, exactly fulfilling required conditions; successful, felicitous: *a happy retort, speech, thought, emendation*; *the happy mean*. **2.** (of persons) **a** Mentally at ease, in a contented frame of mind, cheerful: *to be happy at school, in one's home, in one's work*; Phrs. *as happy as the day is long*; *as happy as a king*, very happy; *I shall be happy to serve you, to accept your invitation*, polite formulae; *a happy family*, collection of disparate animals of incompatible habits, trained to live together peaceably; **b** specif. (colloq.) slightly tipsy. **3.** **a** Causing, promoting, conducing to, happiness: *in happier circumstances*; *a happy event*; **b** expressing happiness: *happy laughter*; *a happy letter*.

happy-go-lucky, adj. Careless, haphazard, imprudent, irresponsible, relying on luck: *to live in a happy-go-lucky fashion*.

hara-kiri, hari-kari, n. [1. hára kíri, hári kári; 2. hǽrə kiri, hǽri kǽri]. Vulg. Jap. fr. *hara*, 'belly', & *kiri*, 'to cut', rendering of classical *seppuku*, fr. Chinese w. same meaning. Suicide by slitting open the abdomen, practised in Japan by nobles and samurai, especially to avert disgrace, or, formerly, by command instead of execution.

harangue (I.), n. [1. haráng; 2. hərǽŋ]. M.E. *arang*, fr. O. Fr. *arenge*; reintroduced into Engl. fr. Mod. Fr. **harangue**, fr. Low Lat. *harenga*, Span. *arenga*, Ital. *aringa*, orig. 'speech made in ring of people' (cp. Ital. *aringo*, 'hustings, place of declamation'); of Gmc. origin, cp. O.H.G. *hring*. See **ring (I.)**. Speech made to crowd; public, formal speech; popular, declamatory, loud or ranting address, tirade; also a long, pompous, private utterance.

harangue (II.), vb. trans. & intrans., fr. prec. Cp. Fr. *haranguer*, Ital. *aringare*. **a** trans. To make an harangue to, address as in an harangue; **b** intrans., to pronounce an harangue.

haras, n. [1. háras, aráh; 2. hǽrəs, ærá]. M.E. 'stud', fr. O. Fr. *haras*, *haraz*, Mod. Fr. *haras*, 'stud'; of unknown origin. (rare) Stud-farm.

harass, vb. trans. & n. [1. háras; 2. hǽrəs]. O. Fr., Mod. Fr. *harasser*, prob. extension of O. Fr. *harer*, 'to incite, set on (dog)' (cp. O. Fr. *har*, 'cry to dog'), perh. fr. O.H.G. *harēn*, 'to cry out'. **1.** vb. **a** To worry, vex, weary by prolonged or often repeated molestation or importunity; to distract, exhaust: *harassed by anxiety*; **b** (mil.) to annoy, fatigue by incessant attacks, surprises, skirmishes, or raids. **2.** n. (obs. or rare) Action of harassing, raiding.

harassment, n. [1. hárasment; 2. hǽrəsmənt]. Prec. & **-ment.** Act of harassing; state of being harassed.

harbinger, n. & vb. trans. [1. hárbinjer; 2. hā́bindžə]. Formed w. insertion of *n* (cp. *messenger*), fr. M.E. *herbergeour*, fr. O. Fr. *herbergeor*, 'provider of lodgings', fr. O. Fr. *herbergier* (Mod. Fr. *héberger*), 'to provide lodgings', fr. O. Fr. *herberge*, 'shelter' &c. See **harbour.** **1.** n. **a** (hist.) Officer who travelled in advance of court, army &c. to provide lodgings; **b** (fig.) forerunner, precursor, herald: *the cuckoo is the harbinger of spring*. **2.** vb. To precede, as harbinger.

harbour (I.), n. [1. hárbur; 2. hā́bə]. M.E. *hereberȝe*, *herburȝe*, *herbor*, fr. O.N. *herbergi*, *herbyrgi*, 'inn, lodging', orig. 'army-shelter', fr. O.N. *her-r*, 'army', O.E. *here* (see **harry (I.)**), & *bjarga*, cogn. w. O.E. *beorgan*, 'to protect, defend' (see **bury, borough**). **1.** (archaic or rare) Shelter, place of protection and safety, refuge; covert. **2.** Natural or artificial inlet of sea or other body of water, affording to vessels protection from weather; haven, port. Phr. *harbour of refuge*, harbour, usually on dangerous coast, maintained to afford shelter to ships in storms.

harbour (II.), vb. trans. & intrans. M.E. *hereberȝen*, *herberwen*. See prec. **A.** trans. **1.** To shelter, afford lodging or protection to, give refuge to; conceal: *the woods harbour much game*; *dirt harbours vermin*. **2.** To foster, cherish, esp. secretly and illegally; **a** (in lit. sense) *to harbour a spy, the king's enemies* &c.; **b** (of mental act) to cherish, hold in the mind &c.: *to harbour treacherous designs, revenge, base thoughts*. **3.** To track (quarry) to its harbour or covert. **B.** intrans. **a** To lodge, take shelter or refuge: *deer harbour in the fern*; **b** (of ships &c.) to anchor in harbour.

harbourage, n. [1. hárburij; 2. hā́bəridž]. **harbour (I.)** & **-age.** Shelter, protection; esp. shelter in port, for ships; place in which to anchor in port.

harbour-due, n. **harbour (I.)** & **due (III.)**. (gen. pl.) Fee paid for anchoring ship in harbour.

harbourer, n. [1. hárburer; 2. hā́bərə]. **harbour (II.)** & **-er.** **1.** Person, community &c., that gives shelter or protection. **2.** Person who tracks deer to its harbour to assist hunters.

harbourless, adj. [1. hárburles; 2. hā́bəlis]. **harbour (I.)** & **-less.** Without a harbour.

harbour-master, n. Officer in charge of harbour, appointed to enforce rules regarding mooring of ships &c.

harbour-seal, n. Small species of seal, frequenting coasts and estuaries in northern hemisphere.

hard (I.), adj. [1. hard; 2. hād]. O.E. *heard*, *hard*, M.E. *hard*, Common Gmc., cp. O.S. *hard*; O.H.G. *harti*, *herti*, *hart*, *hert*, Mod. Germ. *hart*; Goth. *hard-us*, O.N. *harð-r*; Gmc. **harduz* is cogn. w. Gk. *kratús*, 'strong', *krátos*, *kártos*, 'strength' &c. (see **-cracy** & **-crat**); Scrt. *kratu*, 'strength'. Referring to material qualities: **1.** Firm to the touch, offering resistance to pressure, not easily compressed or pierced; contrasted with *soft*. Specific uses: *hard ground*, dense, heavy, difficult to dig or plough up; *a hard apple*, variety having hard flesh; *a hard mouth* (of a horse), not sensitive to the bit; *a hard bed, mattress*, one densely packed, consisting of unyielding, non-resilient materials; *hard food*, corn, as distinct from mash or green stuff, for horses; coarse, plain, unpalatable food for human beings. Phrs. *as hard as a brick*, very hard; *hard cash*, coin, actually paid down; ready money; *a hard nut to crack*, difficult problem; *hard and fast* (*custom, rule* &c.), rigid, inflexible, unadaptable; *hard of hearing*, rather deaf; *prices are hard* (commercial), settled at high level, or not tending to fall. **2.** (of bodily condition) Having firm, tense, muscles; vigorous, robust: *to get hard by taking regular exercise*; *in hard condition*. Phr. *as hard as nails*, very strong, muscular; fit, capable of endurance &c. **3.** (of physical activity, movement &c.) **a** Exhibiting strong effort and force; vigorous, powerful, violent: *a hard blow*; *a hard game, gallop* &c.; *hard riding*; **b** requiring vigorous effort to accomplish; laborious, strenuous, exacting, difficult: *hard work*; *hard exercise*; *a hill hard to climb*. Phrs. *hard labour*, that imposed as a punishment, on criminals; *hard drinking*, frequent and excessive consumption of strong drink. **4.** (of physical conditions, weather &c.) Severe, rigorous, inclement; cold, stormy: *a hard winter, season*. Phr. *hard frost*, one accompanied by very low temperature. **5.** (of chemical conditions) *Hard water*, containing an excess of lime. **6.** (popular phon.) Misleading and vague term applied a to [k] or [g] sounds, as distinct from [tʃ, s] or [dž] respectively: *hard* c *and* g *in* cat *and* get; **b** to voiceless as distinguished from voiced consonants: th *is hard in think*. (This term should be avoided in either sense.) **7.** Referring to qualities: **a** (of colour, outline &c.) too vivid, too clear and distinct, too sharply defined; **b** (of musical sounds) clear and ringing, but metallic; lacking sweetness and mellowness: *a hard voice, tone, timbre* &c. Referring to non-material or spiritual qualities: **8.** **a** (of human disposition, character &c.) Harsh, stern, severe, exacting; not open to pity; not accessible to the gentler emotions: *a hard heart, nature* &c.; **b** (of persons) possessing such a character: *a hard master*; *I never thought he could be so hard*. Phrs. *to be hard on a person*, severe with him; *a hard look, expression of face, eye* &c., one betokening a hard nature. **9.** (of human actions) Severe, merciless, relentless; inflicting pain and hardship on others: *hard discipline*; *hard measures*; *the law is hard on wrongdoers*. Phrs. *hard words*, expressing unkindness, bitterness, anger; *a hard bargain*, one which is severe to point of unfairness. **10.** (of conditions of life) Causing pain, hardship, discomfort, distress &c.: *a hard life, fate*; *hard times*. Phrs. *to have hard luck*, be unfortunate; be harshly, unfairly, treated; *it's rather hard on me that* &c., unfair to me &c. **11.** (of mental activities) Difficult, requiring an effort: **a** (of the intellect) *hard to understand*; *a hard problem, language, study*; *a hard saying*; **b** (of the imagination) *hard to conceive, picture, imagine* &c.; **c** (of the will) *it is hard to make up one's mind*.

hard (II.), adv. O.E. *hearde*, 'severely, sorely, very much', M.E. *herde*, *harde*, fr. prec. **1.** So as to be hard, solid, or firm; to a degree that produces hardness: *it froze hard last night*; *to boil an egg hard*; *to bake hard*.

2. **a** With great energy or effort; strenuously, urgently, vehemently: *to pull, hold, ride, run, struggle, try, work, think, hard; to be hard driven; to rain, blow, hard*; Phrs. *to stare, gaze, look, hard at one*, fixedly; *hard a-port* &c. (naut., of tiller), to the utmost; **b** severely, painfully, against great resistance, with difficulty: *to be hard pressed; to bear hard on; the wheels drag hard*; Phrs. *hard put to it*, embarrassed, hard pressed; *hard hit*, severely affected, esp. (i.) pecuniarily; (ii.) emotionally, deeply smitten with love, grief &c.; *to die hard*, to die only after a hard struggle; (fig.) to resist stubbornly to the last, to be very slow in dying out: *superstitions die hard* (cp. *die-hard*); *it will go hard with him* (*if he is found out*), he will get into serious trouble; *it will go hard but* (*he will succeed*), unless the obstacles are overwhelming; **c** excessively, immoderately: *to drink, swear, hard*; **d** closely, immediately: *to follow hard after, behind, upon*. Phr. *hard by*, close by.

hard (**III.**), n., fr. **hard** (**I.**). **a** Firm, solid, part of shore, suitable for landing, now only in local uses; **b** (colloq.) hard labour: *five years hard*.

hardbake, n. [1. hárdbāk; 2. hā́dbeik]. **hard** (**I.**) & **bake**. Almond toffee.

hard-baked, adj. [1. hárd bákt; 2. hā́d béikt]. Baked until hard.

hardbeam, n. [1. hárdbēm; 2. hā́dbīm]. **hard** (**I.**) & **beam** (**I.**), in obs. sense 'tree'. Species of tree, hornbeam.

hard-bitted, adj. [1. hárd bíted; 2. hā́d bítid]. **hard** (**II.**) & **bit** (**III.**) & **-ed**. (of horses) Not responsive to the bit, hard-mouthed; (fig.) stubborn.

hard-bitten, adj. [1. hárd bítn; 2. hā́d bítn]. Perh. variant of prec., or **hard** (**II.**) & **bitten**, P.P. of **bite** (**I.**). Stubborn, dogged, able to resist toughly.

hard-boiled, adj. **hard** (**II.**) & **boil** (**I.**) & **-ed**. (of egg) Boiled until contents are solid. (*N.B.* accentuation: *a hard-boiled egg* [1. hárd boild ég; 2. hā́d bɔild ég], but, *I like my egg hard boiled* [1. hárd bóild; 2. hā́d bóild].)

hard core, n. **hard** (**I.**) & **core** (**I.**). Stones, clinker, brick-bats, and the like, used as bottom layer for road or foundation.

hard-earned, adj. [1. hárd érnd; 2. hā́d ə́nd]. **hard** (**II.**) & **earn** & **-ed**. Earned with difficulty or hard toil.

harden, vb. trans. & intrans. [1. hárdn; 2. hā́dn]. M.E. *hardnen*, fr. O.N. *harðna*. See **hard** (**I.**) & **-en**. **A.** trans. **1.** To make hard or harder; to make firm, solidify. **2.** (fig.) **a** To make hardy or robust, inure; invigorate, brace: *to harden troops by long marches*; Phr. *to harden off*, to make (seedlings &c.) hardy by gradual exposure to cold; **b** to make resolute, courageous, or self-reliant; **c** to make insensitive, callous, obdurate: *to harden the heart; a hardened offender*. **B.** intrans. **1.** To become hard or harder, grow solid. **2.** (fig.) **a** To become hardy, robust, resolute; **b** to become callous; **c** to become set, definite, decided: *public opinion is hardening*; **d** (of prices &c.) to cease to fluctuate, maintain a steady high level.

hardener, n. [1. hárdner; 2. hā́dnə]. **harden** & **-er**. Person or thing that hardens something; specif., person who hardens steel tools.

hardening, n. [1. hárdening; 2. hā́dəniŋ]. **harden** & **-ing**. **1.** Process of making or becoming hard. **2.** Material used for making hard.

hard-favoured, adj. **hard** (**II.**) & **-favoured**. Having a hard or harsh face.

hard-featured, adj. [1. hàrd féchurd; 2. hàd fítʃəd]. **hard** (**II.**) & **feature** & **-ed**. Having hard or harsh features.

hardfern, n. [1. hárdfërn; 2. hā́dfə̄n]. **hard** (**I.**) & **fern**. One of several ferns of genus *Lomaria*.

hard-fisted, adj. **hard** (**II.**) & **-fisted**. Miserly, niggardly, close-fisted.

hard-fought, adj. **hard** (**II.**) & **fought**. Strenuously contested.

hard-gotten, adj. [1. hárd gotn: 2. hā́d gɔtn]. **hard** (**II.**) & *gotten*, P.P. of **get**. Obtained, won, earned, with difficulty or toil.

hard-grained, adj. [1. hárd grānd; 2. hā́d greind]. **hard** (**II.**) & **grain** (**I.**) & **-ed**. **a** (of wood &c.) Having a hard or close grain; **b** (fig., of human character &c.) stern, harsh; insensitive, obdurate.

hard-handed, adj. **hard** (**II.**) & **handed**. **1.** Having hard hands, esp. as result of manual labour. **2.** (fig.) Oppressive, severe.

hard-head, n. **hard** (**I.**) & **head** (**I.**). **1.** Hard-headed person. **2.** One of several kinds of fish.

hard-headed, adj. **hard** (**II.**) & **headed**. **a** Having a hard head; **b** (fig.) shrewd, practical, business-like, not swayed by sentiment.

hard-hearted, adj. **hard** (**I.**) & **hearted**. Having a hard heart; unfeeling, merciless, pitiless, heartless.

hard-heartedly, adv. Prec. & **-ly**. In a hard-hearted manner.

hard-heartedness, n. See prec. & **-ness**. Quality of being hard-hearted.

hardihood, n. [1. hárdihood; 2. hā́dihud]. **hardy** (**I.**) & **-hood**. Boldness, hardiness.

hardiness, n. [1. hárdines; 2. hā́dinis]. M.E. *hardinesse*, fr. **hardy** (**I.**) & **-ness**. Quality of being hardy; **a** resolute boldness; audacity, impudence; **b** robustness.

hardish, adj. [1. hárdish; 2. hā́diʃ]. **hard** (**I.**) & **-ish**. Rather hard.

hardly, adv. [1. hárdli; 2. hā́dli]. O.E. *heardlīce*, 'sorely, harshly, stoutly', fr. *heardlīc*, 'severe, strict'; see **hard** (**I.**) & **-ly**; M.E. *hardliche, hardeliche*. Cp. O.S. *hardlīko*. **1.** Severely, harshly, unkindly: *to be hardly treated*. **2.** **a** Strenuously, vehemently, with great energy: *the battle was hardly contested*; **b** with difficulty, only by great effort: *victory was hardly won*. **3.** **a** Scarcely, barely, only just: *I had hardly spoken to him when he was gone*; **b** (by litotes, ironically or politely) insufficiently, not at all, by no means: *his conduct hardly corresponded with the dignity of his position; you can hardly expect me to do that*.

hard-mouthed, adj. [1. hárd móudhd, hárd moudhd; 2. hā́d máuðd, hā́d mauðd]. **hard** (**I.**) & **mouth** (**I.**) & **-ed**. **1.** (of horse &c.) Having an insensitive mouth, not responsive to the bit; (fig.) intractable. **2.** (fig.) Prone to harsh, rough speech.

hardness, n. [1. hárdnes; 2. hā́dnis]. O.E. *heardness*, M.E. *hardnesse*. **hard** (**I.**) & **-ness**. Quality or condition of being hard (in variety of senses).

hardpan, n. [1. hárdpan; 2. hā́dpæn]. **hard** (**I.**) & **pan** (**I.**). (Am.) Hard, but not rocky, subsoil, consisting of partially indurated clay, gravel, or sand.

hards, n. pl. [1. hardz; 2. hādz]. O.E. *heordan*, (pl.) 'hards of flax'; M.E. *herdes, hyrdys*; cp. M. Du. *heerde, herde*; fr. Gmc. **hizdṓ-*, **haizdṓ-*, Aryan **kis-(tṓ-)*, **kois-(tṓ-)* &c.; cp. Lat. *caesaries*, 'hair'; Scrt. *késaraš*, 'hair, mane', O.E. *hād-* in *hād-swǣpe*, 'bridesmaid', lit. 'one who brushes bride's hair', fr. **haizd-*; cp. Lith. *kaiszti*, 'to shave'. Orig. sense 'hair, fibre'. Refuse of flax or hemp, tow. Phr. *flocks and hards*, fibrous waste used for stuffing mattresses.

hard-set, adj. **hard** (**I.**) & **set** (**III.**). Firmly fixed, stiff, rigid; specif. **a** (of egg) having contents solidified by incubation; **b** determined, stubborn.

hardshell, adj. [1. hárdshel; 2. hā́dʃel]. **hard** (**I.**) & **shell** (**I.**). **1.** Having a hard shell. Phr. *hard-shell crab*, one that has not lately moulted. **2.** (fig., Am. colloq.) That cannot be influenced by argument, uncompromising; *Hardshell Baptist*, member of rigid Baptist sect in America.

hardship, n. [1. hárdship; 2. hā́dʃip]. M.E. *heardschipe*, fr. **hard** (**I.**) & **-ship**. **1.** **a** Physical rigour, privation, great discomfort; arduous, hard, conditions of life: *polar exploration involves many hardships*; **b** some specific circumstance or condition producing discomfort or privation: *early rising is not a hardship in summer*. **2.** **a** Something hard to bear; circumstance, condition, regulation &c. which is oppressive or unfair; **b** suffering or disability arising from this.

hard-tack, n. **hard** (**I.**) & Engl. dial. *tack*, 'bad food', see **tack** (**III.**). (naut.) Ship's biscuit.

hard-up, adj. **hard** (**I.**) & **up** (**I.**). (only pred., colloq.) Badly needing, in want of; specif. **a** of money: *I'm very hard-up just now*; **b** hard put to it to find, completely lacking: *hard-up for something to say, do* &c.

hardware, n. [1. hárdwār; 2. hā́dweə]. **hard** (**I.**) & **ware** (**I.**). (coll.) Goods, such as tools or kitchen utensils, made of iron or other common metal; ironmongery.

hardwareman, n. [1. hárdwārman; 2. hā́dweəmən]. Prec. & **man**. Maker of, dealer in, hardware.

hardwood, n. & adj. [1. hárdwood; 2. hā́dwud]. **hard** (**I.**) & **wood**. **1.** n. **a** Heavy, close-grained wood; specif. **b** that of any deciduous timber tree; contrasted with that of pines. **2.** adj. Made, consisting of, pertaining to, hardwood.

hard-working, adj. **hard** (**II.**) & **working**. Working hard, industrious.

hardy (**I.**), adj. [1. hárdi; 2. hā́di]. M.E. *hardi*, fr. Fr. *hardi*, orig. P.P. of O. Fr. *hardir*, 'to make bold'; of Gmc. origin. See **hard** (**I.**). **1.** **a** Bold, resolute, daring; **b** rash, audacious, over-confident: *a hardy assertion*. **2.** **a** Capable of enduring, inured to, fatigue, privations, and pain; robust; **b** specif. (hort.) resisting frost and all weather changes; flourishing all the year without protection. Phr. *hardy annual*, (i.) annual plant that can be grown in exposed position; (ii.) (fig., facetious) question that is brought up for discussion annually or periodically.

hardy (**II.**), n. Prob. **hard** (**I.**) & **-y**. Short chisel of hard iron or steel fixed upright in blacksmith's anvil for cutting iron.

hare, n. [1. hār; 2. heə]. O.E. *hāra*, M.E. *hāre*, O.H.G. *haso*, Mod. Germ. *hase*, fr. Gmc. type **hazón-*. Cp. O.E. *hasu*, 'grey', wh. is cogn. w. Lat. *cānus*, 'hoary, grey', fr. **caznos*; also Lat. *cas-cus*, 'old'; further, Scrt. *šašá-*, 'hare'. *Hare* is thus 'the grey animal'. **1.** One of several widely distributed, swift rodents (genus *Lepus*), resembling rabbit, but larger, with long ears, short tail, and powerful hind legs. *Belgian hare*, large species of rabbit. Phrs. *mad as a* (*March*) *hare*, very mad, eccentric, or wild; *first catch your hare* (*then cook him*), make sure of person or thing with which you propose to deal; *to start a hare*, to raise a side issue in a discussion; *to run with the hare and hunt with the hounds*, endeavour to maintain good relations with two opposing parties, to play a double game; *as timid as a hare*, very shy and nervous. **2.** (zool.) Member of family of *Leporidae*, which includes the rabbit.

hare and hounds, n. Paper-chase; game in which two persons ('hares'), being given a start, run across country, dropping trail of paper, and are pursued by number of others; a paper-chase.

harebell, n. [1. hā́rbel; 2. héəbel]. M.E. *harebelle*, fr. **hare** & **bell** (**I.**). Round-leaved wild Campanula, with slender stalk and blue flowers; in Scotland called bluebell.

hare-brained, adj. [1. hā́r brānd; 2. héə breind]. **hare** & **brain** (**I.**) & **-ed**. Volatile, erratic, inconsequent, flighty, scatter-brained.

harefoot, n. [1. hā́rfoot; 2. héəfut]. **hare** & **foot** (**I.**). **1.** Thing resembling foot of hare; specif. **a** long narrow foot of some kinds of dog; **b** one of several plants: avens; hare's-foot trefoil. **2.** Person swift of foot; specif., surname of King Harold I. of England (d. 1040).

hare-lip, n. **hare** & **lip**. (med.) Congenital fissure of human upper lip, often combined with cleft palate.

harem, n. [1. hā́rem, háhrēm; 2. héərem, hārīm, -em]. Arab. *ḥarīm, ḥarām*, 'thing forbidden', fr. *ḥarama*, 'to forbid'. **1.** **a** Part of Oriental, esp. Mohammedan, house, in which women are secluded; seraglio; **b** (coll.) occupants of harem.

hare's-ear, n. European umbelliferous plant (*Bupleurum*) with yellow flowers and leaves like hare's ear.

hare's-foot, n. Common wild British clover, with whitish flowers resembling foot of hare; also called *hare's-foot trefoil*.

haricot, n. [1. hárikō; 2. hǽrikou]. O. Fr. *hericoq* (*de mouton*; 14th cent.), Fr. *haricot* in both senses, **a** & **b**, the former older; of unknown origin. **a** Stew of mutton or lamb, prepared with kidney beans, turnips &c.; **b** haricot bean.

haricot bean, n. Kidney bean; esp. the edible seed-pod and seeds; called by greengrocers and others *French bean*.

hark, vb. trans. [1. hark; 2. hāk]. M.E. *herkien*, of Continental L.G. origin. Cp. **hearken**. **1.** To listen (chiefly in imperat. *hark!*, and as interj.). **2.** Followed by preposition or adverb. *Hark away!*, cry to hounds. *Hark back*, to return, **a** (in space) come back to place whence one started; **b** (in thought, speech &c.) to revert to a subject, idea &c. which has already been discussed and passed; **c** *hark back to*, revert, return to. *Hark to*, (archaic, colloq., or poet.) to listen to: *just hark to him* (iron., also *hark at*); *let us hark to the sweet song of the birds* &c.

harl, harle, n. [1. harl; 2. hāl]. M.E. *herle*, 'fibre'; cp Fris. *harl, harrel*, M.L.G. *herle, harl*, 'fibre of flax or hemp'. Flax, or hempen fibre; barb of a feather.

harlequin, n. & adj. [1. hárlekwin; 2. hálikwin]. Obs. Fr. *harlequin* (16th cent.), later *arlequin*, fr. or affected by Ital. *arlecchino* = Span. *arlequin*. Earlier, name of a demon, Low Lat. *Harlequinus*, Ital. *Alichino* (Dante), O. Fr. *Hierlekin, Hellequin*, M.E. *Hurlewayn*, leader of a demon troop called in O. Fr. *la maisnie Hierlekin* &c. Proposed etymologies are mere speculations. **1.** n. **a** (cap.) Leading male character in the old Italian comedy and in modern pantomime; servant of Pantaloon, lover of Columbine; agile and given to tricks; wearing mask and parti-coloured spangled tights; **b** a practical joker. **2.** adj. Parti-coloured; having variegated plumage: *harlequin duck*.

harlequinade, n. [1. hàrlekwinā́d; 2. hàlikwinéid]. **harlequin** (**I.**) & **-ade**. Cp. Fr. *arlequinade*. **a** Scene, in pantomime, in which harlequin plays leading part; **b** buffoonery; droll, roguish frolic or prank.

harlot, n. [1. hárlut; 2. hálət]. M.E. *harlot, herlot*, 'vagabond, disorderly person' (of either sex), fr. O. Fr. *harlot, herlot, arlot*; cp. Provenç. *arlot*, Span. *arlote*, 'vagabond'; Ital. *arlotto*, 'hedge-priest', (*arlotta*, 'harlot'). Origin entirely dubious, perh. Gmc. Woman of bad life, prostitute.

harlotry, n. [1. hárlutri; 2. hálətri]. M.E. *harlotrie*, fr. prec. & **-ry**. Behaviour of a harlot; rascality.

harm (**I.**), n. [1. harm; 2. hām]. O.E. *hearm, herm*, 'injury, grief, insult'; M.E. *herm, harm* &c.; cp. O.S., O.H.G. *harm*, 'grief, injury, insult', O.N. *harm-r*, 'grief', fr. Gmc. **harm-*, cogn. w. O. Slav., Russ. *sram*, 'shame', Scrt. *śrama*, 'toil, fatigue'. Injury, hurt, damage, physical or moral. Phr. *to do harm*, cause injury; *to do harm to*, to injure; *no harm done*, all is well, no one injured &c.; *out of harm's way*, in safety; *there's no harm in doing so-and-so*, no reason for not doing &c.; *where's the harm in . . .*, how is it wrong?

harm (**II.**), vb. trans. O.E. *hearmian*, 'to hurt, injure'; M.E. *hermen, harmen*, fr. prec. To cause harm to, injure, hurt, physically or morally.

harmattan, n. [1. hàrmatán; 2. hàmətǽn]. Fr., fr. Fanti *haramata*. Dry, parching wind, charged with fine sand, blowing from Sahara to Atlantic coast from December to February.

harmful, adj. [1. hármfool; 2. hámful, -fəl]. In M.E., fr. **harm** (**I.**) & **-ful**. Causing harm and injury; injurious.

harmfully, adv. Prec. & **-ly**. In a harmful manner.

harmfulness, n. See prec. & **-ness**. Quality of causing harm or being harmful.

harmless, adj. [1. hármles; 2. hámlis], fr. **harm** (**I.**) & **-less**. **a** Incapable of doing harm, innocuous: *a harmless drug, habit, amusement*; **b** doing no harm, inoffensive, innocent; *the bullet struck a harmless passer-by*.

harmlessly, adv. Prec. & **-ly**. In a harmless manner; without doing injury.

harmlessness, n. See prec. & **-ness**. Quality, condition, of being harmless.

harmonic, adj. & n. [1. harmónik; 2. hāmɔ́nik]. Lat. *harmonic-*(*us*), fr. Gk. *harmonikós*; fr. **harmony** & **-ic**. **1.** adj. **a** Pertaining to harmony; **b** (mus.) harmonious, concordant; pertaining to harmonics; **c** (math.) *harmonic progression, series*, series of numbers whose reciprocals are in arithmetical progression; *harmonic proportion*, relation between three consecutive terms of a harmonic progression; *harmonic quantities*, those in harmonic progression. **2.** n. **a** (science of mus.) One of the components of a complex musical tone; **b** (wireless, pl.) secondary frequencies to which an oscillating circuit may respond.

harmonica, n. [1. harmónika; 2. hāmɔ́nikə]. Lat. *harmonica*, fem. of *harmonicus*, **harmonic**. Instrument consisting of series of **a** glasses which emit musical notes when touched with a damp finger; **b** small glass or metal plates struck by a hammer.

harmonical, adj. [1. harmónikl; 2. hāmɔ́nikl]. **harmonic** & **-al**. Harmonic.

harmonically, adv. Prec. & **-ly**. In a harmonic manner.

harmonicon, n. [1. harmónikon; 2. hāmɔ́nikən]. Gk. *harmonikón*, neut. sing. of *harmonikós*, **harmonic**. Small mouth-organ.

harmonics, n. pl. [1. harmóniks; 2. hāmɔ́niks]. Science or art of musical harmony.

harmonious, adj. [1. harmṓnius; 2. hāmóuniəs]. **harmony** & **-ous**. **1.** (mus.) Having or producing harmony; melodious, not discordant. **2.** (of form) Justly proportioned, having all parts well fitted, well adapted in size and shape to each other: *a*(*n*) *harmonious arrangement of lines*; *a*(*n*) *harmonious room*. **3.** (of moral conditions) Congruous, agreeing well together, free from strife and disagreement: *a*(*n*) *harmonious family, meeting* &c.

harmoniously, adv. Prec. & **-ly**. In a harmonious manner, in harmony.

harmoniousness, n. See prec. & **-ness**. Quality, condition, of being harmonious; harmony.

harmoniphon, harmoniphone, n. [1. harmónifon, -fōn; 2. hāmɔ́nifən, -foun]. **harmony** & **-phone**. Obsolete wind instrument with keyboard.

harmonist, n. [1. hármunist; 2. hámənist]. Fr. *harmoniste*; fr. **harmony** & **-ist**. **1. a** Person skilled in science of musical harmony; **b** musical composer who has special gifts of harmony. **2.** Person who forms full and consecutive narrative out of, and reconciles apparent inconsistencies in, the Gospels.

harmonistic, adj. & n. [1. hàrmunístik; 2. hàmənístik]. Prec. & **-ic**. **a** adj. Pertaining to a harmonist or to harmony; **b** n., study of Biblical harmony.

harmonium, n. [1. harmṓnium; 2. hāmóuniəm]. Lat. *harmonia*, **harmony**, & Lat. neut. termination *-um*. Small organ, having bellows by which air is forced through free reeds, played from finger-board.

harmonization, n. [1. hàrmunīzā́shun; 2. hàmənaizéiʃən]. Next word & **-ation**. Action or process of harmonizing.

harmonize, vb. trans. & intrans. [1. hármunīz; 2. hámənaiz]. **harmony** & **-ize**. **1.** trans. To make harmonious, bring into harmony, concord, congruity, agreement **a** (in music), **b** (in form), **c** (in moral and intellectual sphere). **2.** intrans. To form, constitute, harmony, be harmonious (in music, physical form, morals, or logic).

harmonizer, n. [1. hármunīzer; 2. hámənaizə]. Prec. & **-er**. One who harmonizes or produces harmony.

harmonometer, n. [1. hàrmunómeter; 2. hàmənɔ́mitə]. **harmony** & **-meter**; Fr. *harmonomètre*. Instrument determining harmonic relations of musical sounds.

harmony, n. [1. hármuni; 2. háməni]. Lat. *harmonia*, 'agreement of sounds, melody, concord', fr. Gk. *harmonía*, 'a fitting together; a joint; musical concord; agreement' (in temper &c.). Connected w. Gk. *harmós*, 'a joining', and *harmózein*, 'to fit together, join; join in marriage' &c. Suggestions of connexion between this & the Lat. group *arma*, 'weapons of war, arms', cannot be accepted on account of the initial *h-*. Undoubted cognates outside Gk. are unknown. The original, & most of derived senses are seen in the Gk. A fitting together, joining, adaptation of parts, or of things, to each other in combination; specif. **1.** (in a work of art) Due proportion and adaptation of parts to each other in relation to the whole so as to make a pleasing aesthetic impression: *harmony of colour and design in a picture*. **2.** (on mental and moral plane) Agreement, coincidence, concordance, of ideas, tastes, opinions &c.: *to live in harmony with one's neighbours*. **3.** (mus.) **a** Concord in musical tone, simultaneous combination of notes so as to form a chord; opposite of *discord*; **b** music in general, considered as a series of pleasing combinations of sounds. **4.** A work in which various narratives, descriptions, accounts, of an event, or series of events are brought together in such a way as to display their essential unity and agreement: *a harmony of the Gospels*.

harness (**I.**), n. [1. hárnes; 2. hánis]. M.E. *harneis*, fr. O. Fr. *harneis, herneis, harnes*, 'armour'; Fr. *harnais*, 'harness' (in series **1** and **2**), cp. Ital. *arnese*; borrowed in M.H.G. *harnasch*, Germ. *harnisch* &c. Of unknown origin. **1.** (chiefly archaic or liter.) Complete body armour or military defensive equipment of man or horse. Phrs. *to die in harness*, to die while still actively engaged in one's work; *in harness*, at one's daily work. **2.** Gear or equipment, usually of leather, of draught horse, mule &c., including both those parts by which the animal is driven, and those by which it is attached to the vehicle, plough &c., which it is required to draw. Phrs. *double harness*, for two animals harnessed abreast to one vehicle; *to work, run, in double harness*, (fig.) to work with a partner, said esp. of husband and wife.

harness (**II.**), vb. trans. M.E. *harneisen*, fr. O. Fr. *harneschier* (mod. *harnacher*), fr. prec. **1.** (archaic or liter.) To array, dress, in armour, equip with armour. **2. a** To put harness on to a horse or other animal: *to harness a horse*; **b** to attach by means of harness: *to harness a horse to a carriage*. **3.** (fig.) To put to routine work: *to harness to a profession*.

harness-cask, n. **harness** (**I.**) & **cask**. (naut.) Cask containing salt meat for immediate use.

harnessed, adj. [1. hárnest; 2. hánist]. P.P. of **harness** (**II.**). **a** Wearing harness; **b** (of animal) having markings on body resembling harness: *harnessed antelope*.

harnessry, n. [1. hárnesri; 2. hánisri]. **harness** (**I.**) & **-ry**. **a** (coll.) Parts of harness; **b** shop or store for sale of harnesses.

haro, interj. & n. [1. harṓ; 2. hæróu]. O. Fr. *haro, harou* (whence M.E. *haro, harou*, obs. Mod. Engl. *harrow*), 'cry for help'; of uncertain origin; cp. possibly O.H.G. *hara*, variant of *hera*, 'hither'. In Channel Islands, formal cry for legal redress, constituting appeal against encroachment on property.

harp (**I.**), n. [1. harp; 2. hāp]. O.E. *hearpe*, M.E. *harpe*, O.H.G. *harpha, harfa*, Mod. Germ. *harfe*. The word is almost certainly cogn. w. Lat. *carpere*, 'to pluck', q.v. under **carpel**, **carpet**; the *-p* in O.E. (& Gmc.) corresponding to *-p* in Lat. may be explained by assuming original Gmc. **harpp-* w. doubling due to a suff. *-*nā* &c., in Aryan, & accentuation on suff., the series fr. Aryan to Gmc. being **karpnā* < Gmc. **harbnó*, whence, later, **harbbó* < **harppo*. See also **harvest**. Musical instrument, consisting of open upright triangular frame, on which are stretched strings that are set in vibration by being plucked by fingers.

harp (**II.**), vb. intrans. O.E. *hearpian*, M.E. *harpien*, intrans., fr. prec. **1.** To play the harp. **2.** (fig.) *Harp on, upon*, to refer repeatedly or with tedious reiteration to; to dwell upon in the mind tediously: *to harp upon the glories of a former day*; *are you still harping on your troubles?* Phr. *to be always harping on the same string*, always dwelling on, referring to, the same theme.

harper, n. [1. hárper; 2. hā́pə]. O.E. *hearpere*, M.E. *harpere*; cp. O.H.G. *harfere*, O.N. *harpari*. Prec. & **-er.** Performer on the harp.

harping(**s**), n. pl. [1. hárping(z); 2. hā́piŋ(z)]. (usually pl., naut.) Strips or strakes on bow of a ship, to give extra strength.

harpist, n. [1. hárpist; 2. hā́pist]. **harp** (**I.**) & **-ist.** Harper, esp. modern professional.

harpoon (**I.**), n. [1. hàrpōōn; 2. hāpū́n]. Early Mod. Engl. *harpon*, fr. Fr. *harpon*, 'clamp, grappling iron, harpoon' (whence Du. *harpoen*, Germ. *harpune*), fr. Fr. *harpe*, 'claw, clamp', obs. 'grappling-iron' (cp. *harper*, 'to claw, grip, grapple'), prob. fr. L. Lat. *harpē*, 'curved sword', fr. Gk. *hárpē*, 'sickle', cogn. w. O. Lat. *sarpere*, 'to prune', & Russ. *serp*, 'sickle', O.H.G. *sarf*, 'rough, sharp, acrid'. Barbed spear with rope attached, used in whaling.

harpoon (**II.**), vb. trans., fr. prec. To strike with a harpoon.

harpooner, n. [1. hàrpōōner; 2. hāpū́nə]. Prec. & **-er.** One who uses harpoon.

harpoon gun, n. Gun used for firing a harpoon.

harp-seal, n. **harp** (**I.**) & **seal** (**I.**). Arctic seal with black harp-shaped mark on each side.

harpsichord, n. [1. hárpsikord; 2. hā́psikōd]. Early Mod. Engl. *harpsechord*, fr. O. Fr. *harpechorde*; cp. Ital. *arpicordo*. See **harp** (**I.**) & **chord.** Obsolete musical instrument, forerunner of the piano, resembling harp placed horizontally upon legs, the strings being plucked by quills set in jacks worked from a keyboard, instead of being struck by hammers.

harpy, n. [1. hárpi; 2. hā́pi]. Fr. *harpie*, fr. Lat. *harpȳia*, fr. Gk. pl. *hárpuiai*, connected w. *harpázein*, 'to snatch, seize'. Cognates outside Gk. are quite uncertain. See **hearse.** **1.** (cap., Gk. mythol.) Horrible, cruel, winged monster, with head and bust of a woman, and the tail, legs, and talons of a bird of prey. **2.** A greedy, merciless person who preys upon his or her kind.

harpy eagle, n. Large, powerful bird of prey, of tropical America, resembling an eagle, but having a double crest.

harquebus, n. See **arquebus.**

harridan, n. [1. háridan; 2. hǽridən]. Of unknown origin, perh. connected w. obs. Fr. *haridelle*, 'worn-out horse'; cp. O. Fr. *harrebanne*, 'debauched woman', (Godefroi). Worn out, disreputable, old woman; hag, vixen.

harrier (**I.**), n. [hárier; 2. hǽriə]. Formerly also *harier*, fr. **hare** & **-ier.** **a** Hound of breed used for hunting hares, like the foxhound, but smaller; (in pl.) pack of such hounds with huntsman; **b** (fig.) member of club for game called hare and hounds, or for cross-country running; (pl.) such a club.

harrier (**II.**), n. **harry** (**I.**) & **-er.** **1.** One who harries. **2.** One of genus of low-flying hawks, like buzzards, but bolder, as *hen harrier, marsh harrier.*

Harris tweed, n. [1. háris twēd; 2. hǽris twīd], fr. name of island in Hebrides. A hand-woven tweed made in this island.

harrow (**I.**), n. [1. hárō; 2. hǽrou]. M.E. *haru, harwe, harowe*; not recorded in O.E., but apparently Gmc. word, cp. N. Fris. *harwe*, & cognates in Du. & Scand. languages. Origin obscure. Agricultural implement, consisting of frame or chain network, with teeth, spikes, or tines below, dragged over ground, for levelling and breaking up soil &c. Phr. (*a toad*) *under the harrow*, (fig.) in great distress or tribulation.

harrow (**II.**), vb. trans. & intrans., fr. prec. **A.** trans. **1.** To use a harrow upon: *to harrow a field.* **2.** (fig., of moral action) To wound the feelings, cause mental distress and torment to: *to harrow one's feelings.* Also *harrow up*, in both senses. **B.** intrans. To permit of harrow being used, be amenable to harrow: *the land won't harrow very well, it is too rocky.*

harrower, n. [1. hárōer; 2. hǽrouə]. **harrow** (**II.**) & **-er.** Person who harrows.

harrowing (**I.**), adj. [1. hárōing; 2. hǽrouiŋ], fr. Pres. Part. of **harrow** (**I.**). Acutely distressing, wounding, to the feelings; heart-rending.

harrowing (**II.**), vbl. n., fr. old variant of **harry.** (obs.) *Harrowing of Hell*, M.E. name for descent of the Saviour to hell and the release by Him of souls. In this use the word means ravaging, despoiling.

harry (**I.**), vb. trans. [1. hári; 2. hǽri]. O.E. *herġian*, 'to lay waste', M.E. *herȝien*; cp. O.H.G. *hariōn, heriōn*, Germ. (*ver*)*heeren*, O.N. *herja*; all connected w. O.E. *here*, O.H.G. *hēr*, 'army, predatory band', cp. **heriot.** Cogn. w. Lith. *karas*, 'war', O. Prussian *karjis*, 'army', O. Slav. *kara*, 'strife'. **1.** To ravage, lay waste, raid, pillage, despoil: *the Danes harried many parts of England continuously for several generations.* **2.** To harass, annoy, worry, persecute (persons).

Harry (**II.**), n. **1.** The devil, in Phrs. *to play old Harry with*, to destroy, throw into confusion; *by the Lord Harry.* **2.** A vulgar, loud young cad, esp. a cockney; commonly *'Arry*, from the manner in which this class of person pronounces the Christian name.

harsh, adj. [1. harsh; 2. hāʃ]. M.E. *harsk*, 'rough to touch', Scand., M. Swed., Dan. *harsk*, Swed. *härsk*, Germ. *harsch.* The word is prob. fr. same base as **hard** (**I.**); Aryan *-tk-* becomes *-sk-* in Gmc., so that Aryan **krat-ko* (with adj. suff.), wd. become Gmc. **hrask-*, **harsk-*. **1.** (of material texture) Disagreeably rough, coarse, irritating to the touch: *a harsh texture, cloth* &c. **2.** (of sound, voice, musical instrument) Discordant, producing jarring notes, grating &c. **3.** (of colours) Crude, offensively glaring, not subdued; inharmonious. Phr. *harsh contrast*, one that is too abrupt and violent. **4.** (in moral sense) **a** (of character and disposition, manners &c.) Rugged, stern, hard, severe; **b** (of features, expression) betokening such character; rough-hewn, coarse; **c** (of action) severe, oppressive, animated by sternness and rigour: *a harsh judgement, punishment.*

harshly, adv. Prec. & **-ly.** In a harsh manner.

harshness, n. See prec. & **-ness.** Quality, condition, of being harsh.

hart, n. [1. hart; 2. hāt]. O.E. *heorot, heort*, M.E. *hert*; cp. O.S. *hirot*, O.H.G. *hiruz*, Mod. Germ. *hirsch*, O.N. *hjört-r.* The word meant orig. 'the horned animal'. The Aryan base **k̑er-*, 'head, horn', occurred also in Lat. *cervus*, 'stag', see **cervine**, & many other words, q.v. under **cerebral, cervical, horn.** Adult male of deer, usually of red deer, more than five years old; stag; (archaic Phrs.) *hart of grease*, fat hart; *hart of ten*, with ten tines on each antler; *hart royal*, hart that has been chased by a royal person.

hartal, n. [1. hártal; 2. hā́tæl]. Anglicized form of Hind. *hathtal*, fr. *hath*, 'market', & *talna*, 'stop, prevent'. Stoppage of all work, business &c., as a sign of humiliation or protest; adopted by Indian Nationalists for political purposes.

hartebeest, hartbeest, n. [1. hárt(e)bēst; 2. hā́t(ə)bist]. S. Afr. Du. See **hart** & **beast.** Large S. African antelope, of reddish colour, with long curved horns; any species of same genus.

hartshorn, n. [1. hárts-horn; 2. hā́tshōn]. **hart** & **horn.** Ammonium carbonate, sal volatile, formerly distilled from antlers of hart; Phrs. *salt of hartshorn*, the impure carbonate in solid form, smelling salts; *spirit of hartshorn*, aqueous solution of this.

hart's-tongue, hartstongue, n. [1. hárts tung; 2. hā́ts taŋ]. British fern with long narrow leaves; so called from shape of these.

hartwort, n. [1. hártwërt; 2. hā́twʌt]. One of several European umbelliferous plants, of genera *Laserpitium*, allied to cicely, and *Tordylium.*

harum-scarum, adj. [1. hárum skárum; 2. héərəm skéərəm]. Orig. Scots, perh. for *hare 'em, scare 'em*, obs. *hare*, 'to frighten'. (colloq.) Reckless, rash, irresponsible; extremely careless, hasty, or unmethodical.

haruspex, n. [1. háruspeks; 2. hǽrəspeks]. Lat., lit. 'gut-seer'. The first element is fr. Aryan **g̑her-*, **g̑hor-* &c., 'intestine', cp. Lat. *hira*, 'empty gut', *hīllae* (for **hīr-ulae*), 'small intestines'; also Gk. *khor-dḗ*, 'gut', (see **chord**). The Gmc. cognates are O.E. *ġearn*, **yarn**, O.H.G. *garn*, 'entrails'. For second element see **species, spy**, & second element of **auspice.** Ancient Roman soothsayer, who took auguries from an inspection of the entrails of animals sacrificed.

harvest (**I.**), n. [1. hárvest; 2. hā́vist]. O.E. *hærfest*, 'season of crops, autumn, harvest'; M.E. *hervest* &c. Cp. O.H.G. *herbist, herbest*, Germ. *herbst*, 'harvest, autumn', fr. Gmc. base **herƀ-*, Aryan **kerp-*, 'to cut, shear, pluck', wh. occurs also in Lat. *carpere*, 'to pluck' &c., also in Gk. *karp-ós*, 'fruit', *krṓp-ion*, 'sickle'. See **carpel, carpet, harp.** **1.** Gathering in of seed crops: *wheat harvest, rice harvest*; of other produce, as apples, honey. **2.** Season when crops are gathered in; early autumn. **3. a** Crops or other produce when gathered or ready to be gathered; yield of the land: *the harvest is ripe*; *the harvest looks well this year*; *harvest of the sea*, fish; **b** (fig.) result of work, reflection, conduct: *researches have yielded a rich harvest of information*; '*The harvest of a quiet eye*' (Wordsworth); consequences of conduct: *the drunkard reaps a bitter harvest of misery.*

harvest (**II.**), vb. trans. & intrans. M.E. *hervesten*, fr. prec.; cp. M. Du. *herfsten*, M.H.G. *herbesten.* **1.** trans. **a** To gather in, reap, (crop); **b** to store, when gathered. **2.** intrans. To gather crops; to work as harvester.

harvest-bug, n. Harvest-mite.

harvester, n. [1. hárvester; 2. hā́vistə]. **harvest** (**II.**) & **-er.** **1. a** Person employed to gather crop, esp. of corn; **b** machine for cutting standing crop, or for cutting and binding. **2.** Labourer who reaps and gathers in the harvest. **3.** Harvest-mite.

harvester ant, n. Prec. & **ant.** One of several species of ant that store seeds for food.

harvest festival, n. Service of thanksgiving held in Christian Churches after the harvest has been safely gathered in.

harvest home, n. Words formerly shouted or sung by the reapers bringing last load home. **a** Song of reapers accompanying last load; **b** festivities provided by farmer for reapers on completion of wheat harvest; **c** completion of harvest.

harvesting, n. [1. hárvesting; 2. hā́vistiŋ]. **harvest** (**I.**) & **-ing.** Act or process of gathering in harvest.

harvest-louse, n. Harvest-mite.

harvest-man, n. **harvest** (**I.**) & **man** (**I.**). Labourer employed in harvesting.

harvest-mite, n. **harvest** (**I.**) & **mite.** Harvest-tick; small insect like a louse, infesting grass stalks &c., which burrows into the skin of men and animals, during harvest.

harvest moon, n. **harvest** (**I.**) & **moon** (**I.**). Moon which is full nearest to autumnal equinox, and which is supposed to help in ripening the corn.

harvest-mouse, n. Very small field mouse, which attaches its nest to growing cornstalks.

harvest-tick, n. **harvest (I.)** & **tick (III.)**. Harvest-mite.

hash (I.), n. [1. hash; 2. hæʃ]. Abbr. fr. Early Mod. Engl. *hachey, hachee*, fr. O. Fr. *hachis*, P.P. of *hacher*, 'to chop up', fr. O. Fr., Fr. *hache*, 'axe'. Prob. Gmc. See **hack (I.)**, **hatch (IV.)** & **hatchet**. **1.** Dish of meat cut small, reheated, and served with vegetables and gravy. **2.** (fig., colloq.) **a** Trite subject presented afresh in disguised form; **b** medley, jumble, muddle, mess: *to make a hash of (a job* &c.). Phr. *to settle one's hash*, to overwhelm, defeat, silence one completely.

hash (II.), vb. trans. Prec., or directly fr. Fr. *hacher*. **a** To chop up (meat), make into a hash; **b** (fig.) to make a mess, a muddle of.

hashish, n. [1. háshēsh; 2. hǽʃīʃ]. Arab. *hashīsh*, 'dried hemp', cp. **assassin**. Intoxicating and narcotic drug made from Indian hemp; smoked, drunk, or chewed in the East.

haslets, harslets, hastelets, n. pl. [1. hárslets; 2. hā́slits]. M.E. *hastelets, hastlettes*, fr. O. Fr. *hastelet* (Fr. *hâtelette*), 'meat roasted on spit', fr. O. Fr. *haste*, 'spit', & **-let**, fr. Lat. *hasta*, 'spear, spit', see **hastate**. Heart, liver, or other edible viscera of animal, esp. of a pig, formerly roasted on a spit.

hasp (I.), n. [1. hahsp; 2. hāsp]. O.E. *hæpse, hæsp*, M.E. *haspe, hespe*, & in other W. Gmc. languages, also O.N. *hespa*, 'hasp'. With metathesis, fr. **hap-s-*, fr. base **hap-*, as in N. Fris. *happe*, 'to snatch, clutch', & formative **-sōn-*. **1.** Metal clasp, or hinged flap, for fastening closed lid, door, window, book &c., held when closed by catch, staple, or other device. **2.** Spindle for winding thread. **3.** Skein, hank.

hasp (II.), vb. trans. O.E. *hæpsian*, M.E. *haspen*, fr. prec. To fasten or lock with hasp.

hassock, n. [1. hásuk; 2. hǽsək]. O.E. *hassuc, hassoc*, '(clump of) coarse grass', M.E. *hassok*, mod. dial. *hassock*, 'large tuft of coarse grass, rushes, or sedges'; of unknown origin, prob. w. dimin. suff. **-ock**. Is there any connexion w. Lat. *cārex*, 'sedge'? The origin of this is said by Walde to be unexplained. Does it stand for **kāzik-*? Small hard cushion for kneeling, probably from resemblance in shape to a tuft of grass &c.

hastate, adj. [1. hástāt; 2. hǽsteit]. Lat. *hastāt-(um)*, 'armed with spear', fr. *hasta*, 'spear'; cogn. w. Goth. *gazds*, O.E. *ġierd*. See **yard (I.)** & **-ate**. (bot.) Shaped like the head of a spear.

haste (I.), n. [1. hāst; 2. heist]. M.E., fr. O. Fr. *haste*, Mod. Fr. *hâte*; a Gmc. loan-word, cp. O.E. *hǣst*, 'violence, fury'; O.H.G. *heisti*, 'violent'. The word has lost an *f*, cp. Goth. *háifst-s*, 'strife', O.N. *heipt* (for **heift*), 'war'. The etymol. of the Gmc. forms is not clear. The word implies intentional, volitional, actions. **a** Speed, rapidity; quick motion, or action, of person or animal; Phrs. *to make haste*, to hasten, hurry: *make haste to come, or and come*; **b** excessive speed, precipitancy, hurry; inconsiderateness, rashness: *to act in haste*; '*I said in my haste, "All men are liars"*'; Phr. *more haste less speed*; **c** state of being urged or forced to act quickly: *I write in great haste*; *marry in haste, repent at leisure*.

haste (II.), vb. trans. & intrans. M.E. *hasten*, fr. O. Fr. *haster*, fr. *haste*, see prec. (now chiefly liter.; superseded in popular speech by *hasten*) **1.** trans. To cause to move or act with speed, to urge on, speed up, hurry, accelerate. **2.** intrans. (of animate beings) To move or act with speed, to be rapid, quick, to hurry: *haste away*, to depart with speed.

hasten, vb. intrans. & trans. [1. hā́sn; 2. héisn]. Prec. & **-en**. **A.** intrans. **1.** (of animate beings) **a** To move rapidly, in a definite direction, go or come quickly, and with speed; to hurry: *he hastened over to France, to his mother's death-bed*; **b** to act with rapidity, without delay: *I hasten to let you know the good news*. **2.** (of non-material things) To advance rapidly: *life, the year &c., is hastening to its close*. **B.** trans. **1.** To impart haste to, cause to hurry, accelerate, speed up (a movement, action, process): *to hasten the growth of plants, one's preparations, one's pace*. **2.** To cause to come on more rapidly, cause to occur earlier; put forward: *to hasten one's departure, arrival* &c.

hastily, adv. [1. hā́stili; 2. héistili]. **hasty** & **-ly**. In a hasty manner, with haste, hurriedly, inconsiderately.

hastiness, n. [1. hā́stines; 2. héistinis]. M.E. *hastinesse*, fr. **hasty** & **-ness**. Quality or condition of being hasty, in senses **a** rapidity; **b** precipitancy, rashness; **c** shortness of temper.

hasty, adj. [1. hā́sti; 2. héisti]. M.E. *hastif, hasty*, fr. O. Fr. *hastif*. **haste (I.)** & **-ive**. The loss of final *-f* was frequent in M.E., & later, cp. **jolly**; but there is little doubt that in adjs. the *-if* suff. was identified w., & influenced by, O.E. *-iġ*. See **-y**. **1.** (of persons, their movements and actions) **a** Exhibiting, characterized by, rapidity; **b** exhibiting undue haste; hurried, precipitate: *a hasty judgement*; *a hasty glance was all he bestowed upon me*; **c** exhibiting impatience, shortness of temper, rashness: *he regretted his hasty words*; *I apologize for what I said—I've been too hasty*. **2.** (of processes) Moving, advancing, coming about, with swiftness; rapid, quick-moving: *the growth of the crops has been very hasty during the hot weather*.

hasty pudding, n. Pudding rapidly concocted by stirring flour in boiling water and milk until it becomes thick.

hat (I.), n. [1. hat; 2. hæt]. O.E. *hæt(t)*, M.E. *hat*; cp. O.N. *hatt-r*, 'hat', *hǫtt-r*, 'hood', Swed. *hatt*, Dan. *hat*; Gmc. type **hattuz*, perh. for **had-n-uz*, related by gradation to **hood**; perh. cogn. w. Lat. *cassis* (for **katt-*), 'helmet'; cp. **chasuble**. Covering for head, usually of somewhat stiff material, and distinguished from cap or bonnet by continuous brim: *a beaver, bowler, chimney-pot, cocked, high, opera, silk, hat*; *top-hat*. Phrs. *as black as my hat*, very, quite, black; *to receive a cardinal's hat, the red hat*, to be made a cardinal, from this as part of official dress of cardinals; *picture hat*, lady's hat with very broad bent brim, as in pictures by old masters; *to hang up one's hat*, to settle down, pay long visit in a house; (*to come*) *hat in hand*, obsequiously, with servile air as though to solicit a favour; *to pass, send, round, go round with, the hat*, to collect contributions of money; *to raise, take off, touch, one's hat to*, salute thus; *to talk through one's hat* (colloq., slang), to talk nonsense in the belief that one will be taken seriously by one's hearers; *my hat!* (slang), exclamation of surprise &c.

hat (II.), vb. trans., fr. prec. To supply with a hat; (chiefly in P.P.) *hatted*, wearing a hat.

hatable, adj. [1. hā́tabl; 2. héitəbl]. **hate (II.)** & **-able**. Capable of being hated.

hatband, n. [1. hátband; 2. hǽtbænd]. Band surrounding hat immediately above brim; *broad hatband*, black band worn as sign of mourning.

hatblock, n. [1. hátblok; 2. hǽtblɔk]. Block or mould on which a hat is shaped or ironed.

hatbox, n. [1. hátboks; 2. hǽtbɔks]. Box, generally of leather, in which a hat or hats are kept or conveyed.

hatbrush, n. [1. hátbrush; 2. hǽtbrʌʃ]. Soft brush for smoothing a top-hat.

hatch (I.), n. [1. hach; 2. hætʃ]. O.E. *hæc* (gen. *hæċċe*), 'grating, gate of lattice-work', M.E. *hacche, hecche* (fr. oblique cases, cp. **hack (IV.)**). Cp. M. Du. *hek*. **1. a** Door or gate with open space above; lower part of divided door; wicket; **b** movable covering, of cross-bars or solid, to opening in floor or roof of building; (naut.) in deck of ship; Phr. *under hatches* (naut.), confined below deck, as prisoners or slaves; also, off duty; (fig.) in bondage or repression; put away out of sight; dead; **c** kind of door in weir, drawn up to open flood-gate, or trap fish. **2.** Opening fitted with hatch; (naut.) hatchway.

hatch (II.), vb. trans. & intrans. M.E. *hacchen*, cp. M.H.G. Germ. *hecken*, Swed. *häcka*, Dan. *hække, hekke*; of doubtful origin. **A.** trans. **1. a** To produce (young) from egg whether by natural or artificial process of incubation: *to hatch chickens*; **b** to produce young from (egg): *hatch 12 out of 13 eggs*. **2.** (fig.) To originate, contrive, bring to maturity, esp. by meditation or secretly: *to hatch a plot, design, theory*. **B.** intrans. **1.** (often *hatch out*) **a** (of birds, fish &c.) To produce young from egg; **b** (of young birds &c.) to emerge from egg; **c** (of egg) to produce young; to develop embryo. **2.** (fig., of plot, design &c.) To be in process of elaborating.

hatch (III.), n., fr. prec. **a** Action of hatching; **b** brood, of chickens &c., hatched.

hatch (IV.), vb. trans. & n. Fr. *hacher*, 'to chop, hatch', fr. *hache*, 'axe'. See **hash (I.)**, **hatchet, hachures**. **1.** vb. **a** To engrave or draw upon with very fine parallel or cross lines, esp. as shading; **b** to inlay, decorate, with thin bands. **2.** n. **a** Line of hatching; **b** hatched moulding as architectural ornament.

hatch-boat, n. **hatch (I.)** & **boat (I.)**. Kind of cargo-boat chiefly decked with hatches.

hatcher, n. [1. hácher; 2. hǽtʃə]. **hatch (II.)** & **-er**. **1. a** Animal that hatches eggs; person that superintends hatching; **b** incubator. **2.** Contriver, plotter: *a great hatcher of plots*.

hatchery, n. [1. hácheri; 2. hǽtʃəri]. **hatch (II.)** & **-ery**. Place or establishment for hatching fish.

hatchet, n. [1. háchet; 2. hǽtʃit]. M.E. *hachet*, fr. Fr. *hachette*, dimin. of *hache*, 'chopper', prob. formed fr. H.G. vb. *hacken* (Meyer-Lübke). Cp. **hash (I.)**, **hatch (IV.)**. Small axe, for one hand, for chopping firewood &c.; tomahawk. Phr. *to bury the hatchet*, to make peace, compose a quarrel; *to dig up, take up, the hatchet*, to make war.

hatchet face, n. Thin narrow face with prominent nose and jaw, suggesting shape of hatchet.

hatchet-faced, adj. Prec. & **-ed**. Having a hatchet face.

hatching, n. [1. háching; 2. hǽtʃiŋ]. **hatch (IV.)** & **-ing**. (in graphic arts) Process or method of marking shade by fine parallel lines.

hatchment, n. [1. háchment; 2. hǽtʃmənt]. Early Mod. Engl. *atcheament*, abbr. form of **achievement**. Escutcheon painted on square panel, hung diamondwise on front of house to notify decease, and afterwards hung in church; an heraldic achievement.

hatchway, n. [1. háchwā; 2. hǽtʃwei]. **hatch (I.)** & **way**. (chiefly naut.) Rectangular opening in deck of vessel or floor of building, closed when required by a hatch.

hate (I.), n. [1. hāt; 2. heit]. O.E. *hete*, M.E. *hete*, altered to *hāte* through influence of vb. (see next word), & perh. of O.N. *hat-r*; Common Gmc., O.S. *hete*, O.H.G. *haz*, Mod. Germ. *hass*; Goth. *hatis*, neut.; Gmc. type **hat-*, fr. Aryan **kəd-*, wk. grade of **kēd-*, 'destroy' &c., whence also Gk. *kēdein*, 'to trouble, vex'; Scrt. *kadanam*, 'destruction'; prob. also Lat. *cadere*, 'to fall' (see **cadency**), & more certainly *calamitas*, 'injury, misfortune' &c., for **cadamitas*, w. Sabine *l* for *d* (see **calamity**). **a** Strong feeling of dislike, detestation, repugnance, against person or thing; hatred; extreme ill-will; loathing; **b** (rare) object of hatred.

hate (II.), vb. trans. O.E. *hatian*, M.E. *hatien, haten*, fr. Gmc. type **hatōjan-*. See prec. **a** To entertain feelings of hatred for, to bear extreme ill-will against, desire evil to (persons); **b** to loathe, detest, abhor, abominate (things); (colloq.) regret, dislike strongly: *I hate to trouble you*; *I hate that you should think so*.

hateful, adj. [1. hā́tfool; 2. héitfəl]. **hate (I.)** & **-ful**. **1.** Arousing hatred; worthy to be hated; loathsome, abominable, odious. **2.** (rare) Filled with feelings of hatred; malignant.

hatefully, adv. Prec. & **-ly**. In a hateful manner.

hatefulness, n. See prec. & **-ness**. Quality of being hateful.

hatful, n. [1. hátfool; 2. hǽtfəl]. **hat (I.)** & **-ful**. Quantity that will fill a hat.

hatless, adj. [1. hátles; 2. hǽtlis]. **hat (I.)** & **-less**. Not having or wearing a hat; bareheaded.

hatpeg, n. [1. hátpeg; 2. hǽtpɛg]. Wooden peg or metal hook for hanging hat.

hatpin, n. [1. hátpin; 2. hǽtpin]. Long pin, usually with ornamental head, used to fasten woman's hat to her hair.

hatrack, n. [1. hátrak; 2. hǽtræk]. Series of pegs or hooks for hanging hats.

hatred, n. [1. hā́tred; 2. héitrid]. M.E. *haterēden*, fr. **hate (I.)** & O.E. *rǣden*, 'rule, direction, condition', used as substantival suff. (as in O.E. *frēondrǣden*, 'friendship', *mannrǣden*, 'allegiance', cp. **kindred**), fr. source of **ready**, **ride**. **a** Vehement or profound ill-will; settled feeling of malignity or rancour towards person or thing; **b** loathing, abomination, detestation; (colloq.) strong dislike.

hatstand, n. [1. hátstand; 2. hǽtstænd]. Piece of furniture consisting of movable frame or post standing on floor with pegs to hang hats on.

hatter, n. [1. háter; 2. hǽtə]. **hat (I.)** & **-er**. Person whose occupation is to sell or make hats; colloq. Phr. *as mad as a hatter*, very mad; very angry.

hat trick, n. **a** (cricket) Feat of taking three wickets with successive balls (originally rewarded by present of new hat); **b** (association football) feat of player who scores three goals in match.

hauberk, **hawberk**, n. [1. háwběrk; 2. hɔ́bāk]. M.E. *hauberc*, *hauberghe*, fr. O. Fr. *hauberc*, *halberc* (Fr. *haubert*), fr. O.H.G. *halsberc*, fr. *hals*, 'neck' (cp. **hawse**), & *bergan*, 'to protect' (cp. **borough**, **bury**); O.E. *healsbeorg*, O.N. *hālsbjōrg* (cp. **habergeon**). Mediaeval coat of armour, esp. one of chain-mail, or of cloth covered with rings, scales, or small plates of steel.

haugh, n. [1. haw; 2. hɔ̄]. Prob. identical w. *-halgh*, *-hall* in place-names, fr. O.E. *h(e)alh*, 'corner, hiding-place, bay'. Possibly fr. Aryan **k*ʷ*olk*ʷ*o-*, & perh. cogn. w. Gk. *kólpos*, 'bosom, lap, bay of the sea' (but see **gulf**). The word may, however, be cogn. w. Lat. *calx*, 'heel', q.v. under **calceolaria**. (chiefly Scots and N. Engl.) Alluvial flat in river-valley.

haughtily, adv. [1. háwtili; 2. hɔ́tili]. **haughty** & **-ly**. In a haughty manner.

haughtiness, n. [1. háwtines; 2. hɔ́tinis]. Next word & **-ness**. Quality of being haughty.

haughty, adj. [1. háwti; 2. hɔ́ti]. Early Mod. Engl. *hauty*; the spelling w. *gh* has no historical justification, but due to anal. of such words as *naught*; prob. extension w. suff. **-y**, fr. early Mod. Engl. *haut*, *hault*, *haught*, 'exalted, noble, haughty', fr. O. Fr. *halt*, *haut* (Fr. *haut*), 'high', fr. Lat. *altus* (see **altitude**), influenced by O.H.G. *hōh*, **high**. Perh. affected in meaning by M.E. *hautein*, *hautyn*, fr. O. Fr. *(h)autain*, Fr. *hautain*, 'haughty', fr. *haut* & suff. *-ain*, fr. Lat. *-ān-us*. **a** (of persons) Proud and disdainful, supercilious; arrogant; **b** (of manner, speech, looks &c.) expressing disdain or arrogance.

haul (I.), vb. trans. & intrans. [1. hawl; 2. hɔ̄l]. M.E. *haulen*, variant of *hālen* (see **hale (II.)**), Fr. *haler*, 'to haul, tow'. **A.** trans. **1.** To pull, drag, esp. with effort or force; to transport by pulling; specif., *to haul timber*, convey it from place where it is felled to sawmill. Phr. *to haul over the coals*, (colloq., from punishment of heretics) to reprimand, find fault with; *to haul down one's flag, colours*, (fig.) to surrender. **2.** (naut.) To bring up (ship) close to the wind (from hauling sheets; cp. *close-hauled*). Phr. *to haul the wind*, haul ship; (fig.) to withdraw, draw back; *to haul up*, (fig., colloq.) check irregularities of, call to account. **B.** intrans. **1.** **a** To pull: *to haul at, upon, a rope*; **b** to pull apart, as two horses harnessed abreast. **2.** (naut.) **a** To alter sailing course: *to haul off, round*; Phrs. *to haul up*, sail near or into wind, stop course; *to haul upon the wind*, haul the wind; **b** (of wind) to shift.

haul (II.), n., fr. prec. **1.** **a** Hauling, pulling with effort or force; **b** length along which a thing is hauled. **2.** Catch of fish; (fig.) capture, acquisition, quantity secured as result of a venture: *a good, big, haul*.

haulabout, n. [1. háwlabout; 2. hɔ́ləbaut]. Kind of steel coal-barge furnished with transporters.

haulage, n. [1. háwlij; 2. hɔ́lidž]. **haul (I.)** & **-age**. **1.** **a** Action or process of hauling; esp. of carting, conveying goods &c.; **b** force employed in hauling. **2.** Charge made for hauling, or for use of railway.

hauler, n. [1. háwler; 2. hɔ́lə]. **haul (I.)** & **-er**. Person who hauls.

haulier, n. [1. háwlier; 2. hɔ́liə]. **haul (I.)** & **-ier**. Hauler, specif. **a** carter; **b** man who hauls coal in mine to foot of shaft.

haulm, **halm**, n. [1. hawm, hahm; 2. hōm, hām]. O.E. *healm*, *halm*, 'straw, grass stem', M.E. *halm*; cp. O.S., O.H.G. *halm*, O.N. *hālm-r*; cogn. w. Gk. *kálamos*, 'reed', *kalámē*, 'cornstalk', Lat. *calamus*, 'reed, cane', *culmus*, 'stalk, esp. of grain'; W. *calaf*, 'stalk'; O. Slav. *slama*, Russ. *soloma*, 'straw'. **a** Stalk, stem, of plant; **b** stalks, esp. of peas, beans, cereals; also of other crops, e.g. of potatoes, esp. after gathering; litter, straw, used for thatching &c.

haunch (I.), n. [1. hawnsh; 2. hɔnʃ]. M.E., fr. O. Fr. *hanche*, apparently fr. W. Gmc. source, cp. M. Du. *hancke*, *hencke*. Etymol. obscure. Could the word be fr. *ham* (see **ham (I.)**), w. dimin. suff.? **a** Part in man and quadrupeds, including projection formed by the hip, together with the thickest part of the thigh and the buttock; hind quarter: *to squat on one's haunches*; **b** (of meat) the above parts together with loin of the animal: *a haunch of venison*.

haunch (II.), n. Perh. fr. prec. Hance.

haunch-bone, n. Hip-bone; also called innominate bone.

haunched, adj. [1. hawnsht; 2. hɔnʃt]. **haunch (I.)** & **-ed**. Having haunches.

haunching, n. [1. háwnshing; 2. hɔ́nʃiŋ]. **haunch (II.)** & **-ing**. Material or backing for haunch of arch.

haunt (I.), vb. trans. [1. hawnt; 2. hɔnt]. M.E. *ha(u)nten*, 'to haunt, practise', fr. Fr. *hanter* (aspirated), 'to frequent, haunt', of uncertain origin, perh. fr. a Low Lat. type **ambitāre*, 'to go about', fr. *ambitus*, 'a going about' (see **ambit**), owing *h-* to anal. of Lat. *habitāre*, 'to dwell' (see **habit**). **1.** **a** To frequent, visit (place) often or habitually: *to haunt the lowest resorts*; **b** to associate with (persons): *to haunt bad company*. **2.** Specif. (of ghosts, goblins, spirits, spooks) **a** to frequent, reside, appear repeatedly in, to infest (places): *the place was said to be haunted by the ghost of its former owner*; **b** to appear frequently to; to obsess, accompany constantly (persons): *to be haunted by the ghost of a dead friend*; **c** (of persons) to annoy by constantly repeated visits, pester by appearing frequently to; importune with one's company: *I seem to be haunted by undesirable foreigners*. **3.** (of non-material things) **a** (of thoughts, ideas, emotions &c.) To occupy the mind, recur frequently to, obtrude upon persistently; obsess: *I am haunted by the thought that I might have saved him*; *remorse haunts him continually*; *to be haunted by fears* &c.; **b** to be associated with, evoked by, cluster round, pervade: *memories and visions of bygone events seem to haunt such buildings as Westminster Hall*.

haunt (II.), n. M.E. *hant*, 'usage, haunt', fr. O. Fr. *hant*; fr. vb., see prec. **a** Place which person frequents; resort: *haunts of vice and crime*; *haunts of one's youth*; *back in one's old haunts*; *a low haunt*; *a haunt of fashion*; also (fig.) *his heart is the haunt of base thoughts*; **b** lair, habitat, feeding-place of animal: '*haunts of coot and hern*' (Tennyson's 'Brook').

haunted, adj. [1. háwnted; 2. hɔ́ntid]. **haunt (I.)** & **-ed**. Repeatedly or habitually subject to ghostly or psychic manifestations: *a haunted house*.

haunter, n. [1. háwnter; 2. hɔ́ntə]. **haunt (I.)** & **-er**. Person, ghost &c. that haunts.

haunting (I.), n. [1. háwnting; 2. hɔ́ntiŋ]. **haunt (I.)** & **-ing**. **a** Action of frequenting or often resorting to place; **b** habitual or repeated appearance of ghost &c. in place.

haunting (II.), adj., fr. Pres. Part. of **haunt (I.)**. Often or persistently recurring to the memory; not easily forgotten: *a haunting melody, cadence, rhyme* &c.

hauntingly, adv. Prec. & **-ly**. In a haunting manner.

haurient, **-ant**, adj. [1. háwrient; 2. hɔ́riənt]. Lat. *haurient-*, stem of Pres. Part. of *haurīre*, 'to draw up, drain, swallow'. See **exhaust**. (her.) Of fish, having head pointing upwards towards the top (chief) of the shield (as if rising to breathe air).

Haussmannize, vb. trans. & intrans. [1. hóusmanīz; 2. háusmənaiz]. Baron G. E. Haussmann (1809–91), who rebuilt much of Paris. To reconstruct or alter (town or quarter) by drastic or ruthless reconstruction.

hautboy, n. [1. hṓboi; 2. hóubɔi]. Fr. *hautbois*, fr. *haut*, 'high', & *bois*, 'wood'. Cp. **haughty**, **bush (I.)**, **oboe**. **a** Oboe; **b** reed-stop or organ with thin tone.

hauteur, n. [1. hōtḗr; 2. houtā́]. Fr., fr. *haut*, 'high' (cp. **haughty**), & *-eur*. See **-or** & **-our**. Haughtiness, haughty aloofness; manner as of one dealing with an inferior.

Havana, n. [1. havána; 2. həvǽnə]. Span. Habana, capital of Cuba. Havana cigar.

have, vb. trans. & auxil. [1. hav; 2. hæv], & auxil. [həv, əv, v]; only [hæv] when specially emphasized. O.E. *habban*, 'to hold, take, possess, have', M.E. *habben* & *hāven*, fr. type *haf-* as in O.E. *hafast* &c.; Common Gmc.; O.S. *habbian*, *hebbian*, fr. W. Gmc. type **habbj-*, Gmc. **hab-ējan-*, cp. O.H.G. *habēn*, Germ. *haben*, Goth. *haban*, O.N. *hafa*. Not connected w. Lat. *habēre*, 'to have' &c., in spite of resemblances of form & meaning. Almost certainly fr. same base as Lat. *capere*, 'to seize, take', q.v. under **captive**, & cogn. w. **heave**, **haft**, & perh. w. **hawk (I.)**. **A.** trans. In the present and past tenses, the colloquial language generally uses construction *have got* instead of the simple *have*, in several of the senses in which the word is used. This alternative usage is indicated in all cases where it may occur. **1.** (of persons) **a** To possess, hold, own, as a material possession, to be in possession of: *to have a large fortune, a house in the country, a polo pony, a motor-car* &c.; also, *I've got a house* &c.; **b** to control, keep, be in enjoyment of, have attached to one, enjoy services, affection, of &c.: *to have a large staff of servants, a butler*; *to have a wife and family, a friend* &c.; also, *I've got a friend* &c.; **c** (of things) to be closely associated with, in proximity to, to be in position of having something attached, or appertaining to as a part or accessory: *this house has an excellent garden*; *my room has three windows*; *such a book ought to have a fine binding*. **2.** (of persons) To possess and exhibit, **a** as a physical trait, feature, characteristic: *to have a bald head, a red nose, lovely blue eyes* &c.; also, *I've, he's &c., got a red nose* &c.; **b** as a mental characteristic, quality &c.: *to have a bad temper, a powerful intellect, a good memory* &c.; also, *I've, he's &c., got a bad temper* &c. Phrs. *will you have the goodness, kindness &c., to do so-and-so?*, be so kind as to, please do, so-and-so; *to have the cheek, impudence &c., to do, say* &c., to be so impudent &c. as to. **3.** (of mental activity) **a** To retain, hold, in the mind; to entertain, feel, intellectually or emotionally: *to have in one's mind*; *to have a notion, an idea, hope, fear*; also, *I've got a notion* &c.; **b** to exercise a function of the mind, exert some mental or spiritual quality: *to have an affection for*; *to have regard to*; *to have care, charge, of*; *to have mercy, pity, compassion* &c.;

to have responsibility for &c. **4.** (of persons) **a** To be concerned with, enjoy, experience: *to have some fun, a lark, a pleasant time, an adventure* &c.; **b** to undergo, to suffer from: (i.) *to have an illness, an attack of gout*; also with *got*; (ii.) *to have a bad night*; **c** (after *shall* or *will*) to be in position of expecting, awaiting; to cause, experience, as result of an action, or of something that has happened or may happen: *if you don't take care you'll have the police down upon you; we shall have all the beggars in the town here.* **5.** (of persons and animals) To take, receive, obtain, consume: *what will you have?; to have a good breakfast, a glass of beer, a cigarette* &c.; *horse had better have a warm mash.* **6. a** (of persons) To be under an obligation to do something, go somewhere, be compelled to do: *I shall have to go to the dentist's; he has (got) to be in by ten; you may not want to go but you'll have to*; **b** (of inanimate things) to require, be in need of: *the library clock will have to be mended; your collar will have to be ironed.* **7.** (followed by P.P.) To cause to be done, get done: *to have one's hair cut; to have a house built, done up; to have a book bound.* **8. a** To take in, deceive, trick, disappoint: *I'm afraid you've been had over your bargain; I was badly had when I just missed the train*; **b** to defeat in a game, in argument, to place in a dilemma: (i.) *he had you completely in the first game*; (ii.) *you've (got) no reply to that, he has (got) you there.* **9.** To assert, maintain, say: *rumour has it that there will be a divorce*; '*to waste its sweetness on the desert air*', *as Gray has it.* Various Phrs. and idioms: *to have and to hold*, to possess and retain; *to have a hat* &c. *on*, to be wearing; *to have nothing on*, to be naked; *to have (a question, matter) out with someone*, to discuss, and come to an understanding with; *to have to do with*, to be concerned with, relate to; *to have nothing to do with a person*, to shun his society; *this has nothing to do with you*, does not concern you; *you have my apologies, sympathy* &c., I apologize &c.; *to have a baby*, give birth to; *to have a person in*, to invite him in; *to be had up*, to be prosecuted, charged, before a magistrate; *I won't have it, such conduct* &c., won't stand, tolerate, it; *to have everything one's own way*, to get what one wants &c.; *I would have you to know*, I desire that you should know &c. **B.** (auxil.) *Have* in its pres. and past tenses, followed by P.P. of vbs., is used to form perf. and pluperf. tenses of these; **a** forming perf. indic.: *I have shot a duck*; **b** pluperf. indic.: *I had just finished dinner when he came*; **c** perf. conditional: *I had started yesterday but for an accident* (archaic); now *I should have* &c.; *had I only known I would not have gone.*

havelock, n. [1. hávlok; 2. hǽvlɔk]. After Sir Henry Havelock (1795–1857), English general during Indian Mutiny. Light cloth covering cap and neck, used as a protection against sun.

haven, n. [1. hāv(e)n; 2. héiv(ə)n]. O.E. *hæfen*, 'harbour', M.E. *havene*; cp. numerous cognates, M. Du., M.L.G. *havene*, Du., L.G. *haven*, M.H.G. *habene*, Germ. (fr. L.G.) *hafen*; prob. fr. same base as **have**, & meaning orig. 'protection, security'. In this case, in the group of words meaning 'sea', e.g. O.E. *hæf*, O.N., Swed. *haf*, Dan. *hav*, M.H.G. *hap*, Germ. *haff*, this latter sense is apparently secondary. **a** Inlet of sea or other body of water forming place of shelter for ships; harbour; **b** (fig.) shelter, refuge: *a haven of refuge from life's storms* &c.

haversack, n. [1. háversak; 2. hǽvəsæk]. Fr. *havresac*, 'wallet, tool-bag', fr. Germ. *hafersack, habersack*, 'sack for oats', fr. Germ. *hafer, haber*, 'oats', fr. O.S. *havoro, havero*, O.H.G. *habaro, habero*, 'oats', cp. Du. *haver*, M.E. *havere*, O.N. *hafri*, Swed. *hafre*, Dan. *havre*, & **sack (I.)**. Small bag or wallet in which soldier or traveller carries his provisions.

havildar, n. [1. hávildar; 2. hǽvəldā]. Pers. *hawāldār*, fr. Pers., fr. Arab. *hawālah*, 'duty, charge', & Pers. *dār*, 'holder'. Sergeant in native regiment in Indian army; hence, *havildar-major*, sergeant-major.

having, n. [1. háving; 2. hǽviŋ]. **have** & **-ing**. **a** Act or state of holding or possessing; **b** thing possessed; possession, estate.

havoc, n. & vb. trans. [1. hávuk; 2. hǽvək]. M.E., A.-Fr. *havok*, fr. O. Fr. *havot*, 'plunder', esp. in phrase *crier havot*, 'to cry havoc', conn. w. O. Fr. *havée*, 'handful, booty', orig. P.P. fem. of *haver*, 'to hook, grapple', prob. fr. Gmc. **haf-*, 'to lift up, seize'. Cp. **heave.** **1. n. a** Destruction of a serious kind, such as that caused by the violence of the elements or other natural forces, by the turbulence of a mob or of any brutal and ill-disciplined body: *terrible havoc was caused by the storm, the waves, the earthquake* &c.; *the invading army wrought havoc throughout the whole province*; **b** injury, harm, inflicted in non-material sphere; disintegration, breaking-up, of religious beliefs, morals, law &c. Phr. *to play havoc with*, to destroy, ruin, bring to confusion; to cause distress to. **2.** vb. trans. (archaic or obs.) To lay waste, ravage (also absol.).

haw (I.), n. [1. haw; 2. hɔ̄]. O.E. *haga*, 'enclosure, messuage', M.E. *hage, hawe*; cogn. w. **hedge.** (hist., obs., or provinc.) Enclosure, close, yard; house with yard, messuage.

haw (II.), n. O.E. *haga*, prob. abbr. fr. **haguberige*, 'hedge berry, hawthorn berry', fr. prec. & **berry.** Cp. **hawthorn.** Berry of hawthorn.

haw (III.), n. Origin unknown. **a** Nictitating membrane, third eyelid, as of horse or dog; **b** (often pl.) inflammation of haw.

haw (IV.), vb. intrans. & n. Imitative. **1.** vb. intrans. To make inarticulate sound like 'haw' when speaking, through hesitation, embarrassment, or affectation; chiefly in phr. *to hum and haw.* **2.** n. Inarticulate murmur like 'haw' in course of speech: *hums and haws.*

hawfinch, n. [1. háwfinsh; 2. hɔ̄finʃ]. **haw (II.)** & **finch.** Large British finch with very stout beak; common grosbeak.

haw-haw (I.), interj., n., & vb. intrans. [1. háw haw; 2. hɔ̄ hɔ̄]. Redupl. fr. **haw (IV.)**. Variant of **ha ha (I.)**.

haw-haw (II.), n. Variant of **ha-ha (II.)**.

hawk (I.), n. [1. hawk; 2. hɔ̄k]. O.E. *h(e)afoc, heafuc*, M.E. *havec, hauk*; M.L.G. *havek*, Du. *havik*, O.H.G. *habuh, hapuh*, O.N. *hauk-r*; prob. fr. Gmc. base **haf-*, 'to seize' (see **have** & **heave**); cp. Lat. *(ac)cipiter, (ac)ceptor*, 'hawk', Low Lat. *capus*, 'falcon', fr. *capere*, 'to take, seize' (see **captive**). **1. a** Any one of the falcon family, excluding larger kinds as eagles and vultures; **b** (in narrower sense) any of the short-winged, long-tailed falcons, without notch in upper mandible, including sparrow-hawk and goshawk. **2.** (fig.) Person who preys on others; a shark, sharper, swindler.

hawk (II.), vb. intrans. & trans. M.E. *hauken*, fr. prec. **1.** intrans. **a** To hunt birds or quadrupeds by means of trained falcon or hawk, to practise falconry; **b** (of bird of prey) to attack prey by flying at it or swooping on it. **2.** trans. To hunt (prey) as hawk.

hawk (III.), vb. intrans. & trans. & n. Prob. imitative. **1.** vb. **a** intrans. To clear the throat audibly, cough up phlegm; to make noise in throat in attempting to clear it; **b** *to hawk up* (trans.), to cough up. **2.** n. Effort to clear throat; noise thus made.

hawk (IV.), vb. trans. Back-formation fr. **hawker (II.)**; cp. Du. *heuken*, 'to retail'. **a** To cry for sale, offer for sale in streets, peddle (also absol.); **b** (fig.) to spread about, vulgarize: *to hawk news about.*

hawk (V.), n. Etymol. unknown. Square board with handle underneath, used by plasterer to carry plaster or mortar.

hawkbit, n. [1. háwkbit; 2. hɔ̄kbit]. Kind of composite flower resembling dandelion.

hawker (I.), n. [1. háwker; 2. hɔ̄kə]. **hawk (I.)** & **-er.** Person who pursues game with hawk, falconer.

hawker (II.), n. Cp. M. Du. *hucker*, Du. *heuker*, L.G., Germ., Dan. *höker*, **huckster**, also (fr. L.G.) M.E. *hokkerye, hukkerye*, 'huckster's trade'; prob. fr. Gmc. base meaning 'to stoop, crouch' (as pedlar with pack), cp. M. Du., L.G. *huken*, Du. *huiken*, M.H.G. *hūchen*, M.L.G., Germ. *hocken*, O.N. *hūka*, 'to crouch, squat', also Germ. *hocken*, 'to carry on one's back', O.N. *hokra*, 'to go bent'. See **huckaback.** Person who cries or sells goods in the streets; itinerant vendor; legally distinguished from pedlar by the use of an animal or other means of carrying wares.

hawk-eyed, adj. **hawk (I.)** & **eyed.** **a** Having very keen sight, like hawk; **b** vigilant.

hawking, n. [1. háwking; 2. hɔ̄kiŋ]. **hawk (II.)** & **-ing.** Hunting with hawk; falconry.

hawk-moth, n. **hawk (I.)** & **moth (I.)**, fr. habit of hovering. One of family (*Sphingidae*) of thick-bodied, mostly large, moths, with long pointed fore-wings and long curled proboscis.

hawk-nosed, adj. Having curved, aquiline nose, like hawk's beak; hook-nosed.

hawk-owl, n. One of several owls resembling hawks.

hawk's-beard, n. [1. háwks bērd; 2. hɔ̄ks bīəd]. Composite herb, of which some species are wild in Britain, mostly with pinnatifid leaves, yellow or orange flowers, and abundant pappus.

hawksbill, n. [1. háwksbil; 2. hɔ̄ksbil]. **hawk (I.)** & **bill (II.)**. Also *hawksbill turtle* or *tortoise*. Small marine turtle of warmer seas, furnishing best tortoise-shell.

hawkweed, n. [1. háwkwēd; 2. hɔ̄kwīd]. One of many species of genus (*Hieracium*) of composite perennial herbs, common in Britain, with yellow or orange flowers.

hawse, n. [1. hawz; 2. hɔ̄z]. Early Mod. Engl. *halse, haulse*, prob. fr. O.N. *hāls*, 'neck, part of bow of ship'; Common Gmc., cp. O.E. *heals, hals*, 'neck, prow'; M.E., O.S., O.H.G., Goth. *hals*, 'neck'; cogn. w. Lat. *collus, collum*, fr. **cols-om*, 'neck'. See **collar.** (naut.) Part of ship's bows containing hawse-holes; the hawse-holes themselves.

hawse-hole, n. Hole in ship's bows through which cables of anchors pass.

hawse-pipe, n. (naut.) Iron or steel pipe lining hawse-hole.

hawser, n. [1. háwzer; 2. hɔ̄zə]. Early Mod. Engl. *halser*, fr. M.E. *halse(n)*, 'to raise, hoist', fr. O. Fr. *halcier*, Fr. *hausser*, 'to raise', fr. Low Lat. **altiāre*, fr. Lat. *altus*, 'high' (cp. **altitude, haughty**), & **-er**; or directly fr. Fr. *haussière*, 'hawser', fr. *hausser.* Wrongly associated w. **hawse.** (naut.) Large rope or small cable, often of steel, used for warping, mooring &c.

hawser-laid, adj. Made of three small ropes twined together, like hawser.

hawthorn, n. [1. háwthorn; 2. hɔ̄þɔn]. O.E. *haguþorn, hægþorn*, fr. *haga*, 'enclosure, hedge' (**haw (II.)**), & **thorn**, M.E. *haʒ(e)-, haweþorn*; M.H.G. *hagedorn*, O.N. *hagþorn.* Spiny tree of rose family bearing clusters of white or red flowers and dark-red berries; much used for hedges; white-thorn, may.

hay (I.), n. [1. hā; 2. hei]. O.E. *hīeg, hēg* &c., M.E. *heiʒ, hei*, cogn. w. O.E. *hēawan*, 'to cut' (see **hew**), Common Gmc. **a** Grass mown and dried for fodder &c.; Phrs. *to look for a needle in a bundle of hay* (or *in a haystack*), to engage in an almost hopeless search; *to make hay*, to dry mown grass by tossing and exposing to sun and air; *to make hay of*, (fig.) to reduce to confusion; *to make hay while the sun shines*, (fig.) to make best use of opportunities, esp. of enriching oneself; **b** grass grown for mowing: *to put a field under hay.*

hay (II.), vb. trans. & intrans., fr. prec. **1.** trans. **a** To supply with hay; **b** to grow grass on, for hay; **c** to turn (grass) to hay. **2.** intrans. To make hay.

hay (III.), n., fr. O. Fr. *haye.* Origin uncertain. (obs.) Kind of country-dance with winding movement; recently revived in this sense, and in that of a similar figure in other country-dances.

haybote, n. [1. hábōt; 2. héibout]. O.E. *hege*, M.E. *hei*, *hai*, Early Mod. Engl. *hay*, 'hedge' (cp. Fr. *haie*, 'hedge', fr. L.G.), fr. Gmc. type **hagiz* (cp. **haw (I.)**, **hedge (I.)**). The second element is fr. O.E. *bōt*, 'remedy, compensation' &c. See **boot (III.)**, **booty**. (law) **a** Right of tenant or commoner to take wood or thorns for mending hedge or fence; **b** wood or thorns thus taken.

hay-box, n. Air-tight box packed with hay, so constructed that hot food placed within it does not lose heat but continues to undergo process of cooking.

haycock, n. [1. hákok; 2. héikɔk]. Pile or cock of hay in field, ready for carting.

hay fever, n. Feverish catarrh affecting the eyes, and the mucous membrane of the nose and throat, occurring in early summer, probably due to irritation caused by pollen or dust.

hayfield, n. [1. háfēld; 2. héifīəld]. Field in which grass is grown for hay; one in which hay is actually being made.

hay-fork, n. Large two-pronged fork for turning, and picking up hay.

hay-knife, n. Long knife for cutting blocks of hay from the rick.

hayloft, n. [1. hálawft; 2. héilɔ̄ft]. Loft, generally above stable or shed, for storing hay for immediate use.

haymaker, n. [1. hámāker; 2. héimeikə]. Person who, machine that, makes hay.

haymow, n. [1. hámou; 2. héimau]. **hay (I.)** & **mow (I.)**. (provinc.) Haycock.

hayrick, n. [1. hárik; 2. héirik]. Rick of hay.

hayseed, n. [1. hásēd; 2. héisīd]. **1. a** Grass seed; **b** small particles of mown hay. **2.** (slang, U.S.A.) A countryman, country bumpkin, rustic.

haystack, n. [1. hástak; 2. héistæk]. Stack or rick of hay.

hayward, n. [1. háward; 2. héiwəd]. M.E. *heiward*, fr. *hei*, 'hedge' (cp. **haybote**), & **ward (I.)**. (largely obs.) Official who inspects the hedges and fences of a parish, and impounds stray beasts.

hazard, n. & vb. trans. [1. házard; 2. hǽzəd]. M.E. *hasard*, fr. Fr. *hasard*, 'game at dice' (12th cent.), 'risk, chance', perh. fr. Span. *azar*, 'unfortunate card or throw at dice, unforeseen accident', perh. fr. Arab. *al zar*, 'the die', but whole history of word is doubtful. **1. n. a** Name of various games of chance played with the dice; hence, **b** chance, risk, danger; Phr. *at all hazards*, whatever the risk, under all circumstances; **c** name applied to certain strokes in billiards, tennis &c. **2. vb. a** To risk, venture, expose to danger: *to hazard one's life*; **b** (fig.) to venture on: *to hazard a remark, conjecture* &c.

hazardous, adj. [1. házardus; 2. hǽzədəs]. **hazard** & **-ous**. Involving hazard; risky.

hazardously, adv. Prec. & **-ly**. In a hazardous manner.

haze (I.), n. [1. hāz; 2. heiz]. Origin unknown; word has no history in Engl., & is apparently borrowed fr. a L.G. dial. **a** Slight, thin fog, or mist; vapour; also thin cloud of smoke; **b** (of mental state) lack of clarity in ideas; slight confusion of thought.

haze (II.), vb. intrans. & trans., fr. prec. (rare) **a** intrans. To become hazy, to produce haze; **b** trans., to make hazy.

haze (III.), vb. trans. Prob. O. Fr. *haser*, 'to irritate, vex, insult'. **a** (naut.) To harass, worry, overwork; **b** (Am. colloq., esp. univ.) to harass by practical jokes &c.; to 'rag'.

hazel, n. & adj. [1. hāzl; 2. héizl]. O.E. *hæsel*, *hæsl*, M.E. *hasel*, O.H.G. *hasal*, O.N. *hasl*. Cogn. w. Lat. *corulus* for **kozulus*, 'hazel, filbert tree'. Origin doubtful. **1. n. a** European tree, *Corylus*, with edible nuts; **b** colour of these nuts, light brown: *eyes of hazel*. **2. adj. a** Made of hazel wood; pertaining to hazel; **b** of colour of hazel.

hazelly, adj. [1. hāzeli; 2. héizəli]. **hazel (I.)** & **-ly**. **a** Abounding in hazels; **b** of hazel colour.

hazel-nut, n. Nut of the hazel.

hazily, adv. [1. házili; 2. héizili]. **hazy** & **-ly**. In hazy manner, dimly, vaguely.

haziness, n. [1. házines; 2. héizinis]. **hazy** & **-ness**. State of being hazy; dimness, vagueness.

hazing, n. [1. házing; 2. héiziŋ]. **haze (III.)** & **-ing**. Action of one who hazes (III.). **a** (naut.) Infliction of excessive or disagreeable task; **b** (Am. colloq., esp. univ.) teasing or harassing by practical jokes &c., 'ragging'.

hazy, adj. [1. hāzi; 2. héizi]. **haze (I.)** & **-y**. **a** Pertaining to, covered with, resembling, haze: *a hazy sky, day; hazy view; hazy weather*; **b** (of mental state) obscure, not clear, confused, vague: *a hazy notion* &c.

he, pron. [1. hē; 2. hī]. Pron. of 3rd pers. masc. nom. O. & M.E. *hē*. The same base is seen in the other cases of the masc., in *it*, q.v., & in the fem. *her*; also in the O.E. pl. *hī*, 'they' &c. The other old Gmc. languages have mostly some traces at least of prons. in *h-*, & the whole group was orig. demonstr., the sense being 'this one here'. The base is seen also in **here**, **hither**; & is cogn. w. Lat. *ci-s* &c., 'on this side', in the particle *-ce*, e.g. in *hicce* &c., 'this one here', & in Gk. *kei-nos*, 'that one'. **1.** Denotes male human being, and male animal. **2.** (colloq., used as n.) *A he*, a male. **3.** As prefix *he-* denotes male animal: *he-goat*.

head (I.), n. [1. hed; 2. hɛd]. O.E. *hēafod*, M.E. *hēved*, *hēd* &c., O.S. *hōbid*; O.H.G. *haupit*, *houbit*, Mod. Germ. *haupt*; Goth. *haubiþ*; O.N. *haufoð*. All these forms point to a Gmc. **hauƀ-iþ*, wh. wd. presuppose an Aryan **koupit-* &c., or, at any rate, a form having **koup-* in first syll. But outside Gmc. the words for 'head', wh. most closely resemble the Gmc. type, have no diphthong, but a simple vowel, cp. Lat. *caput* (see **capital**); w. different formative element, Gk. *kephalḗ* (see **cephalic**); Scrt. *kapuc-chalam* for *kaput-*, 'hair at back of the head'. These point to Aryan **kep-*, **kap-*, whence the Gmc. type w. *au* cannot be derived. It has been suggested that the Gmc. diphthong is due to the influence of another base orig. independent, wh. has been associated w. the word for 'head', either in Aryan or the earliest Gmc., namely Aryan **koup-*, **kūp-* &c., meaning orig. 'to swell, bulge', wh. developed its meaning along two different lines—(1) 'something swelling, rising from the ground, a pile, heap' &c.; & (2) a bulging, swelling, hollow vessel'. The latter of these is seen in Lat. *cūpa*, 'tub, cask' (see **cup**), & O.E. *hȳf*, 'hive', fr. Gmc. **hūbi-* (see **hive**); the former sense is seen in Lith. *kaũpas*, 'pile', cogn. w. O.E. *hēap*, fr. Gmc. **kauppa-*, 'heap, troop' (see **heap**); & w. O.H.G. *houf*, same sense. There is no incongruity in regarding the head as a kind of pot, vessel, receptacle, an anal. wh. wd. be supported at once by its shape, & by the fact that it contains the brains. O.E. has also another word for 'head', *hafola*, wh. retains the old vowel in the first syll., & agrees in this respect, & on account of the *-ol-* element, very closely w. Scrt. *kapāla-*, 'cup, bowl, brain-pan, head'. Cp. also the form of the Gk. word above cited. **1.** That part of the body in man and the lower animals situated on the spinal column, above, or in quadrupeds, anterior to, the shoulders, consisting of bony cavity containing the brain; specif. **a** the whole of this part including the skull, jaws, face &c.: *to cut off the head*; *a drawing of a head*; *to put one's head in at the door* &c.; Phrs. *to eat one's head off*, to eat a great deal, and do very little work; *to go to the head*, (of liquor) to intoxicate; (fig.) to render excited; *over head and ears*, or *head over ears*, (chiefly fig.) deeply involved in, plunged in, esp. *in love, in debt*; (*to turn*) *head over heels*, execute a somersault; *to fall head first*; (*to be promoted*) *over the head(s) of*, in spite of claims of others, passing over them; *above the heads of* (*an audience* &c.), beyond their comprehension, too difficult for them; *to do something on one's head*, easily, without effort; (of several people) *to put their heads together*, to consult, deliberate; (*to have*) *a head on one's shoulders*, have practical ability, and common sense; *to take something into one's head*, come to believe it; (*to be unable*) *to get something out of one's head*, cease to think of, believe it; **b** the upper part of the skull in man covered by the hair, in which the brain is situated: *to have a bump on one's head*; *to hit a man on the head*; *to cut one's head open* &c.; **c** the part corresponding to **a** in lower forms of animal life: *the head of a butterfly, beetle* &c.; **d** that side of a coin bearing sovereign's head; in Phr. *heads or tails*. **2. a** (of persons) A single one of a number of individuals, thought of as severally distinguished by the head: *dinner at five shillings a, per, head*; *to count heads*; **b** individual animal in a herd or flock: *fifty head of cattle*; *so many head of game* &c. **3.** The highest part of something; top, upper portion; variously applied: **a** *head of a mountain, ladder, staircase* &c.; **b** (i.) source of spring, river &c., chiefly in *fountain head* &c.; (ii.) also *head of water*, height from which water descends before reaching outlet in pipe &c., hence (iii.) degree of pressure; **c** froth floating on liquid when newly poured out: *the head on a glass of ale* &c.; **d** the upper growth, boughs &c. of a tree; **e** blossom, or cluster of flowers, or leaves at top of a plant, stalk: *head of a flower, of a cabbage* &c.; **f** *the head of a page, sheet of paper, column of figures* &c.; Phrs. *at the head of the list*, first or successful candidate in a competition; *at the head of the poll*, successful in parliamentary election. **4.** Projecting object, or part of an object; **a** jutting mass of cliff: *Great Orme's Head*; **b** foremost part, front, of an object or body: *to march at the head of a regiment*; *head of a pier*, end farthest from land; **c** forepart of a ship; **d** *head of a cask, drum*, end uppermost at given moment; **e** the end of an object adapted for holding, handling, pressing: *head of a pin, nail, walking-stick* &c.; **f** *head of an axe*, cutting part; *head of a hammer*, part used for striking; **g** *head of a bed, bed-head*, end occupied by head of sleeper. **5.** Point or projection rising from surface of an inflammatory swelling in the flesh, when about to burst; Phrs. *to form, come to, a head*, (i.) be about to burst; (ii.) (fig., of events) *come to a head*, reach decisive or critical stage; *bring matters to a head*, produce crisis, decisive issue. **6.** Section, logical division of a subject, or of a treatise on a subject; heading: *to treat a question under several heads*. **7.** (fig.) The head considered as the seat of the mind; intelligence, intellect, reason, reasoning capacity: *a poor head for business*; *it does more credit to his heart than to his head*; Phrs. *to lose one's head*, become flustered, confused; *to keep one's head*, to preserve self-possession; *weak in the head*, of poor intelligence; imbecile; *off one's head*, (i.) excited; (ii.) deranged in intellect, mad; *two heads are better than one*, desirable to have views and advice of a second person. **8. a** Chief position, principal seat of authority and control: *at the head of affairs, of a business*; **b** seat, place, of honour, seat of person presiding: *to take the head of the table* (at dinner). Phr. *at the head of the class*, top of class. **9. a** Chief, leader, ruler, director: *head of a clan*; *head of a college*; Phr. *the Head*, (colloq.) headmaster; **b** senior member: *the head of the family*. **10.** (attrib.) Principal, chief: *head waiter* &c.

head (II.), vb. trans. & intrans., fr. prec. **A.** trans. **1.** To use the head upon, strike, touch, guide, with head; specif. (association football) *to head the ball*. **2.** To be, appear, at the head of; specif. **a** *his name headed the list*; **b** *to head a procession*. **3.** To act as head, leader, director, of: *to head a rebellion*. **4.** To guide as by the head; **a** to divert course of: *to head a crowd through the proper door*; also *head off*, to get in front of and intercept: *to head a crowd off from the wrong exit*; **b** (fig.) to divert thought, attention, from; to prevent a given action: *I headed him off (from) making a speech; to head off a person's attack* &c. **5.** (rare or techn.) To furnish a head, put a head on: *to head a pin, nail* &c. **B.** intrans. **1.** To direct one's course towards; make for, go in, a certain direction: *to head straight for the open country.* **2.** (of plants &c.) To develop, form a head; generally *head up*: *the cabbages are heading up nicely.*

-head, suff. O.E. *hād*, 'rank, condition, nature', forming common suff., becoming in M.E. (1) *-hōd*, Mod. Engl. **-hood**; (2) *-hēde, hēd*, the form of wh. is prob. due to the influence of suff. *-rēde*, Mod. Engl. *-red* as in *hatred, kindred*; or possibly to an unrecorded O.E. form w. mutation **-hǣd*. State, nature, only in *godhead, maidenhead*, 'state of virginity', and a few archaic or obs. words, as *lustihead*.

headache, n. [1. hédāk; 2. hédeik]. O.E. *hēafodece*, M.E. *hēavedeche*. See **head (I.)** & **ache**. Ache or continuous pain felt in the forehead or back of the head.

headachy, adj. [1. hédāki; 2. hédeiki]. Prec. & **-y**. **a** Suffering from, having tendency to, headache; **b** tending to cause headache: *headachy wine.*

headband, n. [1. hédband; 2. hédbænd]. Band worn round the head.

headboard, n. [1. hédbord; 2. hédbɔ̄d]. **a** Board forming, or placed at, head of structure, as bed; **b** board at head of pen, to which beast is fastened by rope.

head-boom, n. (naut.) Jib-boom or flying jib-boom.

headborough, n. [1. hédburo; 2. hédbarə]. M.E. *hēdborwe*. See **head (I.)** & **borrow**. (hist.) **a** Head of frankpledge, tithing man; hence, **b** petty constable.

headchair, n. [1. hédchār; 2. hédtʃεə]. Chair with high back and rest for head.

head-dress, n. Covering for head, esp. when ornamental or elaborate; mode of dressing the hair.

headed, adj. [1. héded; 2. hédid]. **head** & **-ed**. Having a head, usually qualified, as *blackheaded, long-headed, two-headed* &c.

header, n. [1. héder; 2. hédə]. **head** & **-er**. **1.** (rare) Person who **a** cuts off heads; **b** acts as head or leader. **2.** A dive, plunge, head first into water; a fall resembling such a plunge: *to take a header off a ladder.* **3.** A stone or brick laid across at right angles to face of a wall, as a tie or bond.

headfast, n. [1. hédfahst; 2. hédfāst]. Rope at ship's head making her fast to wharf &c.

head first, adv. With the head in front, head foremost.

head foremost, adv. Head first.

head-gate, n. Gate admitting water to lock &c.

headgear, n. [1. hédgēr; 2. hédgiə]. **a** Covering or ornament worn on head; a hat, cap &c.; **b** horse's bridle.

head-hunter, n. Member of savage tribe which collects and preserves human heads.

head-hunting, n. Custom of collecting the heads of one's enemies, and preserving them as trophies.

headily, adv. [1. hédili; 2. hédili]. **heady** & **-ly**. In a heady manner.

headiness, n. [1. hédines; 2. hédinis]. **heady** & **-ness**. Quality, condition, of being heady.

heading, n. [1. héding; 2. hédiŋ]. **head** & **-ing**. **1.** Action or process, **a** of furnishing or forming a head; **b** of directing, pointing, or turning the head (of a ship, a flock &c.); also, direction in which thing is pointed or turned; **c** of beheading or lopping; **d** (association football) of propelling ball with the head. **2.** Thing which forms or constitutes a head; specif., running title, or inscription, at head of chapter, page, or section in book &c. **3.** Brick or stone laid with one of its smaller ends outwards.

heading course, n. Course in which all the stones or bricks are laid at right angles to face of wall; course consisting of headers.

headland, n. [1. hédland; 2. hédlənd]. **head (I.)** & **land (I.)**. Cp. O.E. *hafudland*, in sense **b**. **a** Cape, esp. one rising steeply, and jutting out into sea, lake &c.; a promontory; **b** strip of unploughed land at end of ploughed field.

headless, adj. [1. hédles; 2. hédlis]. O.E. *hēafodlēas*, M.E. *hēvedlēs*. **head (I.)** & **-less**. Having no head (in various senses).

headlight, n. [1. hédlīt; 2. hédlait]. **a** Lamp fixed in front of locomotive, motor-car &c.; **b** lantern at masthead of ship.

headline, n. [1. hédlīn; 2. hédlain]. **1.** Line of print at head of page, or of chapter, section, or paragraph, in book or newspaper, giving indication of subject-matter &c. **2.** (naut.) One of ropes at head of sail, fastening it to yard.

headlong, adv. & adj. [1. hédlong; 2. hédlɔŋ]. M.E. *hēvedlinge, hēdlinge(s)*, adv.; M.H.G. *houbetlingen*; fr. **head (I.)** & O.E. advbl. suff. *-lunga, -linga* (M.E. *-linge, -linges*), formed by blending the O.E. advbl. suffs. *-ling* (as in *on bæcling*), 'backwards', & *-unga, -inga*; confused in Mod. Engl. w. the adj. *long*. Cp. **darkling**, **sidelong**. **1.** adv. **a** Head first: *to fall headlong*; **b** (fig.) rashly, impetuously, precipitately: *to rush headlong into danger.* **2.** adj. **a** Having the head in front or foremost: *a headlong fall*; **b** (rare) precipitous, steep: *a headlong rock*; **c** (fig.) precipitate, impetuous, rash, excessive, hurried.

headman, n. [1. hédman; 2. hédmæn]. O.E. *hēafodman*, 'chief, leader' &c., M.E. *hǣfedman*; cp. O.H.G. *haubitman*, Mod. Germ. *hauptmann*, 'captain'. **a** Man recognized as leader or chief in a village or other community, esp. in uncivilized or semi-civilized people; chief of tribe; **b** head worker, foreman.

headmaster, n. [1. hédmáhster; 2. hédmāstə]. Chief master, director, in a school.

headmistress, n. [1. hédmístres; 2. hédmístris]. Woman who is chief teacher in, and directress of, a school.

head-money, n. **1.** Capitation tax, poll-tax. **2.** **a** Prize-money for capture of persons at sea, reckoned at so much a head; **b** reward for producing head of enemy or proscribed person.

headmost, adj. [1. hédmōst; 2. hédmoust]. **head (I.)** & **most**. (rare) Most ahead, most to the front, foremost.

head-moulding, n. (archit.) Moulding over the head of an arch.

head note, n. See **head tone**.

headnote, n. [1. hédnōt; 2. hédnout]. Note at head of document; specif. (law) summary prefixed to law report, of rulings and, usually, principal facts connected with judicial decision.

head-on, adv. & adj. **head (I.)** & **on (II.)**. **1.** adv. (of ships, or vehicles) Head to head in collision; head first: *to strike an iceberg head-on.* **2.** adj. Occurring head to head (of collision).

headphones, n. pl. [1. hédfōnz; 2. hédfounz]. See **head (I.)** & **-phone**. In telephony, or esp. in wireless, apparatus with ear-pieces or receivers fitting on to the head.

headpiece, n. [1. hédpēs; 2. hédpīs]. **1.** **a** Covering for the head, specif., helmet or other defensive headgear; **b** headstall. **2.** **a** Head itself; **b** this considered as seat of intelligence; brain: *to have a good headpiece*; **c** person possessing intelligence. **3.** Decorative engraving or design at head of chapter or page in book.

headquarters, n. pl., often used as sing. [1. hédkwórterz; 2. hédkwɔ̄təz]. **head (I.)** & **quarter (I.)**. **1.** **a** Official residence of commander-in-chief of army, or of commander of lesser military unit; of chief of police; also of other official head of an organization; **b** central office from which any organization is directed; **c** headquarters' staff. **2.** (fig.) Best, most authoritative and reliable source of information, knowledge &c.

headquarters' staff, n. Prec. & **staff (I.)**. (mil.) Staff attached to commander-in-chief.

headrace, n. [1. hédrās; 2. hédreis]. Part of mill-race above wheel; flume supplying engine &c.

headreach, vb. intrans. & n. [1. hédrēch; 2. hédritʃ]. **head (I.)** & **reach (I.)**. (naut.) **1.** vb. Of ship, to move ahead while tacking. **2.** n. Distance travelled by head-reaching.

head register, n. Register or series of tones produced by the upper or head voice in singing or speaking.

headrest, n. [1. hédrest; 2. hédrest]. Small curved bar, fixed to back of chair, to steady the head, used by dentists, photographers &c.

headrope, n. [1. hédrōp; 2. hédroup]. **1.** Rope attached to beast's head, by which it is tethered or led. **2.** (naut.) Part of bolt rope sewn along head of sail.

headsail, n. [1. hédsāl; 2. hédseil]. (naut.) Any of the sails set forward of foremast.

head sea, n. Sea that flows or rolls directly against course of vessel.

headship, n. [1. hédship; 2. hédʃip]. **head (I.)** & **-ship**. Office, dignity, of head or chief; leading position.

headsman, n. [1. hédzman; 2. hédzmən]. **head (I.)** & **man (I.)**. **1.** One whose office it is to execute criminals by beheading. **2.** Man in command of whaling boat after whale is struck. **3.** Collier who brings coal from working to horseway.

headspring, n. [1. hédspring; 2. hédspriŋ]. **head (I.)** & **spring (II.)**. **1.** **a** Chief source of river; **b** (fig.) chief source. **2.** Gymnastic feat consisting of a leap on to the feet from a recumbent position, the head and shoulders being used in starting.

headstall, n. [1. hédstawl; 2. hédstɔ̄l]. **head (I.)** & **stall (I.)**; cp. **finger-stall**. Light leather or webbing harness, without a bit, but furnished with rings, passed over head of horse or beast, for leading, or tying it up.

headstock, n. [1. hédstok; 2. hédstɔk]. **head (I.)** & **stock (I.)**. Bearing, supporting moving part or head of machine.

head stone, n. **head (I.)** & **stone**. Chief, principal stone in foundation of a building.

headstone, n. [1. hédstōn; 2. hédstoun]. Upright stone at head of grave.

headstrong, adj. [1. hédstrong; 2. hédstrɔŋ]. **head (I.)** & **strong**. **a** Vehemently, impetuously, rashly, self-willed or obstinate; having a will uncontrolled by reason; **b** (of action) directed by or arising from a headstrong will.

head tone, n. Tone produced by head voice.

head voice, n. Quality of voice depending upon adjustment and condition of vocal chords, produced in singing or speaking in the head register; the tones of this are mostly higher in pitch than those of chest-voice.

headwater, n. [1. hédwawter; 2. hédwɔ̄tə]. (chiefly in pl.) One of streams in upper part of river-basin, which combine to form river.

headway, n. [1. hédwā; 2. hédwei]. **1.** **a** Progress, rate of progress, esp. that made by ship; **b** (fig.) progress. **2.** Clear space overhead in door, under arch, on staircase &c.

headwind, n. [1. hédwind; 2. hédwind]. Wind blowing directly against vessel's course.

headword, n. [1. hédwērd; 2. hédwə̄d]. **1.** Word used as heading in book &c.; often in heavier type. **2.** (gram.) Word forming principal element in compound.

head-work, n. **1.** Mental work, brain-work. **2.** (archit.) Figure of human or other head, or other ornament, carved on keystone.

heady, adj. [1. hédi; 2. hédi]. **head (I.)** & **-y**. **1.** Violently wilful, acting passionately or rashly on sudden impulse; ungovernable, headstrong. **2.** **a** (of alcoholic liquors) Apt to intoxicate, strong, affecting the head; inebriating; **b** (fig.) apt to disturb the judgement, tending to inflame the passions.

heal, vb. trans. & intrans. [1. hēl; 2. hīl]. O.E. *hǣlan*, M.E. *hǣlen, hēlen*; fr. Prim. O.E. **hāl-jan*, fr. Gmc. type **hailjan*, cp. O.E. *hāl*, 'whole, healthy'. See **whole** & **hale (I.)**. **A.** trans. **1.** (of physical action) **a** (archaic) To cure, restore to health: *to heal the sick*; *to heal a man of his disease*; **b** to cure (a disease, or diseased or injured part): *to* *heal diseases, injuries*; specif., to cause (a wound, sore &c.) to cicatrize: *the ointment healed his wounds.* **2. a** To restore to moral or spiritual health or peace of mind: *time heals most troubles*; **b** to make up, compose, appease: *to heal dissensions, breaches* &c. **B.** intrans. (of wounds, sores, abrasions &c.) **a** To form a skin over, cicatrize, become healthy and sound; also, *to heal up*, become completely healthy and covered by a new skin; *heal over*, to become covered by a new skin; **b** also in moral sense.

healable, adj. [1. hḗlabl; 2. hílәbl]. **heal & -able.** Capable of being healed.

heal-all, n. **1.** Universal remedy; panacea. **2.** Popular name of several plants supposed to have healing virtues, specif. **a** self-heal; **b** figwort.

heald, n. [1. hēld; 2. hīәld]. O.E. *hefeld.* Cp. **heddle.** Heddle.

healer, n. [1. hḗler; 2. hílә]. **heal & -er.** Person who heals; specif., person who professes to heal by Christian Science; faith-healer.

healing (I.), n. [1. hḗling; 2. hílíŋ]. **heal & -ing.** Action of person or thing that heals; cure, remedy.

healing (II.), adj., fr. Pres. Part. of **heal. a** Tending to heal: *a healing ointment, touch* &c.; **b** concerned with process of healing: *the healing art.*

healingly, adv. **Prec. & -ly.** In a healing manner.

health, n. [1. helth; 2. helþ]. O.E. *hǣlð*, fr. Prim. O.E. **hāl-iþu*, fr. *hāl*, 'whole, healthy', M.E. *hēlðe*; cp. O.H.G. *heilida.* See **heal, whole, & -th. 1. a** State of bodily or mental wellbeing; normal condition of mind or body in which all parts and faculties perform their functions duly, easily, satisfactorily; soundness, freedom from disease, disorder, pain, or weakness: *health of body and mind*; **b** moral or spiritual soundness or wellbeing: *the soul's health.* (theol.) state of grace. **2. a** Bodily condition, whether good or bad: *to be in good, bad, poor, ill health*; Phr. *a (clean) bill of health*; *public health*, state of health prevalent in community; **b** study or science of conditions of health; hygiene: *Ministry of Health*, government department in charge of public hygiene and other matters of local government. **3.** Healing power: *there is health in the sea-breezes and sunshine.*

healthful, adj. [1. hélthfool; 2. hélþfәl]. **Prec. & -ful. 1.** Tending to maintain, promote, or restore bodily, mental, or spiritual health or wellbeing; salubrious, salutary. **2.** Enjoying, displaying, good health; in sound condition, healthy.

healthfully, adv. **Prec. & -ly.** In a healthful manner.

healthfulness, n. See **prec. & -ness.** Quality or condition of being healthful.

health-giving, adj. [1. hélth giving; 2. hélþ givíŋ]. Tending to promote health; having quality of imparting health.

healthily, adv. [1. hélthili; 2. hélþili]. **healthy & -ly.** In a healthy manner.

healthiness, n. [1. hélthines; 2. hélþinis]. **healthy & -ness.** Healthy condition; health.

health officer, n. Officer appointed by public body to enforce regulations relating to public health.

health resort, n. Place frequented by persons desiring to improve their health, on account of its climate, waters, curative establishments &c.

healthy, adj. [1. hélthi; 2. hélþi]. **health & -y. 1. a** (of persons and living organisms generally) Having good health; in a sound, vigorous, hearty, normal condition: *a healthy infant, apple-tree, skin*; also *a healthy mind, society* &c.; **b** (of conditions, functions &c.) indicating, exhibiting, health, physical or moral: *a healthy colour, appetite*; *a healthy state of public opinion.* **2. a** Tending to promote and maintain, conducive to, physical health; wholesome, healthful, salubrious: *a healthy climate, exercise, mode of life* &c.; **b** mentally or morally wholesome; salutary: *healthy reading for the young.*

heap (I.), n. [1. hēp; 2. hīp]. O.E. *hēap*, 'troop, band, multitude, association'; M.E. *heap, heep*, 'troop, heap, number'; cogn. w. O. Fris. *hāp, hepe*, O.S. *hōp*, Du. *hoop* (cp. **forlorn hope**), O.H.G. *hufo, houf, hauf*, Germ. *haufe*; fr. Gmc. type **haub-n-az*, Aryan **koup-*, whence also Lith. *kaupas*, 'heap', Russ. *kupa*, 'heap, crowd'. For orig. sense of this base see under **head, hive, cup. 1.** Pile, mass of things lying one on the top of another; accumulation; mound: *a heap of stones, of ruins, of slain*; colloq. Phr. *struck, knocked, all of a heap*, overwhelmed; reduced suddenly to utter powerlessness. **2. a** (chiefly colloq.) Throng, crowd, collection, of persons or animals; large number of things, material or non-material: *to go to a heap of places*; *a heap of work*; *to have heaps of money*; *heaps of people*; Phrs. *heaps of times*, often; *heaps of time*, plenty of time, time to spare; **b** (often as adv.) very much: *I am heaps better.*

heap (II.), vb. trans. O.E. *hēapian*, formed fr. n., M.E. *hēpe(n).* See **prec. 1.** (also *heap up*) **a** To pile up, throw or place (together) in a heap: *to heap (up) sand*; **b** to form by piling material: *to heap up a mound*; (fig.) *to heap favours, insults, on one*; **c** (fig.) to amass, accumulate: *to heap up riches*; Phr. *to heap coals of fire on a person's head*, reward bad treatment with good. **2. a** To load, cover, fill, or encumber with a heap or heaps: *to heap a waggon with hay*; *to heap a table with books*; *the street was heaped with dead*; (fig.) to load: *to heap a person with favours*; **b** to fill (measure) so that contents rise in heap above brim: *to heap a bushel*; to pile (contents of measure): *a heaped spoonful.*

hear, vb. trans. & intrans. [1. hēr; 2. hiә], fr. O.E., non-W. Sax. *hēran* (W. Sax. form *hīeran*), M.E. *hēren*; Common Gmc., cp. O. Fris. *hōra, hēra*, O.S. *hōrian*; O.H.G. *hōrjan, hōren*, Mod. Germ. *hōren*; Goth. *hausjan* & *hausjōn*; O.N. *heyra.* Gmc. type **hauzjan-*, fr. Aryan **kous-*, whence also Gk. *akoúein*, 'to hear', fr. *-*kous-*. See **acoustic. A.** trans. **1. a** To receive an impression of sound upon auditory nerves; receive sensation of sound through the ear; to perceive sound produced by: *to hear the sound of laughter*; *to hear a loud noise*; *to hear a person speak(ing), a watch tick(ing)* &c.; Phrs. *to hear say, tell of*, to hear some one, people, say &c.; *to make one's self heard*, (fig.) obtain a hearing, secure attention to one's views &c.; **b** to be able to hear, not to be deaf to: *I hear what is said if you speak loud*; *he doesn't hear a word that is said.* **2. a** To listen to, attend to: *you had better hear what I have to say*; Phrs. *to hear a person out*, to listen to all he has to say; *to hear a child his lesson*, listen while he repeats it, test his knowledge of it; **b** (i.) to attend, be present at performance of: *to hear Mass*; (ii.) to listen to lecture or sermon given by: *to go to hear the great professors and preachers of the day*; to listen to artistic performance by: *to hear Kreisler, a famous singer* &c.; **c** to attend habitually: *to hear a course of lectures* &c.; **d** to give audience to, listen to officially: *the court heard the witnesses*; *to hear a deputation*; **e** (law) to preside at hearing of, to try: *the magistrate, judge, heard the case*; **f** to allow to speak: *you cannot be heard on that subject now*; **g** to be influenced by listening to; accede to, grant: *hear my prayer.* **3.** To learn of, be told: *you mustn't believe everything that you hear.* **4.** (obs. classicism) To be addressed as, be called: '*Or hear'st thou rather pure Ethereal stream*' (Milton, 'P.L.' iii. 7). **B.** intrans. **1.** To perceive sound; to have the ability to perceive it; to possess and exercise function of hearing: *the deaf do not hear.* **2.** Listen! take heed!; Phr. *hear! hear!*, exclamation, expressing approval of something said in speech; sometimes ironical. **3.** Specif. **a** to receive a communication by letter: *I hear from India every week*; **b** to receive information, be informed, learn, (that): *I heard that he was engaged*; also, *hear about*, be informed concerning. Phrs. *you will hear about this*, be censured for; *hear of*, to receive a report about, get news of; *I won't hear of such a thing*, won't allow, refuse to tolerate it. **4.** (obs. classicism, with adv.) To be reputed, talked of: '*Corruption, for which England hears ill abroad*' (Milton, 'Areopagitica').

hearable, adj. [1. hḗrabl; 2. híәrәbl]. **Prec. & -able.** That may or can be heard.

heard, vb. [1. hërd; 2. hǡd]. O.E. *hērde*, M.E. *herde.* Pret. & P.P. of **hear.**

hearer, n. [1. hḗrer; 2. híәrә]. **hear & -er.** One that hears; specif., auditor; one of an audience at a sermon, lecture &c.

hearing, n. [1. hḗring; 2. híәriŋ]. **hear & -ing. 1. a** (i.) Sense by which sound is perceived; (ii.) fact of perceiving sound; audition: *it was said in my hearing*; **b** audience; attention given to a speaker; opportunity of being heard: *to give one a hearing*; *to gain a hearing*; **c** action by judge or magistrate of investigating and trying a case at law, esp. without jury. **2.** Distance within which one can hear; range of hearing, earshot: *within hearing.*

hearken, vb. intrans. [1. hárken; 2. hǡkәn]. O.E. *heorcnian*, M.E. *herknien, hercnen*; related to **hark & hear.** (only liter.) **1.** To listen, hear, attend to what is said. **2.** To take heed, listen, **a** with intention of granting: *to hearken to a supplication*; or **b** of obeying: *just hearken to what you are told.*

hearkener, n. [1. hárkener; 2. hǡk(ә)nә]. **Prec. & -er.** (only liter.) Person who hearkens.

hearsay, n. [1. hḗrsā; 2. híәsei]. **hear & say (I.). a** What one hears said; report, rumour: *this is mere hearsay*; **b** (attrib.) *hearsay evidence* (law), evidence consisting of what witness has heard said, inadmissible in court of law as establishing that the statement is true, though it may prove that the statement was made.

hearse (I.), n. [1. hërs; 2. hǡs]. M.E. *herce, herse*, 'frame for candles or for pall over bier or tomb', fr. O.F. *herce*, 'harrow; frame with upright pins' (whence Fr. *herse*, 'harrow'); fr. Med. Lat. *herpica, hercia*, 'frame for candles in church', Ital. *erpice*, 'harrow', fr. Lat. *(h)irpic-*, stem of *(h)irpex*, 'harrow', perh. fr. Gk. *hárpax, harpag-*, 'thing that grips or seizes, grappling-iron', cp. Gk. *harpágē*, hook, rake'. Cp. **harpy, rehearse, & herse. 1. a** Carriage for conveyance of body to grave; **b** (poet., obs.) bier. **2.** (hist.) **a** Triangular frame resembling harrow, with spikes for candles, used in church at *Tenebrae*; frame, bearing candles, over coffin in church; **b** temporary framework over coffin bearing pall, or heraldic insignia &c.; **c** (obs.) sepulchral monument.

hearse (II.), vb. trans., fr. prec. (rare) To place in a hearse.

hearse-cloth, n. **hearse (I.) & cloth.** Pall.

heart (I.), n. [1. hart; 2. hǡt]. O.E. *heorte*, fem., M.E. *heorte, herte*; Common Gmc., cp. O. Fris. *herte, hirte*, O.S. *herta*; O.H.G. *herza*, Mod. Germ. *herz*; Goth. *hairtō*; O.N. *hjarta*; fr. Gmc. **hertōn-*, orig. neut. fr. Aryan **k̑erd-* &c., whence also Lat. *cord-*, base of *cor*, 'heart' (see **cordate**); Gk. *kradiē, kardiā*; O. Slav. *srŭd-itse.* **1.** Hollow muscular organ in animal body, which by rhythmical contractions propels blood through arteries and veins. Phrs. *smoker's heart*, weakness of heart caused by smoking; *to do the heart good, rejoice the heart*, give great joy to; *to wear one's heart on one's sleeve*, proclaim one's feelings openly; *to have the heart in the right place*, to have true, kind, humane, feelings; *(my) heart leaps up*, throbs or bounds with joy; *to have one's heart in one's mouth*, to be startled, suddenly terrified; *one's heart sinks* (colloq., *into one's boots*), one feels suddenly dismayed or discouraged; *one's heart leaps into one's mouth.* **2.** The heart considered as the seat or organ of emotions or moral and mental qualities; a inmost, deepest part of one's nature; soul, consciousness, conscience; Phrs. *change of heart*, (theol.) conversion, regeneration; *from one's heart*, in perfect sincerity, with the deepest feeling; *in one's heart* (*of hearts*), in the depths of one's soul; *heart and soul*, with all one's energies engaged, enthusiastically; *to lay, take, to heart*, accept and profit by (advice, reproof &c.); *take to heart*, also, to grieve over, feel strongly about; *a new heart*, (theol.) regenerate nature; *to search the heart*, search for, examine, ultimate motives; b vital energy, zeal, ardour, courage, fortitude; Phrs. *in* (*good*) *heart*, in state of confidence, cheerfulness, courage; *to lose heart*, to become depressed, faint-hearted, timid; *out of heart*, discouraged; *to pluck up heart*, to take courage, be emboldened; *to take heart*, to summon up courage, feel more confident; *to take heart of grace*, to pluck up courage to act; c emotional nature; temperament, sensibility, the affections, intimate feelings: *a hard, stony, tender, heart*; *a heart of flint*; Phrs. *to move, stir, touch, the heart*; *to set one's heart at rest*; *to steel the heart*; *to break the heart*, to crush with grief; to cause profound sorrow: *to die of a broken heart*; *to cry one's heart out*, to weep bitterly and without restraint; *to devour one's heart, eat one's heart out*, to pine, brood, over one's grief, to grieve bitterly in secret; *to find it in one's heart to do a thing*, to be inclined to do it; *not to have the heart to do a thing*, to be too tender-hearted to do it; *to have* (*plenty of*) *heart*, to have humane feelings; *a man of heart*, a humane man; *heart of gold*, a sincere, kindly, unselfish nature; *heart and hand*, with goodwill and energy; *heart-to-heart*, intimate(ly), without reservations or reticences: *a heart-to-heart talk*; *to speak to the heart*, to appeal to, stir, the deeper feelings; *to take to heart*, to grieve over, be greatly affected by; Phrs. *an affair of the heart*, love affair; *after one's* (*own*) *heart*, according to one's desire, such as one can love; *to give one's heart to*, to bestow one's love on; *to have at heart*, to be devoted to, deeply interested in; *to one's heart's content*, to the full extent of one's desire; *to lose one's heart to*, to fall in love with; *near one's heart*, very dear to one; *to set one's heart on*, to make the object of one's desire; *to steal one's heart*, to capture one's affection; *to win one's heart*, to gain one's love; (*to love*) *with all one's heart*, with the full strength of one's affections; d intellect, understanding, mind; memory; Phrs. *at the bottom of one's heart* (*one knows* &c.), in the depths of one's mind; (*to get, know, learn, say*) *by heart*, by memory, by rote. 3. Inmost part, centre, core; (in material sense) a dense part in centre of vegetable growth: *heart of a tree, of timber*; *heart of a cabbage, lettuce* &c.; Phr. *heart of oak*, (i.) oak timber of toughest kind from centre of trunk; (ii.) (fig.) man of strong, resolute character; b central area, interior, of a region, country &c.: *in the heart of Africa*; Phr. *the heart of the country*, remote, rural spot or area; c (of non-material things) the most fundamental, important, essential part; essence; inner meaning: *the heart of a mystery, problem, subject*; *to go to the heart of matters*. 4. Applied to persons, a as term of endearment: *dearest heart*; b courageous, spirited person: *a noble, gallant, heart*. 5. a Fertility of soil: *the field is out of heart*; b condition of soil: *in good heart, poor heart*. 6. Representation of a heart; heart-shaped object; specif. a conventional figure with two lobes, representing a heart; ornament or other object of this shape; b kinds of cherry: *a white, black, heart*; c heart-shaped figure on playing-cards; *hearts*, the red suit bearing this figure.

heart (II.), vb. intrans., fr. prec. (3. a). (of certain vegetables) Usually *heart up*, to form a heart: *the lettuces are hearting up well*.

heart-ache, n. Continuous mental or emotional distress; sorrow, anguish.

heart-beat, n. Pulsation of the heart; throb.

heart-blood, n. Heart's-blood (q.v.).

heart bond, n. (building) Bond consisting of two headers placed in one line, and third over their joint.

heartbreak, n. [1. hártbrāk; 2. hátbreik]. Sorrow that breaks the heart; overwhelming grief.

heartbreaker, n. [1. hártbrāker; 2. hátbreikə]. Person or thing that breaks hearts; specif., a ruthless coquette.

heartbreaking, adj. [1. hártbrāking; 2. hátbreikiŋ]. Causing the heart to break; producing acute sorrow; (colloq.) tedious; causing boredom or fatigue: *a heartbreaking job*.

heartbroken, adj. [1. hártbrōken; 2. hátbroukən]. Having a broken heart; deeply wounded, overwhelmed by grief.

heartburn, n. [1. hártbërn; 2. hátbʌ̄n], fr. an obs. vb. *heartburn*, 'to affect with heart-burning'. Burning sensation, caused by acidity of the stomach; formerly referred to region of the heart.

heartburning, n. [1. hártbërning; 2. hátbʌ̄niŋ]. Prec. & **-ing**. (often pl.) Envious, discontented feeling, esp. one due to secret disappointment.

heart cherry, n. One of several kinds of sweet cherry, as *black heart, white heart*; so called from the shape.

heart disease, n. Any organic or functional malady of the heart.

heart-easing, adj. [1. hárt ēzing; 2. hát īziŋ]. Giving ease to the heart; consoling, yielding relief.

-hearted, adj. [1. hárted; 2. hátid]. Only in composition, preceded by adj.: *faint-hearted*.

hearten, vb. trans. & intrans. [1. hárt(e)n; 2. hát(ə)n]. **heart** (I.) & **-en**. 1. trans. To give heart to, cheer up, encourage; also *hearten up*. 2. intrans. (rare) To take courage.

heartfelt, adj. [1. hártfelt; 2. hátfelt]. Deeply, sincerely, felt.

heart-free, adj. Having the affections disengaged; not being in love.

hearth, n. [1. harth; 2. hāþ]. O.E. *heorð*, M.E. *herð*; cogn. w. O. Fris. *herth*, O.H.G. *hert, herd*, Mod. Germ. *herd*; fr. Gmc. type **herđaz*; cp. Goth. *haúri*, 'coal', for **huri-*, O.N. *hyr-r*, 'embers'; fr. Aryan **ker-* &c., 'burn', whence also Lat. *carbo*, 'charred wood, embers' (see **carbon**), & *cremāre*, 'to burn' (see **cremate**). 1. a Hard, flat stone surface beneath fireplace, or on which fire is made; b floor of smith's or other furnace; *open hearth*, bottom of a blast-furnace in which the ore is exposed directly to the flame, hence 'open-hearth steel', made in such furnace. 2. (fig.) This considered as centre of home life; fireside, home, domestic circle: *to fight for hearth and altar*; *hearth and home*.

hearth-brush, n. Brush for sweeping hearth.

hearth-money, n. Former English tax on hearths.

hearth-rug, n. Rug or thick mat spread on the floor of a room before the hearth.

hearthstone, n. [1. hárthstōn; 2. háþstoun]. 1. Slab of stone forming hearth. 2. Soft kind of stone, or composition, rubbed with water over hearth, doorstep &c. to whiten them.

heartily, adv. [1. hártili; 2. hátili]. **hearty** & **-ly**. In a hearty manner; cordially; sincerely; vigorously.

heartiness, n. [1. hártines; 2. hátinis]. **heart** & **-ness**. State or quality of being hearty.

heartless, adj. [1. hártles; 2. hátlis]. O.E. *heortlēas*, M.E. *hertelēs*, fr. **heart** (I.) & **-less**. Having no heart (only in fig. sense); specif. a unfeeling, callous, cruel: *a heartless man*; b (of actions &c.) exhibiting, indicating, these qualities: *a heartless speech, bargain, fraud* &c.

heartlessly, adv. Prec. & **-ly**. In a heartless manner.

heartlessness, n. See prec. & **-ness**. Quality of being heartless.

heart-rending, adj. [1. hárt rending; 2. hát rendiŋ]. **heart** (I.) & **rend**. Causing vehement grief; intensely distressing; grievous.

heart-rot, n. Fungoid disease of tree, causing heart-wood to decay.

heart's-blood, n. a (rare) Blood in or flowing from heart; b (fig.) (i.) life; (ii.) deepest feelings; (iii.) most precious possession.

heart-searching, adj. Trying, testing, the thoughts, desires, motives.

heartsease, n. [1. hártsēz; 2. hátsīz]. **heart** (I.) & **ease** (I.). 1. (obs.) Tranquillity or peace of mind. 2. a Common wild pansy (*Viola tricolor*), a preparation of which was supposed to cure pangs of love; b one of many cultivated varieties of pansy.

heart-shaped, adj. Having approximately the form of a heart, or of its conventional representation.

heart-sick, adj. Greatly depressed in spirits; deeply wounded in the affections.

heart-sickness, n. Prec. & **-ness**. State of being heartsick.

heartsome, adj. [1. hártsum; 2. hátsəm]. **heart** (I.) & **-some**. (rare, chiefly Scots) Cheering, enlivening; cheerful, merry.

heart-sore, n. & adj. M.E. *heortesōr*. a n. Sorrow or grief of heart; b adj., sore at heart; feeling aggrieved.

heartstricken, adj. [1. hártstriken; 2. hátstrikən]. Stricken to the heart; wounded in the affections; oppressed with grief.

heart-string, n. a Tendon formerly believed to brace the heart; b (chiefly pl.) deepest affections or feelings; Phr. *to pull at one's heart-strings*, to stir one's deepest feelings.

heart-whole, adj. 1. Having, keeping, the heart or affections unmoved by love for one of opposite sex. 2. Whole-hearted, devoted to one object.

heart-wood, n. Hard wood in centre of tree-trunk; wood of the heart of a tree; duramen.

hearty, adj. [1. hárti; 2. háti]. M.E. *herti*, fr. **heart** (I.) & **-y**. Pertaining to, proceeding from, the heart (in fig. senses). 1. a Vigorous, healthy, robust; lusty, spirited: *a hearty fellow*; also as noun: *my hearties*, stout fellows; b indicating, proceeding from, vigour or strong vitality: *a hearty appetite, meal*. 2. Sincerely and deeply felt; cordial: *hearty approval, dislike, detestation, support*. 3. Warm-hearted, genial, affectionate, friendly: *a hearty welcome, cheer*. 4. (of land) Fertile, in good heart.

heat (I.), n. [1. hēt; 2. hīt]. O.E. *hǣtu* &c. (fr. earlier **hāti-*), M.E. *hēte*, cogn. w. O. Fris. *hēte*, O.S. *hēt*; O.H.G. *heizi*, fr. Gmc. **haiti-*, whence also, without mutation, O.E. *hāt*, q.v. under **hot**. The Gmc. type is fr. Aryan **kaid-*, whence Lat. *caelum*, fr. **kaidlom*, 'sky, heavens'. See **ceiling**. The original sense of the base appears to be 'bright, shining, glowing'. 1. (phys.) Formerly regarded as an independent substance, now held to be a form of energy associated with molecular agitation: *latent heat*; *radiant heat*. 2. (ordinary use) A condition of material substances accompanied, and characterized, by high temperature; warmth, hotness, reverse of cold: *the heat of the sun, the weather, day* &c. 3. This condition of external bodies as perceived by the sense of touch; sensation of burning, or of considerable warmth produced by contact with, or proximity to, bodies containing heat: *to bask in, enjoy, the heat*. 4. Sensation resembling burning produced by certain substances such as mustard, pepper, and other condiments upon sense of taste. 5. Condition of animal body arising from high, or too high, temperature in the blood; feverish, inflammatory condition of the body: *his face was flushed with sudden heats*. 6. Degree of heat, in any of above senses: *the heat of the sun, blood* &c.; *red, white, heat* &c. 7. Appetence in female mammals; period of duration of this. An animal in this condition is said to be *on heat*. 8. (in moral sense) Strong, vehement feeling; fierceness; a fervour, ardour, impetuosity: *the heat of an attack*; *the heat of eloquence*; b vehemence of temper;

indignation, anger, ruffled feelings: *to repel an accusation with some heat*; *the heat of argument, controversy* &c. **9.** Action performed in a single burst or effort; specif. (athletics) single part, stage, round, of a contest, the object of which is to eliminate all but the best competitors from the final trial or test: *the preliminary heats, the final heat,* in a race &c.

heat (II.), vb. trans. & intrans. O.E. *hǣtan*, M.E. *hēten* &c. See prec. & cp. **hot. 1.** trans. To make hot; **a** (i.) *to heat an iron, some water*; *to heat oneself by running* &c.; (ii.) *heat up*, bring to a high degree of heat; esp. of something grown cold: *heat up the cold mutton*; **b** (in moral sense) chiefly pass., to excite, inflame, animate; irritate, make angry: *heated with dispute, argument, battle*; *heated by opposition*; *heated with wine* &c. **2.** intrans. To become hot (rare in moral sense).

heat apoplexy, n. **heat** (I.) & **apoplexy.** Sunstroke.

heated, adj. [1. hḗted; 2. hītid]. **heat** (II.) & **-ed. 1.** Made hot, warmed up. **2. a** (of the mind) Excited, inflamed: *a heated imagination, brain*; **b** accompanied by passion, strong feeling, anger: *a heated discussion.*

heatedly, adv. [1. hḗtedli; 2. hītidli]. Prec. & **-ly.** In a heated manner.

heat-engine, n. **heat** (I.) & **engine.** Any kind of engine that converts heat into mechanical energy, as steam-engine, petrol motor &c.

heater, n. [1. hḗter; 2. hītə]. **heat** (II.) & **-er.** One of various devices for heating, warming up, food, rooms &c.

heath, n. [1. hēth; 2. hīþ]. O.E. *hǣð*, fem., 'waste land, heath plant', M.E. *hēðe*; cogn. w. O.H.G. *heida*, Mod. Germ., & Du. *heide*, Goth. *háiþi*, 'waste place'; O.N. *heið-r*; fr. Gmc. type **haiðjō-*; perh. cogn. w. Gaulish **cētum* in Lat. *bū-cētum*, 'cow pasture', W. *coed*, 'wood', fr. Aryan base **koit-*. **1.** Tract of waste land, moor; esp. barren land overgrown with any kind of heath. **2.** Any plant or species of an Old World genus, *Erica*, of narrow-leaved, tough-stemmed, herbaceous or shrubby plants, with numerous small white, purple, or pink bell-shaped flowers, esp. the common ling, *Calluna vulgaris*, and the purple heather, *Erica cinerea.*

heath-berry, n. **heath** & **berry.** Any small berry-bearing plant commonly growing on heaths or moors, as whortleberry, cranberry, crowberry; fruit of same.

heath-cock, n. **heath** & **cock** (I.). Blackcock, male of black grouse.

heathen (I.), n. [1. hḗdhen; 2. hīðən]. O.E. *hǣðen*, *hǣðena*, M.E. *hēðen-*, Common Gmc.; cp. O. Fris. *hēthen*, O.S. *hēðin*; O.H.G. *heidan*; O.N. *heiðin-n*; prob. fr. **heath. 1.** In the Old Testament (in pl., translating Heb. *goyyim*) applied to all nations and races other than the Jews; hence those who worship other gods than the God of Israel. **2. a** At present chiefly applied to believer in, worshipper of, the gods of savage tribes; or to adherent of any other religion than Christianity, Judaism, Hinduism, Mohammedanism; irreligious person, infidel: *we don't want our children to grow up heathens*; **b** (colloq.) person of outlandish or uncivilized habits.

heathen (II.), adj. Same as prec. **a** Pertaining to a heathen or the heathen: *a heathen man, temple, rite*; **b** irreligious; **c** (colloq.) barbarous, outlandish.

heathendom, n. [1. hḗdhendum; 2. hīðəndəm]. O.E. *hǣðendōm*, M.E. *heaðendom*, 'paganism'. See **heathen** (I.) & **-dom. 1.** (coll.) The heathen; the heathen parts of the world. **2.** (archaic) Paganism, heathen religion.

heathenesse, n. [1. hḗdhenés; 2. hīðənés]. O.E. *hǣþen-nes*, 'paganism; district inhabited by heathens'. (archaic) Used by Tennyson in sense of regions inhabited by the heathen. Probably a new coinage w. **-ess**, and not derived direct from old word.

heathenish, adj. [1. hḗdhenish; 2. hīð(ə)niʃ]. O.E. *hǣðenisc*, fr. **heathen** & **-ish**; cp. O.H.G. *heidanisc*, Germ. *heidnisch.* **a** Pertaining to the heathen, characteristic of heathen peoples or religions; **b** unchristian, barbarous, outlandish.

heathenishly, adv. Prec. & **-ly.** In a heathenish manner.

heathenishness, n. See prec. & **-ness.** Condition, quality, of being heathenish.

heathenism, n. [1. hḗdhenizm; 2. hīðənizəm]. **heathen** (II.) & **-ism. 1.** Religion or religious practices of heathen; paganism. **2. a** Disregard of religion, condition of being without a religion; **b** barbarism, barbarity.

heathenize, vb. trans. [1. hḗdheniz; 2. hīðənaiz]. **heathen** (II.) & **-ize.** To render heathen.

heathenry, n. [1. hḗdhenri; 2. hīðənri]. **heathen** (II.) & **-ry. 1.** State or character of the heathen; heathenism. **2.** Heathendom, the heathen world.

heather, n. [1. hédher; 2. héðə]. M.E. (Scots) *haddyr*, Early Mod. Engl. *hadder*, later altered through influence of **heath**, relation to wh. is obscure. There seems to be an O.E. formative suff. *-re* in plant-names, e.g. *ampre, clāfre, mædere*; M.E. *doder.* See **clover. a** Plant of heath family, esp. *Calluna vulgaris*, with very small light-purplish flowers, common heath, ling; or purple heath, *Erica cinerea*; **b** expanse of moor covered with it. Phrs. *to set the heather on fire*, to make a disturbance; *to take to the heather*, to become an outlaw (in Scottish mountains).

heather ale, n. Kind of ale flavoured with flowers of heather, formerly brewed in Scotland.

heather bell, n. Bell-shaped flowers of the heather.

heather mixture, n. Woollen fabric woven of threads of various colours, producing speckled effect somewhat like that of heather.

heather tweed, n. Tweed cloth consisting of heather mixture.

heathery, adj. [1. hédheri; 2. héðəri]. **heather** & **-y.** Abounding in, or covered with, heather.

heath-fowl, n. **heath** & **fowl** (I.). Black grouse.

heath-game, n. **heath** & **game** (I.). Black grouse.

heath-hen, n. **heath** & **hen.** Hen of black grouse; grey hen.

heath-pea, n. **heath** & **pea.** Kind of wild pea with small edible tubers.

heathy, adj. [1. hḗthi; 2. hīþi]. **heath** & **-y.** Pertaining to, resembling, covered with, heather; abounding in heath or moor.

heating, vbl. n. & adj. [1. hḗting; 2. hītiŋ]. **a heat** (II.) & **-ing**; **b** fr. Pres. Part. of **heat** (II.). **a** n. Method of warming a building: *the heating of the church is very imperfect*; **b** adj., tending to promote heat: *a heating drink*; *maize is too heating for hens in summer.*

heat lightning, n. Distant sheet lightning, seen by reflection from clouds; summer lightning.

heat ray, n. Ray producing effects of heat; used formerly esp. of ray near the red end of spectrum.

heat spot, n. **1.** Sensory organ in skin, consisting of end of nerve, sensitive to heat. **2.** Pimple, slight skin-eruption, supposed popularly to be produced by heat.

heat stroke, n. Attack of prostration, with various symptoms such as unconsciousness and fever, syncope; slight apoplectic attack, caused by exposure to excessive heat.

heat tone, n. Quantity of heat produced by chemical reaction.

heat unit, n. Unit in quantitative measurement of heat; thermal unit, calorie.

heat wave, n. **1.** Undulation of ether in radiant heat. **2.** Supposed movement of hot weather across part of earth's surface; resulting period of heat in a particular region.

heaume, n. [1. hōm; 2. houm]. Fr., fr. O. Fr. *helme*, fr. Gmc. source. See **helm** (II.). Large, heavy, mediaeval helmet, completely covering head, and often resting on shoulders, much used in tilting.

heave (I.), vb. trans. & intrans. [1. hēv; 2. hīv]. Pret. & P.P. in naut. senses *hove.* O.E. *hebban* (*hef-*), M.E. *hebben, haben, heven*, orig. a strong vb. of *a-ō* type, but wk. forms appear already in late O.E.; & both strong & wk. Pret. & P.P. appear in M.E. Common Gmc., cp. O. Fris. *heva*, O.S. *hebbian*, M. Du. *haven*, Du. *heffen*, O.H.G. *heffan*, M.H.G. *heben, haben*, Mod. Germ. *heben*, Goth. *hafjan*, O.N. *hefja* &c. The Mod. Engl. Pret. *hove* is not lineal descendant of O.E. *hōf*, wh. wd. give **hoof*, **hoove*, but is either formed on anal. of *broke, bore* &c., or borrowed fr. a L.G. source. Gmc. base **hað-*, **hōð-*, Aryan base **kəp-*, **kēp-*, **kōp-*, wh. appear in Lat. *capere* (*capio*), Pret. *cēpi*, 'to take', Gk. *kṓpē*, 'handle'. See further under **captive, haft. A.** trans. **1. a** To raise, lift; swing with movements of the arms: *to heave an axe*; **b** to lift, haul, drag, or push up with effort: *to heave the anchor*; **c** to cause to rise or swell: *the wind heaves the waves*; *to heave one's chest, bosom, breast*; Phr. *to heave the gorge*, to retch; **d** to emit (sound) from chest as if with effort or pain: *to heave a sigh, a groan.* **2. a** (of heavy weights and bulky objects) To move, shift, propel, upward and forward, or in any direction, with effort: *to heave coal*; **b** (naut.) to move by hauling rope or cable; to haul in (cable &c.): *to heave a line taut*; hence, to move (ship &c.) by engines or any method: *to heave a ship ahead, astern.* In numerous nautical Phrs., e.g. *to heave a ship apeak*, to haul her forward at anchor until cable is nearly vertical; *to heave a ship down*, to careen her; *to heave keel out*, to careen ship until keel is out of water; *to heave out sail*, to unfurl it; *to heave a ship to*, to stop her headway, by bringing her into wind &c. **3.** (naut. and colloq.) To throw, cast, hurl: *to heave the lead, the log*; *to heave a brick.* **4.** (geol.) To fracture and displace (stratum or vein). **B.** intrans. **1. a** To rise, esp. slowly or laboriously; **b** to rise with rhythmical movement as of waves, to swell: *the billows heave*; *one's bosom heaves* (with sobs, sighs &c.); **c** to suffer from spasmodic, convulsive, movements of the throat and stomach, as with nausea; to retch; **d** (fig.) to make strenuous or convulsive efforts, as if struggling to throw off weight or burden; **e** (poet., of the ground) to roll, swell, undulate, form mounds: '*Where heaves the turf in many a mouldering heap*' (Gray). **2.** (naut.) **a** To haul rope or cable, by hand or with windlass or capstan; Phr. *heave away, heave ho!*, seamen's call to heave; **b** (of ship) to be moved, by hauling or otherwise, to proceed, draw: *the ship hove alongside*; *she hove out of the harbour.* Phrs. *to heave down*, to be careened; *to heave in sight*, to come into view above horizon (of approaching ships, and by extension, of other moving or fixed objects); *to heave to*, to be hove to.

heave (II.), n., fr. prec. **1. a** Action of heaving, lifting, or hauling with effort; effort to raise weight; **b** upward movement, process of swelling: *the heave of the sea*; **c** heaving of stomach; retching. **2.** (geol., min.) Amount of displacement caused by fault in stratum or vein, measured horizontally. **3.** Kind of throw in wrestling. **4.** (pl.) *The heaves*, (veter.) lung disorder of horse, a kind of asthma; emphysema, broken wind.

heaven (I.), n. [1. hévn; 2. hévn]. O.E. *heofon, hiofon, hefon*, masc., also *heofene* fem., M.E. *heovene, heven*; O.S. *heban, heben*, L.G. *heben, heven*, O.N. *hifin-n.* Origin unknown; connexion w. **heave** (I.), or w. the other Gmc. names for heaven, viz. (1) Goth. *himin-s*, O.N. *himin-n*, (2) O. Fris. *himul*, O.S., O.H.G. *himil*, Germ. *himmel*, is doubtful. **1.** (chiefly liter.) **a** The apparent blue vault or dome spread over the earth; the firmament, sky: '*hills whose heads touch heaven*' (Shakespeare, 'Oth.', I. iii. 141); '*the floor of heaven*' (Shakespeare, 'M. Ven.', V. i. 58); '*the starry cope of heaven*' (Milton, 'P.L.', iv. 992); Phr. *the eye of heaven*, the sun; **b** the open space above the earth, apparently enclosed by the dome of heaven: *the winds, clouds, fowls, of heaven*; *rain* *from heaven*; **c** part of sky over a region, climate, clime: *Italy has a brighter heaven than ours*; **d** canopy with stars, over stage. **2.** (obs. or hist.) Any one of the concentric spheres (often seven or nine) in which, according to Ptolemaic astronomy, the heavenly bodies are fixed. Phrs. *the seventh heaven, the heaven of heavens*, (Bib.) the highest of the heavens; (fig.) *seventh heaven of delight*, state of greatest happiness. **3.** (often pl.) The expanse in which the earth, planets, sun, and stars move, the interstellar space, physical universe: *to search the heavens with a telescope*; *the starry heavens*. **4. a** The abode of a god or of a class of spiritual beings; in some religions regarded as one of many: *the Buddhist heavens*; **b** (in Jewish and Christian theology) Paradise, the abode of God, of angels, and (after the Judgement or, according to some, after death) of the redeemed, regarded either as a place where God's glory is immediately manifest, or as a state of eternal life, perfection, and supreme bliss; the immediate presence of God: '*Heaven lies about us in our infancy*' (Wordsworth); Phrs. *to go to heaven*, to die; *in heaven*, dead; **c** (coll.) the inhabitants of heaven: *all heaven rejoices*. **5.** (fig.) **a** State of extreme felicity or blessedness, ecstatic bliss: *a heaven on earth*; '*to be young was very heaven*' (Wordsworth); perfection of goodness or love: '*heaven in her eye*' (Milton); '*love is heaven and heaven is love*' (Scott, 'Last Minstrel'); **b** the sublimest height of imagination: '*the brightest heaven of invention*' (Shakespeare, 'Henry V.', Prol. 2). **6. a** (transf., usually cap.) God, Providence: *the will, decrees, justice of Heaven*; *would to Heaven*; *Heaven forbid*; (in pl.) the supernal powers, the gods; **b** (in oaths) *by Heaven!*; in exclamations of surprise or pity: *good Heavens!*; *gracious Heavens!*

heaven (II.), vb. trans., fr. prec. (rare) To place in heaven or in bliss; to make blessed.

heaven-born, adj. **heaven** (I.) & **born.** Produced or originating in heaven; of heavenly descent.

heavenliness, n. [1. hévnlines; 2. hévnlinis]. Next word & **-ness.** Quality or condition of being heavenly.

heavenly (I.), adj. [1. hévnli; 2. hévnli]. O.E. *heofonlič*, M.E. *hevenlīch*; fr. **heaven** (I.) & **-ly. 1.** Pertaining to, situated in, proceeding from, or resembling heaven; celestial; **a** of the physical heavens, interstellar space, or sky: *heavenly influence*; Phr. *heavenly body*, a star, planet, comet &c.; **b** connected with, coming from, heaven considered as the abode of God or the gods: *a heavenly angel, spirit, vision*; *the heavenly kingdom*; Phr. *the heavenly city, the heavenly Jerusalem*, the new Jerusalem, described in Rev. xxi. as coming down from heaven. **2. a** Transcendently or divinely good, holy; inspired by, or aspiring to, heaven: *a heavenly mind, heavenly thoughts*; **b** of more than earthly beauty or glory; **c** (colloq.) supremely, or intensely, delightful; causing, characterized by, great pleasure; highly enjoyable; delicious, blissful.

heavenly (II.), adv. **heaven** (I.) & **-ly.** Cp. O.E. *heofonlīče*. (archaic) In a heavenly manner; by the act of heaven.

heavenly minded, adj. Prec. & **minded.** Having the mind and aspirations directed to heavenly things; holy.

heavenly mindedness, n. Quality of being heavenly minded.

heavenward, heavenwards, adv. & adj. [1. hévnward(z); 2. hévnwəd(z)]. M.E. *heveneward*, adv. **heaven** (I.) & **-ward. a** adv. Towards heaven; **b** adj., *heavenward*, advancing towards heaven: *the heavenward journey*.

heave-offering, n. **heave** (I.) & **offering.** (Mosaic law) Contribution to maintenance of priest, priestly due, 'heaved' or lifted out of rest of offering, as tenth part of tithe; shoulder or thigh of animal offered in sacrifice.

heaver, n. [1. hḗver; 2. hívə]. **heave** (I.) & **-er. 1.** Person who heaves or moves heavy goods. **2.** (naut.) Lever for twisting rope &c.

heavily, adv. [1. hévili; 2. hévili]. O.E. *hefiglīce*, M.E. *heviliche, -ly*, fr. **heavy** (I.) & **-ly.** In a heavy manner; ponderously, weightily. **1.** With weight, with heavy pressure: *a heavily loaded waggon*; *to press, weigh, fall, heavily*. **2.** (fig.) **a** As if supporting or moving a heavy weight; slowly and laboriously: *to move, drag, heavily*; **b** in a burdensome, grievous, oppressive manner: *anxiety presses heavily on me*; *food taxes fall heavily on the poor*; **c** to a high degree; severely: *to be punished, fined, heavily*; *to suffer heavily* (chiefly of financial losses); **d** (archaic) gloomily, dejectedly, sorrowfully.

heaviness, n. [1. hévines; 2. hévinis]. O.E. *hefigness*, M.E. *hevinesse*, fr. **heavy** (I.) & **-ness.** Quality or condition of being heavy. **1.** (of physical weight). **2.** (fig.) **a** Languor, inertness, sluggishness, torpor, dullness; **b** clumsiness, lack of grace or lightness: *heaviness of movement*; **c** oppression, grievousness; **d** depression, grief: *heaviness of heart*.

heaving, n. [1. hḗving; 2. híviŋ]. O.E. *hefung*, fr. **heave** (I.) & **-ing.** Action or process of lifting, propelling, or throwing with effort; specif. **a** (archaic or hist.) former English custom of lifting or tossing aloft persons of opposite sex on Easter Monday or Tuesday, in allusion to the Resurrection; hence (attrib.) *heaving day, Monday, Tuesday*; **b** (attrib. in naut. phrs.) *heaving line*, light line to which hawser or other heavy line is attached, thrown to or from ship to establish connexion with wharf &c.; *heaving line bend*, clove hitch.

Heaviside layer, n. [1. hévisīd lāer; 2. hévisaid léiə], fr. A. W. Heaviside, British physicist, d. 1923. Theoretical layer of ionized particles, from 50 to 100 miles above the earth, acting as a reflector of wireless waves and compelling them to follow the contour of the earth.

heavy (I.), adj. [1. hévi; 2. hévi]. O.E. *hefiġ*, M.E. *hĕvi*, O.S. *hebig*, O.H.G. *hebīc, hevīg*. Cp. O.E. *hefe*, 'a weight'. All these represent Gmc. **habīg*, the base being the same as in **heave** (I.). **1.** (of material things) **a** Possessing weight; weighty, ponderous, difficult to lift or to move; having high specific gravity, as gold, lead; (opposite of *light*) *a heavy load, too heavy to lift*; Phr. (fig.) *to have a heavy hand*, (i.) to be clumsy, unskilful; (ii.) to be severe, inclined to punish harshly; **b** specif., *heavy guns, artillery*, of the largest class; *heavy cavalry*, consisting of heavy men and horses; *heavy brigade*, one heavily armed; Phrs. (fig.) *heavy guns, artillery*, overwhelming, conclusive, facts or arguments; *heavy metal*, (of persons) possessing moral or intellectual weight; (colloq.) *a heavy swell*, man who from magnificence of his dress, or loftiness of bearing appears (or is) a person of importance and distinction; **c** (as n., pl.) *the Heavies*, Dragoon Guards. **2. a** (fig.) Burdensome, oppressive, grievous, hard to bear, exacting: *heavy task, work*; causing sorrow, lamentable: *heavy tidings*; severe, dangerous: *a heavy wound*; **b** overwhelming, delivered with force, violent, producing physical shock: *a heavy blow*; *a heavy fall*. **3.** (of mental and moral effect) Depressed, borne down, filled, with sorrow; sad: *a heavy heart*. **4.** (of various physical conditions suggestive of weight) **a** (of the sky) Overcast, lowering; **b** (of food generally) rich, indigestible; **c** (of bread &c.) imperfectly aerated, doughy; **d** (of drink) thick, loaded with alcohol; **e** (of land, soil) stiff, clayey, hard to work; **f** (of a road) having a soft, sticky surface, making travelling difficult; **g** (of odours) penetrating, not easily dispelled, clinging. **5. a** Clumsy, lumbering: without spring (of gait and movements): *a heavy tread*; **b** (of mental processes) slow, dull; lacking animation and sprightliness: *a heavy type of wit*; Phr. (of persons) *to be heavy on hand*, sticky in conversation, a bore; **c** (theatr.) serious, solemn, pompous, sententious: *the part of heavy father*; **d** (arts) over-ornamented, lacking lightness and grace, ponderous: *heavy style of architecture*; **e** (of writing and writers) dull: *a heavy style*; *a heavy book, author*; **f** (of physiological states) languid, lethargic, inert; torpid: *heavy with sleep, with wine*; *to look, feel, heavy*.

heavy (II.), adv. See prec. Cp. O.E. *hefiġe*. Heavily. In composition, as *heavy-laden*, and in a few phrases, as: *to lie heavy on*, to press heavily on; *to find time hang heavy on one's hands*, not to know what to do with one's time, oneself.

heavy (III.), adj. [1. hḗvi; 2. hívi]. **heave** (II.) 4 & **-y.** (veter.) Affected by the heaves.

heavy-armed, adj. (of troops) Carrying heavy weapons; wearing heavy armour.

heavy-browed, adj. [1. hévi broud; 2. hévi braud]. Having heavy, overhanging, or frowning brows.

heavy-handed, adj. Acting with a heavy hand; specif. **a** lacking lightness and fineness of touch; awkward, clumsy, unskilful; **b** oppressive, tyrannical.

heavy-hearted, adj. Filled with grief, or anxiety; dejected, sad.

heavyish, adj. [1. héviish; 2. hévi-iʃ]. **heavy** (I.) & **-ish.** Rather heavy.

heavy-laden, adj. Bearing a heavy load; oppressed, afflicted.

heavy-spar, n. **heavy** (I.) & **spar** (II.). Native sulphate of barium; also called barite.

heavy-weight, n. Person or animal of more than the average weight, esp. a heavy jockey or wrestler; boxer weighing more than 11 st. 4 lb., one between this weight and 12 st. 7 lb. being sometimes called a *light heavy-weight*.

hebdomad, n. [1. hébdomad; 2. hébdəmæd]. Lat. *hebdomad-*, stem of *hebdomas*, fr. Gk. *hebdomás, -ádos*, fr. *hébdomos*, 'seventh'. See **hepta-, seven,** & **-ad.** Lit., group of seven things or persons; specif., a week.

hebdomadal, adj. [1. hebdómadal; 2. hɛbdɔ́mədəl]. Lat. *hebdomadālis*. Prec. & **-al.** Weekly; *Hebdomadal Council*, supreme governing body in Oxford University, which meets weekly.

hebdomadary, adj. [1. hebdómadari; 2. hɛbdɔ́mədəri]. L. Lat. *hebdomadārius*; **hebdomad** & **-ary.** Weekly, hebdomadal.

Hebe, n. [1. hḗbi; 2. híbi]. Lat. *Hēbē*, 'goddess of youth', fr. Gk. *hḗbē*, 'youth, youthful strength', personified as the cup-bearer of gods, and goddess of youth; cp. Lith. *jėgiù*, 'I have power'. (colloq.) Waitress, barmaid.

hebetate, vb. trans. [1. hébetāt; 2. hébiteit]. Lat. *hebetāt-(um)*, P.P. type of *hebetāre*, 'to make blunt', fr. *hebet-*, stem of *hebēs*, 'blunt', cp. *hebēre*, 'to be blunt, dull'. Etymol. unknown. To make mentally blunt or dull.

hebetude, n. [1. hébetūd; 2. hébɛtjūd]. Fr., fr. Lat. *hebetūdo*, fr. *hebet-*, stem of *hebēs*, 'blunt, dull'. See prec. Mental inertness.

Hebraic, adj. [1. hēbrā́ik; 2. hībréi-ik]. Lat. *Hebrāicus*, fr. Gk. *hebraikós*, fr. *hebraîos*, **Hebrew** & **-ic.** Pertaining to the Hebrews; Hebrew.

Hebraically, adv. [1. hēbrā́ikali; 2. hībréi-ikəli]. Obs. *Hebraical*, fr. prec. & **-al** & **-ly.** In a Hebraic manner; like a Hebrew.

Hebraism, n. [1. hḗbrāizm; 2. híbrei-izəm]. See prec. & **-ism.** Cp. Fr. *hébraïsme*. **a** A Hebrew idiom or figure of speech; **b** the Hebrew character and mode of thought; the Hebrew religion, Judaism.

Hebraist, n. [1. hḗbrāist; 2. híbrei-ist]. See **Hebraize** & **-ist.** Cp. Fr. *hébraïste*. **a** One skilled in the Hebrew language, literature, and institutions; **b** person who adheres or inclines to Hebrew thought or religion.

Hebraistic, adj. [1. hēbrāístik; 2. hībrei-ístik]. Prec. & **-ic.** Pertaining to Hebraism or a Hebraist.

Hebraistically, adv. [1. hēbrāístikali; 2. hībrei-ístikəli]. Prec. & **-al** & **-ly.** In a Hebraistic manner.

Hebraize, vb. trans. & intrans. [1. hḗbrāiz; 2. híbrei-aiz]. L. Lat. *hebraīzāre*, fr. Gk. *hebraïzein*, 'to speak Hebrew', fr. *hebraîos*,

Hebrew, & **-ize**. **1.** trans. **a** To translate into Hebrew; **b** to make like a Hebrew. **2.** intrans. To become Hebrew; to act or think in the Hebrew manner.

Hebrew, n. & adj. [1. hḗbrōō; 2. híbrū]. M.E. *Hebreu, Ebreu*, fr. O. Fr. *Hebreu*, Fr. *Hébreu*, fr. Lat. *Hebraeus*, fr. Gk. *hebraîos*, fr. Aramaic *hebrai*. **1.** n. **a** Member of the people or nation of Israel, or of the tribe or group of tribes which became that people; Israelite; (in plain Mod. Engl. interchangeable with *Jew*); **b** ancient language of the Hebrews; Phr. *it's Hebrew to me*, unintelligible. **2.** adj. Pertaining to the Hebrews or their language.

hecatomb, n. [1. hékatōm; 2. hékətoum]. Fr. *hécatombe*, fr. Lat. *hecatombē*, fr. Gk. *hekatómbē*, fr. *hekatón*, **hundred**, & *boûs*, 'ox'. Cp. **bovine, cow (I.)**. **a** (Gk. antiq.) Sacrifice of a hundred oxen; **b** (fig.) great sacrifice, massacre, slaughter, of human, or other living beings.

heck, n. [1. hek; 2. hɛk]. O.E. *hæc*, 'gate, grating'; M.E. *hek, heke*, M.L.G., M. Du. *heck*, Du. *hek*, Dan. *hekke* &c. Variant of **hatch (I.), hack (IV.)**. (provinc.) Frame on a loom for holding the warp threads.

heckle, vb. trans. [1. hékl; 2. hékl]. M.E. *hekelin*, cp. Du. *hekelen*, & **hackle (II.)**. **1.** To hackle. **2.** (fig.) To address difficult, searching, or inconvenient questions to public speaker, esp. candidate at election meetings.

heckler, n. [1. hékler; 2. héklə]. Prec. & **-er**. Person who heckles a speaker.

heckling, n. [1. hékling; 2. héklıŋ]. **heckle** & **-ing**. Action of one who heckles speaker; process of being heckled.

hectare, n. [1. héktār; 2. héktɛə]. Fr., fr. **hecto-** & **are (II.)**. Metric measure equal to 100 ares, or 2·471 acres.

hectic, adj. & n. [1. héktik; 2. héktik]. Fr. *hectique*, fr. Gk. *hektikós*, 'habitual; consumptive', w. suff. **-ic**, fr. adj. stem *hekt-*, found in *héxis*, 'being in a certain condition, or habit, of body', fr. stem *hekh-* for **sekh-*, 'have, hold', cp. Gk. *ékhein*, 'to have, hold' (see **epoch**); fr. Aryan base **segh-*, 'to hold, overpower', whence Scrt. *sah*, 'to hold in, stop', *sáhaš*, 'victory'; cogn. w. Goth. *sigis*, O.E. *sige*, 'victory'. The same base underlies also **scheme** & **school**. **1.** adj. **a** Pertaining to, suffering from, arising from, slowly wasting disease; consumptive: *a hectic patient, fever* &c.; **b** (in popular usage) feverish, unhealthily flushed: *a hectic appearance*; **c** (colloq., fig.) feverish, agitated; exciting: *a hectic time*. **2.** n. (rare) Hectic, feverish, consumptive person.

hecto-, before vowel **hect-**, pref. Form, used in compounds, of Gk. *he-katón* for **se-katón*, '100'; the first syll. is supposed to represent earlier Gk. **ha-* for **sa-*, Aryan *sm̥-*, cp. Scrt. *sa-hasran*, 'group of a thousand', & Gk. *hen*, 'one', for **sen-*; **-katón* is the common Aryan numeral for 'hundred'. **a** A hundred, as in *hectogram* &c.; **b** a large number, as in *hectograph* &c.

hectocotylization, n. [1. hèktōkōtilīzā́shun; 2. hèktoukòtilaizéiʃən]. See next word & **-ation**. Process of forming a hectocotylus.

hectocotylize, vb. trans. [1. hèktōkótilīz; 2. hèktoukótilaiz]. **hectocotylus** & **-ize**. To modify arm or tentacle of cephalopod, so as to form hectocotylus.

hectocotylus, n. [1. hèktōkótilus; 2. hèktoukótiləs]. Mod. Lat. (Cuvier, orig. generic name of supposed parasite), fr. **hecto-** & Gk. *kotúlē*, 'cup' (cp. **cotyledon**). One of arms or tentacles of certain cephalopods, such as the octopus, cuttlefish, argonaut, which undergoes modification as copulative organ, and in some species impregnates female after being detached from male.

hectogram, hectogramme, n. [1. héktōgram; 2. héktougræm]. Fr. *hectogramme*, fr. **hecto-** & **gramme**. Metric weight of 100 grammes, equivalent to 3·527 oz. av.

hectograph, n. & vb. trans. [1. héktōgrahf; 2. héktougrāf]. **hecto-** & **-graph**. **1.** n. Device for multiplying copies of writing or drawing, from a gelatine surface, upon which the writing &c., to be multiplied, has previously been impressed. **2.** vb. To multiply copies of, by hectograph.

hectolitre, n. [1. héktōlēter; 2. héktoulītə]. Fr. **hecto-** & **litre**. Measure of one hundred litres.

hectometre, n. [1. héktōmēter; 2. héktoumītə]. Fr., fr. **hecto-** & **metre (II.)**. Measure of length, 100 metres.

hector (I.), n. [1. héktor; 2. héktə]. Lat., fr. Gk. *Héktōr*, lit. 'he who holds fast' (fr. base seen in *ékhein*, 'to hold', q.v. under **hectic, epoch**), name of a Trojan hero, son of Priam; in mediaeval romances represented as below. Blustering bully, swashbuckler.

hector (II.), vb. trans. & intrans., fr. prec. **a** trans. To bully, browbeat, scold, bluster at; **b** intrans., to behave as a hector.

heddle (I.), n. [1. hédl; 2. hédl]. Apparently through intermediate **held-* by metathesis of *l*, fr. O.E. *hefeld, hebeld, hefel, hebel*, 'thread for weaving', fr. **haf-ild* (see base of **heave, heavy (I.)**). Cp. also O.E. *hefeldġyrd*, 'weaver's shuttle', O.N. *hefald*, 'one of perpendicular thrums holding weft'. (weaving) One of series of parallel cords or wires, fixed in shafts, and furnished with eyes through which warp threads pass in weaving.

heddle (II.), vb. trans., fr. prec. Cp. O.E. *hefeldian*, 'to fix the weft or woof'. (weaving) To pass (warp thread) through heddle eyes.

heddle eye, n. Loop or metal eye in heddle through which warp thread passes.

hedge (I.), n. [1. hej; 2. hedž]. M.E. *hegge*, O.E. *heċġ*; cp. M. Du. *hegghe*, M.L.G., Du. *hegge, heg*, O.H.G. *hecka*, Mod. Germ. *hecke*, 'hedge', cp. O.N. *hegg-r*, 'kind of tree used in hedges'. The Gmc. type seems to be **haȝ-jō*; the meaning of base **haȝ-*, Aryan **kogh-*, was apparently 'seize, grasp, encompass'. Walde compares the Lat. *in-coh-āre*, 'to lay foundations of; begin', orig. 'take in hand, set about'. Cp. Scrt. *kakša*, 'girdle, ring-fence'. Cp. also **haw (I.)**. **1.** Line of bushes, shrubs, or small trees, usually quick (thorn, privet, yew &c.), planted close, trimmed level in height, and cut back on both sides, so as to form a continuous fence, or boundary (esp. of a field or garden): *a dead, quickset, hedge*; *to pleach, plash, lay, a hedge*, thicken and stiffen it, by interweaving new shoots. Phr. *to come down on wrong side of the hedge*, make wrong decision, do wrong thing, from idea of a fall when jumping a hedge in hunting. **2. a** Anything acting as a hedge; a barrier, formed by row of persons or things; **b** (fig.) something which restricts one's freedom of action: *a hedge of etiquette, of convention*. **3.** (colloq., fr. vb. **hedge (II.) 2**). Act of hedging.

hedge (II.), vb. trans. & intrans. M.E. *heggen*, fr. prec., cp. M. Du. *hegghen*, O.E. *heġeġian*. **A.** trans. **1.** To provide or surround with a hedge; to separate by a hedge or hedges. **2.** (fig.) To obstruct movements of, put obstacle in way of, barrier round: *to hedge a person about, round, in, with rules, restrictions, prohibitions*; *to hedge a person's path with difficulties* &c. **3.** (fig.) **a** To protect by surrounding with barrier; *to hedge round with care and affection* &c.; **b** to safeguard (bet, speculation) by making provision which will indemnify one in event of loss. **B.** intrans. **1.** To make, trim, or plash a hedge; to work at hedges. **2.** (fig.) To shelter, as if behind hedge; specif. **a** to protect oneself in a bet or speculation; to reduce financial obligations, risk; **b** (in bad sense) to qualify what one has said, esp. in unobtrusive or underhand way, so as to safeguard oneself against contradiction or exposure; to shilly-shally in action, hesitate in what one has promised, or begun, to do.

hedge-bill, hedging-bill, n. **hedge (I.)** & **bill (I.)**. Bill, often with long handle, used for trimming hedges, chopping small boughs &c.

hedgebote, n. [1. héjbōt; 2. hédžbout]. **hedge (I.)** & **boot (III.)**. Haybote (q.v.).

hedgehog, n. [1. héj(h)og; 2. hédž(h)ɔg]. **hedge (I.)** & **hog**. **1.** Common British insectivorous nocturnal mammal, *Erinaceus europaeus*, about 10 in. long, with pointed snout, and body covered, on upper surface, with spines, which defends itself by rolling up into ball, with spines erect. **2.** (colloq., fig.) Irritable, spiky, ill-natured person.

hedge priest, n. Illiterate or disreputable priest; pretender to priesthood.

hedger, n. [1. héjer; 2. hédžə]. **hedge (II.)** & **-er**. **1.** Man who makes, trims, or repairs hedges: commonly *hedger and ditcher*. **2.** Person who hedges, in any figurative sense.

hedgerow, n. [1. héjrō; 2. hédžrou]. **hedge (I.)** & **row (I.)**. Cp. O.E. *heġerǣwe*. Row of bushes or small trees forming hedge.

hedge-school, n. School of the humblest class, formerly conducted in open air, often under a hedge.

hedge-schoolmaster, n. Master of hedge-school.

hedge-sparrow, n. One of the commonest British warblers, *Accentor modularis*, brown above and grey below.

hedge-writer, n. Mean, beggarly scribbler.

hedging, n. [1. héjing; 2. hédžiŋ]. **hedge (II.)** & **-ing**. Action of one who hedges (in any sense); (attrib.) *hedging bill*.

hedonic, adj. & n. [1. hēdónik; 2. hidónik]. Gk. *hēdonikós*, fr. *hēdoné*, 'pleasure', fr. *hēdús*, 'sweet', & **-ic**. Gk. *hēdu-*, 'sweet', for **swēdw-*, is cogn. w. Lat. *suāvis* for **swād-wis*, & O.E. *swēte*, fr. Gmc. **swōti-*. See **suave** & **sweet**. **1.** adj. **a** Pertaining to pleasure; **b** hedonistic. **2.** n. (pl., *hedonics*) **a** Branch of ethics treating of pleasure in its moral aspects; **b** branch of psychology treating of pleasure and pain.

hedonism, n. [1. hḗdunizm; 2. hídənizəm]. Gk. *hēdoné*, 'pleasure' (see prec.), & **-ism**. **a** (philos.) Ethical theory or doctrine that pleasure is the chief good; **b** devotion to pleasure.

hedonist, n. [1. hḗdunist; 2. hídənist]. Gk. *hēdon-*, as in prec., & **-ist**. **a** Adherent of hedonism; **b** person who lives for pleasure; self-indulgent person.

hedonistic, adj. [1. hēdunístik; 2. hìdənístik]. Prec. & **-ic**. Pertaining to hedonism.

hedonistically, adv. [1. hēdunístikali; 2. hìdənístikəli]. Prec. & **-ally**. In a hedonistic manner.

-hedral, adj. suff., fr. Gk. *hédra*, 'side, face' &c., fr. base seen in *hézomai*, 'I seat myself, sit down', cogn. w. Lat. *sedēre*, see **sedentary**, & **sit**. In *polyhedral* &c.

-hedron, n. suff., see prec., as *polyhedron*.

heed (I.), vb. trans. & intrans. [1. hēd; 2. hīd]. O.E. *hēdan*, M.E. *hēden*, cp. O. Fris. *hōda*, O.S. *hōdian*, O.H.G. *huotan*, M.H.G. *hüeten*, Germ. *hüten*, all fr. Gmc. **hōdjan*, fr. **hōdō*, fem., 'care, protection', whence O.E. *hōd*, 'hood', & O. Fris. *hōde, hūde*, Du. *hoede*, O.H.G. *huota*, Mod. Germ. *hut*, 'hat'. Another cogn. is prob. O.E. *heaðerian*, fr. **haðor-*, 'to confine, restrain'; & possibly Goth. *hēþjō*, 'a room'. Outside Gmc. cp. Lat. *cassis*, 'helmet', for **cattis*, & perh. Gk. *kótulos*, 'pan', though this is doubtful & may belong to another group of words. Connexion w. O.E. *hȳd*, 'skin', Lat. *cutis* is still more doubtful. See **hood, hide (I.), cuticle**. **1.** trans. To attend to, observe, take notice of, regard carefully: *heed what I say, my warning*. **2.** intrans. To attend, take notice: *they were warned, but did not heed*.

heed (II.), n. M.E. *hēde*, fr. prec. Attention, notice, regard, care: *to give heed to advice*; *to take no heed of danger, of what is said*.

heedful, adj. [1. hḗdfool; 2. hídful]. **heed (II.)** & **-ful**. Attentive; careful.

heedfully, adv. Prec. & **-ly**. In a heedful manner.

heedfulness, n. See prec. & **-ness**. Care, attention.

heedless, adj. [1. hḗdles; 2. hídlis]. **heed (II.)** & **-less**. Taking no heed, inattentive; careless, thoughtless.

heedlessly, adv. Prec. & **-ly**. In a heedless manner.

heedlessness, n. See prec. & **-ness**. State or quality of being heedless; inattention; carelessness.

heehaw, hee-haw, n. & vb. intrans. [1. hḗhaw; 2. hī́hɔ̄]. Imitative; cp. Germ. *i-a*. **1.** n. **a** Bray of ass; **b** (fig.) loud senseless laugh, guffaw. **2.** vb. **a** To bray like an ass; **b** (fig.) to guffaw.

heel (I.), n. [1. hēl; 2. hīəl]. O.E. *hēla, hǣla*, M.E. *hēle*; cp. O. Fris. *hēla, heila*, Du. *hiel*, O.N. *hǣl-l*, Swed. *häl*, Dan. *hæl*; perh. contracted fr. O.E. ***hōhila*, fr. *hōh*, '**hough** (I.), heel', & dimin. *-ila*, see **-le**. **1. a** Hinder part of foot, below ankle, of human being; corresponding part of hind-foot of a flat-footed animal; Phrs. *at, on, upon, one's heels*, close behind, in hot pursuit; *to clap, lay, by the heels*, to arrest, imprison (properly, fetter); *to cool, kick, one's heels*, to be kept waiting; *down at heel*, treading down the back of one's shoes; hence, slipshod, slovenly, shabby; *head over heels, heels over head*, turning a somersault, upside-down; (fig.) in reckless haste; *over head and heels* (*in love* &c.), intensely, deeply; *heel!*, (*come, keep*) *to heel*, call to dog to walk close behind one; (fig.) *to come to heel*, consent to conform to discipline, rules, another's will &c.; to cease opposition; *to heel*, in close attendance; *to leave the house heels foremost*, (colloq.) to be carried out dead; *out at heel*, with one's socks or stockings worn through at the heel; shabby, beggarly; *to show one's heels, a clean pair of heels, to take to one's heels*, to run away, take to flight; *to kick up one's heels*, to be lively, skittish, frisky; indulge in a frolic; *to tread on one's heels*, to crowd one; (often fig.) *disasters come treading on each other's heels*; *to turn on one's heel*, to swing or turn round abruptly; *two for his heels*, (in cribbage) two points scored for turning up knave before playing; *under the heel*, crushed or stamped upon; (fig.) *under the heel of a ruthless tyranny*; **b** (compar. anat.) projecting joint, anatomically corresponding to the heel, half-way down hind-leg of hoofed animals, popularly called the hock; **c** hoof; hinder part of either hind-foot of horse &c. just above hoof. **2. a** Part of boot or shoe supporting heel, usually forming projection below sole: *to wear high heels*; **b** one of the projections, or calks, on back portions of horse-shoe; **c** part of stocking or sock covering heel. **3.** Part of various objects bearing real or fancied resemblance to a heel, as lower or hinder end, or projection at such part; e.g. **a** part of implement next handle or shaft, as of ploughshare, golf-club &c.; **b** lower end of post, rafter, mast, boom, bowsprit, stern-post; **c** part of cutting for graft containing piece of bark of stem; **d** fag end of thing: *heel of a loaf or a cheese*; **e** tail, rear: *heel of a hunt*; **f** (hort. phr.) *to lay in tree, or plant, by the heels*, to cover roots temporarily with earth before finally planting; to heel in.

heel (II.), vb. trans. & intrans., fr. prec. **1.** To furnish (boot or shoe) with heel. **2. a** (Rugby football) Usually *heel out*: to pass (ball) out of scrummage with heel; **b** (golf) to strike (ball) with heel of club. **3.** (hort. phr.) *To heel in* (*tree, plant*), to cover roots temporarily with earth before planting finally.

heel (III.), vb. intrans. & trans. O.E. *h(i)eldan*, 'to incline, bend down &c.', fr. ***heald-jan*, cp. *heald*, 'protection', *heldan*, 'to slope', M.E. *helden*, obs. Mod. Engl. *heeld*, E. Fris. *hella*, O.S. (*af-*)*heldian*, O.H.G. *heldian, heldan*, 'to slant, slope'; fr. O.E. *heald*, cp. O. Fris., O.H.G. *hald*, 'sloping', fr. Gmc. ***haldaz*, cp. Goth. (*wilja-*)*halþei*, 'inclination (of will), graciousness'. Related to O.E., O. Fris., O.S., O.H.G., Mod. Germ. *hold*, 'faithful, gracious', Goth. *hulþ-s*, 'gracious', Gmc. ***hulþaz*. This base in its various forms ***k̑el-, *k̑ol-, *k̑l̥-, *k̑l-*, 'slope', has given rise to a large number of words, including Lat. *clīnāre*, 'bend, bow' (see **decline, clement** &c.), & in O.E. *hlǣnan, hlǣdder, hlid* &c., see **lean** (II.), **ladder, lid**. **1.** intrans. To incline, slope, tilt, steadily to one side, esp. of ship or boat: *to heel over*. **2.** trans. To make (ship &c.) heel.

heel (IV.), n., fr. prec. (chiefly naut.) State or condition of heeling or sloping; amount of heeling, list.

heel-and-toe, adj. Pertaining to walking race or walk in which foot touches ground with heel and leaves it with toe.

heel-ball, n. **heel** (I.) & **ball** (I.). Mixture of hard wax and lamp-black, used by bootmakers for polishing leather of boots and shoes; also used for taking rubbings of brasses, coins, inscriptions &c.

heeler, n. [1. hḗler; 2. hī́lə]. **heel** (II.) & **-er**. Person or animal that heels; specif. (Am. slang) one that follows at the heels of another; hanger-on of politician.

heeling, n. [1. hḗling; 2. hī́liŋ]. **heel** (III.) & **-ing**. Condition of vessel that heels; list. Phr. *heeling error*, deviation of compass caused by heeling of vessel.

heel-piece, n. **a** Piece that forms, or that is fitted to, the heel of a shoe; **b** (fig.) end-piece, tail-piece.

heeltap, n. [1. hḗltap; 2. hī́əltæp]. **heel** (I.) & **tap** (IV.). **a** (rare, or trade term) Tap or layer of leather for heel of boot or shoe; **b** (fig.) small quantity of liquor left in the heel or bottom of a glass after drinking: *no heeltaps!*, drink every glass to the bottom.

heft (I.), n. [1. heft; 2. heft]. **heave** (I.) & n. suff. *-t*. Cp. **haft**. (obs. or provinc.) Action of heaving, retching (Shakespeare, 'Winter's Tale', II. i. 45).

heft (II.), vb. trans., fr. prec. (Am.) To judge weight of, by lifting.

hefty, adj. [1. héfti; 2. héfti]. **heft** (I.) & **-y**. (colloq.) Capable of powerful effort; muscular, powerful.

Hegelian, adj. & n. [1. hāgélian; 2. heigī́liən]. G. W. F. Hegel, German philosopher (1770–1831), & **-ian**. **a** adj. Pertaining to the idealist philosophy of Hegel; **b** n., adherent of the philosophy of Hegel.

Hegelianism, n. [1. hāgélianizm; 2. heigī́liənizəm]. Prec. & **-ism**. Hegel's system of philosophy.

hegemonic, adj. [1. hègemónik; 2. hìgimɔ́nik]. Gk. *hēgemonikós*, fr. *hēgemon-*, stem of *hēgemṓn*, 'leader, guide', w. agent-suff. *-mon-*, fr. *hēge-ésthai*, 'to go before, lead', all fr. base ***sēg-* for ***sāg-*, wh. occurs also in Lat. *sāg-ire*, 'to perceive quickly', *sāgus*, 'prophetic', *sāgax*, 'wise, having keen senses' (see **sagacious**); & further Goth. *sōk-jan*, O.E. *sēcan* (see **seek**). Pertaining to hegemony; leading, predominant.

hegemonical, adj. [1. hègemónikl; 2. hìgimɔ́nikl]. Prec. & **-al**. Hegemonic.

hegemony, n. [1. hēgémuni, hēgémuni; 2. hīgímənì, hīgéməni]. Gk. *hēgemonia*. See **hegemonic** & **-y**. Leadership, political preponderance, used esp. of most powerful state in a league, federation, or geographical group: *the Prussian hegemony in Germany*.

hegira, n., also **hejira, hijra** [1. héjira; 2. hédžirə]. Arab. *hijra*, 'separation'. **a** Flight of Mohammed from Mecca, July 15th-16th (conventional date, actually Sept. 20th), 622; hence, the latter date, adopted as Mohammedan era; **b** (fig.) any similar flight.

hegumen, n. [1. hēgū́men; 2. hīgjū́mən]. Gk. *hēgoúmenos*, prop. 'leading, guiding', Pres. Part. of *hēgeésthai*. See **hegemonic**. In Orthodox Eastern Church, first or second official in monastery, of lower rank than archimandrite; corresponding to abbot or prior.

heifer, n. [1. héfer; 2. héfə]. O.E. *hēahfore*, M.E. *hayfare*. A purely Engl. compound, of wh. the first element is *hēah*, '**high**, full-grown' (cp. O.E. *hēahdēor*, 'stag'); the second is same word as O.E. *fearr*, 'bull', O.H.G. *farri, farro*, M.H.G. *varre*, Mod. Germ. *farre*, wh. are cogn. w. Gk. *póris, pórtis*, 'young heifer, female calf; any young animal'; also w. Lat. *parere*, 'to bring forth, breed, produce', & *parent-*, fr. Pres. Part. of this, 'father or mother' (see **parent**). Young cow that has not yet calved.

heigh, interj. [1. hā, hī; 2. hei, hai]. Natural sound. Exclamation calling attention, making inquiry, or expressing joy, encouragement &c.

heigh-ho, interj. [1. hā́ hṓ; 2. héi hóu]. Prec. & **ho**. Exclamation expressing weariness, boredom, or dejection.

height, n. [1. hīt; 2. hait]. O.E. *hīehðu*, M.E. *hēhðe, highte*; Early Mod. Engl. (Milton) also *highth* (now only dial. or vulg.). Cp. O.H.G. *hōhida*, Goth. *hauhiþa*; fr. Gmc. ***hauhiþō*; fr. O.E. *hēah*, **high**, & *-t* for **-th**. Cp. **drought**. **1.** State of being high; loftiness, elevation, altitude: *to rise to a great height*. **2. a** Amount or measure of upward extension of object from bottom to top; vertical dimension: *the height of a box, tower, mountain, person* **b** distance measured vertically from base line, such as ground or sea level; altitude: *the height of a cloud, aeroplane, town*; **c** altitude measured by angular distance, angle subtended by perpendicular from object to horizon: *the sun's height was 20°*. **3.** (fig., of non-material things) **a** Loftiness, elevation, sublimity: *the height of his genius, imagination; to reach great heights of eloquence*; **b** extreme degree, culmination, summit: *expectation was at its height; the height of the storm, wind, fever, season, summer, of folly, fashion* (cp. *depth of winter, ignorance*). **4.** (of material objects) **a** Elevated place or position, high ground; hill: *castles on the heights; the Heights of Abraham*; **b** (Bib., fig.) the heavens: *praise him in the heights* (Ps. cxlviii. 1).

heighten, vb. trans. & intrans. [1. hītn; 2. háitn]. Prec. & **-en**, after *lengthen* &c. **1.** trans. **a** To make high or higher; **b** (fig.) (i.) to make more prominent, intensify, augment, enhance: *to heighten a colour, an effect, one's guilt*; (ii.) to exaggerate: *to heighten a description*. **2.** intrans. (lit. and fig.) To become higher, more prominent.

heinous, adj. [1. hā́nus; 2. héinəs]. M.E. *hainous, heinous*, fr. O. Fr. *hainos*, Mod. Fr. *haineux*, 'full of hate', fr. *haïne* (Fr. *haine*), 'hatred', fr. *haïr*, 'to hate', a Gmc. loan-word, cp. O. Frankish *hatjan*. See **hate** (I.) & **-ine** & **-ous**. (of wrongdoing) Lit., hateful; abominable, extremely wicked, atrocious: *a heinous crime*.

heinously, adv. Prec. & **-ly**. In a heinous manner, abominably.

heinousness, n. See prec. & **-ness**. Quality of being heinous.

heir, n. [1. ār; 2. ɛə]. M.E., fr. O. Fr. *heir, heyr, eir* &c., fr. L. Lat. *hērem* for Lat. *hērēdem*, fr. *hēres*, 'heir'. See **heredity**. **1.** (law) One who succeeds, on the death of another, to the possession of landed property by the operation of the law, as being the son, or kinsman, of previous owner; also called *heir-at-law, legal heir*; contrasted with one who succeeds by will. **2.** (popular usage) **a** One, generally a male, who succeeds to another's property (real or personalty) on the death of the latter, whether he be the *heir-at-law*, or whether the property be left him by will; **b** one who is entitled to succeed to property by the action of law, or to whom property has been left; the term is often applied to a person who expects to succeed to property in the future by will or otherwise: *to make a person one's heir; to be heir to lands and money; he expects to be his uncle's heir.* **c** the term is used, followed by *of* or *to*, to denote reference either to the person from whom property is inherited, or, followed by *to*, to that which is inherited: *heir to, of, one's father; heir to one's father's property*. **3.** (fig.) One who succeeds to, inherits, from his parents and ancestors, or from earlier generations, **a** some spiritual quality, advantage, tradition, ideal &c.: *Englishmen are the heirs of liberty*; '*the heir of all the ages*' (Tennyson); *heirs of salvation, of grace* &c.; or **b** some physical quality transmitted through his parents: *heir to his father's strength and his mother's grace.*

heir apparent, n. **a** The next in succession by law to property, which cannot, if he survives the actual holder, pass to anyone but him; **b** specif., the next in descent to the reigning monarch of England, who is bound to succeed to the throne on the death of the latter.

heir-at-law, n. Transl. of Lat. *heres ad legem.* Legal heir on death of ancestor; person who inherits by operation of law and not by provision of a will.

heirdom, n. [1. árdum; 2. ɛədəm]. **heir** & **-dom.** **a** Succession by inheritance; **b** state of being an heir.

heiress, n. [1. áres; 2. ɛəris]. **heir** & **-ess.** **a** Female heir (lit. and fig.); **b** (colloq.) *an heiress*, woman who has inherited or will inherit money or other property: *he was fortunate enough to marry an heiress*; there is no precisely corresponding use of *heir.*

heirless, adj. [1. árles; 2. ɛəlis]. **heir** & **-less.** Having no heir.

heirloom, n. [1. árlōōm; 2. ɛəlūm]. **heir** & **loom (I.)** in obs. sense, 'implement, vessel, piece of furniture'. **a** (law) Chattel, such as deed, piece of armour or furniture, monument &c., which descends as trust from heir to heir, by custom or settlement, and which cannot be sold or given away; **b** (popular use) object inherited from ancestors.

heir presumptive, n. One who at a given moment is actually the next in succession to property, or title, but who may at any time cease to be so by the birth of a child nearer to, or more direct in descent from, original ancestor; e.g. one who will succeed his elder brother should the latter die childless.

heirship, n. [1. árship; 2. ɛəʃip]. **heir** & **-ship.** **a** State of being an heir; **b** right of inheritance.

hejira, n. See **hegira.**

helcosis, n. [1. helkṓsis; 2. helkóusis]. Gk. *hélkōsis*, fr. *hélkos*, 'ulcer, festering sore', & **-osis**; *hélkos*, cogn. w. Lat. *ulcus*, 'swelling', wh. is perh. connected w. *ulciscere*, 'to take vengeance on', Scrt. *arśaś*, 'haemorrhoids', must owe its initial *h* to association w. Gk. *hélkein*, 'to drag, draw', cp. **hulk.** See **ulcer.** (med.) Ulceration.

held, vb. [1. held; 2. held]. O.E. *hēold*, M.E. *hěld.* Pret. & P.P. of **hold.**

heliacal, adj. [1. hēlíakl; 2. hiláiəkl]. Gk. *hēliakós*, fr. *hēlios*, 'sun', & **-ac** & **-al.** *Hélios* stands for earlier **sāwĕl-ios*, Aryan **sāwĕl-*, cp. Lat. *sōl*, 'sun' (see **sol (I.)**), & Goth. *sauil*, 'sun'. Pertaining to, near, the sun; solar; esp. in Phrs. *heliacal cycle*, solar cycle; *heliacal rising, setting, of a star*, first rising visible after period when it is lost in light of sun; last setting before this; *heliacal year*, Sothic year, q.v.

helianthus, n. [1. hēliánthus; 2. hìliǽnþəs]. Mod. Lat., fr. Gk. *hélios*, 'sun', see prec., & *ánthos*, 'flower'. See **anthology.** (bot.) Genus of plants which includes the common sunflower.

helical, adj. [1. hélikl; 2. hélikl]. Lat. *helic-*, stem of **helix**, & **-al.** Having the form of a spiral.

helically, adv. Prec. & **-ly.** Spirally.

helicogyre, n. [1. hélikōjìr; 2. hélikoudžàiə]. See prec. & **gyre.** An improved form of helicopter.

helicoid, adj. & n. [1. hélikoid; 2. hélikɔid]. Gk. *helikoeidḗs*, 'spiral', cp. Fr. *hélicoïde.* See **helical** & **-oid.** **1.** adj. Shaped like a spiral; resembling a snail shell. **2.** n. (geom.) Surface generated by straight line moving in spiral at constant angle with its axis.

helicoidal, adj. [1. hèlikóidl; 2. hèlikɔ́idl]. Prec. & **-al.** Helicoid. Phr. *helicoidal saw*, endless band or belt of twisted wire used to cut through marble &c.

Helicon, n. [1. hélikon; 2. hélikɔn]. Gk. *Helikṓn*, a mountain in Boeotia. **1.** Greek mountain supposed to be th abode of Apollo, and sacred to the Muses; hence, (fig.) seat of poetic inspiration. **2.** (Either from above, or from Gk. *helikón*, 'twisted, winding' &c., see **helix.**) Large brass wind instrument of deep tone made so as to be carried round the body while being played.

helicopter, n. [1. hèlikópter; 2. hèlikɔ́ptə]. Fr. *hélicoptère*, fr. *helico-*, see **helix**, & Gk. *pterón*, 'wing'. See **ptero-** & **feather.** Type of flying machine, made to rise and sink vertically, by means of horizontal propellers and revolving vanes.

helio-, pref., fr. Gk. *hélios*, 'sun'. See **heliacal.** (combining form) Pertaining to the sun.

heliocentric, adj. [1. hēliōséntrik; 2. hìliouséntrik]. Prec. & **-centric.** Pertaining to, referred to, the sun as centre (of the planetary system), as opposed to *geocentric*: *the heliocentric theory of Copernicus.*

heliocentricism, n. [1. hēliōséntrisizm; 2. hìliouséntrisizəm]. Prec. & **-ism.** The heliocentric theory.

heliochrome, n. [1. héliōkrōm; 2. hílioukroum]. **helio-** & **-chrome.** Photograph in natural colours.

heliochromic, adj. [1. hēliōkrṓmik; 2. hìlioukróumik]. Prec. & **-ic.** Pertaining to heliochromy.

heliochromy, n. [1. héliōkrṑmi; 2. híliokròumi]. See prec. & **-y.** Photography in natural colours.

heliogram, n. [1. héliōgram; 2. híliougræm]. **helio-** & **-gram**, after **telegram.** Message conveyed by heliograph.

heliograph (I.), n. [1. héliōgrahf; 2. híliougrāf]. **helio-** & **-graph.** Name of various instruments, **a** for signalling to distance, by flashing sun's rays from a mirror; **b** for taking photographs of sun; **c** for determining intensity of sunlight.

heliograph (II.), vb. trans., fr. prec. To use a heliograph, **a** for transmitting message; **b** for photographing a heavenly body.

heliographic, adj. [1. hēliōgráfik; 2. hìliougrǽfik]. **helio-** & **graphic.** Pertaining to a heliograph, or to heliography.

heliography, n. [1. hēliógrafi; 2. hìliɔ́grəfi]. **helio-** & **-graphy.** **a** (astron.) Description of sun's surface; **b** process of taking a photograph on a prepared metal plate, which is afterwards engraved; **c** art of signalling by heliograph.

heliogravure, n. [1. hēliōgrávūr; 2. hìliougrævjuə]. Fr., fr. **helio-** & **-gravure**, formed on model of **photogravure.** Process of photo-engraving.

heliology, n. [1. hēliólojí; 2. hìliɔ́lədži]. **helio-** & **-logy.** Science of the sun.

heliometer, n. [1. hēliómeter; 2. hìliɔ́mitə]. Fr. *héliomètre*, fr. **helio-** & **-meter.** (astron.) Instrument for taking various celestial measurements.

heliometry, n. [1. hēliómetri; 2. hìliɔ́mitri]. **helio-** & **-metry.** (astron.) Measurement with heliometer.

helioscope, n. [1. héliōskōp; 2. hílioskoup]. **helio-** & **-scope.** (astron.) Device, usually attached to telescope, for observing the sun without injuring the eye.

heliosis, n. [1. hēliósis; 2. hìlióusis]. Gk. *hēlíōsis*, 'injury by the sun'. See **helio-** & **-osis.** Injury caused to living organisms by exposure to sun's rays; sunstroke.

heliostat, n. [1. héliōstat; 2. hílioustæt]. **helio-** & **-stat.** Cp. Fr. *héliostat.* Spectroscopic instrument for directing sunbeam continuously in one direction, by means of mirror turned by clockwork.

heliotherapy, n. [1. héliōthérapi; 2. híliouþérəpi]. **helio-** & **-therapy.** Treatment of disease by exposure to the sun's rays.

heliothermometer, n. [1. hēliōthermómeter; 2. hìliouþəmɔ́mitə]. **helio-** & **thermometer.** Special thermometer, for measuring amount of absorption of the sun's heat by the atmosphere.

heliotrope, n. & adj. [1. héliotrōp; 2. héliətroup]. Fr., fr. Lat. *hēliotropium*, fr. Gk. *hēliotrópion*, fr. **helio-** & Gk. *tróp-os*, 'turn, direction'. See **trope.** **1.** **a** Plant that turns to the sun, specif., herbaceous, greenhouse and garden plant of borage family, with spikes of small, fragrant, light purple flowers; cherry-pie; **b** (also as adj.) colour of this, pale purple; **c** scent of, or like that of, heliotrope flower, resembling odour of cooked cherries. **2.** Instrument, resembling heliograph, by which sunbeams are reflected for a long distance.

heliotropic, adj. [1. hēliōtrópik; 2. hèlioutrɔ́pik]. **helio-** & **-tropic.** Pertaining to heliotropism.

heliotropism, n. [1. héliotropìzm; 2. hèliɔ́trəpizəm]. See prec. & **-ism.** (physiol.) Tendency of growing organ of plant to respond to action of sun's rays, by moving or turning towards them.

heliotype, n. & vb. [1. héliōtīp; 2. híloutaip]. **helio-** & **-type.** **a** n. Print produced by heliotypy; **b** vb., to print by this process.

heliotypography, n. [1. hēliōtīpógrafi; 2. hìloutaipɔ́grəfi]. **helio-** & **typography.** Process of photo-engraving.

heliotypy, n. [1. héliōtīpi; 2. hílioutaipi]. **heliotype (I.)** & **-y.** Process in which the gelatine film of a negative is hardened, so that prints can be made direct from it.

heliozoan, n. & adj. [1. hēliōzṓan; 2. hìliouzóuən], fr. Mod. Lat. *heliozoa*, fr. **helio-** & Gk. *zôa*, 'animals' (see **zoo-**), & **-an.** **1.** n. Member of the order *Heliozoa*, protozoan animalcules inhabiting fresh water, generally spherical, with numerous radiating pseudopods; sun animalcule. **2.** adj. Pertaining to the *Heliozoa.*

helium, n. [1. hélium; 2. híliəm]. Scientific concoction, fr. Gk. *hélios*, 'sun', see **heliacal**, & **-um.** Gaseous, light, non-inflammable element occurring in atmosphere of sun and earth and in radio-active minerals &c.; discovered as an actual substance by Ramsay in 1895.

helix, n., pl. **helices** [1. héliks, hélisēz; 2. héliks, hélisīz]. Lat., fr. Gk. *hélix* (stem *helik-*), 'coil, spiral, screw, volute', fr. *helissein* for **welikj-ein*, 'to wind, roll, coil', cp. *eíluein* for **welw-ein*, 'to roll round'; cogn. w. Lat. *volvere*, 'to roll round' (see **volute**), & w. **wallow** & **well (I.)**, 'spring'. **1.** **a** Spiral line, in plane, or travelling round surface of cylinder, cone &c.; **b** (math.) any curve on developable surface, which becomes straight line when surface is developed. **2.** Object convoluted or coiled in spiral form, as a wire spring; **b** electric conducting coil; **c** volute in Ionic or Corinthian capital; **d** rim of external ear.

hell, n. [1. hel; 2. hel]. O.E. *hel(l)*, fem., also *helle*, M.E. *helle*; cp. O. Fris. *hille*, Du. *hel*, O.S. *hellia*, *hel*, O.H.G. *hella*, M.H.G. *helle*, Germ. (fr. Aleman. dial.) *hölle*, Goth. *halja*, O.N. *hel* (gen. *heljar*); in O.E., O.H.G., O.N., also 'goddess of the dead'; fr. Gmc. **haljā*, fr. **hal-*, grade of **hel-*, base of O.E., O.S., O.H.G. *helan*, O. Fris. *hela*, Germ. *hehlen*, 'to hide, cover'; cogn. w. Lat. *cēlare*, 'to hide', *cella*, **cell.** **1.** As translating in A.V. Heb. *Sheol* & Gk. *Hades*; abode of spirits of dead, primitively regarded as region below the earth; Sheol, Hades: *He descended into hell* (Apost. Creed). **2.** Abode of devils and of the impenitent dead; place or state of damnation and torment; infernal regions; Phrs. used as imprecation, expressing annoyance, surprise: *go to hell*; *oh hell!*; *what the hell are you doing?* **3.** (fig.) **a** Place, condition, society, marked by intense suffering, misery, cruelty, or wickedness: *to make one's life a hell*; *to suffer hell*; *a regular hell on earth*; (colloq. Phr.) *a hell of a (noise)*, intense, intolerable; **b** vicious haunt, esp. gambling den.

hellbender, n. [1. hélbender; 2. hélbendə]. **hell** & **bend (I.)** & **-er.** Large salamander inhabiting streams in eastern U.S.A.; mud puppy.

hellbroth, n. [1. hélbrawth; 2. hélbrɔþ]. **hell** & **broth.** Mixture brewed by witches for magical purposes; (facet.) a nasty compound.

hellcat. n. [1. hélkat; hélkæt]. Fierce, violent, bad-tempered woman.

hellebore, n. [1. hélebōr; 2. hélibō]. Fr., fr. Lat. *helleborus*, fr. Gk. *helléboros*, of uncertain origin. Name of two distinct groups of plants. **1. a** Christmas Rose (*black hellebore*); **b** poisonous plant whose root is powdered and used for destroying insects (*white hellebore*). **2.** Purgative drug prepared from **1, a.**

helleborine, n. [1. helebōrin; 2. hélibōrin], fr. Gk. *helleborínē*, fr. prec. & **-ine.** One of several British plants of orchid tribe.

Hellenic, adj. [1. helénik; 2. helínik], fr. Gk. *Hellēnikós*, 'Greek'. Connected with, relating to, Greece, the Greeks, and their language.

Hellenism, n. [1. hélenizm; 2. hélinizəm]. Gk. *Hellēnismós*, fr. prec. & **-ism. 1.** Idiom or phrase of Greek origin. **2. a** Greek culture; the Greek mind or spirit; **b** Greek nationality. **3.** Adoption of Greek speech, culture, or manners.

Hellenist, n. [1. hélenist; 2. hélinist]. Gk. *Hellēnistḗs*. See **Hellenize** & **-ist. 1. a** One who adopted and used Greek speech and manners; **b** (N.T.) a Greek Jew. **2.** Student of, expert in, ancient Greek culture, language, literature, and institutions.

Hellenistic, adj. [1. hèlenístik; 2. hèlinístik]. Prec. & **-ic. a** Pertaining to Hellenism or Hellenists; specif., **b** *Hellenistic Greek*, that of the N.T., Greek as written and spoken by Jews.

Hellenize, vb. trans. & intrans. [1. hélenīz; 2. hélinaiz]. Gk. *hellēnízein*, 'to imitate the Greeks, speak Greek', fr. *Héllēnes*, 'descendants of *Hellēn*', who were the first inhabitants of Thessalian Hellas, & **-ize. 1.** trans. To make Greek in character. **2.** intrans. To adopt Greek speech, customs, &c.

heller, n. [1. héler; 2. hélə]. Germ., M.H.G. *haller*, prob. because first coined at Hall in Suabia. **a** (hist.) Former German copper coin of value of half a pfennig; **b** Austrian bronze coin, current until Great War, of value of one-hundredth of krone, or about a tenth of a penny.

hellfire, n. [1. hélfīr; 2. hélfáiə]. O.E. *hellefȳr*, M.E. *helle fīr*. **hell** & **fire.** Fire of hell; *hellfire club*, club of profligate atheists, esp. in 18th century.

hellhound, n. [1. hélhound; 2. hélhaund]. O.E., M.E. *hellehund*. **hell** & **hound. a** Demon in form of hound, such as Cerberus; **b** an abominable, malignant, atrocious person.

hellish, adj. [1. hélish; 2. héliʃ]. **hell** & **-ish. a** Pertaining to, resembling, worthy of, hell; infernal, devilish; **b** (colloq., term of reprobation) inspiring great antipathy; detestable, disgusting, horrible &c.

hellishly, adv. Prec. & **-ly.** In a hellish manner.

hellishness, n. See prec. & **-ness.** Quality of being hellish.

hello, interj. Normally [1. húlṓ; 2. hálóu]. Variant of **hallo, hollo,** & **hullo.** Exclamation used to draw attention, esp. by telephone operators.

helm (I.), n. [1. helm; 2. helm]. O.E. *helma*, M.E. *helme*; cp. O.H.G. *halmo*, O.N. *hjálm*; cp. M.E. *halm*, Germ. *helm*, 'handle'; fr. Gmc. base **halƀ-*, 'to hold'? Cp. **halter** & **helve.** Handle of rudder, tiller; steering wheel of vessel; whole steering apparatus, including rudder: *the ship answers the helm*; (fig.) *helm of state*, government, directing power or principle in a state.

helm (II.), n. O.E., M.E. *helm*, Common Gmc., O.S., Du., O.H.G., Germ. *helm*, Goth. *hilm-s*, O.N. *hjálm-r*; cp. also O.E. *helmian*, 'to cover'; see **hall, hell, hole.** Aryan base **k̑el-*, 'to cover, hide, protect', see **cell** & **conceal,** & substant. suff. *-mo-*. (Now only poet.) Helmet.

helm-cloud, n. Prec. & **cloud (I.).** Cloud gathering round mountain-top before and during storm.

helmed, adj. [1. hélmd; 2. hélmd]. **helm (II.)** & **-ed.** (poet.) Wearing a helm; helmeted.

helmet, n. [1. hélmet; 2. hélmit]. O. Fr., fr. *helme*, 'heaume', itself a loan-word fr. Gmc. *helm*. See **helm (II.)** & **-et. 1. a** Metal cap or covering for the head; part of defensive armour while this was worn; **b** bright metal head-covering worn (in peace) by certain mounted regiments; **c** hat of toughened steel, worn by troops in Great War; **d** cover of wire mesh protecting face in fencing; **e** protective headpiece worn by firemen, policemen, divers; **f** large thick helmet-shaped hat of pith &c., worn by Europeans in hot climates. **2.** (her.) Representation of mediaeval helmet, in armoured bearings, placed above shield, and bearing crest. **3.** Various objects shaped like a helmet, specif. (bot.) hood-shaped upper part of calyx or corolla of some flowers &c.

helmeted, adj. [1. hélmeted; 2. hélmitid]. Prec. & **-ed.** Wearing a helmet.

helminthic, adj. & n. [1. helmínthik; 2. helmínþik]. Gk. *helminth-*, stem of *hélmins*, 'worm', esp. 'intestinal worm', of doubtful origin; perh. for **wel-*, 'roll, wind' &c. See **helix** & **-ic. 1.** adj. Of, pertaining to, parasitic intestinal worms. **2.** n. Drug which expels or destroys such worms.

helminthology, n. [1. hèlminthóloji; 2. hèlminþólədži]. See prec. & **-logy.** Branch of zoology treating of parasitic worms.

helmless (I.), adj. [1. hélmles; 2. hélmlis]. **helm (I.)** & **-less.** (of vessel) Having no helm.

helmless (II.), adj. **helm (II.)** & **-less.** Having no helmet.

helmsman, n. [1. hélmzman; 2. hélmzmən]. **helm (I.)** & *'s-* (possess.) & **man (I.).** Man at the helm; steersman.

helot, n. [1. hélot; 2. hélət]. Gk. *heilōt-*, stem of *heilōs*, 'serf of the Spartans', prob. orig. a 'captive', fr. **hel-jō*, cp. *helein*, 'to take, seize', fr. base **sel-*, **sol-* &c., cp. Goth. *saljan*, 'to give, bring as an offering', O.E. *sellan*, 'to give; sell'. See **sell (I.). a** In Greek sense; Phr. *drunken Helot*, Helot made drunk as object-lesson to Spartan boys, hence, person used as warning example; **b** (fig.) member of a class that is kept in subjection, despised, regarded as outcast.

helotage, n. [1. hélotij; 2. hélətidž]. Prec. & **-age.** Condition of helot; serfdom.

helotry, n. [1. hélotri; 2. hélətri]. **helot** & **-ry.** (coll.) Helot class (lit. and fig.).

help (I.), vb. trans. & intrans. [1. help; 2. help]. O.E. *helpan*, M.E. *helpen*; Common Gmc., O.S. *helpan*, O.H.G. *helfan*, Goth. *hilpan*, O.N. *hjálpa*; cogn. w. Lith. *szelp-ti*, 'to help'. **A.** trans. **1. a** To undertake part of work of (another) for his benefit; to work jointly with; aid, assist in doing something: *help me find it*, or *to find*; Phrs. *God* (or *Heaven*) *help him!*, exclamation of pity or irony, i.e. no one else can; *so help me God*, formula of solemn oath; **b** specif., to give financial assistance to, help with money: *he helps his parents a great deal out of his small income.* **2. a** To promote improvement in, to mitigate, alleviate: *to help a cough*, cure it; **b** to contribute (to), facilitate, conduce to: *to help to ruin a man*; *to help his ruin.* **3. a** To serve, supply (person) with food or drink at table: *let me help you to some sherry*; **b** (colloq.) to serve out (food &c.): *to help the potatoes*; Phr. *to help oneself*, to take for one's own use; make oneself free of: *help yourself to food, wine, cigarettes, or anything you want.* **4.** *Can't help, can help* (probably developed from **2**); **a** to be unable, or able, to avoid, avert, prevent (something happening): *I can't help your being a fool, his bad language, the rain* &c.; Phr. *I can't help it*, it's not my fault, I am powerless under the circumstances; **b** (i.) to be unable to refrain from doing something: *I can't help thinking, wishing, wondering* &c.; (ii.) to be unable to resist: *this peach looks so nice I can't help eating it now*; **c** (after neg. imperat. with neg. omitted after *can*) *don't do, don't tell him, more than you can help*, i.e. than you are obliged to do, to tell. **B.** intrans. To co-operate, render assistance, be of use, avail, contribute to result: *that doesn't help much.* Phr. *every little helps.* **C.** Followed by various adverbs or prepositions. *Help down, downstairs, in, off, over, through, up* &c., trans., to help person in getting down &c. *Help along, forward, on*, trans., to help in advancing. *Help out*, trans., to help in getting out, emerging, escaping, solving difficulty, supplying what is wanting. *Help to*, trans., to help in reaching, attaining, finding: *this clue helped me to the solution.*

help (II.), n. O.E. *help*, fem. & masc., *helpe* fem., M.E. *help(e)*, fr. same base as prec. **1. a** Act of helping; aid, assistance; succour, relief: *thanks for your kind help*; **b** thing that helps or avails: *your advice, work &c. is a great help*; **c** remedy, means of prevention or mitigation: *there's no help for it*; **d** colloq. and vulg. for *helping* (of food). **2. a** Person who helps; helper: '*Thou art my help*' (Ps. xl. 17); **b** (chiefly Am.) domestic servant. Phr. *lady help, mother's help*, superior maid or nursemaid.

helper, n. [1. hélper; 2. hélpə]. M.E. *helpere*; cp. O.S. *helpere*, M.H.G. *helfare*; fr. **help (I.)** & **-er.** Person who helps; assistant, supporter.

helpful, adj. [1. hélpfool; 2. hélpful]. **help (I.)** & **-ful.** Affording help; of service, useful.

helpfully, adv. Prec. & **-ly.** In a helpful manner.

helpfulness, n. See prec. & **-ness.** Quality of being helpful.

helping, n. [1. hélping; 2. hélpiŋ]. **help (II.)** & **-ing.** Various possible usages; chiefly portion of food, given to, or set aside for, one person.

helpless, adj. [1. hélples; 2. hélplis]. **help (I.)** & **-less. a** Lacking help, not helped; **b** unable to help one's self, powerless: *a helpless infant*; **c** shiftless, inefficient, incompetent.

helplessly, adv. Prec. & **-ly.** In a helpless manner; impotently, feebly, shiftlessly.

helplessness, n. See prec. & **-ness.** Quality of being helpless; feebleness, inefficiency.

helpmate, n. [1. hélpmāt; 2. hélpmeit]. Corrupt. of next, as if fr. **help (II.)** & **mate (I.).** Helpmeet.

helpmeet, n. [1. hélpmēt; 2. hélpmīt]. **help (II.)** & **meet (III.)**, after Gen. ii. 18, 'an help meet for him', perh. through confusion w. *mate*, as prec. Fitting helper, comrade, partner, esp. wife.

helter-skelter, adv., adj., & n. [1. hélter skélter; 2. héltə skéltə]. Imitative jingle (cp. *harum-scarum*). **1.** adv. In tumultuous, disorderly haste: *to run helter-skelter.* **2.** adj. (rare and colloq.) Hurried, bustling; moving or acting hastily and without plan. **3.** n. Tumultuous hurry and confusion.

helve, n. & vb. trans. [1. helv; 2. helv], n. fr. O.E. *hielf*, also *helfe*, M.E. *helve, hilve*; cp. O.H.G. *helbe* &c.; of dubious origin; perh. fr. Gmc. base **halƀ-*, 'to hold'; cp. **halter, helm (I.)**; vb., M.E. *helven*, fr. n. **1.** n. Handle of tool, esp. of an axe; obs. Phr. *to throw the helve after the hatchet*, reject, cast away, impatiently what little remains after loss. **2.** vb. To fit a helve to.

hem (I.), n. [1. hem; 2. hem]. O.E. *hem(m)*, M.E. *hem*, perh. orig. 'enclosure'. Cp. O.E. *ham*, O. Fris. *ham, hem*, 'piece of land enclosed by ditch or fence', Germ. *hamm*, 'fence', *hamme*, 'border', also Germ. *hemmen*, 'to check, restrain', O.N. *hemja*, Swed. *hämma*, 'to withhold, keep in'. **a** Edge of cloth or woven material turned up and stitched, to prevent fraying; **b** fig. in Phr. *the hem of a garment*, edge, border, whether actually hemmed or not.

hem (II.), vb. trans. M.E. *hemmen*, fr. prec.; cp. Germ. *hemmen*. **1.** To furnish (cloth &c.) with hem (also absol.). **2.** (fig.) *Hem in, about, round*, to enclose, confine.

hem (III.), interj., n., & vb. intrans. Imitative. **1.** interj. & n. Conventionalized form to represent sound of slight cough, or clearing of throat; specif. such sound, **a** due to hesitation in speech; **b** one deliberately made to arrest attention, esp. as sarcastic comment. **2.** vb. To utter this sound.

hema-, hemat-, hemato-. See **haema-, haemat-, haemato-.**

hematite, n. See **haematite**.

hemi-, pref. Gk. *hēmi-*, 'half', for **sēmi-*, cogn. w. Lat. **semi-**. Prefix in words of Greek origin, denoting half.

hemicycle, n. [1. hèmisíkl; 2. hèmisáikl]. Lat. *hēmicyclus*, fr. Gk. *hēmíkuklos*; fr. **hemi-** & **cycle**. Semicircle; semicircular structure, as room, part of room, wall.

hemiplegia, n. [1. hèmiplḗjia; 2. hèmiplídžiə]. Mod. Lat. after Gk. *paraplēgía*, 'hemiplegia', fr. Gk., fr. **hemi-** & *plēgḗ*, Doric *plāgā́*, 'blow' &c.; cp. *plḗksis* for **plā́ksis*, 'stroke, concussion'; cp. *plḗssō* for **plā́k-jō*, 'strike with lightning, stun' &c.; cp. Goth. *flōkan*, 'complain', O.E. *flōcan*, 'applaud, clap', O.H.G. *fluohhōn*, 'to curse' &c.; Lat. *plāga*, 'blow, stroke', whence **plague**, is borrowed fr. the Gk. Paralysis of one side of the body.

hemipterous, adj. [1. hemípterus; 2. hεmíptərəs], fr. **hemi-** & Gk. *pterón*, 'wing'. See **ptero-**, **feather**, & **-ous**. Of, pertaining to, order of insects *Hemiptera*, having a beak-like proboscis for piercing and sucking; they include cicadas, bugs, aphides &c.; the name is due to the fact that many kinds have half-horny, half-transparent wing-cases.

hemisphere, n. [1. hémisfēr; 2. hémisfiə]. Fr. *hémisphère*, fr. Lat. *hēmisphaerium*, fr. Gk. *hēmisphaírion*. See **hemi-** & **sphere**. **1.** Half of a sphere. **2. a** Any half of the surface of the earth bounded by an imaginary circle; the Eastern, Western, Northern, Southern hemispheres; **b** specif., one half of the brain.

hemispherical, adj. [1. hèmisférikl; 2. hèmisférikl]. **hemi-** & **spherical**. Of, pertaining to, like a hemisphere.

hemistich, n. [1. hémistik; 2. hémistik]. Lat. *hēmistichium*, fr. Gk. *hēmistíkhion*, fr. **hemi-** & Gk. *stíkhos*, 'row, verse'; see **stichic** & cp. **acrostic, distich, stair, sty (I.), vestige**. A metrical half-line.

hemlock, n. [1. hémlok; 2. hémlək]. O.E. *hymblīce, hymlīce, hemlīc*, M.E. *humlok(e), homelok, hemlok*; of unknown origin, apparently found in no other language, & of obscure history; for second element cp. O.E. *ċyrlic, ċerlic*, M.E. *carlok*, **charlock**. **1. a** Umbelliferous British herb, *Conium maculatum*, with finely divided leaves and small white flowers, dangerously resembling cow-parsley in appearance, yielding virulent alkaloid poison; **b** powerful sedative drug made from this. **2.** (fig., poet.) As symbolical of sleep.

hemlock spruce, n. Prec. & **spruce (I.)**. One of several drooping coniferous forest trees valuable for timber, found in Asia and America, genus *Tsuga*.

hemmer, n. [1. hémer; 2. hémə]. **hem (II.)** & **-er**. **a** One who hems; **b** appliance for hemming on sewing-machine.

hemo-, pref. See **haemo-**.

hemorrhage, n. See **haemorrhage**.

hemorrhoid, n. See **haemorrhoid**.

hemp, n. [1. hemp; 2. hεmp]. O.E. *hænep, henep*, M.E. *hemp*; cp. Du. *hennep*, O.H.G. *hanaf*, Mod. Germ. *hanf*, O.N. *hamp-r*, Swed. *hampa*, Dan. *hamp*; fr. Gmc. type **hanap-az*, a very early loan fr. Lat. *cannabis, cannabum*, fr. Gk. *kánnabis, -bos*, wh. is prob. fr. a Semitic source. Cp. Arab. *kinnub*, & see **canvas**. **a** Name applied to various plants whence a fibre is obtained for manufacture of ropes and of coarse cloth; **b** plant related to the mulberry, which yields a resin of narcotic properties, and fibre having commercial value; **c** narcotic drug made from this; **d** (rare and obs.) a hangman's rope.

hempen, adj. [1. hémpen; 2. hémpən]. M.E., fr. **hemp** & **-en**. Cp. O.H.G. *hanafīn*. Made of hemp. Phrs. *a hempen collar*, hangman's noose; *hempen widow*, woman widowed by its means.

hemstitch, vb. trans. & n. [1. hémstich; 2. hémstitʃ]. **hem (I.)** & **stitch**. **a** vb. To decorate border of woven material (esp. in handkerchiefs, table-napkins &c.) by pulling out several contiguous threads, and tying or otherwise separating the cross-threads in series of bundles in the gap thus made; **b** n., ornamental hem made by this process.

hen, n. [1. hen; 2. hεn]. O.E. *hæn, hen(n)*, M.E. *hen*; O.H.G. *henna*, M.L.G., Mod. Germ. *henne* &c.; fr. Gmc. type **hanjō*, fem. of **hanon*, 'cock', lit. 'singer', cp. O.E., & Goth. *hana*, O.S., O.H.G. *hano*, Mod. Germ. *hahn*; cogn. w. Gk. *kanássein*, 'to sound', *kanakhḗ*, 'ringing sound', Lat. *canere*, 'to sing', O. Ir. *canim*, 'I sing', perh. Scrt. *kaṅkaṇi*, 'bell'. See **cant (I.)**, **chant**. **a** Female of domestic fowl; **b** female bird of any kind, as contrasted with, and distinguished from a male: *we saw a pair of eagles, and shot the hen*; (in apposition) *hen bird, sparrow* &c.

hen and chickens, n. Popular name given to various proliferous plants.

henbane, n. [1. hénbān; 2. hénbein]. M.E., fr. **hen** & **bane**. Cp. O.E. name of it, *hænnewōl*, 'hen's pest'. Virulently poisonous British herb, *Hyoscyamus niger*, of nightshade family, with brownish flowers and downy leaves, whence the drug hyoscine is got.

hence, adv. [1. hens; 2. hεns]. M.E. *hennes, hens*, extension w. advbl. (genit.) suff. *-es* (as in *once, else, since, thence* &c.), fr. O.E. *hinan, heonan, heonane*, M.E. *hennene, henne*; cp. O.S., O.H.G. *hinan, hinane*, Mod. Germ. *hinnen*; also O.E. *heona*, M.E. *hine*, O.H.G. *hina*, Mod. Germ. *hin*, fr. demonstr. base **hi-* (see **here, hither**). See also **thence, whence**. **1. a** (of place, archaic, gen. replaced by (*away*) *from here*) Away from here, from this place: *to go (depart) hence*, (fig.) to die; *hence!*, go away, begone!; *hence with it!*, away with it!; **b** (of time) from this time, from now, chiefly in *a year, month, week* &c., *hence*; **c** (of origin) from this source, by descent, derivation, from this (often with ellipsis of vb.): *Jacob had twelve sons, hence (came) the twelve tribes*. **2.** As a result of what has been said, for this reason, consequently, therefore: *he has neither ear nor voice, hence he cannot sing*; *hence we infer* &c.

henceforth, adv. [1. hènsfórth; 2. hènsfɔ́þ]. O.E. *heonan forð*, M.E. *heonne forð*, see prec. & **forth**. From this time on, forward.

henceforward, adv. [1. hènsfórward; 2. hènsfɔ́wəd]. **hence** & **forward**. Henceforth.

henchman, n. [1. hénshman; 2. hén(t)ʃmən]. M.E. *henxtman, henksman, hencheman* (Latinized *hengestmannus*), 'page of honour', orig. 'groom', fr. O.E. *hengest*, O.H.G. *hengist*, O. Fris., Du., Germ. *hengst*, 'male horse, stallion', fr. Gmc. type **hang-ist-*, prob. connected w. vb. **hang**, & **man**. Revived by Scott in erroneous sense of 'haunch-man', attendant who stands at side of chief, hence modern uses. **a** Trusty male retainer, attendant, or follower; **b** staunch political supporter; **c** often in derogatory sense, satellite, creature.

hen-coop, n. **hen** & **coop (I.)**. Coop for poultry.

hendeca-, pref. Gk. *héndeka*, 'eleven', fr. *hén* for **sem*, neut. of *heîs* for **sem-s*, 'one', fr. Aryan base **sem-*, 'together', (cp. Gk. *homoû*, 'together', Lat. *semel*, 'once'), & *déka*, 'ten'. See **simple, deci-**, & **ten**. Combining form denoting eleven, in words of Greek origin.

hendecagon, n. [1. hèndékagon; 2. hèndékəgən]. Prec. & **-gon**. (geom.) Figure with eleven angles and eleven sides.

hendecasyllabic, adj. & n. [1. héndèkasilábik; 2. héndèkəsilǽbik]. Gk. *hendekasúllabos*, 'having eleven syllables', fr. **hendeca-** & *sullabḗ*, **syllable**, & **-ic**. **a** adj. Containing eleven syllables; **b** n., a verse of this form.

hendiadys, n. [1. hèndíadis; 2. hèndáiədis]. Med. Lat. corrupt. of Gk. *hén dià duoîn*, 'one thing by means of two'. Rhetorical figure by which idea ordinarily conveyed by noun and epithet is expressed by two nouns connected by *and*, as: *to put to death with the sword and with the steel*.

henequen, n. [1. héneken; 2. hénikin]. Span., also *jenequén*, fr. Mexican native name. Sisal hemp.

hen-harrier, n. **hen** & **harrier (II.)**. A species of hawk or harrier, of bluish-grey colour, which preys on poultry.

henna, n. [1. héna; 2. hénə]. Arab. (*al-*) *ḥinnā'*. **a** Thorny Asiatic shrub of loosestrife family, with fragrant white flowers, the so-called Egyptian privet, *Lawsonia*; **b** reddish dye made from leaves of this, applied by Oriental women to the finger nails &c.

hennery, n. [1. héneri; 2. hénəri]. **hen** & **-ery**. Enclosed place where domestic fowls are kept.

henotheism, n. [1. hènōthḗizm; 2. hènouþíizəm]. (Gk. *heno-*, form of *heîs* (genit. *henós*), 'one', used in compounds; see **hendeca-**, & **-theism**. System of religion, religious practice, which singles out one of several gods for special veneration.

henotheistic, adj. [1. hènōthēístik; 2. hènouþiístik]. As prec. & **-theistic**. Pertaining to henotheism.

hen party, n. (colloq.) Party attended only by women.

henpeck, vb. trans. [1. hénpek; 2. hénpεk]. **hen** & **peck**. To domineer over (husband).

henpecked, adj. [1. hénpekt; 2. hénpεkt]. Prec. & **-ed**. Tamely submissive to wife.

hen-roost, n. O.E. *henna hrōst*; fr. **hen** & **roost (I.)** Place where poultry roost.

henry, n. [1. hénri; 2. hénri]. After Joseph Henry (1797–1878), American physicist. (elect.) International unit of inductance.

henwife, n. [1. hénwīf; 2. hénwaif]. **hen** & **wife**. Woman who tends poultry.

hepatic, adj. [1. hepátik; 2. hεpǽtik]. Gk. *hēpatikós*, fr. *hēpat-*, stem of *hêpar*, fr. **jēkwərt-*, 'liver', cogn. w. Scrt. *yákṛt*, genit. *yakn-áś*, Lith. pl. *jeknos*, Lat. *jecur* (genit. *jecinor-is*), & **-ic**. **1.** Pertaining to the liver: *hepatic artery, duct* &c.; *hepatic colic*, that caused by passage of gallstone through bile-duct. **2.** Of a brownish colour, like that of liver: *hepatic cinnabar*. **3.** (bot.) Pertaining to the liverworts, *Hepaticae*.

hepatica, n. [1. hepátika; 2. hεpǽtikə]. Specific name of plants, fem. of Lat. *hēpaticus*. See prec. So called from lobed shape of leaves. European species of anemone, cultivated in gardens, bearing blue, red, mauve, and white flowers in early spring.

hepato-, pref. See **hepatic**. Form used in compounds of Greek origin, denoting 'pertaining to the liver'; *hepato-cirrhosis*, cirrhosis of the liver &c.

hephaestic, adj. [1. hefḗstik; 2. hifístik], fr. Gk. *Hḗphaistos*, god of fire and of smith's craft; cp. Gk. *haphḗ*, 'kindling', *háptein*, 'to touch, kindle'. Cognates in other languages not known. (med.) Pertaining to smiths; esp. in *hephaestic cramp*, caused by excessive use of hammer.

Hepplewhite, adj. & n. [1. hép(e)lwīt; 2. héplwait]. **a** adj. Relating to a graceful style of late 18th-cent. furniture, from designer's name: *the Hepplewhite style*; **b** n. furniture of this type: *a piece of Hepplewhite*.

hepta-, pref. Gk. *heptá*, 'seven', for **septṃ*. See **seven**. Form used in compounds of Greek origin; denoting seven.

heptachord, n. [1. héptakord; 2. héptəkōd]. Gk. *heptákhordos*, 'seven-stringed', fr. prec. & **chord**. (mus.) **a** Diatonic system of seven tones; **b** interval of major seventh.

heptad, n. [1. héptad; 2. héptæd]. Gk. *heptás*, (*heptad-*). See **hepta-**. **a** Sum, group, collection, of seven things; **b** (chem.) atom, element, having valence of seven.

heptagon, n. [1. héptagun; 2. héptəgən]. Gk. *heptágōnos*, fr. **hepta-** & **-gon**. (geom.) Figure with seven angles and seven sides.

heptagonal, adj. [1. heptágunal; 2. hεptǽgənəl]. Prec. & **-al**. Having seven angles.

heptahedron, n. [1. hèptahḗdron; 2. hèptəhídrən]. **hepta-** & Gk. *hédra*, 'seat, foundation, base', for **sed-*, 'sit'; see **sedentary, sedate, seat**, & **sit**. The ending perh. due to influence of *-gon*. (geom.) Solid figure having seven faces.

heptarch, n. [1. héptark; 2. héptăk]. **hepta-** & **-arch**. One of the rulers in a heptarchy.

heptarchy, n. [1. héptarki; 2. héptəki]. **hepta-** & **-archy**. Government by seven rulers; specif., supposed system of seven kingdoms, existing at one time in Anglo-Saxon England.

heptateuch, n. [1. héptatūk; 2. héptətjūk]. L. Lat. *Heptateuchos*, formed fr. **hepta-** & Gk. *teûkhos*, 'tool, implement; book'; cp. Gk. *téukhein*, 'make, fashion, prepare'; cp. Goth., O.E. &c. *dugan*, 'to avail, suit' &c., q.v. under **doughty**. First seven books of Old Testament.

her (I.), pers. pron. [1. hĕr; 2. hā, hə]. O.E. *hire*, dat. sing. of *hēo*, 'she', fem. of *hē*, see **he**; cp. O. Fris. *hire*; fr. demonstr. base **hi*; M.E. *hire*, *here*, extended, like other datives of pers. prons., to direct object, replacing O.E. acc. *hīe*. **a** Accusative of **she**, expressing direct object; **b** dative, expressing indirect object; **c** (archaic or poet.) herself (direct or indirect): *she leaned her o'er the saddle-bow*; **d** (colloq. or vulg., emphatic) she: *it's her, sure enough.*

her (II.), possess. pronominal adj. O.E. *hire*, genit. sing. of *hēo*, 'she' (see prec.), also indeclinable pronominal adj., M.E. *hire, hir, her*. See also **hers** & **herself**. Of, pertaining, or belonging to, her.

herald (I.), n. [1. hérald; 2. hérəld]. M.E. *herald, heraud*, fr. O. Fr. *heralt, heraut*, Ital. *araldo*. The first element is apparently that seen in O.H.G. *harēn, herēn*, 'to proclaim, cry aloud', cp. also O.H.G. *fora-haro*, 'one who proclaims; a herald' (cp. **haro**); cogn. w. Goth. *hazjan*, O.E. *herian*, 'to praise'. The second element is fr. O.H.G. *-waldo, -walto*, fr. *waltan*, 'to manage, govern', q.v. under **wield**. **1. a** Official who makes public announcements, esp. in proclaiming king's death or accession, or other solemn public news; **b** official of the College of Arms charged with care of genealogies and armorial bearings. **2.** (by extension) Any person who proclaims news; a person or thing whose appearance imports the coming of some other person or of an event; forerunner, harbinger.

herald (II.), vb. trans., fr. prec. **a** To announce, proclaim; to act as a herald to; **b** to usher in, make known coming of: *the song of birds heralds the approach of spring.*

heraldic, adj. [1. heráldik; 2. herǽldik]. **herald** (I.) & **-ic**. Pertaining to herald or to heraldry.

heraldically, adv. [1. heráldikali; 2. herǽldikəli]. Prec. & **-al** & **-ly**. In a heraldic manner; according to the rules of heraldry.

heraldry, n. [1. héraldri; 2. hérəldri]. **herald** (I.) & **-ry**. **a** Office or functions of herald; **b** art of recording genealogies, of determining precedence, the right to arms, and of blazoning; **c** blazonry, armorial bearings.

Heralds' College, n. **herald** (I.) & **college**. Corporation with authority from the Crown, to grant and record armorial bearings, to decide who is entitled to arms, and to which arms, and to keep records of pedigrees &c.

heraldship, n. [1. héraldship; 2. hérəldʃip]. **herald** (I.) & **-ship**. Office of herald.

herb, n. [1. hĕrb; 2. hāb]. M.E., O. Fr. *herbe, erbe*, fr. Lat. *herba*, 'grass, herb'; etymol. quite uncertain. Derivation has been suggested fr. a dial. form of O. Lat. *forbea*, 'fodder', wh. is fr. Gk. *phorbḗ*, 'pasture', connected w. *phérbein*, 'to feed, nourish'. This is perh. fr. base **bher-*, 'to nourish'. See **bear** (I.). **a** Low plant, without woody tissue, usually dying down in winter; **b** plant, wild or cultivated, with aromatic or other property, for which it is used in flavouring food, for medicine, for scent &c.; a simple: *a herb garden, pot herbs*; **c** (archaic or poet.) grass, herbage.

herbaceous, adj. [1. hĕrbáshus; 2. hābéiʃəs]. Lat. *herbāce-us*, 'grassy'; see prec. & **-aceous**. **1.** Pertaining to, of nature of, herb or herbs; dying down in winter; *herbaceous border*, garden border stocked with herbaceous plants. **2.** Resembling leaf: *herbaceous sepals.*

herbage, n. [1. hĕrbij; 2. hābidž]. Fr., fr. L. Lat. *herbāticum*. See **herb** & **-age**. **1.** (coll.) **a** Grass and other field plants; pasture; **b** tender leaves, tops, of herbs. **2.** (law) Right of pasturage.

herbal, adj. & n. [1. hĕrbal; 2. hābəl]. Lat. *herbāl-(is)*; fr. **herb** & **-al**. **a** adj. Pertaining to herb or herbs; **b** n., descriptive treatise on herbs and their uses.

herbalist, n. [1. hĕrbalist; 2. hābəlist]. Prec. & **-ist**. **a** Writer of a herbal; early descriptive botanist; **b** dealer in herbs, esp. as curatives of disease.

herbarium, n. [1. hĕrbárium; 2. hābéəriəm]. L. Lat. *herbārium*; fr. **herb** & **-arium**. **a** Systematized collection of preserved plants; **b** building or room for storing this.

herbary, n. [1. hĕrbari; 2. hābəri]. Herbarium.

herb beer, n. Non-alcoholic drink made from herbs.

herb bennet, n. [1. hĕrb bénet; 2. hāb bénit]. O. Fr. *herbe beneite*, fr. Lat. *herba benedicta*, 'blessed herb'. See **benediction**. Yellow avens, the astringent root of which was used medicinally.

herb grace, n., also *herb of grace*. Rue.

herbiferous, adj. [1. hĕrbíferus; 2. hābífərəs]. Lat. *herbifer*, fr. *herba* (**herb**) & **-ferous**. Producing herbs.

herbivore, n. [1. hĕrbivōr; 2. hābivɔ̄]. Fr., fr. Lat. *herbi-*, combining form of *herba* (**herb**), & *vorāre*, 'devour'. See **voracious**. Mammal that feeds mainly on grass.

herbivorous, adj. [1. hĕrbívorus; 2. hābívərəs]. Prec. & **-ous**. Feeding on herbage or vegetable food.

herborist, n. [1. hĕrborist; 2. hābərist]. Fr. *herboriste*, see **herborize** & **-ist**. (archaic or rare) **a** Collector of plants; **b** herbalist.

herborization, n. [1. hĕrborizáshun; 2. hābəraizéiʃən]. See next word & **-ation**. (archaic or rare) **a** Action of herborizing; **b** a collection of plants.

herborize, vb. intrans. [1. hĕrborīz; 2. hābəraiz]. Fr. *herboriser*, fr. Lat. *herba*, for *herbal-*; confused w. *arbor*, 'tree', & **-ize**. (archaic or rare) To collect plants.

herb paris, n. Perennial liliaceous herb, native of Britain, bearing green flowers in a whorl of large oval leaves.

herb robert, n. [1. hĕrb róbert; 2. hāb róbət]. Common British geranium with red flowers and an unpleasant odour.

herb tea, n. Drink made from aromatic or medicinal herb.

herby, adj. [1. hĕrbi; 2. hābi]. **herb** & **-y**. **a** Pertaining to, resembling, a herb or herbs; **b** covered with, abounding in, herbs or grass.

Herculean, adj. [1. hĕrkūléan; 2. hākjulíən]. Lat. *Herculeus*, fr. **Hercules** & adj. suff. *-eus*, & **-an**, cp. Fr. *herculéen*. **a** Pertaining to or resembling Hercules; of extreme bodily strength or size: *a man of Herculean build*; **b** needing the strength of a Hercules; laborious, and of great magnitude: *a Herculean labour, task.*

Hercules, n. [1. hĕrkūlēz; 2. hākjulīz]. Lat., for **Herclēs*, fr. Gk. *Hēraklês*, Greek hero renowned for his strength and the number and magnitude of his labours. Man of extraordinary strength: *a regular Hercules.*

Hercules beetle, n. Brazilian beetle, of which male is very large and has long horns.

Hercules powder, n. Kind of dynamite used for blasting.

herd (I.), n. [1. hĕrd; 2. hād]. O.E. *heord*, M.E. *heorde, herd*; cp. O.H.G. *herta*, Mod. Germ. *herde*, Goth. *hairda*, O.N. *hjörd*; cp. also Gk. *kórthus*, 'heap, pile', & Scrt. *śárdhaš*, 'troop, host'. From Aryan base **k̂er-*, 'to make, grow' &c. See also **create, crescent**. **1. a** Collection, group, flock, of large gregarious animals, such as cattle, deer, whales, living, feeding, and moving about together; **b** collection of beasts, esp. cattle or swine, of one stock or breed: *the Chillingham herd.* **2.** (fig., contempt.) Mass, aggregate, of human beings; rabble, crowd; esp. *the herd, the common, vulgar, herd.*

herd (II.), vb. trans. & intrans. M.E. *herdien*, fr. prec. **1.** trans. To gather into, put into, a herd; to drive, tend, as a herd: *to herd sheep, cattle.* **2.** intrans. **a** To assemble or associate as a herd: *to herd together*; **b** to join a herd or company, live in a herd; **c** to gather together into a crowd; flock, throng together.

herd (III.), n. O.E. (non-W.S.) *herde*, cp. W.S. *hierde*, fr. **hirdja-*, 'shepherd', M.E. *herde*; cp. O.S. *hirdi*, O.H.G. *hirti*, Mod. Germ. *hirt(e)*, Goth. *hairdeis*, O.N. *hirðir*, fr. same base as **herd** (I.). (archaic, liter., or dial. except in composition, as *cow-herd*) Man who herds beasts, or tends a herd; herdsman.

herd-book, n. Book containing records of pedigree cattle or sheep.

herd-instinct, n. (psychol.) Instinctive tendency to feel, act, and think in accordance with the crowd or community; susceptibility to mass-suggestion.

herdman, n. [1. hĕrdman; 2. hādmən]. **herd** (I.) & **man** (I.). (rare) Herdsman.

herdsman, n. [1. hĕrdzman; 2. hādzmən]. Man who tends herd, esp. of cattle; owner of herd.

here (I.), adv. [1. hēr; 2. hiə]. O.E., M.E. *hēr*; Common Gmc., cp. O.H.G. *hiar*, Germ. *hier*, O.S., Goth., O.N. *hēr*, Swed. *här*, Dan. *her*, fr. demonstr. base **hi-* (see **he, her**), & advbl. suff. *-r*. See **there, where**. **1. a** In this place where now I am; near, round about me; in my hand: *I live here*; *here is what you ask for, take it*; Phrs. *here!*, present (reply at roll-call); *here below*, on earth; *here and there*, sparsely, dispersed; *here, there, and everywhere*, (i.) moving constantly between many places; (ii.) in many places; *neither here nor there*, not to the point, irrelevant, without significance; *here's (a health) to . . .*, I drink to the health of . . .; *here you are*, (colloq.) this is what you want; (colloq.) *my friend here*, whom you see here; **b** at this place (on map &c.) which I indicate: *here is where the battle was fought* &c.; **c** at this point which I have reached in my narrative, remarks &c.: *here we will pause for a few moments*; *here he glanced at me*; *here I think he is wrong.* **2.** Hither, towards me, to where I am: *come here (to me)*; *look here*; *here he comes.*

here (II.), n. **1.** This place: *far from here, near here.* **2.** (philos.) Immediacy in space: *we are conscious of a here and a now.*

hereabout, hereabouts, adv. [1. hérabout(s); 2. híərəbaut(s)]. Prec. & **about** & M.E. advbl. suff. *-es, -s*, orig. genit. Near this place, in this neighbourhood.

hereafter, adv. & n. [1. hēráhfter; 2. hiərάftə]. O.E. *hērǽfter*, M.E. *hērafter*, fr. **here** & **after**. **1.** adv. **a** After this time, in the future; **b** for the future, henceforth; **c** in the future life. **2.** n. The future life, the world to come: *the unknown hereafter.*

hereat, adv. [1. hērát; 2. hiərǽt]. At this, upon this, when this happened.

hereby, adv. [1. hērbí; 2. hiəbái]. **a** (archaic) By, near, this place; **b** by means, reason, of this.

hereditability, n. [1. herèditabíliti; 2. hirèditəbíliti]. See next word & **-ity**. Quality, condition, of being hereditable.

hereditable, adj. [1. heréditabl; 2. hiréditəbl]. O. Fr., fr. L. Lat. *hērēditābilis*, fr. L. Lat. *hērēditāre*. See **heredity** & **-able**. (law) Heritable; capable of being inherited.

hereditament, n. [1. herèditament; 2. hèridítəmənt]. L. Lat. *hērēditāmentum*, as prec. & **-ment**. (law) Any kind of property that may be inherited.

hereditarily, adv. [1. heréditarili; 2. hiréditərili]. **hereditary** & **-ly**. In a hereditary manner; by or through heredity: *hereditarily afflicted.*

hereditary, adj. [1. heréditari; 2. hiréditəri]. Lat. *hērēditāri-us*, fr. *hērēditas*. See next word & **-ary**. **1.** (biol., of bodily and mental features and characteristics) Derived from, transmitted by, ancestors; not acquired: *hereditary characters, disease* &c. **2.** (legal and constitutional) **a** (of rights, titles, offices

&c.) Derived, handed on, descending by inheritance, from ancestors: *hereditary monarchy* &c.; **b** (of property) transmitted, acquired, by inheritance; ancestral, patrimonial: *hereditary estates, succession*; **c** of persons, holding hereditary office: *hereditary monarch.* **3.** (of habits, customs, beliefs &c.) Learnt, accepted, made current, by continued tradition; inveterate, traditional: *hereditary feud, friendship, religion.*

heredity, n. [1. herédity; 2. hirédití]. Fr. *hérédité*, fr. Lat. *hērēditāt-(em)*, 'heirship', fr. *hērēd-*, stem of *hērēs* (cp. **heir**), an old compound, lit. 'heritage-receiving', & **-ity.** The first element is cogn. w. Scrt. *jáhāti*, 'gives up, leaves', *jíhītē*, 'goes forth', Gk. *khêros*, 'deprived', *khôros*, 'empty space, land', see under **chori-**. The second element, **ēd-*, is prob. fr. a prep. **ē*, 'to, at, by', & **dhō-*, **dhə-* &c., 'to give', q.v. under **date (I.)**, **do (I.)**. (biol.) **a** Tendency of living organism to transmit its bodily and mental characters to its offspring or descendants; **b** the body of theory and doctrine concerning this principle.

Hereford, n. & adj. [1. hériford; 2. hérifəd], fr. county of Hereford, England. **a** n. Beast of breed of red and white beef cattle, first bred in Herefordshire; **b** adj., pertaining to, derived from, this breed.

herefrom, adv. [1. hērfróm; 2. hiəfrɔ́m]. From this.

herein, adv. [1. hērín, hérin; 2. hiərín, híərin]. O.E. *hērinne.* In this.

hereinafter, adv. [1. hērináhfter; 2. hiərinấftə]. (esp. in legal documents) Henceforth in this document: *hereinafter called the vendor.*

hereinbefore, adv. [1. hērinbefór; 2. hiərinbifɔ́]. Hitherto in this document &c.

hereinto, adv. [1. hēríntōō; 2. hiəríntū]. Into this.

hereof, adv. [1. hēróv, -of; 2. hiərɔ́v, -ɔ́f]. Of this.

hereon, adv. [1. hērón; 2. hiərɔ́n]. On this.

heresiarch, n. [1. herḗziark; 2. herízīāk]. Lat. *haeresiarcha*, fr. Gk. *hairesiárkhēs*, fr. **heresy** & **-arch.** Founder or leader of heresy or heretical sect.

heresiologist, n. [1. hèrēziólojist; 2. hèrīziɔ́lədžist]. Next word & **-ist.** Student of heresy and heresies.

heresiology, n. [1. hèrēzióloji; 2. hèrīziɔ́lədži]. Gk. See **heresy** & **-logy.** Systematic knowledge of heresies; treatise on heresies.

heresy, n. [1. héresi; 2. hérisi]. M.E., O. Fr. *(h)eresie*, fr. Lat. *haeresis*, fr. Gk. *hairesis*, 'a taking for oneself; choice, sect, heresy', fr. *hairé-esthai*, Middle Voice of *hairé-ein*, 'to take', & Gk. suff. *-sis*, fr. Aryan **-tis*, forming abstract n. fr. vb. Origin of word unknown. **1. a** An erroneous religious belief, especially one specifically condemned and denounced as such by the Christian Church: *the Arian heresy*; **b** doctrinal error, heterodoxy: *to fall into heresy.* **2.** Opinion on any matter, differing from the received, official, established, or prevalent teaching: *the anti-vaccinationist heresy.*

heretic, n. [1. héretik; 2. héritik]. M.E. *heretike*, fr. Fr. *hérétique*, fr. L. Lat. *haereticus*, fr. Gk. *hairetikós*, 'able to choose, heretical', fr. *hairetós*, 'to be chosen', as prec. & **-ic.** Person guilty of religious heresy; one holding a heresy of any kind; also attrib.: *a heretic bishop.*

heretical, adj. [1. herétikl; 2. herétikl]. Prec. & **-al.** Pertaining to, tainted with, believing, containing, heresy; pertaining to a heretic.

heretically, adv. Prec. & **-ly.** In a heretical manner.

hereticate, vb. trans. [1. herétikāt; 2. herétikeit]. Low Lat. *haereticāt-*, P.P. stem of *haereticāre*, fr. **heretic** & **-ate.** (rare) To declare, esp. officially, to be heretical.

hereto, adv. [1. hērtṓō; 2. hiətū]. M.E. *hēr tō*, fr. **here** & **to.** Hitherto, hereunto; to this.

heretofore, adv. [1. hèrtoofór; 2. hiətufɔ́]. **here** & O.E. *tōforan*; 'before', M.E. *tōfōren*; cp. O.S. *teforan*; fr. **to** & **fore.** (archaic) **a** Hitherto, up to the present; **b** formerly.

hereunder, adv. [1. hērúnder; 2. hiərándə]. **here** & **under.** Under, below, this (in document &c.).

hereunto, adv. [1. hèruntōō; 2. hiərantū́]. **here** & **unto.** (archaic) Hitherto, to this place or time.

hereupon, adv. [1. hèrupón; 2. hiərəpɔ́n]. **here** & **upon.** Upon this; immediately after this.

herewith, adv. [1. hērwíth, -wídh; 2. hiəwíþ, -wíð]. With, accompanying, this; upon this occasion, now.

heriot, n. [1. hériot; 2. hériət]. A.-Fr., M.E. *heriet*, fr. O.E. *heregeat*, *hergeat*, 'military equipment; heriot', fr. *here*, 'army', see **harry**, & *geatwa*, earlier *ge-tāwe*, pl. 'apparatus, arms', fr. *tāwian*, 'to prepare'. (Engl. law) Feudal due or fine paid to lord of manor on tenant's death; originally, equipment previously lent to the latter, now, some chattel prescribed by custom of manor, or money equivalent.

heritability, n. [1. hèritabíliti; 2. hèritəbíliti]. Next word & **-ity.** Capacity for being inherited.

heritable, adj. & n. [1. héritabl; 2. héritəbl]. Fr. *héritable*, fr. *hériter.* **inherit** & **-able**; cp. **hereditable.** **1.** adj. **a** Capable of being inherited, inheritable; Phr. (Scots law) *heritable security*, kind of mortgage; **b** capable of inheriting. **2.** n. (usually pl.) Heritable property, real estate.

heritably, adv. Prec. & **-ly.** By right of inheritance.

heritage, n. [1. héritij; 2. héritidž]. M.E., O.F. *(h)eritage*, fr. Lat. *hērēd-*. See **heredity.** **1. a** Inherited property, inheritance, patrimony; **b** (Scots law) realty. **2.** (fig.) **a** Anything material or non-material, to which one succeeds by birth; e.g. (i.) a right, privilege; (ii.) a burden; (iii.) a characteristic, derived from parents, ancestors, or predecessors: *debts were his only heritage*; *English literature is a glorious heritage*; *a heritage of disease, of woe*; **b** (Bib. phr.) *God's heritage*, the chosen people, Israel; the Church.

heritor, n. [1. héritor; 2. héritə]. M.E. *heriter*, Fr. *héritier*, fr. Lat. *hērēd-*, see **heredity** & **-ier**, assimilated to **-or.** **a** Inheritor, heir; **b** (Scots) landholder in a parish.

herm, n. [1. hērm; 2. hām]. Lat. *Herma*, fr. Gk. *Hermês*, earlier *Herméīas*, god of luck, roads, trade, eloquence &c.; also 'herm'. Of doubtful origin. In ancient Greece, squared pillar, terminating in a head of Hermes, set up in the street, gymnasium &c.

hermaphrodite, n. & adj. [1. hērmáfrodīt; 2. hāmǽfrədait]. Lat. *hermaphrodītus*, fr. Gk. *Hermaphróditos*, properly son of Hermes (see **herm**) as male principle, and of Aphrodite (see **aphrodisiac**) as female, who was united in one body with a nymph. **1.** n. **a** Animal or plant capable at once of fertilizing and of being fertilized; **b** loosely, a human being or animal who has traces of both male and female sexual organs. **2.** adj. Hermaphroditic.

hermaphroditic, adj. [1. hērmàfrodítik; 2. hāmæ̀frədítik]. Prec. & **-ic.** Having character of hermaphrodite (lit. or fig.).

hermaphroditism, n. [1. hērmáfrodītìzm; 2. hāmǽfrədaitìzəm]. **hermaphrodite** & **-ism.** (biol.) Condition of being an hermaphrodite; bisexuality.

hermeneutic, adj. & n. [1. hērmenū́tik; 2. hāminjū́tik]. Gk. *hermēneutikós*, fr. *hermēneutês*, 'interpreter', fr. *hermēneúein*, 'to interpret', perh. fr. *Hermês* (see **herm**) as god of speech, or cogn. w. Lat. *sermo* (stem *sermōn-*, see **sermon**), 'discourse', & *-tēs*, suff. of agent-n., & **-ic.** **a** adj. Interpretative (esp. in theol.); **b** n., pl. *hermeneutics*, science of principles of interpretation, specif., of Bible.

hermetic, adj. [1. hērmétik; 2. hāmétik]. L. Lat. *hermēticus*, 'alchemic' (whence Fr. *hermétique*), irreg. fr. Hermes (Trismegistus), supposed author of *Hermetic books* on magic and alchemy. **a** (cap.) Pertaining to Hermes Trismegistus or his alleged works: *the Hermetic art, philosophy*; **b** (without cap.) having external air excluded; air-tight.

hermetically, adv. [1. hērmétikali; 2. hāmétikəli]. Prec. & **-al** & **-y.** In a hermetic manner; esp. so as to be airtight: *hermetically sealed.*

hermit, n. [1. hérmit; 2. hámit]. M.E. *(h)ermite*, fr. O. Fr. *hermite*, fr. L. Lat. *herēmīta*, fr. Lat. *erēmīta*, fr. Gk. *erēmítēs*, 'hermit', fr. *érēmos*, 'solitary, isolated', cogn. w. Gk. *araiós*, 'rare, scattered', & w. Lat. *rārus*, 'thin, not dense', q.v. under **rare (I.)**. **1. a** Person, usually man, living alone in cell, usually in secluded or desert place, for meditation and prayer; an eremite; an anchoret; **b** man who avoids all society; a recluse. **2.** One of several humming-birds inhabiting recesses of forests.

hermitage, n. [1. hérmitij; 2. hámitidž]. M.E., fr. Fr. Prec. & **-age.** **1. a** Cell or other abode of hermit; **b** any secluded dwelling. **2.** (cap.) Kind of wine from place called l'Hermitage, near Valence, France.

hermit crab, n. One of group of crabs with long soft bodies, inhabiting abandoned shells of gasteropod molluscs.

hermitess, n. [1. hérmites; 2. hámites]. **hermit** & **-ess.** (rare) Female hermit.

hernia, n. [1. hérnia; 2. hániə]. Lat., prob. cogn. w. O.E. *gearn.* See **yarn (I.)**. (med.) Protrusion, through natural or accidental opening, of part of internal organ of the body, esp. of part of the bowel; rupture.

hernial, adj. [1. hérnial; 2. hániəl]. Prec. & **-al.** (med.) Pertaining to hernia.

herniated, adj. [1. hérniāted; 2. hánieitid]. **hernia** & **-ate** & **-ed.** (med.) Affected by hernia.

herniotomy, n. [1. hērniótomi; 2. hāniɔ́təmi]. *hernio-*, form of **hernia** used in compounds, & **-tomy.** (surg.) Operation of cutting for hernia.

hernshaw, n. [1. hérnshaw; 2. hánʃɔ]. M.E. *heronsew*, fr. O.F. *heronceau*, dimin. of *harion*, *hairon*, see **heron.** (obs. or provinc.) A heron.

hero, n. (1. hḗrō; 2. híərou]. M. Fr. *heroe* (Mod. Fr. *héros*), fr. Lat. *hērōem*, acc. of *hērōs*, fr. Gk. *hḗrōs*, fr. **wer-*; cogn. w. Lat. *vir*, O.E. *wer*, 'man', &c.; cp. **virile, werewolf.** **1.** Man, often worshipped as demigod, celebrated by any community, esp. among primitive peoples, for warlike exploits, or credited with the introduction of arts &c. **2. a** Male person conspicuous for valour, fortitude, and endurance in danger and difficulty, and for such romantic qualities as outstanding personal strength and beauty, success in war, chivalry, magnanimity, perfect courtesy &c.: *Bruce and Wallace are Scotland's national heroes*; **b** any person whose character, reputation, exploits, and personality strike the imagination, and cause one to regard him as the ideal of manly virtue: *one of my heroes*; *a schoolboy's hero.* **3.** Leading male character in a literary work, or in a narrative: *the hero of an anecdote, of an adventure.*

heroic (I.), adj. [1. herṓik; 2. hiróuik]. Fr. *héroïque*, fr. Lat. *hērōicus*, fr. Gk. *hērōikós*, fr. prec. & **-ic.** **1. a** Pertaining to a primitive hero or heroes; *the heroic age*, legendary age of Greek or other primitive heroes; **b** (of person or action) resembling, worthy of, a hero; dauntless, inflexibly courageous and steadfast; possessing and exhibiting the virtues of a hero; **c** daring, hazardous, but advisable in last resort; esp. in med.: *heroic measures*; *heroic medicine, remedy, treatment.* **2. a** (art, of human figure) Of size larger than life, but less than colossal: *on a heroic scale*; (also fig.); **b** pertaining to epic, or to poetry dealing with heroes: *heroic poem, poetry*, epic; **c** *heroic verse*, metre customary in epic, hence, specif., classical hexameter, French alexandrine, English line of ten syllables and five stresses in rhyming couplets; *heroic couplets*; **d** (of language) grandiloquent, bombastic.

heroic (II.), n., fr. prec. **a** (sing. or pl.) Heroic poetry or verse; **b** (pl.) *heroics*, grandiloquent, high-flown, bombastic, theatrical, talk, or behaviour.

heroical, adj. [1. herṓikl; 2. hiróuikl]. Prec. & **-al**. (archaic or rare) Heroic.

heroicomic(al), adj. [1. herṓikómík(l); 2. hiróuikómik(l)]. *Heroi-* combining form of **hero** & **comic** (& **-al**). (of poem or prose narrative) Combining heroic and comic elements.

heroin, n. [1. héroin, herṓin; 2. hérouin, hɛróuin]. Invented word. Dangerous sedative drug derived from morphine.

heroine, n. [1. héroin; 2. hérouin]. Fr. *héroïne*, fr. Lat. *hērōina*, fr. Gk. *hērōínē*, fr. **hero** & **-ine**. Female hero in any sense.

heroism, n. [1. hérōizm; 2. hérouizəm]. Fr. *héroïsme*, fr. **hero** & **-ism**. Heroic qualities or conduct.

heroize, vb. trans. & intrans. [1. hḗrōiz; 2. híərouaiz]. **hero** & **-ize**. (rare) **1.** trans. **a** To treat as hero; **b** to make heroic. **2.** intrans. To play the hero, pose as hero.

heron, n. [1. hérun; 2. hérən]. M.E. *heiroun, heroun, hern*, fr. O. Fr. *hairon*, Mod. Fr. *héron*, borrowed, w. addition of *-on* (see **-oon**), fr. O.H.G. *heigir, -er*, 'heron'; cogn. w. Gk. *kissa* (for **kikja*), 'magpie', or 'jay', Lat. *cicōnia*, 'stork', all imitative of cry. Cp. **aigrette, egret.** Large British wading bird, *Ardea cinerea*, with long legs, neck, and beak, grey and white plumage and crest; any bird of same family, as the bittern &c.

heronry, n. [1. hérunri; 2. hérənri]. Prec. & **-ry**. Group of herons' nests in tree-tops.

hero-worship, n. **a** Cult of hero or demigod; **b** veneration of great man or men; **c** extravagant admiration, adulation, of a person.

hero-worshipper, n. One addicted to hero-worship.

herpes, n. [1. hḗrpēz; 2. hə́piz]. Lat. *herpēs*, fr. Gk. *hérpēs*, 'shingles', fr. *hérpein*, 'to creep'. Cogn. w. Scrt. *srp*, Lat. *serpere*, 'to creep'. See **serpent.** (pathol.) One of several inflammatory skin-diseases, marked by spreading vesicles; shingles.

herpetic, adj. [1. hērpétik; 2. həpétik]. Gk. *herpēt-*, stem of prec., & **-ic**; cp. Fr. *herpétique*. (pathol.) Pertaining to, resembling, herpes or shingles.

herpetologist, n. [1. hērpetólojist; 2. həpitóladžist]. Next word & **-ist.** Student of herpetology.

herpetology, n. [1. hērpetóloji; 2. həpitóladži]. Fr. *herpétologie*, fr. Gk. *herpetón*, 'creeping animal, reptile', fr. *hérpein*, 'to creep'. See **herpes.** Science of reptiles.

herring, n. [1. héring; 2. hériŋ]. O.E. *hǣrin(c)g*, M.E. *hering*; cp. O.H.G., Du. *hāring*, Germ. *häring*; of unknown origin. **a** Marine fish, *Clupea harengus*, related to sprat, frequenting coasts of N. Atlantic, North Sea &c., in vast shoals, valued as food, fresh, salted, or dried; *kippered herring*, kipper; Phr. *packed as close as herrings*; *red herring*, smoke-cured herring; Phrs. *neither fish, flesh, nor good red herring*, thing of indefinite character; *to draw a red herring across the path*, to divert attention from awkward subject by introducing some other, interesting but irrelevant, subject (metaphor from drag hunting); **b** fish more or less resembling herring, as *lake herring*, an edible white fish of the Great Lakes of N. America.

herring-bone, n., adj., & vb. trans. **1.** n. **a** Spine of herring with ribs attached; **b** pattern resembling this; series of two or more courses in wall, in which tiles or bricks are laid on end, sloping opposite ways in successive courses; **c** kind of cross-stitch. **2.** adj. Pertaining to, resembling, herring-bone pattern: *herring-bone bond, stitch, strutting, twill.* **3.** vb. To apply herring-bone stitch or pattern to.

herring-gull, n. Large white gull of N. Atlantic, with black tips to wings.

herring-pond, n. (facet.) Ocean, esp. N. Atlantic.

hers, pron. [1. hērz; 2. həz]. Late M.E. *hires, heres*, fr. possess. adj. *hire, here* (**her (II.)**), & *-s*, on anal. of **his.** Cp. **ours, yours.** Used absolutely. **1.** That or those which belong to her: *his hair is darker than hers*; *my mother and hers.* **2.** After *of*, her (pers. pron.): *that heart of hers* (cp. **his**).

herse, n. [1. hērs; 2. həs]. See **hearse.** **a** Portcullis, resembling a harrow in shape; **b** a *cheval de frise*, like an upturned harrow; **c** old formation of troops.

herself, pron. [1. hērsélf; 2. həsélf]. O.E. *hire selfum*, dat. sing. of *hīe self*, M.E. *hire self*, fr. **her** (**I.** & **II.**), acc., genit. & dat., & **self.** See **myself, himself.** (fem., sing. pron.) **1.** (reflex.) *She persuades herself, asks herself a question, works for, hurts herself.* Phr. (*all*) *by herself*, alone. **2.** Emphatic form corresponding to **she, her** (**I.**), in every sense corresponding to emphatic **myself, himself**: *she told me so herself*, &c. **3.** (as quasi-noun) Her normal, healthy self: *she is not herself*; *she has come to herself.*

Hertzian waves, n. pl. [1. hḗrtsian wā́vz; 2. hə́tsiən wéivz], fr. H. Hertz, German physicist (d. 1894). Electric wave movements in the ether, investigated first by Hertz and subsequently adapted to wireless telegraphy &c.

hesitance, hesitancy, n. [1. hézitans(i); 2. hézitəns(i)]. Lat. *haesitantia*, 'stammering', fr. *haesitāre*, **hesitate** & **-ance, -ancy.** Quality of hesitating; hesitation.

hesitant, adj. [1. hézitant; 2. hézitənt]. Fr. *hésitant*, fr. Lat. *haesitant-(em)*, Pres. Part. of *haesitāre*. See **hesitate.** Inclined to hesitate; hesitating, undecided.

hesitantly, adv. Prec. & **-ly.** In a hesitant manner.

hesitate, vb. intrans. & trans. [1. hézitāt; 2. héziteit], fr. Lat. *haesitāt-(um)*, P.P. type of *haesitāre*, 'to stick fast, stammer, hesitate', fr. *haes-(um)*, P.P. type of *haerēre*, 'to cleave, stick'. See **adhere, cohere.** **1.** intrans. **a** To pause in speech, movement, or action through indecision; to falter, to be irresolute; **b** (followed by *to*) to be reluctant, scruple: *I hesitate to affirm.* **2.** trans. (rare) To utter, assert, express, with hesitation: '*Just hint a fault and hesitate dislike*' (Pope).

hesitatingly, adv. [1. hézitātingli; 2. héziteitiŋli]. Prec. & **-ing** & **-ly.** In a hesitating manner.

hesitation, n. [1. hèzitā́shun; 2. hèzitéiʃən]. Fr. *hésitation*, fr. Lat. *haesitātiōn-(em)*, fr. *haesitāre*, 'to hesitate', see prec. & **-ation.** **a** Act of hesitating, condition of one who hesitates; deliberate delay, indecision; reluctance; **b** impediment, defect, in speech.

hesitative, adj. [1. hézitativ; 2. hézitətiv]. **hesitate** & **-ive.** Inclined to hesitate.

Hesperian, adj. & n. [1. hespérian; 2. hɛspíəriən]. Lat. *hesperi-us*, fr. Gk. *hespérios*, fr. *hésperos* for **wesperos*, 'evening, the evening star', cogn. w. **vesper** & **west.** (poet.) **a** adj. Western; belonging to Hesperia, Italy; **b** n., inhabitant of the West.

Hesperus, n. [1. hésperus; 2. héspərəs]. See prec. The evening star.

Hessian, adj. & n. [1. héshan; 2. héʃən]. **1.** adj. Of, pertaining to, Hesse, in Germany, specif. **a** *Hessian boot*, a high military boot worn by Hessian soldiers, employed as mercenaries during 18th cent.; **b** *Hessian fly*, insect, the larvae of which are a wheat pest. **2.** n. Coarse cloth made of hemp or of hemp and jute.

hest, n. [1. hest; 2. hɛst]. Same as **behest.**

hetaira, n. [1. hetíra; 2. hɛtáiərə]. Gk. *hetaira*, earlier *hetárē*, orig. 'female companion', perh. fr. *étēs*, fr. *wétēs*, 'kinsman, townsman, neighbour'; cogn. w. Lith. *svētis*, 'host, guest', fr. base **swĕ-ta*; cp. parallel base **sĕ-t-* &c., in O. Slav. (*po*)*sĕtiti*, 'to visit', Lat. *satelles*, 'bodyguard', see **satellite.** (in ancient Greece) Concubine, mistress; one of class of superior courtesans.

hetairism, n. [1. hetírizm; 2. hɛtáiərizəm]. Gk. *hetairismós*; fr. prec. & **-ism.** **a** Recognized concubinage; **b** (anthrop.) supposed institution of communal marriage within tribe.

heter- = **hetero-**, before vowel.

hetero-, pref. Gk. *héteros*, earlier *háteros*, 'the other, different, unusual', perh. fr. Aryan demonstr. stem **so-* (Gk. *ho*, 'the') & suff. *-tero-*, expressing contrast, comparison &c.; cp. Lat. *al-ter*, Goth. *an-þar*, **other**, also **dexter.** Form in compounds of Greek origin, denoting **a** different from type, abnormal, irregular; **b** of more than one kind; contrasted w. *homo-*.

heteroclite, adj. & n. [1. héteroklīt; 2. hétərəklait]. Fr. *hétéroclite*, fr. Lat. *heteroclitus*, fr. Gk. *heteróklitos*, fr. **hetero-** & *-klitós*, vbl. adj. w. pass. sense fr. *klīnein*, 'to bend, decline, inflect'. See **clinical.** **a** adj. Irregular, anomalous; specif., irregularly inflected; **b** n., (gram.) irregular noun.

heterodox, adj. [1. héterodoks; 2. hétərədɔks]. Gk. *heteródoxos*, fr. **hetero-** & *dóxa*, 'opinion', fr. *dokein, doké-ein*, 'to think', cogn. w. Lat. *docēre*, 'to teach'. See **doxology, dogma** & cp. **docile.** **1.** (theol.) **a** (of opinions, beliefs) Differing from those generally taught and accepted as sound; verging towards heresy; unorthodox; **b** (of persons) holding such opinions. **2.** (gen., of persons, views &c.) Differing from what is commonly received, held, or believed.

heterodoxy, n. [1. héterodoksi; 2. hétərədɔksi]. Gk. *heterodoxia*; fr. prec. & **-y.** **a** Body or system of heterodox opinion; **b** state of mind which is imbued with this.

heterodyne, adj. [1. héterodīn; 2. hétərədain]. See **hetero-** & **dyne.** In wireless telephony, of a method of producing audible sounds by differences in beat between transmitted waves and waves produced in the receiver: *heterodyne receiver, circuit.*

heterogamous, adj. [1. hèterógamus; 2. hètərɔ́gəməs]. **hetero-** & **-gamous.** **a** (biol.) Changing mode of reproduction from asexual to sexual from generation to generation; **b** (bot.) having an irregular formation of stamens and pistils.

heterogeneity, n. [1. hèterōjenḗiti; 2. hètəroudžiníiti], fr. Fr. *hétérogénéité.* See next word & **-ity.** Quality or condition of being heterogeneous; diversity.

heterogeneous, adj. [1. hèterojḗneus; 2. hètərədžíniəs]. L. Lat. *heterogene-us*, fr. Gk. *heterogenḗs*, 'of different kinds', fr. **hetero-** & *génos*, 'race, kind'. See **genus, kin,** & **-ous.** **a** Differing in kind from associated object; dissimilar, diverse: *heterogeneous elements in a society*; (math.) incommensurable: *heterogeneous quantities*; **b** composed of parts or elements of different, unrelated, kinds; not homogeneous; disparate: *a heterogeneous collection of rubbish.*

heterogeneously, adv. Prec. & **-ly.** In heterogeneous manner.

heterogenesis, n. [1. hèterōjénesis; 2. hètəroudžénisis]. **hetero-** & **genesis.** Production of a new organism otherwise than from a parent of same kind; spontaneous generation.

heterogenetic, adj. [1. hèterōjenétik; 2. hètəroudžinétik]. **hetero-** & **-genetic.** Connected with, produced by, heterogenesis.

heteromorphic, heteromorphous, adj. [1. hèteromórfik, -fus; 2. hètərəmɔ́fik, -fəs]. See **hetero-** & **-morphic, -morphous.** Differing in form and shape; exhibiting an abnormal form or shape.

heteronomous, adj. [1. heterónomus; 2. hɛtərɔ́nəməs]. See next word & **-ous.** **a** Under the rule of another, converse of *autonomous*; **b** (biol.) subject to divergence of type.

heteronomy, n. [1. heterónomi; 2. hɛtərɔ́nəmi]. **hetero-** & **-nomy.** **1.** Subjection to the rule of another, converse of *autonomy*; specif. **a** political subordination; **b** (philos.) subjection of desires to will, or of will to external force; deterministic ethics. **2.** (biol.) Divergence from type, specialization of different kind.

hetman, n. [1. hétman; 2. hétmən]. Pol., prob. fr. Germ. *hauptmann*, 'headman, captain', fr. *haupt*, see **head,** & *mann*, **man**; cp. Russ. *atamán*, 'hetman'. **a** (hist.) Polish commander-in-chief; **b** leader, commander, of Cossacks.

heuchera, n. [1. hū́kera; 2. hjúkərə], fr. German botanist Heucher. Kind of American saxifrage, a species of which, having slender stems and red flowers, is cultivated in English gardens.

heuristic, adj. & n. [1. hūrístik; 2. hjuərístik]. Formed fr. Gk. *heuri-*, stem of *heurískein*, 'to find, discover', w. suff. **-ist** & **-ic**. Cogn. w. O. Ir. *fūar*, 'I found'; fr. base, **wewr-* &c., 'find', redupl. fr. **wer-*, 'to find, take', seen in Armenian *gerem*, 'I take'. **a** adj. Enabling one to find out or discover; esp. *the heuristic method of education*; **b** n. (usually pl.) method in which the pupil learns by being trained gradually to find things out for himself; heuristic method.

hew, vb. trans. & intrans. [1. hū; 2. hjū]. O.E. *hēawan*, 'to cut, strike, hew', M.E. *hēwen*, cogn. w. O.S. *hauwan*, Du. *houwen*, O.H.G. *houwan*, Mod. Germ. *hauen*, O.N. *hǫggva*; Gmc. type **hau(ʒ)wan-*, fr. Aryan base **kou-*, **kəu-* &c., 'strike, beat', as in Lith. *káu-ti*, 'to beat, forge, fight', *kúgis*, 'hammer', *kowà*, 'battle'; O. Slav. *kovati*, 'to hammer, forge'; cp. also Lat. *cū-d-ere*, 'to strike, beat, knock' &c., chiefly in compounds, cp. Engl. words ending in *-cute* & *-cuss*, e.g. **concuss**. See **hay** (I.), **hoe**. **A.** trans. **1.** To cut, hack, chop, by striking with edged instrument; often followed by preposition or adverb: *to hew to pieces, asunder, down, off.* **2. a** To make or shape by cutting or hollowing out: *to hew out a tomb in the rock*; Phr. *to hew (out) a path, hew out a career, for oneself*, to make, shape, arrange, one's own career, or walk in life. **B.** intrans. (rare) To carry out act of hewing.

hewer, n. [1. húer; 2. hjúə]. Prec. & **-er**. Person who hews; specif., collier who cuts coal from seam. Phr. '*Hewers of wood and drawers of water*' (Joshua ix. 21), members of servile class; drudges, menials.

hewn, adj. [1. hūn; 2. hjūn]. O.E. *hēawen*, M.E. *hewen*, P.P. of **hew**. Cut, roughly shaped, by blows, as of axe or adze: *hewn timber, stone.*

hex-, hexa-, pref. Gk. *héx*, 'six', *hexa-*, combining form. See **six**. Form in compounds of Greek origin, denoting six, sixth.

hexachord, n. [1. héksakord; 2. héksəkōd]. Fr. *hexacorde*. See **hexa-** & **chord**. (mus.) **1.** (hist.) Ancient and mediaeval diatonic series of six tones. **2.** Major sixth.

hexagon, n. [1. héksagun; 2. héksəgən]. Lat. *hexagōnum*, fr. Gk. *hexágōnos*, 'having six angles'; fr. **hexa-** & **-gon**. Figure of six angles and six sides.

hexagonal, adj. [1. hekságunal; 2. heksǽgənəl]. Prec. & **-al**. Pertaining to, having form of, a hexagon.

hexagram, n. [1. héksagram; 2. héksəgræm]. **hexa-** & **-gram**. Figure formed of six lines; specif., figure composed of two equilateral triangles, so placed that the points coincide with those of a regular hexagon.

hexahedral, adj. [1. hèksahédral; 2. hèksəhídrəl]. Next word & **-al**. Having form of a hexahedron.

hexahedron, n. [1. hèksahédron; 2. hèksəhídrən]. **hexa-** & **-hedron**. Solid figure having six faces, such as cube.

hexameter, n. [1. hèksámeter; 2. hèksǽmitə]. Lat., fr. Gk. *hexámetros*, 'having six measures'; fr. **hexa-** & **-meter**. (metre) **a** Classical verse of six feet; specif., that in which first four feet are dactyls or spondees, fifth a dactyl, and sixth a spondee; **b** accentual verse in modern language of similar structure; (also attrib.) *hexameter verses.*

hexametric, adj. [1. hèksamétrik; 2. hèksəmétrik]. Prec. & **-ic**. Pertaining to hexameter; consisting of hexameters.

hexapla, n. [1. héksapla; 2. héksəplə]. Mod. Lat., fr. Gk. *hexaplâ*, neut. pl. of *hexaplóos*, *-ploûs*, 'sixfold', fr. **hexa-** & base *-plo-*, '-fold', cogn. w. Lat. *plicāri*, 'to fold'. See **ply** (I.). Edition of six texts or versions, esp. of O.T., in parallel columns.

hexapod, n. [1. héksapod; 2. héksəpɔd]. Gk. *hexapod-*, stem of *hexápous*, 'six-footed', fr. **hexa-** & *-pod-*, stem of Gk. *poús*, 'foot'. See **pedal**. (zool.) Any member of the class *Hexapoda*, the six-footed or true insects.

hexateuch, n. [1. héksatūk; 2. héksətjūk]. Formed fr. **hexa-** & Gk. *teûkhos*, 'tool, implement; book', on anal. of *Pentateuch*; the Gk. vb. *teúkhein* means 'to make, fashion, construct, build, weave, cause'. The Aryan base is **dheugh-*, **dhugh-*, wh. is found also in O.E. Pret. Pres. *dēah*, 'avails, is worth something, is of use', & *duguð*, 'mature, grown men', hence 'body of retainers' &c. See **doughty**. First six books of the O.T.

hey, interj. [1. hā; 2. hei]. M.E. *hei*; imitative, cp. Du., Germ. *hei*. Exclamation calling attention, or expressing interrogation, joy, surprise &c. Phrs. *hey for . . .*, hurrah for . . .; *hey presto*, conjuror's command when performing trick; hence used in narrative to announce a sudden or unexpected event: *hey presto! he escaped.*

hey-day, interj. [1. há dá; 2. héi déi], fr. Germ. *heida*, or Du. *hei daar*, 'hey there'. Exclamation of joy or wonder.

heyday, n. [1. hádā; 2. héidei]. First element prob. a dialectal variant of **high**. *Hay, hait*, as pronunciations for *high, height*, are recorded as late as 17th & 18th cents. respectively. Time of greatest vigour, prosperity, or triumph; prime, acme, flush: *in the heyday of youth.*

hi, interj. [1. hī; 2. hai]. Imitative of cry. Cp. **hey**. Exclamation, used for drawing attention or calling a person.

hiatus, n. [1. hiátus; 2. haiéitəs]. Lat. *hiātus*, fr. *hiāt-(um)*, P.P. type of *hiāre*, 'to yawn'. See **yawn**. Gap, lacuna; specif. **a** gap or break in manuscript or other writing where part is lost; **b** juxtaposition of two vowels without contraction or elision.

hibernate, vb. intrans. [1. híbernāt; 2. háibəneit]. Lat. *hībernāt-(um)*, P.P. type of *hībernāre*, 'to pass the winter', fr. *hībernus*, 'wintry', for **heimrinos*, cogn. w. Gk. *kheimerinós*, fr. Aryan base **gheiem-*, 'winter'; cp. Scrt. *héman*, 'in winter', also *himáś*, 'cold, winter', wh. is the first element in *Himalaya*, O. Slav. *zima*, Lith. *žëma*, 'winter'; Gk. *kheîma*, Lat. *hiem-s*, 'winter'; O.N. *gymb-r*, 'ewe of one winter', is also cogn. **a** (of some animals) To pass winter in state of torpidity and suspended animation; **b** to retire into warm winter quarters.

hibernation, n. [1. hìbernáshun; 2. hàibənéiʃən]. Prec. & **-ion**. Habit or state of hibernating.

Hibernian, adj. & n. [1. hībérnian; 2. haibə́niən]. Lat. *Hibernia*, 'Ireland', altered prob. by association w. *hībernus* (see **hibernate**), fr. *Iverna, Juverna* = Gk. *I(w)érnē*, fr. O. Celt. **Iverin* (whence Ir. *Erin*), & **-an**. **a** adj., Irish; **b** n., Irish person.

hibernicism, n. [1. hībérnisizm; 2. haibə́nisizəm]. Prec. & **-ic** & **-ism**. Irish peculiarity, esp. idiom or figure of speech.

hibiscus, n. [1. hibískus; 2. hibískəs]. Lat., fr. Gk. *ibiskos*, 'marsh mallow'. One of a genus of widely distributed plants cultivated in gardens; rose mallow.

hiccup, hiccough, n. & vb. intrans. & trans. [1. híkup; 2. híkəp]. Early Mod. Engl. *hickock, hicket*, n., w. dimin. suffs. **-ock**, **-et** (cp. Fr. *hoquet*, Walloon *hikett*), fr. imitative base **hik-*, cp. provinc. Engl. *hick*, 'to hiccup', also M. Du. *huckup*, Du. *hik*, Dan. *hikke*, W. *ig*, Bret. *hīk*, 'hiccup', n.; the spelling *hiccough* is assimilated to **cough**, *hiccup* perh. to **up**; vb. fr. n. **1.** n. Spasmodic contraction of the diaphragm, often accompanied by sudden closure of glottis, at the moment of drawing in the breath; sound accompanying this. **2.** vb. **a** intrans. To make a hiccup; **b** trans., to utter with a hiccup or hiccups.

hic jacet, n. [1. hík jáset; 2. hík džéisεt]. Lat. *hic jăcet*, 'here lies', first words of epitaph. Epitaph.

hick, n. [1. hik; 2. hik]. Origin doubtful. (Am. slang) A rustic, countryman; usually contemptuous, cp. *hay-seed.*

hickory, n. [1. híkori; 2. híkəri]. Earlier *pohickery*, fr. native Am. word. American tree with tough, hard wood; wood of this; stick made from this; (also attrib.).

hid, vb. [1. hid; 2. hid]. O.E. *hȳdde*, M.E. *hid*. Pret. of **hide** (III.).

hidage, n. [1. hídij; 2. háididž]. See **hide** (IV.) & **-age**. (hist.) Former English land-tax levied on each hide.

hidalgo, n. [1. hidálgō; 2. hidǽlgou]. Span., fr. O. Span. *fidalgo*, contr. fr. *fijo de algo*, 'son of something', i.e. 'son who inherits something', fr. O. Span. *fijo* (Mod. *hijo*), fr. Lat. *fīlius*, 'son' (see **filial**), & *de*, fr. Lat. *dē*, 'down from, of' (see **de-**), & *algo* fr. Lat. *aliquō*, abl. of *aliquod*, 'something' (see **aliquot**). Spanish gentleman by birth.

hidden, adj. [1. híd(e)n; 2. híd(ə)n]. P.P. of **hide** (III.). M.E. *hidden*, new str. P.P., cp. O.E. (*ge*)*hȳdd*. Concealed, secret.

hiddenly, adv. Prec. & **-ly**. Secretly.

hide (I.), n. [1. hīd; 2. haid]. O.E. *hȳd, hīd*, 'skin', fr. **hūdi-*, M.E. *hide* &c., O.S. *hūd*, O.H.G. *hūt*, Mod. Germ. *haut*; O.N. *hūð*; cognates outside Gmc., Gk. *kútos*, Lat. *cutis*, 'skin'. See **cutis**. **a** Skin of large living beast, such as ox, horse &c.; **b** skin of a beast when stripped off, raw or dressed; esp. as article of commerce; **c** (vulg.) applied to human skin. Phrs. *to tan, dress, a person's hide*, give him a thrashing; *to have a thick hide*, to be morally insensitive, lacking in sensibility &c.

hide (II.), vb. trans., fr. prec. **a** To flay, skin; **b** (colloq.) to flog; to take the hide off; now only in colloquial special sense of, to flog, thrash severely.

hide (III.), vb. trans. & intrans. O.E. *hȳdan*, M.E. *hūden, hīden*, fr. **hūd-jan*; perh. cogn. w. Gk. *keúthein*, 'to hide'. See **cutis**. **A.** trans. **1.** (as affecting material objects) To conceal; **a** to prevent from being found: *to hide the family plate where burglars cannot find it*; **b** to prevent from being seen, shut off from sight: *clouds hid the sun*; *his face was hidden by a beard*; *the walls are hidden by ivy*; *he hid his face in his hands*. Phr. *to hide one's face, head*, to withdraw from observation through shame. **2.** (as affecting non-material things) **a** To prevent from being known; to keep secret, not to reveal: *to have nothing to hide*; *to hide one's intentions*; *the future is fortunately hidden from us*; *he deliberately hid the facts from the jury*; **b** to prevent from being understood, render obscure to the mind: *the author's meaning is hidden by the ambiguity of his style*. **B.** intrans. To conceal oneself from sight, observation, notice.

hide (IV.), n. O.E. *hīgid, hīd*, M.E. *hīd*. The word is fr. earlier **hīʒw-*, 'household' &c., & *-(i)d*, a suff. forming abstract ns. The base is found in O.E. *hīwa, hīga*, 'member of a family', *hīwen*, 'family, household', & the pref. *hīw-* as in *hīw-cūþ*, 'familiar, intimate' &c. Other Gmc. cognates are O.H.G. *hīwo*, 'husband, member of a household', Goth. *heiwa-*, 'household', as in *heiwa-frauja*, 'master of a household'. Outside Gmc. the nearest cogn. in form & sense is Lat. *cīvis*, 'citizen' &c. See **civil**. The Aryan base is **k̑ei-*, **k̑oi-*, meaning 'to lie down, settle' &c. See further under **hind** (II.) & **home**. (hist.) A variable measure of land, formerly one sufficient to support a family or household, and varying in extent from 60 to 100 acres.

hide-and-seek, n. Children's game in which some hide themselves, and others try to find them.

hidebound, adj. [1. hídbound; 2. háidbaund]. **hide** (I.) & **bound** (VI.). **1. a** (of an animal) Having the hide too closely adhering to back and ribs; **b** (of a tree) constricted by bark; also, more usually, *bark-bound*. **2.** (in fig. sense) Rigidly conventional, pedantically attached to rules, habits, traditions.

hideous, adj. [1. hídius; 2. hídiəs]. M.E. *hidous*, fr. O. Fr. *hi(s)dous* (Mod. Fr. *hideux*), fr. O. Fr. *hi(s)de*, 'fright, dread', unless this is a back-formation, cp. O. Fr. *hisdor*, 'fear'; perh. fr. Lat. *hisp-id-us*, 'bristly, rough', connected w. *hircus*, 'he-goat'. See **hir-**

sute & -(e)ous. a Repulsive to the senses of sight or hearing; frightful: *a hideous grimace, building, uproar*; **b** morally or mentally revolting; horrible, dreadful: *hideous crime, cruelty; a hideous story*; '*Hideous ruin and combustion*' (Milton).

hideously, adv. Prec. & **-ly.** In a hideous manner.

hideousness, n. See prec. & **-ness.** Quality or state of being hideous.

hiding (I.), vbl. n. [1. híding; 2. háidiŋ]. **hide (II.)** & **-ing.** (colloq.) Flogging, thrashing: *I'll give you a good hiding.*

hiding (II.), vbl. n. **hide (III.)** & **-ing.** **a** Action of one who hides; **b** place where one hides; concealment: *to be in hiding.*

hiding-place, n. Place where person or thing is, or can be, hidden.

hidrosis, n. [1. hidrṓsis; 2. hidróusis]. Mod. Lat., fr. Gk. *hidró-ein*, 'to sweat', fr. *hidrṓs*, 'sweat', fr. **hid-* for **swid-*, fr. base **swoid-*, **swid-*, whence Lat. *sūd-āre* for **swoid-āre.* See **sudorific** & **sweat** & **-osis.** **a** (physiol.) Perspiration; **b** (med.) excessive perspiration; malady of which this is a symptom.

hidrotic, adj. [1. hidrótik; 2. hidrɔ́tik]. Gk. *hidrōtikós*, fr. *hidrōt-*, stem of *hidrṓs*, as prec. & **-ic.** (med.) **a** adj. Producing perspiration; **b** n., medicine producing perspiration; sudorific.

hie, vb. intrans. & reflex. [1. hī; 2. hai]. O.E. *hīgian* or *hīgian*, 'to hasten, strive, pant', M.E. *hīȝhen, hīen*; cogn. w. Lat. *ciēre*, 'to move, put in motion, shake', see **cite**; Gk. *kíein*, 'to go', & *kīnein*, 'to move, set in motion'. See **cinema** & **kinetic.** (chiefly poet. or facet.) **1.** intrans. To go in haste, hasten. **2.** reflex. To hasten: *he hied him homeward.*

hierarch, n. [1. hírark; 2. háiərāk]. L. Lat. *hierarcha*, fr. Gk. *hierárkhēs*, fr. *hierós*, 'sacred' (see **hiero-**), & *árkhein*, 'to lead, rule' (see **arch-**). Chief, leader or ruler, of a sacred order or society; high priest.

hierarchal, adj. [1. hīrárkal; 2. haiərā́k(ə)l]. Prec. & **-al.** Pertaining to a hierarchy or hierarch.

hierarchic, hierarchical, adj. [1. hīrárkik(l); 2. haiərā́kik(l)]. **hierarch** & **-ic** & **-al.** Cp. Fr. *hiérarchique.* Pertaining to a hierarchy.

hierarchy, n. [1. hírarki; 2. háiərāki]. Gk. *hierarkhía*, 'office of a hierarch', whence L. Lat. *ierarchia*, Fr. *hiérarchie.* **hierarch** & **-y.** **1. a** Rank, order, or class of sacred persons; specif., one of the three divisions of angels; **b** government by these as conceived of by mediaeval writers: *celestial hierarchy.* **2.** System, organized body of persons, especially of sacred persons, graded so that those of each rank control or direct those below them; specif. **a** system, society, of graded ecclesiastical officers; organized government in religious matters; government by ecclesiastics; **b** any graded system, or body of officials: *to advance a step in the hierarchy of the Civil Service.*

hieratic, adj. & n. [1. hīrátik; 2. haiərǽtik]. Lat. *hierāticus*, fr. Gk. *hierātikós*, cp. *hierāteia*, 'priest's office', fr. *hierós*, 'sacred, holy'. See **hiero-.** **a** adj. Pertaining to sacred things; priestly, sacerdotal: *hieratic art*; *hieratic writing*, form of ancient Egyptian cursive writing intermediate between hieroglyphic and demotic, in later age used only by priests; **b** n., hieratic writing.

hiero-, pref. Gk. *hierós*, 'sacred', for **wiseros*; cp. also *hiereús*, 'priest'. In the history of this word there appear to have been several influences in operation. Walde connects it w. a base **ais-, is-*, meaning 'honour, worship', wh. appears in Lat. *aestumāre*, 'to honour' &c. (see **esteem**), in Etrusc. *aesar*, 'god', an Italic loan-word, & in O.H.G. *era*, Mod. Germ. *ehre*, 'honour', fr. **aisa*, also in Goth. *aistan*, 'to heed, regard'. The *h-* in Gk. *hierós* is due to confusion & association w. another word *hīerós*, wh. occurs as *wieros* in inscriptions, & means 'alert, active, lively'. This is related to a vb. *hiemai*, 'to put, place; utter'; & fig. 'to desire, yearn after, feel an impulse towards', cogn. w. Lat. *via*, 'way', see **via.** The force of the prefix in compounds is holy, priestly, connected with priests, with sacrifice, or with sacred things.

hierocracy, n. [1. hīrókrasi; 2. haiərɔ́krəsi]. Prec. & **-cracy.** Government by sacred persons; rule of priests.

hierocratic, adj. [1. hīrōkrátik; 2. haiərou-krǽtik]. **hiero-** & **-cratic.** Connected with, based on, characterized by, priestly rule.

hierodule, n. [1. hírodūl; 2. háiərədjūl]. Lat. *hierodūlus*, fr. Gk. *hieródoulos*, fr. **hiero-** & Gk. *doûlos*, 'slave', cogn. w. Goth. *taujan*, O.H.G. *zouwen*, 'to make, prepare'. Cp. **tool.** Temple slave, dedicated to a deity, esp. in ancient Greece.

hieroglyph, n. [1. híroglif; 2. háiərəglif]. Fr. *hiéroglyphe*, back-formation fr. *hiéroglyphique.* See next word. **a** Character in the sacred script of the ancient Egyptians, originally a form of picture-writing; hence, symbol or character used in any picture-writing, as that of the Mexicans; **b** (fig.) secret or generally unintelligible written symbol; (facet.) badly written word: *I can't read his hieroglyphs.*

hieroglyphic, adj. & n. [1. hīroglífik; 2. haiərə-glífik]. Lat. *hieroglyphicus*, fr. Gk. *hiero-gluphikós.* **hiero-** & Gk. *glúphein*, 'to carve' (see **glyph**), & **-ic.** **a** adj. Pertaining to hieroglyphs or writing in hieroglyphs; **b** n. pl. *hieroglyphics*, (coll.) writing in hieroglyphs (in any sense).

hieroglyphically, adv. [1. hīroglífikali; 2. haiə-rəglífikəli]. Prec. & **-al** & **-ly.** In a hieroglyphic manner, in hieroglyphs.

hierogram, n. [1. hírogram; 2. háiərəgræm]. **hiero-** & **-gram.** Sacred character or written symbol.

hierographic, adj. [1. hīrográfik; 2. haiərə-grǽfik]. Gk. *hierographikós.* See **hiero-** & **-graphic.** Pertaining to sacred writing.

hierolatry, n. [1. hīrólatri; 2. haiərɔ́lətri]. **hiero-** & **-latry.** Worship of saints.

hierology, n. [1. hīróloji; 2. haiərɔ́lədži]. Gk. *hierologia*, 'sacred language'. See **hiero-** & **-logy.** Body of religious tradition and literature of a race or people; sacred lore.

hierophant, n. [1. hírofant; 2. háiərəfænt]. Gk. *hierophántēs*, 'priest conducting initiation into the mysteries', fr. **hiero-** & *phaínein*, 'to show'. See **phantasm.** Person who reveals or explains religious mysteries, or who professes to do so.

hierophantic, adj. [1. hīrofántik; 2. haiərəfǽn-tik]. Gk. *hierophantikós*; fr. prec. & **-ic.** Pertaining to, resembling, a hierophant or his acts.

higgle, vb. intrans. [1. hígl; 2. hígl]. Prob. a weakened form of **haggle.** To haggle, chaffer; to drive a hard bargain.

higgledy-piggledy, adv., adj., & n. [1. hígldi pígldi; 2. hígldi pígldi]. **a** adv. In complete disorder; in utter confusion; **b** adj., mixed up, jumbled up, completely disordered and confused; **c** n., complete muddle, confusion, disorder.

higgling, n. [1. hígling; 2. hígliŋ]. **higgle** & **-ing.** Action of one who higgles. Phr. *higgling of the market*, (econ.) process of bargaining by which current prices are determined.

high (I.), adj. [1. hī; 2. hai]. O.E. (non-W.S.) *hēh*, (W.S.) *hēah*, M.E. *heigh, hȳ*; fr. Common Gmc. **hauh-*, cp. O. Fris. *hāch*, O.S., O.H.G. *hōh*; Goth. *hauh-s*, O.N. *hā-r.* Other Gmc. cognates are Germ. *hügel*, 'hill', O.N. *haug-r*, 'mound'. Prob. fr. same Aryan base as Lat. *cumulus*, 'pile, mound' &c., w. quite other formative elements (see **cumulus**), & Lith. *kugis*, 'great pile of hay'. **1. a** (i.) Extending upwards far above a given level or base; having great altitude; tall, lofty, elevated (not of persons or animals, of which *tall* is used): *a high mountain, tower, tree, collar, flagstaff, pole; to fire at a high angle*; Phr. *(to ride) the high horse*, assume lofty, arrogant bearing; *high neck*, part of woman's dress covering shoulders and part of neck; *high relief*, (in sculp. &c.) bold relief; (ii.) having a specified degree or amount of height: *a house 40 ft. high*; **b** (i.) situated at great distance above the surface of the earth or sea: *a high flight, tableland; the highest floor; the sun was high*; (ii.) situated at a specified distance above surface of earth or sea: *the cloud is three miles high*; Phrs. *high and dry* (of vessel) aground out of water; (fig.) (i.) isolated, left in the lurch; (ii.) out of date, not in the swim or movement; *with a high hand*, (i.) (fig.) in an arbitrary, overbearing manner; (ii.) (Bib.) mightily; *high place*, (O.T.) place of worship on hill-top; *high tide*, (i.) tide at its greatest height; time of this; (ii.) culmination, climax; **c** pertaining to the higher part of the country: *High German*, dialects of S. Germany; literary German; **d** (phon., of tongue position) raised towards roof of mouth; also of sound so formed: *a high back vowel.* **2.** (fig.) **a** (of persons, societies &c.) Elevated, exalted in office, rank, dignity, power &c.: *a high caste, family, official*; *high life*, aristocratic or fashionable society; also in titles: *High Commissioner*; *Lord High Chancellor*; Phrs. *high and low*, all classes; *high and mighty*, (i.) very exalted; (ii.) haughty, disdainful; *high place, office*, exalted official position; *the Most High* (Bib., also *the Most Highest*), God; **b** (i.) chief, main; most important: *high altar, festival, road, street* (usually with caps.); (ii.) specially solemn: *High Celebration* (of Eucharist), *High Mass*; Phrs. *high table*, table on dais in hall of college &c., where seniors dine; *high treason*, that against the sovereign or state; **c** of the best quality; superior, very good, excellent: *a high quality, class*; *high art*; *to have a high opinion of one*; *in high feather*, in good spirits; joyous, merry, frolicsome: *a high* (colloq., *high old*) *time*; *high jinks, spirits*; rich, luxurious: *high feeding, living, liver*; **d** morally or intellectually lofty, noble, sublime: *high thinking, aims*; *a high character, resolve, tone, calling*; **e** (Bib.) arrogant, haughty: *a high stomach*; *high looks*; **f** of a High Church character: *high sacramental doctrine*; *a High Anglican*; (colloq.) *a high service*; **g** *higher*, more developed or differentiated: *the higher mammals*; more advanced: *the higher mathematics, arithmetic* &c. Phrs. *the higher criticism*, that of a literary document which is not purely textual criticism; *on a higher plane*, in a condition of fuller or richer existence; at a superior level of thought; *higher space*, that of more than three dimensions. **3. a** (i.) Intense, extreme, very great: *a high wind, explosive, polish, temperature*; *high velocity, speed, tension, frequency* (elect.); *high mettle*; *a high Tory*; *a high percentage, figure, price, cost*; (ii.) costly: *wheat is high today*; Phrs. *a high area*, (meteor.) of high barometric pressure; *high change*, state of money market when exchange is highest; *a high colour*, ruddy complexion, flush; *high farming*, intensive cultivation; *high latitudes*, those near the poles; *high lights*, (in graphic arts) areas which have the greatest illumination; *the high seas*, seas outside national jurisdiction; *high words*, angry speeches: *high words passed between them*; **b** (of time) (i.) advanced, full: *high noon, day, summer*; *it is high time you were gone*; (ii.) remote: *of high antiquity.* **4.** (of sound) Shrill, acute, sharp: *a high voice, key, pitch, note.* **5.** (of meat) Slightly tainted.

high (II.), n. **1.** (meteor.) High area, anticyclone. **2.** (cards) Highest card dealt or drawn. **3.** Heaven, in Phrs. *on high*; *from on high*, from heaven.

high (III.), adv. See prec. **a** At, to, a high level, or place (lit. or fig.): *to fly, mount, climb, aim high*; Phrs. *to hold one's head high*, to bear oneself resolutely, proudly, haughtily; *the sea runs high*, is at high tide with strong current; *passions run high*, are deeply stirred; *to search, hunt, high and low*, in all sorts of places; *to stand high in popular esteem* &c., to occupy a good position; **b** intensely, vehemently, to a high degree: *the wind blows high*; *to play high*, to play for high stakes; to play a high card; at a high price: *to pay, be* *sold, high*; **c** luxuriously: *to live high*; **d** at or to a high pitch: *to sing, speak, high*; *his voice rose high*; **e** with a high flavour.

high-angle, adj. Proceeding from a gun raised to a high angle: *high-angle fire*.

highball, n. [1. hībawl; 2. háibōl]. Origin doubtful. (Am. colloq.) A whisky and soda.

high-blower, n. Horse that flaps its nostrils noisily when breathing.

high-blown, adj. Highly inflated; puffed up with pride.

high-born, adj. Of high birth, of exalted parentage.

high-bred, adj. **1.** Of high birth; of superior stock; having qualities of a good race or stock. **2.** Educated or trained in a superior, refined, or aristocratic manner; showing good breeding.

highbrow, n. & adj. [1. hībrou; 2. háibrau]. (colloq., orig. Am.) **1.** n. Person who assumes airs of superior intellect or culture; (derisively) intellectual or cultured person lacking broad human sympathies. **2.** adj. Pertaining to, characteristic of, a highbrow: *a highbrow play*.

High Church, n. [1. hī chĕrch; 2. hái tʃə̄tʃ], & adj. [1. hī chĕrch; 2. hái tʃə́tʃ]. **1.** n. Party, tendency, in the Church of England, or other Church, which lays great stress upon the episcopal and priestly offices, and emphasizes sacramental grace and ecclesiastical tradition. **2.** adj. Pertaining to, of the nature of, the High Church.

High-Churchman, n. Adherent of High Church principles.

High-Churchmanship, n. Quality, principles of a High-Churchman.

high-coloured, adj. **a** Having a high, bright, or glaring colour; **b** (fig.) vividly descriptive; exaggerated, overdone.

High Court, n. The Supreme Court of Judicature.

high-day, n. Festival, holiday; esp. in Phr. *high-days and holidays*.

high explosive, n. An explosive, detonating very rapidly and of powerful action, as used in shells in heavy artillery.

highfalutin, highfaluting, adj. & n. [1. hīfalōōtin; 2. háifəlū́tin]. Of doubtful origin. **1.** adj. Bombastic, high-flown, extravagantly rhetorical. **2.** n. Bombast, fustian.

high-fed, adj. Richly fed, pampered.

high-flier, high-flyer, n. **a** Bird &c. that flies high; **b** (fig.) person who talks, behaves, or thinks in an extravagant, extreme, or over-ambitious manner; also a brilliant, talented, person; **c** (hist.) extreme Tory or High Church partisan.

high-flown, adj. Soaring, flighty, ambitious; extravagant, bombastic.

high-flying, adj. Flying high; (fig.) of the nature of a high-flier.

high-frequency, n. (elect.) An alternating current whose periods exceed 1000 per second; see **frequency**.

high-handed, adj. Acting with a high hand; arbitrary, domineering, overbearing.

high-handedness, n. Character of one who is high-handed; arbitrary conduct.

high-hearted, adj. Courageous, full of high resolve.

high-heartedness, n. Quality of being high-hearted.

highland, n. & adj. [1. hīland; 2. háilənd]. **high (I.)** & **land (I.)**. Cp. O.E. *hēahlond*. **1.** n. **a** (often pl.) Elevated or mountainous region: *the highlands of Turkey*; specif. **b** (pl., cap.) *the Highlands*, the mountainous or hilly north and north-west part of Scotland. **2.** adj. Pertaining **a** to a highland; **b** to the Scottish Highlands: *a Highland fling, Highland pony* &c.

highlander, n. [1. hīlander; 2. háiləndə]. Prec. & **-er**. **a** Inhabitant of a highland; **b** specif. (cap.) inhabitant, native, of the Scottish Highlands; **c** (cap.) soldier in a Highland regiment of the British army.

high-lows, n. pl. [1. hī lōz; 2. hái louz]. (archaic or obs.) Laced shoes or boots reaching to the ankle.

highly, adv. [1. hīli; 2. háili]. O.E. *hēaliċe*, M.E. *heihlice*, fr. **high (I.)** & **-ly**. **a** (rare or archaic in lit. sense) To or at a height: *a highly walled city*; **b** (fig.) in a high place: *a highly placed official*; **c** in or to a high degree; greatly; extremely, very: *to favour, commend, esteem, colour, season, highly*; *highly pleased, educated, paid*; *highly original, satisfactory, daring, dangerous*; **d** favourably, with esteem or honour: *to think, speak, highly of one*; **e** nobly: *highly connected, descended*.

high-mettled, adj. High-spirited, gallant.

high-minded, adj. **a** Having a lofty or noble mind, principles, or character; highly honourable; **b** (Bib.) proud, haughty.

high-mindedness, n. Quality of being high-minded.

high-necked, adj. [1. hī nékt; 2. hái nékt]. (of woman's dress) Having a high neck.

highness, n. [1. hīnes; 2. háinis]. O.E. *hēahness*, M.E. *hēhnesse, hīnesse*, fr. **high (I.)** & **-ness**. **1.** Quality, fact, of being high (esp. as contrasted with *lowness*); elevation, loftiness: *the highness of prices*; *I complained of the highness of the wall* (not the particular height); *the highness of his aims*. **2.** (with cap.) Title, in England, bestowed only on princes of the blood royal: always *His, Her, Your, Royal Highness*; in speaking of foreign princes, various: *His, Her &c., Highness*; *Serene, Imperial, Highness* &c.

high-pitched, adj. **1.** (of sound, voice) Having a high pitch, shrill. **2.** (of roof) Steep. **3.** (fig.) **a** Lofty, aspiring: *a high-pitched aim, character*; **b** haughty; **c** highly strung.

high-pressure, adj. **a** (of engine, machine &c.) Having, driven by or at, a high pressure of steam, air, water &c.; **b** (fig.) urgent, carried on at great speed.

high-priced, adj. Offered for sale at a high price; expensive, dear.

high-priest, n. Chief priest; specif., head of the ancient Jewish priesthood.

high-priesthood, n. Office of high-priest.

high-principled, adj. Imbued with lofty principles of conduct; highly honourable.

high road, n. Main road, highway; (fig.) easy or direct way: *the high road to fame, success*.

high school, n. Secondary school, usually of superior kind, non-proprietary, but having a governing body, and giving instruction in special subjects, technical or other.

high seas, n., pl. The seas, ocean, outside territorial waters.

high-seasoned, adj. [1. hī sézund; 2. hái sízənd]. **a** Highly flavoured, as with spice &c.; **b** piquant, spicy.

high-souled, adj. Having a lofty or noble soul.

high-sounding, adj. (of style, titles) Pompous, inflated, ostentatious.

high-spirited, adj. Having a lofty spirit; daring; ardent: *a high-spirited person* or *action*; (of a horse) mettlesome, frisky.

high-stepper, n. **a** Horse that steps high; **b** person of lofty spirit and courage; of distinguished bearing and manners; of soaring, powerful intelligence.

high-strung, adj. In a state of nervous tension; sensitive, easily worked up, excitable.

hight, vb. trans., pass. [1. hīt; 2. hait]. Only trace of pass. vb. in Engl., M.E. *highte*, 1st & 3rd Pres. & Pret. Pass., formed by fusion of O.E. *hātte* (Goth. *haitada*), Pres. & Pret. Pass., w. O.E. *hēht*, fr. orig. reduplicating (cp. Goth. *haihait*) Pret. active of *hātan*, 'to call, name, command', Common Gmc.; cp. O.S. *hētan*, Du. *heeten*, O.H.G. *heizan*, Mod. Germ. *heissen*, Goth. *háitan*, O.N. *heita*, fr. Gmc. type **haitan-*. As P.P. (**2**) for M.E. *hōten*, by confusion w. **1**. Cogn. w. Lat. *ciēre*, one sense of wh. is 'to invoke, summon'. See **cite** & **hie**. **1.** (obs.) Is, was, called or named: '*This grisly beast, which Lion hight by name*' (Shakespeare). **2.** (archaic or facet.) Called, named: '*Childe Harold was he hight*' (Byron).

high tension, n. (wireless) Current supplied to anode circuits of receivers and transmitters.

high-toned, adj. Elevated, lofty, in moral or intellectual character or in sentiment: *a high-toned journal*; often iron.: *this book is too high-toned for me*.

highty-tighty. See **hoity-toity**.

high water, n. & adj. **1.** n. **a** Highest level ordinarily attained by body of water subject to fluctuations; specif. **b** state of tidal water at high tide, immediately before it turns; time of this: *it is high water today at 4 p.m at London Bridge*. **2.** adj. **a** Pertaining to high water; Phr. *high-water mark*, mark made along shore or bank by high water; **b** (fig.) highest point of success or excellence reached: *the high-water mark of English poetry* &c.

highway, n. [1. hīwā; 2. háiwei]. M.E. *heiȝwai*, fr. **high (I.)** & **way**. **1.** High or main road: *the king's highway* (orig. road where the king's peace was maintained); contrasted with *byway* in Phr. *highways and byways*, chief roads and minor roads. **2. a** Public thoroughfare, by land or water; traffic route: *the highways of the Empire*. **b** (fig.) (i.) direct line or road towards a non-material aim: *highway to success*; (ii.) best-known, chief part of a subject of study &c.: *the highways of literature*.

highwayman, n. [1. hīwàman; 2. háiwèimən]. Robber, generally mounted, who formerly extorted money from travellers on the public roads by threats of violence or murder.

high-wrought, adj. (rare or obs.) Worked up to a high pitch of skill, perfection, or intensity.

hijacker, n. [1. hījaker; 2. háidžækə]. Origin unknown. (U.S.A. slang) Person who preys on boot-leggers and takes from them the alcoholic liquor they are attempting to smuggle into, or deal with in, the United States.

hijra, n. See **hegira**.

hike, vb. intrans. & n. [1. hīk; 2. haik]. Possibly a dialectal variant of **hitch**. (colloq) **a** vb. To tramp, to go on a walking tour through the country; **b** n., a tramp, country walking excursion.

hilarious, adj. [1. hilārius; 2. hiléəriəs]. Lat. *hilaris, hilarus*, fr. Gk. *hilarós*, 'cheerful, glad' (cp. *híla(w)os*, 'propitious, kind', *hilénai*, 'to be gracious'); prob. cogn. w. Goth. *sēls-*, 'kind', O.E. *sǣl*, 'season, happiness' (see **silly**), & w. Lat. *salvus*, 'safe, unhurt, sound' (see **safe (I.)**), & **-ous**. **a** Merry, blithe, gay; **b** noisily, boisterously merry, as with drink.

hilariously, adv. Prec. & **-ly**. In a hilarious manner.

hilariousness, n. See prec. & **-ness**. Hilarity.

hilarity, n. [1. hilárity; 2. hilǽriti]. Fr. *hilarité*, fr. Lat. *hilaritāt-(em)*, fr. *hilaris*. See **hilarious** & **-ity**. Quality or state of being hilarious; mirth, merriment, jollity.

Hilary, adj. [1. hílari; 2. híləri]. St. Hilarius or Hilary of Poitiers (d. 367), whose festival is Jan. 13th. Applied formerly to one of the terms in the English law-courts, Jan. 11th-31st: *Hilary sittings, term* (now abolished); also to University term between Christmas and Easter.

hilding, n. & adj. [1. hílding; 2. hílding]. **Prob.** fr. O.E. *hyldan, heldan*, 'to incline, bend'. See **heel (III.)** & **-ing**. (archaic) **a** n. Base, servile wretch; **b** adj., base, mean.

hill (I.), n. [1. hil; 2. hil]. O.E. *hyll*, M.E. *hull, hil*; cogn. w. Lith. *kalnas*, Gk. *kolōnós, kolṓnē*, Lat. *collis*, 'hill', fr. Aryan base **kel-* &c., 'to be elevated, rise'. See **holm, column, culminate, excel**. **a** Small elevation of the earth's surface, intermediate between a knoll or mound, and a mountain, the limits varying with the more or less mountainous nature of the country, in Britain usually up to about 2000 ft.: *the Malvern Hills*; Phr. *up hill and down dale*, high and low, everywhere, far and wide; **b** artificial mound or heap of earth &c., chiefly in compounds, e.g. *dunghill, molehill* &c.

hill (II.), vb. trans. & intrans., fr. prec. (rare) **1.** trans. **a** To make into a hill, pile up; **b** (Am.) to surround with a bank of earth: *to hill potatoes*. **2.** intrans. **a** To form a hill; **b** to resort to hills, as birds.

hill country, n. Rugged or undulating elevated district.

hilliness, n. [1. hílines; 2. hílinis]. **hilly** & **-ness**. Quality of being hilly.
hillman, n. [1. hílman; 2. hílmæn]. Man living in the hills; member of a hill tribe.
hillo, hilloa. See **hollo**.
hillock, n. [1. híluk; 2. hílək]. **hill (I.)** & **-ock**. Little hill, mound, knoll; heap.
hillocky, adj. [1. híluki; 2. híləki]. Prec. & **-y**. Diversified by hillocks.
hill-side, n. Side, slope, of a hill.
hill-top, n. Top of a hill.
hilly, adj. [1. híli; 2. híli]. **hill (I.)** & **-y**. **a** Containing, full of, hills: *hilly country*; **b** having the nature of a hill.
hilt, n. & vb. trans. [1. hilt; 2. hilt]. O.E. *hilt*, *hilte*, M.E. *hilt*; cp. O.H.G. *helza*, O.N. *hjalt*; perh. related to **helve**, cp. L.G. *helft*, 'axe-handle'. **1.** n. **a** Handle of sword or dagger; Phr. (*up*) *to the hilt*, completely: *the charge was proved up to the hilt*; **b** handle of miner's pick. (rare) **2.** vb. To furnish with a hilt.
hilum, n. [1. hílum; 2. háiləm]. Lat. *hīlum*, 'very small thing, trifle', according to Festus, 'that which adheres to a bean', perh. same word as second element in Lat. *ni-hil*, 'nothing', on wh. see **nihil**. Scar on seed where it was attached to the pod or vessel.
him, pers. pron. [1. him; 2. him]. O.E. *him*, dat. sing. of **he**, in M.E. also replacing acc. *hine* to form obj. case. **1.** Objective case of *he*; **a** referred to another person than subject; **b** reflexive where there is no ambiguity: *he looked about him*; *he bethought him of his danger*; (archaic and poet.) as general reflexive: *he made him ready.* **2.** (colloq. and vulg.) Emphatic form of nominative: *that's him.*
himation, n. [1. hīmátion; 2. haimǽtiən]. Gk. *himátion*, Attic form for *heimátion*, fr. **wes-ma*; cp. Gk. *hénnūmi*, 'clothe', fr. **wes-nu-*; see further on this base under **wear (I.)**, **vest**. (anct. Gk.) The typical Greek outer garment worn over the chiton.
himself, pron. [1. himsélf; 2. himsélf]. O.E. *him selfum*, dat. sing. of *hē self*. See **he**, **self**, M.E. *himself, himselve*. (masc. sing. pron.) **1.** (reflex.) *He supports himself*; *he gave himself much trouble*; *he kept it for himself*. Phr. (*all*) *by himself*, alone; unaided. **2.** Emphatic, **a** for pers. pron.; as obj.: *the money I gave him is for himself*; (archaic) as subj.: *himself will be there*; **b** in apposition to subj. or obj.: *the King himself says so*; *he says so himself*; *I saw him himself.* **3.** (as quasi-n.) His normal self: *he is himself again*; *he came to himself*, recovered his senses.
hind (I.), n. [1. hīnd; 2. haind]. O.E. *hind*, M.E. *hinde*, O.H.G. *hinta*, Mod. Germ. *hinde*, O.N. *hind*; Gmc. type **hinđjō*, perh. cogn. w. Gk. *kemás*, 'young deer, gazelle'. Female of the (red) deer.
hind (II.), n. M.E. *hīne*, fr. O.E. *hīna*, contracted fr. *hīwna, hīgna*, genit. pl. of *hīwa, hīga*, 'member of household, domestic servant'. See **hide (IV.)**. The new O.E. nom. *hīna* perh. arose fr. such phrases as *hīna man*, 'man of the domestics'. For the added *d* cp. **sound**, **lend**. **a** (archaic) Farm servant; peasant, rustic; **b** (Nthn. Engl. and Scots) skilled farm servant having charge of two horses; farm bailiff.
hind (III.), adj. Perh. back-formation fr. **hinder (I.)**, **hindmost**, or fr. O.E. *hindan*, M.E. *hind*, 'behind', or abbr. fr. **behind**. Hinder, situated behind, at the back, in the rear; posterior: *the hind legs, feet, of a beast*; *hind wheels, quarters.*
hinder (I.), adj. [1. hínder; 2. háində]. O.E. *hinder*, adv., 'back, behind'; M.E. *hindre*, adj., fr. O.N. *hindri*, O.H.G. *hintaro*, O.H.G. *hintar*, Mod. Germ. *hinter*, prep., 'behind'; Goth. *hindar*, prep., 'behind, beyond', fr. Gmc. demonstr. stem **hin-* (see **hence**), fr. base **hi*, 'that' (see **he**), & suff. *-der*, denoting motion to a place (see **hither**), identical w. compar. suff., as in Gk. *-ter-os*. Cp. O.E. *hindan*, adv., 'behind', O.H.G. *hintan*, Mod. Germ. *hinten*, 'behind', Goth. *hindana*, prep., 'behind'. See **behind**. Situated at the back, in the rear; posterior; (more general than *hind*): *the hinder parts, end.*
hinder (II.), vb. trans. & intrans. [1. hínder; 2. híndə]. O.E. *hindrian*, 'to repress'; M.E. *hind(e)ren*, O.H.G. *hintarōn*, *hintarian*, Mod. Germ. *hindern*, O.N. *hindra*, fr. O.E. *hinder*. (see prec.), orig. sense being to 'keep back'. **1.** trans. **a** To keep back, prevent, stop: *I was hindered from coming*; **b** to delay, impede, thwart, embarrass: *to be hindered in one's work.* **2.** intrans. To cause or be a hindrance.
hinderer, n. [1. hínderer; 2. híndərə]. M.E. *hindrer*, fr. prec. & **-er**. Person who hinders.
hindermost, adj. [1. híndermōst; 2. háindəmoust]. Superl. of **hinder (I.)**. See **-most**. Hindmost.
hind-foremost, adv. **hind (III.)** & **foremost**. With the hinder part in front.
Hindi, adj. & n. [1. híndē; 2. híndī]. Hind., fr. *Hind*, 'India', see **Hinduism**. **1.** adj. Pertaining to N. India or the dialect of this part. **2.** n. The Aryan dialect of Northern India.
hindmost, adj. [1. hín(d)mōst; 2. háin(d)moust]. Superl. of **hind (III.)**; see **-most**; cp. Goth. *hindumist-s*. Most to the rear, farthest behind, hindermost.
hind quarters, n. pl. **hind (III.)** & **quarter (I.)** & **-s**, pl. ending. Lower part of back of human being, posterior part of animal's back; posteriors, buttocks.
hindrance, n. [1. híndrans; 2. híndrəns]. **hinder (II.)** & **-ance**. **a** Action or process of hindering; **b** thing or person that hinders; impediment, obstacle.
Hinduism, n. [1. hindōōizm; 2. hindúizəm]. Pers. *Hindū*, 'Indian', fr. *Hind*, 'India', fr. O. Pers. *Hindu*, 'land on the river Indus', fr. Scrt. *sindhu*, 'river', specif., 'the Indus'. See **Indian** & **-ism**. Religion of the Hindus.
Hindustani, adj. & n. [1. hindoostáhnē; 2. hindustáni]. Pers. *Hindū*, see prec., & *stan*, 'place'. **1.** adj. Pertaining to the people or language of Hindustan. **2.** n. Dialect consisting of Hindi with an admixture of Arabic, Persian &c., developed after the Mohammedan conquest of India; Urdu.
hinge (I.), n. [1. hinj; 2. hindž]. M.E. *henge*, fr. *hengen*, 'to hang', a form affected by O.N. *hengja*. See **hang**. **1.** **a** Joint, usually of metal, on which door, gate, lid, or the like, hangs and turns; Phr. *off the hinges* (fig.), mentally or physically disordered, unhinged, unable to function; **b** thing resembling, and serving purpose of, hinge; specif., joint of bivalve shell, as oyster; (also attrib.): *hinge joint.* **2.** (fig.) Principle, fact, on which matters turn or depend; cardinal point.
hinge (II.), vb. intrans. & trans., fr. prec. **1.** intrans. **a** To swing, turn on a hinge; **b** (fig.) to depend on, be contingent on: *everything hinges on his wishes.* **2.** trans. **a** To supply with a hinge or hinges; **b** (obs.) to bend as by a hinge: '*hinge thy knee*' (Shakespeare).
hinged, adj. [1. hinjd; 2. hindžd], fr. P.P. of prec. Furnished with a hinge or hinges.
hinny, n. [1. híni; 2. híni]. Lat. *hinnus*, fr. Gk. *hinnos*, earlier *ginnos*, perh. imitative, cp. Lat. *hinnīre*, 'to neigh, whinny'. Offspring of stallion and she-ass, resembling small mule.
hint (I.), n. [1. hint; 2. hint]. Early Mod. Engl. (Dunbar), 'sudden seizure', fr. O.E. *hentan*, M.E. *henten, hinten*, 'to take, seize'; cp. Goth. (*fra-*)*hinþan*, 'to capture', cp. **hunt** & perh. **hand**. **1.** **a** Slight, indirect, or unobtrusive intimation of fact, desire &c.; covert suggestion or allusion: *to drop, let fall, a hint*; *to take a hint*, act on a slight suggestion; *a delicate, strong, broad, hint*; **b** brief piece of advice: *hints on housekeeping.*
hint (II.), vb. trans. & intrans., fr. prec. **a** trans. To intimate indirectly or covertly; to give a hint of: *to hint disapproval*; *he hinted that he knew more*; **b** intrans., to give, utter, a hint: *to hint at foul play.*
hinterland, n. Anglicized [1. hínterland; 2. híntəlænd]. Germ., fr. *hinter*, 'behind' (see **hinder (I.)**), & *land*, **land (I.)**. **a** Land lying behind strip of coast or the bank of a large river; held to lie within sphere of influence of state occupying coast &c.; **b** area served by a port.
hintingly, adv. [1. híntingli; 2. híntiŋli]. **hint (II.)** & **-ing** & **-ly**. In the manner of one who hints.
hip (I.), n. [1. hip; 2. hip]. O.E. *hype*, M.E. *hīpe, hupe*; Common Gmc., cp. O.H.G. *huf*, Goth. *hup-s*, O.N. *hupp-r*; Gmc. type **hupiz*, cogn. w. Lith. *kumpis*, 'ham', & prob. w. Gk. *kúbos*, 'hollow above hip of cattle'; perh. connected w. **hop (I.)**. **1.** Projecting part on either side of human or animal body, formed by edge of pelvis and upper end of thigh-bone, together with the covering muscular tissue &c.; haunch. Phr. *to have, get, one on the hip*, to tackle, control, effectively (fig., from wrestling); *to smite* (*enemies*) *hip and thigh*, (Bib.) relentlessly, utterly. **2.** Sloping line of junction of two adjacent sides of roof meeting at an external angle.
hip (II.), n. O.E. *hēope*, M.E. *hēpe*, Mod. Engl. dial. *hep*, Gmc. type **hiupōn-*; cp. O.E. *hīopa*, 'briar', O.S. *hiopo*, O.H.G. *hiufo*. Seed vessel of the wild rose or briar: *hips and haws.*
hip (III.), n. & vb. trans. Abbr. fr. **hypochondria**. (colloq., rare) **1.** n. Melancholy, depression of spirits. **2.** vb. To depress the spirits of: (chiefly in P.P.) *to feel hipped.*
hip (IV.), interj. Sound made twice as signal for a united cheer: *hip, hip, hurrah!*
hip-bath, n. Portable bath in which one sits but cannot lie.
hip-belt, n. Mediaeval sword-belt, worn slanting down from right to left side.
hip-bone, n. Haunch bone, innominate bone.
hip-disease, n. Tubercular or other disease of the hip-joint.
hipe, n. & vb. trans. [1. hīp; 2. haip]. Possibly connected w. **hip (I.)**. **a** n. Kind of throw in wrestling in which opponent's thigh is struck up from behind; **b** vb., to throw by a hipe.
hip-joint, n. Joint between pelvis and thigh bones.
hippish, adj. [1. hípish; 2. hípiʃ]. **hip (III.)** & **-ish**. (colloq.) Somewhat melancholy or depressed.
hippo-, pref. Gk. *híppos*, 'horse', dial. *íkkos*, cogn. w. Scrt. *áśvaš*, O. Pers. *aspa-*, Lith. *aszvà*, Goth. *aihwa-* (for **ehwa*), O.E. *eoh*, Lat. *equus*, Gaulish *epo-*, O. Ir. *ech*, fr. Aryan type **ekʷwo-s*. See **equine**. Form in compounds of Greek origin, denoting horse.
hippocampus, n. [1. hìpōkámpus; 2. hìpoukǽmpəs], pl. **hippocampi** [1. hìpōkámpī; 2. hìpoukǽmpai]. Gk. *hippokámpos*, fr. **hippo-** & *kámpos*, 'sea-monster', prop., 'writher, coiler', cp. *kámpē*, 'caterpillar', *kámp-t-ein*, 'to bend'. See **gambol, ham (I.)**. **1.** (class. mythol.) Sea-horse with hinder part in form of long curling tail, represented as drawing car of a sea-god. **2.** Small fish called sea-horse. **3.** (anat.) One of two curved ridges on each lateral ventricle of brain.
hippocras, n. [1. hípōkras; 2. hípoukræs]. M.E., O. Fr., *ipocras, ypocras*, Mod. Fr. *Hippocras*, fr. name of *Hippokrátēs*, Gk. physician of 5th cent. B.C., fr. whom a wine-strainer called *Hippocrates' sleeve* was named. Wine spiced with ginger, cinnamon &c., strained, and used as cordial.
Hippocrene, n. [1. hípōkrēn; 2. hípoukrīn]. Gk., fr. *híppos*, 'horse', see **hippo-**, & *krḗnē*, 'spring, fountain'. Etymol. doubtful. **a** (Gk. mythol.) Fountain of Mt. Helicon, sacred to the Muses, produced by the hoof of Pegasus; **b** poetic inspiration: '*the true, the blushful Hippocrene*,' Keats, 'Nightingale.'
hippodrome, n. [1. hípodrōm; 2. hípədroum]. Fr., fr. Lat., fr. Gk. *hippódromos*, fr. **hippo-** & *drómos*, 'course', see **dromedary**. **a** Ancient Greek or Roman course for horse or chariot races; **b** circus, arena, for equestrian displays.

hippogriff, hippogryph, n. [1. hípōgrif; 2. hípougrif]. Fr. *hippogriffe,* fr. Ital. *ippogrifo,* fr. **hippo-** & Ital. *grifo,* **griffin (I.).** Fabulous monster, consisting of horse with head and wings of griffin.

hippophagous, adj. [1. hipófagus; 2. hipɔ́fəgəs]. **hippo-** & **-phagous.** Eating horse-flesh.

hippophagy, n. [1. hipófaji; 2. hipɔ́fədži]. **hippo-** & **-phagy.** Practice of eating horseflesh.

hippopotamic, adj. [1. hìpōpotámik; 2. hìpoupətǽmik]. Next word & **-ic.** Pertaining to, resembling, a hippopotamus; unwieldy, clumsy.

hippopotamus, n. [1. hìpopótamus; 2. hìpəpɔ́təməs], pl. *hippopotamuses,* learned pl. *hippopotami.* Lat., fr. Gk. *hippopótamos,* fr. **hippo-** & *potamós,* 'river', see **potamo-;** prob. fr. Aryan base **pet-,* 'to fall, fly, hasten towards'; cp. Gk. *pét-esthai,* 'to fly', *poté,* 'flight', Lat. *pet-ere,* 'to seek' &c.; see **ptero-, feather.** Very large ungainly amphibious African pachydermatous ungulate mammal, having large muzzle and short legs; related to swine; the river-horse.

hipshot, adj. [1. hípshot; 2. hípʃɔt]. **hip (I.)** & **shot (II.).** Having a dislocated hip.

hirable, adj. [1. hírabl; 2. háiərəbl]. **hire (II.)** & **-able.** That may be hired.

hircine, adj. [1. hérsīn; 2. hʌ́sain]. Lat. *hircīn-us,* fr. *hircus, hirquus,* 'he-goat', q.v. under **hirsute,** & **-ine.** **a** Pertaining to, resembling, a he-goat; **b** having a rank smell.

hire (I.), n. [1. hīr; 2. haiə]. O.E. *hȳr,* 'wages, usury'; M.E. *hȳre,* Du. *huur,* Germ. dial. *heuer,* Swed. *hyra,* Dan. *hyre;* origin unknown. **1.** Right acquired, in return for payment of an agreed sum, **a** to make use of a person's services in performing a piece of work; or **b** to enjoy use of a thing belonging to another. **2.** The act of employing a person, or making use of a thing, in return for payment: *to let out on hire.* **3.** Money paid or received **a** for person's services: *the labourer is worthy of his hire; to work for hire;* **b** for use of another's property: *to pay for the hire of a motor-car.*

hire (II.), vb. trans. O.E. *hȳrian,* M.E. *hīren, hūren,* fr. prec. **1. a** To engage and pay (a person) to do work; **b** to secure services of (person) in return for wages; **c** to obtain the use of (a thing) by payment to owner: *to hire a gardener, cheap labour, a flat, a cab* &c.; *a hired assassin; to hire a man to do one's dirty work* &c. **2.** Generally *hire out,* **a** to let out to others for their use, to permit use of by others, in return for payment: *to hire out horses, bicycles &c. by the hour;* **b** (reflex.) *to hire oneself out as a hack writer* &c.

hireling, n. [1. hírling; 2. háiəliŋ]. O.E. *hȳrling,* M.E. *hūrling, hīrling.* **hire (I.)** & **-ling.** **a** Person who works for hire; (now usually contemptuous) mercenary person: *the hirelings of the press;* (also attrib.) *hireling scribblers* &c.; **b** thing hired: *this horse is only a hireling.*

hire-purchase, n. & adj. **a** n. Contract by which thing, as house, furniture, motor-car &c., is hired on condition that after payment of hire to a date or amount agreed upon, it becomes the property of the hirer; purchase by instalments; **b** adj., pertaining to hire-purchase: *the hire-purchase system; a hire-purchase agreement.*

hirer, n. [1. hírer; 2. háiərə]. **hire (II.)** & **-er.** Person who hires.

hirsute, adj. [1. hérsūt; 2. hʌ́sjūt]. Lat. *hirsūt-us,* for earlier *hirsus,* cp. the form *hirtus,* also *hircus,* 'he-goat'; connected w. *hispidus,* 'bristly' (cp. **hideous**), & *horrēre,* 'to bristle'. See **horrid.** Shaggy, bristly, hairy; bearded.

hirsuteness, n. Prec. & **-ness.** State or quality of being hirsute.

hirundine, adj. [1. hirúndīn; 2. hirʌ́ndain], fr. Lat. *hirundo, hirundin-is,* 'swallow', & **-ine;** normal form wd. be *hirundin-ine.* The etymol. is very doubtful. Pertaining to, of the nature of, a swallow.

his, pronominal adj. [1. hiz; 2. hiz]. O.E. *his,* gen. sing. of masc. & neut. See **he, it.** Possessive pronoun, of 3rd pers. masc.; also used absolutely: *the book is his.*

hispid, adj. [1. híspid; 2. híspid]. Lat. *hisp-id-us.* See **hideous** & **hirsute.** (bot., zool.) Bristly, covered with stiff hairs.

hiss (I.), vb. intrans. & trans. [1. his; 2. his]. ME. *hissin,* imitative; cp. O.E. *hūsć,* 'insult', an entirely different word. **1.** intrans. **a** (of a person) To make a noise like that heard in prolonging the sound of *s,* esp. as a sign of strong disapproval or anger; **b** (of geese and snakes) to make a similar noise, the sign of fear or anger; **c** (of air, steam &c.) to produce such a sound in escaping from a narrow opening; **d** (of liquid) to bubble, sizzle, when falling on a hot surface. **2.** trans. **a** To express disapproval of, or anger at, by hissing; *to hiss off,* to drive (actor) from the stage by hissing; **b** (very rare) to utter with a hissing sound, as in rage: *to hiss disdain.*

hiss (II.), n., fr. prec. Noise produced in any of the ways mentioned in prec. word; sound of the voiceless open consonants *s, sh* [*s,* ʃ].

hissing, n. [1. hísing; 2. hísiŋ]. **hiss (I.)** & **-ing.** Action of person or thing that hisses.

hist, interj. & vb. trans. [1. hist; 2. hist]. Imitative. **a** interj. (archaic or liter.) Hush, silence; **b** vb., to summon or incite by calling 'hist'.

histo-, pref. Gk. *histós* for **sistos,* 'web, tissue', earlier 'ship's mast, upright beam of loom', fr. *histēnai* for **sistēnai,* 'to make to stand'. See **stand (I.)** & **state (I.).** (anat., bot., physiol.) Form used in compounds of Greek origin, denoting tissue.

histogenesis, n. [1. hìstōjénesis; 2. hìstoudžénisis]. Prec. & **genesis.** Formation and development of organic tissue.

histogenetic, adj. [1. hìstōjenétik; 2. hìstoudžinétik]. **histo-** & **-genetic.** Pertaining to histogenesis.

histologic(al), adj. [1. hìstolójik(l); 2. hìstəlɔ́džik(l)]. **histo-** & **logic, -logical.** Pertaining to histology.

histologist, n. [1. histólojist; 2. histɔ́lədžist]. **histo-** & **-logist.** Person who studies or is skilled in histology.

histology, n. [1. históloji; 2. histɔ́lədži]. **histo-** & **-logy.** Study of the structure of organic tissue.

histolysis, n. [1. histólisis; 2. histɔ́lisis]. **histo-** & **-lysis.** Dissolution of organic tissue; specif., that of the tissues of certain organs of larva during pupal stage.

histolytic, adj. [1. histōlítik; 2. histoulítik]. **histo-** & **-lytic.** Pertaining to histolysis.

historian, n. [1. histṓrian; 2. histṓriən]. Fr. *historien.* **history** & **-an.** Writer of history; student of, one learned in, history.

historiated, adj. [1. histṓriāted; 2. histṓrieitid]. L. Lat. *historiāt-(um),* P.P. of *historiāre,* 'to narrate, depict', fr. Lat. *historia,* **history** & **-ed.** Decorated with figures of flowers, animals, persons &c., as a capital letter or border in a mediaeval manuscript.

historic, adj. [1. histórik; 2. histɔ́rik]. Lat. *historicus,* fr. Gk. *historikós,* fr. **history** & **-ic.** **1. a** Pertaining to history; historical: *the historic sense; historic times,* those within scope of recorded history; contrasted with *prehistoric;* **b** now usually restricted to certain senses: famous, notable, having importance, associations, in history: *a(n) historic spot; this speech will become historic.* **2.** (gram., esp. Gk. and Lat.) *Historic infinitive,* that used in narration instead of indicative; *historic present,* present tense used for past in vivid narrative; *historic tenses,* those ordinarily used in narrating past events, the imperfect and pluperfect.

historical, adj. [1. histórikl; 2. histɔ́rikl]. Prec. & **-al.** **1.** Pertaining to the science and art of history: *the historical science, method; a(n) historical training* &c. **2.** Pertaining to written history, to a record of events and actions; **a** serving as a source, furnishing evidence, for a fact in history: *a(n) historical document;* **b** established by, recorded in, history; authentic, not legendary: *a(n) historical event, personage* &c.; **c** based on, referring to, suggested by, some person or event recorded in history: *a(n) historical picture, novel* &c. **3.** Connected, concerned, with, exhibiting, tracing, a gradual development or evolution; contrasted with what is merely descriptive of a single phase: *a(n) historical treatment of literature; a(n) historical account of a language.*

historically, adv. Prec. & **-ly.** In an historical manner; specif. **a** according to the methods of historical science; **b** so as to exhibit the gradual development and changes which have arisen from age to age.

historicity, n. [1. hìstorísiti; 2. hìstərísiti]. **historic** & **-ity.** Historical character, authenticity.

historico-, pref., fr. Gk. *historikós.* See **historic.** Used in a few compounds, such as *historico-philosophical,* combining historical and philosophical character.

historied, adj. [1. hístorid; 2. hístərid]. **history** & **-ed.** Having a history; recorded in history.

historiette, n. [1. hìstoriét; 2. hìstəriét]. Fr. **history** & **-ette.** Short history, short story.

historify, vb. trans. [1. histórifī; 2. histɔ́rifai]. **history** & **-fy.** To treat of as in history; make subject of history.

historiographer, n. [1. hìstoriógrafer; 2. hìstəriɔ́grəfə]. Lat. *historiograph-us,* fr. Gk. *historiográphos,* fr. *historio-,* combining form denoting **history, & -graph & -er.** Writer of a history; specif., one officially commissioned to record historical events: *Historiographer to the King.*

historiographic(al), adj. [1. històriográfik(l); 2. histɔ̀riəgrǽfik(l)]. See prec. & **-ic, -al.** Pertaining to historiography, or to a historiographer.

historiography, n. [1. hìstoriógrafi; 2. hìstəriɔ́grəfi]. See **historiographer** & **-y.** Act of writing history; specif., official history.

history, n. [1. hístori; 2. hístəri]. Lat. *historia,* 'narrative of past events; any narrative, story, account', fr. Gk. *historía,* 'learning by inquiry; knowledge gained by inquiry; narration of what is learnt, historical narrative', fr. *histōr,* 'knowing, acquainted; versed in; one who knows'. These words stand for **wistoria* &c., & are derived fr. the base **wid-, *woid-* &c., cp. Gk. *oîda,* 'I know' &c. (see **idea**), & Gmc., O.E. &c., *witan,* 'to know'. See **wit;** see also **story.** **1. a** That branch of knowledge which is concerned with the study of the development of man as a social and political being; **b** the science of dealing systematically with the records whence information about human action in the past is derived, and of sifting and co-ordinating the evidence which these records yield: *it has often been disputed whether history is a science or an art. Natural history* is the study of the phenomena of external nature; the term is now often restricted to the study of animate nature, in particular to zoology. **2. a** The series of events and actions which occur in the life of peoples: *the early history of Scotland was extremely agitated;* Phr. *to make history,* to do something which is of importance in the history of a country, or of mankind; **b** the events and experiences of an individual life: *Tamburlane had an amazing history.* **3.** The whole series of gradual changes and modifications which occur during the development of philosophy, religion, arts, institutions, laws, languages, and other products of the human mind and of society; development, evolution: *the history of religious beliefs, of laws and customs, of language* or *a language* &c. **4.** A systematic, reasoned, consecutive, written narrative of the life of a people, an institution, or an individual, or of any series of human activities: *a history of Greece, England* &c.; *a history of the stock exchange, of criminal law; a history of war in the Middle Ages; a history of scientific dis-*

covery &c. Phrs. *a matter of history*, something recorded by history ; *a question of history*, one for history to decide ; *to become history*, subject-matter for history. **5.** An account of the evolution of a language, and of the gradual phases through which it passes, of the various tendencies which arise among the speakers of it at different times, and the changes which it exhibits in each period throughout the whole time during which records of it exist : *a history of English*.

histrionic, adj. [1. histriónik ; 2. histriɔ́nik]. Lat. *histriōnic-us*, fr. *histriōn-(em)*, 'stage-player, actor', fr. early Lat. *hister*, said to be fr. Etruscan, & **-ic**. **a** Pertaining to, resembling, an actor or acting ; dramatic ; also in derogatory sense, artificial, affected, theatrical ; **b** (med.) pertaining to the facial muscles : *histrionic paralysis* ; **c** as n. in pl., *histrionics*, (i.) theatrical display ; (ii.) deliberate play-acting for effect.

histrionically, adv. [1. histriónikali ; 2. histriɔ́nikəli]. Prec. & **-al** & **-ly**. In a histrionic manner ; theatrically.

hit (I.), vb. trans. & intrans. [1. hit ; 2. hit]. Late O.E. *hyttan* for *hittan*, M.E. *hitten*, fr. O.N. *hitta*, 'to light on, meet with'. **A.** trans. **1. a** To reach, touch, strike (object aimed at): *to hit the target* ; Phr. *to hit the* (*right*) *nail on the head*, to get to the root of a matter, seize on vital and essential point ; to express a shrewd judgement in a telling manner ; **b** to light upon, fall in with, find, by design or luck : *to hit the right path*. **2.** (fig.) **a** To attain (one's aim) ; to guess right ; suit exactly : *to hit a likeness* ; *you've hit it*, are perfectly right ; **b** to strike, appeal to : *to hit one's fancy* ; Phrs. *to hit it off with*, to get on well with ; *to hit off*, to portray, describe, tellingly in a few strokes or words. **3. a** To knock, smite : *to hit a ball to the boundary* ; Phr. *to hit a man when he's down*, *hit below the belt*, (fig.) take unfair advantage of, treat unfairly ; **b** to deal (stroke) : *he hit him a heavy blow on the head* ; **c** to bring into collision : *to hit one's head against a beam* ; **d** to wound, hurt, injure feelings of : *you don't know whom your sarcasm may hit*. Phr. *hard hit*, gravely affected. **B.** intrans. **a** To aim (lit. or fig.) ; **b** *to hit on*, *upon*, to light upon, find, meet with casually : *to hit on a gold reef* ; *to hit upon a passage in a book* ; **c** to strike : *to hit against a wall* ; Phr. *to hit out*, to strike boldly or vigorously, esp. with the fists ; (also fig.) to attack or repel attacks with vigour ; **d** to smite hard as at cricket &c. : *go in and hit*, make runs quickly.

hit (II.), n., fr. prec. **1.** Stroke, blow, or shot that hits what is aimed at : *to register a hit on the target* ; (cricket) *a good hit* ; *a hit for three*, batsman's stroke resulting in three runs. **2.** Success, attainment of purpose ; a something that pleases popular taste, which gains wide approval : *his last novel was, made, a great hit* ; **b** piece of good luck, successful stroke, of business, in affairs ; **c** allusive remark, joke, quip, sarcasm, aimed at, directed against, person or thing : *the play contained some clever hits at public characters* ; '*Punch' has many good hits at the fashions of the day*.

hitch (I.), vb. trans. & intrans. [1. hich ; 2. hitʃ]. M.E. *hicchen*, 'to remove', Mod. Engl. dial. *hike*, *hoick*, 'to move with a jerk' ; cp. L.G. *hicken*, of uncertain origin, perh. connected w. **hook**. **1.** trans. **a** To move, pull, twitch, with a jerk : *to hitch up one's trousers* ; *to hitch one's chair to the table* ; **b** (i.) to secure by a hitch, hook, projecting part &c. ; to fasten temporarily or loosely : *to hitch a rope over, round, a bough* ; (ii.) to harness or yoke : *to hitch a horse to a whipple-tree*. **2.** intrans. **a** To move, advance, jerkily ; **b** to be fastened or secured by a hitch ; to catch on a nail, hook &c.

hitch (II.), n., fr. prec. **1.** Jerk, jerky movement. **2.** Kind of nautical knot for fastening rope temporarily. **3.** Entanglement, catch ; (fig.) something which delays, hinders, renders difficult ; an obstacle, hindrance, to action ; a check : *a hitch in the negotiations*. Phr. *without a hitch*, smoothly, easily, successfully.

hithe, n. [1. hīdh ; 2. haið]. O.E. *hȳð*, M.E. *hȳðe*, *hīthe* &c., fr. Gmc. **hunþj-* ; cogn. w. Goth. *hinþan*, 'to take, seize,' & w. **hand**. (archaic, rare, except in Place-Names) Landing place for vessels on coast or river.

hither, adv. & adj. [1. hídher ; 2. híðə]. O.E., M.E. *hider* ; cp. Goth. *hidrē*, O.N. *heðra* for **hiðra*, fr. Gmc. demonstr. base **hi-* (see **he**, **here**) & suff. **-đer-*, as in **hinder**, **other** &c. ; Aryan **-ter-* ; cogn. w. Lat. *citrā*, 'on this side'. **1.** adv. (archaic, now gen. replaced by *here*) In this direction, towards this place, towards me, to the place where I am : *come hither*. Phr. *hither and thither*, in various directions. **2.** adj. Nearer, on this side, on the side where I am : *the hither side*.

hitherto, adv. [1. hìdhertóō ; 2. hìðətú]. **hither** & **to**. **a** Up to this time, to this moment, so far ; **b** (obs.) hither, up to this point.

hitherward, adv. [1. hídherward ; 2. híðəwəd]. O.E. *hiderweard*. **hither** & **-ward**. (obs. or rare) Hither.

hit-or-miss, adj. Careless, happy-go-lucky, casual, haphazard, chancy.

hitter, n. [1. híter ; 2. hítə]. **hit** (I.) & **-er**. Person who hits : *this cricketer is a hard hitter*.

hive (I.), n. [1. hīv ; 2. haiv]. O.E. *hȳf*, M.E. *hīve* ; Du. *huif*, 'hood, hive', M.L.G. *huve*, 'hive', O.N. *hūf-r*, 'hull' ; Gmc. type **hūfi-* ; cogn. w. Lat. *cūpa*, 'tub' ; fr. Aryan base **keup-* &c., 'to bulge, swell out' ; cp. O.E. *cofa*, 'chamber', fr. **kufan-* (see **cove** (I.)). See further under **cup** & **heap** ; also **head**. **1. a** Hut-shaped receptacle, of plaited straw, or of wood, provided for swarm of bees to live and store honey in ; also *beehive* ; **b** (fig.) place where human beings swarm ; scene of busy life : *a hive of industry*. **2. a** Swarm of bees inhabiting hive ; **b** (fig.) busy community.

hive (II.), vb. trans. & intrans., fr. prec. **1.** trans. **a** To gather (bees) into a hive ; **b** (of bees) to store (honey) in a hive ; (fig.) to store up, garner. **2.** intrans. To enter, live in, a hive ; (fig.) to form, live in, a community.

hive-nest, n. Common nest built and used by several pairs of birds.

hives, n. [1. hīvz ; 2. haivz]. Scots ; origin uncertain. One of several maladies ; **a** eruptive disease like chicken-pox ; nettle-rash ; **b** laryngitis ; croup.

ho, interj. [1. hō ; 2. hou]. Cp. O.N. *ho*, Du. *hou* ; not in O.E. **a** As a call or cry to excite attention &c. : *ho ! there* ; *what ho !* &c. ; **b** as expression of various feelings, as surprise, weariness &c. : *ho ! ho !* ; *heigh-ho !* &c.

hoactzin, n. See **hoatzin**.

hoar, adj. [1. hōr ; 2. hɔ̄]. O.E. *hār*, M.E. *hōr* ; O.H.G., M.H.G. *hēr*, 'old, proud, lofty', Mod. Germ. *hehr*, 'exalted, august', orig. 'grey-haired, venerable' (cp. **younker**) ; O.N. *hār-r*, 'grey' ; Gmc. type **hair-az*, 'shining, white', fr. base **hai-*, cp. Goth. *hai-s*, 'torch', O.N. *hei-ð*, 'brightness', O.E. *hādor*, Germ. *hei-ter*, 'bright' ; perh. cogn. w. Gk. *koíranos*, 'lord'. (archaic or poet.) **a** (of the head or hair) Hoary, white, grey, esp. with age ; **b** (of the ground) white with frost.

hoard (I.), n. [1. hord ; 2. hɔ̄d]. O.E., M.E. *hord*, Common Gmc. **huzda-* ; O.S. *hord* ; O.H.G., Mod. Germ. *hort* ; Goth. *huzd* ; O.N. *hodd* ; Aryan **kuzdho-* for **kudh-dho-*, 'thing hidden', fr. **kudh-*, wk. grade of **keudh-*, 'to hide' ; whence also Gk. *keúthein*, 'to hide', *kústhos*, 'a hollow'. See **hide** (III.), **house**. **a** Store of treasure, esp. one that is hidden or guarded : *a hoard of coins was unearthed* ; **b** secret accumulation, as of food : *a squirrel's winter hoard* ; **c** (fig.) mass of material, stored in memory ; fund : *a hoard of witty stories*.

hoard (II.), vb. trans. & intrans. O.E. *hordian*, M.E. *horden*, fr. prec. ; cp. Goth. *huzdian*. **a** trans. To amass and secrete, store up, make a hoard of ; **b** intrans., to practise hoarding, to store up, accumulate, wealth, goods &c.

hoarder, n. [1. hórder ; 2. hɔ́də]. **hoard** (I.) & **-er**. Person or animal that hoards.

hoarding (I.), n. [1. hórding ; 2. hɔ́diŋ]. **hoard** (II.) & **-ing**. **1.** Action of one who hoards. **2.** Store of hoarded goods.

hoarding (II.), n. Obs. Engl. *hoard*, 'hoarding', either fr. O. Fr. *hourd*, *hourt*, 'scaffold', fr. Du. or Germ. *horde*, cogn. w. **hurdle**, **crate**, or direct fr. Du., & **-ing**. **a** Temporary fence or screen of boards round waste land, or in front of place where building &c. is being carried on ; **b** similar screen for display of posters ; **c** (mil. hist.) projecting wooden scaffold on top of wall of fortress.

hoar-frost, n. M.E. *hoorfrost*. **hoar** & **frost** (I.). Deposit of minute needles of ice on the ground, surface of leaves &c. ; white frost, rime.

hoarhound, n. See **horehound**.

hoariness, n. [1. hórines ; 2. hɔ́rinis]. **hoary** & **-ness**. State of being hoary ; whiteness (of the hair) ; antiquity, age.

hoarse, adj. [1. hors ; 2. hɔ̄s]. O.E. *hās*, M.E. *hōs*, *hors*, w. *-r-* through association w. **harsh** ; cp. O.H.G. *heis*, Mod. Germ. *heiser*, O.N. *hāss* ; Gmc. type **hais-az* or **hairs-az*. **a** (of the voice) Rough, husky, harsh ; lacking clearness and ring, as when affected by a cold &c. in the throat ; **b** (of person or animal) having a hoarse or husky voice : *the hoarse raven* ; Phr. *as hoarse as a crow* ; **c** (of inanimate things) discordant, harsh, grating : *hoarse breakers*, *thunder*.

hoarsely, adv. Prec. & **-ly**. In a hoarse manner.

hoarseness, n. O.E. *hāsnysse*, M.E. *hoo(r)snesse*. See prec. & **-ness**. Quality, condition, of being hoarse.

hoar-stone, n. **hoar**, in sense of 'aged', & **stone**. Prehistoric monolith, sometimes used to mark boundary.

hoary, adj. [1. hōri ; 2. hɔ́ri]. M.E. *hori*. **hoar** & **-y**. **1.** White or grey ; specif. **a** white-haired or grey-haired with age : *a hoary head* ; Phr. *a hoary sinner*, an old reprobate ; **b** (bot.) covered with white downy hairs ; canescent : *hoary plantain*. **2.** (fig.) Ancient, venerable : *hoary antiquity*, *eld*.

hoary-headed, adj. Having a head hoary or white with age : '*some hoary-headed swain*' (Gray's 'Elegy').

hoatzin, **hoactzin**, n. [1. hōátsin ; 2. houǽtsin], fr. native name. A bird of tropical S. America, of unique skeletal structure and forming a group, *Opisthocomus* ; its plumage is olive with yellow-tipped feathers and yellow crest ; the young have claws on the wings, with which they climb.

hoax, vb. trans. & n. [1. hōks ; 2. houks]. Earlier *hocus*. See **hocus-pocus**. **1.** vb. To deceive, dupe, take in, by misrepresentation ; to play off a practical joke upon. **2.** n. **a** A deception, misleading statement ; esp. one calculated to induce action based upon a misconception of facts ; **b** a practical joke.

hoaxer, n. [1. hókser ; 2. hóuksə]. See prec. & **-er**. Person who hoaxes.

hob, n. [1. hob ; 2. hɔb]. Formerly, 'a projection, boss, knob' ; prob. a variant of **hub**. **1.** Horizontal ledge or shelf on either side of a fire grate and level with its top, forming stand for a kettle, saucepan &c. **2. a** Peg set as mark in quoits, or other game ; **b** game in which coin laid on peg is target. **3.** Shoe on the runner of a sledge.

hob and nob. See **hobnob**.

hobble (I.), vb. intrans. & trans. [1. hóbl ; 2. hɔ́bl]. M.E. *hobelen* ; cp. Du. *hobbelen*, 'to rock from side to side ; ride hobby-horse ; stammer', provinc. Germ. *hoppeln*, 'to hobble' ; freq. (see **-le**) of a weakened form of **hop**, as Du. *hobben*, 'to toss up and down' ; cp. O. Fr. *hober*, 'to move, bestir oneself', & cp. **hopple**. **1.** intrans. **a** To walk lamely or in an awkward, clumsy manner, as if the feet were painful or partially useless ; to walk with a kind of stumbling limp ; also *hobble along* ; **b** (fig., of verse) to halt, run lamely. **2.** trans. To impede movement of (horse &c.) by connecting two legs by rope ; to hopple.

hobble (II.), n., fr. prec. **1.** Limping, stumbling, gait. **2. a** Rope used to hobble animal; **b** (fig., colloq., rare) difficulty, dilemma, straits: *I'm in rather a hobble.* *Hobble skirt,* woman's skirt made very narrow round the knees.

hobbledehoy, hobbadehoy, hobbedehoy, n. [1. hòbldehói; 2. hɔ̀bldihɔ́i]. Early Mod. Engl. *hobledehoye, hoberdihoie* &c., of unknown origin, possibly connected w. **hobble.** Awkward, clumsy, gawky, overgrown, rather ill-mannered boy or youth; youth between boyhood and manhood.

hobbledehoyish, adj. [1. hòbldehói - ish; 2. hɔ̀bldihɔ́i-iʃ]. Prec. & **-ish.** Having appearance, manners &c. of a hobbledehoy.

hobbler (I.), n. [1. hóbler; 2. hɔ́blə]. **hobble** (I.) & **-er.** Person or animal that hobbles.

hobbler (II.), n. M.E., O. Fr. *hobeler,* cp. Fr. *hobereau,* 'squire', apparently connected w. O. Fr. *hobin, hobi-,* 'a nag', cp. **hobby** (I.). (hist.) Retainer bound to maintain a hobby or horse for war; light-armed soldier mounted on a small horse or hobby.

hobblingly, adv. [1. hóblingli; 2. hɔ́bliŋli], fr. Pres. Part. of **hobble** (I.) & **-ly.** In a hobbling manner.

hobby (I.), n. [1. hóbi; 2. hɔ́bi]. M.E. *hobin,* 'nag', *Hobin,* name for horse (cp. *Dobbin*), perh. fr. O. Fr. *hobin, hobi,* 'nag, small horse', *Hobin* being an Engl. (& perh. Fr.) variant of Fr. *Robin,* familiar form of *Robert.* **1.** (obs.) Middle-sized, active horse for riding; a nag. **2.** Hobby-horse, **1**; hence: **3.** (fig.) **a** (obs.) Idea on which one dwells or expatiates to excess; craze, fad: *to ride a hobby* (*to death*); **b** favourite occupation of one's leisure, subject that one studies as an amateur: *his hobby is collecting old china.*

hobby (II.), n. M.E. *hobi, hoby,* fr. O. Fr. *hobé, hobe,* cp. the dimin. forms *hobet, hobereau,* perh. fr. O. Fr. *hober,* 'to move, bestir oneself', fr. a L.G. source; cp. M. Du. *hobben,* 'to toss, move up and down'. See **hobble.** Small European species of falcon, formerly used for hawking.

hobby-horse, n. See **hobby** (I.). **1.** Figure representing a saddle-horse; specif. **a** in the morris dance, figure of horse attached to dancer, so that he appears to be riding it; also the dancer himself; **b** stick with head of horse, which child bestrides in imitation of rider; **c** wooden horse for riding, as a rocking-horse, or horse in roundabout. **2.** (very rare) Favourite occupation, hobby.

hobgoblin, n. [1. hòbgóblin; 2. hɔ̀bgɔ́blin]. Early Mod. Engl. *hob,* 'kind of fairy', fr. *Hob,* familiar form of *Robert.* See **hobby** (I.), & cp. such names for similar supernatural beings as *Robin Goodfellow,* fr. *Robin.* For second element see **goblin. a** A sprite, a hideous bogey; conceived of as a mischievous creature of the male sex; **b** an ugly, mischievous child, or small ugly person.

hobnail, n. & vb. trans. [1. hóbnāl; 2. hɔ́bneil]. **hob,** 'peg', & **nail** (I.). **1.** n. Nail with large projecting head, used to stud soles of boots; also attrib., *hobnail liver,* (med.) form of cirrhosis of the liver, in which the shrunken surface is studded with nodules. **2.** vb. To stud with hobnails.

hobnailed, adj. [1. hóbnāld; 2. hɔ́bneild]. Prec. & **-ed. a** Set with hobnails; **b** (rare) wearing hobnailed boots; rustic, clownish.

hobnob, vb. intrans. [1. hóbnób; 2. hɔ́bnɔ́b]. Early Mod. Engl., also *hab nab,* 'whatever may happen', fr. O.E. *hæbban,* 'to have', & *nabban* for *ne habban,* 'not to have'; also *hob and nob.* **1.** vb. To associate familiarly with, be on intimate terms, behave as close friends: *to hobnob with strangers.* **2.** n. (rare and vulg.) A friendly talk.

hobo, n. [1. hṓbō; 2. hóubou]. Etymol. unknown. (Am. slang) Tramp, vagrant.

Hobson's choice, n. [1. hóbsunz chóis; 2. hɔ́bs(ə)nz tʃɔ́is]. Thos. Hobson (d. 1631), carrier and keeper of livery stables at Cambridge, who let out his horses by strict rotation; the *University Carrier* of Milton's verses. Sham choice; offer with no alternative; 'take it or leave it'.

hock (I.), n. & vb. trans. [1. hok; 2. hɔk]. Southern form of **hough** (I.), or back-formation fr. obs. *hox,* n. & vb., O.E. *hōhsinu,* M.E. *houȝsenu, hox,* fr. **hough** (I.) & **sinew.** Cp. O. Fris. *hōxene, hōxne,* M.H.G. *hahse,* Mod. Germ. *hechse,* O.N. *hāsin.* **1.** n. **a** Joint in middle of the hind leg of a horse, ass, ox &c., corresponding anatomically to human ankle and heel; hough; **b** butcher's term for flesh on fore or hind leg immediately above foot, esp. of swine. **2.** vb. To hough, hamstring.

Hock (II.), n. Abbr. fr. *hockamore,* ad. fr. Germ. *Hochheimer,* 'wine of Hochheim', village near Mainz, Germany. (usually cap.) Any white Rhenish wine: *still, sparkling, Hock.*

hockey, n. [1. hóki; 2. hɔ́ki]. Of doubtful origin; perh. fr. obs. or dial. Fr. *hoquet,* 'bent club, shepherd's crook', dimin. fr. a L.G. source, cogn. w. **hook** (I.). **a** Game played with a ball, and sticks with curved ends, in a field or on ice, between two teams, each of which tries to drive ball through opponent's goal; **b** (attrib.) as in *hockey ball, club* (society), *stick.*

Hock-tide, n. Second element *tide,* 'season'; etymol. of *hock* unknown; not in O.E.; no connexion w. Germ. *hoch,* 'high'. An old festival and holiday held on the second Monday and Tuesday after Easter; it was celebrated with feasting and much rough horseplay.

hocus, n. & vb. trans. [1. hókus; 2. hóukəs]. Abbr. fr. next word. **1.** n. Drugged drink. **2.** vb. **a** To hoax, dupe, swindle; **b** to put drug in another's drink; to give drugs to a person, horse &c. in drink.

hocus-pocus, n. [1. hṓkus pṓkus; 2. hóukəs póukəs]. Meaningless magic formula; bogus 17th cent. Lat. Cp. **hoax** (I.). Meaningless talk &c., intended to deceive or divert attention from the facts; mystification, claptrap; jugglery, swindling.

hod, n. [1. hod; 2. hɔd]. Early Mod. Engl. *hodd,* obs. *hot*; M. Du. *hodde,* 'basket', Germ. *hotte,* 'wooden vessel, basket for the back', whence Fr. *hotte*; perh. fr. Gmc. source & a form of base ***heud-,* 'to hide, cover'. See **hide** (III.), **hut.** Wooden receptacle, open above and at sides, with long handle underneath, for carrying over the shoulder; used by bricklayers to convey bricks, mortar &c.

hodden, n. & adj. [1. hód(e)n; 2. hɔ́d(ə)n]. Scots; etymol. unknown. **a** n. Coarse undyed woollen fabric; **b** adj., clad in hodden; rustic; *hodden grey* (also *hoddengrey*), hodden cloth of mixed black and white wool.

Hodge, n. [1. hoj; 2. hɔdž]. Used as name of servant in comedy 'Gammer Gurton's Needle' (1575); familiar form of the name *Roger.* Cp. **hobby** (I.). (colloq.) The agricultural labourer: *Gladstone gave the vote to Hodge.*

hodge-podge. See **hotchpotch.**

hodiernal, adj. [1. hòdiérnal; 2. hɔ̀diʌ́n(ə)l]. Lat. *hodiern-us,* fr. *hodie,* 'today', for *hoc die,* 'on this day' (see **dies non**), & *-ern-us,* adjectival suff., & **-al.** Pertaining to, of, today; of the present day.

hodman, n. [1. hódman; 2. hɔ́dmən]. **a** Man who carries a hod; bricklayer's assistant; **b** (fig.) one whose function is merely to provide materials for, or to wait on, another.

hodometer, n. [1. hodómeter; 2. hɔdɔ́mitə]. Gk. *hodós* for ***sod-ós,* 'way, path', fr. Aryan base ***sed-,* q.v. under **sit,** & for sense 'go' under **cede,** & **-meter.** Instrument attached to wheel of vehicle to measure the distance traversed.

hoe (I.), n. [1. hō; 2. hou]. Norm. Fr. *hoe,* Fr. *houe,* fr. O.H.G. *houwa* (Mod. Germ. *haue*), connected w. **hew.** Implement of various makes and shapes, consisting mainly of small blade attached transversely at various angles to long handle, used for uprooting weeds, breaking up hard surface of ground &c.

hoe (II.), vb. trans. & intrans., fr. prec., cp. Fr. *houer.* **a** trans. To treat (soil, crop) with hoe; to uproot (weeds) with hoe; *to hoe a row of onions* &c., break up and loosen earth round the plants; Phr. *a long row to hoe,* a tedious task; **b** intrans., to work with hoe.

hog (I.), n. [1. hog; 2. hɔg]. O.E. *hogg, hocg* (?), M.E. *hog, hogge*; prob. orig. meaning 'cut or castrated animal', cp. O.N. *hӧggva,* cogn. w. **hew. 1. a** Castrated boar; **b** adult domestic swine or pig generally; rarely, wild swine. Phrs. *to eat, behave, like a hog,* eat greedily, behave rudely; *hog in armour,* (colloq.) awkward, ungainly person; person ill at ease in fine dress &c.; *to go the whole hog,* (colloq.) to carry action or opinion to logical conclusion; go all lengths; *to bring one's hogs to the wrong market,* (colloq.) make proposals &c. in unsuitable quarters. **2.** (fig.) Greedy, selfish, coarse, or filthy person. **3.** Young sheep before its first shearing. **4.** Kind of brush for scraping ship's bottom under water.

hog (II.), vb. trans. & intrans., fr. prec. **A.** trans. **1.** To arch (back) like that of hog. **2.** To seize (food &c.) greedily. **3.** To clip (horse's mane, or man's moustache) short and close. **4.** To scrape (ship's bottom) with hog. **5.** (rare) To keep (lamb) till it is a hog. **B.** intrans. **1.** (of horse &c.) To arch the back and lower the head. **2.** To be humped in middle, as stranded ship with broken back.

hogback, n. [1. hógbak; 2. hɔ́gbæk]. Ridge sloping abruptly on each side.

hogbacked, adj. [1. hógbakt; 2. hɔ́gbækt]. Prec. & **-ed.** Having a hogback; shaped like a hog's back.

hogfish, n. [1. hógfish; 2. hɔ́gfiʃ]. One of several fishes with back, body, or head somewhat like that of a hog; esp. a W. Indian fish related to wrasse.

hog-frame, n. Trussed frame extending along ship's deck to prevent hogging.

hogged, adj. [1. hogd; 2. hɔgd]. **hog** (II.) & **-ed. 1. a** Having a narrow ridge like a hogback; **b** sloping towards front and back. **2.** (of horse's mane &c.) Clipped short.

hoggery, n. [1. hógeri; 2. hɔ́gəri]. **hog** (I.) & **-ery. 1.** Place where hogs are reared; herd of hogs. **2.** Hoggish behaviour.

hoggin, n. [1. hógin; 2. hɔ́gin]. Etymol. unknown. Mixture of screened gravel and sand.

hoggish, adj. [1. hógish; 2. hɔ́giʃ]. **hog** (I.) & **-ish.** Resembling a hog; swinish, beastly; greedy, selfish.

hoggishly, adv. Prec. & **-ly.** In a hoggish manner.

hoggishness, n. See prec. & **-ness.** Hoggish behaviour; quality of being hoggish.

Hogmanay, n. [1. hógmani; 2. hɔ́gməni]. Scots, fr. O. Fr., *hoguinané, hoquinano* &c., refrain of song on New Year's Eve, a corrupt. of Lat. *hoc in anno,* 'in this year' (*-ané* influenced by Fr. *année,* 'year'). (in Scotland) New Year's Eve; the festivities then observed.

hogmane, n. [1. hógmān; 2. hɔ́gmein]. **hog** (I.) & **mane.** Hogged mane of horse.

hogmaned, adj. [1. hógmānd; 2. hɔ́gmeind]. Having a hogmane.

hog's back, n. See **hogback.**

hogshead, n. [1. hógz-hed; 2. hɔ́gzhed]. M.E. *hogsheved, hogges - hede,* apparently 'hog's head', though the reason for this designation is unknown. **a** Large cask; **b** liquid measure equal to 52½ imperial gallons, or 54 in the case of beer or cider.

hogsty, n. [1. hógstī; 2. hɔ́g(z)stai]. Pigsty.

hogwash, n. [1. hógwosh; 2. hɔ́gwɔʃ]. **a** Kitchen refuse &c. mixed with water and given to hogs; **b** (fig., vulg.) silly, vapid, or low talk; poor, contemptible, writing.

hoicks, hoick, interj. [1. hoiks; 2. hɔiks]. Cp. **yoicks.** Call to hounds.

hoiden, n. See **hoyden.**

hoi polloi, n. pl. [1. hói pólloi; 2. hɔ́i pɔ̀lɔi]. Gk., 'the many'; see **poly-.** The common people, the majority; the rabble.

hoise, vb. trans. [1. hoiz; 2. hɔiz]. Obs. form of **hoist** (I.). Only in P.P., *hoist with his own* *petar* (petard), (Shakespeare, 'Hamlet', III. iv. 207), blown up with his own bomb, caught in his own trap.

hoist (I.), vb. trans. [1. hoist; 2. hɔist]. Late M.E. *hyse, hysse, hoise,* prob. fr. M. Du. *hÿssen* (Mod. Du. *hijschen*); L.G. *hīsen, hiessen,* Germ. *hissen,* of doubtful origin; the form *hoist* for *hoise* is prob. due to the P.P. **a** To raise, pull up with effort (sail, flag, load), by cord, pulley &c.; to raise weights with a crane; **b** to heave, lift, fling up.

hoist (II.), n., fr. prec. **a** Action of hoisting; **b** appliance for raising heavy goods from lower to higher level; kind of lift, esp. on board ship: *ammunition hoist.*

hoistway, n. [1. hóistwā; 2. hɔ́istwei]. Opening in floor or floors for hoist or lift.

hoity-toity, interj., adj., & n. [1. hóiti tóiti; 2. hɔ́iti tɔ́iti]. Exclamatory jingle. Cp. **hoots, tut.** (archaic or facet.) **a** interj. Exclamation expressing irritable, contemptuous, derisive, or surprised protest; **b** adj., given to exclaiming 'hoity-toity', hence, irritable, fussy, easily offended, touchy, petulant: *a hoity-toity kind of person; he was very hoity-toity;* **c** n., this exclamation.

hokey-pokey, n. [1. hṓki pṓki; 2. hóuki póuki]. Perh. fr. **hocus-pocus.** (gutter colloq.) Cheap ice-cream sold in streets.

hold (I.), vb. trans. & intrans. [1. hōld; 2. hould]. O.E. (Anglian) *haldan,* M.E. *hōlden,* Common Gmc.; Goth. *haldan,* 'to tend, feed, sheep'; O.S., 'hold'; O. Fris., O.N. *halda;* O.H.G. *haltan;* prob. not cogn. w. Lat. *colere,* 'till, tend, take care of' &c. (see **colony, cult** &c.); but perh. fr. same base as Lat. *celer,* 'swift, rapid' &c. (see **celerity**), also Gk. *kélēs,* 'race-horse', & *kéllein,* 'to drive, urge on, push ashore', & (*bou-*)*kólos,* 'cow-herd'; further Lith. *keliù,* 'I lift'. The specialized sense of the word in Goth. & the various other meanings seen in the other words might be reduced to a common basal meaning such as 'to run after, follow, and drive, a flock or herd', hence 'to tend, guard a flock; to guard, keep, hold', in more general sense. **A.** trans. **1. a** Specif., to grasp with, and retain in, the hand: *to hold a pen, brush; to hold a gun, spade* &c.; **b** to grip, keep, retain, by any bodily means: *to hold a pipe between the teeth;* **c** to clasp, embrace: *to hold a child in one's arms.* Phr. *to hold* (*a person or thing*) *in the hollow of one's hand,* to have complete power and control over. **2.** To maintain, support, in a given place or position, **a** the body, or a part of it, by muscular action: *to hold one's hands before one's face, the head straight, on one side; to hold oneself upright;* **b** (of external objects) *to hold a shield in front of one;* **c** (of function of inanimate things) to keep in place, yield support to, bear weight of, resist strain of: *this beam holds the whole weight of the next storey; this wall won't hold a hook bearing a heavy picture.* **3.** To keep oneself, or something else, in a certain state, or condition, of preparedness for action or use: *to hold oneself ready to start at a moment's notice.* **4. a** To have and keep, enjoy possession of, have in keeping or possession; to own: *to hold land; to hold shares in a company; to hold a brief for,* (law) be entrusted with defence of; (fig.) be favourably disposed to, be prepared to support and justify; **b** specif. (mil.) to occupy and fortify, protect, maintain against assault; retain in spite of attack: *to hold a fortress, position, trench* &c.; Phrs. *to hold one's own, one's ground,* (fig.) (i.) preserve one's position, maintain one's point, in argument &c.; not to retract; (ii.) maintain strength, in illness &c.; *lightly won, lightly held,* easily obtained, soon lost. **5.** To contain, enclose, **a** (material things) *this box holds all my securities; this house holds everything I love on earth;* **b** (non-material things) *we cannot tell what sorrows the future may hold* (*in store*) *for us.* **6. a** To be able to contain, have capacity for containing so much, or so many: *this jug holds a quart; the room won't hold more than a hundred persons;* Phr. *to eat as much as one can hold,* to one's utmost limit; **b** to be able to retain a certain kind of substance: *a leather receptacle will hold water but not petrol;* Phr. (fig., of statement, argument &c.) *to hold water,* be perfectly consistent, logically unassailable. **7. a** (of mental action) To have, keep, retain, in the consciousness: *I can't hold all these details in my head, memory, at once;* **b** to have an opinion or belief concerning; to consider, regard: *to hold a man to be a fool, a thing to be impossible;* Phr. *to hold in great esteem, contempt,* to esteem highly, have contempt for; **c** to cherish, entertain (ideas, notions &c.): *to hold strange views;* **d** specif. (law) to lay down as a principle, enunciate as legally binding, decide judicially, or authoritatively: *the evidence was held by the court to be inadmissible.* **8.** To restrain, control, dominate, check; **a** (by physical effort) *to hold a restive horse; to hold a man prisoner;* Phr. (fig.) *to hold a man to his promise,* compel him to fulfil it; Phrs. *to hold one's breath,* not to breathe; *to hold one's hand,* to cease, or delay action; *neither to hold nor to bind,* uncontrollable; *to hold one's peace* (archaic); *to hold one's tongue,* to be silent; (colloq. and vulg.) *hold your noise, row, jaw,* stop making a noise, stop talking. **b** (by moral influence) *he held the mob by the power of his eye and the dignity of his gesture;* **c** to attract and keep by intellectual appeal: *to hold the attention of one's audience; to hold an audience spellbound.* **9.** To bring about, institute, take part in, conduct, carry out, esp. a public or official function: *to hold a meeting, discussion, religious service* &c. **B.** intrans. **1.** To stand, be equal to, a strain, not to give way: *I doubt if the rope will hold much longer.* **2.** (of non-material things) To be valid, be in force, apply: *the principle, bargain, promise, still holds;* also *to hold good.* **3.** To continue in existence, last: *if the frost holds we shall have skating tomorrow; I fear this beautiful weather won't hold much longer.* **4.** Phr. *hold, enough!,* (archaic) that will do, no more of that!; *hold hard!,* stop a moment, don't be in a hurry &c. **C.** Followed by adverb or preposition. *Hold back,* **a** trans., to restrain, deter; **b** intrans., to refrain, hesitate, delay. *Hold by,* intrans., (i.) to adhere to: *to hold by one's decision;* (ii.) follow advice of, be guided, abide, by: *to hold by one's teachers* &c., *by what So-and-so says* &c. *Hold forth,* **a** trans., to offer as inducement or encouragement: *to hold forth a hope;* **b** intrans., to declaim, make harangue, speak publicly (often contempt.). *Hold in,* **a** trans., to restrain, check, confine; **b** intrans., to restrain oneself. *Hold off,* **a** trans., keep back, prevent from attacking &c.: *to hold a dog off;* **b** intrans., to keep aloof, hold back, delay. *Hold on,* intrans., **a** persist, continue in: *to hold on one's course;* **b** to maintain grip: *can you hold on?;* **c** to cling: *to hold on by one's hands;* **d** (fig.) to persist, endure, hold out: *things will come right if you can only hold on a bit. Hold out,* **1.** trans., **a** to stretch forth; **b** to offer, promise: *to hold out a prospect of promotion;* **2.** intrans., to maintain one's position against difficulties or assaults; to endure to the end: *the garrison could hold out no longer on account of starvation. Hold over,* **1.** trans., **a** to postpone, keep in reserve or abeyance: *to hold over a decision for a week;* **b** (fig.) to threaten with: *to hold a threat of disclosure over one's head;* **2.** intrans., (law) to keep possession beyond expiry of term. *Hold to,* intrans., to abide by, adhere to: *I still hold to my former views. Hold together,* **a** trans., to cause to cohere, keep united; **b** intrans., to cohere, remain united. *Hold up,* **1.** trans., **a** to exhibit, display: *to hold up as a model, to ridicule;* **b** to sustain, support, uphold; **c** (colloq., orig. Am.) to stop (train, vehicle, passenger) by violence or threats, for the purpose of robbery; hence, **d** (colloq.) to stop, delay (traffic &c.): *the car was held up by fog;* **2.** intrans., **a** to avoid falling, as horse, when slipping or stumbling; **b** to keep up, maintain, speed; **c** (of weather) to keep fine. *Hold with,* intrans., **a** to agree with, hold the same views as; **b** to approve of: *I don't hold with Sunday dancing.*

hold (II.), n. O.E. (*ǵe*)*heald, -hāld,* 'holding, protection, rule', M.E. *hōld.* See prec. **1. a** Action, manner, power, of holding; grasp, grip, clutch: *to take, lose, hold of, keep a firm hold on, a thing;* Phrs. *to get hold of,* obtain possession of; also specif., *to get hold of a person,* exercise undue influence over him; *to lay hold of,* to grasp; **b** (fig.) power, control, authority: *the government maintained, relaxed, its hold over the province;* **c** (fig.) mental grasp, apprehension: *to lose one's hold of,* or *on, realities.* **2.** Means of holding, something to hold on by: *these rocks afford no hold for hand or foot.* **3.** (archaic) Thing that holds, confines; specif. **a** place of custody, prison: *to put a man in hold;* **b** place of protection or refuge, fastness, stronghold. **4.** (law) Tenure (only in compounds, as *copyhold, freehold* &c., q.v.). **5.** (mus.) Pause; (in notation) mark (𝄐) indicating that note or rest is prolonged.

hold (III.), n. Du. *hol,* 'hole, cavity, ship's hold'. See **hole** (I.), confused w. prec. **a** Space within ship below lower deck, in which cargo is placed; **b** specified part of this when divided.

hold-all, n. **hold** (I.) & **all.** Large unwieldy bag or case for carrying traveller's effects.

hold-back, n. **1.** Hindrance, check. **2.** Stop on shaft of vehicle which prevents this from touching horse when he stops or backs.

holden, vb. [1. hṓlden; 2. hóuldən]. Old P.P. of **hold** (I.). Archaic, except in official Phr. *a meeting &c. will be holden* &c., held.

holder, n. [1. hṓlder; 2. hóuldə]. M.E. *hāldere.* **hold** (I.) & **-er.** **1.** Thing in or by which something is held; esp. in composition, as *cigarette-holder, pen-holder.* **2.** Person who holds; specif. a tenant, occupier, esp. in composition, as *small-holder* &c.; **b** person in (legal) possession of bill, promissory note &c.: *a holder for value.*

holdfast, n. [1. hṓldfahst; 2. hóuldfāst]. Thing that holds fast; specif. **a** clamp, staple, or nail securing object to wall; **b** (bot.) disk-like organ attaching seaweed or climbing plant to rock &c.

holding, n. [1. hṓlding; 2. hóuldiŋ]. M.E. *hōldinge.* **hold** (I.) & **-ing.** **1.** Action of person who holds; specif. **a** (Scots) legal tenure; **b** (football, boxing &c.) irregular seizing of opponent. **2.** Thing held; specif. **a** land held, tenement: *small holdings;* **b** property owned, as bonds or shares.

hold-up, n. (colloq., chiefly Am.) **a** Detention, by violence or threats, of train, vehicle, or passenger for purpose of robbery; **b** stoppage, delay, in traffic &c.

hole (I.), n. [1. hōl; 2. houl]. O.E. *hol,* orig. neut. of adj. *holh* (see **hollow**). M.E. *hōle;* cp. O.H.G. *hol,* M.H.G. *hohl,* adj., 'hollow'; O.N. *hol-r* adj., *hol* n.; cp. Goth. *hul-undi,* 'cave'; Gmc. type **hul-,* wk. grade of **hel-,* 'to hide, cover', cp. O.E. *helan;* fr. Aryan base **k̑ĕl-,* **k̑l̥-* &c., q.v. under **conceal, cell, colour, hall, hell.** **1.** Cavity, depression, in solid body; various specific uses: **a** cavity in the ground; pit: *to dig a hole;* Phr. *to be, put, in a hole,* in a position from which escape is difficult; a fix, dilemma; **b** specif., cavity hollowed out by an animal, his burrow: *the hole of a badger;* Phrs. *like a rat in a hole,* driven to last refuge from which there is no escape; *every hole and corner,* every obscure, secret place; cp. **hole-and-corner;** **c** hollow, empty space, depression in any solid body: *a hole in an apple;* Phrs. *make a hole in,* (colloq.) reduce in size &c., consume, use, a large amount of; *hole in one's head* &c., wound; **d** small hollow in golf green into which players putt their balls: *to win the first three holes;* **e** (fig., contempt.) poky, stuffy, squalid, little house; nasty little place: *a beastly hole to live in.* **2.** Break, gap, aperture in a flat surface; a *hole in a wall, roof, window (pane)* &c.; **b** tear, rent, in fabric: *a hole in a sheet, heel of a stocking, coat,* &c. Phr. *to pick holes in (a man's character; in a plan, argument, performance* &c.), to find fault with, criticize adversely. **3.** An outlet, vent, **a** natural orifice of animal body, such as eye, mouth, ear; **b** outlet or inlet in vessel, pipe &c.: *air hole; bung-, vent-hole* in a cask &c. Phr. *square peg in a round hole,* person whose occupation or surroundings are unsuited to his capacities, and uncongenial to his character.

hole (II.), vb. trans. & intrans. See prec. **A.** trans. **1.** To make hole or holes in, or through: **a** *the shot holed his hat*; specif. **b** to undercut (coal); **c** to make hole through, pierce, excavate: *to hole a tunnel.* **2.** To drive, put, into a hole: *to hole a rabbit; to hole (out) one's ball,* in golf; *to hole the red,* put red ball into pocket, in billiards. **B.** intrans. To drive, put, ball into hole; (golf) in Phr. *to hole out in four* &c., to get the ball into the hole in four strokes.

hole-and-corner, adj. (colloq.) Secret, underhand, furtive: *hole-and-corner methods, procedure.*

holey, adj. [1. hṓli; 2. hóuli]. **hole (I.) & -y.** (rare) Having a hole or holes.

holiday, n. [1. hólidi; 2. hɔ́lidi]. O.E. *hāliġdæġ*; M.E. *hălizdei, hŏlidei* &c., w. vowel of first element shortened. See **holy & day.** **1.** **a** (eccles.) Feast day, day of rejoicing, festival, in commemoration of a saint, or sacred personage, or of some great event in the Church calendar; **b** a cessation from work combined with festivity: *to make a holiday of it.* **2.** Day on which work is wholly or partially suspended; day of recreation and amusement: *to have a holiday every Saturday, on one's birthday* &c. *Bank holiday,* statutory holiday throughout England, on which banks are closed, and all public offices as far as possible suspend work, and shops and business offices &c. are closed. **3.** **a** Period of time during which recreation is taken, and rest from the ordinary, regular, duties and tasks is enjoyed: *to take a month's holiday*; **b** specif. (pl.) *the holidays,* period during which certain large sections of the community enjoy rest from their regular work: *the Easter, summer, holidays*; esp. regularly recurring periods when schools close, and teachers and taught cease teaching and learning and go home; contrasted with *the term.* **4.** (attrib.) Pertaining to, connected with, a holiday, or holidays: *holiday mood, spirit; holiday behaviour* &c.; *holiday task,* piece of work prescribed by a school, to be carried out by pupils during the holidays.

holiday-maker, n. **a** Person out on a holiday; festive person; **b** (contemptuous) noisy, vulgar tripper.

holily, adv. [1. hṓlili; 2. hóulili]. M.E. *hōliliche.* **holy & -ly.** In a holy manner.

holiness, n. [1. hṓlines; 2. hóulinis]. O.E. *hāliġness,* M.E. *hōliznesse.* **holy & -ness.** Quality of being holy; sanctity, sacred character; *His Holiness,* title of the Pope, or of a bishop of the Eastern Church; formerly of the East Roman Emperor.

holism, n. [1. hṓlizm; 2. hóulizəm]. See **holo- & -ism.** Theory which regards nature as a unity, made up of 'wholes' which are more than a mere aggregation of disparate elements.

holla, interj. [1. hulṓ; 2. halóu]. Fr. *holà,* 'ho there', fr. **ho** & Fr. *là,* fr. Lat. *illāc,* 'in that (place), there', abl. fem. sing. (agreeing with *parte,* 'part') of *illic,* fr. *ille,* 'that', & demonstr. particle *-ce*; now indistinguishable fr. **hallo, hollo** &c. (obs.) Call to attract attention, answer call, or make person stop.

Holland, n. & adj. [1. hóland; 2. hɔ́lənd]. *Holland,* district in Netherlands, also the Netherlands, fr. Du. *holt,* 'wood'. See **holt & land.** **a** n. A coarse linen or linen and cotton textile, unbleached and usually undyed or dyed brown; **b** adj., made of holland: *a brown holland coat.*

hollandaise, adj. & n. [1. hòlandáz; 2. hɔ̀ləndéiz]. Fr., fem. of adj. *hollandais,* 'pertaining to Holland'. See prec. **a** adj. Only in *hollandaise sauce,* sauce made of yolk of egg and butter, with seasoning; **b** n., hollandaise sauce.

hollands, n. [1. hólandz; 2. hɔ́ləndz]. Du. *hollandsch (genever),* 'Hollandish (gin)', fr. **Holland & -sch, -ish.** Gin distilled in Holland.

hollo, interj., vb., & n. See **hallo, holla.**

hollow (I.), n. [1. hólō; 2. hɔ́lou]. O.E. *holh,* 'a hollow, hole', M.E. *holwe.* See **hole (I.)** & words there referred to. **1.** A cavity, vacant space, in a solid body; **a** (in the ground) cavity, cup-shaped depression; small valley: *a hollow in the ground; a wooded hollow*; **b** hole, groove, depression, scooped out, in wood or other solid substance; **c** cavity, hole, formed by decay, in tree-trunk. **2.** A depression in the surface of the body: **a** *hollow of the back,* area just above buttocks; **b** depression in soft tissues of the face, e.g. round the eyes or below cheek-bone.

hollow (II.), adj., fr. prec. **1.** (of solid bodies) Having a hollow or cavity; **a** one formed by decay: *a hollow tree*; **b** having cavity artificially scooped out; **c** *hollow cheeks,* sunk, cavernous, having depression below cheek-bone; **d** *hollow eyes,* deep-set, having deep orbit round them. **2.** **a** (of spheres) Not solid, consisting of thin shell with empty space inside: *a hollow vessel, ball* &c.; **b** (of body of troops &c.) not massed together: *a hollow square.* **3.** (fig., of sound) Resembling one made in a hollow; re-echoing, reverberating; muffled; *hollow voice,* one producing such a sound. **4.** (fig., of non-material things) Unreal, unsubstantial, having but a slender foundation, short-lived: *hollow joys; hollow pleasures; hollow affection* &c. **5.** (as adv.) In a hollow manner, as though hollow: *his laughter rang hollow.*

hollow (III.), vb. trans. M.E. *holzen, holwen*; fr. **hollow (I.).** Generally *hollow out,* to make hollow, make a hole, or hollow in, excavate, scoop out: *the river hollows its banks; to hollow out a turnip; to hollow a cave.*

hollow-eyed, adj. Having deep-set eyes.

hollow ground, adj. **hollow (I.) & ground (III.),** P.P. of **grind.** (of razor &c.) Ground with concave surface on either side of blade, so as to allow an extra fine edge.

hollow-hearted, adj. **hollow (II.) & hearted.** Having a hollow, insincere, faithless heart.

hollowly, adv. [1. hólōli; 2. hɔ́louli]. **hollow (II.) & -ly.** (rare) In a hollow manner.

hollowness, n. [1. hólōnes; 2. hɔ́lounis]. M.E. *holounesse.* **hollow (II.) & -ness.** Quality, state, of being hollow.

holly, n. [1. hóli; 2. hɔ́li]. O.E. *hole(ġ)n,* M.E. *holi(n),* cp. O.H.G. *hul(i)s* (whence Fr. *houx*), Du., Germ. *hulst,* cogn. w. Gael. *cuilionn,* Ir. *cuileann.* Origin unknown. **a** Evergreen tree with dark-green, glossy, prickly leaves, white flowers and bright-red, more rarely yellow, berries; **b** (coll.) branches of this, used for decorations.

hollyhock, n. [1. hólihok; 2. hɔ́lihɔk]. M.E. *holihoc,* fr. **holy** & O.E. *hoc(c),* 'mallow', M.E. *hoc, hoke.* Perennial garden plant of Asiatic origin, related to mallow, with tall hairy stem, large leaves, and flowers of various colours growing in form of a spike.

holm, n. [1. hōm; 2. houm]. O.E. (poet.) *holm,* 'wave, sea', later O.E., M.E., through influence of cogn. O.N. *holm-r,* in sense 'island, rising land by water', wh. is also the meaning of O.S., Germ. *holm*; Gmc. type **hulmaz,* fr. base **hel-,* Aryan **kel,* 'to raise up'. See **hill, culminate.** (provinc.) **a** Low-lying land on bank of a river; **b** islet, esp. in river or estuary.

holm-oak, n. Obs. *holm,* 'holly', also 'holm-oak', the leaves of wh. resemble those of holly, prob. corrupt. of M.E. *holin,* 'holly', & **oak.** Ilex, evergreen oak.

holo-, pref. Gk. *holo-,* stem of *hólos,* 'whole, entire', for **sólw-os,* cogn. w. Scrt. *sarva-ś* O. Pers. *haurva-,* Lat. *sollus* for **solu-os,* 'whole, entire', cp. Lat. *salvus,* 'whole, safe', *sōlus,* 'alone'. See **safe (I.).** Form in compounds of Greek origin, denoting whole, entire, entirely, as *holocene,* adj.; (geol.) pertaining to the most recent strata.

holocaust, n. [1. hólokawst; 2. hɔ́ləkɔ̄st]. Fr. *holocauste,* fr. Lat. *holocaustum,* fr. Gk. *holókauston,* lit. 'thing wholly burnt'. See prec. & **caustic.** **a** Sacrifice entirely consumed by fire, whole burnt-offering; **b** (fig.) wholesale destruction, esp. of human lives by fire &c.

holograph, n. & adj. [1. hólograhf; 2. hɔ́ləgrāf]. Fr. *holographe,* fr. Lat. *holographus,* fr. Gk. *hológraphos,* fr. **holo- & -graph.** **1.** n. Document, esp. of legal character, written entirely by the hand of the person from whom it proceeds. **2.** adj. Written as a holograph: *holograph will.*

holographic, adj. [1. hòlográfik; 2. hɔ̀ləgrǽfik]. Prec. & **-ic.** Pertaining to a holograph.

holothurian, n. [1. hòlothū́rian; 2. hɔ̀ləþjúəriən]. Mod. Lat. *Holothūria,* generic name, fr. Lat. *holothūria,* neut. pl., fr. Gk. *holothoúrion,* marine zoophyte or polyp. Any of the sea-cucumbers or sea-slugs, including the trepang or bêche-de-mer.

holpen, vb. [1. hṓpen; 2. hóupən]. O.E., M.E. *holpen,* old P.P. of **help (I.).** Survives in the Magnificat: '*He hath holpen His servant Israel*'.

holster, n. [1. hṓlster; 2. hóulstə]. Prob. borrowed in 17th cent. wars fr. Swed. *holster,* fr. O.N. *hulstr,* 'case, sheath'; cp. the cognates Goth. *hulistr* & O.E. *helustr, heolstor,* 'covering, veil'. The base **hel-,* **hul-,* meant 'to cover, hide'. See **hole (I.)** & words there referred to. The suff. *-(s)tr* expresses idea of instrumentality. Leather case for pistol, attached to saddle-bow or worn on the belt.

holstered, adj. [1. hṓlsterd; 2. hóulstəd]. Prec. & **-ed.** Furnished with holsters.

holt, n. [1. hōlt; 2. hoult]. O.E., M.E. *holt*; O.S., O. Fris. & O.N. *holt*; Mod. Germ. *holz,* 'wood'; Gmc. type **hulta-,* fr. Aryan **kḷdo-,* whence also Gk. *kládos,* 'young branch, shoot', & Lat. *clāvus,* 'nail', orig. 'peg of wood'. See **iconoclasm.** (chiefly liter. or poet., also in Place-Names) Small wood, grove; wooded hill.

holus-bolus, adv. [1. hṓlus bṓlus; 2. hóuləs bóuləs]. Mock Lat., as if fr. **whole & bolus.** At one gulp, all at once.

holy, adj. & n. [1. hṓli; 2. hóuli]. O.E. *hāliġ,* earlier *hālæġ,* M.E. *hāli, hōli* (**whole, hale (I.), & -y**); Common Gmc.; O.S. *hēlag,* O.H.G. *heilig, heilag*; Goth. *heilag-s,* O.N. *heilag-r, helg-r.* The base **hail-* is that seen also in **heal, health,** & means ultimately 'whole, entire, unimpaired', hence, in moral sense, 'unsullied'. Cp. further Scrt. *kévalaš,* 'complete'; O. Slav. *čelŭ,* 'whole, complete'. **A.** adj. **1.** Pertaining to God, to the saints; having a religious function; hallowed, sacred; held in religious awe or reverence: *holy ground; a holy season, vessel, well* &c.; *holy war,* one waged to defend or extend a religion; *holy writ,* the Old and New Testaments. **2.** **a** Of exalted spiritual excellence or purity; divine: *the Holy Trinity*; Phrs. *the Holy One,* God; the Saviour; *the Holy Spirit,* the Holy Ghost; **b** devoted to God; deeply pious, saintly: *a holy life, man.* **3.** (slang) As intensive, in Phr. *a holy terror,* intensely disagreeable, trying, exasperating person. **B.** n. A holy place, now only in *Holy of Holies,* the innermost part of the Jewish tabernacle and Temple containing the Ark of the Covenant and entered only by the High Priest once a year; hence (fig.) any very sacred place.

Holy Alliance, n. (hist.) An alliance of European powers formed to check or suppress revolution in 1815.

Holy Father, n. The Pope.

Holy Ghost, n. The Third Person of the Holy Trinity; the Holy Spirit, Paraclete.

Holy Land, n. Palestine.

Holy Office, n. The Inquisition.

holy orders, n. See **order** (I.).

holystone, n. & vb. trans. [1. hṓlistōn; 2. hóulistoun]. Etymol. doubtful; prob. fr. **holy** (because used for Sunday cleaning) & **stone** (I.). **1.** n. Kind of soft stone used for scrubbing decks of ships. **2.** vb. To scrub with holystone.

holy water, n. **a** Water blessed by priest, and used to sprinkle persons and things; **b** (attrib.) *holy water stoup; holy water sprinkler.*

Holy Week, n. The week before Easter Sunday.

homage, n. [1. hómij; 2. hɔ́midž]. M.E. *homāge*, fr. O. Fr. *homage, (h)ommage*, fr. L. Lat. *hom(in)āticum*, fr. Lat. *homo* (stem *homin-*), 'man' (see **humus, human**), in Low Lat. also 'vassal', cogn. w. Goth. & O.E. *guma*, 'man' (see (**bride**)**groom**), & **-age**. **1.** (hist.) Ceremonial act by which a man became the vassal of the king, or other superior lord, or acknowledged his obligations and claimed his rights as such; declaration of allegiance: *to do, pay, homage.* **2.** (fig.) Expression of reverence, respect, or devotion offered to person of recognized superiority and merit of any kind; deference to merits of person: *a reigning beauty expects homage; to pay homage to the genius of a poet.*

home (I.), n. [1. hōm; 2. houm]. O.E. *hām*, 'home, house, dwelling', M.E. *hōm*; O.S. *hēm*; O.H.G. *heim*, 'residence, homestead'; Goth. *haims*, 'village'; O.N. *heimr*. Prob. cogn. w. Gk. *kṓmē*, 'village' (fr. **k̑ōim-*), related to Gk. *-keîmai*, 'lie down, rest'; cp. further Lith. *kēmas*, 'village'. From same Aryan base, though w. other formative elements, come Lat. *cīvis*, 'citizen' &c. See **civil** & also **hide** (IV.), 'measure of land'. **1. a** House where one is born and bred; house of one's parents and family: *the home of one's fathers; ancestral home; one's own home, the old home* &c.; **b** residence, house, place, in which one lives: *to make one's home in the country, abroad* &c.; *every man returned to his own home*; **c** house which one regards as one's home, where one is received as a member of the family: *my friend's house was my second home.* Phrs. *at home*, in one's house; (*I am*) *not at home today*, not receiving visitors; *to be, feel, make oneself, at home*, at one's ease, as though in one's own house; (fig.) *at home in* (a position &c.), accustomed to, familiar with; *one's long home*, the grave; future life. **2. a** Household, family, occupants of a home: *the War brought sorrow to many homes*; **b** domestic life: *the joys of home.* **3. a** Native country, as distinct from foreign parts: *to leave India for home*; **b** place from which one sets out on an expedition, and to which one will return: *having reached the goal of our journey, we had better turn and set out for home.* **4.** Place of rest, asylum; **a** institution where medical care is given: *nursing home*; **b** charitable or other institution for the indigent, sick, unfortunate &c.: *a home for orphans, idiots, inebriate gentlewomen, lost dogs* &c. **5. a** Habitat; habitual haunt of an animal or plant: *the Indian jungle is the home of the tiger and the elephant*; **b** place where an idea, institution &c. rises, is cherished and fostered: *England is the home of constitutional government; Oxford has been called the home of lost causes.* **6.** Base, goal, in certain children's games, where a player is safe, and cannot be caught.

home (II.), adj., fr. prec. **1.** Connected with the house, family, home &c.: *home interests, ties; home joys* &c. **2.** Connected with one's own country; **a** connected with internal affairs and government: *Home Office* &c.; **b** specif., pertaining to native country as distinct from foreign country: *home rails* (Stock Exchange).

home (III.), adv., fr. **home** (I.); *hām*, indecl., as adv. in O.E. **1.** Towards home: *to go home*, also (colloq.) to die. Phr. *curses come home to roost*, react on their author. **2.** (of material objects) So as to fit in place made for it; as far as it will go: *to shoot a bolt home; drive a nail home* &c. Phrs. *to drive an argument home; the shaft went home* (fig.). **3.** So as to touch the feelings acutely, appeal to reason: *this comes home to me; to bring home to*, to convince. Phr. *to bring a crime &c. home to a person*, prove he did it.

home affairs, n. pl. Internal affairs of nation, esp. those of England and Wales as sphere of one of the Government State Departments, the Home Office.

home-born, adj. Born at home, native.

home-bred, adj. **a** Bred at home, not foreign: *home-bred mutton*; **b** homely, unpolished.

home-brewed, adj. & n. [1. hṓm brṓōd; 2. hóum brūd]. **a** adj. Brewed at home; **b** n., ale brewed at home.

home-coming, n. Coming, return, to one's home.

home counties, n. The counties lying round London.

home farm, n. Farm attached to the residence of the occupier of an estate.

home-keeping, adj. Accustomed to stay at home.

homeless, adj. [1. hṓmles; 2. hóumlis]. O.E. *hāmlēas*. **home** & **-less**. Having no home.

homelike, adj. [1. hṓmlīk; 2. hóumlaik]. **home** & **-like**. Like (a) home.

homelily, adv. [1. hṓmlili; 2. hóumlili]. **homely** & **-ly**. (rare) In a homely manner.

homeliness, n. [1. hṓmlines; 2. hóumlinis]. Next word & **-ness**. Quality or state of being homely.

homely, adj. [1. hṓmli; 2. hóumli]. **home** & **-ly**. **1.** Resembling, reminding one of, home; homelike, evoking memories of home: *the place had a homely air.* **2. a** Simple, unpretentious: *homely fare; quite a homely sort of person*, or *body*; **b** of everyday usage, familiar; not far-fetched, elaborate, or aiming at a high degree of elegance: *if I may use a homely phrase, expression* &c. **3.** (of persons; only Am.) Plain, ugly.

home-made, adj. Made at home: *home-made bread.*

Home Office, n. One of the principal State Departments, dealing with the home affairs of England and Wales, such as the police &c., under the Home Secretary.

homeopath &c. Variants of **homoeopath** &c.

homer (I.), n. [1. hṓmer; 2. hóumə]. Heb. *khōmer*, 'measure', also 'heap, mound', fr. *khāmar*, 'to swell up'. (Bib.) Ancient Hebrew measure of capacity, equal to 10 ephahs, or about 11 bushels.

homer (II.), n. See **homing** & **-er**. Homing pigeon.

Homeric, adj. [1. hōmérik; 2. houmérik]. Lat. *Homēric-us*, fr. Gk. *Homērikós*, fr. *Hómēros*, 'Homer', lit. 'hostage', traditional author of the Gk. epics, the 'Iliad' & 'Odyssey'. **a** Pertaining to Homer, resembling something described by him; Phrs. *a Homeric battle, conflict*, one characterized by feats of individual heroism; *Homeric laughter*, loud, irrepressible laughter; **b** pertaining to the poems of Homer, their style, language &c.

Home Rule, n. **home** (I.) & **rule**. Self-government, autonomy, for nation or province; originally, specif., for Ireland.

Home Secretary, n. British Secretary of State for Home Affairs, ministerial head of the Home Office.

homesick, adj. [1. hṓmsik; 2. hóumsik]. Ardently desiring to go home; pining, longing, for one's home.

homesickness, n. Prec. & **-ness**. Condition of one who is homesick; nostalgia.

homespun, adj. & n. [1. hṓmspun; 2. hóumspan]. **home** & **spun**, P.P. of **spin**. **1.** adj. **a** Spun at home; woven of thread spun at home; **b** (fig.) coarse, plain, homely: *a homespun proverb.* **2.** n. Cloth woven of homespun thread; home-made cloth: *hempen homespun*, plain home product.

homestead, n. [1. hṓmsted; 2. hóumstid, -sted]. O.E. *hāmstede*, 'residence'; cp. O.N. *heimstǒð*. **home** & **stead**. **1.** Home, dwelling-house, with the enclosed land surrounding it; farm. **2.** (Am. and colonial) Area of farm land granted to settler, on conditions regarding residence, cultivation &c.; (also attrib.) *homestead lease* &c.

homethrust, n. [1. hṓmthrust; 2. hóumþrast]. **a** Thrust with a weapon that is driven home; **b** (fig.) remark aimed at a person and felt by him to be painfully true.

homeward, adv. & adj. [1. hṓmward; 2. hóumwəd]. O.E. *hāmweard*, M.E. *hāmward*. **home** & **-ward**. **1.** adv. Towards home: *homeward bound.* **2.** adj. Tending towards home: *the homeward way.*

homewards, adv. [1. hṓmwardz; 2. hóumwədz]. **home** & **-wards**. Homeward.

homicidal, adj. [1. hòmisī́dl; 2. hɔ̀misáidl]. Lat. *homicīdāl-(is)*. **homicide** (I.) & **-al**. **a** Pertaining to, of the nature of, homicide; murderous; **b** having a tendency to homicide: *a homicidal lunatic.*

homicidally, adv. Prec. & **-ly**. In a homicidal manner.

homicide (I.), n. [1. hómisīd; 2. hɔ́misaid]. Fr., fr. Lat. *homicīda*, fr. *homi-* for *homin-*, stem of *homo*, 'man' (see **homage** & words there referred to), & *-cīda*. See **-cide**. Person who kills another; manslayer.

homicide (II.), n. Fr., fr. Lat. *homicīdium*, fr. *homi-*, see prec., & *-cīdium*. See **-cide**. Action of person who kills another, intentionally or accidentally, whether with, or without justification: *felonious, justifiable, excusable, homicide.*

homiletic, adj. & n. [1. hòmilétik; 2. hɔ̀milétik]. Gk. *homīlētikós*, fr. *homīléein*, 'to converse with', fr. *homīlós*, 'assembly'. See **homily**. **1.** adj. Pertaining to sermons or to homiletics; hortatory. **2.** n. pl. *Homiletics*, art of preaching.

homiletical, adj. [1. hòmilétikl; 2. hɔ̀milétikl]. Prec. & **-al**. Homiletic.

homilist, n. [1. hómilist; 2. hɔ́milist]. **homily** & **-ist**. Preacher or composer of homilies.

homily, n. [1. hómili; 2. hɔ́mili]. M.E. *omelye*, fr. O. Fr. *omelie*, Fr. *homélie*, fr. L. Lat. *homilia*, 'homily', fr. Gk. *homīlía*, 'converse, homily', fr. *hómīlos*, 'assembly, concourse', fr. *hom-*, **homo-**, & *ī́lē, eílē*, 'crowd', fr. *eílein*, 'to press, crowd together', fr. **wel-*; cogn. w. Lith. *veliù*, O. Slav. *valjati*, 'to throng'. **a** Sermon, esp. of a practical or expository nature; **b** tedious moral exhortation; Phr. *to read one a homily*, to address such an exhortation to one.

homing, adj. [1. hṓming; 2. hóumiŋ]. As though fr. Pres. Part. of vb. *to home*, wh. is not used. **a** Bound for home, on the way home; esp. *homing pigeon*; **b** longing for home.

hominy, n. [1. hómini; 2. hɔ́mini]. N. Am. Ind. *auhúminea*, 'parched maize'. Meal made from Indian corn or maize.

homo-, pref., fr. Gk. *homós* for **somos*, 'the same'; cogn. w. Scrt. *sama-*; O. Slav. *samŭ*; Goth. *sama*. See **same**. Form used in compounds, usually of Greek origin; denoting the same, of the same kind; contrasted with *hetero-*.

homoblastic, adj. [1. hòmōblástik; 2. hɔ̀moublǽstik]. See prec. & first element in **blastoderm** & **-ic**. (biol.) Developed from cells of the same kind.

homodont, adj. [1. hómōdont; 2. hɔ́moudɔnt]. **homo-** & Gk. *odont-*, 'tooth'. See **dent-, denti-**. (zool.) Having all the teeth of the same type.

homoeo-, pref. Gk. *homoio-*, form of *hómoios*, used in compounds, 'like, similar', fr. *homós*, 'same'. See **homo-**.

homoeomorphism, n. [1. hòmeōmórfizm; 2. hɔ̀umioumɔ́fizəm]. Prec. & first element in **morphology** & **-ism**. Resemblance of form in unrelated crystals.

homoeomorphous, adj. [1. hòmeōmórfus; 2. hɔ̀umioumɔ́fəs]. See prec. & **-morphous**. **a** (crystal.) Exhibiting homoeomorphism; **b** (pathol.) structurally similar to normal tissue.

homoeopath, n. [1. hṓmeōpath; 2. hóumiou-pæþ]; colloq. [1. -pat; 2. -pæt]. See **homoeopathy**. Physician who practises homoeopathy.

homoeopathic, adj. [1. hòmeōpáthik; 2. hòumioupǽþik]. **homoeopathy** & **-ic**. **1.** Pertaining to, accordant with, homoeopathy. **2.** (fig.) **a** Following the principle that 'like cures like'; **b** supplied in very small quantities; infinitesimal: *instruction in homoeopathic doses.*

homoeopathically, adv. [1. hòmeōpáthikali; 2. hòumioupǽþikəli]. Prec. & **-al** & **-ly**. In a homoeopathic manner; according to homoeopathy.

homoeopathist, n. [1. hòmeópathist; 2. hòumiɔ́pəþist]. **homoeopathy** & **-ist**. One who practises, or believes in, homoeopathy.

homoeopathy, n. [1. hòmeópathi; 2. hòumiɔ́pəþi]. Gk. *homoiopátheia*, 'likeness of feeling', fr. **homoeo-** & **-pathy**. System of medicine based on the theory that a malady is cured by frequent minute doses of a drug which normally produces symptoms like those of the malady itself.

homogamous, adj. [1. homógamus; 2. həmɔ́gəməs]. **homo-** & **-gamous**. Exhibiting homogamy.

homogamy, n. [1. homógami; 2. həmɔ́gəmi]. **homo-** & **-gamy**. (biol.) Interbreeding in a segregated group of similar individuals.

homogeneity, n. [1. hòmōjenḗiti; 2. hɔ̀moudžiníiti]. Fr. *homogénéité*, fr. L. Lat. *homogeneitāt-(em)*. See next word & **-ity**. Quality, state, of being homogeneous.

homogeneous, adj. [1. hòmōjḗneus, -jéneus; 2. hɔ̀moudžíniəs, -džéniəs]. Scholastic Lat. *homogene-us*, fr. Gk. *homogenḗs*, 'of the same kind', fr. **homo-** & *génos*, 'kind', see **genus**, & **-ous**. **a** Consisting of parts or elements of the same kind throughout; uniform; **b** belonging to the same category, having the same nature, as another thing; (math.) commensurable. (Reverse of *heterogeneous*).

homogeneously, adv. Prec. & **-ly**. In a homogeneous manner.

homogeneousness, n. See prec. & **-ness**. Homogeneity.

homogenesis, n. [1. hòmōjénesis; 2. hɔ̀moudžénisis]. **homo-** & **genesis**. (biol.) Form of reproduction in which the successive generations are identical with, or resemble, the parental or ancestral type.

homogenetic, adj. [1. hòmōjenétik; 2. hɔ̀moudženétik]. **homo-** & **genetic**. Pertaining to homogenesis.

homogenous, adj. [1. homójenus; 2. həmɔ́džinəs]. See next word & **-ous**. (biol.) Having structural similarity due to common descent.

homogeny, n. [1. homójeni; 2. həmɔ́džini]. **homo-** & **-geny**. (biol.) Quality of being homogenous.

homograph, n. [1. hómōgrahf; 2. hɔ́mougrāf]. **homo-** & **-graph**. One of two or more words identical in spelling, but different in meaning, e.g. *seal* **a** the animal, **b** a stamp; *present* **a** at hand, **b** a gift.

homographic, adj. [1. hòmōgráfik; 2. hɔ̀mougrǽfik]. Prec. & **-ic**. **1.** Pertaining to homographs. **2.** (of system of spelling) Employing a separate symbol for each sound.

homography, n. [1. homógrafi; 2. həmɔ́grəfi]. **homograph** & **-y**. Homographic spelling.

homoiousian, adj. & n. [1. hòmoióusian; 2. hɔ̀məiáusiən]. Gk. *homoi(o)oúsios*, 'of like substance', fr. *homoio-*, see **homoeo-**, & *ousía*, 'being, substance', fr. *einai*, 'to be', q.v. under **is**, & **-an**. (theol.) **a** adj. Pertaining to, holding, the doctrine that the Son is of like, but not the same, substance with the Father; opposed to *homoousian*; **b** n., (cap.) adherent of this doctrine; semi-Arian.

homologate, vb. trans. [1. homólogāt; 2. həmɔ́ləgeit]. L. Lat. *homologāt-*, P.P. stem of *homologāre*, fr. Gk. *homologeîn*, 'to assent, agree', fr. *homólogos*, 'agreeing'. See **homologue**. (civil and Scots law) To confirm, ratify.

homologation, n. [1. homòlogā́shun; 2. həmɔ̀ləgéiʃən]. Prec. & **-ion**. (law) Action of homologating.

homologize, vb. trans. & intrans. [1. homólojīz; 2. həmɔ́lədžaiz]. **homologue** & **-ize**. **a** trans. To make, show to be, homologous; **b** intrans., to be homologous.

homologous, adj. [1. homólogus; 2. həmɔ́ləgəs]. **homologue** & **-ous**. Corresponding, agreeing, in character, proportion, relative position, structure &c.

homologue, n. [1. hómolōg; 2. hɔ́məloug]. Fr., fr. Gk. *homólogon*, neut. of *homólogos*, 'asserting, agreeing', fr. **homo-** & *lógos*, 'speech, proportion' &c. See **logos**. Thing which is homologous to, or displays homology with, another.

homology, n. [1. homóloji; 2. həmɔ́lədži]. Fr. *homologie*, fr. Gk. *homología*. Prec. & **-y**. Quality of being homologous; identity of relation; correspondence; specif. (biol.) correspondence between parts or organs, in different species, which have the same origin, though differentiated in form and function by the process of evolution.

homomorphic, homomorphous, adj. [1. hòmōmórfik, -fus; 2. hɔ̀moumɔ́fik, -fəs]. See **homo-** & first element in **morphology**. **a** (bot.) Having perfect flowers all of the same type; **b** (zool.) having larva resembling imago.

homomorphy, n. [1. hòmōmórfi; 2. hɔ̀moumɔ́fi]. Prec. & **-y**. (biol.) **a** Superficial resemblance in form between organs which have fundamentally different structure; **b** external resemblance between organisms of different groups.

homonym, n. [1. hómonim; 2. hɔ́mənim]. Fr. *homonyme*, fr. Lat. *homōnym-(um)*, fr. Gk. *homṓnumon*, neut. of *homṓnumos*, 'having the same name'; fr. **homo-** & *ónoma*, 'name', see **name** & **nominal**. **1.** One of several words differing in origin and meaning, but sounded alike, as *pail*, 'bucket'; *pale*, 'stake'; *pale*, 'wan'. **2.** Namesake.

homonymic, adj. [1. hòmonímik; 2. hɔ̀mənímik]. Prec. & **-ic**. Homonymous.

homonymous, adj. [1. homónimus; 2. həmɔ́niməs]. Lat. *homōnym-(us)* (see **homonym**) & **-ous**. **a** Having the same name; **b** related as homonyms; **c** equivocal, ambiguous.

homonymy, n. [1. homónimi; 2. həmɔ́nimi]. Gk. *homōnumía*. **homonym** & **-y**. Quality of being homonymous.

homoousian, homousian, adj. & n. [1. hòm(ō)óusian; 2. hɔ̀m(ou)áusiən]. Gk. *homooúsios*, 'consubstantial', fr. **homo-**, 'same', & *ousía*, 'being, substance', see **homoiousian**, & **-an**. (theol.) **a** adj. Pertaining to, holding, the Catholic doctrine that the Son is of one and the same substance with the Father; contrasted with *homoiousian*; **b** n., (cap.) adherent of this doctrine.

homophone, n. [1. hómōfōn; 2. hɔ́moufoun]. Fr., fr. Gk. *homóphōn-(on)*, 'thing having the same sound'. **homo-** & **phone**. **1.** Written character expressing the same sound as another, as *c*, *s*, or *k*. **2.** Word pronounced exactly like another, but differing in meaning, as *hair, hare.*

homophonic, adj. [1. hòmōfónik; 2. hɔ̀moufɔ́nik]. Gk. *homóphōnos*, 'having the same sound'; see prec. & **-ic**. **1.** Of the nature of a homophone; having the same sound. **2.** (mus.) **a** Monodic, not polyphonic; **b** unisonant, not antiphonic.

homophonous, adj. [1. homófonus; 2. həmɔ́fənəs]. See prec. & **-ous**. Homophonic.

homophony, n. [1. homófoni; 2. həmɔ́fəni]. Fr. *homophonie*, fr. Gk. *homophōnía*; as **homophonic** & **-y**. (mus.) Quality of being homophonic.

homoplastic, adj. [1. hòmōplástik; 2. hɔ̀mouplǽstik]. **homo-** & **plastic**. (biol.) Having organs or parts corresponding or analogous, but of different origin.

homopterous, adj. [1. homópterus; 2. həmɔ́ptərəs]. **homo-** & Gk. *pterón*, 'wing'. See **ptero-** & cp. **feather** & **-ous**. (entom.) Belonging to a class of insects, Homoptera, one of the suborders of Hemiptera, including the green-flies, cicadas &c.

homosexual, adj. [1. hòmōsékshooal; 2. hɔ̀mousékʃuəl]. **homo-** & **sexual**. Morbidly attracted to person(s) of one's own sex.

homuncular, adj. [1. hōmúngkūlar; 2. houmáŋkjulə]. See next word & **-ar**. Pertaining to a homunculus.

homunculus, n. [1. hōmúngkūlus; 2. houmáŋkjuləs]. Lat., fr. *homin-*, stem of *homo*, 'man, human being' (see **homage**), & dimin. *-culus*. See **-cule**. **a** Little man; mannikin, dwarf; specif. **b** small, animated, intelligent being, supposed to be produced by magic.

homy, adj. [1. hṓmi; 2. hóumi]. **home (I.)** & **-y**. (colloq.) Homelike.

hone (I.), n. [1. hōn; 2. houn]. O.E. *hān*, only recorded in sense 'stone', M.E. *hoone*, 'hone'; cp. O.N. *hein*, 'hone'; Gmc. type **hainō*, cogn. w. Scrt. *śāṇa-ś*, 'whetstone', fr. *-śa-*, 'to sharpen, whet'; Gk. *kônos*, 'peak, peg, cone' (see **cone**); Lat. *cuneus*, 'wedge' (see **cuneiform**); fr. Aryan base **k̑ō-*, 'to sharpen'. Piece of hard, fine-grained stone or similar substance used for putting a keen edge on cutting instrument, esp. razors.

hone (II.), vb. trans., fr. prec. To sharpen, set, with a hone.

honest, adj. [1. ónest; 2. ɔ́nist]. M.E., fr. O. Fr. *honeste*, Mod. Fr. *honnête*, fr. Lat. *hones-tus*, 'honourable, worthy, handsome', fr. *honos*. See **honour**. **1. a** (archaic) Honourable, of high repute, free from reproach; decent; **b** (of a woman) chaste; Phr. *to make an honest woman of*, to marry after seduction; **c** (patronizing or slightly contemptuous) worthy, respectable, decent: *a very honest fellow.* **2.** (of persons, character &c.) Upright, conscientious, straightforward; specif. **a** not inclined to defraud, to deceive, or to claim what does not belong to one, or more than one is entitled to receive; not given to stealing; trustworthy: *this man is perfectly honest and might be trusted with untold gold*; **b** just, fair-minded, scrupulous in judgement and action, not dissembling; honourable: *to be strictly honest in one's dealings with oneself and others*; **c** impartial, sincere; willing to face facts; veracious, not given to distorting the truth: *he was perfectly honest in admitting the difficulties of the problem, and the conjectural character of his proposed solution.* **3.** Exhibiting, springing from, an honest mind: *it was hardly honest to make you pay so much*; *he made an honest attempt to understand my point of view*; *an honest piece of work*, one conscientiously performed; *an honest face*, one betokening honesty of character; *an honest living*, one honestly earned. Phr. *to turn an honest penny*, take opportunity of making a profit by justifiable means.

honestly, adv. M.E. *honestelīche*. Prec. & **-ly**. In an honest manner.

honesty, n. [1. ónesti; 2. ɔ́nisti]. M.E. *honestē*, fr. O. Fr. *honesté*, fr. Lat. *honestāt-(em)*, 'honour'. See prec. & **-y**. **1.** Quality of being honest; **a** honour, seemliness of behaviour; **b** chastity; **c** uprightness of character; freedom from deceit and fraud; integrity, trustworthiness. **2.** Common garden herb, *Lunaria biennis*, having purple flowers, and seed-pods with translucent oval membrane; so called, perhaps, because the pods are transparent.

honey, n. [1. húni; 2. háni]. O.E. *huniġ*, M.E. *huniȝ*, *honi*, O.S. *honeg*; O.H.G. *honang*, *honag*, O.N. *hunang*, fr. Gmc. **huna(n)gan*; cogn. w. Gk. *knēkós*, 'pale yellow'; Scrt. *kanaka-m*, 'gold'. **1. a** Pale yellow, sweet, sticky, translucent, edible substance, produced by bees from nectar of flowers, and stored in a comb; *virgin honey*, that which drips naturally from the comb; **b** syrup resembling honey: *maple honey.* Phr. *as sweet as honey*, very sweet; (fig.) very delightful. **2.** (fig.) **a** Anything very sweet or pleasant: *his words were honey to my soul*; **b** term of endearment, sweetheart, darling: *my honey.* **3.** (attrib.)

a Pertaining to honey: *a honey cell*; *honey-bag, honey sac*, organ in bee in which honey is prepared; **b** (i.) producing honey: *honey ant*, N. American species, of which the workers store honey in abdomen; (ii.) yielding honey or other sweet substance: *honey flower*, one of several flowers rich in nectar; *honey locust*, one of several locust trees with sweet fruit; **c** feeding on honey: *honey creeper*, one of a family of W. Indian birds.

honey-bear, n. Popular name of the kinkajou.

honey-bee, n. **a** Common bee kept in hive for production of honey and wax; **b** any social bee that produces honey.

honey-buzzard, n. British hawk which feeds on grubs of bees and wasps, *Pernis apivorus*.

honeycomb (I.), n. & adj. [1. húnikōm; 2. hánikoum]. O.E. *huniģcamb*, M.E. *huni-comb*; fr. **honey** (I.) & **comb** (I.). **1.** n. **a** Structure of wax made by bees, consisting of a mass of cells to hold honey or larvae; **b** something resembling a honeycomb in appearance or structure; such as the cavity forming a flaw in metal casting; surface &c. covered with hexagonal pattern. **2.** adj. Pertaining to, resembling, honeycomb; having many small perforations or cavities; decorated with hexagonal pattern: *honeycomb coral, quilt, stitch.*

honeycomb (II.), vb. trans., fr. prec. **a** To pierce with many holes or tunnels; to riddle; *the rock is honeycombed with galleries*; **b** (fig.) to sap the strength, solidarity, or loyalty of, by plots &c.: *the army was honeycombed with disaffection.*

honeydew, n. [1. húnidū; 2. hánidjū]. **1. a** Sweet viscid juice exuding from leaves punctured by insects &c.; **b** sweet excretion of aphids and allied insects; **c** imaginary delicious food, ambrosia: '*For he on honeydew hath fed*' (Coleridge, 'Kubla Khan'). **2.** Name given to kind of tobacco, sweetened with molasses.

honey-eater, n. Member of family of Australasian birds, with thin, curved bills with which they extract nectar from flowers; also called *honey-sucker.*

honeyed, honied, adj. [1. húnid; 2. hánid]. **honey** & **-ed.** Sweet as honey; (chiefly fig.) pleasant, flattering, ingratiating: *honeyed words.*

honey-guide, n. Member of group of African and Asiatic birds, resembling cuckoo, supposed to indicate the presence of wild honey by their movements and cries.

honeymoon, n. & vb. intrans. [1. húnimōōn; 2. hánimūn]. **honey** & **moon** (I.), referring to the waning of the moon. **1.** n. Period, of varying length, immediately after marriage, spent by the couple alone, away from home. **2.** vb. To spend one's honeymoon: *to honeymoon in Italy.*

honey-mouthed, adj. Soft of speech; speaking blandly, flatteringly.

honey-pot, n. **1. a** Pot to hold honey; **b** (fig.) thing or person possessing sweetness, attraction, charm &c. **2.** (pl.) Infant's game, in which child is swung by its arms with its hands clasped below the knees.

honeysuckle, n. [1. húnisukl; 2. hánisakl]. M.E. *honisocle, hunisuccle*, extended, perh. as dimin. (see **-le**), fr. O.E. *huniģsūce, -sūge*, 'privet'; fr. **honey** & **suck. a** Climbing shrub (*Lonicera*), of which one species is British, bearing clusters of fragrant tubular yellow or reddish flowers; woodbine; **b** in America and Australasia, one of various plants unrelated to above.

honey-sweet, adj. O.E. *huniģswēte.* Sweet as honey (lit. and fig.).

honey-tongued, adj. Having a sweet, attractive mode of speech; persuasive, eloquent.

honeywort, n. [1. húniwērt; 2. hániwāt]. Plant related to borage, cultivated to supply bees with honey.

hong, n. [1. hong; 2. hɔŋ]. Cantonese, 'factory', fr. Chinese *hang*, 'row'. Mercantile establishment, factory, warehouse for foreign trade, in China or Japan.

honk, n. & vb. intrans. [1. hongk; 2. hɔŋk]. Imitative. **1.** n. **a** Cry of wild goose; **b** similar sound, as that made by horn of motor-car. **2.** vb. To cry as wild goose; to make similar sound.

honorarium, n. [1. (h)ònorárium; 2. (h)ɔnəréəriəm, -áriəm]. Lat. *honōrārium* (*dōnum*), 'gift made on reception of an honour', properly neut. of *honōrārius*, 'pertaining to honour'. See next word & **honour.** Payment made voluntarily in return for services for which no fee is either claimed, or legally obtainable; gratuity.

honorary, adj. [1. ónorari; 2. ɔ́nərəri]. Lat. *honōrāri-(us).* **honour** & **-ary. 1.** Pertaining to, having the nature of, honour. **2.** Recognized by honourable persons, but not by law: *an honorary debt.* **3. a.** Bestowed, held, as an honour without obligations or remuneration: *an honorary fellowship, office, colonelcy*; **b** conferred as an unsolicited honour without fees, examination &c.: *an honorary degree*; **c** holding an honorary office or other position: *an honorary secretary, member of a society.*

honorific, adj. & n. [1. ònoríflk; 2. ɔnərífik]. Lat. *honōrific-(us,)* fr. *honōri-*, combining form of *honos*, **honour**, & *-ficus*, 'doing, making', fr. *facere*, 'to make'. See **fact. a** adj. Conferring, expressing, honour: *honorific titles*; **b** n., word or phrase conventionally used, esp. in Oriental style, to express respect.

honour (I.), n. [1. ónor; 2. ɔ́nə]. M.E., fr. O. Fr. *honūr, honeur* (Mod. Fr. *honneur*), fr. Lat. *honōr-(em)*, stem of *honos, honor*, 'official dignity, office &c.; repute, esteem; reward, recompense' &c.; of uncertain origin. **1. a** Good name, reputation for high standard of moral or conventional qualities esteemed in a particular class, varying greatly, but including loyalty, chivalry, courage, and integrity at least within the class: *knightly, military, professional, business honour*; *honour among thieves*; Phrs. *debt of honour*, honorary debt; *on, upon, my honour*, asseveration that speaker's good name is at stake; *to put one on one's honour*, to indicate that this will be forfeit if promise is broken, or obligation disregarded; so, *to pledge one's honour, give one's word of honour*; *to accept a bill for the honour of*, in order to save his credit; specif. **b** (in woman) reputation for chastity; **c** (in connexion with duelling) reputation for sensitiveness to personal affronts or disgrace. Phrs. *point of honour*, scruple regarding such acts; *affair, code, court, law, of honour*; *honour is satisfied*, affront &c. has been atoned for, esp. by duel or apology. **2.** Fine sense of what the standard of honour demands; self-respect, moral dignity, high-mindedness, high moral rectitude: *a man of unblemished honour*; *I am bound in honour to refuse.* **3. a** (i.) High respect, esteem, or veneration accorded to person or thing on the ground of great merit, high rank &c.: *to have, hold, in honour*; *to pay, give, honour to the king, the law*; *in honour of the fallen*; *a guard of honour*; Phrs. *maid of honour*, one in attendance upon a great, esp. a Royal, personage; Phrs. *may I have the honour* (of doing, to do, something), polite formula for request; *I have the honour to inform you*, formal mode of intimating something by letter; *I have the honour to be* (*your obedient servant* &c.), formal mode finishing letter; (ii.) something felt by recipient to confer honour; tribute, compliment: *I take your visit as a great honour*; **b** dignity; exalted rank: *the sovereign is the fountain of honour.* Phrs. *His Honour, Your Honour*, mode of referring to, or addressing (i.) British County Court judge; (ii.) in U.S.A., any judge; *your honour* (in Ireland), respectful mode of addressing gentleman by inferiors. **4. a** Mark of honour, such as title, order, decoration, conferred on person; *birthday honours*, conferred by sovereign on his birthday; (attrib.) *the honours list*; **b** badge of such distinction: *Nelson wore all his honours at Trafalgar*; **c** (pl.) act or acts expressing honour; Phrs. *to render the last honours*, perform or attend funeral rites; *military honours*, ceremonies at funeral of soldier; *the honours of war*, privilege granted to defeated enemy to retain weapons, colours, and music; *to receive, drink, a toast with musical honours*, to accompany it with laudatory song; *to do the honours* (*of the table, house, town* &c.), to act as host; **d** (pl., univ.) award for proficiency, usually after more specialized examination than that for ordinary degree: *first-class honours in history*; (attrib.) *an honours man*; **e** person or thing that confers honour on the community &c.: *he is an honour to his country, family*; **f** (pl.) playing-cards to which a special value is assigned; (in whist &c.) court cards in trumps; **g** (golf) right of playing first from the tee. **5.** Designation for an important barony or group of manors; (hist.) also, jurisdiction over this.

honour (II.), vb. trans. M.E. *honouren*, fr. O. Fr. *honourer* (Mod. Fr. *honorer*), fr. Lat. *honōrāre*, fr. *honōr-*. See prec. **1. a** To show honour to, confer honour on, raise to honour, dignify; **b** to feel honour or high respect for; to venerate, revere. **2.** To treat as valid, accept, pay when due: *to honour a bill, draft, cheque, signature.*

honourable, adj. [1. ónorabl; 2. ɔ́n(ə)rəbl]. In M.E., fr. O. Fr., fr. Lat. *honōrābil-(em).* See **honour** (II.) & **-able. 1. a** Possessing, animated by, principles of honour and probity; upright, conscientious, high-minded: *an honourable gentleman*; **b** based on, exhibiting, arising from, such principles and qualities: *honourable conduct*; *an honourable understanding.* **2.** Conferring honour; distinguished, reputable, reflecting glory: *to win honourable distinctions*; *an honourable duty.* **3.** Reflecting honour upon; creditable, meritorious: *such sentiments are entirely honourable to you*; *long years of honourable service.* **4. a** *Honourable*, courtesy title prefixed to name &c.: *the Honourable* (*Honble.*) *John Jones, Mary Brown* &c., usual form of address on envelope for the children of barons, younger children, or eldest child, if a daughter, of viscounts, younger sons of earls; *the Honble. Mrs.*, married daughter of a Baron &c., or wife of one using this courtesy title; *the Honourable gentleman, my Honourable friend*, mode of referring to members in House of Commons; used also of members of legislative bodies in British Dominions; also of members of U.S.A. Congress and of judges and members of State legislatures; *the Honourable Mr. Justice Robinson*, mode of addressing in writing a High Court judge; *the Honourable Lord X*, mode of addressing judge of High Court (of Session) of Scotland; *the Honble. Mary Z*, mode of addressing Royal Maid of Honour; **b** *Right Honourable* (*the Earl of X, the Viscount So-and-so* &c.), title used in style of earls, viscounts, and barons; of Privy Councillors, of Lords Justices and Lords of Appeal, and of the Lord Mayor of London and Lord Provost of Edinburgh; **c** *Most Honourable*, style of Marquis, also of the Order of the Bath.

honourably, adv. M.E. *honourabilī.* Prec. & **-ly.** In an honourable manner.

honourer, n. [1. ónorer; 2. ɔ́nərə]. **honour** (II.) & **-er.** Person who honours.

hooch, n. [1. hōōch; 2. hūtʃ]. Said to be fr. *hoochinoo*, Alaskan Indian name for illicitly distilled spirits. (Am. slang) Any alcoholic liquid made or obtained contrary to the prohibition law.

hood (I.), n. [1. hood; 2. hud]. O.E., M.E. *hōd*, O.S., O.H.G. *huot*, Mod. Germ. *hut*, 'hat'; prob. fr. Gmc. base **hōd-, *had-*, 'to protect, guard', whence also **heed, hat. 1. a** Garment of flexible material covering head (except face) and neck, often attached, or attachable, to cloak, mantle, or the like, and hanging down behind when not in use; cowl; **b** part of full academic dress, in form of loose elongated cowl, always worn hanging behind, varying according to the degree of which it is a symbol and the university conferring the degree. **2.** (fig.) Thing resembling hood in shape or use; specif. a covering for head of hawk or horse; b covering or folding roof of carriage, bath-chair &c.; c cover to prevent escape of fumes &c. during chemical operations; d projecting plate above grate to improve draught; e cowl of chimney; f (naut.) erection with door above companion hatch.

hood (II.), vb. trans., fr. prec. To furnish or cover with a hood; (fig.) to cover, veil.

-hood, suff. O.E. *hād*, 'person, sex, degree, state, condition, nature', M.E. *hād, hōd*, Common Gmc. **haid-*; cp. O.H.G. *heit*, Goth. *haidus*, O.N. *heið-r* &c., cogn. w. Scrt. *kētúš*, 'sign by which a thing is known, form', connected w. *kit*, 'to perceive'. Used in O.E., as O.H.G., Mod. Germ. *-heit* &c., to form abstract ns. in same way as **-head** & cogn. forms. The Mod. Engl. form *-hood* is not satisfactorily explained. The normal form, unless shortened in M.E., wd. be *-hode* [houd], or if shortened *-had* [həd], *-hod* [həd]. The present pronunciation may be due to the spelling, wh. formerly expressed a long vowel of a different kind fr. that now usually written *oo*. Suffix forming: **1.** Abstract nouns denoting quality, condition, state, **a** with nouns, chiefly names of persons or living things: *childhood, manhood*; (in this sense a living suffix: *puppyhood*); **b** rarely with adjectives: *falsehood, hardihood, likelihood*; sometimes in concrete sense: *to tell falsehoods*. **2.** Collective nouns fr. other nouns: *priesthood, brotherhood, neighbourhood*.

hooded, adj. [1. hóoded; 2. húdid]. **hood** (II.) & **-ed**. **a** Wearing, furnished with, a hood; having a hood drawn over the head; **b** (zool.) having crest or other appendage, or markings, resembling hood, on the head: *hooded crow*, common British crow with grey body and black head and wings; Royston crow; *hooded gull*, black-headed gull; *hooded merganser, seal* &c.

hoodie, n. [1. hóodi; 2. húdi]. **hood** (I.) & Scots *-ie*, **-y**. (provinc.) Hooded crow.

hoodless, adj. [1. hóodles; 2. húdlis]. **hood** (I.) & **-less**. Having no hood; having lost, discarded a hood.

hoodlum, n. [1. hóōdlum; 2. húdləm]. Origin unknown. (Am. slang) Young rowdy, rough, hooligan.

hoodman-blind, n. [1. hóodman blínd; 2. húdmən bláind]. Obs. *hoodman*, 'blindfolded man', fr. **hood** (I.), **man** (I.), & **blind** (I.). (obs.) Blindman's-buff.

hoodmould(ing), n. [1. hóodmōld(ing); 2. húdmould(iŋ)]. Projecting moulding over an arch; dripstone.

hoodoo. See **voodoo**.

hoodwink, vb. trans. [1. hóodwingk; 2. húdwiŋk]. **hood** (I.) & **wink**. **1. a** To cover, or cover partially, the eyes of a horse; **b** (obs.) to blindfold (a person). **2.** (fig.) To deceive, impose upon, mislead by falsehood.

hoof (I.), n., pl. *hoofs, hooves*, [1. hōōf; 2. hūf]. O.E. *hōf*, M.E. *hoof, hūf*, O.H.G. *huof*, Mod. Germ. *huf*, O.N. *hōf-r*; cogn. w. Scrt. *śaphāś*, Russ. *kopyto*, 'hoof'. Further connexions are doubtful; the suggested relation of the word w. Lat. *caballus*, 'horse' (see **cavalier**), is not clearly established. **1. a** Modified form of the toe-nail in ruminants, swine, horses, and allied animals, forming horny curved sheath, sometimes divided, covering the lower part of one or more toes, a *cloven hoof* being in reality the nails of two or more toes (for Phr. see **cloven**); Phr. *on the hoof*, (of cattle) alive; **b** (facet. or contempt.) human foot; Phrs. *to pad the hoof*, (slang) to walk; *under the hoof*, down-trodden. **2.** (fig.) Hoofed animal.

hoof (II.), vb. trans., fr. prec. Chiefly in vulg. Phr. *to hoof out*, (slang) to kick out, eject with contumely; also, *to be hoofed*, turned out of post, employment &c.; (slang and rare) *to hoof it*, to walk, tramp.

hoof-bound, adj. (of horse &c.) Suffering from a contracted hoof, which causes lameness.

hoofed, adj. [1. hōōft; 2. hūft]. **hoof** (I.) & **-ed**. Having hoofs; ungulate.

hoof-pad, n. Pad attached to hoof to protect it.

hoof-pick, n. Instrument for extracting stones from horse's hoof.

hoof-rot, n. Inflammatory disease in feet of cattle, sheep &c.

hook (I.), n. [1. hook; 2. huk]. O.E. & M.E. *hōk*; cogn. w. Du. *hoek*, fr. Gmc. **hōk-*, another form of wh. base is **haka-*, cp. O.E. *haca*, 'hook'. Cp. **hake** (I.). **1.** Piece of curved metal with one free end which is often pointed; one of various metal objects made in this form, for catching or hanging; a small piece of metal curved and barbed, with very sharp point for catching fish: *fish-hook*; **b** piece of curved metal one end of which is fastened to a wall, or attached to a chain &c., leaving the other end free for hanging things on: *a clothes-hook*; *pot-hook*, one shaped like letter S for hanging a pot from a chain over a fire; **c** small metal catch or clasp with bent, blunt end which goes into a metal loop (eye), for fastening clothes together: *hooks and eyes*. Phrs. *by hook or by crook*, somehow or other, by any means at all; *to go off the hooks*, (i.) to become mentally deranged; (ii.) to lapse from normal, moral, conduct; (iii.) to die; *to take, sling, one's hook*, (slang) to go away. **2.** One of several strongly curved cutting instruments; **a** *a reaping-hook*, sickle; **b** similarly shaped, but smaller implement for rough cutting and hacking, hedge-trimming, reed-cutting &c.: *fagging-hook, bagging-hook*; **c** short stout chopping implement with partially straight blade having curved end, and short or long handle, for cutting thickish objects, such as small branches &c. **3.** (rare) Sharp bend in a river. **4. a** Side blow with bent arm in boxing; **b** stroke in hooking a ball at cricket, golf &c.

hook (II.), vb. trans. & intrans. See prec. With sense **A 4**, cp. M.E. *hōken*, 'to run away', perh. a different word. **A.** trans. **1.** To make, bend, into form of a hook: *to hook one's finger*. **2. a** To seize, hold, with a hook, or something shaped like a hook: *to hook a fish, a branch*; Phr. *to hook one's fish*, catch, secure, beguile person for one's own purposes, persuade him to consent to some proposed course; **b** (slang) to seize furtively, steal; **c** to fasten, secure, with a hook or hooks: *to hook a dress*; *to hook up, on, in, a thing*. **3. a** (boxing) To strike on the side with the bent arm; **b** (cricket) to play (ball) from off-side round to square-leg; **c** (golf) to drive (ball) so that it swerves round far to the left. **4.** Phr. *to hook it* (slang), to go, run, away, decamp. **B.** intrans. **1.** To form a hook or curve, be bent. **2.** To be attached or fastened by a hook or hooks: *this dress is made to hook up the back*.

hookah, hooka, n. [1. hóoka; 2. húkə]. Arab. *ḥuqqa(h)*, 'casket, bowl', fr. *ḥuqq*, 'hollow place'. Oriental tobacco pipe with long flexible tube, and water-bottle through which the smoke passes; narghile.

hooked, adj. [1. hookt; 2. hukt]. **hook** (II.) & **-ed**. **a** Furnished with a hook or hooks; **b** having the shape of a hook: *a hooked nose*.

hookedness, n. [1. hóokednes; 2. húkidnis]. Prec. & **-ness**. (rare) Quality of being hooked.

hooker, n. [1. hóoker; 2. húkə]. Du. *hoeker*, fr. *hoek*, **hook** (I.), & **-er**. **a** Dutch fishing-boat with two masts; **b** English or Irish fishing smack.

hook-nosed, adj. **hook** (I.) & **nosed**. Having a hooked, aquiline nose.

hook-pin, n. Iron pin with hook at end, used in constructing floors and roofs.

hookworm, n. [1. hóokwërm; 2. húkwām]. Intestinal worm with hooks about mouth; (attrib.) *hookworm disease*, ankylostomiasis.

hooky, adj. [1. hóoki; 2. húki]. **hook** (I.) & **-y**. **a** (rare) Having a hook or hooks; **b** having the nature or shape of a hook.

hooligan, n. [1. hōōligan; 2. húligən], fr. Ir. surname *Houlihan*, used as name of rowdy family in music-hall song c. 1885. Member of gang of street roughs; rowdy, ruffian.

hooliganism, n. [1. hōōliganizm; 2. húligənizəm]. Prec. & **-ism**. Character or behaviour of a hooligan; brutal savagery, rowdiness.

hoop (I.), n. [1. hōōp; 2. hūp]. O.E., M.E. *hōp*; apparently Gmc. word, cp. M. Du. *hoep*, though this might be a loan-word; no other cognates traced. **1.** Circular band or ring of metal, wood, or other material; specif. **a** one of series of bands used to bind together the staves of cask, tub &c.; **b** one of the cylindrical forgings shrunk on to cannon; **c** one of set of rings of whalebone &c. formerly used to expand lady's skirt; **d** large ring of wood or iron bowled along by child as toy; **e** flattened finger-ring. **2.** Small iron arch through which croquet-ball is driven.

hoop (II.), vb. trans. M.E. *hōpen*, fr. prec. To bind with a hoop or hoops; (fig.) to encircle, clasp.

hoop (III.), vb. intrans. M.E. *houpen*, fr. O. Fr. *houper* (cp. Fr. *houp!*, interj., call to animal), prob. imitative, but cp. Goth. *hwōpan*, 'to boast', also **whoop**, w. wh. it has been confused. To utter a cry or sound like 'hoop', as a swan, or a person with hooping-cough.

hooped, adj. [1. hōōpt; 2. hūpt]. **hoop** (II.) & **-er**. Having hoops: *a hooped petticoat, gun*.

hooper (I.), n. [1. hōōper; 2. húpə]. **hoop** (II.) & **-er**. Person who makes or affixes hoops; cooper.

hooper (II.), n. **hoop** (III.) & **-er**. Common wild swan; also called *hooper-swan* or *whooper*.

hooping-cough, whooping-cough, n. [1. hōōping kawf; 2. húpiŋ, húpiŋ kōf]. **hoop** (III.) & **-ing** & **cough** (I.). Infectious disease, esp. of the young, marked by paroxysmal cough followed by difficult inspiration, and vomiting, producing sound like 'hoop'.

hoop-iron, n. Iron in thin strips for hooping barrels &c.

hoopoe, n. [1. hōōpōō; 2. húpū]. Imitative; the Mod. form, like obs. Engl. *hoopoop*, L.G. *huppupp*, O. Fr. *pupu*, is a nearer approximation to the bird's cry than Early Mod. Engl. *houpe*, fr. O. Fr. *huppe*; fr. Lat. *upupa*; cp. Gk. *épop-s*. Insectivorous bird of S. Europe and N. Africa &c., rare in Britain, with handsome erectile crest and plumage, and long, curved bill, *Upupa epops*.

hoot (I.), vb. intrans. & trans. [1. hōōt; 2. hūt]. Imitative. M.E. *hūten, houten, hōten*, fr. a Scand. source, cp. Mid. & Mod. Swed., Norw. *huta* (cp. Norm.-Fr. dial. *houter*, 'to whoop'), orig. 'to utter the sound *hūt*', i.e. 'off, begone' (see **hoots**). Cp. **hue** (II.). **1.** intrans. **a** To utter a prolonged deep, hollow sound, usually expressing contempt, derision, or anger; **b** to cry as an owl; **c** to sound as a steam-whistle, siren, foghorn, or motor-horn. **2.** trans. To assail or mock with hoots. Phrs. *to hoot down*, to silence by hoots; *to hoot off, out*, to drive out &c. by hoots.

hoot (II.), n., fr. prec. Sound made in hooting: *a hoot, hoots, of rage, joy* &c., cry expressing these.

hooter, n. [1. hōōter; 2. hūtə]. Prec. & **-er**. Person, animal, or thing that hoots; specif., siren or steam-whistle sounded as signal to workers.

hoots, interj. [1. hōōts; 2. hūts]. See **hoot** (I.) & cp. **hue** (II.). (Scots & N. Engl.) Exclamation of impatience or disgust; pshaw!, tut!

hoove, n. [1. hōōv; 2. hūv]. Perh. fr. O.E. **hōf-*, strong grade of *hebban*, 'to lift up' &c. See **heave**; cp. perh. O.E. *hofer*, 'hump'. Distension of stomach of cattle by gas.

hop (I.), vb. intrans. & trans. [1. hop; 2. həp]. O.E. *hoppian*, M.E. *hoppen, huppen*, 'to hop, dance', fr. Gmc. **hup-*; cp. Du., L.G. *hoppen*, M.H.G. *hüpfen, hopfen*, Germ. *hüpfen*, O.N., Swed. *hoppa*; perh. connected w. **hip** (I.). **A.** intrans. **1.** (of human beings) **a** To leap or spring with one leg only; to advance by series of short, jerky leaps from one foot: *to hop along*; **b** (slang) to dance. **2. a** (of birds) To spring, to make one or more short light springs from both legs at once: *to hop about*, move along ground, bough &c. by series of such short springs; **b** (of frogs) to advance by leap or leaps from both hind-legs. **B.** trans. **a** To hop over, cross with a hop;

to hop a stick, ditch; Phrs. *to hop the twig*, (vulg. slang) (i.) to evade one's creditors; (ii.) to die; *to hop it* (slang), to depart hastily; **b** to cause to hop or skip, as cricket-ball; also of a punch or other tool making a series of strokes.

hop (II.), n., fr. prec. **a** Action of person or animal that hops; short leap with one leg (human beings), or with both legs together (birds &c.); Phrs. *a hop, skip* (or *step*), *and jump*, (i.) attempt to cover greatest possible distance with these actions in succession, as game or contest; (ii.) (fig.) short distance; *to catch on the hop*, (colloq.) to catch at the moment of departure; **b** (slang) a dance, ball; **c** (cricket) ball which comes to batsman with a hop, usually *long-hop*.

hop (III.), n. Late M.E. *hoppe*, fr. O. Du. *hoppe* (Mod. Du. *hop*); cp. O.S. *hoppo, hupo*, O.H.G. *hopfo*, Germ. *hopfe-n*; of uncertain origin; Mod. Fr. *houblon*, 'hops', comes through Walloon fr. Du. **1.** n. **a** Perennial climbing plant of hemp family, *Humulus Lupulus*, cultivated for its clusters of greenish cone-shaped female flowers, which have a bitter, aromatic flavour; **b** (pl., as a crop, or article of commerce) female flowers of this plant, dried in kiln, and used for flavouring beer and other drinks; also used medicinally. **2.** (attrib.) **a** Pertaining to hops: *hop-garden, hop-bine, -pole* &c.; resembling hop: *hop clover*; **b** preying on hop: *hop-borer*, kind of moth or its larva; *hop-flea, hop-fly* or *-louse, hop-moth*.

hop (IV.), vb. intrans. & trans., fr. prec. **1.** intrans. **a** To gather hops; **b** to produce hops (as vine). **2.** trans. To flavour with hops.

hop-back, n. **hop** (III.) & **back** (V.). (brewing) Back or vat which strains hops from boiled wort.

hop-bine, n. **hop** (III.) & **bine**. Twining stem of hop.

hope (I.), n. [1. hōp; 2. houp]. O.E. *hopa*, M.E. *hōpe*; Du. *hoop*, cp. M.H.G. *hoffe*, Swed. *hopp*; of uncertain origin, perh. fr. Gmc. base **huð-n-*, <**hupp-*, & connected further w. Lat. *cupere*, 'to desire', q.v. under **cupid**. **1.** State, quality, of mind in which one expects confidently that what one desires will come about; the opposite of *despair*: '*Hope springs eternal in the human breast*' (Pope); one of the Christian virtues: *Faith, Hope, and Charity*. **2.** Expectation, confident anticipation, conviction, that some specific thing that one desires will happen, or be obtained: *to cherish the hopes that . . . ; I have good hopes now that he will recover*; Phr. '*hope deferred maketh the heart sick*' (proverb), prolonged disappointment destroys a man's confidence. **3.** Probability, likelihood, that something desired will happen or be secured: *there is no hope of success; there is now a hope of improvement*. Phr. *while there is life there is hope*, until the worst has actually happened, there is always a chance that it may be avoided; *past hope*, hopeless, affording no basis for hope. **4.** Person, thing, circumstance, action, which inspires hope, on whom or which expectation of success is based: *Mr. Gladstone was at one time considered to be the hope of the Tory party; the British Navy was the great hope of the Allies*.

hope (II.), vb. intrans. & trans. O.E. *hopian*, M.E. *hōpen* &c. See prec. **A.** intrans. **1.** To entertain hope; to desire that something shall happen, and at same time expect, feel confident, that it will: *I hope to be able to come; I thought at one time that things would improve, but now I hope no longer*; *to hope in*, place reliance upon. Phrs. *to hope for the best, to hope against hope*, to retain hopefulness where there seems to be no basis for hope. **2.** To desire strongly that certain things should come about, that certain circumstances should arise: *I hope you will be able to come to dinner; I hope you won't hurt yourself*. **B.** trans. (rare) To hope for, desire (something), and expect to attain it: '*Wait better Winds, and hope a calmer Sea*' (Dryden, Æn. iv. 623).

hope (III.), n., fr. Du. *hoop*, 'troop' &c. See **heap** (I.); popularly confused & identified w. **hope** (I.). Only in Phr. **forlorn hope** (q.v.).

hopeful, adj. & n. [1. hṓpfool; 2. hóupfl]. M.E. **hope** (I.) & **-ful**. **1.** adj. Full of hope; **a** feeling, or inclined to feel, hope; sanguine: *I feel hopeful about a settlement*; **b** affording, promising, encouraging hope: *a hopeful sign, prospect, pupil*. **2.** n. Person, esp. boy or girl, who gives good promise: *a young hopeful* (often ironical).

hopefully, adv. Prec. & **-ly**. In a hopeful manner.

hopefulness, n. See prec. & **-ness**. Hopeful state of mind; hope.

hopeless, adj. [1. hṓples; 2. hóuplis]. **hope** (I.) & **-less**. **1.** (of persons) Having no hope; unable to hope; desperate: *I am hopeless of effecting anything*. **2. a** (of circumstances) Affording, promising, or exciting, no hope: *a hopeless case, situation*; **b** (of persons) irreclaimable, incurable: *a hopeless idiot, waster*.

hopelessly, adv. Prec. & **-ly**. In a hopeless manner.

hopelessness, n. See prec. & **-ness**. **1.** Hopeless state of mind; despair. **2.** Condition of affairs which gives no ground for hope.

hop-garden, n. Enclosed field in which hops are grown and trained on wires or poles.

hop-kiln, n. Kiln in which hops are dried; oast-house.

hoplite, n. [1. hóplīt; 2. hɔ́plait]. Gk. *hoplītēs*, 'heavy-armed', also n., fr. *hóplon* for **sop-l-on*, 'tool, piece of armour, heavy shield', prob. in grade relation w. *hépein*, 'to be about or with', cogn. w. Lat. *socius*, 'companion' (see **social**), fr. Aryan base **sekʷ-*, **sokʷ-* &c., 'to accompany' (see **sequela**), & *-l-*, instrumental suff., & **-ite**. (anct. Gk. hist.) Heavy-armed foot-soldier.

hop-o'-my-thumb, n. [1. hóp o mi thùm; 2. hɔ́p ə mi þàm]. Mannikin, dwarf, pigmy; (originally hero of French nursery tale, 'Le petit Poucet').

hopper (I.), n. [1. hóper; 2. hɔ́pə]. M.E. *hoppere*. **hop** (I.) & **-er**. **1.** Person, animal, or thing that hops; specif. **a** leaper, dancer; **b** any small hopping animal, as *leaf-hopper* &c.; **c** piano jack. **2.** Vessel, usually in form of funnel or inverted pyramid with orifice at bottom, through which loose material is passed, originally by agitating it; specif. **a** box through which grain is poured into mill, coal into furnace or truck, or the like; **b** vessel from which grain is mechanically dropped into furrow; **c** barge with collapsible bottom for disposing of mud from dredger; railway truck with similar device.

hopper (II.), n. **hop** (IV.) & **-er**. Hop-picker.

hop-picker, n. **a** Person who helps to get in hop crop; **b** mechanical device for picking hops.

hop-pillow, n. Pillow stuffed with hops, supposed to induce sleep.

hopple (I.), vb. trans. [1. hópl; 2. hɔ́pl]. **hop** (I.) & freq. or instrumental suff. **-le**; cp. M. Du. *hoppelen*, L.G. *hoppeln*. See **hobble**. To hobble (animal); (fig.) to impede, hamper.

hopple (II.), n., fr. prec. Rope or thong used to hobble horse or other animal.

hop-pocket, n. Sack holding $1\frac{1}{2}$ cwt. of hops; used as measure.

hop-pole, n. **a** Pole up which hops are trained; **b** a tall, lanky person.

hoppy, adj. [1. hópi; 2. hɔ́pi]. **hop** (III.) & **-y**. Having the flavour of hops.

hopscotch, n. [1. hópskoch; 2. hɔ́pskɔtʃ]. **hop** (I.) & **scotch** (II.), 'notch, mark'. Children's game in which player, while hopping, kicks a pebble in succession into series of compartments marked on the ground.

hop-vine, n. Hop-bine.

hopyard, n. [1. hópyard; 2. hɔ́pjād]. Hop-garden.

horal, adj. [1. hṓral; 2. hṓrəl]. Lat. *hōrāl-(is)*. See **hour** & **-al**. Pertaining to an hour or hours; hourly.

horary, adj. [1. hórari; 2. hɔ́rəri]. L. Lat. *hōrāri-(us)*. **hour** & **-ary**. **a** Pertaining to an hour or hours; **b** hourly; **c** lasting an hour or a very short time.

Horatian, adj. [1. horā́shun; 2. hɔréiʃ(i)ən]. Lat. *Hōrātiān-(us)*, fr. *Hōrāti-us*, 'Horace', & **-an**. Pertaining to, written in the manner of, the Roman poet Horace (*Q. Horatius Flaccus*, 65–8 B.C.): *an Horatian ode*.

horde (I.), n. [1. hord; 2. hōd]. Fr., fr. Turk. *ordū*, fr. Tatar *yurt, urdu*, 'tent, royal court, camp', cp. **Urdu**. **1.** Aggregate of nomads on or from the steppes of Central Asia, loosely organized for war: *the Golden Horde*, body of Tatars who invaded Europe in 13th cent., and set up a Khanate in Russia. **2. a** Any large predatory band; **b** (contempt.) rough crowd, gang; **c** pack of animals: *a horde of wolves*.

horde (II.), vb. intrans., fr. prec. To gather or live in a horde.

horehound, hoarhound, n. [1. hórhound; 2. hṓhaund]. O.E. *hārhūne*, M.E. *hōrehūne*, fr. **hoar** & O.E. *hūne*, 'horehound', of uncertain origin, possibly cogn. w. Gk. *konīlē*, Lat. *cunīla*, 'wild marjoram'; the final *-d* is excrescent as in **sound** (I.). **a** Kind of mint (also called *white horehound*), wild in Britain, with white down on leaves (whence the name) and bitter flavour; **b** medicinal extract from same used for cough &c.; **c** one of several similar plants, as *black horehound*.

horizon, n. [1. horízn; 2. həráizn]. Fr., fr. Lat. *horīzōn*, fr. Gk. *horízōn* (*kúklos*), lit. 'bounding (circle)', Pres. Part. masc. of *horīzein*, 'to bound, limit', fr. *hóros*, 'boundary', orig. 'furrow'; cogn. w. Lat. *urvus*, 'boundary'. **a** Circle bounding the part of the earth's surface visible from a given point; line at which sky and sea or land appear to meet; **b** (fig.) limits of knowledge, interests, or mental outlook: *beyond the horizon of one's age; science gives us a new horizon*.

horizontal, adj. & n. [1. hòrizóntl; 2. hɔ̀rizɔ́ntl]. Fr., fr. Lat. *horīzont-*, stem of *horīzōn*. Prec. & **-al**. **1.** adj. **a** (obs.) Pertaining to the horizon: '*the horizontal air*' (Milton, 'P.L.'); **b** parallel to the horizon; at right angles to the vertical; flat, level: *a horizontal line, plane*; *horizontal bar*, one fixed thus a few feet above floor, for gymnastics. **2.** n. **a** Horizontal thing, as a line, bar; **b** horizontal position: *out of the horizontal*.

horizontality, n. [1. hòrizontáliti; 2. hɔ̀rizɔntǽliti]. Prec. & **-ity**. Quality of being horizontal.

horizontally, adv. [1. hòrizóntali; 2. hɔ̀rizɔ́ntəli]. **horizontal** & **-ly**. In a horizontal manner or direction.

hormone, n. [1. hórmōn; 2. hṓmoun]. Irregularly formed fr. Gk. *hormáein*, 'to urge, stimulate', fr. *hormḗ*, 'onset, impulse'. (physiol.) Internal secretion which passes into the blood and stimulates functional activity.

horn (I.), n. [1. horn; 2. hōn]. O.E. & M.E. *horn*; in all Gmc. languages, fr. **hurna-*, cogn. w. Lat. *cornu*, 'horn'; Gk. *kéras*, see **keratin**. See further under **hart, cervine, cerebrum**. **1. a** One of a pair of permanent, hard, pointed, curved projections on the head of oxen, sheep, goats &c.; Phrs. *to take the bull by the horns*, to confront an emergency boldly, act promptly and resolutely; *on the horns of a dilemma*; **b** one of pair of branched, bony appendages on the head of deer, which fall and grow again each year; an antler; **c** thick, pointed growth, resembling the horn of an ox in structure, on the nose of rhinoceros; **d** (obs.) *the horns*, represented, and referred to, as growing on the head of a cuckold; symbol of a cuckold. **2.** Various organs or excrescences on heads of animals, somewhat resembling true horns in appearance, e.g. tufts of feathers on heads of certain birds; projecting tentacles of a snail &c.; Phr. *to draw in one's horns*, diminish one's zeal, activity &c. **3.** The substance which composes the horns **a** of oxen &c.; **b** of deer; esp. considered as a material from which various articles are manufactured: *a knife with a handle of horn* (i.e. a piece of the horn either of an ox &c., or of a stag); *spectacle frames of horn*; Phr. *the gate of horn*, in classical mythology, that through which true dreams pass, as contrasted with *the gate of ivory*.

4. Any of various objects, made from or formerly made from, or resembling in shape, a horn of an ox, ram &c.; a drinking-cup made from horn of an ox: *drinking horn*; b receptacle for gunpowder: *powder horn*; c a cornucopia, or *horn of plenty*, i.e. representation of a horn with flowers, fruit &c., flowing from it, the conventional symbol of abundance, wealth &c.; d (i.) one of various wind instruments, formerly of horn, now of metal, capable of emitting musical notes: *huntsman's horn*; a bugle, and other musical instruments; (ii.) instrument for uttering loud, harsh note of warning &c.: *foghorn, motor-horn* &c.; e hollowed piece of horn used for putting shoes on to the feet: *shoe horn* &c. 5. Either of the pointed extremities of the crescent moon. 6. Projecting horn-shaped device at each corner of Jewish altar, to which the victim was bound for the sacrifice. 7. (attrib., or adj.) Made of horn: *a horn handle*; *horn spectacles*, those having frames made of horn.

horn (II.), vb. trans., fr. prec. 1. a (rare) To furnish with horns; b (obs., fig.) to cuckold. 2. To remove the horns of: *to horn cattle.* 3. (rare) To use the horns upon, to gore with the horns.

hornbeam, n. [1. hórnbēm; 2. hɔ́nbīm]. **horn (I.)** & **beam** (tree); prob. fr. its tough, close-grained wood. Deciduous European tree, *Carpinus betulus*, resembling beech, grown for hedges, and for charcoal; one of several allied trees.

hornbill, n. [1. hórnbil; 2. hɔ́nbil]. Member of family of large tropical Old World birds, mostly bearing large horny protuberance on top of the head and bill.

hornblende, n. [1. hórnblend; 2. hɔ́nblɛnd]. Germ. See **horn** & **blende**. Mineral, generally black or dark green, found in granite and other igneous rocks.

hornbook, n. [1. hórnbook; 2. hɔ́nbuk]. Sheet with alphabet &c., on small board covered with transparent horn, formerly used by children for learning to read.

horned, adj. [1. hornd; 2. hɔ̄nd]. **horn (I.)** & **-ed.** 1. a Provided with, having, horns: *horned cattle*; b having tufts or excrescences resembling horns upon the head: *horned owl, pheasant, adder, toad*; c (of the crescent moon, poet.) *the horned moon*; d (of certain plants) having a spike: *horned poppy, violet.* 2. P.P. of **horn (II.)**. Having been deprived of the horns.

horner, n. [1. hórner; 2. hɔ́nə]. **horn (I.)** & **-er.** (rare or obs., except as family name) a Person who makes articles of horn, esp. spoons; b one who blows a horn.

hornet, n. [1. hórnet; 2. hɔ́nit]. O.E. *hyrnet, hyrnetu*, M.E. *harnette* &c., associated w. **horn**, fr. its droning note, or fr. its sting (cp. its names in O.S., *horno-bero*, lit. 'horn-bearer', & M. Du. *horener*, lit. 'horner'), but not derived fr. *horn* in Gmc. period. Cp. O.H.G. *hornuz*, M.H.G. *horniz*, Mod. Germ. *hornisse*; Gmc. type **hurz-nut, -nit* &c., fr. base **hurz-* 'to buzz' (cp. Du. *horzel*, 'hornet', *horzelen*, 'to buzz'), cogn. w. O. Slav. *sreš-ene*, Serb. *sřš-ljen*, Lith. *szirsz-û*, Lat. *crābrō* for **crās-rōn-*, 'hornet'. Possibly fr. a base remotely connected w. **horn**, Aryan **k'eres-*, q.v. under **cerebrum.** a Large species of wasp, *Vespis crabro*, dark brown and yellow, with powerful sting; b (fig.) persistently annoying or pugnacious person; Phrs. *to stir up a nest of hornets*; *to bring a hornets' nest about one's ears*, to provoke a widespread outburst of angry feeling.

hornfish, n. [1. hórnfish; 2. hɔ́nfiʃ]. O.E. *hornfisc*; O.N. *hornfisk-r*, Dan. *hornfisk*, fr. **horn (I.)** & **fish (I.)**. Garfish.

horn-fly, n. Small European fly infesting base of horns of cattle.

hornful, n. [1. hórnfool; 2. hɔ́nful]. **horn (I.)** & **-ful.** Quantity that will fill a (drinking) horn.

horniness, n. [1. hórnines; 2. hɔ́ninis]. **horny** & **-ness.** Quality of being horny.

horning, n. [1. hórning; 2. hɔ́niŋ]. **horn (I.)** & **-ing.** (Scots law) a (hist.) Action of outlawing person by three blasts of horn; b execution against debtor; Phr. *letters of horning*, direction to debtor to comply with law under penalty of arrest.

hornless, adj. [1. hórnles; 2. hɔ́nlis]. **horn (I.)** & **-less.** Having no horns: *hornless sheep.*

horn-mad, adj. Orig. used in reference to cattle whose horns were growing. Furiously angry.

horn-owl, n. Horned owl.

hornpipe, n. [1. hórnpīp; 2. hɔ́npaip]. 1. Obsolete reed instrument of wood, sometimes with horn opening at larger end. 2. a Kind of lively dance for one or more persons, originally accompanied by hornpipe, popular with sailors; b musical composition for such dance.

hornplate, n. [1. hórnplāt; 2. hɔ́npleit]. Axle-guard on railway carriage &c.

hornwork, n. [1. hórnwërk; 2. hɔ́nwʌ̄k]. 1. Working in horn; (coll.) objects made of horn. 2. (fort.) Outwork consisting of two half-bastions connected by a curtain.

horny, adj. [1. hórni; 2. hɔ́ni]. **horn (I.)** & **-y.** a Consisting of, having structure and texture of, horn: *a horny growth* &c.; b hard and tough like horn.

horny-handed, adj. Prec. & **handed.** Having hands with a tough, horny skin, esp. fr. hard work: *horny-handed son of toil.*

horologe, n. [1. hórolōj, -loj; 2. hɔ́rəloudž, -lɔdž]. M.E., fr. O. Fr. (& Mod. Fr.) *horologe*, fr. Lat. *hōrologium*, fr. Gk. *hōrológion*, fr. *hōro-*, combining form of *hṓra*, see **hour**, & *-logion.* See **-logue.** (rare) Any instrument for indicating the hours, such as a sundial or clock.

horologer, n. [1. horólojer; 2. hɔrɔ́lədžə]. Prec. & **-er.** (rare) One who makes horologes or is skilled in horology.

horologic(al), adj. [1. hòrolójik(l); 2. hɔ̀rəlɔ́džik(l)]. **horologe** & **-ic, -al.** (rare) Pertaining to horology or horologes.

horologist, n. [1. horólojist; 2. hɔrɔ́lədžist]. **horologe** & **-ist.** Horologer.

horology, n. [1. horóloji; 2. hɔrɔ́lədži]. Gk. *hōro-*, as in **horologe**, & **-logy.** (i.) Art of indicating the hours or of measuring time; (ii.) construction of instruments for this purpose.

horopter, n. [1. horópter; 2. hɔrɔ́ptə]. Gk. *hóros*, 'limit, boundary' (see **horizon**), & *optḗr*, 'one who looks', fr. base *op-*, 'to see' (see **optic**), & *-tēr*, agent-suff. Range of line and surface seen as single vision when both eyes are directed and fixed upon a given point.

horoscope, n. [1. hóroskōp; 2. hɔ́rəskoup]. Fr., fr. Lat. *hōroscop-(us)*, fr. Gk. *hōroskópos*, adj., 'observing hours', n., 'horoscope', fr. *hōro-*, form of *hṓra.* See **hour** & **-scope.** (astrol.) a Calculation of positions of heavenly bodies at particular moment, esp. of person's birth, in order to predict fortune; b diagram indicating such positions: *to cast a horoscope.*

horoscopic, adj. [1. hòroskópik; 2. hɔ̀rəskɔ́pik]. Lat. *hōroscopicus.* **horoscope** & **-ic.** Pertaining to a horoscope or horoscopy.

horoscopist, n. [1. hóróskopist; 2. hɔrɔ́skəpist]. **horoscope** & **-ist.** Person who casts a horoscope, or studies horoscopy.

horoscopy, n. [1. horóskopi; 2. hɔrɔ́skəpi]. **horoscope** & **-y.** a Art of casting horoscopes; b aspect of the stars at a particular moment.

horrent, adj. [1. hórent; 2. hɔ́rənt]. Lat. *horrent-*, stem of *horrens*, Pres. Part. of *horrēre*, 'to bristle'. See **horror.** (rare or liter.) Bristling: '*With bright emblazonry and horrent arms*' (Milton, 'P.L.').

horrescent, adj. [1. horésent; 2. hɔrésənt], fr. Lat. *horrescent-(em)*, Pres. Part. of *horrescere*, 'to shudder', inceptive fr. *horrēre*, 'to stand on end, bristle; to shiver' &c. See **horror.** Bristling; shuddering with terror &c.

horrible, adj. [1. hóribl; 2. hɔ́ribl, -əbl]. M.E., O. Fr. (& Mod. Fr.), fr. Lat. *horribil-is*, fr. *horrēre* for **hors-ēre*, 'to stand on end, bristle, shudder'. See **horror.** a Such as to make one shudder; causing, of such a nature as to cause, physical fear, disgust, or moral repulsion; dreadful, shocking, revolting: *a horrible din, sound, sight*; *horrible crime, depravity* &c.; b (colloq.) extremely unpleasant or vexatious: *a horrible bore.*

horribleness, n. Prec. & **-ness.** Quality of being horrible.

horribly, adv. See prec. & **-ly.** In a horrible manner; to a horrible degree.

horrid, adj. [1. hórid; 2. hɔ́rid]. Lat. *horrid-us*, 'rough, bristly, frightful', fr. *horrēre.* See **horror.** 1. (obs., or archaic) Rough, bristling, shaggy. 2. a Repulsive, frightful, disgusting, horrifying; b (colloq.) disagreeable, rude, annoying: *how horrid of him*; *what a horrid man, nuisance* (milder than *horrible*).

horridly, adv. Prec. & **-ly.** In a horrid manner.

horridness, n. See prec. & **-ness.** Quality of being horrid.

horrific, adj. [1. horífik; 2. hɔrífik]. Lat. *horrific-(us)*, lit. 'making the hair to stand on end', fr. *horri-*, combining form of *horrēre.* See **horrible** & **horror** & **-fic.** (liter.) Horrifying, frightful.

horrify, vb. trans. [1. hórifī; 2. hɔ́rifai]. Lat. *horrificāre*, as **horrific**; on anal. of words derived through Fr. vbs. in *-fier.* See **-fy.** To affect, fill, with horror, excite horror in; (colloq.) to shock, scandalize: *I was horrified to see her wearing such a hat.*

horrifying, adj. [1. hórifiing; 2. hɔ́rifai-iŋ]. Prec. & **-ing.** That horrifies; shocking.

horripilate, vb. trans. & intrans. [1. horípilāt; 2. hɔrípileit]. Lat. *horripilāt-(um)*, P.P. of *horripilāre*, intrans., fr. *horri-*, as in **horrific**, & *pilus*, 'hair', see **pile (VII.)**. (rare) 1. trans. To cause (the hair) to bristle or stand on end; to frighten. 2. intrans. To bristle, stand on end.

horripilation, n. [1. hòripiláshun; 2. hɔ̀ripiléiʃən]. Lat. *horripilātiōn-(em).* Prec. & **-ion.** Bristling of the hair; gooseflesh.

horror, n. [1. hóror; 2. hɔ́rə]. M.E., O. Fr. *horrour* (Mod. Fr. *horreur*), fr. Lat. *horrōr-(em)*, 'a standing on end, bristling; roughness, rudeness; a trembling; fear, dread, terror' &c. This & the associated words *horrēre, horribilis* &c., fr. **hors-*, all have, to start w., a purely physical sense. The base **ghars-* &c., meaning orig. simply 'rough', is hardly found outside Lat., but in that language has several derivatives; *hircus*, 'he-goat', see **hircine**, & *hirsūtus*, 'shaggy, prickly', see **hirsute.** Other cognates in Engl. are **horrent, horrid, horrible.** Hardly used now in other than moral sense, except in med. (direct fr. Lat.), where the word is still used for the severe trembling & shuddering before fever. Even this is archaic. 1. Powerful emotion of terror and disgust; repulsion, moral shrinking from, loathing: *his mind*, or *he, was filled with horror at the thought, sight* &c. Phr. *to have a horror of*, to loathe, be disgusted by. Specif. use, *the horrors*, uncontrollable fit of unreasoning terror, esp. in delirium tremens. 2. Something which provokes horror in the mind; a something horrible, disgusting, repellent: *the papers are full of murders and horrors of every sort*; *the horrors of war*; b (colloq.) an ugly sight; something, or some person, that inspires mild repulsion and ridicule: *she thought her elderly beau a perfect horror*; *chamber of horrors*, department of a wax-work show filled with effigies of criminals, and objects associated with crimes.

horror-stricken, -struck, adj. [1. hóror strikn, -struk; 2. hɔ́rə strikn, -strak]. Prec. & *stricken, struck*, P.P. of **strike (I.)**. Stricken, seized or overwhelmed with horror.

hors de combat, pred. adj., Anglicized pronunciation [1. ór de kómbah; 2. ɔ̄ di, də, kɔ̄bā]. Fr., 'out of fight', fr. *hors*, 'outside', fr. Lat. *foris*, 'out of doors', abl. pl. of **fora* (see **forum** & **door**), & *dē*, 'of' (see **de-**), & **combat.** a Precluded from fighting; b disabled, out of action.

hors d'œuvre, n. [1. ór dêvr; 2. ɔ̄ dʌ́vr]. Fr., 'outside of (the) work', fr. *hors de* as prec. & *œuvre*, 'work', fr. Lat. *opera*, 'works'. See **opera.** Small dish, consisting of a selection of highly flavoured or salted fish, meats, and cold vegetables, olives &c., served before a meal as appetizer or relish.

horse (I.), n. [1. hors; 2. hōs]. O.E. *hros, hors*, M.E. *hors*, O.S. *hros*, O.H.G. *hros(s)*, M.H.G. *ros, ors*, Mod. Germ. *ross*, O.N. *hross*, Gmc. type **hross-an*, prob. 'leaper' or 'runner'; cp. O.E., O.H.G. *horsc* (for **hors-isc*), 'swift, brisk', cogn. w. Lat. *currere* for **curs-ere*, 'to run'. See more on this base under **current, course. 1. a** Large, powerful, solid-hoofed, domesticated mammal, with long, coarse, flowing mane and tail, used for carrying burdens, draught, and riding; Phrs. *to take horse*, to mount or ride a horse; *to horse!*, command to mount; *to work like a horse*, very hard, with great energy; *a horse of another colour*, quite a different matter; *to put the cart before the horse*, to reverse the order of things, events; take the effect for the cause; *a dark horse*, person or thing whose character and qualities have still to be discovered; *dead horse* (slang), a piece of work for which one is paid in advance; *to flog a dead horse*, to argue about a question which has been already settled, to waste one's efforts; *to look a gift horse in the mouth*, i.e. to look for signs of old age in it; hence, to criticize a gift or favour received; *to mount, ride, the high horse*, to assume airs of importance, to behave haughtily; *to spur a willing horse*, to incite without need: **b** (zool.) member of horse family, including ass, zebra, and extinct genera; **c** full-grown male of the species contrasted with a *mare*, or a *foal*. **2.** (coll.) Mounted troops, cavalry. Phrs. *horse and foot*, cavalry and infantry, (fig.) with all one's resources; *light horse*, lightly armed mounted troops. **3.** One of several objects, made of wood, with legs, some of them bearing rough resemblance to trunk and legs of a horse; used for various purposes: specif. **a** *vaulting-horse*, vaulting-block for gymnastic exercises; **b** (hist.) frame on which a soldier had to sit as punishment: *to ride the wooden horse*; **c** sawing frame; **d** frame on which clothes &c. are hung: *clothes-horse, towel-horse* &c.; **e** currier's trestle. **4.** (techn.) Any of various tools or appliances, as clamp, wedge. **5.** (attrib. or adj.) **a** Pertaining to a horse or horses: *horse hoof, trappings, artillery*; **b** before certain nouns, expressing large, strong, or coarse variety of thing referred to: *horse ant, mackerel, mussel, mushroom, plum, radish*. Cp. also *horse-laugh, horse-play, horse-sense* &c.

horse (II.), vb. trans. & intrans. O.E. *horsian*, M.E. *horsen*, 'to provide with a horse or horses', fr. prec. **1.** trans. **a** To provide (person, troop, vehicle) with a horse or horses: *to horse a squadron, a carriage*; *to be well horsed*; **b** (rare) to put on the back of a person, wooden horse &c. for the purpose of flogging; to flog; **c** (rare) to carry on one's back; **d** to cover (mare). **2.** intrans. (rare or obs.) To mount, ride, a horse.

Horse Artillery, n. Light field artillery with mounted gunners, capable of rapid movement.

horseback, n. [1. hórsbak; 2. hṓsbæk]. M.E. *horsbak*. Back of a horse; chiefly in Phr. *on horseback*, riding, mounted.

horse-bean, n. Coarse variety of bean used for feeding horses &c.

horse-block, n. Low platform of stone &c. with step, used as aid in mounting horse.

horse-boat, n. **1.** Boat in which horses are transported. **2.** Boat towed by a horse.

horse-box, n. **a** Railway-van specially adapted for carrying horses; **b** kind of cage in which horse is slung on board ship; stall for horse on ship.

horse-boy, n. Stable boy.

horse-chestnut, n. **a** European and Asiatic tree, *Aesculus hippocastanum*, superficially resembling the true chestnut, bearing spikes of white or red flowers, seed-vessels with large reddish-brown nuts, and palmate leaves, cultivated for ornament; **b** nut of this, said to have been ground and used as food for horses, whence the name.

horse-cloth, n. Specially shaped blanket, covering horse's back and loins, kept in place by strap and buckle at the breast, and a girth passing round the belly; worn in stable, or in the open air when the animal is being exercised gently.

horse-collar, n. Padded collar of leather &c. worn by draught horse, bearing the hames, to which the traces are attached. Phr. *to grin through a horse-collar*, formerly a competitive game in rustic sports.

horse-coper, n. **horse & coper** (I.). Horse-dealer, esp. one of doubtful honesty.

horse-doctor, n. (colloq.) Farrier, veterinary surgeon.

horse-drench, n. Dose of medicine for horse.

horse-flesh, n. **1.** Flesh of horse, as article of food. **2.** (collectively) Horses: *a good judge of horse-flesh*.

horse-fly, n. M.E. *hors fleȝe*. **horse & fly** (I.). One of several species of large flies that torment horses and cattle; gadfly, breeze-fly.

Horse Guards, n. pl. **1.** (mil.) Household cavalry, esp. the cavalry brigade of the British Guards; consisting of 1st and 2nd Life Guards and specif., *the Royal Horse Guards*, the Blues. **2.** Headquarters of British household cavalry in Whitehall, London, formerly used as offices of commander-in-chief's branch of War Department, now headquarters of the Commander-in-chief of the Home Forces and of the London district.

horsehair, n. [1. hórs-hār; 2. hṓsheə]. M.E. *horshēr*. **horse & hair. a** Long hair of horse's mane or tail, as used in upholstery; **b** cloth woven of this.

horse-latitudes, n. pl. A sailor's name; origin unknown. One of two oceanic zones about 30° N. and S., esp. that in North Atlantic, distinguished by frequent calms and high barometric pressure.

horse-laugh, n. Loud, coarse laugh; guffaw.

horse-leech, n. **1. a** Kind of leech supposed to enter mouth or nostrils of a horse when drinking; **b** (fig.) insatiable person (see Prov. xxx. 15). **2.** (rare) Horse-doctor, veterinary surgeon.

horse-litter, n. Litter borne on poles between two horses.

horse-mackerel, n. Spiny fish somewhat like mackerel; scad; also tunny, or one of several other fishes.

horseman, n. [1. hórsman; 2. hṓsmən]. **1.** Man who rides a horse; mounted man. **2. a** Variety of carrier pigeon; **b** W. Indian land crab.

horsemanship, n. [1. hórsmanship; 2. hṓsmənʃip]. Prec. & **-ship.** Art of riding horses; skill in this.

horse-marines, n. pl. (facet.) Imaginary force of naval cavalry, chiefly in Phr. *tell that to the horse-marines*, said as comment on incredible statement.

horse-master, n. **1.** One who besides having skill in riding, can manage, school, and train horses. **2.** Man who owns horses; esp. one who keeps horses for hire; job-master.

horse pistol, n. Large pistol carried in holster.

horse-play, n. Violent, rough, or boisterous play; noisy romping.

horse-pond, n. Small, shallow pond in which horses are watered or washed.

horse-power, n. Unit of work or power exerted by machine &c., equivalent to the force required to raise 550 lb. one ft. per sec.; abbreviated *h.p.*

horse-race, n. One between horses carrying riders.

horse-racing, n. Act of organizing, riding in, or frequenting, horse-races.

horse-radish, n. Plant, *Cochlearia armoracia*, with hot, pungent, white root, which is grated down and made into a sauce.

horse-rake, n. Rake drawn by horse.

horse-sense, n. Rough, instinctive, practical common sense.

horseshoe, n. [1. hórsshōō; 2. hṓsʃū]. **1.** Flat strip of iron shaped to fit horse's hoof, open at the back, placed when hot upon the under surface of hoof and fastened on with nails. **2.** Thing shaped like a horseshoe. **3.** (attrib. or adj.) Shaped like a horseshoe: *horseshoe arch*.

horse-tail, n. **1.** Tail of horse, esp. as Turkish standard or badge of rank. **2.** A genus, *Equisetum*, of an order *Pteridophyta*, of flowerless plants which resemble a horse's tail in appearance, allied to ferns, but having jointed hollow stem and whorls of leafless branches.

horse-trainer, n. Person who trains horses.

horsewhip, n. & vb. trans. [1. hórswip; 2. hṓswip]. **1.** n. Whip used for driving horses. **2.** vb. trans. To thrash (person) with horse-whip.

horsewoman, n. [1. hórswooman; 2. hṓswumən]. Woman rider, esp. one who rides well.

horsily, adv. [1. hórsili; 2. hṓsili]. **horsy & -ly.** In a horsy manner.

horsiness, n. [1. hórsines; 2. hṓsinis]. Next word & **-ness.** Quality of being horsy, fondness for horses and everything connected with them; fact of being associated with horse dealing, racing &c.

horsy, adj. [1. hórsi; 2. hṓsi]. **horse** (I.) & **-y. a** (of persons) (i.) Fond of horses, having much to do with horses, their use and management; (ii.) fond of, having to do with, horse-racing; **b** (of manners, appearance, dress &c.) suggesting familiarity with horses, riding, horse-racing &c.; sporting.

hortation, n. [1. hortā́shun; 2. hōtéiʃən]. Lat. *hortātiōn-(em)*, fr. *hortāt-(um)*, P.P. of *hortāri*, 'to urge, incite, instigate; encourage, cheer', freq. of *hori*, 'to urge, incite', cogn. w. Gk. *khairō*, 'I rejoice', fr. **khar-jō*; cp. also *kháris*, 'grace' &c., q.v. under **eucharist**, fr. Aryan base **ǵher-*, wh. is found also in O.E. *ġeornian*, 'to desire' (see **yearn**). Action of inciting, encouraging, or exhorting.

hortative, adj. [1. hórtativ; 2. hṓtətiv]. Lat. *hortātīv-us*, fr. *hortāt-*, as in prec., & **-ive.** Pertaining to exhortation; admonitory.

hortatory, adj. [1. hórtat(o)ri; 2. hṓtət(ə)ri]. Lat. *hortātōr-(ius)*, fr. *hortāt-*, as in **hortation**, & **-ory.** Hortative.

horticultural, adj. [1. hòrtikúlchural; 2. hòtikáltʃərəl]. **horticulture & -al.** Pertaining to horticulture: *a horticultural society, show* &c.

horticulturalist, n. [1. hòrtikúlchuralist; 2. hòtikáltʃərəlist]. Popular and usual form for **horticulturist.**

horticulture, n. [1. hórtikulchur; 2. hṓtikaltʃə]. Lat. *horti-*, fr. *hortus*, 'garden', q.v. under **hortus siccus**, & *cultūra*, 'tilling, husbandry' &c., q.v. under **culture.** Art of cultivating gardens; art of producing flowers, fruits, and vegetables.

horticulturist, n. [1. hòrtikúlchurist; 2. hòtikáltʃərist]. Prec. & **-ist.** Person who practises horticulture; expert in gardening.

hortus siccus, n. [1. hórtus síkus; 2. hṓtəs síkəs]. Lat., 'dry garden'; Lat. *hortus* means 'an enclosed space for plants, a garden', cogn. w. Gk. *khórtos*, 'feeding-place'. The essential primitive meaning is 'enclosure', fr. Aryan base **ǵhert-, *ǵhort-*, 'to surround, enclose'; see discussion under **cohort, court.** From same base comes O.E. *gyrdan*, 'to put a girdle on' (see **gird**), & O.E. *gyrdel*, 'belt' &c. (see **girdle**), both fr. Gmc. **gurð-*. Further O.E. *ġeard*, 'enclosure' &c.; see **yard** (II.), fr. Gmc. **garð-*, Aryan **ǵhort-*, exactly equiv. to Lat. *hortus*. Of Lat. *siccus*, 'dry', there are several suggested explanations, q.v. under **siccative.** A collection of dried and preserved plants; a herbarium.

hosanna, interj. & n. [1. hōzána; 2. houzǽnə]. L. Lat., fr. Gk. *hōsanná*, fr. Heb. *hōshā'nā*, abbr. fr. *hōshī'āh nnā*, 'save, we pray'. Hebrew exclamation of praise or adoration.

hose (I.), n. pl. [1. hōz; 2. houz]. Never used in sing. sense. The old pl. *hosen*, used as late as 17th cent., now purely provinc., if still existing. O.E. *hosa*, 'covering for the leg; gaiter', M.E. *hōse*, O.H.G., Mod. Germ. *hose*,

O.N. *hosa*. The primitive meaning of the word was 'sheath, covering, husk' &c.; cp. the closely related O.E. *hos*, 'husk, pod'. If these words are fr. a Gmc. **hus(s)a*, fr. Aryan **kut-so-*, or **kudh-so-*, they might belong to the group to wh. O.E. *hȳd*, 'skin' &c. (see **hide (II.)**), & Lat. *cutis*, 'skin' (see **cuticle**) belong, also ultimately related to **hoard, house, hut.** **1.** Formerly, garment covering leg or part of it, specif. (hist.) close-fitting trousers or breeches reaching from waist to foot, ankle, or knee. **2.** Now, stockings, but purely a tradesman's word.

hose (II.), n. Same word as prec., but apparently introduced in sense of 'water-pipe', fr. Du. *hoos*, wh. has similar sense. **1.** (rare or provinc.) Socket in head of implement, as spade, golf-club, in which shaft is fixed. **2.** Flexible tube or pipe of india-rubber or leather for conveying water; used esp. for extinguishing fire, watering garden &c.

hose-cart, n. Cart in which fire-hose is carried, wound upon a drum or reel.

hoseman, n. [1. hṓzman; 2. hóuzmən]. Fireman in charge of hose.

hose-pipe, n. Flexible pipe used as hose.

hose-reel, n. Reel on which garden or fire-hose is wound.

hosier, n. [1. hṓzher; 2. hóuž(i)ə]. **hose (I.)** & **-ier**. 1. (obs. sense) Maker of hose. 2. (now) A dealer in men's stockings, socks, collars, underclothing &c.

hosiery, n. [1. hṓzheri; 2. hóuž(i)əri]. Prec. & **-y**. **a** (coll.) Hosier's wares; **b** business, shop, of hosier; **c** factory for hosier's wares.

hospice, n. [1. hóspis; 2. hɔ́spis]. Fr., fr. Lat. *hospitium*, 'hospitality, inn', fr. *hospit-*, stem of *hospes* (see **host (II.)**), 'guest'. **1.** House of entertainment and refuge for travellers, esp. one maintained by a religious order: *the Hospice of the Great St. Bernard.* **2.** Home, asylum, for infirm or destitute.

hospitable, adj. [1. hóspitabl; 2. hɔ́spitəbl]. Fr., fr. L. Lat. *hospitāre*, 'to be a host to', fr. *hospit-*, stem of *hospes*, see **host (II.)**, & **-able**. **a** Ready to entertain guests or strangers in a friendly, generous manner without expecting reward; fond of giving, ready to give, hospitality; **b** affording, expressing, hospitality: *a hospitable roof, board, speech*; **c** (rare, fig.) receptive: *a mind hospitable to new ideas.*

hospitableness, n. Prec. & **-ness**. Quality of mind which inclines to giving hospitality.

hospitably, adv. See prec. & **-ly**. In a hospitable manner.

hospital, n. [1. hóspit(a)l; 2. hɔ́spit(ə)l]. M.E., O. Fr. *hospital*, fr. L. Lat. *hospitāle*, 'guest-house', neut. of Lat. *hospitālis*, 'pertaining to a host or guest', fr. *hospit-*, stem of *hospes*. See **host (II.)** & **-al**. Cp. **hostel** & **hotel**. **1. a** Institution which provides medical and surgical treatment and nursing &c., for the sick or injured; **b** building in which patients are treated medically or surgically, nursed, and generally lodged and fed during illness; **c** (attrib.) *hospital nurse*; *hospital fever*, typhus, formerly common in hospitals; *Hospital Sunday* &c., day appointed for making collections throughout the country &c. for hospitals. **2.** In certain old institutions, **a** educational establishment; *Christ's Hospital*, at Horsham; *Heriot's Hospital*, in Edinburgh; **b** charitable foundation, society, for the entertainment of travellers, maintenance of the aged, infirm, or destitute &c.

hospitality, n. [1. hòspitáliti; 2. hɔ̀spitǽliti]. Fr. *hospitalité*, fr. Lat. *hospitālitāt-*, stem of *-itas*, fr. *hospitālis*. See **hospital** & **-ity**. **1.** Act of receiving with cheerfulness, and of entertaining, feeding, and lodging a guest with liberality; the entertainment &c. thus given and received. **2.** Quality of nature and character which prompts a person to be hospitable.

hospitaller, n. [1. hospítaler; 2. hɔspítələ]. M.E. *hospitaler*, fr. O. Fr. *hospitalier*, fr. Med. Lat. *hospitālārius*. **hospital** & **-ier**. **a** Member or official of a charitable society for care of travellers, aged, infirm, sick &c.; specif. **b** (cap.) member of the military religious order of St. John of Jerusalem, formerly devoted to care of pilgrims in Holy Land, now (where surviving) to ambulance work &c.: *Knights Hospitallers.*

hospodar, n. [1. hóspodar; 2. hɔ́spɔdā]. Rumanian form of O. Slav. *gospodĭ*, 'lord, master'. Cp. **host (II.)**. (hist.) Prince; title of a governor of the provinces of Moldavia and Wallachia of the old Turkish Empire.

host (I.), n. [1. hōst; 2. houst]. M.E., O. Fr., fr. Lat. *host-is*, 'enemy', in Med. Lat., 'army', fr. idea of 'hostile, invading army', cogn. w. O. Slav. *gostĭ*, 'stranger, guest', Goth. *gast-s*, 'guest', O.E. *ġiest, ġest*, 'stranger, guest' (see **guest**); Aryan type **ghost-is*, wh. meant orig. 'stranger', whence developed the ideas either of a friendly stranger, 'guest', or of a hostile stranger, 'enemy', as in Lat. (see **hostile**). Prob. cogn. w. Scrt. *ghasati*, 'injures', cp. **exhaust**. See also next word. **a** (now chiefly poet. or liter.) Army; large armed force marshalled for war; Bib. Phrs. *the Lord of Hosts*, Jehovah, as Lord of the heavenly hosts; *the heavenly hosts, the host(s) of heaven*, the angels; the stars; **b** (fig.) crowd, large body or number of persons or things: *hosts of friends, of troubles.* Phr. *a host in himself*, as useful and effective as a number of ordinary persons.

host (II.), n. M.E. *host(e), ost(e)*, fr. O. Fr. *(h)oste* (Mod. Fr. *hôte*), fr. Lat. *hospit-*, stem of *hospes*, 'host, guest'; an ancient compound, already in Aryan **ghosti-potis*. Cp. O. Slav. *gospodĭ*, 'lord', lit. 'lord of strangers'. For first element, meaning orig. 'stranger, guest', see prec. The second element, Aryan **pot-* &c., is found in Lat. *potis*, 'able', *potens*, 'powerful', Goth. *-faþs*, 'master' &c., Scrt. *pati-*, 'master, lord', O. Slav. *-podĭ*, 'lord', Lith. *pati-s*, 'husband', Gk. *pósis*, fr. **potis*, 'husband', & *(des)pótēs*, lit. 'house-lord'. See **despot** & **potent (I.)**. **1. a** Person, generally a male, who receives, entertains, or welcomes guests or strangers; *to act as host*, preside, take the lead at an entertainment, festivity &c.; **b** keeper or landlord of an inn; hotel-keeper; (archaic or facet.) *mine host (of the Bull).* Phr. *to reckon without one's host*, to forget in one's calculations the influence and possible action of another person, or the effect of some other factor. **2.** (biol.) Animal or plant on which a parasite or similar organism depends for existence.

host (III.), n. M.E. *hōste*, fr. Lat. *hostia*, 'sacrificial victim'; later in present sense; perh. fr. *hostēre*, 'to strike, slay'. The etymol. of the words is very doubtful, as is likewise the possible relation of either of them to *hostis*, 'enemy', q.v. under **host (I.)**. (cap., chiefly R.C. Ch.) Consecrated bread or wafer, offered in sacrifice as the body of Christ in the celebration of the Eucharist.

hostage, n. [1. hóstij; 2. hɔ́stidž]. M.E., O. Fr. *hostāge* (Mod. Fr. *otage*); cp. O. Provenç. *ostatge*, Ital. *ostaggio*, perh. due to confusion between (1) Med. Lat. **hospitāticum*, 'that which pertains to reception of guests' (see **host (II.)** & **-age**), and (2) Med. Lat. **obsidāticum*, fr. L. Lat. *obsidāt-us*, 'hostageship', fr. Lat. *obsid-*, stem of *obses*, 'hostage', wh. is fr. *ob*, 'at', & *sedēre* (see **sit**) & *-ātus*, suff. forming abstract n., & **-ic**. **a** Person belonging to enemy state or party, handed over after conclusion of hostilities as pledge for observance of terms, or seized and kept during hostilities to induce compliance with demands; **b** (fig.) pledge, security. Phr. *hostages to Fortune*, wife and children (Bacon).

hostel, n. [1. hóstel; 2. hɔ́stel]. M.E., fr. O. Fr., fr. L. Lat. *hospitāle*. See **hospital**, & cp. **hotel**. **a** (archaic) Inn; **b** (i.) house for the board and lodging of students, workers, or young people, esp. one conducted on a non-commercial, philanthropic basis: *a Y.M.C.A. hostel*; (ii.) residential hall at university.

hosteler, n. [1. hósteler; 2. hɔ́stilə]. Prec. & **-er**. Student in a hostel.

hostelry, n. [1. hóstelri; 2. hɔ́stəlri]. M.E., O. Fr. *hostellerie*. **hostel** & **-ry**. Inn, hotel.

hostess, n. [1. hṓstes; 2. hóustis]. M.E., O. Fr. *hostesse*. **host (II.)** & **-ess**. **a** Female host or entertainer of guests; wife of host; **b** female innkeeper.

hostile, adj. [1. hóstīl; 2. hɔ́stail]. Fr., fr. Lat. *hostīlis*, fr. *hostis*, 'enemy', see **host (I.)**, & **-ile**. **a** Pertaining to an enemy, consisting of enemies; enemy: *a hostile army, country*; **b** behaving or feeling as an enemy; unfriendly, inimical, adverse; indicating or expressing ill will or opposition: *a hostile crowd, demonstration, witness*; *a man hostile to reform*, opposed to reform.

hostilely, adv. Prec. & **-ly**. In a hostile manner.

hostility, n. [1. hostíliti; 2. hɔstíliti]. Fr. *hostilité*, fr. Lat. *hostīlitāt-(em)*. See **hostile** & **-ity**. **1.** Feeling of enmity, hatred, antagonism; ill will: *I have no hostility towards him.* **2. a** Expression, by acts, of enmity and ill will; active opposition; attack, hostile act; **b** specif. in pl., state of war between states or parties: *to open, suspend, hostilities.*

hostler, n. Same as **ostler**.

host-plant, n. (bot.) Plant on which parasite or commensal depends for existence.

hot (I.), adj. [1. hot; 2. hɔt]. O.E. *hāt*, M.E. *hāt, hoot*, w. shortening of the vowel in Late M.E. or Early Mod. Engl.; Common Gmc.; O.S. *hēt*, O.H.G. *heiz*, Mod. Germ. *heiss*, O.N. *heit-r*, cp. Goth. *heitō*, 'fever'; cogn. w. Lith. *kaitra*, 'heat'. See also **heat** & **ceiling**. **1. a** Having sensible degree of heat; contrasted with *cold*; **b** striking very warm to the touch, by reason of possessing considerably higher temperature than that of the body: *a hot day, climate*; *hot water*; *running makes me hot*; Phrs. *hot air*, (colloq.) useless or meaningless talk; *hot and hot*, served straight from the cooking as required; *to drop something like a hot potato, chestnut*, (colloq.) to abandon it precipitately; *to get into hot water*, (colloq.) trouble or quarrel, esp. trouble &c. caused by one's own imprudence; *to make a place, the place is getting, too hot to hold one*, unpleasant on account of hostility, opposition &c., which one has aroused; **c** specif. (of food) freshly cooked and retaining heat from fire that has cooked it: *hot meat, a hot joint*; *to eat a joint hot*; *to keep a helping hot for one*; **d** (of colours) too intense, esp. of yellows and reds; conveying impression of heat. **2.** Producing a sensation of burning in tongue and throat: *a hot curry*; *cayenne pepper is very hot.* **3.** (of mental state, temperament) Ardent, vehement, eager, intense; intent, impetuous, fiery: *a hot temper*; *hot anger.* Phr. *to get hot* (over an argument), wrought up, excited. **4.** (of action) Strenuous, violent, arduous; carried out with vigour, intensity &c.: *a hot battle, fight, contest*; *a hot pursuit*; *a hot run* (with hounds). Phr. *a hot place in the battle*, one where fighting is intense. **5. a** Intent on doing something, or attaining an object; keen, eager for: *hot on playing cricket*; **b** approaching attainment of purpose, nearing one's goal: *hot on the track of.* Phrs. *you are getting hot*, you have nearly guessed right, have got close to where something is hidden &c.; *a hot scent*, thick, close to quarry or other object of pursuit (lit. and fig.). **6.** Inflamed with sexual desire; appetent.

hot (II.), adv. O.E. *hāte*, M.E. *hoote*. See prec. In a hot manner; hotly: *the sun shone hot on the head.* Phrs. *to blow hot and cold*, to waver in opinions, shilly-shally; to offer alternate support and opposition; *to give it (him) hot*, (colloq.) to rebuke or scold severely.

hotbed, n. [1. hótbed; 2. hɔ́tbed]. **a** Bed of earth with thick underlying mass of fermenting manure, used for forcing seeds and plants; **b** (fig.) place, conditions, fostering and promoting development of specified evil: *slums are hotbeds of disease and vice.*

hot-blooded, adj. Having hot blood; ardent, passionate.

hot-brained, adj. [1. hót brānd; 2. hɔ́t breind]. Having a fervent imagination; hot-headed.

Hotchkiss (gun), n. [1. hóchkis; 2. hɔ́tʃkis]. Named after the inventor, B. B. Hotchkiss (1826–85). Rapid-firing automatic gun, worked by gas escaping from barrel.

hotchpot, n. [1. hóchpot; 2. hɔ́tʃpɔt]. M.E., Fr. *hochepot*, 'hotchpotch', fr. *hacher*, 'to shake, jumble', & **pot (I.)**. **1.** (law) Pooling of property, esp. of parent dying intestate, for equal redistribution. **2.** (rare) Hotchpotch.

hotchpotch, n. [1. hóchpoch; 2. hɔ́tʃpɔtʃ]. Formed fr. prec. w. assimilation of second to first element. **a** Stew or other dish of many different ingredients; kind of mutton broth with vegetables; **b** (fig.) varied mixture, medley.

hot cockles, n. Childish game.

hot coppers, n. (vulg. slang) Burning sensation in mouth following excessive drinking.

hotel, n. [1. (h)ōtél; 2. (h)outél]. Fr. *hôtel*, variant of **hostel**. See also **hospital**. Inn, esp. large, modern, or superior inn.

hotel-keeper, n. Keeper, proprietor, of hotel.

hotfoot, adv. [1. hótfoot; 2. hɔ́tfut]. **hot (I.)** & **foot (I.)**. (archaic) In hot haste.

hothead, n. [1. hót-hed; 2. hɔ́thɛd]. **hot (I.)** & **head (I.)**. Hot-headed, rash, impetuous, headstrong person.

hot-headed, adj. Prec. & **-ed**. Impetuous, rash, headstrong.

hothouse, n. [1. hót-house; 2. hɔ́thaus]. **1.** a Conservatory, glass-house, artificially heated for growing plants belonging to warmer climate; **b** (fig.) (i.) conditions of life which are over-luxurious and soft; (ii.) unhealthily stimulating moral or intellectual atmosphere. **2.** Hot drying chamber, as for pottery.

hotly, adv. [1. hótli; 2. hɔ́tli]. **hot (I.)** & **-ly**. In a hot manner, with heat; in various senses of hot.

hotness, n. [1. hótnes; 2. hɔ́tnis]. **hot (I.)** & **-ness**. Quality of being hot; heat.

hotpot, n. [1. hótpot; 2. hɔ́tpɔt]. **hot (I.)** & **pot (I.)**. Meat baked in a pot with potatoes.

hot-press, n. & vb. trans. **1.** n. Machine for glossing paper or linen by pressing it with hot plates. **2.** vb. trans. To treat with a hot press.

hot-short, adj. (metal.) Brittle when heated.

hotspur, n. & adj. [1. hótspër; 2. hɔ́tspʌ], fr. Shakespeare's character. **1.** n. Impetuous, headstrong person. **2.** adj. Impetuous, headstrong.

Hottentot, n. & adj. [1. hótntot; 2. hɔ́tntɔt]. Du., prob. for *hot en tot*, '"hot" and "tot"', such sounds being frequent in the language. **1.** n. a Member of a negroid S. African race; **b** language of this race; **c** (fig.) brutish, uncultivated person. **2.** adj. Pertaining to the Hottentots; *Hottentot bread*, elephant's-foot or its edible root; *Hottentot cherry*, Cape shrub with edible fruit.

houdah, n. See **howdah**.

houdan, n. [1. hóodan; 2. húdən]. Name of town in France. A breed of domestic poultry.

hough (I.), n. [1. hok; 2. hɔk]. O.E. *hōh*, *hō*, 'heel', M.E. *hōh* (pl. *hōȝes*); O.N. *hā-(sinn)*; Gmc. type **haŋχaz*. The pronunciation is affected by **hock (I.)**. See also **heel**, **coccyx**. a Middle joint in hind-leg of horse or other quadruped, between knee and fetlock, corresponding to human ankle; **b** in man, back of knee.

hough (II.), vb. trans. M.E. *hou(g)hen*; fr. prec. To hock, hamstring.

hougher, n. [1. hóker; 2. hɔ́kə]. Prec. & **-er**. Person who houghs or hocks cattle.

hound (I.), n. [1. hound; 2. haund]. O.E. *hund*, M.E. *h(o)und*, Common Gmc.; O.S., O. Fris., Germ., Swed., Dan. *hund*, Du. *hond*, O.H.G. *hunt*, Goth. *hund-s*, O.N. *hund-r*. Aryan type **k̑wn̥-tós*, as Armen. *skund*, 'puppy', extended fr. Aryan base **k̑wn̥-*; whence also Scrt. *śván-*, O. Pers. *spa-* in adj. *spa-ka*, Russ. *su-ka*, 'bitch', Lith. *szun-*, Gk. *kun-* (nom. *kúōn*), Lat. *canis*, Ir., Gael. *cu*, W. *ci*. See **canine**, **cynic**. **1.** a (archaic or liter.) Dog, in general; **b** hunting dog, chiefly in composition, as *basset-*, *blood-*, *boar-*, *deer-*, *grey-*, *otter-*, *wolf-hound*; **c** specif., dog that hunts by scent in pack, usually, where not specified, a foxhound, staghound, beagle, or harrier; *the hounds*, pack of hounds; *to follow (the) hounds*, *ride to hounds*, to hunt with a pack; *Master of (Fox) Hounds* (M.F.H.), master of a hunt. **2.** One of the pursuers in the game of hare and hounds or paper-chase. **3.** Applied as term of abuse to male human beings; a mean, contemptible, cowardly, insolent blackguard.

hound (II.), vb. trans., fr. prec. **1.** a (rare) To pursue, hunt, with or as with hounds; generally **b** (fig.) to pursue (person) relentlessly, persecute: *his enemies hounded him to death.* **2.** (fig.) To set on, incite, excite, goad on: *to hound on the rabble.*

hound (III.), n. M.E. *hūn*, fr. O.N. *hūn-n*, M. Du. *hūn*, all in sense **1.** (usually in pl.) **1.** (naut.) Projection at mast-head to support trestle-trees, shrouds &c. **2.** Side bar in vehicle, increasing rigidity of body.

houndfish, n. [1. hóundfish; 2. háundfiʃ]. M.E. *houndfisch*. **hound (I.)** & **fish**. One of several small sharks; dogfish.

hound's-tongue, n. O.E. *hundes tunge*, cp. O.H.G. *huntes-zunga*; *hound's*, possess. of **hound (I.)**, & **tongue**. British herb, of borage family, with tongue-shaped leaves and small reddish flowers.

hour, n. [1. our; 2. auə]. M.E., A.-Fr. *houre*, fr. O. Fr. *hore*, *hure* (Mod. Fr. *heure*), fr. Lat. *hōra*, fr. Gk. *hṓra* for **jōra*, 'season, hour', cp. *hôros*, 'season, year', cogn. w. O. Pers. *yāre*, 'year', O. Slav. *jare*, 'spring', Lat. *hōrnus* for **ho-jōr-inos*, 'belonging to this year'; cogn. w. **year**. **1.** Division of time, forming 24th part of a day and night; 60 minutes; formerly variable, one 12th part of time between sunrise and sunset, or sunset and sunrise. Phr. *the eleventh hour*, latest possible moment for doing anything; *the small hours*, the first few hours after midnight. **2.** a Brief season, moment, occasion; time destined for some specific event; opportunity, juncture: *the hour of temptation, of danger*; Phrs. *in a good, evil, hour*, (orig. astrol.) fortunately, unfortunately; *the hour and the man*, crisis and the man to deal with it; *his hour has come, struck*, (i.) the time for (his) death; (more rarely) (ii.) the great occasion or crisis in (his) life; *the question of the hour*, topic which occupies general attention, excites interest &c., at a given moment; **b** indefinite period of time: *boyhood's hours*; *the happiest hours of one's life.* **3.** a Point or period of time expressed in hours and minutes: *the hour is 2.30, is late*; *the clock strikes the hour*; *at an early hour*; **b** (pl.) fixed or appointed periods in day or night: *surgery hours*; *the office hours are 10-5*; Phrs. *after hours*, after the regular time of work; time when shopkeepers no longer serve customers &c.; *to keep good, late, regular, hours*, to rise and go to bed early, late &c.; **c** (pl., R.C. Ch.) seven fixed periods in day, called *canonical hours*, appointed for prayer in monasteries, convents &c.; **d** the prayers recited on these occasions: *a book of hours.* **4.** (pl., cap., class. mythol., Lat. *Horae*) Personifications of the hours; goddesses presiding over them. **5.** a Distance which takes an hour to travel: *the town is an hour from here*; **b** period of time spent in performing some action: *an hour's work, reading, play* &c. **6.** (astron.) 15° of longitude.

hour-angle, n. (astron.) Angle between heavenly body and meridian.

hour-circle, n. (astron.) a One of twelve great circles passing through poles of celestial sphere, dividing it into hours; **b** graduated circle attached to equatorial telescope or globe, indicating hours.

hour-glass, n. Sand-glass which runs out in one hour.

hour-hand, n. Hand or index on clock or watch which indicates the hours; small hand.

houri, n. [1. hoori; 2. húəri]. Fr., fr. Pers. *ḥūrī*, fr. Arab. *ḥūriya*, fr. *ḥūr*, fem. pl. of *ahwar*, 'having eyes like a gazelle, beautiful black eyes'. a Nymph in the Mohammedan Paradise; **b** (fig.) seductive woman.

hourly, adj. & adv. [1. óurli; 2. áuəli]. **hour** & **-ly**. **1.** adj. a Occurring, performed, every hour and at intervals of an hour: *hourly chimes*; *an hourly dose of medicine*, *service of trains* &c.; **b** occupying, accomplished in the course of, an hour: *the hourly outflow of water*; **c** continuing from hour to hour; continual, frequent: *in hourly dread of death.* **2.** adv. a At intervals of an hour, once an hour: *to be taken hourly*; **b** hour by hour, at any hour: *to expect the end hourly.*

house (I.), n. [1. hous; 2. haus]. O.E. *hūs*, M.E. *hūs*, *hous*; in all Gmc. languages. Gmc. **hūs-*, Aryan **kūs-*, prob. for earlier **kudh-(s)to-*, fr. base **keudh-*, **kudh-* &c., 'to hide, protect, shelter' &c. See further on this base under **hide (III.)**, **hoard**, **hud**. **1.** Structure, of various materials, having walls, roof, door, and usually windows to give light and air, intended as a temporary shelter or permanent dwelling for human beings; also applied (esp. in certain compounds, *cow-house* &c.) to a shelter for animals: *the most primitive races usually construct some kind of houses, if only of mud and straw, or even of frozen snow.* Phr. *as safe as a house*, perfectly secure. **2.** Building designed and used, as a (i.) a human habitation: *a house in town, in the country*; *houses are springing up all over the most beautiful parts of Surrey*; specif. (ii.) boarding-house (q.v.) at public school; Phrs. *house of God*, a church; *to keep the house*, stay at home, stay indoors; *house of call*, (i.) one where carriers call for orders and parcels; (ii.) house, esp. an inn, where a journey is temporarily broken; *disorderly house*, *house of ill-fame*, brothel; **b** an inn, public-house; Phr. *(to take something) for the good of the house*, so as to give a profit to the landlord; **c** theatre, place of entertainment: *every word was heard in all parts of the house.* Phrs. *a full, empty, house*, crowded, empty, theatre; *a good house*, large audience; *to bring down the house*, excite general applause among an audience; to cause sudden burst of amusement or approval in private company. **3.** A house thought of as the scene and centre of domestic life; home, family abode, household: *to receive a stranger into one's house*; *a noisy, cheerful house*; *meals are always late in our house*; *to leave one's father's house.* Phrs. *to keep house*, (i.) to have a permanent abode; (ii.) to superintend, manage, affairs of a household; *to keep house with*, live, reside, in same house and share expenses &c.; *keep a good house*, provide good fare and high standard of comfort in one's household; *to set one's house in order*, (fig.) get one's affairs straight, restore order in place of muddle; *an Englishman's house is his castle*, is sacred, immune, from entry; domestic privacy must be respected. **4.** Family, all the descendants of a common ancestor; lineage, stock: *to spring from an ancient, illustrious, house*; *the king perished with all his house.* **5.** a Building, with hall, used for deliberations of an assembly of certain public bodies: *the Houses of Parliament stand upon the banks of the Thames at Westminster*; **b** the members, collectively, who form national or other deliberative and legislative bodies: *a member of the House of Lords, Commons*; *the Ancient House of Convocation* (Oxford), the body of Masters of Arts whose names are on the books; *the House rose at 9 o'clock*; *the House was greatly excited by the news.* **6.** The members of a college or hall at Oxford or Cambridge, being an independent, self-governing corporation: *the Vice-Chancellor of Oxford is always a Head of a House.* **7.** A mercantile association, business firm: *an ancient trading house in the city.* **8.** *The House*, variously applied, a any specific legislative body while in session, e.g. the House of Lords, Commons; House of Convocation &c.; Phr. *to enter the House*, become a Member of Parliament;

b Christ Church, Oxford; **c** the London Stock Exchange; **d** (popular slang) the workhouse.

house (II.), vb. trans. & intrans. [1. houz; 2. hauz]. O.E. *hūsian,* 'take into a house', fr. *hūs.* See prec. **A.** trans. **1. a** To provide dwelling-place(s), house(s), for: *to house a large population*; **b** to provide house-room for, be large enough to include: *this cottage will never house us all*; **c** to receive into a house, give shelter to; to harbour: *I shall be happy to house you for a night or two*; **d** to store, place, lodge, bestow in shelter and custody: *I must find some place where I can house my books.* **2.** To insert in a housing, i.e. put part of a piece of timber in a cavity cut in another piece to receive it. **B.** intrans. To lodge, dwell, keep house: *you and I may as well house together.*

house-agent, n. Person who negotiates sale or lease of houses.

house-boat, n. Barge with superstructure, moored in river or lake, used as summer residence.

housebote, n. [1. hóusbōt; 2. háusbout]. **house (I.)** & O.E. *bōt,* 'advantage, profit, recompense'. See **boot (III.)** & **booty.** Wood to which tenant is entitled for repairs to house.

housebreaker, n. [1. hóusbrāker; 2. háusbreikə]. **1.** Person who feloniously breaks into a house; a burglar. **2.** Person whose trade is to pull down buildings.

housebreaking, n. [1. hóusbrāking; 2. háusbreikiŋ]. Action of a housebreaker (in both senses).

housecarl, n. [1. hóuskarl; 2. háuskāl]. O.E. *hūscarl,* fr. O.N. *hūskarl,* fr. *hūs,* **house,** & *karl,* 'man' (see **churl**). (hist.) Member of body-guard of a king or nobleman in late Anglo-Saxon times, esp. among the Danes.

house-cat, n. Cat kept in a house; as distinct from stable-cat.

house-dog, n. Dog kept in, or to protect, a house.

houseflag, n. [1. hóusflag; 2. háusflæg]. Ship's flag indicating owner or line to which it belongs.

house-fly, n. Common fly, *Musca domestica,* infesting houses.

houseful, n. [1. hóusfool; 2. háusful]. **house (I.)** & **-ful.** As much or as many as a house will hold or accommodate: *a houseful of furniture, of guests.*

household, n. [1. hóus-(h)ōld; 2. háus-(h)ould]. M.E. *houshold.* **house (I.)** & **hold.** Cp. Germ. *haushalt.* **1. a** (coll.) Persons living together in one house; family and servants; domestic establishment; **b** specif. (with cap.) *the Household,* that of the Sovereign; *the Royal Household*; *Gentlemen of the Household.* **2.** (fig.) Members of same religion, supporters of same cause: *the household of the faith.* **3.** (used attributively) Pertaining to, used in, a household: *household accounts, bread.* Phrs. *Household Brigade,* brigade of guards having duty of protecting person of British sovereign; so *Household cavalry, troops*; *household franchise, suffrage,* that possessed by a person as householder; *household gods,* (Rom. antiq.) lesser deities presiding over a household, or their images; Lares and Penates; hence (fig.) valued family possessions; *household word,* word or phrase in familiar, everyday use: *your name is a household word with us.*

householder, n. [1. hóus-hōlder; 2. háushouldə]. M.E. *housholdere.* **house** & **holder.** Head of household; occupier of tenement.

housekeeper, n. [1. hóuskēper; 2. háuskīpə]. Woman who manages or keeps house in order, and provides for household; specif. **a** mistress of house: (usually with qualifying adj.) *a thrifty, bad, housekeeper*; **b** woman hired to manage a house; head female servant.

housekeeping, n. [1. hóuskēping; 2. háuskipiŋ]. Act, operation, art, of managing household business; domestic economy.

housel (I.), n. [1. hóuzl; 2. háuzl]. O.E. *hūsel, hūsl,* 'the Eucharist', orig. 'the holy thing, service' &c., M.E. *hūsel*; Goth. *hunsl,* 'sacrifice', O.N. *hūsl*; Gmc. type **huns-l-an-,* cogn. w. O. Slav. *svętu* (for **svent-*), Lith. *szwentas,* 'holy'. (archaic) Consecrated elements of the Eucharist; administration of the same.

housel (II.), vb. trans. O.E. *hūslian,* M.E. *hūslen,* Goth. *hunsljan,* O.N. *hūsla.* See prec. (obs. or archaic) To administer the Eucharist to.

houseleek, n. [1. hóuslēk; 2. háuslīk]. M.E. *hūslēk.* **house** & **leek.** Herb, *Sempervivum,* with rosettes of fleshy leaves and pink flowers, growing on old roofs and walls.

houseless, adj. [1. hóusles; 2. háuslis]. **house** & **-less.** Having no house.

housemaid, n. [1. hóusmād; 2. háusmeid]. Female servant who keeps rooms of a house clean, and does other housework.

housemaid's knee, n. Inflammation of sac over knee-cap, due to too much kneeling.

house master, n. Master in charge of a house in a school.

house match, n. Match between houses of a school.

housemate, n. [1. hóusmāt; 2. háusmeit]. One who shares a house with another or others.

house-parlourmaid, n. Housemaid who also does parlourmaid's work.

house party, n. Party of guests entertained for several days in country house.

house-physician, n. Senior physician resident in hospital.

house porter, n. Doorkeeper in house.

house-room, n. **house (I.)** & **room.** Space in a house; capacity of a house for accommodating dwellers.

house sparrow, n. Common sparrow, frequenting neighbourhood of houses.

house-surgeon, n. Senior surgeon resident in hospital.

house-to-house, adj. Carried on, performed, by visiting a number of houses in succession: *a house-to-house canvass, collection, visitation.*

housetop, n. [1. hóustop; 2. háustɔp]. Top, roof, of house. Phr. *to cry, proclaim (something), from the housetop(s),* to publish abroad, give wide publicity to.

house-warming, n. Entertainment given by person or family to celebrate entrance into, taking up residence in, a new home.

housewife, n. [1. hóuswīf, húzif; 2. háuswaif, házif]. M.E. *hūswīf.* **house** & **wife**; cp. **hussy. 1.** Mistress of a house. **2.** (usually pronounced [1. húzif; 2. házif]) Small receptacle for needles, thread, scissors, buttons &c.

housewifely, adj. Prec. & **-ly.** Appropriate to a housewife; domestic; managing well.

housewifery, n. [1. hóuswīfri, húzifri; 2. háuswaifri, házifri]. **housewife** & **-ry.** Business of a housewife; domestic management or economy.

housing (I.), n. [1. hóuzing; 2. háuziŋ]. M.E. *hūsing.* **house (II.)** & **-ing. 1. a** Action of providing with house or houses, with storage; provision of house or shelter; **b** (coll.) accommodation in houses: *it is difficult to provide housing for a rapidly increasing population*; **c** (attrib.) *the housing question,* problem of providing housing. **2.** Cavity, hollow space, notch, cut in timber, into which part of another timber rests or is fitted.

housing (II.), n. Obs. Engl. *house,* n., 'housing', vb., 'to provide with housing', fr. O. Fr. *houce, huche,* Mod. Fr. *housse,* fr. Low Lat. *hūsia, hūcia,* 'mantle, housing', prob. fr. Arab. *ghūshiah, ghushwa,* 'covering, veil', & **-ing.** Prob. confused w. **house (I.).** Cloth covering for horse's body for protection or show; saddle-cloth; (pl.) trappings.

Houyhnhnm, n. [1. hooínm; 2. huínəm]. Invented by Swift to suggest horse's whinny. One of imaginary race of rational, noble horses in Swift's *Gulliver's Travels.*

hovel (I.), n. [1. hóvl; 2. hɔ́vl], formerly [1. húvl; 2. hávl]. M.E. *hovel, hovyl,* of doubtful origin, perh. fr. (1) an A.-Fr. **hovel,* dimin. w. suff. **-el,** fr. O.E. *hof,* 'house, hall', cogn. w. **hover** or (2) A.-Fr. **huvel,* similarly formed fr. O.E. *hūfe,* 'covering for the head', see **hive**; cp. O. Fr. *huvelet,* 'penthouse'. **1.** Hut, shed; cabin or cottage of the meanest sort; a squalid dwelling. **2.** (archit.) Niche for statue. **3.** (pottery) Large brick cone covering kilns for porcelain.

hovel (II.), vb., fr. prec. **1.** To shelter in a hovel. **2.** To make in shape of hovel; to make chimney with covered top.

hoveller, n. [1. hóveler; 2. hɔ́vələ]. Of uncertain origin, dial. also *hobbler, huffler.* **a** Coast boatman who does odd jobs; **b** hoveller's boat.

hover (I.), vb. intrans. [1. hóver; 2. hɔ́və], formerly [1. húver; 2. hávə]. M.E. *hōveren,* 'to hover, linger', freq. w. suff. **-er,** fr. *hōven,* 'to hover, be poised, inhabit, tarry'; cp. M. Du., M.L.G. *hoven*; of uncertain origin; perh. fr. O.E. *hof,* 'house' (see **hovel**), or fr. **hōf,* strong grade of O.E. *hebban* (see **heave**). **a** (of birds and flying insects) To float in the air; to linger, poised aloft, motionless, or slightly moving: *a hawk hovers overhead*; **b** (of persons) to linger, loiter, hang about: *to hover around, about, near one*; **c** (fig.) to remain irresolute; waver: *to hover on the brink of a decision.*

hover (II.), n., fr. prec. Action or state of hovering.

hoverer, n. [1. hóverer; 2. hɔ́vərə]. **hover** & **-er.** Person or thing that hovers.

hovering (I.), n. [1. hóvering; 2. hɔ́vəriŋ]. **hover (I.)** & **-ing.** Action of bird or person that hovers.

hovering (II.), adj., fr. Pres. Part. of **hover (I.).** In state, position, of one that hovers: *hovering butterflies.*

hoveringly, adv. Prec. & **-ly.** With a hovering motion.

how, adv. & n. [1. hou; 2. hau]. O.E., M.E. *hū, hwū,* for **hwō,* fr. Gmc. interrog. base **hwa-,* Aryan **kʷo-*; cp. O. Fris. *hū, hō,* O.S. *hwo,* Du. *hoe,* O.H.G. *hweo, wio,* Mod. Germ. *wie,* Goth. *hwai-wa*; cogn. w. Lith. *kaī,* 'how', Lat. *ceu* for **ce-ve,* 'as, like as'; fr. base **kʷo-* & enclitic particle **wē,* 'or, like as', Scrt. *vā,* 'or, as', Gk. *ēé* for **ē-wè,* 'or', *ēú-(te),* 'as', Lat. *-ve,* 'or'. **A.** adv. **1.** (interrog.) **a** In what manner, way, condition: *how shall I dress?*; *how is the country looking?*; by what name: *how is he called?*; at what price: *how is the franc today?*; Phrs. *how do you do?,* (colloq.) *how-d'y'-do?,* what is the state of your health? (conventional greeting); *how's that?,* (cricket &c.) appeal to umpire to decide whether player is out; **b** by what means: *how did he escape?*; *how on earth (the deuce &c.) do you do it?*; *how dare you?*; *how is it (comes it) that you are here?* **2.** (rel.) **a** In what manner, way, condition: *he knows how to behave*; *to see how matters stand*; *I understood how you feel about it*; by what name: *I don't know how to call him*; at what price: *find out how the exchange is*; **b** by what means: *I don't know how to account for it, to bear it*; Phr. *all you know how,* (vulg. or slang) to the utmost of your power; **c** (in rel. clause) that: *I told him how I had read in the papers*; (obs. Bib.) *how that.* **3.** (interrog. or rel. with adj. or adv.) To what extent, amount, or degree: *how old is he?*; *I wonder how old he is*; *how much time*; *how many people*; *how fast are we going?*; *how far is it?*; (obs.) how ever: '*I never yet saw man how wise . . . but*' (Shakespeare). **4.** (in exclamatory or interjectional sentences or phrases, expressing wonder, surprise, or other feeling, qualifying adj., adv., or vb.) To what an extent, amount, or degree: *how absurd!*; *how kind of you!*; *how like him!*; *how far away!*; *how well you look!*; *how you talk!* **B.** n. Manner, means: *the how and the why of it.*

howbeit, conj. [1. houbḗit; 2. haubī́it]. **how** & **be,** subj., & **it.** (archaic) However it may be, notwithstanding, yet, nevertheless.

howdah, houdah, n. [1. hóuda; 2. háudə]. Hind., Pers. *haudah*, fr. Arab. *haudaj*, 'litter'. Structure, sometimes having a canopy, containing seats for several persons fastened with girths to an elephant's back.

how-d'ye-do, n. [1. hóu de dōō; 2. háu di dú]. *How do you do?* See **how**. (colloq.) Awkward, troublesome, situation; dilemma: *a nice, a pretty, how-d'ye-do.*

however, adv. & conj. [1. houéver; 2. hauévə]. **how** & **ever**. **1.** adv. **a** In whatever manner, by whatever means: *however you do it, the result is the same*; **b** to whatever extent or degree: *however fast he ran*; *his appeals, however just, were disregarded*; **c** (obs.) although: '*Howe'er thou art a fiend*' (Shakespeare). **2.** conj. Nevertheless, still, though, all the same: *I must hurry off now—however, we shall meet tonight*; *I hate concerts—I shall go to this one, however.*

howitzer, n. [1. hóuitser; 2. háuitsə]. Appears to be through corrupt Germ. forms fr. Czech *houfnice*, 'a catapult'. Kind of short cannon used for high angle fire at short range, esp. for shelling trenches.

howl (I.), vb. intrans. & trans. [1. houl; 2. haul]. M.E. *houlen*, cp. Du. *huilen*, O.H.G. *hiuwilōn*, M.H.G. *hiulen*, Mod. Germ. *heulen*, O.N. *ȳla*; imitative, cp. Gk. *huláein*, 'to bark as dog; howl', Lat. *ululāre*, 'to howl', *ulula*, 'screech-owl'. See also **owl, ululation**. **1.** intrans. **a** To utter loud, protracted, dismal cry, as wolf or dog, or as a person expressing pain, rage, complaint or derision; to wail, yell; **b** to laugh loud and heartily; also, *howl with laughter*; **c** (of inanimate things) to emit wailing sound as of howling animal: *the wind howls through the forest*; also of faulty wireless transmission or reception due to oscillation. **2.** trans. **a** To utter with howls: *to howl defiance*; **b** *to howl down*, to drown speech, remarks of (person) with cries of derision or indignation.

howl (II.), n., fr. prec. Sound made by animal or person that howls; **a** protracted, dismal cry of pain, fear, rage &c.; **b** loud burst of laughter; also *howls of laughter, mirth, merriment* &c.

howler, n. [1. hóuler; 2. háulə]. **howl** (I.) & **-er**. **1.** Animal, person, or thing that howls; specif. **a** professional wailer for the dead; **b** howling monkey. **2.** (colloq. or slang) Egregious blunder, esp. in an examination.

howlet, n. [1. hóulet; 2. háulit]. Variant of **owlet**, perh. affected by Fr. *hulotte*, 'owlet'.

howling, adj. [1. hóuling; 2. háuliŋ], fr. Pres. Part. of **howl** (I.). **1.** Producing, uttering, prone to utter, howls: *a howling dog*; *a howling wind*; *a howling baby*; *howling dervish*, one expressing religious madness in this way; *howling monkey*, one of a group of Central and S. American monkeys that howl; *howling wilderness*, one full of wild beasts. **2.** (slang) Immense, tremendous: *a howling success*; *a howling swell.*

howsoever, adv. [1. hòusoéver; 2. hàusouévə]. **how** & **so** & **ever**. However (adv.), in whatsoever manner or degree.

hoy (I.), n. [1. hoi; 2. hɔi]. M.E. *hoye*, fr. M. Du. *hoei*, also *heu, heude*, cp. Flem. *hui*, of uncertain origin. Small coasting vessel or barge, usually sloop-rigged.

hoy (II.), interj. & n. Natural sound of shout; cp. Du., Dan. *hui*. Cp. **ahoy**. Call to attract attention of ship, or to stop cattle.

hoya, n. [1. hóia; 2. hɔ́iə], fr. T. Hoy, horticulturist. The wax-flower or wax-plant.

hoyden, n. [1. hóid(e)n; 2. hɔ́id(ə)n]. In Early Mod. Engl. usually applied to male sex; origin quite uncertain. Ungainly, rough, undisciplined, romping girl; a tomboy.

hoydenish, adj. [1. hóidenish; 2. hɔ́idəniʃ]. Prec. & **-ish**. Resembling a hoyden.

hub, n. [1. hub; 2. hab]. Prob. variant of **hob**. **1. a** Projecting centre of wheel; nave; **b** (fig.) centre of activity or importance: *a hub of industry*; Phr. *hub of the universe*, a place considered by the inhabitants as of world-wide importance. **2.** Mark at which quoits are aimed; hob.

hubble-bubble, n. [1. húbl bubl; 2. hábl babl]. Imitative word; formed w. **bubble** as a basis. **a** Kind of hookah, form of pipe used in India, in smoking which the smoke is drawn through water, causing a bubbling noise; **b** bubbling noise; confused chatter.

hubbub, n. [1. húbub; 2. hábab]. Cp. now obs. *hubbuboo, hubbaboo*, in Spenser ('State of Ireland') *hubbabowe*, prob. representing some Ir. word or phrase; cp. Gael. *ububu*, exclamation of contempt, Ir. *abu*, a war-cry. Confused noise, as of many voices; uproar, tumult.

hubristic, adj. [1. hūbrístik; 2. hjūbrístik], fr. Gk. *hubristikós*, 'insolent; wantonly, overweeningly proud', fr. *húbris*, 'violent, overweening, pride and insolence'; etymol. doubtful. Overweeningly proud and insolent; arrogant, overbearing.

huckaback, n. [1. húkabak; 2. hákəbæk]. Perh. orig. meaning 'pedlar's ware', cp. perh. L.G. *hukkebak*, 'pick-a-back'. The second element may well be *aback*, 'on the back'. First element perh. connected w. **huckster**. Coarse linen or cotton fabric with rough surface, used for towels &c.

huckleberry, n. [1. húklberi; 2. háklbəri, -bəri]. Prob. for *hurtleberry*, dial. form of **whortleberry**. Edible berry or shrub of *Gaylussacia*, N. American plant resembling whortleberry.

huckster (I.), n. [1. húkster; 2. hákstə]. M.E. *hucster, hokester*, fr. M. Du. *heukster*, fr. *heuken*, 'to retail' (cp. M.E. *hucken*, 'to higgle, sell'), prob. orig. 'to carry on bent back', L.G. *huken*, Germ. *hocken*, O.N. *hūka*, 'to crouch, squat, stoop', of uncertain origin, cp. Germ. *hucke*, 'bent back' (see **huckaback**), & **-ster**. See also **hawker** (II.). **a** Retail dealer in small wares; a petty trader; **b** (fig.) person of mean, haggling, mercenary character.

huckster (II.), vb. intrans. See prec. To be a huckster, carry on petty trade; haggle.

hucksteress, huckstress, n. [1. húkstres; 2. hákstris]. **huckster** (I.) & **-ess**. Female huckster.

huckstery, n. [1. húksteri; 2. hákstəri]. M.E. *hoxterie*. **huckster** (I.) & **-y**. Trade, business, methods, of a huckster.

hud, n. [1. hud; 2. had]. Perh. form of *hood*, or fr. base of **hide** (I.), w. shortening. See **husk** (I.). The outer shell or husk of seeds, nuts &c.

huddle (I.), vb. trans. & intrans. [1. húdl; 2. hádl]. Origin doubtful. **1.** trans. **a** To put, throw, drive, squeeze, together in a confused promiscuous crowd or pile: *to huddle clothes into a trunk*; *the sheep were huddled together in a ditch*; **b** to gather, draw, (oneself) together in a heap: *to lie huddled up*; **c** to put on, hastily, carelessly, in a disorderly way: *to huddle on one's clothes*; **d** to do something in a hasty, clumsy, careless way: *to huddle a job through*; *to huddle up a treaty*. **2.** intrans. To crowd, press, together in a mass, heap: *to huddle together for warmth.*

huddle (II.), n., fr. prec. Cluster of objects, closely packed together without plan or arrangement: *a huddle of roofs.*

Hudibrastic, adj. [1. hūdibrástik; 2. hjūdibrǽstik], fr. *Hudibras*, title and hero of mock-heroic satirical poem (1663–78), by Samuel Butler; formed on anal. of *fantastic* &c. Resembling, in the manner of, 'Hudibras'; of the nature of a lampoon, expressing rather coarse satire in rough, cleverly rhymed verses.

hue (I.), n. [1. hū; 2. hjū]. O.E., non-W.S. *hīow, hēow*, W.S. *hīew, hīw*, 'form, kind, appearance; colour, beauty', M.E. *hēou, hew*; cp. Goth. *hiwi*, 'form, appearance'; Swed. *hy*, 'skin, complexion'; cogn. w. Scrt. *chāyā*, 'skin, complexion'. **a** Colour, tint; particular shade or variety of a colour; **b** (fig.) variety of opinion &c.: *Conservative politicians of various hues.*

hue (II.), n. M.E., fr. O. Fr. *hu*, 'cry, shout', cp. *huer*, 'to shout', of imitative origin. Shouting, clamour, of pursuer; now only in *hue and cry*, **a** (hist.) outcry against felon, in which all who heard it were bound to join; **b** (hist.) official proclamation calling for capture of felon &c.; **c** (fig.) popular clamour against unpopular person, fugitive &c.: *to raise a hue and cry.*

hueless, adj. [1. hūles; 2. hjūlis]. **hue** (I.) & **-less**. Colourless.

huer, n. [1. hūer; 2. hjūə], fr. O. Fr. *huer*, 'to cry, shout', see **hue** (II.), & **-er**. (in Cornwall) Man stationed on cliffs to give warning of approach of shoals of pilchards.

huff (I.), vb. trans. & intrans. [1. huf; 2. haf]. In Early Mod. Engl., 'to blow'; imitative. **1.** trans. **a** To behave insolently to, bully, hector; drive by bluster or bullying: *to huff one into silence*; *to huff one out of the room*; **b** to offend, make sullen or petulant: *to be huffed*; **c** (draughts) to remove opponent's piece or man from board as penalty for not taking a piece. **2.** intrans. To fuss, fret, fume, as though offended.

huff (II.), n., fr. prec. **1.** Fit of sulkiness, petulance, or resentment: *to get into a huff.* **2.** (draughts) Action of huffing.

huffily, adv. [1. húfili; 2. háfili]. **huffy** & **-ly**. In a huffy manner.

huffiness, n. [1. húfines; 2. háfinis]. **huffy** & **-ness**. State of being huffy; cross, sulky behaviour of one who has taken offence.

huffish, adj. [1. húfish; 2. háfiʃ]. **huff** (II.) & **-ish**. Inclined to be petulant or sulky.

huffishly, adv. Prec. & **-ly**. In a huffish manner.

huffishness, n. See prec. & **-ness**. Huffish state of mind and behaviour.

huffy, adj. [1. húfi; 2. háfi]. **huff** (II.) & **-y**. **a** In a huff, sulky; **b** liable to be huffy; taking offence easily.

hug (I.), vb. trans. [1. hug; 2. hag]. Origin uncertain; perh. connected w. Icel. *hugga*, 'to soothe, comfort'. **1.** To embrace closely and fondly, clasp tightly in the arms; (of bears) to seize and squeeze with the forelegs. **2.** (fig.) **a** To cling to, cherish, show fondness for; Phrs. *to hug one's chains*, to prefer servitude to freedom; *to hug oneself (on)*, to congratulate oneself, be pleased with oneself; **b** to skirt along by, keep close to; (of ships) *to hug the shore*; (of pedestrians or vehicles) *to hug the side of the road.*

hug (II.), n., fr. prec. **a** Close, affectionate, or amorous embrace; **b** (wrestling) kind of grip: *a Cornish hug.*

huge, adj. [1. hūj; 2. hjūdž]. M.E. *hūge, hōge*, fr. O. Fr. *ahuge, ahoge*, possibly fr. a Gmc. source; cp. Du. *hoog*, O.H.G. *hōh*, **high**. Very great, enormous, gigantic (of size or amount): *a huge animal, building*; *huge profits, delight, enjoyment* &c.

hugely, adv. M.E. *hūgeliche*. Prec. & **-ly**. To a huge extent: *hugely pleased.*

hugeness, n. M.E. *hūgenis*. See prec. & **-ness**. Quality of being huge; vast size.

hugeous, adj. [1. hūjus; 2. hjūdžəs]. **huge** & **-ous**. (obs.) Huge.

hugger-mugger, n., adj., & adv. [1. húger muger; 2. hágə magə]. Origin unknown. **1.** n. **a** (archaic, Spenser), secrecy; **b** muddle, disorder. **2.** adj. Confused, muddled. **3.** adv. Confusedly, in a muddle.

Huguenot, n. [1. hūgenot; 2. hjūgənɔt]. Perh. fr. earlier Fr. *eigenot*, fr. some form of Germ. *eidgenoss*, L.G. *-genoot*, 'confederate'; Germ. *eid*, 'oath,' & *genoss(e)*, 'comrade.' The first syll. perh. influenced by Fr. pers. n. *Hugues*; all more or less speculation. French Protestant of the 16th or 17th cent.

Huguenotism, n. [1. hūgenotizm; 2. hjūgənɔtizəm]. Prec. & **-ism**. Principles of the Huguenots.

hugy, adj. [1. hūji; 2. hjūdži]. (obs. & poet.) Huge.

hulk, n. [1. hulk; 2. halk]. O.E. *hulc*, 'a shed; a lightship', M.E. *hulke*, 'ship'; Du. *hulke*, M.L.G. *holk*, O.H.G. *holcho, holcha*; fr. Med. Lat. *holcas, hulcus*, fr. Gk. *holkás*, 'ship which is towed, trading vessel', fr. **holk-* for **solk-*, strong grade of *hélkein*, 'to drag, tow'; cogn. w. Lat. *sulcus*, 'furrow',

O.E. *sulh*, 'plough'. **a** Heavy, unwieldy ship; **b** old, derelict, dismantled ship; one no longer used for voyages, formerly used as a prison: *condemned to the hulks*; **c** (fig.) big, clumsy, unwieldy person.

hulking, adj. [1. húlking; 2. hálkiŋ]. Dial. *hulk*, 'to act in a clumsy, unwieldy manner'. Prec. & **-ing**. Ungainly, unwieldy, awkward: *a great hulking fellow*.

hull (**I.**), n. [1. hul; 2. hal]. O.E. *hulu*, M.E. *hule, holl, hoole*; cogn. w. Goth. *huljan*, 'to cover'; **hul-* being wk. grade of base seen in O.E. *helan*, 'to conceal, cover'. See **hall, hell, hole**, & **hollow**. Husk, pod, shell, or other covering of fruit, peas, beans or other seeds.

hull (**II.**), vb. trans., fr. prec. To take peas, beans &c. out of the hull; to shell: *to hull beans, peas* &c.

hull (**III.**), n. Prob. special use of **hull** (**I.**); sense perh. derived fr. Du. *hol*, 'ship's hold'. Body of ship or boat; Phr. *hull down*, with the hull below the horizon.

hull (**IV.**), vb. trans., fr. prec. To strike, pierce, hull of (vessel) with projectile.

hullabaloo, n. [1. hùlabalōō; 2. hàləbəlū́]. Imitative; expanded fr. **hullo**. Uproar, hubbub, outcry; confused sound of noisy voices.

hulled, adj. [1. huld; 2. hald]. **hull** (**II.**) & **-ed**. (of grain &c.) Deprived of the hulls or integument: *hulled maize, rice* &c.

huller, n. [1. húler; 2. hálə]. **hull** (**II.**) & **-er**. Machine for hulling grain.

hullo, interj. [1. huló; 2. halóu]. Variant of **hollo, hallo**. Exclamation calling attention or expressing surprise.

hum (**I.**), vb. intrans. & trans. [1. hum; 2. ham]. M.E. *hummen*, imitative, cp. Germ. *hummen*. Cp. **hem** (**III.**) & **humble-bee**. **A.** intrans. **1. a** To utter a musical sound or series of sounds with the lips closed, the vocal chords vibrating and the breath passing through the nose; **b** to make inarticulate sound, as *h'm*, indicating hesitation or embarrassment; Phr. *to hum and haw* (i.) to make such sounds through embarrassment when speaking; (ii.) (fig.) to hesitate, to shilly-shally, be unable to make up one's mind; **c** to produce a continuous buzzing, droning, murmuring sound, such as a bee, a spinning-top, a rapidly revolving piece of machinery &c. Phr. *hum along*, to move along rapidly, esp. in a vehicle propelled by machinery. **2.** (fig., colloq.) Of business, affairs &c., to be in a state of lively activity. Phr. *to make things hum*, stimulate activity. **B.** trans. To sing with closed mouth: *to hum a tune*.

hum (**II.**), n., fr. prec. **1. a** Act of humming with the voice; **b** sound thus produced. **2.** Continuous buzzing of bees &c., murmuring sound of busy machinery &c. **3.** Muffled sound of distant movements, voices, and other activities of crowds of human beings: *the hum of conversation, of traffic* &c. **4.** (fig.) Human activity, business, busy life of mankind: '*the busy hum of men*' (Milton, Il Pens. 118).

hum (**III.**), interj. [1. mm; 2. m̩m]. Attempted graphic representation of inarticulate sound made by one who hesitates in reply, queries what has been said, is dubious or disapproving.

hum (**IV.**), n. Short for **humbug**. (rare) A hoax, take-in, swindle.

human, adj. [1. hū́man; 2. hjū́mən]. Early Mod. Engl. *hūmaine*, fr. Fr. *humain*, fr. Lat. *hūmān-(us)*, 'human, humane', perh. for **humn-ānus*, fr. *homin-*, stem of *homo*, 'man, human being'. See **homage** & **-an** & cp. **humus**. **1. a** Pertaining to mankind, to any being of the race of men; essentially associated with man; esp. contrasted (i.) with *divine*, and (ii.) with *animal*; having the bodily, moral, and intellectual qualities peculiar to man: *a human being, head, voice*; *human nature*; *his form and face seemed scarcely human*; **b** consisting of a human being or beings: *the human race*; *a human sacrifice*. **2.** Having, animated by, expressing, in a marked degree, the characteristic frailties, sympathies, passions, or other qualities of mankind: *a schoolmaster, but human enough nevertheless*; *a very human error*; *he must be more or less than human not to be moved by such a story*.

humane, adj. [1. hūmā́n; 2. hjuméin]. A variant due to different accentuation (Early Mod. Engl. *humáine*) of prec. Often not distinguished in spelling fr. prec. in 16th cent.; perh. direct fr. Lat. *hūmānus*. **1.** Exhibiting the finest qualities of human nature; compassionate, merciful, tender, sympathetic: *a man of humane character*. **2.** Concerned with man and the products of his genius; tending to refine or ennoble; promoting humanism; polite, elegant: *humane learning, studies, letters* &c.

humanely, adv. Prec. & **-ly**. In a humane manner, benevolently.

humaneness, n. See prec. & **-ness**. Quality of being humane.

humanism, n. [1. hū́manizm; 2. hjū́mənizəm]. **human** & **-ism**. Name given to a phase of the intellectual movement which characterizes the transition from the mediaeval to the modern period, that is, of the Renaissance, and which found its ideal system of culture in a return to the study of the classical poets and philosophers; an attitude of mind, system of thought, which concentrates specially upon human interests and the mind of man, rather than upon the external world of nature, or upon religious ideals.

humanist, n. [1. hū́manist; 2. hjū́mənist]. Fr. *humaniste*. **human** & **-ist**. A student of humanism; an adherent of the philosophical and ethical doctrines of humanism; specif., one of the Renaissance scholars who propounded these doctrines.

humanistic, adj. [1. hùmanístik; 2. hjùmənístik]. Prec. & **-ic**. Pertaining to humanism.

humanitarian, adj. & n. [1. hūmanitā́rian; 2. hjūmænitéəriən]. **humanity** & **-arian**. **1.** adj. Pertaining to humanitarianism or humanitarians; having, expressing, devotion to humanity. **2.** n. Adherent or exponent of humanitarianism (in any sense); specif. **a** one who seeks to promote the welfare of humanity, chiefly by attempting to reduce pain and suffering, these being regarded as the chief evils; one who therefore disapproves of severe punishments, esp. such as inflict bodily pain, even upon the most degraded criminals; **b** heretic who emphasizes the human nature of Christ and questions or denies His Divine nature.

humanitarianism, n. [1. hūmànitā́rianizm; 2. hjūmæ̀nitéəriənizəm]. Prec. & **-ism**. **1.** System of thought which holds that pain and suffering are the worst ills incidental to humanity, and which seeks to raise and improve condition of mankind chiefly by the elimination of these. **2.** Form of Unitarianism which lays stress on the perfection of Christ's human character and denies His Divine nature.

humanity, n. [1. hūmániti; 2. hjumǽniti]. M.E. *humanitē*, fr. Fr. *humanité*, fr. Lat. *hūmānitāt-(em)*, 'human nature, mankind, humane conduct, liberal education'. **human** & **-ity**. **1.** Quality or condition of being a human being; human nature: *to be conscious of one's humanity*. **2.** Those possessing human nature; the human race, mankind: *a crime against humanity*; *a friend of humanity*. **3. a** Quality of being humane; benevolence, kindness of heart; sensibility, tenderness of character: *it is an act of humanity to help the oppressed*; **b** exhibition of humane qualities; humane act: *I should have died but for his humanity towards me on that occasion*. **4. a** (Scots universities) *Chair, Professor, of Humanity*, Latin language and literature; **b** *the Humanities*, classical or literary studies.

humanization, n. [1. hùmanīzā́shun; 2. hjùmənaizéiʃən]. Next word & **-ation**. Action of humanizing; state of being humanized.

humanize, vb. trans. & intrans. [1. hū́manīz; 2. hjū́mənaiz]. **human** & **-ize**. **A.** trans. **1.** To make human, give human nature or character to. **2.** To make humane, gentle, or benevolent; to soften and refine. **3.** (med.) To furnish with properties resembling those of a human product: *to humanize cow's milk*. **B.** intrans. To become humane.

humankind, n. [1. hūmankīnd; 2. hjūmənkáind]. Mankind.

humanly, adv. [1. hū́manli; 2. hjū́mənli]. **human** & **-ly**. In a human manner; from a human point of view. Phr. *humanly speaking* (*he cannot recover*), so far as man's knowledge and skill are concerned, apart from Divine help.

humanness, n. [1. hū́mannes; 2. hjū́mənnis]. **human** & **-ness**. (rare) Quality of being human; humanity.

humble (**I.**), adj. [1. húmbl; 2. hámbl]. M.E. *(h)umble*, fr. O. Fr. *humble*, fr. Lat. *humil-(is)*, 'low, base, humble', fr. *humus*, 'earth, ground', see **humus**, & **-le**. **1.** (of an attitude of mind) **a** Lowly in spirit, meek, modest; unassuming, not self-assertive; exhibiting consciousness of one's defects and shortcomings: *a truly humble genius*; *a humble heart*; **b** (of actions and conduct) performed in a humble spirit; betokening, expressing, a humble attitude of mind: *a humble request, prayer, petition*; *a humble obeisance, smile* &c.; **c** shamefaced, apologetic, ashamed of one's conduct: *he was very humble in his manner after the reprimand he received*; **d** (in unfavourable sense) cringing, abject, lacking self-respect. **2. a** (of persons and their external circumstances) Lowly in rank, position, status; not exalted; obscure, unimportant: *a humble dependent*; *humble birth*; *in humble circumstances*; *a humble occupation*; **b** (of objects associated with persons) unpretentious, poor, shabby, mean; betokening lowliness of rank and fortune on part of owner: *a humble dwelling, cot, home*.

humble (**II.**), vb. trans., fr. prec. To bring low, abase, put to shame, lower the pride of, humiliate.

humble-bee, n. M.E. *hombulbē*; cp. M.L.G. *hummelbee*, cp. Du. *hommel*, O.H.G. *humbal*, Germ. *hummel*, 'humble-bee', fr. M.E. *humblen*, 'to hum', fr. **hum** (**I.**) & freq. suff. **-le**, & **bee**. Large, wild, stingless bee, with thick, clumsy body covered with hairs, making loud droning sound; bumble-bee.

humbleness, n. [1. húmblnes; 2. hámblnis]. M.E. *humblenesse*, fr. **humble** (**I.**) & **-ness**. Quality of being humble; humility.

humble pie, n. For *umble pie*, one made of *umbles*, or entrails (of deer); formerly given to dependents after the chase; the *h-* is due to association w. **humble** (**I.**). See **umbles**. Only in Phr. *to eat humble pie*, to submit to humiliation, make abject apology.

humbling, n. [1. húmbling; 2. hámbliŋ]. **humble** (**II.**) & **-ing**. Action of one who humbles; state of being humbled; humiliation.

humbly, adv. [1. húmbli; 2. hámbli]. M.E. *humblīche*. **humble** (**I.**) & **-ly**. In a humble manner.

humbug (**I.**), n. [1. húmbug; 2. hámbag]. No particular history; prob. a provinc. concoction fr. elements w. special dial. meanings. **1.** (of action) **a** Act intended to deceive; a hoax, imposture, fraud; **b** a foolish, thoughtless, futile action. **2.** (of speech and expression) **a** Misleading, dishonest, untrue statement; **b** foolish, empty talk; nonsense; blarney. **3.** (of persons) **a** A dishonest, swindling rogue; **b** (i.) an empty, pretentious, boastful fellow; one whose performance is not equal to his claims or promises; (ii.) an insincere flatterer; one who practises blarney.

humbug (**II.**), vb. trans. & intrans., fr. prec. **1.** trans. To practise humbug upon, impose on; cajole, dupe, bamboozle: *to humbug people into buying rubbish*; *to be humbugged out of one's rights*. **2.** intrans. To act, behave, speak, as a humbug; employ cajolery.

humdrum, adj. & n. [1. húmdrum; 2. hámdram], fr. **hum** & **drum**, suggesting prolonged, monotonous talk. **1.** adj. Commonplace, trite, tedious, dull, unimaginative, monotonous. **2.** n. Tedious, commonplace, unexciting talk, occupation, or surroundings: *to prefer the humdrum in oratory.*

humectation, n. [1. hùmektâshun; 2. hjūmɛktéiʃən]. Fr., fr. Lat. *(h)ūmectātiōn-(em)*, 'act of moistening', fr. *(h)ūmectāre*, 'to moisten', fr. *(h)ūmectus*, 'moist', fr. *(h)ūmēre*, 'to be moist'. See **humour.** Act of moistening; state of being moist.

humeral, adj. & n. [1. hûmeral; 2. hjúmərəl]. L. Lat. *humerāl-(is)*, fr. Lat. *humerus*, 'shoulder', & **-al**. See **humerus. 1.** adj. (anat.) Pertaining to the shoulder: *humeral veil* (R.C.Ch.), oblong scarf worn by priest or subdeacon when holding paten with host; also, a covering wrapped round paten or chalice. **2.** n. Humeral veil.

humerus, n. [1. hûmerus; 2. hjúmərəs]. Lat. *(h)umer-us*, 'shoulder', cogn. w. Scrt. *aṁsa-s*, Gk. *ômo-s*, Goth. *amsa*, 'shoulder'. (anat.) Bone of the upper arm in man, extending from shoulder to elbow; corresponding bone in other vertebrates.

humid, adj. [1. hûmid; 2. hjúmid]. Lat. *(h)ūmid-(us)*, fr. same base as *(h)ūmēre*, 'to be moist, wet'. See **humour.** Moist, damp.

humidify, vb. trans. [1. hūmídifī; 2. hjūmídifai]. See prec. & **-fy.** To render humid; to moisten, damp.

humidity, n. [1. humíditi; 2. hjūmíditi]. Fr. *humidité*. **humid** & **-ity.** a Moisture, damp; **b** degree of moisture, esp. of air.

humiliate, vb. trans. [1. hūmíliāt; 2. hjumílieit]. L. Lat. *humiliāt-(um)*, P.P. of *humiliāre*, 'to humble', fr. *humilis*, q.v. under **humble (I.).** To humble, lower the pride or dignity of; to mortify; wound feelings of, by rendering contemptible or making appear contemptible.

humiliating, adj. [1. hūmíliāting; 2. hjumílieitiŋ], fr. Pres. Part. of prec. Causing one to lose pride or dignity; mortifying: *a humiliating situation.*

humiliation, n. [1. hūmiliáshun; 2. hjumìliéiʃən]. M.E., fr. Fr. *humiliation*, fr. L. Lat. *humiliātiōn-(em).* See **humiliate** & **-ion.** Act of humiliating; state of being humiliated or humbled.

humility, n. [1. hūmíliti; 2. hjumíliti]. M.E., O. Fr. *humilitē*, Lat. *humilitāt-(em).* See **humble** & **-ity.** Humble state of mind; meekness, lowliness of mind.

hummer, n. [1. húmer; 2. hámə]. **hum (I.)** & **-er.** Person or thing that hums; humming-bird.

humming (I.), adj. [1. húming; 2. hámiŋ]. Pres. Part. of **hum (I.).** Producing a hum, or buzzing, droning sound; resembling, of the nature of, a hum or buzz: *a humming sound.*

humming (II.), n. **hum (I.)** & **-ing.** Sound produced by person or thing that hums.

humming-bird, n. **1.** One of large family, *Trochilidae*, of American birds, mostly tropical and extremely small and brilliantly coloured, with long slender curved bill, hovering over flowers with rapidly vibrating and whirring wings. **2.** (attrib.) As *humming-bird (hawk) moth*, small British hawk moth which hovers over flowers like humming-bird.

humming-top, n. Metal spinning-top with device which causes it to produce a loud, humming sound when spinning.

hummock, n. [1. húmuk; 2. hámək]. Orig. naut.; origin doubtful. Knoll, hillock; specif., pile or ridge of ice in icefield.

hummocky, adj. [1. húmuki; 2. hámәki]. Prec. & **-y.** a Like a hummock; **b** containing, abounding in, hummocks.

humoral, adj. [1. (h)ûmoral; 2. (h)júmərəl]. **humour** & **-al.** (archaic or hist.) Pertaining to the humours of the body.

humoralism, n. [1. (h)ûmoralizm; 2. (h)júmərəlizəm]. Prec. & **-ism.** (hist.) Obsolete medical doctrine deriving all diseases from state of the humours of the body.

humoralist, n. [1. (h)ûmoralist; 2. (h)júmərəlist]. **humoral** & **-ist.** (hist). Adherent of humoralism.

humoresque, n. [1. hūmorésk; 2. hjūmərésk]. Germ. *humoreske.* **humour** & **-esque.** (mus.) Composition of a light, playful, quaint, and humorous character.

humorist, humourist, n. [1. (h)ûmorist; 2. (h)júmərist]. Fr. *humoriste*, fr. Med. Lat. *hūmōrista.* **humour (I.)** & **-ist.** Facetious, comical person; one possessing a droll humour &c.; humorous talker or writer.

humoristic, adj. [1. (h)ūmorístik; 2. (h)jūmərístik]. Prec. & **-ic.** Pertaining to, resembling, a humorist.

humorous, adj. [1. (h)ûmorus; 2. (h)júmərəs]. Lat. *(h)ūmōrōsus*, 'moist'. **humour** & **-ous. 1. a** (obs.) Characterized by, subject to, one of the bodily humours; hence, **b** (archaic) capricious, whimsical. **2.** Having, displaying, humour or a sense of humour: *a humorous writer, essay, twinkle of the eye.* **3.** Laughable, funny: *a humorous situation, accident.*

humorously, adv. Prec. & **-ly.** In a humorous manner.

humorousness, n. See prec. & **-ness.** Quality of being humorous; humour.

humour (I.), n. [1. hûmor, ûmor; 2. hjúmə, júmə]. The pronunciation [1. hûmor; 2. hjúmə], influenced by the spelling, is now usual, although it was until recently & is still by many regarded as a vulgarism. M.E., fr. O. Fr. *humor*, fr. Lat. *(h)ūmōr-(em)*, w. *h-* through influence of *humus*, 'earth'. *(H)ūmōr-* is fr. earlier **ugʷmōr* & is connected w. *(h)ūmēre*, 'to be moist'; cp. further Lat. *ūvidus* (& *ūdus*), fr. **ugʷidos*, 'wet, damp, dank', *ūvēre*, 'to be wet' &c.; fr. same base are Scrt. *ukšati*, 'sprinkles'; Gk. *ugrós*, 'wet, moist'; O.E. *ȳce*, 'toad, frog', fr. Gmc. **ūkjō-*, Aryan **ūgʷjā-*. See further under **ox. 1. a** (obs.) Liquid, moisture, vapour: '*The humours of the dank morning*' (Shakespeare); specif. **b** (anct. physiol.) one of the four primary liquids supposed to exist in the human body, and to influence the health, spirits, and temperament; blood, phlegm, choler, and black bile or melancholy: *the cardinal humours*; **c** one of the secondary products of these; now only *aqueous, vitreous, humours*, transparent liquids or semi-liquids in eye; **d** morbid fluid in body. Hence, **2,** a Temperament, disposition, ruling passion: *a man of sanguine humour*; Phr. *the comedy of humours*, class of 17th cent. comedy depicting various, chiefly eccentric, types of character; **b** passing mood, inclination, frame of mind; whim, fancy: *to be in the humour for a talk*; *a grim humour*; *when the humour takes me*; Phr. *in good, bad, humour*, in a genial, sullen, mood; *out of humour*, annoyed; **c** (obs. or archaic) morbid disposition, peevishness, 'vapours'. **3. a** Jocularity, fun, facetiousness, formerly esp. of low sort, as practical joking; the ridiculous or laughable; ludicrous or jocular action or saying; **b** (chief mod. use) playful and indulgent treatment of the absurd, incongruous or ludicrous; sportive fancy or imagination; capacity or habit of mind which apprehends and appreciates the ludicrous sympathetically, cp. *wit*: *a sense of humour.*

humour (II.), vb. trans., fr. prec. **a** To fall in with the humour or humours, whims, idiosyncrasy of; to indulge: *to humour a person's failings*; to manage by adroit or tactful compliance: *a nurse must humour the patient*; **b** to manipulate (thing) gently by adapting one's handling to its peculiarities: *you can't force the lock, you must humour it.*

humourless, adj. [1. (h)ûmorles; 2. (h)júməlis]. **humour (I.)** & **-less.** Having no humour; devoid of a sense of humour.

humoursome, adj. [1. (h)ûmorsum; 2. (h)júməsəm]. **humour (I.)** & **-some.** Capricious, whimsical.

hump (I.), n. [1. hump; 2. hamp]. Only in Mod. Engl., fr. c. 1680; cp. Du. *homp*, L.G. *humpe, hompe*, Norw. *hump.* Origin doubtful. **1.** Protuberance, swelling; specif. **a** abnormal protuberance on human back, due to curvature or other deformity of the spine; **b** normal protuberance on back of animal, as of camel, bison &c.; **c** hillock, mound. **2.** (slang) Fit of mental depression: *to give one, to get, the hump.*

hump (II.), vb. trans., fr. prec. **1.** To stoop, bend the back, gather shoulders into a hump; to arch, hunch: *to hump up the back.* **2.** (slang) To give the hump to, make sulky.

humpback, n. [1. húmpbak; 2. hámpbæk]. **hump (I.)** & **back (I.). 1.** Back with a hump. **2.** Person with humped back; hunchback. **3. a** Large whalebone whale with very long flippers; **b** humpbacked salmon.

humpbacked, adj. [1. húmpbakt; 2. hámpbækt]. Prec. & **-ed.** Having a humped back: *humpbacked salmon*, small salmon of the rivers flowing into the North Pacific.

humped, adj. [1. humpt; 2. hampt]. **hump (I.)** & **-ed.** Having a hump.

humph, interj. & vb. intrans., conventionally [1. humf; 2. hamf] fr. spelling. Attempted graphic representation of an inarticulate nasal grunt. **1.** interj. Exclamation or inarticulate grunt, expressing doubt, dissatisfaction, scorn &c. **2.** vb. To utter this sound.

humpty-dumpty, n. [1. húmpti dúmpti; 2. hámpti dámpti], fr. name of hero of a nursery rhyme, represented pictorially as a grotesque squat figure. Person having a short, squat, or dumpy figure.

humpy, adj. [1. húmpi; 2. hámpi]. **hump (I.)** & **-y.** Having a hump; full of humps.

humus, n. [1. hûmus; 2. hjúməs]. Lat., 'earth, ground, soil'. Lat. *humus* represents an Aryan base **ǵʰzem-* &c., whence also Scrt. *kšāman-*, 'ground, earth'; *kšámi* (loc.), 'on the ground'; Gk. *khthṓn*, 'ground', *khamai*, 'on the ground'; Lith. *žẽme*, 'earth'; O. Slav. *zem-lja.* Further cognates are Lat. *humilis*, 'low-lying, lowly' &c. (see **humble**), *homo*, 'man' (see **homage** & **human**), O.E. *guma*, 'man', see **bridegroom.** Decomposed organic matter forming soil.

Hun, n. [1. hun; 2. han]. O.E *Húne*, M.E. *Hunne*, O.N. *Húnar*, M.H.G. *Huine*, Germ. *Hūne, Hunne*, fr. Low Lat. *Hunnus, Chūnus.* **1.** Member of great horde of predatory nomads from Central Asia who devastated Europe in the 4th and 5th cents. **2.** (fig.) **a** Ruthless, wantonly destructive person; specif. **b** (slang) German soldier; German. (Originated with a speech of the Emperor William II. on the German expedition to China, 1900, and adopted derisively by the Social Democrats; in Great War by the British.)

hunch (I.), n. [1. hunsh; 2. hanʃ]. Prob. fr. a L.G. source. Cp. **hunk (I.). 1.** Hump, protuberance, on back. **2.** Thick, clumsy piece, chunk, of cake, bread, cheese &c. **3.** (Am. slang) Suspicion, intuition, premonition: *to have a hunch that something is going to happen.*

hunch (II.), vb. trans., fr. prec. To bend the back, stoop, and draw shoulders up, so as to form hunch; also *hunch up.*

hunchback, n. [1. húnshbak; 2. hánʃbæk]. **1.** Hunched or humped back, form of spinal curvature. **2.** Person with hunched back.

hunchbacked, adj. [1. húnshbakt; 2. hánʃbækt]. Prec. & **-ed.** Having a hunched back.

hundred (I.), n. [1. húndred; 2. hándrəd]. O.E. *hund*, later *hundred*, fr. O.N. *hundraþ*; M.E. *hundred*; O.S. *hunderod*, O.H.G. *hunterit*, M.H.G., Mod. Germ. *hundert*; the compound has taken the place of the older *hund*, 'decade', also 'hundred', in most Gmc. languages, Gmc. **hundan* for **humđóm*, Aryan **k̑m̥tóm*, 'group of ten', whence Scrt. *śatám*, O. Slav. *sʹto*, Lith. *szimta-*, Gk. *(he)-katón* (one hundred), Lat. *centum*, O. Ir. *cēt*, W. *cant*; abbr. fr. the neut. ordinal **d(e)k̑m̥tóm* (see **decade, decimal, ten, twenty**). The use of the word in the sense '100' is due to abbreviation, the full form being retained in Goth. *taihuntē-hund* (or **taihuntaihund* ?), 'decade of tens, hundred'. The element *-red* &c. is cogn. w. Goth. *raþjō*, 'reckoning, number', & w. O.E. *rǣdan*, q.v. under **read (I.)** & **riddle (I.). 1.** The cardinal number ten multiplied by ten; ten decades; in singular always preceded by indefinite article or adjective: *a hundred, a bare hundred, one hundred, the second hundred; some hundred,* about 100; uninflected in plural when preceded by another number or adjective expressing number: *two hundred; a few, several, hundred of them; great, long, hundred,* 120, six score. Phrs. *to lend a man a hundred (pounds); to live to a hundred,* to age of 100 years; here *hundred,* though apparently a noun, is really an adjective with following noun understood. **2.** Large, indeterminate number: *hundreds of people; hundreds and hundreds,* a very large number. Phr. *to have hundreds in the bank,* hundreds of pounds, a large sum. **3.** Old administrative division of English or Irish county; perhaps originally an area supporting a hundred free families or containing 100 hides.

hundred (II.), adj. See prec. **1. a** Ten times ten: *a hundred men; two, a few, many, hundred men;* **b** (in composite ordinal numbers): *the hundred and first.* **2.** *A hundred,* very many: *to have a hundred things to do.* Phrs. *a hundred and one things,* a large, indefinite number; *not a hundred miles away,* comparatively close.

hundreder, hundredor, n. [1. húndreder; 2. hándridə]. Med. Lat. *hundredārius.* Prec. & **-er.** (hist., obs.) **a** Chief officer of a hundred; **b** freeman of a hundred.

hundredfold, adj., adv., & n. [1. húndredfōld; 2. hándrədfould]. M.E. *hundredfald.* **hundred & -fold.** **1.** adj. (rare) Multiplied by a hundred: *a hundredfold return on one's money.* **2.** adv. (preceded by *a* or archaic *an*) A hundred times as much or many: *the seed increased a hundredfold.* **3.** n. Amount a hundred times as great: *to yield a hundredfold.*

hundredth, adj. & n. [1. húndredth; 2. hándrədþ]. **hundred & -th.** **1.** adj. **a** Last in series of a hundred; **b** forming one part in a hundred. **2.** n. **a** Last object in series of a hundred; **b** hundredth part.

hundredweight, n. [1. húndredwāt; 2. hándrədweit]. **hundred & weight.** A weight; formerly (and still in U.S.A.) of 100 lb., now of 112 lb. avoirdupois, or one-twentieth of a ton; abbr. *cwt.*

hung, vb. [1. hung; 2. haŋ]. Pret. & P.P. of **hang.**

hunger (I.), n. [1. húngger; 2. háŋgə]. O.E. *hungor,* M.E. *hunger,* Common Gmc.; O.S., O.H.G. *hungar,* M.H.G., Mod. Germ. *hunger,* Goth. *hūhrus,* O.N. *hungr,* Gmc. type **húŋχ-r-uz, huŋgrúz,* cogn. w. Lith. *kankà,* 'suffering'. **1.** Bodily condition of discomfort, weakness, extreme exhaustion, and emaciation, ending in death, caused by lack of nourishment; famine: *to die of hunger.* **2. a** Appetite, desire for food after fasting: *to satisfy one's hunger with a mutton chop;* **b** any physical craving. **3.** Spiritual desire, craving, eagerness, for: *a hunger for the truth, for affection.*

hunger (II.), vb. intrans. O.E. *hyngr(i)an,* M.E. *hingren, hungren.* See prec. **a** To be without food; to lack nourishment; starve; **b** *hunger for, hunger after* (chiefly of spiritual wants), to desire strongly, yearn for: *to hunger after a little kindness.*

hunger strike, n. Refusal of political or other prisoner to eat.

hungrily, adv. [1. húnggrili; 2. háŋgrili]. **hungry & -ly.** In a hungry manner.

hungriness, n. [1. húnggrines; 2. háŋgrinis]. **hungry & -ness.** Quality of being hungry; hunger: *the hungriness of the soil.*

hungry, adj. [1. húnggri; 2. háŋgri]. O.E. *hungriġ,* M.E. *hungriȝ.* **hunger & -y.** **1. a** (of living beings) Suffering from lack of nourishment; starving: *crowds of hungry children followed the travellers; to go hungry,* go without food, starve; Phr. *the hungry forties,* decade from 1840, during which there was famine in parts of Great Britain and Ireland; **b** (of land, soil) poor, requiring much manure. **2. a** Having a keen appetite for food: *I'm hungry today and shall enjoy my dinner;* **b** expressing, suggesting, hunger: *a hungry look.* **3.** Experiencing spiritual hunger, keenly desirous of, yearning after: *hungry for home and friends, for knowledge* &c.

hunk, n. [1. hungk; 2. haŋk]. Cp. W. Flem. *hunke,* of obscure origin; cp. the older **hunch.** Large hunch, lump, thick slice, chunk, esp. of bread.

hunkers, n. pl. [1. húngkerz; 2. háŋkəz], fr. Scots dial. *hunker,* 'to squat on one's hams'; origin doubtful, possibly nasalized form of O.N. *huka,* 'to squat, crouch'. See **huckster.** (dial., esp. Nthn. and Scots) Hams, buttocks, esp. in Phr. *on one's hunkers,* squatting, crouching.

hunks, n. [1. hungks; 2. haŋks]. Origin doubtful. (colloq. or slang) A mean, selfish, niggardly, disagreeable old fellow.

Hunnish, adj. [1. húnish; 2. hániʃ]. **Hun & -ish.** **a** Pertaining to, resembling, the Huns; **b** (fig.) wantonly destructive, barbarous; **c** (slang) pertaining to the Germans.

hunt (I.), vb. trans. & intrans. [1. hunt; 2. hant]. O.E. *huntian,* M.E. *hunten, honten,* only Engl. This base is prob. variant **a** of Gmc. **hunþ-,* wk. grade of base **hinþ-,* 'to seize'; cp. Goth. *-hinþan,* 'to seize', *hunþ-s,* 'captivity'. See **hand** (I.). **A.** trans. **1. a** To follow, chase, pursue (wild animal) with object of shooting or catching: *to hunt antelope, big game;* specif. **b** to pursue (a fox, stag, or hare) with horses and hounds; **c** phrase in names of various children's games in which person or thing is sought: *hunt the fox, hare, squirrel* &c. **2. a** To follow the chase through or in (district): *to hunt a country;* **b** to employ (horse) in hunting: *to hunt one's horse in winter and put it out to grass for the summer;* **c** to act as master, or huntsman, to a pack of hounds: *he hunts the hounds himself.* **3.** To pursue, cause to run away; to chase, drive away: *to hunt cats (away).* **4.** To pursue (person), follow pertinaciously; to harry, persecute: *to hunt a thief, heretics.* **5.** To search through, scour, ransack: *to hunt half London for a book.* **B.** intrans. **1.** To engage in hunting, follow the chase; to ride to hounds: *to hunt with the Beaufort; to go out hunting.* **2.** To search assiduously for a thing: *to hunt high and low.* **3.** (of part of machine) To oscillate or move excessively. **C.** Followed by preposition or adverb. *Hunt down,* trans., to pursue vigorously and remorselessly until caught; to track down: *to hunt down a murderer. Hunt for,* intrans., to seek, search assiduously for. *Hunt out,* trans., to seek something which has been put away and hidden from sight, to rout out: *to hunt out some old clothes; to hunt out a person's address and visit him. Hunt up,* trans., to look for, find, something which is hard to discover through being buried in scattered documents, among disparate matter &c.; hunt out: *to hunt up one's family history, a reference* &c.

hunt (II.), n., prec. **1.** Action of hunting; chase after fox or hare: *to have a good hunt twice a week.* **2. a** (cap.) Local association of persons who engage in hunting: *the Quorn Hunt;* **b** party engaged in hunting; riders, horses, and hounds; **c** district hunted over by particular pack. **3.** Assiduous search: *a hunt for a job, for a missing key.*

hunter, n. [1. húnter; 2. hántə]. O.E. *hunta,* w. different suff., M.E. *huntere.* **hunt** (I.) & **-er.** **1.** Person or animal that pursues, hunts &c. (not used of a person who hunts foxes &c. on horseback): *a mighty hunter; Red Indians are hunters and fishers; the leopard is a skilful hunter; hunter's moon,* full moon after harvest moon. **2.** Horse used for hunting; horse of a breed adapted for fox-hunting. **3.** (rare) Person who seeks persistently for a thing: *a hunter after glory.* **4.** Kind of watch of which the dial is protected by metal cover, suitable for hunting-man.

hunting (I.), adj. [1. húnting; 2. hántiŋ], fr. Pres. Part. of **hunt** (I.). (of person or animal) That hunts: *hunting-spider; hunting-dog,* S. African animal resembling dog, hunting in packs. See also **hunting** (II.).

hunting (II.), n. O.E. *huntung,* M.E. *huntunge.* **hunt** (I.) & **-ing.** **a** Action of person or animal that hunts; chase, pursuit; specif., fox-hunting: *to be fond of hunting;* Phr. *hunting-man,* one addicted to fox-hunting; **b** (attrib.) used in hunting: *hunting-cap, dog, knife* &c.; *hunting-cat, leopard,* cheetah.

hunting-box, n. Small house in hunting district used for residence during season.

hunting-case, n. Metal case for watch, protecting glass and dial.

hunting-crop, n. Riding whip, with thong and lash, sometimes furnished with longish handle at right angles to stock, for pulling gates open and shut; used by persons riding to hounds.

hunting-field, n. Country over which one hunts; *killed in the hunting-field,* while out hunting.

hunting-ground, n. **a** District to which hunters resort for game; Phr. *happy hunting-grounds,* future life as conceived of by N. American Indians; **b** place where one searches for, and sometimes finds, what one wants: *old bookstalls are his (happy) hunting-ground.*

hunting-horn, n. **1.** Horn or bugle giving signals during hunt. **2.** (rare) Second pommel on near side of side-saddle.

huntress, n. [1. húntres; 2. hántris]. **hunter & -ess.** (liter.) Woman or goddess who hunts.

huntsman, n. [1. húntsman; 2. hántsmən]. Possess. of **hunt** (II.) & **man.** **a** Hunter; **b** hunt servant, in charge of hounds during a hunt.

huntsmanship, n. [1. húntsmanship; 2. hántsmənʃip]. Prec. & **-ship.** **a** Office of huntsman; tenure of this; **b** skill and abilities as a huntsman.

hunt's-up, n. [1. húnts úp; 2. hánts áp], fr. Phr. '*the hunt is up*', i.e. started. (archaic) Tune played on hunting-horn or bugle in early morning to arouse hunters; reveille.

hunt-the-slipper, n. Children's game in which one standing inside a close circle formed by other players sitting on floor, tries to find a slipper passed rapidly round below their knees.

hurdle (I.), n. [1. hěrdl; 2. hə́dl]. O.E. *hyrdel,* M.E. *hurdel, hirdel,* fr. W. Gmc. **hurd-il-;* cp. O.H.G., M.H.G. *hurt,* 'basket-work structure'; Goth. *haurd-s,* 'door'; cogn. w. Scrt. *krt-,* 'to spin', *crt-,* 'to bind, connect'; Gk. *kártalos,* 'kind of basket', *kurtía,* 'wicker-work'; Lat. *crātis,* 'hurdle, wickerwork'; fr. Aryan base **kert-* &c., 'to weave, plait'. See **crate, grate** (II.), **hoarding** (II.). **1. a** Movable oblong frame made of osier &c., generally with three uprights, four or five rails, and a cross Λ-shaped stay, used to form section of light, temporary fence, of pen for sheep &c.; one of a series of light, wooden rails, used in a hurdle-race; also *iron hurdle,* section of railing made of iron, used in fencing; **b** (hist.) rough structure resembling a hurdle on which condemned persons were dragged to execution. **2.** (pl.) Hurdle-race.

hurdle (II.), vb. trans. & intrans., fr. prec. **A.** trans. **1. a** To make, supply, hurdles; **b** to place hurdles round, to enclose (space) or fill (gap) with hurdles. **2.** To leap over in race. **B.** intrans. To leap over barrier in race; to jump an obstacle in special manner, as though striding, adopted in jumping hurdles.

hurdler, n. [1. hěrdler; 2. hə́dlə]. Prec. & **-er.** **1.** Maker of wooden hurdles. **2.** Person who leaps hurdles in a race; an expert at this.

hurdle-race, n. Foot-race or horse-race in which the course is crossed by series of fences or hurdles which have to be leapt.

hurdy-gurdy, n. [1. hěrdi gěrdi; 2. hə́di gə́di]. Imitative. **a** An obsolete stringed instrument, in which the place of the bow was taken by a wheel turned by a handle; **b** loosely applied to various forms of hand-organ, especially as played in the street.

hurl (**I.**), vb. trans. & intrans. [1. hĕrl; 2. hāl]. M.E. *hurlen, horlen*. Of L.G. or Scand. origin; cp. E. Fris. *hurreln*, 'to blow in gusts', Norw. *hurla*, 'to buzz', Dan. *hurle*, 'to whir'. **1.** trans. **a** To throw, cast, fling, with vigour and force: *to hurl a javelin*; *to hurl a person downstairs*. Phr. *to hurl abuse at*, abuse loudly; **b** (reflex.) *hurl oneself at, upon*, to rush. **2.** intrans. **a** To throw (something) with force; **b** (archaic, cp. *hurtle*) to rush noisily through the air; to whiz; **c** to play the game of hurling.

hurl (**II.**), n., fr. prec. Act of hurling.

hurlbat, n. [1. hĕrlbat; 2. hálbæt]. Stick or club used in the game of hurling.

hurler, n. [1. hĕrler; 2. hálə]. **hurl** (**I.**) & **-er**. Person who hurls; specif., one who plays at hurling.

hurley, n. [1. hĕrli; 2. háli]. **hurl** (**I.**) & **-ey**. (Ir.) **a** Game of hurling; **b** stick or club used in hurling.

hurling, n. [1. hĕrling; 2. háliŋ]. **hurl** (**I.**) & **-ing**. **1.** Action of person or machine that hurls. **2. a** Irish ball game, like hockey, played with crooked sticks or clubs between two goals; **b** Cornish game in which ball is thrown or carried to opponents' goal.

hurly, n. [1. hĕrli; 2. háli]. O. Fr. *hurlee*, 'great noise', orig. fem. P.P. of *hurler*, 'to howl, yell', for earlier *huller*; cp. Ital. *urlare, ululare*, fr. Lat. *ululāre*, cp. *ulula*, 'owl'. See **ululation**. (obs.) Tumult, uproar (Shakespeare).

hurly-burly, n. [1. hĕrli bĕrli; 2. háli báli]. Relation, if any, to Fr. *hurlu-berlu*, obs. *hurlu-brelu*, 'giddy, extravagant person', is doubtful. Uproar, tumult, commotion.

hurrah, hurra, interj., n., & vb. intrans. & trans. [1. hooráh; 2. hurá]. Prob. fr. Du. *hoera* or Germ. *hurra*, replacing the older **huzza**; cp. M.H.G. *hurrā*; imitative. Cp. **hurry**. **1.** interj. Exclamation or shout of joy, applause, or welcome: *hurrah for the king!, for the holidays!*; often given as cheer by number of persons together at word of command: *hip, hip, hurrah!* **2.** n. A shout of 'hurrah': *listen to the hurrahs of the crowd*. **3.** vb. **a** intrans. To shout hurrah; **b** trans., to greet, applaud, with hurrah.

hurray, interj., n., & vb. [1. hoorá; 2. huréi]. Variant of prec.

hurricane, n. [1. húrikan, -ān; 2. hárikin, -ein]. Formerly *hurricano*, 'water-spout' (Shakespeare), fr. Span. *huracan*, fr. Carib. *huracan*. Cp. Fr. *ouragan*. **1. a** Extremely violent cyclonic storm in W. Indies or tropical Atlantic; **b** any wind of extreme violence: *it blew a regular hurricane*. **2.** (fig.) Sudden vehement outburst of passion, strong feeling &c.: *a hurricane of popular fury, of applause*.

hurricane-bird, n. Frigate-bird.

hurricane-deck, n. (chiefly Am.) Light upper deck on steamboat.

hurricane-lamp, -lantern, n. Lamp or lantern with the light well protected against wind.

hurried, adj. [1. húrid; 2. hárid]. P.P. of **hurry** (**II.**). **a** Urged, impelled, to move, act &c., in haste: *a hurried speaker*; **b** done, performed, carried on, in a hurry; hasty, perfunctory: *a hurried glance*; *a few hurried notes*; *a hurried meal*.

hurriedly, adv. Prec. & **-ly**. In a hurried manner.

hurry (**I.**), n. [1. húri; 2. hári]. Scand. Cp. Swed. *hurr*, 'great haste'; prob. imitative in origin. **1. a** Action of hastening; expedition, haste; undue haste; bustle, hasty movement: *all was hurry and confusion*; Phrs. *in a hurry*, (i.) impatient, anxious to get something done quickly; *in a hurry to be rich*; *an old man in a hurry*; (ii.) (colloq.) readily, easily, soon: *he won't do that again in a hurry*; **b** (colloq., chiefly in interrog. or neg. sentence) reason for haste; urgency, immediate need: *is there any hurry about it?*; *don't go yet, there's no hurry*. **2.** (mus.) Tremolo played by violins &c. to accompany rapid action on stage. **3.** Chute on quay or stage for loading ship with coal or ore.

hurry (**II.**), vb. trans. & intrans. See prec. **A.** trans. **1. a** To cause to move or to act rapidly, or more rapidly; to increase speed of, expedite, movement or action: *the police hurried the prisoner into a closed car*; Phr. *hurry no man's cattle*, don't be impatient; **b** to cause movement to become more rapid, to accelerate motion; to get action performed, or work done, with greater speed: *to hurry one's movements*; *to walk with hurried steps*; *dictionary-making is work which cannot be hurried beyond a certain point*. **2.** To dispatch, send hastily: *troops were hurried to the threatened point*. **3.** To hasten unduly; to do, cause something to be done, with precipitation; to bustle: *I have been hurried into error*; *it is easy to see that you were hurried when you wrote that*; *it would be a pity to hurry the work*. **B.** intrans. To move or act, quickly, with great, or increased, speed: *I wish you would hurry a bit, you'll be late if you don't*; *don't hurry, there's plenty of time*. **C.** With adverbs. *Hurry along*, **a** intrans., to move along with haste; **b** trans., to cause (a person &c.) to hasten; to urge on; to expedite, speed up (an action, piece of work). *Hurry away*, **a** intrans., to depart in haste; **b** trans., to compel (a person) to depart with speed, take away with one. *Hurry off*, hurry away. *Hurry over*, intrans., to carry out, do, perfunctorily. *Hurry up*, **a** intrans., to make haste, increase one's speed of movement or action; **b** trans., to expedite; to cause (a person) to move or act more rapidly; to cause (action) to be done more quickly.

hurry-scurry, adv., n., & vb. intrans., fr. **hurry** (**I.**) & **scurry**. **1.** adv. In extreme hurry, in wild, disorderly haste. **2.** n. Disorderly haste. **3.** vb. To act with extreme, disorderly haste.

hurst, n. [1. hĕrst; 2. hāst]. O.E. *hyrst*, 'wood, thicket', M.E. *hurst*, 'wood', O.H.G., M.H.G. *hurst*, 'thicket', M.L.G., M. Du., Germ. *horst*, 'thicket; eyrie; sandbank'. Prob. fr. Aryan base **ker-*, 'grow', whence also Lat. *creāre*, q.v. under **create**, *crēscere*, 'to grow', see **crescent**; see further under **herd** (**I.**). Survives chiefly in Place-Names. Wood, copse, wooded hill.

hurt (**I.**), vb. trans. & intrans. [1. hĕrt; 2. hāt]. M.E. *hurten, hirten*, 'to dash, push, injure', fr. O. Fr. *hurter* (Mod. Fr. *heurter*), 'to knock, strike against', fr. Romance type *urtāre*, as in Ital., late formation fr. P.P. stem **urt-* of Lat. *urgēre*, 'to press, push'. See **urge**; also **work**. **A.** trans. **1. a** To cause bodily smart or pain to: *a mustard plaster hurts you, but does good at the same time*; *I won't hurt you*; **b** to do bodily harm to, inflict injury upon: *his back was permanently hurt by his fall*. **2.** (fig.) To wound the feelings of; to pain, distress: *he was, felt, hurt by what was said*. **3.** To damage, tend to destroy, injure, or to make less efficient; to cause deterioration of, check progress of; to be bad for: *the drought has hurt the roses this year*; *strikes often hurt the strikers more than the employers*; *the reports hurt his reputation*. **4.** (impers.) *It hurts*, causes pain, does damage, to; in all senses of **1, 2, 3**: *it hurts the eyes to expose them to the sun*; *it hurts the feelings to be laughed at*; *it hurts the amenities of social life when there is mutual distrust*. **B.** intrans. **1.** To cause bodily or mental pain: *nothing hurts worse at the time than a slight burn*; *systematic contempt and neglect hurt worse than actual insults*. **2.** To be the seat of pain (colloq.): *my tooth still hurts a little*. **3.** (impers.) To do harm, cause pain or injury: *it didn't hurt a bit*. Phr. *it won't hurt*, no harm will come of it. **4.** (colloq.) To come to harm, suffer injury: *he won't hurt by himself for a few hours*.

hurt (**II.**), n., fr. prec. Injury, wound; harm, mischief (physical or mental): *to do hurt to* &c.

hurter, n. [1. hĕrter; 2. hátə]. Fr. *heurtoir*, 'buffer, fender', fr. *heurter*, 'to knock'. See **hurt** (**I.**) & **-er**. **a** Shoulder on axle of wheel; **b** timber on gun-platform acting as buffer to gun-carriage.

hurtful, adj. [1. hĕrtfool; 2. hátful]. **hurt** (**II.**) & **-ful**. Causing bodily or spiritual hurt; injurious, harmful: *hurtful to the health, to the morals*.

hurtfully, adv. Prec. & **-ly**. In a hurtful manner.

hurtfulness, n. See prec. & **-ness**. Quality of being hurtful.

hurtle (**I.**), vb. intrans. & trans. [1. hĕrtl; 2. hátl]. M.E. *hurtlen*, fr. **hurt** (**I.**) & freq. **-le**. **1.** intrans. **a** (archaic or liter.) To clash, collide, jostle, crash; **b** to rush, fly, fall, be hurled violently or rapidly: *the shot hurtled through the air*; *a chimney-pot came hurtling down*. **2.** trans. (rare) To cause to hurtle.

hurtle (**II.**), n., fr. prec. **a** Clash, collision, shock; **b** noise of this.

hurtleberry, n. See **whortleberry**.

hurtless, adj. [1. hĕrtles; 2. hátlis]. **hurt** (**II.**) & **-less**. **a** Causing no hurt; **b** suffering no hurt.

husband (**I.**), n. [1. húzband; 2. házbənd]. O.E. *hūsbonda*, 'householder', M.E. *husbonde*, 'householder, small farmer, husband', fr. O.N. *hūsbōndi*, fr. *hūs* (see **house**) & *būandi*, Pres. Part. of *būa*, 'to dwell, inhabit'. See **bondage**; & cp. **boor**, & **bower** (**I.**). **1. a** (obs. or archaic) Person who manages a household, estate, or other concern; specif. **b** *ship's husband*, agent managing the business of a ship for owners. **2. a** Man to whom a woman is married: *Prince George of Denmark was Queen Anne's husband*; **b** man as thought of in relation to his wife: *he was a good, bad, husband to her*.

husband (**II.**), vb. trans. M.E. *husbonden*. See prec. **1. a** To manage thriftily; to spend economically: *to husband one's resources*; **b** (obs.) to cultivate (ground, plants). **2.** (rare) **a** To supply with a husband; **b** to be a husband to; to marry (woman).

husbandage, n. [1. húzbandij; 2. házbəndidž]. **husband** (**I.**) & **-age**. (naut.) Commission paid to ship's husband.

husbandless, adj. [1. húzbandles; 2. házbəndlis]. **husband** (**I.**) & **-less**. Having no husband; having lost a husband.

husband-like, adj. **husband** (**I.**) & **-like**. Resembling, characteristic of, a husband.

husbandly, adj. [1. húzbandli; 2. házbəndli]. **husband** (**I.**) & **-ly**. Belonging to a husband; befitting a husband: *husbandly rights and duties*.

husbandman, n. [1. húzbandman; 2. házbəndmən]. M.E. **husband** (**I.**) & **man** (**I.**). (archaic) Farmer; cultivator of the soil.

husbandry, n. [1. húzbandri; 2. házbəndri]. M.E. *husbonderie*. **husband** (**I.**) & **-ry**. **1.** (archaic) Domestic management, control of household expenditure and affairs; economy, thrift. **2.** Work of husbandman, management of land and crops; farming, agriculture.

hush (**I.**), vb. trans. & intrans. [1. hush; 2. haʃ]. Of imitative origin. Similar words occur in other Gmc. languages. The starting-point was prob. the exclamatory [ʃ] enjoining silence. Mod. *hush!* may perh. be regarded as imperat. of the vb. **1.** trans. **a** (i.) To make silent or quiet: *all strife and clamour were hushed*; *to hush a baby to sleep*; (ii.) (archaic, also reflex.) *O hush thee, my baby!*; **b** (fig.) to lull, calm, soothe; **c** (fig.) to suppress, procure silence concerning, usually *hush up*: *to hush up a scandal*. **2.** intrans. To become silent or quiet; (imperat., as quasi-interj.) silence!

hush (**II.**), n. See prec. Silence, stillness: *the hush of evening*.

hush (**III.**), interj., imperat. of **hush** (**I.**) if pronounced [haʃ]; as [ʃ], prob. the starting-point of the group. Be silent, don't speak; be quiet, don't make a noise; don't, you mustn't, say that!

hushaby, interj. [1. húshabī; 2. háʃəbai]. **hush** (**I.**); cp. **lullaby**. Word in nursery rhymes used to hush an infant.

hush money, n. Money paid to induce one to keep silence regarding a scandal.

husk (I.), n. [1. husk; 2. hask]. M.E. *huske*, of doubtful origin. Perh. related to **hud**, formed w. *-sk*, adj. suff. **a** Dry tough covering of certain fruits or seeds, esp. that of cereals; contrasted with *grain*; **b** (fig., pl.) dry, uninteresting aspect, or treatment, of a subject, lacking soul and imagination.

husk (II.), vb. trans. See prec. To remove husks from.

husk (III.), n., also *hoose*, cp. O.E. *hās*, M.E. *hoos*, Engl. dial. *hask, husk*, 'dry, **hoarse**'. Prob. associated w. **husk (I.)**. Cp. **husky (II.)**. Dry cough in cattle, caused by small worms in bronchial tubes.

husker, n. [1. húsker; 2. háskə]. **husk (II.)** & **-er**. Person or instrument that removes husks.

huskily, adv. [1. húskili; 2. háskili]. **husky (II.)** & **-ly**. With a husky voice.

huskiness, n. [1. húskines; 2. háskinis]. **husky** & **-ness**. Quality or condition of being husky (II.).

husky (I.), adj. [1. húski; 2. háski]. **husk (I.)** & **-y**. **1.** Resembling, covered with, husks. **2.** (slang) Coarse, rough; exhibiting a rude vigour: *a fine husky fellow*.

husky (II.), adj. Associated w. prec., but prob. ultimately for Engl. dial. *hask, husk*, 'hoarse'. See **husk (I. & III.)**, **hoarse**. Hoarse; **a** (of the voice) harsh, rasping, rough; **b** having a dryness or roughness in the throat; having a husky voice.

husky (III.), n. Variant or corruption of **Eskimo**. **a** Eskimo; **b** Eskimo dog; **c** Eskimo language.

hussar, n. [1. hoozár; 2. huzá]. Germ. *husar*, fr. Hung. *huszar*, fr. O. Serb. *khusar*, 'freebooter, pirate', fr. Ital. *corsaro*, or Med. Gk. *koursários*, fr. Low Lat. *cursārius*. See **corsair**. **a** (hist.) One of the light cavalry of Hungary or Croatia; **b** soldier of regiment of light cavalry, with distinctive uniform, in British or continental army.

hussif, n. See **housewife**.

Hussite, n. [1. húsīt; 2. hásait]. Follower of John Huss, Bohemian Reformer (burnt 1415).

hussy, n. [1. húzi; 2. házi], fr. M.E. *huswīf*, w. loss of final *-f* as in **hasty**. See **housewife**. **a** Pert, forward, or ill-mannered young woman or girl; a minx; **b** woman of doubtful character.

hustings, n. pl. [1. hústingz; 2. hástiŋz]. O.E. *hūsting*, 'council', of Danes, M.E. *hūsting*, fr. O.N. *hūsþing*, fr. *hūs* (see **house (I.)**) & *þing*, 'assembly, council'; cp. Swed., Dan. *ting*, 'assize'. See **thing**. **1.** Court formerly held in some English cities and boroughs, now only in city of London: *the court of hustings*. **2. a** (hist.) Platform in London Guildhall where court of hustings was formerly held; **b** (hist.) platform where parliamentary candidates were nominated, and from which they spoke; **c** *the hustings*, electioneering platform; election proceedings.

hustle (I.), vb. trans. & intrans. [1. húsl; 2. hásl]. Cp. Du. *hutselen, husselen*, 'to shake up and down in a vessel', freq. (see **-le**) fr. M. Du. *hutsen*, 'to shake, jog, jolt'. **1.** trans. **a** To push, shove, jostle (person) roughly or rudely, as in crowd: *to be hustled by a pickpocket; the mob was hustled along, hustled out of, the street by cavalry; he was hustled into a cab*; **b** (fig.) to impel, hurry, rush, bustle, (person) into acting: *to be hustled into a decision; I won't be hustled*; **c** (colloq.) to cause to be carried on or completed quickly: *to hustle something through*, get it done; also *hustle up*. **2.** intrans. **a** To push, press, roughly (against person); to press forward: *to hustle against one; to hustle through the streets*; to move about hurriedly; **b** (Am. colloq.) to act rapidly and energetically.

hustle (II.), n., fr. prec. Action of one who hustles; a rapid, energetic action; esp. such action when it results in something being done; push, drive; **b** fussy, restless movement or action.

hustler, n. [1. húsler; 2. háslə]. **hustle (I.)** & **-er**. Person who hustles; one who acts with nervous rapidity and energy, but tends to get things done.

hut (I.), n. [1. hut; 2. hat]. M.E. *hotte*, rare & doubtful, Fr. *hutte*, fr. O.H.G. *huttea, hutta* (Mod. Germ. *hütte*), Gmc. type **hudjō*, W. Gmc. **huddjō*, fr. Gmc. **hud-*, wk. grade of base **heud-* &c., 'to protect, hide, shelter' &c. See **hide (III.)**, **house**. **a** Small rude shelter; poor dwelling; hovel, cabin; **b** light temporary building, used by soldiers in camp, workmen &c.

hut (II.), vb. trans. & intrans., fr. prec. **a** trans. To provide with, shelter in, huts; **b** intrans., to lodge in a hut or huts.

hutch (I.), n. [1. huch; 2. hatʃ]. M.E. *huc(c)he, hoche* (also *whucche, whyche*), fr. O. Fr. *huche*, 'chest, bin', fr. Low Lat. *hūtica*. Origin doubtful. **1. a** Box, bin, chest, as for grain; bin into which flour is bolted; **b** truck in which coal is conveyed to bottom of shaft and hauled up; **c** baker's kneading trough; **d** trough for washing ore. **2. a** Coop or cage for small animals, esp. for rabbits or ferrets, consisting of box with bars or wire netting in front; **b** (colloq.) cabin, small cottage.

hutch (II.), vb. trans., fr. prec. **1.** (obs. or archaic) To store in a hutch or chest (Milton). **2.** (min.) To wash (ore) in hutch.

hutment, n. [1. hútment; 2. hátmənt]. **hut (I.)** & **-ment**. (mil.) **a** Housing in huts; **b** collection or camp of huts.

huzza, interj., n., & vb. intrans. & trans. [1. hoozáh; 2. huzá]. Germ. *hussa*; imitative. (archaic) Hurrah.

huzzy, n. See **hussy**.

hyacinth, n. [1. híasinth; 2. háiəsinþ]. Fr. *hyacinthe*, fr. Lat. *hyacinth-(us)*, fr. Gk. *huák-inth-os*, possibly cogn. w. Lat. *vaccīnium*, 'whortleberry'; the earlier Engl. form was **jacinth**. **1. a** Fabulous blue flower supposed by ancient Greeks to have sprung from blood of the youth, Hyacinthus, slain by Apollo; **b** plant nearly related to the squills, cultivated for its handsome spikes of flowers of various colours; **c** common English bluebell or wild hyacinth &c.; **d** one of several related plants, as *Cape hyacinth*, Galtonia; *grape hyacinth*. **2.** Precious stone usually of a blue or dark colour; **a** jacinth of ancient writers; **b** red or brownish variety of zircon; **c** brownish variety of garnet; cinnamon-stone.

hyacinthine, adj. [1. hīasínthīn; 2. haiəsínþain]. Lat. *hyacinthinus*, fr. Gk. *huakinthinos*. **hyacinth** & **-ine**. **a** Pertaining to hyacinth flower; **b** resembling it in colour; traditional rendering of Homeric epithet applied to hair; perhaps dark and glossy: *hyacinthine locks* (Milton).

Hyades, Hyads, n. pl. [1. híadēz, híadz; 2. háiədiz, háiædz]. Lat., fr. Gk. *Huádes*, orig. prob. 'little pigs', fr. *hûs* (see **sow (I.)** & **-ad**), but associated w. *húein*, 'to rain'. See **hyeto-**. Group of five stars in Taurus, anciently supposed to indicate rain when they rose with the sun.

hyaena, n. See **hyena**.

hyaline (I.), n. [1. híalin, -in; 2. háiəlain, -in]. Lat. *hyalinus*, fr. Gk. *huálinos*, 'glassy', fr. *húalos, húelos*, 'crystal, glass', said to be an Egyptian word. **1.** (poet., Milton) The glassy sea. **2.** Opalescent nitrogenous compound, found in hydatid cysts.

hyaline (II.), adj. See prec. Crystalline, glassy, transparent, translucent.

hyalite, n. [1. híalīt; 2. háiəlait]. **hyalo-** & **-ite**. Fr. *hyalite*. Colourless variety of opal.

hyalitis, n. [1. hīalítis; 2. haiəláitis]. **hyalo-** & **-itis**. (pathol.) Inflammation of the vitreous humour of the eye.

hyalo-, pref. Gk. *húalos*, 'crystal, glass'. See **hyaline**. Form used in combination, denoting 'glassy, transparent, translucent'.

hyaloid, adj. & n. [1. híaloid; 2. háiəlɔid]. Gk. *hualoeidés*. Prec. & **-oid**. **1.** adj. Resembling crystal or glass; transparent, translucent; *hyaloid membrane*, that enclosing the vitreous humour of the eye. **2.** n. Hyaloid membrane.

hybrid (I.), n. [1. híbrid; 2. háibrid]. Lat. *hibrida, hybrida*, 'offspring of domesticated sow and wild boar; mongrel; person of mixed race', of doubtful, but prob. Gk. origin; perh. fr. Gk. *hûs* (see **sow (I.)**) & **ibro-*, 'wild boar' (?), assumed fr. the compound *ibríkalos*, 'hog', & **-ide**; otherwise fr. Gk. *húbrid-, húbris*, 'insolence', see **hubristic**. **1.** Animal or plant (rarely of human being) produced by parents of different species; crossbreed, mongrel (sometimes excluding offspring of parents of different varieties, which is then termed *crossbreed*). **2.** Thing of mixed origin, specif., compound word with elements from two languages, such as *sociology, starvation*.

hybrid (II.), adj., fr. prec. Having the nature of a hybrid: *a hybrid race; hybrid rose*.

hybridism, n. [1. híbridizm; 2. háibridizəm]. **hybrid (I.)** & **-ism**. **a** Condition, nature, of a hybrid; **b** production of hybrids.

hybridist, n. [1. híbridist; 2. háibridist]. See prec. & **-ist**. Person who practises hybridization.

hybridity, n. [1. hībríditi; 2. haibríditi]. **hybrid (I.)** & **-ity**. Quality, state, of being hybrid.

hybridizable, adj. [1. hìbridízabl; 2. hàibridáizəbl]. **hybridize** & **-able**. Capable of hybridization, of producing a hybrid.

hybridization, n. [1. hìbridīzáshun; 2. hàibridaizéiʃən]. Next word & **-ation**. Act, process, of producing a hybrid.

hybridize, vb. trans. & intrans. [1. híbridīz; 2. háibridaiz]. **hybrid (I.)** & **-ize**. **1.** trans. To cause (animals or plants) to produce hybrids; to cross, cross-fertilize: *to hybridize sweet peas*. **2.** intrans. To produce hybrids; to interbreed.

hydatid, n. [1. hídatid; 2. háidətid]. Gk. *hudatid-*, stem of *hudatís*, 'drop of water, watery vesicle', fr. *húdat-*, stem of *húdōr*, 'water'. See **hydro-**. Cyst or sac in animal body, containing watery fluid.

hydr-, pref. Form used in combination for **hydro-** before vowel or *h*.

hydra, n. [1. hídra; 2. háidrə]. Lat. *hydra*, fr. Gk. *húdra*, 'water-serpent'; fr. *húdōr*, 'water'. See **hydro-**. **1. a** (cap., Gk. mythol.) Serpent slain by Hercules at Lernae near Argos, having nine heads, any one of which, when struck off, was replaced by two; **b** (cap. or l.c., fig.) evil which tends to reappear after each effort to extirpate it. **2.** (zool.) Small, sessile, freshwater polyp, of which any severed part will grow into complete animal.

hydraemia, n. [1. hīdrémia; 2. haidrímiə]. Prec. & Gk. *haîma*, 'blood'. See **haemal** & **-ia**. (pathol.) Excessively watery condition of the blood.

hydragogue, adj. & n. [1. hídragog; 2. háidrəgɔg]. Lat. *hydragōgus*, adj., fr. Gk. *hudragōgós*, fr. **hydr-** & Gk. *agōgós*, 'leading, drawing forth', fr. *ágein*, 'to lead'. See this base under **agent**. (med.) **1.** adj. Expelling water from the body; diuretic. **2.** n. Medicine having this property.

hydrangea, n. [1. hīdránja; 2. haidréin(d)žə]. Generic name, fr. **hydr-** & Gk. *aggeîon*, 'vessel, capsule'. Cp. Gk. *ággos*, 'ware'; cogn. w. O. Ir. *aigen*, 'dish'. One of genus of Asiatic and N. American shrubs, cultivated in gardens and greenhouses for its handsome globular clusters of pink, white, or blue flowers.

hydrant, n. [1. hídrant; 2. háidrənt]. **hydr-** & **-ant**; orig. an Am. usage. Pipe, termination of pipe, from water-main, usually in street pavement, with valve and screw to which hose or standard with nozzle can be attached; fire-plug.

hydrate, n. & vb. trans. & intrans. [1. hídrāt; 2. háidreit]. **hydr-** & **-ate**. (chem.) **1.** n. Compound, usually a neutral salt, formed by union of water with another substance. **2.** vb. **a** trans. To make into a hydrate; **b** intrans., to become a hydrate.

hydration, n. [1. hīdráshun; 2. haidréiʃən]. Prec. & **-ion**. (chem.) Process of forming a hydrate.

hydraulic, adj. [1. hīdráwlik; 2. haidrɔ́lik]. Lat. *hydraulicus*, fr. Gk. *hudraulikós*, fr. *húdraulis*, 'water-organ', fr. **hydr-** & *aulós*, 'pipe, tube', formed w. instrumental formative *-l-*, fr. Aryan base **we-*, 'to blow, breathe'. See **air, weather, wind** (I.), & **-ic. 1.** Pertaining to, operated by, water or other liquid flowing through a pipe, channel, or orifice; pertaining to hydraulics.: *a hydraulic brake, buffer, crane, engine, lift* &c. **2.** (loosely) **a** Containing water: *hydraulic joint, valve*, one that prevents escape of gas from pipe by an enclosing vessel containing water; **b** consolidating in water: *hydraulic cement.*

hydraulically, adv. Prec. & **-al** & **-ly.** By means of water power; by means of hydraulics.

hydraulics, n. pl., used as sing. [1. hīdráwliks; 2. haidrɔ́liks]. See **hydraulic.** Science of liquids as motive power; art of applying water-pressure to engineering.

hydric, adj. [1. hídrik; 2. háidrik]. **hydr-** & **-ic.** (chem.) Pertaining to, containing, hydrogen.

hydride, n. [1. hídrīd; 2. háidraid]. **hydr-** & **-ide.** (chem.) Compound of hydrogen with another element.

hydro-, pref. Lat. *hydro-*, fr. Gk. *hudro-*, combining form of *húdōr*, 'water', cogn. w. Scrt. *an-udraš*, 'waterless' &c.; extended fr. Aryan base **wed-* &c. See further under **water, wet, otter, vodka, whisky.** Form used in combination with scientific terms, mostly of Greek origin, denoting **a** water, liquid, fluid, as *hydroelectric*, pertaining to the generation of electricity by water-power; *hydro-extractor*, apparatus for extracting water from yarn &c.; *hydromancy*, divination by water; *hydromechanics*, mechanics of liquids; *hydrophyte* (bot.), plant which grows in water; *hydrotechnical*, pertaining to the employment of water in engineering; *hydrotherapy*, treatment of disease by bathing and drinking waters; **b** (chem.) meaning hydrogen, as *hydrocyanic, -fluoric, -quinone, sulphuric* &c.

hydro, n. Popular abbreviation of *hydropathic (establishment).*

hydrocarbon, n. [1. hìdrōkárbun; 2. hàidroukáːbən]. See **hydro-** & **carbon.** Compound of hydrogen and carbon, as coal-gas &c.

hydrocele, n. [1. hídrōsēl; 2. háidrousīəl]. Gk. **hydro-** & *kḗlē*, 'tumour', see **-cele.** Dropsy of the scrotum, spermatic cord &c.

hydrocephalic, adj. [1. hìdrōsefálik; 2. hàidrousefǽlik]. See **hydro-** & **cephalic.** Pertaining to, suffering from, water on the brain; having abnormally and excessively large head.

hydrocephalous, adj. [1. hìdrōséfalus; 2. hàidrouséfələs]. See prec. & **-ous.** Hydrocephalic.

hydrocephalus, n. [1. hìdrōséfalus; 2. hàidrouséfələs]. Mod. Lat., fr. Gk. *hudroképhalon*, fr. **hydro-** & Gk. *kephalḗ*, 'head'. See **cephalic.** Disease of the brain, esp. in infant, causing accumulation of liquid in and around the brain, often enormously enlarging the head, and causing mental degeneration; dropsy of the brain; water on the brain.

hydrochloric, adj. [1. hìdrōklórik; 2. hàidrouklɔ́rik]. (chem.) Compounded of hydrogen and chlorine; *hydrochloric acid*, that formed by these elements; muriatic acid.

hydrodynamic, adj. & n. [1. hìdrōdīnámik; 2. hàidroudainǽmik]. **hydro-** & **dynamic. 1.** adj. Pertaining to the dynamics of fluids. **2.** n. pl. *Hydrodynamics*, science of the dynamics of fluids, comprising hydraulics and hydrostatics.

hydrogen, n. [1. hídrojen; 2. háidrədžin]. Fr. *hydrogène.* **hydro-** & **-gen.** Inflammable gaseous element, the lightest known substance; constituent, with oxygen, of water.

hydrogenation, n. [1. hìdrōjenáshun; 2. hàidroudženéiʃən]. Prec. & **-ation.** Formation of higher hydrocarbons (e.g. petrol) from lower hydrocarbons (e.g. powdered coal) treated with hydrogen under heat and pressure.

hydrogenize, vb. trans. [1. hīdrójenīz; 2. haidrɔ́džinaiz]. Prec. & **-ize. a** To combine with hydrogen; **b** to treat with hydrogen.

hydrogenous, adj. [1. hīdrójenus; 2. haidrɔ́džinəs]. **hydrogen** & **-ous.** Pertaining to, containing, hydrogen.

hydrographer, n. [1. hīdrógrafer; 2. haidrɔ́grəfə]. **hydro-** & **-graph** & **-er.** Person versed in hydrography.

hydrographic, adj. [1. hìdrográfik; 2. hàidrəgrǽfik]. **hydro-** & **-graphic.** Pertaining to hydrography.

hydrography, n. [1. hīdrógrafi; 2. haidrɔ́grəfi]. **hydro-** & **-graphy**; cp. Fr. *hydrographie.* **a** Descriptive science treating of the bodies of water on the earth's surface; art of surveying and mapping them; **b** representation in map of oceans, seas &c.

hydroid, adj. & n. [1. hídroid; 2. háidrɔid]. **hydr-** & **-oid. 1.** adj. Resembling the hydra, polyp-like. **2.** n. Animal resembling the hydra.

hydrologic, adj. [1. hīdrolójik; 2. haidrəlɔ́džik]. **hydro-** & **-logic.** Pertaining to hydrology.

hydrologist, n. [1. hīdrólojist; 2. haidrɔ́lədžist]. **hydro-** & **-logist.** Person versed in hydrology.

hydrology, n. [1. hīdróloji; 2. haidrɔ́lədži]. **hydro-** & **-logy**; cp. Fr. *hydrologie.* Science treating of water, esp. in relation to its subterranean distribution.

hydrolyse, vb. trans. [1. hídrolīz; 2. háidrəlaiz]. See next word. (chem.) To subject to hydrolysis.

hydrolysis, n. [1. hīdrólisis; 2. haidrɔ́lisis]. **hydro-** & **-lysis.** (chem.) Decomposition of a substance by the combination of one of its elements with one of those in water.

hydrolytic, adj. [1. hīdrolítik; 2. haidrəlítik]. **hydro-** & **-lytic.** (chem.) Pertaining to hydrolysis.

Hydromedusae, n. pl. [1. hìdrōmedúsē; 2. hàidroumidjúsī]. **hydro-** & **medusa.** (zool.) A subclass of Hydrozoa, including the marine jellyfish.

hydromel, n. [1. hídromel; 2. háidrəmel]. Lat. *hydromeli*, fr. Gk. *hudrómeli*; **hydro-** & Gk. *méli*, 'honey'. See **melliferous** & **mildew.** Drink composed of honey and water.

hydrometer, n. [1. hīdrómeter; 2. haidrɔ́mitə]. **hydro-** & **-meter. 1.** Instrument for measuring specific gravity and strength of liquids, or of solids. **2.** Instrument for measuring velocity of water.

hydrometric(al), adj. [1. hìdrométrik(l); 2. hàidrəmétrik(l)]. **hydro-** & **-metric** & **-al.** Pertaining to hydrometry or to the hydrometer.

hydrometry, n. [1. hīdrómetri; 2. haidrɔ́mitri]. **hydro-** & **-metry.** Measurement of the specific gravity of liquids; use of the hydrometer.

hydropath, n. [1. hídropath; 2. háidrəpæþ]. **hydro-** & **-path.** Hydropathist.

hydropathic, adj. & n. [1. hìdropáthik; 2. hàidrəpǽþik]. **hydro-** & **-pathic. 1.** adj. Pertaining to hydropathy; *hydropathic establishment*, hotel with special baths and other facilities for hydropathy. **2.** n. (colloq.) Hydropathic establishment.

hydropathist, n. [1. hīdrópathist; 2. haidrɔ́pəþist]. **hydro-** & **-pathist.** Physician who practises hydropathy.

hydropathy, n. [1. hīdrópathi; 2. haidrɔ́pəþi]. **hydro-** & **-pathy.** System of treating diseases by internal and external application of water; water cure.

hydrophane, n. [1. hídrofān; 2. háidrəfein]. **hydro-** & Gk. *phainein*, 'to show'. See **phantasm.** Variety of opal which becomes transparent when wetted.

hydrophobia, n. [1. hìdrofóbia; 2. hàidrəfóubiə]. Lat., fr. Gk. *hudrophobia*, fr. **hydro-** & **-phobia. a** Dread of water, esp. as symptom of disease; **b** rabies, in animals or human beings, which is marked by convulsions on patient attempting to swallow liquid.

hydrophobic, adj. [1. hìdrofóbik; 2. hàidrəfóubik]. Lat. *hydrophobicus*, fr. Gk. *hudrophobikós*; fr. **hydro-** & **-phobic.** Pertaining to hydrophobia.

hydrophone, n. [1. hídrofōn; 2. háidrəfoun]. **hydro-** & **-phone.** Instrument for detecting sound **a** made by submarine moving in the neighbourhood; **b** of water flowing through pipe.

hydropic, adj. [1. hīdrópik; 2. haidrɔ́pik]. M.E. *ydropike*, fr. O. Fr. *idropique* (Mod. Fr. *hydropique*), fr. Lat. *hydrōpic-(us)*, fr. Gk. *hudrōpikós*, fr. *húdrōps*, see **dropsy, & -ic.** Dropsical.

hydroplane, n. [1. hídroplān; 2. háidrəplein]. **hydro-** & **-plane. 1. a** Plane projecting from submarine, enabling it to be steered upwards or downwards; **b** plane attached to motor-boat enabling it to skim along surface of water; **c** motor-boat fitted with such planes. **2.** Specif., waterplane; aeroplane which can alight and float on water.

hydroscope, n. [1. hídroskōp; 2. háidrəskoup]. **hydro-** & **-scope.** Instrument for observing the bottom of a body of water.

hydrosphere, n. [1. hídrosfēr; 2. háidrəsfiə]. **hydro-** & **sphere**, after **atmosphere. a** The aqueous vapour of the atmosphere; **b** waters of the earth's surface collectively.

hydrostat, n. [1. hídrostat; 2. háidrəstæt]. **hydro-** & **-stat.** Appliance indicating irregularities in level of water in reservoir or boiler.

hydrostatic(al), adj. [1. hìdrostátik(l); 2. hàidrəstǽtik(l)]. **hydro-** & **-static** (& **-al**). Pertaining to hydrostatics, or to the properties of liquids in equilibrium; *hydrostatic press*, machine for compressing materials by transmitting water pressure from small to large cylinder.

hydrostatics, n. pl., used as sing. [1. hìdrostátiks; 2. hàidrəstǽtiks], fr. prec. Science treating of liquids in equilibrium; statics in relation to liquids.

hydrotropism, n. [1. hīdrótropizm; 2. haidrɔ́trəpizəm]. **hydro-** & **-tropism.** (biol.) Tendency of organism to grow either towards or away from moisture: *positive and negative hydrotropism.*

hydrous, adj. [1. hídrus; 2. háidrəs]. **hydro-** & **-ous.** Containing water, esp. chem., in combination.

Hydrozoa, n. pl. [1. hìdrozóa; 2. hàidrəzóuə]. Mod. Lat., fr. **hydro-** & Gk. *zôa*, 'animals'. See **zoo-.** (zool.) Animals forming a class of coelenterates including jellyfishes and polyps.

hydrozoan, adj. & n. [1. hìdrozóan; 2. hàidrəzóuən]. Prec. & **-an. 1.** adj. Pertaining to the Hydrozoa. **2.** n. Member of the class Hydrozoa.

hyena, hyaena, n. [1. hīḗna; 2. haiínə]. Lat. *hyaena*, fr. Gk. *húaina*, 'hyena', lit. 'sow', fr. its bristly mane, fem. of *hûs*, 'swine'. See **sow** (I.) & **swine.** One of a family of carnivorous mammals, allied to the dog, of Asia and Africa, strong, but cowardly, feeding on carrion by night.

hyena-dog, n. Cape hunting dog.

hyeto-, pref. Gk. *huetós*, 'rain', cp. *húei*, 'it rains'; for **sū-*, fr. wh. base comes also O.E *sēaw*, 'sap', *sūgan*, 'to suck'; Lat. *sūcus*, 'juice'. See **succulent**; cp. also O. Prussian *suge*, 'rain'. Form used in combination, denoting rain, as *hyetograph*, chart showing annual rainfall; *hyetography*, scientific description of distribution of rain; *hyetology*, science of atmospheric precipitation; *hyetōmeter*, rain-gauge.

hygiene, n. [1. híjēn; 2. háidžīn]. Fr. *hygiène*, fr. Gk. *hugieinḗ* (*tekhnḗ*), '(art) of health', *hugíeia*, 'health'; fem. sing. of *hugieinós*, 'pertaining to health'; cp. Gk. *hugiḗs*, 'healthy', cogn. w. Scrt. *ugráš*, 'vigorous' &c., & **-ine**; fr. base **weg-* &c., whence also Lat. *vegēre*, 'to quicken, arouse, be brisk', also *vegetus*, 'lively, vigorous' &c. See further under **vegetable.** Science or art of maintaining the health of the individual or community; sanitary principles and methods.

hygienic, adj. [1. hìjḗnik; 2. haidžínik]. Prec. & **-ic.** Pertaining to hygiene, or to the laws of health; conducive to health; healthy.

hygienically, adv. [1. hĭjĕ́nikali; 2. hàidžíni-kəli]. **hygienic** & **-al** & **-ly**. In a hygienic manner.

hygienics, n. pl., used as sing. [1. hĭjĕ́niks; 2. hàidžíniks]. See **hygienic**. Laws, principles, methods, of preserving health.

hygienist, n. [1. hī́jinist; 2. háidžinist]. **hygiene** & **-ist**. Person versed in hygiene.

hygro-, pref. Gk. *hugrós*, 'moist', cogn. w. Lat. *ūvēre*, 'to be moist', *hūmidus*, 'moist', fr. **ugʷ-*. See **humid, humour**. Form used in combination with words of Greek origin, denoting moist, humid, as *hygrograph*, instrument recording changes in atmospheric humidity; *hygrology*, science treating of humidity &c.

hygrometer, n. [1. hīgrómeter; 2. haigrómitə]. **hygro-** & **-meter**. Instrument for measuring the humidity of the atmosphere.

hygrometric, adj. [1. hìgrométrik; 2. hàigrəmétrik]. **hygro-** & **-metric**. Pertaining to hygrometry or the hygrometer.

hygrometry, n. [1. hīgrómetri; 2. haigrómitri]. **hygro-** & **-metry**. Science of measuring the humidity of bodies, esp. of the atmosphere.

hygroscope, n. [1. hī́groskōp; 2. háigrəskoup]. **hygro-** & **-scope**. Cp. Fr. *hygroscope*. Instrument showing variations in atmospheric humidity.

hygroscopic, adj. [1. hìgroskópik; 2. hàigrəskópik]. Prec. & **-ic**. **1.** Pertaining to the hygroscope. **2. a** Absorbing or attracting moisture, as salt; **b** indicating the absorption of moisture: *hygroscopic movements*.

hyle, n. [1. hīl; 2. hail]. Gk. *húlē*, *súlē* 'wood, matter', prob. for *(*k*)*suluwā*, & cogn. w. Lat. *silva*, 'wood'. See **savage, silvan**. (philos.) Matter, as distinguished from form.

hylic, adj. [1. hī́lik; 2. háilik]. Gk. *hūlikós*, fr. prec. & **-ic**. (philos.) Material, corporeal.

hylo-, pref. Gk. *hūlo-*, form of **hyle** used in combination with words of Greek origin denoting **a** wood, as *hylophagous, hylotomous*, (zool.) eating, cutting, wood; *hylophyte*, (bot.) plant living in woods; **b** (philos.) matter, material, as *hylomorphism*, doctrine that nothing exists but matter and material forms; *hylopathism*, doctrine that matter is sentient, or that matter and spirit are interdependent; *hylotheism*, doctrine identifying God with matter; *hylozoism*, doctrine that all matter is living.

hymen, n. [1. hī́men; 2. háimen]. Mod. Lat., fr. Gk. *hūmḗn*, 'thin skin, membrane', prob. for **syūmēn*, cogn. w. Scrt. *syū́man-*, 'band', fr. *sīv-*, 'to sew'; Aryan base **sieu*, 'to sew'. See **seam, suture**, & cp. **hymn**. **1. a** (anat.) Virginal membrane in the vagina; **b** (bot.) pellicle surrounding flower in bud. **2.** (fig., cap.) Marriage (from Lat. *Hȳmēn*, from Gk. *Hūmēn*, god of marriage rites).

hymenal, adj. [1. hī́menal; 2. háiminəl]. Prec. **1** & **-al**. (anat.) Pertaining to the hymen.

hymeneal, adj. [1. hìmenḗal; 2. hàiminíəl]. Lat. *hymenae-(us)*, fr. Gk. *huménaios*, 'wedding song; wedding', also 'the god Hymen'. See **hymen** & **-al**. Pertaining to a wedding or to marriage.

Hymenoptera, n. pl. [1. hìmenóptera; 2. hàiminóptərə]. Mod. Lat., fr. Gk. *hūmenópteros*, 'membrane-winged', fr. *hūmḗn*, 'membrane' (see **hymen**), & *pterón*, 'wing'; fr. base **pet-*, 'fly' &c. See **ptero-** & **feather**. Highest order of insects, including bees, wasps, ants, sawflies &c., having four membranous wings.

hymenopterous, adj. [1. hīmenópterus; 2. hàiminóptərəs]. Prec. & **-ous**. Pertaining to the Hymenoptera.

hymn (I.), n. [1. him; 2. him]. M.E. *ympne*, fr. O. Fr. *ymne* (later Fr. & Engl. *hymne* through Lat. influence), fr. Lat. *hymn-(us)*, fr. Gk. *húmnos*, 'festal song, hymn'. Origin doubtful, perh. orig. 'nuptial song' & connected w. **hymen**. **a** Solemn song of praise or triumph, addressed to God, a god or gods, or other exalted being; **b** specif., religious song performed in Christian churches during divine service.

hymn (II.), vb. trans. & intrans., fr. prec.; cp. L. Lat. *hymnēre*. **1.** trans. To address or praise in a hymn or hymns; to celebrate (an event &c.), proclaim (glory, merits of), in hymns: *to hymn the Redeemer's praise*. **2.** intrans. To sing a hymn or hymns.

hymnal, adj. & n. [1. hímnal; 2. hímnəl]. **hymn (I.)** & **-al**. **1.** adj. Pertaining to, consisting of, hymns. **2.** n. Collection of hymns; hymn-book.

hymnary, n. [1. hímnari; 2. hímnəri]. L. Lat. *hymnārium*. **hymn (I.)** & **-ary**. Hymnal, hymn-book.

hymn-book, n. Book consisting of collection of hymns, esp. for public worship.

hymnic, adj. [1. hímnik; 2. hímnik]. **hymn (I.)** & **-ic**. Cp. Fr. *hymnique*. Pertaining to, resembling, a hymn.

hymnist, n. [1. hímnist; 2. hímnist]. **hymn (I.)** & **-ist**. Composer of a hymn or hymns.

hymnodist, n. [1. hímnodist; 2. hímnədist]. See next word & **-ist**. Person versed in hymnody.

hymnody, n. [1. hímnodi; 2. hímnədi]. Gk. *humnō(i)dia*; **hymn (I.)** & *aeídein*, 'to sing' (see **ode**), & **-y**. **a** Singing of hymns; **b** hymns collectively; **c** study of history and classification of hymns; hymnology.

hymnographer, n. [1. himnógrafer; 2. himnógrəfə]. *hymno-*, combining form of **hymn (I.)** & **-graph** & **-er**. Cp. Gk. *humnográphos*, 'writing hymns'. **1.** Person who writes on subject of hymns. **2.** Writer of hymns.

hymnography, n. [1. himnógrafi; 2. himnógrəfi]. See prec. & **-y**. **1.** Descriptive and historical treatment of hymns and their composition. **2.** Composition of hymns.

hymnologist, n. [1. himnólojist; 2. himnólədžist]. See next word & **-ist**. **1.** Student of hymnology. **2.** Composer of hymns.

hymnology, n. [1. himnóloji; 2. himnólədži]. Eccles. Gk. *humnología*. See **hymn (I.)** & **-logy**. **1. a** Study of hymns; treatise on this; **b** hymns collectively. **2.** Composition of hymns.

hyoid, adj. & n. [1. hī́oid; 2. háioid]. Gk. *huoeid-és*, 'shaped like the Greek letter U' (which, when the initial of a word, is always written with aspirate), fr. the name of the letter & **-oid**. **1.** adj. (anat.) U-shaped; *hyoid bone*, small, U-shaped bone at base of tongue. **2.** n. Hyoid bone.

hyoscin(e), n. [1. hī́osēn; 2. háiəsīn]. Term formed fr. first element in Gk. *hyoskúamos*, 'henbane', & **-in(e)**; the Gk. word is fr. *hûs*, 'pig' (see **sow (I.)**), & *kúamos*, 'bean', the origin of wh. is doubtful. A poisonous alkaloid found in the datura or thorn apple, also in henbane &c., used in medicine as a powerful nerve sedative &c.

hypaethral, adj. [1. hīpḗthral; 2. haipíþrəl]. Lat. *hypaethr-(us)*, fr. Gk. *húpaithros*, 'under the open sky, or aether', fr. **hypo-**, 'under', & *aithḗr*, 'sky'. See **ether**. (archit.) Open to the sky: *an hypaethral court*.

hypallage, n. [1. hīpálaji; 2. haipǽlədži]. Lat. *hypallagē*, fr. Gk. *hupallagḗ*, fr. *hupallássein*, 'to exchange', fr. **hypo-** & *allássein*, 'to change', fr. base **all-*, 'other'. See **alien, alter, else**. (rhet.) Figure of speech by which the syntactic relation of terms in sentence is reversed, as *the ground hit me in the face*, instead of *my face hit the ground*.

hyper-, pref. Lat. *hyper-*, fr. Gk. *hupér*, 'above, beyond', orig. a compar. adv., fr. *hupó*, 'under, beneath, up to', see **hypo-** & cp. **sub-, up**; cogn. w. Scrt. *upári*, Lat. *s-uper*, Goth. *ufar*, q.v. under **above, over**; Aryan type **uper-*. Prefix generally equivalent to **super-**, properly, but not always, with words of Greek origin, denoting: **a** above, beyond, in excess of, the normal or usual, as *hyper-Calvinism*; frequent in physiology and pathology, as *hyperaesthesia*, abnormally keen power of sensation; *hyperaesthetic*; *hyperalgesia*; *hyperkinesis*, spasm; *hyperpnoea* (Gk. *pnoié*, 'breath'), excessively rapid breathing; *hypersthenia* (Gk. *sthénos*, 'strength'), excessive vigour of body or of any part; **b** transcending, as *hyperphenomenal, hyperphysical*; (geom. and math.) transcending conditions of three dimensions, as *hypergeometry, hyperplane, hypersolid, hyperspace, hypersphere*; **c** superimposed, as *hyperparasite*, parasite of parasite.

hyperbatic, adj. [1. hīperbátik; 2. haipəbǽtik]. Gk. *huperbatikós*. See next word & **-ic**. Pertaining to, marked by, hyperbaton.

hyperbaton, n. [1. hīpĕ́rbaton; 2. haipə́bətən]. Lat., fr. Gk. *hupérbaton*, fr. *huperbatós*, 'transposed', vbl. adj., fr. *huperbaínein*, 'to go over', fr. **hyper-** & *baínein*, 'to go'. See **basis**. (gram.) Inversion of natural order of words, e.g. '*All that beauty, all that wealth e'er gave, Awaits alike the inevitable hour*' (Gray's 'Elegy'), for *the inevitable hour awaits all that beauty* &c.

hyperbola, n. [1. hīpĕ́rbola; 2. haipə́bələ]. Lat., fr. Gk. *huperbolḗ*, 'throwing beyond, excess, hyperbola', vbl. n., fr. *huperbállein*, 'to throw beyond, exceed', fr. **hyper-** & *bállein*, 'to throw'. See **ballistic**. (geom.) 'Curve formed by section of cone when the cutting plane makes greater angle with base than sides of cone make' (Webster's 'Internat. Dict.').

hyperbole, n. [1. hīpĕ́rboli; 2. haipə́bəli]. Lat., fr. Gk. *huperbolḗ*, 'an overshooting, excess'. See prec. (rhet.) **a** Figure of speech which consists of obvious over- or under-statement, intended to give emphasis and not to deceive; **b** fantastic, extravagant, exaggeration in statement, made in excitement, from enthusiasm &c.

hyperbolic, adj. [1. hìperbólik; 2. hàipəbólik]. Lat. *hyperbolicus*, fr. Gk. *huperbolikós*. See prec. & **-ic**. **1.** (math., geom.) Pertaining to the hyperbola. **2.** Of the nature of hyperbole.

hyperbolical, adj. [1. hìperbólikl; 2. hàipəbólikəl]. Prec. & **-al**. Pertaining to hyperbole; rhetorically or poetically exaggerated.

hyperbolically, adv. Prec. & **-ly**. **1.** In the manner of hyperbole. **2.** In the manner of the hyperbola.

hyperbolist, n. [1. hīpĕ́rbolist; 2. haipə́bəlist]. **hyperbole** & **-ist**. Person who employs hyperbole.

hyperborean, adj. & n. [1. hìperborḗan; 2. hàipəbɔríən]. L. Lat. *hyperboreānus*, fr. Gk. *huperbóreos*, 'belonging to a region far north'. See **hyper-**, 'beyond', & **boreal**. **1.** adj. Northern; bitterly cold. **2.** n. Inhabitant of the North.

hypercatalectic, adj. [1. hìperkataléktik; 2. hàipəkætəléktik]. L. Lat. *hypercatalēcticus*, fr. Gk. *huperkatálēktos*. See **hyper-** & **catalectic**. (prosody) Having a redundant syllable at the end of the verse.

hypercritic, n. [1. hìperkrítik; 2. hàipəkrítik]. **hyper-** & **critic**. Person who is hypercritical.

hypercritical, adj. [1. hìperkrítikl; 2. hàipəkrítik(ə)l]. Prec. & **-al**. Excessively critical; addicted to severe judgement; carping, captious.

hypercritically, adv. Prec. & **-ly**. In a hypercritical manner.

hypercriticism, n. [1. hìperkrítisizm; 2. hàipəkrítisizəm]. **hyper-** & **criticism**. Excessive or captious criticism.

hypercriticize, vb. trans. & intrans. [1. hìperkritisiz; 2. hàipəkrítisaiz]. **hyper-** & **criticize**. To criticize excessively or captiously.

hypermetrical, adj. [1. hìpermétrikl; 2. hàipəmétrik(ə)l]. Gk. *hupérmetros*, 'going beyond measure'. **hyper-** & **metric** & **-al**. (prosody) **a** Redundant; **b** having a redundant syllable at the end.

hypermetropia, n. [1. hìpermetrṓpia; 2. hàipəmetróupiə]. Gk. *hupérmetros*, see prec., & Gk. *ṓps*, 'eye'. See **optic**. Excessively long sight; reverse of *myopia*.

hypermetropic, adj. [1. hìpermetrópik; 2. hàipəmetrópik]. Prec. & **-ic**. Having excessively, morbidly, long sight.

hypertrophic, adj. [1. hìpertrófik; 2. hàipətrófik]. **hypertrophy** & **-ic**. Pertaining to, of the nature of, affected with, hypertrophy.

hypertrophied, adj. [1. hīpértrofid; 2. haipṓtrəfid]. Next word & **-ed**. **a** (pathol., biol.) Affected with hypertrophy; **b** (fig., of non-material things) over-developed, morbidly excessive: *hypertrophied self-esteem.*

hypertrophy (I.), n. [1. hīpértrofi; 2. haipṓtrəfi], fr. **hyper-** & Gk. *trophḗ*, 'nourishment', cogn. w. Gk. *tréphein*, 'become fat, be nourished' &c. See second element of **atrophy**. **a** (pathol., biol.) Excessive development, abnormal or morbid enlargement, of any part of an organism; reverse of *atrophy*; **b** (fig.) excessive development of a faculty.

hypertrophy (II.), vb. trans. & intrans., fr. prec. **1.** trans. To affect with hypertrophy. **2.** intrans. To be affected with hypertrophy.

hyphen, n. & vb. trans. [1. hífen; 2. háifən]. Lat., fr. Gk. *huphén* for *huph' hén*, 'under one (head)', fr. **hypo-** & *hén*, neut. of *heîs*, 'one'; see first element in **hendeca-**. **1.** n. Short horizontal stroke (-) used in writing and printing, to connect the two parts of a compound word, as in *Anglo-Indian, dining-table*; or to connect the parts of a word divided at the end of a line of writing or printing; also sometimes to indicate the division of a word into syllables or etymological elements, as *co-operate*. **2.** vb. To connect by a hyphen, to hyphenate.

hyphenate, vb. trans. [1. hífenāt; 2. háifəneit]. Prec. & **-ate**. To connect with a hyphen; to write with a hyphen or hyphens. Phr. *hyphenated American*, (colloq.) one of foreign origin, not fully assimilated, as *German-American.*

hypnagogic, adj. [1. hipnagójik; 2. hipnəgódžik]. Gk. *húpn-(os)*, 'sleep', see **hypno-**, & *agōgós*, 'leading, eliciting', fr. *ágein*, 'to lead', see **agent**, & **-ic**. Pertaining to drowsiness; ushering in sleep; *hypnagogic illusions*, dream-like images seen before falling asleep.

hypnic, adj. & n. [1. hípnik; 2. hípnik]. Gk. *hupnikós*, 'pertaining to sleep'. See **hypno-** & **-ic**. **1.** adj. Inducing sleep. **2.** n. Soporific.

hypno-, pref. Gk. *húpnos*, 'sleep', for **swəpno-*, cogn. w. Scrt. *svap-naš*, 'sleep', Lith. *sāp-nas*, 'dream', Lat. *som-nus* for **sop-nus*, fr. **swepnos*, 'sleep', O.E. *swef-en*, 'sleep, dream'; fr. Aryan base **swep-*, 'to sleep'. See further under **somnolent, soporific**. Form used in combination with words of Greek origin, denoting, **a** sleep, ordinary or hypnotic; as *hypnogenetic, hypnogenic*, producing hypnotic sleep; *hypnophobia*, morbid dread of sleep; **b** dormant condition, as *hypnospore*, (bot.) hibernating spore of certain algae.

hypnoid, adj. [1. hípnoid; 2. hípnɔid]. Prec. & **-oid**. Resembling hypnosis; partially or imperfectly hypnotic.

hypnosis, n. [1. hipnṓsis; 2. hipnóusis]. Mod. Lat., fr. Gk. *hupnóein*, 'to put to sleep'. **hypno-** & **-osis**. **1.** Induction of sleep. **2.** Hypnotic state; condition resembling profound sleep, usually artificially induced, marked by subconscious activity and sensitiveness to suggestion.

hypnotic, adj. & n. [1. hipnótik; 2. hipnɔ́tik]. Lat. *hypnōticus*, fr. Gk. *hupnōtikós*, 'drowsy, soporific', fr. *hupnóein*, 'to put to sleep'. See prec. **1.** adj. **a** Inducing sleep, soporific; **b** pertaining to, inducing, subject or susceptible to, hypnosis: *the hypnotic state; a hypnotic subject.* **2.** n. **a** Drug or other agent that induces sleep; soporific, narcotic; **b** person susceptible to hypnotism.

hypnotism, n. [1. hípnotizm; 2. hípnətizəm]. See **hypnotize** & **-ism**. **a** Induction of hypnosis **2**; practice of inducing it; **b** (loosely) hypnosis; **c** (fig.) power of dominating or controlling a person's feelings and will; fascination, power of suggestion.

hypnotist, n. [1. hípnotist; 2. hípnətist]. See **hypnotize** & **-ist**. Person who practises hypnotism.

hypnotization, n. [1. hìpnotīzā́shun; 2. hìpnətaizéiʃən]. See next word & **-ation**. Action or process of hypnotizing.

hypnotize, vb. trans. [1. hípnotīz; 2. hípnətaiz]. Gk. *hupnōt-*, adj. stem fr. *hupnóein* (see **hypnotic**) & **-ize**. **a** To put into the hypnotic state by suggestion; **b** (fig.) to dominate the feelings and will of; to fascinate: *hypnotized by the speaker's eloquence.*

hypnotizer, n. [1. hípnotīzer; 2. hípnətaizə]. Prec. & **-er**. One who hypnotizes; a hypnotist.

hypnotoid, adj. [1. hípnotoid; 2. hípnətɔid]. See **hypnotize** & **-oid**. Resembling hypnosis.

hypo, n. [1. hípō; 2. háipou]. Abbr. fr. *hyposulphite.* Sodium hyposulphite, used in solution for fixing photographs.

hypo-, pref. Lat. *hypo-*, fr. Gk. *hupó*, 'under, below', also 'from below', cogn. w. Scrt. *úpa*, 'near, on, under, up to', Lat. *s-ub* (see **sub-**), Goth. *uf*, 'under'. See **above, over**. Prefix generally equivalent to **sub-**, but used with words of Greek origin, denoting, **a** below, under, on the lower or inner side, as *hypobasal*; *hypoblast*, inner germ-layer of embryo; *hypoblastic, hypobranchial, hypogastric*; *hypogastrium* (Gk. *hupogástrion*), lowest median abdominal region; *hypogeal* (Gk. *gê*, 'the earth'; see **geo-**), subterranean; *hypogene*, (geol.) produced underground; *hypogenous*, (bot.) growing on the underside; *hypogeous*, (bot.) subterranean; **b** subordinate, subordinately, as *hypotactic, hypotaxis*; in a minor degree, somewhat, a little, as *hypothermal*; (chem.) combined with less oxygen, as *hypochlorous, hypophosphate, hypophosphoric*; **d** deficient, as *hypobulia* (Gk. *boúlesthai*, 'to will'), deficient will-power.

hypocaust, n. [1. hípokawst; 2. háipoukɔ̄st]. Lat. *hypocaustum*, fr. Gk. *hupókauston*, lit. 'burnt below'. See **hypo-** & **caustic**. **a** Space beneath pavement of ancient Roman house or bath filled with hot air from furnace; **b** modern heating apparatus beneath floor of hothouse &c.

hypochondria, n. [1. hìpokóndria; 2. hàipoukóndriə]. Lat. pl., fr. Gk. *hupokhóndria*, pl., 'upper parts of abdomen', anciently considered seat of the malady, prop. neut. pl. of adj. *-ios*, 'pertaining to the region below the cartilage' (of the breastbone), fr. **hypo-** & *khóndros*, 'grain, groat, gristle', perh. cogn. w. **grind**; & cp. **gristle**. Morbid depression of spirits, usually with anxiety regarding health.

hypochondriac, n. [1. hìpokóndriak; 2. hàipɔkɔ́ndriæk]. Gk. *hupokhondriakós*. Prec. & **-iac**. Person who suffers from hypochondria.

hypochondriacal, adj. [1. hìpokondríakl; 2. hàipɔkəndráiəkl]. Prec. & **-al**. Suffering from, liable to, hypochondria; due to hypochondria.

hypocoristic, adj. [1. hìpokorístik; 2. hàipəkərístik]. Gk. *hupokoristikós*, fr. *hupokorízesthai*, 'to use childish language, call by an endearing name', fr. *hupo-* (**hypo-**), in sense 'secretly, privately', & *koríz-esthai*, 'to caress, coax', fr. *kóros*, 'child', fr. base **ker-*, 'to grow'. See further under **create, herd**. (gram.) Endearing, familiar. *Hypocoristic name*, one abbreviated or otherwise altered from the full name; familiar, pet, name: e.g. *Bill* for *William* &c.

hypocrisy, n. [1. hipókrisi; 2. hipɔ́krəsi]. M.E., O. Fr. *ipocrisie* (later *hypo-*), on model of Lat. *hypocrisis*, fr. Gk. *hupókrisis*, 'an acting on the stage', hence 'hypocrisy', fr. *hupokrin-esthai*, 'to answer, speak in dialogue, play a part', fr. **hypo-**, 'subordinately', & *krinesthai*, 'to contend, dispute', middle voice of *krínein*, 'to judge, decide'. See **critic**. Action or practice of feigning to be better than one is; simulation of virtue or piety; insincere profession of goodness, affection &c.

hypocrite, n. [1. hípokrit; 2. hípəkrit]. M.E., O. Fr. *ipocrite* (later *hypo-*, as prec.), fr. Lat. *hypocrita*, fr. Gk. *hupokritḗs*, 'actor, hypocrite', fr. *hupokrínesthai*, as prec. Person who practises hypocrisy; one who feigns virtue or piety, affection &c.; a dissembler, a double-faced person.

hypocritical, adj. [1. hipokrítikl; 2. hipəkrítik(ə)l]. Gk. *hupokritik-(ós)*. See prec. & **-ic** & **-al**. Pertaining to a hypocrite or to hypocrisy; simulating virtue or piety; double-faced, insincere, false.

hypocritically, adv. Prec. & **-ly**. In a hypocritical manner.

hypodermic, adj. & n. [1. hìpōdérmik; 2. hàipoudámik]. **hypo-** & **derm(a)** & **-ic**. **1.** adj. (lit.) Under the skin; pertaining to, applied to, some part of the body beneath the skin: *a hypodermic injection, syringe.* **2.** n. **a** Drug injected beneath the skin; **b** hypodermic injection of drug.

hypodermically, adv. [1. hìpōdérmikali; 2. hàipoudámikəli]. Prec. & **-al** & **-ly**. So as to enter below the skin.

hypophosphate, -ite, n. [1. hīpofósfāt, -īt; 2. haipəfɔ́sfeit, -ait]. See **hypo-** & **phosphate, -ite**. (chem.) Salts of hypophosphoric and of hypophosphorous acid.

hypophosphoric, -phosphorous, adj. [1. hìpofosfórik, -fósforus; 2. hàipəfɔsfɔ́rik, -fɔ́sfərəs]. See **hypo-** & **phosphoric, -ous**. (chem.) Pertaining to two types of acids of phosphorus.

hypostasis, n. [1. hipóstasis; 2. haipɔ́stəsis]. Lat., fr. Gk. *hupóstasis*, 'underlying nature, substance', fr. *huphístasthai*, 'to stand under, subsist', fr. **hypo-** & *histasthai*, 'to stand', middle voice of *histánai*, 'to cause to stand'. See **state** (I.), **stand** (I.). **1.** (philos.) **a** Substance, reality, or essence which underlies attributes; **b** concept hypostatized, or regarded as having real existence. **2.** (theol.) Any one of the persons of the Holy Trinity.

hypostatic(al), adj. [1. hìpostátik(l); 2. hàipəstǽtik(l)]. Gk. *hupostatik-(ós)*, fr. *hupostat-*, adj. stem fr. *huphístasthai*. See prec. & **static**. **1.** (obs. or archaic) Underlying, fundamental. **2.** (theol.) Pertaining to an hypostasis or divine person; *hypostatic union*, union of the human and divine natures in Christ.

hypostatization, n. [1. hìpostatīzā́shun; 2. hàipəstætaizéiʃən]. Next word & **-ation**. **a** Action of hypostatizing; state of being hypostatized; **b** object hypostatized.

hypostatize, vb. trans. [1. hīpóstatīz; 2. haipɔ́stətaiz]. Gk. *hupostat-*. See **hypostatic** & **-ize**. **a** To regard as a substance, essence, or thing with real independent existence; **b** to regard as a person; to personify.

hypostyle, adj. [1. hípostīl; 2. háipəstail]. Gk. *hupóstūlos*, fr. **hypo-** & *stûlos*, 'pillar'. See **style** (III.). (archit.) Having pillars to support the roof: *a hypostyle hall.*

hypotenuse, n. [1. hīpótenūz; 2. haipɔ́tinjūz]. Fr. *hypoténuse*, fr. Lat. *hypotēnūsa*, fr. Gk. *hupoteinousa (grammḗ)*, 'subtending (line)', Pres. Part. fem. of *hupoteínein*, 'to stretch under, subtend', fr. **hypo-** & *teínein*, 'to stretch'. See **tenuous** & **thin**. (geom.) Side of right-angled triangle opposite the right angle.

hypothec, n. [1. hípothek; 2. háipəþek]. Fr. *hypothèque*, fr. L. Lat. *hypothēca*, fr. Gk. *hupothḗkē*, 'pledge, mortgage', fr. *hupotithénai*, 'to put under, pledge', fr. **hypo-** & *tithénai*, 'to put'; base **dhē-*. See **thesis**. (Roman and Scots law) Security held by creditor over debtor's property.

hypothecary, adj. [1. hīpóthekari; 2. haipɔ́þikəri]. L. Lat. *hypothēcārius*. Prec. & **-ary**. (law) Pertaining to a hypothec.

hypothecate, vb. trans. [1. hīpóthekāt; 2. haipɔ́þikeit]. L. Lat. *hypothēcāt-*, P.P. stem of *hypothēcāre*, 'to pledge', fr. *hypothēca*, see **hypothec**, & **-ate**. (law) To subject to a hypothec; to pledge, mortgage, without transferring possession or title.

hypothecation, n. [1. hìpòthekā́shun; 2. haipɔ̀þikéiʃən]. L. Lat. *hypothēcātiōn-(em)*. See prec. & **-ion**. Action of hypothecating; obligation thus created.

hypothecator, n. [1. hīpóthekātor; 2. haipɔ́þikeitə]. **hypothecate** & **-or**. Person who hypothecates.

hypothesis, n. [1. hīpóthesis; 2. haipɔ́þisis]. Mod. Lat., fr. Gk. *hupóthesis*, 'foundation, supposition', vbl. n. fr. *hupotithénai*, 'to put under'. See **hypo-** & **thesis.** Supposition; admittedly unproved assumption adopted as basis of inference, or for the sake of argument. Phr. *working hypothesis*, supposition provisionally maintained as long as it accords with observed facts.

hypothesize, vb. intrans. & trans. [1. hīpóthesīz; 2. haipɔ́þisaiz]. Prec. & **-ize. a** intrans. To make an hypothesis; **b** trans., to assume, suppose.

hypothetic(al), adj. [1. hīpothétik(l); 2. haipəþétik(l)]. Gk. *hupothetik-(ós)*, fr. *hupothet-*, adj. stem fr. *hupotithénai.* See **hypothesis** & **-ic** & **-al. a** Of the nature of an hypothesis; assumed for purpose of reasoning; **b** given to making hypotheses.

hypothetically, adv. [1. hīpothétikali; 2. haipəþétikəli]. Prec. & **-ly.** By way of (an) hypothesis.

hypso-, pref. Gk. *húpsos*, 'height', *húpsi*, 'on high', connected w. **hyper-** & **hypo-.** Form used in combination with words of Greek origin, denoting high, height, as *hypsodont*, having, pertaining to, teeth with high crowns and short roots; *hypsophobia*, morbid dread of heights.

hypsographic, adj. [1. hìpsōgráfik; 2. hìpsougræ̃fik]. Prec. & **-graphic.** Pertaining to hypsography.

hypsography, n. [1. hipsógrafi; 2. hipsɔ́grəfi]. **hypso-** & **-graphy. 1.** Scientific description of the contours of the earth's surface; delineation of this in map. **2.** Hypsometry.

hypsometer, n. [1. hipsómeter; 2. hipsɔ́mitə]. **hypso-** & **meter.** Instrument for determining altitudes.

hypsometric, adj. [1. hipsométrik; 2. hipsəmétrik]. **hypso-** & **-metric.** Pertaining to hypsometry or to an hypsometer.

hypsometry, n. [1. hipsómetri; 2. hipsɔ́mitri]. **hypso-** & **-metry.** Determination of altitudes.

hyrax, n. [1. hīraks; 2. háiəræks]. Mod. Lat., fr. Gk. *húrax*, 'shrew-mouse', cogn. w. Lat. *sorex*, 'shrew-mouse' (see **soricine**). One of several small ungulate mammals of Africa and Syria, superficially resembling the guinea-pig; coney, rock-rabbit.

hyson, n. [1. hīson; 2. háisən]. Chinese, 'blooming spring'. Kind of green China tea.

hyssop, n. [1. hísop; 2. hísəp]. Fr. *hys(s)ope*, fr. Lat. *hys(s)ōpum*, fr. Gk. *hússōpos*, fr. Heb. *'ēzōbh.* **1. a** (Bib.) Unknown plant, perhaps caper, of which twigs were used for sprinkling in ancient Jewish rites; bunch of these twigs, hence, **b** (R.C.Ch.) holy-water sprinkler. **2.** Kind of aromatic, pungent mint cultivated for medicinal properties; one of several related plants, as *hedge hyssop.*

hysterectomy, n. [1. histeréktumi; 2. histəréktəmi], fr. **hystero-** & Gk. *ektomé*, 'excision', fr. *ek-* (see **ex-**) & *tomé*, 'a cutting', fr. *témnein*, 'to cut'. See **tome.** (surg.) Excision of the uterus.

hysteresis, n. [1. hìsterésis; 2. hìstərísis]. Invented word, fr. Gk. *hústeros*, 'later', see **hysteron proteron.** (magnetism) Measure of response of steel or iron to a magnetizing force; the lag in the magnetic force produced behind the magnetizing force producing it.

hysteria, n. [1. histéria; 2. histíəriə]. Mod. Lat., back-formation fr. **hysteric** & **-ia. a** Functional nervous disorder, most frequent in young women ; accompanied with extreme emotional excitability and loss of will-power; **b** (fig.) uncontrolled excitement or emotionalism.

hysteric(al), adj. & n. [1. histérik(l); 2. histérik(l)]. Lat. *hysteric-(us)*, fr. Gk. *husterikós*, 'pertaining to the womb', anciently considered the seat of hysteria, fr. *hustéra*, 'womb', cogn. w. Lat. *uterus*, 'womb'. See **uterus.** More commonly *hysterical* when adj. **1.** adj. **a** Pertaining to, arising from, suffering from, hysteria; **b** (fig.) uncontrolledly emotional. **2.** *Hysterics*, n. pl., (colloq.) **a** hysteria, fit of hysteria: *to go into hysterics*; **b** (fig.) excited, uncontrolled ravings.

hysterically, adv. Prec. & **-ly.** In an hysterical manner.

hysteritis, n. [1. hìsterítis; 2. hìstəráitis]. **hystero-** & **-itis.** (med.) Inflammation of the uterus.

hystero-, pref. Gk. *hustéra*, 'womb'. See **hysteric.** Form used in combination with medical words of Greek origin, denoting **a** the womb, uterus, as *hysterology*, science of diseases of the uterus; *hysterotomy*, cutting of the womb; **b** of the nature of, due to, hysteria, hysteric, as *hysterocatalepsy, hysteroepilepsy, hysteroid, hysteromania.*

hysteron proteron, n. [1. hísteron próteron; 2. hístərɔn prɔ́tərɔn]. L. Lat., fr. Gk. *hústeron próteron*, 'latter (treated as) former', fr. *hústeros*, 'later' (a comp. form cogn. w. Scrt. *uttaraś*, 'superior', comp. of *úd*, 'high'), & *próteros*, 'former' (see **protero-**). **1.** (gram., rhet.) Inversion of the natural and logical order of words or clauses and ideas. **2.** Logical fallacy of begging the question.

I

I, i [1. ī; 2. *ai*]. The ninth letter of the English and other alphabets; for use in abbreviations see end of Dictionary.

I, pers. pron. [1. ī; 2. *ai*]. O.E. *ić*, M.E. *ich, i.* Cp. O.H.G. *ih*; Mod. Germ. *ich*; O.N. *ek*; Goth. *ik*; also Lat. *ego*; Gk. *egṓ*; O. Prussian *es*; Scrt. *ahám.* Aryan base **eĝ-, *eĝh-*, 'I'. Nominative case of the personal pronoun used by a speaker or writer in referring to himself.

-i-. Vowel connecting the two elements of a Latin compound word, or of a compound modelled on a Latin word. The *-i-* is the stem-vowel of the first element of the compound, or a reduced (unstressed) form of it: *auricula* (fr. *auri-s*), *argentiferous, curvilinear, equidistant.* The vowel is sometimes introduced merely as a connective: e.g. *diamantiferous.*

-ia, suff. [1. ia; 2. iə]. **1.** Suff. (fr. Lat. & Gk. *-ia*) forming abstract ns. fr. vbl. bases: *anaesthesia, militia.* Very common in Mod. Lat. scientific terms: *hysteria, morphia*; also in anct. & mod. geographical names: *Phœnicia, Nigeria, Australia* &c. Used to form names of flowers fr. that of introducer: *fuchsia, zinnia* &c. **2.** Pl. suff. of Gk. & Lat. neut. ns., in *-ion* & *-ium* respectively: *effluvia*, pl. of *effluvium*; used in modern formations fr. Lat. to designate classes in zoology: *Reptilia.*

-ial, suff. [1. ial; 2. iəl], representing Lat. *-iālis*, forming adjs. fr. Lat. ns. in *-ia, -io, -ium*: *remedial, ceremonial, imperial, judicial*; & in Fr. & Engl. forming adjs. fr. Lat. adjs. in *-is, -ius*; & fr. ns. in *-ium*: *colloquial, aerial, celestial, terrestrial.*

iamb, n. [1. íamb; 2. áiæmb], fr. Fr. *iambe*, fr. Lat. *iambus.* See **iambus.** Iambus.

iambic, adj. & n. [1. īámbik; 2. aiǽmbik], fr. Fr. *iambique*, fr. Lat., fr. Gk. *iambikós*, fr. *iamb-(os)*, 'iambus'. See next word & **-ic. 1.** adj. Pertaining to, containing, composed of, iambuses. **2.** n. Iambic verse.

iambus, n. [1. īámbus; 2. aiǽmbəs]. Lat. *iambus*, fr. Gk. *íambos*, 'a metrical foot consisting of a short syllable followed by a long'. Etymol. doubtful; possibly an Eastern loanword. A metrical foot consisting either **a** of a short syllable followed by a long syllable, or **b** of an unstressed syllable followed by a stressed syllable.

-ian, suff. [1. ian; 2. iən] representing Lat. *-iānus*, adj. suff. *-ānus* (see **-an**) added to a first element having as a stem-vowel *-i-*; mostly in adjs. formed fr. proper names: *Virgilian, Grecian*; *meridian.* Now forming adjs. fr. proper names, & fr. scientific ns. in *-ia* &c.: *Athenian, Cartesian, Baconian*; *reptilian, tellurian*; many of these adjs. are also ns.

-iasis, suff. [1. íasis; 2. áiəsis], fr. Gk., used to indicate state or condition, esp. a pathological or morbid condition, e.g. *elephantiasis, psoriasis* &c.

-iatric, -iatro, -iatry, suffs. Used to form compound words, as *psychiatry* &c., fr. Gk. *iātrós*, 'healer, physician', *iatreía*, 'healing'; cogn. w. Gk. *iaínein*, 'to refresh, revive; to excite', fr. base **is-n̥j-* &c., 'to stir, cause to move'; cp. Scrt. *iṣáyati*, 'to be fresh, animated', & see further under **ire.**

Iberian, adj. & n. [1. ībérian; 2. aibíəriən], fr. Lat. *Ibēria* & **-ian. 1.** adj. **a** Pertaining to Iberia; anciently, Spain, Portugal, and part of S.-W. France; **b** pertaining to Spain and Portugal; **c** (anthropol.) belonging to a short, dark, long-headed prehistoric race, probably the neolithic builders of prehistoric stone monuments, as dolmens &c. of N. Africa, France, Spain, and Britain &c. **2.** n. **a** An inhabitant of ancient Iberia; **b** (anthropol.) member of the prehistoric race of **c** above; **c** the language of ancient Iberia.

ibex, n. [1. íbeks; 2. áibeks]. Lat. *ibex*, 'a kind of goat, the chamois'. Etymol. doubtful. The wild goat of the Alps, Pyrenees &c., with very long recurved horns.

ibidem, adv. [1. ibídem; 2. ibáidem]. Lat., 'in the same place', fr. *ibi*, 'there', & the demonstrative suff. *-dem.* For the adv. *ibi*, cp. Scrt. *i-ha*, 'here'; fr. the pronominal stem *i-*. See **it.** (abbr. to *ib.* or *ibid.*) From the same author, passage; on the same page, line &c. previously quoted; used to avoid repeating a reference.

ibis, n. [1. íbis; 2. áibis]. Lat. *ībis*, fr. Gk. *îbis*, 'ibis', prob. of Egypt. origin. A wading bird with a long curved bill, found in many tropical and sub-tropical countries; *Sacred Ibis*, the white ibis, revered in ancient Egypt.

-ible, adj. suff. [1. ibl; 2. ibl] representing Lat. *-ībilis*, forming adjs. fr. vbs., w. the sense of 'capable of being, able to be'. Cp. **-able.** Adjs. in *-ible* include **a** Lat. adjs. formed fr. the infin. or P.P. stems of vbs. in *-ēre, -īre*: *terrible, edible, legible, discernible, visible, plausible, divisible, sensible*; **b** later or modern formations fr. such vbs.: *dirigible, exhaustible, audible, fallible, responsible* &c.

-ic, suff. [1. ik; 2. ik] representing Gk. *-ik-(os)* or (more rarely) Lat. *-ic-(us)*, forming (1) adjs. fr. ns.; (2) ns. fr. these adjs. The adjs. have the sense of 'like, pertaining to': e.g. (fr. Gk.) *barbaric, heroic, fantastic, frantic*; (fr. Lat.) *aquatic, rustic.* The suff. is still in use to form adjs. fr. ns., chiefly **a** scientific, fr. Gk. or Lat. stems: *encephalic, kinematic, magnetic, acetic, carbonic*; **b** fr. proper names: *Druidic, Icelandic, Napoleonic*; **c** fr. ns. in *-ist*: *artistic, realistic, journalistic.* Ns. in *-ic* represent **a** Gk. or Lat. adjs.: *elastic, sceptic, enteric, climacteric, public, classic*; **b** Gk. ns. in *-ikḗ, -ika*, chiefly names of arts and sciences: *music, rhetoric*; **c** modern formations fr. adjs. in *-ic*, denoting 'the art or science of', end in *-ics*, as *acoustics, physics, dynamics* &c.; **d** as contrasted w. *-ous*, having a higher valency than the equivalent in *-ous*: *nitric, nitrous, acid.*

-ical [1. ikl; 2. ikl], adj. suff. **-al** added to ns. or adjs. in **-ic**: *logical, magical, empirical.*

ice (I.), n. [1. īs; 2. ais]. O.E. *īs*, M.E. *īs*; cp. O.H.G., O. Fris. *īs*, Mod. Germ. *eis*, O.N. *īss.* **1.** Frozen water; Phrs. *to break the ice*, (i.) to overcome reserve, formality; (ii.) take the first steps in a delicate matter; *to* *cut no ice*, to effect little or nothing; *on thin ice*, in a delicate situation, touching upon matters best avoided. 2. Frozen water, cream &c., sweetened and flavoured: *a water ice*; *strawberry ices*.

ice (II.), vb. trans., fr. prec. 1. a To freeze; b to chill (wine, coffee &c.) with ice. 2. To cover with ice: *the shallow pond was soon iced over*. 3. To cover (cake &c.) with sugar icing.

-ice, suff. [1. is; 2. *is*] forming a abstract ns., fr. O. Fr. *-ice*, fr. Lat. *-itia*: *justice, malice*; b ns., fr. Lat. ns. in *-itium*: *precipice, hospice*.

ice-age, n. (geol.) Part of the tertiary era, characterized by extensive movements of ice-fields.

ice-axe, n. Axe used in Alpine climbing, for cutting footholds &c. in the ice.

iceberg, n. [1. ísbĕrg; 2. *áisbʌ̄g*]. Cp. Du. *ijsberg*, Dan. *iisbierg*, fr. Germ. *eisberg*, where second element is Gmc. **berg*, 'hill'. See **ice** & **berg**. Large mass of floating ice broken from glacier.

iceblink, n. [1. ísblingk; 2. *áisbliŋk*]. Light on the horizon caused by reflection from ice-field.

ice-boat, n. Light boat fitted with long runners and sails for sailing on ice.

icebound, adj. [1. ísbound; 2. *áisbaund*]. Obstructed by, frozen up in, ice.

ice-cap, n. Large, perennial sheet of ice; especially one covering mountain top.

ice-cream, n. Frozen mixture of sweetened and flavoured cream &c.

ice-field, n. Extensive sheet of floating ice.

ice-foot, n. Wall of ice along the shore, in Polar regions.

ice-house, n. Building for storing ice.

Icelander, n. [1. íslander; 2. *áisləndə*]. Iceland, island in N. Atlantic, & **-er**. An inhabitant of Iceland.

Icelandic, adj. & n. [1. īslándik; 2. *aislændik*]. See prec. & **-ic**. 1. adj. Pertaining to Iceland. 2. n. The language of Iceland.

Iceland moss, n. [1. ísland mòs; 2. *áislənd mɔ̀s*]. Kind of edible, medicinal, lichen found in Iceland, Norway &c.

Iceland poppy, n. Perennial yellow poppy growing in Arctic regions, nearly related to Alpine poppy.

Iceland spar, n. A transparent variety of calcite used for making prisms.

iceman, n. [1. ísman; 2. *áismən*]. One experienced in traversing, or walking among, ice.

ice-pack, n. Expanse of broken masses of ice formed into solid mass by pressure.

ice-plant, n. A species of Mesembryanthemum, the leaves of which are covered with small vesicles shining like specks of ice.

ichneumon, n. [1. iknúmon; 2. *iknjúmən*]. Lat., fr. Gk. *ikhneúmōn*, lit. 'the tracker', name given to a spider-hunting wasp, and to the ichneumon; fr. *ikhneúein*, 'to track, trace, hunt for', fr. *íkhnos*, 'track, footprint'. See **ichno-**. 1. Small animal resembling a weasel, inhabiting Asia and Africa, which digs up and destroys the eggs of the crocodile; the Indian variety is known as the mongoose. 2. An ichneumon-fly.

ichneumon-fly, n. A parasitic insect which deposits its eggs in the living tissues of another insect.

ichno-, pref., fr. Gk. *íkhno-(s)*, 'track, footprint' (fr. **iksmno-*); cp. Gk. *iksalos*, 'bounding' (of the wild goat). Cp. also Lith. *ìzo*, 'splits'; fr. Aryan base **aiĝ-*, **iĝ-*, 'to jump'; hence, on the one hand, 'the mark left on the ground by a jump or rapid movement', on the other hand, 'to spring apart, split'. Of tracks, traces, footprints.

ichnography, n. [1. iknógrafi; 2. *iknɔ́grəfi*]. Prec. & **-graphy**. The art of drawing ground-plans.

ichnolite, n. [1. íknolīt; 2. *íknəlait*]. **ichno-** & **-lite**. (geol.) A fossil footprint.

ichnology, n. [1. iknóloji; 2. *iknɔ́lədži*]. **ichno-** & **-logy**. The study of fossil footprints.

ichor, n. [1. íkor; 2. *áikɔ̄*]. Gk. *īkhṓr*, 'ichor; any watery fluid'. Etymol. unknown. 1. (Gk. mythol.) Fluid, answering to human blood, supposed to flow in the veins of the gods. 2. (pathol.) Watery matter discharged from wounds and sores.

ichthus, n. See **ichthys**.

ichthy(o)-, pref., fr. Gk. *ikhthū́-(s)*, 'fish'. Alleged cognates fr. Baltic languages (Lith. *żuvis* &c.) throw no light on primitive meaning, & leave the form doubtful. Of, pertaining to, fish.

ichthyography, n. [1. ìkthiógrafi; 2. *ìkþiɔ́grəfi*]. Prec. & **-graphy**. A treatise on, description of, fish.

ichthyoid, adj. & n. [1. íkthioid; 2. *íkþiɔid*]. **ichthy(o)-** & **-oid**. 1. adj. Like a fish. 2. n. A fish-like vertebrate.

ichthyolatry, n. [1. ìkthiólatri; 2. *ìkþiɔ́lətri*]. **ichthy(o)-** & **-latry**. The worship of a god in the form of a fish.

ichthyolite, n. [1. íkthiolīt; 2. *íkþiəlait*]. **ichthy(o)-** & **-lite**. (geol.) A fossil fish.

ichthyologist, n. [1. ìkthiólojist; 2. *ìkþiɔ́lədžist*]. See next word & **-ist**. One who studies ichthyology.

ichthyology, n. [1. ìkthióloji; 2. *ìkþiɔ́lədži*]. **ichthy(o)-** & **-logy**. Branch of zoology which deals with fish.

ichthyophagous, adj. [1. ìkthiófagus; 2. *ìkþiɔ́fəgəs*]. **ichthy(o)-** & **-phagous**. Fish-eating; living on fish.

ichthyornis, n. [1. ìkthiórnis; 2. *ìkþiɔ́nis*]. **ichthy(o)-** & Gk. *órnis*, 'bird'. See **ornitho-**. A kind of fossil bird with fish-like teeth.

ichthyosaurus, n. [1. ìkthiosórus; 2. *ìkþiəsɔ́rəs*]. **ichthy(o)-** & Gk. *saûros*, 'lizard', q.v. under **saurian**. A fossil, marine, carnivorous reptile with a long tail, large head, and four limbs like paddles.

ichthyosis, n. [1. ìkthiósis; 2. *ìkþióusis*]. **ichthy(o)-** & **-osis**. A skin disease characterized by a dry, scaly formation.

ichthyotic, adj. [1. ìkthiótik; 2. *ìkþiɔ́tik*]. **ichthy(o)-** & **-otic**. Pertaining to, resembling, affected with, ichthyosis.

ichthys, n. [1. íkthis; 2. *íkþis*]. Fr., fr. Gk. *ikhthū́s*, 'fish'. See **ichthy(o)-**. Name of an early Christian emblem in the form of a fish, the initial letters in Greek of 'Jesus Christ, Son of God, Saviour', spelling the Greek word.

-ician, suff. [1. íshan; 2. *íʃən*]. Suff. **-ian** added to ns. & adjs., in **-ic(s)**, forming ns. denoting 'person connected with, learned in': *mathematician, musician, physician, mechanician, academician*.

icicle, n. [1. ísikl; 2. *áisikl*]. O.E. *īs-ġicel*, M.E. *īsikel*, cp. O.N. *īs-jökull*; cp. also O.N. *jagi*, 'ice'; Ir. *aig*; Pers. *yagh*. A spear-shaped piece of ice hanging from an edge or projection, formed by the freezing of drops of dripping or slowly trickling water.

icily, adv. [1. ísili; 2. *áisili*]. **icy** & **-ly**. In an icy manner (lit. and fig.).

iciness, n. [1. ísines; 2. *áisinis*]. **icy** & **-ness**. The quality of being icy (lit. and fig.).

icing, n. [1. ísing; 2. *áisiŋ*]. **ice (II.)** & **-ing**. A mixture of sugar, white of egg, and other ingredients, used for coating, or forming a layer in, a cake &c.

icon, n. [1. íkon; 2. *áikən*]. L. Lat., fr. Gk. *eikṓn*, 'a likeness, image, portrait; picture, statue'; cp. Gk. **eik-ein*, 'to be like; to appear, seem'; *oikós*, 'likely, probable'; *íkelos*, 'like, resembling'; also, Lith. *(pa)véiksla s*, 'example'; Aryan base, **weiḱ-*, **woiḱ-*, **wiḱ-*, 'to be like'. 1. Image, likeness, portrait, whether picture or statue &c. 2. Specif. (Gk. Ch.) sacred portrait, mosaic &c., representing the figure of Christ, or of a saint or martyr, usually having the face, and sometimes the hands, painted, or made in enamel, the rest of the figure being moulded in metal which is placed above the enamel, so that the face &c. appear through openings in the metal.

iconic, adj. [1. īkónik; 2. *aikɔ́nik*], fr. L. Lat., fr. Gk. *eikonikós*, 'pertaining to a portrait, representation'. Prec. & **-ic**. 1. Pertaining to, of the nature of, a portrait. 2. (of sculpture) Following a conventional type.

icono-, pref. representing Gk. *eikṓn*, 'image'. See **icon**. Image, icon.

iconoclasm, n. [1. īkónoklazm; 2. *aikɔ́nəklæzəm*]. Prec. & Gk. *klásma*, 'something broken', fr. *kláein*, 'to break, break off'. Cp. Gk. *klêma*, 'a cutting (of a plant)'; *klá-d-os*, 'a slip, shoot, for grafting'; *kladarós*, 'fragile'; *kólos*, 'cut off, truncated'; Lat. *clādēs*, 'harm, damage'; *(per)cellere*, 'to overthrow'; O. Slav. *kladivo*, 'hammer'; Ir. *claidim*, 'I dig'; Lith. *kálti*, 'beat, forge'; Aryan base **klā-(d)-*, **klə-(d)-*, **kēl-(d)*, **kŏl-(d)-*, 'to cut; hence, to destroy, harm'. See further **holt, gladiator, cataclasm**. 1. The destruction of images. 2. (fig.) The destruction of popular idols, of established belief, illusions, objects of admiration &c.

iconoclast, n. [1. īkónoklast; 2. *aikɔ́nəklæst*], fr. Gk. *eikṓn*, 'image' (see **icon**), & *klast-*, fr. *kláein*, 'to break'. See prec. 1. A breaker of images; esp. one of a religious party in the Eastern Church of the 8th and 9th cents., who attacked the worship of images. 2. (fig.) One who attacks traditional or cherished beliefs, superstitions, institutions &c.

iconoclastic, adj. [1. īkònoklástik; 2. *aikɔ̀nəklǽstik*]. Prec. & **-ic**. Pertaining to an iconoclast, or to iconoclasm.

iconography, n. [1. īkonógrafi; 2. *àikənɔ́grəfi*]. **icono-** & **-graphy**. 1. a The study of portraits, statues &c.; b specif., study of the portraits of a particular person: *the iconography of Christ, Shakespeare* &c. 2. The art of illustration by means of figures, diagrams &c.

iconolatry, n. [1. īkonólatri; 2. *àikənɔ́lətri*]. **icono-** & **-latry**. The worship of images.

iconology, n. [1. īkonóloji; 2. *àikənɔ́lədži*]. **icono-** & **-logy**. The study of icons, images &c.

iconomachy, n. [1. īkonómaki; 2. *àikənɔ́məki*]. **icono-** & **-machy**. Hostility to the devotional use of images.

iconostasis, n. [1. īkonóstasis; 2. *àikənɔ́stəsis*]. **icono-** & Gk. *stásis*, 'the act of placing, setting, standing; position'. See **state (I.)**. (Gk. Ch.) Screen, adorned with icons, separating the sanctuary from the rest of the church.

icosahedron, n. [1. īkosahédron, -hédron; 2. *àikɔsəhídrən, -hédrən*], fr. Gk. *eikosáedron*, 'a body with twenty surfaces', fr. *eíkosi*, 'twenty', fr. **e-wikati*; cp. Scrt. *viśati*; Lat. *vīginti*; O. Ir. *fiche*, 'twenty'. From **wī-*, 'two' (cp. Scrt. *vi*, 'separately, separating', *vi-tarám*, 'farther'; Goth. *wiþra*, 'against' (see **with**)), & **(d)ḱm̥t-i-*, 'ten'. Aryan base **deḱem-t-*, **dḱm̥-t* &c., 'ten'. See **deca-, ten, hundred**, & **-hedron**. Polyhedron with twenty planes.

-ics, suff. **-ic** & pl. ending *-s*; forming ns. w. sense of 'art, science, of': *dynamics, optics, politics*.

ictus, n. [1. íktus; 2. *íktəs*]. Lat. *ictus*, 'a blow, stroke; metrical stress'; P.P. type of *īcere*, 'to strike, wound'; cogn. w. Gk. *aikhmḗ*, 'lance-point'; Lith. *ëszmas*, Lett. *ësms*, 'roasting-spit'. Rhythmical stress.

icy, adj. [1. ísi; 2. *áisi*]. **ice (I.)** & **-y**. 1. a Covered with, abounding in, ice: *icy waters*; *the icy North*; b very cold: *the icy blast*. 2. (fig.) Cold, frigid, distant in manner; lacking cordiality: *icy politeness*.

id, n. [1. id; 2. id]. (biol.) Term proposed by Weissmann for the smallest visible unit of life, assumed hypothetically to be made up of a group of still smaller, and invisible, particles of living matter called biophores.

-id (I.), suff. representing Lat. *-id-(us)*, forming adjs., a fr. vbs. w. *ē-* stems, *horrid, frigid, fluid, fervid*; b fr. ns.: *turbid, morbid*. Words in *-id* **(I.)**, are borrowed either directly fr. Lat., or through Fr.

-id (II.), suff. representing a Gk. n. stem: *pyramid, orchid, caryatid*.

-idae, suff. [1. idē; 2. *idī*], fr. Lat. pl., fr. Gk. patronymic suff. *-idēs*, used as termination of zoological families, as *Felidae* &c.

ide, n. [1. īd ; 2. *aid*], fr. Swed. *id.* A fresh-water fish of the carp family.

-ide, suff. used in chemistry to form names of compounds of two elements : *oxide, bromide, carbide* &c. ; *sodium chloride, oxide of zinc* &c.

idea, n. [1. īdēa ; 2. *aidíə*]. L. Lat., fr. Gk. *idéā*, 'form, look, semblance ; kind, nature ; class, species ; ideal form, archetype', earlier **widesā* ; cp. Gk. *eidos*, 'outward form, idea', fr. base **weid-*, **woid-*, **wid-* wh. appears in Lat. *vidēre*, 'to see', *vīsio*, 'sense of seeing, sight' &c. (see **vision**) ; & in O.E. *witan*, 'to know' (see **wit (I.)**), & O.E. *wīs* (see **wise**). For other Gk. forms see **idol** & **-oid**. Used in various and differing senses by philosophers : **1.** (Gk. philos.) Self-activity which is manifested in life and mind ; self-active cause of life ; permanently existing model of which all individual things are but imperfect reproductions. **2.** (mod. philos.) Purely subjective notion ; immediate object of thought, perception, and understanding. **3.** (popular usage) **a** Notion, mental conception : *to form an idea of virtue* ; *to have a poor idea of a man's abilities* ; **b** plan, scheme, formed in the mind ; proposed, suggested course of action ; realization of this : *my idea is to close up the windows looking west, and to open out new ones to the south* ; *that was a good idea of yours to plant a clump of trees on the sky-line* ; Phrs. *full of ideas, a man of ideas*, fertile in suggestions and expedients ; resourceful ; **c** vague premonition, intuition, instinct, fancy ; sense of the probability of some coming event : *I have an idea somehow, that he will come today* ; Phrs. *to get ideas into one's head*, to cherish illusions ; *the idea of such a thing !*, such conduct is preposterous ; such things are highly improbable ; **d** opinion, aspiration : *to force one's ideas on others* ; **e** thought, knowledge ; imagination : *I haven't an idea what you mean* ; *he hasn't an idea in his head.*

idea'd, ideaed, adj. [1. īdēad ; 2. *aidíəd*]. **idea** & **-ed.** Full of, rich in, ideas.

ideal (I.), adj. [1. īdēal ; 2. *aidíəl*], fr. Fr. *idéal*, fr. L. Lat. *ideālis*, 'of an idea'. **idea** & **-al.** **1.** Of the highest, most perfect, type ; in accordance with one's most exalted imagination, or conception ; realizing one's highest standard of excellence : *an ideal companion* ; *an ideal place for a holiday.* **2. a** Representing, embodying, giving visible form to, an idea ; created by the imagination : *an ideal portrait* ; **b** existing only as an idea, having no substance or reality ; visionary : *ideal schemes for the reformation of the world* ; contrasted with *real.*

ideal (II.), n., fr. prec. **1. a** Conception, standard, formed in the mind, of the highest excellence ; supreme perfection, as of something to be aimed at, aspired to, or most to be desired, in material and non-material things : *few of us realize our ideals* ; *an ideal of conduct, of happiness, of comfort, of physical beauty* &c. ; **b** this contrasted with actuality : *the Ideal and the Real.* **2.** Something which comes up to and embodies a conception of the highest attainable excellence : *lovers believe each other to be the ideal of everything desirable* ; *he was the very ideal of an English gentleman.*

idealism, n. [1. īdēalizm ; 2. *aidíəlizəm*]. **ideal** & **-ism.** **1.** (philos.) Conception of the universe which regards mind as the ultimate reality, and ideas as the only objects of perception. **2.** Habit of mind which tends to form ideals, or to idealize. **3.** (art and liter.) Doctrine and practice emphasizing and embodying imaginative treatment of life and nature.

idealist, n. [1. īdēalist ; 2. *aidíəlist*]. **ideal** & **-ist.** **a** An adherent of idealism as a conception of the universe ; **b** one who tends to set up, and be influenced by, ideals ; **c** practitioner of idealism in art or literature.

idealistic, adj. [1. ìdēalístik ; 2. *àidiəlístik*]. Prec. & **-ic.** Pertaining to, of the nature of, based upon, idealism (in all senses).

ideality, n. [1. ìdēáliti ; 2. *àidiǽliti*]. **ideal** & **-ity.** **1.** The quality of being ideal. **2.** Tendency, power, to form, habit of forming, ideals. **3.** An idealization.

idealization, n. [1. idēalīzāshun ; 2. *aidìəlai-zéiʃən*]. See next word & **-ation.** **a** The act of idealizing ; **b** state of being idealized ; something resulting from the act of idealizing.

idealize, vb. trans. & intrans. [1. īdēalīz ; 2. *aidíəlaiz*]. **ideal** & **-ize.** **A.** trans. **1.** To render ideal ; to regard as coming up to an ideal : *to idealize a person's character.* **2.** To represent in accordance with an ideal, rather than in accordance with strict reality : *a son writing the biography of his father is apt to idealize his subject.* **B.** intrans. **1.** To practise, be in the habit of, forming ideals. **2.** To practise representation according to an ideal : *he is a good painter, but tends to idealize.*

ideally, adv. [1. īdēali ; 2. *aidíəli*]. **ideal** & **-ly.** In an ideal manner ; in accordance with ideals, or an ideal.

ideate, vb. trans. & intrans. [1. īdēāt ; 2. *aidí-eit*]. **idea** & **-ate.** **1.** trans. To form an idea of ; imagine. **2.** intrans. To form ideas, have mental conceptions.

ideation, n. [1. ìdēāshun ; 2. *àidiéiʃən*]. Prec. & **-ion.** The act of ideating ; state of being ideated.

ideational, adj. [1. ìdēāshunal ; 2. *àidiéiʃənəl*]. Prec. & **-al.** Pertaining to ideation.

idée fixe, n. [1. ēdā fēks ; 2. *idei fíks*]. Fr., 'fixed idea'. Idea occupying the mind to the exclusion of other ideas ; an obsession.

idem, n. & adv. Lat. *īdem* (masc.), *idem* (neut.), fr. pronominal stem *is*, 'he', & *-dem*, a particle cogn. w. Aryan pronominal stem **dŏ-*, **dĕ-* ; see **to.** **1.** n. & adv. [1. īdem ; 2. *aidem*]. (In) the same author &c. **2.** n. [1. ídem ; 2. *ídem*]. The same word, book, authority &c.

identic, adj. [1. īdéntik ; 2. *aidéntik*], fr. Med. Lat. *identic-(us)*, fr. Lat. *ident-(itas)*, 'identity'. See **identity** & **-ic.** Identical. Specif., *identic note*, dispatch sent simultaneously from two or more states to another, making the same statement or request, or expressing the same opinion in exactly the same terms.

identical, adj. [1. īdéntikl ; 2. *aidéntikl*]. Prec. & **-al.** **1.** Actually the same, the very same, that one and no other : *the identical room where Shakespeare was born.* **2.** (of different objects &c.) Alike in every respect, agreeing absolutely : *the handwriting on both cheques is identical.*

identically, adv. Prec. & **-ly.** In an identical manner.

identifiable, adj. [1. īdéntifīabl ; 2. *aidénti-faiəbl*]. **identify** & **-able.** Capable of being identified.

identification, n. [1. ìdèntifikāshun ; 2. *aidèn-tifikéiʃən*], fr. L. Lat. *identific-(āre)*, 'to identify'. See **identify** & **-ation.** The act of identifying, state of being identified.

identification, also **identity, disk**, n. Small metal disk, inscribed with owner's name, regimental number &c., and worn by member of fighting force while on active service, as a means of identifying him when dead or severely wounded &c.

identify, vb. trans. [1. īdéntifī ; 2. *aidéntifai*], fr. L. Lat. *identificāre*, 'to identify', fr. stem of *identi-(tas)*, 'identity', see next word, & **-fy.** **1.** To regard as identical ; to proclaim, establish, identity of : *to identify a prisoner, lost property* &c. **2.** To show (oneself &c.) to be interested in, play a prominent part in, be associated with : *to identify oneself, be identified, with a movement* &c.

identity, n. [1. īdéntiti ; 2. *aidéntiti*], fr. L. Lat. *identitāt-(em)*, 'identity', fr. *īdem*, 'the same', see **idem**, & **-ity.** **1.** The state of being identical; absolute agreement, sameness. **2.** The state of being some specific person or thing ; individuality : *to prove, recognize, a person's identity.*

ideo-, pref., fr. Gk. *idé-(ā)*, 'form ; kind ; idea'. See **idea.** Idea.

ideogram, n. [1. ídēōgram ; 2. *ídiougræm*]. Prec. & **-gram.** A symbol used in writing, e.g. in Chinese, which represents a picture of the thing itself, or which symbolizes an idea, and not, as in a phonetic system, the sounds which make up the name of these.

ideograph, n. [1. ídeogràhf ; 2. *ídiəgràf*]. **ideo-** & **-graph.** Ideogram.

ideography, n. [1. ìdeógrafi ; 2. *ìdiɔ́grəfi*]. Prec. & **-y.** Study of ideographs ; employment of these in writing.

ideological, adj. [1. īd-, ìdiōlójikl ; 2. *àid-*, *ìdioulɔ́džikl*]. **ideology** & **-ic** & **-al.** Connected with, pertaining to, ideology.

ideologist, n. [1. īd-, ìdiólojist ; 2. *àid-*, *ìdiɔ́lədžist*]. See next word & **-ist.** A student of ideology.

ideology, n. [1. ìdeóloji ; 2. *àidiɔ́lədži*]. **ideo-** & **-logy.** **1. a** Inquiry into the origin of ideas ; specif. **b** theory deriving them from sensations. **2.** Visionary theorizing. **3.** (political jargon) The idea or ideas at the basis of some political or economic theory or system.

Ides, n. [1. īdz ; 2. *aidz*], fr. Fr., fr. Lat. *īdūs*, 'Ides'. Etymol. disputed & doubtful. One of the three days in each month in the Roman calendar, from which dates were reckoned ; the fifteenth of March, May, July, October ; the thirteenth day of other months.

id est, phr. [1. id est ; 2. *id ɛst*]. Lat. *id est*, 'that is'. Commonly abbr. to *i.e.*, that is.

idio-, pref., fr. Gk. *idios*, 'one's own, private, personal ; peculiar, separate, distinct', fr. earlier **widio-s* ; cogn. w. Scrt. *vi*, 'separately' ; Goth. *wiþra*, 'against' (see **with**). Aryan base **wi-*, 'two'. Separate, distinct, independent.

idiocy, n. [1. ídiosi ; 2. *ídiəsi*], fr. Gk. *idiōteia*, 'private life or business ; lack of education, uncouthness', fr. *idiṓt-ēs*, 'a private person ; a layman ; an ignorant, untrained person'. See **idiot.** **1.** State of being an idiot ; extreme defectiveness of mind, and absence of reasoning faculty ; imbecility. **2.** Action and behaviour resembling that of an idiot ; foolish, irrational action or behaviour.

idiom, n. [1. ídium ; 2. *ídiəm*], fr. Lat., fr. Gk. *idiōma*, 'a peculiarity in language', fr. *idió-omai*, 'make one's own'. See **idio-.** **1.** Special mode of expression, use or grouping of words, peculiar to a specific language. **2.** General way of expressing ideas in a language ; the language itself.

idiomatic, adj. [1. ìdiomátik ; 2. *ìdiəmǽtik*], fr. Gk. *idiōmatik-ós*, fr. *idiōmat-(os)*, genit. of *idiōma*, 'a peculiarity of a language'. See prec. & **-ic.** **1.** In accordance with the idioms peculiar to a given language : *to speak idiomatic French.* **2.** Characterized by, containing, rich in, peculiar idioms : *an extremely idiomatic language.*

idiomatically, adv. [1. ìdiomátikali ; 2. *ìdiə-mǽtikəli*]. Prec. & **-al** & **-ly.** In an idiomatic manner.

idiomorphic, -morphous, adjs. [1. ìdiō-mórfik, -fus ; 2. *ìdioumɔ́fik*, *-fəs*]. **idio-** & **-morphic, -ous.** **a** Having its own proper shape or form ; specif. **b** (of crystals) not having its shape or form altered by intrusion of other constituents.

idiopathic, adj. [1. ìdiōpáthik ; 2. *ìdioupǽþik*]. **idiopathy** & **-ic.** (of disease) Developing independently, not as result of another disease ; primary.

idiopathically, adv. [1. ìdiōpáthikali ; 2. *ìdiou-pǽþikəli*]. Prec. & **-al** & **-ly.** In an idiopathic manner.

idiopathy, n. [1. ìdiópathi ; 2. *ìdiɔ́pəþi*]. **idio-**, 'independent' &c., & **-pathy**, 'suffering'. State of disease not caused by and following upon another, but independent and primary.

idiosyncrasy, n. [1. ìdiōsíngkrasi ; 2. *ìdiousíŋ-krəsi*], fr. Gk. *idiosugkrāsía*, 'peculiarity of temperament', see **idio-** & **syn-**, 'together with', & Gk. *krās-(is)*, 'a blending', see **crasis**, & **-y.** **1.** Temperament, mental constitution, habit of mind, manner of thought, peculiar to an individual. **2.** Mode of expression peculiar to an individual ; personal mannerism. **3.** (med.) Physical constitution of specific person.

idiosyncratic, adj. [1. ìdiōsingkrátik; 2. ìdiousiŋkrǽtik], fr. Gk. *idiosugkrās-ia*, 'peculiarity of temperament'. See prec. Arising from, connected with, an idiosyncrasy; peculiar.

idiot, n. [1. ídiut; 2. ídjət], fr. Fr., fr. Lat. *idiōta*, 'an uneducated, inexperienced person', fr. Gk. *idiṓtēs*, 'a private person, one not engaged in public affairs; one without professional knowledge, a layman; an ignorant, uneducated, person', fr. *idio-(s)*, 'one's own, private'. See **idio-**. **1.** A human being of such defective intellect as to be incapable of rational judgement or action; an imbecile. **2.** (colloq.) A foolish, flighty, unbalanced person; a silly fool.

idiotic, adj. [1. ìdiótik; 2. ìdiɔ́tik]. Prec. & **-ic**. **1.** Pertaining to, characteristic of, an idiot. **2.** Utterly foolish.

idiotically, adv. [1. ìdiótikali; 2. ìdiɔ́tikəli]. Prec. & **-al** & **-ly**. In an idiotic manner.

idle (I.), adj. [1. ídl; 2. áidl]. O.E. & M.E. *idel*, 'empty, vain, idle'; O.S. *īdal*, O.H.G. *ītal*. Orig. meaning was apparently 'empty' then 'worthless'; etymol. doubtful, but Kluge suggests connexion w. base **aidh-*, 'to burn' (see **aedile**); in this case the starting-point of meaning was 'burnt out', hence 'empty'. **1. a** (of persons) Doing no work; unemployed, unoccupied, inactive: *to stand idle while a man is drowning; the strike has rendered thousands idle; to have one's hands idle*; **b** (of machines, workshops &c.) disused, not active; Phr. *to lie idle*, to be disused; **c** (of time) not spent in doing something, not filled with activity: *I have not an idle moment*, one during which I am idle. **2.** Lazy, slothful, disinclined for work; habitually doing nothing: *a thoroughly idle and useless fellow.* **3. a** (of action and thought) Futile, ineffective, vain, yielding no result: *to make an idle attempt; it is idle to expect help from him; an idle conceit*; **b** (of statements, talk &c.) empty, baseless, trivial, irresponsible, trifling, shallow: *idle rumours, conversation, chit-chat.*

idle (II.), vb. intrans. & trans., fr. prec. **1.** intrans. Also *idle about*, **a** to be idle, to remain inert and inactive; **b** to waste one's time, to loaf, saunter. **2.** trans. Chiefly, *to idle away* (*one's time, life* &c.), to spend in idleness.

idleness, n. [1. ídlnes; 2. áidlnis]. **idle** (I.) & **-ness**. The quality, state, of being idle; unemployment.

idler, n. [1. ídler; 2. áidlə]. **idle** (II.) & **-er**. **a** One who idles; a lazy, slothful person; **b** a trivial, frivolous, superficial, ineffective person.

idle wheel, n. Wheel placed, and revolving, between two others, so that its cogged edge functions against the edges of each and imparts motion from one to the other.

idly, adv. [1. ídli; 2. áidli]. **idle** (I.) & **-ly**. In an idle manner.

Ido, n. [1. ḗdō; 2. ídou]. Invented word. An artificial universal language, a modified form of Esperanto.

idol, n. [1. ídl; 2. áidl], fr. O. Fr. *idole*, fr. Lat. *īdōl-(um)*, fr. Gk. *eidōlon*, 'an image, phantom; a likeness; idol', fr. base **weid-* &c., 'to see', q.v. under **idea** & words there referred to; & cp. **eidolon**. **1. a** Image, statue &c. representing a deity and worshipped as such; **b** a false god. **2.** Person or thing regarded with extravagant affection, admiration, or reverence; object of extreme devotion: *to make an idol of wealth; a popular idol.* **3.** (obs.) **a** Representation, effigy; **b** an appearance, or image without substance; e.g. reflection in a mirror; **c** (in Baconian logic, usually in Lat. pl. *idola*, see **idolum**), a fallacy: *the idols of the market-place* &c.

idolater, n. [1. ìdólater; 2. aidɔ́lətə], fr. O. Fr. *idolâtre*, contracted fr. L. Lat. *īdōlolatres*, fr. eccles. Gk. *eidōlolátrēs*, 'an idol-worshipper', fr. *eídōlo-(n)*, 'an image, phantom; an idol' (see prec.), & *látris*, 'a hired workman, servant', fr. *látr-(on)*, 'hire, payment' (see **-latry**). **1.** One who worships idols; a worshipper of false gods; pagan, heathen. **2.** A fervent, devoted admirer, adorer.

idolatress, n. [1. ìdólatres; 2. aidɔ́lətris]. Prec. & **-ess**. Fem. of prec.

idolatrous, adj. [1. ìdólatrus; 2. aidɔ́lətrəs]. **idolater** & **-ous**. **1.** Of the nature of, pertaining to, idolatry: *idolatrous worship.* **2.** (of persons) Addicted to idolatry.

idolatrously, adv. Prec. & **-ly**. In an idolatrous manner.

idolatry, n. [1. ìdólatri; 2. aidɔ́lətri]. **idol** & **-latry**. **1. a** The worship of idols, images &c.; **b** the worship of false gods, natural objects &c. **2.** Excessive devotion, admiration.

idolization, n. [1. ìdolīzā́shun; 2. àidəlaizéiʃən]. **idolize** & **-ation**. The act of idolizing; state of being idolized.

idolize, vb. trans. & intrans. [1. ídolīz; 2. áidəlaiz]. **idol** & **-ize**. **1.** trans. (chiefly fig.) To make an idol of; to be excessively devoted to; to love, admire, venerate, to an extreme degree: *to idolize wealth; to idolize a hero.* **2.** intrans. (rare) To worship idols.

idolum, n., pl. **idola** [1. īdólum, -la; 2. aidóuləm, -lə]. L. Lat. *īdōlum*, fr. Gk. *eidōlon*, 'a phantom; an image, likeness; a mental image, idea'. See **eidolon**. **1.** An idea, conception, mental image. **2.** (Baconian logic, usually pl.) Source of error in reasoning; fallacy: *idola theatri* &c.

idyl(l), n. [1. ídil, ídil; 2. áidil, ídil], fr. Lat. *īdyll-(ium)*, fr. Gk. *eidúllion*, lit. 'a little picture', hence 'a short, descriptive, pastoral poem'; same base as **idol**. **1. a** A short, simple, descriptive or narrative poem, esp. one treating, in a manner tinged with romance, of familiar, or pastoral scenes; of incidents of everyday life; **b** *prose idyll*, similar description or narration in prose. **2.** Incident, rural scene &c. forming a suitable subject for an idyll.

idyllic, adj. [1. īdílik; 2. aidílik]. Prec. & **-ic**. Of, pertaining to, an idyll; suitable to, having the qualities of, an idyll.

idyllically, adv. [1. īdílikali; 2. aidílikəli]. Prec. & **-al** & **-ly**. In an idyllic manner.

idyllist, n. [1. ídilist; 2. áidilist]. **idyll** & **-ist**. A writer of idylls.

idyllize, vb. trans. [1. ídilīz; 2. áidilaiz]. **idyll** & **-ize**. To represent as an idyll, make the subject of an idyll.

-ier, suff. Fr., fr. Lat. *-ārius* (see **-eer**), used in forming ns. denoting person's occupation. Words in *-ier* include, **a** early formations found already in M.E. & now accented on first syll.: *glazier, hosier*; & **b** later formations accented on suff.: *gondolier, grenadier* &c.

if, conj. [1. if; 2. if]. O.E. *ġif*, M.E. *ʒif, if.* **1.** On the supposition that, supposing that, provided that, on the condition that: **a** (with reference to present time): *if you like we will go straight home*; **b** (with reference to future) *if you get back before I do, wait for me here; I shall see him if he comes; if he gets a fair chance he will win*; **c** (implying conditions which are hypothetical; doubt, uncertainty): *if I had known, I wouldn't have done it; if he had caught the train he would be here by now; if you knew how I suffered, you would pity me.* **2.** Even though, granting that: *I will do it if it kills me!*; *if I am wrong, you are at least not absolutely right.* **3.** Whenever: *if I do not understand what he says, I always question him.* **4.** Whether: *I don't know if he is here; he asked if you were at home.* **5.** (in exclamatory clause expressing surprise) *If he hasn't kicked his football through the window!* Phr. *as if*, as though fulfilling the conditions indicated: *he looks as if he were angry; he talks as if he knew everything.*

igloo, **-u**, n. [1. íglōō; 2. íglū]. Eskimo. Winter hut, with domed roof, made of blocks of frozen snow.

igneous, adj. [1. ígneus; 2. ígniəs], fr. Lat. *igne-(us)*, 'of fire, fiery', fr. *ign-(is)*, 'fire', cogn. w. Scrt. *agniš*, O. Slav. *ognĭ*, Lith. *agnìs*, 'fire'. **1.** Consisting of, resembling, pertaining to, fire; fiery. **2.** (geol.) *Igneous rock*, produced by the action of fire or great heat.

ignis fatuus, n. [1. ígnis fátūus; 2. ígnis fǽtjuəs]. Lat. *ignis*, 'fire' (see prec.), & *fatuus*, 'foolish'. See **fatuous**. **1.** Phosphorescent light sometimes seen hovering above stagnant water or a marsh; so called because it is supposed to lead travellers out of their way; will-o'-the-wisp. **2.** (fig.) A misleading object of pursuit; mistaken ideal; hope, aspiration, eagerly followed and never attained.

ignitable, adj. [1. ignítabl; 2. ignáitəbl]. See next word & **-able**. Capable of being ignited.

ignite, vb. trans. & intrans. [1. ignít; 2. ignáit], fr. Lat. *ignīt-(um)*, P.P. type of *ignīre*, 'to set on fire', fr. *ignis*, 'fire'. See **igneous**. **1.** trans. To set on fire, to kindle, light. **2.** intrans. To take fire, be kindled.

igniter, n. [1. igníter; 2. ignáitə]. Prec. & **-er**. One who, that which, ignites; specif., device for starting ignition in an internal-combustion engine.

ignition, n. [1. ignishun; 2. igníʃən]. Prec. & **-ion**. **a** The process of igniting; **b** state of being ignited; specif. **c** (of internal combustion engine in a motor-car &c.) the igniting of explosive mixture in the cylinder; also device for so doing, igniter.

ignoble, adj. [1. ignṓbl; 2. ignóubl], fr. Fr., fr. Lat. *ignōbilis*, 'unknown; obscure, undistinguished; of low birth', fr. **in-** (II.) & O. Lat. *gnōbilis*, 'known; famous, renowned; high-born'. See **noble**. **1.** (rare or archaic) Not of noble birth; plebeian. **2. a** (of character, conduct, actions) Mean, base, degraded, despicable; **b** (of persons) possessing and exhibiting mean qualities in character, actions &c.; **c** (of events) humiliating, shameful.

ignobleness, n. Prec. & **-ness**. The quality of being ignoble.

ignobly, adv. See prec. & **-ly**. In an ignoble manner, shamefully.

ignominious, adj. [1. ìgnomínius; 2. ìgnəmínjəs]. **ignominy** & **-ous**. **1.** Deserving disgrace, dishonourable, shameful; contemptible, mean, unworthy: *ignominious conduct.* **2.** Involving disgrace and contempt, bringing dishonour; humiliating: *an ignominious dismissal, death, end.*

ignominiously, adv. Prec. & **-ly**. In an ignominious manner.

ignominy, n. [1. ígnumini; 2. ígnəmini], fr. Lat. *ignōminia*, 'disgrace, dishonour'; orig. 'deprivation of one's good name', fr. **in-** (II.) & *nōmen*, 'name'. See **nominal**. **1.** Disgrace, dishonour, degradation. **2.** Base, ignoble, conduct; degrading action.

ignoramus, n. [1. ìgnorámus; 2. ìgnəréiməs]. Lat., 'we do not know'; (legal) 'we disregard, do not recognize', as written on bill of indictment, thrown out by a grand jury for want of evidence, fr. *ignōrāre*, 'to have no knowledge of; to disregard'. See **ignore**. An ignorant person.

ignorance, n. [1. ígnorans; 2. ígnərəns]. Fr., fr. Lat. *ignōrantia*, 'want of knowledge', fr. Pres. Part. stem of *ignōr-(āre)*, 'to have no knowledge of'. See **ignore** & **-ance**. **1.** Lack of cultivation or education; want of knowledge; inexperience: *he sinned rather from ignorance than from actual wickedness; to live in a state of ignorance.* **2.** Want of knowledge of particular subject, fact &c.: *I am in complete ignorance of his intentions; his total ignorance of foreign languages.*

ignorant, adj. [1. ígnorant; 2. ígnərənt], fr. Fr., fr. Lat. *ignōrant-(em)*, Pres. Part. type of *ignōr-(āre)*, 'not to know'. See **ignore** & **-ant**. **1. a** (of persons) Knowing little or nothing; uneducated, uncultivated, illiterate: *an ignorant man*; **b** (of actions, conduct &c.) springing from, due to, betokening, ignorance: *an ignorant letter; ignorant behaviour.* **2.** Uninformed with regard to a specific subject; unaware, unconscious, of a specific fact: *to be ignorant of Latin, of a person's intentions; I was ignorant of the time.*

ignorantly, adv. Prec. & **-ly**. In an ignorant manner; in, on account of, ignorance.

ignoratio elenchi, n. [1. ignoráshiō eléngkī; 2. ignəréiʃiou iléŋkai]. Lat., 'ignorance of the argument; refutation'; second word fr. Gk. See **elenchus.** (log.) Apparent refutation of an argument which in reality only disproves something which was never maintained.

ignore, vb. trans. [1. ignṓr; 2. ignɔ́], fr. Fr. *ignorer*, fr. Lat. *ignōrāre*, 'not to know; to have no knowledge of; to take no notice of, disregard', fr. **in-** (**II.**) & *gnō-r-, 'knowing'; cp. *gnārus*, 'knowing, acquainted with; expert'; Gk. *gnōrízein*, 'make known, explain'. Cp. also Lat. *nōscere*, 'to know'; Gk. *gnōtós*, 'known'; Aryan base *ĝnō-, *ĝnē-, &c., 'to know'. See **gnostic, know. 1.** To take no notice of, disregard, refuse to consider: *to ignore a person and his remarks.* **2.** (law, of Grand Jury) To reject, throw out (an indictment).

ignotum per ignotius, phr. [1. ignṓtum pĕr ignṓtius; 2. ignóutəm pǟr ignóutiəs]. Lat., (to explain) 'the unknown by something still less known'.

iguana, n. [1. igūáhna; 2. igjuánə]. Span., fr. Carib. *iwana.* A large, arboreal, herbivorous lizard, with crest on the back, found in tropical America and W. Indies.

iguanodon, n. [1. igūánodon; 2. igjuǽnədɔn], fr. **iguana** & Gk. *odón-(tos)*, genit. of *odoús*, 'tooth'. See **odont-.** A very large, extinct, herbivorous lizard, with long, heavy tail, small fore-limbs, and large hind-limbs used in walking.

ihlang-ihlang, n., also *ilang-ilang* & *ylang-ylang* [1. iláng iláng; 2. ilǽŋ ilǽŋ]. Malay., 'flower of flowers'. **a** A tree of Malay Archipelago &c., with large fragrant yellow flowers; **b** strong perfume distilled from these flowers.

il-, pref., representing **in-** (**I.**) & (**II.**) before *-l.*

-il(e), suff., forming adjs. & ns.; (1) adjs., representing **a** O. Fr. *-il* (fem. *-ile*), fr. Lat. *-īlis*: *civil, virile, senile, servile*; **b** later Fr. loanwords fr. Lat. *ĭlis*: *docile, agile, fragile, sterile, versatile*; **c** Fr. or Engl. formations fr. Lat. stems: *prehensile, protractile*; **d** Engl. borrowings fr. Lat. adjs. in *-ĭlis*: *futile, puerile.* (2) Nouns in *-ile, -il* represent Lat. ns. or adjs. in *-ĭlis*, either directly fr. Lat.: *aedile, missile, textile*; or through Fr.: *fossil, utensil.*

ilang-ilang, n. See **ihlang-ihlang.**

ileac, iliac, adj. [1. íleak; 2. íliæk], fr. **ileum** & **-ac**, cp. **iliac.** (anat.) Of, pertaining to, affecting, the ileum.

ileo-, pref. used to form compounds, fr. **ileum**, as *ileo-caecal*, pertaining to the ileum and the caecum.

ileum, n. [1. íleum; 2. íliəm]. Lat., also *īle*, lower part of abdomen from lower ribs to groin. Variant of **ilium.** (anat.) The lower part of the small intestine.

ilex, n. [1. íleks; 2. áileks]. Lat. *īlex*, 'holm-oak'; the Romance forms indicate a Lat. form *ĭlex*, in distinction to the poetical *īlex.* The word is prob. pre-Aryan. Holm-oak, evergreen oak.

iliac, adj. [1. íliak; 2. íliæk], fr. Fr. *iliaque*, fr. L. Lat. *īliacus*, fr. *īlia*, pl. of *īlium*, 'flank' (sing. only in glosses). See **ilium.** (anat.) **a** Of, near, pertaining to, the ilium or flattened upper bone of the pelvis: *iliac artery* &c.; **b** of, pertaining to, the ileum; ileac.

Iliad, n. [1. íliad; 2. íliəd]. Lat. *Iliad-(is)*, stem of *Ilias*, 'the Iliad of Homer', fr. Gk. *Iliás (poiēsis)*, 'the Iliad', fr. *Ili-(os, -on)*, 'Troy', & **-ad.** Greek epic attributed to Homer, telling of the siege of Troy. Phr. *Iliad of woes* (transl. fr. Gk. proverb. phr. *Iliás kakôn*), 'succession of misfortunes, sorrows'.

ilium, n. [1. ílium; 2. íliəm]. Lat. *īlium*, pl. *īlia* (sing. only in glosses), 'the flanks'; prob. cogn. w. O. Fris. *ili*, 'swelling'; O.E. *île*, O.N. *il*, 'sole of the foot'. Aryan base *ĭl, 'to swell, spread out'. Cp. **iliac** & **ileum.** (anat.) One of the flattened upper bones of the pelvis, forming part of the hip-bone.

ilk, adj. [1. ilk; 2. ilk]. O.E. *ilca*, M.E. *ilke*, 'same', prob. fr. pronominal *i-* (cp. Goth. *is*, Lat. *is*, 'he'); & *-līc*, 'like'. See **like** (**I.**). (Scots) **a** *Of that ilk*, of the place or estate bearing the same name as that of the owner: *Anstruther of that ilk=Anstruther of Anstruther*; **b** used also ignorantly, in England, as meaning 'of the same class, set' &c.: *and others of that ilk* &c.

ill (**I.**), adj. [1. il; 2. il]. M.E. *ille*; fr. O.N. *illr*, 'ill, bad'; prob. connected w. O.N. *ylr*, 'heat', & *ylja*, 'to burn', & w. O.E. *ǣlan*, 'to burn, to kindle', & *ǣled*, 'fire, fire-brand'. The latter may be fr. Aryan *aidh-l-, developed by an extending process wh. is not very clear, fr. base *alē-t-, whence Lat. *adolēre*, 'to burn', esp. as a sacrifice, & *altāre* &c., see **altar.** The connexion of the Gmc. & Lat. words must, however, still be considered doubtful. **1.** (pred., replacing *sick*) In bad health, affected with disease, ailing: *to look, be, ill, be taken ill* &c. Rarely attributive in this sense, the more common word being *sick*, as *sick people.* **2.** Morally bad, of evil character: *of ill repute.* **3.** Unfriendly, hostile: '*this ill mansion*' (Milton, 'P.L.'); malevolent, unkind: *ill usage*; *ill will, ill blood*, hatred, enmity, malevolence. Phr. *an ill turn*, action which injures another. **4.** Unfavourable, unpropitious; promising or expressive of evil: *birds of ill omen*; *ill news*; *ill luck.* Phr. *an ill wind* (fig.). **5.** Irritable, morose, gloomy, sullen: *ill temper, humour.* **6.** Poor, unsatisfactory, imperfect, defective: *to meet with ill success.* **7.** (archaic) Difficult, hard, troublesome: *an ill man to please.*

ill (**II.**), adv., fr. prec. Badly; in a wrong, faulty, incorrect manner: *to behave ill*; (in various Phrs.) *to take a thing ill*, to be offended by, be indignant at; *to speak ill of*, to disparage, discredit, speak unfavourably of; *it ill becomes* (*you, him* &c.), it is unsuitable, improper, for you &c.; *ill at ease*, uncomfortable, uneasy, in body or mind; *to go ill with*, be unfavourable to, be disastrous; *ill equipped, provided*, inadequately; *I can ill afford*, with difficulty.

ill (**III.**), n., fr. **ill** (**I.**). **1.** Evil, wickedness, wrongdoing, wrongful action: *to do ill.* **2.** Misfortune, unfavourable circumstance; annoyance, difficulty: '*all the ills that flesh is heir to*'; *to suffer various ills.*

ill-advised, adj. Unwise, rash, imprudent: *an ill-advised proceeding*; *you would be ill-advised to do so and so.*

ill-advisedly, adv. Prec. & **-ly.** In a rash, imprudent manner.

ill-affected, adj. Not favourably disposed towards; having feelings of disapprobation for.

illation, n. [1. iláshun; 2. iléiʃən], fr. L. Lat. *illātiōn-(em)*, 'deduction', fr. *illāt-(um)*, used as P.P. of *inferre*, 'to bring, carry in; to produce, bring forward; to cause, give rise to, occasion; to infer, conclude'. See **il-**, & for *-lātum* (for *tlātum), second element of **elate**, & first syll. of **tolerate. 1.** Deduction, inference, conclusion. **2.** Something deduced or inferred.

illative, adj. [1. ilátiv; 2. iléitiv], fr. L. Lat. *illātīv-(us).* See prec. & **-ive. 1.** (gram.) **a** (of words) Introducing an inference; **b** (of phrase) expressing an inference. **2.** Of the nature of, pertaining to, deduction; inferential.

illatively, adv. Prec. & **-ly.** In an inferential manner.

ill-bred, adj. Imperfectly trained in, or acquainted with, the traditions and manners of good and polite society; churlish in character; common, discourteous, in manner.

ill-breeding, n. Lack of instruction in, and experience of, the traditional ways of regarding, and behaving to, one's fellows which are current in polite society; general or specific exhibition of bad manners and conduct due to such defects of education; ignorant boorishness, rudeness, discourtesy; commonness of manner and behaviour.

ill-conditioned, adj. **1.** Having a bad disposition; **a** inclined to wickedness; **b** ill-tempered, surly, cantankerous. **2.** In bad physical condition.

ill-disposed, adj. [1. íl dispṓzd; 2. íl dispóuzd]. **1.** Inclined to evil, having propensity to behave badly; malicious, malevolent: *ill-disposed persons.* **2.** Having unfavourable bias towards, unfavourable to: *ill-disposed towards a person, plan* &c.

illegal, adj. [1. ilḗgal; 2. ilígəl], fr. Med. Lat. *illēgāl-(is)*, 'illegal'; **il-** & **legal.** Not according to law, in opposition to, forbidden by, the law; not legal; unlawful.

illegality, n. [1. ilēgáliti; 2. iligǽliti]. Prec. & **-ity. 1.** The quality of being illegal. **2.** An illegal action.

illegally, adv. [1. ilḗgali; 2. ilígəli]. **illegal** & **-ly.** In an illegal manner.

illegibility, n. [1. ilèjibíliti; 2. ilèdžibíliti]. **il-** & **legibility.** The quality of being illegible.

illegible, adj. [1. iléjibl; 2. ilédžibl]. **il-** & **legible.** Difficult or impossible to read; not legible.

illegibly, adv. Prec. & **-ly.** In an illegible manner.

illegitimacy, n. [1. ilejítimasi; 2. ilidžítiməsi]. **il-** & **legitimacy.** The state or quality of being illegitimate.

illegitimate (**I.**), adj. [1. ilijítimat; 2. ilidžítimət]. **il-** & **legitimate. 1.** (of actions) Without legal authority; unlawful. **2.** (of persons) Not born in lawful wedlock. **3.** (of deductions, conclusions) Not logically possible; wrongly deduced.

illegitimate (**II.**), vb. trans. [1. ilijítimāt; 2. ilidžítimeit], fr. prec. To pronounce, declare, render, illegitimate.

illegitimately, adv. **illegitimate** (**I.**) & **-ly.** In an illegitimate manner.

illegitimation, n. [1. ilijitimáshun; 2. ilidžitiméiʃən]. **illegitimate** (**II.**) & **-ion.** The act of illegitimating; state of being declared, or rendered, illegitimate.

ill-fated, adj. **1.** Fated, destined, to misfortune. **2.** Bringing misfortune.

ill-favoured, adj. (of person, looks &c.) Unpleasing, unprepossessing, not pleasant to look at; ugly.

ill-gotten, adj. [1. íl gótn; 2. íl gɔ́tn]. See **got** for old P.P. Gained by unscrupulous or unlawful means: chiefly in *ill-gotten gains.*

ill-humour, n. [1. il ū́mur; 2. il jū́mə]. Bad temper.

ill-humoured, adj. [1. il ū́murd; 2. il jū́məd]. Prec. & **-ed.** Bad-tempered, irritable.

illiberal, adj. [1. ilíberal; 2. ilíbərəl], fr. Lat. *illīberāl-(is)*, 'unworthy of a free man; low, mean'. **il-** & **liberal. 1.** Not generous; parsimonious, niggardly. **2. a** Characterized by lack of broad and humane culture; **b** narrow-minded, bigoted, intolerant.

illiberality, n. [1. iliberáliti; 2. ilibərǽliti]. Prec. & **-ity.** The quality of being illiberal; **a** niggardliness; **b** narrow-mindedness.

illiberally, adv. [1. ilíberali; 2. ilíbərəli]. **illiberal** & **-ly.** In an illiberal manner.

illicit, adj. [1. ilísit; 2. ilísit], fr. Fr., fr. Lat. *illicitus*, 'not allowed, illegal'; **il-** & **licit.** Not lawful, prohibited.

illicitly, adv. Prec. & **-ly.** In an illicit manner.

illimitability, n. [1. ilimitabíliti; 2. ilimitəbíliti]. See next word & **-ity.** The quality of being illimitable.

illimitable, adj. [1. ilímitabl; 2. ilímitəbl]. **il-** & **limit** & **-able.** Without real or apparent limits; unlimited, boundless, limitless, vast: *illimitable space*; *the illimitable ocean*; *illimitable wealth.*

illimitableness, n. Prec. & **-ness.** The quality of being illimitable.

illimitably, adv. See prec. & **-ly.** In an illimitable manner.

illiteracy, n. [1. ilíterasi; 2. ilítərəsi]. See next word & **-acy.** The quality, state, of being illiterate; specif., inability to read and write.

illiterate (**I.**), adj. [1. ilíterat; 2. ilítərət], fr. Lat. *illīterāt-(us)*, 'unlearned, ignorant'. **il-** & **literate. 1.** Lacking humane learning and knowledge of literature. 2. Specif., unable to read or write; lacking the elements of education: *the illiterate voter.*

illiterate (**II.**), n., fr. prec. An illiterate person, specif., one unable to read or write.

illiterateness, n. **illiterate** (**I.**) & **-ness.** The quality of being illiterate.

ill-judged, adj. [1. il júјd; 2. il džádžd]. (of conduct, action) Springing from lack of sound judgement; imprudent, mistaken; inopportune.

ill-luck, n. Misfortune; an unfortunate, unhappy, experience.

ill-mannered, adj. Having bad, vulgar manners.

ill-natured, adj. [1. il náchurd; 2. il néitʃəd]. Bad-tempered, surly, cross-grained.

ill-naturedly, adv. Prec. & **-ly.** In an ill-natured manner.

illness, n. [1. ílnes; 2. ílnis]. **ill** (**I.**) & **-ness.** **1.** Unhealthy, morbid condition of the body; less frequently of the mind; disease; opposite of *health*: *there is no serious illness in the city.* **2.** **a** A specific form of disease: *to suffer from a serious illness*; **b** attack, fit, bout, of illness: *to be suddenly seized with illness.*

illogical, adj. [1. ilójikl; 2. ilódžikl]. **il-** & **logical.** Not logical; **a** (of arguments, statements), not in accordance with logical processes of thought; irrational; **b** (of persons) not reasoning in a logical manner; given to reasoning in a way that is not logical; **c** (of actions) based upon, arising from, imperfect reasoning.

illogicality, n. [1. ilojikáliti; 2. ilɔdžikǽliti]. Prec. & **-ity.** The quality of being illogical.

illogically, adv. [1. ilójikali; 2. ilódžikəli]. **illogical** & **-ly.** In an illogical manner.

ill-omened, adj. [1. il ómend; 2. il óumend]. Accompanied by, associated with, unfavourable omens; destined to misfortune; unfortunate.

ill-starred, adj. Born under an evil star; doomed to misfortune; unlucky.

ill-tempered, adj. Bad-tempered, irritable, surly.

illth, n. [1. ilth; 2. ilþ]. **ill** (**I.**) & **-th.** Formed on anal. of **wealth.** (rare) Absence of prosperity, unhappy state; opposed to *welfare, well-being.*

ill-timed, adj. [1. il tímd; 2. il táimd]. Unwise or inappropriate at a particular time; inopportune: *an ill-timed jest, remark* &c.

ill-treat, vb. trans. To treat badly, unkindly.

ill-treatment, n. Cruelty.

illume, vb. trans. [1. ilúm; 2. iljúm]. Shortened fr. **illumine.** (poet., lit., and fig.) To shed light upon, make clear or bright.

illuminant, adj. & n. [1. ilúminant; 2. iljúminənt]. **illumine** & **-ant.** **1.** adj. Giving light, brightening, illuminating. **2.** n. Something that illuminates or gives light.

illuminate, vb. trans. [1. ilúminăt; 2. iljúmineit], fr. Lat. *illūmināt-(um)*, P.P. type of *illūmināre*, 'to make light, brighten'; fig. 'to adorn (speech &c.)', fr. **il-** & *lūmin-(is)*, stem of *lūmen*, 'light'. See **luminous.** **1.** To give light to, make light: *the room was poorly illuminated by one candle.* **2.** To light up brilliantly, adorn with lights: *to illuminate a house, town, street, for a festivity* &c. **3.** To decorate (manuscript &c.) with coloured designs, letters &c. **4.** **a** To give mental or spiritual light to (a person, mind &c.): *many heathen have now been illuminated by the Gospel*; **b** to shed light on, give clarity to, help to explain: *the test of a commentator is how far he illuminates his author's obscurities*; **c** to lend prestige to, make illustrious: *the roll of citizens was illuminated by many famous names.*

Illuminati, n. pl. [1. ilúminátī; 2. iljúminéitai]. Lat. *illūmināti*, nom. pl. masc. of P.P. of *illūmināre*, 'to light up'. See prec. **1.** Persons professing to possess remarkable endowments or perception. **2.** One of several religious sects, e.g. Rosicrucians. **3.** A secret deistic and republican society founded in Bavaria in 1776.

illumination, n. [1. iluminάshun; 2. iljúminéiʃən]. **illuminate** & **-ion.** **1.** Act or process of illuminating; state of being illuminated. **2.** (often pl.) Festive lighting up and decoration of buildings &c. by means of coloured lights &c. **3.** Coloured and gilded decorations in a manuscript.

illuminative, adj. [1. ilúminativ; 2. iljúminətiv]. **illuminate** & **-ive.** Tending to illuminate (in material and non-material senses).

illumine, vb. trans. [1. ilúmin; 2. iljúmin], fr. Fr. *illuminer*, fr. Lat. *illūmināre*, 'to light up'. See **illuminate.** **1.** To give light to, light up. **2.** (fig.) **a** To give mental or spiritual light to, enlighten; **b** to brighten, cheer, relieve (gloom &c.).

Illuminism, n. [1. ilúminizm; 2. iljúminizəm]. Prec. & **-ism.** The principles, doctrines, of the Illuminati.

Illuminist, n. [1. ilúminist; 2. iljúminist]. **illumine** & **-ist.** A supporter of, believer in, Illuminism.

ill-use, vb. trans. To use in an improper way; **a** to ill-treat, cause to suffer, behave cruelly to (sentient beings); **b** to make a wrong use of, injure, do harm to (inanimate objects).

illusion, n. [1. ilúzhun; 2. iljúžən], fr. Fr., fr. Lat. *illūs-(um)*, P.P. type of *illūdere*, 'to play with; to mock at; to deceive', fr. **il-** & *lūdere*, 'to lay', see **ludicrous**, & **-ion.** **1.** **a** (physical) Sensuous perception which conveys an impression other than true of what is perceived; as when a number of lines of equal length are so arranged as to convey the impression that they are of varying length &c.: *optical illusion*; **b** loosely, any visual image, or other sensuous impression which misleads; deceptive appearance: *illusion of the senses*; e.g. distant view of water which travellers in the desert fancy they see when none is there. **2.** Belief not in accordance with actual facts; baseless opinion held about anything; state of mind in which one is deceived; delusion.

illusional, adj. [1. ilúzhunal; 2. iljúžənəl]. Prec. & **-al.** Connected with, of the nature of, an illusion.

illusionary, adj. [1. ilúzhunari; 2. iljúžənəri]. **illusion** & **-ary.** **a** Illusional; **b** subject to illusions.

illusionism, n. [1. ilúzhunizm; 2. iljúžənizəm]. Prec. & **-ism.** Doctrine that the external world exists entirely and only in illusions of the senses.

illusionist, n. [1. ilúzhunist; 2. iljúžənist]. **illusion** & **-ist.** **1.** A supporter of illusionism. **2.** A public performer who produces illusions; a conjurer.

illusive, adj. [1. ilúsiv; 2. iljúsiv], fr. Lat. *illūs-(um)*, P.P. type of *illūdere*, 'to play with; to mock at; to deceive'. See **illusion** & **-ive.** Producing, based on, illusion; deceptive, delusive.

illusively, adv. Prec. & **-ly.** In an illusive manner.

illusiveness, n. See prec. & **-ness.** The quality of being illusive.

illusorily, adv. [1. ilúsorili; 2. iljúsərili]. **illusory** & **-ly.** In an illusory manner.

illusoriness, n. [1. ilúsorines; 2. iljúsərinis]. Next word & **-ness.** The quality of being illusory.

illusory, adj. [1. ilúsori; 2. iljúsəri], fr. Lat. *illūs-(us)*, see **illusion**, & **-ory.** Illusive, deceptive; unreal, based on illusion.

illustrate, vb. trans. [1. ílustrăt; 2. íləstreit], fr. Lat. *illustrāt-(um)*, P.P. type of *illustrāre*, 'to make light; to bring to light, make known; to explain; to make illustrious, celebrate'. **il-** & **lustre.** **1.** To make clear (a statement, argument) by giving specific examples and comparisons &c. **2.** To furnish (book, lecture) with figures and pictures of persons and things dealt with.

illustration, n. [1. ilustráshun; 2. iləstréiʃən], fr. Lat. *illustrātiōn-(em)*. See prec. & **-ion.** **1.** **a** An example; **b** a picture, esp. one in a book. **2.** Act of giving, providing, illustrations (in either sense).

illustrative, adj. [1. ilústrativ; 2. ilástrətiv]. **illustrate** & **-ive.** Serving as, intended as, an illustration, example.

illustratively, adv. Prec. & **-ly.** In an illustrative manner.

illustrious, adj. [1. ilústrius; 2. ilástriəs], fr. Lat. *illustri-(s)*, 'light, bright, brilliant; clear, evident; famous, renowned', fr. **il-** & *lustr-*, 'to make bright, illumine', see **lustre** (**II.**), & **-ous.** Famous, celebrated, distinguished.

illustriously, adv. Prec. & **-ly.** In an illustrious manner.

illustriousness, n. See prec. & **-ness.** The state of being illustrious.

im-, pref. Form of *in-* used before the lip consonants *b, m, p.* See **in-.** (1) = not; (2) = in; also as prefix having intensive force.

image (**I.**), n. [1. ímij; 2. ímidž], fr. Fr., fr. Lat. *imāgin-(em)*, nom. *imāgo*, 'a representation, portrait, statue; a likeness; an appearance, pretence; mental representation, idea'; cp. *im-itāri*, 'to copy; to be like; to represent, depict'; *aem-ulus*, 'rivalling'; Aryan base **aim-*, **im-*, 'to be like, resemble'. See **emulate, emulous.** **1.** **a** Material representation of person or thing; carved or painted figure; statue, effigy: *an image of a saint*; **b** specif., such a carved representation of person or animal to which superstitious reverence or worship is accorded: *to worship images*; *graven images.* **2.** Person or thing exactly like, or bearing a striking resemblance to, another; counterpart: *he is the image of his father.* **3.** (optical) Visual impression of an object made upon a mirror, or upon the retina of the eye. **4.** Figurative expression; simile, metaphor: *to speak in images.* **5.** (psychol.) A revival, reproduction by memory, in the mind, of some sensuous experience undergone in the past, including the visual, auditive, tactile, and other impressions associated with it; an idea.

image (**II.**), vb. trans., fr. prec. **1.** To make an image, representation, of. **2.** To reflect, present a counterpart of; to mirror. **3.** To present to the imagination, recall to the mental vision; to figure, imagine. **4.** To portray, describe, in a life-like manner.

imageable, adj. [1. ímijabl; 2. ímidžəbl]. **image** (**II.**) & **-able.** Capable of being imaged; capable of being imagined.

imagery, n. [1. ímijeri; 2. ímidžəri], fr. Fr. *imagerie.* **image** (**I.**) & **-ery.** **1.** (in plastic arts) Representation of objects; statues, carving. **2.** (in liter.) Figurative representation, metaphorical description; system, mode, of employing images in writing or speaking.

imaginable, adj. [1. imájinabl; 2. imǽdžinəbl], fr. L. Lat. *imāginābilis*, 'imaginable'. **image** & **-able.** Capable of being imagined.

imaginably, adv. Prec. & **-ly.** In an imaginable manner.

imaginal, adj. [1. imájinal; 2. imǽdžinəl], fr. Lat. *imāgin-(em).* See **image** & **-al.** (entom.) Pertaining to the imago of an insect.

imaginarily, adv. [1. imájinarili; 2. imǽdžinərili]. See next word & **-ly.** In an imaginary manner.

imaginary, adj. [1. imájinari; 2. imǽdžinəri], fr. Lat. *imāginări-(us)*, 'imaginary', fr. Lat. *imāgin-*, stem of *imāgo*, see **image**, & **-ary.** Having no actual existence, existing only in the imagination.

imagination, n. [1. imajináshun; 2. imædžinéiʃən], fr. Lat. *imāginātiōn-(em)*, 'imagination, fancy'. **imagine** & **-ation.** **1.** Function or power of the mind of calling up images; specif. **a** power of recalling to the mind, and reproducing in more or less detail, experiences already undergone in the past; **b** power of creating, constructing, mental images of things not previously experienced, but merely suggested or hinted at. **2.** **a** A mental image, or group of these, recalled or created by the imagination; **b** a fanciful idea, foolish notion.

imaginative, adj. [1. imájinativ; 2. imǽdžinətiv], fr. O. Fr., fr. L. Lat. *imāginātīv-(us)*, 'imaginative', fr. *imāgināt-(um)*, P.P. type of *imāginārī*, 'to imagine, picture to oneself'. See **imagine** & **-ive**. **1.** Pertaining to, depending on, springing from, exhibiting, imagination: *imaginative poetry*. **2.** (of persons) Possessing, and in the habit of employing, strong powers of imagination &c.

imaginatively, adv. Prec. & **-ly**. In an imaginative manner.

imaginativeness, n. See prec. & **-ness**. The quality of being imaginative.

imagine, vb. trans. & intrans. [1. imájin; 2. imǽdžin], fr. Fr. *imaginer*, fr. Lat. *imāginārī*, 'to imagine, picture to oneself', fr. *imāgin-*, stem of *imāgo*. See **image**. **A.** trans. **1.** To form a mental picture of, conceive in the mind, form an idea or notion of, construct mentally: *such sufferings as we cannot even imagine*; *I imagine King Richard I. as a tall, strong, handsome man*. Phr. *to imagine the king's death*, to contrive or attempt to kill the king, one of the offences constituting high treason. **B.** intrans. **a** To form an idea, opinion: *I cannot imagine who the man is*; **b** to suppose, conjecture: *I hardly imagine that the Income Tax will be abolished this year*.

imago, n. [1. imágō; 2. iméigou]. pl. **imagines, imagos** [1. imájinēz, imágōz; 2. imǽdžinīz, iméigouz]. Lat. See **image** (I.). (zool.) Final, fully developed, stage of an insect, esp. of a winged insect.

imam, imaum, n. [1. imáhm; 2. imā́m]. Arab. *imam*, fr. *amma*, 'to precede'. **1.** Religious leader or head of the Moslem state. **2.** The official leader of prayer and preacher in a Moslem mosque.

imbecile, adj. & n. [1. ímbesēl; 2. ímbisīl], fr. Fr. *imbécile*, fr. Lat. *imbēcillus*, 'weak, feeble', prob. fr. earlier **im-baccillus*, 'unsupported'; cp. *baculum*, 'a staff'; Gk. *báktron*, *baktēriā*, 'a staff, cane'. See **bacillus**. **1.** adj. **a** Mentally deficient, weak in intellect; **b** unwise, stupid, foolish. **2.** n. **a** A person of feeble intellect; **b** a foolish person.

imbecilely, adv. Prec. & **-ly**. In an imbecile manner.

imbecility, n. [1. ìmbesíliti; 2. ìmbisíliti]. **imbecile** & **-ity**. **1.** The state of being imbecile. **2.** An imbecile action, speech &c.

imbibe, vb. trans. [1. imbíb; 2. imbáib], fr. Fr. *imbiber*, fr. Lat. *imbibere*, 'to drink in; to conceive (an opinion, idea &c.); to resolve upon', fr. **im-** & *bibere*, 'to drink; drink in, absorb'. See under **bibulous**. **1.** (of living organisms) **a** To take in nourishment, or air, into the system; **b** (colloq.) to drink; to drink alcoholic beverages to excess. **2.** (of inanimate objects) To soak up, absorb, moisture: *the earth imbibes the rain*. **3.** (fig.) To receive into the mind, drink in, assimilate (ideas, theories, opinions &c.).

imbibition, n. [1. ìmbibíshun; 2. ìmbibíʃən], fr. Lat. *imbibit-(um)*, P.P. type of *imbibere*, 'to receive mentally, drink in'. See prec. & **-ion**. (rare) Act of imbibing; absorption.

imbricate (I.), vb. trans. & intrans. [1. ímbrikāt; 2. ímbrikeit], fr. Lat. *imbricāt-(um)*, P.P. type of *imbricāre*, 'to shape like a tile', fr. *imbric-*, stem of *imbrex*, 'a hollow roofing-tile to carry off the rain', fr. *imber*, 'a shower of rain'; cogn. w. Scrt. *abhrāš*, 'dull weather'; Gk. *aphrós*, 'foam'. Cp. also, w. different grade of vowel, Scrt. *ambhaš*, 'water', Gk. *ómbros*, 'rain' (see **ombro-**). Aryan base **m̥bh-*, **embh-*, **ombh-* &c., 'rain', earlier **enebh-*, **onebh-* &c. See **nebula**. (zool. and bot.) **1.** trans. (of scales &c.) To place so as to overlap. **2.** intrans. To overlap.

imbricate (II.), adj. [1. ímbrikāt; 2. ímbrikeit], fr. Lat. *imbricāt-(um)*, P.P. type of *imbricāre*, 'to shape like a tile'. See prec. (zool. and bot.) Overlapping, arranged like tiles.

imbrication, n. [1. ìmbrikáshun; 2. ìmbrikéiʃən]. **imbricate** (I.) & **-ion**. The process of imbricating; state of being imbricated; specif., arrangement of scales &c. so that they overlap.

imbricative, adj. [1. ímbrikativ; 2. ímbrikətiv]. See prec. & **-ive**. Tending to overlap.

imbroglio, n. [1. imbróliō; 2. imbróuliou]. Ital., fr. **im-** & *broglio*, 'confusion, hurly-burly'. See **broil** (II.). (rare in material sense) A confusion of ideas; complicated situation.

imbrue, vb. trans. [1. imbrōō; 2. imbrū́], fr. O. Fr. *embreuver*, *embeuvrer*, 'to moisten', fr. **em-**, **im-**, & Lat. **biberāre*, 'cause to drink, moisten', fr. *bibere*, 'to drink'. See **bibulous**. To stain, discolour, soil: (chiefly fig.) *to imbrue one's hands with blood*, be guilty of, responsible for, bloodshed.

imbrute, embrute, vb. trans. [1. imbrōōt; 2. imbrū́t]. **im-** & **brute**. To make like a brute; brutalize.

imbue, vb. trans. [1. imbū́; 2. imbjū́], fr. Lat. *imbuere*, 'to moisten, steep, saturate; to stain, taint; to accustom, inure'; prob. cogn. w. Gk. **aphúein*, *aphússein*, 'to draw, pour out (liquid)'; Aryan base **m̥bhu-*, 'liquid', fr. **m̥bh*, 'rain, water', whence Lat. *imber*, 'rain'; Gk. *aphrós*, 'foam'. See **imbricate**. **1.** To moisten thoroughly, steep, saturate. **2.** To steep in colouring matter, dye. **3.** To stain, taint, imbrue. **4.** (fig.) To inspire, instil into, fill the mind of with: *imbued with hatred, with socialistic doctrines, with a love of piety*.

imitability, n. [1. ìmitabíliti; 2. ìmitəbíliti]. See next word & **-ity**. The quality of being imitable.

imitable, adj. [1. ímitabl; 2. ímitəbl], fr. Lat. *imitābilis*, 'imitable', fr. *imit-ārī*, 'imitate'. See **imitate** & **-able**. Capable of being imitated.

imitate, vb. trans. [1. ímitāt; 2. ímiteit], fr. Lat. *imitāt-(um)*, P.P. type of *imitārī*, 'to imitate, copy; to be like, resemble; to replace, be substitute for; to represent, depict'. Cp. *im-āgo*, 'likeness, representation' (see **image**); *aemulus*, 'rivalling' (cp. **emulate**). Aryan base **aim-*, **im-* &c., 'be like, resemble'. **1.** (of human action) **a** (in moral sense) To follow example of, take as model of conduct; to act, behave in same way as: *we ought to imitate the wise and good in all things*; to reproduce: *to imitate the virtues of*; **b** (in material sense) to copy external appearance of; reproduce, assume, manners, style, bearing, speech &c. of: *vulgar people often try to imitate their betters*; specif. **c** to mimic, take off, burlesque; to copy in a ludicrous way, to caricature: *Garrick used to amuse his friends by imitating Johnson*. **2.** **a** To produce upon the senses an impression of resemblance or identity between two things; to make a thing resemble another by producing through one medium sensuous impressions similar to those produced by something else; to make or do something which looks, sounds, feels, like some other thing, action &c.: *to imitate diamonds in paste*; *to imitate oak by graining*; *to imitate a bird's cry with the lips*; **b** to copy fraudulently, with intent to deceive; to counterfeit: *dishonest dealers sometimes imitate the worm-holes in old wood*. **3.** **a** (of inanimate objects) To resemble in appearance, look like, have same appearance and other qualities as: *fabric is now made from cellulose to imitate silk*; **b** (biol., of animals) to acquire similar appearance to: *the colour of many animals imitates that of their natural environment*.

imitation, n. [1. ìmitáshun; 2. ìmitéiʃən], fr. Lat. *imitātiōn-(em)*. See prec. & **-ion**. **1.** The act of imitating: *painters lacking originality often spend their lives in the imitation of the great masters*. **2.** **a** That which imitates; something constructed as a copy of something else: *wood may be painted as an imitation of marble*; **b** a fraudulent copy, a counterfeit; **c** mimicry, burlesque: *Charles Mathews used to give imitations of other actors*. **3.** (attrib.) *Imitation antiques*; *imitation pearls* &c.

imitative, adj. [1. ímitativ; 2. ímitətiv]. **imitate** & **-ive**. **1.** Imitating, following a model. Phrs. *imitative arts*, painting, sculpture; *imitative word*, one reproducing approximately the sound which it signifies, e.g. *buzz, flick, plop*; or intended to give an impression of the quality which it denotes, e.g. *flimsy, blob*. **2.** **a** (of persons) Tending to imitate others rather than to behave naturally; tending to reproduce ideas of others, instead of having one's own; **b** (of actions, artistic products &c.) not original; modelled on, reproducing, those of others: *imitative poetry* &c.

imitatively, adv. Prec. & **-ly**. In an imitative manner.

imitativeness, n. See prec. & **-ness**. The quality of being imitative.

immaculacy, n. [1. imákūlasi; 2. imǽkjuləsi]. See next word & **-acy**. The state or quality of being immaculate; freedom from stain or defect (in material and non-material senses).

immaculate, adj. [1. imákūlat; 2. imǽkjulit], fr. **im-** & Lat. *maculāt-(um)*, P.P. type of *maculāre*, 'to make spotted, stain; to defile, pollute', fr. *macula*, 'a spot, mark; the mesh of a net; a blemish, fault'. See **macula**. **1.** **a** (in material sense) Unsoiled, perfectly clean, spotless, stainless: *an immaculate robe, shirt-front*; **b** scrupulously correct, faultless: *an immaculate style in dress*; **c** specif. (zool.) not spotted. **2.** (in non-material sense) Pure, unsullied by sin; without fault; spotless, innocent, irreproachable: *immaculate life and conduct*.

Immaculate Conception, n. Doctrine that the Blessed Virgin Mary was born free from original sin.

immaculately, adv. [1. imákūlatli; 2. imǽkjulətli]. **immaculate** & **-ly**. In an immaculate manner.

immaculateness, n. [1. imákūlatnes; 2. imǽkjulətnis]. See prec. & **-ness**. The state or quality of being immaculate.

immanence, n. [1. ímanens; 2. ímənəns], fr. L. Lat. *imman-(ēre)*, 'to dwell in'. See **immanent** & **-ce**. The state of being immanent; specif. (theol.) that of God in the universe.

immanency, n. [1. ímanensi; 2. ímənənsi], fr. L. Lat. *imman-(ēre)*, 'to dwell in'. See next word & **-cy**. Immanence.

immanent, adj. [1. ímanent; 2. ímənənt], fr. L. Lat., fr. **im-** & *manent-(em)*, Pres. Part. of *manēre*, 'to remain, stay; to endure, last'. See this base under **remain**. **1.** Remaining within; inherent, indwelling. Specif. **2.** (theol., of the Deity) Pervading, present, throughout the universe.

immarcessible, adj. [1. imarsésibl; 2. imāsésibl]. Lat.; **im-** & *marcessere*, 'to fade, wither, pine away', fr. *marcēre*, 'to shrink, shrivel', & **-ible**. The Lat. vb. contains same base as *mor(t-)*, 'death'. See **mortal**. Unfading, imperishable: '*the immarcessible crown of glory*' (Edward VI.'s First Prayer Book); altered to *never-fading* after the Second P.B.

immaterial, adj. [1. imatḗrial; 2. imətíəriəl]. **im-** & **material**. **1.** Without bodily form or substance; not corporeal; spiritual, insubstantial. **2.** Unimportant, having no weight or consequence.

immaterialism, n. [1. imatḗrializm; 2. imətíəriəlizəm]. Prec. & **-ism**. Theory that matter has no objective existence.

immaterialist, n. [1. imatḗrialist; 2. imətíəriəlist]. **immaterial** & **-ist**. Believer in immaterialism.

immateriality, n. [1. ìmatēriáliti; 2. ìmətiəriǽliti]. **immaterial** & **-ity**. The state of being immaterial.

immaterialize, vb. trans. [1. ìmatḗrialīz; 2. ìmətíəriəlaiz]. **immaterial** & **-ize**. To make immaterial.

immature, adj. [1. ìmatū́r; 2. ìmətjɔ́], fr. Lat. *immātūr-(us)*, 'unripe, immature; untimely'. **im-** & **mature**. Not completely formed or developed; not ripe, (in material and non-material sense): *immature stock, fish* &c.; *an immature mind, literary work* &c.

immaturity, n. [1. ìmatū́riti; 2. ìmətjɔ́riti]. Prec. & **-ity**. The state of being immature.

immeasurability, n. [1. imèzhurabíliti; 2. imèžərəbíliti]. Next word & **-ity**. The quality of being immeasurable.

immeasurable, adj. [1. imézhurabl ; 2. iméžərəbl]. **im-** & **measurable**. Not capable of being measured ; very great, vast.

immeasurableness, n. Prec. & **-ness**. The quality of being immeasurable.

immeasurably, adv. See prec. & **-ly**. In an immeasurable manner ; to an immeasurable degree.

immediacy, n. [1. imédiasi ; 2. imídjəsi]. See next word & **-acy**. The state of being immediate, of being free from a medium, or something intervening ; directness.

immediate, adj. [1. imédiat ; 2. imídiit], fr. Med. Lat. *immediāt-(us)*. See **im-** & **mediate**. Having no intermediary, nothing coming between ; **1.** (in space) **a** Next to, in direct contiguity : *immediate contact* ; **b** adjacent to, near, close : *the immediate neighbourhood.* **2.** (in time) Without intervening interval, following directly and without pause or delay : *to take immediate action.* **3.** (of other relations) **a** Direct, next in relation, succession &c. ; not remote : *immediate heir* ; **b** (of non-material things or conditions) direct ; first-hand : *immediate information.*

immediately, adv. Prec. & **-ly**. **1.** Without the intervention of anything, without a medium ; directly. **2.** (of time) Without loss of time, at once, without delay.

immediateness, n. See prec. & **-ness**. The state of being immediate.

immemorial, adj. [1. imemórial ; 2. imimórial], fr. Med. Lat. *immemoriāl-(is)*. **im-** & **memorial**. **1.** Beyond the limit of living memory ; exceedingly remote : *from time immemorial* ; *immemorial use, custom* &c. **2.** Hence, very ancient, of great age : *immemorial oaks.*

immemorially, adv. Prec. & **-ly**. From time immemorial.

immense, adj. [1. iméns ; 2. iméns], fr. Fr., fr. Lat. *immensus*, 'immeasurable, boundless, vast', fr. **im-** & *mens-(um)*, P.P. of *mētīri*, 'to measure'. See **measure** & **mete**. **1.** Very large, enormous, vast. **2.** (slang) Splendid, first-rate ; deserving highest praise &c. : *he was simply immense as the comic mother.*

immensely, adv. Prec. & **-ly**. **1.** To an immense degree. **2.** (colloq.) Very much, greatly : *immensely pleased* &c.

immensity, n. [1. iménsiti ; 2. iménsiti]. **immense** & **-ity**. **a** The state or quality of being immense ; vastness ; huge size, extent, degree ; **b** infinite space.

immerse, vb. trans. [1. imérs ; 2. imə́s], fr. Lat. *immers-(um)*, P.P. type of *immergere*, 'to plunge into', fr. **im-** & *mergere*, 'to dip into ; to sink down ; to overwhelm'. See **merge**. **1.** To plunge, dip, into water or other liquid, esp. so as to cover completely. **2.** (in non-material sense) **a** To absorb mind (of) completely, occupy exclusively ; fix attention and interest of ; engross : *immersed in thought, a book, conversation* &c. ; also reflex. : *to immerse oneself in study, in gaieties* &c. ; **b** to entangle, involve, implicate : *immersed in difficulties, debt* &c.

immersion, n. [1. imérshun ; 2. imə́ʃən], fr. L. Lat. *immersiōn-(em)*, 'immersion'. Prec. & **-ion**. **1.** The act of immersing ; state of being immersed (in material and non-material senses) ; specif., *total immersion*, complete covering with water, as in some forms of baptism. **2.** (astron.) Concealment of one heavenly body behind, or by the shadow of, another.

immigrant, adj. & n. [1. ímigrant ; 2. ímigrənt]. See **im-** & **migrant**. **a** adj. Coming into a country as a settler ; **b** n., one who comes into a foreign country as a settler.

immigrate, vb. intrans. & trans. [1. ímigrāt ; 2. ímigreit], fr. Lat. *immigrāt-(us)*, P.P. type of *immigrāre*, 'to remove into'. See **im-** & **migrate**. **1.** intrans. To enter a foreign country for the purpose of settling there. **2.** trans. To bring (a settler) into a foreign country.

immigration, n. [1. imigráshun ; 2. imigréiʃən]. Prec. & **-ion**. **a** The act of immigrating ; **b** state of being immigrated ; **c** number of immigrants settling in a country over a certain specified period.

imminence, n. [1. íminens ; 2. íminəns], fr. Lat. *immin-(ēre)*, 'to hang, project, over ; (fig.) to threaten, be imminent'. See next word & **-ce**. The state of being imminent.

imminent, adj. [1. íminent ; 2. íminənt], fr. Pres. Part. of Lat. *immin-(ēre)*, 'to hang, project, over ; (fig.) to threaten, be imminent', fr. **im-** & *minēre*, 'to project, overhang'. See **menace, minatory**. (of future events, esp. danger &c.) About to happen, threatening, impending.

imminently, adv. Prec. & **-ly**. In an imminent manner.

immiscibility, n. [1. imisibíliti ; 2. imisibíliti]. See next word & **-ity**. The quality of being immiscible.

immiscible, adj. [1. imísibl ; 2. imísibl], fr. **im-** & Lat. *misc-(ēre)*, 'to mix, mingle' (see **mix**), & **-ible**. Not capable of being mixed.

immiscibly, adv. Prec. & **-ly**. In an immiscible manner.

immitigable, adj. [1. imítigabl ; 2. imítigəbl], fr. **im-** & **mitigable**. Not capable of being mitigated, moderated, or alleviated.

immitigably, adv. Prec. & **-ly**. To an immitigable degree.

immixture, n. [1. imíkschur ; 2. imíkstʃə]. See **im-** & **mixture**. **1.** The act of mixing ; state of being mixed. **2.** (fig.) The state of being a sharer in, concerned, involved in.

immobile, adj. [1. imóbil ; 2. imóubail], fr. Fr., fr. Lat. *immōbil-(is)*, 'immovable'. **im-** & **mobile**. **1.** Incapable of movement, or of being moved ; immovable. **2.** Not moving ; motionless.

immobility, n. [1. imōbíliti ; 2. imoubíliti]. Prec. & **-ity**. The state or quality of being immobile.

immobilization, n. [1. imóbilīzáshun ; 2. imoubilaizéiʃən]. See next word & **-ation**. The act of immobilizing ; state of being immobilized.

immobilize, vb. trans. [1. imóbilīz ; 2. imóubilaiz]. **immobile** & **-ize**. **1.** To make immobile ; to fix, establish immovably. **2.** To withdraw (coin) from circulation.

immoderate, adj. [1. imóderat ; 2. imɔ́dərit], fr. Lat. *immoderāt-(um)*, 'without measure, endless ; intemperate, unrestrained'. **im-** & **moderate**. Not kept within limits ; lacking in moderation ; extravagant, unrestrained : *immoderate expressions of gratitude* ; *immoderate indulgence* &c.

immoderately, adv. Prec. & **-ly**. In an immoderate manner, to an immoderate extent.

immodest, adj. [1. imódest ; 2. imɔ́dist], fr. Lat. *immodest-(us)*, 'intemperate'. **im-** & **modest**. **1.** Lacking modesty ; indecent, unseemly, unbecoming, indelicate. **2.** Bold, forward, presumptuous, pert.

immodestly, adv. Prec. & **-ly**. In an immodest manner.

immodesty, n. [1. imódesti ; 2. imɔ́disti], fr. Lat. *immodestia*, 'intemperate conduct ; insubordination'. **im-** & **modesty**. The quality of being immodest.

immolate, vb. trans. [1. ímōlāt ; 2. ímouleit], fr. Lat. *immolāt-(um)*, P.P. of *immolāre*, 'to sprinkle (sacrificial victim) with meal ; to sacrifice'. **im-** & Lat. *mola*, 'mill-stone ; meal'. See **molar** & **mill**. **1.** To kill, offer up (a sacrificial victim). **2.** (fig.) To sacrifice : *to immolate one's ambitions on the altar of duty.*

immolation, n. [1. imoláshun ; 2. iməléiʃən]. Prec. & **-ion**. The act of immolating ; state of being immolated.

immoral, adj. [1. imóral ; 2. imɔ́rəl]. **im-** & **moral**. **1.** (of persons) **a** Not guided by principles of morality and rectitude ; unprincipled, unscrupulous in conduct ; **b** specif., lawless and irregular in sexual habits ; unchaste, incontinent. **2.** (of conduct) **a** Not directed by moral sense ; **b** specif., exhibiting lawlessness and lack of restraint in exercise of sexual functions ; licentious, loose. **3.** (of books, pictures &c.) Expressing, depicting, conceptions at variance with morality ; specif., impure, obscene.

immorality, n. [1. imoráliti ; 2. imərǽliti]. Prec. & **-ity**. **1.** The quality or state of being immoral (in all senses). **2.** Immoral conduct.

immorally, adv. [1. imórali ; 2. imɔ́rəli]. **immoral** & **-ly**. In an immoral manner.

immortal (I.), adj. [1. imórtl ; 2. imɔ́tl], fr. Lat. *immortāl-(is)*, 'deathless, immortal ; everlasting, immeasurable'. **im-** & **mortal**. **a** Never dying ; living for ever : *the immortal gods* ; **b** imperishable, undying, everlasting : *immortal fame* ; *an immortal poem* ; **c** enjoying everlasting fame and enduring renown : *an immortal poet, hero* &c.

immortal (II.), n., fr. prec. One who is immortal ; **a** one who will not die ; **b** famous person, one whose fame endures.

immortality, n. [1. imortáliti ; 2. imɔtǽliti], fr. Lat. *immortālitāt-(em)*, 'immortality ; everlasting renown'. **im-** & **mortality**. The quality of being immortal.

immortalization, n. [1. imòrtalīzáshun ; 2. imɔ̀təlaizéiʃən]. See next word & **-ation**. The act of immortalizing ; state of being immortalized.

immortalize, vb. trans. [1. imórtalīz ; 2. imɔ́təlaiz]. **immortal** & **-ize**. To confer immortality upon ; (chiefly in fig. sense) to make famous for ever, give undying fame to.

immortally, adv. [1. imórtali ; 2. imɔ́təli]. **immortal** & **-ly**. **1.** Without dying ; eternally, for ever. **2.** (archaic slang) Very, exceedingly.

immortelle, n. [1. imortél ; 2. imɔtél]. Fr., fem. of *immortel*, 'immortal'. See **immortal**. Bright-coloured aster-like flower, naturally devoid of moisture, which preserves its shape and colour when dried.

immovability, n. [1. imōōvabíliti ; 2. imūvəbíliti]. See next word & **-ity**. The quality of being immovable.

immovable, adj. & n. [1. imōōvabl ; 2. imúvəbl]. **im-** & **movable**. **1.** adj. **a** Not capable of being moved ; (i.) in physical sense ; (ii.) (of the mind, resolution &c.) unshakable, unflinching ; **b** not moving, stationary, motionless ; **c** (law) *immovable estate, property*, such as is incapable of being moved, e.g. land, trees &c. **2.** n. (law, usually pl.) Immovable possessions, such as land, and everything naturally pertaining and adhering to it, as permanent buildings, also trees and crops.

immovableness, n. Prec. & **-ness**. The quality of being immovable.

immovably, adv. See prec. & **-ly**. In an immovable manner.

immune, adj. [1. imūn ; 2. imjún], fr. Lat. *immūn-(is)*, 'exempt from tax, military service &c. ; free, exempt'. See **im-** & **municipal**. Not liable to be attacked by ; secure, safe from attack, infection, poison &c.

immunity, n. [1. imūniti ; 2. imjúniti], fr. Lat. *immūnitāt-(em)*, 'exemption from public offices or burdens'. Prec. & **-ity**. **1.** (law) Non-liability to, exemption from, taxation &c. **2.** Safety, security, freedom, **a** from disease, infection, poison &c. ; **b** from molestation or attack, physical, mental, or spiritual.

immunization, n. [1. imūnīzáshun ; 2. imjūnaizéiʃən]. See next word & **-ation**. The act of immunizing ; state of being immunized.

immunize, vb. trans. [1. ímūnīz ; 2. ímjūnaiz]. **immune** & **-ize**. To make immune, give immunity to, protect from liability to (disease &c.).

immure, vb. trans. [1. imūr ; 2. imjɔ́], fr. Med. Lat. *immūrāre*, fr. **im-** & Lat. *mūr-(us)*, 'a wall'. See **mural**. To shut up, enclose, imprison ; (also fig.) *to immure oneself*, to shut oneself up, live solitary existence.

immurement, n. [1. imūrment ; 2. imjɔ́mənt]. Prec. & **-ment**. Act of immuring ; state of being immured.

immutability, n. [1. imūtabíliti ; 2. imjūtəbíliti], fr. Lat. *immūtābilitāt-(em)*, 'immutability'. See next word & **-ity**. The quality of being immutable; changelessness; specif. (biol.) *immutability of species*, incapacity to become modified, to change into another.

immutable, adj. [1. imū́tabl; 2. imjū́təbl], fr. Lat. *immūtābil-(is)*, 'unchangeable'. **im-** & **mutable**. Not liable to change, or variation; unchangeable, unalterable.

immutably, adv. Prec. & **-ly**. In an immutable manner.

imp (I.), n. [1. imp; 2. imp]. O.E., M.E. *impe*, 'scion, graft; young tree'. See next word. **1.** Little devil, demon. **2.** (playful) Mischievous child.

imp (II.), vb. trans. O.E. *impian*, M.E. *impen*, 'to graft', fr. Gk. *emphúein*, to implant', fr. **em-** & *phúein*, 'to grow', q.v. under **-phyte**. **1.** To mend or strengthen by inserting something; specif., in falconry, *to imp the wing of a hawk* &c., mend or strengthen by inserting feather(s). **2.** (rare) To help out, add to, increase.

impact (I.), n. [1. ímpakt; 2. ímpækt], fr. Lat. *impact-(um)*, P.P. type of *impingere*, 'to strike against; to press upon one'. See **impinge**. Collision; shock of sudden, violent encounter; striking, dashing, against.

impact (II.), vb. trans. [1. impákt; 2. impǽkt]. See prec. To press, pack, tightly together; to fix, wedge firmly.

impaction, n. [1. impákshun; 2. impǽkʃən]. Prec. & **-ion**. The act of impacting; state of being impacted.

impair, vb. trans. [1. impā́r; 2. impɛ́ə], fr. O. Fr. *empeirer*, fr. **em-** & L. Lat. *pējorāre*, 'to make worse', fr. *pējor*, 'worse'. See **pejorative**. To lessen in strength, vigour, quality, value &c.; to cause to diminish or deteriorate; to injure; to reduce: *to impair one's health, means, usefulness*.

impairment, n. [1. impā́rment; 2. impɛ́əmənt]. Prec. & **-ment**. The act of impairing; state of being impaired.

impale, vb. trans. [1. impā́l; 2. impéil], fr. Fr. *empaler*, fr. Med. Lat. *impālāre*, fr. **im-** & Lat. *pāl-(us)*, 'a stake'. See **pale** (I.). **1. a** To pierce, transfix (body) with sharp-pointed instrument: *to impale oneself upon one's enemy's sword, upon a spike* &c.; **b** to transfix with a stake as capital punishment. **2.** (her.) To blazon (two coats of arms) on one shield, divided by vertical line in pale. **3.** (archaic) To enclose, fence round, with stakes.

impalement, n. [1. impā́lment; 2. impéilmənt]. Prec. & **-ment**. **1.** Act of impaling; state of being impaled, esp. as a form of capital punishment. **2.** (her.) Union of two coats of arms on one shield.

impalpability, n. [1. impàlpabíliti; 2. impælpəbíliti]. Next word & **-ity**. The quality of being impalpable.

impalpable, adj. [1. impálpabl; 2. impǽlpəbl]. **im-** & **palpable**. **1. a** Not perceptible to the touch; not distinguishable by touch: *impalpable powder*, one so fine ground that no grittiness is perceptible; **b** not material; incorporeal: *impalpable forms and shadows*. **2.** (in non-material sense) Not perceptible to, not to be apprehended by, the mind: *impalpable distinctions of meaning*.

impalpably, adv. Prec. & **-ly**. In an impalpable manner; imperceptibly.

impaludism, n. [1. impálūdizm; 2. impǽljūdizəm], fr. **im-** & Lat. *palūd-*, stem of *palus*, 'a marsh'. See **paludal** & **-ism**. Malarial disease to which inhabitants of marshy country are liable.

impanate, adj. & vb. trans. [1. impánāt; 2. impéineit], fr. Med. Lat. *impānāt-(um)*, P.P. type of *impānāre*, fr. **im-** & Lat. *pān-(is)*, 'bread'. See **panification** & words there referred to. (of the Eucharist) **1.** adj. Present in the consecrated bread. **2.** vb. To embody, present, in the form of bread.

impanation, n. [1. ìmpānā́shun; 2. ìmpeinéiʃən]. Prec. & **-ion**. Inclusion of Christ's material body in bread at the Eucharist.

impanel, vb. trans. See **empanel**.

imparadise, emparadise, vb. trans. [1. impáradis; 2. impǽrədais]. **im-** & **paradise**. **1.** To bring into a state of bliss resembling paradise: '*Imparadised in one another's arms*' (Milton, 'P.L.'). **2.** To make into a paradise.

imparisyllabic, adj. & n. [1. impàrisilábik; 2. impæ̀risilǽbik]. **im-** & **parisyllabic**. (Gk. and Lat. gram.) **1.** adj. Having more syllables in genitive than in nominative; e.g. nom. *dens*, genit. *dentis*. **2.** n. Imparisyllabic noun.

impark, vb. trans. [1. impárk; 2. impā́k], fr. O. Fr. *emparquer*. **im-** & **park**. **1.** To enclose (animals) in a park. **2.** To enclose (land) for a park, convert into park-land.

imparkation, n. [1. ìmparkā́shun; 2. ìmpākéiʃən]. Prec. & **-ation**. The act of imparking; state of being imparked.

impart, vb. trans. [1. impárt; 2. impā́t], fr. O. Fr. *empartir*, fr. Lat. *impartīre*, 'to impart, communicate, share', fr. **im-** & *partīre*, 'to divide, distribute'. See **part** (II.). **a** To bestow, give, produce sense of: *to impart comfort, warmth, colour*; **b** to communicate, tell, transmit: *to impart a secret, news*.

impartation, n. [1. ìmpartā́shun; 2. ìmpātéiʃən]. Prec. & **-ation**. (rare) Act of imparting; state of being imparted.

impartial, adj. [1. impárshal; 2. impā́ʃl]. **im-** & **partial**. Not biassed; unprejudiced; just, fair.

impartiality, n. [1. impàrshiáliti; 2. impāʃiǽliti]. Prec. & **-ity**. The quality of being impartial; fairness, justice.

impartially, adv. [1. impárshali; 2. impā́ʃəli]. See prec. & **-ly**. In an impartial manner.

impartible, adj. [1. impártibl; 2. impā́tibl], fr. L. Lat. *impartibilis*, 'impartible'. **im-** & **part** & **-ible**. (of an estate) Indivisible.

impartment, n. [1. impártment; 2. impā́tmənt]. **impart** & **-ment**. (rare) Impartation.

impassability, n. [1. impàhsabíliti; 2. impā̀səbíliti]. See next word & **-ity**. The state of being impassable.

impassable, adj. [1. impáhsabl; 2. impā́səbl]. **im-** & **passable**. Not capable of being crossed, passed over, traversed: *an impassable swamp, road* &c.

impassableness, n. Prec. & **-ness**. The state of being impassable.

impasse, n. [1. ampáhs; 2. ǣpā́s]. Fr., fr. **im-** & *passer*, 'to pass'. See **pass**. **1.** Passage open at one end only; blind alley. **2.** Unsurmountable difficulty, inextricable entanglement; position from which one cannot escape; stage of negotiation in which no further progress can be made because neither side will yield; deadlock.

impassibility, n. [1. ìmpasibíliti; 2. ìmpæsibíliti], fr. eccles. Lat. *impassibil-(is)*, 'impassible'. See next word & **-ity**. The quality of being impassible.

impassible, adj. [1. impásibl; 2. impǽsibl], fr. eccles. Lat. *impassibilis*, 'impassible'. **im-** & **passible**. **1.** Not liable to, incapable of, suffering. **2.** Not capable of being touched or roused; insensitive, unfeeling; apathetic.

impassibleness, n. Prec. & **-ness**. The quality of being impassible.

impassibly, adv. See prec. & **-ly**. In an impassible manner.

impassion, vb. trans. [1. impáshun; 2. impǽʃən], fr. Ital. *impassionare*, fr. **im-** & *passione*, 'passion'. See **passion**. To arouse, inflame, excite, the passions of; stir deeply.

impassioned, adj. [1. impáshund; 2. impǽʃənd], fr. P.P. of prec. **a** Animated with passion; having the feelings stirred; ardent, fiery; **b** expressing passion; glowing: *impassioned glances, oratory*.

impassive, adj. [1. impásiv; 2. impǽsiv]. **im-** & **passive**. **1.** Not subject to, not liable to, suffering. **2. a** Lacking emotion, without feeling, unemotional; calm, unmoved; **b** expressing no feeling, emotion, passion; apathetic.

impassively, adv. Prec. & **-ly**. In an impassive manner.

impassiveness, n. See prec. & **-ness**. Impassivity.

impassivity, n. [1. ìmpasíviti; 2. ìmpæsíviti]. **impassive** & **-ity**. The quality of being impassive.

impaste, vb. trans. [1. impā́st; 2. impéist], fr. Ital. *impastare*. See **im-** & **paste**. **1.** To cover, envelop, with, or as with, paste. **2.** To cover with paint in thick layers, paint in impasto.

impasto, n. [1. impástō, impáhstō; 2. impǽstou, impā́stou]. Ital. See prec. Laying on of colours thickly in painting.

impatience, n. [1. impā́shens; 2. impéiʃəns], fr. O. Fr., fr. Lat. *impatientia*, 'impatience', fr. *impati-(entem)*. See **im-** & **patience**. State or quality of mind marked by incapacity to endure delay, restraint, opposition, pain &c.; specif. **a** eagerness, strong desire to go somewhere, or to do or get something; **b** irritability of mind, intolerance.

impatient, adj. [1. impā́shent; 2. impéiʃənt], fr. O. Fr., fr. Lat. *impatient-(em)*, 'unable to endure, impatient'. See **im-** & **patient**. **1. a** pred. Not enduring easily, unable to brook delay, strongly eager to move, do, obtain object of desires &c.: *impatient to start, to begin*; *impatient to see one's parents*; *impatient to get rich*; also *impatient of*, (i.) not tolerating, chafing under, restraint, opposition &c.: *impatient of reproof, discipline*; (ii.) (archaic) not bearing, incapable of conveying, not intended to convey, not patient of: *this clause is impatient of the interpretation put upon it*; **b** expressing impatience: *an impatient gesture, exclamation* &c. **2. a** Irritable, fretful; **b** restless, uneasy.

impatiently, adv. Prec. & **-ly**. In an impatient manner; with, so as to express, impatience.

impawn, vb. trans. [1. impáwn; 2. impɔ́n]. **im-** & **pawn**. **1.** To put in pawn, pledge. **2.** (fig.) To pledge, plight.

impayable, adj. [1. impā́abl; 2. impéiəbl], or as Fr. [ǣpejābl]. **im-** & **payable**. **1.** (rare) Not capable of being paid; admirable. **2.** (Fr., colloq.) Comic beyond measure.

impeach, vb. trans. [1. impḗch; 2. impítʃ], fr. O. Fr. *empechier*, 'to hinder, impede', fr. L. Lat. *impedicāre*, 'to hinder', fr. **im-** & *pedica*, 'a fetter, snare'. See **impede**. **1. a** To charge, accuse, indict: *to impeach a person of, with, a crime, fault* &c.; specif. **b** to bring before a court on a charge of high treason. **2. a** To express unfavourable opinion of, disparage; **b** to complain of, find fault with. **3.** Still used by Spenser (*em-, impeach*) in orig. sense of 'to hinder': '*There was no barre to stop, nor foe him to empeach*' ('F.Q.').

impeachable, adj. [1. impḗchabl; 2. impítʃəbl]. Prec. & **-able**. Liable to be impeached, deserving impeachment.

impeachment, n. [1. impḗchment; 2. impítʃmənt]. **impeach** & **-ment**. **1. a** The act of impeaching, state of being impeached; **b** specif., prosecution for high treason &c. **2.** Accusation, reproach; in Phr. (Sheridan) *soft impeachment*.

impeccability, n. [1. impèkabíliti; 2. impèkəbíliti], fr. L. Lat. *impeccābil-(is)*, 'impeccable'. Next word & **-ity**. The quality of being impeccable.

impeccable, adj. [1. impékabl; 2. impékəbl], fr. L. Lat. *impeccābil-(is)*, 'impeccable', fr. **im-** & *peccā-(re)*, 'to sin'. See **peccavi**. **a** Incapable of, not liable to, sin; **b** beyond reproach, faultless.

impeccably, adv. Prec. & **-ly**. In an impeccable manner.

impeccant, adj. [1. impékant; 2. impékənt]. See prec. & **-ant**. Impeccable.

impecuniosity, n. [1. ìmpekūniósiti; 2. ìmpikjūniɔ́siti]. Next word & **-ity**. Condition of being without money; poverty.

impecunious, adj. [1. ìmpekū́nius; 2. ìmpikjū́njəs]. On model of Fr. *impécunieux*, 'lacking money', fr. Lat. *pecuniōsus*, 'rich', fr. *pecunia*, 'money', see **pecuniary**. Without money, lacking means; poor, hard-up.

impedance, n. [1. impḗdans; 2. impídəns]. Next word & **-ance**. (elect.) Resistance, due to self-induction, to current in a circuit, particularly in an alternating current circuit.

impede, vb. trans. [1. impḗd; 2. impíd], fr. Lat. *impedīre*, 'to entangle, ensnare; hamper, embarrass', fr. **im-** & *ped-*, 'foot', q.v. under **pedal**. **1.** To obstruct, prevent, hamper, bodily movement. **2.** To embarrass, hinder, delay, thwart, offer opposition to.

impediment, n. [1. impédiment; 2. impédimənt], fr. Lat. *impedīment-(um)*, 'hindrance', fr. *impedī-(re)*, 'to hinder, detain'. See prec. & **-ment**. **a** Cause of delay, hindrance, obstruction, check, obstacle, to movement or action; **b** specif., defect in utterance; stammer: *an impediment in one's speech.*

impedimenta, n. [1. impèdiménta; 2. impèdiméntə]. Lat., neut. pl., 'hindrances; encumbrances; specif., travelling equipment; baggage, supplies (of an army, &c.)', pl. of *impedīmentum*, 'hindrance'. See prec. Travelling equipment, baggage.

impedimental, adj. [1. impèdiméntl; 2. impèdiméntl]. **impediment** & **-al**. Of the nature of an impediment; hindering.

impel, vb. trans. [1. impél; 2. impél], fr. Lat. *impellere*, 'to push, strike against; to drive forward, urge on; to incite, instigate, persuade', fr. **im-** & *pellere*, 'to beat, strike; to thrust, push, drive'. See **pulse**. **a** To push, drive forward, urge on, cause to move forward; **b** to exercise moral influence; to urge, constrain, force into action: *I felt impelled to take sides in the quarrel.*

impellent, adj. [1. impélent; 2. impélənt]. Prec. & **-ent**. Tending to impel; driving.

impend, vb. intrans. [1. impénd; 2. impénd], fr. Lat. *impend-(ēre)*, 'to hang over; to impend, be imminent, threaten'. See **im-** & **pendant**. (chiefly in Pres. Part.) **1. a** To overhang, hang above, be suspended over; **b** to be about to manifest itself: *an impending storm.* **2.** (of events and conditions) **a** To be about to happen, develop, or be realized: *an impending marriage; impending happiness*; **b** (in bad sense) to threaten: *impending disaster, danger* &c.

impendence, -cy, n. [1. impéndens(i); 2. impéndəns(i)]. Prec. & **-ence** & **-cy**. The state of being impendent.

impendent, adj. [1. impéndent; 2. impéndənt]. **impend** & **-ent**. About to happen; imminent, threatening, impending.

impenetrability, n. [1. impènetrabíliti; 2. impènitrəbíliti]. **im-** & **penetrability**. The quality of being impenetrable; **a** incapability of being pierced (of hard substance, and fig., of darkness &c.); **b** inscrutability of mind.

impenetrable, adj. [1. impénetrabl; 2. impénitrəbl], fr. Fr., fr. Lat. *impenetrābilis*, 'that cannot be penetrated; unyielding, unconquerable'. **im-** & **penetrable**. **1.** (of material things) Not capable of being penetrated; dense; **a** unyielding, solid, not to be pierced: *impenetrable rock*; **b** that cannot be passed through: *impenetrable forests*; **c** incapable of being seen through: *impenetrable shade, darkness* &c. **2.** (of non-material things) **a** Not capable of being penetrated by the intelligence; not to be solved, understood; obscure, inscrutable, unfathomable: *an impenetrable mystery*; **b** not to be broken through; unyielding: *impenetrable reserve, silence*; **c** impervious to, not allowing the introduction of, not giving passage to, ideas &c.; obtuse: *a mind impenetrable by, to, new ideas* &c.

impenetrableness, n. Prec. & **-ness**. The quality of being impenetrable.

impenetrably, adv. See prec. & **-ly**. In an impenetrable manner.

impenetrate, vb. trans. [1. impénetrāt; 2. impénitreit]. **im-** & **penetrate**. To sink deep into, penetrate deeply.

impenitence, -cy, n. [1. impénitens(i); 2. impénitəns(i)], fr. Lat. *impaenitentia*, 'impenitence'. **im-** & **penitence**. Impenitent state of mind; failure, refusal, to repent.

impenitent, adj. [1. impénitent; 2. impénitənt], fr. Lat. *impaenitent-(em)*, 'not repenting'. **im-** & **penitent**. Not penitent; unrepentant.

impenitently, adv. Prec. & **-ly**. In an impenitent manner.

imperatival, adj. [1. impèratívl; 2. impèrətáivl]. See next word & **-al**. (gram.) Pertaining to, expressing, the imperative mood.

imperative (I.), adj. [1. impérativ; 2. impérətiv], fr. L. Lat. *imperātīv-(us)*, 'of, proceeding from, a command', fr. *imperāt-(um)*, P.P. type of *imperāre*, 'to command'. See **imperator** & **-ive**. **1.** Authoritative, peremptory, not to be disobeyed: *an imperative command, gesture.* **2.** (of action, circumstances) Urgent, essential, important: *it is imperative that we should act at once.* **3.** (gram.) Expressing a command: *imperative mood, sentence.*

imperative (II.), n., fr. prec. **1.** (gram.) The imperative mood. **2.** Word, sentence &c., expressing an imperative; a command, order: *a categorical imperative.*

imperatively, adv. **imperative** (I.) & **-ly**. In an imperative manner.

imperativeness, n. See prec. & **-ness**. The quality of being imperative.

imperator, n. [1. ìmperā̀tor; 2. ìmpəréitə]. Lat., 'commander-in-chief; title conferred on general after important victory; emperor', fr. *imperāt-(um)*, P.P. type of *imperāre*, 'to command', fr. **im-** & *parāre*, 'to prepare' (see **pare**), & **-or**. See **emperor**. **1.** Title conferred on Roman general, under the Republic, after an important victory. **2.** Supreme ruler, emperor.

imperatorial, adj. [1. ìmpèratórial; 2. ìmpèrətóriəl]. Prec. & **-ial**. Pertaining to an imperator.

imperceptible, adj. [1. ìmperséptibl; 2. ìmpəséptibl]. **im-** & **perceptible**. **a** Not capable of being perceived; **b** very slight; gradual.

imperceptibly, adv. Prec. & **-ly**. In an imperceptible manner; so as not to be perceptible; by imperceptible degrees, gradually.

impercipient, adj. [1. ìmpersípient; 2. ìmpəsípiənt]. **im-** & **percipient**. Lacking in perception; not perceiving.

imperfect, adj. [1. impérfekt; 2. impǽfikt], fr. Lat. *imperfect-(us)*, 'unfinished, incomplete'. **im-** & **perfect**. **1.** (of material things) Not complete; defective, lacking in some part. **2. a** (of non-material things) Not full; incomplete, not reaching a given standard: *to have but an imperfect knowledge of a subject*; **b** (of character &c.) defective, faulty, blemished, not morally perfect. **3.** (gram.) **a** *Imperfect tense*, that expressing an action still in progress and not completed; **b** as n., the imperfect tense.

imperfection, n. [1. imperfékshun; 2. impəfékʃən], fr. Lat. *imperfectiōn-(em)*, 'imperfection'. **imperfect** & **-ion**. **1.** The state of being incomplete, defective; inadequacy, deficiency. **2.** The state of being morally imperfect, faulty, blemished. **3.** Something that mars, detracts from, perfection; fault, weakness, blemish.

imperfectly, adv. [1. impérfektli; 2. impǽfiktli]. **imperfect** & **-ly**. In an imperfect manner.

imperforate, adj. [1. impérforat; 2. impǽfərət]. **im-** & **perforate**. Not perforated; **a** (anat.) without an opening, completely closed; lacking a natural or normal opening; **b** (of postage stamps) without perforations.

imperial (I.), adj. [1. impḗrial; 2. impíəriəl], fr. O. Fr., fr. Lat. *imperiāl-(is)*, 'of the empire or emperor'. Cp. **imperator** & **imperium**. **1. a** Pertaining to an empire; specif. **b** pertaining to the British Empire: *imperial trade, preference*; **c** fixed by a statute of Great Britain; standard: *imperial pint* &c.; **d** relating, belonging, to Great Britain as a whole; contrasted with local: *imperial taxes.* **2.** Of, belonging to, pertaining to, an emperor: *imperial purple, crown.*

imperial (II.), n., fr. prec. **1.** Small beard or tuft below lower lip, so called from the Emperor of the French, Napoleon III. **2.** A former Russian gold coin.

imperialism, n. [1. impḗrializm; 2. impíəriəlizəm]. **imperial** (I.) & **-ism**. **1.** Doctrine that it is at once the duty, and to the advantage, of the members of a State, and of the government of a State, to preserve the integrity, secure the safety, and protect the interests and welfare of the State, and its dependencies, and of the dominions united to it, by all legitimate means. **2.** Travesty, or misconception, of this principle, which affirms the aim of statecraft to be unscrupulous aggrandizement of the State, and the increase by fair or foul means of its territories and influence.

imperialist, n. [1. impḗrialist; 2. impíəriəlist]. See prec. & **-ist**. **1.** Supporter of an emperor or of imperial rule, in distinction to other forms of government. **2.** An advocate of imperialism.

imperialistic, adj. [1. impèrialístik; 2. impìəriəlístik]. Prec. & **-ic**. Pertaining to, imbued with, imperialism.

imperialize, vb. trans. [1. impḗrialīz; 2. impíəriəlaiz]. **imperial** (I.) & **-ize**. To render imperial; **a** to bring under, or into, an empire; **b** to spread or apply imperialist principles of government to.

imperially, adv. [1. impḗriali; 2. impíəriəli]. **imperial** (I.) & **-ly**. In an imperial manner; **a** like, befitting, an emperor; **b** according to, in harmony with, the principles of sound imperialism: *we should learn to think imperially.*

imperil, vb. trans. [1. impéril; 2. impéril]. **im-** & **peril**. To expose to peril, bring into danger.

imperious, adj. [1. impḗrius; 2. impíəriəs], fr. Lat. *imperiōsus*, 'possessed of power, far-ruling, puissant; tyrannical, domineering', fr. *imperi-(um)*, 'command; dominion; empire'. See **imperium** & **-ous**. **1. a** Commanding, dominating, lofty, masterful; **b** domineering, arrogant, tyrannical; dictatorial. **2.** Imperative, urgent, pressing.

imperiously, adv. Prec. & **-ly**. In an imperious manner; **a** in a masterful, commanding manner; **b** arrogantly.

imperiousness, n. See prec. & **-ness**. The quality of being imperious.

imperishability, n. [1. impèrishabíliti; 2. impèriʃəbíliti]. See next word & **-ity**. The quality of being imperishable; (chiefly referring to non-material things) durability, lastingness; immortality.

imperishable, adj. [1. impérishabl; 2. impériʃəbl]. **im-** & **perishable**. (chiefly in non-material sense) Not liable to perish or pass away; enduring, indestructible, permanent: *imperishable glory, renown* &c.

imperishableness, n. Prec. & **-ness**. Imperishability.

imperishably, adv. See prec. & **-ly**. In an imperishable manner; everlastingly.

imperium, n. [1. impḗrium, impérium; 2. impíəriəm, impériəm]. Lat. *imperium*, 'a command, order; sovereignty, dominion; realm, empire', fr. *imper-āre*, 'to command'. See **imperator**. **1. a** Imperial sovereignty, authority of an emperor; **b** absolute authority, supreme power. **2.** Right of jurisdiction in an empire.

impermanence, -cy, n. [1. impérmanens(i); 2. impǽmənəns(i)]. **im-** & **permanence, -cy**. The quality of being impermanent; lack of durability; transitoriness.

impermanent, adj. [1. impérmanent; 2. impǽmənənt]. **im-** & **permanent**. Temporary, lasting only for a time, not permanent.

impermeability, n. [1. impèrmeabíliti; 2. impǽmiəbíliti]. See next word and **-ity**. The quality of being impermeable.

impermeable, adj. [1. impérmeabl; 2. impǽmiəbl], fr. Lat. *impermeābil-(is)*, 'impermeable'. **im-** & **permeable**. Not capable of being permeated, passed through; impervious, impenetrable (in material and non-material senses).

impermissible, adj. [1. impérmísibl; 2. impə̄mísibl]. **im- & permissible.** Not permissible, not to be allowed.

imperscriptible, adj. [1. impērskríptibl; 2. impə̄skríptibl], fr. **im-** & Lat. *perscript-(um)*, P.P. type of *perscrīb-(ere)*, 'to write out; to enter, register'; see **per-** & *scrībere*, 'to write' (see **scribe**), & **-ible.** Not supported by documentary authority; unofficial.

impersonal, adj. [1. impérsunal; 2. impə́sənəl], fr. L. Lat. *impersōnāl-(is)*, 'impersonal'; **im- & personal.** **1.** (of verbs) Used only in 3rd pers. sing., without referring to a person or a definite subject; e.g. *it is raining*. **2.** Without direct reference to oneself, or to any specific person: *an impersonal point of view; to write in an impersonal manner.* **3.** Having no personality; not distinctive or individual.

impersonality, n. [1. impērsunáliti; 2. impə̄sənǽliti]. Prec. & **-ity.** The quality of being impersonal.

impersonally, adv. [1. impérsunali; 2. impə́sənəli]. See prec. & **-ly.** In an impersonal manner.

impersonate, vb. trans. [1. impérsunāt; 2. impə́səneit]. **im- & person & -ate.** **1.** To represent in material form, to embody, give bodily substance to. **2. a** To assume appearance or character of, pretend to be, with fraudulent intent; **b** to act, play, take the rôle of (character in drama &c.).

impersonation, n. [1. impērsunā́shun; 2. impə̄sənéiʃən]. Prec. & **-ion.** **1. a** The act of impersonating; **b** state of being impersonated. **2. a** The assumption of another's appearance, manner &c. (i.) with fraudulent intent to pass for him; (ii.) with the innocent intention of mimicry and burlesque; **b** the mode of interpreting a character in a play.

impersonative, adj. [1. impérsunativ; 2. impə́sənətiv]. **impersonate & -ive.** Pertaining to impersonation; capable of impersonating.

impersonify, vb. trans. [1. impērsónifī; 2. impə̄sónifai]. **im- & personify.** To personify.

impertinence, n. [1. impértinens; 2. impə́tinəns], fr. Lat. *impertin-(entem)*, 'not pertinent'. See next word & **-ence.** **1.** The quality of being impertinent; **a** irrelevancy; **b** impudence, insolence, rudeness. **2.** Act, speech, which is impertinent.

impertinent, adj. [1. impértinent; 2. impə́tinənt], fr. L. Lat. *impertinent-(em)*, 'not belonging, not pertinent'. **im- & pertinent.** **1. a** Not pertinent, not to the point, irrelevant; **b** not suitable to the occasion, inopportune. **2.** Not in accordance with good manners; lacking in consideration and respect; officious; impudent, insolent.

impertinently, adv. Prec. & **-ly.** In an impertinent manner.

imperturbability, n. [1. impertērbabíliti; 2. impətə̄bəbíliti], fr. L. Lat. *imperturbābil-(is)*, 'that cannot be disturbed'. See next word & **-ity.** The quality of being imperturbable.

imperturbable, adj. [1. impertérbabl; 2. impətə́bəbl], fr. L. Lat. *imperturbābil-(is)*, 'that cannot be disturbed'. See **im- & perturb & -able.** Not liable to be agitated, disconcerted, disturbed, or excited; unruffled, calm.

imperturbableness, n. Prec. & **-ness.** The quality of being imperturbable.

imperturbably, adv. See prec. & **-ly.** In an imperturbable manner.

impervious, adj. [1. impérvius; 2. impə́viəs], fr. Lat. *impervi-(us)*, 'that cannot be passed through'. **im- & pervious.** **1.** Not permitting the passage of; impenetrable, impermeable: *impervious to rain, to light* &c. **2.** (of the mind &c.) Not affected by, proof against, deaf to, insensible to; obtuse: *impervious to reason, criticism* &c.

imperviously, adv. Prec. & **-ly.** In an impervious manner.

imperviousness, n. See prec. & **-ness.** The state of being impervious.

impetiginous, adj. [1. impetíjinus; 2. impitídžinəs], fr. Lat. *impetīgin-(is)*, genit. of *impetīgo*. See next word & **-ous.** Afflicted with, of the nature of, impetigo.

impetigo, n. [1. impetígō; 2. impətáigou]. Lat., 'an eruption on the skin', fr. *impet-(ere)*, 'to attack', fr. **im-** & *petere*, 'to fall upon, rush at; to seek, make for'. See **petition.** An eruptive and pustular disease of the skin, resembling eczema.

impetrate, vb. trans. [1. ímpetrāt; 2. ímpitreit], fr. Lat. *impetrāt-(um)*, P.P. type of *impetrāre*, 'to accomplish, effect, obtain, procure', fr. **im-** & *patrāre*, 'to obtain, gain, bring about'; prob. fr. base **pad-*, 'grasp, contain', whence also O.E. *fetel*, 'swordhilt', *fæt*, 'tub, cauldron, vessel', q.v. under **vat**, & cp. **perpetrate.** (theol.) To ask for and obtain; obtain by prayer.

impetration, n. [1. impetrā́shun; 2. impitréiʃən]. Prec. & **-ion.** The act of impetrating.

impetratory, adj. [1. ímpetrātori; 2. ímpitreitəri]. **impetrate & -ory.** Of the nature of an impetration.

impetuosity, n. [1. impètūósiti; 2. impètjuósiti], fr. Lat. *impetuōs-(us)*. See next word & **-ity. a** The quality of being impetuous; **b** an impetuous action.

impetuous, adj. [1. impétūus, -choous; 2. impétjuəs, -tʃuəs], fr. Lat. *impetuōs-(us)*, 'impetuous, violent', fr. *impetu-(s)*, 'attack'. See **impetus & -ous.** **1.** Rushing, moving, with force; violent; furious: *an impetuous gale, torrent, charge, movement.* **2. a** (of persons) Inclined to act on sudden impulse; (i.) eager, ardent, vehement; (ii.) rash, hasty, precipitate; **b** (of action) performed as result of sudden impulse.

impetuously, adv. Prec. & **-ly.** In an impetuous manner; impulsively.

impetuousness, n. See prec. & **-ness.** The quality of being impetuous.

impetus, n. [1. ímpetus; 2. ímpitəs]. Lat., 'attack, onset; impulse, vigour, force; ardour, passion'; fr. **im-** & *pet-(ere)*, 'to rush towards; to seek'. See **petition.** **1.** (mechan.) Property in a moving body derived from its weight, and rate of motion; tendency to continue in motion in a certain direction; momentum. **2.** Intellectual and spiritual stimulus, or incitement, to action, or activity; that which provides such stimulus.

Impeyan, adj. [1. ímpian; 2. ímpiən]. After Lady, the wife of Sir Elijah, Impey, d. 1787. *Impeyan pheasant*, a brilliantly coloured Himalayan pheasant.

impi, n. [1. ímpi; 2. ímpi]. Zulu. A regiment; large organized body of Zulu warriors.

impiety, n. [1. impíeti; 2. impáiiti], fr. Lat. *impietāt-(em)*, 'want of reverence'. **im- & piety.** **1. a** Lack of piety; ungodliness; **b** an impious, wicked, action. **2.** Disrespect for, inattention to, traditional duties and virtues; disregard of parents or their memories, and of one's country and its institutions &c.

impinge, vb. intrans. [1. impínj; 2. impíndž], fr. Lat. *impingere*, 'to push, drive, thrust against', fr. **im-** & *pangere*, P.P. *pact-(um)*, 'to drive in, fix, plant; to settle, determine'. See **pact** & cp. **impact.** **1.** (of physical process) To strike, fall, on, upon, against: *rays of light impinge upon the retina.* **2.** (of non-material process) To infringe, encroach upon, come into contact or collision with: *to impinge upon a person's authority.*

impingement, n. [1. impínjment; 2. impíndžmənt]. Prec. & **-ment.** The process or act of impinging.

impious, adj. [1. ímpius; 2. ímpiəs], fr. Lat. *impi-(us)*, 'irreverent', & **-ous. im- & pious. a** Wanting in respect and regard for God; **b** without piety; wicked.

impiously, adv. Prec. & **-ly.** In an impious manner.

impish, adj. [1. ímpish; 2. ímpiʃ]. **imp (I.)** & **-ish.** Like an imp, mischievous.

impishly, adv. Prec. & **-ly.** In an impish manner.

impishness, n. See prec. & **-ness.** The quality of being impish.

impiteous, adj. [1. impíteus; 2. impítjəs]. **im- & piteous.** (rare) Unpitying, pitiless.

implacability, n. [1. implàkabíliti; 2. implæ̀kəbíliti], fr. Lat. *implācābil-(is)*, 'unappeasable'. Next word & **-ity.** The quality of being implacable.

implacable, adj. [1. implákabl, implā́kabl; 2. implǽkəbl, impléikəbl], fr. Lat. *implācābil-(is)*, 'unappeasable'. **im- & placable.** Not capable of being appeased; inexorable, relentless.

implacably, adv. Prec. & **-ly.** In an implacable manner; inexorably.

implacental, adj. [1. implasénti; 2. implæséntl]. **im- & placental.** Having no placenta; referring to certain division of mammals which includes marsupials.

implant, vb. trans. [1. impláhnt; 2. implánt], fr. Fr. *implanter*. **im- & plant. a** To fix firmly, insert; but chiefly in metaphorical sense; **b** to impress, fix deeply, inculcate (into the mind), imbue: *to implant a hope, aspiration, ideal, doubt &c. (in the mind).*

implantation, n. [1. implahntā́shun; 2. implāntéiʃən]. Prec. & **-ation.** The act of implanting; something which is implanted.

impledge, vb. trans. [1. impléj; 2. implédž]. **im- & pledge.** To pledge, pawn.

implement (I.), n. [1. ímplement; 2. ímplimənt], fr. Lat. *implē-(re)*, 'to fill up; to fulfil, discharge', & **-ment.** See **plenum, plenty.** **1.** Article for performing some form of work; tool, instrument. Phr. *agricultural implements* includes certain types of machines for reaping, binding, sowing &c. **2.** (Scots law) Performance, fulfilment, carrying out (of covenant, promise &c.).

implement (II.), vb. trans. [1. ímplement; 2. ímpliment], fr. prec. **1.** To complete, accomplish. **2.** (Scots law) To carry out, perform, fulfil (an engagement, contract &c.).

impletion, n. [1. implḗshun; 2. implíʃən], fr. L. Lat. *implētiōn-(em)*, 'filling up; fulfilment', fr. *implēt-(um)*, P.P. type of *implēre*, 'to fill up; to fulfil', & **-ion.** See **plenum, plenty.** The act of filling; state of being full.

implicate (I.), n. [1. ímplikāt; 2. ímplikeit], fr. Lat. *implicāt-(um)*, P.P. type of *implicāre*, 'to enfold, entwine, enwrap'; fig. 'to involve'. **im- &** *plicāre*, 'to fold'; see **plicate, ply (I.).** Thing that is implied.

implicate (II.), vb. trans., fr. Lat. *implicāt-(um)*, P.P. type of *implicāre*, 'to enfold; involve'. See prec. **1.** (of material process) To entangle, entwine, envelop, enfold. **2.** (of non-material process) **a** To involve, imply, infer; necessitate a particular inference; **b** to involve, entangle (persons); show to have a share in or connexion with; to inculpate: *to be implicated in a crime.*

implication, n. [1. implikā́shun; 2. implikéiʃən]. Prec. & **-ion.** **1.** The act of implicating; state of being implicated (in crime &c.). **2. a** Act of implying; **b** something that is implied.

implicative, adj. [1. implíkativ; 2. implíkətiv]. **implicate (II.) & -ive.** Tending to imply.

implicit, adj. [1. implísit; 2. implísit], fr. Lat. *implicit-(um)*, occasional P.P. type of *implicāre*, 'to enfold, entangle; to involve, entail, imply'. See **implicate.** **1.** Involved in, inhering in, to be inferred from, something stated, or that is known to exist, though not ostensible or definitely expressed; reverse of *explicit.* **2.** Complete, absolute; unquestioning, unreserved: *implicit obedience; implicit faith*, acceptance of Church's doctrine without full personal understanding. **3.** (obs. and poet.) Entangled in.

implicitly, adv. Prec. & **-ly.** In an implicit manner.

implicitness, n. See prec. & **-ness.** The quality of being implicit.

implode, vb. intrans. & trans. [1. implṓd; 2. imploud], fr. Lat. elements, **im-** & *plōdere, plaudere*, 'to clap'. See **plaudit,**

applaud, explode &c. (rare; only of speech sounds, cp. *implosive*) **1.** intrans. (of stop consonants) To be formed and opened without audible off-glide. **2.** trans. To utter (a stop consonant) without a following off-glide.

implore, vb. trans. [1. implṓr; 2. *implɔ́*], fr. Lat. *implōrāre*, 'to invoke with tears, beseech, implore', fr. **im-** & *plōrāre*, 'to weep aloud, cry out, lament'; perh. an imitative word. Cp. **deplore**. **a** To ask for earnestly; to beg, demand insistently: *to implore a person's help, protection* &c.; **b** to entreat, beseech, call upon (a person) with insistence, to do or grant something: *I implore you to stay with me, to help me, to grant my request* &c.

imploring, adj. [1. implṓring; 2. *implɔ́riŋ*], fr. Pres. Part. of prec. Expressing earnest entreaty: *an imploring glance.*

imploringly, adv. Prec. & **-ly**. With urgent entreaty; so as to express entreaty.

imploringness, n. See prec. & **-ness**. Quality of being imploring.

implosion, n. [1. implṓzhun; 2. *implóužən*]. See **implode** & **-ion**, & cp. **explosion**. (phon.) Fact or process of imploding; utterance of an implosive consonant.

implosive, adj. & n. [1. implṓsiv; 2. *implóusiv*]. See prec. & **-ive**. (phon.) **1.** adj. Term used to describe a stop (also called *plosive*) consonant which is formed by closing the mouth passage as for *b, d, g*, and retaining the closure till, in voiced stops, an audible muffled effect is produced, without releasing the air-stream and thus obtaining the characteristic puff of air (off-glide) which follows a stop consonant uttered in the usual way. Voiceless stops produced implosively are inaudible. **2.** n. An implosive consonant.

implosively, adv. Prec. & **-ly**. As, so as to form, an implosive.

impluvium, n. [1. implóōvium; 2. *implúviəm*]. Lat. *impluvium*, fr. **im-** & *pluvi-(us)*, 'rain'. See **pluvial**. Rain-water tank in central court (atrium) of an ancient Roman house.

imply, vb. trans. [1. implī́; 2. *implái*], fr. O. Fr. *emplier*, fr. Lat. *implicāre*, 'to entangle, enfold; to involve, imply'. See **implicate**. **1.** To involve, include, contain, by implication; to mean, have certain bearing, as interpreted by legitimate inference: *do you realize fully what your words imply? your statement implies more than it definitely expresses.* **2.** To suggest indirectly, hint, insinuate: *I do not imply that you are deliberately dishonest.* **3.** To contain, enclose, enfold: '*For in themselves eternal moisture they* (i.e. plants) *imply*' (Spenser, 'F. Q.', III. 6. 34).

impolicy, n. [1. impólisi; 2. *impɔ́lisi*]. **im-** & **policy**. Bad policy; action, or proposed action, which is impolitic.

impolite, adj. [1. impolī́t; 2. *impəláit*], fr. Lat. *impolīt-(us)*, 'rough, unpolished; inelegant, unrefined'. **im-** & **polite**. Not polite; ill-mannered, rude, discourteous.

impolitely, adv. Prec. & **-ly**. In an impolite manner.

impoliteness, n. See prec. & **-ness**. The quality of being impolite; rudeness.

impolitic, adj. [1. impólitik; 2. *impɔ́litik*]. **im-** & **politic**. Not politic; injudicious, unwise, inexpedient.

impoliticly, adv. Prec. & **-ly**. In an impolitic manner.

imponderability, n. [1. impònderabíliti; 2. *impɔ̀ndərəbíliti*]. See next word & **-ity**. State, condition, of being imponderable.

imponderable, adj. & n. [1. impónderabl; 2. *impɔ́ndərəbl*]. **im-** & **ponderable**. **1.** adj. **a** Not capable of being weighed; without sensible weight; **b** very light; **c** (in non-material sense) not capable of being estimated, valued, or calculated: *the effect on the public mind of such an event is imponderable.* **2.** n. An imponderable object or substance &c.

imponent, adj. & n. [1. impṓnent; 2. *impóunənt*], fr. Lat. *impōnent-(em)*, Pres. Part. of *impōnere*, 'to place, put'. See **impose**. (rare) **1.** adj. Having power of imposing. **2.** n. He who, that which, imposes.

import (I.), vb. trans. [1. impórt; 2. *impɔ́t*], fr. Lat. *import-(āre)*, 'to bring into; to bring about, cause'; in Med. Lat., 'to be of importance'. See **im-** & **port** (IV.). **1. a** To bring in; specif., to bring (goods) from abroad into one's own country; **b** to introduce, obtrude: *to import personal feelings into a discussion.* **2.** To carry with it as a meaning; signify, indicate, be significant of, imply: *I should like to know what his action imports.*

import (II.), n. [1. ímport; 2. *ímpɔt*], fr. prec. **1.** Something that is imported; imported goods (often in pl.). **2.** Significance, meaning, thing implied: *the full import of one's words.* **3.** Interest, consequence, importance: *a matter of great import.*

importability, n. [1. impòrtabíliti; 2. *impɔ̀təbíliti*]. See next word & **-ity**. The quality of being importable.

importable, adj. [1. impórtabl; 2. *impɔ́təbl*]. **import** (I.) & **-able**. Capable of being imported.

importance, n. [1. impórtans; 2. *impɔ́təns*], fr. Fr., fr. Med. Lat. *importantia*. See **import** (II.) & **-ance**. **1.** Quality of being important; significance, outstanding consequence, interest, value; essentialness, noteworthiness: *a matter, fact, business, of great importance.* Phr. *to attach importance, no importance, to*, regard as important, significant, or the reverse. **2.** State of being important; condition of playing significant or distinguished part; eminence, pre-eminence, notability, consideration: *a person of importance; of no importance; position of importance.* Phr. *conscious of, knowing, having good idea of, one's own importance*, self-satisfied, conceited, pompous.

important, adj. [1. impórtant; 2. *impɔ́tənt*], fr. Fr., fr. Med. Lat. *important-(em)*. **import** (I.) & **-ant**. **1.** (of persons) **a** Eminent, distinguished; occupying distinguished, prominent, position, playing a distinguished or essential part in affairs; **b** behaving as though one were important; pompous; officious: *to look important.* **2.** (of things, ideas, facts, events) Of consequence, momentous, possessing significance; on which something vital depends; essential.

importantly, adv. Prec. & **-ly**. In an important manner.

importation, n. [1. ìmportáshun; 2. *ìmpɔtéiʃən*]. **import** (I.) & **-ation**. **a** The act of importing; **b** something imported.

importer, n. [1. impórter; 2. *impɔ́tə*]. **import** (I.) & **-er**. One who imports; merchant, shipper of goods from abroad for sale in his own country; contrasted with *exporter.*

importunate, adj. [1. impórchunat; 2. *impɔ́tʃunit*], fr. Lat. *importūn-(us)*, 'inconvenient, unsuitable, troublesome', & **-ate**; orig. meaning of adj. is 'hard to get at, difficult of access', fr. *porta*, 'gate, passage, entrance'. See **port** (II.). **a** (of persons) Perpetually entreating; wearisomely insistent in soliciting or addressing; **b** (of demands) persistently and repeatedly made; insistent and inopportune.

importunately, adv. Prec. & **-ly**. In an importunate manner.

importune, vb. trans. [1. ìmportū́n, impórchoon; 2. *ìmpɔtjū́n, impɔ́tʃun*], fr. Fr. *importuner*, fr. Med. Lat. *importunāri*. See **importunate**. To persist in addressing and asking for something; to waylay at inconvenient moments and accost; to pester with pertinacious and troublesome demands.

importunity, n. [1. ìmportū́niti; 2. *ìmpɔtjū́niti*], fr. Lat. *importūnitāt-(em)*, 'unsuitableness; want of consideration; rudeness'. See **importunate** & **-ity**. **1.** (rare) The quality of being importunate. **2.** Persistent, reiterated, and wearisome demand, or act of accosting, esp. at inopportune moment.

impose, vb. trans. & intrans. [1. impṓz; 2. *impóuz*], fr. Fr. *imposer*, fr. **im-** & *poser*, 'to place', fr. Lat. *pausāre*, 'to cease, pause', confused w. *posit-(um)*, P.P. type of *pōnere*, 'to put, place'. See **pose, pause**. **A.** trans. **1. a** (archaic) To place, put, lay upon; **b** (print.) to arrange (pages of type) in a chase. **2.** To make responsible for, cause to assume obligation of; to exact: *to impose a tax, a duty, task.* **3.** To persuade to accept by unfair means; to palm off, foist, upon: *to impose bad wine on customers.* **B.** intrans. **1.** (rare) To produce an effect, exert an influence upon, impress by virtue of character, appearance &c. **2.** *Impose on, upon*, to deceive, take in, mislead deliberately: *his plausible talk completely imposed upon his hearers; I was imposed upon when I bought that horse.*

imposing, adj. [1. impṓzing; 2. *impóuziŋ*], fr. Pres. Part. of prec. Making a forcible impression, inspiring admiration; striking, impressive; majestic.

imposingly, adv. Prec. & **-ly**. In an imposing manner.

imposingness, n. See prec. & **-ness**. The quality of being imposing.

imposition, n. [1. impozíshun; 2. *impəzíʃən*], fr. Lat. *impositiōn-(em)*, 'laying on, application'. **im-** & **position**. **1. a** The act of laying on, imposing; specif. **b** (eccles.) *imposition of hands*, by bishop in ordination or confirmation. **2. a** The act of imposing a tax, burden &c.; **b** that which is imposed; (i.) a tax, burden &c.; (ii.) specif., task set as school punishment. **3. a** The act of imposing upon; **b** that which imposes upon; a take-in, a swindle.

impossibility, n. [1. impòsibíliti; 2. *impɔ̀sibíliti*], fr. Lat. *impossibilitāt-(em)*, 'impossibility'. See next word & **-ity**. **1.** The state of being impossible. **2.** Something that is impossible.

impossible, adj. [1. impósibl; 2. *impɔ́sibl*], fr. Lat. *impossibil-(is)*, 'impossible'. See **im-** & **possible**. **1.** Not capable of being done, not feasible: *an impossible task.* **2. a** Not capable of existing or happening: *an impossible circumstance, event*; **b** expressing, dealing with, what cannot exist or happen: *an impossible story, account.* **3.** (colloq.) Intolerable, insufferable, not to be endured; not reaching a recognized standard: *an impossible person.*

impossibly, adv. Prec. & **-ly**. In an impossible manner.

impost (I.), n. [1. ímpōst; 2. *ímpoust*], fr. O. Fr., fr. Med. Lat. *impost-(um)*, Lat. *imposit-(um)*, P.P. of *impōnere*, 'to place, lay upon'. **im-** & *pōnere*, 'to place'; see **position**. **1.** Tax, duty. **2.** (racing) Weight carried by horse in handicap.

impost (II.), n., fr. Fr. *imposte*, fr. Ital. *imposta*, fr. Lat. *imposit-(a)*. See prec. (archit.) Upper part of pillar from which an arch springs.

impostor, n. [1. impóstor; 2. *impɔ́stə*]. L. Lat., 'deceiver', cp. Fr. *imposteur*, fr. *imposit-(um)*, P.P. type of Lat. *impōnere*, 'to put, place; to impose upon; to deceive'. See **impose**. **a** One who fraudulently impersonates another; one who pretends, from interested motives, to be what he is not: *Perkin Warbeck was shown to be an impostor*; **b** one who practises imposition; a deceiver, cheat, swindler; charlatan, quack.

impostrous, adj. [1. impóstrus; 2. *impɔ́strəs*]. Prec. & **-ous**. (rare) Of the nature of, pertaining to, an impostor.

impostume, imposthume, n. [1. impóstūm; 2. *impɔ́stjūm*], fr. O. Fr. *empostume*, formed, w. different suff., fr. Gk. *apóstēma*, 'abscess', lit. 'something which stands away from', fr. *aphístēmi*, 'stand away, aloof, apart; stand out', fr. **apo-** & *hístēmi*, 'I stand'. See under **state** (I.), **stand** (I.). (archaic and rare) A swelling, abscess.

imposture, n. [1. impóschur; 2. *impɔ́stʃə*], fr. Fr., fr. L. Lat. *impostūra*, 'deceit, imposture'. See **impose, impostor**, & **-ure**. Fraudulent deception, a swindle.

impotence, -cy, n. [1. ímpotens(i); 2. *ímpətəns(i)*], fr. Lat. *impot-(ens)*, 'powerless, weak'. See **impotent** & **-ence**. The state of being impotent; specif., sexual incapacity.

impotent adj. [1. ímpotent; 2. ímpətənt], fr. Lat. *impotent-(em)*, 'powerless, weak; uncontrolled, passionate'. See **im-** & **potent**. **1.** Physically feeble, weak, decrepit; specif. (of males) lacking sexual capacity. **2.** Feeble in mind. **3.** Unable, powerless, to act.

impotently, adv. Prec. & **-ly**. In an impotent manner.

impound, vb. trans. [1. impóund; 2. impáund]. **im-** & **pound (III.)**. **1. a** To shut up (animal) in pound; hence **b** to enclose, imprison, shut up (person or thing) as in a pound. **2.** To take possession of by legal authority; to confiscate.

impoverish, vb. trans. [1. impóverish; 2. impɔ́vəriʃ], fr. O. Fr. *empoveriss-*, Pres. Part. stem of *empoverir*, fr. **em-** & *povre*, 'poor' (see **poor**), & **-ish**. **1.** To render poor, reduce to poverty, deprive of means, wealth &c. **2. a** To deprive of goodness or richness, to render less fertile; to make barren, exhaust: *impoverished land, soil*; **b** to weaken, debilitate: *impoverished health*; **c** to divest of interest, variety, charm; to render dull: *to banish art and literature from life would be to impoverish it greatly*; *an impoverished existence, mind* &c.

impoverishment, n. [1. impóverishment; 2. impɔ́vəriʃmənt]. Prec. & **-ment**. The act of impoverishing; state of being impoverished.

impracticability, n. [1. impràktikabíliti; 2. impræ̀ktikəbíliti]. See next word & **-ity**. **a** The quality of being impracticable; **b** something which is impracticable.

impracticable, adj. [1. impráktikabl; 2. impræ̀ktikəbl]. **im-** & **practicable**. **1.** Not capable of being put into practice; not feasible; unworkable, impossible: *an impracticable scheme*. **2.** (of person or character) Unmanageable, intractable, stubborn, difficult to deal with. **3.** (of roads &c.) Not fit to be used; impassable.

impracticableness, n. Prec. & **-ness**. The quality of being impracticable.

impracticably, adv. See prec. & **-ly**. In an impracticable manner.

imprecate, vb. trans. [1. ímprekāt; 2. ímprikeit], fr. Lat. *imprecāt-(um)*, P.P. type of *imprecāri*, 'to invoke, call down, upon', fr. **im-** & *precāri*, 'to pray'. See **pray**. To invoke, summon, call down (misfortune &c.): *to imprecate evil upon a person*.

imprecation, n. [1. imprekáshun; 2. imprikéiʃən]. Prec. & **-ion**. **1.** The act of imprecating, of calling down evil. **2.** Something uttered in imprecating; malediction, curse.

imprecatory, adj. [1. ímprekàturi; 2. ímprikèitəri]. See prec. & **-ory**. Like, pertaining to, of the nature of, an imprecation.

impregnability, n. [1. imprègnabíliti; 2. imprègnəbíliti]. See next word & **-ity**. The quality, state, of being impregnable.

impregnable, adj. [1. imprégnabl; 2. imprégnəbl]. **im-** & **pregnable**. **1.** Not capable of being taken by force; proof against seizure, strong enough to resist attack: *an impregnable fortress*. **2.** (in moral sense) Not capable of being shaken, not yielding to persuasion, moral pressure, or attack: *impregnable virtue*.

impregnably, adv. Prec. & **-ly**. In an impregnable manner.

impregnate (I.), adj. [1. imprégnāt; 2. imprégneit], fr. L. Lat. *impraegnāt-(um)*, 'pregnant'; P.P. type of *impraegnāre*, 'to render pregnant'. **im-** & **pregnant**. **1.** Impregnated, pregnant. **2.** Permeated, saturated.

impregnate (II.), vb. trans. [1. imprégnāt; 2. imprégneit]. See prec. **1. a** To make pregnant; **b** (biol.) to fertilize, fecundate. **2. a** To permeate, saturate, fill: *air impregnated with disease-germs*; **b** to imbue, impress; implant in, instil into (the mind).

impregnation, n. [1. impregnáshun; 2. impregnéiʃən]. Prec. & **-ion**. The act of impregnating; state of being impregnated.

impresario, n. [1. impresáhriō; 2. impresáriou]. Ital., fr. *impresa*, 'undertaking, enterprise'. See **emprise**. Manager and organizer of an operatic company, of concerts, and other forms of public entertainment.

imprescriptible, adj. [1. impreskríptibl; 2. impriskríptibl]. **im-** & **prescript** & **-ible**. Not to be challenged or withdrawn; inviolable, inalienable: *an imprescriptible right*.

impress (I.), vb. trans. [1. imprés; 2. imprés], fr. Lat. *impress-(um)*, P.P. type of *imprimere*, 'to press into, impress, imprint', fr. **im-** & *premere*, 'to press'. See **press (I.)**, & **print (II.)**. **1.** To imprint, stamp: *to impress a mark upon a surface*. **2.** To mark by means of pressure: *to impress a surface with a mark*. **3. a** To cause, produce, a vivid and lasting mental impression; to fix firmly in the mind, implant in the memory: *I want to impress upon you the necessity for hard work*; **b** to strike the mind, make powerful appeal to the judgement or emotions, create vivid impression; fill with sense of importance, significance &c.; to stir, move deeply: *to be much impressed by a book, speech, sight* &c.; *to be favourably, unfavourably, impressed*; *he did not impress me at all*, did not create a strong (favourable) impression; did not strike me as remarkable &c.

impress (II.), n. [1. ímpres; 2. ímpres]. See prec. **1.** The act of pressing; pressure. **2. a** Mark produced by physical pressure; stamp, imprint; **b** result produced on the mind or character by intellectual or moral force or influence: *to leave an impress upon one's age*; *a work bearing the impress of genius*.

impress (III.), vb. trans. **im-** & **press (III.)**. **1.** To compel (men) to serve in army or navy; to press. **2.** (of goods) To seize, confiscate, commandeer for the public service. **3.** (fig.) To introduce, bring in, make use of: *to impress a fact into one's service for argument* &c.

impressible, adj. [1. imprésibl; 2. imprésibl]. **impress (I.)** & **-ible**. Easily impressed, susceptible to mental or emotional impressions.

impression, n. [1. impréshun; 2. impréʃən], fr. Lat. *impressiōn-(em)*, 'impression'. **impress (I.)** & **-ion**. **1.** The act of impressing; state of being impressed. **2.** (print.) **a** Number of copies of single edition of book &c. printed at one time; **b** reprint of edition of book &c. without alteration. **3.** Mark left by physical pressure; stamp, imprint: *the impression of a hand, foot, of fingers* &c. **4.** Effect, result, produced by effort, labour: *the efforts of philanthropists and legislators make but little impression on the mass of human misery*. **5. a** Effect produced upon the senses by external stimuli: *sensuous, visual, auditive, impressions*; *the impression of light on the eye*; **b** immediate effect of external stimuli on the consciousness. **6.** A vague idea, ill-defined notion: *I have an impression that we've taken the wrong road*. Phr. *to be under the impression*, to have an idea, think, have a vague belief.

impressionability, n. [1. imprèshunabíliti; 2. imprèʃənəbíliti]. See next word & **-ity**. The quality of being impressionable.

impressionable, adj. [1. impréshunabl; 2. impréʃənəbl], fr. Fr., fr. *impressionner*, 'to impress'. See **impression** & **-able**. Capable of receiving, liable to receive, and be affected by, impressions; specif. **a** (of nervous system) affected by external stimuli; sensitive: *an eye no longer impressionable by light*; **b** easily accessible to, influenced, moulded, by, intellectual, emotional, or moral, impressions; emotionally or morally susceptible: *an impressionable nature, heart*; *youth is an impressionable age*.

impressionary, adj. [1. impréshunari; 2. impréʃənəri]. **impression** & **-ary**. Pertaining to, of the nature of, impressionism.

impressionism, n. [1. impréshunizm; 2. impréʃənizəm]. **impression** & **-ism**. (arts) **1. a** Doctrine started in France in first half of 19th cent., that a picture should record the immediate sensuous impressions made upon the painter when he looks at the objects which he is representing, and should not be a conventional representation of extraneous facts which may be known from sources other than direct visual experience; **b** the embodiment of this doctrine in the practice of the painter. **2.** Extension of the doctrine and practice, so far as possible, to literature.

impressionist, n. [1. impréshunist; 2. impréʃənist]. **impression** & **-ist**. Painter or writer who practises impressionism.

impressionistic, adj. [1. imprèshunístik; 2. imprèʃənístik]. Prec. & **-ic**. Pertaining to, of the nature of, based on, embodying, the ideals of, impressionism.

impressive, adj. [1. imprésiv; 2. imprésiv]. **impress (II.)** & **-ive**. Producing a deep moral or intellectual impression; affecting strongly, arousing, the mind or emotions: *an impressive speech, gesture, scene* &c.

impressively, adv. Prec. & **-ly**. In an impressive manner.

impressiveness, n. See prec. & **-ness**. The quality of being impressive.

impressment, n. [1. imprésment; 2. imprésmənt]. **impress (III.)** & **-ment**. The act of impressing; state of being impressed.

imprest, n. [1. ímprest; 2. ímprest]. Ital. *impresto*, 'a loan', fr. Lat. *praestāre*, 'to act as surety for', fr. *prae*, 'before' (see **pre-**), & *stāre*, 'to stand' (see **state (I.)**). Advance of money made to an individual by the State to enable him to perform duties for the State.

imprimatur, n. [1. imprīmátur; 2. impraiméitə]. Mod. Lat., 'let it be printed', fr. Lat. *imprimere*, 'to impress, imprint'. See **impress (II.)**. **1.** Licence to print a book &c.; esp. official licence granted by authority of Roman Catholic Church. **2.** Authority, sanction, guarantee, approval: *an organization whose work has received the imprimatur of the Government*.

imprimis, adv. [1. imprímis; 2. impráimis]. Lat. *imprīmis*, 'among the first; chiefly, especially; in the first place', fr. *in prīmis*, 'among the first things'; **in-** & *prīmus*, 'first'. See **primus**. Firstly, in the first place.

imprint (I.), vb. trans. [1. imprínt; 2. imprínt], fr. O. Fr. *empreinter*, fr. P.P. type of *empreindre*. See **im-** & **print**. **1. a** To produce, reproduce, apply, by pressure, stamp: *to imprint a mark on a surface*; **b** to press, apply: *to imprint a kiss on a person's brow* &c. **2.** To mark by pressure, apply mark or design to: *to imprint a surface with a mark* &c. **3.** To fix firmly, establish, impress in the mind: *words, a scene &c. for ever imprinted on one's heart, mind*.

imprint (II.), n. [1. ímprint; 2. ímprint], fr. prec. **a** That which is imprinted; an impression, mark, stamp: *printer's, publisher's, imprint*, details of name, place of business, date &c. printed on title-page or at end of book &c.; **b** (fig.) distinctive character, impress: *the imprint of care, anxiety* &c.

imprison, vb. trans. [1. imprízn; 2. imprízn], fr. O. Fr. *emprisoner*. See **im-** & **prison**. **1.** To put in prison. **2.** (fig.) To shut up, enclose, confine, restrain.

imprisonment, n. [1. impríznment; 2. impríznmənt]. Prec. & **-ment**. **a** The act of imprisoning; **b** state of being imprisoned.

improbability, n. [1. impròbabíliti; 2. imprɔ̀bəbíliti]. See next word & **-ity**. The quality of being improbable.

improbable, adj. [1. impróbabl; 2. imprɔ́bəbl], fr. Lat. *improbābil-(is)*, 'not deserving of approbation; exceptionable'. See **im-** & **probable**. **1.** Not probable, not likely to happen. **2.** Not likely to be true, not possessing verisimilitude, unlikely: *an improbable story*.

improbably, adv. Prec. & **-ly**. In an improbable manner.

improbity, n. [1. impróbiti; 2. imprɔ́biti], fr. Lat. *improbitāt-(em)*, 'wickedness, dishonesty'. See **im-** & **probity**. Lack of probity or uprightness; dishonesty.

impromptu, adv., adj., & n. [1. imprómptū; 2. imprómptjū], fr. Lat. *in promptu*, 'in readiness'. See **in-** & **prompt. 1.** adv. Without preparation, extempore: *to speak impromptu.* **2.** adj. Unprepared, performed or given extempore: *an impromptu speech.* **3.** n. **a** An impromptu performance, speech &c.; **b** a musical composition designed to give an impression of improvisation.

improper, adj. [1. impróper; 2. imprópə]. **im-** & **proper. 1. a** Not suited or adapted to the circumstances; unsuitable for purpose in view: *behaviour, speech &c. improper to the occasion*; *to put something to an improper use*, to one different from that for which it was intended; **b** not in accordance with wisdom, knowledge, truth &c: *improper treatment of disease*; *an improper rendering, statement* &c. **2.** Not in accordance with decorum, good breeding, decent feeling and convention; unbecoming, unseemly, indecent: *improper language*; *an improper word, book* &c.; *an improper person*, one of loose, bad character. **3.** (arith.) *Improper fraction*, one in which the numerator is greater than the denominator.

improperly, adv. Prec. & **-ly.** In an improper manner; unsuitably; wrongly; indecently.

impropriate (I.), vb. trans. [1. impróприāt; 2. impróupriеit], fr. Med. Lat. *impropriāt-(um)*, P.P. type of *impropriāre*, fr. **im-** & Lat. *propri-(āre)*, 'to appropriate', fr. *propri-(us)*, 'own'. See **proper. 1.** To transfer, take over, annex as private property (esp. ecclesiastical benefice &c.); to appropriate. **2.** To transfer (ecclesiastical property, such as tithe &c.) to layman.

impropriate (II.), adj. [1. imprópriat; 2. impróupriət], fr. prec. (of eccles. property) Having been impropriated.

impropriation, n. [1. impròpriáshun; 2. impròupriéiʃən]. **impropriate (I.)** & **-ion. a** The act of impropriating; **b** that which is impropriated.

impropriator, n. [1. imprópriātor, ìmpropriátor; 2. impróupriеitə, ìmprəpráiətə]. See prec. & **-or.** Person to, or by, whom something has been impropriated; specif., layman in possession of ecclesiastical property, such as tithe &c.

impropriety, n. [1. ìmprōpríeti; 2. ìmprouprái̇iti]. Lat. *improprietāt-(em)*, 'impropriety'. **im-** & **propriety. 1. a** Unsuitableness, incorrectness, unfitness: *impropriety of manners, expression, diction* &c.; **b** specific exhibition of this; a mistake, error. **2. a** Unseemliness, indecorum, indecency; **b** improper act, piece of misconduct.

improvability, n. [1. impròòvabíliti; 2. imprûvəbíliti]. See next word & **-ity.** The quality of being improvable.

improvable, adj. [1. impròòvəbl; 2. imprûvəbl]. **improve** & **-able.** Capable of being improved.

improvableness, n. See prec. & **-ness.** The quality of being improvable.

improve, vb. trans. & intrans. [1. impròòv; 2. imprûv], fr. A.-Fr. *emprouwer*, fr. O. Fr. *prod, prou*, 'profit, advantage'. See **prowess. 1.** trans. To make better, increase value, strength &c. of; to ameliorate. Phrs. *to improve the occasion, opportunity*, to use to advantage, make good use of, take advantage of; also, to use as text for a moral dissertation; *improve away*, get rid of (a good quality) in attempting to improve; *improve upon*, (something already done, made) make, produce, something better than. **2.** intrans. To become better; to increase in any good or desirable quality; to acquire more strength, value, beauty, excellence &c.: *to improve in health, manners, looks* &c.

improvement, n. [1. impròòvment; 2. imprûvmənt]. Prec. & **-ment. 1.** The act or process of improving; state of being improved; amelioration. **2.** Something which constitutes a gain in usefulness, beauty &c.: *I am putting some improvements into my house.*

improver, n. [1. impròòver; 2. imprûvə]. **improve** & **-er. a** One who, that which, improves; **b** specif., apprentice working for small wage to gain knowledge of his trade.

improvidence, n. [1. imprόvidens; 2. imprɔ́vidəns]. **im-** & **providence.** The quality of being improvident; improvident conduct.

improvident, adj. [1. imprόvident; 2. imprɔ́vidənt]. **im-** & **provident.** Wanting in foresight; not given to looking ahead, and providing for the future; unthrifty.

improvidently, adv. Prec. & **-ly.** In an improvident manner.

improvisation, n. [1. impròvizáshun; 2. imprɔ̀vizéiʃən]. **improvise** & **-ation. a** The act of improvising; **b** something improvised.

improvisator, n. [1. ímprovizātor; 2. ímprɔvizeitə]. (rarely used) Improvisatore.

improvisatore, n. [1. impròvizatóre; 2. imprɔ̀vizətɔ́ri]. Ital. See **improvise** & **-ate** & **-or.** One who improvises.

improvisatorial, adj. [1. impròvizatórial; 2. imprɔ̀vizətɔ́riəl]. **improvisator** & **-ial.** Pertaining to improvization.

improvisatory, adj. [1. ìmprovízaturi; 2. ìmprɔváizətəri]. See prec. & **-y.** Improvisatorial.

improvise, vb. trans. & intrans. [1. improvíz, ímproviz; 2. imprəváiz, ímprəvaiz], fr. Fr. *improviser*, fr. Ital. *improvisare*, fr. Lat. *imprōvīs-(um)*, 'not foreseen'. See **im-** & **provision, proviso. 1.** To compose and produce (verse, music &c.) extempore, on the spur of the moment, without preparation. **2.** To contrive, arrange, or construct as a makeshift, esp. hastily, without previous warning that this would be necessary, and without proper materials: *to improvise a bed on a sofa.*

imprudence, n. [1. impròòdens; 2. imprûdəns], fr. Lat. *imprūdentia*, 'lack of foresight'. **im-** & **prudence. a** Quality of being imprudent; rashness, indiscretion; **b** an imprudent act, utterance &c.

imprudent, adj. [1. impròòdent; 2. imprûdənt], fr. Lat. *imprūdent-(em)*, 'not foreseeing, imprudent'. **im-** & **prudent.** Without thought of consequences; not cautious; rash, indiscreet, incautious.

imprudently, adv. Prec. & **-ly.** In an imprudent manner.

impudence, n. [1. ímpūdens; 2. ímpjudəns], fr. Lat. *impudentia*, 'shamelessness', fr. *impud-(entem)*, 'impudent'. See next word & **-ence. 1.** The quality of being impudent. **2.** Impudent words or actions.

impudent, adj. [1. ímpūdent; 2. ímpjudənt], fr. Lat. *impudent-(em)*, 'without shame, impudent', fr. **im-** & *pudent-(em)*, 'bashful, modest', fr. *pudēre*, 'to be ashamed' (see **pudency**) & **-ent. 1.** Forward, bold, audacious, shameless; **a** (of persons) *an impudent rogue, beggar* &c.; **b** (of actions, words &c.) *an impudent charge, lie, speech.* **2.** Insolent, rude, saucy: *impudent young rascal* &c.

impudently, adv. Prec. & **-ly.** In an impudent manner.

impudicity, n. [1. ìmpūdísiti; 2. ìmpjudísiti], fr. Fr., fr. Lat. *impudīc-(us)*, 'shameless, immodest'. See base in prec., & **-ic** & **-ity.** Immodesty, shamelessness.

impugn, vb. trans. [1. impún; 2. impjún], fr. Fr. *impugner*, fr. Lat. *impugnāre*, 'to attack, assail', fr. **im-** & *pugnāre*, 'to fight, contend with'. See **pugnacious. a** To attack with criticism, argument &c.; **b** to challenge, call in question, deny.

impugnable, adj. [1. impúnabl; 2. impjúnəbl]. Prec. & **-able.** Capable of being impugned, open to attack.

impugnment, n. [1. impúnment; 2. impjúnmənt]. **impugn** & **-ment.** The act of impugning; state of being impugned.

impuissance, n. [1. impwísans; 2. impwísəns]. Fr. See **im-** & **puissance.** Weakness, feebleness, want of power.

impuissant, adj. [1. impwísant; 2. impwísənt]. **im-** & **puissant.** Feeble, weak, powerless, ineffective.

impulse, n. [1. ímpuls; 2. ímpals], fr. Lat. *impuls-(us)*, 'a pressure, shock; incitement, instigation', fr. *impuls-(um)*, P.P. type of *impellere*, 'to push'. See **impel** & **pulse (I.)**. **1.** Physical act of impelling; a push, thrust, propulsion. **2.** Intellectual or moral stimulus from without; instigation to action. **3. a** Intellectual or emotional propensity, or incitement to act, coming from within; **b** sudden access of this kind of propensity, often occurring in madness and appearing to be irresistible.

impulsion, n. [1. impúlshun; 2. impálʃən], fr. Lat. *impulsiōn-(em)*, 'external pressure; instigation', fr. *impuls-(um)*, P.P. type of *impellere*, 'to push'. See prec. & **-ion. 1. a** Act of impelling; **b** process of driving, or being driven, forward; impetus. **2.** Mental impulse.

impulsive, adj. [1. impúlsiv; 2. impálsiv]. **impulse** & **-ive. 1.** Tending, serving, to impel. **2. a** (of persons) Prone, liable, to act on sudden impulse, without reflection; **b** (of actions) performed as result of an impulse.

impulsively, adv. Prec. & **-ly.** In an impulsive manner.

impulsiveness, n. See prec. & **-ness. a** The quality of being impulsive; **b** impulsive tendency or action.

impunity, n. [1. impúniti; 2. impjúniti], fr. Lat. *impūnitāt-(em)*, 'freedom or safety from punishment', fr. *impūn-(is)*, 'without punishment', fr. **im-** & *poena*, 'punishment, penalty'. See **penal** & **-ity.** Freedom, safety, exemption, from penalty, punishment, injury &c.; esp. in Phr. *with impunity.*

impure, adj. [1. impúr; 2. impjɔ́], fr. Lat. *impūr-(us)*, 'unclean'. **im-** & **pure. 1.** Not clean; dirty, filthy. **2. a** Mixed with other substances, adulterated; not pure: (also fig.) not disinterested: *impure motives*; **b** specif. (of colour) mixed with another colour. **3.** Unchaste, immodest, immoral; obscene: *an impure mind, life*; *an impure book.*

impurely, adv. Prec. & **-ly.** In an impure manner.

impurity, n. [1. impúriti; 2. impjɔ́riti], fr. Lat. *impūritāt-(em)*, 'impurity'. **impure** & **-ity. 1.** The quality or state of being impure (in physical and moral senses). **2. a** An impure thing; foreign substance occurring in another: *impurities in the air, in food* &c.; **b** impure, unchaste, conduct.

imputability, n. [1. impûtabíliti; 2. impjûtəbíliti]. See next word & **-ity.** The state of being imputable.

imputable, adj. [1. impûtabl; 2. impjûtəbl]. **impute** & **-able.** Capable of being imputed; attributable, ascribable.

imputation, n. [1. ìmpūtáshun; 2. ìmpjutéiʃən]. **impute** & **-ation. 1.** The act of imputing; ascription, attribution (esp. in bad sense) of responsibility for; accusation: *imputation of dishonesty, cowardice* &c. **2.** Slur, aspersion: *to cast an imputation on a person's character.*

imputative, adj. [1. impûtativ; 2. impjûtətiv]. **impute** & **-ative.** Pertaining to imputation; imputed.

imputatively, adv. Prec. & **-ly.** As an imputation.

impute, vb. trans. [1. impût; 2. impjût], fr. Fr. *imputer*, fr. Lat. *imputāre*, 'to reckon, charge, ascribe', fr. **im-** & *putāre*, 'to clean, cleanse; to clear up, settle; to come to a reckoning; to reflect, consider'. See **putative. 1.** (chiefly in bad sense) To consider as belonging to; attribute, ascribe to; credit with, regard as guilty of: *I impute no evil motives or improper conduct to him.* **2.** (theol.) To ascribe to, put vicariously to credit of: *the superabundant merits of Christ are imputed to ransomed mankind.*

in (I.), prep. [1. in; 2. in]. O.E., M.E. *in*; O.H.G., O.S., Goth. *in*; O.N. *ī*, 'in'; Lat. *in*, 'in, on, among, into'; Gk. *en, eni*; O. Prussian *en*. **1. a** Expressing position within enclosed space or specified area; inside of, within: *in the house*; *in a box*; *two horses* *in a field*; *to live in England*; *in London*: **b** held by, supported by, partly surrounded by, framed by: *to have a stick in one's hand and a pipe in one's mouth*; *a candle in a candlestick*; *a plant in the window*. **2.** Expressing relation to physical circumstances and surroundings: *out in a storm*; *in the rain*; *to sit in the sun*; *buried in the sand*; *in the dark*; *in chains*; *in prison*. Phrs. *in clover*, in pleasant, profitable state; *in hot water*, in trouble. **3.** Expressing action, nature of activity: *engaged in reading*; *in search of truth*. **4.** Of immediate physical surroundings, covering, dress, or part of dress: *dressed in velvet, in rags*; *upholstered in leather*; *in green*; *in mourning*; *in a top hat*; *in uniform*. **5.** Physical condition: *in bad health*; *in a state of collapse*; *her dress was in rags*. **6.** Inclusion in printed or written composition, or in an utterance: *in the second chapter*; *in a speech*; *in Shakespeare*. **7.** Expressing sphere or scope of activity: *in his sight*; *in one's power*; *in my opinion*. **8.** Mental or moral state or circumstances: *in a rage*; *in despair*; *in difficulties*; *in an uproar*; *in the greatest excitement*; *in tears*. **9.** Expressing relation to time: **a** within the limits of, during: *in the meanwhile*; *in his absence*; *in June*; *in the winter*; **b** at the end of: *to be ready in an hour, a week*. **10.** Implying membership of, existence among, a group, party &c.; indicating occupation: *in the army*; *in society*; *in trade*; *in the Cabinet*. **11.** Limitation, **a** to particular part: *to be blind in one eye*; *a wound in the head*; **b** to physical quality, or amount: *to vary in size, colour* &c.; *his equal in strength*; *a foot in length*. **12.** Limitation with respect to specific mental or moral quality, capacity, accomplishment &c.; as regards: *lacking in faith*; *weak in Latin*. **13.** Relation to capacity, character, ability: *I didn't think he had it in him*. **14.** Conditional; having regard to; should certain things happen: *in the circumstances*; *in that case*. **15.** Expressing means, medium, mode of expression: *to paint in oils*; *printed in colours*; *written in pencil*; *in English*; *in a few words*. **16.** Expressing mode of arrangement, order &c.: *sitting in rows*; *in groups*; *grouped in tens*; *hair in ringlets*. **17.** Expressing reason of, motive for, action: *to cry out in alarm*; *to rejoice in one's recovery*. **18.** Expressing object of action: *to speak in reply, in a person's defence*; *to urge a thing in excuse*. **19.** Expressing direction of action, motion &c.; into: *to put one's hands in one's pockets*; *to dip a pen in the ink*.

in (**II.**), adv. O.E., O.S. *in*, *inn*; Goth., O.N. *inn*; Gmc. **in*, fr. prep. **in*. See prec. Becomes an adv. after a vb. in certain idiomatic uses: *to come in* (*the house, room* &c. understood); *to take in what is said* (*into the mind* understood); also after certain vbs., as *to live in*, i.e. in the house where one's work is.

in (**III.**), adj. Interior, internal; in a few Phrs.: *in patient*, one who lives in the hospital where he is being treated; *the in side*, at cricket, the side having an innings.

in (**IV.**), n., fr. **in** (**II.**). **1.** *The ins*, (polit.) members of party in office. **2.** *Ins and outs*, **a** (often fig.) twists and turns, nooks and corners; **b** full details, complexities: *the ins and outs of a question, subject, situation* &c.

in (**V.**), prep. Lat. *in*, 'in, on, among, into'. See under **in** (**I.**). In various Phrs., *in commendam* &c., q.v.

in- (**I.**), pref. Lat., fr. prep. *in*; in composition, this becomes, in Lat. itself, **il-** before *l*; **im-** before *b*, *m*, *p*; **ir-** before *r*. Often remains unaltered in words of recent formation, esp. if the word w. wh. it is compounded is of Engl. origin—*inmate*, *inlay* &c. It is sometimes difficult to distinguish fr. the O.E. pref. *innan-*, *inne-*, 'within', cogn. w. **in** (**I., II.**), e.g. in **inward**. The force of the pref. in composition is 'in, upon', before vbs. implying rest; 'into, against, towards', before those implying motion. In O. Fr. the pref. becomes **en-**, **em-**.

in- (**II.**), pref., fr. Lat. *in-*, 'not', neg. pref., cogn. w. Gk. *a-*; Goth., O.H.G., O.E. *un-*. See **un-**. Living pref., giving neg. sense to adjs. & words derived fr. adjs., esp. of Lat. origin: *inappropriate*, *inconclusive*, *indestructible* &c. Becomes *il-*, *im-*, *ir-* under same conditions as **in-** (**I.**).

-in, suff., used in chemical terminology. See **-ine** (**VII.**).

-ina (**I.**), suff. [1. ḗna; 2. ína]. Lat. fem. suff.: *regina*. In Engl., used to form fem. titles: *czarina*; & female names: *Georgina* &c.; also in names of musical instruments: *concertina*, *ocarina*.

-ina (**II.**), suff. representing neut. pl. of Lat. adjs. (usually mod. scientific Lat.), forming names of groups of animals &c. related to a specific genus.

inability, n. [1. inabíliti; 2. inəbíliti]. **in-** (**II.**) & **ability**. Lack of ability, power, resources, opportunity; condition of being unable to do something: *inability to help, stand, pay, visit* &c.

inaccessibility, n. [1. inaksesibíliti; 2. inæksɛsibíliti]. See next word & **-ity**. The state or quality of being inaccessible.

inaccessible, adj. [1. inaksésibl; 2. inæksésibl], fr. Fr., fr. L. Lat. *inaccessibilis*, 'unapproachable'. **in-** (**II.**) & **accessible**. **1.** **a** (of material things) Not easily accessible; hard to approach or reach; remote, out-of-the-way: *an inaccessible dwelling, peak* &c.; **b** (of non-material things) not easily attained; unattainable, beyond attainment: *the inaccessible object of one's ambition*. **2.** (of persons) Not easy of access; unapproachable; distant, reserved in manner and nature.

inaccessibly, adv. Prec. & **-ly**. In an inaccessible manner.

inaccuracy, n. [1. inákūrasi; 2. inǽkjurəsi]. **in-** (**II.**) & **accuracy**. **1.** The quality of being inaccurate. **2.** Something that is inaccurate; an error; a mistake.

inaccurate, adj. [1. inákūrat; 2. inǽkjurət]. **in-** (**II.**) & **accurate**. Incorrect, wrong; inexact, not accurate.

inaccurately, adv. Prec. & **-ly**. In an inaccurate manner.

inaction, n. [1. inákshun; 2. inǽkʃən]. **in-** (**II.**) & **action**. Absence of mental or of physical action; rest, quiescence, passiveness; inactivity, idleness, inertness.

inactive, adj. [1. ináktiv; 2. inǽktiv]. **in-** (**II.**) & **active**. **a** Incapable of physical or mental activity; sluggish, inert, dull; **b** not actually engaged in action or motion; motionless, quiescent; **c** (i.) not industrious; idle; (ii.) not busy; unemployed.

inactively, adv. Prec. & **-ly**. In an inactive manner.

inactivity, n. [1. inaktíviti; 2. inæktíviti]. **in-** (**II.**) & **activity**. **1.** The state of being inactive. **2.** **a** Absence of action, motion, or movement; immobility, quiescence; state of unemployment; **b** lack of energy; sluggishness, inertness, lethargy.

inadaptability, n. [1. inadaptabíliti; 2. inədæptəbíliti]. **in-** (**II.**) & **adaptability**. Lack, absence, of adaptability.

inadaptable, adj. [1. inadáptabl; 2. inədǽptəbl]. **in-** (**II.**) & **adaptable**. Incapable of adapting oneself; not capable of being adapted.

inadequacy, n. [1. inádekwasi; 2. inǽdikwəsi]. **in-** (**II.**) & **adequacy**. The quality of being inadequate; a insufficiency, incompleteness; **b** incompetence.

inadequate, adj. [1. inádekwat; 2. inǽdikwət]. **in-** (**II.**) & **adequate**. **a** Not fulfilling requirements; **b** insufficient, incompetent.

inadequately, adv. Prec. & **-ly**. In an inadequate manner.

inadhesive, adj. [1. inad-hḗsiv; 2. inædhísiv]. **in-** (**II.**) & **adhesive**. Not adhesive, not sticking.

inadmissibility, n. [1. inadmisibíliti; 2. inædmisibíliti]. See next word & **-ity**. The quality of being inadmissible.

inadmissible, adj. [1. inadmísibl; 2. inædmísibl]. **in-** (**II.**) & **admissible**. Not to be admitted; not permissible, that cannot be granted.

inadvertence, **-cy**, n. [1. inadvḗrtens(i); 2. inədvə́təns(i)]. See next word & **-ce**, **-cy**. The quality of being inadvertent; a result, effect, of inadvertence; oversight, error.

inadvertent, adj. [1. inadvḗrtent; 2. inədvə́tənt]. **in-** (**II.**) & obs. *advertent*, fr. **advert** & **-ent**. **1.** Inattentive, unheedful; negligent. **2.** (of actions) Due to oversight; unintentional, undesigned.

inadvertently, adv. Prec. & **-ly**. **1.** Negligently, heedlessly. **2.** Unintentionally, accidentally.

inalienability, n. [1. inālienabíliti; 2. inèiliənəbíliti]. **in-** (**II.**) & **alienability**. The quality of being inalienable.

inalienable, adj. [1. inā́lienabl; 2. inéiliənəbl]. **in-** (**II.**) & **alienable**. Not alienable, not capable of being separated, transferred, or taken away: *an inalienable right*.

inalienably, adv. Prec. & **-ly**. Inseparably; so as to be incapable of being alienated.

inalterability, n. [1. inawlterabíliti; 2. inɔ̀ltərəbíliti]. **in-** (**II.**) & **alterability**. The quality of being inalterable.

inalterable, adj. [1. ináwlterabl; 2. inɔ́ltərəbl]. **in-** (**II.**) & **alterable**. Not capable of being altered; unchangeable.

inalterably, adv. Prec. & **-ly**. In an inalterable manner.

inamorata, n. [1. inàmoráhta; 2. inæ̀mərɑ́tə]. Ital., fem. of P.P. of *inamorāre*, 'to fall in love', fr. **in-** (**I.**) & *amorāre*, 'to fall in love', fr. *amore*, fr. Lat. *amor*, 'love'. See **amorous**. Lady with whom one is in love.

inamorato, n. [1. inàmoráhtō; 2. inæ̀mərɑ́tou]. Masc. of prec. Man with whom a woman is in love.

in-and-in, adj. [1. ìn and ín; 2. ìn ənd ín]. In Phr. *in-and-in breeding*, mating of animals or human beings, repeatedly, with individuals of same stock, sprung from common ancestors.

inane (**I.**), adj. [1. inā́n; 2. inéin], fr. Lat. *inān-*(*is*), 'empty, void; worthless, vain, unprofitable'. Etymol. doubtful. **1.** (rare in physical sense) Empty, void, vacant. **2.** (of the mind and its operations) Foolish, trivial, frivolous, silly.

inane (**II.**), n., fr. prec. *The inane*, infinite space: '*Pinnacled dim in the intense inane*' (Shelley).

inanely, adv. **inane** (**I.**) & **-ly**. In an inane manner.

inanimate, adj. [1. inánimat; 2. inǽnimət], fr. L. Lat. *inanimāt-*(*us*), 'lifeless'. **in-** (**II.**) & **animate**. **1.** Deprived of life; lifeless, dead. **2.** Not endowed with organic life: *inanimate matter*; *inanimate nature*. **3.** Without animation; spiritless, listless, dull.

inanimately, adv. Prec. & **-ly**. In an inanimate manner.

inanimation, n. [1. inànimā́shun; 2. inæ̀niméiʃən]. See prec. & **-ion**. The state of being inanimate.

inanition, n. [1. inaníshun; 2. inəníʃən], fr. Lat. *inānītiōn-*(*em*), 'emptiness', fr. *inānīt-*(*um*), 'emptied'. See next word & **-ion**. Emptiness; exhaustion from lack of food or nutriment.

inanity, n. [1. ináníti; 2. inéiniti], fr. Lat. *inānitāt-*(*em*), 'emptiness; uselessness', fr. *inān-*(*is*), 'empty; foolish, trifling'. See **inane** & **-ity**. **1.** The quality of being inane. **2.** Something that is inane; foolish triviality.

inappeasable, adj. [1. inapḗzabl; 2. inəpízəbl]. **in-** (**II.**) & **appeasable**. Not capable of being appeased.

inappellable, adj. [1. inapélabl; 2. inəpéləbl]. **in-** (**II.**) & Lat. *appell-*(*āre*), 'to address, accost; to entreat, appeal to' (see **appeal**), & **-able**. Not able to be appealed against; unappealable.

inappetence, n. [1. inápetens; 2. inǽpitəns]. **in-** (**II.**) & **appetence**. Lack of appetence, absence of desire.

inapplicability, n. [1. inàplikabíliti; 2. inæ̀plikəbíliti]. **in-** (**II.**) & **applicability**. The state of being inapplicable.

inapplicable, adj. [1. ináplikabl; 2. *inǽplikəbl*]. **in- (II.)** & **applicable**. Not capable of being applied, unsuitable to, either generally or under particular circumstances.

inapplicably, adv. Prec. & **-ly**. In an inapplicable manner.

inapposite, adj. [1. inápozit; 2. *inǽpəzit*]. **in- (II.)** & **apposite**. Not apposite; out of place, ill-timed; irrelevant, not pertinent.

inappositely, adv. Prec. & **-ly**. In an inapposite manner.

inappreciable, adj. [1. inaprḗshabl; 2. *in*əprīʃəbl]. **in- (II.)** & **appreciable**. So small or slight as to be incapable of being appreciated; imperceptible, negligible.

inappreciably, adv. Prec. & **-ly**. In an inappreciable manner; very slightly.

inappreciation, n. [1. ìnaprēsiā́shun; 2. *in*əprīsi*éi*ʃən]. **in- (II.)** & **appreciation**. Lack of appreciation.

inappreciative, adj. [1. inaprḗshativ; 2. *in*əprī́ʃətiv]. **in- (II.)** & **appreciative**. **a** Not appreciating; not estimating at just value: *inappreciative of*; **b** not alive to, indifferent to, merit, good qualities &c.

inapprehensible, adj. [1. inàprehénsibl; 2. *in*æprihénsibl]. **in- (II.)** & **apprehensible**. Not capable of being apprehended, not intelligible.

inapproachable, adj. [1. inaprṓchabl; 2. *in*əpróutʃəbl]. **in- (II.)** & **approachable**. (chiefly in moral sense) Inaccessible, unapproachable; reserved, distant.

inappropriate, adj. [1. inaprṓpriat; 2. *in*əpróupriət]. **in- (II.)** & **appropriate**. Not appropriate; unsuitable, incongruous.

inappropriately, adv. Prec. & **-ly**. In an inappropriate manner.

inappropriateness, n. See prec. & **-ness**. The quality of being inappropriate.

inapt, adj. [1. inápt; 2. *inǽpt*]. **in- (II.)** & **apt**. **a** Unskilful, unqualified; not deft or dexterous; **b** inappropriate, irrelevant, unsuitable, not to the point.

inaptitude, n. [1. ináptitūd; 2. *inǽptitjūd*]. **in- (II.)** & **aptitude**. **a** Incapacity, lack of aptitude; **b** unsuitability.

inaptly, adv. [1. ináptli; 2. *inǽptli*]. **inapt** & **-ly**. In an inapt manner; unsuitably.

inaptness, n. [1. ináptnes; 2. *inǽptnis*]. **inapt** & **-ness**. Unsuitability, incongruousness.

inarch, vb. trans. [1. inárch; 2. *inā́tʃ*]. **in- (I.)** & **arch (II.)**. To graft (a shoot, bud) without separating from parent stem.

inarm, vb. trans. [1. inárm; 2. *inā́m*]. **in- (I.)** & **arm (I.)**. (poet.) To take into one's arms, clasp, embrace.

inarticulate, adj. [1. ìnartíkūlat; 2. *inātí*kjulit], fr. L. Lat. *inarticulāt-(us)*, 'indistinct, inarticulate', fr. **in- (II.)** & *articulāt-(us)*, 'jointed, distinct'. See **articulate**. **1.** (anat.) Not joined. **2. a** (of speech) Indistinct, not articulate, not distinguishable; **b** (of persons) not capable of speaking distinctly. **3.** Incapable of expressing one's ideas and feelings; having no fluency in speech; not given to talking much, reticent.

inarticulately, adv. Prec. & **-ly**. In an inarticulate manner.

inarticulateness, n. See prec. & **-ness**. The quality of being inarticulate.

inartificial, adj. [1. inàrtifíshal; 2. *inàtifíʃəl*], fr. L. Lat. *inartificiāl-(is)*, 'inartificial, inartistic'. **in- (II.)** & **artificial**. **1.** (archaic) Not in accordance with artistic principles; inartistic. **2.** Natural, artless, not artificial.

inartificially, adv. Prec. & **-ly**. In an inartificial manner.

inartistic, adj. [1. ìnartístik; 2. *inātístik*]. **in- (II.)** & **artistic**; cp. **unartistic**. **a** Not in accordance with the principles of art, not showing and expressing a sense of form, proportion, symmetry, colour &c.: *an inartistic arrangement, style* &c.; **b** (of persons, mind &c.) devoid of artistic sense and culture.

inartistically, adv. [1. ìnartístikali; 2. *inātístikəli*]. Prec. & **-al** & **-ly**. In an inartistic manner.

inasmuch, adv. [1. ìnazmúch; 2. *in*əzmátʃ]. **in** & **as** & **much**. *Inasmuch as*, **a** (archaic) in so far as; **b** since, because, seeing that.

inattention, n. [1. inaténshun; 2. *in*əténʃən]. **in- (II.)** & **attention**. **1.** Lack of attention, absence of concentration of mind; heedlessness. **2.** Neglect, lack of care, consideration, absence of polite solicitude.

inattentive, adj. [1. inaténtiv; 2. *in*əténtiv]. **in- (II.)** & **attentive**. **a** Not attending, heedless, without concentration of mind; **b** lacking in assiduity; careless, neglectful.

inattentively, adv. Prec. & **-ly**. In an inattentive manner.

inattentiveness, n. See prec. & **-ness**. The quality of being inattentive.

inaudibility, n. [1. inàwdibíliti; 2. *inɔ̄di*bíliti], fr. Lat. *inaudībil-(is)*, 'inaudible'. Next word & **-ity**. The quality of being inaudible.

inaudible, adj. [1. ináwdibl; 2. *inɔ́dibl*], fr. Lat. *inaudībil-(is)*, 'inaudible'. **in- (II.)** & **audible**. Not capable of being heard.

inaudibly, adv. Prec. & **-ly**. In an inaudible manner.

inaugural, adj. & n. [1. ináwgūral; 2. *inɔ́g*jurəl], fr. stem of **inaugurate** & **-al**. **1.** adj. Pertaining to, uttered on occasion of, inauguration: *an inaugural lecture, address* &c., (i.) delivered at a ceremonial opening, e.g. of a congress &c.; (ii.) by a person, e.g. president, professor &c., on assuming office. **2.** n. An inaugural address.

inaugurate, vb. trans. & intrans. [1. ináwgūrāt; 2. *inɔ́gjureit*], fr. Lat. *inaugurāt-(um)*, P.P. type of *inaugurāre*, 'to practise augury; to consecrate, inaugurate; to install', fr. **in- (I.)** & *augurāre*, 'to examine omens', fr. *augur*, 'augur, soothsayer'. See **augur**. **A.** trans. **1.** To admit (a person) to office ceremoniously; induct, introduce formally. **2. a** To make a formal, ceremonious, entrance upon; **b** to open, begin: *to inaugurate a new era*. **3.** To open publicly with formality and ceremony (a building, exhibition &c.). **B.** intrans. To deliver an inaugural address.

inauguration, n. [1. inàwgūrā́shun; 2. *inɔ̀g*juréiʃən]. Prec. & **-ion**. The act of inaugurating; state of being inaugurated.

inauguratory, adj. [1. ináwgūraturi; 2. *inɔ́g*jurətəri]. See prec. & **-ory**. Inaugural.

inauspicious, adj. [1. ìnawspíshus; 2. *inɔ̄s*píʃəs]. **in- (II.)** & **auspicious**. Ill-omened, unpropitious; unlucky, untoward.

inauspiciously, adv. Prec. & **-ly**. In an inauspicious manner.

inauspiciousness, n. See prec. & **-ness**. The quality of being inauspicious.

inboard, adv. & adj. [1. ínbord; 2. *ínbɔ̄d*]. **in (I.)** & **board**. (naut.) In the interior of, near centre of, ship.

inborn, adj. [1. ínborn; 2. *ínbɔ̄n*]. **in (II.)** & **born**. Born in one; natural, inherent, innate.

inbreathe, vb. trans. [1. inbrḗdh; 2. *inbrīð*]. **in (II.)** & **breathe**. (lit. and fig., rare) To breathe in, take in, inhale.

inbred, adj. [1. ínbred; 2. *ínbred*]. **in (II.)** & **bred**; see **breed (I.)**. **1.** Innate, inherent, natural, hereditary. **2.** Bred from parents who have common ancestors; derived from one or more unions of near kin.

inbreeding, n. [1. ínbrēding; 2. *ínbrīdiŋ*]. **in (II.)** & **breeding**. Breeding from closely related stocks.

Inca, n. [1. íngka; 2. *íŋkə*]. Peruvian. **a** A king of ancient Peru; **b** member of royal family of Peru before the Spanish conquest.

incalculability, n. [1. inkàlkūlabíliti; 2. *in*kælkjuləbíliti]. See next word & **-ity**. The quality of being incalculable.

incalculable, adj. [1. inkálkūlabl; 2. *inkǽlk*juləbl]. **in-** & **calculable**. **1.** Too great to be calculated, computed. **2.** Not to be foretold, predicted, or reckoned beforehand. **3.** (of person or character) Not to be relied upon, not to be understood, uncertain; liable to behave in an incalculable manner.

incalculably, adv. Prec. & **-ly**. In an incalculable manner.

in camera. See **camera**.

incandesce, vb. intrans. & trans. [1. inkandés; 2. *in*kændés], fr. Lat. *incandesc-(ere)*, 'to become hot, glow', fr. **in- (I.)** & *candēre*, 'to shine, glisten; to glow with heat'. See **candescent** & **candid**. **1.** intrans. To become glowing, be made luminous, by heat. **2.** trans. To cause to glow, make luminous, with heat.

incandescence, n. [1. ìnkandésens; 2. *in*kændésəns]. See next word & **-ce**. Process of becoming, state of being, incandescent.

incandescent, adj. [1. ìnkandésent; 2. *inkæn*désənt]. **incandesce** & **-ent**. **a** Glowing, luminous, white, with heat; **b** shining, brilliant, gleaming; specif., *incandescent light*, that derived from a substance in a state of incandescence, as a mantle or network of fibre coated with oxide of thorium and cerium in gas lamp, or of tungsten wire in electric bulb.

incantation, n. [1. ìnkantā́shun; 2. *inkæntéi*ʃən], fr. Fr., fr. Lat. *incantātiōn-(em)*, 'enchantment', fr. *incantāre*, 'to bewitch with spells', fr. **in- (I.)** & *cantāre*, 'to sing'. See **chant**. Magic words or formula; spell, charm.

incapability, n. [1. inkàpabíliti; 2. *inkèipə*bíliti]. **in- (II.)** & **capability**. The state of being incapable.

incapable, adj. [1. inkā́pabl; 2. *inkéipəbl*]. **in- (II.)** & **capable**. Lacking the capacity, ability, power, quality, necessary for some specific end or purpose; **a** (physical) *incapable of speech, movement* &c.; **b** (intellectual) inefficient, incompetent: *an incapable person*; *incapable of understanding*; Phr. *drunk and incapable*, so drunk as to be helpless; dead drunk; **c** (moral) (i.) *incapable of telling a lie*, too truthful ever to do so; (ii.) *incapable of speaking the truth*, utterly untruthful.

incapably, adv. Prec. & **-ly**. In an incapable manner.

incapacitate, vb. trans. [1. ìnkapásitāt; 2. *in*kəpǽsiteit]. See **incapacity** & **-ate**. **1.** To render incapable of, unfit for; to deprive of power to, make unequal to: *to incapacitate one from working, for work* &c. **2.** To disqualify: *to be incapacitated from voting by lack of fixed domicile*.

incapacitation, n. [1. ìnkapasitā́shun; 2. *in*kəpæsitéiʃən]. Prec. & **-ion**. **a** Act of incapacitating; **b** state of being incapacitated.

incapacity, n. [1. inkapásiti; 2. *inkəpǽsiti*], fr. Fr. *incapacité*. **in- (II.)** & **capacity**. **1.** Want of physical or mental capacity; inability, powerlessness; incompetence. **2.** Legal disqualification.

incarcerate, vb. trans. [1. inkárserāt; 2. *in*kā́səreit], fr. Med. Lat. *incarcerāt-(um)*, P.P. type of *incarcerāre*, fr. **in- (I.)** & L. Lat. *carcerāre*, 'to imprison', fr. Lat. *carcer*, 'an enclosed place; a prison'; perh. cogn. w. O.E. *hearg*, 'heathen temple'; cp. O.N. *hǫrgr*, 'stone mound; heathen altar'; orig. meaning 'piled-up stones, whether as mound or as enclosing wall'. Cp. Gael. *carn*, 'pile of stones'. See **cairn**. (lit. and fig.) To imprison, shut up, confine.

incarceration, n. [1. inkàrserā́shun; 2. *in*kāsəréiʃən]. Prec. & **-ion**. The act of incarcerating; state of being incarcerated.

incarnadine (I.), adj. [1. inkárnadin; 2. *in*kā́nədin], fr. Fr., fr. Ital. *incarnadino*, fr. *incarnato*, 'in the flesh', fr. Lat. *incarnāt-(us)*. See **incarnate**. (poet.) Flesh-coloured, reddish.

incarnadine (II.), vb. trans., fr. prec. (poet.) To redden; cause to turn red or crimson: '*(my hand will) The multitudinous seas incarnadine*' (Shakespeare, 'Macbeth').

incarnate (I.), adj. [1. inkárnit; 2. *inkā́nit*], fr. Lat. *incarnāt-(um)*, P.P. type of Lat. *incarnāre*, 'to make flesh', fr. **in- (I.)** & *carn-(is)*, genit. of *caro*, 'flesh'. See **carnal**. **a** Having a body; invested with flesh: *an incarnate fiend*; **b** (of an ideal, an abstraction &c.) given, appearing in, a concrete, tangible form.

incarnate (II.) vb. trans. [1. inkárnāt; 2. *inkǻneit*]. See prec. **a** To invest with flesh, give bodily form to; to embody; **b** to give concrete, tangible form to; make concrete (a plan, vision, idea &c.).

incarnation, n. [1. ìnkarnáshun; 2. *ìnkānéiʃən*]. Prec. & **-ion**. **1.** Process, act, of enclosing in flesh, of giving bodily form to; specif., *the Incarnation*, the taking on of human form and nature by Christ. **2.** Embodiment in concrete form; something which embodies, expresses, typifies, an abstract quality &c.: *the incarnation of health.*

incautious, adj. [1. inkáwshus; 2. *inkɔ́ʃəs*]. **in- (II.)** & **cautious**. Not cautious; rash, imprudent.

incautiously, adv. Prec. & **-ly**. In an incautious manner.

incautiousness, n. See prec. & **-ness**. The quality of being incautious.

incendiarism, n. [1. inséndiarizm; 2. *inséndjərizəm*]. See next word & **-ism**. **1.** Deliberate, malicious burning of property; arson. **2.** (fig.) Stirring up of dissension; wilful incitement to violence, rioting &c.

incendiary, adj. & n. [1. inséndyari; 2. *inséndjəri*], fr. Lat. *incendiāri-(us)*, 'causing a fire', fr. *incendi-(um)*, 'a fire, conflagration', fr. *incend-(ere)*, 'to set fire to'. **in- (I.)** & cp. *candēre*, 'to gleam, burn, glow'; see **candescent** & **candid**. **1.** adj. **a** Pertaining to, given to, guilty of, incendiarism; **b** tending to arouse dissension, sedition, strife. **2.** n. **a** Person who deliberately and maliciously sets fire to property; **b** one who stirs up violence, strife, rebellion; an agitator.

incense (I.), n. [1. ínsens; 2. *ínsens*], fr. O. Fr. *encens*, fr. Lat. *incensum*, 'something burnt, incense', fr. *incens-(um)*, P.P. of *incendere*, 'to set fire to'. See prec. **1. a** Pungent, fragrant smoke arising from burning herbs and spices; specif., this used ceremonially in religious worship; **b** herbs &c. used for this purpose. **2.** (fig.) Pleasing homage; adulation, flattery.

incense (II.), vb. trans. [1. inséns; 2. *inséns*], fr. prec. **a** To fumigate, perfume, make fragrant, with incense; to cense; **b** to offer incense to; to burn it in honour of.

incense (III.), vb. trans., fr. Lat. *incens-(um)*. Same word as prec. Lat. *incendere* has fig. meaning 'to irritate, enrage'. See **incendiary**. To anger, enrage, make indignant.

incense burner, n. Stationary vessel for burning incense; in contrast to a *censer*, which is swung.

incensory, n. [1. insénsuri; 2. *insénsəri*], fr. Med. Lat. *incensōrium*, 'censer'. **incense (I.)** & **-ory**. A censer.

incentive, adj. & n. [1. inséntiv; 2. *inséntiv*], fr. Lat. *incentīv-(us)*, 'setting the tune, giving the note', fr. *incent-(um)*, P.P. type of *incinere*, 'to sound, sing', fr. **in- (I.)** & *canere*, 'to sing, sound, play'. See **chant** & **-ive**. **1.** adj. Tending to incite, stir up, urge. **2.** n. Something that incites to action; stimulus, motive.

incept, vb. trans. & intrans. [1. insépt; 2. *insépt*], fr. Lat. *incept-(um)*, P.P. type of *incipere*, 'to begin, take in hand', fr. **in- (I.)** & *capere*, 'to take'. See **captive**. **A.** trans. **1.** (obs.) To begin: *to incept the Psalms*, to sing opening words as solo. **2.** (biol.) To take in (foreign matter) and convert it into organic tissue. **B.** intrans. **a** (Oxford Univ.) *To incept in arts*, to complete the exercises prescribed for the B.A. degree, thus qualifying for degree of Master of Arts, or one in a higher Faculty; **b** (Cambridge) complete taking Master's or Doctor's degree.

inception, n. [1. insépshun; 2. *insépʃən*], fr. Lat. *inceptiōn-(em)*, 'beginning'. Prec. & **-ion**. **1.** Beginning, commencement, start. **2.** (Cambridge Univ.) Taking of full Master's or Doctor's degree.

inceptive, adj. & n. [1. inséptiv; 2. *inséptiv*], fr. Lat. *incept-(um)*, P.P. type of *incipere*, 'to begin'. See **incept** & **-ive**. **1.** adj. **a** Beginning, marking the beginning; initial, introductory; **b** specif. (gram., of vb.) expressing the beginning of an action. **2.** n. An inceptive verb.

incertitude, n. [1. insértitūd; 2. *insǻtitjūd*], fr. Fr., fr. Lat. *incert-(us)*, 'uncertain' (fr. **in- (II.)**, & *cert-(us)*, see **certain**), & **-tude**. Uncertain state of mind; uncertainty; absence of conviction, or assurance; doubtfulness, dubiety.

incessancy, n. [1. insésansi; 2. *insésənsi*]. See next word & **-cy**. The state of being incessant.

incessant, adj. [1. insésant; 2. *insésənt*], fr. L. Lat. *incessant-(em)*, 'unceasing', fr. **in- (II.)** & *cessant-(em)*, Pres. Part. of *cessāre*, 'to stop, cease'. See **cease**. Never ceasing, continual, uninterrupted.

incessantly, adv. Prec. & **-ly**. Ceaselessly, without stopping.

incest, n. [1. ínsest; 2. *ínsest*], fr. Lat. *incest-(us)*, 'unchastity, incest', fr. **in- (II.)** & *castus*, 'chaste'. See **chaste**. Crime consisting in sexual intercourse between closely related persons.

incestuous, adj. [1. inséstūus; 2. *inséstjuəs*], fr. Lat. *incestuōs-(us)*, 'incestuous'. Prec. & **-ous**. **a** Of the nature of incest; **b** guilty of incest.

incestuously, adv. Prec. & **-ly**. So as to constitute incest.

inch (I.), n. [1. inch; 2. *intʃ*]. O.E. *ynće*; M.E. *inche*; fr. Lat. *uncia*, 'a twelfth part; the twelfth part of a pound; an ounce; twelfth part of a foot; an inch'; orig. 'unit', fr. Lat. *ūn-(us)*, 'one'. See **uni-** & cp. **ounce (I.)**. **1. a** The twelfth part of a foot; *an inch of rain*, amount sufficient to cover surface to depth of one inch; **b** *inches*, height, stature. **2.** A small amount, distance, degree; in various Phrs. *by inches*, a small bit at a time; *inch by inch*, by degrees; *every inch*, completely, entirely; *not to yield an inch* (lit. and fig.), not to give way in the smallest degree; *if you give him an inch he'll take an ell*, will take unjustifiable advantage of any concessions.

inch (II.), n., fr. Gael. *innis*, 'island'. (Scots) A small island; hill, or other piece of land isolated from surroundings.

-incher, n. suff. [1. íncher; 2. *íntʃə*], fr. **inch (I.)** & **-er**. Thing measuring so many inches (in length, breadth &c.): *six-incher* &c.

inchoate, (I.) adj. [1. inkōāt; 2. *inkóueit*], fr. Lat. *inc(h)oāt-(um)*, P.P. type of *inc(h)oāre*, *incohāre*, 'to begin', fr. **in- (I.)** & **kagh-*, **kogh-*, 'to take hold of, fasten together, lay together'. Cp. Lat. *cohus*, 'a strap fastening plough-beam to yoke'. In the first stages, just beginning; undeveloped, rudimentary.

inchoate (II.), vb. trans. [1. ínkōāt; 2. *ínkoueit*]. See prec. (rare) To begin, be author of, originate, initiate.

inchoation, n. [1. ìnkōáshun; 2. *ìnkouéiʃən*]. Prec. & **-ion**. (rare) Beginning, origin.

inchoative, adj. [1. inkōativ; 2. *inkóuətiv*]. **inchoate (II.)** & **-ive**. (gram.) *Inchoative verb*, one expressing beginning of an action.

incidence, n. [1. ínsidens; 2. *ínsidəns*], fr. Fr., fr. Lat. *incid-(entem)*, 'falling upon'. Next word & **-ence**. **1.** Fact, mode, of falling or affecting; scope, range, of occurrence: *incidence of taxation, of a particular disease* &c. **2.** Direction in which one body falls on, or strikes another; *angle of incidence*, that made with the falling or moving body, and the plane struck.

incident (I.), adj. [1. ínsident; 2. *ínsidənt*], fr. Fr., fr. Lat. *incident-(em)*, Pres. Part. of *incidere*, 'to fall upon; to happen, occur', fr. **in- (I.)** & *cadere*, 'to fall'. See **cadence**. **1.** Naturally belonging to, liable to occur in connexion with; attendant on: *diseases incident to childhood*; *weaknesses incident to human nature*. **2.** (law) Dependent on, naturally involved in, attached to, something else: *rights, duties &c., incident to a settled estate.* **3.** (phys.) Falling, striking upon, meeting: *a line, ray of light &c., incident upon a surface.*

incident (II.), n., fr. prec. **1. a** Something that happens; an event, occurrence; **b** a subordinate event; detail, minor episode; esp. one apart from the main design in a composition. **2.** (law) Something attaching to, dependent on, something else; esp. a privilege or burden attached to an estate.

incidental, adj. & n. [1. ìnsidéntl; 2. *ìnsidéntl*]. Prec. & **-al**. **1.** adj. **a** Occurring as a result of, consequent on, liable to occur in, attaching to; incident: *the dangers incidental to a soldier's career*; **b** forming an unimportant part; unessential, casual. **2.** n. Something which is incidental.

incidentally, adv. Prec. & **-ly**. In an incidental manner.

incinerate, vb. trans. [1. insínerāt; 2. *insínəreit*], fr. Med. Lat. *incinerāt-(um)*, P.P. type of *incinerāre*, 'to reduce to ashes', fr. **in- (I.)** & *ciner-*, stem of *cinis*, 'ashes'. See **cinerary**. To burn up, reduce to ashes.

incineration, n. [1. insìneráshun; 2. *insìnəréiʃən*]. Prec. & **-ion**. Reduction to ashes, burning up.

incinerator, n. [1. insínerātor; 2. *insínəreitə*]. **incinerate** & **-or**. Furnace for burning rubbish &c.

incipience, -cy, n. [1. insípiens(i); 2. *insípiəns(i)*]. See next word & **-ce, -cy**. The state of being incipient; beginning, first stages.

incipient, adj. [1. insípient; 2. *insípiənt*], fr. Lat. *incipient-(em)*, Pres. Part. of *incipere*, 'to begin'. See **in- (I.)** & **captive**. Beginning, not fully developed, in the early stages: *incipient lunacy.*

incipiently, adv. Prec. & **-ly**. As a beginning.

incipit, vb. [1. ínsipit; 2. *ínsipit*]. Lat. *incipit*, 'begins', 3rd sing. pres. of *incipere*, 'to begin'. See **incipient** & **incept**. (Here) begins (book &c.).

incise, vb. trans. [1. insíz; 2. *insáiz*], fr. Fr. *inciser*, fr. Lat. *incīs-(um)*, P.P. type of *incīdere*, 'to cut into, cut through; to carve, engrave', fr. **in- (I.)** & *caedere*, 'to cut; to cut down, hew; to strike, kill'. See **Caesar** & **cement**. **1.** To cut into, make a cut or gash in. **2.** To carve, engrave: **a** *to incise a stone surface*; **b** *to incise a design &c. on a surface.*

incision, n. [1. insízhun; 2. *insížən*]. Prec. & **-ion**. **a** The act of incising; **b** that which results from incising; a cut, gash; specif., one made in a surgical operation.

incisive, adj. [1. insísiv; 2. *insáisiv*]. **incise** & **-ive**. **1.** (rare) Cutting into; sharp, keen, penetrating. **2. a** (of the mind &c.) Alert, acute, keen, penetrating, active; **b** (of modes of expression) vigorous; cutting, pointed, caustic, sarcastic.

incisively, adv. Prec. & **-ly**. In an incisive manner.

incisiveness, n. See prec. & **-ness**. The quality of being incisive in mind or expression.

incisor, n. [1. insízor; 2. *insáizə*], fr. Med. Lat. *incīsor*, 'cutting tooth'. **incise** & **-or**. Any one of front teeth, between canines, in upper or lower jaw of mammals.

incitation, n. [1. ìnsītáshun; 2. *ìnsaitéiʃən*]. See next word & **-ation**. Incitement, stirring up.

incite, vb. trans. [1. insít; 2. *insáit*], fr. Fr. *inciter*, fr. Lat. *incitāre*, 'to set in motion; to encourage, urge; to rouse, stir up', fr. **in- (I.)** & *citāre*, 'to put in motion, stimulate'. See **cite**. To stir up, inflame; to encourage, urge, rouse.

incitement, n. [1. insítment; 2. *insáitmənt*]. Prec. & **-ment**. **1.** The act of inciting; state of being incited. **2.** Something that incites; spur, stimulus, motive to action.

incivility, n. [1. ìnsivíliti; 2. *ìnsivíliti*], fr. Fr., fr. L. Lat. *incīvīlitāt-(em)*, 'incivility'. **in- (II.)** & **civility**. **1.** Discourtesy, impoliteness, unmannerliness. **2.** Discourteous act.

incivism, n. [1. ínsivizm; 2. *ínsivizəm*], fr. Fr. *incivisme*, fr. **in- (II.)** & Lat. *cīv-(is)*, 'citizen', see **civil**, & **-ism**. **a** Neglect of civic duties, uselessness as citizen; lack of good citizenship, disloyalty to the state; **b** specif., term applied to the principles of Frenchmen hostile to the French Revolution.

in-clearing, n. [1. ín klèring; 2. ín klìəriŋ]. Amount payable by bank on cheques presented through clearing-house.

inclemency, n. [1. inklémensi; 2. inklémənsi], fr. Lat. *inclēmentia*, 'rigour, harshness, severity'. **in-** (II.) & **clemency.** (of weather and climate) Quality of being inclement.

inclement, adj. [1. inklément; 2. inklémənt], fr. Lat. *inclēment-(em)*, 'severe, rough, harsh'. **in-** (II.) & **clement. 1.** (of weather, climate) Reverse of calm, fine, warm; rough, boisterous, cold, severe. **2.** (rare, of character &c.) Harsh, severe, lacking mercifulness.

inclinable, adj. [1. inklínabl; 2. inkláinəbl]. **incline** & **-able.** Followed by *to*: **a** Disposed, inclined, willing, ready; **b** favourable to, approving.

inclination, n. [1. inklináshun; 2. inklinéiʃən], fr. Lat. *inclīnātiōn-em*, 'bending, leaning, inclining, inclination, tendency'. Next word & **-ation. 1. a** Act or process of bending; a bowing, leaning, sloping; **b** state of being inclined; slope, slant. **2.** (geom.) Angle formed by the intersection of two lines or planes. **3. a** (of mental state or process) Tendency, willingness, disposition, propensity (to do something); **b** liking, fondness, partiality, preference, predilection (for something); **c** physical or bodily propensity or tendency: *an inclination to stoutness.*

incline (I.), vb. trans. & intrans. [1. inklín; 2. inkláin], fr. O. Fr. *encliner*, fr. Lat. *inclīnāre*, 'to cause to lean; to bend, bow; to be favourably disposed', fr. **in-** (I.) & *clīnāre*, 'to bend, incline'. See base under **decline, clinical, lean** (II.). **A.** trans. **1.** To cause to assume a position out of the vertical, to cause to slope, slant, lean; *inclined plane*, one up which a body too heavy to lift may be rolled, one of the mechanical powers. **2. a** To bend, bow, stoop: *to incline one's head* &c. Phr. *to incline one's ear (to)*, give one's attention to, listen to, be favourable to; **b** (of non-material process) to direct, dispose: '*incline our hearts to keep this law*'. **3.** (in P.P. after *to be, feel*) *To be, feel, inclined*, to be, feel, disposed, predisposed, drawn to; to tend, in feeling, thought, or habit: *to be inclined to think, believe; inclined to drink too much; inclined to grow fat* &c. **B.** intrans. **1.** To lean, slope, be on a slant, be out of the vertical. **2.** (of mental process) To tend, be disposed towards: *to incline to think that; to incline to an opinion.* **3.** To have an habitual tendency, be naturally disposed; to be prone: *to incline to leanness.*

incline (II.), n. [1. inklín, ínklīn; 2. inkláin, ínklain], fr. prec. An inclined plane; a slope, slant, in the ground; ascent or descent.

inclinometer, n. [1. inklinómeter; 2. inklinɔ́mitə]. **incline** & **-meter.** Apparatus furnished with magnetic needle, for measuring the force, and the direction relative to the plane of the horizon, of magnetic attraction exercised by the earth.

inclose, vb. trans. See **enclose.**

include, vb. trans. [1. inklóod; 2. inklúd], fr. Lat. *inclūd-(ere)*, 'to shut up, shut in, enclose; to include, insert, enclose', fr. **in-** (I.) & *claudere*, 'to shut'. See **close** (I.). **1.** To contain, comprise, embrace, have, as a part of the whole: *the greater includes the less; a good text-book ought to include a bibliography of the subject.* **2.** To reckon, regard, consider, take into account, as part of a whole, as member of a body &c.: *he includes everything in his survey; I include you among my friends.*

including, prep. [1. inklóoding; 2. inklúdiŋ]. Pres. Part. of **include.** Inclusive of, reckoning in; with, among these: *five members were present at the meeting, including the chairman.*

inclusion, n. [1. inklóozhun; 2. inklúžən], fr. Lat. *inclūsiōn-(em)*, 'a shutting up, confinement', fr. *inclūs-(um)*, P.P. type of *inclūd-(ere)*, 'to shut up' &c. See **include** & **-ion.** The act of including; state of being included.

inclusive, adj. [1. inklóosiv; 2. inklúsiv], fr. Med. Lat. *inclūsīv-(us)*, fr. Lat. *inclūs-(um)*, P.P. type of *inclūdere.* See prec. & **include** & **-ive. 1. a** Including, comprising, not omitting: *a party of ten, inclusive of the host;* **b** including the extremes, or limits stated: *chapters i. to v. inclusive; from January 1st to 31st inclusive.* **2.** Including, reckoning in, everything: *inclusive terms* (at hotel &c.).

inclusively, adv. Prec. & **-ly.** So as to include everything.

inclusiveness, n. See prec. & **-ness.** The state of being inclusive.

incognito, adj., n., & adv. [1. inkógnitō; 2. inkɔ́gnitou]. Ital. *incognito*, 'unknown', fr. Lat. *incognit-(us)*, fr. **in-** (II.) & *cognit-(us)*, P.P. type of *cognoscere*, 'to know, learn, recognize'. See **cognition. 1.** adj. Passing under an assumed name or character. **2.** n. Assumed name or character. **3.** adv. (abbr. *incog.*): under an assumed name or title: *the king travelled incognito.*

incognizable, adj. [1. inkó(g)nizabl; 2. inkɔ́(g)nizəbl]. **in-** (II.) & **cognizable.** Not capable of being perceived, apprehended, by the senses or mind.

incognizance, n. [1. inkó(g)nizans; 2. inkɔ́(g)nizəns]. **in-** (II.) & **cognizance.** The state of being incognizant.

incognizant, adj. [1. inkó(g)nizant; 2. inkɔ́(g)nizənt]. **in-** (II.) & **cognizant.** Not recognizing; unconscious, unaware (of).

incoherence, n. [1. inkōhérens; 2. inkouhíərəns]. **in-** (II.) & **coherence.** The state of being incoherent; incoherent utterance or ideas.

incoherent, adj. [1. inkōhérent; 2. inkouhíərənt]. **in-** (II.) & **coherent. a** (of ideas and expression) Lacking logical sequence; not coherent; rambling, disconnected; **b** (of person) exhibiting incoherence of thought or expression.

incoherently, adv. Prec. & **-ly.** In an incoherent manner.

incohesive, adj. [1. inkōhésiv; 2. inkouhísiv]. **in-** (II.) & **cohesive.** Not cohesive.

incombustibility, n. [1. inkumbustibíliti; 2. inkəmbastibíliti]. **in-** (II.) & **combustibility.** The quality of being incombustible.

incombustible, adj. [1. inkumbústibl; 2. inkəmbástibl]. **in-** (II.) & **combustible.** Not inflammable; incapable of burning.

income, n. [1. ínkum, íngkum; 2. ínkam, íŋkam, íŋkəm]. **in** (II.) & **come. 1.** (obs.) Entrance, coming-in. **2.** Money periodically received whether as rent, interest on property or investments, derived from commercial activities and operations, or paid as salary for performance of services; for purposes of taxation, classified as *earned* or *unearned income.*

incomer, n. [1. ínkúmer; 2. ínkámə]. **in** (II.) & **come** & **-er. a** One who enters or comes in; **b** an immigrant, settler; **c** successor.

income-tax, n. Tax levied on annual income.

incoming (I.), n. [1. ínkùming; 2. ínkàmiŋ]. **in** (II.) & **come** & **-ing. 1.** The act of coming in; entrance. **2.** (pl.) Revenue, income.

incoming (II.), adj. [1. ínkùming; 2. ínkàmiŋ]. **in-** (I.) & Pres. Part. of **come. 1.** Coming in, or back; returning: *the incoming tide.* **2.** Succeeding, following; just entering upon possession, office &c.: *the incoming tenant.* **3.** Coming, falling due, accruing: *incoming payments.*

incommensurability, n. [1. ínkumènsūrabíliti; 2. ínkəmènsjərəbíliti]. **in-** (II.) & **commensurability.** Quality of being incommensurable.

incommensurable (I.), adj. [1. inkuménsūrabl; 2. inkəménsjərəbl]. **in-** (II.) & **commensurable. 1. a** Not comparable with, not capable of being measured along with; having extreme inequality of size; **b** not deserving comparison with. **2.** Of quantities, magnitudes: **a** (of two quantities) having no common measure; **b** (of one quantity) irrational.

incommensurable (II.), n. fr. prec. A thing, amount &c. which is incommensurable with something else.

incommensurably, adv. Prec. & **-ly.** In an incommensurable manner.

incommensurate, adj. [1. inkuménsūrat; 2. inkəménsjərət]. **in-** (II.) & **commensurate. 1.** Unequal, inadequate, disproportionate (*with* or *to*). **2.** Incommensurable.

incommensurateness, n. Prec. & **-ness.** The quality of being incommensurate.

incommode, vb. trans. [1. inkumṓd; 2. inkəmóud], fr. Fr. *incommoder*, fr. Lat. *incommodāre*, 'to be inconvenient, troublesome', fr. **in-** (II.) & *commodāre*, 'to make suitable, adapt, accommodate', fr. *commod-(us)*, 'suitable, convenient'. See **commode** & further under **meditate.** To inconvenience, annoy, disturb, make uncomfortable.

incommodious, adj. [1. inkumṓdyus; 2. inkəmóudjəs]. **in-** (II.) & **commodious.** Not spacious, lacking adequate space; inconvenient, uncomfortable.

incommodiously, adv. Prec. & **-ly.** In an incommodious manner.

incommodiousness, n. See prec. & **-ness.** Quality of being incommodious.

incommunicability, n. [1. inkumūnikabíliti; 2. inkəmjùnikəbíliti]. **in-** (II.) & **communicability.** The quality of being incommunicable.

incommunicable, adj. [1. inkumūnikabl; 2. inkəmjúnikəbl]. **in-** (II.) & **communicable.** Not capable of being communicated to another.

incommunicableness, n. Prec. & **-ness.** The quality of being incommunicable.

incommunicably, adv. See prec. & **-ly.** So as to be incommunicable.

incommunicative, adj. [1. inkumūnikativ; 2. inkəmjúnikətiv]. **in-** (II.) & **communicative.** Not communicative; not ready to impart information; unwilling to express thought and feelings; reticent.

incommunicativeness, n. Prec. & **-ness.** Quality of being incommunicative.

incommutable, adj. [1. inkumūtabl; 2. inkəmjútəbl]. **in-** (II.) & **commutable.** Not capable of being exchanged; unchangeable.

incommutably, adv. Prec. & **-ly.** In an incommutable manner.

incompact, adj. [1. inkumpákt; 2. inkəmpǽkt]. **in-** (II.) & **compact.** Not compact.

incomparable, adj. [1. inkómparabl; 2. inkɔ́mpərəbl], fr. Lat. *incomparābil-(is)*, 'that cannot be equalled'. **in-** (II.) & **comparable. 1.** Not to be, not capable of being, compared. **2.** Without equal; peerless, matchless, unique.

incomparableness, n. Prec. & **-ness.** Quality of being incomparable.

incomparably, adv. See prec. & **-ly.** In an incomparable manner; beyond measure or comparison.

incompatibility, n. [1. ínkumpàtibíliti; 2. ínkəmpæ̀tibíliti]. **in-** (II.) & **compatibility.** Quality of being incompatible.

incompatible, adj. [1. inkumpátibl; 2. inkəmpǽtibl]. **in-** (II.) & **compatible. 1.** Disagreeing, opposed, in nature or temperament; inharmonious, discordant. **2.** Not consistent with, disagreeing with; logically opposed to.

incompetence, -cy, n. [1. inkómpetens(i); 2. inkɔ́mpitəns(i)]. **in-** (II.) & **competence** & **-cy.** The quality of being incompetent; powerlessness, inability, incapacity.

incompetent, adj. [1. inkómpetent; 2. inkɔ́mpitənt], fr. L. Lat. *incompetent-(em)*, 'insufficient'. **in-** (II.) & **competent. 1. a** Lacking requisite knowledge, skill, ability, for specified task: *incompetent as an administrator; an incompetent cook* &c.; **b** generally unskilful, incapable, ineffective, futile: *a thoroughly incompetent person;* **c** (of work, action &c.) displaying incompetence of author or performer: *an incompetent lecture, book; incompetent leadership, acting* &c. **2.** Legally unqualified.

incompetently, adv. Prec. & **-ly**. In an incompetent manner.

incomplete, adj. [1. inkumplḗt; 2. inkəmplít], fr. L. Lat. *incomplēt-(us)*, 'incomplete'. **in- (II.)** & **complete**. Not complete; **a** imperfect, defective; **b** not completed, not brought to state of perfection.

incompletely, adv. Prec. & **-ly**. Not completely, imperfectly.

incompleteness, n. See prec. & **-ness**. State of being incomplete.

incomprehensibility, n. [1. inkòmprehènsibíliti; 2. inkɔ̀mprihènsibíliti]. **in- (II.)** & **comprehensibility**. The quality of being incomprehensible.

incomprehensible, adj. [1. inkòmprehénsibl; 2. inkɔ̀mprihénsibl], fr. L. Lat. *incomprehensibil-(is)*, 'that cannot be seized; incomprehensible'. **in- (II.)** & **comprehensible**. **1.** Not capable of being grasped by the mind, not to be understood; unintelligible. **2.** Not capable of being limited, confined; illimitable, boundless, infinite; esp. as attribute of God; also as noun: '*not three incomprehensibles . . . but one incomprehensible*' (Athanasian Creed).

incomprehensibleness, n. Prec. & **-ness**. The quality of being incomprehensible.

incomprehensibly, adv. See prec. & **-ly**. In an incomprehensible manner.

incomprehension, n. [1. inkòmprehénshun; 2. inkɔ̀mprihénʃən]. **in- (II.)** & **comprehension**. Lack of comprehension.

incompressibility, n. [1. ínkomprèsibíliti; 2. ínkəmprèsibíliti]. **in- (II.)** & **compressibility**. The quality of being incompressible.

incompressible, adj. [1. inkumprésibl; 2. inkəmprésibl]. **in- (II.)** & **compressible**. Not capable of being compressed; hard, unyielding.

incomputable, adj. [1. inkumpū́tabl; 2. inkəmpjū́təbl]. **in- (II.)** & **computable**. Not capable of being computed.

inconceivability, n. [1. inkunsèvabíliti; 2. inkənsìvəbíliti]. **in- (II.)** & **conceivability**. Quality of being inconceivable.

inconceivable, adj. [1. inkunsḗvabl; 2. inkənsívəbl]. **in- (II.)** & **conceivable**. **a** Not capable of being conceived by the mind; unimaginable, unthinkable; **b** (colloq.) hard to believe; hence, very unlikely.

inconceivably, adv. Prec. & **-ly**. In an inconceivable manner; to an inconceivable extent.

inconcinnity, n. [1. inkunsíniti; 2. inkənsíniti]. **in- (II.)** & **concinnity**. Unsuitableness, incongruity; lack of concinnity; inelegance.

inconclusive, adj. [1. inkunklṓōsiv; 2. inkənklū́siv]. **in- (II.)** & **conclusive**. Not leading to a conclusion; not carrying conviction; indeterminate; not settling point under discussion.

inconclusively, adv. Prec. & **-ly**. In an inconclusive manner.

inconclusiveness, n. See prec. & **-ness**. Quality of being inconclusive.

incondensable, adj. [1. inkundénsabl; 2. inkəndénsəbl]. **in- (II.)** & **condensable**. Not capable of being condensed.

incondite, adj. [1. inkóndīt; 2. inkɔ́ndait], fr. Lat. *incondit-(um)*, 'unformed, uncouth, rude, artless', fr. **in- (II.)** & *condit-(um)*, P.P. type of *condere*, 'to put together, form into a whole, construct'. See **condition**. **a** (of liter. composition) Not well put together, badly constructed; **b** rough, unpolished.

inconformity, n. [1. inkunfórmiti; 2. inkənfɔ̄miti]. **in- (II.)** & **conformity**. Lack of conformity.

incongruity, n. [1. inkonggrṓōiti; 2. inkɔŋgrū́iti]. **in- (II.)** & **congruity**. **1.** Quality of being incongruous. **2.** Something that is incongruous.

incongruous, adj. [1. inkónggrōōus; 2. inkɔ́ŋgruəs], fr. Lat. *incongru-(us)*, 'inconsistent, unsuitable'. **in- (II.)** & **congruous**. **a** Inconsistent, not in keeping, with; **b** out of place, unsuitable, inappropriate.

incongruously, adv. Prec. & **-ly**. In an incongruous manner.

incongruousness, n. See prec. & **-ness**. Quality of being incongruous; incongruous thing or action.

inconsecutive, adj. [1. inkunsékūtiv; 2. inkənsékjutiv]. **in- (II.)** & **consecutive**. Not following in natural order; lacking consecutiveness.

inconsecutively, adv. Prec. & **-ly**. In an inconsecutive manner.

inconsecutiveness, n. See prec. & **-ness**. Quality of being inconsecutive.

inconsequence, n. [1. inkónsekwens; 2. inkɔ́nsikwəns], fr. L. Lat. *inconsequentia*, 'want of logical connexion'. **in- (II.)** & **consequence**. Quality of being inconsequent.

inconsequent, adj. [1. inkónsekwent; 2. inkɔ́nsikwənt], fr. Lat. *inconsequent-(em)*, 'not logically consequent'. **in- (II.)** & **consequent**. Without logical connexion, not following naturally; irrelevant, beside the mark.

inconsequential, adj. [1. inkònsekwénshl; 2. inkɔ̀nsikwénʃl]. **inconsequent** & **-ial**. Illogical, not following logically; inconsequent.

inconsequentially, adv. Prec. & **-ly**. In an inconsequential manner.

inconsequently, adv. [1. inkónsekwentli; 2. inkɔ́nsikwəntli]. **inconsequent** & **-ly**. In an inconsequent manner.

inconsiderable, adj. [1. inkunsíderabl; 2. inkənsídərəbl]. **in- (II.)** & **considerable**. **a** Not worth considering, unimportant; **b** of small proportions; small.

inconsiderate, adj. [1. inkunsíderat; 2. inkənsídərit], fr. Lat. *inconsiderāt-(us)*, 'thoughtless, inconsiderate'. **in- (II.)** & **considerate**. **a** Not showing regard for the wishes, feelings, of others; thoughtless; **b** ill-considered, rash.

inconsiderately, adv. Prec. & **-ly**. In an inconsiderate manner.

inconsiderateness, n. See prec. & **-ness**. Quality of being inconsiderate.

inconsideration, n. [1. inkunsideráshun; 2. inkənsidəréiʃən]. **inconsiderate** & **-ion**. (rare) Inconsiderateness.

inconsistency, n. [1. inkunsístensi; 2. inkənsístənsi]. **in- (II.)** & **consistency**. **a** Quality of being inconsistent; **b** something that is inconsistent.

inconsistent, adj. [1. inkunsístent; 2. inkənsístənt]. **in- (II.)** & **consistent**. **1.** Not consistent in kind or character, not agreeing; incompatible, not in keeping, (with). **2.** Not logically consistent; contradictory, not holding together: *an inconsistent narrative*. **3.** (of persons and character) Not consistent in principle; not showing uniformity of feeling, habit &c.; changeable.

inconsistently, adv. Prec. & **-ly**. In an inconsistent manner.

inconsolable, adj. [1. inkunsṓlabl; 2. inkənsóuləbl], fr. Lat. *inconsōlābil-(is)*, 'inconsolable'. **in- (II.)** & **consolable**. **a** (of person) Not to be consoled; **b** (of grief) not yielding to consolation.

inconsolably, adv. Prec. & **-ly**. In an inconsolable manner.

inconsonance, n. [1. inkónsunans; 2. inkɔ́nsənəns]. **in- (II.)** & **consonance**. The state of being inconsonant; inharmoniousness.

inconsonant, adj. [1. inkónsunant; 2. inkɔ́nsənənt]. **in- (II.)** & **consonant (I.)**. Not agreeing; inharmonious, inconsistent.

inconspicuous, adj. [1. inkunspíkūus; 2. inkənspíkjuəs], fr. L. Lat. *inconspicu-(us)*, 'inconspicuous'. **in- (II.)** & **conspicuous**. **a** Not easily seen, not attracting attention; specif. **b** (bot., of flowers) small and green.

inconspicuously, adv. Prec. & **-ly**. In an inconspicuous manner.

inconspicuousness, n. See prec. & **-ness**. Quality of being inconspicuous.

inconstancy, n. [1. inkónstansi; 2. inkɔ́nstənsi], fr. Lat. *inconstantia*, 'fickleness'. **in- (II.)** & **constancy**. Quality of being inconstant; **a** changeableness of character, fickleness; infidelity; **b** variability, lack of uniformity.

inconstant, adj. [1. inkónstant; 2. inkɔ́nstənt], fr. Lat. *inconstant-(em)*, 'changeable'. **in- (II.)** & **constant**. **1. a** Changeable in character and purpose, unsteadfast; vacillating, capricious; **b** changeable, not constant in feelings and affections; unfaithful. **2.** Subject to change, variable; not constant; irregular, alterable.

inconstantly, adv. Prec. & **-ly**. In an inconstant manner.

inconsumable, adj. [1. inkunsū́mabl; 2. inkənsjū́məbl]. **in- (II.)** & **consume** & **-able**. Not capable of being consumed.

incontestable, adj. [1. inkuntéstabl; 2. inkəntéstəbl]. **in- (II.)** & **contest** & **-able**. Not to be contested or disputed; undeniable.

incontestably, adv. Prec. & **-ly**. In an incontestable manner.

incontinence, -cy, n. [1. inkóntinens(i); 2. inkɔ́ntinəns(i)], fr. Lat. *incontinentia*, 'incontinence'. **in- (II.)** & **continence** & **-cy**. The quality of being incontinent; lack of restraint, inability to control; specif. **a** inordinate indulgence of sexual appetite, unchastity; **b** (med.) inability to restrain natural evacuations: *incontinency of urine*. Phr. *incontinence of speech*, loquacity.

incontinent (I.), adj. [1. inkóntinent; 2. inkɔ́ntinənt], fr. Lat. *incontinent-(em)*, 'incontinent'. **in- (II.)** & **continent (I.)**. **1.** Incapable of self-restraint; specif., given to unlawful indulgence of sexual passion; unchaste. **2.** (med.) Not capable of retaining natural evacuations.

incontinent (II.), adv. & adj., fr. O. Fr., fr. L. Lat. *incontinenti* (*tempore*), 'without interruption, instantly', fr. **in- (I.)** & *continent-(em)*, 'continual, uninterrupted', Pres. Part. of *continēre*, 'to hold, keep, together; to contain, enclose; to continue'. See **contain**. (archaic) **a** adv. Immediately, forthwith, straightway; **b** adj., immediate.

incontinently, adv. Prec. & **-ly**. Forthwith.

incontrovertible, adj. [1. inkòntrōvḗrtibl; 2. inkɔ̀ntrouvā́tibl]. **in- (II.)** & **controvert** & **-ible**. Not to be controverted or disputed; unquestionable, unassailable.

incontrovertibly, adv. Prec. & **-ly**. In an incontrovertible manner.

inconvenience (I.), n. [1. inkunvḗnyens; 2. inkənvínjəns], fr. O. Fr., fr. L. Lat. *inconvenientia*, 'incongruity, lack of harmony'. **in- (II.)** & **convenience**. **1.** The state of being inconvenient; lack of convenience, unsuitability; discomfort. **2.** Something that is inconvenient; cause of discomfort.

inconvenience (II.), vb. trans., fr. prec. To cause inconvenience to, render uncomfortable; to disturb.

inconvenient, adj. [1. inkunvḗnyent; 2. inkənvínjənt], fr. Fr., fr. Lat. *inconvenient-(em)*, 'unsuitable'. **in- (II.)** & **convenient**. **a** Not adapted to comfort, to easiness of action, &c.; causing trouble and difficulty; awkward, ill-arranged; **b** (archaic, in moral sense) unfitting, unbecoming.

inconveniently, adv. Prec. & **-ly**. In an inconvenient manner.

inconvertibility, n. [1. inkunvërtibíliti; 2. inkənvā̀tibíliti]. **in- (II.)** & **convertibility**. The state of being inconvertible.

inconvertible, adj. [1. inkunvḗrtibl; 2. inkənvā́tibl]. **in- (II.)** & **convertible**. **a** Not convertible; unexchangeable for something else; **b** specif. (of paper-money) not capable of being exchanged for coin.

inconvertibly, adv. Prec. & **-ly**. In an inconvertible manner.

inconvincible, adj. [1. inkunvínsibl; 2. inkənvínsibl]. **in- (II.)** & **convincible**. Not capable of being convinced.

inco-ordination, n. [1. inkōōrdináshun; 2. inkouɔ̄dinéiʃən]. **in- (II.)** & **co-ordination**. Lack of co-ordination.

incorporate (I.), adj. [1. inkórporit; 2. inkɔ̄pərit]. Lat. *incorporātus*. See **in- (II.)** & **corporate**. Incorporeal, spiritual, not bodily.

incorporate (II.), adj., fr. L. Lat. *incorporāt-(um)*, P.P. type of *incorporāre*, 'to incorporate', fr. in- (I.) & *corporāre*, 'to make into a body, furnish with a body', fr. *corpor-*, stem of *corpus*, 'a body'. See **corpus**. **1.** United, combined, in one body, group, or corporation. **2.** Constituted as a legal corporation.

incorporate (III.), vb. trans. & intrans. [1. inkórporāt; 2. inkɔ́pəreit]. See prec. **A.** trans. **1.** To include, combine, assimilate, into a unity: *a book which incorporates the newest information.* **2. a** To add, join (a person), to a body or society; make a member of: *to be incorporated a member of a college*; **b** to blend, mingle with: *to incorporate a chemical substance with others.* **3.** To form into, recognize as, a legal corporation. **B.** intrans. To be capable of blending in with; to mix, unite, with.

incorporating, adj. [1. inkórporàting; 2. inkɔ́pərèitiŋ], fr. Pres. Part. of **incorporate** (III.). (of languages) Expressing modifications of meaning by the incorporation of formative elements into the body of words.

incorporation, n. [1. inkòrporáshun; 2. inkɔ̀pəréiʃən]. Prec. & **-ion**. Act or process of incorporating; state of being incorporated.

incorporative, adj. [1. inkórporativ; 2. inkɔ́pərətiv]. **incorporate** (II.) & **-ive**. Tending to incorporate.

incorporator, n. [1. inkórporātor; 2. inkɔ́pəreitə]. **incorporate** (III.) & **-or**. Member of one university who is incorporated in the membership of another.

incorporeal, adj. [1. inkorpóreal; 2. inkɔ̄pɔ́riəl]. See **in-** (II.) & **corporeal**. **1.** Having no bodily form; spiritual, unsubstantial, immaterial. **2.** Pertaining to incorporeal beings. **3.** (law) Of something not having physical existence, but existing as a right attached to corporeal property: *incorporeal hereditaments.*

incorporeally, adv. Prec. & **-ly**. In an incorporeal manner.

incorporeity, n. [1. inkorporḗiti; 2. inkɔ̄pəríiti]. See **incorporeal** & **-ity**. The quality of being incorporeal.

incorrect, adj. [1. inkorékt; 2. inkərékt], fr. Lat. *incorrect-(us)*, 'uncorrected, unfinished'. **in-** (II.) & **correct**. **1. a** Not adhering strictly to rules or a model: *incorrect drawing, incorrect grammatical construction*; **b** not in accordance with facts; inaccurate, wrong: *an incorrect statement.* **2.** Not in accordance with a recognized standard; not conforming to custom or convention: *incorrect behaviour.*

incorrectly, adv. Prec. & **-ly**. In an incorrect manner.

incorrectness, n. See prec. & **-ness**. The state of being incorrect; a inaccuracy; **b** breach of convention or decorum.

incorrigibility, n. [1. inkòrijibíliti; 2. inkɔ̀ridžibíliti]. See next word & **-ity**. The state of being incorrigible.

incorrigible, adj. [1. inkórijibl; 2. inkɔ́ridžibl], fr. L. Lat. *incorrigibil-(is)*, 'not to be improved'. **in-** (II.) & **corrigible**. (of person, character, quality, behaviour) Not capable of correction, amendment, improvement, or reform.

incorrigibly, adv. Prec. & **-ly**. In an incorrigible manner.

incorruptibility, n. [1. inkuruptibíliti; 2. inkəraptibíliti]. See next word & **-ity**. The quality of being incorruptible.

incorruptible, adj. & n. [1. inkurúptibl; 2. inkəráptibl], fr. Lat. *incorruptibil-(is)*, 'incorruptible'. **in-** (II.) & **corruptible**. **1.** adj. **a** Not liable to decay; imperishable; **b** not to be influenced by bribery and corruption. **2.** n. (archaic) Incorruptible thing or substance.

incorruptibly, adv. Prec. & **-ly**. In an incorruptible manner.

incorruption, n. [1. inkurúpshun; 2. inkərápʃən], fr. Lat. *incorruptiōn-(em)*, 'incorruptibility'. **in-** (II.) & **corruption**. Nonliability to decay; imperishability.

incrassate, adj. [1. inkrásat; 2. inkrǽsət], fr. Lat. *incrassāt-(um)*, P.P. type of *incrassāre*, 'to make thick, fat, stout', fr. **in-** (I.) & *crass-(us)*, 'thick, solid'. See **crass**. (zool., bot.) Thick, stout, swollen.

increase (I.), vb. intrans. & trans. [1. inkrḗs; 2. inkríːs]. M.E. *encrēsen*, fr. O. Fr. *encreiss-*, stem of *encreistre*, fr. Lat. *incrēscere*, 'to grow; to augment, increase', fr. **in-** (I.) & *crēscere*, 'to grow'. See **crescent**. **A.** intrans. **1. a** To grow larger in bulk or amount; **b** to grow in numbers, become more numerous, to multiply. **2.** (of qualities) To become more pronounced, to be intensified: *one's vanity, wisdom, skill &c. increases.* **B.** trans. **1.** To make greater, extend: *to increase one's dominions, wealth.* **2.** (with reference to qualities &c.) **a** To make more pronounced, aggravate, intensify; **b** in various Phrs. *to increase (one's) speed*, go, move, faster; *to increase one's pace*, walk faster; *increase one's efforts*, work harder, make greater exertions.

increase (II.), n. [1. ínkrēs; 2. ínkrīs], fr. prec. **1.** Growth, enlargement, multiplication, enhancement, in size, amount, numbers, intensity &c.: *a steady increase in the population.* Phr. *on the increase*, growing, increasing. **2.** Amount by which a thing increases: *his weight showed an increase of 3 lbs. in a month.* **3.** (archaic) Something that has grown; crops: *the earth yields her increase.*

increasingly, adv. [1. inkrḗsingli; 2. inkrísiŋli]. Pres. Part. of **increase** (I.) & **-ly**. More and more; to an increasing extent or degree.

incredibility, n. [1. inkrèdibíliti; 2. inkrèdibíliti]. See next word & **-ity**. The quality of being incredible.

incredible, adj. [1. inkrédibl; 2. inkrédibl], fr. Lat. *incrēdibil-(is)*, 'incredible'. **in-** (II.) & **credible**. **1.** Not to be, incapable of being, believed; passing belief. **2.** (colloq.) Marvellous, extraordinary, remarkable.

incredibly, adv. Prec. & **-ly**. To an incredible degree; used colloq. as mere intensive, very: *incredibly easy, lazy, offensive &c.*

incredulity, n. [1. inkredúliti; 2. inkridjúliti], fr. L. Lat. *incrēdulitāt-(em)*, 'incredulity'. **in-** (II.) & **credulity**. The state of being incredulous.

incredulous, adj. [1. inkrédūlus; 2. inkrédjuləs], fr. L. Lat. *incrēdul-(us)*, 'unbelieving'. **in-** (II.) & **credulous**. **a** Unbelieving; finding difficulty in believing: sceptical; **b** expressing unbelief: *an incredulous laugh.*

incredulously, adv. Prec. & **-ly**. In an incredulous manner.

increment, n. [1. íngkrement; 2. íŋkrimənt], fr. Lat. *incrēment-(um)*, 'growth, increase', fr. *incrē-(scere)*, 'to grow'. See **increase** & **-ment**. **1.** Act or process of increasing; growth, increase. **2.** The amount by which a thing increases; specif. **a** profit, increase, gain; **b** (math.) regular amount of increase of variable quantity.

incriminate, vb. trans. [1. inkríminãt; 2. inkrímineit], fr. Med. Lat. *incrīmināt-(um)*, P.P. type of *incrīmināre*, 'to incriminate', fr. **in-** (I.) & *crīmināre*, 'to accuse'. See **criminate**. **1.** To accuse, make a charge against, attribute a crime to. **2.** To indicate guilt of, make guilt of appear probable, render liable to accusation; (often reflex.): *to incriminate oneself*, as by admissions &c.

incriminating, adj. [1. inkríminãting; 2. inkrímineitiŋ], fr. Pres. Part. of prec. Tending to incriminate.

incriminatory, adj. [1. inkríminaturi; 2. inkríminətəri]. Prec. & **-ory**. Tending, serving, to incriminate.

incroach, vb. intrans. See **encroach**.

incrustation, n. [1. inkrustáshun; 2. inkrastéiʃən], fr. L. Lat. *incrustātiōn-(em)*, 'covering (of walls &c.) with plaster'. **encrust** & **-ation**. **1.** The act of encrusting; state of being encrusted. **2. a** Outer coat, crust, deposit; **b** inlay, mosaic facing.

incubate, vb. trans. & intrans. [1. ínkūbāt; 2. ínkjubeit], fr. Lat. *incubāt-(um)*, P.P. type of *incubāre*, 'to lie, sit; to sit on eggs, brood', fr. **in-** (I.) & *cubāre*, 'to lie down'. See **cubicle**. **A.** trans. **1. a** (of bird) To hatch, develop (eggs) for hatching, by sitting on them; **b** to hatch (eggs) by artificial heat. **2.** (fig.) To meditate upon, bring to maturity, hatch (schemes &c.). **B.** intrans. **a** To sit on eggs; **b** (of eggs) to undergo process of incubation.

incubation, n. [1. inkūbáshun; 2. inkjubéiʃən], fr. Lat. *incubātiōn-(em)*, 'a sitting on eggs, brooding'. Prec. & **-ion**. **1.** The act or process of incubating; state of being incubated. **2.** (pathol.) Stage through which disease-germs pass, or a disease itself passes, between the moment of infection and the development of the first symptoms.

incubative, adj. [1. ínkūbātiv; 2. ínkjubèitiv]. **incubate** & **-ive**. Pertaining to incubation.

incubator, n. [1. ínkūbātor; 2. ínkjubeitə]. **incubate** & **-or**. Artificially heated apparatus, **a** for hatching eggs; **b** for rearing prematurely born infants; **c** for developing bacteria.

incubatory, adj. [1. ínkūbàturi; 2. ínkjubèitəri]. **incubate** & **-ory**. Incubative.

incubus, n. [1. ínkūbus; 2. ínkjubəs]. L. Lat. *incubus*, 'nightmare', fr. *incub-(āre)*, 'to lie, lie down'. See **incubate**. **1. a** Evil spirit supposed to materialize and to obsess sleeping persons; **b** bad dream, nightmare. **2.** Tedious, burdensome, oppressive, person or thing that cannot be shaken off or got rid of.

inculcate, vb. trans. [1. ínkulkāt; 2. ínkalkeit], fr. Lat. *inculcāt-(um)*, P.P. type of *inculcāre*, 'to tread down; press, stuff, in; to urge, impress, upon', fr. **in-** (I.) & *calcāre*, 'to tread on, trample on', fr. *calc-*, stem of *calx*, 'heel'. See **calceolaria**. To impress, implant, instil, establish firmly, in the mind of another; to enforce, urge upon: *to inculcate a doctrine, an idea, obedience, patience &c.*

inculcation, n. [1. inkulkáshun; 2. inkalkéiʃən]. Prec. & **-ion**. The act of inculcating.

inculpate, vb. trans. [1. ínkulpāt; 2. ínkalpeit], fr. **in-** (I.) & Lat. *culpāt-(um)*, P.P. type of *culpāre*, 'to reproach, blame, censure'. See **culpable**. **1.** To accuse, make a charge against; to censure, blame. **2.** (of circumstances, evidence &c.) To involve in, associate (person) with, a crime, or accusation of crime; to incriminate.

inculpation, n. [1. inkulpáshun; 2. inkalpéiʃən]. Prec. & **-ion**. The act of inculpating.

incult, adj. [1. inkúlt; 2. inkált], fr. Lat. *incult-(us)*, 'untilled; unpolished, rough; unadorned', fr. **in-** (II.) & *cult-(um)*, P.P. type of *colere*, 'to till'. See **cult**. (rare or archaic) **1.** (of land) Untilled, uncultivated. **2.** (of person, manners, products of intellect) Rough, unpolished, unrefined, inelegant.

incumbency, n. [1. inkúmbensi; 2. inkámbənsi]. **incumbent** (II.) & **-cy**. **1.** The fact of holding, tenure of, period of tenure of, an ecclesiastical benefice. **2.** An ecclesiastical benefice.

incumbent (I.), n. [1. inkúmbent; 2. inkámbənt]. See next word. **a** One who holds an ecclesiastical benefice; **b** (more rarely) holder of any office.

incumbent (II.), adj., fr. Lat. *incumbent-(em)*, Pres. Part. of *incumbere*, 'to lie, lean, recline, upon; to apply oneself to, pay attention to', fr. **in-** (I.) & *cumbere*, 'to lie'; cp. *cubāre*, 'to lie down'. See **cubicle**. **1.** (archaic) Lying, resting, upon: '*incumbent on the dusky air*' (of Satan) (Milton, 'P. L.'). **2.** *Incumbent upon*, resting upon one as an obligation, due from one as a duty; morally obligatory.

incunabula, n. pl. [1. inkūnábūla; 2. inkjūnǽbjulə]. Lat. *incūnābula*, 'swaddling-clothes; the cradle; childhood; origin, beginning', fr. **in-** (I.) & *cūnābula* (pl.), 'cradle', fr. *cūnae* (pl.), 'cradle', fr. **koinā*. See base under **civic, hide** (measure of land), **home**. **1.** The beginning, origin, first stages, of anything. Specif. **2.** Early printed books; books printed before 1500.

incur, vb. trans. [1. inkḗr; 2. inkə́ː], fr. Lat. *incurr-(ere)*, 'to run towards, rush at, assail', fr. **in-** (I.) & *currere*, 'to run'. See **current**.

To run into, bring upon oneself, meet with, become liable to: *to incur debt, loss* &c.

incurability, n. [1. inkûrabíliti; 2. *i*nkjɔ̄r-əb*i*l*i*ti]. See next word & **-ity**. The quality of being incurable.

incurable, adj. & n. [1. inkûrabl; 2. *i*nkjɔ̄r-əbl], fr. L. Lat. *incūrābil-(is)*, 'incurable', fr. **in- (II.)** & **curable**. **1.** adj. Not capable of being cured, ameliorated, or corrected; not yielding to treatment; inveterate: *an incurable disease, habit* &c. **2.** n. Person suffering from an incurable complaint.

incurableness, n. Prec. & **-ness**. The quality or state of being incurable.

incurably, adv. See prec. & **-ly**. In an incurable manner.

incuriosity, n. [1. inkùriósiti; 2. *i*nkjɔ̄r*i*ós*i*ti]. **in- (II.)** & **curiosity**. Lack of curiosity.

incurious, adj. [1. inkûrius; 2. *i*nkjɔ̄r*i*əs], fr. Lat. *incūriōs-(us)*, 'careless, indifferent, negligent'. **in- (II.)** & **curious**. **1.** (archaic) Careless, heedless, negligent, indifferent. **2.** Not curious or inquisitive; not seeking, indifferent to, information. **3.** Devoid of interest, uninteresting; chiefly *not incurious*.

incuriously, adv. Prec. & **-ly**. In an incurious manner.

incursion, n. [1. inkérshun; 2. *i*nkʌ́ʃən], fr. Lat. *incursiōn-(em)*, 'assault, inroad', fr. *incurs-(um)*, P.P. type of *incurrere*, 'to attack'. See **incur**. Attack, invasion, inroad, raid.

incursive, adj. [1. inkérsiv; 2. *i*nkʌ́s*i*v], fr. Lat. *incurs-(um)*, P.P. type of *incurrere*, 'to attack'. See prec. & **-ive**. Assailing, invading.

incurvation, n. [1. inkërváshun; 2. *i*nkʌ̄véiʃən], fr. L. Lat. *incurvātiōn-(em)*, 'a bending, curving', fr. *incurvāt-(um)*, P.P. type of *incurvāre*, 'to bend, crook, curve'. See next word. The act of incurving; state of being incurved.

incurve, vb. trans. [1. inkérv; 2. *i*nkʌ́v], fr. Lat. *incurv-(āre)*, 'to bend, curve, crook', fr. **in- (I.)** & *curvāre*, 'to bend, curve'. See **curve**. To bend, curve, inwards: *an incurved beak.*

incus, n. [1. ínkus; 2. *í*nkəs]. Lat. *incūs*, 'anvil', fr. *incūd-*, cp. *incūdere*, 'to forge with a hammer', fr. **in- (I.)** & **caudere*, 'to strike, beat; to forge'; cp. *caudex*, 'split wood; wood block; tablet'. See **codex**. A bone in the middle ear, to which vibrations are transmitted by the malleus; called also *anvil bone.*

incuse (I.), adj. & n. [1. inkúz; 2. *i*nkjúz], fr. Lat. *incūs-(um)*, P.P. type of *incūdere*, 'to forge with a hammer'. See **incus**. **1.** adj. Stamped, hammered in, impressed by stamping. **2.** n. Impression stamped on coin &c.

incuse (II.), vb. trans. See prec. **1.** To impress, stamp (a mark, design &c.), on a coin &c. **2.** To mark (a coin &c.) by stamping a design &c. on it.

indaba, n. [1. indáhbah; 2. *i*nd*á*bā]. Bantu, 'business, affair.' A tribal council or meeting among the Zulus and other Bantu tribes of S. Africa.

indebted, adj. [1. indéted; 2. *i*ndét*i*d], fr. P.P. of M.E. *endetten*, 'to put under an obligation', fr. O. Fr. *endetter*; w. substitution of Lat. *in-* for **en-**, & *dette*, 'debt'. See **debt**. **1.** Owing money, being in debt. **2.** Under moral obligation; owing gratitude, being obliged: *to be greatly indebted to one for help, kindness* &c.

indebtedness, n. Prec. & **-ness**. The state of being indebted.

indecency, n. [1. indésensi; 2. *i*ndísəns*i*], fr. Lat. *indecentia*, 'impropriety'. **in- (II.)** & **decency**. **1.** The quality of being indecent. **2.** Something that is indecent; impropriety; obscenity.

indecent, adj. [1. indésent; 2. *i*ndísənt], fr. Lat. *indecent-(em)*, 'unseemly, immodest, improper'. **in- (II.)** & **decent**. **1.** Unbecoming, unseemly, improper, not fitting or suitable: *indecent haste.* **2.** Immodest, obscene: *indecent story, picture* &c.

indecently, adv. Prec. & **-ly**. In an indecent manner.

indeciduous, adj. [1. indesídūus; 2. *i*nd*i*síd-juəs]. **in- (II.)** & **deciduous**. Not deciduous.

indecipherable, adj. [1. indesíferabl; 2. *i*nd*i*sáifərəbl]. **in- (II.)** & **decipherable**. Not capable of being deciphered; not to be read; illegible.

indecision, n. [1. indesízhun; 2. *i*nd*i*síʒən]. **in- (II.)** & **decision**. Want of decision; irresoluteness, hesitation.

indecisive, adj. [1. indesísiv; 2. *i*nd*i*sáis*i*v]. **in- (II.)** & **decisive**. **1.** Not settling a thing definitely; inconclusive. **2.** Hesitating, undecided, irresolute.

indecisively, adv. Prec. & **-ly**. In an indecisive manner.

indecisiveness, n. See prec. & **-ness**. The quality of being indecisive.

indeclinable, adj. [1. indeklínabl; 2. *i*nd*i*kláinəbl]. **in- (II.)** & **declinable**. (gram.) Not capable of being declined; uninflected.

indecomposable, adj. [1. indēkumpózabl; 2. *i*ndīkəmpóuzəbl]. **in- (II.)** & **decompose** & **-able**. Not capable of being split up or separated into its constituent parts.

indecorous, adj. [1. indekórus; 2. *i*nd*i*kɔ́rəs], fr. Lat. *indecōr-(us)*, 'unseemly', & **-ous**. **in- (II.)** & **decorous**. Not in accordance with good taste or manners; unbecoming.

indecorously, adv. Prec. & **-ly**. In an indecorous manner.

indecorousness, n. See prec. & **-ness**. The quality of being indecorous.

indecorum, n. [1. indekórum; 2. *i*nd*i*kɔ́rəm]. Lat., neut. form of *indecōrus*, 'unseemly'. **in- (II.)** & **decorum**. **1.** The quality of being indecorous. **2.** Indecorous behaviour, proceeding &c.; impropriety.

indeed (I.), adv. [1. indéd; 2. *i*ndíd]. **in (I.)** & **deed**. **1.** In fact, in reality, in truth. **2.** Giving emphasis: *very cold indeed; yes, indeed!* **3.** Concessive; it is true; I grant, admit: *I may, indeed, be wrong.*

indeed (II.), interj., fr. prec. Expressing incredulity, indignation, irony, interrogation &c.

indefatigability, n. [1. indefàtigabíliti; 2. *i*nd*i*fætigəbíl*i*ti]. See next word & **-ity**. The quality of being indefatigable.

indefatigable, adj. [1. indefátigabl; 2. *i*nd*i*fǽtigəbl], fr. Lat. *indēfatigābil-(is)*, 'that cannot be wearied', fr. **in- (II.)** & *dēfatīg-(āre)*, 'to tire, exhaust', fr. **de-** & *fatīgāre*, 'to weary'. See **fatigue** & **-able**. Not capable of being wearied; unwearying, untiring, unremitting.

indefatigably, adv. Prec. & **-ly**. In an indefatigable manner.

indefeasibility, n. [1. indefèzibíliti; 2. *i*nd*i*fìz*i*bíl*i*ti]. See next word & **-ity**. The quality of being indefeasible.

indefeasible, adj. [1. indefézibl; 2. *i*nd*i*fízibl]. **in- (II.)** & **defeasible**. Not liable to be annulled, forfeited, taken away: *indefeasible rights.*

indefeasibly, adv. Prec. & **-ly**. In an indefeasible manner.

indefectible, adj. [1. indeféktibl; 2. *i*nd*i*fékt*i*bl]. **in- (II.)** & **defect** & **-ible**. **1.** Not liable to become imperfect; unfailing. **2.** Not liable to defects; perfect.

indefensibility, n. [1. indefensibíliti; 2. *i*nd*i*fensib*í*l*i*ti]. See next word & **-ity**. The quality of being indefensible.

indefensible, adj. [1. indefénsibl; 2. *i*nd*i*féns*i*bl]. **in- (II.)** & **defensible**. **1.** Not capable of being defended, liable to capture by force of arms. **2.** (of conduct, argument &c.) Not capable of being justified; inexcusable.

indefensibly, adv. Prec. & **-ly**. In an indefensible manner; so as to be indefensible.

indefinable, adj. [1. indefínabl; 2. *i*nd*i*fáinəbl]. **in- (II.)** & **definable**. Not admitting of definition; vague, indescribable: *an indefinable air of distinction.*

indefinably, adv. Prec. & **-ly**. In an indefinable manner.

indefinite, adj. [1. indéfinit; 2. *i*ndéf*i*n*i*t], fr. L. Lat. *indēfinīt-(us)*, 'indefinite'. **in- (II.)** & **definite**. **1.** Not having clearly or sharply defined limits or outlines; not precise; **a** (of sensuous impressions) indistinct, blurred, of indeterminate character; **b** (of ideas &c.) not clear and precise; vague, ill-defined; **c** (of number, amount, size) not specifically stated, not strictly limited, undetermined; **d** (of modes of expression) lacking clearness and precision. **2.** (gram.) **a** (of pron. and adj.) Not giving exact indication of the number, person &c. to which they refer; e.g. *some, any, few*; *indefinite article*, **a**, an; **b** (of vb. inflexion) not specifying whether the action or occurrence is completed, or still continuing at the moment at which it is referred to.

indefinitely, adv. Prec. & **-ly**. In an indefinite manner; to an indefinite extent.

indefiniteness, n. See prec. & **-ness**. The quality of being indefinite.

indefinitude, n. [1. indefínitūd; 2. *i*nd*i*fín*i*tjūd]. **indefinite** & **-tude**. Indefiniteness.

indehiscent, adj. [1. indehísent; 2. *i*nd*i*hísənt]. **in- (II.)** & **dehiscent**. (bot., of seed-vessels) Not bursting or splitting open.

indelibility, n. [1. indèlibíliti; 2. *i*ndèl*i*bíl*i*ti]. See next word & **-ity**. Quality of being indelible.

indelible, adj. [1. indélibl; 2. *i*ndél*i*bl], fr. Lat. *indēlēbil-(is)*, 'indelible, imperishable', fr. **in- (II.)** & *dēl-(ēre)*, 'to abolish, destroy; blot out, efface'. See **delete** & **-ible**. **a** (physical sense) Not capable of being erased, effaced, blotted out; **b** producing an indelible mark: *indelible pencil*; also **c** (of non-material things) not to be done away: *indelible disgrace, shame, impression* &c.

indelibly, adv. Prec. & **-ly**. In an indelible manner.

indelicacy, n. [1. indélikasi; 2. *i*ndél*i*kəs*i*]. **in- (II.)** & **delicacy**. **a** Quality of being indelicate; **b** indelicate action, behaviour, utterance &c.; impudicity.

indelicate, adj. [1. indélikat; 2. *i*ndél*i*k*i*t]. **in- (II.)** & **delicate**. Lacking delicacy of feeling; specif., offending against modesty and decency; unrefined, coarse; suggestive of immodesty.

indelicately, adv. Prec. & **-ly**. In an indelicate manner.

indemnification, n. [1. indèmnifikáshun; 2. *i*ndèmn*i*f*i*kéiʃən], fr. Lat. *indemni-(s)*, 'uninjured'. See next word & **-fication**. The act of indemnifying; state of being indemnified.

indemnify, vb. trans. [1. indémnifī; 2. *i*ndémn*i*fai], fr. Lat. *indemni-(s)*, 'uninjured', fr. **in- (II.)** & *damn-(um)*, 'loss, injury'. See **damn** & **-fy**. **1.** To make safe, secure, against; prevent liability to: *to indemnify one from, against, loss.* **2.** To give legal security against, give freedom from responsibility or penalty for: *to indemnify one for an action.* **3.** To compensate, make up to, make good: *to indemnify one for loss* &c.

indemnity, n. [1. indémniti; 2. *i*ndémn*i*ti], fr. Fr. *indemnité*, fr. L. Lat. *indemnitāt-(em)*, 'security from damage, loss', fr. *indemn-(is)*, 'uninjured'. See prec. & **-ity**. **1.** Safety, security, from, non-liability for, loss, injury, damage &c. **2.** Legal security from blame, penalty, punishment &c., for an action. **3.** Compensation for loss or damage. **4.** **a** Amount paid as compensation for loss, damage &c.; esp. **b** sum demanded as compensation by victorious nation &c. at conclusion of war.

indemonstrable, adj. [1. indémunstrabl, indemónstrabl; 2. *i*ndémənstrəbl, *i*nd*i*mɔ́nstrəbl]. **in- (II.)** & **demonstrable**. Incapable of demonstration.

indent (I.), vb. trans. & intrans. [1. indént; 2. *i*ndént], fr. Fr. *indenter*, fr. **in- (I.)** & Lat. *dent-(em)*, 'a tooth'. See **denti-**. **A.** trans. **1.** **a** To cut pointed pieces from the edge of, notch; **b** to make curves, recesses, in, carve out: *an indented coast-line.* **2.** **a** To cut (a document drawn up in duplicate) in two along a zigzag line, so as to form an 'indenture'; **b** to draw up in duplicate. **3.** (print.) To print (first line of paragraph &c.) further from left-hand margin than remaining lines of paragraph &c., or further than is normal. **B.** intrans. To present an official demand for, make requisition for, usually by means of a written order of which a duplicate is retained: *to indent upon a person, stores &c. for goods.*

indent (II.), n. [1. indént, índent; 2. indént, índent], fr. prec. **1.** A cut, notch, indentation. **2.** Indented document, indenture. **3.** Indenting, official demand, for goods &c. **4.** Commercial order for goods (esp. for abroad).

indent (III.), vb. trans. [1. indént; 2. indént]. **in-** (I.) & **dent**. **1.** To make a dent, depression, small hollow, in. **2.** To impress, imprint, stamp (a mark &c.).

indent (IV.), n. [1. índent; 2. índent], fr. prec. Small hollow, depression, dent.

indentation, n. [1. indentâshun; 2. indentéiʃən]. **indent** (I.) & **-ation**. **1.** The act of indenting; state of being indented. **2. a** Space left as by cutting out of pointed piece from edge; a notch, cut; **b** an inward curve, recess.

indention, n. [1. indénshun; 2. indénʃən]. **indent** (I.) & **-ion**. **1.** (print.) The act of indenting; state of being indented. **2.** Indentation.

indenture (I.), n. [1. indénchur; 2. indéntʃə], fr. O. Fr. *endenture*. **indent** (I.) & **-ure**. **1.** An indented document; one cut into two parts along a zigzag line, as a means of future identification. Hence, **2.** Any document, deed, contract, drawn up in duplicate and sealed; esp. contract binding apprentice to employer. **Phr.** *to take up, be out of, one's indentures,* complete one's apprenticeship. **3.** Indentation; notch.

indenture (II.), vb. trans., fr. prec. To make an agreement, contract, with, bind as apprentice by means of an indenture.

independence, n. [1. indepéndens; 2. indipéndəns]. **in-** (II.) & **dependence**. **1.** The state or quality of being independent. **2.** An independent income.

independency, n. [1. indepéndensi; 2. indipéndənsi]. **in-** (II.) & **dependency**. **1.** An independent state. **2.** (cap.) Congregationalism.

independent (I.), adj. [1. indepéndent; 2. indipéndənt]. **in-** (II.) & **dependent**. **1.** Not subject to the control of another; not dependent or subordinate; able to act on one's own authority; not having to rely on another person or thing: *independent of authority; a motor-car makes one independent of trains.* **2.** Unwilling to be subject to, or under obligation to, another; resenting control; shunning advice: *rather an independent young woman.* **3.** Uninfluenced by any other person or thing; standing by itself; not depending on, not related to, anything else: *independent proof, witness, account.* **4. a** (of income) Large enough to obviate the necessity for owner to earn his living; **b** (of persons) (i.) having such an income: *an independent gentleman*; (ii.) not dependent on another for support; either possessing or earning means of support: *his elder sons are now quite independent (of their father).*

independent (II.), n., fr. prec. **1.** Person who acts without professing allegiance to any party in politics &c. **2.** (cap.) A Congregationalist.

independently, adv. **independent** (I.) & **-ly**. In an independent manner.

indescribability, n. [1. indeskrîbabíliti; 2. indiskraibəbíliti]. See next word & **-ity**. The quality of being indescribable.

indescribable, adj. [1. indeskríbabl; 2. indiskráibəbl]. **in-** (II.) & **describable**. **1.** Making too vague an impression on the mind or senses to allow of adequate description, or definition; indefinable: *an indescribable sensation.* **2.** Possessing some quality in a degree too great to be described; too intense &c. to be described: *indescribable charm; indescribable sufferings.*

indescribably, adv. Prec. & **-ly**. In an indescribable manner; to an indescribable degree.

indestructibility, n. [1. indestrùktibíliti; 2. indistràktibíliti]. See next word & **-ity**. The quality of being indestructible.

indestructible, adj. [1. indestrúktibl; 2. indistráktibl]. **in-** (II.) & **destructible**. Not capable of being destroyed.

indestructibly, adv. Prec. & **-ly**. In an indestructible manner; so as to be indestructible.

indeterminable, adj. [1. indetẽrminabl; 2. inditə́minəbl], fr. L. Lat. *indēterminābil-(is)*, 'that cannot be defined'. **in-** (II.) & **determinable**. Not capable of being ascertained, fixed, determined.

indeterminate, adj. [1. indetẽrminat; 2. inditə́minit], fr. L. Lat. *indēterminăt-(us)*, 'undefined'. **in-** (II.) & **determinate**. **1.** Not determined or fixed; uncertain, doubtful, vague; of undetermined character &c. **2.** (math., of quantity) Not fixed in value.

indeterminately, adv. Prec. & **-ly**. In an indeterminate manner.

indeterminateness, n. See prec. & **-ness**. The quality of being indeterminate.

indetermination, n. [1. indetẽrminâshun; 2. inditəminéiʃən]. **in-** (II.) & **determination**. **1.** The quality of being indeterminate. **2.** Lack of decision; irresolution; want of fixed purpose or intention.

indeterminism, n. [1. indetẽrminizm; 2. inditə́minizəm]. **in-** (II.) & **determinism**. (metaph.) Doctrine that human will and choice of action are free, and not determined by external causes, and that the choice of motives of action is free.

indeterminist, n. [1. indetẽrminist; 2. inditə́minist]. **in-** (II.) & **determinist**. Adherent of indeterminism.

index (I.), n. [1. índeks; 2. índeks], pl. *indexes* or, in learned usage, *indices* [1. índisēz; 2. índisīz]. Lat., 'a pointer, indicator; the forefinger; a sign, mark, indication; a list, table, catalogue; a guide, witness, informer'. See **in-** (I.), & the base in **diction**, & words there referred to. **1.** Anything that indicates, points out, draws the attention to something; esp. a pointer on an instrument for indicating measurement &c. **2.** The forefinger; also *index finger.* **3.** (fig.) An indication, guide, witness: *style is an index of the mind.* **4. a** Alphabetical list of subjects treated, words found &c., in a book; **b** specif., *the Index, Index expurgatorius,* or *Index librorum prohibitorum,* list of books forbidden by the Roman Catholic Church to be read, or permitted to be read only in expurgated editions. **5.** (alg.) The exponent of a power.

index (II.), vb. trans., fr. prec. **a** To supply (a book) with an index; **b** to enter (word &c.) in an index.

indexer, n. [1. índekser; 2. índeksə]. Prec. & **-er**. Compiler of an index to a book.

index number, n. (in statistics) A percentage number, based on prices, wages &c. taken as 100 at a certain time, showing rise and fall.

India, n. [1. índia; 2. índiə]. Lat., fr. Gk., fr. *Indós*, 'the river Indus', fr. Pers. *hind*, Scrt. *sindhu*, 'river'. S. Asiatic peninsular country between the Indus, the Himalayas, and the Brahmaputra. *Further India,* country between N.E. India and China, including Burmah, Siam, Indo-China &c.; *India Office,* British Government department dealing with Indian affairs; *East India Company,* a once rich and important company incorporated in 1600 for trading with India and East Indies.

Indiaman, n. [1. índiaman; 2. índiəmən]. Prec. & **man**. Ship engaged in trade with India.

Indian, adj. & n. [1. índian; 2. índiən]. **India** & **-an**. **1.** adj. Of, pertaining to, India or an Indian. **2.** n. **a** A native of India; **b** European long domiciled in India; **c** aboriginal inhabitant of N. or S. America.

indian club, n. Bottle-shaped wooden club held in the hand and swung as gymnastic exercise.

indian corn, n. Maize.

indian file, n. Single file, one behind the other.

indian ink, n. Very black fluid for writing, drawing &c., made in China and Japan.

Indianize, vb. trans. [1. índianīz; 2. índiənaiz]. **Indian** & **-ize**. **1.** To make into, cause to resemble, an Indian. **2.** To alter the character of government, administration, the army, education, and other public institutions in British India by placing them more and more under the control of Indians.

indian meal, n. Maize meal.

Indian summer, n. **a** Period of warm, dry weather in late autumn; **b** (fig.) revival of vigour or passion late in life.

India paper, n. **a** Thin, soft paper made in China and Japan, used for fine impressions of engravings; **b** a thin, opaque paper used for printing books such as Bibles &c.

India proofs, n. Proofs of engravings on India paper.

india-rubber, n. **a** Commercial product made from solidified juice of rubber plant; **b** specif., small piece of this used for rubbing out pencil marks.

indicate, vb. trans. [1. índikāt; 2. índikeit], fr. Lat. *indicāt-(um)*, P.P. of *indicāre*, 'to point out, indicate; to show, declare, make known', fr. **in-** (I.) & *dicāre*, 'to proclaim, make known; to dedicate, consecrate; to set apart, appropriate'. See **diction**. **1. a** To point to, point out, direct attention to; show, make known: *to indicate the required road*; **b** to give a sign, hint, of what is in the mind; to intimate, to make known in outline: *to indicate one's intentions; to indicate assent,* signify it by some outward gesture; **c** to imply, suggest necessity of, require: *severe illness indicates drastic treatment.* **2.** To be a sign of, give grounds for an inference, give a hint of: *snow indicates the coming of winter.*

indication, n. [1. indikâshun; 2. indikéiʃən]. Prec. & **-ion**. **1.** The act of indicating; state of being indicated. **2.** That which indicates; a sign, evidence; **a** (in material sense) *a thermometer gives indication of changes in temperature*; **b** (in non-material sense) *his manner is no indication of his feelings*; **c** an intimation, suggestion, hint, foreshadowing: *an indication of one's intentions.*

indicative, adj. & n. [1. indíkativ; 2. indíkətiv]. **indicate** & **-ive**. **1.** adj. **a** [also 1. índikātiv; 2. índikeitiv] Serving to indicate, giving a hint, intimation, of; suggestive of; **b** (gram.) *indicative mood,* that which states an action or state as a fact; contrasted with conditional, imperative &c. **2.** n. Indicative mood.

indicatively, adv. Prec. & **-ly**. In an indicative manner.

indicator, n. [1. índikātor; 2. índikeitə]. **indicate** & **-or**. One who, that which, indicates; esp. a pointer on a dial, in an instrument, or engine &c., which denotes measurement of some kind, amount of pressure, speed &c.

indicatory, adj. [1. indíkaturi; 2. indíkətəri]. **indicate** & **-ory**. Tending, serving, to indicate.

indicium, n. [1. indísium; 2. indísiəm]. Lat. *indicium*, 'information, discovery, disclosure; sign, mark, token', fr. *indic-*, stem of *index*, 'a pointer, indicator; a witness'. See **index**. A sign, mark, indication, token.

indict, vb. trans. [1. indít; 2. indáit]. Spelling influenced by Lat.; fr. M.E. *endīten*, fr. A.-Fr. *enditer*, 'to indict', fr. O. Fr. *enditer*, 'to indict; indite', fr. Low Lat. **indictāre*, 'to declare, make known, proclaim in writing', fr. **in-** (I.) & *dictāre*, 'to pronounce, declare; to express in writing; prescribe, order, dictate'. See **diction** for etymol. of base. To make a formal accusation against: *to indict a person for, on a charge of, manslaughter.*

indictable, adj. [1. indítabl; 2. indáitəbl]. Prec. & **-able**. **a** (of person) Liable to indictment; **b** (of action) rendering one liable to be indicted: *an indictable offence.*

indiction, n. [1. indíkshun; 2. *indíkʃən*], fr. Lat. *indictiōn-(em)*, 'a declaration; imposition of a tax; fiscal period of fifteen years', fr. *indīcere*, 'declare, proclaim' &c. See **in- (I.)** & **diction**. **a** Edict of Roman Emperor (first made by Constantine in A.D. 312) establishing a valuation of property for purposes of taxation; this was done at the beginning of a period of fifteen years; **b** tax levied under such an edict.

indictment, n. [1. indítment; 2. *indáitmənt*]. **indict** & **-ment**. **1. a** Act of indicting; **b** state of being indicted. **2.** Document embodying formal statement of offence with which a person is charged.

Indies, n. pl. [1. índiz; 2. *índiz*]. Pl. of old *Indy*, 'India', cp. Fr. *les Indes*. Old, general collective term for India and the Far East, generally thought to have been reached by the early discoverers of America; specif., *East Indies*, India, Further India, and Malay Archipelago &c.; *West Indies*, group of Islands in or about the Caribbean Sea, off the east coast of Central America.

indifference, -cy, n. [1. indíferens(i); 2. *indíf(ə)rəns(i)*], fr. Lat. *indifferentia*, 'want of distinction; similarity', fr. *indifferent-(em)*, 'indifferent'. See next word & **-ce**, **-cy**. **1.** State characterized by lack of interest in; state of not being intellectually, emotionally, or morally stirred by; unconcern, callousness, insensitiveness: *indifference to suffering, danger, art, pleasure.* **2.** Unimportance, insignificance, absence of material consequence: *a matter of indifference.*

indifferent (I.), adj. [1. indíferent; 2. *indífərənt*], fr. Lat. *indifferent-(em)*, 'not different, similar; regarding indifferently; neither good nor evil'. **in- (II.)** & **different**. **1. a** Not affected, not intellectually stimulated; uninterested: *indifferent to politics, religion*; **b** not emotionally or morally stirred; callous, unfeeling: *indifferent to the suffering of others*; impassive, heedless, unmoved, regardless: *indifferent to pleasure, danger, discomfort* &c.; **c** unbiassed in judgement, not swayed by partiality; neutral, impartial, dispassionate: *to remain indifferent in a dispute*; (archaic) *an indifferent judge.* **2.** Arousing no interest, passion, emotion: *success and failure are alike indifferent to me.* **3. a** Neither good nor bad; of medium quality, commonplace, mediocre: *an indifferent play*; *indifferent acting*; **b** below the average, unsatisfactory, inferior: *an indifferent player, cook, performance, meal* &c. **4.** (elect.) Neutral.

indifferent (II.), n., fr. prec. Person who is indifferent, esp. in politics.

indifferentism, n. [1. indíferentizm; 2. *indífərəntizəm*]. **indifferent (I.)** & **-ism**. Attitude of habitual, systematic indifference; specif. to religious or political principles.

indifferentist, n. [1. indíferentist; 2. *indífərəntist*]. **indifferent (I.)** & **-ist**. One who professes indifferentism.

indifferently, adv. [1. indíferentli; 2. *indífərəntli*]. **indifferent (I.)** & **-ly**. In an indifferent manner. **1.** With indifference; impassively, without interest, unfeelingly: *to look on indifferently at a match.* **2.** In a mediocre manner; rather badly: *to play but indifferently.* **3.** (archaic) Impartially, dispassionately: '*that they may truly and indifferently minister justice*' (Prayer for Church Militant).

indigence, n. [1. índijens; 2. *índidžəns*], fr. Lat. *indigentia*, 'need, want; insatiable desire'; **indigent** & **-ce**. Poverty, destitution.

indigene, n. [1. índijēn; 2. *índidžīn*]; or as Fr. [ǣdižēn], fr. Fr. *indigène*, fr. Lat. *indigena*, 'a native', fr. *indu*, 'in' (chiefly in compounds), older *endo*; cp. Gk. *éndon*, 'within' (see **endo-**); the second element is the base **ĝen-*, 'to produce'. See **genus.** A native.

indigenous, adj. [1. indíjenus; 2. *indídžinəs*], fr. Lat. *indigen-(a)*, 'native'. See **indigene** & **-ous**. (of forms of life, customs, products) Native, autochthonous, aboriginal; belonging from beginning; not exotic, or immigrant: *marsupials are indigenous to Australia.*

indigenously, adv. Prec. & **-ly**. Aboriginally.

indigent, adj. [1. índijent; 2. *índidžənt*], fr. Lat. *indigent-(em)*, 'needy', fr. *indig-(ēre)*, 'to need, want, require, long for', fr. *indu-*, 'in', see **indigence**, & *egēre*, 'to be needy, be in want'; cogn. w. O.E. *ācan*, 'to ache'. See **ache (II.)**. Poor, needy, poverty-stricken.

indigested, adj. [1. indijésted; 2. *indidžéstid*], fr. obs. *indigest*, fr. Lat. *indīgest-(us)*, 'unarranged, confused', fr. **in- (II.)** & *digest-(um)*, P.P. type of *dīgerere*, 'to divide, distribute; set in order'. See **digest** & **-ed**. Not digested; chiefly used **a** of results of mental activity; crude, chaotic, confused, ill-arranged, improperly thought out; less commonly **b** (of food) undigested in stomach.

indigestibility, n. [1. indijestibíliti; 2. *indidžɛstibíliti*]. Next word & **-ity**. The quality of being indigestible.

indigestible, adj. [1. indijéstibl; 2. *indidžéstibl*], fr. Lat. *indīgestibil-(is)*, 'indigestible'. **in- (II.)** & **digestible.** (lit. and fig.) Not capable of being digested; not easily digested.

indigestion, n. [1. indijéschun; 2. *indidžéstʃən*], fr. L. Lat. *indīgestiōn-(em)*, 'indigestion'. **in- (II.)** & **digestion**. **1.** The state of not being digested. **2.** Inability to digest food; dyspepsia.

indigestive, adj. [1. indijéstiv; 2. *indidžéstiv*]. **in- (II.)** & **digestive.** Suffering from, tending to promote, indigestion.

indign, adj. [1. indín; 2. *indáin*], fr. Fr. *indigne*, fr. Lat. *indignus*, 'unworthy, undeserving; shameful, disgraceful'; fr. **in- (II.)** & *dignus*, 'worthy, honourable'. See **dignity.** (archaic) Unworthy, derogatory, shameful.

indignant, adj. [1. indígnant; 2. *indígnənt*], fr. Lat. *indignant-(em)*, Pres. Part. of *indign-(āri)*, 'to be displeased at, regard as unworthy, improper', fr. *indign-(us)*, 'unworthy'. See **dignity.** Feeling, expressing, fierce, angry scorn; esp. roused to anger by, smarting under, injustice, cruelty, meanness, insolence &c.

indignantly, adv. Prec. & **-ly**. In an indignant manner.

indignation, n. [1. indignáshun; 2. *indignéiʃən*], fr. Lat. *indignātiōn-(em)*, 'indignation, displeasure', fr. *indign-(āri)*, 'to be annoyed'. See **indignant** & **-ation**. Righteous anger aroused by injustice and baseness.

indignation-meeting, n. Meeting held to express public indignation.

indignity, n. [1. indígniti; 2. *indígniti*], fr. Lat. *indignitāt-(em)*, 'unworthiness, heinousness; insulting treatment', fr. *indign-(us)*, 'unworthy'. See **indign** & **-ity**. A slight; a profound affront; any conduct towards another which humiliates him, and tends to affect or destroy his personal dignity.

indigo, n. [1. índigō; 2. *índigou*]. Fr., fr. Lat. *Indicum*, fr. Gk. *Indikón*, 'a blue (Indian) pigment', fr. *Indikós*, 'Indian', fr. **India** & **-ic**. **a** A blue dye obtained from decomposition of certain substances in indigo plant; **b** the indigo plant, genus *Indigofera.*

indigo-blue, n. The blue obtained from the indigo plant; a deep bluish violet.

indigotic, adj. [1. indigótik; 2. *indigɔ́tik*]. **indigo** & **-ic**. Pertaining to, resembling, indigo.

indigo-white, n. Deoxidized indigo, a colourless, crystalline powder.

indirect, adj. [1. indirékt; 2. *indirékt*]. **in- (II.)** & **direct**. **1.** Not direct, not going straight; circuitous, roundabout, devious: *an indirect route.* **2.** (of expression, behaviour &c.) Not straightforward, not seeking to attain object aimed at by nearest, directest means: *an indirect reference, allusion*; *indirect methods.* **3.** Not what is primarily aimed at; secondary, consequential: *an indirect result, effect* &c. **4.** (gram.) **a** *Indirect speech*, oblique narration, reported speech, with first person changed to third: *he said that he was ill*; (cp. *he said, 'I am ill'*); **b** *indirect object*, person, or thing indirectly affected by action denoted by verb, as *me* in *give me the book.* **5.** (polit. econ.) *Indirect taxation*, that paid in form of increased price of goods by consumer, which covers both actual price of article and the duty, not as direct payment to government.

indirection, n. [1. indirékshun; 2. *indirékʃən*]. Prec. & **-ion**. (Shakespeare, 'Hamlet,' II. i. 66). Dishonest action; crookedness, dishonesty, deceit.

indirectly, adv. [1. indiréktli; 2. *indiréktli*]. **indirect** & **-ly**. In an indirect manner.

indirectness, n. [1. indiréktnes; 2. *indiréktnis*]. See prec. & **-ness**. Quality of being indirect.

indiscernible, adj. & n. [1. indisérnibl; 2. *indisə́nibl*]. **in- (II.)** & **discernible**. **1.** adj. Not capable of being discerned; imperceptible, invisible. **2.** n. An indiscernible thing.

indiscernibly, adv. Prec. & **-ly**. In an indiscernible manner; to an indiscernible degree.

indiscerptibility, n. [1. indisērptibíliti; 2. *indisə̄ptibíliti*]. See next word & **-ity**. The quality of being indiscerptible.

indiscerptible, adj. [1. indisḗrptibl; 2. *indisə́ptibl*]. **in- (II.)** & **discerptible**. Not capable of being resolved into component parts.

indisciplinable, adj. [1. indisiplínabl; 2. *indisipláinəbl*]. **in- (II.)** & **disciplinable**. (rare) Not capable of being disciplined.

indiscipline, n. [1. indísiplin; 2. *indísiplin*]. **in- (II.)** & **discipline**. Absence of discipline.

indiscreet, adj. [1. indiskrḗt; 2. *indiskrít*]. **in- (II.)** & **discreet**. Not discreet; injudicious, imprudent; esp. in discussing and handling delicate questions.

indiscreetly, adv. Prec. & **-ly**. In an indiscreet manner.

indiscrete, adj. [1. indískrēt; 2. *indískrīt*], fr. Lat. *indiscrēt-(us)*, 'undivided, closely connected'. **in- (II.)** & **discrete**. Not consisting of distinct and separate parts or elements; homogeneous.

indiscretion, n. [1. indiskréshun; 2. *indiskréʃən*], fr. L. Lat. *indiscrētiōn-(em)*, 'lack of discernment, indiscretion'. **in- (II.)** & **discretion**. **1.** Lack of the quality of discretion. **2.** An indiscreet action; specif. **a** offence against conventional good behaviour or morality; **b** unjustifiable discussion of private matters.

indiscriminate, adj. [1. indiskríminat; 2. *indiskríminit*]. **in- (II.)** & Lat. *discrīmināt-(um)*, P.P. type of *discrīmināre*, 'to divide; distinguish'. See **discriminate**. Not based on, or resulting from, the exercise of discrimination; random, promiscuous: *indiscriminate abuse, praise* &c.; *indiscriminate blows*, dealt to all and sundry.

indiscriminately, adv. Prec. & **-ly**. In an indiscriminate manner.

indiscriminateness, n. See prec. & **-ness**. Quality of being indiscriminate; lack of prudent judgement.

indiscrimination, n. [1. indiskrimináshun; 2. *indiskriminéiʃən*]. **indiscriminate** & **-ion**. Lack of discrimination.

indiscriminative, adj. [1. indiskríminativ; 2. *indiskríminətiv*]. **in- (II.)** & **discriminative**. Not discriminating; not tending, or serving, to discriminate.

indispensability, n. [1. indispensabíliti; 2. *indispɛnsəbíliti*]. See next word & **-ity**. Quality of being indispensable.

indispensable, adj. [1. indispénsabl; 2. *indispénsəbl*]. **in- (II.)** & **dispensable**. **1.** Not capable of being dispensed with; essential to, necessary, urgently required for, purpose in hand. **2.** (of law, duty, obligation &c.) From which no exemption, or dispensation, can be given; not capable of being set aside.

indispensableness, n. Prec. & **-ness**. Quality of being indispensable.

indispensably, adv. See prec. & **-ly**. In an indispensable manner.

indispose, vb. trans. [1. indispṓz; 2. *indispóuz*]. **in- (II.)** & **dispose**. **1.** To make unwilling, to disincline; dissuade from. **2.** To make unfit, unable, incapable.

indisposed, adj. [1. indispózd; 2. indispóuzd], fr. P.P. of prec. **1.** Not in good health, ill. **2.** Unwilling, averse, disinclined.

indisposition, n. [1. indispōzíshun; 2. indispouzíʃən]. **in-** (II.) & **disposition. 1.** Slight ailment; illness; ill health. **2.** (followed by *to*) Disinclination, unwillingness, reluctance, aversion.

indisputability, n. [1. indispūtabíliti; 2. indispjutəbíliti]. See next word & **-ity.** Quality of being indisputable.

indisputable, adj. [1. indispūtabl; 2. indíspjutəbl], fr. L. Lat. *indisputābil-(is)*, 'indisputable'. **in-** (II.) & **disputable.** Not to be disputed; not open to question; certain.

indisputableness, n. Prec. & **-ness.** Quality of being indisputable.

indisputably, adv. See prec. & **-ly.** In an indisputable manner; certainly, undoubtedly.

indissolubility, n. [1. indisolūbíliti; 2. indisəljubíliti]. See next word & **-ity.** Quality of being indissoluble.

indissoluble, adj., fr. Lat. *indissolūbil-(is)*, 'that cannot be dissolved'. **in-** (II.) & **dissoluble. 1.** (of material things) [1. indisólūbl; 2. indisóljubl]. Not capable of being dissolved or broken up into component parts. **2.** (of non-material things) [1. indísolūbl; 2. indísəljubl] Not to be destroyed; permanent, lasting; imperishable: *an indissoluble bond, friendship.*

indissolubly, adv. Prec. & **-ly.** In an indissoluble manner.

indistinct, adj. [1. indistíngkt; 2. indistíŋkt], fr. Lat. *indistinct-(us)*, 'not distinct; confused, obscure'. **in-** (II.) & **distinct.** Not distinct, not conveying a clear impression to the senses or mind; obscure, dim, subdued, confused, indefinite: *an indistinct murmur of voices; an indistinct recollection; objects grew indistinct in the twilight.*

indistinctive, adj. [1. indistíngktiv; 2. indistíŋktiv]. **in-** (II.) & **distinctive.** Not distinctive or characteristic; not capable of serving as a distinction.

indistinctively, adv. Prec. & **-ly.** In an indistinctive manner.

indistinctly, adv. [1. indistíngktli; 2. indistíŋktli]. **indistinct** & **-ly.** In an indistinct manner.

indistinctness, n. [1. indistíngktnes; 2. indistíŋktnis]. See prec. & **-ness.** The quality of being indistinct.

indistinguishable, adj. [1. indistínggwishabl; 2. indistíŋgwiʃəbl]. **in-** (II.) & **distinguishable.** Not capable of being distinguished.

indistinguishably, adv. Prec. & **-ly.** So as to be indistinguishable.

indistributable, adj. [1. indistríbūtabl; 2. indistríbjutəbl]. **in-** (II.) & **distributable.** Not capable of being distributed.

indite, vb. trans. [1. indīt; 2. indáit]. Variant of **indict. 1.** To compose, write, express in words: *to indite a poem.* **2.** To write, draw up, express in writing: *to indite a letter, complaint.*

indium, n. [1. índium; 2. índiəm], fr. **India**, w. Latinized termination. A rare, malleable silvery metallic element, found in zinc ores.

indivertible, adj. [1. indivértibl; 2. indivə́tibl]. **in-** (II.) & **divert** & **-ible.** Not capable of being diverted, or turned aside; not to be hindered from taking its course.

indivertibly, adv. Prec. & **-ly.** In an indivertible manner.

individual (I.), adj. [1. individūal, -víjooal; 2. individjuəl, -vídžuəl], fr. Med. Lat. *indīviduāl-(is)*, 'individual', fr. Lat. *indīvidu-(us)*, 'undivided', fr. **in-** (II.) & *dīviduus*, 'divisible', fr. *dīvidere*, 'to divide'. See **divide** & **-al. 1.** Single, separate, distinct: *each individual person, word, tree* &c. **2.** Marking a thing out as separate, unique; characteristic, peculiar, distinctive: *an individual style, method, mode of dress* &c. **3.** Pertaining to, derived from, performed by, a single person: *to receive individual attention; my individual labours; individual subscriptions.*

individual (II.), n., fr. prec. **a** A single member of class or group of persons, animals, plants, or inanimate things; **b** (colloq.) a person, human being: *an agreeable individual*, a nice man.

individualism, n. [1. individūalizm; 2. individjuəlizəm]. **individual** (I.) & **-ism. 1.** Tendency to regard oneself as the paramount interest in one's life; egoism. **2.** Social doctrine which emphasizes the rights of individuals rather than those of society and of the State as a whole.

individualist, n. [1. individūalist; 2. individjuəlist]. See prec. & **-ist.** An upholder of individualism.

individualistic, adj. [1. individūalístik; 2. individjuəlístik]. Prec. & **-ic.** Pertaining to, based on principles of, individualism.

individuality, n. [1. individūáliti; 2. individjuǽliti]. **individual** (I.) & **-ity. 1.** Individual character; group, sum, of essential distinctive traits, or characteristics which belong to an individual and mark him out from others. **2.** (philos.) The fact of having separate existence, of being an individual; separate existence, distinct personality.

individualization, n. [1. individūalīzáshun; 2. individjuəlaizéiʃən]. See next word & **-ation.** The act of individualizing; state of being individualized.

individualize, vb. trans. [1. individūalīz; 2. individjuəlaiz]. **individual** (I.) & **-ize. 1.** To mark out, stamp, as an individual; be distinctive of. **2.** To particularize, specify, state definitely and in detail.

individually, adv. [1. individūali; 2. individjuəli]. **individual** (I.) & **-ly. 1.** As an individual person or thing, separately; as concerned with each one of a group or series; reverse of *collectively*: *to address each member of a class individually.* **2.** Displaying individual characteristics; distinctively.

individuate, vb. trans. [1. individūāt; 2. individjueit], fr. Med. Lat. *indīviduāt-(um)*, P.P. type of *indīviduāre*, 'to individualize', fr. Lat. *indīvidu-(us)*, 'undivided'. See **individual** & **-ate.** To individualize, give individuality to.

individuation, n. [1. individūáshun; 2. individjuéiʃən]. Prec. & **-ion.** The act of individuating; state of being individuated.

indivisibility, n. [1. indivizibíliti; 2. indivizibíliti]. See next word & **-ity.** Quality of being indivisible.

indivisible, adj. & n. [1. indivízibl; 2. indivízibl], fr. L. Lat. *indīvīsibil-(is)*, 'indivisible'. **in-** (II.) & **divisible. 1.** adj. Not capable of being divided. **2.** n. Something which is indivisible; an infinitely small thing or quantity.

indivisibly, adv. Prec. & **-ly.** So as to be indivisible.

Indo-, pref., fr. Gk. *Indó-(s)*, 'Indus'. See **India.** Indian.

Indo-Chinese, adj. [1. índō chīnḗz; 2. índou tʃainíz]. Pertaining to Further India.

indocile, adj. [1. indósīl; 2. indóusail], fr. Lat. *indocilis*, 'that cannot be taught'. **in-** (II.) & **docile.** Not docile; not willing to be taught or trained; difficult to manage, intractable.

indocility, n. [1. indōsíliti; 2. indousíliti]. Prec. & **-ity.** Quality of being indocile.

indoctrinate, vb. trans. [1. indóktrināt; 2. indóktrineit]. **in-** (I.) & **doctrine** & **-ate.** Cp. Fr. *endoctriner.* To teach, instruct; to imbue with particular doctrines, opinions &c.

Indo-European, n. & adj. [1. índō ūropḗan; 2. índou jūərəpíən]. **1.** n. **a** (frequently *Aryan*) The family of languages, with many subdivisions, including most of those spoken in Europe and in part of western Asia, India, and Persia; **b** the parent language of this family. **2.** adj. Pertaining to Indo-European, or Aryan.

Indo-Germanic, n. & adj. [1. índō jermánik; 2. índou džəmǽnik]. Indo-European.

indolence, n. [1. índolens; 2. índələns], fr. Lat. *indolentia*, 'freedom from pain; insensibility', fr. **in-** (II.) & *dol-(ēre)*, 'to feel pain; to grieve', q.v. under **dole** (III.), & **-ence.** The state or quality of being indolent; idleness.

indolent, adj. [1. índolent; 2. índələnt], fr. Lat. **in-** (II.) & *dolent-(em)*, *dol-(ēre)*, 'to feel pain; to grieve'. See prec. & **-ent. 1.** Idle, lazy, slothful, indisposed to action; inactive. **2.** (med.) Not giving pain: *an indolent abscess* &c.

indolently, adv. Prec. & **-ly.** In an indolent manner.

indomitable, adj. [1. indómitabl; 2. indómitəbl], fr. L. Lat. *indomitābil-(is)*, 'indomitable', fr. **in-** (II.) & *domit-(āre)*, 'to tame', fr. *domit-(um)*, P.P. type of *domāre*, 'to blame', q.v. under **daunt, tame,** & **-able.** Not to be subdued; unconquerable, unyielding: *indomitable courage.*

indomitably, adv. Prec. & **-ly.** In an indomitable manner.

Indonesian, adj. [1. indōnḗshan; 2. indouníʃən], fr. **Indo-** & Gk. *nēs-os*, 'an island', possibly cogn. w. Gk. *né-khein*, 'to swim, float', & Lat. *nāre*, 'to swim'. See **natation.** Pertaining to the East Indian Archipelago.

indoor, adj. [1. indōr; 2. índō]. **in-** (I.) & **door.** Belonging to the inside of a house; performed, carried on, inside a house: *indoor games; indoor repairs; indoor relief*, support given to paupers in a workhouse.

indoors, adv. [1. indórz; 2. indṓz]. Prec. & genitival *-s* used to form adv. Inside a house, or building; in the house: *to stay, keep, go, indoors.*

indorsation, n. [1. indorsáshun; 2. indōséiʃən], fr. Med. Lat. *indors-(āre)*, 'to endorse'. See **endorse** & **-ation.** Endorsement.

indorsee, n. [1. indorsḗ; 2. indōsí]. **endorse** & **-ee.** The person in whose favour a bill &c. is endorsed.

indorsement, n. See **endorsement.**

indraught, indraft, n. [1. índrahft; 2. índrāft]. **in-** (I.) & **draught. 1.** Process of drawing inwards. **2.** Inward current, of air or water.

indrawn, adj. [1. índrawn; 2. índrōn]. **in-** (I.) & **drawn.** Drawn in, as of breath &c.

indri, n. [1. índri; 2. índri], fr. Malagasy *indry*, 'behold', mistaken for animal's name. A kind of lemur found in Madagascar.

indubitable, adj. [1. indúbitabl; 2. indjúbitəbl], fr. Lat. *indubitābil-(is)*, 'that cannot be doubted'. **in-** (II.) & **dubitation** & **-able.** Not capable of being doubted; beyond doubt.

indubitably, adv. Prec. & **-ly.** In an indubitable manner; without doubt.

induce, vb. trans. [1. indús; 2. indjús], fr. Lat. *indūcere*, 'to lead, bring in; to bring forward, exhibit; to persuade; to resolve, determine', fr. **in-** (I.) & *dūcere*, 'to lead', q.v. under **duct. 1.** To persuade, lead, prevail upon: *to induce a person to do something.* **2.** To cause, produce, have as a consequence, bring about: *weakness induced by starvation.* **3.** (rare) To infer, make an induction. **4.** (elect.) To produce by induction.

inducement, n. [1. indúsment; 2. indjúsmənt]. Prec. & **-ment.** Something that serves, or tends, to induce one to do something; an attraction, incentive, motive.

induct, vb. trans. [1. indúkt; 2. indákt], fr. Lat. *induct-(um)*, P.P. type of *indūcere*, 'to lead, bring in; to persuade'. See **induce. 1.** To lead, or bring with ceremony to, to establish, install: *to induct a person into a seat.* **2.** To install formally, introduce with ceremony into an official position: *to induct a clergyman to a benefice.*

inductance, n. [1. indúktans; 2. indáktəns]. See **induction** & **-ance.** (elect.) The coefficient of induction, particularly of self-induction in magnetic circuits.

inductile, adj. [1. indúktīl; 2. indáktail]. **in-** (II.) & **ductile.** Not ductile.

induction, n. [1. indúkshun; 2. indákʃən], fr. Lat. *inductiōn-(em)*, 'a leading into, introduction; a purpose, resolve; a method of reasoning from the particular to the general', fr. *induct-(um)*, P.P. type of *indūcere*, 'to lead or bring in; to persuade'. See **in- (I.)** & **duct** & **-ion**, & cp. **induce** & **induct**. **1. a** The act of inducting; state of being inducted; introduction, installation; **b** the ceremony of inducting a person to an office. **2.** Method of reasoning from particular, or individual cases, to general conclusions. **3.** The introduction, statement, production (of facts &c.) to support a conclusion, theory. **4.** (elect.) Transference of magnetic or electric force without physical contact; magnetization at a distance.

induction-coil, n. Apparatus for transforming electric energy from low to high pressure by induction.

inductive, adj. [1. indúktiv; 2. *in*dáktiv], fr. Lat. *inductīv-(us)*, 'inductive'. **induct** & **-ive**. **1.** Pertaining to, based on, of the nature of, induction: *inductive reasoning* &c. **2.** (elect.) Producing electric energy by induction.

inductively, adv. Prec. & **-ly**. By induction.

inductiveness, n. See prec. & **-ness**. The quality of being inductive.

inductor, n. [1. indúktor; 2. *in*dáktə]. **induct** & **-or**. **1.** One who inducts to an ecclesiastical benefice, or other office. **2.** Part of electric apparatus which produces induction.

indulge, vb. trans. & intrans. [1. indúlj; 2. *in*dáldž], fr. Lat. *indulgēre*, 'to be kind, tender, indulgent to; to take pleasure in, give oneself up to, yield to', orig. 'to be long-suffering, patient, enduring'. Cogn. w. Gk. *dolikhós*, 'long' (see **dolichocephalic**), Goth. *tulgus*, 'firm, constant'. **A.** trans. **1. a** To give way, yield to, gratify, give a loose rein to (tastes, desires, passions &c.); **b** to allow (a person, oneself) to gratify his, one's, desires; to favour unduly, to pamper, cocker, spoil. **2.** To bestow upon as a favour, confer a benefit upon, give pleasure to, favour: *to indulge the company with a song*. **B.** intrans. (colloq.) To partake freely, too freely, of intoxicating drink: *I'm afraid he indulges too much.* Phrs. (vulg.) *will you indulge?*, will you have a drink?; *indulge in*, **a** to give way to, permit oneself to enjoy: *to indulge in a nap, glass of wine*; **b** to treat oneself to: *to indulge in a new suit.*

indulgence, n. [1. indúljens; 2. *in*dáldžəns], fr. Lat. *indulgentia*, 'complaisance, gentleness, remission', fr. *indulgēre*. See prec. **1.** The act of indulging; state of being indulged. **2.** Constant gratification of one's desires; self-indulgence. **3.** Privilege, advantage, exemption, remission, granted as a favour; specif., *Declaration of Indulgence*, promise of religious toleration proclaimed, **a** by Charles II. in 1672; **b** by James II. in 1687. **4.** (R.C.Ch.) Specif. **a** remission or reduction of punishment due for sins, granted through the Church, and effected by the infinite merits of Christ, and the superabundant merits of the saints; these are held to release those who can take advantage of them from part of the period of Purgatory which they would otherwise undergo; **b** (loosely) remission, exemption.

indulgenced, adj. [1. indúljenst; 2. *in*dáldžənst]. Prec. & **-ed**. (R.C.Ch.) Securing indulgence.

indulgent, adj. [1. indúljent; 2. *in*dáldžənt], fr. Lat. *indulgent-(em)*, 'indulgent, kind, tender'. **indulge** & **-ent**. Merciful, tolerant; not severe; exhibiting indulgence to others; tender, regardful of feelings and desires of others: *an indulgent parent.*

indulgently, adv. Prec. & **-ly**. In an indulgent manner.

induline, n. [1. índūlin; 2. *í*ndjulin]. Formed fr. **indigo**, w. dimin. suff. *-ule* & **-ine**. (chem.) Name given to a group of blue, grey, and black aniline dyes.

indult, n. [1. indúlt; 2. *in*dált], fr. Lat. *indult-(um)*, 'grace, favour, indulgence', fr. P.P. type of *indulgēre*, 'to be kind to; to be pleased with'. See **indulge**. Dispensation granted by the Pope giving authority for something not ordinarily sanctioned by the law of the Church.

induna, n. [1. indōōna; 2. indúnə]. Zulu. The chief leader of a Zulu impi or regiment; one of the elders or councillors of a Zulu tribe.

indurate, vb. trans. & intrans. [1. índūrāt; 2. *í*ndjureit], fr. Lat. *indūrāt-(um)*, P.P. type of *indūrāre*, 'to make, become, hard', fr. **in- (I.)** & *dūrāre*, 'to harden', fr. *dūr-(us)*, 'hard'. See **durable**. **1.** trans. **a** (of material action) To make hard, cause to become hard, firm; **b** (of non-material action) to harden; make callous, obdurate. **2.** intrans. **a** (of material things) To become hard; **b** (of non-material things) to become obdurate, callous.

induration, n. [1. ìndūráshun; 2. *ì*ndjuréiʃən]. Prec. & **-ion**. The act or process of indurating; state of being indurated.

indurative, adj. [1. índūrativ; 2. *í*ndjurətiv]. **indurate** & **-ive**. Tending to indurate.

indusium, n. [1. indúzium; 2. *in*djúziəm]. Lat. *indūsium*, 'a tunic', fr. *indu-(ere)*, 'to put on'. See **exuviae**. **1.** (bot.) **a** Outer case of spore-cluster of ferns; **b** hairy covering of stigma. **2.** (entom.) Case enclosing larva, esp. larva-case of fossilized insect.

industrial, adj. & n. [1. indústrial; 2. *in*dástriəl]. **industry** & **-al**. **1.** adj. Pertaining to, connected with, industries. *Industrial school*, one to which destitute children, those living in criminal surroundings, or themselves guilty of offences, are committed by the magistrates. **2.** n. Person engaged in industry.

industrialism, n. [1. indústrializm; 2. *in*dástriəlizəm]. Prec. & **-ism**. Social system in which industrial occupations form an important or basal element.

industrialist, n. [1. indústrialist; 2. *in*dástriəlist]. **industrial** & **-ist**. **a** A supporter of industrialism; **b** one engaged in industry.

industrialize, vb. trans. [1. indústrialīz, 2. *in*dástriəlaiz]. **industrial** & **-ize**. To devote to industrial pursuits.

industrially, adv. [1. indústriali; 2. *in*dástriəli]. **industrial** & **-ly**. In an industrial manner; based on, considered from point of view of, industry.

industrious, adj. [1. indústrius; 2. *in*dástriəs], fr. Lat. *industriōs-(us)*, 'diligent', fr. *industri-(us)*, 'diligent', fr. *industri-(a)*, 'industry'. See **industry** & **-ous**. Paying attention to one's work; hard-working, diligent, assiduous, painstaking.

industriously, adv. Prec. & **-ly**. In an industrious manner.

industry, n. [1. índustri; 2. *í*ndəstri], fr. Lat. *industria*, 'diligence, activity, industry', earlier *indostrum*, prob. fr. *indu*, 'in', q.v. under **indigent**, & *stru-ere*, 'to build, erect, make'. See **structure**. **1.** The quality or state of being industrious; diligence, assiduity; painstaking, laborious activity. **2. a** Human exertion devoted to creation of wealth, or capital; **b** specif., labour devoted to manufactures; often contrasted with *trade* or *commerce*. **3.** Specific branch of trade, or manufacture: *shipping industry*; *iron industry* &c.

induviae, n. pl. [1. indúviē; 2. *in*djúviī]. Lat., 'things put on, clothes', fr. *induere*, 'to put on'. See **exuviae**. (bot.) Leaves which remain attached to the stem after withering.

indwell, vb. trans. & intrans. [1. indwél; 2. *ì*ndwél]. **in- (I.)** & **dwell**. **1.** trans. To occupy, dwell in, inhabit, abide in (the mind, soul). **2.** intrans. *Indwell in*, to dwell, have an abiding-place, in.

indweller, n. [1. índweler; 2. *í*ndwelə]. Prec. & **-er**. Inhabitant.

-ine (I.), adj. suff. representing Lat. *-īnus* (Fr. *in(e)*, Engl. *in, ine*). The suff. gives the sense of 'like, pertaining to, of the nature of', & forms adjs. fr. ns.; **a** w. suff. stressed, pronounced [*ain*]: *divine*; **b** w. suff. unstressed, pronounced [*ain*]: *serpentine, saline, ferine, canine, leonine* &c.; **c** when stressed, in words recently borrowed fr. Fr. [īn]: *marine*; **d** unstressed [*in*]: *feminine, genuine* &c. Lat. adjs. in *-īnus*, were also formed fr. proper names, unstressed [*ain*]: *Byzantine* &c. Modern formations are mostly scientific: *alkaline, lacustrine* &c.; or fr. proper names: *Levantine, Caroline, saturnine*.

-ine (II.), adj. suff. representing Lat. *-inus*, fr. Gk. *-inos*, 'of the nature of, pertaining to': *adamantine, crystalline, hyaline, elephantine.*

-ine (III.), suff. forming fem. ns., representing Lat. *-īna*, fr. Gk. *-īnē*: *heroine.*

-ine (IV.), n. suff. representing Lat. *-īna*, forming abstract ns. fr. vbs. & other ns.: *doctrine, famine, rapine.*

-ine (V.), n. suff. representing Lat. adjs. in *-īnus, -īna*, used as ns.: *lupine.*

-ine (VI.), n. suff. representing Fr. *-ine*, **a** forming names of derivative products: *brilliantine*; **b** fr. Ital. dimin. suff. *-ino, -ina*: *mandoline, figurine.*

-ine (VII.), also **-in**, n. suff. forming names of chemical bases: *aniline, caffeine, creatine* &c.; occurs also in the names of the four elements, *bromine, chlorine, fluorine, iodine*; the *-in* form is seen in *casein, insulin.*

inebriate (I.), adj. & n. [1. inébriat; 2. *in*íbriit], fr. Lat. *inēbriāt-(um)*, P.P. type of *inēbriāre*, 'to make drunk', fr. **in- (I.)**, intens., & *ēbriāre*, 'to intoxicate', fr. *ē-brius*, 'drunk'. See **ebrious**. **1.** adj. Drunken, intoxicated. **2.** n. **a** Intoxicated person; **b** habitual drunkard.

inebriate (II.), vb. trans. [1. inébriāt; 2. *in*íbrieit], fr. Lat. *inēbriāt-(um)*, P.P. type of *inēbriāre*, 'to make drunk'. See prec. **1.** To make drunk, intoxicate. **2.** (fig.) To intoxicate, exhilarate, stir powerfully with excitement &c.: *inebriated by success.*

inebriation, n. [1. inèbriáshun; 2. *in*ìbriéiʃən]. Prec. & **-ion**. The act or process of inebriating; state of being inebriated.

inebriety, n. [1. inēbríeti; 2. *in*ibráiiti]. **in- (I.)** & **ebriety**. **a** Intoxication; **b** habitual drunkenness.

inedibility, n. [1. inèdibíliti; 2. *in*èdibíliti]. **in- (II.)** & **edibility**. Quality of being inedible.

inedible, adj. [1. inédibl; 2. *in*édibl]. **in- (II.)** & **edible**. Not suitable to be eaten.

inedited, adj. [1. inédited; 2. *in*éditid]. **in- (II.)** & **edit** & **-ed**. **1.** Not published. **2.** Published in original form, without editor's alterations.

ineffable, adj. [1. inéfabl; 2. *in*éfəbl], fr. Lat. *ineffābil-(is)*, 'unutterable, unpronounceable', fr. **in- (II.)** & *effābilis*, 'utterable', fr. *effāri*, 'to speak', fr. **ef-** for **ex-** & *fāri*, 'to say, speak', q.v. under **fable**. Not to be described or expressed in words; unutterable; inexpressibly great, marvellous, or sacred.

ineffably, adv. Prec. & **-ly**. In an ineffable manner.

ineffaceability, n. [1. ìnefàsabíliti; 2. *ì*nifèisəbíliti]. See next word & **-ity**. Quality of being ineffaceable.

ineffaceable, adj. [1. ìnefásabl; 2. *ì*niféisəbl]. **in- (II.)** & **effaceable**. Not capable of being effaced; indelible.

ineffaceably, adv. Prec. & **-ly**. In an ineffaceable manner.

ineffective, adj. [1. ìneféktiv; 2. *ì*niféktiv]. **in- (II.)** & **effective**. **1. a** Not producing the required effect; useless; **b** not producing an artistic effect; not striking. **2.** (of persons) Incompetent, inefficient, incapable.

ineffectively, adv. Prec. & **-ly**. In an ineffective manner.

ineffectiveness, n. See prec. & **-ness**. Quality of being ineffective.

ineffectual, adj. [1. ìneféktūal; 2. *ì*niféktjuəl]. **in- (II.)** & **effectual**. Having no result; unsuccessful, failing, fruitless.

ineffectually, adv. Prec. & **-ly**. In an ineffectual manner.

ineffectualness, n. See prec. & **-ness**. Quality of being ineffectual.

inefficacious, adj. [1. ìnefikáshus; 2. ìnefikéiʃəs]. **in- (II.)** & **efficacious**. Not efficacious; not producing desired effect.

inefficiency, n. [1. ìnefíshensi; 2. ìnifíʃənsi]. **in-** (II.) & **efficiency**. The quality of being inefficient.

inefficient, adj. [1. ìnefíshent; 2. ìnifíʃənt]. **in-** (II.) & **efficient**. **1.** (of persons) **a** Incompetent, generally incapable; **b** not skilled in, or qualified to do, some particular thing: *an inefficient plumber.* **2.** Not performing required and expected functions, not working properly: *an inefficient pump.*

inefficiently, adv. Prec. & **-ly**. In an inefficient manner.

inelastic, adj. [1. ìnelástik; 2. ìnilǽstik]. **in-** (II.) & **elastic**. **1.** Not elastic. **2.** (fig.) **a** (of mind &c.) Not resilient; unadaptable; **b** (of rules, systems &c.) fixed, rigid, not allowing of modification or exceptions.

inelasticity, n. [1. ìnēlastísiti; 2. ìnīlæstísiti]. Prec. & **-ity**. Quality of being inelastic; rigidity; unadaptability.

inelegance, -cy, n. [1. inélegans(i); 2. inéligəns(i)]. **in-** (II.) & **elegance**, & **-cy**. **1.** The state of being inelegant; lack of elegance; clumsiness. **2.** Something that is inelegant; inelegant action, speech; harshness of style &c.

inelegant, adj. [1. inélegant; 2. inéligənt], fr. Lat. *inēlegant-(em)*, 'without taste, judgement, discrimination'. **in-** (II.) & **elegant**. **1.** Wanting in physical elegance; lacking charm, shapeliness, grace; ungainly. **2.** (of non-material things, actions, mode of expression &c.) Unrefined, uncouth, awkward, unpolished, crude.

inelegantly, adv. Prec. & **-ly**. In an inelegant manner.

ineligibility, n. [1. inèlijibíliti; 2. inèlidžibíliti]. See next word & **-ity**. State of being ineligible.

ineligible, adj. & n. [1. inélijibl; 2. inélidžibl]. **in-** (II.) & **eligible**. **1.** adj. Not eligible; **a** not capable of being chosen or elected; **b** not qualified or suitable. **2.** n. An ineligible person; specif., an undesirable, unsuitable candidate for a lady's hand.

ineligibly, adv. Prec. & **-ly**. So as to be ineligible.

ineluctable, adj. [1. ìnelúktabl; 2. ìnilʌ́ktəbl]. Fr., fr. Lat. *inēluctābil-(is)*, 'unavoidable, inevitable', fr. **in-** (II.) & *ēluctā-(ri)*, 'to struggle out of; to surmount', fr. **e-** & *luctāri*, 'to struggle, wrestle'; cp. *lucta*, 'wrestling match'; cogn. w. Gk. *lugizein*, 'to bend, twist; to writhe; to throw in wrestling', cp. Gk. *lúgos*, 'withy', *lúginos*, 'plaited'; cp. also Lith. *lugnas*, 'supple, pliant'; O.N. *lokkr*, O.H.G. *loc*, O.E. *locc*, 'lock of hair'. See **lock**. Not capable of being overcome, not to be escaped from; inescapable.

inept, adj. [1. inépt; 2. inépt], fr. Lat. *inept-(us)*, 'unsuitable; absurd; tactless'; fr. **in-** (II.) & *aptus*, 'fit, apposite, appropriate'. See **apt**. **1.** (rare) Inapt, inapposite; inappropriate, out of place. **2.** Absurd, foolish, fatuous, senseless.

ineptitude, n. [1. inéptitūd; 2. inéptitjūd]. Prec. & **-tude**. **1.** Quality of being inept; folly, futility of mind. **2.** Something that is inept; inept conduct, remark &c.

ineptly, adv. [1. inéptli; 2. inéptli]. **inept** & **-ly**. In an inept manner.

ineptness, n. [1. inéptnes; 2. inéptnis]. See prec. & **-ness**. Quality of being inept.

inequality, n. [1. ìnēkwóliti; 2. ìnīkwóliti], fr. Med. Lat. *inaequālitāt-(em)*, 'inequality'. **in-** (II.) & **equality**. **1.** Absence of equality; dissimilarity, difference, in size, amount, quality, rank &c. **2.** Tendency to change; variableness, unevenness. **3.** (of surface) Roughness, unevenness, irregularity. **4.** (astron.) Deviation in motion.

inequilateral, adj. [1. ìnēkwiláteral; 2. ìnīkwilǽtərəl]. **in-** (II.) & **equilateral**. Having sides of unequal length or area.

inequitable, adj. [1. inékwitabl; 2. inékwitəbl]. **in-** (II.) & **equitable**. Unjust, not equitable, not fair.

inequitably, adv. Prec. & **-ly**. Unjustly.

inequity, n. [1. inékwiti; 2. inékwiti]. **in-** (II.) & **equity**. Injustice, unfairness.

ineradicable, adj. [1. ìnerádikabl; 2. ìnirǽdikəbl]. **in-** (II.) & **eradicable**. (chiefly in fig. sense) Not to be rooted out, or uprooted; fixed firmly and deeply; deep-rooted, deep-seated: *ineradicable habits, hatred, contempt.*

ineradicably, adv. Prec. & **-ly**. So as to be ineradicable.

inerrability, n. [1. inêrabíliti; 2. inʌ̀rəbíliti], fr. L. Lat. *inerrābil-(is)*, 'unerring'. See next word & **-ity**. Quality of being inerrable; incapacity to err, infallibility.

inerrable, adj. [1. inêrabl; 2. inʌ́rəbl], fr. L. Lat. *inerrābil-(is)*, 'unerring', fr. **in-** (II.) & *err-āre*, 'to err' (see **err**), & **-able**. Not liable to error; unerring, infallible.

inerrably, adv. Prec. & **-ly**. Infallibly.

inerrancy, n. [1. inéransi; 2. inérənsi], fr. **in-** (II.) & Lat. *err-āre*, 'to wander; to err' (see **err**), & **-ancy**. Inerrability.

inerrant, adj. [1. inérant; 2. inérənt], fr. **in-** (II.) & Lat. *err-āre*, 'to wander; to err' (see prec.), & **-ant**. Not erring, not liable to err.

inert, adj. [1. inêrt; 2. inʌ́t], fr. Lat. *inert-*, stem of *iners*, 'unskilled; inactive', fr. **in-** (II.) & *ars*, 'skill'. See **art**. **1. a** (phys.) Having no power of independent motion: *inert mass, matter* &c.; **b** (chem.) without active chemical properties. **2.** Not disposed to mental or bodily activity; slow, sluggish, inactive, heavy, dull, in mind or body.

inertia, n. [1. inêrshia; 2. inʌ́ʃiə]. Lat. *inertia*, 'unskilfulness, ignorance; inactivity, idleness'. See prec. **1.** (phys.) Property of matter by which when in rest it continues without motion, and when moved it continues to move in the direction originally imparted to it, until a new direction is given to it from without. **2.** Inactivity, sluggishness, inertness, dullness, torpor, of mind or body.

inertly, adv. [1. inêrtli; 2. inʌ́tli]. **inert** & **-ly**. In an inert manner.

inertness, n. [1. inêrtnes; 2. inʌ́tnis]. See prec. & **-ness**. Tendency to remain inactive; sluggishness, dullness, torpor, of mind or body.

inescapable, adj. [1. ìneskápabl; 2. ìniskéipəbl]. **in-** (II.) & **escape** (I.) & **-able**. From which there is no escape; not to be escaped or avoided.

inessential, adj. & n. [1. ìnesénshal; 2. ìnisénʃl]. **in-** (II.) & **essential**. **1.** adj. Not essential, not indispensable; not absolutely necessary; not important. **2.** n. Something that is inessential.

inestimable, adj. [1. inéstimabl; 2. inéstiməbl]. **in-** (II.) & **estimable**. Not to be estimated; possessing a degree of size, or merit beyond computation; invaluable: *inestimable magnitude*; *an inestimable benefit*; *of inestimable value.*

inestimably, adv. Prec. & **-ly**. To an inestimable degree.

inevitability, n. [1. inèvitabíliti; 2. inèvitəbíliti]. See next word & **-ity**. Quality of being inevitable.

inevitable, adj. [1. inévitabl; 2. inévitəbl], fr. Lat. *inēvītābil-(is)*, 'unavoidable', fr. **in-** (II.) & *ēvītābilis*, 'avoidable', fr. *ēvīt-(āre)*, 'to avoid, shun', fr. **e-** & *vītāre*, 'to seek to escape, avoid'. Etymol. doubtful. **1.** Not to be avoided, put off, turned aside; bound to happen or to appear: '*the inevitable hour*' (Gray's 'Elegy'), that of death. **2. a** Bound to happen as a necessary consequence of some earlier event or action: *after several of the contending states had mobilized their armies, war was inevitable*; **b** following as a logical necessity from something already accepted as proved; logically irresistible; *in view of the facts, the conclusion is inevitable that ...*

inevitableness, n. Prec. & **-ness**. Quality of being inevitable.

inevitably, adv. See prec. & **-ly**. In an inevitable manner; unavoidably; necessarily, as a matter of course.

inexact, adj. [1. ìnegzákt; 2. ìnigzǽkt]. **in-** (II.) & **exact**. Not exact; not absolutely accurate.

inexactitude, n. [1. ìnegzáktitūd; 2. ìnigzǽktitjūd]. **in-** (II.) & **exactitude**. Inexactness.

inexactly, adv. [1. ìnegzáktli; 2. ìnigzǽktli]. **inexact** & **-ly**. In an inexact manner.

inexactness, n. [1. ìnegzáktnes; 2. ìnigzǽktnis]. See prec. & **-ness**. The state or quality of being inexact.

inexcusable, adj. [1. ìnekskúzabl; 2. ìnikskjūzəbl], fr. Lat. *inexcūsābil-(is)*, 'inexcusable'. **in-** (II.) & **excusable**. Not to be excused; unpardonable; unjustifiable.

inexcusably, adv. Prec. & **-ly**. In an inexcusable manner.

inexecutable, adj. [1. ìnegzékūtabl; 2. ìnigzékjutəbl]. **in-** (II.) & **execute** & **-able**. Not capable of being performed, or carried out.

inexhaustibility, n. [1. ìnegzàwstibíliti; 2. ìnigzɔ̀stibíliti]. See next word & **-ity**. State of being inexhaustible.

inexhaustible, adj. [1. ìnegzáwstibl; 2. ìnigzɔ́stibl]. **in-** (II.) & **exhaustible**. **1.** Not capable of being exhausted, or used up; copious, abundant, unfailing: *an inexhaustible supply.* **2.** Unwearied, indefatigable.

inexhaustibly, adv. Prec. & **-ly**. To the point of being inexhaustible.

inexhaustive, adj. [1. ìnegzáwstiv; 2. ìnigzɔ́stiv]. **in-** (II.) & **exhaustive**. **a** Inexhaustible; **b** not exhaustive.

inexorability, n. [1. inèksurabíliti; 2. inèksərəbíliti]. See next word & **-ity**. Quality of being inexorable.

inexorable, adj. [1. inéksurabl; 2. inéksərəbl], fr. Lat. *inexōrābil-(is)*, 'not to be moved by entreaty; rigorous, inexorable', fr. **in-** (II.) & *exōrābilis*, 'easily entreated', fr. *exōr-(āre)*, 'to prevail upon, persuade', fr. **ex-** & *ōrāre*, 'to pray, entreat' (see **oration**), & **-able**. Relentless, stern, ruthless, rigorous; not to be turned from one's, its, path or purpose.

inexorably, adv. Prec. & **-ly**. In an inexorable manner.

inexpectant, adj. [1. ìnekspéktant; 2. ìnikspéktənt]. **in-** (II.) & **expectant**. Not expecting.

inexpediency, n. [1. ìnekspḗdyensi; 2. ìnikspídjənsi]. **in-** (II.) & **expediency**. State of being inexpedient.

inexpedient, adj. [1. ìnekspḗdyent; 2. ìnikspídjənt]. **in-** (II.) & **expedient**. Not expedient; unsuitable, impolitic, under given circumstances; tending to defeat desired end.

inexpensive, adj. [1. ìnekspénsiv; 2. ìnikspénsiv]. **in-** (II.) & **expensive**. Not costing much, cheap; not tending to extravagance.

inexpensively, adv. Prec. & **-ly**. In an inexpensive manner; without great expense, cheaply.

inexpensiveness, n. See prec. & **-ness**. State or quality of being inexpensive.

inexperience, n. [1. ìnekspḗriens; 2. ìnikspíəriəns]. **in-** (II.) & **experience**. Lack of experience.

inexperienced, adj. [1. ìnekspḗrienst; 2. ìnikspíəriənst]. Prec. & **-ed**. Lacking experience; unpractised.

inexpert, adj. [1. ìnekspêrt; 2. ìnikspʌ́t], fr. Lat. *inexpert-(us)*, 'unpractised, unaccustomed'. **in-** (II.) & **expert**. Not expert; unskilful; clumsy.

inexpertly, adv. Prec. & **-ly**. In an inexpert manner; unskilfully.

inexpiable, adj. [1. inékspiabl; 2. inékspiəbl], fr. Lat. *inexpiābil-(is)*, 'that cannot be atoned for; implacable'. **in-** (II.) & **expiable**. **1.** (of action) Not capable of being expiated or atoned for. **2.** Unappeasable, relentless, implacable: '*thou, who tookst the way To raise in me inexpiable hate*' (Milton, 'Samson').

inexpiably, adv. Prec. & **-ly**. In an inexpiable manner.

inexplicability, n. [1. inèksplikabíliti; 2. inèksplikəbíliti]. See next word & **-ity**. Quality of being inexplicable.

inexplicable, adj. [1. inéksplikabl; 2. inéksplikəbl], fr. Lat. *inexplicābil-(is)*, 'inexplicable', fr. **in-** (II.) & **explicable**. Not capable of being explained; incomprehensible, unintelligible.

inexplicably, adv. Prec. & **-ly**. In an inexplicable manner.

inexplicit, adj. [1. ìneksplísit; 2. ìnɪksplísɪt], fr. Lat. *inexplicit-(us)*, 'not to be traced'; (poet.) 'unexplained, obscure'. **in- (II.)** & **explicit**. Not explicit; **a** lacking definiteness; not precisely defined; **b** (of persons) not making explicit statement; not defining fully, using vague or merely general terms.

inexplicitly, adv. Prec. & **-ly**. In an inexplicit manner.

inexplicitness, n. See prec. & **-ness**. Quality of being inexplicit.

inexplosive, adj. [1. ìneksplṓsiv; 2. ìnɪksplóusɪv]. **in- (II.)** & **explosive**. Not explosive; not able or liable to explode.

inexpressible, adj. & n. [1. ìnekspr ésibl; 2. ìnɪksprésɪbl]. **in- (II.)** & **expressible**. **1.** adj. Greater than, beyond anything that, can be expressed; unutterable, indescribable. **2.** n. pl. *Inexpressibles*, (facetious, archaic) trousers.

inexpressibly, adv. Prec. & **-ly**. To an inexpressible degree.

inexpressive, adj. [1. ìneksprésiv; 2. ìnɪksprésɪv]. **in- (II.)** & **expressive**. **1.** Not expressive; conveying little or no meaning; not significant. **2.** Not capable of expressing oneself; reticent.

inexpressively, adv. Prec. & **-ly**. In an inexpressive manner.

inexpressiveness, n. See prec. & **-ness**. Quality of being inexpressive.

inexpugnable, adj. [1. ìnekspúgnabl; 2. ìnɪkspʌ́gnəbl], fr. Lat. *inexpugnābil-(is)*, 'not to be taken by assault', fr. **in- (II.)** & *expugnābil-(is)*, 'that may be captured', fr. *expugn-(āre)*, 'to take by assault', fr. **ex-** & *pugnāre*, 'to assault; fight'. See **pugnacious** & **-able**. (lit. and fig.) Not capable of being overcome by attack; not yielding to force; impregnable; unconquerable.

inextensible, adj. [1. ìnekstén sibl; 2. ìnɪksténsɪbl]. **in- (II.)** & **extensible**. Not capable of being extended.

inextinguishable, adj. [1. ìnekstínggwishabl; 2. ìnɪkstíŋgwɪʃəbl]. **in- (II.)** & **extinguishable**. (lit. and fig.) Not to be extinguished; unquenchable, indestructible.

inextricable, adj. [1. inékstrikabl; 2. inékstrɪkəbl], fr. Lat. *inextrīcābil-(is)*, 'that cannot be disentangled, disengaged'. **in- (II.)** & **extricable**. (chiefly fig.) Not to be disentangled, or smoothed out; incapable of being reduced to order: *inextricable confusion, difficulties.*

inextricably, adv. Prec. & **-ly**. In an inextricable manner.

infallibilism, n. [1. infálibilizm; 2. ɪnfǽlɪbɪlɪzəm], fr. Med. Lat. *infallibil-(is)*, 'infallible'. See **infallible** & **-ism**. The doctrine of the infallibility of the Pope.

infallibilist, n. [1. infálibilist; 2. ɪnfǽlɪbɪlɪst]. See **infallible** & **-ist**. A believer in the Pope's infallibility.

infallibility, n. [1. infàlibíliti; 2. ɪnfæ̀lɪbílɪti]. **infallible** & **-ity**. Quality of being infallible; freedom, exemption, from liability to error; specif., *Papal Infallibility*, the dogma of the Roman Catholic Church laid down by the Vatican Council, 1870, that the Pope, when, speaking *ex cathedra* in virtue of his office, he lays down a doctrine concerning faith and morals, possesses the same exemption from liability to error as that with which Christ endowed the Church.

infallible, adj. [1. infálibl; 2. ɪnfǽlɪbl], fr. Med. Lat. *infallibil-(is)*, 'infallible'. See **in- (II.)** & **fallible**. **1.** (of person) Incapable of error in thought or action; invariably and unquestionably right; never mistaken. **2.** (of thought and action) Not liable to fail; certain to be right; incapable of going, or leading, astray; unerring. **3.** Occurring without fail; inevitable; always occurring under given circumstances: *the infallible result of such conduct will be . . .*

infallibly, adv. Prec. & **ly**. In an infallible manner: without fail.

infamize, vb. trans. [1. ínfamīz; 2. ínfəmaiz]. See next word & **-ize**. (rare) To render infamous, defame.

infamous, adj. [1. ínfamus; 2. ínfəməs], fr. Med. Lat. *infāmōs-(us)*, fr. Lat. *infām-(is)*, 'ill spoken of, notorious'. See **in- (II.)** & **famous**. **1.** Commonly known and reputed as scandalous and disgraceful; notorious: *a name infamous in history.* **2. a** Disgraceful, odious, shameful, scandalous; specif. (of medical practitioner) *infamous conduct*, such conduct as may be considered professionally disgraceful by the General Medical Council; **b** (colloq.) very bad of its kind, not coming up to desired standard of excellence: *an infamous pen, dinner, horse, house* &c. **3.** (law) Deprived of some civic or professional right or status through being convicted of crime.

infamously, adv. Prec. & **-ly**. In an infamous manner.

infamy, n. [1. ínfami; 2. ínfəmɪ], fr. Lat. *infāmia*, 'bad repute, dishonour, infamy', fr. *infām-(is)*, 'infamous'. See **infamous** & **-y**. **a** The state or quality of being infamous; (i.) dishonour, disgrace, evil repute; (ii.) moral depravity; **b** infamous conduct.

infancy, n. [1. ínfansi; 2. ínfənsɪ], fr. Lat. *infantia*, 'inability to speak; early childhood; lack of eloquence'. **infant** & **-cy**. **1.** The state or period of being an infant; earliest years, early childhood. **2.** Legal minority. **3.** The beginning, earliest stages, of anything: *in the infancy of the arts and sciences.*

infang(en)thief, n. [1. ínfang(en)thēf; 2. ínfæŋ(ən)þīf]. O.E. *infangenþēof*, see **in-** & **outfang(en)thief**. The right of a lord to judge a thief taken within his jurisdiction.

infant (I.), n. [1. ínfant; 2. ínfənt], fr. Lat., *infant-(em)*, 'a young child, babe', lit. 'unable, not yet able, to speak', fr. **in- (II.)** & *fant-*, Pres. Part. stem of *fāri*, 'to speak'. See **fable, fate**. **1.** Very young child, baby. **2.** Legal minor; person under the age of 21.

infant (II.), adj., fr. prec. Of, pertaining to, infants: *infant voices.*

infante, infanta, n. [1. infántā, infánta; 2. ɪnfǽntei, ɪnfǽntə]. Span., masc. & fem., fr. Lat. *infant-(em)*, 'infant'. See prec. Any son or daughter of a sovereign of Spain, formerly also of Portugal and Brazil, excluding the heir to the throne, who in Spain is *Prince of Asturias.*

infanticidal, adj. [1. infàntisídl; 2. ɪnfæ̀ntɪsáidl]. See next word & **-al**. Pertaining to infanticide.

infanticide, n. [1. infántisīd; 2. ɪnfǽntɪsaid], fr. L. Lat. *infanticīd-(ium)*, 'infanticide', fr. *infanticīda*, 'child-murderer'. See **infant** & **-cide**. **1.** n. **a** The crime of child-murder; murder of a new-born infant; **b** custom among some tribes of killing new-born children. **2.** (fr. L. Lat. *infanticīda*, 'child-murderer') One guilty of the crime of child-murder.

infantile, adj. [1. ínfantīl; 2. ínfəntail], fr. L. Lat. *infantil-(is)*, 'of infants'. **infant** & **-ile**. **1.** Connected with, affecting, infants; childish. **2.** In the first stages, elementary; incipient, rudimentary.

infantine, adj. [1. ínfantīn; 2. ínfəntain]. **infant** & **-ine (I.)**. Infantile, childish.

infantry, n. [1. ínfantri; 2. ínfəntrɪ], fr. Fr. *infanterie*, fr. Ital. *infanteria*, fr. *infante*, 'youth; servant; foot-soldier'. **infant** & **-(e)ry**. Foot-soldiers; *mounted infantry*, foot-soldiers mounted for rapidity of movement.

infantryman, n. [1. ínfantriman; 2. ínfəntrɪmən]. Soldier in an infantry regiment.

infant-school, n. School for very young children.

infatuate, vb. trans. [1. infátūāt; 2. ɪnfǽtjueit], fr. Lat. *infatuāt-(um)*, P.P. type of *infatuāre*, 'to make a fool of, infatuate', fr. **in- (I.)** & *fatu-(us)*, 'foolish, simple'. See **fatuous**. **1.** To make foolish, deprive of sane judgement. **2.** To inspire with a blind, unreasoning passion.

infatuated, adj. [1. infátūāted; 2. ɪnfǽtjueitɪd], fr. P.P. of prec. **1.** Foolish, silly, demented, incapable of rational judgement. **2.** Possessed with blind, extravagant, unreasoning passion.

infatuatedly, adv. Prec. & **-ly**. In an infatuated manner.

infatuation, n. [1. infàtuáshun; 2. ɪnfæ̀tjuéiʃən]. See **infatuate** & **-ion**. **a** The act of infatuating; **b** an engrossing, absorbing passion.

infect, vb. trans. [1. infékt; 2. ɪnfékt], fr. Lat. *infect-(um)*, P.P. type of *inficere*, 'to dip into; to stain, tinge; to taint, infect', fr. **in- (I.)** & *facere*, 'to make, do'. See **fact**. **1. a** To convey disease germs into, to contaminate with disease: *water infected with cholera*; **b** to cause to suffer from a disease, communicate disease to (a living organism). **2.** (fig.) **a** To affect morally by example; to inspire with, impart to: *to infect a person with one's laziness, high spirits* &c.; **b** to influence intellectually; to instil (idea &c.) into, imbue with, cause to adopt: *to infect a person with a theory, belief* &c.

infection, n. [1. infékshun; 2. ɪnfékʃən], fr. L. Lat. *infectiōn-(em)*. See prec. & **-ion**. **1.** The act of infecting, process of being infected; communication, or absorption, of germs of disease, transmission or acquirement of disease. **2.** (fig.) **a** Bad moral influence, contamination, vitiation; **b** intellectual or moral influence: *the infection of another's excitement, enthusiasm* &c.

infectious, adj. [1. infékshus; 2. ɪnfékʃəs]. **infect** & **-ious**. **1. a** (of person or thing) Suffering from, contaminated by infection, and in a condition which makes him or it liable to communicate disease; having the property of infecting; **b** (of disease) (i.) arising from, due to, infection; (ii.) capable of being, liable to be, communicated from one person to another. **2.** (of moral, emotional, or intellectual influence &c.) Easily communicated by, and picked up from others: *laughter, good manners, habits, are infectious.*

infectiously, adv. Prec. & **-ly**. In an infectious manner.

infectiousness, n. See prec. & **-ness**. State or quality of being infectious.

infective, adj. [1. inféktiv; 2. ɪnféktɪv]. **infect** & **-ive**. Liable to infect; infectious.

infectively, adv. Prec. & **-ly**. In an infective manner; by infection.

infectiveness, n. See prec. & **-ness**. Quality or state of being infective.

infelicific, adj. [1. ìnfēlisífik; 2. ìnfīlɪsífɪk]. **in- (II.)** & **felicific**. (rare) Causing unhappiness.

infelicitous, adj. [1. ìnfelísitus; 2. ìnfɪlísɪtəs]. **in- (II.)** & **felicitous**. **1.** Unhappy. **2.** (of style, speech &c.) Inappropriate, not happy, inapt; not well expressed.

infelicity, n. [1. ìnfelísiti; 2. ìnfɪlísɪtɪ], fr. Lat. *infēlīcitāt-(em)*, 'ill-luck, misfortune'. **in- (II.)** & **felicity**. **a** Unhappiness, misery, misfortune; **b** inappropriateness; inapt, inelegant turn of phrase &c.

infer, vb. trans. [1. infér; 2. ɪnfʌ́], fr. Lat. *inferre*, 'to bring, carry in; to introduce, bring forward; to deduce, infer', fr. **in- (I.)** & *ferre*, 'to carry, bear'. See **-ferous & bear (I)**. **1.** To deduce, derive, as a consequence; draw conclusions: *what am I to infer from your remarks?*; *from the way he behaved I should infer that the man was drunk.* **2.** To imply, involve, lead to as a conclusion: *your silence infers consent.*

inferable, adj. [1. ínferabl; 2. ínfərəbl]. Prec. & **-able**. Capable of being inferred.

inference, n. [1. ínferens; 2. ínfərəns], fr. Med. Lat. *inferentia*, 'inference'. **infer** & **-ence**. **1.** Act of inferring. **2.** Something inferred; deduction, conclusion. **3.** Something implied; implication.

inferential, adj. [1. inferénshal; 2. ɪnfərénʃəl]. See prec. & **-ial**. Of, pertaining to, an inference; inferred.

inferentially, adv. Prec. & **-ly**. By inference; as an inference.

inferior (I.), adj. [1. infḗrior; 2. infíəriə], fr. Lat. *inferior*, compar. of *infer-(us)*, 'lower'. See **infra**; cogn. w. **under**. **1.** At a lower level in space; near the bottom or base, beneath; specif. (typog.) placed below normal line of print. **2.** *Inferior to*, (expressing specif. comparison) **a** of a lower quality or degree of excellence than, not so good as: *foreign mutton is inferior to home-grown in flavour*; **b** of lower status or rank than: *a colonel is inferior to a general in the army*. **3. a** Of poor quality; second-rate, mediocre: *this wine is very inferior stuff*; **b** of low or humble rank or status: *the inferior classes, ranks*; *an inferior clerk*; *the inferior clergy*, the unbeneficed; those below the rank of prebendary or canon. Phr. *inferior planets*, those revolving between the earth and the sun.

inferior (II.), n., fr. prec. Person **a** of lower rank, or **b** of less ability &c.: *to be condescending to one's inferiors*.

inferiority, n. [1. inferióriti; 2. infìəriɔ́riti]. **inferior** (I.) & **-ity**. The state of being inferior; *inferiority complex*, a term of psycho-analysis, for a complex or abnormal mental state, due to the sense of being inferior to others, which often results in exaggerated self-assertion &c.

inferiorly, adv. [1. infḗriorli; 2. infíəriəli]. See **inferior** (I.) & **-ly**. In an inferior manner.

infernal, adj. [1. infẽrnl; 2. infʌ́nl], fr. Lat. *infernāl-(is)*, 'belonging to the lower regions', fr. *infern-(us)*, 'lying beneath; underground; infernal', fr. *infer-(us)*, 'lower'. See **inferior**. **1.** Of, pertaining to, hell: *the infernal regions*. **2.** Devilish, fiendish, abnormally wicked, inhuman: *infernal cruelty* &c.; *infernal machine*, explosive bomb. **3.** (colloq.) Outrageous, confounded: *an infernal nuisance*.

infernality, n. [1. ìnfẽrnáliti; 2. ìnfʌnǽliti]. Prec. & **-ity**. The quality of being infernal.

infernally, adv. [1. infẽrnali; 2. infʌ́nəli]. **infernal** & **-ly**. **a** In an infernal manner; to an infernal degree; **b** (colloq., as intens.) very.

inferno, n. [1. infẽrnō; 2. infʌ́nou]. Ital., fr. Lat. dat. of *infernus*, 'beneath'. See **infernal**. **a** Hell; specif. (cap.) the first part of Dante's 'Divina Commedia'; **b** (by transf.) something which can be likened to hell: *the burning building became an inferno*.

inferrable, adj. [1. infẽrabl; 2. infʌ́rəbl]. **infer** & **-able**. Inferable.

infertile, adj. [1. infẽrtīl; 2. infʌ́tail], fr. L. Lat. *infertil-(is)*, 'unfruitful'. **in-** (II.) & **fertile**. Not fertile; barren, sterile.

infertility, n. [1. ìnfẽrtíliti; 2. ìnfʌtíliti]. Prec. & **-ity**. The quality of being infertile.

infest, vb. trans. [1. infést; 2. infést], fr. Lat. *infestāre*, 'to attack, trouble, molest', fr. *infest-(us)*, 'attacking; unsafe, unquiet; hostile'; cp. *manifestus*, 'able to be grasped by the hand' (see **manifest**); the second element is perh. cogn. w. Scrt. *dharš-aṇam*, 'attack', *dhṛšṇóti*, 'dares', O.E. *dearr*, 'dare'; see **dare**. (gen. of undesirable persons or animals) To swarm in, frequent in large numbers: *brigands infest the mountains*; *infested with bats, vermin*.

infestation, n. [1. ìnfestā́shun; 2. ìnfestéiʃən]. Prec. & **-ation**. The act of infesting; state of being infested.

infeudation, n. [1. ìnfūdā́shun; 2. ìnfjūdéiʃən], fr. Med. Lat. *infeudātiōn-(em)*, fr. *infeudāt-(um)*, P.P. type of *infeudāre*, 'to enfeoff', fr. **in-** (I.), **feud** (II.), & **-ation**. **1.** The granting of a fief; enfeoffment. **2.** The granting of tithes to a layman.

infibulation, n. [1. infibūlā́shun; 2. infìbjuléiʃən], fr. Lat. *infibul-(āre)*, 'to close with a clasp' (fr. **in-** (I.) & **fibula**), & **-ation**. The act of securing, fastening; specif. of the sexual organs, to prevent intercourse, as practised among certain primitive tribes and races.

infidel (I.), n. [1. ínfidl; 2. ínfidl], fr. O. Fr. *infidèle*, fr. Lat. *infidēl-(is)*, 'faithless; unbelieving', fr. **in-** (II.) & *fidēlis*, 'faithful'. See **fidelity**. **1.** Person who believes in no religion; unbeliever, atheist. **2.** (hist.) Person who does not believe in Christianity; (among Mohammedans) adherent of some other religion; pagan, heathen.

infidel (II.), adj., fr. prec. Connected with infidels; unbelieving.

infidelity, n. [1. ìnfidéliti; 2. ìnfidéliti], fr. Lat. *infidēlitāt-(em)*, 'unfaithfulness'. See **infidel** & **-ity**. **1.** Disbelief in the Christian religion. **2.** Faithlessness, esp. of husband or wife.

infield, n. [1. ínfēld; 2. ínfīəld]. **in** (II.) & **field**. **1.** Farm-land lying nearest to farm-buildings. **2.** Arable land; land under regular cultivation. **3. a** (cricket) Ground near and surrounding the pitch; the fielders near the wicket, contrasted with *outfield*; **b** (baseball) space between the base lines.

infiltrate, vb. trans. & intrans. [1. infíltrāt; 2. infíltreit]. **in-** (I.) & **filtrate**. **A.** trans. **1.** To filter (fluid) into; cause to filter into or through something. **2.** To pass, filter, through, permeate. **B.** intrans. (of fluid) To penetrate, permeate, be diffused.

infiltration, n. [1. ìnfiltrā́shun; 2. ìnfiltréiʃən]. Prec. & **-ion**. The act or process of infiltrating; state of being infiltrated.

infinite (I.), adj. [1. ínfinit; 2. ínfinit], fr. Lat. *infīnīt-(us)*, 'boundless, unlimited'. **in-** (II.) & **finite**. **1.** Boundless, unlimited, endless, illimitable; very great, measureless: *infinite space*; *an infinite number*; *infinite kindness, gratitude* &c. **2.** (with pl. n.) Very many, numerous, countless. **3.** (gram., of parts of vb.) Not limited by number and person.

infinite (II.), n., fr. prec. *The Infinite*, **a** the Creator, God; **b** infinite space.

infinitely, adv. **infinite** (I.) & **-ly**. To an infinite extent, degree.

infinitesimal, adj. & n. [1. ìnfinitésimal; 2. ìnfinitésiməl], fr. **infinite**, on anal. of **centesimal**. **1.** adj. Minute, very small; infinitely small. **2.** n. Infinitesimal amount.

infinitesimally, adv. Prec. & **-ly**. In an infinitesimal manner; minutely.

infinitival, adj. [1. ìnfinitívl; 2. ìnfinitáivl]. See next word & **-al**. Of, with, pertaining to, an infinitive: *an infinitival construction*.

infinitive, adj. & n. [1. infínitiv; 2. infínitiv], fr. Lat. *infīnītīv-(us)*, 'indefinite', fr. *infīnīt-(us)*. See **infinite** & **-ive**. (gram.) **1.** adj. Connected with that form of a verb which denotes action or existence without limitation of person, number, or tense. **2.** n. Infinitive form, or mood, of verb.

infinitude, n. [1. infínitūd; 2. infínitjūd]. See **infinite** & **-tude**. **1.** The state of being infinite; boundlessness, endlessness. **2.** Infinite extent, number.

infinity, n. [1. infíniti; 2. infíniti], fr. Lat. *infīnītāt-(em)*, 'boundlessness', fr. **in-** (II.) & *fīn-(is)*, 'limit, boundary'. See **finis** & **-ity**. **1.** The state of being infinite; boundlessness. **2.** (math.) Infinite quantity.

infirm, adj. [1. infẽrm; 2. infʌ́m], fr. Lat. *infirm-(us)*, 'weak, feeble; inconstant, weak-minded', fr. **in-** (II.) & *firmus*, 'strong, firm'. See **firm** (I.). **1. a** (of persons) Reverse of active, robust; physically weak, feeble, debilitated; esp. through old age; **b** (of movements) characterized by, resulting from, weakness; characteristic of an infirm person. **2.** Mentally or morally weak; unstable, vacillating.

infirmary, n. [1. infẽrmari; 2. infʌ́məri], fr. Med. Lat. *infirmāria*; prec. & **-ary**. **a** Hospital, esp. one attached to a poor-law institution; **b** building, room, set aside for the sick in an institution, school &c.

infirmity, n. [1. infẽrmiti; 2. infʌ́miti], fr. Lat. *infirmitāt-(em)*, 'weakness; sickness', **infirm** & **-ity**. **1.** The state of being infirm. **2. a** Specific form of bodily weakness; ailment; **b** moral defect; immoral habit.

infirmly, adv. [1. infẽrmli; 2. infʌ́mli]. **infirm** & **-ly**. In an infirm manner.

infix (I.), vb. trans. [1. infíks; 2. infíks]. **in** (II.) & **fix**. **1. a** To fix, set firmly, fasten; **b** (fig.) fix in the mind. **2.** (gram.) To insert (a sound, formative element) in the body of a word.

infix (II.), n. [1. ínfiks; 2. ínfiks], fr. prec. Sound, formative element, inserted in body of a word.

inflame, vb. trans. & intrans. [1. inflā́m; 2. infléim], fr. O. Fr. *enflammer*, fr. Lat. *inflammāre*, 'to set alight, kindle; to rouse, excite'. See **in-** (I.) & **flame**. **A.** trans. **1.** (rare) To cause to blaze, burn, flame; to set on fire, set alight. **2.** To cause rise of temperature in; render hot, feverish, angry, red: *an inflamed eye, pimple* &c. **3.** (fig.) **a** To rouse, excite, passion, strong feeling, anger &c. in; **b** to stimulate, rouse (passion, feeling &c.); to increase intensity of (feelings); to exacerbate. **B.** intrans. **1.** (rare) To blaze up, take fire, break into flame. **2.** To become congested, feverish, sore. **3.** (fig., of feelings &c.) To become heated, roused, excited, agitated.

inflammability, n. [1. inflàmabíliti; 2. inflæ̀məbíliti]. See next word & **-ity**. **a** Liability, tendency, to catch fire, to burst into flame; **b** excitability of mind and feelings.

inflammable, adj. & n. [1. inflámabl; 2. inflǽməbl], fr. Lat. *inflamm-(āre)*, 'to set alight; to excite'. See **inflame** & **-able**. **1.** adj. **a** (of material substance) Easily set on fire; liable to catch fire, tending to burn quickly; combustible; **b** (of temperament, feelings &c.) easily roused, excitable, fiery. **2.** n. Inflammable substance.

inflammableness, n. Prec. & **-ness**. Quality of being inflammable (lit. and fig.).

inflammation, n. [1. ìnflamā́shun; 2. ìnfləméiʃən], fr. Lat. *inflammātiōn-(em)*, 'kindling, conflagration; inflammation of part of the body', fr. *inflammāre*, 'to set on fire; to excite'. See **inflame** & **-ation**. (chiefly of bodily conditions) **a** Act or process of inflaming; **b** state of being inflamed; congestion accompanied with abnormal increase of temperature in some part of the body, e.g. *inflammation of the lungs*, pneumonia.

inflammatory, adj. [1. inflámaturi; 2. inflǽmətəri], fr. Lat. *inflammāt-(um)*, P.P. type of *inflammāre*, 'to kindle; to rouse, excite'. See **inflame** & **-ory**. **1.** Pertaining to, tending to produce, inflammation of part of the body. **2.** (fig.) Tending to rouse, excite to, passion; tending to inflame passions of anger and hostility: *inflammatory speeches*.

inflate, vb. trans. [1. inflā́t; 2. infléit], fr. Lat. *inflāt-(um)*, P.P. type of *inflāre*, 'to blow into, inflate; to puff up, make haughty', fr. **in-** (I.) & *flāre*, 'to blow', q.v. under **flatus**. **1. a** To blow out, or up, cause to swell out, fill to fullest extent, to distend, with air or gas: *to inflate a balloon*; **b** (commerc.) To raise (price of goods, shares &c.) artificially, otherwise than as natural result of supply and demand; **c** to increase the amount of money, especially paper money, in circulation, leading thus to an increase in prices. **2.** (fig.) To make haughty, proud, overweening; to puff up: *inflated with pride*.

inflated, adj. [1. inflā́ted; 2. infléitid], fr. P.P. of prec. (of style, language) High-flown, grandiose, turgid, bombastic.

inflation, n. [1. inflā́shun; 2. infléiʃən], fr. Lat. *inflātiōn-(em)*, 'a swelling up, distension'. **inflate** & **-ion**. Act or process of inflating; state of being inflated (in all senses).

inflect, vb. trans. [1. inflékt; 2. inflékt], fr. Lat. *inflect-(ere)*, 'to bend, curve; to alter, change; (gram.) to mark, pronounce, with a circumflex accent; (mus.) to modulate', fr. **in-** (I.) & *flectere*, 'to bend'. See **flex** (I.). **1.** To bend, curve inwards; incurve. **2.** (gram.) To modify forms of words by inflexion. **3.** To modulate (the voice).

inflection, n. See **inflexion**.

inflective, adj. [1. infléktiv; 2. infléktiv]. Prec. & **-ive**. Subject to inflexion.

inflexibility, n. [1. inflèksibíliti; 2. inflèksibíliti]. See next word & **-ity**. (lit. and fig.) The quality of being inflexible.

inflexible, adj. [1. infléksibl; 2. infléksibl], fr. Lat. *inflexibil-(is)*, 'inflexible', fr. *inflex-(um)*, P.P. type of *inflectere*, 'to bend'. See **inflect** & **-ible**. Not flexible; **a** (in moral sense) (i.) not to be diverted from purpose: *inflexible determination*; (ii.) unshakable, unflinching: *inflexible courage*; **b** (of material things; rare) not to be bent; rigid.

inflexibly, adv. Prec. & **-ly**. In an inflexible manner.

inflexion, n. [1. inflékshun; 2. infléks̆ən], fr. Lat. *inflexiōn-(em)*, 'bending; inflexion, modification', fr. *inflex-(um)*, P.P. type of *inflectere*, 'to bend'. See **inflect** & **-ion**. **1.** The act of bending; state of being bent. **2.** Modulation of the voice; intonation. **3.** (gram.) **a** Variation of words, by addition of suffixes, alteration of vowel of base &c., so as to express number, person, case, tense &c.; **b** a suffix used in inflexion; inflexional ending.

inflexional, adj. [1. inflékshunal; 2. inflékʃənəl]. Prec. & **-al**. Pertaining to, of the nature of, inflexion, or of an inflexion.

inflexionless, adj. [1. inflékshunles; 2. inflékʃənlis]. See prec. & **-less**. Without inflexion.

inflict, vb. trans. [1. inflíkt; 2. inflíkt], fr. Lat. *inflict-(um)*, P.P. type of *inflīgere*, 'to strike, dash, against; to impose', fr. **in-** (**I.**) & *flīgere*, 'to strike, strike down'. Cogn. w. O. Slav. *blizŭ*, 'struck'; *blizna*, 'scar'; Lett. *blaiſīt*, 'to beat, strike'; Gk. *phlíbein*, 'to press, crush'. **a** To strike, deal, perpetrate upon, cause to undergo: *to inflict a blow, stroke, wound, pain &c. upon a person*; **b** to impose: *to inflict a penalty, loss, suffering.*

inflictable, adj. [1. inflíktabl; 2. inflíktəbl]. Prec. & **-able**. Capable of being inflicted.

infliction, n. [1. inflíkshun; 2. inflíkʃən]. **inflict** & **-ion**. **1.** The act of inflicting; state of being inflicted. **2.** Something that is inflicted; punishment, suffering, tribulation &c.

inflorescence, n. [1. infloresens; 2. inflərésəns]. **in-** (**I.**) & **florescence**. (bot.) **1.** The character and arrangement of flowers of a plant. **2.** The whole number of flowers of a plant, considered collectively. **3.** (lit. and fig.) The process of flowering, blossoming forth.

inflow, n. [1. ínflō; 2. ínflou]. **in** (**II.**) & **flow**. The process of flowing in; influx.

inflowing, adj. & n. [1. ínflōing; 2. ínflouiŋ]. Prec. & **-ing**. **1.** adj. Flowing in. **2.** n. Inflow.

influence (**I.**), n. [1. ínflooens; 2. ínfluəns], fr. Fr., fr. Lat. *influ-(ere)*, 'to flow into', fr. **in-** (**I.**) & *fluere*, 'to flow'. See **fluent** & **-ce**. **1.** (astrol.) Effect supposed to be exerted by the heavenly bodies upon human affairs and human character. **2. a** Effect, consequence, result, of non-physical action; mental or spiritual effect of power exerted upon a person by precept or example: *the Salvation Army has a civilizing influence upon strata of society which are often not reached by the Churches.* **b** effect produced upon mind or body by some external agency, material or non-material: *to be under the influence of terror, of drugs, of drink*; *to feel the influence of music, of kindness* &c. **3.** Power of producing a mental or spiritual effect; ability to modify another's will, behaviour &c.; mental or moral ascendancy; suasion, advocacy: *to have influence with the Government*; *to exercise one's influence in a person's behalf*; *a person of influence*, one able to affect the minds or conduct of others, esp. of those in high places. **4.** Human, or supernatural being, exerting influence: *influences for good or for evil are all around us.*

influence (**II.**), vb. trans., fr. prec. To exert influence upon; especially, to affect action or thought of, guide, move, incline, predispose, by intellectual or moral suasion or appeal.

influent, adj. & n. [1. ínflooent; 2. ínfluənt]. See **influence** & **-ent**. **1.** adj. (lit. and fig.) Flowing in. **2.** n. Tributary stream, affluent.

influential, adj. [1. inflooénshal; 2. influénʃəl]. fr. Lat. *influent-(em)*, Pres. Part. of *influ-(ere)*, 'to flow in'. See **influence** & **-ial**. **a** Exerting influence; providing an inducement or motive: *circumstances which were influential in one's decision*; **b** (of persons) possessing and exerting influence; able to effect something by exerting influence.

influentially, adv. Prec. & **-ly**. By means of influence; so as to exert influence.

influenza, n. [1. inflooénza; 2. influénzə]. Ital. See **influence**. Epidemic disease caused by bacteria, characterized by catarrh, high fever, and extreme weakness in patient.

influx, n. [1. ínfluks; 2. ínflaks], fr. L. Lat. *influx-(us)*, 'a flowing in', fr. *influx-(um)*, P.P. type of *influ-(ere)*, 'to flow in'. See **in-** (**I.**) & **flux**. **1.** The process of flowing in; that which flows in. **2.** The act of coming in, entrance; a rapid, constant, copious, flow: *an influx of aliens, visitors, patients*; *influx of gold, wealth, of correspondence* &c.

inform, vb. trans. & intrans. [1. infórm; 2. infɔ́m], fr. O. Fr. *enformer*, fr. Lat. *inform-(āre)*, 'to give form to, shape; to represent, delineate; to instruct', fr. **in-** (**I.**) & *formāre*, 'to shape, form'. See **form** (**II.**). **A.** trans. **1.** To fill, imbue, animate, with a moral or physical quality; pervade: *informed with new life, with beauty* &c. **2.** To tell, instruct, impart knowledge to, acquaint with: *to inform a person of a fact, that he must do something* &c. **B.** intrans. *Inform against*, to bring a charge, complaint, against; to give information leading to a charge: *to inform against a person.*

informal, adj. [1. infórmal; 2. infɔ́məl]. **in-** (**II.**) & **formal**. **1.** Not in accordance with usual form or procedure; not in order; irregular. **2.** Without formality and ceremony.

informality, n. [1. informáliti; 2. infɔmǽliti]. Prec. & **-ity**. **1.** The state of being informal. **2.** An informal proceeding.

informally, adv. [1. infórmali; 2. infɔ́məli]. See prec. & **-ly**. In an informal manner.

informant, n. [1. infórmant; 2. infɔ́mənt]. **inform** & **-ant**. Person who gives information.

information, n. [1. informáshun; 2. infəméiʃən]. Cp. O. Fr. *enformacion*, fr. Lat. *informātiōn-(em)*, 'representation, outline, sketch; idea, conception'. **inform** & **-ation**. **1.** The act of informing; state of being informed. **2. a** Something told, communicated, or acquired; imparted knowledge of a fact: *I have no information on the point.* **b** knowledge instruction, facts learnt; learning: *to be a mine of information*; *to pick up useful information.* **3.** (law) Accusation lodged with magistrate or court.

informational, adj. [1. informáshunal; 2. infəméiʃənəl]. Prec. & **-al**. Pertaining to information.

informative, adj. [1. infórmativ; 2. infɔ́mətiv], fr. Lat. *informāt-(um)*, P.P. type of *informāre*, 'to give shape to'. See **inform** & **-ive**. Imparting information; instructive.

informatory, adj. [1. infórmaturi; 2. infɔ́mətəri]. See prec. & **-ory**. Informative.

informed, adj. [1. infórmd; 2. infɔ́md], fr. P.P. of **inform**. Chiefly *well-*, or *ill-informed*; having, lacking, information; **a** in general, knowledgeable: *a very well-informed man*; **b** possessing, lacking, information on a specific matter: *ill-, well-informed as to another's intentions.*

informer, n. [1. infórmer; 2. infɔ́mə]. **inform** & **-er**. Person who informs, brings accusation, against another; *common informer*, one who makes a business of collecting evidence of infringement of the law for the purpose of bringing a charge.

infra, adv. [1. ínfra; 2. ínfrə]. Lat. *infrā*, 'below, underneath'; fr. earlier **ŋdhra* & cogn. w. **under**. See also **inferior**. **a** Below, further down, underneath; **b** (in references) later, below, further on (in the book), as *see infra p. 40* &c.

infra-, pref., fr. Lat. *infrā*, 'below'. See prec. Below; specif. (physics) *infra-red*, of invisible rays of the spectrum, below the red rays, the limit of visibility. Cp. *ultra-violet.*

infraction, n. [1. infrákshun; 2. infrǽkʃən], fr. Lat. *infractiōn-(em)*, 'a breaking'. See **in-** (**I.**) & **fraction**; also **infringe**. Infringement, breaking, violation of, offence against (the law &c.).

infra dig., adj. [1. ínfra díg; 2. ínfrə díg]. Abbr. of Lat. *infrā dignitātem*, 'below the dignity (of)'. **infra** & **dignity**. (pred.) Beneath one's dignity; derogatory.

infralapsarian, n. & adj. [1. infralapsárian; 2. infrəlæpséəriən]. **infra-** & Lat. *laps-(us)*, 'a fall', see **lapse**, & **-arian**. **1.** n. One of a school of Calvinists which holds that the decrees and purposes of God for the salvation of the Elect, were formed after, and in consequence of, the Fall of man; contrasted with *supralapsarian.* **2.** adj. Pertaining to this doctrine.

infrequency, n. [1. infrékwensi; 2. infríkwənsi]. **in-** (**II.**) & **frequency**. The state of being infrequent; rarity of occurrence.

infrequent, adj. [1. infrékwent; 2. infríkwənt], fr. Lat. *infrequent-(em)*, 'seldom occurring, rare, unusual, uncommon; unfrequented'. **in-** (**II.**) & **frequent**. **a** Not frequent; uncommon, seldom occurring; **b** occurring at considerable intervals; sparse.

infrequently, adv. Prec. & **-ly**. Not often; seldom, rarely.

infringe, vb. trans. [1. infrínj; 2. infríndʒ], fr. Lat. *infring-(ere)*, 'to break, crack, snap off; to mitigate, assuage', fr. **in-** (**I.**) & *frangere*, 'to break'. See **fraction**. To fail to obey or keep; to violate, break: *to infringe the law, a rule, an oath, promise, copyright* &c.

infringement, n. [1. infrínjment; 2. infríndʒmənt]. Prec. & **-ment**. The act of infringing; act which infringes.

infructuous, adj. [1. infrúktūus; 2. infráktjuəs], fr. Lat. *infructuōs-(us)*, 'unfruitful; useless, fruitless'. See **in-** (**II.**) & **fructuous**. **1.** Unfruitful, barren. **2.** (fig.) Fruitless, useless, yielding no result, unprofitable.

infundibular, adj. [1. infundíbūlar; 2. infandíbjulə], fr. Lat. *infundibul-(um)*, 'a funnel', fr. *infund-(ere)*, 'to pour in'. See **infuse** & **-ar**. Funnel-shaped.

infuriate, vb. trans. [1. infúriāt; 2. infjɔ́rieit], fr. Med. Lat. *infuriāt-(um)*, P.P. type of *infuriāre*, 'to enrage', fr. **in-** (**I.**) & Lat. *furiāre*, 'to enrage', fr. *furia*, 'fury'. See **fury**. To render furious; to enrage, madden, drive to frenzy.

infuse, vb. trans. [1. infúz; 2. infjúz], fr. Lat. *infūs-(um)*, P.P. type of *infundere*, 'to pour into or upon; to wet, moisten; to communicate, impart', fr. **in-** (**I.**) & *fundere*, 'to pour'. See **fuse** (**I.**). **1.** To pour, introduce, transfer (liquid into vessel &c.). **2.** To steep, soak (organic, esp. vegetable substance) in liquid, so as to extract its properties: *to infuse tea.* **3.** (fig.) To introduce, inspire, cause to pass into, permeate: *to infuse* (*the mind, a person*) *with new hope*; *to infuse fresh courage into one.*

infuser, n. [1. infúzer; 2. infjúzə]. Prec. & **-er**. Vessel for infusing herbs &c.

infusibility, n. [1. infūzibíliti; 2. infjūzibíliti]. See next word & **-ity**. **a** The quality of being infusible; **b** quality of not being fusible.

infusible, adj. [1. infúzibl; 2. infjúzibl]. **infuse** & **-ible**. **1.** Capable of being infused. **2.** (**in-** negative pref., & **fusible**) Not fusible; not capable of being melted or dissolved.

infusion, n. [1. infúzhun; 2. infjúʒən], fr. Lat. *infūsiōn-(em)*, 'a pouring into'. See **infuse** & **-ion**. **1.** Act or process of infusing; state of being infused. **2.** Liquid solution of properties of a vegetable substance, obtained by infusion. **3.** Something added to, blended with, something else; a mixture.

Infusoria, n. [1. infūzória; 2. infjūzɔ́riə]. See **infuse** & **-ory** & **-ia**. One of several groups of Protozoa found in infusions of decaying organic matter.

infusorial, adj. [1. infūzórial; 2. infjūzɔ́riəl]. Prec. & **-al**. Of, containing, composed of, infusoria.

infusorian, adj. & n. [1. infūzórian; 2. infjūzɔ́riən]. **Infusoria** & **-an**. **a** adj. Infusorial; **b** n., one of the Infusoria.

infusory, adj. [1. infúzuri; 2. infjúzəri]. **infuse** & **-ory**. Infusorial.

-ing (**I.**), suff. [1. ing; 2. iŋ] representing

O.E., M.E. *-ung, -ing*; Gmc. **-unga*, forming ns. of action. In M.E. & Mod. Engl. these ns. have the vbl. property of being modified by an adv., and (if trans.) of governing an object: *the expectation of probably receiving a fortune in the future.* **1.** Besides denoting merely the vbl. action (*dancing, hunting* &c.), esp. as occupation or trade (*stock-broking, gardening*), ns. in *-ing* have the senses of **a** material used: *railing, clothing, facing*; **b** thing produced: *painting, facings, smocking*; **c** thing that is to be acted upon: *sewing, a sitting of eggs*; **d** character of: *colouring.* **2.** Ns. in *-ing* are derived also fr. other ns., usually w. the senses of **a** employment: *clerking, soldiering*; **b** thing used as: *grating, paling, carpeting, flooring.*

-ing (II.), suff. forming Pres. Part., wh. during 14th cent. gradually ousted the older *-ende, -inde* &c. The origin of the suff. is uncertain, but it is perh. identical w. prec.

-ing (III.), suff. O.E., M.E. *-ing*, fr. Gmc. **-ing-*, forming patronymics (*king, Atheling*), & ns. denoting 'thing related to, connected with, resembling, composed of' (*stocking, farthing* &c.).

ingathering, n. [1. ín-gàdhering; 2. íngæðəriŋ]. **in- (I.)** & **gather** & **-ing (I.)**. Gathering, bringing in, collecting, harvesting.

ingeminate, vb. trans. [1. injéminàt; 2. indžémineit], fr. Lat. *ingeminăt-(um)*, P.P. type of *ingemināre*, 'to redouble, repeat, reiterate', fr. **in- (I.)** & *gemināre*, 'to double', fr. *gemin-(us)*, 'twin'. See **gemini**. To repeat, say or do over again, reiterate: '*he* (Lord Falkland) *would . . . ingeminate the word Peace, Peace . . .*' (Clarendon, 'Hist. of the Rebellion').

ingenious, adj. [1. injénius; 2. indžínjəs], fr. Lat. *ingeniōs-(us)*, 'intellectual, gifted, clever; skilfully made, ingenious', fr. *ingeni-(um)*, 'nature; disposition; ability', fr. **in- (I.)** & stem **ĝen-*, 'to produce; to be born'. See **genus**. **a** (of person, the mind &c.) Clever, resourceful; skilled in, possessing faculty of, inventing, contriving; **b** (of things contrived or devised) exhibiting originality, resourcefulness, and skill; skilfully contrived: *an ingenious device, excuse* &c.

ingeniously, adv. Prec. & **-ly**. In an ingenious manner.

ingénue, n. [1. ánzhanū; 2. æ̃ʒeny]. Fr. See **ingenuous**. **a** An artless, inexperienced, simple, girl; **b** actress representing such a character.

ingenuity, n. [1. ìnjenúiti; 2. indžinjúiti], fr. Lat. *ingenuităt-(em)*, 'frankness, ingenuousness, nobility', fr. *ingenu-(us)*, 'free-born'. See next word & **-ity**. The Engl. meaning is due to confusion w. **ingenious**. **a** Resourcefulness in invention, power and skill in devising; **b** originality of design, cleverness.

ingenuous, adj. [1. injénūus; 2. indžénjuəs], fr. Lat. *ingenu-(us)*, 'native; free-born; noble, upright', fr. **in- (I.)** & **ĝen-*, 'to beget; to be born' (see **genus**), & **-ous**. **1.** Frank, straightforward; open, concealing nothing; candid, sincere. **2.** Simple, artless, unsophisticated, unaffected.

ingenuously, adv. Prec. & **-ly**. In an ingenuous manner.

ingenuousness, n. See prec. & **-ness**. The quality of being ingenuous.

ingest, vb. trans. [1. injést; 2. indžést], fr. Lat. *ingest-(um)*, P.P. type of *ingerere*, 'to bring, put, carry, in; to press, force, upon', fr. **in- (I.)** & *gerere*, 'to carry'. See **-gerous**. To swallow, take into the stomach.

ingestion, n. [1. injéschun; 2. indžéstʃən], fr. Lat. *ingestiōn-(em)*, 'a pouring in, introduction'. Prec. & **-ion**. Process of ingesting; state of being ingested.

ingestive, adj. [1. injéstiv; 2. indžéstiv]. **ingest** & **-ive**. Serving, tending, to ingest.

ingle, n. [1. íngl; 2. íŋgl]. Gael. & Ir. *aingeal*, 'fire'. **a** Fire on hearth; **b** fire-place.

ingle-nook, n. Prec. & **nook**. Corner by fire, chimney-corner.

inglorious, adj. [1. in-glórius; 2. inglɔ́riəs], fr. Lat. *inglōriōs-(us)*, 'inglorious, without repute'. See **in- (II.)** & **glorious**. **1.** Unrenowned, obscure, unknown to fame: '*Some mute, inglorious Milton*' (Gray's 'Elegy'). **2.** Dishonourable, ignoble, ignominious.

ingloriously, adv. Prec. & **-ly**. In an inglorious manner.

ingoing, adj. & n. [1. ín-gōing; 2. íngouiŋ]. **in (II.)** & **go** & **-ing (I., II.)**. **1.** adj. Going in, just entering: *ingoing tenant.* **2.** n. Act of going in; entrance.

ingot, n. [1. ínggut; 2. íŋgət], fr. **in- (I.)** & an element prob. cogn. w. Mod. Germ. *guss*, 'a casting, mould', cp. O.E. & M.E. *goten*, P.P. type of O.E. *gēotan*, M.E. *ȝēten*, 'to pour; to shed; to cast (metal)'; cp. O.S. *giotan*; O.H.G. *giozan*; Goth. *giutan*, 'to pour'; Mod. Germ. *giessen*. Cogn. w. Gk. *khéein* (fr. **khew-ō*), 'to pour'; *khūlos*, 'sap' (cp. **chyle**), *khúsis*, 'effusion'; Lat. *fundere*, 'to pour', P.P. *fūs-um*; Scrt. *juhṓti*, 'pours into the fire, sacrifices'. See **fuse** & perh. **gut**. Mass, lump, or bar of metal, esp. gold or silver, cast in a mould.

ingrain, adj. [1. ín-grān; 2. íngrein] before n., [1. ingrán; 2. ingréin] after n. or pred. **in (I.)** & **grain (I.)**. **1.** Dyed in the yarn or fibre, before being manufactured into goods. **2.** (fig.) Inveterate, ingrafted, ingrained.

ingrained, adj. [1. ín-grānd, in-gránd; 2. íngreind, ingréind]. Same as **engrained**. Penetrating and permeating the whole; fully established, inveterate, inherent, innate. In both material and non-material senses: *ingrained dirt; ingrained habits, wickedness* &c.

ingrate, adj. & n. [1. ín-grāt; 2. íngreit], fr. Lat. *ingrāt-(us)*, 'unpleasant; ungrateful', fr. **in- (II.)** & *grāt-(us)*, 'pleasing; grateful'. See **grateful, grace**. (archaic) **1.** adj. Ungrateful, thankless. **2.** n. Ungrateful person.

ingratiate, vb. trans. [1. in-gráshiāt; 2. ingréiʃieit]. Prob. through Ital. fr. Lat. Phr. *in gratiam*, 'for the favour (of)'; see **in- (I.)** & **grace** & **-ate**. (reflex.) To obtain another's goodwill; to bring (oneself) into another's good graces or favour: *to try to ingratiate oneself with a person.*

ingratiating, adj. [1. in-gráshiāting; 2. ingréiʃieitiŋ], fr. Pres. Part. of prec. Serving, tending, to ingratiate, or propitiate; attractive, charming, winning: *an ingratiating smile, manner* &c.

ingratiatingly, adv. Prec. & **-ly**. In an ingratiating manner.

ingratitude, n. [1. in-grátitūd; 2. ingrǽtitjūd], fr. Fr., fr. L. Lat. *ingrātitūdo*, 'ingratitude'. **in- (II.)** & **gratitude**. Want of gratitude; thanklessness.

ingravescence, n. [1. ìn-gravésens; 2. ingrəvésəns]. See next word & **-ce**. The state of being ingravescent; process of growing worse.

ingravescent, adj. [1. ìn-gravésent; 2. ìngrəvésənt], fr. Lat. *ingravescent-(em)*, Pres. Part. of *ingravescere*, 'to grow worse', fr. **in- (I.)** & *gravis*, 'heavy, severe'. See **grave (IV.)**. (med., of disease) Becoming more serious.

ingredient, n. [1. in-grédyent; 2. ingrídjənt], fr. Lat. *ingredient-(em)*, Pres. Part. of *ingredīri*, 'to go into, enter; to enter upon, engage in', fr. **in- (I.)** & *gradīri*, 'to step, walk, go', fr. *grad-us*, 'a step'. See **gradus**. Material or non-material thing entering into a mixture, forming part of a compound; component, constituent part, element: *the ingredients of a cake; an important ingredient in a character.*

ingress, n. [1. ín-gres; 2. íngres], fr. Lat. *ingressus*, 'entrance; way in', fr. *ingress-(um)*, P.P. type of *ingredīri*, 'to enter; to engage in'. See prec. **1.** The act of going in, entrance: *the right, means, of ingress.* **2.** Right of entrance.

ingrowing, adj. [1. ín-grōing; 2. íngrouiŋ]. **in (II.)** & **grow** & **-ing (II.)**. **a** Growing inwards; **b** (of nail, esp. toe-nail) growing into the flesh.

ingrowth, n. [1. ín-grōth; 2. íngrouþ]. **in (II.)** & **growth**. **a** The process of growing inwards; **b** amount of inward growth.

inguinal, adj. [1. ín-gwinal; 2. íngwinəl], fr. Lat. *inguināl-(is)*, 'of the groin', fr. *inguin-*, stem of *inguen*, 'the groin; a swelling in the groin; the abdomen'. Cogn. w. Gk. *adḗn*, 'gland', fr. **n̥gʷén-*. See **adenoid**. Of, relating to, the groin.

ingurgitate, vb. trans. [1. in-gérjitāt; 2. ingʌ́džiteit], fr. Lat. *ingurgitāt-(um)*, P.P. type of *ingurgitāre*, 'to pour in like a flood; to flood, fill; to gorge oneself'; (fig.) 'to be absorbed in, devoted to', fr. **in- (I.)** & *gurgitāre*, 'to flood, surge'. See **gurgitation**. **1.** To swallow up voraciously, devour greedily. **2.** (fig.) To engulf, absorb.

ingurgitation, n. [1. in-gèrjitáshun; 2. ingʌ̀džitéiʃən], fr. Lat. *ingurgitātiōn-(em)*, 'immoderate eating and drinking'. Prec. & **-ion**. Act of ingurgitating; state of being ingurgitated.

inhabit, vb. trans. [1. inhábit; 2. inhǽbit]. O. Fr. *enhabiter*, fr. Lat. *inhabitāre*, 'to dwell in', fr. **in- (I.)** & *habitāre*, 'to dwell'. See **habit**. **1.** To dwell in, live in (a house, place, region &c.). **2.** (of non-material things) To occupy, abide in; pervade.

inhabitable, adj. [1. inhábitabl; 2. inhǽbitəbl]. Prec. & **-able**. Able, fit, suitable, to be lived in.

inhabitancy, n. [1. inhábitansi; 2. inhǽbitənsi]. **inhabit** & **-ancy**. Residence, state of being an inhabitant, esp. as qualification, or to obtain some right.

inhabitant, n. [1. inhábitant; 2. inhǽbitənt]. **inhabit** & **-ant**. Person who lives in some specific place, house, region &c.

inhabitation, n. [1. inhàbitáshun; 2. inhæ̀bitéiʃən]. **inhabit** & **-ation**. **1.** The act of inhabiting; state of being inhabited. **2.** Dwelling-place, habitation, residence.

inhalation, n. [1. ìnhaláshun; 2. ìnhəléiʃən]. See next word & **-ation**. The act of inhaling; that which is inhaled.

inhale, vb. trans. [1. inhál; 2. inhéil], fr. Lat. *inhālāre*, 'to breathe upon', fr. **in- (I.)** & *hālāre*, 'to breathe'. See **exhale**. To breathe in, draw into the lungs: *to inhale air, tobacco smoke, fumes of remedial substance* &c.; *to inhale* (without object), specif. **a** to make a practice of inhaling tobacco smoke; **b** to inhale medicinal vapour.

inhaler, n. [1. inhāler; 2. inhéilə]. Prec. & **-er**. Apparatus for inhaling medicated vapour.

inharmonic, adj. [1. inharmónik; 2. inhāmɔ́nik]. **in- (II.)** & **harmonic**. Not harmonic.

inharmonious, adj. [1. inharmónius; 2. inhāmóuniəs]. **in- (II.)** & **harmonious**. (lit. and fig.) Not in harmony; discordant.

inharmoniously, adv. Prec. & **-ly**. In an inharmonious manner.

inhere, vb. intrans. [1 inhḗr; 2 inhíə], fr. Lat. *inhaer-(ēre)*, 'to cling, cleave to; to inhere in, be closely connected with', fr. **in- (I.)** & *haerēre*, 'to stick, cling, adhere'. See **adhere**. **1.** (of qualities &c.) To be, reside in, be inseparable from, natural to, innate in: *a quality inhering in a person* &c. **2. a** (of rights &c.) To be vested in, be inseparably associated with; **b** (of meaning) to be involved in (a form of words, formula), be implicit in.

inherence, -cy, n. [1. inhḗrens(i); 2. inhíərəns(i)]. See next word & **-ce, -cy**. The state of being inherent.

inherent, adj. [1. inhḗrent; 2. inhíərənt]. **inhere** & **-ent**. Naturally, and inseparably, associated with: *an inherent property of matter.*

inherently, adv. Prec. & **-ly**. In an inherent manner.

inherit, vb. trans. & intrans. [1. inhérit; 2. inhérit], fr. O. Fr. *heriter*, 'to put in possession', fr. L. Lat. *inhērēditāre*, 'to appoint an heir', fr. **in- (I.)** & *hērēditāre*, 'to inherit', fr. *hērēd-*, stem of *hēres*, 'an heir'. See **heredity**. **A.** trans. **1.** (law, in connexion with property, rights &c.) To receive by inheritance: *to inherit an estate, a fortune, title* &c. **2.** (in relation to physical and mental characters) To derive, have transmitted to one, from one's parents or ancestors: *an* *inherited quality, tendency* &c. ; (in biol.) contrasted with *acquired*. B. intrans. To receive property as heir ; to be, become, the heir.

inheritability, n. [1. inhèritabíliti ; 2. *in*hèrit*ə*bíl*i*t*i*]. See next word & **-ity.** The quality of being inheritable.

inheritable, adj. [1. inhéritabl ; 2. *in*hérit*ə*bl], fr. A.-Fr. *enheritable.* **inherit & -able.** 1. a Capable of being transmitted to heirs ; b capable of being transmitted to descendants. 2. Capable of becoming heir to, of receiving as a birthright ; *inheritable blood*, lineage, descent, which entitles a person to become an heir.

inheritance, n. [1. inhéritans ; 2. *in*hérit*ə*ns], fr. A.-Fr. *enheritance.* **inherit & -ance.** 1. (law) Act of inheriting ; specif., acquisition, as an heir, of any kind of property ; strictly, acquisition as heir of land in fee simple. 2. a That which is acquired by a person as heir to another ; b (fig.) anything which comes to an individual from another, esp. from a forbear, predecessor : *an inheritance of disease, enmity.* 3. (biol.) Process of transmission by descent to offspring of the natural physical or mental characters of the parents.

inheritor, n. [1. inhéritor ; 2. *in*hérit*ə*, -tō]. **inherit & -or.** Person who inherits.

inheritress, n. [1. inhéritres ; 2. *in*hérit*ri*s]. Prec. & **-ess.** Female who inherits.

inheritrix, n. [1. inhéritriks ; 2. *in*hérit*ri*ks]. See **inheritor & -trix.** Inheritress.

inhesion, n. [1. inhézhun ; 2. *in*hížn], fr. L. Lat. *inhaesiōn-(em)*, 'adhering', fr. *inhaes-(um)*, P.P. type of *inhaerēre*, 'to cling to'. See **inhere & -ion.** Inherence.

inhibit, vb. trans. [1. inhíbit ; 2. *in*híb*i*t], fr. Lat. *inhibit-(um)*, P.P. type of *inhibēre*, 'to keep back, check ; to hinder, prevent', fr. **in- (I.)** & *habēre*, 'to have, hold, possess'. See **habit (I.).** 1. (esp. in eccles. law) a To prevent, prohibit, restrain, forbid (a person from doing) ; b specif., to prohibit (a priest &c.) from performing ecclesiastical functions. 2. a To hinder, restrain, delay, obstruct : *to inhibit an action* &c. ; b specif. (psychol. and physiol.) to control by inhibition.

inhibition, n. [1. inhibíshun ; 2. *in*h*i*bíʃ*ə*n]. Prec. & **-ion.** The act of inhibiting ; state of being inhibited ; prohibition ; specif. 1. a (psychol.) Restraint exerted by the will, or instinctively and subconsciously, upon an emotional impulse, or other psychic condition ; b (physiol.) suspension of an organic function by the will, or by involuntary physiological action. 2. (law) a Decree by higher court prohibiting further proceeding in an inferior court ; b (eccles.) command of a bishop prohibiting a clergyman from exercising ministerial functions.

inhibitory, adj. [1. inhíbitori ; 2. *in*híb*i*t*ə*r*i*]. **inhibit & -ory.** Tending, serving, to inhibit ; prohibitory ; of the nature of an inhibition.

inhospitable, adj. [1. inhóspitabl ; 2. *in*hɔ́sp*i*t*ə*bl]. **in- (II.) & hospitable.** a (of persons, behaviour &c.) Not hospitable, unwelcoming ; showing no kindness to guest or stranger ; b (of place, country &c.) giving no refuge, affording no means of shelter ; exposed, bleak, uninviting.

inhospitableness, n. Prec. & **-ness.** Inhospitality.

inhospitably, adv. See prec. & **-ly.** In an inhospitable manner.

inhospitality, n. [1. inhòspitáliti ; 2. *in*hɔ̀sp*i*tǽl*i*t*i*], fr. Lat. *inhospitālitāt-(em)*, 'inhospitality'. **in- (II.) & hospitality.** Quality of being inhospitable.

inhuman, adj. [1. inhúman ; 2. *in*hjúm*ə*n], fr. Lat. *inhūmān-(us)*, 'inhuman ; savage, barbarous ; discourteous', fr. **in- (II.)** & *hūmān-(us)*, 'human ; humane'. See **human.** 1. (of persons, conduct &c.) Lacking humanity ; not being or acting in accordance with the character or habits of human beings ; cruel, unfeeling, brutal. 2. Not belonging to, or resembling, the human species.

inhumanity, n. [1. inhūmániti ; 2. *in*hjūmǽn*i*t*i*], fr. Lat. *inhūmānitāt-(em)*, 'inhumanity ; inhuman conduct'. **in- (II.) & humanity.** 1. The quality of being inhuman ; cruelty, barbarity, brutality. 2. Inhuman conduct.

inhumanly, adv. [1. inhúmanli ; 2. *in*hjúm*ə*nl*i*]. **inhuman & -ly.** In an inhuman manner.

inhumation, n. [1. inhūmáshun ; 2. *in*hjūméiʃ*ə*n]. See next word & **-ation.** Act of inhuming, burial ; state of being inhumed.

inhume, vb. trans. [1. inhúm ; 2. *in*hjúm], fr. Lat. *inhum-(āre)*, 'to bury', fr. **in- (I.)** & *humāre*, 'to bury', fr. *hum-(us)*, 'ground'. See **humus.** To put into the ground ; to bury, inter.

inimical, adj. [1. inímikl ; 2. *in*ímikl], fr. L. Lat. *inimīcāl-(is)*, 'hostile', fr. *inimīc-(us)*, 'enemy', fr. **in- (II.)** & *amīcus*, 'a friend'. See **amicable, amative, & -al.** a Hostile, unfriendly : *nations inimical to one another* ; b unfavourable, harmful, disadvantageous ; antagonistic : *circumstances inimical to success.*

inimically, adv. Prec. & **-ly.** In an inimical manner.

inimitable, adj. [1. inímitabl ; 2. *in*ím*i*t*ə*bl], fr. Lat. *inimitābil-(is)*, 'inimitable', fr. **in- (II.)** & *imitābil-(is)*, 'imitable', fr. *imit-(āre)*, 'to imitate'. See **imitate & -able.** Not capable of being imitated, so good as to defy imitation ; unrivalled, unique, supreme.

inimitableness, n. Prec. & **-ness.** Quality of being inimitable.

inimitably, adv. See prec. & **-ly.** In an inimitable manner.

iniquitous, adj. [1. iníkwitus ; 2. *in*íkw*i*t*ə*s], fr. Lat. *inīquit-(ātem)*, 'iniquity'. See **iniquity & -ous.** Displaying iniquity, wicked.

iniquitously, adv. Prec. & **-ly.** In an iniquitous manner.

iniquity, n. [1. iníkwiti ; 2. *in*íkw*i*t*i*], fr. Lat. *inīquitāt-(em)*, fr. *inīqu-(us)*, 'unequal ; uneven ; unfair ; hostile ; unwilling', fr. **in- (II.)** & *aequus*, 'level ; fair'. See **equal & -ity.** 1. Injustice, wickedness, sin. 2. Iniquitous conduct ; an iniquitous action.

initial (I.), adj. [1. iníshal ; 2. *in*íʃ*ə*l], fr. L. Lat. *initiāl-(is)*, 'initial, incipient, original', fr. *initi-(um)*, 'beginning'. See **initio & -al.** 1. Of, occurring at, pertaining to, the beginning : *the initial stages* ; *initial expenditure.* 2. (of sound, or letter) Occurring at the beginning of a word.

initial (II.), n., fr. prec. An initial letter ; specif., the first letter(s) of one's name or names.

initial (III.), vb. trans., fr. prec. To write one's initials on ; mark with one's initials.

initially, adv. **initial (I.) & -ly.** At the beginning.

initiate (I.), vb. trans. [1. iníshiāt ; 2. *in*íʃieit], fr. Lat. *initiāt-(um)*, P.P. type of *initiāre*, 'to originate ; to initiate, consecrate, admit', fr. *initi-(um)*, 'beginning'. See **initio & -ate.** 1. To originate, make a beginning in, set going, be instrumental in the starting of. 2. a To introduce, admit, esp. with appointed rites and ceremonies : *to initiate a person into a society, Freemasonry* ; specif., to admit to first degree in Freemasonry ; Phr. *to initiate a person into a secret* ; b to instruct (person) in the rudiments of, help him over the difficulties of beginning, a new occupation &c.

initiate (II.), adj. & n. [1. iníshiat ; 2. *in*íʃi*ə*t], fr. Lat. *initiāt-(us).* See prec. 1. adj. Having been initiated into a society, secret &c. 2. n. Initiated person.

initiation, n. [1. inishiáshun ; 2. *in*iʃiéiʃ*ə*n], fr. Lat. *initiātiōn-(em)*, 'participation in secret rites', fr. *initiāt-(um)*, P.P. type of *initiāre*, 'to initiate'. See **initiate (I.) & -ion.** a Act of initiating, starting, setting going ; b specif., ceremonial act of initiating ; c state of being initiated.

initiative (I.), adj. [1. iníshyativ ; 2. *in*íʃj*ə*t*i*v]. **initiate & -ive.** Beginning, incipient.

initiative (II.), n., fr. prec. 1. Initial step, introductory measure, first move. Phrs. *to have the initiative*, have the power or right of making the first move ; *to take the initiative*, take the lead. 2. (polit.) Right to introduce legislative measures : *the Commons have the initiative in respect of money bills.* 3. Mental capacity for originating ; ability to start something new, to make new departure ; enterprise, originality.

initiator, n. [1. iníshiātor ; 2. *in*íʃieit*ə*]. **initiate (I.) & -or.** One who performs the ceremony of initiation.

initiatory, adj. [1. iníshyaturi ; 2. *in*íʃj*ə*t*ə*r*i*]. **initiate & -ory.** Connected with, of the nature of, initiation.

initio, adv. [1. iníshiō ; 2. *in*íʃiou]. Lat. *initiō*, abl. of *initium*, 'beginning ; origin ; element, constituent', fr. *init-(um)*, P.P. type of *in-(īre)*, 'to go into, enter ; to enter upon, begin', fr. **in- (I.)** & *īre*, 'to go'. See **iterate.** Abbreviated to *init.*, at the beginning (with reference to page, paragraph &c. in book). Phr. *ab initio*, from the beginning.

inject, vb. trans. [1. injékt ; 2. *in*džékt], fr. Lat. *inject-(um)*, P.P. type of *injicere*, 'to throw or fling in ; to inspire, occasion', fr. **in- (I.)** & *jacere*, 'to throw, fling, cast ; to lay, set, found'. See **jactitation.** 1. To introduce, drive in (fluid, drug &c.), by pressure, as by means of a syringe, hypodermic needle &c. 2. To fill (a cavity, as blood-vessel &c.) by injection.

injection, n. [1. injékshun ; 2. *in*džékʃ*ə*n]. Prec. & **-ion.** 1. The act of injecting. 2. Liquid, solution of drug &c., to be injected.

injector, n. [1. injéktor ; 2. *in*džékt*ə*]. **inject & -or.** Apparatus for injecting fluid.

injudicious, adj. [1. injoodíshus ; 2. *in*džudíʃ*ə*s]. **in- (II.) & judicious.** Not wise, imprudent ; inexpedient, ill-judged, ill-timed : *injudicious remarks.*

injudiciously, adv. Prec. & **-ly.** In an injudicious manner.

injudiciousness, n. See prec. & **-ness.** Quality of being injudicious.

injunction, n. [1. injúngkshun ; 2. *in*džáŋkʃ*ə*n], fr. L. Lat. *injunctiōn-(em)*, 'a command, injunction', fr. *injunct-(um)*, P.P. type of *injungere*, 'to join, fasten into something ; to unite ; to inflict, occasion ; to impose upon, charge, enjoin', fr. **in- (I.)** & *jungere*, 'to join, attach, connect'. See **enjoin & junction.** 1. That which is enjoined ; an order, command, instruction, charge. 2. (law) Writ issued by a court, requiring that something shall be, or shall not be, done.

injure, vb. trans. [1. ínjur ; 2. índž*ə*]. Back-formation fr. **injury.** 1. To do harm to, offend against ; act unjustly, wrongfully, malevolently, towards : *to injure a person, his feelings, reputation* &c. 2. To cause material or bodily harm to ; to hurt, damage, impair, spoil, be detrimental to : *to injure one's eyes, leg* &c. ; *crops injured by rain* ; *a picture injured by damp.*

injured, adj. [1. ínjurd ; 2. índž*ə*d], fr. P.P. of prec. 1. Wronged, having suffered wrong ; offended, aggrieved, misjudged : '*Erasmus, that great injured name*' (Pope, 'Essay on Criticism') ; *the injured party.* Phr. *injured innocence.* 2. Expressing sense of injury : *an injured look.*

injurious, adj. [1. injóorius ; 2. *in*džɔ́ri*ə*s], fr. Lat. *injūriōs-(us)*, 'wrongful, criminal ; harmful, noxious', fr. *injūr-(ia)*, 'injury, wrong ; affront ; damage'. See **injury & -ous.** 1. a (of actions) Wrongful, iniquitous, unjust ; b (of language) tending to injure ; slanderous, detracting ; insulting. 2. Harmful, detrimental, noxious : *a climate injurious to health.*

injuriously, adv. Prec. & **-ly.** In an injurious manner.

injuriousness, n. See prec. & **-ness.** Quality of being injurious.

injury, n. [1. ínjuri ; 2. índž*ə*r*i*], fr. Lat. *injūria*, 'injury, wrong, violence ; injustice ; insult, affront ; damage, harm', fr. **in- (II.)** & *jūr-*, stem of *jūs*, 'right, justice, duty', q.v. under **jurist, jus.** 1. Harm, detriment, hurt, a (to the body) something causing pain, impairing functions; a wound: *an injury to the head, the eyes* &c.; **b** (to material, inanimate objects) damage, something destroying or impairing usefulness, beauty &c.: *injury to a roof, to a picture* &c. **2. a** Act inflicting moral hurt; insult, outrage, detraction, slander: *injury to one's feelings, reputation, character* &c.; **b** moral harm or detriment suffered. **3.** (law) Act constituting violation of another's rights, in respect of which legal action can be taken.

injustice, n. [1. injústis; 2. indžástis], fr. Lat. *injustitia*, 'injustice, unjust proceeding'. See **in- (II.)** & **justice**. **1.** Lack of justice; violation of another's rights. **2.** Unjust action. Phr. *to do a person an injustice*, not to appreciate merits of; to misjudge.

ink (I.), n. [1. ingk; 2. iŋk], fr. O. Fr. *enque*, fr. L. Lat. *encaustum*, fr. Gk. *égkauston*, 'the purple ink used by the later Roman emperors', fr. *égkaustos*, (of colours &c.) 'burnt in'. See **encaustic**. **1. a** Black or coloured fluid used in writing; Phr. *as black as ink*, very black; **b** thick black or coloured paste used in printing; also *printer's ink*. **2.** Black viscous liquid squirted out by a cuttle-fish when alarmed.

ink (II.), vb. trans., fr. prec. To mark, stain, cover, with ink.

ink-bag, n. Sac from which cuttle-fish's ink is ejected.

ink-bottle, n. Bottle for holding ink.

inker, n. [1. íngker; 2. íŋkə]. **ink (II.)** & **-er**. (print.) Roller for coating type with ink.

ink-horn, n. Horn vessel formerly used for holding and carrying ink.

inkiness, n. [1. íngkines; 2. íŋkinis]. **inky** & **-ness**. The state of being inky; deep blackness.

inkless, adj. [1. íngkles; 2. íŋklis]. **ink** & **-less**. Without ink.

inkling, n. [1. íngkling; 2. íŋkliŋ]. Origin uncertain. A faint notion, slight suspicion; hint, intimation.

ink-pot, n. Vessel holding ink into which the pen is dipped for writing.

ink-sac, n. Ink-bag.

ink-stand, n. Stand for holding one or more ink-pots, sometimes with tray for pens &c.

inky, adj. [1. íngki; 2. íŋki]. **ink** & **-y**. **1.** Marked, stained, or covered, with ink. **2.** Resembling ink in colour; very dark.

inland (I.), n. [1. ínland; 2. ínlənd, ínlænd]. **in (II.)** & **land**. The interior of a country.

inland (II.), adj., fr. prec. **1.** Situated in, belonging to, the interior of a country; remote from the sea: *an inland town*. **2. a** (of trade &c.) Carried on within the country itself, not foreign; **b** *inland revenue*, that derived from taxes and duties levied in country itself.

inland (III.), adv. [1. inlánd, ínland; 2. inlǽnd, ínlænd]. In, towards, the interior of a country: *to live, go, look, inland*.

inlander, n. [1. ínlander; 2. ínləndə]. **inland** & **-er**. Person living inland.

inlay (I.), vb. trans. [1. inlā́; 2. inléi]. **in- (I.)** & **lay (III.)**. **1.** To lay, sink, imbed, one or more substances in another, by way of ornament, so as to produce a level upper surface. **2.** To ornament by inserting inlaid material of different kind or colour: *an inlaid table*; *ivory inlaid with gold*.

inlay (II.), n. [1. ínlā; 2. ínlei], fr. prec. Inlaid ornamentation.

inlet, n. [1. ínlet; 2. ínlet]. **in (II.)** & **let (II.)**. **1.** An arm of the sea; narrow recess, creek &c. in coast-line. **2.** Something let in, inlaid.

inlier, n. [1. ínlīer; 2. ínlaiə]. **in (II.)** & **lie (III.)** & **-er**. (geol.) Rock formation completely covered by overlying stratum.

inly, adv. [1. ínli; 2. ínli]. O.E. *innlīce*, M.E. *inlīche, inli*, 'inly, sincerely'. **in (I.)** & **-ly**. (poet.) **a** Inwardly; **b** deeply, sincerely.

inlying, adj. [1. ínlīing; 2. ínlaiiŋ]. **in (II.)** & **lie (III.)** & **-ing**. Lying inside, inward.

inmate, n. [1. ínmāt; 2. ínmeit]. **in- (I.)** & **mate**. The inhabitant of a house, or place; one of several inhabitants of house, place, institution, asylum &c.

inmost, adj. [1. ínmōst; 2. ínmoust]. **in- (II.)** & **-most**. **1.** Most inward, farthest in, most remote. **2.** Most intimate, most private or secret: *one's inmost thoughts, feelings* &c.

inn, n. [1. in; 2. in]. O.E., M.E. *in(n)*, 'house; lodging', fr. **in (II.)**. **1.** (archaic and poet.) Abode, dwelling, resting-place: '*Here is the port of rest from troublous toil, The world's sweet inn from pain*' (Spenser, 'F. Q.'). **2.** House of entertainment for travellers; hostelry. **3.** *Inns of Court*, **a** four legal societies through one of which persons are admitted to the bar; **b** buildings belonging to these societies.

innate, adj. [1. innā́t; 2. innéit], fr. Lat. *innāt-(us)*, 'inborn, inherent', fr. P.P. type of *innasci*, 'to be born in; to arise, originate, in'. See **in- (I.)** & **natal**. Native, instinctive, inborn, inherent.

innately, adv. Prec. & **-ly**. In an innate manner.

innateness, n. See prec. & **-ness**. The quality of being innate.

innavigable, adj. [1. innávigabl; 2. innǽvigəbl], fr. Lat. *innāvigābil-(is)*, 'unnavigable'. **in- (II.)** & **navigable**. Not navigable.

inner, adj. & n. [1. íner; 2. ínə]. O.E. *innera, inra*, M.E. *inre*, compar. of **in (II.)**. **1.** adj. Inside, interior. Phr. *the inner man*, **a** the soul and mind, contrasted with the body; **b** (facetious) the stomach, appetite: *to warm the inner man*. **2.** n. **a** Ring of target next to bull's-eye; **b** shot hitting this ring.

innermost, adj. [1. ínermōst; 2. ínəmoust]. Prec. & **-most**. Inmost.

innervate, vb. trans. [1. inérvāt; 2. inə́veit]. **in- (I.)** & **nerve** & **-ate**. **a** To supply with nerves; **b** to furnish with nervous energy, stimulate.

innervation, n. [1. inervā́shun; 2. inəvéiʃən]. Prec. & **-ion**. The act of innervating; state of being innervated.

innings, n. [1. íningz; 2. íniŋz]. Orig. pl., fr. **in (II.)** & **-ing (I.)**. **1.** (cricket) Period during which a given player or given side is batting. **2.** (fig.) Period of active life, of supremacy, power, good fortune; turn, opportunity: *after all, he has had a good long innings*.

innkeeper, n. [1. ínkēper; 2. ínkīpə]. **inn** & **keeper**. Person who keeps an inn; licensed victualler.

innocence, n. [1. ínusens; 2. ínəsəns], fr. Lat. *innocentia*, 'harmlessness; blamelessness; uprightness', fr. *innoc-(entem)*, 'harmless; guiltless'. **innocent** & **-ce**. The quality or state of being innocent.

innocency, n. [1. ínusensi; 2. ínəsənsi], fr. Lat. *innoc-(entem)*, 'harmless; guiltless'. See next word & **-cy**. (archaic) Innocence.

innocent (I.), adj. [1. ínusent; 2. ínəsənt], fr. Lat. *innocent-(em)*, 'harmless; blameless, guiltless; upright', fr. **in- (II.)** & *nocent-(em)*, Pres. Part. of *nocēre*, 'to hurt, harm, injure', q.v. under **noxious**. **1. a** Devoid of moral stain or blemish; blameless, immaculate; **b** not guilty of some specific sin, crime, or fault charged against one. **2.** Not tending to evil; morally harmless: *innocent pleasures, games* &c. **3. a** Ignorant of evil; simple, artless, ingenuous, guileless: *an innocent child*; **b** foolishly simple, ignorant: *not quite so innocent as to believe that*. **4.** Free from hurtful properties, innocuous: *few drugs are completely innocent*.

innocent (II.), n., fr. prec. **1.** A simple, artless, guileless person or child. Phr. *Holy Innocents' Day*, Dec. 28th; commemoration by the Church of Herod's massacre of children. **2.** Half-witted person; congenital idiot.

innocently, adv. [1. ínusentli; 2. ínəsəntli]. **innocent (I.)** & **-ly**. In an innocent manner.

innocuity, n. [1. inokū́iti; 2. inəkjúiti]. See next word & **-ity**. Quality of being innocuous.

innocuous, adj. [1. inókūus; 2. inókjuəs], fr. Lat. *innocu-(us)*, 'harmless; inoffensive', fr. **in- (II.)** & stem **noc-*, 'to harm'. See **noxious** & **-ous**. Harmless, inoffensive, not tending to injure, without hurtful effect.

innocuously, adv. Prec. & **-ly**. In an innocuous manner.

innocuousness, n. See prec. & **-ness**. Quality of being innocuous.

innominate, adj. [1. inóminăt; 2. inómineit], fr. Lat. *innōmināt-(us)*, 'unnamed', fr. **in- (II.)** & *nōmināt-(um)*, P.P. type of *nōmināre*, 'to name, call by name'. See **nominate**. **1.** Unnamed; without a name. **2.** (anat.) *innominate bone*, the hip-bone, as made up of three originally separate bones with specific names.

innovate, vb. intrans. [1. ínuvāt; 2. ínəveit], fr. Lat. *innovāt-(um)*, P.P. type of *innovāre*, 'to renew, alter', fr. **in- (I.)** & *novāre*, 'to make new; to change'. See **novel (I.)**. To introduce innovations, bring in new methods.

innovation, n. [1. inōvā́shun; 2. inouvéiʃən], fr. Lat. *innovātiōn-(em)*, 'an alteration; innovation'. Prec. & **-ion**. **1.** The process of innovating. **2.** Something newly introduced; a change, novelty; new-fangled practice.

innovatory, adj. [1. ínōvāturi; 2. inouvéitəri]. **innovate** & **-ory**. Introducing something new; tending to make changes.

innoxious, adj. [1. inókshus; 2. inókʃəs], fr. Lat. *innoxi-(us)*, 'harmless; blameless'. See **in- (II.)** & **noxious**. Harmless, without ill effect, innocuous.

innoxiously, adv. Prec. & **-ly**. In an innoxious manner.

innoxiousness, n. See prec. & **-ness**. The quality of being innoxious.

innuendo, n. & vb. intrans. [1. inūéndō: 2. injuéndou]. Lat. *innuendo*, gerund of *innuere*, 'to nod to; to give a sign, hint', fr. **in- (I.)** & *nuere*, 'to nod, wink', q.v. under **nutate**. **1.** n. **a** (in unfavourable sense) An indirect reference or suggestion; hint, intimation, insinuation; specif. **b** (law) in actions for libel and slander, term used in pleadings, of an averment by plaintiff of the construction which he wishes to be placed on the words &c., of the defendant; the word is properly placed in parenthesis equivalent to 'meaning that.' **2.** vb. To make innuendos.

innumerable, adj. [1. inúmerabl; 2. injúmərəbl], fr. Lat. *innumerābil-(is)*, 'countless'. See **in- (II.)** & **numerable**. Too many to be reckoned; countless.

innutrition, n. [1. inūtríshun; 2. injutríʃən]. **in- (II.)** & **nutrition**. Lack of nutrition.

innutritious, adj. [1. inūtríshus; 2. injutríʃəs]. **in- (II.)** & **nutritious**. Not nourishing, supplying no nutriment.

inobservance, n. [1. inobzérvans; 2. inəbzə́vəns], fr. Lat. *inobservantia*, 'inattention, negligence'. **in- (II.)** & **observance**. **a** Heedlessness, inattention; **b** negligence of, failure to observe or keep: *inobservance of a rule, of Sunday*.

inoccupation, n. [1. inokūpā́shun; 2. inəkjupéiʃən]. **in- (II.)** & **occupation**. Want of occupation.

inoculate, vb. trans. [1. inókūlāt; 2. inókjuleit], fr. Lat. *inoculāt-(um)*, P.P. type of *inoculāre*, 'to engraft, to implant', fr. **in- (I.)** & *ocul-(us)*, 'an eye; a bud'. See **ocular**. **1.** To introduce a specific germ or germ-culture, virus &c., into the system so as to secure immunity from particular disease &c. **2.** To introduce, implant (disease &c.), in a person's system as a safeguard: *to inoculate a disease into, upon, a person*. **3. a** To insert, engraft (a bud, shoot &c.) into another plant; **b** to insert a bud, shoot &c. into (a plant).

inoculation, n. [1. inokūlā́shun; 2. inəkjuléiʃən]. Prec. & **-ion**. **1.** The act of inoculating; state of being inoculated. **2.** Method of securing immunity from a bacterial disease, by introducing into the system the germs of the disease itself in a special form, or germs closely allied to them.

inoculative, adj. [1. inókūlativ; 2. inókjulətiv]. **inoculate** & **-ive**. Pertaining to inoculation.

inoculator, n. [1. inókūlātor; 2. inókjuleitə]. **inoculate** & **-or**. Person who practises inoculation.

inodorous, adj. [1. inṓdurus; 2. inóudərəs], fr. Lat. *inodōr-(us)*, 'without smell', & **-ous**.

in- (II.) & **odorous**. Having no smell; without odour.

inoffensive, adj. [1. inofénsiv; 2. inəfénsiv]. **in-** (II.) & **offensive** (I.). **1.** Giving, causing, no offence; harmless, innocent. **2.** Neither positively offensive, nor actively pleasing; unnoticeable, negative.

inoffensively, adv. Prec. & **-ly**. In an inoffensive manner.

inoffensiveness, n. See prec. & **-ness**. Quality of being inoffensive.

inofficious, adj. [1. inofíshus; 2. inəfíʃəs], fr. Lat. *inofficiōs-(us)*, 'undutiful'. **in-** (II.) & **officious**. **1.** Without office or function. **2.** (law) Undutiful; negligent of duty, forgetful of moral obligations.

inoperative, adj. [1. inóperativ; 2. inɔ́pərətiv]. **in-** (II.) & **operative**. (chiefly of laws) Not in operation, not working, having no force.

inopportune, adj. [1. inópurtūn; 2. inɔ́pətjūn], fr. L. Lat. *inopportūn-(us)*, 'unfitting'. **in-** (II.) & **opportune**. Ill-timed, unseasonable.

inopportunely, adv. Prec. & **-ly**. In an inopportune manner.

inopportuneness, n. See prec. & **-ness**. Quality of being inopportune.

inordinate, adj. [1. inórdinat; 2. inɔ́dinit], fr. Lat. *inordināt-(us)*, 'not arranged; disorderly, irregular', fr. **in-** (II.) & *ordināt-(um)*, P.P. type of *ordināre*, 'to set in order, arrange; to ordain, appoint'. See **ordain**. Not properly restrained; immoderate, extravagant, excessive: *inordinate passions, appetites, pride, demands.*

inordinately, adv. Prec. & **-ly**. To an inordinate degree.

inorganic, adj. [1. inorgánik; 2. inɔgǽnik]. **in-** (II.) & **organic**. Not organic. **1.** Consisting, made up of, non-living, inanimate, matter; *inorganic chemistry*, that dealing with substances other than those composing animal or vegetable matter; specif., that dealing with all substances other than hydrocarbons. **2.** (of forms of society, political institutions &c.) Not resembling an organism in structure; showing absence of design, lack of relation and co-ordination of parts.

inorganically, adv. [1. inorgánikali; 2. inɔgǽnikəli]. Prec. & **-al** & **-ly**. So as to be inorganic.

inorganization, n. [1. inòrganīzáshun; 2. inɔ̀gənaizéiʃən]. **in-** (II.) & **organization**. Lack of organization.

inornate, adj. [1. inornát; 2. inɔnéit], fr. Lat. *inornāt-(us)*, 'unadorned'. **in-** (II.) & **ornate**. Not ornate; plain, simple.

inosculate, vb. intrans. & trans. [1. inóskūlāt; 2. inɔ́skjuleit], fr. **in-** (I.) & Lat. *osculāt-(um)*, P.P. type of *osculāre*, 'to supply with a mouth, opening', fr. *oscul-(um)*, dimin. of *ōs*, 'mouth'. See **osculum** & **oral**. **A.** intrans. **1.** (of vessels, ducts &c. in human or animal body) To unite at the ends by contact. **2.** (of fibres &c.) To intertwine, become blended, so as to form one substance; also of non-material things, to blend, amalgamate. **B.** trans. To cause to intertwine, to join (fibres &c.).

inosculation, n. [1. inòskūláshun; 2. inɔ̀skjuléiʃən]. Prec. & **-ion**. The act, process, or method of inosculating; the state of being inosculated.

in-patient, n. [1. ín pàshent; 2. ín pèiʃənt]. **in** (III.) & **patient**. Patient lodged and boarded in a hospital &c. when undergoing treatment.

inpouring, n. [1. ínpōring; 2. ínpɔ̄riŋ]. **in** (II.) & **pour** & **-ing**. Pouring in, addition.

inquest, n. [1. ínkwest; 2. ínkwɛst], fr. O. Fr. *enqueste*, fr. Med. Lat. *inquesta*, fr. P.P. type of Romance **inquērere*, 'to inquire'. See **inquire**. **1. a** Legal or judicial inquiry before a jury to ascertain facts; specif. **b** *coroner's inquest*, inquiry into cause of death. Phr. *the Last, Great, Inquest*, Last Judgement. **2.** Court before which an inquest is held.

inquietude, n. [1. inkwíetūd; 2. inkwáiitjūd], fr. L. Lat. *inquiētūdo*, 'restlessness, disquietude'. **in-** (II.) & **quietude**. Restlessness, uneasiness, disturbance, discomposure, of mind or body.

inquire, enquire, vb. trans. & intrans. [1. inkwír; 2. inkwáiə]. M.E. *enquere*, fr. O. Fr. *enquerre*, fr. Romance **inquērere*, fr. Lat. **in-** (I.) & *quaerere*, 'to seek, to ask'. See **query**. *Inquire* has *-i-* through influence of Lat. *inquīrere*, 'to inquire'. See **inquisition**. **A.** trans. To ask; to seek information about by questioning: *to inquire one's way, a person's name* &c. **B.** intrans. To make inquiries, ask questions, seek for information: *when I don't know I inquire.* **C.** Followed by preposition. *Inquire after*, to ask about the health of (a person &c.). *Inquire for*, **a** to ask about the health of, inquire after; **b** to ask for, try to obtain by request: *to inquire for a particular book at a bookseller's. Inquire into*, to examine, investigate.

inquiring, adj. [1. inkwíring; 2. inkwáiəriŋ], fr. Pres. Part. of prec. **a** Expressive of inquiry: *an inquiring look*; **b** seeking information, curious: *an inquiring mind.*

inquiringly, adv. Prec. & **-ly**. In an inquiring manner.

inquiry, enquiry, n. [1. inkwíri; 2. inkwáiəri]. **inquire** & **-y**. **1.** The act of inquiring, asking: *to find out by inquiry.* **2.** A question, interrogation. Phr. *to make inquiries*, ask questions, investigate. **3.** Investigation, examination, especially of an official character: *to make a searching inquiry; to hold an official inquiry.*

inquisition, n. [1. inkwizíshun; 2. inkwizíʃən], fr. Lat. *inquīsītiōn-(em)*, 'a seeking or searching for; an inquiry, examination; legal inquiry', fr. *inquīsīt-(um)*, P.P. type of *inquīrere*, 'to seek after, inquire into', fr. **in-** (I.) & *quaerere*, 'to seek; to ask'. See **inquire**. **1.** Searching examination, investigation, inquiry; esp. legal, official, investigation. **2.** *The Inquisition* (R.C. Ch.), ecclesiastical tribunal for the discovery and suppression of heresy; in full, *the Congregation of the Holy Inquisition*, or *the Holy Office.*

inquisitional, adj. [1. inkwizíshunal; 2. inkwizíʃənəl]. Prec. & **-al**. **1.** Pertaining to, making, inquiries. **2.** Of, pertaining to, resembling, the Inquisition.

inquisitive, adj. [1. inkwízitiv; 2. inkwízitiv], fr. L. Lat. *inquīsītīv-(us)*, 'making inquiry', fr. *inquīsīt-(um)*, P.P. type of *inquīrere*, 'to inquire into'. See **inquisition** & **-ive**. Curious; desirous of finding out what one does not know; given to asking questions, making inquiries, attempting to gain information by questions; often in derogatory sense; curious about what does not concern one; prying.

inquisitively, adv. Prec. & **-ly**. In an inquisitive manner.

inquisitiveness, n. See prec. & **-ness**. Quality of being inquisitive.

inquisitor, n. [1. inkwízitor; 2. inkwízitə], fr. O. Fr. *inquisiteur*, fr. Lat. *inquīsītōr-(em)*, 'one who searches for a suspected person; a detective; an investigator', fr. *inquīsīt-(um)*, P.P. type of *inquīrere*, 'to inquire, investigate'. See **inquisition**. **1.** Person who asks questions, makes inquiries, investigates; especially an official investigator. **2.** Specif., member of a court of the Inquisition; *Grand Inquisitor*, head of this court; *Inquisitor-General*, head of court of Inquisition in Spain.

inquisitorial, adj. [1. inkwizitórial; 2. inkwizitɔ́riəl]. Prec. & **-ial**. **1.** Of, pertaining to, resembling, an inquisitor, or an inquisition. **2.** Over-curious, inquisitive, prying.

inquisitorially, adv. Prec. & **-ly**. In an inquisitorial manner.

inroad, n. [1. ínrōd; 2. ínroud]. **in-** (I.) & **road**, in obs. sense 'riding'. **1.** An attack, invasion, incursion. **2.** (fig.) Attack, encroachment: *inroads upon one's time, into one's resources* &c.

inrush, n. [1. ínrush; 2. ínraʃ]. **in-** (I.) & **rush** (III.). The act of rushing in, irruption.

insalivate, vb. trans. [1. insálivāt; 2. insǽliveit]. **in-** (I.) & **saliva** & **-ate**. To mix (food) with saliva.

insalivation, n. [1. insàliváshun; 2. insæ̀livéiʃən]. Prec. & **-ion**. The act of insalivating; state of being insalivated.

insalubrious, adj. [1. insalúbrius; 2. insəljúbriəs], fr. Lat. *insalūbri-(s)*, 'unwholesome; unhealthy'. **in-** (II.) & **salubrious**. (of place, climate) Unhealthy; not favourable or beneficial to health.

insalubrity, n. [1. insalúbriti; 2. insəljúbriti], fr. Lat. *insalūbr-(is)*, 'unhealthy'. See prec. & **-ity**. Quality of being insalubrious.

insane, adj. [1. insán; 2. inséin], fr. Lat. *insān-(us)*, 'mad, insane; outrageous, extravagant, excessive'. **in-** (II.) & **sane**. **1.** Of unsound mind; mad. **2.** Of such a kind or character as to suggest madness; senseless, extravagant: *an insane proposal.* **3.** as n. *The insane*, mad persons.

insanely, adv. Prec. & **-ly**. In an insane manner.

insanitary, adj. [1. insánitari; 2. insǽnitəri]. **in-** (II.) & **sanitary**. Not sanitary; unhealthy, likely to cause disease.

insanity, n. [1. insániti; 2. insǽniti]. **insane** & **-ity**. Unsoundness of mind; madness, lunacy.

insatiability, n. [1. insāshabíliti; 2. inseiʃəbíliti], fr. Lat. *insatiābilitāt-(em)*, 'insatiability', fr. *insatiābil-(is)*, 'insatiable'. See next word & **-ity**. Quality of being insatiable.

insatiable, adj. [1. insáshabl; 2. inséiʃəbl], fr. Lat. *insatiābil-(is)*, 'that cannot be satisfied', fr. **in-** (II.) & **satiable**. Not capable of being satisfied; unappeasable, unquenchable.

insatiably, adv. Prec. & **-ly**. In an insatiable manner.

insatiate, adj. [1. insáshiāt; 2. inséiʃieit], fr. Lat. *insatiāt-(us)*, 'unsatisfied', fr. **in-** (II.) & *satiāt-(um)*, P.P. type of *satiāre*, 'to satisfy'. See **satiate**. Never satisfied; insatiable.

inscribable, adj. [1. inskríbabl; 2. inskráibəbl]. See next word & **-able**. (geom., of figure) Capable of being inscribed (within another figure).

inscribe, vb. trans. [1. inskríb; 2. inskráib], fr. Lat. *inscrīb-(ere)*, 'to write in or on anything; to furnish with an inscription; to inscribe', fr. **in-** (I.) & *scribere*, 'to write'. See **scribe**. **1. a** To write, engrave, make written symbols, trace designs upon: *to inscribe a stone, a page &c., with one's name*; **b** to engrave on, upon, write down on, or in: *to inscribe one's name in a book, on a page* &c. **2.** To draw (a geometrical figure) within (another). **3.** To enter (name of shareholders, subscribers) on register, list &c.: *inscribed stock.*

inscription, n. [1. inskrípshun; 2. inskrípʃən], fr. Lat. *inscriptiōn-(em)*, 'inscription', fr. *inscript-(um)*, P.P. type of *inscrībere*, 'to inscribe'. See prec. That which is inscribed; anything, words &c., written or engraved; specif. (i.) name, words, records, cut on stone; (ii.) those stamped upon a coin.

inscriptional, adj. [1. inskrípshunal; 2. inskrípʃənəl]. Prec. & **-al**. Pertaining to, of the character of, an inscription.

inscriptive, adj. [1. inskríptiv; 2. inskríptiv], fr. Lat. *inscript-*, see **inscription**, & **-ive**. Inscriptional.

inscrutability, n. [1. inskrōōtabíliti; 2. inskrūtəbíliti], fr. Lat. *inscrūtābil-(is)*, 'inscrutable'. See next word & **-ity**. Quality of being inscrutable; that which is inscrutable.

inscrutable, adj. [1. inskrōōtabl; 2. inskrūtəbl], fr. Lat. *inscrūtābil-(is)*, 'inscrutable', fr. **in-** (II.) & *scrūt-(āri)*, 'to search, examine, investigate'. See **scrutiny** & **-able**. Not capable of being searched out, interpreted, understood; impenetrable, mysterious; enigmatic: *the inscrutable decrees of Providence; an inscrutable smile, expression* &c.

inscrutably, adv. Prec. & **-ly**. In an inscrutable manner.

insect, n. [1. ínsekt; 2. ínsɛkt], fr. Lat. *insect-(um) (animal)*, 'animal notched or cut into; insect', fr. P.P. type of *insecāre*, 'to cut into', fr. **in-** (**I.**) & *secāre*, 'to cut'. See **section**. **1. a** (entom.) Any member of the class *Insecta*, of arthropods, with segmented bodies, six paired legs, usually winged in the adult state, and breathing through tracheae; more loosely used of other small arthropods, as spiders, woodlice &c.; **b** (popularly and inaccurately) any small creeping or flying animal. **2.** Abusive term applied to a contemptible, insignificant person, esp. one who is small, and misshapen, or malevolent.

insectarium, n. [1. insektárium; 2. insɛktéəriəm]. Mod. Lat., fr. prec. & **-arium**. Place for keeping living insects.

insecticide, n. [1. inséktisīd; 2. inséktisaid]. **insect** & **-cide**. Substance for killing insects.

Insectivora, n. [1. insektívora; 2. insɛktívərə]. Mod. Lat. neut. pl. See **insect** & **-vorous**. Order of mammals who prey upon insects, including moles, shrews, hedgehogs &c.

insectivore, n. [1. inséktivōr; 2. inséktivɔ̄]. Anglicized sing. of prec. Insect-eating animal.

insectivorous, adj. [1. insektívorus; 2. insɛktívərəs]. Prec. & **-ous**. Living on, given to eating, insects.

insectology, n. [1. insektóloji; 2. insɛktɔ́lədži]. **insect** & **-o-** & **-logy**. Systematic study of insects.

insecure, adj. [1. insekúr; 2. insikjɔ̄]. See **in-** (**II.**) & **secure**. **1.** Exposed to, not proof against, danger, harm, loss &c.; not safe; in perilous position or circumstances. **2. a** Likely to give way: *insecure footing, hold*; **b** not to be depended upon, unreliable: *insecure hopes, promises* &c.

insecurely, adv. Prec. & **-ly**. In an insecure manner; not safely.

insecurity, n. [1. insekúriti; 2. insikjɔ́riti]. See prec. & **-ity**. State or quality of being insecure.

inseminate, vb. trans. [1. inséminàt; 2. inséminet], fr. Lat. *insēmināt-(um)*, P.P. type of *insēmināre*, 'to sow, implant', fr. **in-** (**I.**) & *sēmināre*, 'to sow'. See **semination**. (lit. and fig.) To implant, impregnate.

insemination, n. [1. inseminā́shun; 2. insemineíʃən]. Prec. & **-ion**. The act of inseminating; state of being inseminated.

insensate, adj. [1. insénsat; 2. insénsət], fr. L. Lat. *insensāt-(us)* 'foolish, irrational', fr. **in-** (**II.**) & *sensātus*, 'intelligent, sensible', fr. *sens-(us)*, 'sense, perception; sensation'. See **sense** & **-ate**. **1.** Not possessed of, incapable of experiencing, bodily sensation; inanimate: '*the silence and the calm of mute insensate things*' (Wordsworth). **2.** (rare) Having lost consciousness; insensible. **3.** Unreasoning; lacking sense, irrational: *insensate rage*.

insensately, adv. Prec. & **-ly**. In an insensate manner.

insensibility, n. [1. insensibíliti; 2. insɛnsibíliti], fr. L. Lat. *insensibilitāt-(em)*, 'insensibility'. See next word & **-ity**. **1. a** Lack of sensuous perception or sensation: *insensibility to pain*; **b** unconsciousness; condition of being senseless: *the patient lapsed into insensibility*. **2. a** Lack of moral feeling, incapacity for emotion or sympathy; obtuseness, callousness; **b** lack of intellectual or aesthetic perception; want of power of appreciation.

insensible, adj. [1. insénsibl; 2. insénsibl], fr. Lat. *insensibil-(is)*, 'imperceptible; incomprehensible; not able to feel, senseless'. **in-** (**II.**) & **sensible**. **1. a** Lacking power of physical perception or sensation: *insensible to pain*; **b** unconscious, senseless: *insensible from wounds* &c. **2.** Lacking intellectual, moral, or aesthetic perception and discrimination; unaware of, indifferent to: *insensible of the beauties of art*; *insensible of past kindnesses*. **3.** So slight, so small, as to be imperceptible; inappreciable: *by insensible degrees*.

insensibly, adv. Prec. & **-ly**. Too gradually to be perceived; imperceptibly.

insensitive, adj. [1. insénsitiv; 2. insénsitiv]. **in-** (**II.**) & **sensitive**. Not sensitive to, unaffected by, not alive to, physical, mental, or moral impressions: *insensitive to light, beauty* &c.

insensitiveness, n. See prec. & **-ness**. The quality of being insensitive.

insentient, adj. [1. insénshient; 2. insénʃiənt]. **in-** (**II.**) & **sentient**. Not capable of perception; inanimate.

inseparability, n. [1. insèparabíliti; 2. insèpərəbíliti], fr. L. Lat. *insēparābilitāt-(em)*. See next word & **-ity**. Quality of being inseparable.

inseparable (**I.**), adj. [1. inséparabl; 2. insépərəbl], fr. L. Lat. *insēparābil-(is)*, 'inseparable'. **in-** (**II.**) & **separable**. **1. a** Not capable of being separated; firmly united one to another; **b** constantly found together; intimately associated in friendship: *inseparable companions*. **2.** (gram., of particles, prefixes &c.) Not existing as separate word.

inseparable (**II.**), n., fr. prec. (in pl.) Things or persons that cannot be separated; esp. *inseparables*, inseparable friends.

inseparably, adv. [1. inséparabli; 2. insépərəbli]. **inseparable** (**I.**) & **-ly**. In an inseparable manner.

insert, vb. trans. [1. insért; 2. insə́t], fr. Lat. *insert-(um)*, P.P. type of *inserere*, 'to put or bring in; to introduce, mix with', fr. **in-** (**I.**) & *serere*, 'to join, bind together; to connect, combine', q.v. under **series**. **a** To put, place, slip, push, into, within something else: *to insert a key in a lock*; **b** to introduce, interpolate: *to insert a word in a line* &c.; **c** to cause to appear in: *to insert an advertisement in a newspaper*.

insertion, n. [1. insérshun; 2. insə́ʃən], fr. Lat. *insertiōn-(em)*, 'a putting in; grafting'. Prec. & **-ion**. **1.** The act of inserting; state of being inserted. **2.** Something that is inserted; e.g. a word, paragraph &c., introduced in written or printed matter; **b** advertisement &c. in newspaper. **3.** Strip of embroidery, lace &c. let into another kind of material.

inset (**I.**), n. [1. ínset; 2. ínset]. **in-** (**I.**) & **set** (**II.**). **1.** Leaf or group of leaves inserted in a book between the sheets or pages. **2.** Small picture, diagram &c. drawn or printed within larger one. **3.** Piece of material let into larger one.

inset (**II.**), vb. trans. [1. insét; 2. insét]. **in-** (**I.**) & **set** (**I.**). To insert, fix or place in.

inshore, adv. & adj. [1. inshór; 2. inʃɔ̄]. **in** (**II.**) & **shore** (**I.**). **1.** adv. Near the shore. **2.** adj. Situated near the shore: *inshore fisheries*. Phr. *inshore of*, nearer the shore than.

inside (**I.**), n. [1. ínsíd, insíd, ínsīd; 2. insáid, insáid, insaid]. **in** (**III.**) & **side**. **1.** The inner part, interior, part situated within: *the inside of a box, envelope* &c. Phr. *the inside of a week*, middle, Monday to Friday &c.; *to turn (a thing) inside out*, so that the inside becomes the outside. **2.** Inner surface: *the inside of a window, wall* &c. **3. a** (of path &c.) Part farthest from road; **b** (of road, track &c.) part lying on inner edge of curve. **4.** Passenger travelling inside carriage &c. **5.** (colloq.) Digestive organs, stomach: *something wrong with, a pain in, one's inside*.

inside (**II.**), adj. [1. ínsīd; 2. ínsaid], fr. prec. Situated on the inner side, within, inside: *an inside cabin, seat, passenger* &c.

inside (**III.**), prep. [1. ínsíd; 2. ínsáid]. Within; on, to, the inner side: *inside the house*.

inside (**IV.**), adv. [1. insíd; 2. insáid]. Within; on the inner side; in the interior: *to go, look, stay, inside*; colloq. Phr. *inside of*, within, in less than: *inside of a week, year* &c.

insider, n. [1. insíder; 2. insáidə]. **inside** & **-er**. Person admitted to, belonging to, a specific society, circle, organization &c.; an initiate; one possessing special knowledge, privileges &c.

insidious, adj. [1. insídius; 2. insídiəs], fr. Lat. *insidiōs-(us)*, 'artful, deceitful, dangerous', fr. *insidi-(ae)*, 'an ambush; stratagem; artifice, snare', fr. *insid-(ēre)*, 'to sit in or on; to occupy, stand on', fr. **in-** (**I.**) & *sedēre*, 'to sit'. See **sedentary**, **sit**. **1.** Cunning, crafty, treacherous; serving to ensnare, deceive, entrap: *insidious wiles*. **2.** Progressing, developing, advancing, gaining upon one, imperceptibly, stealthily: *the insidious approach of age*.

insidiously, adv. Prec. & **-ly**. In an insidious manner.

insidiousness, n. See prec. & **-ness**. The quality of being insidious.

insight, n. [1. insīt; 2. ínsait]. **in** (**II.**) & **sight**. **1.** Faculty of mental perception, observation, discernment, vision. **2.** Knowledge, enlightenment, acquaintance, familiarity: *to gain an insight into a person's mind, into the working of an organization* &c.

insignia, n. [1. insígnia; 2. insígniə]. Lat. *insignia*, pl. of *insigne*, 'distinctive mark; sign or badge of office, honour' &c., fr. *insignis*, 'distinguished, remarkable', fr. **in-** (**I.**) & *sign-(um)*, 'a sign, mark, token'. See **sign**. Signs, tokens, symbols, badges, of office, honour, of an order of knighthood &c.

insignificance, **-cy**, n. [1. insignífikans(i); 2. insignífikəns(i)]. **in-** (**II.**) & **significance, -cy**. The quality of being insignificant.

insignificant, adj. [1. insignífikant; 2. insignífikənt]. **in-** (**II.**) & **significant**. **1.** Without significance, conveying no meaning: *insignificant phrases* &c. **2.** Unimportant, trivial, immaterial: *to waste time on insignificant points*. **3.** Unimposing; without dignity; conveying an impression of futility, feebleness, or meanness: *an insignificant person*.

insignificantly, adv. Prec. & **-ly**. In an insignificant manner.

insincere, adj. [1. insinsér; 2. insinsíə], fr. Lat. *insincēr-(us)*, 'not genuine, adulterated; not candid'. **in-** (**II.**) & **sincere**. (of person, character, action, words &c.) Not sincere; not expressing genuine feeling; hypocritical, dissembling, disingenuous.

insincerely, adv. Prec. & **-ly**. In an insincere manner.

insincerity, n. [1. insinsériti; 2. insinsériti]. **in-** (**II.**) & **sincerity**. **1.** The quality of being insincere. **2.** Insincere words, actions &c.

insinuate, vb. trans. [1. insínūāt; 2. insínjueit], fr. Lat. *insinuāt-(um)*, P.P. type of *insinuāre*, 'to wind, twist, oneself into; to ingratiate oneself', fr. **in-** (**I.**) & *sinuāre*, 'to bend, wind, curve', fr. *sinu-(s)*, 'a bend, curve, hollow'. See **sinus**. **1.** (referring to physical movement; reflexive) To force its way, penetrate, by gradual and imperceptible degrees: *the ivy insinuates itself into every crevice*. **2.** (referring to behaviour; reflexive) To gain entrance by subtle means, by furtive, cunning contrivance; to manœuvre, worm, oneself: *to insinuate oneself into a person's favour, into good society* &c. **3.** To suggest indirectly, hint, imply, convey by way of innuendo: *to insinuate that a man is dishonest*.

insinuating, adj. [1. insínūāting; 2. insínjueitiŋ], fr. Pres. Part. of prec. Tending to insinuate; ingratiating: *an insinuating smile, manner* &c.

insinuatingly, n. Prec. & **-ly**. In an insinuating manner.

insinuation, n. [1. insinūā́shun; 2. insinjuéiʃən], fr. Lat. *insinuātiōn-(em)*, 'entrance through a narrow or twisted passage; ingratiating'. **insinuate** & **-ion**. **1.** The act of insinuating. **2.** A hint, indirect allusion, subtle suggestion, implication, innuendo.

insinuative, adj. [1. insínūātiv; 2. insínjuətiv]. **insinuate** & **-ive**. **1.** Tending to gain another's favour, confidence, by insinuating manners &c. **2.** Making use of indirect hints and innuendo.

insinuatory, adj. [1. insínūaturi; 2. insínjuətəri]. See prec. & **-ory**. (rare) Insinuative.

insipid, adj. [1. insípid; 2. insípid], fr. L. Lat. *insipid-(us)*, 'tasteless', fr. **in-** (**II.**) & *sapidus*, 'savoury, tasty'. See **sapid**. **1.** (of material things) Lacking kick and pungency of flavour; tasteless, flat. **2.** (fig.) Arousing no interest; not stimulating, lacking in point, spice, bite, spirit; dull, vapid: *insipid conversation*; *an insipid beauty*.

insipidity, n. [1. insipíditi; 2. insipíditi]. Prec. & **-ity**. **1.** Tastelessness, lack of flavour. **2.** (fig.) Lack of animation; dullness, flatness.

insipidly, adv. [1. insípidli; 2. insípidli]. **insipid** & **-ly**. In an insipid manner.

insipidness, n. [1. insípidnes; 2. insípidnis]. See prec. & **-ness**. Insipidity.

insist, vb. intrans. & trans. [1. insíst; 2. insíst], fr. Lat. *insist-(ere)*, 'to stand, tread upon; to pursue; to devote oneself to; to press upon, urge; to dwell upon', fr. **in-** (**I.**) & *sistere*, 'to stand; to place', by reduplication fr. *stāre*, 'to stand'. See **state** (**I.**). **1. a** *Insist* (*up*)*on*, to dwell upon; enlarge, dilate, upon; to emphasize, bring into prominence continually: *to insist on a point, on the importance of*; **b** to assert, affirm, declare confidently: *to insist upon one's innocence*, or *that one is innocent*. **2.** To demand urgently, require with compelling force: *to insist on obedience, acceptance*; *to insist on something being done, that something shall be done*; (absol.) *I will have another glass if you insist*.

insistence, -cy, n. [1. insístens(i); 2. insístəns(i)]. See next word & **-ce, -cy**. **1. a** Act of insisting; continued dwelling upon, repetition of, emphasizing of: *his insistence upon the necessity of cold baths*; **b** reiterated, confident assertion, affirmation; resolute maintaining: *insistence upon one's innocence*. **2.** Act of insisting; enforcing, requiring, exacting: *insistence upon strict obedience*.

insistent, adj. [1. insístent; 2. insístənt], fr. Lat. *insistent-(em)*, Pres. Part. of *insistere*. See **insist**. **1.** Urgent, compelling, persistent, imperative: *insistent demands* &c. **2.** (of colours, sounds, tones &c.) Prominent, dominant, conspicuous, enforcing attention.

insistently, adv. Prec. & **-ly**. In an insistent manner.

insobriety, n. [1. insōbríeti; 2. insoubráiiti]. **in-** (**II.**) & **sobriety**. Intemperance, drunkenness.

insolation, n. [1. insolā́shun; 2. insəléiʃən], fr. L. Lat. *insōlātiōn-(em)*, 'a setting in the sun', fr. *insōlāt-(um)*, P.P. type of *insōlāre*, 'to expose to the sun', fr. **in-** (**I.**) & *sōl*, 'sun'. See **sol** & **-ation**. Exposure to the rays of the sun.

insolence, n. [1. ínsolens; 2. ínsələns], fr. Lat. *insolentia*, 'unusualness, novelty; want of moderation; pride, haughtiness'. See next word & **-ce**. **1.** The state or quality of being insolent. **2.** Insolent behaviour, or utterance; insulting arrogance, impudence.

insolent, adj. [1. ínsolent; 2. ínsələnt], fr. Lat. *insolent-(em)*, 'contrary to custom, unusual; immoderate; haughty, arrogant', orig. 'puffed up', fr. **in-** (**I.**) & base **sol-*, fr. Aryan **swel-*, **swḷ-* &c., 'to swell'; see **swell** (**I.**). Haughtily, contemptuously, insulting in behaviour or utterance; hubristic.

insolently, adv. Prec. & **-ly**. In an insolent manner.

insolubility, n. [1. insòlūbíliti; 2. insòljubíliti]. See next word & **-ity**. (of substances) Property of being insoluble.

insoluble, adj. [1. insólūbl; 2. insɔ́ljubl], fr. Lat. *insolūbil-(is)*, 'that cannot be loosed; incontestable', fr. **in-** (**II.**) & *solūbilis*, 'that may be loosed, taken apart'. See **soluble**. **1.** Not capable of being dissolved: *an insoluble substance*. **2.** Admitting of no solution; not capable of being solved, explained, interpreted: *an insoluble problem, mystery*.

insolubleness, n. Prec. & **-ness**. Quality of being incapable of solution.

insolubly, adv. See prec. & **-ly**. In an insoluble manner.

insolvency, n. [1. insólvensi; 2. insɔ́lvənsi]. **in-** (**II.**) & **solvency**. The state of being insolvent; bankruptcy.

insolvent, adj. & n. [1. insólvent; 2. insɔ́lvənt]. **in-** (**II.**) & **solvent**. **1.** adj. Unable to pay debts, to meet liabilities; bankrupt. **2.** n. Insolvent person.

insomnia, n. [1. insómnia; 2. insɔ́mniə]. Lat., 'want of sleep', fr. *insomn-(is)*, 'sleepless', fr. **in-** (**II.**) & *somn-(us)*, 'sleep'. See **somnolent** & **-ia**. Inability to sleep; want of sleep; sleeplessness.

insomuch, adv. [1. insōmúch; 2. insoumátʃ]. **in** (**I.**) & **so** & **much**. To such a degree that.

insouciance, n. [1. ansṓōsiahns; 2. ǽsúsiãs]. Fr., 'carelessness, indifference'. See next word & **-ce**. Careless indifference; heedlessness.

insouciant, adj. [1. ansṓōsiahn; 2. ǽsúsiã]. Fr., 'heedless, indifferent', fr. **in-** (**II.**) & Pres. Part. of *soucier*, 'to care'. See **solace**, **solicit**. Careless, heedless, indifferent.

inspan, vb. trans. & intrans. [1. ínspan; 2. ínspæn]. S. Afr., fr. Du. *inspannen*, fr. **in** (**II.**) & *spannen*, 'to span; to fasten, join'. See **span** (**I.**). **1.** trans. To harness to waggon &c., yoke up: *to inspan oxen*. **2.** intrans. To perform action of inspanning.

inspect, vb. trans. [1. inspékt; 2. inspékt], fr. Lat. *inspect-(um)*, P.P. type of *inspicere*, 'to look at, look into; to contemplate, examine', fr. **in-** (**I.**) & *specere*, 'to look'. See **spectrum**, **species**. **a** To look carefully at, examine closely; specif. **b** to perform duties of an official inspector.

inspection, n. [1. inspékshun; 2. inspékʃən], fr. Lat. *inspectiōn-(em)*, 'a looking into, inspection; examination, investigation'. Prec. & **-ion**. **a** Careful scrutiny, close examination; **b** official examination or investigation.

inspector, n. [1. inspéktor; 2. inspéktə]. **inspect** & **-or**. Person who inspects; specif., official appointed by higher authority to investigate, test, examine, and report (in schools, factories &c.); *police-inspector*, officer between sergeant and superintendent.

inspectoral, adj. [1. inspéktoral; 2. inspéktərəl]. Prec. & **-al**. Of, pertaining to, an inspector.

inspectorate, n. [1. inspéktorat; 2. inspéktərit]. **inspector** & **-ate**. **1.** The office of inspector. **2.** The body of inspectors as a whole. **3.** District under supervision of inspector.

inspectorial, adj. [1. inspektórial; 2. inspektɔ́riəl]. **inspector** & **-ial**. Of, pertaining to, an inspector.

inspectorship, n. [1. inspéktorship; 2. inspéktəʃip]. **inspector** & **-ship**. **a** Office of inspector; **b** tenure of inspector's office.

inspectress, n. [1. inspéktres; 2. inspéktris]. See prec. & **-ess**. Woman inspector (of schools &c.).

inspiration, n. [1. inspirā́shun, inspīrā́shun; 2. inspiréiʃən, inspairéiʃən], fr. L. Lat. *inspīrātiōn-(em)*, 'inspiration'; fr. *inspīrāre*, 'to breathe into, blow upon; to excite; inspire'. See **inspire** & **-ation**. **1.** Act of breathing in, inhaling, drawing breath into the lungs. **2. a** Influence arousing creative power in the mind; instinctive, mental stimulus; creative impulse; afflatus: *the inspiration of a poet, artist* &c.; **b** thoughts, ideas, due to such an impulse: *to have a sudden inspiration*. **3.** The act of inspiring; imparting of power and will to create; intellectual stimulus: *the inspiration of one's teacher*. **4.** Divine influence; esp. divine guidance, direction, in the writing of the Scriptures; *verbal inspiration*, in which exact words are inspired; *plenary inspiration*, in which every idea is inspired; *moral inspiration*, limited to moral teaching, and not including historical narration &c.

inspirational, adj. [1. inspirā́shunal; 2. inspiréiʃənəl]. Prec. & **-al**. Pertaining to inspiration.

inspirationism, n. [1. inspirā́shunizm; 2. inspiréiʃənizəm]. **inspiration** & **-ism**. Belief in divine inspiration.

inspirationist, n. [1. inspirā́shunist; 2. inspiréiʃənist]. **inspiration** & **-ist**. One who believes in the inspiration of the Scriptures, esp. in plenary inspiration.

inspirator, n. [1. ínspirātor; 2. ínspireitə]. Lat., fr. *inspīrāt-(um)*, P.P. of *inspīrāre*. See **inspire** & **-or**. Device for drawing in air, vapour &c.

inspiratory, adj. [1. inspirā́turi, inspíraturi; 2. inspiréitəri, inspáiərətəri]. Prec. & **-y**. Pertaining to the inspiration of air &c.

inspire, vb. trans. [1. inspír; 2. inspáiə], fr. Lat. *inspīr-(āre)*, 'to breathe into, blow upon; to excite, inflame; to arouse by divine influence', fr. **in-** (**I.**) & *spīrāre*, 'to breathe'. See **spirant**, **spirit**. **1.** To breathe in, draw into the lungs, inhale. **2. a** To fill, animate, with, as though by breathing into; to influence the mind from without, by, or as though by, supernatural agency: *to inspire the mind with terror, hope, love*; *with a sense of beauty* &c.; **b** to instil, infuse into, impart to (the mind): *his words inspired new courage*; **c** specif., to breathe into, fill with, as by supernatural power; animate with creative genius: *the muse does not inspire all poets equally*.

inspired, adj. [1. inspírd; 2. inspáiəd], fr. P.P. of prec. **1. a** (i.) Divinely influenced; dominated by divine power; specif., roused to a state of intense mental emotion, endowed with knowledge &c., by divine revelation: *an inspired propheteess*; (ii.) moved with creative impulse: *inspired poet*; **b** produced under the guidance of divine influence: *the inspired books of the Bible*; *inspired words*; **c** characterized by inspiration: *an inspired moment*. **2.** Special use, *an inspired article, statement* &c., e.g. in a newspaper, dictated by one possessing inside knowledge in politics, or affairs generally.

inspiring, adj. [1. inspíring; 2. inspáiəriŋ]. **inspire** & **-ing** (**II.**). Tending to inspire; animating, stimulating.

inspirit, vb. trans. [1. inspírit; 2. inspírit]. **in-** (**I.**) & **spirit**. To animate, exhilarate, put spirit into, infuse life into, instigate to action.

inspiriting, adj. [1. inspíriting; 2. inspíritiŋ], fr. Pres. Part. of prec. Tending to inspirit, animate; encouraging, stimulating: *inspiriting words*; *an inspiriting example*.

inspissate, vb. trans. [1. inspísāt, ínspisāt; 2. inspíseit, ínspiseit], fr. L. Lat. *inspissāt-(us)*, 'thickened', fr. **in-** (**I.**) & *spissāt-(um)*, P.P. type of *spissāre*, 'to thicken, condense', fr. *spiss-(us)*, 'thick, compact; slow, late; protracted; hard, difficult', fr. **spid-s-o*. Cogn. w. Gk. *spidés*, 'extended, protracted'; Lett. *spaidit*, 'to press'. See also **spike**, **spoke** (**I.**), **spine**. To thicken, make thick, as by evaporation &c.; also in P.P. as adj., in transferred sense, dense: *inspissated gloom*.

inspissation, n. [1. inspisā́shun; 2. inspiséiʃən]. Prec. & **-ion**. The act or process of inspissating; state of being inspissated.

instability, n. [1. instabíliti; 2. instəbíliti], fr. Lat. *instabilitāt-(em)*, 'unsteadiness'. See **in-** (**II.**) & **stability**. **a** Lack of steadiness; shakiness; **a** tottering, unsteady condition; **b** unsteadiness of character; liability to change, unreliability; inconstancy, irresolution.

install, vb. trans. [1. instáwl; 2. instɔ́l], fr. Med. Lat. *install-(āre)*, 'to introduce formally', fr. **in-** (**I.**) & *stall-(um)*, 'stall, seat', fr. Gmc. source. See **stall** (**I.**). **1.** To introduce, induct, to an office &c., with formality, ceremony; to invest with a dignity &c.: *to install a person in an office*. **2.** To establish, settle, introduce: *comfortably installed in a seat by the fire*. **3.** To place (apparatus &c.) in position, and prepare for use: *to install electric light*.

installant, n. [1. instáwlant; 2. instɔ́lənt]. Prec. & **-ant**. Person conducting official ceremony of installation.

installation, n. [1. instawlā́shun; 2. instɔléiʃən]. **install** & **-ation**. **1.** Act of installing; state of being installed. **2.** Complete mechanical apparatus, e.g. for system of lighting or heating.

instalment, n. [1. instáwlment; 2. instɔ́lmənt]. In early, obs. sense fr. **install** & **-ment**;

in the other senses, the word is prob. fr. obs. *estall, stall*, 'to arrange (payments) for', cp. O. Fr. *estallement*, fr. *astallere*, 'to arrange on a stall', see **stall** (I.). **1.** (archaic, obs.) Installation. **2.** Sum of money paid as one of a series of payments, forming part of a total sum of money due; esp. in hire-purchase contracts. **3.** Each portion of a thing appearing, supplied, in parts at different times: *an instalment of a serial story; the first instalment of goods ordered.*

instance (I.), n. [1. ínstans; 2. ínstəns], fr. Fr., fr. Lat. *instantia*, 'the state of being near or close, presence; force, earnestness, urgency', fr. *inst-(āre)*, 'to stand in or on; to be near; to follow, press upon; to solicit, insist upon', fr. **in-** (I.) & *stāre*, 'to stand'. See **state** (I.), **stand** (I.). **1.** Single example, individual case, fact, illustrating general statement. Phr. *for instance*, by way of example, as an illustration. **2.** Request, solicitation, suggestion; esp. in Phr. *at the instance of; at his instance* &c. **3.** (law) **a** Institution of a process, suit, proceeding: *court of first instance;* **b** a step, stage, in a legal suit; hence Phr. *in the first instance*, to start with, as a beginning.

instance (II.), vb. trans., fr. prec. To cite, adduce, refer to, as an example or illustration.

instancy, n. [1. ínstansi; 2. ínstənsi], fr. Lat. *inst-(āre)*, 'to be near, press upon; to urge, insist'. See **instance** (I.) & **-cy**. Pressing character, urgency, insistency.

instant (I.), adj. [1. ínstant; 2. ínstənt], fr. Lat. *instant-(em)*, 'present; pressing, importunate, urgent', fr. *inst-(āre)*, 'to be near; to press upon; to urge, insist'. See **instance** (I.) & **-ant**. **1.** Urgent, active; ready, unceasing, unwearied: '*continuing instant in prayer*'. **2.** Immediate, without delay; occurring or acting at once: *an instant response.* **3.** (with specified date) Of the current month: *the 13th instant* (abbr. *inst.*).

instant (II.), n., fr. prec. **1.** Exact point of time, precise moment: *obey me this instant; at that very instant a shot was fired.* Phr. *on the instant*, immediately, straightway, without delay; *the instant*, as soon as: *the instant you call.* **2.** Very short space of time: *don't waste an instant; I shall be ready in an instant.*

instantaneous, adj. [1. ìnstantáneus; 2. ìnstəntéiniəs]. **instant** & **-aneous**. **1. a** Done, or occurring, in an instant; **b** (of two actions or events) occurring at the same instant, without interval of time; immediate: *the dose produced an instantaneous effect; the two movements were almost instantaneous.* **2.** (mechanics, of position &c.) At, referring to, a particular instant.

instantaneously, adv. Prec. & **-ly**. In, at, the same instant; without an instant's delay; without an interval.

instantaneousness, n. See prec. & **-ness**. The quality of being instantaneous.

instanter, adv. [1. instánter; 2. instǽntə]. Lat. *instanter*, 'urgently, pressingly', fr. *instant-(em)*, 'present; urgent'. See **instant** (I.). Immediately, without delay.

instantly, adv. [1. ínstantli; 2. ínstəntli]. **instant** (I.) & **-ly**. At once, immediately.

instauration, n. [1. ìnstawráshun; 2. ìnstɔ̄réiʃən], fr. Lat. *instaurātiōn-(em)*, 'renewal, restoration', fr. *instaurāt-(um)*, P.P. type of *instaurāre*, 'to renew, repeat; restore'. See second element of **restore** & **-ation**. Process of bringing a thing back to its former condition; renewal, restoration.

instead, adv. [1. instéd; 2. instéd]. **in** (I.) & **stead**. In place of, as substitute for, as an alternative to: *give me this instead of that; give me that instead.*

instep, n. [1. ínstep; 2. ínstɛp]. Etymol. uncertain; *instop* occurs also as an early form; prob. fr. **in** & **stop**, but origin is not clear. **a** Curved upper surface of human foot in front of ankle; **b** part of shoe, stocking &c. which covers the instep.

instigate, vb. trans. [1. ínstigāt; 2. ínstigeit], fr. Lat. *instīgāt-(um)*, P.P. type of *instīgāre*, 'to urge, stimulate, incite', fr. **in-** (I.) & **stīg-(āre)*, 'to prick, goad'; see further under **stigma**, **stick** (I.), & **stimulus**. **1.** To stimulate, urge, incite, goad: *to instigate (a person) to do something.* **2.** To be an active agent of; to stir up, foment, urge: *to instigate a rebellion* &c.

instigation, n. [1. ìnstigáshun; 2. ìnstigéiʃən], fr. Lat. *instīgātiōn-(em)*, 'urging, incitement'. Prec. & **-ion**. Act of instigating; state of being instigated.

instil(l), vb. trans. [1. instíl; 2. instíl], fr. Lat. *instill-(āre)*, 'to pour in drop by drop; (fig.) to infuse, introduce', fr. **in-** (I.) & *stillāre*, 'to drop, trickle, distil'. See **distil**, **still** (V.). **1.** (rare). To pour in drop by drop: '*from the well of life three drops instilled*' (Milton, 'P.L.'). **2.** To inculcate, implant gradually; infuse: *to instil ideas into the mind* &c.

instilment, n. [1. instílment; 2. instílmənt]. Prec. & **-ment**. Act or process of instilling; state of being instilled.

instinct (I.), n. [1. ínstingkt; 2. ínstiŋkt], fr. Lat. *instinct-(us)*, 'instigation, impulse', fr. P.P. type of *instinguere*, 'to incite, impel', fr. **in-** (I.) & **stinguere*, 'to urge on, goad', w. infixed *-n-*, fr. Aryan base **stig-* &c., 'to prick.' See **instigate**. **1.** Natural, involuntary propensity or tendency, not arising from reason or experience, of an organism possessing consciousness to behave in a certain way, which tends to some specific end, e.g. the safety, welfare, preservation, of the individual or of the species: *the instinct of self-preservation; to do something by instinct; to act on instinct.* **2.** Natural aptitude, impulse, intuition: *an instinct for doing the right thing.*

instinct (II.), adj. [1. instíngkt; 2. instíŋkt], fr. Lat. *instinct-(um)*, P.P. type of *instinguere*, 'to incite, impel'. See prec. (followed by *with*) Animated by; filled, imbued, with: *a picture instinct with life.*

instinctive, adj. [1. instíngktiv; 2. instíŋktiv]. **instinct** (I.) & **-ive**. **a** Connected with, arising from, instinct or innate tendency or propensity; not the result of reasoning or experience: *an instinctive horror of spiders; an instinctive movement;* **b** intuitional, not due to knowledge or instruction: *an instinctive sense of danger; an instinctive taste for art.*

instinctively, adv. Prec. & **-ly**. In an instinctive manner; by instinct.

institute (I.), n. [1. ínstitūt; 2. ínstitjūt], fr. Lat. *institūt-(um)*, P.P. type of *instituere*, 'to place, fix; to found, establish'. See next word. **1.** Formal organization or society established with a scientific, social, or educational or other object. **2.** Building forming headquarters of such society &c., or in which its work is carried on. **3.** (pl.) Summary, digest, of fundamental principles, precepts, elements, esp. of jurisprudence; *Institutes of Justinian*, summary of Roman Law compiled by order of Justinian.

institute (II.), vb. trans., fr. Lat. *institūt-(um)*, P.P. type of *instituere*, 'to put, fix, plant; to set up, erect, construct; to found, organize, establish; to appoint, ordain'; fr. **in-** (I.) & *statuere*, 'to cause to stand, erect, set up; to establish, constitute'. See **statute**. **1.** To establish, set up, found, introduce, originate: *to institute a custom, rule* &c. **2.** To begin, take initial proceedings in, set going: *to institute an inquiry.* **3.** To appoint, install, induct: *to institute a person into a benefice.*

institution, n. [1. ìnstitúshun; 2. ìnstitjúʃən], fr. Lat. *institūtiōn-(em)*, 'arrangement, disposition; principles, elements; appointment'. See **institute** (II.) & **-ion**. **1. a** Act of instituting; state of being instituted; setting up, founding, establishment, introduction; **b** specif., induction into a benefice. **2. a** Something that has been instituted; established custom, order, principle, system, law &c.; **b** (colloq., fig.) person, esp. one possessing well-marked characteristic or eccentricity, who is widely known and admired, or at least tolerated. **3.** Society, organization &c. established for some scientific or social purpose; organized body supplying some public or educational need. **4.** Building in which the work of an institution is carried out.

institutional, adj. [1. ìnstitúshunal; 2. ìnstitjúʃənl]. Prec. & **-al**. Pertaining to, of the nature of, an institution.

instruct, vb. trans. [1. instrúkt; 2. instrákt], fr. Lat. *instruct-(um)*, P.P. type of *instruere*, 'to build, erect, construct; to set in order, draw up; to prepare, provide; to teach'. See **in-** (I.) & **structure**. **1. a** To impart information or knowledge to; teach, train: *to instruct the young; to instruct a person in a subject;* **b** specif. (law) to give directions to, state facts as to, or law, concerning, a case. **2.** To direct, give orders to, command.

instruction, n. [1. instrúkshun; 2. instrákʃən], fr. Lat. *instructiōn-(em)*, 'a building, construction; arrangement, disposition; teaching'. Prec. & **-ion**. **1.** Act of instructing; state of being instructed. **2.** Knowledge, information, imparted to another; teaching, training: *to give instruction in Latin, swimming* &c. **3.** (pl.) **a** Directions, commands, orders; **b** specif., directions given by a judge to a jury, or by a solicitor to counsel.

instructional, adj. [1. instrúkshunal; 2. instrákʃənəl]. Prec. & **-al**. Of, pertaining to, for the purpose of, instruction.

instructive, adj. [1. instrúktiv; 2. instráktiv]. **instruct** & **-ive**. Containing instruction or information; conveying knowledge.

instructively, adv. Prec. & **-ly**. In an instructive manner.

instructiveness, n. See prec. & **-ness**. The quality of being instructive.

instructor, n. [1. instrúktur; 2. instráktə]. **instruct** & **-or**. **a** One who instructs; a teacher, trainer; **b** book giving instruction on some particular subject.

instructress, n. [1. instrúktres; 2. instráktris]. Prec. & **-ess**. A female instructor.

instrument (I.), n. [1. ínstroomənt; 2. ínstrumənt], fr. Lat. *instrūment-(um)*, 'tool, implement; apparatus, stock, material, furniture; document, record; provision, supply', fr. base seen in *instru-(ere)*, 'to build, erect; to provide, furnish; to teach'. See **instruct** & **-ment**. **1. a** Thing by means of which something is done; thing used in carrying out an operation, esp. a tool, implement, used for scientific purposes: *surgical instrument;* **b** one of various mechanical contrivances for the production of musical sounds: *musical instrument.* **2.** Formal, legal, document, deed, record. **3. a** Person by whose agency something is done: *to be the instrument of a person's death;* **b** one employed to do work planned by another; a tool: *he is the leader, the others are merely his instruments; the instrument of vengeance.*

instrument (II.), vb. trans., fr. prec. To arrange (musical composition) for performance by musical instruments.

instrumental (I.), adj. [1. ìnstrooméntl; 2. ìnstruméntl]. **instrument** (I.) & **-al**. **1.** (of persons) Serving as means or instrument by which something is done: *instrumental in obtaining an appointment for a friend.* **2. a** Arising from, produced by, a mechanical device or instrument: *instrumental errors in measurement* &c.; **b** produced by, arranged for, musical instruments: *instrumental music.* **3.** (gram.) Denoting, expressing, indicating, means, agent, instrument.

instrumental (II.), n., fr. prec. (gram.) Instrumental case.

instrumentalist, n. [1. ìnstrooméntalist; 2. ìnstruméntəlist]. **instrumental** (I.) & **-ist**. Performer on musical instrument.

instrumentality, n. [1. ìnstroomentáliti; 2. ìnstrumentǽliti]. **instrumental** (I.) & **-ity**. Means, agent, agency, whereby something is done.

instrumentally, adv. [1. ìnstrooméntali;

2. instruméntəli]. See prec. & **-ly.** **a** By means of, as, an instrument; **b** by means of musical instruments.

instrumentation, n. [1. instroomentáshun; 2. instrumentéiʃən]. **instrument (II.)** & **-ation.** **1.** Arrangement of a musical composition for instrumental performance. **2.** The use of scientific instruments. **3.** (obs. or rare) Agency, instrumentality.

insubordinate, adj. [1. insubórdinat; 2. insəbɔ́dinət]. **in- (II.)** & **subordinate.** Resisting authority; disobedient, unruly.

insubordination, n. [1. insubordináshun; 2. insəbɔ̄dinéiʃən]. Prec. & **-ion.** The state, quality, of being insubordinate; disobedience, rebelliousness, unruliness.

insubstantial, adj. [1. insubstánshal; 2. insabstǽnʃl]. **in- (II.)** & **substantial.** Lacking in substance; unreal, illusory.

insubstantiality, n. [1. insubstanshiáliti; 2. insabstænʃiǽliti]. Prec. & **-ity.** Quality of being insubstantial.

insufferable, adj. [1. insúferabl; 2. insáfərəbl]. **in- (II.)** & **sufferable.** Not to be endured; intolerable, detestable: *an insufferable person, nuisance; insufferable insolence.*

insufferably, adv. Prec. & **-ly.** To an insufferable degree.

insufficiency, n. [1. insufíshensi; 2. insəfíʃənsi], fr. L. Lat. *insufficientia*, 'insufficiency'. **in- (II.)** & **sufficiency.** **a** State of being insufficient; **b** an insufficient quantity, a lack, dearth.

insufficient, adj. [1. insufíshent; 2. insəfíʃənt], fr. L. Lat. *insufficient-(em)*, 'insufficient'. **in- (II.)** & **sufficient.** Not sufficient; inadequate.

insufficiently, adv. Prec. & **-ly.** To an insufficient degree or extent.

insufflate, vb. trans. [1. insuflāt; 2. ínsafleit], fr. Lat. *insufflāt-(um)*, P.P. type of *insufflāre*, 'to blow, breathe, into or upon', fr. **in- (I.)** & *sufflāre*, 'to blow'. See **suf-** & **flatus.** **1.** To blow or breathe (air, vapour &c.) into body, cavity in body &c. **2.** To fill (cavity &c.) with air &c., breathed or blown into it.

insufflation, n. [1. insufláshun; 2. insafléiʃən], fr. L. Lat. *insufflātiōn-(em)*, 'a blowing into'. Prec. & **-ion.** The act of insufflating; state of being insufflated; specif. **a** act of breathing upon, as symbolical of a new spiritual life, in baptism; **b** (med.) blowing of air or gas into the lungs to stimulate respiratory action.

insufflator, n. [1. ínsuflātur; 2. ínsəfleitə]. **insufflate** & **-or.** Mechanical apparatus for injecting air, vapour &c. into a cavity of the body &c.

insular, adj. [1. ínsūlar; 2. ínsjulə], fr. Lat. *insulār-(is)*, 'of, belonging to, an island', fr. *insul-(a)*, 'an island', & **-ar**; according to Walde, perh. for **en sālo*, '(that which is) in the sea', cp. Lat. *sāl*, 'salt; the sea'. See **sal (I.).** **1.** Of, pertaining to, of the nature of, an island. **2.** Of, pertaining to, characteristic of, the inhabitants of an island; specif., narrow-minded, illiberal, intolerant, as being cut off from the current of ideas in the world at large: *insular habits, prejudices* &c.

insularism, n. [1. ínsūlarizm; 2. ínsjulərizəm]. Prec. & **-ism.** Quality of being insular; narrow-mindedness, prejudice.

insularity, n. [1. insūláriti; 2. insjulǽriti]. **insular** & **-ity.** **1.** The state of being an island, or like an island. **2.** Quality of being insular; narrowness, illiberality of mind.

insularly, adv. [1. ínsūlarli; 2. ínsjuləli]. See prec. & **-ly.** **a** In an insular manner, as an island; **b** in a prejudiced manner, so as to exhibit insularism.

insulate, vb. trans. [1. ínsūlāt; 2. ínsjuleit], fr. Lat. *insul-(a)*, 'an island'. See **insular** & **-ate.** **1.** To make (land) into an island, surround by water. **2.** To separate, detach (person or thing) from surroundings; place in detached position; cut off from communication with, dependence on, surroundings; isolate. **3.** (phys. and elect.) To isolate, cut off, by means of non-conducting substance, to prevent the passage of electricity, heat, or sound.

insulation, n. [1. insūláshun; 2. insjuléiʃən]. Prec. & **-ion.** Act or process of insulating; state of being insulated.

insulator, n. [1. ínsūlātur; 2. ínsjuleitə]. **insulate** & **-or.** That which insulates; specif. (elect.) a substance of low conductivity, loosely a non-conductor.

insulin, n. [1. ínsūlin; 2. ínsjulin], fr. Lat. *insulae*, 'islands', see **insular,** & **-in.** An extract made from the pancreas of sheep or other animals, containing the special secretion of the small masses of ductless cells known as 'the islets of Langerhans', used as a specific for diabetes.

insult (I.), n. [1. ínsult; 2. ínsalt], fr. L. Lat. *insult-(us)*, 'insult, reviling', fr. **in- (I.)** & *saltus*, 'a leap, spring, bound'. See next word. Word or act which wounds the feelings of another, which tends to humiliate, and offend another; insolence, affront.

insult (II.), vb. trans. [1. insúlt; 2. insált], fr. Lat. *insult-(āre)*, 'to spring, leap, upon; to behave insolently towards, revile, taunt', fr. **in- (I.)** & *saltāre*, 'to leap repeatedly, to dance'. See **saltant** & **salient.** To treat with contempt and insolence; to wound feelings of, to affront, by word or act.

insulting, adj. [1. insúlting; 2. insáltiŋ], fr. Pres. Part. of prec. Conveying, expressing, an insult; wounding, insolent.

insultingly, adv. Prec. & **-ly.** In an insulting manner.

insuperability, n. [1. insūperabíliti; 2. insjūpərəbíliti], fr. Lat. *insuperābil-(is)*, 'unsurmountable'. See next word & **-ity.** Quality of being insuperable.

insuperable, adj. [1. insúperabl; 2. insjúpərəbl], fr. Lat. *insuperābil-(is)*, 'unsurmountable, unconquerable'. **in- (II.)** & **superable.** (chiefly fig.) Not capable of being surmounted, not to be overcome; impassable: *an insuperable difficulty, obstacle.*

insuperably, adv. Prec. & **-ly.** In an insuperable manner.

insupportable, adj. [1. insupórtabl; 2. insəpɔ́təbl]. **in- (II.)** & **supportable.** Not capable of being supported or endured; unbearable, intolerable.

insupportably, adv. Prec. & **-ly.** To an insupportable extent or degree.

insurable, adj. [1. inshórabl; 2. inʃɔ́rəbl]. **insure** & **-able.** Capable of being insured.

insurance, n. [1. inshórans; 2. inʃɔ́rəns]. **insure** & **-ance.** **1.** Act of insuring; state of being insured. **2. a** Premium paid for insuring; **b** insurance policy.

insurance policy, n. Written contract of insurance.

insurant, n. [1. inshórant; 2. inʃɔ́rənt]. Next word & **-ant.** One who pays premium for insurance.

insure, vb. trans. [1. inshór; 2. inʃɔ́]. Variant of **ensure.** See also **assure.** **1.** (referring to action of insured) To contract, arrange for, secure, payment of sum of money, as compensation for loss of, damage to (one's property, life &c.), by payment of premium: *to insure oneself, one's life; to insure one's property against fire, burglary* &c. **2.** (referring to act of the insurer) To contract to pay a sum of money to (person or his heirs), in consideration of specified premium, upon certain contingencies, e.g. loss of life, damage to person or property &c. **3.** (by extension) To secure certain benefits, under Health or Unemployment Insurance Acts, by weekly payments of employed and employer with State contributions.

insured, n. [1. inshórd; 2. inʃɔ́d], fr. P.P. of prec. *The insured*, person to whom payment is to be made.

insurer, n. [1. inshórer; 2. inʃɔ́rə]. **insure** & **-er.** Person or company contracting to pay money as compensation for, or in case of, loss or damage to person or property &c.

insurgency, n. [1. insérjensi; 2 insə́dʒənsi], fr. Lat. *insurg-(ere)*, 'to rise, rise up'. See next word & **-cy.** State of being insurgent.

insurgent, adj. & n. [1. insérjent; 2. insə́dʒənt], fr. Lat. *insurgent-(em)*, Pres. Part. of *insurgere*, 'to rise; to rise up, rouse; to rise against, revolt; to rise in flood', fr. **in- (I.)** & *surgere*, 'to rise'. See **surge.** **1.** adj. **a** Rising against established authority, actively rebellious, resisting forcibly; **b** (poet., of natural phenomena) rising, surging, rushing in: *insurgent waves, sea* &c. **2.** n. A rebel, revolutionary.

insurmountable, adj. [1. insérmóuntabl; 2. insəmáuntəbl]. **in- (II.)** & **surmountable.** Not capable of being surmounted.

insurmountably, adv. Prec. & **-ly.** In an insurmountable manner.

insurrection, n. [1. insurékshun; 2. insərékʃən], fr. Lat. *insurrectiōn-(em)*, 'a rising up, revolt', fr. *insurrect-(um)*, P.P. type of *insurgere*, 'to rise up'. See **insurgent.** Organized and active opposition, resistance, to established authority; revolt, rebellion.

insurrectional, adj. [1. insurékshunal; 2. insərékʃənl]. Prec. & **-al.** Of, pertaining to, insurrection.

insurrectionary, adj. [1. insurékshunari; 2. insərékʃənəri]. **insurrection** & **-ary.** Insurrectional.

insurrectionist, n. [1. insurékshunist; 2. insərékʃənist]. **insurrection** & **-ist.** One who incites or takes part in, approves of, insurrection.

insusceptibility, n. [1. insuseptibíliti; 2. insəseptibíliti]. See next word & **-ity.** The quality or state of being insusceptible.

insusceptible, adj. [1. insuséptibl; 2. insəséptibl]. **in- (II.)** & **susceptible.** Not susceptible; not capable of being affected; **a** (physically) *insusceptible of medical treatment;* **b** (emotionally) incapable of being stirred, moved; inaccessible, insensible: *a heart insusceptible of,* or *to, mercy.*

intact, adj. [1. intákt; 2. intǽkt], fr. Lat. *intact-(us)*, 'untouched, uninjured, intact; untried, unattempted', fr. **in- (II.)** & *tact-(um)*, P.P. type of *tangere*, 'to touch; to reach, arrive at; to affect; to impress'. See **tact.** Untouched, uninjured undiminished, unimpaired, whole, entire, complete.

intagliated, adj. [1. intágliāted; 2. intǽglieitid], fr. Ital. *intagliat-(o)*, P.P. of *intagliare*, 'to incise', fr. **in- (I.)** & *tagliare*, 'to cut'. See next word. Carved in intaglio, incised on a hard surface.

intaglio (I.), n. [1. intágliō, intáhliō; 2. intǽgliou, intáliou]. Ital., fr. *intagli-āre*, 'to incise'; **in-** & Med. Lat. *tāleāre*, 'to cut', fr. *tālea*, 'a cutting, layer; stake'. See **tailor.** **1.** Design carved, engraved, in hard surface; incised figure. **2.** Gem with incised design; cp. *cameo.*

intaglio (II.), vb. trans., fr. prec. **a** To engrave design on (surface); **b** to incise (design) on hard surface.

intake, n. [1. íntāk; 2. ínteik]. **in (II.)** & **take.** **1. a** Point at which water or air flows into a narrow channel, pipe &c.; **b** air-shaft in a mine. **2.** (provinc.) Piece of enclosed land, esp. portion reclaimed from a moor or swamp.

intangibility, n. [1. intànjibíliti; 2. intændʒibíliti]. See next word & **-ity.** Quality of being intangible.

intangible, adj. [1. intánjibl; 2. intǽndʒibl]. **in- (II.)** & **tangible.** **1.** Not perceptible to the touch; not to be touched or grasped; impalpable, incorporeal, insubstantial. **2.** Not capable of being grasped by the mind; vague, indefinite; not capable of clear, precise, definition.

intangibly, adv. Prec. & **-ly.** In an intangible manner, so as to be incapable of being grasped, or understood.

integer, n. [1. íntejer; 2. íntidʒə]. Lat. *integer*, adj., 'unhurt, untouched, unchanged; whole, entire, undiminished; sound, fresh; honest, blameless; unbiassed, impartial', fr. **in-** (II.) & *tag-, stem of *tangere*, 'to touch'. See **tact** & **tangent**. **1.** An undivided whole; anything complete, entire. **2.** (arith.) A whole number; opposed to *fraction*.

integral (I.), adj. [1. íntegral; 2. íntigrəl], fr. L. Lat. *integrāl-(is)*, 'whole, complete'. Prec. & **-al.** **1.** a Necessary to completeness; essential, intrinsic: *an integral part of object, scheme* &c.; b containing all that is necessary for completeness, having all constituent parts; whole, entire. **2.** (math., of quantity &c.) Denoted by, composed of, pertaining to, integers.

integral (II.), n., fr prec. A whole, totality.

integrality, n. [1. ìntegráliti; 2. ìntigrǽliti]. **integral** (I.) & **-ity.** Quality of being integral.

integrally, adv. [1. íntegrali; 2. íntigrəli]. **integral** (I.) & **-ly.** In an integral manner; as an integral part.

integrant, adj. [1. íntegrant; 2. íntigrənt], fr. Lat. *integrant-(em)*, Pres. Part. of *integrāre*, 'to make whole, renew; to supply, keep full; to refresh', fr. **integer.** Forming a complete whole; constituent, component, essential to completeness.

integrate (I.), adj. [1. íntegrat; 2. íntigrət]. See next word. a Made up of component parts; b complete, whole.

integrate (II.), vb. trans. [1. íntegrāt; 2. íntigreit], fr. Lat. *integrāt-(um)*, P.P. type of *integrāre*, 'to make whole, renew; to refresh', fr. **integer.** **1.** a To combine (parts) into a whole, put together to form a whole; b to make into a whole by adding, putting together, constituent parts; to complete, make entire. **2.** To give total sum of, mean value of, average of (temperature, velocity of wind, area of irregular figure &c.).

integration, n. [1. ìntegráshun; 2. ìntigréiʃən]. Prec. & **-ion.** The act of integrating; state of being integrated.

integrative, adj. [1. íntegrativ; 2. íntigrətiv]. **integrate** (II.) & **-ive.** Of, pertaining to, integration; integrant.

integrator, n. [1. íntegrāter; 2. íntigreitə]. **integrate** (II.) & **-or.** One who, that which, integrates; specif., mechanical device for obtaining numerical value of irregular figure &c.

integrity, n. [1. intégriti; 2. intégriti], fr. Lat. *integritāt-(em)*, 'completeness, soundness; blamelessness, innocence'. **integer** & **-ity.** **1.** Unimpaired condition; state of being untouched, undiminished; wholeness, original completeness. **2.** Wholeness of mind; honesty, probity, uprightness, sincerity.

integument, n. [1. intégūment; 2. intégjumənt], fr. Lat. *integument-(um)*, 'a covering', fr. **in-** (I.) & *teg-(ere)*, 'to cover'. See **tegument.** Outer covering, case, envelope; esp. natural covering of animal or vegetable body, skin, shell, husk, rind &c.

integumentary, adj. [1. intègūméntari; 2. intègjuméntəri]. Prec. & **-ary.** Of, pertaining to, forming, an integument.

intellect, n. [1. íntelekt; 2. íntilɛkt], fr. Lat. *intellect-(us)*, 'perception, discernment; faculty of understanding', fr. P.P. type of *intellegere, -ligere*, 'to perceive; to understand, comprehend', fr. **inter-** & *legere*, 'to pick out, choose; read'. See **lecture** & cp. **legend.** **1.** The faculty of perceiving, knowing, and thinking; reasoning power, mind, as distinguished from the emotional faculties. **2.** Intellectual persons, collectively: *the whole intellect of the country approved the measure.*

intellection, n. [1. ìntelékshun; 2. ìntilékʃən], fr. Lat. *intellect-(um)*, P.P. type of *intelligere*, 'to perceive, understand'. See **intelligent** & **-ion.** The process of thinking, understanding; activity of the intellect.

intellective, adj. [1. ìntelékti v; 2. ìntiléktiv]. **intellect** & **-ive.** Of, pertaining to, the intellect.

intellectual (I.), adj. [1. ìnteléktūal, ìntelékchooal; 2. ìntiléktjuəl, ìntiléktʃuəl], fr. Lat. *intellectuāl-(is)*, 'of the understanding', fr. *intellectu-(s)*, 'perception; understanding'. See **intellect** & **-al.** **1.** Of, pertaining to, appealing to, exercising, the intellect: *intellectual effort, pursuits* &c. **2.** (of persons) Of trained intelligence, having capacity for high degree of mental effort; habitually exercising the intellect; inclined to mental activity.

intellectual (II.), n., fr. prec. Intellectual person.

intellectualism, n. [1. ìnteléktūalizm; 2. ìntiléktjuəlizəm]. **intellectual** & **-ism.** **1.** Addiction to intellectual pursuits. **2.** a Doctrine that knowledge is entirely derived through the exercise of pure reason; b tendency to over-estimate the rational and disregard the other faculties of the human mind.

intellectualist, n. [1. ìnteléktūalist; 2. ìntiléktjuəlist]. **intellectual** & **-ist.** One who tends to over-emphasize the rational faculties at the expense of others.

intellectuality, n. [1. ìntelektūáliti; 2. ìntilɛktjuǽliti]. **intellectual** & **-ity.** Quality of being intellectual; intellectualism.

intellectualization, n. [1. ìntelèktūalīzáshun; 2. ìntilèktjuəlaizéiʃən]. See next word & **-ation.** The act or process of intellectualizing; state of being intellectualized.

intellectualize, vb. trans. & intrans. [1. ìnteléktūalīz; 2. ìntiléktjuəlaiz]. **intellectual** & **-ize.** **1.** trans. a To give intellectual character to; reduce to an intellectual form; b to treat intellectually. **2.** intrans. To use or develop the intellect.

intellectually, adv. [1. ìnteléktūali, -chooali; 2. ìntiléktjuəli, -tʃuəli]. See **intellectual** (I.) & **-ly.** In an intellectual manner.

intelligence, n. [1. intélijens; 2. intélidžəns], fr. Lat. *intelligentia*, 'power of understanding, discernment'. See **intelligent** & **-ce.** **1.** a The faculty of understanding; power of perceiving, knowing, reasoning; intellect, mental ability; b readiness, quickness of understanding, mental alertness. **2.** (of animals) Mental quality resembling the power of reasoning; sagacity. **3.** Communicated information; general information on any subject; *intelligence service, department*, one collecting, filing, interpreting, information of value to the staff of an army, navy, to the police &c. **4.** Intelligent being.

intelligencer, n. [1. intélijenser; 2. intélidžənsə]. Prec. & **-er.** Person supplying information or news; specif., a spy.

intelligent, adj. [1. intélijent; 2. intélidžənt], fr. Lat. *intelligent-(em)*, Pres. Part. of *intelligere, -legere*, 'to perceive, discern; to understand, comprehend', fr. **inter-** & *legere*, 'to gather, collect; to choose, select; to observe, survey; to read'. See **lecture** & cp. **intellect.** **1.** Endowed with faculty of understanding, with reasoning power; rational. **2.** Having an alert mind; of active intellect, acute: *an intelligent child; an intelligent reader* &c. **3.** Revealing intelligence, indicating the exercise of mental activity: *an intelligent question, reply* &c.

intelligential, adj. [1. intèlijénshal; 2. intèlidžénʃəl]. Prec. & **-ial.** Of, pertaining to, the intellect.

intelligently, adv. [1. intélijentli; 2. intélidžəntli]. See prec. & **-ly.** In an intelligent manner.

intelligentsia, n. [1. intèligéntsia; 2. intèligéntsiə], fr. Russ. *intelligentsiya*, fr. Ital. *intelligenza*, or direct fr. Lat. *intelligentia.* See **intelligence.** A term applied, originally by Russian revolutionaries, to the scientific, learned, or intellectual classes collectively, as contrasted with the bourgeoisie on the one hand and the proletariat on the other.

intelligibility, n. [1. intèlijibíliti; 2. intèlidžibíliti]. See next word & **-ity.** Quality of being intelligible.

intelligible, adj. [1. intélijibl; 2. intélidžibl], fr. Lat. *intelligibil-(is)*, 'that can be understood', fr. *intellig-(ere)*, 'to perceive, understand', q.v. under **intelligent**, & **-ible.** **1.** Capable of being understood; clear in meaning. **2.** (philos.) Capable of being grasped by the intellect only, not to be perceived by the senses.

intelligibly, adv. Prec. & **-ly.** In an intelligible manner.

intemperance, n. [1. intémperans; 2. intémpərəns], fr. Lat. *intemperantia*, 'immoderation, excess'. **in-** (II.) & **temperance.** a Lack of moderation, control, restraint; extravagance; b over-indulgence, excess; specif., excessive indulgence in intoxicating liquor; drunkenness.

intemperate, adj. [1. intémperat; 2. intémpərit], fr. Lat. *intemperāt-(us)*, 'immoderate'. **in-** (II.) & **temperate.** **1.** (of person, conduct) Unrestrained, immoderate, excessive. **2.** Given to excess, addicted to over-indulgence, esp. in strong drink.

intemperately, adv. Prec. & **-ly.** In an intemperate manner.

intend, vb. trans. [1. inténd; 2. inténd], fr. Fr. *entendre*, fr. Lat. *intendere*, 'to stretch out, extend; to aim, direct; to apply oneself to; to purpose, intend', fr. **in-** (I.) & *tendere*, 'to stretch out'. See **tend** (II.) & words there referred to. **1.** a (i.) To purpose, to have in mind as object; to contemplate, mean, design: *he does not intend to obey you; he intends to go; what do you intend doing?; 'I intended an ode'*; (ii.) to plot, plan, scheme: '*intend at home . . . what best may ease the present misery*' (Milton, 'P.L.' ii. 457 &c.); b to have as a deliberate, set, purpose: *I didn't intend to hurt you.* **2.** To design, destine: *the gift was intended for you; his son was intended for the army; where did you intend him to go?* **3.** a To mean, signify; to mean, desire, to convey: *what do you intend by your words?*; b to design to represent: *that portrait is intended for me.*

intendancy, n. [1. inténdansi; 2. inténdənsi]. See next word & **-cy.** The office or status of an intendant.

intendant, n. [1. inténdant; 2. inténdənt], fr. Fr. See **intend** & **-ant.** Director, superintendent, manager, of a business or some branch of public administration &c.; the term is obsolete in English usage but survives in French and Spanish; specif. (Fr. hist.) a one of the four financial controllers under Francis I.; b chief administrator of a province.

intended, n. [1. inténded; 2. inténdid], fr. P.P. of **intend.** (colloq. preceded by poss. pron. or n.) Future wife or husband; fiancé(e).

intendment, n. [1. inténdment; 2. inténdmənt], fr. Fr. *entendement*, fr. *entend-(re)*, 'to mean, intend, hear, understand', fr. Lat. *intendere*, 'to extend; to aim; to intend'. See **intend** & **-ment.** (rare) Precise meaning (of document &c.) as fixed or accepted by law.

intense, adj. [1. inténs; 2. inténs], fr. Fr., fr. Lat. *intens-(us)*, alternative to *intent-(us)*, P.P. type of *intendere*, 'to stretch out, extend; to aim, direct; to enlarge, magnify; to apply oneself; to endeavour, purpose, intend'. See **intend.** **1.** (of quality &c.) Existing, present, in a high, marked, extreme, degree; deep, extreme, violent, excessive, vivid: *intense cold, heat, colour; intense obstinacy, stupidity.* **2.** (of feeling or action) Fervent, ardent, eager, extreme: *an intense longing, hatred*, &c.; zealous: *intense devotion to duty.* **3.** Experiencing and exhibiting intensity or exuberance of feeling; highly emotional: *an intense young lady.*

intensely, adv. Prec. & **-ly.** **1.** In a high degree; extremely, excessively. **2.** In an intense manner, with strong feeling.

intenseness, n. See prec. & **-ness.** Quality of being intense.

intensification, n. [1. intènsifikáshun; 2. intènsifikéiʃən]. **intense** & **-fication.** The act or process of intensifying; state of being intensified.

intensify, vb. trans. & intrans. [1. inténsifī; 2. inténsifai]. **intense** & **-fy.** **1.** trans. To make, cause to become, more intense; to heighten, to deepen, increase in degree. **2.** intrans. To become more intense.

intension, n. [1. inténshun; 2. intén∫ən], fr. Lat. *intensiōn-(em)*, 'a stretching out, straining; increase, intensifying'. **intense** & **-ion.** **1.** Vigorous effort, straining, exertion, esp. of mind. **2.** Intensity, high degree; violence, vehemence. **3.** (log.) Collective attributes of a general term or general notion; cp. *extension.*

intensity, n. [1. inténsiti; 2. inténsiti]. **intense** & **-ity.** The quality of being intense; high degree, intenseness, of quality, feeling, force &c.; strength, depth.

intensive, adj. [1. inténsiv; 2. inténsiv]. **intense** & **-ive.** **1.** Of, pertaining to, characterized by, intensity and concentration: *intensive study*; intensifying; admitting of intensification. **2.** (gram.) Giving added intensity or force; expressing intensity, emphasizing. **3.** (econ. &c.) Pertaining to the production of large results, by concentration of labour and care upon a small area of operation: *intensive cultivation, gardening* &c. **4.** (med., of inoculation) Characterized by increasing strength of successive injections.

intensively, adv. Prec. & **-ly.** In an intensive manner.

intent (I.), n. [1. intént; 2. intént], fr. O. Fr. *entent*, fr. Lat. *intent-(us)*, 'a stretching out, extending', fr. P.P. type of *intendere*, 'to extend; to aim, direct; to purpose, intend'. See **intend.** Aim, purpose, design, intention; result desired; esp. in Phrs. *with good, evil, intent*; *with intent to kill, defraud* &c.; *to all intents and purposes,* in every respect, practically.

intent (II.), adj. fr., Lat. *intent-(us)*, alternative to *intens-(um)*, P.P. type of *intendere*, 'to extend; to aim; to apply oneself'. See **intend. 1. a** Having the mind and will firmly fixed and concentrated upon, directed towards: *intent on an object*; *intent on pleasing everyone*; **b** with the desires directed towards; occupied by, given up to: *to be intent on pleasure* &c. **2.** (of faculty, look &c.) Firmly directed upon some object, giving full attention to; fixed, earnest: *a mind intent upon study*; *an intent look.*

intention, n. [1. inténshun; 2. intén∫ən], fr. Lat. *intentiōn-(em)*, 'a straining, tension; effort, exertion; attention, application; design, purpose', fr. *intent-(um)*, P.P. type of *intendere*, 'to extend; to aim; to exert; to apply oneself to, intend'. See **intend** & **-ion. 1.** Something intended; **a** something implicit; import, bearing: *the intention of a clause*; **b** something resolved upon in the mind; determination to do something; contemplated act: *my intention is to go abroad in the vacation*; specif. **c** (eccles.) special concentration of the will towards accomplishment of particular purpose; e.g. *to say a mass for a person's intention*, in the hope, and with the earnest desire, that the act may benefit him. **2.** (philos.) Concept, notion. **3.** (surg.) Mode of healing of wounds, or fractures: *to heal with first intention*, heal at once.

intentional, adj. [1. inténshunal; 2. intén∫ənəl]. Prec. & **-al.** Intended, designed, premeditated, done on purpose.

intentionally, adv. Prec. & **-ly.** In an intentional manner; on purpose.

-intentioned, adj. [1. inténshund; 2. intén∫ənd]. **intention** & **-ed.** Having intentions of specified kind: *well-intentioned* &c.

intently, adv. [1. inténtli; 2. inténtli]. **intent** (II.) & **-ly.** In an intent manner.

intentness, n. [1. inténtnes; 2. inténtnis]. See prec. & **-ness.** The quality of being intent.

inter (I.), vb. trans. [1. intér; 2. intə́], fr. O. Fr. *enterrer*, fr. Low Lat. *interrāre*, fr. **in-** (I.) & *terra*, 'earth'. See **terra.** To place in the earth or in a tomb; to bury, inhume.

inter (II.), prep. [1. ínter; 2. íntə]. Lat. *inter*, 'between, among'; cogn. w. Scrt. *antár*; O.H.G. *untar*, 'between'; O.H.G. *untorn*, O.S. *undorn*, 'mid-day'; O.E. *undorn*, 'morning'. Orig. comparative of ***en**, 'in'. See **in** (I.). (in Lat. Phrs.) *Inter alia*, among other things; *inter nos, se*, among ourselves, themselves; *inter vivos*, between living persons, esp. (law) of gifts.

inter-, pref. See prec. Very common in words derived fr. Lat., & also as a living pref., forming ns., adjs., & vbs.; (1) w. sense of 'between, among': *intercollegiate, interoceanic* &c.; (2) expressing mutual relation, reciprocal action: *interconvertible, intergrowth, interknit* &c.; (3) in scientific words, esp. adjs., w. sense of 'between': *intercostal, interglacial, interstellar* &c.

interact (I.), n. [1. ínterakt; 2. íntərækt]. **inter-** & **-act** (I.), on anal. of Fr. *entr'acte.* **a** Interval between two acts of a play; **b** performance given in such an interval; interlude.

interact (II.), vb. intrans. [1. interákt; 2. intərǽkt]. **inter-** & **act** (II.). To act and react one upon another; have reciprocal effect.

interaction, n. [1. interákshun; 2. intərǽk∫ən]. Prec. & **-ion.** The process of interacting; reciprocal effect, action, influence.

interactive, adj. [1. interáktiv; 2. intərǽktiv]. See prec. & **-ive.** Acting upon each other.

interblend, vb. trans. & intrans. [1. interblénd; 2. intəblénd]. **inter-** & **blend. 1.** trans. To mix (two or more things) one with another. **2.** intrans. To blend one with another.

interbreed, vb. trans. & intrans. [1. interbréd; 2. intəbríd]. **inter-** & **breed. 1.** trans. To breed together (animals or plants) of different species. **2.** intrans. To breed with each other.

intercalary, adj. [1. intérkaleri; 2. intə́kələri], fr. Lat. *intercalāri-(us)*, 'intercalary', fr. *intercal-(āre)*, 'to insert, intercalate'. Next word & **-ary. 1.** (of day(s) or month) Added to calendar, sometimes periodically, to make civil year correspond to solar year. **2.** (of year) Having an intercalary period added. **3.** Inserted, interpolated, intervening: *intercalary strata.*

intercalate, vb. trans. [1. intérkalāt; 2. intə́kəleit], fr. Lat. *intercalāt-(us)*, P.P. type of *intercalāre*, 'to proclaim insertion of intercalary day &c.', fr. **inter-** & *calāre*, 'to call out, proclaim, call together'. See **calendar. 1.** To insert, add (intercalary period) to calendar. **2.** To insert, interpolate.

intercalation, n. [1. intérkaláshun; 2. intə̀kəléi∫ən], fr. Lat. *intercalātiōn-(em).* Prec. & **-ion. a** The act of intercalating; **b** something intercalated; an insertion.

intercede, vb. intrans. [1. intersḗd; 2. intəsíd], fr. Lat. *intercēd-(ere)*, 'to go between, intervene; to interpose, interfere, on another's behalf', fr. **inter-** & *cēdere*, 'to go; to depart, withdraw; to give place to; to yield'. See **cede.** To put forward a plea on another's behalf; mediate, plead for: *to intercede with (a person), for another, for mercy* &c.

intercept, vb. trans. [1. intersépt; 2. intəsépt], fr. Lat. *intercept-(um)*, P.P. type of *intercipere*, 'to seize while passing; to interrupt, cut off', fr. **inter-** & *capere*, 'to take'. See **captive. 1.** To seize, take, stop (person, object), between starting-point and destination; to prevent arrival at destination: *to intercept a letter, messenger* &c. **2.** To interrupt, hinder, prevent passage, or progress of; to get, or put something, in the way of; to obstruct, cut off: *to intercept rays of light, a view* &c. **3.** (math.) To include between, cut off by, two points, lines &c.

interception, n. [1. intersépshun; 2. intəsép∫ən]. Prec. & **-ion.** The act of intercepting; state of being intercepted.

interceptive, adj. [1. interséptiv; 2. intəséptiv]. See prec. & **-ive.** Tending to intercept.

intercession, n. [1. interséshun; 2. intəsé∫ən], fr. Lat. *intercessiōn-(em)*, 'a coming between, intervention', fr. *intercess-(um)*, P.P. type of *intercēdere*, 'to go between, to intervene, interpose'. See **intercede. 1.** The act or process of interceding; mediation, entreaty on behalf of another. **2.** Intercessory prayer.

intercessor, n. [1. intersésur; 2. intəsésə]. Lat. *intercessor*, 'one who intervenes; mediator', fr. stem *intercess-(um).* See prec. & **-or.** One who intercedes.

intercessorial, adj. [1. intersesṓrial; 2. intəsesṓriəl]. Prec. & **-ial.** Of, pertaining to, intercession, an intercessor.

intercessory, adj. [1. intersésuri; 2. intəsésəri]. **intercessor** & **-y.** Making intercession; interceding.

interchange (I.), n. [1. ínterchānj; 2. íntə-t∫eindž], fr. O. Fr. *entrechange.* **inter-** & **change** (I.). **1.** Mutual exchange between two persons &c.: *the interchange of greetings.* **2.** Alternate succession; alternation.

interchange (II.), vb. trans. & intrans. [1. interchā́nj; 2. intət∫éindž], fr. O. Fr. *entrechangier.* **inter-** & **change** (II.). **A.** trans. **1.** (of two persons) To exchange with each other, give and receive. **2.** To put each in place of the other; to change about. **3.** To alternate, cause to occur alternately. **B.** intrans. **1.** (of two things) To take each other's places, change about. **2.** To follow alternately.

interchangeability, n. [1. interchānjabíliti; 2. intət∫eindžəbíliti]. See next word & **-ity.** Quality of being interchangeable.

interchangeable, adj. [1. interchā́njabl; 2. intət∫éindžəbl]. **interchange** & **-able.** Capable of being interchanged.

interchangeableness, n. Prec. & **-ness.** Interchangeability.

interchangeably, adv. See prec. & **-ly.** So as to be interchangeable.

intercollegiate, adj. [1. interkolḗjiat; 2. intəkəlídžiit]. **inter-** & **collegiate.** Occurring &c. between different colleges.

intercolonial, adj. [1. interkulṓnial; 2. intəkəlóuniəl]. **inter-** & **colonial.** Occurring &c. between different colonies.

intercolumnar, adj. [1. interkulúmnar; 2. intəkəlámnə]. **inter-** & **columnar. a** (archit.) Situated, placed, between columns; **b** (anat.) between the columns of the abdominal ring.

intercolumniation, n. [1. interkulùmniáshun; 2. intəkəlàmniéi∫ən]. **inter-** & **column** & **-ation.** (archit.) The clear space left between columns; the arrangement of columns in respect of their spacing.

intercommunicate, vb. intrans. [1. interkumū́nikāt; 2. intəkəmjū́nikeit]. **inter-** & **communicate. 1.** To communicate, have intercourse, with each other. **2.** (of rooms &c.) To lead from, open, one into the other.

intercommunication, n. [1. interkumūnikáshun; 2. intəkəmjūnikéi∫ən]. Prec. & **-ion.** Mutual intercourse; communication with, between, each other.

intercommunion, n. [1. interkumū́niun; 2. intəkəmjū́niən]. **inter-** & **communion.** Mutual, intimate, communion; specif., reciprocal spiritual relations and ministrations between different religious bodies.

intercommunity, n. [1. interkumū́niti; 2. intəkəmjū́niti]. **inter-** & **community.** Quality of being common to several.

interconnect, vb. trans. & intrans. [1. interkunékt; 2. intəkanékt]. **inter-** & **connect. 1.** trans. To connect, link, join together, esp. in P.P. *interconnected.* **2.** intrans. To be connected, linked, together.

interconvertible, adj. [1. interkunvértibl; 2. intəkənvə́tibl]. **inter-** & **convertible.** Capable of being converted each into other; interchangeable.

intercostal, adj. [1. interkóstal; 2. intəkóstəl]. **inter-** & **costal. a** (anat.) Occurring between the ribs: *intercostal muscles*; *intercostal rheumatism* &c.; **b** (bot.) between the veins of a leaf.

intercourse, n. [1. ínterkors; 2. íntəkōs], fr. O. Fr. *entrecours*, fr. Lat. *intercurs-(um)*, P.P. type of *intercurrere*, 'to run between to mingle with, be among'. See **inter-** & **course. 1. a** Social dealings, communication, association (between individuals); **b** mutual dealings, relations, communication (between countries &c.). **2.** Spiritual or mental communion. **3.** Sexual connexion.

intercross, vb. trans. & intrans. [1. interkráws; 2. intəkrṓs]. **inter-** & **cross** (II.). **1. trans. a** To cause (lines &c.) to lie across each other; **b** to cause to interbreed. **2.** intrans. **a** (of lines &c.) To lie across each other; **b** to interbreed.

intercurrence, n. [1. ìnterkúrens; 2. ìntəkárəns]. Next word & **-ce**. The state or condition of being intercurrent.

intercurrent, adj. [1. ìnterkúrent; 2. ìntəkárənt], fr. **inter-** & **current (I.)**. **1.** Coming between, intervening. **2.** (med., of disease) **a** Affecting person suffering from another disease; **b** recurring at intervals.

interdenominational, adj. [1. ínterdenòmináshunal; 2. íntədinòminéiʃənəl]. **inter-** & **denominational.** Carried on by, shared by, different religious denominations.

interdepend, vb. intrans. [1. ìnterdepénd; 2. ìntədipénd]. **inter-** & **depend.** To depend upon each other.

interdependence, -cy, n. [1. ìnterdepéndens(i); 2. ìntədipéndəns(i)]. Prec. & **-ence.** Mutual dependence.

interdependent, adj. [1. ìnterdepéndent; 2. ìntədipéndənt]. **inter-** & **dependent.** Mutually dependent; depending one upon another.

interdependently, adv. Prec. & **-ly.** In an interdependent manner.

interdict (I.), n. [1. ínterdikt; 2. íntədikt], fr. Lat. *interdict-(um)*, 'a prohibition'. See **inter-** & **dictum.** **1.** Prohibitive decree, authoritative order forbidding something; prohibition. **2.** (eccles.) Decree excluding person(s) from taking part in the rites of the Church.

interdict (II.), vb. trans. [1. ìnterdíkt; 2. ìntədíkt]. See prec. **1. a** To stop by authority, forbid, prevent by decree, prohibit (an action &c.); **b** to forbid use of (thing). **2.** To stop, restrain, hinder (a person from an action &c.).

interdiction, n. [1. ìnterdíkshun; 2. ìntədíkʃən], fr. Lat. *interdictiōn-(em)*, 'prohibition'. Prec. & **-ion.** The act of interdicting; state of being interdicted.

interdictory, adj. [1. ìnterdíkturi; 2. ìntədíktəri]. **interdict** & **-ory.** Pertaining to, of the nature of, uttering, an interdict.

interdigital, adj. [1. ìnterdíjitl; 2. ìntədídžitl]. **inter-** & **digital.** Between the fingers or toes.

interdigitate, vb. intrans. [1. ìnterdíjitāt; 2. ìntədídžiteit]. **inter-** & **digit** & **-ate.** To interlock, be interlocked, in a way resembling the interlocking of the fingers of clasped hands.

interesse termini, n. [1. ínteresi términī; 2. íntərεsi tə́minai]. Low Lat., 'interest of a term'. See next word. The common law right of entry conferred on a lessee by grant of a lease.

interest (I.), n. [1. ínterest; 2. íntərεst]. Lat. *interest*, 'it concerns, is important to', 3rd sing. Pres. of *interesse*, 'to be, lie, between; to differ; to take part in; to be of interest', fr. **inter-** & *esse*, 'to be'. See **esse.** **1. a** Proprietary right, share; legal concern, claim: *interest in an estate* &c.; **b** pecuniary concern, right of benefiting from: *interest in a business.* **2.** Profit, advantage, benefit, good: *to look after one's own interests.* **3. a** State of keenly arrested attention; preoccupation, pleasurable concern; intellectual curiosity: *to feel, take, interest in politics*; **b** object of such concern or curiosity: *to have no interests outside one's business*; **c** importance, consequence, moment: *a matter of no little interest in such a connexion.* **4.** Influence, controlling power: *to have interest with the authorities.* Phr. *to make interest with*, bring influence to bear on. **5.** Group of persons engaged in similar occupation, those concerned in the same branch of industry &c.: *the agricultural interest*; *the landed interest* &c. **6. a** Payment made for use of money; *simple interest*, reckoned on principal; *compound interest*, sum accumulating by addition of each periodic payment of interest to principal, thereby increasing principal gradually; **b** (fig.) addition, something more than an exact equivalent, given in returning something: *to return a blow with interest.*

interest (II.), vb. trans., fr. prec. **1.** To cause to take a share in, engage in, induce to participate, to be concerned in: *to be interested in the rubber industry.* **2.** To arouse interest; attract, engage, rivet, attention; to excite the curiosity or sympathy of: *to be interested by a book*; *what you tell me interests me very much.*

interested, adj. [1. ínt(e)rested, ínterèsted; 2. ínt(ə)rəstid, ínt(ə)rεstid, íntristid], fr. P.P. of prec. **1. a** Having one's attention, curiosity, sympathy, aroused; taking an interest: *interested spectators*; **b** exhibiting, expressing, interest: *an interested look.* **2.** Influenced by personal concern; biassed: *an interested witness*; *interested motives.*

interestedly, adv. Prec. & **-ly.** In an interested manner.

interesting, adj. [1. ínteresting, ínterèsting; 2. íntrəstiŋ, ínt(ə)rεstiŋ], fr. Pres. Part. of **interest (II.).** Arousing interest, holding the attention.

interestingly, adv. Prec. & **-ly.** In an interesting manner.

interfacial, adj. [1. ìnterfáshial; 2. ìntəféiʃiəl]. **inter-** & **facial.** Included between two plane faces or surfaces, esp. of angles of crystals.

interfenestration, n. [1. ìnterfenestráshun; 2. ìntəfεnistréiʃən]. **inter-** & **fenestration.** (archit.) Arrangement of windows in a building in regard to the spaces between them.

interfere, vb. intrans. [1. interfḗr; 2. intəfíə], fr. O. Fr. *s'entreférir*, 'to strike against each other', fr. **inter-** & *férir*, 'to strike', fr. Lat. *ferīre*, 'to strike, smite; to slay, kill; to affect'. See **ferule**; cogn. w. **bore (I.).** **1.** (of persons) **a** To intervene, esp. in matters which do not concern one; to meddle: *to be always interfering*; **b** to interpose, intervene, mediate: *matters have reached such a state of confusion that it is time to interfere.* **2.** (of horses) To knock feet together in going. **3.** (of heat or light waves &c.) To interact, affect each other reciprocally. **4.** (of circumstances, events, actions) To hinder, prevent, act as an obstacle. **5.** *Interfere with*, **a** to annoy, pester, molest; to hinder, interrupt (persons): *I shall never finish my work if you interfere with me like this*; **b** to thwart, prevent, interrupt, be an obstacle to: *pleasure must not be allowed to interfere with business*; **c** to affect prejudicially, injure: *sedentary habits often interfere with health.* **6.** *Interfere in*, to meddle, intermeddle with: *I refuse to interfere in what does not concern me.*

interference, n. [1. ìnterfḗrens; 2. ìntəfíərəns]. Prec. & **-ence.** Act or process of interfering; **1. a** Meddlesome, unjustifiable, intervention; **b** hindrance, interruption, impediment, obstruction. Specif. **2.** (phys.) interaction of two streams of vibrations or wave motions, as of light, sound &c., tending, if similar, to increase, or, if dissimilar, to neutralize each other; cp. *atmospherics.*

interferential, adj. [1. ìnterferénshal; 2. ìntəfərέnʃəl]. See prec. & **-ial.** (phys.) Pertaining to interference of light, sound &c.

interfering, adj. [1. ìnterfḗring; 2. ìntəfíəriŋ], fr. Pres. Part. of **interfere.** Given to interference; officious, meddlesome.

interferingly, adv. Prec. & **-ly.** In an interfering manner.

interferometer, n. [1. ìnterferómeter; 2. ìntəfiərɔ́mitə]. **interfere** & **-meter.** Apparatus for measuring the interference of light waves.

interflow, vb. intrans. [1. ìnterfló; 2. ìntəflóu]. **inter-** & **flow.** To flow into each other; to intermingle.

interfluent, adj. [1. ìnterflōōent; 2. ìntəflúənt]. See **inter-** & **fluent.** Flowing together, into each other.

interfuse, vb. trans. & intrans. [1. ìnterfúz; 2. ìntəfjúz], fr. Lat. *interfūs-(um)*, P.P. type of *interfundere*, 'to pour between'. See **inter-** & **fuse.** **1.** trans. **a** To cause to blend, intermix: *to interfuse one substance with another*; **b** to mix together, penetrate, permeate, with. **2.** intrans. (of two things) To become blended, mingle.

interfusion, n. [1. ìnterfúzhn; 2. ìntəfjúžən], fr. Lat. *interfūsiōn-(em)*, 'a flowing, or pouring, between'. Prec. & **-ion.** Act or process of interfusing; state of being interfused.

interglacial, adj. [1. ìntergláshial; 2. ìntəgléiʃiəl]. **inter-** & **glacial.** (geol.) Pertaining to, occurring in, a period between two glacial periods or ice-ages.

intergradation, n. [1. ìntergradáshun; 2. ìntəgrədéiʃən]. **inter-** & **gradation.** **a** Passage, transition, through a series of grades, kinds, or forms; **b** a transition step or stage in such process.

interim, adj. & n. [1. ínterim; 2. íntərim]. Lat. *interim*, adv., 'meanwhile, in the meantime; for a time', fr. **inter-** & *-im*, old acc. masc. of *is*, 'he', personal pron. **1.** adj. Belonging to, occurring, done, in an intervening period or interim; temporary, for the meantime: *an interim dividend.* **2.** n. **a** Intervening, intermediate, period; interval; esp. in Phr. *in the interim*; **b** (hist.) an edict or decree, having temporary force, of the Holy Roman Empire.

interior (I.), adj. [1. intḗrior; 2. intíəriə]. Lat. *interior*, 'inner, within; inland', compar. of **inter (II.)** **1.** Situated, existing, on the inside; inner, internal: *the interior wall of a building* &c. **2.** Of, pertaining to, the inside: *interior repairs*; *the interior dimensions of a room* &c. **3.** (of place &c.) At a distance from the coast, boundary, frontier; inland. **4.** (of affairs of state, &c.) Domestic, internal, as opposed to foreign. **5.** (of the mind, heart, soul) Inward, spiritual.

interior (II.), n., fr. prec. Inside, inner part; specif. **1.** Part of country remote from coast or frontier; inland district. **2. a** Home affairs of a country; **b** government department dealing with these. **3. a** Inner nature, inward feelings, true character; **b** (colloq.) the inside of the body, the digestive organs.

interiorly, adv. **interior (I.)** & **-ly.** Inwardly; in, towards, the interior.

interjacent, adj. [1. interjásent; 2. intədžéisnt], fr. Lat. *interjacent-(em)*, Pres. Part. of *interjacēre*, 'to lie between', fr. **inter-** & *jacēre*, 'to lie'. See **adjacent.** Lying between, intervening, intermediate.

interject, vb. trans. [1. ìnterjékt; 2. ìntədžékt], fr. Lat. *interject-(um)*, P.P. type of *interjacere*, 'to throw, set, place, between; to join, add to,' fr. **inter-** & *jacere*, 'to throw'. See **jactitation.** To interpose, interrupt by, introduce suddenly, break in with: *to interject a remark* &c.

interjection, n. [1. ìnterjékshun; 2. ìntədžékʃən], fr. Lat. *interjectiōn-(em)*, 'a throwing between, insertion; (gram.) an interjection'. Prec. & **-ion.** **1.** Exclamation, ejaculation. **2.** (gram., as part of speech) Word expressing sudden emotion, such as surprise &c., and having no syntactical relation to sentence.

interjectional, adj. [1. ìnterjékshunal; 2. ìntədžékʃənəl]. Prec. & **-al.** Of, pertaining to, of the nature of, an interjection.

interjectionally, adv. Prec. & **-ly.** In an interjectional manner; as, by way of, an interjection.

interjectory, adj. [1. ìnterjékturi; 2. ìntədžéktəri]. **interject** & **-ory.** Interjectional.

interlace, vb. trans. & intrans. [1. interlás; 2. ìntəléis], fr. Fr. *entrelacer.* **inter-** & **lace (II.).** **1.** trans. To intertwine, twist together, interweave. **2.** intrans. To twine together, be interwoven, to pass over and under each other: *interlacing branches.*

interlacement, n. [1. ìnterlásment; 2. ìntəléismənt]. Prec. & **-ment.** The act or process of interlacing; something interlaced.

interlard, vb. trans. [1. ìnterlárd; 2. ìntəlád], fr. Fr. *entrelarder.* **inter-** & **lard**, vb. To mix, diversify: *to interlard one's speech with foreign phrases* &c.

interleaf, n. [1. ínterlēf; 2. íntəlīf]. **inter-** & **leaf.** Blank leaf inserted or bound up between leaves of book &c.

interleave, vb. trans. [1. ìnterlḗv; 2. ìntəlív], fr. *interleaves*, pl. of prec. To furnish (book &c.) with blank leaves inserted, bound up, between the pages.

interline, vb. trans. [1. ìnterlín; 2. ìntəláin], fr. Med. Lat. *interlīneāre*, 'to interline', fr. **inter-** & Lat. *līnea*, 'a line'. See **line**. **1.** To write between the lines of (a text, manuscript &c.). **2.** To insert between the lines of a text: *to interline corrections, a translation* &c.

interlinear, adj. [1. ìnterlínear; 2. ìntəlíniə], fr. Med. Lat. *interlīneār-(is)*. **inter-** & **linear**. Written, inserted, between the lines of a written or printed text: *an interlinear gloss.*

interlineation, n. [1. ìnterlineáshun; 2. ìntəliniéiʃən], fr. Med. Lat. *interlīne-(āre)*, 'to interline'. See **interline** & **-ation**. **1.** Act of interlining; state of being interlined. **2.** Word, passage, correction &c., inserted between the lines.

interlock, vb. intrans. & trans. [1. ìnterlók; 2. ìntəlɔ́k]. **inter-** & **lock (III.)**. **1.** intrans. To lock, join, together, engage, become fastened, by reciprocal action, clasp each other, become linked; *interlocking signals*, on railways &c.; (also in transferred sense) *interlocking directorate*, of trusts, combines &c., in which seats on the boards are interchanged between the various companies. **2.** trans. To cause to interlock.

interlocution, n. [1. ìnterlokúshun; 2. ìntələkjúʃən], fr. Lat. *interlocūtiōn-(em)*. See **inter-** & **locution**. A dialogue, conversation, interchange of speech.

interlocutor, n. [1. ìnterlókūter; 2. ìntəlɔ́kjutə], fr. Lat. *interlocūt-(um)*, P.P. type of *interloqui*, 'to interrupt in speaking'. See prec. & **-or**. Person taking part in dialogue.

interlocutory, adj. [1. ìnterlókūturi; 2. ìntəlɔ́kjutəri]. See prec. & **-ory**. **1.** Of, pertaining to, of the nature of, consisting of, dialogue. **2.** (law) Intermediate, of proceedings under order of the court, taken during the preliminary stages of an action, before trial.

interlocutress, n. [1. ìnterlókūtres; 2. ìntəlɔ́kjutris]. **interlocutor** & **-ess**. Woman taking part in conversation.

interlocutrix, n. [1. ìnterlókūtriks; 2. ìntəlɔ́kjutriks]. See prec. & **-trix**. Interlocutress.

interlope, vb. intrans. [1. interlṓp; 2. intəlóup]. Hybrid word fr. **inter-**, & O.N. *hlaupa*, 'to leap, run'; cogn. w. **leap**. (rare) To act as an interloper.

interloper, n. [1. ínterlṑper; 2. íntəlòupə]. Prec. & **-er**. **1.** Person who pushes himself into the affairs of others, or into a position to which he has no right; an intruder. **2.** (hist.) Unlicensed, unauthorized, trader, esp. one who attempts to interfere in the trade of a chartered company or monopoly.

interlude, n. [1. ínterlūd; 2. íntəl(j)ūd], fr. Med. Lat. *interlūd-(ium)*, 'interlude', fr. **inter-** & *lūd-(us)*, 'game, play', q.v. under **ludicrous**. **1.** (hist.) Short dramatic performance between the acts of a mystery- or morality-play. **2. a** Time intervening between two acts of play; interval; **b** performance during such an interval. **3. a** Intervening period, interval differing in character from preceding and following periods; **b** action, incident, event, regarded as occurring in the course of other proceedings, or between two more important events &c. **4.** (mus.) Instrumental passage played between verses of song, vocal passages &c.

intermarriage, n. [1. ìntermárij; 2. ìntəmǽridž]. **inter-** & **marriage**. **1.** Marriage between persons of different races, tribes, families &c. **2.** Marriage of related persons.

intermarry, vb. intrans. [1. ìntermári; 2. ìntəmǽri]. **inter-** & **marry**. (of families, tribes, races &c.) To marry amongst, with, each other.

intermeddle, vb. intrans. [1. ìntermédl; 2. ìntəmédl]. **inter-** & **meddle**. To occupy oneself, concern oneself, interfere, meddle: *to intermeddle with what does not concern one, in other people's affairs.*

intermediary (I.), adj. [1. ìntermḗdiari; 2. ìntəmídiəri], fr. Lat. *intermedi-(us)*, 'intermediate'. See **inter-** & **mediate** & **-ary**. **1.** Acting between two persons, parties &c.; acting as agent, as means of communication, mediator &c. **2.** Situated or coming between; intervening, intermediate.

intermediary (II.), n., fr. prec. Intermediary person or thing, esp. mediator.

intermediate (I.), adj. & n. [1. ìntermḗdiat; 2. ìntəmídiit], fr. Lat. *intermedi-(us)*, 'lying between, intermediate', fr. **inter-** & *medius*, 'middle', see **medium**, & **-ate**. **1.** adj. Situated, existing, occurring, between two things, in time, space, order, degree &c.: *intermediate rank*; *intermediate types in a series* &c.; specif., *Intermediate examination*, one between that of Matriculation at a University, and the Final, or Degree examination. **2.** n. **a** Something that is intermediate; **b** Intermediate examination.

intermediate (II.), vb. intrans. [1. ìntermḗdiāt; 2. ìntəmídieit]. **inter-** & **mediate**. (rare) To act as intermediary, intervene.

intermediately, adv. [1. ìntermḗdiatli; 2. ìntəmídiətli]. **intermediate (I.)** & **-ly**. In an intermediate position; as an intermediate.

intermediation, n. [1. ìntermēdiáshun; 2. ìntəmīdiéiʃən]. **intermediate (II.)** & **-ion**. The act of intermediating.

intermediator, n. [1. ìntermḗdiātur; 2. ìntəmídieitə]. **intermediate (II.)** & **-or**. Person who intermediates; intermediary.

intermedium, n. [1. ìntermḗdium; 2. ìntəmídiəm]. Lat. *intermedium*, neut. form of *intermedi-(us)*, 'intermediate'. See **inter-** & **medium**. Intervening agent, means of communication or transmission; medium.

interment, n. [1. intẽrment; 2. intʌ́mənt]. **inter (I.)** & **-ment**. Burial, inhumation.

intermezzo, n. [1. ìntermétsō; 2. ìntəmétsou]. Ital., fr. Lat. *intermedi-(us)*, 'intermediate'. See **intermediate (I.)**. **1.** Short dramatic performance, burlesque &c. between acts of play, opera &c.; interlude. **2.** (mus.) Short composition connecting main movements of sonata, symphony &c., or played between the acts or scenes of an opera.

intermigration, n. [1. ìntermīgráshun; 2. ìntəmaigréiʃən]. **inter-** & **migration**. Reciprocal migration between two countries or areas.

interminable, adj. [1. intẽrminabl; 2. intʌ́minəbl], fr. L. Lat. *interminābil-(is)*, 'endless'. See **in- (II.)** & **terminable**. **a** Lasting for ever; endless; **b** unduly prolonged; unending, ceaseless; wearisome: *an interminable discourse.*

interminableness, n. Prec. & **-ness**. The state of being interminable.

interminably, adv. See prec. & **-ly**. In an interminable manner; to an interminable extent.

intermingle, vb. trans. & intrans. [1. ìntermínggl; 2. ìntəmíŋgl]. **inter-** & **mingle**. **1.** trans. To mix, mingle, blend, together. **2.** intrans. To mingle, become blended.

intermission, n. [1. ìntermíshun; 2. ìntəmíʃən], fr. Lat. *intermissiōn-(em)*, 'a breaking off, interruption, cessation, pause', fr. *intermiss-(um)*, P.P. type of *intermittere*, 'to leave off, omit, neglect; to cease, pause'. See next word & **-ion**. Temporary cessation, pause, interval, interruption; esp. in Phr. *without intermission.*

intermit, vb. trans. & intrans. [1. ìntermít; 2. ìntəmít], fr. Lat. *intermitt-(ere)*, 'to leave off, omit, suspend; to cease, pause', fr. **inter-** & *mittere*, 'to send', q.v. under **mission**. **1.** trans. To stop for a time; suspend, interrupt, cease temporarily. **2.** intrans. To cease temporarily, pause, be interrupted.

intermittence, n. [1. ìntermítens; 2. ìntəmítəns]. Prec. & **-ence**. The state of being intermittent.

intermittent, adj. [1. ìntermítent; 2. ìntəmítənt]. **intermit** & **-ent**. Having periods of intermission; pausing at intervals; relaxing in violence, strength, or degree from time to time: *an intermittent pulse*; *intermittent fever, pain* &c.

intermittently, adv. Prec. & **-ly**. In an intermittent manner, with occasional or periodic pauses.

intermix, vb. trans. & intrans. [1. ìntermíks; 2. ìntəmíks]. **inter-** & **mix**. To mix together, intermingle.

intermixture, n. [1. intermíkschur; 2. intəmíkstʃə]. **inter-** & **mixture**. A compound, mass, blend, formed by mixing things together.

intern, vb. trans. [1. intẽrn; 2. intʌ́n], fr. Fr. *interner*, fr. Lat. *intern-(us)*, 'inward, internal', fr. same base as **inter (II.)**, **interior**; cp. O.S. *undorn*, 'mid-day'. To put under restraint, confine to specified area: *to intern aliens.*

internal (I.), adj. [1. intẽrnal; 2. intʌ́n(ə)l], fr. Lat. *intern-(us)*, 'inner'. See prec. & **-al**. **1.** Of, pertaining to, situated on, the inside; interior; inner, inward: *to receive internal injuries.* **2.** Of, pertaining to, based on, derived from, the substance, content, nature, of anything; intrinsic, inward. Phr. *internal evidence*, derived from the thing itself. **3.** Pertaining to one's inner nature; inward. **4.** Of, pertaining to, the home affairs of a country; domestic, civil; contrasted with *foreign.*

internal (II.), n., fr. prec. (pl.) Natural, internal, qualities.

internal-combustion engine, n. Type of engine in which the motive power is produced by the explosion of gas or oil vapour in the cylinder, as in stationary gas engines or petrol-driven motor vehicles &c.

internality, n. [1. intẽrnáliti; 2. ìntʌ̄nǽliti]. **internal (I.)** & **-ity**. State or quality of being internal.

internally, adv. [1. intẽrnali; 2. intʌ́nəli]. See prec. & **-ly**. **a** In the inside; so as to affect the interior or inner part; inwardly; **b** mentally or spiritually.

international (I.), adj. [1. ìnternáshunal; 2. ìntənǽʃənəl]. **inter-** & **national**. Existing between, carried on between, relating to, representing, different nations: *international peace, trade*; *an international code, conference*; *international games* &c.; *international law*, the law of nations, the body of rules regarded by the nations of the world as binding on them in their relations with each other, in peace and war; styled *public*, in distinction from *private, international law*, which deals with the rights and obligations of private citizens in a foreign country or with the conflict of laws of different countries.

international (II.), n., fr. prec. **1.** Person who takes part in international contest, esp. in athletics, football &c. **2.** Name of a socialist political organization, the *International Working Men's Association*, the first of which lasted from 1864 to 1874; the second, founded in 1882, still meets; the third, the Communist or Moscow organization, founded 1919, repudiates the second as reactionary.

internationalism, n. [1. internáshunalizm; 2. intənǽʃənəlizəm]. **international** & **-ism**. Political doctrine and policy which, claiming to be based on the principle of the universal brotherhood of man, tends to minimize or ignore the differences of interests, character, and ideals which exist between races and nations.

internationalist, n. [1. internáshunalist; 2. intənǽʃənəlist]. **international** & **-ist**. **1.** Student of international law. **2.** Adherent of the doctrine of internationalism.

internationality, n. [1. ìnternàshunáliti; 2. intənæ̀ʃənǽliti]. **international** & **-ity**. The state of being international.

internationalization, n. [1. ìnternàshunalīzáshun; 2. ìntənæ̀ʃənəlaizéiʃən]. See next word & **-ation**. The act of internationalizing; state of being internationalized.

internationalize, vb. trans. [1. internáshunalīz; 2. intənǽʃənəlaiz]. **international** & **-ize**. To make international, bring under control of different nations.

internationally, adv. [1. internáshunali; 2. *in*-tənǽʃənəli]. **international (I.) & -ly.** From an international point of view; in a manner affecting different nations.

internecine, adj. [1. internésīn; 2. intənísain], fr. Lat. *internecīn-(us)*, 'deadly, destructive', fr. *internec-(āre)*, 'to kill, destroy', fr. **inter-** & *necāre*, 'to kill'; cogn. w. Gk. *nekrós*, 'dead' (see **necro-**), also w. Lat. *nocēre*, 'to harm' (see **noxious**), & **-ine**. **a** Deadly, involving destruction; **b** mutually destructive.

internment, n. [1. intérnment; 2. intə́nmənt]. **intern & -ment.** The act of interning; state of being interned.

internuncial, adj. [1. internúnsial; 2. intənánsiəl], fr. Lat. *internunti-(us)*, 'a messenger'. See next word & **-al.** (of nerves) Communicating, acting as messengers, between different organs or parts of body.

internuncio, n. [1. internúnsiō; 2. intənánsiou], fr. Ital. *internunzio*, fr. Lat. *internuntius*, 'messenger', fr. **inter-** & *nuntius*, 'a messenger'. See **nuncio.** Papal representative of lesser rank than, and acting in absence of, a nuncio.

interoceanic, adj. [1. interōsheánik; 2. intərouʃiǽnik]. **inter- & oceanic.** Between, joining, oceans: *interoceanic canal, traffic* &c.

interosculate, vb. intrans. [1. interóskūlāt; 2. intərɔ́skjuleit]. **inter- & osculate.** To intermix; specif. (of species) to have certain characters in common.

interosculation, n. [1. interoskūláshun; 2. intərɔskjuléiʃən]. Prec. & **-ion.** Act or process of interosculating.

interpage, vb. trans. [1. interpáj; 2. intəpéidž]. **inter- & page (III.).** To insert on intermediate pages.

interpellate, vb. trans. [1. intérpelāt, interpélāt; 2. intə́pileit, intəpéleit], fr. Lat. *interpellāt-(um)*, P.P. type of *interpellāre*, 'to interrupt by speaking'. See **inter-** & second element of **appeal**, also **spell (I.).** (in foreign, esp. French, legislative bodies) To demand statement or explanation from (a minister), a form of challenge to the Government, corresponding to a motion for adjournment; involving usually a debate, and vote of confidence, or the reverse.

interpellation, n. [1. interpeláshun, interpeláshun; 2. intə̀piléiʃən, intəpeléiʃən], fr. Lat. *interpellātiōn-(em)*, 'interruption'. Prec. & **-ion.** The act of interpellating; state of being interpellated.

interpenetrate, vb. trans. & intrans. [1. interpénetrāt; 2. intəpénitreit]. **inter- & penetrate. 1.** trans. To pervade, penetrate, pass into, be diffused through, all parts of; to permeate. **2.** intrans. (of two things) To penetrate, pervade, each other.

interpenetration, n. [1. interpenetráshun; 2. intəpenitréiʃən]. Prec. & **-ion.** The act or process of interpenetrating; state of being interpenetrated.

interpenetrative, adj. [1. interpénetrativ; 2. intəpénitrətiv]. **interpenetrate & -ive.** Tending to, able to, interpenetrate.

interplay, n. [1. ínterplā; 2. íntəplei]. **inter- & play.** Reciprocal action; effect of two things upon each other; action and reaction.

interplead, vb. intrans. [1. interpléd; 2. intəplíd]. **inter- & plead.** (law) To initiate trial of an action under an interpleader.

interpleader, n. [1. interpléder; 2. intəplídə]. Prec. & **-er.** (law) Form of action in which, when two or more parties are suing a third for recovery of goods or money in his possession but in which he has no interest, he may compel them to have the issue tried between themselves only.

interpolate, vb. trans. [1. intérpolāt; 2. intə́pəleit], fr. Lat. *interpolāt-(um)*, P.P. type of *interpolāre*, 'to give a new appearance to; to polish up; to falsify; to insert, interpolate', fr. **inter-** & **pol-*, stem of *polīre*, 'to polish'. See **polish. 1.** To insert (spurious words, passages &c.) in document, book &c. **2.** To insert such passages in (book &c.). **3.** (math.) To insert (intermediate term) in a series.

interpolation, n. [1. interpoláshun; 2. intə̀pəléiʃən]. Prec. & **-ion. 1.** The act of interpolating; state of being interpolated. **2.** Something interpolated; words or passages added by another, usually later, author, scribe &c.

interpolator, n. [1. intérpolātor; 2. intə́pəleitə]. See prec. & **-or.** One who makes interpolations in book, manuscript &c.

interposal, n. [1. interpózl; 2. intəpóuzl]. See next word & **-al.** (rare) Interposition.

interpose, vb. trans. & intrans. [1. interpóz; 2. intəpóuz], fr. Fr. *interposer*. See **inter-** & **pose. A.** trans. **1.** To cause to come between, make intervene, put between, insert: *to interpose a barrier &c. between two things.* **2.** To put forward, offer, introduce, as intervention, interference: *to interpose an objection.* **3.** To interrupt by means of, break in with: *to interpose a remark.* **B.** intrans. **1.** To come between, introduce oneself, intervene, interfere: *to interpose between opponents* &c. **2.** To interrupt, break in upon, conversation, proceedings &c.

interposition, n. [1. interpozíshun; 2. intəpəzíʃən], fr. Lat. *interpositiōn-(em)*, 'a putting between, insertion, introduction'. **inter- & position. 1.** The act of interposing; state of being interposed; intervention. **2.** Something that is interposed.

interpret, vb. trans. & intrans. [1. intérpret; 2. intə́prit], fr. Fr. *interpréter*, fr. Lat. *interpretāri*, 'to explain, expound; translate', prob. orig. 'to act as agent between two parties in a bargain', the second element being the base in Lat. *pretium*, 'price, value' &c. See **precious & price. A.** trans. **1.** To explain, show the meaning of, by deciphering or elucidating: *to interpret an obscure passage, an inscription* &c. **2.** To represent objectively, reveal meaning of, bring out character of: *a musician interprets the work of a composer; an actor interprets a character in a play* &c. **3.** To understand in specific way, construe, take meaning to be: *to interpret a person's silence unfavourably.* **4.** To translate (speech) in a foreign language as interpreter. **B.** intrans. To act as interpreter.

interpretable, adj. [1. intérpretabl; 2. intə́pritəbl]. Prec. & **-able.** Capable of being interpreted.

interpretation, n. [1. interpretáshun; 2. intə̀pritéiʃən], fr. Lat. *interpretātiōn-(em)*, 'explanation, exposition, translation'. **interpret & -ation. 1.** The act of interpreting; result of this; explanation, exposition, elucidation. **2.** Sense, meaning, given by an expositor; significance; construction. **3.** Dramatic or artistic representation of a character in a play, the spirit of a piece of music &c. in accordance with performer's conception of it.

interpretative, adj. [1. intérpretativ; 2. intə́pritətiv], fr. Lat. *interpretāt-(um)*, P.P. type of *interpretāri*, 'to explain; to translate'. See **interpret & -ive.** Intended, tending, to interpret; containing an interpretation; explanatory.

interpreter, n. [1. intérpreter; 2. intə́pritə], fr. Fr. *interprétateur*, fr. L. Lat. *interpretātōr-(em)*, 'explainer', fr. *interpretāt-(um)*, P.P. type of *interpretāri*, 'to explain; to translate'. See **interpret & -or. 1.** One who explains, expounds, interprets. **2.** One whose business it is to translate foreign languages orally, as they are being spoken.

interpretership, n. [1. intérpretership; 2. intə́pritəʃip]. Prec. & **-ship.** The office of interpreter.

interregnum, n. [1. interégnum; 2. intərégnəm]. Lat. *interregnum*, fr. **inter-** & *regnum*, 'reign'. See **reign. 1.** Time between two reigns; interval between the death, abdication &c. of one sovereign and the accession of his successor. **2.** Any period forming a break in continuity; interval.

interrelation, n. [1. interelāshun; 2. intəriléiʃən]. **inter- & relation.** Mutual relation.

interrogate, vb. trans. [1. intérugāt; 2. intérəgeit], fr. Lat. *interrogāt-(um)*, P.P. type of *interrogāre*, 'to ask, question, examine', fr. **inter-** & *rogāre*, 'to ask'. See **rogation.** To question, ask questions of, esp. searchingly, as in a formal examination.

interrogation, n. [1. interugáshun; 2. intèrəgéiʃən], fr. Lat. *interrogātiōn-(em)*, 'a questioning, inquiry, examination'. Prec. & **-ion. 1.** The act of interrogating; specif., an official examination of a witness by question and answer. **2.** A question, inquiry, query: *note, mark, point, of interrogation*, the punctuation mark (?) used to indicate a direct question.

interrogative, adj. & n. [1. interógativ; 2. intərɔ́gətiv], fr. Lat. *interrogātīv-(us)*, 'of a question'. **interrogate & -ive. 1.** adj. **a** Of, pertaining to, of the nature of, indicating, a question; inquiring; **b** (gram., of pron. &c.) used in asking questions. **2.** n. An interrogative pronoun.

interrogatively, adv. Prec. & **-ly.** In an interrogative manner.

interrogatory, adj. & n. [1. interógaturi; 2. intərɔ́gətəri], fr. Lat. *interrogātōri-(us)*, 'interrogatory'. **interrogate & -ory. 1.** adj. Pertaining to, expressing, a question. **2.** n. **a** Inquiry, questioning, interrogation; **b** series, formal set, of questions, esp. (pl., law) written questions to be answered on oath sent from one party to another in the proceedings of ar action before trial.

interrupt, vb. trans. [1. interúpt; 2. intərápt], fr. Lat. *interrupt-(um)*, P.P. type of *interrumpere*, 'to break up, break to pieces; to break off, interrupt', fr. **inter-** & *rumpere*, 'to break'. See **rupture. 1.** To break in upon; cause to stop, temporarily or permanently: *to interrupt a conversation, a train of thought, a person speaking; to interrupt the proceedings*; (also absol.) *children must learn not to interrupt.* **2.** To get in the way of, hinder, obstruct: *the wall interrupts the view.* **3.** To cut off, cut through, break, destroy, the continuity of: *to interrupt an electric current* &c.

interrupted, adj. [1. interúpted; 2. intəráptid], fr. P.P. of prec. Broken by interruptions; not continuous: *interrupted sleep.*

interruptedly, adv. See prec. & **-ly.** In an interrupted manner; with interruptions.

interruption, n. [1. interúpshun; 2. intərápʃən], fr. Lat. *interruptiōn-(em)*, 'an interruption, interval'. **interrupt & -ion. 1.** The act of interrupting; state of being interrupted. **2.** Something that interrupts.

interruptory, adj. [1. interúpturi; 2. intəráptəri]. **interrupt & -ory.** Tending to interrupt; acting as an interruption.

interscapular, adj. [1. interskápūlar; 2. intəskǽpjulə]. **inter- & scapular.** Situated between the scapulars or shoulder-blades, esp. of feathers of birds.

intersect, vb. trans. & intrans. [1. intersékt; 2. intəsékt], fr. Lat. *intersect-(um)*, P.P. type of *intersecāre*, 'to cut asunder, separate', fr. **inter-** & *secāre*, 'to cut'. See **section. 1.** trans. To divide by cutting into, or passing across; to cut through, pass across. **2.** intrans. (of lines, surfaces &c.) To cut, cut into, cross, one another.

intersection, n. [1. intersékshun; 2. intəsékʃən]. Prec. & **-ion. 1.** The act of intersecting; state of being intersected. **2.** (geom.) Point or line of contact between two lines, planes &c.

intersectional, adj. [1. intersékshunal; 2. intəsékʃənəl]. Prec. & **-al.** Of, pertaining to, intersection.

interspace, n. & vb. trans. **inter- & space. 1.** n. [1. ínterspās; 2. íntəspeis]. Space between two things; interval between two events or points of time. **2.** vb. [1. interspás; 2. intəspéis]. To put, leave, spaces between.

intersperse, vb. trans. [1. interspérs; 2. intəspə́s], fr. Lat. *interspers-(us)*, 'strewn, sprinkled upon', fr. **inter-** & *spars-(um)*, P.P. type of *spargere*, 'to scatter'. See **sparse.**

1. To set here and there, scatter among: *poppies interspersed among the corn; a few passages of humour interspersed in a dull book.* 2. To diversify by objects &c. scattered here and there: *sky interspersed with stars.*

interspersion, n. [1. interspérshun; 2. intəspʌ́ʃən]. Prec. & **-ion.** The act of interspersing; state of being interspersed.

interstate, adj. [1. ínterstát; 2. íntəstéit]. **inter-** & **state** (I.). Pertaining to relations between, connecting, the states of a federal government, as of Australia, United States of America &c.: *interstate railways, commerce* &c.

interstellar, adj. [1. ínterstélar; 2. íntəstélə]. **inter-** & **stellar.** Situated, passing, between the stars: *interstellar space* &c.

interstice, n. [1. intérstis; 2. intʌ́stis], fr. Lat. *interstiti-(um)*, fr. *interstit-(um)*, P.P. type of *intersistere*, 'to stand between', fr. **inter-** & *sistere*, 'to stand'. See **state** (I.) & **stand** (I.). **a** Intervening space, interval; **b** small opening, chink, crack, crevice.

interstitial, adj. [1. interstíshial; 2. intəstíʃiəl], fr. Lat. *interstiti-(um)*, 'space between, interval'. Prec. & **-al.** Of, pertaining to, occurring in, forming, an interstice.

intertribal, adj. [1. intertríbl; 2. intətráibl]. **inter-** & **tribal.** Existing between different tribes: *intertribal warfare, marriage* &c.

intertropical, adj. [1. intertrópikl; 2. intətrɔ́pikl]. **inter-** & **tropical.** Lying, situated, within or between the tropics.

intertwine, vb. trans. & intrans. [1. intertwín; 2. intətwáin]. **inter-** & **twine**, vb. **1.** trans. To twine, twist, wreathe together, interlace. **2.** intrans. To become twined or twisted together, interlace.

intertwinement, n. [1. intertwínment; 2. intətwáinmənt]. Prec. & **-ment.** The act or process of intertwining; state of being intertwined.

interval, n. [1. ínterval; 2. íntəvəl], fr. Lat. *intervall-(um)*, 'open space between ramparts, palisades; space between, interval; intermission, pause; difference, dissimilarity', fr. **inter-** & **vallum. 1.** Intervening space, distance between two objects, points &c. Phr. *at intervals*, at a series of points, with spaces between. **2.** Amount of separation, extent of difference, in degree, quality, capacity &c. **3.** Intervening period of time between two fixed periods; a portion of time, distinguished in some way from those before and after it: *lucid intervals between fits of madness; the interval between birth and death.* **4.** (mus.) Difference of pitch between two tones.

intervallic, adj. [1. intervális; 2. intəvǽlik]. Prec. & **-ic.** Of, pertaining to, forming, existing in, an interval.

intervene, vb. intrans. [1. intervén; 2. intəvín], fr. Lat. *interven-(īre)*, 'to come between, come upon, interrupt; to happen, occur, during other things; to prevent, hinder; to interfere', fr. **inter-** & *venīre*, 'to come'. See **venue. 1.** To come in, appear, as something irrelevant or extraneous. **2. a** (of events) To occur, take place, between other events: *Lent intervenes between Christmas and Easter*; **b** (of things) to be placed, be situated, lie: *a small part of Bucks intervenes between Middlesex and Berkshire.* **3. a** (of events, circumstances) To come, be interposed, happen, as preventive, hindering influence: *I will see you tomorrow, should nothing intervene*; **b** (of persons) to interfere, make intervention, step in, take part: *to intervene in a dispute.* **4.** (law) To become a party to an action at law.

intervener, n. [1. intervéner; 2. intəvínə]. Prec. & **-er.** One who intervenes, esp. in a lawsuit.

intervenient, adj. [1. intervénient; 2. intəvíniənt], fr. Lat. *intervenient-(em)*, Pres. Part. of *intervenīre*, 'to come between, intervene'. See prec. Coming between, intervening, interposing.

intervention, n. [1. intervénshun; 2. intəvénʃən], fr. Lat. *interventiōn-(em)*, 'interposition', fr. *intervent-(um)*, P.P. type of *intervenīre*, 'to come between, interpose'. See **intervene** & **-ion.** Act of intervening; **a** act of interference or interposition; **b** mediation.

interview (I.), n. [1. íntervū; 2. íntəvjū], fr. Fr. *entrevue*, fr. P.P. of *(s')entrevoir*, fr. **inter-** & **view. a** Formal meeting and conversation between two persons or parties; conference; **b** specif., meeting between a journalist and a person upon whose conversation, opinions, habits &c. he wishes to report.

interview (II.), vb. trans., fr. prec. To have an interview with; specif., to meet and question (person) in order to report on his opinions.

interviewer, n. [1. íntervûer; 2. íntəvjûə]. Prec. & **-er.** One who interviews; specif., newspaper reporter who interviews a person in order to elicit an expression of his opinions &c. for publication.

intervolve, vb. trans. [1. intervólv; 2. intəvɔ́lv], fr. **inter-** & Lat. *volvere*, 'to roll'. See **volute.** To coil, roll up (two things) together, into each other.

interweave, vb. trans. [1. interwév; 2. intəwív]. **inter-** & **weave.** To weave, twine, wreathe, together; interlace; intermingle.

interwind, vb. trans. & intrans. [1. interwínd; 2. intəwáind]. **inter-** & **wind** (IV.). To wind together, twist into or through one another.

intestacy, n. [1. intéstasi; 2. intéstəsi]. See next word & **-cy.** Fact of, result of, one's dying intestate.

intestate, adj. & n. [1. intéstat; 2. intéstət], fr. Lat. *intestāt-(us)*, 'having made no will', fr. **in-** (II.) & *testāt-(us)*, P.P. type of *testāri*, 'to witness; to make a will'. See **testament. 1.** adj. **a** Having made no will; esp. in Phr. *to die intestate*; **b** not disposed of by will: *an intestate estate.* **2.** n. Person who has died intestate.

intestinal, adj. [1. intéstinal; 2. intéstinəl]. See next word & **-al. 1.** Pertaining to, situated in, the intestines. **2.** (rare) Internal, not foreign, domestic.

intestine, n. & adj. [1. intéstin; 2. intéstin], fr. Lat. *intestīna*, pl. 'entrails'; fr. *intestīnus*, 'inward, internal'. Cp. *interus*, 'inward'. See **interior. 1.** n. That part of the alimentary canal below the stomach; bowel, gut. **2.** adj. (fig.) Arising from, existing, within; specif. (of war, strife) civil, domestic.

intimacy, n. [1. íntimasi; 2. íntiməsi]. See next word & **-cy. a** The state or quality of being intimate; confidential, affectionate, intercourse; familiarity; familiar, intimate acquaintance; specif. **b** sexual relations.

intimate (I.), adj. [1. íntimat; 2. íntimit]. Earlier *intime*, fr. Fr.; present form has adj. suff. *-ate.* See **intimate** (III.). **1.** Deep-seated, inward, pertaining to innermost nature: *one's intimate feelings.* **2. a** Closely bound up; knit together in close physical or spiritual relation: *intimate friends, friendship*; **b** private, personal: *intimate details*; **c** penetrating to the essence: *intimate knowledge.*

intimate (II.), n., fr. prec. Intimate friend.

intimate (III.), vb. trans. [1. íntimāt; 2. íntimeit], fr. L. Lat. *intimāt-(um)*, P.P. type of *intimāre*, 'to bring, put, press, into; to announce, make known'; fr. *intim-(us)*, 'inmost', superl. form of Lat. *in*, adv. & prep., see **in** (V.). **1.** To declare, announce, give notice. **2.** To hint, imply, suggest.

intimately, adv. [1. íntimatli; 2. íntimətli]. **intimate** (I.) & **-ly.** In an intimate manner.

intimation, n. [1. intimáshun; 2. intiméiʃən]. **intimate** (III.) & **-ion. 1.** Act of intimating. **2.** That which is intimated; **a** notification, information; **b** hint, suggestion.

intimidate, vb. trans. [1. intímidāt; 2. intímideit], fr. Med. Lat. *intimidāt-(um)*, P.P. type of *intimidāre*, 'to intimidate', fr. **in-** (I.) & Lat. *timid-(us)*, 'timid'. See **timid** & **-ate. a** To strike fear into, scare; to terrorize, cow; **b** to restrain or coerce by threats or violence.

intimidation, n. [1. intimidáshun; 2. intimidéiʃən]. Prec. & **-ion. a** Act of intimidating; specif., the use of threats or violence to restrain or coerce another; **b** state of being intimidated.

intimidator, n. [1. intímidātur; 2. intímideitə]. See prec. & **-or.** One who intimidates.

intimidatory, adj. [1. intímidāturi; 2. intímideitəri]. **intimidate** & **-ory.** Tending to intimidate; using threats.

intimity, n. [1. intímiti; 2. intímiti], fr. Lat. *intim-(us)*, 'inmost', see **intimate** (II.), & **-ity. a** The state or quality of being intimate; intimacy; **b** privacy, seclusion.

intinction, n. [1. intíngkshun; 2. intíŋkʃən], fr. Lat. *intinctiōn-(em)*, see **in-** (I.) & **tinction.** Act of the priest at the Eucharist in dipping a Host into the consecrated wine before reception or administration.

intitule, vb. trans. [1. intítūl; 2. intítjūl], fr. O. Fr. *intituler*, fr. L. Lat. *intitulāre*, 'to give a name to', fr. **in-** (I.) & *titulāre*, 'to entitle', fr. *titul-(us)*, 'a name'. See **title.** To give a name to, entitle; chiefly used in P.P., and applied to an Act of Parliament.

into, prep. [1. íntoo; 2. íntu]. **in** (I.) & **to. 1.** Expressing direction of action or motion towards a point within an enclosed space or specified area; (in material and non-material sense) *to put a cake into the oven; to go into the garden; to look into one's eyes; to look into one's antecedents; to inquire into a matter; to get into difficulties.* **2.** Expressing passage, change from one state, condition, quality, arrangement &c. to another: *to make flour into bread; to convert water into ice; to put Latin into English; a caterpillar turns into a butterfly; to harden into a mass.*

intoed, adj. [1. íntōd; 2. íntóud]. **in** (II.) & **toe** & **-ed.** Having the toes turned inwards.

intolerable, adj. [1. intólerabl; 2. intɔ́lərəbl], fr. Lat. *intolerābil-(is)*, 'that cannot be borne'. **in-** (II.) & **tolerable.** Not to be borne, unendurable; insupportable, unbearable.

intolerableness, n. Prec. & **-ness.** The quality of being intolerable.

intolerably, adv. See prec. & **-ly.** In an intolerable manner, to an intolerable degree.

intolerance, n. [1. intólerans; 2. intɔ́lərəns], fr. Lat. *intolerantia*, 'impatience'. **in-** (II.) & **tolerance.** Quality of being intolerant.

intolerant, adj. [1. intólerant; 2. intɔ́lərənt], fr. Lat. *intolerant-(em)*, 'impatient, intolerant'. **in-** (II.) & **tolerant.** Not able or willing to endure or consider, impatient of, beliefs, opinions, conduct &c. at variance with one's own; bigoted, illiberal.

intolerantly, adv. Prec. & **-ly.** In an intolerant manner.

intonate, vb. trans. [1. íntonāt; 2. íntəneit], fr. Lat. *intonāt-(um)*, P.P. type of *intonāre*, 'to thunder; to resound'. See **intone.** To intone.

intonation, n. [1. intonáshun; 2. intənéiʃən]. Prec. & **-ion. 1.** The act of intoning. **2.** Modulation of the voice; rise and fall in pitch of the voice in speaking. **3.** (mus.) **a** Production of musical tones; **b** opening phrase in plain-song.

intone, vb. trans. & intrans. [1. intón; 2. intóun], fr. Lat. *intonāre*, 'to thunder; to resound; to sound', fr. **in-** (I.) & *tonāre*, 'to thunder, resound', fr. *ton-(us)*, 'tone'. See **tone. 1.** trans. **a** To recite, utter (prayer &c.) in musical recitative, utter with singing voice; **b** to give specific intonation to, utter in specified tones. **2.** intrans. To practise intonation.

intoxicant, adj. & n. [1. intóksikant; 2. intɔ́ksikənt]. See next word & **-ant. 1.** adj. Intoxicating. **2.** n. Intoxicating liquor.

intoxicate, vb. trans. [1. intóksikāt; 2. intɔ́ksikeit], fr. Med. Lat. *intoxicāt-(um)*, P.P. type of *intoxicāre*, 'to dip into or smear with poison'. See **in-** (I.) & **toxic. 1.** To make drunk, to inebriate. **2.** To cause great emotional excitement in; to work on the passions of to the point at which complete self-control is lost.

intoxicating, adj. [1. intóksikāting; 2. *in*tɔ́ks*i*keitiŋ], fr. Pres. Part. of prec. Tending to intoxicate.

intoxication, n. [1. intòksikáshun; 2. *in*tɔ̀ksikéiʃən]. **intoxicate** & **-ion.** The act of intoxicating; state of being intoxicated.

intra-, pref. representing Lat. *intrā*, 'within, on the inside, inwardly', contracted fr. **interā*, fr. *inter-(us)*, 'inner'. See **interior** & **inter- (II.)**. The pref. is used chiefly in scientific words, e.g. *intracardiac*, within the heart; *intracellular*, inside the cells of a body; *intraglacial*, deposited inside a glacier &c.

intractability, n. [1. intràktabíliti; 2. *in*træ̀ktəbíl*i*ti]. See next word & **-ity.** Quality of being intractable.

intractable, adj. [1. intráktabl; 2. *in*trǽktəbl], fr. Lat. *intractābil-(is)*, 'unmanageable'. **in- (II.)** & **tractable.** **a** (of living beings, character) Not capable of being controlled, not docile; refractory; **b** (of inanimate things) Difficult to deal with, unmanageable; hard, awkward, to manipulate; not amenable to treatment.

intractableness, n. Prec. & **-ness.** The quality of being intractable.

intractably, adv. See prec. & **-ly.** In an intractable manner.

intrados, n. [1. intrádos; 2. *in*tréidɔs]. Fr., fr. **intra-** & *dos*, 'back', fr. Lat. *dorsum*, 'back'. See **dorsal.** (archit.) The lower curve or interior of an arch.

intramural, adj. [1. ìntramū́ral; 2. *in*trəmjɔ́rəl]. **intra-** & **mural.** Within the walls of a city, building &c.; specif., *intramural burial*, within the walls of, inside, a church.

intransigent, adj. & n. [1. intráhnsijent, intránsijent; 2. *in*trɑ́nsidžənt, *in*trǽnsidžənt], fr. Fr. *intransigeant*, fr. Span. *intransigentes*, political revolutionary party refusing compromise, fr. **in- (II.)** & Lat. *transigent-(em)*, Pres. Part. of *transigere*, 'to transfix, pierce through; to carry through, accomplish, settle; to come to an agreement, understanding', fr. **trans-** & *agere*, 'to act, do, perform'. See **agent** & **act.** **1.** adj. Refusing to compromise, or come to an understanding; irreconcilable. **2.** n. Intransigent person.

intransitive, adj. & n. [1. intráhnsitiv, intránsitiv; 2. *in*trɑ́nsitiv, *in*trǽnsitiv], fr. Lat. *intransitīv-(us)*, 'intransitive'. **in- (II.)** & **transitive.** (gram.) **1.** adj. Not governing a direct object. **2.** n. Intransitive verb.

intransitively, adv. Prec. & **-ly.** As an intransitive verb.

intrant, n. [1. íntrant; 2. íntrənt], fr. Lat. *intrant-(em)*, Pres. Part. of *intrāre*, 'to enter'. See **enter.** Person who enters, esp. one entering on public duty or membership of society &c.

intrench, vb. See **entrench.**

intrepid, adj. [1. intrépid; 2. *in*trépid], fr. Lat. *intrepid-(us)*, 'unshaken, undaunted', fr. **in- (II.)** & *trepidus*, 'restless, agitated, alarmed'. See **trepidation.** Not to be frightened; brave, dauntless, fearless.

intrepidity, n. [1. ìntrepíditi; 2. ìntrɛpíditi]. Prec. & **-ity.** Quality of being intrepid; courage, fearlessness.

intrepidly, adv. [1. intrépidli; 2. *in*trépidli]. See prec. & **-ly.** In an intrepid manner.

intricacy, n. [1. íntrikasi; 2. íntr*i*kəsi]. See next word & **-cy.** **1.** Quality of being intricate. **2.** Something that is intricate; convolution, complication.

intricate, adj. [1. íntrikat; 2. íntr*i*kit], fr. Lat. *intrīcāt-(um)*, P.P. type of *intrīcāre*, 'to entangle, perplex', fr. **in- (I.)** & *trīc-(ae)*, 'wiles, tricks, hindrances', cogn. w. Lat. *torquere*, 'to twist'. See **torque, torture.** Difficult to follow; involved, entangled, perplexing, complicated: *the intricate windings of a path*; *an intricate pattern, plot*; *intricate directions.*

intricately, adv. Prec. & **-ly.** In an intricate manner.

intrig(u)ant, n., Fr., hardly naturalized in Engl. [1. antrēgahn; 2. ǣtrīgɑ̃]. Pres. Part. of *intriguer*. See **intrigue (I.)** Person given to intrigue.

intrig(u)ante, n. [1. antrēgáhnt; 2. ǣtrīgɑ̃t]. Fr., fem. form of prec. Woman given to intrigue.

intrigue (I.), vb. intrans. [1. intrḗg; 2. *in*tríg], fr. Fr. *intriguer*, 'to intrigue', fr. Lat. *intrīcāre*, 'to entangle, embarrass'. See **intricate.** **1.** To plot, scheme, have underhand dealings. **2.** To engage in an illicit love-affair, to have a liaison. [*Note*: The trans. use, in sense of 'to puzzle, attract, fascinate, mystify' &c., as, *his curious character has intrigued many biographers*; *a most intriguing piece of news* &c., is a modern journalistic usage, taken from the French.]

intrigue (II.), n. Fr., fr. Ital. *intrigo*, fr. *intrigare*, 'to intrigue', fr. Lat. *intrīcāre*, 'to entangle, embarrass'. See **intricate.** **1.** Secret, underhand, method or plot. **2.** Illicit love-affair, liaison.

intrinsic, adj. [1. intrínsik; 2. *in*trínsik], fr. Fr. *intrinsèque*, fr. L. Lat. *intrinsec-(us)*, 'inward', fr. Lat. *intrinsecus* (adv.), 'on the inside, inwardly', fr. **intrim*, cp. **intra-**, & *secus*, 'according to, following', fr. base of *sequi*, 'to follow'. See **sequela.** Pertaining to the real nature of a thing; inherent, essential, not dependent on outer circumstances: *intrinsic qualities, worth, value* &c.

intrinsically, adv. [1. intrínsikali; 2. *in*trínsikəli]. Prec. & **-al** & **-ly.** In an intrinsic manner.

intro-, pref. representing Lat. *intrō* (fr. **interō*; see **interior**), 'to the inside'; e.g. *introgression*, 'entrance'; *introflexion*, 'a bending inward'; *intropulsive*, 'driving inward.'

introduce, vb. trans. [1. ìntrodū́s; 2. ìntrədjū́s], fr. Lat. *intrōdūc-(ere)*, 'to lead or bring in; to introduce a person or subject; to institute, originate', fr. **intro-** & *dūcere*, 'to lead'. See **duct.** **1.** To put, place, in, or within; to insert: *to introduce a tube into a wound.* **2. a** To bring into a given place or position: *to introduce a touch of colour into a room, a romantic situation into a novel*; **b** to impart to: *to introduce an acrimonious spirit into a discussion.* **3.** To bring into use, give currency to, inaugurate: *to introduce a new method, an improvement, a strange custom.* **4. a** To make known to, bring to the notice of, make acquainted with, present to formally: *let me introduce my brother (to you)*; **b** to give experience of, initiate into: *to introduce a person to a strange mode of life, into a whirl of gaiety.* **5.** To lead, conduct, usher, in; present, announce: *to introduce a person into an anteroom*; *to introduce a person into a company.* **6. a** To bring forward, present formally for consideration: *to introduce a bill into Parliament*; **b** to bring up, bring before, raise, moot: *to introduce a subject of conversation.*

introduction, n. [1. ìntrodúkshun; 2. ìntrədákʃən], fr. Lat. *intrōductiōn-(em)*, 'introduction', fr. *intrōduct-(um)*, fr. *intrōdūcere.* See **introduce** & **-ion.** **1.** Act or process of introducing; state of being introduced; **a** insertion: *the rapid introduction of a probe into a wound*; **b** bringing into use or currency: *the introduction of a new fashion*; **c** formal presentation of one person to another. **2. a** Something that leads up to, introduces, prepares the way for, something else; specif. **b** preliminary statement, section in book &c., defining or explaining subject &c. **3.** Elementary text-book or treatise.

introductory, adj. [1. ìntrodúkturi; 2. ìntrədáktəri], fr. Lat. *intrōductōri-(us)*, 'introductory', fr. *intrōduct-(um)*. See prec. & **-ory.** Serving as an introduction; preliminary.

introit, n. [1. intrṓit; 2. intróuit], fr. Fr. *introït*, fr. Lat. *introitus*, 'entrance', fr. *introit-(um)*, P.P. type of *introīre*, 'to enter', fr. **intro-** & *īre*, 'to go', q.v. under **itinerate.** Hymn &c., sung as the priest goes up to the altar to celebrate Mass.

intromission, n. [1. intromíshun; 2. *in*trəmíʃən], fr. Lat. *intrōmiss-(um)*, P.P. type of *intrōmittere*, 'to send or let in'. **intro-** & **mission.** The act of intromitting; state of being intromitted.

intromit, vb. trans. [1. ìntromít; 2. ìntrəmít], fr. Lat. *intrōmitt-(ere)*, 'to send or let in', fr. **intro-** & *mittere*, 'to send'. See **mission.** **1.** To allow to enter, let in, admit. **2.** To put or place in, insert.

intromittent, adj. [1. intromítent; 2. *in*trəmítənt], fr. Lat. *intrōmittent-(em)*, Pres. Part. of *intrōmittere*, 'to send or let in'. See prec. Admitting, conveying inwards.

introspect, vb. intrans. [1. ìntrospékt; 2. ìntrəspékt], fr. Lat. *intrōspect-(um)*, P.P. type of *intrōspicere*, 'to look into, observe closely', fr. **intro-** & *specere*, 'to look', q.v. under **species.** To practise introspection.

introspection, n. [1. ìntrospékshun; 2. ìntrəspékʃən]. Prec. & **-ion.** Observation, analysis, of, dwelling upon, one's own thoughts and feelings; self-analysis, self-examination.

introspectionist, n. [1. ìntrospékshunist; 2. ìntrəspékʃənist]. Prec. & **-ist.** One who practises introspection.

introspective, adj. [1. ìntrospéktiv; 2. ìntrəspéktiv]. **introspect** & **-ive.** Of, pertaining to, characterized by, based on, dealing with, introspection.

introspectively, adv. Prec. & **-ly.** In an introspective manner; by means of introspection.

introspectiveness, n. See prec. & **-ness.** Quality of being introspective; introspection.

introversible, adj. [1. ìntrovérsibl; 2. ìntrəvʌ́sibl], fr. **intro-** & Lat. *vers-(um)*, P.P. type of *vertere*, 'to turn'. See **version** & **-ible.** Capable of being introverted.

introversion, n. [1. ìntrovérshun; 2. ìntrəvʌ́ʃən]. **intro-** & **version.** Act of introverting; state of being introverted.

introversive, adj. [1. ìntrovérsiv; 2. *in*trəvʌ́siv], fr. **intro-** & Lat. *vers-(um)*, P.P. type of *vertere*, 'to turn'. See **version** & **-ive.** Tending to introvert, taking an inward direction.

introvert (I.), vb. trans. [1 ìntrovért; 2. ìntrəvʌ́t]. **intro-** & Lat. *vert-(ere)*, 'to turn'. See prec. **1.** To direct inwards, cause to take an inward direction: *to introvert the thoughts.* **2.** (zool.) To draw (organ) inwards upon itself.

introvert (II.), n. [1. íntrovërt; 2. íntrəvʌ̄t], fr. prec. Person who is naturally and habitually disposed to mental, psychological, introversion or introspection, as distinguished from *extrovert.*

introvertive, adj. [1. introvértiv; 2. *in*trəvʌ́tiv]. **introvert (I.)** & **-ive.** Introversive.

intrude, vb. trans. & intrans. [1. intrṓōd; 2. intrū́d], fr. Lat. *intrūd-(ere)*, 'to thrust in', fr. **in- (I.)** & *trūdere*, 'to thrust, push'; cogn. w. O.E. *þrēatian*, 'to oppress, threaten'. See **strut (I.), thrust,** & **threat**; cp. O. Slav. *trudŭ*, 'distress'. **A.** trans. **1. a** To thrust, force, push in; specif. **b** (geol.) to force into another series or stratum: *intruded rocks.* **2.** To thrust, force, introduce, without invitation or permission: *to intrude oneself, one's views, upon a person.* **B.** intrans. To come into, enter, join a company, without leave, invitation, or welcome: *I hope I am not intruding.*

intruder, n. [1. intrṓōder; 2. intrū́də]. Prec. & **-er.** One who intrudes; one who pushes himself in where he is not invited or desired.

intrusion, n. [1. intrṓōzhun; 2. intrū́žən], fr. Lat. *intrūs-(um)*, P.P. type of *intrūdere*, 'to thrust in'. See prec. & **-ion.** **1.** The act of intruding, state of being intruded: *the intrusion of one's opinions upon another.* **2.** The act of entering a place, forcing oneself upon a person &c., without leave or welcome: *an intrusion upon one's privacy.* **3.** (geol.) The forcing of masses of melted rock between strata or beds of different rock.

intrusive, adj. [1. intrṓōsiv; 2. intrū́siv], fr. Lat. *intrūs-(um)*, P.P. type of *intrūdere*, 'to thrust in'. See **intrude** & **-ive.** Intruding, tending to intrude, given to intrusion.

intrusively, adv. Prec. & **-ly.** In an intrusive manner.

intrusiveness, n. See prec. & **-ness.** The quality of being intrusive.

intubate, vb. trans. [1. íntūbāt; 2. íntjubeit], fr. **in-** (I.) & Lat. *tub-(us)*, 'a pipe, tube'. See **tube** & **-ate.** (med.) To insert a tube into (a wound, passage of the body).

intuit, vb. trans. & intrans. [1. íntūit; 2. íntjuit], fr. Lat. *intuit-(um)*, P.P. type of *intuēri*, 'to look at; to regard, consider', fr. **in-** (I.) & *tuēre*, 'to look at, watch'. See **tuition** & **tutor.** (rare) **1.** trans. To know by intuition. **2.** intrans. To acquire knowledge by intuition.

intuition, n. [1. ìntūíshun; 2. ìntjuíʃən], fr. Fr., fr. Med. Lat. *intuitiōn-(em)*, 'intuition'. Prec. & **-ion.** **a** Faculty of the mind whereby there is immediate apprehension or cognition without the process of conscious reasoning; instinct, flair; **b** knowledge derived in this manner.

intuitional, adj. [1. ìntūíshunal; 2. ìntjuíʃənəl]. Prec. & **-al.** Pertaining to, derived from, of the nature of, intuition.

intuitionalism, n. [1. ìntūíshunalizm; 2. ìntjuíʃənəlizəm]. Prec. & **-ism.** Philosophical doctrine that a knowledge of truth and of moral distinctions is derived by intuition.

intuitionalist, n. [1. ìntūíshunalist; 2. ìntjuíʃənəlist]. **intuitional** & **-ist.** A believer in intuitionalism.

intuitionism, n. [1. ìntūíshunizm; 2. ìntjuíʃənizəm]. **intuition** & **-ism.** Doctrine that the reality of perceived objects is known by intuition.

intuitionist, n. [1. ìntūíshunist; 2. ìntjuíʃənist]. **intuition** & **-ist.** A believer in intuitionism.

intuitive, adj. [1. intū́itiv; 2. intjū́itiv]. **intuit** & **-ive.** Of, pertaining to, perceived or known by, intuition.

intuitively, adv. Prec. & **-ly.** In an intuitive manner; by intuition.

intuitiveness, n. See prec. & **-ness.** Quality of being intuitive.

intuitivism, n. [1. intū́itivizm; 2. intjū́itivizəm]. **intuitive** & **-ism.** Intuitionalism.

intuitivist, n. [1. intū́itivist; 2. intjū́itivist]. **intuitive** & **-ist.** A believer in intuitivism.

intumescence, n. [1. ìntūmésens; 2. ìntjumésəns]. See next word & **-ce.** **1.** Process of swelling; state of being swollen. **2.** A swelling.

intumescent, adj. [1. ìntūmésent; 2. ìntjumésənt], fr. Lat. *intumescent-(em)*, Pres. Part. of *intumescere*, 'to swell up', fr. **in-** (I.) & *tumescere*, 'to swell'. See **tumescent** & **tumid.** Swelling up, becoming inflated.

intussusception, n. [1. ìntususe̅pshun; 2. ìntəsəsépʃən], fr. Lat. *intus*, 'within' (fr. **in-** (V.) & abl. suff. *-tu(s)* & *susceptiōn-(em)*, 'a taking in hand, undertaking; acceptance', fr. *suscept-(um)*, P.P. type of *suscipere*, 'to support; to undertake; to take, receive'. See **susceptible** & **-ion.** **1.** The reception of foreign matter, i.e. food, by an organism, and conversion of it into tissue. **2.** Introversion of part of intestine into adjacent part. **3.** (fig.) Reception, taking in, assimilation, of ideas &c.

inulin, n. [1. ínūlin; 2. ínjulin], fr. Lat. *inula*, see **elecampane**, & **-in.** **a** (chem.) A starch-like substance obtained from the root of *Inula* (elecampane) and other plants; **b** (med.) a decoction of the extract of *Inula* used for various purposes; also a laevulose sugar used in cases of diabetes.

inunction, n. [1. inúngkshun; 2. ináŋkʃən], fr. Lat. *inunctiōn-(em)*, 'anointing'. **in-** (I.) & **unction**, & cp. **ointment.** The act of anointing; state of being anointed; rubbing of ointment, oil &c. into the skin.

inundate, vb. trans. [1. ínundāt; 2. ínəndeit], fr. Lat. *inundāt-(um)*, P.P. type of *inundāre*, 'to overflow, flood', fr. **in-** (I.) & *undāre*, 'to rise in waves, surge, swell', fr. *unda*, 'a wave'. See **undulate.** **1.** (of water) To cover by overflowing; to flood, swamp, deluge. **2.** (fig.) To fill to abundance; overwhelm: *a place inundated with visitors; inundated with invitations, correspondence* &c.

inundation, n. [1. ìnundā́shun; 2. ìnəndéiʃən], fr. Lat. *inundātiōn-(em)*, 'overflowing, inundation'. Prec. & **-ion.** **1.** **a** The act of inundating; **b** state of being inundated. **2.** A flood, deluge, overflow, influx. (Also fig.)

inurbane, adj. [1. ìnërbā́n; 2. ìnābéin], fr. Lat. *inurbān-(us)*, 'rustic, unpolished, unmannerly'. **in-** (II.) & **urbane.** (rare) Reverse of urbane; unpolished, discourteous, unmannerly; inelegant, lacking grace.

inurbanity, n. [1. ìnërbániti; 2. ìnābǽniti]. Prec. & **-ity.** (rare) Quality of being inurbane.

inure, enure, vb. trans. & intrans. [1. inū́r; 2. injṓ], fr. **in-** (I.) & obs. *ure*, 'use, work', fr. O. Fr. *œuvre*, fr. Lat. *opera*, 'work'. See **opus.** **1.** trans. To accustom, give experience, harden, habituate: *to be inured to exposure, cold, heat* &c. **2.** intrans. (law) To take effect, become operative; come into use, serve for the use or benefit of.

inurement, n. [1. inū́rment; 2. injṓmənt]. Prec. & **-ment.** The act or process of inuring; state of being inured.

inurn, vb. trans. [1. inërn; 2. inā́n]. **in-** (I.) & **urn.** To enclose, place, in a cinerary urn.

inutile, adj. [1. inū́tīl; 2. injū́tail], fr. Lat. *inūtil-(is)*, 'useless', fr. **in-** (II.) & *ūtilis*, 'useful'. See **utility.** Useless, unprofitable.

inutility, n. [1. inūtíliti; 2. ìnjutíliti], fr. Lat. *inūtilitāt-(em)*, 'uselessness'. **in-** (II.) & **utility.** Quality of being inutile; uselessness.

invade, vb. trans. [1. invā́d; 2. invéid], fr. Lat. *invād-(ere)*, 'to go into, enter upon; to fall upon, make an attack on', fr. **in-** (I.) & *vādere*, 'to go, step, move', fr. *vadum*, 'shoal, ford', cogn. w. **wade.** **1.** **a** (of hostile army, enemy &c.) To enter with hostile intent, to overrun, make an inroad into; **b** (fig.) to rush into, overwhelm, crowd into, throng: *my house was invaded by a crowd of visitors.* **2.** (fig.) **a** To assail, attack, take possession of: *terror invaded our minds*; **b** to encroach upon, infringe: *to invade another's rights.*

invader, n. [1. invā́der; 2. invéidə]. Prec. & **-er.** One who, that which, invades; assailant, intruder.

invaginate, vb. trans. [1. invájināt; 2. invǽdzineit], fr. **in-** (I.) & **vagina** & **-ate.** **1.** To put into, receive into, a sheath. **2.** To withdraw (part of tube) into itself, introvert.

invagination, n. [1. invàjinā́shun; 2. invæ̀dzinéiʃən]. Prec. & **-ion.** **a** Act of invaginating; **b** state of being invaginated.

invalid (I.), adj. & n., fr. Fr. *invalide*, fr. Lat. *invalid-(us)*, 'weak, infirm; inefficient, inadequate'. **in-** (II.) & **valid.** **1.** adj. [1. ínvalēd; 2. ínvəlīd]. **a** Disabled by illness; weak, infirm, suffering from ill-health: *he supports an invalid mother*; **b** suitable for illness or sick person: *an invalid diet; invalid chair* &c. **2.** n. [1. ìnvalḗd, ínvalēd; 2. ìnvəlíd, ínvəlīd]. A sick person; one permanently or temporarily ailing: *a resort of invalids.*

invalid (II.), vb. trans. [1. ìnvalḗd, ínvalēd; 2. ìnvəlíd, ínvəlīd], fr. prec. **a** To make into an invalid, disable by illness; specif. **b** to consider, treat, as an invalid, put on sick-list, remove from active service on account of ill-health: (esp. of soldier or sailor) *to be invalided home, invalided out of the army.*

invalid (III.), adj. [1. inválid; 2. invǽlid], fr. Lat. *invalid-(us)*, 'weak, infirm; inadequate'. See **invalid** (I.). **a** Without value, weight, effect; not valid: *invalid arguments* &c.; **b** without legal force or soundness: *invalid claims; to declare a marriage invalid.*

invalidate, vb. trans. [1. inválidāt; 2. invǽlideit]. Prec. & **-ate.** To render invalid, deprive of legal force; to deprive of weight, cogency: *to invalidate a claim* &c.

invalidation, n. [1. invàlidā́shun; 2. invæ̀lidéiʃən]. Prec. & **-ion.** Act of invalidating; state of being invalidated.

invalidhood, n. [1. ìnvalḗd-hood; 2. ìnvəlíd-hud]. **invalid** (I.) & **-hood.** State of being an invalid.

invalidism, n. [1. ìnvalḗdizm; 2. ìnvəlídizəm]. **invalid** (I.) & **-ism.** Invalidhood.

invalidity, n. [1. ìnvalíditi; 2. ìnvəlíditi]. **invalid** (I., III.) & **-ity.** **1.** Lack of validity, of legal or binding force. **2.** (rare) Infirmity, invalidism.

invalidly, adv. [1. inválidli; 2. invǽlidli]. **invalid** (III.) & **-ly.** Without validity.

invaluable, adj. [1. inválūabl; 2. invǽljuəbl]. **in-** (II.) & **valuable.** Beyond estimation; priceless, of the greatest value.

invar, n. [1. invā́r; 2. invā́ə], fr. **invariable.** An alloy of steel and nickel, used for making scientific instruments &c., as not liable to expand or shrink under changes of temperature.

invariability, n. [1. invàriabíliti; 2. invèəriəbíliti]. **in-** (II.) & **variability.** State or quality of being invariable.

invariable, adj. & n. [1. invā́riabl; 2. invéəriəbl]. **in-** (II.) & **variable.** **1.** adj. **a** Not capable of being varied; unchangeable, unalterable: *an invariable rule*; **b** not varying; unchanging, remaining constant; **c** (math.) constant, fixed. **2.** n. An invariable thing, substance, property.

invariableness, n. Prec. & **-ness.** Invariability.

invariably, adv. See prec. & **-ly.** **a** Uniformly, regularly, without change or exception; always; **b** unalterably, without liability to change.

invasion, n. [1. invā́zhun; 2. invéižən], fr. L. Lat. *invāsiōn-(em)*, 'attack', fr. *invās-(um)*, P.P. type of *invādere*, 'to go into; to fall upon'. See **invade** & **-ion.** Act of invading; state of being invaded: *Julius Caesar's invasion of Britain*; incursion, violation, encroachment: *an invasion of one's privacy, prerogatives* &c.

invasive, adj. [1. invā́siv; 2. invéisiv]. See prec. & **-ive.** Pertaining to, of the nature of, invasion; encroaching.

invective, n. [1. invéktiv; 2. invéktiv], fr. Med. Lat. *invectīva (oratio)*, fr. L. Lat. *invectīvus*, 'reproachful, abusive', fr. *invect-(um)*, P.P. type of *invehere*, 'to carry or bring in; to enter, penetrate; to attack, assail; to inveigh against'. See next word & **-ive.** **a** Abusive speech or writing, vituperation, wordy onslaught or attack: *he was a master of invective but a shallow reasoner; invective may score a cheap success*; **b** (usually in pl.) abusive words, abuse: *a stream of coarse invectives.*

inveigh, vb. intrans. [1. invā́; 2. invéi], fr. Lat. *invehi*, pass. of *invehere*, 'to carry, bring, into; to enter, penetrate; to fall upon, assail; to attack with words', fr. **in-** (I.) & *vehere*, 'to carry'. See **vehicle** & **way.** (followed by *against*) To attack violently in words; to censure vehemently; utter invective against.

inveigle, vb. trans. [1. invḗgl, invā́gl; 2. invígl, invéigl], fr. **in-** (I.) & O. Fr. *avugler*, Mod. Fr. *aveugler*, 'to blind, delude', fr. Lat. **ab-** & *oculus*, 'eye'. See **ocular.** To persuade by deceptive or underhand means, delude, lure, trick into, entice, seduce: *to inveigle a person into a place, into doing something.*

inveiglement, n. [1. invḗglment; 2. invíglmənt]. Prec. & **-ment.** Act of inveigling; state of being inveigled.

invent, vb. trans. [1. invént; 2. invént], fr. Lat. *invent-(um)*, 'a device, contrivance', P.P. of *invenīre*, 'to find, come upon, meet with; to find out, discover; to contrive, devise, invent', fr. **in-** (I.) & *venīre*, 'to come'. See **venue.** **1.** To contrive, discover use or form of, by thought or imagination; to originate, construct or use for the first time: *to invent a new method, new form of verse; to invent the steam engine, telephone* &c. **2.** To fabricate, concoct, make up: *to invent an excuse, explanation* &c.

invention, n. [1. invénshun; 2. invénʃən], fr. Lat. *inventiōn-(em)*, 'invention', fr. *invent-(um)*, P.P. type of *invenīre*, 'to find; to find out, discover; to devise, invent'. See prec. & **-ion**. **1.** The act of inventing; state of being invented: *the invention of the telescope.* **2.** Something that is invented; new method &c.; new mechanical device or contrivance; a discovery: *a most useful invention has just been patented.* **3.** Fabrication, concoction, fiction; fictitious statement, narrative &c.: *the report was an invention of the sensational newspapers.* **4.** Capacity for inventing; inventiveness; creative faculty: *necessity is the mother of invention.* **5.** The act of finding, fact of being found; discovery; only in Phr. *Invention of the Cross*, festival (May 3rd) commemorating the discovery of the True Cross by St. Helena in 326.

inventive, adj. [1. invéntiv; 2. invéntiv]. **invent** & **-ive**. Pertaining to invention; given to, capable of, invention; originative.

inventively, adv. Prec. & **-ly**. In an inventive manner.

inventiveness, n. See prec. & **-ness**. Quality of being inventive.

inventor, n. [1. invéntor; 2. invéntə]. **invent** & **-or**. One who invents; discoverer of new methods, or of new mechanical contrivances.

inventory (I.), n. [1. ínventuri; 2. ínvənt(ə)ri], fr. Med. Lat. *inventori-(um)*. See **invent** & **-ory**. **1.** Detailed list, descriptive enumeration, catalogue: *an inventory of household furniture.* **2.** Articles named in an inventory; stock.

inventory (II.), vb. trans., fr. prec. To make an inventory of.

inveracity, n. [1. inverásiti; 2. invərǽsiti]. **in-** (II.) & **veracity**. Lack of veracity; untruthfulness; cp. *unveracious.*

inverness, n. [1. invernés; 2. invənés], fr. name of town in Scotland. Also *Inverness cloak, coat, cape*, kind of long coat or ulster with wide, sometimes removable, cape.

inverse, adj. [1. invêrs; 2. invʌ́s] & n. [1. ínvêrs; 2. ínvʌs], fr. Lat. *invers-(um)*, P.P. type of *invertere*, 'to turn upside-down; to turn up, turn over; to transpose, change, pervert', fr. **in-** (I.) & *vertere*, 'to turn'. See **version**. **1.** adj. Opposed, reversed, contrary: *in inverse order of merit*; *inverse ratio, proportion*, of two quantities, one of which increases in proportion to decrease in the other. **2.** n. **a** State of being inverted; **b** thing that is direct opposite of another, that has contrary effect: *evil is the inverse of good.*

inversely, adv. [1. invêrsli; 2. invʌ́sli]. Prec. & **-ly**. In inverse order or manner, contrariwise; in inverse ratio.

inversion, n. [1. invêrshun; 2. invʌ́ʃən], fr. Lat. *inversiōn-(em)*, 'inversion, transposition'. See **inverse** & **-ion**. **1.** The act of turning upside-down; state of being upside-down. **2.** The act of reversing, transposing, changing, natural order of anything; state of being reversed, transposed; esp. (gram.) reversal of normal order of words. **3.** (mus., of intervals) Transference of lower note of interval to that an octave above.

inversive, adj. [1. invêrsiv; 2. invʌ́siv]. **inverse** & **-ive**. Pertaining to, causing, inversion.

invert (I.), vb. trans. [1. invêrt; 2. invʌ́t], fr. Lat. *invertere*, 'to turn upside-down, turn about, turn up; to transpose, change, reverse', fr. **in-** (I.) & *vertere*, 'to turn'. See **version**. **1.** To turn upside-down. **2.** To change, transpose, reverse the order or position of; to put into reverse, contrary, order or relation. **3.** (mus.) To change relation of notes in (interval) by transferring lower note to position an octave higher. **4.** (phon.) To turn the point (of tongue) upwards and backwards; *inverted consonant*, one uttered with this position of the tongue.

invert (II.), n. [1. ínvêrt; 2. ínvʌt], fr. prec. **1.** Inverted arch, vault, esp. that at bottom of sewer. **2.** Person with inverted or reversed sexual disposition. **3.** (attrib.) Inverted; specif., *invert sugar*, cane-sugar rendered laevulose by acid or yeast.

invertebrate, adj. & n., fr. **in-** (II.) & **vertebrate**. **1.** adj. [1. invêrtibrat; 2. invʌ́tibrit]. **a** (zool.) Having no backbone or spinal column; **b** (fig., of person, character &c.) without firmness, weak, irresolute. **2.** n. [1. invêrtibrāt; 2. invʌ́tibreit]. Invertebrate animal.

inverted, adj. [1. invêrted; 2. invʌ́tid], fr. P.P. of **invert** (I.). **a** Turned upside-down; reversed, transposed; **b** (phon.) see **invert** (I.), **4**.

invest, vb. trans. [1. invést; 2. invést], fr. Lat. *invest-(īre)*, 'to clothe, cover', fr. **in-** (I.) & *vestīre*, 'to clothe'. See **vest** (II.). **1. a** To put a covering on, clothe, dress; **b** specif., to array, decorate, with dress, insignia, badge &c., symbolical of office, rank, honour. **2.** To endue, clothe, surround (with qualities &c.): *a person invested with an air of dignity, mystery* &c. **3.** To lay siege to, surround, beleaguer. **4.** To use, lay out, money, in such a way as to obtain a return upon it. *Invest in*, **a** to spend money in the purchase of, put money into, a business, stocks &c.; **b** (colloq.) to spend money on, buy.

investigate, vb. trans. [1. invéstigāt; 2. invéstigeit], fr. Lat. *investīgāt-(um)*, P.P. type of *investīgāre*, 'to track, trace out; to search, examine, inquire, into', fr. **in-** (I.) & *vestīgāre*, 'to track out, search after', fr. *vestīg-(ium)*, 'footprint, track'. See **vestige**. To inquire into, make careful search into, examine systematically; research into.

investigation, n. [1. invèstigáshun; 2. invèstigéiʃən], fr. Lat. *investīgātiōn-(em)*, 'a searching, inquiring into'. Prec. & **-ion**. **a** Act of investigating; inquiry, examination; research; **b** treatise consisting of statement of results of research.

investigative, adj. [1. invéstigàtiv; 2. invéstigèitiv]. **investigate** & **-ive**. Pertaining to, concerned with, investigation.

investigatory, adj. [1. invéstigàturi; 2. invéstigèitəri]. **investigate** & **-ory**. Investigative.

investiture, n. [1. invéstichur; 2. invéstitʃə], fr. Med. Lat. *investitura*, fr. Lat. *investīt-(um)*, P.P. type of *investīre*, 'to clothe'. See **invest** & **-ure**. **1.** Process, formal ceremony, of investing a person with an office, benefice &c., or with symbol, badge, insignia, of an office, order, benefice &c. **2.** State of being invested, endued with (a quality &c.).

investment, n. [1. invéstment; 2. invéstmənt]. **invest** & **-ment**. **1. a** The act of investing money; **b** (of money) state of being invested. **2. a** Money that is invested; **b** property, stocks &c., in which money is invested: *a good investment*, one making a profitable return. **3.** The act of laying siege to; state of being besieged. **4. a** Clothing, array, covering; **b** formal investing, investiture.

inveteracy, n. [1. invéterasi; 2. invétərəsi]. **inveterate** & **-cy**. The state or quality of being inveterate.

inveterate, adj. [1. invéterat; 2. invétərət], fr. Lat. *inveterāt-(us)*, 'preserved for a long time; of long standing; deep-seated', fr. P.P. of *inveterāre*, 'to give age to, render old; to grow old, endure', fr. **in-** (I.) & *veter-*, stem of *vetus*, 'old'. See **veteran**. **1.** (rare) Ancient, long established: *an inveterate feud, enmity.* **2.** (of feeling, disease &c.) Deeply rooted, persistent, obstinate. **3.** (of persons) Long confirmed, and persisting, in a habit &c., thorough-paced, out-and-out: *an inveterate liar, humbug, smoker, gambler* &c.

inveterately, adv. Prec. & **-ly**. In an inveterate manner.

invidious, adj. [1. invídius; 2. invídiəs], fr. Lat. *invidiōs-(us)*, 'envious; enviable', fr. *invidia*, 'envy', & **-ous**; cp. *invidēre*, 'to look askance at; to envy', fr. **in-** (I.) & *vidēre*, 'to see'. See **vision**; cp. **envy**. (of conduct, speech, quality &c.) **a** Arousing hostile feelings, giving offence, provoking ill-will, by injustice; **b** fussily but undiscerningly and unjustly discriminating, and hence tending to create ill-will: *invidious distinctions.*

invidiously, adv. Prec. & **-ly**. In an invidious manner.

invidiousness, n. See prec. & **-ness**. Quality of being invidious.

invigilate, vb. intrans. [1. invíjilāt; 2. invídžileit], fr. Lat. *invigilāt-(um)*, P.P. type of *invigilāre*, 'to be watchful, to watch over', fr. **in-** (I.) & *vigilāre*, 'to watch over'. See **vigil**. To watch over, to keep order, secure good and honest behaviour among, candidates during a written examination.

invigilation, n. [1. invìjiláshun; 2. invìdžiléiʃən]. Prec. & **-ion**. Act or process of invigilating.

invigilator, n. [1. invíjilātor; 2. invídžileitə]. See prec. & **-or**. One who invigilates at an examination.

invigorate, vb. trans. [1. invígorāt; 2. invígəreit], fr. **in-** (I.) & Lat. *vigor*, 'strength'. See **vigour** & **-ate**. To make strong and vigorous; to brace, refresh, physically or mentally; to strengthen, animate, encourage.

invigorating, adj. [1. invígoràting; 2. invígərèitiŋ], fr. Pres. Part. of prec. Tending to invigorate; bracing, stimulating; cheering.

invigorative, adj. [1. invígorativ; 2. invígərətiv]. See prec. & **-ive**. Tending to invigorate; stimulating, refreshing.

invincibility, n. [1. invinsibíliti; 2. invìnsibíliti], fr. Lat. *invincibil-(is)*, 'unconquerable'. See next word & **-ity**. Quality of being invincible.

invincible, adj. & n. [1. invínsibl; 2. invínsibl], fr. Lat. *invincibil-(is)*, 'unconquerable'. **in-** (II.) & **vincible**. **1.** adj. Not capable of being overcome; unconquerable: *an invincible army*; insuperable: *invincible opposition*; Phr. *invincible ignorance*, that which cannot be overcome by human powers, and for which the possessor cannot be held responsible. **2.** n. (cap.) Name taken by a rebel Irish association in the eighties of 19th cent.

invincibly, adv. Prec. & **-ly**. In an invincible manner; to a degree that renders invincible.

inviolability, n. [1. inviolabíliti; 2. invàiələbíliti], fr. Lat. *inviolābil-(is)*, 'indestructible; invulnerable; inviolable'. See next word & **-ity**. Quality, state, of being inviolable.

inviolable, adj. [1. invíolabl; 2. inváiələbl], fr. Lat. *inviolābil-(is)*, 'invulnerable; inviolable, hallowed'. **in-** (II.) & **violable**. **1.** Not violated, unprofaned, kept free from physical or moral damage. **2.** Not to be, not permitted to be, violated or profaned; not susceptible of violation.

inviolably, adv. Prec. & **-ly**. In an inviolable manner.

inviolacy, n. [1. invíolasi; 2. inváiələsi]. See next word & **-acy**. State or quality of being inviolate.

inviolate, adj. [1. invíolat; 2. inváiəlit], fr. Lat. *inviolāt-(us)*, 'unhurt, inviolate', fr. **in-** (II.) & *violāt-(um)*, P.P. type of *violāre*, 'to violate'. See **violate**. Not violated; strictly preserved; kept sacred; unbroken, uninjured: *to keep one's faith, a promise, a rule &c. inviolate.*

inviolately, adv. Prec. & **-ly**. In an inviolate manner.

inviolateness, n. See prec. & **-ness**. State or quality of being inviolate.

invisibility, n. [1. invìzibíliti; 2. invìzibíliti], fr. L. Lat. *invīsibilitāt-(em)*, 'invisibility', fr. *invīsibil-(is)*, 'invisible'. Next word & **-ity**. State or quality of being invisible.

invisible (I.), adj. [1. invízibl; 2. invízibl], fr. Lat. *invīsibil-(is)*, 'invisible, unseen'. **in-** (II.) & **visible**. **1.** Not capable of being seen, on account of remoteness, lack of size, external conditions, insubstantiality &c.: *many stars are invisible without a telescope*; *an invisible particle*; *invisible in the dark*; *an invisible presence*; Phr. *invisible ink*, one which does not show up until heated. **2.** Refusing to show oneself, remaining withdrawn from society: *he remains invisible when out of spirits.*

invisible (**II.**), n., fr. prec. *The invisible*, the unseen world.

invisibleness, n. **invisible** (**I.**) & **-ness**. State or quality of being invisible; invisibility.

invisibly, adv. See prec. & **-ly**. In an invisible manner, so as to be invisible.

invitation, n. [1. invitáshun; 2. invitéiʃən], fr. Lat. *invītātiōn-(em)*, 'an invitation, challenge, incitement'. **invite** & **-ation**. **1.** The act of inviting. **2.** Message, request, which invites; specif., message offering hospitality, requesting a visit, or the acceptance of an honour or favour &c.

invitatory, adj. [1. invítatori; 2. inváitətəri], fr. Lat. *invītāt-(um)*, P.P. type of *invītāre*, 'to invite'. Next word & **-ory**. Expressing, containing, an invitation.

invite, vb. trans. [1. invít; 2. inváit], fr. Lat. *invīt-(āre)*, 'to invite; to entertain; to challenge; to attract'. Etymologies suggested appear to be quite uncertain. **1. a** To make a polite request to (person) to be present at a place, ceremony, function, social gathering &c.: *to invite a person to one's house, to dinner* &c.; **b** to request, urge, to do something: *to invite one to sing, to be seated; I invite you to consider ...* **2.** To allure, attract: '*And every scene invites the ravished eye*'. **3. a** To ask for, make a request for, solicit: *to invite questions*; **b** to induce, court, encourage: *his manner does not invite confidences.* **4.** To bring upon, lay open to, provoke, call for: *to invite attack.*

inviting, adj. [1. inviting; 2. inváitiŋ], fr. Pres. Part. of prec. Tempting, attractive, alluring.

invitingly, adv. Prec. & **-ly**. In an inviting manner; alluringly, temptingly.

invocation, n. [1. invokáshun; 2. invəkéiʃən], fr. Lat. *invocātiōn-(em)*, 'invocation'. See **invoke** & **-ation**. **1.** Act of invoking; specif., calling upon, prayer to, God, the saints, a deity, the Muses &c. for help, inspiration &c. **2.** Words, prayer, passage in poem &c. expressing invocation.

invocatory, adj. [1. invókatori; 2. invɔ́kətəri]. See prec. & **-ory**. Of, pertaining to, containing, expressing, invocation.

invoice, n. & vb. trans. [1. ínvois; 2. ínvɔis]. Prob. orig. *invoyes*, pl. of *invoy*, 'something sent', fr. O. Fr. *envoi*. See **envoy, voyage**. **1.** n. List of goods dispatched, with details of price &c. **2.** vb. To make an invoice of (goods &c.).

invoke, vb. trans. [1. invṓk; 2. invóuk], fr. Fr. *invoquer*, fr. Lat. *invocāre*, 'to invoke, call upon, appeal to', fr. **in-** (**I.**) & *vocāre*, 'to call'. See **vocal** & **vocation**. **1.** To call upon, address, make supplication to, for help, protection, or as witness &c.: *to invoke the gods.* **2.** To appeal to, summon, demand support from: *to invoke the power of the law.* **3.** To ask for earnestly or solemnly, implore, demand insistently: *to invoke aid, protection, vengeance* &c. **4.** To summon up, conjure up (spirits &c.).

involucre, involucrum, n. [1. ínvolûker, involûkrum; 2. ínvəljûkə, invəljûkrəm], fr. Fr., fr. Lat. *involūcrum*, 'wrapper, covering, case, envelope', fr. *involū-(tum)*, P.P. stem of *involvere*, 'to roll up.' See **involve**. **1.** (chiefly anat.) Covering, case, membranous envelope. **2.** (bot.) Group of bracts surrounding base of flower or cluster of flowers.

involuntarily, adv. [1. invóluntarili; 2. invɔ́ləntərili]. **involuntary** & **-ly**. In an involuntary manner; without deliberate exercise of the will.

involuntariness, n. [1. invóluntarines; 2. invɔ́ləntərinis]. **involuntary** & **-ness**. State or quality of being involuntary.

involuntary, adj. [1. invóluntari; 2. invɔ́ləntəri], fr. L. Lat. *involuntāri-(us)*, 'involuntary'. **in-** (**II.**) & **voluntary**. **a** Not depending on, or resulting from, exertion of the will; unintentional; automatic, instinctive; **b** not done willingly; unwished for.

involute, adj. [1. ìnvolût; 2. ìnvəljût], fr. Lat. *involūt-(um)*, P.P. type of *involvere*, 'to roll upon; to roll up, wrap up, infold, envelop'. See next word. **1.** Intricate, involved, complicated. **2.** (bot.) Having the edges rolled inwards. **3.** (zool.) Arranged in a spiral curve.

involution, n. [1. ìnvolûshun; 2. ìnvəljûʃən], fr. Lat. *involūtiōn-(em)*, 'a rolling up', fr. *involūt-(um)*, P.P. type of *involvere*, 'to roll up'. See next word & **-ion**. **1.** The act of involving; state of being involved. **2.** Something that is involute or involved; **a** inward curve or curl; **b** complication, intricacy, entanglement. **3.** (math.) Act of raising a quantity to any given power.

involve, vb. trans. [1. invólv; 2. invɔ́lv], fr. Lat. *involv-(ere)*, 'to wrap or roll up; to cover, infold, envelop, surround, entangle'; fr. **in-** (**I.**) & *volvere*, 'to roll'. See **volute**. **1.** (archaic and rare) To wrap up, roll up, envelop, enfold: '*And Night with sable Clouds involves the Main*' (Dryden, 'Æneid', III. 227). **2. a** To surround, entangle in, mix up with, so as to hamper movement: *to get involved with one's fishing-line*; **b** (fig.) to surround, entangle with, draw into, overwhelm &c.: *involved in intrigues, debt, disaster.* **3.** To imply, have as necessary or logical consequence; to entail: *lavish hospitality involves great expense on the giver; to accept the appointment would involve living in London.*

involved, adj. [1. invólvd; 2. invɔ́lvd], fr. P.P. of prec. **1.** (of thought and expression) Complicated; lacking in clearness, obscure; confused, muddled. **2.** (of pecuniary affairs) Embarrassed.

involvement, n. [1. invólvment; 2. invɔ́lvmənt]. Prec. & **-ment**. **1.** The act of involving; state of being involved. **2.** That in which one is involved; embarrassment, perplexity, difficulty.

invulnerability, n. [1. invùlnerabíliti; 2. invàlnərəbíliti], fr. Lat. *invulnerābil-(is)*, 'invulnerable'. See next word & **-ity**. Quality of being invulnerable.

invulnerable, adj. [1. invúlnerabl; 2. inválnərəbl], fr. Lat. *invulnerābil-(is)*, 'invulnerable'. **in-** (**II.**) & **vulnerable**. **a** Not capable of being wounded; **b** (fig.) not liable to injury; proof against attack; unassailable.

invulnerably, adv. Prec. & **-ly**. In an invulnerable manner.

inward, adj. & n. [1. ínward; 2. ínwəd]. O.E. *innanweard*, M.E. *inneward*, fr. *innan*, 'within'. See **in** (**II.**) & **-ward**. **1.** adj. **a** (in both physical and non-material senses) Situated within; internal, inner: *the inward parts, organs; inward thoughts*; **b** towards the inside: *an inward curve*; **c** not outward or material; mental, spiritual: *inward nature.* **2.** n. (colloq., gen. [1. ínardz; 2. ínədz]). Entrails, bowels, the guts: *a pain in the in'ards*; internal organs of animals as food: *I can't eat tripe nor any sort of in'ards.*

inward(s), adv. [1. ínward(z); 2. ínwəd(z)], fr. prec. **a** Towards the inside; **b** in the mind, heart, soul.

inwardly, adv. [1. ínwardli; 2. ínwədli]. **inward** & **-ly**. **a** In or towards the inside, centre, interior; **b** so as not to have outward expression; secretly, to oneself; **c** in the inner being, mind, soul.

inwardness, n. [1. ínwardnes; 2. ínwədnis]. **inward** & **-ness**. **1.** Essential, inherent character or meaning; real nature, true quality. Phr. *the true inwardness.* **2.** The state of being inward; spirituality.

inweave, enweave, vb. trans. [1. inwḗv; 2. inwív]. **in** (**II.**) & **weave**. (lit. and fig.) To weave into, intertwine, work in.

inwrought, adj. [1. inrawt, inráwt; 2. inrɔ̄t, inrɔ́t]. **in** (**I.**) & **wrought**, P.P. of **work**. **1.** (of pattern, design) Worked into, forming an adornment on, a fabric; interwoven. **2.** (of material, fabric, background) Having a design worked into or impressed upon it. **3.** (fig.) Closely blended, interwoven.

inyala, n. [1. inyáhla; 2. injálə]. Native Bantu name. A harnessed antelope or bushbuck of Central Africa.

iodic, adj. [1. iódik; 2. aiɔ́dik]. See **iodine** & **-ic**. Of, pertaining to, containing, iodine: *iodic acid*, compound of iodine and oxygen, formed by treating iodine with nitric acid.

iodide, n. [1. íodīd; 2. áioudaid]. See prec. & **-ide**. (chem.) Compound of iodine with another element or radical, as *iodide of potassium*, used medicinally, *iodide of silver*, in photography &c.

iodine, n. [1. íodīn, -ēn; 2. áioudain, -īn], fr. Fr. *iode*, fr. Gk. *ioeidḗs*, 'like the violet', fr. *ío-(n)*, 'violet' (see **iolite**), & *eidēs*, 'like' (q.v. under **-oid**), fr. the colour of its fumes. A non-metallic element widely diffused in nature but seldom in the free state; obtained from the ashes of seaweed and from the mother-liquor of Chile saltpetre; used in medicine as an antiseptic, also in photography and dyeing.

iodism, n. [1. íodizm; 2. áioudizəm]. See prec. & **-ism**. Iodine poisoning.

iodize, vb. trans. [1. íodīz; 2. áioudaiz]. See **iodine** & **-ize**. To treat with, impregnate with, expose to fumes of, iodine.

iodoform, n. [1. iódoform; 2. aióudəfɔ̄m]. See **iodine** & **formic**. A crystalline compound of iodine used as an antiseptic.

iolite, n. [1. íolīt; 2. áiəlait], fr. Gk. *ío-(n)*, 'violet' (fr. **wion*, etymol. doubtful, cogn. w. **violet**), & **-lite**. A blue or violet-coloured mineral.

ion, n. [1. íon; 2. áiən], fr. Gk. *ión*, neut. sing. Pres. Part. of *iénai*, 'to go', cogn. w. Lat. *ī-re*, 'to go', see **itinerate**. (phys.) A particle of matter, moving in an electric field, either in a gas or a liquid, carrying an electric charge. See **electron, ionize**.

-ion, suff. representing Lat. *-iōn-(em)*, forming ns. denoting state, condition, action, fr. adjs. (*union, potion*); fr. present stems of vbs. (*region, legion, religion*); or, most commonly, fr. P.P. stems of vbs., often through O. Fr. (*mission, question, fashion, lesion, flexion, inflation, nutrition* &c.).

Ionian, adj. & n. [1. īṓnian; 2. aióuniən], fr. Lat. *Iōni-(us)*, 'Ionian', fr. Gk. *Iṓnios* & **-an**. **1.** adj. **a** Of, belonging to, Ionia; **b** (mus.) *Ionian mode*, one of the six mediaeval, ecclesiastical modes. **2.** n. Member of one of the chief divisions of the ancient Greeks, originally settled in Attica and the neighbourhood.

Ionic, adj. [1. iónik; 2. aiɔ́nik], fr. Lat., fr. Gk. *Iōnik-(ós)*, 'Ionian'. See prec. & **-ic**. Of, pertaining to, originating in, Ionia; esp. **a** *Ionic dialect*, that spoken in Ionia, including Attica and most of the Aegean islands; **b** (archit.) *Ionic order*, characterized by fluted columns, and capitals with four spiral scrolls; **c** (prosody) *Ionic a majore*, foot consisting of two long followed by two short syllables; *Ionic a minore*, with two short followed by two long syllables.

ionization, n. [1. ìonīzáshun; 2. àiənaizéiʃən]. See next word & **-ation**. The state of a liquid (electrolyte) or gas through which an electric current is passing.

ionize, vb. trans. [1. íonīz; 2. áiənaiz]. **ion** & **-ize**. To charge the particles or ions of a liquid (electrolyte) with electricity; also applied to gases.

-ior (**I.**), suff. [1. ier; 2. iə]. Variant of **-iour**, later than this, & influenced by Lat. spelling, as *warrior*.

-ior (**II.**), suff. representing Lat. compar. ending *-ior*: *superior, interior, junior* &c.

iota, n. [1. īṓta; 2. aióutə]. Gk. *iōta*, loan-word fr. Phoenician; cp. Heb. *yōd* & cp. **jot**. **1.** The Greek letter *i*. **2.** Insignificant part, jot, atom: *not an iota of truth in this statement.*

iotacism, n. [1. íōtasizəm; 2. aióutəsizəm], fr. Lat. *iōtacism-(us)*, fr. Gk. *iōtakismós*, fr. prec. **1.** Too frequent use of the Greek letter *i*, substitution of this letter for others.

2. Greek tendency to level a number of originally different vowels and diphthongs under the sound (ī); ē, ei, oi, all underwent this change.

IOU, n. [1. ī ō ū; 2. ái ou jû], = I owe you. Formal acknowledgement of debt, consisting of signed paper with these letters and statement of sum owed.

-iour, suff. [1. ier; 2. iə], representing O. Fr. *-eour*, *-ieur*, forming ns. denoting the agent: *saviour*, *paviour*. Chiefly fr. Lat. ns. in *-or*. See **-our**.

-ious, adj. suff. [1. (i)us; 2. (i)əs], representing Lat. *-iōsus*, Fr. *-ieux*, w. sense 'characterized by, full of, exhibiting', found in a words representing Lat. adjs. in *-iōsus*, formed fr. ns. ending in *-ia(e)*, *-ius*, *-ium*, *-io*, *-ies*: *delicious, furious, precious, fastidious, prodigious, religious, factious*; or by anal., fr. ns. in *-a*: *curious*; **b** new formations fr. Lat. adjs. in *-ius*: *conscious, dubious*; or *-us*: *delirious*; **c** new formations fr. Lat. ns. in *-io*, *-ia*: *rebellious, penurious*. See also **-ous**.

ipecacuanha, often abbr. **ipecac.**, n. [1. ípekàkūána, ípekak; 2. ípikækjuǽnə, ípikæk]. Port., fr. native Brazilian word. Root of a S. American herbaceous or shrubby plant, used as an emetic and expectorant, esp. in cases of bronchitis and laryngitis.

ipse dixit, n. [1. ípse díksit; 2. ípsi díksit]. Lat., 'he himself has said it'. Dogmatic statement, assertion; dictum.

ipso facto, adv. [1. ípsō fáktō; 2. ípsou fǽktou]. Lat., 'by the fact itself'. By the fact itself, by that very fact.

ir- = **in-** (**I., II.**) before *-r*.

iradé, n. [1. iráhde; 2. irǽde]. Turkish, fr. Arab. *iradah*, 'will'. Written decree of Sultan of Turkey.

Iranian, adj. & n. [1. īrānian; 2. airéiniən]. Pers. *Irān*, 'Persia', & **-ian**. Cp. **Aryan**. **1.** adj. **a** Of, pertaining to, Persia; **b** belonging to that branch of the Aryan languages which includes Old Persian, Zend, and their descendants. **2.** n. **a** Member of Persian race; **b** Iranian language.

irascibility, n. [1. iràsibíliti; 2. iræ̀sibíliti], fr. Lat. *īrascibil-(is)*, 'irascible'. See next word & **-ity**. The quality of being irascible.

irascible, adj. [1. irásibl; 2. irǽsibl], fr. Lat. *īrascibil-(is)*, 'irascible', fr. *īrasc-(i)*, 'to be angry', fr. *īra*, 'anger'. See **ire**. Easily angered; irritable, petulant, crusty.

irascibly, adv. Prec. & **-ly**. In an irascible manner.

irate, adj. [1. īrāt; 2. airéit], fr. Lat. *īrāt-(us)*, 'angry, violent, furious', fr. P.P. of *īrasci*, 'to grow angry'. See **ire**. Angry, enraged, wrathful.

ire, n. [1. īr; 2. áiə], fr. O. Fr. fr. Lat. *īra*, 'anger', fr. base *is-*. Cogn. w. Gk. *oîma*, 'impetus', fr. **oisma*, cp. *oistros*, 'gadfly; frenzy, madness, vehement impulse' (see **oestrus**); Scrt. *ēsati*, 'urges', *isyati*, 'sets in motion', *isirás*, 'lively, strong'; Gk. *ierós*, 'strong'; O.N. *eisa*, 'hasten forward'; O.E. *(of)-ost*, O.S. *(ob)-ast*, fr. **-aist*, 'haste, eagerness'. (chiefly poet.) Anger, wrath.

ireful, adj. [1. īrfool; 2. áiəful]. Prec. & **-ful**. Wrathful, angry.

irefully, adv. Prec. & **-ly**. In an ireful manner.

irenic(al), adj. [1. īrḗnik(l), īrénik(l); 2. airíːnik(l), airénik(l)], fr. Gk. *eirēnik-(ós)*, 'peaceful', fr. *eirḗnē*, 'peace', etymol. uncertain, & **-ic** (& **-al**). **a** Of the nature of peace; peaceful; **b** tending towards, promoting, peace; pacific.

irenicon, n. See **eirenicon**.

iridescence, n. [1. iridésens; 2. iridésəns]. See next word & **-ce**. The state or quality of being iridescent.

iridescent, adj. [1. iridésent; 2. iridésənt], fr. Gk. *irid-*, stem of *iris*, 'rainbow'. See **iris** & **-escent**. Showing the colours of the rainbow; changing in colour as light falls from different angles.

iridium, n. [1. irídium; 2. irídiəm], fr. Gk. *irid-*, stem of *iris*, 'rainbow'. See next word & **-ium**. Hard, silvery, metallic element, related to platinum.

iris, n. [1. íris; 2. áiəris]. Gk. *îris*, 'rainbow', fr. **wīrid-s*. Orig. prob., 'the bent, curved thing', & fr. base **wi-*, 'to bend, twist'; cp. Lat. *viēre*, 'to bend, twist together, weave'. See further cognates under **viti-** & **withy**. **1.** Coloured portion of the eye pierced by the pupil in the centre. **2.** Genus of plants, called also flags, with sword-shaped leaves and stiff, erect stems with large flowers, usually blue, purple, yellow, or white.

Irish, adj. & n. [1. írish; 2. áiəriʃ]. M.E. *Irisch*, fr. O.E. *Ir-(as)*, 'the Irish', fr. Irish *Eire*, 'Ireland', & **-ish**. **1.** adj. Of, pertaining to, originating in, Ireland; *Irish point*, a kind of point-lace; *Irish stew*, mutton cutlets boiled with potatoes and onions. **2.** n. **a** The language of the Irish; **b** *the Irish*, people of Ireland.

Irishism, n. [1. írishizm; 2. áiəriʃizəm]. Prec. & **-ism**. Idiom characteristic of the Irish language, or of English as spoken in Ireland; e.g. *I'm after having my dinner*, I've just had it.

Irishize, vb. trans. [1. írishīz; 2. áiəriʃaiz]. **Irish** & **-ize**. To make Irish, give Irish character to.

Irishman, n. [1. írishman; 2. áiəriʃmən]. **Irish** & **man**. Native of Ireland.

Irish terrier, n. A large breed of terrier, with rough, wiry coat of a reddish-brown colour.

Irish wolfhound, n. A large, heavily built, rough-coated breed of hound, resembling a deer-hound.

Irishwoman, n. [1. írishwoòman; 2. áiəriʃwùmən]. **Irish** & **woman**. Woman of Irish birth.

iritis, n. [1. irítis; 2. aiəráitis]. **iris** & **-itis**. Inflammation of iris of the eye.

irk, vb. trans. [1. ërk; 2. ʌ̄k]. M.E. *irken*, 'to be distasteful, to weary'. Origin doubtful. (archaic) To weary, fatigue, be tiresome to, worry; esp. in Phr. *it irks me, him* &c.

irksome, adj. [1. ërksum; 2. ʌ́ksəm]. Prec. & **-some**. Wearisome, tedious, toilsome, tiresome; oppressive.

irksomely, adv. Prec. & **-ly**. In an irksome manner.

irksomeness, n. See prec. & **-ness**. The quality of being irksome.

iron (**I.**), n. [1. íern; 2. áiən]. O.E. *īren* (& *īsen*), M.E. *īren*, & rarely, *īsen*; cp. also O.E. *isern*, O.S., O.H.G. *īsarn*; Goth. *eisarn*. These appear to be all cogn. w. Goth. *ais*, 'brass, money'; O.H.G. *ēr*, O.E. *ār*, *ǣr*, 'brass, copper' (see **ore**), & further w. Lat. *aes*, 'copper ore' &c. The base prob. meant orig. 'to shine, glow', & is seen also, in extended form, in Lat. *aedes*, 'hearth; house', q.v. under **aedile**, **edify**, & Lat. *aestas*, 'summer heat' (see **aestival**). **1.** A silvery, malleable, metallic element, very hard and tough; the most common metal used, with an admixture of carbon in various proportions, to make tools, weapons, utensils &c. Phrs. *to strike while the iron is hot*, act promptly, and while circumstances are favourable; *to rule with a rod of iron*, with extreme severity; *as hard as iron*, very hard, very severe; *man of iron*, hard, unyielding man; *will of iron*, inflexible will; *muscles of iron*, very hard muscles. **2.** Tool, implement, instrument, made of iron; often in compounds: *grappling-iron, fire-irons, stirrup-iron* &c.; specif. **a** *irons*, fetters, shackles; **b** tool with smooth, flat surface for smoothing linen &c.; Phrs. *to have a number of irons in the fire*, have many enterprises afoot at one time; *too many irons in the fire*, excessive number and variety of projects; **c** (golf) club with iron head laid back. **3.** Preparation of iron used in medicine as tonic.

iron (**II.**), adj., fr. prec. **1.** Made of iron; consisting wholly or chiefly of iron: *iron bars* &c. Phrs. *iron horse*, railway engine; *iron ration*, emergency ration. **2.** (fig.) Like iron; very strong, firm, unyielding, hard: *an iron will, constitution, grip* &c.

iron (**III.**), vb. trans., fr. **iron** (**I.**). **1.** To smooth (linen &c.) with a heated iron. **2.** To put into irons, fetter, shackle. **3.** To furnish, cover, with iron, put iron parts to.

iron age, n. Period in human history, succeeding bronze age, characterized by the use of iron implements and weapons.

iron-bark, n. Kind of eucalyptus tree with solid bark.

iron-bound, adj. **1. a** Bound with iron; **b** (in fig. sense) inflexible, unyielding. **2.** (of coast) Rugged, rocky, edged with cliffs.

ironclad, adj. & n. [1. íernklad; 2. áiənklæd]. **1.** adj. Covered with, protected by, iron; armoured. **2.** n. Vessel protected by iron plates.

iron-foundry, n. Establishment for the production of cast-iron.

iron-grey, adj. Of the colour of newly broken iron.

ironic(al), adj. [1. īrónik(l); 2. airɔ́nik(l)], fr. Gk. *eirōnik-(ós)*, 'ironic', fr. *eirōn-(eía)*, 'dissimulation'. See **irony** & **-ic**. Of, pertaining to, given to, expressing, irony.

ironically, adv. Prec. & **-ly**. In an ironical manner.

ironing, n. [1. íerning; 2. áiəniŋ]. **iron** (**III.**) & **-ing** (**I.**). **1.** The process of smoothing linen &c. with a heated iron. **2.** Clothes, linen &c., to be ironed.

ironing-board, n. Smooth, cloth-covered board on which clothes &c. are spread for ironing.

ironist, n. [1. íronist; 2. áiərənist], fr. Gk. *eirōn*, 'dissembler'. See **irony** & **-ist**. One given to the use of irony.

ironmaster, n. [1. íernmàhster; 2. áiənmàstə]. Manufacturer of articles and appliances of iron.

ironmonger, n. [1. íernmùngger; 2. áiənmàŋgə]. Dealer in iron and other metal goods.

ironmongery, n. [1. íernmùnggeri; 2. áiənmàŋgəri]. Iron and other metal goods.

iron-mould, n. & vb. trans. & intrans. **1.** n. Stain made on textiles by iron-rust or ink. **2.** vb. To stain with iron-mould.

ironsides, n. [1. íernsīdz; 2. áiənsàidz]. Man of courage and resolution; esp. (pl.) Cromwell's troopers.

ironstone, n. [1. íernstōn; 2. áiənstoun]. Rock or mineral containing iron.

ironwork, n. [1. íernwërk; 2. áiənwʌ̀k]. Iron parts of a structure; castings, mouldings &c. made of iron.

ironworks, n. [1. íernwërks; 2. áiənwʌ̀ks]. Establishment for smelting iron or making iron goods.

irony (**I.**), adj. [1. íerni; 2. áiəni]. **iron** (**I.**) & **-y**. Made of, consisting of, like, iron.

irony (**II.**), n. [1. íruni: 2. áiərəni], fr. Lat. *īrōnīa*, 'irony', fr. Gk. *eirōneia*, 'irony, assumed ignorance', fr. *eírōn*, 'dissembler', either fr. base **wer-*, 'to say', as in Gk. *eírō*, 'I say', fr. **werjo*, & cogn. w. **word**; or for **erjōn* for **werjōn*, fr. base seen in Lat. *errāre*, 'to go astray, err' &c. See **err**, **error**. In the first case the original meaning would be '*said*, but not meant'; in the latter 'that which leads astray'. **1.** Use of words, with humorous or sarcastic intention, so that the meaning is the direct opposite of what is actually said: e.g. *this is a nice, pleasant sort of weather* = the weather is perfectly detestable. **2.** Course of events, combination of circumstances, line of conduct, the result of which is the direct opposite of what is, or might be, expected, as though directed by malice, or the perversity of fate, and produced in mockery; chiefly, *irony of fate, circumstances*; *life's ironies*. **3.** *Socratic irony*, assumption of ignorance for the purpose of confounding an opponent in dispute.

irradiance, n. [1. irādians; 2. iréidiəns]. **ir-** = **in-** (**I.**) & **radiance**. The quality or state of being irradiant.

irradiant, adj. [1. irādiant; 2. iréidiənt], fr. Lat. *irradiant-(em)*, Pres. Part. of *irradi-(āre)*, 'to illumine; to cast forth rays of light'. See next word. Radiating light; luminous.

irradiate, vb. trans. & intrans. [1. irādiāt; 2. iréidieit], fr. Lat. *irradiāt-(um)*, P.P. type of *irradiāre*, 'to illumine; to cast forth rays of light'. See **ir-** = **in-** (I.) & **radiate**. **A.** trans. **1.** To radiate light upon, shine upon, illumine. **2.** (fig.) **a** To throw intellectual light upon, make clear, illuminate; **b** to light up, give sweetness, animation, to: *a face irradiated by a smile.* **3.** To diffuse, scatter, shed: *to irradiate goodness and happiness.* **B.** intrans. To give out light.

irradiation, n. [1. irādiáshun; 2. irèidiéiʃən]. Prec. & **-ion**. **1.** (lit. and fig.) **a** The act of irradiating; **b** state of being irradiated; **c** ray of light. **2.** (phys.) Apparent enlargement of bright object seen against a dark background.

irradiative, adj. [1. irádiātiv; 2. iréidieitiv]. **irradiate** & **-ive**. Having the property of irradiating; illuminating.

irrational (I.), adj. [1. iráshunal; 2. iræʃənəl], fr. Lat. *irratiōnāl-(is)*, 'without reason, irrational'. **ir-** = **in-** (II.) & **rational**. **1.** Without power of reasoning: *man sometimes behaves like an irrational animal.* **2.** Contrary to reason; not in accordance with, or resulting from, reasoning; illogical; foolish, extravagant: *such conduct is quite irrational.* **3.** (math., of number) Not capable of being expressed by integer, or by vulgar fraction; surd.

irrational (II.), n., fr. prec. (math.) Irrational number.

irrationality, n. [1. iràshunáliti; 2. iræʃənæliti]. Prec. & **-ity**. Quality of being irrational.

irrationalize, vb. trans. [1. iráshunalīz; 2. iræʃənəlaiz]. **irrational** & **-ize**. To make irrational.

irrationally, adv. [1. iráshunali; 2. iræʃənəli]. See prec. & **-ly**. In an irrational manner.

irreclaimable, adj. [1. ìreklámabl; 2. ìrikléiməbl]. **ir-** = **in-** (II.) & **reclaimable**. Not capable of being reclaimed.

irreclaimably, adv. Prec. & **-ly**. In an irreclaimable manner.

irrecognizable, adj. [1. irèkognízabl; 2. irèkəgnáizəbl]. **ir-** = **in-** (II.) & **recognizable**. Not capable of being recognized; unrecognizable.

irreconcilability, n. [1. irèkonsīlabíliti; 2. irèkənsailəbíliti]. **ir-** = **in-** (II.) & **reconcilability**. Quality of being irreconcilable.

irreconcilable, adj. & n. [1. irèkonsílabl; 2. irèkənsáiləbl]. **ir-** = **in-** (II.) & **reconcilable**. **1.** adj. **a** (of persons &c.) Not capable of being reconciled, permanently hostile; intransigent; **b** (of facts, ideas &c.) not capable of being harmonized; inconsistent, conflicting, incompatible. **2.** n. (in politics &c.) One who will not agree to any plan but his own, who will not come to a compromise; an intransigent.

irreconcilableness, n. Prec. & **-ness**. Quality of being irreconcilable.

irreconcilably, adv. See prec. & **-ly**. In an irreconcilable manner; to an irreconcilable degree.

irrecoverable, adj. [1. ìrekúverabl; 2. ìrikávərəbl]. **ir-** = **in-** (II.) & **recoverable**. Not capable of being recovered or got back, specif., of debt; not to be redeemed, or regained; irretrievable.

irrecoverably, adv. Prec. & **-ly**. In an irrecoverable manner; beyond recall.

irrecusable, adj. [1. ìrekúzabl; 2. ìrikjúzəbl], fr. L. Lat. *irrecūsābil-(is)*, 'not to be refused', fr. **ir-** = **in-** (II.) & *recūs-(āre)*, 'to refuse'. See **recusant** & **-able**. Not to be refused or rejected; that must be accepted.

irredeemable, adj. [1. ìredémabl; 2. ìridíməbl]. **ir-** = **in-** (II.) & **redeemable**. **1.** Not to be redeemed, beyond redemption, irreclaimable. **2.** **a** (of government loans &c.) Not to be terminated by repayment; **b** (of paper-notes &c.) not to be converted into coin.

irredeemably, adv. Prec. & **-ly**. In an irredeemable manner.

irredentism, n. [1. iredéntizm; 2. ìridéntizəm]. See next word & **-ism**. Policy of the irredentists.

irredentist, n. [1. ìredéntist; 2. ìridéntist], fr. Ital. *irredentist(a)*, fr. *(Italia) irredenta*, 'unredeemed (Italy)', fr. **ir-** = **in-** (II.) & *redempt-(a)*, P.P. type of *redimere*, 'to redeem'. See **redeem**. Member of Italian political party which demands the return to, and inclusion with, Italy of all Italian-speaking areas.

irreducibility, n. [1. ìredūsibíliti; 2. ìridjūsibíliti]. **ir-** = **in-** (II.) & **reducibility**. State or quality of being irreducible.

irreducible, adj. [1. ìredúsibl; 2. ìridjúsibl]. **ir-** = **in-** (II.) & **reducible**. **1.** Not capable of being reduced; incapable of being brought to desired form, arrangement, state, degree &c. **2.** Not capable of being lessened, diminished: *irreducible minimum*, smallest amount, lowest degree, to which anything can be reduced; point beyond which further reduction would render it useless, or unacceptable.

irrefragable, adj. [1. iréfragabl; 2. iréfrəgəbl], fr. L. Lat. *irrefrāgābil-(is)*, 'irrefragable', fr. **ir-** = **in-** (II.) & *refrāg-(āri)*, 'to oppose, resist', fr. **re-** & *frāg-(or)*, 'noise, crash, sound'. The base *frāg-* is prob. connected w. *frangere*, 'to break' (see **fraction**), & w. Engl. **break** (I.). Not capable of being refuted; incontrovertible, unanswerable; not to be denied or gainsaid.

irrefragably, adv. Prec. & **-ly**. In an irrefragable manner.

irrefrangible, adj. [1. ìrefránjibl; 2. ìrifrændžibl]. **ir-** = **in** (II.) & **refrangible**. **1.** (of law &c.) Not capable of being broken; inviolable. **2.** (opt.) Not capable of being refracted.

irrefutability, n. [1. ìrefūtabíliti; 2. ìrifjūtəbíliti], fr. L. Lat. *irrefūtābil-(is)*, 'irrefutable'. See next word & **-ity**. State or quality of being irrefutable.

irrefutable, adj. [1. ìrefútabl, iréfūtabl; 2. ìrifjútəbl, iréfjutəbl], fr. L. Lat. *irrefūtābil-(is)*, 'irrefutable'. **ir-** = **in-** (II.) & **refutable**. Not capable of being disproved; indisputable.

irrefutably, adv. Prec. & **-ly**. In an irrefutable manner.

irregular (I.), adj. [1. irégūlar; 2. irégjulə]. **ir-** = **in-** (II.) & **regular**. Not regular. Various specific uses: **1.** Not in accordance with rule, not conforming to recognized standards; **a** (of act) not in accordance with law, not statutory; informal; invalid: *an irregular marriage*; **b** (of conduct) disorderly, undisciplined; not in accordance with moral principles; **c** (eccles.) *irregular orders*, not lawfully conferred; **d** not under the regulations, not trained according to, or fulfilling the requirements of, some particular, recognized body: *irregular troops.* **2.** (of form, arrangement &c.) Not symmetrical; uneven, not according to a systematic plan; broken, out of order, not evenly disposed or distributed: *an irregular outline, irregular group of buildings, trees* &c. **3.** (gram.) not inflected in normal way; specif., *irregular verb*, one that is anomalous in the way it forms its tenses; popular name in English for a strong verb.

irregular (II.), n., fr. prec. A member of an irregular military force.

irregularity, n. [1. irègūláriti; 2. irègjulæriti]. **irregular** & **-ity**. **1.** State or quality of being irregular; divergence from normal conditions; lack of symmetry, order, method, constancy of recurrence &c. **2.** Something that is irregular; **a** irregular action, conduct, method; **b** unevenness, roughness.

irregularly, adv. [1. irégūlarli; 2. irégjuləli]. **irregular** (I.) & **-ly**. In an irregular manner.

irrelative, adj. [1. irélativ; 2. irélətiv]. **ir-** = **in-** (II.) & **relative**. Not relative; unconnected, unrelated; without relations.

irrelatively, adv. Prec. & **-ly**. In an irrelative manner.

irrelevance, -cy, n. [1. irélevans(i); 2. iréləvəns(i)]. **ir-** = **in-** (II.) & **relevance**. **1.** State or quality of being irrelevant. **2.** Something that is irrelevant; irrelevant remark, question, statement &c.

irrelevant, adj. [1. irélevant; 2. iréləvənt]. **ir-** = **in-** (II.) & **relevant**. Off the point, not relevant, not applicable to matter in hand, not pertinent.

irrelevantly, adv. Prec. & **-ly**. In an irrelevant manner.

irreligion, n. [1. ìrelíjun; 2. ìrilídžən], fr. L. Lat. *irreligiōn-(em)*, 'irreligion'. **ir-** = **in-** (II.) & **religion**. Indifference, opposition, hostility, to religion.

irreligious, adj. [1. ìrelíjus; 2. ìrilídžəs], fr. L. Lat. *irreligiōs-(us)*, 'impious'. **ir-** = **in-** (II.) & **religious**. **a** (of person &c.) Indifferent to, hostile to, religion; **b** (of thought, action, &c.) not in accordance, out of harmony, with religion; impious.

irreligiously, adv. Prec. & **-ly**. In an irreligious manner.

irremeable, adj. [1. irémeable; 2. irímiəbl]. Fr., fr. Lat. *irremeābilis*, 'not returning'; **ir-**, **re-**, and stem of *meāre*, 'to go', see **meatus**, and **-ble**. From which there is no return; rare and poet.: '*My three brave brothers in one mournful day All trod the dark, irremeable way*' (Pope, 'Iliad').

irremediable, adj. [1. ìremédiabl; 2. ìrimídiəbl], fr. L. Lat. *irremediābil-(is)*, 'incurable'. **ir-** = **in-** (II.) & **remediable**. Not capable of being remedied or redressed; irreparable.

irremediably, adv. Prec. & **-ly**. So as to be irremediable.

irremissible, adj. [1. ìremísibl; 2. ìrimísibl], fr. L. Lat. *irremissibil-(is)*, 'unpardonable'. **ir-** = **in-** (II.) & **remissible**. Not capable of being remitted, not to be excused; unpardonable.

irremissibly, adv. Prec. & **-ly**. In an irremissible manner.

irremovability, n. [1. ìremōōvabíliti; 2. ìrimūvəbíliti]. **ir-** = **in-** (II.) & **removability**. State or condition of being irremovable.

irremovable, adj. [1. ìremōōvabl; 2. ìrimúvəbl]. **ir-** = **in-** (II.) & **removable**. (lit. and fig.) Not capable of being removed, not to be blotted out; specif., not liable to removal from office, permanent.

irremovably, adv. Prec. & **-ly**. In an irremovable manner.

irreparable, adj. [1. iréparabl; 2. irépərəbl], fr. L. Lat. *irreparābil-(is)*, 'irreparable'. **ir-** = **in-** (II.) & **reparable**. **a** Not capable of being repaired; incapable of being restored to original condition, or of being made good; past cure: *irreparable damage, injury*; **b** not be rectified, recovered from; irretrievable: *irreparable disaster, loss* &c.

irreparableness, n. Prec. & **-ness**. The state or quality of being irreparable.

irreparably, adv. See prec. & **-ly**. To such a degree &c. as to be irreparable.

irreplaceable, adj. [1. ìreplásabl; 2. ìripléisəbl]. **ir-** = **in-** (II.) & **replaceable**. Not capable of being replaced; leaving nothing, no one, to take the place of.

irrepressible, adj. [1. ìreprésibl; 2. ìriprésibl]. **ir-** = **in-** (II.) & **repress** & **-ible**. Not capable of being repressed, restrained, controlled; inextinguishable: *an irrepressible child; irrepressible laughter, spirits* &c.

irrepressibly, adv. Prec. & **-ly**. In an irrepressible manner.

irreproachability, n. [1. ìreprōchabíliti; 2. ìriproutʃəbíliti]. See next word & **-ity**. State or quality of being irreproachable.

irreproachable, adj. [1. ìrepróchabl; 2. ìripróutʃəbl], fr. Fr. *irréprochable*. **ir-** = **in-** (II.) & **reproach** & **-able**. Not liable to be found fault with; immaculate, blameless; above criticism, unexceptionable.

irreproachably, adv. Prec. & **-ly**. In an irreproachable manner; faultlessly.

irresistibility, n. [1. ìrezistibíliti; 2. ìrizistibíliti]. **ir-** = **in-** (II.) & **resistibility**. State or quality of being irresistible.

irresistible, adj. [1. ìrezístibl; 2. ìrizístibl]. **ir-** = **in** (II.) & **resistible**. **a** (of physical force) Overpoweringly great, not to be withstood; carrying all before it; **b** (of emotion, or emotional influence) overmastering: *ir-*

resistible desire, impulse; overpoweringly attractive: *irresistible charms*; **c** carrying intellectual conviction; compelling assent to, concurrence with, its cogency: *an irresistible argument*; *irresistible proofs* &c.

irresistibleness, n. Prec. & **-ness**. Property, quality, of being irresistible.

irresistibly, adv. See prec. & **-ly**. In an irresistible manner.

irresolute, adj. [1. irézolūt; 2. irézəljūt]. **ir-**=**in-** (**II.**) & **resolute**. Wanting in resolution, firmness, decision; hesitating, vacillating, undecided.

irresolutely, adv. Prec. & **-ly**. In an irresolute manner.

irresoluteness, n. See prec. & **-ness**. State or quality of being irresolute.

irresolution, n. [1. irèzolúshun; 2. irèzəljúʃən]. **ir-**=**in-** (**II.**) & **resolution**. State or quality of being irresolute; lack of decision.

irresolvable, adj. [1. irezólvabl; 2. irizólvəbl]. **ir-**=**in-** (**II.**) & **solvable**. **a** Not capable of being resolved, analysed, broken up, into parts; **b** not capable of being solved by the intellect.

irrespective, adj. [1. irespéktiv; 2. irispéktiv]. **ir-**=**in-** (**II.**) & **respective**. (followed by *of*) Without regard or reference to, independent of; not taking into account, putting aside: *irrespective of other claims*; *irrespective of what has been said*; also used as quasi-adverb: *done irrespective of other things*.

irrespectively, adv. Prec. & **-ly**. In an irrespective manner.

irresponsibility, n. [1. irresponsibíliti; 2. irispɔnsibíliti]. **ir-**=**in-** (**II.**) & **responsibility**. Quality or state of being irresponsible; freedom from responsibility.

irresponsible, adj. [1. irespónsibl; 2. irispɔ́nsibl]. **ir-**=**in-** (**II.**) & **responsible**. **a** Not responsible, not accountable, or answerable (for); **b** not feeling, lacking sense of, incapable of taking, responsibility; not based on sense of responsibility, unauthorized, arbitrary: *an irresponsible person*; *irresponsible conduct, action*.

irresponsibly, adv. Prec. & **-ly**. In an irresponsible manner.

irresponsive, adj. [1. irespónsiv; 2. irispɔ́nsiv]. **ir-**=**in-** (**II.**) & **responsive**. Giving no response to; not able, not inclined, to respond.

irresponsively, adv. Prec. & **-ly**. In an irresponsive manner.

irresponsiveness, n. See prec. & **-ness**. State or quality of being irresponsive.

irretentive, adj. [1. ireténtiv; 2. iriténtiv]. **ir-**=**in-** (**II.**) & **retentive**. Lacking power to retain.

irretentiveness, n. Prec. & **-ness**. Quality of being irretentive.

irretrievability, n. [1. iretrēvabíliti; 2. iritrīvəbíliti]. **ir-**=**in-** (**II.**) & **retrievability**. Quality of being irretrievable.

irretrievable, adj. [1. iretrévabl; 2. iritrívəbl]. **ir-**=**in-** (**II.**) & **retrievable**. Not capable of being recovered, restored, remedied, made good; irreparable.

irretrievably, adv. Prec. & **-ly**. In an irretrievable manner.

irreverence, n. [1. iréverens; 2. irévərəns]. **ir-**=**in-** (**II.**) & **reverence**. **1.** State or quality of being irreverent. **2.** Irreverent frame of mind; irreverent conduct or utterance.

irreverent, adj. [1. iréverent; 2. irévərənt], fr. Lat. *irreverent-(em)*, 'disrespectful, irreverent'; **ir-**=**in-** (**II.**) & **reverent**. Feeling, exhibiting, irreverence; esp. showing no veneration for sacred things, or respect for the noble and sublime.

irreverential, adj. [1. irèverénshal; 2. irèvərénʃl]. Prec. & **-ial**. Irreverent.

irreverently, adv. [1. iréverentli; 2. irévərəntli]. See prec. & **-ly**. In an irreverent manner.

irreversibility, n. [1. ireversibíliti; 2. irivʌ̄sibíliti]. **ir-**=**in-** (**II.**) & **reversibility**. State or quality of being irreversible.

irreversible, adj. [1. irevérsibl; 2. irivʌ́sibl]. **ir-**=**in-** (**II.**) & **reversible**. **1.** Not capable of being reversed, inverted, turned inside out; not capable of being made to work, or run, backwards. **2.** Not capable of being annulled, revoked; unalterable.

irreversibly, adv. Prec. & **-ly**. In an irreversible manner.

irrevocability, n. [1. irèvokabíliti; 2. irèvəkəbíliti]. See next word & **-ity**. The state or quality of being irrevocable.

irrevocable, adj. [1. irévokabl; 2. irévəkəbl], fr. Lat. *irrevocābil-(is)*, 'irrevocable'; **ir-**=**in-** (**II.**) & **revocable**. Not capable of being recalled, beyond recall; not to be annulled; final, unalterable.

irrevocableness, n. Prec. & **-ness**. Irrevocability.

irrevocably, adv. See prec. & **-ly**. In an irrevocable manner.

irrigable, adj. [1. írigabl; 2. írigəbl]. See next word & **-able**. (of land &c.) Capable of being irrigated.

irrigate, vb. trans. [1. írigāt; 2. írigeit], fr. Lat. *irrigāt-(um)*, P.P. type of *irrigāre*, 'to convey, conduct, water to; to water, irrigate; to wet, moisten; to refresh, nourish', fr. **ir-**=**in-** (**I.**) & *rigāre*, 'to wet, moisten, bedew', possibly cogn. w. **rain**. **1. a** To water, make fertile by watering: *a land irrigated by many streams*; **b** to convey water to (land) by system of artificial channels, ditches: *to irrigate the desert or karoo*. **2.** (med.) To wash, keep moist (wound &c.) with spray, or constant jet, of water.

irrigation, n. [1. irigáshun; 2. irigéiʃən], fr. Lat. *irrigātiōn-(em)*, 'a watering, irrigating'. Prec. & **-ion**. **a** Process of irrigating; act of irrigating artificially; **b** state of being irrigated.

irrigative, adj. [1. írigativ; 2. írigətiv]. **irrigate** & **-ive**. Connected with, tending to supply, intended for, irrigation.

irriguous, adj. [1. irígūus; 2. irígjuəs], fr. Lat. *irriguus*, 'moist', see **irrigate** & **-ous**. (poet.) Moist, well watered: '*some irriguous valley*' (Milton, 'P. L.').

irritability, n. [1. iritabíliti; 2. iritəbíliti]. See next word & **-ity**. State or quality of being irritable.

irritable, adj. [1. íritabl; 2. íritəbl], fr. Lat. *irrītābil-(is)*, 'easily excited or enraged', fr. *irrīt-(āre)*, 'to excite, provoke, stimulate'. See **irritate** & **-able**. **1.** (of persons, temper) Easily angered, readily excited and exasperated; petulant, irascible, touchy. **2.** (of parts of the body, wounds &c.) Undergoing, liable to, unhealthy excitability; excessively sensitive to stimuli; inflamed, sore.

irritably, adv. Prec. & **-ly**. In an irritable manner.

irritancy (**I.**), n. [1. íritansi; 2. íritənsi], fr. Lat. *irrīt-(āre)*, 'to excite, provoke, stimulate'. **irritant** & **-cy**. State of being irritated; annoyance; that which irritates; provocation.

irritancy (**II.**), n., fr. L. Lat. *irrīt-(āre)*, 'to invalidate'. See **irritate** (**II.**) & **-ancy**. (law) Act of annulling, invalidating; state of being annulled.

irritant (**I.**), adj. & n. [1. íritant; 2. íritənt], fr. Lat. *irrītant-(em)*, Pres. Part. of *irrītāre*, 'to excite, stimulate'. See **irritate** (**I.**). **1.** adj. Causing irritation. **2.** n. **a** Irritant substance; **b** circumstance which causes irritation of mind.

irritant (**II.**), adj. See **irritate** (**II.**). (law) Rendering null and void: *irritant clause*, one which provides for nullification under specified conditions.

irritate (**I.**), vb. trans. [1. íritāt; 2. íriteit], fr. Lat. *irrītāt-(um)*, P.P. type of *irrītāre*, 'to excite, stimulate'. The uncompounded **rītāre* is not recorded; the etymol. is doubtful, but the base is perh. fr. **wrīt-* & cogn. w. O.E. *wrīðan*, 'to twist'. See **writhe** & **wrath**. **1.** To annoy, anger, exasperate; to excite, inflame the mind and temper of; to provoke. **2.** To cause excessive, unhealthy and painful excitement, and disquiet in some part or organ of the body; to inflame, make sore &c. **3.** (physiol.) To excite to action by stimulus.

irritate (**II.**), vb. trans., fr. Lat. *irrĭtāt-(um)*, P.P. type of *irrĭtāre*, 'to invalidate', fr. *irrĭt-(us)*, 'invalid, void, ineffectual', fr. **ir-**=**in-** (**II.**) & *ratus*, 'fixed, established, valid'. See **rate** (**I.**). (law) To make null and void; to cause forfeiture.

irritating, adj. [1. íritāting; 2. íriteitiŋ], fr. Pres. Part. of **irritate** (**I.**). **a** Causing physical irritation; irritant; **b** exasperating, provoking, annoying, vexing.

irritatingly, adv. Prec. & **-ly**. In an irritating manner; provokingly.

irritation, n. [1. iritáshun; 2. iritéiʃən], fr. L. Lat. *irrītātiōn-(em)*, 'irritation; stimulation; vexation'. **irritate** (**I.**) & **-ion**. (of both physical and mental conditions) **a** Act or process of irritating; **b** state of being irritated; specif., distressing sensation of excitement, or itching on surface of the body; **c** something which irritates.

irritative, adj. [1. íritātiv; 2. íriteitiv]. **irritate** (**I.**) & **-ive**. Causing irritation, tending to irritate.

irruption, n. [1. irúpshun; 2. irápʃən], fr. Lat. *irruptiōn-(em)*, 'a bursting in, irruption, invasion', fr. *irrupt-(um)*, P.P. type of *irrumpere*, 'to break, burst, rush in', fr. **ir-**=**in-** (**I.**) & *rumpere*, 'to break'. See **rupture**. Sudden, violent incursion; invasion.

is, vb. [1. iz; 2. iz]. 3rd sing. pres. indic. of **be**. See also **am** & **are** (**I.**). Aryan **es-ti*, cp. Scrt. *as-ti*, Gk. *es-ti* Lat. *est*, Germ. *ist*. The suff. *t* has been lost in English.

isabella, n. & adj. [1. izabéla; 2. izəbélə], fr. the female name; origin doubtful. **1.** n. Greyish yellow, dull straw colour. **2.** adj. Of this colour.

isabelline, adj. [1. izabélīn; 2. izəbélain]. Prec. & **-ine**. Isabella-coloured.

isagogic, adj. & n. [1. isagójik; 2. àisəgɔ́džik], fr. Lat. *isagōgic-(us)*, fr. Gk. *eisagōgikós*, 'introductory', fr. *eisagōgḗ*, 'introduction', fr. *eis*, 'into' (fr. **ens*, cp. **in** (**I.**)), & *agōgḗ*, 'a leading, carrying', fr. *ágein*, 'to lead, carry, bring', see **agent**, **agonistic**. **1.** adj. Introductory. **2.** n. pl. Study of the literary history, authorship &c. of the Bible.

isatin, n. [1. ísatin; 2. áisətin], fr. Lat. *īsat-(is)*, fr. Gk. *isátis*, 'woad', fr. **wisat-*, possibly cogn. w. **woad**, & **-in**. Yellowish or reddish crystalline substance obtained by oxidizing indigo.

ischiatic, **ischiadic**, adj. [1. iskiátik, -ádik; 2. iskiǽtik, -ǽdik], fr. Med. Lat. *ischiatic-(us)*, Lat. *ischiadicus*, 'of sciatica', fr. Gk. *ischiadik-(ós)*, fr. *iskhíon*, 'hip-joint'. See **sciatic**. Of, pertaining to, the hip; sciatic.

-ise (**I.**), n. suff. representing O. Fr. *-ise*, fr. Lat. *-itia*, *-itium*, *-icium*. Words in Fr. & Engl. derived straight fr. Lat. are now spelt **-ice**: *justice, service*; those formed in Fr. itself w. the old suff. preserve spelling **-ise**: *merchandise*. But Engl. has the latter in *exercise*, Fr. *-ice*.

-ise (**II.**), vbl. suff. See **-ize**.

-ish (**I.**), adj. suff. [1. ish; 2. iʃ] representing O.E. *-isć*; cp. Mod. Germ. *-isch*. Adjs. w. this suff. in O.E. have the sense of 'of, belonging to, of the nature of', esp. in national, racial names: *English, Irish, Cornish, heathenish*. Later formations have the sense of **a** having, in accordance with, the natural qualities of: *fiendish, foolish, feverish*; **b** having the bad qualities of: *childish, monkish* &c.; **c** somewhat, fairly: *brownish, coldish, thinnish*.

-ish (**II.**), vbl. suff. representing O. Fr. **-iss-**, appearing in some parts of O. Fr. vbs. in *-ir*, & formed as though derived fr. Lat. vbs. in *-isc-ĕre*: *finish, polish, punish, abolish*.

Ishmael, n. [1. íshmāl; 2. íʃmeiəl]. Son of Hagar, with reference to Gen. xvi. 12. An outcast, general enemy; one at war with society.

Ishmaelite, n. [1. íshmālīt; 2. íʃmeiəlait]. Prec. & **-ite** (**I.**). An Ishmael.

isinglass, n. [1. ízingglàhs; 2. áiziŋglàs]. Modified fr. O.D. *huizenblas*, fr. *huso*, 'sturgeon', & *blas*, 'bladder'. Semi-transparent, gelatinous substance made from viscera of certain fish, esp. the sturgeon, and used for glue, jellies &c.

Islam, n. [1. ízlam, -lahm; 2. ízləm, -lām]. Arab., 'surrender, obedience', fr. *salām*, 'peace, safety', fr. *salama*, 'he became safe'. Cp. **Moslem** & **salaam**. **1.** Mohammedan religion. **2.** Mohammedans collectively; countries under Mohammedan rule.

Islamic, adj. [1. izlámik; 2. izlǽmik]. Prec. & **-ic**. Of, pertaining to, Islam.

Islamism, n. [1. ízlamizm; 2. ízləmizəm]. **Islam** & **-ism**. Mohammedanism.

Islamite, n. [1. ízlamīt; 2. ízləmait]. **Islam** & **-ite (I.)**. Mohammedan.

island (I.), n. [1. íland; 2. áilənd]. O.E. *īgland*, *ēgland*; M.E. *īland*; fr. O.E. *ēğ*, *īğ*, 'island', & **land**. Cp. O.N. *ey*, M. Du. *ei*. The modern spelling has *s* by anal. w. **isle**. **1.** Piece of land entirely surrounded by water. **2.** Anything resembling an island; detached or isolated mound, patch &c. **3.** (anat.) Group of cells of different formation from those surrounding them; cp. *insulin*.

island (II.), vb. trans., fr. prec. **1.** To make into an island. **2.** To dot, intersperse, with or as with islands.

islander, n. [1. ílander; 2. áiləndə]. **island (I.)** & **-er**. Native of, inhabitant of, an island.

isle, n. [1. īl; 2. ail]. M.E. *ī(s)le*, fr. O. Fr. *i(s)le*, fr. Lat. *insula*, 'island'. See **insular**. Island, esp. poetical or in proper names.

islet, n. [1. ílet; 2. áilit], fr. Fr. *islette*. Prec. & **-et**. **a** Small island; **b** small isolated patch, mound, spot &c.

ism, n. [1. izm; 2. izəm]. Popular abbr. of one of many words having this suff. A doctrine, system, theory, or practice; often derisive.

-ism, suff. representing Fr. *-isme*, fr. Lat., fr. Gk. *-ism-(os)*, *-ism-(a)*, fr. vbl. suff. **-ize** & *-m*; forming abstract ns., **a** of action, corresponding to vbs. in **-ize**: *baptism, catechism, ostracism*; **b** of action, conduct, state, condition, process, of specified kind: *heroism, antagonism, metabolism, alcoholism*; **c** system, doctrine, belief: *deism, Calvinism, scepticism*; **d** characteristic, peculiarity: *mannerism, Irishism, witticism*.

iso-, pref. representing Gk. *íso-(s)*, 'equal', fr. **wis-wo-s*, cogn. w. Gk. *eîdos*, 'appearance' (fr. **weid-wo-*; see **idol, eidolon**), *idéā*, 'form' (see **idea**). See also **wise, wit (I.)**. The pref. is used chiefly to form scientific ns. & adjs., e.g. *isomerism*, (chem.) the property of compound substances having the same elements in same proportion but with different qualities; *isometric*, of equal measure; *isomorphous*, having the property of crystallizing in identical or nearly identical forms.

isobar, n. [1. ísōbar; 2. áisoubā]. See prec. & **baro-**. Line on map joining places at which the barometric pressure is the same on an average, or at a specified time.

isoclinic, adj. [1. ìsōklínik; 2. àisouklínik]. **iso-** & **clinic**. (magnetism) Of lines, *isoclinic lines*, on a map where the magnetic needle has the same inclination.

isogonic, adj. [1. ìsōgónik; 2. àisougɔ́nik]. **iso-** & **-gon** & **-ic**. (magnetism) Of lines, *isogonic lines*, on a map where the dip or declination of the magnetic needle is the same.

isolate, vb. trans. [1. ísolāt; 2. áisəleit]. Orig. as P.P., fr. Ital. *isolato*, fr. Lat. *insulāt-(um)*, 'made into an island', fr. *insula*, 'an island'. See **insular** & **-ate**. **1.** To place alone, apart, set in a detached position, separate from others of same kind; specif., to put (person) into quarantine; separate (infectious patient) from others &c. **2.** (elect.) To insulate. **3.** (chem. and bacter.) To recognize, detect, and separate out an element, constituent substance, from a compound; to perform this process in respect of a germ or bacillus.

isolation, n. [1. ìsoláshun; 2. àisəléiʃən]. Prec. & **-ion**. Act of isolating; state of being isolated; also attrib., as *isolation hospital*, one in which patients suffering from infectious diseases may be treated.

-ison, suff. representing O. Fr. *-aison*, *-eison*, *-ison*, fr. Lat. *-ātiōnem*, *-ētiōnem*, *-itiōnem*, fr. P.P. stems of vbs. & **-ion**: *venison, orison, malison*; also by anal. in ns. first found in O. Fr.: *garrison*.

isopod, n. [1. ísōpod; 2. áisoupɔd]. **iso-** & Gk. *pod-*, stem of *poûs*, 'foot'. See **-pod, pedal**. Crustacean with pairs of thoracic legs similar and similarly placed.

isosceles, adj. [1. īsóselēz; 2. aisɔ́səlīz]. L. Lat. *īsosceles*, fr. Gk. *isoskelés*, fr. **iso-** & *skélos*, 'leg', cogn. w. Gk. *skoliós*, 'twisted, oblique, bent', *skalēnós*, 'crooked, lame' (see **scalene**), & w. Lat. *scelus*, 'crime'. *Isosceles triangle*, one having two sides equal.

isotherm, n. [1. ísōthĕrm; 2. áisouþām]. See **iso-** & **therm**. Line on map joining places which have the same mean annual or monthly temperature.

Israel, n. [1. ízrael; 2. ízriəl], fr. Lat., fr. Gk. *Israēl*, fr. Heb. *yisrael*, 'one who strives with God', w. reference to Gen. xxxii. 28. The Jewish people.

Israelite, n. [1. ízraelīt; 2. ízriəlait]. Prec. & **-ite**. Descendant of Israel; a Jew.

Israelitish, adj. [1. ízraelītish; 2. ízriəlaitiʃ]. Prec. & **-ish**. Of, pertaining to, the Jews.

issuable, adj. [1. ísūabl; 2. ísjuəbl]. **issue (II.)** & **-able**. Capable of issuing or being issued.

issuance, n. [1. ísūans; 2. ísjuəns]. **issue (II.)** & **-ance**. The act of issuing; state of being issued; giving out, distribution, promulgation.

issue (I.), n. [1. ísū, íshū; 2. ísjū, íʃjū], fr. O. Fr. *issue*, fr. Low Lat. **exūta*, corresponding to Lat. *exitus*, 'a coming or going out', fr. *exit-(um)*, P.P. type of *exīre*, 'to go out'. See **exit**. **1.** Point at which a passing outward, outward flow, takes place; exit, egress: *an issue of water*. **2.** That which passes or flows out: *an issue of blood, bloody issue*. **3. a** Act of emitting, of putting forth, sending out; delivery; publication: *the issue of stamps, coinage*; *issue of a newspaper* &c.; **b** something issued, sent out, published, esp. at one time, or as part of a set or batch: *a new issue*, e.g. of coinage, bank notes, printed matter, goods to troops by the government &c. **4. a** A point or head of debate, controversy, or dispute: *to raise a new issue*; **b** some question concerning which there is debate or dispute; subject debated; debate, discussion, controversy: *to debate an issue*; Phrs. *at issue*, under discussion; *to join issue with*, start an argument with. **5.** Result of a series of events; outcome, upshot: *to abide the issue*. **6.** Offspring, progeny, child or children born from particular parent or parents: *to die without issue*.

issue (II.), vb. intrans. & trans., fr. prec. **A.** intrans. **1.** To come, go, flow, pour, out; proceed forth, emerge: *water issuing from the rock, smoke from a chimney*; *no words, sound, issued from his lips*. **2. a** To proceed, be derived, emanate, spring from: *whence do these reports issue?*; **b** to be descended from, have as parent or ancestor (archaic). **3.** (rare) To result, end, in, turn out. **B.** trans. **1.** To send forth, circulate, make public, give out, pronounce: *to issue an order*. **2.** To give out, distribute: *to issue ammunition &c. to troops*. **3.** To publish, put into circulation (book, paper &c.).

issueless, adj. [1. ísūles; 2. ísjulis]. **issue (I.)** & **-less**. Without issue.

-ist, suff. [1. ist; 2. ist] representing Fr. *-iste*, fr. Lat. *-ista*, fr. Gk. *-istēs*; fr. vbl. suff. **-ize**, & *-tēs* denoting agent. The suff. forms **a** agent ns. corresponding to vbs. in **-ize**: *evangelist, rhapsodist*; **b** ns. denoting adherent of, supporter of, some doctrine, custom, practice &c.: *atheist, socialist, polygamist* &c.; **c** ns. denoting person connected with, devoted to, some specific subject, occupation &c.: *pianist, botanist, zoologist, dentist, florist, novelist*. Many of the ns. in *-ist* are new formations fr. Engl., Fr., Lat., or Gk. stems.

-ister, n. suff. representing O. Fr. *-istre*, prob. a variant of **-ist** by anal. w. *(min)istre* (see **minister**): *chorister*.

isthmian, adj. [1. ístmian, ísmian; 2. ístmiən, ísmiən], fr. Lat. *isthmi-(us)*, 'of an isthmus'. See next word & **-an**. **a** Of, pertaining to, an isthmus; **b** (cap., in ancient Greece) of, pertaining to, the Isthmus of Corinth, esp. *Isthmian Games*, held there in alternate years.

isthmus, n. [1. ístmus, ísmus; 2. ístməs, ísməs]. Lat. *isthmus*, fr. Gk. *isthmós*, 'neck, narrow passage; neck of land between two seas'. The original sense seems to have been 'passage', & the base is prob. an extension of *i-* &c., 'to go'. See **itinerate**. **1.** Narrow strip of land connecting two continents, or a peninsula with the mainland. **2.** (anat., bot., zool.) Narrow part or passage joining two larger parts.

istle, n. [1. ístli; 2. ístli], fr. Mexican *ixtli*. Fibre obtained from certain tropical American plants, and used for cord &c.

it (I.), pron. [1. it; 2. it]. O.E. *hit*, M.E. *hit*, *it*, neut. pron. of 3rd pers. Cp. O. Fris. *hit*, Du. *het*, also Goth. *hita*, 'this'. Nom. & acc. sing. neut. of *he*. From pronominal stem **hi*, fr. older demonstr. part. **k i-*, **k̑ ŏ-*, **k̑ jo-*, see **he**, & neut. ending *-t*, as in **what, that**. **1.** Used for an inanimate object, of a very young child, or of a lower animal. **2.** Referring, with slight demonstrative force, to person, thing, circumstance, event, action, which one has in mind, or which is under discussion, whether already, or about to be, expressed, or merely implied: *who is it that I see?*; *it is your money that we want*; '*It was a lover and his lass*'; *I should like to have a horse, to go out hunting, but I can't afford it*. (Note current construction *it's me*; earlier, but now archaic or obs., *it is I*; O.E. & M.E. *(h)it am I*.) **3.** As subject of an impersonal verb: *it is going to rain*; *it will snow before long*. **4.** Referring to general and vague terms, circumstances, state of things, affairs, the weather, temperature &c.: *how goes it with you today?*; *don't let it come to a breach between us*; *you are cutting it rather fine*; *what can you do about it?*; *there it is, do what you like*; *it is getting very hot*; *it looks like snow*. **5.** In such constructions as: *it is easy to be wise after the event* = to be wise &c. . . . is easy; *I take it that you will act at once*, it = the fact (to be); *we shall have to run for it*, it = our purpose, in order to escape, or the like. **6. a** In some colloquial phrases as the object of verbs which are normally intransitive, *to foot it*, to walk; *hook it!*, be off!; **b** after nouns exceptionally used as verbs: *to queen it*, behave like, play the part of, a queen; *to lord it*, play the lord.

it (II.), n., fr. prec. (colloq. and recent) Usually written in italics, and uttered with special emphasis; the ideal, the last word, absolute perfection, *the* thing: *he really looked it in his new clothes*.

It (III.), n. Abbreviation of *Italian*. (slang) Italian vermouth, in Phr. *gin and It*.

itacism, n. [1. ḗtasizm; 2. ítəsizəm], fr. Gk. *ēta*, the letter *ē* (see **etacism**), on anal. of **iotacism**. **1.** Pronunciation of Greek *ē* (orig. [ē]), as [ī], as in Modern Greek and English pronunciation of Greek. **2.** Substitution of Greek *i* for *ē*, *ei*, *oi*, in MS.

Italian, adj. & n. [1. itályan; 2. itǽljən], fr. Lat. *Italia*, 'Italy', & **-an**. **1.** adj. Of, pertaining to, originating in, Italy; *Italian greyhound*, a small, delicate breed of greyhound; *Italian iron*, narrow, rounded iron for goffering; *Italian warehouseman*, one who deals in olive oil, macaroni, and other Italian goods. **2.** n. **a** Inhabitant of Italy; **b** the language of Italy.

Italianism, n. [1. itályanizm; 2. itǽljənizəm]. Prec. & **-ism**. Custom, peculiarity, characteristic of Italy or Italian; an Italian idiom, or mode of speech.

Italianize, vb. trans. [1. itályanīz; 2. itǽljənaiz]. **Italian** & **-ize**. To make Italian, give Italian character to.

italic, adj. & n. [1. itálik; 2. itǽlik], fr. Lat. *Italic-(us)*, 'of Italy', fr. *Ital-(ia)*, 'Italy', & **-ic**. **1.** adj. **a** (cap.) Of Italy, esp. ancient Italy as distinct from Rome; *italic type*, printing type with letters sloping upwards to the right; first used by Aldus Manutius of Venice, c. 1500; **b** specif. (cap., philol.) referring to that branch of Aryan speech spoken in Italy, including Latin, Oscan &c. **2.** n. **a** In pl., *italics*, italic type, used chiefly to indicate emphasis, or for other purposes of distinction; **b** Italic speech.

italicize, vb. trans. [1. itálisīz; 2. itǽlisaiz]. Prec. & **-ize**. To print in italics for emphasis &c.

Italiot, Italiote, n. [1. itáliȯt, -ōt; 2. itǽliɔt, -iòut], fr. Gk. *Italiṓt-(ēs)*, 'Italiot', fr. Lat. *Itali(a)* & **-ot**. Inhabitant of one of the Greek colonies in Italy.

itch (I.), n. [1. ich; 2. itʃ], O.E. *ġiċċe*, 'itch'. Cp. M.H.G. *jucke*, & next word. **1.** An irritating sensation in the skin. **2.** (pathol.) A contagious skin disease, accompanied by intense irritation, caused by the itch-mite, which burrows under the surface of the skin. **3.** (fig.) Restless longing; uneasy, irritating desire: *an itch for money, gain* &c.

itch (II.), vb. intrans. O.E. *ġiċċean*, M.E. *ȝicche, icche*; cp. O.H.G. *juckan*, 'to itch'. **1.** To have an irritating sensation on surface of the skin. **2.** (fig.) To have a restless longing, a teasing desire: *itching to get one's hands on a person*. Phr. *to have an itching palm*, of person greedy of money.

itchiness, n. [1. íchines; 2. ítʃinis]. See next word & **-ness**. The state of being itchy.

itchy, adj. [1. íchi; 2. ítʃi]. **itch (I.)** & **-y**. Inclined to itch, irritating; having, suffering from, the, or an, itch.

-ite (I.), suff. [1. īt; 2. ait] representing Fr. *-ite*, fr. Lat. *-ita*, fr. Gk. *-ítēs*, forming ns. & adjs., **a** denoting person connected with, coming from, adherent of: *Semite, Israelite, Darwinite*; **b** very common in scientific names of kinds of rock (e.g. *dolomite*), fossils (e.g. *trilobite*), chemical salts (e.g. *selenite*), explosives (e.g. *dynamite*) &c.

-ite (II.), **-it**, suff. representing Lat. *-ĭt-* in P.P. types; found **a** in adjs. fr. Lat. P.P. types in *-ĭt-(um)*: *polite, finite, definite*; **b** in ns. fr. Lat. P.P. types in *-ĭt-(um)*: *appetite*; **c** in vbs. fr. Lat. P.P. types in *-īt-(um)*: *unite*; those vbs. fr. Lat. *-ĭt-* stems gen. end in *-ite* in Engl., these fr. the *-ĭt-* type, in *-it*, e.g. *deposit*.

item (I.), n. [1. ítem; 2. áitɛm]. See next word. **1.** Single detail, particular article, included in a list, detailed account: *to number each item in a catalogue*. **2.** Piece of news, subject of newspaper paragraph &c.

item (II.), adv. Lat. *item*, adv., 'just so, in like manner, likewise', fr. Lat. *ita*, 'thus'; cp. Scrt. *ittham*, 'so, thus', *ittha*, 'there'. From pronominal stem **i-*, 'that one' &c. (in enumeration) Also, likewise, further; used to introduce each new article.

itemize, vb. trans. [1. ítemīz; 2. áitɛmaɪz]. **item (I.)** & **-ize**. (Am. usage) To set out (an account) in items or details.

iterance, -cy, n. [1. íterans(i); 2. ítərəns(i)]. See next word & **-ance**. The act of iterating; state of being iterated; iteration.

iterate, vb. trans. [1. íterāt; 2. ítəreit], fr. Lat. *iterāt-(um)*, P.P. type of *iterāre*, 'to do over again, to repeat; to say again, rehearse', fr. *iter-(um)*, 'again', fr. pronominal stem **i-*, as in *id*, 'that', & **item**, & compar. suff. *-ter*. Cp. Scrt. *itaraš*, 'the other', & **interior**. To say over again, repeat, reiterate: *to iterate a warning, accusation* &c.

iteration, n. [1. iteráshun; 2. itəréiʃən], fr. Lat. *iterātiōn-(em)*, 'repetition'. Prec. & **-ion**. The act of iterating; that which is iterated; repetition.

iterative, adj. [1. íterativ; 2. ítərətiv]. **iterate** & **-ive**. Characterized by, expressing, repetition.

ithyphallic, adj. & n. [1. ìthifálik; 2. ìþifǽlik], fr. Lat. *ithyphallic-(us)*, 'ithyphallic', fr. Gk. *ithúphall-(os)*, 'phallus carried erect in the Bacchic ceremonies', fr. *ithú-(s)*, 'straight', & **phallus**. *Ithús* is cogn. w. Scrt. *sidhyati*, 'to attain one's ends, succeed', *sā́dhati*, 'cause to succeed'; Aryan base **sāidh-, *sīdh-, *sidh-*, 'straight, direct'. **1.** adj. **a** Of, pertaining to, the phallus carried in the rites of Bacchus; **b** (of verse) in the metre used in the Bacchic hymns. **2.** n. Poem in ithyphallic metre.

itineracy, n. [1. ī-, itínerasi; 2. (a)itínərəsi]. See next word. Itinerancy.

itinerancy, n. [1. ī-, itíneransi; 2. (a)itínərənsi]. See next word & **-cy**. The state or condition of being itinerant; practice of travelling from place to place.

itinerant, adj. [1. ī-, itínerant; 2. (a)itínərənt], fr. Lat. *itinerant-(em)*, Pres. Part. of *itinerāri*, 'to travel'. See **itinerate**. **a** Travelling from place to place, wandering, wayfaring: *itinerant musicians*; **b** (of justices) travelling on circuit; **c** (of Methodist ministers) preaching on circuit.

itinerary (I.), adj. [1. ī-, itínerari; 2. (a)itínərəri], fr. L. Lat. *itinerāri-(us)*, 'belonging to a journey', fr. *itiner-(is)*, stem of *iter*, 'a journey'. See **itinerate** & **-ary**. Of, pertaining to, a journey or route.

itinerary (II.), n., fr. L. Lat. *itinerāri-(um)*, 'account of a journey', fr. neut. form of prec. **1.** Way, course, path, followed in going from place to place; route. **2.** Account, description, record, indication, of route followed, or to be followed; record of travel; book of directions for traveller, guide-book.

itinerate, vb. intrans. [1. ī-, itínerāt; 2. (a)itínəreit], fr. Lat. *itinerāt-(um)*, P.P. type of *itinerāri*, 'to travel', fr. *itiner-*, stem of *iter*, 'a journey'. This word contains the base **i-* &c., 'to go'; cp. Lat. *īre*, 'to go'; Gk. *eî-mi*, 'I go'; Scrt. *ēti*, 'he goes'; Goth. *iddja*, 'he went'. It is doubtful whether O.E. *gā*, 'I go', is fr. **ga-i-*, containing this base as has been suggested. The Lat. *ex-i-tium* (see **exit**) & *in-i-tium* (see **initial**) certainly contain the base; further Lat. *jānua*, 'door', fr. **i-ān-* (see **janitor** & **Janus**). To travel from place to place; specif., to travel on a circuit for specific purpose.

itineration, n. [1. ī-, itineráshun; 2. (a)itìnəréiʃən]. Prec. & **-ion**. Act of itinerating; itinerancy.

-ition, suff. [1. ishun; 2. iʃən] forming ns. expressing action or condition, fr. Lat. P.P. stems in *-ĭt-(um)* & **-ion**; e.g. *petition, definition*.

-itious, suff. [1. ishus; 2. iʃəs] forming adjs., **a** fr. Lat. P.P. stems in *-ĭt-(um)*, & representing Lat. *-itiōsus*, or *-itius*, *-icius* (*c* & *t* confused in many Lat. MSS.), e.g. *ambitious, adventitious*; **b** fr. Lat. adj. stems in *-it*, e.g. *propitious*. In many Engl. words the ending *-icious* represents *-itious*, e.g. *malicious*. **-ous** always represents an additional Lat. suff. *-ōsus*.

-itis, suff. [1. ītis; 2. aitis] representing Gk. *-ītis*, fem. form of *-ítēs* (see **-ite (I.)**), used w. *nósos*, 'disease' (often understood), to denote 'characterized by, of the nature of'. The suff. is now used to denote especially diseases characterized by inflammation; e.g. *neuritis, arthritis*.

-itous, adj. suff. [1. itus; 2. itəs] formed fr. n. stem *-it-* & **-ous**: *iniquitous, felicitous*.

itself, pron. [1. itsélf; 2. itsélf]. **it** & **self**. **a** Emphatic form of *it*, used in apposition with noun to emphasize the latter: *even the well itself was empty*; **b** reflexive form of *it*; Phrs. *by itself*, alone, apart from other things; *in itself*, independently of external circumstances.

-ity, suff. [1. iti; 2. iti]. Fr. *-ité*, Lat. *-itāt-(em)*, used to form abstract ns. fr. adjs.; e.g. Lat. *probus*, 'good, upright', *probitas*, acc. *probitāt-(em)*, 'uprightness, probity'.

-ium, suff. [1. ium; 2. iəm] representing Lat. neut. adj. suff., **a** in adjs. & ns. fr. Lat.: *medium, premium, solatium*; **b** in new formations as names of metallic elements: *sodium, radium, iridium* &c.

-ive, suff. [1. iv; 2. iv] representing Fr. *-if, -ive*, fr. Lat. *-īvus*, forming adjs. w. the sense 'with a tendency to, in the manner of, having the character of', **a** fr. P.P. stems: *native, captive, nominative, extensive*; **b** fr. ns.: *festive, furtive*. Modern & mediaeval formations are fr. **a** vb. stems: *restive, sportive*; **b** ns.: *massive*; **c** Lat. P.P. stems: *aggressive, punitive*. In some cases these adjs. are used also as ns.: *captive, motive*; in others only as ns.: *initiative, invective*.

ivied, adj. [1. ívid; 2. áivid]. See **ivy** & **-ed**. Covered, overgrown, with ivy.

ivory, n. [1. ívori; 2. áivəri], fr. O. Fr. *ivurie*, fr. Lat. *eboreus*, 'of ivory', fr. *ebur*, 'ivory', perh. fr. Egyptian *āb, ābu*, 'elephant, ivory'. **1.** Hard white substance composing tusks of elephant, hippopotamus, narwhal, and walrus. Phr. *black ivory*, African negro slaves; *vegetable ivory*, hard albuminous substance obtained from the ivory-nut. **2.** (slang) *The ivories*, **a** things made of ivory, e.g. billiard-balls, piano-keys &c.; **b** teeth. **3.** Colour of ivory. **4.** (attrib.) Made of ivory.

ivory-black, n. Black pigment obtained from burnt ivory.

ivory-nut, n. Seed of a tropical American palm, resembling ivory when dried and polished.

ivy, n. [1. ívi; 2. áivi]. O.E. *īfiġ*, M.E. *īvi*; cp. Germ. *epheu*; etymol. doubtful. A climbing, evergreen shrub, *Hedera helix*, with dark-green, glossy, usually five-angled leaves.

-ix, suff. [1. iks; 2. iks], fr. Lat., variant of *-iss-*. Suff. used to form the fem. fr. masc. ns. in *-or*, as *executrix, executor*. Cp. **-ess**.

ixia, n. [1. íksia; 2. íksiə], fr. Gk. *ixós*, 'mistletoe, its berry; bird-lime'; for **wixos*, & cogn. w. Lat. *viscum*, in same sense, & O.H.G. *wihsela*, 'wild cherry'. See **viscous** & **viscera**. Genus of South African plants, of the iris family, cultivated in English gardens.

izard, n. [1. ízard; 2. ízəd], fr. Fr. *isard*; etymol. doubtful. Kind of chamois of the Pyrenees.

-ize, -ise, vbl. suff. [1. īz; 2. aiz] representing O. Fr. *-iser*, fr. L. Lat. *-izāre*, fr. Gk. *-izō, -izein*, wh. was used to form trans. & intrans. vbs. w. the sense of 'to act, treat, in a specified way; put into a specified state'. As a living pref., *-ize* is chiefly used to form vbs. fr. proper ns. & scientific names. **1.** To act in specified way: *sympathize, diarize, diplomatize, soliloquize*. **2.** To treat in certain way: *organize, catechize, characterize*. **3.** To bring, come into, specific state: *equalize, Gallicize, civilize, decimalize*. **4.** To act like, treat in the way of, treat on system of: *Darwinize, Bowdlerize*. **5.** To treat with: *chloralize, oxidize*.

J

J, j [1. jā; 2. džei]. **a** Tenth letter in Engl. alphabet; formerly written *i*; for use in abbr. see end of Dictionary; **b** broad-pointed pen-nib.

jaal-goat, n. [1. jáal, yáhl gōt; 2. džéiəl, jɑ́l gout], fr. Heb. *ya'el*, 'wild-goat'. Long-horned wild goat of Arabia, Upper Egypt, and Abyssinia.

jab (I.), vb. trans. [1. jab; 2. džæb]. Prob. imitative. **1.** To poke suddenly and violently. **2.** To thrust roughly.

jab (II.), n., fr. prec. A sudden rough thrust or poke.
jabber (I.), vb. intrans. & trans. [1. jáber; 2. džǽbə]. Imitative. 1. intrans. a To speak rapidly and indistinctly; b (of monkeys &c.) to chatter. 2. trans. To utter rapidly and indistinctly.
jabber (II.), n., fr. prec. Chatter, gabble, voluble speech.
jabiru, n. [1. jábiroo; 2. džǽbirū]. Brazil. Large stork of tropical America, allied to the adjutant-bird.
jaborandi, n. [1. jàborándi; 2. džæ̀bərǽndi]. Brazil. *jaburandi*. Dried leaflets of a tropical American shrub, used in medicine.
jabot, n. [1. zhábō; 2. žǽbou]. Fr.; etymol. doubtful. a Frill of lace on front of woman's bodice; b (hist.) frill or ruffle on man's shirt-front.
jacamar, n. [1. jákamar; 2. džǽkəmā]. Brazil. name. A tropical American insectivorous bird, with long sharp bill and deep metallic bronze and green plumage.
jacana, n. [1. jákanah; 2. džǽkənā]. Brazil. name. A wading bird of Central and S. America, allied to the rails.
jacaranda, n. [1. jakaránda; 2. džækərǽndə]. Brazil. A tropical American tree, with hard, scented wood.
jacinth, n. [1. jásinth, jásinth; 2. džǽsinþ, džéisinþ], fr. O. Fr. *iacinte*, fr. Lat. *hyacinthus*, 'hyacinth; a precious stone'. See **hyacinth**. A reddish-orange variety of zircon, used as gem.
Jack (I.), n. [1. jak; 2. džæk], prob. fr. O. Fr. *Jacques*, 'James', fr. Lat., fr. Gk. *Iakōbos*. See **Jacob**. 1. Used as popular or familiar form of *John*; also in general sense of fellow, man. Phrs. *every man jack*, everyone, one and all; *Jack Frost*, personification of frost; *Jack Ketch*, hangman; *before you could say Jack Robinson*, very quickly, in a moment; *Jack of all trades*, one who can turn his hand to anything; *Jack-in-office*, pompous, self-important official; *cheap-jack*, hawker, pedlar; *Yellow Jack*, yellow fever. 2. Specif. (of persons) a common sailor, jack-tar; b (archaic) workman: *Jack wants to be as good as his master*; c hence, knave on playing-cards. 3. Name for various machines, contrivances; esp. a device for turning spit; b machine for raising heavy weights; c device for raising axle of carriage, motor &c. in order to free wheel(s); d boot-jack; e (elect.) socket forming a terminal in an electric circuit, adapted to receive a plug connector. 4. (bowls) Ball used as mark. 5. Young pike.
jack (II.), n. Prob. fr. prec. National flag flown at bow of ship on a jack-staff; *Union Jack*, properly the Union flag when flown at bow of ship.
jack (III.), n. Fr. *jaque*, cp. **jacket**. 1. Sleeveless, padded leather coat worn by mediaeval foot-soldier. 2. Leather vessel, bottle, usually *black jack*.
jack (IV.), vb. trans., fr. **Jack** (I.). Also *jack up*, to raise with a jack; (colloq. slang) to give up, abandon, to chuck up: *he threatened to jack up his job*.
jack (V.), n., fr. Port. *jaca*, fr. Malayalam *chakka*. Kind of East Indian coarse bread-fruit.
jack-a-dandy, n. (obs.) Dandy, fop.
jackal, n. [1. jákawl; 2. džǽkōl], fr. Turk. *chakal*, fr. Pers. *shagāl*. 1. Animal of dog family, *Canis aureus*, about the size of a fox, with a bushy tail, and greyish yellow in colour; found chiefly in Southern Asia and Northern Africa; the jackal was formerly supposed to act as scout for the lion in hunting. Hence, 2. (fig.) Person who does menial, base work for another; a servile tool.
jackanapes, n. [1. jákanāps; 2. džǽkəneips]. 16th-cent. *Jackanapes*, also *a napes, jack napis*, in sense of 'a fool'. *Jack Napes* was a nickname of William de la Pole, Duke of Suffolk (d. 1450), whose badge was a clog and chain as attached to tame apes. The name may also have contained an allusion to Naples, as Suffolk had advocated the marriage of the King with the daughter of the King of Naples. See Skeat. 1. (archaic) Monkey. 2. Impertinent, insolent, monkey-like, mischievous, person; pert child. 3. A conceited, insignificant, vulgar fop, a coxcomb.
jackaroo, n. [1. jákaroo; 2. džǽkərū]. Australian slang name for a new hand or pupil on a sheep farm.
jackass, n. [1. jákahs; 2. džǽkās]. 1. a Male donkey; b stupid person; fool, ass, dolt. 2. *Laughing jackass*, large Australian kingfisher.
jack-boot, n. Large top-boot reaching above the knee, as worn by fishermen &c., and formerly by cavalry &c. for defensive purposes.
jackdaw, n. [1. jákdaw; 2. džǽkdō]. See **daw**. British bird of corvine order, *Corvus monedula*, rather smaller than the ordinary crow.
jacket (I.), n. [1. jáket; 2. džǽkit], fr. O. Fr. *jaquet*, dimin. of *jaque*. See **jack** (III.). 1. Short, sleeved outer garment worn by man or woman. Phr. *to dust a person's jacket for him*, to beat him. 2. Covering for pipes, boiler &c. to prevent radiation of heat. 3. Any outer coat or covering, skin &c.; e.g. animal's coat, skin of potatoes, paper cover of book &c.
jacket (II.), vb. trans., fr. prec. a To provide cover with, a jacket; b (slang) to thrash.
Jack-in-office, n. Self-important, dictatorial official; one magnifying office as his sole claim to notice.
jack-in-the-box, n. Child's toy consisting of small box enclosing a figure on a spring, which leaps up when the lid is unfastened.
jack-in-the-green, n. Man enclosed in framework of laths covered with branches, as a character in May-day sports.
jack-knife, n. Large clasp-knife.
jack-o'-lantern, n. [1. ják o lántern; 2. džǽk ə lǽntən]. Will o' the wisp.
jack-plane, n. Large plane for rough work.
jack-pot, n. A pool or pot, in poker, which can only be played for if a player opens the game holding a pair of knaves, 'jacks', or something better.
jack-pudding, n. Buffoon.
jack-rabbit, n. Large, long-legged, long-eared American hare.
jack-snipe, n. Small species of snipe.
jack-tar, n. Sailor.
jack-towel, n. Roller-towel.
Jacob, n. [1. jákub; 2. džéikəb], fr. Lat., fr. Gk. *Jakōbos*, fr. Heb. *Ya'aqob*. *Jacob's ladder*, a blue-flowered, cultivated herb, *Polemonium*, with ladder-like arrangement of leaves; b (naut.) rope ladder with wooden rungs for climbing into rigging; *Jacob's staff*, surveyor's staff for supporting compass &c.
Jacobean, adj. & n. [1. jàkobēan; 2. džæ̀kəbīən], fr. L. Lat. *Jacobae-(us)*, fr. *Jacob-(us)*. See **Jacob** & **-an**. 1. adj. Belonging to, made in, the reign of James I.: *Jacobean poets, architecture, furniture* &c. 2. n. Personage belonging to this period.
Jacobin (I.), n. & adj. [1. jákobin; 2. džǽkəbin]. Fr., fr. Med. Lat. *Jacobin-(us)*. **Jacob** & **-in(e)**. 1. n. a French Dominican friar; named from original establishment of the order in a convent near the church of St. Jacques in Paris; b member of a revolutionary society formed in Paris in 1789; so called from headquarters of society in the old Jacobin convent. 2. adj. Extreme, wild, violent, revolutionary.
jacobin (II.), n., fr. Fr. *jacobine*, fr. fem. form of prec. Kind of pigeon, with arrangement of feathers on back of neck suggesting a hood or cowl.
Jacobinic(al), adj. [1. jàkobínik(l); 2. džæ̀kəbínik(l)]. **Jacobin** (I.) & **-ic** & **-al**. Of, pertaining to, the Jacobins or Jacobinism.
Jacobinism, n. [1. jákobinizm; 2. džǽkəbinizəm]. See prec. & **-ism**. Principles of the Jacobins; violent opposition to established government.
Jacobinize, vb. trans. [1. jákobinīz; 2. džǽkəbinaiz]. **Jacobin** (I.) & **-ize**. To imbue with principles of Jacobinism.
Jacobite, n. [1. jákobīt; 2. džǽkəbait], fr. Lat. *Jacōb-(us)*, 'James'. See **Jacob** & **-ite**. Adherent of James II., after his abdication, and of the Stuart cause; in more recent times a theoretical advocate of the claims of the elder Stuart line to the English throne.
Jacobitical, adj. [1. jàkobítikl; 2. džæ̀kəbítikl]. Prec. & **-ic** & **-al**. Connected with, holding political principles of, the Jacobites.
Jacobitism, n. [1. jákobītizm; 2. džǽkəbaitizəm]. **Jacobite** & **-ism**. Political principles of the Jacobites.
Jacobus, n. [1. jakṓbus; 2. džəkóubəs]. Lat. *Jacōbus*, 'James'. See **Jacob**. English gold coin of reign of James I., worth twenty to twenty-five shillings.
jaconet, n. [1. jákunet; 2. džǽkənet], fr. Hind. *Jagannathi*, name of town in Bengal. a Kind of soft white cotton fabric of medium thickness; b dyed cotton cloth, glazed on one side.
Jacquard loom, n. [1. jákard loom; 2. džǽkād lūm], fr. name of French inventor (d. 1834). A loom for weaving silk or cotton textiles with figured patterns by use of an endless belt of cards punched with holes arranged to form the pattern required.
jacquerie, n. [1. zhak(w)erḗ; 2. žæk(w)ərī]. Fr., fr. *Jacques*, 'James; used as general term for peasant', & **-ery**. Peasants' revolt; specif., rising of French peasants in 1358.
jactitation, n. [1. jàktitáshun; 2. džæ̀ktitéiʃən], fr. Med. Lat. *jactitātiōn-(em)*, fr. *jactitāt-(um)*, P.P. type of *jactitāre*, 'to toss about', fr. Lat. *jact-(um)*, P.P. type of *jacere*, 'to throw, cast, toss'. See **jet** (III.). 1. (med.) Frequent jerky movements of the body and limbs, uncontrollable restlessness, generally in delirium. 2. (law) Ill-founded assertion that some event, esp. a marriage, has taken place &c., made to the prejudice of another.
jade (I.), n. [1. jād; 2. džeid], fr. Fr. *le jade*, orig., *l'ejade*, fr. Span. *(piedra de) ijada*, 'stone for curing disease in the side', fr. Lat. *ilia*, 'the flanks'. See **iliac**. Hard, fibrous, nephrite or jadeite, silicate, varying in colour from pure white to green, cut and polished for ornaments.
jade (II.), n. O.N. *jalda*, 'mare'. a Wretched, worn-out, horse: *a sorry jade*; b (disparagingly) a battered, ill-tempered, and, usually, disreputable woman; c (playfully) a wench, woman: *a saucy jade*.
jade (III.), vb. trans., fr. prec. (rare, except in P.P. as adj.) See next word.
jaded, adj. [1. jáded; 2. džéidid], fr. P.P. of prec. Weary, worn-out, harassed; showing effects of overwork or of worry.
jadeite, n. [1. jádīt; 2. džéidait]. **jade** (II.) & **-ite**. A variety of jade, an aluminium sodium silicate.
jaeger (I.), **jäger**, n. [1. yáger; 2. jéigə]. Germ., 'huntsman, hunter', fr. *jagen*, 'to hunt'. A member of a rifle regiment in German and Austrian armies; sharpshooter.
jaeger (II.), n., fr. name of scientist who adduced hygienic value of wool clothing: used as trade mark by The Jaeger Co. Ltd., London.
jag (I.), n. [1. jag; 2. džæg]. 15th cent. *iagge*, 'a rough cut or tear'. Origin doubtful. Sharp-pointed projection, or corresponding indentation; tooth; notch; a rough, pointed tear in cloth &c.
jag (II.), vb. trans., fr. prec. To cut into notches, tear unevenly, give a ragged edge to.
jagged, adj. [1. jáged; 2. džǽgid], fr. P.P. of prec. Having rough indentations, uneven, notched, serrated; roughly, raggedly torn.
jaggedly, adv. Prec. & **-ly**. In a jagged manner.
jaggedness, n. See prec. & **-ness**. The state or quality of being jagged.
jaggy, adj. [1. jági; 2. džǽgi]. **jag** (I.) & **-y**. Rough-edged, uneven, notched.
jaguar, n. [1. jágwar, jáguar; 2. džǽgwə, džǽgjuə], fr. Brazil. *yaguara*. Large, spotted, yellowish-brown, carnivorous mammal, *Felis onca*, of the cat family, found in the forests of Central and S. America.

Jah, n. [1. jah; 2. džā]. Heb. *Yah*, fr. *Yahweh*. See **Jehovah**. Jehovah.

jail, n. [1. jāl; 2. džeil]. See **gaol**.

jailbird, n. [1. jálbērd; 2. džéilbād]. See **gaolbird**.

Jain, n. & adj. [1. jān, jīn; 2. džein, džain], fr. Hind., fr. Sert. *jaina*, 'of a Buddha'; cogn. w. *jina*, 'saint, hero', *jayáś*, 'victory, *jináti*, 'conquers'; cogn. w. Gk. *bía*, 'force', *biáein*, 'to compel'. **1.** n. Member of Hindu religious sect having doctrines common both to Brahminism and Buddhism. **2.** adj. Of, pertaining to, the Jains.

Jainism, n. [1. jánizm; 2. džéinizəm]. Prec. & **-ism**. The religious system of the Jains.

jalap, n. [1. jálap; 2. džǽləp], fr. Fr., fr. Span. *jalapa*, fr. Xalapa, town in Mexico. Dried root of a Mexican plant, used as purgative.

jalousie, n. [1. zhálooze; 2. žǽluzī]. Fr., fr. O. Fr. *gelosi*, 'jealousy, suspicion'. See **jealousy**. External window-shutter with sloping slats to keep out the sun.

jam (I.), vb. trans. & intrans. [1. jam; 2. džæm]. Prob. orig. a variant of **champ**. **A.** trans. **1.** To press tightly, ram roughly, into constricted space. **2.** To fill (space) by crowding or pressing into it; block up, fill up. **3.** To catch, block, fix (part of machine &c.) so as to prevent movement. **B.** intrans. (of movable parts of machine) To become wedged, cease to work.

jam (II.), n., fr. prec. Number of persons or things wedged tightly together, esp. so as to prevent movement; crush, squeeze.

jam (III.), n. & vb. trans. Origin doubtful; prob. fr. **jam (I.)**. **1.** n. Preserve of fruit, boiled with sugar, poured into jars, and allowed to become firm. **2.** vb. To make into jam: *to jam all one's fruit.*

jamb, n. [1. jam; 2. džæm], fr. Fr. *jambe*, 'leg', fr. L. Lat. *gamba*, 'hoof'. See **gambol**, **gambit**. Side-post or side of doorway, window, or fire-place.

jamboree, n. [1. jàmborḗ; 2. džæmbəri]. Origin unknown. **a** A frolic, a spree; **b** a social gathering; specif., of boy-scouts.

jam-jar, -pot, n. Glass or earthenware vessel for holding jam.

jangle (I.), vb. intrans. or trans. [1. jánggl; 2. džǽŋgl], fr. O. Fr. *jangler*; prob. imitative. **A.** intrans. **1.** To make a harsh, discordant, clanging sound. **2.** To speak noisily, angrily, harshly; to wrangle, bicker. **B.** trans. To ring (bells) out of tune.

jangle (II.), n., fr. prec. **1.** Harsh, discordant sound; noisy clash. **2.** (archaic) Quarrel, dispute, bickering.

janitor, n. [1. jánitor; 2. džǽnitə]. Lat. *jānitor*, 'door-keeper', fr. *Jān-(us)*, 'the deity presiding over doors' &c. See **Janus**. **a** Door-keeper, porter; **b** member of the lowest of the minor orders in Roman Catholic Church.

janizary, janissary, n. [1. jánisari; 2. džǽnisəri], fr. Turk. *yenitsheri*, lit. 'new soldiers'. **1.** Member of troop of infantry formerly forming bodyguard of Sultan of Turkey. **2.** Turkish soldier.

jannock, adj. [1. jánuk; 2. džǽnək]. Northern dial., esp. Lancs. & Yorks. Origin doubtful. Straightforward, genuine, thorough; term used generally of persons or things one can trust or approve of.

Jansenism, n. [1. jánsenizm; 2. džǽnsənizəm], fr. name of Cornelius Jansen, Bishop of Ypres (d. 1638), & **-ism**. Doctrines of Jansen, which closely resembled those of Calvin, touching the means whereby man could obtain Divine Grace; they were declared heretical by the Roman Catholic Church.

Jansenist, n. [1. jánsenist; 2. džǽnsənist]. See prec. & **-ist**. Adherent of Jansenism.

Jansenistic, adj. [1. jànsenístik; 2. džænsənístik]. Prec. & **-ic**. Pertaining to, based on, Jansenism.

January, n. [1. jánūari; 2. džǽnjuəri], fr. Lat. *Jānuāri-(us)*, month dedicated to *Jānu-(s)*. See next word. First month of the year.

Janus, n. [1. jánus; 2. džéinəs]. Lat. *Jānus*, 'deity presiding over doors'; whence Lat. *jānua*, 'door', as the seat of his activity. Formed fr. **ei-*, **i-*, 'to go', as in Lat. *īre*, 'to go'. See **itinerate**. Ancient Italian deity, presiding over beginnings and entrances; he was represented with two faces, one at the front and one at the back of his head.

Jap, adj. & n. [1. jap; 2. džæp]. Colloq. abbr. Japanese.

japan (I.), n. [1. japán; 2. džəpǽn]. Name of island country off east coast of Asia; prob. fr. Chinese *Jih-pun*, 'sunrise'. **1.** Hard, black, resinous varnish, lacquer, as used originally in Japan. **2.** Japanned or other work in Japanese style.

japan (II.), vb. trans., fr. prec. To lacquer with japan, or similar black varnish.

Japanese, adj. & n. [1. jàpanḗz; 2. džæpəníz]. **Japan (I.)** & **-ese**. **1.** adj. Of, pertaining to, Japan. **2.** n. **a** Native of Japan; **b** language of Japan.

Japanesque, adj. [1. jàpanésk; 2. džæpənésk]. **Japan (I.)** & **-esque**. In the Japanese style.

jape, vb. intrans. & n. [1. jāp; 2. džeip]. Perh. fr. Fr. *japper*, 'to bark, yap, as a dog'. (archaic and facet.) **a** vb. To make a mock, to joke, jest; **b** n., joke, jest, quip.

Japhetic, adj. [1. jāfétik; 2. džeifétik]. *Japheth*, third son of Noah, & **-ic**. Of, descended from, Japheth; contrasted with Semitic and Hamitic; Aryan, Indo-European.

Japonic, adj. [1. japónik; 2. džəpónik], fr. Fr. *Japon*, 'Japan'. Japanese.

japonica, n. [1. japónika; 2. džəpónikə]. Mod. Bot. Lat. Prec. used as fem. adj. One of several varieties of a Japanese bright-flowered shrub, esp. *Pyrus* or *Cydonia Japonica*.

jar (I.), n. [1. jar; 2. džā], fr. next word. **1.** Harsh, discordant sound. **2.** a Shock, friction, vibration, caused by sudden collision, impact, of two bodies; **b** (fig.) discord, clash of opinions or temperaments, quarrel. **3.** a Bodily shock; *a jar to one's spine*; **b** mental shock, perturbation, discomfiture, disconcerting effect: *the news gave me a nasty jar.*

jar (II.), vb. intrans. & trans. Probably imitative; but Skeat suggests derivation fr. the very rare O.E. *ċeorian*, 'to creak'; cp. also perh. M. Du. *karren*, *kerren*, 'to creak like a cart'. **A.** intrans. **1.** a To emit a harsh, creaking sound, as of one hard substance rubbing against another; **b** to cause slight shaking, and vibration, by impact. **2.** a To produce, be a cause of, disagreement and friction; **b** to cause disgust, wound susceptibilities, excite feelings of disapproval; *to jar on* (a person), to wound feelings of, irritate, annoy; **c** to produce bodily or mental shock. **B.** trans. **1.** To shake, cause to tremble, throw out of gear, by sudden violent impact. **2.** a To cause bodily shock to, by sudden fall, blow, or the like; **b** to cause mental shock, as by sudden grief, disaster &c.

jar (III.), n., fr. Fr. *jarre*, fr. Span. *jarra*, *jarro*, fr. Arab. *jarrah*. Deep, usually cylindrical, vessel of stone, glass, or earthenware, with no spout, sometimes without handles, sometimes with two.

jardinière, n. [1. zhàrdinyấr; 2. žādinjéə]. Fr., fr. *jardin*, 'garden', q.v. Ornamental flower-pot, often mounted on stand.

jarful, n. [1. járfool; 2. džáful]. **jar (III.)** & **-ful**. Contents of a jar; amount which a jar will contain.

jargon (I.), n. [1. járgun; 2. džágən]. O. Fr.; etymol. doubtful. **a** Confused, unintelligible speech, gibberish; **b** a debased, vulgar dialect; **c** set of highly technical terms used by members of particular profession or trade, by students of particular branch of learning &c.

jargon (II.), jargoon, n. [1. járgun, jargóōn; 2. džágən, džāgún], fr. Arab. *zargūn*, 'gold-coloured'. Variant of **zircon**. Transparent, usually colourless or slightly brownish-yellow variety of zircon, found in Ceylon.

jargonelle, n. [1. jàrgunél; 2. džāgənél]. Fr., dimin. of prec., fr. its colour. A sweet, early pear.

jargonize, vb. intrans. & trans. [1. járgunīz; 2. džágənaiz]. **jargon (I.)** & **-ize**. **a** intrans. To talk in a jargon; **b** trans., to convert into a jargon.

jarl, n. [1. yarl; 2. jāl]. O.N. *jarl*, 'man of noble birth'. See **earl**. (hist.) Scandinavian chieftain.

jarrah, n. [1. jára; 2. džǽrə], fr. Australian native name *jerrhyl*. **a** Kind of eucalyptus tree of S.-W. Australia, with very durable wood; **b** timber from this tree.

jarring, adj. [1. járring; 2. džáriŋ], fr. Pres. Part. of **jar (II.)**. **1.** (lit. and fig.) Harsh, discordant, inharmonious: *a jarring note.* **2.** Causing a mental or physical shock: *jarring to the nerves.*

jarringly, adv. Prec. & **-ly**. In a jarring manner.

jarvey, n. [1. járvi; 2. džávi], fr. surname *Jarvis*. Hackney-coachman, cab-driver; esp. driver of Irish jaunting-car.

jasmin(e), jessamin(e), n. [1. jásmin, jésamin; 2. džǽsmin, džésəmin], fr. Fr. *jasmin*, *jessemin*, fr. Arab., fr. Pers. *yāsmīn*. Genus of ornamental, usually climbing, shrubs, with small, often fragrant, white or yellow flowers.

jasper, n. [1. jásper; 2. džǽspə], fr. O. Fr. *jaspre*, fr. Lat. *iaspis*, fr. Gk. *íaspis*, 'a bright-coloured, esp. green, chalcedony'; oriental loan-word; cp. Arab. *yasf*, Heb. *yashpheh*. Opaque variety of quartz, reddish, yellow, or brown.

jaundice (I.), n. [1. jáhndis, jáwndis; 2. džándis, džóndis], fr. O. Fr. *jaunice*, fr. *jaune*, 'yellow', fr. Lat. *galbinus*, 'greenish-yellow', fr. *galbus*, 'yellow', & **-ice**. **1.** Disease caused by obstruction of bile, and characterized by weakness, nausea, and temporary yellow pigmentation of the skin and the whites of the eyes. **2.** (fig.) Mental state produced by prejudice, jealousy; condition in which the judgement is biassed.

jaundice (II.), vb. trans., fr. prec. **1.** (rare) To affect with jaundice. **2.** (fig.; chiefly in P.P.) To affect with envy, jealousy, or gloom; to prejudice: *to take a jaundiced view.*

jaunt (I.), n. [1. jawnt, jahnt; 2. džónt, džánt]. Origin doubtful. A pleasure-trip, excursion.

jaunt (II.), vb. intrans., fr. prec. To take a short excursion for pleasure.

jauntily, adv. [1. jáwntili; 2. džóntili]. **jaunty** & **-ly**. In a jaunty manner.

jauntiness, n. [1. jáwntines; 2. džóntinis]. **jaunty** & **-ness**. Quality of being jaunty; careless, cheerful, easy, good nature; self-confidence, perkiness, esp. as exhibited in manner.

jaunting-car, n. [1. jáwnting kar; 2. džóntiŋ kā]. Irish two-wheeled vehicle, with seats on either side back to back.

jaunty, adj. [1. jáwnti; 2. džónti]. Not connected with **jaunt**. Earlier *jantee*, fr. Fr. *gentil*. See **genteel** & **gentle**. Feeling, or affecting, careless ease; sprightly; swaggering, perky: *a jaunty manner, gait.*

javelin, n. [1. jávlin; 2. džǽvlin], fr. Fr. *javeline*, prob. Celtic. Light spear for throwing; dart.

jaw (I.), n. [1. jaw; 2. džō]. Perh. fr. M.E. *jowe*, fr. O. Fr. *joue*, 'cheek, jaw', influenced in vowel sound by M.E. *chawl*, fr. O.E. *ċeafl*, 'jaw' (see **jowl**); *joue* was earlier *jode*, fr. Lat. *gabata*, 'dish, platter'. The word is difficult & doubtful. See **jowl**. **1.** One of the two bones forming the framework of the mouth in vertebrates. **2.** (pl.) a Mouth, including jaw-bones and teeth. Phrs. (vulg.) *hold your jaw*, stop talking; **b** (fig.) grip: *jaws of death.* **3.** (pl.) Parts of a machine &c. between which material is held or crushed. **4.** (pl.) Narrow entrance to, mouth of, a valley &c. **5.** (colloq. and vulg.) **a** Talk, garrulity, loquacity; **b** lengthy and tedious reproof; warning lecture, admonition.

jaw (II.), vb. intrans. & trans., fr. prec. **1.** intrans. (vulg.) **a** To talk; **b** to utter reproof. **2.** trans. To lecture, reprove, admonish.

jawbation, n. [1. jàwbáshun; 2. džōbéiʃən], fr. **jobation**, by association with **prec.** Lengthy tirade, reproof, moral allocution.

jaw-bone, n. One of the bones of the jaws.

jaw-breaker, n. (slang.) Word composed of sounds difficult to pronounce.

jaw-breaking, adj. (of words) Containing strange, harsh sounds; difficult to pronounce.

jay, n. [1. jā; 2. džei]. M.E., fr. O. Fr. Origin doubtful. **a** One of a genus of noisy, crow-like birds, with brilliant colouring, longish tail, and short, rounded wings; **b** (fig.) foolish, chattering person; *jay-walker* (Am. slang), person who walks the streets and roads, carelessly or absent-mindedly, without looking out for the traffic.

jazz, n. [1. jaz; 2. džæz]. Invented word. Noisy, discordant, usually syncopated, or rag-time music, played as accompaniment to dancing; originally of negro origin; also attrib., as *jazz band* &c.

jealous, adj. [1. jélus; 2. dželəs], fr. O. Fr. *gelos*, fr. L. Lat. *zēlōs-(us)*, fr. *zēl-(us)*, 'zeal, emulation; jealousy'. See **zeal** & **-ous**. **1.** Eager to uphold, solicitous for, guarding watchfully: *to be jealous of one's rights, honour* &c. **2.** (Bib., of God) Requiring whole-hearted worship and service. **3. a** Apprehensive of being supplanted, outdone, by a rival in love, or in the favour of another: *jealous of one's friend*; *a jealous wife*; **b** apprehensive of influence of rival; grudging, suspicious: *to be jealous of another's influence*. **4.** Envious, feeling ill-will on account of another's possessions, happiness, success &c. **5.** Zealously vigilant; solicitous: *a jealous guardian*.

jealously, adv. Prec. & **-ly**. In a jealous manner.

jealousy, n. [1. jélusi; 2. dželəsi], fr. O. Fr. *gelosi*. **jealous** & **-y**. **1.** Watchful, solicitous care, esp. in guarding. **2.** Envious, grudging suspicion and dislike of another, or of his achievements, advantages, possessions &c.

jean, jane, n. [1. jān; 2. džein], fr. M.E. *Gene*, fr. O. Fr. *(drap de) Gênes*, Genoa. **a** Strong, twilled, cotton fabric; **b** pl. (Am. slang.) trousers, overalls.

jeer (I.), n. [1. jēr; 2. džiə]. Origin unknown. (naut.) *Jeers*, tackle for hoisting and lowering lower yards.

jeer (II.), vb. intrans. & trans. Not found before mid-16th cent.; perh. a form of **cheer**. **1.** intrans. To mock, scoff, speak contemptuously, derisively: *you may jeer, but can you do any better?* *Jeer at*, to mock, throw contempt on. **2.** trans. (rare) To taunt, deride.

jeer (III.), n., fr. prec. Derisive speech, taunt, gibe.

jehad, n. See **jihad**.

Jehovah, n. [1. jehṓva; 2. džihóuvə], fr. Heb. *Yahweh*. Hebrew name of God, in Old Testament.

Jehovist, n. [1. jehṓvist; 2. džihóuvist]. See prec. & **-ist**. Author(s) of certain parts of the O.T. in which God is called Jehovah.

Jehovistic, adj. [1. jèhōvístik; 2. džihouvístik]. Prec. & **-ic**. Of, pertaining to, written by, a Jehovist.

jehu, n. [1. jéhū; 2. džíhjū]. With reference to 2 Kings ix. 20. A driver, a skilful driver (of horses).

jejune, adj. [1. jejṓōn; 2. džidžū́n], fr. Lat. *jējūn-(us)*, 'fasting, hungry; barren, unproductive; meagre, spiritless, dull'. Origin dubious. **1.** (lit. and fig.) Poor, unproductive, barren. **2.** Dull, dry, void of interest.

jejunely, adv. Prec. & **-ly**. In a jejune manner.

jejuneness, n. See prec. & **-ness**. The quality or state of being jejune.

jellied, adj. [1. jélid; 2. dželid]. **jelly** & **-ed**. Stiffened, thickened, into a jelly.

jelly (I.), n. [1. jéli; 2. dželi], fr. Fr. *gelée*, 'frost', fr. Lat. *gelāta*, fem. P.P. of *gelāre*, 'to freeze'. See **gelid**. **1.** Soft, semi-transparent, gelatinous, resilient substance; specif. **a** an edible material of this consistency, obtained by boiling down bones, and fleshy tissue, and allowing the liquid to cool; **b** substance of similar consistency obtained by boiling down fruit and sugar, and straining out the skins, stones &c. **2.** Fruit jelly flavoured with wine &c., moulded into a symmetrical shape and served as a sweet.

jelly (II.), vb. intrans. & trans., fr. prec. To turn into, set as, jelly.

jelly-bag, n. Pointed bag through which jelly is strained.

jelly-fish, n. Marine animal, umbrella-shaped, and consisting chiefly of a whitish, jelly-like substance, with hanging tentacles; medusa.

jemadar, n. [1. jémadar; 2. džémədā]. Hind., fr. Arab. *jama'dar*, fr. *jama'*, 'an aggregate'; the compound indicates generally 'the leader of a troop of individuals'. (Indian Army) Title of second rank of native officer in a company of sepoys.

jemimas, n. [1. jemímaz; 2. džimáiməz], fr. woman's name. (obs. and colloq.) Elastic-sided boots.

jemmy, n. [1. jémi; 2. džémi], fr. man's name, popular form of *James*. Burglar's short, sectional crowbar.

je ne sais quoi, n. [1. zhenesākwáh; 2. žənəseikwá, -kwɔ̃]. Fr., 'I don't know what'. Something too elusive for exact description or specification: *there is a je ne sais quoi of distinction about him*.

jennet, n. [1. jénet; 2. dženit], fr. Fr. *genet*, fr. Span. *jinete*, 'light horseman', fr. Arab. Small Spanish breed of horses.

jenneting, n. [1. jéneting; 2. dženitiŋ], fr. Fr. name *Jeannet*, dimin. of *Jean*, 'John', so called because it is supposed to be ripe on St. John Baptist's Day, June 24. Kind of very early summer apple; by popular etymology, also known as *June eating*.

jenny, n. [1. jéni, jíni; 2. dženi, džíni]. Dimin. of *Jane*. **1.** Travelling crane. **2.** (usually *spinning-jenny*) Machine for spinning several cotton threads at once. **3.** Stroke at billiards, off the object ball placed near a cushion, into a pocket on the same side of the table.

jenny-wren, n. Female wren.

jeopardize, vb. trans. [1. jépardīz; 2. džépədaiz]. Next word & **-ize**. To bring into danger, put into jeopardy, imperil.

jeopardy, n. [1. jépardi; 2. džépədi]. M.E. *je-, jeo-, juparti*, fr. O. Fr. *jeu parti*, 'even game', fr. Lat. *jocus*, 'game', see **joke**, & *partīt-(us)*, P.P. type of *partīre*, 'to divide'. See **part**. Hazard, peril, danger.

jequirity, n. [1. jekwíriti; 2. džikwíriti], fr. Fr., fr. native *jekiriti*. Indian shrub with coloured, poisonous seeds, used for ornament and in medicine.

jerboa, n. [1. jĕrbṓa; 2. džəbóuə], fr. Arab. *yarbū'*. Small Arabian & N. African rodent with long hind-legs adapted for jumping; somewhat resembling a miniature kangaroo in appearance.

jeremiad, n. [1. jèremíad; 2. džèrimáiæd], fr. Fr. *jérémiade*, fr. *Jérémie*, fr. Lat. *Jeremias*, 'Jeremiah', & **-ad**; w. reference to *Lamentations of Jeremiah*. Lamentation, mournful complaint; tale of woe.

Jericho, n. [1. jérikō; 2. džérikou]. Town in S. Palestine. Phr. *go to Jericho*, to the devil.

jerid, jereed, n. [1. jerḗd; 2. džərīd], fr. Arab. *jarid*. **1.** Javelin used in Turkey, Arabia, Persia. **2.** Kind of mock tournament in which the jerid is used.

jerk (I.), n. [1. jĕrk; 2. džə̄k]. Not found before 16th cent.; spelt also *girk, yerk* & *jert*, & has the meanings, 'blow, stroke, nip'; the vb. at first means 'to beat'. Origin unknown, though Skeat suggests a possible connexion w. **gird** (II.). **1.** Sudden, sharp, staccato, movement; quick, sudden, pull or twitch; sudden arrest of motion: *a jerk of the head, wrist* &c.; *to give the rope a jerk*; *the carriage stopped with a jerk*. **2. a** Involuntary, spasmodic, muscular contraction; specif. **b** *the jerks*, spasmodic twitchings of limbs &c., esp. as accompanying powerful emotional excitement.

jerk (II.), vb. trans. & intrans., fr. prec. **1.** trans. To move, pull, throw, twitch &c., with a jerk. **2.** intrans. To move with a jerk.

jerk (III.), vb. trans., fr. S. Am. Span. *charquear*, fr. Peruv. *ccharqui*, 'dried meat'. To cure (meat) by cutting into long slices and drying in the sun or over a fire; esp. in P.P. *jerked beef*.

jerkily, adv. [1. jĕrkili; 2. džə́kili]. **jerky** & **-ly**. In a jerky manner.

jerkin, n. [1. jĕrkin; 2. džə́kin]. Origin doubtful. Short, close-fitting coat, usually of leather.

jerkiness, n. [1. jĕrkines; 2. džə́kinis]. **jerky** & **-ness**. Quality of being jerky.

jerky, adj. [1. jĕrki; 2. džə́ki]. **jerk** (I.) & **-y**. Moving in jerks, characterized by jerks, spasmodic, jumpy.

jerry, n. [1. jéri; 2. džéri], fr. Jeremiah. (schoolboy slang) A chamber utensil.

jerry-builder, n. Prob. fr. man's name Jerry, abbr. fr. Jeremiah. Builder of cheap, trumpery houses.

jerry-building, n. Hasty, careless, flimsy mode of construction.

jerry-built, adj. Built hastily and roughly of poor, flimsy materials.

jersey, n. & adj. [1. jĕrzi; 2. džə́zi]. Name of one of the Channel Islands. **1.** n. **a** Knitted or woven sleeved garment reaching from neck to waist; **b** animal of Jersey breed. **2.** adj. Derived from Jersey; specif., *Jersey cow* &c.

Jerusalem artichoke, n. [1. jerṓōsalem ártichōk; 2. džirū́sələm átitʃouk], by popular etymol., fr. Ital. *girasole*, 'sun flower'. See **girasole**. The edible tuber, or plant itself, of a species of sunflower. See **artichoke**.

Jerusalem pony, n. (facet.) A donkey.

jess, n. & vb. trans. [1. jes; 2. džes], fr. O. Fr. *ges*, fr. Lat. *jactus*, 'a throw', fr. *jact-(um)*, P.P. type of *jacere*, 'to throw'. See **jet** (III.) **1.** n. (falconry, usually in pl. *jesses*) Short strap for putting round leg of hawk, with a ring at one end to which a leash is fastened. **2.** vb. To put jesses on (hawk).

jessamine, n. See **jasmine**.

Jesse, n. [1. jési; 2. džési]. Name of the father of David in the Bible, from whom the genealogy of Jesus Christ is traced in Matt. &c., whence *Tree of Jesse*, representation of this genealogy by a tree growing from the body of Jesse, with various figures in the branches, and crowned with the figure of Christ at the top, frequently found in stained-glass windows &c.

jest (I.), n. [1. jest; 2. džest]. M.E. *jeste, geste*, 'deed, exploit', fr. O. Fr. *geste*, fr. Lat. *gesta*, 'deeds, acts', neut. pl. of P.P. of *gerere*, 'to do'. See **gerent, gest**, & **gesture**. **1.** Something said or done to excite mirth, laughter; joke, witticism, a merry quip. Phr. *(to speak) in jest*, for fun, not in earnest. **2.** Object of ridicule, derision; laughing-stock: *to be a standing jest*.

jest (II.), vb. intrans., fr. prec. **a** To make jests; to speak or act in a comical, ludicrous manner; **b** to behave with levity, and irresponsibility, to trifle.

jest-book, n. Book containing collection of jests.

jester, n. [1. jéster; 2. džéstə]. **jest** (II.) & **-er**. One who jests, a funny fellow; specif., professional mirth-maker formerly attached to royal and noble households.

jesting, adj. [1. jésting; 2. džéstiŋ]. **jest** (II.) & **-ing**. Of the nature of, expressing, a jest; given to jests; spoken in jest.

jestingly, adv. Prec. & **-ly**. In a jesting manner; not in earnest.

Jesuit, n. [1. jézūit; 2. džézjuit], fr. Fr. *Jésuite*, fr. Mod. Lat. *Jesuita*, fr. Lat. stem *Jesu-*, 'Jesus' & **-ite**. **1.** Member of Society of Jesus, Roman Catholic religious order founded in 1539 by Ignatius Loyola; *Jesuit's bark*, cinchona. **2.** (opprobriously, as used by Protestant opponents) A crafty, insidious intriguer; a dissembler; a casuist.

Jesuitical, adj. [1. jèzūítikl; 2. džèzjuítikl]. Prec. & **-ic** & **-al**. Resembling a Jesuit in principles and methods; specif. (in opprobrious use, as above) crafty, intriguing;

using cunning, insidious methods; subtle; prevaricating.

Jesuitically, adv. Prec. & **-ly**. In a Jesuitical manner.

Jesuitism, n. [1. jézūitizm; 2. džézjuitizəm]. **Jesuit & -ism**. Alleged principles and methods of the Jesuits; craftiness, subtlety, duplicity.

Jesuitize, vb. trans. & intrans. [1. jézūitīz; 2. džézjuitaiz]. See prec. & **-ize**. To treat, act, Jesuitically.

Jesuitry, n. [1. jézūitri; 2. džézjuitri]. **Jesuit & -ry**. Jesuitism.

jet (I.), n. [1. jet; 2. džet], fr. O. Fr. *jaiet*, fr. Lat., fr. Gk. *gagátēs*, 'jet', prob. fr. *Gagas* in Lycia. **1.** Rich, black, hard variety of lignite, capable of being highly polished, and used for ornaments. **2.** Colour of jet.

jet (II.), adj., fr. prec. Of jet, of the colour of jet.

jet (III.), vb. trans. & intrans., fr. Fr. *jeter*, 'to throw', fr. L. Lat. *jectāre*, fr. Lat. *jactāre*, 'to throw, toss', fr. *jact-(um)*, P.P. type of *jacere*, 'to throw', cogn. w. Gk. *hiēmi*, 'I send' (fr. **jijēmi*), aor. *hēka*. Cp. also **jactitation**, & cp. **adjacent**. **1.** trans. To emit, shoot out, in a thin stream. **2.** intrans. To spirt forth in a jet.

jet (IV.), n. Fr. See prec. **1.** Stream, rapid, continuous flow, spirt, emission, of water, steam, gas &c., driven upwards or forwards from a small opening. **2.** Spout, pipe &c., emitting gas, water &c.

jet(t)on, n. [1. jéton; 2. džétən]. Fr. *jeton*, fr. *jeter*, see **jet** (III.). Counter, with value stamped on it, used in gambling.

jetsam, n. [1. jétsam; 2. džétsəm]. Variant of next word. **a** Goods thrown overboard to lighten vessel; **b** such goods when washed ashore; in Phr. *flotsam and jetsam*; **c** (fig.) person tossed about by fate.

jettison, n. & vb. trans. [1. jétisun; 2. džétisən], fr. A.-Fr. *getteson*, fr. Lat. *jactātiōn-(em)*, 'a throwing, shaking', fr. *jact-(āre)*, 'to throw', see **jet** (III.), & **-ation**. **1.** n. The act of throwing goods overboard to lighten a ship. **2.** vb. **a** To throw (cargo &c.) overboard to lighten ship in distress; **b** (fig.) to abandon, get rid of, free oneself from (an encumbrance).

jetty, n. [1. jéti; 2. džéti]. M.E. *jettey*, O. Fr. *jetée*, n., fr. fem. P.P. of *jeter*, 'to throw'. See **jet** (III.). Lit. 'something thrown, or built out'. **1.** Structure of wood or stone built out into water to form a rampart or mole to protect harbour or end of a pier. **2.** Landing-pier.

jeu de mots, n. [1. zhē de mṓ; 2. žʌ̄ də móu]. Fr., 'play of words'. Play on words, a pun.

jeu d'esprit, n. Anglicized to [1. zhē despré; 2. žʌ̄ dεsprí]. Fr., 'play of wit'. Witticism, humorous sally, play of fancy.

Jew (I.), n. [1. jōō; 2. džū], fr. O. Fr. *giu*, fr. Lat. *Jūdaeus*, fr. Gk. *Ioudaîos*, fr. Aramaic *y'hudai*, fr. Heb. *y'hudah*, 'Judah'. **a** Member of Hebrew race; **b** (fig.) avaricious, extortionate person, usurer.

jew (II.), vb. trans., fr. prec. (colloq.) To cheat, outwit, defraud.

jewel (I.), n. [1. jōōel; 2. džūil], fr. A.-Fr. *juel*, *jouel*, O. Fr. *joiel*, *jouel* &c., fr. Low Lat. *jocālia* (pl.), 'playthings, trinkets', fr. Lat. *jocus*, 'play, jest'. See **joke & joy**. **1. a** Personal ornament set with precious stone(s); **b** precious stone, gem. **2.** Highly valued person or thing; precious object.

jewel (II.), vb. trans., fr. prec. **1.** To adorn, set, with jewels. **2.** To fit (watch) with precious stone, crystal &c. for pivot-holes.

jewel-box, -case, n. Small box, usually lined with velvet, and fitted with trays and divisions, for keeping jewels.

jewel-house, n. Building in Tower of London where crown jewels are kept.

jeweller, n. [1. jōōeler; 2. džūilə]. **jewel & -er**. Tradesman having a shop for the sale of jewels.

jewellery, jewelry, n. [1. jōōelri; 2. džūilri]. **jewel & -ery**. Jewels collectively; ornaments set with gems.

jewelly, adj. [1. jōōeli; 2. džūili]. **jewel & -y**. Like jewels, brilliant.

Jewess, n. [1. jōōes; 2. džūis]. **Jew & -ess**. Female of Jewish race.

jewing, n. [1. jōōing; 2. džūiŋ]. **Jew**, w. reference to Jew's hooked nose, & **-ing**. Wattles at base of beak of some pigeons.

Jewish, adj. [1. jōōish; 2. džūiʃ]. **Jew & -ish**. Of, pertaining to, the Jews; like, of the nature of, a Jew.

Jewry, n. [1. jōōri; 2. džūəri], fr. O. Fr. *juerie*. **Jew & -ery**. **1.** The Jewish people. **2.** That quarter of a town in which alone Jews were formerly allowed to live; ghetto.

jew's-ear, n. Kind of edible fungus growing on the elder tree.

Jews'-harp, n. Earlier called *Jews' trump*; origin of name unknown. Small harp-shaped musical instrument, held against the teeth and played by striking a metal tongue with the finger.

Jezebel, n. [1. jézebl; 2. džézibl]. Name of Ahab's wife. Vicious, abandoned, or shameless woman. Phr. *painted Jezebel*.

jib (I.), n. [1. jib; 2. džib]. Perh. connected w. **gibbet**. (naut.) Triangular sail set on a stay, and extending from jib-boom to foretopmast head. Phr. *cut of one's jib*, external appearance, mode of dress &c.

jib (II.), vb. intrans. & trans. Prob. of Du. origin; variant of **gybe**. (naut.) **1.** intrans. (of sail) To swing across the vessel as the wind or course of vessel changes. **2.** trans. To pull (sail &c.) round, in tacking.

jib (III.), vb. intrans. Etymol. doubtful; perh. same as prec. fr. sudden movement of sail. **1.** (of horse) **a** To stop suddenly, balk; **b** to move restively sideways or backwards. **2.** (fig.) To come to a standstill, refuse to proceed. Phr. *to jib at*, to hesitate to do; to show reluctance, boggle at.

jibber, n. [1. jíber; 2. džíbə]. Prec. & **-er**. Horse given to jibbing.

jib-boom, n. Spar used to prolong bowsprit.

jib-door, n. Origin doubtful. Door set flush with wall, usually painted or papered for concealment.

jibe. See **gibe**.

jiff(y), n. [1. jíf(i); 2. džíf(i)]. Etymol. unknown. (colloq.) A moment, instant: *I'll come in half a jiff(y)*.

jig (I.), n. [1. jig; 2. džig]. O. Fr. *gigue*, 'a musical instrument; a lively dance'; cp. Ital. *giga*, 'fiddle'; cp. M.H.G. *gīge*, Mod. Germ. *geige*, 'fiddle'. The origin is very doubtful; Meyer-Lübke derives all the Romance words of this group fr. Gmc., & connects also Fr. *gigot*, 'leg of mutton'. **a** Quick, lively dance; **b** music for such a dance.

jig (II.), vb. intrans. & trans. See prec. **1.** intrans. **a** To dance a jig; **b** to move jerkily up and down: *to jig up and down*. **2.** trans. **a** To move, jerk, shake, up and down; specif. **b** to separate (coarse and fine ores &c.) by shaking in sieves under water.

jigger (I.), n. [1. jíger; 2. džígə]. **jig** (II.) & **-er**. **1. a** One who jigs ore; **b** apparatus for this. **2.** (naut.) **a** Kind of old-fashioned fishing-sloop; **b** small tackle consisting of double and single block. **3.** Rest for billiard-cue.

jigger (II.), n. Variant of **chigoe**. Kind of mite, found in tropical countries, which burrows into, and lays its eggs in, the skin of men and animals, especially in the foot, causing sores.

jiggered, adj. [1. jígerd; 2. džígəd]. Mild and meaningless expletive: *well, I'm jiggered!*

jiggle, vb. trans. [1. jígl; 2. džígl]. **jig** (II.) & **-le**. To shake lightly, joggle.

jihad, jehad, n. [1. jehấd; 2. džihấd]. Arab., 'contest, war'. **a** Mohammedan war against unbelievers, campaign against the enemies of Islam; **b** (fig.) campaign against a doctrine, policy &c.

jill. See **gill** (IV.).

jilt (I.), n. [1. jilt; 2. džilt]. Prob. fr. obs. *gillot*, dimin. of **gill** (IV.). **a** Woman who heartlessly rejects a lover after encouraging him; **b** (rare) man who treats a woman in this way.

jilt (II.), vb. trans., fr. prec. To reject, discard (a lover, suitor), after encouraging him.

Jim Crow, n. [1. jím krṓ; 2. džím króu]. American contemptuous name for a negro; *Jim Crow car*, railway carriage, tram car, set apart for exclusive use of negroes.

jimp, adj. [1. jimp; 2. džimp]. Etymol. unknown. (Scots) **a** Slender, elegant; **b** skimpy, scanty.

jingal. See **gingall**.

jingle (I.), n. [1. jínggl; 2. džíŋgl]. Imitative. **1.** Light, ringing, tinkling sound, as of small bells or light metal objects shaken together. **2.** Words or verses in simple rhythm with frequent repetition of sounds, designed to catch the attention or remain in the memory. **3.** (obs., except in Cornwall) Light two-wheeled, covered or open, cart.

jingle (II.), vb. intrans. & trans., fr. prec. **A.** intrans. **1.** To make a thin, ringing, tinkling sound. **2.** (of words, verses &c.) To give an effect of easy rhythm and constant repetition of sounds. **B.** trans. To cause to jingle.

jingo, n. & adj. [1. jínggō; 2. džíŋgou], fr. popular patriotic song current in late seventies of 19th cent., beginning, 'We don't want to fight, but by Jingo if we do . . .' **1. a** Fiery, blustering person who professes vehement patriotism of a vulgar and rather frothy kind; a chauvinist; **b** term sometimes applied by political opponents to those who insist on taking every possible legitimate means to ensure national security and preparedness against attack. **2.** *By Jingo*, mild and meaningless expletive.

jingoism, n. [1. jínggōizm; 2. džíŋgouizəm]. Prec. & **-ism**. Attitude of mind, political principles, of jingoes.

jingoist, n. [1. jínggōist; 2. džíŋgouist]. See prec. & **-ist**. Supporter of jingoism; a jingo.

jingoistic, adj. [1. jinggōístik; 2. džiŋgouístik]. Prec. & **-ic**. Of, pertaining to, jingoism.

jinks, n. [1. jingks; 2. džiŋks]. Imitative of rapid movement? *High jinks*, boisterous merrymaking; sport, fun, jollification.

jinnee, n. [1. jinḗ; 2. džiní], fr. Arab. *jinnī*. Often confused w. **genie**. One of a class of spirits in Mohammedan mythology able to assume the forms of men or animals, and having certain supernatural powers; genie.

jinricksha, jinrikisha, n. [1. jinrík(i)shaw; 2. džinrík(i)ʃɔ], Jap. *jin*, 'man', *riki*, 'power', *sha*, 'carriage'. Small two-wheeled Japanese carriage, with a hood, and drawn by one or two men; often abbreviated 'ricksha'.

jitney, n. [1. jítni; 2. džítni]. Origin doubtful. (Am. slang) **a** A five-cent piece; **b** motor-car plying for hire over fixed route for a small sum.

jiu-jitsu, n. See **ju-jutsu**.

job (I.), n. [1. job; 2. džɔb]. Etymol. unknown. **1.** Piece of work, either independent, or as part of larger undertaking: *to do a job well*; *to finish one's job*; *to give a person a job*. Phrs. *to make a good job of it*, do it well; *to do his job for him*, to destroy, ruin, him; *odd jobs*, disconnected pieces of miscellaneous work; *job lot*, miscellaneous collection of things bought cheaply; *by the job* (of engagement to work, payment &c.), for single piece of work; *a good job too*, a good thing; *that's a good job*, that is fortunate. **2.** Unscrupulous transaction which is profitable to private person at the expense of the public; specif., appointment of an unsuitable, incompetent person to a post from interested motives. **3.** (colloq.) Habitual work, employment, profession, occupation, post, billet: *he's got a nice job as private secretary to a rich man*.

job (II.), vb. intrans. & trans., fr. prec. **A.** intrans. **1.** To work irregularly at different kinds of employment; do odd jobs. **2.** To use an official position as opportunity for private gain, or unmerited advancement of friends. **3.** To act as broker. **B.** trans. **1. a** To let out (horse or carriage) for hire; **b** to hire, employ, by the job. **2.** To buy and sell, deal in (goods, stocks &c.), as broker. **3.** To carry (a transaction) through by unscrupulous means from interested motives. Phr. *to job (a person) into a post* &c., put him there by unscrupulous means, by using undue influence &c.

job (III.), vb. trans. & n. Variant of **jab**. **1.** vb. To strike, poke, prod, suddenly; to jab. Phr. *to job at*, make a stab, thrust, jab, at. **2.** n. Sudden jab, poke, prod.

Job (IV.), n. [1. jōb; 2. džoub]. Name of Hebrew patriarch who gave his name to Book of Job in Old Testament; used as type of patience. Phr. *Job's comforter*, one who aggravates person's distress under pretext of comforting him.

jobation, n. [1. jōbáshun; 2. džoubéiʃən], fr. obs. *jobe*, 'to reprove', fr. prec., & **-ation**; often taken as **jawbation**, & connected w. **jaw**. Lengthy reproof, tedious scolding.

jobber, n. [1. jóber; 2. džóbə]. **job** (II.) & **-er**. One who jobs; **a** an occasional workman who does odd jobs; **b** dealer in Stock Exchange securities, distinguished from *broker*; **c** man who lets out horses by the day; **d** person who carries out unscrupulous transactions in an underhand way, in public business.

jobbernowl, n. [1. jóbernōl; 2. džóbənoul]. Cp. Fr. *jobard*, 'a dupe', & *nol*, obs. or provinc. form of **noddle**. Stupid person, blockhead.

jobbery, n. [1. jóberi; 2. džóbəri]. **job** (I.) & **-ery**. **a** Fraudulent method of gaining private advantage, esp. in public, official, transactions; **b** unscrupulous action, exertion of undue influence, to further one's own ends.

jobbing, adj. [1. jóbing; 2. džóbiŋ], fr. Pres. Part. of **job** (II.). Doing occasional, odd work, not regularly employed: *jobbing gardener*.

jobmaster, n. [1. jóbmàhster; 2. džóbmàstə]. One who lets out horses and carriages to hire.

Jock, n. [1. jok; 2. džɔk]. See next word. A Highland or Scottish soldier.

jockey (I.), n. [1. jóki; 2. džóki], fr. Scots *Jock* = **Jack** (I.), & **-y**. Man, esp. professional, riding in horse-races. *Jockey Club*, society for promotion and regulation of horse-racing.

jockey (II.), vb. trans. & intrans., fr. prec., in obs. sense 'cheat'. **1.** trans. To cheat, outwit; to persuade, coerce, by trickery; also *jockey* (person) *into* (doing something); *jockey out of* (property). **2.** intrans. To play the cheat; manœuvre cunningly.

jockeydom, n. [1. jókidum; 2. džókidəm]. **jockey** & **-dom**. Jockeys collectively.

jockeyship, n. [1. jókiship; 2. džókiʃip]. **jockey** & **-ship**. The art of the jockey, skill in horse-racing.

jocko, n. [1. jókō; 2. džókou], fr. Fr., fr. native *engeco*. A chimpanzee.

jocose, adj. [1. jōkṓs; 2. džoukóus], fr. Lat. *jocōs-(us)*, 'humorous, jocose', fr. *joc-(us)*, 'a jest'. See **joke** & **-ose**. Facetious, playful, jesting; given to jesting; spoken in jest.

jocosely, adv. Prec. & **-ly**. In a jocose manner.

jocoseness, n. See prec. & **-ness**. The state or quality of being jocose; jocose behaviour or talk; jocosity.

jocosity, n. [1. jōkósiti; 2. džoukósiti]. **jocose** & **-ity**. Jocoseness.

jocular, adj. [1. jókūlar; 2. džókjulə], fr. Lat. *joculār-(is)*, 'facetious', fr. *jocul-(us)*, dimin. of *jocus*, 'a jest'. See **joke** & **-ar**. Humorous, facetious, mirthful.

jocularity, n. [1. jòkūláriti; 2. džòkjulǽriti]. Prec. & **-ity**. The state or quality of being jocular.

jocularly, adv. [1. jókūlarli; 2. džókjuləli]. See prec. & **-ly**. In a jocular manner.

jocund, adj. [1. jókund, jókund; 2. džóukand, džókənd]. O. Fr., fr. L. Lat. *jōcundus*, through the influence of *jocus*, 'a jest' (see **joke**), fr. Lat. *jūcundus*, 'pleasant, delightful', fr. **juvicondos*, cogn. w. *juv-āre*, 'to help, support; to please, delight'. See **coadjutor**. Merry, cheerful, blithe; pleasant, gay, genial.

jocundity, n. [1. jōkúnditi; 2. džoukánditi]. Prec. & **-ity**. State or quality of being jocund.

jocundly, adv. [1. jókundli; 2. džóukandli]. See prec. & **-ly**. In a jocund manner.

Joe Miller, n. [1. jō míler; 2. džóu mílə]. Comedian (d. 1738) whose name was connected with a book of humorous stories published in 1739. Old, stale joke, a chestnut.

joey, n. [1. jói; 2. džóui], fr. native (Australian) *joé*. Young kangaroo.

jog (I.), vb. trans. & intrans. [1. jog; 2. džɔg]. Etymol. doubtful. **A.** trans. **1. a** To give a slight shake, jerk, push, to; to knock, shove; **b** to nudge, in order to attract attention: *to jog a person's elbow*. **2.** (fig.) To stimulate, stir up: *to jog one's memory*. **B.** intrans. **a** To move along at a slow trot, move heavily at a steady pace; to proceed slowly and heavily, but steadily; *to jog on, along*; **b** to move on, go on one's way; **c** (fig.) to proceed, get on with, continue steadily in, one's occupation &c.: *we jog along quietly*.

jog (II.), n., fr. prec. **1.** Nudge, push, slight shake, shove. **2.** Slow, jolting trot; also *jog trot*.

joggle (I.), vb. trans. & intrans. [1. jógl; 2. džógl]. Prec. & **-le**. **1.** trans. To shake slightly, give a push, jerk, or jolt to. **2.** intrans. To shake, have a jolty or jerky motion.

joggle (II.), n., fr. prec. Slight, jerky shake, jolt.

joggle (III.), n. Etymol. doubtful, perh. same as prec. (mason's term) Method of jointing stone so that one piece is made to fit into another.

jog-trot, n. **jog** (II.) & **trot**. **a** Regular, slow, heavy trot; **b** (fig.) monotonous, humdrum, mode of life, method, or procedure.

Johannine, adj. [1. jōhánīn; 2. džouhǽnain], fr. L. Lat. *Jōhann-(es)*, fr. Lat. *Jōannes*, 'John'. See **John** & **-ine**. Of, written by, the apostle St. John.

Johannisberger, n. [1. yōhánisbërger; 2. jouhǽnisbɜ̄gə]. German Place-Name & adj. suff. **-er**. Kind of white Rhine wine or Hock from Johannisberg, near Wiesbaden.

John, n. [1. jon; 2. džɔn], fr. O. Fr. *Jehan*, fr. Lat. *Jōannes*, fr. Gk. *Iōannēs*, fr. Heb. *Yokhanan*. Man's Christian name: *John Barleycorn*, personification of malt liquor; *John Bull*, a typical Englishman; the English nation; *John Bullism*, typically English character, conduct, policy &c.; *John Chinaman*, Chinaman; *John Company*, the old East India Company; *John Doe*, fictitious plaintiff in legal action; *John Dory* (see **dory**).

Johnian, adj. & n. [1. jṓnian; 2. džóuniən]. **John** & **-ian**. **a** adj. Of St. John's College, Cambridge; **b** n., member of this.

johnny, n. [1. jóni; 2. džóni]. **John** & **-y**. (slang) **a** Fellow, chap; **b** a dandy, man about town; Phr. *Johnny Raw*, beginner, novice, recruit.

johnny-cake, n., fr. *Jonathan*? **a** (U.S.A.) Flat cake made from maize flour; **b** (Australia) wheat-meal cake.

Johnsonese, n. [1. jònsonḗz; 2. džònsəníz], fr. name of Samuel Johnson, writer and lexicographer, d. 1784. **a** Literary style of Dr. Johnson; **b** feeble imitation of this, reproducing its least admirable mannerisms; ponderous, verbose, inflated style, abounding in words of Latin origin.

Johnsonian, adj. [1. jonsṓnian; 2. džɔnsóuniən], fr. name of Samuel Johnson. See prec. & **-ian**. Pertaining to, resembling, Dr. Johnson or his style.

join (I.), vb. trans. & intrans. [1. join; 2. džɔin], fr. O. Fr. *joign-*, stem of *joindre*, 'to join', fr. Lat. *jungere*, 'to join, unite, connect'; cogn. w. Scrt. *yunákti*, 'harnesses'; *yuktá-s*, 'harnessed'; Gk. *zeúgnūmi*, 'to yoke, harness' (see **zeugma**); Lith. *jùngiu*, 'to yoke'; O.E. *ġeoc*, 'yoke'. See **yoke** & cp. **coadjutor**. **A.** trans. **1.** To fasten, connect, attach; put together so as to form a whole; to combine: *to join two pieces of material together, one piece on to another*; Phr. *to join battle*, begin fighting, engage; *to join hands*, **a** to clasp hands; **b** to combine with another in action, unite for an undertaking. **2.** To give connecting link, way, road, to; unite: *to join two points by a line*; *to join two towns by a railway, banks of a river by a bridge* &c. **3.** To unite, bring together, bring into close association with: *to join persons, one person with another, in friendship, marriage* &c.; Phr. *to join forces (with)*, to unite in action, act in concert with. **4. a** To come up to, come into company of, associate oneself with: *I will wait here till you join me*; *to join a person in a walk, a drink* &c.; **b** to become a member of: *to join a society* &c.; **c** to take one's place in, go, or return, to: *to join one's ship, regiment* &c. **5.** To come into connexion with, meet and form one with, flow, or run, into: *the stream joins the river*; *the lane joins the high-road*. **B.** intrans. **1. a** To be united, come together, meet: *the two roads join at that point*; **b** to be in contact, be adjacent: *the two estates join*. **2.** To associate oneself with, take part, in common with another, in: *join with me in buying him a present*; *if you are raising a subscription, I'll join (in)*.

join (II.), n., fr. prec. Place or line of contact or fastening; junction.

joinder, n. [1. jóinder; 2. džóində], fr. Fr. *joindre*, 'to join', see **join** (I.), infin. used as n. (law) Act of joining, uniting; state of being joined; union.

joiner, n. [1. jóiner; 2. džóinə], fr. O. Fr. *joigneor*, fr. *joigner*, 'to join', fr. *joign-*, stem of *joindre*, 'to join'. See **join** (I.) & **-er**. **1.** One who, that which, joins. **2.** Specif., skilled workman doing the lighter kinds of work in wood; cp. *carpenter*.

joinery, n. [1. jóineri; 2. džóinəri]. **join** & **-ery**. **1.** The art, occupation, of the joiner. **2.** Woodwork, furniture &c. made by joiner.

joint (I.), n. [1. joint; 2. džɔint]. O. Fr., P.P. of *joindre*, 'to join'. See **join** (I.). **1. a** Place, line, surface &c. where two things are joined; articulation, junction; **b** method, structure, contrivance, by means of which two things are joined. **2.** (anat.) Place where two bones join; method or structure by which two bones fit together, either immovably, or so as to permit of movement: *to put (knee &c.) out of joint*, to dislocate it. Phrs. *to put one's nose out of joint*, supplant one in another's favour &c.; '*the times are out of joint*' (Shakespeare), disordered. **3.** One of the parts into which butcher divides a carcass, esp. as prepared for cooking: *a joint of beef*. **4.** (bot.) Point at which leaf or branch springs from stem. **5.** (geol.) One of a series of more or less parallel cracks traversing a mass of rocks. **6.** (book-binding) Hinge of leather &c. between back and sides of book. **7.** (slang, U.S.A.) **a** A low, illegal drinking saloon, gambling hell &c.; **b** an institution, a building, house.

joint (II.), adj., fr. prec. **1.** Of, pertaining to, done by, involving, produced by, two or more persons: *joint efforts, action, ownership* &c. **2.** (of persons) United in some action; sharing, participating: *joint owners, heirs* &c.

joint (III.), vb. trans., fr. **joint** (I.). **1.** To unite, connect, fasten, fit together, by joints: *a jointed fishing-rod, doll* &c. **2. a** To divide into joints; **b** cut at joints, disjoint. **3.** (masonry) To fill joints of (brickwork) with mortar. **4.** To give a true edge to, plane edge of (board &c.), preparatory to fitting it to another.

jointer, n. [1. jóinter; 2. džóintə]. Prec. & **-er**. **1.** Plane for jointing. **2.** Bent iron bar for riveting stones together. **3.** Mason's tool for pointing.

jointless, adj. [1. jóintles; 2. džɔ́intlis]. **joint** (I.) & **-less**. Without joints.

jointly, adv. [1. jóintli; 2. džɔ́intli]. **joint** (II.) & **-ly**. Together, unitedly, in combination.

jointress, n. [1. jóintres; 2. džɔ́intris], fr. obs. *jointer*, 'joint holder', & **-ess**. Widow on whom a jointure is settled.

joint stock company, n. Association of persons who carry on a business with a common capital.

jointure (I.), n. [1. jóinchur; 2. džɔ́intʃə], fr. Fr., fr. Lat. *junctūra*, 'jointure', fr. *junct-(um)*, P.P. type of *jungere*, 'to join'. See **join** (I.) & **-ure**. Estate settled upon a woman at her marriage.

jointure (II.), vb. trans., fr. prec. To settle jointure upon.

joist, n. [1. joist; 2. džɔist], fr. M.E. *gīste*, early Mod. (16th cent.) *jiste*, fr. O. Fr. *giste*, fr. *gesir*, 'to lie', fr. Lat. *jacēre*, 'to lie', fr. *jacĕre*, 'to throw'. See **jet** (III.). One of the parallel timbers resting upon beams, to which floor-boards or laths of ceiling are nailed.

joisted, adj. [1. jóisted; 2. džɔ́istid]. Prec. & **-ed**. Provided with joists.

joke (I.), n. [1. jōk; 2. džouk]. Only fr. 17th cent.; fr. Lat. *jocus*, 'a jest', cogn. w. Lith. *jŭkas*, 'jest'; the orig. meaning was prob. 'jesting speech'; cogn. w. Scrt. *jăčati*, 'asks, begs'; O.H.G. *jĕhan*, 'to say, declare'; O.N. *jā*, 'to declare, confess'. Something said or done to cause amusement, laughter &c.; incident, circumstance, exciting laughter; jest, witticism, amusing speech. Phrs. *no joke*, a serious matter; *practical joke*, trick played on person to give amusement to others.

joke (II.), vb. intrans. & trans., fr. prec. **1.** intrans. To make jokes; to jest; to be merry, witty, humorous. **2.** trans. To make fun of, make merry with, banter.

joker, n. [1. jṓker; 2. džóukə]. Prec. & **-er**. **1. a** One who jokes; **b** (slang) man, fellow, chap. **2.** (cards) Odd card in pack, used in some games, as euchre, as highest trump, or in poker as any card the holder chooses to suit his hand.

jokingly, adj. [1. jṓkingli; 2. džóukiŋli], fr. Pres. Part. of **joke** (II.) & **-ly**. As a joke.

jokul, jökull, n. [1. yṓkool, yḗkool; 2. jóukul, jǽkul]. Icel. *jōkull*, 'icicle', dimin. of *jaki*, 'ice'; cp. O.E. *gicel*, 'icicle'. See **icicle**. Snow-covered peak in Iceland.

joky, adj. [1. jṓki; 2. džóuki]. **joke** (I.) & **-y**. Fond of, given to, joking; of the nature of a joke.

jollification, n. [1. jòlifikáshun; 2. džɔ̀lifikéiʃən]. See next word & **-fication**. **a** The act of jollifying; **b** festivity, revel, merry-making.

jollify, vb. trans. & intrans. [1. jólifī; 2. džɔ́lifai]. **jolly** & **-fy**. **a** trans. To make jolly; **b** intrans., to become jovial, make merry.

jollily, adv. [1. jólili; 2. džɔ́lili]. **jolly** & **-ly**. In a jolly manner.

jollity, n. [1. jóliti; 2. džɔ́liti], fr. O. Fr. *jolivete*, fr. *jolif*, 'pretty, gay'. See **jolly** & **-ty**. State or condition of being jolly; mirth, merriment, gaiety.

jolly (I.), adj., n., & vb. trans. [1. jóli; 2. džɔ́li]. M.E. *joli(f)*, fr. O. Fr. *joli(f)*, 'merry, gay, pretty'. Etymol. doubtful. **1.** adj. **a** Gay, merry, jovial, mirthful; **b** slightly intoxicated; Phr. *the jolly god*, Bacchus; **c** (colloq.) agreeable, pleasant, delightful, enjoyable: *jolly weather*. **2.** n. (slang) A Royal Marine. **3.** vb. To treat with good humour; to flatter, cajole, into good temper or acquiescence; also *jolly along, up*.

jolly (II.), adv., fr. prec. (colloq.) Very, thoroughly: *a jolly good fellow*; *you will be jolly late*; *jolly well do what I tell you*.

jolly-boat, n. Origin doubtful; possibly fr. Du. *jolle*. See **yawl**. Small ship's boat.

jolt (I.), vb. trans. & intrans. [1. jōlt; 2. džoult]. Etymol. unknown. **1.** trans. To shake with sudden jerk or shock, give a jog to, e.g. in a moving vehicle. **2.** intrans. (of vehicle) To move along jerkily, bump along, as on rough surface.

jolt (II.), n., fr. prec. Sudden, rough, jerk, jog, or bump.

jolterhead, n. [1. jṓlterhed; 2. džóultəhed]. Earlier *jolthead*; etymol. doubtful. Stupid person, fool, blockhead.

jolty, adj. [1. jṓlti; 2. džóulti]. **jolt** (II.) & **-y**. Causing, accompanied by, jolts; bumpy.

Jonah, n. [1. jṓna; 2. džóunə], fr. name of the Hebrew prophet. Person supposed, or appearing, to bring bad luck and disaster upon an enterprise in which he takes part.

Jonathan, n. [1. jónathan; 2. džɔ́nəþən]. Perh. fr. name of a governor of Connecticut, Jonathan Trumbull, d. 1785. Also *Brother Jonathan*, **a** citizen of U.S.A.; **b** American nation personified.

jongleur, n. [1. zhonglḗr; 2. žɔ̃glǽr]. Fr., variant of O. Fr. *jo(u)gleor*. See **juggler**. (hist.) Wandering minstrel.

jonquil, n. [1. jóngkwil; 2. džɔ́ŋkwil], fr. Fr. *jonquille*, fr. dimin. of Lat. *juncus*, 'rush', fr. **joini-cos*; cp. O. Ir. *aoine*, 'rush'. Plant growing from bulb, with sweet-smelling flowers, a variety of narcissus.

Jordan almond, n. [1. jórdan áhmund; 2. džɔ́dn ámənd]. Origin of *Jordan* doubtful; prob. corrupt. of Fr. *jardin*, 'garden'. Fine variety of almond.

jorum, n. [1. jṓrum; 2. džɔ́rəm], fr. King Joram. **a** Large drinking-vessel; **b** contents of drinking-vessel, large quantity of drink.

joss, n. [1. jos; 2. džɔs]. Prob. fr. Port. *deos*, fr. Lat. *deus*, 'god'. See **deity**. Chinese idol.

josser, n. [1. jóser; 2. džɔ́sə]. Etymol. unknown. (slang, vulg.) Fellow.

joss-house, n. Chinese temple.

joss-stick, n. Stick of fragrant gum mixed with clay, burned as incense in Chinese temples.

jostle (I.), vb. trans. & intrans. [1. jósl; 2. džɔ́sl]. Earlier *justle*, fr. **joust** & **-le**. **1.** trans. To push against, knock, elbow, push roughly, hustle. **2.** intrans. To perform act of jostling.

jostle (II.), n., fr. prec. Rough push, elbowing.

jot (I.), n. [1. jot; 2. džɔt], fr. Lat., fr. Gk. *iōta*, 'letter *i*'. See **iota**. Trifle, negligible quantity, esp. with negative: *not a jot*.

jot (II.), vb. trans. Prob. fr. prec. To write down briefly, make a note of: esp. *jot down*.

jotting, n. [1. jóting; 2. džɔ́tiŋ]. Prec. & **-ing**. Rapidly made, brief, note.

joule, n. [1. jool; 2. džūl], fr. J. P. Joule, d. 1889; English physicist. (physics) Unit of electrical energy, amount of work done per second by a current of one ampere flowing at a potential of one volt = 10 million ergs.

jounce, vb. trans. & intrans. [1. jouns; 2. džauns]. Perh. mixture of **jaunt** or **jump** & **bounce**. To bump, jolt.

journal (I.), n. [1. jḗrnl; 2. džǽnl], fr. O. Fr. *jornal*, fr. Lat. *diurnāl-(is)*, 'daily'. See **diurnal**. **1. a** Book containing private record of events as they occur day by day; diary; **b** (parl.) *the Journals*, daily record of proceedings. **2.** (naut.) *Ship's journal*, log-book. **3.** (book-keeping) Book in which each day's transactions are entered. **4. a** Daily newspaper; **b** any periodical publication: *a monthly journal*. **5.** (origin doubtful) Part of shaft resting on bearings; also *journal box*, part of machine in which the journal revolves or moves.

journal (II.), adj. See prec. (archaic) Daily; cp. Spenser: '*Whiles from their journal labours they did rest*'.

journalese, n. [1. jḗrnalḗz; 2. džǽnəlīz]. **journal** & **-ese**. Written style characteristic of inferior journalists; careless, unpolished style produced in a hurry; high-flown style with cheap effects.

journalism, n. [1. jḗrnalizm; 2. džǽnəlizəm]. **journal** & **-ism**. Profession of a journalist.

journalist, n. [1. jḗrnalist; 2. džǽnəlist]. **journal** & **-ist**. One who regularly writes for, or edits, a periodical publication, esp. a newspaper.

journalistic, adj. [1. jḗrnalístik; 2. džǽnəlístik]. Prec. & **-ic**. Pertaining to, characteristic of, journalism or journalists.

journalize, vb. trans. & intrans. [1. jḗrnalīz; 2. džǽnəlaiz]. **journal** & **-ize**. **1.** trans. To enter, record, in a journal. **2.** intrans. To keep a journal, write a diary.

journey (I.), n. [1. jḗrni; 2. džǽni], fr. O. Fr. *jornee*, 'day; day's work; day's journey', fr. Low Lat. *diurnāta*, 'day, day's work', fr. Lat. *diurn-(us)*, 'daily', see **diurnal**, & *-āta*, ending of fem. P.P. of vbs. in *-āre*, & cp. **journal**. **1.** Expedition, esp. of some duration, or to a place at a considerable distance; travels. **2.** Distance traversed, or that may be traversed, in specified time: *a day's journey from here*.

journey (II.), vb. intrans., fr. prec. To take a journey, travel.

journeyman, n. [1. jḗrniman; 2. džǽnimən]. **a** Formerly, one hired to work by the day; **b** now, man who has learnt his craft, contrasted with an *apprentice*.

journey-work, n. **a** Work done by a journeyman, for hire; **b** routine, hack work.

joust, just, vb. intrans. & n. [1. joost, joust, just; 2. džūst, džaust, džast], fr. O. Fr. *juste(r)*, fr. L. Lat. *juxtāre*, 'to approach', fr. *juxtā*, 'near, close', fr. **jugistā*, adv. formed fr. superl. of adj. **jŭg-(os)*, 'bound fast, closely', cogn. w. *jugum*, 'yoke'. See **jugate** & **yoke**. **1.** vb. intrans. To take part in a tournament or joust; to tilt. **2.** n. **a** Encounter between two armed and mounted knights at a tournament; **b** (often pl.) display of jousting, a tournament.

Jove, n. [1. jōv; 2. džouv], fr. Lat. *Jov-(em)*, acc., O. Lat. *Diov-(em)*, 'Jupiter', fr. orig. vocative **djew-* of base **dejewo-*, 'shining, brilliant'. See **deity** & **dies non**. Jupiter; chiefly in Phr. *by Jove!*

jovial, adj. [1. jṓvial; 2. džóuviəl], fr. Fr., fr. Lat. *joviāl-(is)*, 'of Jupiter', fr. *Jov-(em)*, 'Jupiter'. See prec. & **-al**. Cheery, merry, hearty; festive, convivial; originally considered as being under the influence of the planet Jupiter, cp. and contrast *saturnine*.

joviality, n. [1. jòviáliti; 2. džòuviǽliti]. Prec. & **-ity**. State or quality of being jovial.

jovially, adv. [1. jṓviali; 2. džóuviəli]. See prec. & **-ly**. In a jovial manner.

Jovian, adj. [1. jṓvian; 2. džóuviən]. **Jove** & **-ian**. **a** Pertaining to, resembling, Jupiter; august, majestic; **b** of the planet Jupiter.

jowl, n. [1. joul; 2. džaul]. O.E. *ceafl*, 'jaw', M.E. *chaul*; this wd. give Mod. Engl. [tʃōl]; it is probable that both the initial cons. & the vowel have been influenced by O. Fr. & M.E. *joue*, 'jaw', q.v. under **jaw**. **1.** Jaw, jawbone; more usually of lower part of face including cheeks and chin, and esp. of a thick, fat, heavy face. Phr. *cheek by jowl*, close together, side by side. **2. a** Outside of neck, dewlap, of cattle &c.; **b** head and shoulders of salmon.

joy (I.), n. [1. joi; 2. džɔi], fr. M.E., fr. O. Fr. *joie*, fr. Low Lat. **gaudia*, fem. sing. n., fr. Lat. *gaudia*, pl. of *gaudium*, 'joy'. See **gaud** & **gaudy** (I.) **1.** Great pleasure, gladness, delight, rejoicing. **2.** Thing which provokes delight: '*A thing of beauty is a joy forever*' (Keats, 'Endymion').

joy (II.), vb. intrans. & trans., fr. O. Fr. *joir*, 'rejoice', fr. Lat. *gaudēre*, 'to rejoice'. See prec. (poetical) **1.** intrans. To take pleasure, rejoice in, to feel joy at: *I joy to see you happy*. **2.** trans. **a** To give joy to, delight; **b** (archaic) to enjoy.

joy-bells, n. pl. Church bells rung to celebrate a joyful occasion, or to announce a festivity, triumph &c.

joyful, adj. [1. jóifool; 2. džɔ́iful]. **joy** & **-ful**. Feeling, expressing, bringing, joy; happy, glad.

joyfully, adv. Prec. & **-ly**. In a joyful manner.

joyfulness, n. See prec. & **-ness**. State or quality of being joyful.

joyless, adj. [1. jóiles; 2. džóilis]. **joy** & **-less.** Without joy, giving no joy; dismal, gloomy.

joylessly, adv. Prec. & **-ly.** In a joyless manner.

joylessness, n. See prec. & **-ness.** State or quality of being joyless.

joyous, adj. [1. jóius; 2. džóiəs]. M.E., fr. O. Fr. *joyeux.* See **joy** & **-ous.** Full of joy; happy, merry, gay, joyful.

joyously, adv. Prec. & **-ly.** In a joyous manner.

joyousness, n. See prec. & **-ness.** State or quality of being joyous.

joy-ride, n. (colloq.) An unnecessary, irresponsible, trip in a motor-car, esp. in one belonging to someone else, and without his knowledge or permission.

joy-stick, n. (airman's slang) Controlling lever of an aeroplane.

jubé, n. [1. zhōōbā; 2. žūbe]. Fr., fr. Lat. *jube,* imper. of *jubēre,* 'to command, bid', fr. first word of Lat. prayer, said before the reading of the Gospel fr. the rood-loft. Lat. *jubēre,* O. Lat. *joub-,* P.P. *jussum,* seems to have meant orig. 'to put in action, cause to move', fr. base **jeudh-* &c., 'to shake'; cp. Scrt. *yōdhati,* 'fights'; Lith. *júdinu,* 'shake, move'. A gallery or loft over the rood screen in a Church; a rood-loft.

jubilance, -cy, n. [1. jōōbilans(i); 2. džūbiləns(i)], fr. Lat. *jūbil-(āre),* 'to shout for joy'. See next word & **-ce.** (rare) Joy, exultation, triumphant delight.

jubilant, adj. [1. jōōbilant; 2. džūbilənt], fr. Lat. *jūbilant-(em),* Pres. Part. of *jūbil-(āre),* 'to shout for joy'. See **jubilate.** Triumphant, exultant, elated.

jubilantly, adv. Prec. & **-ly.** In a jubilant manner.

jubilate (I.), vb. intrans. [1. jōōbilāt; 2. džūbileit], fr. Lat. *jūbilāt-(um),* P.P. type of *jūbil-(āre),* 'to shout for joy', fr. *jūbil-(um),* 'cry of joy, shout'; the stem **jū-* is cogn. w. M.H.G. *jū(ch),* 'cry of joy', *jūchezen,* 'to shout', Mod. Germ. *jauchzen.* Cp. Gk. *iūgḗ,* 'outcry'. To exult, triumph; to hug oneself, shout with delight, jump for joy.

jubilate (II.), n. [1. jōōbiláhti; 2. džūbiláti]. Lat. *jūbilāte,* 'cry out with joy', imperat. pl. of *jubilāre,* 'to shout for joy'. See prec. **1.** Hundredth psalm, beginning 'O be joyful', used as canticle, as alternative to Benedictus, in Anglican matins. **2.** Joyful outcry.

jubilation, n. [1. jōōbiláshun; 2. džūbiléiʃən]. **jubilate** & **-ion.** Act of jubilating; exultation, triumphant rejoicing.

jubilee, n. [1. jōōbilē; 2. džūbilī], fr. Fr. *jubilé,* fr. L. Lat. *jūbilaeus (annus),* 'year of jubilee', fr. Gk. *iōbēlai-(os),* adj., fr. Heb. *yōbel,* 'ram; ram's horn trumpet; rejoicing, jubilee', w. vowel assimilated in Lat. to that of *jūbilum,* 'joyous outcry'. See **jubilate (I.).** **1.** Festival of emancipation, kept by Jews every fiftieth year. **2.** (R.C. Ch.) Year of indulgence, granted at fixed intervals, or at time specially appointed. **3.** Fiftieth anniversary of a notable event: *silver jubilee,* twenty-fifth anniversary; *(the) diamond jubilee,* sixtieth anniversary, specif., of the accession of Queen Victoria. Phr. *jubilee port,* name given to the '87 vintage on account of Queen Victoria's first jubilee. **4.** Festival, festive season or occasion.

Judaic, adj. [1. jōōdāik; 2. džūdéiik], fr. Lat. *Jūdaic-(us),* fr. Gk. *Ioudaik-(ós),* 'Jewish', fr. *Ioudaî-(os),* 'a Jew'. See **Jew** & **-ic.** Jewish.

Judaism, n. [1. jōōdāizm; 2. džūdeiizəm], fr. Lat. *Jūdae-(us),* 'Jewish', fr. Gk. *Ioudaî-(os),* 'a Jew'. See **Jew** & **-ism.** Religion of the Jews.

Judaist, n. [1. jōōdāist; 2. džūdeiist]. See prec. & **-ist.** Adherent of Judaism.

Judaize, vb. trans. & intrans. [1. jōōdāiz; 2. džūdeiaiz], fr. L. Lat. *jūdaiz-(āre),* 'to Judaize', fr. Gk. *ioudaizein,* fr. *Ioudaî-(os),* 'a Jew'. See **Jew** & **-ize.** **1.** trans. To make Jewish, convert to Judaism. **2.** intrans. To follow Jewish customs &c.

Judas, n. [1. jōōdas; 2. džūdəs, -æs]. Name of disciple who betrayed Christ. **1.** Traitor, infamous betrayer. **2.** (without cap.) A small peep-hole in a door.

Judas-coloured, adj. From colour of Judas's hair, according to tradition. (of hair) Red.

Judas-kiss, n. Act of treachery, performed under the pretence of friendship.

Judas-tree, n. Tree of S. Europe and Asia Minor, with reddish-purple flowers appearing before the leaves; traditionally said to be the tree on which Judas hanged himself.

Judenhetze, n. [1. yōōdnhètse; 2. júdnhètsə]. Germ. Persecution of Jews.

judge (I.), n. [1. juj; 2. dža̋dž], fr. O. Fr. *juge,* fr. Lat. *jūdic-(em),* nom. *jūdex,* 'judge', fr. **jous-dic-(s),* 'he who declares what is just', fr. **jous,* 'law, justice'. See **jus** & **dic-,** cogn. w. *dīc-ere,* 'to say, declare'; see **diction.** **1.** a Official appointed to preside over court of justice, and to hear and decide cases: *Judge of the High Court* &c.; as title, only of County Court judges, in English usage; cp. *justice.* Phr. *as grave as a judge,* very solemn; **b** (of God) supreme and absolute arbiter. **2.** (Jewish hist.) **a** Supreme magistrate having civil and military authority before time of the kings; **b** (pl., cap.) book of Old Testament recording events in the time of the judges. **3.** Person appointed to settle dispute, controversy. **4.** **a** Person able to give authoritative opinion on a point or thing: *a judge of dogs, wine, men* &c.; **b** person specially appointed to apportion merit, to award success in a competition, or exhibition; e.g. at a race, horse-show &c.

judge (II.), vb. trans. & intrans., fr. O. Fr. *juger,* fr. Lat. *jūdicāre,* 'to judge, decide', fr. *jūdic-,* stem of *jūdex,* 'judge'. See prec. **A.** trans. **1.** **a** To hear, try (a case) in a court of justice; to pronounce judgement; **b** to try (a person) and pronounce sentence: *God will judge all men;* **c** to pass moral or intellectual judgement upon, appraise critically merits and demerits of: *it is not for me to judge you, your conduct.* **2.** To give a final opinion upon the relative merits of competitors in a contest of any kind; to decide authoritatively who has won a game, match &c.; to discriminate between the claims of candidates and award prize: *to judge horses, cattle* &c. **3.** To hold the opinion, deem: *I judge him to be a very honest sort of man.* **B.** intrans. **1.** To act as a judge, pass judgement, award; **a** in a court of law; **b** at a competition, exhibition &c.; **c** to pass moral judgement, esp. unfavourable judgement, or appraise moral or intellectual values: '*judge not that ye be not judged*'. **2.** To draw conclusions from facts, form an opinion, come to a decision: *whether he was right or not I am unable to judge; to judge by appearances.*

Judge Advocate General, n. Legal official appointed to advise the Crown on matters of military law and court-martial, a deputy, *judge advocate,* appearing for him in court.

judge-made, adj. *Judge-made law,* that based on the interpretation put upon statutes &c. by judges.

judg(e)ment, n. [1. jújment; 2. dža̋džmənt]. **judge** & **-ment.** **1.** **a** Authoritative decision given by a judge sitting officially in court; **b** decree, decision, of a court as to what is just or legal in a given case. **2.** (theol.) Final award, sentence, of God as supreme judge of all things: *the Day of Judgement.* **3.** Result of a Divine decree, or something regarded as such; a calamity sent by God as a punishment: *his misfortunes were a judgement upon him for his wickedness.* **4.** Intellectual process of judging, of comparing, discriminating, relating, material, moral, or intellectual facts, and reaching a rational conclusion. **5.** Capacity for forming an intellectual judgement, esp. a right one; discrimination, discernment, prudence, sagacity: *a man of good heart but poor judgement.* **6.** Result of the process of judging (**4**); an opinion, a view; conclusion: *in my judgement you are wrong.*

judg(e)ment-day, n. Day on which God will pronounce final judgement on all mankind.

judg(e)ment-seat, n. Judge's seat; court of justice, tribunal.

judgeship, n. [1. jújship; 2. dža̋džʃip]. **judge** & **ship.** Office of a judge.

judgmatic(al), adj. [1. jujmátik(l); 2. dža̋džmǽtik(l)], fr. **judge,** on anal. of **dogmatic.** (colloq.) Showing sound judgement; judicious.

judgmatically, adv. Prec. & **-ly.** (colloq.) In a judgmatic manner.

judicature, n. [1. jōōdikachur; 2. džūdikətʃə], fr. Med. Lat. *jūdicātūra,* fr. Lat. *jūdicāt-(um),* P.P. type of *jūdicāre,* 'to judge'. See **judge (II.)** & **-ure.** **1.** Judges collectively; body of those employed in the state administration of justice. **2.** Administration of justice: *Supreme Court of Judicature,* used as full official title of the various Courts of Justice composing the High Court, as determined by the *Judicature Acts.*

judicial, adj. [1. jōōdíshal; 2. džūdíʃəl], fr. Lat. *jūdiciāl-(is),* 'judicial', fr. *jūdici-(um),* 'legal investigation, trial; judgement', fr. *jūdic-,* stem of *jūdex.* See **judge** & **-al.** **1.** Pertaining to a judge, or to a court of justice; or to administration of justice: *the judicial bench; judicial proceedings.* Phr. *judicial murder,* unjust sentence of death pronounced after legal trial. **2.** Judging, discriminating, apt at reasoning, and deciding; capable of forming an impartial judgement: *a judicial mind, intellect.*

judicially, adv. Prec. & **-ly.** In a judicial manner.

judiciary, adj. & n. [1. jōōdíshari; 2. džūdíʃəri], fr. Lat. *jūdiciārius.* See **judicial** & **-ary.** **1.** adj. Pertaining to a court of law; judicial: *judiciary proceedings* &c. **2.** n. Judges collectively; judicature: *an impartial and incorruptible judiciary.*

judicious, adj. [1. jōōdíshus; 2. džūdíʃəs], fr. Fr. *judicieux,* fr. Lat., fr. stem *jūdic-.* See **judge** & **-ous.** Wise, prudent, showing sound judgement; discerning.

judiciously, adv. Prec. & **-ly.** In a judicious manner.

judiciousness, n. See prec. & **-ness.** Quality of being judicious.

jug (I.), n. [1. jug; 2. dža̋g]. Etymol. unknown. **1.** Deep vessel of earthenware, glass &c., with handle and spout, for holding liquids. **2.** (slang) *(Stone) jug,* prison; *in jug,* in gaol.

jug (II.), vb. trans., fr. prec. **a** To stew (hare, rabbit) in covered jar; **b** (slang) to put into gaol.

jug (III.), also **jug-jug**, n. & vb. intrans. Imitative. **a** n. Notes in song of nightingale; **b** vb., to utter this note.

jugate, adj. [1. jōōgāt; 2. džūgeit], fr. Lat. *jugāt-(um),* P.P. type of *jugāre,* 'to connect, join', fr. *jug-(um),* 'yoke', cogn. w. **yoke.** (bot.) Having the leaflets in pairs.

jugful, n. [1. júgfool; 2. dža̋gful]. **jug (I.)** & **-ful.** **a** Contents of a jug; **b** amount which a jug will hold.

Juggernaut, n. [1. júgernawt; 2. dža̋gənɔ̄t], fr. Hind. *Jagannath,* 'lord of the universe', fr. Scrt. *Jagannātha,* fr. *jagat,* 'world', & *nātha,* 'lord'. **1.** Form of Hindu god Vishnu; the image of the god at Orissa was formerly dragged through the streets on a car, before and under which devotees were said to hurl themselves, allowing themselves to be crushed to death. **2.** (fig.) Irresistible, relentless, ruthless force which destroys all that comes in its way; (also in same sense) *Juggernaut's car.*

juggins, n. [1. júginz; 2. dža̋ginz]. Etymol. unknown. (slang) Inexperienced, simple person who allows himself to be easily duped.

juggle (I.), vb. intrans. & trans. [1. júgl; 2. dža̋gl], fr. O. Fr. *jogler,* fr. L. Lat. *joculāre,* fr. Lat. *joculāri,* 'to joke, jest', fr. *jocul-(us),* dimin. of *jocus,* 'jest'. See **joke.** **A.** intrans. **1.** To perform conjuring tricks, exhibit manual dexterity, sleight-of-hand. **2.** (fig.) *Juggle with,* **a** to misrepresent, distort (facts); **b** to practise artifice upon, deceive (person); *to juggle with words*, use them for purposes of deception and misrepresentation. **B.** trans. To overcome by trickery, fraud, cunning; outwit, cheat: *to juggle a person out of his money.*

juggle (II.), n., fr. prec. **1.** Feat of manual dexterity, sleight-of-hand. **2.** Cunning trick, artifice, imposture; verbal deception, misuse of words for purpose of misleading.

juggler, n. [1. júgler; 2. džáglə], fr. O. Fr. *jo(u)gleor*, fr. Lat. *joculātōr-(em)*, 'jester', fr. *joculāt-(um)*, P.P. type of *joculāri*, 'to jest'. See **juggle** (I.) & **-er.** One who juggles; **a** one who performs feats of manual dexterity; **b** a cheat, trickster; prevaricator.

jugglery, n. [1. júgleri; 2. džágləri]. **juggle** & **-ery.** **1.** The art, act, or practice, of juggling. **2.** Imposture, fraud, cunning trick; misrepresentation.

Jugo-Slav, n. [1. ūgō slàhv; 2. júgou slàv]. Serb., 'Southern Slav'. Inhabitant, subject, of Jugo-Slavia, the kingdom of the Serbs, Croats, and Slovenes, formed by union of the former Serbia with the Hungarian Croatia &c.

jugular, adj. & n. [1. júgūlar, jōōgūlar; 2. džágjulə, džūgjulə], fr. Lat. *jugul-(um)*, 'collar-bone', cogn. w. *jug-um*, 'yoke'. See **yoke** & **-ar.** **1.** adj. **a** Of, pertaining to, head and neck; *jugular veins*, four large veins conveying blood from head and face; **b** (of fish) with ventral fins in front of pectoral. **2.** n. Jugular vein.

jugulate, vb. trans. [1. júgūlāt, jōōgūlāt; 2. džág-, džūgjuleit], fr. Lat. *jugulāt-(um)*, P.P. type of *jugulāre*, 'to cut the throat of, kill; to destroy', fr. *jugul-(um)*, 'collar-bone; throat'. See **jugular.** **a** To cut throat of, strangle; **b** (med.) to check (disease) by drastic remedy.

juice, n. [1. jōōs; 2. džūs], fr. Fr. *jus*, fr. Lat. *jūs*, 'broth, soup', cogn. w. Scrt. *yūš*, 'broth'; Lith. *júszė*, 'soup', fr. base **jūs-*, 'broth, mixture', connected w. **jew-*, **ju-* &c., 'to join together', whence Lat. *jungere*, 'to join'. See **join** & **yoke.** **1.** Fluid part of animal or vegetable tissue: *digestive juices*; *lemon juice.* **2.** (fig.) Essence, essential meaning, best part, of anything. **3.** (slang or colloq., U.S.A.) **a** Electric current as motive power &c.; **b** petrol, gasoline, for motor-car.

juiceless, adj. [1. jōōsles; 2. džūslis]. Prec. & **-less.** Without juice.

juiciness, n. [1. jōōsines; 2. džūsinis]. See next word & **-ness.** Quality of being juicy.

juicy, adj. [1. jōōsi; 2. džūsi]. **juice** & **-y.** **1.** Containing much juice, succulent. **2.** (slang) Full of interest, not dull or dry; spicy.

ju-ju, n. [1. jōō jōō; 2. džū džū]. Etymol. doubtful; native word is *gru-gru.* (W. Afr.) **1.** Charm, magic, spell, fetish. **2.** Ban, prohibition, effected by such a charm; taboo.

jujube, n. [1. jōōjōōb; 2. džūdžūb], fr. Fr., fr. Med. Lat. *jujuba*, fr. Gk. *zizuphon*, an Eastern plant. **1.** Small plum-like fruit of an Eastern shrub. **2.** Lozenge made of sugar, gelatine &c., originally in imitation of this.

ju-jutsu, jiu-jitsu, n. [1. jōō jítsōō; 2. džū džítsū]. Jap. *ju-jutsu.* Japanese art and style of wrestling.

julep, n. [1. jōōlep; 2. džūlɛp], fr. Fr., fr. Arab. *jūlāb*, fr. Pers. *gūlāb*, fr. *gūl*, 'rose', & *ab*, 'water'. Sweet, syrupy, soothing, medicated drink.

Julian, adj. [1. jōōlian; 2. džūliən], fr. Lat. *Jūliān-(us)*, adj., fr. *Jūli-(us)*, 'Julius', & **-an.** Of Julius Caesar; *Julian Calendar*, calendar as reformed by Julius Caesar.

julienne, n. [1. zhūlién; 2. žyliɛn]. Fr., fr. personal name. Clear soup containing finely chopped herbs and vegetables.

July, n. [1. jōōlí; 2. džulái]. M.E. *Jule*, fr. O. Fr. *Jule*, fr. Lat. (*mensis*) *Jūlius*, named after Julius Caesar. Seventh month of year.

jumble (I.), vb. trans. & intrans. [1. júmbl; 2. džámbl], fr. blend of *jump* (or *join* ?) & *tumble* ? **1.** trans. To mix up, shake up, confuse together without any order; put together things which are disparate and unrelated; esp. *to jumble up*, or *together.* **2.** intrans. To be mixed confusedly; to jostle.

jumble (II.), n., fr. prec. Confused mixture, miscellaneous collection; muddle, confusion.

jumble (III.), n. Kind of thin, sweet, sticky cake.

jumble-sale, n. Bazaar at which all kinds of miscellaneous articles are sold at very low prices, the proceeds being applied to charitable purposes.

jumbly, adj. [1. júmbli; 2. džámbli]. **jumble** (II.) & **-y.** Jumbled together, confused.

jumbo, n. [1. júmbō; 2. džámbou], fr. name of celebrated elephant sent fr. London Zoo to U.S.A. in the early eighties of 19th cent., whose departure caused great popular interest. Very large clumsy animal or person.

jump (I.), vb. intrans. & trans. [1. jump; 2. džamp]. First recorded in 16th cent. Origin uncertain. **A.** intrans. **1.** (of human beings and animals) **a** To propel oneself suddenly into the air from the feet, by exertion of muscular energy; to spring, leap, bound; Phrs. *to jump for joy*, (i.) to leap, dance, skip about under influence of exultant feelings; (ii.) to feel and show strong emotions of pleasure and exultation; to jubilate; *his eyes were jumping out of his head*, were very prominent, or were staring intently; **b** specif. (of animals) to spring into the air and propel the body forwards so as to clear an obstacle: *this horse is no good as a hunter, he can't jump.* **2.** **a** To make a sudden, brusque, involuntary movement, with the whole or part of the body; to start, give sudden, convulsive movement; to twitch, as from a sudden physical or emotional shock of surprise, fright &c.: *you made me jump when you came in so suddenly*; *my heart jumped as I heard the news*; **b** to throb, as an abscess, bad tooth &c. **3.** (of inanimate objects) **a** (when stationary) To be propelled suddenly, be jerked, from position, as by strong impact or oscillation: *he hit the table so hard that he made all the tea-cups jump*; **b** (when moving) to be hurled into the air, and diverted from course by a sudden check: *the car struck a stone and jumped clear of the pedestrian.* **4.** (of mental action) To pass rapidly and suddenly from a subject or thought &c.: *to jump from one topic to another.* **B.** trans. **1.** **a** (of men and animals) To pass over, cross, clear, by jumping: *to jump a gate, a stream* &c.; **b** (of inanimate objects in motion) to be propelled, jerked, shot, over, or away from: *the engine jumped the rails*; **c** to compel to jump: *to jump a horse over a fence* &c. **2.** To leave out, skip, pass over without considering: *to jump a chapter in a book.* **3.** To hoodwink, dupe, bamboozle, persuade by misrepresentations: *to be jumped into doing something.* Phr. *to jump a claim*, to obtain land, right of mining &c., to which another had a prior claim. **4.** To dandle, toss in one's arms: *to jump a baby on one's knee.* **C.** Followed by adverb or preposition. *Jump about*, to cut capers, skip, leap about, with excitement, pleasure, pain &c.; to be restless. *Jump at*, to accept, adopt, seize upon, with eagerness: *to jump at an offer, suggestion, idea* &c. *Jump down*, **a** intrans., to spring to lower level by single muscular effort; **b** trans., to help (child, &c.) to jump down. *Jump in, into, out, over* &c., to get in (to) or out of quickly: *jump over*, to clear with a bound. *Jump up*, to get up quickly, rise hurriedly to one's feet: *to jump up from one's chair*; *he jumped up as I went in*; *jump up!*, get on to your horse, seat of carriage &c. *Jump upon, on*, to make a sudden attack on; specif., to scold severely, blame, reprimand. *Jump with*, to agree, coincide with, correspond to: *your statement doesn't altogether jump with the facts.*

jump (II.), n., fr. prec. **1.** Voluntary spring from ground, leap, bound: *high, long, jump*, as athletic exercise or test. **2.** **a** Sudden involuntary movement, start, caused by shock &c.; **b** (slang) *the jumps*, nervous twitchings, restless, jerking movements; the fidgets. **3.** Sudden upward movement, rise, increase (in price, temperature &c.). **4.** Interruption, break, gap, abrupt transition, in a series &c.

jumpable, adj. [1. júmpabl; 2. džámpəbl]. **jump** & **-able.** Capable of being jumped.

jumper (I.), n. [1. júmper; 2. džámpə]. **jump** (I.) & **-er.** **1.** One who, that which, jumps; specif. **a** one of a sect of Welsh Methodists (c. 1760) who leapt about under influence of religious emotion; **b** insect that jumps. **2.** (naut.) Rope to keep yard &c. in position.

jumper (II.), n. Etymol. uncertain; possibly corruption of Fr. *jupe, jupon*, 'skirt'. **1.** Sailor's loose tunic of canvas &c. **2.** Woman's loose blouse or jersey, extending over top of skirt.

jumping-bean, n. [1. júmping bēn; 2. džámpiŋ bín]. Seed of tropical American plant, containing larva which causes it to move as though jumping.

jumping-deer, n. Black-tailed deer of N. America.

jumping-hare, n. S. African rodent, a kind of jerboa.

junction, n. [1. júngkshun; 2. džáŋkʃən], fr. Lat. *junctiōn-(em)*, 'a joining', fr. *junct-(um)*, P.P. type of *jungere*, 'to join', see **join**, & **-ion.** **1.** Act or process of joining. **2.** **a** Place, line, point, at which two things join; specif. **b** station where two or more lines or branches of railway meet. **3.** Means, method, by which two things join; joint, connexion.

juncture, n. [1. júngkchur; 2. džáŋktʃə], fr. Lat. *junctūra*, 'a joining', fr. *junct-(um)*, P.P. type of *jungere*, 'to join'. See **join** & **-ure.** **1.** Position of affairs, circumstances; critical point, esp. in Phr. *at this juncture.* **2.** (rare) **a** Act or process of joining; **b** place, point, where things join; joint.

June, n. [1. jōōn; 2. džūn], fr. Lat. (*mensis*) *Jūnius*, 'June', fr. name of a Roman gens; prob. fr. same base as **Juno.** Sixth month of year.

jungle, n. [1. júnggl; 2. džáŋgl], fr. Hind. *jangal*, 'desert; forest'. Uncultivated land, overgrown with forest, brushwood &c.

jungled, adj. [1. júnggld; 2. džáŋgld]. Prec. & **-ed.** Overgrown with jungle.

jungle-fever, n. Severe malarial fever.

jungle-fowl, n. One of several varieties of game bird living in the jungle.

jungly, adj. [1. júnggli; 2. džáŋgli]. **jungle** & **-y.** Overgrown with jungle; pertaining to, like, the jungle.

junior (I.), adj. [1. jōōnior; 2. džūniə]. Lat. *jūnior*, fr. **juveniōs*, compar. of *jūven-is*, 'young'. See **juvenile.** **1.** Younger, esp. of two brothers, or of son with same names as his father: *Thomas Brown, junior.* **2.** Of less standing; subordinate: *junior partner, Fellow (of a College).*

junior (II.), n., fr. prec Person who is younger or of lower standing: *one's juniors*, those younger than oneself.

juniorate, n. [1. jōōniorāt; 2. džūniəreit]. **junior** & **-ate.** Two-year course of instruction demanded of Jesuits before entering the priesthood.

juniority, n. [1. jōōnióriti; 2. džūnióriti]. **junior** & **-ity.** State or condition of being junior.

juniper, n. [1. jōōniper; 2. džūnipə], fr. Lat. *jūniper-(us)*, 'juniper tree'; etymol. doubtful. Genus of coniferous evergreen trees, with dark, rough berries from which an essential oil is obtained, used in medicine and for flavouring gin.

junk (I.), n. [1. jungk; 2. džaŋk]. Etymol. unknown. **1.** **a** Old cables &c., used for making oakum &c.; **b** (slang) rubbish, useless stuff; nonsense. **2.** (naut.) Salt meat. **3.** Tissue in head of sperm-whale, from which spermaceti is obtained. **4.** Lump, piece, chunk, of anything.

junk (II.), vb. trans., fr. prec. **a** To make into junk; **b** to cut into chunks.

junk (III.), n. Port. *junco*, adaptation of Malay. *jōng*. Large, flat-bottomed, usually three-masted vessel, used in China sea.

junker, n. [1. yóongker; 2. júŋkə]. Germ. *junker*, fr. M.H.G. *junkher*, 'young lord'. Cp. **younker**. **1. a** German landed gentleman, a squire; **b** member of political party in Prussia representing the conservative and landed interest.

junket (I.), n. [1. júngket; 2. džáŋkit]. Perh. fr. A.-Fr. *jonquette*, 'rush-basket' (for making junket in), fr. Lat. *juncus*, 'rush'. See **jonquil**. **1.** Milk thickened into soft curd with rennet; often eaten with cream. **2.** Merry-making &c., usually *junketing*.

junket (II.), vb. intrans., fr. prec. To feast, make merry.

junketing, n. [1. júngketing; 2. džáŋkitiŋ]. Prec. & **-ing**. Feasting, merrymaking, jollification.

junk-shop, n. **junk (I.)** & **shop**. Marine store.

Juno, n. [1. jóonō; 2. džúnou]. Lat. *Jūno*; etymol. uncertain; prob. fr. **Jusn-*, cogn. w. Scrt. *yóša*, genit. *yōšnáš*, 'young wife', & ultimately fr. same base as Lat. *juvenis*, 'young'; see **juvenile**. **1.** (Roman mythol.) Wife of Jupiter. **2.** Majestic, stately woman. **3.** Name of one of the smaller planets.

junta, n. [1. júnta; 2. džántə]. Span., fr. Lat. *juncta*, P.P. fem. of *jungere*, 'to join'. See **join**. **1.** Spanish or Italian administrative assembly, council of state. **2.** Junto.

junto, n. [1. júnto; 2. džántou]. Variant of prec. Body of confederates, intriguers; political faction, cabal.

Jupiter, n. [1. jóopiter; 2. džúpitə]. Lat. *Juppiter*, fr. **Jū-piter*, orig. a vocative **djēw pəter*, fr. **diēus*, 'deity', see **deity**, & **pətér*, 'father'. See **pater** & **father**. Cp. **Jove**. **1. a** (Roman mythol.) Supreme deity, king of the gods and ruler of heaven; *Jupiter Pluvius*, name under which Jupiter was worshipped as god of rain; **b** archaic expletive: *By Jupiter*. **2.** Largest planet of solar system.

jural, adj. [1. jóoral; 2. džórəl, džúərəl], fr. Lat. *jūr-*, stem of *jūs*, 'law, right'. See **jus** & **-al**. **1.** Pertaining to law; legal. **2.** Pertaining to moral obligation, right, duty.

Jurassic, adj. [1. joorásik; 2. džurǽsik], fr. Fr. *Jurassique*, fr. *Jura* (Mts.), on anal. of *liassic* &c. (of rocks &c.) Of the geological character of the Jura Mountains; *Jurassic period*, one of the three divisions of the Mesozoic era, including the lias and the oolites.

jurat, n. [1. jóorat; 2. džúəræt], fr. Med. Lat. *jūrāt-(us)*, fr. Lat. *jūrāt-(um)*, P.P. type of *jūrāre*, 'to swear', cogn. w. *jūr-(em)*, 'right, law, justice' (see **jus**); lit. 'person under oath'. **a** Municipal officer in the Cinque Ports; **b** life magistrate in Channel Islands.

juridical, adj. [1. jooridikl; 2. džurídikl], fr. Lat. *jūridic-(us)*, 'judicial', fr. *jūr-(em)*, 'right, law' (see **jus**), & *-dic-(us)*, cogn. w. *dīcere*, 'to say'. See **diction** & **-al**. Connected with, pertaining to, the administration of the law; judicial, legal.

jurisconsult, n. [1. jóoriskónsult; 2. džōr-, džùəriskónsʌlt], fr. Lat. *jūrisconsult-(us)*, 'lawyer', fr. *jūris*, genit. of *jūs*, 'law' (see **jus**), & *consultus*, P.P. of *consulere*, 'to consider, consult'. See **consult**. One who can give authoritative opinions on legal points; jurist.

jurisdiction, n. [1. jóorisdíkshun; 2. džōr-, džùərisdíkʃən], fr. Lat. *jūrisdictiōn-(em)*, 'judicial authority', fr. *jūris*, genit. of *jūs*, 'law'. See **jus** & **diction**. **1.** Administration of justice. **2. a** Legal authority; right of exercising authority; **b** extent of authority of person, court of justice &c. **3.** District over which a person, court &c. exercises authority.

jurisdictional, adj. [1. jóorisdíkshunal; 2. džōr-, džùərisdíkʃənəl]. Prec. & **-al**. Connected with jurisdiction.

jurisprudence, n. [1. jóorisproódens; 2. džōr-, džùərisprúdəns], fr. Lat. *jūrisprūdentia*, 'science of law', fr. *jūris*, genit. of *jūs*, 'law'. See **jus** & **prudence**. Science and philosophy of law and of legal principles.

jurisprudent, adj. & n. [1. jóorisproódent; 2. džōr-, džùərisprúdənt], fr. Lat. *jūris-prūdent-(em)*, 'one skilled in the law', fr. *jūris*, genit. of **jus**, & **prudent**. **1.** adj. Skilled in the law. **2.** n. Jurist, student of law.

jurisprudential, adj. [1. jóorisproodénshal; 2. džōr-, džùərisprūdénʃəl]. Prec. & **-ial**. Of, pertaining to, jurisprudence.

jurist, n. [1. jóorist; 2. džúərist], fr. Med. Lat. *jurista*, 'jurist', Fr. *jūr-(is)*, genit. of *jūs*, 'law'. See **jus** & **-ist**. One learned in the law; student of, writer on, law.

juristic(al), adj. [1. jooristik(l); 2. džurístik(l)]. Prec. & **-ic** & **-al**. Of, pertaining to, jurists.

juristically, adv. Prec. & **-ly**. In a juristic manner; legally.

juror, n. [1. jóoror; 2. džórə, džúərə], fr. O. Fr. *jureor*, fr. Lat. *jūrātōr-(em)*, 'one who swears', fr. *jūrāt-(um)*, P.P. type of *jūrāre*, 'to swear', fr. *jūr-*, stem of *jūs*, 'law, right'. See **jus** & **-or**. **1.** Member of jury, juryman. **2.** One who binds himself by an oath; cp. *non-juror*.

jury, n. [1. jóori; 2. džóri, džúəri], fr. O. Fr. *jurée*, 'oath; legal inquiry', fr. Med. Lat. *jūrāta*, fem. P.P. of Lat. *jūrāre*, 'to swear'. See **jurat**. **1. a** Body of citizens summoned, and sworn to decide impartially on the facts of a case tried before a judge, and to give a verdict thereon; **b** similar body who decide on the cause of death at an inquest in a coroner's court. **2.** (fig.) The whole body of the public who form and express an opinion on public matters: *the jury of public opinion*.

jury-box, n. Enclosed space where jury sit in a court of justice.

juryman, n. [1. jóoriman; 2. džórimən]. Member of jury; juror.

jury-mast, n. Origin uncertain; possibly for *ajury*, fr. O. Fr. *ajuirie*, 'aid', fr. Lat. *adjutāre*, 'to help'. See **adjutant**; it is not a shortened form of 'injury-mast'. Temporary mast erected in place of one broken &c.

jus, n. [1. jus; 2. džas]. Lat. *jūs*, 'law, right, equity', O. Lat. *jous*, fr. **jouros*, cogn. w. Scrt. *yōš*, 'safety'; other cognates are doubtful. Law, right, equity; *jus civile*, civil law; *jus divinum*, divine right of kings; *jus gentium*, law of nations.

just (I.), adj. [1. just; 2. džast]. Fr. *juste*, fr. Lat. *jūst-(us)*, 'just, upright; fair, equitable', fr. Lat. *jūs*, 'law, right' (see **jus**); perh. cogn. w. O. Slav. *istŭ*, 'true.' **1.** (of person, conduct, action) Fair, right, equitable, upright. **2.** (of emotion, opinion &c.) well-grounded, felt with good reason, having a sound basis: *just indignation* &c. **3. a** Accorded, obtained, rightly, and according to justice; well-deserved, due, fairly earned: *just reward, deserts* &c.; **b** due, proper, fitting, to the right amount: *the payment is just*.

just (II.), adv., fr. prec. **1.** Exactly, precisely: *just what I said*; *that is just right*; *just so*. **2.** Hardly, barely, scarcely: *I just caught the train*; *only just enough*. **3. a** At that precise moment: *just then*; *he has just come*; *just at that moment*; **b** a short time before, not long ago; Phr. *just now*, (i.) at this moment; (ii.) not long ago; (iii.) presently. **4.** (colloq.) Quite, absolutely: *just perfect*.

just (III.). See **joust**.

justice, n. [1. jústis; 2. džástis], fr. Lat. *justitia*, 'justice'; **just** (I.) & **-ice**. **1.** Principle of rectitude and integrity of conduct in the dealings of men with each other; just conduct, fairness, equity; one of the cardinal virtues: *to treat a man with justice*. **2.** Quality of being right, just, equitable; conformity with what is just; rightness, righteousness: *he complained with justice of his treatment*. **3. a** The law; administration of the law as it affects rights and wrongs of persons; **b** punishment for crime inflicted by the law: *to bring a murderer to justice*; Phr., specif., *to administer justice*, to punish an offender. **4.** Person appointed by authority to hold courts, try cases and administer justice; **a** (i.) a judge of the Supreme Court; referred to as *Mr. Justice Jones* &c.; (ii.) a Lord of Appeal; referred to as Lord Justice X.; **b** one holding a commission of the peace, a magistrate, also called *Justice of the Peace*. See also **eyre**.

justiceship, n. [1. jústisship; 2. džástisʃip]. Prec. & **-ship**. Office, rank, term of office, of justice.

justiciable, adj. & n. [1. justíshyabl; 2. džastíʃjəbl], fr. O. Fr., *justici-(er)*, 'to bring to trial', fr. Med. Lat. *justitiāre*, fr. *justitia*, 'justice'. See **justice** & **-able**. **1.** adj. Subject to jurisdiction: *justiciable offences* &c. **2.** n. Person subject to another's jurisdiction.

justiciar, n. [1. justíshiar; 2. džastíʃiə], fr. Med. Lat. *justitiār-(ius)*, 'officer of justice'. See next word. Highest judicial officer in time of Normans and Early Plantagenets.

justiciary, n. & adj. [1. justíshyari; 2. džastíʃjəri], fr. Med. Lat. *justitiāri-(us)*, 'officer of justice', fr. *justitia*, 'justice', & **-ary**. **1.** n. **a** Officer, administrator, of justice; **b** justiciar. **2.** adj. Of, pertaining to, administration of justice; judicial.

justifiability, n. [1. jústifiabíliti; 2. džástifaiəbíliti]. See next word & **-ity**. State or quality of being justifiable.

justifiable, adj. [1. jústifiabl; 2. džástifaiəbl]. **justify** & **-able**. That can be justified.

justifiably, adv. Prec. & **-ly**. In a justifiable manner.

justification, n. [1. jùstifikáshun; 2. džàstifikéiʃən]. See **justify** & **-fication**. **1. a** Act of justifying; state of being justified; **b** specif. (print.) spacing out of type. **2.** Something that justifies; plea, argument in favour of person or action; vindication.

justificative, justificatory, adj. [1. jústifikàtiv, jùstifikátori; 2. džástifikèitiv, džàstifikéitəri]. See prec. & **-ive, -ory**. Having the power of justifying.

justifier, n. [1. jústifier; 2. džástifaiə]. One who justifies; specif. (print.) man, or machine, that spaces out type.

justify, vb. trans. [1. jústifī; 2. džástifai], fr. Fr. *justifier*, fr. L. Lat. *justificāre*, 'to justify'. **just** (I.) & *-i-* & **-fy**. **1.** To prove, assert, to be just; vindicate; show to be in accordance with reason and fitness: *to justify one's action*. Phr. *to be justified in doing something*, act in accordance with what is right and proper. **2.** To show a rational or moral sanction for; to exonerate, excuse: *I cannot justify his strange conduct to you*. **3.** To set, arrange, in proper order, straighten &c.: specif. (print.) *to justify a line of type*, space it out properly.

jut, n. & vb. intrans. [1. jut; 2. džat]. Variant of **jet** (III.). **1.** n. Projection; piece, point, jutting out. **2.** vb. To project, protrude, stick out; often *jut out*.

jute (I.), n. [1. joot; 2. džūt], fr. Bengali *jhoṭo*, fr. Scrt. *juṭa*, cogn. w. *jaṭa*, 'braid of hair, tress'. Fibre of Indian plant, *Corchorus*, used for coarse canvas, rope &c.

Jute (II.), n. O.E. *Iote, Yte*; Lat. *Iuta*. Ancient inhabitant of Jutland. Member of one of the Germanic tribes invading Britain in 5th century.

juvenescence, n. [1. jóovenésens; 2. džùvənésəns], fr. Lat. *juvenescent-(em)*, Pres. Part. of *juvenescere*, 'to grow up to youth', fr. stem *juven-(is)*, 'young'. See **juvenile** & **-ence**. **1.** State of being young; youth. **2.** State or process of growing up to youth, or of becoming young.

juvenescent, adj. [1. jóovenésent; 2. džùvənésənt]. See prec. **1.** Growing into a youth. **2.** Becoming young.

juvenile, adj. & n. [1. jóovenīl; 2. džúvənail], fr. Lat. *juvenīl-(is)*, 'youthful', fr. *juven-(is)*, 'young', & **-ile**. See **young** & **youth**. **1.** adj. Young, youthful; of, pertaining to, suited to, characteristic of, youth. **2.** n. Young person, youth.

juvenilely, adv. Prec. & **-ly**. In a juvenile manner.

juvenility, n. [1. jōōveníliti, -íliti; 2. džūvəníliti, -áiliti]. **juvenile** & **-ity**. State or quality of being juvenile.

juxtapose, vb. trans. [1. jukstapṓz; 2. džakstəpóuz], fr. Lat. *juxtā*, 'next, close by'; fr. **jugistā*, adv. fr. superl. of adj. **jug-os*, 'closely connected', cogn. w. *jug-(um)*, 'yoke'. See **jugate**; for the second element see **pose**. (in material and non-material senses) To place side by side.

juxtaposition, n. [1. jùkstapozíshun; 2. džàkstəpəzíʃən]. Prec. & **-ition**. The act of placing side by side; state of being juxtaposed.

K

K, k [1. kā; 2. kei]. The eleventh letter of the English alphabet; for use in abbreviations see end of Dictionary.

ka, n. [1. kah; 2. kā]. (anct. Egyptian religion) The soul, represented on monuments by a bird.

Kaaba, Caaba, n. [1. káhba; 2. kā́bə]; also [1. káh-abah; 2. kā́əbā]. Arab. *ka'ba*, 'building', fr. *ka'b*, 'cube'. Shrine at Mecca, containing sacred 'black stone' to which Moslems make pilgrimage.

kaama, n. [1. káhma; 2. kā́mə]. Native name of S. African antelope; hartebeest.

kabala, kabbala, n. See **cabala**.

kabyle, n. [1. kabíl; 2. kæbáil]. Fr., fr. Arab. *qabail*, pl. of *qabilah*, 'tribe'. **a** Member of Berber tribes in N.E. Algeria and Tunis; **b** dialect of Berber language spoken by Kabyles.

kaddish, n. [1. káhdish; 2. kā́diʃ]. Aramaic, 'holy'. The doxology in Jewish ritual.

kadi, n. See **cadi**.

Kaffir (I.), n. [1. káfer; 2. kǽfə]. Arab. *kafir*, 'infidel'. **1. a** Member of a S. African division of the Bantu race, esp. one inhabiting the Transkei territory between Natal and Cape Colony; **b** name given generally by whites to all coloured people in S. Africa. **2.** (pl.) *Kaffirs* (Stock Exchange slang) S. African mining shares.

Kaffir (II.), adj., fr. prec. Of or pertaining to Kaffirs or their country; *Kaffir-corn*, kind of millet; *Kaffir-date*, kind of plum; (Stock Exchange) *Kaffir-market*, that dealing in S. African mining shares.

kaftan, n. See **caftan**.

kagu, n. [1. káhgōō; 2. kā́gū]. Native name. Crested bird found in New Caledonia.

kaid, n. [1. kād; 2. keid]. N. Afr. variant of Arab. *kadi*, 'cadi', q.v. Chief of a tribe or group of tribes in Morocco, Algeria, and Tunis.

kail, n. See **kale**.

kaimakam, n. [1. kímakahm; 2. káiməkām]. Turk. *qāimāqam*, 'deputy'. Title of military rank in Turkish and Egyptian armies, equivalent to lieutenant-colonel.

kainite, n. [1. kánīt; 2. kéinait]. Germ. *kainit*, formed fr. Gk. *kainós*, 'new'; the base occurs in second syll. of Lat. *(re)cent-(em)*, 'new, recent'. See **recent**. Compound of sulphates of magnesium and potassium, used as manure.

Kainozoic, adj. [1. kànōzṓik; 2. kèinouzóuik], fr. Gk. *kainós*, 'new', see prec., & Gk. *zōḗ*, 'life', see **zoo-**, & **-ic**. (geol.) Denoting a period or era which followed the Mesozoic to the present age, including the Tertiary and Quaternary eras.

Kaiser, n. [1. kízer; 2. káizə]. Germ. form of 'Caesar', q.v. Emperor of the old Holy Roman, the Austrian, and the German empires. Until recently the word in English always referred to the German Emperor, *the Kaiser*.

kaka, n. [1. káhkah; 2. kā́kā]. Imitative Maori name. New Zealand parrot.

kakapo, n. [1. káhkahpō; 2. kā́kāpou]. Maori. Owl-parrot of New Zealand.

kakemono, n. [1. kàkemṓnō; 2. kæ̀kimóunou]. Japanese. A hanging picture, usually painted on silk and provided with a roller at lower end on which it can be rolled up.

kale, kail, n. [1. kāl; 2. keil]. Scots variant of **cole**, also found in *sea-kale*. **1.** Species of cabbage with curly leaves; cole, colewort. **2.** Broth made of cabbage or other vegetables.

kaleidophone, n. [1. kalídofōn; 2. kəláidəfoun]. Mod. invention. See next word & suff. **-phone**. Instrument for making sound waves visible by reflection from a sound plate or bar.

kaleidoscope, n. [1. kalídoskōp; 2. kəláidəskoup]. Mod. word formed fr. Gk. *ká(l)los*, 'beautiful' (see first element in **calligraphy**), *eidos*, 'shape, form' (see **eidograph** & cp. **idea**), & suff. **-scope**. **1.** Tube containing pieces of coloured glass and reflectors, showing, through an eyepiece, on being turned, constantly varying patterns. **2.** (fig.) Any frequently changing scene: *the kaleidoscope of life*; *sun and cloud made the landscape a kaleidoscope of colour and pattern.*

kaleidoscopic(al), adj. [1. kalìdoskópik(l); 2. kəlàidəskɔ́pik(l)]. Prec. & **-ic** (& **-al**). Resembling the patterns and colours of a kaleidoscope; constantly changing.

kalendar, n. See **calendar**.

kalends, n. See **calends**.

kaleyard, kailyard, n. [1. kályard; 2. kéiljād]. Cabbage or kitchen garden; *kailyard school*, referring to writers of stories or sketches of lowland Scottish peasant life told in dialect.

Kali, n. [1. káhlē; 2. kā́li]. Scrt., 'black'. (Hindu mythol.) Consort of Siva, as goddess of death.

kali, n. [1. kálī; 2. kéilai]. Arab. *qali*. See **alkali**. The glasswort or saltwort from which soda-ash is obtained by burning.

kaligenous, adj. [1. kalíjenus; 2. kəlídžənəs]. Prec. & suff. **-genous**. Producing or supplying alkalis.

kalium, n. [1. kálium; 2. kéiliəm]. Formed fr. **kali**. (chem.) The element potassium, whence its symbol K.

kalmia, n. [1. kálmia; 2. kǽlmiə]. Formed fr. name of Swed. botanist, Kalm. (bot.) Genus of evergreen flowering N. American shrubs.

Kalmuck, Kalmuk, n. [1. kálmuk; 2. kǽlmak]. Tatar name. **1.** Member of various wandering Mongol tribes in Russia and N.W. China. **2.** Coarse woolly kind of cloth.

kalong, n. [1. kálong; 2. kǽlɔŋ]. Malay name. (zool.) Large fruit-eating bat or flying-fox.

Kama, n. [1. káhma; 2. kā́mə]. Scrt., 'love', cogn. w. Lat. *cārus*, 'dear', q.v. under **charity**. (Hindu mythol.) **a** The god of love; **b** sexual desire, sensual passion.

kame, n. [1. kām; 2. keim]. Scots & Nthn. Engl. variant of **comb**. (geol.) High, narrow ridge of glacial gravel deposit; eskar.

kamptulicon, n. [1. kamtū́likon; 2. kæmtjúlikən]. Trade name concocted fr. Gk. *kamptós* (q.v. under **campus**), 'bent, bending', *oûlos*, 'thick, fleecy' (q.v. under **lanate**), & suff. *-icon*. Early form of linoleum; now obs. together with the material.

kamsin, n. See **khamsin**.

Kanaka, n. [1. kanáka, kánaka; 2. kənǽkə, kǽnəkə]. Hawaiian, 'man'. General name for a native of South Sea Islands, esp. one formerly shipped for forced or indentured labour to Australia.

Kanarese, n. [1. kànarḗz; 2. kæ̀nəríz]. **a** Member of a Dravidian race living in the districts of Kanara, in Bombay and Madras, India; **b** language spoken by the Kanarese.

kangaroo, n. [1. kànggarṓō; 2. kæ̀ŋgərū́]. Prob. anct. Australian aboriginal name. **1.** A pouched (marsupial) herbivorous mammal, genus *Macropus* &c.; only found in or near Australia, with short, weak fore-limbs, but long, powerful hind-limbs, giving great leaping capacity, and a thick tail which acts as support when the animal stands erect. **2.** Specific uses: **a** *kangaroos*, (Stock Exchange slang) Australian mining shares; **b** *kangaroo closure*, a rule of procedure in House of Commons, which gives chairman of committee power of selecting for debate amendments on a bill and closuring or jumping over others. **3.** (in compounds, esp. bot. and zool.) Indicating some relation to or with the kangaroo: *kangaroo-acacia (thorn)*, shrubby, thorny plant used for hedges; *kangaroo-apple*, plant and its edible fruit, found in Australia and New Zealand; *kangaroo-beetle*, bright-coloured beetle with long hind-legs; *kangaroo-dog*, dog used for hunting kangaroos; *kangaroo-grass*, native Australian fodder grass; *kangaroo-rat*, **a** Australian marsupial, resembling a rat; **b** N. American jumping rodent with cheek pouches.

kantar, cantar, n. [1. kantár; 2. kæntā́], fr. Arab. *qintar*. See **quintal**. Egyptian weight, equivalent roughly to hundredweight.

Kantian, adj. [1. kántian; 2. kǽntiən]. Belonging to the philosophic system of Immanuel Kant.

Kantianism, n. [1. kántianizm; 2. kǽntiənizəm]. Prec. & **-ism**. The system of Kant's philosophy.

kaolin, n. [1. káolin; 2. kéiəlin]. Through Fr. *kaoline*, fr. Chinese *kao-ling*, 'high mountain', name of mountain wh. was chief source of the material for the Chinese. **a** China-clay, forming the paste in manufacture of porcelain, used also for sizing paper, loading cheap textiles &c.; **b** (chem.) hydrous silicate of aluminium, formed by decomposition of felspar.

kapellmeister, n. [1. kapélmister; 2. kæpélmaistə]. Germ., 'chapel master', *kapelle*, 'chapel', *meister*, 'master'. **a** Director, conductor, composer, of music in the private chapel or at the court of a German ruling prince; **b** conductor of a choir or orchestra, esp. contemptuously, as meaning an academic conductor or composer of music which will please his patron. Phr. *kapellmeister music*, academic, old-fashioned, or stereotyped music.

kapok, n. [1. káhpok; 2. kā́pɔk]. Malay. *kapoq*, 'cotton tree'. Soft cotton-like fibre obtained from the seeds of the cotton tree; it is non-absorbent and lighter than cork, and is used in life-belts &c.

Karaism, n. [1. káraizm; 2. kéərəizəm]. See next word & **-ism**. Doctrine or system of the Karaites.

Karaite, n. [1. kárait; 2. kéərəait], fr. Heb. *qara*, 'to read'. Member of Jewish heretical sect holding to literal meaning of the Scriptures, without Talmudic or other interpretation.

Karlsbad plum, n. [1. kárlzbad plúm; 2. kā́lzbæd plám]. Large preserved plum or prune.

Karlsbad salts, n. Aperient salts obtained from the mineral springs of Karlsbad, town in Czechoslovakia (Bohemia).

karma, n. [1. káma; 2. kā́mə]. Scrt., 'deed, act', cp. Scrt. *karóti*, 'makes'; cogn. w. Lith. *kuriù*, 'to build', & perh. ultimately w. Lat. *corpus* (q.v.). An act considered in its causal relation to a person's fate or destiny; (in Buddhist philos.) the sum of a man's acts, words, and deeds which decides his fate in each stage of existence; sometimes used as synonym of fate, destiny.

karoo, karroo, n. [1. karṓō; 2. kərū́], fr. Hottentot *karusa*, 'hard, dry'. Waterless table-land in S. Africa; specif., the 'Great Karoo', the largest of such table-lands in Cape Colony.

kaross, n. [1. karós; 2. kərɔ́s]. S. Afr. word; etymol. unknown. Cloak of skin, with wool or fur left on, worn by S. African natives; the leopard-skin kaross is worn only by chiefs.

karri, n. [1. kári; 2. kǽri]. Native name. An Australian tree, a species of eucalyptus, or blue-gum, with hard timber.

kartell, n. See **cartel**.

karyo-, pref. in comb., fr. Gk. *káruon*, 'nut, kernel', cogn. w. Lat. *carīna*, 'keel'. See **careen**. Used to form biological terms relating to the nucleus of a cell.

karyoplasm, n. [1. kárioplazm; 2. kǽriəplæzəm], fr. prec. & **-plasm**. (biol.) Nuclear protoplasm, as differentiated from *cytoplasm*, cell-plasm.

kata-, kat-, kath-. See **cata-**.

katabolism, n. [1. katábolizm; 2. kətǽbəlizəm], fr. Gk. *katabolḗ*, lit. 'throwing down', fr. **cata-**, 'down', & *-bol-*, stem of *bállein*, 'to throw'. See **ballistic** & **-ism**. (biol. and physiol.) Process of change in organic bodies by which more complex elements are broken down into simpler ones; destructive metabolism.

Katherine-wheel, n. See **Catherine-wheel**.

katydid, n. [1. kā́tidid; 2. kéitidid]. Imitative of sound made by the insect. Large green American grasshopper of several varieties.

kauri, n. [1. kóuri; 2. káuri]. Maori name. New Zealand conifer valued for its hard timber and resin: *kauri-gum*.

kava, n. [1. káhva; 2. kávə]. Native Polynesian name. Intoxicating drink of the South Sea Islands, made from pounded root of a shrubby pepper plant.

kavass, n. [1. kavás; 2. kəvǽs]. Turk. *qawwas*, 'bow-maker'; Arab. *qaws*, 'bow'. Turkish military policeman, esp. one serving as armed guard for foreign travellers.

kayak, n. [1. kíak; 2. káijæk]. Eskimo. Decked canoe used by Eskimo men, made of sealskin stretched on wooden frame; cp. *umiak*.

kea, n. [1. káa; 2. kéiə]. Native Maori name. New Zealand mountain parrot, destructive to sheep.

keck, vb. intrans. [1. kek; 2. kɛk]. Imitative. To retch, heave, make sound as if vomiting.

keddah, n. [1. kéda; 2. kédə]. Malay., fr. Arab. *qada*, 'hole'. Trap for wild elephants.

kedge (I.), vb. trans. & intrans. [1. kej; 2. kedž]. Etymol. doubtful; perh. variant of **cadge**, 'to catch'. **a** trans. To move a ship by warping against an anchor dropped for that purpose; **b** intrans., (of the ship) to move by kedging.

kedge (II.), n., fr. prec. Small anchor, properly *kedge-anchor*, dropped for warping a ship.

kedgeree, n. [1. kéjerē; 2. kédžərī]. Hind. *khichri*. Anglo-Indian breakfast dish of boiled rice, fish, and eggs.

keek, vb. intrans. [1. kēk; 2. kīk]. Scots & Nthn. Engl.; cp. L.G. *kiken*, Du. *kijken*, 'to peep'. To peep, spy.

keeker, n. [1. kḗker; 2. kíkə]. Prec. & **-er**. (colloq.) **a** Inquisitive person, inspector; **b** (pl.) eyes, cp. *peeper*.

keeking, n. [1. kḗking; 2. kíkiŋ]. Act of spying or peeping: *keeking-glass*, looking-glass.

keel (I.), n. [1. kēl; 2. kiəl]. Scand., fr. O.N. *kjǫlr*; cp. Swed. *köl*, Dan. *kjöl*, Du. & Germ. *kiel*. The O.E. cogn. *ċēol* wd. produce 'cheel' in Mod. Engl. The word is prob. fr. Aryan **geul-*, 'a bulging, swelling, hollow thing'; cp. Lat. *vola*, fr. **gwola-*, 'hollow of the hand'; cp. further, Gk. *guálē*, 'goblet', *gaulós*, 'beehive', & O.N. *kūla*, 'a swelling'. **1. a** Lowest, basal timber or set of plates of a ship on which framework is built; **b** a ship; specif., flat-bottomed craft used on Tyne. (This is probably direct, by late borrowing, from Dutch.) Phrs. *to lay down a keel*, start building a boat or ship; *on an even keel*, without movement to one side or the other; (fig.) evenly, calmly. **2.** (bot. and zool.) Ridge-like projection, resembling the keel of a boat, in the structure of leaf or bird; cp. *carinate*.

keel (II.), vb. trans. & intrans. See prec. To turn a ship over on one side for cleaning or repairing the bottom; *keel over*, to capsize.

keel (III.), vb. trans. O.E. *cēlan*, fr. earlier **kōljan*, fr. O.E. *cōl*. See **cool**. (obs.) To keep cool or off the boil: *to keel the pot*, keep it from boiling over.

keelage, n. [1. kḗlij; 2. kílidž], fr. **keel (I.)** & **-age**. Toll on ship entering port.

keeled, adj. [1. kēld; 2. kiəld]. **keel (I.)** & **-ed**. Provided with, having, a keel.

keelhaul, vb. trans. [1. kḗlhawl; 2. kíəlhɔ̄l]. **keel (I.)** & **haul**; prob. borrowed fr. Du. *kielhallen*. To drag a man from one side of a ship to the other under the keel, as a punishment; (fig.) to rebuke or reprimand severely.

keelless, adj. [1. kḗlles; 2. kiəlles]. **keel (I.)** & **-less**. Without a keel.

keelson, kelson, n. [1. kḗlsun, kélsun; 2. kiəlsn, kélsn], fr. **keel (I.)**; the origin of second element is unknown in spite of various guesses. Set of timbers or plates running parallel to and above the keel of a ship, fastening it by bolts to upper framework or flooring.

keen (I.), n. & vb. trans. & intrans. [1. kēn; 2. kin]. Ir. *caoine*, 'wail, dirge'. **1.** n. Hideous, dismal wailing or howling practised in Ireland among the humbler classes in token of grief, at funerals, and on hearing news of a death or other calamity. **2.** vb. To set up a keen (for): *they keened the corpse tonight*; *the women were keening*.

keen (II.), adj. O.E. *cēn(e)*, 'bold; wise', M.E. *kēne* &c., 'sharp; bold'; fr. Gmc. **kōnja-*, cp. O.H.G. *chuoni*; prob. an extension of Aryan **ĝen-* &c., 'to know', q.v. under **gnosis, can (I.)**, & **ken (I.)**. The concrete meaning in Mod. Engl. is derivative. **1. a** (of points and edges) Sharp, capable of cutting or piercing: *a keen arrow, spear, sword, knife* &c.; *a knife with a keen edge*; **b** (fig., of other things) producing effects and sensations resembling cutting or piercing; painfully acute, penetrating: *a keen east wind*; *a keen frost*; *a keen hunger*. **2.** (of physical, bodily senses) Acute, very sensitive: *keen sight, hearing* &c. **3. a** (of the mental faculties) Penetrating, incisive, acute: *a keen intelligence, wit, understanding, sense of humour* &c.; **b** (of mental activities) vigorously, energetically, pursued: *a keen mental struggle*; *keen intellectual exertion*; **c** (of emotions) strongly felt, intense: *keen sorrow, anguish, delight, pleasure, disappointment* &c. **4.** (of other non-material things) **a** Rapid, sharp, penetrating: *a keen glance*; **b** strongly, vigorously, contested; proceeding from animated, powerful feelings: *a keen contest, fight, competition, bargain* &c.; **c** designed to probe and try; shrewd, searching: *a keen cross-examination*. **5.** (of persons and their character and disposition) **a** Eager, zealous, animated, spirited; filled with healthy spirit of emulation; desirous to do or be: *a keen man of business, athlete*; *he takes no interest in anything, I wish he were keener*; **b** wishful, desirous: (followed by infin.) *keen to go abroad*; *keen to see one's friends*. Phr. *keen on*, (i.) anxious, desirous, eager for, ambitious of: *keen on promotion, on passing an examination*; (ii.) fond of, delighting in: *I'm not very keen on strawberries*; *keen on hunting, cricket* &c., (iii.) zealous in prosecution of: *keen on one's work*.

keener, n. [1. kḗner; 2. kínə], fr. **keen (I.)** & **-er**. Person who keens at Irish funerals &c.; often a paid mourner.

keep (I.), vb. trans. & intrans. [1. kēp; 2. kīp]. O.E. *cēpan*, M.E. *kēpe(n)*; etymol. unknown. (gen. senses) To retain, preserve. **A.** trans. **1. a** (of physical action) To retain in one's hold or grasp: *keep that stick in your hand*; Phr. *to keep hold of*; **b** (of mental action) to retain in the mind, remember: *to keep in mind*. **2. a** To retain in one's possession, care, guardianship: *you may keep the book for a month*; **b** to retain as a permanent possession, constitute oneself, or become, the owner of: *since you have found a watch you may as well keep it*; *to keep something that doesn't belong to one*; *what I have won fairly I intend to keep*; **c** to preserve, take care of, not to discard or throw away: *to keep old letters, one's old clothes* &c. Phr. *to keep one's temper*, not to get angry. **3. a** To hold, maintain, continue to hold, in a certain position or relation: *to keep one's hands in one's pockets*; *to keep one's eyes fixed on a person's face*; *to keep a revolver in one's pocket*; *to keep things separate*; *to keep persons apart*; Phrs. *to keep oneself to oneself*, live apart from, refuse to associate with, one's neighbours; *to keep one's eye on*, look after thoroughly and carefully; *to keep one's hand, eye, in*, to preserve some art, form of dexterity &c., by practice; **b** to preserve in a certain condition: *to keep meat fresh by refrigeration*; *to keep a house in a state of repair*; *to keep a razor sharp*; Phrs. *to keep one's head cool*, remain calm, not to get flustered; *to keep something going*, in working order as an effective concern; *to keep (a person) going*, (i.) preserve his life; (ii.) assist him financially; *to keep a stiff face*, not to allow one's expression to alter, not to smile; also *to keep one's, my, countenance*, preserve one's gravity. **4. a** To maintain at one's own cost, to support: *to keep a wife and family*; **b** specif., to maintain, retain, under one's direction, at one's orders or disposal: *to keep a butler, houseful of servants*; *to keep a hunter, dog, motor-car* &c. **5.** To manage, direct, run: *to keep a shop, public-house*; *keep a school*; *to keep house*; *keep great state*. **6. a** To preserve, adhere to, be faithful to: *to keep faith with*; *keep one's word, promise*; **b** to obey, observe: *to keep the law, the rules*. **7.** To honour by special observances, celebrate: *to keep Christmas, one's birthday*; *keep holy the Sabbath day*. **8. a** To guard, inviolate, defend: *to keep the road, a town* &c. *against the enemy*; **b** to withhold, refuse to give up or communicate, to conceal (things from or to persons): *to keep knives away from children*; *you are keeping something from me*; Phr. *to keep things, news* &c. *to oneself*, retain for one's own use, not to divulge; **c** to prevent access of persons or things; prevent person from doing something: *to keep a child away from the fire*; *to keep a person from knowing too much, from hurting himself* &c. **B.** intrans. **1.** To be and remain in a certain condition; **a** (physical) *how are you keeping?*; *to keep well*, remain in good health; *the weather keeps fine*; *the kettle is keeping hot on the hob*; *to keep cool*, (i.) not get hot; (ii.) not get flustered; *keep quiet*, remain silent or still; **b** (of mental states) *to keep cheerful, happy*. Phr. *to keep to oneself*, remain solitary, not to mix in society. **2.** Specif., to remain in a sound condition, to be free from taint, putrescence, sourness &c.: *mutton doesn't keep this weather*; *eggs will keep for months in water-glass*. Phr. *that news will keep*, can be told later. **3.** To remain in a certain place, to stay: *to keep at home, keep indoors* &c. **C.** Followed by preposition or adverb. *Keep at*, trans. & intrans.: **1.** trans., to compel to remain at, stick to, work: *keep people at their job*; *we were kept at it the whole day*; *keep at it*, stick to, persist in, what one is doing; **2.** intrans., **a** to pester constantly with entreaties, complaints &c.: *they kept at me with their appeals for subscriptions, for payment of income-tax* &c.; **b** to stick to, pursue diligently: *to keep (hard) at work*. *Keep down*, trans. & intrans.: **1.** trans., **a** to suppress by physical means: *keep down revolt*; **b** to suppress, master, overcome (feelings &c.): *keep down one's anger*; **2.** intrans., to refrain from rising or jumping up, remain sitting or lying down. *Keep in*, trans. **a** to restrain: *to keep in one's feelings*; **b** to compel to stay in a house &c.: *the doctor kept me in for a week*; Phr. *to be kept in* (of schoolboy), to suffer detention as a punishment. *Keep on*, trans. & intrans.: **1.** trans., **a** to retain something on one's person: *to keep on one's overcoat*; *to keep one's hat on, keep all one's clothes on*; **b** retain a person in particular office &c.: *keep on one's cook*; *keep him on at his old job*; **2.** intrans., to continue to follow some particular occupation: *I'm sick of my work, but I still keep on*; Phrs. *keep on* (followed by Pres. Part.), repeat an action; do a thing continuously, or at repeated short intervals: *keep on blowing one's nose*;

keep on scolding. Keep on at, intrans., (colloq.) to upbraid continuously, to nag. *Keep out*, trans. & intrans.: **1.** trans., (i.) to exclude, shut out: *keep out undesirable aliens, foreign foodstuffs*, &c.; (ii.) (fig.) to restrain from: *to keep children out of mischief*; **2.** intrans., (fig.) to remain outside, not be mixed up in, or concerned with: *keep out of quarrels, intrigues* &c. *Keep up*, trans. & intrans.: **1.** trans., **a** to maintain: *keep up a large establishment*; **b** to continue a line of action: *keep up an attack*; **c** to preserve, *keep up appearances*; *keep up one's spirits*; Phr. *to keep one's end up*, hold one's own; **2.** intrans., to show fortitude, maintain dignified and calm bearing in the face of fatigue, anxiety, adversity &c.: *in spite of the cold they kept up wonderfully*.

keep (II.), n., fr. prec. **1.** Central, most strongly fortified part of a castle; donjon. **2.** That which supports or maintains a person or animal; **a** food, sustenance; cost of living: *to earn one's keep*, do enough work to be worth employment; *pigs now are hardly worth their keep*, do not pay the cost of keeping them; **b** specif., fodder &c. stored for cattle or horses &c.: *this late grass will make some useful keep for the winter*. **3.** (colloq.). In Phr. *for keeps*, permanently.

keeper, n. [1. kḗper; 2. kípə], fr. **keep (I.)** & **-er.** One who keeps, guards &c. (in various senses). **1.** (in gen. sense) Guardian, protector, one in charge of, or responsible for, another: '*Am I my brother's keeper?*'; specif. **a** attendant in charge of lunatic; **b** one who protects preserves against poachers; a game-keeper (usually with defining term prefixed, see **3** below); **c** (at Eton College) title of captain of various games, as *keeper of the field, of the fives, of the racquets* &c. **2.** Title of holder of various offices, now mainly historical or obsolete: *Lord Keeper*, i.e. of the Great Seal, now the Lord Chancellor; *Keeper of Privy Purse, petty bag* &c.; *Keeper of Crown Jewels*, official at Tower of London; *Keeper of Printed Books* &c. (at British Museum &c.). Phr. *Keeper of the King's Conscience*, the Lord Chancellor, formerly the Lord Keeper, as responsible for the King's acts of State. **3.** (in compounds) **a** Of one who guards, watches, attends to special duty &c.: as *game-, lighthouse-, park-keeper* &c.; *time-keeper*, official who records the time at races, in boxing &c.; **b** of one who manages, runs shop, business &c.: *shopkeeper, innkeeper* &c.; **c** (games) one who protects, guards &c.: (as at association football) *goal-keeper*; (at cricket) *wicket-keeper*. **4.** Ring worn on finger above another, esp. a wedding ring, to prevent slipping off: (also attrib.) *keeper ring*.

keepership, n. [1. kḗpership; 2. kípəʃip]. Prec. & **-ship.** Office, function, of a keeper.

keeping, n. [1. kḗping; 2. kípiŋ], vbl. n. fr. **keep (I.)** & **-ing. 1.** Act of retaining, holding, preserving &c. Phr. *finding is keeping*, indicating the illegal idea that if one finds or picks up an object, dropped, lost, or mislaid, one has the right to retain it in one's possession. **2.** Guardianship, care, protection, custody: *to have valuables in safe keeping*; *we are all safe in God's keeping*. **3.** *In keeping*, **a** congruity, consistency, agreement, harmony: *his acts are not in keeping with his promises*; **b** suitability, commensurability: *your expenses should be in keeping with your income*.

keepsake, n. [1. kḗpsāk; 2. kípseik], fr. **keep (I.)** & **sake**; a late word in Engl. Object kept or retained for the sake or memory of or association with another; memento.

kef, n. See **kief.**

keg, n. [1. keg; 2. kɛg]. Scand., cp. Icel. *kaggi*, Swed. & Norw. *kagge*. Small barrel or cask.

kelp, n. [1. kelp; 2. kɛlp]. M.E. *culp*; etymol. unknown. Large kind of brown seaweed; the burnt ashes of seaweed from which iodine is extracted.

kelpie, kelpy, n. [1. kélpi; 2. kélpi]. Etymol. doubtful. Skeat suggests connexion w. Gael. *culpach*, 'heifer, colt'. **a** (in Scots folklore) Water-sprite, in form of a horse, which drowns or foretells death by drowning; **b** (gen.) a grotesque sprite.

kelson, n. See **keelson.**

Kelt (I.), n. See **Celt (I.).**

kelt (II.), n. [1. kelt; 2. kɛlt]. Scots; etymol. unknown. Salmon or sea-trout in bad condition after spawning; one which has not yet reached the sea.

kemp, n. [1. kemp; 2. kɛmp]. Scand., cp. O.N. *kampr*, 'beard'. Coarse hair or wool, esp. pl. *kemps*, coarse fibres picked out as not fit for felting or dyeing.

ken (I.), vb. trans. [1. ken; 2. kɛn]. O.E. *cennan*, 'declare, make known', fr. **kannjan*, a form still surviving in Goth. in sense, 'to make known'; O.S. *-kennian*; O.H.G. *-chennan* &c., 'to know'; O.N. *kenna*, 'inform, get to know'. From same base as **can** (I.), fr. Aryan base **ĝen-, ĝṇ-, *ĝnā-* &c., 'to know', whence also Lat. *nōscere*, 'to know', for **gnōscere, gnārus*, 'knowing, acquainted with', *ignōrāre*, 'not to know' (see **ignore**); Gk. *gnōtós*, 'known'; *gnôsis*, 'knowledge, wisdom'. See **gnosis**; cp. also Scrt. *jānāmi*, 'I know'; O. Slav. *znati*, 'to know'. **ken (II.)** is fr. same base. (obs. or provinc.) To recognize, know, be acquainted with.

ken (II.), n. See prec. **a** Range of bodily vision: '*like some watcher of the skies, When a new planet swims into his ken*' (Keats); **b** range of knowledge or intelligence; esp. in Phr. *beyond, outside, one's ken*.

ken (III.), n. Prob. abbr. of **kennel (I.).** (slang) Thief's den or hiding-place.

kennel (I.), n. [1. kénl; 2. kénl]. M.E. *kenil*, prob. fr. A.-Fr. form of O. Fr. *chenil*, fr. O. Fr. *chen*, Mod. Fr. *chien*, 'dog'; Lat. *canis*. See **canine. 1. a** Hut or shelter for a dog; lair or refuge of an animal; Phr. *to go to kennel*, to go into hiding, take refuge; **b** *the kennels*, headquarters of a Hunt, set of kennels where the hounds are kept. **2.** Poor, mean hovel or dwelling.

kennel (II.), vb. trans. & intrans. See prec. **1.** trans. To put or keep (dog) in kennel, bring hounds back to kennels. **2.** intrans. To remain, live, in a kennel.

kennel (III.), n. M.E. *canel, cannel*, doublet of **channel**; & cp. **canal.** Gutter, open drain or sewer.

kenosis, n. [1. kenṓsis; 2. kinóusis]. Gk. *kénōsis*, lit. 'emptying', fr. *kenós*, 'empty'; etymol. obscure. See **cenotaph** & **-osis.** (theol.) Action of the Saviour in humbling Himself by becoming Man and accepting human limitations.

Kentish, adj. [1. kéntish; 2. kéntiʃ]. Of, or belonging to, the county of Kent, England. *Kentish fire*, continued round of applause or dissent at a public meeting. *Kentish man*, native of the county other than one born or living east of the river Medway who is a 'Man of Kent'. *Kentish rag*, kind of hard building stone.

kentledge, n. [1. kéntlej; 2. kéntlidž]. Etymol. unknown. Permanent ballast of pig-iron in a ship.

kephalic, adj. See **cephalic.**

kepi, n. [1. kā́pē; 2. képi]. Fr. *képi*, fr. S. Germ. *käppi*, dimin. of *kappe*, 'cap', q.v. Typical form of peaked cap worn by French soldiers with a flat top sloping forward.

kept, vb. [1. kept; 2. kɛpt]. M.E. *kepte, kept*, Pret. & P.P. of **keep (I.).**

keramic, adj. See **ceramic.**

kerat(o)-, cerat(o-), pref. Cartilaginous, horny, used to form compounds. See next word.

keratin, n. [1. kératin; 2. kérətin], fr. Gk. *kerat-*, stem of *kéras*, 'a horn', cogn. w. Scrt. *śiraś*, 'head', & w. different formative element, Lat. *cornu*, 'horn'. See **corn** (on foot), & further under **cerebral, cervine, & horn.** (chem.) Basic substance of horns, nails, feathers, and hair in animals.

keratitis, n. [1. kèratítis; 2. kèrətáitis] See **kerat(o)-** & **-itis.** (pathol.) Inflammation of the cornea of the eye.

keratose, n. & adj. [1. kératōs; 2. kérətous]. See **kerat(o)-** & **-ose.** (chem.) **a** n. Horny substance in sponges; **b** adj., horny.

kerb, n. [1. kërb; 2. kʌ̄b]. Variant spelling of **curb (I.).** The stone-edging, *kerbstone*, of a pavement in a street. Phr. *kerbstone broker*, outside broker who is not a member of the Stock Exchange.

kerchief, n. [1. kërchif; 2. kʌ́tʃif]. M.E. *kerchef, coverchef*, fr. O. Fr. *covrechef*, O. Fr. *covrir*, Mod. Fr. *couvrir*, see **cover**, & *chef*, 'chief, head', see **chief. a** Square piece of cloth, lace, or other material worn as a covering for the head by women; **b** wrap, scarf, for the neck.

kerf, n. [1. kërf; 2. kʌ̄f]. O.E. *cyrf*, 'a cutting', fr. **kurfi-*, fr. base **kurf-*, reduced grade of O.E. *ċeorfan*, 'to cut'. See **carve.** The wedge-shaped notch made by an axe or saw in that side of tree-stem in the direction in which it is to be felled.

kermes, n. [1. kërmēz; 2. kʌ́mīz]. Arab. *qirmiz*. See **crimson. 1. a** Dried bodies of a genus of insects, yielding a crimson dye; **b** crimson dye obtained from these insects. **2.** Bright-red mineral, a compound of antimony.

kermess, -mis, n. [1. kërmes, -mis; 2. kʌ́mes, -mis]. Du. fr. *kerkmes*, 'church mass'. A fair held on the feast day of the patron saint of a church in Holland, Flanders &c.

kern, kerne, n. [1. kërn; 2. kʌ̄n]. Irish *ceatharn*, 'troop of soldiers', also 'a soldier'. Cp. **cateran. a** Light-armed soldier of ancient Irish military levies; **b** wild Irish peasant.

kernel, n. [1. kërnl; 2. kʌ́n(ə)l]. O.E. *cernel*, the S.E. dial. type of a word wh. in W.S. appears as *cyrnel*, 'kernel, seed; hard swelling', fr. earlier **kurnil-*, fr. **kurn-*, same base as O.E. *corn*, 'grain' &c., fr. **kurna-*. See **corn (I.)** & **-el. 1.** The germinating part or seed of a fruit, esp. one contained in a fruit-stone. **2.** (fig.) The essential, vital, central part, aspect, element of a problem, subject, controversy &c.; gist. **3. a** (obs. or provinc.) Hard swelling in glands of neck; **b** the centre, nucleus, of an abscess or other inflammatory swelling.

kerosene, n. [1. kérosēn; 2. kérəsīn]. Mod. word, formed fr. Gk. *kērós*, 'wax'. See **cere.** Illuminating oil, originally distilled from waxy product of bituminous coal or shale, now obtained from petroleum.

Kerry, n. [1. kéri; 2. kéri], fr. Co. Kerry in Ireland. **1.** Small breed of black cattle, good for milking; also *Kerry cow*. **2.** Breed of large Irish terrier; also *Kerry blue* or *blue Kerry*.

kersey, n. [1. kërzi; 2. kʌ́zi], fr. Kersey, in Suffolk, Engl., formerly seat of cloth-making. Coarse, ribbed, woollen cloth.

kerseymere, n. [1. kërzimēr; 2. kʌ́zimiə]. Popular form of **cashmere**, earlier *cassimere*, doubtless influenced by prec. word. Fine, twilled, smooth-faced cloth, cashmere; *kerseymeres*, tight-fitting breeches or trousers made of this cloth.

kestrel, n. [1. késtrel; 2. késtrəl]. Earlier *castrel* for *casrel, casserel*, fr. O. Fr. *quercerelle*, Mod. Fr. *crécerelle*, dimin. of **carcelle*, cp. Mod. Fr. *sarcelle*, 'teal'; name perh. imitative of bird's note. Small, migratory falcon or hawk, the wind-hover.

ketch, n. [1. kech; 2. kɛtʃ]. Earlier *cache, catch*, fr. **catch**, 'to take, chase'. Small sailing-vessel with fore and aft rigged main and small mizzen mast; *ketch bomb* or *bomb ketch*, similar vessel, used to carry mortars for throwing bombs in early navy.

ketchup, n. [1. kéchup; 2. kétʃəp]. Also earlier *catchup, catsup*, fr. Malay. *kĕchup*, 'sauce', prob. fr. Chinese *ke-tsiap*, 'pickled fish-sauce'. Sauce made from mushrooms, tomatoes &c., usually with name of chief ingredient prefixed, as *mushroom ketchup* &c.

ketone, n. [1. kḗtōn; 2. kítoun]. (chem.) Name of group of organic compounds of which acetone, q.v., is representative type and to which it gives its name. They are derived by oxidation of a secondary alcohol or distillation of a fatty acid.

kettle, n. [1. kétl; 2. kétl]. Scand., cp. O.N. *ketill*; the cogn. O.E. *ċetel*, M.E. *chetel*, wd. have produced *chettle*; Common Gmc., cp. Du. *ketel*, Germ. *kessel*; all apparently borrowed fr. Lat. *catillus*, 'small, shallow dish', dimin. of *catīnus*, 'large cooking-bowl'; cp. Gk. *kotúlē*, 'cavity, hollow cup', & Scrt. *čatvālaš*, 'cavity', wh. are cognates of the Lat. Vessel of iron or other metal, with spout and handle, used for boiling water. Phr. *a pretty, nice, kettle of fish*, a muddle, mess, awkward affair.

kettle-drum, n. **1.** Small hemispherical drum of brass or copper with parchment head, used by cavalry bands and orchestras in pairs tuned to low and high compass respectively. **2.** Afternoon party or reception, 19th cent., now obsolete, probably from *tea-kettle* and *drum*, 'reception', as if assembled by beat of drum.

kettle-holder, n. Small, square piece of cloth, for protecting hand when holding a hot kettle handle.

kevel, n. [1. kévl; 2. kévl]. O. Nthn. Fr. *keville*; cp. Mod. Fr. *cheville*, fr. L. Lat. *clavicula*. See **clavicle**. (naut.) Peg, cleat, bollard, to which a rope is fastened.

kex, n. [1. keks; 2. keks]. Prob. fr. unrecorded O.E. **cēsċ*, **cēx*, earlier **kōsci-*, fr. Gmc. **kanski-*, Aryan **g̑ont-ki*, lit. 'jointed (stem)'; fr. same base as Gk. *gónat-*, 'knee, joint', cp. *gonátion*, 'joint of plant stem', also Lat. *geniculātus*, 'jointed', of plants, fr. *genu*, 'knee'. See further under **kneel**, **genual**. Stalks of hemlock or of other plants with jointed stems, especially when dried up.

key (I.), n. [1. kē; 2. kī]. O.E. *cǣġ* (fr. Gmc. **kaigi-*), M.E. *keye*; etymol. unknown. **1. a** Portable metal, usually steel, instrument, which, operating by its flanges on the wards and levers or tumblers of a lock, turns a bolt backwards or forwards to open or close door, box &c.: *latch-key*, key of front door of this house; this as symbol of being free to come in and out as one pleases: *I don't give my daughter a latch-key*; *master key*, one that opens a set of locks, as in an hotel &c.; *skeleton key*, filed so that it can open a variety of locks; Phr. *to get the key of the street*, to be evicted, locked out of house; **b** representation of a key, as symbol or badge of power, authority, control, office &c.; *the cross keys*, in arms of the Pope, as successor of St. Peter, to whom was given the power of binding and loosing; *the power of the keys*, power given to St. Peter to forgive or retain sins; *gold key*, badge of office of the Lord Chamberlain; *House of Keys*, representative chamber of the Isle of Man. **2.** Dominating position which commands or controls free movement of troops, ships &c., as a fortified place, hill, railway junction &c.; one which controls political or other action: *the key to the Channel*; *key to political situation* &c. **3.** (fig.) **a** That which unlocks a mystery, secret &c.; solution, answer, clue to a problem, puzzle, cipher &c.: *the key to a difficulty, mystery* &c.; **b** a literal translation of a foreign book; set of answers to mathematical or other questions set in an examination. **4.** Name of various devices, implements &c. similar to a key in use or in mode of working; **a** instrument for winding up a clock or watch: *watch-key*; **b** wrench, spanner, for turning a bolt or nut: *bed-key*; **c** wedge of wood or metal for tightening joints &c.; **d** first layer of plaster on laths of a wall; **e** small knob or button pressed by finger, used for working a typewriter, or telegraphic instrument; **f** keystone, q.v. **5.** (in musical instruments) Lever pressed by finger for making a hammer strike against a string: *the keys of a pianoforte*; or for opening and closing valves, as in wind instruments, organ, oboe &c., so as to produce a special note or sound. **6.** (mus.) a Group, system, of notes considered in relation to one another as based on a particular note, the tonic or keynote, q.v.: *key of C major*; *major, minor key*; **b** tone, pitch of voice: *in a high, low, key*. **7.** (fig., on musical anal.) **a** (of feelings and modes of expression) *In a minor key*, plaintively, sadly; *all in the same key*, monotonously; **b** (of colour) predominating shade or tone: *a picture painted in a low key*, i.e. in subdued colours. **8.** (attrib.) *Key-bugle*, bugle with valves worked by keys by which variety of notes can be played. *Key industry*, dominating industry; one concerned with articles that are essential to many other industries. *Key money*, money paid as illegal or unauthorized premium or commission for securing occupation of house, set of rooms &c. from outgoing tenant. *Key pattern*, ornamental design of short straight lines or bars, meeting at right angles; fret. *Key-ring*, split ring of metal, for carrying a bunch of keys. *Key signature*, (mus.) a sign, marking number of sharps or flats and thus the key in which a musical composition is written.

key (II.), vb. trans., fr. prec. **1.** To fasten, tighten together, with a key or wedge. **2.** To attach a clue, mark of origin, to, esp. to an advertisement in a newspaper. **3.** To tune up to a particular key, raise tone or pitch, also *to key up*, **a** to tune up the string of an instrument; **b** (fig.) *to key up expectation, courage* &c., to raise, excite, by anticipation of some event or emergency believed to be about to happen.

key (III.), n. Variant spelling of **cay**; see also **quay**.

keyboard, n. [1. kébord; 2. kíbɔ̄d]. **a** The series of notes or keys of a pianoforte, the manual of an organ, or similar musical instrument, which being struck by the fingers operate levers working the hammers which strike the strings, or open valves allowing air to pass through pipes or reeds, thus producing musical notes; **b** set of keys for operating typewriter, linotype, etc.

keyhole, n. [1. kéhōl; 2. kíhoul]. Hole in lock in which a key is inserted for locking or unlocking a door &c. Phr. *to spy through, listen at, the keyhole*, or *keyholes*, play spy on. *Keyhole-saw*, fine saw for cutting out or round a keyhole or for other delicate work.

keyless, adj. [1. kéles; 2. kílis]. **key** (I.) & **-less**. Without a key; specif., of watch or clock, capable of being wound up by a special apparatus attached to it, thus not requiring a key.

keynote, n. [1. kénōt; 2. kínout]. **a** Tonic, fundamental, final note of a key in music; **b** (fig.) predominant note, tone, topic, style, of a speech &c.; chief motive of an action &c.: *to strike, sound, the keynote of policy* &c.

keystone, n. [1. késtōn; 2. kístoun]. **a** (archit.) The central voussoir, or wedge-shaped stone in an arch or vault, serving as a bond or tie for the other stones or members; **b** (fig.) essential, binding, supporting element in plan, policy, course of action &c.

khaki (I.), adj. [1. káhkē; 2. kákī]. Hind. *khākī*, 'dusty, dust-coloured', fr. Pers. *khāk*, 'dust'. Of a dull brown colour, resembling dust or earth.

khaki (II.), n., fr. prec. Cloth of this colour, of cotton, wool, or a mixture, used, originally in India, by British army for military uniforms as indistinguishable in colour from the ground and so adopted by other countries in various shades for field-service uniforms. Phrs. *khaki election*, Parliamentary Election, 1902, at close of Boer War, when appeal was made to the imperialistic, military instincts of the electorate; *to get into khaki*, enlist in the army.

khalif, khalifa, n. See **caliph**.

khamsin, kamsin, n. [1. kámsin; 2. kǽmsin]. Arab., fr. *khamsūn*, 'fifty'. Hot south wind, simoom, blowing for about fifty days, from March to May, in Egypt.

khan (I.), n. [1. kahn; 2. kān]. Pers., 'lord, prince', of Tartar origin, cp. Turk. *khagan*, 'king'; early Engl. form is *Cham*, as in 'the Great Cham of Tartary'. **a** Title of ruler in various states in Central Asia; **b** part of name, signifying 'of royal or gentle birth', in Moslem countries in Central Asia or N. India.

khan (II.), n. Arab. & Pers. Caravanserai, inn.

khanate, n. [1. káhnat; 2. kánət]. **khan** (I.) & **-ate**. District, tribe &c., ruled by a khan (I.).

khansamah, n. [1. káhnsamah; 2. kánsəmā]. Hind., Pers. *khansaman*, fr. *khan*, 'lord', & *saman*, *sumun*, 'stores, household gear'. House steward, butler, esp. of an Anglo-Indian household.

khedival, adj. [1. kedéval; 2. kidívəl]. See next word & **-al**. Of or belonging to the powers of the Khedive.

Khedive, n. [1. kedév; 2. kidív]. Through Fr. *khédive*, fr. Turk., fr. Pers. *khadiv*, 'prince, ruler'. Title of the ruler of Egypt as viceroy of the Sultan of Turkey; the office and title no longer exist, as the ruler of Egypt is now an independent sovereign.

khitmatgar, n. [1. kítmatgar; 2. kítmətgā]. Hind., fr. Pers. *khidmadgar*, fr. *khidmat*, 'service'. Male servant in India who waits at table; butler in Anglo-Indian households.

kibe, n. [1. kīb; 2. kaib]. Origin unknown. Chilblain, esp. a broken one on the heel.

kiblah, n. [1. kíblah; 2. kíblā]. Arab. *qiblah*, fr. *qabala*, 'to be or lie opposite'. Direction of the sacred 'black stone', *kaaba*, at Mecca, to which Moslems turn in prayer.

kibosh, n. [1. kíbosh; 2. káibɔʃ]. Origin unknown. (slang) In Phr. *to put the kibosh on*, to put an end to, once for all.

kick (I.), vb. trans. & intrans. [1. kik; 2. kik]. M.E. *kike*. Origin uncertain. **A.** trans. **a** To strike with the foot (of man or animal): *he kicked my shins, the ball* &c.; *the horse kicked the rider's head as they fell*; **b** (of inanimate objects) to strike violently on recoil: *the rifle kicked his shoulder*. Phrs. *kick the beam*, (i.) of unloaded or lighter scale in a balance, to fly up and hit the beam; (ii.) (fig.) to be found wanting; (colloq., vulg.) *kick the bucket*, to die; *kick a man when he's down*, to strike at a man when he is beaten and at one's mercy (lit. & fig.); *kick one's heels*, to waste time in waiting for no purpose; *to kick up one's heels*, to have a fling; indulge in festivity and gaiety, esp. after a spell of monotonous, tedious work; *to kick up a row, dust, fuss, shindy* &c., to cause, raise, a disturbance; *kick upstairs*, to give promotion to, not on merits, but for some other motive, so of Minister made a peer as method of shelving or getting rid of him. **B.** intrans. **a** To strike out with the foot: *the horse began to kick*; **b** to move back suddenly, as a rifle or gun on discharge, to recoil: *the modern rifle hardly kicks at all*; **c** (colloq.) to object, resist: *put up the price of beer and the workman will kick*; **d** to rise up, rebound off the ground to an unusual height, as a ball in cricket: *the fast bowler made the ball kick dangerously*. **C.** Followed by preposition. *Kick against, at*, intrans., resist, resent, object to; *the rising generation kicks against, at, all old-fashioned restrictions*; Phr. *kick against the pricks*, originally of ox resenting the prick of a goad; to resist uselessly something which will hurt more than you hurt it. *Kick back*, trans., to retaliate: *do him an injury and he will kick (you) back*; intrans., to recoil. *Kick off*, **a** trans., to remove quickly, get rid of, as shoes &c.; **b** intrans., to start game of football by kicking the ball from centre of ground, also at half-time and after a goal has been scored. *Kick out*, trans., **a** (colloq.) to eject, remove by physical or other means; dismiss, sack: *the fellow was rude so I kicked him out*; **b** (football) to kick (ball) into touch and so out of play. *Kick up*, trans., to lift, raise, with the foot, stir up with the foot; cp. Phr. *kick up a dust* &c. above.

kick (II.), n., fr. prec. **a** Blow with the foot; **b** act or result of kicking: *kick of horse, gun, ball &c. was a hard one*; *the bruise was caused by a kick*; **c** (football) one who kicks: *he was a splendid kick*; **d** (colloq.) pungency, bite: *this whisky has no kick in it* (also fig.); **e** (slang) sixpence: *two and a kick*, two shillings and sixpence. Phrs. *more kicks than halfpence*, more trouble, loss, punishment than reward; *to get the kick*, (slang) to be dismissed, get the 'sack'. *Kick off, kick out*, (football) act or result of kicking ball as under **kick** (I.).

kick (III.), n. Etymol. doubtful, prob. not connected w. prec. Deep dent or hollow at bottom of a glass bottle.

kicker, n. [1. kíker; 2. kíkə], fr. **kick** (I.) & **-er**. **1.** Horse with habit of kicking. **2.** (colloq., Canadian and Am.) A person who persistently objects to, resents, or resists anything; one who criticises, runs down, or depreciates; as contrasted with a 'booster'.

kicking-strap, n. [1. kíking strap; 2. kíkiŋ stræp]. Strap round hind-quarters of draught-horse fastened to shafts to check kicking.

kickshaw, n. [1. kíkshaw; 2. kíkʃɔ]. Properly *kickshaws*, pl. *kickshawses*, as 'Twelfth Night', I. iii. 122, quoted by Skeat; fr. Fr. *quelque-chose*, 'something, anything'. **a** Fancy dish, sweetmeat, delicacy; **b** fantastic, trifling thing; frippery, useless adornment.

kicksies, n. pl. [1. kíksiz; 2. kíksiz], fr. **kick** (I.). (slang) Wide-bottomed trousers as worn by costermongers, adorned with pearl buttons.

kickup, kick-up, n. [1. kíkup; 2. kíkap]. Cp. **kick** (I.). (colloq.) a Row, fuss, shindy; **b** a festivity, merry party; **a** do, a jamboree.

kid (I.), n. [1. kid; 2. kid]. In M.E.; Scand.; cp. O.N. *kið*, Dan. *kid*. **1. a** The young of a goat, also of antelopes, and formerly, of deer, now 'fawn'; **b** the flesh, meat, of a kid; **c** (astron.) *the Kids*, group of three stars, in the constellation Auriga, whose rising foretells storms. **2.** Leather made from skin of a kid: *boots, shoes, gloves of kid*; *bound in kid*. **3.** (vulg. slang) **a** A child; **b** (Am. slang) prefixed to name of young boxer &c.: *Kid O'Flannigan*.

kid (II.), vb. intrans., fr. prec. (of goats) To bring forth young.

kid (III.), vb. trans. & n. Etymol. unknown. (vulg. slang) **1.** vb. To delude, humbug, swindle: *he kidded me the horse wasn't going to run*. **2.** n. (vulg.) Hoax: *the threat of a lock-out (strike) was all a kid*.

kid (IV.), n. Perh. variant of **kit** (I.). Small tub, used as a mess-tub by sailors.

Kidderminster, adj. & n. [1. kíderminster; 2. kídəminstə]. **a** adj. Made at Kidderminster, town in Worcestershire, England, esp. of a strong coarse kind of two-ply carpet made there; **b** n., a Kidderminster carpet.

kiddle, n. [1. kídl; 2. kídl], fr. O. Fr. *quidel, guidel*, possibly connected w. **kid** (IV.). Basket-work barrier, with nets, used for catching fish in a river.

kiddy, n. [1. kídi; 2. kídi]. Dimin. of **kid** (I.), 3. (colloq.) Child.

kid glove, n. **kid** (I.) & **glove**. **a** Glove made of kid-skin; **b** (fig.) method or manner of treating or dealing with any problem, softly, delicately, or without severe measures, as if wearing kid gloves: *one cannot suppress a revolution in kid gloves*; also attrib.: *kid-glove methods* &c.

kidnap, vb. trans. [1. kídnap; 2. kídnæp], fr. **kid** (I.), 3, 'child'; & *nap*, variant of **nab**, 'to catch, steal'. **a** To abduct or steal a child; **b** carry away a person illegally by force or fraud against his will.

kidnapper, n. [1. kídnaper; 2. kídnæpə]. Prec. & **-er**. One who kidnaps or practises kidnapping.

kidney, n. [1. kídni; 2. kídni]. Early forms are pl., *kidneris, kidneers*; origin of first element is unknown; second element prob. fr. M.E. *eire*, pl. *eiren*, 'egg'. M.E. *nere*, cogn. w. Germ. *niere*, 'kidney' is a different word. **1. a** One of a pair of oval or bean-shaped glandular internal organs, in mammals, birds, and reptiles, excreting urine and removing other, esp. nitrogenous, waste products from the blood; **b** this organ, of sheep, ox, or pig, as article of food: *kidneys and bacon*; **c** (fig.) kind, type, character: *a man of this kidney*. **2.** (attrib.) Various things resembling a kidney in shape: *kidney-bean*, dwarf French bean; scarlet runner bean; *kidney-potato*, variety so called from shape; *kidney-stone*, nephrite.

kief, kef, n. [1. kēf, kef; 2. kīf, kef]. Arab. *kaif, kef*, 'ease, well-being'. **a** State of dreamy tranquillity or drowsiness, produced by smoking or chewing Indian hemp or bhang; **b** Indian hemp or bhang so used.

kieselguhr, n. [1. kézelgōōr; 2. kízəlguə]. Germ., fr. *kiesel*, 'flint', & *guhr*, 'earthy sediment'. A fine white siliceous powder, containing the fossilized remains of algae, used for polishing and as an absorbent in various manufactures.

kikumon, n. [1. kíkoomon; 2. kíkumən]. Jap. Imperial Japanese emblem, representing open chrysanthemum flower.

kilderkin, n. [1. kílderkin; 2. kíldəkin]. Origin doubtful; apparently a form of Du. *kindeken*, dimin., fr. *kind*, child, as name of similar liquid measure. **a** Barrel, containing 16 or 18 gallons of beer or other liquid; **b** measure of this quantity, two firkins.

kilerg, n. [1. kílĕrg; 2. kílʌg]. Fr. **kilo-** & **erg**. Physical unit of work, one thousand ergs.

Kilkenny, adj. [1. kilkéni; 2. kilkéni], fr. name of town in Ireland. Only in Phr. *to fight like Kilkenny cats*, referring to legend of two cats who fought till only their tails were left.

kill (I.), vb. trans. & intrans. [1. kil; 2. kil]. M.E. *killen*, earlier *cullen*, 'beat, kill'. Etymol. unknown. Connexion w. **quell**, fr. O.E. *cwellan*, 'to kill', has been suggested, but is extremely improbable. **A.** trans. **1.** To deprive of life, put to death, slay; **a** (of human action) implying deliberate violence and intention to destroy life: *Cain killed Abel*; *to kill a man in a duel*; *the Turks killed thousands of Armenians*; Phrs. *to kill with kindness*, overwhelm, oppress with; *to kill time*, devise means of spending it without boredom; **b** (implying no intention) to cause death of: *he had the misfortune, as a child, to kill a playfellow with a toy pistol*; **c** to slaughter (animals): *our butcher kills his own sheep every day*; **d** to put (animals) to death in sport, by giving to hounds, shooting, spearing &c.: *to kill a fox, a brace of pheasants, an otter, a salmon*; Phr. *to kill two birds with one stone*, produce two separate results by a single action. **2. a** (of disease, accident, war &c.) To cause death of, cut short the life of: *tuberculosis killed him at last*; *killed in a motor-smash, in battle* &c.; **b** to cause to shrivel up, blight, wither, die down, waste away: *the frost has killed the seedlings*; **c** (fig., of action on affections, feelings) to extinguish, blight, destroy, check, suppress: *to kill a person's love, hopes, ambitions* &c. **3.** To sap strength or vitality of, tend to shorten life; of physical and moral agencies: *the hardships and privations of his youth are killing him*; *she is being slowly killed by grief*. Phr. *to kill by inches*, slowly drain life away from. **4.** To destroy effect of by sharp contrast: **a** (of colour) to neutralize: *the violent vermilion kills the blue in the picture*; **b** (of sounds) deaden, swamp, be too loud for: *the drums killed the strings*. **5.** To put an end to, finish, cause failure of, defeat: *to kill a bill, proposal* &c., cause its withdrawal; *to kill a play, novel* &c., prevent its success, by criticism &c. **6. a** (tennis, racquets &c.) To play a ball so that it cannot be returned; **b** (print., editing) to delete, strike out, cancel. **7. a** (colloq.) To create a strong impression, sensation; (of glance, dress, manners): *made, dressed, to kill*; **b** to produce violent emotion of mirth: *a screamingly funny play, it nearly killed me*; cp. *to make one die with laughter*. **B.** intrans. To have the effect, perform action of, killing: *strychnine kills by violent action on the muscles*; *thou shalt not kill*; *it is easy to kill but impossible to restore life*. **C.** Followed by preposition or adverb. *Kill off*, trans., to eliminate, get rid of **a** (of material things) as superfluous animals, plants &c.: *the late frost has done some good in killing off insect pests, weeds* &c.; **b** (fig.) in a novel or play: *in 'Hamlet' Shakespeare kills off practically all the characters before the curtain falls*. *Kill out*, trans., to destroy entirely, eliminate, weed out: *an epidemic often kills out the weaklings*.

kill (II.), n., fr. prec. **a** Act of killing, esp. fox-hunting: *we lost our fox, so there was no kill*; **b** that which is killed, number of animals killed in hunting by man or beast: *a plentiful kill*.

killer, n. [1. kíler; 2. kílə]. **kill** (I.) & **-er**. One who, or that which, kills, esp. **a** instrument, such as a pole-axe, used for slaughtering animals for food: *humane killer*, special device for slaughtering animals without unnecessary pain; **b** person who does not scruple to kill another; **a** murderer.

killer-whale, n. Kind of dolphin, with strong jaws and teeth, killing and feeding on seals and, if in sufficient numbers, on whales, esp. (zool.) *Orca gladiator*, grampus, of Atlantic and Pacific Oceans.

killing (I.), adj. [1. kíling; 2. kíliŋ], fr. Pres. Part. of **kill**. **1.** Having property of causing death, tending to kill, fatal: *a killing frost*. **2.** (fig.) **a** Causing strong emotions of mirth; highly comical, laughable: *a perfectly killing play*; **b** of a kind to excite strong feelings of admiration; ravishing: *she looked killing in an old-fashioned hat*.

killing (II.), n. **kill** & **-ing**. Slaughtering, slaying.

killjoy, kill-joy, n. [1. kíljoi; 2. kíldžɔi], fr. **kill** & **joy**. One who kills, casts gloom on, damps, enjoyment, merriment &c.; a wet-blanket.

kiln, n. [1. kiln; 2. kiln], fr. O.E. *cyln, cylene*, fr. Lat. *culīna*, 'kitchen'. See **culinary**. Furnace or oven, for burning, as *lime-kiln*; for baking, as *brick-kiln*; for drying, as *hop-kiln*, place for drying hops; oast-house.

kilo-, pref. Through Fr., fr. Gk. *khilioi*, 'a thousand', prob. for **khislioi* or **kheslioi*, cp. Scrt. *sáhásram*, for *sa-*g'heslo-*, 'a thousand', perh. connected w. Scrt. *sáhaš*, 'power, victory', cp. Goth. *sigis*, O.E. *sige*, 'victory'. cp. **epoch**. Combining form, meaning 'one thousand', in metric system.

kilo, n. [1. kélō; 2. kílou]. See prec. (abbr.) A kilogramme, kilometre &c., leaving unit of weight or measure to be understood.

kilogram(me), n. [1. kílogram; 2. kíləgræm]. **kilo-** & **gram(me)**. One thousand grammes, equivalent to about 2 lbs.

kilolitre, -liter, n. [1. kíloléter; 2. kíləlītə]. **kilo-** & **litre**. One thousand litres, one cubic metre.

kilometre, -meter, n. [1. kílomēter; 2. kíləmītə]. **kilo-** & **metre** (II.). One thousand metres, about five-eighths of a mile.

kilowatt, n. [1. kílowot; 2. kílowɔt]. **kilo-** & **watt**. Unit of electrical power, one thousand watts.

kilt (I.), vb. trans. [1. kilt; 2. kilt]. Scand. Cp. Dan. *kilte*, Swed. *kilta*, vbs., & Icel. *kilting*, n.; not an early word in Scots or Engl. vernacular. To tuck, gird up, of a skirt, a loose garment or cloak, so that the lower folds fall in pleats.

kilt (II.), n. See prec. Short pleated skirt or petticoat, fastened round waist and reaching to the knee, worn by Scottish Highlanders, and by Highland regiments as uniform. Phr. *the kilt*, Highland costume.

kilted, adj. [1. kílted; 2. kíltid]. Prec. & **-ed**. Provided with, wearing, a kilt: *kilted regiments*, Highland regiments wearing the kilt as uniform.

kimono, n. [1. kimṓnō; 2. kimóunou]. Japanese. **a** Loose robe, with short, very wide, sleeves; the typical national garment of both sexes in Japan; **b** dressing-gown of this type, as adopted by Western peoples.

kin, n. [1. kin; 2. kin]. O.E. *cynn*, 'kind, species, race, family', M.E. *cunn(e)*, *kinn(e)* &c., fr. Gmc. **kunja-*, W. Gmc. **kunnj-*, cp. O.H.G. *kunni*; O.N. *kynn*; Goth. *kuni*; fr. Aryan base **ĝen-*, 'to produce' &c.; whence Lat. *genus*, 'birth, origin, descent'. See **genus**; see also **kind (I.)** & **kith**. **1. a** Family, stock; group of persons connected by blood, or by descent from a common ancestor; **b** (collectively) relatives, kindred; relationship, connexion by blood or marriage; Phrs. *kin to*, (i.) related by blood &c.; (ii.) alike, akin (q.v.); *of good kin*, of good birth; *near of kin*, closely related or similar to; *next of kin*, nearest relative(s) by blood; *more kin than kind*, though related to, or of kin with, yet not kindly or friendly. **2.** Identity of essential character and constituents as belonging to same order in nature: *a diamond is of the same kin as coal.*

kin-, pref. fr. Gk. *kīnein*, 'to move, set in motion, set going' &c., fr. base *kī-*, as in Gk. *kíein*, 'to go', cogn. w. Lat. *ciēre*, 'to move, shake, put in motion', *citus*, 'rapid, swift', cp. also *citāre*, 'to put in motion, stimulate; to call, summon' (see **cite**); further cognates are Goth. *haitan*, 'command', O.E. *hātan*. See **hight** & **hest**. Prefix used in a large number of words from Greek, some borrowed from Greek itself, as *kinesis*, others being modern scientific concoctions from Greek elements, as *kinaesthesis*. The force of the prefix is 'moving, movement'.

-kin, dimin. suff. Prob. fr. Du. *-kijn*, *-ken*, cp. Ger. *-chen*, as in *mädchen*, 'girl, little maid'. Many words w. this termination are direct borrowings fr. Du., as *firkin*, *kilderkin*, *mannikin*; *lambkin* seems an exception. The suff. appears also in dimin. & familiar modifications of names, e.g. *Simkin*, fr. *Simon* or *Samuel*, *Jenkin*, fr. *John*.

kinaesthesis, kinesthesis, n. [1. kinesthḗsis; 2. kinisþísis], fr. **kin-** & Gk. *aisthēsis*, 'perception'. See **aesthetic**. (psychol.) Perception of muscular movement or effort; sum or total of such perceptions as affecting will to perform them.

kinaesthetic, kinesthetic, adj. [1. kinēsthétik; 2. kinispétik]. **kin-** & **aesthetic**. Pertaining to kinaesthesis or perception of muscular movement: *kinaesthetic image, memory, sensation* &c.

kinchin, n. [1. kínchin; 2. kíntʃin]. Possibly fr. Germ. *kindchen*, 'little child', fr. *kind*, 'child', & dimin. *-chen*, cp. **-kin**. (old thieves' slang) Child, esp. in Phr. *kinchin lay*, stealing from a child in the streets.

kincob, n. [1. kíngkob; 2. kíŋkəb]. Pers. *kinkhab*. East Indian brocade, embroidered with gold or silver thread.

kind (I.), n. [1. kīnd; 2. kaind]. O.E. *(ĝe-)cÿnd*, 'kind, species, nature, quality, offspring'; fr. Gmc. **kundi-*, fr. Aryan type **ĝn̥ti-*; exactly cogn. w. Lat. *genti-*, stem of *gens*, 'family, nation, race, breed' (see **gentile**). From Aryan base **ĝen-*, 'to produce' (see **generate** & **genus**); fr. this base is also derived Lat. *nātūra* for **gnātūra* (see **nature**); other Engl. cognates are **kin** & **kith**. **1. a** (archaic) Natural group of animals or plants, closely related by descent, and considered as derived from a common origin; breed, species, genus: '*tree yielding fruit after his kind*'; *to be fond of one's kind*, i.e. of other human beings; **b** (in popular usage) sort, class, variety: *the wrong kind of umbrella*; *the best kind of coat for the country*; *a queer kind of person*; *apples of several kinds*; (also colloq.) *what kind of man is he?*, for *of what kind is this man*; *he is the kind of man who . . .*, for *he is a man of the kind who . . .*; (familiar) *these kind of people* &c. Various Phrs. (*I won't*) *stand this kind of thing*, disapprovingly or contemptuously, of conduct, circumstances &c.; *this is the kind of thing I want*, something like but not exactly what I want; *a kind of gentleman, gentleman of a kind* = a bad kind; *nothing of the kind*, form of emphatic denial; *to pay back, answer, in kind*, (fig.) to behave to, reply to, a person according to the treatment &c. he has accorded; *kind of*, (with advbl. force): *I kind of thought this would happen*, half expected it. **2.** Essential character, nature; **a** esp. in Phr. *to differ in degree but not in kind*; **b** specif. (eccles.) one of the elements, bread or wine, in the Eucharist: *to receive in both kinds*. **3.** Natural products, fruits of labour; now only in Phr. *to pay in kind*, i.e. in goods instead of in money.

kind (II.), adj. O.E. *(ĝe-)cÿnde*, 'innate, natural, suitable', lit. 'according to nature'. See prec. **1. a** (of persons) Possessing, exhibiting, natural feelings; hence, benevolent, affectionate, tender, gentle, considerate, obliging, indulgent: *a kind mother, friend, heart* &c.; **b** (of actions, conduct, utterances &c.) expressing kindness of feeling: *kind deeds, words, looks*; in various polite Phrs.: *you are very kind; it is so kind of you to call*; in letters &c. as form of courteous address, often of no real significance: *with kind regards*; *your kind attention will oblige*; ironically: *be kind enough to hold your tongue.* **2.** Easy to handle, tractable: *this stone is kind for dressing*; *horse kind in harness.*

kindergarten, n. [1. kíndergàrten; 2. kíndəgàt(ə)n]. Mod. Germ., lit. 'garden of children'; *kinder*, 'children', pl. of *kind*, cogn. w. **kind (I.)**, & *garten*, 'garden', q.v. School for very young children conducted on a system invented by Froebel, the fundamental idea of which is to educate mind and body in such a way as to arouse interest instead of fatigue or boredom; the instruction consists of a series of highly organized games accompanied by songs and actions, of the making of simple objects out of modelling clay &c.

kind-hearted, adj. [1. kīnd hárted; 2. káind hátid]. Having a kind heart; humane, charitable, sympathetic.

kind-heartedly, adv. Prec. & **-ly**. In a kind-hearted manner.

kind-heartedness, n. See prec. & **-ness**. Quality of being kind-hearted.

kindle, vb. trans. & intrans. [1. kíndl; 2. kíndl]. Scand., prob. fr. O.N. *kynda*, 'to light a fire', & **-le**. **A.** trans. **1. a** To set fire to, light, start (a fire), cause to ignite: *to kindle a fire*; **b** (fig.) to light up, make to glow: *the setting sun kindled the sky.* **2.** (fig.) To inflame, rouse, provoke passion, enthusiasm &c.: *to kindle an audience, the interest of an audience, by one's words.* **B.** intrans. **1. a** To take, catch, fire; to burn, light up, glow, grow warm: *the fire is kindling at last*; also *kindle up*; **b** (fig.) *his face kindled*, grew warm, blushed; *eyes kindled*, grew bright, flashed; *day kindles in the east.* **2.** (fig.) To be roused, excited, to grow warm, flame up: *to kindle at an insult.*

kindler, n. [1. kíndler; 2. kíndlə]. Prec. & **-er**. One who, that which, kindles; specif., a fire-lighter, kindling-wood.

kindless, adj. [1. kīndles; 2. káindlis], fr. **kind (II.)** & **-less**. (obs. or poet.) Not kind or gentle; unkind, cruel, without pity or mercy.

kindliness, n. [1. kīndlines; 2. káindlinis]. **kindly** & **-ness**. **a** Quality, state, of being kind; kindness, benevolence; **b** a kind act or deed.

kindling, n. [1. kíndling; 2. kíndliŋ]. **kindle** & **-ing**. **1.** Act of setting fire to or of taking fire at. **2.** Material such as small pieces of wood &c. used for lighting a fire.

kindling-wood, n. Kindling.

kindly (I.), adj. [1. kīndli; 2. káindli]. O.E. *ĝe-cÿndlić*, 'natural'. See **kind (I.)** & **-ly**. **1.** (archaic) Pertaining to, resulting from, the processes of nature; natural: *the kindly fruits of the earth.* **2.** Kind, benevolent, considerate: *a kindly heart*; expressing benevolence: *a kindly smile, act* &c.

kindly (II.), adv. O.E. *(ĝe)-cÿndelīće*, 'naturally'. See **kind (II.)** & **-ly**. **1. a** In a kind manner: *to speak kindly*; **b** (in polite formulae) *would you kindly tell me the time?*; *kindly forward all letters*; also ironical: *kindly behave properly.* **2.** Naturally, easily: *to take kindly to one's new duties.*

kindness, n. [1. kīndnes; 2. káin(d)nis]. **kind (II.)** & **-ness**. **1.** (quality of mind) Goodness, benevolence, gentleness, amiability: *kindness of heart.* Phr. *to have a kindness for (a person)*, to be fond of, have an affection for him. **2.** A kind act, deed of benevolence; an obliging action: *to do a personal kindness*; *it would be a great kindness to call upon the bereaved family.*

kindred (I.), n. [1. kíndred; 2. kíndrid]. M.E. *kinrede(n)*, formed fr. O.E. *cynn*, 'family' &c. (see **kin**), & suff. *-rǣden*, indicating condition &c. (cp. **ready**). **1. a** Blood relationship; also **b** (loosely) relationship, connexion by marriage. **2.** Group of persons related through descent from common ancestor; family, clan. **3.** (coll., with pl. vb.) Whole group of one's blood relations and family connexions; family to which one belongs.

kindred (II.), adj., fr. prec. **1.** Belonging to same family, related in blood: *kindred races, tribes* &c. More usually **2. a** (in spiritual sense) congenial, having similar character, possessing affinity in disposition &c.: *kindred souls, natures, spirits*; **b** related by origin from common source; bearing more or less close resemblance; showing similarity of structure, character &c.: *kindred languages, institutions* &c.

kindredship, n. [1. kíndredship; 2. kíndridʃip]. **kindred (I.)** & **-ship**. State of being related; affinity, relationship.

kine, n. [1. kīn; 2. kain]. M.E. *kīn*, irreg. pl., fr. O.E. *cÿ*, M.E. *kī* &c., mutated pl. of *cū*, **cow (I.)**, cp. Scots **kye**, & weak pl. suff. *-en*, as in *oxen*. (provinc. or poet.) Cows, cattle.

kinema, n. See **cinema**.

kinematic, adj. [1. kinemátik; 2. kinimǽtik], fr. Gk. *kīnēmat-(os)*, 'motion', & **-ic**. See account of this base under **kin-**. Of or belonging to the science of kinematics.

kinematics, n., fr. prec. [1. kinemátiks; 2. kinimǽtiks]. (phys.) Branch of science dealing with phenomena of motion, in relation to velocity, distance travelled, and time occupied.

kinematograph, n. Formerly so written, and pronounced by some [1. kīnēmatograhf; 2. kainímətəgrāf]. For usual form, and sense see **cinematograph**.

kinesis, n. [1. kin-, kīnḗsis; 2. kin-, kainísis]. Gk. *kīnēsis*, 'motion, movement'. See account of base under **kin-**. Physical movement.

kinetic, adj. [1. kin-, kīnétik; 2. kin-, kainétik]. Gk. *kīnētikós*, 'putting in motion, exciting', fr. base *kī-* in Gk. *kīnein*, 'to move'. See under **kin-**. **a** (phys.) Of or belonging to, caused by, or due to, motion: *kinetic energy, theory of gases* &c.; **b** (fig.) having moving force, powerful, dynamic, as metaphorical borrowing from scientific usage: *a man of kinetic energy, force* &c.

kinetics, n. [1. kin-, kīnétiks; 2. kin-, kainétiks]. (phys. and mechan.) Science dealing with principles and forces underlying the motion of bodies.

kineto-, pref. Form of Gk. *kīnētós*, 'movable', used in compounds; fr. base *kin-*, 'to move'. See **kin-**.

kinetoscope, n. [1. kīnētoskōp; 2. kainítəskoup]. See prec. & **-scope**. Instrument which produced the visual effect of objects in continuous motion, by passing rapidly before the eye a series of pictures each recording a particular position momentarily assumed by the moving object before passing to the next; primitive form of cinematograph.

king (I.), n. [1. king; 2. kiŋ]. O.E. *cyning*, *cyng*, 'king', fr. base **kun-*, 'family, race, tribe' &c., see **kin**, & patronymic **-ing**. **1.** A man who is the supreme, usually hereditary, governor and head of a nation, state, tribe &c.: *the King of England*; *His Majesty the King*; *King George V.*; *king of beasts*, the lion; *king of misrule*, ruler of revels, who often wore mock crown and sceptre; *King of Kings*, (i.) Almighty God; (ii.) title assumed by some Oriental monarchs; *king of terrors*, death. **2. a** Person who by force of character, or by his social position and wealth, exerts great influence and power in a particular sphere or area; a territorial magnate: *a king of men*; *king of the country-side*; **b** person who dominates and controls, or who is enormously successful in, some branch of industry: *an oil king, soap king* &c. **3. a** (cards) One bearing conventional figure of a king, ranking below the ace and above the queen; **b** (chess) principal piece, usually having a small crown on the top, which has to be guarded against mate or checkmate; *king's pawn, bishop* &c., piece on right hand of king on chess-board; **c** (draughts) piece which on reaching opponent's base is 'crowned' by piece of same colour which has been previously taken by opponent, and may then move backwards or forwards. **4.** (her.) One of the three principal officers or Kings-of-Arms (in full (*Garter*) *King-of-Arms*) in the College of Heralds of England immediately below the Earl Marshal; the corresponding official in Scotland and Ireland, Lyon King-of-Arms, and Ulster King-of-Arms respectively.

king (II.), vb. intrans. & trans., fr. prec. To rule, play the king, behave as a king; chiefly in such Phrs. as *to king it over one's associates* &c.

king-, pref. In composition this prefix indicates predominance in size or function.

King-at, more correctly **of, -Arms**. See **king** (I.), **4.**

king-bird, n. **a** American bird, the tyrant flycatcher; **b** variety of bird of paradise.

king-bolt, n. Large, important bolt in a building or vehicle.

King Charles's spaniel, n. [1. kìng chárlzez spányel; 2. kìŋ tʃálziz spǽnjəl]. A small breed of spaniel, usually black and tan in colour, kept as pet; so named from Charles II., who made them fashionable.

king-crab, n. One of a group, *Limulus*, of marine animals having a shell somewhat resembling that of a crab, and a long spiked tail; placed by zoologists between spiders and crustaceans.

king-craft, n. Art of ruling, statecraft, as shown by a king.

king-cup, n. **a** Country name for the marsh marigold; **b** (loosely) a large buttercup.

kingdom, n. [1. kíngdum; 2. kíŋdəm]. O.E. *cynedōm*, 'royal power, empire', *cyningdōm* being rare. See **king (I.)** & **-dom. 1. a** Realm; territory ruled by a king or queen: *the United Kingdom*; *Kingdom of Sweden* &c.; **b** dominion, power, authority of a king: *Louis XI. by statecraft established the kingdom in France.* **2.** (in religious, spiritual, things) Dominion, rule, of God and Christ. the Messiah, in this world or the hereafter: *Thy Kingdom come*; *the kingdom of heaven is within you.* Phrs. *kingdom come*, heaven, future life; *gone to kingdom come*, dead. **3.** (nat. hist., popular or archaic) One of the three primary divisions, or realms, of nature: *the animal, vegetable and mineral kingdoms.*

king-fish, n. Popular local name of various marine food fishes of N. America, Australia &c.

kingfisher, n. [1. kíngfisher; 2. kíŋfiʃə]. Bird of family *Alcedinidae*, with long beak and brilliant colouring, especially blue, green, red, black and white, frequenting streams and rivers, and feeding on fish; specif. (in Engl. usage) *Alcedo ispida*, or common kingfisher.

kingless, adj. [1. kíngles; kíŋlis]. **king (I.)** & **-less.** Without a king or ruler; in a state of anarchy.

kinglessness, n. Prec. & **-ness.** Condition of being kingless.

kinglet, n. [1. kínglet; 2. kíŋlit], fr. **king** & **-let. 1.** Petty king; king of an insignificant dominion. **2.** (zool.) The golden-crested wren.

kinglike, adj. & adv. [1. kínglīk; 2. kíŋlaik]. **king (I.)** & **-like. a** adj. Like a king in bearing, appearance, character; kingly, regal; majestic, august; **b** adv., (rare and poet.) in a kingly manner.

kingliness, n. [1. kínglines; 2. kíŋlinis]. **kingly** & **-ness.** State or condition of being kingly; **a** in appearance, bearing, demeanour, character; **b** in external circumstances and splendour.

King Log, n., fr. Æsop's Fable of the Frogs who asked Jupiter for a king. Person in position of nominal authority, who remains passive and inactive, and exerts no influence.

kingly, adj. & adv. [1. kíngli; 2. kíŋli]. **king** (I.) & **-ly. a** adj. Kinglike, becoming, suitable to, a king; regal; pertaining to a king; royal, majestic, splendid: '*his state Is kingly. Thousands at his bidding speed*' (Milton, 'On his Blindness'); *he pledged his kingly word*; **b** adv. (archaic) in a kingly manner.

king-maker, n. One who is the chief agent in establishing a king on his throne by deposing another; specif. used of Richard Beauchamp, Earl of Warwick (1428–71).

King-of-Arms. See **king** (I.), **4.**

king-post, n. Main upright beam or post supporting the angle or ridge of a roof, and resting on a horizontal tie or girder.

King's Bench, n. One of the divisions of the High Court of Justice of England; generally called *King's Bench Division*, which consists of the Lord Chief Justice and 17 judges. The name derives from the fact that the king formerly sat in this court on a raised bench.

King's Counsel, n. (abbr. to K.C. [kèi sí]). Senior member of the English Bar appointed to this honorary office by the Crown on nomination of the Lord Chancellor; he wears a silk gown in court, and is thence called *a silk*; he always sits within the bar of the court and takes precedence of all junior barristers, who sit outside the bar; he cannot appear alone in a case, but must always have a junior barrister with him.

king's evidence, n. A criminal who volunteers to give evidence against his accomplices in the crime with which he is charged. Phr. *to turn king's evidence*, to give such evidence.

king's evil, n. Old name for scrofula; so called because the disease was believed to be cured by the touch of the king of England's, or of Scotland's, hand.

kingship, n. [1. kíngship; 2. kíŋʃip]. **king (I.)** & **-ship.** State, condition, office, of a king.

king-wood, n. Brazilian wood, used for furniture, having fine grain and purple colouring.

kinit, n. [1. kínit; 2. kínit]. Formed fr. Gk. base **kin-**, 'motion'. (phys.) Unit of force; that amount of force which, acting for a second, will impart to a pound weight a velocity of one foot per second.

kink (I.), n. [1. kingk; 2. kiŋk]. Scand.; cp. same word in Swed. & Norw., meaning 'a twist in a rope'. Perh. related to **kick. a** An irregular, unexpected twist, hitch, bend, or curl in a rope, length of wire &c.; **b** (fig.) twist in mind or character; eccentricity, perversity.

kink (II.), vb. trans. & intrans., fr. prec. **a** trans. To make a kink in; **b** intrans., to develop, form into, a kink.

kinkajou, n. [1. kíngkajōō; 2. kíŋkədžū]. Imitative native Am. name, through Fr. *quincajou.* Small racoon-like animal, of S. and Central America, living in trees and nocturnal in habit; sometimes called 'honey-bear' or potto.

kinkle, n. & vb. trans. & intrans. [1. kíngkl; 2. kíŋkl]. Formed fr. **kink** & **-le** on anal. of *wrinkle.* **1.** n. A small kink, curl, or wave, in hair &c. **2.** vb. **a** trans. To make kinkles in; **b** intrans., to form into kinkles.

kinnikinic, n. [1. kínikìnik; 2. kínikìnik]. N. Am. Ind. Mixture of dried leaves and bark, smoked instead of tobacco.

kino, n. [1. kḗnō, kínō; 2. kínou, káinou]. Native name. Astringent gum, obtained from various tropical trees, used in tanning and medicine.

kinoplasm, n. [1. kín-, kínōplàzm; 2. kín-, káinouplæ̀zəm]. Form fr. Gk. **kin-**, & **plasm.** (biol.) Active element of protoplasm which produces movement.

kinsfolk, n. [1. kínzfōk; 2. kínzfouk]. **kin** & **folk.** (coll.) Relatives, kindred, family.

kinship, n. [1. kínship; 2. kínʃip]. **kin** & **-ship. a** State of being kin to, of the same blood as, another; relationship, affinity; **b** (fig.) close resemblance; similarity in character.

kinsman, n. [1. kínzman; 2. kínzmən]. Male relative, one belonging to, or closely allied to, one's family.

kinswoman, n. [1. kínzwooman; 2. kínzwumən]. Female relation, esp. a blood relation; (more loosely) a female allied by marriage to one's family.

kiosk, kiosque, n. [1. kiósk; 2. kiɔ́sk], fr. Turk. *kiaskh*, Pers. *kaskh.* **1.** Lightly built open Turkish summer-house; a summer villa in Turkey: *Yildiz Kiosk*, formerly the name of the Sultan's palace; also formerly the seat of Turkish government and diplomacy. **2.** In France and England, an open building supported on pillars and built in a supposed Turkish or Oriental style; such a building used as an open-air band-stand, a refreshment booth, or one for the sale of newspapers &c.

kip, n. [1. kip; 2. kip]. Etymol. unknown. **a** Hide of a calf or other young beast; **b** leather made from such a hide.

kipper (I.), n. [1. kíper; 2. kípə]. O.E. *cypera*, 'kind of salmon'; etymol. doubtful. **1.** Salmon during or after spawning. **2.** Smoked and salted herring. **3.** (slang) Person, usually with appropriate adjective prefixed: *saucy young kipper, merry old kipper.*

kipper (II.), vb. trans., fr. prec. To cure (fish) by smoking and salting.

kirimon, n. [1. kírimon; 2. kírimən]. Jap. Imperial Japanese emblem, representing the leaves and buds of the Paulownia tree.

kirk, n. [1. kĕrk; 2. kɜ̄k], fr. O.N. *kirkja*, 'church'; same word as O.E. *ċiriċe.* See **church.** (Nthn. Engl. and Scots) **a** Church, place of worship in Scotland; jocularly used in England: *to go to kirk* &c.; **b** members, congregation, of a kirk: *The (Auld) Kirk*, the Church of Scotland. This is now regarded in Scotland as an English term.

kirsch, n. [1. kērsh; 2. kiəʃ], fr. Mod. Germ. *kirsche*, 'cherry', O.H.G. *kirsa*, fr. a Romance form *ceresia*, whence also **cherry**, fr. O. Fr. *cherise.* Short for *kirschwasser*, 'cherry water', a perfectly clear potent spirit distilled from cherries together with the stones and kernels.

kirschwasser, n. [1. kḗrshvahser; 2. kiəʃvāsə]. Prec. & *wasser*, 'water'. Kirsch.

kirtle, n. [1. kḗrtl; 2. kɜ̄tl]. O.E. *cyrtel*, 'gown, tunic', cp. Icel. *kyrtill*, Swed. *kjörtel*, 'skirt'; prob. dimin. formed fr. Lat. *curtus*, 'short' (see **curt**), & *-il* (see **-le**). **a** Woman's skirt or petticoat; **b** (archaic) man's or woman's short outer garment; tunic.

kismet, n. [1. kízmet; 2. kízmɛt]. Turk., fr. Arab. *qismat*, 'fate', fr. *qismah*, 'divide, apportion'. Destiny, fate, esp. as exclamation expressing resignation to the will of Allah.

kiss (I.), n. [1. kis; 2. kis]. The O.E. n. is *coss*, M.E. *coss* &c.; the present n. is formed on anal. of vb. The Gmc. type is **kussa-*, whence W. Gmc. **koss*, as in O.E. *coss* & O.S. *kos*; O.H.G. *kus* & the same form in O.S. must owe their *u* to anal. of vb. wh. preserves this vowel through influence of the *-ja-* suff. The word prob. represents Aryan **gʷ(ə)t-to-* fr. base **gʷet-* &c., 'to speak, address, greet', whence also O.E. *cweþan*, 'to speak', q.v. under **quoth**(a) & second element of **bequeath**; cp. also O. Ir. *bēl*, 'mouth', lit. 'the speaker', fr. Aryan **gʷet-lo.* The orig. sense of *kiss* wd. thus be 'greeting'. **1. a** Pressure of the lips, often accompanied by slight drawing-in of the air which produces a faint smacking sound; **b** this pressure applied to face or hand of another as a form of greeting, or as a caress, expressing love, affection, or respect. Phrs. *Judas' kiss*, treacherous, hypocritical kiss or greeting of pretended affection; *kiss of peace*, that exchanged between the clergy during the celebration of the Mass in Greek Church as symbol of reconciliation. **2. a** (fig., poet.) Light touch or pressure, as of breeze on flowers, hair &c., or of waves on sand &c.; **b** slight contact between moving balls in billiards. **3.** (children's expression) Froth or bubbles on tea or milk.

kiss (II.), vb. trans. O.E. *cyssan*, M.E. *cusse(n)*, *kisse(n)* &c., fr. W. Gmc. **kussjan*. See prec. **1.** To give a kiss to; to caress, or touch with the lips. Phrs. *to kiss the book*, i.e. Bible, or New Testament, as formal act when taking an oath in law court, swearing an affidavit &c.; *kiss the dust, ground*, as formal act of submission; to suffer or submit to humiliation; to be slain or killed; *kiss hands*, to perform the ceremonial act of kissing the sovereign's hand on appointment to office; *kiss the rod*, submit to discipline humbly or without complaint. **2.** (of the wind, waves &c.) To touch lightly, gently, caressingly. **3.** (billiards, of moving balls) To touch lightly in passing: *kiss-cannon*, one made with such slight impact that the two other balls are not moved from their relative positions by that of the player.

kiss-in-the-ring, n. An old country game in which a ring is formed round a player, who is chased and kissed by one of the opposite sex on whom he or she drops a handkerchief.

kist (I.), n. [1. kist; 2. kist]. O.N. *kista*, 'chest'. See **chest (I.)**. (Nthn. Engl. and Scots) Chest.

kist (II.), n. (archaeol.). See **cist**.

kit (I.), n. [1. kit; 2. kit]. Prob. fr. M. Du. *kitte*, 'tub', cp. Norw. *kitte*, 'bin'; ultimate etymol. unknown. **1.** Small wooden tub, for butter, water, fish &c. **2.** Receptacle, bag or box, in which a soldier or sailor packs the clothes, equipment &c. which he does not carry on his person; similar receptacle for workman's tools; valise, a kit-bag, q.v. **3. a** (mil.) Equipment, other than arms, of a soldier or sailor: *kit inspection*, examination of the clothes &c. of a soldier by an officer; **b** equipment generally, esp. that required for carrying on a particular trade or occupation; **c** outfit, equipment for sport, travelling, or other special purpose: *hunting, shooting, golfing kit*.

kit (II.), n. Etymol. unknown. Small fiddle used formerly by a teacher of dancing.

kit (III.), n. Abbr. of **kitten (I.)**.

kit-bag, n. fr. **kit (I.)** & **bag**. **a** Long canvas bag in which a soldier carries his kit; **b** large leather travelling hand-bag with wide opening or mouth.

kit-cat, adj. & n. **a** adj. Of or belonging to the Kit-Cat Club, founded by Whigs in 1703 and held at a tavern in London, kept by Christopher (Kit) Catling or Cat: esp. *Kit-cat portrait*, a small, less than half-length, portrait of the members of the club, of head, bust, and hands; of any portrait of this size; **b** n., portrait of this size.

kitchen, n. [1. kíchen; 2. kítʃin]. O.E. *cyċene*, M.E. *kuchen(e)*, *kichen(e)* &c.; loan-word of the Continental period fr. L. Lat. *coquīna*; cp. fr. same source O.H.G. *kuchina*, Mod. Germ. *küche*; M. Du. *kokene*; fr. Lat. base *coq-*, as in *coquere*, 'to cook'. See **cook (I.)**. Place or apartment in a house in which cooking takes place.

kitchener, n. [1. kíchener; 2. kítʃenə]. Prec. & **-er**. **1.** A cooking-range or stove. **2.** Official in charge of the cooking of a monastery.

kitchen-garden, n. Piece of ground enclosed by a wall or fence in which vegetables are grown for the house, or for market.

kitchen-maid, n. Domestic servant who does a great part of the cook's work.

kitchen-midden, n. In techn. sense ad. fr. Dan. *kjökken-mödding*. **a** Household rubbish-heap; **b** specif. (archaeol.) prehistoric rubbish-heap of a type found in parts of Denmark near the coast, containing bones of men and animals, shells, tools, household implements, pottery &c.; the refuse of a primitive settlement.

kite, n. [1. kīt; 2. kait]. O.E. *cȳta*, M.E. *kīte*; etymol. doubtful. **1. a** Bird of prey, genus *Milvus*, belonging to the hawk family, distinguished from other members of the order by forked tail and long wings; **b** (fig.) one who preys on others; shark. **2. a** Contrivance, carried by wind into the air, consisting usually of a triangular framework of wood or cane, covered with paper or thin textile material, balanced by a tail, and connected with the ground by a string or cord; similar contrivance, of box shape, 'box-kite', with open sides, used for meteorological observation; **b** bill, promissory note, or other negotiable instrument of fictitious or worthless security; accommodation bill. Phr. *fly a kite*, (i.) see how the wind blows, set rumour current as to forthcoming political or other action as a test of public opinion, cp. Fr. *ballon d'essai*; (ii.) to attempt to raise money on worthless security.

kite-balloon, n. (mil.) Fixed or captive observation balloon, with kite attachments to check wind-pressure.

kith, n. [1. kith; 2. kiþ]. O.E. *cȳþþo*, 'relationship; lineage', fr. **kunþ-jō*; fr. anct. variant of ancestral form of **kind (I.)**, q.v. for cognates; Aryan **ĝn̥t-jā*, 'family, race' &c. Some derive *kith* fr. **kunþja*, 'known', connecting it w. O.E. *cȳðan*, 'to make known' &c. The O.E. *cȳþþo* has also the sense of 'acquaintance'. It is possible that there were two words, one derived fr. **kun-*, 'to know', the other fr. **kun-*, 'to produce', & that the senses were blended just as the forms were identical. It is probable that Aryan **ĝen-* &c., meaning 'know', & **ĝen-*, 'produce', were ultimately one & the same. See **know** & **can (I.)**. Now only in Phr. *kith and kin*, family and relations, those of one's own blood and lineage.

kitling, n. [1. kítling; 2. kítliŋ]. Prob. Scand.; cp. O.N. *ketlingr*, 'kitten; young of other animals', dimin. of *köttr*, 'cat'; this is earlier in Engl. than *kitten*. A small kitten.

kitten (I.), n. [1. kítn; 2. kítn]. M.E. *kyton*, *kitoun*, fr. O. Fr. *chitoun*, 'kitten'; cp. obs. Mod. Fr. *chaton*, dimin. of *chat*, 'cat'. The older Engl. word was **kitling**. A young cat.

kitten (II.), vb. intrans., fr. prec. To bear, bring forth, kittens.

kittenish, adj. [1. kítenish; 2. kítəniʃ], fr. **kitten (I.)** & **-ish**. Like a kitten, playful, frisky; often applied to a young girl or, disparagingly, to an older woman who pretends to be much younger than she is.

kittiwake, n. [1. kítiwāk; 2. kítiweik]. Imitative, fr. its cry. A sea-gull, common to both sides of N. Atlantic; (zool.) a gull belonging to the genus *Rissa*.

kittle (I.), vb. intrans. [1. kítl; 2. kítl]. **kit (III.)** & **-le**. (obs. or dial.) To bring forth kittens; to kitten.

kittle (II.), adj. M.E. *kytelle*, 'to tickle'; etymol. doubtful. Ticklish, difficult, troublesome, now only in Scots Phr. *kittle cattle*, (i.) difficult cattle to drive; (ii.) (fig., of persons) uncertain in temper and behaviour.

kitty, n. [1. kíti; 2. kíti]. Dimin. **kit (I.)** & **-y**. **1.** Child's or pet name for a kitten. **2.** Pool of stakes in various card games, as poker &c.

kiwi, n. [1. kḗwē; 2. kíwī]. Maori, imitative, fr. its cry. Tailless New Zealand bird with rudimentary wings; the apteryx.

kleisto-, pref. See first element in **cleistogamic**.

klepht, n. [1. kleft; 2. klɛft]. Mod. Gk. *klephtēs*, Gk. *kléptēs*, 'robber, thief'; cp. Gk. *kleptein*, 'to steal', *klopḗ*, 'theft', *klopós*, & *klōps*, 'thief'; cogn. w. Lat. *clepere*, 'to steal'; Goth. *hlifan*, 'to steal', & *hliftus*, 'thief'. See **lift (I.)**. **a** Member of various bands of Greeks who, after the conquest of Greece by Turkey, maintained a kind of independence in the mountains; **b** a Greek brigand.

kleptomania, n. [1. klèptōmánia; 2. klèptouméiniə]. Invented word fr. Gk. **klepto-*, *kléptēs*, 'thief'. See prec. & **mania**. Uncontrollable propensity to steal due to pathological causes and not arising from criminal instincts, often affecting those who have not the incentive of poverty.

kleptomaniac, n. [1. klèptōmániak; 2. klèptouméiniæk]. Prec. & **-ac**. Person addicted to kleptomania.

klino-, pref. See **clino-**.

klipspringer, n. [1. klípsprìnger; 2. klípspriŋə]. S. Afr. Du., fr. *klip*, 'rock, cliff', & *springer*, 'leaper, springer'. Small S. and E. African mountain antelope, resembling European chamois.

kloof, n. [1. kloof; 2. klūf]. S. Afr. Du. Connected w. **cleave, cleft**. Deep gorge, gully, ravine.

knack, n. [1. nak; 2. næk]. Imitative; cp. **knock** & **knap (II.)**; Norw. & Swed. have *knaka*, 'to crack'. **1.** (orig.) Snap, click of the fingers against each other, hence, a jester's, juggler's trick. **2.** Specif., skill, dexterity, esp. as acquired by habit or practice; **a** (in bodily actions) *splitting wood with a beetle and wedge seems easy enough when you have the knack of it*; **b** (of intellectual exercises) *a happy knack of ingenious rhyming*. **3.** (rare) Trifle, toy, worthless object, knick-knack, q.v.

knacker, n. [1. náker; 2. nǽkə]. Etymol. doubtful; possibly fr. prec. **1.** One who buys and slaughters worn-out horses: *fit only for the knacker's yard*. **2.** Buyer and breaker-up of old ships or houses.

knackery, n. [1. nákeri; 2. nǽkəri]. Prec. & **-y**. A knacker's yard, slaughter-house for old horses.

knag, n. [1. nag; 2. næg]. M.E. *knagge*; cp. Swed. & Norw. *knagg*. Knot in wood, projection left after lopping branch from a tree, peg.

knaggy, adj. [1. nági; 2. nǽgi], fr. prec. & **-y**. Full of knags or knots.

knap (I.), n. [1. nap; 2. næp]. O.E. *cnæp*, 'top, mountain-top'; cp. O.N. *knappr*, 'knob'. Cp. **knop**. Top, crest, of a hill; still surviving in English Place-Names, as *Knap-hill*, in Surrey.

knap (II.), vb. trans. Imitative; cp. Du. *knappen*, 'to crack'. **1.** (obs.) To break with a sharp blow, esp. flints or stones; earlier, to snap, cp. Ps. xlvi. 9 (Prayer Book from 16th cent. version): '*He knappeth the spear in sunder*', where A.V. has *cutteth*. **2.** (obs.) To bite: '*knapped ginger*' (Shakespeare, 'Merchant of Venice').

knapper, n. [1. náper; 2. nǽpə], fr. prec. & **-er**. One who fashions flints for flint-locks &c.: *flint-knapper*.

knapsack, n. [1. nápsak; 2. nǽpsæk], fr. Du. *knapzak*, 'bag for food', fr. *knappen*, 'to bite, eat', & *zak*, **sack (I.)**. Canvas or leather sack, for food, spare clothing &c., carried by soldiers or travellers, slung by straps over one shoulder or strapped across the shoulder-blades.

knapweed, n. [1. nápwēd; 2. nǽpwīd]. Earlier *knopweed*, fr. **knop**, 'knob', & **weed**. Common weed resembling thistle, with round, purple flowers.

knar, n. [1. nar; 2. nā]. M.E. *knarre*, cp. Du. *knar*; cp. **gnarled**. Rough, hard knot or protuberance in wood.

knave, n. [1. nāv; 2. neiv]. The ordinary O.E. form is *cnapa*, 'boy, servant', but *cnafa* also occurs, whence M.E. *knāve* & the present word; cp. O.H.G. *knabo*, Mod. Germ. *knabe*, 'lad, boy', wh. is parallel w. O.E. *cnafa* & O.H.G. *knappe* (fr. L.G. source ?); perh. derived fr. Aryan base **ĝen-*, 'produce, beget', q.v. under **kind (I.)**. **1.** (archaic and obsolesc.) Boy, lad, esp. a serving lad, servant. **2.** A rogue; a dishonest, swindling rascal. **3.** (cards) Lowest of so-called court cards, bearing conventional representation of a court page and ranking below the queen and above the ten; cp. Fr. *valet*, Germ. *knecht*, for same card.

knavery, n. [1. nắveri; 2. néivəri]. Prec. & **-ery**. Behaviour of a knave; roguery, dishonesty, underhand dealing.

knavish, adj. [1. nắvish; 2. néiviʃ]. **knave** & **-ish**. Characteristic of a knave; tricky, dishonest, mischievous, untrustworthy.

knavishly, adv. Prec. & **-ly**. In a knavish manner.

knavishness, n. See prec. & **-ness**. **a** Quality of being knavish; **b** the behaviour of a knave; trickery, dishonesty.

knead, vb. trans. [1. nēd; 2. nīd]. O.E. *cnedan*, M.E. *knēde(n)*; orig. a strong vb.; Gmc. cognates are O.H.G. *chnetan*, Mod. Germ. *kneten*; Du. *kneden*, O.N. *knoða*, fr. Aryan base **gnet-* &c., whence also O. Slav. *gnesti*, 'squeeze, press'. **1. a** To work thoroughly by squeezing and pressing with the hands; used specially of working dough in bread-making; also **b** to use hands and knuckles upon other material in similar manner, as upon the body in massage. **2.** (fig., of action upon character) To mould, shape, by discipline and training.

kneadable, adj. [1. nédabl; 2. nídəbl]. Prec. & **-able**. Capable of being worked by kneading.

kneading-trough, n. [1. néding trawf, truf; 2. nídiŋ trɔ̄f, traf]. Baker's trough in which dough is kneaded.

knee (I.), n. [1. nē; 2. nī]. O.E. *cnēo*, M.E. *knē*, O.S. & O.H.G. *kneo*, O.N. *knē*, Goth. *kniu*; the Aryan base is **ǵenewo-* &c. w. many possible gradational variants, some of wh. appear in most of the derived families; cp. Scrt. *jānu*, Gk. *gónu* for **ǵonwo-*, also *gōnia*, 'corner, angle' (see **-gon**), Lat. *genu* (see **genual, genuflect**), *geniculum*, 'little knee, or joint, the joint on plant stem' (see **geniculate(d)**. **1. a** Joint and parts surrounding it between upper and lower parts of the human leg; **b** joint in some other animals, similar in appearance or position to that of man, esp. that in a horse's foreleg, in reality the *carpal*, or wrist joint; in birds, the *tarsal* or ankle. Phrs. *to bend the knee to*, (i.) supplicate, pray to; (ii.) to show great respect and submission to; *on the knees*, kneeling as in act of submission or supplication; *to go on one's knees*, (i.) kneel down; (ii.) to pray; *go on one's knees to*, to beg urgently, implore; *to bring a person to his knees*, force him to submit; *to give a knee to*, to aid, support, originally of second to a boxer between rounds; *up to one's knees*, knee-deep; *gone at the knees* (colloq.), broken-down, decrepit, of a broken-kneed horse. **2.** Object resembling a bent knee, as branch of tree, obtuse-angled timber or metal beam in ship or other building.

knee (II.), vb. trans. & intrans., fr. prec. **1.** trans. **a** To strike, knock, with the knee; **b** to stretch, distort, cause bagginess in (trousers) at the knee. **2.** intrans. (obs. and rare) To kneel, go, on one's knees: *I'll knee to no man.*

knee-breeches, n. pl. Breeches reaching to, and fitting close about, the knee, as in court-dress.

knee-cap, n. **a** Flat bone covering of the knee-joint; patella; **b** padded or other covering to protect the knee.

knee-deep, adj. Up to the knees; (also fig., rare) deeply involved, immersed in.

knee-high, adj. Reaching to the knees.

knee-hole, n. Space for the knees; esp. one in a writing-table or bureau.

knee-joint, n. **a** Joint of the knee in man and other animals; **b** (mach.) movable, right-angled joint between two pieces of metal &c.

kneel, vb. intrans. [1. nēl; 2. nīəl]. O.E. *cnēowlian*, M.E. *knelen*. See **knee**. To rest upon one's knees; to support the body from the knees, which are bent so that they rest upon the ground; also *kneel down*. *Kneel to*, to go on one's knees before, in supplication, or as token of respect; to pray to.

kneeler, n. [1. néler; 2. nílə]. Prec. & **-er**. **1.** Hassock, stool for kneeling on. **2.** (building) A stone so shaped to fit an angle between a coping and a gable or arch.

knee-pan, n. Knee-cap, patella.

knell (I.), n. [1. nel; 2. nɛl]. O.E. *cnell*, the S.E. type, W.S. *cnyll*, 'sound of a bell'; of imitative origin. Similar words occur in other Gmc. languages; O.H.G. *knallen*, 'to resound'; Du. *knal*, 'a clap, report' &c. Sound made in tolling a church-bell; specif., this sound as signal of a death, funeral, or other mournful event. Phrs. *to sound a knell*, to toll so as to announce a death &c.; (fig.) *to sound the knell of*, be an omen of the passing away of existing order, conditions &c.

knell (II.), vb. intrans. & trans., fr. prec. **1.** intrans. (of bell) To make the sound of a knell; to give forth a dismal note. **2.** trans. **a** To announce by, or as though by, a knell; to summon by a knell; **b** (fig.) to proclaim, bode: *to knell the downfall of an empire.*

knelt, vb. [1. nelt; 2. nɛlt]. Pret. & P.P. of **kneel**.

knew, vb. [1. nū; 2. njū]. O.E. *cnēow*, M.E. *knew*, Pret. of **know**.

Knickerbocker, n. [1. níkerbòker; 2. níkəbɔ̀kə], fr. *Diedrich Knickerbocker*, fictitious Du. author of Washington Irving's burlesque *History of New York*, 1809. **a** An original Dutch settler in or descendant in New York (New Amsterdam); **b** as adj., *Knickerbocker family*, one claiming descent from such settler.

knickerbockers, n. pl. Prob. fr. illustrations of Dutchmen in wide, loose knee-breeches in later (1859) editions of Washington Irving's work. Loose, baggy breeches reaching to the knees and fastened below them; similar breeches reaching above the knee and not fastened, shorts; similar breeches worn by women as undergarments.

knickers, n. pl. [1. níkerz; 2. níkəz]. Abbr. of prec. (shoppy or vulgar).

knick-knack, n. [1. ník nak; 2. ník næk]. Reduplication of **knack, 3**, & far more commonly used. Toy, trifle; small tasteful article of jewellery, dress &c.; small ingenious contrivance; article of virtu as ornament &c.

knife (I.), n. [1. nīf; 2. naif]. O.E. *cnīf*, M.E. *knīf*, cogn. w. Du. *knijf*, O.N. *knífe*, Swed. *knif*; etymol. unknown. Fr. *canif* is borrowed fr. a Gmc. source. **a** Cutting implement with a long fixed one-edged blade and short handle; or one with a short blade made on a hinge, to fold into handle; **b** also of various objects or parts of machines designed to cut; e.g. *the knives of a mowing-machine*. Various idiomatic uses: *the surgeon's knife*, surgical treatment by cutting; *the assassin's knife*, attack, murder; (of wind &c.) *to cut like a knife*; *war to the knife*, relentless opposition; *to get one's knife into*, (fig.) to make an onslaught upon, submit to searching criticism; *before one could say knife*, without a moment's delay.

knife (II.), vb. trans., fr. prec. **a** To use a knife upon; specif., to attack, wound, cut, stab with a knife; **b** to assassinate by stabbing.

knife-board, n. **1.** Wooden board treated with emery-powder upon which domestic table-knives are cleaned. **2.** (colloq.) Two benches placed back to back, longitudinally, on the roof of the old-fashioned horse-drawn omnibus.

knife-edge, n. **a** Edge of a knife; **b** sharp-edged metal fulcrum of a balance, devised to lessen friction.

knife-rest, n. Silver or glass support for blade of carving knife or prongs of fork, used on sideboard &c. to protect the cloth.

knight (I.), n. [1. nīt; 2. nait]. O.E. *cniht*, 'boy, servant, retainer'; M.E. *knight* &c. in Mod. sense, corresponding to Lat. *eques*, Fr. *chevalier*; O.H.G. *kneht*, 'lad, servant'. The other Gmc. languages if they have the word have apparently borrowed it fr. O.H.G. Only Engl. uses it in connexion w. chivalry. As regards the etymol. it has been suggested w. some plausibility that the word is derived fr. Gmc. base **ken-*, **kun-* &c., 'family, tribe' &c., see **kin** & words there referred to, & the adj. suff. *-iht*, thus meaning orig., 'of the tribe', perh. later 'admitted as full member of the tribe, full-grown'. This, however, is purely speculative. **1. a** (in feudal times) A man, usually of noble birth, who, having acquitted himself valiantly in war, was raised, by the King or his representatives, to the status above that of esquire by receiving the accolade, that is, having a sword laid upon his shoulder and being invested with spurs, together with other ceremonies, and the taking of certain vows by the recipient of the honour, who generally further received a grant of land; **b** (in modern times) a man who receives the non-hereditary title of honour, known as a knighthood, being admitted to it by the sovereign who gives him the accolade; a knight prefixes the title *Sir* to his Christian and surname, *Sir John Jones* &c., and is thus addressed and referred to, or simply, more familiarly, as *Sir John*; Phrs. *knight of the pen*, a journalist; *of the road*, highwayman; *knight of the rueful countenance*, Don Quixote; **c** member of one of the Orders of Knighthood, *the Garter*; *Thistle*; *St. Michael and St. George* &c.; also member of any of several organizations which confer the designation of *knight* on their members without however conferring the right to a title; **d** (Gk. and Rom. hist.) word used for a member of class of citizen, Gk. *hippeús*, Lat. *eques*, in Athens and Rome respectively; in each case the original class formed the cavalry of the city and army and provided their own horses. **2.** (fig.) One who performs loyal and chivalrous service to a person or a cause; specif. (poet.) a devoted attendant upon a lady. **3.** (chess) A piece or man surmounted by a horse's head.

knight (II.), vb. trans., fr. prec. To make a knight of, confer honour of knighthood upon.

knightage, n. [1. nít j; 2. náitidž]. **knight** (I.) & **-age**. **a** The body of knights collectively; **b** book of reference giving a list of these.

knight-bachelor, n. Knight of lowest class of British knights, who is not a member of an Order of Knighthood.

knight-banneret, n. Knight who is such as being member of special class in an Order of Knighthood.

knight-errant, n. **a** Knight wandering in search of adventure; **b** (fig.) (i.) a Don Quixote, an enthusiastic supporter of lost or neglected causes, ideas &c.; (ii.) one who travels and speaks in support of a special cause.

knight-errantry, n. Prec. & **-ry**. Condition, character, act, of a knight-errant; quixotic action or behaviour.

knighthood, n. [1. nít-hood; 2. náithud]. **knight** (I.) & **-hood**. **a** Character, dignity, rank, of a knight; **b** body of knights collectively: *his name would do honour to the knighthood.*

knightly, adj. & adv. [1. nítli; 2. náitli]. **knight** (I.) & **-ly**. **a** adj. (i.) Connected with or pertaining to, befitting, suitable to a knight; (ii.) specif., exhibiting a lofty courtesy; chivalrous, magnanimous; **b** adv., (archaic) in a knightly manner, like a knight.

knight's fee, n. (feudal law) Amount of land held by a knight, the tenure of which implied specific amount of service.

knight's service, knight-service, n. **1.** The military service performed by a knight or holder of a knight's fee, as a condition of holding his land. **2.** Service such as a knight ought to render; good and useful service.

knit, vb. trans. & intrans. [1. nit; 2. nit]. O.E. *cnyttan*, 'to tie, knot'; M.E. *knitten*, fr. **knutt-jan*, cp. O.N. *knytja*, 'to tie'. There appear to be no cognates in other Gmc. or Aryan languages. The base is the same as that of **knot** (I.). **A.** trans. **1. a** To interweave and fasten together, by series of loops and knots, cotton or silk threads, or woollen yarn, into a fabric or article of such fabric, by hand or knitting-machine: *to knit wool into stockings*; **b** to make, weave, fashion, by this process: *to knit stockings out of wool.* **2.** To join, fasten together, unite; **a** (of physical process) *mortar knits bricks together*; *a surgeon knits broken bones together again*; **b** (of spiritual process) to unite, link, together by ties of affection, interest &c.; *knit together in bonds of affection* &c. **3. a** To draw together, contract; esp. in Phr. *to knit the brows,* to frown; **b** (only in P.P.) to make compact, to brace together firmly: *a well-knit frame,* of human body; (also fig.) *a closely knit argument* &c. **B.** intrans. **1.** To perform the act of knitting: *to knit from morning to night.* **2.** To unite, come together, join up: (often) *knit together*; *the ends of a broken bone often knit (together) naturally.* **C.** Followed by preposition. *Knit in,* **a** trans., to incorporate in knitting: *to knit in the blue with the green wool*; **b** intrans., to be capable of being knitted in. *Knit up,* **a** trans., to pick up and fasten dropped or broken stitches in knitting; **b** intrans., to become united, linked or joined up.

knitter, n. [1. níter; 2. nítə], fr. **knit** & **-er.** **a** One who knits; **b** a knitting-machine.

knitting, n. [1. níting; 2. nítiŋ]. **knit** & **-ing.** **a** Act of one who knits; **b** knitted fabric or article.

knitting-machine, n. Machine used for manufacture of stockings and other articles otherwise made by hand.

knitting-needle, n. An eyeless needle of bone, metal, or wood used for knitting by hand; similar object in a knitting-machine.

knob, n. [1. nob; 2. nɔb]. M.E., cp. L.G. *knobbe,* 'knob', & Engl. variants **knap (I.),** **knop.** **a** Rounded protuberance, as on branch of tree, club, stick &c.; **b** ball-shaped protuberance, serving as handle of a door, a 'door-knob', or of a drawer, or as top of bed-post &c.; **c** round lump (of coal, sugar &c.). Phr. (slang) *with knobs on,* signifying something additional, esp. to already existing pain, discomfort &c.

knobby, adj. [1. nóbi; 2. nɔ́bi]. Prec. & **-y.** Furnished with, full of, knobs; rough.

knobkerrie, n. [1. nóbkèri; 2. nɔ́bkèri]. S. Afr. Du. *knobkirie,* fr. Du. *knob(be),* 'knob', & Hottentot *kerrie, kirrie,* 'stick, club'. Kaffir club, used as a weapon for striking and throwing, with heavy knobbed head; a knobstick.

knobstick, n. [1. nóbstik; 2. nɔ́bstik]. **a** Knobbed stick, knobkerrie; **b** (slang) workman who refuses to join a trade union or a strike; blackleg.

knock (I.), vb. trans. & intrans. [1. nok; 2. nɔk]. O.E. *cnocian,* M.E. *knokken,* cp. O.N. *knoka,* 'to knock', possibly imitative of sound. (gen. sense) To hit, strike, usually followed by prepositions, adverbs &c. See **C** below. **A.** trans. **1. a** To strike, rap, a door, head, ball &c.: *I knocked (at) the door several times*; *knock one's head (against)*; *knock (cricket) ball hard*; Phrs. *knock to pieces,* destroy, demolish, as an argument; *knock home,* drive (a nail &c.) firmly in; also (fig.) of argument; **b** (colloq.) to surprise, impress: '*Knocked 'em in the Old Kent Road*'; *his cool impudence knocked me completely*; **c** (Am. slang) to depreciate, criticize adversely, run down; opposed to *boost*: *to knock one's own town is unforgivable.* **B.** intrans. **1. a** To perform act of knocking, hitting, striking; specif., to strike with the knocker at or on a door &c. as signal or call for entrance: *do not knock unless an answer is required*; '*Knock, knock, knock!*' (the Porter in 'Macbeth'); **b** to rattle, make a bumping noise, as parts of machinery not working smoothly: *engine (of car) is knocking badly.* **C.** Followed by preposition or adverb. *To knock about,* **a** trans., to hit repeatedly, or in several places: *you've no business to knock your wife about like this*; *he was badly knocked about*; **b** intrans., to wander, travel, in careless, irresponsible fashion: *knock about the world*; (absol.) *knock about,* lead a dissipated life. *Knock against,* **a** trans., to strike, hit, against: *knock one's foot against a stone*; Phr. *to knock one's head against a brick wall,* to struggle uselessly against insuperable difficulty; **b** to meet (a person) unexpectedly: *I knocked against X yesterday in the street.* *Knock at,* to beat, rap, tap: *to knock at a door, window* &c., as call or signal; Phr. *to knock at an open door,* to exert useless effort to attain an object already accessible. *Knock down,* **a** to beat, strike, to the ground, cause to fall by striking: *if you are insolent I'll knock you down*; *knocked down by a motor-car*; **b** destroy, demolish: *house-breakers are knocking the house down*; (fig.) to upset, refute: *to knock an argument down like a house of cards*; Phr. *you might have knocked me down with a feather,* implying, I was so overcome and incapacitated by the shock of amazement &c.; **c** to beat down, force to reduce in price: *knock dealer, tender for contract &c. down 10%*; **d** specif. (of auctioneer) to rap with hammer as sign of acceptance of final bid; to accept bid for object at an auction: *the picture was knocked down to X.* *Knock in, into,* **a** trans., to drive, beat, hammer in, as a nail &c.; Phrs. (fig.) *knock into the head,* to instil, impress, lesson, rule &c., so that it shall not be forgotten; *knock into a cocked-hat,* to defeat, demolish, disconcert (person, argument, plan &c.); **b** intrans., to enter a college &c. by knocking after the gates are closed. *Knock on,* to strike, beat upon; Phr. *to knock on the head,* to destroy, demolish, do for, scotch, a proposal, plan, scheme &c. *Knock off,* **a** to strike, brush away: *knock a wasp off one's hand*; **b** to reduce, take off from price, rate of speed &c.: *knock two shillings off the bill*; *accident knocked ten knots an hour off the vessel's speed*; Phr. *to knock off work,* cease one's occupation, stop work; **c** to finish, complete, quickly, hastily, or roughly: *to knock off a leading article in half an hour*; *knock off runs,* (at cricket) make a number of runs to win a match. *Knock out,* **a** to strike, hammer, an object out of its position, e.g. nail out of a board; Phr. *knock the bottom out of,* demolish, refute entirely an argument &c.; **b** (boxing) to deal opponent blow rendering him incapable of continuing the fight when 'time' is called; (fig.) to overwhelm, stun; Phr. *knock out of time* (fig., from boxing phrase), render another incapable of action; **c** (auctioneering) to sell privately by dealers among themselves after a sale where they have agreed not to bid against each other; depreciate price at sale by a knock-out, q.v.; **d** to make a rough, preliminary plan, sketch: *knock out an idea of, for, a play* &c. *Knock together,* to hit, strike, one thing against another; to put, fit, together, hastily or roughly, cp. *to knock off* or *up*; Phr. *knock their heads together,* make two quarrelling people agree by strong measures. *Knock up,* **a** to hit, strike, upwards: *knock up his arm, hand* &c.; **b** *to knock up runs,* make runs, score, at cricket; **c** to rouse by knocking, at door, window &c.: *knock me up at 7 o'clock*; **d** to tire, wear out, fatigue: *the long climb knocked me up*; also intrans., to be worn out, to break down: *he knocked up after influenza*; **e** to put together roughly and hastily: *knock up some sort of a shelter.*

knock (II.), n., fr. prec. **a** Stroke, blow, hit, rap: *a knock on the head*; (also fig.) *knocks and blows of this work-a-day world*; Phr. (colloq.) *to get the knock,* to be dismissed from employment; (of actor &c.) get a bad reception; **b** specif., action of rapping on a door, with knocker or with knuckles &c.; sound made by this: *the postman's knock*; *a double knock*; *did you hear a knock?* Phr. *runaway knock,* one given as a hoax, the person who knocks not waiting till the door is opened.

knock-about, adj. & n. **1.** adj. **a** Consisting of knocks, blows, as in a comic turn on the stage: *knock-about performance*; **b** made for knocking about, for rough wear: *a knock-about suit* &c. **2.** n. A rough, noisy, boisterous farce enlivened by horseplay.

knock-down, adj. **a** Of blow which fells recipient to the ground; **b** (fig.) *knock-down blow,* a moral shock that stuns, overwhelms, or stupefies; *knock-down price,* lowest price at which anything can be sold or bought.

knocker, n. [1. nóker; 2. nɔ́kə], fr. **knock (I.)** & **-er.** **1.** Person who, thing which, knocks; specif., device in form of a metal hammer attached by hinge to a door, which is struck upon a metal plate or knob to call for admission. **2.** (Am. slang) One who criticizes, runs down anything; opposed to *booster.*

knocker-up, n. Person hired to rouse workmen for early work by knocking at window or door.

knock-knee, n. Condition of having the knees turned inwards so that they knock against each other in walking.

knock-kneed, adj. [1. nók nēd; 2. nɔ́k nīd]. **a** Having knock-knees; shambling in gait; **b** (fig.) feeble, lacking moral courage and fibre.

knock-out, n. & adj. **1.** (boxing) Final decisive blow, as on point (of jaw) or solar plexus, which prevents recipient from continuing the fight; (also fig. and as adj.) *knock-out blow.* **2.** (auction) Agreement among ring of dealers not to bid against particular dealer, and after the auction to hold private sale, dividing difference between fictitious and real price among themselves; sale conducted on such system.

knoll (I.), n. [1. nōl, nol; 2. noul, nɔl]. O.E. *cnoll,* 'hillock, mound'; cp. Du. *knol,* Germ. *knolle,* 'lump, mound'. Top of a small hill; a hillock, mound.

knoll (II.), vb. trans. & intrans. [1. nōl; 2. noul]. Variant of **knell.** To knell; to ring, toll, a bell; to sound as a bell tolling for a death, as signal &c.

knoll (III.), n., fr. prec. Sound of a tolling bell.

knop, n. [1. nop; 2. nɔp]. M.E. *knop(pe),* cp. Du. *knop,* Germ. *knopf,* 'knob, button'; prob. variant of **knob.** Knob, protuberance, esp. of ornament in shape of the rounded bud of a flower, on stem of a cup or on a crocket or pinnacle in architecture.

knot (I.), n. [1. not; 2. nɔt]. O.E. *cnotta,* M.E. *knotte*; cp. O.N. *knut,* Du. *knot,* fr. unmutated form of Gmc. base whence **knit** is derived. **1.** Fastening of rope, cord, string &c., one free end being passed through loop and drawn tight; of various kinds, as *slip-knot,* one that slides up and down and can be unfastened by a pull; *fool's, granny's, knot,* one insecurely tied so that it comes unfastened at once. **2.** Bow, tie, of ribbon, twist of gold braid &c., worn as ornament: *shoulder-knot, sword-knot.* **3.** (fig.) **a** That which joins or unites; a bond of union, tie: *the nuptial, marriage, knot*; *to tie the knot,* to marry; **b** complicated problem, difficulty, entanglement. Phrs. *to cut the knot,* evade problem, get out of difficulty by means which provide no real solution; cp. **Gordian;** *to tie oneself (up) in(to) knots,* to get entangled in difficulties or complications. **4. a** Hard lump on tree where a branch sprang; **b** rounded cross-grained mark on sawn timber left by this; **c** representation in wood or stone of a knot or series of knots, as in a moulding; often called *knotwork.* **5.** Small group, cluster, of persons in close proximity to each other: *to gather, stand about, in knots.* **6.** (naut.) **a** Unit of measurement of speed of a ship (from the spaced knots in a long line), always signifying number of nautical miles travelled in an hour: *vessel of 35 knots,* one capable of attaining speed at rate of 35 nautical miles in an hour; **b** (loosely) a nautical mile.

knot (II.), vb. trans. & intrans., fr. prec. **1.** trans. **a** To tie, make, form, a knot in rope, string &c.; **b** to fasten, tie up or together by means of a knot; to work thread &c. into loose fringe, 'knotting'. **2.** intrans. **a** To perform act of knotting or tying knot;

b to become knotted, entangled, tied together in knots.

knot (III.), n. Etymol. unknown. Small wading sea-bird, one of the many varieties of the sandpiper.

knot-grass, n. Popular name of various common weeds with jointed stems.

knotted, adj. [1. nóted; 2. nɔ́tid], fr. P.P. of **knot** (II.). Full of knots; twisted, entangled.

knotting, n. [1. nóting; 2. nɔ́tiŋ]. **knot** (II.) & **-ing**. Loose fringe made of thread &c. knotted together.

knotty, adj. [1. nóti; 2. nɔ́ti], fr. **knot** (I.) & **-y**. **a** (chiefly of wood) Full of knots; knotted; **b** (fig.) full of difficulty, complicated: *a knotty problem.*

knout (I.), n. [1. nout, nōōt; 2. naut, nūt]. Through Fr. *knout* [nūt], fr. Russ. *knut*, prob. fr. Scand. *knut*, 'knot, knotted whip'. Russian whip or scourge, with short handle and a lash of several leather thongs knotted, or bound with wire. Phr. *the knout*, severe physical or other punishment, as typical of Russian severity.

knout (II.), vb. trans., fr. prec. To whip, lash, with a knout.

know (I.), vb. trans. & intrans. [1. nō; 2. nou]. O.E. *cnāwan*, M.E. *cnōwe(n)*; O.H.G. *(bi-) knāan*; cogn. w. Lat. *(g)nō-scere*; Gk. *(gi-) gnṓ-skō*, 'know'; Scrt. *jānāmi*, 'I know'; O. Slav. *znajǫ*, 'I know'; all fr. Aryan base **g̑nē-, *g̑nō-*, 'to know, have mental potency' &c., fr. other grades of wh. are derived also **can**, 'am able'; **ken** (I.) & (II.); the second syll. of **uncouth**. It is possible, though the relation is uncertain, that this base is ultimately identical w. that meaning 'to produce, beget' &c., discussed under **kin**, **kind** (I.), **genus, generate** &c., **nature, natal**; **kith** is usually connected w. **know**, but may equally well be related to **kind**. **A.** trans. **1. a** To have in the mind as an element of knowledge, possess as essential information; be cognizant of: *to know the facts of the case*; *to know the way*; *to know one's faults*; *know (that) the man was dead*: *to know (that) it is going to rain, that one has made a fool of oneself*; **b** to understand thoroughly, have intellectual command of as a result of study or practice: *to know a language*; *to know the law, banking* &c. Phrs. *to know one's own business*, not to interfere with affairs of others; *to know how many beans make five, a thing or two, the ropes, what's what* &c., all meaning that one has sharp wits, understanding, common sense &c.; *to know better than*, to be wise enough to avoid doing; also *know better than that.* **2.** To recognize, identify, a person or thing as being familiar to one, or as belonging to a particular category; to be able to distinguish, discriminate, persons and things from others by attributes perceived by the senses: *to know a friend from a foe*; *to know a man by sight*; *to know a good horse when one sees him*; *should never have known you again*; *not to know one tune from another*; *to know apart, from*, distinguish one thing from another. Phrs. *to know B from a bull's foot, black from white, chalk from cheese, on which side one's bread is buttered*, all implying capacity of understanding, or discriminating by mother-wit and common sense. **3.** To be personally acquainted with (persons); to enjoy greater or less familiarity with them: *I know the man by sight, but I don't know him personally*; *should like to know Mr. Jones*; *you two ought to know one another*; *I don't know your father.* **4.** To have experience of, to experience, get to understand by experience: *a man who has known poverty and sorrow*; *to know life*; *he knows his Oxford thoroughly.* **5.** (Bib. and legal, of a man) To have sexual intercourse with. **B.** intrans. To be in the condition of knowing; to have knowledge; to be aware, understand: *what I say is not mere conjecture, I know*; *my father has just died*; *yes, I know.* **C.** Followed by preposition or adverb. *Know about*, have knowledge, information, concerning: *knew about the trouble long ago*; *know all about him*, know the character, antecedents &c. of a person. *Know of*, to be aware of existence of (thing), be acquainted with, a fact, event &c.: *know of a shop where you can get things cheaper*; *knew of the engagement before it was announced.*

know (II.), n., fr. prec. (colloq.) Knowledge, only in Phr. *in the know*, having special information.

knowability, n. [1. nōabíliti; 2. nòuəbíliti]. Next word & **-ity**. Knowableness.

knowable, adj. [1. nóabl; 2. nóuəbl]. **know** & **-able**. **1.** Capable of being known, within the scope of human knowledge. **2.** (of persons) Easy to know or get on with: *knowable sort of people.*

knowableness, n. [1. nṓablnes; 2. nóuəblnis]. Prec. & **-ness**. Quality of being knowable.

knowing, adj. [1. nṓing; 2. nóuiŋ], fr. Pres. Part. of **know** (I.). Cunning, smart, shrewd, artful; skilful, intelligent: *a knowing fellow*; *knowing hand at the game*; *a knowing dog*; *knowing look.*

knowingly, adv. Prec. & **-ly**. **1.** With full knowledge and intention; intentionally: *he would not knowingly injure me.* Legal Phr. *knowingly kill*, deliberately murder. **2.** In a knowing, smart manner: *he managed the trick very knowingly.*

knowledge, n. [1. nólij; 2. nɔ́lidž]. M.E. *knōweleche, knowlege*, fr. **know** (I.) & *-ledge*, the origin of wh. is uncertain. Act, process, of knowing; result of knowing, that which is known. **1.** Comprehension, understanding, perception: *knowledge of good and evil, of the truth* &c. **2.** Learning; mastery of a subject; body of facts known or ascertained by study, science &c.: *knowledge is spreading*; *knowledge of chemistry, music, French* &c.; *man's knowledge of nature.* **3.** Familiarity with, experience of, acquaintanceship with, information concerning, person, place, fact, event &c.: *knowledge of life*; *my knowledge of X is slight*; *a good knowledge of London*; *knowledge of the victory soon spread.* Phrs. *to the best of (one's) knowledge and belief*, as far as one knows; *not to my knowledge*, not so far as I know. **4.** (law) **a** Cognizance, acceptance of fact in court of law as proved by evidence: *court has no knowledge of that*, will take no notice of, as not proved; **b** sexual intercourse, esp. in Phr. *carnal knowledge of.*

knuckle (I.), n. [1. núkl; 2. nákl]. M.E. *knokyl* &c.; derived either fr. Scand. or L.G.; cp. Dan. & Du. *knokkel*; the suff. is dimin. (see **-le**); cp. also Mod. Germ. *knöchel*, dimin. of *knochen*, 'a bone'. Perh. cogn. w. **knock**. **a** Joint of a finger, esp. where it joins the hand, protruding in a rounded knob at the back of the hand; also one of the other joints at back of fingers; (usually pl.) *the knuckles*, the series of four such joints at back of hand; Phr. (fig.) *(to give, get) a rap on, over, the knuckles*, a snub, rebuff, reproof; **b** joint of meat, as veal, pork &c., taken from between the upper and lower part of a leg.

knuckle (II.), vb. trans. & intrans., fr. prec. **a** To use the knuckles or clenched hand on or against a person or object, as in fighting or in playing marbles; **b** to clench the hand so as to show the knuckles. Phrs. *knuckle to, down to (work* &c.), settle down determinedly to; *knuckle under*, to submit, to yield.

knuckle-bone, n. Bone of the joints, knuckles, in the fingers; joint, knuckle, of veal, pork &c.; specif., small bone from leg of a sheep, cleaned and bleached; *knuckle-bones*, boys' game played with these.

knuckle-duster, n. Device used in fighting with the fists by low blackguards, consisting of a strap held in the palm, furnished with spikes or weighted knobs, which protrude between the fingers of the clenched fist.

knur, n. [1. nër; 2. nʌ̄]. M.E. *knorre*; origin doubtful. (rarely used) **a** Rough projection or knob on trunk or branch of tree; **b** wooden ball, used in old game of *knur and spell*, struck as it is thrown up from the 'spell' or trap.

knurl, n. [1. nërl; 2. nʌ̄l]. Prob. variant of prec. Knur, rough protuberance, ridge in wood or metal.

koa, n. [1. kṓa; 2. kóuə]. Native name. Hawaiian acacia, much used for furniture-making and building.

koala, koolah, n. [1. kōáhla, kōōla; 2. kouálə, kūlə]. Native name. Small arboreal pouched mammal of Australia allied to the wombat, called also 'the native bear' or 'sloth'.

kobold, n. [1. kóbold; 2. kɔ́bəld]. Mod. Germ., etymol. unknown. (Germ. folklore) Mischievous dwarfish spirit, supposed to dwell in mines; a gnome, brownie.

kodak (I.), n. & vb. [1. kṓdak; 2. kóudæk]. Word invented and used as trade mark by the Eastman Kodak Co., U.S.A. **1.** n. **a** Small hand camera used with sensitized films, so called from name of firm which first introduced this type; **b** photograph taken with such a camera. **2.** vb. To take photographs with a kodak.

koh-i-noor, n. [1. kṓ i nór; 2. kóu i nɔ̄]. Pers., 'mountain of light'. **a** Famous diamond, now one of British Crown jewels; **b** (fig.) something extremely valuable or priceless.

kohl, n. [1. kōl; 2. koul]. Arab. See **alcohol**. Powder of antimony, used by Eastern, esp. Moslem, women to darken the eyelids.

kohlrabi, n. [1. kṓlràhbi; 2. kóulràbi]. Apparently ad. through Mod. Germ., fr. Ital. *cavoli*, 'rape'. Cp. **cole**, 'kale', & **rape** (III.). Kind of cabbage with fleshy, turnip-shaped stem.

kola, cola, n. [1. kṓla; 2. kóulə]. W. Afr. name for the tree. Bitter, stimulating extract of the *kola-nut*, nut of a W. African tree, cultivated in S. America.

kolinsky, n. [1. kolínski; 2. kəlínski]. Russ., adj. fr. Kola, district in N.W. Russia. Fur of various kinds of mink, often confused with or styled 'sable'.

koodoo, n. See **kudu**.

koolah, n. See **koala**.

kopeck, n. See **copeck**.

kopje, n. [1. kópi; 2. kɔ́pi]. S. Afr. Du., dimin. of Du. *kop*, 'head, hill'. Small hill or hillock in S. Africa.

Koran, n. [1. koráhn, kṓran; 2. kərán, kɔ̄rən], fr. Arab. *qaran*, 'the book'. The sacred book of the Mohammedans, containing the teachings revealed to and written down by Mohammed.

koranic, adj. [1. koráhnik, -ánik; 2. kəránik, -ǽnik]. Prec. & **-ic**. Of or belonging to, derived from, the Koran.

kosher, adj. [1. kṓsher; 2. kóuʃə]. Heb. *kāshēr*, 'proper, fit, right'. Ceremonially fit, pure or clean; specif. **a** of meat used as food, killed in the form laid down by Jewish law; **b** of shop where such meat or other ceremonially pure things are sold.

kotow. See **kowtow**.

koumiss, kumiss, n. [1. kōōmis; 2. kúmis]. Through Fr. *koumis*, fr. Russ. *kumys*, Tatar *kumiz*. Fermented mare's or camel's milk, used as a drink; similar stuff made of cow's milk.

kourbash, kurbash, n. [1. kōōrbash; 2. kúəbæʃ]. Turk. *qirbach*, 'whip'. Whip, scourge of leather thongs, formerly used in Turkey and Egypt in punishment, or as an encouragement to work &c. Phr. *under the kourbash*, by forced labour.

kouskous, kuskus, couscous, n. [1. kōōskōōs; 2. kúskūs]. Through Fr., fr. Arab. *kuskus*, fr. *kuskasa*, 'pound, bruise'. Boiled mutton or other meat, mixed with semolina, a favourite dish in N. Africa.

kowtow, kotow, n. & vb. intrans. [1. kóutóu; 2. káutáu]. Chinese, lit. 'to knock the head'. **1.** n. Humble salutation, made by touching ground with the forehead in sign of submission and respect. **2.** vb. **a** To make a kowtow; **b** (fig.) to show great humility and submission to a person; to defer to in a very obsequious, servile, fashion.

kraal, n. & vb. trans. [1. krahl, krawl; 2. krāl, krōl]. S. Afr. Du., 'village, pen', fr. Port. *curral*, 'pen for cattle'. See **corral**. **a** n. Native (S. Africa) fenced village, or collection of huts; fenced enclosure for cattle &c.; **b** vb., to enclose (cattle &c.) within a kraal.

krait, n. [1. krīt; 2. krait]. Hind. *karait*. Venomous Indian snake.

kraken, n. [1. kráhken; 2. krā́kən]. Norw. *krake*, n. Legendary sea-monster of northern seas, probably a giant octopus.

krantz, kranz, n. [1. krants; 2. kræmts]. S. Afr. Du., fr. Du. *krans*, 'garland, wreath, coronet'. This word appears during the historical period in several Gmc. languages, e.g. M.H.G. & Late O.N. Its origin is a subject of speculation. Steep cliff encircling a ravine or gorge; often found in S. African Place-Names, e.g. *Vaalkrantz*.

krater, n. [1. kráter; 2. kréitə]. Gk. *krātḗr*, 'a bowl'. See **crater**. (archaeol.) Large, double-handled bowl or vessel used for mixing wine with water.

Kremlin, n. [1. krémlin; 2. krémlin]. Fr., fr. Russ. *kreml*, 'citadel'. Fortress, citadel; specif., *the Kremlin*, Imperial palace, and the cathedral of Moscow.

kreutzer, n. [1. króitzer; 2. krɔ́itzə]. Germ., fr. *kreuz*, 'cross', fr. bearing figure of a cross. See **cross (I.)**. Copper coin formerly current in Germany and Austria and equivalent to a farthing.

kriegspiel, n. [1. krḗgspēl; 2. krígspīl]. Mod. Germ., fr. *krieg*, 'war', & *spiel*, 'game'. Kluge can suggest no etymol. for either word. The former is confined to H. Germ., & appears late, being almost unknown in O.H.G.; the latter occurs in O.H.G. meaning 'play, merriment', together w. the vb. *spilōn*, a cogn. of wh. *spelen* is used in Du.; otherwise the word does not exist in Gmc. languages. War game, played for strategical or tactical instruction, on map with blocks, flags, counters &c., representing military or naval units.

kris, creese, n. [1. krēs; 2. krīs]. Malay name. A Malay dagger with a wavy blade.

Krishnaism, n. [1. kríshnaizm; 2. kríʃnəizəm], fr. *Krishna* & **-ism**. Worship, cult, of the Hindu God Krishna, the cowherd god, incarnation of Vishnu as god of fertility and happiness.

krone, n. [1. króner; 2. króunə]. Scand. & H. Germ. form of Lat. *corōna*, 'crown'. See **crown**. **a** Scandinavian monetary unit and coin, =1s. 1½d.; **b** German 10-mark gold coin; **c** pre-war Austrian silver coin.

krooboy, krooman, kruman, n., pl. *-men*, [1. krōōboi, krōōman; 2. krū́bɔi, krū́mæn], fr. *Kru*, native W. Afr. name. One of a seafaring race of W. African (Liberian) coast, employed as sailors, boatmen &c., by European vessels in tropical waters.

krummhorn, krumhorn, n. [1. króomhorn; 2. krúmhɔ̄n]. Mod. Germ., fr. *krumm*, 'curved', & **horn**. Musical curved wind-instrument.

krypto-, pref. See **crypto-**.

krypton, n. [1. krípton; 2. kríptɔn]. Invented fr. Gk. *kruptós*, 'hidden'. See **crypto-**. An inert gas, forming an element of the atmosphere.

kudos, n. [1. kū́dos; 2. kjū́dɔs]. Gk. *kûdos*, 'glory, fame'; cp. also Gk. *kūdainō*, 'glorify'; cogn. w. O. Slav. *čudo*, 'miracle'. (colloq.) Credit in popular estimation, honour and glory gained by some achievement.

kudu, n. [1. kōōdōō; 2. kū́dū]. Hottentot. Large S. African antelope, *Strepsiceros kudu*, greyish brown in colour, with white markings and spiral horns.

Ku-Klux-Klan, n. [1. kū́ klúks klán; 2. kjū́ kláks klǽn]. Invented name. Secret society of Southern States of U.S.A., formed after Civil War; similar society recently revived working against Roman Catholics, Jews, and other supposed alien elements in American civilization.

kukri, n. [1. kóokri; 2. kúkri]. Hindi word. Knife, sword, with short, wavy blade, used by Gurkha soldiers.

kultur, n. Anglicized to [1. kooltóōr; 2. kultúə]. Mod. Germ. See **culture**. System, rule, order, mode of life, in all aspects, moral, religious, intellectual, political, or practical, adopted by a nation or race as best suited to its development and success; civilization.

kultur-kampf, n. [1. kooltóōr kamf; 2. kultúə kæmf]. Mod. Germ. *kultur* & *kampf*, 'battle, fight'. See **camp & champion**. (hist.) Name given to the struggle on question of State control of religious education, civil marriage, appointment of priests &c., between the Papacy and Germany, under Bismarck (1873–87).

kumiss, n. See **koumiss**.

kümmel, n. Anglicized to [1. kíml; 2. kíml]. Mod. Germ., 'cumin, caraway seed'. See **cumin**. Liqueur flavoured with tincture or essence of caraway (cumin) seeds.

kummerbund, n. See **cummerbund**.

Kuomintang n. [1. kōōmintang; 2. kūoumintæŋ], Chinese *kuo*, 'kingdom, nation', *min*, 'people', *tang*, 'party'. The Chinese Nationalist revolutionary party.

kurbash, n. See **kourbash**.

kursaal, n. Anglicized to [1. kōōrsahl; 2. kúəsāl]. Mod. Germ., fr. *kur*, see **cure**, & *saal*, 'hall'. See **saloon**. Building containing public reception, music, dancing rooms at a health resort; casino.

kvass, n. [1. kvas; 2. kvæs]. Russ. *kvas*. Beer made from rye.

ky, kye. See **kine**.

kyanize, vb. trans. [1. kíaniz; 2. káiənaiz], fr. name of inventor, J. H. Kyan. To preserve (wood) from dry rot by special treatment with solution of corrosive sublimate.

kyle, n. [1. kīl; 2. kail]. Gael. *caol*. Narrow channel, strait, between sea and lake, as *Kyles of Bute*, in Scotland.

kylin, n. [1. kílin; 2. káilin]. Chinese, 'hybrid', fr. *ch'i*, 'man', *lin*, 'woman'. (Chinese and Japanese art) Grotesque figure, in bronze, pottery or porcelain, of hybrid animal or monster.

kyloe, n. [1. kílō; 2. káilou]. Etymol. unknown. A breed of small, long-horned Highland cattle.

kymograph. See **cymograph**.

kyrie, n. [1. kḗrii; 2. kíərii]; popularly [1. kíri; 2. káiəri]. Gk. voc. of *kū́rios*, 'authority, power, lord'; cp. Scrt. *śū́raś*, 'strong, brave'; Gaulish *kauaros*, Ir. *caur*, 'hero', W. *cawr*, 'giant'; all fr. base **k̑ew-* &c., whence Gk. *kúein*, 'to swell, become pregnant', q.v. under **cave (I.)**. The orig. sense is 'the big, strong, important person'. Abbreviation of *Kyrie eleison*; specif., musical setting for the versicle.

kyrie eleison, n. [1. kḗrii eláison; 2. kíərii iléiisɔn]. Gk. *kū́rie eléison*, 'Lord, have mercy upon us'. Versicle as response in liturgy of the Church occurring esp. in the Mass.

L

L, l, [1. el; 2. ɛl]. The twelfth letter of the English alphabet; as a Roman numeral L=50, in origin a corruption of Greek ν; for use in abbreviations see end of Dictionary.

la (I.), interj. [1. lah, law; 2. lā, lɔ̄]. See **lo**. (obs. or archaic) Exclamation of surprise.

la (II.), n. [1. lah; 2. lā]. (mus.) Syllable used for the sixth tone of the scale in tonic sol-fa system.

laager, n. & vb. intrans. [1. láhger; 2. lā́gə]. S. Afr. Du. *lager*, 'camp'. See **leaguer**. **1.** n. Temporary camp, composed of enclosure of waggons; chiefly S. African Dutch. **2.** vb. To form a laager; settle down temporarily in a laager.

labarum, n. [1. lábarum; 2. lǽbərəm]. Lat., also in Gk. *lábaron*; etymol. dubious. Originally a cavalry standard of the late Roman Empire; under Constantine the Great it bore the first two letters of the name of Christ, XP, as a sacred monogram, and it became the standard of the Christianized Empire.

labefaction, n. [1. làbifákshun; 2. læ̀bifǽkʃən]. Lat. *labefact-(um)*, P.P. type of *labefacere*, 'to shake, cause to totter', & **-ion**. See **labour & -faction**. **a** Process of shaking, ruining; **b** state of being shaken, ruined; downfall.

label (I.), n. [1. lā́bel; 2. léibəl]. M.E., fr. O. Fr. earlier *lambel*; Mod. Fr. *lambeau*, 'a strip'; origin unknown. **1.** Slip of card, paper &c., used as a means of identification; **a** such a slip attached to parcels, boxes &c., with name and address of owner or of person for whom they are intended; **b** a paper slip, bearing name of station, pasted on to passengers' luggage by railway officials; **c** a slip bearing name and description of a museum specimen. **2.** (fig.) A brief descriptive phrase applied to persons, schools of thought &c. Specif. **3. a** (archit.) projecting stone moulding or dripstone over doors and windows; **b** (her.) fillet with pendants introduced into a family coat of arms as mark of cadency of eldest son.

label (II.), vb. trans., fr. prec. **a** To attach a label to; **b** to indicate identity and category of, by means of a label.

labellum, n. [1. lābélum; 2. leibéləm]. Lat., 'little lip'; dimin. of *labium*, 'lip', q.v. under next word. (bot.) One of the three parts which form the corolla in orchidaceous plants.

labial, adj. & n. [1. lā́bial; 2. léibiəl], fr. Lat. *labia, -ium*, 'lip', & **-al**; cogn. w. **lip**; all further connexions uncertain. **1.** adj. Connected with, formed by, the lips; specif. (phon.) of speech sounds, formed by, associated with, activity of the lips; e.g. [m, b, p]. **2.** n. A labial, or lip sound.

labialism, n. [1. lā́bializm; 2. léibiəlizəm]. Prec. & **-ism**. **a** (of sounds) Condition of being formed by the lips; **b** tendency to labialize.

labialize, vb. trans. [1. lā́bializ; 2. léibiəlaiz]. **labial & -ize**. To modify character of, to pronounce with lip action; to make into a labial sound.

labiate, adj. & n. [1. lā́biāt; 2. léibieit], fr. Lat. *labium*, 'lip'. See **labial & -ate**. **1.** adj. Like a lip in shape or function; **a** (bot.) with calyx or corolla divided into two parts, one projecting over the other, like lips of a mouth; **b** (anat.) with thick, fleshy margins. **2.** n. Plant of the order *Labiatae*, which includes the mints, thymes &c.

labile, adj. [1. lā́bil; 2. léibail]. Lat. *lābilis*, 'unsteady, wavering'; fr. *lābi*, 'to slip, slide' &c. See **labefaction & labour**. (chem.) Unstable, liable to chemical change.

labio-, pref. Form of Lat. *labium*, 'lip' (see **labial**), used in compounds. (phon.) Implies the use of the lips or one of them, in combination with some other speech organ.

labio-dental, adj. & n. [1. lā́biō déntal; 2. léibiou déntəl]. Prec. & **dental**. **1.** adj. Formed between the lower lip and the teeth; also called *lip-teeth*; e.g. [f, v]. **2.** n. A sound formed in this way.

labium, n., pl. **labia** [1. lā́bium, -ia; 2. léibiəm, -iə]. Lat., 'lip'. See **labial**. **a** (anat.) External fold of female pudendum; **b** inner lip of a single valved shell; **c** the lip of a labiate plant.

laboratory, n. [1. lā́buraturi, labóraturi; 2. lǽb(ə)rət(ə)ri, ləbɔ́rət(ə)ri]. Med. Lat.

labōrātōrium, 'workshop' &c., fr. *labōrāt-*, P.P. type of *labōrāre*, 'to work' (see **labour**), & *-ōrium* (see **-ory**). **a** Place, building, where experiments and investigations in the natural sciences are carried out; **b** room set apart and equipped with books and documents for research in history, philology &c.; Phr. *laboratory of the mind*, critical thought.

laborious, adj. [1. labṓrius; 2. ləbɔ́riəs]. Lat. *labōriōsus*, 'toilsome, wearisome; industrious'. **labour (I.)** & **-ous**. **1.** (of work, action &c.) **a** Involving great effort; toilsome, strenuous, wearisome, tedious; **b** performed with pains and accuracy; exact. **2.** (of persons) Inclined to work hard; industrious, hardworking; painstaking, conscientiously diligent, accurate.

laboriously, adv. Prec. & **-ly**. In a laborious manner.

laboriousness, n. See prec. & **-ness**. Quality of being laborious; **a** toilsomeness, tediousness; **b** diligence, industriousness.

labour (I.), n. [1. lā́bor; 2. léibə]. O. Fr. *labor*, M.E. *labóur*, fr. Lat. *labōr-(em)*, 'hardship, fatigue; toil', connected w. Lat. *labāre*, 'to totter, be ready to fall, hesitate, waver', & *lābi*, 'to slip, slide, glide'; the primitive meaning of Lat. n. is 'slipping, tottering, under a burden'. See also **labefaction** & **lapse**. **1. a** Work, toil, exertion, esp. when severe, of body or mind; Phr. *labour of love*, work undertaken from inclination rather than for reward; *hard labour*, work imposed upon criminals as a punishment; **b** (in pl.) the ordinary affairs of life, e.g. *his labours are over*, his life is finished. **2. a** The body of those who engage in manual work: *the claims of labour*, as contrasted with those of the community who perform other kinds of work or none at all; *Ministry of Labour*, Government department responsible for administration of various laws &c. regarding arbitration, unemployment &c.; **b** general term for the body of employed, as opposed to employers, esp. regarded as representative of Capital: *Labour and Capital*; **c** (usually with caps.) the Labour Party, q.v., also electorate voting for that party: *how will Labour fare at the next election?* **3.** Pains of childbirth: *to be in labour*, of woman while in act of parturition.

labour (II.), vb. intrans. & trans. Fr. *labourer*, Lat. *labōrāre*, 'to labour, take pains; to work out; cultivate'. See prec. **A.** intrans. **1.** To perform mental or bodily work, esp. of a hard, painful kind; to work strenuously: *to labour in the fields, at a dictionary*. **2. a** To exert oneself, work hard, make strenuous efforts, in order to do or to get something; to strive: *I am labouring to get finished, to understand what is said*; *to labour for breath*, have difficulty in breathing; *to labour for peace*; *to labour after wealth*; **b** to move, advance, slowly, and with difficulty: *to labour along a bad road*; *to labour through a heavy sea*; '*The line too labours, and the words move slow*' (Pope, 'Ess. on Crit.'); Phr. *to labour under a delusion*, to be misinformed, be in error. **3.** (of women) To travail, be in pangs of childbirth. **B.** trans. **1.** (archaic) To cultivate: *to labour the land*. **2.** To elaborate unduly, work out in unnecessary detail, develop minutely: *to labour an argument, a point*.

laboured, adj. [1. lā́burd; 2. léibəd], fr. P.P. of prec. **1.** (of style) Producing the effect of, resulting from, strenuous effort; reverse of *easy*; over-elaborate, heavy, cumbersome; *a laboured joke, compliment* &c., far-fetched, made with effort, not natural and spontaneous. **2.** Performed painfully and with difficulty; hard, painful, slow: *laboured breathing, movements* &c.

labourer, n. [1. lā́burer; 2. léibərə]. **labour (II.)** & **-er**. One who labours, a worker; specif., one who toils with his hands; manual worker; esp. of those employed on the land.

Labour Exchange, n. A bureau, established by Government, in towns and districts for finding employment for unemployed workmen.

labouring, adj. [1. lā́buring; 2. léibəriŋ], fr. Pres. Part. of **labour (II.)**. Habitually engaged in labour, esp. in manual work: *a labouring man*, one who works with his hands; *the labouring classes*, those who engage in manual labour for their living.

Labour Party, n. Organized political party, to some extent composed of, and primarily intended to represent the claims of, the labouring classes.

labour-saving, adj. Applied to methods and appliances designed to reduce the amount and severity of manual labour involved in agriculture, industry, household economy &c.

Labrador dog, n. [1. lábrador dòg; 2. lǽbrədɔ̄ dɔ̀g], fr. Labrador, peninsula on the N.E. of British N. America. A special breed of Newfoundland dog.

Labradorite, n. [1. làbradṓrīt; 2. læ̀brədɔ́rait]. See prec. & **-ite**. A variety of felspar, showing when polished a blue or bluish green and grey iridescence.

Labrador tea, n. A heathy shrub of N. and Arctic America, a species of *Ledum*, the young leaves of which are dried and used as a substitute for tea.

labret, n. [1. lā́bret; 2. léibrit], fr. Lat. *labrum*, 'lip', fr. same base as *labium* (see **labial**), & **-et**. Ornament, such as a piece of wood, bone, or shell, inserted in a hole pierced through the lip.

laburnum, n. [1. labérnum; 2. ləbə́nəm]. Lat., etymol. obscure. Tree of genus *Cytisus*, with pendulous clusters of yellow flowers.

labyrinth, n. [1. lábirinth; 2. lǽbərinþ], fr. Gk. *labúrinthos*, 'maze; large building with intricate passages'. Etymol. unknown, apparently a foreign loan-word. **a** Any group or system of complicated, winding, intricate paths or passages; a maze; **b** (fig.) applied to spiritual and intellectual difficulties and complexities.

labyrinthine, adj. [1. làbirínthīn; 2. læ̀bərínþain], fr. prec. & **-ine**. Connected with, resembling, in form of, a labyrinth; complicated, intricate, mazy.

lac (I.) or **lakh**, n. [1. lak; 2. læk]. Hind. *lākh*, 'one hundred thousand (rupees)', about £7500.

lac (II.), n. Hind. *lākh*, fr. Scrt. *rākšā*. A red resinous substance used as a dye, and in manufacture of varnish &c.

lace (I.), n. [1. lās; 2. leis]. O. Fr. *laz*, *las*, 'noose', Lat. *laqueus*, 'noose, snare', perh. related to *lacio*, 'draw gently', whence *allicio*, 'entice'; fundamental meaning seems to be a noose for snaring. **1.** A string or cord which binds or holds together, esp. garments such as boots, gaiters, stays &c. **2.** A fine net-like fabric, often elaborately wrought with designs made of linen or silk thread: *Brussels lace, Alençon lace* &c.; *gold lace*, ornamental trimming of gold wire, plaited or worked into designs, and used on diplomatic, naval, and military uniforms. **3.** Dash of brandy, gin &c. taken with another liquid.

lace (II.) vb. trans. & intrans., fr. prec. **A.** trans. **1.** To fasten together with laces, as boots &c. **2.** To adorn with lace: *a laced coat*. Phr. *to lace a person's jacket*, i.e. give him a thrashing. **3.** To mingle spirits with (another liquid, esp. coffee). **B.** intrans. To be fastened with a lace, or with laces: *to lace up the back*.

lace boots, n. Boots fastening with laces.

laced, adj. [1. lāst; 2. leist], fr. P.P. of **lace (II.)**. **1. a** Fastened, kept together, with a lace or laces; **b** trimmed, ornamented, with lace: *a laced hat, coat* &c. **2.** Fortified by having a dash of spirits mixed with it: *laced coffee*.

lace paper, n. Paper with open-work design at the edge resembling lace.

lace-pillow, n. Cushion used in making lace.

lacerable, adj. [1. láserabl; 2. lǽsərəbl], fr. base of next word & **-able**. Capable of being, liable to be, torn.

lacerate, vb. trans. [1. láserāt; 2. lǽsəreit]. Lat. *lacerāt-(um)*, P.P. type of *lacerāre*, 'to tear', fr. *lacer*, 'torn'; prob. fr. **wlac-*, n.; perh. related to Lat. *vulnus*, 'wound', & *vellere*, 'to tear, tear off'; cp. also *lāna*, 'wool'. See **lanate** & **wool**. **a** To tear, mangle, esp. flesh or soft tissue; **b** (fig.) to wound the feelings; distress, harass, afflict grievously.

laceration, n. [1. làserā́shun; 2. læ̀səréiʃən]. **lacerate** & **-ion**. **a** Act of lacerating; **b** state of being lacerated; a torn, jagged wound; injury to the feelings.

lacertian, lacertine, adj. [1. lasérshian, -tīn; 2. læsə́ʃiən, -tain], fr. Lat. *lacerta*, 'lizard', wh. is supposed to be fr. same base as Lat. *lacertus*, 'forearm', lit. 'that which bends, twists' &c.; cp. further Gk. *loxós*, 'bent, crooked'; O.N. *leggr*, whence **leg**, is fr. same base; for suff. see **-ian, -ine**. Belonging to lizards; lizard-like.

laches, n. [1. lā́chez; 2. léitʃiz]. O. Fr. *lachesse*, fr. Lat. *lascus* for *laxus*, 'slack', cp. Lat. *laxāre*, 'to make wide, slacken, relax' &c.; connected w. *languēre*, 'to be slack'. See **languid** & cp. **lax**. Formerly, negligence; now, (legal) such unreasonable delay in asserting an equitable right that the court will refuse relief.

Lachryma Christi, n. [1. lákrima krísti, -ī; 2. lǽkrimə krísti, -ai]. Lat., 'Tear of Christ'. A strong, sweet Italian wine.

lachrymal, adj. & n. [1. lákrimal; 2. lǽkriməl]. Lat. *lacrima*, 'tear from the eye', & adj. suff. *-ālis*, O. Lat. *dacruma*, cogn. Gk. *dákru*, cogn. w. Goth. *taggr*, O.E. *tēar*, 'tear'. See **tear (III.)**. **1.** adj. Pertaining to tears; *lachrymal gland*, (med.) tear-secreting gland. **2.** n. Small vase, found in ancient sepulchres, in which tears of the mourners were collected.

lachrymation, n. [1. làkrimā́shun; 2. læ̀kriméiʃən]. Lat. *lacrimātiōn-(em)*, fr. *lacri-māt-(um)*, P.P. type of *lacrimāre*, 'to weep'. See prec. & **-ion**. Weeping, flow of tears.

lachrymatory, adj. & n. [1. lákrimaturi; 2. lǽkrimətəri]. Lat. *lacrimāt-*, see prec., & **-ory**. **a** adj. Pertaining to, causing, flow of tears: *lachrymatory gas, gas-shell* &c.; **b** n., a lachrymal vase.

lachrymose, adj. [1. lákrimōs; 2. lǽkrimous]. Lat. *lacrimōsus*, 'tearful'; *lacrima*, 'tear', see **lachrymal**, & **-ous**. Tearful, addicted to weeping, mournful.

lachrymosely, adv. Prec. & **-ly**. Tearfully, as though weeping.

laciniate(d), adj. [1. lasíniāt(ed); 2. læsínieit(id)]. Lat. *lacinia*, 'lappet, flap, of a garment', connected w. *lacer*, 'torn', see **lacerate**, & **-ate** (& **-ed**). **a** Fringed; **b** specif. (bot.) having petals cut into deep lobes.

lack (I.), n. [1. lak; 2. læk], fr. L.G., cp. M. Du. *lak*, 'deficiency'. Want, deficiency, shortage, absence, need: *a lack of wit, intelligence*; *no lack of food*.

lack (II.), vb. trans. & intrans., fr. prec. **1.** trans. To be deficient in, short of: *to lack money, intelligence* &c. **2.** intrans. To show deficiency, be wanting; only in Pres. Part.: *nothing is lacking for your comfort* &c.

lackadaisical, adj. [1. lakadā́zikl; 2. lækədéizikl]. Next word & **-ic** & **-al**; suggestive of one who in a crisis wd. merely utter an exclamation of dismay or surprise instead of acting. Affectedly languid; full of airs and graces; vague, absent-minded, dreamy.

lackadaisy, interj. [1. lákadāzi; 2. lǽkədéizi]. Popular refashioning of obs. *(a)lackaday*.

lackaday, interj. [1. lákadā; 2. lǽkədéi]. Cp. **alack**. (obs.) Expression of sorrow, surprise and dismay or impatience.

lackey, lacquey, n. & vb. trans. [1. láki; 2. lǽki]. Fr. *laquais*, fr. Span. *lacayo*. Origin unknown. **1.** n. **a** Manservant, footman in livery; **b** (fig.) a servile, insignificant fellow who takes his ideas from others. **2.** vb. To play, act, the lackey to; to attend on, escort.

lack-lustre, adj. **lack (II.)** & **lustre**. Dull, dim, lacking fire and brilliance: *lack-lustre eyes*.

laconic(al), adj. [1. lakónik(l); 2. ləkɔ́nik(l)]. Fr. *laconique*, Lat. *Lacōnicus*, fr. Gk. *Lakōnikós*, 'belonging to, characteristic of, Lacedemon, or Lacedemonians, or Spartans'. **a** (of style, expression) Brief, concise, abrupt; expressing meaning in few words; **b** (of persons) given to laconic utterance.

laconically, adv. Prec. & **-ly**. In a laconic manner; briefly, in few words.

laconicism, n. [1. lakónisizm; 2. ləkónisizəm]. **laconic** & **-ism**. Laconic mode of utterance or expression.

laconism, n. [1. lákonizm; 2. lǽkənizəm]. Gk. *Lakōnismós, Lakōn*, 'a Spartan', & **-ism**. **a** Brief mode of expression; **b** a laconic utterance.

lacquer, lacker, n. & vb. trans. [1. láker; 2. lǽkə]. Fr. *lacre*, 'kind of sealing-wax'. See **lac (II.)**. **1.** n. Hard, bright, smooth, variously coloured varnish composed of shellac. **2.** vb. To coat, cover, with lacquer.

lacquering, n. [1. lákering; 2. lǽkəriŋ]. Prec. & **-ing**. **a** Act of applying lacquer; **b** style, mode, in which this has been done; **c** lacquer itself.

lacrosse, n. [1. lahkrós; 2. lākrós]. Fr. *crosse*, 'crozier; curved stick, club &c. used in certain games'; fr. Med. Lat. *crucea*, fr. Lat. *cruci-*, stem of *crux*, 'cross'. See **cross (I.)**. A game, played originally in Canada, in which the ball is caught in, and thrown by, a long-handled racquet, called a crosse.

lactarine, n. [1. lákterēn; 2. lǽktərīn]. For etymol. see under **lacteal**. Material made from casein of milk, used by calico-printers.

lactate, vb. intrans. [1. láktāt; 2. lǽkteit], fr. Lat. *lactāt-(um)*, P.P. type of *lactāre*, 'to suckle young'. See **lacteal**. To secrete milk; to suckle young.

lactation, n. [1. laktáshun; 2. læktéiʃən]. Prec. & **-ion**. **a** Process of secreting milk; **b** act of suckling.

lacteal, adj. [1. lákteal; 2. lǽktiəl]. Mod. formation fr. Lat. *lac*, genit. *lact-is*, 'milk', & **-al**. The base *lact-*, earlier **glact-*, is cogn. w. Gk. *gálakt-*, 'milk'. See **galacto-**. **a** Resembling milk; milky; **b** pertaining to milk: *lacteal fluid*; *lacteal gland*, one secreting milk.

lactescence, n. [1. laktésens; 2. læktésəns], fr. Lat. *lactescent-(em)*, Pres. Part. of *lactescere*, 'turn to milk'. See prec. & **-ce**. Process of becoming milky.

lactic, adj. [1. láktik; 2. lǽktik], fr. stem *lact-* as in **lacteal**, & **-ic**. (chem.) Belonging to milk; *lactic acid*, derived from sour milk.

lactiferous, adj. [1. laktíferus; 2. læktífərəs]. Lat. *lacti-*, see **lacteal**, & **-ferous**. Milk-yielding.

lactose, n. [1. láktōs; 2. lǽktous]. See **lacteal** & **-ose**. (chem.) Sugar of milk.

lacuna, n., pl. *lacunae* or *-as* [1. lakúna; 2. ləkjúnə]. Lat., 'pit, hole, pool, pond, chasm'; conn. w. *lacus*, 'basin, tank, lake', see **lake**. Cp. also **lagoon**. A gap or hiatus, vacancy, omission, esp. in a book, manuscript, list &c.; a gap in one's knowledge.

lacustrine, adj. [1. lakústrīn; 2. lækástrain], fr. Lat. *lacus*, 'lake'; late formation on anal. of *paluster, -ustris*, 'marshy' (fr. *palus*, 'swamp, marsh'), & **-ine**. Belonging to lakes; *lacustrine dwellings*, lake-dwellings.

lacy, adj. [1. lási; 2. léisi]. **lace (I.)** & **-y**. Made of, resembling, having structure of, lace.

lad, n. [1. lad; 2. læd]. M.E. *ladde*, 'serving-man, youth'. Origin doubtful. **a** Young boy, youth, young man: *the lads of the village* &c.; used specif. of older men employed in racing stables: *stable lad*; **b** (colloq., slang) (i.) a man of character and vigour; (ii.) also (in detrimental sense) of a man of somewhat loose and wild habits: *he's a bit of a lad*.

ladanum, n. [1. ládanum; 2. lǽdənəm]. Lat., fr. Gk. *ládanon*, also *lédanon*, mastic obtained fr. a shrub, *lédon*, prob. fr. Pers. *lādan*. A dark, fragrant, bitter resin, obtained from various species of Cistus or rock rose, formerly used in medicine; the name was transferred to laudanum, q.v.

ladder (I.), n. [1. láder; 2. lǽdə]. O.E. *hlǣd(d)er*, M.E. *ládder*; O.H.G. *hleitara*; Gmc. form **hlaid(d)ir*; prob. fr. Aryan base **k̑lei-, *k̑loi-, *k̑li-*, 'to slope, incline'; this base, w. different formative elements, is seen in Gk. *klīnō*, 'I slope, lean', & *klîmax*, 'ladder, staircase' (see **climax**); also in O.E. *hlǣnan*, 'to cause to lean' (see **lean (II.)**). Less probable is the suggestion that O.E. *hlǣdder* is for **hlaiwid-dr*, cogn. w. Gk. *kleîthron*, 'a bolt, a bar', fr. **kleiwidh-*, the base being **klei-* &c., cp. Gk. *kleiō*, 'I shut', & *kleis*, 'instrument for shutting, a bolt; a key'. The latter is cogn. w. Lat. *clāvis*, 'a key' (see under **clavicle**). If this etymol. be accepted, *ladder* meant orig. 'a set of bars or spars'. **1. a** An instrument of wood, iron, or rope for climbing, consisting of two parallel pieces connected by cross-pieces (*rungs*) at regular intervals which serve as foothold; **b** something resembling a ladder in appearance, esp. an accidental vertical break in the mesh of silk or other fine material, particularly of a stocking, due to one or more slipped threads. **2.** (fig.) *Ladder of fame, success* &c., means by which success, fame &c. are attained. Phr. *to get one's foot on the ladder*, to make a beginning; *to kick away the ladder by which one rose*, despise persons or means by whose help one began.

ladder (II.), vb. intrans., fr. prec. (only of stockings &c.) To become affected by a ladder or vertical break in the mesh.

laddie, n. [1. ládi; 2. lǽdi]. Dimin. of **lad**. A little boy; affectionate mode of address, **a** for a small boy; **b** (slang) old chap, old man &c.

lade, vb. trans. [1. lād; 2. leid]. O.E. *hladan*, 'to put upon as a burden, load; to pile up; to draw water'; also in O.S. & O.H.G.; Goth. *(af-)hlaþan*. Cp. O.E. *hlōð*, 'booty'. Apparently unconnected w. **load** in origin, though partly identical in meaning. **1. a** To put freight into a vessel, to place a load in a waggon: *to lade a ship, cart* &c.; **b** to put into a ship, on to waggon &c., as a freight or load: *to lade hay* &c. **2.** In P.P. *laden*, **a** freighted, loaded; **b** (fig.) burdened, oppressed; now only as adjective. See **laden**. **3.** To draw, dip, out with a ladle &c.: *to lade water out of a hole* &c.

laden, adj. [1. ládn; 2. léidn], fr. old P.P. of prec. O.E. *hladen*. **1.** Piled, loaded, up; filled with cargo; loaded with burden: *heavily laden ship*; *well-laden mules*; *cart completely laden with hay*. **2.** Morally burdened, oppressed, weighed down: *mind laden with sin, sorrow, guilt*.

ladida, n. & adj. [1. làhdidáh; 2. lādidā́]. No history; prob. coined in the music halls; occurred in refrain of song once popular. (obs. and vulg. slang) **a** n. Used in eighties of 19th cent. for an affected, swaggering, overdressed person; a vulgar swell; **b** adj., equivalent to *foppish*.

ladies' chain, n. [1. ládiz chān; 2. léidiz tʃéin]. Figure in a country dance or other square dance, as the lancers.

lading, n. [1. láding; 2. léidiŋ]. **lade** & **-ing**. Cargo, freight, of a vessel; *bill of lading*, see **bill (III.)**.

ladle, n. & vb. trans. [1. ládl; 2. léidl]. O.E. *hlǣdel*, M.E. *lādel*. See **lade** & **-le**. **1.** n. Spoon with a long handle for serving liquids, esp. gravy, punch &c. **2.** vb. **a** To draw, scoop, out with, or as with, a ladle; *ladle out*, to take (liquid) out of a vessel with a ladle; also **b** (fig., colloq.) to distribute, award, esp. indiscriminately: *to ladle out honours, praise*.

ladleful, n. [1. ládlfool; 2. léidlful]. Prec. & **-ful**. The contents of a ladle; as much as a ladle will hold.

lady (I.), n. [1. ládi; 2. léidi]. O.E. *hlǣfdige*, 'mistress of a house; female of rank', often used in L.O.E. as a kind of title, applied to females of royal blood, equiv. to 'princess'; M.E. *lēfdi, lēuedi, lāuedi, lādi* &c. The first syll. is fr. O.E. *hlāf*, 'loaf, bread'; see also **loaf (I.)** & **lord**. The origin of *-dige* is doubtful. A favourite suggestion is that it means 'kneader', fr. a vb. **dīgan*, 'knead', not found in O.E., but occurring as *deigan* in Goth. See the cognates of this under **dough**. **1. a** Female of birth, breeding, good manners, and refinement; also *Our Lady*, the B.V.M.; **b** a woman who, apart from her birth, has good manners and a kind, generous, and honourable character: *not (quite) a lady* means either (i.) not well born and bred, or (ii.) not generous and straightforward; shabby, mean in behaviour; **c** often used now, esp. by themselves and their friends, in referring to females who have neither birth, breeding, education, nor manners, the term *woman* being felt by them as derogatory, as implying, perhaps, a person of light conduct; **d** (euphemistically) *lady of easy virtue, of pleasure*, a courtesan. **2. a** Title of respect accorded by custom to the wives of all peers below rank of duke, to wives of lords by courtesy, baronets, and knights, and to daughters of peers above the rank of viscount; **b** used specifically in reference to women who bear the title, esp. in combination *lords and ladies*. **3. a** Woman who was the special object of a knight's devotion in the age of chivalry; **b** in imitation of this, object of a man's attachment, lady-love; Phr. (vulg.) *my, his, young lady*, fiancée; (archaic or provinc.) *my, your, good lady*, wife.

lady (II.), adj. (attrib.) **1.** Woman, female; **a** in *lady doctor, lady president, lady secretary*; **b** (as euphemism) *lady dog* for *bitch*. **2.** In *lady cook, lady-help*, implying superior status, education, and refinement.

lady-bird, n. = Our Lady's bird. *Lady* in this and several of the following is a survival of an old (M.E.) uninflected possessive of feminine nouns. Small flying beetle, red or reddish brown, with dark spots on back.

Lady Chapel, n. = Our Lady's Chapel. Chapel dedicated to B.V.M., attached to large churches and cathedrals; generally built eastward of the high altar, and often projecting from main building.

Lady Day, n. = Our Lady's Day; Feast of Annunciation, March 25th; one of the quarter days.

lady-fern, n. Lat. *filix femina*. Common tall, slender variety of fern.

lady-help, n. Female of rather superior position and education who undertakes domestic duties for wages.

ladyhood, n. [1. ládihood; 2. léidihud]. See **-hood**. Status, condition, of a lady.

lady-in-waiting, n. One in attendance on royalty.

lady-killer, n. A conceited, foppish coxcomb, who endeavours to excite admiration in the opposite sex, esp. by the supposed attractions of his person and dress.

ladykin, n. [1. ládikin; 2. léidikin]. **lady** & **-kin**. A little lady; also term of endearment.

ladylike, adj. [1. ládilīk; 2. léidilaik]. **lady** & **like**. **a** (of female persons) Having appearance and manners of a lady; refined, elegant; **b** applied also, derisively, to men having an effeminate, feeble, over-sensitive character, and a fastidious, finical, and affected bearing.

lady-love, n. Woman admired and courted by a man; sweetheart.

lady mayoress, n. Wife of a lord mayor, or one permanently acting as hostess &c. for a lord mayor during his term of office; a woman elected as Lord Mayor styles herself so, and not Lady Mayoress.

lady's bedstraw, n. See **bedstraw**.

ladyship, n. [1. ládiship; 2. léidiʃip]. See **-ship**. Rank, quality, of a lady; used in addressing, or referring to, one having title of lady: *your, her, ladyship*; obsolete or archaic among equals except on formal occasions.

lady's laces, n. [1. ládiz lásiz; 2. léidiz léisiz]. Kind of ribbon grass.

lady's maid, n. Female servant whose business is to assist her mistress in her toilet.

lady's man, n. One who is fond of society of ladies and who makes efforts to attract and please them by being particularly polite and obliging.

lady's-slipper, n. **a** A wild orchid, genus *Cypripedium*; **b** the cultivated calceolaria.

lady's smock, n. The cuckoo-flower.

laevo-, form used in compounds in scientific terminology, w. force of 'on, towards, the left side', as *laevo-rotatory*, 'turning, rotating, to the left' &c. (contrast **dextro-**); fr. Lat. *laevus*, 'left' (a poetic word, the commoner word being *sinister*), cogn. w. Gk. *laiós*, 'left', fr. ***laiwos*, cp. Russ. *levo*, 'left'.

laevulose, n. [1. lḗvūlōs; 2. līvjulous], fr. Fr. *lévulose*. See prec. word, w. dimin. suff. in *-ul-*, & **-ose**. (chem.) Fruit-sugar present in honey, most sweet fruits &c.; it is laevo-rotatory, that is, turns the plane of polarized light to the left (cp. *dextrose*), and is sweeter than cane sugar.

lag (I.), n. & vb. trans. [1. lag; 2. læg]. Swed. *lagg*. **1.** n. Stave of a cask; narrow board used for covering boiler. **2.** vb. To cover with lags.

lag (II.), n. & vb. trans. Origin unknown. **1.** n. A convict: *old lag*, one accustomed to jail, one often in prison. **2.** vb. **a** To arrest; **b** to put in jail.

lag (III.), vb. intrans. Origin uncertain. To loiter, linger, behind others; to walk or move along slowly; often *lag behind*.

lag (IV.), n. See prec. **1.** (archaic and provinc.) The last. **2.** Retardation: *the lag of the tide.* Specif. **3.** A technical term in mechanics and electricity, indicating retardation by the influence of various forces, as when the value of an alternating current reaches its maximum after the electromotive force is at its maximum; cp. **phase**.

lagan, n. [1. lágan; 2. lǽgən]. A.-Fr.; of Gmc. origin, fr. base ***lag-*. See **lay** (III.) & **lie** (III.). Ship's wreckage or cargo when sunk to and lying on the bed of the sea; cp. and contrast *flotsam and jetsam.*

lager (**beer**), n. [1. láhger; 2. lágə]. Germ. *lager*, 'storehouse, warehouse'; cogn. w. O.E. *leġer*. See **lair** & cp. **laager**. Light German beer; similar beer made in other countries; so called because it is stored for some months before being drunk.

laggard, n. [1. lágard; 2. lǽgəd]. **lag** (III.) & **-ard**. One who is slow to action; one without energy and courage.

lagoon, n. [1. lagōōn; 2. ləgūn]. Fr. *lagune*, fr. Ital. *laguna*, 'fen, bog'; another Ital. form is *lagone*, 'fen, pool, lake'; fr. Lat. *lacūna*, 'hole, pool' &c. See **lacuna** & **lake** (I.). Shallow lake or channel near river or sea, esp. one communicating with the latter as at Venice.

laic, adj. & n. [1. lā́ik; 2. léi-ik]. Fr. *laïque*, Lat. *laicus*. See **lay** (II.). (obsolesc.) **1.** adj. Belonging to the laity. **2.** n. A layman.

laicize, vb. trans. [1. lā́isīz; 2. léi-isaiz]. Prec. & **-ize**. To secularize; to render laic; to open to laymen.

laid, vb. [1. lād; 2. leid]. P.P. of **lay** (III.), used as adj. (of paper) Having parallel lines in watermark.

lain, vb. [1. lān; 2. lein]. O.E. (*ġe*)*leġen*, M.E. *lein*. P.P. of **lie** (III.).

lair, n. & vb. intrans. [1. lār; 2. lɛə]. O.E. *leġer*, 'bed, couch, resting-place' &c.; M.E. *leir* &c.; O.H.G. *leger*, Mod. Germ. *lager*; Goth. *ligrs*; fr. same base as O.E. *liċġan*, 'to lie down'. See **lie** (III.) & cp. **lager**. **1.** n. Resting-place, bed, den, esp. of wild animals; retreat, home, habitual resort (of human beings). **2.** vb. To rest, stop, in a lair.

laird, n. [1. lārd; 2. lɛəd]. Nthn. Engl. & Scots form of **lord**, w. specialized meaning. Scottish landowner; originally one holding direct from the king.

lairdship, n. [1. lā́rdship; 2. lɛ́ədʃip]. Prec. & **-ship**. **a** Status or condition of a laird; **b** extent of landed property held by a laird.

Lais, n. [1. lā́is; 2. léi-is]. Name of a celebrated courtesan of ancient Greece, noted for her beauty and avarice. A courtesan possessing beauty and some cultivation of mind.

laissez-faire, n. [1. lā́sā fā́r; 2. léisei fɛ́ə]. Fr., 'let be, leave alone, let them do what they like'. Policy of non-interference; freedom from, or the minimum of, state interference in economic or industrial affairs, esp. by tariffs, restrictions on individual competition &c.

laity, n. [1. lā́iti; 2. léi-iti]. **lay** (II.) & **-ity**. **a** Whole body of persons not in Holy Orders, as distinct from the clergy; **b** persons outside a particular profession or occupation, and not possessing some special knowledge.

lake (I.), n. [1. lāk; 2. leik]. M.E. *lac*, *lāke*, fr. O. Fr., fr. Lat. *lacus*, 'basin, tank; pool'; cogn. w. Gael. *loch*, Ir. *lough*, 'lake'; also O.E. *lagu*, 'sea'; O.N. *logr*, 'sea, moisture'. Walde suggests connexion w. the large group of words fr. base ***lak-* &c., meaning 'bend, twist' (see **lacertian**), & assumes the orig. meaning of *lacus* &c. to be 'hollow, dip in the ground; marshy, wet hollow &c.' Sheet of water of considerable size, usually entirely surrounded by land.

lake (II.), n., fr. Fr. *laque*. See **lac** (II.). Reddish, purplish pigment made from cochineal mixed with a metallic substance.

lake-dweller, n. Inhabitant of a lake-dwelling.

lake-dwelling, n. Prehistoric habitation built upon piles some way from the shore of a lake; found esp. in Switzerland and Ireland.

Lake poets, n. Group, school, of English poets of whom the chief were Wordsworth and Coleridge, who lived near each other in the English lake district in the early 19th cent.; Southey, who lived in this region, though not one of the school, is sometimes included.

lakh, n. See **lac** (I.).

laky, adj. [1. lā́ki; 2. léiki]. **1. lake** (I.) & **-y**. Abounding in lakes; resembling, pertaining to, coming from, a lake. **2. lake** (II.) & **-y**. Having the colour of the pigment lake; pale crimson; of the blood in certain pathological conditions.

lam, vb. trans. [1. lam; 2. læm], fr. O.N. *lama*, 'to beat'. See **lame**. (schoolboy slang) To beat, flog, thrash.

lama, n. [1. láhma; 2. lámə], fr. Tibetan *blama*, 'priest'; the *b* is not sounded. Buddhist priest in Tibet: *Grand Lama*, the chief priest; called also *Dalai Lama.*

lamaism, n. [1. láhmaizm; 2. láməizəm]. Prec. & **-ism**. The form of the Buddhist religion practised among the lamas.

Lamarckian, adj. & n. [1. lamárkian; 2. læmákiən], fr. name of Fr. naturalist Lamarck (1744–1829). **1.** adj. Pertaining to, based on, the teachings of Lamarck and his doctrine of organic evolution; Lamarck held that species were gradually modified by the inherited results of environment upon the individual. **2.** n. A follower of Lamarck.

Lamarckism, n. [1. lamárkizm; 2. læmákizəm]. Prec. & **-ism**. Evolutional doctrines of Lamarck.

lamasery, n. [1. láhmaseri; 2. láməsəri]. Fr. *lameserie*. See **lama**. Monastery of lamas.

lamb (I.), n. [1. lam; 2. læm]. O.E. *lămb*, M.E. *lămb*, *lōmb*. Occurs in most Gmc. tongues, cp. O.N. *lamb*, Du. *lam*, Germ. *lamm*, but cannot be traced outside these w. any certainty. **1. a** The young of the sheep; Phr. *Lamb of God*, the Saviour; (proverb) '*You may as well be hung for a sheep as (for) a lamb*', as well act (sin) boldly and thoroughly while you are about it; **b** flesh of lamb as food. **2.** Applied as term of affection to young children.

lamb (II.), vb. intrans., fr. prec. To bring forth lambs.

lambda, n. [1. lámda; 2. lǽmdə]. Name of letter *l* in Gk. alphabet; borrowed fr. Semit.; cp. Heb. *lamed.*

lambdacism, n. [1. lámdasizm; 2. lǽmdəsizəm]. Gk. *lambdakismós*. Substitution of sound of *l* for original *r*, as when Chinese pronounce [véli] for *very* &c.

lambdoid(al), adj. [1. lámdoid, làmdóidal; 2. lǽmdɔid, læ̀mdɔ́idəl]. **lambda** & **-oid** (& **-al**). **a** Shaped like the Greek letter lambda (Λ); **b** specif. (anat.) *lambdoidal suture*, that between the bones of the skull.

lambency, n. [1. lámbensi; 2. lǽmbənsi]. Next word & **-cy**. Fact, quality, of being lambent.

lambent, adj. [1. lámbent; 2. lǽmbənt], fr. Lat. *lambent-(em)*, Pres. Part. type of *lambere*, 'to lick' (of flame). Cogn. w. O.E. *lapian*, 'drink, lap'. See under **lap** (III.). **a** (of flame, light) Lightly moving about, playing on the surface, twinkling, flickering; **b** (fig., of wit and humour) gently and playfully brilliant.

lambing, vbl. n. [1. láming; 2. lǽmiŋ]. **lamb** (II.) & **-ing**. **a** Act of bringing forth lambs; **b** assistance rendered to ewes at lambing season; *lambing coat*, garment worn by shepherds when assisting ewes; *lambing hut*, small wooden hut used for shelter during lambing season.

lambkin, n. [1. lámkin; 2. lǽmkin]. **lamb** (I.) & dimin. **-kin**. **a** Very young lamb; **b** affectionate mode of address or reference to a young child.

lamblike, adj. [1. lámlīk; 2. lǽmlaik]. Like the supposed character of a lamb; gentle, meek, unresisting.

lambrequin, n. [1. lámberkin; 2. lǽmbəkin]. Fr., fr. Du. *lamperkin*, 'small veil'; etymol. doubtful. **1.** (obs.) Small scarf or veil used to protect a helmet from heat or wet. **2.** Drapery surrounding top of door or window; drapery round top of bed-posts, or hanging from mantelpiece &c. **3.** (her.) Flowing drapery or scroll-work displayed on either side of the helmet; mantling.

lambskin, n. [1. lámskin; 2. lǽmskin]. **a** Dressed hide of a lamb with wool preserved; **b** leather made from this skin.

lamb's-wool, n. [1. lámz wool; 2. lǽmz wul]. **a** Wool of lamb; **b** cloth &c. made from this; **c** hot ale, sugared and spiced, and mixed with pulp of roasted apples.

lame (I.), adj. [1. lām; 2. leim]. O.E. *lam(a)*, M.E. *lāme*. The base ***lam-* occurs in most Gmc. languages in sense of 'lame, paralysed', & O.N. has vb. *lama*, 'to beat' (cp. **lam**); cogn. w. Russ. *lomat*, 'to break'; orig. sense is 'broken, bruised'; perh. connected w. **limp** (II.). **1.** Disabled, having imperfect use of limbs, esp. of feet and legs. Phr. *lame duck*: **a** lame person, disabled vessel &c.; **b** defaulter on Stock Exchange. **2.** (of a speech, argument, excuse) Halting, unconvincing; *lame metre*, bad verse.

lame (II.), vb. trans., from prec. To make lame.

lamella, n., pl. **lamellae** [1. laméla, -lē; 2. læmélə, -lī]. Lat. *lāmella*, 'small thin plate', dimin., connected w. *lāmina*, 'thin plate of metal, wood' &c. Etymol. doubtful. Thin plate, layer, scale, usually applied to a thin plate of bone, or other tissue in animals.

lamellar, lamellate, adj. [1. lamélar, lámelāt; 2. læmélə, lǽmileit]. Prec. & **-ar**, **-ate**. (zool.) Composed of, arranged in, thin plates, scales, or layers.

lamellibranchiate, adj. [1. lamèlibrángkiāt; 2. læmèlibrǽŋkieit]. See **lamella** & **branchiate**. (zool.) Belonging to a class, *Lamellibranchia*, of molluscs which have lamellate gills, as clams, mussels, oysters &c.

lamelliform, adj. [1. laméliform; 2. læmélifɔ̄m]. See prec. & **-form**. Having form or structure of a lamella; scale-like.

lamely, adv. **lame** (I.) & **-ly**. In a lame or halting manner.

lameness, n. See prec. & **-ness**. Condition of being lame.

lament (I.), vb. intrans. & trans. [1. lamént; 2. ləmént]. Lat. *lāmentāre*, late formation fr. *lāmentum*, 'wailing, moaning, weeping'; the base of first syll. is prob. ***lā-*, found in Lat. *lātrāre*, 'to bark'; cp. also Gk. *láskein*, 'to crash; creak; shriek; bark'; O. Slav. *lajati*, 'to bark, scold'; & perh. Goth. *laian*, 'to revile'. **1.** intrans. **a** To utter cries, sobs, &c., expressive of grief; to complain aloud; **b** to feel grief, to mourn; bewail a calamity; *lament for*, to bewail, mourn for. **2.** trans. To bewail, mourn for; feel grief at; feel and express deep regret at; to deplore: *to lament a person's death*; *to lament a person's folly*. Phr. (ironical) *the late lamented*, the deceased; specif., late husband.

lament (II.), n. See prec. Older than vb. in Engl. a Passionate outward expression of sorrow or grief; b a dirge, elegy, composed, and sung or played on the occasion of some specific death, or calamity: *the lament of David over Saul and Jonathan*; *a coronach or lament for the bagpipes*.

lamentable, adj. [1. lámentabl; 2. lǽmintəbl]. **lament** (I.) & **-able**. 1. Worthy, of a nature, to be lamented; grievous, causing sorrow; disastrous. 2. (poet.) Expressive of sorrow; mournful: *a lamentable voice, shriek*. 3. (contemptuous) Wretched, mean, paltry; of very inferior quality: *a lamentable performance, meal* &c.

lamentableness, n. Prec. & **-ness**. State or quality of being lamentable.

lamentably, adv. See prec. & **-ly**. a In a lamentable manner; b (as intens.) *lamentably ugly*.

lamentation, n. [1. làmentáshun; 2. lǽmen-, lǽmintéiʃən]. **lament** (I.) & **-ation**. 1. a Outward, audible expression of grief; b inward grieving, sorrow. 2. *Lamentations*, book of Old Testament, attributed to the Prophet Jeremiah.

lamenting, adj. [1. laménting; 2. ləméntiŋ], fr. Pres. Part. of **lament** (I.). Feeling, expressing, grief; grieving, complaining.

lamentingly, adv. Prec. & **-ly**. In a manner expressive of grief, regret, or complaint.

lamia, n. [1. lámia; 2. léimiə]. Lat., fr. Gk. *lámia*, 'a vampire, bogey'; cp. also Gk. *lamós*, 'maw, crop', cogn. w. Lat. *lemurēs*, 'phantoms'. (class. mythol.) Alluring and devouring monster with head and breast of a woman and the body and tail of a serpent; vampire, witch.

lamina, n., pl. **laminae** [1. lámina, -nē; 2. lǽminə, -nī], Lat., 'thin piece of metal, wood &c.; a plate, veneer'. Cp. **lamella**. Etymol. doubtful. Thin layer, plate, flake, scale, of metal, or of bone, or other animal or vegetable tissue; specif., one of the plates of sensitive vascular tissue on the hoof of a horse.

laminal, laminar, adj. [1. láminal, -ar; 2. lǽminəl, -nə]. Prec. & **-al, -ar**. Arranged in layers; having form of, resemblance to, laminae.

laminate, vb. trans. & intrans. [1. láminät; 2. lǽmineit]. **lamina** & **-ate**. 1. trans. a To cause to form, or split, into laminae; b to form (metal) into thin plates; c to cover with thin plates. 2. intrans. To split, divide up, into thin layers.

laminated, adj. [1. láminàted; 2. lǽminèitid]. Prec. & **-ed**. Formed of, arranged in, thin layers.

lamination, n. [1. làmináshun; 2. lǽminéiʃən]. **laminate** & **-ion**. 1. Process of laminating; state of being laminated. 2. (elect.) Thin sheet or strip of soft iron used in building up cores or armatures of dynamos and electric motors.

laminiferous, adj. [1. làminíferus; 2. lǽminífərəs]. **lamina** & **-ferous**. Having laminae.

laminitis, n. [1. làminítis; 2. lǽminάitis]. **lamina** & **-itis**. Inflammation of the lamina in a horse's hoof.

Lammas, n. [1. lámas; 2. lǽməs]. O.E. *hlāfmæsse, hlāmmæsse*, M.E. *lāmmasse*. See **loaf** (I.) & **mass** (III.). Old name for feast celebrated on 1st of August; so called because a loaf was offered to represent first fruits.

Lammas lands, n. pl. (legal hist.) Fields or meadows thrown open to the commoners from Lammasday to the spring, sown and held in severalty during the rest of the year.

Lammas tide, n. Season of Lammas.

lammergeier, n. [1. lámergīer; 2. lǽməgάiə]. Germ. *lämmergeier*, fr. *lämmer*, 'lambs' (see **lamb**), & *geier*, 'vulture', O.H.G. *gīr*, wh. is fr. same base as Lat. *hiāre*, 'to be open, to gape'. See **hiatus** & **chaos**. Largest European bird of prey, now only found in Pyrenees; also called *bearded vulture*.

lamp, n. [1. lamp; 2. læmp]. Fr. *lampe*, fr. Gk. *lampás*, 'torch, light, lamp', connected w. *lámpō*, 'I shine'; orig. meaning 'that which shines, a torch'. The primitive sense is still preserved in Lett. *lápa*, 'pine torch'. 1. a A vessel burning a wick in oil, used for illumination; b any kind of light-giving contrivance, e.g. *gas lamp, electric lamp*; c (fig.) source of spiritual light or knowledge; Phr. *to smell of the lamp*, reference to highly wrought style which suggests that the night has been spent on it; *to hand on the lamp*, to further knowledge or other cause, phrase derived from the ancient Greek torch-race, *lampadephoria*, q.v. 2. Vessel with wick burning spirit, esp. for heating food: *spirit lamp*.

lampadephoria, n. [1. làmpadefória; 2. lǽmpædifɔ́riə]. Gk. *lampadēphoria*, fr. *lampád-(os), lampás*, see **lamp**, & **-phore**. Race in ancient Greece in which a lighted torch was handed on from runner to runner, as in relay racing.

lampas (I.), n. [1. lámpaz; 2. lǽmpəz]. Fr. *lampas*. Origin unknown. (veter.) Disease in horses accompanied by swelling of gums and roof of mouth.

lampas (II.), n. Fr.; origin unknown. Material of silk and wool.

lamp-black, n. a Soot formed from burning of carbonaceous matter, or deposited by smoke of a lamp; b pigment made from this.

lamp-burner, n. Part of oil-lamp which holds the wick, and from which light proceeds.

lamp-chimney, n. Glass funnel or tube placed round flame of oil or gas lamp.

lampern, n. [1. lámpern; 2. lǽmpən], fr. O. Fr. *lamprion*, see **lamprey**. A young lamprey.

lampion, n. [1. lámpiun; 2. lǽmpiən]. Ital. *lampione*. See **lamp**. Coloured glass vessel containing oil and floating wick, hung up for purposes of illumination, esp. in the open air.

lampless, adj. [1. lámples; 2. lǽmplis]. Having no lamp.

lamplight, n. [1. lámplīt; 2. lǽmplait]. Light from an oil-lamp; *by lamplight*, by artificial light.

lamp-lighter, n. Man who lights the lamps in public streets. Phr. *to run like a lamplighter*, run very fast.

lampoon, n. & vb. trans. [1. làmpōōn; 2. lǽmpūn]. Fr. *lampon*, 'drinking song', perh. fr. *lampons*, 'let us drink', fr. vulg. *lamper*, 'to guzzle', wh. is prob. a variant of **lap** (III.). 1. n. Satirical attack, generally of a scurrilous but humorous character, in prose or verse. 2. vb. To write a lampoon against; to attack by lampoons.

lampooner, n. [1. lampōōner; 2. læmpūnə]. Prec. & **-er**. Writer of lampoons.

lampoonist, n. [1. lampōōnist; 2. læmpūnist]. **lampoon** & **-ist**. Lampooner.

lamp-post, n. Iron support for street lamps.

lamprey, n. [1. lámpri; 2. lǽmpri]. Fr. *lamproi*, Ital. *lampreda*, earlier *lampedra*, fr. Lat. *lampetra*, fr. *lambere*, 'lick', & *petra*, 'rock', the latter borrowed fr. Gk. *pétra*. See **petro-**. A marine and freshwater fish somewhat resembling an eel, with sucker lips by which it attaches itself to rocks.

lamp-shade, n. Globe of glass or porcelain, screen of silk, paper &c., placed round flame of lamp to shade direct light from the eyes.

lanate, adj. [1. lánāt; 2. lǽneit]. Lat. *lānātus*, 'woolly', fr. *lāna*, 'wool, soft hair, down' &c., for **wlāna*; cp. also Gk. *lēnos*, 'wool'; cogn. w. Scrt. *ū́rṇā* for **wl̥nā*; Lith. *vilna*, O. Slav. *vlŭna*; Goth. *wulla*, fr. **wl̥na-*, O.E. *wull* (see **wool**); all cogn. w. Lat. *vellus*, 'wool shorn off, fleece', *vellere*, 'to pluck, pluck off, twitch' &c., & further, w. different vowel grade, Gk. *oûlos* for **wolsos*, or **wolnos*, 'woolly, fleecy'; the orig. sense seems to be 'that which is plucked, or shorn off'. Woolly; covered with wool or fine hair.

Lancastrian, adj. & n. [1. langkástrian; 2. læŋkǽstriən]. Lancaster & **-ian**. 1. adj. a Belonging to, coming from, Lancaster or Lancashire; b sprung from, connected with, adhering to, the royal house of Lancaster, descended from John of Gaunt. 2. n. a Inhabitant, native, of Lancaster or Lancashire; b member, adherent, of Lancastrian royal house, or of party supporting this in the Wars of the Roses, opposed to *Yorkist*.

lance (I.), n. [1. lahns; 2. lāns]. M.E. *launce, lance*, fr. O. Fr. *lance*, fr. Lat. *lancea*, 'light spear'; prob. a Celt. word; connected w. base seen in M. Ir. *do-lēcim*, 'I fling, let fly'; if this is fr. **plenk-*, then we may also connect O.N. *flengja*, 'to hurl' (see **fling**); Gk. *lógkhē*, 'spear-head', according to Walde, is for earlier **lakhē*, fr. Celt. *lagīna*, 'sword', but influenced in form & meaning by *lógkhē*, 'the long thing', cogn. w. Lat. *longus*, 'long'. See also **launch**. 1. Weapon of offence and defence consisting of a pointed iron head fixed to a long shaft, used for thrusting and parrying; a modern cavalry lance has a handle or shaft 9 or 10 feet in length. 2. Man armed with a lance; lancer (esp. in pl.).

lance (II.), vb. trans. O. Fr. *lancier, lancer*, 'pierce with a lance'. See prec. 1. To pierce, attack, with a lance. 2. To cut, open, with a lancet: *to lance an abscess* &c.

lance-corporal, n. The old obs. name was *lance-pesade*, a Fr. term borrowed fr. Ital. *lancia spezzata*, lit. 'broken or half lance', used of intermediate class of lancer. (mil.) Acting corporal, with or without additional pay.

lancelet, n. [1. láhnslet; 2. lánslit]. **lance** (I.) & dimin. **-let**. Small marine animal, the lowest form of vertebrate, *Amphioxus*, a few inches long, which burrows into sand in shallow water.

lanceolate, adj. [1. láhnseolāt; 2. lánsiəleit]. Lat. *lanceolātus*, 'lance-shaped', fr. *lanceola*, 'little lance'. See **lance** (I.) & **-ate**. (zool. and bot.) Lance-shaped, tapering to a point.

lancer, n. [1. láhnser; 2. lánsə]. O. Fr. *lanceor*, Mod. Fr. *lancier*, 'man armed with lance'. **lance** & **-er**. 1. Soldier armed with lance; specif., member of a cavalry regiment thus armed, and known as *Lancers*; also *Lancer Regiment*. 2. *Lancers*, a a square dance, kind of quadrille, or figure dance; b music for this.

lance-sergeant, n. See **lance-corporal** for origin of term. (mil.) Corporal acting as sergeant.

lancet, n. [1. láhnset; 2. lánsit]. Fr. *lancette*, dimin. of **lance** (I.). 1. Small surgical cutting instrument, of various form, often two-edged, used for opening veins, abscesses &c. 2. Lancet-window, or arch.

lancet arch, n. Narrow, pointed arch.

lanceted, adj. [1. láhnseted; 2. lánsitid]. **lancet** & **-ed**. Having lancet windows or arches.

lancet fish, n. Large deep-sea fish with lancet-shaped teeth.

lancet window, n. Narrow, pointed window.

lancewood, n. [1. láhnswood; 2. lánswud]. Tough, elastic wood from American or W. Indian tree, used for making lance-shafts, bows, fishing-rods &c.

lanciform, adj. [1. láhnsiform; 2. lánsifɔ̄m]. **lance** (I.) & **-form**. Narrow and pointed, like head of a lance in shape.

lancinate, vb. trans. [1. láhnsināt; 2. lánsineit]. Lat. *lancināt-(um)*, P.P. type of *lancināre*, 'to tear to pieces, mangle'; connected w. Lat. *lacer*, 'torn, rent'. See **lacerate**. To tear; to pierce, stab.

lancinating, adj. [1. láhnsināting; 2. lánsineitiŋ], fr. Pres. Part. of prec. Stabbing, shooting: *lancinating pains*.

lancination, n. [1. làhnsináshun; 2. lànsinéiʃən]. **lancinate** & **-ion**. Fact or process of lancinating; a stabbing, shooting, of pain.

land (I.), n. [1. land; 2. lænd]. O. & M.E.; in all Gmc. languages; cogn. w. W. *llan*, 'tract, region' &c. 1. Solid surface of the earth, as distinct from, and contrasted with, *water* or *sea*: *to spy, come to, reach, land*. Phr. (*to see*) *how the land lies*, state of affairs; *dry land*, the shore, earth, contrasted with water. 2. Specific area, or region of the earth, country; nation, state: *to visit far-off lands*;

one's native land. Phrs. *Land of Promise, Promised Land,* Canaan; *land o' the leal,* heaven; *land o' cakes, of the thistle,* Scotland; *land of dreams,* beautiful, imaginary country which is never seen; *land of the living,* this present life; *land of Nod,* sleep. **3. a** Ground, soil, considered from point of view of its character, quality, the crops which it bears &c.: *rich, poor, boggy, clayey, land; good corn land; cultivated, arable, land;* **b** this contrasted with urban area; country, rural district; Phrs. *to go on, work on, the land,* become, be, a farm labourer; *back to the land,* return to country life. **4.** Area, tract, considered as property; estate, including everything annexed to it by nature, timber, water &c.: *to own land; how far does your land go?; to live on one's own land;* (also in pl.) *houses and lands,* estates.

land (II.), vb. trans. & intrans., fr. prec. **A.** trans. **1. a** To put (persons and things) on shore: *to land troops in France;* **b** (fig.) to bring, put, a person in unfavourable or undesired situation, conditions or circumstances: *this lands me in great difficulties;* Phr. *to be nicely landed; to land a man with coat that doesn't fit* &c. **2. a** To bring (a fish) to shore; **b** (fig., colloq.) to secure a person's support, his consent to act in desired way; **c** to obtain what one desires as result of effort: *to land a prize.* **3. a** To set down from train or other vehicle or from a ship, aeroplane &c.: *to be landed at a roadside station, in the desert, on a lonely island* &c.; **b** to place, deposit; cause to reach particular spot: *to land a ball in the middle of the field;* **c** (colloq.) to place, deal, strike: *I landed him one, a blow, on the nose.* **B.** intrans. **1.** To come to land from the sea, air &c.; disembark: *to land at Dover, Croydon aerodrome* &c. **2. a** To reach, arrive at, come to, a particular place, or in a specified condition or manner: *I landed at midnight at King's Cross;* **b** to come down after a fall or jump: *to land on the opposite bank; to land on one's feet, all doubled up* &c.

land agency, n. Office and business of a land agent.

land agent, n. Person employed to manage landed estates.

landau, n. [1. làndáw; 2. lǽndɔ̄], fr. place in Germany. Four-wheeled horse carriage, with top made in two portions to fold back.

landaulet, n. [1. làndawlét; 2. lændɔ̄lét]. Prec. & **-let. a** Small type of landau; **b** now a type of motor-car with movable back part of covering.

land breeze, n. One blowing from the land towards the sea, esp. after sundown, owing to the more rapid cooling of ground surface.

land crab, n. One of several sorts inhabiting warm coasts, which live mostly on land, but breed in the sea.

landed, adj. [1. lánded; 2. lǽndid]. **land** (I.) & **-ed. 1.** Consisting of land, or real estate: *landed property.* **2.** Possessing land: *landed interest; the landed classes.*

lander, n. [1. lánder; 2. lǽndə]. **land** (II.) & **-er. 1.** One who lands, disembarks. **2.** Person who receives, and superintends unloading of, ore at mouth of mine-shaft.

landfall, n. [1. lándfawl; 2. lǽndfɔ̄l]. Sighting and calculation of distance and position of land from a ship at sea.

land-grabber, n. **a** One who possesses himself of land illegally; **b** specif. (Ireland) person taking up land from which a tenant has been evicted.

landgrave, n. [1. lándgrāv; 2. lǽndgreiv]. Germ. *landgraf,* fr. *land* (see **land**) & *graf,* 'count, earl', etymol. of wh. is doubtful. Cp. **reeve** (II.). Title of head of one of the smaller semi-independent states of the former German Empire.

landgravine, n. [1. lándgràvēn; 2. lǽndgrèivīn]. Germ. *landgräfin.* Wife of a landgrave.

landholder, n. [1. lánd-hòlder; 2. lǽndhòuldə]. Landed proprietor.

landing, n. [1. lánding; 2. lǽndiŋ]. **land** (II.) & **-ing. 1. a** Act of coming, or bringing, to land; **b** act of arriving or alighting; **c** place, spot, at which one arrives, or on which one alights. **2.** Flat part between two sets of stairs; floor, passage, at top of a staircase on to which the rooms open.

landing-net, n. Bag-shaped net with long handle used for getting fish ashore when they have been caught with rod and line, and brought close to water's edge.

landing-stage, n. **a** Small stone pier or jetty, built out from the land into the water alongside of which boats can float while landing passengers; **b** large wooden structure, or platform, at which passengers land from larger vessels; built over the water, connected at one side with a pier or with the land; often floating, and made to rise and fall with the tide.

landlady, n. [1. lándlādi; 2. lǽndleidi]. **1.** (rare) Proprietress of an estate who lets the land to tenants. **2. a** Proprietress of a house which is let to tenants; **b** specif., proprietress, mistress, of an inn or hotel; **c** woman who keeps and lets out lodgings.

Land League, n. Association or league of tenant farmers formed in Ireland by M. Davitt in 1879 to obtain reduction of rents.

Land Leaguer, n. Prec. & **-er.** Member of Land League.

landless, adj. [1. lándles; 2. lǽndlis]. **land** (I.) & **-less. 1.** Not owning land; destitute of land. **2.** (of area in a large body of water) Not having land near it.

land-locked, adj. [1. lánd lòkt; 2. lǽnd lɔ̀kt]. (of bay, harbour &c.) Enclosed, or nearly enclosed, by land.

landloper, -louper, n. [1. lándlòper, -lòuper; 2. lǽndlòupə, -làupə]. Second element prob. Du. fr. *loopen,* 'to run', cogn. w. **leap.** See **interloper.** A vagabond.

landlord, n. [1. lándlord; 2. lǽndlɔ̄d]. **1.** Proprietor of land; landowner. **2.** Owner of a house which is let to a tenant or tenants. **3.** Owner, keeper, of an inn or public-house.

landlordism, n. [1. lándlordizm; 2. lǽndlɔ̄dizəm]. Prec. & **-ism. 1. a** Habits of thought and conduct of landlords as a class; **b** condition of being a landlord. **2.** System of private ownership of land whereby rent for its use is paid to an individual.

landlordly, adj. [1. lándlordli; 2. lǽndlɔ̄dli]. See prec. & **-ly.** Belonging to, characteristic of, the position of landlord: *landlordly rights and duties.*

land-lubber, n. **land** (I.) & **lubber.** Sailor's word for one unaccustomed to the sea, who is clumsy and unhandy at everything connected with ships.

land-lubberly, adj. Prec. & **-ly.** Pertaining to, characteristic of, a land-lubber.

landmark, n. [1. lándmark; 2. lǽndmāk]. O.E. *landmearc,* 'boundary'. **1.** Boundary, line of division, object or objects indicating this, esp. between two estates or separate holdings: *to move one's neighbour's landmarks.* **2. a** Some object, whether a natural feature or a structure of any kind, serving to indicate a particular locality; esp. one visible from a distance which acts as a guide whereby direction or position may be ascertained; **b** (fig.) some outstanding event or episode which marks an epoch in time, a period in history, a stage in human life, turning-point in a career &c.

land measure, n. System of square measure used in measuring land.

landowner, n. [1. lándòner; 2. lǽndòunə]. Owner of landed property; landed proprietor, landlord.

landowning, n. & adj. [1. lándòning; 2. lǽndòuniŋ]. **1.** n. Ownership of land; fact, system, of owning land. **2.** adj. **a** Having landed property: *landowning classes;* **b** pertaining to the ownership of land, or to landowners: *landowning worries.*

landrail, n. [1. lándrāl; 2. lǽndreil]. **land** (I.) & **rail** (I.). Bird which utters a continuous series of harsh, loud staccato notes; corncrake.

landscape, n. [1. lán(d)skip; 2. lǽn(d)skip], now, by some, pronounced [1. lán(d)skāp; 2. lǽn(d)skeip]. Cp. O.E. *landscipe,* 'region', & *landsceap,* 'land'; the present word, however, is not derived fr. either of these, but is a 17th cent. borrowing fr. Du. *landschap,* 'landscape; province', but was applied primarily to painting; the 17th & 18th cent. spelling was *landskip(p),* a form retained by many good speakers, in pronunciation; this form of the suff. appears to be a compromise between Engl. **-ship,** w. *k* fr. attempted imitation of Du. *sch-*; the modern spelling must be due to association w. **shape.** The pronunciation of the second element as [skeip], quite recent, is based on the spelling, & has no tradition. **1.** Pictorial representation of inland scenery; **a** pictorial reproduction of a specific piece of country; **b** the branch of pictorial art which deals with scenery. **2.** Actual tract of inland country and all its features, considered as scenery, and from the visual impression which it creates; prospect.

landscape gardener, n. One whose profession it is to design and lay out gardens, parks &c., so as to utilize to the utmost the natural features, such as large trees, slopes, hollows, distant views, vistas &c., and so to relate them to the general scheme that a pleasing unity is secured, that woodland, lawns, paths, isolated trees, shrubberies &c. are all placed in the most telling relations, with a view to the general effect desired.

landscape painter, n. Artist who devotes himself to painting natural (inland) scenery.

landscapist, n. [1. lándskāpist; 2. lǽn(d)-skeipist]. Landscape painter.

landslide, n. [1. lándslīd; 2. lǽndslaid]. **1.** Fall of considerable portion of land from the side of a mountain or edge of a cliff. **2.** (fig.) Sudden trend of public opinion in a new direction, esp. sudden great change in strength of parties in a parliamentary election.

landsturm, n. [1. lándstoorm; 2. lǽndstuəm]. Germ. *land,* 'country', & *sturm,* 'storm', here used in sense of 'rushing together, struggling'. See **storm.** The German compound goes back to 1813. Last line of defence in pre-War Germany, consisting of all men under sixty who were not engaged already in the army or navy; this levy could only be made in the gravest national emergency.

land-tag, n. Germ. Engl. pronunciation usually [1. lánd tàhg; 2. lǽnd tàg]. The second element is Germ. equiv. of **day**; the secondary meanings are 'fixed day, day for transaction of some specified business; business; assembly of those taking part in this'; hence 'council' &c. Cp. **diet** (I.) in same sense. Legislative assembly in a German state.

landward, adj. & adv. [1. lándward; 2. lǽndwəd]. See **-ward.** Situated near the land; towards the land.

landwehr, n. [1. lándvàr; 2. lǽndvèə]. Mod. Germ., fr. O.H.G. *landweri,* 'army for protection of the country'; cp. O.H.G. *werian,* Goth. *warjan,* O.E. *werian,* 'to protect' &c.; cp. also O.E. *wēr,* 'dam' &c., q.v. under **weir.** Troops corresponding to militia, called out for national defence in time of war.

lane, n. [1. lān; 2. lein]. O.E. *lāne,* M.E. *lāne*; cp. Du. *laan,* 'alley'; provinc. Engl. *loan* &c. is fr. the O.E. type *lōne,* M.E. (W. Midl.) *lōne.* Etymol. unknown. A narrow road or track, generally between fields, often lower than these, and usually having hedges, walls, or banks on either side; sometimes used of an alley or narrow road between buildings in towns, in which case the term has survived from earlier times, and become gradually transferred in meaning. Phrs. *it is a long lane that has no turning,* things are sure to change sometime for the better; *red lane,* throat.

langrage, -idge, n. [1. lánggrij; 2. lǽŋgridž]. Origin unknown. Kind of canister shot formerly used to damage enemy's rigging in a sea battle.

lang syne, adv. & n. [1. làng sín; 2. læŋ sáin]. Scots. See **long** & **since**. **1.** adv. Long since, in the old days. **2.** n. Long ago, ancient times.

language, n. [1. lánggwij; 2. læŋgwidž]. M.E., fr. O. Fr. *language*, fr. Lat. *lingua*, 'tongue, speech'. See **lingual** & **-age**. **1. a** The expression of thoughts and emotions by means of articulate sounds formed by the vocal organs; rational vocal utterance, human speech in general: *articulate language appears to be confined to man*; **b** the set of inarticulate vocal sounds whereby the lower animals express their wants and feelings. **2. a** Particular, characteristic form, or mode of speech current among a specific large group of human beings; the speech of a nation, race, tribe &c.: *the languages of Europe*; **b** any of these when expressed in graphic symbols: *written language*. **3. a** (i.) Given mode of using and arranging the elements of speech, particular selection of these, in uttered or graphic expression; style, diction; individual style of writer or orator: *the language of poetry*; *Browning speaks of Wordsworth's 'great language'*; Phrs. *fine language*, over-elaborate, flowery style; *bad language*, profanity, obscenity, abuse &c.; *strong language*, forcible expression of vehement feeling; (ii.) (vulg.) abuse, obscenity, profanity: *I won't have any language here*; *complained that her master used language to her*, swore at her; **b** special set of terms and expressions in use among, peculiar to, members of a particular profession &c.: *the language of the law, of science* &c. **4.** Any set of symbols or gestures used to express meaning: *the language of flowers*; *sign language*.

langued, adj. [1. langd; 2. læŋd]. Fr. *langue*, 'tongue'. See prec. & **-ed**. (her.) Applied to beasts in heraldry to imply that they are represented with a tongue of different tincture from the rest: *langued gules*, &c.

langue d'oc, n. [1. láhngg dók; 2. lãŋg dɔ́k]. Fr. *langue*, 'speech', & *oc*, 'yes', fr. Lat. *hoc*, 'this thing'. Romance languages of S. France; so called from their word for 'yes'.

langue d'oïl, n. [1. láhngg dóil; 2. lãŋ dɔ́il]. O. Fr. *oïl*, Mod. Fr. *oui*, 'yes', fr. Lat. *hoc illud*, 'that's it'. Romance languages of France other than those of S. France.

languid, adj. [1. lánggwid; 2. læŋgwid], fr. Lat. *languidus*, 'faint, weak, dull, sluggish', fr. *languēre*, 'to be faint, weary; to droop, wither' &c.; cogn. w. Lat. *laxus*, 'slack', Gk. *lagarós*, 'slack, hollow', Scrt. *langaš*, 'lame'. See **lax**. Weak, slack, flagging, listless, in body or mind: *languid attempts*, half-hearted.

languish, vb. intrans. [1. lánggwish; 2. læŋgwiʃ]. M.E. *languischen*, fr. Fr. *languiss-*, Pres. Part. stem of *languir*, fr. Lat. *languēre*. See prec. **1.** To become languid; **a** to droop, fail in health and vigour, pine: *flowers languish in drought*; *young children languish in slums*; **b** to grow faint, wane, diminish: *my interest in the subject has greatly languished*. **2.** To pass through a period of external discomfort and mental uneasiness; to droop gradually from misery and restless longing: *to languish for years in a dungeon*. **3.** To adopt a look of melancholy, wistful, sentimental tenderness and unfulfilled longing.

languishing, adj. [1. lánggwishing; 2. læŋgwiʃiŋ], fr. Pres. Part. of prec. **1.** Drooping, growing faint; diminishing. **2.** Melancholy, sentimental, amorous: *a languishing look*.

languishingly, adv. Prec. & **-ly**. In a languishing manner.

languor, n. [1. lánggor; 2. læŋgə]. M.E. *langour*, Lat. *languor*, 'feebleness, weariness, lassitude', fr. same base as **languid**. **1.** State of bodily or mental weariness; lassitude; inertia. **2.** Sentimental dreaminess: '*The lilies and languors of virtue*' (Swinburne). **3.** Stagnation, lack of life and movement.

languorous, adj. [1. lánggorus; 2. læŋgərəs]. Prec. & **-ous**. Feeling, affected by, languor; causing languor.

languorously, adv. Prec. & **-ly**. In a languorous manner.

langur, n. [1. lunggóor; 2. laŋgúə]. Hind. A long-tailed monkey of India and Asia, esp. the sacred monkey, *hanuman*, the scientific name of which is *Entellus*.

laniferous, adj. [1. laníferus; 2. læníferəs]. Lat. *lānifer*, 'wool-bearing'. See **lanate** & **-ferous**. Wool-bearing, fleecy.

lanigerous, adj. [1. laníjerus; 2. lænídžərəs], fr. Lat. See **lanate** & **-gerous**. Laniferous.

lank, adj. [1. langk; 2. læŋk]. O.E. *hlanc*, 'lank, lean', M.E. *lank*; origin doubtful, but Skeat suggests connexion w. Germ. *lenken*, 'to turn', & thinks the orig. meaning was 'bending', hence 'weak'. This wd. connect the word w. O.E. *hlenċe*, 'link'. See further under **link (I.)**. **1.** (of bodily shape and condition) Slender, long and thin, lean. **2.** (of hair) Straight, not curled.

lankiness, n. [1. lángkines; 2. læŋkinis]. **lanky** & **-ness**. Quality of being lanky.

lankness, n. [1. lángknes; 2. læŋknis]. **lank** & **-ness**. Quality of being lank.

lanky, adj. [1. lángki; 2. læŋki]. **lank** & **-y**. Tall and slim of figure; esp. long and lean as though overgrown.

lanner(et), n. [1. láner(et); 2. lǽnə(rit)]. O. Fr. *lanier*, 'cowardly', & **-et**; Mod. Fr. *laneret*, 'kind of falcon', & *lanier*, 'the female bird'; perh. fr. Lat. *lānārius*, 'connected with wool; worker in wool', fr. *lāna*, 'wool' (see **lanate**); the steps in meaning are not very clear. A kind of long-tailed falcon of S.E. Europe, N. Africa &c., formerly much used for hawking, the female being a *lanner* and the male *lanneret*.

lanolin(e), n. [1. lánolēn; 2. lǽnəlīn], fr. Lat. *lāna*, 'wool' (see **lanate**), & *ol-*, fr. Lat. *oleum*, 'oil' (see **oil**), & **-ine**. Natural grease in sheep's wool; purified form of this used as a soothing ointment.

lansquenet, n. [1. lánskenet; 2. lǽnskənɛt]. Fr., fr. Germ. *landsknecht*, 'foot soldier'. See **land** & **knight**. **1.** German mercenary in 16th and 17th cents. **2.** German card game.

lantern, n. [1. lántern; 2. lǽntən], fr. Fr. *lanterne*, fr. Lat. *lanterna*, fr. Gk. *lamptḗr* (see **lamp**), influenced by Lat. *lucerna*, 'oil lamp', fr. *luc-*, stem of *lux*, 'light'. See **lucent**. **1.** Lamp, in various forms, which has the flame enclosed and protected by glass or horn, and is provided with a handle, used for carrying in the open air; *dark lantern*, one with a sliding shutter for hiding the light. **2.** Chamber of a lighthouse in which the lights are. **3.** Open structure at the top of a tower made to give light and air to the upper chamber, or centre of church.

lantern-jawed, adj. [1. lántern jàwd; 2. lǽntən džɔ̀d]. Having long thin jaws and hollow emaciated cheeks.

lantern-jaws, n. pl. Thin cadaverous jaws and face.

lanthanum, n. [1. lánthanum; 2. lǽnþənəm]. Coined fr. stem of Gk. *lanthánein*, 'to lie hid' (q.v. under **latent**); so called from lateness of its discovery. Rare element, one of the metallic earths, allied to aluminium.

lanthorn, n. [1. lántern; 2. lǽntən]. Old spelling of **lantern**, due to association with *horn*, of which the sides were often made.

lanuginous, adj. [1. lanújinus; 2. lænjúdžinəs]. Lat. *lānūginōsus*, fr. *lānūgo*, 'down'; cp. *lāna*, 'wool'. See **lanate** & next word. Downy; covered with soft, fine hair.

lanugo, n. [1. lanúgō; 2. lænjúgou]. Lat., 'down, on cheeks, or on plants', see prec. (anat.) Soft downy hair which covers the fetus in the womb, and often the infant for some time after birth.

lanyard, n. [1. lányard; 2. lǽnjəd]. Fr. *lanière*, 'rope, line', Lat. *lānārius*, '(made) of wool'. See **lanate**. The addition of a final *-d* after *-r* &c. is frequent in Engl. fr. 15th cent. onwards. Cp. *visard* fr. **visor**, & the vulg. *schollard* fr. **scholar** &c. The final syll. of such a form as *lanyard* wd. easily be associated w. *yard* (of a ship). **a** Short thick rope, esp. as used on board ship; **b** cord used by sailors to fasten their knives round their necks.

Laodicean, adj. & n. [1. làodisḗan; 2. lèiədisíən], fr. Laodicea, cp. Rev. iii. 15, 16. **a** adj. Lukewarm, lacking strong feeling for or against anything; **b** n., person who is lukewarm and indifferent.

lap (I.), n. [1. lap; 2. læp]. O.E. *læppa*, 'tag, skirt'; cogn. w. **lobe**. **1.** Flap of cloth, of a garment. **2. a** That part, of a person who is sitting, from waist to knees; this part in women and portion of the skirt covering it: *to sit on, in, a person's lap*. Phrs. *in the lap of Fortune*, fortunate; *lap of luxury*, luxurious circumstances; **b** (poet.) surface, bosom: '*brooks, On whose fresh lap*' &c. (Milton, 'Lyc.', 138); '*earth's freshest, softest lap*' ('P. L.'). **3.** Stage in a game; one circuit of course in a race which consists of several circuits.

lap (II.), vb. trans. & intrans., fr. prec. **A.** trans. **1. a** To wrap, enfold, embosom: *lapped in velvet*; *a house lapped in woods*; **b** (fig.) to surround, enfold (with): *lapped in luxury*. **2.** *Lap over*, to cause to overlap, place something so that it projects beyond something else. **B.** intrans. To lap over, turn, fold, over or back; (of things lying one on the other) to come, be, even with.

lap (III.), vb. trans. & intrans. O.E. *lapian*, 'to drink, lap'; O.H.G. *laffan*, cp. O.H.G. *leffil*, Mod. Germ. *löffel*, 'a spoon'; cogn. w. O. Slav. *lobŭzŭ*, 'kiss'; Lat. *lambere*, 'to lick'. See **lambent**. **1.** trans. **a** To drink by scooping (liquid) into the mouth with the tongue, esp. as animals do; *lap up*, consume by lapping; **b** (of human beings, vulg.) *lap up, lap down*, (i.) to drink, consume, greedily or excessively; (ii.) to swallow, accept, listen eagerly to (flattery, compliments, tales &c.). **2.** intrans. **a** To carry out the action of lapping; to drink by lapping; **b** to make a sound resembling that of an animal drinking: *the brook laps upon the stones*.

laparotomy, n. [1. làparótomi; 2. læpərɔ́təmi], fr. Gk. *lapárā*, 'the soft part of the body between the ribs and hips; the flanks, loins', fr. *laparós*, 'soft, flaccid, hollow', & **-tomy**. Cp. Gk. *alapázein*, 'to empty'; cogn. w. Scrt. *álpaš*, 'small'. A surgical operation involving an incision into the abdominal wall.

lap-dog, n. Small pet dog of any breed, as nursed on a woman's lap; (contemptuously) any pampered, badly behaved, small dog.

lapel, n. [1. lapél; 2. læpél]. Dimin. of **lap (I.)**. Part of a coat forming a continuation of the collar, turned back on the chest.

lapelled, adj. [1. lapéld; 2. læpéld]. Prec. & **-ed**. Having lapels; in form of a lapel.

lapidary, adj. & n. [1. lápidari; 2. lǽpidəri]. Lat. *lapidārius*, 'worker in stone', fr. *lapid-*, stem of *lapis*, 'stone'. See under **lapis lazuli** & **-ary**. **1.** adj. **a** Connected with, pertaining to, stones; **b** connected with the cutting, polishing, or engraving of precious stones or gems: *lapidary work, lathe* &c.; **c** pertaining to, suitable for, inscriptions engraved on monuments: *a neat lapidary style*. **2.** n. **a** One skilled in the cutting and polishing of precious stones or the engraving of gems; **b** an expert, connoisseur, of precious stones; **c** treatise on gems.

lapidate, vb. trans. [1. lápidāt; 2. lǽpideit]. Lat. *lapidāt-(um)*, P.P. type of *lapidāre*, 'pelt with stones'. See prec. To pelt with stones; to stone.

lapidation, n. [1. làpidáshun; 2. læ̀pidéiʃən]. Prec. & **-ion**. Act of stoning.

lapilli, n. pl. [1. lapílī; 2. ləpílai]. Lat. pl. of *lapillus*, dimin. of *lapis*, 'stone'. See next word. Small stones, fragments of lava &c. erupted by a volcano.

lapis lazuli, n. [1. lápis lázūlī; 2. lǽpis lǽzjulai]. Lat. *lapis*, 'stone', cogn. w. Gk. *lépas*, 'bare rock, crag'; cp. also *lépein*, 'to strip off, to peel'; & Med. Lat. *lāzuli*, genit. of *lāzulum*, wh. is formed fr. Arab. *lājward*, the name of the stone, also '**azure**'. See

azure. Semi-precious stone of a bright-blue colour.

Laplander, Lapp, n. [1. láp(lander); 2. lǽp(lәndә)]. Inhabitant of Lapland.

lappet, n. [1. lápet; 2. lǽpit]. **lap (I.)** & dimin. **-et.** Loose fold or flap of a garment; flap of flesh.

Lappish, adj. & n. [1. lápish; 2. lǽpiʃ]. Prec. & **-ish.** 1. adj. Belonging to Lapland, or the Lapps. 2. n. Language of the Lapps.

lapse (I.), n. [1. laps; 2. læps]. Lat. *lapsus,* 'a slipping, a fall, a flowing', fr. same base as *labāre,* 'to totter' &c. See **labour.** 1. A slip, fall; **a** an error, failure: *lapse of the pen, of memory;* **b** departure, falling away from strictness of conduct: *a lapse from virtue; moral lapse; a lapse into crime.* 2. A gliding, passing away, passage: **a** *the lapse of a stream;* **b** *the rapid lapse of time.* 3. That which has passed away; a period of time: *a long lapse of time.* 4. (law) **a** Termination of right through disuse; **b** failure of legacy to take effect, through death of legatee.

lapse (II.), vb. intrans., fr. Lat. *lapsāre,* 'slide', or direct fr. prec. 1. (not used in physical sense) To fall away from, fail to maintain, a standard of conduct; **a** followed by *into,* to slide, pass, into a worse state, go back morally: *to lapse into idleness, crime, vice, barbarism;* **b** (absol.) to commit an offence, be guilty of, fall back into, misconduct &c.: *I fear he has lapsed again.* 2. (law, of privileges, offices &c.) **a** (followed by *to*) To pass away from one person to another, owing to negligence, non-fulfilment of stipulated conditions &c.: *the estate of a person dying without heirs or successors lapses to the Crown;* **b** to be extinguished, cease to be enjoyed: *tenure of the office has lapsed, at the expiry of the term of appointment.*

lapsus calami, n. [1. lápsus kálamī; 2. lǽpsәs kǽlәmai]. Lat., 'a slip of the pen'.

lapsus linguae, n. [1. lápsus línggwē; 2. lǽpsәs líŋgwī]. Lat., 'a slip of the tongue'.

lapwing, n. [1. lápwing; 2. lǽpwiŋ]. O.E. *hlēapewince;* the first element is **leap,** & the second perh. fr. the same base as **wink,** wh. orig. implied merely 'rapid movement, wavering'; the name is apparently descriptive of the bird's flight; another O.E. name for the bird was *lǣpewince,* the first element of wh. can have nothing to do w. 'leap'. Crested plover or peewit, *Vanellus,* a bird common in England, noted for its irregular flight and shrill wailing cry, which the name 'peewit' not imperfectly imitates.

lar, n., pl. **lares** [1. lar, lárēz; 2. lā, léәrīz]. Lat., 'household deities; home'. Walde gives several speculative etymologies, none of wh. is perfectly satisfactory. Chiefly pl. and in Phr. *lares and penates,* home and familiar, treasured belongings.

larboard, n. & adj. [1. lárbord; 2. lábәd]. M.E. *laddeborde;* second element **board;** origin of first element unknown, assimilated to *starboard.* (naut. obs., superseded by *port*) **a** n. Left-hand side of a ship when one is looking towards the bows; **b** adj., pertaining to, towards, this side.

larcener, larcenist, n. [1. lársener, -ist; 2. lásәnә, -ist]. O. Fr. *larrecin* & **-er,** & **-ist.** See **larceny.** One guilty of larceny.

larcenous, adj. [1. lársenus; 2. lásәnәs]. *larcen-* as in prec. & **-ous.** Of the nature of larceny; guilty of larceny, thievish.

larceny, n. [1. lárseni; 2. lásәni]. O. Fr. *larrecin,* 'theft', fr. Lat. *latrocinium,* 'service of mercenaries', then 'freebooting, highway robbery', fr. *lātrō,* 'a mercenary soldier', then 'a highway robber', prob. fr. Gk. *látris,* 'hired servant'. This word is connected w. Gk. *látron,* 'reward, pay'. The base *la-, *lē- is found in other Gk. words & in Goth. *lētan,* O.E. *lǣtan,* 'leave behind, bequeath'. Unlawful removal of another's possessions with intent to deprive him of them, and to convert them to one's own use; theft; *petty larceny,* formerly, theft of goods below the value of twelve pence.

larch, n. [1. larch; 2. lātʃ]. Germ. *lärche,* fr. Lat. *larici-* stem of *larix* for **darix,* w. *l-* for *d-* as in *lacrima* for *dacruma* (see **lachrymal**), fr. old base **dlerewo-* &c., 'tree, wood', whence Scrt. *dāru,* Gk. *dóru,* 'wood, spear', also *drūs,* 'tree, oak' (see **dryad**); Goth. *triu,* O.E. *trēo,* whence **tree.** **a** Deciduous, coniferous tree, genus *Larix;* **b** timber of this tree.

lard, n. & vb. trans. [1. lard; 2. lād]. Fr. *lard,* fr. Lat. *lāridum, lardum,* 'fat of bacon, bacon', cogn. w. Gk. *lārī-nós,* 'fat'. 1. n. Refined, rendered, fat of the pig; esp. the internal fat of the abdomen. 2. vb. **a** To insert small portions of bacon or bacon fat into meat before cooking, to increase its richness and flavour; **b** (fig.) to overlay, enrich, embellish (style) with: *he lards his conversation with Latin words, with quotations, oaths* &c.

lardaceous, adj. [1. lardāshus; 2. lādéiʃәs]. Prec. & **-aceous.** Consisting of, resembling, lard; fatty, esp. of animal tissue in state of degeneration.

larder, n. [1. lárder; 2. ládә]. O. Fr. *lardier,* 'tub in which bacon was pickled and kept'; in Engl. applied formerly to room in which bacon and meat generally was kept, see **lard.** Place in dwelling-house, or near it, where meat of all kinds for the household is kept.

larderer, n. [1. lárderer; 2. ládәrә]. Prec. & **-er.** (archaic) Servant in charge of a larder.

lardon, lardoon, n. [1. lárdon, lardōōn; 2. ládәn, lādūn]. **lard** & **-oon.** Strip of bacon used for larding.

lardy, adj. [1. lárdi; 2. ládi]. **lard** & **-y.** Resembling, having consistency of, lard.

lares. See **lar.**

large (I.), adj. [1. larj; 2. lādž]. M.E., fr. O. Fr., fr. Lat. *largus,* 'abundant, copious, plentiful; profuse, liberal'. Etymol. very doubtful; various suggestions, e.g. connexions w. **lar,** 'household divinity', considered a personification of wealth &c., & w. *lāridum,* 'fat of bacon', fr. idea of copiousness, richness &c., are rejected by Walde. 1. (of material things) **a** Occupying much space; of considerable size; great, big, bulky: *a large dog, tree, rock, building;* **b** enclosing, containing, much space; spacious, roomy: *a large room, house* &c.; **c** considerable in number, numerous; or in amount, extent; broad; copious: *a large income; a large property, field* &c.; *a large congregation, population; a large supply; a large meal.* 2. **a** Big contrasted with other things of the same kind; great of its kind: *large eyes, ears; a large mouth; a large needle, table; to write in large letters;* **b** too big for its purpose: *this coat is a trifle large for me.* Phr. *on the large side,* rather too large. 3. (in spiritual sense) **a** Liberal, broad; generous, magnanimous; reverse of petty or mean: *a large heart, toleration, kindness;* **b** far-reaching, embracing a wide range, unrestricted, not confined within narrow limits: *large ideas, insight, conceptions.*

large (II.), adv., fr. prec. 1. In a large way; in large form: *to write large.* 2. Boastfully, pompously: *to talk large.*

large (III.), n., fr. **large (I.).** Liberty, freedom; only in Phr. (i.) *at large,* free, not in prison; (ii.) *to talk at large,* diffusely.

large-handed, adj. Free, liberal, inclined to generous giving.

large-handedness, n. Generosity, liberality.

large-hearted, adj. Charitable, tolerant; loving, kindly disposed to, one's fellow-men.

large-heartedness, n. Kindness of nature and disposition; sympathetic attitude of mind.

largely, adv. [1. lárjli; 2. ládžli]. **large (I.)** & **-ly.** In a large manner; **a** to a great extent: *largely engaged in writing;* **b** abundantly, generously: *to give largely;* **c** on a big scale, extensively: *to spend, build, largely.*

large-minded, adj. Tolerant; broad in sympathies and ideas.

large-mindedness, n. Prec. & **-ness.** Breadth of mental outlook and sympathies.

largeness, n. [1. lárjnes; 2. ládžnis]. **large (I.)** & **-ness.** 1. **a** Bulk, magnitude; **b** great size. 2. Breadth of view; generosity, magnanimity of mind and character; absence of narrowness in ideas. 3. Moral greatness in human beings, or in their achievements.

largess(e), n. [1. lárjes; 2. ládžes]. M.E., fr. O. Fr., 'liberality'. See **large** & **-ess.** Something, esp. money, freely and generously given; liberality, charity.

larghetto, adj. & adv. [1. largétō; 2. lāgétou]. Ital. Dimin. of **largo,** 'slow'. (musical direction) Rather slow; not so slow as *largo.*

largish, adj. [1. lárjish; 2. ládžiʃ]. **large** & **-ish.** Rather large.

largo, adv. & n. [1. lárgō; 2. lágou]. Ital., fr. Lat. See **large.** 1. adv. (musical direction) Very slow. 2. n. Musical composition with a slow, stately movement.

lariat, n. & vb. trans. [1. láriat; 2. lǽriәt], fr. Span. *la reata,* 'the rope'. 1. n. Long rope with running noose which is flung over the heads of animals such as bulls, horses &c.; a lasso. 2. vb. To catch with a lariat.

lark (I.), n. [1. lark; 2. lāk]. O.E. *lāverce,* M.E. *larke;* cp. O.H.G. *lērahha,* Mod. Germ. *lerche,* O.N. *lǣvirki.* Origin unknown. 1. Any bird of various species of genus *Alauda,* or of the large family *Alaudidae,* esp. the skylark, *A. arvensis,* a bird with clear, sweet note, which flies upwards to a great height and sings as it mounts. 2. A jest, sport, frolic; a merry, waggish bout, a piece of fun. Phrs. *to have a lark,* to carry out a merry prank; *he only did, said, it for a lark,* in jest, as a joke.

lark (II.), vb. intrans., fr. prec. To jest, play, amuse oneself; *to lark about,* to play somewhat noisily and roughly.

larkspur, n. [1. lárkspĕr; 2. lákspā]. The delphinium, esp. the annual species; so called from shape of its leaves.

larky, adj. [1. lárki; 2. láki]. **lark** & **-y.** Inclined for a jest; given to larking; frolicsome.

larrikin, n. [1. lárikin; 2. lǽrikin]. Origin doubtful. Said to be from an Irish pronunciation of *larking.* (Australian slang) A noisy, blackguardly street rough; a rowdy, a hooligan.

larrup, vb. trans. [1. lárup; 2. lǽrәp]. Cp. Du. *larpen,* 'to thrash'. (slang) To administer a thrashing to; to beat soundly.

larva, n., pl. **larvae** [1. lárva, -ē; 2. lávә, -ī]. Lat. *larva,* 'spectre, mask'; prob. connected w. **lar.** 1. A kind of uncanny, supernatural monster; an elemental. 2. (entom.) Caterpillar, or worm-like stage of butterfly, moth, fly &c.; also (zool.) animal, e.g. tadpole, not yet arrived at final stage of change.

larval, adj. [1. lárvl; 2. lávәl]. Prec. & **-al.** Pertaining to a larva: *in the larval stage.*

laryngeal, adj. [1. lȧrinjḗal; 2. lǽrindžiәl], fr. **larynx** & **-al.** Pertaining to the larynx.

laryngitis, n. [1. lȧrinjítis; 2. lǽrindžáitis]. **larynx** & **-itis.** Inflammation of the larynx.

laryngoscope, n. [1. laringgoskōp; 2. lәríŋgәskoup]. See **larynx** & **-scope.** Instrument with mirrors for examining the larynx in a living person.

laryngoscopist, n. [1. lȧringgóskopist; 2. lǽriŋgóskәpist]. Prec. & **-ist.** One skilled in the use of the laryngoscope.

laryngoscopy, n. [1. lȧringgóskopi; 2. lǽriŋgóskәpi]. Art of using the laryngoscope.

larynx, n. [1. láringks; 2. lǽriŋks], fr. Gk. *lárugx, lárugg-(os),* 'throat, upper part of windpipe'; perh. cogn. w. Lat. *lurcāre,* 'devour', *lurco,* 'devourer'; cp. also O.N. *slark,* 'a noisy riot', orig. perh. 'a drinking bout'. The back of the throat, upper part of windpipe, containing the vocal chords.

Lascar, n. [1. láskar; 2. lǽskā]. Hind., fr. Pers. *lashkar,* 'army, camp'. Foreign sailor, esp. a native of East Indies, employed on European ships.

lascivious, adj. [1. lasívius; 2. lәsíviәs]. L. Lat. *lasciviōsus,* Lat. *lascivus,* 'wanton'. Cogn. w. Scrt. *lašati,* 'he desires', *lasati,* 'plays, delights'; Gk. *li-laiomai,* fr. -**las-*

jomai, 'desire'; Goth. *lustus*, q.v. under **lust. a** Lustful, wanton; **b** expressing wantonness: *a lascivious glance* &c.; **c** provoking, inciting to, wantonness.

lasciviously, adv. Prec. & **-ly.** In a lascivious manner.

lasciviousness, n. See prec. & **-ness.** Lewd, lustful feeling and desire; wantonness, voluptuousness.

lash (**I.**), vb. trans. & intrans. [1. lash; 2. læʃ]. Etymol. dubious; sense **1** perh. fr. **lash** (**II.**). **A.** trans. **1. a** To strike violently, as with a whip; to flog, thrash: *to lash a man across the face*; **b** (fig.) to strike violently upon: *the waves lashed the shore*; *hail lashed the window pane*; **c** (fig.) to excite violently, provoke powerfully: *to lash a person to fury by one's remarks*; *to lash oneself into a rage*, to become more and more angry with indignation which increases as one broods on wrongs, insults, or the like. **2.** To move rapidly backwards and forwards as though in anger: (of animals) *to lash the tail.* **3.** To vituperate, attack violently, heap invective on; to satirize, scold fiercely: *to lash a person with one's tongue, pen.* **4.** To bind, fasten securely, with a thong, rope &c.: *to lash one piece to another*; *to lash two pieces together.* **B.** intrans. **1.** To make rapid violent movement; gen. *lash out* (*at*), (of horse) to kick out, suddenly and fiercely; also (fig.) to burst into a sudden, violent attack in words. **2.** (of rain &c.) To fall violently: *to come lashing down.*

lash (**II.**), n. M.E. *lasche*, 'lash of a whip; blow'; cp. Germ. *lasche*, 'thong' &c., wh. is fr. Ital. *laccio*, 'a string, lace' &c. The Engl. word is fr. O. Fr. *laz*, 'cord, snare', Mod. Fr. *lacs*, fr. Low Lat. *lacium*, Lat. *laqueus*, 'noose, snare'. See **lace. 1.** Flexible thong, forming part of a whip; that part with which the stroke is given. Phr. *under the lash*, suffering corporal punishment; also (fig.) incurring severe, biting censure. **2. a** Blow, stroke, given with a whip or scourge: *to receive so many lashes*; **b** stroke of satire, cutting reproof. **3.** An eyelash.

lasher, n. [1. lásher; 2. lǽʃə]. **lash** (**I.**) & **-er.** Opening in a weir through which the water rushes.

lashing, n. [1. láshing; 2. lǽʃiŋ]. See **lash** (**I.**) & **-ing. 1.** Action of one who lashes; a thrashing. **2.** Arrangement of cords &c. with which anything is fastened; the cords which fasten things together. **3.** In pl., *lashings* (possibly separate word, origin obscure), also in Phr. *lashin's*, or *lashions, and leavin's*, a great deal, plentiful supply, esp. of food and drink.

lashkar, n. [1. láshkar; 2. lǽʃkā]. Hind. 'army'. A body of armed tribesmen on the N.W. Frontier of India.

laspring, n. [1. láspring; 2. lǽspriŋ]. Perh. fr. O.E. *leax*, 'salmon', & *pink*, Engl. dial., 'young salmon'. Young salmon.

lass, n. [1. las, lahs; 2. læs, lās]. M.E. *lasse.* Origin doubtful. (chiefly Scots and Nthn.) **a** Young girl; **b** female child; **c** familiar and affectionate mode of address to women, who are the equals, inferiors, or juniors of speaker (prov. or vulg.)

lassie, n. [1. lási; 2. lǽsi]. Dimin. of prec. **a** Young or small girl; **b** affectionate mode of address to such.

lassitude, n. [1. lásitūd; 2. lǽsitjūd]. Lat. *lassitūdo*, fr. *lassus*, 'faint, exhausted'; fr. **lad-to-*; the base (reduced grade of **lē-*, see **lenient**) is cogn. w. Goth. *lats*, 'slothful'; O.E. *læt*, 'sluggish'; see **late** &c. Bodily or mental weakness, weariness, exhaustion.

lasso, n. & vb. trans. [1. láso; 2. lǽsou]. Span. *lazo.* See **lace. a** n. Long strip of untanned hide with noose at one end, used by Spaniards in S. America for throwing over necks of cattle and horses which they wish to catch; **b** vb., to catch (animal) with a lasso.

last (**I.**), adj. [1. lahst; 2. lāst]. O.E. *latost*, superl. of *læt*, q.v. under **late**; M.E. *latst*, *laste.* **1.** Coming at the end of a series, after all others in place; furthest from the first; hindmost: *the last chair in the row*; *the last carriage on a train*; *the last page of a book.* **2. a** Coming, occurring, after all others in time; furthest from the beginning, latest: *the last day of the year*; *to see something for the last time*; Phr. *at last*, in the end, finally: *I hope to succeed at last*; after a long time; **b** done, performed, as the final one of a series of actions: *the last words he uttered*; *his last act was to provide for his children*; **c** sole remaining, surviving &c.: *last breath*; *last hope*; *one's last shilling, crust* &c. **3. a** Immediately before the present, or before some specified time: *last night, week, year*; *last vacation*; *last summer*; *as we saw in the last chapter*, i.e. the one before this; **b** most recent: *his last letter came a week ago*; *the last news I heard was that he was married*; also elliptically: *I hope you received my last* (letter); *the last I heard* &c.; **c** newest, most up-to-date: *the last thing in hats.* **4.** Most remote from what is postulated, desired, expected; most unlikely; most unsuitable: *the last man I want to see*; *the last person I expected to see*; *the last thing I should do*; *he is the last man to consult in such matters.* **5. a** Final, conclusive; leaving nothing more to be said, done, learnt &c.: *the last word in science*; **b** supreme, utmost: *of the last importance.*

last (**II.**), adv., fr. prec. **1.** In the last place, finally; after all others in place or turn: *to come last*; *to speak last*; also in combinations: *last-mentioned.* **2.** At a time immediately before the present; the last time or occasion: *when did you last go abroad?*; *I last met him in Oxford*; *when did you see her last?*

last (**III.**), n., fr. **last** (**I.**). **1.** That which is last **a** in a series, or succession: *the last of the Stewarts*; **b** in time: *I thought every moment would be my last*; **c** the last one of certain acts: *to breathe, look, one's last.* **2. a** The end; *to hold on to the last*; **b** final manifestation, appearance, mention &c.: *to see the last of*; *I shall never hear the last of that.*

last (**IV.**) n. O.E. *lāst*, 'sole of foot; track, footstep'; *lǣst*, 'boot'; O.H.G. *leist*, 'track'; Goth. *laists*, 'track'; fr. Gmc. **lais-*, cp. Goth. *laisjan*, 'to teach', O.E. *lǣran*, earlier **lār-jan*, fr. O.E. *lār*, 'teaching, doctrine', q.v. under **lore** (**I.**); cogn. w. Lat. *līra*, 'furrow', for **līsa*; cp. Lat. *de-līrāre*, 'to draw the furrow away; deviate from straight line'; (fig.) 'to be crazy'. See **delirium.** Mould, model of foot, upon which a shoemaker makes his boots and shoes. Phr. *to stick to one's last*, attend to one's business and duties.

last (**V.**), vb. intrans. O.E. *lǣstan*, trans., 'to follow; to help; to carry out, perform'; intrans. 'to continue, last, suffice'; M.E. *lesten*, *lasten*, 'to perform', but chiefly intrans. 'to last, continue, endure'. The orig. meaning is 'to track out, follow a track', hence, 'to pursue, carry out' &c., whence, 'to continue' &c. The O.E. vb. is fr. **lāst-jan*, fr. *lāst*, 'track' &c. See prec. **1. a** To continue in existence; to hold out, endure: *as long as life lasts*; *he can't last till morning*; *the frost has lasted a month*; **b** to keep on, continue: *how long will the performance last?*; *the sermon lasted an hour.* **2. a** To remain unimpaired, to suffer no exhaustion or diminution: *his strength lasted to the end of the journey*; *if my health lasts I will finish my work*; **b** to wear well, remain in good condition, be durable: *good woollen cloth lasts much longer than shoddy.* **3.** To suffice, be adequate: *a pound of tobacco only lasts me a fortnight*; *you must make your money last till you get home*; also *last out*: *our supply of coal will hardly last out the winter.*

last (**VI.**), n., fr. prec. Capacity for lasting; staying power, power of resistance.

last (**VII.**), n. O.E. *hlæst*, 'burden', fr. **hlædst*, fr. base of *hladan*, 'to load', q.v. under **lade.** Measure of weight or quantity, the amount of which varies according to the commodity; *last of meal* = ten barrels; *last of corn* = ten quarters, or eighty bushels.

lasting, adj. [1. láhsting; 2. lāstiŋ], fr. Pres. Part. of **last** (**V.**). Permanent, durable, enduring: *a lasting comfort, sorrow* &c.

lastingly, adv. Prec. & **-ly.** In a lasting manner.

lastingness, n. See prec. & **-ness.** Quality of being lasting; durability; permanence.

lastly, adv. [1. láhstli; 2. lāstli]. **last** (**I.**) & **-ly.** In the last place, finally.

latakia, n. [1. làtakéa; 2. lætəkíə]. Turk., fr. place of origin, the ancient Laodicea. A kind of strong Syrian tobacco used in smoking mixtures.

latch (**I.**), n. & vb. trans. & intrans. [1. lach; 2. lætʃ]. Etymol. doubtful; M.E. has *lacche*, 'catch, fastening', fr. *lacchen*, 'to seize, catch hold of', O.E. *læċċan*, prob. to be referred to same base as in Lat. *laqueus*, 'snare'. See **lace**; cp. **latchet. 1.** n. **a** Fastening for doors and windows; **b** special lock affixed to principal door of a house in addition to main lock, which can be opened by small key from the outside: *the door is on the latch*, fastened only by latch, and capable of being opened by small key from without. **2.** vb. **a** trans. To fasten (door or window) with a latch; **b** intrans., to be capable of being fastened with a latch.

latchet, n. [1. láchet; 2. lǽtʃit]. M.E. *lachet*, fr. O. Fr. *lachet*, 'thong', dial. variant of *lacet*, dimin. of **lace.** (obs. and Bib.) Leathern thong for fastening a shoe.

latch-key, n. Small, light key for opening a house door from without; *latch-key voter*, derisive name for a person who obtained a vote as a householder on rather slender grounds.

late (**I.**), adj. [1. lāt; 2. leit]. O.E. *læt*, 'behindhand; sluggish, slow'; M.E. *lāte*; cogn. w. O.H.G. *lazz*, 'lazy, slow'. Cp. also Lat. *lassus*, fr. **lad-tos*, 'languid, sluggish' (see **lassitude**). See further **let**, 'to hinder'. **1.** (predic.) **a** After the time expected, after the suitable, or agreed, fixed hour; behindhand: *the post is late today*; *late for one's own wedding*; *late for breakfast*; also preceded by *too* without adding much to the force: *too late for the train*; **b** after natural period or season; backward: *the crops are late this year*; Phrs. (*rather, very*) *late in the day*, too late; *to keep late hours*, go to bed and get up late. **2.** (attrib.) Occurring in an advanced stage, towards the end; typical of latter part of a period of time, of a season, or of an historical epoch: *the late afternoon*; *late summer*; *late eighteenth-century poetry*; *late Middle English*, that of 14th cent.; *late Gothic architecture.* Phr. *late dinner*, taken at night; comparative used in same sense but with loss of definiteness: *the later Middle Ages*; *the later Plantagenets*; *in the later spring.* **3.** (of a system, régime, form of activity, condition) Former; earlier than present; having recently come to an end: *the late Government*; *my late illness.* Phr. *of late years.* **4.** (of persons) **a** No longer living; dead before date of speaking, or that to which reference is made: *my late father*; *the late king*; **b** no longer holding specified office or status: *the late headmaster of X has gone to live in London.* **5.** (superl.) **a** Expressing novelty, what is most recent: *the latest news*, information. Phr. *the latest thing*, a novelty, up-to-date invention &c.; **b** referring to time: *at* (*the*) *latest*; *we must be there by 10 at* (*the*) *latest*, not later than 10.

late (**II.**), adv., fr. prec. **1. a** After the time or period fixed, expected, or regarded as suitable or natural: *to come late*; *to develop, blossom, ripen, late*; Phr. *better late than never*; **b** too late: *to arrive late for the train.* **2. a** At an advanced hour; towards the end of a given period of time: *to get up, go to bed, late*; Phr. *to dine late*, dine in the evening, not at midday; **b** to, up, down, to, an advanced hour: *to stay, sit, late.* **3.** Recently, lately, in Phr. *of late*: *I've been rather ill of late.*

lateen, adj. & n. [1. latén; 2. lætín], fr. Fr. *voile latine*, lit. 'Latin sail'. **a** adj. *Lateen sail*, triangular sail as used on small boats in Mediterranean; **b** n., vessel rigged with such a sail.

lately, adv. [1. lā́tli ; 2. léitli]. **late (I.)** & **-ly.** Of late, recently, during recent period.

laten, vb. trans. & intrans. [1. lā́t(e)n ; 2. léit(ə)n]. **late** & **-en. a** trans. To make late, or later; **b** intrans., to become late, or later.

latence, -cy, n. [1. lā́tens(i) ; 2. léitəns(i)]. **latent** & **-ce, -cy.** Quality, condition, of being latent.

lateness, n. [1. lā́tnes ; 2. léitnis]. **late (I.)** & **-ness.** Quality, condition, of being late : *lateness of arrival, of the season.*

latent, adj. [1. lā́tent ; 2. léitənt], fr. Lat. *latent-(em)*, Pres. Part. type of *latēre*, 'to lie hid, to lurk' ; fr. base **lə-* reduced grade of **la-* ; cp. Gk. *léthē*, 'forgetfulness, oblivion'. See **Lethe.** Cp. nasalized form in Gk. *lanthánein*, 'to be hidden' (cp. **lanthanum**). Hidden, concealed ; dormant ; present but not fully developed and apparent : *latent qualities, defects, disease* &c. ; specif., *latent heat*, e.g. of steam, quantity of heat absorbed by a liquid just before boiling-point, without an increase of temperature.

-later, suff. [1. later ; 2. lətə]. Gk. *látris*, 'worshipper'. See under **-latry.** Suffix forming nouns expressing an agent : *idolater* &c.

lateral (I.), adj. [1. láteral ; 2. lǽtərəl]. Lat. *laterālis*, 'pertaining to the side', fr. *later-*, stem of *latus*, 'side, flank' ; the connexions are doubtful, but cp. O. Ir. *leth*, 'side', W. *lled*, 'half'. **1.** Pertaining to, situated at, the side : *lateral branches.* **2.** (phon.) *Lateral consonant*, one formed by partial closure of air-passage by the tongue, which, however, is so placed as to allow the air-stream to pass out at one or both sides of point of contact during articulation; [l] is a lateral consonant. Also called *divided.*

lateral (II.), n., fr. prec. **1.** Something having a lateral position ; something springing, growing, from side ; e.g. a lateral shoot of a plant &c. **2.** A lateral consonant.

lateralize, vb. trans. [1. láteralīz ; 2. lǽtərəlaiz]. Prec. & **-ize.** To direct towards one side.

laterally, adv. [1. láterali ; 2. lǽtərəli]. **lateral** & **-ly.** From, on, towards the side.

Lateran, n. & adj. [1. láteran ; 2. lǽtərən], fr. name *Laterani* of the ancient family whose palace stood on site of the present church. **1.** n. *The Lateran*, Church of St. John Lateran in Rome. **2.** adj. Connected with, held in, the Lateran : *Lateran Council*, one of the General Councils of the Western Church.

latero-, pref. Form of Lat. *latus*, 'side', used in compounds, see **lateral** ; *latero-abdominal*, connected with the sides of the abdomen &c.

latex, n. [1. lā́teks ; 2. léiteks]. Lat., any fluid or liquid ; prob. fr. Gk. *látax*, 'drop of wine' ; cogn. w. O.N. *leþja*, 'filth' ; M. Ir. *laith*, 'beer'. (bot.) White, milky juice of plants, such as the rubber plant.

lath, n. [1. lahth ; 2. lāþ]. O.E. *lætt, læþþa* ; M.E. *latthe* ; related to O.H.G. *latta*, Mod. Germ. *lathe.* Origin doubtful. Thin, narrow, strip of wood ; specif., one of the thin pieces of wood nailed to rafters or joints, in building, to form basis for plastering, of ceilings, and partitions, or for fixing roofing tiles or slates &c. Phr. *thin as a lath* (of persons) very thin ; *lath painted to look like iron*, of a weak, timid man who affects an imposing, resolute expression and bearing.

lathe (I.), n. [1. lādh ; 2. leið]. Origin uncertain. Machine used in turning, by means of which a piece of wood or metal is rotated while the edge of a chisel is held against it, so as to cut the wood or metal into required shape.

lathe (II.), n. O.E. *lǣd*, 'landed estate' ; cp. **-latry.** One of the five, formerly six, administrative districts of the county of Kent.

lather (I.), n. [1. ládher ; 2. lǽðə]. O.E. *lēaþor*, 'washing soap', cogn. w. Gk. *loutrón*, 'bath, water for bathing', fr. *loú-ein*, 'bathe' &c. The base is found in Lat. *lavāre* &c., q.v. under **lave. a** Froth from soap and water ; **b** foamy sweat of a horse.

lather (II.), vb. intrans. & trans., fr. prec. **1. a** To form lather ; **b** to cover with lather. **2.** (colloq.) To thrash severely.

lathi, n. [1. lahtē ; 2. lā́tī]. Hind. A stout wooden staff, shod and bound with iron, used as a weapon by natives in India.

laticlave, n. [1. lā́tiklāv ; 2. léitikleiv], fr. Lat. *lāticlāvus*, fr. *lātus*, 'broad' (see **latitude**) & *clāvus*, 'nail, stripe', see **clavicle.** (Roman antiq.) A broad purple stripe down the two front edges of the toga, worn by senators &c., as a badge of their rank.

latifundia, n. pl. [1. lātifúndia ; 2. lèitifándiə]. Lat., pl. of *lātifundium*, fr. *lātus*, 'broad' (see **latitude**), & *fundus*, 'bottom, foundation; farm', see **fund (I.).** Large landed estates carried on by slave labour and owned by absentee capitalists &c., in ancient Italy.

Latin, adj. & n. [1. látin ; 2. lǽtin]. Fr., fr. Lat. *lingua Latīna*, 'Latin language' ; *Latīnus*, pertaining to Latium', i.e. part of Italy where this dialect was spoken. **1.** adj. **a** Belonging to Latium ; **b** pertaining to, written in, the language of Ancient Rome ; **c** pertaining to the languages descended from this, or to the races and peoples speaking the languages ; **d** pertaining to the Christian Church of the West. **2.** n. **a** Language of Ancient Rome ; *Old Latin*, before c. 75 B.C. ; *classical Latin*, literary language fr. c. 75 B.C. to c. A.D. 175 ; *Late Latin*, post-classical literary language to c. A.D. 600 ; *Low* or *Vulgar Latin*, popular speech in post-classical period ; *Mediaeval Latin*, from c. 600 to c. 1500 ; **b** member of one of the Latin races.

Latine, adv. [1. latī́ni ; 2. lætáini]. Lat. In Latin ; used in giving Latin equivalent of English word or expression.

Latinism, n. [1. látinizm ; 2. lǽtinizəm]. **Latin** & **-ism.** An idiom peculiar to Latin introduced into the style of another language.

Latinist, n. [1. látinist ; 2. lǽtinist]. **Latin** & **-ist.** A Latin scholar.

Latinistic, adj. [1. làtinístik ; 2. lætinístik]. Prec. & **-ic.** Pertaining to, of the nature of, characterized by, Latinism.

latinity, n. [1. latíniti ; 2. lətíniti]. Lat. *latīnitāt-(em).* **Latin** & **-ity.** Style, quality, of one's Latin scholarship.

latinize, vb. trans. & intrans. [1. látinīz ; 2. lǽtinaiz]. **Latin** & **-ize. 1.** trans. **a** To give a Latin form or character to word or style ; to put into Latin ; **b** to assimilate (peoples) to ancient Rome in ideas and mode of life ; **c** to render conformable to Latin Christianity ; specif., to diffuse the beliefs and practices of the Roman Church. **2.** intrans. To make use of Latin idioms.

latitude, n. [1. látitūd ; 2. lǽtitjūd]. Lat. *lātitūdo*, 'breadth', fr. *lātus*, 'broad, extensive' ; for **stlātus* ; cp. *stlātārius*, 'kind of broad ship' ; cogn. w. O. Slav. *steljǫ*, 'I spread out'. **1.** (geog.) Distance north and south from equator. **2.** Region of the earth considered in relation to its latitude : *cold latitudes.* **3.** Freedom of judgement, thought, action ; permitted freedom from restrictions ; specif., in religious opinions.

latitudinal, adj. [1. làtitū́dinal ; 2. lætitjū́dinəl]. Lat. *lātitūdin-*, stem of *lātitūdo.* See prec. & **-al.** (geog.) Pertaining to latitude ; in direction of latitude.

latitudinarian, adj. & n. [1. làtitūdinā́rian ; 2. lætitjūdinéəriən], fr. Lat. *lātitūdin-*, stem of *lātitūdo.* See prec. & **-arian. 1.** adj. Broad, liberal, in interpretation of rules and principles of conduct ; specif., untrammelled by literal or rigid interpretation of religious dogma ; generally used to imply a certain laxity or indefiniteness of belief. **2.** n. Person of latitudinarian principles.

latitudinarianism, n. [1. làtitūdinā́rianizm ; 2. lætitjūdinéəriənizəm]. Prec. & **-ism.** Latitudinarian system of religious beliefs ; liberal interpretation of dogma.

latrine, n. [1. latrḗn ; 2. lətrī́n]. Lat. *lātrīna*, 'a privy', fr. earlier *lavatrīna*, 'bath', fr. *lavāre*, 'to wash' (see **lave**) ; for development of meaning cp. **lavatory.** Privy, esp. in an institution or a camp.

-latry, suff. [1. latri ; 2. lətri], fr. Gk. *-latria, latreia*, 'worship', as in *eidōlatria*, 'worship of idols'. The base is seen in Gk. *latreúein*, 'to serve', *látris*, 'servant, worshipper', *látron*, 'pay', cogn. w. Lat. *latrōn-*, 'paid servant, mercenary' ; the orig. base **lē(i)-* is supposed to have meant 'grant, possession'. Cp. further, O.E. *lǣd*, 'landed property' ; Goth. *(un)lēds*, 'poor'. The suffix occurs not only in original Greek words such as *idolatry*, but in new formations such as *bibliolatry, Mariolatry* &c. It has the force of 'exaggerated devotion, false worship'.

latten, n. & adj. [1. láten ; 2. lǽtin]. M.E. *laton, latoun*, fr. O. Fr. *laton, laiton* ; etymol. uncertain. (obs.) **a** n. Yellow alloy of copper and zinc formerly used for making vessels, candle-sticks &c. ; **b** adj., made of latten.

latter, adj. [1. láter ; 2. lǽtə]. O.E. *lætra*, 'later', compar. of *læt*, 'late'. See **late.** The short vowel (cpd. w. that of *late*) is due to its position before *-tr-* ; *later* is a more recent formation straight fr. *late.* **1.** (obs.) Later : *the latter rain.* Phr. *these latter days*, recent and present periods of the world. **2.** (obs.) Latest, final ; now only in *latter end*, last moment of life ; death. **3.** Further removed in time from the beginning : *the latter half, part, of the year, latter end of June* &c., second half, part towards the end. **4.** The second of two, last mentioned of two ; contrasted with *former* : *I know both John and his brother, and I prefer the latter.*

Latter-day Saint, n. A Mormon.

latterly, adv. [1. láterli ; 2. lǽtəli]. **latter** & **-ly. a** Of late, lately ; in a time shortly before the present ; **b** towards the end of some period referred to.

lattice (I.), n. [1. látis ; 2. lǽtis]. M.E. *latis*, fr. O. Fr. *lattis* ; cp. Fr. *latte*, 'lath' ; of Gmc. origin, cp. **lath. 1.** Framework of wood or other material composed of thin laths or strips crossed diagonally, fastened together at each point where one crosses another, so as to form a net-like structure. **2.** Window or other opening protected by a lattice ; window with diagonal strips of lead, in form of a lattice, to hold the panes. **3.** (her.) Representation of a lattice having the strips crossed horizontally and vertically.

lattice (II.), vb. trans., fr. prec. To provide with, cover with, a lattice.

latticed, adj. [1. látist ; 2. lǽtist], fr. P.P. of prec. **a** Made in form of a lattice ; **b** provided with a lattice.

lattice-work, n. Latticing ; trellis-work.

latticing, n. [1. látising ; 2. lǽtisiŋ]. **lattice (II.)** & **-ing.** Lattice ; structure in form of a lattice.

laud, n. & vb. trans. [1. lawd ; 2. lɔ̄d]. O. Fr. *laude*, fr. Lat. *laud-(em)*, 'praise', acc. of *laus* ; prob. cogn. w. Goth. *liuþōn*, 'to sing', O.E. *lēoþ*, 'song, poem' ; O.H.G. *liod*, Mod. Germ. *lied*, 'song'. **1.** n. **a** Praise ; **b** in pl., *lauds*, the first of the 'hours' of the Christian Church, the office recited at daybreak. **2.** vb. To praise, extol ; to express approbation of.

laudability, n. [1. làwdabíliti ; 2. lɔ̄dəbíliti]. Next word & **-ity.** Praiseworthiness.

laudable, adj. [1. láwdabl ; 2. lɔ̄́dəbl]. **laud** & **-able.** Praiseworthy.

laudably, adv. Prec. & **-ly.** In a praiseworthy manner.

laudanum, n. [1. lódanum ; 2. lɔ́d(ə)nəm]. Transf. fr. Lat. *lādanum*, a juice obtained from a gum-resin. See **ladanum.** Tincture of opium.

laudation, n. [1. lawdā́shun ; 2. lɔ̄déiʃən]. Lat. *laudātiōn-(em)*, fr. *laudāt-(um)*, P.P. type of *laudāre*, 'to praise', fr. *laud-.* See **laud** & **-ion.** Action of lauding, or of being lauded ; high praise, commendation, eulogy.

laudative, adj. [1. láwdativ ; 2. lɔ̄́dətiv]. Lat. *laudātīvus*, 'expressing praise', fr. *laudāt-*, as in prec., & **-ive.** Expressing, signifying, praise.

laudatorily, adv. [1. láwdatorili ; 2. lɔ̄́dət(ə)rili]. See next word & **-ly.** In a manner expressing approbation and commendation.

laudatory, adj. [1. láwdatori; 2. lɔ́dət(ə)ri]. Lat. *laudāt-*, as in **laudation** &c., & **-ory**. Expressing praise and approbation, eulogistic; tending to commend.

Laudian, adj. [1. láwdian; 2. lɔ́diən], fr. name of Archbishop Laud (1573–1645). Pertaining to, connected with, the Archbishop, or with his character and principles.

laugh (I.), vb. intrans. & trans. [1. lahf; 2. lāf]. O.E. *hleahhan* &c., M.E. *lahen, laughen* &c.; O.S. *hlahan*; O.H.G. *hlahhan*, Mod. Germ. *lachen*; Goth. *hlahjan*; prob. imitative in origin, & connected w. Gk. *klázein*, for **klag(g)-j-*, 'to make a sharp, shrill sound; to rattle; scream, screech; to bark'; also to Gk. *klaggé*, 'a sharp, shrill sound'; Lat. *clangere*, 'to resound', *clangor*, 'noise' (see **clangour**); further, cp. Lith. *klegeti*, 'to laugh'. **A.** intrans. **1. a** To utter, often involuntarily, an inarticulate, usually voiced, sound, or series of such sounds, with the vocal organs, expressive of merriment, amusement, happiness, or contempt &c.; the sounds are frequently accompanied by a characteristic expression of the facial features, as in smiling; Phrs. *he laughs best who laughs last*; *to laugh in a person's face*, deride, defy him openly; *to laugh in one's sleeve*, be secretly amused; enjoy secret triumph; *to laugh on the wrong*, or, *on the other, side of one's mouth*, experience sudden disappointment and annoyance, esp. at failure of arrogant pretensions; **b** to be merry, crack jokes; **c** to feel amusement, gratification, triumph &c.: *I should laugh if he turned out to be wrong after all.* **2.** To typify, convey an impression of, thoughtless happiness, placid peace, prosperity &c.; said of waves (partly in reference to the sound of movement), of a landscape, and of nature generally. **3.** *Laugh at*: **a** to be amused, be made to laugh, by: *to laugh at a joke*; **b** to deride, treat as an object of ridicule, or contempt; make fun of: *to laugh at a person's appearance*; **c** to disregard, be unmoved by, be heedless of: *to laugh at threats, danger, fate, misfortune* &c. **4.** *Laugh over*, to consider, discuss, with laughter: *to laugh over a letter* &c. **B.** trans. **1.** Chiefly in certain phrases with preposition or adverb: *Laugh down*, to silence, render inaudible, by laughing: *to laugh down a speech. Laugh away*, to dismiss, dispel, with laughter: *to laugh away a person's fears. Laugh off*, to pass off, escape from, an embarrassing remark, situation &c. with laughter, or a joke. **2.** To utter with a laugh: *to laugh a reply.*

laugh (II.), n., fr. prec. **1.** The action of laughing: *to have a good, a hearty, laugh at the joke.* Phr. *to have the laugh of*, get the better of, score off. **2.** Sound made in laughing; burst of laughter: *someone gave a loud laugh*; individual quality, character, of a laugh: *a musical, harsh, ugly, laugh.* Phr. *to raise a laugh*, cause amusement.

laughing (I.), vbl. n. [1. láhfing; 2. láfiŋ], fr. **laugh** (I.) & **-ing**. Laughter: *too much laughing and talking.*

laughing (II.), adj., fr. Pres. Part. of **laugh** (I.). **1. a** Expressing merriment, amusement, happiness &c. by laughter, or by facial expression: *a laughing countenance*; **b** (fig.) conveying impression of peace, joy, prosperity &c. by external appearance: *the laughing face of nature*; *laughing wavelets* &c. **2.** Giving cause for, rise to, laughter or amusement; in Phr. *no laughing matter*, a very serious matter, not one for laughter.

laughing gas, n. Nitrous oxide used as an anaesthetic by dentists.

laughing hyena, n. Spotted hyena.

laughing jackass, n. Kind of kingfisher found in Australia, which utters a harsh cackling note.

laughing-stock, n. Person or thing that excites general ridicule.

laughter, n. [1. láhfter; 2. láftə]. O.E. *hleahtor*, M.E. *lahter* &c. See **laugh** (I.). Sound of laughing; burst of merriment. Phr. *Homeric laughter*, loud, uproarious, inextinguishable laughter.

launch (I.), vb. trans. & intrans. [1. lawnch, lahnch; 2. lɔntʃ, lāntʃ]. M.E. *lanchen, launchen*, variant of *lancen* &c., 'to drop, leap, shoot'. See **lance**. **A.** trans. **1. a** To hurl, fling, cast, cause to fly from hand &c. through the air: *to launch a spear, projectile* &c.; **b** to strike, aim: *to launch a blow*; **c** (fig.) to utter with force: *to launch an invective.* **2.** To cause to become active; to initiate, start, begin, some form of physical movement or activity: **a** specif. (mil.) *to launch an attack*; **b** (fig.) *to launch a campaign of abuse.* **3.** To cause a vessel to pass from the land into the water; to thrust it out: **a** (of any ship or boat, on any occasion) *to launch one's skiff from a landing-stage*; **b** to cause a newly built ship to pass into the water for the first time: *it is hoped that the new liner will be launched this year.* **4.** To start some form of activity for first time, cause to begin operations, set going: *to launch an enterprise, a new undertaking* &c. **B.** intrans. Followed by preposition or adverb. *Launch into*, plunge, embark on, throw oneself into with enthusiasm, vigour, recklessness &c.: *to launch into an argument*; *launch into dissipation, extravagance*; also *launch out into. Launch out*, (i.) to put out to sea, esp. on an adventurous voyage: *to launch out into the deep, on a voyage of discovery* &c.; (ii.) (fig.) to start, embark upon, some new enterprise: *he is launching out into a series of agricultural experiments*; (iii.) (absol.) to spend money freely and extravagantly.

launch (II.), n., fr. prec.; in sense **2** possibly a different word, fr. Span. *lancha*, 'pinnace', fr. Malay. *lanchar*, 'swift, speedy'. **1. a** Movement of vessel in being thrust, or of sliding, into the water; **b** act of launching a vessel. **2. a** Large boat carried by warship, used for transporting men, stores &c. to and from ship, driven by steam, oil, or petrol; **b** boat of any size driven by various means, used for short journeys of business or pleasure: *pleasure launch, motor launch* &c.

launder, vb. trans. & intrans. [1. láhnder, láwnder; 2. lándə, lɔ́ndə], fr. obs. M.E. n. *lavender*, O. Fr. *lavandier*, fr. Lat. *lavandus*, 'to be washed', fr. *lavāre*, 'to wash'. See **lave**. (obs. except in P.P.) To wash linen, carry on trade of a laundress: *beautifully laundered linen.*

laundress, n. [1. láhndres, láwndres; 2. lándris, lɔ́ndris], fr. prec. & **-ess**. Woman who washes clothes.

laundry, n. [1. láhndri, láwndri; 2. lándri, lɔ́ndri]. M.E. *lavenderie*, O. Fr. *lavanderie*. **launder** & **-y**. **1. a** Place, establishment, where clothes are washed; **b** process of washing clothes. **2.** (colloq.) Clothes sent to, or returned from, a laundry.

laureate, adj. & n. [1. lóreat, láwreat; 2. lɔ́riət, lɔ́riət]. Lat. *laureus*, 'laurel'; see next word & **-ate**. **1.** adj. Crowned with a laurel wreath. **2.** n. (usually cap.) In full, *Poet Laureate*, a poet appointed by the Crown, officially attached to the royal household, and nominally expected to write Court odes, and poems on great national occasions.

laurel, n. [1. lórel; 2. lɔ́rəl]. M.E. *lorer, laurer, lorel*; O. Fr. *laurier, lorier*, Lat. *laureus*, 'of laurel', fr. *laurus*, 'bay-tree, laurel; laurel crown; a triumph'; etymol. doubtful; Gk. *laûros* is fr. the Lat. **1.** One of several kinds of evergreen shrub, allied to the bay. **2.** (fig.) Recognition for services rendered; reward; chiefly in Phr. *to win, gain, laurels*, to gain approbation, recognition, prestige; *rest on one's laurels*, be content with what one has already done or gained.

laurelled, adj. [1. lóreld; 2. lɔ́rəld]. Prec. & **-ed**. **a** Crowned with laurel; **b** honoured, decorated, for merit and services rendered.

laurel water, n. Liquor containing prussic acid, distilled from leaves of the laurel.

laurustinus, n. [1. lòrus-, làwrustínus; 2. lɔ̀rəs-, lɔ̀rəstáinəs], fr. Lat. *laurus* (see **laurel**) & *tīnus*, 'a plant of the laurel tribe'; perh. named fr. its purging qualities, in wh. case the name may be cogn. w. O. Slav. *tina*, 'mud, mire'; O.E. *þīnan*, 'to become moist'; & w. first syll. of Gk. *tílos*, 'a purging'. Spring-flowering shrub of guelder rose tribe, *Viburnum tinus*, with pinkish-white blossoms.

lava, n. [1. láhva; 2. lávə]. Ital., connected w. *lavāre*, 'to wash'. See **lave**. Matter which flows in a fluid, molten state from a volcano and hardens as it cools.

lavabo, n. [1. laváhbō; 2. lævéibou]. Lat., 'I will wash', opening word of Ps. xxvi. 6. **1.** Ritual of washing celebrant's hands at the offertory, accompanied by repetition of the above-mentioned verse. **2.** Fixed basin in lavatories for washing hands (from Fr. *lavabo*, with transferred sense of 'basin').

lavation, n. [1. laváshun; 2. lævéiʃən]. Lat. *lavātiōn-(em)*, 'a washing, bathing', fr. *lavāt-(um)*, P.P. type of *lavāre*, 'to wash'. See **lave** & **-ion**. Process or act of washing; water for washing.

lavatory, n. [1. lávatori; 2. lǽvət(ə)ri]. Lat. *lavātōrium*, fr. *lavāt-(um)*, P.P. type of *lavāre*, 'to wash'. See **lave** & **-ory**. **a** Place or room for washing; room in house, hotel &c., esp. for washing hands; often associated with a privy; **b** euphemism for a privy.

lave, vb. trans. & intrans. [1. lāv; 2. leiv]. O.E. *lafian*, 'wash, pour'; this word is cogn. w. (or borrowed fr. ?) Lat. *lavāre*, 'wash, bathe' &c., whence Fr. *laver*, 'wash'. The vb. *lāve(n)*, 'pour out, wash', is fairly common in M.E. So far as the form goes the Mod. Engl. word might come fr. either the O.E. or the Fr. The sense of the two was nearly the same, though that of 'pour' belongs rather to the O.E.; prob. the two words have been blended in M.E., & subsequently. The Gk. cogn. is *loúein*, 'wash, bathe', fr. **lowein*; cp. also O.N. *laug*, 'warm bath', O.E. *lēag*, 'lye, ashes and water for washing', & *lēaþor*, 'lather'. See also **lather**. (chiefly poet.) **1.** trans. **a** To wash, bathe: '*With nectar pure his oozy locks he laves*' (Milton, 'Lycidas'); **b** (of a stream) to flow past or against, lap against. **2.** intrans. (rare) To bathe.

lavement, n. [1. lávment; 2. léivmənt]. Fr. See prec. & **-ment**. **a** A washing; **b** a clyster, an enema.

lavender, n. & adj. [1. lávender; 2. lǽvində]. M.E., fr. O. Fr. *lavendre*, L. Lat. *lavendula*. Origin uncertain. **1.** n. **a** Plant with very pungent, agreeably scented, pale purple flowers, growing on long, stiff, rather dry stalks, which have narrow greyish-green leaves growing from them at intervals; the strong characteristic perfume pervades the leaves and stalks as well as the flowers; **b** pale purple colour approximating to that of lavender flowers. **2.** adj. **a** Of, pertaining to, the lavender plant or its flowers; **b** of colour of lavender.

lavender-water, n. Scented liquid used as an article of toilet, distilled from lavender plant.

laver (I.), n. [1. láver; 2. léivə], fr. O. Fr. *laveoir*; fr. Lat. *lavātōrium*. See **lavatory**. Basin or other vessel for washing.

laver (II.), n. Lat. *laver*, 'a water plant', connected w. *lavāre*, 'to wash', see **lave**. Kind of edible seaweed.

laverock, n. [1. láverok; 2. lǽvərək]. Archaic, provinc. variant of **lark**.

lavish (I.), adj. [1. lávish; 2. lǽviʃ]. Perh. fr. O. Fr. *lavasse, lavache*, 'deluge of rain'; connected w. **lave**. **1.** (of persons) Profuse, generous, free: *lavish in, of one's, expenditure, hospitality, kindness*; *lavish of one's time, trouble, help, praise* &c.; *lavish in one's ideas, habits*, extravagant; (also absol.) *he's rather too lavish*, given to extravagance. **2.** (of something provided, given, offered &c.) **a** Abundant, generous, ample: *a lavish supply*; *lavish hospitality* &c.; **b** too profuse, superabundant, extravagant: *lavish expenditure.*

lavish (II.), vb. trans., fr. prec. **a** To bestow freely, generously: *to lavish money on the poor*;

to lavish care upon one's children; *to lavish one's affection on unworthy objects*; **b** to expend with prodigality, to squander: *to lavish one's money in self-indulgence*; *upon one's pleasures*.

lavishly, adv. **lavish (I.)** & **-ly**. In a lavish manner; generously, copiously; extravagantly.

lavishness, n. See prec. & **-ness**. **a** Quality of being lavish; **b** abundance, profusion; extravagance.

law, n. [1. law; 2. lɔ̄]. O.E. *lagu*, M.E. *lawe*. The O.E. word is fr. a primitive Scand. form wh. later in O.N. itself became *lōg*; the cogn. *lag* is found in O.S.; the base is that of the vbs. **lay (III.)** & **lie (III.)**, the fundamental meaning being 'something set, placed, fixed, laid down' &c. Cp. a similar development of meaning in Germ. *gesetz*, 'law'. **1.** Rule of action and conduct imposed by superior authority, enjoining what is right and prohibiting what is wrong: *the laws of God*; *law of Moses*. Phrs. *laws of the Medes and Persians*, system, practice &c. which never varies; *necessity knows no law*, is superior to, is compelled to override, ordinary rules. **2. a** Body of customary or enacted rules and practices, the observance of which is sanctioned and enforced by the supreme governing body in a State, and which are recognized by the community as binding: *the laws of England, the law of the land*; *the law of contract* &c.; **b** a specific act or enactment of the legislature; **c** law considered as a branch of knowledge; jurisprudence, legal science; Phr. *to lay down the law*, to assert one's opinions dictatorially; to hector; **d** the legal profession: *to follow the law, go in for law*; **e** the operation of law as a means of preserving rights and redressing wrongs; litigation: *to go to law*. Phrs. *to have the law of a person*, to prevent him from, or punish him for, inflicting an injury, by appealing to the law; *to take the law into one's own hands*, to decide on and pursue a line of action, in defence of one's rights, inflict punishment &c., without legal authority. **3.** Body of rules, usages or principles; procedure, action, behaviour, recognized and observed by custom and usage as correct; **a** (in morals) *laws of honour*; **b** (in art of all kinds) *the laws of perspective, painting, harmony, metre* &c.; **c** (in sport, games &c.) *the laws of the chase*; *the laws of golf* &c.; **d** *laws of thought*, principles of logical reasoning. **4.** (in science) **a** (i.) A sequence of natural processes or events in nature, a series of causes and effects observed to occur uniformly when the same conditions are present: *a law of nature*; *the law of gravity, of the conservation of energy* &c.; *phonetic law*; (ii.) a generalized statement or formulation of such a sequence of events and of the conditions under which they occur: *Dalton's Law, Grimm's Law* &c.; **b** (i.) a sequence of what are believed to be causes and effects observable in the relations of one set of human activities to another set, or to external conditions: *the law of supply and demand*; *economic laws*; (ii.) formulation of these causes and effects. **5.** Propensity, inherent, instinctive tendency of sentient beings to behave in a particular way under given conditions: *the law of self-preservation*. **6. a** Allowance of time, or distance granted to a competitor in a contest, or to an animal about to be hunted; start; **b** indulgence, grace: *to give a person five minutes' law before beginning dinner*.

law-abiding, adj. Adhering to, observing, the law; well-behaved, peaceable.

law agent, n. (Scotland) Solicitor acting for a party in a lawsuit or trial.

law-calf, n. Natural-coloured leather with roughish surface in which law books, ledgers &c. are bound.

law court, n. One in which legal causes are tried.

law-French, n. Form of Norman French in which proceedings in law courts were conducted from the Conquest to 1363.

lawful, adj. [1. láwfool; 2. lɔ́fəl]. **law** & **-ful**. **a** In accordance with the law; allowed by law, legitimate: *lawful authority*; *a lawful act*; **b** recognized, authorized, appointed, by law: *a lawful occasion*; *lawful possessor*. Phrs. *lawful age*, that at which full legal rights are enjoyed; majority; *lawful money*, legal tender.

lawfully, adv. Prec. & **-ly**. In a lawful manner; rightly, legally.

lawfulness, n. See prec. & **-ness**. Quality of being lawful.

lawgiver, n. [1. láwgiver; 2. lɔ́givə]. One who makes and promulgates laws; legislator.

lawgiving, adj. & n. [1. láwgiving; 2. lɔ́giviŋ]. **1.** adj. Legislative. **2.** n. Legislation.

law-Latin, n. That used in legal documents; Late, Low, Latin.

lawless, adj. [1. láwles; 2. lɔ́lis]. **law** & **-less**. **a** Not subject to, not observing, the law; **b** not in accordance with, not conforming to, the law; **c** not controlled or regulated by the law; unruly.

lawlessly, adv. Prec. & **-ly**. In a lawless manner.

lawlessness, n. See prec. & **-ness**. **a** Quality of being lawless; **b** lawless action, conduct; unruliness.

law-lord, n. Member of House of Lords who acts there in judicial capacity, and is qualified to sit as member of the highest court of appeal, as being one of the Lords of Appeal in Ordinary or as having held high judicial office.

law merchant, n. (hist.) Body of customs and regulations dealing with commerce and trade, as distinguished from the Common Law.

lawn (I.), n. [1. lawn; 2. lɔ̄n]. Formerly *laune lynen*, 'linen from Laon', fr. name of French town. **a** Fine, thin linen fabric; **b** a symbol of episcopal office, from the wide sleeves of this material worn by English bishops: '*Chicane in furs, and casuistry in lawn*' (Pope, 'Dunciad').

lawn (II.), n. M.E., fr. O. Fr. *launde*, Mod. Fr. *lande*, 'great stretch of uncultivated, barren land, heath'; fr. Celt.; cp. W. *llan*, 'clear, open space'; cogn. w. **land**. **1.** (poet.) Open space in wood or forest; glade. **2. a** Stretch of grass kept closely cut and rolled, in gardens; **b** specif., such a stretch of grass used for some game; often qualified: *croquet, tennis, lawn* &c.

lawn-mower, n. Machine furnished with blades fixed on a revolving cylinder, cutting against a fixed, flat blade, used for cutting lawns.

lawn-tennis, n. Form of tennis played upon an open court, on grass, gravel &c., or in covered court on a wooden floor, between either one or two players on each side, with racquets and felt-covered, hollow, india-rubber balls.

lawny (I.), adj. [1. láwni; 2. lɔ́ni], fr. **lawn (I.)** & **-y**. Made of, resembling, lawn.

lawny (II.), adj. **lawn (II.)** & **-y**. **1.** Abounding in lawns. **2.** Of the nature of a lawn.

law officer, n. Legal functionary and adviser of the Government; applied to *Attorney-General* and *Solicitor-General*.

law-sheep, n. Thick leather of sheepskin used in binding law books.

lawsuit, n. [1. láwsūt; 2. lɔ́sjūt]. **law** & **suit (I.)**. Action at law; case heard in a court of law.

law term, n. **a** Word or expression of technical meaning used in legal parlance; **b** period of year in which the courts are sitting.

lawyer, n. [1. láwyer; 2. lɔ́jə]. **law** & **-ier**. **1.** Member of the legal profession; esp. a solicitor: *I must consult my lawyer*; *family lawyer*, solicitor doing legal business for private persons; legal adviser on family business. **2.** Student of legal science; one skilled, learned, in this; a jurist: *a good advocate but a poor lawyer*.

lawyer-like, adj. After the manner of, like, becoming, a lawyer.

lawyerly, adj. [1. láwyerli; 2. lɔ́jəli]. Lawyer-like.

lax (I.), adj. [1. laks; 2. læks]. Lat. *laxus*, 'loose, wide'; cogn. w. **languid** & **slack (I.)**. **1.** Reverse of tense or firm; slack; (chiefly, fig., of morals, conduct, principles &c.), not rigid, remiss; licentious, dishonourable. **2.** (of bowels) Relaxed, open, free in action.

lax (II.), n., fr. prec. Looseness of intestines.

lax (III.), n. Scand.; cp. O.E. *leax*, 'salmon'. Smoke-dried salmon of Norway and Sweden.

laxative, adj. & n. [1. láksativ; 2. lǽksətiv], fr. Lat. *laxāt-(um)*, P.P. type of *laxāre*, 'to open, relax', see **lax (I.)**, & *-īvus* (see **-ive**). **1.** adj. **a** Tending to open or relax; **b** specif., tending to cause looseness of the bowels. **2.** n. A laxative medicine.

laxity, n. [1. láksiti; 2. lǽksiti]. **lax (I.)** & **-ity**. **1.** Want of exactness (in expression or style). **2. a** Lack of moral principle, of strictness, or firmness of character; **b** dissoluteness (of morals, or conduct).

laxness, n. [1. láksnes; 2. lǽksnis]. **lax** & **-ness**. Slackness.

lay (I.), n. [1. lā; 2. lei]. M.E., fr. O. Fr. *lai*; perh. fr. Celt. source; cp. O. Ir. *loid, laid*, 'poem'. Prob. unrelated to O.E. *lēoþ*, 'song, poem', q.v. under **laud**. **a** Short song; poem of a lyrical character; brief narrative poem, a ballad; **b** bird's song.

lay (II.), adj. M.E., fr. Fr. *lai*, fr. Lat. *lāicus*, fr. Gk. *laikós*, 'of, belonging to, the people', fr. *lāós*, 'people'; perh. for **lāwos*, & possibly orig. connected w. O.E. *lǣwede*, 'lay, layman', q.v. under **lewd**. **1.** Belonging to the laity as distinct from the clergy; not clerical. **2.** Not of, or connected with, some particular profession; non-professional.

lay (III.), vb. trans. & intrans. M.E. *leyen* &c., new formation by the side of orig. *leggen*, fr. O.E. type *leġ-(e)þ*, M.E. *ley(e)þ* &c., 3rd pers. sing. of *leċġan*, 'to lay, put in position'. The O.E. infin. is fr. earlier **læġ-jan*, the base being identical w. *læġ*, wh. is the normal Pret. of the strong vb. *liċġan*. See **lie (I.)**. General meanings: to place, put, set, dispose, impose; to place in a recumbent position. **A.** trans. **1.** To place, set, put down, deposit, in a certain place or position; to cause to lie; to apply: *to lay something on a shelf, on the ground*; *lay one's hand upon a person's shoulder*; *to lay one's head on a pillow*; *the axe is laid to the root of the tree*; *to lay the flattering unction to one's soul*, claim the merit of. Phrs. *to lay stress upon*, to emphasize; *to lay field to field*, to keep adding to one's possessions, acquire continually more land; *to lay one's finger on*, to detect and indicate; *don't dare to lay a finger on me*, don't touch me ever so lightly; *to lay eyes on*, catch sight of; *to lay hands on*, (i.) to ordain as priest or deacon, consecrate as bishop; (ii.) to get possession of, get hold of, grasp, seize: *he sticks to everything he can lay his hands on*; *I can't lay my hands on it*, can't find, get hold of; *to lay hold of*, seize, grasp; *to lay one's bones*, be buried; to die; *to lay to heart*, take, consider, seriously; *to lay heads together*, discuss, arrive at a common plan; *to lay oneself out for*, make arrangements to do; *to lay something at a person's door*, hold him responsible for, charge him with it. **2.** To cause to fall and lie prostrate by use of force; to strike down; in such Phr. as *to lay a man in the dust with a single blow*; &c.; Phr. *to lay by the heels*: **a** to put in the stocks, in prison; **b** (fig.) to put out of action, deprive of liberty of movement. **3.** To cause to abate, subside; to calm down, appease; to suppress: *to lay the dust*. Phr. *to lay a ghost*, exorcise, cause it to disappear. **4.** (of birds) To produce and deposit: *to lay eggs*. **5. a** To put in order, prepare (table) for a meal by placing cloth, silver, glass &c. upon it: *to lay a (the) table for dinner*; also **b** *to lay the cloth*, spread it upon the table; *to lay the plates* &c., put them in suitable places upon the table, for a meal. **6.** To stake, wager, bet: *to lay heavy odds that* &c.; specif., *to lay the odds*; (also absol.) of bookmaker, who accepts bets from 'backers'. **7. a** To ascribe to, charge with responsibility for: *to lay an accusation against*; *to lay a* *crime to one's charge*; **b** to present, exhibit, as evidence, produce as a deposition: *to lay information against*. **8.** To impose as a burden, duty, punishment: *to lay a tax upon*; *lay strict injunctions on* &c. **9.** To layer, pleach: *to lay a hedge*. **10.** To deposit, place, in proper position for desired purpose: *to lay bricks, a foundation stone*. Phr. *to lay the foundations of*, (fig.) to start going, make a beginning, found: *to lay a trap for*; *to lay one's plans*, make arrangements. **11.** To put, bring, into a given situation or condition: *to lay one's chest bare*; *to lay one's cheek open with a cut*; *to lay a country waste*. Phr. *to lay one's heart, one's plans, bare*, to speak one's mind openly; to divulge plans. **12.** To allege, put forward, assert: *to lay claim to*. **B.** intrans. **1.** To produce eggs: *the hens don't lay this cold weather*. **2.** To make a bet: *I'll lay you never saw anything better than that*. **C.** Followed by preposition or adverb. *Lay about* (*one*), intrans., to fight vigorously, hit out in all directions (lit. and fig.). *Lay aside*, trans., **1. a** to set aside, save, hoard: *lay aside money*; **b** to store up for future use, preserve: *to lay aside leaf-mould for the garden*; **c** set apart, dedicate: *to lay aside a day for golf*; **2. a** to give up, abandon, discontinue: *to lay aside the prejudices, bad habits &c. of a lifetime*; **b** to neglect, discard, forsake: *to lay aside old friends*; **3.** to incapacitate, put out of active participation in affairs &c., esp. of effects of illness: *he was laid aside for six months by an accident*. *Lay before*, trans., to exhibit, give exposé of, explain, bring to notice of: *to lay one's ideas, scheme &c. before a person*. *Lay by*, trans., **1.** same as *lay aside*; **2.** same as *lay to* (naut.). *Lay down*, trans., **1. a** to place in recumbent position; **b** specif., to place in a cellar &c. for storing; to acquire and deposit: *to lay down wine*; **2.** to assert as a fact or principle, maintain: *to lay it down as an axiom that* &c.; Phr. *to lay down the law*, talk dogmatically, dictate; **3.** to discard, abandon, relinquish: *to lay down arms, an office*; *to lay down one's life*, sacrifice, give it up voluntarily; **4.** to plan out, start construction of, sketch out scheme for; construct: *to lay down a plan, a battleship*; **5.** to plant: *to lay a field down in grass* &c. *Lay in*, trans., **1.** to gather together and preserve a stock or store: *to lay in provisions, coal, for the winter*; Phr. (colloq.) *to lay in a good meal*, to eat; **2.** (gardening) **a** esp. *lay in by the heels*, to plant temporarily in shallow soil and tread in; **b** to train, arrange shoots &c. in desired positions: *to lay in a hedge*. *Lay off*, trans. & intrans., (naut.) to steer (a vessel) further away from shore or another ship. *Lay on*, trans. & intrans., **1.** trans., **a** to apply with violence, inflict: *to lay on strokes, blows* &c.; Phr. *to lay it on*, administer a sound thrashing; **b** to apply, spread: *to lay on paint, plaster* &c.; Phr. *to lay it on*, (fig.) to bestow excessive, or fulsome, praise; also *to lay it on with a trowel*; **2.** intrans., to make an attack: '*lay on, Macduff*'; to perform act of beating. *Lay open*, trans., **1. a** to open up, uncover; **b** (fig.) to reveal, expose, lay bare; **2.** *lay oneself open* (*to attack* &c.) to expose to, incur risk of, render liable. *Lay out*, trans., **1. a** to spread out, in order, for use: *to lay out one's evening clothes*; **b** specif., to arrange, compose, limbs decently for burial: *to lay out a corpse*; **c** (colloq.) to knock down, knock out, cause to fall prone and helpless by use of violence: *to lay a man out with a blow under the jaw*; **2.** to plan out, scheme out, devise; trace, mark out lines, proportions, disposition of: *to lay out an orchard, a garden*; Phr. *lay oneself out* (*for*), prepare (oneself), be disposed; **3.** to expend, invest: *to lay out one's money*. *Lay to* (naut.), **a** trans., to bring (ship) into the wind and hold still; **b** intrans., (of ship &c.) to lie with head to wind without moving. *Lay up*, trans., **1.** to amass, put by, store up: *to lay up treasure*; **2. a** to put aside temporarily from use, active service: *to lay up a ship for repairs*; **b** to put out of action, incapacitate through illness: *laid up with gout*.

lay (IV.), n., fr. prec. **1.** (slang) Course, plan, of action; field of operations; job, business: *to start a new lay*. **2.** Way in which something lies in relation to other things; mode of arrangement; disposition: *the lay* (also *lie*) *of the land*.

lay (V.), vb. O.E. *læġ*, M.E. *lei*, *lay*, Pret. of **lie**.

lay days, n. pl. For *delay days*. Days allowed for loading or unloading a vessel within which no charge is made for demurrage.

layer (I.), n. **lay** (III.) & **-er**. **1.** (usually [1. lār; 2. lɛə)] One thickness of a substance lying upon another; stratum. **2.** [1. lắer; 2. léiə]. **a** One who lays odds; **b** female bird which lays eggs: *Rhode Islands are excellent layers*. **3.** [1. lār; 2. lɛə] Shoot of plant or branch of growing shrub bent down and partly covered with earth to encourage rooting, without being detached from parent stem.

layer (II.), vb. trans. [1. lār; 2. lɛə], fr. prec. To treat (plants) by layering.

layerage, n. [1. lắrij; 2. léərídž]. **layer** (I.) & **-age**. Propagation by layering.

layering, n. [1. lắring; 2. léəriŋ]. Process of causing branch of growing shrub &c., to strike by bending down and covering with earth at one point; layerage.

layette, n. [1. lāyét; 2. lèi(j)ét]. Fr., dimin. fr. *laie*, 'box, coffer', fr. Germ. *lade*, 'drawer', & **-ette**. Set of clothes, blankets &c. for a newly born baby.

lay figure, n. Formerly *layman*, fr. Du. *ledeman*; *lede* means 'joint, limb', & is cogn. w. O.E. *liþ*, Goth. *liþus*; Germ. *glied*, fr. *ga-lied*. The base **li-* is found again in **limb** (I.). **a** Model of human figure with joints to all the limbs, used by painters, in absence of human model, to hang drapery upon; **b** person who has no individuality and plays no active part in affairs with which he and his name are connected.

laying, n. [1. lắing; 2. léi-iŋ]. **lay** (III.) & **-ing**. **1.** Action of person who lays, in various senses. **2.** A clutch of eggs.

laylock, n. & adj. [1. lắlok; 2. léilɔk]. An old and now provincial variant of lilac, q.v.

layman, n. [1. lắman; 2. léimən]. **lay** (II.) & **-man**. **1.** One not in holy orders; contrasted with *priest, clergyman* &c. **2. a** One who is not a member of a particular profession; **b** one who is not an expert in some special branch of knowledge.

layout, n. [1. lắout; 2. lèiáut]. **a** Act of laying out or planning (a garden &c.); **b** plan, mode in which something, esp. a garden, estate &c., is designed, laid out, arranged.

lay shaft, n. Secondary shaft of a machine; one driven and working independently of main parts of machine.

lazar, n. [1. lázar; 2. lǽzə]. Fr. *lazare*, fr. *Lazarus*. **a** Diseased, filthy beggar; one in lowest stage of poverty and misery; also **b** (archaic) a leper.

lazaret, n. [1. lazaret; 2. lǽzərət]. Fr., fr. Ital. See next word. Lazaretto.

lazaretto, n. [1. làzarétō; 2. lǽzərétou]. Ital., fr. name *Lazarus*. **1.** Public institution for the poor suffering from leprosy or contagious diseases; a pest-house. **2.** (naut.) Space between decks in stern of a vessel, often used as storehouse.

laze, vb. intrans. [1. lāz; 2. leiz]. Formed fr. **lazy**. **1.** To spend time in a lazy, idle manner; to loaf about, waste one's time in idleness. **2.** To take it easy after strenuous effort.

lazily, adv. [1. lắzili; 2. léizili]. **lazy** & **-ly**. In a lazy, slothful manner.

laziness, n. [1. lắzines; 2. léizinis]. See next word & **-ness**. State of being lazy; sloth, disinclination to work.

lazy, adj. [1. lắzi; 2. léizi]. Not found before 16th cent. Origin uncertain. Disinclined for activity; idle, slothful.

lazy-bones, n. (colloq.) A lazy person.

lazy-tongs, n. Device for grasping small objects which are just out of reach of the arm, consisting of a series of strips of jointed metal in form of trellis-work, with loops like those of scissors for finger and thumb at one end, and flattened pieces of metal at right angles to the general structure at the other; when the finger and thumb are brought together the metal strips straighten at the joints so that the grasping ends are thrust out to a distance of two or three feet from the hand.

-le. Formative suff., fr. M.E. *-el*, *-il*, of various origins. See also **-el** & **-al**. **1.** From O.E. *-ol*, *-ul*, *-el*; **a** in ns. expressing an agent, or instrument; formed fr. vbl. stems: *beadle*, O.E. *bydel*, 'messenger'; *girdle*, O.E. *gyrdel*; *stile*, O.E. *stigol*, 'place for climbing over a fence', fr. *stīgan*, 'to climb' &c.; *ladle*, O.E. *hlædel*; *bridle*, O.E. *brīdel*, fr. **briġdil*, fr. base *bregd-*, 'to draw, pull' &c.; **b** in ns. where the suff. had orig. a dimin. force: *thimble*, O.E. *þȳmel*, fr. *þūma*, 'thumb'; *hurdle*, O.E. *hyrdel*, fr. **hurðil*, cp. Goth. *haurds*, 'a door', O.H.G. &c., *hurt*; *icicle*, O.E. *-ġycel*, 'small piece of ice', cp. O.N. *jökul* & *joki*, 'piece of ice'. **2.** In adjs. fr. vbs. the suff. expresses tendency towards action or process expressed by the vb.: *brittle*, fr. O.E. *brēotan*, 'to break'; *fickle*, O.E. *ficol*, 'treacherous', fr. (*be-*)*fician*, 'to betray'. **3.** In vbs. the suff. often represents the O.E. *-lian*, formerly freq., though this force is often considerably weakened: *wrestle*, O.E. *wrǣstlian*; many of the vbs. in *-le* in Mod. Engl. are new formations, such as *sprinkle, nestle, snuggle, frizzle, guzzle* &c. **4.** (i.) O. Fr. *-el*, Lat. *-ellum*: *castle*, O. Fr. *castel*, Lat. *castellum*; (ii.) O. Fr. *-el*, Lat. *-āle*: *cattle*, M.E. fr. O. Fr. *cattel*, Lat. *cap(i)tāle*; (iii.) O. Fr. *-aille* &c., Lat. *-ālia*, *battle*; (iv.) O. Fr. *-eille* &c., Lat. *-icula*, *bottle* &c. **5.** Lat. dimin. *-ulus* &c.: *angle*, Lat. *angulus*. **6.** Fr. *-ille*: *cockle* (shell).

lea (I.), n. [1. lē; 2. lī]. O.E. *lēah*, 'field', M.E. *lēi*, *lēh* &c., O.H.G. *lōh*, cogn. w. Lat. *lūcus*, 'grove', fr. **leukos*, & Lith. *laũkas*, 'open field'; fr. base in Lat. *lūx*, 'light'. See **lucent, lucus**. A *lea* was originally a clearance, in a forest, or land cleared of forest, contrasted with **field**. (poet.) Stretch of open grassy country. Common in place-names, spelt *-ley*, *-leigh*, *-ly* &c.

lea (II.), n. Prob. new formation fr. *leas*, taken as pl., fr. O. Fr. *lier*, 'to bind'. See **ligature**. Length of yarn, varying in different districts.

leach (I.), vb. trans. & intrans. [1. lēch; 2. lītʃ]. O.E. *leċċan*, 'to water, lave'; connected w. O.E. *lacu*, 'stream' &c. See **lake** (I.). **1.** trans. **a** To moisten; cause (liquid) to percolate through some material; **b** to saturate, steep, (bark, ashes &c.), with a percolating fluid. **2.** intrans. To melt, dissolve.

leach (II.), n., fr. prec. Perforated vessel used in leaching.

lead (I.), n. [1. led; 2. lɛd]. O.E. *lēad*, M.E. *lēde*; M.L.G. *lōd*, 'weight, plummet'. **1.** A heavy, pliable white metal, which soon tarnishes and becomes dull grey in colour. Phr. *as heavy as lead*, very heavy. **2.** Lump of lead, plummet, used in sounding; *to heave the lead*, take soundings. **3.** (obs.) Vessel, kettle, cauldron made of some alloy of lead. **4.** *Leads*, (coll.) roofs, passages between roofing, flat tops of building &c., covered with lead. **5.** Strip of metal placed between lines of type. **6. a** Black-lead, used for polishing grates &c.; **b** the marking material in a pencil; graphite; small length of this material for insertion into a metal pencil-case; **c** red lead, red oxide of lead, minium.

lead (II.), adj., fr. prec. Made of lead.

lead (III.), vb. trans., fr. **lead** (I.). To cover, fill, stop, with lead.

lead (IV.), vb. trans. & intrans. [1. lēd; 2. līd]. O.E. *lǣdan*, 'to lead, guide, convey' &c.; M.E. *lēden*; the O.E. vb. is fr. **lād-jan*, cp. O.E. *lād*, 'path, track, way, course', q.v. under **load** (I.); cp. also O.H.G. *leiten*, O.S *lēdian*; w. a different grade, but closely related, are O.E. *līþan*, 'to travel, sail'; O.S. *līthan*; Goth. *(ga)leiþan*, 'to go', *(af)leiþan*, 'to go away'; connexion w. Lat. *lītus*, 'shore', wh. was formerly suggested, is now no longer believed in. **A.** trans. **1. a** To conduct, guide, direct course of by physical contact: *to lead a person by the hand*; *to lead a horse by his bridle*; **b** specif., *to lead a horse*, to walk, or ride beside him, holding a rein or lead attached to him, as contrasted with riding on his back. Phrs. *the blind leading the blind*, (fig.) one ignorant, ill-informed person instructing another; *to lead astray*, mislead, set bad example to; *to lead the way*, to go first, show the path, direction &c.; *to lead by the nose*, to dominate and persuade to do anything one wishes; *to lead (a woman) to the altar*, marry her. **2. a** To induce to follow a line of action by persuasion or example: *he may be led but won't be coerced*; **b** to persuade to think in a particular way, induce to come to a certain logical conclusion; to incline; predispose: *I am led from all I hear to agree with you*; *I am led to believe*, I have information which causes me to believe; *what you say leads me to refuse*; Phr. *to lead one to expect*, raise expectations in; **c** to be the motive of an action; to prompt: *fear led him to tell lies*; *curiosity led me to look again.* **3. a** To have direction, act as chief of; conduct, guide: *to lead a polar expedition*; **b** to direct, govern, unify, the activities of a company of performers, indicate the part of each in relation to all: *to lead an orchestra, a ballet* &c.; **c** (mil.) to command, act as chief officer, direct operations of: *to lead an army.* Phr. *to lead the House*, act as official spokesman. **4. a** (of road, track &c.) To give access to, serve one as a passage to, bring one to: *that path will lead you straight to the house*; **b** to convey, act as conductor, conduit to: *gutters lead the water away from the roof.* **5. a** To pursue, pass, spend; *to lead a happy life*; **b** to cause to spend: *to lead a person a dog's life.* **6.** To go first, precede, go in front: *the choir leads the procession, the bishop comes last.* **7.** (cards) To begin a round by playing: *to lead trumps.* **8.** (Scots law) To tender, testify, state on oath: *to lead evidence.* **B.** intrans. **1.** To act as guide, director, commander; specif., to act as principal counsel in law case: *to lead for the prosecution, defence* &c. **2.** n. **a** To be ahead, be first, outstrip others, in a race or contest: *the big chestnut was leading by several lengths*; *the Conservative candidate appeared to lead from the first*; **b** (fig.) to be superior to others, to excel: *as a preacher he certainly leads.* **3.** (of road &c.) To extend, go, pass, run, form mode of approach to: *where does this road lead?* Phrs. *all roads lead to Rome*, there are many ways of attaining the same end; *to lead nowhere*, to have no result. **C.** Followed by preposition or adverb. *Lead out*, trans. & intrans., **1.** trans., to conduct (lady) from her place, to begin a dance &c.; **2.** intrans., *lead out of* (of rooms &c.), to communicate with directly: *my room leads out of the hall. Lead off*, intrans., to start, begin, make a beginning: *he led off by making an apology. Lead to*, intrans., **1.** to go, extend to, reach: *what place does this road lead to?*; **2.** to result in, produce, have as a result, as an effect: *poverty often leads to crime*; *to lead to a poor result. Lead up to*, intrans., to approach gradually, prepare the way for, by preliminary remarks in conversation: *to lead up to a favourite story, to a subject of discussion.*

lead (V.), n., fr. prec. **1. a** Action of leading; direction, command; power of initiation: *to take the lead in planning a campaign* &c.; **b** directions, instructions, suggestion, how to act: *I wish you would give me a lead in this business*; **c** specif., hunting, encouragement given to a rider or horse by leaping a fence in front of him: *a lead over a hedge.* **2.** Position (in contest &c.) in advance of others, priority; amount by which one leads: *to gain the lead in a race*; *a lead of several yards.* **3.** (cards) **a** Right of playing first in a round or game; **b** card, suit, which a player leads. **4.** (theatr.) **a** Principal part or rôle in a play; **b** person who plays this. **5.** Strap, cord, for leading a horse or dog. **6.** Watercourse leading to a mill. **7.** (elect.) **a** An electrical conductor; **b** a term indicating acceleration, converse of *lag.*

leaden, adj. [1. léd(e)n; 2. léd(ə)n]. **lead** (I.) & **-en. 1. a** Made of lead; **b** having colour of lead, of a dull grey. **2.** (fig.) **a** Heavy, sluggish, dull: *leaden slumber*; **b** inert, unresponsive: *a leaden heart, mind.*

leadenness. n. [1. lédnnes; 2. lédnnis]. Prec. & **-ness.** Quality of being leaden (chiefly fig.).

leader, n. [1. léder; 2. lídə]. **lead** (IV.) & **-er. 1.** Person who leads (in various senses); specif. **a** *leader of the House*, official member of Government who acts as conductor of business, and who initiates discussion in Parliament; **b** principal, senior, counsel on either side who conducts case in a law court; senior counsel on circuit. **2.** One of the two horses of a team of four who are farthest from driver; foremost horse in a tandem. **3. a** The highest and most recent growth of the main stem of a tree; **b** strongest, and longest shoot from a branch. **4.** One of the principal and longer articles in a newspaper; leading article. **5.** A sinew, tendon.

leaderette, n. [1. lèderét; 2. lìdərét]. Prec. **4** & **-ette.** Short editorial paragraph in a newspaper, printed in same type as leading articles.

lead-in, n. **lead** (IV.) & **in.** (wireless) Wire or other conductor connecting an aerial to a receiver.

leading (I.), n. [1. léding; 2. lédiŋ]. **lead** (I.) & **-ing.** Leadwork; e.g. strips of lead holding small panes in casement windows.

leading (II.), n. [1. léding; 2. lídiŋ]. **lead** (IV.) & **-ing.** Direction, guidance; leadership. Phr. *men of light and leading*, of recognized authority and influence.

leading (III.), adj. Pres. Part. of **lead** (IV.). Directing, controlling; giving guidance; foremost, pre-eminent: *a leading writer*; *the leading topics of the hour*; *a leading light in popular theology.* Phr. *leading lady, man*, actress, actor, playing a principal part.

leading article, n. Editorial article in a newspaper, either political, expressing the paper's policy, or social.

leading case, n. Legal case the decision in which serves as a precedent for subsequent cases involving same points of law.

leading question, n. (law) Question so framed as to suggest the answer that the questioner wishes to receive.

leading-rein, n. Strap or cord attached by one end to horse's bit, the other end being held in the hand of a rider on another horse.

leading-strings, n. pl. Straps or tapes for supporting and guiding young children just learning to walk. Phr. (fig.) *in leading strings*, in undue dependence, under excessive control by another, in a state of childish dependence.

lead-off, n. **lead** (IV.) & **off.** Start, beginning.

lead pencil, n. See **lead** (I.). Pencil composed of graphite enclosed in wooden casing.

lead poisoning, n. Pathological condition due to the absorption of lead into the human organism; plumbism.

leady, adj. [1. lédi; 2. lédi]. **lead** (I.) & **-y.** Containing, resembling, lead.

leaf (I.), n. [1. lēf; 2. lif]. O.E. *lēaf*, M.E. *lēf(e)*; O.S. *lōf*, O.H.G. *loub*, 'leaf, foliage'; Goth. *laufs*; cp. Lith. *lùbas*, 'rind of a tree'; O. Slav. *lubu*, 'bast, inner rind of a tree'. With these we may prob. equate Lat. *liber*, fr. **luber*, 'inner rind of a tree; this material used for writing upon; collection of writings consisting of several leaves; a book' (see **library**). Cp. also Gk. *lopós*, 'shell, husk, bark, peel', & *lépein*, 'to strip off rind, to peel'. The vowels of the last two words are difficult to equate w. the *ou, u* series seen in the other words. The final consonant of the base is also doubtful. There may have been two closely related bases, **leup-*, **lup-* &c., & **leubh-*, **lubh-* &c. **1.** (bot.) **a** One of the lateral growths from plant stem which occur at definite intervals along extent of this; **b** (popularly) one of the flat, expanded, green, most abundant organs of a plant, as distinguished from the flowers, which serve to absorb nourishment from the air (strictly, these are called *foliage leaves*); **c** (coll.) leaves as a whole, foliage. Phrs. *in leaf*, having the leaves expanded; *the fall of the leaf*, autumn; *to come into leaf*, to have leaf-buds open. **2.** The leaves of a plant considered collectively as an article of commerce, as of tea, tobacco. **3.** Any of various thin, flat objects suggestive of a leaf in shape; **a** sheet of paper, esp. a page of a book: *to turn over the leaves, cut the leaves* &c.; Phrs. *to take a leaf out of somebody's book*, to copy him, follow his example; *to turn over a new leaf*, make a fresh start, behave better for the future; **b** hinged flap of a table; portion of top of a table which can be inserted or removed; **c** exceedingly thin sheets of metal, thinner than *foil*, e.g. *gold leaf.*

leaf (II.), vb. intrans., fr. prec. (of trees &c.) To come into leaf.

leafage, n. [1. léfij; 2. lífidž]. **leaf** (I.) & **-age.** Leaves collectively, foliage.

leaf-bud, n. Bud which develops into a leaf and not a flower.

leafiness, n. [1. léfines; 2. lífinis]. **leafy** & **-ness.** Condition of having (abundance of) leaves.

leaf insect, n. An orthopterous insect of the E. Indies &c., which resembles a leaf.

leafless, adj. [1. léfles; 2. líflis]. **leaf** (I.) & **-less.** Devoid, bare, of leaves.

leaflessness, n. Prec. & **-ness.** Condition of being bare of leaves.

leaflet, n. [1. léflet; 2. líflit]. **leaf** (I.) & **-let. 1.** A little leaf; a division of a compound leaf. **2.** A folded, unstitched printed sheet, containing a notice, advertisement &c.

leaf-mould, n. Mould consisting of fallen leaves piled up and allowed to rot down, used for manuring garden soil.

leafy, adj. [1. léfi; 2. lífi]. **leaf** (I.) & **-y. 1. a** Bearing leaves freely; **b** covered with, having an abundance of, leaves. **2.** Consisting of, produced by, leaves: *leafy shade.*

league (I.), n. [1. lēg; 2. līg]. O. Fr. *legue*, whence Fr. *lieue*, Low Lat. *leuga, leuca*; prob. Gaulish. An old measure of distance varying in different times and countries; an English league was three miles.

league (II.), n. Fr. *ligue*, 'confederacy' &c., fr. Lat. *ligāre*, 'to bind'. See **ligament. a** Compact, alliance, made between individuals or nations for mutual protection and support, for promotion of peace, common interests &c.; **b** body of individuals who are parties to such a compact; group of clubs, as football or cricket, for playing each other for a championship.

league (III.), vb. trans. & intrans., fr. prec. **1.** trans. To form into a league, cause to become allied &c. **2.** intrans. To become a league, to unite with others in forming a league: *to league together against a common enemy.*

leaguer (I.), n. [1. léger; 2. lígə]. Prec. & **-er.** Member of a league (of individuals).

leaguer (II.), n., fr. Du. *leger*, 'camp'; cp. Germ. *lager*; cogn. w. **lair.** Cp. **beleaguer.** (archaic) A camp, esp. a siege camp.

leak (I.), vb. intrans. [1. lēk; 2. lik], fr. O.N. *leka*, 'to drip, leak'; cogn. w. O.E. *leċċan*, 'to moisten, water'. See **leach** (I.). **1. a** (of a boat or ship) To allow water to flow slowly in through a fissure, flaw, chink: *the boat is leaking*; **b** (of other things) to allow liquid, steam, gas, to drip or flow, pass slowly, out through a crack or chink: *the cistern, kettle, boiler &c. is leaking*; the word always implies an undesired and unintentional passage of liquid in or out. **2. a** (of liquid, steam, gas) *leak in, leak out*, to pass, drip, ooze, into, or out of, a receptacle, vessel &c., through a chink, flaw, crack &c.; **b** (fig., of news, a secret, information &c.) *leak out*, to become known improperly through carelessness or treachery.

leak (II.), n. A new formation fr. prec. vb. **1. a** The hole, crack, flaw, or crevice caused by accident, wear &c., through which liquid passes from vessel containing it: *a leak in a boiler*; **b** hole, crack &c. in a ship through which water passes into interior of vessel: *a leak in a ship*. Phr. *to start, spring, a leak*, to begin leaking. **2.** The water, steam &c. or other liquid, or gas, which passes through a chink or flaw in a receptacle, or ship; the amount which passes. **3. a** (elect.) Escape of electric charge from an incompletely insulated conductor, e.g. in a condenser; **b** (wireless) also *grid-leak*, high resistance providing a path for leakage of positive current from grid electrode of valve.

leakage, n. [1. lékij; 2. líkidž]. **leak** (I.) & **-age. a** Process of leaking; leak; **b** the amount of liquid, steam, gas &c. which passes through a leak; **c** (fig.) unauthorized, undesired transpiring of information, secrets &c.

leakiness, n. [1. lékines; 2. líkinis]. **leaky** & **-ness**. Condition of having a leak, of being leaky.

leaky, adj. [1. léki; 2. líki]. **leak** (II.) & **-y**. Having a leak; inclined to leak.

leal, adj. [1. lēl; 2. līəl]. Variant of **loyal**; O. Fr. *leal*, fr. Lat. *legālis*. (obs. or liter.) Loyal, true, faithful; *land of the leal*, heaven.

lean (I.), adj. & n. [1. lēn; 2. līn]. O.E. *hlǣne*, M.E. *lēne*, 'lean, thin'; prob. orig. 'bending, inclined to droop'; hence 'slender, thin, lean'. See **lean** (II.). **1.** adj. **a** Thin, reverse of fat (of persons and animals); **b** containing no fat (of meat); **c** (fig.) unproductive, impoverished: *lean years*. **2.** n. **a** The muscular part of meat, as contrasted with the *fat*; **b** (fig.) what is unproductive or unprofitable.

lean (II.), vb. intrans. & trans. O.E. *hlǣnan*, fr. **hlānjan*, 'to cause to incline' (trans.); M.E. *lēnen*; O.H.G. *hleinen*; cp. Goth. *hlains*, 'hill or slope'; O.N. *hlein*, 'cliff'. From another grade of same base comes O.E. *hleonian*, fr. **hlinōjan*, 'to slope'; O.S. *hlinōn*. The base is **klein-*, **kloin-*, **klin-*, whence Lat. *acclīnāre*, 'to lean against'; *inclīnāre*, 'to bend, cause to bend' (see **incline**); *declīnāre*, 'turn aside from' &c. (see **decline**). See further under **climate, climax, clinic**, &, w. different formative elements, **clement, ladder, lid. A.** intrans. **1.** To be out of, deviate from, the perpendicular; to incline: *the wall, tower, leans somewhat; to lean to the right*. **2. a** (i.) To press downwards upon, prop oneself upon, support one's weight on: *to lean on a person's arm, upon one's elbow, on a gate*; (ii.) (fig.) to rely, depend upon (person) for moral support; **b** to stand in a sloping position, pressing against; to rest against: *to lean against a wall, a tree* &c.; **c** *lean forward*, to sit or stand with upper part of body inclined forward; **d** *lean out* (*of the window*), to thrust upper portion of the body forward so that it projects beyond the sash, while standing or sitting inside. **3.** To be inclined to in opinions, desires &c.; to prefer: *I rather lean to your view*; *to lean towards staying where one is*. **B.** trans. To cause to lean, incline, or rest against: *to lean one's stick against a wall*; *to lean one's back against a tree*.

lean (III.), n., fr. prec. A slope, deviation from perpendicular: *a wall with a slight lean*.

leaning, n. [1. léning; 2. líniŋ]. **lean** (II.) & **-ing**. Act of one who, that which, leans (in various senses); (chiefly in non-material sense) inclination of the mind, desires, opinions &c.; predilection, tendency, penchant: *a leaning to ritualism*; *a distinct leaning towards the law as a profession*; (also pl.) *literary leanings*.

lean-to, adj. & n. [1. lén tōō; 2. lín tū]. (building) **a** adj. Having only one slope, the upper part of which meets a perpendicular wall: *a lean-to roof, shed*; **b** n., building constructed in this way.

leap (I.), vb. intrans. & trans. [1. lēp; 2. līp]. O.E. *hlēapan*, M.E. *lēpen*; O.S. *hlōpan*; O.H.G. *hlaupan, loufen*; Germ. *laufen*, 'to run'; O.N. *hlaupa*; perh. cogn. w. Lith. *klupti*, 'to stumble', orig. 'to scramble along on the knees', cp. *klúpoti*, 'to bend the knees, kneel'. **1.** intrans. To propel oneself from the ground by muscular effort of the legs; to spring, jump; *jump* is now the usual word. Phrs. *look before you leap*, consider well before taking action; *leap at*, (fig.) show great eagerness to get something, to accept or avail oneself of, offer, opportunity &c. **2.** trans. **a** To pass over, across, by leaping: *to leap a fence, a brook*; when said of a horse, often pronounced [1. lep; 2. lɛp]; **b** to cause, compel, to leap: *to leap* [lɛp] *a horse*.

leap (II.), n., fr. prec. **1.** Act of leaping; a spring, jump, bound; height or distance covered in leaping. Phrs. *a leap in the dark*, action the result of which cannot be foreseen; *by leaps and bounds*, with very rapid rate of advance. **2.** (fig.) A sudden, considerable movement upwards or forwards: *his income went up with a leap*.

leaper, n. [1. léper; 2. lípə]. One who leaps; (of a horse) *a good leaper*; often [1. léper; 2. lépə].

leap-frog, n. Game in which players stand in a line, several yards apart, with heads bent down and hands resting on knees or thighs, the last in the line vaulting in succession over each of those in front, and taking his stand at the head of the line.

leap year, n. One in which February has 29 days, making 366 days in the year.

learn, vb. trans. & intrans. [1. lērn; 2. lɜ̄n]. O.E. *leornian*, M.E. *lernen*; O.H.G. *lernēn*; fr. same base as O.E. *lār*, 'learning, knowledge, doctrine', & *lǣran*, 'to teach'. See **lore. A.** trans. **1. a** To acquire as knowledge, to get to know; become familiar with by study or by being taught: *to learn Latin, one's lesson*; Phrs. *learn by heart*, commit to memory; (fig.) *to learn one's lesson*, profit by experience; **b** to acquire skill in practice of any art, exercise, game: *to learn to skate, to ride*; *to learn cricket*. **2.** To receive instruction in, to be taught: *I am learning French from an excellent teacher*. **3.** To try to acquire, become possessed of, be able to display (some moral quality): *you must learn patience*. **B.** intrans. **1.** To acquire knowledge, become instructed; to gain skill, experience &c.: *he learns very slowly*; *he is very ignorant, but he will learn in time*. **2.** To acquire and practise a moral habit or attitude of mind: *learn to be more careful, tolerant, polite*.

learned, adj. [1. lérned; 2. lɜ́nid]. Prec. & **-ed**. Properly P.P. of prec. in obs., but still vulg. or provinc. use in sense of 'to teach'. **1. a** Possessing much knowledge; well-informed, erudite: *a learned man*; **b** possessing some special knowledge, deeply read in some branch of knowledge: *a learned theologian*. **2. a** Pertaining to scholarship and study: *learned activities*; **b** resulting from, exhibiting, learning: *a learned book*.

learnedly, adv. Prec. & **-ly**. In a learned manner.

learning, n. [1. lérning; 2. lɜ́niŋ]. O.E. *leornung*, 'study, reading', M.E. *lerning*. **1.** Knowledge, information, acquired by study; erudition; used esp. in sense of considerable or special knowledge, and more particularly in reference to literary, historical, philological knowledge as distinct from scientific. **2.** Act, process, of acquiring knowledge by study.

lease (I.), vb. trans. [1. lēs; 2. līs]. O. Fr. *laissier*, 'to leave, transmit', fr. Lat. *laxāre*, 'to make wide; to slacken, relax; to set free, relieve', fr. *laxus*, 'wide, loose; slack'. See **lax** (I.). To grant possession of lands or tenements for a term of years under a contract.

lease (II.), n. O. Fr. *lais*. See prec. **1.** Contract whereby possession of land or buildings &c. is granted by owner for specified term of years, usually subject to payment of rent. Phr. *on lease*. **2. a** The rights enjoyed under such a contract: *I have a long lease of this house*; **b** (fig.) time during which life or health are enjoyed: *a new lease of life*, expectation of living owing to recovered health.

leasehold, adj. & n. [1. lés-hōld; 2. líshould]. **lease** & **hold. a** adj. Held on a lease; **b** n., land &c. held on a lease for a term of years.

leaseholder, n. [1. lés-hōlder; 2. líshouldə]. Person who holds a lease; lessee.

leash, n. & vb. trans. [1. lēsh; 2. līʃ]. M.E. *lēs* &c., fr. O. Fr. *lesse*, Mod. Fr. *laisse*; Lat. *laxus*, 'loose' &c. See **lax** (I.). **1.** n. **a** Chain or strap with which coursing dogs are held; Phr. *to strain at the leash*, to be eager to get freedom in order to do what one desires, impatiently awaiting moment when permission is granted to go somewhere or do something; **b** set of three coursing dogs held in leash; set of three hares. **2.** vb. To attach leash to, put on, control by, a leash.

leasing, n. [1. lézing; 2. líziŋ]. O.E. *lēasung*, 'falsehood, deception'; fr. *lēas*, 'devoid of; false, feigned; untruthful'; cp. O.S. & O.H.G. *lōs*, 'free; bare of, empty'; Goth. *laus*, 'empty, vain'; cogn. w. O.E. *lēosan*, 'to lose', q.v. under **lose**. See also **-less**. (obs., Bib.) Lies, falsehoods, deceit.

least (I.), adj. & adv. [1. lēst; 2. līst]. O.E. *lǣsest, lǣst*, 'smallest'; superl. of *lǣssa*, 'less'. See **less. 1.** adj. Smallest, in size, degree, extent, amount, importance: *there is not the least wind today*; *the least sum, breadth* &c.; '*the least of the apostles*'. **2.** adv. To the smallest extent; less than any others: *those who work hardest are sometimes paid least*; *least of all do I want to hurt you*.

least (II.), n., fr. prec. The least, smallest amount, lowest degree &c. Phrs. *not in the least*, not at all; *to say the least of it*, not to exaggerate, not to overstate; *at* (*the*) *least*: **a** at lowest estimate: *it will cost at least five pounds*; **b** at any rate: *you might at least be polite*.

leastways, adv. [1. léstwāz; 2. lístweiz]. **least** & **-ways**. (illit., vulg.) Leastwise; at least, or rather.

leastwise, adv. [1. léstwīz; 2. lístwaiz]. **least** & **-wise**. (rare) At least.

leat, n. [1. lēt; 2. līt]. O.E. *ġelæt*, 'junction of roads', connected w. *lǣtan*, 'let', here in sense of allowing a passage fr. one road to another. See **let** (I.). Open trench for conducting water from mill.

leather, n. & vb. trans. [1. lédher; 2. léðə]. O.E., M.E. *leðer*; O.H.G. *ledar*; O.N. *leðr*. Further connexions outside Gmc. unknown. **1.** n. **a** Skin of animals preserved and toughened by tanning; Phr. *nothing like leather*, one's own things are the best, one's own interests the most important; **b** any of various things made of leather; e.g. strap holding stirrup iron; cricket ball or football; tip of billiard cue &c.; pl., *leathers*, riding breeches; **c** (slang) one's skin. **2.** vb. (colloq.) To beat, thrash soundly.

leatherette, n. [1. lèdherét; 2. lèðərét]. Prec. & **-ette**. Cheap material made to look like leather, and used as a substitute for it.

leathering, n. [1. lédhering; 2. léðəriŋ]. **leather**, vb., & **-ing**. (slang) A beating.

leather-jacket, n. Tough-skinned larva of the crane-fly or daddy-long-legs, which eats roots of vegetables.

leathern, adj. [1. lédhern; 2. léðən]. **leather** & **-en**. Made of leather.

leatheroid, n. [1. lédheroid; 2. léðərɔid]. **leather** & **-oid**. Tough material made in thin sheets, of paper, scraps of leather &c.

leathery, adj. [1. lédheri; 2. léðəri]. **leather** & **-y**. Resembling leather in dryness and toughness.

leave (I.), n. [1. lēv; 2. līv]. O.E. *lēaf*, 'permission, licence', M.E. *lēve*; cp. Du. *oorlof*, 'permission'. From the O.E. n. is formed *ģelīefan*, ' to allow ', cp. the cognates O.H.G. *irlouben*, ' to allow, permit ' ; Goth. *uslaubjan*, ' allow ' &c. The orig. meaning is ' favour, favourable disposition ', hence ' sanction '. A different shade of meaning is seen in O.E. *ģelēafa*, ' belief ', whence *ģelīefan*, ' to believe ', Goth. *galaubjan*, q.v. under **belief, believe**, wh. are fr. the same Gmc. base **laub*-. Another grade of this is **leub*-, as in O.E. *lēof*, ' dear ', q.v. under **lief**. See also **libidinous. 1.** Permission: *leave to do what one likes, to go where one pleases.* Phrs. *leave out*, permission to go out, or away from given place ; *leave off*, permission to absent oneself from, to take respite from, one's duties ; *neither with your leave nor by your leave*, whether you like it or not ; *I take leave to say*, politely ironical formula, implying intention to say something with or without approval of hearers. **2. a** Permission to be away from duty : *to have, go on, leave* ; *a month's leave* (used esp. in Army, Navy, Civil Service), invariably called ' leaf ' by private soldiers and by sailors; (usual expression) *leave of absence*; **b** time spent away from regiment, ship &c. : *to spend one's leave in London.* **3.** Farewell, greeting, on departure; departure : *to take one's leave*, to go away ; *to take leave of*, bid farewell to. Phr. *French leave*, departure without obtaining permission, or without farewell.

leave (**II.**), vb. trans. & intrans. O.E. *lǣfan*, trans., ' not to take away, to leave ; to bequeath ' ; intrans., ' to remain ', fr. **lāfjan*, fr. *lāf*, ' what is left, remnant ' ; cp. Goth. *(bi)laibjan*, ' to survive, be left over ' ; M.E. *lēven* ; cogn. w. O.S. *belīfan*, ' to remain ' ; O.S. *bilīban*, O.H.G. *(bi)līban*, Mod. Germ. *bleiben*, Goth. *bileiban*. Closely connected w. these words, & fr. same base, are O.E. *libban, leofian*, ' to live, be alive ' (see **live** (**I.**)), & *līf*, ' life ' (see **life**). The development of meaning is ' to remain, remain in existence, subsist, live '. The fundamental sense ' remain, allow to remain ', wh. is the starting-point of all words fr. this base in Gmc., seems to be largely peculiar to this family, except for Gk. *leípein*, ' leave, leave remaining, leave behind ' &c., & *loipós*, ' what is left over, the rest '. The orig. meaning wh. has to be inferred fr. the various cognates in the languages outside Gmc. appears at first sight very remote fr. that developed in the latter. Etymologists identify the Gmc. base w. Scrt. *liptaš*, ' sticky, adhesive ', & *lēpaš*, ' something smeared on, dirt ' ; cp. Gk. *lípos*, ' grease, fat ', & *aloiphḗ*, ' anything for smearing, grease, lard, unguent ' ; Lith. *lipti*, ' to stick, remain '. Although it is possible to see a connexion in sense between ' smear, stick, remain ' &c., it is prob. that the last was helped by a very early association between this base & that in Lat. *linquere*, ' to leave behind ' &c., q.v. under **relinquish.** See also **loan. A. 1. a** To allow, or cause, to remain ; to let lie, depart without taking : *leave the book on the table* ; *leave things where you can find them again* ; **b** to omit, forget, to take, or bring with one : *I've left my umbrella in the train* ; also *to leave behind* ; **c** to allow to remain unaltered, undisturbed : *to leave things as they are, as one found them* ; Phrs. *to leave* (person, animal) *alone*, not to molest, interfere with, or disturb ; *to leave* (thing, business) *alone*, not to meddle with, not to touch, spoil &c. : *leave my car alone* ; *I should leave that question alone if I were you* ; *to leave well alone*, not to try to improve what is already good ; *to leave severely alone*, be scrupulous not to molest, interfere, or meddle with ; *to leave a person to himself, to his own devices*, not to direct or control his action ; *leave go*, to loosen one's hold (of). **2.** (of persons &c.) To cause, or allow, to remain behind one ; to let stay when one goes away, not to cause to accompany : *to leave one's horse at the door* ; *leave one's family in India.* **3. a** To go away from, quit, cease to reside in : *to leave one's house, the country* &c. ; also **b** intrans., when used absol., to go away, depart : *we have been here a month and it's time we left* ; specif. **c** to quit for good : (of boys at school) *leaving at the end of next term.* **4.** To forsake, abandon, desert ; cease to live with : *he has gone to Australia leaving his wife and family.* Phrs. *to be (nicely) left*, deceived, taken in, duped ; *to leave in the lurch, stranded*, placed in awkward predicament. **5. a** To die having a family : *to leave a wife and five children* ; **b** to die having heirs : *to leave no heir to one's property.* **6. a** To die possessing, own at one's death : *to leave a large fortune* ; **b** to bequeath by will at death : *to leave a legacy to an old friend* ; **c** to provide for by will : *to leave one's widow comfortably, badly, off.* **7.** To commit, entrust, to ; rely on to do : *I leave you to settle up*, or *I leave it to you to settle up* ; *leave it to me, in my hands.* Phr. *I'll leave that to you*, in answer to question, what is the fare, price, your proper payment &c. = give me what you please, as much as you like &c. **8.** To deposit, hand over, before departing : *the postman left three letters and a parcel* ; *to leave one's bag in the cloak-room.* Phr. *to leave cards on*, pay formal call on. **9.** To allow to remain over, yield as a remainder, surplus, after process of subtraction, deduction, expenditure, or the like : *2 from 5 leaves 3* ; *I hope you've left me something to eat* ; *the payment of his debts left him nothing to live upon.* Phr. *to leave something, much, to be desired*, be unsatisfactory, inadequate. **10.** To put into, and cause to remain in, a specified condition : *malaria had left him a wreck* ; *the insult left him speechless.* Phr. *to leave one cold*, not to excite, rouse no interest in. **11.** To pass, go beyond (an object), keeping in a specified direction relative to it : *you leave the village on your right and go up the hill.* **12.** (archaic) To cease, discontinue, bring to an end : *it is time to leave talking and begin doing.* **B.** Followed by adverb. *Leave off*, **1.** trans., **a** to discontinue, cease to do : *leave off biting your nails, bad habits, going to church* &c. ; **b** to cease to wear, cast : *to leave off one's winter clothes* ; **2.** intrans., to cease, come to an end of any action, stop : *I left off at the end of Chapter III.* ; *to begin where one's father left off*, start life in same social or financial position as that secured by one's father at end of his career. *Leave out*, trans., **1. a** to omit, cut out : *to leave out half one's words* ; *you must leave out this epithet* ; **b** to avoid consideration of, fail to consider, omit to reckon with : *you have left out the probability that he will refuse to discuss the matter at all.* **2.** To neglect, pass over, overlook : *leave out in the cold.*

leaved, -leaved, adj. [1. lēvd ; 2. līvd]. **leaf** & **-ed.** Having leaves ; having specified number or kind of leaves : *four-leaved shamrock.*

leaven (**I.**), n. [1. lévn ; 2. lévn]. Fr. *levain*, fr. Lat. *levāmen*, ' alleviation, mitigation ', but in orig. physical sense, ' something which lightens, raises ', fr. *levāre*, ' mitigate, lighten, relieve ; to raise ', fr. *levis*, ' light ', q.v. under **levant** (**I.**). Cp. also second syll. of **relieve. 1.** Yeast; substance due to fermentation which added to dough causes bread to rise. **2.** (fig.) A spiritual influence which permeates the mind and reacts forcibly on thought and conduct (in a good and bad sense).

leaven (**II.**), vb. trans., fr. prec. **a** To cause fermentation in by addition of leaven ; to mix leaven with ; **b** (fig.) to permeate with ; to induce change in for good or bad.

leavening, n. [1. lévening ; 2. lévəniŋ]. **a** (in physical and spiritual sense) Process of permeating and acting by fermentation ; **b** leaven.

leaving, n. [1. lēving ; 2. līviŋ]. **leave** (**II.**) & **-ing.** (chiefly in pl.) *Leavings*, things left, remnants ; esp. things cast off, or aside, as superfluous or worthless : *I don't care for other men's leavings.*

lecher, n. [1. lécher ; 2. létʃə]. O. Fr. *lecheur*, ' glutton, libertine ', lit. ' licker ', fr. *lechier*, ' to lick ' ; of Gmc. origin. See **lick** & **lickerish.** One inordinately given to illicit sexual indulgence.

lecherous, adj. [1. lécherus ; 2. létʃərəs]. Prec. & **-ous.** Lustful, salacious.

lecherously, adv. See prec. & **-ly.** In a lecherous manner.

lechery, n. [1. lécheri ; 2. létʃəri]. **lecher** & **-y.** Lust, lubricity ; inordinate lustfulness.

lecithin, n. [1. lésithin ; 2. lésiþin], fr. Gk. *lékithos*, ' yolk of an egg ', etymol. unknown. & **-in.** (physiol.) A waxy substance containing nitrogen and phosphorus found in tissues of the brain and nerves of animals, also in yolk of egg and in plants, used in medicine in treatment of nervous ailments.

lectern, n. [1. léktern ; 2. léktən, léktʌn]. M.E., fr. O. Fr. *lettrun*, fr. L. Lat. *lectrum*, ' reading-desk ', fr. base **leg*-, ' read '. See **lecture.** Reading-desk in church, esp. that from which the lessons are read.

lectionary, n. [1. lékshunari ; 2. lékʃən(ə)ri]. Lat. *lectiōn*-, stem of *lectio*, ' reading ', & *-ārium.* See next word & **-ary.** Sequence of lessons appointed by authority to be read in churches each day at divine service ; list of such lessons and of days upon which they are to be read.

lecture (**I.**), n. [1. lékchur ; 2. léktʃə]. Fr., fr. Lat. type *lect*-, fr. base *leg*-, ' read ', & *-ūra* (see **-ure**) ; Lat. *legere* means ' to gather, collect ; to pick out, choose ; to survey, observe ; to read, read aloud, recite ' ; cp. Gk. *légein*, ' to pick out, choose ; to relate, speak, utter, declare ' ; also Gk. *léxis*, ' speech ; diction ', & w. different grade, *lógos*, ' word expressing thought ; thought, reason ' ; see **elect, elegant, legion**, & possibly **legal.** Discourse, whether read or extempore, upon a set subject, delivered with a view to instruction, to a class or other audience. Phr. *to read one a lecture*, admonish or reprove him.

lecture (**II.**), vb. intrans. & trans., fr. prec. **a** intrans. To deliver lectures, or a lecture : *to lecture twice a week* ; *to lecture to a class* ; *to lecture on a particular subject* ; **b** trans., to deliver a lecture to ; esp. to admonish, reprove : *his wife lectured him severely on his late hours.*

lecturer, n. [1. lékchurer ; 2. léktʃərə]. Prec. & **-er.** One who delivers lectures ; esp. a professional teacher at a university or college.

lectureship, n. [1. lékchurship ; 2. léktʃəʃip]. **lecture** & **-ship.** Office or post of lecturer, generally one held at a university or college.

lecythus, n. [1. lésithus, lékithus ; 2. lésiþəs, lékiþəs], fr. Gk. *lékuthos*, ' oil-flask ', etymol. doubtful. (Gk. antiq.) A tall slender type of vase with narrow neck and single handle.

led, vb. [1. led ; 2. led]. O.E. *lǣdde*, M.E. *lědde* ; Pret. & P.P. of **lead** (**IV.**).

ledge, n. [1. lej ; 2. ledž]. M.E. *legge* meant apparently ' support, bar ' ; prob. orig. ' something laid ', fr. Pr. O.E. **læg-jo*, cp. type *læġ*, Pret. of O.E. *liċġan* (see **lay** & **lie** (**I.**)) ; the word meant perh. ' bracket or support ', then ' something supported by a bracket, a shelf '. **a** Narrow shelf projecting from surface of wall ; **b** projection from face of cliff, rock &c.

ledger (**I.**), n. [1. léjer ; 2. ledžə]. Prob. formed fr. O.E. *leċġan*, M.E. *leggen*, ' to lay '. See prec. **1.** An account book ; esp. one used in a business institution. **2.** (archit.) **a** A large flat stone ; **b** large horizontal timber in scaffolding.

ledger (**II.**), as adj., formed fr. base **lag*-, ' to lay '. See **lay** (**III.**), & **lie** (**III.**). Not moving, stationary ; placed in position, and remaining there. Only used in following few compounds.

ledger-bait, n. Bait for fish, anchored, and allowed to float over given spot.

ledger-blade, n. Large, flat, fixed blade in machine for cutting chaff, shearing cloth &c., against which the revolving blade works.

ledger-hook, n. One attached to ledger-line.

ledger-line, n. **a** Fishing line used with ledger-bait ; **b** (mus.) an additional line above or below the staff.

ledger-tackle, n. Line, hook &c. used in ledger-bait fishing.

lee (**I.**), n. & adj. [1. lē ; 2. lī]. O.E. *hlēo(w)*, ' covering, shelter ; protection ', also adj. *ġehlēo*, ' sheltered, warm ' ; O.H.G. *lāo*, *lāwer*, Mod. Germ. *lau*, 'warm'; O.N. *hlǣr*, 'warm, mild'; cogn. w. Lat. *calēre*, 'to be warm, to glow'. See **cauldron** & **calm**. **1.** n. **a** Shelter, protection: *under the lee of a house*; **b** sheltered place, one protected from the wind; *on the lee*, lee side. **2.** adj. (naut.) Said of the side, or part of ship farthest removed from that from which the wind is blowing: *the lee side, rail* &c.

lee (**II.**), n. Fr. *lie*; origin doubtful; perh. of Celt. (Gaulish) origin. Chiefly *lees*, pl., that which settles at bottom of wine-cask; sediment, dregs: *wine on the lees*; *to drink a cup to the lees*, (fig.) to undergo the last extremes of suffering.

lee-board, n. **lee** (**I.**) & **board**. Wooden frame fastened over lee side of flat-bottomed ship to prevent her losing leeway when close-hauled.

leech (**I.**), n. [1. lēch; 2. lītʃ]. O.E. *lǣċe*, 'physician; leech (the animal)'; O.H.G. *lāhhi*, Goth. *lēkeis*, 'physician, healer', orig. 'magician, exorcist'; cp. O.E. *lācnian*, 'to heal'; O.H.G. *lāhhinōn*, 'to exorcise, heal'; Goth. *lēkinōn*, 'to heal'. **1.** (archaic) Physician. **2. a** Blood-sucking worm living in ponds, used in medicine for blood-letting. Phr. *to stick like a leech*; **b** (fig.) blood-sucker, usurer.

leech (**II.**), n., fr. Du. *lijk*, 'bolt rope'. Free edge of a sail.

leechcraft, n. [1. lḗchkrahft; 2. lítʃkrāft]. O.E. *lǣċecræft*. See **leech** (**I.**) & **craft**. (archaic) Medical skill and practice.

leechdom, n. [1. lḗchdum; 2. lítʃdəm]. O.E. *lǣċedōm*, 'remedy, medicine'. **leech** (**I.**) & **-dom.** (obs.) Remedy, medical recipe.

leek, n. [1. lēk; 2. lik]. O.E. *lēac*, 'vegetable, leek, garlic'; O.S. *lōk*, O.H.G. *laoh*, O.N. *laukr*; connexions outside Gmc. doubtful. Cp. **garlic**. A vegetable, somewhat resembling an onion in structure and flavour, but with cylindrical stem instead of a globular bulb; national emblem of Wales. Phr. *to eat the leek*, suffer humiliation.

leer (**I.**), n. [1. lēr; 2. liə]. O.E. *hlēor*, 'cheek'; O.S. *hlior*; origin uncertain. The original sense is 'face, expression of face', then a particular kind of expression; cp. similar usage of **face**. A sly, furtive, smirking, grin, denoting and expressing esp. either lubricity or malignity, or sometimes mere inanity, as in an idiot.

leer (**II.**), vb. intrans., fr prec. To assume a leer; *to leer at*, to leer with face turned to.

leer (**III.**), n. Etymol. unknown. Place in which glass is cooled and annealed in process of manufacture.

leering, adj. [1. lḗring; 2. líəriŋ], fr. Pres. Part. of **leer** (**II.**). **a** Wearing, constantly assuming, a leer: *a leering ruffian*; **b** addicted to assuming leers.

leeringly, adv. Prec. & **-ly**. As though wearing a leer.

leery, adj. [1. lḗri; 2. líəri]. Given to leers; having a leer on the face; esp. (slang) cunning, knowing: *a leery old bird*.

lees, n. pl. [1. lēz; 2. līz]. See **lee** (**II.**).

leet, n. [1. lēt; 2. līt]. In L. Lat. *lēta*, origin uncertain, possibly connected w. O.E. *lǣð*, 'estate', wh. survives in *lathe*, an old administrative district of Kent. See **lathe** (**II.**). (legal hist.) An old annual manorial court of record, in full, *court leet*, with jurisdiction over minor criminal offences.

leeward, adj., adv., & n. [1. lóoard; 2. lúəd]. **lee** (**I.**) & **-ward.** **1. a** adj. On side away from that from which wind is coming; **b** adv., towards the lee. **2.** n. Side away from the wind.

leewardly, adj. Tending to fall off to lee.

leeway, n. [1. lḗwā; 2. líwei]. **lee** (**I.**) & **way**. **1.** Deviation from her true course, as indicated by line of her keel, which a vessel makes in drifting to leeward. **2.** (fig.) Loss of time, diminution, retarding, of progress: *to have a great deal of leeway to make up* (in one's studies, in execution of a piece of work &c.).

left (**I.**), adj., adv., & n. [1. left; 2. lɛft]. Rare in O.E. in wh. the usual word is *winstre*; *left* is apparently a S.E. type, of wh. the W.S. wd. be *lyft*; M.E. *luft, lift, left*; orig. meaning 'weak, infirm'; cp. O.E. *lēf*, 'infirm, diseased', *ġelēfed*, 'weak, old', fr. **lēafi-*? If Walde is right in connecting O.E. *lēf* distantly w. Lat. *lētum*, 'death' (see **lethal**), Gk. *loimós*, 'pestilence', *līmós*, 'hunger', Lith. *lḗsas*, 'thin', the vowel in the O.E. words wd. require a different explanation fr. that suggested above. **1.** adj. Connected with, pertaining to, that part of the body which is situated to the west when one faces north; the opposite of *right*; **a** primarily applied to the hand, and the whole of the body, its parts and organs on this side: *left hand, shoulder, arm, leg* &c.; **b** (by extension) applied to direction or position generally, relative to speaker or spectator: *left bank of a river*, that on one's left hand as one looks downstream; *to look, turn, neither to the left hand nor to the right*, look, go, straight ahead. **2.** adv. Towards the left, in direction of one's left hand: *to turn left*. **3.** n. **a** That position or direction which is on, or nearest to, one's left side; left hand: *turn to the left*; *keep to the left*; *will you sit on my left?*; **b** (politics, usually cap.) group of members, party, belonging to legislative body, who sit on the left hand of the speaker, or president, as he faces the house; hence, the extreme radicals who by custom occupy this position. The term originates from the horse-shoe arrangement of the seats in most continental chambers.

left (**II.**), vb. M.E. *lafte, lefte*, Pret. & P.P. of **leave**.

left-hand, adj. **1.** Situated nearer to the left hand than to the right: *left-hand side of the street*. **2.** Performed, done, with the left hand: *a left-hand blow, stroke* &c.

left-handed, adj. **left** (**I.**) & **handed**. **1.** (of persons) Addicted to using, able to, preferring to, use the left hand in those more complex acts such as writing, drawing, shaving, cutting with knife &c., for which most persons use the right hand. **2.** Dubious, ambiguous, insincere, esp. *a left-handed compliment*. **3.** (of a marriage) Morganatic, pertaining to one in which a person of royal blood marries one of inferior rank.

left-handedly, adv. Prec. & **-ly**. In a left-handed manner; with the left hand.

left-handedness, n. See prec. & **-ness**. State, condition, of being left-handed.

left-hander, n. [1. léft hánder; 2. léft hǽndə]. **left-hand** & **-er**. **a** Person using the left hand and not the right; **b** blow, stroke, with the left hand.

leg (**I.**), n. [1. leg; 2. lɛg], fr. O.N. *leggr*, fr. Gmc. **lag-ja-*. This word is cogn. w. Lat. *lacertus*, 'the arm from shoulder to elbow', &, w. different grade, w. Lat. *lōcusta*, 'locust', lit. 'the jumper'. See **locust** & **lobster**. We may further connect Gk. *láx*, 'with the heel, or foot', *lakizein*, 'to kick with the foot'; cp. also Lith. *lakstýti*, 'to leap, spring, hop'. **1. a** One of the limbs of any animal which serve for support in standing, and for progression; that part of such a limb between the hip and the ankle; Phrs. *not to have a leg to stand on*, no justification or excuse, no argument in one's favour; *to pull a person's leg*, to chaff, fool him; *to stretch one's legs*, to walk, esp. after a prolonged sitting; *(to be) on one's legs*, (i.) to be kept standing about; (ii.) to stand up ready to make a speech at public meeting; (also facetious) *on one's hindlegs*; *to shake a (loose) leg*, to dance; *to stand on one's own legs*, to be independent; *to set a man on his legs (again)*, afford him financial or other assistance; to restore him to health; *to walk a man off his legs*, make him walk too far, tire him out; *run off one's legs*, exhausted by excessive number of duties and occupations; *on one's, its, last legs*, approaching death, nearly worn out or done for; *as fast as one's legs would carry one*, at full speed; *to make a leg*, (archaic) to bow, bend the knee in salutation; *to give a person a leg up*, help him to climb; (fig.) do him a good turn, afford assistance; **b** imitation limb worn as a support: *cork, wooden, leg*; **c** part of the leg of an animal prepared as food: *leg of mutton, pork*; *leg-of-mutton sail*, triangular sail; *leg-of-mutton sleeve*, one broad at shoulder and tapering towards the wrist. **2. a** A part of certain articles which serves as a support, upon which they stand: *leg of a chair, stool, table*; **b** one side of a pair of compasses; **c** either side of a triangle other than its base. **3.** Part of a garment covering the leg: *leg of a stocking, of trousers*. **4.** (cricket) **a** That part of the field on batsman's left, or to rear of this, as *short, square, long leg*, of fieldsmen in these positions; **b** (attrib.) on, towards, the legs of batsman, as *leg-bye*, bye off the batsman's leg; *leg-stump* &c. Phr. *leg before wicket*, abbreviated *l.b.w.*, stopping by batsman's legs of ball which otherwise would have bowled him. **5.** Distance covered by ship in one tack. **6.** (slang) Swindler, sharper, short for blackleg, q.v.

leg (**II.**), vb. intrans., fr. prec. (colloq.) *Leg it*, to go on one's legs, to walk; to run away.

legacy, n. [1. légasi; 2. légəsi]. O. Fr. *legacie*, in sense of 'office of legate'. See **legate** (**II.**) & **-cy**. The Lat. *lēgātum* meant 'bequest, legacy', fr. P.P. of *lēgāre*, in sense of to appoint by will, to bequeath'; the Mod. Fr. word is *legs*. Bequest, gift of personal property by will; also (fig.) *a legacy of hatred, ill-will* &c.

legacy-hunter, n. One who toadies another in hopes of getting a legacy.

legal, adj. [1. lḗg(a)l; 2. líg(ə)l]. Lat. *lēgālis*, 'belonging to the law', fr. *lēg-*, base of *lēx*, 'law'; the etymol. is doubtful, but connexion w. Lat. *legere*, 'to select', is possible; cp. **lecture**. **1.** Belonging, pertaining, relating, to the law: *legal profession*; *legal adviser*. **2.** In accordance with, not forbidden by, the law; lawful, permissible: *it is perfectly legal to fish on Sunday*. **3.** Enjoined, defined, by statute and therefore binding, compulsory: *legal payment, fare* &c. **4.** According to a definition made by the law: *a legal offence*, an act which the law has recognized as unlawful and defined as an offence.

legalism, n. [1. lḗgalizm; 2. líg(ə)lizəm]. Prec. & **-ism**. Magnification of letter of the law; excessive fondness for legal forms; red tape.

legalist, n. [1. lḗgalist; 2. lígəlist]. See prec. & **-ist**. One who attaches undue importance to the strict letter of the law, or to legal forms.

legality, n. [1. lēgáliti; 2. ligǽliti]. Fr. *légalité*. See **legal** & **-ity**. Lawfulness; state of being according to, sanctioned by, the law.

legalization, n. [1. lēgalīzā́shun; 2. ligəlaizéiʃən]. See next word & **-ation**. Act or process of legalizing.

legalize, vb. trans. [1. lḗgalīz; 2. lígəlaiz]. **legal** & **-ize**. To render legal; to make lawful.

legate (**I.**), n. [1. légat; 2. légit]. Lat. *lēgātus*, 'ambassador, envoy', fr. P.P. of *lēgāre*, 'to send as ambassador', fr. the base seen in **legal**. Ecclesiastical envoy, appointed to represent the Pope outside Rome.

legate (**II.**), vb. trans. [1. lēgā́t; 2. ligéit]. Lat. *lēgāt-um*, P.P. of *lēgāre*, 'to bequeath by will'. See prec. To bequeath by will: *give and legate*.

legatee, n. [1. lègatḗ; 2. lègətí]. Prec. & **-ee**. One to whom a legacy is bequeathed.

legatine, adj. [1. légatīn; 2. légətain]. **legate** (**I.**) & **-ine**. Pertaining to a legate.

legation, n. [1. legā́shun; 2. lɛgéiʃən]. Lat. *lēgātiōn-(em)*, 'embassy'. See **legate** (**I.**) & **-ion**. **1. a** Diplomatic body, inferior in rank to embassy, sent to foreign country; **b** the chief of such a body and his staff, including secretaries, attachés &c. collectively. **2. a** Official residence of chief diplomatic agent; **b** office where the business of a legation is carried on.

legato, adv. [1. legáhtō; 2. ligátou]. Ital., P.P., 'tied together', fr. Lat. *ligāt-um, -o*, fr. *ligāre*, 'to bind'. See **ligament**. (mus. direction, of a series of notes) (To be played) smoothly, without intervals or breaks.

legator, n. [1. legátor; 2. legéitō]. **legate (II.)** & **-or.** Person who bequeathes.

legend, n. [1. léjend; 2. lédžənd]; more rarely and affectedly [1. léjend; 2. lídžənd]. Fr. *légende*, fr. Lat. *legenda*, 'things to be read', fr. *legere*. See **lecture**. **1.** Originally, **a** an account of a saint's life which was read aloud as a duty; **b** extended to include stories of other kinds, generally of a marvellous character. **2. a** A traditional, popular tale; **b** a tale of doubtful authenticity and veracity. **3.** An inscription, esp. on medal or coin.

legendary, adj. & n. [1. léjendari; 2. lédžəndəri]. Prec. & **-ary.** **1.** adj. **a** Surviving only in legends; **b** fabulous, mythical. **2.** n. Collection of legends.

legendry, n. [1. léjendri; 2. lédžəndri]. **legend** & **-ry.** Traditional, mythical, stories collectively.

legerdemain, n. [1. lèjerdemán; 2. lèdžədiméin]. Fr. *léger de main*, 'light of hand'. Conjuring tricks; applied also to specious argument, or clever unscrupulous action.

legged, adj. [1. legd; 2. legd]. **leg** & **-ed.** (chiefly in compounds) Having legs of a specified kind: *bow-legged, thick-legged* &c.

legginess, n. [1. légines; 2. léginis]. **leggy** & **-ness.** **a** State of being leggy, of having disproportionately long legs; **b** state (in plants) of having long bare stems.

legging, n. [1. légin(g); 2. légiŋ, -in]. **leg** & **-ing.** (gen. pl.) Covering of leather or canvas to protect leg below the knee, fastened with buttons or straps.

leggy, adj. [1. légi; 2. légi]. **leg** & **-y.** **a** Having disproportionately long legs, as of young animal, boy, girl &c.; **b** applied also to shrubs and climbing plants, having long bare stems near the base, with leaves and blossom on the top.

leghorn, n. [1. legórn, lég-horn; 2. legɔ́n, léghɔ̄n]. **1.** Plaited straw used in making hats, from Leghorn (*Livorno*), in Italy; also attrib., *leghorn hat*. **2.** A hat made from this straw. **3.** Breed of domestic fowl: *white leghorn* &c.

legibility, n. [1. lègibíliti; 2. lèdžibíliti]. See next word & **-ity.** Quality of being legible.

legible, adj. [1. léjibl; 2. lédžibl]. Fr. *légible*, 'readable', fr. Lat. *legibilis*, see *leg-* under **lecture**, & **-ible.** Capable of being read; clear, easy to read, readable.

legibleness, n. Prec. & **-ness.** Quality of being legible; legibility.

legibly, adv. See prec. & **-ly.** In a legible manner.

legion, n. [1. léjun; 2. lídžən]. Lat. *legiōn-(em)*, fr. base *leg-*, 'to pick out, collect, gather', see **lecture**, & **-ion.** **1.** Unit in ancient Roman army of from 3000 to 6000 men, together with complement of cavalry; hence, (large) body of troops in general. **2.** (only pred.) A host, multitude, large number: *my foes, anxieties, are legion.* **3. a** *British Legion*, a federation of the various societies of soldiers who had served in the Great War, formed for their assistance and protection; **b** *Foreign Legion*, corps of the French army recruited by voluntary enlistment from foreigners for service in the Colonies, esp. in N. Africa. **4.** *Legion of Honour*, a French Order of chivalry and merit, having various grades of distinction, founded by Napoleon I., bestowed for civil or military services.

legionary, adj. & n. [1. léjunari; 2. lídžənəri]. Lat. *legiōnārius.* **1.** adj. Belonging to, consisting of, a legion or of legions. **2.** n. Member of a legion.

legislate, vb. intrans. [1. léjislāt; 2. lédžisleit]. Back-formation fr. **legislator.** To make, enact, laws.

legislation, n. [1. lèjisláshun; 2. lèdžisléiʃən]. L. Lat. *lēgislātiōn-(em)*, fr Lat. *lēgis*, genit. of *lēx*, 'law' (see **legal**), & *lātiōn-(em)*, 'bringing (forward), proposing'. See **tolerate.** **1.** Act of making laws. **2.** The laws that are enacted.

legislative, adj. [1. léjislativ, -lātiv; 2. lédžislətiv, -leitiv]. See prec. & **-ive.** **1.** Having the duty and power to make laws: *legislative assembly.* **2.** Pertaining to the enactment of laws.

legislator, n. [1. léjislātor; 2. lédžisleitə]. Lat. *lēgis lātor*, 'proposer of a law' (see **legislation**); *lāt-* for **tlāt-*, 'to bear' (see **tolerate**). Member of body which makes laws; a lawgiver.

legislature, n. [1. léjislāchur; 2. lédžisleitʃə]. See **legislate** & **-ure.** Body of persons in a state whose function is to make and alter laws; legislative body.

legist, n. [1. léjist; 2. lídžist], fr. *lēg-* (see **legal**) & **-ist.** Student of, one skilled in, the science of law.

legitimacy, n. [1. lejítimasi; 2. lidžítiməsi]. See next word & **-cy.** State, status, fact, of being legitimate; **a** (of children) fact of being born, (of birth) fact of occurring, in lawful wedlock; **b** (of a sovereign or ruler) fact of being lawful heir to his throne by right of descent.

legitimate (I.), adj. [1. lejítimat; 2. lidžítimit]. Formed fr. Lat. *lēgitimus*, 'lawful', fr. *lēg-*, 'law' (see **legal**), & **-ate.** **1.** Lawful, permitted; **a** in accordance with law: *a legitimate claim, purpose*; **b** in accordance with recognized principles; reasonable, justifiable: *a legitimate argument. Legitimate drama*, body of plays of recognized and accepted merit. **2.** Specif. **a** (of children) born in lawful wedlock; **b** (of birth, descent) derived from lawful marriage. **3.** (of kings) Lawfully descended from royal line, representing the direct senior line, and holding throne by such lawful hereditary right; with this conception is often associated the theory of Divine Right.

legitimate (II.), vb. trans. [1. lejítimāt; 2. lidžítimeit]. Etymol. as prec. **a** To render legitimate and lawful; **b** specif., to confer legitimacy of birth, by a legal act, upon one born out of lawful wedlock; to recognize as legitimate, give status of a legitimate offspring to.

legitimately, adv. [1. lejítimatli; 2. lidžítimitli]. **legitimate (I.)** & **-ly.** In a legitimate manner (in all senses).

legitimation, n. [1. lijìtimáshun; 2. lidžìtiméiʃən]. **legitimate** & **-ion.** Act of legitimating.

legitimatize, vb. trans. [1. lejítimatīz; 2. lidžítimətaiz]. **legitimate (I.)** & **-ize.** To legitimate.

legitimism, n. [1. lejítimizm; 2. lidžítimizəm]. Lat. *lēgitim(us)*, 'lawful' (see **legitimate (I.)**), & **-ism.** Principles and aims of legitimists.

legitimist, n. [1. lejítimist; 2. lidžítimist]. Lat. *lēgitim-(us)*, see prec., & **-ist.** One who supports the principle of monarchy based upon strict hereditary descent; specif., supporter of claims of Bourbon line to the throne of France.

legitimize, vb. trans. [1. lejítimīz; 2. lidžítimaiz]. *Legitim-*, as in prec., & **-ize.** To legitimate.

legume, legumen, n. [1. légūm, legúmen; 2. légjūm, legjúmen]. Fr. *légume*, 'vegetable', Lat. *legūmen*, 'pulse, or other leguminous plant, a pea', fr. *legere*, 'to gather'. See **lecture.** **1. a** Seed of a leguminous plant, pea, bean &c.; **b** the plant itself. **2.** A seed pod of leguminous plant.

legumin, n. [1. legúmin; 2. legjúmin]. Prec. & **-in.** Proteid substance forming a constituent of the pea and other leguminous plants.

leguminous, adj. [1. legúminus; 2. legjúminəs]. Lat. *legūmin-*, stem of *legūmen* (see **legume**), & **-ous.** Connected with, of the nature of, the pea, bean, and other kindred plants.

Leibnitzian, adj. & n. [1. lībnítsian; 2. laibnítsiən], fr. name of Gottfried Wilhelm Leibnitz (1646–1716). **a** adj. Pertaining to, based on, the philosophical doctrines of Leibnitz; **b** n., adherent of those doctrines.

Leicester, n. [1. léster; 2. léstə], fr. name of county of Leicestershire. A breed of sheep.

leister, n. & vb. trans. [1. léster; 2. lístə]. O.N. *ljostr*, fr. *ljosta*, 'strike'. **a** n. Salmon-spear; **b** vb., to spear with a leister.

leisure, n. [1. lézhur; 2. léžə], or, obsolesc. or provinc. [1. lézhur; 2. lížə]. M.E. *leisere*, &c., O. Fr. *leisir*; orig. an infin., fr. Lat. *licēre*, 'to be lawful, to be allowed'. See **licence.** **a** Freedom from occupation, esp. from compulsory duties or business; **b** time which is free and unoccupied. Phrs. *to be at leisure*, to be free, unoccupied; (*to do something*) *at one's leisure*, at a convenient moment, implying no immediate urgency; (attrib.) *leisure hour*, time of leisure; regularly recurring period of leisure; *leisure time*, spare time, between hours of business.

leisured, adj. [1. lézhurd; 2. léžəd]. Prec. & **-ed.** Possessing leisure, being master of one's own time; specif., having no regular business, no obligatory duties to perform.

leisureliness, n. [1. lézhurlines; 2. léžəlinis]. Next word & **-ness.** **a** Absence of hurry or bustle; deliberateness of movement or action; **b** excessive slowness in action; dilatoriness.

leisurely, adj. [1. lézhurli; 2. léžəli]. **leisure** & **-ly.** **a** Unhurried, deliberate; not characterized by urgency: *leisurely movements*; **b** not exhibiting signs of haste, not hurrying: *leisurely in one's movements.*

leitmotif, n. [1. lítmōtēf; 2. láitmoutīf]. Mod. Germ. *leit*, 'leading', cogn. w. **lead (IV.)** & Fr. *motif.* See **motive.** **a** Recurring phrase, or short passage, in a musical composition, always associated with the same sentiment, situation, or personage; **b** (fig.) dominant aim, sentiment, ideal, consistently exhibited throughout a course of action.

leman, n. [1. léman; 2. lémən]. M.E., first found as compound in Layamon's 'Brut', earlier text, c. 1200, *leofmon, leouemon*; later text, c. 1250, *lemman, -mon*, 'mistress', fr. O.E. *lēof*, 'dear' (see **lief**), & **man.** Lover, sweetheart; usually in bad sense, paramour.

lemma, n., pl. **lemmata** [1. léma, lémata; 2. lémə, lémətə]. Gk. *lêmma*, 'something received, premise taken for granted', cp. (*ei*)*lēmmai*, perf. pass. of *lambánein*, 'to seize, take'. See **dilemma.** **a** Proposition taken for granted, or immediately demonstrated, used in an argument; **b** subject of a literary article or argument; **c** headline or head-word in a dictionary.

lemming, n. [1. léming; 2. lémiŋ]. Norw., fr. Lapp. *luomek.* (zool.) Small, rat-like, migratory animal found in arctic regions.

lemon, n. [1. lémun; 2. lémən]. Fr. *limon*, Span. *limón*, fr. Arab. *laimūn.* Cp. also **lime**, the fruit. **1.** n. **a** Moderate-sized, very acid, pale yellow fruit, chiefly used for flavouring, or for making cooling drinks; *salts of lemon*, see **salt**; **b** tree, *Citrus Limonum*, which bears this fruit. **2.** adj. Having the colour of the rind of lemons.

lemonade, n. [1. lèmunád; 2. lèmənéid], fr. Fr. *limonade.* See **lemon** & **-ade.** Sweet drink made from lemon juice, sugar, and water, or soda-water.

lemon-drop, n. Small hard lozenge made of sugar strongly flavoured with lemon.

lemon-sole, n. Fr. *limande.* A flat fish resembling a sole in appearance, but inferior in taste and texture.

lemon-squash, n. Beverage made of juice of lemon and soda-water, usually sweetened.

lemur, n. [1. lémur; 2. límə], fr. Lat. *lemures*, 'spirits of the dead'; cogn. w. Gk. *lámia*, 'spectre'. See **lamia.** Small arboreal animal found in Madagascar, somewhat resembling a monkey, having thick, soft fur, a bushy, furry tail, and a pointed muzzle like that of a fox; the name is due to the nocturnal habits of the animal.

lend, vb. trans. [1. lend; 2. lend]. O.E. *lǣnan*, 'to lend, grant', M.E. *lēnen*, fr. **lān-jan*, cp. *lān*, q.v. under **loan.** **1.** To grant a person temporary use of anything: (with *to* before indirect object if direct object not expressed) '*whoso giveth to the poor lendeth to the Lord*'; but *lend me a sovereign.* Phrs. *lend me your ears,* listen; *to lend a hand* (*in, at*), be of use in, help; *to lend a helping hand,* act as a benefactor to; *lend countenance to,* tolerate, acquiesce in; support (a person or a line of conduct). **2.** To let out money at interest. **3.** To impart, contribute, add to: *this fact lends probability to the story*; '*'Tis distance lends enchantment to the view*' (Campbell, 'Pleasures of Hope'). **4.** (reflex.) **a** (of persons) *To lend oneself to,* (usually in bad sense) stoop to: *lend oneself to dishonest means*; **b** (of things) be useful for, serve for: *a fork does not lend itself to the purposes of a corkscrew.*

lender, n. [1. lénder; 2. léndə]. Prec. & **-er.** One who lends; (in compound) *money-lender,* one who lets out money at exorbitant interest.

lending-library, n. [1. lénding lībrari; 2. léndiŋ laibrəri]. Institution which lets out books temporarily, at a price.

length, n. [1. length; 2. lɛŋþ]. O.E. *lengþu,* M.E. *lengthe*; fr. **langiþa,* fr. O.E. *lang,* 'long' (see **long (I.)**), & formative suff. **-th.** **1. a** A dimension of space; the measurement of anything from one end to another: *the length of a line, rod, house, field, road*; **b** extent of distance, *length of a journey.* **2. a** Total duration (of time): *length of a visit, stay, holiday*; **b** duration of utterance, and of the acoustic effect: *the length of a syllable, of a vowel*; *the length of a musical note.* **3.** Range, scope, compass, extent: *length of a book, paragraph, sermon* &c. Phrs. *at length,* (i.) finally, at last; *he came at length*; (ii.) in detail, thoroughly, fully: *to explain something at length*; (iii.) for a long time: *to speak at length*; *at full length,* stretched straight out; (*to speak* &c.) *at some length,* rather long; *to go the length of,* to go so far, take such extreme measures as (followed by Pres. Part.); *to go all lengths,* be prepared to do anything, stick at nothing to attain one's object; *at arm's length,* as far away as possible; (fig.) *keep a man at arm's length,* behave with marked coldness as discouraging intimacy; *to have, get, know, the length of a person's foot,* form an estimate of his character; *length of days,* long life; *to win by a length,* of a boat, horse &c., in a race, i.e. by its own length, as measure of distance.

lengthen, vb. trans. & intrans. [1. léngthen; 2. léŋþən]. Prec. & **-en.** **1.** trans. To prolong, extend, make longer; *lengthen out,* prolong unduly. **2.** intrans. **a** To grow longer: *the days are lengthening*; *the shadows lengthen,* (i.) evening is coming on; (ii.) one is growing older, life is nearing its close; **b** to extend, pass, into: *summer lengthens into autumn.*

lengthily, adv. [1. léngthili; 2. léŋþili]. **lengthy** & **-ly.** In a lengthy manner.

lengthiness, n. [1. léngthines; 2. léŋþinis]. **lengthy** & **-ness.** Quality of being lengthy; excessive length; (specif. of speech) prolixity.

lengthwise, adv. [1. léngthwīz; 2. léŋþwaiz]. **length** & **-wise.** In the direction of the length.

lengthy, adj. [1. léngthi; 2. léŋþi]. **length** & **-y.** Having excessive length; **a** (of duration in time) lasting too long, spun out; hence, **b** (of speech) prolix; **c** (of persons) given to lengthiness in speaking; verbose.

lenience, -cy, n. [1. lḗniens(i); 2. līniəns(i)]. Next word & **-ce, -cy.** Quality of being lenient; indulgence, mercy, clemency.

lenient, adj. [1. lḗnient; 2. līniənt], fr. Lat. *lēnient-(em),* Pres. Part. type of *lēnīre,* 'to soften, alleviate; to allay, pacify', fr. *lēnis,* 'smooth, soft, gentle'; prob. cogn. w. O. Slav. *lenŭ,* 'slothful, inactive', fr. base **lē-,* for the reduced grade of wh. see **lassitude.** **1.** (archaic) Tending to assuage, or allay: '*With lenient arts extend a mother's breath*' (Pope). **2.** Clement, mild, merciful; **a** (of persons) not exacting or imposing full retribution; **b** (of punishment) light in proportion to the offence.

lenify, vb. trans. [1. lénifī, lḗnifī; 2. lénifai, līnifai]. Lat. *lēni-,* as in prec., & **-fy.** To assuage, alleviate.

lenitive, adj. & n. [1. lé-, lénitiv; 2. lí-, lénitiv]. See next word & **-ive.** **a** adj. Tending to mitigate or assuage; emollient; **b** n., a medicine which soothes and eases pain or irritation.

lenity, n. [1. lé-, léniti; 2. lí-, léniti]. Lat. *lēnitāt-(em),* 'softness, mildness', fr. *lēni-,* see **lenient,** & **-ity.** Quality or condition of being lenient; mercy, clemency.

leno, n. [1. lḗnō; 2. līnou]. Fr. *linon,* 'soft fabric, lawn'. See **linen.** Soft, light cotton fabric.

lens, n. [1. lenz; 2. lɛnz]. Lat. *lens, -tis,* 'lentil'; Mod. sense fr. the shape. See **lentil.** A piece of glass or crystal cut or ground so as to affect in various ways the rays of light, and modify vision. *Crystalline lens,* (anat.) transparent body in interior of the eye having shape and function of a lens.

Lent (I.), n. [1. lent; 2. lɛnt]. O.E. *lencten, lengten,* 'spring, Lent', M.E. *lenten, lente*; O.H.G. *lengizin.* The first element is a mutated form of O.E. *lang,* 'long', as in **length**; the ending *-ten* may represent an old word for 'day', seen in Goth. *sin-teins,* 'daily', cogn. w. O. Slav. *dĭni,* 'day', & Scrt. *dina-,* 'day'. The name wd. in this case refer to the lengthening of days in spring. That period of ecclesiastical year (forty days) extending from Ash Wednesday until Easter Day, kept as a time of fasting and abstinence to commemorate the Temptation, Trial, and Crucifixion of the Saviour. *Lent lily,* the daffodil; *Lent term,* term at school or university following the Christmas vacation, ending about Easter.

lent (II.), vb. Pret. & P.P. of **lend.**

-lent, suff. [1. lent; 2. lənt], fr. Lat. adjs. ending in *-lentus,* e.g. *succulent, virulent*; the equiv. Engl. suff. is *-ful.*

Lenten, adj. [1. lénten; 2. léntən]. O.E. *lencten*; but present word fr. **lent** (I.) & adj. suff. **-en.** Belonging to, connected with, Lent: *Lenten fast, fare, services* &c.

lenticular, adj. [1. lentíkūlar; 2. lɛntíkjulə]. See next word & **-ar.** **1.** Shaped like a lens or a lentil. **2.** Connected with the crystalline lens of the eye.

lentil, n. [1. léntil, -tl; 2. léntil, -tl]. Fr. *lentille,* fr. Lat. *lenticula,* dimin. of *lens* (stem *lenti-*), 'pulse' &c., & dimin. suff. *-cul* (see **-cule**). The stem perh. meant orig. 'pliable', & may be identical w. that in next word. Seed of a leguminous plant; specif., the seed of one of several varieties of bean, dried and used as a vegetable.

lentisk, n. [1. léntisk; 2. léntisk], fr. Lat. *lentiscus,* fr. *lentus,* 'flexible'. See next word. The mastic tree; mastic.

lentitude, n. [1. léntitūd; 2. léntitjūd]. Lat. *lentitūdo,* 'slowness, sluggishness', fr. *lentus,* 'flexible, twining; slow, immovable'; cogn. w. O.H.G. *lindi,* 'soft, mild' &c., O.E. *līþe.* See **lithe.** (rare) Slowness, sluggishness.

lentoid, adj. [1. léntoid; 2. léntɔid]. See **lens** & **-oid.** Lens-shaped.

Leonid, n. [1. lḗōnid; 2. līounid]. Fr., fr. Lat. *leōnidēs,* fr. *leo, leōn-(is),* 'lion', & **-id.** Shooting star apparently radiating from the constellation Leo.

leonine (I.), adj. [1. lḗōnīn; 2. līounain]. Lat. *leōnīnus,* fr. *leōn-,* stem of *leo,* 'lion'. Like a lion: *a leonine type of face* &c. Phrs. *leonine partnership,* (law, fr. Lat. *leonīna societas*) a partnership in which one gets all the profits and the other has to bear the losses or most of them; cp. 'a lion's share'.

Leonine (II.), adj., fr. name *Leo.* **a** Connected with one of the popes called Leo: *Leonine city,* that part of Rome in which the Vatican is, as walled by Leo IV.; **b** connected with any person of this name; *Leonine verse,* elegiac hexameters and pentameters, with the last word of the line rhyming with that just before the caesura; invented in 12th cent. by a Benedictine of the name.

leopard, n. [1. lépard; 2. lépəd]. M.E. *leoparde, leparde, libbard* &c.; O. Fr. *leopard,* fr. Lat. *leopardus.* See **lion** & **pard** (I.). **1.** Large spotted animal, *Felis pardus,* of cat tribe, found in Africa and Asia; *American leopard,* the jaguar; *snow leopard,* the ounce. **2.** (her.) A lion depicted sideways but with face turned full towards one.

leopardess, n. [1. lépardes; 2. lépədis, -ɛs]. Prec. & **-ess.** Female of the leopard.

leopard moth, n. A moth, genus *Zeuzera,* the burrowing larvae of which destroy timber.

leper, n. [1. léper; 2. lépə]. M.E., fr. O. Fr. *lepre,* 'leprosy', Lat. *leprae, lepra,* fr. Gk. *léprā,* 'leprosy', fr. *leprós,* 'scaly', cp. *lepís, lépos,* 'scale'; cp. *lépein,* 'to peel, strip'; cogn. w. O. Slav. *lupiti,* 'to peel'; further Lat. *liber,* 'inner bark of a tree'. See **library** & cp. **leaf.** **1.** (obs., Bib.) Leprosy: '*He . . . will surely strike his hand over the place, and recover the leper*' (2 Kings v. 11). **2.** (with transference of sense) One afflicted with leprosy.

lepido-, pref. Form used in compounds, fr. Gk. *lepid-,* stem of *lepis,* 'scale', see prec.

Lepidoptera, n. pl. [1. lèpidóptera; 2. lèpidɔ́ptərə]. Prec. & Gk. *pterón,* 'feather', see **ptero-** & **feather.** Insects with four scaly wings; moths and butterflies.

lepidopterous, adj. [1. lèpidópterus; 2. lèpidɔ́ptərəs]. Prec. & **-ous.** Pertaining to the Lepidoptera.

leporine, adj. [1. léporīn; 2. lépərain]. Lat. *leporīnus,* fr. *lepor-,* stem of *lepus,* 'hare', & **-ine.** Etymol. very doubtful. Belonging to the hare family.

leprechaun, n. [1. léprehawn; 2. léprəhɔ̄n]. Ir. *luchorpān, lupracān,* lit. 'having a small body'. A sprite in the form of a small wizened old man.

leprosy, n. [1. léprosi; 2. léprəsi]. **leprous** & **-y.** Infectious chronic disease caused by a micro-organism, occurring chiefly in Asia, Africa, parts of Northern Europe &c., affecting the skin, tissues, or nerves; (fig.) *moral leprosy,* contagious demoralization and corruption.

leprous, adj. [1. léprus; 2. léprəs]. **leper** & **-ous.** Afflicted with leprosy.

lepto-, pref., fr. Gk. *leptós,* 'cleaned; fine, delicate, slender; thin, small', cp. Lat. *lepidus,* 'fine, elegant; pleasant, agreeable'; prob. fr. same base as Gk. *lépein,* 'to peel, take the husk off'. See under **leper.**

leptodactyl, n. [1. lèptōdáktil; 2. lèptoudǽktil]. See prec. & **dactyl.** (zool.) Bird or animal having thin, slender toes.

Lesbian, adj. [1. lézbian; 2. lézbiən]. Gk. *Lésbios,* 'pertaining to Lesbos', w. substitution of Lat. suff. *-an.* **a** Connected with the island of Lesbos (now Mytilene); **b** specif., pertaining to a type of sexual perversion among women.

lese-majesty, n. [1. lēz májesti; 2. līz mǽdžisti]. Fr. *lèse-majesté,* Lat. *laesa majestas,* 'violated majesty'. See next word & **majesty.** High treason; an offence against the dignity of the sovereign power of a state; specif., offence against the person or dignity of the king or other ruler as representing the sovereign power.

lesion, n. [1. lḗzhun; 2. līžən]. Lat. *laesiōn-(em),* 'injury; attack', fr. *laes-(um),* P.P. type of *laedere,* 'to injure, damage; to offend, aggrieve; to insult'. Etymol. doubtful, but perh. cogn. w. Gk. *líthos* 'stone' (see **litho-**). The orig. meaning in this case wd. be 'cut, bruised &c. with a stone'. Cp. similar connexion of meaning between Lat. *secāre,* 'to cut', & *saxum,* 'large rough stone, rock'. Damage, injury; **a** specif. (med.) harmful alteration in the tissue or in the function of an organ; also **b** moral injury.

less, adj., adv., n., & prep. [1. les; 2. lɛs]. O.E. *lǣs,* adv., 'less'; *lǣssa,* adj., 'smaller', used as compar. of *lȳtel,* 'little'. Etymol. unknown. **1.** adj. Smaller in size, fewer in number; not so much, not so long; of minor importance: *the height of English mountains is less than that of the Alps*; *less people go to* church than to theatres; *drink less wine*; *he spends less time at work than a' play*; *I want less noise, please!* Phrs. *may your shadow never grow less*, may you continue to flourish; *your shadow hasn't grown any less*, you have not grown thinner; *no less a person than*, no other than; so important a person as. **2.** adv. To a smaller extent, to an inferior degree: *the heat grows less intense*; *he is less fat than he was*. Phr. *to expect no(thing) less*, at least that, at least as much. **3.** n. A smaller amount: *he won't take less*; *I had less to eat than I needed*; *less of your nonsense*; *less of a fool than he looked*. **4.** prep. Omission made of; with the deduction of: *five pounds less half-a-crown*.

-less, suff. [1. les; 2. lis], forming adjs. O.E. *-lēas*, identical w. *lēas*, 'devoid of; sham, false, vain'; O.S., O.H.G. *lōs*, 'free from'; O.N. *laus*; fr. same base as that of O.E. *lēosan*, 'lose'. See **lose** & **loss**. **1.** (after ns.) Lacking, devoid of, free from, not possessing: *fatherless, sinless, sunless*. **2.** (after vbs.) Not performing, or undergoing, incapable of performing, not suffering, the action or process expressed by the verb: *tireless, fadeless, ceaseless, relentless*.

lessee, n. [1. lesé; 2. lɛsí]. See **lease (I.)** & **-ee**. Person to whom the lease of a house or land is granted; tenant under a lease.

lessen, vb. intrans. & trans. [1. lésn; 2. lésn], fr. **less**, adv., & vbl. suff. *-en*. **1.** intrans. To grow less, diminish, shrink, contract: *light lessens as evening comes on*. **2.** trans. **a** To make less, take away from, reduce in size or extent: *this circumstance lessens the danger*; **b** to belittle, depreciate, minimize, disparage: *he is inclined to lessen the difficulties*; *I don't wish to lessen the services he has rendered*.

lesser, adj. [1. léser; 2. lésə]. Compar. of **less**. Often used instead of *less*: *the lesser of two evils*; esp. archaic and poet.: '*the lesser light to rule the night*' (Gen. i. 16).

lesson, n. [1. lésn; 2. lésn]. M.E. *lessoun*, O. Fr. *lecon*, fr. Lat. *lectiōn-(em)*, 'a reading', fr. base *leg-*, q.v. under **lecture**. **1. a** Anything learnt or taught; piece of instruction given or received: *to give, take, a lesson in riding, music, Latin* &c.; Phr. *to read a person a lesson*, to admonish, reprove, him. **b** (pl.) course of instruction: *to have music lessons*; *lessons in fencing* &c. **2.** Definite piece of information, set of facts &c., appointed to be mastered at a given time: *the boy doesn't know, hasn't learnt, his lessons properly today*. **3.** (pl.) Whole course of instruction, and systematic education generally, as imparted to the young: *not very bright at his lessons*; *fond of his lessons*. **4.** Something learnt by observation or experience which should preserve one from repetition of error: *he has had a severe lesson*; *let this be a lesson to you*. **5.** Portion of Scripture appointed to be publicly read in churches on particular days: *the lesson for the day*; *here endeth the first lesson*.

lessor, n. [1. lesór; 2. lɛsɔ́]. See **lease (I.)** & **-or**. The person who grants a lease.

lest, conj. [1. lest; 2. lɛst]. O.E. *þȳ lǣs þe*, 'lest', lit. 'by that the less that'; *þ* after *s* normally changes to *t*. For fear that, so that . . . not, in case: '*take heed lest ye fall*'; *I hid it lest he should see it*.

let (I.), vb. trans. & n. [1. let; 2. lɛt]. Pret. *letted*, P.P. *let*; O.E. *lettan*, fr. **lættjan*; O.S. *lettian*, O.H.G. *lezzan*, 'to hinder'; Goth. *latjan*, 'to make late; to tarry'. See **late**. **1.** vb. (archaic) To hinder, prevent, thwart: '*I purposed to come unto you, but was let hitherto*' (Rom. i. 13); chiefly, *to let and hinder*. **2.** n. **a** A hindrance, stoppage; Phr. *without let or hindrance*; **b** (in lawn-tennis &c.) an accidental obstruction of the ball in serving, as by the top of the net, not counted as a fault, a repetition of the service being allowed.

let (II.), vb. trans., & auxil. O.E. *lǣtan*, 'to leave behind; bequeath; depart from, leave; to permit; to cause to happen; to lease (land)'; M.E. *lēten*, 'to leave, relinquish'; O.S. *lātan*; O.H.G. *lāzan*; Goth. *lētan*, 'to permit, suffer, allow'; cogn. w. Gk. *lēdein*, 'to be idle, tired'; also w. Lat. *lassus* (fr. **lad-to*), 'tired, exhausted' (see **lassitude**); fr. same base as Goth. *lats*, 'idle' &c. See **late**. **A.** trans. **1.** To leave: *to let be, let alone*; **a** to refrain from molesting or disturbing: *let me be, let me alone*; **b** not to touch, not to interfere with: *let my things alone*; **c** not to interfere, or intermeddle, with; not to take part in: *I should let this business alone if I were you*; Phrs. *let me alone for taking care of myself*, rely on me to; *let alone*, not to mention, to say nothing of: *I can't afford to hunt, let alone to play polo*. **2.** To allow, cause, to flow; (in archaic phr.) *to let (him &c.) blood*, to bleed; *he was let blood*, was bled. **3. a** To give temporary use of (house, land) in return for rent; to lease, hire out: *I shall let my house for the winter*; *I let all my land for grazing*; *to let lodgings*; **b** *to let out*, (not confined to houses and land) to let on hire: *to let out horses and carriages &c. by the day*. **B.** auxil. (followed by another vb. in infin., but not preceded by *to*). **1. a** To allow by act of volition; to allow, permit: *will you let me smoke?*; *do let me have one more shot*; *I won't let you waste your time like this*; Phrs. *to let a person hear, know, (the news, what has happened* &c.), to inform him; *to let a person hear from one*, to write to, communicate with him; **b** (with second vb. understood but not expressed) *he wanted to go but his wife wouldn't let him*. **2.** To allow through indifference or carelessness, incapacity &c.; to take no steps to prevent: *to let a prisoner escape*; *to let a dish fall*; *to let the fire (go) out*. **3.** (in imperat.) Expressing desire, command, exhortation: *let us (let's) go at once*; *let us (let's) have a good time while we are here*; *let me hear you sing*; *let him try his best*; (ironical) *let him do his worst*. **C.** Idiomatic uses before certain verbs. *Let be*, leave alone; Phr. *let bygones be bygones*, forgive and forget. *Let drive at*, to strike violently, aim a powerful blow at. *Let drop, fall (a word, remark* &c.), to blurt out, utter inadvertently. *Let fly*, to discharge, hurl forth, violently. *Let go*, to release one's hold; *let oneself go*, to abandon oneself to one's emotions or passions, relax self-control. *Let pass*, to overlook, disregard, forgive. *Let (things) slide*, to show indifference. **D.** Followed by preposition or adverb. *Let down*, to lower: *let down the window*; Phrs. *to let a man down*, deceive, betray, place him in awkward position; *to let a business, school &c. down*, lower its prestige, injure its reputation; *let a man down easily*, show him consideration and leniency. *Let in*, allow to pass, flow in: *to let in light and air*; *to let a person in*, **a** give him admission; **b** to deceive, betray, put in a fix: *I was badly let in over that business*. *Let loose*, release, remove restraint from. *Let off*, **a** to fire off: *to let off a gun*; **b** to excuse, pardon, show clemency to, mete out lenient punishment to: *to let a man off what he owes*; *let him off lightly, with light sentence* &c. *Let on*, to admit, reveal, make admission &c.: *he knew the facts all the time but he never let on*. *Let out*, **a** allow to flow, run, away: *to let the water out of the bath*; **b** to release: *to let a man out (of prison), on bail*; **c** to make (a garment) wider, looser, longer: *the trousers must be let out round the waist*; **d** to divulge, esp. by inadvertence: *in the course of conversation he let out that he had lost all his money*; *let out at*, aim a violent blow at; attack violently in words.

let (III.), n., fr. prec. (colloq.) A letting, lease, or renting of a house, room &c.

-let, dimin. suff. [1. let; 2. lit], fr. Fr. dimin. **-el** & **-et**. *Chaplet, hamlet*; *streamlet* &c.

lethal, adj. [1. léthl; 2. líþl]. Fr. *léthale*, fr. Lat. *lētālis*, 'deadly, fatal'; cp. *lētum*, 'death'; the base **lēi-*, **li-* occurs in Scrt. *li-yatē*, 'vanishes, disappears'; Gk. *limós*, 'hunger'; Lith. *leilas*, 'thin, worn out', *lēsas*, 'slim, thin'; for connexion between the ideas of *hunger* & *death* cp. **famish** & **starve**. Spelling perh. influenced by fancied connexion w. **lethe**. The base may ultimately be the same as that in O.E. *lēf*, 'worn out', see **left (I.)**. Cp. also **oligo-**. Fatal, deadly, mortal: *lethal weapon*, one causing death; *lethal chamber*, place where dogs and cats are painlessly put to death.

lethargic(al), adj. [1. letháriik(l); 2. lɛþádžik(l)]. **lethargy** & **-ic**. **a** Resembling, connected with, lethargy; **b** in a state of lethargy; drowsy; **c** inclined to lethargy; dull, heavy, slow of movement, inactive in body or mind; apathetic.

lethargy, n. [1. létharji; 2. léþədži]. Fr. *léthargie*, Lat., fr. Gk. *lēthargía*, 'forgetfulness', fr. *lēthargos*, 'idle, forgetful'; fr. *lēthe*, 'forgetfulness' (see **Lethe**), & *argós*, 'idle, not working; lying fallow', for **awergos*, fr. **a-**, neg. pref., & base **werg-*, 'work' &c. See **ergon**, **erg**, & **work**. **a** State of abnormal drowsiness; inertness, torpidity, inactivity of body; **b** state of mental torpor; indifference, apathy.

Lethe, n. [1. léthē; 2. líþi]. Gk. *lēthē*, 'forgetfulness, oblivion'; name in Gk. mythol. of a river in Hades the water of which the souls of the dead were obliged to taste, with the effect of complete forgetfulness of the past. This word & Gk. *lēthō*, 'escape notice, be unseen' &c., *lēthargos*, 'forgetfulness', & other related words are cogn. w. *láthrios*, 'stealthy, secret, furtive'; connected w. *lanthánein*, 'to escape notice'; cp. Lat. *latēre*, 'to lie hidden', q.v. under **latent**. Oblivion, forgetfulness.

let-off, n. **let (II.)** & **off**. Act of letting off, or excusing; an escape from punishment which is deserved.

Lett, n. [1. let; 2. lɛt]. Inhabitant of former Russian duchy of Kurland, now the republic of Latvia; one of a Baltic people related to the Lithuanians in race and language.

letter (I.), n. [1. léter; 2. létə]. Lat. *littera*, 'letter of the alphabet; handwriting'; in pl. *litterae*, 'epistle, document'; the etymol. is not perfectly certain; the alternative form *lītera* is apparently not the older. The word is therefore not directly connected w. Lat. *litūra*, 'smear', esp. 'smearing of wax on writing tablet', wh. is related to *linere*, 'to daub, smear, spread over' &c. Walde, following others, considers *littera* as a loan-word fr. Gk. *diphthéra*, 'leather, dressed hide' (see **diphtheria**), w. *l* for *d*, due to association w. *linere*, & *legere*, 'to read'. If this be correct it wd. seem that the word must have been applied in Lat., first of all, to the skin used for writing, & then transferred to the symbols written upon it. Cp. **literal**. **1. a** Graphic symbol engraved or written, expressing a sound of speech: *letter of the alphabet*; Phr. *the letter of the law*, exact, precise, rigidly accurate meaning; often contrasted with *spirit*: '*the letter killeth, but the spirit giveth life*' (2 Cor. iii. 6); **b** a printed type. **2.** Written document conveying message, greeting &c. to another person; epistle, missive; various specific meanings in Phrs. *letter of credit*, document in which a banker intimates to his agents that a given person, named in the document, is entitled to draw upon him up to an amount stated; *letters of business*, authorization, command, from the sovereign to the ecclesiastical authorities to take a certain action; *letters of marque*, authorization to a private person to fit out and arm a vessel to seize foreign ships and merchandise; *letters of administration*, legal document authorizing executors of a deceased person to administer his estate; *letters of orders*, certificate of ordination granted by a bishop; *letters patent*, legal document issued by supreme authority granting the right to an individual to do certain things, or enjoy certain privileges. **3.** (in pl.) Elements of the art of reading: *to teach a child his letters*. **4.** (in pl.) Literary culture, literature, learning: *art and letters*; *a man of letters*, a writer, scholar; *the profession of letters*, that of an author, or scholar.

letter (II.), vb. trans., fr. prec. To mark with letters, impress letters on.

letter book, n. Book in which copies of letters are preserved.

letter-box, n. Receptacle for holding letters intended for, or delivered by, the post, having an opening, usually protected by movable flap, through which letters are passed.

letter-card, n. Device used in correspondence, consisting of a thin sheet of pasteboard folded in the middle, having postage stamp engraved on outside, with gummed edge on the inner side by which it can be kept closed.

letter carrier, n. Person who takes round, and distributes letters; a postman.

letter-case, n. Folding case for holding letters &c. in the pocket; pocket-book.

lettered, adj. [1. léterd; 2. létəd]. **letter** & **-ed**. **1.** Having education; learned in literature. **2.** Having letters written, stamped, or engraved upon it: *a book lettered in gold*.

lettering, n. [1. létering; 2. létəriŋ]. Series of letters written or engraved, inscription; style and form of these.

letter-perfect, adj. Knowing the words of a part in a play, of a piece for recitation &c., with complete accuracy.

letter-press, n. Device for copying letters by pressing them under plate of metal worked by a screw.

letterpress, n. [1. léterpres; 2. létəpres]. **a** Printed words, print; **b** specif., printed words on page of a book, as distinct from illustrations.

letter-weight, n. Block of some heavy substance, often fashioned into a fanciful or artistic shape, used to prevent loose papers from blowing away; paper-weight.

Lettic, adj. & n. [1. létik; 2. létik]. See **Lett** & **-ic**. **a** adj. Belonging to a certain branch of Balto-Slavonic languages; pertaining to the Letts or their language; **b** n., the Lettic branch of languages.

Lettish, adj. & n. [1. létish; 2. létiʃ]. See prec. & **-ish**. **a** adj. Pertaining to the Letts or their language; **b** n., the language of the Letts.

Letto-, pref. Form of Lett, or Lettish, used in compounds: *Letto-Lithuanian*.

lettre de cachet, n. [1. létr de káshā; 2. létr də kǽʃei]. Fr., 'sealed letter'. **a** Sealed letter coming from, and signed by, a sovereign; specif. **b** a letter of this kind authorizing imprisonment for no alleged offence, formerly issued by the kings of France.

lettuce, n. [1. létis; 2. létis]. Fr. *laitue*, Lat. *lactūca*, 'lettuce', fr. *lact-*, milk, referring to white juice of the root and stems of the plant. See **lacteal**. Plant with bright green succulent leaves, of a slightly bitter taste, used for salads.

leucaemia, leukaemia. See **leucocythaemia**.

leucite, n. [1. lūsīt; 2. ljúsait], fr. Gk. *leukós*, 'white'. See **leuco-** & **-ite**. A crystalline rock-forming mineral, a silicate of aluminium and potassium, found chiefly in volcanic lavas.

leuco-, pref. Form in combinations meaning 'white', used in scientific terminology, fr. Gk. *leukós*, 'white, shining'; cogn. w. Scrt. *rōkáš*, 'bright', Lat. *lūc-(em)*, *lux*, 'light', *lūcēre*, 'to shine', *lūna*, 'moon', see **lunar**; Goth. *liuhaþ*, 'light', O.E. *lēoht*. See further under **lea** (I.), **light** (I.), **lucent**.

leucocyte, n. [1. lúkosīt; 2. ljúkəsait]. See prec. & **-cyte**. White blood corpuscle. Cp. *phagocyte*.

leucocythaemia, n. [1. lùkōsīthḗmia; 2. ljùkousaiþímiə], fr. **leucocyte** & Gk. *haima*, 'blood'. See **haemal**. (pathol.) Disease marked by an abnormal excess of the leucocytes or white corpuscles in the blood, accompanied by enlargement of the spleen or lymphatic glands and changes in the bone marrow; also called *leukaemia*.

leucocytosis, n. [1. lùkōsītṓsis; 2. ljùkousaitóusis]. **leucocyte** & **-osis**. An abnormal increase in the number of leucocytes in the blood stream.

leucoderma, n. [1. lùkōdérma; 2. ljùkoudə́mə]. See **leuco-** & **derm**. A skin affection in which white patches appear often surrounded by dark patches.

leucoma, n. [1. lūkṓma; 2. ljūkóumə], fr. Gk. *leúkōma*, 'anything whitened; white tablet for notices'. See **leuco-**. Disease of the eye causing white opaque patch on the cornea.

leucopathia, -pathy, n. [1. lùkōpáthia, lūkópathi; 2. ljùkoupǽþiə, ljūkɔ́pəþi]. See **leuco-** & **-pathy**. (med.) **a** Albinism; **b** leucoderma.

leucorrh(o)ea, n. [1. lùkoréa; 2. ljùkəríə]. See **leuco-** & **rheo-**. A disease in women accompanied by inflammation and a white discharge from the vagina.

Levant (I.), n. [1. levánt; 2. livǽnt]. Fr. *levant*, Ital. *levante*, 'point where sun rises, the east', fr. Lat. Pres. Part. *levant-(em)*, 'rising', fr. *levāre*, 'to raise'; fr. same base as *levis*, 'light in weight'; for **legʷhis*; cogn. w. Gk. *elakhús*, 'small', fr. **elnghus*; Goth. *leihts*, O.E. *lēoht*. See **light** (IV.). Eastern part of Mediterranean and the countries washed by it.

levant (II.), vb. intrans. Prob. fr. Span. Phr. *levantar el campo*, 'break up camp'. Cp. *decamp*. To run away, disappear unexpectedly, without leave-taking, and esp. without paying one's debts.

levanter, n. [1. levánter; 2. livǽntə]. **Levant** (I.) & **-er**. Strong easterly wind prevalent in the Mediterranean.

Levantine, adj. & n. [1. levántin, lévantīn; 2. levǽntain, lévəntain]. **Levant** (I.) & **-ine**. **a** adj. Connected with, belonging to, coming from, the Levant; **b** n., a person born in, or inhabiting, the Levant.

levator, n. [1. levā́tor; 2. livéitə]. Lat., fr. *levāt-*, P.P. type of *levāre*, 'to raise'. See **Levant** (I.) & **-or**. (anat.) Muscle which serves to raise a limb or other part of the body.

levee (I.), n. [1. lévi; 2. lévi]. Fr., P.P. of *lever*, 'to raise'. See **Levant** (I.). Reception held by the sovereign or his representative, attended only by men; originally a term of the French court where the sovereign held his morning reception on rising from bed.

levee (II.), n. [1. lévi, levḗ; 2. lévi, livī́]. See prec.; the usage is that of the Southern states of the U.S.A. A natural embankment of alluvium deposited by a slow-moving river in a flat plain, esp. of such rivers as the Mississippi &c.; also an artificial embankment raised to prevent inundations.

levée en masse. See **levy** (I.).

level (I.), n. [1. lévl; 2. lév(ə)l]. M.E., fr. O. Fr. *livel*, *level*, fr. Lat. *lībella*, 'level, plummet line'; dimin. of *lībra*, 'a balance; measure of liquids, pound weight'. See **libra**. **1. a** A plane surface; **b** a flat area of ground. **2. a** Degree of elevation equal to that of something else: *on a level with*; **b** usual, customary height: *water finds its level*. **3. a** Social, moral, or intellectual standard: *a high level of excellence*; **b** state of moral or intellectual equality with another: *to find one's (own) level*. **4.** Instrument for ascertaining a level, for testing whether objects are on same horizontal line, or whether different parts of a surface are horizontal: *a spirit level*.

level (II.), adj., fr. prec. **1. a** Having no part higher than another; horizontal; even; of same height; **b** (of a musical note, of the voice &c.) produced with equal force, remaining at same pitch throughout its entire duration or utterance; *level stress*, a degree of emphasis that is constant, neither increasing nor diminishing. **2.** (fig.) **a** Having same quality as another to an equal degree: *the two brothers were almost level in intelligence*; **b** of equal rank, condition &c. **3.** (of the mind &c.) Not exhibiting sudden inequalities or disparities; well-balanced, equable, impartial. Phr. *one's level best*, utmost, most energetic effort of which one is capable.

level (III.), adv., fr. prec. In a level manner; so as to be level: *to run level with another*; *to fill a basin level with the brim*.

level (IV.), vb. trans., fr. **level** (II.). **1. a** To reduce to a level, make flat: *to level a tennis lawn*; **b** to lower, throw down: *to level a building with the ground*. **2.** To bring to a horizontal position; to aim: *to level a gun at*. **3.** (philol., of process of sound change) To reduce two or more originally distinct sounds to a single sound: *the two M.E. long vowel sounds expressed by e have been levelled under a single sound in present-day English*. **4.** (fig.) To reduce to social, moral, intellectual, equality: *death levels the monarch with the clown*; *level up*, to raise the value, quality &c. of some person or thing, so as to make it equal with that of another; *level down*, to equalize by lowering to inferior condition.

leveller, n. [1. léveler; 2. lévələ]. Prec. & **-er**. Political enthusiast who aims at securing equality among men chiefly by reducing all to a common level of mediocrity; specif., member of a democratic party in Parliament in 1647, which advocated the abolition of all distinctions of rank.

levelness, n. [1. lévlnes; 2. lévəlnis]. **level** (II.) & **-ness**. Quality, condition, of being level.

lever (I.), n. [1. lḗver; 2. lívə]. O. Fr. *levere*, Mod. Fr. *levier*, lit. 'a lifter', fr. *lever*, 'to lift'; Lat. *levāre*, q.v. under **Levant** (I.). **1.** (mechan.) **a** A rigid bar which rests, and moves, at one point upon a fulcrum or prop, and lifts a weight at a second point by means of power brought to bear upon a third; e.g. a crowbar, which is the simplest form of lever; **b** any device for transmitting and modifying force and motion in which these fundamental principles are applied. **2.** (fig.) A means whereby moral influence is exerted; circumstance which enables moral influence to be effectively exerted.

lever (II.), vb. trans. & intrans., fr. prec. To use a lever upon; to move or lift by means of a lever; also, with sense determined by adverb, *lever out*, *lever over*, *lever up* &c.

leverage, n. [1. lḗverij; 2. lívəridʒ]. **lever** (I.) & **-age**. **1. a** Action of a lever; **b** set, system, of levers; **c** advantage gained in moving or lifting by use of lever. **2.** (fig.) Means and power of exerting moral influence; means, advantage possessed, whereby a purpose can be accomplished.

lever de rideau, n., anglicized [1. lévā de rēdṓ; 2. lévei də rīdou]. Fr., 'lifting of the curtain'. Small play performed before the main piece; curtain-raiser.

leveret, n. [1. léveret; 2. lévrit]. O. Fr. *levre*, 'hare', fr. Lat. *lepor-(em)*, *lepus*, 'hare' (cp. **leporine**), etymol. of wh. is very doubtful, & dimin. **-et**. Young hare.

leviable, adj. [1. léviabl; 2. léviəbl]. **levy** (II.) & **-able**. **a** (of a tax) Capable of being levied, of being assessed and collected; **b** (of goods &c.) capable of being, liable to be, taxed.

Leviathan, n. [1. levíathan; 2. liváiəþən], fr. Heb. *levyāthān*. See Job xli. 1. **a** (Bib.) A water-monster, probably a crocodile; **b** (fig.) something of enormous size, esp. a huge ship.

levigate, vb. trans. [1. lévigāt; 2. lévigeit], fr. Lat. *lēvigāt-(um)*, P.P. type of *lēvigāre*, 'to make smooth; to pulverize', fr. Lat. *lēvis*, 'smooth'; cp. Gk. *leios*, 'smooth, flat', for **leiwos*; perh. ultimately fr. base **slei-*, & connected w. O.E. *slīm*, q.v. under **slime**; a further cogn. may be Lat. *līma*, 'file', implement for smoothing, & *līmax*, 'snail', lit. 'the slimy creature' (see **limax**). To grind to fine powder; to reduce to a smooth paste.

levigation, n. [1. lèvigā́shun; 2. lèvigéiʃən]. Prec. & **-ion**. Act or process of levigating.

levin, n. [1. lévin; 2. lévin]. M.E. *levene*, 'flash of lightning'; not found in O.E., prob. fr. O.N. *lȳvna*, *lȳgna*, 'lightning', connected w. Goth. *lauhmuni*, 'lightning', & w. O.E. *līeget(u)* in same sense. The precise relationship between these words is by no means clear. The starting-point is apparently the base **leuk-*, 'light, bright' &c. See further under **lucent**, **light** (I.), **leuco-**. (poet.) Flash of lightning.

levirate, n. [1. lévirāt; 2. lévireit]. Lat. *lēvir*, 'husband's brother', earlier **dēvir*, *daewir, & -ate: cp. Gk. dāêr for *dāwēr, Scrt. devár, O. Slav. deverĭ; these forms all mean 'brother-in-law'. Germ. cognates are O.E. tācor, fr. Gmc. *taikwor, fr. wh. also O.H.G. zeihhur; fr. an Aryan *daikʷ-(ōr), & w. k by association w. word for wife's brother, cp. Lith. laigōvas. Ancient system or custom among the Jews and some other races, according to which a dead man's brother married the widow.

levitate, vb. intrans. & trans. [1. lévitāt; 2. léviteit]. Formed fr. stem levitāt-(em), 'buoyancy, lightness'. See **levity** & **-ate**. **1.** intrans. To tend to rise, become buoyant; opposite of *gravitate*. **2.** trans. To raise, cause to rise; the word in both senses is used by modern spiritualists in reference to the alleged rising and raising of bodies from the ground through spiritual agency.

levitation, n. [1. lèvitāshun; 2. lèvitéiʃən]. Prec. & **-ion**. Action or process of rising or raising from the ground, esp. in sense as used by spiritualists.

Levite, n. [1. lévīt; 2. lívait]. Heb. proper name Lēvī & **-ite**; through Lat. fr. Gk. Leuítēs. **1.** One belonging to the tribe of Levi; descendant of Levi; member of the tribe appointed to assist the priest. **2.** (popular) A Jew. **3.** (obs.) Woman's garment with a belt, worn in 18th cent.

Levitic(al), adj. [1. levítik(l); 2. livítik(l)]. Prec. & **-ic** (& **-al**). **1.** Connected with a Levite, or with Levites. **2.** Relating to, prescribed by, the law contained in the book of Leviticus.

Leviticus, n. [1. levítikus; 2. livítikəs]. Lat., fr. Levi. The third book of the Old Testament which contains the laws relating to priests and Levites.

levity, n. [1. léviti; 2. léviti], fr. O. Fr. levité, fr. Lat. levitāt-(em), fr. levis, 'light'. See **Levant** (I.) & **light** (IV.). **1.** (in physical sense, rare) Lightness, tendency to rise, buoyancy. **2.** (fig., of conduct, character, behaviour &c.) Irresponsible flippancy, lack of gravity; unbecoming, frivolous gaiety.

levulose, n. See **laevulose**.

levy (I.), n. [1. lévi; 2. lévi]. Fr. levée. See **levee**, **lever** (I.), & **Levant** (I.). **1. a** Imposition, collection, of a tax or other compulsory payment, by authority or by force; **b** sum of money thus exacted. **2. a** Forced enrolment of men for military service; **b** body of troops thus raised or enrolled. *Levy en masse*, enrolment of all able-bodied men liable by law for military service.

levy (II.), vb. trans. & intrans., fr. prec. **1.** trans. **a** To impose a tax, tribute, fine; **b** to raise troops by forced enlistment. **2.** intrans. To raise money by a levy.

lewd, adj. [1. lūd; 2. ljūd]. O.E. lǣwede, 'lay, layman'; M.E. lēwed, 'lay; ignorant; vile'; origin doubtful, but perh. borrowed fr. Lat. lāicus. See **lay** (II.). **1.** Indecent, unchaste (of persons and conduct). **2.** (Bib. and obs.) Low, ignorant, base &c.: *'lewd fellows of the baser sort'* (Acts xvii. 5).

lewdly, adv. Prec. & **-ly**. In a lewd manner.

lewdness, n. See prec. & **-ness**. Quality of being lewd; indecency, unchastity, in conduct or expression.

lewis, n. [1. lōōis; 2. lūis]. Etymol. unknown. **1.** Device of iron dovetailed in to heavy blocks of stone by which these can be lifted. **2.** Son of a freemason (origin obscure).

Lewis gun, n., fr. name of inventor. A light form of automatic machine-gun, which can be fired from the shoulder, like a rifle.

lexical, adj. [1. léksikl; 2. léksikl]. See **lexicon** & **-al**. **1.** Pertaining to the vocabulary of a language; contrasted with *grammatical*. **2. a** Pertaining to lexicons or dictionaries; **b** pertaining to lexicography.

lexico-, pref. Form of Gk. lexikón used in compounds. See **lexicon**. Pertaining to dictionaries.

lexicographer, n. [1. lèksikógrafer; 2. lèksikógrəfə]. Gk. lexikográphos. Prec. & **-graph** & **-er**. Compiler of a dictionary.

lexicographic(al), adj. [1. lèksikōgráfik(l); 2. lèksikougrǽfik(l)]. **lexico-** & **graphic** (& **-al**). Pertaining to lexicography.

lexicography, n. [1. lèksikógrafi; 2. lèksikógrəfi]. **lexico-** & **-graphy**. **a** Act, process, of dictionary-making; **b** principles and methods of the art of making dictionaries.

lexicon, n. [1. léksikon; 2. léksikən]. Gk. lexikón, neut. sing. of lexikós, 'pertaining to words', fr. léxis, 'speech; way of speaking, diction', fr. base *leg-, 'to speak', &c., common to Lat. & Gk. See further under **legend**, **lecture**. Book containing the words of a language in alphabetical order; esp. a book giving the meanings of each word in some other language; a dictionary. The word is applied particularly to dictionaries of Greek or Hebrew.

lexigraphy, n. [1. leksígrafi; 2. leksígrəfi]. Gk. léxis, 'speech', see **lexicon**, & **-graphy**. Mode of writing in which each symbol represents a word.

lex talionis, n. [1. léks tàliṓnis; 2. léks tæ̀lióunis]. Lat. See **legal** & **talion**. Law of retaliation; an eye for an eye, a tooth for a tooth.

Leyden jar, n. [1. lídn jar; 2. láidn džā], fr. place in Holland where it was invented. Glass jar coated with tinfoil inside and out, having a lid through which passes a brass rod surmounted by a knob, used for accumulating an electric charge.

li, n. [1. lē; 2. lī]. Chinese. A Chinese measure of length, slightly more than one-third of a mile, about 633 yards.

liability, n. [1. līabíliti; 2. làiəbíliti]. Next word & **-ity**. **1. a** Responsibility, fact of being answerable for: *limited liability*, see **limited**; **b** the sum for which one is liable, amount which one is bound to pay; **c** (in pl.) debts. **2.** Proneness, tendency, predisposition: *liability to disease*.

liable, adj. [1. líabl; 2. láiəbl], fr. Fr. lier, 'to bind', fr. Lat. ligāre (see **ligature**), & **-able**. **1.** Answerable; responsible for, legally bound: *to be liable for a debt*; also absol. **2.** Inclined, apt, predisposed, subject to; in the habit of catching (disease) &c.: *liable to catch cold, to be sea-sick*; *liable to fits of temper*.

liaison, n. [1. liázon; 2. liéizɔ̃], semi-Fr. pronunciation. Fr., fr. Lat. ligātiōn-(em), 'act of binding', fr. ligāt-(um), P.P. type of ligāre, 'to bind' (see **ligament**), & **-ion**. **1.** Connexion, relation; **a** generally used of an illicit association between unmarried pair; **b** relation, link, established between two individuals or parties; esp. (mil.) link between one unit and another, between higher and lower command, or between the commands of two allied armies in the field. **2.** Applied to French pronunciation of final consonant of a word before the initial vowel of the next, e.g. *il se fait aimer* [ils fɛteme].

liaison officer, n. (mil.) Staff officer employed to form a link between the commands of units of the same army, or between those of his own and of allied forces.

liana, n. [1. liáhna; 2. liánə]. Fr. liane, S. American climbing plant; prob. connected w. lien, 'bond', Lat. ligāmen, 'band, tie', fr. ligāre, 'to bind'. See **ligament**. Any climbing tropical plant with woody stems found in S. American forests or Indian jungles.

liar, n. [1. líar; 2. láiə]. M.E. līere. See **lie** (II.) & -ar = **-er**, on anal. of **-ar**. One who does not speak the truth, who tells falsehoods, whether habitually or on a particular occasion. Thus *you're a liar* may mean, according to circumstances, either, you are one who always tells falsehoods, or merely, I do not believe that statement.

lias, n. [1. lías; 2. láiəs]. Fr. liais, 'a fine-grained limestone'; origin unknown. (geol.) **a** Blue limestone; **b** lower, oldest strata of Jurassic series, a blue fossiliferous limestone.

liassic, adj. [1. liásik; 2. laiǽsik]. Prec. & **-ic**. Pertaining to, consisting of, lias.

libation, n. [1. libāshun; 2. laibéiʃən]. Lat. lībātiōn-(em), 'drink-offering', fr. lībāt-(um), P.P. type of lībāre, 'to take a little from; eat sparingly of; to taste, sip; to pour out in honour of a deity'; cp. Gk. libás, 'anything that drops; fount, stream', also leíbein, 'to pour, pour out as a libation'. The base in these words is prob. an extension of that seen in O. Slav. lĭjã, 'I pour', &, w. a different formative element; cp. also Goth. leiþu, O.E. līþ, 'strong drink'. **a** Drink-offering to a god; **b** (facetious) a drink, a drinking bout, potation.

libel (I.), n. [1. líbl; 2. láib(ə)l]. Lat. libellus, 'little book; document, pamphlet; placard; lampoon, libel', dimin. of liber, 'book' &c. See **library**. **1.** (law) **a** A statement, or allegation, concerning a person, made openly and publicly, being neither privileged nor made in the public interest, of a nature calculated to damage in any way the character and reputation of the person about whom the statement is made, or to bring him into ridicule and contempt; any action, such as the publication of a graphic representation of the person, likely to have this effect; **b** the act of publishing such a statement or representation. **2.** (esp. eccles. law) The writ which contains plaintiff's allegations in a law case. **3.** (popular usage) **a** Injurious statement about a person; **b** anything which gives an impression of a person's character, abilities, appearance, below the merits of these; an unflattering statement, portrait &c.: *portraits are often absolute libels upon those whom they represent.*

libel (II.), vb. trans., fr. prec. **1.** To publish a libel concerning; to defame character, detract maliciously from reputation of. **2.** (colloq.) To represent a person as possessing less excellence of character, ability, good looks &c. than he actually does possess; not to do full justice to.

libellant, n. [1. líbelant; 2. láibələnt]. Prec. & **-ant**. One who brings forward allegations in form of a libel (2), which constitute the basis of an action at law.

libellee, n. [1. lìbelḗ; 2. làibelī]. **libel** (II.) & **-ee**. Party in a lawsuit against whom allegations (a libel, 2) are brought; defendant.

libeller, n. [1. líbeler; 2. láibələ]. **libel** (II.) & **-er**. One who libels, defames, another.

libellous, adj. [1. líbelus; 2. láibələs]. **libel** (I.) & **-ous**. **a** (of statements &c.) Expressing, constituting, of the nature of, a libel; defamatory; **b** (of persons) given to uttering libels, inclined to defame others.

libellously, adv. Prec. & **-ly**. In such a way as to constitute libel.

liberal (I.), adj. [1. líberal; 2. líbərəl]. Lat. līberālis, 'of, belonging to, freedom, or freemen; honourable, gracious; generous; plentiful', fr. līber, 'free'; also name of an anct. Italic god of plenty & fruitfulness, Pr. Italic form *leufero-, fr. *leudhero-, whence also Gk. eleútheros, 'bountiful, free'. See **liege**. **1.** Open-minded, wide in sympathy; opposite of narrow-minded. **2.** (of persons) **a** Open-handed, generous, of money, time &c.; **b** (of things) plentiful, copious, abundant: *a liberal share, helping, diet*; *a liberal table*, plentiful food, generous hospitality. **3.** Suitable for a gentleman; enlightened, refined: *liberal education*. **4.** (polit.) Connected with Liberals, belonging to the party bearing this name.

liberal (II.), n., fr. prec. (polit., usually cap.) Member of a party which in England inherits, with considerable modification, the traditions of the old Whigs, and which is reputed to stand for religious toleration and democratic institutions, and generally to be in sympathy with new ideas and methods; the Liberals were formerly one of the two great parties in the State, and in opposition to the *Tories*, or *Conservatives*.

liberalism, n. [1. líberalizm; 2. líb(ə)rəlizəm]. **liberal** (II.) & **-ism**. Principles and ideals of the Liberal party.

liberalist, n. [1. líberalist; 2. líbərəlist]. **liberal** & **-ist**. One who supports the ideas and principles of liberalism.

liberalistic, adj. [1. lìberalístik; 2. lìb(ə)rəlístik]. Prec. & **-ic**. Inclined to, tinged with, approximating to, liberalism.

liberality, n. [1. lìberáliti; 2. lìbərǽliti]. Lat. *līberālitāt-(em)*, 'manner of thought and behaviour befitting a freeman; nobleness, affability; generosity; a gift'. See **liberal** & **-ity**. **1.** Quality of being liberal; **a** generosity, open-handedness; **b** breadth of understanding and sympathy; enlightenment of mind, catholicity. **2.** Something given, a gratuity.

liberalization, n. [1. lìberalīzáshun; 2. lìbərəlaizéiʃən]. Next word & **-ation**. **a** Act of liberalizing; **b** condition of being liberalized.

liberalize, vb. trans. & intrans. [1. líberalīz; 2. líbərəlàiz]. **liberal (I.)** & **-ize**. **1.** trans. **a** To make liberal in sympathies and outlook; to broaden, render more refined and catholic; **b** to make liberal in political sense. **2.** intrans. To become liberal (in all senses).

liberate, vb. trans. [1. líberāt; 2. líbəreit], fr. *līberāt-(um)*, P.P. type of Lat. *līberāre*, 'to release from slavery, make free'; fr. *līber*, 'free' &c. See **liberal**. **1.** (in material and non-material sense) To set free, release from restraint, duty &c.: *to liberate from prison, from a task, from anxiety, from cares of office.* **2. a** (chem., of gases &c.) To set free, allow to escape; **b** (of physical forces) allow to operate.

liberation, n. [1. lìberáshun; 2. lìbəréiʃən]. Lat. *līberātiōn-(em)*, 'a setting free, deliverance'. See prec. & **-ion**. Act of freeing, of setting free; state of being set free.

liberationism, n. [1. lìberáshunizm; 2. lìbəréiʃənizəm]. Prec. & **-ism**. Doctrine that the Church should not be established; advocacy of Church disestablishment.

liberationist, n. [1. lìberáshunist; 2. lìbəréiʃənist]. **liberation** & **-ist**. One who advocates separation of Church and State by disestablishing the former.

liberator, n. [1. líberātor; 2. líbəreitə]. Lat. *līberātor*, 'one who sets free, deliverer'. **liberate** & **-or**. One who sets free; esp. (polit.) one who releases his country from foreign domination or political oppression.

libertarian, adj. & n. [1. libertárian; 2. lìbətéəriən], fr. **liberty** & **-arian**. **1.** adj. Believing in, advocating, the doctrine of the freedom of the will; contrasted with *necessitarian*. **2.** n. Believer in the doctrine of the freedom of the will.

libertarianism, n. [1. libertárianizm; 2. lìbətéəriənizəm]. Prec. & **-ism**. Principles, beliefs, doctrine, of the libertarians.

liberticidal, adj. [1. libêrtisídl; 2. lìbʌ̂tisáidl]. See next word & **-al**. Tending to destroy liberty.

liberticide, n. [1. libértisīd; 2. lìbʌ́tisaid]. **liberty** & **-cide**. **1.** Destruction of liberty. **2.** A destroyer of liberty.

libertinage, n. [1. líbertināj; 2. líbətineidʒ]. See next word & **-age**. Conduct of a libertine.

libertine, n. [1. líbertīn; 2. líbətain]. Lat. *lībertīnus*, 'a freedman', fr. *lībertus*, 'manumitted slave, one freed from slavery', & **-ine**. See **liberty** & **liberal**. **1. a** (usually in bad sense, of a person of loose, unrestrained habits and conduct) A licentious man, a rake, a debauchee; **b** (in playful sense) without disparagement: *a chartered libertine* (man or woman), one whose eccentricities and mild irregularities are tolerated by public opinion. **2.** (rare) A free-thinker, sceptic, agnostic.

liberty, n. [1. líberti; 2. líbəti]. Fr. *liberté*, fr. Lat. *lībertāt-em*, 'civil freedom, condition of freedmen', fr. *līber*, 'free, not a slave'. See **liberal**. **1. a** Freedom from restraint, condition of being a free man; contrasted with *slavery*; **b** condition of being untrammelled in action, free from compulsory occupation; Phr. *at liberty*, (of persons) unoccupied, not busy; (of things) not bespoke, not in use. **2.** (pl.) Certain privileges, rights, franchise conferred by prescription or grant: *the liberties of the city of London.* **3.** Place or area, manor within which certain rights, privileges, and jurisdiction are exercised. **4.** Excessive freedom of, lack of restraint in, conduct which oversteps reasonable limits and becomes an affront; offensive, insulting act or remark. Phrs. *to take liberties with*, treat in too free a manner, to act offensively towards; *to take liberties with a text*, alter it; *to take the liberty of doing so and so*, to presume to do. **5.** Free choice, freedom from compulsion, discretion, permission; esp. in Phr. *you are at liberty to make any use of this which you please* &c.; *liberty of choice.*

libidinous, adj. [1. libídinus; 2. libídinəs]. Lat. *libīdinōsus*, 'full of desire, lustful', fr. *libīdin-*, stem of *libīdo*, 'pleasure; desire, eager longing; sensual passion', & **-ous**; earlier *lubīdo*, cogn. w. Lat. *libet, lubet*, 'it pleases, is agreeable'; cp. same base in Scrt. *lubhyati*, 'he desires, longs eagerly for', & *lōbhaś*, 'desire'; O. Slav. *ljuby*, 'love', *ljubŭ*, 'dear', *ljubiti*, 'to love'; O.E. *lufu* (see **love (I.)**); Goth. *liufs*, O.E. *lēof*, 'dear' (see **lief**). **a** (of persons) Habitually or constitutionally lustful; sensual; **b** (of books &c.) tending to, provoking, lust.

libidinously, adv. Prec. & **-ly**. In a libidinous manner.

libidinousness, n. See prec. & **-ness**. Quality of being libidinous; lustfulness.

libra, n. [1. líbra; 2. láibrə]. Lat., 'Roman pound; pair of scales; the constellation Libra'. Earlier form **līpra*, whence Gk. *lítra*, later, Doric, *lîtra*. Etymol. unknown; prob. borrowed fr. some anct. Mediterranean language. **1. a** A pound weight, only as abbreviated to *lb.*; **b** pound sterling, £. **2.** Seventh sign of the zodiac; called also *the Scales.*

librarian, n. [1. lībrárian; 2. laibréəriən]. Lat. *librārius*, 'transcriber of book, copyist, secretary'; fr. Lat. *liber*, 'book', see **library**, & **-ian**. The keeper of a library.

librarianship, n. [1. lībrárianship; 2. laibréəriənʃip]. Prec. & **-ship**. Office of a librarian.

library, n. [1. líbrari; 2. láibrəri]. Fr. *librairie*, now 'bookshop', fr. Lat. *librārium*, 'place to keep books in, bookcase, or chest', fr. Lat. *liber*, 'book', earlier *luber*; orig. 'the inner bark of a tree', then fr. use made of this for writing on, 'a collection of leaves of writing', & so 'a book, treatise'; cogn. words in other Aryan languages fr. bases **lubh-*, **lup-*, **lep-*, signify some part of a tree, or objects made fr. these. Lat. *dēlibro* means 'strip off bark of a tree, peel'; O. Slav. *lubinŭ*, 'made of bark'; Russ. *lub*, 'bast', O. Pruss. *lubbo* & Lith. *lubà*, 'board'; *lùbas* in same language is 'a wooden roof or ceiling of a room'. With a different final cons., but prob. orig. connected, there is Gk. *lepís*, 'scale, shell', *lopós*, 'shell, husk, bark, peel' (see **lepido-**). A further group of cognates is Goth. *laufs*, 'leaf' &c., q.v. under **leaf**; cp. also **leper**. **1. a** A collection of books; **b** the room or place where this is lodged. **2.** Collection of books temporarily let out to subscribers: *circulating library.* **3.** Series of books of the same kind, or on related subjects, issued by the same publisher: *a library of fiction* &c.

librate (I.), n. [1. líbrāt; 2. láibreit]. L. Lat. *librāta*. See **libra** & **-ate**. (hist.) Amount of land worth a pound in the year.

librate (II.), vb. intrans., fr. *librāt-(um)*, P.P. type of *librāre*, 'to weigh; to hold in equilibrium, as a balance'. See **libra** & **-ate**. **a** To vibrate to and fro as a balance before coming to rest; hence, **b** to remain poised.

libration, n. [1. lībráshun; 2. laibréiʃən]. Prec. & **-ion**. **a** Oscillation, poising, as of a balance; **b** apparent similar oscillation in a heavenly body: *libration of the moon.*

librettist, n. [1. librétist; 2. librétist]. See next word & **-ist**. Writer, author, of a libretto or librettos.

libretto, n. [1. librétō; 2. librétou], pl. *librettos* or *libretti* [1. librétē; 2. librétī]. Ital., dimin. of *libro*, 'a little book'; Lat. *liber*. See **library**. Words of an opera.

lice, n. [1. līs; 2. lais]. Pl. of **louse**.

licence, license (I.), n. [1. lísens; 2. láisəns]. Fr. *licence*, fr. Lat. *licentia*, 'freedom, leave to do as one pleases', fr. *licent-(em)*, Pres. Part. type of impers. vb. *licet* &c., 'it is permitted, lawful, one is at liberty' &c.; the etymol. of the base is quite uncertain. **1. a** Permission, legal authorization, to do some specified thing, esp. to perform some act which without such formal, authoritative permission would be illegal: *licence to fish, shoot, to sell tobacco*, esp. *to sell alcoholic liquor; license to preach*, granted by diocesan bishop to unbeneficed clergy in his own diocese, or to those belonging to other dioceses; **b** official document granting authorization to have, or to do something: *dog-, fishing-licence.* **2.** Excess of freedom, abuse of liberty; undisciplined, irregular conduct, unlawfulness: '*Licence they mean when they cry Liberty*' (Milton); *the invading troops displayed the most unbridled licence.* **3.** Tolerated irregularity, accepted departure from strict rule in form, structure; deviation from meticulous accuracy, which an artist practises in the hope of securing some advantage for his work: *poetic licence.*

license (II.), vb. trans., fr. prec. To grant permission, authorize, to do something which requires a licence to render the act legal: *to license a man to practise as a doctor, to keep a beer-shop; to license the letting of lodgings.*

licensed, adj. [1. lísenst; 2. láisənst], fr. P.P. of prec. **1.** Possessed of a licence, legally authorized by a licence, to do a specific thing: *licensed to sell beer and spirits; licensed victualler*, public innkeeper. **2.** Privileged, enjoying special freedom in some specific capacity: *a licensed buffoon.*

licensee, n. [1. lìsensḗ; 2. làisənsí]. **license (II.)** & **-ee**. Person holding a licence, esp. to sell alcoholic liquor.

licenser, -or, n. [1. lísenser; 2. láisənsə]. **license** & **-er**. One who grants licences.

licentiate, n. [1. lìsénshiāt; 2. laisénʃieit]. Med. Lat. *licentiātus*, P.P. of *licentiāre*, 'to allow, license'. See **licence (I.)**. One in possession of a licence; specif., person holding a licence from a learned, scientific, or professional body, entitling him to practise his profession: *Licentiate in Dental Surgery, of the Society of Apothecaries* &c.

licentious, adj. [1. lìsénshus; 2. laisénʃəs]. Lat. *licentiōsus*, 'wanton' &c., fr. stem *licenti-* (see **licence (I.)**) & **-ous**. **1.** (rare and archaic) Irregular, exhibiting licence, not according to best or traditional usage: *a licentious rhyme, construction* &c. **2.** (of persons and conduct) Unrestrained, dissolute, immoral, debauched.

licentiously, adv. Prec. & **-ly**. In a licentious manner.

licentiousness, n. See prec. & **-ness**. Loose conduct, debauchery; profligacy.

lichen, n. [1. líken; 2. láikin]. Lat., fr. Gk. *leikhḗn*, 'a mossy plant; eruption of the skin'; said to be connected w. *leíkhein*, 'to lick', though connexion in sense is not clear. See **lick (I.)**. **1.** Species of mosslike or scaly cryptogamous plant which grows chiefly on tree-trunks, rock, stones, and buildings; it is a fungus and alga combined. **2.** (med.) A kind of pustular disease of the skin.

lichenous, adj. [1. líkenus; 2. láikinəs]. Prec. & **-ous**. Resembling or pertaining to lichen; infested by lichen.

lichgate, lychgate, n. [1. líchgāt; 2. lítʃgeit]. O.E. *līc*, 'living body; corpse', & *ġeat*, q.v. under **gate (I.)**; *līc* corresponds to O.S. *līk*, 'body, flesh, corpse', O.H.G. *līh*, 'external form, body; corpse', Mod. Germ. *leiche*, 'corpse'. The orig. sense is 'form'. See **like (I. & II.)**. Porch or roofed gateway leading into a churchyard, under which the coffin was placed at a funeral to await arrival of the clergyman.

licit, adj. [1. lísit; 2. lísit]. Fr. *licite*, fr. Lat. *licitus*, 'permitted, lawful', fr. P.P. of *licēre*, 'to be permitted'. See **licence**. (rare) Permissible, lawful.

licitly, adv. Prec. & **-ly.** Lawfully.

lick (I.), vb. trans. [1. lik; 2. lĭk]. O.E. *liccian*; cp. O.S. *liccōn*; O.H.G. *leckōn*; Du. *likken*; Gmc. **lik-* is fr. earlier **ligná-*; cp. Goth. *(bi-)laigōn*, 'to lick'; cogn. w. these are Gk. *likhneúein*, 'to lick', *líkhnos*, 'dainty, greedy'; also *leikhein*, 'to lick'; cp. Lat. *ligurrīre*, 'to lick', & *ligula*, 'little tongue', lit. 'licker', also *lingula*; *lingere*, 'to lick up'. Lat. *lingua*, 'tongue', is not historically connected (see **lingual**), though it is pretty certain that the Romans must have associated *lingua* & *lingere*. Fr. *lécher* is borrowed fr. a Gmc. language. **1. a** To pass the tongue over: *a dog licks one's hand*; Phrs. *to lick one's lips*, (fig.) to show eagerness, greed, in anticipation of pleasure, or satisfaction, or in remembering past pleasures; *to lick into shape*, to bring unpromising material (person or thing) into some degree of smartness, efficiency &c.; to bring a piece of work to something like its final form; *to lick the dust*, (i.) to be sent sprawling on the ground; to be slain; (ii.) behave abjectly: *to lick a person's boots, shoes*, show him abject submission, toady him; **b** *lick up*, to consume by licking or lapping. **2.** To play, flicker, round, touch lightly, as waves of the sea, or darting flames. **3.** (colloq.) **a** To thrash, beat, soundly: *a cowardly, sneaking boy deserves to be well licked*; **b** to triumph over, be superior to, excel, in a fight or other contest or competition. Phrs. *that licks everything, licks creation*, surpasses everything; *that licks me*, is beyond my comprehension; *to go as hard as one can lick*, run at one's top speed.

lick (II.), n., fr. prec. **1. a** Act of licking; Phr. *a lick and a promise*, inadequate, perfunctory, attempt at washing or cleaning; **b** small portion of something, as much as can be licked up with one motion of the tongue: *a lick of butter*. **2.** (colloq.) **a** Severe blow; **b** rapid pace: *to go at a tremendous lick*; *(at) full lick*.

lickerish, liquorish, adj. [1. líkerish; 2. líkərĭʃ]. M.E. *likerous*, 'dainty, lecherous', fr. A.-Fr. variant of O. Fr. *licherous, lecherous*, of Gmc. origin. In the sense 'dainty', the first element was apparently influenced by Engl. *lick*; there has also been a substitution of the Engl. suff. for older *-ous*. Dryden has *liquorish*. (archaic) **1. a** Lecherous, lustful; **b** eager or greedy to devour. **2.** Fastidious, dainty, nice.

lickerishness, n. M.E. *likerousnes*, 'lecherousness'. See prec. & **-ness.** Quality of being lickerish.

licking, vbl. n. [1. líking; 2. líkiŋ]. **lick** (I.) & **-ing. 1.** Act of touching or lapping with the tongue; a lick. **2.** (colloq.) **a** A beating, thrashing; **b** infliction of a defeat in any fight or contest.

lickpenny, n. [1. líkpeni; 2. líkpeni]. (obs.) A needy, greedy person. Cp. Lydgate's *London Lickpenny* (c. 1420).

lickspittle, n. [1. líkspitl; 2. líkspĭtl]. A servile, toadying, abject rascal.

licorice, n. See **liquorice.**

lictor, n. [1. líktor; 2. líktō]. Lat., fr. base *lig-* as in *ligāre*, 'bind', q.v. under **ligament**, & **-tor.** An officer who attended a Roman magistrate; so called from their occupation of binding prisoners; they bore bundles of rods or *fasces*, in which an axe was bound up, as emblems of their powers and office.

lid, n. [1. lid; 2. lĭd]. O.E. *hlid*, 'cover for a vessel or cup; a lid'; O.H.G. *lit*; cogn. w. O.E. *hlīdan*, 'to cover with a lid'; cp. further Goth. *hleiþra*, 'tent, hut'. The starting-point is the Aryan base **klei-* &c., 'to slope, lean' &c., whence come a large number of words. See **clinical, lean (II.). 1.** A cover for the open top of a hollow vessel: *the lid of a kettle, saucepan, teapot*; movable flap, sometimes on hinges, for covering top and closing a box: *lid of a chest* &c. Phr. (colloq.) *to put the lid on (a plan, action* &c.), to come as culminating obstacle, to put a stop to it, bring it to an end, destroy. **2.** One of the fleshy, movable coverings of the eyes; eyelid.

lidded, adj. [1. líded; 2. lídĭd]. Prec. & **-ed.** Provided with a lid or with lids; covered with, protected by, a lid or lids.

lidless, adj. [1. lídles; 2. lídlĭs]. **lid** & **-less.** Lacking a lid or lids.

lie (I.), vb. intrans. [1. lī; 2. lai]. O.E. *lēogan*, M.E. *līȝen, līen*; O.S., O.H.G. *liogan*; O.N. *ljūga*; Goth. *liugan*, 'to lie', cp. also O.H.G. *louginēn*, Mod. Germ. *leugnen*, 'to deny, disavow', cp. O.E. *līegnan*, 'to deny'; O.E. *lyġe*, 'a lie', fr. **lugi* (cp. **lie (II.)**), is fr. the weak grade of this base; outside Gmc. the base appears in O. Slav. *lŭgati*, 'to tell lies'. To utter an untruth; specif., to utter wilful and deliberate falsehood, with intention to deceive, or for an unrighteous purpose. Phr. *to lie in one's throat*, utter gross falsehoods.

lie (II.), n. O.E. *lyġe*. See prec. A deliberate untruth; statement made to hide the truth for some sinister purpose: *to tell a lie*, utter an untruth; *give the lie to*, accuse one to his face of telling a lie, and disprove his statement. *White lie*, a statement not in strict accordance with truth, uttered from benevolent motives, or without any sinister intent.

lie (III.), vb. intrans. O.E. *liċgan*, M.E. *liggen*, & *līen*. The latter, a new formation on the pattern of the O.E. 3rd sing. Pres. *liġeþ*, is the ancestor of the mod. form; O.S. *liggian*, O.H.G. *liggan*; cogn. w. Lat. *lectus*, 'couch, bed'; Gk. *lékhos*, 'bed', & *lókhos*, 'lair'; O. Slav. *lěžati*, 'to lie'. See also **lay (III.). A. 1.** To be, or put oneself, in a recumbent position, recline: *to lie still*; '*Lying robed in snowy white . . . She floated down to Camelot*' (Tennyson); often with *down*: *I lay down in peace and took my rest*. Phrs. *lie doggo*, keep quiet and hidden; *lie low*, **a** be dead (poet.); **b** keep quiet, so as not to attract attention; *lie at one's door, the blame lies at your door*, you are responsible; *lie close*, pressed together. **2.** In general sense of to remain, be placed, be: *the book lies on the table*; *let it lie*, let it stay where it is; *it lies with you to decide*. **3. a** To be situated, occupy fixed position: *Ireland lies to the west of England*; **b** to stretch, be spread out, to open out: *the valley lies at our feet*; (fig.) *the world lies all before you*; *life lies in front of you*. **4.** To be buried: *that great temple where lie the bones of so many kings and heroes*. **5.** (archaic) To stay for a while, lodge, pass the night, sleep: *we lay at Bristol that night*. **6.** (legal) To be admissible, capable of being sustained: *the appeal does not lie*. **B.** Followed by adverb or preposition. *Lie down*, Phrs. *lie down under (an insult* &c.), to submit without protest or resistance; *to take (slight &c.) lying down*, without protest or resistance; *to go and lie down*, rest on a bed, without entering it. *Lie in*, to be in childbed. *Lie under*, to be liable to, suffer, incur: *to lie under suspicion*. *Lie up*, to take to one's bed on account of ill-health, keep one's room. *Lie with*, (archaic and Bib.) to have sexual intercourse with.

lie (IV.), n., fr. prec. Direction, position: *the lie of the land*; (also fig.) position, state, of affairs.

lief, adv. & adj. [1. lēf; 2. līf]. O.E. *lēof*, 'dear, beloved', M.E *lēf*, O.S. *liof*, O.H.G. *liob*, Mod. Germ. *lieb*, 'dear'; Goth. *liufs*; fr. same base as O.E. *lufu* (see **love**); Lat. *libet, lubet*, 'it pleases', *libīdo, lubīdō*, 'pleasure, lust' (see **libidinous**). **1.** adv. (rare and obsolesc.) Gladly, willingly; chiefly in such Phr. as *I would as lief go there as anywhere else*; also in compar., rather, sooner: *I would liefer die than live dishonoured*. **2.** adj. (rare and archaic) '*As thou art lief and dear*' (Tennyson, 'Morte d'Arthur').

liege, adj. & n. [1. lēj; 2. līdž]. M.E. *lēge, līge*, fr. O. Fr. *liege*, fr. Low Lat. *leudes*, O. Fr. *leudes*, 'fief-holders, great vassals', fr. O.H.G. *liut*, 'people, Mod. Germ. *leute*; cp. O.S. *liud*, O.E. *lēod*. These are cogn. w. O. Slav. *ljudŭ*, 'people', & w. Gk. *eleútheros*, 'free', & prob. also w. Lat. *līber*, 'free' (see **liberal**). The form of O. Fr. is due to association w. Lat. *ligāre*, 'to bind', q.v. under **ligament.** (feud.) **1.** adj. **a** (of an overlord) Entitled to receive homage: *liege lord, sovereign*; **b** (of vassals) bound to render homage, service, allegiance: *liege man, subject*; **c** pertaining to the homage of a vassal rendered to his lord: *liege service*. **2.** n. **a** Feudal superior entitled to homage and allegiance; **b** feudal vassal bound to do homage and render service to his overlord: *His Majesty's lieges*.

lien (I.), vb. [1. līn; 2. lain]. Obs. P.P. of **lie (III.)**, fr. M.E. *līen, līȝen*, formed direct fr. the new M.E. infin. type. The O.E. P.P. *leġen*, M.E. *leyn(e)*, is the ancestor of the type *lain* now used.

lien (II.), n. [1. lēn, léen; 2. līn, líən]. Fr., fr. Lat. *ligāmen*, 'band, tie'. See **ligament.** (legal) Right to hold and control property of another until a debt is paid or legal claim discharged.

lienee, n. [1. lēnḗ; 2. līnī]. Prec. & **-ee.** Owner of property upon which another holds a lien.

lienor, n. [1. lénor; 2. línō]. See prec. & **-or.** One who holds a lien on another's property.

lierne, n. [1. liérn; 2. laiə̄n]. Etymol. unknown. (archaic) Short rib in Gothic vaulting which connects bosses and intersections of larger ribs.

lieu, n. [1. lū, lōō; 2. ljū, lū]. Fr., fr. Lat. *locus*, 'place'. See **locus.** Place; only in Phr. *in lieu of*, instead of.

lieutenancy, n. [1. lefténansi; 2. lefténənsi]. See next word & **-cy. a** Office, status, rank of a lieutenant; **b** tenure of this office.

lieutenant, n. [1. lefténant; 2. lefténənt]. Fr. See **lieu** & **tenant. 1.** Deputy, substitute. **2. a** Rank of a junior officer in navy; **b** rank of an officer in the army immediately below that of captain; used as mode of address for naval officer holding this rank (*Lieutenant Jones, R.N.*), but not for a military officer.

lieutenant-colonel, n. **a** Military officer immediately above the rank of major, commanding a battalion; **b** used as title and mode of address on letters &c.

lieutenant-colonelcy, n. Status, rank, of a lieutenant-colonel.

lieutenant-commander, n. **a** Naval officer immediately above the rank of lieutenant and below that of commander; **b** used as title and mode of address.

lieutenant-general, n. Military officer immediately above rank of major-general and below that of general.

lieutenant-governor, n. Official ruling a district or province in a British dominion or colony under a governor-general.

lieutenant-governorship, n. Office of a lieutenant-governor.

life, n. [1. līf; 2. laif]. O. & M.E. *līf*; the other old Gmc. languages have the word in the sense of 'body', as well as 'life', O.H.G. *līp*, 'body, life'; Mod. Germ. *leib*, 'body'; Du. *lijf*, 'body'; O.N. *līf*, 'life, body'. These words are derived fr. a base **leip-*, **lip-*, 'to last, endure, remain', as in Gk. *leípein*, 'to leave, remain' &c. See further under **leave (II.)**, & cp. **live (I.). 1.** Principle which pervades organic matter and which enables animals and plants to transform food into energy, to grow, to adapt themselves to their environment, and to propagate their kind: *the origin of life*. **2.** Animated nature; living organisms generally: *life retreated before the advancing ice-age*. Phrs. *drawn, imitated, to the life*, so as exactly to reproduce the living person or thing; *as large as life*, life-size; (facetious) evident, unmistakable &c.: *there he was as large as life*. **3. a** Period, state, of existence in the world as a living being; time spent by an individual man, lower animal or plant, between birth and death: *life is sweet*; *to spend one's life in doing good*; *to lose one's life*; *to save a person's life*. Phrs. *to take a person's life*, to kill him; *take one's own life*, to commit suicide; *a matter of life and death*, circumstance on which it depends whether one will live or die; (fig.) a matter of highest importance; *to choke the life out of*, kill by choking; *for dear life, for very life*, in order to preserve one's life, implying that even this is difficult; *for the life of me I can't tell you* &c., even though I were to be killed for it; *to come to life (again)*, assume, resume, the functions and ways of a living being, begin to live; *(to take, get) a new lease of life*, (i.) fresh health and strength, such as seem to promise an extended duration of life; (ii.) of inanimate, or of non-material things, capacity for extended existence; *the struggle for life*, effort necessary to provide for human needs; competition for success; **b** conscious existence after bodily death: *the life of the world to come*; *eternal life*. **4.** Mode of existence, way of living; **a** in regard to circumstances, conditions, surroundings: *a comfortable life*; *a happy life*; *low life*; **b** in relation to one's actions and conduct: *to lead a good, saintly life*; *his life will hardly bear investigation*. **5. a** Human life thought of in relation to society; the relations of human beings to each other, and social experience generally; one's career in the world: *to see, learn, something of life*; *to enter upon life*; *a successful, active, life*; **b** specif., social activity, bustling, stirring, existence: *there is not much life in a small country village*. **6.** Account of a person's life and career; a biography: *Boswell's 'Life of Johnson'*; *the Lives of the Poets*. **7. a** Vital energy, vigour; exuberance; vivacity, liveliness, animation: *full of life*; *he infused new life into what seemed a dying cause*; *to put life into a portrait*; *put more life into your movements*; **b** source, cause, of energy or liveliness; inspiration: *he was the life of the whole party*; **c** source of physical health and strength: *plenty of sleep is the life of young children*. **8.** (archaic) Person or thing that is very dear or precious; form of endearment: *my dear life* &c. **9.** Period during which an institution, organization, or an inanimate object will last and continue to exist in a state of activity or usefulness: *the life of a state, a government*; *the life of a steamship, of a popular novel*. **10.** (insurance) Person whose life is insured.

life-belt, n. Belt made of, or lined with, some buoyant material which keeps the human body afloat.

life-blood, n. **1.** (poet.) The blood in the veins of a living creature; blood which has flowed from a living creature. **2.** (fig.) Source of strength and vigour: *research is the life-blood of science and learning*.

life-boat, n. **1.** Specially constructed, highly buoyant boat, used for saving life from a shipwrecked vessel. **2.** Small boat carried by larger vessel to be used in case this has to be abandoned.

life-buoy, n. A life-belt.

life-giving, adj. [1. lif giving; 2. láif giviŋ]. **a** Imparting, having power to impart, life; **b** refreshing, invigorating.

life-guard, n. **a** Military body-guard; **b** specif., *Life Guards*, two cavalry regiments whose function is to guard the person of the sovereign.

life-insurance, or **-assurance**, n. System of contract by which a certain sum becomes payable to a person at a stated age, or to his heirs at his death, on condition of the payment of an annual premium down to the time when the specified age is reached, or the death of the insured occurs.

life-interest, n. Interest in an estate enjoyed by a person during his life, but not transmissible by will.

lifeless, adj. [1. lífles; 2. láiflis]. **life** & **-less**. **1.** Having no life; **a** having lost life, dead; **b** having never possessed life; inanimate. **2.** Not lively, not animated; dull.

lifelessly, adv. Prec. & **-ly**. In a lifeless manner.

lifelessness, n. See prec. & **-ness**. Condition of being lifeless (in all senses).

life-like, adj. **life** & **-like**. **a** Resembling life, resembling a living being; **b** (of a portrait) resembling closely the person whom it represents.

life-line, n. **1.** Line fired by means of a rocket from the shore to or over a ship in distress, by which a stout rope is passed on board. **2.** Rope fastened to a buoy, or a ship, to make it easier to reach it.

lifelong, adj. [1. liflong; 2. láiflɔŋ]. **life** & **-long**. Lasting, continuing, continued, for a lifetime: *a lifelong friend, friendship*.

life-office, n. Insurance business; office of this, which deals with life-insurance.

life-peerage, n. One granted to an individual for his lifetime and not hereditary.

life-preserver, n. Weapon in the form of a short, heavy bludgeon, or of a heavily weighted cane &c.

lifer, n. [1. lífer; 2. láifə]. (colloq.) Person who has received a sentence of imprisonment for life.

life-saving, adj. Designed for, used for, having property of, saving or protecting human life.

life-size(d), adj. (of portraits, statues &c.) Having natural size and proportions of the living objects they represent.

life-table, n. Table used by actuaries &c. showing expectation of duration of life at different ages.

life-tenant, n. (law) One who has a life-interest in an estate.

lifetime, n. [1. líftīm; 2. láiftaim]. Period during which the life of an individual continues.

life-work, n. Work, task, occupying one's whole life; one to which a lifetime is devoted.

lift (I.), vb. trans. & intrans. [1. lift; 2. lift]. M.E. *lyften, liften*, 'to raise', fr. O.N. *lypta, lyfta*, 'to raise'; cogn. w. O.N. *lopt, loft*, 'sky; upper room' (see **loft**); cp. O.E. *lyft*, 'air, cloud'; O.H.G. *luft*, Goth. *luftus*. Further etymol. doubtful. **A.** trans. **1.** To raise from lower to a higher level, set higher up, elevate, hoist: *to lift a child over a ditch*; *steam cranes easily lift several tons at a time*; also *lift up*; Phrs. *lift one's hand against*, strike, threaten to strike; *lift up one's eyes*, look up; *lift (up) one's, its, head*, (i.) to show oneself, become apparent; (ii.) to show signs of regaining strength; (iii.) to feel pride or self-respect; (iv.) (of mountains, big buildings &c.) to tower up, rise; *lift up one's voice*, speak, cry out; *lift (up) one's voice against*, protest. **2. a** To pick up, grasp, and raise by a muscular effort: *the box is too heavy for you to lift*; **b** (slang) to steal. **3.** To cause (a ball) to rise by an upward stroke. **4.** To take up, get (root crops) out of the ground: *to lift potatoes*. **5. a** To raise to a higher moral or intellectual level: *to lift a conversation out of the commonplace*; **b** to raise to a higher social position, or to superior surroundings: *to lift a person from obscurity and poverty*. **B.** intrans. (of clouds, mist, rain, darkness) To rise, disperse, be dissipated, pass away.

lift (II.), n., fr. prec. **1.** Act of lifting, a heave: *to give a stone a lift*; *the lift of an axe*. Phr. *to give a person a lift*, to take him into a vehicle, and carry him in the direction in which he wishes to travel, for a part or the whole of his journey. **2. a** Upward trend, movement, tendency: *the lift of a branch*; **b** lofty carriage of the body: *a characteristic lift of the head*. **3. a** A rise in one's position or fortunes; source of advantage, aid to progress: *his knowledge of languages gave him a great lift in his career*; **b** profitable help, a good turn, a helping hand: *he gave me many a lift when I was a young man*. **4.** Means by which something is lifted; specif. **a** an apparatus for carrying passengers or goods to different floors of a building; an elevator, hoist; **b** rope running from the masthead of a ship to the yard below, for supporting or squaring this; **c** a layer of leather in the heel of a boot or shoe.

ligament, n. [1. lígament; 2. lígəmənt]. Lat. *ligāmentum*, 'band, bandage', fr. base of *ligāre*, 'to bind, tie, fasten'; etymol. & connexions outside Lat. of the base *lig-*, 'to bind', are very dubious. Cp. **lien (II.)**, **lictor**, **ligature**. **a** A tie, band &c. connecting one thing with another; **b** specif. (anat.) tough, flexible band of fibrous tissue connecting the extremities of two bones, or holding an organ in place.

ligamental, adj. [1. ligaméntl; 2. lìgəmént(ə)l]. Prec. & **-al**. Pertaining to, of the nature of, forming part of, a ligament.

ligamentary, adj. [1. ligaméntari; 2. lìgəméntəri]. See prec. & **-ary**. Ligamental.

ligamentous, adj. [1. ligaméntus; 2. lìgəméntəs]. See prec. & **-ous**. Ligamental.

ligate, vb. trans. [1. lígāt; 2. láigeit], fr. Lat. *ligāt-(um)*, P.P. of *ligāre*, 'to bind together, bandage'. See **ligament**. (surg.) To bandage; to tie with a ligature.

ligature, n. & vb. trans. [1. lígachur; 2. lígətʃə]. Lat. *ligātūra*, fr. *ligāt-*, as in prec., & **-ure**. **1.** n. **a** Something that binds, or connects; a bond &c.; **b** (mus.) curved line connecting several notes, slur; **c** (surg.) a tie of silk, catgut &c. used for tying the ends of a cut blood-vessel to stop haemorrhage &c.; **d** (typog.) character containing two letters united. **2.** vb. To tie with a ligature.

light (I.), n. [1. līt; 2. lait]. O.E. *lēoht*, 'light'; O.S., O.H.G. *licht*; Goth. *liuhaþ*; cogn. w. Lat. *lūcēre*, 'to shine' (see **lucent, lucid**), *lūx*, 'light' (see **Lucifer, lucus**; see further **lunation, lunar, luminous**); cogn. also w. Gk. *leukós*, 'bright, shining, white' (see **leuco-**); cp. also O. Slav. *luči*, 'light', & see **lea (I.)**. **1.** (nat. sc.) Form of energy consisting of vibrations in the ether which act upon the optic nerve and make vision possible: *the theory of light*; *light year*, astronomical unit for measuring the distance of stars, being the distance travelled by light in a year. **2. a** Sensation imparted to the sight organs by any natural or artificial luminosity; brightness, gleam, radiance: *the light of the sun, stars, of a candle, a lamp, a fire*; *a good light*, one which enables one to see well; *a bad light*, inadequate for seeing; Phrs. *to stand in one's own light*, (fig.) injure oneself, retard one's progress, by one's own conduct, folly, lack of judgement &c.; *get out of the light*, (colloq.) don't hinder, get out of the way (lit. and fig.); *the light of one's countenance*, favour; *light of one's eyes*, beloved person or thing; *to bring to light*, reveal; **b** light afforded by the sun; daylight: *let's leave before the light fails*; *the light won't last much longer*; **c** specific localized manifestation of light: *a wonderful light lay upon the landscape*. **3. a** A bright, shining body: *'the greater light to rule the day, and the lesser light to rule the night'* (Gen. i. 16); **b** source of light, illuminating agency: *bring in the lights*; *lights on the altar*; *the Admiralty provide lights all round the coast as a guide to seamen*; Phr. *ancient lights*, absence of obstruction of daylight by buildings; right to preserve light, falling on windows, unobstructed by other buildings. **4.** Means of producing, communicating, or kindling light or fire; a match, spill &c.: *to put a light to the fire, to the lamp*; *give me a light for my pipe*. **5.** Aperture through which light passes; division of a window. **6. a** Spiritual and moral illumination or enlightenment: *the children of light*; *the light of the Gospel*; *a man of light and leading*; *'sweetness and light'* (M. Arnold (fr. Swift)); **b** intellectual enlightenment; elucidation, interpretation, explanation; clarity of meaning: *to throw, shed, light on a subject*; *to get light on a difficulty*; Phrs. *in the light of past events, of what you say* &c., with the knowledge gained from; *the light of nature*, intuition, unaided intelligence; **c** key word in acrostic. **7.** Way in which anything impresses one; aspect, complexion: *I can't see the affair in that light*; *to put things in a favourable, unfavourable, light*, make them appear favourable &c.; *to throw a new light upon*, cause to appear different. **8.** (paint., pl.) The brighter parts of a picture; contrasted with shade, shadow; *high lights*, the brightest parts of a picture; Phr. (fig.) *light and shade*, strong contrasts, differing degrees of intensity in emotion, varieties in conduct &c. **9.** Look, expression, on human face, suggestive of brightness, animation, liveliness of spirits, happiness, or other strong emotion: *the light died out of her face*; *the light of battle shone in his eye.*

light (**II.**), vb. trans. & intrans. O.E. *līhtan*, 'to shine, give light'. See prec. **A.** trans. **1. a** To cause to give light by applying a light to: *to light the lamp, gas*; also *light up*; **b** to cause to burn, start burning; to kindle: *to light a fire.* **2.** To illuminate: *to light up a room*, make it light; give it a cheerful appearance; (fig.) to render (a face &c.) cheerful, cause to appear animated &c.: *a charming smile lighted up his features.* **B.** intrans. **1.** (of a lamp, fire &c.) To begin burning; also *light up.* Phr. (colloq.) *to light up*, (of a person) to begin smoking. **2.** (of face and expression) To become cheerful; to express animation, intelligence &c.; to sparkle: *his face lights up when he becomes interested.*

light (**III.**), adj. O.E. *lēoht.* See **light** (**I.**). **1.** Not dark, pervaded with light, rather bright: *a light room*; *a light day*; *a light evening*, one in which daylight lasts. **2.** (of colour) Pale, not intense, whitish; often used before name of colour to denote a pale shade of this: *light blue, brown* &c.

light (**IV.**), adj. O.E. *lēoht*; O.H.G. *līhti, līht*; Goth. *leihts*, 'not heavy, light'; fr. earlier **liŋχta-*; cp. Lith. *lengvùs.* Lat. *levis*, 'light in weight', either fr. an orig. variant **leghwi-*, without nasalization, or, as has been suggested, formed on anal. of *brevis, gravis*; O. Slav. *lĭgŭkŭ*, 'light', Gk. *elakhús*, 'small', for *(*e*)*lŋgkwús*, & *elaphrós*, 'light, active', for *(*e*)*lŋghʷrós*, are derived fr. the nasal type. Cp. also **lights & lung. 1. a** Not heavy, not having much weight; Phrs. (*to have*) *a light hand*, delicacy of touch, skill, dexterity; (fig.) skill in handling a situation, tact: *as light as a feather, as air*, very light; **b** lacking proper, normal, weight, not weighing enough; below legal weight: *a light coin*; *to give light weight*, to cheat by supplying goods below legal standard of weight; **c** not encumbered with heavy arms and accoutrements: *light infantry, cavalry* &c. **2. a** (of soil) Easily pulverized, loose, friable, not dense; **b** (of pastry, bread &c.) well risen, not sticky; **c** (of food generally) easy of digestion. **3. a** (in physical sense) Active, agile, easy, graceful; not ponderous or clumsy: *light movements, step, bound* &c.; **b** (in non-material sense) delicate, exhibiting sensibility and grace: *a light vein of humour*; *light persiflage.* **4. a** Not severe; (i.) devoid of rigour; mild, clement: *a light sentence, punishment*; (ii.) not onerous or exacting: *light duties, work* &c.; **b** (in physical sense) slight in degree, not violent or intense: *a light frost*; *a light attack of measles.* **5.** Lacking moral or intellectual weight; **a** superficial, trivial; unimportant: *a light novel*; *light remarks*; Phrs. *one's lightest word, wish*, most trivial utterance, whim; *to make light of*, represent as unimportant; **b** irresponsible, flighty, immoral: *a person of light character*; *light conduct*; *a light woman*, one of bad character. **6. a** Superficially gay, careless: *light laughter*; *a light jest*; **b** happy, cheerful, buoyant, free from care: *light spirits*; *a light heart.*

light (**V.**), adv., fr. prec. **a** Lightly: *to sit, ride, light*; Phr. *to travel light*, without heavy baggage; **b** easily, without incurring severe punishment: *to get off light.*

light (**VI.**), vb. intrans., for **alight** (**I.**). O.E. *līhtan*, 'to alight'; orig. sense, 'to make lighter; relieve from burden'; connected w. prec. **1.** (archaic, gen. followed by *off, down, from*) To dismount, get off, down from: *to light off a horse*; '*he lighted down from the chariot*' (2 Kings v. 21); also (rarely) *to light at one's door* &c., arrive, and alight at. **2.** To land, settle, alight upon, fall upon: *to light on one's feet*; *the bird lighted upon the bough*; *my eye lighted on a friendly face among the crowd.* **3.** To come upon, discover as by chance, happen to find: *to light on a passage in a book.*

light-armed, adj. Bearing only light weapons.

lighten (**I.**), vb. trans. & intrans. [1. lītn; 2. láitn]. M.E. *lihtenen.* See **light** (**I.**) & **-en. 1.** trans. To make light, illuminate: '*Lighten our darkness, we beseech Thee, O Lord*'. **2.** intrans. **a** To grow light, become brighter: *the day lightens in the east*; **b** to flash out, as lightning.

lighten (**II.**), vb. trans. & intrans. See **light** (**IV.**) & **-en. 1.** trans. **a** To make less heavy; to relieve of a burden; **b** to make more cheerful, enliven. **2.** intrans. **a** To become lighter, less heavy; **b** to become more cheerful, less gloomy.

lighter (**I.**), n. [1. līter; 2. láitə]. **light** (**II.**) & **-er. a** One who lights, kindles; **b** device, object, for producing light, or for kindling.

lighter (**II.**), n. & vb. trans. & intrans. Du. *lichter*, fr. *lichten*, 'to lighten, unload', cogn. w. **light** (**IV.**). **1.** n. Flat-bottomed boat used for unloading vessels anchored at a distance from the wharf. **2.** vb. To use a lighter for unloading and conveying goods from a vessel.

lighterage, n. [1. līterij; 2. láitəridž]. Prec. & **-age.** Sum charged for unloading ship with a lighter.

light-fingered, adj. **1.** Light of touch, delicate; skilful, in using the hands. **2.** Skilful at using the hands to steal; inclined to pilfer; dishonest.

light-foot(ed), adj. Light of foot; nimble, active: '*The light-foot squyre*' (Spenser).

light-handed, adj. **a** Having a light, delicate, dexterous touch; **b** having nothing heavy in the hands.

light-headed, adj. **a** Delirious, disordered in mind; giddy; **b** thoughtless, forgetful.

light-headedly, adv. **a** As though delirious; **b** thoughtlessly.

light-headedness, n. **a** State of giddiness; delirium; **b** thoughtlessness.

light-hearted, adj. Free from care and anxiety; gay, debonair, cheerful.

light-heartedly, adv. Without misgiving; gaily, merrily.

light-heartedness, n. Condition of being free from care; gaiety, high spirits.

light-heeled, adj. [1. līt hḗld; 2. làit híld]. Brisk in movement; agile, nimble.

light-horseman, n. Trooper in a regiment of light cavalry.

lighthouse, n. [1. līt-hous; 2. láithaus]. Lofty structure built at the edge of a cliff by the sea, or on a rock in the sea, provided with a powerful light which serves as a guide to vessels at sea, warning them of dangerous rocks &c.; a beacon, pharos.

lightish, adj. [1. lītish; 2. láitiʃ]. **a light** (**III.**); **b light** (**IV.**), & **-ish. a** Rather light, or pale, in colour; **b** rather light in weight.

lightly, adv. [1. lītli; 2. láitli]. **light** (**IV.**) & **-ly.** In a light manner; **a** not heavily, so as not to press upon; **b** nimbly, with agility; **c** without ponderousness or pedantry; **d** not severely or violently; **e** carelessly, flippantly, not seriously; **f** without difficulty, easily; Phr. *lightly come, lightly go*, what is obtained easily is lost easily; **g** cheerfully, without complaining; **h** slightly: *lightly cooked.*

lightness, n. [1. lītnes; 2. láitnis]. **light** (**IV.**) & **-ness.** Quality of being light, in various senses: **a** absence of weight; **b** nimbleness, power of rapid, active movement; **c** delicacy, skilfulness of touch (lit. and fig.); **d** lack of seriousness; flippancy; **e** absence of density, or stiffness of consistency; **f** digestibility; **g** mildness; absence of severity, intensity &c.

lightning, n. [1. lītning; 2. láitniŋ], fr. **lighten** (**I.**) & **-ing.** Electric discharge from the atmosphere in the form of a vivid flash of light. Phrs. *like lightning*; *like greased lightning*, very fast, with great rapidity; *with lightning speed.*

lightning-conductor, or **-rod**, n. Metal rod projecting above roof of building and connected with the earth, to prevent building from being struck by lightning.

light-o'-love, n. [1. līt o lúv; 2. làit ə láv]. Wanton woman; a paramour.

lights, n. pl. [1. līts; 2. laits], fr. **light** (**IV.**). **a** The lungs of a slaughtered animal; **b** (archaic and vulg.) lungs of a human being.

lightship, n. [1. līt-ship; 2. láitʃip]. Vessel anchored near a shoal, or other dangerous ground, bearing lights at the masthead at night as a guide and warning to seamen.

lightsome (**I.**), adj. [1. lītsum; 2. láitsəm]. **light** (**III.**) & **-some.** Pervaded with light; bright, not gloomy.

lightsome (**II.**), adj. **light** (**IV.**) & **-some. 1.** Nimble, agile; graceful, airy. **2.** Gay, cheerful, light-hearted.

light-weight, adj. **a** Below normal weight; (of boxer) not weighing more than 9 st. 9 lb.; **b** (fig.) intellectually unimportant, lacking weight and authority.

lightwood, n. [1. lītwood; 2. láitwud]. Wood abounding in resin, and therefore inflammable and suitable for torches &c.

lign-aloes, n. [1. līn álōz; 2. làin ǽlouz], fr. Lat. *lignum*, 'wood', see **lignum vitae.** Aloes, aloes-wood, as a drug.

ligneous, adj. [1. lígneus; 2. lígniəs]. Lat., *ligneus*, 'woody', fr. *lignum*, 'wood' (see prec.), & **-ous.** (bot.) Woody; of the nature of, resembling, wood.

ligni-, pref. Form of Lat. *lignum*, 'wood' (see **lignum vitae**), used in compounds.

lignification, n. [1. lìgnifikáshun; 2. lìgnifikéiʃən]. See prec. & **-fication.** Process of becoming woody, or like wood.

lignify, vb. trans. & intrans. [1. lígnifī; 2. lígnifai]. See **ligni-** & **-fy. a** trans. To make into wood; **b** intrans., to become wood.

lignite, n. [1. lígnīt; 2. lígnait]. **ligni-** & **-ite.** Imperfectly formed coal, still showing woody structure; brown coal.

lignum vitae, n. [1. lígnum vítē; 2. lígnam váiti]. Lat., 'wood of life'; *lignum* is prob. fr. base of *legere*, 'to pick out, select; collect', the orig. meaning being 'collected, gathered, wood'. See **legend**; see also **vital.** S. American tree, of genus *Guaiacum*; hard wood of this.

ligula, ligule, n. [1. lígūl(a); 2. lígjul(ə)]. Lat. *ligula* & *lingula*, 'a spoon, a little tongue; a strap'. See **lick.** No doubt there was also association w. *ligāre*, 'to bind' &c. See **ligament.** (bot.) So-called strap-shaped petal at the base of composite flower.

ligulate(d), adj. [1. lígūlāt(ed); 2. lígjuleit(id)]. Prec. & **-ate. a** Like a strap or bandage; **b** having ligules.

likable, adj. [1. líkabl; 2. láikəbl]. **like** (**III.**) & **-able.** Of a kind to provoke liking, worthy to be liked; of a kind that is liked; attractive, pleasant, genial.

like (**I.**), adj. & adv. [1. līk; 2. laik]. O.E. *ġe-līċ*, 'similar, equal'; *ġe-līċe*, adv., 'in the same, in a similar way'; O.H.G. *galīh*, 'similar' &c.; cp. Mod. Germ. *gleich*, 'equal' &c. The word is the same as O.E. *līċ*, 'body, form' (see **lichgate**), & means ultimately, 'having the same form, or appearance, as'. See also **alike, each, such, which. 1.** adj. **a** Resembling, having the same, or similar, qualities, character, appearance &c.: *the two brothers are very like each other*; *a voice like a trumpet*; *eyes like stars*; '*Like angels' visits, few and far between*'; Phrs. *like master like man*, as the one is, so the other will be; *as like as two peas*, exactly similar; *what is he, it, like?*, what kind of man, what sort of thing, is he, it?; (*it cost*) *something like £50*, about, pretty nearly; *like nothing on earth*, queer, very strange, remarkable; **b** resembling, reproducing closely an original or model: *I didn't think his portrait was very like*; **c** having, manifesting, the qualities which were to be expected: *it is just like you to help a friend*; *it was like him to fail us at the last minute*; Phrs. *like your impudence*, what might be expected from your known impudent character; *I am surprised* *that a man like you should behave in this way*, of your character, abilities &c.; *something like*, (colloq.) what one might hope for, expect, desire: *ah, that's something like!*; *something like a dinner!*, a very good one; **d** of same degree or amount, equal: '*We are men of like passions with you*' (Acts xiv. 15); *I spent £50 on travelling, and a like sum on books*; (golf) *like as we lie*, having played same number of strokes; **e** probable, likely, (archaic): '*tis like we shall see him no more.* **2.** adv. **a** In the same, or a similar, way as; in a way resembling: *I wish I could play like you*; *don't speak to me like that*; '*Like as a father pitieth his children*' (Ps. ciii. 13); *you speak like a fool*; in various adverbial Phrs.: *to run like mad, like fun*; *to work like blazes*; *to cry like anything*; *it's raining like the devil*, all meaning with great speed, violence; vigorously, in a violent, extreme, manner &c., the force of *like* itself seems largely adverbial; so also in such Phrs. as *off like a shot*, with great rapidity; *I'll do it like a bird*, very willingly, with alacrity &c.; **b** in the following, *like* has almost the force of a preposition: *like the stars in number*; *like a mountain in bulk* &c.; **c** (provinc. or illit.) as it were, so to say: *he was all of a tremble like*; *very particular like*; *like enough*, very likely, probably.

like (II.), n., fr. prec. That which resembles, is of the same nature as, is equal or equivalent to, something else: *we shall not look upon his like again*; *like attracts like*; *did you ever hear the like (of that)?*, specif., anything so remarkable, so preposterous; *like cures like*. Phrs. *and the like*, after an enumeration, and other things of the same kind, and so forth; *not for the likes of me*, (colloq.) such a humble, unimportant person.

like (III.), vb. trans. O.E. (*ǵe*)-*līcian*, impers. 'to be pleasing to', *hit mē ǵelīcaþ*, 'it pleases me'; fr. base *līč*, 'body, form' &c. See **like** (I.), orig. sense 'to be like, equal'; thence 'to be harmonious, suitable, agreeable' &c. **1.** To be fond of, to feel attracted to, have a preference, or taste for; be pleased by; less forcible than *love*: *to like dancing, dogs, fruit* &c.; *she likes him but does not love him*; *I like to see young people enjoying themselves*; *how do you like your tea?*; *I don't like it too sweet.* Phrs. (ironical) *I like that*, implying that something startling and provocative has been said; *I like your impudence*, implying that this is so preposterous as to be amusing; *I should like to see you do it*, implying I don't believe you can. **2.** (in negative sentence, followed by infin.) To be reluctant, unwilling to do; only in such Phrs. as *I don't like to disturb him*; *I didn't like to interrupt you.* **3.** (obs. or liter.) Survival of old impersonal construction: *it likes me well*, I am pleased by it; *it liked her not*, she did not like it. **4.** To suit the health of; only in such Phr. as *I like port, but it doesn't like me.*

like (IV.), n., fr. prec. Thing that one likes; only in Phr. *likes and dislikes*, predilections and prejudices; fads and fancies &c.

-like, adj. & adv. suff. Same as **like** (I.). **1.** adj. *Godlike, cowlike*, like a god, cow &c. **2.** adv. In a way resembling that of: *she, womanlike, was afraid of mice.*

likelihood, n. [1. líklihood; 2. láiklihud]. **likely** & **-hood.** **a** Probability; **b** (rare) promise of excellence: *a young man of great likelihood.*

likeliness, n. [1. líklines; 2. láiklinis]. **likely** & **-ness.** (rare) Probability, likelihood.

likely, adj. & adv. [1. líkli; 2. láikli]. **like** (I.) & **-ly.** **1.** adj. **a** Probable, credible; such as might well be, or happen, reasonably to be expected: *he tells a likely story, gives a likely account*; *should he come, which is quite likely*; *I am likely to be in London next week*; **b** such as will probably suit, or be satisfactory; promising: *I couldn't find a likely house*; *he seemed a likely young fellow.* **2.** adv. Probably (often preceded by *very*): *I shall very likely see you again*; *he'll forget all about it as likely as not.*

like-minded, adj. Having the same ideas, opinions, aims, ideals; in agreement.

like-mindedness, n. Quality, condition, of being like-minded.

liken, vb. trans. [1. líken; 2. láikən]. **like** (I.) & **-en.** **1.** (archaic) To compare with, point out resemblance to: *I know not to what I can liken it.* **2.** To make like (rare): *cannot you liken the portrait a little more to the sitter?*

likeness, n. [1. líknes; 2. láiknis]. O.E. *ǵelīcnes*, 'quality of being like; resemblance; image'. See **like** (I.) & **-ness.** **1.** Resemblance: *I see no likeness whatever between him and his brother.* **2.** A portrait of a person: *to have one's likeness taken*; *a good likeness*, a portrait that resembles the original. **3.** (archaic) Form, guise, similitude: '*Satan in likeness of an angel bright*' (Milton, 'P. L.').

likewise, adv. & conj. [1. líkwīz; 2. láikwaiz]. See **like** (I.) & **-wise.** **1.** adv. In like manner, in the same way, similarly: '*go thou and do likewise*'. **2.** conj. Moreover, in addition, also: '*Likewise after supper He took the cup*'.

likin, n. [1. lēkḗn; 2. līkín]. Chinese. Chinese tax levied on articles in transit.

liking, vbl. n. & adj. [1. líking; 2. láikiŋ]. **like** (II.) & **-ing.** **1.** n. Feeling of affection, favourable disposition (for persons); predilection, taste (for things): *to have a great liking for the clergy*; *a liking for cigars.* **2.** adj. (obs.) In a certain condition: '*Fat and well liking*' (Psalms).

lilac, n. & adj. [1. lílak; 2. láilək]. Earlier Fr. *lilac* (Mod. Fr. *lilas*), fr. Span. *lilac*, fr. Arab. *līlak*, fr. Pers. *līlaj*, variant of *nīlaj*, 'indigo plant', fr. *nīl*, 'blue'. **1.** n. (bot.) Well-known flowering tree with pale or dark purple, or white blossoms in pendulous clusters, genus *Syringa*; name applied both to the tree and the flower. **2.** **a** n. A pale purple or mauve colour; **b** adj. having this colour.

liliaceous, adj. [1. liliáshus; 2. liliéiʃəs]. See **lily** & **-aceous.** (bot.) Belonging to the lily family.

Lilliputian, adj. & n. [1. lilipúshan; 2. lilipjúʃən]. **1.** adj. **a** Belonging to *Lilliput*, fabulous country where men were 6 in. high, and everything else proportionally small, described by Swift in 'Gulliver's Travels'; hence **b** diminutive. **2.** n. An inhabitant of *Lilliput.*

lilt, vb. intrans. & trans. & n. [1. lilt; 2. lilt]. M.E. *lulte*; etymol. uncertain, perh. connected w. **lull.** **1.** vb. To sing sweetly and simply, but with spirit and go. **2.** n. **a** A song thus sung; **b** the beat, cadence, or rhythm of a song, tune, or rhyme; specif., a well-marked beat or rhythm, swing.

lily, n. [1. líli; 2. líli]. O.E. & M.E. *lilie*, 'lily flower', fr. Lat. *līlium*, wh. is borrowed fr. Gk. *leírion*; it has been suggested (1) that the name is connected w. Gk. *leirós*, 'delicate, pale', wh. is cogn. w. Lat. *lētum*, 'death' (see **lethal**), w. Lith. *leilas*, 'thin, worn out', & perh. O.E. *lēf*, 'weak' (see **left** (I.)); or (2) that the name is borrowed fr. a primitive Mediterranean language. One of a large class of flowers grown from bulbs, typically trumpet-shaped and white, but occurring also in various colours, shapes, and sizes. Phrs. *fair as a lily*; *pure as a lily*. *The lilies of France*, heraldically *fleurs-de-lis*, the emblem of the old Bourbon dynasty.

lily-iron, n. Harpoon with peculiarly shaped detachable head, used in killing sword-fish.

lily of the valley, n. Low-growing plant, *Convallaria*, having broad leaves, and bearing nodding sprays of small, strongly scented, bell-shaped flowers.

lily-white, adj. White like a lily, very white, pure white; applied to *hands* and *brow* in old popular ballads.

limaceous, adj. [1. līmáshus; 2. laiméiʃəs]. Lat. *līmāc-*, stem of *līmax*, 'slug, snail'. See **limax** & **-eous.** Limacine.

limacine, adj. [1. límasīn; 2. líməsain]. See next word & **-ine.** Pertaining to snails or slugs.

limax, n. [1. límaks; 2. láimæks]. Lat., 'snail, slug', stem *līmāc-*, cogn. w. Gk. *leímax*, 'slug'; cp. Lat. *līmus*, 'slime, mud' (see **lime** (I.)); prob. cogn. w. **slime.** (zool.) Genus containing slugs or shell-less snails.

limb (I.), n. [1. lim; 2. lim]. O. & M.E. *lim*, O.N. *limr*, 'limb, branch of a tree'; prob. cogn. w. Lith. *lēmů*, 'trunk, stature'; fr. same base, w. different formative element, as O.E. *liþ*, 'joint, limb', Goth. *liþus*, 'limb, member'. Cp. **lay figure.** **1.** **a** An extremity of the body; a member, leg, arm; wing of a bird; **b** bough of a tree; Phr. *limb of the law*, member of legal profession. **2.** (colloq. and obsolesc.) A naughty child; formerly *limb of Satan*: *a regular (young) limb* (cp. *lively member*).

limb (II.), also **limbus**, n. [1. lim, límbus; 2. lim, límbəs]. Lat. *limbus*, 'hem, border'; cogn. w. Scrt. *lambatē*, 'hangs down'; O.E. *limpan*, 'to happen, befall'; O.H.G. *limfan*, 'to be adapted to'. Cp. **limp** (I.). Edge or border; **a** of the surface of a heavenly body; **b** upper, spreading portion of the corolla, or of the calyx of a flower; **c** margin of leaf in mosses when different from stem in colour and structure; **d** marked edge of a quadrant.

limbate, adj. [1. límbāt; 2. límbeit]. Prec. & **-ate.** (biol.) Bordered, edged; e.g. of a moss which has an edging of a different colour.

limbec, n. [1. límbek; 2. límbek]. Poet. variant of **alembic.**

-limbed, adj. **limb** (I.) & **-ed.** Having limbs of kind specified: *clean-limbed, strong-limbed.*

limber (I.), n. & vb. trans. [1. límber; 2. límbə]. Cp. Fr. *limonière*, 'litter, or cart with shafts', fr. *limon*, 'shaft' &c. Origin unknown. (mil.) **1.** n. Part of a gun-carriage, consisting of front wheels, axle, and pole, generally fitted with chest for ammunition, with a lid upon which the driver sits. **2.** vb. To fasten to a limber; often *limber up.*

limber (II.), adj. Origin doubtful. Pliant, easily bent, supple, pliable.

limberness, n. Prec. & **-ness.** Flexibility, suppleness.

limbers, n. pl. [1. límberz; 2. límbəz]. Etymol. doubtful. Holes cut through floor boards of a ship close to the keel or kelson, to allow of water draining into the ship's well.

limbless, adj. [1. límles; 2. límlis]. **limb** (I.) & **-less.** Lacking limbs.

limbo, limbus, n. [1. límbō, -us; 2. límbou, -əs]. Lat. *limbus*, 'border, hem, edge'. See **limb** (II.). **1.** Intermediate condition, or region, between heaven and hell, to which, according to scholastic theology, the souls of unbaptized infants pass at death; *Limbus Patrum*, intermediate place where souls of the prophets and patriarchs awaited coming of the Messiah. **2.** (fig.) A place of neglected and forgotten things.

lime (I.), n. [1. līm; 2. laim]. O.E., O.H.G., O.N. *līm*, 'anything which causes adhesion, mortar, bird-lime'; cogn. w. Lat. *līmus*, 'slime, mud', fr. base **leim-*, **loim-*, 'mud'; cp. O.E. *lām*. See **loam** & also **slime.** **1.** Substance, calcium oxide, got by burning limestone, used in making mortar, and for manure &c.: *slaked lime*, watered lime. **2.** Sticky substance for catching birds, usually *bird-lime.*

lime (II.), vb. trans., fr. prec. **a** To mix, dress (land), treat (hides &c.) with lime; **b** to smear with bird-lime.

lime (III.), n. Fr., fr. Span. *lima*. See **lemon.** Round, very acid fruit, allied to lemon.

lime (IV.), n. Earlier *line*. See **linden.** Linden tree; one with smooth roundish leaves, and sweet-smelling flowers.

lime juice, n. A cordial made from the juice of the lime fruit much sweetened.

lime-kiln, n. Kiln for burning lime.

limelight, n. [1. límlīt; 2. láimlait]. Very bright light produced by the incandescence of a rod or cylinder of lime in a flame of oxygen and hydrogen; used for lighting the stage in theatres; Phrs. *in the limelight*, a on that part of stage so lighted; **b** (fig.) occupying important or prominent position; *fond of the limelight*, fond of publicity.

limen, n. [1. līmen; 2. láimen]. Lat. *līmen, līmin-is*, 'threshold, the lintel or sill of a door'; perh. orig. 'cross-bar', & cogn. w. Lat. *līmus*, 'oblique; squinting'; *līmes*, 'balk; boundary'; see **limit, oblique.** (psychol.) The threshold of consciousness, the lowest stage at which sensation becomes noticeable; used to translate the German technical term *schwelle*; cp. *subliminal*.

lime-pit, n. **a** Limestone quarry; **b** pit where lime is slaked; **c** pit where hides are steeped and limed.

Limerick, n. [1. límerik; 2. límərik]. A nonsense verse of five lines rhyming a, a, b, b, a, or in last line simply repeating last words of the first line. Invented by Edward Lear (1812–88) in his *Book of Nonsense*, and so called (not by Lear) on account of refrain, '*Won't you come up, come up, won't you come up to Limerick?*', which is said to have been sung or recited after each verse, but which is now never heard.

lime-tree, n. Same as **lime (IV.)**.

lime-twig, n. One smeared with bird-lime.

lime-wash, vb. trans. & n. **a** vb. To whitewash (walls &c.) with lime dissolved in water; **b** n., solution used for this purpose.

limewater, n. [1. límwawter; 2. láimwōtə]. Medicinal preparation of water impregnated with lime, calcium, used as an antacid.

limit (I.), n. [1. límit; 2. límit]. Lat. *līmit-*, stem of *līmes*, 'cross path, balk, between fields; boundary'; fr. base of *līmus*, 'aslant, sidelong', cp. **oblique**, & ***it-**, 'go'. See **itinerary**. Boundary, border, extreme edge or point, confine (in material and non-material sense, of space, time, thought, feeling). Phrs. (fig.) *within limits*, in moderation; *without limit*, without restriction; (slang) *that's the limit*, the utmost of what can be tolerated, or rather beyond.

limit (II.), vb. trans., fr. prec. To set a boundary to; to curb; raise an obstacle, hinder further progress: (chiefly fig.) *his activities were limited only by his opportunities*; *to limit one's desires*; *to limit the amount of work a man may do in a day.*

limitarian, n. [1. lìmitárian; 2. lìmitéəriən]. Prec. & **-arian**. One who limits, restricts; specif., supporter of the view that salvation is limited to that part of mankind which is predestined for it.

limitary, adj. [1. límitari; 2. límitəri]. **limit (II.)** & **-ary**. **a** Confined within limits; limited; **b** serving as a boundary; restrictive.

limitation, n. [1. limitáshun; 2. limitéiʃən]. Lat. *līmitātiōn-(em)*. **limit** & **-ation**. **1. a** Act of limiting; **b** circumstance which limits; **c** state of being limited, in space, time; also in action. **2.** (fig., of understanding, intelligence, capacity, powers &c.) *To have one's limitations*, be rather stupid; *to know one's limitations*, have a just estimate of one's rather moderate ability. **3.** (law) **a** Specific legal restriction of power, or right: *a peerage granted with limitation to heirs male*; **b** legally fixed period after the expiry of which legal action cannot be brought, a claim cannot be made, a law is no longer operative, and so on: *statute of limitations*, one fixing such period.

limitative, adj. [1. límitativ; 2. límitətiv]. See prec. & **-ive**. Serving to limit or restrict.

limited, adj. [1. límited; 2. límitid], fr. P.P. of **limit (II.)**. **1.** Having limits, circumscribed, narrow, restricted (of material and non-material things): *our space, accommodation, is very limited*; *to have a limited intelligence*; *limited ideas, sympathies.* **2.** (polit.) Having constitutional restrictions and limitations on power of action: *a limited monarch, monarchy.* **3.** (commerc.) *Limited* (*liability*) *company*, one in which the liability of shareholders is limited to the amount actually invested; *limited liability*, such as is subject to specific limitations.

limitless, adj. [1. límitles; 2. límitlis]. **limit** & **-less**. Without limits; boundless, vast: *the limitless ocean*; *limitless ambition, credulity* &c.

limitrophe, adj. [1. límitrōf; 2. límitrouf]. Hybrid formation fr. Lat. *līmit-* (see **limit (I.)**) & Gk. *trophḗ*, 'nourishment, food, maintenance'. See **trophic** & **atrophy**. Original, or literal meaning, is, set apart for nourishing and sustaining troops on a frontier; hence, of territory, pertaining to a borderland or frontier; on or adjacent to the frontier between two countries or districts.

limn, vb. trans. [1. lim; 2. lim]. M.E. *limnen*, fr. *luminen*, fr. Fr. *enluminer*. See **illuminate.** (archaic) **a** To decorate, illuminate (manuscripts); **b** to paint, depict, portray.

limner, n. [1. límner; 2. límnə], fr. prec. & **-er.** (archaic) **a** One who illuminates manuscripts &c.; **b** one who portrays, draws, paints.

limnetic, adj. [1. limnétik; 2. limnétik]. Gk. *limnḗtēs*, 'living in marshes', & **-ic**; fr. *límnē*, 'marsh, lake'; cp. Gk. *leimṓn*, 'damp, marshy place'; prob. for **sleim-*, **slim-*. See **slime** & cp. **limax.** Belonging to, inhabiting, fresh water.

limnology, n. [1. limnóloji; 2. limnólədži]. See prec. & **-logy**. Scientific study of fresh waters, especially of lakes and ponds, from every point of view, chemical and biological.

limonite, n. [1. límunīt; 2. láimənait]. Gk. *leimṓn*, 'moist place, meadow'. See **limnetic** & **-ite**. Brown haematite, iron ore of a dark, or yellowish brown colour; it is the colouring matter of brown rocks and clays.

limosis, n. [1. līmósis; 2. laimóusis], fr. Gk. *līmós*, 'hunger', q.v. under **lethal**, & **-osis**. (med.) Ravenous, excessive, morbid appetite for food.

limousine, n. [1. límoozēn; 2. límuzīn]. Fr., adj. fem., fr. Limousin, name of province in Central France. Motor-car with permanent top which projects over the driver's seat, and closed back, and sides with windows like a brougham.

limp (I.), adj. [1. limp; 2. limp]. O.N. *limpa*, 'limpness, weakness'; prob. cogn. w. **limb (II.)**. **1.** Relaxed, wanting in stiffness; flabby, flaccid. **2.** (fig.) **a** (of bodily conditions) Lacking strength and stamina; also **b** of character.

limp (II.), vb. intrans. & n. Cp. O.E. *lemphealt*, 'lame, halt'; prob. connected w. **lame**. **1.** vb. **a** To walk stiffly and lamely, to halt, drag a leg; **b** (fig., of verse) to halt, have a rough, uneven movement; to scan imperfectly. **2.** n. Lameness, impediment in walking: *to walk with a limp*; *he has a decided limp.*

limpet, n. [1. límpet; 2. límpit]. O.E. *lempedu*, fr. Low Lat. *lampreda*. See **lamprey**. A marine gastropod mollusc with a single, flattish, conical shell, which clings tightly to rocks. Phr. *to stick like a limpet*, of a tenacious or importunate person.

limpid, adj. [1. límpid; 2. límpid]. Lat. *limpidus*, 'clear'; perh. connected w. **lymph**, q.v. Clear, transparent; **a** of water and liquids generally; esp. *limpid waters, brooks* &c.; also **b** (fig.) of literary and oratorical style.

limpidity, n. [1. limpíditi; 2. limpíditi]. Prec. & **-ity**. Quality, state, of being limpid; clearness.

limpidly, adv. [1. límpidli; 2. límpidli]. See prec. & **-ly**. In a limpid manner; clearly.

limpidness, n. [1. límpidnes; 2. límpidnis]. **limpid** & **-ness**. Limpidity.

limping, adj. [1. límping; 2. límpiŋ], fr. Pres. Part. of **limp (II.)**. Going with, characterized by, a limp.

limply, adv. [1. límpli; 2. límpli]. **limp (I.)** & **-ly**. In a limp manner; flabbily, slackly.

limpness, n. [1. límpnes; 2. límpnis]. **limp (I.)** & **-ness**. Quality, condition, of being limp; flabbiness, slackness.

limulus, n. [1. límūlus; 2. límjuləs]. Lat. dimin. of *līmus*, 'aslant'. See **limit**. (zool.) Genus of large marine arachnids, the king crabs.

limy, adj. [1. līmi; 2. láimi]. **lime (I.)** & **-y**. **a** Of the nature of lime; **b** covered with lime; **c** impregnated with lime.

linage, n. [1. línij; 2. láinidž]. **line (I.)** & **-age**. **a** Number of printed lines on a page; **b** payment for this.

linchpin, n. [1. línshpin; 2. línʃpin]. For *lins-*, cp. O.E. *lynis*, 'axle-tree'; O.S. *lunisa*, late M.H.G. *lunse*, Mod. Germ. *lünse*, 'linchpin'; prob. fr. base seen in O.E. *linnan*, 'to desist, cease from'; cp. also *ālinnan*, 'to pull out, set free', fr. same base comes O.E. *līþe*, 'soft, mild', fr. **linþ-*; O.H.G. *lindi*; see further **lithe.** *Linchpin* thus meant 'releasing pin', a device enabling the wheel to be taken off. Metal pin or peg passing through the outer end of an axle-tree outside the wheel, and preventing this from coming off.

Lincoln green, n. [1. língkun grēn; 2. líŋkən grīn]. Bright-green cloth manufactured at Lincoln, formerly worn by, and associated with, hunters in Sherwood Forest.

linctus, n. [1. língtus, língktus; 2. líŋtəs, líŋktəs]. Lat. *linctus*, 'a licking', fr. *linct-(um)*, P.P. type of *lingere*, 'to lick'. See **lick**. Syrupy medicine, usually taken from a spoon, for soothing throat and bronchial tubes.

linden (tree), n. [1. línden (trē); 2. líndən (trī)]. O.E. *lind*, 'lime tree', O.H.G. *linta*, & adj. suff. **-en**; prob. cogn. w. Gk. *elátē* for **elntā*, 'fir tree'. For transference of old tree-names from one species to another, cp. **beech.** The lime tree.

line (I.), n. [1. līn; 2. lain]. O.E. *līn*, 'flax', q.v. under **Linum**. See also next word. (obs.) Flax plant, flax fibre, flax thread.

line (II.), n. [1. līn; 2. lain]. Fr. *ligne*, fr. Lat *linea*, 'a linen thread, string, cord; mathematical line; boundary-line', fr. Lat. *līnum*, 'flax, linen'. Cp. **linen** & **Linum**. **1. a** String, cord: *clothes-line*; specif. **b** long, fine, very strong cord used in fishing: *with rod and line*; Phr. *to throw a good line*, be an expert fisherman; **c** cord used for measuring and levelling &c. **2.** Very thin, thread-like mark or indentation; esp. **a** one straight or curved, of appreciable length, drawn on paper, a slate &c., or cut on any hard substance; **b** thread-like furrow resembling a line on the skin of face &c.; one of the marks in form of fine lines traversing palms of the hands and soles of feet. **3. a** Mark made on the ground to indicate some position, boundary, starting-point &c.; Phrs. *to toe the line*, to submit to discipline, obey orders; *to find it hard to draw the line*, to distinguish between; *to draw the line at*, object to, refuse to tolerate, or to do; *one must draw the line somewhere*, there is a limit to toleration, endurance &c.; *to know when, where, to draw the line*, keep one's actions within bounds of discretion or decency; hence, **b** a border, boundary, dividing limit between two territories; **c** division, demarcation, between two conditions, degrees of excellence &c.; Phrs. *to go over the line*, pass permitted limits (lit. and fig.); *below the line*, not reaching a specified standard; *just on the line*, on the border between two conditions, between two classes, standards &c. **4.** Contour, outline: *he has good lines in his face*; *the severe lines of Norman architecture.* **5.** A row, continuous series of objects at approximately the same level, or presenting a more or less uniform surface; **a** a straight row of words, letters, figures, written or printed, occupying a definite space in length and breadth on a page: *the stroke of d extends above the line, the tail of g below it*; Phrs. *to read between the lines*, find more in a written statement &c. than is actually expressed; also (fig.) to infer more than is actually said in an uttered statement; *a few lines*, a short note; *marriage lines*, certificate of marriage; **b** a straight row of persons standing side by side, or one in front of another: *to stand in (a) line*; Phrs. *come into line (with)*, agree with, accept views of, co-operate, act in accord with; specif., *line of troops, line of battle*; *ship of the line*, battleship; **c** area occupied and defended by an army in a campaign, esp. that portion facing the enemy, and the troops actually ready to fight: *the front lines*; *to go into the line*; *behind the line*; *the enemy's lines* &c.; **d** any series of objects extending for some distance and so placed in relation to each other as to form a unity to the eye: *a line of trees, houses, hills* &c. **6.** (mil.) *The line, regiments of the line*, all those of the regular army except the Guards and the Artillery. **7.** Metrical unit, consisting of a definite number of feet, usually written or printed in a separate line; a metrical verse: *lines*, piece of poetry. Phr. *lines*, punishment, imposition, inflicted on schoolboys, consisting formerly of so many hundred lines of Greek or Latin verse to be written out. **8. a** Organized group of trains or steamers under a single management: *the Great Western line*; *the Cunard line* &c.; **b** (railways) the rails, track, upon which trains run: *to fall from the platform on to the line.* **9.** (geog.) *The line*, the equator: *to cross the line.* **10.** (math.) That which has length, but not breadth or thickness. **11.** Imaginary straight line determined by the relative position of objects: *the house is on a direct line to the church.* **12. a** Course, mode, of action, way of behaving, manner of dealing with a given situation: *to take a strong line*, act energetically; *a mistaken line*; *a poor line to take*, unsatisfactory mode of action or attitude of mind; *you are going on wrong lines*, pursuing erroneous method; **b** trend, direction, tendency of events: *things are going on thoroughly sound lines*; **c** (in pl.) conditions of life, circumstances, fortune: *my lines have fallen in pleasant places*; *hard lines*, bad luck. **13. a** Succession of generations in a family, course of descent: *the direct line*, descent from eldest son to eldest son; *a long line of kings*; *the last of his line*, of his family; **b** all the individuals, at a given moment, descended from a common ancestor: *he perished with all his line*; **c** stock, lineage: *to come of an illustrious line.* **14. a** Trade, profession, business: *his line is stockbroking, medicine, grocery* &c.; *in the drapery line*; **b** ordinary, favourite pursuits, tastes, and predilection; object of interest; subject on which one has special knowledge: *cards are not much in my line*; *geology is his particular line.* **15.** (commerc.) Series of goods of particular kind and quality offered for sale by a tradesman: *a cheap line in hats.* **16.** (unit of measurement) The twelfth of an inch.

line (III.), vb. trans. and intrans., fr. prec. **A.** trans. **1. a** To mark, rule, with lines: *to line a paper, book*; also *to line through*, to cross out by drawing a line through it; **b** to furrow, mark with lines: (usually in P.P.) *face lined with pain.* **2. a** To place, form in line: *to line troops along a road* &c.; also *line up*; **b** to place troops, objects &c. along: *to line a wall with troops*; *to line a street with trees*; **c** (of troops, objects &c.) to be placed along: *troops lined the streets*; *the side of the lake was lined by trees.* **B.** intrans. Also *line up*, to take position, draw up in line.

line (IV.), vb. trans., fr. **line** (I.). Lit. to put *linen* in or on a thing. **1.** To put a covering or second layer of material, generally different from that of which the article is made, on the inside of any hollow receptacle, or on the reverse or inner side of anything made of cloth: *to line a box, drawer*; *to line a coat with silk* &c. Phr. (colloq.) *to line one's pockets*, to make money. **2.** (from Fr. *ligner*) To impregnate; esp. of a bitch.

lineage, n. [1. líneij; 2. líniidž]. M.E. *linage*, O. Fr. *lignage.* See **line** (II.) & **-age.** Descent in straight line, ancestry generally; pedigree. Generally confined to a distinguished ancestry: *a man of ancient, lofty, illustrious lineage.*

lineal, adj. [1. líneal; 2. líniəl]. Fr., fr. Lat. *līneālis*, 'pertaining to a line'. See **line** (II.) & **-al.** In direct line of descent: *lineal descendant.*

lineally, adv. Prec. & **-ly.** By direct ancestry or descent.

lineament, n. [1. líni(a)ment; 2. líni(ə)mənt]. Lat. *līneāmentum*, 'stroke made with a pen; feature, cast of countenance', fr. *līnea.* See **line** (II.). (pl., except after *each, every*) **a** Features of the face; **b** external lines, contours, of the body; **c** distinguishing peculiarities of character &c.

linear, adj. [1. línear; 2. líniə]. Lat. *līneāris*, fr. *līnea.* See **line** (II.) & **-ar.** Pertaining to, consisting of, resembling, a line or lines; drawn in lines.

lineate, adj. [1. líneāt; 2. línieit]. Lat. *līneātum*, P.P. of *līneāre*, 'to make into a straight line', fr. *līnea*, 'line'. See **line** (II.) & **-ate.** Traversed, marked, by lines.

lineation, n. [1. lineáshun; 2. liniéiʃən]. Prec. & **-ion.** **a** Act of marking with lines; **b** system, series, of lines.

lined (I.), adj. [1. līnd; 2. laind], fr. P.P. of **line** (IV.). Provided with a lining.

lined (II.), adj. **line** (II.) & **-ed.** Traversed by, marked with, lines.

line-engraving, n. **a** One, usually upon a copper plate, in which the effects of light and shade, and contour, are obtained by lines of varying thickness and nearness to each other; **b** print made from a plate so engraved.

linen, n. & adj. [1. línen; 2. línin]. O.E. *līnen*, 'made of flax or of linen', fr. *līn*, 'flax, linen cloth'. See **line** (I. & II.) & **Linum** & suff. **-en.** **1.** n. **a** Cloth made of flax; **b** (coll.) personal clothing and household articles made from this; specif., underclothes, and tablecloths, napkins, sheets &c. Phr. *to wash one's dirty linen in public*, discuss one's private or domestic affairs, esp. those of an unpleasant character, publicly or before strangers. **2.** adj. Made of linen.

linen-draper, n. Retail dealer in linen and cotton goods and in women's apparel of various kinds.

linen pattern, n. Design carved or moulded, used esp. in panelling, consisting of vertical grooves separated by rounded flutings supposed to resemble pleats or folds in linen.

liner, n. [1. líner; 2. láinə]. **line** (II.) & **-er.** Ship belonging to a steamship line.

linesman, n. [1. línzman; 2. láinzmən]. **a** Soldier in a regiment of the line; **b** man employed to examine and test safety of the rails on a railway line; **c** assistant umpire at football or lawn-tennis who determines whether a ball crosses the line or not.

ling (I.), n. [1. ling; 2. liŋ]. M.E. *lenge*; perh. fr. Du. *leng*; cp. O.N. *langa*, apparently connected w. **long** (I.). Species of coarse seafish, allied to the cod, with long body; usually split and dried and used for food under the name of 'stock fish'.

ling (II.), n. O.N. *lyng*, 'heather'. Kind of heather, with small pink or white bells, *Calluna vulgaris.*

-ling (I.). Gmc. suff. forming ns., fr. *-il-*, dimin. suff., see **-el**, & **-ing.** Expresses diminutive sense, *pigling, gosling* &c., or disparagement, as in *princeling, underling.*

-ling (II.). Gmc. suff. used in O.E. & M.E. for forming advs., as *-linge, -linges*, also *-lunga.* Cp. *grovelling, flatling*; now replaced by **-long**, as in *headlong.*

linga(m), n. [1. língga(m); 2. líŋgə, -gæm]. Scrt. *linga.* A phallic emblem, in worship of Siva, in India.

linger, vb. intrans. [1. língger; 2. líŋgə]. Cp. O.E. *lengan*, 'to prolong, delay', fr. *lang*; see **long** & **-er**, perh. on anal. of *loiter.* **1.** To put off departure unduly, remain after proper time for going; show reluctance to depart: *to linger after others have left*; *linger about*, to hang idly about (a place); *linger on*, continue to stay, continue to live or exist; *linger out one's days, life* (trans.), continue to live after health, strength, and capacity for usefulness and enjoyment have gone. **2.** To delay, loiter, dawdle, be too slow, over: *to linger over one's work.*

lingerie, n. [1. lánzherē; 2. lǣžəri]. Fr. (tradesman's word) Formerly, collection of linen articles, now women's underclothes of linen, silk &c.

lingering, adj. [1. língering; 2. líŋg(ə)riŋ]. **linger** & **-ing.** **1.** Long, spun-out, protracted: *lingering illness*, one which kills slowly. **2.** (of an action) Protracted through reluctance to bring it to an end: *a lingering look, touch*, regretfully, slowly and reluctantly withdrawn.

lingeringly, adv. Prec. & **-ly.** In a lingering manner into which regret enters: *the travellers gazed lingeringly at the fast-fading coast of their native land.*

lingo, n. [1. línggō; 2. líŋgou]. Provenç. *lingo, lengo*, 'language', fr. Lat. *lingua*, 'tongue, language'. See **lingual.** A rude, barbarous, outlandish jargon; used, in contempt, of foreign languages generally.

lingua franca, n. [1. línggwa frángka; 2. líŋgwə frǽŋkə]. Ital., 'language of the Franks'. See next word & **Frank.** **a** A mixed language with Spanish, Italian, French, Greek elements, used as a means of intercourse among the mixed European and Oriental peoples of the Levant; **b** any mixed jargon which has a wide currency.

lingual, adj. & n. [1. línggwal; 2. líŋgwəl]. Lat. *lingua*, 'tongue', & **-al**; Lat. *lingua* is fr. earlier **dingua* & is cogn. w. O.E. *tunge*, Goth. *tuggō* &c. See **tongue.** **1.** adj. Pertaining to the tongue; (of speech sounds) made with the tongue. **2.** n. (popular or obs. phon.) Any of the sounds [d, l, n], from the notion that these were more characteristic of the tongue than other sounds.

linguiform, adj. [1. línggwiform; 2. líŋgwifōm]. Lat. *lingua*, 'tongue'. See prec. & **-form.** Tongue-shaped.

linguist, n. [1. línggwist; 2. líŋgwist]. Lat. *lingua*, see **lingual**, & **-ist.** One possessing knowledge of languages; generally of one specially skilled in use of foreign tongues: *he's quite a linguist*; *a good linguist*; *a poor, bad, linguist*, one who has a poor command of foreign languages.

linguistic, adj. [1. linggwístik; 2. liŋgwístik]. Prec. & **-ic.** Concerned with study of languages or with problems relating to human language in general: *linguistic method, studies, problems.*

linguistics, n. pl., fr. prec. Philology, esp. that side which has to do with phonetics and changes of sound.

lingulate, adj. [1. línggūlāt; 2. líŋgjuleit], fr. Lat. *lingula*, dimin. of *lingua*, 'tongue'. See **lingual** & **-ate.** Shaped like a tongue.

linguo-, pref. [1. línggwō; 2. líŋgwou]. Form of Lat. *lingua*, 'tongue', used in compounds; (chiefly in old-fashioned phonetics) *linguo-dental*, consonant made by (point of) tongue against the teeth; often applied indiscriminately to all kinds of [t, d, n] sounds, e.g. to English varieties which are not formed against the teeth at all.

liniment, n. [1. líniment; 2. línimənt]. Lat. *linimentum*, fr. *linīre*, 'to smear', & **-ment.** *Linīre* is fr. base *(*s*)*lei-*, *(*s*)*li-*, 'slippery', wh. appears also in **limax** & **slime.** Medicated, oily liquid for rubbing on a painful or inflamed part of the body; an embrocation.

lining, n. [1. līning; 2. láiniŋ], fr. **line** (III.) & **-ing.** **a** Substance or material used to cover the inner surface of anything; **b** (fig.) something which resembles a lining, e.g. a cloud of a different colour apparently behind another and projecting beyond it, presenting a contrast in colour Phr. *every cloud has a silver lining*, misfortune, unhappiness, is often followed by happier times.

link (I.), n. [1. lingk; 2. liŋk]. M.E. *linke*; prob. Scand.; cp. Swed. *länk*, 'ring', O.N. *hlekkr*, cogn. w. O.E. *hlence*; cp. also Germ. *gelenk*, 'joint', M.H.G. *lenken*, 'to bend'. **1. a** Any one in a series of metal rings or loops from which a chain is made; **b** any one of the small metal rings or loops forming a coat of chain mail armour; **c** one of a pair of buttons or disks of metal, pearl &c. joined by a small chain, for fastening the cuffs of a shirt &c.: *sleeve-*, *cuff-link(s)*; **d** any single section of anything forming a chain, as of sausages &c. **2.** Specif. **a** (mach.) a short connecting rod for transmitting motive power (cp. *linkage*); and also sliding bar in reversing gear (cp. *link-motion*); **b** (surv.) one of the hundred parts of a measuring chain, as a unit of length, (i.) in English usage, 7·92 in., being $\frac{1}{100}$ of Gunter's chain of 22 yds.; (ii.) American usage, 1 ft. in chain of 100 ft. **3.** (by transf.) Any person, individual, or thing forming a bond of union between other persons &c. or groups, or forming a connecting section in a series: *Johnson was a link between the age of Pope and that of Cowper*; *a link of Empire*. Phr. *missing link*, that which is lacking to complete a series, esp. (but now obsolesc.) specimen or remains of man in early stage of evolution from the ape. **4.** (fig.) An important point or stage in an argument or investigation which joins two inferences: *connecting links*. Phr. *a chain is no stronger than its weakest link*, one discrepancy destroys the whole argument.

link (II.), vb. trans. & intrans., fr. prec. **1.** trans. To join together, connect, unite, as with a link or series of links; (often in fig. sense) *to be linked together by interest in a common cause*; *these events were all subtly linked together*. **2.** intrans. Usually *link up*, to join together with, be knitted together; *to link up with*, to join with another or others in common action &c.

link (III.), n. Origin unknown; possibly, according to O.E.D., derived fr. **link (I.)**, as being sold in lengths of tow and pitch. A torch; *link-boy*, (obs.) one who carried a link and guided people through badly lighted streets at night.

link (IV.), n. O.E. *hlinč*, 'ridge, slope, hill'; prob. fr. same base as O.E. *hlǣnan*, 'to cause to lean' (see **lean (II.)**), & *hlinian*, 'to recline'. See also **clinical.** (usually pl.) Grassy, undulating land, a grassy slope, esp. grassy sandhills near the sea; specif., course laid out for golf, without reference to character of situation; often *a links* as singular.

linkage, n. [1. língkij; 2. líŋkidž]. **link (I.)** & **-age.** Arrangement, esp. (mach.) system of connecting rods for transmitting motion.

link-motion, n. Reversing gear of steam engines; specif., the sliding bar or rod connecting two eccentric rods.

linn, n. [1. lin; 2. lin]. O.E. *hlynn*, 'torrent'; cp. also W. *llyn*, 'pool, pond', perh. borrowed fr. this. (provinc. and in Pl.-Ns.) **a** Waterfall; **b** pool of water.

Linn(a)ean, adj. [1. linéan; 2. liníən], fr. *Linnaeus*, Latinized form of Linné, name of Swedish botanist (1707–78), who established system of botanical classification and nomenclature. Of, pertaining to, *Linné* or *Linnaeus*: *Linnaean system*; *Linnean Society*, chief botanical society in England.

linnet, n. [1. línet; 2. línit]. O. Fr. *linette*, fr. *lin*, Lat. *līnum*, 'flax'. See **Linum.** The bird is so called because it feeds on the seeds of this plant. Small brown singing bird, with crimson neck and breast and whitish belly, genus *Linota*.

linoleum, n. [1. linóleum; 2. linóuliəm], fr. Lat. *līnum*, 'flax' (see **Linum**), & *oleum*, 'oil' (see **oleo-** & **oil**). A kind of washable covering or carpet for floors, made of a hard, shiny composition of linseed-oil, with canvas backing.

linotype, n. [1. línotīp; 2. láinətaip], = *line o' type*. See **line (II.)** & **type. a** Machine used for setting up type matrices and casting bars of type in complete lines therefrom; **b** bar, or slug, thus produced.

linsang, n. [1. línsáng; 2. línsǽŋ]. Jav. Long-tailed, cat-like animal found in S. Asia and the E. Indies.

linseed, n. [1. línsēd; 2. línsīd]. O.E. *līnsǣd*. See **line (I.)** & **seed.** Seeds of flax.

linseed cake, n. Solid mass of oily husks of linseed which remains after crushing to extract the oil, used as cattle food.

linseed-meal, n. Meal ground from linseed.

linseed-oil, n. Oil pressed out of linseed.

linseed-poultice, n. Soothing poultice made of boiled linseed enclosed in a muslin bag.

linsey-woolsey, n. [1. línzi wóolzi; 2. línzi wúlzi], fr. O.E. *līn*, 'linen, flax' (see **line (I.)**), & *say*, of doubtful origin. See **say (III.)** & **wool**, w. ending on anal. of first element. Coarse fabric made of wool and cotton.

linstock, n. [1. línstok; 2. línstɔk], fr. Du. *lontstok*, cp. Scots *lunt*, 'a slow match', Dan. *lunte*, & **stock (I.)**. (obs.) Staff with iron point to hold a lighted match, used for applying fire to touchhole of a cannon.

lint, n. [1. lint; 2. lint]. Late M.E. *lynt*, & *lynnette*, fr. Lat. *linteum*, 'linen cloth', fr. *linteus*, 'of linen'. See **linen** & **Linum.** Soft linen with one side scraped to a woolly surface, used for dressing wounds.

lintel, n. [1. líntl; 2. líntl], fr. O. Fr., fr. Low Lat. *lintellus*, fr. *limitellus*, dimin. fr. Lat. *līmit-*, 'boundary'. See **limit.** (archit.) Piece of stone or timber over doorway or window, supporting superstructure.

Linum, n. [1. línum; 2. láinəm]. Lat., 'flax', cogn. w. O.E., Goth. &c. *līn*, O. Ir. *līn*, 'flax'; Gk. *linon*, O. Slav. *līnŭ*, Lith. *linaĩ*, 'flax'. (bot.) The genus of plants which includes the flax, *Linum utilissimum*, from the fibres of which linen is made; specif., a species cultivated in gardens for its blue or red flowers.

liny, adj. [1. líni; 2. láini]. **line (II.)** & **-y.** Marked with, crossed by, lines.

lion, n. [1. líun; 2. láiən]. Fr.; Lat. *leōn-*, Gk. *léōn*, cp. *léaina* for **le-aina*, 'lioness'; prob. of Semitic origin, cp. Heb. *lābi*, 'lion', Egypt. *lawai*, 'lioness'; the word has passed into Gmc., cp. O.H.G. *lewo*, Germ. *lōwe*, & Slav., cp. Russ. *lev*. **1.** (zool.) Large, powerful, tawny-coloured animal of the cat tribe, *Felis leo*, with mane and tufted tail, found in Africa and S. Asia; known as *the king of beasts* from its courage, size, and imposing appearance. Phrs. *like a lion*, fiercely, powerfully, bravely; *brave as a lion*, very brave, fearless; *the lion's share*, biggest share of anything; *put one's head into the lion's mouth*, run great risk; *a lion in the path*, a difficulty or danger which has to be overcome; *March comes in like a lion and goes out like a lamb*. **2.** (fig., pl.) *The lions*, objects of interest and celebrity in a place; (of a person) one who has fame or notoriety, or who arouses public interest for the moment, and passes for a celebrity: *to make a lion of one*. **3. a** (astron.) The constellation *Leo*; also fifth sign of the zodiac; **b** (her.) representation of a lion in armorial bearings, cp. *leopard*: *the lions of England*; (fig.) *the (old), the British lion*, England, Great Britain.

lioncel, n. [1. líunsel; 2. láiənsel], fr. O. Fr., 'young lion', w. dimin. ending, Mod. Fr. *lionceau*. See prec. **a** Young lion, lion whelp; **b** (her.) if two or more lions appear on a shield they are regarded as whelps, and called *lioncels*.

lionesque, adj. [1. līunésk; 2. làiənésk]. **lion** & **-esque.** Resembling a lion in appearance; rugged and imposing.

lioness, n. [1. líunes; 2. láiənis]. **lion** & **-ess.** Female lion.

lion-hearted, adj. Bold, brave, dauntless.

lion-hunter, n. Person who pursues, and tries to make the acquaintance of, celebrities.

lionism, n. [1. líunizm; 2. láiənizəm]. **lion** & **-ism. 1. a** Practice of lionizing; **b** state of being lionized. **2.** Lion-like appearance of face in late stages of leprosy.

lionization, n. [1. līunīzáshun; 2. làiənaizéiʃən]. See next word & **-ation.** Act of lionizing.

lionize, vb. trans. & intrans. [1. líunīz; 2. láiənaiz]. **lion** & **-ize. 1.** trans. To make a lion of, to regard, treat, as a celebrity. **2.** intrans. To visit the sights, or lions, of a place, to go sight-seeing.

lion-like, adj. Brave as a lion; magnanimous.

lion-tamer, n. Man who trains lions to perform and puts them through their tricks.

lip (I.), n. [1. lip; 2. lip]. O.E. *lippa*, M.E. *lippe*; cogn. w. Lat. *labium*, 'lip' (see **labial**); all further connexions uncertain. **1. a** One of the fleshy, highly mobile flaps of muscular tissue which cover the teeth and serve to open the mouth and close it from outer air: *upper, lower, lip*; **b** the lips considered primarily as organs of speech. Phrs. *to refuse to open one's lips*, refuse to speak, or to tell what one knows; *to hang on a person's lips*, pay great attention, attach great importance to what he says; *my lips are sealed*, I refuse to, I must not, tell what I know; *a curl of the lip*, a sneer; *not a word passed his lips*, he said nothing; *not a drop, no food, has passed my lips all day*, I have drunk, have eaten, nothing; *to put (a glass &c.) to one's lips*, to taste; *to smack, lick, one's lips*, (fig.) to express a gloating satisfaction, in anticipation, or at recollection, of pleasure; *steeped to the lips in*, (fig.) saturated in, thoroughly habituated to (vice, crime, treachery) &c. **2.** (vulg. slang) Chatter; impudence, impertinence, insolent abuse: *none of your lip!* **3. a** Edge, rim, of a hollow vessel, esp. a projecting portion of this: *the lip of a jug* &c.; **b** edge of a cavity: *the lip of a crater*; **c** edge(s) of a wound.

lip (II.), vb. trans., fr. prec. **a** To touch, caress, with the lips; to kiss; **b** (rare) to utter with the lips, speak, repeat.

lip-, pref. Used in certain phonetic terms, implying formed, articulated, with the lips: *lip-back (consonant)*, one in which the lips are sufficiently close together to produce slight consonant friction, while the back of the tongue is raised, as [w, w̥]; *lip-front (cons.)*, one formed with the lips, while the front of the tongue is raised, as [β, ɸ], sound of *u* in Fr. *buis, puis*; *lip-open (cons.)*, one formed with the lips alone, which are brought near together but not closed, as in Span. or Mod. Gk. *b* [b]; *lip-teeth (cons.)*, one made with lower lip against upper teeth, as [v, f]; *lip-rounding*: **a** act of bringing lips near together in speech in such a way as to modify the sounds formed by the tongue; **b** rounded position of lips; e.g. in [ū, ō, ɔ] &c.

lip-deep, adj. Superficial; expressed but not felt.

lip-homage, n. Insincere expression of respect; flattery.

lip-language, n. Speech which is intelligible through the movements of the lips, and not by speech sounds.

lipless, adj. [1. líples; 2. líplis]. **lip (I.)** & **-less.** Having no lip or lips.

lipo-, pref., fr. Gk. base *leip-, lip-*, 'to be lacking', cogn. w. **leave (II.)**, expressing lack, deficiency: *lipography*, omission of a letter or word in writing.

lipped, adj. [1. lipt; 2. lipt]. **a** Having a projection in rim for pouring: *a lipped jug*; **b** *-lipped*, having lips of specified kind: *thick-lipped* &c.

lipper, n. [1. líper; 2. lípə]. Perh. connected w. **lap (III.)** (of waves &c.). (naut.) **a** Slight ruffling of surface of the sea; **b** light spray.

lip-reading, n. Art of interpreting the movements of another's lips when he speaks, and following the words he utters, without hearing the sounds; a method taught to the deaf.

lip-salve, n. Greasy substance used for healing sore, cracked, lips.

lip-service, n. Insincere expressions of affection, respect, devotion, admiration &c.; insincere promises.

lip-stick, n. Cosmetic used by women for heightening the colour of the lips.

liquate, vb. trans. [1. líkwāt; 2. líkweit]. Lat. base *liqu-*, as in **liquid**, & **-ate.** To separate two combined substances of differing fusibility from each other by melting.

liquation, n. [1. likwáshun; 2. likwéiʃən]. Prec. & **-ion.** Process of separating by liquating.

liquefaction, n. [1. likwefákshun; 2. likwifǽkʃən], fr. Lat. *liquefact-(um)*, P.P. type of *liquefacere* (see **liquefy**), & **-ion. a** Process of liquefying; **b** state of being, or becoming, liquefied.

liquefiable, adj. [1. líkwefìabl; 2. líkwifàiəbl]. **liquefy** & **-able**. Capable of being liquefied.

liquefier, n. [1. líkwefìer; 2. líkwifaiə]. **liquefy** & **-er**. Apparatus for liquefying gases.

liquefy, vb. trans. & intrans. [1. líkwefī; 2. líkwifai]. Lat. *liquefacere*, 'to make liquid, to dissolve'. See **liquid** & **-fy**. **1.** trans. To turn solids into a liquid condition. **2.** intrans. To become liquid.

liquescent, adj. [1. likwésent; 2. likwésənt], fr. Lat. *liquescent-(em)*, Pres. Part. of *liquescere*, 'to become liquid, to melt'. See **liquid**. In process of becoming liquid; tending to liquefy.

liqueur, n. [1. likĕr, likúr; 2. likə́, likjə́]. Fr., fr. Lat. *līquor-(em)*, 'a fluid, liquid'. See **liquid (I.)**. Strong, sweet, syrupy, pungent, alcoholic liquid, generally drunk in sips from small glasses: *liqueur brandy, whisky*, one of special quality for drinking as a liqueur; *liqueur-glass*, very small glass from which liqueurs are sipped.

liquid (I.), adj. [1. líkwid; 2. líkwid]. Lat. *liquidus*, 'fluid, flowing'; cp. Lat. *liquāre*, 'to melt, dissolve, liquefy'; *liquēre*, 'to be fluid'; also *lix*, stem *līc-*, 'lye'; the etymol. is uncertain, & the only cognates outside Lat. appear to be Celt., cp. O.W. *gulip*, 'moist', fr. base **wleikʷ-* &c. **1. a** Fluid, flowing; in a condition between a solid and a gas; Phr. *liquid eyes, sky*, bright and moist; **b** capable of being poured or of flowing, having a thin watery consistency: *liquid mud, cement* &c.; **c** (fig., of principles, convictions, opinions) not fixed, unstable, liable to change. **2. a** (fig., of sounds, verse &c.) Flowing smoothly and easily; **b** (phon.) conventionally applied indiscriminately to the sounds [l, r] which have little in common and are better otherwise described (see **divided, trill**). **3.** (finance) *Liquid securities, assets* &c., readily convertible into cash.

liquid (II.), n., fr. prec. **1.** A liquid substance, a fluid; contrasted with a *solid*. **2.** (phon.) Name given in antiquated but still current terminology to the different varieties of the sounds [l, r], which are better called respectively *divided consonants*, and *trills*.

liquid air, gas, ns. Air, gas, reduced to a liquid state under high pressure and low temperature; used in refrigerating &c.

liquidambar, n. [1. líkwidámbar; 2. líkwidǽmbə]. Mod. Lat., fr. **liquid** & Med. Lat. *ambar*, see **amber**. An American tree with fine-grained wood, yielding an aromatic gum.

liquidate, vb. trans. & intrans. [1. líkwidāt; 2. líkwideit]. **liquid** & **-ate**. **1.** trans. **a** To pay, settle, a debt; **b** to wind up affairs of a commercial concern and apportion assets and debts. **2.** intrans. (of commerc. concern) To have its business wound up, undergo liquidation; become bankrupt.

liquidation, n. [1. likwidáshun; 2. likwidéiʃən]. Prec. & **-ion**. **a** Process of winding up financial affairs; **b** state in which this has been done: *go into liquidation*, become bankrupt.

liquidator, n. [1. líkwidàtor; 2. líkwidèitə]. **liquidate** & **-or**. Person legally appointed to wind up the affairs of a bankrupt business or one in course of liquidation.

liquid gas, n. See **liquid air**.

liquor, n. & vb. intrans. [1. líker; 2. líkə]. Lat. See **liqueur** & **liquid**. **1.** n. **a** Liquid substance, esp. of alcoholic drink; Phrs. *liquor traffic*, trade in, sale of, strong drink; *in liquor*, drunk; *under the influence of liquor*, partly drunk; **b** [1. líkwŏr; 2. láikwɔ] a pharmaceutical term for a solution in water of some substance. **2.** vb. Generally *liquor up*, to take liquor, consume strong drink.

liquorice, licorice, n. [1. líkeris; 2. líkəris]. A.-Fr. *licorys*, L. Lat. *liquirītia*, fr. Gk. *glukúrrhiza*, fr. *glukús*, 'sweet' (see **glyco-, gluco-**), & *rhíza*, 'root' (see **rhizo-**). The form of the Lat. word is prob. influenced by Lat. *liquēre*, 'to be fluid' &c. See **liquid**. Black, pungent, very sweet substance extracted from the dried root of plant of same name; used in medicine, brewing &c., and also as a sweetmeat.

liquorish, adj. [1. líkerish; 2. líkəriʃ]. Ad. fr. **lickerish**, as if fr. **liquor** & **-ish**. Fond of, inclined for, liquor.

liquorishness, n. Prec. & **-ness**. Fondness for liquor.

lira, n. [1. lḗra; 2. líra, líərə]. Ital., fr. Lat. **libra**. Italian silver coin, and monetary unit, equivalent to French *franc*, = 100 centesimi, nominal value about tenpence in English money.

liripipe, n. [1. líripīp; 2. líripaip], fr. Late or Med. Lat. *liripipium*. (hist.) A long pendent tail to a hood.

lisle thread, n. [1. līl thred; 2. láil þred]. Old spelling for Lille in France. Strong, fine thread made at Lille; fabric made from this.

lisp (I.), vb. intrans. & trans. [1. lisp; 2. lisp]. O.E. *wlispian, wlipsian*, 'to stammer, lisp'. M.E. *(w)lispen, (w)lipsen*. Prob. imitative. **1.** intrans. **a** To speak imperfectly, esp. to substitute *th* [þ, ð], for *s, z*; **b** (poet., of a child) to begin to speak: '*I lisped in numbers, for the numbers came*' (Pope, To Arbuthnot). **2.** trans. To utter with a lisp.

lisp (II.), n. O.E. *wlisp*. See prec. **a** The defect referred to in prec.: *to speak with a lisp*; **b** imperfect utterance.

lisping, vbl. n. [1. lísping; 2. líspiŋ]. **lisp (I.)** & **-ing**. Speech uttered with a lisp; imperfect, hesitating, halting speech: *childish lispings*.

lissom, adj. [1. lísum; 2. lísəm]. For **lithesome**. Supple, flexible, active.

list (I.), n. [1. list; 2. list]. O.E. *līste*, 'hem, border'; O.H.G. & O.N. *līsta*, 'edge, border, hem'. Origin uncertain. (formerly) Border, selvage of a piece of cloth; hence, the material of which such selvage is made, detached, and used for making cheap common articles of apparel: *list slippers*.

list (II.), n. Same word as prec. (in pl.) **a** Palisades placed as boundary of piece of ground; **b** ground so enclosed; specif., ground where tournaments were held. Phr. *to enter the lists*, (i.) to ride on to the ground ready for the tournament, and challenge an adversary; (ii.) to take part in a contest or competition of any kind.

list (III.), n. & vb. trans. Same word as **list (I.)**. **1.** n. An enumeration, roll, catalogue; inventory, of names, words, books, or other objects. Phr. *to make a list of*, enumerate (names &c.) in form of a list. **2.** vb. **a** To inscribe in, place upon, enter in a list; make a list or catalogue of; **b** intrans. (popular) to enlist as a soldier.

list (IV.), n. & vb. intrans. Perhaps fr. next word in sense of inclination towards. **a** n. An inclination, leaning, slope (of a vessel, building, tree &c.) towards one side; **b** vb., to lean, incline away from the horizontal.

list (V.) vb. intrans. E. Midland form of vb. **lust**; O.E. *lystan*, M.E. *lusten* (Sthn. & W. Midl.), *listen* (E. Midl. & Nthn.), 'desire'. (obs.) To have pleasure in; to desire: *let him do what he lists*; '*The wind bloweth where it listeth*' (John iii. 8).

list (VI.), vb. intrans. & trans. O.E. *hlystan*. See **listen**. (poet.) To listen, hark: '*List, Lady, be not coy*' (Milton, 'Comus'); to listen to.

listen, vb. intrans., rarely trans. [1. lísn; 2. lísn]. O.E. *hlysnan*; cp. also *hlyst*, 'sense of hearing; attention'; a large number of words in the Gmc. & other languages spring fr. this old base **k̑lew-*, **k̑lu-*, 'to hear'; e.g. O.E. *hlēoþor*, 'sound, melody'; Goth. *hliuþ*, 'attention, silence'; Goth. *hliuma*, 'hearing'; cp. O.H.G. *hliumunt*, Mod. Germ. *leumund*, 'fame'. See further under **loud**. Outside Gmc., Lat. *cluēre*, 'to hear oneself called, to be spoken of, reputed'; *(in)clutus*, 'famous'; Gk. *klutós*, 'famous, glorious'; *klúein*, 'to hear, listen'; *kléos*, 'rumour, report; fame'; Scrt. *śṛnōti*, 'he hears'; *śrōtram*, 'ear'; *śrómat-am*, 'good report', fr. **k̑leumn̥t* (cp. O.H.G. *hliumunt*, 'fame'); O. Slav. *sluchŭ*, 'hearing'; *slyšati*, 'to hear' &c. **1.** (followed by *to*) To direct the sense of hearing upon, to hearken: *to listen to a sermon, to conversation, to music*. **2. a** To pay attention to, have regard to: *you didn't listen to what was said*; **b** to receive and accept advice; yield to persuasion: *he is fooling you, don't listen to him*. Phr. *listen in*, **a** to intercept message &c. by tapping telephone wire; **b** preferably *listen*, listen to sounds, speeches, music, transmitted by wireless telephony.

listener, n. [1. lísner; 2. lísnə]. Prec. & **-er**. One who listens.

listening, adj. [1. lísning; 2. lísniŋ]. Directing sense of hearing upon, attentive; preoccupied: '*There was a listening fear in her regard*' (Keats, 'Hyperion', I.).

listless, adj. [1. lístles; 2. lístlis], fr. M.E. *list*, 'desire, wish'. See **list (V.)** & **-less**. Lacking interest and animation; languid, indifferent, spiritless.

listlessly, adv. Prec. & **-ly**. In a listless manner.

listlessness, n. See prec. & **-ness**. State of being listless; indifference, spiritlessness.

lit, vb. [1. lit; 2. lit]. Pret. & P.P. of **light (II.)**.

litany, n. [1. lítani; 2. lítəni]. M.E., fr. O. Fr. *letanie*; Lat. *litania*, fr. Gk. *litaneía*, 'entreaty, supplication', fr. *litē*, 'prayer'. Etymol. doubtful. Form of earnest prayer and supplication, recited by priest, with same recurring response repeated by the congregation: '*We beseech Thee to hear us, Good Lord*' &c.

litany desk, n. Desk at which priest kneels with his back to congregation when reciting the litany.

litchi, n. [1. lèché; 2. lìtʃí]. Chinese. Chinese tree bearing aromatic, edible fruit.

-lite, suff., fr. Fr. *-lithe*, fr. Gk. *lithos*, 'stone', see **litho-**, used to designate certain objects composed of stone, also stones, rocks, and minerals.

literacy, n. [1. líterasi; 2. lítərəsi]. **literate** & **-cy**. Condition of being literate; usually employed in contrast with *illiteracy*.

literae hūmāniorēs, n. [1. líterē hūmànióréz; 2. lítərī hjūmèiniɔ́rīz]. Lat., 'humane, or polite letters'; also abbr. to *Lit. Hum.* [lit hám]. Name of Classical Honour School, or examination for the B.A. degree in this, at Oxford.

literal, adj. [1. líteral; 2. lítərəl]. Fr., fr. Lat. *litterālis*, fr. *littera*, 'letter of the alphabet; handwriting; epistle', & **-al**. The older etymologists derived *littera* fr. the base *lit-*, fr. Lat. *linere*, 'to smear, daub', P.P. *litum*. This, however, is rejected by Walde, who regards the word as borrowed fr. Gk. *diphthéra*, 'leather, dressed hide', w. *l-* fr. *d-* through association w. Lat. *linere*, 'to smear' &c., & *legere*, 'to read'; *diphthéra* is connected w. *dépheín*, 'to soften by working by hand, to render supple; to tan (hides)' (see **diphtheria**). Boisacq connects the Gk. words w. O.N. *tifa*, 'to trample'. According to the above etymol., therefore, *littera* meant first 'a mark made on parchment', & became associated popularly w. the idea of 'daubing', & then of 'reading', the mark. Cp. **letter**. **1.** Having to do, connected, with, based on, pertaining to, a letter of the alphabet: *a purely literal error in printing*; also as n., *a literal*; *literal marking* (of examination papers), expressed by letters instead of numerically. **2.** According to the letter; **a** based on what is actually written or expressed; adhering to the actual words; not fanciful, metaphorical &c.: *a literal interpretation of a document*; **b** giving an exact rendering, word for word; reverse of *free*: *a literal translation*. **3.** Inclined to take words in their narrowest and baldest sense, thus apt to miss the real spirit and meaning; hence, unimaginative, matter-of-fact: *a literal, rather barren mind*. **4. a** Adhering to actual fact, perfectly accurate; not heightened; unvarnished: *a literal account of what happened*; *the literal truth*; **b** capable of being described in a specified way without exaggeration or departure from truth: *the gale has made a literal desert of my garden.*

literalism, n. [1. líteralizm; 2. lítərəlizəm]. **literal & -ism.** System, habit of mind, practice, of slavishly following the letter; tendency to accept literal interpretation; exaggerated realism.

literalist, n. [1. líteralist; 2. lítərəlist]. **literal & -ist.** One who adheres to literalism in theory and practice.

literalistic, adj. [1. literalístik; 2. litərəlístik]. Prec. & **-ic.** Based on, inspired by, literalism.

literality, n. [1. literáliti; 2. litərǽliti]. **literal & -ity.** Quality of being literal; a literal interpretation.

literalize, vb. trans. [1. líteralīz; 2. lítərəlaiz]. **literal & -ize.** To render literal; to interpret literally.

literally, adv. [1. líterali; 2. lítərəli]. **literal & -ly. 1.** In accordance with the strict letter; not freely; not metaphorically: *to translate literally; to interpret a remark, an order, literally.* **2.** Used to qualify, or tone down slightly, an epithet or statement which is rather forcible or somewhat exaggerated: *literally starving,* very hungry; *literally the ugliest woman I know; literally drenched to the skin.*

literalness, n. [1. líteralnes; 2. lítərəlnis]. **literal & -ness.** Quality of being literal; **a** (of statements, interpretation) use of words in their plain and natural meaning; strict adherence to this; absence of metaphor; straightforwardness; **b** quality of mind, practice, which understands and expresses things literally; lack of imagination, matter-of-factness.

literary, adj. [1. líterari; 2. lítərəri]. Lat. *litterārius,* 'connected with, pertaining to, reading and writing.' See **literal & -ary. 1.** Pertaining to letters and learning: *literary labours, studies; literary works, writings.* **2.** Devoted to, skilled in, learning and literature: *a literary man; quite a literary person,* fond of books, versed in literature; a producer of literature. **3.** *Literary dialect, language,* that form of a given language which is used as the common vehicle for literary expression, that in which the literature of a people is written; that used in a given country for writing generally. **4.** *Literary property,* right of an author, his heirs and assigns, to enjoy profit arising from his literary works.

literate, adj. & n. [1. líterit; 2. lítərit]. See **literatus. 1.** adj. Educated, instructed; specif., able to read and write; contrasted with *illiterate.* **2.** n. An educated person; one who can read and write.

literati, n. pl. [1. literátī; 2. litəréitai]. See **literatus.** Men of letters; the learned world.

literatim, adv. [1. literátim; 2. litəréitim]. Lat., 'literally'. See **literal, literatus**; the suff. is an old acc. used adverbially. Letter by letter; literally.

literature, n. [1. lít(e)rachur; 2. lít(ə)rətʃə]. Lat. *litterātūra,* 'writing; grammar; erudition, scholarship'. See **literal & -ure. 1. a** Writings in prose or verse, without regard to their standard of merit, esp. of an imaginative, descriptive, or critical, character; drama, fiction, essays, and treatises of a general character (as distinct from special and technical works) and all kinds of poetry: *every age produces both good and bad literature.* **b** the study, practice, of literature: *to take to, devote oneself to, literature,* as a hobby, or profession. **2.** Writings of acknowledged excellence and beauty of form, possessing permanent value: *much of the current writing of the present day is clever and competent without being literature; journalistic writing often reaches the dignity of literature.* Phr. *light literature,* works of transitory value. **3.** (archaic) Learning, erudition, literary taste and knowledge: *he is an astute man, but he has very little literature.* **4.** Special treatises or monographs on scientific or technical subjects: *philological, mathematical, literature.*

literatus, n. [1. literátus; 2. litəréitəs]. Lat., 'liberally educated', fr. *littera,* 'letter, learning'. See **literal & -ate.** A learned person, scholar, man of letters, usually in pl., literati.

-lith, suff., fr. Gk. *líthos,* 'a stone'. See **litho-.** Used with same force as **-lite**: *monolith,* single stone, or block of stone.

litharge, n. [1. lítharj; 2. líþādž]. M.E. *litarge,* 'white lead', fr. Fr., fr. Lat. *lithargyrus,* fr. Gk. *lithárguros,* 'vitrified lead, collected in the process of separating lead from silver'; fr. *líthos,* 'stone' (see **litho-**), & *árguros,* 'silver'. See **argent & argil.** Hard, yellowish-red crystalline substance obtained by melting lead; used in manufacture of some kinds of glass.

lithe, adj. [1. līdh; 2. laið]. O.E. *līþe,* 'soft, mild, gentle, pleasant', fr. **linþi-,* cp. O.S. *līthi,* O.H.G. *lindi*; cogn. w. Lat. *lentus,* 'pliant, flexible; slow'. See **lentitude**; & cp. **linchpin.** Easily bent, supple, flexible, limber, sinuous: '*lithe proboscis*', applied to the trunk of the elephant by Milton, 'P. L.'; *lithe movements* &c.

lithely, adv. Prec. & **-ly.** In a lithe manner.

litheness, n. See prec. & **-ness.** Quality of being lithe.

lithesome, adj. [1. lídhsum; 2. láiðsəm]. **lithe & -some.** Lithe, lissom.

lithia, n. [1. líthia; 2. líþiə]. Formed fr. Gk. *litheion,* 'of stone', neut. sing. on anal. of *soda* &c. See **litho-.** (chem.) Crystalline substance obtained from lithium.

lithia water, n. Mineral water containing lithium salts.

lithic, adj. [1. líthik; 2. líþik]. Gk. See **litho- & -ic. a** Of stone; **b** of lithium.

lithium, n. [1. líthium; 2. líþiəm]. Latinized, fr. Gk. *líthos,* 'stone'. See **litho-.** White metallic element of alkali group.

litho-, pref. Form used in compounds, of Gk. *líthos,* 'stone'; origin uncertain, but see **lesion.** In many medical words it refers to calculus or stone in the bladder or kidneys.

lithograph, n. & vb. intrans. & trans. [1. líthograhf; 2. líþəgrāf]. **litho- & graph. 1.** n. Writing or designs of any kind made upon a flat, specially treated surface of stone, whence the design is printed off. **2.** vb. **a** intrans. To print, or make designs by lithographic process; **b** trans., to reproduce (writing, pictures &c.) by such a process.

lithographer, n. [1. lithógrafer; 2. liþógrəfə]. Prec. & **-er.** One who makes lithographs.

lithographic, adj. [1. lithográfik; 2. liþəgrǽfik]. **lithograph & -ic. a** Of, pertaining to, lithographs or lithography: *lithographic stone,* a finely ground limestone; **b** of the nature of a lithograph; reproduced by lithography.

lithography, n. [1. lithógrafi; 2. liþógrəfi]. **lithograph & -y.** Art or process of making designs on prepared stone, and taking impressions or prints from this.

lithologic(al), adj. [1. litholójk(l); 2. liþəlódžik(l)]. See next word & **-ic & -al.** Pertaining to lithology; pertaining to rocks.

lithology, n. [1. lithóloji; 2. liþólədži]. **litho- & -logy.** Scientific study of formation, structure, and character of rocks.

litholysis, n. [1. litholísis; 2. liþəláisis]. **litho- & -lysis.** (med.) Solution, destruction of calculi in the bladder &c. by drugs or injections.

lithontriptic, adj. & n. [1. lithontríptik; 2. liþəntríptik]. Gk. *lithōn,* gen. pl. of *líthos,* 'stone' (see **litho-**), & base of *thrúptein,* 'to crush' (q.v. under **drop**), & **-ic**; second element confused w. *triptós,* 'rubbed, pounded', fr. *tríbein,* 'to rub, grind' (q.v. under **trite**). (med.) **a** adj. Tending to destroy, used for destroying, calculi in the bladder; **b** n., drug, or remedy, used for this purpose.

lithophyte, n. [1. líthōfīt; 2. líþoufait]. Gk. See **litho- & -phyte,** fr. *phutón,* 'that which grows; a plant'. (zool.) Plant-like organism with a hard stony skeleton, e.g. a coral.

lithosphere, n. [1. líthosfēr; 2. líþəsfiə]. See **litho- & sphere.** (geol.) The solid part of the earth, as distinct from the *atmosphere* and *hydrosphere.*

lithotomist, n. [1. lithótomist; 2. liþótəmist]. See next word & **-ist.** Surgeon who practises lithotomy.

lithotomy, n. [1. lithótomi; 2. liþótəmi]. Gk. See **litho-,** 'stone', & *tomía,* 'a cutting' (see **-tomy**). Operation of cutting into the bladder and removing calculi.

lithotrity, n. [1. lithótriti; 2. liþótriti]. Hybrid fr. Gk. **litho-,** 'stone', & Lat. *trīt-(um),* P.P. type of *terere,* 'to bruise, crush'. See **trite & triturate.** (surg.) Operation of crushing a stone in the bladder to very small pieces capable of being voided naturally, without cutting into the bladder.

Lithuanian, adj. & n. [1. lithūánian; 2. liþju-éiniən]. **a** adj. Belonging to Lithuania, its people or language; **b** n., language of Lithuania; native of that country.

litigant, n. & adj. [1. lítigant; 2. lítigənt]. Fr., fr. Lat. *lītigant-(em),* Pres. Part. of *lītigāre,* 'to dispute'. See next word. **1.** n. A party in a lawsuit. **2.** adj. Engaged in a lawsuit.

litigate, vb. intrans. & trans. [1. lítigāt; 2. lítigeit]. Lat. *lītigāt-(um),* P.P. of *lītigāre,* fr. *līt-,* stem of *līs,* 'dispute, strife', wh. stands for **stlīt-*; fr. same base comes Goth. *sleiþs,* 'hurtful, bad'; O.E. *slīþe,* 'painful, cruel'; O.S. *slīđi,* 'cruel, wicked'; cp. also Gk. *(a)litein,* 'to sin against, transgress'. Another series of related words without *s-*, & nearer in form to the Lat. *līt-,* are O.H.G. *leid,* 'suffering, sorrow'; O.E. *lāþ,* 'hostile; hateful' &c. See **loathe. 1.** intrans. To go to law, carry on legal proceedings. **2.** trans. **a** To make the subject of a lawsuit; **b** (fig.) to dispute, canvass.

litigation, n. [1. litigáshun; 2. litigéiʃən]. Lat. *lītigātiōn-(em).* See prec. & **-ion. a** Act or process of litigating; **b** a lawsuit; a legal dispute.

litigatory, adj. [1. lítigātori; 2. lítigeitəri]. **litigate & -ory.** Pertaining to, of the nature of, litigation.

litigious, adj. [1. litíjus; 2. litídžəs]. Lat. *lītigiōsus,* 'full of disputes, fond of disputes, quarrelsome; contentious', fr. *lītig-(ium),* 'dispute'. See **litigate & -ous. a** Fond of going, inclined to go, to law; quarrelsome, disputatious; **b** capable of being disputed at law.

litigiously, adv. Prec. & **-ly.** In a litigious manner.

litigiousness, n. See prec. & **-ness.** Quality of being litigious.

litmus, n. [1. lítmus; 2. lítməs]. A.-Fr. *lytemoise*; said to be fr. Early Du. *lakmoes,* fr. *lak,* 'lacquer', *moes,* 'fruit pulp'. (chem.) Substance obtained from lichens which becomes red when acted on by acids, and blue by action of alkalis.

litmus paper, n. Paper steeped in litmus used for testing presence of acids or alkalis.

litotes, n. [1. lítotēz; 2. láitətīz]. Gk. *litótēs,* 'plainness, simplicity'; in rhet., 'diminution', fr. *lītós,* 'plain, simple'; connected w. *leios,* 'smooth, polished', for **sleiwos*; cp. also Gk. *leimax,* 'meadow'; prob. connected w. O.H.G. *slīmen,* 'to polish' (see **slime**), & cp. **lime (I.) & loam.** Figure of rhetoric which consists in softening or diminishing the form of expression by understatement, or by putting a negative for its opposite; meiosis; as *Turner is rather a good painter; not bad,* very good; *I shan't be sorry,* shall be very glad.

litre, n. [1. lḗter; 2. lītr, lītə]. Fr., fr. L. Lat., fr. Gk. *lītra,* 'pound', fr. Lat. **līþra,* later **libra.** Metric unit of capacity, equivalent to c. 1¾ pints.

litter (I.), n. [1. líter; 2. lítə]. Fr. *litière,* Low Lat. *lectāria,* fr. *lectus* 'bed', cogn. w. **lair, lay (III.), lie (III.). 1. a** A vehicle consisting of a kind of bed or couch, furnished with poles for carrying, or shafts; **b** contrivance for carrying wounded and sick; a stretcher.

2. **a** Straw, hay, bracken &c. used as bedding for animals; **b** similar material used to protect plants from the cold. **3.** All the young of a sow, bitch &c. brought forth at one birth; (so called from the nature of the bedding). **4. a** Miscellaneous odds and ends scattered about, e.g. loose papers, books out of place, small personal belongings &c.; discarded rubbish of all sorts; **b** state of untidiness and confusion caused by such things.

litter (II.), vb. trans. & intrans., fr. prec. **A.** trans. **1.** To supply (animals) with (often *litter down*), cover (plants) with, litter. **2.** To make untidy with a litter of miscellaneous, scattered articles: *to litter a table, room*; also *litter up*. **3.** (archaic and rare) To give birth to as part of a litter. **B.** intrans. To bring forth a litter of young, **a** of certain animals; **b** (vulg.) to give birth to a child.

litterateur, n. [1. lìterahtẽr; 2. lìtəratə́]. Fr. A literary person, writer, man of letters.

littery, adj. [1. líteri; 2. lítəri]. **litter** (I.) & **-y. a** Of the nature of litter or bedding; **b** covered with litter, strewn with odds and ends; untidy.

little (I.), adj. [1. lítl; 2. lítl]. O.E. *lȳtel*, 'small', M.E. *lūtel, lītel*; O.H.G. *luzzil*, M.H.G. *lützel*. The etymol. of the base of this word is very doubtful; Goth. *leitils*, 'small', must be an entirely different word in spite of its similarity of form & meaning; it is impossible to connect the O.E. & O.H.G. forms w. another having *ī* in the first syllable. The Goth. form may be connected w. **least, less. 1.** Small in size, of inconsiderable bulk, dimensions, height &c.; idiomatic antithesis of *big*: *a little piece, bit, book, house, hill*; various special uses: *little finger, toe*, the smallest, situated on the outside of each hand or foot; *little ones*, children, young of animals; *little rabbits* &c., young ones, not fully grown; *little family*, of young children; *a little man*, short, not tall; *a little war*, with comparatively few fighting on each side; *his, your, their little game*, (expressing amused contempt) intrigue, design to get the better of one &c.; *little ways*, undesirable habits, laughable eccentricities &c.; (disparagement) *my poor little efforts*; *little woman*, affectionate, slightly patronizing mode of address; *(my) little man*, familiar mode of address to a child; *quite a* (or *the*) *little gentleman*, contemptuous or patronizing reference to a polite but rather insignificant little man; *my, your, little people*, children; *the little Browns*, the Browns' children; *a little place*, small landed estate; *a little thing*, unimportant circumstance; (of persons) *a nice little thing* &c., young, smallish woman (often slightly contemptuous); *little things*, trifling objects; trivial, unimportant actions &c. **2.** (of duration of time) Brief, not lasting long; transitory: *life's little day*; '*They fall, and leave their little lives in air*' (Pope); *a little while, time*. **3.** (of distance, extension in space) Not far, going only a short way: *come a little way with me*; *only a little distance from here*. Phr. *to go but a* (*very*) *little way to*, not to suffice, be inadequate to. **4.** (in moral sense) Petty, mean, narrow: *little things amuse little minds*. **5.** Small in degree, amount, quantity, measure; **a** *a little drop*; *a little glass of whisky*; *little or no comfort*; **b** in many phrases in which *little* is felt as, and functions apparently as, an adjective, the noun construction, *a little of*, with ellipse of *of* may underlie the form of construction; or, more probably, *little* may be a true adjective and the ellipse may be of the words *amount of*: *do take a little trouble, pains, with your work*; *give me just a little bacon, please*; **c** *no little*, very much, a great amount of: *I took no little pains over it*; **d** *very little*, often means not enough, none at all: *he had very* (or *precious*) *little knowledge of the subject*; *I must say you show very little interest*; *he takes very little trouble about his work*; **e** *little* may be merely a polite formula, and may mean merely *some*, without any idea of limiting the amount: *let me give you a little mutton*; *may I have a little claret, please?*

little (II.), adv. **1.** To a slight extent, not much, only slightly; **a** (qualifying vbs.) *to eat, smoke, little*; *I see him very little*; *little understood*; *a little known poet*; **b** (qualifying adj.) *little more than half an hour*. **2.** Not at all; chiefly with *know, imagine, dream, think, guess*, and the like: *he little thought it was his last visit here*; *little did I dream that I should never see him again*.

little (III.), n., fr. **little** (I.). A small amount, not much: *I can only eat a little*; *I'll give you a little, I can't afford much*; *every little helps*; *I must keep what little I get*. Phrs. *not a little*, a great deal: *I lost not a little over cards alone*; *little by little*, gradually; *for a little*, a short time; *little or nothing*, hardly anything; *in little*, on a small scale.

little-ease, n. **a** A prison cell in which the prisoner could neither stand upright nor lie at full length; **b** discomfort, wretchedness.

Little-endian, n. [1. lìtl éndian; 2. lìtl éndiən]. School or party in Lilliput (Swift's 'Gulliver's Travels') who maintained that eggs should be cracked at the *little end*, as opposed to the *Big-endians*, who maintained the contrary view; used derisively of those who dispute about trivialities.

Little-Englander, n. [1. lítl íngglander; 2. lítl íŋgləndə]. One who holds that Great Britain should reduce her commitments and responsibilities, and limit her political aims and Empire, and concentrate more upon purely home affairs; antithesis of *Imperialist*.

little-go, n. (colloq.) The first examination for a pass B.A. degree at Cambridge University, corresponding to 'smalls' or responsions at Oxford.

Little Masters, n. pl. School of designers and engravers on wood and copper of 16th and 17th cents.; so called because their designs were on a small scale.

littleness, n. [1. lítlnes; 2. lítlnis]. **little** (I.) & **-ness.** Quality of being little; **a** small size: *the littleness of English mountains compared with the Alps*; **b** pettiness, paltriness, insignificance; meanness: *the littlenesses of human nature*.

littoral, adj. & n. [1. lítoral; 2. lítərəl]. Fr., fr. Lat. *lītorālis*, 'pertaining to the seashore', fr. *lītor-*, stem of *lītus*, 'seashore'; etymol. doubtful, but perh. fr. base **lei-*, 'to flow', whence also Lat. *lībāre*, 'pour out' &c. See **libation. 1.** adj. **a** Pertaining to the seashore; **b** pertaining to the strip of land along the sea-coast. **2.** n. **a** Space between high and low water mark on seashore; **b** margin of sea near coast; **c** coastal region.

liturgic(al), adj. [1. litẽrjik(l); 2. litə́džik(l)]. **liturgy** & **-ic** (& **-al**). Connected with, of the nature of, a liturgy.

liturgically, adv. Prec. & **-ly**. According to, from the point of view of a, or the, liturgy.

liturgics, n. [1. litẽrjiks; 2. litə́džiks]. See **liturgic(al)**. Science of public worship; study of the history, doctrine &c. of liturgies.

liturgiological, adj. [1. litẽrjiolójikl; 2. litə̀džiəlódžikl]. **liturgiology** & **-ic** & **-al.** Pertaining to liturgiology.

liturgiologist, n. [1. litẽrjiólojist; 2. litə̀džiólədžist]. Next word & **-ist.** Student of, one skilled in, liturgiology.

liturgiology, n. [1. litẽrjióloji; 2. litə̀džiólədži]. **liturgy** & **-logy.** Systematic study of, treatise on, liturgies.

liturgist, n. [1. líturjist; 2. lítədžist]. **liturgy** & **-ist.** One who advocates the use of a prescribed liturgy in public worship; one who practises, and desires to enforce, strict adherence to a prescribed liturgy.

liturgy, n. [1. líturji; 2. lítədži]. Fr. *liturgie*, L. Lat. *līturgia*, fr. Gk. *leitourgía*, 'a public service; a burdensome public office; divine service'; fr. *leîtos*, 'of the people', & a form of the Gk. base *érgon*, 'work, business, employment'; the first element is fr. Gk. *leṓs*, 'people'; for the second see **ergon.** Established and prescribed formularies used in churches at public worship; esp. the office of the Mass.

livable, adj. [1. lívabl; 2. lívəbl]. **live** (I.) & **-able. 1.** (of life) Worth living, endurable. **2.** (of houses, places, rooms) Fit, pleasant, to live in. **3.** (of persons) Easy to live with; pleasant, companionable.

live (I.), vb. intrans. & trans. [1. liv; 2. liv]. O.E. *lifian, libban*, M.E. *liven* &c.; cp. O.N. *lifa*, 'to remain behind, to live'; O.H.G. *(be)līban*; Germ. *leben* &c. See **life. A.** intrans. **1.** To be possessed of life; to exist; to carry on, exercise, the functions of a living organism; generally replaced by *to be alive*, except in certain constructions, and in poetry. Phr. *live and let live*, exercise the same toleration towards others that one desires for oneself. **2. a** To continue in life, remain alive: *to live to be old*; *so badly hurt that he can't live*; *to live through the night* (of a person seriously ill); *to live to see one's grandchildren*; *to live happily ever after*, conventionally of the hero and heroine of fairy story, also facetiously of one who has come through an agitated period to happier conditions; *we shan't live to see it*, it will never happen; **b** (of inanimate things) to remain uninjured, escape destruction: *no ship could live in such a storm*. **3.** To regulate, order, one's life; lead one's life in a specified manner: *to live virtuously, happily, free from care* &c.; Phrs. *to live carefully*, **a** economically, **b** abstemiously; *to live in the past*, to dwell upon, be preoccupied with the past, and take but little interest in the present; *live hard*, **a** lead a dissolute life, **b** to endure hardships; *to live rough*, without luxury, in hardship; *to live in a small way*, meanly, in poverty; *to live from hand to mouth*, precariously; *live like a fighting-cock*, luxuriously; *to live well*, **a** lead a pious life, **b** to live in great luxury; *to live beyond one's means*, more extravagantly than one can afford. **4.** (followed by *on*) **a** To subsist, feed on, have as one's diet: *to live on bread and water*; *to live chiefly on milk*; Phr. *live on the fat of the land*, to have the most expensive and delicate food obtainable; **b** to preserve life, supply one's needs generally, support oneself; *to live on one's salary, on a small income*; *to have very little to live on*; *to live on others, on such and such a person*, to be supported at another's expense; *to live on, by, one's wits*, by dishonest means. **5.** (followed by *in, at*, or an adv. phr.) To inhabit, make one's dwelling; to reside: *to live in England, at the seaside*; *to live abroad*; also absol. in interrog. sentences: *where do you live?* Phrs. *live in*, to lodge under same roof as, in same house as, one's business; *live out*, to lodge away from this; said esp. of shop assistants &c. **6.** To enjoy life, lead a life of varied emotions and experiences: *I don't want to spend all my days in a small village, I want to live.* **7.** (of imaginative and intellectual creations) To be filled with vigour and vitality, to be vivid; to impress one as possessing life: *to make a historical character live*; '*The groves of Eden vanished now so long, Live in description, and look green in song*' (Pope). **B.** trans. **1.** To spend, pass; in such Phr. as *to live one's life*. **2.** To live, behave, in accordance with; to regulate one's life in such a manner as to experience, or make actual: *to live romance*; *he doesn't merely preach religion, but lives it as well.* **C.** Followed by prepositions, with special sense. *Live down*, trans., to dispel, do away with reproach, or memory, of, rehabilitate oneself after: *to live down a former offence, bad reputation, scandal* &c. *Live out*, trans., to live as long as, last out: *he will never live out another month. Live through*, trans., to experience and survive: *to live through a political crisis. Live up to*, intrans., to fulfil expectation, reach a specified standard: *to live up to one's reputation*; to be worthy of, to show an equal degree of merit: *his wife was so distinguished that he felt he could never live up to her.*

live (II.), adj. [1. līv; 2. laiv], fr. **alive**, 'in life', q.v. (only used attrib., with same general meanings as *living*) **1.** Having life: *a live fish*; contrasted with a dead one. **2.** (of embers, coal &c.) Still glowing or burning, alight. Phr. *live wire*, electrified wire; (fig.) a forcible, lively person.

-lived, adj., properly [1. līvd; 2. laivd], now almost universally [1. livd; 2. livd]. **life** & **-ed.** Possessing life of specified duration, esp. *long-lived*, inclined to live long: *a long-lived family* &c.; *short-lived*, tending, likely, to live for a short time only; passing away in a short time, transient: *his triumph was short-lived.*

livelihood, n. [1. līvlihood; 2. láivlihud]. O.E. *līf-ġelād*, 'course of life, lifetime'; M.E. *livelode*, often 'biography, account of a person's life'. See **life** & **lead** (IV.), **lode**; modern form as though fr. **lively** & **-hood.** Means of subsistence, of supporting life. Phrs. *to make a decent livelihood*; *to pick up a scanty livelihood*; *to earn an honest livelihood.*

liveliness, n. [1. līvlines; 2. láivlinis]. **lively** & **-ness.** Quality or condition of being lively; **a** spiritedness, sprightliness, animation, vivacity, of mind and character; **b** briskness, activity, vigour, of movement; **c** (of events) tendency to move, change; absence of stagnation.

livelong, adj. [1. lívlong, līvlong; 2. lívlɔŋ, láivlɔŋ]. First element confused w. **live** (II.) or **life**, but orig. M.E. *lēve*, fr. O.E. *lēof*, 'dear'; cp. Mod. Germ. *den lieben langen tag* &c. See **lief** & **-long. a** Only in *livelong day, night*, lasting throughout the whole of; **b** lasting, enduring; cp. Milton's '*Thou . . . hast built thyself a livelong monument*', on Shakespeare.

lively, adj. [1. līvli; 2. láivli], fr. O.E. *līflic*, 'living, life-giving'; in most mod. senses prob. new formation fr. **life** & **-ly. 1. a** (of persons) Full of vitality, spirited, vivacious, merry; active, vigorous; **b** (of the mind) active, alert, responding freely to stimuli; acute, penetrating: *a lively imagination, intellect* &c. **2.** Expressing, suggesting, inspiring, liveliness and sprightliness; gay, cheerful: *a lively tune, dance, tone of voice.* **3.** (of inanimate things) **a** Moving rapidly: *a lively ball*; **b** fresh, stimulating, brisk: *a lively breeze*; **c** causing, promoting, rapidity of movement: *a lively pitch* (at cricket); a billiard table, cushion, may be *lively* or *slow.* **4. a** (of sensuous impressions) Brilliant, vivid, intense: *a lively colour*; **b** (of emotions &c.) strongly felt, powerful, intense: *a lively sense of gratitude*; *a lively faith.*

liven, vb. trans. & intrans. [1. līvn; 2. láivən]. **live** (II.) & **-en.** Usually *liven up.* **a** trans. To enliven, render more lively, brighten, cheer up: *to liven things up*; to make more alert and active; **b** intrans., to become more lively, be cheered &c.

liver (I.), n. [1. liver; 2. livə]. **live** (I.) & **-er. a** One who lives; (obsolesc.) except in archaic Phr. *evil-liver, free liver*; **b** (rare) an inhabitant, dweller: *a liver in cities.*

liver (II.), n. O.E. *lifer*, O.H.G. *lebara*, O.N. *lifr*; either fr. orig. **ljekʷr̥(t)*, & cogn. w. Scrt. *yákr̥t*, Lat. *jecur*, & Gk. *hêpar*, genit. *hépat-os* (see **hepatic**), all for **ljekʷr̥t-*; or fr. base **lip-* & cogn. w. Gk. *lipos*, 'fat'. **1.** (anat.) Large, dark reddish-brown organ in the abdomen, which secretes bile and plays an important part in digestion. **2.** The flesh of this organ, as of calves, pigs, chicken &c., cooked as food.

liver-coloured, adj. Dark reddish-brown: esp. *liver-coloured spaniel.*

liveried, adj. [1. liverid; 2. livərid]. **livery** (II.) & **-ed.** Wearing livery.

liverish, adj. [1. liverish; 2. livəriʃ]. **liver** (II.) & **-ish.** (colloq.) Suffering from a derangement of the liver; bilious.

liverwort, n. [1. liverwērt; 2. livəwʌt]. Flowerless plant of Hepatica tribe, somewhat resembling a moss.

livery (I.), adj. [1. liveri; 2. livəri]. **liver** (II.) & **-y. 1.** Resembling liver in appearance &c. **2.** Suffering from deranged liver; liverish.

livery (II.), n. M.E. *liverē*, 'allowance of food', fr. O. Fr. *livrée*, 'allowance, something allowed free; an allowance, gift of clothes from a master to his servants', fr. Lat. *līberāt-*, P.P. type of *līberāre*, 'release'. See **liberate. 1.** Allowance or provision of food or clothing provided for retainers. **2.** Allowance of food for horses: *livery and bait*; *at livery*, of a horse, stabled, groomed, and fed at a fixed charge. **3. a** Distinctive uniform worn (i.) by member of city company, and esp. (ii.) by a private person's man-servant: *livery-servant*, one wearing livery; Phr. (fig.) *the livery of woe*, mourning garments; **b** (poet.) the characteristic colour, foliage, plumage, appearance, of trees and birds at certain seasons: *the livery of spring*; *the sombre liveries of the rooks* &c. **4.** (law) Delivery of possession of lands of a ward released by Court of Chancery. Phr. *to sue for (one's) livery.*

livery company, n. One of the London city companies, formerly trade guilds.

liveryman, n. [1. liveriman; 2. livəriman]. **1.** Member of a city company entitled to wear the distinctive dress of his guild and to vote for the Lord Mayor and sheriffs. **2.** Keeper of a livery stable.

livery stable, n. Stable where horses of private owners are fed and cared for at a fixed payment, and where horses and vehicles are kept for hire.

live-stock, n. **live** (II.) & **stock** (I.). Domestic animals kept on farm &c.

livid, adj. [1. livid; 2. livid]. Lat. *līvidus*, 'bluish, livid', for *slīvidus*, cogn. w. O. Slav. *sliva*, 'plum'; cp. O.E. *slāh*, 'sloe'; O.H.G. *slēha*, Mod. Germ. *schlehe.* Cp. **sloe.** Of a bluish colour, of the colour of lead, of a bruise. Phr. *livid with anger, with cold.*

lividity, n. [1. lividiti; 2. lividiti]. Prec. & **-ity.** Lividness.

lividness, n. [1. lividnes; 2. lividnis]. **livid** & **-ness.** State, condition, of being livid.

living (I.), adj. [1. living; 2. liviŋ], fr. Pres. Part. of **live** (I.). **1.** Alive, not dead: '*Some maintain that to this day, She is a living child*' (Wordsworth); *a living language*, one still spoken. Phrs. *living death*, state of hopeless misery or bodily suffering; *within living memory*, that of those still living; *living wage*, one upon which he who earns it can just live. **2. a** Full of vitality and interest: *his discourse was living and impressive*; **b** lifelike, closely resembling a person: *the child is the living image of his father*, exactly like him. **3.** *Living rock*, in its natural place. **4.** as n. *The living*, those who are still alive.

living (II.), vbl. n. [1. living; 2. liviŋ]. **live** (I.) & **-ing. 1.** Livelihood, maintenance: *to work for, earn, one's living*; *make an honest living.* **2.** Mode of existence in the world: *the art of living*; *plain, high, living*; *standards of living.* **3.** An ecclesiastical benefice or incumbency: *a poor, good, rich, living.*

living-room, n. Sitting-room, contrasted with a bedroom.

livre, n. [1. lēvr; 2. livr]. Fr., fr. Lat. *lībra*, 'pound'. See **libra.** Ancient French monetary unit, about equivalent to a franc; coin of this value.

lixiviate, vb. trans. [1. liksíviāt; 2. liksívieit]. Lat. *lixivius*, 'made into lye', & **-ate**, fr. *lix*, 'ashes, lye', see **lye**; related to **liquid.** To separate a soluble from an insoluble substance by steeping and soaking in water.

lixiviation, n. [1. liksiviáshun; 2. liksiviéiʃən]. Prec. & **-ion.** Process of separating soluble from insoluble substance by washing in water.

lizard, n. [1. lizard; 2. lizəd]. O. Fr. *lesard*, fr. Lat. *lacertus.* See **lacertian.** Kind of reptile, with four legs, a longish tail, and scaly hide, order Lacertilia.

llama, n. [1. láhma; 2. lámə]. Span., fr. Peruvian. S. American ruminant animal allied to the camels, but having no hump; it has a thick woolly coat, stands about 3 ft. high, and is domesticated and used as a beast of burden.

llanero, n. [1. lyahnárō; 2. ljānéərou]. Span. See next word. Inhabitant of the *llanos* of S. America.

llano, n. [1. láhnō, lyáhnō; 2. lánou, ljánou]. Span., 'plain, even', fr. Lat. *plānus.* See **plain** (I.). One of the extensive plains or steppes in S. America.

Lloyd's, n. [1. loidz; 2. lɔidz]. Association of marine underwriters; so called from *Lloyd's Coffee House* (opened 1688), where business was originally transacted. Phr. *A1 at Lloyd's*, (lit. of ship, and fig. of anything) among the best of its kind.

lo, interj. [1. lō; 2. lou]. O.E. *lā*; possibly connected w. **look.** Obs., except in Phr. *lo and behold!*, see!

loach, n. [1. lōch; 2. loutʃ]. M.E., fr. Fr. *loche*; origin unknown. Small freshwater edible fish allied to the carp.

load (I.), n. [1. lōd; 2. loud]. O.E. *lād*, 'way, course, journey; act of carrying goods'; M.E. *lōde*; for etymol. see **lead** (IV.); the modern meanings have been influenced by the quite unrelated **lade. 1. a** Something which is carried, a burden, esp. a heavy weight: *to bear a load on one's shoulders, back*; **b** (fig.) something which weighs upon, oppresses, the mind, spirits &c.: *a load of care, grief, anxiety*; *a load off one's mind*, relief from anxiety &c. **2.** A vague measure; that which can be put into and contained by a cart, waggon, ship: *a (cart) load of hay, coal* &c. **3.** (mechan.) Work imposed on an engine, motor, dynamo &c.: esp. in Phr. *working load.*

load (II.), vb. trans. & intrans., fr. prec. **A.** trans. **1.** To place a load or burden upon, in, any conveyance: *to load a cart, ship* &c. **2. a** To bestow, esp. upon a person, in great abundance, so as to overwhelm and weigh him down; esp. *to load with favours, honours* &c.; also *to load with reproaches, insults* &c.; **b** to overburden, overcharge with food: *to load the stomach.* **3.** To place the charge in a firearm: *to load a gun, firearm, cannon.* **4. a** To add weight to, as *a loaded cane*, one with lead introduced at one end; *to load dice*, (i.) weight them so that sixes come uppermost; (ii.) (fig.) *to load the dice*, prepare a case in one's favour, prejudice a case, so as to obtain an unfair advantage; **b** to add drugs to drink, to doctor: *this wine has been loaded.* **B.** intrans. **1.** (of a gun) To receive its charge; permit of being loaded. **2.** *Load up*, **a** to place a load on vehicle designed for it; perform act of loading a cart &c., in preparation for departure; **b** (colloq.) to eat and drink copiously; make a good meal while the opportunity offers.

loaded, adj. [1. lōded; 2. loudid], fr. P.P. of prec. Excessively burdened; weighted, clogged; in various special senses: **a** *a loaded stomach*, overcharged with food; **b** *loaded dice*, fraudulently weighted so that they fall with the sixes uppermost; **c** *a loaded stick*, one with the handle filled with lead, used as a bludgeon; *a loaded whip*, one having lead pellets fixed to the lash; **d** *loaded wine*, (i.) adulterated, fortified with spirit, so as to make it appear rich and generous; (ii.) drugged, doped.

loader, n. [1. lōder; 2. loudə]. **load** (II.) & **-er. 1.** Mechanical device, **a** for charging a firearm, also in combination indicating method of loading, as *breech-loader* &c.; **b** for loading a cart &c. **2.** Person who loads a gun, esp. one employed in shooting game.

load-line, n. Line on sides of a ship marking the depth at which she floats when fully loaded.

loadstar, n. See **lodestar.**

loadstone, n. [1. lōdstōn; 2. loudstoun], fr. O.E. *lād* (see **load** (I.)), with retention of something like the old meaning. Magnetic oxide of iron; magnet.

loaf (I.), n. [1. lōf; 2. louf]. O.E. *hlāf*, 'bread, loaf'; O.H.G. *hleip, leip*, Mod. Germ. *laib*; O.N. *hleifr*, Goth. *hlaifs*; O. Slav. *chlebŭ*,

Russ. *chljeb* &c., 'bread', are borrowed fr. anct. Gmc. The word in the gen. sense of 'baked dough' has now been displaced by the cogn. of **bread** in all Gmc. languages. **1.** A mass or cake of bread of definite size and weight, in the form in which it is baked: *a quartern loaf.* Phrs. *the loaf*; esp. in reference to price of bread, *the loaf has risen,* or *fallen, in price*; *loaves and fishes,* material benefit, contrasted with spiritual gain; *half a loaf is better than no bread,* take what you can get, or what is offered, rather than risk losing everything. **2.** Large conical mass of sugar shaped in a mould; (attrib.) *loaf sugar.*

loaf (II.), vb. intrans. & n. Origin uncertain; possibly fr. Du. or Germ. dial.; cp. Germ. *laufen*, 'to run'. See **leap.** **1.** vb. **a** To loiter about idly without any definite occupation; to fritter away one's time in trivial pursuits; **b** to work very slowly and without energy: also *loaf about*; *to loaf away one's time*; *to loaf through life.* **2.** n. Action of loafing.

loafer, n. [1. lṓfer; 2. lóufə]. Prec. & **-er.** One who loafs; idler; lounger; one who refuses to work and lives by begging, and sponging on others; vagrant, tramp.

loafing, vbl. n. [1. lṓfing; 2. lóufiŋ]. Prec. & **-ing.** Action of a loafer; idling.

loam, n. [1. lōm; 2. loum]. O.E. *lām*, 'clay'; cogn. w. **lime (I.).** Soil composed of clay with a mixture of lighter, more friable earth.

loamy, adj. [1. lṓmi; 2. lóumi]. Prec. & **-y.** Consisting of, resembling, loam.

loan, n. & vb. trans. [1. lōn; 2. loun]. O.E. *lān*, 'loan', whence M.E. *lōne*, is very rare, the usual form being *lǣn*, 'lending, loan, thing lent'; cp. also *lǣnan*, 'to lend' (see **lend**). The base **lī-*, **lai-*, is found in O.E. *lēon*, 'to lend', fr. **līhan*, cogn. w. O.H.G. *līhan*, Mod. Germ. *leihen*, 'to lend'; Goth. *leihwan.* The orig. sense was 'to leave, abandon', then 'abandon to another's use'. The base is further seen in Gk. *leipein*, 'to leave'; cp. Lat. *līqui*, 'I have left, abandoned' &c., perf. of *linquere* (see **leave**). **1.** n. Something lent to another for his temporary use: *the loan of a book*; *not a gift, only a temporary loan*; specif., sum of money lent to another, with or without interest being payable. Phrs. *on loan*, as a loan; *Government Loan*, sum of money borrowed by a State from another State, or from individuals in return for an agreed rate of interest. **2.** vb. To make a loan of, allow use of as a loan; an American usage; *lend* is generally felt to be preferable.

loanable, adj. [1. lṓnəbl; 2. lóunəbl]. Prec. & **-able.** Capable of being lent.

loan-collection, n. Collection of pictures &c. lent temporarily for purposes of exhibition.

loan-word, n. Modelled on Mod. Germ. *lehnwort.* Word borrowed by the speakers of one language from another, and incorporated into their own.

loath, loth, adj. [1. lōth; 2. louþ]. O.E. *lāþ*, 'hostile, hateful, unpleasant'; cp. O.H.G. *leit*, Mod. Germ. *leid*, cogn. w. Lat. *līs* for **līt-s*, 'dispute' &c. (see **litigate**). A common O.E. construction is *mē is lāþ*, 'it is hateful, unpleasant, to me—I am reluctant'. Unwilling, reluctant: *to be loath to go, loath to part with a person* &c.

loathe, vb. trans. [1. lōdh; 2. louð]. O.E. *lāþian*, (impers.) 'to be distasteful, hateful to'. See prec. **a** To hate, detest, be filled with horror at, or disgust by; feel strong aversion to: *to loathe cruelty*; *to loathe the sight of food*; **b** (colloq.) expressing mere dislike or mild aversion: *I loathe tea for breakfast.*

loathing, n. [1. lṓdhing; 2. lóuðiŋ]. Prec. & **-ing.** Great disgust, detestation, repulsion: *to be filled with loathing.*

loathingly, adv. **loathe & -ing (II.) & -ly.** With horror or detestation.

loathliness, n. [1. lṓdhlines; 2. lóuðlinis]. See next word & **-ness.** Hatefulness.

loathly, adj. [1. lṓdhli; 2. lóuðli]. O.E. *lāþlīc*, 'hateful, horrible'. See **loath & -ly.** Abominable, disgusting; also hideous, inspiring disgust by appearance.

loathsome, adj. [1. lṓthsum; 2. lóuþsəm]. **loath & -some.** **a** Nauseating, disgusting, esp. to the taste or sense of smell; **b** revolting; shocking to the moral sense.

loathsomely, adv. Prec. & **-ly.** In a loathsome manner.

loathsomeness, n. See prec. & **-ness.** Quality, state, of being loathsome.

lob (I.), n. [1. lob; 2. lɔb]. Cp. O. Fris. *lobbe*, 'thick lump of flesh or fat'. **1.** A loutish, clumsy person. **2.** A high-pitched, slow ball bowled underhand in cricket; similar ball struck so as to fall at back of court over opponent's head at lawn-tennis.

lob (II.), vb. intrans. & trans., fr. prec. **1.** intrans. To move, walk or run along with a heavy, clumsy action; also *lob along.* **2.** trans. To pitch, strike, a ball high in the air at cricket or lawn-tennis.

lobar, adj. [1. lṓbar; 2. lóubə]. **lobe & -ar.** Of, pertaining to, a lobe or lobes, esp. of the lung: *lobar pneumonia.*

lobate, adj. [1. lṓbāt; 2. lóubeit]. See **lobe & -ate.** (bot.) Lobed, having lobes or projecting divisions; esp. of leaves such as those of the oak.

lobby (I.), n. [1. lóbi; 2. lɔ́bi], fr. Low Lat. *laubia, lobia*, 'portico, gallery, covered way'; this is apparently borrowed fr. M.H.G. *loube*, 'arbour, bower, way leading to a house'. Mod. Germ. *laube*, 'a shady, leafy bower'; cogn. w. Engl. **leaf.** See also **lodge. 1.** Hall, ante-room, waiting-room. **2.** Specif., *the Lobby (of House of Commons)*, large hall open to the public in which members of the House interview their constituents and others; also *Division lobby*, corridor to which members go to vote on a division.

lobby (II.), vb. trans. & intrans., fr. prec. **a** To discuss privately (in the Lobby) with members of a legislative or deliberative body, in order to secure their support for a given object; **b** (gen.) to bring influence to bear privately, in advance, on those who have subsequently to decide public questions.

lobe, n. [1. lōb; 2. loub]. Fr., fr. Gk. *lobós*, 'lobe of the ear', also 'seed pod', as of peas &c.; cogn. w. Gk. *léb-inthioi*, 'peas', *lebēris*, 'peel or husk of fruits', & Lat. *legūmen*, 'plant with pods'. The words are perh. cogn. w. Scrt. *lag-*, 'hang', & in that case the fundamental idea wd. seem to be 'that which hangs down, something pendulous'. Hence the application to the lobe of the ear & to a seed pod. Further extension of usage prob. arises fr. a fancied resemblance in shape to the lobe of the ear &c. On the other hand, the base may be unconnected w. *lag-*, 'hang', & may have a direct connexion in meaning w. the *ear.* Lat. *legere* means amongst other things 'to pick up by ear, hear', cp. *legula*, 'ear', that wh. picks up, hears (sounds). In this case the application is first to the ear, then to the lower part of the ear, finally to the seed pods of certain plants on account of fancied resemblance in shape, and in being pendulous. **1. a** The flat pendulous part which terminates the human ear at its lowest point; **b** any projection or division of an organ, esp. of a rounded shape: *a lobe of the lungs, of the liver.* **2.** (bot.) *Lobe of a leaf*, rounded, projecting division.

lobed, adj. [1. lōbd; 2. loubd]. Prec. & **-ed.** Furnished with lobes.

lobelia, n. [1. lōbḗlia; 2. loubíljə], fr. proper name (M. de l'Obel, physician to James I.). One of many species of herbaceous plants, with red, blue, or white flowers, cultivated in gardens.

loblolly boy, man, n. [1. lòblóli; 2. lɔblɔ́li]. (naut.) Surgeon's mate; *loblolly (loplolly)* was sailors' name for gruel. It is recorded by Mrs. Piozzi (*Anecdotes of Dr. Johnson*, No. 142) that Dr. Johnson once visited a man-of-war and was informed, on inquiring the use of some part of the ship that it was 'where the *loplolly man keeps his loplolly*'. This reply he considered, probably erroneously, 'disrespectful, gross, and ignorant'.

lobscouse, n. [1. lóbskous; 2. lɔ́bskaus]. Origin unknown. Sea dish of meat, vegetables, ship's biscuit &c., usually stewed.

lobster, n. [1. lóbster; 2. lɔ́bstə]. O.E. *lopustre, lopestre*, form of Lat. *locusta*, 'locust', also 'lobster, crayfish'. See **locust. 1. a** Large edible marine crustacean, genus *Homarus*, with powerful claws; greyish black when alive, bright red when boiled; **b** its flesh as food. **2.** (obs. slang, colloq.) A British soldier, from old scarlet uniform.

lobster-pot, n. Kind of basket trap in which lobsters are caught.

lobular, adj. [1. lóbūlar; 2. lɔ́bjulə]. See next word & **-ar.** Connected with, resembling, lobules, or a lobule.

lobule, n. [1. lóbūl; 2. lɔ́bjūl]. Fr. *lobule*, L. Lat. *lobulus*, dimin. of *lobus.* See **lobe & -ule.** A small lobe.

lobworm, n. [1. lóbwërm; 2. lɔ́bwām]. See **lob (I.) & worm.** Earthworm or marine worm used as bait for fishing.

local (I.), adj. [1. lṓkl; 2. lóukl]. Lat. *locālis*, adj., 'belonging to a place', fr. *locus*, 'place'. See **locus.** Belonging to, residing in, or confined to, a particular place, region, or neighbourhood: *local affairs*; *the local clergyman, doctor*; *a local habit, dialect*; *local examination*, one held by a university in a locality for granting certificates to the pupils of secondary schools; *local injury*, one affecting only a specific area of the body; *local train*, one running but a short distance from its starting-point; *a bird, animal, plant* &c. is said to be *(quite) local*, i.e. not widely distributed. Phr. *local colour*, details characteristic of place or time, added to a story to give a sense of reality. Specific uses: *local government*, administration of local affairs by councils or other bodies elected by the inhabitants of the locality, such as county councils, boroughs &c.; *Local Government Board*, former state department concerned with such administration, now absorbed in Ministry of Health; *local option*, scheme whereby the inhabitants of a place or district decide the number of public-houses which shall be licensed in their area, the regulations as to sale of liquor &c.; *local veto*, right of inhabitants of a locality to forbid sale of alcoholic liquor.

local (II.), n., fr. prec. Something belonging to some definite place; short for *local train*; *local news*, as given in a newspaper &c.

locale, n. [1. lōkáhl; 2. loukál]. Fr. Scene, theatre, of some specified event or action.

localism, n. [1. lṓkalizm; 2. lóukəlizəm]. **local (I.) & -ism. 1. a** Habit of mind which favours what is local, or characteristic of a particular place or area; **b** narrowness, limitation of ideas. **2.** Local mode of speech, pronunciation, idiom; a provincialism.

locality, n. [1. lōkáliti; 2. loukǽliti]. **local (I.) & -ity. 1.** Position or place in which a thing exists. **2.** Place, district, neighbourhood. Phr. *bump, sense, of locality*, faculty of visualizing objects and landmarks in relation to others in any region and thus of finding one's way.

localizable, adj. [1. lṓkalīzabl; 2. lóukəlaizəbl]. **localize & -able.** Capable of being localized.

localization, n. [1. lòkalīzáshun; 2. lòukəlaizéiʃən]. See next word & **-ation.** Act of localizing; state of being localized.

localize, vb. trans. [1. lṓkalīz; 2. lóukəlaiz]. **local & -ize. 1.** To assign to a particular place or area, locate. **2.** To confine within, restrict to, prevent from spreading beyond, a particular area: *to localize a disturbance*; *to localize infection.* **3.** To make local, give a local character to.

locally, adv. [1. lṓkali; 2. lóukəli]. **local & -ly.** Within a given place, neighbourhood, or area.

locate, vb. trans. [1. lōkát; 2. loukéit], fr. Lat. *locāt-(um)*, P.P. type of *locāre*, 'to place, put, arrange, dispose' &c. See **locus & -ate.**

1. **a** To place, set in, assign to, a particular place or position; **b** to lodge, take up residence in; esp. in P.P., *to be located in.* **2.** To discover with certainty the exact position of anything: *to locate the source of a pain.*

location, n. [1. lōkā́shun; 2. loukéiʃən]. Lat. *locātiōn-(em)*, 'a placing, arrangement'. See prec. & **-ion.** **a** Act, process, of locating; **b** state of being located; **c** situation, place of residence.

locative, adj. & n. [1. lókativ; 2. lɔ́kətiv]. **locate** & **-ive.** (gram.) **a** adj. Connected with the case which expresses place where; **b** n., the case itself, word having locative ending, or expressing place where.

loch, n. [1. logh; 2. lɔχ]. Gael. *laough*, 'lake'. A lake, esp. in Scotland.

Lochaber-axe, n. [1. loghā́ber áks; 2. lɔχǽbər ǽks]. An axe attached to a long handle with a hook at the end, as formerly used by Scottish Highlanders in fighting; fr. *Lochaber*, Inverness-shire.

lock (I.), n. [1. lok; 2. lɔk]. O.E. *locc*, 'lock of hair; hair'; O.H.G. *loc*; O.N. *lokkr*, all fr. **lugná*; cogn. w. Gk. *lúgos*, 'a pliant twig or rod; a withy', cp. Gk. *lugízein*, 'to bend, twist'; also Lat. *luctāre, -āri*, 'to wrestle, struggle', referring to the twisting & intertwining, whence Fr. *lutter*, 'struggle, wrestle'; Lith. *lugnas*, 'flexible, pliant, docile'. **1.** **a** A small tress, tuft, ringlet, of hair as it grows upon the head; one that has been cut from the head; **b** tuft of hair or wool on an animal. **2.** pl. (poet. or liter.) The hair as a whole: *grizzled, golden, locks.*

lock (II.), n. O.E. *loc*, 'lock, bolt, bar; something enclosed; an enclosure, a prison'; cp. also *loca*, 'enclosure'; cogn. w. *lūcan*, trans. 'to close, confine; interlace'; intrans. 'to intermingle, join together in single mass'; the base is perh. ultimately the same as in **lock** (I.). **1.** Contrivance for closing doors, the lids of chests, drawers &c., consisting of a system of levers and a strong spring, which act upon a bolt or bolts; the mechanism is enclosed in a metal or wooden case, and is worked by a key. Phr. *under lock and key*, secured by being placed in locked receptacle. **2.** Mechanism of levers worked by a trigger, by means of which a gun is fired. **3.** Mode of grappling in wrestling. **4.** **a** Enclosure on a river or canal, with movable, water-tight gates, through which vessels pass, and proceed from one water-level to another; **b** similar enclosure at entrance to a tidal dock. **5.** A lock hospital, q.v.

lock (III.), vb. trans. & intrans., fr. prec. **A.** trans. **1.** **a** To close, make fast, prevent opening, by shooting the bolts of a lock: *to lock a door, a drawer.* Phr. *to lock the stable door after the horse has been stolen*, take precautions too late; **b** (fig.) to retain firmly fixed, and inviolate in the mind: *knowledge, secrets, safely locked in one's breast.* **2.** To embrace closely: *to lock a person in one's arms*; *locked in a close embrace.* **3.** **a** To fix firmly and rigidly: *jaws tightly locked*; **b** (of machinery, wheels &c.) to jam, render immovable, prevent from revolving. **4.** To intertwine, interlace: *to lock fingers, arms, together.* **B.** intrans. To become locked: *the door locks automatically*; to be capable of being locked: *the door won't lock, locks quite easily.* **C.** Followed by adverb or preposition. *Lock away*, trans., to put away in a locked receptacle. *Lock in*, trans., to confine (person) in a room &c., the door of which is locked on the outside to prevent exit. *Lock into*, trans., to put (person, or animal) into a room, stable &c., and lock the door on the outside. *Lock out*, trans., to prevent from entering by locking door or gate on inside; specif., to prevent workmen from entering workshop &c. to carry on their work, in an industrial dispute. *Lock up*, **a** make secure, shut up, by locking doors &c.: *to lock up one's house*; *to lock up for the night*; *to lock up one's papers*, enclose them in locked drawer, box, desk &c.; Phr. *to lock oneself up in one's room* &c., refuse to see anyone, hold oneself aloof and inaccessible; specif., *to lock a person up*, put him in prison, or in a lunatic asylum; *to lock up one's money*, put it into securities that cannot easily be converted into cash; **b** intrans., to secure house &c. by locking doors &c.

lockage, n. [1. lókij; 2. lɔ́kidž]. **lock** (II.) & **-age.** **a** Amount of change in elevation effected by lock of canal, dock, or river; **b** charge for passing vessel through a lock; **c** apparatus and works forming a lock.

locker, n. [1. lóker; 2. lɔ́kə]. **lock** (III.) & **-er.** **1.** Person who locks. **2.** **a** Cupboard, drawer &c. which can be locked; specif., one for private property, the owner of which keeps the key; **b** chest, compartment in a ship's cabin &c. used to keep clothes &c. in. Phr. *to go to, be in, Davy Jones's locker*, to be drowned at sea.

locket, n. [1. lóket; 2. lɔ́kit], fr. O. Fr. *locquet*, of Gmc. origin. See **lock** (II.) & **-et.** Small metal case containing a miniature, lock of hair, or other relic, usually hung on a chain from neck, or from watch-chain.

lock hospital, n. Prob. fr. name of an old leper's hospital in London. A hospital for the treatment of venereal diseases.

Lockian, adj. [1. lókian; 2. lɔ́kiən]. Connected with John Locke (1632–1704) or his philosophy.

lock-jaw, n. Tetanic, spasmodic closure of the jaws, which remain locked; trismus.

lock-out, n. Refusal by employer to allow work to continue, in an industrial dispute, until employees accept his terms; reverse of a workmen's strike.

locksmith, n. [1. lóksmith; 2. lɔ́ksmiþ]. Skilled workman who makes and repairs locks.

lock-stitch, n. Stitch made by a sewing-machine, in which two threads are firmly fastened together.

lock-up, n. & attrib. adj. **1.** n. **a** Time for locking up, stopping work &c.; **b** place where arrested persons are temporarily confined. **2.** adj. Capable of being locked up: *a lock-up shed.*

loco citato. See **locus.**

locomotion, n. [1. lòkōmṓshun; 2. lòukoumóuʃən]. Lat. *loco*, abl. case of *locus*, 'place' (see **locus**), & *mōtiōn-(em)*, 'a moving'. See **motion.** Act or process of moving from one place to another; power to do this: *capacity for, power of, locomotion*, of walking; *means of locomotion*, of being transported from place to place.

locomotive, adj. & n. [1. lòkōmṓtiv; 2. lòukoumòutiv]. Lat. *loco-*, as in prec. & **motive,** (II.) **1.** adj. Endowed with power of locomotion: *locomotive power*; *locomotive engine*, one which moves under its own power from place to place, as distinct from a stationary engine, esp. one which draws trains along a railway. **2.** n. A locomotive engine; specif. an engine driven by steam, used for drawing trains on a railway.

locomotivity, n. [1. lòkōmōtíviti; 2. lòukoumoutíviti]. Prec. & **-ity.** Capacity for locomotion.

locomotor, n. & adj. [1. lókōmòtor; 2. lóukoumòutə]. See prec. & **-or.** **1.** n. Person or thing having power of locomotion. **2.** adj. Pertaining to locomotion; chiefly in *locomotor ataxy* (see **ataxia**), a progressive disease of the nervous system, *tabes dorsalis*, affecting lower part of spinal cord, and characterized by loss of control of lower limbs, and of power to co-ordinate movements, which produces peculiarities of gait.

locomotory, adj. [1. lòkōmṓtori; 2. lòukoumóutəri]. See prec. & **-y.** Pertaining to, possessing, locomotion.

locular, adj. [1. lókūlar; 2. lɔ́kjulə]. Next word & **-ar.** Pertaining to, resembling, having, loculi.

loculus, n., pl. **loculi** [1. lókūlus, -lī; 2. lɔ́kjuləs, -lai]. Lat., 'a little place'. See **locus.** (biol.) One of a number, or series of small cells.

locum tenens, n. [1. lókum tḗnenz; 2. lóukəm tínenz]. Lat., 'holding the place'. See **locus** & **tenant.** One holding another's office temporarily, and acting as his deputy; esp. of a doctor or clergyman.

locus, n. [1. lókus; 2. lóukəs]. Lat. *locus*, 'place', older Lat. *stlocus*; the word is prob. derived fr. base **stel-*, 'to place', cp. Scrt. *sthalī*, 'place, locality'; Gk. *stéllein*, 'set in order, arrange, array' &c.; *stḗlē*, 'pillar', *stólos*, 'an expedition'; O.E. *stela*, 'stalk, support'; *stellan*, 'to set, place', further *stille*, 'at rest, quiet', O.H.G. *stilli* (see **still** (I.)); **stel-* is itself an extension of base **st(h)ā-*, 'to stand'. See **stand** (I.) & **state** (I.). *Loco citato* [1. lókō sitā́tō; 2. lóukou saitéitou], in the passage quoted, abbrev. *loc. cit.* *Locus classicus* [1. lókus klásikus; 2. lóukəs klǽsikəs], stock, standard, most authoritative passage in illustration of specified point or subject. *Locus poenitentiae* [1. lókus pēniténshiē; 2. lóukəs pīniténʃiī], 'place, opportunity, for repentance'; opportunity permitted for withdrawing from a line of action before being finally committed to it. *Locus sigilli* [1. lókus sijílī; 2. lóukəs sidžílai], 'place for the seal,' on documents. *Locus standi* [1. lókus stándī; 2. lóukəs stǽndai], 'place of standing', right to intervene in a lawsuit; recognized position.

locust, n. [1. lókust; 2. lóukəst]. Lat. *locusta*, 'grasshopper, locust'; cogn. w. *lacertus*, 'lizard'. See **lacertian**; further w. Gk. *láx*, adv. 'with the heel', & *laktízein*, 'to kick with the heel, to trample on'; cp. Lith. *lakstýti*, 'to hop'; also O.N. *leggr*, q.v. under **leg.** *Locust*, therefore, means orig., either 'the creature with long legs', or, 'the hopping insect'. Large insect allied to grasshopper, which migrates in vast swarms in hot climates, and is specially destructive to crops of all kinds; (fig.) a person of greedy, destructive tendencies.

locust bean, n. Sweet edible pod of carob tree.

locust-tree, n. **a** The false acacia, *Robinia*; **b** carob tree.

locution, n. [1. lokū́shun; 2. lɔkjúʃən]. Lat. *locūtio*, fr. *loqui*, 'to speak'. See **loquacious.** Style of speech; phrase, idiom.

locutory, n. [1. lókūtori; 2. lɔ́kjutəri]. Med. Lat. *locūtōrium*, fr. same base as prec., & **-ory.** Room for conversation, esp. in monasteries.

lode, n. [1. lōd; 2. loud]. Variant spelling of **load** (I.); see also **lead** (IV.). **1.** Course, way. Obsolete, except in English Place-Names, usually in form *lade*, e.g. *Lechlade* &c. **2.** Vein (of ore).

lodestar, loadstar, n. [1. lṓdstar; 2. lóudstā]. **a** Star by which one steers; **b** (fig.) object of attraction and pursuit; guiding ideal or principle.

lodestone, n. See **loadstone.**

lodge (I.), n. [1. loj; 2. lɔdž]. Fr. *loge*, Ital. *loggia*, fr. Low Lat. *laubia*; doublet of **lobby,** q.v. for further etymol. **1.** Habitation, dwelling, esp. a small house at entrance to a park, or drive leading to a large house. **2.** The set of rooms in the chief gateway or entrance to a college or other important building, as at Oxford, e.g. *the Porter's Lodge.* **3.** **a** Local branch of certain societies and associations such as the Freemasons; **b** the building or actual room in which these hold their meetings; **c** the meeting itself. **4.** **a** The wigwam, a tent, of a N. American Indian; **b** the lair or den built by a beaver or otter.

lodge (II.), vb. intrans. & trans., fr. prec. **A.** intrans. **1.** To dwell temporarily; occupy lodgings: *to lodge over a baker's.* **2.** To enter and remain embedded or fixed (in): *the bullet lodged in his brain.* **B.** trans. **1.** **a** To afford lodging to; to house: *I can lodge you for a day or two*; **b** *to lodge a stag*, to drive it to covert. **2.** To place, implant, land: *to lodge a blow*; *to lodge a bullet.* **3.** To deposit (money, securities &c.) for safe custody: *to lodge money in the bank.* **4.** To lay a statement or accusation before legal authorities: *to lodge an accusation, complaint, charge (against a man)*; *to lodge information.*

lodged, adj. [1. loj'd ; 2. lɔdžd], fr. P.P. of prec. (her., of a stag) Lying on the ground with head erect.

lodg(e)ment, n. [1. lójment ; 2. lɔ́džmənt]. **lodge** & **-ment**. **1.** Place in which to lodge; lodgings, quarters. **2.** Accumulation of matter which has been deposited and become impacted and arrested ; e.g. in a pipe or conduit. **3.** Act, process, of lodging ; mode of coming to rest.

lodger, n. [1. lójer ; 2. lɔ́džə]. **lodge** & **-er**. One who lodges in or inhabits a house ; specif., a person who occupies premises or a portion of a house temporarily, on payment of weekly rent, the rest of the house being used by the owner or actual lessee : *to take in lodgers*.

lodging(s), n. [1. lójing(z) ; 2. lɔ́džiŋ(z)]. See prec. & **-ing**. Room(s) in a house let temporarily to a lodger. *The Lodgings* is sometimes the designation of an official residence, e.g. of certain heads of Oxford Colleges.

lodging-house, n. One in which rooms are let by the week ; *common lodging-house*, one in which a man or woman can hire a bed for the night.

loess, n. [1. lṓes, lës ; 2. lóuis, lɜs]. Germ. *löss*. Fine siliceous and calcareous earth of brownish-yellow colour found esp. in N. China, Central U.S.A., and Central Europe.

loft (I.), n. [1. lawft, loft ; 2. lɔ̄ft, lɔft]. M.E., fr. O.N. *lopt*, 'air ; upper room', cogn. w. O.H.G. *luft*, O.E. *lyft*, Goth. *luftus*, 'air' ; origin unknown. **1. a** Chamber immediately below the roof of a building and above the ceilings of top floor ; **b** space above stables, immediately under roof, chiefly used for storing hay and straw. **2.** (golf) **a** Slope on edge of golf-club which causes the ball to rise when struck ; **b** a stroke which causes the ball to rise ; lofting stroke.

loft (II.), vb. trans., fr. prec. **1.** To place, store, in a loft. **2.** (golf) **a** To give a slope to the face of (a golf-club) ; **b** to strike (a ball) so as to cause it to rise and pass over an obstacle.

lofter, n. [1. láwfter ; 2. lɔ̄́ftə]. Prec. & **-er**. Golf-club for lifting ball high into the air.

loftily, adv. [1. láwftili ; 2. lɔ̄́ftili]. **lofty** & **-ly**. In a lofty manner ; **a** reaching to, situated at, a great height ; **b** in a dignified or haughty manner.

loftiness, n. [1. láwftines ; 2. lɔ̄́ftinis]. See prec. & **-ness**. Condition of being lofty ; **a** great height ; **b** nobility, elevation of aims and ideals ; **c** pride, haughtiness, of manner.

lofting, n. [1. láwfting ; 2. lɔ̄́ftiŋ]. Timber used to form roof in a mine.

lofty, adj. [1. láwfti ; 2. lɔ̄́fti]. **loft (I.)** & **-y**. **1.** Of great height (of objects, not of persons) : *a lofty mountain, spire, room, tree.* **2.** (fig.) **a** (of style, language, ideals, thoughts &c.) Elevated, noble, dignified, sublime : *lofty diction ; lofty principles, aims ; lofty contempt* &c. ; **b** (of bearing, manners) superior, dignified, with a touch of haughtiness or arrogance.

log (I.), n. [1. log ; 2. lɔg]. M.E. *logge* ; cp. Swed. *logg*, 'log', esp. as naut. term. Origin unknown. **1.** Rough mass of wood, strictly speaking unhewn, though it may be sawn into lengths, great or small. Phrs. *to lie, fall, sleep like a log*, immovable or unconscious ; *in the log*, rough, unhewn ; *to roll logs for a person*, whence *log-rolling*, q.v. ; *King Log*, an inert, idle fellow in a position of command or leadership ; refers to Æsop's fable of Jupiter and the Frogs. **2.** Apparatus used to measure and record speed of a ship through the water, originally a piece of floating wood attached to a knotted cord thrown out and reeled in at intervals. Phr. *to heave the log*, take speed of a ship by means of the log. **3.** (also *log-book*) Record or journal kept on board a ship of the chief events connected with voyage, including results of reading the log ; a ship's log doubtless began simply as a record of speed, longitude &c., and was extended to include other notable incidents of the trip.

log (II.), vb. trans., fr. prec. **1. a** To cut (timber) into logs ; **b** to haul (cut timber). **2. a** To enter in log-book, as distance run by ship and other details of day's run ; **b** (of ship) to cover (so many knots, distance) in day's run.

log (III.), n. Abbr. of **logarithm**.

loganberry, n. [1. lṓganberi ; 2. lóugənbɛri], fr. name of Judge Logan, U.S.A., who first produced the fruit in 1881. Plant bearing large dark-red fruit much resembling the raspberry in appearance and taste ; a hybrid between the raspberry and blackberry.

logan-stone, n. [1. lógan stṑn ; 2. lɔ́gən stòun]. Provinc. dial. *log*, 'to rock'. Large stone so nicely balanced upon another that it can be rocked by touching.

logarithm, n. [1. lógaridhm ; 2. lɔ́gəriðəm], fr. Gk. *lógos*, 'word, ratio' &c. (see **logos**), & *arithmós*, 'number' (see **arithmetic**). (math.) Exponent of power to which a given invariable number must be raised in order to produce another given number ; logarithms are tabulated and are used to facilitate calculations.

logarithmic(al), adj. [1. lògaríthmik(l) ; 2. lɔ̀gəríþmik(l)]. Prec. & **-ic**. Pertaining to, consisting of, logarithms.

logarithmically, adv. Prec. & **-ly**. By means of logarithms.

log-book, n. Record of ship's log ; ship's diary or journal.

log-cabin, -house, -hut, n. Small dwelling, house, made of undressed logs, as built in backwoods of America and Canada &c.

-loger, suff. formed by adding *-er* to Lat. *-logus* & Gk. *lógos* (see **-logy**), now, except in *astrologer*, replaced by **-logist**.

logged, adj. [1. logd ; 2. lɔgd], fr. P.P. of **log (II.)**. Made heavy ; esp. *water-logged* : (of wood, boats) saturated with water so as to lose buoyancy ; (of land) soaked, heavy, with water ; marshy.

loggerhead, n. [1. lógerhed ; 2. lɔ́gəhɛd]. **1.** (obs.) Variant of obs. *log-head*. A fool, stupid fellow, blockhead. Phr. *to be at loggerheads with*, to fall out, have a disagreement, with a person. **2.** A small species of turtle.

loggia, n. [1. lója ; 2. lɔ́dža]. Ital. See **lodge (I.)** & cp. **lobby**. Kind of roofed verandah built on to front of house, and used as an out-of-doors sitting-room.

logging, n. [1. lóging ; 2. lɔ́giŋ], fr. **log (II.)** & **-ing**. Business of felling, sawing up, and marketing timber.

logic, n. [1. lójik ; 2. lɔ́džik]. M.E. *logike* ; Fr. *logique*, fr. Lat. *logica*, fr. Gk. *logikḗ* (*tekhnḗ*), 'logic art', that is, the art of speaking and reasoning, fr. adj. *logikós*, 'belonging to speech or reasoning'. See **logos** & **-ic**. **1. a** Science of formal thought and of the laws according to which pure reasoning should be conducted. Phr. *to chop logic*, engage in pedantic argument, bandy words ; **b** treatise on logic : *Bradley's Logic.* **2.** Mode of reasoning, chain of argument, good or bad : *his logic is unsound, shaky.* **3.** Sound reasoning : *if that's not logic I don't know what is.* **4.** Natural and necessary chain of causes and effects : *the logic of fate, of events.*

logical, adj. [1. lójikl ; 2. lɔ́džikl]. Prec. & **-al**. **a** Belonging to, imbued with, in accordance with, the principles of logic : *a logical mind ; logical argument* ; **b** necessary as result of what has gone before : *the logical result of one's acts* &c. ; **c** consistent : *logical conduct, action.*

-logical, suff. to form adjs. fr. ns. ending in **-logy**, as *geological* &c.

logically, adv. [1. lójikali ; 2. lɔ́džik(ə)li]. See **logical** & **-ly**. In a logical manner.

logician, n. [1. lojíshan ; 2. lɔdžíʃən]. Fr. *logicien*. See **logic** & **-ian**. One skilled in logic ; a professor of, writer on, the science.

logie, n. [1. lṓgi ; 2. lóugi]. Prob. fr. name of inventor. Ornament of sham jewellery used in theatres.

logion, n., pl. **logia** [1. lógion, lógia ; 2. lɔ́giɔn, lɔ́giə]. Gk., 'a saying', fr. **logos**. Saying of Jesus Christ preserved elsewhere than in the Gospels.

-logist, suff. to form ns. by addition of **-ist** to words w. suff. **-logy**, as *geologist* &c.

logistic, adj. & n. [1. lojístik ; 2. lɔdžístik]. Gk. *logistikós*, 'skilled in calculation ; skilled in reasoning'. See **logos**, **-ist**, & **-ic**. **a** adj. Skilled in logic ; **b** n., art of calculation.

logistics, n. pl., fr. Fr. *logistique*, fr. *loger*, 'to lodge'. See **lodge (II.)**. (mil.) Science and practice of moving, lodging, and supplying troops.

logo-, pref. Form of Gk. *lógos* (see **logos**) used in compounds ; denoting speech, discourse, thought.

logodaedaly, n. [1. lògōdḗdali ; 2. lɔ̀goudídəli]. Gk. *logodaidalía*. See prec. & **daedal** & **-y**. (rare) Skill in playing with words ; verbal juggling ; used by Coleridge.

logogram, n. [1. lógōgram ; 2. lɔ́gougræm]. **logo-** & **-gram**. Sign or letter representing a word.

logograph, n. [1. lógōgrahf ; 2. lɔ́gougrāf]. **logo-** & **-graph**. Logogram.

logogriph, n. [1. lógōgrif ; 2. lɔ́gougrif]. **logo-** & Gk. *grîphos*, 'fishing-net ; something intricate ; a riddle'. Etymol. doubtful. Word puzzle.

logomachy, n. [1. logómaki ; 2. lɔgɔ́məki]. **logo-** & **-machy**. A dispute in, or concerning, words.

logometric, adj. [1. lògōmétrik ; 2. lɔ̀goumétrik]. **logo-** & **-metric**. (chem.) Serving to represent graphically chemical equivalents.

logos, n. [1. lógos ; 2. lɔ́gɔs]. Gk. *lógos*, 'word by which inward thought is expressed ; a story ; eloquence ; the thought itself ; reason ; calculation ; proportion' ; cogn. w. Gk. *légein*, 'to pick out ; to count, reckon ; to tell, narrate, to speak' ; near cogn. of Lat. *legere*, 'to pick out, choose ; read' &c. See **legend**, **lecture**, **legate**, **legible**. (theol.) The Divine Word, Christ.

logotype, n. [1. lógōtīp ; 2. lɔ́goutaip]. **logo-** & **type**. (typog.) Several letters, or a word cast in a single body.

log-roll, vb. trans. See **log (I.)**. To pursue the art of log-rolling, q.v.

log-roller, n. Prec. & **-er**. One who log-rolls.

log-rolling, n. See prec. & **-ing**. Act or process in which a group of friends and professed admirers of each other's literary or artistic talents combine to praise and puff each other, by word of mouth and in reviews, thus establishing a fictitious reputation for all members of the coterie.

-logue, suff. derived through Fr. fr. Gk. words ending in *-logos, -logon* (cp. **-logy**), as *epilogue, dialogue* &c.

log-wood, n. So called because it reaches this country in large logs. Also called *Campeachy wood* ; **a** tree from Central America and W. Indies of order of Leguminosae ; **b** chips of this tree used for producing **a** black dye, and also, it is supposed, for imparting a rich colour to inferior port wine.

-logy, suff., fr. Gk. *-logia*, fr. *lógos*, 'speech' &c., used in many compounds, old and recent, to denote, **a** pronouncement, utterance, speech, as in *eulogy, tautology* ; **b** treatise, science, doctrine, as in *physiology, philology.*

loimic, adj. [1. lóimik ; 2. lóimik]. Gk. *loimikós*, adj., fr. *loimós*, 'pestilence', cogn. w. Gk. *līmós*, 'hunger', fr. base **lēi-*, whence also Lat. *lētum*, 'death, destruction'. See **lethal**. Pertaining to plague or pestilence.

loin(s), n. [1. loin(z) ; 2. lɔin(z)], fr. Fr. *loigne*, Lat. *lumbus*, 'loin', cogn. w. O.E. *lenden(u)*, 'loins'. See also **lumbar**. **1. a** (anat.) That part of an animal or human being, just above the hip, on either side of the spine ; **b** this part of animal considered as a table joint : *loin of mutton, veal.* Phr. *to gird up one's loins*, make ready for action. **2.** (fig.) The loins considered as the region of procreation ; a race, family, or individual is said to be *sprung from the loins* of the founder of the stock.

loin-cloth, n. Strip of material worn round the loins by primitive peoples.

loir, n. [1. loir; 2. lóiə]. Fr., fr. Lat. *glīrem*, acc. of *glīs*, 'dormouse'. Species of large dormouse with a bushy tail like that of a squirrel.

loiter, vb. intrans. & trans. [1. lóiter; 2. lóitə]. Cp. Du. *leuteren*, 'to delay, linger'. **a** intrans. To linger, lag behind; to hang about in an idle manner; to loaf; to delay, dally, over an occupation; **b** trans., *to loiter away one's time*, waste it in idleness and dilatoriness.

loiterer, n. [1. lóiterer; 2. lóitərə]. Prec. & **-er.** One who loiters; lingerer, dawdler.

loll, vb. intrans. & trans. [1. lol; 2. lɔl]. Cp. O.N. *lolla*, 'to act lazily'. **A.** intrans. **1.** To sit, or stand, propped against some support, in an attitude suggestive of idleness and inactivity; to lounge: *to loll in a chair; to loll against a wall; to loll about doing nothing.* **2.** (of the tongue) To hang out, as from exhaustion. **B.** trans. Allow to protrude, or to hang forward: *to loll the tongue (out); to loll the head forward.*

Lollard, n. [1. lólard; 2. lɔ́ləd]. Du. *lollaerd*, 'a mumbler', esp. of prayers & psalms, fr. *lollen*, 'mumble'. See also **lull.** Member of a sect of fanatical heretics who existed in England in 14th and 15th cents. *Lollards* were the followers of John Wyclif (1324–84); their doctrines anticipated some of those of the advanced Protestantism of a later day. *Lollards' Tower*, place of imprisonment formerly attached to Episcopal residences for the convenient keeping of those guilty or suspected of heresy.

Lollardism, Lollardy, ns. [1. lólardizm, -di; 2. lɔ́lədizəm, -di]. Prec. & **-ism, -y.** System of religious doctrine adopted by Lollards.

lollipop, n. [1. lólipop; 2. lɔ́lipɔp]. Childish word, now hardly in actual use among any class of speakers in England; a sweetmeat (usually in pl.).

lollop, vb. intrans. & n. [1. lólop; 2. lɔ́ləp]. Cp. **loll.** **1.** vb. To walk or run in a clumsy, flopping manner; (not a common word); also *lollop along.* **2.** n. A movement of this kind in walking &c.

lolloping, adj. [1. lóloping; 2. lɔ́ləpiŋ]. Characterized by a lollop: *a lolloping walk, movement, action.*

Lombard, n. & adj. [1. lúmbard, lómbard; 2. lámbəd, lɔ́mbəd]. Fr., fr. Lat. *Langobardi*, name of a Germanic people who invaded Italy in 568; the name was traditionally supposed to be derived from the words corresponding to **long** & **beard.** **1.** n. **a** A member of this tribe; **b** an inhabitant of Lombardy; **c** formerly a banker or money-lender, from the fame of the Lombards in these capacities; *Lombard Street* in London is still a great banking centre. **2.** adj. Belonging to, derived from, Lombardy or the Lombards.

Lombardesque, adj. [1. lòmbardésk; 2. lɔ̀mbədésk]. Prec. & **-esque.** Belonging to the Lombard school of Renaissance artists.

Lombardic, adj. [1. lombárdik; 2. lɔmbádik]. See prec. & **-ic.** Pertaining to Lombardy or the Lombards; specif. **a** of early architecture; **b** of Renaissance painters.

Lombardy poplar, n. [1. lúmbardi, lómbardi póplar; 2. lámbədi, lɔ́mbədi pɔ́plə]. A tall graceful kind of poplar, a variety of the black poplar, growing in a pyramidal or cypress-like shape.

loment, n. [1. lóment; 2. lóument]. Lat. *lōmentum*, a cosmetic of bean-meal & rice used by Roman ladies for cleansing & preserving the skin; perh. fr. type *lō-*, as in *lōtum*, P.P. of *lavāre*, 'to wash' (see **lave** & **lotion**), & *-mentum* (see **-ment**). (bot.) Seed pod like that of pea or bean, but containing each seed in the row in a well-marked division separating it from those next it.

lomentaceous, adj. [1. lòmentáshus; 2. lòuméntéiʃəs]. Prec. & **-aceous.** (bot.) Bearing loments; like a loment.

Londoner, n. [1. lúnduner; 2. lándənə]. Inhabitant of London.

Londonism, n. [1. lúndunizm; 2. lándənizəm]. Trick of manner, or (esp.) of speech peculiar to London.

London pride, n. [1. lúndun príd; 2. lándən práid]. A kind of saxifrage, *Saxifraga umbrosa.*

Londres, n. [1. lóndrez; 2. lɔ́ndrez]. Span. for London. Trade name for a cigar of a particular cylindrical shape.

lone, adj. [1. lōn; 2. loun]. Abbr. fr. **alone.** **a** Solitary, by oneself: *a lone female*; **b** remote, separated from others, lying apart: *a lone waste.*

loneliness, n. [1. lṓnlines; 2. lóunlinis]. See next word & **-ness.** The condition of being lonely.

lonely, adj. [1. lṓnli; 2. lóunli]. **lone** & **-ly.** **a** (of persons) Solitary, conscious of solitude; Phr. *to feel lonely*, to be conscious of, and regret, solitude; **b** (of things) isolated, remote from men and life: *a lonely house, inn, wood; a lonely life*, one led apart from society.

lonesome, adj. [1. lṓnsum; 2. lóunsəm]. **lone** & **-some.** Lonely.

lonesomely, adv. Prec. & **-ly.** In a lonesome state.

lonesomeness, n. See prec. & **-ness.** State of being lonesome.

long (I.), adj. [1. long; 2. lɔŋ]. O.E. *lang*, M.E. *lōng*; common to all Gmc. languages, & cogn. w. Lat. *longus*; M. Ir. *long.* The view that the original form was **dlongos*, & that these words were cogn. w. Gk. *dolikhós*, see **dolichocephalic,** is now questioned by Walde, because of the Ir. form, wh. shd. be **dlong*, since *dl-* remains in Celt.; on the other hand, the Ir. form may be a direct loan fr. Lat. & not derived fr. the orig. Celt. **1.** (of distance and length) Extended for a considerable way, having prolonged extension, occupying much space from starting-point to termination; not short: *a long way to go; a long distance; long legs, long hair, a long nose* &c.; *a long journey*, one in which much ground is traversed; Phrs. *the, a, long arm*, far-reaching power; *to make a long arm*, stretch out for, make an effort to reach something; *a long face*, dismal, lugubrious face; *(to make) a long nose*, vulgar, insulting gesture made with the thumb touching the nose, and the fingers spread out; *to have a long tongue*, be inclined to talk too much; *long views*, prevision, foresightedness; *at long range*, from a distance; *to have a long wind*, capacity to run far without getting out of breath; *a long purse*, plenty of money; *long manure*, composed largely of unrotted straw; *long home*, the grave; *long hop*, (cricket) ball which pitches some way in front of the batsman; *long jump*, one estimated by distance covered between taking off and alighting; *long leg*, fielder in outfield on leg side of batsman at cricket; *long pig, pork*, human flesh as eaten by cannibals; *long clothes*, first type of frocks worn by babies; *long clay pipe*, one with long stem. **2.** (of time) **a** Having considerable duration, continued during an extended period; drawn, spun, out, protracted: *a long life, visit, wait, reign, winter, night*; **b** occupying a considerable time, taking much time to enact or complete: *a long war, debate, lecture, play*; also, of speech, diffuse, prolix; Phrs. *in the long run*, as a total result; *to cut a long story short*, abbreviate it and come to the point; *a long look*, lingering; *a long farewell*, one before a long separation; *Long Vacation*, the summer vacation of Law Courts and Universities &c.; **c** appearing to last for considerable time, passing slowly, by reason of impatience, anxiety, difficulties felt or undergone, although the actual period of time may be fixed and definite; hence, tedious, wearisome, too long: *long years of misery; the long hours dragged slowly by; the days never seemed long, so full of interest were they.* **3.** (of a series, list, enumeration) Containing many items; *a long bill*, an excessive, exorbitant bill. **4.** Having a specific extension in time or space: *an hour long; 5 feet long.* **5.** (phon.) *Long vowel, consonant*, one the actual articulation of which continues for a longer space of time than a short vowel or consonant in the same language; *length* applied to sounds of language is a relative term; *long syllable*, one containing a long vowel, a diphthong, or a long or short vowel followed by two consonants; the phrase *long by position*, used of a short vowel in Latin, is inaccurate; the *syllable* is long because it contains two consonants, though the *vowel* remains short. **6.** (prosody) Applied to genuine quantitative metres the terms *long vowel*, or *syllable*, correspond approximately to the phonetic usage; but in stress metres, such as those of English, the terms are often applied to vowels or syllables which have stress, as distinct from the unstressed, or weak. *Long measure*, octosyllabic quatrains with alternate rhymes.

long (II.), adv. See prec. **1.** For a long time: *to live, last, long; I have long been meaning to write; stay (for) as long as you like.* **2.** At a point of time remote from that specified, whether before or after: *long before you were born; long after his death.* Phrs. *long since, long ago*, at a time in the past remote from the present. **3.** (in compar.) After, beyond a specified point of time: *wait a while longer; no longer; any longer*; superl. Phr. *(a week) at longest*, not more than a week at most.

long (III.), n., fr. **long** (I.). **1.** (mus.) A long note; (phon. and prosody) a long sound or syllable. **2.** *The Long*, Long Vacation.

long (IV.), vb. intrans. O.E. *langian*, M.E. *lōngen.* See **long** (I.). **1.** **a** To be filled with a strong yearning for something; to feel a strong regretful desire: *to sit at home and long day after day*; **b** (followed by infin.) to desire earnestly, have continuous and powerful yearning to do something: *to long to go away; to long to see, forget, be told* &c. **2.** *Long for*, to yearn for, desire earnestly to possess or obtain; to desire, want, hanker after, crave for: *to long for something to eat, for a change, for fresh air, for something new* &c; also (archaic) *long after.*

-long, suff. O.N. *-langr*, adv. suff. wh. has now displaced Engl. **-ling**: *headlong, sidelong.*

longanimity, n. [1. lònggannímiti; 2. lɔ̀ŋgənímiti]. L.Lat. *longanimitāt-(em)*, fr. *longus*, see under **long,** & *anima*, 'spirit', see **animal, animus,** & **-ity.** Long-suffering, patient endurance.

long-boat, n. Largest boat carried on a sailing-ship.

longbow, long bow, n. [1. lóngbō; 2. lɔ́ŋbou]. Bow drawn by hand, as distinct from cross-bow; formerly made the same length as the height of the archer. Phr. *to draw the long bow*, make exaggerated statements.

longcloth, n. [1. lóngklawth; 2. lɔ́ŋklɔþ]. A thick, tough cloth of cotton.

long-eared, adj. Having long ears.

longeron, n. [1. lónzheron; 2. lɔ̃žərɔ̃]. Fr. Any one of the longitudinal members of the body or fuselage of an aeroplane.

longevity, n. [1. lonjéviti; 2. lɔndžéviti]. See next word & **-ity.** Prolonged duration of life; specif., prolongation of life beyond the ordinary period.

longevous, longeval, adj. [1. lonjḗvus, -al, 2. lɔndžívəs, -əl]. Lat. *longaevus*, fr. *longus*, 'long' (see **long**), & *aevum*, see **age.** Long-lived.

long firm, n. A fraudulent business which obtains goods on long credit and sells them at once at reduced prices without paying for them.

longhand, n. [1. lóng-hand; 2. lɔ́ŋhænd]. Ordinary handwriting, contrasted with *shorthand.*

long-headed, adj. **1.** Having a skull that is long in proportion to its breadth; dolichocephalic. **2.** (fig.) Shrewd, sensible, wide-awake.

long-headedness, n. Prec. & **-ness.** **a** State of being dolichocephalic; **b** shrewdness, common sense.

longi-, pref. Form of Lat. *longus*, 'long', used in compounds before consonants. See **long.**

longicorn, adj. [1. lónjikorn; 2. lɔ́ndžikɔ̄n]. Prec. & Lat. *cornu*, 'horn'. See **corn (III.).** (zool.) Having long antennae.

longing, vbl. n. [1. lónging; 2. lɔ́ŋiŋ]. **long (IV.) & -ing.** Strong desire, yearning; aspiration.

longipennate, adj. [1. lònjipénāt; 2. lɔ̀ndžipéneit]. See **longi- & pen (III.) & -ate.** Having long wings.

longirostral, adj. [1. lònjiróstral; 2. lɔ̀ndžirɔ́strəl]. See **longi- & rostrum & -al.** (zool.) Having a long bill; belonging to the *Longirostres*, group of birds with long slender bills, such as the curlew, snipe &c.

longish, adj. [1. lóng(g)ish; 2. lɔ́ŋ(g)iʃ]. **long (I.) & -ish.** Rather long.

longitude, n. [1. lónjitūd; 2. lɔ́ndžitjūd]. Lat. *longitūdo*, 'length', fr. *longus*. See **long (I.).** (geog.) Distance in degrees from given meridian, esp. fr. that of Greenwich.

longitudinal, adj. & n. [1. lònjitúdinal; 2. lɔ̀ndžitjúdinəl], fr. Lat. *longitūdin-(em)*. See prec. & **-al. 1. adj.** Pertaining to longitude. **2. n.** Long girder running lengthwise in a ship.

longitudinally, adv. Prec. & **-ly.** According to, in terms of, longitude.

long-lived, adj. Inclined to live long; having a long life; living long; lasting: *a long-lived family*; *long-lived happiness*.

long primer, n. [1. lóng prímer; 2. lɔ́ŋ prímə]. (typog.) A size of type which occupies $7\frac{1}{2}$ lines to the inch.

longshoreman, n. [1. lóngshórman; 2. lɔ́ŋʃɔ̄mən]. For **along- & shore. a** Man who works on wharves at seaport, loading and unloading vessels &c.; **b** a shore, as opposed to a deep-sea, fisherman; **c** (colloq.) man who hangs about the shore at seaside resorts, doing odd jobs, helping with pleasure boats &c.

long-sighted, adj. **a** Able to see objects at a distance; **b** having foresight; far-seeing, sagacious.

long-sightedly, adv. Prec. & **-ly.** In a long-sighted manner.

long-sightedness, n. See prec. & **-ness. a** Capacity for seeing distant objects; **b** foresight.

longspun, adj. [1. lóngspun; 2. lɔ́ŋspan]. Spun out; tedious.

long-suffering, adj. Enduring insult, injuries &c. with patience and resignation.

long-waisted, adj. **a** (of human beings) Long between the lower ribs and the hips; **b** (of garments) having the line of the waist made low down.

long-winded, adj. [1. lòng wínded; 2. lɔ̀ŋ wíndid]. **a** Able to run fast and far without getting out of breath; **b** (fig.) given to speaking at a tedious length; diffuse, prolix.

loo, n. & vb. [1. lōō; 2. lū]. Abbr. of obs. *lanterloo*, fr. Fr. *lanturlu*, orig. the refrain of a song. **1. n. a** A card game for a pool composed of stakes and various forfeits, played with three or five cards dealt to each player from the pack with a 'miss'; **b** forfeit paid for not taking a trick. **2. vb.** To compel to pay loo to the pool.

looby, n. [1. lōōbi; 2. lúbi]. Cp. **lubber.** A fool; a half-witted person.

loofah, n. [1. lōōfa; 2. lúfə], fr. Arab. *lufah*, name of the plant. Fibrous skeleton of tropical plant, *Luffa*, of the pumpkin tribe, used as a means of applying soap and friction to the person in a bath.

look (I.), vb. intrans. [1. look; 2. luk]. O.E. *lōcian*, M.E. *lōkie(n)*, *lōken*, cp. O.S. *lōkōn*, O.H.G. *luogen*, 'spy out'. See **lynx. A. 1. a** To use the eyesight with attention, direct the glance with intention of seeing; gaze, stare: *don't look till I tell you*; *I did it while he wasn't looking*; Phr. *look before you leap*, don't act without full consideration; **b** semi-trans. in *to look unutterable things*, express by one's manner of looking; *to look daggers at*, shoot an angry look at; *look a gift horse in the mouth*, find fault with a present. **2.** To have the appearance of, give the impression of being, seem to be: **a** (followed by adj.) *to look ill, worried, unhappy* &c.; **b** (followed by n.) *look* (*like*), *he looks* (*like*) *a perfect fool, like a gentleman, a clever fellow, an honest man*; Phrs. *to look black*, angry; *to look blue*, discontented, and depressed; **c** (impers. construction) *it looks like*, promises, suggests coming of: *it looks like rain*; *it looks as though*, seems, appears, as though, gives impression of probability that: *it looks as though we should have a storm.* **B.** Followed by adverb or preposition. *Look about*, to glance round; to take one's bearings, examine situation and surroundings; also *look about one.* *Look after*, to take care of, protect, watch over. *Look at*, **1.** to direct glance at, fix attention upon, consider, gaze at: *to look at the view*; Phrs. *a cat may look at a king*; *I, he, &c., wouldn't look at* (*an offer, proposal* &c.), would despise, refuse, reject; **2.** to pay special attention to, examine carefully with the object of improving, repairing, explaining, or the like: *the plumber has come to look at the pipes*; *I wish you would look at this sentence, I can't make it out.* *Look down on, upon*, to despise, be indifferent to. *Look for*, **1.** to seek, try to find, search for; **2.** to expect, anticipate: *I don't look for much profit from the business*; *it is too soon to look for results as yet.* *Look forward to*, to anticipate, expect, await, with pleasure. *Look in* (*on*), to visit, pay a visit to, call on. *Look into*, to inspect, examine, carefully. *Look on*, **1.** intrans., to be a spectator, to watch: *he merely looked on and did nothing*; **2.** trans., (archaic) also *look upon*, to look at, gaze upon, consider; *to look on as*, regard, consider: *to look on a person as an authority.* *Look out*, **a** to be on one's guard, be careful: *I've warned you, so now look out*; **b** to direct sight, attention, outwards or out of: *look out of the window.* *Look to*, **1.** to be careful of, take heed to: *just look to it that this doesn't happen again*; **2.** to appeal to, rely upon, count on, resort to: *I look to you to put things right*; *to look to a person for help.* *Look towards*: (vulg. colloq.) *I look towards you*, drink your health. *Look up*, **1.** intrans., **a** to aspire; **b** to improve, enter upon more prosperous phase: *business is looking up*; **2.** trans., **a** to call upon, drop in on: *look me up when you are in town*; **b** to refer to, turn up (in book of reference &c.): *to look up a date, an address* &c.; *to look a person up and down*, stare at, examine his appearance with most careful scrutiny. *Look up to*, to respect, regard with veneration: *to look up to one's teachers.*

look (II.), n., fr. prec. **1.** Act of looking; **a a** glance: *he shot an angry look at his wife*; **b** an examination, scrutiny, conducted by the eye: *to have a look at the paper, at a passing show* &c. **2. a** Expression of the eyes or countenance generally: *an ugly look in his eye, on his face*; **b** appearance of a person or living thing; impression conveyed by this to, made on, another; mien, demeanour: *I don't like the look of him*; *he has a mean, shabby look*; (also pl.) *good looks*, beauty, handsome appearance; **c** impression produced by inanimate objects: *the house had a dismal look*; **d** appearance of, impression produced by, events, circumstances, a situation &c.: *affairs took on an ugly look.*

looker-on, n. [1. lòoker ón; 2. lùkər ɔ́n]. A spectator; one who watches an action or an event, but takes no active part. Phr. *lookers-on see most of the game.*

looking, adj. [1. lóoking; 2. lúkiŋ], fr. Pres. Part. of **look (I.).** Having a specified appearance; chiefly in compounds, the first element of which is an adj.: *good-looking*; *cross-looking*; *wretched-looking* &c.

looking-glass, n. A glass mirror.

look-out, n. [1. lòok óut; 2. lùk áut]. **1.** State of watchfulness, observation; wary vigilance; esp. in such Phrs. as *to keep a good look-out*, *to be on the look-out* (*for*), to be wary and cautious, to expect, watch for &c.; *that's my look-out*, my business, something only concerning myself. **2. a** Prospect, view: *a wonderful look-out over the sea*; **b** (fig.) prospects for the future, situation of affairs as likely to affect one's fortunes: *it is a bad look-out for me.*

look-see, n. [1. lòok sḗ; 2. lùk sí]. (slang) A hasty glance at, cursory examination of: *you'd better take, have, a look-see round the place before you go.*

loom (I.), n. [1. lōōm; 2. lūm]. O.E. (*ge*)*lōma*, 'tool, utensil', M.E. *lōme*, 'tool, instrument'; cp. also O.E. *andlōman*, (pl.) 'utensils'. Etymol. doubtful, but the word may be cogn. w. Gk. *lôma*, 'hem, border of a garment'; the same base **lō-* may perh. be traced in Lat. *lōdix*, 'a blanket, counterpane'; cp. also O.H.G. *lōdo*, 'coarse cloth'. **1.** Machine for weaving thread or yarn into cloth. **2.** That part of the shaft of an oar which lies when in use between the rowlock and the handle.

loom (II.), vb. intrans. Etymol. unknown. **1. a** To appear gradually and indistinctly, to emerge, come into view, start up, slowly, esp. as a vague and shadowy shape: *the ship loomed through the mist, fog*; *the mountain-tops loom through the clouds*; **b** (of non-material things) to appear and seem to menace: *dangers and anxieties looming ahead.* **2.** *Loom large*, **a** to appear with its size as though distorted and exaggerated by the atmosphere; to seem to menace; **b** (fig., of non-material things) to appear of great importance, fill the mind: *his own private troubles loom very large just now.*

loom (III.), n., fr. O.N. *lōmr.* A guillemot; a puffin; also called 'loon'.

looming, adj. [1. lōōming; 2. lúmiŋ]. **loom (II.) & -ing.** Appearing vaguely; menacing.

loon, n. [1. lōōn; 2. lūn]. Scots, earlier *lown*; cp. Du. *loen*, 'stupid person'. **a** A lout; a clumsy, uncouth fellow; a boor; **b** guillemot, puffin, loom.

loony, n. [1. lōōni; 2. lúni]. For **lunatic.** (colloq.) A crazy, half-witted person.

loop (I.), n. [1. lōōp; 2. lūp]. In M.E.; immediate origin unknown; etymologists cp. Ir. *lub*, 'to bend', & suggest a remote connexion w. **slip. 1.** A fold, bend, in a cord, string, wire, or other long flexible line-like object, formed by bending over one end and making it fast to the line below the bend, leaving a circular opening, through which another cord, or the other end of the same one, can be passed. **2.** (railways) A line, *loop-line*, which branches out of the main line of railway, runs in a curve, and joins the main line again at a point farther on.

loop (II.), vb. trans. & intrans. See prec. **1.** trans. To form, bend, into a loop. Phr. (aeron.) *loop the loop*, to fly in the direction of a curve, down, round, and upwards again, so that the line of the imaginary loop is completely closed; during the operation the machine is for a moment upside-down. **2.** intrans. To form into, become, a loop or loops.

looper, n. [1. lōōper; 2. lúpə]. Prec. & **-er.** Kind of caterpillar of a geometer moth, which in moving along forms a series of arches or loops with its body.

loophole, n. [1. lōōphōl; 2. lúphoul]. Cp. M. Du. *lupen*, 'to peer'. **1.** Slit in masonry of a wall, made to admit light and air; also for looking and firing through. **2.** (fig.) Means of opportunity for evasion or escape; a basis of excuse.

loose (I.), adj. [1. lōōs; 2. lūs]. M.E. *lōs*, also *lous*, in mod. sense; fr. O.N. *lauss*, 'loose, free, unimpeded; not binding; vacant; absolved; dissolute'; the various meanings agree pretty fully w. those of the word in Mod. Engl.; the O.N. word is cogn. w. O.E. *lēas*, 'devoid of; false' &c. (see **-less**); the same base is in Lat. *luere*, 'to atone for, expiate' &c.; Gk. *lúein*, 'to unfasten, slacken; to release, set free'; cp. *lúsis*, 'setting free, deliverance' see **-lysis.** See also lose. 1. Free, not under restraint or confinement; able to move about at pleasure; not tied up: *the pigs are loose in the garden.* Phrs. *to break loose*, escape from confinement; *to let loose*, allow to go free, release, unchain &c.; (fig.) *to let loose one's indignation* &c.; *to get loose*, manage to escape; *shake oneself loose*; *to go loose*, move about without restriction; *loose cash, securities* &c., easily available, not locked up; *to carry things loose in one's hand*, separate, not packed or fastened together. 2. Reverse of tight; **a** not fully stretched, not drawn tight; slack: *a loose collar, belt* &c.; Phr. *(to ride) with a loose rein*, (fig.) to handle, manage, a person mildly and indulgently; **b** giving ample room, not fitting tight or clinging close: *a loose coat, robe, boot* &c. 3. (of the mind and its activities) Not rigidly logical, not strictly accurate; incoherent, ill-defined; (of style and expression) vague, inexact, slipshod. 4. **a** (of conduct) Not properly controlled, not in accordance with morality; lax, dissolute; lewd: *to lead a loose life*; *loose morals*; Phr. *a loose fish*, immoral person; **b** (of principles, character) lax, unscrupulous, dishonourable: *loose morality*; *loose ideas of the truth*; **c** (of physical action) inaccurate, careless: *loose bowling, fielding* &c.; *a loose ball*, one that can be hit freely. 5. **a** (of fabrics) Not dense, not tightly woven or compact; (fig.) *a loose (human) frame, joints*, not closely knit; **b** not closely cohering, having particles separate and distinct: *loose soil* &c.; **c** (of the fleshy tissues) flabby, slack, not braced and tense; pendulous: *loose cheeks, lips.* 6. **a** Not fitting snugly into its place, liable to shake and rattle, having too much play: *a loose window, door*; **b** not firmly embedded: *a loose tooth, nail*; Phrs. *to have a screw loose*, to be somewhat unsound in mind or morals; *there's a screw loose somewhere*, something wrong, underhand, insecure &c.; **c** not properly packed, liable to shift: *eggs loose in a box*; **d** not firmly tied, liable to come unfastened: *a loose package, knot* &c.; Phrs. *to play fast and loose*, to behave unscrupulously or evasively; *a loose end* (of a rope), that which is not attached to anything; *at a loose end*, (fig.) not specifically occupied; perplexed, in disorder. 7. (of the bowels) Relaxed, inclined to diarrhoea.

loose (**II.**), adv., fr. prec. Loosely; chiefly in Phrs. *to sit loose to*, metaphor from riding, to be only slightly affected or influenced by, to maintain attitude of detachment respecting; *to come loose*, come unfastened, untied; *work loose* (of bolt, screw &c.), become loosened by strain, play of movement &c.

loose (**III.**), vb. trans., fr. **loose** (**I.**). 1. To unfasten, untie, undo: *to loose a knot, the fastening of a window* &c. 2. **a** To let loose, release from restraint or control; Phr. (fig.) *his tongue was loosed by drink*; **b** to let go, free, detach (a boat from its moorings, a rope from the object to which it is attached); Phr. *to loose one's hold*, relax, let go. 3. To let fly, discharge (an arrow); to fire (a gun, shot); also *loose off*. 4. (absol.) To absolve, pardon, release from results of sin: *priests have power to bind and to loose.*

loose (**IV.**), n., fr. prec. In Phr. *to give a loose to* (one's passions, feelings, anger &c.), remove restraint from, allow free outlet, expression.

loose-box, n. Stable in which a horse is left free to move about, lie down &c., instead of being tied up as in a stall.

loosely, adv. [1. lo͝osli; 2. lúsli]. **loose** (**I.**) & **-ly**. In a loose manner (various senses).

loosen, vb. trans. & intrans. [1. lo͝osn; 2. lúsn]. **loose** & **-en**. 1. trans. **a** To make loose or looser; to unfasten, untie: *to loosen girths, one's collar*; *loosen the reins* &c.; **b** (fig.) to relax, render less strict and severe: *to loosen discipline*. Phr. *to loosen one's grip of, one's hold on*, to grasp less tightly, let go (physically or intellectually). 2. intrans. To become loose or looser.

loosestrife, n. [1. lo͝osstrīf; 2. lússtraif], fr. translation of Lat. *lysimachia*, fr. Gk. *lūsimákhion*; cp. proper name *Lysimakhos*, as if fr. *lúein*, 'to loose' (see **-lysis**), & *mákhē*, 'battle' (see **-machy**). Popular name of **a** any of several species of primulaceous plants, genus *Lysimachia*, esp. *L. vulgaris*, with erect stem and clusters of yellow flowers; **b** *the purple loosestrife, Lythrum salicaria*, belonging to a different order, with spikes of rosy or purple flowers.

loot, n. & vb. trans. & intrans. [1. lo͞ot; 2. lūt]. Hind. *lūt*, fr. Scrt. *lōtram*, 'booty'. Cp. **lucre**. 1. n. Plunder, spoils of war, booty. 2. vb. **a** To plunder, despoil, sack (a city, camp &c.); **b** to seize as booty in war; to appropriate by a lawless action.

lop (**I.**), vb. trans. & n. [1. lop; 2. lɔp]. Origin unknown; apparently only in Engl. 1. vb. To chop, hew, cut; to shorten by chopping; to trim (trees and bushes); also *lop off* (*a bough* &c.); also to hack, slice, off (an arm, head &c.); expresses the act of chopping off with one stroke. 2. n. **a** Act of lopping; **b** parts of a tree that have been lopped off.

lop (**II.**), vb. intrans. & trans. Prob. imitative. 1. intrans. **a** To hang down, to droop, to flop, esp. of an animal's ears; **b** to move about, or along, with a clumsy or halting gait, resembling that of a rabbit or hare when moving slowly. 2. trans. (rare) To cause, allow (ears), to lop.

lope, vb. intrans. & trans. & n. [1. lōp; 2. loup], fr. O.N. *hlaupa*. See **leap**. 1. vb. **a** intrans. To move with a bounding, cantering pace or gait; **b** trans., to cause to lope. 2. n. An easy, bounding, cantering pace.

lop-eared, adj. Having lop-ears.

lop-ears, n. pl. Pendulous, drooping, ears.

lopho-, pref. Form of Gk. *lóphos*, 'crest, tuft', used in compounds; perh. cogn. w. **alp**.

lophobranchiate, adj. & n. [1. lòfōbrángkiāt; 2. lòufoubrǽŋkieit]. Prec. & **branchiate**. (zool.) **a** adj. Having gills in tufts on the branchial arches. **b** n. Order of small fishes (including sea-horses) having gills so placed.

lophodont, adj. & n. [1. lófōdont; 2. lóufoudɔnt]. **lopho-** & **odont-**. **a** adj. Having transverse ridges on upper surface of molar teeth: **b** n., an animal having teeth of this kind, e.g. the ungulates and rodents.

loppings, n. pl. [1. lópingz; 2. lɔ́piŋz], fr. **lop** (**I.**) & **-ing**. Portions lopped off from trees &c.; trimmings.

lop-sided, adj., fr. **lop** (**II.**) & **-side**. Unevenly balanced, or appearing to be unevenly balanced; larger on one side than on the other; asymmetrical; hanging lower on one side than on the other.

lop-sidedly, adv. Prec. & **-ly**. In a lop-sided manner.

lop-sidedness, n. See prec. & **-ness**. State of being lop-sided.

loquacious, adj. [1. lōkwáshus; 2. loukwéiʃəs]. Lat. *loquāci-*, stem of *loquax*, 'talkative', & **-ous**. Cp. Lat. *loquor*, 'I speak', fr. **laquor*, cogn. w. Gk. *láskein* for **lakj-*, 'to creak, shriek, shout; speak loud'; cp. O.S. *lahan*, O.E. *lēan*, fr. **læhan*, 'to find fault with'. Talkative, inclined to chatter, garrulous.

loquaciously, adv. Prec. & **-ly**. In a loquacious manner.

loquaciousness, n. See prec. & **-ness**. Habit of constant talking; garrulity.

loquacity, n. [1. lōkwásiti; 2. loukwǽsiti]. Lat. *loquāci-*, as in **loquacious**, & **-ty**. Talkativeness, garrulity.

loquat, n. [1. lókwat; 2. lóukwæt], fr. Chin. *lo kwat*, 'medlar'. The Japanese medlar, an evergreen flowering shrub, with small reddish clustered fruit of sharp taste.

loquitur, vb. intrans. [1. lókwiter; 2. lɔ́kwitə]. Lat. 3rd pers. pres. indic. sing. of *loqui*, 'to speak'. See **loquacious**. He, or she, speaks (in stage directions).

lor, interj. [1. lor; 2. lɔ̄]. For **lord**. (colloq.) Chiefly *O Lor!*, exclamation of surprise or annoyance.

loral, adj. [1. lóral; 2. lɔ́rəl], fr. **lore** (**II.**) & **-al**. (zool.) Of, pertaining to, the lore in birds or reptiles.

lorate, adj. [1. lórāt; 2. lɔ́reit], fr. Lat. *lōrātus*, fr. *lōrum*, 'thong, strap'. Cp. **lore** (**II.**). (bot., of leaves) Having the shape of a strap or thong.

lorcha, n. [1. lórcha; 2. lɔ́tʃə]. Port.; possibly corrupt. of Malay word. A light sailing-vessel of the Far East, with lug sails like a junk, but built on European lines.

lord (**I.**), n. [1. lord; 2. lɔ̄d]. O.E. *hlāford*, 'lord, master', fr. *hlāf*, 'loaf, bread', & *weard*, 'guardian'. See **loaf** (**I.**) & **ward** (**I.**); see also **lady**. 1. (gen. sense) Superior, ruler, governor, master; in such Phrs. as *Lord of hosts*; *Lord of all, all things*, God; *Lord of misrule*, master of revels. 2. **a** *The Lord*, the supreme ruler, God; **b** form of invocation of the Deity, *Lord have mercy upon us* &c.; Phrs. *O Lord!*; *Good Lord!*, exclamations of surprise, annoyance &c.; *Lord knows who*, someone or other, no one in particular; **c** *Our Lord*, the second Person of the Trinity, the Saviour; Phrs. *the year of Our Lord*, counted from the birth of Christ, Anno Domini; *the Lord's Supper*, the Eucharist; *Lord's Table*, (i.) altar in a church; (ii.) the Service of the Altar, the Eucharist; *the Lord's Day*, Sunday; *the Lord's Prayer*, 'Our Father', Paternoster. 3. In reference to the king: *our sovereign lord King George*. 4. A feudal superior; person from whom an estate is held: *lord of the manor, of the soil*; *lord paramount*, the sovereign. 5. **a** A peer, a member of the House of Lords; Phrs. *to make a man a lord* usually means to raise him to the peerage; *drunk as a lord*, very drunk; *lords spiritual*, bishops in House of Lords; *lords temporal*, the other peers; **b** person holding the title of *Lord*, whether a peer of Parliament or not, e.g. a Scottish or Irish peer; **c** *my Lord* [1. mi lórd; 2. mi lɔ̄d], form of address to bishops (always), and from inferiors to marquises, earls, viscounts, barons, whether these are peers, or elder sons bearing their fathers' second titles by courtesy; also to lord mayors, lord provosts, to judges of the High Court when on the Bench, and to younger sons of all peers above the rank of earl; *my lord* is now only used on formal and ceremonial occasions, except in addressing bishops, and High Court judges when in Court, and is otherwise omitted by gentlemen meeting lords socially on a basis of equality; **d** persons bearing any of the above titles are usually referred to, as *Lord X* rather than as *the Marquis of, Earl (of)*, or *Viscount X* &c. 6. Prefixed to the names of various officials: *Lord of the Bedchamber, Lord Steward, Lord High Commissioner, Lord President of the Council, Lord Privy Seal, Lord Warden of the Cinque Ports* &c.; also of chief members of certain great departments of state, as *Civil, Naval, Lords of the Admiralty, of the Treasury*.

lord (**II.**), vb., fr. prec. Chiefly *lord it*, to play the lord, assume airs of importance and authority; *lord it over*, to assert authority over, rule; behave arrogantly and dictatorially to.

Lord Chamberlain, n. A peer and privy councillor who governs and directs business connected with Royal household, issues invitations &c.

Lord Chancellor (**of England**), n. (in full, *Lord High Chancellor*) Chief officer of state, president of House of Lords, and Keeper of the Great Seal; ranking, after the Archbishop of Canterbury, immediately below princes of the blood.

Lord Chief Justice (**of England**), n. Presiding judge of the King's Bench Division of the High Court of Justice.

lordless, adj. [1. lórdles; 2. lɔ́dlis]. Without a chief or lord.

Lord-Lieutenant, n. 1. The former Viceroy of Ireland, now Governor-General of the Free State of N. Ireland (Ulster). 2. Head of the magistracy in a county.

lordliness, n. [1. lórdlines; 2. lɔ̄dlinis]. **lordly** & **-ness**. **a** Splendour, magnificence; **b** generosity, lavishness; **c** haughtiness, overbearing demeanour.

lordling, n. [1. lórdling; 2. lɔ̄dliŋ]. **lord** & **-ling**. A young or unimportant lord.

lordly, adj. [1. lórdli; 2. lɔ̄dli]. **lord** & **-ly**. **a** In keeping with the position, wealth &c. of a lord; magnificent; **b** lavish, generous, open-handed: *a lordly banquet, bequest*; **c** haughty, lofty; arrogant, overbearing.

Lord Mayor, n. Chief magistrate, the Mayor, of certain cities, such as London, York, Liverpool, and Manchester &c.; addressed as *my lord*, and referred to as *his lordship*; *Lord Mayor's Day*, Nov. 9th, on which the Lord Mayor of London is installed; *Lord Mayor's Show*, pageant, procession, through streets of City of London to celebrate this.

Lord Provost, n. Chief magistrate in certain important Scottish cities—Edinburgh, Glasgow &c.—corresponding to a lord mayor in England.

Lord Rector, n. The elected honorary head of a Scottish university, corresponding to the *Chancellor* of English and Welsh universities.

Lord's, n., fr. Thomas Lord, maker and proprietor of cricket grounds, d. 1832. In full, *Lord's cricket ground*, in London, headquarters of the Marylebone Cricket Club (M.C.C.) and of the Middlesex C.C.

lords-and-ladies, n. The wild arum, *Arum maculatum*.

lordship, n. [1. lórdship; 2. lɔ̄dʃip]. **1. a** Authority, dominion, jurisdiction; specif., of a feudal lord; **b** (fig.) command, control: *lordship over self*. **2.** *Your, his, lordship*, formal mode of addressing, or referring to, persons bearing title of *Lord*; also in addressing, and referring to, bishops, lord mayors, lord provosts, and judges of High Court when on the Bench. **3.** Territory, area, over which jurisdiction of a feudal lord extended.

lore (I.), n. [1. lōr; 2. lɔ̄]. O.E. *lār*, 'doctrine, teaching, learning', M.E. *loor* &c.; O.H.G. *lēra*, Mod. Germ. *lehre*, 'teaching'; cp. O.E. *lǣran*, 'to teach', fr. *lārjan; exactly corresponding to Goth. *laisjan*, 'to teach', fr. the base *lais-, as in Goth. *lais*, 'I know'. See also **learn**. **1.** (archaic) Teaching, instruction. **2.** Body of special knowledge; esp. either **a** as possessed by a particular group of people, by a profession or class &c.: *the lore of the Egyptians*; *doctors' lore*; *schoolboy lore*; or **b** knowledge of a special kind, relating to some particular group of objects, subject of study: *philological lore, folklore* &c.; often **c** knowledge derived from tradition: *herbal lore*.

lore (II.), n., fr. Lat. *lōrum*, 'strap'. Cogn. w. Gk. *eúlēra*, 'reins'; fr. base *wlēr-, *wlōr-, 'cord, band', apparently orig. 'twisted cord', fr. base *wel-, *wl-, 'to turn, twist', q.v. under **volute**. Space between the eye and upper part of the beak in birds and reptiles.

lorgnette, n. [1. lornyét; 2. lɔ̄njét]. Fr., 'eye-glass', fr. *lorgner*, 'to stare at'. Eyeglass, esp. one held up to the eyes by a long handle.

loricate, adj. [1. lórikāt; 2. lɔ́rikeit]. Lat. *lōrica*, 'leather breast-plate', fr. *lōrum*, 'thong, strap'; see **lore (II.)**, & **-ate**. (zool.) Furnished with, protected by, bony plates or scales, used of such animals as armadillos, crocodiles &c.

lorikeet, loriquet, n. [1. lórikēt; 2. lɔ́rikīt]. Dimin. of **lory**, on anal. of *parakeet*. A small green and blue parrot of the East Indies and Australia, allied to the lory.

loriner, n. [1. lóriner; 2. lɔ́rinə], fr. O. Fr. *lorainier, lorenier*, fr. *lorain*, 'bridle', fr. Lat. *lōrum*, 'thong, strap', see **lore (II.)**. (hist.) A maker of bits, bridles &c., and other metal work for the harness of horses; now only surviving as name of a City Livery Company.

loris, n. [1. lṓris; 2. lɔ̄ris]. Fr., origin doubtful. Small nocturnal lemur found in Ceylon and Malaya &c.

lorn, adj. [1. lorn; 2. lɔ̄n]. O.E. *-loren*, M.E. *lor(e)n*, fr. obs. P.P. of O.E. *lēosan*, M.E. *lēsen*, 'to lose'. See **lose** & cp. **forlorn**. (archaic) **a** Lost, ruined; **b** in a few Phrs., desolate, bereft: *a lone, lorn widow*.

lorry, n. [1. lóri; 2. lɔ́ri]. Etymol. unknown. Large, very strong, low-built, open waggon or truck for transporting heavy goods; formerly horse-drawn; now often used of truck of this kind driven by steam or petrol.

lory, n. [1. lóri; 2. lɔ̄ri]. Malay *lūri*. Small, brightly coloured parrot, found in Australia, New Guinea &c.

lose, vb. trans. & intrans. [1. lōōz; 2. lūz]. O.E. *for-lēosan*, 'to lose, to destroy', M.E. *lēsen*, wh. wd. give mod. *leese; cp. also O.E. *lōsian*, 'to be lost, escape', wh. wd. become mod. [louz]; the vowel of present-day [lūz] has been influenced by **loose**. **A.** trans. **1. a** To be deprived of possession of, suffer loss of, through accident, mischance, carelessness: *to lose one's clothes in the wash*; *to lose one's money*; Phrs. *to lose one's life*, to be killed, suffer death; *to lose one's head*, be decapitated; **b** to get rid of; to suffer from, show signs of, no longer: *I've quite lost my cold*; *she has lost the frightened look*. **2.** To be unable to find, to mislay: *I can't open the box as I have lost the key*; *I am sorry to say I have lost the book you lent me*. Phrs. *to lose one's way*, be unable to discover the right path, miss one's direction, go astray; *to lose one's place in a book*, be unable to find a word, line, passage, forming sequence to that which one has just read. **3.** To bring to destruction, destroy: *to lose one's ship on the rocks*. Phr. *a lost soul*, one that is damned, doomed to perdition. **4. a** To fail to retain, be deprived of, some physical or mental quality or feature by natural process, disease, age &c.: *to lose one's hair, sight, health, good looks, memory* &c. Phrs. *to lose one's head*, to become perplexed, flustered, confused; *to lose one's grip, grasp, of*, to become weak in one's intellectual comprehension of; *to lose one's temper*, get angry; **b** to forget, allow to die out, or to pass out of one's control or habitual use and practice: *to lose the art of pleasing*; *a lost art*, one that has perished; *to lose interest*, cease to feel, or take, interest. **5. a** To fail to obtain, gain, win: *to lose a game, a prize, a reward*; **b** to cause to lose: *his insolence lost him his situation*. **6. a** To be deprived of society, companionship of, esp. by death: *to lose a son in the war*; *to lose one's wife*; **b** to allow to become alienated: *to lose one's friends*. **7.** To fail, be unable, to see, or hear: *to lose the end of a sentence*; *to lose the clear outlines of*. **8.** To arrive, be, too late for, miss: *to lose one's train, the post* &c. **9.** To waste, fail to employ fruitfully, not to make the most of: *there's not a moment to lose*, no time to spare; *you are losing your time trying to teach him*. Phrs. *I shall lose no time in beginning work* &c., I shall begin at once; *to be lost upon*, fail to affect, influence, impress, attract attention of: *good acting is quite lost upon me*; *his eloquence was lost upon his audience*. **10.** *Lose oneself*, **a** to go astray, miss one's way; **b** to become deeply absorbed in: *to lose oneself in abstruse speculations*. **11.** (in P.P.) *Lost to*, oblivious of, insensible to, incapable of feeling: *lost to all sense of decency*. **B.** intrans. **1.** To undergo loss, suffer deprivation: *when I gamble I always lose*. **2.** *Lose by*, to suffer financial or other loss, detriment, disadvantage on account of: *I don't want you to lose by me*; *his honesty did him no good, in fact he lost by it*.

losel, n. [1. lózl; 2. lóuzl]. M.E. *lōsel*, 'worthless fellow', fr. base of O.E. *losian*, 'to perish', weak form of *lēosan*, 'to lose', & **-el**. (archaic) A dissipated, profligate man.

loser, n. [1. lōōzer; 2. lūzə]. **lose** & **-er**. **1. a** Person who loses; Phrs. *a loser by (one's own folly* &c.), sufferer as a result of; *a bad, good, loser*, one who accepts defeat in a game churlishly, or cheerfully; **b** (billiards) losing hazard.

losing, adj. [1. lōōzing; 2. lūziŋ]. Tending, bound, to cause, or result in, loss: *to play a losing game* (lit. and fig.).

losing hazard, n. (billiards) Stroke of pocketing one's own ball off another ball.

losings, n. pl. [1. lōōzingz; 2. lūziŋz]. Losses; specif., losses incurred in speculation or gambling.

loss, n. [1. laws, los; 2. lɔ̄s, lɔs]. O.E. *los*, 'loss, disaster', fr. *lusa-, fr. reduced grade of base seen in O.E. *lēosan*, 'lose'. See **lose**. **1. a** Act or fact of losing in various senses: *the loss of a vessel*; *of one's eyesight, of money* &c.; **b** that which is lost: *my losses this year have been considerable*; **c** amount lost: *a loss of forty pounds*. **2.** Disadvantage, deprivation, detriment, injury, harm caused by the loss of anything: *his absence from the party was not a great loss*; *serious losses in business*. Phrs. *that is my loss*, it is I who suffer; *at a loss (to explain* &c.), nonplussed, unable to come to a conclusion &c.; *at a loss for*, unable to find. **3.** Failure to gain or obtain: *the loss of a race, prize*. **4. a** Waste, failure to utilize, dissipation of: *loss of time, of opportunities*; **b** deprivation, diminution: *loss of blood*; *loss of water through a leak*; (mechan. and elect.) *loss of power, current* &c. **5.** (mil.) Deprivation suffered by an army by the killing, wounding, or capture of soldiers in battle; casualties: *heavy losses of men and material*. **6.** (insurance) Death of person, destruction of property, insured, and consequent liability of person undertaking the risk to pay sum insured: *a total, partial, loss*.

lost, adj. [1. lawst; 2. lɔ̄st], fr. P.P. of **lose**.

lot (I.), n. [1. lot; 2. lɔt]. O.E. *hlot*, 'allotment, portion, share'; cp. also O.E. *hlēotan*, 'cast lots, obtain by lot', cogn. w. O.H.G. *hloz, loz*, Mod. Germ. *los*, 'share; fate, destiny'; Goth. *hlauts*, 'portion, inheritance'; cp. further Lat. *clāva*, 'club', orig. 'a fragment of branch broken off'. See also **clavicle**. **1.** Object used for determining something by chance; obsolete, except in *to cast, draw, lots*, to determine something by the chance fall of a die, by drawing from a receptacle, selecting one of several objects, different in length, markings &c., but so held as to look exactly alike. **2. a** That which comes to one, is obtained, by the casting of lots; **b** hence, that which happens, or is apportioned, to one by chance, fate, providence; destiny, portion in life, luck: *his lot has been a hard one*. **3. a** Portion of a thing, collection of objects, grouped together, to be sold as a single whole; an item to be sold at an auction sale; **b** parcel, portion of land; **c** any group or collection of objects, portion of a substance regarded as a unity. Phr. *my little lot*, that which belongs to me. **4.** (colloq.) A considerable portion, number, amount: *a lot of people, houses*; *to eat a lot of food*; *a whole lot of wine*; (iron.) *a lot you care!*, you don't care at all; also in pl., *lots and lots (of)*, a very large number. **5.** (in bad sense) A person or thing; chiefly *a bad lot*, an evil person.

lot (II.), vb. trans., fr. prec. **a** To divide into lots; **b** (rare) to allot, apportion.

lota(h), n. [1. lṓta; 2. lóutə]. Hind. A round water-vessel, usually of brass.

loth, adj. See **loath**.

Lothario, n. [1. lōtháhriō; 2. louþáriou], fr. name of character in Rowe's 'Fair Penitent'. The name is the same as Fr. *Lothaire* & is of Gmc. origin; cp. O.H.G. *Hlothari*, the mod. form of wh. is *Luther*. The first element means 'famous'. See under **loud**. Usually *gay Lothario* (Rowe's 'F. P.', v. 1), a rake, woman-hunter.

lotion, n. [1. lṓshun; 2. lóuʃən], fr. Lat. *lōt-(um)*, P.P. of *lavāre*, 'to bathe, moisten, bedew' &c., & **-ion**. See **lave**. Medicinal liquid used externally for affections of the skin or for injuries to fleshy tissue.

lottery, n. [1. lóteri; 2. lɔ́təri]. Ital. *lotteria*; of Gmc. origin. See **lot (I.)**. **a** Organized competition for money or other prizes, the winners of which are selected by drawing lots, the funds being subscribed by the competitors; **b** (fig.) a matter of pure chance and uncertainty in which, on the whole, the odds are against success in any given case: *marriage is said to be a lottery*; *a great lottery*, affair in which the chances of success are very uncertain.

lotto, n. [1. lótō; 2. lɔ́tou]. Ital., fr. Gmc. See **lot** (I.). Game of chance played with cards bearing five numbers in a line, and numbered balls drawn from a bag, the object being to cover all the numbers in a line or as many as possible. The right to cover a number on a card is determined by the same number being drawn from the bag.

lotus, n. [1. lṓtus; 2. lóutəs]. Lat., fr. Gk. *lōtós*, 'a kind of clover', also an African shrub, the fruit of which was eaten by the *Lōtophágoi*; prob. a Semitic loan-word. The fruit of the shrub was supposed to produce in those who ate it a complete distaste for active life, and a state of indolent, luxurious enjoyment. **1. a** Egyptian water-lily; **b** (archit.) an ornament based on the form of this, much used in Egyptian capitals; **c** Indian water-lily.

lotus berry, n. **a** A yellow West Indian edible fruit; **b** tree on which it grows.

lotus-eater, n. **a** One of the *Lōtophágoi*, a peaceful nation on the coast of Cyrenaica who were supposed, in Greek legend, as a result of eating the fruits of the lotus, to relapse into a state of sensuous, indolent enjoyment; **b** (fig.) one who abandons ambition and an active life and lives in a world of dreams.

lotus-eating, n. **a** Practice of eating the lotus fruit in search of the pleasant, dreamy indolence which it produced; **b** (fig.) indulgence in dreamy indolence and the pleasures of inaction.

loud (I.), adj. [1. loud; 2. laud]. O.E. & O.S. *hlūd*, M.E. *loud*; O.H.G. *lūt*, Mod. Germ. *laut*, cogn. w. Lat. *in-clutus*, 'famous'; Gk. *klutós*, Scrt. *śrutáś*, 'heard of, celebrated'. The base **klu-*, 'to hear', occurs in Lat. *cluēre*, 'to hear oneself called, be spoken of, reputed' &c. **1. a** Characterized by a full, powerful sound; sonorous, resonant, reverberating: *a loud noise, note, report* &c.; **b** producing much sound; causing a powerful impression upon the sense of hearing: *a loud voice, laugh*; **c** (of persons) noisy, uproarious; blatant, boisterous, blustering. **2.** (of colour) Excessively vivid, flamboyant, gaudy, flaunting, garish; also of clothes, too striking, showy, flashy, florid.

loud (II.), adv. O.E. *hlūde*, 'loudly'. See prec. In a loud manner, so as to produce a volume of sound: *he laughs too loud.*

loudly, adv. [1. lóudli; 2. láudli]. **loud (I.)** & **-ly**. In a loud manner (in various senses); so as to produce a great deal of sound; noisily; gaudily &c.

loudness, n. [1. lóudnes; 2. láudnis]. See prec. & **-ness**. Quality of being loud.

loud speaker, n. Device for amplifying sounds produced by the diaphragm of an electromagnetic apparatus of the telephone type.

lough, n. [1. logh; 2. lɔχ]. Anglo-Ir. See **loch**. A lake, an estuary, in Ireland.

louis, louis d'or, n. [1. lo͞oi (dŏr); 2. lúi (dɔ̄)]. Fr., 'golden louis'. French gold coin worth 20 francs, obsolete, though the name still survives in colloquial speech in France for 20 francs in paper or gold.

louis quatorze, quinze, seize, adj. [1. lo͞oi katórz, kanz, sāz; 2. lúi kætɔ́z, kǣz, seiz]. Fr., Louis XIV., XV., XVI. Applied to furniture, or works of art, made in, or in the style of, the reigns of these monarchs in 17th and 18th cents.

lounge (I.), vb. intrans. [1. lounj; 2. laundž]. Found since 1500 as n., 'a vagabond'; origin extremely doubtful. **a** To loll idly and indolently, with a relaxed position or condition of the body; to crouch propping oneself against the back and sides of a chair, or to stand propped against something; **b** to spend one's time idly and indolently; to abstain from exercise and occupation; also *lounge about*, lie, stand, stroll about in a lounging manner; *lounge away* (one's life, time &c.).

lounge (II.), n., fr. prec. **1.** Act of lounging. **2.** Apartment, esp. in a hotel or club, fitted with comfortable sofas and chairs, used for smoking, conversation &c. **3.** Also *lounge chair, seat*, comfortable easy-chair or other seat.

lounge-coat, suit, n. (tailor's names) Coat for day wear cut short, as distinct from a tail-coat; suit worn with such a coat.

lounge-lizard, n. (slang) A despicable, effeminate, mean-spirited youth, who spends his time in lounges and dancing-halls, esp. one who hires himself out to women as dancing-partner.

lounger, n. [1. lóunjer; 2. láundžə]. **lounge** (I.) & **-er**. One who lounges; a person with no special occupation who is spending his time lazily.

loungingly, adv. [1. lóunjingli; 2. láundžiŋli]. Pres. Part. of **lounge (I.)** & **-ly**. As one who lounges or lolls.

lour, lower, vb. intrans. [1. lour; 2. láuə]. M.E. *louren*; cp. O.N. *lūra*, 'to slumber'. See **lurk**. **a** To look, glare, threateningly or sullenly; to frown; also **b** (fig., of the sky &c.) to grow dark, look threatening; (of clouds, thunder) to show signs of approaching; to menace.

louringly, adv. [1. lóuringli; 2. láuəriŋli]. Pres. Part. of prec. as adj. & **-ly**. **a** In a frowning manner, with sullen looks; **b** threateningly.

louse, n., pl. **lice** [1. lous, līs; 2. laus, lais]. O.E., O.H.G., O.N. *lūs*; etymol. uncertain. Minute creeping parasite infesting the skin and hair of human beings and animals.

lousiness, n. [1. lóuzines; 2. láuzinis]. **lousy** & **-ness**. Condition of being lousy.

lousy, adj. [1. lóuzi; 2. láuzi]. **louse** & **-y**. **a** Infested with lice; **b** (fig.) mean, contemptible, vile.

lout (I.), n. [1. lout; 2. laut]. Perh. dialectal, & either fr. *lout*, 'to bow' (see next word), or obs. *lout*, 'to lurk'. A clumsy, mannerless, ill-bred boor; a bumpkin.

lout (II.), vb. intrans. O.E. *lūtan*; cp. O.N. *lúta*. Cp. Goth. *liuts*, 'hypocrite', *lutōn*, 'to deceive'. Prob. cogn. w. O. Slav. *luditi*, 'to deceive', *ludŭ*, 'foolish'. (archaic and poet). To bow, prostrate oneself: '*He humbly louted in meeke lowlinesse*', Spenser, "F.Q.," I. x. 44.

loutish, adj. [1. lóutish; 2. láutiʃ]. **lout (I.)** & **-ish**. Like a lout; awkward, clumsy, boorish.

loutishness, n. Prec. & **-ness**. Quality of being loutish.

louver, n. [1. lo͞over; 2. lúvə]. M.E. *lover*, fr. O. Fr. *lovier*, Med. Lat. *lodārium*, fr. *lōdium*; orig. an opening over a fireplace; prob. of Gmc. origin, cp. O.N. *hlōð*, 'hearth'. This, according to Skeat, is another grade of the base seen in **lade**. **a** Lantern-shaped, open turret in the roof of an ancient hall &c. through which the smoke escaped from the open hearth; **b** an unglazed opening in the wall of a loft, tower &c., closed or opened by means of a series of slats or boards, to admit air and light.

louver-board, n. One of the movable slats fixed in a louver.

lovable, adj. [1. lúvabl; 2. lávəbl]. **love (II.)** & **-able**. Possessing qualities which endear, which evoke love; deserving love; engaging.

lovableness, n. Prec. & **-ness**. Quality of being lovable.

lovage, n. [1. lúvij; 2. lávidž]. O. Fr. *levesche*, Fr. *livèche*; M.E *loveache*, as though fr. **love** (I.) & **-age**, or *-ache* [ātʃ]; Low Lat. *livisticum*, fr. *ligusticum*, 'belonging to Liguria'. Popular name of a herb, formerly used in medicine &c.

love (I.), n. [1. luv; 2. lav]. O.E. *lufu*, 'love, affection, friendliness', M.E. *luve, lōve*; cogn. w. O.E. *lēof*, 'dear' (see **lief**); cp. also Lat. *lubet*, 'it pleases', *libīdin-*, stem of *libīdo* (see **libidinous**); Scrt. *lúbhyati*, 'he desires strongly'; O. Slav. *ljubiti*, 'to love', *ljuby*, 'love', n. See further under **leave** (I.). **1.** Affection, friendliness, strong liking; tenderness, attachment, devotion: *love for one's children, parents, friends, for one's profession*; *the love of a man for his brother*; *to bear love to, towards, a person*; *to have a love of learning*. Phrs. *there's no love lost between them*, they dislike each other; *to send one's love to*; *give my love to*, affectionate greeting; *not to be had for love or money*, impossible to get; *a labour of love*, task undertaken without hope of reward; *love of country*, patriotism. **2. a** The infinite benevolence, goodwill, mercifulness, of the Creator towards mankind; **b** the sense of veneration, devotion, humble attachment, borne by human beings to God. **3.** Feeling of benevolence, charity, brotherliness, borne by human beings towards others of mankind: *to live in love and charity with one's neighbour*. **4. a** Sexual passion; strong, passionate affection, attachment felt for person of opposite sex; amorous desire; Phrs. *to fall in love (with)*, conceive passionate attachment (for); *to be in love (with)*, to entertain a passionate attachment (for), to be enamoured of; *all's fair in love and war*; *love in a cottage*, marriage on inadequate means; *to make love to*, to court; **b** object of passionate attachment, person who inspires this: '*Come ye whose loves are dead*' (Beaumont and Fletcher); *her own true love*; Phr. *my love*, affectionate mode of address to object of affections, or to a child or young person. **5. a** Personification of the god of love, Cupid, represented as a plump, winged boy with a bow and arrow: '*What though no weeping loves thy ashes grace?*' (Pope, 'Unfortunate Lady,' 59); **b** an attractive, lovely person or thing: *a little love of a child*; *a regular love of a kitten, cottage* &c. **6.** (tennis) No score, nothing: *love forty*, meaning that the server has scored nothing, and his opponent forty points; *a love game, set*, one in which the beaten party scores nothing; also in other games, as *won by four goals to love.*

love (II.), vb. trans. & intrans. O.E. *lufian*, M.E. *luvie(n), lōve(n)*. See prec. **A.** trans. **1. a** To entertain a strong affection for, be fond of: *to love one's mother*; **b** to feel strong passion for, to desire. **2. a** To regard with veneration and humble devotion; to worship: *to love God*; **b** to consider with goodwill, benevolence, merciful kindness: *God so loved the world* &c.; **c** to entertain feelings of charity and kindliness towards: *to love one's fellow-men*. **3.** To have a strong liking for, enjoy, delight in: *to love the country*; *love one's work*. Popular usage: *I simply love new-laid eggs, sea-bathing* &c. =am very fond of; *to love playing bridge*; *I should love to come to dinner*, for *like*. **B.** intrans. To entertain the feeling or passion of love, in various senses: '*I cannot understand—I love*' (Tennyson, 'In Mem.' xcvi. 9); '*her sins . . . . are forgiven, for she loved much*' (Luke vii. 47).

love-affair, n. Amour.

love-apple, n. Popular name of a tomato.

love-bird, n. Kind of small African bright-coloured parrot.

love-child, n. Illegitimate offspring.

love-feast, n. Agape.

love-in-a-mist, n. Fennel flower, *Nigella*.

love-in-idleness, n. Pansy, heartsease.

love-knot, n. Bow of ribbon interlaced in a special way.

Lovelace, n. [1. lúvlis; 2. lávlis], fr. name of character in Richardson's 'Clarissa Harlowe'. Heartless libertine, a seducer of women.

loveless, adj. [1. lúvlis; 2. lávlis]. **love** & **-less**. **a** Not giving, feeling, expressing, or attracting love; **b** not based on love: *a loveless union.*

love-letter, n. One written to a sweetheart.

love-lies-bleeding, n. [1. lúv līz blḗding; 2. láv laiz blīdiŋ]. Popular name of *Amaranthus caudatus*, with long drooping spikes of purple flowers.

loveliness, n. [1. lúvlines; 2. lávlinis].

lovely & **-ness.** Quality of being lovely; physical or moral beauty, charm, enchantment.

lovelock, n. [1. lúvlok; 2. lávlɔk]. Curl or tress of hair trained to lie flat on the forehead, or hanging down upon the cheek.

love-lorn, adj. **love** & **lorn.** Pining hopelessly for love; abandoned by one's love.

lovely, adj. [1. lúvli; 2. lávli]. O.E. *luflīc*, 'loving, amiable, pleasant'. **love** & **-ly. 1.** (of sensuous impressions) Beautiful, charming, delightful, highly pleasing, enchanting, alluring: *a lovely sight, landscape, scene* &c.; *a lovely woman; a lovely melody, scent*; also (colloq.) *a lovely taste*, delicious; *a perfectly lovely time*, enjoyable. **2.** (of non-material things) Appealing to, pleasing, the moral sense; morally elevated, noble, pure: '*Whatsoever things are lovely, whatsoever things are of good report*,' Philippians iv. 8.

love-making, n. Courtship.

love-match, n. Marriage made entirely from motives of love.

love-philtre, n. Magic potion supposed to incline the affections of the person drinking it in a desired direction.

love-potion, n. Love-philtre.

lover, n. [1. lúver; 2. lávə]. **love (II.)** & **-er. 1.** One who is fond of, who delights in, a specified thing: *a lover of pictures, of horses, of the country* &c. **2.** (chiefly used of a man, except in pl.) **a** An admirer, sweetheart, fiancé: '*a lover and his lass*', *two happy lovers*; **b** paramour: *the guilty lovers* &c. **3.** In obsolete formula, at end of letter &c.: *your true lover*, friend, supporter &c.

loverlike, adj. [1. lúverlīk; 2. lávəlaik]. Resembling, behaving like, a lover.

loverly, adj. [1. lúverli; 2. lávəli]. Like, befitting, a lover; loving.

lovesick, adj. [1. lúvsik; 2. lávsik]. Strongly affected by, languishing on account of, love.

love-song, n. One expressing, or on the subject of, love.

love-story, n. One with love as its chief theme.

love-token, n. Object given as a symbol of affection.

loving, adj. [1. lúving; 2. láviŋ], fr. Pres. Part. of **love (II.)**. **a** Animated by, feeling, expressing, love; affectionate; **b** dutiful, loyal, in formula: *His Majesty's loving subjects.*

loving-cup, n. Large drinking-vessel, usually of silver, with two or more handles, passed from one person to another, each of whom drinks in turn.

loving-kindness, n. Affectionate solicitude; clemency, favour.

low (I.), vb. intrans. & trans. [1. lō; 2. lou]. O.E. & O.S. *hlōwan*; M.E. *lōwen*; O.H.G. *hluojen*; cogn. w. the base in Lat. *clā-māre*, 'to call, shout, cry out' (see **clamour, claim**); cp. also *clārus*, 'loud, distinct' (see **clear**); Gk. *ki-klḗ-skein*, 'to call on, invoke'. Another form of the same base as in Lat. *calāre*, 'to cry out'; Gk. *kalein*, 'to call, invoke; proclaim' (see **calends**). **a** intrans. To make the characteristic cry of a cow; **b** trans., to utter with lowing.

low (II.), n., fr. prec. The cry uttered by the cow.

low (III.), adj. Scand., M.E. *lōuh, lōw*, fr. O.N. *lāgr*; fr. same base as **lay (III.)** & **lie (III.)**. **1. a** Reverse of high; not elevated, not extending far upwards from the ground, not lofty: *a low wall, fence, range of mountains*; not placed far from ground or floor: *a low roof, ceiling*; special uses: *a low dress*, one cut so as to expose part of shoulders, chest, and back; *a low neck*, part of dress near the neck or throat cut so as to expose these; *low relief*, (sculpture or moulding) bas-relief; *a low brow, forehead*, measuring but little between roots of hair and top of nose; **b** near the horizon: *a low moon*; **c** of mercury in a barometer or thermometer, not marking high atmospheric pressure or temperature: *the glass is low*; also *a low temperature.* **2.** Of less than normal height: *the water* (or by transference, *the well*) *is low*; less than full height, far from the shore: *low tide, low water.* Phr. *in low water*, short of money, hard up. **3.** (phon., of position of tongue in speaking) Not raised, depressed, relatively far from roof of mouth; also *a low vowel*, one produced by the tongue in the low position. **4.** (of sounds &c.) **a** Reverse of loud; soft, not resonant: *a low whisper*; *in a low voice*; **b** (of musical notes) not high or shrill in pitch: *a low note.* **5. a** Lacking force or intensity: *low pressure* (of steam &c.); *a low fever*; **b** lacking physical energy and vitality; feeble, enfeebled: *a low pulse*; *a low state of health*; **c** (of state of mind) depressed, despondent, melancholy: *low spirits.* **6.** Lacking nourishing qualities, not rich; plain, simple: *a low diet.* **7.** Inferior, undistinguished; occupying a humble, unimportant position; **a** in order of merit: *low in one's class, in the list*; *a low standard*; **b** in social position; plebeian: *of low birth, origin*; *low life*; *the lower orders*; Phr. *brought low*, humbled; **c** racially inferior, not highly civilized: *lower tribes, races*; **d** (biol.) not high in the scale of organisms; not highly evolved, not showing complexity of structure or function: *low forms of life.* **8.** Not refined; ill-bred, coarse, vulgar: *low manners*; *a low fellow.* **9.** Morally degraded; ignoble, vile, mean; ribald, lewd, obscene: *low tastes, ideals, mind*; *low conduct, talk, jests*; also (colloq.) *low-down*, degraded, dishonourable, mean: *low-down behaviour.* **10.** Unfavourable, tending to disparage: *to have, hold, form, a low opinion of*, not to rate or esteem highly. **11.** Belonging to, characteristic of, the Low Church.

low (IV.), adv., fr. prec. **1. a** In a low position, near the ground; so as not to reach high: *to crouch low*; *to aim, shoot, low*; Phr. *I hope I shall never fall as low as that*, shall not stoop to, be so degraded as to; *to run low*, (of supplies) to fail, give out; *the sands are running low* (in the glass), (in various senses) (i) the time is nearly up; (ii) life is coming to an end; *to lie low*, (i.) to be prostrate; to be dead; (ii.) to keep quiet, remain inconspicuous, lie hidden; *to be laid low*, (i.) to be killed; to be knocked down; (ii.) to be incapacitated; obliged to keep one's bed, by illness; **b** *low-down*, in a very low position; Phr. *to play it low-down*, behave dishonourably, shamefully; *play it low-down on*, treat meanly. **2. a** In a low voice; softly, not loudly: *to speak low*; **b** in a low key, not high pitched: *I can't sing, get down, so low as that.* **3.** At a small price; cheaply: *to buy low.*

low-born, adj. Of mean or humble birth.

low boy, n. [1. lō boi; 2. lóu bɔi]. Chest of drawers with short legs. Cp. *tallboy.*

low-bred, adj. Ill-bred, rude, mannerless; characteristic of one born and bred in a mean rank of life.

low-brow, n. & adj. (colloq., orig. Am.) **1.** n. Person who does not pretend to superior intellect or culture; opposed to *high-brow.* **2.** adj. Pertaining to, characteristic of, a low-brow: *such low-brow amusements.*

low-browed, adj. [1. lṓ broud; 2. lóu braud]. Having low brows, that is, a forehead which is short from the eyebrows to the roots of the hair.

Low Celebration, n. Celebration of the Eucharist without music; Low Mass.

Low Church (I.), n. [1. lṓ chērch; 2. lóu tʃɜ̄tʃ]. *The Low Church*, opposed to *High Church*, the Evangelical, Protestant party in the Church of England.

Low-church (II.), adj. [1. lȍ chérch; 2. lòu tʃɜ́tʃ]. Belonging to, characteristic of, that party, also called Evangelical, in Church of England, which lays comparatively little emphasis upon sacramental doctrine.

Low Churchman, n. [1. lȍ chérchman; 2. lòu tʃɜ́tʃmən]. Member of Low-church party.

low comedy, n. Type of drama characterized by farce and burlesque, aiming at laughable situations and dialogue.

Low Countries, n. The Netherlands; Holland, Belgium and Grand Duchy of Luxembourg.

lower (I.), vb. trans. & (rarely) intrans. [1. lṓer; 2. lóuə], fr. **lower (III.)**. **1. a** (i.) To cause, allow, to descend; esp. to allow to slide down gradually by its own weight while held suspended; to let down, haul down: *to lower a boat, a sail*; (ii.) (colloq., slang) to swallow, put down, (food and drink); *to lower a sandwich and a glass of beer*; **b** to reduce height of: *to lower a roof, ceiling.* **2.** (fig.) **a** To humble, render less lofty: *to lower one's pride*; **b** *lower oneself*, condescend, stoop to, abandon some of one's self-respect: *to lower oneself to ask a favour.* **3.** To reduce bodily strength and vitality of: *to lower the system.* **4.** To make cheaper, reduce price (of goods &c.). **5. a** To reduce loudness of: *to lower one's voice*; **b** to reduce pitch of.

lower (II.), vb. intrans. See **lour.**

lower (III.), compar. of **low (III.)**. *Lower animals, creation*, (coll.) all mammals except man; more rarely used of birds. *Lower-case*, (print., of type, letters) small, not capitals; abbreviated l.c.; so called from being kept in a lower case. *Lower Chamber*, popular chamber of the legislature; House of Commons. *Lower House*, House of Commons. *Lower classes*, the proletariat. *Lower form*, one below the middle of a school; *lower boy*, one in such a form. *Lower regions*, (i.) Hell, Hades; (ii.) (facet.) basement of a house; kitchen premises, servants' quarters.

low frequency, n. (elect.) An alternating current whose periods are below 1000 per second; see **frequency.**

lowing, n. [1. lṓing; 2. lóuiŋ]. **low (I.)**. Sound made by a cow that lows.

lowland, n. & adj. [1. lṓland; 2. lóulənd]. **1.** n. Country which is low, flat, level, compared with surrounding country; *the Lowlands*, the southern counties of Scotland, contrasted with *the Highlands.* **2.** adj. **a** Belonging to low, flat country; **b** (cap.) belonging to southern counties of Scotland.

lowlander, n. [1. lṓlander; 2. lóuləndə]. Prec. & **-er. a** Inhabitant of lowland country; **b** (cap.) inhabitant of Scottish Lowlands.

Low Latin, n. Late, popular, spoken Latin, contrasted with *Classical Latin.*

lowliness, n. [1. lṓlines; 2. lóulinis]. See next word & **-ly.** Quality, state, of being lowly; humility

lowly (I.), adj. [1. lṓli; 2. lóuli]. **low (III.)** & **-ly. 1.** Of humble rank; of mean or low degree. **2.** Humble of heart; meek, modest.

lowly (II.), adv. In a lowly manner.

Low Mass, n. Low Celebration.

low-necked, adj. [1. lṓ nekt; 2. lóu nɛkt]. (of woman's dress) Cut so as to expose throat and neck.

low-spirited, adj. Dejected, depressed; lacking proper pride and courage.

low tension, n. (elect.) Term loosely used for any circuit where the potential is comparatively small; cp. *high tension.*

loxo-, pref. Form of Gk. *loxós*, 'slanting, crooked, bent', used in compounds; cogn. w. Gk. *lékhrios*, 'inclined, bent', & w. Lat. *lacertus*, 'arm', *lacerta*, 'lizard', q.v. under **lacertian.**

loxodromic, adj. [1. lȍksōdrómik; 2. lɔ̀ksoudrɔ́mik]. Prec. & **-drome** & **-ic.** (naut.) Of, pertaining to, sailing on, an oblique course by the *rhumb line.*

loyal, adj. [1. lóial; 2. lɔ́iəl]. O. Fr. *loial*, fr. Lat. *lēgālis*; variant of legal & leal. **1.** Faithful, true, to one's allegiance; observant of one's obligation **a** to one's king and country: *a loyal subject, citizen*; **b** to other persons: *a loyal husband, friend* &c.; **c** to a cause, ideal, institution: *a loyal supporter of the Church, of progress* &c. **2.** Upright, honourable, staunch.

loyalist, n. [1. lóialist; 2. lɔ́iəlist]. Prec. & **-ist. a** One who habitually practises loyalty to the sovereign; **b** one who remains loyal to the sovereign and the established government in times of rebellion and revolt.

loyally, adv. [1. lóiali; 2. lóiəli]. **loyal** & **-ly**. In a loyal manner; with fidelity.

loyalty, n. [1. lóialti; 2. lóiəlti]. **loyal** & **-ty**. Quality of being loyal in all senses; fidelity, trustworthiness, staunchness.

lozenge, n. [1. lózinj; 2. lózindž]. Fr. *losange*; origin quite uncertain. **1.** Figure having two acute, and two obtuse angles. **2.** A small thin cake or tablet composed of medicinal substances, often sweetened and flavoured to make it palatable. **3.** Any of various lozenge-shaped figures or objects; **a** (her.) a form of the escutcheon, esp. used by women; figures of this shape upon an escutcheon; **b** one of the lozenge-shaped facets upon a cut gem; **c** a small lozenge-shaped pane of glass.

lozengy, adj. [1. lózenji; 2. lózindži]. (her., of the escutcheon) Divided into, covered with, lozenge-shaped figures.

L.s.d., n. [1. èl es dḗ; 2. èl ɛs dī]. For Lat. *librae, solidi, denarii*. **a** Pounds, shillings, and pence; **b** (colloq.) money: *a question of £.s.d.*

lubber, n. [1. lúber; 2. lábə]. Swed., prob. related to **lob** & obs. *looby*, M.E. *loby*. **a** A clumsy, awkward, unhandy fellow; specif. **b** a clumsy, inexperienced seaman, also *land-lubber*.

lubberliness, n. [1. lúberlines; 2. lábəlinis]. See next word & **-ness.** Quality of being a lubber; clumsiness, lack of skill.

lubberly, adj. [1. lúberli; 2. lábəli]. **lubber** & **-ly**. Like a lubber.

lubra, n. [1. lo͞obra; 2. lūbrə]. Native Australian. A female aboriginal; black woman.

lubricant, adj. & n. [1. lū́brikant; 2. ljū́brikənt], fr. Lat. *lūbricant-(em)*, Pres. Part. of *lūbricāre*, 'to make smooth'. See next word. **a** adj. Having the property of making slippery, diminishing friction, esp. in the movable parts of machinery; **b** n., greasy substance used for this purpose; (fig.) something which facilitates action, speech &c.

lubricate, vb. trans. & intrans. [1. lū́brikāt; 2. ljū́brikeit], fr. Lat. *lūbricāt-(um)*, P.P. of *lūbricāre*, 'to make smooth or slippery'; fr. *lūbricus*, 'slippery'; fr. **sloib-* & cogn. w. **lisp. 1.** trans. **a** To treat, rub, smear, with a lubricant to diminish friction and facilitate smooth working; **b** (fig., colloq.) to do something to render conversation easy, or action more readily performed, e.g. to ply with drink; to tip or bribe: *to lubricate a person's tongue, palms.* **2.** intrans. To perform the functions of a lubricant.

lubrication, n. [1. lūbrikā́shun; 2. ljūbrikéiʃən]. Prec. & **-ion. a** Act or process of lubricating; **b** state of being lubricated.

lubricator, n. [1. lū́brikātor; 2. ljū́brikeitə]. **lubricate** & **-or. a** One who lubricates; **b** automatic device for lubricating machinery.

lubricity, n. [1. lūbrísiti; 2. ljūbrísiti]. Fr. *lubricité*, fr. Lat. *lūbricitāt-(is)*, 'slipperiness'. See **lubricate. 1.** Lubricating property. **2.** (fig., rare) Slipperiness, instability of character. **3.** Lewdness, lasciviousness, lustfulness, salaciousness.

lubricous, adj. [1. lū́brikus; 2. ljū́brikəs]. Lat. *lūbricus*. See **lubricate** & **-ous. a** Smooth, slippery; **b** elusive; **c** given to lubricity.

Lucan, Lukan, adj. [1. lū́kan, lo͞okan; 2. ljū́kən, lū́kən]. Lat. *Lūcas*, 'Luke' & **-an.** Pertaining to St. Luke.

luce, n. [1. lūs; 2. ljūs]. O. Fr. *lus*, Lat. *lūcius*, 'a pike' (fish), etymol. doubtful. **a** Full-grown pike; **b** (her.) figure of a pike borne as a charge in a coat of arms.

lucence, -cy, n. [1. lū́sens(i); 2. ljū́səns(i)]. See next word & **-ce, -cy.** Quality, property, of being lucent.

lucent, adj. [1. lū́sent; 2. ljū́sənt]. Lat. *lūcent-(em)*, Pres. Part. of *lūcēre*, 'to shine', fr. base *lūc-*, 'light, shine', as in *lūc-em*, acc. of *lūx*, 'light'; for further cognates see under **leuco-** & **light** (I.), also **luminous, lune. a** Giving forth light; bright; **b** clear, transparent.

lucerne, n. [1. lo͞osern, lo͞osérn; 2. lū́sən, lūsə́n]. Fr. *luzerne*, fr. Provenç. *luserno*; etymol. dubious. Plant much used for forage, with trifoliate leaves and bluish pink flowers resembling those of clover; alfalfa.

lucid, adj. [1. lū́sid; 2. ljū́sid]. Lat. *lūcidus*, 'full of light, clear, bright'. See base in **lucent. 1.** (archaic or poet.) **a** Bright, shining; **b** clear, transparent: '*Abbana and Pharpar, lucid streams*', Milton, 'P.L.,' 1. 469; **c** (fig.) normal as to intellectual faculties. Phr. *a lucid interval*, one between paroxysms of madness, or rage. **2.** Thinking clearly: *a lucid mind*; expressing meaning with clearness, and without ambiguity; clear, easy to understand: *a lucid explanation, argument.*

lucidity, n. [1. lūsíditi; 2. ljūsíditi]. Prec. & **-ity.** Quality of being lucid.

lucidly, adv. [1. lū́sidli; 2. ljū́sidli]. See prec. & **-ly.** In a lucid manner; clearly.

Lucifer, n. [1. lū́sifer; 2. ljū́sifə]. Lat., lit. 'light-bearing'; *lūci-*, 'light', see **lucent**, & **-ferous. 1.** The planet Venus appearing as the morning star. **2.** Satan, as identified with the rebel archangel who lost heaven through pride. Phr. *as proud as Lucifer.* **3.** (archaic or obs., not cap.) A match which ignites by friction; also *lucifer match.*

lucifugous, adj. [1. lūsífūgus; 2. ljūsífjugəs]. Lat. *lūcifugus*, 'avoiding light', & **-ous.** See **lucent** & **fugitive.** Avoiding, turning away from, the light.

luck, n. [1. luk; 2. lak]. Prob. fr. Du. *luk*, also *geluk*, 'fate, happiness', cp. Germ. *glück*, in same sense; prob. connected w. O.H.G. *lockōn*, 'to attract, entice'; further connexions are doubtful. **1.** Fate, chance regarded as bringer of good or ill fortune; series of events, occurring as though by chance, which affect the individual: *good luck, bad luck.* Phrs. *to have hard luck*, to be unfortunate; *to try one's luck*, test one's fortune in an enterprise the upshot of which is uncertain. **2.** Good fortune, favourable series of events; happiness: *a great piece of luck*; *to have no luck.* Phrs. *to be off one's luck*, to have ill fortune; *in luck*, fortunate, favoured by fate; *for luck*, in order to bring good fortune &c. **3.** (archaic) Some object embodying, and closely associated with, the fortunes of an individual or family: *luck of Eden Hall*, goblet of the Musgrave family.

luckily, adv. [1. lúkili; 2. lákili]. **lucky** & **-ly.** In a lucky, fortunate manner; by good fortune, fortunately: *luckily I was out when he called*; *most luckily for you he didn't see you.*

luckless, adj. [1. lúkles; 2. láklis]. **luck** & **-less.** Unfortunate, unhappy, ill-starred, turning out disastrously.

lucklessly, adv. See prec. & **-ly.** Unfortunately; without any good luck.

luck-money, -penny, n. **a** Small coin kept as being thought lucky or likely to bring good luck; **b** small sum of money, returned for luck by seller to a purchaser.

lucky, adj. [1. lúki; 2. láki]. **luck** & **-y. a** (of persons) Favoured by fate, having good luck, fortunate; **b** (of events and actions) resulting in, associated with, good luck; bringing good fortune: *a lucky move, journey* &c.; **c** (of times and seasons) connected with good luck in the past, and held to be auspicious of the same in the future: *my birthday is one of my lucky days*; **d** (of objects) supposed to influence events favourably, likely to bring good luck on the possessor; Phr. *a lucky sixpence*, weighted so as to turn up always the same side when spun or tossed.

lucky bag, n. Receptacle containing various objects, one of which is selected by touch, by a person who pays for the privilege of dipping.

lucrative, adj. [1. lū́krativ; 2. ljū́krətiv]. Lat. *lūcrāt-(um)*, P.P. of *lūcrāri*, 'to gain, acquire', fr. *lūcrum*, 'gain, profit, advantage', see **lucre**, & **-ive.** Yielding material advantage; profitable: *a lucrative employment, trade* &c.

lucratively, adv. Prec. & **-ly.** So as to produce gain.

lucrativeness, n. See prec. & **-ness.** Quality of being lucrative.

lucre, n. [1. lū́ker, lo͞oker; 2. ljū́kə, lū́kə]. Lat. *lūcrum*, 'gain, profit, advantage', said to be for **lutlom*, & cogn. w. Scrt. *lōtram*, 'booty, stolen property' (see **loot**). Variants of the base **lau-*, **lu-*, 'to gain, enjoy', are seen also in Gk. *apo-láuein*, 'to enjoy', *láia*, 'booty'; O. Slav. *loviti*, 'to pursue, seize'; & perh. in Goth. *laun*, O.E. *lēan*, 'reward'. Material profit, gain; money, riches; always now in unfavourable sense. Phr. *filthy lucre.*

lucubrate, vb. intrans. [1. lū́kūbrāt; 2. ljū́kjubreit], fr. Lat. *lūcubrāt-(um)*, P.P. type of *lūcubrāre*, 'to work by lamplight; work at night', fr. base *lūc-*, 'light'. See **lucent.** To work at night; to work laboriously.

lucubration, n. [1. lūkūbrā́shun; 2. ljūkjubréiʃən]. Lat. *lūcubrātiōn-(em)*, 'nocturnal study; something composed at night'. See prec. & **-ion. a** Hard, laborious study and meditation; **b** the product of such study, esp. some laborious, over-elaborated work, one which 'smells of the lamp'.

luculent, adj. [1. lū́kūlent; 2. ljū́kjulənt]. Lat. *lūculentus*, 'full of light; burning brightly; excellent'; fr. *lūc-*, 'light'. See **lucent. a** Clear, shining, transparent; **b** (fig.) clear to the understanding; lucid.

lucus a non lucendo, n. [1. lū́kus ā nòn lūséndō; 2. ljū́kəs ei nɔ̀n ljūséndou]. Often *lucus a non.* Lat., 'a grove because it is not light'; a gibe at whimsical & paradoxical etymologies; *lūcus*, 'grove', is fr. Lat. base *lūc-*, cp. *lūx*, 'light', & see **lucent.** The word means, not 'a place with no light', but 'a place into which light has been allowed to enter; a clearing in a forest'. The older form was **loukos*, & is exactly cogn. w. O.E. *lēah*, 'open, cleared country' (see **lea (I.)**), & Lith. *laŭkas*, 'field, open country' A fanciful etymology; an absurd, illogical, inconsequent statement or explanation; **a** *non sequitur.*

Luddite, n. [1. lúdīt; 2. ládait], fr. Ludd, name of a person who broke stocking-frames in 1779. One of a band of fanatics who in 1811–16 attempted to prevent the use of machinery by smashing it and burning factories.

ludicrous, adj. [1. lo͞odikrus, lū́dikrus; 2. l(j)ū́dikrəs]. Lat. *lūdicer, lūdicrus*, 'serving for sport, sportive; pertaining to stage-plays or players'; cp. *lūdus*, 'pastime, sport, play; stage-play'; & *lūdere*, 'to play, sport, frolic'; The etymol. is quite uncertain. Calculated to provoke laughter; absurd, laughable, ridiculous, comical.

ludicrously, adv. Prec. & **-ly.** In a ludicrous manner, to a ludicrous extent &c.

ludicrousness, n. See prec. & **-ness.** Quality, fact, of being ludicrous.

ludo, n. [1. lo͞odō; 2. lū́dou]. Lat., 'I play'. See **ludicrous.** Name of a simple game played on a checkered board with counters which are moved according to throw of dice.

lues, n. [1. lo͞oēz; 2. lūiz]. Lat., 'a plague, pestilence, contagious disease', cp. *luere*, 'to wash', wh. base see under **lave, lather, alluvium. a** A pestilential disease; **b** syphilis, also *lues venerea.*

luff, n. & vb. intrans. [1. luf; 2. laf]. Prob. borrowed fr. Du. *loef*, n., *loeven*, vb. The highly ingenious speculations & suggestions of Skeat are not convincing, since it is uncertain what the object called in M.E. *lof* was, whether it be the same as *luff*, or what purpose it served. **a** n. Act of sailing a ship close to the wind; **b** vb., to sail nearer the wind.

lug (I.), vb. trans. & intrans. & n. [1. lug; 2. lag]. Scand., cp. Swed. *lugga*, 'to pull the hair'. (colloq.) **1.** vb. **a** To drag, pull, roughly, violently, or with effort; also *lug about, lug along*; **b** (fig.) *lug in*, to introduce unnaturally and irrelevantly a subject, name, story &c., into a conversation. **2. n.** Act, labour, of lugging; pull, tug.

lug (II.), n. Prob. fr. Swed. *lugg*, 'forelock', cp. prec. **1.** (Scots.) The ear. **2.** Something which projects like an ear, as projection on rim of a pot or pan for lifting it; one of the leather loops in harness through which the shafts of a cart or other vehicle pass.

luge, n. [1. lūzh; 2. lyž]. Fr. A small raised toboggan for one person.

luggage, n. [1. lúgij; 2. lágidž], fr. **lug** (I.) & **-age**. Travellers' baggage; impedimenta, packages containing personal effects carried about with one when travelling.

lugger, n. [1. lúger; 2. lágə]. See next word. Small ship rigged with lug-sails.

lug-sail, n. [1. lúg sāl, lúgsl; 2. lág seil, lágsl]. Origin of *lug-* in this word is uncertain. One of several types of four-cornered sails, slung from a yard at a third or quarter of its length from forward end.

lugubrious, adj. [1. lōō-, lūgū́brius; 2. l(j)ugjū́briəs]. Lat. *lūgūbris*, 'connected with mourning; doleful, plaintive'; cp. Lat. *lūgēre*, 'to mourn, lament; wear mourning'; cogn. w. Gk. *lugrós*, 'mournful, sad, dismal', & *leugaléos*, 'wretched, pitiful, dismal'. Further connexions wh. have been suggested are possible but somewhat obscure. Mournful, dismal, woe-begone, depressed; funereal.

lugubriously, adv. Prec. & **-ly**. In a lugubrious manner; mournfully.

lugubriousness, n. See prec. & **-ness**. State, quality, of being lugubrious.

lug-worm, n. Origin doubtful. Worm-like marine animal used as bait in sea fishing, found buried in the wet sand after the tide has gone down.

lukewarm, adj. [1. lŏŏkworm; 2. lúkwɔ̄m]. M.E. *leuk, luke*, 'tepid, warm', wh. is prob. fr. Du. *leuk*, 'warm'. The other M.E. word *lew*, 'tepid', O.E. (*ge*)*hlēo*(*w*), is not connected, but prob. influenced the sense. For this see **lee**. *Lew-warm* may still be heard in dialects. **a** Moderately warm, less than hot; tepid: *lukewarm water*; **b** (fig., of sentiments, character &c.) not ardent, tending to indifference; torpid, phlegmatic, half-hearted: *lukewarm support, agreement*; *a lukewarm champion of a cause* &c.

lukewarmly, adv. Prec. & **-ly**. Half-heartedly.

lukewarmness. n. See prec. & **-ness**. Absence of ardour or enthusiasm.

lull (I.), vb. trans. & intrans. [1. lul; 2. lal]. Prob. fr. Swed. *lulla*, 'to sing to sleep', & imitative of soothing, crooning sound. **A.** trans. **1. a** To soothe, compose, calm down, by crooning or rocking: *to lull a baby to sleep*; **b** (fig.) to persuade, cajole: *to lull a person into a false sense of security*. **2.** (fig.) To assuage, mitigate, render less intense: *to lull a person's suspicions to sleep*; *to lull pain*. **B.** intrans. (rare) To abate, grow calmer, become less violent: *the violence of the storm had lulled to some extent*.

lull (II.), n., fr. prec. Temporary cessation, pause, stoppage; interval of silence, or inactivity: *a lull in the wind, traffic*; *a lull in the conversation*.

lullaby, n. [1. lúlabī; 2. láləbai]. **a** A soothing song to lull infants to sleep; cradle-song; **b** (fig.) a gentle, soothing sound made by the wind, falling water &c.

lumbago, n. [1. lumbā́gō; 2. lambéigou]. L. Lat., fr. *lumbus*, 'loin'. See next word. Rheumatic pain in the loins or lower part of the spine in the region of the hips.

lumbar, adj. [1. lúmbar; 2. lámbə]. Lat. *lumbus*, 'loin', & **-ar**; orig. form **londhwos*; cp. O.E. *lenden*, 'loin', O.H.G. *lenti*, fr. **landi-*; O. Slav. *lĕdvija*, 'loin, kidney'; ultimate meaning perh. 'hollow, depression', cp. O.N. *lundr*, 'grove', & O. Prussian *lindan*, 'valley'. Pertaining to, situated near, the loins: *lumbar nerves, region*.

lumber (I.), n. [1. lúmber; 2. lámbə]. Variant of **Lombard**. Used orig. for a pawnbroker's shop, fr. the fact that these were often kept by Lombards. **1. a** Miscellaneous articles, odds and ends of furniture &c. stored away; hence, **b** superfluous, useless, objects in general; rubbish. **2.** Timber, esp. trees cut up ready for the market.

lumber (II.), vb. trans. & intrans., fr. prec. **A.** trans. **1. a** To fill with useless articles; **b** to crowd with furniture; **c** to encumber, hamper, embarrass, obstruct, with odds and ends; also *lumber up*, encumber. **2.** To cut down (trees) as lumber for the market. **B.** intrans. **1.** To overcrowd; cause embarrassment with piles of lumber or rubbish. **2.** To cut down and prepare timber for the market.

lumber (III.), vb. intrans. Cp. Swed. dial. *loma*, 'to walk heavily'; also *lomra*, 'to resound'; prob. connected w. **lame** & **limp** (II.). **a** To walk, move, along painfully, clumsily, heavily; **b** (of heavy vehicles) to move along heavily and noisily; to rumble along; also *lumber along, by, past*.

lumbering (I.), n. [1. lúmbering; 2. lámbəriŋ], fr. **lumber** (II.) & **-ing**. Act of cutting and selling timber; timber-trade.

lumbering (II.), adj., fr. **lumber** (III.). Moving heavily and clumsily; moving heavily and noisily.

lumberman, n. [1. lúmberman; 2. lámbəmən], fr. **lumber** (I.). One who fells and dresses timber for the market.

lumber-mill, n. Saw-mill.

lumber-room, n. One in which lumber, rubbish, is kept.

lumber-yard, n. Timber yard.

lumbo-, pref. Form of Lat. *lumbus*, 'loin', used in compounds. See **lumbar**. *Lumbo-dorsal* &c. indicates connexion with lumbar regions.

lumbrical, adj. & n. [1. lúmbrikl; 2. lámbrikl], fr. Lat. *lumbrīcus*, 'earthworm' &c., & **-al**; cogn. w. W. *llyngyr*, 'earthworm'. **a** adj. Connected with the small muscles which move the fingers and toes; **b** n., one of these muscles. The name is derived from the supposed resemblance of the muscles in shape to worms.

Lumière process, n. [1. lōōmiār prōses; 2. lýmiɛ̄r próusɛs], fr. name of inventors. Method of colour-photography, in which a special plate is used in an ordinary camera.

lumin-, pref. Form used in compounds, fr. oblique cases of Lat. *lūmen*, 'a light, a lamp', genit. *lūmin-is*. The word stands for **lūcmen*. See base *lūc-* under **lucent**.

luminary, n. [1. lū́minari; 2. ljū́minəri]. O. Fr. *luminarie*, fr. Low Lat. *lūminārium*, 'a light, candle, torch'. See prec. & **-ary**. **a** Light-giving body; esp. **a** heavenly body; **b** (fig.) an enlightened person; an eminent authority on some branch of learning.

luminescence, n. [1. lūminésens; 2. ljūminésəns]. See next word & **-ence**. Quality of being luminescent.

luminescent, adj. [1. lūminésent; 2. ljūminésənt]. See **lumin-** & **-escent**. Giving light, shining, esp. of phosphorescent objects &c.

luminiferous, adj. [1. lūminíferus; 2. ljūminífərəs]. **lumin-** & **-ferous**. Yielding, transmitting, light.

luminosity, n. [1. lūminósiti; 2. ljūminɔ́siti]. **luminous** & **-ity**. Quality, property, of being luminous.

luminous, adj. [1. lū́minus; 2. ljū́minəs]. Lat. *lūminōsus*, 'full of light'. See **lumin-** & **-ous**. **a** Radiating light; bright, glowing, clear; **b** (fig., of non-material things) brilliant, enlightening; intelligible: *a luminous discourse, exposition*.

luminously, adv. Prec. & **-ly**. In a luminous manner.

luminousness, n. See prec. & **-ness**. Quality of being luminous.

lump (I.), n. [1. lump; 2. lamp]. *Lompe*, 'lump, mass', occurs in O.D.; *lump* in Swed. & Norw. dialects; origin doubtful. **1.** Shapeless, cohesive mass; clod, block: *a lump of clay, pudding, rock, ice*. Phrs. *in the lump*, in the aggregate, as a whole, taken all together; *a lump of sugar*, small, specially shaped, piece or cube used in tea and coffee; *lump sum*, amount of money paid at one time for several items, contrasted with separate payments. **2.** A swelling, excrescence, bump, on the body: *a lump on the forehead*. Phr. *a lump in the* (*one's*) *throat*, sensation of constriction caused by strong emotion. **3.** A gross, unshapely, clumsy person.

lump (II.), vb. trans. & intrans., fr. prec. **1.** trans. To put all together as it were in one lump; to include under one head, consider, without distinguishing, as belonging to the same class or kind; generally *lump together*; *lump this with that*; *lump several things under one name*. Phr. *if you don't like it, you can, will have to, lump it*, put up with it. **2.** intrans. **a** To form into lumps; **b** to walk, move, along in a clumsy, awkward, laborious manner; chiefly *lump along*.

lumper, n. [1. lúmper; 2. lámpə]. Prec. & **-er**. Labourer employed in loading and unloading vessels.

lumpfish, n. [1. lúmpfish; 2. lámpfiʃ]. Greenish or purplish, clumsily shaped marine fish found in North Atlantic; it has a sucker enabling it to cling to stones.

lumping, adj. [1. lúmping; 2. lámpiŋ]. **lump** & **-ing**. (colloq.) Copious, plentiful, piled up: *a lumping great helping of pudding*.

lumpish, adj. [1. lúmpish; 2. lámpiʃ]. **lump** & **-ish**. **a** Like a lump; thick and shapeless; **b** (of persons) thickset and heavy; of sluggish mind, unresponsive.

lumpy, adj. [1. lúmpi; 2. lámpi]. See prec. & **-y**. **a** Covered with, full of, lumps; **b** lumpish.

lunacy, n. [1. lōōnasi; 2. lúnəsi], fr. Lat. *lūn-*, 'moon' (see **lune**), & **-acy**; orig. an intermittent form of insanity supposed to vary in intensity with the phases of the moon. **a** Insanity, madness; **b** great foolishness; a foolish act.

lunar, adj. [1. lōōnar, lū́nar; 2. lū́nə, ljū́nə]. Lat. *lūnāris*, 'pertaining to the moon'. See **lune** & **-ar**. **a** Pertaining to the moon: *lunar rainbow*, one formed by moon's rays; **b** determined by the moon: *a lunar month*, one of four weeks; contrasted with *calendar month*.

lunarian, n. [1. lūnā́rian; 2. ljūnéəriən]. Prec. & **-ian**. **a** Inhabitant of the moon; **b** person having special knowledge of the moon.

lunate, adj. [1. lū́nāt; 2. ljū́neit]. Lat. *lūnātus*, 'crescent-shaped'. See **lune** & **-ate**. (zool., bot.) Shaped like the crescent moon.

lunatic, n. & adj. [1. lōōnatik; 2. lū́nətik]. Lat. *lūnāticus*, 'affected by the moon; temporarily insane'. See **lunacy**. **1.** n. Person suffering from lunacy, an insane person. **2.** adj. **a** (obs.) Moonstruck; **b** mad, insane.

lunation, n. [1. lūnā́shun; 2. ljūnéiʃən]. **lune** & **-ation**. Period of time between new moons.

lunch, n. & vb. intrans. & trans. [1. lunsh; 2. lanʃ]. For **luncheon**. **1.** n. Luncheon. **2.** vb. **a** intrans. To partake of luncheon; **b** trans., to give luncheon to: *to lunch a friend at one's club*.

luncheon, n. [1. lúnshun; 2. lánʃən], fr. dial. *lunch*, 'lump, lump of food'; a word w. no definite origin, & on a par w. *lump, hunch*, & such forms; prob. influenced by obs. **nuncheon**. **a** Lightish meal consumed between breakfast and dinner; **b** (among labourers) hunch of bread and cheese or bacon, eaten at about 10 a.m.

lune, n. [1. lūn; 2. ljūn]. Fr., fr. Lat. *lūna*, 'moon', wh. is fr. **lūc-na*, fr. base *lūc-*, 'to shine' &c. See **lucent** & **lucus**. Object or figure shaped like a half-moon or crescent.

lunette, n. [1. lūnét; 2. ljūnét]. Fr., lit. 'little moon', applied to a number of objects having a round or half-round form; used esp. in sense of 'eye-glass'. Prec. & **-ette**. Applied to various crescent-shaped objects: **a** an opening in a vaulted roof to admit light; **b** (fort.) a projecting work having an inner open base, and two external faces formed by two walls running parallel for some distance and then sloped towards each other and meeting to form an angle; **c** watch-glass with flattened centre.

lung, n. [1. lung; 2. laŋ]. O.E. *lungen*, 'lungs'; O.H.G. *lungun*. Connected w. **light (IV.)**, 'not heavy'; cp. **lights**. **1.** One of the organs of respiration in air-breathing animals; gen. used in pl., *the lungs*: *inflammation of the lungs*, pneumonia; but also *the right, left, lung*. Phr. *to have good lungs*, a powerful voice. **2.** (fig.) A large open space pervaded with pure fresh air, esp. in or near a big city.

lunge (I.), n. & vb. trans. [1. lunj; 2. landž]. Fr. *longe*, 'strap, line, for leading a horse', fr. Lat. *longus*, 'long'. See **long (I.)**. **a** n. Long line attached to a horse's head-piece for breaking him in; **b** vb., to train by means of a lunge; to cause to leap while attached to a lunge: *to lunge a horse (over a fence)* &c.

lunge (II.), n. & vb. intrans. Earlier *allonge*, Fr., cp. *allonger*, 'to lengthen, stretch out'; fr. Lat. *longus*, 'long'. See **long**. **1.** n. **a** A thrust in fencing; **b** a sudden thrust, or thrusting blow delivered with any kind of weapon. **2.** vb. To make a lunge, to thrust.

lungfish, n. [1. lúngfish; 2. láŋfiʃ]. A kind of fish, belonging to group known as Dipnoi, q.v., which have lungs as well as gills; also called mud-fish.

lunkah, n. [1. lúngkah; 2. láŋka], fr. Hind. *lañka*. Kind of cheroot.

lupin, n. [1. lōōpin, lúpin; 2. lúpin, ljúpin]. Fr., fr. Lat. *lūpīnus*; same as next word; reason for the name not clear. Plant much cultivated in gardens for its long spiky clusters of white, yellow, pink or purple blossom.

lupine, adj. [1. lúpin, lōōpin; 2. ljúpain, lūpain]. Lat. *lūpīnus*, 'of, connected with, a wolf', fr. *lŭpus*, 'wolf', wh. is fr. **wḷkʷos*, & cogn. w. Goth. *wulfs*, O.E. *wulf*. See **wolf**, & cp. **vulpine**. Wolf-like, fierce, ravenous.

lupus, n. [1. lōōpus; 2. lúpəs]. Lat. *lūpus*, 'wolf'. See prec. Tuberculous disease which destroys the skin and soft tissues of the face.

lurch (I.), n. & vb. intrans. [1. lërch; 2. lǟtʃ]. Origin doubtful. **1.** n. A sudden staggering movement, a pitching forward or sideways, caused by loss of balance, as in the walk of drunken man, or one who walks on deck of a rolling ship. **2.** vb. To pitch forward or sideways with a lurch.

lurch (II.), n. Fr. *lourche*, obsolete game something like backgammon, apparently used formerly to denote a critical phase in a game. Obs., except in Phr. *to leave one in the lurch*, desert him at moment of danger; leave him in awkward position.

lurcher, n. [1. lércher; 2. lǟtʃə]. For *lurker*, see **lurk** & **-er**. Dog of nondescript breed, something between collie and greyhound, esp. one used by poachers.

lurdan, n. [1. lérdan; 2. lǟd(ə)n]. O. Fr. *lourdin*, fr. *lourd*, 'heavy', fr. Lat. *lūridus*, 'pale, wan'. See **lurid**. This etymol., in spite of doubts wh. have been raised, is upheld by Meyer-Lübke, who takes the development of meaning to be, 'pale, fainting, perturbed in mind, foolish'. The sense 'heavy' in Fr. & Mod. Provenç. is derived fr. the physical effects of fainting, in loss of control of the movements &c. (archaic and poet.) A dull, heavy, stupid person.

lure (I.), n. [1. lūr; 2. ljō, ljuə], fr. O. Fr. *loevre* &c., Mod. Fr. *leurre*, fr. Frankish *lōpr*, 'bait, carrion', O.H.G. *luoder*, Mod. Germ. *luder*, 'decoy' &c.; prob. connected w. O.E. *laþian*, O.H.G. *ladōn*, Goth. *laþōn*, 'to invite'; cp. also Goth. *laþōns*, 'invitation; consolation'. **1. a** Device consisting of a bunch of feathers and a bait, attached to a long cord, used for recalling hawks; **b** decoy used for attracting wild animals. **2. a** Anything which invites, draws on, attracts, by an apparent promise of gain or pleasure; **b** airs and graces, charms, witcheries.

lure (II.), vb. trans. & intrans., fr. prec. **1.** trans. **a** To recall (falcon); **b** to attract, entice, decoy; (often in bad sense) *to lure a person to his death*; *to lure on*, persuade, entice, cause to proceed on a disastrous course of action. **2.** intrans. To recall a hawk to its lure.

lurid, adj. [1. lúrid; 2. ljórid]. Lat. *lūridus*, 'pale yellow, sallow, wan, ghastly, lurid'; cogn. w. Gk. *khlōrós*, 'pale green, bright green, pale, pallid' (see **chloro-**). **1.** Glowing, appearing bright like fire: *a lurid sky, sunset*; (of pictures) highly coloured, garish. **2.** (in moral sense) Characterized by sensational, tragic, events, startling actions; filled with passion or crime: *a lurid career*.

luridly, adv. Prec. & **-ly**. In a lurid manner.

luridness, n. See prec. & **-ness**. State, quality, of being lurid.

lurk, vb. intrans. [1. lërk; 2. lǟk]. Origin doubtful. **1.** To remain hidden, lie privily and furtively retired, to skulk in a corner, as though shunning observation; to lie in wait. **2.** (fig.) To be latent in, exist unsuspected, reside in unperceived: *a strange beauty lurks in the autumn woodland*.

lurking-place, n. [1. lérking plās; 2. lǟkiŋ pleis]. Secret haunt, lair, hiding-place.

lurry, n. [1. lúri; 2. lári]. Variant of **lorry**.

luscious, adj. [1. lúshus; 2. láʃəs]. Origin doubtful; perh. fr. *delicious*, influenced by **lush**. **1. a** Appealing strongly to the taste and smell; highly flavoured; having a rich fragrance; **b** possessing these qualities to excess; cloying to the palate, too sweet and full-flavoured. **2.** Suggestive of sensuous delight and richness: *luscious colouring, style*.

lusciously, adv. Prec. & **-ly**. In a luscious degree; in a luscious manner or style.

lusciousness, n. Quality of being luscious.

lush, adj. [1. lush; 2. laʃ]. M.E. *lusch*, 'loose', Mod. dial. *lash*, 'soft and watery'; O. Fr. *lasche*, 'relaxed, loose', fr. Lat. *laxus*. See **lax (I.)**. **a** (of herbage &c.) Juicy, abundant, luxuriant in growth; **b** exhibiting lush growth: *lush pastures*.

lust (I.), n. [1. lust; 2. last]. O.E., O.S., O.H.G. *lust*, 'pleasure; desire, lust'; Goth. *lustus*; cp. Lat. *lascīvus*, 'unrestrained, wanton, playful; lustful'; (see **lascivious**); cp. also Russ. *lásyj*, 'full of desire, covetous'. **a** Bodily appetite: *the lusts of the flesh*; **b** specif. (i.) sexual appetite; (ii.) unlawful, excessive, degrading sensual passion.

lust (II.), vb. intrans. O.E. *lystan*, 'to desire strongly'. See prec. **1.** To feel strong physical desire. **2.** *Lust after, for*, to desire passionately; to long for with excessive sexual passion.

lustful, adj. [1. lústfool; 2. lástfəl]. **lust (I.)** & **-ful**. Filled with, strongly moved by, powerful sexual appetite; lascivious, lewd.

lustfully, adv. Prec. & **-ly**. In a lustful manner.

lustfulness, n. See prec. & **-ness**. Condition, quality, of being lustful.

lustihood, n. [1. lústihood; 2. lástihud]. **lusty** & **-hood**. Condition of being lusty.

lustily, adv. [1. lústili; 2. lástili]. **lusty** & **-ly**. With vigour, powerfully, forcefully: *to shout, lay about one, lustily*.

lustiness, n. [1. lústines; 2. lástinis]. See prec. & **-ness**. Strength, vigour; flourishing health.

lustral, adj. [1. lústral; 2. lástrəl]. Lat. *lustrālis*, 'pertaining to purification from guilt; expiatory'. See **lustrum** & **-al**. Connected with, used in, ceremonial purification: *lustral season*; *lustral water*.

lustrate, vb. trans. [1. lústrāt; 2. lástreit]. Lat. *lustrāt-um*, P.P. of *lustrāre*, 'to purify'. See **lustrum**. To cleanse, purge, from guilt by propitiatory offerings and ceremonies.

lustration, n. [1. lustráshun; 2. lastréiʃən]. Prec. & **-ion**. Purificatory, expiatory, ceremony.

lustre (I.), n. See **lustrum**.

lustre (II.), n. [1. lúster; 2. lástə]. Fr. *lustre*, as fr. Lat. **lūstrum* for **lūcstrom*, 'illumination', cp. Lat. *lustrāre*, 'to illumine', fr. base **lūc-*, 'light'. See **lucent**. **1. a** Brilliance, gloss, sheen, beauty; specif. **b** iridescence, metallic sheen, gloss, imparted by a glaze to pottery, or by special process to the surface of fabrics. **2.** Moral or intellectual brilliance or splendour; distinction, renown, fame, prestige: *to give new lustre to an honoured name*.

lustreless, adj. [1. lústerles; 2. lástəlis]. Prec. & **-less**. Lacking brightness or lustre.

lustre-ware, n. Kind of pottery the surface of which has a metallic sheen resembling silver, pewter, copper &c.

lustring, also **lutestring**, n. [1. lústring, lútstring; 2. lástriŋ, ljútstriŋ]. Fr. *lustrine*, fr. **lustre (II.)** & **-ine**. Silk fabric with glossy, sheeny surface.

lustrous, adj. [1. lústrus; 2. lástrəs]. **lustre (II.)** & **-ous**. Luminous, brilliant, shining, resplendent.

lustrously, adv. Prec. & **-ly**. With lustre.

lustrum, lustre, n. [1. lústrum, lúster; 2. lástrəm, lástə]. Lat. *lūstrum*, 'purificatory sacrifice, made every five years, after a census', hence 'period of five years', fr. base of *luere*, 'to wash'. See **lave**. Period of five years.

lusty, adj. [1. lústi; 2. lásti]. **lust** & **-y**. Vigorous, powerful, as with the strength of youth and health.

lusus naturae, n. [1. lúsus nātúrē; 2. ljúsəs neitjúəri]. Lat., 'sport, freak, of nature', fr. *lūs-(um)*, stem of *lūdere*, 'to play, sport'. See **ludicrous**. A remarkable, abnormal, natural object.

lutanist, n. [1. lútanist; 2. ljútənist]. Low Lat. *lutanista*. See next word. Lute-player.

lute (I.), n. [1. lūt, lōōt; 2. ljūt, lūt]. O. Fr. *leut*, Ital. *liuto*, Span. *laud*; prob. fr. Arab. *al 'ūd*, 'the timber, wood; harp'. Stringed instrument resembling a guitar in shape, played by plucking with the fingers; conventionally associated with poets and poetry. Phr. *rift within the lute*; see **rift**.

lute (II.), n. & vb. trans. Lat. *lutum*, 'mud, clay'; cp. Gk. *lûma*, fr. **lut-ma*, 'filth, dirt; disgrace'; Lith. *lutynas*, 'puddle'. **a** n. Cement or other cohesive substance used for rendering air-tight joints in pipes or other apparatus, for sealing vessels &c.; also called *luting*; **b** vb., to stop, make air-tight, with lute.

luteo-, pref. Form of Lat. *lūteus*, 'yellow', used in compounds. See next word. Yellow-coloured.

luteous, adj. [1. lúteus; 2. ljútiəs]. Lat. *lūteus*, 'dyed yellow, golden, or orange-yellow', fr. *lūtum*, 'weed used by dyers in dying yellow', & **-ous**; prob. fr. **wlūt-* & cogn. w. **weld (II.)**, an old name for this plant wh. represents a different grade of the base. Of a deep orange-yellow colour.

lutestring, n. [1. lútstring; 2. ljútstriŋ]. Popular form of **lustring**, as though fr. **lute (I.)** & **string**.

Lutetian, adj. [1. lūtéshan; 2. ljutíʃən], fr. old name *Lutetia*, 'Paris', & **-an**. Parisian.

Lutheran, adj. & n. [1. lōōtheran; 2. lúþərən], fr. name of Martin Luther the German reformer (1483–1546) & **-an**. **1.** adj. Connected with, holding doctrines taught by, Luther: *Lutheran Church*, Protestant Evangelical Church of Germany &c. **2.** n. Adherent of Luther's doctrines; member of Lutheran Church.

Lutheranism, n. [1. lōōtheranizm; 2. lúþərənizəm]. Prec. & **-ism**. System of religion and religious and ecclesiastical theory founded by Luther.

luting, n. [1. lúting; 2. ljútiŋ]. See **lute (II.)**.

lutist, n. [1. lútist; 2. ljútist]. **lute (I.)** & **-ist**. Lute-player, lutanist.

luxate, vb. trans. [1. lúksāt; 2. lákseit]. Lat. *luxāt-(um)*, P.P. type of *luxāre*, 'to dislocate'; cp. Lat. *luxus*, 'dislocated'; connected w. Gk. *lugizein*, 'to bend', *lúgos*, 'withy'. To displace, dislocate; to put out of joint.

luxation, n. [1. luksáshun; 2. lakséiʃən]. Prec. & **-ion**. Act or process of dislocating; state of being dislocated.

luxe, n. [1. looks; 2. luks, lyks]. Fr., 'luxury', fr. Lat. *luxus*, 'excess, debauchery, luxury; pomp, magnificence'; perh. fr. base *lūc-*, 'to shine, be brilliant' &c. See **lucent.** Elegance, sumptuousness; in various Phrs. *articles de luxe*; *édition de luxe*, splendidly printed and produced edition of a book.

luxuriance, -cy, n. [1. lukzúrians(i); 2. lakzjʃ́riəns(i)]. Fr. See **luxuriant & -ce.** Prolific growth, excessive abundance; exuberance; (also fig.) *luxuriance of imagination.*

luxuriant, adj. [1. lukzúriant; 2. lakzjʃ́riənt]. Lat. *luxuriant-(em)*, Pres. Part. of *luxuriāre*. See next word. **1.** Extremely productive, abundantly fertile: *luxuriant soil.* **2. a** Excessively prolific, growing and thriving abundantly; exuberant, growing lush: *luxuriant growth, pasture, foliage* &c.; **b** (also of intellectual and emotional production) copious, exuberant: *luxuriant imagination.* **3.** (of expression and style) Flowery, florid, lacking in restraint and austerity.

luxuriate, vb. intrans. [1. lukzúriāt; 2. lakzjʃ́rieit]. Lat. *luxuriāt-(um)*, P.P. type of *luxuriāre*, 'to be rank; to have in abundance; to be too fruitful; to revel, be wanton', fr. *luxuria*, 'rankness, luxury', fr. *luxus*, 'excess'. See **luxe & luxury. 1.** To grow luxuriantly, grow rankly and exuberantly. **2.** To indulge in, dwell upon, take delight in exhibiting, run riot in: *some writers luxuriate in horrors.* **3.** To revel in, take delight in, enjoy: *to luxuriate in sunshine, in the sea-air* &c.

luxurious, adj. [1. lukzúrius; 2. lakzjʃ́riəs]. Lat. *luxuriōsus*, 'luxuriant; voluptuous', fr. *luxuria.* See **luxury & -ous. 1.** (of persons and habits) Delighting in, exhibiting a love of, luxury; self-indulgent, extravagant. **2.** (of things) Contributing to extreme comfort; sumptuous, splendid: *a luxurious house; luxurious furniture, bed, food* &c.

luxury, n. [1. lúkshuri; 2. lákʃəri]. Lat. *luxuria*, 'luxuriance; riotous living, extravagance; redundancy', fr. *luxus.* See **luxe. 1. a** State, mode, of life characterized by great ease and comfort, and by availability of the means to gratify one's tastes and desires: *to live in luxury.* Phr. *in the lap of luxury*, surrounded by every comfort and gratification; **b** habits of indulgence in costly pleasure: *made effeminate by luxury.* **2.** Something, an object or circumstance, which contributes to comfort and enjoyment; esp. something which is not an essential necessity of life; often specif. contrasted with *necessity*: *his means sufficed for a meagre existence, but could not procure him any luxuries; a few small luxuries and comforts; what is, economically, a luxury today is the necessity of tomorrow.* **3.** An intellectual or emotional enjoyment, also that which produces these: *the luxury of a good book, of leisure, of a holiday after prolonged work.*

-ly, suff. [1. li; 2. li]. **1.** Suff. forming adjs., chiefly fr. ns.; O.E. *-līc*, M.E. *-lich, -ly*, same as the independent word meaning 'body, shape' &c. See first element in **lichgate & like (I.).** The force is 'resembling in appearance; having the nature and character of': *kingly, manly, motherly, daughterly, fleshly, bodily*; also added to adj. w. slight modification of sense: *goodly.* **2.** Suff. forming advs. fr. adjs. & parts. used as such, & occasionally fr. ns., O.E. *-līce*, a dat. of *līc.* Examples: *badly, wrongly, smilingly, contentedly, luxuriously* &c.; fr. ns.: *monthly, yearly*, by the month, year &c.

lycanthropy, n. [1. līkánthropi; 2. laikǽnþrəpi]. Gk. *lúkos*, 'wolf', cogn. w. **lupus & wolf**, & *ánthrōpos*, 'man'. See under **anthropology. 1.** Transformation of a human being into a wolf which, according to ancient legend, took place as the result of magic spells. See **werewolf. 2.** Disease, form of insanity, in which the patient believes himself to be a wolf and attempts to behave like one.

lycée, n. [1. lésā; 2. līsei]. Fr. See **lyceum.** French State secondary school.

lyceum, n. [1. līseum; 2. laisíəm]. Latinized form of Gk. *lúkeion*, a gymnasium with covered walks in Athens, where Aristotle taught, named after the neighbouring temple of *Apollo Lúkeios*; the latter word means 'wolf-slaying', & was an epithet of Apollo. See first element in **lycanthropy.** Building serving as headquarters of a literary society, usually containing library, reading and lecture rooms.

lychgate, n. See **lichgate.**

lychnis, n. [1. líknis; 2. líknis]. Gk. *lukhnís*, cp. *lúkhnos*, 'a lamp', fr. Gk. base *leuk-, luk-*, 'bright, shining'. See **leuco-**; also **lucent** &c. One of several related kinds of scarlet or white flowering plants; ragged robin.

lycopodium, n. [1. līkopṓdium; 2. laikəpóudiəm]. Latinized form, fr. Gk. *lúkos*, 'wolf' (see **lycanthropy**), & *pod-, poús*, 'foot' (see **pedal**). Large genus of evergreen plants; ground pine, club-moss.

lycopodium powder, n. Powder composed of spores of lycopodium; highly inflammable and used in manufacture of fireworks; also used medicinally.

lyddite, n. [1. lídīt; 2. lídait], fr. Lydd in Kent, where it was manufactured. High explosive, of picric acid, used in shells.

Lydian, adj. & n. [1. lídian; 2. lídiən], fr. *Lydia*, ancient country in Asia Minor. **1.** adj. **a** Belonging to Lydia or its inhabitants; **b** soft, effeminate, voluptuous (referring to character of Lydian culture), esp. of one of the modes of ancient Greek music. **2.** n. **a** Inhabitant of Lydia; **b** language of Lydia.

lye, lie, n. [1. lī; 2. lai]. O.E. *lēah*, M.E. *leȝe, leye*, O.H.G. *louga*, O.N. *laug*, 'hot bath; hot spring'; ultimately fr. base **lau-, *lu-*, 'to wash'. Cp. **lave, lixiviate, lather.** Strong alkaline solution made by soaking woodashes in water, used in washing, and soapmaking.

lying, adj. [1. líing; 2. lái-iŋ], fr. Pres. Part. of **lie (II.).** False; stating, expressing, an untruth: *a lying prophet, story, rumour* &c.

lying-in, n. [1. líing ín; 2. lái-iŋ ín]. State attending childbirth, confinement; *lying-in hospital*, one which receives women about to be confined.

lyme-grass, n. [1. lím grahs; 2. láim grās]. Origin unknown. Grass which grows on sand-dunes and binds the sand, preventing it from shifting.

lymph, n. [1. limf; 2. limf]. Lat. *lympha, lumpha, lumpa*, 'pure spring water'. Etymol. unknown; the only suggestion seems to be that the word is borrowed, w. dissimilation, fr. Gk. *númphē.* See **nymph. 1.** (poet.) Spring of water; something pure and clear like water. **2. a** (physiol.) A colourless fluid found in the lymphatic vessels, somewhat similar to the blood in character, but containing no red corpuscles; **b** (med.) clear substance which exudes from inflamed tissues; **c** substance exuding from the vesicles formed in certain diseases such as cow-pox, or produced artificially in certain media, and used for inoculations against smallpox.

lymphatic, adj. & n. [1. limfátik; 2. limfǽtik], fr. prec. **1.** adj. **a** Pertaining to, containing, secreting lymph: *lymphatic glands, ducts* &c.; **b** having a complexion and temperament of a kind formerly supposed to be due to excess of lymph, i.e. pale, bloodless; sluggish, inactive, heavy. **2.** n. (usually in pl.) Lymphatic vessel or gland of the body.

lympho-, pref. Form of Lat. *lympha* used in mod. compounds; used in medical terms, e.g. *lymphocele*, tumour containing lymph; *lymphocyte*, cell found in lymph.

lyncean, adj. [1. linsḗan; 2. linsíən]. See **lynx & -an. a** Connected with the lynx; **b** having sharp sight.

lynch, vb. trans. [1. linsh; 2. linʃ]. Origin obscure. See **Lynch law.** To execute judgement, esp. capital punishment, upon, without the formalities of a legal trial and sentence; to hang, or put to death by any means, as a result of popular indignation and impatience, the punishment being inflicted by the mob.

lynchet, n. [1. línchet; 2. líntʃit], fr. O.E. *hlinċ*, 'slope', q.v. under **link (IV.). 1.** Strip of grassland left unploughed. **2.** Terrace formed on slope of downs &c. as result of ploughing in prehistoric times.

lynching, n. [1. línshing; 2. línʃiŋ]. Act of executing a suspected person according to the principles of Lynch law.

Lynch law, n. Formerly *Lynch's law*; supposed to be derived from name of a magistrate (d. 1796), in Virginia, U.S.A., who started the practice which goes by his name. Rapid, summary justice, carried out by an indignant and impatient mob, who will not wait for the formalities of a trial.

lynx, n. [1. lingks; 2. liŋks]. Lat., fr. Gk. *lúgx*, prob. connected w. *leússein*, 'to see, look at'; cp. Scrt. *lōkáyati*, 'he looks at'; Lith. *laukti*, 'to await, look out for'; O.H.G. *luogen*, 'to watch'; O.E. *lōcian.* See **look (I.).** The name is derived fr. the animal's keen sight. Animal of the cat tribe, greyish, or pale brown in colour, having a short thick tail and tufted ears.

lynx-eyed, adj. Keen-sighted.

Lyon, n. [1. líun; 2. láiən]. Old spelling of *lion*, fr. the Royal Arms of Scotland: *Lord Lyon, Lord Lyon King of Arms*, title of the chief Herald of Scotland.

Lyra, n. [1. líra; 2. láiərə]. Lat., fr. Gk. *lúrā.* See **lyre.** Name of a Northern constellation, supposed to represent the lyre of Orpheus.

lyrate(d), adj. [1. lírāt, lirā́ted; 2. láiəreit, laiəréitid]. **lyre & -ate.** Shaped like a lyre.

lyre, n. [1. lír; 2. laiə]. Lat. *lyra*, Gk. *lúrā*; perh. fr. base **lu-, *leu-*, wh. occurs in an extended form in Lat. *laud-*, stem of *laus*, 'praise' (see **laud**); cp. O.E. *lēoþ*, 'song'; O.H.G. *liod*, Mod. Germ. *lied*; O.E. *lēodan*, Goth. *liuþōn*, 'to sing'. Form of harp with seven strings, used by the ancient Greeks for accompanying song and recitation.

lyre bird, n. Small Australian bird whose tail feathers are long and curved into the shape of a lyre.

lyric, n. [1. lírik; 2. lírik]. See **next word.** A lyrical poem; words for a song.

lyric(al), adj. [1. lírik(l); 2. lírik(l)]. Gk. *lurikós*, 'singing to the lyre; a lyric poet'. See **lyre & -ic (& -al). a** Pertaining to a lyre; adapted for singing to the lyre; hence, **b** (of poet.) composed in the form of a song, usually in regular stanzas; *lyrical poetry* expresses the poet's emotion rather than a description of events; *lyrical poet*, composer of lyrics. Phr. (of persons) *to become quite lyrical*, give emotional expression to strong feeling.

lyricism, n. [1. lírisizm; 2. lírisizəm]. **lyric & -ism. a** Lyrical quality or character in a poetical composition; **b** lyrical expression; emotional expression.

lyrist, n. [1. lírist, lírist; 2. láiərist, lírist]. **lyre & -ist. a** A player on the lyre; **b** a lyrical poet.

-lysis, suff. Gk. *lúsis*, 'a loosing', fr. *lúein*, 'to loose'; cogn. w. Scrt. *lunā́ti*, 'to cut'; Lat. *luere*, 'to pay', *solvere* (fr. **se-lu-*), 'to loose, separate' (see **solve**); Goth. *laus*, 'empty', O.E. *lēas*, 'free from' (see **-less**). The base is **lŭ, *lēu-*, 'to cut, loosen'; n. suff. signifying 'a loosing, dissolving, solution' &c.: *electrolysis.*

lysol, n. [1. lísol; 2. láisɔl], fr. Gk. *lúsis*, 'loosening', fr. *lúein*, 'to loose', see prec. & **-ol.** (med.) A dark, oily liquid, soluble in water, obtained by mixing cresol with castor or linseed oil, and saponifying with caustic potash and alcohol; used as a powerful antiseptic and disinfectant.

-lytic, suff. Gk. *-lutikós*, 'loosing', fr. *lúein*, 'to loose'; adj. suff. corresponding to **-lysis**, wh. forms ns.: *analytic*; *paralytic.*

M

M, m [1. em; 2. ɛm], the thirteenth letter of the English alphabet; as Roman numeral = 1000, *mille*; for abbreviations see list at end of Dictionary.

-m, -ma, -me, n. suff. representing Gk. *-ma*, forming ns. denoting result of vbl. action: *poem, phantasm, diaphragm, theme, drama.* Adjs. fr. these ns. have *-mat-*, as in the stem of the Gk. ns.: *dramatic* &c.

ma, n. [1. mah; 2. mā]. Abbr. fr. **mamma.** (vulg.) Mother.

ma'am, n. [1. mam, mahm, mm; 2. mæm, mām, m(a)m]. Contracted fr. **madam.** Form of address, used esp. to royal ladies [mæm], or by servant to mistress &c.

macabre, adj. [1. makáhbr; 2. mækábr]. Fr.; O. Fr. *Macabré.* Origin much disputed; prob. for *Maccabé*, fr. *Maccabeus* (see **Maccabean**), a character in an old French morality play. Gruesome, terrible; *danse macabre*, dance of death.

macaco, n. [1. makáhkō; 2. məkákou]. Port., 'monkey'. Cp. **macaque.** A species of lemur, esp. the black lemur.

macadam, n. [1. makádam; 2. məkǽdəm], fr. name of John Loudon McAdam, inventor (d. 1836). Material for making surface of roads, consisting of hard stone broken small and rolled in with some binding material; (also attrib.) *macadam road* &c.

macadamization, n. [1. makàdamīzáshun; 2. məkædəmaizéiʃən]. See next word & **-ation.** Process of treating surface of roads by McAdam's method.

macadamize, vb. trans. [1. makádamīz; 2. məkǽdəmaiz]. **macadam** & **-ize.** To cover surface (of road) with macadam.

macaque, n. [1. makáhk; 2. məkák]. Fr., fr. Port. *macaco*, 'monkey'. See **macaco.** Etymol. unknown, prob. fr. a native S. Am. word. Any monkey belonging to the genus *Macacus*, with short tails; they belong to Asia and the Far East, except the Barbary ape of N. Africa.

macaroni, n. [1. màkaróni; 2. mækəróuni]. Ital. *maccaroni.* Etymol. unknown. **1.** Thin, tough paste made from wheat flour, formed into long tubes and dried; these are used as food when boiled. **2.** Young dandy of 18th cent., affecting continental manners and fashions.

macaronic, adj. & n. [1. màkarónik; 2. mækərónik]. Prec. & **-ic. 1.** adj. (of verse) Written in a burlesque style, with foreign, usually Latin, words, and modern words with Latin endings. **2.** n. (usually in pl.) **a** Macaronic verse; **b** mixture, medley, jumble.

macaroon, n. [1. màkaróōn; 2. mækərún], fr. Fr. *macaron*, fr. Ital. *maccaroni.* See **macaroni.** Small, flat, crisp, sweet cake made of ground almonds.

macartney, n. [1. makártni; 2. məkátni], fr. Lord Macartney (d. 1806). Kind of pheasant.

macassar, n. [1. makásar; 2. məkǽsə], fr. *Mangkasara*, island in Celebes group. Also *macassar oil*, kind of oil imported from the East, widely used formerly for dressing the hair.

macaw (I.), n. [1. makáw; 2. məkɔ́]. Port. *macao*, prob. fr. native S. Am. name. Genus of large, brightly coloured parrots, native to tropical America.

macaw (II.), n., fr. Carib. Kind of tropical American palm.

Maccabean, adj. [1. màkabéan; 2. mækəbíən], fr. Lat. *Maccabae-(us)*, fr. Gk. *Makkabaî-os*, fr. Hebrew. Of, belonging to, the Jewish family of the Maccabees, who resisted the oppression of their nation by the Greek kings of Syria, in the 2nd cent. B.C.

maccaboy, maccabaw, n. [1. mákaboi, -baw; 2. mǽkəbɔi, -bɔ], fr. Macouba, in Martinique. Kind of scented snuff.

mace (I.), n. [1. mās; 2. meis], fr. O. Fr. *mace*, fr. assumed Lat. **matea*; cp. Lat. dimin. *mateola*, 'tool for digging in the ground'; cogn. w. Scrt. *matyám*, 'implement'; O. Slav. *motyka*, 'hatchet'; O.H.G. *medela*, 'plough'; orig. 'edged tool'. **1.** (hist.) Weapon consisting of a heavy iron club with spiked head. **2.** Symbol of authority shaped like mace, borne before mayors, heads of universities &c., when acting in an official capacity; specif., *the Mace*, symbol of the Speaker's authority in the House of Commons, placed on the table when he is in the chair. **3.** Flat-headed stick used in bagatelle.

mace (II.), n., fr. Fr. *macis.* Etymol. unknown. Outer layer of nutmeg, dried and used as spice.

mace-bearer, n. Person carrying official mace in procession &c.

macédoine, n. [1. màsādwáhn; 2. mæseidwán]. Fr. A dish consisting of fruit or vegetables embedded in jelly.

macerate, vb. trans. & intrans. [1. máserāt; 2. mǽsəreit], fr. Lat. *mācerāt-(um)*, P.P. type of *mācerāre*, 'to soak in water; to weaken, reduce', orig. 'to knead in; to press'; cp. Gk. *mássein*, 'to knead', fr. **makj-*; Scrt. *mácatē*, 'he grinds'; also O.E. *mengan*, 'to mix'. See **mingle**; cp. **magma. 1.** trans. **a** To steep, soften by soaking; **b** (fig.) to mortify, torment: *to macerate the soul.* **2.** intrans. To become emaciated through fasting.

maceration, n. [1. màseráshun; 2. mæsəréiʃən]. Prec. & **-ion.** Act or process of macerating.

machete, n. [1. machátā; 2. matʃéitei]. Span. A large, heavy knife, used in S. America &c. as cutting implement and as a weapon.

-machia, suff. See **-machy.**

Machiavel(li), n. [1. màkiavél(i); 2. mækiəvél(i)], fr. Niccolo Machiavelli (d. 1527), of Florence, author of 'Il Principe', which advocates the principle that any political means, no matter how unscrupulous, are justifiable, which strengthen the central government of a State. Crafty, subtle person, who sacrifices moral scruples to the attainment of power, or furtherance of his ends.

Machiavellian, adj. [1. màkiavélian; 2. mækiəvéliən]. Prec. & **-ian.** Following, based on the principles of, Machiavelli; subtle and unscrupulous in attaining ends.

Machiavellism, n. [1. màkiavélizm; 2. mækiəvélizəm]. **Machiavel** & **-ism.** Principles and methods advocated by Machiavelli.

machicolate, vb. trans. [1. machíkolāt; 2. mætʃíkəleit], fr. Med. Lat. *machicolāt-(um)*, P.P. type of *machi-colāre*; the origin of first element is doubtful; for the second see **coulisse** & **portcullis.** To provide with machicolations.

machicolation, n. [1. màchikoláshun; 2. mætʃikəléiʃən]. Prec. & **-ion.** Opening in the floor of a projecting gallery or parapet, at the top of a wall or tower, made between the corbels which support the parapet; the purpose of machicolations is to enable the garrison of a fortified place to hurl missiles, or pour boiling liquid, upon the attackers.

machicoulis, n. [1. màhshikóōli; 2. maʃikúli]. Fr. *mâchicoulis.* See prec. Machicolation.

machinate, vb. intrans. [1. mákināt; 2. mǽkineit], fr. Lat. *māchināt-(um)*, P.P. type of *māchinārī*, 'to invent, devise'; fr. *māchin-(a)*, 'machine; device'. See **machine.** To plot, scheme, intrigue, contrive.

machination, n. [1. màkináshun; 2. mækinéiʃən]. Prec. & **-ion.** Act, process, of machinating; plot, intrigue, subtle contrivance.

machinator, n. [1. mákinātŏr; 2. mǽkineitə]. See prec. & **-or.** Plotter, schemer.

machine (I.), n. [1. mashén; 2. məʃín]. Fr., fr. Lat. *māchina*, 'machine; military engine; device, trick', fr. Gk. *mēkhanḗ*, 'means, expedient; machine, engine', fr. *mêkh-(os)*, 'contrivance'; cogn. w. Goth. *magan*, 'to be able'; O.E. *mæg*, 'I can', see **may** (I.); O.E. *meaht*, 'power', see **might**; O.E. *mægen*, 'strength', see **main (I.).** See also **mechanic. 1. a** Apparatus consisting of several parts, some of which move in specific manner and direction, and each of which is adapted for a special function, designed to produce a desired effect; device for transmitting and modifying power so as to direct motion and perform a certain kind of work; a machine is the intermediary between the motive power and those parts which actually carry out the movements necessary to the required work: *sewing, mowing, reaping, machine*; **b** (more gen.) a material contrivance designed for any purpose; Phr. *the god from the machine* (fr. Lat. *deus ex machina*), from use in ancient Greek tragedy of a god appearing suddenly to solve a plot &c., hence any sudden intervention to solve a difficulty. **2.** (of persons) One who acts like a machine, performing certain functions as it were automatically, without the exercise of reason or emotion: *to become a mere machine.* **3.** An organized system under definite control for carrying out specific functions, together with the persons engaged in the work, and the prescribed methods according to which they act: *the machine of government*; *the social machine*; *the political, party, machine.*

machine (II.), vb. trans., fr. prec. **a** To apply a machine to, so as to effect its purpose; to shape, form, by use of a machine or machinery: *to machine cloth, steel* &c.; **b** to print by a printing machine &c.

machine-gun, n. Quick-firing small-arm gun with mechanism for loading and firing, operated by the recoil on discharge, or by the explosion of the gas.

machine-made, adj. Made by machinery; contrasted with *hand-made.*

machinery, n. [1. mashéneri; 2. məʃínəri]. **machine** & **-ery. 1.** Machines collectively. **2. a** The moving parts of a machine; the various devices contained in it by means of which the work is accomplished; mechanism; **b** organized methods by which a political or other system is carried on. **3.** Series of mechanical or supernatural devices, used for development of the plot or dénouement in a drama, poem &c.

machine-tool, n. A cutting, shaping, turning tool worked not by hand but by machinery.

machinist, n. [1. mashénist; 2. məʃínist]. **machine** & **-ist. 1. a** Person who makes machines; **b** one skilled in control of machinery. **2.** One who works a machine, specif., sewing-machine.

-machy, -machia, suff. meaning 'battle, war', fr. Gk. *mákhē*, 'battle'; the base is seen also in *mákhomai*, 'I fight'; the etymol. is disputed, but the word is prob. connected w. Goth. *mēkeis*, O.E. (poet.) *mēce*, O.S. *māki*, 'sword', although the *-k-* of the Gmc. words offers difficulties.

macintosh, mackintosh, n. [1. mákintosh; 2. mǽkintɔʃ], fr. name of inventor, Charles Macintosh (d. 1843). **1.** Cotton or other fabric made waterproof by treating with a solution of rubber, or with lining of a layer of rubber. **2.** Garment made of such material; a waterproof coat.

mackerel, n. [1. mákerel; 2. mǽk(ə)rəl], fr. O. Fr. *makerel*, Mod. Fr. *maquereau.* Etymol. unknown. Edible fish, genus *Scomber*, of the Atlantic and the coasts of Europe, having a silvery belly, and a greenish grey back with dark bluish stripes.

mackerel-breeze, -gale, n. Strong breeze, as favourable to mackerel-fishing.

mackerel-sky, n. One streaked like the back of a mackerel.

mackle, n. [1. mákl; 2. mǽkl]. Variant of

macle, fr. Lat. *macula*, 'spot'. **a** A printer's term for a blurred impression; **b** a spot of deeper colour on a lighter background.

mackled, adj. [1. mákld; 2. mǽkld]. Prec. & **-ed.** Of the edges of books, spotted with irregular-shaped blotches of deeper colour than the ground.

macle, n. [1. mákl; 2. mǽkl]. Fr., fr. Lat. *macula*, 'spot'; origin doubtful. A twinned crystal.

Maconochie, n. [1. makónoki; 2. məkɔ́nəki], fr. maker's name. A tinned stew of meat and vegetables, issued as army rations during the Great War.

macramé, n. [1. makráhmi; 2. məkrā́mi]. Perh. fr. Turk. *maqrama*, 'towel'. Fringe or other ornamental work of knotted thread.

macro-, pref. representing Gk. *makró-(s)*, 'long; large', orig. of things long in proportion to their thickness; cogn. w. Lat. *macer*, 'thin'; O.N. *magr*; O.E. *mæger*, 'thin'. See **meagre.** Long, large; *macrocephalous*, having a long or large head; *macropod*, long-footed or long-legged animal; *macroscopic*, visible to the naked eye.

macrocosm, n. [1. mákrōkozm; 2. mǽkroukɔzəm]. See prec. & **cosmos.** The great world, the universe, contrasted with *microcosm*.

macron, n. [1. mákron; 2. mǽkrɔn]. Gk. *makrón*, neut. form of *makrós*, 'long'. See prec. Short horizontal line placed over vowel (*ā*) to show that the sound is long.

macrurous, adj. [1. makrṓorus; 2. mækrúərəs]. Formed fr. Neo-Lat. *macrura*, fr. **macro-** & Gk. *ourá*, 'tail', see **-ure** & **-ous.** (zool.) Having a long tail; specif., belonging to the division Macrura of crustaceans which includes the lobsters, crayfish, prawns, shrimps &c.

macula, n. [1. mákūla; 2. mǽkjulə]. Lat. *macula*, 'spot, mark'. Etymol. doubtful. Dark spot **a** on surface of sun or moon; **b** flaw, fault, in minerals; **c** spot, blemish, permanent mark, on surface of skin.

macular, adj. [1. mákūlar; 2. mǽkjulə]. See prec. & **-ar.** Of, pertaining to, of the nature of, bearing, spot(s) or stain(s).

maculation, n. [1. màkūláshun; 2. mækjuléiʃən], fr. Lat. *maculāt-(um)*, P.P. type of *maculāre*, 'to make spotted', see **macula,** & **-ion.** **a** State of being spotted; **b** spot, stain, blemish.

mad (I.), adj. [1. mad; 2. mæd]. O.E. *(ġe)mǣded*, P.P. of *(ġe)mǣdan*, 'to drive mad'; M.E. *mad(de)*; cp. O.S. *gimēd*, O.H.G. *gameit*, 'foolish'; Goth. *gamaiþs*, 'weak, crippled', *maidjan*, 'to change, alter; to spoil, mar'. Cogn. w. Lat. *mūtāre*, fr. **moit-*, 'to change' &c. See **mutate**; see also **mis-.** **1. a** Out of one's mind, insane, disordered in intellect; Phr. *to go mad*, become mad; *to drive one mad*, madden; *to work, run &c. like mad*, furiously, with very great energy; **b** beside oneself, temporarily out of one's senses; highly wrought up: *mad with pain, rage, drink* &c. **2.** (of dog &c.) Affected with rabies. **3.** Proceeding from a disordered mind: *mad ravings, laughter* &c. **4.** Having an uncontrollable desire, excited by strong passion; vehemently eager, infatuated: *to be mad for, after, about, on, something.* **5.** (of person or conduct) Foolish, rash, irrational; extravagant, wild: *a mad enterprise.* **6.** Annoyed, angry, furious. **7.** Extravagantly gay, wildly hilarious.

mad (II.), vb. trans. & intrans., fr. prec. (rare) **1.** trans. To cause to become mad, madden. **2.** intrans. To be mad, act madly, be distracted, esp. in Pres. Part. as in Phr. '*the madding crowd*' (Gray's 'Elegy').

madam, n. [1. mádam; 2. mǽdəm]. Fr. *ma dame*, 'my lady'. See **dame.** Polite, formal, mode of addressing women, in speaking, and in beginning letters (to strangers); formerly used before surname, instead of Mrs., in speaking to, and of, women of superior birth or position.

madame, n. [1. madáhm; 2. mædā́m]. Semi-French spelling and pronunciation used in speaking to, and of, and in writing to French ladies; also prefixed to surnames, and used before titles: *Madame Dubois, Madame la Baronne* &c.

madcap, n. [1. mádkap; 2. mǽdkæp]. Rash, high-spirited, impulsive girl.

madden, vb. trans. & intrans. [1. mádn; 2. mǽdn]. **mad** (I.) & **-en.** **1.** trans. **a** To drive mad, distract, make demented; **b** to irritate, infuriate. **2.** (rare) intrans. To become mad.

maddening, adj. [1. mádening; 2. mǽdn-iŋ]. Prec. & **-ing.** **a** Tending to excite powerfully, tending to render distracted; **b** tending to infuriate.

maddeningly, adv. Prec. & **-ly.** In a maddening manner.

madder (I.), n. [1. máder; 2. mǽdə]. O.E. *mædere*; M.E. *mader*; cp. Swed. *madra*; cogn. w. Scrt. *madhura-*, 'sweet, tender', also *madhurā*, plant-name. See further under **mead** (I.). **1.** Yellow-flowered plant, *Rubia*, whose roots yield a red dye. **2. a** Dye obtained from madder; **b** artificial colouring matter as substitute for natural madder; alizarin.

madder (II.), adj. Compar. of **mad.**

mad-doctor, n. One skilled in treatment of the insane; alienist.

made, adj. [1. mād; 2. meid]. P.P. of **make**; O.E. *macod*, M.E. *maked, made.* Special uses, **a** *made dish*, food prepared from several ingredients, often of meat recooked, contrasted with a plain joint; **b** (of person, figure &c.) *well, slightly made* &c., formed, built; **c** *a made man*, one who has attained success.

Madeira, n. [1. madḗra; 2. mədíərə]. Port. Name of island in the Atlantic; fr. Lat. *māteria*, 'timber', see **material.** **1.** A tawny-coloured wine from Madeira. **2.** *Madeira cake*, rich, sweet cake without fruit.

Madelenian. See **Magdalenian.**

mademoiselle, n. [1. màdmezél; 2. mædməzél]. Fr. See **damsel.** Title used in speaking to or of unmarried French women; applied also, in England, to unmarried women of foreign nationalities other than French.

madhouse, n. [1. mád-hous; 2. mǽdhaus]. Lunatic asylum.

madly, adv. [1. mádli; 2. mǽdli]. **mad** (I.) & **-ly.** In a mad manner, as though one were mad; wildly, furiously.

madman, -woman, n. [1. mádman, -wòoman; 2. mǽdmən, -wumən]. One who is mad, a lunatic. Phr. *to behave, talk, like a madman*, wildly, excitedly, irresponsibly.

madness, n. [1. mádnes; 2. mǽdnis]. **mad** & **-ness.** **1.** State of being mad; insanity; intense temporary excitement, perturbation of mind. **2.** Mad action, conduct, proceeding.

Madonna, n. [1. madóna; 2. mədɔ́nə]. Ital. *ma-*, fr. *mia*, 'my', & *donna*, 'lady', fr. Lat. *domina*, 'lady', q.v. under **dame.** **a** The Virgin Mary; **b** picture, statue &c. of the B.V.M.

Madonna lily, n. The white lily, as often depicted in paintings of the Annunciation.

madrasah, medresseh, n. [1. madrása; 2. mədrǽsə]. Arab. *madrasa*, fr. *daras*, 'to read'. Moslem college.

madrepore, n. [1. màdrepṓr; 2. mædrəpɔ́], fr. Ital. *madrepora*, fr. *madre*, 'mother', fr. its rapid rate of production, fr. Lat. *māter* (see **mater**), & *porus*, 'pore' (see **pore** (I.)); or Gk. *pôros*, 'soft, friable stone', etymol. doubtful. **a** Any of several kinds of perforated coral; **b** animal producing this.

madreporic, adj. [1. madrepórik; 2. mædrəpɔ́rik]. Prec. & **-ic.** Of, composed of, of the nature of, madrepore.

madreporiform, adj. [1. màdrepóriform; 2. mædrəpɔ́rifɔ̄m]. See prec. & **-form.** Like madrepore.

madrigal, n. [1. mádrigl; 2. mǽdrigl], fr. Ital. *madrigale*; etymol. doubtful. **a** Short love lyric; **b** music in several parts, for such a song, sung without accompaniment.

madrigalian, n. [1. màdrigálian; 2. mædrigéiliən]. Prec. & **-ian.** Of, of the character of, a madrigal.

madrigalist, n. [1. mádrigalist; 2. mǽdrigəlist]. See prec. & **-ist.** Composer, singer, of madrigals.

Maecenas, n. [1. mēsḗnas; 2. misínæs]. Name of patron of Horace and Virgil. Patron of art or literature.

maelstrom, n. [1. málstrom; 2. méilstrəm], fr. Maelström, a whirlpool in Lofoden Islands, off west coast of Norway; cp. Dan. *male*, 'to grind', cogn. w. **meal**, 'flour' &c., & *strōm*, see **stream.** **a** A whirlpool; specif., *the Maelstrom*, the whirlpool mentioned above; **b** (fig.) turbulent, violent condition of mind, circumstances &c.: *maelstrom of passion, war* &c.

maenad, n. [1. mḗnad; 2. mínæd], fr. Lat. *maenad-(em)*, fr. Gk. *mainád-*, stem of *mainás*, 'raving', as n., 'a mad woman; bacchante', fr. *máinomai*, 'I rave, rage', fr. **man-jō-*. See **mania.** Nymph attendant upon Dionysus; a bacchante.

maestoso, adv. [1. màh-estṓzō; 2. mɑ̄estóuzou]. Ital., fr. Lat. *mājest-(as)*, 'majesty'. See **majesty** & **-ose.** (musical direction) With dignity; majestically.

maestro, n. [1. mah-éstrō; 2. mɑ̄éstrou]. Ital. *maestro*, 'master; maestro', fr. Lat. *magist-(er)*, 'master'. See **master.** Eminent musical composer, conductor, or teacher.

maffick, vb. intrans. [1. máfik; 2. mǽfik]. Back-formation fr. Mafeking, town in S. Africa, held by the British and besieged for many months by the Boers; its relief in 1900 was celebrated uproariously throughout England. To indulge in uproarious and riotous rejoicing.

mafia, n. [1. máhfia; 2. mɑ́fiə]. Sicilian *maffia*; etymol. doubtful. Organized hostility to law and order in Sicily; those taking part in such lawless hostility; esp. *the Mafia*, the secret organization of this hostility.

magazine, n. [1. magazḗn; 2. mægəzín], fr. Fr. *magasin*, fr. Arab. *makhaçia*, 'storerooms', fr. *khazana*, 'to store up'. **1.** (mil.) **a** Building &c. for storing ammunition, food, equipment &c.; **b** storehouse or store-room for explosives; **c** the chamber holding cartridges in a 'magazine rifle'. **2.** Periodical publication containing articles on various subjects by different writers.

magazine rifle, n. Rifle automatically reloaded from cartridge chamber attached to it.

magdalen(e), n. [1. mágdalēn; 2. mǽgdəlin], fr. Mary Magdalene (Luke viii. 2, identified w. the sinner of Luke vii. 37); Magdalen College, Oxford, & Magdalene College, Cambridge, are pronounced [1. máwdlin; 2. mɔ̄́dlin]. Reformed prostitute.

Magdalenian, Madelenian, adj. [1. ma(g)dalḗnian; 2. mæ(g)dəlíniən], fr. Fr. *ma(g)dalenien*, fr. La Madeleine, Vézère, France (see prec.), where discoveries were first made. Denoting a period and culture of the latest palaeolithic age, following the Solutrian.

mage, n. [1. māj; 2. meidž], fr. Lat. *magus*, 'learned man, magician'. See **magus.** (archaic) Magician.

magenta, n. [1. majénta; 2. mədžéntə]. Named after battle of Magenta (N. Italy) in 1859, in which year the dye was discovered. **a** Deep, purplish red aniline dye; **b** colour derived from this.

maggot, n. [1. mágot; 2. mǽgət]. M.E. *magot*, prob. a modification of M.E. *maddok*, 'flesh-worm', cp. Early M.E. *maðek*, fr. O.N. *maðkr*, see **mawkish.** **1.** Larva, esp. of a house-fly or blow-fly, also of cheese-mite, feeding on animal substance. **2.** (fig.) Whim, fad, crotchet.

maggoty, adj. [1. mágoti; 2. mǽgəti]. Prec. & **-y.** Full of maggots.

Maghzen, n. [1. máhgzen; 2. mɑ́gzen], fr. Arab. *makhzan*. Cp. Arab. *makhaçia*, see **magazine.** The executive, administrative Council of Morocco.

Magi, n. [1. mắjī; 2. méidžai], pl. of **magus.** Magicians; specif., *the Magi*, the 'wise men' who visited the infant Saviour (Matt. ii.); the word is used in the Vulgate.

Magian, adj. & n. [1. mắjian; 2. méidžiən]. Prec. & **-an.** **1.** adj. Of the Magi. **2.** n. **a** One of the Magi; **b** magician, magus.

Magianism, n. [1. mắjianizm; 2. méidžiənizəm]. Prec. & **-ism.** Doctrines, philosophy, of the Persian Magi.

magic (I.), n. [1. májik; 2. mǽdžik]. M.E. *magike*, fr. Lat. *magicē* or (*ars*) *magica*, fr. Gk. (*tékhnē*) *magikḗ*, 'magic art'. See next word. **1.** Feigned superhuman mastery over natural forces and objects, and control of events; sorcery, witchcraft, enchantment; *black magic*, performed by the aid of wicked spirits; *white magic*, performed with help from beneficent spirits. Phr. *to act like magic*, in a mysterious but effectual manner. **2.** Unexplained influence, or method, which produces remarkable and apparently mysterious results; applied to modern conjuring &c. **3.** (fig.) Mysterious charm, unanalysable witchery, produced upon the senses and emotions by certain kinds of beauty in external objects, or works of art: *the magic of the woodlands in spring, of Turner's pictures, of great poetry* &c.

magic (II.), adj., fr. Fr. *magique*, fr. Lat. *magic-(us)*, fr. Gk. *magik-(ós)*, 'magical', fr. *mág-(os)*, 'magician'. See **magus & -ic.** Not used predicatively. **1.** Of, pertaining to, produced by, used in, magic; producing the effects of magic: *magic arts, words*; *magic lantern*, instrument for projecting magnified and illuminated pictures on to a white screen; *magic square*, a square divided into smaller squares with numbers so arranged that the totals of the horizontal, vertical, and diagonal rows are the same; *magic wand*, small staff, supposed to have mysterious powers, used by magicians and conjurers. **2.** Working in a mysterious manner; **a** exerting an influence, producing results, which seem to resemble those produced by occult means: *the magic skill of the modern surgeon*; **b** mysteriously impressive, beautiful: *the magic influence of the past.*

magical, adj. [1. májikl; 2. mǽdžikl]. Prec. & **-al.** Same as prec., but can be used predicatively as well as attributively: *the effect of the treatment upon the patient was magical.*

magically, adv. Prec. & **-ly.** In a magical manner; by or as if by magic.

magician, n. [1. majíshan; 2. mədžíʃən], fr. Fr. *magicien*, **magic & -ian.** Worker of, one skilled in, magic; wizard, enchanter, sorcerer; a conjurer.

magisterial, adj. [1. màjistḗrial; 2. mæ̀džistíəriəl], fr. Med. Lat. *magisteriāl-(is)*, fr. L. Lat. *magister-(ius)*, 'pertaining to a master', fr. Lat. *magister*, 'a master', see **master**, & **-ial.** **1.** Of, pertaining to, a master. **2.** Of, pertaining to, conducted by, a magistrate: *magisterial rank* &c. **3.** **a** (of persons) Impartial, judicial; **b** (of words, opinions &c.) weighty, of moment, authoritative.

magisterially, adv. Prec. & **-ly.** In a magisterial manner.

magistracy, n. [1. májistrasi; 2. mǽdžistrəsi]. See **magistrate & -cy.** **1.** Office or rank of magistrate; magistrate's tenure of office. **2.** Magistrates collectively.

magistral, adj. [1. majístral; 2. mədžístrəl], fr. Lat. *magistrāl-(is)*, 'of a master', fr. *magistr-(i)*, genit. of *magister*, 'master', see **master, & -al.** **1.** Of, pertaining to, a master. **2.** (med., of remedies) Specially devised, prescribed, by individual practitioner, to meet requirements of particular case; opposed to *officinal*, or *official.*

magistrate, n. [1. májistrit, -āt; 2. mǽdžistrit, -eit], fr. Lat. *magistrāt-(us)*, 'office of magistrate; high civil official, magistrate', fr. *magistr-*, stem of *magister*, 'master', see **master, & -ate.** **1.** Person wielding public judicial authority; a judge. **2.** Specif. in England, person, usually unpaid, appointed to try minor offences and small civil cases; one holding the Commission of the Peace, Justice of the Peace; such a person is addressed as *your Worship* in court; *Police Magistrate*, paid judicial officer sitting in a Police Court, also *Stipendiary Magistrate.*

magistrateship, n. [1. májistritship; 2. mǽdžistritʃip]. Prec. & **-ship.** Office, rank, term of office, of magistrate.

magistrature, n. [1. májistrachur; 2. mǽdžistrətʃə]. **magistrate & -ure.** Magistracy.

magma, n. [1. mágma; 2. mǽgmə]. Lat., fr. Gk. *mágma*, 'dough', cogn. w. *mássein*, 'to knead dough', fr. **mŋkʷ-jō*; cp. O. Slav. *męknati*, 'to soften'; Lith. *minkyti*, 'to knead'; O.E. *mengan*, 'to mix together'. See **mingle**, also **macerate.** **1.** Soft doughy, pasty mass of mineral or other matter. **2.** Molten rock supposed to lie beneath earth's crust.

Magna C(h)arta, n. [1. mágna chárta, kárta; 2. mǽgnə tʃátə, kátə]. Med. Lat., 'Great Charter.' See **magnum & chart.** Great charter obtained from King John in 1215; one of the charters upon which English personal and political liberty is based.

magnanimity, n. [1. màgnanímiti; 2. mæ̀gnənímiti], fr. Lat. *magnanimitāt-(em)*, 'greatness of soul', fr. *magnanim-(us)*, 'high-minded'. See next word & **-ity.** State or quality of being magnanimous.

magnanimous, adj. [1. magnánimus; 2. mægnǽniməs], fr. Lat. *magnanim-(us)*, 'high-minded, generous', fr. *magn-(us)*, 'great', see **magnum, & animus & -ous.** (of person, conduct &c.) Having, showing, greatness of soul; of generous, noble character; above all that is petty, mean, and base.

magnanimously, adv. Prec. & **-ly.** In a magnanimous manner.

magnate, n. [1. mágnat; 2. mǽgnit], fr. L. Lat. *magnāt-(em)*, *magnas*, 'magnate', fr. *magn-(us)*, 'great'. See **magnum.** Man of high position, wealth, authority, power &c.; often with reference to specified class, occupation &c.: *territorial, financial, magnates* &c.

magnesia, n. [1. magnḗshia; 2. mægníʃiə]. Med. Lat. *magnēsia*, fr. Gk. *magnēsía* (*líthos*), 'stone from Magnesia (in Thessaly), loadstone'. **a** Oxide of magnesium; **b** white alkaline powder obtained from magnesium carbonate and used in medicine as a mild aperient and antacid; *sulphate of magnesia*, Epsom salts.

magnesian, adj. [1. magnḗshan; 2. mægníʃən]. Prec. & **-an.** Of, containing, magnesia.

magnesium, n. [1. magnḗzium; 2. mægníziəm]. See **magnesia & -ium.** Silvery-white metallic element, producing a brilliant white light when burnt.

magnet, n. [1. mágnet; 2. mǽgnit], fr. Lat. *magnēt-*, stem of *magnēs*, 'loadstone', fr. Gk. *magnêtis* (*líthos*), 'stone from Magnesia, loadstone'. **1.** Piece of iron or steel which has the property of attracting steel; *natural magnet*, the loadstone or magnetic oxide of iron; *artificial magnet*, one given the property by contact with another magnet or by passing electric current through coil of copper wire wrapped round it. **2.** (fig.) Person or thing that possesses power of attraction.

magnetic, adj. [1. magnétik; 2. mægnétik]. Prec. & **-ic.** **1.** Having the properties of a magnet; capable of acting as a magnet, or of transmitting such properties to other substances: *magnetic field*, sphere of influence of a magnet; *magnetic needle*, piece of magnetized steel on a pivot, as in a compass, which always points to the north; *magnetic pole*, direction north or south to which the magnetic needle points, the difference between the true and the magnetic pole being the *magnetic declination* or *deviation*; *magnetic storm*, disturbance of terrestrial magnetism. **2.** (fig.) Exercising powerful attraction: *a magnetic personality*; mesmeric: *magnetic eyes.*

magnetically, adv. [1. magnétikali; 2. mægnétikəli]. **magnetic & -al & -ly.** In a magnetic manner; by magnetism; also (fig.) so as to attract.

magnetics, n. pl. [1. magnétiks; 2. mægnétiks], fr. **magnetic.** Science of magnetism.

magnetism, n. [1. mágnetizm; 2. mǽgnitizəm]. **magnet & -ism.** **1.** **a** Natural agency closely connected with electricity, and all the phenomena associated with it; **b** the science of these phenomena; *terrestrial magnetism*, magnetic properties of phenomena displayed by the earth; **c** *animal magnetism*, mesmerism. **2.** (fig.) Power of intellectual or moral attraction.

magnetist, n. [1. mágnetist; 2. mǽgnitist]. **magnet & -ist.** Student of magnetism.

magnetite, n. [1. mágnetīt; 2. mǽgnitait]. **magnet & -ite.** A black, brittle mineral, magnetic oxide of iron; loadstone.

magnetization, n. [1. màgnetīzáshun; 2. mæ̀gnitaizéiʃən]. See next word & **-ation.** Process of magnetizing; state of being magnetized.

magnetize, vb. trans. [1. mágnetīz; 2. mǽgnitaiz]. **magnet & -ize.** **1.** To turn into a magnet, by means of a loadstone, by passing electric current through &c. **2.** (fig.) To exercise powerful intellectual, moral, or emotional attraction upon. **3.** (obs.) To mesmerize.

magneto-, pref., fr. **magnet.** Magnetic; *magneto-electricity*, produced by magnetic action; *magnetograph*, device for recording magnetic variations; *magnetophone*, kind of microphone.

magneto, n. [1. magnḗtō; 2. mægnítou]. A magneto-electric machine; specif., magneto-dynamo used to generate electric ignition spark in internal-combustion engine, as of motor-car &c.

magnific(al), adj. [1. magnífik(l); 2. mægnífik(l)], fr. Fr. *magnifique*, fr. Lat. *magnificus*, 'distinguished, lofty, splendid', fr. *magn-(us)*, 'great', see **magnum, & -fic & -al.** (archaic) Splendid, noble, sublime.

Magnificat, n. [1. magnífikat; 2. mægnífikæt]. Lat. *magnificat* (first word of Latin version of hymn), 3rd sing. pres. of *magnificāre*, 'to magnify, praise highly'. See **magnify.** Hymn of B.V.M. beginning, '*My soul doth magnify the Lord*' (St. Luke i. 46-55), used as canticle at Evensong.

magnification, n. [1. màgnifikáshun; 2. mæ̀gnifikéiʃən]. See **magnify & -fication.** Act of magnifying; state of being magnified.

magnificence, n. [1. magnífisens; 2. mægnífisəns], fr. Lat. *magnificentia*, 'loftiness; splendour; munificence', fr. *magnific-(us)*, 'lofty, splendid', see **magnific, & -ence.** State or quality of being magnificent.

magnificent, adj. [1. magnífisent; 2. mægnífisənt], fr. Lat. *magnificent-(ior)*, compar. of *magnific-(us)*, 'lofty, splendid'. See **magnific.** **1.** Of surpassing beauty, splendour, size, quality, generosity &c.: *a magnificent chorus, building, robe, voice, host* &c. **2.** (colloq.) Excellent, splendid.

magnificently, adv. Prec. & **-ly.** In a magnificent manner.

magnifico, n. [1. magnífikō; 2. mægnífikou]. Ital., fr. Lat. *magnific-(us)*, 'splendid'. See **magnific.** Venetian nobleman; magnate, grandee.

magnifier, n. [1. mágnifīer; 2. mǽgnifaiə]. See next word & **-er.** Person who, thing, instrument, which, magnifies.

magnify, vb. trans. [1. mágnifī; 2. mǽgnifai]. M.E. *magnifien*, fr. O. Fr. *magnifier*, fr. Lat. *magnificāre*, 'to prize highly', fr. *magn-(us)*, 'great', see **magnum, & -fy.** **1.** (archaic) To praise, laud, extol: '*My soul doth magnify the Lord*'. **2.** (rare) To enlarge, increase, make greater. **3.** To cause to appear larger, increase apparent dimensions of, esp. by means of lens &c. **4.** (of non-material things) To exalt unduly, to attribute an excessive degree of importance to; to exaggerate: *to magnify losses, difficulties, one's office.*

magniloquence, n. [1. magnílokwens; 2. mægnílәkwәns], fr. Lat. *magniloquentia*, 'elevated language; boastful language', fr. *magnilo-qu-(us)*, 'pompous or boastful in talk', fr. *magn-(us)*, 'great' (see **magnum**), & *-loquus*, 'speaking', fr. *loqu-(or)*, 'I speak' (see **loquacious**), & **-ence**. **1.** State or quality of being magniloquent. **2.** Magniloquent speech or style.

magniloquent, adj. [1. magnílokwent; 2. mægnílәkwәnt], fr. Lat. *magniloqu-(us)*, 'pompous or boastful in talk', see prec., & **-ent.** Speaking in a pompous or grandiose style; bombastic, boastful.

magniloquently, adv. Prec. & **-ly.** In a magniloquent manner.

magnitude, n. [1. mágnitūd; 2. mǽgnitjūd], fr. Lat. *magnitūd-(o)*, 'greatness, size; high degree; importance', fr. *magn-(us)*, 'great', see **magnum**, & **-tude**. **1. a** State of being large; great size; **b** size generally; extent, dimensions. **2.** One of the classes to which the fixed stars are assigned according to degree of brilliancy; fig. Phr. *of the first magnitude*, of great importance.

magnolia, n. [1. magnṓlia; 2. mægnóuliә]. Named after Pierre Magnol, botanist (d. 1715). Genus of North American and Asiatic trees and shrubs with fine foliage and large showy flowers, often highly perfumed.

magnum, n. [1. mágnum; 2. mǽgnәm]. Lat. *magnum*, neut. form of *magnus*, 'great'; cogn. w. Gk. *mégas*, 'large'; Goth. *mikils*, O.E. *myčel*, 'large' (see **much**); Scrt. *mahánt-*, 'great'. **a** Bottle, vessel, holding two quarts of liquor, esp., but not exclusively, of champagne, port, or claret; **b** amount of liquor contained in such a bottle.

magnum bonum, n. [1. mágnum bṓnum; 2. mǽgnәm bóunәm]. Lat. neut. adjs., fr. *magnus*, 'large' (see **magnum**), & *bonus*, 'good' (see **bonus**). **a** Kind of large yellow plum; **b** a variety of potato.

magpie, n. [1. mágpī; 2. mǽgpai], fr. *Mag*, abbr. of *Margaret*, & **pie (I.)**; cp. Fr. *Margot*, in same sense. **1.** European bird, *Pica caudata*, of the crow family, with black and white plumage, long, tapering tail, harsh, chattering cry, and predatory habits. **2.** Idle, noisy chatterer. **3. a** Outermost ring but one of target; **b** shot striking this.

maguey, n. [1. mágwā; 2. mǽgwei]. Span., fr. Mexican word. The agave or century plant, also called American aloe, of Mexico and Central America.

magus, n. [1. mágus; 2. méigәs]. Lat. *magus*, fr. Gk. *mágos*, 'member of Persian priestly caste; magician'. Iranian loan-word. **1.** Priest of ancient Persia; (pl.) *the Magi*; see **Magi**. **2.** Magician, sorcerer.

Magyar, n. [1. mágyar; 2. mǽgjā]; Hungarian [1. módyor; 2. mɔ́djɔ̄r], native name. **1.** Member of the ruling race of Hungary, of Mongolian origin. **2.** Language of the Magyars; Hungarian.

Mahabharata, n. [1. màhhahbáhrata; 2. màhābā́rata]. Scrt.; for first element cp. next word. One of the ancient Hindu epics.

maharaja(h), n. [1. màhharáhja; 2. mā̀hәrā́dʒә]. Hind. *maha*, 'great', cogn. w. **magnum**, & **rajah**. **a** Title given to certain sovereign Indian princes of a higher degree than rajah; **b** prince having this title.

maharanee, n. [1. màhharáhnē; 2. mā̀hārā́nī]. See prec. & **ranee**. Wife of a maharajah; princess of this rank in her own right.

Mahatma, n. [1. ma-hátma; 2. mәhǽtmә], fr. Scrt. *mahatman*, fr. *maha*, 'great' (cp. prec.), & *atman*, 'soul'. Indian adept, believed to be possessed of special occult knowledge.

Mahdi, n. [1. máhdi; 2. mā́di], fr. Arab. *mahdiy*, 'one who is guided aright'. **1.** Mohammedan leader and prophet expected by Islam to appear before the end of the world. **2.** Name assumed at different times by various leaders of insurrection in the Sudan &c.

Mahdi(i)sm, n. [1. máhd(i)izm; 2. mā́d(i)izәm]. Prec. & **-ism**. Belief in the coming of a Mahdi.

mah-jongg, n. [1. mah jóng; 2. mā dʒɔ́ŋ]. Chinese. A game for four persons played with 144 small decorated domino-shaped bricks or 'tiles', introduced from China, where it has long been played.

mahlstick, n. See **maulstick**.

mahogany, n. [1. ma-hógani; 2. mәhɔ́gәni], fr. West Indian native name. **1. a** Wood of a tropical American tree, taking a fine polish, and much used for furniture; **b** tree producing this wood. **2.** Deep reddish brown, colour of mahogany. **3.** (fig.) Dining-table: *to put, stretch, one's legs under a man's mahogany*, enjoy his hospitality.

Mahometan. See **Mohammedan**.

Mahound, n. [1. ma-hŏŏnd; 2. mәhū́nd], fr. O. Fr. *Mahun*, abbr. of *Mahomet*. (archaic) Mohammed, the founder of Islam.

mahout, n. [1. ma-hóut; 2. mәháut], fr. Hind. *mahaut*. Indian elephant-keeper and driver.

mahseer, n. [1. máhsēr; 2. mā́siә]. Hind. A large game fish of the rivers of India, allied to the barbel.

maid, n. [1. mād; 2. meid]. Contracted form of **maiden**. **1.** Young girl. **2.** Unmarried woman; a virgin; a spinster; *old maid*, **a** elderly spinster; **b** round game of cards. **3.** Female indoor-servant: *to keep three maids*; (often in compounds) *parlour-maid, kitchen-maid, house-maid* &c.

maidan, n. [1. mīdáhn; 2. maidā́n]. Hind., Pers., & Arab. *maidān*. An open space in an Indian town, used as a market-place, promenade, for military parades &c.

maiden (I.), n. [1. mā́dn; 2. méidn]. O.E. *mæġden*, M.E. *meiden*; dimin. corresponding to O.E. *mæġ(e)ð*, 'virgin'; cp. Goth. *magaþs*, O.H.G. *magad*, Du. *maagd*; cp. further Goth. *magus*, O.E. *magu*, 'son, boy, servant'; perh. cogn. w. Avesta *magana-*, 'unmarried'. **1.** Girl, young unmarried woman, spinster. **2.** (hist.) Instrument like the guillotine, formerly used in Scotland for capital punishment.

maiden (II.), adj., fr. prec. (only attrib.) **1.** (of woman) Unmarried. **2.** Various special uses: **a** horse which has never won a race; *maiden race*, one for horses which have never won a prize; **b** *maiden speech*, one made in Parliament by member speaking for the first time; **c** *maiden assize*, one at which no cases are brought for trial; **d** *maiden battle*, first in which particular soldier takes part; **e** *maiden over*, (cricket) one in which no runs are made; **f** *maiden castle*, one that has never been captured by an enemy.

maidenhair, n. [1. mā́denhàr; 2. méidnhɛ̀ә]. Kind of fern, genus *Adiantum*, with small, delicate fronds on hair-like stalks.

maidenhead, n. [1. mā́dnhed; 2. méidnhɛd]. O.E. *mæġþhād*. **maiden & -head.** **a** (archaic) Virginity, maidenhood; **b** the hymen.

maidenhood, n. [1. mā́dnhòod; 2. méidnhùd]. **maiden & -hood.** State of being a maiden; spinsterhood.

maidenish, adj. [1. mā́dnish; 2. méidn-iʃ]. **maiden & -ish.** Of, like, a maiden.

maiden-like, adj. **maiden & -like.** Pertaining to, resembling, suitable to, becoming in, a maiden; modest, coy.

maidenliness, n. [1. mā́dnlines; 2. méidnlinis]. See next word & **-ness.** Quality of being maidenly.

maidenly, adj. [1. mā́dnli; 2. méidnli]. **maiden & -ly.** Maiden-like.

maiden-name, n. Woman's family name before marriage.

maidish, adj. [1. mā́dish; 2. méidiʃ]. **maid & -ish.** Of, like, a maid.

maid-of-all-work, n. [1. mā̀d uv áwl wërk; 2. mèid әv ɔ̄l wā̆k]. Servant doing general household duties.

maid-of-honour, n. [1. mā̀d uv ónor; 2. mèid әv ɔ́nә]. **1.** Unmarried lady attending on a queen or princess. **2.** Kind of almond cheesecake.

maidservant, n. [1. mā́dsërvant; 2. méidsāvәnt]. A female domestic servant.

maieutic, adj. [1. māū́tik; 2. meijū́tik], fr. Gk. *maieutik-(ós)*, 'obstetric', fr. *maieú-omai*, 'act as midwife', fr. *maîa*, 'mother: nurse', fr. *mâ*, 'mother'; cp. redupl. form *mámmē*, 'mother', q.v. under **mam(m)a (I.)**. (of method of Socrates) Serving to elicit people's ideas.

maihem. See **mayhem**.

mail (I.), n. [1. māl; 2. meil], fr. Fr. *maille*, fr. Lat. *macula*, 'spot, mark; mesh'. See **macula**. **1.** Armour composed of steel rings or links: *chain-mail, ring-mail, coat of mail.* **2.** Defensive armour in general.

mail (II.), vb. trans., fr. prec. To cover, protect, with, or as with, mail; fig. Phr. *the mailed fist*, physical force.

mail (III.), n., fr. O. Fr. *male*, 'bag', Mod. Fr. *malle*, 'trunk, bag', fr. O.H.G. *malha*, 'wallet'. **1. a** Bag for conveyance of letters &c. by post; **b** *mail, mails*, all letters &c. conveyed at one time (esp. of foreign letters): *the mail is late*; *the mails were lost.* **2.** System of conveying letters; means, vehicle, boat &c. whereby these are conveyed; the post: *His Majesty's Mail*; *air mail*, conveyed by aeroplane &c.

mail (IV.), vb. trans., fr. prec. (chiefly Am.) To send by post.

mail-bag, n. Bag for conveying letters; mail.

mail-cart, n. **a** Cart for carrying road-borne mail; **b** small light carriage for children, usually pushed by hand; kind of perambulator.

mail-clad, adj. **mail (I.) & clad.** Covered, protected, by, wearing, armour.

mail-coach, n. Formerly, a stage-coach carrying public mails and passengers; mail-cart.

mail order, adj. & n. (Am. usage) **a** adj. Pertaining to system of ordering and purchasing goods by post; **b** n., an order for goods to be sent by post.

mail train, n. Train conveying the mails, usually with a sorting-van attached.

maim, vb. trans. [1. mām; 2. meim]. M.E. *maime, maine*, fr. O. Fr. *mahaigner*, 'to cripple'; etymol. doubtful, cp. **mayhem.** To injure, cripple, lame, mutilate; render unfit for usage.

main (I.), n. [1. mān; 2. mein]. O.E. *mæġen*, 'strength, power'; M.E. *main*; cp. O.S., O.H.G. *megin*, O.N. *magn*; cogn. w. **may (I.)**, & **might (II.)**. **1.** Physical strength, might, force; only in Phr. *with might and main*, to the utmost of one's strength. **2.** Mainland, only in *Spanish Main*, **a** north coast of S. America from Panama to the Orinoco; hence, **b** Caribbean Sea, off this coast; **c** (poet.) the high sea. **3.** Principal part, only in Phr. *in the main*, for the most part, on the whole. **4.** Principal pipe or conduit conveying gas, water, sewage &c.: *water straight from the main*, as contrasted with that drawn from a pipe supplied from a cistern.

main (II.), adj., fr. O.N. *meginn*, 'strong', cogn. w. prec. **1.** (of physical force) Effective, fully exerted, vigorous: *by main force.* **2.** Forming the chief or largest part: *the main body (of troops* &c.). **3. a** Most important, principal, leading: *the main points of an argument*; *the main features of a dialect*; Phr. *to have an eye to the main chance*, look after one's own material interests; **b** *main drain*, that into which the sewage from a whole area of a town is conveyed; *main road*, high road running through principal places in an area; *main line*, railway line passing through important towns; principal line of a system.

main (III.), n. Etymol. doubtful; possibly extension of meaning fr. prec. **a** Any number from 5 to 9 called by the thrower in games of dice, such as hazard; **b** a match between two birds in cock-fighting.

main-brace, n. (naut.) Brace of main-yard. Phr. *to splice the main-brace*, (naut.) to serve out spirits; to drink; to get drunk.

main-deck, n. Principal, uppermost deck of a ship.

mainland, n. [1. mā́nland; 2. méinlәnd]. Principal or larger part of a country, continent &c. as distinct from neighbouring islands &c.

mainly, adv. [1. mănli; 2. méinli]. **main (II.)** & **-ly**. **a** Chiefly, to the greatest extent, in the main: *you are mainly responsible for our misfortunes*, you more than anyone else; **b** for the most part: *the audience consisted mainly of women*, the largest portion were women.

mainmast, n. [1. mănmahst; 2. méinmāst]. Principal mast of ship.

mainpernor, n. [1. mănpernor; 2. méinpānə]. A.-Fr. law term; first element as in next word; second element fr. Fr. *preneur*, fr. *prendre* (see **prize**). One who gives 'mainprize' for another's appearance.

mainprize, n. [1. mănprīz; 2. méinpraiz]. O. Fr., A.-Fr. law term, *main*, 'hand' (fr. Fr., fr. Lat., see **manual**), & *prise*, 'a taking, seizing' (see **prize**). (legal) Undertaking to be responsible for the appearance of a released prisoner in court on a day appointed.

mainsail, n. [1. mănsl; 2. méinsl]. Principal sail of ship, differing in shape according to ship's rig.

mainspring, n. [1. mănspring; 2. méinspriŋ]. **a** Chief spring of watch, through the gradual uncoiling of which the whole works are kept in motion; **b** principal source of, leading motive for, action.

mainstay, n. [1. mănstā; 2. méinstei]. **1.** Rope from top of mainmast to foot of foremast. 2. (fig.) Chief support.

maintain, vb. trans. [1. māntắn; 2. meintéin]. M.E. *maintene, menteine*, fr. O. Fr. *maintenir*, fr. Lat. *manu tenēre*, 'to hold in the hand'. See **manual** & **tenacious**. **1.** To keep up, continue in, retain: *to maintain a position, an attitude of defiance*; carry on: *to maintain a correspondence*. **2. a** To support, preserve, keep in certain condition or position: *food is necessary to maintain life*; *to maintain a large establishment*; **b** to keep up, keep in repair: *to maintain roads* &c. **3.** To support, provide for: *to maintain a wife and family*. **4.** To preserve, retain, keep: *to maintain an open mind, a smiling countenance*. **5.** To lend support to; defend, give assistance, or countenance, to: *to maintain a cause, an argument, point of view, opinion* &c. **6.** To assert, defend as an opinion, affirm, state to be true: *to maintain that the earth is flat*.

maintainable, adj. [1. māntắnabl; 2. meintéinəbl]. Prec. & **-able**. Capable of being maintained.

maintenance, n. [1. mắntenans; 2. méintinəns]. In O. Fr. See **maintain** & **-ance**. **1.** Act of maintaining or preserving; state of being maintained. **2.** Means of support; livelihood. **3.** (law) A common law offence, a lesser form of champerty, q.v., in which a person intermeddles in a suit which does not concern him by assisting, by money &c., in the prosecution or defence. **4.** (her.) *Cap of maintenance*, cap of scarlet velvet lined with ermine, borne by, or before, sovereign princes; also represented instead of a torse or crest wreath in some crests.

main-top, n. Platform at top of lower mainmast.

main-yard, n. Yard on which the mainsail is extended.

maize, n. [1. māz; 2. meiz], fr. Span. *maiz*, fr. Cuban. **a** Plant, *Zea mays*, grown in warm climates, producing an edible grain; **b** the seed of this plant; Indian corn.

maizena, n. [1. māzḗna; 2. meizínə], fr. prec. Corn-flour made from maize.

majestic, adj. [1. majéstik; 2. mədžéstik]. **majesty** & **-ic**. Having, expressing, majesty; stately, dignified, august.

majestically, adv. [1. majéstikali; 2. mədžéstikəli]. Prec. & **-al** & **-ly**. In a majestic manner.

majesty, n. [1. májesti; 2. mǽdžisti], fr. Fr. *majesté*, fr. Lat. *mājestāt-(em), mājestas*, 'dignity, grandeur; honour, excellence', fr. base seen in *mājor*, 'greater'. See **major (II.)**. **1.** Stateliness, dignity, elevation, sublimity. **2.** Sovereignty, royal power. **3.** Title given in addressing and referring to a sovereign: *Your, His, Her, Majesty*. **4.** Pictorial, symbolical, representation of the Deity enthroned.

majolica, **maiolica**, n. [1. majólika, mayólika; 2. mədžɔ́likə, məjɔ́likə]. Ital. *maiolica*, perh. fr. island of Majorca. **a** Kind of decorative, enamelled, Italian pottery; **b** pottery made in imitation of this.

major (I.), n. [1. mấjor; 2. méidžə]. Perh. a major, or senior captain. See next word. **a** Military officer between captain and lieutenant-colonel in rank, acting as second-in-command of a battalion, or commanding a company; **b** used as title immediately before surname.

major (II.), adj. Lat. *mājor*, 'greater', earlier **majjor*, fr. **mag-jōs*, used as compar. of, & fr. same base as, *mag-nus*, 'great', also in *magis*, 'more, rather'. See **magnum**. Greater or more important of two things, groups, portions &c.: *Major Prophets*; *major epilepsy*. Various special uses: *Jones &c. major*, the elder of two brothers at same school; *major part*, chief, larger, part; *major premise*, the first of a syllogism, containing a statement of the general rule; *major term*, the predicate of the conclusion of a syllogism; *major interval*, (in mus.) semitone greater than minor interval; *major scale*, having a major third; *major key*, represented by major scale.

major (III.), n., fr. prec. Person of full age; contrasted with *minor*.

major-domo, n. [1. mấjor dṓmō; 2. méidžə dóumou]. Low Lat. *majordomus*, Ital. *maggiordomo*. **a** Chief steward of a royal or princely household; **b** (facetiously) principal manservant, steward, butler, in a private household.

major-general, n. Army officer ranking next above a brigadier or colonel, and below a lieutenant-general; used as title immediately before the surname; major-generals are commonly addressed as *General*.

majority, n. [1. majóriti; 2. mədžɔ́riti], fr. Fr. *majorité*, fr. Med. Lat. *mājōritāt-(em)*, 'majority'. **major (II.)** & **-ity**. **1.** Greater number: *the majority of people*. Phr. *to join the majority*, die. **2. a** Greater or greatest number of votes: *to gain a majority*; *absolute majority*, in which number of votes gained exceeds half of total number of votes cast; **b** number of votes gained in excess of opponent or opposed party: *a large majority*; *a majority of 100* &c. **3.** Rank of major in army. **4.** Full age: *to attain one's majority*.

majorship, n. [1. mấjorship; 2. méidžəʃip]. **major (I.)** & **-ship**. Office or rank of major.

majuscular, adj. [1. majúskūlar; 2. mədžáskjulə]. See next word & **-ar**. Of, resembling, written in, majuscules.

majuscule, n. & adj. [1. májuskūl; 2. mǽdžəskjūl]. Lat. *mājuscula (litera)*, fr. *mājuscul-(us)*, 'somewhat greater', dimin. of *mājor*, 'greater'. See **major (II.)**. (palaeography) **1.** n. Large letters, capital or uncial; contrasted with *minuscule*. **2.** adj. Of, of the nature of, written in, majuscules.

make (I.), vb. trans. & intrans. [1. māk; 2. meik]. O.E. *macian*, M.E. *māken*; O.S. *makōn*, 'to make, build'; O.H.G. *mahhōn*, 'construct' &c. There appear to have been two Aryan bases, **mag-*, whence O.E. *macian* &c., & **mak[w]-*, both meaning 'to knead, press, work into shape, construct' &c. From the former we get Gk. *magís*, 'dough, paste', *mageús*, 'one who kneads'; O. Slav. *mazati*, 'to smear'; fr. **mak[w]-* come Lat. *mācerāre*, 'to soften by steeping' (see **macerate**), *māceria*, 'garden wall', orig. 'a mud bank' (cp. relation in meaning between Gk. *teîkhos*, 'wall', & Goth. *deigan*, 'to knead', *daigs*, 'dough' (see **dough**), & Lat. *fingere*, 'to frame, make' (see **figure**)); further Gk. *mássō*, 'I knead', fr. **mak-jō*; Scrt. *máčatē*, 'he grinds'; Lith. *minkyti*, 'to knead', & so on. The word expresses gen. construction, action, behaviour. **A.** trans. **1. a** To fashion, frame, construct, put together out of constituent parts or elements so as to produce a new object or material: *to make a machine*; *to make hurdles*; *to make bricks, bread, a cake, a coat* &c.; **b** to form, build up, cause to develop: *to make bone and sinew*; **c** to form, cause to develop intellectually and morally: *to make a person's character*; *to make oneself*, develop knowledge and character. Phr. *to make one's own life*, shape, direct, one's way of living, or the course of one's destiny. **2. a** To prepare, get ready for use, bring into a desired condition, treat in such a way as to render fit for its purpose: *to make tea, hay*; Phrs. *to make hay while the sun shines*, seize a favourable opportunity to obtain some advantage; *to make hay of (a room &c.)*, put into a state of confusion; *to make the cards*, shuffle them; **b** to arrange, put in order: *to make a bed*. Phr. *as you make your bed, so you must lie upon it*. **3. a** To create by an intellectual effort; to compose: *to make a poem, play*; *make a joke, a speech*; **b** to devise, think out, arrive at, by mental effort: *to make a scheme, a plan, an invention*; *to make one's will*. **4.** To produce, bring about, be the cause of, a certain condition of affairs: *to make a mess, a fuss, a terrible to-do*. **5. a** To earn, gain, win, acquire: *to make money, a profit*; *to make one's, a, living*; Phr. *to make a good thing of*, to derive a profit or benefit from; **b** (in non-material sense) *to make friends, enemies*; *make an ally*. **6. a** To carry out, perform, a specific action: *to make war*; **b** to execute a specific physical movement: *to make a bow, curtsey, a gesture*. **7.** To cause to become, to produce specified effect; to put into specified condition: *too much wine makes men drunk*; *to make one sick, ill, happy, comfortable* &c. **8. a** To constitute, be an element in, be recognized as: *four members make a quorum*; *cold tea makes an excellent drink in summer*; **b** to amount to, result in, add up to such a sum: *twenty shillings make a pound*; *two and two make four*; Phr. *one swallow does not make a summer*; **c** to prove, turn out, to be, develop into, be shown to be: *he will make an excellent husband*; *to make a bad headmaster*. **9. a** To force, compel, to do something, coerce into doing something (followed by vb. without *to*): *I'll make him do it whether he wants to or not*; *I can't make you come if you refuse to*; **b** to induce, persuade, force conviction upon; in Phrs. *it makes me think you are right*; *I can make him believe anything I choose*. **10. a** To cause to happen, be the means of producing; to bring about: *to make the grass grow, the fire burn, the kettle boil*; **b** to cause, get, procure, a certain physical or mental process to take place; cause a person to do something: *to make a man hear, understand, laugh, sit up* &c. **11.** To reach, arrive at, be able to reach: *the ship will never make port in such a storm*. **12.** To reckon, calculate, compute at; arrive at an opinion concerning by calculation: *how large do you make the congregation?*; *what time do you make it?*; *I make the score fifty for both sides*. **13.** To represent as being or doing, appearing: *this portrait makes him too old*; *the author makes the villain cut his own throat*. **14.** To appoint, constitute; put (a person) into a specified rank or position: *to make a man king, a judge, a peer, a general* &c. **15.** *Make* is used with a large number of nouns in such a way that the pair are equivalent to the verb connected with the noun or implied by this: *to make (an) answer, reply* &c.; *make a pause*; *make haste*, hasten; *make a denial*, to deny; *make a journey*, to journey, travel; *make progress*, to progress; *make a start*, to start; *make a mistake, blunder*, to be wrong, commit an error. **16.** To behave in a certain way indicated by the sentence: *to make an ass, fool, beast, of oneself*, behave like an ass &c. **17.** In a large number of idiomatic phrases *make* has such a very general meaning that it is impossible to classify and define it apart from the context; a few only can be given here, as many occur elsewhere, under other words: *to* *make a face,* to grimace, distort the features; *to make eyes (at),* to glance at significantly, esp. in a coquettish manner; to ogle; *make mischief,* cause ill-feeling, anger, quarrels; *make good,* **a** restore, make reparation for (damage); **b** vindicate one's character, approve oneself; *make headway,* progress; *make love (to),* to court, behave as a lover to; *make it one's business,* regard it as one's duty, proper occupation, as incumbent upon one; *make place, way,* give room; *make fun of,* to mock, deride; to chaff; *make the best of,* **a** use to greatest advantage; **b** speak as favourably of as possible; **c** not to complain of; *make sure,* **a** to ascertain beyond doubt; **b** to render secure against failure; **c** to feel convinced; *make a good dinner, meal,* eat heartily; *make water,* **a** (of a ship) to leak; **b** (of persons) to urinate; *make ready,* to prepare; *make fast,* to tie, fasten; *make bold to,* be so bold as to, take the liberty of. **B.** intrans. **1. a** To start, begin, to do something: *he made to reply when I stopped him;* **b** to behave as though about to do something: *he made as though to strike me; he made as if he would escape.* **2. a** To mature, get into condition of ripeness; esp. *the hay ought to make well in this drying breeze;* **b** (of the tide) to flow, rise: *the tide is making fast.* **3.** To point, tend, go to show: *all the evidence makes in the same direction.* **C.** Followed by adverb or preposition. *Make away with,* intrans., to destroy, remove, cause to disappear; steal; kill. *Make after,* intrans., to pursue. *Make for,* intrans., **1.** to tend towards, contribute to: *to make for righteousness;* **2.** to direct one's course towards, approach: *to make for home, the open sea* &c.; **3.** to rush violently at, attack, go for: *the bull made for him. Make off,* intrans., to go, run away, depart, escape. *Make out,* trans., **1. a** to see, discern, decipher, manage to see or read: *to make out a dim figure through the mist; to make out an inscription;* **b** to understand, contrive to grasp import of: *to make out the meaning of;* **2.** to represent that, convey suggestion that: *to make out that one is badly treated. Make over,* trans., to give, hand over, entrust: *he made over most of his property to his son. Make up,* trans., **1.** to invent, compose: *to make up a story, account;* (in unfavourable sense) to invent an untruth with intent to deceive; **2.** to compose a quarrel, dispute: *to make up one's differences;* Phr. *to make it up (with),* become reconciled, become friends again after falling out; **3.** to apply cosmetics &c. to (person, face, &c.), for purpose of disguise, on stage &c.; **4.** (print.) to prepare and arrange material for (page, column &c.). *Make up to,* intrans., **1.** compensate, indemnify: *I want to make up to you for what you have suffered;* **2.** to flatter, try to gain favour of: *to make up to important people.*

make (II.), n., fr. prec. **a** (i.) Way in which something is made; style, shape, mode of structure; composition, texture: *a new make of motor; a coat of first-class make;* (ii.) (fig.) *a man of quite another make,* different character &c.; **b** process, act, of making: *our own make,* made by us (tradesman's phrase). Phr. *on the make,* (of persons) bent on, striving for, gain, success &c.

make-believe, n. Pretence, feigning.

makepeace, n. [1. mákpēs; 2. méikpīs]. Peacemaker.

maker, n. [1. máker; 2. méikə]. **make** & **-er.** **1.** One who, that which, makes; a manufacturer: specif., *our, his* &c. *Maker,* the Creator, God. **2.** (obs. or liter.) A poet.

makeshift, n. [1. mákshift; 2. méikʃift]. Device, contrivance, used as temporary substitute or expedient.

make-up, n. **a** Facial and other disguise used by actors &c.; materials used to effect this; **b** (fig.) pose; **c** (print.) action of making up; material so arranged.

makeweight, n. [1. mákwāt; 2. méikweit]. **1.** Small quantity added to make up required weight. **2.** (fig.) Single person or thing, unimportant argument &c. to supply deficiency.

making, n. [1. máking; 2. méikiŋ]. **make** & **-ing.** **1.** The act or process of forming, constructing; process or course of development: *mankind in the making;* specif. in Phr. *to be the making of,* cause to develop satisfactorily, ensure success of. **2.** (pl.) Gains, profit, earnings. **3.** (pl.) **a** Elements out of which a specified thing can be made: *the makings of a good garden;* **b** necessary qualities, essential characteristics: *the makings of a fine character, of a good soldier.*

mal-, pref. representing Fr. *mal-,* fr. Lat. *male,* 'badly', fr. adj. *mal-(us),* 'bad', perh. orig. 'mean, base', & cogn. w. O. Slav. *malŭ,* 'small'; Goth. *smals,* O.E. *smæl,* 'little' (see **small**); Gk. *mēlon,* 'small cattle'. The pref. forms ns., adjs., & vbs. w. the sense of **a** bad, badly: *malnutrition, malformed, maltreat;* **b** not, un-: *malapert, malcontent.*

Malacca, n. [1. maláka; 2. məlǽkə]. Name of district in Malaya. Also *Malacca cane,* walking-stick made from stem of kind of bamboo.

malachite, n. [1. málakīt; 2. mǽləkait], fr. Gk. *malákh-(ē),* 'mallow'; perh. cogn. w. Lat. *malva,* 'mallow'. See **malvaceous.** Green mineral composed chiefly of carbonate of copper, which takes a high polish; used for ornaments, vases, tops of tables &c.

malaco-, pref. representing Gk. *malakó-(s),* 'soft', cogn. w. Lat. *molere,* 'to grind', *mollis,* 'soft' (see **mollify**). See also **meal (I.).** E.g. *malacoderm,* soft-skinned animal, esp. sea-anemone; *malacology,* study of molluscs &c.

maladjustment, n. [1. màlajústment; 2. mæ̀lədʒʌ́stmənt]. **mal-** & **adjustment.** Wrong adjustment.

maladministration, n. [1. màladministráshun; 2. mæ̀lədministréiʃən]. **mal-** & **administration.** Faulty administration; bad management of public affairs.

maladroit, adj. [1. màladróit; 2. mæ̀lədrɔ́it], fr. Fr., fr. **mal-** & **adroit.** **a** Clumsy, unskilful; **b** tactless.

maladroitly, adv. Prec. & **-ly.** In a maladroit manner; clumsily; tactlessly.

maladroitness, n. See prec. & **-ness.** Quality of being maladroit.

malady, n. [1. máladi; 2. mǽlədi], fr. Fr. *maladie,* fr. *malade,* 'sick', fr. L. Lat. *male habitus,* 'ill'. Cp. **mal-** & **habit.** Sickness, disease, ailment.

mala fide, adv. & adj. [1. mála fídi; 2. méilə fáidi]. Lat. *malā fidē,* 'in bad faith'. See **mal-** & **fidelity.** **1.** adv. In bad faith. **2.** adj. Done, acting, in bad faith.

Malaga, n. [1. málaga; 2. mǽləgə]. Name of port in south of Spain. White wine exported from Malaga.

Malagasy, adj. & n. [1. màlagázi; 2. mæ̀ləgǽzi]. **1.** adj. Of Madagascar. **2.** n. **a** Language of Madagascar; **b** native of Madagascar.

malaise, n. [1. màláz; 2. mæ̀léiz]. Fr., 'discomfort'. See **mal-** & **ease.** Slight physical discomfort.

malapert, adj. & n. [1. málapërt; 2. mǽləpʌ̄t]. O. Fr., fr. **mal-** & *appert,* variant of *espert,* 'experienced, skilful, deft'. See **expert.** **1.** adj. Forward, impudent, saucy. **2.** n. Impudent person.

malapropian, adj. [1. màlapróp̆ian, -própian; 2. mæ̀ləpróupiən, mæ̀ləprɔ́piən], fr. *Mrs. Malaprop,* a character in Sheridan's *The Rivals,* fr. **malapropos** & **-ian.** Of the nature of a malapropism.

malapropism, n. [1. málapropìzm; 2. mǽləprɔpìzəm], fr. Mrs. Malaprop. See prec. Ridiculous misuse of a word, esp. through confusion with one resembling it; e.g. *derangement of epitaphs,* for arrangement of epithets.

malapropos, adv., adj. & n. [1. màlapropó; 2. mæ̀læprəpóu], fr. Fr. *mal à propos.* See **mal-** & **apropos.** **1.** adv. Inopportunely, unseasonably, inappropriately. **2.** adj. (chiefly predic.). Out of place, untimely, inopportune. **3.** n. Thing done or said inopportunely.

malar, adj. & n. [1. málar; 2. méilə], fr. Lat. *māl-(a),* 'jaw-bone, cheek', prob. fr. **mandslā-,* cogn. w. *mand-(ere),* 'to chew'. See **mandible** & **-ar.** **1.** adj. Of, pertaining to the cheek. **2.** n. Cheek-bone.

malaria, n. [1. malária; 2. məléəriə], fr. Ital. *mal' aria,* 'bad air'. See **mal-** & **aria** & **air.** **1.** Intermittent fever produced by bite of a germ-bearing mosquito, genus *Anopheles.* **2.** Poisonous air arising in marshy districts; noxious exhalations, miasma; formerly considered the cause of the fever.

malarial, adj. [1. malárial; 2. məléəriəl]. Prec. & **-al.** Of, pertaining to, of the nature of, malaria.

malarian, adj. [1. malárian; 2. məléəriən]. **malaria** & **-an.** Malarial.

malarious, adj. [1. malárius; 2. məléəriəs]. **malaria** & **-ous.** Malarial.

Malay, adj. & n. [1. malá; 2. məléi], fr. native *malayu.* **1.** adj. Of race inhabiting Malaya and Eastern Archipelago. **2.** n. **a** Member of this race; **b** Malay language.

Malayalam, n. [1. màlááhlam; 2. mæ̀leiάləm]. Native. A Dravidian language of Malabar, S. West Coast of India.

Malayan, adj. [1. maláan; 2. məléiən]. **Malay** & **-an.** Of, pertaining to, Malay race, language, or archipelago.

malcontent, adj. & n. [1. málkontent; 2. mǽlkəntɛnt]. O. Fr., fr. **mal-** & **content (II.)** **1.** adj. Discontented, dissatisfied; rebellious. **2.** n. **a** Discontented person; one inclined to rebel against authority; **b** state of discontent.

male (I.), adj. [1. māl; 2. meil], fr. O. Fr. *masle,* Mod. Fr. *mâle,* fr. Lat. *masculus,* 'male', dimin. of *mās,* 'male'. See **masculine.** **1. a** Belonging to, connected with, that sex, or with individuals of it, in human beings, the lower animals, and plants, which procreates, begets, offspring by fructifying the female: *a male animal;* **b** suitable to, characteristic of, a male; virile, masculine: *male vigour, voices* &c.; **c** composed, consisting of, males: *male choir.* **2.** Various terms and expressions: **a** *male fern,* European fern used internally as a remedy against worms: **b** *male screw,* one that fits into a hollow shaped to receive it.

male (II.), n., fr. prec. Male person, animal, or plant; generally used specifically in contrast to *female.*

male-, pref. representing Lat. *male,* 'evil, ill', adv. See **mal-.**

malediction, n. [1. màledíkshun; 2. mæ̀lidíkʃən], fr. Lat. *maledictiōn-(em),* 'reviling'. See **male-** & **diction.** Curse, reviling, imprecation.

maledictory, adj. [1. màledíktori; 2. mæ̀lidíktəri], fr. Lat. *maledict-(um),* P.P. type of *maledīcere,* 'to abuse', fr. **male-,** & *dīcere,* 'to say', see **diction,** & **-ory.** Of the nature of, expressing, a malediction.

malefaction, n. [1. màlefákshun; 2. mæ̀lifǽkʃən], fr. Lat. *malefact-(um),* P.P. type of *malefacere,* 'to injure', fr. **male-,** & *facere,* 'to do', see **fact,** & **-ion.** Crime, evil deed, wrongdoing.

malefactor, n. [1. málefaktor; 2. mǽlifæktə]. Lat. *malefactor,* 'evil-doer'; **male-** & **factor.** Criminal, evil-doer.

malefic, adj. [1. maléfik; 2. məléfik], fr. Lat. *malefic-(us),* 'malicious'; **male-** & **-fic.** Doing harm; mischievous, hurtful (esp. of sorcery &c.).

maleficence, n. [1. maléfisens; 2. məléfisəns]. Prec. & **-ence.** Quality of being maleficent; harmfulness, mischief.

maleficent, adj. [1. maléfisent; 2. məléfisənt]. **malefic** & **-ent.** **a** Harmful, hurtful, malicious; **b** criminal, evil.

malevolence, n. [1. malévolens; 2. məlévələns], fr. Lat. *malevolentia,* 'ill-will', fr. *malevol-(entem).* See next word & **-ence.** Malice, ill-will, hatred; quality of being malevolent.

malevolent, adj. [1. malévolent; 2. məlévələnt], fr. Lat. *malevolent-(em)*, 'malevolent', fr. **male-** & Pres. Part. of *velle*, 'to wish'. See **volition.** Wishing evil to others; ill-disposed, malicious, vindictive.

malevolently, adv. Prec. & **-ly.** In a malevolent manner.

malfeasance, n. [1. màlfézans; 2. mælfízəns], fr. O. Fr. *malfaisance*, fr. *malfais-(ant)*, 'doing evil'. See next word & **-ance.** (law) Wrongdoing, illegal act, esp. in connexion with official business; cp. *misfeasance.*

malfeasant, adj. & n. [1. màlfézant; 2. mælfízənt], fr. O. Fr. *malfaisant*, 'doing evil', fr. **mal-** & Pres. Part. of *faire*, 'to do', fr. Lat. *facere*, 'to do'. See **faction. 1.** adj. Criminal, illegal; doing, involving, evil. **2.** n. Wrongdoer.

malformation, n. [1. màlformáshun; 2. mælfōméiʃən]. **mal- & formation.** Wrong formation; defect, deformity.

malformed, adj. [1. màlfórmd; 2. mælfɔ̄md]. **mal- & form & -ed.** Badly formed, distorted, having a structural defect.

malic, adj. [1. málik; 2. méilik], fr. Fr. *malique*, fr. Lat. *māl-(um)*, 'apple', fr. Gk. *mêl-(on)*, Doric *mâlon*, 'apple'; etymol. unknown. *Malic acid*, obtained from juice of apple and other fruits.

malice, n. [1. mális; 2. mælis], fr. Fr., fr. Lat. *malitia*, 'wickedness, malice', fr. *mal-(us)*, 'bad'. See **mal- & -ice. 1.** Desire to harm others; vindictiveness, ill-will, spite; Phr. *to bear malice*, have malicious feelings, have a spite against, be resentful. **2.** (law) State of mind evinced by commission of an illegal act, or by intention to commit ono; *(with) malice aforethought, malice prepense*, implying wicked intention, and an act deliberately planned beforehand.

malicious, adj. [1. malíshus; 2. məlíʃəs]. See prec. & **-ous. a** (of persons) Ill-disposed towards others; spiteful, harbouring ill-will; **b** (of thoughts and actions) inspired by, evincing, malice.

maliciously, adv. Prec. & **-ly.** In a malicious manner; with malice.

malign (I.), adj. [1. malín; 2. məláin], fr. O. Fr. *maligne*, fr. Lat. *malign-(us)*, 'ill-disposed', fr. **mal-** & base **g̑no-, *g̑eno-*, 'to be born, to be of a specific nature'. See **genus. a** Chiefly *malign influence*, baleful, injurious, sinister; **b** (of persons) malevolent, malicious; reverse of *benign.*

malign (II.), vb. trans., fr. O. Fr. *malignier*, fr. Lat. *malignāre*, 'to act maliciously', fr. *malign-(us)*, 'malicious'. See prec. **a** To speak evil of, maliciously of; to defame, traduce; **b** to attribute lower degree of merit to than is deserved.

malignancy, n. [1. malígnansi; 2. məlígnənsi]. **malignant & -cy.** State or quality of being malignant.

malignant (I.), adj. [1. malígnant; 2. məlígnənt], fr. L. Lat. *malign-(āre)*, 'to act maliciously'. See **malign & -ant. 1.** Evilly disposed, willing to do harm, desiring evil rather than good; filled with hatred. **2.** (of disease) Likely to prove fatal; virulent; contrasted with *benignant*: *malignant growth, tumour*, cancer.

malignant (II.), n., fr. prec. Name given by Parliamentary party to supporter of Charles I. in Civil War.

malignantly, adv. **malignant (I.) & -ly.** In a malignant manner.

malignity, n. [1. malígniti; 2. məlígniti], fr. Fr., fr. Lat. *malignitāt-(em)*, 'malice'; **malign & -ity. 1.** Ill-nature, spite, malice, intense ill-will. **2.** (of disease) Quality of being malignant.

malignly, adv. **malign (I.) & -ly.** In a malign manner.

malinger, vb. intrans. [1. malíngger; 2. məlíŋgə], fr. Fr. *malingre*, 'ailing'; etymol. doubtful. (esp. of soldier or sailor) To feign illness in order to escape duty.

malingerer, n. [1. malínggerer; 2. məlíŋgərə]. Prec. & **-er.** One who malingers; a shirker.

malism, n. [1. málizm; 2. méilizəm], fr. Lat. *mal-(us)*, 'bad'. See **mal- & -ism.** Doctrine that evil predominates over good in the world.

malison, n. [1. málizn, málisn; 2. mælizn, mælisn], fr. O. Fr. *maleison*, 'curse', fr. Lat. *maledictiōn-(em)*, 'abuse'. See **malediction**; cp. **benison & benediction.** (archaic) Curse.

mall, n. [1. mal, mawl; 2. mæl, mɔ̄l]. Variant of **maul (I.)**, mallet used in game of pall-mall. **1.** Level, sheltered walk, esp. as public promenade; specif., *the Mall* (now usually [mæl]), broad shady street in St. James's Park, London, originally an alley for the game of pall-mall, q.v. **2.** (hist.) **a** Game of pall-mall; **b** mallet used in this.

mallard, n. [1. málard; 2. mæləd], fr. O. Fr. *mallart*; etymol. doubtful. The common wild duck, *Anas boschus*; the drake has a bright green head and neck with white collar.

malleability, n. [1. màleabíliti; 2. mæliəbíliti]. **malleable & -ity.** State or quality of being malleable.

malleable, adj. [1. máleabl; 2. mæliəbl], fr. Lat. *malle-(āre)*, 'to hammer', fr. *malle-(us)*, 'a hammer'. See **malleus & -able. 1.** (of metal &c.) Capable of being hammered, beaten, or pressed to a different form. **2.** (of character &c.) Pliable, docile, amenable.

mallee, n. [1. málē; 2. mælī]. Native Australian name. A scrubby, dwarf species of eucalyptus, growing in the dry plains of Australia.

mallemuck, n. [1. málemuk; 2. mælimak], fr. Du. *mallemoke*; possibly corrupt. of an Eskimo word meaning 'follower'. Sailor's name for the fulmar or petrel.

malleolar, adj. [1. maléolar; 2. mælfələ]. See next word & **-ar.** Pertaining to, connected with, a malleolus or the malleoli of the ankle.

malleolus, n. [1. máleolus; 2. mæliələs]. Lat. dimin. of *malleus*, 'hammer', see **malleus.** (anat.) One of the two round projecting bones on each side of the ankle.

mallet, n. [1. málet; 2. mælit], fr. Fr. *maillet*, dimin. of *mail*, 'hammer'. See **maul (I.) & malleus. a** Hammer with heavy wooden head used for driving a chisel &c.; **b** type of this with a long handle used for driving heavy wooden balls in croquet; **c** similar lighter stick used in polo.

malleus, n. [1. máleus; 2. mæliəs]. Lat. *malleus*, 'hammer'; possibly fr. **madlei-os*, fr. base **mad-*, 'to strike, hew'; cp. O.H.G. *(stein)mezzo*, 'mason'. Small bone of middle ear, transmitting vibrations of tympanum.

mallow, n. [1. málō; 2. mælou]. O.E. *mealu, mealwe*, M.E. *mal(o)we*; fr. Lat. *malva*, 'mallow', perh. cogn. w. Gk. *malákhē*, 'mallow', cp. **malachite & malvaceous.** One of several species of plant, of genus *Malva* or family *Malvaceae*, with hairy stems, broad, downy leaves, and large pinkish-purple flowers, esp. the common wild mallow, *Malva sylvestris.*

malm, n. [1. mahm; 2. mām]. O.E. *m(e)alm*, 'sand'; cp. O.N. *malmr*, Dan. *malm*; O.H.G. *melm*, 'dust'; Lat. *molere*, 'to grind'; O.E. *melu*, 'meal'. See **meal (I.).** Soft chalky loam.

malmaison, n. [1. malmázon; 2. mælméizɔ̄]. Name of palace of Empress Josephine. **a** Kind of carnation; **b** kind of blush rose.

malmsey, n. [1. máhmzi; 2. mámzi], fr. Med. Lat. *malmasia*, fr. Gk. *Monembasia*, in the Morea, cp. O. Fr. *malvoisie*, fr. Ital. form of the name, *Napoli di Malvasia.* Sweet white wine, made formerly in Greece, now also in Spain and Canary Islands.

malnutrition, n. [1. màlnūtríshun; 2. mælnjūtríʃən]. **mal- & nutrition.** Inadequate, defective nutrition.

malodorous, adj. [1. màlódorus; 2. mælóudərəs]. **mal- & odorous.** Ill-smelling.

Malpighian, adj. [1. malpígian; 2. mælpígiən], fr. Malpighi, Italian anatomist, d. 1694. (anat. and zool.) Pertaining to certain glands and other bodies discovered by Malpighi, esp. the *Malpighian bodies, capsules*, in the kidney; *Malpighian tubes*, supposed urinary organs in insects &c.

malpractice, n. [1. màlpráktis; 2. mælpræktis]. **mal- & practice. 1.** Wrongdoing, irregularity. **2.** (law) **a** Improper, unskilful treatment of patient by medical attendant; **b** improper, dishonest use of an official position for purpose of enriching oneself.

malt (I.), n. [1. mawlt; 2. mɔ̄lt]. O.E. *m(e)alt*, 'malt', M.E. *malt*; cp. Du. *mout*, O.H.G. *malz*, 'malt'; cogn. w. O.H.G. *malt*, 'soft'; cp. Lat. *mollis*, 'soft', fr. **moldwis*; Scrt. *mr̥diš*, 'soft, tender'; O. Slav. *mladu* for **moldu-*, 'young, tender'. See further under **melt, mould (II.), moulder (II.).** Barley or other grain steeped in water, allowed to sprout and then roasted in a kiln; used in brewing; *malt liquor*, made from fermented malt (e.g. beer), not by distillation; *extract of malt*, used as nourishing food for children &c.

malt (II.), vb. trans. & intrans., fr. prec. **1.** trans. To make (grain) into malt. **2.** intrans. (of grain) To come into a condition resembling malt.

Malta, n. [1. máwlta; 2. mɔ́ltə]. Island in Mediterranean. *Malta fever*, Mediterranean relapsing fever, at one time endemic in Malta, due to germ conveyed by goats' milk.

Maltese, adj. & n. [1. màwltéz; 2. mɔ̀ltíz]. Prec. & **-ese. 1.** adj. Of, pertaining to, Malta; *Maltese cat*, a blue-grey, short-haired variety; *Maltese dog*, kind of small spaniel; *Maltese cross*, with four equal limbs, with broad, indented ends, and narrowing towards the centre, the badge of the Knights of Malta, of the Order of St. John of Jerusalem. **2.** n. **a** Native of Malta; **b** Semitic language spoken by natives of Malta, much influenced by Italian.

maltha, n. [1. máltha; 2. mælþə]. Lat., fr. Gk. *máltha*, 'mixture of wax and pitch'; cp. Gk. *malthakós*, 'soft, tender, gentle'; cogn. w. Goth. *-milds*; O.N. *mildr*, 'gentle', see **mild.** Mixture of wax, pitch &c., used as cement.

malt-house, n. Building in which malt is made.

Malthusian, adj. & n. [1. malthúzian; 2. mælþjúziən], fr. name of Thomas Malthus, d. 1834; who advocated restriction of increase of population when this threatened to exceed means of support. **1.** adj. Connected with, pertaining to, the principles of Malthus. **2.** n. Follower of Malthus.

Malthusianism, n. [1. malthúzianizm; 2. mælþjúziənizəm]. Prec. & **-ism.** Doctrine of Malthus.

malting, n. [1. máwlting; 2. mɔ́ltiŋ]. **malt & -ing. 1.** Process of making malt. **2.** Establishment for making malt; malt-house.

maltose, n. [1. máwltōs; 2. mɔ́ltous]. **malt & -ose.** Sugar obtained by action of the ferments or enzymes in malt on starch.

maltreat, vb. trans. [1. màltrét; 2. mæltrít]. **mal- & treat.** To use roughly, unkindly; to ill-treat.

maltreatment, n. [1. maltrétment; 2. mæltrítmənt]. Prec. & **-ment.** Act of maltreating; state of being maltreated.

maltster, n. [1. máwl(t)ster; 2. mɔ́l(t)stə]. **malt & -ster.** One who makes malt.

maltworm, n. [1. máwltwērm; 2. mɔ́ltwə̄m]. (archaic) Heavy drinker, tippler.

malty, adj. [1. máwlti; 2. mɔ́lti]. **malt (I.) & -y.** Connected with, arising from, resembling, malt: *a malty taste, smell* &c.

malvaceous, adj. [1. malváshus; 2. malvéiʃəs], fr. L. Lat. *malvaceus*, fr. Lat. *malva*, 'mallow'. See **mallow & -aceous.** (bot.) Of, pertaining to, the family *Malvaceae*, which includes the mallows, the hibiscus &c.

malversation, n. [1. màlvērsáshun; 2. mælvə̄séiʃən]. Fr., fr. *malverser*, fr. **mal- & Lat.** *versāri*, 'to turn round, turn about; **to** behave, to take part in', fr. *vers-(um)*, P.P. type of *vertere*, 'to turn', see **version, & -ation.** Corrupt conduct in official position; maladministration, misuse, of public funds.

mamelon, n. [1. mámelon; 2. mǽmilən]. Fr. *mamelon*, 'nipple', fr. *mamelle*, 'breast', fr. Lat. *mamilla*, 'breast'. See **mamma (II.)**. Small rounded hillock.

mameluke, n. [1. mámelōōk; 2. mǽməl(j)ūk], fr. Arab. *mamluk*, 'slave'. **1.** (hist.) Member of military force, originally of Caucasian slaves, who made themselves masters of Egypt in 1254 till their massacre in 1811. **2.** A slave.

mamilla, n. [1. mamíla; 2. məmílə]. Lat. *mamilla*, 'breast', dimin. of *mamma*, 'breast'. See **mamma (II.)**. **1.** Nipple, forming termination of mammary gland. **2.** Nipple-shaped organ.

mamillary, adj. [1. mámilari; 2. mǽmiləri]. Prec. & **-ary**. Of, pertaining to, resembling, a mamilla.

mamillate(d), adj. [1. mámilāt(ed); 2. mǽmileit(id)]. See prec. & **-ate, -ed**. **a** Having a mamilla, or mamilliform projection; **b** (geol.) formed of small rounded crystals.

mamilliform, adj. [1. mamíliform; 2. mæmílifōm]. See **mamilla** & **-form**. Having the shape of a mamilla.

mam(m)a (I.), n. [1. mamáh; 2. məmá]. Cp. Lat. *mamma*; Gk. *mámmē*; Lith. *mãma*, 'mother'; also, without reduplication, Scrt. *mā*; Gk. *mâ*, 'mother'. Word prob. derived orig. fr. infants' babbling; at the basis of most Aryan words for 'mother'. Mother (used esp. by children, now obsolesc).

mamma (II.), n., pl. **mammae** [1. máma, mámē; 2. mǽmə, mǽmī]. Lat., prob. fr. **madmā*, fr. base seen in *mad-(ēre)*, 'to flow, to be wet'; cp. Gk. *madáein*, 'to flow', *mastós*, 'breast' (see **mastoid**); Scrt. *mádati*, 'is drunk'. **a** Milk-secreting organ of female mammal; mammary gland; **b** rudimentary mammary gland in males.

mammal, n. [1. máml; 2. mǽml], fr. next word. One of class Mammalia.

Mammalia, n. [1. mamália; 2. məméiliə]. Lat. *mammālia*, neut. pl. of L. Lat. *mammālis*, 'mammalian', fr. **mamma (II.)** & **-al**. Class of warm-blooded vertebrates, having milk-secreting organs for nourishing their young.

mammalian, adj. & n. [1. mamálian; 2. məméiliən]. **mammal** & **-ian**. **1.** adj. Of, pertaining to, a mammal. **2.** n. Mammal.

mammaliferous, adj. [1. màmaliferus; 2. mæ̀məlífərəs]. **mammal** & **-ferous**. (geol.) Containing mammalian remains.

mammalogist, n. [1. mamálojist; 2. mæmǽlədžist]. **mammal** & **-logist**. Student of mammalogy.

mammalogy, n. [1. mamáloji; 2. mæmǽlədži]. **mammal** & **-logy**. Study of mammals.

mammary, adj. [1. mámari; 2. mǽməri]. **mamma (II.)** & **-ary**. Pertaining to the breasts or mammae.

mammee, n. [1. mamḗ; 2. mæmí], fr. Span. *mamey*, fr. Haitian. **a** Tropical American and West Indian tree, producing a sweet fruit with yellow flesh; **b** this fruit.

mammiferous, adj. [1. mamíferus; 2. mæmífərəs]. **mamma (II.)** & **-ferous**. Having mammae.

mammiform, adj. [1. mámiform; 2. mǽmifōm]. **mamma (II.)** & **-form**. Having the shape of a mamma.

mammon, n. [1. mámun; 2. mǽmən], fr. L. Lat. *mammona*, fr. Gk. *mamōnâs*, fr. Aram. *mamon*, 'riches'; as proper name, that of the false god of cupidity, as in Milton's *Paradise Lost*. Personification of wealth, conceived of as an ignoble object of desire and pursuit.

mammonish, adj. [1. mámunish; 2. mǽmənıʃ]. Prec. & **-ish**. Of, pertaining to, Mammon; money-loving.

mammonism, n. [1. mámunizm; 2. mǽmənizəm]. **mammon** & **-ism**. Devotion to wealth.

mammonist, n. [1. mámunist; 2. mǽmənist]. **mammon** & **-ist**. Person devoted to the acquisition of wealth.

mammoth, n. [1. mámuth; 2. mǽməþ], fr. Russ. *mammot*, *mamant*; etymol. doubtful. **1.** n. Gigantic extinct species of elephant, with long hairy coat and curved tusks, whose fossil and frozen remains are preserved in Middle and Northern Europe, Northern Asia, and North America. **2.** (attrib.) Very large, enormous.

mammy, n. [1. mámi; 2. mǽmi]. Familiar form of **mamma (I.)**. **1.** (child's word) Mother. **2. a** (U.S.A.) Coloured nurse; **b** in many parts of Africa, an old negress.

man (I.), n. [1. man; 2. mæn]. O.E. *mann*, 'human being; male, man'; M.E. *man*; cp. Goth. *manna*; O. Fris. *man*, *mon*; O.H.G. *man*; O.N. *maðr*, fr. *mannr*; cogn. w. Scrt. *manuš*, 'human being'; O. Slav. *mąžĭ*, 'man'; perh. fr. orig. **ghmon-*, & cogn. w. Goth. *guma*, 'man', & Lat. *homo*. Cp. **homage, human, humus**. **1. a** Human being, as distinct from the lower animals and from angels or the Divine Being; **b** person, individual: *any man, no man, all men*; Phr. *to a man*, every individual; **c** (indefinite) one: *you don't give a man a chance*. **2.** Adult male human being, as distinct from *woman* or *boy*. Phrs. *man and boy*, from boyhood; *man in the moon*, legendary man whose features are traced on the moon's surface; *man of the world*, one with knowledge of life and mankind; *one's man of business*, (i.) agent; (ii.) solicitor; *man of letters*, writer and scholar; *to be one's own man*, be at liberty to do as one pleases; to be in possession of one's senses, energies &c.; *the man in the street*, the ordinary, average man, as distinct from experts; representative of general public opinion. **3.** Human race, mankind: '*Man never Is, but always To be blest*' (Pope, 'Essay on Man', i. 96). **4.** One having manly qualities, virility, courage &c.: *to be a man*; *to play the man*; *only half a man*. **5. a** Male attendant, manservant; **b** workman, employee. Phr. *like master, like man*. **6.** Husband: *man and wife*. **7.** (pl.) **a** Soldiers; **b** rank and file, contrasted with *officers*. **8.** (hist.) Vassal. **9.** Piece used in playing chess, draughts &c. **10.** In combination, **a** denoting occupation: *postman, dustman, clergyman* &c.; **b** ship: *merchantman, Indiaman* &c.

man (II.), vb. trans., fr. prec. **1.** To supply with men for defence, service &c.: *to man a fort, the walls*; *to man a ship*; *to man the pumps*. **2.** (fig.) To strengthen, encourage, fortify: *to man oneself*.

manacle, n. & vb. trans. [1. mánakl; 2. mǽnəkl], fr. O. Fr. *manicle*, 'handcuff', fr. Lat. *manicula*, dimin. of *man-(us)*, 'hand'. See **manual**. **1.** n. **a** Fetter, esp. for hand; handcuff; **b** (fig.) a restriction, impediment. **2.** vb. To confine with manacles; to fetter, handcuff.

manage (I.), vb. trans. & intrans. [1. mánij; 2. mǽnidž], fr. Ital. *maneggiare*, fr. Low Lat. *manidiāre*, fr. Lat. *man-(us)*, 'hand'. See **manual**. **A.** trans. **1.** To wield, guide, control, by the use of the hands; to handle: *to manage a boat, an oar*. **2. a** To control behaviour of, bring under one's influence: *to manage a spoilt child, a spirited horse* &c.; **b** to have one's way with, gain one's ends with: *to manage a person successfully*. **3.** To conduct, control; be at the head of, direct the working of: *to manage a business, a household, one's own affairs* &c. **4. a** To deal with, cope with (a thing, piece of work &c.): *I can't manage it alone*; **b** (of food &c.) to eat: *can you manage another bun?* **B.** intrans. **1.** To deal with affairs, to cope with a situation, piece of work &c.: *I'll manage with the tools I have*; *I shall manage somehow*. **2.** To contrive to, succeed in: *he managed to get home somehow*; (often ironical) *the housemaid managed to smash the best Crown Derby tea-pot*.

manage (II.), n. See prec. (archaic) Training, management, of a horse; now usually manège, q.v.

manageability, n. [1. mànijabíliti; 2. mæ̀nidžəbíliti]. See next word & **-ity**. State or quality of being manageable.

manageable, adj. [1. mánijabl; 2. mǽnidžəbl]. **manage** & **-able**. Capable of being managed.

manageableness, n. Prec. & **-ness**. State or quality of being manageable.

manageably, adv. See prec. & **-ly**. In a manageable manner.

management, n. [1. mánijment; 2. mǽnidžmənt]. **manage (I.)** & **-ment**. **1.** Act of managing; state of being managed: *the care and management of the insane*. **2.** Artful, ingenious, methods or treatment: *it took a good deal of management to get him to leave the house*. **3.** *The management*, body of persons managing a business.

manager, n. [1. mánijer; 2. mǽnidžə]. **manage (I.)** & **-er**. **1.** Person who manages, controls, directs a business, or other undertaking &c.: *general manager*, principal working official of a business, company &c. **2.** (usually qualified) *Good, bad, manager*, one who manages money, domestic affairs &c., successfully, unsuccessfully: *she is not much of a manager*. **3.** Specif. **a** person appointed by Court of Chancery to manage a business in the interests of the creditors; **b** one of committee of House of Lords or Commons, appointed to discuss and arrange business in which both Houses are concerned.

manageress, n. [1. mánijeres; 2. mǽnidž(ə)res]. Prec. & **-ess**. Woman manager.

managerial, adj. [1. mànijḗrial; 2. mæ̀nidžíəriəl]. **manager** & **-ial**. Of, pertaining to, a manager, or to management.

managership, n. [1. mánijership; 2. mǽnidžəʃip]. **manager** & **-ship**. Office of manager.

managing, adj. [1. mánijing; 2. mǽnidžiŋ]. **manage** & **-ing**. **1.** (in gen. sense of vb.) *Managing director*, director of a company with functions of a general manager. Specif. **2. a** Wishing to, inclined to, domineer over, and control, others; meddlesome, officious; **b** inclined to conduct money affairs with excessive care and economy; hence, niggardly.

manakin, n. [1. mánakin; 2. mǽnəkin], fr. Du. *manneken*, 'manikin'; also used of various small birds. See **manikin**. Name given to a group of brightly coloured small birds, the *Pipridae*, of Central and S. America.

man-at-arms, n. [1. màn at ármz; 2. mæ̀n ət ámz]. Soldier, esp. the mounted, fully armed soldier of mediaeval armies.

manatee, n. [1. mànatḗ; 2. mæ̀nətí], fr. Span. *manati*, fr. Carib. *manattoui*. Genus of aquatic, herbivorous mammals of America and West Africa, the sea-cow, allied to the dugong of East Indies.

Manchester, adj. [1. mánchester; 2. mǽntʃistə]. Town in Lancashire, centre of cotton-trade. Of, pertaining to, Manchester: *Manchester goods*, cotton textiles of every description; *Manchester School*, of economic and political theory and practice, the Free Trade, individualist, *laissez-faire* school of Mill and Cobden and the Liberal party.

Manchesterism, n. [1. mánchesterizm; 2. mǽntʃistərizəm]. Prec. & **-ism**. Principles of the *Manchester School* in economics and politics. See above.

manchet, n. [1. mánchet; 2. mǽntʃit]. M.E. *manchete*, fr. O. Fr. *manchette*; etymol. uncertain. (archaic) **a** Bread of the finest wheat flour; **b** a loaf of such bread.

man-child, n. Male child, boy.

manchineel, n. [1. mànchinḗl; 2. mæ̀ntʃiníl], fr. Fr. *mancenille*, fr. Span. *manzanilla*, dimin. of *manzana*, fr. Lat. *matiāna*, 'an apple', fr. name of Roman gens *Matia*. Tropical American tree with poisonous, yellowish-green fruit and blistering, milky sap.

manciple, n. [1. mánsipl; 2. mǽnsipl]. O. Fr., fr. Med. Lat. *mancipium*, 'office of buyer', fr. Lat. *mancip-(em)*, *manceps*, 'buyer', fr. *man-(us)*, 'hand', see **manual**, & *cap-(ere)*, 'to take', see **capable**. Official who buys provisions for a college &c.; a steward.

-mancy, suff. representing O. Fr. *-mancie*, fr. L. Lat., fr. Gk. *manteíā*, 'oracle; divination', fr. *mánti-s*, 'prophet, diviner'; cogn. w. Scrt. *múniš*, 'inspired'; Goth. *muns*, 'thought'; Lat. *mens*, 'mind'. See **mental**.

The suff. forms ns. w. the sense of 'divination by means of': *geomancy, necromancy* &c.

mandamus, n. [1. màndámus; 2. mændéiməs]. Lat., 'we command', 1st pers. pl. of pres. indic. of *mandāre*, 'to command; to entrust to, to commit to the charge of', fr. *man-(us)*, 'hand', see **manual**, & *dare*, 'to give', see **date (I.)**. **1.** Formerly, royal writ commanding performance of some service. **2.** Now, writ from High Court conveying an order to an inferior court.

mandarin (I.), n. [1. mándarin; 2. mændərin], fr. Port. *mandarim*, fr. Malay., fr. Hind. *mantri*, fr. Scrt. *mantrin*, 'counsellor'; cp. Scrt. *mantiš*, 'thought'; cogn. w. Lat. *mens*, 'mind', see **mental (I.)**; O.E. *(ge)mynd*, 'thought, memory', see **mind**. **1. a** European name for Chinese civil or military official; **b** that form of the Chinese language spoken by officials and educated persons and used in official documents &c. **2.** (by transf., ironically) Any high government official, or bureaucrat; one whose opinions, edicts &c. must never be questioned. **3.** Porcelain figure of Chinaman, with nodding head.

mandarin(e) (II.), n. Same as prec., fr. yellow robes of Chinese officials. **1. a** Small Chinese orange, also cultivated in N. Africa &c.; it is the origin of the *tangerine*; **b** liqueur made from this. **2.** Deep orange dye, resembling the orange in colour, obtained from coal-tar.

mandarin duck, n. A brightly plumaged duck of China and the Far East; the drake has a ruff of deep chestnut colour, and green, white and brown crest.

mandatary, n. [1. mándatari; 2. mændətəri]. See next word & **-ary** & cp. **mandatory**. Person, state, to whom or to which a mandate is given.

mandate (I.), n. [1. mándat, -āt; 2. mændit, -eit], fr. Lat. *mandātum*, 'commission, order', fr. P.P. of *mandāre*, 'to entrust to, to command'. See **mandamus**. **1. a** Authoritative command from a superior; **b** (by transf.) a general command, as by a body of electors, the members of a corporate body, as a trade union &c., ordering a representative to act in a certain way, without allowing him independence of judgement. **2. a** (Roman law) A form of contract by which a person undertakes to do something for another without reward, but with an indemnity against loss; **b** (Engl. law) a bailment of personal property without consideration; **c** (Canon law) a papal rescript. **3.** Specif., a commission given by the League of Nations to one of the States comprising it, to administer, as mandatary, certain of the colonies or portions of the dominions of the defeated enemy powers in the Great War for the benefit of the inhabitants.

mandate (II.), vb. trans. [1. mandát; 2. mændéit]. Back-formation fr. **mandated**. To entrust (state &c.) to a mandatary.

mandated, adj. [1. mandáted; 2. mændéitid]. **mandate (I.)** & **-ed**. Committed, entrusted to, under a mandate: *the mandated colonies of Germany.*

mandatory, adj. & n. [1. mándatori; 2. mændətəri]. See prec. & **-ory**. **1.** adj. Of, pertaining to, containing, expressing, a command. **2.** n. Mandatary.

mandible, n. [1. mándibl; 2. mændibl], fr. L. Lat. *mandibula*, 'jaw', fr. *mand-(ere)*, 'to chew'; cogn. w. Gk. *masâsthai*, 'to chew', *mástax*, 'mouth'; perh. also, more remotely, w. Goth. *munþs*, O.E. *mūð*, 'mouth'. See **mawkish, mouth**, & cp. **malar**. **1.** (of mammal or fish) Jaw, esp. lower jaw. **2.** (of birds) Upper or lower part of beak. **3.** (of insects) Either half of upper pair of jaws.

mandibular, adj. [1. mandíbūlar; 2. mændíbjulə], fr. Lat. *mandibul-(a)*, 'jaw'. See prec. & **-ar**. Of, pertaining to, a mandible.

mandibulate, adj. [1. mandíbūlāt; 2. mændíbjulət], fr. Lat. *mandibul-(a)*, 'jaw'. See **mandible** & **-ate**. Having a mandible.

mandola, mandora, n. [1. mándola, mándora; 2. mændələ, mændərə]. Ital. *mandola, mandora*, 'lute', variant of **pandora**. Large type of mandolin.

mandolin(e), n. [1. mándolin; 2. mændəlin], fr. Fr. *mandoline*, fr. Ital. *mandolino*, dimin. of prec. Musical stringed instrument of guitar type with fretted handle, deep melon-shaped body and metal strings, in four or six pairs, played with a plectrum.

mandragora, n. [1. màndrágora; 2. mændrǽgərə]. L. Lat. fr. Gk. *mandragórās*; etymol. unknown. See next word. Mandrake, esp. with reference to Shakespeare's use in *Othello* &c.

mandrake, n. [1. mándrāk; 2. mændreik]. M.E. *mandragge*, fr. prec.; mod. form shows association w. **man & drake (II.)** in sense of 'dragon, monster'. European herbaceous plant, narcotic and emetic, with a root formerly supposed to resemble the human form; said to shriek when pulled out of the ground.

mandrel, -il, n. [1. mándril; 2. mændril]. Earlier *manderil*; apparently corrupted form of Fr. *mandrin*; etymol. doubtful. **1.** Iron bar or lathe on which articles are fixed while being turned. **2.** Rod for shaping metal in forging &c.

mandrill, n. [1. mándril; 2. mændril]. Prob. fr. **man, & drill (VII.)**, wh. is of native origin. Kind of large, powerful, baboon, *Papio maimon*, of Western Africa, with highly coloured patches and callosities on face and hindquarters.

manducate, vb. trans. [1. mándūkāt; 2. mændjukeit], fr. L. Lat. *mandūcāre*, 'to chew', fr. *mand-(ere)*, 'to chew'. See **mandible** & **manger**. (rare) To chew, eat, devour.

manducation, n. [1. màndūkā́shun; 2. mændjukéiʃən]. Prec. & **-ion**. (rare) Act of chewing; state of being chewed.

manducatory, adj. [1. màndū́katori; 2. mændjū́kətəri]. **manducate** & **-ory**. (rare) Of, pertaining to, manducation.

mane, n. [1. mān; 2. mein]. O.E. *manu*; M.E. *māne*; cp. O.H.G. *mana*, O.N. *mōn*; also O.E. *mene*; O.N. *men*; O.H.G. *menni*, 'neck ornament'; cogn. w. Lat. *monīle*, 'necklace, collar; neck'. See **moniliform**. **a** Long hair on neck of horse &c., or lion; also **b** human hair when thick and long.

man-eater, n. **a** Cannibal; **b** animal, esp. tiger, which has tasted human flesh.

maned, adj. [1. mānd; 2. meind]. **mane** & **-ed**. Having a mane.

manège, n. [1. mánāzh, manā́zh; 2. mæneiž, mænéiž]. Fr., fr. Ital. *maneggio*, fr. *maneggiare*. See **manage (I.)**. **1.** Training, management, of a horse. **2.** Exercises used in training horse; action, movements, of trained horse. **3.** Riding-school.

maneless, adj. [1. mā́nles; 2. méinlis]. **mane** & **-less**. Without a mane.

manes, n. pl. [1. mā́nēz; 2. méinīz]. Lat. *mānēs*, 'ghosts, shades of the dead'. Origin doubtful. **a** Spirits of the dead; the shades of ancestors revered as gods and objects of reverence; **b** the gods of the underworld regarded as benevolent.

manful, adj. [1. mánfool; 2. mænful]. **man** & **-ful**. Bold, courageous, resolute.

manfully, adv. Prec. & **-ly**. In a manful manner; stoutly, boldly, vigorously.

manfulness, n. See prec. & **-ness**. Quality of being manful; manly courage and resolution.

mangabey, n. [1. mánggabā; 2. mæŋgəbei]. Name of district in Madagascar, though the genus is not found there. Genus, *Cercocebus*, of small, long-tailed, agile W. African monkeys.

manganese, n. [1. mànggané̄z; 2. mæŋgəníz], fr. Fr. *manganèse*, fr. **magnesia**. **1.** Brittle, greyish-white, metallic element. **2.** Oxide of manganese, a black mineral used in manufacture of glass, and as an alloy for steel &c.

manganesian, adj. [1. mànggané̄zian; 2. mæŋgəníziən]. Prec. & **-ian**. (rare) Manganic.

manganic, adj. [1. manggánik; 2. mæŋgǽnik]. See **manganese** & **-ic**. Pertaining to, containing, of the nature of, manganese.

mange, n. [1. mānj; 2. meindž]. M.E. *manjewe*, fr. O. Fr. *manjue*, 'itch', fr. *manjuer*, 'to eat', fr. L. Lat. *mandūcāre*, 'to chew'. See **manducate**. Eruptive skin disease, due to a parasitic mite which destroys the hairy coats of animals, esp. dogs.

mangel, mangold-, mangel-wurzel, n. [1. mánggl wĕrzl; 2. mæŋgl wǽzl], fr. Germ. *mangold wurzel*, fr. *mangold*, 'beet', M.H.G. *mangolt* (etymol. doubtful), & *wurzel*, 'root', q.v. under **wort**. The form *mangel-wurzel* ('root of scarcity') is due to popular etymology. Large variety of beet, cultivated as food for cattle.

manger, n. [1. mā́njer; 2. méindžə], fr. Fr. *mangeoire*, cp. *manger*, 'to eat', fr. Low Lat. **mandūcātōria*, 'feeding-trough'. See **manducate**. Raised trough in stable, cow-house &c., for horses or cattle to eat from. Phr. *dog in the manger*, see under **dog**.

mangily, adv. [1. mā́njili; 2. méindžili]. **mangy** & **-ly**. In a mangy manner.

manginess, n. [1. mā́njines; 2. méindžinis]. See prec. & **-ness**. State or quality of being mangy.

mangle (I.), n. & vb. trans. [1. mánggl; 2. mæŋgl], fr. Du. *mangel*, fr. Low Lat. *manganum*, 'instrument for throwing stones', fr. Gk. *mágganon*, 'engine for defending fortifications'. See **mangonel**. **1.** n. Machine with rollers for pressing linen &c. **2.** vb. To press by means of a mangle.

mangle (II.), vb. trans., fr. A.-Fr. *mahangler*, prob. fr. *mahaigner*, 'to maim'; perh. connected w. **maim**. **1.** To cut roughly, cut and bruise, mutilate, lacerate, hack. **2.** (fig.) To spoil, misrepresent, garble (a version of a text, pronunciation &c.).

mango, n. [1. mánggō; 2. mæŋgou], fr. Port. *manga*, fr. Tamil *mankay*, fr. *man*, 'mango-tree', & *kay*, 'fruit'. **a** Large tree of tropical Asia; **b** its fruit, eaten ripe, or used unripe for preserves, pickles &c.; *mango trick*, Indian juggler's trick, in which a mango-tree appears to grow from a seed, and to bear flowers and fruit almost under the eyes of the spectators.

mango-fish, n. Kind of yellow Indian fish.

mangold (-wurzel), n. See **mangel**.

mangonel, n. [1. mánggunel; 2. mæŋgənel], fr. O. Fr. dimin. of L. Lat. *mangōn-(em)*, fr. Gk. *mágganon*, 'a means of tricking, a philtre, charm; an engine for hurling stones'. See **mangle (I.)**. (hist.) A mediaeval military engine for hurling stones &c.

mangosteen, n. [1. mánggustēn; 2. mæŋgəstīn], fr. Malay. *mangustan*. **a** East Indian tree with dull red flowers and bearing a fruit with thick, reddish-brown rind, and white, juicy pulp; **b** fruit of this.

mangrove, n. [1. mánggrōv; 2. mæŋgrouv]. Earlier *mangle*, fr. Fr. *manglier*, fr. Malay. *manggi-manggi*; second element due to influence of **grove**. Genus of trees and shrubs which grow in swamps along river-banks in the tropics, spreading by means of aerial roots.

mangy, adj. [1. mā́nji; 2. méindži]. **mange** & **-y**. **1.** Affected with mange. **2.** (fig.) Squalid, sordid, mean.

man-handle, vb. trans. **man** & **handle (II.)**. **1.** To move by man's strength without mechanical aid. **2.** To treat roughly.

man-hole, n. Opening in the ground or floor, usually provided with a movable iron cover, giving access to drains or other pipes, or to cables &c. laid below ground.

manhood, n. [1. mánhood; 2. mænhud]. **man** & **-hood**. **1.** Time of life of a male human being after maturity is reached: *to arrive at manhood.* **2.** Manly qualities; courage, manliness: *to appeal to a person's manhood.* **3.** Men collectively, the male population: *the manhood of the country, nation.*

mania, n. [1. mā́nia; 2. méiniə]. Lat. *mania*, fr. Gk. *maniā*, 'madness'; cp. Gk. *maínesthai*, 'to be mad'; orig. 'to have one's mind in action, aroused, excited', cogn. w. O. Slav. *minją*, 'to think'; Lat. *meminisse* 'to remember'; Scrt. *mányatē*, 'to think'; O.H.G. *minna*, 'love'; O.E. *myne*, 'thought', (*ge*)*mynd*, 'thought, remembrance'. See **mind, mental (I.)**, & words there referred to. **1.** Violent madness; form of insanity characterized by excessive excitement or hallucination, sometimes on one subject only. **2.** Extreme or excessive enthusiasm, absorbing interest in, extravagant preoccupation with, obsession for, some object or pursuit: *a mania for amateur theatricals*; *her interest in Girl Guides had become a mania.*

-mania, suff., fr. prec., forming ns. denoting **a** specific type of mental disease, e.g. *kleptomania*; **b** excessive enthusiasm for specified object, occupation &c.; e.g. *bibliomania*; **c** excessive admiration for, e.g. *gallomania*; reverse of **-phobia.**

maniac, adj. & n. [1. máníak; 2. méiniæk], fr. L. Lat. *maniac-(us)*, 'maniac'. **mania** & **-ac. 1.** adj. Of, pertaining to, caused by, mania; mad, raving. **2.** n. Madman, person affected with mania.

-maniac, suff. forming ns. & adjs. referring to persons, fr. ns. in **-mania**; *kleptomaniac* &c.

maniacal, adj. [1. manfakl; 2. mənáiəkl]. **maniac** & **-al.** Of, pertaining to, of the nature of, mania; violently mad, exhibiting, characterised by, unrestrainable impulses of violence: *maniacal fury, cruelty.*

maniacally, adv. Prec. & **-ly.** In a maniacal manner; as a maniac.

Manich(a)ean, adj. & n. [1. mànikéan; 2. mæ̀nikíən]. See next word & **-an. a** adj. Of, pertaining to, a Manichee or Manichaeism; **b** n., a Manichee.

Manichee, n. [1. mánikē; 2. mǽnikī], fr. L. Lat. *Manichae-(us)*, fr. Gk. *Manikhaîos*, Mani, Persian founder of sect (d. A.D. 276). Follower of a system of religion, founded by Mani in the 3rd cent. on the doctrine of the existence in the universe of two fundamental principles of good and evil.

Manich(a)eism, n. [1. mánikēizm; 2. mǽnikī-izəm]. Prec. & **-ism.** Religious system, doctrine, of the Manichees.

manicure, n. & vb. trans. [1. mánikūr; 2. mǽni-kjɔ̄], fr. Fr., fr. Lat. *man-(us)*, 'hand', see **manual**, & *cūra*, 'care', see **cure (I.). a** n. The treatment, care, of the hands and nails; **b** vb., to pare, clean, polish, the nails.

manicurist, n. [1. mánikūrist; 2. mǽnikjɔ̄r-ist]. Prec. & **-ist.** Person practising manicure as a profession.

manifest (I.), n. [1. mánifest; 2. mǽnifest], fr. Fr. *manifeste*, fr. *manifester*, 'to show'. See next word. Detailed list of ship's cargo for use of customs officials.

manifest (II.), adj., fr. Lat. *manifest-(us)*, 'clear, evident', orig., 'capable of being seized by the hand, near at hand'; cp. *infestus*, 'attacking, hostile' (see **infest**); first element is *man-(us)*, 'hand', see **manual**; *-fest-* is perh. cogn. w. Scrt. *dharšayati*, 'attacks; conquers'; O. Prussian *adaršnaus*, 'he dared'. Clear, evident, distinct, obvious, to the mind or senses.

manifest (III.), vb. trans. & intrans., fr. Fr. *manifester*, fr. Lat. *manifestāre*, 'to show clearly', fr. *manifest-(us)*, 'clear'. See prec. **A.** trans. **1.** To show clearly, make plain or distinct. **2.** To give expression to (feeling &c.) by word or action; to exhibit, evince: *to manifest impatience, dissatisfaction* &c. **3.** To prove, put beyond doubt: *manifest the truth of.* **4.** (reflex.) To appear, show itself. **5.** To enter in ship's manifest. **B.** intrans. (of spirit, ghost &c.) To appear, make presence felt.

manifest (IV.), vb. intrans. [1. mànifést; 2. mæ̀nifést]. Back formation fr. **manifesto. a** To give a public manifestation of political or other opinion; **b** to issue a manifesto.

manifestation, n. [1. mànifestáshun; 2. mæ̀ni-festéiʃən]. **manifest (III.)** & **-ation.** Act or process of manifesting; state of being manifested.

manifestative, adj. [1. mànifèstativ; 2. mæ̀ni-féstətiv]. **manifest** & **-ative.** Of, pertaining to, of the nature of, a manifestation.

manifestly, adv. [1. mánifestli; 2. mǽnifɛstli]. **manifest (II.)** & **-ly.** In a manifest manner; clearly, obviously.

manifesto, n. [1. mànifésto; 2. mæ̀niféstou]. Ital., fr. Lat. *manifest-(us)*, 'clear'. See **manifest (II.).** Public statement issued by a prince, leader of a party, or other person in authority, of principles and future policy.

manifold (I.), adj. [1. mánifōld; 2. mǽni-fould]. O.E. *manigfald*, M.E. *manifold.* **many** & **-fold. 1.** Numerous. **2.** Various, of several different kinds, multifarious.

manifold (II.), vb. trans., fr. prec. To multiply copies of a document by a mechanical device.

manifoldly, adv. **manifold (I.)** & **-ly.** In manifold form; in various ways.

manifoldness, n. See prec. & **-ness.** State or quality of being manifold.

manikin, n. [1. mánikin; 2. mǽnikin], fr. Du. *manneken*, dimin. of **man. 1.** Small, undersized man, dwarf. **2. a** Anatomical model of the human body; **b** lay figure, for artists &c.; **c** a mannequin, q.v. **3.** Small bird of tropical America, more usually manakin, q.v.

Manil(l)a (I.), n. [1. maníla; 2. mənílə]. Name of capital of Philippine Islands. **1. a** *Manilla hemp*, stiff, durable fibre obtained from a tree of the Philippine Islands, used for making rope &c.; **b** *Manilla paper*, stout, brownish wrapping paper of Manilla hemp &c. **2.** Cigar, cheroot, made from a special tobacco leaf of the Philippines.

manilla (II.), n. Span., fr. Lat. *monīlia*, pl. of *monīle*, 'collar, neck-ring'. See **moniliform.** Ring, bracelet, worn as ornament or used as money by West African tribes.

manilla (III.), also **manille**, n. [1. maníl(a); 2. məníl(ə)], fr. Span. *malilla*, dimin. of *mala*, 'bad', Lat. *malus*. See **mal-.** Second highest trump or honour in ombre or quadrille.

manioc, n. [1. mániok; 2. mǽniɔk], fr. native Brazilian *mandioca*. **1.** Tropical plant, cassava, yielding a starchy meal. **2.** Farinaceous substance obtained from manioc; tapioca.

maniple, n. [1. mánipl; 2. mǽnipl], fr. O. Fr., fr. Lat. *manipul-(us)*, 'a handful; division of Roman army', fr. *man-(us)*, 'hand', see **manual**, & a form of the base **plē-* &c. as in *plēre*, 'to fill', *plēnus*, 'full' &c. See **plenary. 1.** Division of Roman army, one-third of cohort. **2.** Short scarf or stole worn on left arm by celebrant at the Eucharist.

manipulate, vb. trans. [1. manípūlāt; 2. mənípjuleit]. As though fr. Low Lat. **manipulāt-(um)*, P.P. of **manipulāre*, 'to handle', fr. *manipulus*, 'handful'. See **maniple. a** To work, mould, operate, with the hands; **b** (fig.) to influence (a person or opinions) by dexterous or unscrupulous management.

manipulation, n. [1. manìpūláshun; 2. mənìpjuléiʃən]. Prec. & **-ion.** Act of manipulating; state of being manipulated.

manipulative, adj. [1. manípūlativ; 2. mənípjulətiv]. **manipulate** & **-ive.** Of, pertaining to, done by, manipulation.

manipulatory, adj. [1. manípūlatori; 2. mənípjulətəri]. **manipulate** & **-ory.** Manipulative.

manitou, n. [1. mánitōō; 2. mǽnitū]. Algonquin *manito.* Spirit dominating the forces of nature, among N. American Indians.

mankind (I.), n. [1. mankínd; 2. mænkáind]. O.E. *manncynn.* See **man** & **kin**; w. substitution for second element of **kind (I.).** Human race, man, human beings.

mankind (II.), n. [1. mánkìnd; 2. mǽn-kaind], w. contrasting stress when opposed to *womenkind.* Perh. formed direct fr. **man** & **kind (I.).** Male sex; men as opposed to *women.*

manless, n. [1. mánles; 2. mǽnlis]. **man** & **-less.** Without a man or men.

manlike, adj. [1. mánlīk; 2. mǽnlaik]. **man** & **-like. a** Like, characteristic of, having the qualities of, a man; **b** (of a woman) masculine.

manliness, n. [1. mánlines; 2. mǽnlinis]. See next word & **-ness.** State or quality of being manly.

manly, adj. [1. mánli; 2. mǽnli]. **man** & **-ly. 1. a** Becoming to, befitting, a man; characteristic of a man; **b** having the qualities of a man; bold, resolute, courageous, virile. **2.** (of a woman) Like a man; mannish.

manna, n. [1. mána; 2. mǽnə]. L. Lat., fr. Gk. *mánna*; fr. Heb. & Arab. *mān.* **1.** Food miraculously provided for the Israelites in the Wilderness. **2. a** Sweet sap of manna-ash, used as mild laxative; **b** gummy, sweet exudation from a species of tamarisk in Arabia, which solidifies into small hard drops in the cold of early morning.

manna-ash, n. Flowering ash of Southern Europe and Asia Minor, exuding a thick, sweetish juice.

manna-croup, n. [1. mána krōōp; 2. mǽnə krūp]. **manna** & Russ. *krupa*, 'groats'. Coarse meal made in Russia from wheat or other grain.

mannequin, n. [1. mánekin; 2. mǽnikin, mǽnkæ̃]. Fr. form of **manikin. 1. a** A lay figure of wax &c. used for exhibition in shop windows &c. of ladies' clothes &c.; **b** specif., person employed by dressmakers to show off clothes by walking about in them before possible purchasers.

manner, n. [1. máner; 2. mǽnə], fr. O. Fr. *manière*, fr. Low Lat. **man(u)aria*, 'method of handling', fr. Lat. *man-(us)*, 'hand'. See **manual** & **-ary. 1.** Way, mode, method, style, fashion, in which a thing is done, happens: *in such a manner*; *after this manner.* Phrs. *to the manner born*, accustomed from birth to the practice indicated; *in a manner of speaking*, so to speak; (gram.) *adverb of manner*, word or phrase indicating or asking how something is done. **2. a** Personal bearing, behaviour; style of acting or speaking: *to have an awkward manner*; specif. **b** (i.) (pl.) personal behaviour in social intercourse: *good, bad, manners*, in accordance, not in accordance, with polite social conventions. Phr. *to have no manners*, no good manners; (ii.) (sing.) specif., distinguished, self-possessed bearing, affable, easy, dignified style of behaviour which bespeaks familiarity with the usages of good society: *to have a great deal of manner*; *he had fair manners, but no manner.* **3.** (pl.) Habits, customs, mode of life, social conditions: *the manners of our ancestors.* **4. a** Style, characteristic method, in art, music, literature &c.; **b** mannerism. **5.** (archaic) Kind, sort, character: *what manner of man is this?*; *all manner of*, all kinds of; *by no manner of means*, by no means, under no circumstances; *no manner of*, none at all; *in a manner*, to some extent.

mannered, adj. [1. mánerd; 2. mǽnəd]. Prec. & **-ed. 1.** Having manners of specified character: *ill-mannered, well-mannered* &c. **2.** (of style) Characterized by mannerism; affected.

mannerism, n. [1. mánerizm; 2. mǽnərizəm]. **manner** & **-ism.** Peculiarity; distinctive, often affected method or trick of style, speech, behaviour, gesture &c.

mannerist, n. [1. mánerist; 2. mǽnərist]. **manner** & **-ist.** Person addicted to mannerism.

manneristic(al), adj. [1. manerístik(l); 2. mænərístik(l)]. Prec. & **-ic** & **-al.** Of, pertaining to, of the nature of, characterized by, mannerism.

mannerless, adj. [1. mánerles; 2. mǽnəlis]. **manner** & **-less.** Without manners, unmannerly; ill-bred.

mannerliness, n. [1. mánerlines; 2. mǽnəli-nis]. See next word & **-ness.** Quality of being mannerly.

mannerly, adj. [1. mánerli; 2. mǽnəli]. **manner** & **-ly.** Showing good manners; polite, civil, urbane, well-bred.

mannish, adj. [1. mánish; 2. mǽniʃ]. **man & -ish.** (chiefly used of women) Masculine, not like a woman.

mannishness, n. Prec. & **-ness.** Quality of being mannish.

mannite, n. [1. mánīt; 2. mǽnait]. **manna & -ite.** Sweet, crystalline substance obtained from manna (**2. a**).

manœuvre (I.), n. [1. manōōver; 2. mənúvə], fr. Fr., fr. Low Lat. *manopera*, fr. *manoperāre*, fr. Lat. *manū operāri*, 'to work by hand'. See **manual & opera.** Cp. **manure**, wh. comes fr. same source. **1. a** Strategic movement of troops or warships; **b** (pl.) series of movements of troops or ships &c. organized in peace-time as means of training. **2.** (fig.) **a** Skilful, dexterous, adroit management of affairs; **b** disingenuous action, intrigue.

manœuvre (II.), vb. intrans. & trans., fr. Fr. *manœuvrer*, fr. L. Lat. *manoperāre*, 'to work by hand'. See prec. **A.** intrans. **1.** (of troops or ships) To perform manœuvres, carry out planned strategic or tactical movements. **2.** To arrange affairs to suit one's purposes; to use artifice and cunning. **B.** trans. **1.** To move or cause (troops &c.) to move according to a tactical or strategic plan. **2.** *Manœuvre* (person) *into, out of*, **a** (a room &c.), to inveigle him, into, persuade him to go in or out: **b** *manœuvre a person into an awkward position, oneself into a good billet*, to jockey (oneself or another) into, out of, use unscrupulous means to effect this.

manœuvrer, n. [1. manōōvrer; 2. mənúvrə]. Prec. & **-er.** **a** One who manœuvres or directs manœuvres; **b** a shifty trickster.

man-of-war, n. [1. màn uv wór; 2. mæ̀n əv wɔ́]. War-ship.

manometer, n. [1. manómeter; 2. mənɔ́mitə], fr. Fr. *manomètre*, fr. Gk. *mānó-(s)*, 'thin, porous, not dense', fr. **manwos*, & **-meter**; cogn. w. Scrt. *mandk*, 'a little'; Lith. *meñkas*, 'small, inferior'; & perh. w. O. Ir. *menb*, fr. **menw*, 'small'. Instrument measuring elastic force of gases; pressure gauge.

manometric, adj. [1. mànométrik; 2. mænəmétrik]. See prec. & **-metric.** Of, pertaining to, a manometer.

manor, n. [1. mánor; 2. mǽnə], fr. O. Fr. *manoir*, 'manor', n. fr. Lat. infin. *manēre*, 'to remain'. See **mansion** & second element in **remain. 1.** Under feudalism a term of somewhat vague import, and connoting **a** a certain territorial and agricultural unit; **b** a fiscal unit; **c** a jurisdictional unit. **2.** In recent times the term is applied to a specific estate, generally having a principal residence, the owner or lord of which still retains certain ancient manorial rights over the land.

manor-house, n. House of a lord of the manor.

manorial, adj. [1. manórial; 2. mənɔ́riəl]. Prec. & **-ial.** Connected with, pertaining to, a manor: *manorial rights, customs* &c.

mansard, n. [1. mánsard; 2. mǽnsād], fr. Fr. *mansarde*, fr. name of architect, François Mansarde (d. 1666). A garret. Also *mansard roof*, form of roof in which each face has two slopes, the lower one steeper than the upper.

manse, n. [1. mans; 2. mæns], fr. Med. Lat. *mans-(us)*, 'house', fr. Lat. *mans-(um)*, P.P. type of *manēre*, 'to remain'. Cp. **manor** & see **mansion.** Residence of a Scottish Presbyterian minister.

mansion, n. [1. mánshun; 2. mǽnʃən], fr. O. Fr., fr. Lat. *mansiōn-(em)*, 'sojourn; halting-place', fr. *mans-(um)*, P.P. type of *manēre*, 'to remain', see **remain, & -ion. 1.** Large dwelling-house; capacious, imposing, residence. **2.** (pl.) Often used as name for large building divided into flats.

mansion-house, n. **a** Mansion, esp. manor-house; **b** (cap.) official residence of Lord Mayor of London.

manslaughter, n. [1. mánslàwter; 2. mǽnslɔ̄tə]. **man & slaughter.** Unlawful, though unpremeditated, killing of a human being; unlawful homicide short of wilful murder, as in the heat of passion, or accidentally, in the course of another illegal act.

mansuetude, n. [1. mánswetūd; 2. mǽnswitjūd], fr. Lat. *mansuētūdin-(em)*, *mansuētūdo*, fr. *mansuēt-*, stem of *mansuescere*, 'to tame', fr. *man-(us)*, 'hand', see **manual**, & *suescere*, 'to accustom'. See **ethical.** (rare or archaic) Gentleness, mildness, meekness of character or temperament.

mantel, n. [1. mántl; 2. mǽntl]. Variant of **mantle. a** Also *mantelpiece*, structure of wood, stone &c. framing fireplace; **b** also *mantelshelf*, shelf projecting above fireplace.

mantel-board, n. Wooden board covering mantelshelf.

mantelpiece, n. [1. mántlpēs; 2. mǽntlpīs]. **a** The whole structure framing a fireplace; also **b** mantelshelf: *put the clock on the mantelpiece.*

mantelshelf, n. [1. mántlshelf; 2. mǽntlʃɛlf]. Mantel, **b.**

mantel-tree, n. Lintel of a fireplace whether of wood or stone.

mantic, adj. [1. mántik; 2. mǽntik], fr. Gk. *mantik-(ós)*, 'prophetic, oracular', fr. *mánt-(is)*, 'soothsayer'. See **mantis** & cp. **-mancy.** Of, pertaining to, divination; prophetic.

mantilla, n. [1. mantíla; 2. mæntílə]. Span., dimin. of *manta*, 'cloak', fr. Lat. *mant-(um)*, 'cape'. See **mantle. 1.** Kind of shawl or wrap worn by Spanish women round the neck so as to cover the head and shoulders. **2.** Short cape.

mantis, n. [1. mántis; 2. mǽntis]. Gk. *mántis*, 'prophet'; the normal form wd. be **matis*; the *n* is due to anal. of Gk. *mani-*, as in *maínomai*, 'I rage, am furious', fr. **manjomai*; cogn. w. Lat. *mens*, see **mental (I.)**; O.E. *gemynd*, see **mind**; cp. also Goth. *muns*, 'thought'. Genus of orthopterous insects; *praying mantis*, species which holds up its fore-legs as if in prayer, while lying in wait for its prey.

mantissa, n. [1. mantísa; 2. mæntísə]. Lat., 'useless addition, makeweight', said to be of Etruscan origin. Decimal part of logarithm.

mantle (I.), n. [1. mántl; 2. mǽntl], fr. O. Fr. *mantel*, fr. Lat. *mantellum*, 'cloak, veil', wh. is prob. fr. Lat. *mantum*, 'cloak', but may be influenced by Lat. *mantēlum*, 'towel, napkin', fr. *manus*, 'hand', see **manual**, & base *terg-*, 'to wipe, cleanse', see **detergent & trite. 1.** Loose sleeveless, flowing, outer garment; cloak. **2.** (fig.) Something that covers, enfolds &c.: *spring's mantle of green.* **3.** (zool.) Thin, fleshy, membranous lining of mollusc's shell. **4.** Hollow cover of fine mesh made of cotton treated with fire-resisting material which placed over a flame becomes incandescent, and increases the light.

mantle (II.), vb. trans. & intrans., fr. prec. **A.** trans. To cover as with a mantle; to envelop, clothe, conceal, wrap. **B.** intrans. **1.** To form a covering; to overspread, gather on, a surface; **a** to flush: *blushes mantled on her cheek*; also *her cheeks mantled with blushes*; **b** *water-weeds mantle on a pool.* **2.** (of hawks) To cover the legs with the wings.

mantlet, mantelet, n. [1. mántlet; 2. mǽntlit], fr. O. Fr. *mantelet*, dimin. of **mantle (I.). 1.** Small cloak, short mantle. **2.** (mil.) Temporary shelter, screen, to protect attacking force, guns in action &c.

man-trap, n. Trap set to catch trespassers, consisting of two iron half-hoops hinged together at the ends, which close when a spring is released.

mantua, n. [1. mántūa; 2. mǽntjuə], fr. Fr. *manteau*, 'mantle', associated w. the place-name *Mantua*, by popular etymol.; used in 17th & 18th cents. (obs.) Woman's gown, mantle.

mantua-maker, n. See prec. (obs.) Dress-maker.

manual (I.), adj. [1. mánūal; 2. mǽnjuəl], fr. Lat. *manuāl-(is)*, 'relating to the hand', fr. *man-(us)*, 'hand'; prob. cogn. w. O.N. *mund*, O.E. *mund*, 'hand'; Goth. *manwus*, 'ready'; & w. Gk. *márē*, 'hand'. It has been suggested that the word contains a form of the base **am-*, **m̥-* &c., 'to seize', cp. Lat. *amplus*, 'much embracing, comprehensive, spacious, large', also *amplector*, 'to embrace'. See **ample.** Connected with, pertaining to, done by, formed by, the hand: *manual labour*; *manual alphabet*, finger alphabet; *manual exercises*, drill with rifle and other arms; *sign manual*, person's own signature written by himself.

manual (II.), n., fr. prec. **1.** Keyboard of organ. **2.** Small textbook, handbook.

manually, adv. **manual (I.) & -ly.** With, by means of, the hands.

manucode, n. [1. mánūkōd; 2. mǽnjukoud]. Fr., fr. Malay. *manuk dēwāta*, 'bird of the gods'. A bird of Papua and Queensland, with bright, iridescent, steel-blue plumage and clear, ringing voice; allied to the bird of paradise.

manufactory, n. [1. mànūfákchuri; 2. mænjufǽktʃəri], the usual pronunciation, due to influence of *manufacture*; [1. mànoofáktori; 2. mænjufǽktəri] is less commonly heard; fr. Fr., fr. Lat. *manū*, 'by hand', fr. *man-(us)*, 'hand', see **manual, & factory.** Place, building, set of workshops, where articles, fabrics &c. are manufactured.

manufacture (I.), n. [1. mànūfákchur; 2. mænjufǽktʃə]. Fr., fr. Lat. *manū*, 'by hand', see **manual**, & *factūra*, 'a making'. See **fact & -ure. 1. a** Process of making articles, wares, goods, whether by hand or by machinery, esp. on a large scale, with highly organized division of labour; **b** any specific branch of industry: *steel, cloth, hardware &c. manufacture.* **2.** Anything manufactured from raw products; pl. *manufactures*, manufactured goods collectively.

manufacture (II.), vb. trans., fr. prec. **1.** To produce (goods, articles) from raw material by manual or mechanical labour, esp. on large scale as commercial undertaking. **2.** (fig.) **a** To produce (literary work &c.) mechanically in large quantities without inspiration or originality; **b** to fabricate, concoct (story, account &c.).

manufacturer, n. [1. mànūfákchurer; 2. mænjufǽktʃərə]. Prec. & **-er.** One occupied in manufacturing, esp. owner of factory.

manuka, n. [1. máhnooka; 2. mánukə]. Maori name. An Australasian shrub or tree, with aromatic leaves, from which a kind of tea is made.

manul, n. [1. máhnool; 2. mánul]. Mongol name. A small wild cat of Tibet, Mongolia, and Siberia, with grey fur and black stripes.

manumission, n. [1. mànūmíshun; 2. mænjumíʃən], fr. Lat. *manūmissiōn-(em)*, 'manumission', fr. *manūmiss-(um)*, P.P. type of *manūmittere*, 'to release'. See next word. **1.** Act of freeing, state of being freed, from bondage; used esp. of the freeing of slaves and serfs. **2.** Formal document liberating a serf or slave.

manumit, vb. trans. [1. mànūmít; 2. mænjumít], fr. Lat. *manūmit-(tere)*, 'to release', fr. *manū*, 'by the hand', see **manual, &** *mittere*, 'to send, send off, dismiss'. See **mission.** (hist.) To release, set free (slave or serf) from bondage.

manure (I.), n. [1. manúr; 2. mænjɔ́], fr. **next** word. Any substance spread on surface of ground, or forked into it, as a fertilizer.

manure (II.), vb. trans., fr. A.-Fr. *maynoverer*, fr. L. Lat. *manoperāre*, 'to work with the hand.' See **manœuvre.** To apply manure to (land &c.).

manurial, adj. [1. manúrial; 2. mənjɔ́riəl]. Prec. & **-ial.** Connected with, pertaining to, consisting of, manure.

manuscript, adj. & n. [1. mánūskript: 2. mǽnjə-, mǽnjuskript], fr. Lat. *manū scriptus*, Med. Lat. *manuscriptum*, n., 'written with the hand, manuscript'. See **manual &**

script. **1.** adj. Written by hand: *manuscript notes.* **2.** n. a Book, text, document, written by hand, not printed or typed, abbreviated MS., (pl.) MSS.; **b** handwriting as opposed to printing or typing: *a work still in manuscript,* not yet printed.

manward, adj. [1. mánward; 2. mǽnwəd]. **man** & **-ward.** Directed towards man.

Manx, adj. & n. [1. mangks; 2. mæŋks], fr. O.N. *manskr,* 'of (Isle of) Man'. **1.** adj. Of, belonging to, coming from, the Isle of Man. *Manx cat,* tailless breed. **2.** n. Language of Isle of Man, a branch of Gaelic.

Manxman, n. [1. mángksman; 2. mǽŋksmən]. Native of Isle of Man.

many (I.), adj. [1. méni; 2. méni]. O.E. *manig*; M.E. *mani*; cp. O.H.G. *manag*; Goth. *managș*; the present pronunciation is influenced by that of *any.* **a** Numerous; indicating a number of persons or things: *many people*; *many times*; *how many,* what number; *as many,* the same number; *his virtues were many, his faults few*; Phr. *to be one too many for,* to get the better of, be more than a match for; also **b** in construction, *many a time,* on many occasions; *many a one* (earlier, *an one*). Phr. *for many a long day,* for a very long time.

many (II.), n., fr. prec. Group comprising a number of persons or things: *many are called but few are chosen*; *the many,* the multitude, majority; *a good many,* fair number; *a great many,* large number; (archaic) *there's a many would be glad to go* &c.

many-headed, adj. Having many heads: '*The many-headed monster of the pit*' (Pope, 'To Augustus', 305), the common people, the mob, populace.

many-sided, adj. **a** (geom.) Having many sides; **b** having a variety of interests, qualities, accomplishments: *a many-sided man*; *many-sided question,* of many aspects.

many-sidedness, n. Prec. & **-ness.** Quality of being many-sided.

Maori, n. [1. móuri; 2. máuəri]. Native, New Zealand. **a** Member of aboriginal race of New Zealand; **b** language spoken by this race.

map (I.), n. [1. map; 2. mæp], fr. Med. Lat. *mappa,* usually *mappa mundi,* 'map' (of the world), fr. Lat. *mappa,* 'napkin; cloth'; prob. a Punic loan-word. **1.** Plane representation of earth's surface or a part of this, indicating physical features, political boundaries &c. **2.** Similar representation of heavens, showing position of stars &c.

map (II.), vb. trans., fr. prec. **1.** To represent, show, in form of a map, make a map of. **2.** *Map out,* to plan, arrange, draw up a scheme for: *to map out one's time, a piece of work* &c.

maple, n. [1. mápl; 2. méipl]. O.E. *mapel* (*trēow*), 'maple tree'; cp. O.S. *mapulder.* **1.** Tree of genus *Acer,* found in Europe, Asia, and America, cultivated for timber, maple-sugar, or ornament. **2.** Wood of maple.

maple-sugar, -syrup, n. Sugar, syrup, got by evaporation from sap of a species of maple.

maqui, n. [1. máhkē; 2. mákī]. Native Chilean name. An evergreen shrub of Chile; the bark yields a stringy fibre and from its berries a medicinal wine is made.

maquis, n. [1. máhkē; 2. mákī]. Fr., fr. Corsican dial., Ital. *macchia* 'thicket'. A dense, scrubby forest of various dwarfed evergreen trees and shrubs in Corsica &c.

mar, vb. trans. [1. mar; 2. mā]. O.E. *merran*; M.E. *merre, marre,* 'to hinder, injure'; cp. O.H.G. *merren*; O.S. *merrian,* 'to hinder'; Goth. *marzjan,* 'to offend'. Origin dubious. To injure, spoil, damage, ruin, detract from: *clouds later marred the beauty of the day.* Phr. *to make or mar,* either to make a brilliant success of, or to ruin irretrievably.

marabou, n. [1. márabōō; 2. mǽrəbū], fr. Fr., prob. fr. Arab. **a** West African stork; **b** down from wings or tail of this bird, used as trimming.

marabout, n. [1. márabōōt; 2. mǽrəbūt], fr. Arab. *murabit.* **a** Mohammedan saint or hermit; **b** tomb, shrine, of a marabout.

maranatha, n. [1. maranáhtha; 2. mærənáþə]. Aramaic, *maran atha,* 'the Lord cometh' or 'O Lord come'. Wrongly combined with *anathema,* q.v. in 1 Corinthians xvi. 22, as if an intensified imprecation or curse.

maraschino, n. [1. màraskḗnō; 2. mærəskínou]. Ital., fr. (*a*)*marasca,* 'small sour cherry', fr. *amara,* 'bitter', fr. Lat. *amār-(us),* 'bitter'; cogn. w. Du. *amper,* 'sharp, bitter'; O.N. *apr,* 'sharp'; Scrt. *am-láș,* 'sour'; cp. further, w. a different grade of vowel, Gk. *ōmós,* 'rough'; Scrt. *āmáș,* 'rough, raw, unripe'. Strong, sweet, mawkish liqueur made from small black cherry grown in Dalmatia.

marasmic, adj. [1. marázmik; 2. mərǽzmik]. Next word & **-ic.** Of, pertaining to, of the nature of, marasmus.

marasmus, n. [1. marázmus; 2. mərǽzməs], fr. Gk. *marasmós,* 'consumption', fr. *maraínein,* 'to consume; to be exhausted'; cogn. w. Scrt. *mṛṇāti,* 'to crush'; O.H.G. *maro,* 'ripe, tender'. Cp. **marble.** (pathol.) Wasting away of the body; atrophy.

Marathon race, n. [1. márathon rās; 2. mǽrəþon rèis], fr. name of place, twenty-six miles north of Athens, scene of great victory of the Athenians over the Persians, 490 B.C., the news of which was brought by a runner who dropped dead on arrival. A long-distance race, usually of about twenty-six miles.

maraud, vb. intrans. & trans. [1. maráwd; 2. mərɔ́d], fr. O. Fr. *marault,* 'vagabond', Fr. *maraud,* 'rogue, thief', & *marauder,* 'to pilfer'; etymol. disputed. **1.** intrans. To rove in search of booty, make raids for plunder: *marauding hordes.* **2.** trans. (rare) To plunder, rob, pillage.

marauder, n. [1. maráwder; 2. mərɔ́də]. Prec. & **-er.** Plunderer, roving thief, robber, raider.

maravedi, n. [1. màravā́di; 2. mærəvéidi]. Span., fr. Arab. *Murābitīn,* name of a Moorish dynasty in Spain, 1086–1147. Connected w. **marabout.** (hist.) **a** Spanish gold coin, worth about 14s.; **b** Spanish copper coin, ⅛d.

marble, n. [1. márbl; 2. mábl], fr. Fr. *marbre,* fr. Lat. *marmor,* 'marble', fr. Gk. *mármaros,* 'stone, rock, hard substance', later 'marble', through association w. *marmaírein,* 'to shine', cogn. w. Lat. *merus,* 'pure, unmixed', see **mere (II.)**; Gk. *mármaros* is cogn. w. Scrt. *mṛṇāti,* 'to crush, grind'. See **marasmus** & **Mars. 1.** Crystalline form of limestone, occurring in various colours, and often beautifully streaked, with close, even grain, and capable of taking a high polish, used in building and sculpture. Phr. *as hard, as cold, as marble.* **2.** (pl. *marbles*) Group, collection, of figures &c. sculptured in marble: *the Elgin Marbles.* **3.** Small ball of marble, glass &c. used in childish games. **4.** (attrib.) Denoting **a** hardness, insensibility, immovability, smoothness &c.; (fig.) *marble breast* (insensible); **b** white like marble: *a marble brow*; **c** marked, streaked, like marble: *marble paper.*

marbled, adj. [1. márbld; 2. mábld]. Prec. & **-ed.** Stained, veined, painted, so as to look like marble: *marbled paper, edges of book* &c.

marbly, adj. [1. márbli; 2. mábli]. **marble** & **-y.** Resembling marble.

marc, n. [1. mark; 2. māk]. Fr., connected w. *marcher,* 'to walk', in sense 'tread', fr. Lat. *marcus,* 'large hammer'; ultimately 'something trodden, beaten, out'. Mass left after the juice has been pressed out of fruit.

marcasite, n. [1. márkasīt; 2. mákəsait], fr. Med. Lat. *marcasita*; etymol. unknown. Kind of iron ore, white iron pyrites.

marcel wave, n. [1. mársel wāv; 2. másel wèiv], fr. name of inventor. A kind of artificial wave in hair.

marcescence, n. [1. màrsésens; 2. màsésəns]. See next word & **-ce.** State of being marcescent.

marcescent, adj. [1. marsésent; 2. māsésənt], fr. Lat. *marcescent-(em),* Pres. Part. of *marcescere,* 'to droop', fr. *marc-(ēre),* 'to wither'; cp. *marcidus,* 'languid, faded', *marcor,* 'decay', fr. an Aryan base **merek-,* 'to wear out, fade, droop'; to injure, crush'. Cp. Scrt. *marcáyati,* 'injured'; Goth. *gamaurgjan,* 'to shorten'; O.E. *myrġe,* 'pleasant'. See **merry.** (bot., of part of plant) Withering, dying back, though still attached to plant.

March (I.), n. [1. march; 2. mātʃ], fr. O. Fr., fr. Lat. *Martius* (*mensis*) '(month) of Mars', fr. *Mart-,* stem of **Mars.** Third month of year. Phr. *mad as a March hare,* see **hare.**

march (II.), n., fr. Fr. *marche*; Gmc. See **mark (I.).** (hist.) **1.** Boundary, limit, frontier. (pl., often specif.) Border of England and Wales or Scotland: *the Marches.* **2.** Tract of debatable land lying between frontiers of two countries.

march (III.), vb. intrans., fr. prec. (of countries, areas of land, estates &c.) Often *march with,* to be adjacent to, border on, lie alongside of.

march (IV.), n., fr. Fr. *marche,* fr. *marcher,* 'to walk'. See next word. **1.** (mil.) Act of marching; Phr. *on the march,* marching; *line of march,* route followed by troops on the march; *march past,* marching of troops past reviewing officer &c. **2. a** Long, esp. fatiguing, walk; steady, resistless, monotonous, advance; **b** (fig.) progress, advance, forward movement: *the march of time, events, intellect* &c. **3.** Distance covered by troops in one day; Phr. *forced march,* day's march longer than normal distance, undertaken for strategic purposes, or in an emergency &c. **4.** Uniform step taken by soldiers &c., marching: *quick, slow, march.* **5.** (mus.) Composition fitted or intended to accompany march; Phr. *dead march,* one played at a funeral service.

march (V.), vb. intrans. & trans., fr. Fr. *marcher,* 'to walk', fr. Low Lat. *marcare*; prob. fr. Lat. *marcus,* 'hammer'. The orig. sense of the vb. wd. thus be 'to hammer, beat, the ground with the feet'. Lat. *marcus* is prob. a back-formation fr. *marculus,* 'a hammer', w. dissimilation fr. Aryan **mal-tlo-,* whence also Russ. *molotŭ,* O. Slav. *mlatŭ,* 'hammer'. **A.** intrans. **1.** To walk in steady, rhythmical step, esp. of uniform step of troops in formation: *to march away, off*; *to march into the town* &c. **2.** To proceed, advance, walk, steadily. **B.** trans. **a** To cause (troops &c.) to march; **b** to compel to walk swiftly, to hustle, hurry: *to march a man off to gaol.*

marchioness, n. [1. márshunis; 2. máʃənis], fr. Med. Lat. *marchionissa,* fr. *marchiōn-(em),* 'ruler of march'. See **march (II.)** & **-ess.** & cp. **marquis. 1. a** Title given to wife, or widow, of marquis; **b** lady having this title. **2.** Lady holding in her own right rank equal to that of marquis.

marchpane, marzipan, n. [1. márchpān, márzipan; 2. mátʃpein, mázipæn]. Cp. Germ. *marzipan,* Fr. *massepain*; etymol. doubtful. Thick paste of ground almonds, sugar &c.

marconigram, n. [1. markṓnigram; 2. mākóunigræm], fr. name of Italian inventor, G. Marconi, b. 1874, & **-gram.** Message sent by wireless telegraphy.

mare (I.), n. [1. māri; 2. méəri]. Lat. *mare,* 'sea'; cogn. w. O. Slav. *morje,* 'sea'; Goth. *marei,* 'sea'; O.N. *marr,* O.E. *mere,* 'sea, lake'. See **mere (I.).** *Mare clausum,* sea protected by authority of specific nation; *mare liberum,* sea open to ships of all nations.

mare (II.), n. [1. mār; 2. mɛə]. O.E. *mere,* M.E. *mere, mare*; cp. Mod. Germ. *mähre*; Du. *merrie*; O.N. *merr.* Cp. further O.E. *mearh*; O.H.G. *marah*; O.N. *marr,* 'horse'; O. Ir. *mare,* 'horse'. See **marshal.** Female of horse. Phrs. *shanks's mare,* one's own legs, as means of travelling; *the grey mare is the better horse,* of wife who is more capable and masterful than her husband.

maremma, n. [1. maréma; 2. mərémə]. Ital., fr. Lat. *maritima*, neut. pl. See **maritime.** Low, unhealthy, marshy land near sea-shore, esp. in Western Italy.

mare's nest, n. Supposed discovery which turns out to be illusory.

mare's tail, n. **1. a** Tall slender plant, *Hippuris vulgaris*, growing in marshy ground; **b** the horsetail, q.v. **2.** Long straight bars of cirrus cloud.

margaric, adj. [1. margárik; 2. māgǽrik]. Fr. *margarique*, fr. Gk. *márgaron*, 'pearl', also *margarítēs*, cp. Lat. *margarīta*, 'pearl', cp. *marguerite*, & name *Margaret*; of Oriental origin, fr. Pers. *murwārīd*, 'pearl'. (chem.) Pertaining to, designating, a fatty acid, *margaric acid*, with a pearly appearance, found in various animal and vegetable fats.

margarine, n. [1. márgarèn; 2. mā́gərīn], popularly [1. márjarèn; 2. mā́džərīn]. Fr., formed fr. prec. word & **-ine**, owing to a mistaken notion that all oils and fats contained margaric acid. Artificial butter, or butter substitute, composed of various vegetable and animal oils and fats.

margay, n. [1. márgā; 2. mā́gei]. Fr., fr. native word *mbaracaia*. Small, spotted wild-cat of South America.

marge, n. [1. marj; 2. mādž], fr. Fr., fr. Lat. *margo*, 'edge'. See next word. (poet.) Edge, border, margin.

margent, n. [1. márjent; 2. mā́džənt]. Variant, with 'excrescent *-t*', of **margin**, found in Lyly's 'Euphues' (1580), and revived by Tennyson.

margin, n. [1. márjin; 2. mā́džin], fr. Lat. *margin-(em)*, *margo*, 'edge', cogn. w. Goth. *marka*, 'border, borderland'; O.E. *mearc*, 'border'. See **mark (I.)**. **1.** Edge, border, rim, limit of surface. **2.** Space, usually blank, surrounding central body of printed or written matter &c., on page &c. **3.** Extra amount of anything (time, money &c.) beyond what is strictly necessary; specif. **a** (commerc.) the lowest amount of profit possible for a business to be run without loss or insolvency; **b** (Stock Exchange) difference between the buying and selling prices of stocks and shares; esp. as deposited as cover for speculative dealings.

marginal, adj. [1. márjinal; 2. mā́džinl]. **margin** & **-al.** Of, pertaining to, near, placed in, the margin: *marginal notes.*

marginalia, n. pl. [1. màrjinā́lia; 2. mādžinéiliə]. Mod. Lat., neut. pl., fr. prec. Marginal notes.

marginally, adv. [1. márjinali; 2. mā́džinəli]. **marginal** & **-ly.** In the margin.

marginate(d), adj. [1. márjināt(ed); 2. mā́džineit(id)]. **margin** & **-ate** & **-ed.** Having a margin.

margosa, n. [1. margṓsa; 2. māgóusə], fr. Port. *amargoso*, 'bitter'. East Indian tree with bitter bark, used medicinally as a tonic.

margrave, n. [1. márgrāv; 2. mā́greiv], fr. M. Du. *markgrave*; Germ. *markgraf*; fr. *mark*, 'border', see **march (II.)**, & *grave*, 'count'; cp. O.E. *ġe-rēfa*. See **reeve (II.)**, & **sheriff.** (hist.) Title of certain princes of Holy Roman Empire, originally title of military governor of border district.

margravine, n. [1. márgràvin; 2. mā́grèivin]. Prec. & **-ine.** Wife of margrave.

marguerite, n. [1. márgerēt; 2. mā́gərīt], fr. Fr., fr. L. Lat. *margarīta*, 'a pearl', fr. Gk. *margarítēs*, fr. *márgar-(on)*, 'pearl'. See **margaric** & **-ite.** Ox-eye daisy.

mariage de convenance, n. [1. máriahzh de kónvenàhns; 2. mariaž də kɔ̃vənɑ̃s]. Fr. Marriage arranged from prudential motives.

Marian, adj. & n. [1. mārian; 2. méəriən], fr. Lat. *Maria*, 'Mary', & **-an. 1.** adj. Pertaining to, connected with, **a** the B.V.M.; **b** Mary, Queen of England; **c** Mary Queen of Scots. **2.** n. Supporter, advocate, of Mary Queen of Scots.

marigold, n. [1. márigōld; 2. mǽrigould], fr. *Mary*, prob. the B.V.M., & **gold. 1.** One of several herbs, genera *Calendula* and *Tagetes*, with bright yellow, red or orange composite flowers. **2.** The marsh marigold.

marinade, n. & vb. trans. [1. màrinā́d; 2. mæ̀rinéid], fr. Fr., fr. Span. *marinada*, 'to pickle in brine', fr. Lat. *marīn-(us)*, 'of the sea'. See **marine** & **-ade. 1.** n. **a** Mixture of vinegar, wine, spice &c.; **b** fish, meat, &c., pickled or steeped in this mixture. **2.** vb. To pickle (fish &c.) in marinade.

marinate, vb. trans. [1. márināt; 2. mǽrineit]. Prec. & **-ate.** To marinade.

marine (I.), adj. [1. marḗn; 2. mərín], fr. Lat. *marīn-(us)*, 'of the sea', fr. *mar-(e)*, 'sea'. See **mare (I.)** & **-ine**, & cp. **mere (I.)**. **1. a** Of, pertaining to, found in, connected with, the sea: *marine animals*; *marine painting* &c.; **b** of, pertaining to, shipping, sea trade &c.: *marine insurance*; *marine stores.* **2.** (of soldier) Serving on man-of-war.

marine (II.), n., fr. prec. **1.** Country's fleet of ships, naval or mercantile. **2.** Soldier serving on war-ship; *Royal Marines*, corps of soldiers for service at sea. Phrs. *tell that to the marines*, expressing incredulity in an impossible story; *horse marines*, an imaginary body.

mariner, n. [1. máriner; 2. mǽrinə], fr. A.-Fr., fr. Med. Lat. *marinarius*, 'sailor', fr. Lat. *marīn-(us)*, 'of the sea'. See **marine** & **-ary.** Sailor, seaman; *master mariner*, captain in merchant service; *mariner's compass*, ordinary compass as used on ships.

Marinism, n. [1. marḗnizm; 2. mərínizəm], fr. name of Italian poet Marini, d. 1625, & **-ism.** Artificial, high-flown style of writing, as that of Marini.

Marinist, n. [1. marḗnist; 2. mərínist]. See prec. & **-ist.** Writer affecting Marinism.

Mariolatry, n. [1. màriólatri; 2. mèəriɔ́lətri], fr. Gk. *María*, 'Mary', & **-latry.** Worship of the B.V.M.; a term used by opponents of the Roman Catholic Church.

marionette, n. [1. màrionét; 2. mæ̀riənét], fr. Fr. *marionnette*, fr. *Marion*, dimin. of personal name *Marie*, & **-ette.** Figure of man or woman, made of wood, &c., moved by strings; puppet.

marischal, n. [1. márshal; 2. mā́ʃl], fr. Fr. *maréchal*. See **marshal.** The old Scottish form of marshal, q.v.

marish, n. & adj. [1. márish; 2. mǽriʃ], fr. M.E. *mares, mareis*, fr. O. Fr. *mareis*, 'marsh', fr. Med. Lat. *marisc-(us)*, 'marsh'. See **marsh.** (rare or archaic) **1.** n. Marsh, swamp, morass. **2.** adj. Pertaining to a marsh.

Marist, n. [1. mārist; 2. méərist], fr. Fr. *Mariste, Marie* & **-ist.** Member of Society of Mary, Roman Catholic teaching community.

marital, adj. [1. máritl, marītl; 2. mǽritl, məráitl], fr. Lat. *marītāl-(is)*, 'of marriage', fr. *marīt-(us)*, 'married', cogn. w. Scrt. *máryaš*, 'man, youth, lover'; cp. Lith. *marti*, 'bride'; O. Prussian *martin*, 'bride'; Gk. *meîrax*, 'boy, girl'. **1.** Pertaining to a husband. **2.** Of, pertaining to, marriage.

maritally, adv. Prec. & **-ly.** In a marital manner, according with the duties &c. of marriage.

maritime, adj. [1. máritīm; 2. mǽritaim], fr. Lat. *maritim-(us)*, 'of or near the sea', fr. *mar-(e)*, 'sea'. See **mare (I.)**, w. superl. suff. on anal. of *intimus*, *ultimus* &c.; cp. **ultimate. 1.** Pertaining to, connected with, the sea or navigation: *maritime trade.* **2. a** Situated, lying, near the sea; littoral: *maritime region, province*; **b** living near the sea; **c** having a navy and mercantile fleet, having sea-borne trade; having connexions with the sea: *maritime nation.*

marjoram, n. [1. márjuram; 2. mā́džərəm], fr. O. Fr. *majorane*, fr. Med. Lat. *majorana*; etymol. doubtful. Genus, *Origanum*, of aromatic herbs of Europe and Western Asia, used in medicine and cookery.

mark (I.), n. [1. mark; 2. māk]. O.E. *mearc*, 'mark; limit of space or time; end, boundary; district'; M.E. *mark*; cp. O.H.G. *mark*; M. Du., O.H.G. *mark*, O.N. *mark*, *merki*, 'sign; boundary'; O.N. *mork*, 'forest'. Cogn. w. Lat. *margo*, 'edge, border'. See **margin. 1. a** Anything destroying, diverging from, breaking, uniformity, normal colouring, design &c., of a surface; spot, stain, smear, scar &c.: *to leave a mark on the new paint*; *the mark of a wound*; **b** distinctive feature of colouring &c.; physical trait, peculiarity: *a horse with a white mark on its nose*; **c** (fig.) impress, result, modification, imparted to thought, habits, external conditions of life &c.: *great men leave their mark on the thought and life of their age.* Phr. *to make one's mark* (*as a scholar* &c.), to attain distinction. **2.** Sign, symbol; engraved, stamped, drawn or printed figure &c., having specific meaning: *to put a mark on a thing as a means of identification*; specif. **a** symbol, e.g. cross, inscribed in place of signature by person unable to write: *to make one's mark*; **b** distinguishing symbol, sign, imprint, esp. in compounds: *trade-mark, hall-mark* &c.; *the marks on china*, indicating place of manufacture &c. **3.** Thing aimed at; object of aim; target &c. Phr. *beside, wide of, the mark*, failing to hit; (fig.) not to the point; astray, at fault; *to hit, miss, the mark*, to attain, fail to attain, one's object; (*God*) *save the mark!*, expressing astonishment, irony, apology &c. **4. a** Any natural, or other, distinguishing sign, feature, characteristic or quality: *grey hair is not always a mark of age*; *jealousy is one of the marks of a petty character*; Phr. *mark of mouth*, indentation in horse's tooth indicating age; **b** distinction, repute, celebrity: *a man of mark.* **5.** Limit, boundary; line indicating measure, extent, position. Phr. *to be below, up to, the mark*, be below, up to, a standard. **6.** Numerical or other symbol expressing a judgement of the merits of candidates in a competition of any kind, or of value of performance in school or university examinations &c.; the degree of merit actually implied by a mark: *high marks for Latin prose* &c. **7.** (hist.) **a** Common land held by all members of community, among Germanic tribes; **b** frontier district: *the Mark of Brandenburg*; cp. **margrave. 8.** (Rugby football) Heel-mark made by player who has secured a fair catch.

mark (II.), vb. trans., fr. prec. **A. 1.** To put or leave a mark on; to stain, scar &c. **2. a** To stamp, write, draw, engrave &c., a mark having a specific meaning; specif. **b** to put name, number &c. on (linen &c.) as means of identification; **c** to put label indicating price on (goods &c.). **3.** To show, indicate, draw attention to, by means of a sign, dot, line &c.: *to mark a place, mark a river &c. on a map*; *to mark the accents in a line of verse.* **4. a** To record, put down, make a note of: *to mark the score in a game* &c.; **b** to assign marks to, record the number of marks awarded for: *to mark a paper, an exercise* &c. **5.** To observe, pay attention to, take note of, notice: *mark my words*; *to mark well what is said*; Phr. *a marked man.* **6.** To distinguish, single out, make remarkable: *great advances in applied science marked the course of the 19th century.* **7.** *Mark time*, to move feet up and down in march rhythm, without advancing; (fig.) to remain idle or unprogressive. **B.** Followed by adverbs and prepositions. *Mark off*, to put, indicate, point or line as limit, put a boundary to: *to mark off a section of a surface*; *to mark off six-inch lengths on a four-foot pole.* *Mark out*, **a** to trace, draw line(s) indicating boundary &c. on: *to mark out a lawn for tennis* &c.; **b** to plan out and indicate by visible signs: *to mark out a course for a race* &c.; **c** (fig.) to destine, indicate as suitable to receive: *to be marked out for promotion.*

mark (III.), n. Prob. same as **mark (I.)**. **1.** (obs.) **a** Mediaeval unit of weight applied to gold and silver, equal to about 8 oz.; **b** mediaeval coin worth about 13s. 4d. **2. a** Monetary unit of the modern German

Reich, worth as stabilized about 1s.; **b** coin or note representing this.

marked, adj. [1. markt; 2. mākt]. **mark (II.)** & **-ed**. **1.** Having marking(s). **2. a** Distinct, appreciable, considerable: *a marked difference, improvement*; **b** deliberately intended, noticeable: *he paid her marked attentions*; *his coldness was rather marked.*

markedly, adv. [1. márkedli; 2. mákidli]. Prec. & **-ly**. In a marked manner.

markedness, n. [1. márkednes; 2. mákidnis]. See prec. & **-ness**. State of being marked.

marker, n. [1. márker; 2. mákə]. **mark (II.)** & **-er**. One who, that which, marks; specif. **a** person marking score in game, e.g. *billiard-marker* &c.; **b** device for marking a score; **c** a book-marker.

market (I.), n. [1. márket; 2. mákit], fr. A.-Fr., fr. Lat. *mercāt-(us)*, 'trade, business; public place of business, market', fr. P.P. type of *mercāri*, 'to carry on trade, to buy'. See **mercantile**. **1. a** Public assembly of people for buying and selling (esp. live-stock and provisions); **b** open space or building to which people come for buying and selling, esp. provisions, cattle, horses &c. Phrs. *to put on the market*, offer for sale; *to come into the market*, be offered for sale; *to bring one's eggs, hogs, to a bad, the wrong, market*, fail in an undertaking through directing one's efforts in wrong quarter, approaching unsuitable persons. **2.** Fixed time at which a market is held. **3.** Trade in specific commodity: *corn market*; *money-market* &c. **4.** Demand, call, for, opportunity of selling, goods, in trade: *there is no market for that class of goods in England*; *to find a market*, be in demand. **5.** Rate of purchase and sale; present value: *the market rose.*

market (II.), vb. intrans. & trans., fr. prec. **1.** intrans. To buy or sell in market: *to go marketing*. **2.** trans. **a** To take to, place on the, market; **b** prepare (goods, produce &c.) for the market.

marketable, adj. [1. márketabl; 2. mákitəbl]. **market (II.)** & **-able**. Fit, suitable, for the market; salable.

marketably, adv. Prec. & **-ly**. In a marketable manner.

market-cross, n. Cross standing in mediaeval market-place.

market-day, n. Fixed day on which periodic markets are held.

market-garden, n. Garden in which vegetables are grown for the market.

market-overt, n. See **overt**.

market-place, n. Open space in which market is held.

market-price, n. Price for which a thing is sold in open market.

market-town, n. Town legally privileged to hold a market.

markhor, n. [1. márkor; 2. mákō]. Pushtu name, lit. 'snake-eater'. Goat with spiral horns, *Capra falconeri*, of the Himalayas.

marking, n. [1. márking; 2. mákiŋ]. **mark (I.)** & **-ing**. Distinctive mark, patch or streak of colour &c. on skin, feathers &c. of animal or bird.

marking-ink, n. Indelible ink, for marking linen &c.

marksman, n. [1. márksman; 2. máksmən]. **mark (I.)** & **man**. One skilled in accurate shooting; sharpshooter.

marksmanship, n. [1. márksmanship; 2. máksmənʃip]. Prec. & **-ship**. **a** Accuracy in shooting, skill in hitting a mark; **b** state of being a marksman.

marl, n. & vb. trans. [1. marl; 2. māl], fr. O. Fr. *marle*, fr. L. Lat. *margila*, dimin. of Lat. *marga*, 'marl'; prob. a Celtic word. **1.** n. Soil consisting of clay and carbonate of lime, often used as fertilizer. **2.** vb. To cover, fertilize, with marl.

marline, n. [1. márlin; 2. málin], fr. Du. *marlijn*, fr. *marren*, 'to bind', & *lijn*, 'line'. (naut.) Thin two-ply line used for binding shrouds &c.

marlinespike, n. [1. márlinspīk; 2. málinspaik]. (naut.) Spiked iron tool for separating strands in splicing a rope.

marlite, n. [1. márlīt; 2. málait]. **marl** & **-ite**. Variety of marl which does not become pulverized by the action of air.

marly, adj. [1. márli; 2. máli]. **marl** & **-y**. **a** Like, of the nature of, marl; **b** containing, abounding in, marl.

marmalade, n. [1. mármalād; 2. máməleid]. Fr., fr. Port. *marmelada*, fr. *marmelo*, 'quince', fr. Lat. *melimēlum*, fr. Gk. *melimēlon*, fr. *méli*, 'honey', q.v. under **melliferous**, & *mēlon*, 'apple'. See **melinite**. Preserve generally made of bitter oranges, less commonly of lemons, cut up and boiled with the peel and sugar.

marmolite, n. [1. mármolīt; 2. máməlait], fr. Gk. *marm-(airein)*, 'to shine', cogn. w. Lat. *merus*, 'pure, unmixed', see **mere (II.)**, & **-lite**. Pale-green variety of serpentine.

marmoreal, adj. [1. marmóreal; 2. māmɔ́riəl], fr. Lat. *marmore-(us)*, 'of, like, marble', fr. *marmor*, 'marble', see **marble**, & **-al**. (poet.) Of, like, marble.

marmoset, n. [1. mármozèt; 2. máməzèt], fr. Fr. *marmouset*, 'grotesque carved figure'; etymol. doubtful. Very small, bushy-tailed monkey of tropical America.

marmot, n. [1. mármot; 2. mámət], fr. Fr. *marmotte*, fr. Rhaeto-Romanic *murmont*, fr. Lat. *mūr-(em)*, stem of *mūs*, 'mouse', q.v. under **mouse**, & *mont-(is)*, 'of the mountain', see **montane**. **1.** Genus of burrowing, hibernating rodents of squirrel family, inhabiting Northern Asia, North America, and Europe, esp. Alps and Pyrenees. **2.** Kind of bathing-cap.

marocain, n. [1. márokān; 2. mǽrəkein]. Fr., 'Moroccan'. A heavy, crêpe dress material, made of silk or other textiles.

Maronite, n. [1. máronīt; 2. mǽrənait], fr. L. Lat. *Maronita*, fr. *Maron*, founder of sect in 4th century, & **-ite**. Member of sect of Eastern Christians living in neighbourhood of Mt. Lebanon, Syria.

maroon (I.), n. & adj. [1. maro͞on; 2. mərún], fr. Fr. *marron*, 'chestnut', fr. Ital. *marrone*. **1.** n. & adj. Brownish-crimson. **2.** n. Kind of firework producing loud report.

maroon (II.), n., fr. Fr. *marron*, perh. fr. Span. *cimarron*, 'wild', fr. *cima*, 'mountain-top', possibly fr. Gk. *kûma*, 'wave'. See **cyma**. **1.** One of class of negroes, originally fugitive slaves, living in mountains of West Indies. **2.** Marooned person.

maroon (III.), vb. trans. & intrans., fr. prec. **1.** trans. To put ashore, and abandon, on a desert island or other uninhabited spot. **2.** intrans. To loaf, loiter.

marplot, n. [1. márplot; 2. máplɔt]. **mar** & **plot**. One who hinders a scheme or enterprise by officious interference.

marque, n. [1. mark; 2. māk]. Fr., fr. Provenç. *marca*, fr. *marcar*, 'to seize as pledge'. *Letter(s) of marque*, licence given to private person to fit out and use armed ship for the purpose of attacking enemy's vessels.

marquee, n. [1. markḗ; 2. mākí]. Supposed sing., fr. **marquise**, taken as pl. Large tent, esp. one used at fêtes, flower-shows &c., or constructed in private grounds for dancing, refreshments &c.

marquet(e)ry, marqueterie, n. [1. marketri; 2. mákitri], fr. Fr. *marqueterie*, fr. *marqueter*, 'to vary; to inlay', fr. *marque*, 'mark'. See **mark (I.)**. **a** Method used in cabinet-making of producing designs, of flowers and fruits or figures, on wood by inlaying with other woods of different colours; **b** designs produced by this method.

marquis, marquess, n. [1. márkwis; 2. mákwis], fr. O. Fr. *marchis*, Ital. *marchese*, 'governor of the marches'. See **march (II.)** & **-ese**. **a** Title of nobility ranking between duke and earl, or, in foreign countries, above a count; also as courtesy title of the eldest son of a duke; **b** man holding this title.

marquisate, n. [1. márkwizat; 2. mákwizit]. Prec. & **-ate**. Office, rank, of marquis.

marquise, n. [1. markḗz; 2. mākíz]. Fr., fem. of **marquis**. **1. a** Foreign title corresponding to English *marchioness*; **b** lady holding this rank and title. **2.** Ring set with cluster of stones arranged in pointed oval.

marquois scale, n. [1. márkwoiz skāl; 2. mákwɔiz skeil], fr. name of supposed inventor, 18th cent. Device for drawing equidistant parallel lines.

marram, n. [1. máram; 2. mǽrəm], fr. O.N. *maralmr*, 'sea straw', fr. *marr*, 'sea', see **mare (I.)**, & *halmr*, 'straw', see **haulm**. A coarse, tough, binding grass growing on sand-dunes by the sea-shore.

marriage, n. [1. márij; 2. mǽridž], fr. Fr. *mariage*, fr. Low Lat. **maritāticum*, fr. *marīt-(us)*, 'husband'. See **marital** & **-age**. **1. a** Legal and social contract involving, in Christian countries, the permanent union of two persons of opposite sex as husband and wife; wedlock; **b** relation between married pair, married life. Phrs. *to give, take, in marriage*, give or take, as husband or wife; *marriage articles*, agreement concerning property &c. made by two persons before marriage; *marriage lines*, certificate of marriage; *marriage settlement*, arrangement whereby part of the property of either spouse is settled, for the benefit of the other, or for that of the children of the marriage. **2.** Act of marrying; ceremony by means of which a man and woman become husband and wife; *civil marriage*, one performed by government official, without religious ceremony; *religious marriage*, one solemnized with religious rites; *marriage licence*, official permit for two persons to marry. **3.** (fig.) Intimate association, close union: '*Let me not to the marriage of true minds Admit impediments*' (Shakespeare, Sonnet cxvi). **4.** (cards) Declaration of king and queen of same suit, in certain games.

marriageable, adj. [1. márijabl; 2. mǽridžəbl]. Prec. & **-able**. **1.** (of persons) Of an age suitable for marriage. **2.** (of age) Suitable for marriage.

married, adj. [1. márid; 2. mǽrid], fr. P.P. of **marry (I.)**. (of person(s)) **a** Having a husband or a wife: *married man, woman*; **b** joined in matrimony, united by marriage: *married couple*; **c** arising from the state of marriage; connected with, undertaken, enjoyed, by persons joined together in marriage, and as a result of this: *married love, life, happiness, misery.*

marrow, n. [1. márō; 2. mǽrou]. O.E. *mearg*; M.E. *merȝ*, *marou*; cp. O. Fris. *merg*; O.N. *mergr*; O.H.G. *maerg*, Germ. *mark*. **1.** Fatty substance enclosed in the hollow of bones. Phr. *to the marrow of one's bones*, to one's innermost soul; *frozen to the marrow*, frozen through and through. **2.** (fig.) Essential or best part of anything; substance, essence. **3.** Also *vegetable marrow*, species of edible gourd.

marrowbone, n. [1. márōbōn; 2. mǽroubоun]. Bone containing marrow; specif., section of shin of beef served hot for the sake of the marrow; Phr. *to go down on one's marrowbones*, to kneel down.

marrowfat, n. [1. márōfat; 2. mǽroufæt]. Kind of large green pea.

marrowless, adj. [1. márōles; 2. mǽroulis]. **marrow** & **-less**. Without marrow.

marrow spoon, n. Large narrow spoon for extracting marrow from bones.

marrowy, adj. [1. márōi; 2. mǽroui]. **marrow** & **-y**. (lit. and fig.) Containing marrow; rich.

marry (I.), vb. trans. & intrans. [1. mári; 2. mǽri], fr. Fr. *marier*, fr. Lat. *marītāre*, 'to marry', fr. *marīt-(us)*, 'of marriage'. See **marital**. **A.** trans. **1.** To take in marriage, take as husband or wife, wed. **2.** (of parent or guardian &c.) To give in marriage, cause to be married: *to marry one's daughter to a stockbroker*. **3.** (of priest) To perform the ceremony of marriage for: *the happy pair were married by the bishop of the diocese*. **4.** (fig.) To unite closely, join intimately:

to marry intellect with sensibility. **B.** intrans. To take a husband or wife, enter the state of matrimony: *to marry late in life.*

marry (II.), interj. = *Mary* (the Virgin). (archaic) Expressing surprise, indignation &c. Phr. *marry come up*, expressing surprise, incredulity &c.

Mars, n. [1. marz; 2. māz]. According to Walde, cogn. w. Gk. *márnamai*, 'I fight'; Scrt. *mṛṇāti*, 'strikes, crushes'. See **marasmus, marble.** **1. a** Roman god of war; hence, **b** war personified. **2.** Planet nearest to the earth and fourth in order from the sun.

Marsala, n. [1. marsáhla; 2. māsálə]. Name of town in Sicily. Kind of light, sweetish, white wine, produced in Sicily.

Marseillaise, n. [1. màrsāyáz; 2. màseijéiz]. Fr., fr. fem. adj. *Marseillaise*, 'of Marseilles'. See next word & **-ese.** French national Republican song, composed by Rouget de Lisle in 1792, and first sung by volunteers from Marseilles in French Revolution.

Marseilles, n. [1. marsálz; 2. màséilz]. Town on south coast of France. Kind of stiff cotton material.

marsh, n. [1. marsh; 2. māʃ]. O.E. *mersč*, M.E. *mersh*; cp. M.L.G. *mersch*; fr. Gmc. **mari-*, 'sea'. See **mere** (I.) & **-ish**, & cp. **marish.** Tract of low-lying land, more or less permanently water-logged; bog, morass.

marshal (I.), n. [1. márshal; 2. máʃəl], fr. O. Fr. *mareschal*, Mod. Fr. *maréchal*, fr. Med. Lat. *mariscalcus*, fr. O.H.G. *marahscalh*, fr. *marah*, 'horse', cp. O.E. *mearh*, 'horse', see **mare** (II.), & *scalh*, 'servant', cp. O.E. *sčealc*; O. Fris. *skalk*; O.N. *skalkr*; Goth. *skalks*, 'servant, man'. A marshal was orig. **a** person in charge of horses, then a high officer in a royal household, a master of the horse. A term used of certain officials, civil and military, of various rank and dignity. **1.** An official of a royal household, or court &c. directing ceremonies &c.; in England, *the Earl-Marshal*, q.v.; *the City Marshal*, official of the Corporation of London. **2.** (mil.) **a** A general officer of the highest rank in certain foreign countries, as *Marshal of France*; also as title of address, as *Marshal Foch*; in British army *Field-Marshal*; **b** as part of the title of various officers of high rank in the British Royal Air Force: *Air-Marshal* &c., see under **air**; **c** a chief officer of military police: *provost-marshal.* **3.** (judicial and administrative) **a** An official, with certain ceremonial and personal duties, who accompanies a High Court judge on circuit: *a judge's marshal*; **b** the principal attendant of a university proctor, colloquially known as a *bulldog*; **c** (U.S.A.) the executive official of the Federal Courts in each judicial district, with the functions of a sheriff.

marshal (II.), vb. trans., fr. prec. **1. a** To bring into order, arrange in appointed positions: *to marshal persons in procession, at banquet* &c.; **b** (fig.) to set out in an orderly manner, arrange clearly: *to marshal facts* &c. **2.** To lead, conduct, with ceremony: *to marshal a person into his place.* **3.** (her.) To put in due order the quarterings &c. on an escutcheon. **4.** (law) To arrange, fix, in order according to priority of the claims of creditors, in distribution of an estate of a bankrupt or deceased person: *to marshal the assets.*

Marshalsea, n. [1. márshalsē; 2. máʃəlsī], fr. earlier *marshalcy.* **marshal** & **-cy.** **a** Court formerly held in Southwark by the marshal of the royal household; **b** a prison in Southwark for debtors &c., under the marshal of the King's Bench, who was responsible for their safe custody, abolished 1849.

marshalship, n. [1. márshalship; 2. máʃəlʃip]. **marshal** & **-ship.** Office, rank, of marshal.

marsh-gas, n. Light inflammable gas, product of decomposed vegetable matter, as in marshes; methane.

marshiness, n. [1. márshines; 2. máʃinis]. **marshy** & **ness.** State of being marshy.

marsh-mallow, n. **a** Herb of the mallow family with pink flowers, growing in damp ground: **b** sweetmeat made from root of this.

marsh-marigold, n. Genus of plants of Ranunculus family, growing in low-lying marshy ground, and having bright golden flowers.

marshy, adj. [1. márshi; 2. máʃi]. **marsh** & **-y.** Of, like, a marsh; abounding in marshes; wet, boggy, swampy.

marsupial, adj. & n. [1. marsûpial; 2. māsjúpiəl], fr. Lat. *marsūpi-(um)*, 'purse, pouch', fr. Gk. *marsúpion*, dimin. of *már-sipos*, 'bag, purse'; perh. of Oriental origin. **1.** adj. **a** Pertaining to, like, a pouch: e.g. *marsupial muscle, bone* &c.; **b** (of animal) belonging to subclass, *Marsupialia*, of mammals having a pouch in which to carry their young, which are born in an immature condition. **2.** n. A marsupial animal, as the kangaroo, wombat &c.

mart, n. [1. mart; 2. māt], fr. Du. *markt*, fr. Lat. *mercātus*, 'market'. See **market.** **1. a** (poet.) Market-place; **b** trading centre. **2.** Auction room.

martello tower, n. [1. martélō tóur; 2. mātélou táuə]. Distortion of name of Cape Mortella in Corsica, where a tower of this kind was unsuccessfully attacked by a landing party. Small round fort or fortified tower with a single gun, a number of which were erected on the E., S.E., and S. sea-coast of England to guard against invasion in the Napoleonic wars.

marten, n. [1. márten; 2. mátin], fr. O. Fr. *martrine*, adj. fr. *martre*, 'marten', of Gmc. origin; cp. O.E. *mearþ*; Mod. Germ. *marder*, 'marten'. A carnivorous mammal, genus *Mustela*, resembling a weasel, valued for its fur; the two best-known species are the pine marten and the sable.

martial, adj. [1. márshal; 2. máʃəl], fr. Fr., fr. Lat. *martiāl-(is)*, 'of Mars'; fr. *Mart-is*, genit. of **Mars**, & **-ial.** **1.** Pertaining to, suitable for, war: *martial music*; *martial law*, temporary government by military officers, during which ordinary civil and criminal law ceases to act, as in time of war, rebellion &c. **2.** Warlike, militant; ready, eager, to fight: *the true martial spirit.* **3.** (cap., rare) Of, pertaining to, planet Mars.

martialize, vb. trans. [1. márshaliz; 2. máʃəlaiz]. Prec. & **-ize.** To make suitable for, prepare for, warfare; impart martial spirit to.

martially, adv. [1. márshali; 2. máʃəli]. **martial** & **-ly.** In a martial manner.

Martian, n. [1. márshian; 2. máʃiən], fr. Lat. *Mart-(ius)*, 'of Mars', & **-ian.** Inhabitant of the planet Mars.

martin, n. [1. mártin; 2. mátin], fr. personal name *Martin.* Name given to several birds of swallow family, esp. the house-martin, *Hirundo urbica*, building its nest of mud or clay under eaves &c., and the sand-martin, *H. riparia*, in sandy banks.

martinet, n. [1. màrtinét; 2. màtinét], fr. name of officer in the army of Louis XIV. Strict, rigid, rather pedantic disciplinarian, esp. naval or military; any stickler for regulations and discipline.

martinet(t)ish, adj. [1. màrtinétish; 2. màtinétiʃ]. Prec. & **-ish.** Of, pertaining to, a martinet; strict, rigorously exacting.

martinetism, n. [1. màrtinétizm; 2. màtinétizəm]. **martinet** & **-ism.** Strict discipline.

martingale, n. [1. mártinggāl; 2. mátiŋgeil], fr. Fr.; etymol. doubtful. **1.** Part of horse's harness consisting of a strap having one end fastened to the girth, passing thence between the forelegs; the strap is double at the breast, and the upper ends have rings through which the reins pass, thus preventing the horse tossing its head up or rearing. **2.** Stay for a jib-boom. **3.** The doubling of amount of a preceding stake which has been lost.

martini cocktail, n. [1. martḗni kóktāl; 2. mātíni kókteil]. Origin doubtful. A cocktail made of vermouth, orange bitters, and gin.

Martini-Henry rifle, n. [1. martḗni hénri rífl; 2. mātíni hénri ráifl], fr. name of inventors. A breech-loading rifle, superseded in 1886.

Martinmas, n. [1. mártinmas; 2. mátinmæs], fr. name of St. Martin, Bishop of Tours (d. 397), & **mass** (I.). St. Martin's day, Nov. 11th.

martlet, n. [1. mártlet; 2. mátlit], fr. Fr. *martelet*, perh. fr. *martinet*, dimin. of **martin.** **1.** Bird of swallow family, esp. martin. **2** (her.) Representation of a bird of rather vague species without feet; used as a charge, and also as a difference for a fourth son.

martyr (I.), n. [1. márter; 2. mátə], fr. eccles. Lat., fr. Late Gk. *mártur*, fr. Gk. *mártur-*, stem of *mártus*, 'a witness'; cp. Gk. *mérimna*, 'care, solicitude, thought'; cogn. w. Scrt. *smárati*, 'to remember'; Lat. *memor*, 'mindful', see **memory**; Goth. *maurnan*, O.E. *murnan*, 'to care for, be anxious about; to lament over', see **mourn.** **1.** One who voluntarily suffers pain, punishment, or death for the sake of some cause or principle; specif., one who suffers death on account of his adherence to Christian faith, or to the doctrine of specific branch of Church: *a Christian martyr*; *a martyr in the cause of science* &c. **2.** Sufferer, esp. in Phr. *a martyr to*, suffering from: *a martyr to gout* &c.; Phr. *to make a martyr of oneself*, to make a show of self-sacrifice.

martyr (II.), vb. trans., fr. prec. To put to death by martyrdom.

martyrdom, n. [1. márterdum; 2. mátədəm]. **martyr** (I.) & **-dom.** **1.** State of being a martyr. **2. a** Suffering or death of martyr; **b** (fig.) pain, torment; severe suffering.

martyrize, vb. trans. [1. mártiriz; 2. mátiraiz]. **martyr** (I.) & **-ize.** To make a martyr of.

martyro-, pref., fr. **martyr** (I.). Of martyrs; e.g. *martyrolatry*, worship of martyrs; *martyrology*, history, study, record, of martyrs.

martyry, n. [1. márteri; 2. mátəri], fr. Late Gk. *martúrion*, fr. *mártur*, 'martyr'. See **martyr** (I.) & **-y.** Martyr's shrine.

marvel (I.), n. [1. márvl; 2. mávl], fr. O. Fr. *merveille*, fr. Lat. *mīrābilia*, 'wonders', neut. pl. of *mīrābilis*, 'wonderful', fr. *mīrā-(ri)*, 'to wonder at'. See **miracle, admire,** & **-ble.** **1.** Something wonderful, thing arousing astonished admiration. **2.** Person or thing exhibiting specific quality in very high and uncommon degree: *a marvel of patience, beauty* &c. Phr. (colloq.) *he's a perfect marvel*, an admirable person, one possessing some exceptional quality or accomplishment. **3.** (archaic) Astonishment, wonder.

marvel (II.), vb. intrans., fr. O. Fr. *merveiller*, fr. *merveille*, 'wonder'. See prec. **a** *Marvel at*, to be roused to wonder and admiration by: *to marvel at a person's courage, impudence* &c.; **b** to be surprised and bewildered: *as they listened to his words, they marvelled greatly.*

marvellous, adj. & n. [1. márvelus; 2. mávələs], fr. O. Fr. *merveillos.* **marvel** (I.) & **-ous.** **1.** adj. Arousing admiration and wonder; surprising, because uncommon or exceptional. **2.** n. *The marvellous*, phenomena lying outside ordinary experience, which excite surprise and awe; mysterious, uncanny, almost incredible event, or series of events.

marvellously, adv. Prec. & **-ly.** In a marvellous manner.

marvellousness, n. See prec. & **-ness.** Quality of being marvellous.

marzipan, n. See **marchpane.**

mascot, n. [1. máskut; 2. mǽskət], fr. Fr. *mascotte*; etymol. doubtful. Person or thing supposed to bring good luck; talisman, charm.

masculine (I.), adj. [1. máhskūlin, máskūlin; 2. máskjulin, mǽskjulin(e)], fr. Fr. *masculin(e)*, fr. Lat. *masculīn-(us)*, 'of the male sex', fr. *mās*, 'male', perh. cogn. w. Scrt. *(pú)mans*, 'man', & **-cule,** & **-ine.** **1.** (gram.) Of the gender to which nouns denoting males usually belong. **2. a** Of the male sex; **b** having the qualities of a male; virile, vigorous; **c** (of a woman) having qualities more suitable to a man than to a woman.

3. (prosody) **a** *Masculine rhyme*, (in French verse) between the final syllables of words; **b** *masculine ending*, (of verse-line) one rhyming in this way.

masculine (**II.**), n., fr. prec. **a** Masculine gender; **b** masculine noun, pronoun &c.

masculineness, n. **masculine** (**I.**) & **-ness.** (rare) Masculinity.

masculinity, n. [1. màhskūlíniti; 2. màskjulíniti]. **masculine** & **-ity.** Quality, state, of being masculine; virility.

mash (**I.**), n. [1. mash; 2. mæʃ]. O.E. *māsc*, 'mash'; cp. Mod. Germ. *meisch*, 'pulp, crushed grapes', &c.; perh. cogn. w. O.E. *miscian*, 'to mix'. See **mix.** **1.** (brewing) Mixture of malt and hot water. **2.** Mixture of bran or grain steeped in boiling water, given to horses &c. **3.** Any soft substance, e.g. potatoes, crushed or beaten to a pulp.

mash (**II.**), vb. trans., fr. prec. **1.** To make an infusion of (malt) with hot water. **2.** To reduce to a mash.

mash (**III.**), vb. trans. & n. (obsolesc. or obs. slang) **1.** vb. To make love to, attempt to excite admiration and affection of (one of opposite sex); Phr. *mashed on*, in love with. **2.** n. Person being mashed.

masher, n. [másher; 2. mǽʃə]. Prec. & **-er.** **a** A lady-killer, a coxcomb; **b** a fop, a swell; a man who affects excessive smartness, esp. of a second-rate style, in his dress.

mashie, mashy, n. [1. máshi; 2. mǽʃi]. Perh. fr. Fr. *massue*, 'club'. Kind of golf-club with short, iron head.

mash-tub, n. Tub in which mash is made in breweries.

masjid, n. [1. músjid; 2. másdžid]. Arab. Mohammedan mosque.

mask (**I.**), n. [1. mahsk; 2. māsk], fr. Fr. *masque*, prob. fr. Span. *mascara*, 'mask'; etymol. doubtful. **1. a** Small piece of silk, velvet &c. worn so as partially, or entirely, to conceal face; Phr. *to throw off one's mask*, (fig.) to abandon pretence and concealment, to reveal one's true character or intentions; **b** covering of wire gauze stretched on framework, worn to protect face in fencing &c.; **c** form of protective covering with respirator attachment for face and head, against poisonous gas in war &c.: *a gas-mask.* **2. a** Representation of human head and face, esp. as worn by Greek and Roman actors; **b** impression taken in clay or other plastic material from the human face, esp. after death: *death-mask.* **3.** Person wearing mask and other disguise, as at a masked ball &c.; a masker. **4.** Head and face of a fox, cut off and kept as a hunting trophy.

mask (**II.**), vb. trans. & intrans., fr. prec. **A.** trans. **1. a** To cover with a mask; **b** (fig.) to disguise, conceal, dissemble: *to mask one's real character, intentions &c. behind an assumed manner.* **2.** (mil.) To conceal from the enemy: *to mask the batteries, guns* &c., to cover, protect from the enemy's attack. **B.** intrans. To assume a mask; to disguise oneself.

masked, adj. [1. mahskt; 2. māskt], fr. P.P. of prec. **1. a** Wearing a mask, disguised; **b** *masked ball* &c., one at which masks are worn. **2.** (mil.) Hidden from enemy: *masked guns.*

masker, masquer, n. [1. máhsker; 2. máskə]. **mask** & **-er.** **a** One who wears a mask, esp. person taking part in masquerade; **b** performer in masque.

maskinonge, n. [1. máhskinonj; 2. máskinəndž]. Am. Indian word. Kind of large pike of N. American lakes.

maslin, n. [1. mázlin; 2. mǽzlin]. M.E. *mestlyon*, fr. O. Fr. *mestillon*, fr. L. Lat. *mestilliōn-(em)*, fr. Lat. *mixt-(um)*, P.P. type of *miscere*, 'to mix'. See **mix.** A mixture of different kinds of grain, such as wheat and rye, for bread-making.

masochism, n. [1. mázokizm; 2. mǽzəkizəm], fr. L. von Sacher-Masoch, Austrian novelist, d. 1895, who described a case in one of his works. A form of sexual perversion, in which gratification is derived from physical suffering, mental humiliation &c.; contrasted with *sadism.*

mason (**I.**), n. [1. másn; 2. méisn], fr. O. Fr. *maçon*, fr. Med. Lat. *machio*; prob. fr. Gmc. base **mak-*. See **make.** **1.** Artificer who cuts and prepares stone for building, and who builds with stone. **2.** Member of society of Freemasons.

mason (**II.**), vb. trans., fr. prec. To construct (building) of, or partly of, masonry.

masonic, adj. [1. masónik; 2. məsɔ́nik]. **mason** & **-ic.** Of, pertaining to, Freemasonry.

masonry, n. [1. másunri; 2. méisənri]. **mason** & **-ery.** **1.** Occupation or trade of a mason. **2.** Work done by mason; that part of a building made of stone, brick &c. and mortar; stonework. **3.** (cap.) Freemasonry.

Mas(s)ora(h), n. [1. masóra; 2. mæsɔ́rə], fr. Heb. *masoreth.* Body of accumulated tradition concerning Hebrew text of Old Testament, forming critical commentary.

Mas(s)orete, Mas(s)orite, n. [1. másorēt, -rīt; 2. mǽsərīt, -rait], fr. Heb. *masoreth.* See prec. Jewish scribe contributing to Massorah.

Mas(s)oretic, adj. [1. màsorétik; 2. mæ̀sərétik]. Prec. & **-ic.** Of, pertaining to, the Massorah, or to a Massorete.

masque, n. [1. mahsk; 2. māsk], fr. Fr. *masque.* See **mask** (**I.**). **1.** Dramatic performance, largely spectacular, originally in dumb show, later having a dialogue, which, however, is somewhat subordinate to the pageantry. **2.** Literary composition written to be performed as a masque.

masquerade, n. & vb. intrans. [1. màhskeràd; 2. màskəréid], fr. Span. *mascarada*, fr. *mascara*, 'mask'. See **mask** & **-ade.** **1.** n. Assembly in the nature of an amusing frolic, in which those taking part wear masks and other disguises. **2.** vb. intrans. **a** To take part in a masquerade; **b** (fig.) *to masquerade as*, give oneself out to be, assume character of.

Mass (**I.**), n. [1. mas; 2. mæs]. O.E. *messe*, *mæsse*, M.E. *masse*; fr. Low Lat. *messa*, fr. words of dismissal at end of service: *ite, missa est*; fem. P.P. of *mittere*, 'to send'. See **mission.** **1.** Celebration of the Eucharist; ancient name often confined, among strict Protestants, to the Roman Catholic service: *to go to, hear, Mass*; *High Mass*, one accompanied by full ceremonial and music; *Low Mass*, one without elaborate ceremonial and music. **2.** Office, liturgy, of the Mass. **3.** Musical setting for part of this office.

mass (**II.**), n., fr. Fr. *masse*, fr. Lat. *massa*, 'lump, mass', fr. Gk. *mâza*, 'barley-cake', prob. connected w. Gk. *mássein*, 'to knead'. See **macerate** & **make** (**I.**). **1.** Coherent body of matter of indefinite shape: *a mass of cloud, of earth, iron* &c. **2.** (phys.) Quantity of matter in a body. **3.** Closely compacted group, large amount, of individual objects: *a mass of particles, flowers* &c. **4.** Large number, great quantity: *masses of people.* Phr. *to be a mass of*, exhibit large numbers of, be covered with: *to be a mass of bruises* &c. **5. a** *The mass*, greater part, majority; Phr. *in the mass*, in the main, in the aggregate; **b** pl., *the masses*, the lower classes of society.

mass (**III.**), vb. trans. & intrans., fr. prec. **1.** trans. **a** To bring, put, gather, together into a mass; **b** (mil.) to bring together at one point, concentrate: *to mass troops.* **2.** intrans. To come together into a mass.

massacre, n. & vb. trans. [1. másaker; 2. mǽsəkə], fr. Fr., fr. O. Fr. *macecle*, 'slaughter'; fr. Lat. *macellum*, 'provision market where flesh and fish are sold'; according to Walde, not related to *mactāre*, 'to sacrifice, destroy', but fr. Semitic; cp. Heb. *makhela*, 'hurdle, enclosure'. **1.** n. Indiscriminate slaughter, carnage, butchery, esp. of persons. **2.** vb. To put to death by a massacre; to slaughter indiscriminately.

massage, n. & vb. trans. [1. másahzh; 2. mǽsāž], fr. Fr., fr. *masser*, 'to massage', fr. Port. *amassar*, 'to knead', fr. *massa*, 'dough', fr. Lat. *massa*, 'lump; barley-cake'. See **mass** (**II.**). **1.** n. Remedial treatment consisting of rubbing and kneading a part of the body with the fingers to rectify morbid conditions, muscular injury &c. **2.** vb. To treat with massage.

massé, n. [1. masá; 2. mæséi], fr. Fr., P.P. of *masser*, 'to make a massé', fr. *mace*, 'club'. See **mace** (**I.**). (billiards) Stroke made with cue held perpendicularly.

masseur, n. [1. masér; 2. mæsʌ́]. Fr., fr. *mass-(er)*, 'to massage', see **massage**, & **-or.** Man who practises massage.

masseuse, n. [1. maséz; 2. mæsʌ́z]. Fem. of prec. Woman who practises massage.

massif, n. [1. másēf; 2. mǽsīf]. Fr. See **massive.** (physical geog.) Group of mountains connected together forming a unit, either in an isolated mass or as distinctive part of a mountain range.

massiness, n. [1. másines; 2. mǽsinis]. **massy** & **-ness.** State or quality of being massy.

massive, adj. [1. másiv; 2. mǽsiv], fr. Fr. See **mass** (**II.**) & **-ive.** **1.** Large, substantial, solid, heavy, bulky, ponderous. **2. a** (of features, figure, build) Of large proportions, of generous mould; strong and heavy; **b** (of the mind) powerful, solid.

massively, adv. Prec. & **-ly.** In a massive manner.

massiveness, n. See prec. & **-ness.** State or quality of being massive.

mass-meeting, n. **mass** (**II.**) & **meeting.** Large public meeting, esp. political.

massor, n. [1. máser; 2. mǽsə]. See **massage** & **-or.** Masseur.

massy, adj. [1. mási; 2. mǽsi]. **mass** (**II.**) & **-y.** Solid, bulky, massive.

mast (**I.**), n. [1. mahst; 2. māst]. O.E. *mæst*, M.E. *mast*; cp. Du. *mast*, O.H.G. *mast*; O.N. *mastr*; cogn. w. Lat. *mālus*, 'mast', fr. **mādus*, fr. **mazdos*; cp. O. Slav. *mostŭ*, 'bridge'. Long pole of wood, iron &c. set upright **a** in ship to support sails, rigging &c.; **b** for wireless, decorations &c. Phrs. *before the mast*, as ordinary seaman; *half-mast* (*high*), (of flag) lowered by amount equal to width of flag, as sign of mourning.

mast (**II.**), n. O.E. *mæst*, M.E. *mast*; cp. O.H.G. *mast*, 'mast, fodder'; cogn. w. Gk. *mazós*, *mastós*, 'breast', see **mastoid**, Scrt. *mēdaš*, 'fat', *mēdana-m*, 'fodder'; Goth. *mats*, 'food'; O.E. *mete*, 'food'. See **meat.** Fruit of beech, oak, chestnut &c., esp. as food for swine.

mastaba, n. [1. mástaba; 2. mǽstəbə]. Arab. *maçtabah*, 'stone bench'. (archaeol.) A primitive form of tomb in ancient Egypt with sloping sides and flat roof, containing mummy chamber.

master (**I.**), n. [1. máhster; 2. mástə], fr. O.E. *mægester*, O. Fr. *maistre*, fr. Lat. *magister*, 'master'; the word is formed fr. stem **mag-*, 'great', as in *magnus*, 'great', see **magnum**, w. a double compar. suff., cp. Lat. *magis*, 'more', & see suff. in **inter** (**II.**), &c. The word has the general senses of (male) director, controller, leader, person having authority, employer, owner, & is used in various connexions. Further, the word may imply spiritual mastery or intellectual grasp. **1.** *Master of a ship, ship's master*, the captain (of merchantman); *the master of the house*, head of the household; Phrs. *to be master in one's own house*, manage one's own affairs and allow no interference from others; *a servant's, workman's, master*, person who employs and pays him; *master and man*; *the young master*, son of employer; *a dog knows his own master*, his owner; *master of a fortune*, having it at one's disposal. **2. a** Title given to the Heads of certain Colleges at Oxford and Cambridge: *the Master of Balliol, of Peterhouse* &c.; **b** title given to eldest son and heir of some ancient Scottish baronies: *the Master of Borthwick, of Lovat* &c.; **c** *Master of the*

Temple, (i.) (hist.) title of the Chief of the Knights Templars, usually *Grand Master*; (ii.) title of the priest in charge of the Temple Church, London; **d** form of address employed by inferiors to boys and youths of superior station: *Master Charles, young master Jones* &c. **3. a** Teacher, instructor, esp. in a school, also *school-master*; in many compounds designating an instructor in some specific art or accomplishment: *riding-, music-, dancing-master* &c.; **b** leader, teacher, in philosophy, religion &c., specif., *The Master,* Christ. **4.** Skilled artificer, esp. one having a business of his own: *master builder, potter, carpenter* &c. **5.** Great painter, esp. *old master,* **a** one of the leading artists of 13th to 18th centuries; **b** picture painted by one of these. **6.** Person holding the second degree in the Faculty of Arts or Science at Oxford or Cambridge, *Master of Arts* (abbr. M.A.) [èm éi], which entitles the holder to teach and examine in the university; *Master in the Schools,* a University examiner; in other Universities, also *Master of Science* (M.Sc.), *of Engineering* (M.Eng.) &c. **7.** Name of holder of various offices: **a** *Master of Ceremonies,* person presiding over arrangements, forms observed &c., on state occasions or at social gathering; **b** *Master of foxhounds* (abbr. M.F.H.), person having control of a pack; **c** *Master of the Horse,* officer in English royal household; **d** *Master of the Rolls,* principal judge of Court of Appeal and head of the Record Office; **e** *Master of the High Court,* a subordinate judicial official of the Supreme Court, dealing with the preliminaries of cases in chambers &c. **8.** Person possessing some special aptitude, art, accomplishment, or quality of mind to a pre-eminent degree: *a master of satire, persiflage, cajolery* &c.; *Milton was a master of majestic harmonies in verse.* **9.** In various Phrs. implying spiritual or intellectual control and mastery: *master of oneself,* having one's emotions and passions and actions perfectly under the control of one's reason; *master of a subject, language* &c., knowing it thoroughly; *master of the situation,* (i.) dominant or victorious figure in a contest; (ii.) able to deal successfully with given circumstances; *master of one's fate,* independent of circumstances, and able to control and determine one's destiny. **10.** (attrib.) Equivalent to 'of a master'; implying supremacy, domination: *a master mind*; or pre-eminence: *a master stroke.*

master (II.), vb. trans., fr. prec. **1.** To become master of, overcome, defeat, subdue: *to master a naughty boy, a horse.* **2.** To acquire knowledge of, skill in, facility in using: *to master a subject, the art of fly-fishing* &c.

master-at-arms, n. [1. máhster at ármz; 2. mástər ət ámz]. Police officer on man-of-war.

masterful, adj. [1. máhsterfool; 2. mástəful]. **master & -ful.** Inclined and able to take the lead; inclined to impose one's will on others; imperious, domineering.

masterfully, adv. Prec. & **-ly.** In a masterful manner.

masterfulness, n. See prec. & **-ness.** Quality of being masterful.

Master-General, n., in full, *Master-General of the Ordnance.* Title of the head of the Ordnance department at the War Office.

masterhood, n. [1. máhsterhood; 2. mástəhud]. **master & -hood.** State of being a master.

master-key, n. Key made to open many different locks.

masterless, adj. [1. máhsterles; 2. mástəlis]. **master & -less.** Without a master.

masterliness, n. [1. máhsterlines; 2. mástəlinis]. See next word & **-ness.** Quality of being masterly.

masterly, adj. [1. máhsterli; 2. mástəli]. **master & -ly.** **a** (of persons) Displaying supreme executive or creative power and ability; **b** (of actions or works) performed with the skill of a master.

master-mariner, n. Captain of merchant or fishing-vessel.

master-mason, n. **1.** Stone-mason who has passed his apprenticeship. **2.** Freemason who has attained to the third degree.

masterpiece, n. [1. máhsterpēs; 2. mástəpīs]. Piece of work of supreme excellence.

mastership, n. [1. máhstership; 2. mástəʃip]. **master & -ship.** **1.** Office of master, esp. schoolmaster. **2.** Dominion, rule, control.

masterstroke, n. [1. máhsterstrōk; 2. mástəstrouk]. Action in politics, diplomacy &c., of extreme skill, tact, and effectiveness.

mastery, n. [1. máhsteri; 2. mástəri], fr. O. Fr. *maistrie.* **master & -y.** **1. a** Authority, dominion, command; **b** supremacy, ascendancy, the upper hand: *to gain the mastery.* **2. a** Skill, dexterity, worthy of a master; **b** thorough knowledge of, skill in, a subject or use of an instrument.

mast-head, n. & vb. trans. **1.** n. Highest part of ship's mast. **2.** vb. trans. **a** To send (sailor) to mast-head as punishment; **b** to raise (sail) to top of mast.

mastic, n. [1. mástik; 2. mǽstik], fr. Fr., fr. L. Lat. *mastichum,* fr. Gk. *mastíkhē,* 'chewing gum'; cp. *mastikháein,* 'to grind the teeth'. See **masticate.** **1. a** Resin exuding from bark of certain trees, growing esp. in the Levant; **b** tree producing mastic. **2.** Kind of cement made of mastic. **3.** Colour of mastic, pale fawn.

masticability, n. [1. màstikabíliti; 2. mæ̀stikəbíliti], fr. L. Lat. *masticā-(re),* 'to chew', see **masticate, & -bility.** State of being masticable.

masticable, adj. [1. mástikabl; 2. mǽstikəbl], fr. L. Lat. *masticā-(re),* 'to chew', see next word, & **-ble.** Capable of being masticated.

masticate, vb. trans. [1. mástikāt; 2. mǽstikeit], fr. L. Lat. *masticāt-(um),* P.P. type of *masticāre,* 'to chew', prob. fr. Gk.; cp. Gk. *mastikháein,* 'grind the teeth'; *mástax,* 'mouth'; fr. stem **math-to,* fr. **mn̥th-to*; cogn. w. Lat. *mandere,* 'to chew'; Goth. *munþs*; O.N. *munnr*; O.H.G. *munt*; O.E. *mūð,* 'mouth'. See **mastic & mouth.** To grind up with the teeth; to chew.

mastication, n. [1. màstikáshun; 2. mæ̀stikéiʃən]. Prec. & **-ion.** Act of masticating.

masticator, n. [1. mástikātor; 2. mǽstikeitə]. **masticate & -or.** One who, that which, masticates; esp. machine for grinding food.

masticatory, adj. [1. mástikātori; 2. mǽstikeitəri]. **masticate & -ory.** Of, pertaining to, for, mastication.

masticic, adj. [1. mastísik; 2. mæstísik]. Prec. & **-ic.** (chem.) Of, pertaining to, of the nature of, mastic.

mastiff, n. [1. máhstif; 2. mástif], fr. O. Fr. *mastin,* fr. Low Lat. **mansuētīn-(us),* fr. Lat. *mansuēt-(us),* 'tame, quiet', fr. P.P. of *mansuēscere,* 'to tame', fr. *man-(us),* 'hand', see **manual, &** *suēscere,* 'to grow accustomed', q.v. under **desuetude.** Breed of large, thick-set, powerful dogs, with broad muzzle and pendulous lips.

mastitis, n. [1. mastítis; 2. mæstáitis], fr. Gk. *mast-(ós),* 'breast', see **mastoid, & -itis.** Inflammation of the breast.

mastodon, n. [1. mástodon; 2. mǽstədɔn], fr. Gk. *mast-(ós),* 'breast', see **mastoid,** & Gk. *odón-(t)-,* stem of *odoûs,* 'tooth', see **odonto-.** Genus of large extinct mammals allied to the elephant, having nipple-shaped prominences on the molar teeth.

mastodontic, adj. [1. màstodóntik; 2. mæ̀stədɔ́ntik]. Prec. & **-ic.** Of, pertaining to, a mastodon.

mastoid, adj. & n. [1. mástoid; 2. mǽstɔid], fr. Gk. *mast-(ós),* 'breast', fr. **mad-t-os*; cp. Gk. *madáein,* 'to be wet, to flow'. Cogn. w. Lat. *madēre,* 'to drip'; Scrt. *mádati,* 'is drunk'; *médaš,* 'fat'; Goth. *mats,* O.E. *mete,* 'food'. See **meat.** (anat. &c.) **1.** adj. **a** Shaped like female breast; of a process of the bone behind the ear: *mastoid process*; **b** pertaining to, affecting, the mastoid process or its region: *mastoid abscess.* **2.** n. The mastoid process or bone.

masturbate, vb. intrans. [1. másterbāt; 2. mǽstəbeit], fr. Lat. *masturbāt-(um),* P.P. type of *masturbāri,* 'to masturbate'; etymol. doubtful. To practise self-abuse.

masturbation, n. [1. màsterbáshun; 2. mæ̀stəbéiʃən]. Prec. & **-ion.** Act of masturbating.

mat (I.), n. [1. mat; 2. mæt]. O.E., M.E. *matt,* fr. L. Lat. *matta,* 'mat, rough covering'; perh. a Phoenician loan-word. **1. a** Coarse fabric made of straw, rushes &c. or of coconut or other fibre; **b** piece of such material for wiping feet on, to cover part of floor, esp. outside the door of a room; Phr. *to leave* (person) *on the mat,* refuse to receive; **c** any piece or strip of fabric or carpet covering part of the floor; a rug; a disorderly tangle of hair. **2.** Small piece of material of linen, lace, plaited rushes &c., to put dishes on &c.

mat (II.), vb. trans. & intrans., fr. prec. **A.** trans. **1.** To cover, supply, with mat(s). **2.** (esp. in P.P.) To cause to form a confused, tangled mat: *fibres matted together*; *matted hair.* **B.** intrans. To become matted.

mat (III.), adj., fr. Fr., fr. Med. Lat. *mattus,* fr. Arab. *mat,* 'helpless'. Having a dull surface, without lustre.

mat (IV.), n., fr. prec. **1.** Rough or frosted appearance, as on frosted glass. **2.** Dull, lustreless appearance (of metal &c.). **3.** Dull gold border round mount of framed picture.

mat (V.), vb. trans., fr. prec. **1.** To give a dull, dead surface to (metal &c.). **2.** To frost (glass).

matador, n. [1. mátador; 2. mǽtədɔ̄]. Span., fr. Lat. *mactātōr-(em),* 'slayer', fr. *mact-(āre),* 'to kill; to honour by sacrifice', prob. an amalgamation of two vbs.; one cogn. w. Goth. *mēkeis*; O.E. *mēće*; O.N. *mækir,* 'sword'; the other cogn. w. Scrt. *mahāyati,* 'honours, delights'; *maháš,* 'feast, sacrifice'. **1.** Man who kills the bull in Spanish bull-fight. **2.** One of three chief cards in ombre and quadrille. **3.** A variety of dominoes, in which the number seven must be made when one piece is placed against another; the 6/1, 5/2, 4/3, and 0/0 are 'matadors' and can be played at any time.

match (I.), n. [1. mach; 2. mætʃ]. O.E. *(ġe)mæćća,* 'one of a pair; mate'; cp. *mac-ian,* 'to make, form'. See **make.** **1. a** Person able to meet another in contest &c. on equal terms; one able to cope with another: *to meet one's match*; *no match for you*; Phr. *to be more than a match for one,* to have more skill, strength &c. than one can cope with; **b** person equal to another in quality, power &c.; peer, equal. **2.** Thing agreeing in shape, colour, or other details with another; thing exactly, or very nearly, like another; thing corresponding to another in position, so placed as to be symmetrical with another. **3.** Contest of skill, strength &c. in which persons or groups of persons are opposed: *cricket match*; *wrestling match.* **4. a** Marriage; Phr. *to make a match of it,* bring about, enter upon, a marriage; **b** person regarded as possessing eligibility or the reverse: *to be a good, poor, match.*

match (II.), vb. trans. & intrans., fr. prec. **A.** trans. **1.** To bring (person) into conflict with another, to oppose (one person) to another: *to match one person against another.* **2.** To be a match for, be equal to, in a contest. Phr. *well matched* (of persons), (i.) suited to each other; (ii.) able to cope with each other. **3.** To join (person) in marriage with another. **4.** To be identical in size, colour, quality &c. to; correspond with: *the trimming does not match the hat.* **5.** To find, obtain, material &c. to match another: *to match some silk.* **B.** intrans. To be identical to, agree with, each other, in size, colour &c.: *these two shoes don't match*; *the carpets and curtains do not match*; *dress trimmed with braid to match.*

match (III.), n., fr. O. Fr. *mesche,* Mod. Fr. *mèche,* 'wick'; etymol. doubtful. **1.** Small piece of wood, or wax taper, tipped with combustible substance ignited by friction, formerly (now obs.) *lucifer match*; *safety match*, kind which will only light when rubbed on specially prepared surface. **2.** Piece of prepared rope &c., burning uniformly, used to fire gun &c.

match-board, n. **match** (I.) & **board.** Thin board with a groove cut along one edge, and a tongue along the opposite edge, to fit into boards similarly cut.

match-boarding, n. Work, structure, of match-boards.

match-box, n. Box for holding matches.

matchet, n. [1. máchet; 2. mǽtʃit]. See **machete.** Broad, strong knife used in S. America.

matchless, adj. [1. máchles; 2. mǽtʃlis]. **match** (I.) & **-less.** Having no match; incomparable, peerless, unequalled.

matchlessly, adv. Prec. & **-ly.** In a matchless manner.

matchlock, n. [1. máchlok; 2. mǽtʃlɔk]. **match** (III.) & **lock.** **a** Lock of gun holding match for firing it; **b** gun fitted with lock of this kind.

match-maker, n. **match** (I.) & (III.), & **maker.** **1.** One who schemes to bring about marriages. **2.** Person employed in making wooden &c. matches.

matchwood, n. [1. máchwood; 2. mǽtʃwud]. **match** (III.) & **wood.** Wood of suitable size for making matches; small splinters. Phr. *to reduce* (article) *to matchwood*, smash it up, break it into small pieces.

mate (I.), n. & vb. trans. [1. māt; 2. meit]. Shortened fr. **checkmate.** (chess) **1.** n. Checkmate; cp. also *stalemate, fool's mate.* **2.** vb. To checkmate.

mate (II.), n. Perh. fr. M.L.G. *mate*, fr. O.L.G. *gemate*, 'companion, mess-mate', fr. Gmc. pref. **ga-* & **mat-*, 'meat'. See **meat.** **1.** (among working men) **a** Companion, fellow-workman; **b** a general, friendly, form of address. **2. a** Husband or wife; partner, spouse; **b** (of animals, and esp. of birds) one of a pair. **3.** (naut.) **a** Officer second in command on merchant ship; **b** assistant to some official: *boatswain's mate*; *gunner's mate* &c.

mate (III.), vb. trans. & intrans., fr. prec. **A.** trans. **a** To join in marriage; **b** to pair (birds &c.). **B.** intrans. **a** (of persons) To marry; **b** (of birds &c.) to pair.

maté, n. [1. mátā; 2. mǽtei], fr. Span. *mate*, fr. native *mati*, 'vessel for making maté'. **1. a** Infusion of dried and powdered leaves of a species of ilex, of Paraguay and S. Brazil; Paraguay tea; **b** shrub whose leaves are used for making this. **2.** Vessel in which maté is made.

mateless, adj. [1. mâtles; 2. méitlis]. **mate** (II.) & **-less.** Without a mate.

matelote, n. [1. mátelot; 2. mǽtəlɔt]. Fr., fr. *matelot*, 'sailor'. Dish of fish stewed with wine, onions &c.

mater, n. [1. mâter; 2. méitə]. Lat. *māter*, 'mother'; cogn. w. Gk. *mḗtēr*; Scrt. *mātár-*, 'mother'; Lith. *motė̃*, 'wife'; O. Slav. *mati*; O.H.G. *muoter*; O.E. *mōðor*, 'mother'. See **mother.** **1.** (school slang) Mother. **2.** Either of two of the three membranes enveloping brain and spinal cord, *dura mater* and *pia mater*.

materfamilias, n. [1. mâterfamílias; 2. méitəfəmíliæs]. Lat., fr. prec. & old genit. of *familia*. See **family.** Mother of household.

material (I.), adj. [1. matérial; 2. mətíəriəl], fr. L. Lat. *māteriāl-(is)*, 'of matter', fr. *māteria*, 'wood, timber, stuff, matter'. See **matter** & **-al.** **1.** Consisting of matter; contrasted with *spiritual*; substantial, tangible: *the material universe*; *in material form.* **2. a** Based on, derived from, matter; sensuous, not spiritual; corporeal, pertaining to the physical nature of man: *material needs, comforts, delights*; **b** (of persons) not spiritually-minded; of the earth earthy; gross, loving things of the senses. **3. a** Of a weighty, solid character; important, essential, of consequence: *a point material to one's argument*; **b** (law) of such a character as to affect a judgement, necessary to be borne in mind in giving a judicial decision; affecting, or able to affect, the validity of a legal instrument.

material (II.), n., fr. prec. **1.** The stuff of which something is made; the various substances from which a composite thing is built up, or constructed; **a** specif., a textile fabric: *clothes made of good, inferior, material*; **b** (pl.) *a house built of good materials*; *raw materials*, such as are not manufactured, but serve as basis for manufacture. **2.** (fig.) **a** Elements of mental equipment, or of character; **b** human beings regarded as possessing these: *the great Public Schools turn out splendid material for the making of public servants.* **3.** Subject-matter, pieces of knowledge, fact(s), emotional experiences &c., from which the mind constructs something: *material for thought*; *to collect material for an essay, a poem, a dictionary.* **4.** Things, implements, necessary for the carrying out of some specific process or action; esp. *writing materials.*

materialism, n. [1. matérializm; 2. mətíəriəlizəm]. Prec. & **-ism.** **1.** Theory that all the facts and phenomena of the universe can be explained in terms of the nature and behaviour of matter. **2. a** Undue or exclusive insistence, in art, upon the purely material aspects of nature; **b** undue attachment to material aims and needs.

materialist, n. [1. matérialist; 2. mətíəriəlist]. **material** & **-ist.** **1.** One who accepts and supports materialism. **2.** Writer, artist &c. who over-emphasizes the material side of nature. **3.** Person engrossed in material interests.

materialistic, adj. [1. matèrialístik; 2. mətìəriəlístik]. Prec. & **-ic.** Of, pertaining to, of the nature of, materialism or materialists.

materialistically, adv. [1. matèrialístikali; 2. mətìəriəlístikəli]. Prec. & **-al** & **-ly.** In a materialistic manner.

materiality, n. [1. matèriáliti; 2. mətìəriǽliti]. **material** & **-ity.** State or quality of being material.

materialization, n. [1. matèrializáshun; 2. mətìəriəlaizéiʃən]. See next word & **-ation.** **1.** Act or process of materializing; state of being materialized. **2.** Materialized spirit.

materialize, vb. trans. & intrans. [1. matérializ; 2. mətíəriəlaiz]. **material** & **-ize.** **A.** trans. **1. a** To render material; represent in material form; **b** to cause to appear in material form: *to materialize a spirit.* **2.** To make materialistic; to occupy with material aspects or interests. **B.** intrans. **1.** (of spirit) To appear in bodily form, to become substantial and corporeal. **2.** (of wish, plan, hope &c.) To become fact, be realized, carried out.

materia medica, n. [1. matéria médika; 2. mətíəriə médikə]. Med. Lat., fr. Lat. *māteria*, 'stuff', see **matter**, & *medica*, 'medical', see **medical.** **1.** Substances, drugs, used as remedies in medicine. **2.** Science of the properties of drugs and of their application as curative agents.

matériel, n. [1. matāriél; 2. mætεəriél]. Fr., fr. Lat. *māteriāl-(is)*, 'of matter'. See **material.** Complete stock of materials, implements, equipment &c. used in any series of complex operations; available material resources; contrasted with *personnel.*

maternal, adj. [1. matérnal; 2. mətʌ́nəl], fr. Fr., fr. Lat. *mātern-(us)*, 'of a mother', fr. *māter*, 'mother'. See **mater** & **-al.** **1.** Connected with, pertaining to, characteristic of, a mother or of mothers; motherly: *maternal care* &c. **2.** (of relationships) On the mother's side: *maternal grandfather* &c.

maternally, adv. Prec. & **-ly.** In a maternal manner.

maternity, n. [1. maténiti; 2. mətʌ́niti], fr. Fr., fr. Lat. *māternitāt-(em)*, 'motherhood', fr. *mātern-(us)*, 'of a mother', see **maternal**, & **-ity.** **1.** State of being a mother; motherhood; *maternity hospital*, one for women during confinement; *maternity nurse*, midwife. **2.** Character, qualities, of a mother; motherliness.

math, n. [1. math; 2. mæþ]. O.E. *mǣþ*. See **meadow** & **mow** (IV.). A mowing; chiefly in *aftermath*, q.v.

mathematical, adj. [1. màthemátikl; 2. mæþimǽtikl], fr. Lat., fr. Gk. *mathēmatik-(ós)*, 'disposed to learn; mathematical', fr. *mathēmat-*, stem of *máthēma*, 'learning, knowledge', fr. the stem of *manthánein*, 'to learn, observe, understand'; cogn. w. Goth. *mundrei*, 'guardian, watcher'; O.S. *mendian*, 'to rejoice'; O. Slav. *mądrŭ*, 'wise'; fr. **men-dh-*, 'to direct the thought towards', expanded fr. **men-*, 'to think'. See **mental** (I.), **mind.** **1.** Pertaining to, concerned with, of the nature of, mathematics. **2.** Completely accurate, rigorously exact.

mathematically, adv. Prec. & **-ly.** In a mathematical manner; as in mathematics.

mathematician, n. [1. màthematíshan; 2. mæþimətíʃən]. See **mathematics** & **-ian.** Student of, one learned in, mathematics.

mathematico-, pref. Form of next word used in compounds; implying combination of mathematical method with that of some other science.

mathematics, n. [1. màthemátiks; 2. mæþimǽtiks]. See **mathematical** & **-ics.** The abstract science concerned with the properties of, and relations between, quantities; also *pure mathematics*; *applied mathematics*, application of this to the problems of physics.

matico, n. [1. matékō; 2. mətíkou]. Span., dimin. of *Mateo*, 'Matthew'. **a** Peruvian shrub; **b** astringent and styptic prepared from its leaves.

matin, n. [1. mátin; 2. mǽtin], fr. Fr. *matines*, fr. eccles. Lat. *mātūtīnas*, n., fr. fem. pl. adj. fr. *Mātūta*, 'goddess of morning', cp. *mātūrus*, 'ripe' (see **mature**), the orig. meaning being 'at the right time'; the stem **mā-* w. a different suff. appears in Lat. *māne*, 'early', *mānus*, 'good'. **1.** (pl.) Morning service of Church of England; also *Morning Prayer.* **2.** (pl.) One of the seven canonical hours, sung at midnight or daybreak. **3.** (poet.) Birds' morning song.

matinée, n. [1. mátinā; 2. mǽtinei]. Fr.; fr. *matin*, 'morning', see prec., & fem. P.P. ending fr. Lat. *-āta*, see **-ade.** Afternoon theatrical or musical performance.

matrass, n. [1. mátras; 2. mǽtrəs], fr. Fr. *matras*; etymol. doubtful. Glass vessel with long tapering neck, used in chemical processes &c.

matriarch, n. [1. mâtriark; 2. méitriāk], fr. **mater**, on anal. of **patriarch.** Wife of patriarch; woman with status corresponding to that of patriarch.

matriarchal, adj. [1. màtriárkl; 2. mèitriákl]. Prec. & **-al.** Pertaining to, of the nature of, a matriarch or matriarchy.

matriarchy, n. [1. mâtriarki; 2. méitriāki]. **matriarch** & **-y.** Social system in which the mother of the family is regarded as the principal ancestor, descent being traced through the female line.

matric, n. [1. matrík; 2. mətrík]. Shortened form of **matriculation.** Examination for matriculation at a university.

matricidal, adj. [1. mâtrisīdl; 2. méitrisaidl]. See next word & **-al.** Of, of the nature of, matricide.

matricide, n. [1. mâtrisīd; 2. méitrisaid], fr. Lat. *mātricīda*, 'matricide', fr. *mātr-*, stem of **mater**, & **-cide.** **a** The act of killing one's own mother; **b** one who kills his own mother.

matricular, adj. [1. matríkūlar; 2. mətríkjulə]. See next word & **-ar.** Contributed to a central or common fund, esp. of contributions made to the federal treasury of the German Empire by the various states.

matriculate, vb. trans. & intrans. [1. matríkūlāt; 2. mətríkjuleit], fr. L. Lat. *mātri-*

cula, 'register', dimin. of **matrix**, & **-ate**. **1.** trans. To admit to membership of a university. **2.** intrans. To be admitted to privileges of such membership.

matriculation, n. [1. matrikūláshun; 2. mətrìkjuléiʃən]. Prec. & **-ion**. **1.** Act, ceremony, of matriculating; state of being matriculated. **2.** Examination held by universities, which must be passed before admittance; also attrib.: *matriculation examination.*

matriculatory, adj. [1. matríkūlatori; 2. mətríkjulətəri]. **matriculate** & **-ory**. Of matriculation.

matrimonial, adj. [1. màtrimṓnial; 2. mætrimóuniəl]. **matrimony** & **-al**. Of, pertaining to, marriage.

matrimonially, adv. Prec. & **-ly**. In a matrimonial manner.

matrimony, n. [1. mátrimuni; 2. mǽtriməni], fr. O. Fr. *matremoine*, fr. Lat. *mātrimōnium*, 'marriage'; fr. *māter*, 'mother'. See **mater**. **1.** State of being married. **2.** Declaration of king and queen of trumps in some card games.

matrix, n. [1. mā́triks; 2. méitriks]. Lat. *mātrix*, 'womb', fr. *mātr-*, stem of *māter*, 'mother'. See **mater**. **1. a** Womb; **b** place in which anything is formed or developed. **2.** Earthy substance, rock &c. in which minerals, gems &c. are embedded. **3.** Mould in which stamp, type &c. is cast.

matron, n. [1. mā́trun; 2. méitrən], fr. Fr. *matrone*, fr. Lat. *mātrōna*, 'married woman', fr. *mātr-*, stem of *māter*, 'mother'. See **mater**. **1.** Married woman. **2.** Woman who superintends nursing, or domestic staff in a hospital, or other institution; one in charge of the health, personal comfort, and well-being of children at a boarding-school, and of domestic matters affecting them.

matronage, n. [1. mā́trunij; 2. méitrənidž]. **matron** & **-age**. **1.** State of being a matron. **2.** Matrons collectively.

matronal, adj. [1. mā́trunal; 2. méitrənl]. **matron** & **-al**. Of, pertaining to, suitable for, becoming to, a matron.

matronhood, n. [1. mā́trunhood; 2. méitrənhud]. **matron** & **-hood**. State of being a matron.

matronly, adj. [1. mā́trunli; 2. méitrənli]. **matron** & **-ly**. **a** Pertaining to, suitable for, becoming in, a matron: *matronly duties, virtues*; **b** (of women) resembling a married woman in appearance and bearing; staid, mature-looking; portly: *a matronly figure, manner*.

matronship, n. [1. mā́trunship; 2. méitrənʃip]. **matron** & **-ship**. **a** State of being a matron; **b** office of matron, in hospital &c.

mattamore, n. [1. mátamōr; 2. mǽtəmɔ], fr. Fr. *matamore*, fr. Arab. *maṭmurah*, fr. *tamara*, 'to store up'. Subterranean dwelling.

matter (**I.**), n. [1. máter; 2. mǽtə], fr. O. Fr. *matere*, fr. Lat. *māteria*, 'timber; stuff, material'; prob. fr. same base as **mater**. **1.** That of which physical objects are composed; substance. **2.** Pus, morbid discharge from abscess, wound, sore &c. **3.** Substance, subject, what is actually stated, and dealt with, in a book, lecture &c.; contrasted with *style*, or *manner*, that is, the way in which it is said. Phr. *as a matter of fact*, in truth. **4.** That which is the subject of discussion, negotiation, and the like; **a** business, affair, subject, thing; often rather vaguely used: *to speak of sundry matters*; *a matter of slight importance*; *one or two small matters of dispute*; Phr. *a matter of course*, something that is expected, something inevitable; **b** cause, occasion for: *a matter of congratulation, of regret* &c.; Phr. *no laughing matter*, nothing to laugh at, something very serious. **5.** Affair having significance, importance, consequence &c.; in Phrs. *no matter*, it is of no consequence; *what matter?*, of what importance is it?; *what's the matter* (*with you*)?, what do you complain of, what are you suffering from, what disaster has occurred? &c.; *for the matter of that*, so far as that goes, in reference to that &c. **6.** Amount, quantity, space &c.: *a matter of a hundred pounds, of ten miles* &c. **7.** Stuff, objects, things; in various Phrs.: *printed matter, published matter*; *first-class &c. matter* (for the post).

matter (**II.**), vb. intrans., fr. prec. **1.** To signify, be of importance: *it doesn't matter if we are late*. **2.** To discharge pus.

matter-of-fact, adj. Unimaginative, adhering strictly to facts; prosaic, dry, commonplace.

matting, n. [1. máting; 2. mǽtiŋ]. **mat** (**I.**) & **-ing**. Material woven of rushes, hemp, fibre &c., as floor-covering, for wrapping objects in transit &c.

mattock, n. [1. mátuk; 2. mǽtək]. O.E. *mattuc*; M.E. *mattok*; etymol. doubtful. Kind of grubbing axe for loosening soil, cutting roots &c., with one broad cutting edge and one sharp point.

mattress, n. [1. mátres; 2. mǽtrəs], fr. O. Fr. *materas*, fr. Ital. *materasso*, prob. fr. Arab. *almatrah*, 'place where something is thrown'. **a** Case of canvas or other cotton material, stuffed with feathers, wool, straw, horsehair &c. to form a bed; **b** *chain mattress*, series of thin chain-like structures, tightly stretched to frame, supporting hair mattress; **c** *spring mattress*, series of wire springs stretched in framework of wood or steel which is fitted to a bedstead; **d** *wire mattress*, series of wires, sometimes criss-crossed, stretched on a frame, to support a mattress of hair &c.

maturation, n. [1. màtūráshun; 2. mætjuréiʃən], fr. Lat. *mātūrātiōn-(em)*, 'ripening', fr. *mātūr-(āre)*, 'to ripen', fr. *mātūr-(us)*, 'ripe', see **mature**, & **-ation**. **1.** (lit. and fig.) The act of bringing or coming to maturity, ripening. **2.** (med.) **a** The process of suppurating; **b** act of promoting suppuration.

maturative, adj. [1. matū́rativ; 2. mətjɔ́rətiv]. Next word & **-ative**. (med.) Promoting suppuration.

mature (**I.**), adj. [1. matū́r; 2. mətjɔ́], fr. Lat. *mātūr-(us)*, 'ripe, mature, fully developed'; the orig. meaning was prob. 'seasonable, occurring at the right time'. See **matin**. **1. a** (of living organisms) Ripe; fully developed, having reached maximum growth; **b** (of the mind, intelligence) thoroughly formed; developed by care, training, and experience; not superficial, or puerile; **c** (of thought, a decision, plan, action &c.) resulting from well-developed mental faculties; prudent, wise; based upon careful deliberation and wide experience; well thought out; complete in every detail. **2.** (commerc., of bills) Due for payment.

mature (**II.**), vb. trans. & intrans., fr. O. Fr. *maturer*, fr. Lat. *mātūrāre*, 'to ripen; to quicken, hasten', fr. *mātūr-(us)*, 'ripe'. See prec. **A.** trans. **1.** To ripen, bring to maturity, physical or mental; to develop, complete. **2.** To perfect, work out in detail, complete: *to mature schemes* &c. **B.** intrans. **1.** To come to maturity, ripen, reach full development. **2.** (commerc., of bills) To become due for payment.

maturely, adv. **mature** (**I.**) & **-ly**. In a mature manner.

matureness, n. See prec. & **-ness**. State or quality of being mature.

maturity, n. [1. matū́riti; 2. mətjɔ́riti]. **mature** & **-ity**. State or quality of being mature; ripeness, full development.

matutinal, adj. [1. màtūtī́nal; 2. mætjutáinəl], fr. Lat. *mātūtīn-(us)*, 'of, early in, the morning', fr. *Mātūt-(a)*, 'goddess of early morning', see **matin**, & **-al**. **1.** Of, pertaining to, happening in, the early morning. **2.** Early.

maud, n. [1. mawd; 2. mɔ̄d]. Etymol. unknown. **a** Scotch shepherd's grey woollen plaid; **b** travelling-rug made of this.

maudlin, adj. & n. [1. máwdlin; 2. mɔ́dlin], fr. O. Fr. *Madelaine*, 'Magdalen', q.v. **1.** adj. Loquaciously or tearfully sentimental; exhibiting foolish sentimentality, and ill-controlled, vapid emotion. **2.** n. Weak-minded, feeble sentiment.

maugre, prep. [1. máwger; 2. mɔ́gə], fr. O. Fr. *maugré*, 'in spite of', fr. *mal*, 'bad', see **mal-**, & *gré*, fr. Lat. *grātus*, 'pleasing', see **grateful**. (archaic) In spite of.

maul (**I.**), **mall**, n. [1. mawl; 2. mɔ̄l], fr. O. Fr. *mail*, fr. Lat. *malleus*, 'hammer'. See **malleus**. Heavy wooden hammer.

maul (**II.**), vb. trans., fr. prec. **1. a** To injure seriously by tearing or beating; to bruise, lacerate, maltreat: *badly mauled by a tiger, in a fight* &c.; **b** to handle clumsily and coarsely; to paw over, finger, roughly. **2.** (fig.) To tear to pieces by hostile destructive criticism.

maulstick, n. [1. máwlstik; 2. mɔ́lstik], fr. Du. *maalstok*, fr. *malen*, 'to paint', cp. O.H.G. *mālōn*, 'to paint, draw'; O.N. *mǽla*, 'to colour, paint'; Goth. *mēljan*, 'to write', *mēla*, 'letter'; the second element, *stok*, 'stick', is cogn. w. **stock**. Long, thin rod used by painters as rest for the wrist, to steady the hand while putting in fine touches.

maund, n. [1. mawnd; mɔ̄nd], fr. Hind. *mān*. Indian, Persian, and Turkish weight, from about 25 to over 80 lb. avoirdupois.

maunder, vb. intrans. [1. máwnder; 2. mɔ́ndə]. Origin unknown. **1.** To talk aimlessly, to ramble in speech. **2.** *Maunder along, about*, to wander about vaguely and listlessly.

maundy, n. [1. máwndi; 2. mɔ́ndi], fr. O. Fr. *mandé*, fr. Lat. *mandātum*, 'command' (with reference to the 'new Commandment' of St. John xiii.). See **mandate**. **1.** Ceremonial washing of feet of poor people, and distribution of alms, as religious act. **2.** Distribution of alms by royal almoner, as survival of this custom; *maundy money*, money distributed to the poor by royal almoner on *Maundy Thursday*, Thursday before Easter.

Maundy Thursday, n. The day before Good Friday. See **maundy**.

Mauser, n. [1. móuzer; 2. máuzə]. Name of inventor, d. 1882. Kind of magazine rifle, or pistol.

mausoleum, n. [1. màwsolḗum; 2. mɔ̄səlíəm]. Lat. *mausōlēum*, fr. Gk. *Mausōleion*, tomb erected by Queen Artemisia for her husband Mausolos, king of Caria, at Halicarnassus, c. 350 B.C. A large, important, stately tomb.

mauvais, adj. [1. mōvā; 2. mouvei]. Fr. *mauvais*, 'bad'; etymol. doubtful. *Mauvais quart-d'heure*, brief space of time during which one has an unpleasant experience; *mauvais sujet*, worthless fellow, rogue; *mauvaise honte*, false modesty; bashfulness, extreme diffidence.

mauve, n. & adj. [1. mōv; 2. mouv], fr. Fr., fr. Lat. *malva*, 'mallow'. See **malvaceous**. **1.** n. Clear, light, purple colour. **2.** adj. Having, of, this colour.

mavis, n. [1. mā́vis; 2. méivis], fr. O. Fr. *mauvis*, fr. Span. *malviz*; etymol. doubtful, possibly of Celt. origin. (Scots or poet.) Song-thrush.

maw, n. [1. maw; 2. mɔ̄]. O.E. *maga*, M.E. *mawe*; cp. O.H.G. *mago*; O.N. *magi*; Du. *maag*; Germ. *magen*. **a** The stomach, specif. the fourth stomach of a ruminant; **b** (fig.) gulf, abyss, in such Phrs. as *death's maw, the maw of time* &c.

mawkish, adj. [1. máwkish; 2. mɔ́kiʃ], fr. obs. *mawk*, 'maggot', fr. M.E. *maðek*, fr. O.N. *maðkr*; cp. Dan. *maddik*; cp. further Goth. *maþa*; O.E. *maða*; O.H.G. *mado*, 'worm, insect, maggot', cogn. w. Lat. *mandere*, 'to chew, gnaw', see **mandible**; cogn. w. Gk. *mastáomai*, 'I chew, bite'; *mástax*, 'mouth', see **mastic**. **1.** (in physical sense) Having a faint, sweet, sickly taste; insipid. **2.** (of non-material things) Weakly sentimental, feebly emotional.

mawkishly, adv. Prec. & **-ly**. In a mawkish manner.

mawkishness, n. See prec. & **-ness**. State or quality of being mawkish.

mawseed, n. [1. máwsēd; 2. mɔ́sīd], fr. Germ. *mohn*, 'poppy', & **seed**. Seed of opium poppy.

mawworm, n. [1. máwwẽrm; 2. mɔ́wʌ̄m]. **maw** & **worm**. **1.** Intestinal worm. **2.** (cap.)

Dissembler, hypocrite (from name of character in *The Hypocrite*, 1768, a play by Bickerstaffe).

maxilla, n. [1. maksíla; 2. mæksílə]. Lat. *maxilla*, 'jaw-bone', dimin. of *māla*, 'jaw', see **malar** & **mandible**, prob. on anal. of **axilla**. Jaw-bone, esp. upper jawbone of vertebrates.

maxillary, adj. [1. maksílari; 2. mæksíləri]. Prec. & **-ary**. Of, pertaining to, the jaw or jaw-bone.

maxilliform, adj. [1. maksíliform; 2. mæksílifōm]. See **maxilla** & **-form**. Having the shape of a maxilla.

maxim (I.), n. [1. máksim; 2. mǽksim], fr. Fr. *maxime*, fr. Lat. fem. adj. *maxima*, 'greatest'. See **maximum**. **1.** General principle deduced from experience. **2.** Rule of conduct; precept, principle.

Maxim (II.), n., fr. name of inventor, Sir Hiram Maxim (1840–1916). Automatic, quick-firing machine-gun; called also *Maxim gun*.

maximalist, n. [1. máksimalist; 2. mǽksiməlist]. **maximum** & **-al** & **-ist**. Person who insists on the whole of his demands.

maximization, n. [1. màksimīzáshun; 2. mæksimaizéiʃən]. See next word & **-ation**. Act of maximizing; state of being maximized.

maximize, vb. trans. [1. máksimīz; 2. mǽksimaiz], fr. Lat. *maxim-(us)*, 'greatest', see next word, & **-ize**. To raise to the highest possible degree, intensify, increase, magnify.

maximum, n. & adj. [1. máksimum; 2. mǽksiməm]. Lat., neut. form of *māximus* (fr. **magsṃ-mo-*), 'greatest', superl. of stem **mag-*, 'great', seen in *magnus*, 'great'. See **magnum**. **1.** n. Highest point, degree, greatest quantity, size &c.; *maximum thermometer*, one recording highest temperature reached within certain time. **2.** adj. Greatest, highest possible.

may (I.), auxil. vb. [1. mā; 2. mei]. O.E. *mæǵ*; M.E. *mai, mei*; cp. Goth. *magan*, 'to be able'; O.H.G., O.S. *mag*; O. Fris. *mei*, 'may'; Goth. *mahts*, O.H.G. *maht*; O.N. *mättr*, 'might, power'. Prob. cogn. w. Gk. *mêkhos*, 'means, instrument', q.v. under **mechanic**. See **might**. **1.** Expressing possibility: *it may be true*; *I may be late*; *you may perhaps remember the name*; *I hope I may live to see the day*. **2.** Expressing uncertainty: *who may you be?* **3.** **a** Expressing request or permission: *may I come and see you?*; *you may go if you choose*; **b** expressing wish, hope: *may you live long and die happy!*

may (II.), n. Prob. fr. O.E. *mǣǵ*, 'kinswoman', cp. O.H.G. *māg*, O.S. *mēch*, 'relative'; Goth. *mēgs*, 'son-in-law'; etymol. doubtful. (poet.) Maiden.

May (III.), n., fr. Fr. *mai*, fr. Lat. *Māius*, 'the month of May', named after the goddess *Māia*, whose name prob. means 'she who brings increase, growth', & is connected w. *māior*, 'greater'. See **major**. **1.** The fifth month of the year. **2.** (fig.) Youth, prime of life. **3.** Hawthorn blossom. **4.** (pl., Camb. Univ.) **a** Examinations held in May; **b** eight-oared bumping boat-races held late in May or early in June.

maya, n. [1. máh-ya; 2. mádjə]. Scrt. *māyā*. Illusion, esp. the material world as deceptive and unreal.

maybe, adv. [1. mābē; 2. méibī]. **may** (I.) & **be**. Perhaps, possibly.

May Day, n. First of May, esp. as spring festival, on which games, sports &c. are held.

may-fly, n. Species of ephemeral insect; artificial reproduction of this used in fishing.

May games, n. Dances, sports &c. such as are held on May Day.

mayhem, n. [1. māhem; 2. méihem], fr. O. Fr. *mehaing, mahaigne*, 'injury'. See **maim**. (legal hist.) Loss of, injury to, a limb or part of the body, esp. of such as can be used in self-defence, as basis for an action for damages against person causing such loss or injury.

mayonnaise, n. [1. māonáz; 2. meiənéiz]. Fr.; perh. fr. **mahonnaise*, celebrating capture of Mahon, in Minorca, in 1756. **1.** Creamy sauce made of yolk of eggs, oil, vinegar &c. **2.** Cold dish of fish &c. dressed with this sauce: *salmon, lobster, chicken mayonnaise*.

mayor, n. [1. mār; 2. mɛə], fr. Fr. *maire*, 'mayor', fr. Lat. *mājor*, 'greater'. See **major** (II.). Chief officer of municipal corporation; principal magistrate of a town.

mayoral, adj. [1. máoral; 2. méərəl]. Prec. & **-al**. Of, pertaining to, a mayor or mayoralty.

mayoralty, n. [1. máoralti; 2. méərəlti], fr. O. Fr. *mairalté*; **mayor** & **-al** & **-ty**. **a** Office of mayor; **b** period of tenure of this office.

mayoress, n. [1. máores; 2. méəris]. **mayor** & **-ess**. Wife of mayor.

maypole, n. [1. māpōl; 2. méipoul]. Pole decorated with flowers, ribbons &c. set up for dancing round on May Day.

May queen, n. Girl elected for her beauty and charm to be queen of May Day sports.

May Week, n. Week in late May or early June when Cambridge University boat-races are held.

mazard, n. [1. mázard; 2. mǽzəd], fr. M.E. *maser*, 'bowl of maple-wood; maple-wood', fr. O. Fr. *masere*, 'maple-wood', of Gmc. origin. Cp. O.N. *mōsurr*; O.H.G. *masar*, 'knot in maple-wood'. **1.** (archaic) Head, skull. **2.** Kind of wild cherry.

mazarine, n. & adj. [1. màzarḗn; 2. mæzərín]. Perh. fr. Cardinal Mazarin. **1.** n. Deep blue colour. **2.** adj. Of this colour: *mazarine robe*, as worn by aldermen of City of London.

Mazdaism, n. [1. mázdaizm; 2. mǽzdə-izəm], fr. *mazda*, good principle of Persian mythology, & **-ism**. Zoroastrianism.

maze (I.), n. [1. māz; 2. meiz]. See next word. **1.** A series of intricate winding paths with hedges on either side, artificially designed as a puzzle for those who try to find their way in them; a labyrinth. **2.** (fig.) Confusion, perplexity, bewilderment.

maze (II.), vb. trans. M.E. *masen*, 'to confuse, puzzle', cp. O.E. P.P. *amasod*, 'confused, dizzy'. Cp. perh. O.N. *masa*, 'to chatter, prattle'. (esp. in P.P.) To confuse, bewilder.

mazer, n. [1. māzer; 2. méizə]. See **mazard**. A large shallow drinking-bowl of maple wood mounted in silver, with foot, and boss in inside.

mazily, adv. [1. mázili; 2. méizili]. **mazy** & **-ly**. In a mazy manner.

maziness, n. [1. mázines; 2. méizinis]. See prec. & **-ness**. State or quality of being mazy.

mazurka, n. [1. mazérka, mazóorka; 2. məzákə, məzúəkə], fr. Pol. **a** Lively Polish dance for four or eight couples; **b** music for this, in triple time.

mazy, adj. [1. māzi; 2. méizi]. **maze** (I.) & **-y**. **1.** Like a maze, having many windings; intricate, involved. **2.** Puzzled, confused in mind.

me, pron. [1. mē; 2. mī]; unstressed [1. mi; 2. mi]. O.E. *mē*, dat., M.E. *mē*; cp. O. Fris., O.S. *mi*, dat.; O.E. *mēc*; O.H.G. *mih*; Goth. *mik*, acc.; Lat. acc. *mē*, dat. *mihi*; Gk. dat. *moi*, acc. *me*; Scrt. *mām*, acc.; O. Slav. *mę*, acc. **1.** Objective case of singular pronoun of first person. **2.** (colloq.) Used as nominative after verb *to be*: *it's only me*. **3.** (archaic) Reflexive: *I will lay me down and sleep*. **4.** In interjections: *dear me!*

mead (I.), n. [1. mēd; 2. mīd]. O.E. *meodu*; M.E. *mēde*; cp. O. Fris. *mede*; O.H.G. *medo*; O.N. *miöðr*, 'mead'; cogn. w. Gk. *méthu*, 'wine' (cp. **amethyst** & **methyl**); Scrt. *mádhu*, 'honey; sweet wine'; Lith. *medùs*; O. Slav. *medŭ*, 'honey'. Intoxicating drink made of fermented honey and water.

mead (II.), n. O.E. *mǣd, mēd*; M.E. *mēd*; cp. O.E. *māwan*, 'to mow', *mǣþ*, 'harvest, crop'. See **mow** (III.), **aftermath**. (poet.) Meadow.

meadow, n. [1. médō; 2. médou]. O.E. *mǣdwe*, dat. of *mǣd*, 'meadow', see prec.; M.E. *meduwe*. Connected w. **mow** (III.) & **math**. Tract of grass-land; strictly speaking, a field kept for hay; low-lying, rich ground, esp. on river-bank.

meadow-lark, n. American field-lark.

meadow-sweet, n. Herb, genus *Spiraea*, producing large heads of creamy, sweet-smelling flowers, on long slender stalks, common in damp meadows, allied to the dropwort, q.v.

meadowy, adj. [1. médōi; 2. médoui]. **meadow** & **-y**. Resembling, of the nature of, abounding in, meadows.

meagre, adj. [1. mḗger; 2. mīgə], fr. O. Fr. *maigre*, fr. Lat. *macer*, 'thin'; cogn. w. Gk. *makrós*, 'long', see **macro-**; O.E. *mæger*; O.H.G. *magar*, 'lean'. **1.** (of persons &c.) Thin, lean, gaunt. **2.** **a** Poor, scanty, stinted, inadequate: *meagre fare*; *a meagre allowance of time, material* &c.; **b** (also fig., of the intellect and its products) not rich or full; limited, arid.

meagrely, adv. Prec. & **-ly**. In a meagre manner.

meagreness, n. See prec. & **-ness**. State or quality of being meagre; scantiness, poverty.

meal (I.), n. [1. mēl; 2. mīl]. O.E. *melo*; M.E. *mēle*; Du. *meel*; Germ. *mehl*; O.N. *mjǫl*. Cogn. w. Lat. *molere*, 'to grind'; cp. Goth., O.H.G. *malan*, 'to grind'; Goth. *malma*, 'sand'; O.H.G. *melm*, 'dust'; O. Slav. *meljǫ*, 'to grind'; Lith. *miltai*, 'meal'. See also **mill** (I.), **molar** (I.), **mollify**. Any kind of edible grain or pulse rather coarsely ground; contrasted with *flour*, which term implies finer grinding.

meal (II.), n. O.E. *mǣl*, 'mark, sign; measure; fixed time; meal'; cp. O. Fris. *mēl, māl*; Goth. *mēl*, 'appointed time'; Germ. *mahl*, 'meal'; *mal*, 'time'. The orig. meaning was 'sign; written sign; mark'. See **melanism**. **1.** Taking of food; occasion on which food is taken, esp. at fixed or usual time for this: *to have one's meals regularly*. **2.** Amount of food taken on one occasion: *to make a good solid meal*; *a light meal*. Phr. *square meal*, large and satisfying one.

meal (III.), vb. intrans., fr. prec. To have a meal.

mealie, n. [1. mḗli; 2. mīli], fr. Cape Du. *milje*, fr. Port. *milho*, Fr. *millet*. See **millet**. (S. Afr.) Maize; the cob of Indian corn.

mealiness, n. [1. mḗlines; 2. mīlinis]. **mealy** & **-ness**. Quality of being mealy.

meal-time, n. Usual time for a meal.

mealy, adj. [1. mḗli; 2. mīli]. **meal** (I.) & **-y**. **1.** Of meal; resembling meal in texture; producing meal. **2.** (of horses) Covered with small spots. **3.** (of complexion) Pale, sallow.

mealy-bug, n. Small insect found on vines &c. and in greenhouses.

mealy-mouthed, adj. Apt to mince one's words; inclined to avoid forcible or coarse expressions.

mean (I.), n. [1. mēn; 2. mīn]. See next word. **1.** Point, quality, course, action, degree &c. midway between two extremes; esp. in Phr. *the happy* or *golden mean*, moderate course of action. **2.** (math.) Term interpolated between two other terms of a series, and intermediate in value: *arithmetical mean*, number obtained by adding quantities together and dividing the result by number of quantities; average. **3.** (pl.) **a** Mode, method, way, agent, instrument, by which anything is done, brought about, caused: *to be the means of helping others*; *by fair means or foul*; *to lift a weight by means of a lever*; Phrs. *means of grace*, sacraments &c.; *by means of*, through, with the help, agency, instrumentality, of; *by all means*, certainly; *by no (manner of) means*, not at all, in no way; *by no means a pleasant man to deal with*; **b** in above and similar Phrs. often used as a singular: *a means of accomplishing one's object*. **4.** (pl.) **a** Resources, money, available funds: *to live within one's means*; **b** wealth, riches: *a man of means*.

mean (II.), adj. M.E. *mēne*, fr. O. Fr. *men, moien*, fr. L. Lat. *mediān-(us)*, 'middle'. See **median**. **1.** (math., of quantity, point &c.) Intermediate in value, position &c. between two other quantities, points &c.: *mean proportional*, middle term of three quantities of which first is to second as second is to third. **2.** Average, representing the mean: *the mean annual temperature*. **3.** (of time) Intervening, coming between: *in the mean time, while*.

mean (III.), adj. O.E. (*ġe*)*mǣne*, 'common'; M.E. *mene*, 'common, mean'; cp. O. Fris. *mēne*; O.H.G. *gimein*, 'common'; Goth. *gameins*. Cogn. w. Lat. (*com*)*mūnis*, O. Lat. *comoin*[*em*], 'common', see **common**; Lith. *mainýti*, 'to exchange'; O. Slav. *měna*, 'exchange'; further, Lat. *mūnus*, 'gift; office, function, duty', *mūnia*, 'official duties', see **municipal**. Aryan base **mei-(n)-*, **moi-(n)-* &c., 'to exchange'; for the same base w. a different formative element see **mutation**. **1. a** Of low rank, undistinguished: *of mean parentage*; *persons of the meaner sort*; **b** undistinguished in appearance, shabby. **2.** (of natural powers, faculties &c.) Inferior, mediocre. Phr. *of no mean ability* &c., of great ability &c. **3. a** Ignoble, squalid, shabby: *mean streets*; **b** stingy, parsimonious: *mean over money matters*.

mean (IV.), vb. trans. & intrans. O.E. *mǣnan*, 'to mean, signify, intend'; cp. O. Fris. *mēna*; O.S. *mēnian*; O.H.G. *meinen*; cogn. w. O. Slav. *měniti*, 'to think, have an opinion'. **A.** trans. **1.** (of persons) **a** To intend, contemplate; to have in view as an aim or object; in Phr. *to mean business*, intend to act, contemplate doing something; **b** to destine, design, for some specific purpose or use: *I mean this house for my son*; *he was meant to be a barrister*. **2. a** To have in mind and intend to convey or express: *what exactly do you mean by that remark?*; *to mean what one says*; Phr. *what* (*on earth*) *do you mean* (*by behaving like that*)?, how can you justify such conduct?; how dare you behave in such a way?; **b** to intend deliberately to do something, or to produce a particular result: *to mean no harm*; *he is such a vulgar, ill-bred fellow, that he's often rude without meaning it*. Phr. *to mean mischief*, (i.) (of persons) to contemplate some malevolent act; (ii.) (of circumstances) to portend evil. **3.** (in pass.) To be intended, designed, to represent, reproduce: *the portrait is meant for me, though you wouldn't think it*. **4. a** (of verbal or graphic expression) To have as a sense or significance, to imply, convey: *these words mean nothing*; *tell me what this Latin sentence means*; **b** to have a vital significance, to appeal strongly, be highly precious to: *your friendship means a great deal to me*; *modern music means very little to me*. **B.** intrans. **1.** To have the intention to do something, to propose, form a plan to act in a certain way: *I mean to spend my holidays abroad this year*; *what do you mean to do?* **2.** To have a deliberate intention to produce a specific result: *I'm very sorry I hurt you, I never meant to*.

meander (I.), n. [1. miánder; 2. miǽndə], fr. Lat. *Maeander*, fr. Gk. *Maiandros*, a slow, winding river of Caria; hence 'a winding pattern'. **a** Winding course of a stream; **b** rambling, aimless walk; **c** a pattern of winding lines; fret.

meander (II.), vb. intrans., fr. prec. **1.** (of streams) To wind about with a slow, gentle flow. **2.** (fig.) **a** To wander, ramble, aimlessly along; also *meander along*; **b** to ramble in talk; to speak in an inconsequent, discursive way.

meandering, n. & adj. [1. miándering; 2. miǽndəriŋ], fr. Pres. Part. of prec. **1.** n. **a** A winding, bending course; **b** rambling, desultory talk. **2.** adj. Acting as that which, he who, meanders.

meanderingly, adv. Prec. & **-ly**. In a meandering manner; with a meandering course.

meandrine, adj. [1. miándrin; 2. miǽndrin]. **meander** (I.) & **-ine**. (rare) Full of windings or convolutions.

meaning (I.), n. [1. méning; 2. míniŋ]. **mean** (IV.) & **-ing**. What one means, something meant; sense, significance; sense conveyed or intended by something said or done. Phr. *with meaning*, significantly, implying more than is actually expressed.

meaning (II.), adj., fr. Pres. Part. of **mean** (IV.). Full of meaning; significant, expressive: *a meaning look*.

meaningless, adj. [1. méningles; 2. míniŋlis]. **meaning** (I.) & **-less**. Having no meaning or significance; senseless; purposeless, without motive.

meaningly, adv. [1. méningli; 2. míniŋli]. **meaning** (II.) & **-ly**. With meaning; expressively.

meanly, adv. [1. ménli; 2. mínli]. **mean** (III.) & **-ly**. In a mean manner; shabbily, stingily.

meanness, n. [1. ménnes; 2. mínnis]. **mean** (III.) & **-ness**. Quality of being mean (in various senses).

meantime, n. & adv. [1. méntīm; 2. míntaim]. **mean** (II.) & **time**. **1.** n. Intervening time. **2.** adv. In the meantime.

meanwhile, n. & adv. [1. mènwíl; 2. mìnwáil]. Meantime.

measles, n. [1. mézlz; 2. mízlz]. M.E. *maseles*; cp. M. Du. *masel*, 'spot'; O.H.G. *masala*, 'blister'; cp. *māsa*, 'scar'. **1. a** Infectious disease, rubeola, most prevalent among children, characterized by fever, catarrh, and rash; *German measles*, disease resembling a mild form of measles; **b** small red spots characteristic of measles. **2.** Disease of swine and cattle.

measly, adj. [1. mézli; 2. mízli]. See prec. & **-y**. **1.** Connected with, resembling, affected with, measles, esp. of swine or cattle, or the flesh as unfit for food. **2.** (slang) Miserable, worthless, mean; meagre, skimpy.

measurable, adj. [1. mézhurabl; 2. méžərəbl]. **measure** & **-able**. Capable of being measured or estimated. Phr. *within measurable distance of*, close to.

measurably, adv. Prec. & **-ly**. In a measurable degree; to a measurable extent.

measure (I.), n. [1. mézhur; 2. méžə], fr. Fr. *mesure*, fr. Lat. *mensūra*, 'measure', fr. *mens-(um)*, P.P. type of *mētīri*, 'to measure'; cogn. w. Scrt. *mātra-(m)*, 'measure'; *mitiš*, 'measure, weight, worth'; Gk. *mêtis*, 'wisdom, prudence'; O.E. *mǣþ*, 'measure, proportion'. Cp. the related base **med-*, 'to measure', in **meditate, metre** (I.), **mete** (II.). Cp. **commensal** & **mesa**. **1. a** Size, extent, dimension(s), quantity, weight &c. determined or expressed in terms of some unit; **b** specific amount, quantity &c.: *to give full, short, measure*. Phrs. *clothes made to measure*, to fit person's individual measurements; (fig.) *to take one's measure*, find out one's capabilities; *to take the measure of one's foot*, estimate one's character and capacities. **2. a** Method, system, of measuring, series of related units: *dry, liquid, linear, measure*; **b** unit of capacity, e.g. bushel: *a measure of wheat*. **3.** Device for ascertaining measure; **a** marked rod, tape &c. for determining length: *yard measure*; **b** vessel of standard size for measuring liquid &c.: *pint measure*. **4.** (of non-material things) Standard by which a quality of mind or feeling is or may be gauged, estimated, computed: *words do not always give the measure of one's feelings*; *this book shows the measure of the author's intelligence*. **5.** (arith.) Number contained in another an exact number of times: *greatest common measure*, largest quantity exactly dividing each of two or more given quantities. **6.** Limit, fixed extent, degree, quantity: *to set measures to*, to limit. Phr. *beyond measure*, excessively. **7. a** Verse rhythm, metre; **b** time in which piece of music is written; **c** (archaic) dance: '*Now tread we a measure, said young Lochinvar*' (Scott). **8. a** Proceeding, step; course, mode, of action: *to take severe measures*; *to adopt measures*; *measures quite inadequate for the purpose*; **b** enactment, statute, parliamentary bill: *the Government was defeated over the principal measure of their programme*. **9.** (geol., pl.) Series of beds, strata: *the coal measures of S. Wales*.

measure (II.), vb. trans., fr. prec. **1. a** To ascertain dimension(s), or quantity of, by comparison with a fixed unit or with object of specified or known size: *to measure a piece of cloth*; Phr. *to measure swords with*, to see that swords are equal in length, for duel &c., hence to fight with; **b** specif., to ascertain proportions &c. of (person) for clothes &c. Phr. *to measure a person with one's eye*, look over, look up and down. **2.** To estimate, judge (person's character, quality &c.), by some standard. **3.** To mark out, mark off, indicate limits of (given length): *to measure a yard of silk*. Phr. *to measure one's length*, fall flat. **4.** To show measurement of, be of specified length, breadth, height: *the room measures 20 feet across*. **5.** To test by trial against, bring into comparison or competition with: *to measure one's strength, one's wits, with another's*: *to measure oneself with*, pit oneself against. **6.** *Measure out*, to deal out specific or stated quantity: *to measure out a quart of milk, a dose of medicine*. **7.** (poet.) To go, cover, traverse (distance).

measured, adj. [1. mézhurd; 2. méžəd], fr. P.P. of prec. **1.** (of language) Careful, considered, well-weighed. **2.** Steady, uniform, rhythmical, esp. in Phr. *measured tread*.

measureless, adj. [1. mézhurles; 2. méžəlis]. **measure** (I.) & **-less**. Unlimited, boundless.

measurement, n. [1. mézhurment; 2. méžəmənt]. **measure** (I.) & **-ment**. **1.** Act of measuring; state of being measured. **2.** Amount, size, extent, which anything measures; expressed in terms of fixed unit.

meat, n. [1. mēt; 2. mīt]. O.E. *mete*, 'food'; M.E. *mēte*; cp. Goth. *mats*, O. Fris. *mete*; O.S. *meti*; O.N. *matr*, 'food'; perh. cogn. w. Scrt. *médaš*, 'fat'; Lat. *madēre*, 'to be wet, to drip'; O.H.G. *mast*, 'fodder'. See **mast** (II.) & **mastoid**. **1.** (archaic) **a** Food, anything edible, nourishment: '*Thou givest them their meat in due season*' (Ps.); Phrs. *green meat*, vegetables; (fig.) *to be meat and drink to one*, be a source of satisfaction and delight to one; **b** a meal: *before, after, meat*; *to sit at meat*. **2.** Specif., flesh of animals used as food; also *butcher's meat*; as contrasted with fish, and sometimes with poultry. Phr. *white meat*, poultry, veal, pork &c. **3.** (fig.) Substantial, solid intellectual quality: *a book, speech &c. full of meat*.

meatless, adj. [1. métles; 2. mítlis]. **meat** & **-less**. Without, containing no, meat.

meat-offering, n. See **meat**, **1**. (Bib.; rendered *meal* in R.V.) Sacrifice of oil and flour.

meat-safe, n. Cupboard with walls of perforated zinc, wire gauze &c., for storing meat &c.

meatus, n. [1. mēátus; 2. miéitəs]. Lat. *meātus*, 'going, passing; way, passage', fr. P.P. type of *meāre*, 'to go, pass'; cogn. w. O. Slav. *minąti*, 'to go, cross over'; the orig. meaning of the stem **mei-*, **mejā-*, may have been 'to change one's place'; in this case the word is connected w. Aryan base **moi-*, **mei-*, 'to change'. See **mutation** & **mean** (III.). (anat.) External opening of a channel, duct, passage, in the body, as of the internal ear, nose &c.

meaty, adj. [1. méti; 2. míti]. **meat** & **-y**. **1. a** Of meat; **b** full of meat, fleshy. **2.** (fig.) Pithy, substantial.

Mecca, n. [1. méka; 2. mékə]. Birthplace of Mohammed, in the Hedjaz. (fig.) **1.** Goal of one's aspirations or ambitions. **2.** Place in which some cause, pursuit &c. originates.

mechanic (I.), n. [1. mekánik; 2. mikǽnik], fr. Lat. adj., fr. Gk. *mēkhanik-(ós)*, 'inventive, ingenious' (of machines), fr. *mēkhané*, 'means; invention; machine', whence Lat. *māchina*, 'invention', see **machine**; & cp. O.E. *mæg*, 'is able', see **may** (I.). **1.** Artisan, skilled and trained workman, esp. one who specializes in machinery. **2.** (pl.) *Mechanics*: **a** science of machines; **b** science of motion and force, a branch of applied mathematics.

mechanic (II.), adj. (archaic) Mechanical.

mechanical, adj. [1. mekánikl; 2. m*i*kǽn*i*kl]. Prec. & **-al.** **1.** Of, pertaining to, machines; produced by machinery: *mechanical power*; *mechanical products* &c.; *the mechanical powers*, such simple machines as the lever, wedge, pulley &c. **2.** Acting in accordance with, governed by, the laws of mechanics: *mechanical action*; contrasted with *chemical* &c. **3.** Acting like a machine; resulting from machine-like movements or automatic impulse; not due to, or requiring, deliberate exercise of will or intelligence; hence, unintelligent: *dictionary making is not entirely mechanical work.* **4.** (archaic) Pertaining to, characteristic of, artisans; base, ill-bred: *a base, mechanical fellow.*

mechanically, adv. Prec. & **-ly.** In a mechanical manner.

mechanicalness, n. See prec. & **-ness.** State or quality of being mechanical.

mechanician, n. [1. mèkaníshan; 2. mèkən*í*ʃən]. **mechanic** & **-ian.** Artisan, skilled in constructing, repairing, and working machines.

mechanism, n. [1. mékanizm; 2. mékən*i*zəm]. See **mechanic** & **-ism.** **1.** Machinery; combination of parts; the working parts of a machine collectively; system of working of a machine. **2.** Philosophic theory or doctrine that organic life consists solely in material and mechanical forms and operations; opposed to *vitalism.*

mechanist, n. [1. mékanist; 2. mékən*i*st]. See prec. & **-ist.** Upholder of philosophic theory of mechanism.

mechanistic, adj. [1. mèkanístik; 2. mèkən*í*st*i*k]. Prec. & **-ic.** Pertaining to the theory of mechanism and of the mechanists.

mechanize, vb. trans. [1. mékanīz; 2. mékənaiz]. See **mechanic** & **-ize.** To make mechanical, give mechanical character to.

Mechlin, n. [1. méklin; 2. mékl*i*n]. Town in Belgium. A fine pillow lace made at Mechlin.

meconic, adj. [1. mekónik; 2. m*i*kón*i*k], fr. Gk. *mḗkōn*, 'poppy'; etymol. doubtful. *Meconic acid*, acid obtained from opium.

meconium, n. [1. mekónium; 2. m*i*kóuniəm]. Lat., fr. Gk. *mēkṓnion.* See prec. **1.** (obs.) Opium. **2.** (med.) The greenish matter first discharged from the intestines of a new-born infant.

medal, n. [1. médl; 2. médl], fr. Fr. *médaille*, fr. Low Lat. **metallea*, 'metal disk', fr. Lat. *metall-(um)*, 'metal'. See **metal.** Small metal disk resembling a coin, with inscription, device &c., **a** struck to commemorate an historical event, or as portrait of some distinguished person &c.; awarded **b** for services in war; **c** for valour in civil life; **d** for signal distinction in some branch of learning, discovery &c.; **e** as prize in competitions in games, as golf &c.; *medal play*, (in golf) scored by strokes, not holes as in a match. Phr. *the reverse of the medal*, the other side of the question.

medalled, adj. [1. médld; 2. médld]. Prec. & **-ed.** Possessed of, decorated with, medal(s).

medallic, adj. [1. medálik; 2. m*i*dǽl*i*k]. **medal** & **-ic.** Of, pertaining to, like, a medal.

medallion, n. [1. medáliun; 2. m*i*dǽliən], fr. Fr. *médaillon*; **medal** & **-oon.** **1.** Large round metal disk bearing engraved portrait or other device and inscription. **2.** Any round, flat ornament, of metal, stone, wood, lace &c.; round panel, portrait &c.

medallist, n. [1. médalist; 2. médəl*i*st]. **medal** & **-ist.** **1.** Maker, designer, engraver, of medals. **2.** One who has been awarded a special medal for distinction.

meddle, vb. intrans. [1. médl; 2. médl], fr. O. Fr. *medler*, fr. *mesler*, fr. Low Lat. **misculāre*, fr. Lat. *miscēre*, 'to mix'. See **mix.** **1.** To touch unnecessarily, fidget, tamper, with: *don't meddle with the clock.* **2.** To interfere, intervene officiously, occupy oneself with unnecessarily: *to meddle with other people's business*; *to meddle in matters that do not concern one*; *he is always meddling.*

meddler, n. [1. médler; 2. médlə]. Prec. & **-er.** One given to meddling; an officious busybody.

meddlesome, adj. [1. médlsum; 2. médlsəm]. **meddle** & **-some.** Given to meddling; interfering.

meddlesomeness, n. Prec. & **-ness.** State or quality of being meddlesome.

media (I.), n. [1. mḗdia; 2. mídiə]. Lat. *media*, adj., fem. of *medius*, 'middle'; cogn. w. Gk. *méssos, mésos*, 'middle', fr. **medhj-os*; Scrt. *mádhyaš*; Goth. *midjis*; O.H.G. *mitti*; O.E. *midd*, 'middle', see **mid**; O. Slav. *meždu*, 'between'; *mežda*, 'middle, boundary'. See also **meso-.** **1.** (antiquated phon.) Voiced stop consonant [b, d, g]. **2.** (anat.) Middle membrane of artery &c.

media (II.), n., pl. of **medium.**

medi(a)eval, adj. [1. mèdiḗval; 2. mèdiívl], fr. Lat. *medi-(us)*, 'middle', see **media**, & *aev-(um)*, 'age', q.v. under **age**, & **-al.** Of, belonging to, in the spirit of, imitating, the Middle Ages.

medi(a)evalism, n. [1. mèdiḗvalizm; 2. mèdiívəl*i*zəm]. Prec. & **-ism.** **a** Fondness for mediaeval ideals, customs &c.; **b** spirit of the Middle Ages.

medi(a)evalist, n. [1. mèdiḗvalist; 2. mèdiívəl*i*st]. **medi(a)eval** & **-ist.** Student of mediaeval history &c.

medi(a)evalize, vb. trans. & intrans. [1. mèdiḗvalīz; 2. mèdiívəlaiz]. **medi(a)eval** & **-ize.** **1.** trans. To make mediaeval; to give a mediaeval character or tendency to. **2.** intrans. To follow, adopt, mediaeval customs, ideals &c.

medi(a)evally, adv. [1. mèdiḗvali; 2. mèdiívəli]. **medi(a)eval** & **-ly.** In a mediaeval manner.

medial, adj. [1. mḗdial; 2. mídiəl], fr. L. Lat. *mediāl-(is)*, 'middle', fr. *medi-(us)*, 'middle', see **media**, & **-al.** **1.** Situated in, passing through, the middle: *medial line*; *medial consonant*, in middle of word. **2.** **a** Of, pertaining to, an average; **b** of average size.

medially, adv. Prec. & **-ly.** In a medial position.

median, adj. & n. [1. mḗdian; 2. mídiən], fr. L. Lat. *mediān-(us)*, 'middle', fr. *medi-(us)*, 'middle', see **media**, & **-an.** **1.** adj. Of, situated in, passing through, the middle: as *median artery* &c. **2.** n. (anat.) Median artery, vein &c.

mediant, n. [1. mḗdiant; 2. mídiənt], fr. Ital. *mediante*, fr. L. Lat. *mediant-(em)*, Pres. Part. type of *medi-(āre)*, 'to intervene'. See **mediate** & **-ant.** (mus.) Third note of scale.

mediastinal, adj. [1. mèdiastínl; 2. mìdiəstáinl]. See next word & **-al.** Of, pertaining to, the mediastinum.

mediastinum, n. [1. mèdiastínum; 2. mìdiəstáinəm]. Med. Lat., fr. Lat. *medi-(us)*, 'middle'. See **media.** (anat.) Membranous septum between principal portions of an organ, esp. that between right and left lungs.

mediate (I.), adj. [1. mḗdiat; 2. mídiət], fr. L. Lat. *mediāt-(um)*, P.P. type of *mediāre*, 'to intervene', fr. Lat. *medi-(us)*, 'middle'. See **media.** Dependent on, involving the presence or agency of, some other person or thing; not independent or direct.

mediate (II.), vb. intrans. & trans. [1. mḗdiāt; 2. mídieit]. See prec. **A.** intrans. To intervene between two parties, esp. as peacemaker. **B.** trans. **1.** To bring about by one's intervention. **2.** To hold intermediate position, form connecting link, between.

mediately, adv. [1. mḗdiatli; 2. mídiətli]. **mediate (I.)** & **-ly.** In a mediate manner.

mediation, n. [1. mèdiáshun; 2. mìdiéiʃən]. **mediate (II.)** & **-ion.** Act or process of mediating; state of being mediated; reconcilement.

mediatization, n. [1. mèdiatīzáshun; 2. mìdiətaizéiʃən]. See next word & **-ation.** Act of mediatizing; state of being mediatized.

mediatize, vb. trans. [1. mḗdiatīz; 2. mídiətaiz]. **mediate** & **-ize.** To annex (smaller state) to larger one; absorb (principality &c.) into neighbouring state, leaving former ruler his title, as in the former empires of Austria-Hungary and Germany.

mediator, n. [1. mḗdiātur; 2. mídieitə]. **mediate** & **-or.** One who mediates; specif., *the Mediator*, Christ.

mediatorial, adj. [1. mèdiatórial; 2. mìdiətóriəl]. **mediator** & **-ial.** Of, pertaining to, a mediator or to mediation.

mediatory, adj. [1. mḗdiaturi; 2. mídiətəri]. **mediate** & **-ory.** Of, pertaining to, of the nature of, mediation.

mediatrix, n. [1. mèdiátriks; 2. mìdiéitriks]. See **mediator** & **-trix.** Woman who mediates.

medicable, adj. [1. médikabl; 2. méd*i*kəbl], fr. Lat. *medicābil-(is)*, 'curable', fr. *medic-(āre)*, 'to heal, cure', fr. *medic-(us)*, 'doctor', see **medical**, & **-able.** Capable of being cured, yielding to medical treatment.

medical (I.), adj. [1. médikl; 2. méd*i*kl], fr. L. Lat. *medicāl-(is)*, 'of a doctor', fr. *medic-(us)*, 'doctor', & **-al.** Cp. *medēri*, 'to heal'; cogn. w. Avesta (*vī*)-*mad-*, 'physician'. Other cognates uncertain. **1.** Pertaining to, connected with, the art of healing and the treatment of disease in general, and including all branches: *medical knowledge*; *medical schools, practitioners, books* &c.; *medical man*, doctor; *medical jurisprudence*, legal aspects of medicine. **2.** Specif., pertaining to, requiring, treatment by a physician, by means of drugs &c.; contrasted with *surgical*: *medical cases*; *a medical ward*, one in a hospital for the treatment of such cases.

medical (II.), n., fr. prec. (colloq.) Student of medicine.

medically, adv. [1. médikali; 2. méd*i*kəli]. **medical (I.)** & **-ly.** In a medical manner; by means of medicine; from the point of view of medical science.

medicament, n. [1. medíkament, médikament; 2. medíkəmənt, méd*i*kəmənt], fr. Lat. *medicāment-(um)*, 'remedy', fr. *medicā-(re)*, 'to heal', see **medicate**, & **-ment.** Remedy, drug; substance used in medical treatment.

medicaster, n. [1. médikaster; 2. méd*i*kæstə], fr. Lat. *medic-(us)*, 'doctor', see **medical**, & **-aster.** (rare) A quack.

medicate, vb. trans. [1. médikāt; 2. méd*i*keit], fr. Lat. *medicāt-(um)*, P.P. type of *medicāri*, 'to heal, cure', fr. *medic-(us)*, 'doctor'. See **medical.** **1.** To treat with medicine. **2.** To impregnate with medicinal substance: *medicated cotton-wool.*

medication, n. [1. mèdikáshun; 2. mèd*i*kéiʃən]. Prec. & **-ion.** Act of medicating; state of being medicated.

medicative, adj. [1. médikativ; 2. méd*i*kət*i*v]. **medicate** & **-ive.** **a** Of, of the nature of, medication; **b** tending to heal, medicinal.

Medicean, adj. [1. mèdisḗan; 2. mèd*i*síən], fr. Med. Lat. *Medice-(us)*, Latinized form of *Medici*, name of Florentine family who attained to sovereign power in Tuscany in the 15th cent. Of, relating to, the Medici family.

medicinal, adj. [1. medísinl; 2. med*í*s*i*nl]. **medicine** & **-al.** **1.** Pertaining to medicine. **2.** Having healing properties; curative.

medicinally, adv. Prec. & **-ly.** In a medicinal manner, by medicine.

medicine (I.), n. [1. médsn; 2. médsn], fr. O. Fr. *medecine*, fr. Lat. *medicīna*, 'the art of healing', fr. *medic-(us)*, 'physician'. See **medical** & **-ine.** **1.** **a** The science or art of the prevention, treatment, and cure of disease: *Schools of Medicine*; **b** specif., treatment by drugs, dieting &c.; contrasted with *surgery*: *medicine and surgery.* **2.** **a** Any substance or compound taken internally to cure disease; **b** (fig.) salutary experience, punishment for folly or wrong-doing. **3.** Charm, spell, magic, as used by savages, also an object, formula, ritual, supposed to have magic properties; *medicine-man*, magician, witch-doctor.

medicine (II.), vb. trans., fr. prec. To treat medicinally, give medicine to.

medico, n. [1. médikō; 2. médikou]. Ital., fr. Lat. *medic-(us)*, 'doctor'. See **medical.** (facet.) Doctor.

medico-, pref. = 'medical, of medicine and —'; fr. Lat. *medic-(us)*, 'doctor'. See **medical.** *Medico-botanical, medico-legal.*

medieval, adj. See **medi(a)eval.**

mediocre, adj. [1. mèdióker; 2. midióukə], fr. Fr. *médiocre*, fr. Lat. *mediocris*, 'middling, indifferent', orig. 'half-way up a height', fr. *medi-(us)*, 'middle', see **media**, & O. Lat. *ocris*, 'peak, rugged mountain'; cogn. w. Gk. *ókris*, 'peak, point', & w. Lat. *ăcer*, 'sharp'. See **acrid.** Of medium quality, neither good nor bad; indifferent, average; (chiefly in disparaging sense) second-rate, inferior.

mediocrity, n. [1. mēdiókriti; 2. midiókriti], fr. Lat. *mediocritāt-(em)*, 'moderation; inferiority, insignificance'. Prec. & **-ity. 1.** Quality of being mediocre. **2.** A person of mediocre qualities or importance.

meditate, vb. trans. & intrans. [1. méditāt; 2. méditeit], fr. Lat. *meditāt-(um)*, P.P. type of *meditāri*, 'to think over, consider; to reflect'; cp. Lat. *moderāre*, 'to set limits to; moderate', see **moderate**; *modus*, 'measure; size; limit, boundary; manner, mode', see **mode**; *modestus*, 'keeping within bounds', see **modest**; cogn. w. Gk. *médomai*, 'I think of, devise', *médea*, 'plans, counsels'. The Aryan base **měd-*, **mōd-*, meant orig. 'to measure', hence 'to weigh in the mind, reflect on'; other cognates are Goth. *mitan*, O.E. *metan*, 'to measure', see **mete** (II.). See also **measure. 1.** trans. **a** To plan, plot; contemplate: *to meditate revenge*; **b** (rare) to think, dwell, upon; attend assiduously to: '*And strictly meditate the thankless Muse*' (Milton, 'Lycidas'). **2.** intrans. To engage in deep, concentrated thought or contemplation; to ponder.

meditation, n. [1. mèditāshun; 2. mèditéiʃən], fr. Lat. *meditātiōn-(em)*, 'meditation, contemplation'; prec. & **-ion. a** Concentrated thought, pondering; **b** solemn contemplation of, reflection upon, some serious subject; **c** (pl.) treatise embodying such reflections.

meditative, adj. [1. méditātiv; 2. méditeitiv]. **meditate** & **-ive. a** Of the nature of, based on, meditation; **b** given to meditation; contemplative.

meditatively, adv. Prec. & **-ly.** In a meditative manner.

meditativeness, n. See prec. & **-ness.** Quality of being meditative.

mediterranean, adj. & n. [1. mèditerānean; 2. mèditəréiniən], fr. Lat. *mediterrāne-(us)*, 'inland', fr. *medi-(us)*, 'middle', see **media**, & *terra*, 'land', see **terra**, & **-an. 1.** adj. **a** (of land, region) Far from coast; **b** (of sea) inland, land-locked. **2.** n. Specif. (cap.) *the Mediterranean (Sea)*, that lying between Europe and Africa; (also attrib.) *Mediterranean fever*, Malta fever.

medium (I.), n. [1. mēdium; 2. mídiəm], Lat. *medium*, 'the middle', fr. neut. form of *medi-(us)*, 'middle'. See **media. 1.** Middle, intermediate degree, quality &c. **2. a** Substance, e.g. air, in which objects exist, and by means of which sensory impressions are conveyed; **b** (fig.) state, condition, circumstances, of life. **3.** Agency, means, instrumentality, esp. in Phr. *by, through, the medium of*; *medium of circulation.* **4.** (in spiritualism) Person through whom spirits of the departed are supposed to communicate with the material world. **5.** Substance with which pigments are mixed before use in painting.

medium (II.), adj., fr. prec. Moderate, average, middle, not extreme in any direction: *medium size, height* &c.

mediumistic, adj. [1. mèdiumístik; 2. mìdiəmístik]. **medium** (I.) & **-ist** & **-ic.** Having qualities of, pertaining to, a spiritualistic medium.

mediumize, vb. trans. [1. mēdiumīz; 2. mídiəmaiz]. **medium** & **-ize.** To bring into condition of a medium.

medlar, n. [1. médlar; 2. médlə], fr. O. Fr. *medler, mesler*, fr. Lat., fr. Gk. *mespílē*; etymol. unknown. **a** Small brown stone fruit, eaten when half rotten, having a sour and slightly astringent taste; *medlar jelly*, jelly made of the fruit; **b** tree producing this fruit.

medley (I.), n. [1. médli; 2. médli], fr. O. Fr. *medlee*, fr. fem. P.P. of *medler, mesler*, 'to mix up'. See **meddle.** Confused, indiscriminate, assortment of objects; heterogeneous collection of things, persons, compositions &c.; specif. **a** crowd, assembly, of people of various nationalities &c.; mixed company; **b** piece of music consisting of excerpts from a number of different musical compositions; **c** literary miscellany.

medley (II.), adj., fr. prec. Mixed, varied.

Médoc, n. [1. medók; 2. medók]. Wine district of the Gironde in S.W. France. Kind of claret produced in Médoc district.

medulla, n. [1. medúla; 2. medálə]. Lat. *medulla*, 'marrow of bones'; perh. fr. the stem seen in *med-(ius)*, 'middle'. See **media. 1.** Marrow of bones. **2. a** Spinal marrow; **b** continuation of this within the cranium, forming the hindmost part of the brain; called also *medulla oblongata.* **3.** Cellular, central, inner, part, pith, **a** of animal hair; **b** of certain bodily organs such as the kidney; **c** pith of plant stems.

medullary, adj. [1. medúlari; 2. medáləri]. Prec. & **-ary.** Pertaining to, consisting of, of the nature of, medulla or pith.

Medusa, n. [1. medúza; 2. midjúzə]. Lat. *Medūsa*, fr. Gk. *Médousa*, 'guardian'. **1.** (Gk. mythol.) One of the three Gorgons, with snakes for hair, whose gaze had the power of turning to stone all who encountered it. **2.** (zool., *medusa*, pl. *medusae*) Jelly-fish.

medusal, medusan, adj. [1. medúzl, -zn; 2. midjúzl, -zn]. Prec. & **-al, -an.** (zool.) Of, pertaining to, the medusae.

medusoid, adj. [1. medúzoid; 2. midjúzoid]. **Medusa** & **-oid.** (zool.) Of the nature or form of a medusa.

meed, n. [1. mēd; 2. mīd]. O.E. *mēd*; M.E. *mēde*, 'reward'; cp. O.H.G. *mēta, miata*; O. Fris. *mēde*, 'reward, hire'. Cp. further Gk. *misthós*, 'wages, pay'; Scrt. *mīḍha-m*, 'prize'; O. Slav. *mĭzda*, 'salary'; Goth. *mizdō*, O.E. *meord*, 'reward, pay'. (poet.) **a** Reward; what is bestowed upon one; **b** full portion; what one merits: *one's meed of praise, blame* &c.

meek, adj. [1. mēk; 2. mīk]. O.E. *mēoc*, M.E. *mēke*, fr. O.N. *mjūkr*, 'soft, gentle'; cp. M. Du. *muik.* Submissive, mild, gentle; humble in spirit; reverse of *self-assertive.*

meekly, adv. Prec. & **-ly.** In a meek manner.

meekness, n. See prec. & **-ness.** Quality of being meek; lowliness, humility.

meerkat, n. [1. mērkat; 2. míəkæt]. S. Afr. Du., fr. Du. *meerkat*, 'monkey'; cp. Germ. *meerkatze*, O.H.G. *mericazza*, 'monkey', possibly an Eastern loan-word; cp. Scrt. *markaṭa*, 'ape'. The suricate, a kind of ichneumon, of S. Africa.

meerschaum, n. [1. mērsham; 2. míəʃəm]. Germ., fr. *meer*, 'sea', q.v. under **mere** (I.), & *schaum*, 'foam'. **a** Porous, light, whitish clay composed of silicate of magnesia; **b** tobacco pipe made of this.

meet (I.), n. [1. mēt; 2. mīt], fr. next word. Assembly of riders and foxhounds, or harriers, at a fixed place previous to a hunt.

meet (II.), vb. trans. & intrans. O.E. *mētan*; M.E. *mēte*; O.N. *mōta*; O.S. *mōtian.* See **moot. A.** trans. **1. a** To come face to face with, encounter: *to meet a person in the street*; Phr. *to meet a person half-way*, to be ready to make concessions, to respond to another's advances; **b** to come towards, approach, come upon, pass, from opposite directions: *if he comes by this road I shall meet him*; *the two trains coming from the North and South meet at Carlisle.* **2.** (of line, road, river &c.) To join, open, flow into, at a given point: *the Cherwell meets the Thames at Oxford.* **3.** To come into contact with, touch: *his hand met hers.* Phr. *to meet one's eye, ear*, to become visible, audible; to become apparent. **4. a** To come into the company of: *one doesn't often meet him in society*; **b** to make the acquaintance of: *come to lunch to meet my brother*; **c** to come into personal relation with for purposes of discussion, negotiation &c.: *the owners are ready to meet the miners.* **5.** To await arrival of, go beforehand to specific place in order to receive; greet on arrival: *to meet a person at the station*; *meet a train, boat* &c. **6. a** To encounter in conflict, duel &c.; **b** to face, confront, stand up against: *to meet calamities with a smile.* **7. a** To satisfy, comply with, conform to: *to meet a person's wishes, demands*; *to meet the requirements of a situation*; **b** to satisfy by payment: *to meet one's liabilities*; **c** to pay when due: *to meet a bill.* **8.** To refute by argument, to answer satisfactorily: *to meet objections, criticisms* &c. **B.** intrans. **1. a** (of lines, roads &c.) To join, come together, converge, at a given point; Phr. *extremes meet*; **b** (of opposite ends of a line, piece of material &c.) to come into contact, be long enough to join, touch: *this belt won't meet round my waist.* Phr. (fig.) *to make both ends meet*, to make one's means suffice for one's expenses. **2.** (of persons) **a** To come together into one another's company: *we correspond regularly but seldom meet*; **b** to make each other's acquaintance: *he and I know each other by sight, but have never met.* **3.** (of qualities) To be united, to occur, be found, combined, e.g. in the same person, character, or thing: '*And all that's best of dark and bright Meet in her aspect and her eyes*' (Byron). **C.** Followed by adverbs and prepositions. *Meet together*, to come together. *Meet with*, **a** to undergo, experience: *to meet with adventures, ill-treatment, kindness, misfortune* &c.; **b** to come across, meet, encounter: *to meet with a friend in the train*; **c** to come upon, find by chance: *to meet with a striking phrase in a book.*

meet (III.), adj. O.E. *(ge)mǣte*, 'suitable, well-fitting'; M.E. *mēte*, 'suitable, fit, moderate'; cp. O. Fris. *mēte*; O.H.G. *gimāti*, 'fitting'; cp. also Pret. pl. *mǣton*, of O.E. *metan*, 'to measure'. See **mete** (II.) (archaic) Fitting, suitable, proper: '*It is very meet, right, and our bounden duty*' &c. (Communion Service).

meeting, n. [1. mēting; 2. mítiŋ]. **meet** (II.) & **-ing. 1. a** The act of coming face to face, of flocking together; (i.) an encounter, whether friendly or hostile, by accident or design; (ii.) specif., a duel; **b** process or fact of coming together, joining, coming into contact: *the meeting of the waters.* **2. a** Assembly of people for specific purpose: *political meeting, race-meeting*; specif. (cap.) assembly for public worship, esp. of Quakers; **b** persons assembled at a meeting: *to address the meeting.*

meeting-house, n. Building for religious meetings held by Friends.

meeting-place, n. Place fixed on for a meeting; one in which meetings are held.

meetly, adv. [1. mētli; 2. mítli]. **meet** (III.) & **-ly.** In a proper, fitting, seemly, suitable, manner.

meetness, n. [1. mētnes; 2. mítnis]. See prec. & **-ness.** Quality of being meet.

mega-, pref. representing Gk. *méga-(s)*, 'large'; cogn. w. Scrt. *maj-mán-* 'size'; Lat. *magnus*, 'great', see **magnum**; Goth. *mikils*; O.E. *myčel*, see **much.** Great, large, e.g. *megalithic, megapode* &c.

megacephalous, megacephalic, adj. [1. mègaséfalus, -sefálik; 2. mègəséfələs, -sifǽlik]. Prec. & **-cephalous, -ic.** Large-headed.

megaceros, n. [1. megáseros; 2. megǽsərəs]. **mega-** & Gk. *-kerōs*, fr. *kéras*, 'horn'. See **cerato-**. Species of fossil deer, Irish elk.

megalith, n. [1. mégalith; 2. mégəliþ]. **mega-** & Gk. *líthos*, 'stone'. See **litho-**. A large prehistoric stone monument, menhir, dolmen &c.

megalithic, adj. [1. megalíthik; 2. megəlíþik]. See prec. & **-ic**. Made of, pertaining to, large stones or megaliths, esp. as prehistoric monuments: *megalithic circles, structures.*

megalo-, pref. representing Gk. *megál-(ē)*, fem. of *mégas*, 'great, large'. See **mega-**.

megalomania, n. [1. mègalōmánia; 2. mègəloumḗiniə]. See prec. & **mania**. Unfounded belief in one's own greatness; this as form of insanity.

megalomaniac, n. [1. mègalōmániak; 2. mègəloumḗiniæk]. Prec. & **-ac**. Person suffering from megalomania.

megalosaurus, n. [1. mègalōsórus; 2. mègəlousɔ́rəs]. See **megalo-** & **saurian**. Genus of huge, extinct, carnivorous reptiles.

megaphone, n. [1. mégafōn; 2. mégəfoun]. **mega-** & **-phone**. Large speaking-trumpet, used for making the voice travel to a distance.

megapod(e), n. [1. mégapod, -pōd; 2. mégəpɔd, -poud]. **mega-** & Gk. *pod-(ós)*, *poús*, 'foot', see **pedal** & **-pod**. Name of a family of Australasian birds, also known as mound-bird, which leaves its eggs to hatch in a mound of grass, leaves &c.

megaron, n. [1. mégaron; 2. mégərɔn]. Gk., fr. *mégas*, 'great'. See **mega-**. (archaeol.) The great hall of the early Greek palace, as at Mycenae &c., and described in the Homeric poems.

megass, n. [1. megás; 2. migǽs]. Etymol. unknown. Fibre left after sugar is extracted from sugar-cane.

megatherium, n. [1. mègathérium; 2. mègəþíəriəm]. **mega-** & Lat. form of Gk. *thērion*, 'wild animal', fr. *thḗr*, 'wild animal'. See **theriac**. Extinct genus of huge herbivorous, hairy sloths, order *Edentata*, of South America.

megilp, n. [1. megílp; 2. migílp]. Etymol. unknown. Mixture of linseed oil and turpentine, used as medium for oil-paints.

megohm, n. [1. mégōm; 2. mégoum]. **mega-** & **ohm**. (elect.) Unit of resistance, one million ohms.

megrim, n. [1. mḗgrim; 2. mígrim], fr. Fr. *migraine*. See **migraine**. **1.** Severe headache, usually periodical and affecting one side of head only; migraine. **2.** Pl., *the megrims*: **a** depression, low spirits, dejection; **b** the staggers in horses and cattle. **3.** Sudden fancy, whim, caprice.

meiosis, n. [1. mīósis; 2. maióusis]. Gk. *meíōsis*, 'lessening', fr. *meióein*, 'to lessen', fr. *meíōn*, 'less', earlier **meínōn*; cp. *minúthein*, 'to lessen'; cogn. w. Scrt. *minā́ti*, 'to impair'; Lat. *minor*, 'less', see **minor**, & words there referred to; for the second element see **-osis**. Litotes, q.v.

mekometer, n. [1. mekómeter; 2. mikɔ́mitə], fr. Gk. *mêkos*, 'length', cogn. w. *makrós*, 'long', see **macro-**, & **-meter**. A special form of range-finder for artillery or rifle fire.

melancholia, n. [1. mèlankōlia; 2. mèlənkóuliə]. L. Lat. *melancholia*, fr. Gk. *melagkholía*, 'choleric humour', fr. *melan-*, stem of *mélas*, 'black', see **melanism**, & *kholḗ*, 'bile', see **choler**. Form of emotional insanity, characterized by extreme mental depression.

melancholiac, n. [1. mèlankóliak; 2. mèlənkóuliæk]. Prec. & **-ac**. Person suffering from melancholia.

melancholic, adj. [1. mèlankólik; 2. mèlənkɔ́lik], fr. Lat. *melancholic-(us)*, fr. Gk. *melagkholikós*, 'atrabilious'. See prec. & **-ic**. Sad, gloomy, melancholy; given to, caused by, melancholy.

melancholy, n. & adj. [1. mélankoli; 2. mélənkəli], fr. O. Fr. *melancholie*, fr. Lat. *melancholia*. See **melancholia**. **1.** n. **a** Gloom, sadness, depression of spirits, dejection; **b** habitual tendency to this. **2.** adj. **a** Given to expressing melancholy; gloomy, mournful, depressed; **b** causing melancholy; gloomy, depressing, saddening: *a melancholy landscape; a melancholy event.*

mélange, n. [1. māláhnzh; 2. melā̃ž]. Fr., fr. *mêler*, 'to mix', fr. O. Fr. *mesler*. See **meddle**. Mixture, medley.

melanism, n. [1. mélanizm; 2. mélənizəm], fr. Gk. *melan-*, stem of *mélās*, 'black'; cp. Scrt. *malinás*, 'dirty, stained, black'; Lett. *melns*, 'black'; O. Prussian *melne*, 'bluish mark on the body'; fr. base **mel-*, **ml̥-*, 'to soil; stained, dirty; of dark colour'; hence 'marked in any way, bearing marks', cp. Goth. *mēla*, 'letters'; O.E. *mǣl*, 'sign, mark; fixed time', see **meal (II.)**; also 'coloured', cp. Lith. *mélnys*, 'blue pigment'; Lith. *mulvas*, 'reddish'; Lat. *mulleus*, 'red, purple'; Gk. *míltos*, 'reddish'. Abnormal development of dark pigment in skin, hair, nails &c.

melanite, n. [1. mélanīt; 2. mélənait], fr. Gk. *melan-*, stem of *mélās*, 'black', see prec., & **-ite**. Deep black variety of garnet.

melanochroi, n. pl. [1. mèlanókrōī; 2. mèlənɔ́krouai], fr. Gk. *melanókhro-(os)*, 'swarthy', fr. *melan-*, stem of *mélās*, 'black', see **melanism**, & either *khró-(ā)*, 'skin, surface; appearance'; cp. *khroízein*, 'to touch the surface lightly; to tint'; *khrôma*, 'skin; complexion; colour', see **chrome**. Individuals of white race, having exceptionally dark complexion.

melanochroid, adj. [1. mèlanókroid; 2. mèlənɔ́krɔid]. Prec. & **-oid**. Of, of the nature of, melanochroi.

melanosis, n. [1. mèlanósis; 2. mèlənóusis], fr. Gk. *melan-*, stem of *mélās*, 'black', see **melanism**, & **-osis**. **a** Abnormal deposit of black pigment in the tissue, organs &c. of the body; **b** morbid condition arising from this.

melanotic, adj. [1. mèlanótik; 2. mèlənɔ́tik], fr. Gk. *melan-*, see prec., & **-otic**. Of, of the nature of, affected with, melanosis.

mêlée, n. [1. mélā; 2. mélei]. Fr., fr. O. Fr. *medlée*. See **medley**. Confused fight, skirmish, conflict, affray.

melic, adj. [1. mélik; 2. mélik], fr. Gk. *melik-(ós)*, 'of a song', fr. *mél-(os)*, 'limb, joint; part of musical phrase; song, tune'; cogn. w. Corn. *mal*, 'joint, vertebra'; no certain cognates in other languages. Of, pertaining to, intended as, a song: *melic poetry; a melic ode.*

melilot(e), n. [1. mèlilót, mèlilṓt; 2. mèlilɔ́t, mèlilóut], fr. Gk. *melílōt-(on)*, 'kind of clover', fr. *méli*, 'honey', cogn. w. Lat. *mel*, 'honey', see **melliferous**, & *lōtós*, 'lotus', see **lotus**. Genus of white or yellow-flowered plants with sweet, aromatic scent.

melinite, n. [1. mélinīt; 2. mélinait], fr. Fr. *mélinite*, fr. Gk. *mēlin-(ós)*, fr. *mêl-(on)*, 'apple', the etymol. of wh. is unknown. See **malic** & **-ite**. A high explosive containing picric acid.

meliorate, vb. trans. & intrans. [1. mḗliorāt; 2. míliəreit], fr. L. Lat. *meliōrāt-(um)*, P.P. type of *meliōrāre*, 'to improve', fr. Lat. *melior*, 'better'; prob. orig. 'stronger, greater'; cp. Gk. *mála*, 'very'; *mâllon*, 'more'; *malerós*, 'strong'; Lat. *multus*, 'much', see **multi-**; Lett. *milns*, 'very much'; O. Slav. *izmolěti*, 'to rise above'. To improve, amend, make or become better.

melioration, n. [1. mḗliorā́shun; 2. mìliəréiʃən]. Prec. & **-ion**. Improvement, amendment.

meliorative, adj. [1. mḗliorativ; 2. míliərətiv]. **meliorate** & **-ive**. Tending to improve, or to cause improvement; reverse of *pejorative.*

meliorism, n. [1. mḗliorizm; 2. míliərizəm]. Lat. *melior*, 'better', see **meliorate**, & **-ism**. Doctrine that man and human life tend to become better, and that human effort may contribute to this improvement; reverse of *pessimism.*

meliorist, n. [1. mḗliorist; 2. míliərist]. See prec. & **-ist**. Believer in meliorism.

mellay, n. (archaic) See **mêlée**.

melliferous, adj. [1. melíferus; 2. məlífərəs], fr. Lat. *melli-*, stem of *mel*, 'honey'; cogn. w. Gk. *méli*, 'honey', *mélissa*, 'bee'; Goth. *miliþ*, 'honey'; O.E. *mele(dēaw)*, *mil(dēaw)*, 'nectar', see **mildew**, **blithe**, & **-ferous**. Producing honey; sweet.

mellifluence, n. [1. melíflooens; 2. məlífluəns]. See next word & **-ence**. Quality of being mellifluent; sweetness.

mellifluent, adj. [1. melíflooent; 2. məlífluənt], fr. Lat. *melli-*, 'honey', see **melliferous**, & *flu-(ere)*, 'to flow', see **fluent**. Mellifluous.

mellifluous, adj. [1. melíflooùs; 2. məlífluəs]. See prec. & **-ous**. (of words, music, voice &c.) Sweet-sounding, dulcet.

mellifluously, adv. Prec. & **-ly**. In a mellifluous manner.

mellow (I.), adj. [1. mélō; 2. mélou]. M.E. *melwe*, *melowe*, 'ripe, mature'; perh. fr. O.E. *melu*, 'meal, flour', stem *melw-*. See **meal (I.)**. **a** (of fruit) Ripe, soft, sweet; **b** (of wine) well matured; soft and pleasant to the taste; **c** (of voice, sound, colour &c.) rich, full and soft; not harsh or thin; **d** (of earth) rich and moist; **e** (of character &c.) made sympathetic, wise, and gentle by experience; **f** (slang) (i.) jovial, gay; (ii.) intoxicated.

mellow (II.), vb. trans. & intrans., fr. prec. **a** To make mellow; **b** to become mellow.

mellowly, adv. **mellow** & **-ly**. In a mellow manner.

mellowness, n. See prec. & **-ness**. State or quality of being mellow.

melodeon, melodion, melodium, n. [1. melṓdeun, -um; 2. milóudiən, -əm]. Invented word fr. **melody**. **1.** Kind of reed organ; American organ. **2.** Kind of accordion.

melodic, adj. [1. melódik; 2. melɔ́dik]. Lat. *melodicus*, fr. Gk. *melōdikós*. See **melody** & **-ic**. Of the nature of, pertaining to, melody; melodious.

melodious, adj. [1. melṓdius; 2. milóudiəs], fr. O. Fr. *melodieus*. **melody** & **-ous**. **1.** Of, producing, full of, melody. **2.** Sweet-sounding, tuneful, musical.

melodiously, adv. Prec. & **-ly**. In a melodious manner.

melodiousness, n. See prec. & **-ness**. Quality of being melodious.

melodist, n. [1. mélodist; 2. mélədist]. **melody** & **-ist**. Composer, singer, of melodies; specif., a composer whose work excels in melody.

melodize, vb. intrans. & trans. [1. mélodīz; 2. mélədaiz]. **melody** & **-ize**. **a** trans. To render melodious; **b** intrans., to compose melodies.

melodrama, n. [1. mèlōdráhma; 2. mèloudrā́mə], fr. Fr. *mélodrame*, fr. Gk. *mélo-(s)*, 'song, music', see **melic**, & **drama**. **1.** (obs.) A play interspersed with songs. **2.** Play in which the sentiments and emotions displayed are violent and intense, the incidents of a highly sensational and exciting kind, and the style of the dialogue high-flown and bombastic. **3.** Incident, action &c. combining sensational and sentimental elements after the manner of melodrama.

melodramatic, adj. [1. mèlōdramátik; 2. mèloudrəmǽtik]. See prec. & **dramatic**. Resembling melodrama; violently sentimental and sensational.

melodramatically, adv. [1. mèlōdramátikali; 2. mèloudrəmǽtikəli]. Prec. & **-al** & **-ly**. In a melodramatic manner.

melodramatist, n. [1. mèlōdrámatist; 2. mèloudrǽmətist]. See prec. & **dramatist**. Writer of melodrama.

melodramatize, vb. trans. [1. mèlōdrámatīz; 2. mèloudrǽmətaiz]. See prec. & **dramatize**. To put into the form of a melodrama.

melody, n. [1. mélodi; 2. mélədi], fr. O. Fr. *melodie*, fr. L. Lat., fr. Gk. *melōdía*, 'chant, song', fr. *melōd-(ós)*, 'musical', fr. *melōdéō*,

'I sing', fr. *mél-(os)*, 'song', see **melic,** & *ōdḗ*, 'song', see **ode.** A sequence of agreeable musical sounds or notes; specif. **a** an air, tune, in music; also tunefulness; **b** sweet agreeable sounds which give pleasure to the ear: *the melody of brooks and trees.*

melon, n. [1. mélun; 2. mélən], fr. Fr., fr. L. Lat. *melōn-(em),* nom. *melo,* prob. contracted fr. Gk. *mēlopépōn,* wh. is fr. *mēlo-(n),* 'apple', see **melinite,** & *pépōn,* 'ripe'; cp. Gk. *pepaínein,* 'to ripen'; *peptós,* 'cooked', see **pepsin.** Kind of gourd with sweet, tender, juicy flesh, containing a very large number of flat seeds.

melt (I.), n. [1. melt; 2. melt], fr. next word. Molten metal.

melt (II.), vb. intrans. & trans. O.E. *meltan,* 'to melt' (intrans.), *mæltan, meltan* (trans.); M.E. *melten*; cp. O.N. *melta,* 'digest'; cogn. w. Gk. *méldein,* 'to melt, become liquid'; fr. another form of same base comes also Lat. *mollis,* 'soft', & *molere,* 'to grind'. See further under **malt, mild, mill (I.),** & **meal (I.)** & **mould (I.). A.** intrans. **1.** (of ice, snow, wax, rock, metal &c.) **a** To become liquid through heat; **b** also *melt away,* to dissolve and disappear through heat; Phrs. (colloq.) *I'm simply melting (with heat),* am very hot; (of food) *to melt in one's mouth,* to be so tender that it disintegrates quickly. **2. a** To dissolve: *sugar melts in tea*; **b** to disappear, vanish, fade, gradually from sight: *the vision melted away*; (also fig.) *his resources were gradually melting away*; **c** (fig., of person, feelings &c.) to become softened, tender through pity &c.; to relent: '*Look homéward, Angel, now, and melt with ruth*' (Milton, 'Lycidas'); **d** (of courage, determination &c.) to ooze away, be weakened. **3.** To pass by imperceptible degrees into, become indistinguishable from; to blend: *ocean melts into sky on the horizon.* **B.** trans. **1. a** To reduce to liquid, cause to melt, by heat; *melt down,* to reduce (metal articles, plate &c.) to condition of molten metal; **b** to dissolve by immersion in liquid. **2.** (fig.) To soften, make tender, mild; to cause to relent: *her entreaties would melt the hardest heart.*

melting, adj. [1. mélting; 2. méltiŋ], fr. Pres. Part. of prec. **1. a** (of feelings, heart &c.) Strongly affected by emotion; inclined to relent; **b** (of looks, glances) languishing, sentimental. **2.** (of sounds) Provoking gentle, tender, emotions; sweet, soothing, soft.

meltingly, adv. Prec. & **-ly.** In a melting manner.

melton, n. & adj. [1. méltun; 2. méltən]. fr. Melton Mowbray, Leicestershire, a famous hunting centre. **1.** n. **a** A fine, closely woven and fulled wool cloth, with smooth surface, used for overcoats &c.; **b** overcoat of this cloth. **2.** adj. Made of this cloth.

member, n. [1. member; 2. mémbə], fr. Fr. *membre,* fr. Lat. *membrum,* 'limb, member, part', earlier **mems-rom*; cp. Lat. *membrāna,* 'fine skin'. Cogn. w. Gk. *mērós,* 'thigh'; Scrt. *mą̄sá-m,* 'flesh'; O. Slav. *męso,* Goth. *mims,* 'flesh'. **1. a** Part, organ, limb, of human or animal body; Phr. *unruly member,* the tongue; **b** (fig.) *member of Christ,* Christian. **2.** Distinct part of complex whole; single constituent part. **3.** Person belonging to a corporate society, specified group &c.; *Member of Parliament,* elected representative in House of Commons. **4. a** Clause of sentence; **b** group of figures forming part of arithmetical expression.

-membered, adj. [1. mémberd; 2. mémbəd]. Prec. & **-ed.** Having limbs or members.

memberless, adj. [1. mémberles; 2. mémbəlis]. **member** & **-less.** Without members.

membership, n. [1. mémbership; 2. mémbəʃip]. **member** & **-ship. 1.** State of being a member; status as member. **2.** Whole number of members of a society &c.: *to have a large membership.*

membranaceous, adj. [1. mèmbranáshus; 2. mèmbrənéiʃəs]. See next word & **-aceous.** Consisting of, of the character of, membrane.

membrane, n. [1. mémbrān; 2. mémbrein, mémbrin]. Lat. *membrāna,* 'fine skin, membrane; parchment'; cp. Lat. *membrum,* 'limb'. See **member. 1.** (anat.) Fine, supple, usually elastic, skin covering or lining the organs, canals &c. of the body. **2.** (bot.) Fine, film-like skin lining canals, covering seeds &c., of plant. **3.** Single skin of parchment.

membran(e)ous, adj. [1. membráneus, mémbranus; 2. membréiniəs, mémbrinəs]. **membrane** & **-eous.** Of, pertaining to, consisting of, of the character of, membrane.

memento, n. [1. meméntō; 2. miméntou]. Lat. imperat. of *meminisse,* 'to remember', fr. redupl. form of stem **men-,* 'to think', seen in *mens,* 'mind, thought'; see **mental (I.).** Object serving as reminder; memorial, warning. Phr. *memento mori* (Lat., 'remember you must die'), anything serving to remind us that we must die; an emblem of mortality.

memoir, n. [1. mémwar; 2. mémwā], fr. Fr. *mémoire,* masc.; specialized use of *mémoire,* fem., 'memory', fr. Lat. *memoria,* 'memory'. See **memory. 1. a** Biographical account of a person written by another; **b** monograph, dissertation upon some noteworthy subject. **2.** (pl.) *Memoirs,* **a** a narrative of events based on the personal observation and experiences of the writer; account of the writer's own life and adventures; **b** collection of researches published by a learned academy or society.

memorabilia, n. [1. mèmorabília; 2. mèmərəbíliə]. Lat.; neut. pl. of *memorābilis,* 'memorable'. See **memorable.** Things worth remembering; points worthy of note.

memorability, n. [1. mèmorabíliti; 2. mèmərəbíliti]. See next word & **-ity.** Quality of being memorable.

memorable, adj. [1. mémorabl; 2. mémərəbl], fr. Lat. *memorābil-(is),* 'remarkable, memorable', fr. *memor-(āre),* 'to call to mind', fr. *memor,* 'mindful', q.v. under **memory,** & **-able.** Noteworthy, remarkable, worthy to be remembered.

memorableness, n. Prec. & **-ness.** Quality, fact, of being memorable.

memorably, adv. See prec. & **-ly.** In a memorable manner.

memorandum, n. [1. mèmorándum; 2. mèməréndəm], pl. *memoranda, memorandums.* Lat., 'something to be remembered'; neut. sing. gerundive fr. *memorāre,* 'to call to mind'. See **memorable. 1. a** Note made to help the memory; **b** brief record of events &c. **2.** (law) Brief note of a transaction; summary of terms of contract &c.; specif., *memorandum of association,* document to be signed at the formation of a company, whether with limited liability or not, which must state name of proposed company, place of business, the objects for which it is to be carried on &c.

memorial (I.), adj. [1. memórial; 2. mimɔ́riəl], fr. Lat. *memoriāl-(is),* 'of memory'. See **memory** & **-al. 1.** Connected with, relating to, memory. **2.** Bringing to mind, commemorating; serving as reminder: *memorial festival, service, tablet* &c. Phr. *Memorial Day,* (U.S.A.) commemorating those who fell in the Civil War, held on different dates in the various states.

memorial (II.), n., fr. prec. **1.** Object, esp. a monumental structure, serving to commemorate person, event &c.; custom, observance &c., which does this. **2.** (usually pl.) Chronicle, document containing historical narrative, record &c. **3.** Written statement of views in form of petition presented to legislative body &c.

memorialist, n. [1. memórialist; 2. mimɔ́riəlist]. Prec. & **-ist.** Person presenting memorial; signatory to memorial.

memorialize, vb. trans. [1. memórialīz; 2. mimɔ́riəlaiz]. **memorial** & **-ize. 1.** To commemorate by a memorial. **2.** To present a memorial to.

memoria technica, n. [1. memória téknika; 2. mimɔ́riə téknikə]. Lat., 'artificial memory'. See **memory** & **technic.** Formula, system, used to aid the memory.

memorize, vb. trans. [1. mémorīz; 2. méməraiz]. See next word & **-ize. 1.** To note down, record. **2.** To commit to memory, learn by heart.

memory, n. [1. mémori; 2. méməri], fr. O. Fr. *memoire,* fem., fr. Lat. *memoria,* 'memory', fr. *memor,* 'mindful', w. reduplication fr. base **mer-*; cp. O.E. *(ġe)mimor,* 'known'; *māmrian,* 'to plot, design'; Du. *mijmeren,* 'to ponder'; Gk. *merimnān,* 'to be thoughtful', *mérmēra,* 'care'; Scrt. *smárati,* 'to remember'; Goth. *maurnan,* O.E. *murnan,* 'to be anxious for'. See **martyr** & cp. **moratory. 1. a** Faculty of retaining mental and physical impressions in, and of recalling them to the mind; power of remembering; **b** this faculty in individual: *to have a good, bad, memory*; Phr. *living memory,* recollection, remembrance, of those now living. **2.** Something remembered; recollection: *memories of childhood.* **3.** Commemoration, remembrance, esp. in Phr. *in memory of.* **4.** Time within which memory is exercised; period including events which are remembered: *before, within, the memory of man.* **5.** Fame, reputation, remembered character, of dead person: *of famous, blessed, memory.*

mem-sahib, n. [1. mém sàh-ib; 2. mém sā-ib]. **ma'am** & **sahib.** Mode of address used by native Indian speakers to a European woman instead of the proper feminine form *sahiba.*

men, pl. of **man.**

-men, Lat. suff. forming ns. fr. vbs.: *specimen, regimen, stamen* &c.

menace (I.), n. [1. ménas; 2. ménəs]. O. Fr., fr. Lat. *mināciae,* 'threats', fr. *mināc-,* stem of *minax,* 'overhanging; threatening'. See **minatory.** Threat.

menace (II.), vb. trans., fr. prec. To threaten.

menacingly, adv. [1. ménasingli; 2. ménəsiŋli], fr. Pres. Part. of prec. & **-ly.** In a menacing manner.

ménage, n. [1. ménahzh; 2. ménāž]. Fr., fr. O. Fr. *manaige,* fr. Low Lat. *mansionāticum,* 'domain', fr. Lat. *mansiōn-(em),* 'halting-place', see **mansion,** & **-age. 1.** Household. **2.** Management of a household, domestic affairs.

menagerie, n. [1. menájeri, menáhzheri; 2. minǽdžəri, mināžəri], fr. Fr. *ménagerie.* Prec. & **-ery.** Collection of wild animals kept in captivity for exhibition, esp. a travelling show; contrasted with *zoological gardens.*

mend (I.), vb. trans. & intrans. [1. mend; 2. mend]. For **amend. A.** trans. **1. a** To repair, restore to original or sound condition, remove defect in: *to mend a garment, a broken cup, a road*; **b** to repair, remove defect of: *to mend a hole, a tear* &c. **2.** Various specific meanings: **a** To improve, amend, correct: *to mend one's ways*; **b** to improve, rectify: *that won't mend matters*; *least said soonest mended*; **c** to put fuel on, make up: *to mend a fire*; **d** to cut into shape when worn: *to mend a quill pen*; **e** to increase, quicken: *to mend one's pace.* **B.** intrans. **1.** To grow better, recover, improve in health. **2.** To be capable of repair.

mend (II.), n., fr. prec. Hole, broken part &c. that has been repaired. Phr. *on the mend,* recovering, improving in health or condition.

mendable, adj. [1. méndabl; 2. méndəbl]. **mend (I.)** & **-able.** Capable of being mended.

mendacious, adj. [1. mendáshus; 2. mendéiʃəs], fr. Lat. *mendāc-,* stem of *mendax,* 'lying; untrue'; prob. orig. 'faulty, defective', fr. *mend-(um),* 'fault', cogn. w. Scrt. *mindā,* 'physical defect'; O. Ir. *mennair,* 'blemish'; Lat. *mentīri,* 'to lie, be untruthful', wh. seems to have influenced the sense of *mendax,* is fr. the stem **men-,* 'to think', seen in **memento, mental (I.)** &c. For the ending see **-acious.** Lying, untruthful.

mendaciously, adv. Prec. & **-ly.** In a mendacious manner; untruthfully.

mendacity, n. [1. mendásiti; 2. mendǽsiti], fr. Lat. *mendāc-(is)*, stem of *mendax*, 'lying', see **mendacious**, & **-ity**. Untruthfulness, tendency to lie.

Mendelian, adj. [1. mendélian; 2. mendílian], fr. name of Gregor Mendel (d. 1884), abbot of Brünn, Moravia. (biol.) Pertaining to those laws and principles of heredity enunciated by Mendel in 1865, rediscovered in 1900 and generally accepted.

Mendelism, n. [1. méndelizm; 2. méndəlizəm]. See prec. & **-ism**. (biol.) The laws of the inheritance of parental and ancestral characters formulated by Mendel.

mendicancy, n. [1. méndikansi; 2. méndikənsi]. See next word & **-cy**. State of being mendicant; practice of habitual begging.

mendicant, adj. & n. [1. méndikant; 2. méndikənt], fr. Lat. *mendīcant-(em)*, Pres. Part. of *mendicāre*, 'to beg', fr. *mendīc-(us)*, 'beggar', orig. 'undeserving man', fr. *mend-(um)*, 'fault'. See **mendacious** & **-ant**. **1.** adj. Begging; living as beggar; *mendicant orders, friars*, depending on alms for their support. **2.** n. **a** Beggar; **b** mendicant friar.

mendicity, n. [1. mendísiti; 2. mendísiti], fr. Lat. *mendīcitāt-(em)*, 'state of being a beggar', fr. *mendīc-(us)*, 'beggar'. See prec. & **-ity**. State of being a beggar; begging.

menhaden, n. [1. menhádn; 2. menhéidn], fr. a N. Am. Indian word meaning 'fertilizer'. Kind of large herring, found on east coast of North America, yielding oil, and used as manure.

menhir, n. [1. ménhēr; 2. ménhiə], fr. Bret. *men hir*, 'long stone'; cp. W. *maen*, 'rock, stone'; & O. Ir. *sír*, 'long, everlasting'; Corn. *hēs*, 'slow, dull'; cogn. w. Lat. *sērus*, 'late'; see **serotine, since**. A single, upright, large stone or monolith set up as monument by prehistoric races; found in Europe, Asia, and Africa.

menial, adj. & n. [1. mḗnial; 2. míniəl], fr. A.-Fr., fr. O. Fr. *mesnie*, 'household', fr. Low Lat. *mansionāta*. See **mansion**. **1.** adj. **a** (of work) Servile, mean; **b** (of person) doing servile work. **2.** n. **a** Domestic servant, retainer of humble rank; **b** a person of base, servile, character.

menially, adv. Prec. & **-ly**. In a menial manner, as a menial.

meningeal, adj. [1. mèninjḗal; 2. mènindžíəl], fr. Gk. *mēning-*, stem of *mênigx*, 'membrane'. See **meninx**. Of, pertaining to, the meninges.

meninges, n. pl. [1. menínjēz; 2. meníndžīz]. Lat. pl. of *mēnigx*, 'a membrane', see **meninx**. The three membranes covering the brain and spinal cord.

meningitis, n. [1. mèninjítis; 2. mènindžáitis], fr. Gk. *mēning-*, stem of **meninx**, & **-itis**. Inflammation of the membranes enveloping the brain.

meningocele, n. [1. menínjosēl; 2. meníndžəsīl]. See prec. & **-cele**. Tumour on the brain.

meninx, n., pl. **meninges** [1. mḗningks, menínjēz; 2. míniŋks, meníndžīz], fr. Gk. *mênigx*, 'membrane', prob. earlier **mēmsn-*; cp. Gk. *mērós*, 'thigh', fr. **mēmsr-o-*; cogn. w. Lat. *membrum*, 'limb', see **member**; *membrāna*, 'fine skin', see **membrane**. One of the three membranes, meninges, enveloping the brain and spinal cord.

meniscus, n., pl. **menisci** [1. menískus, -kī; 2. menískəs, -kai], fr. Gk. *mēnískos*, 'crescent', fr. *mḗn*, 'moon'. See next word. **1.** Lens with one surface convex and the other concave. **2.** (math.) Crescent-shaped figure.

meno-, pref. representing Gk. *mḗn*, 'month'; cogn. w. Scrt. *mās-*, 'moon, month'; Lat. *mēns-(is)*, 'month', see **menses**; O. Ir. *mī*, 'month'; Goth. *mēna*; O.H.G. *māno*; O.E. *mōna*, 'moon'. See **moon**. **a** Connected with months; **b** connected with the menses.

menology, n. [1. mēnóloji; 2. minólədži], fr. Late Gk. *mēnológion*, fr. *mḗn*, 'month', see prec., & **-logy**. Register or calendar of saints and martyrs, esp. in the Greek Church.

menopause, n. [1. ménōpawz; 2. ménoupōz]. **meno-** & Gk. *paúein*, 'to cause to cease', see **pause**. Period of life, generally between forty and fifty, in women, at which menstruation ceases; change of life in woman, climacteric.

menorrhagia, n. [1. mènorájia; 2. mènouréidžiə]. **meno-** & Gk. *-rhagia*. See second element in **haemorrhage**. Excessive menstruation.

menses, n. [1. mensēz; 2. ménsīz], fr. Lat. *mensēs*, pl. of *mensis*, 'month'. See **meno-, month, moon**. Monthly discharge of blood from the uterus.

Menshevik, n. [1. ménshevik; 2. ménʃəvik]. Russ., lit. 'one of those in a minority', fr. *menshe*, 'smaller, less', opposed to **Bolshevik**. Member of the moderate Socialist party in Russia, which was in a minority and defeated at a Socialist Conference in 1903; at the Revolution of 1917, after being in power a short time, it was overthrown by Lenin and the Bolshevik, Communist, party.

menstrual, adj. [1. ménstrooal; 2. ménstruəl], fr. Lat. *menstruāl-(is)*, 'monthly', fr. *menstru-(us)*, 'monthly', fr. *mens-(is)*, 'month', see **menses**, & **-al**. **1.** Pertaining to the menses. **2.** (astron.) Monthly.

menstruate, vb. intrans. [1. ménstrooāt; 2. ménstrueit], fr. Lat. *menstru-(us)*, 'monthly', see prec., & **-ate**. To discharge the menses.

menstruation, n. [1. mènstrooáshun; 2. mènstruéiʃən]. Prec. & **-ion**. Act or process of menstruating.

menstruous, adj. [1. ménstroous; 2. ménstruəs], fr. Lat. *menstru-(us)*, 'monthly'. See **menstrual** & **-ous**. Menstrual; also, soiled with menstrual blood.

menstruum, n. [1. ménstrooum; 2. ménstruəm]. Neut. form of Lat. *menstruus*, 'monthly'. See **menstrual**. **a** Something to dissolve a solid body, originally a term of alchemy; **b** anything acting as a solvent.

mensurable, adj. [1. ménshurabl; 2. ménʃərəbl], fr. L. Lat. *mensūrābil-(is)*, 'measurable', fr. *mensūrāre*, 'to measure', fr. Lat. *mensūra*, 'measure'. See **measure** and **-able**. **1.** Capable of being measured. **2.** (mus.) Having fixed time or rhythm.

mensural, adj. [1. ménshural; 2. ménʃərəl], fr. Lat. *mensūra*, 'measure'. See **measure** & **-al**. **1.** Of, relating to, measure. **2.** (mus.) Mensurable.

mensuration, n. [1. mènshuráshun; 2. mènʃəréiʃən], fr. L. Lat. *mensūrātiōn-(em)*, 'measuring', fr. *mensūr-(āre)*, 'to measure', see **measure**, & **-ation**. **1.** The act, or art, of measuring. **2.** (math.) The art of determining the length of lines, area of surface, and volume of solid bodies.

-ment, suff. representing Lat. *-mentum*, forming ns. expressing vbl. action or result of this; **a** fr. vb. stems in Lat., Fr., or Engl.: *torment, testament, sentiment, acknowledgement*; **b** rarely fr. adjs.: *oddment*.

mental (I.), adj. [1. méntl; 2. méntl], fr. Fr., fr. L. Lat. *mentāl-(is)*, 'of the mind', fr. Lat. *ment-*, stem of *mens*, 'mind, understanding, reason; thought'; cp. Scrt. *matiš*, 'thought'; Lith. *atmintis*, 'memory'; Goth. *ga-munds*; O.E. *ge-mynd*, 'mind, memory', see **mind**; cp. Lat. *monēre*, 'to remind', & see **memento**. **1.** **a** Of, relating to, the mind: *mental effort*; *mental process*; *mental weakness, excitement* &c.; **b** (colloq.) specif., pertaining to a diseased mind; connected with, afflicted with, insanity: *a mental case, patient*; *mental specialist*, authority on insanity. **2.** Carried out in the mind without aid of graphic figures: *mental arithmetic, calculations* &c.

mental (II.), adj., fr. Lat. *ment-(um)*, 'chin', prob. fr. the stem **men-* &c., 'to project', seen in Lat. *eminēre*, 'to stand out', see **minatory**, & in Lat. *mons*, 'mountain', see **mount**; see **mouth** for other cognates. Pertaining to, situated near, the chin.

mentality, n. [1. mentáliti; 2. mentǽliti]. **mental** (I.) & **-ity**; cp. Fr. *mentalité*. **1.** Mental quality, mode of thinking; intellectual character. **2.** (in loose, journalistic use) Mental attitude, mood, state of mind.

mentally, adv. [1. méntali; 2. méntəli]. **mental** (I.) & **-ly**. In, by means of, as regards, the mind.

mentation, n. [1. mentáshun; 2. mentéiʃən], fr. Lat. *ment-*, stem of *mens*, 'mind'. See **mental** (I.) & **-ation**. Exercise of the mind; mental process or function.

menthaceous, adj. [1. mentháshus; 2. menþéiʃəs], fr. Lat. *mentha*, see **mint** (I.), 'the plant', & **-aceous**. (bot.) Belonging to the group of Labiate herbs and shrubs, which includes the mints, sages &c.

menthol, n. [1. ménthol; 2. ménþɔl], fr. Lat. *ment(h)-(a)*, 'mint', see **mint** (I.), & **-ol**. White crystalline substance derived from essential oil of peppermint cooled to a low temperature; used to relieve neuralgia &c. by its freezing properties.

mention (I.), n. [1. ménshun; 2. ménʃən], fr. Lat. *mentiōn-(em)*, 'a speaking of', fr. *ment-*, stem seen in *mens*, 'mind' &c., see **mental** (I.), & **-ion**. **1.** The act of mentioning, or speaking of; reference to: *to make mention of*; *honourable mention*, award made to candidate, competitor &c. for work which is good, though not entitling him to prize. **2.** A short, cursory reference to, a passing allusion to, or notice of, a person or thing: *he made no mention of this*; *only a bare mention of him in the book*.

mention (II.), vb. trans. Fr. *mentionner*. See prec. To speak of, refer to, specify, name of, in speech or writing. Phr. *not to mention*, to say nothing of: *he was guilty of many notorious crimes, not to mention others known only to the few*.

mentionable, adj. [1. ménshunabl; 2. ménʃənəbl]. Prec. & **-able**. Capable of being mentioned or referred to; fit to be referred to.

mentor, n. [1. méntur; 2. méntə], fr. Gk. *Méntōr*, adviser of Telemachus; cp. Scrt. *mantár-*, 'one who thinks', fr. the stem **men-*, 'to think'. See **mental** (I.). Counsellor, wise and prudent adviser.

menu, n. [1. ménū; 2. ménjū] or as Fr. [məny]. Fr., 'list, detailed list', fr. adj. *menu*, 'small', fr. Lat. *minūtum*, 'small'. See **minute** (III.). **a** Bill of fare; list and specification of courses to be served at a meal; **b** by transf., the meal itself: *we had an admirable menu*.

Mephistophelean, adj. [1. mèfistofélian; 2. mèfistəfílian]. See next word & **-ean**. Of, pertaining to, of, the character of, Mephistopheles.

Mephistopheles, n. [1. mèfistófelēz; 2. mèfistɔ́filīz]. Origin of name doubtful. **a** In German *Faust* legend, specif. in Goethe's *Faust*, an evil spirit to whom Faust sold his soul; hence, **b** evil, malevolent, sinister person.

Mephistophelian, adj. See **Mephistophelean**.

mephitic, adj. [1. mefítik; 2. mifítik]. See next word & **-ic**. Of, of the nature of, mephitis; noxious, pestilential, offensive to the smell.

mephitis, n. [1. mefítis; 2. mifáitis]. Lat. *mephītis*, 'noxious exhalation from the ground'. Etymol. unknown. Poisonous exhalation from the ground, esp. from decomposing vegetable or animal matter; noisome smell.

mercantile, adj. [1. mérkantīl; 2. mə́kəntail], fr. Fr., fr. Ital. *mercantile*, fr. *mercante*, 'merchant', fr. Pres. Part. of Lat. *mercāri*, 'to trade'; cp. *merx*, 'merchandise', *mercēs*, 'pay, reward'. Etymol. doubtful. Perh. cogn. w. Scrt. *mṛčáti*, 'grasps'; Gk. *márptein*, 'to seize'. See **market, mercenary**, & **merchant**. **1.** Connected with, relating to, trade; commercial: *mercantile marine*, ships and men employed in commerce; *mercantile law*, commercial law; *mercantile system*, that based on the old economic theory that money is wealth and that the object of trade is to export goods at highest price &c. **2.** (rare) Eager for gain; mercenary.

mercantilism, n. [1. mĕrkantīlizm; 2. mā́kəntailizəm]. Prec. & **-ism**. **a** The mercantile system; **b** commercialism.

mercantilist, n. [1. mĕrkantīlist; 2. mā́kəntailist]. **mercantile** & **-ist**. Believer in the mercantile system.

Mercator, n. [1. mĕrkā́ter; 2. mākéitə]. Lat. translation of name of Gerard Kremer, Flemish mathematician and geographer (d. 1594), who first employed the method of map projection now known by his name; see **projection**.

mercenariness, n. [1. mĕrsenarines; 2. mā́sinərinis]. See next word & **-ness**. Quality of being mercenary.

mercenary, adj. & n. [1. mĕrsenari; 2. mā́sinəri], fr. Lat. *mercēn(n)āri-(us)*, 'hired, paid', fr. *mercē(s)*, 'hire', see **mercantile**. **1.** adj. **a** Eager for gain, actuated merely by hope of reward, working only for payment; **b** hired, engaged to work, for fixed payment. **2.** n. Soldier hired by foreign country.

mercer, n. [1. mĕrser; 2. mā́sə], fr. Fr. *mercier*, fr. L. Lat. **merciāri-(us)*, 'merchant', fr. *merci-(s)*, genit. of *merx*, 'merchandise'. See **market**, **mercantile**. & **-er**. Dealer in textile, silk, or woollen fabrics.

mercerize, vb. trans. [1. mĕrserīz; 2. mā́səraiz], fr. name of inventor of process, John Mercer, 1791–1866, & **-ize**. To treat (cotton fabrics) with caustic alkali so as to impart a sheen resembling that of silk.

mercery, n. [1. mĕrseri; 2. mā́səri]. **mercer** & **-ery**. **a** Trade or business of a mercer; **b** goods dealt in by a mercer.

merchandise, n. [1. mĕrchandīz; 2. mā́tʃəndaiz], fr. O. Fr. *marchandise*, fr. *marchand*, 'merchant'. See **merchant** & **-ise**. Goods bought and sold; objects of commercial activity; wares.

merchant, n. [1. mĕrchant; 2. mā́tʃənt], fr. O. Fr. *marchand*, fr. *mercātant-(em)*, Pres. Part. type of Low Lat. *mercātāre*, fr. Lat. *mercāt-(um)*, P.P. type of *mercāri*, 'to trade'. See **mercantile** & **market**. **1. a** Wholesale trader, esp. one trading with foreign countries; **b** (slang) person, individual, fellow (chiefly in disparagement): *who's the merchant in a tail-coat and a bowler hat?* (cp. **chap (III.)**). **2.** attrib. Of merchants or commerce: *merchant prince*, one who has made a fortune in commerce; *merchant service*, mercantile marine; *merchant ship*, vessel employed in trade; see also **law merchant**.

merchantable, adj. [1. mĕrchantabl; 2. mā́tʃəntəbl], fr. obs. vb. *merchant*, 'to trade', fr. prec., & **-able**. Suitable for sale; marketable.

merchantman, n. [1. mĕrchantman; 2. mā́tʃəntmən]. Merchant ship.

merciful, adj. [1. mĕrsifool; 2. mā́siful]. **mercy** & **-ful**. **a** Feeling, showing, mercy; compassionate; **b** favourable, fortunate (circumstance); **c** of punishment, lenient, mild, not severe.

mercifully, adv. Prec. & **-ly**. In a merciful manner.

mercifulness, n. See prec. & **-ness**. Quality of being merciful.

merciless, adj. [1. mĕrsiles; 2. mā́silis]. **mercy** & **-less**. Without mercy or compassion; cruel, pitiless, relentless.

mercilessly, adv. Prec. & **-ly**. In a merciless manner.

mercilessness, n. See prec. & **-ness**. Quality of being merciless.

mercurial (I.), adj. [1. mĕrkū́rial; 2. mākjṓriəl]. **mercury** & **-al**. **1.** Of, containing, consisting of, like, the drug mercury. **2.** Active, lively, excitable; changeable, erratic; from supposed influence of planet Mercury, cp. *jovial, saturnine.*

mercurial (II.), n., fr. prec. Preparation of mercury for medicinal use: *mercurial poisoning*, by overdose of a mercurial or by contact with mercury &c.

mercurialism, n. [1. mĕrkū́rializm; 2. mākjṓriəlizəm]. Prec. & **-ism**. Mercurial poisoning.

mercuriality, n. [1. mĕrkūriáliti; 2. mākjṓriǽliti]. **mercurial** & **-ity**. Sprightliness, alertness, excitability.

mercurialize, vb. trans. [1. mĕrkū́rialīz; 2. mākjṓriəlaiz]. **mercurial** & **-ize**. To affect with mercury.

mercurially, adv. [1. mĕrkū́riali; 2. mākjṓriəli]. **mercurial** & **-ly**. In a mercurial manner.

mercuric, adj. [1. mĕrkū́rik; 2. mākjṓrik]. **mercury** & **-ic**. Of, pertaining to, consisting of, mercury, esp. (chem.) of compounds in which mercury has a valency of two: *mercuric chloride*, corrosive sublimate.

mercurous, adj. [1. mĕrkūrus; 2. mā́kjurəs]. See next word & **-ous**. Mercuric; (chem.) of compounds in which mercury has a valency of one: *mercurous chloride*, calomel.

mercury, n. [1. mĕrkūri; 2. mā́kjuri], fr. Lat. *Mercurius*; prob. fr. stem **merc-*, 'trade', seen in *merx*, 'merchandise', *mercēs*, 'reward, pay' &c. See **market, mercantile.** **1.** (cap.) **a** Roman god of oratory, patron of merchants and thieves, and messenger of the gods; hence, **b** (facet.) messenger. **2.** (cap.) Name of the planet nearest to the sun. **3. a** Silvery white, fluid metallic element, quicksilver; specif. **b** column of mercury in barometer &c.; **c** any medical preparation of mercury. **4.** (bot.) Popular name for various plants or herbs, as *Dog's mercury* &c.

mercy, n. [1. mĕrsi; 2. mā́si], fr. O. Fr. *merci*, fr. Lat. *mercēd-(em)*, acc. of *mercēs*, Lat., 'pay, reward', L. Lat., 'favour, pity'. See under **mercantile**. **1.** Forbearance, compassion, leniency, shown to person wholly in one's power; clemency, lenity: *to have, show, mercy on one.* Phrs. *at the mercy of*, wholly in the power of; *left to the tender mercies of*, in the power of, usually of one from whom ill-usage may be expected. **2.** Something to be thankful for; a blessing, a good thing, fortunate circumstance, esp. in Phr. *it's a mercy that ...*; *that's a mercy!*; *thankful for small mercies*, content with little.

mercy-seat, n. Covering of Jewish Ark of the Covenant; the throne of God.

mere (I.), n. [1. mēr; 2. miə]. O.E. *mere*, M.E. *mēre*; cp. O.H.G. *meri*; Germ. *meer*; O.S. *meri*; O.N. *marr*, 'lake, sea'; Goth. *marei*, 'sea'; cogn. w. Lat. *mare*, 'sea', see **marine** (I.); O. Slav. *morje*, 'sea'. Lake, sheet of water.

mere (II.), adj., fr. Lat. *merus*, 'pure, unmixed, esp. of undiluted wine'; cp. O.E. *ā-merian*, 'to purify; to test'; Scrt. *márīciš*, 'ray of light'; Gk. *marmairein*, 'to gleam'; orig. meaning of stem, 'clear, shining'; cp. **marble**. **1.** (obs. or archaic) Undiluted, pure. **2.** Nothing more or less than; sheer, simple, absolute: *a mere blunder*; *a mere pretext.* Phr. (law) *of mere motion*, by one's own volition, without constraint.

merely, adv. Prec. & **-ly**. Purely, simply; only, solely.

meretricious, adj. [1. mèritríshus; 2. mèritríʃəs], fr. Lat. *meretrīci-(us)*, fr. *meretrīc-*, stem of *meretrix*, 'harlot', fr. *mer-(ēri)*, 'to earn'. See **merit** & **-trix** & **-ous**. **1.** (obs. or archaic) Of, pertaining to, a harlot. **2.** (fig.) Specious, tawdry, flashy; making a false show of beauty or merit.

meretriciously, adv. Prec. & **-ly**. In a meretricious manner.

meretriciousness, n. See prec. & **-ness**. Quality of being meretricious.

merganser, n. [1. mĕrgánser; 2. māgǽnsə], fr. Lat. *merg-(us)*, 'diver, gull', q.v. under **merge**, & *anser*, 'goose', see **anserine**. (zool.) A kind of large, fish-eating, diving bird with long, slender, serrated beak, allied to the true ducks; the best-known species is the goosander, *Mergus merganser.*

merge, vb. trans. & intrans. [1. mĕrj; 2. mā́dž], fr. Fr., fr. Lat. *mergere*, 'to plunge, immerse; to sink down'; cp. *mergus*, 'kind of diving bird', see prec.; cogn. w. Scrt. *májjati*, 'dives under'; Lith. *mazgóti*, 'to wash'. **1.** trans. **a** To cause (thing) to be lost, swallowed up, become united with, another: *to merge one's identity in another's*; **b** (legal) to cause to be absorbed by merger, q.v. **2.** intrans. To become lost, swallowed up, indistinguishably united with another thing.

mergence, n. [1. mĕrjens; 2. mā́džəns]. Prec. & **-ence**. Act or process of merging; state of being merged.

merger, n. [1. mĕrjer; 2. mā́džə], fr. **merge**, formed on anal. of other O. Fr. infins. used as ns.; cp. **user**. (law) The absorption of an estate, contract, interest, obligation &c. in a greater; union of several business concerns under a single central management; a combine.

mericarp, n. [1. mérikarp; 2. mérikāp], fr. Gk. *méros*, 'part', see **mero-**, & *karpós*, 'fruit', see **carpel**. (bot.) One of the two carpels, each containing a seed, which split open when ripe, as in the sycamore &c.

meridian (I.), n. [1. merídian; 2. mərídiən], fr. O. Fr. *meridien*, fr. Lat. *merīdiān-(us)*, 'of midday; southern', fr. *merīdi-(ēs)*, 'noon; the south', w. dissimilation fr. earlier **medīdiē-*, fr. *medi-(us)*, 'middle', see **media**, & *diēs*, 'day', see **dies non**. **1.** (geog. and astron.) **a** A great imaginary circle supposed to pass through the poles, and intersecting the equator and the equinoctial at right angles; **b** representation of this on a map or globe. **2.** (by transf.) Noon, midday. **3.** (fig.) **a** Highest, culminating point of success or happiness attained by an individual during his whole career; **b** period of greatest health and vigour; prime of life.

meridian (II.), adj., fr. prec. **1. a** Of, pertaining to, noon; **b** belonging to the highest point attained by a heavenly body in its daily course. **2.** (fig.) Of the highest point or pitch of anything; culminating, supreme.

meridional, adj. & n. [1. merídional; 2. merídiənəl], fr. L. Lat. *merīdionāl-(is)*, 'of noon; of the south'. See **meridian** & **-al**. **1.** adj. **a** Of a meridian; **b** of, relating to, the south of Europe, or the inhabitants of this region. **2.** n. Inhabitant of a southern country, esp. of southern Europe.

meringue, n. [1. meráng; 2. mə-, mirǽŋ]. Fr. Origin unknown. **a** Mixture of sugar and white of egg, baked till crisp and slightly browned, as garnish &c.; **b** thin case of meringue filled with whipped cream.

merino, n. & adj. [1. merḗnō; 2. mərínou]. Span., adj., 'moving from pasture to pasture'; n., 'royal inspector of sheepwalks'; fr. Low Lat. *merinus*, fr. *mājorīnus*, 'steward of a household', fr. *mājor*, 'greater'. See **major** (II.) & **mayor**. **1.** n. **a** Also *merino sheep*, breed of sheep, originally Spanish, noted for long, fine, silky wool; **b** fine woollen fabric, originally made of wool of this kind; **c** fine, soft, woollen yarn. **2.** adj. Made of merino or similar wool.

meristem, n. [1. méristem; 2. méristem], fr. Gk. *meristós*, 'divided', fr. *merízein*, 'to divide', fr. *méros*, 'part'. See **mero-**. (bot.) Cell-tissue capable of dividing and forming new growth.

merit (I.), n. [1. mérit; 2. mérit], fr. O. Fr. *merite*, fr. Lat. *meritum*, 'desert, merit; reward', fr. P.P. type of *merēri*, 'to earn, obtain; to deserve'; cogn. w. Gk. *meíromai*, 'I receive a share'; *méros*, 'part; lot'; cp. *moira*, 'share; fate'. See **mero-**. **1.** Desert; quality or fact of deserving punishment or reward, approbation or censure: *to reward a person according to his merits.* **2.** (law) Intrinsic rights and wrongs of a case; strict legal rights of parties in a suit: *to decide a case on its merits.* **3. a** Good, desirable, praiseworthy quality; excellence: *the merits of a writer, of a horse, house* &c.; *a man of merit*; **b** quality or fact of deserving well; praiseworthy act: *there is less merit in being generous when one is very rich than when one is poor*; *to receive the reward of merit*; *Order of Merit* (abbr. O.M.), an order, limited in membership, for high and distinguished service, civil or military, founded in 1902.

merit (II.), vb. trans., fr. prec. To have earned, to deserve, be worthy of: *to merit attention, reward, punishment* &c.

meritorious, adj. [1. mèritórius; 2. mèritórias], fr. Lat. *meritōri-(us)*, 'that for which hire is paid', fr. *merit-(um)*, 'reward', see **merit**, & **-ory** & **-ous**. **a** Possessing and exhibiting merit; deserving praise, reward, honour &c.; praiseworthy; **b** (slightly depreciatory) well-intentioned, estimable.

meritoriously, adv. Prec. & **-ly**. In a meritorious manner.

meritoriousness, n. See prec. & **-ness**. Quality of being meritorious.

merle, n. [1. mërl; 2. mʌ̄l], fr. Fr. *merle*, fr. Lat. *merula*, 'blackbird', prob. fr. **misula*; cp. O.E. *māse*, O.H.G. *meisa*, O.N. *meisingr*, 'titmouse'. (archaic) Blackbird.

merlin, n. [1. mërlin; 2. mʌ̄lin], fr. A.-Fr. *merilun*, fr. O. Fr. *esmerillon*, fr. Med. Lat. *smerillus*; of Gmc. origin; cp. O.H.G. *smirlin* & *smirl*, Mod. Germ. *schmerl*. The word is prob. identical w. Germ. *schmerle*, the name of a fish, the loach, or groundling, wh. is perh. identical w. Gk. *smarís*, 'a small sea fish'. Kind of small, strong falcon.

merlon, n. [1. mërlun; 2. mʌ̄lən], fr. Fr., fr. Ital. *merlone*, fr. *merlo*, 'battlement', possibly fr. *mergola*, dimin. representing Lat. *mergae*, 'pitchfork'; cp. Lat. *merges*, 'sheaf of corn'; Gk. *amérgein*, 'to gather' (leaves, fruit &c.), *omórgnūmi*, 'I wipe'; Scrt. *mṛjáti*, 'rubs off, wipes'; the orig. meaning of the base **merg-* &c. seems to have been 'to pluck off, rub off', hence 'to gather into bunches, reap'. Solid part of battlemented wall or parapet between two openings or embrasures.

mermaid, n. [1. mërmād; 2. mʌ̄meid]. M.E. *meremaid*. **mere** (I.) & **maid**. Fabulous sea monster represented as having the head and body of a beautiful woman, with a scaly tail.

merman, n. [1. mërman; 2. mʌ̄mən]. M.E. *mereman*. **mere** (I.) & **man**. Male counterpart of a mermaid.

mero-, pref. representing Gk. *méro-(s)*, 'part'; cp. Gk. *meíromai*, 'I obtain a share'; *moîra*, 'part, share; lot, destiny'; *móros*, 'fate, destiny'; cogn. w. Lat. *merēri*, 'to obtain, earn; to deserve'. See **merit**. Partly, partially.

meroblast, n. [1. mérōblahst; 2. méroublāst]. Prec. & Gk. *blastós*, 'bud'. See first element in **blastoderm**. (physiol. and biol.) Ovum in two parts, one of which is germinal and the other nutritive.

-merous, suff. See **mero-** & **-ous**. Having specified number of parts, e.g. *pentamerous*, having five parts; usually written *5-merous*.

Merovingian, adj. & n. [1. mèrōvínjian; 2. mèrouvíndžiən]. L. Lat. *Merovingi*, 'descendants of *Merovaeus*', Lat. form of name of mythical early Frankish king. **1.** adj. Of, pertaining to, the first line of Frankish kings of Gaul, founded by Clovis, and reigning in the 6th, 7th, and 8th cents. **2.** n. King of this dynasty.

merrily, adv. [1. mérili; 2. mérili]. **merry** (II.) & **-ly**. In a merry manner; with merriment.

merriment, n. [1. mériment; 2. mérimənt]. **merry** (II.) & **-ment**. Mirth, hilarity, gaiety.

merriness, n. [1. mérines; 2. mérinis]. **merry** (II.) & **-ness**. State, quality, of being merry.

merry (I.), n. [1. méri; 2. méri], fr. O. Fr. *merise*, 'wild cherry'; etymol. doubtful. The Fr. word was wrongly taken as a pl. The wild black cherry.

merry (II.), adj. O.E. (W.S.) *myr(i)ġe*, 'delightful, pleasant'; M.E. (S.E.) *meri*, 'pleasant, gay, merry'; orig. meaning is perh. 'brief, transitory, passing rapidly', contrasted w. 'long, slow, tedious'; see **mirth**; cp. O.H.G. *murg-*, 'short'; & Goth. *ga-maurgjan*, 'to shorten, cut off'; further prob. cogns. are Lat. *murcus*, 'mutilated'; *marcēre*, 'to shrink, shrivel'. See **marcescent**. **1.** (archaic) Pleasant, esp in Phr. *merry England*. **2.** Gay, cheerful, joyous, lively: *a merry voice, laugh, dance*; *a merry Christmas*; *the merry monarch*, Charles II. Phrs. *to make merry*, to be gay, festive; *to make merry over*, make fun of, ridicule. **3.** (colloq.) Slightly drunk.

merry-andrew, n. [1. méri ándrōō; 2. méri ǽndrū]. Said to be fr. Andrew Boorde, of Henry VIII.'s time, to whom jest books were attributed. **a** Assistant to mountebank; **b** a buffoon; foolish, irresponsible person, without dignity of behaviour.

merry-go-round, n. [1. méri gō ròund; 2. méri-gou-ràund]. Circular structure having wooden horses and seats at intervals, rotated by an engine, usually to the accompaniment of music; used at fairs &c.; a roundabout.

merry-making, n. Gay entertainment; junketing, conviviality, festivity.

merrythought, n. [1. mérithawt; 2. mériþōt]. Forked bone at upper end of breast of bird; the wish-bone.

mesa, n. [1. mása; 2. méisə]. Span., fr. Lat. *mensa*, 'table', apparently fem. P.P. type of *mētīri*, 'to measure', q.v. under **measure**. (phys. geog.) A high plateau or table-land, with steep sides and covered by cap of hard rock.

mésalliance, n. [1. māzaliáhns; 2. mezaliɑ̃s]. Fr. See **mis-** & **alliance**. Marriage with person of lower birth or social position.

mescal, n. [1. meskál; 2. meskǽl], fr. Span. *mezcal*, fr. Mexican *mexcalli*. **1.** A spirit distilled from pulque, the national drink of Mexico, which is obtained from the sap of the maguey or agave. **2.** Also *mescal button*, a succulent kind of cactus, *Mamillaria*, of Mexico and Texas; the natives chew the tops, which have a narcotic effect.

meseems, vb. intrans. [1. mesḗmz; 2. misímz]. *Me*, dat. of 1st pers. pron., & *seems*. See **seem**. (archaic) It seems to me.

mesembryanthemum, n. [1. mèzembriánthemum; 2. mèzembriǽnþimәm], fr. Gk. *mesēmbri-(ā)*, 'noon', & *ánthemon*, 'flower'. The first element is fr. Gk. *més-(os)*, 'middle', see **meso-**, & *êmar, hēméra*, 'day', see **ephemeral**; for the third element see **anther**. A genus, including the ice-plant, of succulent-leaved herbs and shrubs, with bright pink or white flowers.

mesenteric, adj. [1. mèsentérik; 2. mèsəntérik]. **mesentery** & **-ic**. Of, relating to, the mesentery.

mesenteritis, n. [1. mèsenterítis; 2. mèsəntəráitis]. See next word & **-itis**. Inflammation of the mesentery.

mesentery, n. [1. mésenteri; 2. mésəntəri], fr. Gk. *mesentérion*, fr. *més-(os)*, 'middle', see **meso-**, & *énter-(on)*, 'intestine', see **enteric**. Part of the peritoneum supporting the intestines.

mesh (I.), n. [1. mesh; 2. meʃ], fr. O.E. **mesċe*, mutated form corresponding to O.E. *max* for **masc*, 'met'; cp. O.H.G. *masca*, O.N. *mǫskui*, 'net, mesh'; Lith. *mezgù*, 'to knit'; *māzgas*, 'knot'. **1. a** One of the open spaces between the threads of a net; **b** (pl.) threads of net; network. **2.** (fig., pl.) Snares, toils: *caught in the meshes of an enchantress.* **3.** (of wheels of machine &c.) *In mesh*, in gear, engaged.

mesh (II.), vb. trans. & intrans., fr. prec. **1.** trans. (lit. and fig.) To ensnare, catch, in net. **2.** intrans. (of gear-wheels &c.) To engage, interlock.

mesial, adj. [1. mḗzial, mésial; 2. mízial, mésiəl], fr. Gk. *més-(os)*, 'middle', see **meso-**, & **-ial**. Of, pertaining to, lying in, the central line of a figure or body.

mesially, adv. Prec. & **-ly**. In a mesial position.

mesmeric, adj. [1. mezmérik; 2. mezmérik]. See next word & **-ic**. Of, pertaining to, of the nature of, produced by, mesmerism.

mesmerism, n. [1. mézmerizm; 2. mézmərizəm], fr. Mesmer, an Austrian physician (d. 1815), & **-ism**. **a** Method of artificially inducing sleep and other peculiar bodily and mental conditions, practised by Mesmer; hypnotism; **b** hypnotic state induced by this method.

mesmerist, n. [1. mézmerist; 2. mézmərist]. See prec. & **-ist**. Person who practises mesmerism.

mesmerization, n. [1. mézmerīzáshun; 2. mézməraizéiʃən]. See next word & **-ation**. Act of mesmerizing; state of being mesmerized.

mesmerize, vb. trans. [1. mézmerīz; 2. mézməraiz]. See **mesmerism** & **-ize**. **a** To put into a mesmeric state; to hypnotize; **b** (fig.) to fascinate, rivet attention of; to have powerful influence upon.

mesne, adj. [1. mēn; 2. mīn]. O. Fr. See **mean** (II.). (law) Intermediate: *mesne lord*, one who is himself a tenant of a superior lord, but who has tenants holding from him; *mesne profits*, rents and profits from an estate accruing to an occupier in unlawful possession, which are sued for by the true owner on regaining possession; such profits arise when a tenant remains in possession after expiry of a lease.

meso-, pref. representing Gk. *méso-(s)*, 'middle', fr. **medhjo-s*; cp. Scrt. *mádhyaš*; Lat. *medius*, see **media**; Goth. *midjis*; O.H.G. *mitti*; O.E. *midd*, see **mid** (I.); O. Slav. *mežda*. Middle, intervening, intermediate; e.g. *mesocarp*, middle layer of seed-vessel; *mesogastric*, of the membrane supporting the stomach; *mesozoic*, second geological era, between palaeozoic and kainozoic.

mesquit(e), n. [1. méskēt; 2. méskīt]. Span., fr. Mexican *misquitl*. Leguminous shrub of the mimosa family, growing in Mexico and south-west of North America; the seed-pods are used as fodder.

mess (I.), n. [1. mes; 2. mes], fr. O. Fr. *mes*, fr. L. Lat. *missum*, fr. P.P. type of *mitt re*, 'to send'. See **mission**. **1. a** (archaic) Dish of food, esp. soft or liquid food; Phr. *mess of pottage*, material advantage for which something higher is bartered (with reference to Gen. xxv. 29-34); **b** mash prepared for hounds &c. **2.** Mixture, medley, varied concoction. **3.** State of confusion, disorder, dirt &c. Phrs. *to make a mess of things*, to be unsuccessful, fail badly, in doing something; bungle, mismanage; *in a mess*, (i.) dirty, soiled; (ii.) in confusion; (iii.) (fig.) in awkward position, suffering under disastrous circumstances. **4. a** Group of persons who habitually take their meals together, esp. in army or navy: *officers' mess*; *sergeants' mess* &c.; **b** meal served to such a group.

mess (II.), vb. trans. & intrans., fr. prec. **A.** trans. **1.** To make a mess of, soil, mar, make dirty. **2. a** To put into confusion; **b** to mismanage; also *mess up*. **B.** intrans. **1.** *Mess about*, to occupy oneself in a desultory manner, without achieving any definite object; to loiter, potter, about. **2.** To eat at a common table, have one's meals: *to mess with others*; *to mess together.*

message (I.), n. [1. mésij; 2. mésidž], fr. Fr., fr. Low Lat. *missaticum*, 'message', fr. Lat. *miss-(um)*, 'sent', fr. P.P. type of *mittere*, 'to send', see **mission**, & **-age**. **1.** Oral or written communication sent from one person to another through the agency of a third. Phr. *to go on a message*, on an errand. **2.** Inspired utterance of prophet or sage, and the import of this for mankind.

message (II.), vb. trans., fr. prec. (rare) **1.** To send, communicate, as message. **2.** To signal, transmit by signalling.

messenger, n. [1. mésenjer; 2. mésindžə]. M.E., fr. O. Fr. *messager*, prec. & **-er**, w. infixed *-n-*, as in *passenger*, fr. *passager*. **1. a** One who carries a message; **b** person regularly employed to deliver letters and messages by hand. **2.** Rope or chain connecting cable to capstan and used to haul in the former.

Messiah, n. [1. mesía; 2. mesáiə]. Lat., fr. Gk. *Messías*, fr. Heb. *mashiaḥ*, 'anointed'. **1.** Deliverer and Saviour promised to the Jews. **2.** Christ as fulfilling this promise. **3.** Deliverer of oppressed nation; liberator.

Messiahship, n. [1. mesíaship; 2. misáiəʃip]. Prec. & **-ship.** State of being a Messiah; specif., Christ's Messianic office.

Messianic, adj. [1. mèsiánik; 2. mèsiǽnik]. **Messiah** & **-an** & **-ic.** Relating to a, or the, Messiah: *Messianic prophecies.*

Messidor, n. [1. mésidōr; 2. mésidɔ̄]. Fr., fr. Lat. *messi-(s)*, 'harvest', fr. *mess-(um)*, P.P. type of *metere*, 'to reap, mow'; cp. O.W. *medel*, 'reapers'; also, w. a different grade of vowel, O.E. *māwan*; see also **math** & **mow (III.)**; *-dor* is fr. Gk. *dôron*, 'gift'; cogn. w. Lat. *dare*, 'to give', *dōnum*, 'gift'. See **donor.** Tenth month of French revolutionary calendar, June 19th to July 18th.

messieurs, n. [1. mesyē; 2. mɛsjø]. Fr., pl. of **monsieur.**

messmate, n. [1. mésmāt; 2. mésmeit]. **mess** & **mate.** **a** Companion in a mess; chiefly a sailor's word; **b** fellow-workman, associate, friend.

messrs., n. [1. méserz; 2. mésəz]. Abbr. of **messieurs.** **a** Before names of partners in a firm: *Messrs. Jones & Co.*; **b** as pl. of Mr.

messuage, n. [1. méswij; 2. méswidž]. A.-Fr. *messuage*, O. Fr. *mesuage*, 'a tenure of land', fr. Low Lat. *mansuagium, mesuagium*, fr. *mansum*, 'dwelling-house', O. Fr. *més.* See also **manse** & **mansion.** (law) Dwelling-house with adjoining lands and outbuildings appropriated to it.

mestizo, n. [1. mestḗzō; 2. mɛstízou]. Span., fr. Low Lat. *mixticius*, fr. Lat. *mixtus*, P.P. of *miscēre*, 'to mix'. See **mix.** Half-caste Spaniard or Portuguese, esp. person of Spanish and American-Indian parentage.

met, vb. [1. met; 2. mɛt]. Pret. & P.P. of **meet.**

meta-, pref. representing Gk. *metá*, 'between, among; with; after', often used to express change, alternation &c.; cp. Goth. *miþ*; cp. w. different formative element, Aryan **me-dhi-*, 'middle', O.N. *með*; O.H.G. *mit*; O.E. *mid*, see **mid.**

metabasis, n. [1. metábasis; 2. mɛtǽbəsis]. Gk., 'a passing over'. See **meta-** & **basis.** A transition; a passage from one point, or subject, to another.

metabolic, adj. [1. mètabólik; 2. mètəbɔ́lik]. See next word & **-ic.** Pertaining to, of the nature of, metabolism: *metabolic diseases.*

metabolism, n. [1. metábolizm; 2. mɛtǽbəlizəm], fr. Gk. *metabolḗ*, 'change', fr. *metabállein*, 'to turn quickly, throw into a different position; to change, alter', fr. **meta-** & *bállein*, 'to throw', see **ballistics**, & **-ism.** (physiol.) Process of building up and breaking down, continually going on in living organisms, nutritive substances being converted into protoplasm, or protoplasm broken down into simpler substances by chemical change; cp. *anabolism* and *katabolism.*

metabolize, vb. trans. [1. metábolīz; 2. mɛtǽbəlaiz]. See prec. & **-ize.** To change by metabolism, cause to undergo process of metabolism.

metacarpal, adj. [1. mètakárpl; 2. mètəkā́pl]. See next word & **-al.** Of, pertaining to, the metacarpus; *metacarpal bones*, those at the back of the hand between the knuckles and the wrist.

metacarpus, n. [1. mètakárpus; 2. mètəkā́pəs]. **meta-** & **carpus.** Back of the hand, esp. the bones of this, between the wrist and the knuckles.

metacentre, n. [1. mètasénter; 2. mètəséntə]. **meta-** & **centre.** The point in a floating body, as a ship, where the verticals through the centres of buoyancy and gravity intersect, shifting according as the equilibrium is altered; the position of the 'metacentre' indicates the relative stability.

metacentric, adj. [1. mètaséntrik; 2. mètəséntrik]. Prec. & **-ic.** Of, pertaining to the, a, metacentre.

metachrosis, n. [1. mètakrṓsis; 2. mètəkróusis], fr. **meta-** & Gk. *khrôsis*, 'colour, colouring'. See **chrome.** (biol. and zool.) Change of colour, as exhibited in certain reptiles, fishes &c., as the chameleon &c., so as to suit the surroundings.

metage, n. [1. mḗtij; 2. mítidž]. **mete (II.)** & **-age.** **a** Official measuring of coal; **b** fee, price, paid for this.

metagenesis, n. [1. mètajénesis; 2. mètədžénisis]. **meta-** & **genesis.** (biol.) Alternate reproduction of a new individual by an organism by means of processes alternately sexual and asexual, such as by gemmation.

metagenetic, adj. [1. mètajenétik; 2. mètədžinétik]. **meta-** & **-genetic.** Pertaining to, of the nature of, metagenesis.

metal (I.), n. [1. métl; 2. métl], fr. O. Fr., fr. Lat. *metallum*, 'metal; mine, quarry', fr. Gk. *métallon*, 'mine, quarry'; cp. *metalleús*, 'miner'; *metalleúein*, 'to get by mining; to search'; *metalláein*, 'to search after, inquire about'; etymol. doubtful. **1.** One of a class of substances of which gold, silver, lead, tin, copper &c. are examples, which are generally characterized by opacity, ductility or malleability, a lustre which pertains to their smallest part, fusibility under heat, and the property of being good conductors of electricity. **2.** (chem.) Specif., an elementary, unmixed metal, as contrasted with an alloy; one of the metallic elements. **3.** (her.) One of the two metals recognized in heraldry when used as *tinctures*; *or*, gold, whose colour is yellow, and *argent*, silver, whose colour is white. **4.** (techn. uses) **a** *Road metal*, hard stone, broken up and used for making roads; **b** (in pl.) railway lines: *the train ran off the metals*; **c** molten material used in glass-making. **5.** (fig.) Mettle.

metal (II.), vb. trans., fr. prec. **1.** To supply, furnish, with metal; to cover &c. with metal. **2.** To mend (roads) with hard stone or metal: *metalled roads.*

metallic, adj. [1. metálik; 2. mitǽlik]. **metal** & **-ic.** **1.** Pertaining to, consisting of, like, metal: *metallic currency*, consisting of metal coinage, as distinct from paper currency; *metallic salts*, salts having a metal or metallic oxide as base. **2.** Suggestive of, characteristic of, resembling metal: *metallic sound*; *metallic lustre.*

metalliferous, adj. [1. metalíferus; 2. mɛtəlífərəs]. See prec. & **-ferous.** Bearing, producing, metals: *metalliferous mines* &c.

metalline, adj. [1. métalīn; 2. métəlain]. **metal** & **-ine.** Of, like, metal.

metallization, n. [1. mètalīzā́shun; 2. mètəlaizéiʃən]. See next word & **-ation.** Act of metallizing; state of being metallized.

metallize, vb. trans. [1. métalīz; 2. métəlaiz]. **metal** & **-ize.** To make metallic, give metallic properties to.

metallography, n. [1. metalógrafi; 2. mɛtəlɔ́grəfi]. **metal** & **-graphy.** Study, description of metals, their structure and properties, esp. by means of the microscope combined with photography.

metalloid, adj. & n. [1. métaloid; 2. métəlɔid]. **metal (I.)** & **-oid.** **1.** adj. Like, of the nature of, in the form of, metal. **2.** n. An element which in some respects resembles a metal but cannot strictly be classed as such, as tellurium &c.

metallurgic(al), adj. [1. metalérjik(l); 2. mɛtəlā́džik(l)]. **metallurgy** & **-ic** & **-al.** Of, pertaining to, metallurgy.

metallurgist, n. [1. metálerjist; 2. mɛtǽlədžist]. See next word & **-ist.** Person skilled in metallurgy.

metallurgy, n. [1. metálerji; 2. mɛtǽlədži]. **metal** & Gk. *-ourg-(os)*, 'a worker', cp. *érgein*, 'to work', *érgon*, 'work'. See **ergon** & **work.** Science and art of preparing metals for use by smelting, refining, mixing &c.

metamere, n. [1. métamēr; 2. métəmiə]. **meta-** & Gk. *méros*, 'part'. See **mero-.** (zool.) One of a series of identical transverse segments of an animal body, as of a worm &c.; a somite.

metameric, adj. [1. mètamérik; 2. mètəmérik]. Prec. & **-ic.** (zool.) Of, of the nature of, formed of, metameres.

metamerism, n. [1. metámerizm; 2. mɛtǽmərizəm]. **metamere** & **-ism.** (zool.) Segmentation; state of being composed of metameres.

metamorphic, adj. [1. metamórfik; 2. mɛtəmɔ́fik]. **meta-** & Gk. *morphḗ*, 'form, shape', see **morphology**, & **-ic.** **1.** Of, characterized by, subject to, metamorphosis. **2.** (geol., of rocks) Having undergone changes in form or structure through natural agencies, esp. heat, pressure &c.

metamorphism, n. [1. mètamórfizm; 2. mètəmɔ́fizəm]. See prec. & **-ism.** (geol.) State of being metamorphic; specif., the condition in which rocks have become crystalline through heat, pressure &c.

metamorphose, vb. trans. [1. mètamórfōz; 2. mètəmɔ́fouz], fr. Fr. *métamorphoser*, fr. *métamorphose.* See next word. To change the form or character of; to transform.

metamorphosis, n. [1. mètamórfosis; 2. mètəmɔ́fəsis]. Gk. *metamórphōsis*, 'transformation', fr. *metamorphóein*, 'to transform', fr. **meta-** & *morphóein*, 'to give form to', fr. *morphḗ*, 'form'. See **morphology.** **a** Change of form; transformation, alteration in structure, constitution, appearance, by magic, or by natural development, e.g. change of caterpillar to insect &c.; **b** transformation of form or character generally.

metaphor, n. [1. métafor; 2. métəfə], fr. Fr. *métaphore*, fr. Lat., fr. Gk. *metaphorá*, 'transference; metaphor', fr. **meta-** & *phorá*, 'a carrying', q.v. under **-phore**; cp. Gk. vb. *metaphérein*, 'to carry over, transfer'. Figure of speech in which a word or phrase is used to denote or describe something entirely different from the object, idea, action, or quality which it primarily and usually expresses, thus suggesting a resemblance or analogy: *the curtain of night*; *the ocean of life*; '*My heart leaps up when I behold a rainbow in the sky*' (Wordsworth); *all nature smiled.*

metaphorical, adj. [1. metafórikl; 2. mɛtəfɔ́rikl]. Prec. & **-ic** & **-al.** Of the nature of, consisting of, a metaphor; containing metaphors.

metaphorically, adv. Prec. & **-ly.** In a metaphorical manner; in metaphors.

metaphrase, n. & vb. trans. [1. métafrāz; 2. métəfreiz], fr. Gk. *metáphrasis*, 'paraphrase', fr. *metaphrázein*, 'to paraphrase, translate', fr. **meta-** & *phrázein*, 'to show, tell'. See **phrase.** **1.** n. Translation, esp. a literal, word-for-word rendering, as distinct from *paraphrase.* **2.** vb. To translate, put into another language.

metaphrastic, adj. [1. mètafrástik; 2. mètəfrǽstik]. Gk. *metaphrast-*, stem of Part. of *metaphrázein*, 'to translate'. See prec. & **-ic.** **a** Literal in translating; **b** (of translation) literal.

metaphysical, adj. [1. mètafízikl; 2. mètəfízikl]. See **metaphysics** & **-al.** **1.** Connected with, of the nature of, metaphysics. **2.** Not physical; unsubstantial, incorporeal. **3. a** (of theory &c.) Based on abstract reasoning; **b** (of reasoning &c.) making too fine distinctions; over-subtle.

metaphysically, adv. Prec. & **-ly.** In a metaphysical manner; by metaphysics.

metaphysician, n. [1. mètafizíshan; 2. mètəfiziʃən]. See **metaphysics** & **-ian.** Student of metaphysics; one who reasons metaphysically.

metaphysicize, vb. intrans. [1. mètafízisīz; 2. mètəfízisaiz]. See next word & **-ize.** To study metaphysics; to indulge in metaphysical reasoning.

metaphysics, n. [1. mètafíziks; 2. mètəfíziks], fr. Med. Gk. *metaphusiká*, named fr. the works of Aristotle wh. followed his 'Physics': *tà metà tà phusiká*, 'those after the "Physics"'. See **meta-** & **physics.** Branch of abstruse study concerned with the nature of being, and the theory of knowledge.

metaplasm, n. [1. métaplazm; 2. mét*ə*plæz*ə*m]. Gk. **meta-** & *plasmós*, 'something moulded'. See **plasm.** (biol.) That part of the contents of a cell which consists of non-living matter.

metapolitical, adj. [1. mètapolítikl; 2. mèt*ə*p*ə*lít*i*kl]. See **metapolitics** & **-al.** Of, of the nature of, metapolitics.

metapolitician, n. [1. mètapolitíshan; 2. mèt*ə*p*ə*lit*í*ʃ*ə*n]. See next word & **-ic** & **-ian.** Student of metapolitics.

metapolitics, n. [1. metapólitiks; 2. met*ə*pól*i*t*i*ks]. **meta-** & **politics**, on anal. of **metaphysics.** Abstract political theory.

metastasis, n. [1. metástasis; 2. mɛtǽst*ə*s*i*s], fr. L. Lat., fr. Gk. *metástasis*, 'removal, change'. **meta-** & *stásis*, 'a standing, a position'. See **state** (I.), **stand** (I.). **1.** Change, transference of disease from one part of body to another. **2.** (biol.) Metabolism. **3.** Change of spiritual state, as in baptism.

metastatic, adj. [1. mètastátik; 2. mèt*ə*stǽt*i*k], fr. Gk. *metastatikós*. See prec. & **-ic.** Pertaining to, due to, metastasis.

metatarsal, adj. & n. [1. mètatársl; 2. mèt*ə*tάsl]. **metatarsus** & **-al.** **1.** adj. Of, pertaining to, the metatarsus. **2.** n. Metatarsal bone.

metatarsus, n. [1. mètatársus; 2. mèt*ə*tάs*ə*s]. **meta-** & **tarsus.** Group of bones in the upper surface of the foot, between ankle and toes, corresponding to the metacarpal bones of the hand.

metathesis, n. [1. metáthesis; 2. mɛtǽþ*ə*s*i*s]. Gk. *metáthesis*, 'transposition'; fr. **meta-** & *thésis*, 'a setting, placing'. See **thesis.** **1.** (phonol.) Name given to a change in the relative position of the consonants in a word, e.g. O.E. *wyrhta*, 'workman, wright', appears in some forms of M.E. as *wrihte* &c., the word for 'grass' appears in O.E. both as *gærs*, and *græs*, and so on. The change of *-sk-* to *x=ks* in O.E., e.g. *tūx*, from *tūsc*, 'tusk', is a further instance of two consonantal sounds changing places. **2.** (chem.) Substitution of one radical or atom for another in a molecule. **3.** (med.) Change in position of a morbid substance without removal from the body, as when a calculus slips or is pushed from a duct back into the bladder.

métayage, n. [1. métāyahzh; 2. méteiάž]. Fr. See next word & **-age.** System of land tenure in which the owner and farmer divide the yield in varying proportions, stock, seed &c. being provided by the owner of the land.

métayer, n. [1. métāyā; 2. méteiei]. Fr., fr. Med. Lat. *medietārius*, fr. *mediet-(as)*, 'middle, medium; moiety', see **moiety**, & **-ary.** Holder of land on métayage system.

mete (I.), n. [1. mēt; 2. mīt], fr. O. Fr. *mete*; fr. Lat. *mēta*, 'conical or pyramidal figure; goal, end, boundary; column, pillar'; cp. Scrt. *mēthiš*, 'post'; *mít*, 'pillar'; M. Ir. *methos*, 'boundary mark'; O.N. *meiðr*, 'tree, beam'; Aryan base **mēj-*, **mē(i)-*, 'stake, post'; cp., w. different formative elements, Lat. *moenia*, 'wall, stockade', *mūnire*, 'to surround with a wall'; *mūrus*, 'wall'. See **muniment, mural.** Boundary mark or stone; boundary, esp. in legal Phr. *metes and bounds*.

mete (II.), vb. trans. O.E. *metan*, 'to measure'; M.E. *mēte*; O.S. *metan*; O. Fris., O.N. *meta*; O.H.G. *mezzan*; Goth. *mitan*, 'to measure'; cp. Gk. *métron*, 'measure', see **metre** (I.); Lat. *modus*, 'measure, limit; manner, mode', see **mode**; Lat. *modestus*, 'within limits', see **modest**; *meditāri*, 'to measure, weigh mentally, reflect on', see **meditate**; Gk. *médomai*, 'I consider'; O.H.G. *māza*, 'moderation'; O.N. *mjǫtuðr*, O.E. *metod*, 'fate, destiny; God'. See also **measure.** **1.** (poet.) To measure. **2.** (liter., usually *mete out*) To allot, distribute, give out.

metempiric, n. [1. mètempírik; 2. mètɛmpír*i*k]. **meta-** & **empiric.** **1.** Also *metempirics*, philosophy of things outside human experience; transcendental philosophy. **2.** Student of this.

metempirical, adj. [1. mètempírikl; 2. mètɛmpír*i*kl]. Prec. & **-al.** Of, of the nature of, metempiric.

metempiricist, n. [1. mètempírisist; 2. mètɛmpír*i*s*i*st]. **metempiric** & **-ist.** Student of, believer in, metempiric.

metempsychosis, n. [1. metèmsikṓsis; 2. mɛtèms*i*kóus*i*s], fr. L. Lat., fr. Gk., fr. **meta-** & *en*, 'in', see **en-**, & *psūkhḗ*, 'breath, spirit, soul', see **psyche**, & **-osis.** Passing of the soul at death into another body, whether of a human being or of a lower animal.

metempsychosist, n. [1. mètemsikṓsist; 2. mèt*ə*ms*i*kóus*i*st]. See prec. & **-ist.** Believer in metempsychosis.

meteor, n. [1. mḗteor; 2. mít*iə*], fr. Gk. *meteṓr-(os)*, 'raised from the ground; high in air, lofty', fr. **meta-** & **-aworos*, 'raised up'; cp. *aeirein*, 'to raise'; cognates doubtful. **1.** A shooting or falling star; a fire ball, one of the small solid bodies in the solar system which become luminous and visible when passing through the earth's atmosphere. **2.** (obs. or rare) Any phenomenon or appearance in the sky, esp. if transient. **3.** (fig.) Any bright, dazzling, but transient object.

meteoric, adj. [1. mèteórik; 2. mìt*i*ór*i*k]. Prec. & **-ic.** **1.** Of, pertaining to, influenced by, atmosphere or atmospheric conditions. **2.** Of, pertaining to, meteors. **3.** (fig.) Like a meteor; swift, flashing, of dazzling speed and brilliance: *a meteoric career*.

meteorite, n. [1. mḗteorīt; 2. mít*iə*rait]. **meteor** & **-ite.** Meteoric stone.

meteorograph, n. [1. mḗteorograhf; 2. mít*iə*r*ə*grāf]. **meteor** & **-graph.** Instrument recording atmospheric phenomena.

meteoroid, n. [1. mḗteoroid; 2. mít*iə*r*ɔ*id]. **meteor** & **-oid.** Small, solid body in the solar system which becomes a meteor on passing into the atmosphere of the earth.

meteoroidal, adj. [1. mèteoróidl; 2. mìt*iə*róidl]. Prec. & **-al.** Of, of the nature of, a meteoroid.

meteorolite, n. [1. mḗteorolīt; 2. mít*iə*r*ə*lait]. **meteor** & **-lite.** A meteorite.

meteorologic(al), adj. [1. mèteorolójik(l); 2. mìt*iə*r*ə*lɔ́dž*i*k(l)]. **meteor** & **-logic** & **al.** **1.** Of, pertaining to, of the nature of, atmospheric phenomena. **2.** Of meteorology.

meteorologist, n. [1. mèteorólojist; 2. mìt*iə*rɔ́l*ə*džist]. Next word & **-ist.** One skilled in meteorology.

meteorology, n. [1. mèteoróloji; 2. mìt*iə*rɔ́l*ə*dži]. **meteor** & **-logy.** **1.** The study of atmospheric phenomena. **2.** Atmospheric character of specific region &c.

meter, n. [1. mḗter; 2. mít*ə*]. Prob. same as next word; or fr. **mete** (II.) & **-er.** Mechanical device for measuring quantity, volume, velocity &c.: *turn off the gas at the meter*; *a gas-meter, water-meter*.

-meter, suff., fr. Gk. *métron*, 'measure', see **metre** (I.), forming ns. denoting measuring instruments, **a** fr. Gk. ns.: *barometer, thermometer, perimeter*; **b** fr. Lat. ns.: *pedometer, potentiometer*; **c** fr. mod. ns.: *gasometer, speedometer* &c.

mete-wand, -yard, n., fr. **mete** (II.). (fig.) Standard of measurement.

methane, n. [1. méthān; 2. méþein], fr. **methyl** & **-ane.** (chem.) A highly inflammable hydrocarbon gas, the product of decomposition of organic substances, occurring as marsh-gas, fire-damp in mines &c.

metheglin, n. [1. methéglin; 2. mɛþégl*i*n], fr. W. *meddyglyn*, fr. *meddyg*, 'physician', fr. Lat. *medicus* (see **medical**), & *llyn*, 'juice'. Obsolete drink made from fermented honey; a kind of mead.

methinks, impers. vb., 3rd pers. sing. [1. mithíngks; 2. miþíŋks]. O.E. *mē þync(e)þ*, 'it seems to me', fr. **me**, dat. of **I**, & **think.** (archaic) It seems to me.

method, n. [1. méthod; 2. méþ*ə*d], fr. Lat. *methodus*, fr. Gk. *méthodos*, 'pursuit, esp. of knowledge; scientific inquiry; method of inquiry'; fr. **meta-** & Gk. *hodós*, 'way, path; manner; system, method'; for **sodos*, cogn. w. Lat. *cēdere*, 'to go, move, walk', see **cede.** Mode, manner, order, of procedure in accomplishing an end and achieving a desired result; specif. used of a rigidly systematic way of procedure adopted in scientific investigation, or in imparting intellectual training: *philological, biological, method*; *methods of teaching*.

methodic(al), adj. [1. methódik(l); 2. m*i*þɔ́d*i*k(l)]. Prec. & **-ic** & **-al.** **1.** Arranged, planned, carried out, with method; showing systematic planning and orderly procedure. **2.** Of orderly, regular, habits; doing things in an orderly and systematic manner.

methodically, adv. Prec. & **-ly.** In a methodical manner.

Methodism, n. [1. méthodizm; 2. méþ*ə*d*i*z*ə*m]. See **methodist** & **-ism.** Religious teaching and organization of Methodists.

Methodist, n. [1. méthodist; 2. méþ*ə*d*i*st]. **method** & **-ist.** **1.** (cap.) Member of one of several nonconformist religious bodies which have developed from the teaching of John and Charles Wesley. **2.** (usually depreciatory) Person of strict and intolerant religious views. **3.** (rare) One who observes method.

methodistic(al), adj. [1. mèthodístik(l); 2. mèþ*ə*díst*i*k(l)]. Prec. & **-ic** & **-al.** Of, pertaining to, the Methodists.

methodistically, adv. Prec. & **-ly.** In a methodistical manner.

methodize, vb. trans. [1. méthodīz; 2. méþ*ə*daiz]. **method** & **-ize.** To reduce to method or system, bring into order, arrange in an orderly manner.

methodology, n. [1. mèthodóloji; 2. mèþ*ə*dɔ́l*ə*dži]. **method** & **-o-** & **-logy.** Science, study, of method in scientific research.

methought, impers. vb. [1. mithawt; 2. m*i*þɔ́t]. O.E. *mē þūhte*, 'it seemed to me'. Past tense of **methinks.**

methyl, n. [1. méthil; 2. méþ*i*l], fr. Fr. *méthyle*, fr. Gk. *méthu*, 'wine', q.v. under **mead** (I.) & *húlē*, 'wood; forest; timber; material, matter', see **hylo-.** Chemical basis of wood spirit, formic acid, and other organic substances, having a very offensive taste and smell: *methyl alcohol*, wood alcohol.

methylate, vb. trans. [1. méthilāt; 2. méþ*i*leit]. Prec. & **-ate.** To saturate (alcohol) with methyl in order to render it undrinkable and therefore exempt from duty; to denature (alcohol). *Methylated spirit*, spirits of wine denatured by methyl.

methylic, adj. [1. methílik; 2. m*i*þíl*i*k]. **methyl** & **-ic.** Of, of the nature of, methyl.

meticulous, adj. [1. metíkūlus; 2. m*i*tíkjul*ə*s], fr. Lat. *meticulōs-(us)*, 'full of fear', fr. *met-(us)*, 'fear', *metuere*, 'to fear', prob. cogn. w. Ir. *meata*, 'coward'; other cognates are very uncertain. See **-cule** & **-ous.** Mod. Engl. use is fr. Fr. *méticuleux*. Overcareful about minute details; timorously and fussily exact and punctilious.

meticulously, adv. Prec. & **-ly.** In a meticulous manner.

métier, n. [1. métyā; 2. métjei]. Fr., 'trade, business, usual occupation'; earlier *mestier, mistier*, fr. Lat. *ministerium*, 'office' &c. See **minister** (I.). **a** Trade, profession, occupation; **b** that for which one is specially adapted; one's line.

metis, n. [1. mḗtis; 2. mít*i*s], fr. Fr. *métis*, fr. Low Lat. *mixticius*. See **mestizo.** Canadian of mixed white and N. American-Indian parentage.

Metonic, adj. [1. metónik; 2. mɛtɔ́n*i*k], fr. Meton, an Athenian astronomer of the 5th cent. B.C., & **-ic.** Pertaining to, discovered by, Meton; specif., *Metonic Cycle*, of 19 solar years, 235 lunar months, the moon passing through all its changes and the new and full moons recurring at its close on the same days; it forms the basis of modern calendars and is used for fixing movable feast days, such as Easter.

metonymical, adj. [1. metonímikl; 2. metən-ímikl]. Next word & **-ic** & **-al.** Of, of the nature of, metonymy.

metonymy, n. [1. metónimi; 2. mətónimi], fr. L. Lat., fr. Gk. *metōnumia*, fr. **meta-** & *ónoma*, 'name', cogn. w. Lat. *nōmen*, see **name.** Figure of speech which consists in putting the name of one thing for another, the substituted word expressing an object or idea closely associated with that for which it stands; e.g. *fond of the bottle* for *fond of drink*, *wine* &c.; *fur and feathers* for *beasts and birds* &c.

metope, n. [1. métōp; 2. métoup], fr. Gk. **meta-** & *opḗ*, 'opening, hole; hole in frieze for end of beam', fr. earlier **okw-*; cp. O. Slav. *oč-i*, 'eyes'; Lith. *ākas*, 'ice-hole'. See also **ocular.** (class. archit.) Marble slab or tablet filling the space between the triglyphs in a Doric frieze; usually adorned with sculpture.

metre (I.), n. [1. mḗter; 2. mítə], fr. Lat. *metrum*, fr. Gk. *métron*, 'measure, metre', fr. **med-tro-*; cp. Gk. *médomai*, 'I reflect upon, ponder'; Lat. *meditāri*, 'to reflect', see **meditate**; *modus*, 'measure; way, manner', see **mode**; *modestus*, 'within limits', see **modest**; O.E. *metan*, 'to measure', see **mete (II.).** **1.** Any form of poetical rhythm, characterized by fixed arrangement of accented and unaccented, or of long and short syllables. **2.** Group of metrical feet.

metre (II.), n., fr. Fr. *mètre*, fr. Lat. *metrum*, 'measure'. See prec. Unit of length in metric system; 39·37 inches.

metric, adj. [1. métrik; 2. métrik]. Prec. & **-ic.** Measuring by metres: *metric system*, decimal system of weights and measures based on Fr. *mètre*.

metrical, adj. [1. métrikl; 2. métrikl], fr. L. Lat., fr. Gk. *metrik-(ós)*, 'metrical', fr. *métr-(on)*, 'measure', see **metre (I.)**, & **-ic** & **-al.** **1.** Of, composed in, forming, metre. **2.** Of, pertaining to, treating of, measurement: *metrical geometry*.

metrically, adv. Prec. & **-ly.** In a metrical manner; in metre.

metrician, n. [1. metríshan; 2. metríʃən]. **metric** & **-ian.** One who writes in, one skilled in, metre; metrist.

metrics, n. [1. métriks; 2. métriks]. **metre (I.)** & **-ics.** The study of the laws of metre.

metrist, n. [1. métrist; 2. métrist]. **metre (I.)** & **-ist.** **a** Writer skilled in metrical composition; **b** student of poetical metre.

metrological, adj. [1. mètrolójikl; 2. mètrəlɔ́dʒikl]. See next word & **-ic** & **-al.** Of, relating to, metrology.

metrology, n. [1. metróloji; 2. metrɔ́lədʒi]. **metre (I.)** & **-logy.** Science of weights and measures.

metronome, n. [1. métronōm; 2. métrənoum]. **metre** & Gk. *nóm-(os)*, 'law'. See **nomad.** (mus.) Mechanical device for beating time, consisting of a pendulum worked by clockwork.

metronomic, adj. [1. mètronómik; 2. mètrənɔ́mik]. Prec. & **-ic.** Of, like, a metronome.

metronymic, adj. [1. mètrōnímik; 2. mìtrounímik]. Gk. *mētrōnumikós*, fr. *mḗtēr*, 'mother', see **mater**, & *ónoma*, 'name', see **name.** Derived from name of mother or of a female ancestor; contrasted with *patronymic*.

metropolis, n. [1. metrópolis; 2. mitrɔ́pəlis], fr. Lat., fr. Gk. *mētrópolis*, 'mother-state; mother-country; capital', fr. *mētr-*, stem of *mḗtēr*, 'mother', q.v. under **mater**, & *pólis*, 'city', see **policy.** **1.** Capital, chief city, of a country: *the metropolis*, London. **2.** See of metropolitan bishop.

metropolitan (I.), adj. [1. mètropólitan; 2. mètrəpɔ́litən], fr. Gk. *mētropolīt-(ēs)*, 'metropolitan', see prec., & **-ite** & **-an.** **1.** Belonging to a metropolis. **2. a** Of, pertaining to, the see of a metropolitan bishop; **b** *metropolitan bishop*, one having jurisdiction over bishops of a province.

metropolitan (II.), n., fr. prec. **1.** Metropolitan bishop; in England there are two metropolitans, the Archbishops of Canterbury and York. **2.** Inhabitant of metropolis.

metropolitanate, n. [1. mètropólitanāt; 2. mètrəpɔ́litəneit]. Prec. & **-ate.** Office, jurisdiction, of a metropolitan bishop.

-metry, suff. representing Gk. *-metria*, 'measurement', fr. *métr-(on)*, 'measure', see **metre (I.)**, forming ns. denoting measurement & systems of measurement: *geometry*, *psychometry*, *galvanometry*.

mettle, n. [1. métl; 2. métl]. Variant of **metal.** **a** Disposition, quality of mind and character, temperament; **b** spirit, courage, ardour; Phr. *on one's mettle*, roused to do one's best.

mettled, adj. [1. métld; 2. métld]. Prec. & **-ed.** Ardent, high-spirited, courageous.

mettlesome, adj. [1. métlsum; 2. métlsəm]. **mettle** & **-some.** High-spirited.

meum and tuum [1. mḗum and tū́um; 2. míəm ən(d) tjū́əm]. Lat. neut. adjs., 'mine' and 'thine'. Used as phrase, expressing right in property &c.

mew (I.), n. [1. mū; 2. mjū]. O.E. *mǣw*; cp. Du. *meeuw*; Germ. *möwe*; prob. imitative. Usually *sea-mew*, the common gull.

mew (II.), n. & vb. trans., fr. Fr. *mue*, fr. *muer*, 'to moult'. See next word. **1.** n. **a** Cage for hawks, esp. when moulting; **b** process of moulting. **2.** vb. trans. **a** To cage, shut up, in mew; **b** (fig., often *mew up*) to confine, as in a cage.

mew (III.), vb. trans., fr. Fr. *muer*, 'to mew', fr. Lat. *mūtāre*, 'to change'. See **mutation.** (archaic, of birds, esp. of hawks) **a** To shed, to moult (their feathers); **b** (of stags) to shed (their horns).

mew (IV.), vb. intrans. & n. Imitative. **1.** vb. intrans. (of cat) To utter characteristic cry; **b** (of other creatures) to utter cry resembling this. **2.** n. Characteristic cry of cat.

mewl, vb. intrans. [1. mūl; 2. mjūl]. Imitative. **1.** To cry as a cat. **2.** To whimper, cry weakly.

mews, n. [1. mūz; 2. mjūz]. Pl. of **mew (II.).** First of royal stables, built on place where the king's falcons were originally kept. Series of private stables; group of sets of stabling; esp. rows of stabling built on both sides of a long lane, as in towns where there is no room for private stables adjoining houses; stables built round a yard, in which horses are kept for hire.

mezzanine, n. [1. mézanēn; 2. mézənīn], fr. Fr., fr. Ital. *mezzanino*, dimin. of *mezzano*, 'middle', fr. Lat. *mediānus*, 'middle'. See **median.** **1.** Also *mezzanine storey*, low storey between two higher ones. **2.** Floor below stage of theatre from which mechanical contrivances are worked.

mezzo, adv. [1. métsō; 2. métsou]. Ital., fr. Lat. *medius*, 'middle'. See **media (I.).** (mus.) Moderately, fairly: *mezzo forte*, fairly loud &c.

mezzo-rilievo, n. [1. métsō rilyā́vō; 2. métsou riljéivou]. Ital. See prec. & **relief.** Form of relief in which figures stand out in half their real proportions.

mezzo-soprano, n. [1. mètsō sōprā́hnō; 2. mètsou souprā́nou]. **mezzo** & **soprano.** **a** Voice between contralto and soprano; **b** person with such a voice; **c** part for mezzo-soprano in duet, concerted piece &c.

mezzotint, n. & vb. trans. [1. métsōtint; 2. métsoutint], fr. Ital. *mezzotinto*, fr. **mezzo** & **tint.** **1.** n. **a** Form of engraving on copper or steel in which the plate is first roughened all over, the roughness being then scraped away to form the lighter parts of the print; **b** engraving produced by this method. **2.** vb. To engrave in mezzotint.

mho, n. [1. mō; 2. mou]. Anagram of **ohm**, q.v. The reciprocal of the unit of electrical resistance, the ohm.

mi, n. [1. mē; 2. mī], fr. first two letters of Lat. *mīra*, 'wonder', as occurring in the hymn *Sancte Joannes* used by Guido d'Arezzo in drawing up the **gamut.** (mus.) The third tone in the diatonic scale; third note, E, in scale of C.

miaow, **miau**, n. & vb. intrans. [1. mióu; 2. miáu]. Imitative. **a** n. The cry, mew, of a cat; **b** vb., to cry, mew.

miasma, n. [1. miázma; 2. miǽzmə], popular pl. *miasmas*, learned (Gk.) pl. *miasmata* [1. miázmata; 2. miǽzmətə]. Gk. *míasma*, 'stain, defilement', fr. *miainein*, 'to stain, dye, defile'; prob. cogn. w. O. Slav. *myti*, 'to wash'; Lett. *maut*, 'to swim'. Infectious, harmful emanation or effluvium, esp. of damp mists, which formerly were considered the cause of malaria; malarious atmosphere.

miasmatic, adj. [1. miazmátik; 2. miəzmǽtik], fr. Gk. *miásmat-(os)*, as prec., & **-ic.** Of or pertaining to a miasma; malarious.

miau. See **miaow.**

mica, n. [1. míka; 2. máikə]. Lat. *mīca*, 'crumb, tiny morsel', cogn. w. Gk. *mikrós*, 'small', see **micro-**; wrongly connected w. Lat. *micāre*, 'to shine, glisten'. A group of minerals, chiefly aluminium silicates, cleaving readily into thin, elastic plates or leaves, found in glittering scales in crystalline rocks such as granite; the common transparent mica is generally known as talc, q.v. *Mica schist*, a slaty rock, composed of mica and quartz.

micaceous, adj. [1. mīkā́shus; 2. maikéiʃəs]. Prec. & **-aceous.** Of the nature of, pertaining to, mica; containing, resembling, mica.

Michaelmas, n. [1. míklmas; 2. míklməs], fr. Michael, name of the Archangel, Heb. *Mīkāēl*, 'who is like God!', & *-mas*, 'mass'. The festival of St. Michael, Sept. 29th: *Michaelmas Day*; *Michaelmas goose*, as special dish on St. Michael's feast; *Michaelmas daisy*, a perennial variety of aster, flowering in the autumn, with blue, pinkish, or white flowers resembling the daisy.

miching, adj. [1. míching; 2. mítʃiŋ]. Etymol. doubtful; possibly fr. O. Fr. *muchier*, 'to hide', cp. **mooch**; cp. provinc. Engl. *to mitch*, *maich*, 'loaf about' &c. Skulking, hiding: '*miching mallecho*' (Shakespeare, 'Hamlet', iii. 2).

mickle, adj. [1. míkl; 2. míkl], fr. O.N. *mykill*; cogn. w. O.E. *myčel*, *mičel*, 'great', wh. wd. become *muchel*, *michel*, in M.E.; Common Gmc., cp. O.H.G. *mihil*, O.S. *mikil*, Goth. *mikils*, cogn. w. Gk. *megálē*, *mégas*, Lat. *magnus*, 'great'. See **much** & the variant **muckle.** (provinc.) Great; much: '*A man of mickle might*' (Spenser); *every little makes a mickle* (or *muckle*), every little helps.

micro-, pref. [1. míkrō, míkrō; 2. máikrou, mikrou]. Form of Gk. *mīkrós*, 'small', for **smīkros*; used in compounds; cogn. w. **mica**; also w. O.H.G. *smāhi*, 'small, humble' &c., & O.H.G. *smāhen*, 'to reduce'; cp. O.E. *smēalič*, 'searching, subtle'. Used chiefly in scientific terminology; contrasted with *macro-* and *mega-*, meaning **a** small, minute; **b** (elect.) one-millionth part of: *microampère*, *microfarad*, *microhm*.

microbe, n. [1. míkrōb; 2. máikroub]. Modern scientific invented word; fr. prec. & Gk. *bios*, 'life'. See **biology.** A popular name for bacteria, esp. those which are the causes of disease.

microbial, adj. [1. mīkróbial; 2. maikróubiəl]. Prec. & **-ial.** Of, pertaining to, microbes or bacteria.

microbic, adj. [1. mīkróbik; 2. maikróubik]. As prec. & **-ic.** Microbial.

micro-biological, adj. [1. míkrō bīolójikl; 2. máikrou baiəlɔ́dʒikl]. **micro-biology** & **-ic** & **-al.** Connected with, pertaining to, micro-biology; bacteriological.

micro-biologist, n. [1. míkrō bīólojist; 2. máikrou baiɔ́lədʒist]. See prec. & **-ist.** One who studies, specializes, in micro-biology; bacteriologist.

micro-biology, n. [1. míkrō bīóloji; 2. máikrou baiɔ́lədʒi]. **micro-** & **biology.** Study of microbes or bacteria; bacteriology.

microcephalic, adj. [1. mīkrōsefálik; 2. màikrousefǽlik]. **micro-** & **cephalic.** Microcephalous.

microcephalous, adj. [1. mīkrōséfalus; 2. màikrouséfələs]. See prec. & **-ous**. Having an abnormally small head, and consequently small brain capacity; microcephalic: *a microcephalous idiot.*

microcephaly, n. [1. mīkrōséfali; 2. màikrouséfəli]. As prec. & **-y**. State, condition of being microcephalous.

microcosm, n. [1. míkrokozm; 2. máikrəkɔzəm], fr. Fr. *microcosme*, fr. L. Lat. *microcosmus*; fr. Gk. *mīkrós kósmos*, 'little world'. See **micro-** & **cosmos** & cp. **macrocosm**. **a** Man regarded as the summary or epitome of the macrocosm, i.e. of the great world or the universe; **b** community, class &c., considered as representative of humanity as a whole; **c** a representation on a small scale or in miniature.

microcosmic, adj. [1. mīkrokózmik; 2. màikrəkɔ́zmik]. Prec. & **-ic**. **1.** Pertaining to the microcosm. **2.** Specif. *microcosmic salt*, (chem.) a salt of sodium and ammonium phosphates, first identified in human urine.

microfarad, n. [1. mīkrōfárad; 2. màikroufǽræd], fr. **micro-** & **farad**. (elect.) Working unit of capacity, equal to one-millionth part of the scientific unit, the farad, the latter being too large for practical purposes.

micrograph, n. [1. míkrograhf; 2. máikrəgrāf]. **micro-** & **-graph**. A micro-photograph.

micrology, n. [1. mīkróloji; 2. maikrɔ́lədži]. **micro-** & **-logy**. **a** Science or art dealing with microscopic objects; **b** exaggerated attention to small details or minutiae.

micrometer, n. [1. mīkrómeter; 2. maikrɔ́mitə]. **micro-** & **-meter**. Instrument used for making minute and exact measurements.

micrometric, adj. [1. mīkrométrik; 2. màikrəmétrik]. See prec. & **-ic**. Of or pertaining to the micrometer and its use.

micrometry, n. [1. mīkrómetri; 2. maikrɔ́mitri]. As prec. & **-y**. Art, skill in using, use of, the micrometer.

micron, n. [1. míkron; 2. máikrɔn]. Mod. Lat., fr. Gk.; see **micro-**. Thousandth part of a millimetre.

micro-organism, n. [1. mīkrō órganizm; 2. màikrou ɔ́gənizəm]. **micro-** & **organism**. A microscopic organism, used of bacteria.

microphone, n. [1. míkrofōn; 2. máikrəfoun]. **micro-** & **-phone**. (elect.) Instrument used for transforming sound waves into electric current, as in the transmitter of a telephone.

micro-photograph, n. [1. mīkrō fótograhf; 2. màikrou fóutəgrāf]. **micro-** & **photograph**. A photograph of microscopic objects taken through a microscope, and enlarged.

microscope, n. [1. míkroskōp; 2. máikrəskoup]. **micro-** & **-scope**. An instrument with high powers of magnification, used for observing objects, and details of structure, so minute as to be either altogether invisible, or only faintly discernible, to the naked eye.

microscopic, adj. [1. mīkroskópik; 2. màikrəskɔ́pik]. Prec. & **-ic**. **a** Pertaining to the microscope; **b** visible only by means of a microscope; microscopical; **c** very small, minute.

microscopical, adj. [1. mīkroskópikl; 2. màikrəskɔ́pikl]. Prec. & **-al**. Visible only by the microscope.

microscopically, adv. Prec. & **-ly**. **a** By means of the microscope; **b** in a minute, searching way.

microscopist, n. [1. míkroskōpist, mīkróskopist; 2. máikrəskoupist, maikrɔ́skəpist]. **microscope** & **-ist**. One who habitually uses, one skilled in use of, the microscope.

microscopy, n. [1. mīkróskopi; 2. maikrɔ́skəpi]. **microscope** & **-y**. Use of the microscope.

microsome, n. [1. míkrosōm; 2. máikrəsoum]. **micro-** & Gk. *sôma*, body'. See **somatic**. (biol.) One of the minute granules in protoplasm, which constitute an essential element in its structure.

microspore, n. [1. míkrospōr; 2. máikrəspɔ]. **micro-** & **-spore**. (bot.) A minute sexual spore in certain plants.

microtome, n. [1. míkrotōm; 2. máikrətoum], fr. **micro-** & Gk. suff. *-tomia*, 'cutting', connected w. *témnein*, 'to cut'. See **tome**. Instrument used in cutting very thin sections of organic tissue for examination by the microscope.

microtomy, n. [1. mīkrótomi; 2. maikrɔ́təmi]. Prec. & **-y**. Art of cutting and preparing sections for the microscope.

micturate, vb. intrans. [1. míktūrāt; 2. míktjəreit]. Formed wrongly fr. next word. To pass water.

micturition, n. [1. mìktūríshun; 2. mìktjəríʃən], fr. Lat. *micturīt-(um)*, P.P. of *micturīre*, 'to desire to pass water'; formed fr. *mict-(um)*, P.P. type of *mingere*, 'to pass water', & **-ion**. The base occurs also in Gk. *omīkhein*, 'to urinate'; O.E. *mīgan*, 'to urinate', & *miċġe* &c., 'urine'; Goth. *maihstus*, 'dung'. **a** Morbid desire to pass water; **b** act or process of passing water, of urinating.

mid (I.), adj. [1. mid; 2. mid]. O.E. *midd*, fr. **meddj-*; cp. O.S. *middi*, O.H.G. *mitti*, Goth. *midjis*, O.N. *miðr*; cp. Lat. *medius*, Gk. *mésos*, fr. **medhjo-*; Scrt. *madhya*; cp. **media (I.)** & **meso-**, & see **meta-**. Denoting the middle part or position, chiefly used in combination, with or without hyphen: *in mid air*, or *mid-air*; *in mid-Atlantic.*

mid (II.), prep., for **amid**. (poet.) Amid.

midday, n. [1. mìddā́; 2. mìddéi]. O.E. *middæġ*. **mid (I.)** & **day**. **a** The middle of the day, noon; also **b** attrib.: *a midday meal.*

midden, n. [1. mídn; 2. mídn]. M.E. *midding*; of Scand. origin, cp. Dan. *mödding*, earlier *mögdynge*, fr. *mög*, 'dung, muck', & *dynge*, 'heap (of dung)'. **1.** A dunghill. **2.** Specif. (archaeol.) a prehistoric refuse heap, a kitchen-midden (q.v.).

middle (I.), adj. [1. midl; 2. midl]. O.E. *middel*, *midd-*, 'mid', & **-el**, cp. O.H.G. *mittil*, O.N. *meðal*, prep., 'amid'. See **mid (I.)**. **1.** Occupying a central place; half-way between two other points, of space, number, time &c.; equidistant from extremes; intermediate; *the middle house in the row*; *middle hours of the day*; *to take a middle point of view*; *middle finger*, second finger. **2.** Various special uses: **a** (gram.) of a special form of the verb, *the middle voice*, as in Greek, half-way between active and passive, expressing reflexive action of the verb on the subject or intransitive action; **b** (logic) of the term in a syllogism which is common to both premisses: *the middle term.* **3.** (philol., cap.) Of languages, occupying a stage in development between the Old (or oldest) and the Modern forms: *Middle English*; *Middle High German* &c.

middle (II.), n. See prec. **1. a** A middle, central point, part, in position or time: *the middle of the road, of the stage, night*; **b** point between the beginning and end of an action: *in the middle of a meal*; *of a race* &c.; Phr. *in the middle of one's work* &c., (while) fully occupied, engrossed, with work &c. **2.** The middle part of the body; the waist: *a belt round his middle.* **3.** (rare) An intermediary, medium: *to act as a middle between two disputants.* **4.** Specif. uses: **a** (gram.) the middle voice; **b** (logic) a middle term; **c** in various trades, (usually pl.) goods of a grade between an inferior and a higher quality; **d** (cricket) a guard, position, of the bat as covering the middle stump: *to take middle*, to get this guard from the umpire; *middle and leg*, guard for the middle and the leg stump: **e** (Association football) the kicking of the ball from either wing to the centre of the line of forwards.

middle (III.), vb. trans., fr. prec. To place in the middle; specif. (Association football) to kick the ball from the wing to the centre.

middle age, n. The middle period of life, between the end of youth and the beginning of old age; now usually applied to the years between forty and sixty.

middle-aged, adj. Of middle age.

Middle Ages, n. pl. [1. mídl ājiz; 2. mídl éidžiz]. (hist.) The mediaeval period of European history, connecting ancient and modern times, variously calculated, but commonly applied to the period from the fall of the Roman Empire of the West (5th cent.) to the beginning of the Renaissance (middle of 15th cent.).

middle class, n. [1. mídl kláhs; 2. mídl klā́s]. **1.** That class of society regarded as lying between the class of artisans and the aristocracy; the bourgeoisie; including the professional, business, shop-keeping, classes: *the middle classes.* **2.** Attrib. [1. mídl klahs; 2. mídl klās], **a** belonging to, typical of, the middle class in society: *the middle-class vote, mind*; **b** (rare) of ordinary or second-rate quality.

middle distance, n. (paint.) That part of a picture which lies between the foreground and the background.

Middle East, n. A term used in politics for the various States lying between the Near and the Far East, usually including Persia, Iraq (Mesopotamia), Syria, Palestine, Arabia, and parts of Turkestan.

Middle Kingdom, n. The Chinese Empire, translating Chinese *Chang Kuo.*

middleman, n. [1. mídlman; 2. mídlmæn]. **a** An agent or broker who occupies a middle position in dealing with commodities as they pass between the producer and the consumer, or more strictly, between producer and retailer; **b** a go-between, intermediary.

middlemost, adj. [1. mídlmōst; 2. mídlmoust]. Superlative of *middle*; nearest the middle, of two or more persons or things; midmost.

middle passage, n. The part of the Atlantic lying between the West Coast of Africa and the West Indies, used esp. in connexion with the slave trade.

middle watch, n. (naut.) The watch between midnight and 4 A.M.

middle weight, n. & adj. (boxing) **a** n. Boxer of a weight between a light or welter-weight and a heavy-weight, i.e. between 10 st. and 11 st. 4 lb.; **b** adj., being of middle weight.

middling, adj. & n. [1. mídling; 2. mídliŋ]. **middle** & **-ing**. **1.** adj. Of middle size, quality, state &c.; ordinary, second-rate; fairly good: *the place is only of middling size*; *the dinner was middling*; *to feel only middling*, to feel so-so, only pretty well; (also advbl.) *middling tall, hungry.* **2.** n. (usually pl.) *Middlings*, grades of commodities, such as flour, considered of a second quality.

middy, n. [1. mídi; 2. mídi]. (colloq.) Abbreviated form of **midshipman**.

midge, n. [1. mij; 2. midž]. O.E. *myċġ(e)*, M.E. *migge*; O.H.G. *mucca*, *mugga*, L.G. *mugge*, cp. Du. *mug*, 'gnat'; possibly connected w. Gk. *muia*, 'fly'; *múzein*, 'to buzz'; O. Slav. *mucha*, 'fly'. **a** Minute buzzing, biting, flying insect; **b** diminutive person.

midget, n. [1. míjit; 2. mídžit]. Prec. & **-et**. An extremely diminutive person; dwarf.

midinette, n. [1. midinét; 2. midinét]. Fr., fr. *midi*, 'midday', & dimin. **-nette**. A shop-girl in Paris, so called as being generally visible in the streets at luncheon time.

mid-iron, n. (golf) An iron-headed club with a moderate loft.

midland, adj. & n. [1. mídland; 2. mídlənd]. **mid (I.)** & **land**. **1.** adj. **a** In, belonging to, the central district of a country: *the Midland Counties of England*; **b** surrounded by land: *the midland sea*, Mediterranean. **2.** n. **a** (pl.) *The Midlands*, the midland counties of England; **b** (sing.) dialect of these areas.

midmost, adj. [1. mídmōst; 2. mídmoust]. See **middlemost**.

midnight, n. [1. mídnīt; 2. mídnait]. O.E. *midniht*. **mid (I.)** & **night**. **a** Twelve o'clock in the middle of the night; the middle of the night; **b** (material or fig.) deep darkness; **c** (attrib.) during the middle of the night; at midnight: *the midnight hours*; *midnight revels*; Phrs. *dark, black, as midnight*, very dark; *to burn the midnight oil*, to work, study, very late at night. *The Midnight Sun*, visible appearance of the sun at midnight within the Arctic and Antarctic Circles at and about midsummer or midwinter respectively.

mid-off, mid-on, n. [1. mìd áwf, ón; 2. mìd ɔ́f, ɔ́n]. (cricket) Fieldsman standing in the middle of the field not far from the bowler and on the off- or on-side of the batsman.

midrash, n., pl. **midrashim** [1. mídrash, midráshēm; 2. mídræʃ, midrǽʃim]. Heb., 'examination, exposition'. The ancient Jewish explanatory commentary on the Old Testament.

mid-rib, n. A middle or central rib; specif. (bot.) the central nerve or vein of a leaf running from the stem to the apex.

midriff, n. [1. mídrif; 2. mídrif]. O.E. *midhrif*, fr. **mid (I.)** & *hrif*, 'belly', cp. O.H.G. *href*, 'body', O. Fris. *ref*; cogn. w. Lat. **corpus**. The diaphragm; muscular wall which separates the chest cavity from the abdomen.

midship, adj. & n. [1. mídship; 2. mídʃip]. **a** adj. Of or belonging to the middle of a ship; **b** n., the middle part of a ship.

midshipman, n. [1. mídshipman; 2. mídʃipmən]. Prec. & **man**. In the British navy, a junior officer ranking between a naval cadet and a sub-lieutenant; the name is derived from the position amidships of midshipmen's quarters in the old sailing days.

midships, adv. [1. mídships; 2. mídʃips]. The *-s* is the survival of a genit. suff. used adverbially. Amidships.

midst, n. & prep. [1. midst; 2. midst]. For *middest, in middest*, fr. earlier M.E. *in middes*, fr. **mid (I.)** & *-es*, suff. of genit. used adverbially; the *-t* may be intrusive as in *whilst*, or may be due to the supposed superl. **middest* of *mid*. **1.** n. The middle, central part, only now in Phrs. *in, into, from, the midst of, out of the midst of*; also *in, from &c., our, your, their midst*; *in the midst of us* &c. **2.** prep. In the middle of; amidst.

midsummer, n. [1. mídsumer; 2. mídsamə]. O.E. *midsumor*, fr. **mid (I.)** & **summer (I.)**. The middle of summer; period of the summer solstice, June 21; *Midsummer Day*, June 24, the feast of the Nativity of St. John the Baptist, an English quarter-day. Phr. *midsummer madness*, extreme folly, assumed to be due to the midsummer moon and heat.

midway, adj. & adv. [1. mìdwá; 2. mìdwéi]. **mid (I.)** & **way**. Situated in the middle; half-way; in the middle of the way.

midwife, n. [1. mídwīf; 2. mídwaif]. M.E. *midwif*, fr. O.E., M.E. *mid*, 'with', & *wīf*, 'wife, woman', see **wife**; *mid* is cogn. w. O.H.G. *mit*, 'with'; Goth. *miþ*; cp. also Gk. *metá*, see **meta-**. A woman who assists another at childbirth; *midwife toad*, the obstetric toad.

midwifery, n. [1. mídwiferi; 2. mídwifri]. Prec. & **-ery**. Art, practice, of attending or assisting at childbirth; obstetrics.

midwinter, n. [1. midwínter; 2. midwíntə]. The middle of winter; the period of the winter solstice, Dec. 21.

mien, n. [1. mēn; 2. mīn]. Etymol. doubtful; Fr. *mine*, in same sense, is also of doubtful origin & is late; possibly a shortened form of **demean**. (chiefly liter.) Manner, demeanour, bearing; appearance: *of pleasing, angry, haughty, mien*.

miff, n. & vb. trans. & intrans. [1. mif; 2. mif]. Perh. fr. exclamation expressing disgust; cp. Mod. Germ. *muffen*, 'to sulk'. (colloq.) **1.** n. A fit of the sulks; trifling quarrel, huff, tiff. **2.** vb. To put out of humour, cause to be sulky; be out of humour, sulk.

might (I.), vb. [1. mīt; 2. mait]. O.E. *mihte*, past tense of **may (I.)**. Expresses probability, or possibility; also used as optative.

might (II.), n. O.E. *miht*, fr. **mæhti-*; O.H.G. & O.S. *maht*, Goth. *mahts*; fr. Gmc. base **mag-*, 'to be able'. See **may (I.)**. Power, strength, energy, capacity, of body or mind; physical force and power: *might is right*. Phrs. *with all one's might, with might and main*, all one's strength and energy.

mightily, adv. [1. mítili; 2. máitili]. **mighty** & **-ly**. **a** In a mighty manner; powerfully, vigorously; **b** (colloq.) very much, extremely: *mightily bored*; *pleased him mightily*.

mightiness, n. [1. mítines; 2. máitinis]. See next word & **-ness**. Quality, state, of being mighty; greatness; high rank and dignity; also as title, highness, *His Mightiness*; so ironically, *his high and mightiness*, of an exceedingly arrogant person.

mighty, adj. & adv. [1. míti; 2. máiti]. O.E. *mihtiġ*. **might (II.)** & **-y**. **1.** adj. **a** (of persons and things) Having might; strong, powerful: *a mighty man of valour*; '*put down the mighty from their seats*'; *a mighty wind*; *a mighty building*; **b** (colloq.) great, of large amount and size: *made a mighty bother*; *a mighty hit*. Phr. *high and mighty*, very proud, arrogant, haughty. **2.** adv. (colloq.) Very, extremely: *mighty pleasant*; *was mighty pleased*.

mignon, adj. [1. minyon; 2. minjɔ̃]. Fr., 'delicate, sweet, charming'; of Gmc. origin, cp. O.H.G. & O.S. *minna*, 'love', see **minnesinger**; **minion** is a variant. Delicately formed, dainty; small and charming, petite.

mignonette, n. [1. mìnyunét; 2. mìnjənét], fr. Fr. *mignonnette*, dimin. of prec. **a** (bot.) A sweet-scented garden plant, *Reseda odorata*, having grey-green flowers with reddish-brown anthers; **b** colour resembling that of these flowers; **c** a fine, open-work, French pillow lace.

migraine, n. [1. mḗgrān; 2. mígrein]. Fr., through Lat. *hēmicrānium*, fr. Gk. *hēmikrānía*, 'pain on one side of the head', fr. *hēmi-*, 'half', see **hemi-**, & *krānion*, 'head, skull', see **cranium**; cp. variant **megrim**. A periodical, nervous headache, usually on one side only; formerly often called a sick headache.

migrant, adj. & n. [1. mígrant; 2. máigrənt], fr. Lat. *migrant-(em)*, Pres. Part. type of *migrāre*. See **migrate**. **1.** adj. Having the habit of migrating, esp. of birds. **2.** n. One that migrates, esp. a migrating bird.

migrate, vb. intrans. [1. mígrāt; 2. máigreit], fr. Lat. *migrāt-(um)*, P.P. type of *migrāre*, 'to change place, move from one place to another, to change', fr. **migʷr-*, cp. also Gk. *(a)méibein*, 'to change; to quit one place for another', fr. **meigʷ-*; cp. also Gk. *amoibḗ*, 'change', see **amoeba**. The base **moigʷ-*, **meigʷ-* &c., is prob. an extension fr. **moi-*, 'to change', q.v. under **mutate**. **a** To leave one habitation, place, or country and go to another; esp. to leave one's own country and settle abroad; **b** specif. (of birds) to go periodically from one region to another, in search of a different climate, or food, or for breeding.

migration, n. [1. mīgráshun; 2. maigréiʃən], fr. Lat. *migrātiōn-(em)*, 'removal, change'. See prec. & **-ion**. **a** Act of migrating, or changing one's place of residence or abode; used esp. **b** of the periodical movement of birds, fishes &c.; **c** the body of individuals so migrating.

migratory, adj. [1. mígratori; 2. máigrətəri]. **migrate** & **-ory**. Migrating; having the habit of migration; wandering, moving constantly from place to place.

mikado, n. [1. mikáhdō; 2. mikádou]. Jap. name of the gate of the Imperial palace, fr. *mi*, 'honourable, exalted', & *kado*, 'gate', cp. *Sublime Porte* & *Pharaoh*. The title, as used by Europeans, of the Emperor of Japan, is not a Japanese usage.

milage. See **mileage**.

milch, adj. [1. milsh; 2. milʃ]. Late M.E. *milche*, 'milk-giving'. The precise formal connexion w. **milk** is not clear. Yielding, giving milk, now only in *milch cow*, cow kept for milking; (colloq.) a source of profit: *to treat a person as a milch cow*.

mild, adj. [1. mīld; 2. maild]. O.E. *milde*, O.S. *mildi*; O.H.G. *milti*; O.N. *mildr*; cogn. w. Gk. *malthakós*, 'soft, mild'; also w. O. Slav. *mladŭ*, 'tender, young'; ultimately connected w. Lat. *mollis*, 'soft', fr. **moldwis*, see **mollify**, also w. **malt** & **melt**. **1.** (of persons) Gentle, kind, temperate, amiable; not harsh, rude, violent, or severe: *mild of manner, in disposition* &c.; *a mild ruler*. **2.** (of things) Soft, moderate; not harsh, hard, strong, or violent: *mild punishment*; *mild weather*, warm; *a mild medicine*, one that acts gently; *mild ale*, not bitter; Phr. (fig., colloq.) *draw it mild*, a don't exaggerate; **b** behave with moderation and decorum; *mild steel*, malleable and tough, having a low proportion of carbon.

mild-cured, adj. [1. mīld kūrd; 2. máild kjɔ̄d]. (of bacon and ham) Not strongly pickled, not salt.

mildew, n. & vb. trans. & intrans. [1. míldū; 2. míldjū]. O.E. *meledēaw, mildēaw*, 'honeydew', the sugary exudation on leaves of certain plants; M.E. *meldew*, 'mildew, blight'; cogn. w. O.H.G. *militow*, 'mildew'; the first element is cogn. w. Goth. *miliþ*, 'honey'; Lat. *mel*, 'honey', & prob. also w. **blithe**. See **melliferous** & **dew**. **1.** n. **a** Any of various parasitic fungi, destructive to plants, such as cereals, hops &c.; **b** the whitish, spotty discolouration on plants &c. affected by mildew; **c** the white, furry mould forming on leather, paper, food &c., when exposed to damp. **2.** vb. To affect, be affected, by mildew; esp. in P.P. *mildewed*.

mildewy, adj. [1. míldūi; 2. míldjūi]. Prec. & **-y**. Mildewed, affected by mildew; resembling mildew.

mildly, adv. [1. míldli; 2. máildli]. **mild** & **-ly**. In a mild, gentle manner; gently, softly, moderately. Phr. *to put it mildly*, to say the least of it; not to exaggerate.

mildness, n. [1. míldnes; 2. máildnis]. See prec. & **-ness**. State, quality, of being mild; gentleness, softness, kindness.

mile, n. [1. mīl; 2. mail]. O.E. *mīl*, pl. *mīla*, *mile*, M.E. *mile*; early loan-word fr. Lat. *millia, mīlia*, 'a thousand (things), a mile', fr. *mille*, 'thousand'; the Roman mile being 1000 paces, *mille passus* or *passuum*; Lat. *mille* is prob. fr. **smī*, 'one', cp. Gk. *mía*, 'one', for **smia-*, same base as **sem-* in *simplex*, see **simple**, & **gʹhstī-*, whence also Gk. *khīlioi*, 'thousand'; cp. also Scrt. *sa-hásram*, 'one thousand'. A measure of linear distance; the English *statutory mile*, 1760 yds.; the *geographical* or *nautical mile*, one minute of a great circle of the earth, in British Admiralty usage, 6080 ft.; the Roman mile of one thousand military paces, about 1620 yds.

mileage, milage, n. [1. mílij; 2. máilidž]. **mile** & **-age**. **a** Total distance in an aggregate of miles; miles travelled in a certain time; **b** rate of travelling in miles; **c** allowance for expenses &c. reckoned by the miles travelled.

miler, n. [1. míler; 2. máilə]. (colloq.) A runner, man or horse, whose favourite or best distance in a race is a mile.

Milesian, adj. & n. [1. milḗzian; 2. mailíziən], fr. *Milesius*, a legendary Spanish king who conquered Ireland in 14th cent. B.C. **a** adj. Irish; **b** n., an Irishman.

milestone, n. [1. mílstōn; 2. máilstoun], fr. **mile** & **stone**. **1.** A stone indicating the miles on a highway to or from a given place. **2.** (fig.) Important event which marks the end of a stage, or the beginning of a new era, in history or in a human life.

milfoil, n. [1. mílfoil; 2. mílfɔil]. O. Fr., fr. Lat. *millefolium*, name of the plant, fr. *mille*, 'thousand', see **mile**, & *folium*, 'leaf', see **folio**. (bot.) The yarrow, the leaf of which is divided into a large number of small segments.

miliaria, n. [1. miliária; 2. miliḗəriə]. Mod. Lat., fr. Lat. *mil(l)iārius*. See next word. (pathol.) A disease of the sweat-glands, inflammatory and marked by an eruption of small red pustules, resembling millet-seeds

miliary, adj. [1. míliari; 2. míliəri], fr. Lat. *mil(l)iār(ius)*, of or resembling *milium*, **millet**. Resembling the seeds of millet; specif. (med.) *miliary fever*, miliaria, on account of characteristic rash.

militancy, n. [1. mílitansi; 2. mílitənsi]. See next word & **-cy**. State, character, of being militant or warlike; aggressiveness, combativeness, fighting spirit or instinct.

militant, adj. & n. [1. mílitant; 2. mílitənt], fr. Lat. *mīlitant-(em)*, P.P. of *mīlitāre*, 'to serve as a soldier', fr. *mīlit-(em)*, acc. of *mīles*, 'soldier'. See **militia**. **1.** adj. Serving as a soldier; fighting, warlike, combative: *militant suffragettes*; (also fig.) the *Church militant*, considered as at war on earth with the powers of evil; contrasted with the heavenly *Church triumphant*. **2.** n. A fighting, combatant person.

militantly, adv. Prec. & **-ly**. In a militant, combative manner.

militarily, adv. [1. mílitarili; 2. mílitərili]. **military** & **-ly**. In a military way; like a soldier, in army fashion.

militariness, n. [1. mílitarines; 2. mílitərinis]. See prec. & **-ness**. Custom, fashion, of a soldier.

militarism, n. [1. mílitarizm; 2. mílitərizəm]. Cp. Fr. *militarisme*. **military** & **-ism**. **1.** Theory that the safety of a nation is only secured by the maintenance of trained fighting forces, and by a state of preparedness for war. **2.** Combatant spirit, esp. in a nation; disposition to exalt unduly soldierly virtues and military methods; converse of *pacifism*.

militarist, n. [1. mílitarist; 2. mílitərist]. See prec. & **-ist**. **a** Supporter of militarism; **b** an expert or student of war and military matters.

militarization, n. [1. mìlitarīzā́shun; 2. mìlitəraizéiʃən]. Next word & **-ation**. **a** Condition of being militarized; **b** act of militarizing.

militarize, vb. trans. [1. mílitarīz; 2. mílitəraiz], fr. next word & **-ize**. To make military or warlike; to instil the principles of militarism or a warlike spirit into.

military, adj. & n. [1. mílitari; 2. mílitəri], fr. Fr. *militaire*, fr. Lat. *mīlitāris*, of or belonging to a soldier, fr. *mīlit-(em)*, stem of *mīles*, 'soldier'. See **militia** & **-ary**. **1.** adj. Belonging to, suitable to, performed by, consisting of, soldiers, or the army; contrasted with *civil*: *military authority, discipline, band, forces, hospital* &c. *Military age*, the age at which, under compulsory service, a citizen is liable for service in the army, or, under a voluntary system, may enlist; *Military Cross*, a British decoration for bravery in face of the enemy, instituted in 1915; *military fever* (obs.), typhoid or typhus fever; *Military Knights of Windsor*, a body of retired officers attached to the Order of the Garter; *military law*, the body of regulations which governs the soldier in peace and war; *military police*, body of soldiers performing police duties for the army; *military service*, service in the army; (hist.) service as a soldier rendered to a feudal superior by a tenant who holds lands on such (military) tenure; *military testament* or *will*, a nuncupative will made by a soldier on active service. **2.** n. The army; soldiers collectively, soldiery.

militate, vb. intrans. [1. mílitāt; 2. míliteit], fr. *mīlitāt-(um)*, P.P. type of *mīlitāre*, 'to serve as a soldier, to fight', fr. *mīlit-(em)*, *mīles*, 'soldier'. See **militia**. **1.** (obs. or rare) To serve as a soldier; to fight, contend; chiefly followed by *against*. **2.** (followed by *against*) To work against, hinder, be detrimental to: *ill-health militated against his chances of success*.

militia, n. [1. milísha; 2. milíʃə]. Lat. *mīlitia*, 'military service; warfare; soldiery', fr. *mīlit-*, stem of *mīles*, 'a soldier', prob. connected w. the base **mīl-*, seen in Scrt. *mēlaś*, 'an assembly', *miláti*, 'he unites, comes together with others'; *mīles* therefore meant orig. 'one who advances, or marches in a horde or troop'. **1.** A national levy of citizens under arms, undergoing periodical training and embodied as an army in national emergencies. **2.** (in England) An auxiliary infantry force, enlisted by counties, undergoing periodical training, paid, and liable to be called out on emergency; it was merged in the Special Reserve in 1908, but restored with its old name after the Great War.

militiaman, n. [1. milíshaman; 2. milíʃəmən]. A soldier of the militia.

milk (I.), n. [1. milk; 2. milk]. O.E. *meolc*, O. Mercian *milc*, M.E. *milk*; O.S. & O. Fris. *miluk*; O.H.G. *miluh*; Goth. *miluks*, O.N. *mjǫlk*; cogn. w. Lat. *mulgēre*, 'to milk'; Gk. *amélgein*, 'to press, squeeze out; to milk'; Scrt. *mṛkšati*, 'he strokes, rubs' &c.; the orig. meaning wd. appear to be 'something pressed, squeezed out'. **1. a** The white or yellowish fluid secreted by the mammary glands of the female of all mammals as the food of their young; **b** specif. the milk of the domestic cow, universally used as an article of human food; Phr. *land of milk and honey*, of great fertility and abundance; *milk for babes*, (of books, sermons, opinions &c.) of an elementary kind suitable for childish minds; *milk of human kindness*, natural goodness and affection; *it's no good crying over spilt milk*, what is past cannot be helped. **2.** The milk-like fluid of certain plants, as the juice of the coco-nut, the latex of tropical trees such as caoutchouc &c. **3.** Preparation of drugs, herbs &c., resembling milk in appearance: *milk of sulphur, of almonds*. **4.** (obs.) Milt (of fish).

milk (II.), vb. trans. & intrans. O.E. *milcian*. See prec. **A.** trans. **1.** To draw milk, cause milk to flow from the breast or udder (of cows &c.) by pressure of the fingers. **2.** (vulg.) To extract all possible profit from, by illicit or extortionate means. **3.** To tap, or steal a message from, a telegraph wire. **B.** intrans. To yield milk: *cows are milking well this season*.

milk-and-water, adj. [1. milk and wáwter; 2. mílk ən(d) wɔ́tə]. Lacking strength and spirit; emasculated, wishy-washy; reverse of outspoken or pungent.

milker, n. [1. milker; 2. mílkə]. **1.** One who milks cows &c. **2.** Cow in milk, or used for milking.

milk fever, n. A fever to which women are liable after child-birth during lactation.

milkiness, n. [1. mílkines; 2. mílkinis]. **milky** & **-ness**. (of liquids) Quality of being milky; **a** opaqueness, cloudiness as of milk or of water and milk; **b** quality of being white and slightly thick, resembling milk in appearance and consistency.

milk-leg, n. An inflammatory condition of the leg, in women after child-birth, accompanied by white swellings.

milkmaid, n. [1. mílkmād; 2. mílkmeid]. A woman employed to milk cows and to work in a dairy.

milkman, n. [1. mílkman; 2. mílkmən]. **a** A man who sells and distributes milk by retail; a dairyman; **b** a man who milks and attends to cows.

milk pudding, n. A baked pudding made of rice, sago &c., and sweetened milk.

milk-punch, n. A punch made of spirits and sweetened milk.

milk-sickness, n. A cattle-disease prevalent in the Western States of the U.S.A., also transmitted to persons feeding on the meat, milk &c. of the affected cattle.

milksop, n. [1. mílksop; 2. mílksɔp]. **milk** (I.) & **-sop**. A feeble, effeminate, timid man or boy, who shrinks from danger or hardship.

milk-sugar, n. Sugar of milk; lactose.

milk-tooth, n. One of the first, temporary set of teeth in mammals.

milkweed, n. [1. milkwēd; 2. mílkwīd]. Popular name of many common plants having a milky juice or sap, esp. the cow-parsley.

milk-white, adj. Of the colour of milk, white as milk.

milkwood, n. [1. mílkwood; 2. mílkwud]. Popular name of many tropical trees which yield a milk or latex.

milkwort, n. [1. mílkwĕrt; 2. mílkwʌ̄t]. Popular name of a perennial plant, *Polygala*, growing in meadows, formerly said to increase milk in cows eating it.

milky, adj. [1. mílki; 2. mílki]. **milk** (I.) & **-y**. **1.** Like milk, in colour or consistency. **2. a** Mixed with milk; **b** yielding milk, as a plant. *The Milky Way*, the Galaxy, the luminous belt, consisting of countless stars and nebulae, stretching across the night sky.

mill (I.), n. [1. mil; 2. mil]. O.E. *mylen*, *myln*, M.E. *mulne*, *mulle*, *mille* &c., fr. L. Lat. *mulīna*, Lat. *molīna*, 'mill', fr. *mola*, 'millstone'; whence *molere*, 'to grind', see **molar** (I.); cogn. w. Gk. *múlē*, 'mill', see also **meal** (I.). **1. a** Apparatus driven by wind, water, steam &c., for grinding grain into flour; **b** whole building and structure containing and attached to the actual mill. **2.** Small machine, worked by hand, for grinding coffee, or pepper. **3. a** Machinery for manufacturing various materials, and the works or factory in which the work of manufacturing is carried out: *paper-mill, cotton-mill* &c.; also **b** *saw-mill*, large apparatus, and the buildings and yards adjacent to it, for sawing timber. **3.** (slang) A boxing-match, prize-fight, fight with the fists.

mill (II.), vb. trans. & intrans., fr. prec. **A.** trans. **1.** To treat in, put through, a mill or other machinery (in various specif. senses); **a** to grind and reduce to flour, powder, or pulp: *to mill grain, paper*; *to mill ore*, by crushing &c.; **b** *to mill steel*, make it into bars; *to mill cloth*, to full it; **c** *to mill a coin*, to raise its edge and cut it into ridges, to prevent clipping. **2. a** To whip, churn, (chocolate) into a froth; **b** (slang) to strike with the fists. **B.** intrans. **1.** To make use of a mill. **2.** (slang) To fight with the fists. **3.** (of cattle &c.) To move round and round in a circle.

mill (III.), n. Formed on anal. of *cent*, fr. Lat. *millēsimus*, 'thousandth', fr. *mille*, 'thousand'. See **mile**. (Am.) A one-thousandth part of the dollar, as a money of account.

millboard, n. [1. mílbord; 2. mílbɔ̄d]. **mill** (II.) & **board**. Strong stout pasteboard used in book-binding.

mill-dam, n. **mill** (I.) & **dam** (II.). The dam of a mill-pond.

millenarian, adj. & n. [1. milenárian; 2. milinéəriən]. **millenary** & **-an**. **1.** adj. Of, concerning, the millennium: *millenarian prophecies*. **2.** n. A believer in the speedy coming of the millennium; millennialist.

millenarianism, n. [1. milenárianizm; 2. mìlinéəriənizəm]. Prec. & **-ism**. Doctrine of, belief in, the millennium.

millenary, adj. & n. [1. milénari; 2. milénəri], fr. Lat. *millēnārius*, 'containing a thousand', fr. *millēni*, 'a thousand each', fr. *mille*, 'thousand'. See **mile**. **1.** adj. **a** Consisting of a thousand, esp. of a thousand years; **b** of, concerning, the millennium; millennial. **2.** n. **a** Period of a thousand years; **b** a thousandth anniversary; celebration of this.

millennial, adj. [1. milénial; 2. miléniəl]. See **millennium** & **-al**. Of the millennium.

millennialism n. [1. milénializm; 2. miléniəlizəm]. Prec. & **-ism**. Millenarianism.

millennialist, n. [1. milénialist; 2. miléniəlist]. See prec. & **-ist**. Millenarian.

millennium, n. [1. milénium; 2. miléniəm], popular pl. *millenniums*, learned (Lat.) pl. *millennia*. Formed, on anal. of Lat. *biennium*, 'period of two years', fr. Lat. *mille*, 'thousand', see **mile**, & *annum*, 'year', see **annual**. **1. a** A period of a thousand years; **b** specif., that during which Christ at His second Advent will reign on earth, as in Revelation xx. **2.** A period of peace and great prosperity; a golden age, esp. such an age regarded as visionary.

millepede, n. See **millipede**.

millepore, n. [1. mílipōr; 2. mílipō], fr. Lat. *mille*, 'thousand', see **mile**, & **pore** (I.). A genus of coral, with numerous minute pores in a smooth surface.

miller, n. [1. míler; 2. mílə]. **mill** (II.) & **-er**. **a** One who works or owns a flour- or corn-mill; **b** (entom.) the popular name for some varieties of moths whose wings are powdered with a fine white dust.

millerite (I.), n. [1. mílerīt; 2. míləraít], fr. W. H. Miller, d. 1880, British mineralogist, & **-ite**. (mineral.) Nickel sulphide.

Millerite (II.), n., fr. W. Miller, d. 1849, American millenarian, & **-ite**. A follower of Miller, who predicted the coming of the millennium in 1843.

miller's thumb, n. [1. mílerz thùm; 2. míləz þàm]. The popular name of a small fresh-water fish, *Cottus gobio*, allied to the gudgeon, also called the bull-head.

millesimal, adj. & n. [1. milésimal; 2. milésiməl], fr. Lat. *millēsimus*, 'thousandth', fr. *mīlle*, 'thousand', see **mile**, & **-al**. **a** adj. Thousandth; having a thousand parts; **b** n., a thousandth part.

millet, n. [1. mílet; 2. mílit], fr. Fr. *millet*, dimin. of *mil*, fr. Lat. *milium*, 'millet', cogn. w. Gk. *melinē*; etymol. doubtful. **a** An East Indian cereal grass, *Panicum miliaceum*, cultivated in S. Europe, Asia, and N. Africa for the food value of its seeds; **b** the name of various other cereal grasses, cultivated for the same reason or as fodder; **c** a tall North American woodland grass.

mill-hand, n. A worker, operative, in a mill or factory, esp. a cotton-mill.

milli-, pref. Form of Lat. *mīlle*, 'thousand', see **mile**, used in compounds to express a thousandth part of a weight or measure in the metric system.

milliard, n. [1. míliard; 2. míliād]. Fr., fr. Lat. *mīlle*, 'thousand', see **mile**. A thousand millions, the billion of French and American usage.

millibar, n. [1. mílibar; 2. mílibā]. **milli-** & **barometer**. (meteor.) A thousandth part of a *bar* (pressure of mercury column 29·53 inches high), as unit of atmospheric pressure.

milligramme, n. [1. míligram; 2. míligræm]. **milli-** & **gramme**. One-thousandth part of a gramme, ·0154 of a grain.

millilitre, n. [1. mílilèter; 2. míliltə]. **milli-** & **litre**. One-thousandth part of a litre; ·06102 cubic inch.

millimetre, n. [1. mílimèter; 2. mílimītə]. See prec. & **metre**. One-thousandth part of a metre; ·03937 in.

milliner, n. [1. míliner; 2. mílinə]. Earlier form also *millaner*, fr. Milan, town in Italy. **a** Originally a dealer, usually a man, in small wares, such as needles, gloves, ribbons, lace &c. imported from Milan; a haberdasher; **b** a woman who makes up and trims women's hats, and who also sells ribbons and other articles of millinery.

millinery, n. [1. mílineri; 2. mílinəri]. Prec. & **-y**. **a** Articles such as hats, lace, ribbons, and other trimmings &c. sold by a milliner; **b** a milliner's business, and premises.

milling, vbl. n. [1. míling; 2. míliŋ]. **mill** (II.) & **-ing**. **1.** Act, process, occupation, of grinding or working material in a mill, esp. a flour-mill. **2. a** The raising of the edge of a coin in a mill or press and serrating it with raised ridges; **b** milled edge of a coin.

million, n. & adj. [1. mílyun; 2. míljən]. Fr., fr. Ital. *millione*, L. Lat. *mīlliōn-(em)*, fr. Lat. *mīlle*, 'thousand'. See **mile**. **1.** n. **a** A thousand thousand; ten hundred thousand; **b** a million monetary units, pounds, dollars, francs &c.: *worth two millions*; *spent millions*; **c** an extremely large or indefinite number: *millions of reasons* &c.; **d** (with *the*) the majority of people, the masses: *to play down to the million*. **2.** adj. Numbering, amounting to, a million.

millionaire, n. [1. milyunâr; 2. miljənéə]. Fr. *millionnaire*. Prec. & **-aire**. **a** A person whose wealth amounts to a million pounds, dollars, francs &c.; **b** loosely, an extremely wealthy person.

millionairess, n. [1. mìlyunâres; 2. mìljənéəris]. Prec. & **-ess**. A woman millionaire.

millionfold, adj. & adv. [1. mílyunfōld; 2. míljənfould]. **million** & **-fold**. **a** adj. A million times as much; **b** adv., a million times.

millionth, adj. & n. [1. mílyunth; 2. míljənþ]. As prec. & **-th**. **a** adj. Forming one part of that which is divided into a million parts; **b** n., one of a million parts.

millipede, millepede, n. [1. mílipēd; 2. mílipīd], fr. Lat. *millepeda*, 'a wood-louse', fr. *mīlle*, 'thousand', see **mile**, & *ped-(em)*, *pēs*, 'foot'. See **pedal**. Insect with a very large number of legs, having a segmented body, and a pair of legs on either side at each segment, e.g. a wood-louse.

mill-pond, n. **mill** (I.) & **pond**. The pool or pond formed by a mill-dam, whence the water flows to drive a water-wheel. Phr. *calm as, like, a mill-pond*, said of a very, exceptionally, calm sea.

mill-race, n. See prec. & **race** (I.). The stream or current of water which turns a mill-wheel.

Mills bomb, n. [1. mílz bóm; 2. mílz bóm], fr. name of inventor. An oval-shaped hand grenade.

millstone, n. [1. mílstōn; 2. mílstoun]. **mill** (I.) & **stone**. **a** One of the pair of circular stones used for grinding corn &c. into flour, the upper one of which moves upon the immovable nether, lower, bed: **b** stone used for mill-stones. Phrs. *between the upper and the nether millstone*, in an inextricably difficult position, between two merciless forces; *hard as the nether millstone*, merciless, heartless, unfeeling, the lower or bed millstone being of harder stone than the upper, or of iron; *see (look) through a millstone*, have very acute, sharp, senses, esp. of sight. *Millstone grit*, (geol.) a very hard sandstone.

mill-stream, n. A mill-race.

mill-tail, n. The water of a mill after it has turned and passed the mill-wheel.

mill-wheel, n. The wheel which turns the machinery of a water-mill.

millwright, n. [1. mílrīt; 2. mílrait]. One who constructs and fits the machinery of a mill.

milreis, n. [1. mílrās; 2. mílréis]. Port. *mil*, 'thousand', & *reis*, pl. of *real*. See **reis**. **a** A former Portuguese gold coin (value about 4s. 6d.); **b** a Portuguese and Brazilian money of account, one thousand reis.

milt (I.), n. [1. milt; 2. milt]. O.E. *milte*; O.H.G. *milzi*, O.N. *milti*; fr. **meltja-*. See **melt**. The spleen.

milt (II.), n. & vb. trans. Possibly the same word as prec., cp. M. Du. *milte*, 'milt of a fish'; but usually explained as an adaptation of *milk*, 'the milt of fish', to *milt*, 'spleen'; cp. similar use in Germ. & Dan. **a** n. The male roe of fish; (also attrib.) of male fish in the breeding season: *a milt herring*; **b** vb., to impregnate the female roe.

milter, n. [1. mílter; 2. míltə]. A male fish in the breeding season.

mime, n. & vb. intrans. [1. mīm; 2. maim], fr. Lat. *mīmus*, fr. Gk. *mīmos*, 'an imitator, actor'; etymol. unknown. **1.** n. **a** (Gk. and Rom. antiq.) A form of farce, depicting scenes from real life, in which mimicry and dancing played a great part; **b** an actor taking part in a mime; **c** a mimic, buffoon, jester. **2.** vb. To act in a mime; to play the mimic, to act with gestures, as in pantomime.

mimeograph, n. & vb. trans. [1. mímōgrahf; 2. máimougrāf]. Word coined fr. prec. & **-graph**. **1.** n. A device for making a stencil copy of writing from which other copies can be taken. **2.** vb. To make copies of MSS. with a mimeograph.

mimesis, n. [1. mīmēsis; 2. maimísis]. Gk., 'imitation'. See **mime**. (biol.) Imitation, mimicry; the protective resemblance in colour, markings &c. of an animal to its environment, or to another animal.

mimetic, adj. [1. mīmétik; 2. maimétik], fr. Gk. *mīmētikós*, 'imitative'. See **mime**. Imitative; pertaining to, characterized by, mimicry or mimesis.

mimic (I.), adj. & n. [1. mímik; 2. mímik], fr. Lat. *mīmicus*, 'of or belonging to mimes or farces; farcical, feigned, mimic'. See **mime** & **-ic**. **1.** adj. **a** Apt, inclined, to imitate or copy; imitative, mimetic: *the mimic habit* (of animals); '*mimic Fancy wakes to imitate her*' (Milton); *the mimic stage*; **b** imitative; not real, feigned, sham: *mimic eloquence*; *mimic tears*; *mimic colouration*; **c** imitated, copied, mock; (often with dimin. sense) *mimic fleet, battle*. **2.** n. One who imitates, burlesques, caricatures, the characteristic mode of speech, appearance, gestures &c. of another.

mimic (II.), vb. trans., fr. prec. **a** To copy, imitate, burlesque, reproduce in a grotesque manner, ape: *to mimic another's voice, manner* &c.; **b** to resemble closely, have the exact appearance of: *in a mirage the desert will mimic a lake or the sea*; **c** (biol.) to take on the colour, markings, shape &c. of environment, or of another animal or object.

mimicry, n. [1. mímikri; 2. mímikri]. **mimic** (I.) & **-ry**. **a** Act, skill, practice, of imitating, copying, or mimicking; imitation, burlesque; **b** (biol.) resemblance assumed by animals to their environment, in colour &c.

mimosa, n. [1. mimóza; 2. mimóuzə]. Invented word, fr. Lat. *mīmus*, 'mime, mimic', see **mime**. (bot.) A genus of low trees and shrubs, allied to the Acacias, prickly, bearing seeds in a pod, and having clusters of small yellow flowers; some species, as the Sensitive Plant, curl the leaves when touched, whence the name.

mimulus, n. [1. mímūlus; 2. mímjuləs]. Lat., 'little mime'; dimin. of **mime**. (bot.) A genus of flowering plants, including the monkey-flower and musk.

mina (I.), n. [1. mína; 2. máinə]. Lat., fr. Gk. *mnā*; of Semitic origin; cp. the Heb. weight *maneh*. (Gk. antiq.) A weight and a sum of money, equivalent to about 15 oz. troy and £4 respectively.

mina (II.). See **myna**.

minacious, adj. [1. mināshus; 2. minéiʃəs], fr. Lat. *mināc-(em)*, *minax*, 'threatening', fr. *minārī*, 'to threaten'. See **minatory** & **-ous**. Threatening, minatory, menacing.

minaret, n. [1. mínaret; 2. mínərɛt], fr. Span. *minarete*, for Arab. *manārat*, 'tower of a mosque, lighthouse'; also 'candlestick'. (archit.) A tall slender tower, or spire-like erection, attached to a mosque, with balconied top from which the faithful are summoned to prayer.

minatory, adj. [1. mínatori, mínatori; 2. mínətəri, máinətəri], fr. L. Lat. *minātōrius*, fr. *minārī*, 'to threaten'; fr. *minae*, 'projecting points, pinnacles, of walls'; fig. 'threats'; fr. base **men-*, 'to project, stand out', q.v. under **mount** (I.). See also **menace**. Threatening, menacing.

mince (I.), vb. trans. & intrans. [1. mins; 2. mins], fr. O. Fr. *mincier*, *mincer*, fr. Low Lat. **minūtiāre*, 'to make small', fr. L. Lat. *minūtia*, 'a small piece', fr. *minūtus*, 'small'. See **minutiae** & **minute** (I.). **A.** trans. **1.** To cut, chop (meat &c.), into very fine, small, pieces. **2.** (fig.) To express in a mild, feeble, way; to weaken, tone down, palliate. Phr. *not to mince matters, one's words*, to state the plain, blunt truth. **B.** intrans. To move or speak in an affected, finicky manner, with an air of prim delicacy: '*the daughters of Zion . . . mincing as they go*' (Isaiah iii. 16).

mince (II.), n., fr. prec. **a** Meat minced or chopped up fine; **b** dish or course consisting of this.

mincemeat, n. [1. mínsmēt; 2. mínsmīt]. Rich mixture of raisins, currants, candied peel, apples, suet, brandy &c., served, usually hot, in covering of pastry. Phr. *to make mincemeat of*, (i.) to defeat utterly, put out of action (an opponent in a fight); (ii.) to refute, tear to shreds (an argument, claim &c.).

mince-pie, n. Covered pie, usually small, filled with mincemeat.

mincing, adj. [1. mínsing; 2. mínsiŋ]. Pres. Part. of **mince (I.)**. Affectedly delicate or prim, in speech or bearing.

mincingly, adv. Prec. & **-ly**. In an affected, delicate manner; primly.

mincing machine, n. Device consisting of revolving blades for mincing meat &c.

mind (I.), n. [1. mīnd; 2. maind]. O.E. (*ġe*)*mynd*, 'memory', M.E. *mīnd*, 'memory, mind'; O.H.G. *gimunt*; cp. also O.E. (*ġe*)*munan*, 'to remember, think'; cogn. w. Lat. *ment-(em)*, 'mind', see **mental (I.)**; Lith. (*at*)*mintis*; O. Slav. (*pa*)*męti*, 'memory'; Scrt. *mati-*, 'thought, sense, meaning'. **1.** Memory, recollection, remembrance: *to bear, keep, in mind*; *to call to mind*; *put in mind of*, to remind. Phr. *time out of mind*, period outside, beyond, anyone's memory; time immemorial. **2. a** (philos.) Consciousness or intelligence, as contrasted with *matter*; **b** (psychol.) consciousness, subject, source of consciousness, (i.) that part of man which thinks, feels, and wills, as contrasted with *body*; (ii.) that part of consciousness which thinks but does not feel or will, as contrasted with *soul*. **3.** Individual mental faculties, intellect; intellectual capacity or power: *a strong, weak, profound, shallow, mind*. Phrs. *out of one's mind*, mad, insane; *the mind's eye*, mental range, grasp, vision; *to turn one's mind to*, direct one's attention, thoughts, to; *frame of mind*, passing mood; *to keep one's mind on*, concentrate attention on, continue to think of; *to take one's mind off*, distract, distract attention from; *to have something on one's mind*, be anxious, worried, about something; *absence of mind*, absent-mindedness; *presence of mind*, readiness of decision in emergency. **4.** A human being thought of primarily as an intellectual force: *the great minds of the world*; *no two minds work alike*. **5.** Characteristic mode of thought, cast of intellect, mental constitution: *the Greek mind*; *the popular mind* &c. **6.** Opinion, thought, intention, decision, wish, inclination. Phrs. *to read another's mind*, discern what he is thinking of; *to speak one's mind*, declare one's thoughts; *make up one's mind*, come to a decision; *to be of one mind (with)*, agree (with); *to one's mind*, **a** in one's opinion: *to my mind the action was premature*; **b** to one's liking, *he found life in India very much to his mind*; *to change, alter, one's mind*, change one's intentions; *to open one's mind to*, tell one's views, feelings, thoughts, freely and candidly; *to be in two minds*, to hesitate; *to give (person) a piece of one's mind*, (i.) tell him bluntly one's opinion of him and his acts; (ii.) to rate him soundly; *to have half a mind to*, to be rather inclined to do something; *have a good mind to*, feel much disposed, have almost decided, to do something.

mind (II.), vb. trans. & intrans., fr. prec. **A.** trans. **1. a** (obs. or provinc.) To remember, keep in mind: *I mind the time when . . .*; **b** (as command) *mind what was told you*; *mind our appointment next week*. **2. a** To attend to, take heed of, pay attention to; to regard, obey: *mind one's own business*, not interfere with other people's affairs; *to mind rules, regulations* &c.; *mind what I tell you*; *do not mind what other people say*; **b** to watch, be careful of, look out for: *mind the dog, the step, that motor-car*. Phrs. *mind your eye*, (slang) look out!; *to mind one's p's and q's*, to be very careful of what one says and does. **3. a** (in interrog. or neg. constructions) To care, be troubled about, to object to, to dislike: *do you mind my cigar? I don't mind it a bit*; *he doesn't mind what he spends on hunters*; *I don't mind walking*; Phrs. *I should not mind a holiday now*, I should like a holiday; *do you mind holding your tongue?*, you are to hold your tongue; *I don't mind telling you that the man is a swindler*, emphatic assertion; **b** (in declaratory sentences in reply to questions) *do you mind going without dinner? yes, I mind it very much*; (in contrasting) *I don't mind hard work, but I do mind insufficient pay*. **4.** To take care of, look after, attend to: *to mind the house, the children*; *a shepherd minds his sheep*; *the wife minds the household accounts*. **B.** intrans. **1.** To attend, take heed, be careful; *if you don't mind, you'll get run over*; *mind! you'll slip*; *now mind and do what you're told*; *he was often warned of his danger but he never minded*. **2. a** To feel dislike, object: *do you mind if I smoke? I don't mind a bit*; **b** to care, be affected: *he appears not to feel leaving home, but he really minds a great deal*. Phrs. *never mind!*, don't distress yourself; it is of no consequence; *I don't mind if I do*, casual mode of accepting an offer: *will you have some?, some more?* &c.

minded, adj. [1. mínded; 2. máindid]. **mind (I.)** & **-ed**. **1.** Having a mind to, disposed to, inclined: *he was not so minded*, had no such intention. **2.** (usually qualified) Having such or a special kind of mind, character, or disposition: *strong-, weak-minded*; *evil-minded* &c.

minder, n. [1. mínder; 2. máində]. One who minds, attends to, looks after: *the minder of the house*; *a machine-minder*.

mindful, adj. [1. míndfool; 2. máindfəl]. **mind (I.)** & **-ful**. Keeping, bearing in mind; attentive, observant of, careful; taking thought for: *mindful of one's duties*.

mindfully, adv. Prec. & **-ly**. In a mindful manner; attentively, carefully.

mindless, adj. [1. míndles; 2. máindlis]. **mind (I.)** & **-less**. **a** Without mind, thought, or consciousness; unintelligent, stupid: *pass mindless hours in idleness*; *a mindless act, person* &c.; **b** not paying attention to, regardless of; careless, heedless: *mindless of what is to happen*.

mine (I.), possess. adj. [1. mīn; 2. main]. O.E. *mīn*; O.S., O.H.G. *mīn*; Goth. *meins*, declined as adj. in O.E. &c.; orig. genit. sing. of *ić*, 'I', O.E. *mīn*; cp. Goth. *meina*, 'of me'. Cp. **me**. **1.** (obs. or archaic and poet.) **a** Before words beginning with a vowel or *h-*: *mine eyes, mine heart* &c.; **b** in inverted constructions: *lady mine* &c. **2.** (when absol.) **a** (pred.) *That umbrella is mine*, belonging to me, not yours &c.; *the game is mine*, won by me; **b** *a friend of mine*, one of my friends; *no business of mine*, not my business.

mine (II.), n. [1. mīn; 2. main]. In M.E. as vb., fr. Fr. *mine*, n., also *miner*, vb.; etymol. doubtful, perh. Celt.; cp. Ir. & Gael. *mein*, 'ore, vein (of metal)'. **1.** A shaft or passage, or shaft and passages dug or sunk in the earth for the extraction of metal, coal, salt, or any mineral other than stone; *coal-mine, gold-mine, copper-mine, diamond-mine* &c. Phr. (fig.) *a mine of wealth, of information* &c., copious source of. **2. a** The shafts, passages, machinery, plant, and buildings &c. of a mine; **b** the mining industry: (in pl.) *the mines*. **3.** (mil.) **a** An underground passage or sap leading to the foot of a wall or earthwork for making a breach in or destroying these; **b** a charge of explosive used in such a passage for destroying walls or earthworks; similar charge for destroying railways, bridges &c., or for general destructive purpose in war; also *land mine*; Phr. *to spring a mine on one*, to surprise unpleasantly; **c** (fig.) a secret plot, scheme &c.: *to lay a mine for*, to overthrow, surprise, or defeat; **d** a large high-explosive shell, discharged at short distances, as in trench-warfare &c., from a mortar. **4.** (nav.) A charge of high explosive contained in a watertight metal case, exploded on contact or electrically, and either floating on the surface of the water, *surface-mine*, or submerged, *submarine mine*, used in war to protect harbours, rivers, or to block a channel or large area of sea against the enemy fleet.

mine (III.), vb. trans. & intrans. See prec. **A.** trans. **1. a** To dig or excavate a passage or shaft in: *to mine the earth for coal, gold*; **b** to extract (ore &c.) from the earth by a mine: *to mine coal*. **2.** To dig, drive, a passage to, and explode a land mine under; to sap; to explode a floating or submerged mine under: *to mine the wall of a fortress* &c.; *the ship was mined*. **3.** To lay explosive mines in or under: *the navy mined the Channel*. **4.** (fig.) To undermine, destroy, or cause to collapse by secret means, plots &c.: *his political career was mined*. **B.** intrans. **1.** To carry out the operation **a** of sinking a mine; **b** of extracting coal &c. from a mine; **c** to burrow into, scratch, the earth, (said of animals). **2.** To lay explosive mines on land or sea.

minefield, n. [1. mínfēld; 2. máinfīəld]. **a** Area in which coal, gold, or other mines exist; **b** (mil. and nav.) area of land or sea in which mines have been laid.

minelayer, n. [1. mínlàer; 2. máinlèiə]. A vessel specially equipped for laying mines at sea.

miner, n. [1. míner; 2. máinə]. Fr. *mineur*. **mine (II.)** & **-er**. **a** One who works in a mine; properly one who works underground, but also loosely used of one who is employed in or about a mine, either underground or on the surface; *miner's disease*, a form of anaemia, due to an intestinal parasitic worm, the hookworm, to which miners are liable; ankylostomiasis; **b** (mil.) soldier trained to dig tunnels, or sap, in siege work; usually *sapper and miner*, member of Corps of Royal Engineers.

mineral (I.), n. [1. míneral; 2. mín(ə)rəl], fr. Fr. *minéral*, Mod. Lat. *minerālis*, fr. *mināria*, *minara*, O. Fr. *miniere*, 'a mine'. See **mine (II.)**. **1.** (in popular usage) Any substance which is neither animal nor vegetable. **2.** (chem.) Any inorganic element or compound which has a constant chemical composition. **3.** Any substance which is extracted from the earth by mining or from mines, including the metals, stone, and also coal, which is not chemically a **mineral**. **4.** (popular, usually pl.) Mineral water.

mineral (II.), adj., fr. prec. **a** Of, belonging to, minerals; consisting of, containing, mineral; **b** (chem.) inorganic.

mineralization, n. [1. mìneralīzáshun; 2. mìnərəlaizéiʃən]. See next word & **-ation**. Act, process, of mineralizing; state of being mineralized.

mineralize, vb. trans. & intrans. [1. míneralīz; 2. mínərəlaiz]. **mineral** & **-ize**. **1.** trans. **a** To convert into a mineral or into mineral form: *coal is mineralized vegetation*; **b** (chem.) to combine with a metal to form an ore; **c** to impregnate water with mineral salts. **2.** intrans. To search, look, for minerals.

mineralizer, n. [1. míneralīzer; 2. mínərəlaizə]. Prec. & **-er**. **a** (chem.) A substance which combines with a metal to form an ore; **b** one who mineralizes or searches for minerals.

mineralogical, adj. [1. mìneralójikl; 2. mìnərəlɔ́džikl]. **mineral** & **-logic** & **-al**. Of or pertaining to mineralogy: *a mineralogical collection, examination* &c.

mineralogically, adv. Prec. & **-ly**. In a mineralogical way, from a mineralogical aspect: *mineralogically considered*.

mineralogist, n. [1. mìnerálojist; 2. mìnərǽlədžist]. See next word & **-ist**. Student of mineralogy.

mineralogy, n. [1. mìneráloji; 2. mìnərǽlədži], fr. **mineral** & **-logy**. The science of minerals, their classification, structure, and properties.

mineral water, n. **1.** Water naturally impregnated with a mineral, or mineral salts, esp. those of a medicinal character. **2.** (popular) An aerated drink, such as soda-water, lemonade, ginger-beer &c.

mine-sweeper, n. Trawler or other vessel fitted with nets for sweeping up and destroying mines in a minefield at sea.

mine-thrower, n. Transl. of Germ. *minen-*

werfer. Mortar for throwing charges of high explosive in trench-warfare.

minever, miniver, n. [1. míniver; 2. mínivə]. M.E. *meniver*, O. Fr. *menu ver, menu vair*, fr. *menu*, 'small, little', & *vair*, 'a spotted fur', fr. Lat. *varius*, 'variegated, spotted'. See **menu, vair, various.** a A white fur used in ceremonial costume, with symmetrically arranged black patches or tabs; b the fur of the ermine in its winter coat showing the black tips of the tail.

mingle, vb. trans. & intrans. [1. mínggl; 2. míŋgl]. M.E. *mengel*, frequent. form of *mengen*, O.E. *mengan*, fr. same base as **among & mongrel.** 1. trans. To combine with, mix, blend together: *to mingle wine and water; the ashes of saint and king are mingled in the Abbey.* Phr. *mingled feelings*, partly pleasurable, partly the reverse. 2. intrans. a To mix, blend: *the colours don't mingle well*; b to join, mix with: *to mingle in the crowd.*

mingle-mangle, n. Reduplication of prec. A medley, confusion, hodge-podge, olla-podrida: *a mingle-mangle of ideas.*

miniate, vb. trans. [1. míniāt; 2. mínieit]. See next word & **minium.** 1. To paint with vermilion. 2. To decorate, illuminate, as a manuscript, with ornamental letters.

miniature, n., adj., & vb. trans. [1. míni(a)chur; 2. míni(ə)tʃə], fr. Ital. *miniatura*, fr. Lat. *miniāt-(um)*, P.P. type of *miniāre*, 'to paint in red lead or vermilion', esp. used of initial or other letters in MSS. &c. coloured red as mark of distinction. See **minium & -ure.** 1. n. a A coloured initial letter or small coloured picture in an illuminated manuscript; b a small highly finished portrait, usually painted on ivory. Phr. *in miniature*, on a small scale. 2. adj. a Represented, depicted, in the form of a miniature: *a miniature portrait*; b made, planned, formed, on a small scale; having less than usual size of things of the same kind: *a miniature park, quadrangle* &c. 3. vb. To depict, represent, in miniature or on a small scale.

miniaturist, n. [1. mínichurist; 2. mínitʃərist]. Prec. & **-ist.** One who paints miniatures.

Minié bullet, rifle, n. [1. míniā, míni; 2. míniei, míni], fr. Minié, name of French inventor. A conical, expanding bullet; rifle for firing this.

minify, vb. trans. [1. mínifī; 2. mínifai]. Formed w. **-fy,** fr. Lat. *mini-*, as in **minimum.** To make small or smaller; to lessen, diminish, minimize, contrasted with *magnify.*

minikin, n. [1. mínikin; 2. mínikin], fr. O. Du. *minneken*, 'darling, fondling', fr. *minne*, 'love', see **minnesinger,** & dimin. *-ken*, see **-kin.** A diminutive, undersized, delicate, person or object.

minim, n. [1. mínim; 2. mínim], fr. Lat. *minimus*, 'smallest, least', superl. of *minor*, 'smaller, less'. See **minimum.** 1. (mus.) A note, originally that of shortest duration, now of the value or time of half a semibreve or two crotchets. 2. (of liquid measure) One-sixtieth of a fluid drachm; a drop. 3. An object of the smallest size; a particle, jot, tittle. 4. (R.C. Ch., cap.) An order of mendicant friars.

minimal, adj. [1. míniml; 2. míniməl]. Prec. & **-al.** Smallest, least, minimum.

minimalist, n. [1. mínimalist; 2. míniməlist]. Prec. & **-ist.** Person willing to accept a minimum of his demands as a compromise.

minimalize, vb. trans. [1. mínimalīz; 2. míniməlaiz]. Prec. & **-ize.** To minimize.

minimization, n. [1. mìnimīzā́shun; 2. mìnimaizéiʃən]. See next word & **-ation.** Act, process, of minimizing; state of being minimized.

minimize, vb. trans. [1. mínimīz; 2. mínimaiz], fr. **minim & -ize.** 1. To reduce to a minimum, to lessen: *to minimize friction; to minimize danger.* 2. To conceive of, or represent, as being smaller, less important, less severe, less excellent &c., than reality; to understate, underrate: *I don't want to minimize your services, the risks you have run* &c.

minimizer, n. [1. mínimīzer; 2. mínimaizə]. Prec. & **-er.** One who tends to minimize; esp. one who understates, and tries to explain away, religious or philosophical doctrines and difficulties.

minimum, n., pl. **minima** [1. mínimum, -ma; 2. mínimәm, -mə]. Lat. neut. sing. of *minimus*, 'least, smallest', superl. of *minor*, 'less, smaller'; fr. base **mei-*, **mi-*, 'small' &c.; 'to diminish; to change; to injure, impair' &c.; cp. Lat. *minuere*, 'to reduce, lessen' &c.; Scrt. *minā́ti*, 'injures'. Gk. *minúthein*, 'to diminish, weaken' &c., *meiōn*, 'smaller' (see **meiosis**); Goth. *mins*, O.E., O.H.G. *min(n)*, 'small' &c. 1. The smallest, least, quantity, amount, or point possible, usual, necessary, or registered; contrasted with *maximum*: *to reduce demands, wages &c. to a minimum; thermometer reached the minimum for the year; shares stand now at a minimum.* 2. (attrib.) *A minimum supply; minimum price, wage* &c.; *a minimum thermometer*, one graduated for registering the lowest degrees of temperature.

minimus, adj. [1. mínimus; 2. míniməs]. Lat. As prec. Third or youngest of three boys at a school of same family, or having the same name, also termed *tertius*, 'third': *Brown minimus*, the eldest and second being *major* and *minor.*

mining, n. [1. míning; 2. máiniŋ], fr. **mine (II.) & -ing.** 1. n. Act, process, business, of working a mine or mines, as *coal-, gold-, diamond-mining* &c. 2. (attrib.) *Mining engineer*, engineer skilled in developing, sinking, or designing machinery for mines.

minion, n. [1. mínyun; 2. mínjən], fr. Fr. *mignon*, adj., 'small, delicate', also as n. See **mignon.** 1. A darling, favourite; specif., a king or queen's favourite, male or female, at a court: *James the First's minion Robert Carr.* 2. A servile, obsequious agent or partisan: *his minions of the press.* 3. (print.) A form of type between *brevier* and *emerald.*

minish, vb. trans. [1. mínish; 2. míniʃ]. fr. M.E. *menusen*, fr. O. Fr. *menuisier*, 'to lessen', fr. Low Lat. **minūtiāre*, 'to make less', fr. Lat. *minūt-(um)*, *minuere*, 'to make small'. See **minute (I.).** (archaic) To cause to lessen; to lower, make small, depreciate, diminish.

minister (I.), n. [1. mínister; 2. mínistə]. M.E. *menistre, ministre*, fr. O. Fr. *menistre*, Mod. Fr. *ministre*, fr. Lat. *minister*, 'a servant, subordinate', contrasted w. *magister*, 'master'; a double compar. fr. *minus*, 'less'. See **minimum.** 1. A servant, agent, subordinate; one who carries out the orders or purpose of a superior: *to act as minister of, to, another's desires, pleasures, will* &c. 2. Specif., a member of the executive government or ministry of a State, in charge of and responsible for a department, acting as the servant of the king or head of the State, whether a member of the Cabinet (*Cabinet minister*) or not, and holding office only as long as the particular ministry lasts. 3. A diplomatic representative or agent to a foreign state; specif., one next in rank below an ambassador. 4. (eccles.) Also *minister of religion*, one who performs spiritual functions or services, one who conducts the worship or service in a church or chapel; specif. a (in England), a nonconformist clergyman; b (in Scotland) clergyman of the Church of Scotland or other Protestant body. Not generally used now of a clergyman of the English Church, though so used in Prayer Book.

minister (II.), vb. intrans. & trans. M.E. *ministren*, O. Fr. *ministrer*, fr. Lat. *ministrāre*, 'to serve'. See prec. 1. intrans. a To act as a servant or minister; to serve; b to render help to, supply wants of: *to minister to a person's needs*; c to be conducive to: *to minister to one's comfort.* 2. trans. (archaic) To administer, perform (a rite &c.).

ministerial, adj. [1. mìnistḗrial; 2. mìnistíəriəl], fr. Fr. *ministériel*, Lat. *ministeriālis*, 'of a minister or servant'. See prec. & **-ial.** 1. a Of or pertaining to a minister or a ministry; performing the functions of a minister; executive, administrative: *ministerial office, duties, prestige* &c.; *the ministerial benches*, those on the Government side, in House of Commons, as contrasted with *Opposition benches*; *the ministerial arm of the law*, as contrasted with *judicial*; b pertaining to a minister of religion. 2. Serving as an agent or instrument, instrumental, subordinate, contributing: *ministerial services*, as contrasted with *directing* or *principal.*

ministerialist, n. [1. mìnistḗrialist; 2. mìnistíəriəlist]. Prec. & **-ist.** A member of the Ministry or Government; member of the party in power or office.

ministerially, adv. [1. mìnistḗriali; 2. mìnistíəriəli]. **ministerial & -ly.** a As in character or position of a minister, or member of the executive of a Government; b in the capacity of a minister of religion.

ministrant, adj. & n. [1. mínistrant; 2. mínistrənt], fr. Lat. *ministrant-(em)*, Pres. Part. of *ministrāre*, 'to serve'. See **minister (II.).** a adj. Serving, acting, as a minister; ministering; b n., one who ministers; helper, supporter.

ministration, n. [1. mìnistrā́shun; 2. mìnistréiʃən], fr. Lat. *ministrātiōn-(em)*, *ministrātio*, 'service, serving', fr. *ministrāt-(um)*, P.P. type of *ministrāre.* See **minister (II.).** Service, aid, help, ministry, esp. of a minister of religion.

ministrative, adj. [1. mínistrativ; 2. mínistrətiv]. Lat. *ministrāt-*, as in prec., & **-ive.** Ministering, helping, aiding.

ministry, n. [1. mínistri; 2. mínistri], fr. Lat. *ministerium.* **minister (I.) & -y.** 1. Office of a minister: a of religion; b of head of a department of State. 2. a Body of ministers, or heads of branches of a legislature; b specif., the Cabinet. 3. a Body of ministers of religion; b the profession of a minister of religion.

minium, n. [1. mínium; 2. míniəm]. Lat., 'cinnabar, vermilion'; etymol. doubtful; possibly a Span. (Iberian) word. Cp. **miniature.** a Bright red colour, vermilion; b (chem.) red oxide of lead.

miniver, n. See **minever.**

mink, n. [1. mingk; 2. miŋk]. Etymol. doubtful; cp. Swed. *menk.* a A semi-aquatic animal, genus *Putorius*, related to the stoat and weasel, valued for its thick brown fur; b the fur of the various species of mink.

minnesinger, n. [1. mínisinger; 2. mínisiŋə]. Mod. Germ., also *minnesänger*, revived fr. O.H.G. *minne*, 'love'; cp. O.S. *minna*, 'love'; fr. **men-*, 'to think of, remember' &c. See **mental (I.), memory.** One of a circle of German lyric poets of 12th, 13th, and 14th cents. who sang their songs of love and beauty to their own music and accompaniment.

minnow, n. [1. mínō; 2. mínou]. M.E. *menow*, 'small fish'; etymol. doubtful; perh. same as Fr. *menu*, 'small', Lat. *minūtus.* See **minute (III.).** a A small freshwater fish of the carp family; loosely, the stickleback &c; Phrs. *to throw out a minnow to catch a whale; a Triton among minnows*; b an artificial metallic bait for fishing.

Minoan, adj. [1. mīnṓan; 2. mainóuən], fr. Gk. *Mínōs*, the legendary king of Crete. Of or relating to the prehistoric art and culture which, centred in Crete, spread over the Aegean and eastern part of the Mediterranean Seas and their coastlands.

minor (I.), adj. [1. mínor; 2. máinə]. Lat., 'less'. See under **minimum.** 1. a Less, smaller; not important; holding an inferior or subordinate position: *a minor injury; a minor planet, poet; the Minor Prophets; minor canon*, a clergyman attached to a cathedral, but not a member of the chapter, who conducts and assists at the services, esp. those parts that require singing; *minor orders*, (in R.C. Ch.) the lesser orders or grades, ranking below that of subdeacon; b (log.) of the term which forms the subject of the conclusion in a syllogism: *minor* *premise*, the premise which contains the minor term. 2. (mus.) Of intervals, less by a semitone than the corresponding major intervals. Phrs. *in a minor key*, in a key in the minor mode, as contrasted with *major*, see **mode**; (fig.) in a melancholy, sad, depressed mood; in a lower tone. 3. Second or younger of two boys at school having the same name; also *secundus*, 'second': *Brown minor*.

minor (II.), n., fr. prec. 1. Person below the age of twenty-one years. 2. (log.) A minor term or premise. 3. (mus.) A minor key, mode, or scale. 4. (eccles., cap.) A Minorite.

Minorca, n. [1. minórka; 2. minɔ́kə]. Name of one of the Balearic Islands. A breed of domestic fowls, a red-faced variety of the black Spanish fowl.

Minorite, n. [1. mínorīt; 2. mínərait], fr. **minor** (I.) & **-ite**. A Franciscan friar, so called because he regarded himself as of humbler rank than a member of the other religious orders.

minority, n. [1. mīnóriti; 2. mainɔ́riti]. On anal. of *majority*, fr. **minor** (I.) & **-ity**. 1. a A smaller number; specif. b the smaller of two parties or totals, esp. the smaller of two aggregates of votes cast. 2. a State of being a minor or under age; b period of life before attainment of legal age, twenty-one years.

Minotaur, n. [1. mínotōr; 2. máinətɔ̄], fr. Gk. *Mīnṓtauros*, fr. *Mīnōs*, Minos, legendary king of Crete, & *taûros*, 'bull', see **taurine**. (mythol.) A legendary monster, half-bull, half-man, who dwelt in the Labyrinth in Crete, and was killed by Theseus with the help of Ariadne.

minster, n. [1. mínster; 2. mínstə]. O.E. *mynster*, fr. Lat. *monastērium*, fr. Gk. See **monastery**. The church of an abbey or monastery, and so used of large churches that were formerly such, and also of some cathedrals, as *York Minster*.

minstrel, n. [1. mínstrel; 2. mínstrəl]. M.E. *ministral, menestrel*, fr. A.-Fr. *menestrel*, fr. L. Lat. *ministrālis*, 'servant, retainer, jester'. See **minister**. 1. a (hist.) A professional musical entertainer of the Middle Ages, either attached to a great household, or wandering from place to place, singing and playing the harp &c., also reciting poems, juggling, performing acrobatic feats &c.; gleeman, jongleur; *minstrels' gallery*, a high projecting gallery for the minstrels at one end of the hall in a mediaeval or Tudor house; b a poet, singer, musician. 2. An itinerant singer or musician; esp. (pl.) a troupe of singers, banjo players &c., with blackened faces, who sing negro melodies &c.: *negro, nigger, Christy, minstrels*.

minstrelsy, n. [1. mínstrelsi; 2. mínstrəlsi]. A.-Fr. *menestralcie*. See prec. 1. a The singing and playing of a minstrel or minstrels; b the art, songs, poetry, of minstrels; c a body of minstrels. 2. (poet.) a Poetry; b song of birds.

mint (I.), n. [1. mint; 2. mint]. O.E. *minte*, fr. Lat. *menta, mentha*, fr. Gk. *mínthē*, 'mint'. An aromatic herb, belonging to the family *Labiatae*, esp. the spearmint, of kitchen gardens; used for flavouring: *mint sauce*, of chopped mint, sugar, and vinegar; used with roast lamb.

mint (II.), n. O.E. *mynet*, 'coin'; M.E. *minte*, fr. Lat. *monēta*, 'mint, a coin, money'; orig. a name of Juno, in whose temple at Rome money was coined; fr. *monēre*, 'to remind, warn' (see **monition**), or possibly fr. a tribal name. Cf. **money**. 1. The place, esp. one under State control, where money is coined and stamped. Phrs. *a mint of money*, a great quantity; (also fig.) *a mint of trouble*. 2. Source, origin, of ideas, invention, fabrication &c.: *one may guess the mint of these plots and intrigues*.

mint (III.), vb. trans., fr. prec. a To stamp, coin (money); b (fig.) to invent, coin (phrases, words &c.).

mintage, n. [1. míntij; 2. míntidž]. **mint** (II.) & **-age**. a Process, result, of minting; b coinage, money; esp. such as is issued from a particular mint or at a special time; c charge for minting.

mint-julep, n. A drink of brandy or whisky, sugar, and ice, flavoured with sprigs of mint.

mint mark, n. Mark on a coin showing where it was minted.

mint state, n. Fresh, untouched state of a coin as when just minted; also used of fresh, unspoiled states of prints, postage-stamps &c.

minuet, n. [1. mìnūét; 2. mìnjuét], fr. Fr. *menuet*, fr. *menu*, 'small', see **minute** (III.); the dance is performed with short, small steps. a A slow, stately dance, of French origin, dating from the middle of the 17th cent.; b music, in triple measure, composed for this dance.

minus, adj. & n. [1. mínus; 2. máinəs]. Lat., neut. sing. of *minor*, 'less'. See **minimum**, **minor**. 1. adj. a Less; deducted or to be deducted from; subtracted, contrasted with *plus*: *a minus sign* (−), as opposed to *plus sign* (+); b negative, as contrasted with *positive*: *a minus quantity*; (elect.) *minus charge*, a negative charge; c deprived of, wanting: (also used with prepositional force) *minus any profit; minus an eye; minus one's clothes*. 2. n. a A minus sign (−); b a minus quantity; c a minus mark awarded in an examination paper.

minuscule, n. [1. minúskūl; 2. minʌ́skjūl]. Fr., fr. Lat. *minusculus*, 'rather small', dimin. of *minus*, 'less, smaller'. See prec. a A small cursive letter in ancient manuscripts, as distinguished from *majuscule* or *uncial*; b (mod. typog.) a lower-case letter.

minute (I.), n. [1. mínit; 2. mínit]. Fr., fr. Lat. *minūta*, fem. of P.P. *minūtus*, of *minuere*, 'to make smaller, diminish, lessen', fr. base *min-*, as in **minimum**; Lat. has *minūtum*, 'a mite, farthing', but the sense of one 60th part comes fr. Med. Lat. *minuta pars prima* of each of the 60 divisions of the 360 parts into wh. the circumference of a circle was divided, cp. **second** (IV.). 1. a The 60th part of an hour or degree, 60 seconds; b a very short space of time; an instant, moment: *wait half a minute*; *in a few minutes*. Phr. *to the minute*, at the exact time fixed. 2. a A short draft, note, or memorandum containing instructions, authority for certain action &c.; b in pl., *the minutes*, summary, notes made, record taken, of proceedings at a meeting.

minute (II.), vb. trans., fr. prec. a To time, take the time of, accurately or to the minute: *to minute a race, the duration of an eclipse* &c.; b to record in the form of minutes: *to minute the proceedings of a meeting*. Phr. *to minute down*, note down.

minute (III.), adj. [1. mīnū́t; 2. mainjū́t]. Lat. *minūtus*, 'small'. See **minute** (I.). 1. (of size, scale, time &c.) Very small: *minute particles, graduations, periods*. 2. Trifling, petty, insignificant: *to be troubled with minute differences*. 3. Concerned with small details; careful, searching, meticulous, precise: *minute researches, investigation, criticism*.

minute bell, n. Bell tolled at intervals of a minute, as signal of mourning or death.

minute-book, n. A book in which the minutes of a meeting &c. are recorded.

minute-glass, n. A sand-glass for registering minutes.

minute-gun, n. A gun fired at intervals of a minute, as a signal of distress, as by a ship at sea, or of mourning at a death.

minute-hand, n. The long hand of a watch or clock, which marks the minutes and moves round the dial in one hour.

minutely (I.), adj. & adv. [1. mínitli; 2. mínitli]. **minute** (I.) & **-ly**. a Occurring every minute; b minute by minute.

minutely (II.), adv. [1. mīnū́tli; 2. mainjū́tli], fr. **minute** (III.) & **-ly**. In a minute manner; closely, particularly.

minuteness, n. [1. mīnū́tnes; 2. mainjū́tnis]. **minute** (III.) & **-ness**. Quality of being minute; a extreme smallness; b particularity, exactness, care for details.

minutia, n., usually in pl. **minutiae** [1. mīnū́shia, -iē; 2. mainjū́ʃiə, -iī]. Lat., fr. *minūtus*, 'small, minute'. See **minute** (I.) & (III.). a A minute detail; b (in pl.) precise, trifling details; trifles.

minx, n. [1. mingks; 2. miŋks]. Etymol. doubtful; possibly fr. L.G. *minsk*, 'a man,' also, 'an impudent woman'; cogn. w. Germ. *mensch*, 'a man'. See **man** & **-ish**. An impudent, forward, saucy, girl or woman; a hussy.

miocene, adj. [1. míosēn; 2. máiəsīn]. Mod. coinage, fr. Gk. *meíōn*, 'less', see **meiosis**, & *kainós*, 'new, recent', see **kainite**. (geol.) Less recent, of a period of geologic time between the Oligocene and Pliocene periods, the Middle Tertiary period; also as n., the Miocene period.

mir, n. [1. mēr; 2. miə]. Russ. A Russian village community, under the old regime.

miracle, n. [1. mírakl; 2. mírəkl]. O. Fr., fr. Lat. *mīrāculum*, 'wonderful thing, marvel', fr. *mīrāri*, 'to wonder at', fr. *mīrus*, 'wonderful, marvellous'. See **admire** & **marvel**. 1. A strange, wonderful, extraordinary thing or event; a marvel: *his recovery was a miracle*; *a miracle of ingenuity, skill* &c. 2. a An abnormal event or occurrence which cannot be explained by any known natural law of cause and effect, and is therefore assigned to supernatural agency; something transcending the laws of nature; b specif., any one of the marvellous acts of Christ, such as raising the dead, feeding the five thousand &c., as related in the Gospels.

miracle-monger, n. One who pretends or claims to work miracles; wonder-worker.

miracle play, n. A mediaeval form of drama founded on the wonderful works or miracles of the saints or martyrs.

miraculous, adj. [1. mirákūlus; 2. mirǽkjuləs], fr. Fr. *miraculeux*. See **miracle** & **-ous**. Of the nature of a miracle; supernatural; wonderful, marvellous.

miraculously, adv. Prec. & **-ly**. By a miracle; in a miraculous way.

miraculousness, n. See prec. & **-ness**. State, quality, of being miraculous or marvellous.

mirage, n. [1. miráhzh; 2. mirā́ž]. Fr., fr. (*se*) *mirer*, 'look at oneself in a mirror', fr. Lat. *mīrāri*, 'to wonder at'. See **admire** & **miracle**; cp. also **mirror**. 1. An optical illusion, chiefly apparent in deserts, caused by atmospheric conditions, in which a distant object, invisible directly, is reflected so as to be not only visible, but to appear comparatively near at hand; the object thus made visible often appears as though reflected in a sheet of water. 2. (fig.) A misleading fancy or delusion; an unrealisable hope or aspiration.

mire, n. & vb. trans. & intrans. [1. mīr; 2. maiə]. M.E. *myre, mire*; of Scand. origin, fr. O.N. *mýrr*, 'bog, swamp', cogn. w. O.E. *mēos*, 'moss', O.H.G. *mios*, M.H.G. *mies*, 'swamp'. See **moss**. 1. n. a Mud, slush, swampy ground; Phr. *to drag through the mire*, expose to ignominy and contempt; to disgrace; b (fig.) defilement, dirt. 2. vb. a trans. To cover with mud; to drive, plunge, into mud; b intrans., to sink in mud.

miriness, n. [1. mírines; 2. máiərinis], fr. **miry** & **-ness**. Condition of being miry.

mirk, n. See **murk**.

mirror, n. & vb. trans. [1. míror; 2. mírə]. M.E. *mirour*, fr. O. Fr. *mireour*, Mod. Fr. *miroir*, fr. assumed L. or Low Lat. **mīrātōrium*, fr. L. Lat. *mīrāre*, 'to look at', Lat. *mīrāri*, 'to wonder at'. See **admire** & cp. **mirage**. 1. n. a A looking-glass; a polished surface which reflects an image; b (in non-material sense) that which reflects, or gives, a true representation of life &c.; a pattern, example: *a mirror of fashion, of all the virtues*. 2. vb. To reflect as in a mirror (lit. and fig.).

mirth, n. [1. mĕrth; 2. mǝ̄þ]. O.E. *myrigð, mir(i)gð*, M.E. *mirthe, murthe* &c., fr. *myrge*, 'merry', see **merry**, & **-th.** Merriment, joyfulness, gladness; laughter, hilarity.

mirthful, adj. [1. mérthfool; 2. mǽþful]. Prec. & **-ful.** Full of mirth; merry, jolly.

mirthfully, adv. Prec. & **-ly.** Merrily; in a mirthful, jolly manner.

mirthfulness, n. Prec. & **-ness.** Merriment, state of being mirthful; gaiety, joyousness.

mirthless, adj. [1. mérthles; 2. mǽþlis]. **mirth** & **-less.** Without mirth; sad, melancholy, joyless, grim.

mirthlessly, adv. Prec. & **-ly.** In a mirthless manner.

miry, adj. [1. míri; 2. máiəri]. **mire** & **-y.** Muddy, swampy, dirty.

mirza, n. [1. mérza; 2. mǽzə]. Pers., fr. *mirzadeh*, son of a *mir*, or prince, cp. **emir.** A Persian title added to a name as denoting royal descent, or prefixed as denoting official rank.

mis-, pref. meaning *amiss, wrong, wrongly, ill*, or *unfavourable*; w. advbl. force before vbs. & adjs., & w. adjectival force before vbl. ns. & ns.; also, usually archaic, as intens. before a word wh. already has a negative or pejorative meaning, as *misdread, misdoubt.* The pref. has two sources: (1) in words of Engl. origin, O.E. *mis-*, Common Gmc., cp. O.N. *mis-*, Goth. *missa-*, in same sense, as O.E. *misdǣd*, 'misdeed'; Goth. *missa-dēds*, cogn. w. **miss (II.)**; (2) in words of Fr. origin, Engl. *mis-* takes place of O. Fr. *mes*, priv. & pejorative pref., fr. Lat. *minus*, 'less'. See **minor.**

misadventure, n. [1. mìsadvénchur; 2. mìsədvéntʃə], fr. O. Fr. *mesaventure.* **mis-** & **adventure.** Mishap, unlucky chance; ill-luck; accident; mischance, misfortune. Phr. *by misadventure*, by accident, accidentally.

misadvise, vb. trans. [1. mìsadvíz; 2. mìsədváiz]. **mis-** & **advise.** To give bad or wrong advice to.

misalliance, n. [1. mìsalíans; 2. mìsəláiəns], ad. fr. Fr. *mésalliance*; or formed directly fr. **mis-** & **alliance.** Mésalliance.

misanthrope, n. [1. mísanthrōp; 2. mísənþroup], fr. Gk. *mīsánthrōpos*, 'hating mankind', fr. *mīsein*, 'to hate', fr. *mīsos*, 'hatred', origin doubtful, & *ánthrōpos*, 'a man'. See **anthropology.** One who hates mankind; one who shuns his fellow-men; cynic.

misanthropic(al), adj. [1. mìsanthrópik(l); 2. mìsənþrópik(l)]. Prec. & **-ic** & **-al.** Hating mankind; avoiding, despising, mankind or human society.

misanthropically, adv. Prec. & **-ly.** In a misanthropic way or manner.

misanthropist, n. [1. misánthropist; 2. misǽnþrəpist]. See **misanthrope** & **-ist.** A misanthrope, cynic.

misanthropy, n. [1. misánthropi; 2. misǽnþrəpi]. See prec. & **-y.** Hatred, contempt, dislike, of mankind or of human society, contrasted with *philanthropy.*

misapplication, n. [1. mìsaplikáshun; 2. mìsæplikéiʃən]. **mis-** & **application.** A wrong application, use, or employment.

misapply, vb. trans. [1. mìsaplí; 2. mìsəplái]. **mis-** & **apply.** **a** To apply wrongly, make wrong use of: *to misapply one's talents, gifts, opportunities*; **b** to use dishonestly, or for an unlawful purpose: *to misapply money entrusted to one.*

misapprehend, vb. trans. [1. mìsaprehénd; 2. mìsæprihénd]. **mis-** & **apprehend.** To apprehend wrongly; take in a wrong sense; to misunderstand, misconceive.

misapprehension, n. [1. mìsaprehénshun; 2. mìsæprihénʃən]. **mis-** & **apprehension.** **a** Act of misapprehending; **b** misunderstanding.

misapprehensive, adj. [1. mìsaprehénsiv; 2. mìsæprihénsiv]. **mis-** & **apprehensive.** Tending, inclined, to misapprehend.

misappropriate, vb. trans. [1. mìsaprṓpriāt; 2. mìsəpróuprieit]. **mis-** & **appropriate.** **a** To appropriate, take and use wrongly, or for a wrong purpose; to misapply; **b** (law) to use dishonestly, convert to wrong use.

misappropriation, n. [1. mìsaprōpriáshun; 2. mìsəprouprìéiʃən]. **mis-** & **appropriation.** Wrongful appropriation; esp. (law) wrongful conversion to personal use of money entrusted to one, as by a trustee, solicitor &c.

misbecome, vb. trans. [1. mìsbekúm; 2. mìsbikám]. **mis-** & **become.** Not to become, to suit or fit ill; not to be consonant with.

misbecoming, adj. [1. mìsbekúming; 2. mìsbikámiŋ]. **mis-** & **becoming.** Not becoming, not fitting; unbecoming.

misbegotten, adj. [1. mìsbegótn; 2. mìsbigɔ́tn]. **mis-** & **begotten.** Ill-begotten; bastard, illegitimate.

misbehave, vb. reflex. & intrans. [1. mìsbeháv; 2. mìsbihéiv]. **mis-** & **behave.** To behave ill; to be guilty of bad, immoral, or dishonest conduct.

misbehaviour, n. [1. mìsbehávyur; 2. mìsbihéivjə]. **mis-** & **behaviour.** Bad behaviour, ill manners; immoral or dishonest conduct.

misbelief, n. [1. mìsbeléf; 2. mìsbilíf]. **mis-** & **belief.** A wrong, false, mistaken belief or opinion, esp. in religious matters; contrasted with *disbelief* or *unbelief.*

misbeliever, n. [1. mìsbeléver; 2. mìsbilívə]. **mis-** & **believer.** One who believes wrongly, falsely, or mistakenly; heretic, infidel.

misbelieving, adj. [1. mìsbeléving; 2. mìsbilíviŋ]. **mis-** & **believing.** Believing wrongly, falsely, or mistakenly; infidel, heretical.

misbeseem, vb. trans. [1. mìsbesém; 2. mìsbisím]. **mis-** & **beseem.** Not to beseem; to be unseemly, unsuitable.

misbirth, n. [1. mísbërth; 2. mísbǝ̄þ]. **mis-** & **birth.** A miscarriage, abortion.

miscalculate, vb. trans. & intrans. [1. mìskálkūlāt; 2. mìskǽlkjuleit]. **mis-** & **calculate.** **a** trans. To calculate wrongly; to misjudge: *to miscalculate the numbers present, the distance between the two cars*; **b** intrans., to make a miscalculation.

miscalculation, n. [1. mìskalkūláshun; 2. mìskælkjuléiʃən]. **mis-** & **calculation.** A wrong, mistaken, calculation; error in judgement; a wrong reckoning.

miscall, vb. trans. [1. miskáwl; 2. miskɔ́l]. **mis-** & **call.** **a** To call by a wrong or inappropriate name; **b** (provinc. or vulg.) to call by an ill-name; to abuse.

miscarriage, n. [1. miskárij; 2. miskǽridž]. **mis-** & **carriage.** **1.** Failure to be carried out; lack of success; an error, a going astray: *miscarriage of one's plans*; *a miscarriage of justice.* **2.** Failure to reach destination: *miscarriage of goods, a letter, message* &c. **3.** Premature delivery of a child; abortion.

miscarry, vb. intrans. [1. miskári; 2. miskǽri], **mis-** & **carry.** **1.** **a** Not to succeed; not to attain object; to go awry: *all his schemes miscarried*; **b** to go astray, fail to reach destination: *the letter, message, miscarried.* **2.** (of women) To be confined prematurely.

miscegenation, n. [1. mìsejenáshun; 2. mìsidžinéiʃən]. Coinage fr. Lat. *miscēre*, 'to mix, mingle', & *gen-*, as in **genus**, 'kind, race', & **-ation.** The interbreeding of races, esp. of races totally different in type, and in the stage of civilization reached &c., e.g. between the white and black races.

miscellanea, n. [1. mìselánea; 2. mìsəléiniə]. Lat. neut. pl. of *miscellāneus.* See next word. A miscellany.

miscellaneous, adj. [1. mìseláneus; 2. mìsəléiniəs], fr. Lat. *miscellāneus*, 'mixed, made up of all kinds', fr. *miscellus*, 'mixed', fr. *miscēre*, 'to mix'. See **mix.** Mixed; consisting, composed, of various kinds; having various qualities or characters: *a miscellaneous collection of people, pictures* &c.

miscellaneously, adv. Prec. & **-ly.** In a miscellaneous manner.

miscellaneousness, n. See prec. & **-ness.** State, quality, of being miscellaneous; variety.

miscellany, n. [1. míselani, miséláni; 2. mísəlàni, miséləni], fr. Lat. *miscellānea*, as above, & **-y**, or adaptation of Fr. *miscellanée*, fr. same source. **1.** A medley of various kinds of things. Specif. **2.** collection of writings on various subjects, or by various authors.

mischance, n. [1. mischáhns; 2. mistʃáns], fr. O. Fr. *meschance.* **mis-** & **chance.** Ill-luck, accident, misadventure, misfortune.

mischief, n. [1. míschif; 2. místʃif]. M.E., *mes-*, *mys-chef*, fr. O. Fr. *meschef*; fr. *mes-*, **mis-**, & *chef*, 'chief, end', see **chief.** **1.** **a** (in material sense) Damage, harm, injury, destruction, havoc: *great mischief was wrought by the storm.* Phrs. *to do a person a mischief*, injure him physically; *to play the mischief with* (i.) (a person, or any other living organism), injure his health, maim him; (ii.) (a machine &c.) spoil its mechanism; (iii.) (any orderly arrangement or group of objects so arranged): *the wind has played the mischief with my papers*, has disarranged, confused, them; **b** (i.) pathological condition, state of bodily disorder, of injury or destruction to part of the body: *the mischief was more deep-seated than the external injuries to the body showed*; (ii.) in inorganic things: *the mischief is in the mainspring of the watch*; as mild expletive, *what the mischief* (*do you want?* &c.). **2.** (in non-material sense) Moral harm or injury; wicked, immoral influence: *thoughtless, inflammatory speech may work great mischief.* Phr. *to make mischief* (between two persons or parties), to arouse strife, ill-will, cause them to quarrel. **3.** **a** Wilfully destructive action; irresponsible, troublesome, foolish, harmful conduct: *the breaking of the windows is a piece of childish mischief*; *it is difficult to keep children out of mischief*; Phr. *there is mischief brewing*, in contemplation, or in course of perpetration; *up to mischief*, planning, or carrying it out; **b** innocent, light-hearted mirth; frolicsome spirit: *eyes beaming with mischief.* **4.** (colloq.) A mischievous person, esp. a child: *a regular little mischief.*

mischief-maker, n. Person who stirs up strife, causes quarrels, ill-feeling &c.

mischievous, adj. [1. míschivus; 2. místʃivəs]. A.-Fr. *meschevous.* **mischief** & **-ous.** **1.** (chiefly in moral sense) Creating, causing, mischief, injurious, tending to cause trouble: *a mischievous statement, rumour, gossip, action* &c.; *a mischievous person, influence* &c. **2.** **a** Animated by a spirit of mischief; performing thoughtless, irritating actions, doing foolish, mildly harmful acts: *a mischievous boy, monkey* &c.; **b** causing annoyance, effecting needless minor damage: *a mischievous prank.* **3.** Animated by, expressing, light-hearted gaiety, thoughtless frolicsomeness &c., with a spice of innocent malice: *a mischievous glance.*

mischievously, adv. Prec. & **-ly.** In a mischievous manner.

mischievousness, n. See prec. & **-ness.** **a** Mischief; habit of making mischief; **b** quality of being mischievous.

miscibility, n. [1. mìsibíliti; 2. mìsibíliti]. See next word & **-ity.** Capacity of being mixed.

miscible, adj. [1. mísibl; 2. mísibl], fr. Lat. *miscēre*, 'to mix', see **mix** & **-ible.** Capable of being mixed.

misconceive, vb. trans. [1. mìskonsév; 2. mìskənsív]. **mis-** & **conceive.** To conceive wrongly or falsely; to misapprehend, misunderstand, mistake.

misconception, n. [1. mìskonsépshun; 2. mìskənsépʃən]. **mis-** & **conception.** Misapprehension, misunderstanding; mistaken, false, opinion.

misconduct (I.), n. [1. miskóndukt; 2. miskɔ́ndəkt]. **mis-** & **conduct (I.).** **a** Wrong or improper conduct; misbehaviour; specif. **b** irregular sexual intercourse.

misconduct (II.), vb. trans. [1. mìskondúkt; 2. miskəndákt]. **mis-** & **conduct (II.).** **1.** To conduct badly, manage wrongly; mismanage. **2.** (reflex.) *Misconduct oneself*: **a** to behave badly, be guilty of bad conduct; **b** specif., *misconduct oneself with*, to have illicit sexual intercourse with.

misconstruction, n. [1. mìskonstrúkshun; 2. mìskənstrákʃən]. **mis-** & **construction.** **a** Mistaken, wrong construction; **b** wrong interpretation of meaning.

misconstrue, vb. trans. [1. mìskonstrōō; 2. mìskənstrū]. **mis-** & **construe.** **a** To construe, translate (a passage) wrongly; **b** form a wrong notion of meaning of, to put a wrong interpretation on, to misunderstand.

miscount (I.), vb. trans. & intrans. [1. miskóunt; 2. miskáunt]. **mis-** & **count** (I.). To count, calculate, wrongly; make an error in counting.

miscount (II.), n. An error in counting or reckoning.

miscreant, adj. & n. [1. mískriant; 2. mískriənt], fr. O. Fr. *mescreant*, 'unbelieving, unbeliever', *mes-*, see **mis-**, & *creant*, Pres. Part., fr. Lat. *crēdent-(em)*, Pres. Part. of *crēdere*, 'to believe'. See **creed.** **1.** adj. **a** (obs. or archaic) Unbelieving, infidel; **b** villainous, vile. **2.** n. **a** (obs.) Infidel, heretic; **b** one guilty of an atrocious crime; a scoundrel, ruffian; a desperate villain.

miscreated, adj. [1. mìskriā́ted; 2. mìskriéitid]. **mis-**, **create**, & **-ed.** Ill-formed, misshapen.

mis-cue, vb. intrans. & n. [1. mìs kū́; 2. mìs kjū́]. **mis-** & **cue** (II.). **1.** vb. (billiards) To make a faulty stroke so that the tip of cue slips off the ball without striking fairly. **2.** n. A faulty stroke of the cue.

misdate, vb. trans. [1. misdā́t; 2. misdéit]. **mis-** & **date** (II.). **a** To put a wrong date on (a letter &c.); **b** to assign to a wrong date.

misdeal, vb. trans. & intrans. & n. [1. mìsdḗl; 2. misdíəl]. **mis-** & **deal** (I.). **1.** vb. **a** (obs.) To deal wrongly with; **b** to deal playing-cards wrongly. **2.** n. A wrong deal at cards.

misdealing, n. [1. mìsdḗling; 2. mìsdíliŋ]. Prec. & **-ing.** Dishonest, unscrupulous, wicked conduct or action.

misdeed, n. [1. misdḗd; 2. misdíd]. O.E. *misdǣd.* See **mis-** & **deed.** A wicked act, evil deed, a crime.

misdeem, vb. trans. & intrans. [1. misdḗm; 2. misdím]. **mis-** & **deem.** (poet.) To judge wrongly; to form mistaken opinions.

misdemeanant, n. [1. mìsdemḗnant; 2. mìsdimínənt], fr. obs. vb. *misdemean* & **-ant.** A person convicted of a misdemeanour; person guilty of misconduct.

misdemeanour, n. [1. mìsdemḗnur; 2. mìsdimínə]. **mis-** & **demeanour.** **a** (law) An indictable offence or crime other than treason or felony by common law or by statute; **b** (popularly) any offence; misdeed.

misdescription, n. [1. mìsdeskrípshun; 2. mìsdiskrípʃən]. **mis-** & **description.** A wrong, defective, or misleading description, esp. one made in a legal contract.

misdirect, vb. trans. [1. mìsdirékt; 2. mìsdirékt]. **mis-** & **direct.** **1.** To direct wrongly; put a wrong name, title, or address on (a letter). **2.** To give wrong instructions or indications to, as how to find, or go to, a place, building &c. **3.** Specif. (of a judge) to give wrong instructions, a misdirection, to (a jury). **4.** **a** To aim badly, strike feebly, or without precision: *a misdirected blow*; **b** (of non-material action) to direct mistakenly, or into wrong channels: *misdirected energies, talents* &c.

misdirection, n. [1. mìsdirékshun; 2. mìsdirékʃən]. **mis-** & **direction.** **1.** Wrong address (on a letter &c.). **2.** Wrong, misleading, indication of the way to a place &c. **3.** Wrong direction given by a judge in charging a jury.

misdoing, n. [1. mìsdōōing; 2. mìsdúiŋ]. **mis-** & **doing.** Wrongdoing; misdeed.

misdoubt, vb. trans. & n. [1. misdóut; 2. misdáut]. **mis-** & **doubt.** **1.** vb. (archaic) To have doubts, suspicions, misgivings of or about; to suspect. **2.** n. (obs.) Doubt, suspicion, misgiving.

mise, n. [1. mēz, mīz; 2. mīz, maiz]. O. Fr., P.P. fem. of *mettre*, 'to put, lay', fr. Lat. *mittere*, 'to send'. See **missile.** **1.** (hist.) **a** An agreement, pact: *Mise of Lewes*, 1264, between Henry III. and the Barons; **b** an agreed grant or levy paid by the Welsh on entry of a new Prince of Wales. **2.** (gambling) **a** A stake; **b** the lay-out of the cards.

mise-en-scène, n. [1. mēz on sán; 2. mīz ā séin]. Fr., 'setting on the stage'. See prec. & **scene.** **a** A stage-setting, including the costumes, scenery, properties &c. of a play as represented on the stage; **b** (fig.) the general external surroundings and setting of an event or action.

miser (I.), n. [1. mízer; 2. máizə]. Lat. *miser*, 'wretched'. See **miserable.** **1.** (obs.) A miserable, wretched person; a poor wretch. **2.** An avaricious, grasping, covetous person; one who, having wealth or means, lives wretchedly and hoards money for the sake of hoarding.

miser (II.), n. Etymol. unknown. A boring instrument used in mining and well-sinking.

miserable, adj. [1. mízerabl; 2. míz(ə)rəbl], fr. Fr. *misérable*, 'wretched' &c., fr. Lat. *miserābilis*, fr. *miserāri*, 'to pity', fr. *miser*, 'wretched, miserable'; connected w. Lat. *maerēre* for **maesēre*, 'to mourn', *maeror*, 'sadness, grief', & *maestus*, 'sad, sorrowful'; further relations doubtful. **1.** **a** Unhappy; suffering mental pain; wretched, sad, dejected: *to feel, be made, miserable by unkindness*; characterized by, filled with, wretchedness: *a miserable life*; **b** causing unhappiness: *miserable news.* **2.** **a** Suffering extreme bodily pain or discomfort: *miserable with hunger and cold*; **b** (of external surroundings) exhibiting great discomfort and wretchedness; squalid, poverty-stricken: *a miserable hovel.* **3.** **a** Of poor quality: *a miserable dinner*; **b** insufficient in amount, scanty: *you've made a miserable meal, I fear*; **c** contemptible, inadequate, pitiable: *miserable effort, performance*; *a miserable failure*; **d** morally reprehensible; shameful, disreputable, abandoned: *a miserable scoundrel.*

miserably, adv. Prec. & **-ly.** **1.** In a miserable manner: *to live miserably.* **2.** (as pejorative) Very: *miserably inadequate, weak, poor, ill* &c.; *to fail miserably.*

misère, n. [1. mizā́r; 2. mizéə]. Fr., 'misery'. See prec. A call in solo-whist by which the player undertakes not to take a single trick.

miserere, n. [1. mìzerḗri; 2. mìzəríəri]. Lat., imperat., 'have mercy', fr. *miserēri*, 'to have pity, mercy on', fr. *miser*, 'wretched'. See **miserable.** **1.** **a** The 51st Psalm, one of the most commonly used of the Penitential Psalms, of which the first words are *Miserere mei, Deus*, 'Have mercy on me, O God'; **b** a musical setting for this Psalm. **2.** A lamentation, call for mercy. **3.** (a loose use) Also *miserere seat*, misericord (in sense **2.**).

misericord, n. [1. mizérikord; 2. mizérikɔ̄d]. O. Fr. *misericorde*, fr. Lat. *misericordia*, 'mercy, compassion', fr. *miserēri*, 'to have pity for', see **miserable**, & *cor, cordis*, 'heart', see **cordate.** **1.** A room set apart in a monastery, where monks might take special food as an indulgence. **2.** A small projecting bracket or shelf on the under side of a hinged seat in the choir of a monastic church, to allow a slight rest when standing; also loosely called *miserere (seat).* **3.** A thin, pointed dagger, used in mediaeval warfare, for piercing the joints of armour, and giving the *coup de grâce*, or mercy stroke, to a fallen knight.

miserliness, n. [1. mízerlines; 2. máizəlinis]. See next word & **-ness.** Quality of being miserly; avarice.

miserly, adj. [1. mízerli; 2. máizəli]. **miser** (I.) & **-ly.** Like a miser; avaricious, niggardly.

misery, n. [1. mízeri; 2. mízəri], fr. O. Fr. *miserie*, Lat. *miseria*, 'wretchedness, misery'. See **miserable** & **-y.** **1.** Mental suffering, extreme unhappiness: *the miseries of human life.* **2.** **a** Extreme bodily suffering or discomfort: *to suffer great misery from toothache*; **b** (of external conditions) squalor, wretchedness, poverty: *the misery of the slums.* **3.** (solo-whist) Misère.

misfeasance, n. [1. mìsfḗzans; 2. mìsfízəns], fr. O. Fr. *mesfaisance*, fr. *mesfais-ant*, Pres. Part. of *mesfaire*, 'to do wrong', fr. *mes-*, see **mis-**, & *faire*, 'to do', fr. Lat. *facere*, see **faction.** (law) A wrong or trespass by the doing in a wrongful way what is otherwise lawful, as the wrongful use of legal authority, contrasted with *malfeasance.*

misfire, vb. intrans. & n. [1. mìsfír; 2. mìsfáiə]. **mis-** & **fire.** **1.** vb. **a** (of a gun &c.) To fail to go off; **b** (of internal combustion engine of motor-car &c.) to fail to ignite. **2.** n. A failure to explode, or to ignite.

misfit, n. [1. misfít; 2. misfít]. **mis-** & **fit** (V.). **a** A bad fit (of clothes &c.); **b** article of wearing apparel which does not fit.

misfortune, n. [1. misfórchun; 2. misfɔ̄tʃən]. **mis-** & **fortune.** **1.** Bad fortune, adversity, unhappiness; ill luck: '*As though misfortune made the throne her seat, And none could be unhappy but the great*' (Rowe); *his face is his misfortune, not his fault.* **2.** A disastrous event, an unhappy accident: *the early loss of one's parents is a grave misfortune.*

misgive, impers. vb. [1. misgív; 2. misgív]. **mis-** & **give.** To cause, give rise to, fear, doubt, mistrust, suspicion: '*Yet oft his heart, divine of something ill, Misgave him*' (Milton, 'P. L.').

misgiving, n. [1. misgíving; 2. misgíviŋ]. Prec. & **-ing.** Doubt, suspicion, mistrust; scruple.

misgovern, vb. trans. [1. misgúvern; 2. misgávən]. **mis-** & **govern.** To govern ill.

misgovernment, n. [1. misgúvernment; 2. misgáv ə(n)mənt]. Prec. & **-ment.** Bad, evil, incompetent government or rule.

misguidance, n. [1. misgídans; 2. misgáidəns]. **mis-** & **guidance.** Wrong guidance.

misguide, vb. trans. [1. misgíd; 2. misgáid]. **mis-** & **guide.** To mislead, advise wrongly, lead into error: (chiefly as adj. in P.P.) *misguided enthusiasts, opinions* &c.

misguidedly, adv. [1. misgídedli; 2. misgáididli]. P.P. of prec. & **-ly.** In a misguided manner; under misleading, wrong advice.

mishandle, vb. trans. [1. mis-hándl; 2. mishǽndl]. **mis-** & **handle.** **1.** **a** To handle wrongly or clumsily; **b** to handle roughly or rudely; to ill-treat, maltreat. **2.** To manage badly, mismanage: *to mishandle negotiations.*

mishap, n. [1. mis-háp; 2. mishǽp]. **mis-** & **hap.** Mischance, accident, piece of bad luck.

mishna, mishnah, n. [1. míshna; 2. míʃnə]. Heb. *mishnāh*, 'oral teaching, instruction', fr. *shānāh*, 'to repeat'. A collection of rabbinical interpretations, traditions, and precepts on the Mosaic law.

misinform, vb. trans. [1. mìsinfórm; 2. mìsinfɔ̄m]. **mis-** & **inform.** To give wrong or misleading information to.

misinformation, n. [1. mìsinformā́shun; 2. mìsinfəméiʃən]. Prec. & **-ation.** Wrong, misleading information.

misinterpret, vb. trans. [1. mìsintérpret; 2. mìsintə́prit]. **mis-** & **interpret.** To interpret wrongly; to explain, construe wrongly; to misunderstand.

misinterpretation, n. [1. mísintèrpretā́shun; 2. mísintə̀pritéiʃən]. Prec. & **-ation.** Wrong interpretation; misconstruction.

misjudge, vb. trans. [1. misjúj; 2. misdžádž]. **mis-** & **judge.** **1.** **a** To form a wrong judgement or opinion concerning; specif. **b** to estimate (esp. a person or his character) wrongly; (gen.) to underrate; not do justice to. **2.** To form a wrong estimate of, as regards size, length, amount &c.: *to misjudge a distance.*

misjudgement, n. [1. misjújment; 2. misdžádžmənt]. Prec. & **-ment.** A mistaken, erroneous, judgement or opinion.

mislay, vb. trans. [1. mislā́; 2. misléi]. **mis-** & **lay** (III.). To put something where it cannot readily be found; to lose temporarily.

mislead, vb. trans. [1. misléd; 2. misl*í*d]. **mis-** & **lead (IV.)**. **a** To lead astray, cause to err in action or conduct; **b** to cause to form wrong judgement; to deceive, delude.

misleading, adj. [1. misléding; 2. misl*í*diŋ]. Prec. & **-ing**. Tending to mislead, deceptive; giving wrong impression, delusive.

mislike, vb. trans. [1. mislík; 2. misl*ái*k]. **mis-** & **like**. To dislike, disapprove of.

mismanage, vb. trans. [1. mismánij; 2. mismǽnidž]. **mis-** & **manage**. To manage wrongly, or badly, make a muddle of.

mismanagement, n. [1. mismánijment; 2. mismǽnidžmənt]. Prec. & **-ment**. Bad management.

misname, vb. trans. [1. misnám; 2. misnéim]. **mis-** & **name**. To call by a wrong name.

misnomer, n. [1. misnómer; 2. misnóumə], fr. O. Fr. *mesnommer*, 'to misname', *mes-*, see **mis-**, & *nommer*, 'to name', see **name**. A wrong name; term which is an incorrect description or designation.

miso-, pref. Form of Gk. *mīsos*, 'hatred', used in combination; cp. also *mīsein*, 'to hate'.

misogamist, n. [1. misógamist; 2. m*ai*sɔ́gəmist]. Prec. & Gk. *gám-(os)*, see **gamo-**, 'marriage', & **-ist**. A hater of marriage.

misogamy, n. [1. misógami; 2. m*ai*sɔ́gəmi]. As prec. & **-y**. Hatred of marriage.

misogynist, n. [1. mīsóginist, -jinist; 2. m*ai*sɔ́ginist, -džinist], fr. Gk. *mīsogúnēs*, as prec., & *guné*, 'woman', see **gyno-**. A hater of women.

misogyny, n. [1. mīsógini, -jini; 2. m*ai*sɔ́gini, -džini], fr. Gk. *misogunia*, as prec., & **-y**. Hatred of women.

misplace, vb. trans. [1. misplás; 2. mispléis]. **mis-** & **place**. **a** To put in wrong, or unsuitable, place or position; **b** (chiefly in P.P.) to bestow (confidence, affection &c.) mistakenly, upon an unworthy object.

misplacement, n. [1. misplásment; 2. mispléismənt]. Prec. & **-ment**. Act or process of misplacing or placing wrongly; fact of being misplaced.

misprint, vb. trans. & n. [1. misprínt; 2. misprínt]. **mis-** & **print**. **a** vb. To make a mistake in printing; **b** n., letter, or word, wrongly printed.

misprise. See **misprize**.

misprision (I.), n. [1. misprízhun; 2. mispríž∂n]. O. Fr. *mesprison*, *mesprision*, 'mistake, error', fr. *mesprendre*, 'to take amiss', *mes-*, see **mis-**, & *prendre*, 'to take', cp. Fr. *méprise*, 'a mistake', & see **prison**. (law) Mistake, neglect of duty, misdemeanour; now only used in *misprision of treason*, or *of felony*, knowledge and concealment of treason, or of felony, without such assent, however, as would make the person charged an accessory.

misprision (II.), n., fr. **misprize**, confused w. prec. Contempt, depreciation.

misprize, misprise, vb. trans. [1. mispríz; 2. mispráiz]. O. Fr. *mesprisier*, 'to despise', *mes*, see **mis-**, & *prisier*, 'to prize', cp. Fr. *mépris*, 'contempt'; see **prize**. To despise, scorn, undervalue.

mispronounce, vb. trans. & intrans. [1. mìspronóuns; 2. misprənáuns]. **mis-** & **pronounce**. **a** To pronounce with faulty articulation; **b** to utter with wrong sounds.

mispronunciation, n. [1. mispronùnsiáshun; 2. misprənànsiéiʃən]. **mis-** & **pronunciation**. A wrong, bad, pronunciation.

misquotation, n. [1. miskwōtáshun; 2. miskwoutéiʃən]. **mis-** & **quotation**. A wrong, incorrect, quotation.

misquote, vb. trans. & intrans. [1. miskwót; 2. miskwóut]. **mis-** & **quote**. To quote wrongly or inaccurately.

misread, vb. trans. [1. misréd; 2. misríd]. **mis-** & **read**. **a** To read wrongly; **b** to put a wrong construction upon; to misinterpret.

misrepresent, vb. trans. [1. mìsreprezént; 2. misreprizént]. **mis-** & **represent**. To represent wrongly or inaccurately; to give a false, inaccurate, account of what is said; to describe (an occurrence) inaccurately.

misrepresentation, n. [1. mìsreprezentáshun; 2. misreprizentéiʃən]. Prec. & **-ation**. **a** A wrong, false, inaccurate, representation, account, or description; **b** (law) a false statement of fact (not of opinion), which may render a contract voidable.

misrule, vb. trans. & n. [1. misrōōl; 2. misrúl]. **mis-** & **rule**. **a** vb. To rule, govern, badly; to misgovern; **b** n., misgovernment; disorder, tumult. Phr. *Lord of Misrule*, the king, master, of revels at Christmas.

miss (I.), n. [1. mis; 2. mis]. Contraction of **mistress**, only fr. the second half of 17th cent. **1. a** (cap.) Mode of address of an unmarried woman, unless she is entitled to be addressed as *Lady* or *Dame*; prefixed to surname, as *Miss Robinson*, of the elder of two or more unmarried sisters, or to the Christian and surname of the younger sisters, *Miss Joan Robinson*; (in pl.) either *the Miss Robinsons* or (archaic and formal) *the Misses Robinson*; **b** a young girl, an unmarried woman: *a saucy miss*. **2.** (obs.) A mistress, kept woman.

miss (II.), vb. trans. & intrans. O.E. *missan*, 'to fail to hit (a mark); to escape (notice)'; M.E. *missen*; cp. O.N. *missa*; O.H.G. *missen*; the pref. **mis-** is fr. same base. The form *miss-* comes fr. pre-Gmc. **mit-to*, cp. Lat. **miss-(um)**, P.P. of *mittere*, 'to let go, send off' &c., cp. **mittimus** & **mission**. It is further prob. that the following are also derived fr. another grade of same base: O.E. *mīþan*, 'to conceal; be hidden; avoid'; O.S. *mīthan*, O.H.G. *mīdan*, 'to hide; to avoid', Mod. Germ. *meiden*. **A.** trans. **1. a** To fail to hit (what is aimed at): *to miss one's aim*; *to miss a bird* (in shooting); Phr. *to miss the mark* (fig.), not to achieve what is attempted; to fall short of one's endeavours; to be inadequate; **b** to fail to hold, catch, hold on to: *to miss a catch* (at cricket); *to miss one's footing*, slip (in climbing &c.); *to miss one's hold*, loosen, let go one's grip &c.; **c** to fail to reach a given object or position: *he missed the bank and landed in the water*. **2. a** To fail to achieve, obtain, secure, some non-material object, aim, or desire: *he just missed the highest success*; *to miss a prize, promotion* &c.; **b** to fail to attain or reach; to fall short of: *it has just missed being a great picture*; **c** to avoid, escape: *to miss having a nasty accident*. **3. a** To fail to meet, arrive too late to see or catch; not to find at home &c.: *to miss a train, boat* &c.; *I was sorry to miss you when I called*; **b** to fail to see, overlook: *to miss a person in a crowd*; *I must have missed the notice in the paper yesterday*; **c** to be aware of, notice, absence of, to fail to see what one is expecting: '*One morn I miss'd him on the custom'd hill*' (Gray's 'Elegy'). **4.** Also *miss out*, to omit, leave out; *you've missed out some of the best verses in the poem*; *don't miss my name out of your list*. **5. a** To feel the want of, and hanker after, something to which one is accustomed: *I shall miss our pleasant talks when you leave*; **b** to regret, suffer from, the absence or loss of something or someone: *I miss my old friends more each day*. **B.** intrans. **a** To fail to hit one's mark, to go wide of: *aim very carefully or you'll miss*; **b** (fig.) to fail to attain one's object, be unable to do, or obtain what one is striving for: *you've worked so hard for your exam. that I'm sure you won't miss again*. Phr. *it's hit or miss*, success or failure, with nothing between.

miss (III.), n., fr. prec. **a** Failure to hit, gain, obtain, reach &c.; Phr. *a miss is as good as a mile*, a failure is a failure however near to success it may be; specif. **b** (billiards) intentional or unintentional failure to hit the object ball: *to give a miss in balk*; **c** deliberate avoidance: *to give a person a miss*; **d** escape: *a lucky miss*.

missal, n. [1. mísl; 2. mísl], fr. L. Eccles. Lat. *missale*, *missalis liber*, fr. *missa*, 'Mass'. See **Mass (I.)**. (R.C. Ch.) **a** Book containing the service of the Mass for the whole year; **b** (loosely) a book of hours, prayers, or devotions, esp. one that is illuminated.

missel thrush, n. [1. mísl thrush; 2. mísl þraʃ], for *mistle*, as feeding on mistletoe berries, and propagating the plant. See **mistletoe**. A large species of thrush, *Turdus viscivorus*, of grey colour with distinct spots on the under parts.

misshapen, adj. [1. mísshápen; 2. mísʃéipən]. **mis-** & *shapen*, old P.P. of **shape**. Deformed, distorted; ill-shaped.

missile, adj. & n. [1. mís(ī)l; 2. mís(*ai*)l], fr. Lat. *missilis*, 'capable of being thrown', fr. *miss-(um)*, P.P. type of *mittere*, 'to throw, hurl'; etymol. doubtful, but see **miss (II.)**; Lat. has *missile*, neut. sing., as n., 'a missile', see **miss (II.)**. **1.** adj. Capable of, suitable for, being thrown or hurled: *a missile weapon*. **2.** n. A weapon or object which is thrown, or intended for throwing; e.g. a stone, spear &c.

missing, adj. [1. mísing; 2. mísiŋ], fr. Pres. Part. of **miss (II.)**. Wanting; not to be found; lost, absent: *a missing chapter*; *the money was missing*; *killed, wounded, or missing*. Phr. *the missing link*, popular name of a supposed type of animal between the anthropoid apes and man.

mission, n. [1. míshun; 2. míʃən], fr. Lat. *missiōn-(em)*, fr. *missio*, 'a sending, mission, delegation', fr. *miss-(um)*, P.P. type of *mittere*, 'to send'. See **miss (II.)** & **missile**. **1.** Specif. **a** (theol.) The sending out of the Son by the Father, or of the Holy Ghost by the Son; **b** (eccles.) authority given by the Church to a priest to minister the Sacraments, to preach and teach, or to a Bishop to do these things, and further to consecrate other bishops and ordain priests. **2.** The sending out of persons as representatives to a foreign country to conduct political or other negotiations or business; the body of persons so sent, a delegation: *a financial mission to the U.S.A.* **3.** Specif. **a** the sending out by religious organizations of persons as *missionaries*, to preach and teach, either abroad, a *Foreign Mission* (esp. to convert the heathen or unbelievers), or at home, *Home Missions*, *the Missions to Seamen* &c.; **b** a sphere, field of missionary work or effort; a post or settlement of missionaries, esp. in a foreign country; **c** a course, period, of preaching, religious services &c., specially held for a revival of spiritual life in a district. **4.** A settlement for charitable, medical, or social work generally among the poor in a town or district. **5. a** Commission, duty, errand on which a person is sent; **b** calling, vocation; that for which one is specially fitted or destined: *one's mission in life*.

missionary, adj. & n. [1. míshunari; 2. míʃən(ə)ri]. Prec. & **-ary**. **1.** adj. Of, belonging to, missions or missionaries, esp. to religious missions: *missionary meeting, settlement, collection, work* &c. **2.** n. **a** One sent on a mission; specif., one who preaches the Gospel to, and tries to make converts to Christianity; one engaged in missionary work; **b** one who advocates some cause and proclaims a gospel.

missioner, n. [1. míshuner; 2. míʃənə]. **mission** & **-er**. Person in charge of, and conducting, a parochial mission.

missionize, vb. trans. & intrans. [1. míshunīz; 2. míʃənaiz]. **mission** & **-ize**. **1.** trans. To act as a missionary towards; specif. **a** to preach the Gospel to, to attempt to convert to Christianity; **b** to attempt to convert to any cause or ideal. **2.** intrans. To play the part of a missionary.

missis, missus, n. [1. mísiz; 2. mísiz]. Shortened form of **mistress**. **1.** Sometimes so written to express pronunciation of title prefixed to surname of married woman; usual spelling *Mrs.* **2.** (colloq., and familiar) **a** Mistress; used by servants of the lady they serve; **b** wife: *my, his, missis*.

missive, adj. & n. [1. mísiv; 2. mísiv]. Fr., 'letter', as if fr. Lat. **missiva*, 'sent', fr. *miss-(um)*, P.P. type of *mittere*, 'to send', see **missile**, & **-ive**. **1.** adj. (archaic) Sent, in Phr. *letter(s) missive*, letters sent from the sovereign to a special body or to special persons; specif., letter sent to dean and chapter nominating person to be elected bishop. 2. n. a A letter, esp. a formal, official epistle; b (Scots law) formal document setting forth the terms, and the offer or acceptance, of a contract.

mis-spell, vb. trans. [1. mis spél; 2. mis spél]. **mis-** & **spell (II.)**. To spell wrongly or badly: *a mis-spelt letter.*

mis-spend, vb. trans. [1. mìs spénd; 2. mìs spénd]. **mis-** & **spend**. To spend wrongly or wastefully: *a mis-spent fortune; a mis-spent youth.*

mis-state, vb. trans. [1. mìs stát; 2. mìs stéit]. **mis-** & **state (III.)**. To state wrongly or inaccurately.

mis-statement, n. [1. mìs státment; 2. mìs stéitmənt]. Prec. & **-ment**. a Act of stating wrongly and inaccurately; b a wrong, inaccurate, misleading statement; an untruth.

missy, n. [1. mísi; 2. mísi]. **miss (I.)** & **-y**. (familiar) Miss, used in addressing, or referring to, a young girl.

mist (I.), n. [1. mist; 2. mist]. O.E. *mist*, 'darkness'; O.N. *mistr*; cp. Du. & Swed. *mist*, 'fog'; prob. fr. primitive base **migh-*; cp. Lith. *migla*, 'mist'; Gk. *omikhlē*, 'fog, mist', Scrt. *mēgh-a*, 'cloud'. 1. a Visible watery vapour in the air, of less density than a fog; a haze, thin cloud; b *Scotch mist*, heavy, wetting drizzle. 2. A cloudy appearance or film over the eye. 3. Any thing or circumstance which obscures meaning, makes understanding difficult &c. Phr. *in a mist*, mentally perplexed.

mist (II.), vb. intrans. & impers., & trans. 1. impers. To fall as a mist, to produce mist: *it's hardly raining, only misting.* 2. trans. To suffuse, cover, obscure, with, or as with, a mist: *eyes misted with tears.*

mistakable, adj. [1. mistákabl; 2. mistéikəbl]. **mistake (I.)** & **-able**. Liable to be mistaken; capable of being misunderstood.

mistake (I.), vb. trans. [1. misták; 2. mistéik]. M.E. *mistaken*, fr. O.N. *mistaka*, 'to take in error or by mistake'. See **mis-** & **take**. 1. To take or understand wrongly or inaccurately; to make an error in interpreting: *to mistake another's meaning, object, purpose.* Phr. *there is no mistaking*, no possibility of error. 2. To identify wrongly: *to mistake one (person or thing) for another; mistake the road, direction.*

mistake (II.), n., fr. prec. An error, fault; misunderstanding, misconception: *to make a mistake; there is no mistake.* Phrs. (colloq.) *a good thing and no mistake; they have come to grief and no mistake*, without any doubt.

mistaken, adj. [1. mistáken; 2. mistéikən], fr. P.P. of **mistake (I.)**. a Wrong; in error; holding an erroneous opinion: *to be mistaken*, to be wrong; b ill-judged; ill-conceived; due to, exhibiting, an error of judgement: *mistaken act of clemency; mistaken kindness.*

mistakenly, adv. Prec. & **-ly**. In a mistaken manner; wrongly; in error.

mistaught, adj. [1. mistáwt; 2. mistɔ́t]. P.P. of *misteach*, wh. is hardly now used except in this form; fr. O.E. *mistǣcan*. See **mis-** & **teach**. Ill-instructed; taught inaccurately or mistakenly.

mister, n. [1. míster; 2. místə]. Variant of **master**; as the mode of speaking the written contraction *Mr.*, it does not appear before the 16th cent. 1. (usually written Mr.) a Form of address prefixed to a man's name in writing, speaking, and referring to him, when he is not entitled to any other, such as Lord, The Honourable, Sir, Colonel &c.; also b used as formal prefix to certain titles of office, as *Mr. Justice X; Mr. Speaker; Mr. Vice-Chancellor* &c.; c (vulg.) as form of address without any name following: *Look here, mister!* (used by inferiors). 2. Person not entitled to any title other than Mr.: *a plain mister he remained.*

mistery. See **mystery (II.)**.

mistily, adv. [1. místili; 2. místili]. **misty** & **-ly**. (lit. and fig.) With, in, a mist; foggily; through a mist, obscurely.

mistime, vb. trans. [1. mistím; 2. mistáim]. **mis-** & **time**. 1. To do out of time, in bad time or rhythm: *to mistime one's stroke.* 2. To do or say on an unsuitable, improper occasion: *to mistime one's remarks.*

mistimed, adj. [1. mistímd; 2. mistáimd], fr. P.P. of prec. a Done in wrong time; b done, said, (i.) at the wrong time, or (ii.) on an inappropriate occasion.

mistiness, n. [1. místines; 2. místinis]. **misty** & **-ness**. Condition of being misty.

mistletoe, n. [1. míslto, mízlto; 2. mísltou, mízltou]. O.E. *misteltān*; the first element is *mistel*, name of the plant; O.H.G., O.N. *mistil*; perh. allied to O.E. *meox*, Goth. *maihstos*, 'dung', the plant being propagated by seeds carried in the excrement of birds that feed on the berries; see also **micturition**, **mixen**; the second element is O.E. *tān*, 'twig', cp. M.H.G. *zein*, O.N. *teinn*, Goth. *tains*, 'twig'; etymol. uncertain. A parasitic plant, *Viscum album*, with yellowish-white berries filled with a sticky, viscous substance used for making birdlime; it grows chiefly on apple trees.

mistold, adj. [1. mistóld; 2. mistóuld], fr. P.P. of *mistell*, wh. is scarcely used in other forms. Wrongly, inaccurately, told, reported.

mistral, n. [1. místral; 2. místrəl]. Provenç. & Fr.; fr. Lat. *magistrālis*, 'magistral, masterful'. See **magistrate**. A very cold, dry N.W. wind on the Mediterranean coast of France, esp. at the mouth of the Rhone and along its valley.

mistranslate, vb. trans. [1. mìstrahnzlát; 2. mìstrānzléit]. **mis-** & **translate**. To translate wrongly or inaccurately.

mistranslation, n. [1. mìstrahnzláshun; 2. mìstrānzléiʃən]. Prec. & **-ion**. An incorrect translation.

mistress, n. [1. místres; 2. místris], fr. O. Fr. *maistresse*, also so spelt in M.E., fem. of O. Fr. *maistre*, 'master'. See **master** & **-ess**. 1 a A woman who is the head of a household and its servants: *the mistress of the house; is the mistress at home?*; b (cap.) used as form of address, written *Mrs.* and pronounced *missis*, of a married woman other than one having the title of Lady or Dame: *Mrs. Brown; the Honourable Mrs. Y.* 2. (as fem. equiv. of *master*) A woman having some special skill or mastery: *mistress of all the feminine arts.* 3. A woman teacher in a school; *the French mistress; a dancing mistress.* 4. A woman considered as having rule, control, or authority: *mistress of society at the period; 'And mistress of herself, though China fall'* (Pope, 'To a Lady'), having her emotions under proper control, remaining unruffled. 5. (fig.) Something personified as a female ruler: *the moon, the mistress of the night*; specif., *Mistress of the World*, Rome; *Mistress of the Seas*, Great Britain; *Mistress of the Adriatic*, Venice. 6. (poet.) A lady-love, sweetheart: *O, mistress mine!* 7. A man's paramour; kept woman, female favourite.

Mistress of the Robes, n. Title of the chief lady of the Royal Household.

mistrial, n. [1. mìstríal; 2. mìstráiəl]. **mis-** & **trial**. (law) A trial which is void through an error in proceedings.

mistrust (I.), vb. trans. [1. mistrúst; 2. mistrást]. **mis-** & **trust**. To have no trust or confidence in; to suspect, doubt.

mistrust (II.), n., fr. prec. Suspicion, distrust, want of confidence.

mistrustful, adj. [1. mistrústfool; 2. mistrástfəl]. Prec. & **-ful**. Suspicious, distrustful.

mistrustfully, adv. Prec. & **-ly**. Suspiciously, distrustfully.

mistrustfulness, n. See prec. & **-ness**. Mistrust, suspicion, distrust.

misty, adj. [1. místi; 2. místi]. O.E. *mistig*. **mist (I.)** & **-y**. 1. a Covered, hidden, by mist; accompanied by mist: *a misty morning; misty weather*; b (of the eyes) suffused with tears. 2. Intellectually obscure, vague, indistinct: *a misty notion, idea, conception; misty recollections of the past.*

misunderstand, vb. trans. [1. mìsunderstánd; 2. mìsandəstǽnd]. **mis-** & **understand**. To mistake the meaning of; to put a wrong meaning to, or wrong interpretation on.

misunderstanding, n. [1. mìsunderstánding; 2. mìsandəstǽndiŋ]. Prec. & **-ing**. a Mistake, misconception, misinterpretation; b a dispute, disagreement; quarrel.

misusage, n. [1. misúzij; 2. misjúzidž]. See next word & **-age**. a Wrong usage, misuse (of words &c.); b ill-treatment.

misuse (I.), vb. trans. [1. misúz; 2. misjúz], fr. O. Fr. *mesuser*, 'to misuse', fr. *mes-*, see **mis-**, & *user*, 'to use'. See **use**. a To put to a wrong use; to misapply (esp. words); b to treat improperly; to ill-treat.

misuse (II.), n. [1. misús; 2. misjús], fr. prec. Wrong, improper use; misusage.

mite (I.), n. [1. mīt; 2. mait]. M.E. *myte*, *mite*; not in O.E.; fr. M. Du. *mijt*, also in O. Fr. *mite*; prob. not the same word as **mite (II.)**, though fr. same ultimate source. 1. A very small coin, orig. a Flemish copper coin; in popular usage a half-farthing. 2. A small contribution, effort &c., the most or best one can afford or do: *to contribute one's mite; the widow's mite*, small but willing gift of poor person. 3. Any very small thing: *a tiny mite (of a child).*

mite (II.), n. O.E. *mīte*, 'small insect'; O.H.G. *miza*, 'midge, fly', L.G. *mite*; cogn. w. Goth. *maitan*, 'to cut'; prob. cogn. w. Lat. *mutilus*, 'maimed'. See **mutilate**. A small arachnid, of many kinds, found as parasites or in food, esp. *cheesemite*.

Mithraism, n. [1. míthraizm; 2. míþrəizəm], fr. O. Pers. *Mithra*, in Gk. *Míthras*, 'god of light', & **-ism**. The worship or cult of Mithras, an Old Persian deity or demiurge, regarded as the God of Light and helper of mankind.

mithridate, n. [1. míthridāt; 2. míþrideit], fr. Mithridates VI., King of Pontus, d. 63 B.C., who made himself poison-proof. Ancient name for an antidote against poison: *'Thessalian drugs or Mithridate'* (Marlowe).

mitigate, vb. trans. [1. mítigāt; 2. mítigeit], fr. Lat. *mītigāt-(um)*, P.P. type of *mītigāre*, 'to make soft, tender, to tame; pacify, calm, soothe', fr. *mītis*, 'mild, gentle, calm'; etymol. unknown. a To reduce intensity of, alleviate: *to mitigate pain, suffering, grief, anger* &c.; b to make milder, reduce severity of: *to mitigate a punishment.*

mitigation, n. [1. mìtigáshun; 2. mìtigéiʃən]. Prec. & **-ion**. 1. Act of mitigating; state of being mitigated. 2. Abatement, alleviation; extenuation; specif. (law) *mitigation of damages*, a lowering of damages to be assessed by a jury.

mitigatory, adj. [1. mítigāturi; 2. mítigeitəri]. See **mitigate** & **-ory**. Tending to mitigate.

mitosis, n. [1. mitósis; 2. mitóusis]. Modern scientific concocted word, fr. Gk. *mitos*, 'thread', etymol. doubtful, & **-osis**. (biol.) The more usual method of division of animal and plant cells.

mitotic, adj. [1. mitótik; 2. mitɔ́tik]. Prec. & **-ic**. Pertaining to mitosis.

mitrailleuse, n. [1. mètrīyéz; 2. mìtraijə́z]. Fr., fr. *mitraille*, 'small missiles, grape-shot', in O. Fr. 'small coins', fr. *mite*, 'small coin'. See **mite (I.)**. A form of machine-gun, consisting of a collection of breech-loading rifle barrels, arranged to fire bullets in succession or simultaneously.

mitral, adj. [1. mítral; 2. máitrəl]. See next word & **-al**. (anat.) *Mitral valve*, one of the valves of the heart; so called from its shape.

mitre (I.), n. [1. míter; 2. máitə]. Fr., fr. Lat. *mitra*, 'cap, turban', as worn by Asiatics, & by women & effeminate men in Rome, fr. Gk. *mitra*, 'belt; head-band, fillet, chaplet'; also applied to an Asiatic turban; origin doubtful. 1. a (Jewish antiq.) The turban or official head-dress of the High

Priest; **b** (eccles.) official head-dress of a bishop, sometimes also of certain abbots; consisting of a high conical cap of linen, divided by a cleft between back and front, with two fillets hanging from the bottom edge at the back; **c** (fig.) office, dignity, of a bishop: *to confer a mitre upon*, make a bishop of. **2.** (carpentry, perh. of different, though unknown origin) Joint formed by bevelling the ends of two pieces of wood so that they fit exactly to form an angle.

mitre (II.), vb. trans. See prec. **1.** (rare) To confer, bestow, the mitre of a bishop upon; to make (a person) a bishop. **2.** To join two pieces of wood, at an angle, by a mitre.

mitred, adj. [1. míterd; 2. máitəd]. **mitre** (I.) & **-ed.** **a** Wearing a mitre; **b** entitled to wear a mitre: *mitred abbot.*

mitt, n. [1. mit; 2. mit], abbr. of next word. **1.** Mitten. **2.** (slang) **a** (pl.) Boxing-gloves; **b** (sing.) fist, hand.

mitten, n. [1. mítn; 2. mítn], fr. O. Fr. *mitaine*; etymol. unknown. **a** Kind of glove with thumb but no separate fingers, worn as protection for the hand against cold or injury; **b** (i.) a knitted woollen glove covering the palm and back of hand and the wrist, but not the thumb or fingers; worn as protection against cold, often over an ordinary glove; (ii.) similar glove of silk or lace formerly worn by ladies in the evening &c.

mittimus, n. [1. mítimus; 2. mítiməs]. Lat., 'we send'; 1st pers. pl. pres. indic. of *mittere*, 'to send'. See **missile.** **a** (law) A warrant committing a person to prison; **b** (colloq.) notice of dismissal, discharge from employment.

mix, vb. trans. & intrans. [1. miks; 2. miks]. Formed fr. **mixed**, earlier *mixt*; the vb. does not appear before late 16th cent. **A.** trans. **1.** To mingle (things, substances) together; to combine so that the ingredients form a compound: *to mix wine and water*; *to mix sand in* or *with the sugar.* Phrs. *to mix a salad*, to prepare and make it; *to mix a poison*, to prepare, compound, a poison; *to mix up*, (i.) to mix thoroughly; to confuse, combine, inextricably: *to mix up one's ideas*; (ii.) confuse one thing with, mistake it for, another: *mix up one tune with another.* **2. a** To cause (persons) to come together and intermingle: *it does not always do to mix people of different social worlds*; **b** (of non-material things) to combine, mingle: *to mix business with pleasure*; *to mix feelings of love and pity.* **B.** intrans. **1.** To be capable of being mixed or mingled together; to join, combine, blend, with; to go well with: *oil and water will not mix*; *the colours mix well.* **2.** (of persons) **a** To frequent each other's society: *it is good for people with different interests to mix*; Phr. *to mix in society*, to frequent it; **b** to get on well together, associate amicably: *pure scholars do not mix easily with those who care for nothing but sport.*

mixed, adj. [1. mikst; 2. mikst]. Earlier *mixt*, fr. O. Fr. *mixte*, fr. Lat. *mixt-(um)*, P.P. type of *miscēre*, 'to mix', cogn. w. Gk. *misgein*, *mignūnai*, 'to mix, mingle', Scrt. *micra*, 'mixed'; the form *mixed* is late & formed as if P.P. of **mix. 1.** Composed, compounded, blended, of several ingredients, constituents, parts, elements, kinds &c.; not simple; not all of one kind: *mixed biscuits, pickles* &c. Phrs. *mixed motives*, not completely disinterested; *to have mixed feelings*, be partly glad, partly sorry; *mixed up with*, associated with, involved in. **2.** Composed of persons of different classes, ranks &c., esp. of those of uncertain or suspicious antecedents; not select: *a very mixed company, assembly* &c. **3.** Shared, engaged in, by persons of opposite sexes: *mixed bathing*; *mixed doubles* (at lawn tennis &c.). **4.** Confused in mind, muddled, incoherent: *you are getting mixed.*

mixen, n. [1. míksn; 2. míksn]. O.E. *meoxen*, fr. *meox*, 'dung', cogn. w. Goth. *maihstus*, 'dung', Germ. *mist*; fr. same base as O.E. *mīgan*, 'to make water'. See **micturition, mistletoe.** (archaic or dial.) Dung-hill, manure heap.

mixer, n. [1. míkser; 2. míksə]. **mix** & **-er.** **a** Contrivance for mixing; **b** person who mixes; **c** (colloq., U.S.A.) a person who mixes easily, and sociably with others; a sociable, genial person: *a good, a bad, mixer.*

mixture, n. [1. míkschur; 2. míkstʃə], fr. Lat. *mixtūra*, 'mixing'. See **mixed** & **-ure.** **1.** Act of mixing; state of being mixed. **2.** (of material things) That which is mixed; **a** a compound, combination, blend: *a mixture of real and artificial silk, of Indian and China tea* &c.; specif. **b** combination of various kinds of tobacco; also called *smoking mixture*; **c** combination of several drugs in liquid, taken medicinally; a medicine; **d** (chem. and phys.) a combination of two or more substances which, however thoroughly mixed, retain unaltered their properties, as contrasted with *compound.* **3.** Combination of various feelings, emotions &c.: *a mixture of grief and anger* &c.

mix-up, n. [1. miks úp; 2. miks áp]. (colloq.) **a** Confusion, muddle; **b** a confused fight.

mizzen, mizen, n. [1. mízn; 2. mízn], fr. Fr. *misaine*, 'a foresail', prob. fr. Ital. *mezzana*, 'a sail on the poop of a ship', fr. L. Lat. *mediānus*, 'of or in the middle', fr. Lat. *medius*, 'middle'. See **mezzanine. a** The fore-and-aft sail set on the mizzen-mast of a ship; **b** the mizzen-mast.

mizzen-mast, n. The aftermost mast of a three-masted ship, or of a two-masted vessel, as a yawl, where the foremast is the greater of the two.

mizzle (I.), vb. impers. & n. [1. mízl; 2. mízl]. Cogn. w. L.G. *miseln*, M. Du. *mieselen*, 'to drizzle', cp. Fris. *misig*, 'damp'. **a** vb. To drizzle, rain in fine drops; **b** n., a drizzle; fine rain.

mizzle (II.), vb. intrans. Etymol. unknown. (slang) To run away, sneak off; do a bolt or bunk.

mnemonic, adj. & n. [1. nemónik; 2. nemɔ́nik], fr. Gk. *mnēmonikós*, 'of memory; having a good memory', fr. *mnḗmōn*, 'mindful, remembering'; cp. Gk. *mnâsthai*, 'to remember'; cogn. w. Scrt. *mnā*, 'to remember'; fr. base **men-*, 'to think'. See **mental** (I.) & **mind. 1.** adj. Helping, strengthening, the memory: *mnemonic system*; *mnemonic rhymes* &c. **2.** n. pl. *Mnemonics*, **a** art of aiding the memory; **b** a system of rules, methods, precepts &c. for helping or improving the memory.

moa, n. [1. móa; 2. móuə]. Native Maori name. An extinct New Zealand, flightless bird, *Dinornis* &c., somewhat resembling the ostrich.

moan (I.), n. [1. mōn; 2. moun]. M.E. *mōne*; fr. O.E. **mān-*, cogn. w. O.E. *mǣnan*, 'to lament, moan', fr. **mānjan*, M.E. *mēnen*; cp. **mean** (IV.). **a** A low, long-drawn sound expressing pain or sorrow; a groan; **b** (poet.) lament, complaint: '*She . . . made sweet moan*' (Keats, '*Belle Dame Sans Merci*').

moan (II.), vb. trans. & intrans. See prec. **1.** trans. (poet.) **a** To lament, grieve, for: *they moaned their lost ones*; **b** to utter a moan for; usually *bemoan*: *moan one's grief, loss.* **2.** intrans. To utter a moan or sound like a moan: *the wounded moaned ceaselessly*; *the wind moans through the trees.*

moat, n. & vb. trans. [1. mōt; 2. mout]. M.E. *mōte*, O. Fr. *mote*, 'embankment, dike, hill', Mod. Fr. *motte*, 'mound', cp. L. Lat. *motta*, 'mound, mound and ditch'; the word orig. meant an earth rampart including the ditch fr. wh. the earth was thrown up, cp. **dike** & **ditch**; prob. of Gmc. origin & possibly cogn. w. **mud. 1.** n. A ditch or trench, generally filled with water, outside the rampart or wall of a fortification. **2.** vb. To surround with a moat, dig a moat round: *the Moated Grange.*

mob (I.), n. [1. mob; 2. mɔb]. Shortened form of Lat. *mōbile vulgus*, 'the movable, excitable, crowd or rabble'; in 17th & early 18th cent. the full form *mobile* [1. mṓbili, móbili; 2. móubili, mɔ́bili] was used, & Swift regards *mob* as a rather vulgar modernism. **a** A disorderly crowd or rabble; a mixed, promiscuous gathering or assemblage: '*the wits of either Charles's days, The mob of gentlemen who wrote with ease*' (Pope, 'To Augustus'); **b** the lower orders, the rabble, the masses: *mob law*, rule dictated by the mob or masses; lynch law; **c** (slang) gang of pickpockets or thieves: *the swell-mob*, gang of flashily dressed pickpockets.

mob (II.), vb. trans., fr. prec. To jostle, attack, in a mob or crowd; to crowd round either for attack or to applaud &c.: *the crowd mobbed the unpopular minister*; *the returning soldiers were mobbed in the streets.*

mobbish, adj. [1. móbish; 2. mɔ́biʃ]. **mob** (I.) & **-ish.** Like a mob; disorderly, rowdy.

mob-cap, n. Also *mob*; cp. Du. *mopmuts*, 'mob-cap', *mop*, 'a coif', *muts*, 'cap'. A woman's head-dress, consisting of a high frilled cap covering the entire head and tied under the chin.

mobile (I.), adj. [1. mṓbīl; 2. móubail]. Fr., fr. Lat. *mōbilis*, 'movable', for **mōvibilis*, fr. *mŏvēre*, 'to move'. See **move. 1.** Movable, easily moved; moving easily or rapidly: *mobile artillery, troops* &c. **2.** Changing easily, rapidly, constantly: *mobile features*; active, versatile: *a mobile mind*; changeable, fickle: *mobile fancies.*

mobile (II.), n. [1. mṓbili; 2. móubili]. Lat., neut. sing. of *mōbilis*, as prec. **1.** Primum mobile, q.v. **2.** (obs.) Mob (I.), q.v.

mobility, n. [1. mōbíliti; 2. moubíliti]. Fr. *mobilité*, fr. Lat. *mōbilitāt-(em)*, *mōbilitas*, 'mobility'. See **mobile** (I.) & **-ity.** Quality, state, of being mobile; ability, capacity, for rapid and easy movement.

mobilization, n. [1. mòbilīzáshun; 2. mòubilaizéiʃən]. **mobilize** & **-ation. 1.** Specif. (mil.) act of raising a fleet or army from a peace to a war-footing and putting it in a state to move, fully equipped, to the seat of war. **2.** The making liquid or available, of money, assets, property of any kind; the bringing of money &c. into circulation: *the mobilization of the financial resources of a country.*

mobilize, vb. trans. & intrans. [1. mṓbilīz; 2. móubilaiz]. Fr. *mobiliser*, 'to make mobile'. See **mobile** (I.) & **-ize. A.** trans. To make mobile or movable. Specif. **1.** to place a navy or army or portions thereof on a war-footing, furnished with full equipment, stores &c., and able to move to the seat of war. **2.** To render money, property &c. liquid, available; to put money &c. into circulation. **B.** intrans. Specif., to mobilize armed forces.

mobocracy, n. [1. mobókrasi; 2. mɔbɔ́krəsi], fr. **mob** (I.) & **-cracy**, on anal. of *democracy.* Rule by the mob.

moccasin, n. [1. mókasin; 2. mɔ́kəsin]. N. Am. Indian, *makisin*, *mockasin*. **1.** The soft leather, usually deerskin, shoe of the N. American Indians. **2.** (zool.) The popular name of two N. American snakes, of similar appearance, the harmless *Natrix*, and esp. the very venomous water moccasin, *Ancistrodon.*

Mocha, n. [1. mṓka; 2. móukə]. Name of Arab port on the Red Sea. **1.** A fine variety of coffee, originally shipped from Mocha. **2.** A fine leather for gloves, made from the skin of the Arabian goat.

mocha stone, n. Chalcedony, moss-agate.

mock (I.), vb. trans. & intrans. [1. mok; 2. mɔk]. M.E. *mokken*, fr. O. Fr. *mocquer*, Mod. Fr. *moquer*; etymol. doubtful. **A.** trans. **1.** To ridicule, hold up to contempt; to deride, treat with scorn and contempt. **2.** To render futile, defeat, defy: *the river mocked all our efforts to cross.* **3. a** To mimic, so as to bring into contempt; to burlesque (a person); **b** (fig.) to delude, lure on, attract and disappoint: *mocked with false hopes.* **B.** intrans. To jeer, scoff; to express, exhibit, feelings of contempt; to deride; also *mock at*-

mock (II.), n., fr. prec. (archaic) **a** (i.) An act of ridicule or contempt; flout, jeer; (ii.) person or thing ridiculed or mocked; Phr. *to make a mock of*, to ridicule, mock; **b** an imitation, mockery, travesty.

mock (III.), adj., fr. prec. (only in certain combinations) Sham, false, counterfeit: *mock-heroic*, burlesquing the heroic style or manner; *mock-majesty*; *mock-modesty*; *mock auction*, an auction where confederates of the sellers of worthless goods make fictitious bids to encourage the unwary to believe the goods are valuable; *mock-moon*, paraselene; *mock-orange*, the syringa, from the scent of its flowers; *mock-sun*, parhelion; *mock-turtle* (*soup*), soup made of calf's head to imitate real turtle soup.

mocker, n. [1. móker; 2. mɔ́kə]. **mock** (I.) & **-er**. One who mocks.

mockery, n. [1. mókeri; 2. mɔ́kəri], fr. Fr. *moquerie*. **mock** (I.) & **-ery**. **1.** Derision, ridicule; contemptuous, scornful laughter: *to hold a person, thing, up to mockery*. **2.** Object, butt, of derision, ridicule &c.: *to make a mockery of* (person or thing). **3.** Delusion, delusive appearance; bad imitation, travesty: *the performance was a mockery of the great original*. **4.** Disappointment, vain, futile, fruitless attempt: *all our hopes, efforts, struggles, were mockeries*.

mocking-bird, n. [1. móking bērd; 2. mɔ́kiŋ bʌ̄d]. A bird, *Mimus polyglottus*, resembling, and allied to, the thrush, common in the south of North America and in the West Indies, which imitates exactly the notes of other birds.

mockingly, adv. [1. mókingli; 2. mɔ́kiŋli]. **mock** (I.) & **-ing** & **-ly**. In a mocking, jeering manner; derisively; with mockery.

modal, adj. [1. mṓdal; 2. móudəl], fr. Med. Lat. *modālis*, 'of or belonging to a mode', fr. Lat. *modus*, see **mode**, & **-al**. **1.** Of or belonging to a mode or mood; of form as opposed to essence or substance. **2.** (gram.) Expressing mood or manner, as of verbs or particles. **3.** (law) Containing direction as to the mode or manner in which the terms of a document are to be carried out: *a modal will, bequest, legacy*. **4.** (log.) Expressing, marked by, modality: *modal proposition*, a proposition, which affirms or denies with a qualification or modality. **5.** (mus.) Of or belonging to any one of the modes.

modality, n. [1. mōdáliti; 2. moudǽliti]. Prec. & **-ity**. State, condition, quality, of being modal; specif. (log.) the qualification of the assertion or denial of the terms of a proposition, according as they are possible, impossible, necessary, or contingent.

mode, n. [1. mōd; 2. moud], fr. or influenced by Fr. *mode*, 'manner, fashion, style', fr. Lat. *modus*, 'measure, manner, form'; fr. base **med-*, 'to measure'. Cp. **mete** (II.) & see **meditate**. **1.** a Manner, method, form, style, fashion; custom, way of acting, speaking, behaving &c.: *a mode of life*; **b** *the mode*, the prevailing fashion in dress, speech &c.; **c** *modes*, specif., the passing, prevailing fashions in wearing apparel. **2.** (log.) **a** The form in which a proposition qualifies an assertion or denial, as possibility, impossibility, necessity, or contingency; **b** mood. **3.** (mus.) **a** Any one of the forms in the method or system of arranging the scale or octave in the Ancient Greek and mediaeval ecclesiastical music, as the *Lydian, Dorian, modes*; *authentic, plagal, modes*; **b** (mod. mus.) either of the two classes of keys, the *major* and the *minor mode*.

model (I.), n. [1. módl; 2. mɔ́dl], fr. O. Fr. *modelle*, fr. Ital. *modello*, 'pattern, mould', dimin. of *modo*, fr. Lat. *modus*, 'measure, pattern, mode'. See **mode** & cp. **mould** (III.). **1.** a A reproduction or copy in three dimensions, in miniature, but to scale, of some object already in existence: *model of a ship, engine, cathedral* &c.; *a model yacht*; **b** a preliminary three-dimensional reproduction embodying the plan from, and according to which, something is to be constructed, either in miniature or on full scale: *a model for a war memorial, factory* &c.; *of a mechanical invention*; *a working model*, one of a machine, showing the parts at work: *clay, wax, model*, of piece of sculpture to be reproduced later in marble, bronze &c.; **c** (colloq.) a person or thing exactly resembling another: *the boy is a perfect model of his father*. **2.** **a** (of persons or things) A standard, pattern, of excellence; an example, copy, to be followed and imitated: *a model of industry, discretion, beauty* &c.; *a model of delicate construction*; **b** system, method, plan: *advance can be on an evolutionary or a revolutionary model*; *the New Model*, (i.) Cromwell's system of reorganizing the Parliamentary army, 1644–45; (ii.) his army as so reorganized. **3.** **a** A person who poses to a painter or sculptor: *an artist's model*; **b** (i.) a woman who wears and exhibits to customers new costumes, hats &c. in a draper's or milliner's shop; a mannequin; also (ii.) a costume so exhibited. **4.** (attrib.) Serving as a model or pattern to be imitated, or as a standard of excellence: *model behaviour*; *model farm*; *model wife*.

model (II.), vb. trans., fr. prec. **1.** To make a model of; to mould, form (something); specif. **a** to mould (clay or other plastic material into given shape), or (something) out of clay &c.; (also fig.) *delicately modelled features, limbs* &c.; **b** generally, to put into shape, plan out, design: *to model a city, park* &c.; to organize: *to model a household* &c. **2.** **a** To make, plan (something) in a particular way or according to a particular design: *to model a garden after the manner of Kew*; **b** to conform in behaviour, action &c. to, direct one's course of action &c. according to some particular principle or exemplar: *to model one's life according to the ideals of Christianity*; *to model one's manners on those of the old school*. Phr. *to model oneself* (*up*)*on a person*, imitate him, take him as an example.

modeller, n. [1. módeler; 2. mɔ́dələ]. Prec. & **-er**. One who practises modelling, esp. in clay, wax, or other plastic material.

modelling, n. [1. módeling; 2. mɔ́d(ə)liŋ]. **model** (II.) & **-ing**. **1.** Art of the modeller. **2.** The act or process of working in plastic materials, such as clay, wax, &c. **3.** Mode of representation in sculpture or painting of the three dimensions of the forms, contours, outlines, of a solid figure; the way in which this is done; shaping, moulding: *the exquisite modelling of Greek sculpture*, (also fig.) *the modelling of a person's features* &c.

moderate (I.), adj. [1. móderat; 2. mɔ́dərit], fr. Lat. *moderāt-*(*um*), P.P. type of *moderāri*, 'to set bounds or a measure to; to mitigate, lessen, temper, moderate', fr. *modus*, 'measure'. See **mode**. **1.** **a** (of persons) Not going to extremes, keeping within reasonable bounds; not violent; temperate, restrained: *a moderate man*; *moderate in temper, language, in views, policy* &c.; **b** (of actions, ideas, opinions &c.) showing moderation; well-considered, measured, sober: *moderate demands*; *a moderate sentence*, not a severe one. **2.** (of quantity, amount, degree, extent &c.) Not large; limited, on the small side: *moderate means, income, height, distance, weight* &c.; *a moderate appetite*, not a large one; *at moderate speed*, not too fast. **3.** (of quality) Indifferent, fair, medium, only mediocre: *moderate abilities, skill, good looks, success, health*.

moderate (II.), n., fr. prec. A moderate person, esp. in political and religious views.

moderate (III.), vb. trans. & intrans. [1. móderāt; 2. mɔ́dəreit], fr. **moderate** (I.). **1.** trans. **a** To restrain, keep within bounds; to render moderate, make less violent or extreme: *to moderate one's language, appetite, temper* &c.; **b** to temper, qualify, reduce, mitigate: *to moderate the heat, draught*; *to moderate one's policy, views* &c.; *to moderate one's demands*; *to exercise a moderating influence on*. **2.** intrans. **a** To grow, become moderate; to become less violent or extreme: *the gale, the sea, his temper, has moderated*; **b** to act as moderator.

moderately, adv. [1. móderatli; 2. mɔ́dəritli]. See prec. & **-ly**. In a moderate manner; not excessively; to a moderate extent or degree.

moderateness, n. [1. móderatnes; 2. mɔ́dəritnis]. As prec. & **-ness**. State, quality, of being moderate; moderation.

moderation, n. [1. mòderáshun; 2. mɔ̀dəréiʃən]. Fr. *modération*, fr. Lat. *moderātiōn-*(*em*), acc. of *moderātio*, fr. *moderāt-*(*um*), P.P. type of *moderāre*. See **moderate** (I.) & **-ion**. **1.** **a** State or quality of being moderate; **b** act of moderating. **2.** **a** Avoidance of excess in conduct; abstemiousness, temperance; Phr. *in moderation*, moderately; **b** absence of extremes of temper, or violence of disposition; restraint, equability, mildness of character. **3.** (cap., pl.) *Moderations*, the first public examination at Oxford University for the Bachelor of Arts degree; popularly known as *Mods*. **4.** (Presbyterian Churches) The calling of a minister by a congregation and presbytery under the presidency of the Moderator.

moderator, n. [1. móderātor; 2. mɔ́dəreitə]. Lat., 'manager, director'. See **moderate** (III.) & **-or**. **1.** One who or that which moderates; an arbitrator, mediator; regulator; *moderator lamp*, lamp with a mechanism for regulating the flow of oil to the wick. **2.** (eccles.) The presiding ecclesiastical officer at the General Assembly of the Church of Scotland. **3.** **a** An examiner for Moderations at Oxford University; **b** one of the two superintending officials at the examination for the mathematical tripos at Cambridge University.

moderatorship, n. [1. móderātorship; 2. mɔ́dəreitəʃip]. Prec. & **-ship**. Office of a Moderator, in Church of Scotland.

modern (I.), adj. [1. módern; 2. mɔ́dən]. L. Lat. *modernus*, 'modern', formed fr. *modo*, 'just now, lately', fr. *modus*, 'measure, mode'. See **mode**. **1.** **a** Belonging to, characteristic of, the present time; recent: *modern times*; *modern discovery, poetry* &c.; **b** new-fashioned, not old-fashioned or antiquated; up-to-date: *modern ideas, fashions* &c. **2.** **a** Contrasted with *classical*: *modern languages*; *modern school, side*, that division of a school in which science, higher mathematics, modern languages &c. are taught; **b** (specif., philol.) designating the later period of linguistic development, extending from a given approximate date to the present time: *Modern English* (from early 15th cent. onwards); **c** contrasted with *Ancient*, or *Mediaeval*: *Modern History*, history of Europe from the conquest of Constantinople by the Turks (1453).

modern (II.), n., fr. prec. **a** A person living in modern times; **b** a person who holds modern ideas; one who is in sympathy with the beliefs, feelings, and ideals of recent times, or of the present day.

modernism, n. [1. módernizm; 2. mɔ́dənizəm]. **modern** (I.) & **-ism**. **1.** Modern, present-day, usage, thought, customs, practice &c.; a particular example of this. **2.** (usually cap.) The system and methods adopted by a certain advanced school of theologians and historians who attempt to state, or re-state, the dogmas of Christianity in the light of modern criticism and thought, and to test the credibility of the historical facts recorded in the Old and New Testaments by applying to them the results of modern textual and historical research.

modernist, n. [1. módernist; 2. mɔ́dənist]. **modern** & **-ist**. **a** A follower, admirer of, believer in, modern ways, thought, usages &c.; specif. **b** (cap.) one who applies the methods of Modernism in religion.

modernity, n. [1. modérniti; 2. mɔdʌ́niti]. **modern** & **-ity**. State, quality, of being modern; modernness.

modernization, n. [1. mòdernizáshun; 2. mɔ̀dənaizéiʃən]. See next word & **-ation**.

a Act of modernizing or making modern; act of bringing up to date; b state of being modernized.

modernize, vb. trans. [1. módernīz; 2. mɔ́dən-aiz], fr. **modern (I.)** & **-ize**. To make, render, modern; to adapt to modern usage or for present-day use.

modernly, adv. [1. módernli; 2. mɔ́dənli]. **modern** & **-ly**. In a modern manner.

modernness, n. [1. módernnes; 2. mɔ́dənnis]. **modern** & **-ness**. State, quality, of being modern; modernity.

modest, adj. [1. módest; 2. mɔ́dist], fr. Fr. *modeste*, fr. Lat. *modestus*, 'measured, moderate', fr. *modus*, 'measure, mode'. See **mode** & **moderate**. **1.** Moderate; not excessive: *modest expenditure, demands, hopes, requirements, pretentions* &c. **2.** Having and expressing a moderate opinion of one's own abilities and qualities; not boastful, arrogant or self-assertive; diffident, humble, unpretentious: *really great men are essentially modest; modest behaviour.* **3.** (chiefly of women) Chaste in behaviour, speech, bearing, dress &c.; decent, seemly.

modestly, adv. Prec. & **-ly**. In a modest manner.

modesty, n. [1. módesti; 2. mɔ́disti]. Fr. *modestie*, Lat. *modestia*. As prec. & **-y**. Quality of being modest. **1.** Unpretentiousness, humility, unwillingness to put oneself forward; lowly opinion of one's own talents, virtues &c.; reverse of boastfulness, conceit, self-assertiveness. **2.** Female virtue of chastity; purity of sentiment; decency, seemliness, decorum, in speech, behaviour, dress &c. **3.** Proper sense of shame; delicacy of feeling.

modicum, n. [1. módikum; 2. mɔ́dikəm]. Lat. neut. sing. of *modicus*, 'moderate', fr. *modus*, 'measure'. See **mode**. A small amount or quantity: *satisfied with a modicum of sleep; one gets but a modicum of pleasure from such a book.*

modifiability, n. [1. mòdifīabíliti; 2. mɔ̀difai-əbíliti]. See next word & **-ity**. Capacity of being modified.

modifiable, adj. [1. módifīable; 2. mɔ́difaiəbl]. **modify** & **-able**. Capable of being, liable to be, modified.

modification, n. [1. mòdifikáshun; 2. mɔ̀difi-kéiʃən]. Lat. *modificātiōn-(em)*, *modificātio*, 'the making modified or moderate', fr. *modificāre*. See **modify**. **1.** Act or process of modifying; state of being modified. **2.** a Result of such process; change, alteration; b specif. (i.) change wrought in a vowel sound by *mutation*; (ii.) graphic expression of this, e.g. *ö, ü.*

modificatory, adj. [1. mòdifikátori; 2. mɔ̀di-fikéitəri]. As prec. & **-ory**. Modifying, qualifying.

modify, vb. trans. [1. módifī; 2. mɔ́difai], fr. Fr. *modifier*, fr. Lat. *modificāre*, 'to make moderate, modify', fr. *modus*, 'measure'. See **mode** & **-fy**. **1.** To moderate, make less severe; to limit, lessen: *to modify demands, one's tone* &c. **2.** To change, qualify, alter: *to modify the terms in a document; to modify one's ideas, opinions* &c. **3.** (popular gram.) To change a vowel sound, through the influence of one which follows; to cause to undergo vowel mutation; such a Phr. as *the modified ü in Bühne* may refer either to the sound change, or to the graphic representation of it by (¨) placed over the letter.

modillion, n. [1. modíliun; 2. mədíliən]. Fr., fr. Ital. *modiglione*, fr. Lat. See **modulus**. (archit.) A decorated projection or bracket beneath the cornice of an entablature of the Corinthian Order.

modish, adj. [1. módish; 2. móudiʃ]. **mode** & **-ish**. According to the mode or fashion; fashionable.

modishly, adv. Prec. & **-ly**. Fashionably.

modishness, n. See prec. & **-ness**. Quality of being fashionable.

modiste, n. [1. mōdḗst; 2. moudíst]. Fr., 'dress-maker', fr. *mode*, 'fashion', see **mode**, & **-ist**. A dressmaker, milliner.

modular, adj. [1. módūlar 2. mɔ́djulə]. **module** & **-ar**. Of or pertaining to a module or modulus.

modulate, vb. trans. & intrans. [1. módūlāt; 2. mɔ́djuleit], fr. Lat. *modulāt-(um)*, P.P. type of *modulāri*, 'to measure off, regulate, measure rhythmically', fr. *modulus*, dimin. of *modus*, 'measure'. See **mode** & **modulus**. **1.** trans. a To regulate, adapt, adjust; b to vary, change, inflect (voice, tone, pitch &c.). **2.** intrans. (mus.) To pass from one key to another.

modulation, n. [1. mòdūláshun; 2. mɔ̀dju-léiʃən]. Lat. *modulātiōn-(em)*, 'rhythmical measure'. See prec. & **-ion**. a Variation, inflexion of voice, tone, movements, in intensity, or rhythm; specif. b (elect.) the varying of a continuous oscillating current in accordance with the varying frequency and amplitude of sound waves, as in wireless telephony.

modulator, n. [1. módūlàtor; 2. mɔ́djuleitə]. Lat., 'one who measures rhythmically; a musical director'. See **modulate** & **-or**. **1.** One who, that which, modulates. **2.** (mus.) A chart or map showing relations between tones and scales in the tonic sol-fa system.

module, n. [1. módūl; 2. mɔ́djūl]. Fr., fr. Lat. See next word. **1.** A unit or standard of measurement, as for the flow of water. **2.** (archit.) A unit of measurement for determining the proportions of a building, as half the diameter of a column at the base of the shaft.

modulus, n., pl. **moduli** [1. módūlus, -lī; 2. mɔ́djuləs, -lai]. Lat., 'small measure', dimin. of *modus*, 'measure'. See **mode**. (math. and phys.) A constant multiplier or coefficient.

modus, n., pl. **modi** [1. módus, mṓdī; 2. móudəs, móudai]. Lat., 'standard by which anything is measured; a measure'. See **mode**. Method, manner, mode: *modus operandi*, method, system, of working or operating; plan of operations; *modus vivendi*, mode, method, of living, esp. of a scheme or arrangement under which two parties can temporarily carry on while a dispute is being settled.

mofette, n. [1. mōfét; 2. moufét]. Fr., fr. Ital. *mofeta*. Cp. **mephitic**. a A fissure in the earth allowing noxious gases to escape; b discharge of noxious gas from the earth.

mofussil, n. [1. mōfúsl; 2. moufásl]. Hind. *mufassil*, fr. Arab. *mufaççal*, fr. *façala*, 'to divide, separate'. The rural, country, districts in India, as distinguished from the towns, residences, or seats of government.

Mogul, n. [1. mogúl; 2. məgál]. Pers. *mugul*, 'Mongol'. One of the Mongolian invaders of India, follower of Baber or Jenghiz Khan: *the Great Mogul*, the Emperor of Delhi, of the Mogul dynasty which governed all or part of Hindustan from 16th cent. till the Indian Mutiny.

mohair, n. [1. mṓhār; 2. móuhɛə]. Earlier *moekaire*, form influenced by *hair*, fr. Arab. *mukhayyah*, 'a choice hair-cloth', fr. *khayyara*, 'to choose, select'. See also **moire**. **1.** a The fine, silky hair of the Angora goat; b the fine camlet cloth made from this. **2.** Imitation of this made of a mixture of wool and cotton.

Mohammedan, adj. & n. [1. mōhámedan; 2. mouhǽmidən]. Mohammed, fr. name of the Prophet, d. 632, in Arab., *Muḥammad*, lit. 'praiseworthy', & **-an**. **1.** adj. Pertaining to the religion, law, customs founded by Mohammed. **2.** n. A follower of Mohammed; a Moslem.

Mohammedanism, n. [1. mōhámedanizm; 2. mouhǽmidənizəm]. Prec. & **-ism**. System of religion and law founded by Mohammed; Islam.

Mohammedanize, vb. trans. [1. mōhámedanīz; 2. mouhǽmidənaiz]. See prec. & **-ize**. To bring under the influence of Mohammedanism.

Moharram, Muhurram, n. [1. mohúram; 2. məhárəm]. Arab. *muḥarram*, 'sacred, forbidden'. a The first month of the Mohammedan year; b a festival held by the Shī'ite sect in the early part of this month, in remembrance of the deaths of Hosein and Ali.

Mohawk, n. [1. mṓhawk; 2. móuhɔ̄k]. Native name. **1.** a Member of a tribe of North American Indians; b their language. **2.** (skating) A stroke from an edge on one foot to the same edge on the other foot in the opposite direction.

Mohock, n. [1. mṓhok; 2. móuhɔk]. Variant of prec. A member of a gang of ruffianly young men of fashion, who infested the streets of London in the early part of 18th cent. and molested citizens.

mohur, n. [1. mṓhėr; 2. móuhā]. Hind., fr. Pers. *muhr*, 'seal, coin'. A gold coin current in India until 1899, worth 15 rupees.

moidore, n. [1. móidōr; 2. móuidɔ̄], fr. Port. *moeda d'ouro*, 'money, coin of gold'; fr. Lat. *monēta*, 'money' (see **mint (II.)**), *aurum*, 'gold' (see **aurum**). A former Portuguese gold coin, worth 15 rupees, or about 27s.

moiety, n. [1. móieti; 2. mɔ́iəti], fr. A.-Fr. *moyté*, Fr. *moitié*, fr. Lat. *medietāt-(em)*, *medietas*, 'the middle, a half', fr. *medius*, 'middle'. See **medium**. a The half, a half-share, usually legal, of property &c.; b either of two parts into which something is divided.

moil, vb. intrans. [1. moil; 2. mɔil]. M.E. *moillen*, 'to wet; trudge through mud and wet'; O. Fr. *moiller*, Mod. Fr. *mouiller*, 'to moisten', fr. stem *molli-*, of Lat. *mollis*, 'soft'. See **mollify**. To toil, drudge; usually in Phr. *to toil and moil.*

moire, n. [1. mwar, moir; 2. mwā, mɔ́iə]. Fr., variant of **mohair**. a Mohair; b a watered silk or other textile; *moire antique*, a heavy rich watered silk; c metal surface with cloudy, watery appearance.

moiré, adj. [1. mwáhrā; 2. mwā́rei]. Fr., P.P. of *moirer*, 'to water silk', fr. prec. Watered, of silk or other textile material.

moist, adj. [1. moist; 2. mɔist]. M.E. *moiste*, 'fresh, new', of fruit, ale &c.; O. Fr. *moiste*, *moite*, 'wet, moist'; etymol. doubtful; cp. perh. Lat. *mustum*, 'new wine, must', or *mūcidus*, 'mouldy, musty'. See **must (II.)** & **mucus**. Damp, humid, not dry; rather wet; *moist colours*, water-colours put up in the form of a paste; *moist sugar*, sugar of pale brown colour, semi-crystallized and sticky.

moisten, vb. trans. & intrans. [1. móisn; 2. mɔ́isn]. Prec. & **-en**. a trans. To render moist, wet slightly, cover, impregnate, with moisture; b intrans., (rare) to become moist.

moisture, n. [1. móischur; 2. mɔ́istʃə], fr. O. Fr. *moisteur*, Mod. Fr. *moiteur*. See **moist** & **-ure**. Dampness, humidity; watery vapour condensed on a surface.

moistureless, adj. [1. móischurles; 2. mɔ́istʃəlis]. Prec. & **-less**. Without moisture; dry.

moke, n. [1. mōk; 2. mouk]. Etymol. unknown. (slang) A donkey.

molar (I.), adj. & n. [1. mṓlar; 2. móulə], fr. Lat. *molāris*, 'of or belonging to a mill; grinding, of mill-stones and teeth', fr. *mola*, 'mill, millstone'. See **mill (I.)**. **1.** adj. a Grinding, able to grind; specif., of the back teeth, *the molar teeth*; b of, relating, near to the molar teeth: *molar glands.* **2.** n. A molar tooth, grinder.

molar (II.), adj., fr. Lat. *mōlēs*, 'mass', etymol. doubtful; possibly cogn. w. Gk. *mōlos*, 'effort'; O.H.G. *muodi*, Goth. *(af)mauiþs*, 'weary'. (mech.) Of or pertaining to, acting on or by, mass or masses, contrasted with *molecular*.

molasses, n., pl. as sing. [1. molásez; 2. moulǽsiz], fr. Port. *melaço*, cp. Fr. *mélasse*, Span. *melazo*, fr. L. Lat. *mellāceus*, 'like honey, honey-sweet', fr. *mel*, *mellis*, 'honey'. See **melliferous**. The thick non-crystallizable dark syrup which drains from raw sugar during manufacture; thickest kind of treacle.

mold. Alternative spelling for **mould**.

mole (I.), n. [1. mōl; 2. moul]. O.E. *māl*; O.H.G. *meil*, Goth. *mail*, 'spot, blemish'. A dark-coloured spot or blemish on the skin; a small pigmented naevus.

mole (II.), n., fr. Fr. *môle*, fr. Lat. *mōlēs*, 'mass, heap'; see **molar** (II.). **a** A massive structure of stone laid in the sea as a breakwater; **b** a stone pier built out from the land to form a harbour.

mole (III.), n. & vb. trans. M.E. *molle, mulle*, cogn. w. L.G. *mull*, M. Du. *mol*, 'mole'; prob. akin to O.E. *myl*, M.E. *mul*, 'dust'; apparently not connected w. provinc. Engl. *mouldwarp, moldwarp*, lit. 'the mould-thrower', fr. **mould** (II.) & *warpen*, 'to throw', cp. Germ. *werfen*, 'to throw'. **1. n.** A small burrowing animal, genus *Talpa*, with soft, thick, dark, shining fur, small, barely perceptible eyes and ears, and bare paws resembling hands at the end of very short forearms. Phr. *as blind as a mole*. **2. vb.** (rare) To dig, burrow under ground like a mole.

mole (IV.), n. Fr., fr. Lat. *mola*, 'millstone', also in this sense. See **molar** (I.). A false conception, a misbirth.

mole-cricket, n. **mole** (III.) & **cricket**. A burrowing orthopterous insect, *Gryllotalpa*, allied to the true crickets.

molecular, adj. [1. molékūlar; 2. məlékjulə]. **molecule** & **-ar**. Belonging to molecules; produced by, acting in, consisting of, molecules: *molecular weight*, the weight of a molecule of a substance stated in terms of its relation to a molecule of hydrogen.

molecularity, n. [1. molèkūláriti; 2. məlèkjulæriti]. Prec. & **-ity**. State, quality, of being molecular.

molecularly, adv. [1. molékūlarli; 2. məlékjuləli]. As prec. & **-ly**. In the fashion, manner, of molecules.

molecule, n. [1. mólekūl; 2. mɔ́likjūl]. Fr. *molécule*, a dimin. formed fr. Lat. *mōlēs*, 'mass'. See **mole** (II.). (chem. and phys.) The smallest particle of matter that can exist independently without losing the distinctive characters of the substance in its original mass.

molehill, n. [1. mṓlhil; 2. móulhil]. **mole** (III.) & **hill**. The pile of earth which a mole throws up on to the surface of the ground while burrowing. Phr. *to make a mountain out of a molehill*, to exaggerate a petty difficulty or grievance.

mole-rat, n. **mole** (III.) & **rat** (I.). A burrowing rodent, genus *Spalax*, resembling the mole in appearance and habits.

mole-shrew, n. **mole** (III.) & **shrew**. A burrowing shrew, genus *Urotrichus*, resembling a mole in appearance and habit.

moleskin, n. [1. mṓlskin; 2. móulskin]. **mole** (III.) & **skin**. **1. a** The skin of the mole, dressed and used as fur; **b** a kind of cotton fustian, with a thick pile, shaved before dyeing. **2.** (pl.) Trousers made of this kind of fustian.

molest, vb. trans. [1. mōlést; 2. moulést], fr. O. Fr. *molester*, fr. Lat. *molestāre*, 'to annoy, trouble', fr. *molestus*, 'troublesome, annoying', prob. fr. *mōlēs*, 'mass, heavy burden'. See **molar** (II.). **1.** To trouble, annoy, vex persistently. **2.** To accost without justification. **3.** To interfere, meddle with, in hostile manner.

molestation, n. [1. mòlestáshun; 2. mòulestéiʃən]. Prec. & **-ation**. Act of molesting; persistent annoyance; unlawful interference.

molet, n. See **mullet** (II.).

Molinism, n. [1. mólinizm; 2. mɔ́linizəm]. **1.** Religious doctrine taught by the Spanish Jesuit Luiz Molina, d. 1600, that the gifts of grace depended on man's free will. **2.** Doctrine of religious quietism taught by the Spanish mystic Miguel de Molinos, d. 1696.

Molinist, n. [1. mólinist; 2. mɔ́linist]. A follower of Luiz Molina or Miguel de Molinos.

mollification, n. [1. mòlifikáshun; 2. mɔ̀lifikéiʃən]. See next word & **-fication**. Act of mollifying, appeasing &c.

mollify, vb. trans. [1. mólifī; 2. mɔ́lifai], fr. Fr. *mollifier*, fr. Lat. *mollificāre*, 'to make soft, soften', fr. *mollis*, 'soft'. *Mollis* is supposed to mean ultimately 'ground small, reduced to powder', & is connected w. Lat. *molere*, 'to grind in a mill'. See further cognates under **meal** (I.), **malt**, & **-fy**. (rarely used except in non-material sense) To pacify, appease; cause to abate: *to mollify a person, his anger, indignation* &c.

mollusc, n. [1. mólusk; 2. mɔ́ləsk], fr. Fr. *mollusque*, fr. Lat. *molluscus*, adj., esp. *mollusca nux*, 'a soft kind of nut with a thin shell', fr. *mollis*, 'soft'. See **mollify**. One of a subkingdom of invertebrate animals some of which are popularly called shell-fish, which have a soft, unsegmented body, and in many cases a protective shell the molluscs include oysters, mussels, whelks &c., also slugs and snails.

molluscoid, adj. [1. molúskoid; 2. məlʌ́skɔid]. Prec. & **-oid**. Resembling, like, a mollusc.

molluscous, adj. [1. molúskus; 2. məlʌ́skəs]. **mollusc** & **-ous**. Belonging to, resembling, a mollusc or molluscs.

molly, n. [1. móli; 2. mɔ́li], fr. woman's name; a familiar form of *Mary*. A milksop, effeminate person, a molly-coddle.

molly-coddle, n. & vb. trans. **a** n. One who is coddled, or who coddles or pampers himself one who takes excessive care of himself; a milksop, a molly; **b** vb., to coddle, pamper, pet, spoil.

Moloch, n. [1. mólok; 2. móulɔk]. Through Lat., fr. Gk. *Molókh*, fr. Heb. *Mōlek*, variant of *melek*, 'king'. **1.** (cap.) **a** A Semitic god of Palestine propitiated by the sacrifice of children, often the first-born; **b** (fig.) a dreadful power or influence to which everything is sacrificed. **2.** (zool.) An Australian spiny lizard; the thorn-devil.

molt. See **moult**.

molten, adj. [1. mṓlten 2. móultən]. O.E. & M.E. *molten*, P.P. of **melt**. Melted; of metals, in state of being melted, rendered liquid by intense heat: *molten steel*; *a molten image*, one made of molten metal.

moly, n. [1. mṓli; 2. móuli]. Lat., fr. Gk. *mōlu*; cp. Scrt. *mūlam*, 'root'. **a** (mythol.) A magic, fabulous plant, with milk-white flowers and black root, which protected Ulysses against the spells of Circe; sometimes identified with the mandrake; **b** (bot.) wild garlic.

molybdenite, n. [1. molíbdenīt, mòlibdénīt; 2. məlibdinait, mɔ̀libdínait], fr. next word & **-ite**. (mineral.) An ore of molybdenum, molybdenum-sulphide, resembling graphite.

molybdenum, n. [1. molíbdenum, mòlibdénum; 2. məlibdinəm, mɔ̀libdínəm]. Invented word fr. Gk. *mólubdos*, 'lead' (foreign loan-word), first used of graphite. A metallic element, used as an alloy in steel-making.

moment, n. [1. mṓment; 2. móumənt]. Lat. *mōmentum*, 'movement; short space of time', for **movimentum*, fr. base *mov-*. See **move** & **movement**. **1. a** A brief duration or space of time: *the whole operation only lasted a moment*; *just wait here a moment*; Phrs. *half a moment*, an instant, very brief space of time; *in a moment*, directly, very soon **b** (pl.) *moments*, a certain period of time: *how many happy moments have I spent in her company!* **2.** A specific point of time; a given, specified hour, time, occasion; a crisis: *the supreme moment has come*; *we both arrived at the same moment*. Phrs. *go this (very) moment*, now, at once; *to the (very) moment*, up to time, punctually, at the hour agreed on; *(the fashions, rage &c.) of the moment*, of the present time; hence, transient; *the man of the moment*, one very important at present time; *(I have nothing to do) at, for, the moment*, just now, at this particular time; *he's the man for this, the, moment*, for this occasion, crisis. **3.** Importance, consequence, weight: *affairs of great moment*; *of little, no great, moment*. **4.** (mechan.) Measure of power of a force to cause rotation about an axis.

momentarily, adv. [1. mṓmentarili; 2. móuməntərili]. **momentary** & **-ly**. **a** For a brief space of time; **b** every moment; from instant to instant.

momentariness, n. [1. mṓmentarines; 2. móuməntərinis]. See prec. & **-ness**. State, quality, of being momentary.

momentary, adj. [1. mṓmentari; 2. móumənt(ə)ri]. Lat. *mōmentārius*. **moment** & **-ary**. Lasting but a moment; transitory, fleeting, transient.

momently, adv. [1. mṓmentli; 2. móuməntli]. **moment** & **-ly**. (rare) From moment to moment; every moment.

momentous, adj. [1. mōméntus; 2. mouméntəs]. **moment** & **-ous**. Of great moment, of vital importance; grave, weighty: *a momentous question to decide*.

momentously, adv. Prec. & **-ly**. In a momentous manner.

momentousness, n. See prec. & **-ness**. State, quality, of being momentous.

momentum, n. [1. mōméntum; 2. mouméntəm]. Lat., 'movement'. See **moment**. **1. a** (dynamics) The product of the mass of a moving body and its velocity; **b** (popular usage) force imparted to a moving body by its motion; impetus. **2.** (fig., of events) Tendency to move forward, to develop with great force.

Momus, n. [1. mṓmus; 2. móuməs]. Lat., god of mockery and censure, fr. Gk. *mōmos*, 'ridicule'; cp. Gk. *a-mūmōn*, 'irreproachable'; etymol. doubtful. A carping critic.

mon, n. [1. mon; 2. mɔn]. Jap. The circular badge of a family of the Japanese feudal nobility.

monachal, adj. [1. mónakl; 2. mɔ́nəkl], fr. L. Eccles. Lat. *monachālis*, 'of a monk', fr. *monachus*. See **monk** & **-al**. Of or belonging to a monk or the monastic life; monastic.

monachism, n. [1. mónakizm; 2. mɔ́nəkizəm]. See prec. & **-ism**. System of the monastic life; monasticism.

mon-acid, adj. [1. món ásid; 2. mɔ́n ǽsid]. **mono-** & **acid**. (chem.) Having one hydrogen atom replaceable by an acid atom.

monad, n. [1. mónad; 2. mɔ́næd], fr. Lat. *monad-(em), monas*, fr. Gk. *monád-(os), monás*, 'unit', fr. *mónos*, 'alone, single'. See **mono-**. **1.** (biol.) A primary individual organism or organic unit. **2.** (chem.) An element which replaces one atom of hydrogen in a compound. **3.** (philos. of Leibniz) One of the elements, or simple, 'intelligent, substantial', unities into which every compound can be resolved.

monadelphous, adj. [1. mònadélfus; 2. mɔ̀nədélfəs]. **mono-** & Gk. *adelph-(ós)*, 'brother', wh. is fr. *a-* for *ha-*, fr. **sm-*, 'one, the same', whence also Lat. *similis*, 'alike' &c., see **similar**, & *delphús*, 'womb', fr. **gʷelbh-*, **gʷolbh-* &c., whence also Lat. *volva, vulva*, 'womb', see **vulva, calf** (I.), & **-ous**. (bot.) Having the filaments of the stamens united.

monadism, n. [1. mónadizm; 2. mɔ́nædizəm]. **monad** & **-ism**. The philosophic theory of Leibniz that the universe is ultimately composed of many spiritual substances or monads.

monal, monaul, n. [1. mōnáwl; 2. mounɔ́l]. Hind. *monāl, munāl*. A brilliantly plumaged Asiatic pheasant, genus *Lophophorus*, of the Himalayas and mountains of North India and China.

monandrous, adj. [1. mònándrus; 2. mɔnǽndrəs]. **mono-** & Gk. *andr-(ós)*, fr. *anḗr*, 'man', see first element in **androgynous**, & **-ous**. (bot.) Having a single stamen.

monandry, n. [1. mònándri; 2. mɔ̀nǽndri]. See prec. & **-y**. **1.** State, custom, of having only one husband; contrasted with *polyandry*. **2.** (bot.) Condition of having a single stamen.

monarch, n. [1. mónark; 2. mɔ́nək], fr. Lat. *monarcha*, fr. Gk. *monárkhēs, mónarkhos*, 'one who rules alone', **mono-** & *arkhós*, 'chief' &c. See **arch-**. **1.** Supreme ruler, usually an hereditary head of a state; strictly, a king, emperor &c. who is the sole ruler, or *an absolute monarch*; the term is now constantly applied to a limited or constitutional sovereign, and is regarded as synonymous with *king* &c. **2.** (fig.) Person, or other living thing, regarded as the chief or master, or as being pre-eminent, of commanding size &c. in a given place or area: '*I am monarch of all I survey*' (Cowper, 'Alex. Selkirk'); *the monarch of the forest*, oak tree; *monarch of the glen*, the stag. **3.** Large orange-brown butterfly whose wings are veined and bordered with black.

monarchal, adj. [1. monárkl; 2. mənákl]. Prec. & **-al.** (poet.) Of, befitting, a monarch or sovereign; royal, regal: '*Satan . . . with monarchal pride*' (Milton, 'P. L.' II. 427-8).

monarchian, n. [1. monárkian; 2. mənákiən]. L. Lat. *monarchiānus*; **monarch** & **-ian.** A supporter of monarchianism.

monarchianism, n. [1. monárkianizm; 2. mənákiənizəm]. See prec. & **-ism.** A Christian heresy of the 2nd and 3rd cent. A.D., which 'confounded the persons', and opposed the doctrine of the Trinity as infringing strict monotheism or the supremacy of a single God.

monarchic, adj. [1. monárkik; 2. mənákik]. **monarch** & **-ic.** Of, belonging to, having the characteristics or attributes of a monarch or monarchy; monarchical, royal, regal.

monarchical, adj. [1. monárkikl; 2. mənákikl]. Prec. & **-al.** Monarchic.

monarchically, adv. Prec. & **-ly.** Like a monarch; regally, royally.

monarchism, n. [1. mónarkizm; 2. mónəkizəm]. **monarch** & **-ism.** System, principle, of monarchy.

monarchist, n. [1. mónarkist; 2. mónəkist]. Prec. & **-ist.** One who supports a monarchy, or the principles of monarchy; a royalist.

monarchy, n. [1. mónarki; 2. mónəki]. Fr. *monarchie*, fr. Lat. *monarchia*, fr. Gk. *monarkhía*, 'monarchy'. See **monarch** & **-y. 1.** The supreme rule or sovereignty of a single person or monarch. **2.** A state ruled by a single sovereign or monarch. **3.** System of rule by a single sovereign or monarch.

monastery, n. [1. mónastri; 2. mónəstri], fr. L. Eccles. Lat. *monastērium*, fr. L. Eccles. Gk. *monastḗrion*, fr. *monastḗs*, 'living alone', hence later 'a monk', fr. *monázein*, 'to live alone', fr. *mónos*, 'alone', see **mono-.** See also **minster** & **monk.** House used as the regular abode of a community of monks; rarely used of house for religious women, which is usually called a *nunnery* or *convent.*

monastic, adj. [1. monástik; 2. mənǽstik], fr. L. Gk. *monastikós*, 'living alone'. See prec. & **-ic. 1.** Connected with, belonging to, a monastery or monasteries, or to monks and a secluded religious life under vows: *monastic rule, institutions* &c.; *monastic vows*, those taken by monks. **2.** (by extension) Secluded, austere: *to lead a monastic life.*

monastically, adv. [1. monástikali; 2. mənǽstikəli]. Prec. & **-al** & **-ly.** In a monastic way or fashion; like a monk.

monasticism, n. [1. monástisizm; 2. mənǽstisizəm]. **monastic** & **-ism.** The monastic life and system.

Monday, n. [1. múndi; 2. mándi]. O.E. *Mōnandæg.* **moon** & **day.** The second day of the week, the day following Sunday. *Black Monday*, the first day when real work begins at school; *Mad Monday*, (Stock Exchange) the day after the weekly closing on Saturday; characterized, during a boom, by an enormous rush of business.

Mondayish, adj. [1. múndiish; 2. mándiiʃ]. Prec. & **-ish.** (colloq.) As one is supposed to feel on Monday morning, when work begins again; disinclined to work.

monde, n. [mɔ̃d] or Anglicized to [1. mond; 2. mɔnd]. Fr., fr. Lat. *mundus*, 'the world'. See **mundane.** The world of society or fashion; also *beau monde*, contrasted with *demi-monde.*

monetary, adj. [1. múnetari; 2. mánitəri]. Lat. *monētārius*, 'of or belonging to a mint', fr. *monēta*, 'mint, money'. See **mint (II.)** & cp. **money. 1.** Of, relating to, the coinage or currency: *a monetary unit, convention, union* &c. **2.** Of or relating to money; pecuniary, financial: *in monetary difficulties.*

monetization, n. [1. mùnetizáshun; 2. mànitaizéiʃən]. See next word & **-ation.** Act of monetizing.

monetize, vb. trans. [1. múnetīz; 2. mánitaiz], fr. Lat. *monēta*, 'money', see **mint (II.)**, & **-ize.** To coin into money; specif., to give a standard value to a metal, e.g. silver, in the currency of a country.

money, n. [1. múni; 2. máni]. O. Fr. *moneie*, Mod. Fr. *monnaie*, fr. Lat. *monēta*, 'mint, money'. See **mint (II.). 1.** Gold, silver, or other metal coined under State authority to serve as currency; coin or coins in general. **2.** A promissory or other note issued by the State or by an authorized bank, and available as currency: *paper-money.* **3.** (pl., legal or archaic) Sums of money: *moneys belonging to the estate.* **4.** (econ.) Any recognized medium of exchange and measure of value, as the cowrie shells of West Africa, the iron bars of ancient Sparta &c. *Money of account*, a term of value or price, not currency passing from hand to hand, as the English *guinea.* **5.** Wealth, property, one's fortune generally: *to have plenty of money*; *to lose all one's money.* Phrs. *to make money*, acquire wealth; *to marry money*, marry a rich person; *time is money*, every moment well spent is valuable; *one's money's worth*, full value for expenditure.

money-bag, n. **1. a** A bag for holding money; **b** a rich, stingy person. **2.** (pl., fig., colloq.) Riches, wealth.

money bill, n. A bill, originating in the House of Commons, which involves the expenditure or the raising of money for public purposes.

money-box, n. A box with a narrow slit in it for holding coins saved and put aside.

money-changer, n. [1. múni chānjer; 2. máni tʃeindžə]. One who changes money from one currency into another at a fixed rate of exchange.

moneyed, adj. [1. múnid; 2. mánid]. **money** & **-ed.** (only attrib.) Endowed with, possessed of, a considerable amount of money; wealthy: *a moneyed man.*

moneyer, n. [1. múnier; 2. mániə]. O. Fr. *monoier.* See **money** & **-er.** One who coins or mints money.

money-grubber, n. One who is solely bent on accumulating money; an avaricious, miserly person.

money-grubbing, n. [1. múni grubing; 2. máni grabiŋ]. Sordid devotion to the accumulation of wealth.

money-lender, n. A person who makes a business of lending money at interest, generally at a usurious rate.

money-market, n. The market or field of operations where financial business on a large scale is conducted; the body of financial interests which determines the rate of interest on capital lent.

money-order, n. An order for the payment of money, issued by a post-office, enabling a person who purchases one to send money to another to whom it is payable at a specified post-office.

money-spinner, n. Popular name of a small red garden spider, which is supposed to bring good luck.

moneywort, n. [1. múniwërt; 2. mániwʌt]. **money** & **wort (I.).** A creeping herb, with round, opposed leaves and single yellow flower; the Creeping-Jenny.

monger, n. [1. múngger; 2. máŋgə]. O.E. *mangere*, 'merchant'; cp. *mangian*, 'to deal, trade in', fr. Lat. *mango*, 'a dealer who polishes up and sets off his wares; a slave-dealer'; borrowed fr. Gk. *mágganon*, 'any means of tricking, bewitching; a juggler's apparatus'; also *magganeúein*, 'to cheat by sleight of hand', cogn. w. M. Ir. *meng*, 'deceit'; O. Prussian *manga*, 'courtesan'; Scrt. *manjuš*, 'charming'. **a** A dealer, trafficker, trader; now usually preceded by qualifying noun: *ironmonger, costermonger, cheese-monger*; **b** (in derogatory sense, also an unscrupulous trafficker) *newsmonger, scandal-monger* &c.

Mongol, n. & adj. [1. mónggol; 2. mɔ́ŋgɔl]. Native name; usually taken to be fr. *mong*, 'brave'. **1.** n. One of a yellow-skinned, black-haired race inhabiting a wide area, Mongolia, of Central Asia. **2.** adj. Of, pertaining to, this race.

Mongolian, adj. & n. [1. monggólian; 2. mɔŋgóuliən]. Mongolia & **-an. 1.** adj. Of, pertaining to, Mongolia or the Mongols. **2.** n. **a** A Mongol; **b** Mongolian language.

mongoloid, adj. [1. mónggoloid; 2. mɔ́ŋgəlɔid]. **Mongol** & **-oid.** Resembling, of the same type as, a Mongol or the Mongols.

mongoose, n., pl. **mongooses** [1. mónggōōs; 2. mɔ́ŋgūs], fr. Tamil *mangus.* **1.** A small carnivorous, ferret-like animal, the ichneumon of India, allied to the civets, famous for its power of killing snakes and other vermin. **2.** A lemur of Madagascar.

mongrel, n. & adj. [1. múngrel; 2. máŋgrəl]. Also spelt *mungrel*; etymol. doubtful; prob. fr. **mongerel*, fr. O.E. *mengan*, 'to mix'. See **mingle. 1.** n. **a** A dog of mixed, uncertain breed; **b** (as term of contempt) any other animal, or a human being, of mixed race or origin; a cross-breed between varieties of the same species. **2.** adj. Of mixed breeding or origin: *mongrel dog, race* &c.

mongrelism, n. [1. múnggrelizm; 2. máŋgrəlizəm]. Prec. & **-ism.** Condition, state, of being a mongrel.

mongrelize, vb. trans. [1. múnggrelīz; 2. máŋgrəlaiz]. See prec. & **-ize.** To make a mongrel of; to give a mongrel character to.

mongrelly, adj. [1. múnggreli; 2. máŋgrəli]. **mongrel** & **-ly.** Mongrel.

monial, n. [1. mōnial; 2. móuniəl]. O. Fr. See **mullion.** (archit.) A mullion.

moniliform, adj. [1. moníliform; 2. mənílifōm]. Lat. *monīle*, 'necklace', cp. Gk. *mánnos*, 'necklace worn by Celtic people', Scrt. *mani*, 'gem, pearl'; & cp. **mane.** (bot. and zool.) Jointed and beaded as stems or roots of certain plants, antennae of insects &c.

monism, n. [1. mónizm; 2. mónizəm], fr. Gk. *mónos*, 'single, alone', see **mono-**, & **-ism.** (philos.) The doctrine which attributes all the phenomena of the universe, both of mind and matter, to a single principle; contrasted with *dualism* and *pluralism.*

monist, n. [1. mónist; 2. mónist]. See prec. & **-ist.** A believer in monism.

monistic, adj. [1. monístik; 2. mənístik]. Prec. & **-ic.** Of, pertaining to, monism.

monition, n. [1. moníshun; 2. məníʃən], fr. Lat. *monitiōn-(em)*, *monitio*, 'a reminding, advice, warning', fr. *monēre*, 'to call to mind, advise, warn', fr. base seen in Lat. *ment-(em)*, 'mind'. See **mental (I.)** & **mind. 1.** A cautionary intimation or notice; warning, caution. **2.** (eccles. law) Summons, notice, to appear; an episcopal order to do or refrain from doing something.

monitor, n. [1. mónitor; 2. mónitə]. Lat., 'one who reminds or admonishes, counsellor, instructor, teacher'. See prec. & **-or. 1. a** One who reminds, advises, instructs, or warns; **b** specif., a senior pupil in a school who has special disciplinary powers; a prefect. **2.** (naut.) A shallow-draught, heavily armoured, slow-moving vessel, carrying heavy guns for use in coast defence; so called from the name of the first vessel of this type, designed by Captain Ericsson, in the American Civil War, 1862. **3.** (zool.) A member of a genus, *Varanus*, of large lizards of Africa, Australia, and S. Asia.

monitorial, adj. [1. mònitórial; 2. mɔ̀nitɔ́riəl]. Prec. & **-ial. 1.** Admonitory, warning, admonishing. **2.** Connected with, pertaining to, school monitor or monitors: *the monitorial system*; *monitorial duties.*

monitorship, n. [1. mónitorship; 2. mónitəʃip]. **monitor** & **-ship.** Office, position, of a school monitor.

monitory, adj. & n. [1. mónitori; 2. mɔ́nitəri], fr. Lat. *monitōrius*, 'warning'. **monitor** & **-y.** **1.** adj. Warning, admonitory: *a letter monitory.* **2.** n. A letter giving an admonition or warning from an ecclesiastical superior.

monitress, n. [1. mónitres; 2. mɔ́nitris], fr. **monitor** & **-ess.** A female school monitor.

monk, n. [1. mungk; 2. maŋk]. O.E. *munuc*, fr. Lat. *monachus*, 'monk', fr. Gk. *monakhós*, 'living alone, solitary', also as n., 'monk', fr. *mónos*, 'alone', see **mono-**. **1.** (hist.) One who left the world and lived alone and apart, as in the desert, in religious exercises; a hermit, anchorite. **2. a** Member of a Christian religious Order, living according to the Rule of the Order and under vows of poverty, chastity, and obedience, in a community or monastery; contrasted with a *friar*; **b** a member of a similar religious community among the Buddhists of Tibet, the Senussi Moslems of the Eastern Sahara &c.

monkery, n. [1. múngkeri; 2. máŋkəri]. Prec. & **-ery.** Term of disparagement, used esp. by aggressive Protestants; **a** the monastic life and system; **b** monks in general; **c** a monastery.

monkey (I.), n. [1. múngki; 2. máŋki]. Etymol. doubtful; L.G. has *moneke(n)*, apparently a dimin., cp. M. Ital. *monnicchio*; Ital. *monna* for *madonna*, used as form of address to a woman, hence, 'an old woman, monkey'; a connexion w. **monk** has also been suggested as origin. **1.** A term applied to any member of the *Primates*, or highest order of mammals, other than man or the lemurs, but usually and popularly restricted to the small, long-tailed members, as distinguished from the large, tailless apes. Phr. (slang) *to get, put, one's monkey up*, to get, or be made, angry or annoyed. **2.** A mischievous, mimicking, playful young person; an imp, a rogue. **3.** Of various parts of machinery &c., e.g. the head of a pile-driver, a melting-pot in glass-making &c. **4.** (slang) £500.

monkey (II.), vb. intrans. & trans., fr. prec. **a** intrans. To play tricks; to meddle, interfere; also *monkey with, monkey about with*, to fiddle about, play tricks, fool, with; disturb, injure; **b** trans., to upset, injure, by unskilful, mischievous handling.

monkey-bread, n. The fruit of the baobab.

monkey-engine, n. The engine which lifts the monkey or head of a pile-driver.

monkey-flower, n. A plant of the genus *Mimulus*, so called from the flower, which has the appearance of a monkey's face.

monkeyish, adj. [1. múngkiish; 2. máŋkiiʃ]. **monkey** & **-ish.** Like a monkey; mischievous.

monkey-jacket, n. A short, tight-fitting jacket, worn by sailors.

monkey-puzzle, n. The Chile pine, *Araucaria imbricata*, used as a formal ornamental tree; it has broad, prickly spines growing at intervals down the branches, which would make it impossible for a monkey to climb it.

monkey-wrench, n. A wrench or spanner with sliding, adjustable grip or jaw.

monkfish, n. [1. múngkfish; 2. máŋkfiʃ]. Popular name of the angel-fish or shark-ray, so named from its appearance.

monkhood, n. [1. múngkhood; 2. máŋkhud]. **monk** & **-hood.** **a** Condition, character, of a monk; **b** monks, considered as a body.

monkish, adj. [1. múngkish; 2. máŋkiʃ]. **monk** & **-ish.** Of or pertaining to, characteristic of, a monk or monks, or the monastic life.

monk's-hood, n. [1. múngks hood; 2. máŋks hud]. A plant, *Aconitum napellus*, with dark-purple, hood-shaped flowers.

mono- (**mon-** before vowels), pref., fr. Gk. *mónos*, 'alone, single'; used **a** in this sense generally; **b** (chem.) as signifying the presence of a single atom or combining equivalent. Cp. w. *mónos*, Gk. *mânós*, 'isolated' (fr. **manwós*); Scrt. *manâk*, 'a little'; Lith. *meñkas*, 'mediocre'.

monobasic, adj. [1. mònobásik; 2. mɔ̀nəbéisik]. **mono-** & **basic.** (chem.) Of an acid having one hydrogen atom replaceable by a basic atom.

monocarpic, adj. [1. mònokárpik; 2. mɔ̀nəkápik]. **mono-** & Gk. *karp-(ós)*, 'fruit', see **carpel**, & **-ic.** (bot.) Bearing fruit once and then dying, as an annual plant.

monocarpous, adj. [1. mònokárpus; 2. mɔ̀nəkápəs]. See prec. & **-ous.** (bot.) Bearing its seed in a single ovary.

monochord, n. [1. mónokord; 2. mɔ́nəkōd], fr. Lat. *monochordon*, Gk. *monókhordon*. **mono-** & **chord.** An instrument, having a single string or chord stretched across a scale or rule, used for measuring musical sounds.

monochromatic, adj. [1. mònōkrōmátik; 2. mɔ̀noukroumǽtik]. **mono-** & **chromatic.** See also next word. **a** Having only one colour, showing light rays of only one colour; **b** drawn, painted, in monochrome.

monochrome, n. [1. mónokrōm; 2. mɔ́nəkroum]. Fr., fr. Gk. *monókhrōmos*, 'of one colour', fr. **mono-**, & *khrôma*, 'colour', see **chrome.** A drawing or painting in a single colour or tint or in different shades or tints of the same colour.

monocle, n. [1. mónokl; 2. mɔ́nəkl]. Fr., 'single eyeglass'. See **monocular.** A single glass worn fixed into eye-socket.

monoclinal, adj. [1. mònoklínal; 2. mɔ̀nəkláinəl]. **mono-**, Gk. *klín (ein)*, 'to bend', see **clinical**, & **-al.** (geol.) Of strata, having a single dip or fold.

monocotyledon, n. [1. mònokotilḗdun; 2. mɔ̀nəkɔtilídən]. **mono-** & **cotyledon.** (bot.) A plant having a single cotyledon or seed-leaf, as grasses, lilies, palms &c.

monocotyledonous, adj. [1. mònokotilḗdunus; 2. mɔ̀nəkɔtilídənəs]. Prec. & **-ous.** (bot.) Having a single cotyledon.

monocular, adj. [1. monókūlar; 2. mənɔ́kjulə], fr. L. Lat. *monoculus*, 'one-eyed; a one-eyed man'; hybrid word. See **mono-** & **ocular.** Having one eye; fitted or adapted for vision by one eye.

monocyclic, adj. [1. mònosíklik; 2. mɔ̀nəsáiklik]. **mono-** & **cyclic.** Having a single cycle.

monodic, adj. [1. mònṓdik; 2. mɔ̀nóudik], fr. Gk. *monōidikós*. See **monody** & **-ic.** **a** Of or pertaining to, resembling, a monody; **b** (mus.) of, pertaining to monody, for one voice; homophonic.

monodist, n. [1. mónodist; 2. mɔ́nədist]. **monody** & **-ist.** Writer, composer, of monodies.

monodrama, n. [1. mónodràhma; 2. mɔ́nədrāmə]. **mono-** & **drama.** A dramatic piece for performance by a single person.

monody, n. [1. mónodi; 2. mɔ́nədi], fr. Lat. *monōdia*, fr. Gk. *monōidia*, fr. *monōidós*, 'singing alone', *mónos*, 'alone', see **mono-**, & *ōidḗ*, 'song', see **ode.** **1.** An ode or song sung by a single actor in a Greek tragedy; a dirge, lament, funeral ode. **2.** A poem in which the writer mourns for a dead friend; e.g. Milton's *Lycidas*. **3.** (mus.) Method of composition in which the melody is sustained by a single voice.

monoecious, adj. [1. monḗshus; 2. mɔníʃəs]. **mono-** & Gk. *oik(os)*, 'house, dwelling', see first element of **economy**, & **-ous.** (bot. and zool.) Having both female and male sex-organs in the same individual.

monogamist, n. [1. monógamist; 2. mənɔ́gəmist]. **monogamy** & **-ist.** One who practises monogamy.

monogamous, adj. [1. monógamus; 2. mənɔ́gəməs]. See prec. & **-ous.** **1.** Having one wife or husband at a time. **2.** (zool.) Mating with a single female or male at a time.

monogamy, n. [1. monógami; 2. mənɔ́gəmi]. Lat. *monogamia*, Gk. *monogamia*, fr. *monógamos*, 'marrying once or a single time', fr. **mono-**, & *gámos*, 'marriage', see **gamo-.** **a** The principle and practice of having a single husband or wife at a time; marriage with only one person at one time; contrasted with *polygamy* and *polyandry*; **b** (hist.) practice of marrying only once during life.

monogenesis, n. [1. mònōjénesis; 2. mɔ̀noudžénisis]. **mono-** & **genesis.** **1.** Singleness of origin. **2.** (biol.) **a** Doctrine that all living organisms have sprung from a single cell; **b** reproduction by a single parent; asexual reproduction.

monogenetic, adj. [1. mònōjenétik; 2. mɔ̀noudžinétik]. **mono-** & **genetic.** Reproduced by a single parent; asexually reproduced.

monogenism, n. [1. monójenizm; 2. mənɔ́džənizəm]. Next word & **-ism.** Doctrine that all the peoples of the world have descended from a single pair of individuals.

monogeny, n. [1. monójeni; 2. mənɔ́džəni]. **mono-** & **-geny.** **1.** Descent of man from a single pair of parents. **2.** (biol.) Monogenesis.

monoglot, adj. [1. mónoglot; 2. mɔ́nəglɔt]. **mono-** & Gk. *glṓtta, glôssa*, 'tongue', see **gloss (III.)**; formed on anal. of *polyglot.* Speaking one language only.

monogram, n. [1. mónogram; 2. mɔ́nəgræm]. L. Lat. *monogramma*, L. Gk. *monógramma*, of the Christian monogram. See **mono-** & **gram.** A combination of two or more letters intertwined so as to form a device or cipher; *the Christian monogram*, ☧, the first two letters in Greek of the name of Christ.

monogrammatic, adj. [1. mònogramátik; 2. mɔ̀nəgrəmǽtik]. See prec. & **-ic.** In the form of a monogram.

monograph, n. & vb. trans. [1. mónograhf; 2. mɔ́nəgrāf]. **mono-** & **-graph.** **1.** n. A book, pamphlet, or treatise embodying results of investigation on a single subject, or on a single aspect of a subject. **2.** vb. (rare) To treat of, deal with, a subject in a monograph.

monographer, n. [1. monógrafer; 2. mənɔ́grəfə]. Prec. & **-er.** A writer of a monograph.

monographic(al), adj. [1. mònográfik(l); 2. mɔ̀nəgrǽfik(l)]. **monograph** & **-ic** & **-al.** Of the nature of a monograph; treated in a monograph.

monographically, adv. Prec. & **-ly.** In the form of a monograph.

monographist, n. [1. monógrafist; 2. mənɔ́grəfist]. **monograph** & **-ist.** Monographer.

monogynous, adj. [1. monóginus, -jinus; 2. mənɔ́ginəs, -džinəs]. See next word & **-ous.** **1.** (bot.) Having a single pistil. **2.** (zool.) Mating with a single female.

monogyny, n. [1. monógini, -jini; 2. mənɔ́gini, -džini]. **mono-** & **-gyny.** Habit, custom, of mating with one female.

monolatry, n. [1. monólatri; 2. mənɔ́lətri]. **mono-** & Gk. *latreia*, 'service, worship'. See **-latry.** The worship of one only out of several gods whose existence is recognized; distinguished from *monotheism*.

monolith, n. [1. mónolith; 2. mɔ́nəliþ], fr. Lat. *monolithus*, Gk. *monólithos*, 'made of a single stone'. See **mono-** & **litho-.** A pillar, column, monument, consisting of a single block of stone.

monolithic, adj. [1. monolíthik; 2. mɔ̀nəlíþik]. Prec. & **-ic.** Consisting of, having the character of, a monolith: *a monolithic monument.*

monologist, n. [1. monólojist; 2. mənɔ́lədžist]. See **monologue** & **-ist.** **a** One who monologizes; one who monopolizes all the conversation; **b** a monologuist.

monologize, vb. intrans. [1. monólojīz; 2. mənɔ́lədžaiz]. See prec. & **-ize.** To soliloquize, to speak in monologues; to speak at great length in company, so as to monopolize the conversation.

monologizer, n. [1. monólojīzer; 2. mənɔ́lədžaizə]. Prec. & **-er.** One who monologizes.

monologue, n. [1. mónolog; 2. mɔ́nələg]. Fr., fr. Gk. *monólogos*, 'speaking alone'. See **mono-** & **-logos.** **1. a** A form of dramatic composition for one performer only; **b** a long speech in a play by a single actor. **2.** A long speech by a single person, esp. one that interferes with general conversation.

monologuist, n. [1. mónològist; 2. mɔ́nəlɔ̀ugist]. Prec. & **-ist.** a A speaker, reciter, of dramatic monologues; b person given to holding forth in society, and monopolizing the conversation.

monomania, n. [1. mònománia; 2. mɔ̀nəméiniə]. **mono-** & **mania.** a An obsession of the mind by a single idea or interest; a craze; b such an obsession developed to the point of mental derangement.

monomaniac, n. [1. mònomániak; 2. mɔ̀nəméiniæk]. **mono-** & **maniac.** One suffering from a monomania.

monomaniacal, adj. [1. mònomaníakl; 2. mɔ̀nəmænáiəkl]. Prec. & **-al.** a Of the nature of a monomania; b suffering from monomania.

monomial, adj. [1. monómial; 2. mənóumiəl]. **mono-** & *nom-*, 'name', q.v. under **nominal**; formed on anal. of *binomial.* (alg.) Consisting of a single term or expression.

monomorphic, monomorphous, adj. [1. mònomórfik, -mórfus; 2. mɔ̀nəmɔ́fik, -mɔ́fəs]. **mono-** & Gk. *morph-(ḗ)*, 'shape, form', see **morphology**, & **-ic** & **-ous.** (biol.) Keeping the same form or shape through the stages of development from the embryo.

monopetalous, adj. [1. mònopétalus; 2. mɔ̀nəpétələs]. **mono-** & **petal** & **-ous.** (bot.) Having the petals of corolla united.

monophobia, n. [1. mònofóbia; 2. mɔ̀nəfóubiə]. **mono-** & **-phobia.** A morbid dislike or dread of being left alone.

monophthong, n. [1. mónofthong; 2. mɔ́nəfþɔŋ]. Gk. *monóphthoggos*, 'having one sound'. **mono-** & *phthóggos*, 'voice of men, cry of animals; sound'; cp. *phthéggomai*, 'to utter a sound; to speak'; see second element of **diphthong.** A single vowel sound; contrasted with *diphthong.*

monophthongal, adj. [1. mònofthónggal; 2. mɔ̀nəfþɔ́ŋgl]. Prec. & **-al.** Of the nature of a monophthong; consisting of a single vowel sound; contrasted with *diphthongal.*

monophthongize, vb. trans. [1. mónofthonggīz; 2. mɔ́nəfþɔŋgaiz]. See prec. & **-ize.** To reduce (a diphthong) to a monophthong.

Monophysite, n. [1. monófisīt; 2. mənɔ́fisait]. Gk. *monophusítēs*, **mono-** & *phúsis*, 'nature'. See **physic.** One who maintains the heresy (Monophysitism) that the human and divine natures in Christ are united in one single nature, part human, part divine, in opposition to the dogma laid down at the Council of Chalcedon, A.D. 451; (also attrib.) *Monophysite Churches*, i.e. the Armenian, Coptic, and Jacobite Churches.

Monophysitic, adj. [1. monòfisítik; 2. mənɔ̀fisítik]. Prec. & **-ic.** Relating to, maintaining, the doctrine of the Monophysites.

monoplane, n. [1. mónoplān; 2. mɔ́nəplein]. **mono-** & **plane (V.).** An aeroplane with one plane or set of supporting surfaces.

monopolism, n. [1. monópolizm; 2. mənɔ́pəlizəm]. **monopoly** & **-ism.** The system or practice of monopolies or monopolists.

monopolist, n. [1. monópolist; 2. mənɔ́pəlist]. See prec. & **-ist.** One who has a monopoly; a supporter of monopolies.

monopolization, n. [1. monópolīzáshun; 2. mənɔ̀pəlaizéiʃən]. Next word & **-ation.** Act of monopolizing; state, condition, of being monopolized.

monopolize, vb. trans. [1. monópolīz; 2. mənɔ́pəlaiz]. **monopoly** & **-ize.** a To acquire, maintain, a monopoly of; b to engross, enjoy, to the exclusion of others: *to monopolize the conversation*, allow no one else to speak.

monopolizer, n. [1. monópolīzer; 2. mənɔ́pəlaizə]. Prec. & **-er.** One who has a monopoly; monopolist.

monopoly, n. [1. monópoli; 2. mənɔ́pəli], fr. Lat. *monopōlium*, fr. Gk. *monopṓlion*, fr. **mono-** & *pōlein*, 'to sell'; cogn. w. Lith. *pelnýte*, 'to gain'; O.H.G. *fāli*, 'for sale; venal'; & O.N. *falr*, in same sense. 1. An exclusive right of trading in a specified commodity or group of commodities, enjoyed by the State, or granted by it to individuals as a privilege. 2. a Licence, privilege, of a monopoly; b company or group of persons having a monopoly; c the subject controlled under a monopoly. 3. A control of commodities, land, public services &c. of such a kind that free competition is excluded. 4. Exclusive control, domination, enjoyment of anything: *monopoly of the conversation, one's attention.*

monorail, n. [1. mónorāl; 2. mɔ́nəreil]. **mono-** & **rail (IV.).** A railway in which the track consists of a single rail on which the carriages or trucks are carried.

monorhyme, n. [1. mónorīm; 2. mɔ́nəraim]. **mono-** & **rhyme.** A form of verse in which every line has the same rhyme.

monospermous, adj. [1. mònospérmus; 2. mɔ̀nəspə́məs]. **mono-** & Gk. *spérma*, 'seed', see **sperm (I.)**, & **-ous.** (bot.) Having a single seed.

monostichous, adj. [1. mònostíkus; 2. mɔ̀nɔ́stikəs]. **mono-** & Gk. *stikh-(os)*, 'line, row', see **stichic**, & **-ous.** (bot.) Arranged in a single row, as leaflets on one side of a stem.

monostrophe, n. [1. mónostròfe; 2. mɔ́nəstròufi]. Gk. See **mono-** & **strophe.** Poem in which all the strophes have the same metrical form.

monosyllabic, adj. [1. mònosilábik; 2. mɔ̀nəsilǽbik]. See **monosyllable** & **-ic.** a Consisting of one syllable; b (of persons) speaking in, using, monosyllables.

monosyllabically, adv. [1. mònosilábikali; 2. mɔ̀nəsilǽbikəli]. Prec. & **-al** & **-ly.** In monosyllables.

monosyllable, n. [1. mónosìlabl; 2. mɔ́nəsìləbl]. **mono-** & **syllable.** a Unit of utterance consisting of a single syllable; b a word of this nature.

monotheism, n. [1. mónothèizm; 2. mɔ́nəþìizəm]. **mono-** & **theism.** Belief or doctrine that there is only one God; contrasted with *polytheism* or *monolatry.*

monotheist, n. [1. mónothèist; 2. mɔ́nəþìist]. **mono-** & **theist.** Believer in monotheism, or in a single God.

monotheistic, adj. [1. mònothēístik; 2. mɔ̀nəþiístik]. Prec. & **-ic.** Of or pertaining to monotheism; believing in one God.

monotint, n. [1. mónotint; 2. mɔ́nətint]. **mono-** & **tint.** A drawing or painting in a single colour; monochrome.

monotone (I.), n. [1. mónotōn; 2. mɔ́nətoun]. **mono-** & **tone.** 1. (mus.) a A single unvarying pitch or tone; b utterance of succession of notes, or of syllables, words &c. on a single tone. 2. Sameness of colour, style; monotony of any kind.

monotone (II.), vb. trans., fr. prec. To recite, speak, sing, in a monotone.

monotonic, adj. [1. mònotónik; 2. mɔ̀nətɔ́nik]. Prec. & **-ic.** In a monotone, without change of pitch.

monotonous, adj. [1. monótonus; 2. mənɔ́tənəs], fr. L. Gk. *monótonos*, 'of the same or single tone'. **monotone** & **-ous.** 1. (of voice or sound) Continuing in a monotone without variation of pitch. 2. (fig., variously applied) Without variety or change; dull, tedious, wearisome, by reason of monotony: *monotonous occupations*; *a monotonous life.*

monotonously, adv. Prec. & **-ly.** In a monotonous, wearisome manner.

monotonousness, n. See prec. & **-ness.** State, quality, of being monotonous; monotony.

monotony, n. [1. monótuni; 2. mənɔ́təni]. Gk. *monotonía*, 'sameness, singleness of tone'. **monotone** & **-y.** 1. (of sound) Absence of variation of pitch; sameness in tone; monotone. 2. (in general sense) Want of variation or change; wearisome sameness; monotonous state or condition.

monotype, n. [1. mónotīp; 2. mɔ́nətaip]. **mono-** & **type.** 1. (biol.) A single representative or type, as a single species of a genus. 2. (print.) Machine operated by a keyboard which sets up and casts type in single letters.

monotypic, adj. [1. mònotípik; 2. mɔ̀nətípik]. Prec. & **-ic.** (biol.) Having a single representative or type.

monoxide, n. [1. monóksīd; 2. mənɔ́ksaid]. **mono-** & **oxide.** (chem.) An oxide with one oxygen atom in the molecule.

Monroeism, n. [1. munrṓizm; 2. mənróuizəm], fr. James Monroe, President of U.S.A., 1816–1824. The principle that no extension of European influence on the American continent should be tolerated by the United States; as laid down by Monroe in 1823; also known as *the Monroe Doctrine.*

monseigneur, n. [1. monsānyḗr; 2. mɔ̃seinjə́r], abbr. *Mgr.* Fr. *mon*, 'my', *seigneur*, 'lord'. See **seigneur.** 1. A French title, equivalent to 'his grace', prefixed to the title of princes, cardinals, and prelates: *Monseigneur le duc de Richelieu*; also used alone as mode of address. 2. Specif. (hist.) the title of the dauphin of France.

monsieur, n., pl. **messieurs** [1. mesyḗr; 2. məsjǿ, møsjø], abbr. *M.* Fr. *mon*, 'my', *sieur*, 'lord, sir', shortened fr. **seigneur.** 1. The French equivalent of 'Mr.' (mister); as used before names: *M. Briand*; also used alone as polite form of address, equivalent to 'sir'. 2. (hist., cap.) Title of the second son, or of the younger brother, of the kings of France.

monsignor, n. [1. mònsḗnyōr; mònsínjō], abbr. *Mgr.* Ital. *monsignore*, equiv. of Fr. *monseigneur.* See prec. a The honorific title granted by the Pope to chamberlains and other high officials of the Papal household; b *a monsignor*, person bearing this title.

monsoon, n. [1. mònsṓōn; 2. mɔ̀nsúːn], fr. M. Du. *monssoen*, ad. fr. Port. *mançāo*, cp. Ital. *monsone*; prob. fr. Arab. *mausim*, whence Malay. *mūsim*, 'time of the year, season'. a The name of a periodical wind blowing from the Indian Ocean at two seasons of the year, the *wet monsoon* from the S.W., May-Sept., and the *dry monsoon* from the N.E., Oct.-Dec.; b specif., the rainy season in India.

monster, n. [1. mónster; 2. mɔ́nstə]. M.E. *monstre*, fr. O. Fr. *monstre*, Lat. *monstrum*, 'that which teaches; something out of usual course; portent, omen; misshapen man or animal &c., monster'; cp. *monstrāre*, 'to show'; ultimately fr. same base as *monēre*, 'to warn'. See **monition.** 1. Any legendary, fabulous creature, often represented as partly human, partly animal in form, or as a compound of two or more animals, such as a centaur, chimaera, dragon, mermaid, sphinx &c. 2. Any huge, extraordinary animal, esp. an extinct, prehistoric animal, such as the mammoth, ichthyosaur &c. 3. Anything of abnormally large size: *my apples this year were regular monsters.* 4. a A remarkably misshapen man, animal, or plant; a monstrosity, a freak of nature; one abnormal in form; e.g. one having abnormal number, or considerable misplacement, of limbs or organs; or being abnormal in size, e.g. a giant or a dwarf; b an abnormally wicked, cruel, malicious person: *a monster of iniquity.* 5. (attrib.) Huge, very large: *a monster potato, petition* &c.

monstrance, n. [1. mónstrans; 2. mɔ́nstrəns]. O. Fr., fr. L. Lat. *monstrantia*, fr. *monstrant-(em)*, Pres. Part. type of *monstrāre*, 'to show, point out'. See **monster** & **demonstrate.** Receptacle in which the consecrated Host is exposed for adoration, consisting of a glass or crystal case set in an ornamented standing frame, often surrounded with golden rays.

monstrosity, n. [1. monstrósiti; 2. mənstrɔ́siti]. Earlier *monstruosity*, cp. Fr. *monstruosité*, fr. L. Lat. *monstruōsitas*, *monstrōsitas.* See **monstrous** & **-ity.** 1. State, quality, of being monstrous; a in size; b in shape; c in a moral sense. 2. a Man, animal, or plant that is markedly abnormal in shape or size; a freak; b a badly made, hideous object; **c** excessive and abnormally wicked conduct.

monstrous (I.), adj. [1. mónstrus; 2. mónstrəs]. Earlier *monstruous*, fr. O. Fr. *monstrueux*, *monstreux*, L. Lat. *monstruōsus*, *monstrōsus*, fr. *monstrum*. See **monster** & **-ous.** **1.** (in physical sense) Abnormal, unnatural; **a** (of size) huge, gigantic; **b** (of form) misshapen; having the appearance of a monster. **2.** (in moral sense) **a** Intensely and abnormally bad; arousing horror and reprobation; atrocious, outrageous: *monstrous cruelty, crime* &c.; **b** (colloq.) preposterous: *it is perfectly monstrous to keep me waiting like this.*

monstrous (II.), adv., fr. prec. (obs. or liter.) Exceedingly, marvellously, wonderfully: *a monstrous fine woman*; *monstrous good dinner.*

monstrously, adv. **monstrous** (I.) & **-ly.** In a monstrous way; unnaturally; enormously, extravagantly.

monstrousness, n. See prec. & **-ness.** Quality of being monstrous; monstrosity.

montage, n. [1. móntahzh; 2. mɔ̄tāž]. Fr., fr. *monter*, 'to mount', see **mount** (II.), & **-age.** Technical term for the final selection and arrangement of series of photographs in the making of a cinema film.

montane, adj. [1. móntān; 2. mɔ́ntein]. Lat. *montānus*, 'pertaining to a mountain; mountainous; inhabiting a mountain'. See **mount** (I.) & **-ane.** **a** (of country) Mountainous; **b** (of persons &c.) inhabiting such country.

montbretia, n. [1. monbrḗshia; 2. mɔnbríʃiə], fr. A. J. C. de Montbret. A bulbous plant, of the iris family, genus *Tritonia*, with showy orange-red flowers, a native of S. Africa.

mont-de-piété, n. English pronunciation, [1. món de pḗetā; 2. mɔ̄ də píətei]. Fr., lit. 'mount of piety; charitable bank'. A pawnbroker's shop, in France, managed by the State, part of profits going to the poor.

monte, n. [1. mónti; 2. mɔ́nti]. Span., 'mountain; pile of cards remaining after first deal', fr. Lat. *mont-(em)*, 'mountain'. See **mount.** A Spanish-American gambling game of cards; *three-card monte*, a Mexican version of the three-card trick.

monteith, n. [1. muntḗth; 2. məntíþ]. History doubtful. **1.** An 18th-cent. bowl, usually of silver, with scalloped rim, from which punch ladles and glasses could be hung, ready to dip and cool in the water with which it was filled. **2.** Kind of spotted cotton handkerchief made in Glasgow.

montem, n. [1. móntem; 2. mɔ́ntɛm]. For Lat. *Ad Montem*, 'to the hill' (see **mount**). An old ceremony at Eton College, abolished in 1847, held on Whit Tuesday every three years, when the boys assembled at a hill near Slough and collected money from travellers.

month, n. [1. munth; 2. manþ]. O.E. *mōnað*, M.E. *mōneth*; O.H.G. *manōd*, Goth. *mēnōþs*; O.N. *mānaðr*. See **moon** & **-th.** **1.** A period of time reckoned by the moon's revolutions; any one of the twelve parts into which the year is divided, of 30, 31, and 28 (29) days: *calendar month.* **2.** Period occupied by a complete revolution of the moon, reckoned from new moon to new moon, about 29 days 13 hours: *lunar month.* **3. a** A period of four weeks or 28 days; **b** period reckoned from any day in one month to the corresponding day in the next; Phr. (*not once in*) *a month of Sundays*, never; *month's mind*, (hist.) the requiem Mass celebrated one month after a person's death.

monthly (I.), adj. & adv. Prec. & **-ly.** **1.** adj. Occurring, performed, appearing &c., once every month: *a monthly visit*; *monthly payments.* **2.** adv. Once a month, every month: *to pay monthly.*

monthly (II.), n. **1. a** A magazine or periodical which is published once every month; **b** plant, e.g. a monthly rose, which blooms month after month. **2.** (pl.) *Monthlies*, menses.

monthly nurse, n. One who attends a woman in childbirth, and the newly born child, and who stays as a rule for a month.

monthly rose, n. Semi-single pink China rose which flowers month after month throughout summer and autumn.

monticule, n. [1. móntikūl; 2. mɔ́ntikjūl]. Fr. fr. L. Lat. *monticulus*, 'little hill', dimin. fr. *monti-*, stem of *mons*, 'mountain, hill'. See **mount** (I.) & **-cule.** A small hill, a hillock; specif., a subsidiary cone thrown up by a volcano on the slope of the main cone.

monument, n. [1. mónūment; 2. mɔ́njumənt], fr. Lat. *monumentum*, 'that which reminds, recalls; a monument', fr. *monēre*, 'to call to mind, remind, warn'. See **monition.** **1.** An object, such as a tablet, tombstone, column, building &c., constructed, or erected to perpetuate the memory of a person or event; a memorial; *The Monument*, tall column erected to commemorate the Great Fire of London. **2. a** Any structure of historic or artistic interest that is worth preserving as a survival or memorial of the past, such as prehistoric and other fortifications, stone circles, historic, ancient, or beautiful houses, bridges, churches &c.; styled *Ancient Monuments*; **b** a beautiful or striking natural feature, a waterfall, lake; ancient timber &c.; styled *Natural Monuments.* **3.** (obs.) An ancient record or document, now usually *muniment.* **4. a** A work of literature, scholarship, learning, or labour, which has a lasting, permanent value: *a monument of learning, research*; *monument of industry*; **b** (ironic) something which serves as a lasting reminder of the folly or mistaken effort which produced it: *a monument of stupidity and ignorance.*

monumental, adj. [1. mònūméntl; 2. mɔ̀njuméntəl]. Prec. & **-al.** **1.** Serving as a monument, memorial, or record of the past; of or belonging to monuments, esp. of the dead: *monumental brasses, inscriptions* &c.; *monumental mason*, one who carves and erects tombstones. **2. a** Of permanent value; serving as a record of industry, learning &c.; massive in conception and execution: *a monumental work of history* &c.; **b** (of bad qualities) strongly emphasized; extravagant, enormous: *monumental conceit, ignorance, impudence, obstinacy.*

monumentalize, vb. trans. [1. mònūméntalīz; 2. mɔ̀njuméntəlaiz]. **monumental** & **ize.** To commemorate by a monument.

monumentally, adv. [1. mònūméntali; 2. mɔ̀njuméntəli]. **monumental** & **-ly.** **a** By means of a monument or memorial; **b** greatly, excessively.

-mony, suff. Always unstressed; through O. Fr. *-monie*, or direct fr. Lat. *-monia, -monium*, a suff. to form ns., signifying action, result of action, state, condition &c., as *testimony, matrimony, acrimony* &c.

moo, vb. intrans. & n. [1. mōō; 2. mū]. Imitative of cry of the cow. **1.** vb. To low, of cattle. **2.** n. The lowing of a cow.

mooch, mouch, vb. intrans. [1. mōōch, mouch; 2. mūtʃ, mautʃ]. O. Fr. *muchier*, 'to slink, skulk', cp. **miching** & Mod. Fr. *moucheur*, slang for a plain-clothes detective. (slang) To slouch, slink, about; to hang, loiter, idly about the street; often *to mouch round, around.*

moo-cow, n. Child's name for cow.

mood (I.), n. [1. mōōd; 2. mūd]. O.E. *mōd*, 'mind, heart; courage, pride', M.E. *mood*, 'mind; anger'; O.S. *mōd*, O.H.G. *muot*, 'courage', Goth. *mōþs*, O.N. *mōðr*, 'wrath'. Temporary state, disposition, of mind or feeling; temper: *pleasant, jovial, sulky, mood*; *a dreamy, lazy, mood.* Phr. *in the mood for, to do*, disposed, inclined to; *a man of moods*, of variable and uncertain temper.

mood (II.), n. A doublet of **mode,** influenced by association w. prec. **1.** (gram.) Designation, by the choice of form in the conjugation of a verb, of how an act, event &c. is conceived, as a fact, as possible, desirable &c.: *indicative, subjunctive moods* &c. **2.** (logic) Any one of the various classes into which the figures of the syllogism are divided. **3.** (mus.) Mode.

moodily, adv. [1. mōōdili; 2. mūdili]. **moody** & **-ly.** In a moody manner; sullenly, morosely.

moodiness, n. [1. mōōdines; 2. mūdinis]. Next word & **-ness.** State, condition, of being moody; sulkiness, depression.

moody, adj. [1. mōōdi; 2. mūdi]. O.E. *mōdiġ*, 'high spirited, brave; impetuous'. See **mood** (I.) & **-y.** Exhibiting varying moods; (always in unfavourable sense) depressed, sulky, sullen, surly.

moolvie, n. [1. móolvi; 2. múlvi]. Hind., fr. Arab. *maulavi*, cp. **mullah.** One learned in Moslem law in India; a learned person, teacher.

moon (I.), n. [1. mōōn; 2. mūn]. O.E. *mōna*, M.E. *mōne*; O.H.G. *mānō*; Goth. *mēna*, O.N. *māni*; cogn. w. Lat. *mensis*, 'month'; Gk. *mḗnē*, 'moon', *mḗn*, 'month'; also Scrt. *mās*, 'month'; perh. fr. base **mē-*, 'to measure'. See also **mete** (II.) & **month.** **1. a** The earth's satellite, shining by light reflected from the sun and revolving round the earth in the period of a lunar month: *a new moon, full moon* &c. Phrs. *the man in the moon*, the figure or face of a man that can be traced in the markings on the full moon; *know no more about it than the man in the moon*, to know nothing at all; *old moon in new moon's arms*, the faintly visible disk of the moon within the crescent of a new moon, reflection being gained from the earth; *to shoot the moon*, (slang) to do a moonlight flit; *to cry for the moon*, to crave for the unattainable; **b** satellite of another planet, as of Jupiter. **2.** The time taken by moon to make one revolution in its orbit; a lunar month: '*this roaring moon of daffodil And crocus*' (= March) (Tennyson, 'Prefatory Sonnet to the Nineteenth Century'). Phr. *once in a blue moon*, very seldom, rarely if ever. **3.** Light shed by the moon: *the moon is full on my face.*

moon (II.), vb. trans. & intrans., fr. prec. Cp. **moonstruck.** **a** trans. Generally *moon away* (*one's time*) &c., to pass it in a dreamy, listless fashion; **b** intrans., *to moon about*, to loiter, lounge about in an idle, aimless way, with a preoccupied air.

moonbeam, n. [1. mōōnbēm; 2. mūnbīm]. A ray or beam of light from the moon.

moonblind, adj. [1. mōōnblīnd; 2. mūnblaind]. Suffering from moonblindness.

moonblindness, n. Prec. & **-ness.** **1.** A disease of the eye in horses, also called moon-eye. **2.** Night-blindness, formerly attributed to sleeping in the moonlight.

mooncalf, n. [1. mōōnkahf; 2. mūnkāf], fr. supposed influence of the moon on a cow. **a** Misshapen monster; **b** a stupid, doltish person.

moon-eye, n. A periodical inflammation of the eye in horses; moonblindness.

moonflower, n. [1. mōōnflour; 2. mūnflauə]. The ox-eye daisy.

moonless, adj. [1. mōōnles; 2. mūnlis]. **moon** & **-less.** Without a moon; not lighted by the moon: *a moonless night.*

moonlight, n. & adj. [1. mōōnlīt; 2. mūnlait]. **a** n. The light of the moon; **b** (attrib.) of or pertaining to moonlight; performed, occurring, in the moonlight; lit by the moon: *a moonlight ramble*; *moonlight night*; Phr. *a moonlight flit*, a secret removal by night of furniture &c. from a house to avoid its being distrained for rent.

moonlighter, n. [1. mōōnlīter; 2. mūnlaitə]. Prec. & **-er.** An Irish Land Leaguer who committed agrarian outrages by night.

moonlit, adj. [1. mōōnlit; 2. mūnlit]. Lit by the moon.

moonshee, munshi, n. [1. mōōnshē; 2. mūnʃī]. Hind. *munshī.* Native interpreter or teacher of Indian languages; native secretary.

moonshine, n. [1. mōōnshīn; 2. mūnʃain]. **1.** The light of the moon; moonlight. **2.** (fig.) Idea, belief, statement, lacking substance and reality; nonsense. **3.** Illicitly distilled or smuggled spirits, esp. whisky.

moonshiner, n. [1. mōōnshīner; 2. múnʃainə]. Prec. & **-er.** Illicit distiller, smuggler, of spirits.

moonsif, munsif, n. [1. mōōnsif; 2. múnsif], fr. Arab. *munçif*, 'just'. Indian native judge of lowest rank.

moonstone, n. [1. mōōnstōn; 2. múnstoun]. A bluish-green opalescent gem-stone, a variety of feldspar.

moonstruck, adj. [1. mōōnstruk; 2. múnstrak]. Deranged in mind; crazy, wild, and wandering in the wits; a condition supposed formerly to be due to the moon's influence.

moony, adj. [1. mōōni; 2. múni]. **moon** & **-y. 1.** Resembling the moon in shape or appearance. **2.** Dreamy, listless, mooning, as though affected by the moon.

Moor (I.), n. [1. mōr, mōōr; 2. mɔ̄, muə]. Fr. *More, Maure*, cp. Ital. & Span. *Moro*, fr. Lat. *Maurus*, 'inhabitant of Mauretania, N.W. Africa', Gk. *Maûros*. **1.** An inhabitant of Morocco, in N.W. Africa, part of the ancient country of Mauretania, originally of Berber race, now mixed Berber and Arab. **2.** (hist.) One of the conquering Moslem invaders of Spain in the 8th cent. A.D.

moor (II.), n. O.E. *mōr*, M.E. *more*; O.H.G. *muor*, M. Du. *moer*, 'marshy, boggy land'; prob. allied to Goth. *marei*, 'lake'. See **mere** (I.). **a** A stretch or area of waste ground, covered with heather, and marshy or peaty in parts; a heath; specif. **b** such ground used as a preserve for game, esp. grouse.

moor (III.), vb. trans. & intrans. Not in O.E. or M.E.; prob. connected w. O.E. *mārels*, 'mooring rope'; cp. Du. *maaren, meeren*, 'to moor a ship'. **1.** trans. **a** To fasten, secure (a vessel) to the shore, or to buoys, by a cable; to secure (a vessel) head up stream by an anchor on either side of the bows; **b** to secure (an airship) to a mooring mast. **2.** intrans. **a** (archaic, of vessel) To be secured by mooring; **b** to perform the action of mooring a vessel.

moor-cock, n. **moor** (II.) & **cock** (I.). The male bird of the red grouse.

moor-game, n. Grouse, usually the red grouse.

moor-hen, n. **a** The female bird of the red grouse; **b** the water-hen.

mooring-mast, n. A lattice-work mast to which an airship is moored or anchored.

moorings, n. pl. [1. mōringz; 2. mɔ́riŋz]. **moor** (III.) & **-ing. 1.** The cables, ropes, buoys &c. by which a vessel is moored or secured. **2.** Place where a vessel is moored.

Moorish, adj. [1. mōrish; 2. mɔ́riʃ]. **Moor** (I.) & **-ish. a** Pertaining to the Moors; **b** specif., pertaining to the style and design of building introduced by the Moors: *Moorish architecture.*

moorland, n. [1. mórland; 2. mɔ́lənd]. **moor** (II.) & **land.** Land consisting of open moor.

moose, n. [1. mōōs; 2. mūs]. N. Am. Indian name. The North American elk, *Alces machlis americanus*, inhabiting the forests of Canada and of N.E. areas of U.S.A.

moot (I.), n. [1. mōōt; 2. mūt]. O.E. (*ġe*)*mōt*, M.E. *mote*, 'a meeting, discussion'; M.H.G. *muoz*, O.N. *mōt*; etymol. uncertain; fr. n. are derived O.E. *mōtian*, 'to talk, to discuss'; also *mētan*, fr. **mōt-jan*, 'to come upon, discover, meet with'. See **meet** (II.) & **witenagemot. 1.** (Engl. hist.) A meeting or assembly of freemen of a ward, hundred, shire &c., for deliberation and debate on matters of the community's interest. **2.** (law) A meeting of members of an Inn of Court, students, and barristers, to debate and argue a stated legal case or point, as an exercise or practice.

moot (II.), adj., fr. prec. Subject to debate or argument; debatable, arguable: only in Phr. *a moot point, question.*

moot (III.), vb. trans., fr. **moot** (I.). To raise in debate, bring forward for discussion.

mop (I.), n. [1. mop; 2. mɔp]. Earlier *map*; etymol. doubtful; prob. through O. Fr. *mappe*, fr. Lat. *mappa*, 'napkin, cloth'. See **napkin** & **map. 1.** A household implement used for cleaning and washing floors &c., consisting of a loose bundle of coarse yarn fastened to a long handle. **2.** A mass of untidy, loose hair resembling a mop.

mop (II.), vb. trans., fr. prec. **1.** To use the mop on (a floor &c.) in washing it. **2.** To wipe, clean, up (spilled liquid &c.) with a mop or cloth. **3.** To wipe: *to mop one's face, eyes, head*, to wipe away tears, moisture, perspiration. Phr. *to mop up*, (colloq.) (i.) to soak, clean, up, sweep up with a mop; (fig.) (ii.) to pick up, gain (profits &c.); (iii.) to finish off, complete (some piece of work).

mop (III.), vb. intrans. & n. Etymol. doubtful; possibly imitative; cp. Du. *moppen*, 'to pout'. See **mow** (III.). Only in Phrs., **a** *to mop and mow*, to chatter and grimace, e.g. like an idiot or a monkey; **b** *mops and mows*, grimaces &c.

mope (I.), vb. intrans. & trans. [1. mōp; 2. moup]. Etymol. uncertain; cp. Du. *moppen*, 'to pout'. See **mop** (III.). **1.** intrans. To be low-spirited and depressed; to be dull and apathetic; esp. *to mope by oneself*; also *mope about*, to go about in gloomy, listless manner. **2.** trans. In pass. or reflex.: *I was moped to death*; *moping oneself in the house* &c.

mope (II.), n., fr. prec. **a** Person who mopes; **b** gloomy, listless state of mind; chiefly pl.: *to have (a fit of) the mopes.*

mopish, adj. [1. mōpish; 2. móupiʃ]. See prec. & **-ish.** Depressed, inclined to mope.

mopishly, adv. Prec. & **-ly.** In a mopish, depressed way.

mopishness, n. See prec. & **-ness.** State of being mopish.

mopoke, morepork, n. [1. mōpōk, mórpork; 2. móupouk, mɔ́pɔk]. Imitative. Popular name of a small owl in New Zealand, and of the nightjar or goatsucker in Australia; so called from its cry.

moppet, n. [1. mópet; 2. mɔ́pit]. **mop** (I.) & dimin. **-et. a** Child's name for a rag-doll; **b** pet name for a little girl; **c** small lap-dog.

moquette, n. [1. mōkét; 2. moukét]. Fr.; etymol. uncertain. Coarse fabric with a velvety pile, made of wool on a basis of cotton or jute.

moraine, n. [1. morán; 2. mɔréin]. Fr., etymol. uncertain. (geol.) The débris of earth, stones &c. piled up and left in the track of a glacier.

moral (I.), adj. [1. móral; 2. mɔ́rəl]. Fr., fr. Lat. *mōrālis*, 'relating to manners, customs, or morals', fr. *mōr-*, stem of *mōs*, 'manner, way, custom, habit'; pl., 'morals'; etymol. doubtful, possibly connected w. Goth. *mōþs*, 'wrath' &c. See **mood** (I.). **1.** Relating to, concerned with, the difference between right and wrong in matters of conduct; concerned with morality or morals: (*high* or *low*) *moral character, standards* &c.; *moral considerations, judgement* &c., contrasted with *nonmoral.* Phrs. *moral law*, the rules of right conduct; *moral duties, obligations, rights*, such as are based on the moral law; *moral sense*, capacity of differentiating right from wrong; *moral philosophy*, ethics. **2. a** Marked by a high standard in matters of duty and right conduct; obedient to the laws of morality; virtuous; **b** (popularly) virtuous in sexual matters; chaste; contrasted with *immoral.* **3.** Teaching, inculcating, principles of good conduct; proper, seemly: *a moral play, book* &c. **4.** Acting not by physical force, or practical means, but by appeal to reason, sense of right &c.: *moral support, influence, pressure* &c. Phr. *moral victory*, a defeat so narrow or so stimulating to the defeated that it amounts to a victory. **5.** Concerned with the spiritual nature, with the mind and feelings: *to use a word in its moral sense*; contrasted with *material, physical*, or *literal*; *moral courage*, strength of mind, readiness to face ridicule or blame rather than do what is wrong; contrasted with *physical courage.* **6.** Not strictly proved or demonstrable to the reason, but appealing to the moral sense as so probable as to admit of no practical doubt: *a moral certainty*; *moral evidence.*

moral (II.), n., fr. prec. **1.** The real meaning of, practical moral teaching, instruction, guidance, contained in, or to be derived from, a story, fable; or from an experience, circumstance &c.; maxim: '*To point a moral, or adorn a tale*' (Johnson, 'Vanity of Human Wishes'); *the moral of all this is, look before you leap.* **2.** (colloq.) Close resemblance: *the boy is the very moral of his father.* **3.** (pl., *morals*) **a** The principles of right and wrong conduct; science, philosophy, dealing with these principles; ethics; **b** (i.) conduct, habits &c. considered by a standard of right and wrong; morality; (ii.) (popularly) more esp. conduct in regard to sexual matters: *a person of doubtful morals.* **4.** (rare) Morale.

morale, n. [1. moráhl; 2. mɔrál]. Fr. fem. sing. of *moral*, 'moral'; in this sense Fr. uses the masc. *moral*; the necessity of distinguishing the word in the Fr. sense fr. the Engl. word in appearance, as in pronunciation, has led to spelling w. *-e.* The mental state or condition of a body of men, esp. of an army, as evidenced by their discipline, degree of cheerfulness, readiness to endure heavy losses, fatigue &c.

moralism, n. [1. móralizm; 2. mɔ́rəlizəm]. **moral** (I.) & **-ism. 1.** Teaching of morals and morality. **2.** A moral maxim or saying. **3.** Principles of conduct and life based solely on morals, or the distinction between right and wrong, and not on religion.

moralist, n. [1. móralist; 2. mɔ́rəlist]. See prec. & **-ist. 1.** A teacher of, writer on, morals; one who moralizes. **2.** One who practises morality or leads a moral life: *a stern moralist in his own life.*

moralistic, adj. [1. mòralístik; 2. mɔ̀rəlístik]. Prec. & **-ic.** Concerned with morals or moralizing; teaching morality.

morality, n. [1. moráliti; 2. mərǽliti], fr. Fr. *moralité*, Lat. *mōrālitāt-(em), mōrālitas*, 'manner, character', L. Lat., 'morality'. See **moral** (I.) & **-ity. 1.** Doctrines, principles of conduct, based on distinction between right and wrong; moral conduct or character; morals: *the morality of their action is not above question*; *high (low) standard of morality*; *financial, commercial, morality.* **2. a** Conformity with right rules of conduct; moral excellence, virtue; **b** (popularly) virtue in sexual matters; chastity. **3.** (hist.) A form of drama, following the miracle plays or mysteries, in the 16th cent., the principal characters being personifications of the virtues and vices.

moralization, n. [1. mòralīzáshun; 2. mɔ̀rəlaizéiʃən]. Next word & **-ation. a** Act of moralizing; **b** moral reflections.

moralize, vb. trans. & intrans. [1. móralīz; 2. mɔ́rəlaiz], fr. Fr. *moraliser.* **moral** (I.) & **-ize. A.** trans. **1.** To deduce, draw a moral or moral lesson from; to make moral reflections on; to give a moral significance to: '*... he ... stooped to truth, and moralized his song*' (Pope, 'Epistle to Arbuthnot', 341). **2.** To render moral, teach morality to, improve the morals of: *to moralize the heathen.* **B.** intrans. To make moral reflections; write, speak, on the moral aspects of a question: *the author moralizes excessively in this work.*

morally, adv. [1. mórali; 2. mɔ́rəli]. **moral** (I.) & **-ly. 1. a** In a moral sense: *to interpret a statement morally*; **b** according to the principles of sound morality, to what is right; virtuously, uprightly: *to act, live, morally.* **2.** According to probability or moral certainty; virtually, to all intents and purposes: *morally bound to fail, succeed* &c.

morass, n. [1. morás; 2. mərǽs], fr. Du. *moeras*, 'marsh, fen', earlier *maerasch, marasch*, fr. O. Fr. *maresche*, 'marshy', cp. Mod. Fr. *marais*, 'marsh', fr. Low Lat. *mariscus.* See **marsh. a** A bog, marsh, fen, swamp; **b** (fig.) situation, circumstance, of difficulty, embarrassment, perplexity &c.; state of moral degradation.

moratorium, n. [1. mòratórium; 2. mɔ̀rətɔ́riəm]. A modern coinage. See next word. Delay; specif. **a** an act, decree, or ordinance of the legislature giving authority to delay or defer the payment of a debt or obligation; **b** period of delay so authorized.

moratory, adj. [1. móratori; 2. mɔ́rətəri], fr. Lat. *morātōrius*, 'delaying, deferring', fr. *morāt-(um)*, P.P. type of *morāri*, 'to delay', fr. *mora*, 'hesitation, delay'. The etymol. of the latter is doubtful; Walde suggests derivation fr. a base **(s)mer-*, 'to think, to pause and consider', wh. occurs in Lat. *memor*, 'mindful of', *memoria*, 'remembrance', see **memory**; cp. Scrt. *smárati*, 'he remembers'; Gk. *mérmeros*, 'full of care, causing anxiety'; cp. also O.E. *ġemimor*, 'known, familiar'. This & the other words cited show reduplication; the chain of meaning is 'thought, hesitation, pause, delay'. Delaying, deferring, esp. of ordinance authorizing a moratorium.

Moravian, n. [1. morā́vian; 2. mɔréiviən], fr. Moravia, former province of the Austrian Empire. A member of a Protestant sect claiming descent from a branch of the Hussites.

morbid, adj. [1. mórbid; 2. mɔ́bid], fr. Lat. *morbidus*, 'sickly', fr. *morbus*, 'disease', fr. **morodhos*, 'causing death', cp. *mori*, 'to die', *mort-(em)*, 'death'. See **mortal**. **1.** (of the body) **a** Diseased, sickly, not normally healthy; due to disease: *a morbid growth*; **b** concerned or dealing with disease; pathological: *morbid anatomy*. **2.** (of the mind) Abnormally sensitive, unhealthy; inclining to gloominess and depression; tending to dwell on and gloat over unpleasant, horrible subjects.

morbidezza, n. [1. mòrbidétsa; 2. mɔ̀bidétsə]. Ital. See prec. **a** (paint.) Delicacy, fineness, in the representation of flesh-tints; **b** (liter.) sensitiveness, delicacy of expression and feeling.

morbidity, n. [1. mòrbíditi; 2. mɔ̀bíditi]. See **morbid** & **-ity**. State, quality, of being morbid; sickliness; unhealthiness, as in a particular district.

morbidly, adv. [1. mórbidli; 2. mɔ́bidli]. **morbid** & **-ly**. In a morbid manner.

morbidness, n. [1. mórbidnes; 2. mɔ́bidnis]. See prec. & **-ness**. Morbid state of mind.

morbific, adj. [1. morbífik; 2. mɔbífik], fr. Lat. *morbus*, 'disease', see **morbid**, & **-fic**. Causing disease or sickness.

morceau, n. [1. mórsō; 2. mɔ́sou]. Fr. See **morsel**. Literally, piece, bit; specif., a short musical composition or short passage from a longer composition; also a short literary composition or extract.

mordacity, n. [1. mòrdásiti; 2. mɔ̀dǽsiti], fr. Fr. *mordacité*, fr. Lat. *mordācitāt-(em)*, *mordācitas*, 'biting severity, sharpness', fr. *mordax*, 'biting'; cp. *mordēre*, 'to bite'. See next word. Biting sarcasm; sharpness, acridity of temper &c.

mordant (I.), adj. [1. mórdant; 2. mɔ́dənt]. Fr., 'biting', Pres. Part. of *mordre*, 'to bite', fr. Lat. *mordent-(em)*, Pres. Part. type of *mordēre*, 'to bite'; for **smord-*, cp. Gk. *smerdnós*, 'terrible', & Scrt. *márdati*, 'rubs away, crumbles'; prob. cogn. w. **smart**. **1.** (in moral sense) Biting, cutting; sarcastic, caustic: *a mordant wit, tongue* &c. **2. a** (of acid) Acting as a mordant, corrosive; **b** (of disease) causing destruction of tissue, tending to eat away flesh &c.: *a mordant ulcer*.

mordant (II.), n., fr. prec. **1.** (dyeing) A substance used for fixing colours, which in composition with a dye renders this insoluble. **2.** (etching) An acid used for biting into the copperplate.

mordantly, adv. **mordant** (I.) & **-ly**. In a mordant way or manner; bitingly, sarcastically.

mordent, n. [1. mórdent; 2. mɔ́dənt]. Through Mod. Germ. fr. Ital. *mordente*, fr. Lat. See prec. A grace or trill of one note in rapid alternation with the note immediately below it.

more (I.), adj. [1. mōr; 2. mɔ̄]. O.E. *māra*, 'greater in size and number', used as compar. of *miċel*, 'big, much', M.E. *mōre*; O.S. *mēr*; O.H.G. *mēro*, *mēr*; Goth. *maiza*, adj.; *maiz*, adv.; cp. O.N. *meiri*. Cogn. w. O. Ir. *mār*, *mōr*, O.W. *maur*, 'great'; O.H.G. *māri*, 'famous'. See **most** & **much**. A compar., of wh. there is no positive, the positives used being *much, many*; superl. *most*. **1.** Greater, in number, size, amount, degree, quality: *more people than before*; *more money than he needs*; *more knavery than ever*; *more ability than his predecessor*; *make more progress* &c. **2.** Additional, further, other: *there are more books to be written on the subject*; *no more new continents to explore*.

more (II.), adv. In O.E. *mā*, & in M.E. *mō*, were used as comparatives of the adv. *miċele*, 'much'. *Mo* may be found in 16th cent., but is now obs., being replaced by *more*, wh. does duty for the adv. as well as the adj. **1.** In a greater quantity; to a greater degree or extent; *he is growing more now*; *you ought to walk more*. **2.** (forming compar. of adjs. and advs.) *More beautiful*; *more rapidly*. **3.** In addition, further, again: *once more*; *no, never, more*; *any more* &c. Phrs. *more or less*, approximately, nearly, almost, about: *more or less crazy*; *about an hour's walk, more or less*; *more and more*, to an ever increasing degree or extent: *the crowd is growing more and more*; *more and more delighted*; *to be no more*, to die; *the more . . . the more*: *the more he asserted his innocence the more they disbelieved him*.

more (III.), n., fr. **more** (I.). A greater or additional quantity, amount, portion, number &c.: *the more they have, the more they want*; *there is more in his character than simplicity*; *I should like a little more of that excellent mutton*.

moreen, n. [1. morḗn; 2. mɔrín]. Etymol. doubtful; possibly connected w. **moiré**. A woollen or woollen and cotton fabric, with a rib or twill in it, sometimes watered or embossed with a figured pattern.

morel (I.), n. [1. morél; 2. mɔrél], fr. Fr. *morille*; prob. cogn. w. or ad. fr. Germ. *morchel*. An edible fungus, *Morchella esculenta*.

morel (II.), n. O. Fr. *morele*, L. Lat. *morellus*, 'dark-coloured'; etymol. doubtful; possibly fr. Lat. *mōrum*, 'mulberry', wh. is borrowed fr. Gk. *móron*, *mōron*. The black nightshade.

morello, n. [1. morélō; 2. mɔrélou]. Ital., possibly dimin. of Lat. *morum*, see prec. A dark, bitter variety of cherry, used in making cherry-brandy.

moreover, adv. [1. mōrṓver; 2. mɔ̄róuvə]. **more** & **over**. Besides, further(more), also; often used in introducing a new statement.

Moresque, **Mauresque**, adj. [1. mòrésk; 2. mɔ̀résk]. Fr., fr. Ital. *Moresco*, fr. *Moro*; see **Moor** (I.). Moorish, of style or pattern in architecture, art &c.

morganatic, adj. [1. mòrganátik; 2. mɔ̀gənǽtik], fr. Med. Lat. phr. *matrimonium ad morganaticum*; the latter word being an adaptation of Germ. *morgengabe*, 'morning gift', made by a husband to his wife on marriage. Relating to a form of legal marriage, *morganatic marriage*, between a male member of a royal or princely house, in Germany and elsewhere in Europe (not in Great Britain), and a woman not of royal or princely birth; the wife being a legal wife and the children legitimate, but having no rights of succession to the titles of the father or to property other than his private property; also styled a *left-handed marriage*.

morganatically, adv. [1. mòrganátikali; 2. mɔ̀gənǽtikəli]. Prec. & **-al** & **-ly**. By a morganatic marriage.

morgen, n. [1. mórgen; 2. mɔ́gən]. Mod. Germ. & Du. (see **morn**); lit. 'morning', as being amount a man can plough in a morning. An old land measure of area, about two acres, still used in S. Africa.

morgue (I.), n. [1. morg; 2. mɔg]. Fr., perh. same as next word. Place, building, where the bodies of people found dead are kept for identification; a dead-house, mortuary.

morgue (II.), n. Fr., 'disdain, surliness; disdainful look'; also vb. *morguer*, 'to grumble, growl; to behave disdainfully, treat with disdain'; fr. Lat. *mōrigerāri*, 'to comply with, gratify, humour; to accommodate oneself to'; fr. base *mōr-*, fr. *mōs*, 'manner, custom, fashion', see under **moral**, & *gerere*, 'to arrange, govern; to conduct, behave, oneself', see **gerent**. There has been a change of meaning in Fr. compared w. Lat. fr. the accommodation of oneself to another to demanding such compliance fr. another. Pride, hauteur; a chilling, haughty manner or demeanour.

moribund, adj. [1. móribund; 2. mɔ́riband]. Lat. *moribundus*, 'dying', fr. *mori*, 'to die'. See **mortal**. **a** Near to, at the point of, death; in a dying condition; **b** (fig.) about to cease, come to an end; flickering out.

morion, n. [1. móriun; 2. mɔ́riən]. Fr.; etymol. doubtful; cp. Ital. *morione*, Span. *morrion*; possibly connected w. Span. *morro*, 'head'. A late 16th-cent. form of the helmet, shaped like a hat, without visor or neck-guard.

Morisco, n. [1. morískō; 2. mɔrískou]. Span., a dimin. fr. *Moro*; see **Moor** (I.). The name given to the descendants of the Moors who remained in Spain after their expulsion and accepted Christianity.

Mormon, n. [1. mórmun; 2. mɔ́mən]. Invented name; supposed author of the 'Book of Mormon', which contained the revelations on which the sect was founded. **a** A member of a religious sect, founded, 1830, in America by Joseph Smith, a prominent feature of the creed being polygamy; the sect is properly styled *Church of Jesus Christ of Latter-Day Saints*; **b** (fig.) a polygamist.

Mormonism, n. [1. mórmunizm; 2. mɔ́mənizəm]. Prec. & **-ism**. Religious principles and organization of the Mormons.

morn, n. [1. morn; 2. mɔn]. O.E. *morgen*, 'morn, morrow', M.E. *morwe(n)*, O. Fris. *morn*; O.S. *morgan*; Goth. *maurgins*, cp. O.N. *morginn*, prob. fr. base **mergh-*, 'to blink, twinkle', of the light at dawn. Cp. **morrow** & **morning**. **a** (poet. or archaic) The morning, early part of the day; dawn; superseded in Modern English by *morning*; **b** (Scots) Tomorrow, the morrow: *the morn's morn*, tomorrow morning.

morning, n. [1. mórning; 2. mɔ́niŋ]. M.E. *morwening*, 'coming or morn of day', *morwen*, 'morn', & **-ing**. See prec. **1. a** The early part of the day, usually counted from dawn to midday or to the midday meal; Phr. *good morning*, greeting in the morning; **b** (fig.) the early period or beginning of anything: *the morning of life*; **c** (poet.) dawn, esp. as personified, Aurora. **2.** (attrib.) *Morning coat*, a tail-coat, with skirt cut away and fuller tails than a dress-coat; *morning-dress*, dress other than evening-dress; *morning glory*, the name of a flowering twining plant, *Ipomaea*, of the convolvulus family; *Morning Prayer*, the morning service of the English Church; matins; *morning-room*, a sitting-room, other than the dining- or drawing-room, for use in the morning; *morning star*, **a** the planet Venus as seen before sunrise; **b** (hist.) a mediaeval weapon consisting of a spiked iron-ball attached by a chain to a staff or handle; *morning watch*, the watch at sea from 4 A.M. to 8 A.M.

morocco, n. [1. morókō; 2. mərɔ́kou], fr. Morocco, where the leather was originally made. A fine flexible leather, originally made of goat-skin, now of calf- or sheep-skin, specially grained to imitate the true morocco; *Levant morocco*, a large-grained morocco, used for fine bookbinding.

moron, n. [1. móron; 2. mɔ́rɔn], fr. Gk. *mōrós*, 'foolish, stupid', cogn. w. Scrt. *mūraš*, 'idiotic'. A term used by American psychologists and criminologists of children, and of adult persons of feeble, undeveloped, or degenerate mind and character.

morose, adj. [1. morṓs; 2. mərṓus], fr. Lat. *mōrōsus*, 'peevish, capricious, full of whims', fr. *mōs, mōris*, 'custom, habit'. See **moral (I.)** & **-ose**. Surly, sullen, gloomy.

morosely, adv. Prec. & **-ly**. In a morose manner; surlily, sullenly.

moroseness, n. See prec. & **-ness**. State, condition, of being morose; surliness, sullenness.

Morpheus, n. [1. mórfyōōs; 2. mɔ́fjūs]. Lat., fr. Gk. *Morpheús*, 'the god of sleep', lit. 'the maker of shapes or visions', fr. *morphḗ*, 'shape'. See **morphology**. The God of dreams or sleep; hence, sleep itself.

morphia, n. [1. mórfia; 2. mɔ́fiə]. Invented word, fr. prec. An alkaloid of opium, used as a narcotic to relieve pain &c.; morphine.

-morphic, suff. Form fr. Gk. *morphḗ*, 'shape', used in compounds as *anthropomorphic* &c., see first element in **morphology**, & **-ic**.

morphine, n. [1. mórfēn; 2. mɔ́fīn]. Fr. See **morphia** & **-ine**. (chem.) Morphia.

morphinism, n. [1. mórfinizm; 2. mɔ́finizəm]. Prec. & **-ism**. **a** The habitual taking of morphia; **b** diseased condition produced by this habit.

morphinomania, n. [1. mòrfinōmā́nia; 2. mɔ̀finouméiniə]. See prec. & **mania**. Irresistible, morbid craving for morphia.

morphinomaniac, n. [1. mòrfinōmā́niak; 2. mɔ̀finouméiniæk]. **morphine** & **maniac**. One addicted to morphinism; victim of the habit of taking morphia.

morphological, adj. [1. mòrfolójikl; 2. mɔ̀fəlɔ́dʒikl]. **morphology** & **-ic** & **-al**. Pertaining to morphology.

morphologically, adv. Prec. & **-ly**. From the point of view of morphology; structurally.

morphologist, n. [1. mòrfólojist; 2. mɔ̀fɔ́lədžist]. See next word & **-ist**. Student of morphology.

morphology, n. [1. morfóloji; 2. mɔ̄fɔ́lədži], fr. Gk. *morphḗ*, 'shape', the connexion of wh. w. Lat. *forma* is possible, but not altogether clear, see **form**, & **-logy**. **1.** The science and study of external form and structure; applied **a** (biol.) to that of animals and plants; **b** (philol.) to that of languages. **2.** Mode of form or structure itself, **a** (biol.); **b** (philol.).

-morphous, suff. Gk. *morphḗ*, 'form', see prec., & **-ous**, in sense of 'having a specified form or structure'.

morris (I.), n. [1. móris; 2. mɔ́ris]. Earlier *morys*, a form of *Moorish*; the dance was also called *morisco*; the reason for the name is uncertain. An old form of dramatic dance, *morris-dance*, performed in fancy costume, with characters such as Maid Marian &c.

morris (II.), n. Etymol. uncertain; also called *merils*. An old game, played with stones or pegs, on a space marked on the ground, resembling draughts; it was called *five, nine men's morris* &c. according to the number of stones or pegs used.

morris tube, n., fr. inventor's name. A metal tube inserted into the barrel of a rifle to lessen the bore and allow a miniature cartridge to be fired on short ranges or under shelter for practice, now superseded by the miniature rifle.

morrow, n. [1. mórō; 2. mɔ́rou]. M.E. *morwe*, form of *morwen*, 'morn', q.v. **1.** (archaic) Morning: *a radiant morrow*; *good morrow*, good morning, good day. **2.** (liter. or poet.) The next following day: *we will come on the morrow*. **3.** Time immediately following after a specified event: *the morrow of the victory brought disillusionment*.

morse (I.), n. [1. mors; 2. mɔ̄s]. O. Fr. *mors*, fr. Lat. *morsus*, 'biting, the catch of a buckle', fr. *mordēre*, 'to bite'. See **mordant**, **morsel**. A large, round, ornamental brooch, used to fasten a cope; an ouch.

morse (II.), n. Fr., fr. Lapp. *morsha*. A walrus.

Morse (III.), adj. Of or pertaining to a system of signalling by telegraph &c. invented by S. F. B. Morse (d. 1872): *Morse alphabet, code* &c., built up of dots, dashes, and spaces.

morsel, n. [1. mórsl; 2. mɔ́sl]. O. Fr. *morsel*, Mod. Fr. *morceau*, dimin. of *mors*, 'bite', Lat. *mors-(um)*, P.P. type of *mordēre*, 'to bite'. See **mordant**. A small piece, fragment, of food &c.

mort, n. [1. mort; 2. mɔ̄t]. Fr., 'dead; death', fr. Lat. *mort-(em)*, *mors*, 'death'. See next word. Call on hunting horn announcing death of stag or other beast of chase.

mortal (I.), adj. [1. mórtl; 2. mɔ́tl]. O. Fr. *mortal*, Mod. Fr. *mortel*, fr. Lat. *mortālis*, 'subject to death, mortal', fr. *mort-(em)*, 'death'; cp. also Lat. *mori*, 'to die'; the base occurs also in Scrt. *mártaš*, 'mortal, man', *mṛtáš*, 'dead'; Gk. *brotós* for **mrotós*, 'mortal'; O. Slav. *mrěti*, 'to die', *morŭ*, 'pestilence'; Lith. *mirtis*, 'death'; Goth. *maurþr*, 'murder'. See also **murder** & **morbid**. **1.** Liable to die, subject to death; liable to be ended by death; contrasted with *immortal*: *all men are mortal*; *this mortal life*. Phr. *the mortal remains of, all that is mortal of*, the dead body. **2. a** Causing death; deadly, fatal (in physical and spiritual sense): *mortal wound, illness*; *mortal sins*, those incurring perdition unless repented of and forgiven; **b** relating to, concerned with, accompanying, death: *mortal agony*; *mortal fear*, arising from danger or dread of death; (colloq.) *in a mortal funk*. **3. a** Lasting till death; implacable: *mortal enemy*; **b** (colloq.) excessive, lasting a long time, wearisome; very great: *three mortal hours*.

mortal (II.), adv., fr. prec. (colloq. or dial.) Extremely, very: *he was mortal ill*; *mortal sorry* &c.

mortal (III.), n. One subject to death; specif., a human being.

mortality, n. [1. mortáliti; 2. mɔ̄tǽliti], fr. Fr. *mortalité*, fr. Lat. *mortālitāt-(em)*, 'mortality'. **mortal (I.)** & **-ity**. **1.** Quality, condition, of being mortal; liability to die: *none can escape mortality*. **2.** Human nature as subject to death; the human race, humanity: *poor, suffering mortality*. **3.** Number of deaths occurring within given time, in a given place or area; death rate: *the mortality from smallpox is now negligible*. *Mortality tables*, tables giving the expectation of life, or probability of death, over a specified period among specified persons of various ages.

mortally, adv. [1. mórtali; 2. mɔ́təli]. **mortal (I.)** & **-ly**. **1.** So as to cause death; fatally: *mortally wounded*. **2.** Gravely, irrevocably: *mortally offended*.

mortar (I.), n. [1. mórtar; 2. mɔ́tə]. O.E. *mortere*, M.E. *mortir*; cp. O.H.G. *morsari*, 'mortar', fr. Lat. *mortārium*, 'a mortar', also 'cement'; possibly connected w. Lat. *morētum*, 'a salad' (mixture rubbed together), the base being **mer-* &c., 'to rub', as in **marcescent**. A mixture of lime, sand, and water used to bind bricks or stones together in building.

mortar (II.), n. Same as prec. **1.** A metal, stone, or hard porcelain vessel, bowl- or bell-shaped, in which substances, esp. drugs, are pounded and ground to powder by means of a pestle. **2. a** A short cannon, resembling a mortar in shape, used for throwing heavy shells at a high angle for short distances; **b** similar piece of ordnance for throwing life-lines &c. to shipwrecks or for firing heavy fireworks.

mortar (III.), vb. trans., fr. **mortar (I.)**. To bind, join, bricks or stones together with mortar.

mortar-board, n. **1.** A small flat board used by masons or bricklayers for holding mortar. **2.** A college cap, with a stiff, flat, square, projecting top, resembling a mason's mortar-board.

mortgage (I.), n. [1. mórgij; 2. mɔ́gidž]. O. Fr., lit. 'a dead pledge', *mort*, 'dead', see **mortal**, & **gage (I.)**; a translation of Med. Lat. *mortuum vadium*, 'dead pledge'. (law) **1.** A conveyance of property by the owner, *mortgagor*, as security for a debt or money lent by the *mortgagee*, the property remaining in possession of the borrower and being reconveyed on payment of principal and interest by him according to terms stated in the mortgage deed. **2.** The deed conveying property in this way.

mortgage (II.), vb. trans., fr. prec. **1.** To convey property by way of mortgage to another as security for a debt, or for money lent. **2.** (by transf.) To pledge, put under an obligation or claim: *to mortgage one's future career*.

mortgagee, n. [1. mòrgajḗ; 2. mɔ̀gədžī́]. **mortgage** & **-ee**. The person to whom property is conveyed by way of mortgage as security for a debt.

mortgagor, n. [1. mòrgajór; 2. mɔ̀gədžɔ́]. See prec. & **-or**. The person who conveys property by way of mortgage.

mortician, n. [1. mortíshun; 2. mɔ̄tíʃən]. Invented American term, fr. Lat. *mort-*, as in **mortal**, **mortify**, & **-ician**. Vulgar American euphemism for undertaker.

mortification, n. [1. mòrtifikā́shun; 2. mɔ̀tifikéiʃən]. Fr., fr. L. Eccles. Lat. *mortificātiōn-(em)*, *mortificātio*, 'a slaying, putting to death'. See **mortify** & **-ation**. Act of mortifying, state of being mortified. **1.** The subjection, submission, of the body and passions to fasting, penance &c. as a spiritual exercise: *the mortification of the flesh*. **2.** Vexation of spirit; humiliation, chagrin, shame, disappointment: *to have the mortification of acknowledging oneself defeated*. **3.** (pathol.) The death, decay, of a part of the tissues of the body during life; necrosis, gangrene.

mortify, vb. trans. & intrans. [1. mórtifī; 2. mɔ́tifai], fr. O. Fr. *mortifier*, fr. L. Eccles. Lat. *mortificāre*, 'to kill, put to death', fr. *mort-(em)*, *mors*, 'death'. See **mortal (I.)** & **-fy**. **A.** trans. **1.** To submit the body to penance, fasting, and other austerities, so as to reduce, or destroy, the earthly passions and appetites: *to mortify the flesh*. **2.** To humiliate, cause chagrin or mortification to; to hurt, wound: *to be mortified at (by) a former friend's neglect*. **3.** (pathol.) To cause tissues of the body to become gangrenous. **B.** intrans. (of tissues) To become gangrenous.

mortise, mortice, n. & vb. trans. [1. mórtis; 2. mɔ́tis]. M.E. *morteis*, fr. Fr. *mortaise*; etymol. unknown; Span. has *mortaja*; a possible Arab. origin has been suggested. **1.** n. A hole cut in a piece of timber, stone &c. shaped to fit and hold the tenon of another piece which is to be joined to it. *Mortise chisel*, a carpenter's heavy chisel for cutting mortises; *mortise gauge*, carpenter's implement for measuring and laying out mortises; *mortise lock*, door-lock fitted in a mortise. **2.** vb. To join, fasten, by tenon and mortise.

mortmain, n. [1. mórtmān; 2. mɔ́tmein]. O. Fr. *morte main* or *main morte*, Med. Lat. *mortua manus*, 'dead hand', applied to the Church as owner of property held in perpetuity, and incapable of alienation or transfer. See **mortal (I.)** & **manual**. The tenure or possession of land &c. by an ecclesiastical or other corporation not having power of alienation; *in mortmain*, unalienable.

mortuary, adj. & n. [1. mórchooari; 2. mɔ́tʃuəri], fr. Lat. *mortuārius*, 'of, belonging to, the dead', fr. *mortuus*, 'dead', see **mortal (I.)**, & **-ary**. **1.** adj. Of, pertaining to, death, burial, or mourning: *mortuary emblems, monuments* &c.; *mortuary chapel*, one in which the dead are placed prior to Christian burial; chapel attached to public cemeteries; *mortuary urn*, one in which the ashes of a cremated body are placed. **2.** n. **a** A public building in which dead bodies are kept, awaiting burial; or in which bodies of those found dead are kept prior to an inquest &c.; a morgue, dead-house; **b** (hist.) fee formerly paid to the parson of a parish by a dead man's representative for masses &c.

Mosaic (I.), adj. [1. mōzāik; 2. mouzéiik]. Pertaining to Moses, the leader of the Israelites, esp. *Mosaic law*, the Pentateuch.

mosaic (II.), n., fr. Fr. *mosaïque*, fr. L. Lat. *mōsaicus, mūsaicus*, adj., as if fr. a Gk. **mousaikós*, fr. Late (Byzant.) Gk. *mouseîon*, 'mosaic work', as decorating a temple or shrine of the *Moûsai*, the Muses. See **Muse** (I.) & **museum**. **1.** n. **a** A form of surface decoration obtained by fitting together, so as to form a pattern or picture, a number of small pieces of different coloured marble, glass &c.; **b** a picture, design, pattern, made in mosaic. **2.** (fig.) A literary or other work made up of fragments, extracts &c. of other works; a pastiche. **3.** (attrib.) Formed, consisting, of mosaic: *mosaic work, a mosaic pavement* &c.; *mosaic gold*, an imitation gold pigment.

mosaic (III.), vb. trans., fr. prec. To form by or in mosaic; to decorate with mosaics.

mosaicist, n. [1. mōzāisist; 2. mouzéiisist]. Prec. & **-ist**. A worker in mosaic.

mosasaurus, n. [1. mòsasórus; 2. mòusəsɔ́rəs], fr. Lat. *Mosa*, 'the river Meuse', near wh. the first fossil specimen was discovered, & Gk. *saûros*, 'lizard'. See **saurian**. A large extinct lizard.

moschatel, n. [1. mòskatél; 2. mɔ̀skətél], fr. Fr. *moscatelle*. See **musk** & **muscatel**. A small plant, with greenish-white flowers having a musky smell.

moselle, n. [1. mōzél; 2. mouzél]. A dry white wine from the vineyards in the valley of the Moselle.

Moslem, also **Muslim**, n. & adj. [1. mózlem; 2. mɔ́zlɛm], fr. Arab. *muslim*, 'a believer in Islam', Pres. Part. of *salama*, 'to be safe'. See **Islam** & **salaam**, also **Mussulman**. **1.** n. A Mohammedan, Mussulman. **2.** adj. Of, pertaining to, Mohammedans and their faith: *Moslem lands*.

mosque, n. [1. mosk; 2. mɔsk], fr. Fr. *mosquée*, cp. Ital. *moschea*, Span. *mezquita*, fr. Arab. *masjid*, 'temple'. A Mohammedan place of prayer and worship.

mosquito, n., pl. **mosquito**(e)s [1. moskḗtō; 2. mɔs-, məskítou]. Span., dimin. of *mosca*, 'gnat, fly', fr. Lat. *musca*, 'fly', cogn. w. Gk. *muîa*, 'fly'; cp. also O.E. *myċġ*, see **midge**; perh. orig. fr. an imitation of the humming of the insect. Any one of various kinds of dipterous insects or gnats, family *Culicidae*, of which the females have a piercing and bloodsucking proboscis; certain species act as disseminators of the germs of malaria, yellow fever, and other diseases. *Mosquito curtain, net*, a fine-meshed net for keeping mosquitoes from a room, bed &c.; *mosquito fleet, craft*, collective name for the smaller vessels, such as torpedo-boats &c., of a navy.

moss, n. [1. mos; 2. mɔs]. O.E. & M.E. *mos*; O.N. *mosi*; cogn. w. O.E. *mēos*, 'mossy tract of country; swamp', O.H.G. *mios*, see **mire** & **muscology**. O.E. *mēos* has now disappeared except in Place-Names, *moss*, the descendant of O.E. *mos*, doing double duty. **1.** (with sense of O.E. *mēos*) Bog, swamp, morass; still found in names of peaty moorland as *Solway Moss, Chat Moss* &c. **2.** (bot.) The name of various cryptogamous plants, growing in small tufty masses in damp places, on rocks, trees &c.; properly a plant belonging to the class *Musci*, of the *Bryophyta*, but often applied to other plants, e.g. lichens: *Iceland moss*; lycopodia: *club moss* &c. Phr. *a rolling stone gathers no moss*, a restless, changeable sort of person will not prosper or gain wealth.

moss-agate, n. A variety of agate with moss-like markings.

moss-bunker, n. Popular form fr. Du. *marsbanker*. The menhaden, a large kind of Atlantic herring.

mossgrown, adj. [1. mósgrōn; 2. mɔ́sgroun]. **a** Covered, over-grown with moss, as old trees, houses &c.; **b** (fig.) antiquated, old-fashioned.

moss hag, n. **moss** & **hag** (II.). Boggy ground from which peat has been dug.

mossiness, n. [1. mósines; 2. mɔ́sinis]. **mossy** & **-ness**. State of being mossy or covered with moss.

moss-rose, n. A variety of rose, having the calyx and stem covered with a dark-green mosslike growth.

moss-trooper, n., fr. **moss**, 'bog, moor', & **trooper**. A freebooter, cattle lifter, marauder of the Scottish Border, during the 17th cent.

mossy, adj. [1. mósi; 2. mɔ́si]. **moss** & **-y**. Covered with moss; resembling moss.

most, adj., n., & adv. [1. mōst; 2. moust]. O.E. *mǣst*, 'most, greatest', used as superl. of *miċel*, 'great', M.E. *mēst, mōst*; as though fr. O.E. **māst*; the *ā* perh. due to anal. of *māra*, 'more'; O.S. *mēst*; Goth. *maists*, superl. of *maiz*, 'more'. See **more**. **1.** adj. (as superl. of *many, much*) Greatest, in number, quantity, or degree, *to have (the) most soldiers, money* &c.; *to have the most skill, talent* &c.; *most men, people*, the majority of men &c. Phr. *for the most part*, mostly, generally, usually. **2.** n. The greatest number, quantity, amount, degree &c.: *to ask the most for it*, highest price; *most of the loss, profit* &c. Phrs. *to make the most of*, (i.) to make the best use of; (ii.) to represent as of highest possible value, intensity &c.; to exaggerate value &c. of; *at the most, at most*, not more than, at the outside. **3.** adv. **a** To the highest, greatest, degree: *what most pleased me*, or *what pleased me most*; **b** (forming superl. of adjs. and advs.) *most glorious, most famous*; *most truly, most certainly*; also as part of titles: *Most Reverend*, title of archbishops; *Most Gracious King, Queen*; *The Most High*, God; *Most Noble*, for Dukes.

-most, suff. O.E. *-mēst*, a double superl., (1) *-ma*, as O.E. *meduma*, 'midmost', *forma*, 'first'; cp. Lat. superl. in *-mus*; & (2) *-est*. Identified w. *most*, & even in O.E. w. *mǣst*, 'most'. A superl. suff. to form adjs. & advs.: *foremost, topmost, utmost*; also used w. compars.: *lowermost, undermost*.

mostly, adv. [1. mōstli; 2. móustli]. **most** & **-ly**. For the most part, generally, usually, chiefly.

mot, n. [1. mō; 2. mou]. Fr., 'word'. See **motto**. A witty saying or remark; a bon mot.

mote (I.), n. [1. mōt; 2. mout]. O.E. *mot*, M.E. *mōte*, 'atom, mote', prob. cogn. w. Du. *mot*, 'dust, sawdust', & E. Fris. *mut*, 'rubbish'. **1.** A speck, tiny particle, esp. of dust; chiefly used of minute particles of dust in the air: *motes in a sunbeam* &c. **2.** (fig., archaic) Small, trifling blemish or fault: '*The mote that is in thy brother's eye*' (Matt. vii. 3).

mote (II.), vb. O.E. *mōt*, 'can, may', Pres. tense of wh. *mōste* was Pret. See **must** (IV.). (archaic) May, only in Phr. *so mote it be*, so be it, so may it be.

mote (III.). Variant of **moot** (I.).

motet, n. [1. mōtét; 2. moutét]. Fr., dimin. of *mot*, 'word', cp. Ital. *motetto* & see **motto**. A vocal, usually unaccompanied, musical setting to a passage from the Bible, as sung in churches.

moth, n. [1. moth; 2. mɔþ]. O.E. *moððe*, *mohðe*, M.E. *motthe*, cogn. w. O.N. *motti*, Mod. Germ. *motte*; etymol. uncertain; connexion w. O.E. *maðu*, 'maggot', Goth. *maþa*, 'worm', offers difficulties on account of the vowels. Cp. **mawkish**. **a** The popular name for those insects belonging to the Order *Lepidoptera* which are not called *butterflies*, being mostly nocturnal in habit and not having club-ended antennae; **b** the clothes-moth, *Tinea*, or any other insect whose larvae feed on woollen fabrics, furs &c.

moth-eaten, adj. [1. móth ētn; 2. mɔ́þ ītən]. Eaten, destroyed, by clothes-moths or other insects; (fig.) worn-out, decayed.

mother (I.), n. [1. múdher; 2. máðə]. O.E. *mōdor*, M.E. *mōder*; O.S. *mōdar*; O.H.G. *muotar*; O.N. *moðir*; cp. Gael. & Ir. *mathair*; O. Slav. *mati*; Gk. *mḗtēr*; Lat. *māter*; Scrt. *mātṛ*; fr. base **mā*, the meaning of wh. is uncertain. **1.** **a** A female parent; Phrs. *necessity is the mother of invention*; *every mother's son*, (colloq.) everyone, everybody; **b** a motherly person; form of address to an elderly woman. **2.** An incubator, artificial rearing place for chickens, prematurely born animals &c. **3.** The head of a convent or nunnery: *Mother Superior*. **4.** The source, origin of anything: *the House of Commons, Mother of Parliaments*; *our country, mother of heroes* &c. **5.** (attrib.) *Mother Church*, **a** the Church considered as the last resort of all; specif. **b** a cathedral, as principal church of a diocese, also **c** the oldest parish church in a town, district; *mother country*, one's native land, also the original country from which colonies have been founded; *mother tongue*, one's native language; *mother wit*, natural wit, common sense. Phr. *Mother Carey's chicken*, the stormy petrel; *Mother Carey's goose*, the great fulmar; *Mother Carey* is supposed to be a sailor's corruption of Latin *mater cara*, 'the dear Mother', i.e. the Blessed Virgin Mary.

mother (II.), vb. trans., fr. prec. **1.** To look after, tend, cherish, as a mother. **2.** To adopt (a child) as one's own; acknowledge oneself to be the mother of.

mother (III.), n. Origin doubtful; cp. Germ. *mutter*, 'mother, sediment'; M. Du. has *modder*, 'dregs', whence Germ. *moder*, 'mould', cogn. w. **mud**. A thick scum or film produced by fermentation in alcoholic liquors, which is used to turn wine &c. into vinegar, hence called also *mother of vinegar*; also a slimy sticky sediment in vinegar during fermentation.

motherhood, n. [1. múdherhood; 2. máðəhud]. **mother** (I.) & **-hood**. **a** State, condition, of a mother; **b** quality, character, of a mother.

Mothering Sunday, n. [1. múdhering sùndi; 2. máðəriŋ sàndi]. Mid-Lent Sunday, fourth Sunday in Lent; it was formerly the custom to visit the Mother Church of a town or district on this day and present offerings.

mother-in-law, n. [1. múdher in law; 2. máðər in lɔ̄]. Wife's or husband's mother.

motherless, adj. [1. múdherles; 2. máðəlis]. **mother** (I.) & **-less**. Having no mother.

motherlike, adj. [1. múdherlīk; 2. máðəlaik]. See prec. & **-like**. Having the qualities of a mother; motherly.

motherliness, n. [1. múdherlines; 2. máðəlinis]. Next word & **-ness**. Quality of being motherly.

motherly, adj. [1. múdherli; 2. máðəli]. **mother** (I.) & **-ly**. Having the tender, kindly qualities of a mother.

mother-of-pearl, n. The pearly iridescent lining of certain shells, as of oysters, mussels &c., used in making buttons &c.

mothery, adj. [1. múdheri; 2. máðəri]. **mother** (III.) & **-y**. Full of mother or sediment; affected by mother.

motif, n. [1. mōtḗf; 2. moutíf]. Fr. See **motive**. A theme, idea, feature, running through and predominating in an artistic or literary composition; esp. in music, a recurrent melodic phrase or passage.

motile, adj. [1. mṓtīl; 2. móutail]. See **motion** & **-ile**. (physiol.) Capable of movement or motion; moving.

motility, n. [1. mōtíliti; 2. moutíliti]. Prec. & **-ity**. (physiol.) Capacity of movement.

motion (I.), n. [1. mṓshun; 2. móuʃən]. Fr., fr. Lat. *mōtiōn-(em)*, *mōtio*, 'a moving, motion', fr. *mōt-(um)*, P.P. type of *movēre*, 'to move'. See **move**. **1.** **a** Act or process of changing position or place; movement; **b** change in relative position of the parts of anything; mechanical action; Phr. *in motion*, moving, changing position; *to set in motion*, start, set going or moving. **2.** **a** Bodily movement; way, style, of moving the limbs; carriage: *all her motions were graceful*; **b** gesture: *a motion of the hand*; **c** (i.) an action of the bowels; (ii.) matter evacuated. **3.** Mental act; purpose, intention, will, inclination. Phr. *of one's own motion*, without suggestion or influence from another. **4.** A proposal in a legislative or other assembly or meeting: *motion to adjourn, to refer to a committee* &c. **5.** (law) Application to the court for an order or ruling on a specific matter.

motion (II.), vb. trans. & intrans., fr. prec. **1.** trans. To make a significant motion or gesture towards, expressive of wish or intention; to indicate direction by a gesture: *he motioned me away*; *to motion a person to a seat.* **2.** intrans. To make a significant motion or gesture: *he motioned with his head that I should leave him.*

motional, adj. [1. mṓshunal; 2. móuʃənəl]. **motion (I.)** & **-al.** Connected with, of the nature of, causing, motion.

motionless, adj. [1. mṓshunles; 2. móuʃənlis]. See prec. & **-less.** Without motion or movement; at rest; perfectly still.

motion picture, n. (Am. usage) Cinematograph, moving picture.

motivate, vb. trans. [1. mṓtivāt; 2. móutiveit]. Coined word fr. **motive** & **-ate.** (psychol.) To give a motive for; to impel, induce.

motivation, n. [1. mòtiváshun; 2. mòutivéiʃən]. Prec. & **-ion.** Provision of a motive; inducement.

motive (I.), n. [1. mṓtiv; 2. móutiv]. M.E., fr. Fr. *motif*, fr. L. Lat. *mōtīvum*, n., 'cause of movement', fr. *mōt-(um)*, P.P. type of *movēre*. See **move.** **1.** That which influences the desires, incites the will in a particular direction, and induces a specific action; inner force which causes one to act in a particular way: *the motive of a crime* &c. **2.** Predominant feature, idea, or theme underlying or running through an artistic or other composition which determines its form and general development; motif.

motive (II.), adj. Lat. *mōtīvus*, 'moving'. See prec. **1.** Causing, imparting, motion or movement; concerned with, relating to, movement: *motive power, force*, power, force, such as electricity, steam &c., which moves machinery. **2.** Relating to a motive or motives.

motive (III.), vb. trans., fr. prec. To move to action; to impel, incite to action as by a motive; (rare, except in P.P.) *motived by avarice* &c.

motiveless, adj. [1. mṓtivles; 2. móutivlis]. Prec. & **-less.** Without a motive, purpose, or object.

motivity, n. [1. mōtíviti; 2. moutíviti]. **motive (II.)** & **-ity.** Capacity of producing or imparting motion.

motley, adj. & n. [1. mótli; 2. mɔ́tli]. M.E. *mottelee*; etymol. doubtful; apparently Fr.; perh. fr. O. Fr. *motel, mottelet*, 'clod, clot of earth'. Cp. also **mottle. 1.** adj. Of various colours; parti-coloured; of mixed ingredients, parts, or character: *a motley coat*; *motley scene*; *a motley crowd, assembly* &c. **2.** n. A parti-coloured garment, esp. one worn by a jester or fool: *to wear the motley*, to act the jester.

motmot, n. [1. mótmot; 2. mɔ́tmɔt]. Native name; imitative. A tropical S. American bird, resembling the jay.

motor (I.), n. [1. mṓtor; 2. móutə]. Lat., 'a mover', fr. *mōt-(um)*, P.P. type of *movēre*, 'to move', w. agent-suff. **-or.** See **move. 1.** That which imparts motion or gives movement to; **a** a prime mover, such as a steam engine, turbine, water-wheel &c., as source of motive power; **b** (elect.) machine for converting electrical into mechanical power. **2. a** Specif., a compact, powerful engine, now usually an oil- (petrol-) driven internal-combustion engine, used to drive a vehicle, boat, aeroplane, airship &c.; **b** vehicle driven by such an engine; motor-car, motor-boat &c. **3.** (anat.) A muscle moving a part of the body; nerve exciting muscular action. **4.** (attrib.) Driven by a motor: *motor-bicycle, -cycle*; *motor-boat*; *motor-bus, -omnibus*; *motor-car*, the usual term for automobile; *motorman*, one who is in charge of the motor on an electric train, tram &c.; *motor-ship* &c.; *motor-spirit*, petrol.

motor (II.), adj. See prec. Causing, imparting, motion or movement; specif. (physiol.) *motor nerve, muscle.*

motor (III.), vb. intrans. & trans., fr. **motor (I.)**. **a** intrans. To travel by or in a motor-car: *to motor to Brighton*; **b** trans., to convey in a motor-car: *let me motor you to town.*

motorist, n. [1. mṓtorist; 2. móutərist]. Prec. & **-ist.** One who drives, travels by, a motor-car.

mottle, n. & vb. trans. [1. mótl; 2. mɔ́tl]. Earliest form is *mottled*, 'blotched'; prob. fr. **motley. 1.** n. A blotch, spot; a collection, arrangement, of blotches of different colours or shades, as in certain stones, soap, on the face &c. **2.** vb. To stain, mark, with blotches or patches of different colour, or varying degrees of brightness: *mottled surface*, variegated.

motto, n. [1. mótō; 2. mɔ́tou]. Ital., 'saying; device', fr. Low Lat. *mattum*, Lat. *muttum*, 'a mutter, grunt', fr. *mutt-(īre)*, 'to grunt, mutter', prob. imitative, cp. **mutter** & **mot.** **a** A short, pregnant saying, phrase, or word, attached to or inscribed on anything as appropriate to it; specif., one attached to a coat-of-arms, crest &c.; **b** a maxim, rule of conduct expressed in a short pithy sentence; a sentiment: *every man for himself was his motto*; **c** a short quotation prefixed, as indicative or suggestive of the contents, to an essay, chapter in a book &c.

moucharaby, n. [1. mōōshárabi; 2. mūʃǽrəbi]. Fr., fr. Arab. *mashrabīyah*, 'bay window'. (archit.) A projecting latticed oriel window, in Moorish architecture, supported on corbels or brackets.

moufflon, mouflon, n. [1. mṓōflon; 2. mū́flən]. Fr., *mouflon*; L. Lat. *mufron*, cp. Ital. *muffione*, etymol. doubtful. A wild mountain sheep, *Ovis musimon*, of Sardinia and Corsica, the rams having large recurving horns.

moujik, n. [1. mṓōzhik; 2. mū́žik]. Russ. *muzhik.* A Russian peasant.

mould (I.), n. [1. mōld; 2. mould]. Etymol. doubtful; either a variant of **mole (I.)**, 'spot, blemish', or derived as **mouldy**, fr. obs. *moul*, 'to grow mouldy', P.P. *mouled.* **a** A woolly or furry fungoid growth produced on clothes, leather, cheese, bread &c., when kept in the damp: *blue, green, mould*; **b** the fungus which causes mould; *iron-mould*, earlier *yron-mole*, a stain or mark left on linen &c. by rust or ink.

mould (II.), n. & vb. trans. O.E. & M.E. *molde*, 'earth, dust, ground'; O.H.G. *molta*, Goth. *mulda*, 'dust', O.N. *mold*, 'earth', fr. same base as that seen in **mill (I.)**, **meal (I.)**, 'flour'; original sense, 'powdery earth, dust'. **1.** n. **a** Fine, loose crumbling earth or soil; humus; **b** earth, soil generally. **2.** vb. To cover over with mould; also *mould up*, to heap the earth into a mound or ridge over something which has been planted: *to mould up potatoes.*

mould (III.), n. M.E. *molde*, fr. O. Fr. *molle*, earlier *modle*, Mod. Fr. *moule*, fr. Lat. *modulus*, 'a small measure'. See **model. 1. a** Cavity, hollow receptacle, or matrix, within which plastic material such as clay, plaster, molten metal, jelly &c., is cast and shaped into desired form; a plasterer's templet; Phrs. (fig.) *cast in the same mould*, exactly alike in character, disposition &c.; (*cast*) *in a heroic mould*, lofty minded, heroic in character; **b** (in fig. sense) pattern, model: '*The glass of fashion and the mould of form*' (Shakespeare). **2.** Something shaped in a mould; a cast, moulding; specif. **a** a jelly, blancmange &c., moulded into an ornamental shape; **b** (fig.) character, disposition, thought of as directed and modelled in a particular way: *the two were men of quite different mould.*

mould (IV.), vb. trans., fr. prec. **1.** To cause to assume desired shape, **a** by pouring into a mould: *to mould iron*; **b** by kneading, working, pressing, squeezing &c.: *to mould clay into busts.* **2. a** To produce a given object in desired shape by moulding: *to mould a face in, out of, clay*; **b** (fig. and poet., of action of nature) *Nature has moulded her form and features with masterly touch.* **3.** (fig.) To direct, determine, the development of; modify by precept, influence, discipline: *to mould a person's character. Mould on, upon*, to shape according to example or model of: *to mould one's conduct (up)on that of good men*; *to mould one's style upon the best writers.*

mould-board, n. Curved iron plate at back of plough-share which turns the earth over.

moulded, adj. [1. mṓlded; 2. móuldid], fr. P.P. of **mould (IV.)**. Shaped by, or as by, moulding; cast or modelled: *moulded iron, wax* &c.

moulder (I.), n. [1. mṓlder; 2. móuldə]. **mould (IV.)** & **-er.** One who moulds or shapes; one who makes moulds for shaping, casting &c.: *iron-moulder*, in foundry-work, the man who makes the moulds.

moulder (II.), vb. intrans. Freq. of **mould (II.)**. **a** To crumble to dust; to decay: *a mouldering ruin*; **b** (fig.) to decline, degenerate, morally and intellectually; to pass one's life in inactivity and futility: *to remain mouldering in the country. Moulder away*, to fall to dust, disintegrate; fall into ruin and decay.

mouldiness, n. [1. mṓldines; 2. móuldinis]. **mouldy** & **-ness.** State of being mouldy, stale, or fusty.

moulding, n. [1. mṓlding; 2. móuldiŋ], fr. **mould (IV.)** & **-ing. 1. a** Act of shaping, casting, in a mould; **b** manner in which anything is shaped or moulded; modelling. **2. a** Object cast or shaped in a mould or cut or carved according to a pattern; specif. **b** (often pl., *mouldings*) a narrow strip of decorated wood or stone or plaster, used for cornices &c. on buildings, panelling &c.

mouldy, adj. [1. mṓldi; 2. móuldi]. As if fr. **mould (I.)** & **-y**, but prob. orig. fr. *mouled*, P.P. of obs. *moul(en)*, 'to grow musty or mouldy' (of bread &c.), cogn. w. O.N. *mygla*, of same meaning, & allied to **muggy. a** Covered with mould or fungoid growth; musty, fusty: *mouldy bread, cheese* &c.; **b** (fig.) stale, old-fashioned, out of date.

moulin, n. [1. mṓōlan; 2. mūlǽ]. Fr., 'mill', fr. Lat. *molīnum.* See **mill (I.)**. (mountaineering) A vertical shaft in a glacier, formed by a stream of surface water pouring into a crevasse; also the stream which does this.

moult (I.), vb. intrans. & trans. [1. mōlt; 2. moult]. O.E. *bi-mūtian*, 'to exchange', M.E. *mouten* (the *l* is due to some anal. w. *fault*); fr. Lat. *mūtāre*, 'to change'. See **mutable. 1.** intrans. **a** (of birds) To go through periodical process of shedding the old plumage; **b** (more rarely, of other animals) to shed the old hair from their coats. **2.** trans. To shed, lose: *to moult feathers* &c.

moult (II.), n., fr. prec. **a** Process of shedding old plumage; **b** period during which this takes place.

mound (I.), n. & vb. trans. [1. mound; 2. maund]. Origin uncertain. **1.** n. **a** An artificially raised heap of earth, stones &c.; specif., one raised for defensive purposes near a castle; **b** isolated natural hillock, knoll. **2.** vb. To pile, heap up, earth &c. into a mound.

mound (II.), n., fr. Fr. *monde*, Lat. *mundus*, 'the world'. See **mundane.** A globe or ball of gold, surmounted by a cross, forming part of the regalia of a sovereign; orb.

mound-builder, n. **mound** (I.). (ethnol.) Race of N. American aborigines who raised large mounds for burial and defence.

mount (I.), n. [1. mount; 2. maunt]. O.E. *munt*, 'hill, mountain', M.E. *mont, mount*, borrowed fr. Lat. *mont-(em)*, *mons*, 'mountain'; connected w. Lat. *mināri*, 'to jut out, project, tower up'; also 'to threaten'; cp. further Lat. *mentum*, 'chin' (see **mental**

(**II.**)); W. *mynydd*, 'mountain'; all fr. base *men- &c., 'to project'. See **minatory**, **menace**; also **eminent**. **1. a** A hill, mountain; **b** the regular form in names of mountains, as *Mount Everest* (abbr. *Mt.*). **2.** (palmistry) A fleshy protuberance at the base of the fingers.

mount (**II.**), vb. trans. & intrans. M.E. *monten*, *mounten*; fr. Fr. *monter*, lit. 'to go up hill', hence 'to climb, ascend', fr. Lat. *mont-(em)*, *mons*, 'mountain'. See prec. **A.** trans. **1. a** To climb, ascend, go up; get to, or on to, the top of: *to mount a hill, stairs* &c.; Phr. *to mount the throne*, succeed as king; **b** specif., to get on to the back of: *to mount a horse*. **2.** To set (an object) up in a fixed position or on or in something which will serve to hold it in position or securely. Various specific senses: **a** *to mount a gun*, on a gun-carriage; **b** *to mount a picture*, fix to a stretcher, or to a card cut to serve as a margin; **c** *to mount a specimen*, on a slide for microscope work; **d** *to mount jewels*, put them in a setting; **e** to prepare, stuff, and set up the skin of an animal; **f** *to mount a play*, to furnish (a play and actors) with scenery, costumes, properties &c.; to set on the stage. Phrs. *to mount guard*, to go on duty as sentinel or guard; *to mount guard over*, to guard, protect. **B.** intrans. **1. a** To rise, ascend, go up; **b** specif., get up on, seat oneself on, a horse: *he mounted and rode away*. **2.** To increase in amount, rise: *prices continue to mount*; also *mount up*, increase by accumulation: *losses, debts, bills, mount up rapidly*.

mount (**III.**), n., fr. prec. That on which anything is mounted; specif. **a** a horse, mule &c. for riding; **b** a card serving as a margin for a picture; **c** setting for a jewel; **d** a slide for microscopic object; **e** carriage for a gun &c.

mount (**IV.**), vb. trans. In specific sense, fr. prec. **1.** To provide with a mount, lend one a horse to ride: *my friend was good enough to mount me for the day*. **2.** To provide (soldiers) with horses, turn into cavalry: *to mount a regiment*.

mountain, n. [1. móuntin; 2. máuntin]. M.E. *montaine*, fr. O. Fr. *montaigne*, Mod. Fr. *montagne*, fr. Low Lat. *montanea*, Lat. *montānus*, 'of, belonging to, mountains; hilly', fr. *mont-(em), mons*, 'mountain, hill'. See **mount** (**I.**). **1.** A lofty, natural elevation of the earth's surface; generally used to imply something much larger than a *hill*. Phrs. *to make mountains out of molehills*, magnify petty troubles and difficulties; *Old Man of the Mountains*, the founder of the Assassins, Hassan ben Sabbah, living in N. Persia; *the mountain in labour*, a great effort with only a small result or effect. **2.** *The Mountain*, name of the violent extreme party during the French Revolution, *les Montagnards*, from the high seats they occupied in the National Assembly. **3.** (by transf.) **a** Anything of great bulk: *a mountain of flesh*, a very tall, stout person; **b** (fig.) a very large amount or quantity: *a mountain of difficulties, liabilities* &c.; *mountain(s)-high*, (of waves &c.) very high. **4.** (attrib.) *Mountain artillery, battery*, guns which can take to pieces easily and be packed on mules &c. for quick transport in mountain or hilly country; *mountain ash*, the rowan tree; *mountain dew*, Scotch whisky, properly, whisky illicitly distilled in the mountains; *mountain sickness*, a disease, marked by difficulty of breathing, debility, nausea, headache &c., caused by rarefaction of the air at very high altitudes.

mountaineer, n. & vb. intrans. [1. mòuntinḗr; 2. màuntiníə]. Prec. & **-eer**. Cp. Fr. *montanier*. **1.** n. **a** An inhabitant of mountains or of hilly country; **b** a trained climber of mountains. **2.** vb. To climb mountains.

mountaineering, n. [1. mòuntinḗring; 2. màuntiníəriŋ]. Prec. **2** & **-ing**. Practice, sport, of climbing mountains.

mountain finch, n. The brambling.

mountainous, adj. [1. móuntinus; 2. máuntinəs], fr. O. Fr. *montagneux*, fr. L. Lat. *montāneōsus*, Lat. *montānus*. See **mountain** & **-ous**. **1.** Characterized by mountains: *a mountainous district, country* &c. **2.** Resembling a mountain in bulk; very great, huge, enormous: *a mountainous load of debt*.

mountainy, adj. [1. móuntini; 2. máuntini]. See prec. & **-y**. **1.** Mountainous; very hilly. **2.** (an Irishism) Living in, coming from, the mountains or wild hilly districts of Ireland: esp. *mountainy men*.

mountebank, n. [1. móuntibangk; 2. máuntibæŋk]. Ital. *montambanco*, fr. *montare*, 'to mount', *in*, 'on', *banco*, 'bench', fr. the platform or bench fr. wh. quacks &c. addressed their audience. Cheap-jack, quack, charlatan, buffoon.

mounted infantry, n. [1. móunted ínfantri; 2. máuntid ínfəntri]. Soldiers who are mounted for moving from place to place, but who fight on foot.

mounting, n. [1. móunting; 2. máuntiŋ]. **mount** (**II.**) & **-ing**. **1. a** Setting up of a gun on its carriage, of a stuffed animal, microscopical specimen &c.; **b** way in which a thing is mounted. **2.** That which serves as a mount; mount (in various senses). *Mounting-block*, a stone or wooden step, used for mounting on horseback.

mourn, vb. intrans. & trans. [1. morn; 2. mɔ̄n]. O.E. *murnan*, M.E. *mournen*; Common Gmc.; O.H.G. *mornēn*, Goth. *maurnan*, O.N. *morna*; perh. fr. orig. base *(s)mer-, 'to ponder, hesitate' &c., cp. Lat. *mora*, 'delay'. See **moratory** & **memory**. **1.** intrans. To feel and express grief or sorrow; to lament, regret; esp. to lament for loss (of friends &c.) by death: *to mourn for, over, the dead, misfortunes* &c. **2.** trans. To grieve, sorrow, for; to lament, regret: *to mourn the loss of friends*.

mourner, n. [1. mórner; 2. mɔ́nə]. Prec. & **-er**. One who mourns; **a** one mourning loss of relative or friend; specif. **b** one who attends the funeral of a dead person, as relative or friend; **c** an undertaker's assistant who attends a funeral in a professional capacity; a mute.

mournful, adj. [1. mórnfool; 2. mɔ́nfəl]. **mourn** & **-ful**. **a** Full of mourning, grief, or sorrow; **b** expressing grief: *mournful songs*; **c** inspiring sorrow; gloomy, dismal: *a mournful scene*.

mournfully, adv. Prec. & **-ly**. Sadly, sorrowfully.

mournfulness, n. See prec. & **-ness**. State or quality of being mournful.

mourning, n. [1. mórning; 2. mɔ́niŋ]. **mourn** & **-ing**. **1.** Lamentation, grief, sorrow: *sounds of mourning*. **2.** Wearing apparel of black or dark material worn as sign of sorrow and respect for the dead. Phr. *to go into mourning*, to assume clothes of black or other suitable colour as sign of respect for the dead; *in mourning*, wearing such clothes for one recently dead. **3.** Period during which black is worn.

mourning-band, n. Band of black crape or other material worn round the arm as a sign of mourning.

mourning-card, n. Black-edged card giving name, date of birth, and death of a deceased person.

mourning-coach, n. A black carriage drawn by black horses, used at funerals.

mourning-paper, n. Black-edged note-paper.

mourning-ring, n. Ring worn in memory of one dead.

mouse (**I.**), n., pl. **mice** [1. mous, mīs; 2. maus, mais]. O.E. *mūs*, pl. *mȳs*, M.E. *mous*; Common Gmc. & Aryan; cogn. w. O.H.G. & O.N. *mūs*, cp. Germ. *maus*, Du. *muis*; Russ. *muish*; O. Slav. *myšĭ*; Lat. *mūs*, Gk. *mûs*, Scrt. *mūsh*, fr. root *meus-, 'to steal'; Scrt. *mush*, 'to steal', *musha*, 'robber'. **1.** Any one of various species of small rodents belonging to the genus *Mus*, smaller than rats: *common house mouse, field mouse*; also *shrew mouse*. **2.** A timid, quiet, retiring person. **3.** A small leaden weight used in sash-windows. **4.** (slang) A black eye. **5.** (attrib.) *Mouse colour*, a dark-grey colour shaded with buff or yellowish brown.

mouse (**II.**), vb. intrans. [1. mouz; 2. mauz]. To hunt for and catch mice (of cats, owls &c.).

mouse deer, n. The chevrotain.

mouse-ear, n. Hawk-weed.

mouser, n. [1. móuzer; 2. máuzə]. **mouse** (**II.**) & **-er**. An animal, esp. a cat, good at catching mice.

mouse-tail, n. The stone-crop.

mouse-trap, n. Trap for catching mice.

mousquetaire, n. See **musketeer**.

mousse, n. [1. mōōs; 2. mūs]. Fr., 'foam'. A dish of whipped cream and eggs, with various flavourings &c.

mousseline, n. [1. mōōslēn; 2. mūslīn]. Fr., 'muslin', q.v. A fine, soft fabric of wool and cotton, *mousseline-de-laine*, or of silk, *mousseline-de-soie*.

moustache, **mustache**, n. [1. mustáhsh, moostáhsh; 2. məstā́ʃ, mustā́ʃ], fr. Fr.; earlier *mustachio*; fr. Ital. *mostaccio*; fr. Gk. *mústax*, *mástax*, 'that with which one chews; the mouth and jaws, the upper lip, moustache'. Cp. **masticate**. The hair on the upper lip of a man; also used of bristles or hair round the lips and mouths of animals, as cats &c. *Moustache cup*, a drinking-cup with a guard to prevent the moustache from becoming wet.

Mousterian, adj. [1. mōōstḗrian; 2. mūstíəriən], fr. Le Moustier, in S. France, where remains of this type were first found. (palaeont.) Belonging to the last type of culture of the early palaeolithic age.

mouth (**I.**), n. [1. mouth; 2. mauþ]. O.E. *mūð*, M.E. *mouth(e)*; O.S. *mūð*; Goth. *munths*, O.N. *muðr*, *munnr*; fr. base *menth-, *mnth-, 'to chew'. See **mandible**. **1.** The orifice, protected by the lips, in the head or face of man and other animals through which food is taken; also the cavity into which the orifice leads, containing the tongue, teeth &c., and serving as the means both of transmitting vocal sounds, and of mastication of food; Phrs. *down in the mouth*, dejected, depressed; *make one's mouth water*, (i.) make one long to eat, from the action that appetizing, savoury food produces upon the salivary glands; (ii.) make one envious: *to laugh on the wrong side of one's mouth*, to be vexed or disappointed; *to open one's mouth too wide*, to ask, expect, too much, or too high a price; *to put words into one's mouth*, to suggest that one has said what one has not; *to take words out of one's mouth*, to anticipate what one is going to say. **2.** A horse's mouth, considered as susceptible to the pressure and guidance of the bit and reins: *hard, tender, bad, good, mouth*. **3.** (usually pl.) A human being regarded as a consumer of food: *so many mouths to feed*; *useless, hungry mouths*. **4.** Any outlet, opening, or aperture, as **a** of a river, harbour, bottle, cave, bag &c.; **b** the mouthpiece of a musical wind-instrument.

mouth (**II.**), vb. trans. & intrans. [1. moudh; 2. mauð], fr. prec. **A.** trans. **1.** To utter, speak, with a strained, affectedly sonorous or pompous voice; esp. with excessive movement of lips and jaws: *to mouth one's words*. **2.** To take (food) into the mouth and chew it; esp. to make facial contortions while chewing. **3.** To train a horse to answer to the bit and reins. **B.** intrans. **a** To make excessive movements and contortions of lips and jaws while eating or speaking; **b** to speak pompously, with over-emphasis; to declaim, rant.

mouthed, adj. [1. moudhd; 2. mauðd]. **mouth** (**I.**) & **-ed**. Having a mouth; having a particular kind of mouth: *wide-mouthed* &c.

mouther, n. [1. móudher; 2. máuðə]. **mouth** (**II.**) & **-er**. One who mouths; a ranter.

mouthful, n. [1. móuthfool; 2. máuþful]. **mouth** (**I.**) & **-ful**. **1. a** As much food as the mouth will hold; **b** amount of food put into the mouth at one time. **2.** A small portion or quantity; esp. a small portion of food: *have a mouthful of luncheon before you start.*

mouth-organ, n. A small popular wind-instrument, flat in shape, having openings for the various notes, and producing sounds of considerable sonority in proportion to its size; also called the *pan-pipes.*

mouthpiece, n. [1. móuthpēs; 2. máuþpīs]. **1.** That part of a pipe, tube &c., which is placed in the mouth or between the lips, as of a tobacco-pipe, musical wind-instrument &c. **2.** (by transf.) Spokesman; organ, e.g. of the press, which voices current opinion. **3.** An appendage to the orifice of a water-pipe to regulate the flow of water.

mouthy, adj. [1. móudhi; 2. máuði]. **mouth (II.)** & **-y.** Ranting, declamatory, bombastic; garrulous, prolix.

movability, n. [1. mōōvabíliti; 2. mūvəbíliti]. See next word & **-ity.** Quality, condition, of being movable in space.

movable, adj. [1. mōōvabl; 2. mūvəbl]. O. Fr. *movable*; see **move** & **-able**, & cp. **mobile (I.).** **1.** Capable of being moved or of being changed from place to place; not stationary or fixed; *movable property,* chattels, personal property, as contrasted with *real property.* **2.** Changing in time; shifting: *movable feast,* such as Easter, the date of which is different each year.

movableness, n. See prec. & **-ness.** Movability.

movables, n. pl. [1. mōōvablz; 2. mūvəblz]. See prec. Movable property, chattels.

move (I.), vb. trans. & intrans. [1. mōōv; 2. mūv]. M.E. *moeven, mēven, mōven,* fr. O. Fr. *movoir,* Mod. Fr. *mouvoir,* fr. Lat. *movēre,* P.P. *mōtus,* 'to move, set in motion', cogn. w. Scrt. *mīvati,* 'he shifts, presses, moves'; Gk. *ameúomai,* 'I get ahead of, surpass, conquer'; also Corinthian dial., *amoiwá,* 'interchange', cp. also perh. M.H.G. *mouwe,* 'sleeve', apparently 'something drawn on'. **A.** trans. **1.** To change the position of, to shift from one place to another: *to move the furniture; to move troops, goods, traffic* &c.; *to move a piece,* in chess, draughts &c. Phrs. *to move house,* to change one residence for another; *not well enough to be moved,* to be transferred to another house, or place. **2.** To set in motion, start going, stir, shake: *to move one's legs; the wind moves the trees; the engine moves the train*; specif., *to move the bowels,* cause them to function. **3. a** To affect, stir, arouse, the feelings and emotions, touch the heart, of: *the story moves me profoundly; much moved by sights and sounds of misery*; **b** to provoke (persons) to the exhibition of some particular form of emotion: *to move one to tears, laughter, anger* &c.; **c** to urge, provoke, incite, persuade, to act in a particular way: '*the Scripture moveth us . . . to acknowledge and confess*' (General Confession); *I felt moved to go for a ride, to pay a round of visits* &c. **4.** To propose, make a formal proposal for: *to move the adjournment of the House* (*of Commons*); *to move the previous question*; *to move a resolution,* at a committee &c. **B.** intrans. **1.** (of living organisms) **a** To have the faculty or power of voluntary bodily movement; to be able to alter position of the body or its members by exerting the voluntary muscles; to live, have being: '*God created great whales, and every living creature that moveth*' (Gen. i. 21); Phr. *to move in good society,* to frequent it; **b** to exercise the function of movement; to set the body or part of it in motion, alter its position by volitional action: *keep quite still and don't move*; *I'm so stiff I can hardly move*; *he moved uneasily in his sleep*; *there's not a soul moving*; **c** (of bodily members and organs) to be set in motion, to undergo change of position, be brought into state of activity by the action of the will: *his lips moved, but no sound escaped them*; *his fingers moved rapidly over the keyboard*; **d** to move oneself, carry, bear, oneself in a particular way: *to move gracefully.* **2.** (of inanimate objects) **a** To be shifted from one position to another, be agitated, shaken, put into a state of motion, by some external natural force: *so still was the air that not a leaf was moving*; **b** to be set in motion by a mechanical agency, perform a series of continuous movements as result of mechanical action: *a piston moves by steam pressure*; *a pendulum moves slowly backwards and forwards.* **3.** To undergo a change of place; **a** (of persons) (i.) to go from one place to another; shift one's position relatively to surrounding objects: *move nearer this way, out of the light* &c.; (ii.) to change one's habitat or place of residence; go from one place or region to another, and take up one's abode there; to migrate: *nomad peoples constantly move to new areas in search of pasture*; *to move into the country*; (iii.) specif., to go from one house into another to live: *my house is too small for me, so I've made up my mind to move*; **b** (of inanimate things) to be shifted from one place to another; to proceed, pass, be propelled, along, by the action of external forces: *a ship moves before the wind*; *the train moved slowly into the station.* **4. a** (of events, circumstances, external conditions) To progress, advance, change by natural process of development; to exhibit a certain trend or tendency of change: *events are moving rapidly*; *things are not moving quite as I could wish*; '*And one far-off divine event, To which the whole creation moves*' (Tennyson, 'In Memoriam'); **b** (of natural world) to exhibit signs of growth and development; to sprout, grow: *the weather is so cold that nothing is moving in the garden.* **5.** Specif., to make move in chess or draughts: *it is your turn to move.* **6.** To make a formal motion in an assembly, court of law: *to move for an adjournment, papers* &c. **C.** Followed by adverbs. *Move about,* intrans., to move from place to place. *Move away,* intrans., to move from. *Move in,* intrans., to enter, take up residence in, a new house. *Move on,* **a** trans., (of policeman) to keep people, a person, on the move, prevent from loitering; **b** intrans., to go on to another place or position, to keep moving. *Move out,* intrans., to leave, quit, one's house or place of residence.

move (II.), n., fr. prec. **1. a** Act or process of moving; movement; a change of position; Phrs. *to make a move,* (i.) to prepare to depart; to leave place where one is: *it is getting late, it's time to make a move*; (ii.) to take action, begin to act; *on the move,* (i.) continually moving from place to place; (ii.) (of things, events) progressing, advancing, stirring; **b** specif., removal of household effects to a different dwelling; change of residence. **2.** One of recognized movements, alteration in relative position of a piece at chess, draughts &c.: *a knight's move.* **3.** (fig.) An act to effect a given purpose; device, step: *a clever move.*

movement, n. [1. mōōvment; 2. mūvmənt]. O. Fr. *movement,* Mod. Fr. *mouvement*; L. Lat. *movimentum.* See **move (I.)** & **-ment.** **1.** Act, process, fact, of moving or being moved; motion in the abstract; activity, agitation; contrasted with quiescence, passivity, repose, inactivity: *we find movement of one kind and another everywhere in nature.* **2. a** Act of moving the body or members, carried out by man or lower animals; bodily motion whether voluntary or involuntary; gesture: *a faint movement of the lips, eyes*; *a graceful, hesitating, violent, movement of the hand*; *a movement of impatience, of disdain,* gesture expressing these; **b** (pl.) mode of moving the body; deportment, bearing, carriage: *her movements were easy and dignified*; **c** natural extension and expansion of branches, buds, leaves &c., of plants in process of growth. **3.** Sum of a person's activities during a given period, including wanderings from place to place, and general doings: *mind you let me know all your movements while you are away.* **4. a** Motions imparted by mechanical means to parts of a machine; **b** mode of action, way in which a machine works. **5.** Motion, disturbance, agitation, imparted to inanimate objects by natural forces: *the movement of the waves, of boughs in the wind.* **6.** Passage, process of going, from one place to another: **a** by draught or propulsion: *the movement of trains, traffic* &c.; **b** change of habitat, shifting of place of abode by men or animals; migration: *the movement of races, peoples, population.* **7.** Liveliness, activity, increase of business: *considerable movement on the Stock Exchange, in the oil market.* **8. a** Body of opinion, feeling shared by a number of persons, in favour of, or in opposition to, something, esp. such opinion and feeling expressed in words and actions: *a movement to abolish the death penalty*; *the temperance movement*; Phr. *in the movement,* abreast of the times; **b** spiritual or intellectual stirring; tendency, trend of opinion; impetus towards new development: *the great religious movement started by Luther.* **9.** That quality in a play or novel which gives a sense of life and reality; variety of action and sentiment; fire, spirit: *a play that lacks movement.* **10.** A division of a long musical composition, e.g. of a sonata, having a characteristic tempo; *slow movement* or *andante, quick movement* or *allegro.*

mover, n. [1. mōōver; 2. mūvə]. **move (I.)** & **-er.** One who or that which moves; specif. **a** an agency for the production of motion; a motive power or motor; **b** person who is active, who takes the initiative in an enterprise: *he is the chief mover in the scheme of reform*; also *prime mover*; **c** a proposer; one who moves a resolution &c. in an assembly.

movies, n. pl. [1. mōōviz; 2. mūviz]. (vulg. and colloq.) Cinematograph; moving pictures.

moving, adj. [1. mōōving; 2. mūviŋ], fr. Pres. Part. of **move (I.).** **1. a** Changing position; in process of movement; **b** causing motion. **2.** Tending to excite the feelings, and stir the emotions; affecting, pathetic: *a moving appeal*; *a moving account of human suffering.*

movingly, adv. Prec. & **-ly.** In a moving, touching, affecting manner.

moving pictures, n. pl. Cinematograph.

moving staircase, n. A staircase or flight of steps moving on a continuous belt which carries passengers up and down an incline; escalator.

mow (I.), n. [1. mō; 2. mou]. O.E. *mūga,* M.E. *mowe*; cogn. w. O.N. *mūgi.* A heap, stack of hay or straw; stack of sheaves of corn; esp. *barley mow*; the term is usually applied to a stack of hay &c. before being thatched or stored in a barn.

mow (II.), n. & vb. intrans. [1. mō, mou; 2. mou, mau], fr. O. Fr. *moe,* Mod. Fr. *moue,* 'mouth, pout'; etymol. doubtful. **a** n. A grimace, only in Phr. *mops and mows,* gestures and grimaces; **b** vb., to make a grimace.

mow (III.), vb. trans. [1. mō; 2. mou]. O.E. *māwan,* M.E. *mōwen*; O.H.G. *māan,* cp. Du. *maaijen,* Germ. *mähen*; cogn. w. Gk. *amân,* Lat. *metere,* 'to reap'; cp. also **mead (II.), meadow, math.** **1. a** To cut down (grass or other fodder crops) in swathes with a scythe, or with mechanical mower: *to mow the grass, clover* &c.; **b** to cut grass growing on (field, &c.) with a mowing machine: *to mow a field, the lawn.* **2.** (fig.) To cut, sweep down, like grass: *the attacking troops were mown down by machine-gun fire.*

mower, n. [1. mōer; 2. móuə]. O.E. *māwere.* See prec. & **-er.** **a** A person who mows or cuts grass; **b** a mowing machine.

mowing machine, n. [1. mōing mashēn; 2. móuiŋ məʃīn]. A machine used for cutting grass, containing a revolving cylinder furnished with a set of sharp blades, cutting against a flat, fixed blade; drawn by a horse, driven by steam or petrol, or pushed by hand.

moxa, n. [1. móksa; 2. móksə], fr. **Jap.** *mogusa.* A soft downy material made from the leaves of a kind of wormwood, used as a counter-irritant for inflamed joints &c.

Mozarab, n. [1. mōzárab; 2. mouzǽrəb]. Span. *Mozarabe*, fr. Arab. *musťarīb*, 'pretended, would-be Arab'. One of the Christians who submitted to the Moorish conquest of Spain and were allowed to practise their religion.

Mozarabic, adj. [1. mōzárabik; 2. mouzǽrəbik]. Prec. & **-ic.** Pertaining to the Mozarabs; *Mozarabic liturgy*, an ancient Spanish liturgy.

Mpret, n. [1. bret; 2. bret]. Albanian corrupt. of Lat. *imperātor*, 'emperor'. Title of sovereign ruler of Albania, now extinct.

Mr. See **mister.**

Mrs. See **mistress.**

much, adj., n., & adv. [1. much; 2. matʃ]. M.E. *miche, moche, muche*, earlier *michel, mochel, muchel*, O.E. *mičel, myčel*, 'great, big; many'. See **mickle. 1.** adj. **a** Great in quantity, duration: *much snow has fallen*; *much time is wasted*; **b** (archaic) great in number, many: (Bib.) *much people* &c. Phrs. *too much for*, more than one can cope with, more than a match for; *much cry and little wool*, much ado about nothing. **2.** n. A great quantity, a good deal: '*much is omitted . . . much likewise is performed*' (Johnson, Pref. to Dict.); *to gain much* (*advantage* &c. understood); *much of the time was wasted*; *much of what you say*. Phrs. *to make much of*, to treat as of importance; to flatter, cosset; *I don't think much of*, have a poor opinion of; *not much of a linguist* &c., not a good. **3.** adv. **a** (with vbs.) To a great extent, greatly: *much vexed*; *much enduring*; **b** (with compar. and superl. adjs.) *much better*; *much the greatest*; **c** nearly, almost: *much* (*about*) *the same*; also *pretty much* (*alike* &c.).

muchness, n. Prec. & **-ness.** (colloq.) Greatness in quantity; in Phr. *much of a muchness*, much the same, nearly alike.

mucilage, n. [1. músilij; 2. mjúsilidž]. Fr., fr. Lat. *mūcilāgo*, 'musty, mouldy juice'; cp. *mūcēre*, 'to be musty', *mūcidus*, 'musty'. See **mucus. a** A gelatinous, viscous substance found in seaweeds and other plants; **b** gum.

mucilaginous, adj. [1. mùsilájinus; 2. mjùsilǽdžinəs], fr. Lat. *mūcilāgin-(em)*. See prec. & **-ous.** Viscous, gummy, sticky.

muck, n. & vb. trans. [1. muk; 2. mak]. M.E. *muc, muk*, prob. Scand., cp. O.N. *myki*, 'dung'. **1.** n. **a** Dung, manure; **b** filth, dirt; **c** (of material and non-material things) anything disgusting or unclean; **d** rubbish, balderdash: *the last book he wrote was sheer muck*. Phr. *to make a muck of*, to render unclean; to make thoroughly untidy. **2.** vb. **a** To cover with dung or muck; **b** (colloq.) to make untidy, disorderly, or dirty; to bungle, mishandle. Phrs. (colloq.) *to muck about*, to loaf, mouch about, wander aimlessly; *to muck up*, to spoil, ruin, put out of order by unskilful handling.

mucker, n. [1. múker; 2. mákə]. Prec. & **-er.** (slang or colloq.) A cropper, fall, bad mishap: *to come a mucker*, to have a heavy fall or mishap, physically or figuratively.

muckle. Variant of **mickle**, cp. **much.**

muckna, n. [1. múkna; 2. máknə]. Hind. *makhnā*. Male elephant with rudimentary tusks, or tuskless.

muckrake, n. [1. múkrāk; 2. mákreik]. A rake for manure or dung; (fig.) *the man with the muckrake*, from Bunyan's 'Pilgrim's Progress', a man so intent on raking muck that he was blind to the heavenly crown; one who is always looking for evil motives, scandal, and corruption &c.

muckworm, n. [1. múkwërm; 2. mákwām]. A larva or grub breeding in manure; (fig.) a miser.

mucky, adj. [1. múki; 2. máki]. **muck & -y.** Dirty, filthy; unpleasant, distasteful.

mucosity, n. [1. mūkósiti; 2. mjūkɔ́siti]. See next word & **-ity.** State, condition, quality, of being mucous.

mucous, adj. [1. mūkus; 2. mjúkəs], fr. Lat. *mūcōsus*, fr. *mūcus*, 'mucus'. Resembling, containing, secreting, mucus: *mucous membrane*, the moist lining or coating of various inner cavities and passages of the body, as of mouth, nose, alimentary canal &c.

mucro, n. [1. mūkrō; 2. mjúkrou]. Lat., 'point', of a sword. Etymol. doubtful. (bot. and zool.) A sharp point or tip, as on leaf or organ.

mucronate(d), adj. [1. múkrunāt(ed); 2. mjúkrəneit(id)], fr. Lat. *mucrōn-(em)*, see prec., & **-ate.** Having a sharp point or tip.

mucus, n. [1. mūkus; 2. mjúkəs]. Lat., 'slime from the nose', cogn. w. Gk. *múxa* (cp. **myco-**), & stem of Lat. *ēmu(n)gere*, 'to wipe (the nose)'; cp. **emunctory. a** The slimy, moist secretion of the mucous membrane of the body; **b** any slimy, viscous secretion of animals such as slugs, snails &c.

mud, n. [1. mud; 2. mad]. Not in O.E.; of L.G. origin, cp. O.L.G. *mudde*, 'mud', *muddig*, 'muddy', Du. *modder*. See **mother (III.).** Wet, moist earth: *to treat, consider* (person) *as mud, as the mud beneath one's feet*, treat, consider, as something contemptible, despicable; soil in a slimy, semi-liquid condition; Phr. *to throw mud at*, to speak evil of, asperse.

mudar, n. [1. mudár; 2. mədā́]. Hind. *madār*. Kind of East Indian tree, *Calotropis*, yielding fibre.

mud-bath, n. A bath in mud impregnated with various salts, as a remedy for rheumatism &c.

muddily, adv. [1. múdili; 2. mádili]. **muddy & -ly.** (rare) In a muddy manner; with mud.

muddiness, n. [1. múdines; 2. mádinis]. See prec. & **-ness. a** Condition of being muddy; **b** specif., cloudiness in liquids.

muddle (I.), vb. trans. & intrans. [1. múdl; 2. mádl], fr. **mud & -le**, the earliest meaning being 'to dabble in mud', cp. M. Du. *moddelen*, 'to make water muddy'. **a** To bewilder, confuse the mind of, fuddle; **b** to bungle; to cause to go awry or fail by uncertain, confused action: *to muddle a plan, scheme, piece of business* &c.; **c** often *muddle away*, to waste through folly, lack of clearness of purpose: *muddle away one's time, money* &c. Phrs. *to muddle on*, to carry on, proceed, in a confused, indefinite sort of way; *to muddle through*, to get through somehow, to achieve one's purpose only after many failures.

muddle (II.), n., fr. prec. **1. a** Material disorder and confusion: *everything in a muddle*; **b** confused heap of heterogeneous objects; a mess, a litter. **2. a** Confusion of ideas; **b** disorderly arrangement; jumble of disconnected facts or statements &c.

muddle-headed, adj. Incapable of clear, logical thought; confused in mind.

muddy, adj. & vb. trans. [1. múdi; 2. mádi]. **mud & -y. 1.** adj. **a** Full of, covered in, mud; filthy: *muddy water, boots* &c.; **b** mud-coloured, dark-coloured, not clear; opaque: *muddy light, muddy skin*; **c** (of liquids) not clear, cloudy, having particles of solid matter in suspension. **2.** vb. To cloud, fill with mud, make muddy.

mudfish, n. [1. múdfish; 2. mádfiʃ]. The popular name of various fishes which live in muddy water or burrow in mud at the bottom of rivers &c.

mudguard, n. [1. múdgard; 2. mádgād]. A metal or other protective shield to the wheels of a vehicle to catch the mud from the wheels and prevent its flying up.

mudir, n. [1. mōōdēr; 2. mūdíə]. Arab., 'governor'. The governor of an Egyptian province; also of a small Turkish town or village.

mudlark, n. [1. múdlark; 2. mádlāk]. Street urchin who dabbles in the mud of a river at low tide in the hope of finding something of value; one who enjoys dabbling in mud.

mud-pie, n. Small heap of mud shaped like a pie by a child.

mud-volcano, n. A volcano which discharges a muddy mixture of water and ashes.

muezzin, n. [1. mōōezēn; 2. mūezīn]. Arab. *mu'adhdhin*, fr. *adhana*, 'to call, proclaim', *adhan*, 'call'. The official of a Mohammedan mosque who cries the call to prayer from the minaret; cp. '*A Muezzin from the Tower of Darkness cries*' (Fitzgerald, 'Omar Khayyám').

muff (I.), n. [1. muf; 2. maf]. Fr., Du. *mof*, cp. Walloon *mouffe*, fr. Fr. *moufle*. See **muffle (I.).** A warm covering for the hands, made of fur, lined with quilted silk &c., usu. in cylindrical form with the two ends open.

muff (II.), n. & vb. trans. Etymol. doubtful; Engl. dial. has *maffle*, 'to mumble, speak indistinctly'. **1.** n. **a** (i.) A clumsy, awkward person, esp. one who is unhandy at games and sports; (ii.) a cowardly, unmanly fellow, a molly-coddle, a milksop; **b** blunder, failure: *to make a muff of the business*. **2.** vb. To miss, fail to catch; to make a mess of: *to muff a ball, a catch, at cricket*.

muffetee, n. [1. mùfetḗ; 2. màfətí]. A form of **muff (I.).** (obs.) A woollen covering for the wrists and part of the hands; mitten.

muffin, n. [1. múfin; 2. máfin]. Etymol. doubtful; prob. not connected w. O. Fr. (*pain*) *moflet*, 'soft bread'. A light, flat cake of yeast dough, with rounded, brown top, toasted, buttered, and eaten as hot as one can get it. *Muffin bell*, bell rung by a *muffin man*, who sells muffins in the street.

muffineer, n. [1. mùfinḗr; 2. màfiníə]. Prec. & **-eer. 1.** A covered dish for keeping toasted muffins hot. **2.** (old-fashioned) A castor with perforated top, used for sprinkling salt, pepper, or sugar on muffins, cakes &c.; sugar-castor.

muffle (I.), n. [1. múfl; 2. máfl], fr. O. Fr. *moufle, mofle*, 'leather or fur winter glove', in early Med. Lat. *muffula*. Etymol. unknown; the vb. is fr. the n. **1.** (obs., or dial.) A leather glove or mitten. **2.** A chamber or covering in a furnace or kiln which protects the substances heated or baked from direct contact with the fire.

muffle (II.), vb. trans., fr. prec. To wrap with a covering, a for warmth or concealment: *to muffle one's throat, head* &c.; also *muffle up*; **b** to deaden, stifle, sound (of): *to muffle oars, bells, drums*; *a muffled voice*; *muffled curses*.

muffle (III.), n., fr. Fr. *mufle*. Etymol. unknown. The thick fleshy end of the nose and lips of ruminant animals.

muffler, n. [1. múfler; 2. máflə]. **muffle (II.) & -er. 1.** A wrap, scarf, for the throat. **2.** A silencer for a motor-car or motor-cycle. **3.** A pad of felt between hammers and strings of a pianoforte.

mufti, n. [1. múfti; 2. máfti]. Arab., fr. *afta*, 'to expound the law'. **1.** An official expounder of Mohammedan law; a legal assessor. **2.** (mil. and nav.) Civilian clothes; contrasted with *uniform*.

mug (I.), n. [1. mug; 2. mag]. Etymol. unknown. **a** China drinking vessel the top and bottom of which have the same diameter; **b** tankard of silver &c.

mug (II.), n. Perh. fr. prec. (vulg. slang) The face, mouth.

mug (III.), n. Etymol. unknown. (slang) **a** Innocent, inexperienced, person; esp. one who falls a prey to swindler; **b** person who is unacquainted with, and therefore unskilful at, a particular game &c.

mug (IV.), vb. intrans. & trans., & n. Etymol. unknown. **a** vb. (colloq., slang) To study, work hard, cram; also trans.: *to mug up a subject*; **b** n., one who is always at work and takes no recreation; a prig, a superior person.

mugger, muggur, n. [1. múger; 2. mágə], fr. Hind. *magar*, 'broad-snouted crocodile'. The Indian marsh crocodile.

muggins, n. [1. múginz; 2. máginz]. Etymol. doubtful. **a** A simpleton, mug; **b** name of a game of cards and of dominoes.

Muggletonian, n. [1. mùgltṓnian; 2. màgltóuniən]. Member of a schismatic sect, founded by John Muggleton (1609–98).

muggy, adj. [1. múgi; 2. mági]. Prob. Scand.

in origin; cp. O.N. *mugga*, 'drizzling mist'; possibly cogn. w. **mucus.** (of weather) Damp, close, warm, oppressive.

mugwort, n. [1. múgwërt; 2. mágwǝt]. O.E. *myċġwyrt.* See **midge** & **wort (I.).** British plant, a species of wormwood.

mugwump, n. [1. múgwump; 2. mágwamp]. N. Am. Indian, 'chief'. (Am. polit. slang) One who holds himself aloof from, and superior to, party politics; originally used of independent members of the Republican party.

Muhammedan. See **Mohammedan.**

Muharram. See **Moharram.**

mulatto, n. [1. mūlátō; 2. mjulǽtou], fr. Span. & Port. *mulato*, 'of mixed breed', fr. *mulo.* See **mule. 1.** The offspring of a negro and a European or white man. **2.** (attrib.) Of brownish-yellow colour, as mulattoes.

mulberry, n. [1. múlberi; 2. málbǝri]. M.E. *murberie, moolberie*, cp. O.H.G. *mūrberi*; the final element is **berry**; O.E. has *mōrbēam*, 'the mulberry tree', *mōr*, 'mulberry', being fr. Lat. *mōrus*, 'mulberry', cp. Gk. *môron*, cp. **morel (II.). a** A tree, genus *Morus*, with dark-purple or white edible berries, and broad, dark-green leaves on which silkworms feed; **b** the fruit of this tree; **c** a dark-purple colour.

mulch, n. & vb. trans. [1. mulsh; 2. malʃ]. Etymol. doubtful; prob. fr. obs. *mulch*, adj., 'soft'; cp. O.E. *melsċ*, & Germ. dial., *molsch*, 'soft, ripe'. **1.** n. A surface dressing of manure, moist straw, leaves &c. placed round plants, and small, or newly-planted trees &c., to protect the roots from heat, or cold, and to prevent evaporation of moisture. **2.** vb. To put a mulch on or round (plants &c.).

mulct, n. & vb. trans. [1. mulkt; 2. malkt], fr. Lat. *mulctāre*, 'to punish; to fine', cp. *mulcta, multa*, 'fine, penalty', orig. paid in cattle or sheep; cp. Lat. *mulcāre*, 'to beat, cudgel', apparently cogn. w. Lat. *mulcēre*, 'to stroke', the orig. meaning of the base having been 'to touch', cp. **demulcent. 1.** n. A fine imposed by way of penalty for a wrong; a pecuniary penalty. **2.** vb. **a** To fine (a person) for an offence: *to mulct one £10* or *in £10*; **b** to deprive of, take money from: *to be mulcted of £10.*

mule, n. [1. mūl; 2. mjūl]. Fr. *mule*, fem. of *mul*, fr. Lat. *mūlus*, cogn. w. Gk. *múklos, mukhlós*, 'a he-ass'. **1.** A cross or hybrid between the horse and the ass; properly the offspring of an ass-stallion and mare, the name of the offspring of she-ass and horse being *hinny.* Phr. *as obstinate, stubborn, as a mule.* **2.** A stubborn, obstinate person. **3.** A hybrid plant or animal; specif., *mule canary*, a cross between a canary and another bird of the finch family. **4.** A spinning-jenny. **5.** A heelless slipper.

muleteer, n. [1. mùletḗr; 2. mjūlitíǝ], fr. Fr. *muletier*, fr. *mulet*, dimin. of *mul(e)*, 'mule'. See prec. & **-eer.** A mule driver.

muliebrity, n. [1. mùliébriti; 2. mjūliíbriti], fr. Lat. *muliēbritas*, fr. *mulier*, 'woman, wife'; perh. connected w. *mollis*, 'soft'. See **mollify.** Womanhood; effeminacy; contrasted with *virility.*

mulish, adj. [1. mū́lish; 2. mjū́liʃ]. **mule** & **-ish.** Like a mule in character; stubborn, obstinate.

mulishly, adv. Prec. & **-ly.** Stubbornly, obstinately.

mulishness, n. Prec. & **-ness.** Stubbornness, obstinacy.

mull (I.), vb. trans. [1. mul; 2. mal]. Etymol. unknown. To heat and spice wine or beer, esp. in P.P., *mulled claret, ale* &c.

mull (II.), vb. trans. & n. Etymol. unknown. (colloq.) **a** vb. To make a mess or muddle of; **b** n., muddle, mess: *to make a mull of one's work*, to bungle, mismanage it.

mull (III.), n. Gael. *maol*, cogn. w. O.N. *muli*, O.E. *mūle*, Germ. *maul*, 'snout'. A promontory, common in Scottish place-names: *the Mull of Kintyre.*

mull (IV.), n. Etymol. doubtful; possibly fr. S. & W. type of **mill (I.).** A large table snuff-box, made of a ram's horn mounted in silver.

mull (V.), n., fr. Hind. *malmal.* A thin, soft kind of muslin.

mullah, n. [1. múla, móola; 2. málǝ, múlǝ]. Pers. & Hind.; in Turk. *mollah*, fr. Arab. *maulā*, 'judge, magistrate'. One learned in Mohammedan law and religious dogma; a reader and expounder of the Koran; often a spiritual, religious leader, as in Afghanistan, and on the north-west frontier of India.

mullein, n. [1. múlin; 2. málin]. M.E. *moleyn*, fr. A.-Fr. *moleine*, Fr. *molène*, fr. *mol*, 'soft', fr. Lat. *mollis*, 'soft'. See **mollify.** A wild herbaceous plant, genus *Verbascum*, with coarse, woolly leaves and tall spikes of yellow flowers.

muller, n. [1. múler; 2. málǝ]. Perh. variant of **miller**; cp. M.E. *mullere* by side of *millere*; cp. **mill (I.). 1.** A stone or piece of thick glass used for reducing drugs &c. to powder on a slab. **2.** Apparatus for grinding silver, copper, and other ores.

mullet (I.), n. [1. múlet; 2. málit]. M.E. *molet, mulot*, fr. O. Fr. *mulet*, dimin. fr. Lat. *mullus*, in L. Lat. *mulus*, 'the red mullet', cp. Gk. *múllos*, a sea-fish (not the red mullet). An edible sea-fish of two kinds: **a** *the red mullet*, genus *Mullus*, family *Mullidae*, of a bright-red colour, with two barbels suspended from the mouth; **b** the *grey mullet*, genus *Mugil*, family *Mugilidae*, of greenish, silvery colour, of larger size and less esteemed as a food-fish.

mullet, molet (II.), n. M.E. *molet*, O. Fr. *molette*, 'the rowel of a spur'; prob. ultimately fr. Lat. *mola*, 'a mill, mill-wheel'. See **mill (I.).** (her.) A five- or six-pointed star, usually pierced with a round hole in the centre, borne as a charge in a coat of arms.

mulligatawny, n. [1. mùligatáwni; 2. màligǝtɔ́ni], fr. Tamil *milagutannir*, 'pepper-water'. A thick, hot soup, to which rice is usually added, made with curry-powder and hot seasonings; of East Indian origin.

mulligrubs, n. [1. múligrubs; 2. máligrabz]. Invented word. (colloq.) **a** Colic, gripes; **b** a fit of the sulks, the blues.

mullion, munnion, n. [1. múliun, múniun; 2. máliǝn, mániǝn]. Etymol. doubtful; prob. fr. O. Fr. *moignon*, 'stump of a tree, pinion of a wing'; whence also comes **monial.** An upright shaft, or column, usually of stone, dividing the lights in a window.

mullock, n. [1. múluk; 2. málǝk], fr. obs. *mull*, 'dirt, refuse', fr. M.E. *mullen*, 'to grind'. See **muller** & dimin. suff. **-ock.** Dirt, rubbish; specif. (Australian min.) the refuse rock or earth from which gold has been extracted or which contains no gold.

multi-, pref., usually before vowels **mult-**, fr. Lat. *mult(us)*, 'many'; prob. connected w. Gk. *mála*, 'very, very much, exceedingly'; also w. Lat. *melior*, 'better', q.v. under **ameliorate.** Form used as prefix signifying 'many, repeated, several, more than one or two'; many terms thus compounded are explained by reference to the main word, and are not included here, as *multi-coloured*, 'many coloured', *multi-cellular*, 'having many cells', *multipolar* (elect.), having more than two poles, and the like.

multifarious, adj. [1. mùltifárius; 2. màltiféǝriǝs]. L. Lat. *multifārius*, adj., fr. Lat. *multifāriam*, adv., 'in many places', *multifāriē*, 'in many ways', *multi-*, as prec., & *-fāriam*, termination, the origin of wh. is doubtful, possibly connected w. *fāri*, 'to speak'; cp. the equiv. fr. Gk. **poly-**, & the contrasted pref. **mono-.** Consisting of many kinds, various, manifold: *multifarious duties.*

multifariously, adv. Prec. & **-ly.** In many various ways; with great variety.

multifariousness, n. See prec. & **-ness.** State of being multifarious; great variety, diversity.

multiform, adj. [1. múltiform; 2. máltifɔ̄m]. **multi- & form.** Having many forms or shapes; manifold.

multiformity, n. [1. mùltifórmiti; 2. màltifɔ́miti]. Prec. & **-ity.** Variety, diversity of shape or form; contrasted with *uniformity.*

multi-millionaire, n. [1. mùlti milyunár; 2. màlti miljǝnéǝ]. Person who is worth several millions (of pounds, dollars &c.); a millionaire several times over.

multinomial, adj. [1. mùltinómial; 2. màltinóumiǝl]. **multi-** & *-nomial*, as in **binomial.** (alg.) Expressed by more than two terms; polynomial.

multiparous, adj. [1. multíparus; 2. maltípǝrǝs]. **multi- & -parous**, fr. Lat. *parĕre*, 'to produce, bring forth'. See **parent.** Producing more than one at a birth.

multiple, adj. & n. [1. múltipl; 2. máltipl]. Fr., fr. L. Lat. *multiplus.* See **multiply. 1.** adj. **a** Having many component parts or elements; formed of many individual members: *multiple shop*, a retail business which has many branches; *multiple star*, a group of stars which are so close together as to have the appearance of a single star; **b** (specif., elect.) of a circuit with a number of parallel conductors; **c** (math.) repeated, occurring more than once. **2.** n. (math.) A number or quantity which contains another quantity an exact number of times: *12 is a multiple of 4*; *common multiple*, a number which contains two or more numbers an exact number of times; *20 is a common multiple of 2, 4, 5, and 10*; *least common multiple* (abbr. L.C.M.), the smallest number which will do this: *12 is the L.C.M. of 3 and 4.*

multiplepoinding, n. [1. mùltipl-póinding; 2. màltipl-póindiŋ]. Prec. & *poind*, Scots, 'to distrain', fr. O.E. *pyndan*, 'to put in a pound, pen up, enclose'. See **pound (III.).** (Scots law) A form of action to decide between several conflicting claims to property, or to a sum of money; in English law, *interpleader.*

multiplex, adj. [1. múltipleks; 2. máltipleks]. Lat., fr. *multi-* & *-plex*, fr. *plic-(āre)*, 'to fold'. See **multiply.** Manifold, multiple, having many component parts.

multipliable, adj. [1. múltipliabl; 2. máltiplaiǝbl]. **multiply & -able.** Capable of being multiplied; multiplicable.

multiplicable, adj. [1. mùltiplíkabl; 2. màltiplíkǝbl]. Lat. *multiplicābilis.* See **multiply.** Multipliable.

multiplicand, n. [1. mùltiplikánd; 2. màltiplikǽnd]. Lat. *multiplicand-(us)*, 'to be multiplied'. See **multiply.** (maths.) A number which is to be multiplied by another number, the *multiplier.*

multiplication, n. [1. mùltiplikáshun; 2. màltiplikéiʃǝn]. Fr., fr. Lat. *multiplicātiōn-(em).* See **multiply. 1. a** Act, process, of multiplying or increasing the number of; **b** state of being multiplied; increase in number: *the multiplication of the population.* **2.** (arith.) The repeating or adding of any given number or quantity a certain number of times, symbol ×, e.g. $6 \times 4 = 24$; *multiplication table*, a table of a set of numbers, usually 1 to 12, with the products of multiplication by the same numbers successively.

multiplicative, adj. [1. mùltiplíkativ; 2. màltiplíkǝtiv]. See prec. & **-ive.** Having the capacity of multiplying or being multiplied.

multiplicity, n. [1. mùltiplísiti; 2. màltiplísiti]. Lat. *multiplicitāt-(em)*, fr. *multiplic-(em), multiplex*, 'manifold'. See **multiple & multiply & -ity.** Quality, state, of being very numerous or various; a great number or variety: *the multiplicity of his duties.*

multiplier, n. [1. múltiplier; 2. máltiplàiǝ]. **multiply & -er.** That which, one who, multiplies; specif. **a** (arith.) a number by which another number, the *multiplicand*, is multiplied; **b** (elect.) an instrument or device for multiplying or intensifying current, oscillations &c.

multiply, vb. trans. & intrans. [1. múltiplī; 2. máltiplai], fr. O. Fr. *multiplier*, fr. Lat. *multiplicāre, multiplicāt-(um)*, fr. *multiplex, multi-* & *-plex*, '-fold', fr. stem **plic-*, of *plicāre*, 'to fold', cogn. w. Gk. *plikein,* 'to plait, twist'. See **complex** (I.) & **plicate. 1.** trans. **a** To increase, add to the number of; to produce in large numbers, make more numerous; **b** (specif., arith.) to add, by the process of multiplication, a number to itself a specified number of times: *to multiply 5 by 3,* to add 5 to itself 3 times, 5×3=15. **2.** intrans. To increase in number: *cares multiply as one gets older. Multiplying gear,* gear for increasing speed in a machine; *multiplying glass,* (i.) a magnifying glass; (ii.) a lens with a number of facets on one side.

multitude, n. [1. múltitūd; 2. máltitjūd]. Fr., fr. Lat. *multitūdo,* 'a great number, a crowd', fr. *multus,* 'much, many'. See **multi-. 1.** Numerousness; greatness of number: *as the stars in multitude.* **2. a** A large number: *a multitude of flowers;* **b** specif., a large number of persons; a crowd; *the multitude,* the masses.

multitudinous, adj. [1. mùltitúdinus; 2. maltitjúdinəs], fr. Lat. *multitūdin-(em),* stem of *multitūdo.* See prec. & **-ous.** Very numerous; consisting of, pertaining to, a multitude or crowd.

multitudinously, adv. Prec. & **-ly.** In a crowded fashion, in very large numbers.

multitudinousness, n. See prec. & **-ness.** State of being multitudinous.

multum in parvo, n. [1. múltum in párvō; 2. máltəm in pávou]. Lat., 'much in little'. Much contained in a small space.

multure, n. [1. múlchur; 2. máltʃə], fr. O. Fr. *moulture,* fr. L. Lat. *molitūra,* 'grinding of corn', fr. Lat. *molere,* 'to grind (corn)'. See **mill** (I.) & **meal** (I.). (Scots law) A toll or fee paid in grain or flour to a miller.

mum (I.), adj. [1. mum; 2. mam]. Imitative of the smallest sound made by the lips. Silent, dumb; also as noun: *mum's the word!,* silence is the essential thing.

mum (II.), vb. intrans. Cp. Du. *mommen,* 'to mask'; cp. also O. Fr. *momer,* 'to act in dumb show', & Span. *momo,* 'buffoonery'; perh. connected w. **Momus.** To act in dumb show, usually masked or disguised; esp. to take part in popular acting and merry-making at Christmas; esp. in Pres. Part., *to go mumming.* See **mummer.**

mum (III.), n., fr. L.G. *mumme,* cp. Du. *mom.* A kind of strong ale or beer, originally brewed in Brunswick.

mumble, vb. intrans. & trans. & n. [1. múmbl; 2. mámbl]. M.E. *momelen, momele,* fr. **mum** (I.), cp. L.G. *mummeln,* 'to mumble food'; Du. *mommelen,* 'to mutter'. **1.** vb. intrans. **a** To speak, utter indistinctly, to mutter; **b** to chew, bite, esp. of an old toothless person. **2.** vb. trans. **a** To utter (words &c.) in an indistinct manner; **b** to chew or nibble (a crust &c.) with excessive workings of the jaws. **3.** n. A mumbled indistinct sound or utterance.

mumblemattins, mumbletext, n. (archaic) A careless priest whose sense of his duties is satisfied when he has gabbled through his office or his sermon.

Mumbo Jumbo, n. [1. múmbō júmbō; 2. mámbou džámbou]. **a** The supposed name of a negro or African deity or idol; **b** any object of popular superstition.

mumchance, adj. & n. [1. múmchahns; 2. mámtʃāns], fr. **mum** (I.). (obs.) **a** adj. Silent; **b** n., silence.

mummer, n. [1. múmer; 2. mámə], fr. O. Fr. *momeur, mommeur;* as **mum** (II.), 'to act in dumb show', cp. M. Du. *mummen,* 'to act as a mummer'. **a** An actor in an old popular drama played mostly in dumb show; **b** (colloq.) an actor (usually in derogatory sense).

mummery, n. [1. múmeri; 2. máməri], fr. O. Fr. *momerie.* **mum** (II.) & **-ery. a** A performance by mummers; a dumb show; **b** any display of exaggerated and meaningless ceremonial; a mockery, pretentious show.

mummification, n. [1. mùmifikáshun; 2. màmifikéiʃən]. **mummy** & **-fication. a** Act, process, of mummifying or embalming; **b** state of being mummified.

mummiform, adj. [1. múmiform; 2. mámifɔ̄m]. **mummy** & **-form.** Shaped like, in the form of, a mummy.

mummify, vb. trans. & intrans. [1. múmifī; 2. mámifai], fr. Fr. *momifier.* See **mummy** & **-fy. a** trans. To make a mummy of, to embalm; **b** intrans., to shrivel, dry up, become like a mummy; usu. in P.P., *mummified.*

mumming. See **mum** (II.).

mummy, n. [1. múmi; 2. mámi], fr. Fr. *momie,* fr. Ital. *mummia,* in Med. Lat. *mumia,* fr. Pers. (Arab.) *mūmiyā,* 'bitumen, a mummy', fr. Pers. *mūm,* 'wax'. **1.** The body of a human being, or lower animal such as a cat, preserved from decay by embalming; specif., a body so preserved by the ancient Egyptians. **2.** A portion of an ancient mummy, or of materials used in mummification, reduced to powder; formerly used as a medicine, esp. as remedy for wounds. **3.** A dark brown colour obtained from bitumen.

mummy case, n. The case modelled to the shape of the body, with painted or moulded representation of the head and face, in which an Egyptian mummy was placed for burial.

mummy cloth, n. The linen cloth in which a mummy was wrapped for burial.

mummy wheat, n. A variety of Egyptian wheat, *Triticum compositum,* supposed to have come originally from seeds found with mummies.

mump, vb. intrans. [1. mump; 2. mamp]. Imitative, cp. **mum** (I.) & **mumble;** M. Du. has *mompelen,* 'to whine, beg', *mompen,* 'to cheat'. **a** To be sulky, to mope; **b** (old slang) to beg whiningly or cantingly; to play the impostor.

mumper, n. [1. múmper; 2. mámpə]. Prec. & **-er.** An old slang name for a fraudulent beggar.

mumps, n., pl. treated as sing. [1. mumps; 2. mamps], fr. **mump,** fr. sullen appearance of a patient. **a** An infectious disease, accompanied by painful swelling of the glands of the throat and other parts of the body; infectious parotitis; **b** a fit of the sulks.

munch, vb. intrans. & trans. [1. munsh; 2. man(t)ʃ]. Prob. imit.; cp. **mumble;** not connected w. Fr. *manger,* 'to eat'. To chew, masticate, food in a coarse manner, with much moving of the jaws and lips.

Munchausen, n. [1. munchóuzen, muncháwzen; 2. mantʃáuzən, mantʃɔ̄zən], fr. Baron Munchausen, the name of the hero & supposed author of a book of impossible adventures & travels, written in Engl. by a German, Rudolph Raspe, 1785. A wildly impossible story, an incredible yarn.

mundane, adj. [1. múndān; 2. mándein]. Lat. *mundānus,* 'of or belonging to the world', fr. *mundus,* 'order of the world, the universe', fr. *mundus,* 'orderly, neat', & **-ane;** for meaning cp. **cosmos.** Belonging to this world; worldly, earthly, contrasted with *spiritual* or *heavenly.*

mundungus, n. [1. mùndúnggus; 2. màndáŋgəs], fr. Span. *mundungo.* (obs.) A coarse, offensively smelling plug tobacco.

mungo, n. [1. múnggō; 2. máŋgou]. Etymol. unknown. A variety of shoddy, but made from hard spun or felted woollen cloth.

mungoose, n. See **mongoose.**

municipal, adj. [1. mūnísipl; 2. mjunísipl], fr. Lat. *mūnicipālis,* 'of or belonging to a *mūnicipium,* a free town with Roman rights of citizenship', fr. *mūniceps,* 'citizen of a free town', fr. *mūnia,* 'civic duties, functions', & *-cep-,* form of *cap-(ere),* 'to take, undertake', see **captive,** & **-al;** Lat. *mūnia* is fr. *moenia,* earlier **moinia;* cp. *mūnus* (fr. **moin-*), 'a service, office, function, duty', & *mūnis,* 'ready to be of service, obliging'; the base, according to Walde, is **mei-,* **moi-,* 'to change, interchange', w. nasal extension; the base is seen also in Goth. *maiþms,* 'gift, treasure', O.E. *māþum* in same sense; orig. 'that which is changed, which passes from hand to hand'. See also **mutable. 1.** (Roman hist.) Having the rights of a *municipium* or free town. **2. a** Pertaining to the government of a borough, city, or town; **b** carried on, exercised by, the corporation of a city or town, or by the local authority of a district: *municipal trading, tramways* &c. **3.** Of or pertaining to a free state or nation; specif., *municipal law,* the internal, domestic law of a state or nation, as contrasted with *international law.*

municipalism, n. [1. mūnísipalizm; 2. mjunísipəlizəm]. Prec. & **-ism.** System of municipal or local self-government.

municipalist, n. [1. mūnísipalist; 2. mjunísipəlist]. See prec. & **-ist.** A supporter of local self-government.

municipality, n. [1. mūnisipáliti; 2. mjūnisipǽliti], fr. Fr. *municipalité.* See **municipal** & **-ity. 1.** A town, borough, city, district &c. enjoying local self-government. **2.** The corporate body exercising these functions; a local authority.

municipalization, n. [1. mūnìsipalīzáshun; 2. mjunìsipəlaizéiʃən]. See next word & **-ation.** Act, process, of municipalizing; state of being municipalized.

municipalize, vb. trans. [1. mūnísipalīz; 2. mjunísipəlaiz]. **municipal** & **-ize.** To take over and administer under municipal government; to transfer the ownership and management of private industries &c. to municipal or local ownership: *to municipalize the tramways.*

municipally, adv. [1. mūnísipali; 2. mjunísipəli]. **municipal** & **-ly.** By municipal authority or administration; by means of local government, locally: *municipally managed.*

munificence, n. [1. mūnífisens; 2. mjūnífisəns]. Fr., fr. Lat. *mūnificentia,* 'bountifulness, bounty, generosity', fr. *mūnificus,* 'bountiful, liberal'; the first element is *mūnis,* 'obliging' &c., q.v. under **municipal.** See further **-fic, -ent, -ce.** Magnificent, lavish generosity, bounty, or liberality.

munificent, adj. [1. mūnífisent; 2. mjūnífisənt]. Apparently a back-formation fr. prec., on the pattern of *intelligent, intelligence.* Lavishly generous, open-handed.

munificently, adv. Prec. & **-ly.** In a munificent manner.

muniment, n. [1. múniment; 2. mjúnimənt]. Fr., 'defence', fr. Lat. *mūnīmentum,* 'fortification, protection', fr. *mūnīre,* (*moenīre*), 'to defend, protect', fr. *moenia,* 'walls, ramparts'; cogn. w. Lat. *mūrus* (fr. **moir-*), 'wall'; fr. base **mei-,* **moi-,* 'a stake, pile', whence also Scrt. *mayūkhaś,* 'beam, post', *mitáś,* 'makes firm'. See further **mete** (I.). (usually in pl.) Documentary records, archives; specif. (law) the title-deeds to property.

muniment room, n. A specially protected chamber belonging to a cathedral, college, large house &c. in which title-deeds and other valuable documentary records are kept.

munition, n. & vb. trans. [1. mūníshun; 2. mjūníʃən]. Fr., fr. Lat. *mūnītiōn-(em), mūnītio,* 'fortification, defence', fr. *mūnīt-(um), mūnīre,* 'to fortify, defend'. See **muniment** & cp. **ammunition. 1.** n. (usually pl.) **a** Military stores of all kinds, esp. shells, and ammunition for guns and rifles: *munitions of war;* **b** material stored ready for any operation or emergency, esp. money: *munitions for a political campaign.* **2.** vb. To provide, furnish, with munitions: *to munition an army.*

munjeet, n. [1. múnjēt; 2. mándžīt]. Hind. *majīṭh.* Indian variety of madder, yielding a red dye.

munnion, n. See **mullion.**

munshi, n. See **moonshee.**

munsif, n. See **moonsif.**

muntjak, n. [1. múntjak; 2. mántdžæk], fr. native Malay name. A small horned deer, the barking deer, of the East Indies and S.E. Asia.

murage, n. [1. múrij; 2. mjɔ̄ridž]. O. Fr.,

fr. Med. Lat. *mūrāgium*, fr. Lat. *mūrus*, 'wall'. See **mural** & **-age**. An ancient tax levied on citizens for the building and upkeep of city walls and fortifications.

mural, adj. [1. múral; 2. mjŏrəl]. Fr., fr. Lat. *mūrālis*, 'of or belonging to a wall', fr. *mūrus*, earlier *moerus*, for **moiros*, 'wall'; cogn. w. O.E. (*ge*)*mǣre*, 'boundary', fr. **mairi-*, fr. same base as *moenia*, 'town walls, ramparts'. See **muniment**; **munition**. Of or pertaining to a wall or walls: *mural painting*, wall-painting, fresco; *mural decoration*; *mural tower*, one built on ramparts. *Mural crown*, **a** (Roman hist.) one with indentations to represent masonry, and shaped like a battlemented wall, given to the first who scaled the walls of a besieged town; **b** (her.) a charge or badge of this form.

murder (I.), n. [1. mërder; 2. mə́də]. O.E. *morþor*, *morþur*, 'murder; crime, sin', M.E. *morðer*, & also *morder*, through influence of O. Fr. *murdre*, wh. is a Gmc. loan-word; O.E. had also *morþ*, 'murder; death, destruction; crime'; Goth. *maurþr*, O.E., O.S., & O.N. *morð*, 'murder, death'; fr. same base as Lat. *mort-(em)*, *mors*, 'death', *mori*, 'to die' &c., q.v. under **mortal**. **1.** (law) The felonious killing of a human being by another with malice aforethought; unlawful and intentional homicide; distinguished from (*accidental* or *justifiable*) *homicide* and *manslaughter*. Phr. *murder will out*, every murder, or piece of wickedness, is sure to be discovered sooner or later; *to cry 'murder'*, to raise a cry of alarm. **2. a** Unwarranted and unjustifiable sacrifice of the lives of troops: *to send troops on such an errand was sheer murder*; **b** irresponsible and excessive slaughter of wild animals.

murder (II.), vb. trans., fr. prec. **1.** (law) To commit murder upon the person of. **2.** To kill, slaughter; to destroy. **3.** (fig.) To spoil, ruin, through defective skill in execution: *to murder a song, Mozart, the English language* &c.

murderer, n. [1. mërderer; 2. mə́dərə]. Prec. & **-er**. One guilty of murder.

murderess, n. [1. mërderes; 2. mə́d(ə)ris]. See prec. & **-ess**. A female murderer.

murderous, adj. [1. mërderus; 2. mə́d(ə)rəs]. **murder** (I.) & **-ous**. **1. a** Pertaining to, of the nature of, murder; likely to cause murder: *murderous assault*; **b** apt to inflict murder: *a murderous weapon*; **c** capable of, intending to inflict, murder; bloodthirsty: *a murderous ruffian*. **2. a** Deadly, perilous, likely to prove fatal: *a murderous fire from the enemy*; *a murderous climate*; **b** (fig.) extremely severe, intolerable: *murderous heat*.

murderously, adv. Prec. & **-ly**. In a murderous manner; with intent to murder.

mure, vb. trans. [1. mūr; 2. mjō], fr. Fr. *murer*, fr. Lat. *mūrāre*, 'to enclose within walls', fr. *mūrus*, 'wall'. See **mural**. To immure, enclose within walls; shut up, imprison.

murex, n. [1. múreks; 2. mjŏrɛks]. Lat., 'the purple-fish, purple dye'; for **mūsex*; cp. Gk. *múax*, fr. **musax*, 'sea-mussel'; cp. also Lat. *mūsculus*, 'a little mouse; muscle of the body; sea-mussel'. See **muscle**. The name of a marine Gastropod mollusc from which a purple dye was obtained.

muriate, n. [1. múriāt; 2. mjŏrieit]. See next word. A salt of hydrochloric acid; chloride. A commercial, not a chemical, term.

muriatic, adj. [1. mùriátik; 2. mjŏriǽtik], fr. Lat. *muriāticus*, 'pickled in brine', fr. *muria*, 'brine for pickling'; cogn. w. Lat. *mare*, 'sea'. See **marine**. Of or pertaining to hydrochloric (muriatic) acid.

murine, adj. [1. múrīn; 2. mjŏrain]. Lat. *mūrīnus*, 'of mice', for **mūsīnus*, cp. *mūs*, genit. *mūris*, 'a mouse'; Gk. *mûs*; O.E., O.H.G. &c. *mūs*. See **mouse**. Of or belonging to the family of rats and mice, or *Muridae*.

murk, adj. & n. [1. mërk; 2. mə̄k]. Prob. fr. O.N. *myrkr*, 'dark', cp. the cogn. O.E. *myrće*, *mirće*, M.E. *mirke*; O.S. *mirki*. **1.** adj. (archaic and poet.) Dark, gloomy, obscure, murky. **2.** n. Darkness, gloom, murkiness: *the murk of night*.

murkily, adv. [1. mërkili; 2. mə́kili]. **murky** & **-ly**. Gloomily, darkly, obscurely.

murkiness, n. [1. mërkines; 2. mə́kinis]. See prec. & **-ness**. Darkness, gloom.

murky, adj. [1. mërki; 2. mə́ki]. **murk**, n., & **-y**. **a** Dark, gloomy, obscure; misty, cloudy: *a murky night, day* &c.; **b** morally dingy; dubious.

murmur (I.), n. [1. mërmer; 2. mə́mə]. Fr. *murmure*, Lat. *murmur*, 'a murmur, roaring, grumbling sound', cogn. w. Gk. *mormúrein*, 'to roar', of water, Scrt. *marmara*, 'rustle', of wind; reduplication of the imitative base *mur*. **1. a** A low continuous sound, as of wind, water, of subdued talk &c.; **b** beating of the heart &c.; specif. (med.) any typical low sound from the heart, indicative of some disease of the organ. **2.** A half-suppressed grumble or complaint.

murmur (II.), vb. intrans. & trans., fr. Fr. *murmurer*, Lat. *murmurāre*. See prec. **A.** intrans. **1. a** To make a subdued, continuous sound, as trees in the wind, water &c.; **b** to speak in a low voice. **2.** To complain, grumble; often followed by *at*, *against*. **B.** trans. To utter, speak (words &c.) in a low, subdued voice: *to murmur a prayer*.

murmurous, adj. [1. mërmurus; 2. mə́mərəs]. **murmur** (I.) & **-ous**. **1.** Murmuring; full of murmurs or low, subdued sounds: '*the murmurous haunt of flies on summer eves*' (Keats). **2.** Complaining, grumbling.

murmurously, adv. Prec. & **-ly**. Murmuringly; in, with, a low, subdued voice or sound.

murphy, n. [1. mërfi; 2. mə́fi]. Irish name. (colloq.) A potato.

murrain, n. [1. múrin; 2. márin]. M.E. *moreine*, fr. O. Fr. *morine*, cp. Span. *morriña*, Port. *morrinha*; prob. fr. Lat. *mori*, 'to die'. Cp. **mortal**. An infectious disease of cattle; cattle plague. Phr. *a murrain on you!*, (archaic) plague on you!

murrey, adj. & n. [1. múri; 2. mári], fr. O. Fr. *moree*, Lat. *mōrāt-(us)*, 'mulberry coloured', *mōrum*, 'mulberry'; cp. **morel** (II.). **a** adj. (archaic) Of a mulberry or dark purple red; **b** n., a dark-red purple colour.

murrhine, adj. [1. múrīn; 2. márain], fr. Lat. *murr(h)īnus*, 'made of *murr(h)a*', a stone of which precious vases &c. were made, possibly fluor-spar. **a** (Roman antiq.) Made of *murrha*, as *murrhine cups, goblets* &c.; **b** resembling or supposed to resemble the Roman *murrha*; *murrhine glass*, a coloured glass-ware with small particles of gold or other coloured metal embedded in it.

Musca, n., pl. **Muscae** [1. múska, -kē; 2. máskə, -kī]. Lat., 'fly', cogn. w. Gk. *muîa*, 'fly, gnat'. Cp. **mosquito**. (zool.) The genus of dipterous insects which includes the common house-fly. *Muscae volitantes*, Lat., 'flying flies', the medical term for floating specks or dots in the eye.

muscadel, n. See **muscatel**.

muscadine, n. [1. múskadin; 2. máskədin]. Fr., dimin. form fr. Port. *moscado*, or Ital. *moscato*, 'flavoured with musk'. See **muscatel**. **a** Muscatel grape; **b** muscatel wine.

muscardine, n. [1. múskardīn; 2. máskədain]. Fr., fr. Ital. *moscardino*, 'a lozenge flavoured with musk'. See **muscatel**. **1.** The dormouse, so called from its musky smell. **2.** A parasitic disease of silkworms.

muscat, n. [1. múskat; 2. máskæt]. Fr. See **muscatel**. Light-coloured, musky, grape.

muscatel, n. [1. mùskatél, múskatel; 2. màskətél, máskətɛl]. Fr., fr. Ital. *moscatello*, *moscadello*, 'muscatel grape and wine', fr. *moscato*, *moscado*, 'flavoured with musk'. See **musk**. **a** A white grape, of several varieties, having a strong musky scent and flavour; also a raisin of this variety of grape; **b** a strong sweet white wine made from muscatel grapes.

muscle, n. [1. músl; 2. másl]. Fr., fr. Lat. *mūsculus*, 'a little mouse; a sea-mussel; muscle, force', fr. *mūs*, 'mouse'; a muscle in movement being supposed to resemble a creeping mouse. See **mouse** & **mussel**. **1.** A band or mass of elastic fibrous tissue in an animal body, possessing power of contraction by means of which movement is effected. Phr. *not move a muscle*, remain perfectly still, be motionless. **2.** (fig.) Bodily force, strength, or vigour: *a man of muscle*.

muscle-bound, adj. Having the muscles enlarged and overstrained and rendered inelastic by over-exercise.

muscled, adj. [1. músld; 2. másld]. Furnished with strong muscles; muscular.

muscleless, adj. [1. múslles; 2. másəllis]. **muscle** & **-less**. Without muscles; feeble, flabby, flaccid.

muscoid, adj. [1. múskoid; 2. máskoid]. See next word & **-oid**. Moss-like.

muscology, n. [1. mùskóloji; 2. màskɔ́lədži], fr. Lat. *muscus*, 'moss'; cogn. w. O. Slav. *mŭchŭ*, 'moss'; O.E. *mos*; see **moss**. Science, study, of mosses; bryology.

muscovado, muscovato, n. [1. mùskováhdō, -tō; 2. màskəvádou, -tou], fr. Span. *mascabado*, 'of inferior quality, unrefined'. Dark-coloured moist sugar obtained by evaporating the juice of sugar-cane and draining off the molasses.

Muscovite, n. & adj. [1. múskovīt; 2. máskəvait], fr. Fr., fr. *Moscovie*, 'Muscovy, Russia', fr. Russ. *Moskva*, 'Moscow'. **a** n. A Russian; **b** adj., Russian. *Muscovite glass*, common mica, usually colourless.

Muscovy duck, n. [1. múskovi dúk; 2. máskəvi dák]. Corrupt. of 'musk-duck'. A South American duck, *Cairina moschata*, now domesticated, the musk-duck, so called from its slightly musky smell.

muscular, adj. [1. múskūlar; 2. máskjulə]. Earlier *musculous*, now obs., fr. Lat. *mūsculōsus*, fr. *mūsculus*. See **muscle** & **-ar**. **1.** Of, relating to, effected by, affecting, the muscles: *muscular system, energy, strength*; *muscular rheumatism*. **2.** Having well-developed muscles; strong, brawny, powerful. Phr. *muscular Christian*, a term applied, originally somewhat disparagingly, to the active, physically vigorous and healthy religious man, as portrayed in the writings of Charles Kingsley; so *muscular Christianity*, a Christian life of cheerful, physical activity.

muscularity, n. [1. mùskūláriti; 2. màskjulǽriti]. Prec. & **-ity**. Quality, state, condition, of being muscular.

musculature, n. [1. múskūlachur; 2. máskjulətʃə], fr. **muscle** & **-ate** & **-ure**. (anat.) System, arrangement, of muscles in the animal body.

musculo-, pref. Form of Lat. *musculus*, 'muscle' (see **muscle**); used as pref. in anatomical terminology: *musculo-cutaneous*, of muscle and skin, applied to a nerve in the arm and leg.

Muse (I.), n. [1. mūz; 2. mjūz]. Fr., fr. Lat. *Mūsa*, fr. Gk. *Moûsa*, 'a Muse, music', fr. **month-ja*; cogn. w. O.H.G. *mendī*, 'excitement, joy', fr. **manþī-*; cp. also O.S. *mendian*, 'to rejoice'; possibly connected w. base **men-*, 'to think'. See **mental** (I.) & **mind**. See also **museum** & **music**. **1.** (cap., class. mythol.) One of the nine nymphs or goddesses, the Muses, daughters of Zeus, protectors and inspirers of the arts, such as music, poetry, history, dancing &c. **2.** (without cap.) Poetical inspiration or genius; *the muse*, poetry.

muse (II.), vb. intrans. & n., fr. O. Fr. *muser*, 'to loiter, dream, reflect'; cp. *amuser*, 'to gaze, stare at', & see **amuse**; etymol. doubtful; prob. fr. O. Fr. *musc*, 'mouth of an animal, muzzle', Mod. Fr. *museau*; Ital. has *musare*, 'to sniff the air to catch a scent', as a dog, fr. *muso*, 'muzzle'. See **muzzle**. **1.** vb. **a** To ponder deeply, reflect; to be in a state of reverie, be lost in meditation: *to muse a while*; **b** *muse (up)on, over*, to consider silently and raptly, dwell upon meditatively: *to muse upon a distant view, on what one has heard, over past memories* &c. **2.** n. (obs. or archaic) Profound meditation, rapt thought: *lost in a muse* &c.

musette, n. [1. mūzét; 2. mjūzét]. Fr., dimin. of O. Fr. *muse*, 'bagpipe'; etymol. doubtful. **a** A small soft-toned bagpipe or oboe; **b** a musical composition for this instrument, pastoral.

museum, n. [1. mūzēum; 2. mjūzíəm]. Lat., fr. Gk. *Mouseîon*, 'temple, shrine, of the Muses, a philosophical school or library', fr. *Moûsa*, **Muse (I.)**. Cp. **mosaic (II.)**. **a** An institution for the collection, permanent preservation, and exhibition of objects of all kinds, illustrating esp. the development of the arts and sciences, the growth and character of various types of civilization of all ages, and of natural products of every kind, including man and the races of men &c.; **b** the building in which such collections are housed; **c** the actual collections themselves.

mush (I.), n. [1. mush; 2. maʃ]. Variant of **mash (I.)**. **1. a** Any soft, pulpy mass or mess: *mush of snow* &c; **b** (U.S.A.) a porridge made from maize flour. Phr. (colloq.) *to make a mush of*, to make a mess of, to bungle, mishandle. **2.** (fig.) Nonsense, worthless talk or writing.

mush (II.), n. Short for **mushroom.** (slang) An umbrella.

mush (III.), n. & vb. intrans., prob. corrupt. of Fr. *marche*, see **march.** (U.S.A. & Canada) **1.** n. Journey with dog-sleigh. **2.** vb. To make such a journey.

mushroom (I.), n. [1. múshroom; 2. máʃrum]. M.E. *muscheron*, fr. M. Fr. *mouscheron*, Mod. Fr. *mousseron*; etymol. doubtful, perh. fr. *mousse*, 'moss'. **1.** Popular name of any edible fungus, esp. of species *Agaricus campestris*, the common field mushroom, as contrasted with *toadstool*, a poisonous fungus. **2.** (attrib., of various objects) Resembling a mushroom in shape: **a** *mushroom hat*; **b** *mushroom anchor*, a variety of anchor of which the head is shaped like an inverted mushroom. **3. a** An upstart, parvenu; person or institution but newly risen, or recently and rapidly come into prominence; **b** (attrib.) *mushroom millionaire, growth, suburb* &c.

mushroom (II.), vb. intrans., fr. prec. To seek and gather mushrooms: *to go mushrooming*.

mushy, adj. [1. múshi; 2. máʃi]. **mush (I.)** & **-y. a** Soft, pulpy; **b** (fig.) flabby, weakly sentimental, maudlin, rubbishy.

music, n. [1. mūzik; 2. mjūzik]. M.E. *musyk, musik*, fr. Fr. *musique*, fr. Lat. *mūsica*, fr. Gk. *mousikḗ* (sc. *tékhnē*), 'musical art or skill', fr. *Moûsa*, 'Muse', applied to the various arts protected or inspired by the Muses, esp. to lyric poetry accompanied by music. See **Muse (I.)**. **1.** The art of combining sounds or tones for reproduction by the voice or by various kinds of musical instruments in rhythmical, melodic, and harmonic form so as to affect the emotions. Phrs. *to face the music*, (perh. from **4**) to meet an emergency or difficulty boldly; to be ready to take the responsibility for one's conduct, and to face the consequences; *to set to music*, to compose music as accompaniment or setting for words. **2.** A composition of rhythmical, melodic, harmonic sounds or tones, as written or printed; musical compositions collectively or generally. **3.** Any pleasing, rhythmical, or melodious sound in art or nature, as of a voice, of wind, waves, birds &c. *The Music of the Spheres*, the harmony supposed by the Pythagoreans to result from the vibrations set up by the motion of the different planets, inaudible to mortal ears. **4.** (hunting) The sound of a pack of hounds in full cry. **5.** (archaic) A choir or band: *Master of the King's Music*, title of the director of the choirs and music in the Chapels Royal.

musical, adj. [1. mūzikl; 2. mjūzikl]. Fr., fr. Med. Lat. *mūsicālis*, fr. Lat. *mūsica*, 'music'; see prec. & **-al. 1.** Relating to music or its performance; set to, accompanied by, music: *musical intervals, performance, scale* &c.; *musical ride*, a performance on horseback of combined movements executed in time to music. **2.** Having a pleasing sound, melodious, harmonious: *a musical voice, sound* &c. **3. a** (of persons) Skilled in, fond of, music; **b** (of taste, judgement) trained to enjoy and appreciate music.

musical-box, n. A case containing a revolving metal cylinder worked by a clock-work mechanism, furnished with minute pegs which strike on vibrating strips of metal, graduated to produce different notes.

musical chairs, n. A game in which a number of players move round a circle of chairs, less by one in number than the players, while music is played, all trying to gain a seat the moment the music suddenly stops; the player left standing is eliminated from the next round, and a chair is removed.

musical comedy, n. A form of dramatic musical entertainment, consisting of spoken dialogue carrying a comic or farcical plot, interspersed with songs, lyrical or comic, dances &c., with orchestral accompaniment.

musical glasses, n. pl. A set of glasses, graduated in tone, struck by small sticks and used as a musical instrument on which tunes are played; similar instrument with glass bells or tubes; harmonica.

musical instrument, n. Any one of a variety of instruments with which music is produced; usually classified as *stringed, wind*, and *percussion*.

musically, adv. [1. mūzikali; 2. mjūzik(ə)li]. **musical** & **-ly.** In a musical manner; melodiously, harmoniously.

musicalness, n. [1. mūziklnes; 2. mjūziklnis]. See prec. & **-ness.** State, quality, of being musical; melodiousness.

music case, n. Folding case for holding music.

music-hall, n. A theatre in which variety entertainments are given, consisting of songs, dancing, short theatrical sketches, acrobatic and conjuring performances &c.

musician, n. [1. mūzíshan; 2. mjūzíʃən], fr. Fr. *musicien*. See **music** & **-ian. a** A person skilled in the practice and art of music; **b** a performer of vocal or instrumental music; **c** a composer of music.

musicianly, adj. Prec. & **-ly.** Having musical art, skill, or taste.

music master, mistress, n. A teacher of music.

music paper, n. Paper specially ruled for writing music.

music stand, n. A light framework with ledge for holding sheets of music for a player.

music-stool, n. A stool without a back, the seat of which is adjustable to various heights; used while playing a pianoforte.

musing, n. [1. mūzing; 2. mjūziŋ]. **muse (II.)**, vb., & **-ing.** Contemplation, pondering, thoughtful meditation, absorbed brooding.

musingly, adv. [1. mūzingli; 2. mjūziŋli], fr. Pres. Part. of **muse (II.)** & **-ly.** In a contemplative manner; as though musing.

musk, n. [1. musk; 2. mask]. Fr. *musc*, fr. Lat. *muscus*, fr. L. Gk. *móskhos*, 'musk as obtained from animals', fr. Pers. *musk, misk*, prob. cogn. w. Scrt. *mushkaś*, 'scrotum, testicle, musk-gland', orig. 'a little mouse'. See **mouse. 1. a** Substance with very pungent odour, secreted by a gland on the abdomen of the male musk-deer, and of various other animals, and used as a constituent of perfumes; **b** the perfume, odour, of musk. **2.** The name of various plants having a musky scent.

musk-deer, n. A small mountain, hornless deer, *Moschus*, of Central Asia, the male of which has a gland on the stomach secreting the musk of commerce, used in perfumery.

musk-duck, n. **a** The Muscovy duck of S. America; **b** an Australian duck, emitting a musky scent during the pairing season.

musket, n. [1. músket; 2. máskit], fr. Fr. *mousquet*, fr. Ital. *mosquetto, moschetto*, 'a small sparrow-hawk'; a musket, or hand-gun'; etymol. doubtful, possibly fr. Lat. *musca*, 'fly' (see **Musca**), fr. the small size of the hawk; Skeat compares *falconet*, & other fanciful animal names, for the early guns. The name of the early form of hand firearm or gun, in use till the development of the modern rifle. *Musket-shot*, a shot from a musket; range of fire of a musket.

musketeer, n. [1. mùsketḗr; 2. màskətíə], fr. Fr. *mousquetaire*. See prec. & **-eer. a** An infantry soldier armed with a musket; specif., **b** a member of a body of soldiers, *mousquetaires du Roi*, in the French royal service during the 17th and part of the 18th cents.

musketoon, n. [1. mùsketōōn; 2. màskətún], fr. Fr. *mousqueton*, Ital. *moschettone*. **musket** & **-oon.** A short, heavy form of musket with large bore, used by cavalry; a blunderbuss.

musketry, n. [1. músketri; 2. máskitri]. Fr., *mousqueterie*. See **musket** & **-ry. 1.** (obs.) Muskets collectively; troops armed with muskets. **2.** Specif., shooting with, fire from, muskets, a term still in use for rifle-fire and for the art, skill, and practice of firing with small-arms or rifles: *musketry training; school of musketry* &c.

musk-mallow, n. A species of mallow, *Malva moschata*, with white or pink flowers and musk-scented leaves.

musk-ox, n. Kind of ungulate ruminant, with large curved horns, intermediate between the oxen and the sheep, found in Greenland and Arctic America, and having a strong musky smell.

musk-rat, n. Kind of water-rat, the musquash, *Fiber zibethicus*, of N. America, valuable for its fur; both sexes have musk-glands.

musk-rose, n. A variety of climbing rose with very fragrant, rather musky, white flowers.

musk-wood, n. **a** A West-Indian tree with mahogany-like wood; **b** an Australian tree with hard, white wood; both have a musky scent.

musky, adj. [1. múski; 2. máski]. **musk** & **-y.** Having the odour of musk.

Muslim. See **Moslem.**

muslin, n. [1. múzlin; 2. mázlin]. Fr. *mousseline*, fr. Ital. *mussolina*, fr. *Mussolo*, Ital. name of Mosul, town in Iraq, where the material was originally made. A fine, soft, cotton fabric used for women's dresses, curtains &c.

muslinet, n. [1. mùzlinét; 2. màzlinét]. Prec. & **-et.** A coarse kind of muslin.

musquash, n. [1. múskwosh; 2. máskwɔʃ], fr. N. Am. Ind. *muscassus*, 'the musk-rat', lit. 'the red animal'. **a** The musk-rat; **b** specif., the fur of this animal.

muss, n. & vb. trans. [1. mus; 2. mas]. Variant of **mush (I.)**. (U.S.A.) **a** n. A mess, muddle, confusion, disorder; **b** vb., to muddle, bungle, confuse.

mussel, n. [1. músl; 2. másl]. O.E. & M.E. *mūscle*, fr. Lat. *mūsculus*, 'little mouse; muscle; mussel'. See **muscle.** Any of several varieties of marine or freshwater bivalve molluscs, as *Mytilus edulis*, the common, edible sea-mussel, or *Unio*, the freshwater pearl-bearing mussel.

mussuck, n. [1. músuk; 2. másək]. Hind. *masak*. Leathern skin for holding water.

Mussulman, n. & adj. [1. múslman; 2. máslmən], pl. **Mussulmans.** Pers. & Turk. *musulmān*, fr. Arab. *Muslim*, pl. *Muslimin*. See **Moslem.** Mohammedan.

must (I.), n. [1. must; 2. mast]. Prob. formed fr. **musty.** Mould, mustiness.

must (II.), n. In O.E. *must*, fr. Lat. *mustum*, 'new wine', fr. *mustus*, 'fresh, new'; cp. **mustard.** The freshly expressed juice of grapes; new, unfermented wine.

must (III.), adj. & n. Hind. & Pers. *mast*, 'drunk, intoxicated; also of animals, rutting'. **1.** adj. Frenzied, mad; specif., of male elephants and camels at the rutting season. **2.** n. **a** State of frenzy to which male elephants are liable in rutting season; **b** an elephant in this state.

must (IV.), auxil. vb. Defective vb.; past tense used as pres.; O.E. *mōste*, Pret. of a defective vb., *ic mōt* &c., 'I may, can, am free to'; now obs. or archaic; cogn. w. O.H.G. *muozan*, 'to be free to do'; Mod. Germ. *müssen*, 'to be obliged to', O.S. Pres. *ik mōt*, Pret. *mōsta*, 'I must'; cp. Goth. *(ga)mōtan*, 'to have, find, room'; etymol. unknown. The word is followed by the verb direct, without *to*, after the manner of auxiliaries. **1.** Expressing general necessity, arising out of universal conditions: *one must eat to live*; *boys must amuse themselves somehow*. **2. a** Expressing specific compulsion or necessity: *you must do as you are told*; *I must go*; *you mustn't do it*; **b** also absolutely, with no foll. vb. expressed: '*I do but sing because I must*' (Tennyson, 'In Mem.' xxi. 6); *well, go if you must*; *if you must, you must*; **c** (archaic) followed by adv., verb of motion being understood: *I must hence, away*; **d** expressing less emphatic necessity: *I must ask you for your name*. **3. a** Expressing certainty or necessary result: *war must follow*; *if he did that, he must have been mad*; **b** expressing strong conviction of probability, amounting almost to certainty: *why, that must be my old friend.*

mustache, mustachio, n. See **moustache**.

mustang, n. [1. mústang; 2. mástæŋ], either fr. Span. *mestengo, mesteño*, 'belonging to graziers', fr. *mesta*, 'group, company of graziers', fr. Lat. *mixt-(um), miscēre*, 'to mix'; or fr. *mostrenco*, 'straying, wild', fr. Lat. *monstrāre*, 'to point out, show'. A semi-wild horse of the American prairies; broncho.

mustang grape, n. A small red Texas grape.

mustard, n. [1. mústard; 2. mástəd]. O. Fr. *moustarde*, Mod. Fr. *moutarde*, fr. Lat. *mustum*, 'new wine'; so called from must being used in the preparation of mustard. See **must (II.)**. **1.** (bot.) A plant, genus *Sinapis*, with yellow flowers and black or white seeds contained in pods. **2.** A hot pungent powder made from the pounded seeds of the mustard plant, either mixed with water, *English mustard*, or with tarragon vinegar, *French mustard*, and used as a condiment with meat; also as a counter-irritant: *mustard-plaster, poultice* &c.; Phr. *keen as mustard*, (colloq.) very eager, enthusiastic. *Mustard and cress*, a salad made of cress and the young shoots or leaves of the white mustard plant; *mustard gas*, a heavy, sluggish, blistering, irritant chemical gas, used in warfare, so called from its smell and effect; *mustard oil*, essential oil obtained from the seeds of the black mustard; *mustard pot*, vessel for holding mustard at table.

musteline, adj. [1. mústelēn; 2. mástəlīn], fr. Lat. *mustēlīnus*, 'of or belonging to a weasel', *mustēla*, 'weasel'; connected w. Lat. *mūs*, see **mouse**. (zool.) Of or belonging to the family *Mustelidae*, which includes the weasels, skunks, martens, and other animals, many of which have valuable fur.

muster (I.), n. [1. múster; 2. mástə]. M.E. *moustre*, fr. O. Fr. *mostre* for *monstre*, 'show, pattern, muster', fr. Lat. *monstrāre*, 'to show, point out'. See **monster**. **1.** An assembly or parade of soldiers or sailors &c., for numbering, inspection &c.; (gen.) collection, gathering of persons, animals &c. Phr. *to pass muster*, to be considered fit or satisfactory after inspection; to be up to sample, be good enough for required purpose. **2.** The total number of men at a muster; the register or roll of men at a muster: *a muster book*, a register, roll. **3.** *A muster of peacocks*, flock.

muster (II.), vb. trans. & intrans., fr. O. Fr. *mostrer*, as prec. **1.** trans. **a** To cause to assemble, to call together, as troops &c. for parade, roll-call, and inspection; **b** to collect, gather together; usually *muster up*: *to muster up courage, one's energies, strength* &c. **2.** intrans. To come together, assemble. Phr. *To muster in (out)*, to enlist (discharge) troops &c.

mustiness, n. [1. mústines; 2. mástinis], fr. next word & **-ness**. Quality, condition, of being musty.

musty, adj. [1. músti; 2. másti]. Etymol. doubtful; possibly as **moist**, fr. O. Fr. *moiste*, fr. Lat. *mustum*, 'new wine', see **must (II.)**; Provenç. has *mousti, musti*, 'damp, humid', of same origin. **1. a** Mouldy, fusty, smelling or tasting stale or sour, as food, wine &c. kept in a damp place; **b** specif. (of eggs, bacon &c.) having the smell and taste of incipient putrescence from being kept too long. **2.** Stale, antiquated, out of date.

mutability, n. [1. mûtabíliti; 2. mjûtəbíliti]. See next word & **-ity**. Quality, condition, of being mutable; changeability.

mutable, adj. [1. mûtabl; 2. mjûtəbl], fr. Lat. *mūtābilis*, fr. *mūtāre*, 'to change', allied to *mūtuus*, 'borrowed, lent, reciprocal, mutual'; earlier *moit-*; cp. Gk. *moîtos*, 'thanks, return'; cp. Goth. *maiþms*, 'gift'; O.E. *māþm*, 'treasure'; cp. also Goth. *maidjan*, 'to change'; connected also w. **mis-** & **municipal**. Subject, liable, to change; changeable; fitful, inconstant.

mutate, vb. trans. & intrans. [1. mūtát; 2. mjūtéit], fr. Lat. *mūtāt-(um)*, P.P. type of *mūtāre*, 'to change'. See prec. To change, by mutation, esp. in biological or philological senses.

mutation, n. [1. mūtáshun; 2. mjūtéiʃən]. Fr., fr. Lat. *mūtātiōn-(em)*. See prec. & **-ion**. **1.** Change in form or qualities; specif. **a** (biol.) sudden deviation of offspring from parents in some well-marked characters; **b** (philol.) alteration in the quality of a vowel sound through the influence of another vowel in the following syllable, by a prior modification of an intervening consonant; e.g. *tooth, teeth*; O.E. *tōþ, tēþ*, fr. **tōþi*. **2.** Change in conditions of life and fortune; vicissitude.

mutation plural, n. Plural of a noun, the vowel of which has been changed by mutation, this difference between it and the vowel of the singular being the only sign of plural number; e.g. *man, men*; *goose, geese* &c.

mutatis mutandis, phr. [1. mūtátis mūtándis; 2. mjūtéitis mjūtǽndis]. Lat., 'things being changed which should be changed'. With necessary alterations or changes.

mutative, adj. [1. mûtativ; 2. mjûtətiv]. Fr. See **mutate** & **-ive**. (biol.) Liable to mutation or variation.

mutch, n. [1. much; 2. matʃ], fr. M. Du. *mutze*, 'cap', cp. Germ. *mütze*. (Scots) Close-fitting linen cap, worn by old women or babies.

mutchkin, n. [1. múchkin; 2. mátʃkin], fr. M. Du. *mutseken*, prec. & dimin. *-ken*, **-kin**. (Scots) **a** An old liquid measure, equivalent to ¾ of English pint; **b** ¼ of the old Scots pint, which was four English pints.

mute (I.), adj. [1. mūt; 2. mjūt]. M.E. *muet*, fr. O. Fr. *muet*, dimin. of O. Fr. *mu*, fr. Lat. *mūtus*, 'silent, dumb'; fr. same base as Gk. *múein*, 'to shut'; Scrt. *mukhaś*, 'dumb'; perh. imitative of sound made in closing lips; cp. other words of this kind as **mum** (I.), **mutter**. **1. a** Not making a sound: *he stood perfectly mute while I talked to him*; **b** no longer heard, silent: '*some orator renowned In Athens or free Rome, where eloquence Flourished, since mute*' (Milton, 'P. L.' ix. 670-72). **2.** Not capable of speaking; dumb. **3.** Not expressed in words: *a mute appeal*. **4.** (law, of prisoner) Refusing to plead guilty or not guilty to a charge: *mute of malice*, wilfully refusing to answer to a charge, not through physical incapacity. **5.** (popular phon., of letters) Not sounded, although written; e.g. *the* e *in* time *is mute*. **6.** (of consonants) Stopped; produced with a closing at some point in the throat or mouth passage, as *b, d, g* &c.

mute (II.), n., fr. prec. **1.** A dumb person, esp. *a deaf mute*. **2. a** Actor without speaking part in a play; **b** a hired mourner, an undertaker's assistant at a funeral. **3.** (phon.) A mute consonant; better called a *stop*; e.g. *p, d, g*; formed by complete momentary stopping of the air-stream at some part of the throat or mouth. **4.** (mus.) A device made of bone or metal, placed on the bridge of a stringed instrument to deaden or soften the tone; sordino; a pad inserted in the bell of a wind-instrument. **5.** *Mute swan*, the common white swan, *Cygnus olor*.

mute (III.), vb. trans., fr. **mute (I.)**. (mus.) To deaden, soften, the sound of an instrument with a mute: *with muted strings*.

mute (IV.), vb. trans. & intrans., fr. O. Fr. *esmeutir*, earlier *esmeltir*; prob. Gmc. in origin; cp. O. Du. *smelten*, 'to melt, liquefy'. (archaic, of birds) To void excrement.

mutely, adv. [1. mûtli; 2. mjûtli]. **mute (I.)** & **-ly**. Dumbly, silently.

muteness, n. [1. mûtnes; 2. mjûtnis]. **mute (I.)** & **-ness**. Dumbness, silence.

mutilate, vb. trans. [1. mûtilāt; 2. mjûtileit], fr. Lat. *mutilāt-(um)*, P.P. type of *mutilāre*, 'to mutilate', fr. *mutilus*, 'maimed, mutilated'; origin doubtful. **1.** To maim, deprive of a limb or organ; to cripple. **2.** To destroy, remove an essential part of, so as to render imperfect: *to mutilate a book, picture, speech* &c.

mutilation, n. [1. mûtiláshun; 2. mjûtiléiʃən]. Fr., fr. Lat. *mutilātiōn-(em)*. Prec. & **-ion**. **1.** Act of mutilating; state of being mutilated. **2.** Injury resulting from mutilation.

mutilator, n. [1. mûtilātor; 2. mjûtileitə]. **mutilate** & **-or**. One who mutilates.

mutineer, n. & vb. intrans. [1. mûtinḗr; 2. mjûtiníə]. O. Fr. *mutinier*. See **mutiny** & **-eer**. **1.** n. One guilty of mutiny. **2.** vb. To mutiny.

mutinous, adj. [1. mûtinus; 2. mjûtinəs]. See **mutiny** & **-ous**. Guilty of mutiny; rebellious, insubordinate: *mutinous sailors*; *mutinous conduct, acts* &c.

mutinously, adv. Prec. & **-ly**. In a mutinous, rebellious manner.

mutiny, n. & vb. intrans. [1. mûtini; 2. mjûtini]. Formed fr. obs. vb. *mutine* & **-y**. Cp. Fr. *mutin*, 'rebellious, mutinous', fr. O. Fr. *meute*, 'struggle, commotion', Mod. Fr. *émeute*, fr. L. Lat. *mōvita, mōta*, 'movement, struggle', fr. *mō(vi)tum*, P.P. of *movēre*, 'to move; to stir up, disturb'. See **move**. **1.** n. Resistance to lawful authority; rebellion, insubordination; specif., such resistance offered by soldiers or sailors; collective, concerted refusal to obey the orders of a superior officer; *Mutiny Act*, an annual act of Parliament for maintenance of discipline in the Army and Navy, now (since 1881) incorporated in the annual Army Act. **2.** vb. To be guilty of mutiny.

mutism, n. [1. mûtizm; 2. mjûtizəm]. **mute (I.)** & **-ism**. Condition of being mute; dumbness; specif., the condition of a deaf mute.

mutoscope, n. [1. mûtoskōp; 2. mjûtəskoup], fr. *muto-*, fr. Lat. *mūtāre*, 'to change', used in compounds, see **mutable**, & **-scope**. Early apparatus based on the principle afterwards more elaborately applied in the cinematograph, whereby a series of pictures of the same object, each differing slightly from those before and after in representing a slight difference of position, is made to pass rapidly before the sight, thus producing the impression that the object represented is actually moving.

mutt, n. [1. mut; 2. mat]. Origin doubtful; perh. for *mutton-head*? (Am. slang) A fool, duffer.

mutter, vb. intrans. & trans. & n. [1. múter; 2. mátə]. M.E. *moten, mutteren*; prob. imitative; cp. Lat. *mūtīre, mūttīre*, 'to mutter', cp. **mute (I.)**. **1.** vb. **a** To speak or utter sounds below one's breath in a low, indistinct voice; to murmur; **b** to speak indistinctly; **c** to grumble: *to mutter threats*; *mutter to oneself*. **2.** n. Muttered speech, or vocal sounds.

mutton, n. [1. mútn; 2. mátn]. M.E. *motoun, motone*, fr. O. Fr. *moton*, Mod. Fr. *mouton*, 'sheep', fr. Low Lat. *multōn-(em), multo*, 'sheep', prob. a Celt. word, cp. Gael. *mult*, Ir. *molt*, W. *mollt*, 'wether, sheep'. **1.** (obs. or archaic) A sheep. Phr. *to return to our muttons*, to return to the point, from Fr.

revenons à nos moutons, a phrase in an old French farce, 'Maître Pathelin', used by the judge in bringing a wandering witness back to the subject, some sheep, of a case he is trying. **2.** The flesh of sheep, as used for food. Phr. *dead as mutton*, quite dead.

mutton bird, n. Sailor's name for a large petrel of the S. Atlantic and Pacific oceans.

mutton-chop, n. A piece of the rib or loin of mutton served fried or grilled; *mutton-chop whiskers*, short bushy whiskers extending to the corners of the mouth, shaped like a mutton-chop.

mutton-head, n. (colloq.) A stupid, slow-witted person.

mutton-headed, adj. Stupid, slow in the intellect.

muttony, adj. [1. mútuni; 2. mátəni]. **mutton** & **-y.** Like mutton; having the taste, smell, or consistency of mutton.

mutual, adj. [1. mûchooal; 2. mjûtʃuəl], fr. Fr. *mutuel*, fr. Lat. *mūtuus*, 'borrowed, lent, exchanged'; fr. base seen in Lat. *mūtāre*, 'to change'. See **mutable. 1.** Interchanged, reciprocal, reciprocated; given and received by two or more persons to or from each other; felt by each of two or more persons for each other: *mutual gifts, affection, hostility* &c. **2.** Performed by a joint action, done in common: *mutual efforts*; the expression *mutual friend*, one who is a friend of several people, a common friend, is, strictly, against the best usage, but is fairly common since being used by Dickens. **3.** (insurance) *Mutual plan, mutual benefits* &c., referring to a system by which the insured persons are shareholders and members of the company, and share in the profits.

mutualism, n. [1. mûchooalizm; 2. mjûtʃuəlizəm]. Prec. & **-ism. 1.** (biol.) Close association, or symbiosis, between two dissimilar organisms; the term is generally used to imply the mutual advantage of both. **2.** (ethics) Theory that mutual dependence is essential to social well-being.

mutuality, n. [1. mûchooáliti; 2. mjûtʃuǽliti]. **mutual** & **-ity.** Quality, state, of being mutual or reciprocal; reciprocity, interdependence.

mutually, adv. [1. mûchooali; 2. mjûtʃuəli]. **mutual** & **-ly.** In a mutual manner; reciprocally.

mutule, n. [1. mûtūl; 2. mjûtjūl]. Fr., fr. Lat. *mūtulus*; dimin., either, if *mū-*, fr. **moit-*, cogn. w. Lat. *mēta*, 'conical stone'; cp. O.N. *meiðr*, 'a beam, balk' &c. (see **mete (I.)** & **muniment**); or, if *mŭ-*, =*mutilata trabs*, 'truncated beam'. See **mutilate.** (archit.) A flat projecting block under the corona of the cornice of the Doric Order; equivalent to the modillion in the Corinthian Order; the mutule represents the projecting ends of rafters of an earlier wooden structure.

muzhik, n. See **moujik.**

muzzily, adv. [1. múzili; 2. mázili]. See **muzzy** & **-ly.** In a muzzy, dazed manner.

muzziness, n. [1. múzines; 2. mázinis]. See **muzzy** & **-ness.** State, condition, of being muzzy or dazed.

muzzle (I.), n. [1. múzl; 2. mázl]. M.E. *mosel*, fr. O. Fr. *musel, muzel*, now *museau*, fr. Med. Lat. *musellus*, dimin. of L. Lat. *mūsus*, 'snout', etymol. unknown; the vb. is fr. the n. **1.** The projecting nose and mouth of an animal, as of a dog, fox, cat, ape &c.; snout. **2.** Cage-like device made of wire and leather, fastened over the head and muzzle of an animal, esp. of a dog, to prevent it biting or eating. **3.** The mouth or opening of anything, esp. of a fire-arm, as a gun, rifle &c. *Muzzle energy*, energy of a projectile at its discharge from the muzzle of a gun; *muzzle-loader*, a fire-arm loaded at the muzzle, contrasted with *breech-loader*; *muzzle-loading*, adj., loaded at the muzzle; *muzzle velocity*, velocity of a projectile at its discharge from the muzzle of a gun.

muzzle (II.), vb. trans., fr. prec. **1.** To put a muzzle over the jaws and mouth of an animal. **2.** To impose silence upon, restrict freedom of speech of.

muzzy, adj. [1. múzi; 2. mázi]. Etymol. unknown. Confused in mind, dazed, stupid, as from drink.

my, possessive adj. of 1st person singular [1. mī; 2. mai]. O.E. *mīn*, see **mine (I.)**, M.E. *mīn* & *mī*, the latter being used before consonants, the former before vowels. **a** Belonging to me; mine: *my clothes, house, relatives* &c.; **b** as form of address: *my dear*; *my lord* &c.; (colloq.) in friendly way or patronizingly: *my dear fellow*; *my good man* &c.; **c** as interjection: *my goodness!, oh my!*

myalgia, n. [1. mīálјia; 2. maiǽldžiə]. Invented word, fr. Gk. *mûs*, 'muscle', & *álgos*, 'pain', on anal. of neuralgia. See **myo-** & **-algia.** Muscular pain.

myalism, n. [1. mīalizm; 2. máiəlizəm]. Prob. fr. a negro word & **-ism.** A West Indian negro magic or witchcraft.

myall, n. [1. míawl; 2. máiɔ̄l], fr. native Australian *maial*, 'wild'. Any of various Australian acacias with hard, sweet-scented wood.

mycelial, adj. [1. mīsélial; 2. maisíliəl]. See next word & **-al.** Of or belonging to mycelium or fungus spawn: *mycelial spores, threads* &c.

mycelium, n. [1. mīsélium; 2. maisíliəm]. Scientific concoction fr. Gk. *múkēs*, 'fungus'. See **myco-.** Mushroom or fungus spawn.

mycetoma, n. [1. mīsētóma; 2. màisitóumə], fr. Gk. *múkēt-*, stem of *múkēs*, 'fungus', see **myco-**, & **-oma.** A fungoid disease of the bones of the foot and leg, sometimes also of the hand; also known as *madura foot.*

myco-, pref. Form of Gk. *múkēs*, 'fungus', wh. is perh. cogn. w. Gk. *múxa*, 'mucus', & w. **mucus.** Chiefly used of parasitic, or fermentative, fungoid bacteria: *mycoderma*, the fungus which produces 'mother of vinegar' during the fermentation of wine.

mycological, adj. [1. mīkolójikl; 2. màikəlɔ́džikl]. **myco-** & **-logical.** Of, pertaining to, mycology.

mycologist, n. [1. mīkólojist; 2. maikɔ́lədžist]. Next word & **-ist.** A student of mycology.

mycology, n. [1. mīkóloji; 2. maikɔ́lədži]. **myco-** & **-logy.** Scientific study of fungi.

mycosis, n. [1. mīkósis; 2. maikóusis]. **myco-** & **-osis.** Condition in which the body is affected by fungoid growth.

myelitis, n. [1. mīelítis; 2. màiəláitis], fr. Gk. *muelós*, 'marrow', etymol. doubtful, & **-itis.** Inflammation of the spinal cord, or bone-marrow.

mylodon, n. [1. mílodon; 2. máilədɔn], fr. Gk. *múlē*, 'mill', in pl., 'molar teeth', cogn. w. **mill (I.)**, & *odont-*, 'tooth'. See **odonto-.** An extinct genus of giant sloths, found as fossils in S. America.

myna, mina, n. [1. mína; 2. máinə]. Hind. *mainā.* A South Indian passerine bird, the grackle, of glossy black plumage, marked with purple and green, and an orange bill.

mynheer, n. [1. mīnhár; 2. mainhéə]. Du. *mijnheer*, 'sir', *mijn*, 'mine', & *heer*, 'master'; cp. **mine (I.)** & **younker.** A Dutchman.

myo-, pref., fr. Gk. *muós, mûs*, 'muscle', see **muscle**, used in anatomical terminology; *myocardium*, the muscular structure of the heart &c.; *myology*, anatomical study of the muscular system &c.

myope, n. [1. míōp; 2. máioup]. See next word. A short-sighted person.

myopia, n. [1. mīópia; 2. maióupiə], fr. Gk. *múōp-(os), múōps*, 'short-sighted', fr. *múein*, 'to close', see **mystery (I.)**, & base *ōp-* of *ōps*, 'the eye'. See **optic.** Short-sightedness, near-sightedness.

myopic, adj. [1. mīópik; 2. maióupik]. See prec. & **-ic.** Short or near-sighted.

myosis, n. [1. miósis; 2. maióusis], fr. Gk. *múein*, 'to close'. See **myopia** & **-osis.** (pathol.) An unnatural, extreme smallness, or contraction, of the pupil of the eye.

myosotis, n. [1. mīosótis; 2. màiəsóutis]. Lat., fr. Gk. *muosōtis*, the name of the plant, lit. 'mouse's ear', fr. *muós, mûs*, 'mouse', & *ōtós*, genit. of *oûs*, 'ear'. See **oto-. a** The plant forget-me-not; **b** (bot., cap.) a genus of herbs, belonging to the borage family, of which the forget-me-not, *Myosotis palustris*, is a species.

myriad, n. & adj. [1. míriad; 2. míriəd], fr. Gk. *mūriád-(os), mūriás*, 'the number 10,000', fr. *mūrios*, 'infinitely numerous, countless'; etymol. doubtful. **1.** n. **a** The number 10,000; **b** an indefinitely large number, an immense number. **2.** adj. Extremely numerous; countless, numberless.

myriapod, n. [1. míriapod; 2. míriəpɔd]. Prec. & Gk. *pod-(ós)*, 'foot'. See **-pod.** (zool.) Any animal belonging to the subclass Myriapoda, which is composed of the millepedes and centipedes.

myriorama, n. [1. mìriōráhma; 2. mìriourǽmə], fr. Gk. *mūrios*, 'countless', see **myriad**, & *hórāma*, 'a sight, spectacle', see second element in **panorama.** An obsolete form of entertainment, consisting of a large number of pictures and views variously combined.

myrmeco-, pref. [1. mĕrmekō; 2. mǽmikou]. Combining form, fr. Gk. *múrmēk-(os), múrmēx*, 'ant', possibly cogn. w. Lat. *formīca*, 'ant', see **formic**; used in zoological terminology: *myrmecology*, scientific study of ants; *myrmecophaga*, the great ant-eater.

myrmidon, n. [1. mĕrmidon; 2. mǽmidən], fr. Gk. *Murmidónes.* **a** (cap., Gk. antiq.) One of a warlike, savage Thessalian race, the subjects and followers of Achilles; hence, **b** an unscrupulous inferior who carries out orders without compunction; partisan; *the myrmidons of the law*, policemen, bailiffs, sheriff's officers.

myrobalan, n. [1. mīróbalan; 2. mairɔ́bələn]. Lat. *myrobalanum*, Gk. *murobálanon*, 'a sweet balsam made from a palm-nut', fr. *múron*, 'sweet plant juice', see **smear**, & *bálanos*, 'acorn, nut', see **balaniferous.** The dried astringent fruit of certain East Indian trees, *Phyllanthus emblica*, containing tannin; used in dyeing and tanning.

myrrh, n. [1. mĕr; 2. mā̆]. O.E. *myrra*, fr. Lat. *myrrha*, fr. Gk. *múrrha*, 'myrrh, the juice of the Arabian myrtle', fr. Arab. *murr*, 'bitter; the myrtle'; M.E. *mirre* is fr. O. Fr. *mirre*, Mod. *myrrhe*; Mod. Engl. spelling is taken fr. Lat. A resinous gum, bitter in taste and strongly aromatic, obtained from various species of balsams, formerly used for incense and in embalming; also prized for medicinal qualities; now chiefly used as an astringent and antiseptic mouth-wash, & in perfumery.

myrtle, n. [1. mĕrtl; 2. mǽtl], fr. O. Fr. *myrtille*, 'myrtle-berry', dimin. of *myrte*, 'myrtle', fr. Lat. *myrtus*, fr. Gk. *múrtos*, cogn. w. Pers. *murd*, 'the myrtle tree', of Semitic origin, cp. **myrrh.** (bot.) Any shrub belonging to the genus *Myrtus*, esp. *M. communis*, the European myrtle with dark, glossy, evergreen leaves and fragrant white flowers.

myself, pron. [1. mīsélf; 2. maisélf]. **my** & **self. 1.** Emphatic pron. of 1st pers., as subject, after *I*: *I did it myself*; (archaic) *myself I did it*, alone, with my own hands; *I saw it myself*, actually with my own eyes; *I myself was present*, in person. Phr. *I am not myself*, am not in my ordinary, normal state, mentally or physically. **2.** As reflex. pron.: *I have hurt myself*; *I have hit myself on the shin.*

mystagogic, adj. [1. mìstagójik; 2. mìstəgɔ́džik]. Next word & **-ic.** Of, pertaining to, a mystagogue.

mystagogue, n. [1. místagog, -gōg; 2. místəgɔg, -goug], fr. Lat. *mystagōgus*, fr. Gk. *mustagōgós*, 'initiator into the mysteries', fr. *mústēs*, 'an initiate', lit. 'one whose lips are closed', fr. *múein*, 'to close, shut', & *agōgós*, 'leading, a leader', fr. *ágein*, 'to lead' (q.v. under **agent**).

See **mystery** (**I.**). **a** (Gk. antiq.) The teacher or initiator of candidates in the religious mysteries, such as those of Eleusis; **b** a teacher of esoteric or mystical religious doctrines; hierophant.

mysterious, adj. [1. mistérius; 2. mistíəriəs]. See **mystery** (**I.**) & **-ous**. Cp. Fr. *mystérieux.* Full of mystery, secret; difficult to understand; obscure, unexplained, inexplicable: *a mysterious disease, person, murder*; *mysterious hints* &c.

mysteriously, adv. Prec. & **-ly**. In a mysterious manner.

mysteriousness, n. See prec. & **-ness**. Condition or quality of being mysterious.

mystery (**I.**), n. [1. místeri; 2. místəri], fr. Lat. *mystērium*, fr. Gk. *mustḗrion*, wh. is usually pl. *tà mustḗria,* 'secret, religious rites, a secret, mystery', fr. *mústēs*, 'one who is initiated into the mysteries', fr. *mueîn*, 'to initiate, teach', fr. *múein*, 'to close, shut the lips', fr. the imitative stem **mu-*, seen in **mum** (**I.**), **mumble, mutter** &c. **1. a** Any strange, secret, obscure fact, principle, force, motive &c.; something mysterious, unexplained, inexplicable, or puzzling: *the mysteries of nature*; *mystery of a murder, of conduct* &c.; Phr. *to make a mystery of*, to hide, conceal, what is plain, obvious, simple; **b** secrecy, concealment: *wrapped in mystery*. **2. a** (class. antiq., in pl.) Secret lore, rites, and ceremonies only revealed to the initiated, e.g. the Greek *Eleusinian mysteries*; **b** similar secret rites and ceremonies as practised by primitive races. **3.** (eccles.) A doctrine, aspect, ceremony &c. of the Christian religion beyond human understanding; applied to the doctrines of the Trinity, Incarnation, and esp. to the Eucharist: '*these holy mysteries*' (Prayer Book). **4.** A mystery play, q.v.

mystery (**II.**), n. M.E. *mistere*, later *mistery*, fr. confusion w. prec.; fr. O. Fr. *mestier*, Mod. *métier*, 'trade, occupation', fr. Lat. *ministērium*, 'service', fr. *minister*, 'servant'. See **minister**. (obs.) A trade or craft, a handicraft; also the body of persons practising a special trade or craft; a guild.

mystery play, n. A form of mediaeval drama, representing scenes from the Old or New Testament, as the Creation, the Nativity &c., and so called as treating of the *mysteries* of religion; they were frequently staged and managed by a particular craft or trade guild or *mystery* (*mistery*), and the origin of the term has been referred to the latter word without justification. The French term is *mystère*, not *mestier*, for this form of early drama; see also **miracle** and **morality**.

mystic, adj. & n. [1. místik; 2. místik], fr. Fr. *mystique*, fr. Lat. *mysticus*, fr. Gk. *mustikós*, 'of, pertaining to, a *mústēs*, an initiate to the mysteries'. See **mystery** (**I.**). **1.** adj. **a** Relating to mysteries or secret ceremonies; having an inner, secret meaning; esoteric, occult, emblematical: *mystic arts, rites, doctrines* &c.; **b** (poet.) weird, uncanny, strange, mysterious: '*an arm Clothed in white samite, mystic, wonderful*' (Tennyson, 'Morte d'Arthur'); **c** of, relating to, mysticism or mystics: *mystic relations with the spiritual world*. **2.** n. A believer in mysticism.

mystical, adj. [1. místikl; 2. místikl]. Prec. & **-al**. Mystic.

mystically, adv. Prec. & **-ly**. In a mystical manner.

mysticism, n. [1. místisizm; 2. místisizəm]. **mystic** & **-ism**. Cp. Fr. *mysticisme*. Doctrine that a knowledge of ultimate reality, and the divine, can be gained only by immediate intuition, esp. by concentration of the mind on, and absorption in, the divine essence, which leads through ecstasy to the revealing vision.

mystification, n. [1. mìstifikā́shun; 2. mìstifikéiʃən]. Fr. See **mystify** & **-fication**. **1.** Act of mystifying; state of being mystified; bewilderment. **2.** That which mystifies; a mystery, puzzle.

mystify, vb. trans. [1. místifī; 2. místifai], fr. Fr. *mystifier*; as **mystic** & **-fy**. **a** To instil a sense of mystery into the mind of; to puzzle, bewilder; **b** to render mysterious.

myth, n. [1. mith, mīth; 2. miþ, maiþ], fr. Gk. *mûthos*, 'word, speech, tale, legend'; etymol. doubtful. **1.** Sometimes pronounced [1. mīth; 2. maiþ]. A fictitious, traditional story or legend, embodying ancient or primitive beliefs in, and an interpretation of, religious or supernatural phenomena such as the gods and lesser deities, the forces of nature: *Hercules myths*; *the myth of Cupid and Psyche*; *solar, deluge, myth* &c. **2.** Generally [1. mith; 2. miþ]. **a** An imaginary, fictitious, person, event, or thing: *Mrs. Harris was a myth invented by Mrs. Gamp*; *the unicorn is a myth*; **b** a fictitious story.

mythic, adj. [1. míthik; 2. míþik], fr. Lat. *mythic-(us)*, Gk. *muthikós*, 'of, relating to, a myth', see prec. (poet.) Mythical.

mythical, adj. [1. míthikl; 2. míþikl]. See prec. & **-al**. **1.** Of or relating to myths, legends, or fables. **2.** Having no existence except in myth; imaginary, fabulous, legendary.

mythically, adv. Prec. & **-ly**. In a mythical manner; by means of a myth or myths.

mythicize, vb. trans. [1. míthisīz; 2. míþisaiz]. **mythic** & **-ize**. To form a myth of, to turn into, treat as, a myth; to explain as a myth.

mytho-, pref. Combining form fr. Gk. *mûtho(s)*, 'myth', q.v.

mythography, n. [1. mith-, mīthógrafi; 2. miþ-, maiþógrəfi]. Prec. & **-graphy**. The delineation, representation, of myths in painting or sculpture.

mythological, adj. [1. mìtho-, mìthólójikl; 2. mìþə-, màiþəlódžikl]. **mytho-** & **-logical**. Of, relating to, mythology or myths; fabulous, imaginary, mythical.

mythologically, adv. Prec. & **-ly**. In a mythological manner; mythically.

mythologist, n. [1. mith-, mīthólojist; 2. miþ-, maiþólədžist]. **mythology** & **-ist**. Student of mythology and of myths; an inventor of myths or fables.

mythologize, vb. intrans. [1. mith-, mīthólojīz; 2. miþ-, maiþólədžaiz]. See prec. & **-ize**. To treat of myths and mythology; to invent myths or fables.

mythology, n. [1. mith-, mīthóloji; 2. miþ-, maiþólədži], fr. Fr. *mythologie*, fr. Gk. *muthologia*. **mytho-** & **-logy**. **a** Study, science, of myths; **b** collection, body, of myths concerning particular deities &c., or current among a particular race: *mythology of Apollo*; *Scandinavian mythology* &c.

mythopoeic, adj. [1. mìthō-, mìthōpéik; 2. miþou-, màiþoupíik], fr. Gk. *muthopoi-(ós)*, 'myth-making', *mûthos*, see **myth**, & *poieîn*, 'to make'. See **poet**. Creating, tending to produce, myths: *mythopoeic faculty*.

mythopoetic, adj. [1. mìthō-, mìthōpōétik; 2. miþou-, màiþoupouétik]. **mytho-** & **-poetic**. Mythopoeic.

myxoedema, n. [1. mìksēdḗma; 2. mìksīdímə], fr. Gk. *múxa*, 'slime', see **mucus**, & *oidēma*, 'swelling', fr. *oidein*, 'to swell', see **oedema**. (pathol.) A metabolic disease, resembling cretinism in its symptoms, due to deficiency in the thyroid gland.

N

N, n [1. en; 2. en]. The fourteenth letter of the English alphabet; as mathematical symbol, *n* stands for an indefinite quantity or power, as *to the nth power*; for use in abbreviations, see list at end of Dictionary.

nab, vb. trans. [1. nab; 2. næb]. Etymol. doubtful; cp. Swed. *nappa*, 'to catch'. (slang) To catch, seize suddenly, while in the act of doing something, esp. something criminal: *the police nabbed the thief yesterday*.

nabob, n. [1. nā́bob; 2. néibəb]. Ad. fr. Hind. & Arab. *nawwāb*, pl., w. sing. meaning, of *nā'ib*, 'deputy, lieutenant-governor during Mogul Indian Empire'; cp. Fr. *nabab* & cp. **nawab**. **a** Name given in 18th and early 19th cents. to Anglo-Indians who came home with great wealth, after official service, or trade in India; **b** (gen.) person of great wealth.

nacarat, n. [1. nákarat; 2. nækəræt]. Fr., fr. Span. *nacarado*, fr. *nacar*, 'mother-of-pearl'. See **nacre**. **a** A bright orange-red colour; **b** fine crêpe or linen material of this colour.

nacelle, n. [1. nàhsél; 2. nàsél]. Fr., fr. Lat. *nāvicella*, later *naucella*, 'little ship', dimin. of *nāvis*, 'ship'. See **naval**. (aeronautics) **a** The basket attached to a balloon; **b** the framework containing the engines, crew &c. of an airship.

nacre, n. [1. nā́ker; 2. néikə], or as Fr. [1. náhkr; 2. nā́kr]. Fr., cp. Span. *nacar*, Ital. *nacchero*; L. Lat. has *nacrum*, all prob. fr. Arab. *naqrah*, 'hollow, cavity', fr. *naqara*, 'to hollow out'. Cp. **naker**. Iridescent, pearly lining of shell of various molluscs; mother-of-pearl.

nacred, adj. [1. nā́kerd; 2. néikəd]. Prec. & **-ed**. Covered, lined, with nacre.

nacreous, adj. [1. nā́kreus; 2. néikriəs]. **nacre** & **-ous**. **a** Of, pertaining to, resembling, nacre or mother-of-pearl; **b** iridescent, shining.

nadir, n. [1. nā́dēr, nā́der; 2. néidiə, néidə], fr. Arab. *nadir* (*nazir*), 'opposite to', in phr. *nazir-es-semt*, 'opposite to the azimuth or zenith'. **1.** (astron.) Imaginary point in heavens, directly opposite to the zenith, the lowest of the two poles of the horizon; the point directly under one's feet, as the zenith is directly above one's head. **2.** (fig., and by transf.) The lowest point, stage, of depression or decline: *at the nadir of one's career, hopes, ambitions* &c.

naevus, n. [1. nḗvus; 2. nívəs]. Learned (Lat.) pl. **naevi**, [1. nḗvī; 2. nívai] popularly *naevuses*. Lat., 'wart, mole'; for **gnaevus*, fr. root **ĝen-*, as in *nātus* for *gnātus*, 'born', hence 'that which is born with one, birth-mark'. See **genus, kin, kind** (**I.**). (med.) Name given to various stains, marks, or tumours on or under the surface of the skin, caused by enlargement and spreading of the blood-vessels; usually congenital, hence often styled 'birth mark'.

nag (**I.**), n. [1. nag; 2. næg]. M.E. *nagge*, 'horse'. Etymol. doubtful; cp. M. Du. *negge*, Mod. Du. *neg*, in same sense. **a** Small riding-horse, pony; this as sign of an inn: *the Nag's Head*; **b** (usually in derogatory sense) a poor, inferior, kind of horse: *a wretched nag*; *the old nag*.

nag (**II.**), vb. trans. & intrans. Scand., cp. O.N. *gnaga*, 'to gnaw'. See **gnaw**. **1.** trans. To worry, pester, by persistent and continuous scolding, complaints, fault-finding &c., esp. used of a woman: *to nag a man to death*; also *nag at*. **2.** intrans. To scold, complain, find fault persistently and perpetually: *to nag from morning to night*.

nag (**III.**), n., fr. prec. (colloq.) Persistent, continuous scolding, carping, fault-finding: *it is nag, nag all day long*.

nagana, n. [1. nagáhna; 2. nəgā́nə], fr. Bantu *n'gana*, native name for disease. Cattle disease of S. and E. Africa, caused by the tsetse-fly.

nagger, n. [1. náger; 2. nǽgə]. **nag** (**II.**) & **-er** A scold; persistently complaining woman.

nagging, n. & adj. [1. náging; 2. nǽgiŋ]. **nag (II.)** & **-ing**. **1.** n. Persistent worrying, scolding, and complaining: *daily nagging will destroy any man's temper.* **2.** adj. Persistently carping, worrying &c.: *a nagging tongue*; *incessant nagging criticism.*

nagor, n. [1. nágōr; 2. néigō], fr. native name. Kind of West African antelope.

naiad, n. [1. níad; 2. náiæd]. Gk. *nāiád-(os)*, stem of *nāiás* for **snāwjad-*, 'water nymph', usually in pl. *nāiádes*. The base occurs also in Gk. *náein*, 'to flow', wh. stands for **snáw-jein*; cogn. w. Scrt. *snáwti*, 'to drip', also w. Goth. *snīwan*, O.E. *snēowan*, 'to hasten'; & w. Lat. *nāre*, 'to swim', q.v. under **natation.** See also **necto-. a** (class. mythol.) Water-nymph, of river, lake, fountain, or spring; **b** (by transf.) a girl swimmer.

naiant, adj. [1. náant; 2. néiənt]. Prob. for *najant*, fr. Pres. Part. of O. Fr. *nagier*, 'to swim', fr. Lat. *navigāre.* See **navigate.** (her.) Swimming, of a fish represented horizontally.

naïf, adj. See **naïve.**

nail (I.) n. [1. nāl; 2. neil]. O.E. *nægel*, 'nail of the finger; metal nail, peg'; O.H.G. & O.S. *nagal*; O.N. *nagl*; fr. Aryan type **nokʷhló*, a reduced grade of **enekhʷló.* A kindred base, without the *-l* suff. occurs also in Lat. *unguis*, 'nail, claw' (see **ungual**), for **ongʷh-*; & in Gk. *ónux* (see **onyx**), fr. stem **ónukʷh-*, 'claw, nail, hoof'; cp. also O. Slav. *noga*, 'foot', & *nogŭtĭ*, 'nail', & Lith. *nāgas*, 'finger-nail', *nagà*, 'horse's hoof'; Scrt. *nakha-*, 'nail of finger or toe; bird's claw'. The base evidently existed in two types, one in wh. the medial consonant was *kʷh*, & another wh. had *gʷh*. **1.** Thin layer of horny substance covering and growing beyond the upper or outer surface of the tip of the human fingers and toes; applied also to the corresponding growth in some lower animals, esp. in monkeys and apes. Phrs. *(to fight, oppose, something) tooth and nail*, (chiefly in fig. sense) vigorously, implacably, with all the means at one's disposal; *to pay on the nail*, pay ready money, pay on demand. **2. a** Spike or peg (gen. of metal), of various length and thickness, generally with one pointed end, and a flattened head, driven into desired place by blows of a hammer; used for fastening two things or substances, or parts of things, together, or for fixing one thing upon another &c.; *wire nail*, one cut from sheet wire, used for fastening lid on to a wooden packing case &c.; *carpet nail*, for attaching carpet to floor; Phrs. *a nail in one's coffin*, (i.) some thing, or habit, which is considered likely to shorten life: *every glass of spirits you take is a nail in your coffin*; (ii.) action, speech, which hastens or brings about end of a system, institution, period of power, prosperity &c.: *the Government's hesitation in dealing with the crisis was a final nail in its coffin*; *to hit the right nail on the head*, to perceive and state central, essential, point of an argument or situation, to size it up correctly; to give the conclusive and convincing argument; *as hard as nails*, esp. of physical condition, very hard, strong, fit, wiry, and healthy, from physical training and exercise; **b** hard, pointed excrescence on the beak of a duck or other soft-billed birds (from its shape); **c** old measure of length = 2¼ inches.

nail (II.), vb. trans. O. Gmc. vb.; O.E. *næġlan*, also Goth. *(ga-)nagljan*, 'to nail'. See prec. **1.** To fasten together, to fix to, with a nail or nails. Phrs. *to nail one's colours to the mast*, (fig.) (i.) to announce one's views, principles &c. clearly and openly; (ii.) to form a resolution, plan of action &c. and adhere to it with unshakable determination; from the method of naval commanders for making it impossible to haul flag down in token of surrender; *to nail (a lie) to the counter*, to establish, by proof, the falsity of a statement; perhaps from former custom of nailing a false coin to the counter of a shop &c. as a warning. **2.** To provide, stud, with nails: *to have one's boots nailed.* **3.** (colloq. and slang) **a** To catch, seize, take into custody: *police have nailed the thief*; **b** (schoolboy slang) to find out, detect, discover: *some form-masters never nail it when cribbing goes on*; *to be nailed going off without leave.* Followed by preposition or adverb. *Nail down*, trans., **a** to fix by nailing: *to nail down a carpet*; **b** to secure, shut, by nailing; *to nail down the lid of a box*; **c** (fig.) to hold responsible for, pin down: *to nail a man down to his promise, statement* &c. *Nail on (to)*, to fasten one thing on to another by nails: *to nail a notice on (to) the door. Nail together*, to fasten together with nails, esp. of a rough, hasty piece of carpentry &c.: *the shed is just nailed together. Nail up*, to fasten, close up, so that it cannot be opened: *to nail up a door, window* &c.

nail-brush, n. Small brush for cleaning the nails.

nailer, n. [1. náler; 2. néilə]. **nail (I.)** & **-er. 1.** Nail-maker. **2.** (colloq., slang) One who excels in, is extremely good at, or keen on, particular form of sport, game, or other pursuit: *nailer to hounds, at bridge, golf* &c. *on his work* &c.

nail-head, n. Carved representation in wood or stone of head of a nail, used as ornament.

nail-headed, adj. Shaped like a nail, with flat, broad head and tapered, wedge-like body, esp. used of letters in cuneiform (q.v.).

nailing, adj. [1. náling; 2. néiliŋ]. **nail (I.)** & **-ing.** For meaning cp. **nailer, 2.** (slang, colloq.) Excellent, good, topping: *a nailing run, play, stroke* &c.; also as adverb: *nailing good day with the hounds, on the moors* &c.

nailless, adj. [1. nálles; 2. néillis]. **nail (I.)** & **-less. a** Not having a nail or nails on finger or toe; **b** not furnished with or fastened by metal nails.

nail-scissors, n. Scissors with short, strong blades for cutting the nails on human fingers and toes.

nainsook, n. [1. nánsook; 2. néinsuk]. Hind. *nainsukh*, fr. *nain*, 'eye', & *sukh*, 'delight, pleasure'. A striped or plain cotton fabric, finer than cambric and thicker than muslin, made originally in India.

naïve, naive, adj. [1. náh-ēv, nāv; 2. náiv, neiv]. Fr., fem. of *naïf*, fr. Lat. *nātīvus*, 'inborn, natural, not artificial'. See **native.** (of persons, manner, speech) Natural, unaffected, simple, innocent, ingenuous; frank, open, candid; also, foolishly simple.

naïvely, naively, adv. Prec. & **-ly.** In a naïve, artless, simple manner.

naïveté, n. [1. náh-ēvtā; 2. náivtei]. Fr., fr. **naïve**; used in Engl. as Fr. word & usually italicized. See following.

naïvety, naivety, n. [1. náh-ēvti, návti; 2. náivti, néivti]. Anglicized fr. prec. See **naïve** & **-ty.** Natural, unaffected, simple manner; simplicity, ingenuousness; artlessness.

naked, adj. [1. náked; 2. néikid]. O.E. *nacod*, M.E. *nāked*; O.H.G. *nacéot*, Mod. Germ. *nackt*; Goth. *naqaþs*; O.N. *nokkueðr*; fr. Aryan type **nogʷedho-*, whence also Lat. *nūdus*, 'naked'. See **nude. 1. a** (of human beings) Unclothed, bare, having no part of the body covered; nude: *to strip naked*; *to go, run, naked*; **b** (of parts of the body) uncovered, exposed, unprotected: *the naked feet, hands* &c.; Phr. *the naked eye*, unassisted by glasses of any kind. **2. a** (of animals &c.) Not yet covered with natural coat of hair or feathers, as when just born; **b** (bot.) without hairs or down on leaves or stem; without case or other covering for the seeds. **3.** (of various inanimate objects) **a** Without the usual, proper, natural covering; bare: *a naked blade*, of sword, dagger, knife, withdrawn from its scabbard or sheath; *naked branches*, leafless; *with naked fists*, of fight without boxing gloves; *naked light*, as lamp, candle, without glass or other protection from air or wind; **b** uncultivated, bare, barren, denuded of vegetation, soil &c.: *a barren and naked land*; *the naked surface of the desert*; *naked rock*; **c** unfurnished, bare of ornament or decoration: *a naked attic*; *naked walls.* **4.** (in non-material sense) **a** Not concealed or disguised; exposed, plain, obvious: *the naked truth*; *the naked facts*; **b** not supported by evidence, proof, argument &c., bare, bald: *only his naked word, assertion* &c.; **c** (poet.) defenceless, unprotected: '*Left me naked to mine enemies*' (Shakespeare, 'Henry VIII.'); **d** (rare) stripped, deprived, of some spiritual quality: *naked as regards reputation, honour* &c.

nakedly, adv. Prec. & **-ly. 1.** In an unclothed manner, without clothes on. **2.** Openly, plainly, simply, without disguise, directly.

nakedness, n. See prec. & **-ness. 1. a** State of being naked or unclothed; **b** (fig.) plainness, obviousness, absence of concealment or disguise; usually in unfavourable sense: *the truth in all its nakedness.* **2.** (archaic and Bib.) The secret parts of the body. **3.** Defencelessness, barrenness: *the nakedness of the land* (Genesis xlii. 9).

naker, n. [1. náker; 2. néikə]. O. Fr. *nacaire*, fr. Arab. *naqqirah*, 'kettle-drum', fr. *naqara*, 'to hollow out', cp. **nacre.** (archaic) A kettle-drum.

namable, adj. [1. námabl; 2. néiməbl]. **name** & **-able.** Capable of being named.

namby-pamby, adj. & n. [1. nàmbi pámbi; 2. næ̀mbi pǽmbi]. Formed in ridicule fr. name of Ambrose Philips (d. 1749), author of feeble pastoral poems. **1.** adj. Feebly sentimental, insipid, weak, lacking force and virility: *namby-pamby person, conversation, novel* &c. **2.** n. **a** A weak, feeble, effeminate person: *he's a regular namby-pamby*; **b** foolish, twaddling, sickly sentiment, talk, style &c.: *a popular writer of namby-pamby.*

name (I.), n. [1. nām; 2. neim]. O.E. *nama*, M.E. *nāme*, cp. O.S. & O.H.G. *namo*, Mod. Germ. *name*; Goth. *namō*, O.N. *nafn*; all fr. Aryan type **noman-*; the full form of the base was prob. **onoman-*, whence w. varying forms of gradation, Gk. *ónoma*, cp. also *anṓnumos*, 'nameless', fr. **nōmon-* type; Lat. *nōmen*, see **nominal**; Scrt. *nāman.* **1.** The word by which a person, thing, idea &c. is known, called, or spoken of; an appellation, designation; **a** applied in general to a class or to individual as one of class, e.g. *man, horse, town*; **b** applied specif. to particular individual: *Thomas Brown*; *London*; *the Thames* &c.; Phrs. *by name*, (i.) with mention or knowledge of the actual name: *he could speak to, knew, all his soldiers by name*; (ii.) by name and reputation only, not personally or familiarly: *I know you well by name. By, of, under, the name of*, named; *a man by, of, the name of Brown*; esp. of an assumed name or alias: *he goes by, under, the name of X. In the name of*, (i.) as invocation, esp. to the Deity: also gen. as appeal to: *in the name of common honesty*; (ii.) with the authority of: *in the name of the law*; *open! in the King's name. To one's name*, belonging to one: *not a penny to his name. Without a name*, nameless, not to be named: *a deed without a name. A mere name, only a name*, having no reality; hardly known: *these early kings are mere names*; *truth is only a name to him. Give it a name*, (colloq. and slang) of an invitation to drink at one's expense, name what you want. *Take a name in vain* (esp. the Divine name), to use it idly, profanely, irreverently. *Put one's name down for*, to join in a subscription, join a movement, organization &c.; to enter one's name for a school, college, club &c. *Keep one's name on, take name off*, the books of a college &c., as remaining, or ceasing to be, a member. **2. a** (log.) A term; the word denoting a concept; **b** (philos.) the word by which an abstract idea is known; that by which things themselves are known; **c** (gram.) noun. **3. a** That which is commonly attributed to a person, place &c.;

reputation, character: *a good, bad, name; to leave a (great, famous) name behind one; the town has a name as a health resort; hardly deserves the name; he had the name of a mean hunks*; Phrs. *give a dog a bad name and hang him*, to condemn a person on mere reputation or hearsay; *a king in name only*, (i.) one enjoying the legal right of kingship, and the external pomp and circumstance, but too indolent or incapable to exercise the functions of a king; (ii.) one who although a legitimate sovereign, and acknowledged as such by his adherents, has been driven from his throne: *a wife in name only*, woman who, although legally married, does not cohabit as a wife with her husband; **b** famous person, identified with his name: *the great names of history*; '*Erasmus, that great injured name*' (Pope, 'Ess. on Crit.', 693); Phr. *of name*, of reputation, well-known: *people of name flocked to his standard.* **4.** Family, descent, lineage, line, as identified with a particular name: *he upheld the honour of his name; to disgrace one's name; their name goes back to the Conquest; the last of his name.* **5.** Authority, support: *to lend one's name to a proposal, cause* &c. **6.** (usually pl.) Abusive, derogatory epithets; only in Phr. *to call (a person) names*, to abuse, insult &c.

name (II.), vb. trans., fr. prec. **1.** To give a name to, call, designate: *name this child; to name new substances, plants &c. is a difficult task.* Phr. *name after*, to call a person or thing by the same name as another: *to name a child Henry after his father*; to form a name for a person, thing, place &c. from that of another: *the fuchsia is named after the botanist Fuchs.* **2. a** To call, mention by name; identify, distinguish by name: *to name the stars in the sky; name all the flowers in the garden; name all the Archbishops of Canterbury in order*; Phr. *name the day*, (of a woman) to fix the day for her wedding; **b** specif., to call a member (of Parliament) by his name, for refusal to obey a ruling from the chair or for disorderly conduct, as preliminary to suspension (as action of Speaker or Chairman of Committee in House of Commons); *Name! Name!*, (i.) as demand from members for the Speaker to name a member; (ii.) as call from an audience for the name of a person to be given to whom allusion has been made. **3.** To select for, appoint to, nominate, designate for: *X has been named for the vacant bishopric.*

name-day, n. The festival day of the saint, after whom a person is named; (loosely) baptismal day.

nameless, adj. [1. nā́mles; 2. néimlis]. **name (I.)** & **-less.** **1.** Without a name; not named, anonymous: *the nameless author of this book; a well-known person, who shall be nameless, told me.* **2.** Unknown, not identified: *the nameless dead; nameless grave.* **3. a** Not to be named, unfit to be named: *nameless vices*; **b** undefinable, vague: *a nameless horror.*

namely, adv. [1. nā́mli; 2. néimli]. **name (I.)** & **-ly.** To wit, that is to say, *videlicet, viz.*

namer, n. [1. nā́mer; 2. néimə]. **name (II.)** & **-er.** One who names; nominator.

namesake, n. [1. nā́msāk; 2. néimseik]. For *name's sake*, 'for the sake of the name'. **a** One who is called or named after another; **b** one who has the same name as another.

nankeen, nankin, n. [1. nánkḗn; 2. nænkín], fr. Nanking, town in China. **a** Cotton cloth, of yellowish-brown colour, originally made at Nanking; **b** (pl.) trousers made of this.

Nankin, adj. & n. See prec.; this porcelain was not, however, made specially at Nanking. **1.** adj. [1. nánkēn; 2. nǽnkīn]. A trade-name for a class of Chinese porcelain, of blue pattern on white ground, of many varieties and values: *Nankin porcelain, china; a Nankin dish, plate* &c.; *Nankin blue*, the colour seen in Nankin china. **2.** n. [1. nánkḗn; 2. nænkín]. Piece or number of pieces of such porcelain: *he made a fine collection of Nankin.*

nanny-goat, n. [1. náni gōt; 2. nǽni gout], fr. *Nanny*, female name, fr. *Ann*, & **goat.** Cp. *billy-goat*, for the he-goat. A she-goat.

Nantz, n. [1. nants; 2. nænts]. Prob. through Du., fr. Nantes, France, a great wine & spirit port. (obs.) French brandy: *good, right, Nantz.*

nap (I.), n. & vb. trans. [1. nap; 2. næp]. M.E. *nappe*, 'rough surface of cloth', perh. connected w. O.E. *hnæppan*, 'to strike'; cp. M. Du. *noppe*, 'nap of cloth', *noppen*, 'to clip, shear off'. Further connexion unknown. **1.** n. Smooth, hairy, or downy surface of cloth after the pile has been clipped or sheared. **2.** vb. To put, raise, a nap on cloth.

nap (II.), n. & vb. intrans. The n. is not recorded in O. & M.E., except in form *hnapping*, but the vb. *hnappian*, 'to slumber, doze', is found in former & becomes *nappen* &c., in the latter; our present n. is formed fr. the old vb. **a** n. A short sleep or doze; forty winks; **b** vb. (rare, except in Pres. Part.) to doze, take a nap; Phr. *to be caught napping*, (fig.) to be taken unprepared, unawares, be surprised.

nap (III.), n. Abbr. of Napoleon. (colloq.) Name of a card game. Phr. *to go nap*, to call 'nap', i.e. to undertake to win all five tricks in this game; (fig.) *to go nap on*, to be so sure, of a fact, future event &c., as to stake one's reputation upon it.

nape, n. [1. nāp; 2. neip]. Etymol. doubtful, possibly fr. O.E. *cnæp*, 'hill, mountain-top', see **knap (I.)**, referring to the projection at the top of the spine. The back of the neck.

napery, n. [1. nā́peri; 2. néipəri], fr. O. Fr. *naperie*, 'table-linen', fr. L. Lat. *naparia, napparia*, 'linen', also 'keeper of household linen', fr. L. Lat. *nappa*, whence O. Fr. *nappe*, 'cloth', for *mappa*, see **map.** (chiefly Scots) Household, esp. table, linen.

naphtha, n. [1. náf-tha; 2. nǽfþə]. Gk., fr. Pers. *naft*, name given to a liquid inflammable oil found in Persia, fr. Zend, **napta*, 'liquid'. **a** A clear, liquid, inflammable oil found exuding from bitumen beds in district of the Caspian Sea, styled 'native naphtha'; **b** strong-smelling liquid distilled from crude petroleum, used in cleaning and lighting.

naphthalene, n. [1. náf-thalēn; 2. nǽfþəlīn]. **naphtha, -al** & **-ene.** (chem.) A solid hydrocarbon obtained from coal-tar, used in manufacture of dyes &c.

naphthol, n. [1. náf-thol; 2. nǽfþɔl]. **naphtha** & **-ol.** (chem.) A solid substance obtained from naphthalene, used for antiseptics and disinfectants and in making dyes.

napkin, n. [1. nápkin; 2. nǽpkin]. M.E. *napekin*; dimin. suff. **-kin** added to adaptation of Fr. *nappe*, 'table-cloth'. See **napery. a** Small linen cloth used for protecting the clothes at table and for wiping lips or fingers; usually *table-napkin*; **b** small towel or diaper for a baby.

napkin-ring, n. Broad ring of silver, ivory, bone &c. for holding a rolled-up napkin.

napless, adj. [1. náples; 2. nǽplis]. **nap (I.)** & **-less.** (of cloth) Having no nap; having smooth surface; worn threadbare.

napoleon, n. [1. napṓleon; 2. nəpóuliən], fr. Napoleon I., Emperor of the French. **a** Gold coin of the 1st and 2nd French Empires, value 20 francs, equivalent to the louis; **b** name of a card game, now usually abbreviated to nap, q.v.

Napoleonic, adj. [1. napòleónik; 2. nəpòulión-ik]. Prec. & **-ic. a** Of or relating to Napoleon I. or his period; **b** having qualities, attributes &c. resembling those of Napoleon, esp. as a great conqueror, or organizer, or as a colossal figure in the world &c.: *a Napoleonic career; a Napoleonic figure.*

na-poo, adj. [1. nàhpṓō; 2. nāpú]. The British soldier's pronunciation of Fr. *il n'y (en) a plus*, 'there is no more (of it)'; dating fr. the Great War. (obs. or obsolesc.) A common expression of British soldiers in France with a variety of meanings, apart from its proper sense; e.g. 'no good', 'useless', 'not up to much'; of a failure, wasted effort &c.; so, too, of one who has been killed or died: *he's na-poo.*

napu, n. [1. náhpōō; 2. nā́pū]. Malay. A small chevrotain or musk-deer of Java and Sumatra.

narceine, n. [1. nárseēn; 2. nā́s(i)īn]. Fr., fr. Gk. *nárkē*, 'numbness'. See **narcotic** & **-ine.** (chem.) A narcotic alkaloid obtained from opium.

narcissism, n. [1. narsísizm; 2. nāsísizəm]. See **Narcissus (II.)** & **-ism.** A term in psycho-analysis, of a morbid condition characterized by excessive admiration of oneself, one's person, abilities &c.

narcissus (I.), n., pl. **narcissi** [1. narsísus, -sī; 2. nāsísəs, -sai]. Lat., fr. Gk. *nárkissos* 'daffodil', fr. *nárkē*, 'numbness', fr. its effects. See **narcotic. a** Bulbous flowering plant, with white or yellow petals and red or yellow centre, of various kinds; jonquil, daffodil; **b** (bot.) genus of flowering plants belonging to the order *Amaryllidaceae.*

Narcissus (II.), n. **a** (Gk. mythol.) A beautiful youth who died from love of his own beauty as reflected in water, and was changed into the flower bearing the name; **b** a very handsome but vain young man.

narcolepsy, n. [1. nárkolepsi; 2. nā́kəlɛpsi], fr. Gk. *narkṓ-(ein)*, 'to stupefy'. See **narcotic** & second element in **epilepsy.** (med.) A nervous epileptic disease, marked by fits of intense sleepiness or drowsiness.

narcosis, n. [1. narkṓsis; 2. nākóusis]. Gk. *nárkōsis*, 'numbness'. See **narcotic** & **-osis.** (pathol.) State of stupor, insensibility, coma, esp. that induced by narcotic poisoning; narcotism.

narcotic (I.), adj. [1. narkótik; 2. nākɔ́tik]. Gk. *narkōtikós*, 'stupefying, benumbing'; fr. *nárkē* for **snarkē*, 'numbness, stupor; fr. base **snark*ʷ- &c., 'twist, turn, constrain, confine in,' whence also O.E. *snēare*, 'noose', fr. **snærhe.* See **snare.** Having the effect of stupefying, inducing sleep or drowsiness; soothing, soporific: **a** of certain drugs, such as opium; **b** of intellectual soporifics, e.g. tedious books, lectures, sermons &c.

narcotic (II.), n., fr. prec. **a** Substance, drug, which produces drowsiness, sleep, insensibility by acting on the bodily organism; **b** (fig.) any cause of drowsiness which has soothing, soporific effect on the mind.

narcotically, adv. [1. narkótikali; 2. nākɔ́tikəli]. Prec. & **-al** & **-ly.** In the manner of a narcotic.

narcotine, n. [1. nárkotēn; 2. nā́kətīn]. See **narcotic** & **-ine.** (chem.) An alkaloid of opium.

narcotism, n. [1. nárkotizm; 2. nā́kətizəm]. *narcot-*, as in prec. & **-ism.** State of profound stupor, insensibility, produced by narcotic poisoning; narcosis.

narcotization, n. [1. nàrkotīzā́shun; 2. nā̀kət-aizéiʃən]. See next word & **-ation. a** Process of narcotizing; **b** state of being narcotized.

narcotize, vb. trans. [1. nárkotīz; 2. nā́kətaiz]. See **narcotic** & **-ize.** To produce state of insensibility, stupor, or narcosis, as effect of a powerful narcotic.

nard, n. [1. nard; 2. nād], fr. Fr., fr. Lat. *nardus*, Gk. *nárdos*, fr. Heb. *nērd*, the plant fr. wh. an unguent was obtained. A perfumed unguent or balsam, usually called spikenard, q.v.

nares, n. pl. [1. nā́rēz; 2. nέərīz]. Lat., pl. of *nāris*, 'nostril', wh. stands for **nazis.* See **nasal** & **nose.** (anat.) The nostrils.

narghile(h), nargile(h), n. [1. nárgili; 2. nā́gili]. Pers., fr. *nargīl*, 'coco-nut'; the bowls of the earliest narghilehs are said to have been made of coco-nut shells. Hookah, or hubble-bubble, an oriental form of tobacco-pipe in which the smoke is drawn through a bowl, filled with perfumed water, before passing into the mouth.

nark, n. [1. nark; 2. nāk]. Etymol. unknown. (thieves' slang) Spy, informer, esp. one in the service of the police.

narrate, vb. trans. [1. narā́t; 2. nəréit], fr. Lat. *narrāt-(um)*, P.P. type of *narrāre*, 'to make known, relate, tell', prob. fr. *nārus*, **gnārus*, 'acquainted with, aware of, knowing', fr. the same base *g̑no-, as in **know**; the word in Engl. is later than **narration.** To relate, give a connected account, by word of mouth or in writing, of a series of facts or events as they occurred; to recount, tell the story of &c.: *to narrate one's adventures.*

narration, n. [1. narā́shun; 2. nəréiʃən]. Fr., fr. Lat. *narrātiōn-(em)*, 'a relating, narrating of events &c., narrative', fr. *narrāre.* See **narrate. a** Process, act, of narrating, relating, recounting: *the bare narration of the facts in the case took two hours; manner, style, form of narration*; **b** that which is narrated; narrative; esp. a rather diffuse story: *travellers' narrations.*

narrative, n. [1. nárativ; 2. nǽrətiv], fr. Fr. *narratif*, adj., fr. Lat. *narrātīvus*, 'suitable for narration', fr. *narrāre.* See **narrate** & **-ive. 1.** n. **a** Tale, story, account of events in order of time; specif. **b** (Scots Law) recital; that part of a deed which sets out the facts, such as names, reasons for the deed &c. **2.** attrib. **a** In form of a narrative, tale, story; setting out events or facts in order of time: *narrative literature*; **b** connected with narrative: *a writer of great narrative power.*

narratively, adv. Prec. & **-ly.** In form of a narrative or recital of events in order.

narrator, n. [1. narā́tur; 2. nəréitə]. Lat. See **narrate** & **-or.** One who narrates; the teller of a story.

narrow (I.), adj. [1. nárō; 2. nǽrou]. O.E. *nearu*, M.E. *narewe, narowe*; O.S. *naro*; etymol. doubtful; connexion w. base seen in **nerve**, has been suggested, but the etymol. of this is also dubious. **1. a** (of material things) Of small width or breadth in proportion to length; the opposite of *broad* or *wide*: *a narrow road, pass, passage, river* &c.; *narrow plank, margin, ribbon* &c.; *narrow cloth*, of less than 52 in. wide; *narrow gauge*, of railway lines, less than 4 ft. 8½ in. wide; *narrow goods*, ribbons, tapes, braids &c. Phrs. *one's narrow bed*, the grave; *narrow escape*, one accomplished with difficulty, risk, and danger; (colloq.) *a narrow squeak*, something with difficulty, and only just, escaped or avoided; *narrow majority*, one only slightly larger than minority; *the Narrow Seas*, English Channel and Irish Sea; *narrow victory*, one only just gained, nearly a reverse; *the narrow way*, (fig.) the difficult path of virtue, cp. Matt. vii. 14; **b** limited in area, restricted in extent: *our space here is rather narrow*; also fig. (of life, opportunities) confined to limited circle: *a narrow scope for one's energies*; Phr. *narrow means, circumstances*, poverty. **2. a** (of the mind and its processes) Limited in outlook, working only in restricted sphere; confined to one point of view; prejudiced, bigoted: *a narrow mind, interests*; *to take narrow views*; **b** (of persons) possessing such a mind; taking such views. **3.** Mean, parsimonious, hard in bargaining: *very narrow in his dealings*; *narrow with his money.* **4.** Of limited meaning or intent; restricted to literal meaning of the words: *in a narrow, the narrowest, sense.* **5.** (phon.) **a** Ambiguous term implying tenseness of the tongue in utterance; applied also to vowels uttered with a tense tongue; better called *tense*; **b** (of air passage in given utterance) constricted, exiguous.

narrow (II.), n., fr. prec. A narrow channel or strait between two seas or two lakes; narrow pass in mountains; (usually in pl.): *the Narrows.*

narrow (III.), vb. trans. & intrans. **narrow (I.). 1.** trans. To reduce the width of, cause to become narrow (in all senses, lit. and fig.). Phr. *to narrow an argument down*, reduce to single point or to a few essential points. **2.** intrans. **a** To become narrow: *the river narrows at this point*; **b** (of the eyes) to be almost closed, leaving only a narrow slit between the eyelids.

narrowly, adv. [1. nárōli; 2. nǽrouli]. **narrow (I.)** & **-ly. 1.** In a narrow manner or form (in all senses); specif., by a narrow margin; with difficulty, scarcely, hardly: *he narrowly escaped drowning*, was nearly drowned. **2.** In a close, searching manner: *to cross-examine a witness narrowly*; *to look at a thing narrowly*; *to watch a person or process narrowly.*

narrow-minded, adj. Having a narrow mind; prejudiced, bigoted.

narrow-mindedly, adv. Prec. & **-ly.** In a narrow-minded way.

narrow-mindedness, n. See prec. & **-ness.** State or condition of being narrow-minded.

narrowness, n. [1. nárōnes; 2. nǽrounis]. **narrow (I.)** & **-ness.** State or condition of being narrow (in all senses): *the narrowness of the road*; *narrowness of his views, mind* &c.

narthex, n. [1. nártheks; 2. nā́þeks]. Gk. *nárthēx*, 'the giant fennel, small casket for unguents', in L. Gk. applied to the architectural feature, fr. resemblance to the hollow, reed-like stem of the plant; cp. Scrt. *naḍáś*, 'reed'. (archit.) A long arcaded porch at the west end of early Christian churches, forming a place for those, such as penitents or catechumens, not admitted to the body of the church.

narwhal, narwal, n. [1. nárwal; 2. nā́wəl]. Scand., cp. Swed. & Dan. *narhval*, O.N. *nāhvalr*; the last element is 'whale', q.v., O.N. *hvalr*, Swed. &c. *hval*; the first element is doubtful, prob. O.N. *nār*, 'corpse', the animal being of a pale, whitish colour on the under side. A kind of Arctic whale, the male having the left of two tusks developed into a long twisted horn; also called *sea-unicorn.*

nasal (I.), adj. [1. nā́zl; 2. néizl], fr. L. Lat. *nāsālis*, 'belonging to the nose', fr. *nāsus*, 'nose', & **-al**, cogn. w. **nares.** See also **ness** & **nose. a** Of, belonging to, connected with, the nose; **b** (phon.) applied to speech-sounds in the formation and articulation of which the air-stream passes through the nose; **c** to a mode of utterance in which all speech-sounds are to some extent nasalized.

nasal (II.), n., fr. prec. **1.** A straight piece of metal projecting from the early mediaeval helmet to protect the nose. **2.** (phon.) A nasal sound.

nasalism, n. [1. nā́zalizm; 2. néizəlizəm]. Prec. & **-ism.** Nasal pronunciation.

nasality, n. [1. nāzáliti; 2. neizǽliti]. **nasal** & **-ity.** Quality of being nasal; resonance in nose passage.

nasalization, n. [1. nā̀zalīzā́shun; 2. nèizəlaizéiʃən]. See next word & **-ation.** Process, result, of nasalizing speech-sounds.

nasalize, vb. trans. [1. nā́zalīz; 2. néizəlaiz]. **nasal (I.)** & **-ize.** (phon.) To utter (a vowel or consonant) while the air-stream, or part of it, is allowed to pass through the nose.

nasally, adv. [1. nā́zali; 2. néizəli]. **nasal (I.)** & **-ly.** With a nasal sound or accent; through the nose.

nascent, adj. [1. nā́sent; 2. néisənt]. Lat. *nāscent-(em)*, Pres. Part. type of *nāsci*, 'to be born', fr. base *g̑nat- & inceptive suff. *-sk-.* See this base under **natal, native,** & **nature.** Coming to, approaching, birth; beginning to grow or be formed; just appearing; coming into existence.

naseberry, n. [1. nā́zberi; 2. néizbəri]. Corrupt. of Span. *nispero*, fr. Lat. *mespilus*, Gk. *mespílē*, 'medlar', etymol. unknown. A West Indian and Central American tree and its fruit; also called *Sapodilla.*

naso-, pref. Form of Lat. *nāsus*, 'nose', see **nasal (I.)**, used in compounds, indicating connexion with the nose; chiefly anatomical: *naso-labial*, of nose and lips; *naso-palatal*, nose and palate &c.

nastily, adv. [1. náhstili; 2. nā́stili]. **nasty** & **-ly.** In a nasty, dirty, offensive manner.

nastiness, n. [1. náhstines; 2. nā́stinis]. **nasty** & **-ness. a** State, condition, quality, of being nasty; **b** nasty object; dirtiness, foulness; **c** nasty thought or expression; obscenity.

nasturtium, n. [1. nastérshum; 2. nəstə́ʃəm]. Lat., 'cress', for *nāsi-tortium*, 'nose-twister', fr. the hot, pungent smell and taste of leaves and seeds of the plant, fr. *nāsus*, 'nose', see **nasal (I.)**, & *tort-(um)*, P.P. of *torquēre*, 'to twist, twinge', see **torture. a** (bot.) Genus of plants belonging to the order *Cruciferae*, including the watercress; **b** a garden plant, *Tropaeolum*, of many varieties, climbing or dwarf, with red and yellow flowers.

nasty, adj. [1. náhsti; 2. nā́sti]. Etymol. doubtful, cp. possibly Du. *nestig*, 'dirty'; M.E. has *nasky*, wh. may be an earlier form, cp. Swed. dial. *naskug*, 'dirty, foul'. Unpleasant, offensive, revolting, disgusting. **1.** Offensive to the senses, esp. those of taste and smell; nauseous, sickening, repellent: *a nasty smell, taste*; *nasty medicine*; *a nasty sight*, one exciting feelings of physical disgust; *a nasty job*, one which it is physically revolting to perform; Phr. *to leave a nasty taste in the mouth*, (fig.) leave a lasting impression of moral disgust. **2.** Morally offensive and shocking; specif., unpleasantly suggestive; indecent, obscene; morally filthy and unclean: *a thoroughly nasty book, play*; *he has a nasty mind*; *a nasty story*; Phr. (colloq.) *a nasty piece of work*, a person with a nasty mind, and guilty of dishonourable or disgusting conduct. **3.** Exhibiting, imbued with, ill-will and malevolence; angry, spiteful, malicious: *a nasty temper*; *a nasty remark*; Phr. *to turn nasty*, become angry or spiteful; *to play one a nasty trick*, behave to in a treacherous or mean manner; *a nasty piece of work*, a malevolent action or intrigue. **4 a** Threatening, menacing, dangerous: *a nasty look in his eye*; *things look nasty for me*; *a nasty storm is coming on*; **b** painful, severe, dangerous: *a nasty fall*; *a nasty bout of influenza*; **c** difficult to deal with; awkward; precarious: *a nasty rock to climb*; *rather a nasty situation, position* (fig.); *he got himself into a nasty mess*, (fig.) an awkward predicament.

natal, adj. [1. nā́tal; 2. néitəl], fr. Lat. *nātālis*, 'of or belonging to one's birth', fr. *nāt-(um)*, P.P. type of *nāsci*, 'to be born'. See also **nation, nature.** The orig. base is *g̑nā-t-, 'to produce' &c.; whence also Goth. *knōþs*, 'race, stock'; also O.E. *cnōsl*, 'progeny, kindred' &c., fr. *knōss-la, fr. Aryan *g̑nāt-tlō, *g̑nōt-tlō; cp. O.H.G. *chnuosal*; cogn. w. Gk. *gnōtós*, 'relative'; *g̑nōt-, *g̑nāt- &c. are variants of Aryan base *g̑en-, q.v. under **genesis, genus, generate** &c. See also **kin, kind (I.).** Of or belonging to one's birth: *natal day*, birthday; *natal place*, birthplace.

natality, n. [1. nātáliti; 2. neitǽliti]. Fr. *natalité.* See prec. & **-ity.** Birth-rate.

natant, adj. [1. nā́tant; 2. néitənt], fr. Lat. *nātant-(em)*, Pres. Part. type of *natare*, 'to swim, float', freq. form of *nāre*, 'to swim'. See next word. Floating, swimming, as of water-plants whose leaves float on the water.

natation, n. [1. nātā́shun; 2. neitéiʃən], fr. Lat. *natātiōn-(em)*, 'swimming', fr. *natāt-*, P.P. type of *natāre*, extended form of *nāre*, 'to float, swim'. The orig. base was *snā-, *snə-; also *sno-, as in Gk. *nótios* (for *snot-), 'damp'. Cp. also Scrt. *snā́ti*, 'he bathes', & M. Ir. *snaim*, 'I swim', & further O.E. *snēowan* & (w. different suff.) O.N. *snyðja*, 'to hasten'. See also **naiad** & **necto-.** Swimming; art of, skill in, swimming.

natatorial, natatory, adjs. [1. nā̀tatṓrial, nā́taturi; 2. nèitətɔ́riəl, néitətəri]. Lat. *natātor*, 'swimmer'. See prec. & **-ial, -y.** Swimming; pertaining to swimming.

nates, n. pl. [1. nā́tēz; 2. néitīz], fr. Lat. *natēs*, pl. of *natis*, 'rump', prob. cogn. w. Gk. *nōton*, 'back'; other cognates unrecorded. (anat.) Buttocks, rump.

natheless, nathless, adv. [1. nàth(e)lés; 2. nǽþ(ə)lés]. M.E. *natheles*, combination of O.E. *nā, ne*, 'no, not', & *ā*, 'ever', see **aye,** & O.E. *þȳ*, instr. of def. art., & **less** See **nevertheless.** (obs. or poet.) Nevertheless.

nation, n. [1. nā́shun ; 2. néiʃən], fr. Fr. *nation*, Lat. *nātiōn-(em)*, 'breed, race, people' &c.; fr. base **gˇnāt-*, q.v. under **natal**. **1.** A large group of human beings who form an independent political unity, and are subject to a single supreme central government; usually occupying a clearly defined geographical area, and further united by an ancient community of race, customs, traditions, and general spirit, and feeling themselves to be a unity: *the British, French, Dutch, nation* &c.; *the voice of the nation*, opinion of the majority of the inhabitants of a country; *law of nations*, international law; *Battle of the Nations*, Leipzig, 1813. Phr. *most favoured nation*, one whose exports are subject to the lowest rate of tariff charges when they enter given country, the latter having the same terms for its own exports. **2.** A group of people who form, or once formed, an ancient national unity, though at present either geographically scattered (*Jewish nation*), or forming part of a larger national unit (*Scottish, Welsh, nation*), but still presenting distinguishing racial and other characters, such as separate religion or language. **3.** (Bib.) In pl. *the nations*, the Gentiles, the non-Jewish peoples. **4.** (in mediaeval universities) Group of students belonging to the same race or nationality.

national (I.), adj. [1. náshunal; 2. nǽʃənəl]. Prec. & **-al**. **a** Pertaining to, characteristic of, disseminated throughout, springing from, a nation: *national spirit, genius, customs, literature, language* &c.; specif. usages: *national anthem*, State hymn or song, as 'God save the King', the 'Marseillaise' &c.; *National Assembly*, convention of representatives of a nation; *national debt*, the public debt of a State; *national church*, an established church; *national flag*; *national forces*, army, navy and air force; **b** owned, controlled, guaranteed by the State, nationalized: *national railway, bank* &c.; *national theatre*, one subsidized by the State; **c** (gen.) public, popular, (as part of a name or title): *National and Provincial Bank*; the *Grand National* (steeplechase) &c.

national (II.), n., fr. prec. (usually pl.) One who has the full rights, by birth or naturalization, of a citizen of a nation or State; used esp. of those living in a foreign country: *the State's duty is to protect its nationals*.

nationalism, n. [1. náshunalizm; 2. nǽʃənəl-izəm]. **national** (I.) & **-ism**. **1.** Consciousness of, and pride in, the individual character and spirit of a people as felt by themselves; sense of national unity. **2.** Specif., a political movement to foster and assert the right of national independence when this is conceived to be imperilled or suppressed by the predominance of another nation.

nationalist, n. & adj. [1. náshunalist; 2. nǽʃən-əlist]. **national** (I.) & **-ist**. **1.** n. **a** One imbued with a spirit of nationalism; **b** specif., member of a political party or society aiming at the assertion of the national spirit and the rights of nationality. **2.** adj. Supporting, upholding, nationalism: *nationalist ideals, party* &c.

nationality, n. [1. nàshunáliti; 2. næ̀ʃənǽliti]. **national** (I.) & **-ity**. **1.** Status of a member, by birth or naturalization, of a particular State or nation. **2.** State, quality, of belonging by birth to a particular nation. **3.** Nation: *how many nationalities are represented at Geneva?*

nationalization, n. [1. nàshunalīzā́shun; 2. næ̀ʃənəlaizéiʃən]. **nationalize** & **-ation**. **1.** Act, process, of nationalizing or making national; state of being nationalized. **2.** Specif., the process of transferring, fact of transference, from private, to national or State ownership and control, of such things as land, mines, railways &c.: *the nationalization of the railways, of land* &c. **3.** (rare) Naturalization.

nationalize, vb. trans. [1. náshunalīz; 2. nǽʃənəl-aiz]. **national** (I.) & **-ize**. Cp. Fr. *nationaliser* in same sense. **1.** **a** To make into a nation: *the Poles are now nationalized*, have become an independent nation; **b** to make current among a nation, render national: *to nationalize the Gaelic language in Scotland*. **2.** To remove (land, mines, railways &c.) from private ownership and control, and bring under that of the State. **3.** (rare) To naturalize.

nationalizer, n. [1. náshunalīzer; 2. nǽʃənəl-aizə]. **nationalize** & **-er**. One who supports a policy of nationalization, esp. in economic sense.

nationally, adv. [1. náshunali; 2. nǽʃənəli]. **national** & **-ly**. In a national manner; by the nation as a whole; from a national point of view; publicly: *to consider a question nationally*, not from a personal, local, class, or party point of view.

native (I.), adj. [1. nā́tiv; 2. néitiv], fr. Fr. *natif*, masc., *native*, fem., fr. Lat. *nātīvus*, 'born, innate, natural, primitive', fr. *nāt-(um)*, 'born', fr. base of **natal**, & *-īvus*, see **-ive**. **1.** Belonging, pertaining, to a person by birth: *one's native land, language*; *a native word*, one belonging to the ancient vocabulary of a language, and not borrowed from another tongue; contrasted with *loan-word*; *one's native place*, that where one was born. **2.** Of or belonging to the people of a particular country, race &c., usually of non-European people; aboriginal: *native customs, dress* &c.; *native troops*. Phr. *to go native*, (of a European) to adopt the mode of life &c. of a less civilized race among whom he lives. **3.** Born with one, innate; not acquired from others, or by training, education &c.; natural: *native genius, talent, wit*. **4.** (of plants and animals) Growing or living naturally in, indigenous to, a specified region; not introduced from outside; reverse of *exotic*: *oak, ash, and thorn are native English trees*; *the native British black rat is nearly extinct*; specif., *native oysters*, those bred artificially in British waters; **b** (of minerals &c.) in a natural, original state: *native rock, metal*.

native (II.), n., fr. prec. **1.** One born in a particular place, town, country &c.; inhabitant, denizen: *a native of Somerset*; *a native of Hungary*. **2.** A person belonging to a non-European race, as applied to the aborigines of a newly discovered country and so generally by European settlers &c. to the inhabitants of a country with a civilization lower than or different from their own: *South African natives*, the Bantus or Hottentots; *many natives and Europeans lose their lives during Indian riots*. **3.** **a** An indigenous plant or animal: *the eucalyptus and kangaroo are natives of Australia*; specif. **b** a native oyster bred artificially in British waters.

nativity, n. [1. natíviti; 2. nətíviti], fr. Fr. *nativité*, fr. L. Lat. *nātīvitāt-(em)*, 'birth'. See **native** (I.) & **-ity**. **1.** (cap.) **a** Birth, esp. that of Jesus Christ; festival of His Nativity, Dec. 25th, Christmas Day; **b** pictorial or sculptured representation of the same. **2.** Birth, festival, or representation of that of the B.V.M., on Sept. 8th; or of St. John the Baptist, on June 24th. **3.** (astrol.) Horoscope: *to cast a man's nativity*.

natron, n. [1. nā́tron; 2. néitrən]. Fr., through Span., fr. Arab. *nātrūn*, fr. Gk. *nitron*. See **nitre**. (chem. and mineral.) Native carbonate of sodium, found in salt lakes, and used in ancient Egypt for embalming.

natterjack, n. [1. náterjak; 2. nǽtədʒæk]. Provinc. Engl.; first element perh. fr. O.E. *āt(t)or*, 'venom, poison', w. initial *n-* fr. indef. art., cp. **newt**; cp. O.H.G. *eitar*, 'poison', & provinc. Engl. *attercop*, 'spider'. O.E. *āt(t)or* is cogn. w. Gk. *oidos*, 'a swelling, tumour', see **oedema**. Kind of toad with a yellow stripe on the back.

natty, adj. [1. náti; 2. nǽti]. Etymol. doubtful; possibly connected w. Fr. *net*, 'neat'. **1.** Trim, neat, dapper, spruce, esp. of clothes or general appearance: *natty suit, turn-out* &c. **2.** Neat, quick, skilful.

natural (I.), adj. [1. náchural; 2. nǽtʃərəl], fr. Lat. *nātūrālis*, 'by birth, in accordance with nature'. See **nature** & **-al**. **1.** **a** Of, connected with, arising from, nature or the external physical world: *natural forces, phenomena*; specific uses: *natural order* (see *natural system*); *natural religion*, one founded on, and approved by, human reason without the help of divine revelation; hence *natural theology*, based on such religion; *natural selection*, phrase applied by Darwin to the process whereby those individuals and their descendants which fail to adapt themselves to the environment are eliminated; such as can adapt themselves to the conditions of life survive, and are regarded as 'the fittest'; *natural system*, of botanical classification by resemblance of structure, instead of by sexual characteristics; hence *natural order*, a class of plants under this system; **b** concerned with, dealing with, treating of, nature or the physical world: *natural history*, originally, history or science of nature as a whole, dealing with all branches; now, specif. of zoology and botany; *natural historian*, one who studies, writes on, natural history; *natural philosophy*, formerly, moral philosophy, now, science of physics; *natural philosopher*, physicist; *natural science*, formerly, physics, now, including all branches of knowledge of the physical world; **c** in the state, under the condition, produced or provided by nature without man's intervention; wild, uncultivated, unconfined; free, undomesticated: *land in its natural state*; *the buffalo can live its natural life in Yellowstone Park*; *natural growth of timber*; *a natural spring*, of medicinal water; *natural gas*, inflammable gas issuing from oil-bearing beds. **2.** **a** In accordance with the ordinary, observed processes of nature; contrasted with *supernatural* or *miraculous*: *a natural explanation of miracles*; *a natural process*; Phrs. *a natural death*, one due to old age or disease, not to violence; *the term of one's natural life*, as long as one lives; **b** in accordance with logical notions of cause and effect; happening according to reasonable anticipation or expectation; ordinary, normal: *the natural consequences of an action*; *it is only natural for economic distress to follow war*. **3.** True to nature, having a close resemblance to an object in nature; real, life-like: *most natural representation of past time*; *a natural pose in statuary or painting*. **4.** Illegitimate, born out of wedlock: *a natural child*. **5.** **a** (of mental endowments and qualities) Coming as by nature, born with one, innate, inborn; native; contrasted with *acquired*: *natural abilities, parts, charm, skill, capacity, wit, talent, gifts*; **b** (of persons in relation to these) possessing them innately: *a natural poet, linguist, comedian* &c. **6.** In accordance with one's usual habits, not put on, genuine; simple, easy, unstudied; contrasted with *artificial, affected*: *to speak in a natural voice*; *a natural way of speaking*; *a natural manner*; *natural expression of face*. **7.** **a** In accordance with the nature of the individual temperament; characteristic of: *he behaved with the bravery that was natural to him*; **b** in accordance with one's ordinary experience, practice, habits &c.; normal, usual; habitual, familiar: *it seems quite natural to see you once more in your old place*; *it is hardly natural for a lively young man to remain silent in a social gathering*. **8.** In accordance with human nature; springing from impulses implanted in man by nature; arising from circumstances and conditions determined by processes of nature: *natural affection, feeling*; *it is natural for children to love their parents*; Phr. *natural laws, rights, duties, obligations* &c., as binding apart from legislation, customs, or institutions, e.g. the right to life and freedom, duty of parent to child; *natural guardian*, the parent or nearest relative. **9.** In accordance with a person's usual, normal, healthy state of mind or body: *her flushed face didn't look natural to me*; *his pulse was quick, but that is natural to him*; *a* *complexion of the natural colour of health*; *not in a natural state of mind.* **10.** (mus.) Without flats or sharps in the signature: *natural key,* that of C major.

natural (II.), n., fr. prec. **1.** Person born without normal intelligence or sense; an idiot. **2.** (mus.) **a** A white note on the keyboard of a pianoforte or organ; **b** musical note which is not a sharp or flat; **c** graphic expression of this. **3.** (card games) Two cards which on being dealt amount to a winning number without further drawing, as in *vingt et un,* where an ace, counting eleven, plus a ten or court card amount to twenty-one.

naturalism, n. [1. náchuralizm; 2. nǽtʃərəl-izəm]. **natural** & **-ism.** **1. a** Imaginary condition of life and society shaped, as it is supposed, by the free play of the purely natural instincts of man; **b** system of conduct, thought, law &c., based on the natural instincts. **2.** (theol. and philos.) Doctrine that natural or physical laws are sufficient to explain religion and the universe without divine revelation or purpose; denial of the supernatural. **3.** (art and liter.) Attempt to realize absolute fidelity to nature, by a literal and unidealized representation of life, or of natural objects; realism.

naturalist, n. [1. náchuralist; 2. nǽtʃ(ə)rəlist]. **natural** & **-ist.** **1.** Student of external nature, esp. of living organisms; *field naturalist,* one who studies the life and habits of animals and plants in the place where they live or grow. **2.** Adherent of the doctrine of naturalism, **a** in philosophy and religion; **b** in art.

naturalistic, adj. [1. nàchuralístik; 2. nǽtʃərəl-ístik]. Prec. & **-ic.** **a** Closely resembling nature or a natural object; realistic: *naturalistic principles in art*; **b** of or belonging to naturalism in theology and philosophy.

naturalistically, adv. [1. nàchuralístikali; 2. nǽtʃərəlístikəli]. Prec. & **-al** & **-ly.** In a naturalistic, realistic, way or manner.

naturalization, n. [1. nàchuralīzáshun; 2. nǽtʃərəlaizéiʃən]. **naturalize** & **-ation.** Act or process of conferring on or acquiring by an alien the rights, privileges, and duties of a citizen or subject of another State.

naturalize, vb. trans. & intrans. [1. náchuralīz; 2. nǽtʃ(ə)rəlaiz]. **natural** (I.) & **-ize.** Cp. Fr. *naturaliser.* **A.** trans. **1.** To confer rights &c. of citizenship on (an alien), to grant naturalization to. **2. a** (of animals or plants) To make natural or native; to acclimatize: *the grey squirrel is now naturalized in and near London*; *the pine has long been naturalized in southern England*; **b** (of foreign words) to adopt and make part of the native language: *many English sporting terms have been naturalized in French.* **B.** intrans. To become naturalized.

naturally, adv. [1. náchurali; 2. nǽtʃərəli]. **natural** (I.) & **-ly.** **1.** According to one's nature; innately: *naturally clever, morose, indolent.* **2. a** Without artificial aid, treatment, or special cultivation; by virtue of the unassisted processes of nature: *plants, animals, thrive naturally in such climates*; **b** as by natural instinct, without difficulty: *he took to swimming quite naturally.* **3.** Without affectation or mannerisms, in accordance with natural instincts: *drop your airs and graces and behave naturally.* **4.** In the ordinary course of events; as might be expected, as a matter of course: *he was too sanguine, and naturally was disappointed*; *you are going to refuse? naturally.* **5.** In accordance with normal, healthy conditions; after the manner of normal health: *I left him sleeping naturally.*

nature, n. [1. náchur; 2. néitʃə]. M.E., fr. O. Fr., fr. Lat. *nātūra,* 'blood-relationship; natural character of a thing; bent, natural disposition; natural propensity; course, order of things; nature, the universe'; fr. base **g̑nāt-* &c., 'to produce', see under **natal,** & cognates there referred to, & **-ure.** **1. a** The sum of forces and agencies at work in the physical, external world; sum of physical processes, of causes and effects which underlie and produce all existing phenomena: *the laws, processes, of nature*; *miracles are often said to be contrary to nature*; **b** (often with cap.) personification of these forces and processes: '*Nature red in tooth and claw With ravine*' (Tennyson, 'In Mem.', lvi. 4); *Nature, that kindly mother of humanity.* Phrs. *to pay one's debt to nature,* to die; *in the course of nature,* according to the natural course of things; *one of Nature's gentlemen,* person of humble origin with noble instincts, and consideration for others; *one of Nature's noblemen,* (ironical) an uncultivated person with outrageously bad manners. **2. a** The external, material world and its phenomena, considered primarily as these manifest themselves to the senses, without reference to the underlying forces, causes, and processes: *a poet, lover, of nature*; '*Looks through Nature up to Nature's God*' (Pope, 'Ess. on Man', iv. 332); **b** representation, expression, treatment of phenomena of the material universe in art. **3.** Primitive state, mode, of life, or condition of existence conceived of as resulting purely from natural processes, and unmodified by intervention from without; a condition unchanged, whether for good or ill, from the pristine state: *savages were formerly considered as simple children of nature*; *eighteenth-century sentimental writers advocated a return to nature.* Phr. *in a state of nature,* completely naked. **4.** Sum of spiritual and intellectual qualities and propensities which make up the character; essential features and elements of character; disposition; specif. **a** (of man) *a generous, gentle, fierce, revengeful, nature*; *it is not in his nature to be treacherous*; *an artistic nature.* Phrs. *human nature,* sum of qualities, instincts, and propensities, mental and physical, peculiar to mankind; *good nature,* amiability, kindness of heart, indulgence of character; (*a crime*) *against nature,* opposed to innate instincts; **b** (of other sentient beings) innate, essential instincts and qualities of behaviour: *it is in the nature of a dog to be faithful to his master*; *cats and dogs have entirely different natures.* **5.** Sum of essential properties and qualities; characteristic: **a** (of material things) *the nature of iron differs greatly from that of wood*; *the nature of gases, of soil* &c.; **b** (of non-material things) *the nature of evidence*; *the nature of mind.* Phr. *from the nature of the case,* given the facts and circumstances. **6.** (variant meaning from **5,** and often hardly distinguishable from it) Kind, sort, variety: *theft is a different nature of crime altogether from murder,* i.e. a crime of a different nature (**5, b**). Phr. *in the nature of,* resembling, of same kind as.

nature deities, gods, n. pl. The forces and phenomena of external nature, such as sun, moon, winds, ocean &c., personified and worshipped.

nature myth, n. Myth or legend based on natural phenomena, such as rising and setting of the sun &c.

nature study, n. Branch of educational training for children, based on the practical study and observation of plant and animal life in the neighbourhood of the school.

nature worship, n. Worship of the personified forces of nature, of nature gods.

naufrageous, adj. [1. nawfrájus; 2. nōfréidž-əs]. Cp. Fr. *naufrage,* 'shipwreck', fr. Lat. *naufragium,* cp. adj. *naufragus,* 'shipwrecked, causing shipwreck', fr. *nāvis,* 'ship', see **naval,** & base **frag-,* 'to break', see **fragment,** & **-ous.** (poet. and archaic) Causing shipwreck: *the naufrageous sea.*

naught, n. & adj. [1. nawt; 2. nōt]. O.E. *nāwiht, nāht,* 'nothing'; M.E. *nauht* &c., fr. *nā-,* see **no** (I.), & *wiht,* 'thing', see **wight.** Spelling variant of **nought.** **a** n. (archaic and poet.) Nothing, usually only in Phr. *all for naught,* for nothing, for no purpose, idly; *cared naught for him*; *set at naught,* to defy; *thing of naught,* worthless, useless; *bring to naught,* to ruin, defeat, as schemes &c.; **b** adj., worthless, useless: *find one's position, wealth &c. naught.*

naughtily, adv. [1. náwtili; 2. nōtili]. **naughty** & **-ly.** In a naughty manner.

naughtiness, n. [1. náwtines; 2. nōtinis]. Next word & **-ness.** **a** (archaic, Bib.) Wickedness: '*in the naughtiness of thine heart*' (1 Sam. xvii. 28); **b** (of children) misbehaviour, disobedience.

naughty, adj. [1. náwti; 2. nōti]. **naught** & **-y.** **1.** (orig.) **a** Worthless, wicked, bad: '*A naughty person*' (Prov. vi. 12); '*very naughty figs*' (Jer. xxiv. 2); **b** specif., guilty of, exhibiting, indecorum, of speech or conduct; improper, indelicate: *a naughty story.* **2. a** (chiefly of children) Mischievous, unruly, disobedient, badly behaved; reverse of *good*: *a naughty little boy*; *put in the corner for being naughty*; **b** (playfully, of adults) *that's very naughty of you.*

naumachy, naumachia, n. [1. náwmaki, nawmákia; 2. nōməki, nōméikiə]. Lat., fr. Gk. *naumakhía,* 'naval battle', fr. *naûs,* 'ship', see **nautical,** & *makhḗ,* 'battle'. See **-machy.** (Rom. antiq.) Spectacle of a mock sea-fight in a flooded arena.

nausea, n. [1. náwsea, náwshea; 2. nōsiə, nōʃiə]. Lat., 'sea-sickness, vomiting', fr. Gk. *nausía,* fr. **nautia,* 'sea-sickness', fr. *naûs,* 'ship'. See **nautical.** **a** Sensation of sickness from any cause; disposition or inclination to vomit; vomiting; qualm; **b** (fig.) mental disgust, feeling of extreme distaste.

nauseate, vb. trans. [1. náwseāt; 2. nōsieit], fr. Lat. *nauseāt-(um),* P.P. type of *nauseāre,* 'to be or feel sick'. See prec. **1. a** To make sick, cause to vomit, cause feeling of disgust or loathing; **b** (obs.) to detest, dislike extremely, feel nausea at: '*I nauseate walking*' (Congreve, 'Way of the World'). **2.** (fig.) To disgust: *his cant and hypocrisy nauseate one.*

nauseating, adj. [1. náwseāting; 2. nōsieitiŋ], fr. Pres. Part. of prec. Causing nausea; disgusting, sickening.

nauseatingly, adv. Prec. & **-ly.** To a nauseating degree; in a manner to nauseate.

nauseous, adj. [1. náwseus, náwshus; 2. nōsiəs, nōʃəs]. **nausea** & **-ous.** Causing nausea, nauseating; disgusting, nasty to taste or smell, sickening; morally revolting.

nauseously, adv. Prec. & **-ly.** In a disgusting, nauseous way.

nauseousness, n. See prec. & **-ness.** State, quality, of being nauseous.

nautch, n. [1. nawch; 2. nōtʃ]. Hind. *nāch,* 'dance', fr. Scrt. *nṛtya,* 'dancing', fr. *nṛt,* 'to dance'. Entertainment of dancing performed by professional dancers; *nautch girl,* Indian dancing girl.

nautical, adj. [1. náwtikl; 2. nōtik(ə)l], fr. Lat. *nautic-(us),* 'of ships or sailors', & **-al**; fr. Gk. *nautikós,* w. same meaning, fr. *naútēs,* 'sailor', *naûs,* 'ship'. The latter is fr. **nāus,* fr. **nāwos*; cp. Scrt. *nāuš,* Lat. *nāvis,* 'ship'. See further under **naval.** Gk. *naútēs* stands for **nāwit-.* Connected with, pertaining to, ships, sailors, and to art and science of navigation: *a nautical yarn*; *nautical almanac,* astronomical tables for use at sea &c.; *nautical mile,* sea mile, geographical mile, $\frac{1}{60}$ of a degree, equivalent to 6080 ft.

nautically, adv. Prec. & **-ly.** In a nautical way or manner.

nautilus, n. [1. náwtilus; 2. nōtiləs]. Lat., fr. Gk. *nautílos,* 'sailor'; also as name of the animal, fr. base **nāw-,* 'ship', as in **nautical.** (zool.) One of two kinds of small marine cephalopods, inhabiting a shell; **a** *paper nautilus* of Mediterranean, formerly supposed to use tentacles as sails; **b** *pearly nautilus* of Far East.

naval, adj. [1. návl; 2. néivl]. Fr. *naval,* fr. Lat. *nāvālis,* 'of or belonging to ships', fr. *nāvis,* 'ship'; cogn. w. Gk. *naûs,* 'ship', see **nautical**; also w. Scrt. *nāuš*; in Gmc. we have O.E. *nōwend,* 'sailor', O.N. *nór,* 'ship', but further connexions are dubious.

a Of, belonging to, connected with, a **navy**, its ships, officers, or men: *naval barracks, hospital*, for members of the navy on shore; *naval brigade*, unit of troops composed of sailors and marines for service on land; *naval officer*, one holding commissioned rank in the navy; *naval reserve*, reserve of officers and men for the navy for service in war, recruited from mercantile marine or by voluntary enlistment; **b** exercised, performed, by the navy: *naval battle, engagement* &c.; *naval power*, sea power.

navalism, n. [1. nāvalizm; 2. néivəlizəm]. Prec. & **-ism**. **a** Policy of advocating and building a powerful navy; sea-power; **b** aggressive policy in international affairs based on sea power, equivalent of 'militarism' on land.

nave (I.), n. [1. nāv; 2. neiv], fr. Lat. *nāv-(em), nāvis*, 'ship', see **naval**; in L. (eccles.) Lat. in symbolical sense of 'the Church of Christ', as exposed to winds & waves; cp. Fr. *nef*, whence the architectural meaning was borrowed; origin fr. external resemblance of a church to upturned keel of ship has been suggested. (archit.) Central part or body of cathedral or church, extending from main, western, door to the choir or chancel, usually separated by pillars and arches from the aisles.

nave (II.), n. O.E. *nafu*; O.H.G. *naba*, Mod. Germ. *nabe*, Du. *naaf*. See further under **navel, omphalos, umbilical**. The central portion of a wheel, from which the spokes branch out, and to which the axle is fixed.

navel, n. [1. nāvl; 2. néiv(ə)l]. O.E. *nafela*, fr. *nafu*, see prec., cp. Germ. *nabel*, Du. *navel*, O.N. *nafli* &c.; Scrt. *nābhila*, Gk. *omphalós*, Lat. *umbilicus*, all w. same meaning. The orig. sense was 'boss, knob', cp. Lat. *umbo*, 'knob; boss on a shield'. All the above words have the twofold meaning of 'navel' & 'boss'. **a** External depression in centre of abdomen of mammals, left by severance of the umbilical cord at birth: *navel cord, string*, umbilical cord; **b** (fig., rare) central point or middle of anything.

navel orange, n. Kind of seedless orange with another small, undeveloped fruit at junction with the stem.

navicular, adj. [1. navíkūlar; 2. nævíkjulə]. L. Lat. *nāviculāris*, fr. *nāvicula*, 'small boat, skiff', dimin. of *nāvis*, 'ship'. See **naval**. (anat.) Boat-shaped, of bones in fore or hind feet of animals; specif., *navicular bone*, in horse's fore-foot; *navicular disease*, inflammatory condition of this.

navigability, n. [1. nàvigabíliti; 2. nævigəbíliti]. **navigable** & **-ity**. State, condition, of being navigable.

navigable, adj. [1. návigabl; 2. nævigəbl]. Lat. *nāvigābilis*, fr. stem *nāvigā-*. See **navigate** & **-able**. **1.** (of waterway) Capable of being sailed, travelled over, or passed by watercraft &c.: *navigable sea, channel, river, canal* &c. **2.** (of vessels) Capable of being sailed, steered, guided, directed, on water, or through the air: *navigable balloon, ship* &c.

navigate, vb. trans. & intrans. [1. návigāt; 2. nævigeit]. Lat. *nāvigāt-(um)*, P.P. type of *nāvigāre*, 'to sail', lit. 'to drive a ship', fr. *nāvi-*, 'ship', see **naval**, & base **ag-*, 'to drive' &c. See **agent**. **A.** trans. **1.** (of persons) **a** To cause to sail, or travel, in a desired course and direction, any kind of water- or air-craft, on the water, or in the air; to sail, pilot: *to navigate a ship* &c.; **b** (fig.) to direct a measure, negotiation &c. through its various stages: *to navigate a bill through Parliament*. **2. a** (of persons) To pass over the water, through a channel, or in the air; in a vessel: *to navigate the seas* &c.; **b** (of vessels) to be steered, directed, sailed, across the sea, up a river, through a channel &c. **B.** intrans. To engage in navigation; to be navigated.

navigating officer, n. [1. návigāting òfiser; 2. nævigeitiŋ ɔ́fisə]. The officer, esp. on a ship of war, whose business is to direct the course of the ship, and who gives all the orders concerned with her management and handling while at sea.

navigation, n. [1. nàvigā́shun; 2. nævigéiʃən]. Through Fr., fr. Lat. *nāvigātiōn-(em)*, 'sailing, directing, a ship'. See **navigate** & **-ion**. **1.** The act of navigating water- or air-craft. **2.** Art, science, of navigating, of directing the course of ships, or of air-craft, by charts, nautical almanacs, observation of sun and stars &c. **3.** Passage of ships &c. over particular area of sea, air, or through river, canal, or other waterway; process of being navigated; voyage, voyaging: *ice has stopped all navigation*; *inland navigation*, by river or canal; *navigation of the globe*. **4.** That which is navigated; shipping, ships collectively: *navigation through Suez Canal has increased*. **5.** (obs.) Navigable passage.

Navigation acts, laws, n. pl. (hist.) Name of various British measures adopted for protection of national mercantile marine and expansion of trade.

navigator, n. [1. návigātur; 2. nævigèitə]. Lat., 'sailor'. See **navigate** & **-or**. **1.** One who navigates a ship &c.; the navigating officer of a vessel. **2.** A skilled, experienced sailor, one who has taken part in many voyages, esp. of early explorers: *Henry the Navigator*, Portuguese prince, 1394–1460; *Arctic navigators* &c. **3.** Treatise on practical navigation.

navvy, n. [1. návi; 2. nævi]. Abbr. of prec. *Navigator* was the name formerly given to workmen engaged on making canals or 'navigations', i.e. of passages that could be navigated. A labourer engaged in heavy manual, unskilled work of all kinds, as on making of roads, sewers &c.; *steam navvy*, one of various mechanical devices for heavy excavation work. Phrs. *to work like a navvy*, to toil laboriously at some task, esp. at one that is uncongenial; *mere navvy's work*, mechanical, laborious drudgery, which does not demand originality or subtlety of mind.

navy, n. [1. nāvi; 2. néivi], fr. O. Fr. *navie*, 'fleet of ships, ship', Lat. *nāvia*, late variant of *nāvis*, 'ship'. See **naval**. **1. a** Collective name for the warships of a nation or state; **b** the establishment, including ships, officers, men, dockyards, administrative staff &c., of a nation's power at sea: (in both senses **a** and **b**, usually with capital initial letter) *the Royal (British) Navy*. **2.** A fleet of ships, either of war or (now usually historical) of the mercantile marine: *the navies of Venice, of Solomon* &c. **3.** The department of State which administers a nation's power at sea; the Admiralty: *the navy must cut down its cost*.

navy blue, adj. & n. Very dark blue, of shade of naval uniforms.

Navy League, n. Private association formed to advocate, and secure, the maintenance of a powerful British navy.

navy list, n. Official publication containing list of naval officers.

nawab, n. [1. nahwáwb, nahwáhb; 2. nawɔ́b, -ɑ́b]. Hind., fr. Arab. *nāwwāb*, pl. of *nā'ib*, 'lieutenant, deputy-governor'; **nabob** is a variant of this. Differentiated in meaning from *nabob*, and used as a hereditary title conferred upon Indian princes and gentlemen.

nay, particle & n. [1. nā; 2. nei]. Early M.E. *nai*, a Scand. variant of Engl. **no (III.)**, cp. O.N. *nei*, 'no', used in Engl. as an emphatic neg. **1.** particle. **a** (archaic or provinc.) No; **b** (archaic or liter.) vaguely argumentative, or reflective, in introducing a statement or argument, as: *nay, shall we not rather say* &c. Phr. *to say a person nay*, to refuse his request. **2.** n. In Phr. *let your yea be yea and your nay be nay* &c.

Nazarene, n. & adj. [1. nàzarḗn; 2. næzərín]. Lat. *Nazarēnus*, Gk. *Nazarēnós*, 'inhabitant of Nazareth', in Palestine. **a** Name given to Jesus Christ, because His early life was spent in Nazareth; **b** a Christian, as used by Jews and later by Moslems, as follower of Jesus of Nazareth.

Nazarite, n. [1. názarīt; 2. næzərait]. Lat. *Nazaraeus*, Gk. *Nazaraios*, fr. Heb. *nāzar*, 'to separate oneself from, vow to abstain from', & **-ite**. A Hebrew ascetic or devotee, vowed to celibacy, to abstain from wine, and from cutting the hair and beard.

naze, n. [1. nāz; 2. neiz]. O.E. *næss*, 'promontory'; connected w. *nosu*, 'nose'. See also **ness** & **nose**. Promontory; cliff projecting into the sea; headland.

nazim, n. [1. nā́zim; 2. néizim]. Hind. & Arab., 'governor', fr. Arab. *nazm*, 'order'. The title of a high police official in India and Moslem countries.

nazir, n. [1. nā́zēr; 2. néiziə]. Hind. & Arab. *nāzir*, 'overseer', fr. Arab. *nazar*, 'to observe, see'. Title of various Indian, chiefly Moslem, officials in Indian courts.

-nd, suff. forming adjs. & ns.; **a** fr. Lat. gerundives ending in *-nd-(us)*, meaning 'to be (done)'; *dividend*, 'that which is to be divided'; *reverend*, 'to be revered'; **b** fr. Lat. words in gerundial form: *jocund, moribund*; **c** in Engl. ns., fr. old Pres. Part. termination *-and*: *friend*; *fiend*.

-nda, pl. suff. for ns.; Lat. gerundive neut. pl.; in words taken direct fr. Lat.: *propaganda*, 'things to be propagated, published'; *agenda*, 'things to be done'.

neaf, n. [1. nēf; 2. nīf]. Scand., cp. O.N. *knefi*, 'fist'. (obs. or dial.) Hand, fist: '*Give me your neaf*' (Shakespeare, 'Midsummer Night's Dream', IV. i. 20).

Neanderthal, adj. [1. nāándertahl; 2. neiǽndətāl]. (anthrop.) Of or belonging to the Neanderthal, a valley near Düsseldorf, Germany; specif., of very primitive human skull found there: hence, *Neanderthal man*, type of very early palaeolithic man, as represented by this skull.

neap (I.), adj. & n. [1. nēp; 2. nīp]. O.E. *nēp*, in *nēpflōd*, 'neap flood'; etymol. doubtful; possibly connected w. **nip (I.)**, 'pinch', hence 'scanty, low'. **1.** adj. Of tide, *neap tide, neap-tide*, that at end of first or third quarter of the lunar month, when the distance between high and low water marks is shortest; a very low tide; contrasted with *spring tide*. **2.** n. A neap tide: *tides are at the neap*.

neap (II.), vb. trans. & intrans., fr. prec. **a** trans. (usually in pass.) To be caught by a neap tide: *ships are neaped*, i.e. cannot sail till next spring tide; **b** intrans., (of tides) to begin to move towards the neap.

Neapolitan, adj. & n. [1. nēapólitan; 2. nìəpɔ́litən], fr. Lat. *Neāpolītānus*, 'of or belonging to Naples', fr. Gk. *Neāpolis*, 'the new town'. **1.** adj. Of, belonging to, Naples: esp. *Neapolitan ice*, an ice-cream, made in layers of various flavours and colours; *Neapolitan violet*, a very fragrant double variety of the violet. **2.** n. Inhabitant of Naples.

near (I.), adv. & prep. [1. nēr; 2. niə]. O.E. *nēar*, adv., compar. of *nēah*, 'nigh'; M.E. *nēr, neer*; later *near* became a positive adv. w. new compar. *nearer*; this change was helped by O.N. *nǣr*, 'near', also orig. compar. of *nā*, 'nigh'. See further under **nigh**. **1.** adv. **a** Close to, at, within, a short distance from, of; in proximity to, not far from (of place): *to come near*; *the new houses are built too near to us*; (of time) *spring draws near*; *the day of reckoning is getting near*; **b** within a very little of, almost (now obs. or provinc., more usually *nearly*): *near frightened out of their wits*; (with neg.) not anything like: *not near so popular as before*. Phrs. *far and near*, in every direction, everywhere; *near at hand* (of place), close to, within reach; (of time) approximately, not far off: *near upon (six o'clock* &c.), almost six o'clock; *that will go near to (killing him)*, will nearly (kill him). **2.** prep. Close to; expressing **a** propinquity in space: *near the river, the edge of the pavement, the town* &c.: Phr. *to sail near the wind*, to sail close-hauled, close to the wind; (fig.) of just avoiding a breach of the law or dishonourable action &c.; **b** nearness in time: *near sixty years of age*; *near dinner-time*; **c** manner of achievement: *near success, victory* &c.; **d** nearness in condition: *I was very near dead*; **e** nearness in likeness, resemblance or similarity: *the portrait does not come near the original.*

near (**II.**), adj., fr. prec. **1. a** Situated in the neighbourhood, close to in space, adjacent, neighbouring: *the station is quite near*; *how near is the sea from here?*; Phrs. *the Near East*, Turkey and the Balkan States; *the nearest way*, most direct and shortest; *a near thing*, a narrow escape. **2.** Specif., *near side* &c., **a** (of horse) left; the side from which one mounts; **b** left side of a road; **c** side of carriage &c. next to this. **3.** Not far removed in time; approaching, at hand, about to come or happen: *spring is near*; *the end of the struggle is near.* **4.** (of conditions, circumstances) About to be experienced, just coming upon one: *death is near to each of us every day*; *success is nearer than you think.* **5. a** Closely related in blood: *a near relation, connexion*; **b** closely concerned in one's feelings and affections; intimate, familiar: *a near friend*; Phr. *near and dear*, closely connected by ties of relationship and affection; **c** involving one's interests, touching one closely: *that is a very near concern of mine.* **6.** (of persons) Niggardly, mean, parsimonious, close-fisted: *you won't get much out of him, he's very near.*

near (**III.**), vb. trans. & intrans., fr. prec. To approach, come, draw near to: *to near the land* (of ships); *he must be nearing home by now*; *to near one's end*, to be dying.

near by, adv.; **near-by**, adj. Close at hand, adjacent.

Nearctic, adj. [1. nèárktik; 2. niáktik], fr. **neo-** & **arctic**. Term applied to a region including arctic and temperate North America, esp. as applied to botanical and zoological distribution.

nearly, adv. [1. nérli; 2. níəli]. **near** (**II.**) & **-ly**. **1.** Almost, all but, within a short distance, or time &c., of; in large number of usages: *nearly home, nearly there, nearly a mile long*; *nearly five o'clock, nearly time to go*; *nearly killed, nearly done now, nearly enough to eat*; Phr. *not nearly*, by no means, far from, nowhere near. **2.** Closely, intimately: *nearly related*; *nearly concerned* &c.

nearness, n. [1. nérnes; 2. níənis]. **near** (**II.**) & **-ness**. **1.** State, quality, of being near; closeness, proximity, propinquity; **a** (in space) *the nearness of the house to the sea*; **b** (in time) *the nearness of these events to our own time*; **c** in affinity or consanguinity: *nearness of relationship*; **d** in feelings, affections &c.: *his very nearness to her blinded her to his faults.* **2.** Parsimony, stinginess, meanness.

nearsighted, **near-sighted**, adj. [1. nérsíted; 2. niəsáitid]. Shortsighted, myopic.

nearsightedness, n. Prec. & **-ness**. State of being nearsighted; myopia.

neat (**I.**), n. & adj. [1. nēt; 2. nīt]. O.E. *nēat*, M.E. *nēt*; O.N. *naut*, 'cattle'; prob. connected w. O.E. *nēotan*, 'to use, enjoy'; O.H.G. *niozan*, Mod. Germ. (*ge*)*niessen*, 'to enjoy, have the use of'; cogn. w. Lith. *naudà*, 'use, profit'. **1.** n. **a** An animal of the ox kind, as distinguished from sheep, horses &c.; **b** (coll. as pl.) cattle, kine. **2.** adj. Pertaining to the ox kind: *neat cattle*; *neat's foot, neat's tongue*, as articles of food; *neat's foot oil*, an oil from a neat's foot, used for dressing leather, and as lubricant.

neat (**II.**), adj. Earlier *nette*, fr. Fr. *net*, masc., *nette*, fem., 'neat, clean', fr. Lat. *nitid-*(*us*), 'shining, clear; well-favoured, elegant, smart, trim'; cp. *nitēre*, 'to shine'; cp. O. Slav. *gnětiti*, 'to kindle'; prob. also O.E. *gnāst*, 'spark', fr. **gnaist*, fr. **gnaitto*; cp. O.H.G. *gneisto*. **1. a** (of outward appearance) (i.) Elegant, without unnecessary adornment; having every detail carefully arranged; simple, in good taste: *neat costume, dress*; (ii.) well proportioned, trim: *a neat figure*; **b** clean, well kept, orderly: *her house was always very neat*; *neat in one's person.* **2.** Well formed, well proportioned and arranged; carefully finished: *neat handwriting.* **3. a** (of actions) Skilful, dexterous, cleverly done: *a neat stroke*; *a neat piece of work*; *to make a neat job of it*, do something skilfully and satisfactorily; **b** (of utterances) apt, to the point, polished: *a neat speech, retort* &c.; **c** (of persons) doing, speaking, skilfully and aptly, or capable of so doing and speaking: *a neat workman, speaker* &c. **4.** (of alcoholic liquor) Pure, unmixed, not diluted with water. **5.** (obs.) Without deduction, now usually *net.*

'neath, prep. [1. nēth; 2. nīþ]. Poet. for **beneath**.

neat-handed, adj. Clever, quick, with the hands; deft, dexterous.

neat herd, **neat-herd**, n., fr. **neat** (**I.**) & **herd** (**II.**). Cow-herd, tender of cattle.

neatly, adv. [1. nétli; 2. nítli]. **neat** (**II.**) & **-ly**. In a neat manner: *dressed neatly*; *neatly turned verses.*

neatness, n. [1. nétnes; 2. nítnis]. See prec. & **-ness**. Condition or quality of being neat; **a** tidiness; **b** spruceness, smartness of appearance; **c** skill, dexterity; aptness.

neb, n. [1. neb; 2. neb]. O.E. *nebb*, 'beak, snout, face', cogn. w. O.N. *nef*, cp. Dan. *næb*, 'beak, nose'; cp. also **nib** (**I.**). (Scots) Beak, bill, of a bird; nose; point, tip.

nebula, n. [1. nébūla; 2. nébjulə]. Lat., 'mist, fog, cloud', fr. base **nebh-*, 'mist, rain', cogn. w. Gk. *nephélē*, 'cloud', dimin. of *néphos*, 'cloud' (cp. **nephology**), cp. Scrt. *nabhuš*, 'sky, air, cloud'; O.N. *nifl-*, 'mist', O.E. *nifol*, 'dark'. See also **nimbus, imbricate**. **1.** (astron.) A luminous, fixed, cloud-like patch in the sky, consisting of incandescent, gaseous matter; also applied to a cluster of stars having the appearance of a true nebula. **2.** A whitish speck on the cornea of the eye.

nebular, adj. [1. nébūlar; 2. nébjulə]. Prec. & **-ar**. (astron.) Of or pertaining to nebulae; resembling, like, a nebula: specif., *nebular hypothesis*, theory that the planetary and stellar systems originated from nebulae or masses of incandescent, gaseous matter.

nebulé, adj. See **nebuly**.

nebulium, n. [1. nebūlium; 2. nebjúliəm], fr. **nebula**. The name given to an unidentified element indicated by two green lines in the spectra of nebulae.

nebulosity, n. [1. nèbūlósiti; 2. nèbjulósiti]. Fr. *nébulosité*, fr. **nebulous** & **-ity**. **1. a** Condition of being nebulous; something which is nebulous; a nebula. **2.** Cloudiness, vagueness, indefiniteness, in thought and expression.

nebulous, adj. [1. nébūlus; 2. nébjuləs]. Lat. *nebulōsus*, 'cloudy'. See **nebula** & **-ous**. **1.** (astron.) Having the qualities of, resembling, a nebula: *nebulous cluster* (of stars); *nebulous star*, one with a nebula about it or in close proximity. **2. a** Cloudy, clouded, misty; not clear or pellucid; **b** (fig., of state of mind, ideas &c.) hazy, vague, indefinite.

nebuly, **nebulé**, adj. [1. nébūli; 2. nébjuli]. Fr. *nébulé*. See **nebula**. **a** (her.) Of a charge on a coat of arms consisting of a line of rounded curves, supposed to represent clouds; **b** (archit.) undulating, wavy (of a moulding).

necessarian, adj. See **necessitarian**.

necessarily, adv. [1. nésesarili; 2. nésisərili]. **necessary** & **-ly**. Of necessity, as a necessary consequence or result; inevitably; of course.

necessary (**I.**), adj. [1. nésesari; 2. nésisəri]. M.E. *necessarie*, fr. Fr. *nécessaire*, fr. Lat. *necessārius*, 'inevitable, necessary; indispensable, needful', fr. *necesse*, indecl. adj., 'unavoidable, inevitable, necessary' &c.; fr. **ne-cēd-tis*, *ne*, neg. particle, & *cēd-*, as in Lat. *cēdere*, 'to yield', see **cede**; ultimately the word means 'not to be turned aside'. **1. a** Following as the natural effect of a cause; inevitable, certain to happen: *heat is a necessary result of friction*; *the necessary consequence of an action*; Phr. *a necessary evil*, something unpleasant which has to be borne or tolerated; **b** following as logical consequence: *a necessary conclusion, inference.* **2. a** Not to be done without; indispensable, requisite: *food is necessary for life*; *your help is absolutely necessary*; *my friends are necessary to my happiness*; Phr. (archaic) *necessary house*, a privy; **b** obligatory, compulsory, enjoined by law: *passports are necessary for all who visit foreign countries*; *it is necessary that the wicked should be punished.*

necessary (**II.**), n., fr. prec. **1.** That which is necessary or essential for a specific purpose: *a motor-car is a necessary of life nowadays*; *necessaries of existence* &c. **2.** (law) A thing or things which are necessary for the support of a minor, married woman, lunatic, or other dependent in the condition suitable to his or her social position.

necessitarian, n. & adj. [1. nesèsitárian; 2. nisèsitéəriən]. **necessity** & **-arian**. **1.** n. One who believes in the doctrine of necessity; one who holds the ethical doctrine that actions and volitions are determined by preceding causes and motives and not by free-will; determinist. **2.** adj. Of or belonging to the doctrine of necessity.

necessitarianism, n. [1. nesèsitárianizm; 2. nisèsitéəriənizəm]. Prec. & **-ism**. Doctrine held by necessitarians; determinism.

necessitate, vb. trans. [1. nesésitāt; 2. nisésiteit], fr. L. Lat. *necessitāt-*(*um*), P.P. type of *necessitāre*, 'to make necessary'. See **necessity**. **1.** To render necessary or unavoidable; to compel: *the prisoner's violence necessitated his being handcuffed.* **2.** To involve as a logical consequence: *your assumptions necessitate your conclusions.*

necessitous, adj. [1. nesésitus; 2. nisésitəs]. **necessity** & **-ous**. Poor, indigent, needy, destitute: *necessitous persons*; *in necessitous circumstances*; *necessitous areas*, poverty-stricken districts.

necessity, n. [1. nesésiti; 2. nisésiti], fr. Fr. *nécessité*, fr. Lat. *necessitāt-*(*em*), *necessitas*, 'inevitableness; destiny; poverty', fr. *necesse*, see **necessary**, & **-ity**. State, quality, of being necessary. **1.** Set of circumstances compelling something to be, or to be done; especially this regarded as a law of the universe, inseparable from, and directing, human life and action; often, *physical necessity*, compulsion, constraint, fate, destiny: *to bow to necessity*; *there is no necessity* (*to do so and so*), no compulsion to do. Phrs. *necessity knows no law*, conditions of emergency override law; *under the necessity of* (*doing*), compelled to do; *to make a virtue of necessity*, to submit with good grace to that which is inevitable; *necessity is the mother of invention*, if something absolutely must be done a way of doing it will be found; *of necessity*, necessarily, as a matter of course. **2. a** Something which takes place in accordance with the laws of thought, which cannot be conceived as not being or happening: *logical necessity*; *such a conclusion follows as a necessity from the premises*; **b** that which inevitably occurs, as result of natural causation; principle governing this: *heat follows friction as a necessity.* **3.** *Doctrine of necessity*, that which denies the freedom of the will and asserts that all actions are conditioned by the laws of cause and effect. **4. a** Something which is absolutely necessary for human life and cannot be dispensed with: *food and warmth are necessities*; **b** something which has become necessary by custom or habit: *we regard as necessities many things which our fathers had never heard of*; *harmful drugs once indulged in soon become necessities.* **5.** Poverty, want, indigence: *to be in dire necessity.*

neck (**I.**), n. [1. nek; 2. nek]. O.E. *hnecca*, O.N. *hnakki*, 'nape of the neck', cp. Du. *nek*, Germ. *nacken*, 'neck'. **1. a** That part of the body in man and other animals which joins the head to the trunk; **b** often used to include the upper part of a woman's chest and shoulders when these are exposed. Phrs. *to break the neck of* (*a piece of work, job* &c.), to get the worst part over; *to save one's neck*, lit., to escape hanging or execution; to escape the consequences of a mistake, error, or misdeed; *get it in the neck* (slang), (i.) to undergo a severely painful or unfortunate experience of any kind; (ii.) to be severely attacked, injured, punished, censured; *neck and crop*, altogether, bag and baggage: *throw him out neck and crop*; *neck and neck* (orig. of horse-racing), side by side, so close together that there is little to choose between two competitors; *neck or nothing* (orig. of riding to hounds), taking great risks in an emergency, such as involve either complete success or failure; *a stiff neck*, obstinacy, persistency in sin or error; so *stiff-necked*, obstinate; **c** portion of garment, encircling or covering the neck; **d** neck of an animal considered as article of food: *neck of mutton*. **2.** Applied to various objects supposed to resemble a neck in shape; narrow connecting part: **a** *neck of a bottle, retort* &c., the narrow portion below the orifice; **b** *neck of a capital*, a narrow moulding at the lower part; **c** *neck of a golf club*, the part of the head into which the shaft is fitted; **d** *neck of a violin* &c., narrow part between the scroll and the body, the part held by the left hand in playing; **e** *a neck of land*, a narrow connecting strip between two larger areas of land; **f** a narrow channel of water; a strait.

neck (**II.**), n. Etymol. doubtful; prob. not the same as prec. The last sheaf reaped at harvest, formerly carried home with ceremony.

neckband, n. [1. nékband; 2. nékbænd]. That part of a shirt which goes round the neck, to which the collar is attached.

neckcloth, n. [1. nékklawth; 2. nékklɔþ]. (archaic) Scarf for the neck; neckerchief.

neckerchief, n. [1. nékerchif; 2. nékətʃif]. **neck** (**I.**) & **kerchief.** (archaic) Scarf for the neck.

necking, n. [1. néking; 2. nékiŋ]. **neck** (**I.**) & **-ing.** (archit.) The moulding or mouldings round the top of the shaft of a column below the capital.

necklace, n. [1. néklis, -las; 2. néklis, -ləs]. **neck** (**I.**) & **lace.** A string of jewels, or beads, or a chain of gold &c., worn as an ornament round the neck.

necklet, n. [1. néklit; 2. néklit]. **neck** (**I.**) & **-let.** **a** Ornament worn round the neck; necklace; **b** covering for the neck, collar of fur or the like.

necktie, n. [1. néktī; 2. néktai]. **neck** (**I.**) & **tie** (**I.**). A narrow scarf of silk or other material, worn round the neck, over, or within the fold of, shirt-collar, and tied in a bow or knot in front.

neck-verse, n. The verse, usually the first verse of Ps. li., beginning *Miserere mei*, which those who claimed Benefit of Clergy had to read as a test of their learning.

neckwear, n. [1. nékwār; 2. nékwɛə]. **neck** (**I.**) & **wear.** (vulg., or shop term) Collective name for neckties, scarves, and collars.

necro-, pref. Used to form compounds, fr. Gk. *nekrós*, 'dead body, corpse', also *nékus*, cogn. w. Scrt. *naśati* &c., 'is ruined, vanishes'; Lat. *nex*, 'murder, slaughter', *necāre*, 'to kill'; cp. also Lat. *noxius*, 'hurtful', see **noxious.**

necrobiosis, n. [1. nèkrōbīósis; 2. nèkroubaióusis]. Prec. & Gk. *bíōsis*, 'manner of life, living', *bios*, 'life', see **biology.** Decay, atrophy of tissue in a living body.

necrolatry, n. [1. nekrólatri; 2. nɛkrɔ́lətri]. **necro-** & **latry.** Worship of the dead.

necrology, n. [1. nekróloji; 2. nɛkrɔ́lədži]. **necro-** & **-logy.** **a** Register of deaths, esp. of the members of monastery or other society; **b** obituary notices collected together.

necromancer, n. [1. nékromànser; 2. nékrəmænsə]. See next word & **-er.** One who practises necromancy; a wizard, sorcerer.

necromancy, n. [1. nékromànsi; 2. nékrəmænsi]. Gk. *nekromanteíon, -eia*, 'oracle of the dead', fr. *nekrós*, 'a corpse', see **necro-**, & *manteía*, 'oracular response', fr. *mántis*, 'soothsayer', see **-mancy**; M.E. & O. Fr. *nigromancie*, 'magic, black art', show confusion between Gk. *nekro-*, & Lat. *niger*, 'black'. **a** Divination by communication with the spirits of the dead; witchcraft, sorcery; **b** magic, esp. 'black magic'; 'the black art', so called from the early false etymology.

necromantic, adj. [1. nèkromántik; 2. nèkrəmǽntik]. See prec. & **-ic.** Practising necromancy or witchcraft.

necrophagous, adj. [1. nekrófagus; 2. nɛkrɔ́fəgəs]. See **necro-** & **-phagous.** Feeding on dead bodies or carrion; specially used of various insects and bacteria.

necrophobia, n. [1. nèkrofóbia; 2. nèkrəfóubiə]. **necro-** & **-phobia.** **a** Exaggerated dread of death; **b** horror of dead bodies.

necropolis, n. [1. nekrópolis; 2. nɛkrɔ́pəlis]. Gk. *nekrópolis*, 'city of the dead'. See **necro-** & **policy, politic.** **a** A cemetery, esp. one belonging to an ancient city or site of prehistoric habitation; **b** a large modern cemetery.

necropsy, n. [1. nékròpsi; 2. nékrɔ̀psi]. Gk., *nekrós*, 'corpse', see **necro-**, & *ópsis*, 'sight', see **optic.** Examination of a dead body; a post-mortem examination, autopsy.

necroscopy, n. [1. nekróskupi; 2. nɛkrɔ́skəpi], fr. **necro-** & **-scopy.** Necropsy.

necrosis, n. [1. nekrṓsis; 2. nɛkróusis], fr. Gk. *nékrōsis*, 'state of death'. See **necro-** & **-osis.** Death and decay of a portion of bodily tissue, esp. of bone; mortification, gangrene.

necrotic, adj. [1. nekrótik; 2. nɛkrɔ́tik]. See prec. & **-ic.** Mortifying, gangrenous.

nectar, n. [1. néktar; 2. néktə], fr. Gk. *néktar*, 'drink of the gods', prob. fr. base *nek-*, 'death', see **necro-**, as the drink which conferred immortality. **1.** (Gk. mythol.) The drink of the immortal gods. **2.** Any sweet, delicious drink; a wine of very high quality. **3.** Specif. (bot.) the sweet, sugary liquid secreted by the nectaries of plants, from which bees get honey.

nectarean, adj. [1. nektā́rean; 2. nɛktéəriən]. Prec. & **-ean.** Nectareous.

nectared, adj. [1. néktard; 2. néktəd]. **nectar** & **-ed.** Sweet as nectar; filled with nectar.

nectareous, adj. [1. nektáreus; 2. nɛktéəriəs]. Lat. *nectareus*, Gk. *nektáreos*, fr. *néktar*, 'nectar', q.v. Of the nature or quality of nectar; delicious, sweet.

nectariferous, adj. [1. nèktaríferus; 2. nèktəríferəs]. **nectar** & **-ferous.** (bot.) Yielding, secreting, nectar: *nectariferous glands*, of plants, the nectaries.

nectarine (**I.**), adj. [1. néktarin; 2. néktərin]. See **nectar** & **-ine.** (archaic or poet.) Nectareous.

nectarine (**II.**), n., fr. prec., so called from its delicious taste. A fruit closely resembling a peach, but with a thinner, smoother skin, and without the down of the former.

nectary, n. [1. néktari; 2. néktəri], fr. **nectar** & **-y.** **a** (bot.) The organ in flowers which secretes honey, or nectar; **b** (zool.) tube in the aphis or green-fly, formerly thought to collect and secrete the juice from plants.

necto-, pref. Used to form compounds, fr. Gk. *nēktós*, 'swimming', fr. *nḗkhein*, 'to swim', formed w. suff. *-khō*, or *-ghō*, fr. base **snā-*, 'to flow', seen also in Gk. *náein*, Lat. *nāre*, 'to swim'; see **naiad, natation**; *nectocalyx*, the swimming disc or bell of a jelly-fish; *nectogale*, fr. Gk. *galê*, 'weasel', the Tibetan swimming-shrew.

necton. See **nekton.**

Neddy, n. [1. nédi; 2. nédi]. Familiar form of *Edward.* A donkey.

née, adj. [1. nā; 2. nē, nei]. Fr., 'born', P.P. fem. of *naitre*, 'to be born', fr. Lat. *nasci*, *nāt-(a)*, see **natal.** Born, by birth, used to indicate a married woman's maiden name: 'Mrs. Brown, *née* Robinson'.

need (**I.**), n. [1. nēd; 2. nīd]. O.E. *nīed, nēd, nēod* &c., 'inevitableness; compulsion; requirement; hardship'; M.E. *nēde*; O.S. *nōd*; O.H.G. *nōt*; Goth. *nauþs.* **1.** Conditions, state of affairs, circumstances, in which there is a deficiency, or insufficiency of something; **a** urgent necessity, imperative requirement: *there is a great need of money, ships, and men*; *to be in need of help*; *there is need for more patience and goodwill on both sides*; *the hour of need*; *to fail a man in his need*; Phr. *a friend in need is a friend indeed*; **b** a requirement, want; something desired or felt to be necessary: *I'm in need of a match*; *the house is in need of a coat of paint*; *bodily and spiritual needs.* **2.** Felt want of, and desire for something: *to have need of a rest*; *to feel the need of stimulants*; *your need is greater than mine.* **3.** Compelling circumstance, compulsion, obligation, necessity: *is there any need to hurry?*; *there is no need for him to work.* **4.** Lack, insufficiency, of financial means; poverty, indigence, destitution.

need (**II.**), vb. trans. & intrans., fr. prec.; O.E. *nēodian.* See prec. **1.** trans. To want, require, be in need of: *he needs a wash, washing*; *I shall need a new suit for the wedding*; *we shall need every penny we can get*; *the book needs correction*; also ironic: *what he needs is a good thrashing*, that is, what he deserves. **2.** As auxiliary, **a** (uninflected and followed by uninflected infin., in interrog. and neg. sentences) to be necessary, be obliged, must: *need he come?*; *need I obey?*; *you needn't do it if you don't want to*; *we need not go into that now*; **b** (inflected and followed by *to* and infin., in affirmative sentences or neg. and interrog. sentences in periphrastic construction) *one needs to be careful*; *he didn't need to be told twice*; *does he need to know?* **3.** intrans. **a** To be in want or distress: *give to them that need*; **b** (obs. or archaic) to be necessary: *it needs not*; *what needs it?*

needful, adj. [1. nḗdfool; 2. nídfəl]. **need** (**I.**) & **-ful.** **1.** Necessary, requisite; indispensable: *do what is needful*; *the needful equipment.* Phr. *to do the needful*, to do what is necessary in specified case; (slang) *the needful*, money. **2.** (obs. or archaic) Characterized by need: *the needful time of trouble.*

needfully, adv. Prec. & **-ly.** Necessarily.

needfulness, n. See prec. & **-ness.** State or quality of being needful.

neediness, n. [1. nḗdines; 2. nídinis]. **needy** & **-ness.** State of being needy; want, destitution.

needle (**I.**), n. [1. nḗdl; 2. nídl]. O.E. *nǣdl*, M.E. *nēdel*; O.H.G. *nādala*; Goth. *nēþla*; O.N. *nāl*; cogn. w. O.H.G. *nājan*, 'to sew', Mod. Germ. *nähen*; the base is that seen in Lat. *nēre*, 'to spin, weave'; Gk. *néein*, 'to spin', also *nēma*, 'that which is spun, thread', cp. Lat. *nēmen*; perh. fr. *(*s*)*nēi-*, 'to weave, intertwine', cp. Scrt. *snāyati*, 'wraps up', & *snāyu*, 'tendon, sinew, string'; perh. cogn. w. Gk. *neûron*, 'nerve', for **snēuro-* (see **neur(o)-**). **1.** **a** An implement for sewing, consisting of a thin, usually rounded, piece of steel with one end sharpened to a point and the other pierced with a hole or eye, through which the thread is passed; Phrs. *as sharp as a needle*, intellectually penetrating; *to get, have, the needle*, (slang, rare) to have the hump, be depressed; *pass through the eye of a needle*, pass through the narrowest of entrances, from Matt. xix. 24; *look for a needle in bundle of hay*, try to find small thing in a mass of other things, or a person among a crowd; **b** (i.) thin rod or wire of metal, bone, or wood without an eye, or with rounded end, for knitting; (ii.) or with hooked end, for crochet work; **c** the sharp, hollow point of a hypodermic syringe. **2.** **a** The balanced magnetized bar of steel in a compass, pointing to the pole; **b** similar magnetized bar in a telegraphic instrument. **3.** Any of various objects which resemble a needle in being thin and pointed;

a the thin, pointed leaf of the pine or fir; **b** a tapering pinnacle of rock; **c** an obelisk: *Cleopatra's Needle*; **d** a pointed crystal or piece of ice; **e** a small bar of wood or metal used to support a beam in shoring or underpinning.

needle (II.), vb. trans. & intrans., fr. prec. (obs. or rare) **1.** To sew, ply the needle (on); to thread one's way (through). **2.** Specif., to treat (cataract) with an instrument resembling a needle.

needle-bar, n. The bar in a sewing or knitting machine to which the needles are attached.

needle-bath, n. Shower-bath in which the water is forced under pressure in fine jets.

needle-book, -case, n. Book or case for holding needles.

needle-fish, n. A fish, such as the garfish, with thin body and long, pointed head and jaw.

needleful, n. [1. nḗdlfool; 2. nídlful]. Amount of thread carried by a needle at one time.

needle-gun, n. Early form of breech-loading rifle, in which the detonator was a needle or pin acting on the fulminate in the cartridge.

needle-lace, n. Lace made with a needle and not with bobbins.

needle point, n. **1.** The sharp point of a needle, or of instrument sharpened to a similar fine point. **2.** Point-lace made with a needle.

needless, adj. [1. nḗdles; 2. nídlis]. **need (I.)** & **-less**. Unnecessary, superfluous: *needless work; needless to say, he never came*; unprovoked: *needless enmity, abuse* &c.

needlessly, adv. Prec. & **-ly**. Unnecessarily, superfluously.

needlessness, n. See prec. & **-ness**. Quality, condition, of being needless: *the needlessness of their alarm*.

needlewoman, n. [1. nḗdlwooman; 2. nídlwumən]. A woman who sews or does needlework; a seamstress.

needlework, n. [1. nḗdlwērk; 2. nídlwāk]. Work done with the needle; sewing; embroidery.

needments, n., pl. [1. nḗdments; 2. nídmənts]. On anal. of *requirements*. What is needed; things wanted for specific purpose, as luggage &c. for a journey.

needs, adv. [1. nēdz; 2. nīdz]. O.E. *nȳdes, nēdes*, adverbial genit. See **need (I.)**. Of, by, necessity; necessarily; only used before or after *must*: *he needs must* (*do* &c.), he is compelled to; (sarcastic) *he must needs* (*go away just when he was wanted* &c.); Phr. *needs must when the devil drives*.

needy, adj. [1. nḗdi; 2. nídi]. **need (I.)** & **-y**. Poor, indigent, necessitous, in want or need; impecunious: *the poor and needy*.

neem, n. [1. nēm; 2. nīm]. Hind. *nīm*. The margosa.

ne'er, adv. [1. nār; 2. nɛə]. See **never**. (poet.) Never.

ne'er-do-well, -weel, n. [1. nḗr doo wel, -wēl; 2. nɛ́ə du wel, -wiəl]. An improvident, dissipated, worthless, good-for-nothing fellow.

ne exeat (regno), n. [1. nḗ éksiat (régnō); 2. ní ɛ́ksiæt (régnou)]. Lat., 'let him not go out of (the kingdom)'. (law) Name of a High Court writ forbidding a person against whom an action is pending to leave the country.

nef, n. [1. nef; 2. nef]. Fr., 'ship', fr. Lat. *nāvis*. See **nave (I.)**. A table ornament of silver or silver-gilt, in the form of a ship, used in mediaeval and later times for holding salt, napkins, spoons &c.

nefarious, adj. [1. nefā́rius; 2. niféəriəs]. Lat. *nefārius*, 'wicked, impious', fr. *nefās*, 'crime, wrong', fr. *ne-*, negative pref., & *fās*, 'divine law', cogn. w. *fāri*, 'to speak, say'. See this base under **fable**. Unlawful, unjustifiable; wicked, iniquitous: *nefarious ends, purpose* &c.

nefariously, adv. Prec. & **-ly**. Wickedly, iniquitously.

nefariousness, n. See prec. & **-ness**. Wickedness, iniquity.

negate, vb. trans. [1. nēgā́t; 2. nīgéit], fr. Lat. *negāt-(um)*, P.P. type of *negāre*, 'to deny'; formed fr. Lat. **neg*, 'no, not', cp. Lith. *negù, negì*, 'not'. Cp. Germ. *verneinen*, fr. *nein*, 'no'. To deny the existence of; involve or imply that something is not; to nullify, be equivalent to a negative of what has been affirmed.

negation, n. [1. nēgā́shun; 2. nīgéiʃən], fr. Fr. *négation*, fr. Lat. See prec. & **-ion**. **1.** Act of denying; denial; assertion that a thing is not, has not been, will not be; opposite of *affirmation*. **2.** Absence of any positive quality or meaning; destruction; annihilation: *arbitrary action is the negation of order and justice*. **3.** (log.) Definition of a term by stating what it is not, by excluding it from a class; e.g. *no negroes are Europeans*.

negationist, n. [1. negā́shunist; 2. nigéiʃənist]. Prec. & **-ist**. One who is content merely to deny beliefs commonly held without putting anything positive in their place.

negative (I.), adj. [1. négativ; 2. négətiv], fr. Fr. *négatif*, fr. L. Lat. *negātīvus*. See **negate** & **-ive**. **1.** Expressing denial; prohibiting, refusing; saying 'no' to; opposite of 'affirmative': *a negative answer, reply, vote; negative order, command; they assumed a negative attitude; the right of veto only gives negative powers; negative evidence*, such as does not affirm anything or supply a new fact. **2.** Not possessing qualities of which anything can be affirmed; not affirming or proving anything; having the effect of removing, diminishing, denying; privative; opposed to *positive*: *negative value, criticism* &c.; *a negative character; negative qualities; to say 'no news is good news' is a negative sort of comfort*; (colloq.) *a negative quantity*, nothing. **3.** Specif. (elect.) of or belonging to that kind of electricity produced by rubbing resin, wax, or vulcanite, *resinous* or *negative electricity*, anciently supposed to be due to a want of the electric fluid, contrasted with *vitreous* or *positive electricity*; now of electricity where the current flows to a higher potential; *negative pole*, that from which the negative, and to which the positive, current flows; cathode. **4.** (log.) Denying the identity of one term with another: *negative proposition*, one that contains such denial. **5.** (math.) Of or belonging to quantity subtracted from another; minus: *negative sign*, minus sign. **6.** (photog.) Reversing the lights and shades: *negative plate, film*, a negative (q.v.).

negative (II.), n. See prec. **1.** Word or particle expressing denial, contradiction, refusal, prohibition, as *no, not, neither* &c. **2.** Statement, answer, proposition, decision, which denies, refuses, forbids &c.: *I reply with a resolute negative*. Phr. *the answer is in the negative*, that is, 'no'. **3.** Specif. **a** (elect.) the plate in an electric battery opposite to the positive plate; **b** (photog.) prepared plate or film which on exposure to light shows a print in which the dark and light shades of the object are reversed; **c** (math.) a minus quantity.

negative (III.), vb. trans., fr. **negative (I.)**. **1.** To reject, refuse, a proposal, motion &c.; to veto; to reply in the negative to. **2.** To prove untrue, disprove: *experience negatives the theory*. **3.** To make of no effect, render useless; offer opposition to, neutralize: *the deep mud negatived all efforts to advance*.

negatively, adv. **negative (I.)** & **-ly**. **a** In a negative manner; so as to deny or refuse; **b** in a manner involving the absence of something; not positively: *negatively friendly*, i.e. not actively hostile.

negativeness, n. See prec. & **-ness**. State, quality, of being negative.

neglect (I.), vb. trans. [1. neglékt; 2. nigléktl], fr. Lat. *neglect-(um)*, P.P. type of *negligere*, (*neglegere*), 'to be indifferent to, disregard, neglect', fr. **neg-*, **nec-*, 'not', see **negate**, & prob. a word **leg-*, cogn. w. that in Gk. *alégein*, 'to trouble oneself, have a care, heed', cp. *álgos*, 'pain' (see **-algia**), cp. also Lat. *dīligere*, 'to esteem highly', see **diligent**. **1.** To pay no heed or attention to, take no care of; to treat as of no importance; to leave uncared for or unattended; to disregard, slight, pass over: *neglect one's business, duties, appointments, the law, rules, orders, one's family, children, one's friends, supporters; neglect criticism, annoyance, worries; neglect an author's works*. **2.** To omit, fail to do: *he neglected to wind up the clock, to verify his quotations*.

neglect (II.), n. Lat. *neglectus*, n. See prec. **1.** Act of neglecting; want of care or attention; negligence, disregard, carelessness, indifference: *neglect of one's duties, law* &c.; *neglect of home, children* &c.; *neglect of consequences; to treat with neglect*. **2.** State of being neglected; condition showing neglect: *her children were in a terrible state of neglect*.

neglectful, adj. [1. negléktfool; 2. nigléktful]. Prec. & **-ful**. Negligent, careless, heedless: *lazy and neglectful; neglectful of one's family, duties* &c.

neglectfully, adv. Prec. & **-ly**. In a negligent way; negligently.

neglectfulness, n. See prec. & **-ness**. State of being neglectful; negligence.

négligé, negligee, n. & adj. [1. néglizhā; 2. néglizei]. Fr. *négligé*, P.P. of *négliger*. See **neglect (I.)**. **1.** n. A loose robe, such as a dressing-gown; easy, informal style of dress. **2.** adj. Careless, informal, off-hand: *he treated me in a very négligé manner*.

negligeable, adj. See **negligible**.

negligence, n. [1. néglijens; 2. néglidžəns]. Fr. *négligence*, fr. Lat. *neglegentia*, 'negligence'; See next word & **-ce**. **1. a** Conduct springing from a careless, neglectful state of mind; heedlessness, carelessness, lack of attention, indifference to duties and obligations &c.; **b** specif. (law) lack of reasonable care: *culpable negligence*. **2.** Result of such neglectful conduct; state showing inattention and heedlessness; hence, disorder, neglected condition and appearance &c.: *the negligence of one's attire* &c.

negligent, adj. [1. négligent; 2. néglidžənt]. Fr. *négligent*, fr. Lat. *negligent-(em)*, Pres. Part. of *negligere*. See **neglect (I.)**. Neglectful, careless; not attending to duties, appearance &c.; remiss: *negligent in work, in dress; negligent of his duties*.

negligently, adv. Prec. & **-ly**. In a negligent manner.

negligibility, n. [1. nèglijibíliti; 2. nèglidžibíliti]. See next word & **-ity**. Quality of being negligible.

negligible, negligeable, adj. [1. néglijibl; 2. néglidžibl]. Fr. *négligeable* &c.; see **negligent** & **-ible, -able**. That may be neglected; not worth considering; of no importance: *a negligible person; a negligible amount*, a very slight amount.

negotiability, n. [1. negṓshiabíliti; 2. nigòuʃiəbíliti]. See next word & **-ity**. State, quality, of being negotiable.

negotiable, adj. [1. negṓshiabl; 2. nigóuʃiəbl]. See next word & **-able**. **1.** Able to be negotiated; specif. (law) *negotiable instruments*, such as bills of exchange, cheques, promissory notes &c. which are transferable by delivery and give to a *bona fide* holder for value without notice complete title to their value. **2.** Capable of being traversed, of affording a passage (of roads, means of approach &c.).

negotiate, vb. trans. & intrans. [1. negṓshiāt; 2. nigóuʃieit], fr. Lat. *negōtiāt-(um)*, P.P. type of *negōtiāri*, 'to trade, traffic'; fr. *negōtium*, 'lack of leisure; business, employment, trade' &c.; fr. **neg-*, 'not', see **negate**, & *ōtium*, 'leisure', see **otiose**. **A.** trans. **1. a** To arrange, as a matter of business, by discussion, bargaining, and the like: *to negotiate a loan, terms of peace* &c.; **b** to change, get cash for a security: *to negotiate a bill of exchange* &c. **2.** To contrive to surmount an obstacle, or to gain a passage over, or along: *to negotiate a mountain, a bad bit of road* &c. **B.** intrans. **1. a** To engage in trafficking, discussion, bargaining, with a view to arranging a business matter, coming to an agreement &c.; specif. **b** to enter into discussion with an enemy with a view to arranging terms of peace. **2.** *Negotiate with,* **a** to discuss, bargain, carry on business discussions with; **b** to discuss terms of peace with.

negotiation, n. [1. negōshiā́shun; 2. nigouʃiéiʃən]. See prec. & **-ation**. Cp. Lat. *negōtiātio,* 'business by wholesale, banking'. Act of negotiating; conference and discussion of an agreement, treaty, understanding &c.

negotiator, n. [1. negṓshiàtur; 2. nigóuʃièitə]. Lat., 'one who conducts a business; agent, factor, banker'. See **negotiate** & **-or**. One who negotiates; member of one of two parties in conference.

negress, n. [1. nḗgres; 2. nígris]. **negro** & **-ess**. A female of negro race.

negrillo, n. [1. negrílō; 2. nigrílou]. Span., dimin. of **negro**. Member of a pygmy negroid race of Equatorial Africa.

negrito, n. [1. negrḗtō; 2. nigrítou]. Span., dimin. of **negro**. **1.** A member of aboriginal, dark, dwarfish race, inhabiting the Philippines, Andaman Islands, and Malay Peninsula. **2.** (cap.) Name given to a racial stock or group including the negrillos of Africa and the negritos of Asia.

negro, n. & adj. [1. nḗgrō; 2. nígrou]. Span., 'black', fr. Lat. *nigrum,* acc. case of *niger,* 'black'; etymol. doubtful; possibly remotely connected w. O.E. *nīpan,* 'to grow dark', & *ġenip,* 'darkness'. **1.** n. **a** Member of an African race, characterized chiefly by woolly hair, a flat nose, protruding jaw, thick lips, and a skin ranging in colour from dark brown to jet black; **b** (loosely) member of various negroid races of Africa, such as the Bantus &c.; also applied to member of black African races generally whether negroid or not. **2.** adj. Of, or belonging to, negroes: *the negro race; the negro question,* in U.S.A.

negro head, n. A special kind of very dark plug tobacco, treated with molasses.

negroid, adj. & n. [1. nḗgroid; 2. nígroid]. **negro** & **-oid**. **a** adj. Resembling, related to, the negro race by admixture of blood or by having same characteristic features or some of them; **b** n., member of a negroid race.

negroidal, adj. [1. nēgróidal; 2. nīgróidəl]. Prec. & **-al**. Negroid.

negroism, n. [1. nḗgrōizm; 2. nígrouizəm]. **negro** & **-ism**. **1.** Support of the cause of negroes or the negro race. **2.** Negro idiom, custom, habit &c.

negrophil, n. [1. nḗgrōfil; 2. nígroufil]. **negro** & **-phil**. One who supports the cause of negroes or the negro race.

negrophobia, n. [1. nēgrōfṓbia; 2. nìgroufóubiə]. **negro** & **-phobia**. Fear, dislike, of negroes or the negro race.

Negus (I.), n. [1. nḗgus; 2. nígəs], fr. Abyssinian *n'gus,* 'king'. Title of the sovereign of Abyssinia.

negus (II.), n., fr. name of inventor, Colonel Francis Negus, d. 1732. Beverage of sweetened and spiced wine and hot water; esp. *portwine negus.*

neigh, vb. intrans. & n. [1. nā; 2. nei]. O.E. *hnǣġan,* prob. imitative word, cp. O.N. *hneggia,* M.H.G. *negen.* **a** vb. To utter the cry of a horse; **b** n., the cry of a horse.

neighbour (I.), n. [1. nā́bur; 2. néibə]. O.E. *nēahġebūr, nēahbūr,* fr. *nēah,* 'nigh, near', & *ġebūr, būr,* 'husbandman, peasant'; O.H.G. *nāhgibūr,* Mod. Germ. *nachbar.* See **nigh** & **boer** & cp. **boor**. **1. a** One who lives near to one: *a next-door neighbour; one's nearest neighbours;* **b** such a person regarded from point of view of the degree of friendliness which he displays: *a good, bad, neighbour;* **c** one of several objects of similar kind situated near to each other: *a house and its neighbours.* **2.** Person occupying temporarily a place next, or near to one: *one's neighbour at dinner; I had very noisy neighbours last night.* **3.** Member of the society, in widest sense, in which one lives; one to whom one owes duties as a fellow man: *one's duty to one's neighbour.*

neighbour (II.), vb. trans. & intrans., fr. prec. Rare except in Pres. Part. See **neighbouring**. To adjoin, approach, be near to, border on: *the wood neighbours (upon) the lake.*

neighboured, adj. [1. nā́burd; 2. néibəd]. **neighbour** (I.) & **-ed**. (rare) Having neighbours, situated in a neighbourhood, of a specified kind: *a friendly, sparsely, neighboured place.*

neighbourhood, n. [1. nā́burhood; 2. néibəhud]. **neighbour** (I.) & **-hood**. **1.** State of being adjacent, close, near; proximity: *the neighbourhood of the railway is a drawback.* Phr. *in the neighbourhood of,* (of amount, quantity, number &c.) about, nearly: *in the neighbourhood of a thousand tons.* **2. a** District, area, position, adjacent to some specified place or object: *in the neighbourhood of London; meadows in the neighbourhood of the river; I would rather not live in the neighbourhood of the gas-works;* **b** specif., the region adjacent to that in which one lives; country and district surrounding one's house; often specif., *the neighbourhood; our neighbourhood is a beautiful one; we live in a healthy, a good sporting neighbourhood; our new house is good but we don't like the neighbourhood.* **3.** The district in which one lives considered as a social centre; one's neighbours collectively: *a friendly, sociable, lively, dull, neighbourhood; the laughing-stock of the whole neighbourhood.* **4.** (archaic or provinc.) Neighbourly feeling; good fellowship, sociability; neighbourliness: *in a town one misses the neighbourhood of a country village where one knows everybody.*

neighbouring, adj. [1. nā́buring; 2. néibəriŋ]. As though fr. Pres. Part. of *to neighbour.* Adjacent, situated in the neighbourhood; lying, placed, near together: *two neighbouring counties; we live in neighbouring houses.*

neighbourless, adj. [1. nā́burles; 2. néibəlis]. **neighbour** (I.) & **-less**. Without neighbours.

neighbourliness, n. [1. nā́burlines; 2. néibəlinis]. Next word & **-ness**. Quality of being neighbourly; sociability, kindliness, such as one expects from one's neighbours.

neighbourly, adj. & adv. [1. nā́burli; 2. néibəli]. **neighbour** (I.) & **-ly**. **1.** adj. Like a neighbour; displaying the qualities expected in a good neighbour; kind, sociable, friendly. **2.** adv. (rare) In a neighbourly manner, as befits neighbours: *to live neighbourly with others.*

neither, adj., pron., adv., & conj. [1. nídher; 2. náiðə], less usually [1. nḗdher; 2. níðə]. M.E. *neither, neyther, naither;* cp. O.E. *nāhwæðer, nāwðer, nāðor,* 'neither of two', fr. *ne,* 'not', *āhwæðer,* 'either of two', fr. *ā-,* 'always, ever' (see **aye**), & *hwæþer,* 'which of two', see **whether**; the present-day & M.E. forms are not fr. the O.E., but as fr. *ne,* 'not', & *either,* see **either**. Not either; not the one nor the other of two alternatives. **1.** (as adj.) *He took neither side in the dispute; accept neither offer; neither tree must be felled; neither party is confident; neither statement is true.* **2.** (as pron.) *Will you take sherry or hock? Neither; neither of the statements is true; neither of the witnesses knows what happened.* **3.** (as adv.) **a** Followed by co-ordinate sentence or word preceded by *nor,* negativing both of two alternatives: *one can neither stand up nor lie down; neither advancing nor retreating; neither one thing nor the other;* '*She neither hears nor sees*' (Wordsworth). Note—with two nouns or pronouns the verb agrees with the latter: *neither his father nor his mother is living; neither I nor he is, neither he nor I am, aware of;* **b** (archaic or illit., at end of sentence as emphatic neg.) '*Twas not a crown neither*' (Shakespeare, 'Julius Caesar'); *he give me a sovereign? No, nor a shilling neither.* **4.** (as conj.) And not, negativing both clauses: '*They toil not, neither do they spin*'; introducing a negative sentence following another expressed or understood: '*Neither do I tell you by what authority I do these things*' (Mark xi. 33).

nek, n. [1. nek; 2. nɛk]. S. Afr. Du. for 'neck'; cogn. w. **neck**. A neck, pass, col, in a range of mountains, esp. in South African Place-Names, as *Laing's Nek.*

nekton, n. [1. nékton; 2. néktən], fr. Gk. *nēktos,* 'swimming', see **necto-**. Term used, in oceanography, for the free-swimming life of the sea's surface and middle waters, cp. *benthos* and *plankton.*

nelly, n. [1. néli; 2. néli]. Prob. the familiar dimin. of the female name *Ellen* or *Eleanor.* Sailor's name for the giant fulmar.

nemato-, pref., fr. Gk. *nēmat-,* stem of *nēma,* 'thread', fr. *néein,* 'to spin'. See **needle**. (zool.) Form used in compounds. Having, resembling, threads or filaments.

nematocyst, n. [1. nématosist; 2. némətəsist]. Prec. & **cyst**. Cell containing the thread-like sting of a jelly-fish.

nematode, nematoid, n. & adj. [1. némətōd, -toid; 2. némətoud, -toid]. **nemato-** & **-ode, -oid.** (zool.) **a** n. Member of a group of thread-like worms, *Nematoda,* chiefly parasitic, as the guinea-worm; **b** adj., *nematode worm,* a nematode.

Nemesis, n. [1. némesis; 2. némisis]. Gk. *némesis,* 'righteous indignation, anger, at what is unjust'; also personified as the goddess of retribution; fr. *némein,* 'to deal out to, distribute'; cogn. w. Gk. *nómos,* 'anything assigned; custom, convention; law', see **anomo-**; cp. further, Lat. *numerus,* 'number' &c., see **numerous, number**. **1.** (class. antiq.) The goddess of retribution; esp. as visiting with disaster pride arising from undeserved prosperity and good fortune. **2.** Retributive justice, esp. the fate which overtakes folly or misconduct.

nemine contradicente (abbr. *nem. con.*), advbl. phr. [1. némine kòntrādisénte; 2. nímini kɔ̀ntreidaisénti]. Lat. *nēmine,* abl. sing. of *nēmo,* 'no one', fr. *ne hemo,* 'no man', & *contrādicente,* abl. sing. Pres. Part. of *contrādicere,* 'dissent, contradict'. No one dissenting or voting against; said of motion or resolution brought before a meeting &c.: *carried nem. con.*

nemophila, n. [1. nemófila; 2. nemɔ́filə]. Coined fr. Gk. *némos,* 'glade in a wood', & *philos,* 'loving'. Cp. **philo-**. The first element is cogn. w. Lat. *nemus,* 'grove; sacred grove', apparently fr. base *nem- &c., 'vault, curve, arch'; cp. O. Ir. *nem,* 'sky'; Scrt. *namaś,* 'bending; curve; reverence'. **a** Annual garden plant, having bright blue flowers with white centre; **b** (bot., cap.) genus of plants including the above, *N. insignis.*

nenuphar, n. [1. nénūfar; 2. nénjufā]. Fr., L. Lat., fr. Pers. *nīnūfar,* earlier *nīlupar,* 'water-lily, lotus'; Scrt. *nīlōtpala,* 'the blue lotus', *nīla,* 'blue', & *utpala,* 'lotus'. The white or yellow water-lily.

neo-, pref. [1. nḗō; 2. níou], fr. Gk. *néos,* 'new'; for *newo-, cogn. w. O.E. *nēowe* &c., 'new', see **new**. New, recent, later, revived, with or without modification: **a** (as in art) *neo-classic, neo-Gothic,* of revived classic and Gothic art and architecture; **b** (geol. &c.) recent: *Neocomian,* fr. *Neocomium,* Lat. for Neuchâtel, Switzerland, of the Lower Cretaceous system; *Neogene,* geological period including the Miocene and Pliocene; *Neotropical,* of a region and the animals inhabiting it, which includes South and Central America and tropical part of North America; *neozoic,* of the third great period of geological time; **c** (of language) *neo-Latin,* of the Romance languages as descended from Latin; **d** (philos. &c.) *neo-Hegelian,* of modern followers of Hegel; *neo-Lamarckian,* of modern revival and modification of Lamarck's theory of the origin of the variety of species; *neo-Malthusian,* of revival of Malthus and his theory of population. The prefix is used quite freely, sometimes with a slightly derogatory sense, as of new-fangled or of unnecessary revival of old ideas &c.

neolith, n. [1. nḗolith; 2. níəliþ], fr. **neo-** & Gk. *lithos*, 'stone', see **litho-**. A neolithic implement.

neolithic, adj. [1. nèolíthik; 2. niəlíþik]. Prec. & **-ic**. Of or belonging to a primitive period or age of civilization following the *palaeolithic*; of the later Stone Age, characterized by the use of polished, highly finished tools and weapons.

neologian, n. [1. nèolṓjian; 2. niəlóudžiən]. See **neology** & **-an**. (theol.) Adherent of neologism in theology; neologist.

neologism, n. [1. nēólojizm; 2. niɔ́lədžizəm]. **neology** & **-ism**, or direct fr. Fr. *néologisme*. **1. a** Use, invention, introduction, of a new word or idiom, or the use of a common word with a new meaning; **b** (i.) new word or idiom; (ii.) word or idiom used in new sense. **2.** (theol.) Adoption or support of rationalistic new views in theology.

neologist, n. [1. nēólojist; 2. niɔ́lədžist]. **neology** & **-ist**. One who practises neologism or neology.

neologize, vb. intrans. [1. nēólojīz; 2. niɔ́lədžaiz]. **neology** & **-ize**. To practise neologism or neology in either sense.

neology, n. [1. nēóloji; 2. niɔ́lədži]. **neo-** & **-logy**. **1. a** Practice of coining or using new words or idioms; **b** use with new meaning of words already existing. **2.** (theol.) Novelty in theological doctrine, esp. a rationalistic interpretation of a doctrine.

neon, n. [1. nḗon; 2. níɔn]. Gk. *néon*, neut. sing. of *néos*, 'new'. See **neo-**. (chem.) An inert gas in the atmosphere, discovered in 1898. *Neon light*, a glowing, red light, penetrating fog, obtained by ionizing the gas by passing an electric current through a tube or bulb containing this.

neophyte, n. [1. nḗofīt; 2. níoufait], fr. Eccles. Lat. *neophytus*, fr. Gk. *neóphutos*, lit. 'newly planted', hence 'newly initiated into the mysteries', fr. *néo(s)*, 'new', see **neo-**, & *phutón*, 'plant', cp. *phúein*, 'to grow, bring forth, produce', see **-phyte**. **1.** (Church hist.) One newly baptized and received into the primitive Christian Church; a new convert, a proselyte. **2. a** Newly ordained priest in Roman Catholic Church; **b** a novice in a monastic or other religious order. **3.** A beginner in an art, profession, trade &c.; novice, tiro.

neoplasm, n. [1. nḗoplàzm; 2. níouplæ̀zəm]. **neo-** & **plasm.** (med.) A new formation of tissue; specif., a tumour, or other morbid growth.

neoplastic, adj. [1. nèōplástik; 2. nìouplǽstik]. **neo-** & **plastic.** Pertaining to, of the nature of, a neoplasm.

Neo-Platonism, n. [1. nèō plā́tunizm; 2. nìou pléitənizəm]. **neo-** & **Platonism.** A school and system of philosophy, arising in Alexandria in 3rd cent. A.D., combining some of the doctrines of Greek philosophy, including those of Plato, with the mystical religious ideas of the East.

Neo-Platonist, n. [1. nèō plā́tunist; 2. nìou pléitənist]. Adherent of Neo-Platonism.

neoteric, adj. [1. nèōtérik; 2. nìoutérik], fr. Gk. *neōterikós*, 'youthful, fresh', fr. *neṓteros*, compar. of *néos*, 'new', see **neo-**, & **-ic.** Newly invented, modern, new-fangled.

neozoic, adj. [1. nèōzṓik; 2. nìouzóuik]. Gk. See **neo-**, 'new', & **zoo-**, fr. Gk. *zōḗ*, 'life', & **-ic.** (geol.) Belonging to, designating, the whole period of time from the *Mesozoic* to the present geological age.

nepenthe, n. [1. nepénthe; 2. nəpénþi], fr. Lat. *nēpenthes*, n., Gk. *nēpenthés*, adj., 'dispelling pain or grief', applied in Homer to a narcotic drug, possibly opium; fr. *nē-*, neg. pref., & *pénthos*, 'pain, grief', variant of base in Gk. *páthos*, 'pain, suffering'. See **pathos. 1.** Drug which gives relief from pain; (also fig.) that which relieves grief or sorrow or induces forgetfulness. **2.** (bot.) The Pitcher-plant, *Nepenthes distillatoria.*

nepheline, n. [1. néfelin; 2. néfəlin], fr. Gk. *nephélē*, 'cloud', cogn. w. Lat. **nebula,** & **-ine.** A mineral found in form of crystals in volcanic rocks, showing a cloudy appearance when treated with acids.

nephew, n. [1. névū; 2. névju]. M.E., fr. O. Fr. *neveu*, fr. Lat. *nepōt-(em)*, 'grandson, descendant', also later 'nephew'. See **nepotism. 1.** Son of one's brother or sister. **2.** (obs.) **a** Grandchild, as 1 Tim. v. 4 (A.V.); **b** cousin (Shakespeare, 1 Henry VI. II. v.). **3.** Formerly used, euphemistically, of a natural son, esp. of a Pope; cp. *nepotism.*

nephology, n. [1. nefóloji; 2. nefɔ́lədži]. Gk. *néphos*, 'cloud', see **nepheline** & **nebula,** & **-logy.** Branch of meteorology concerned with the study of clouds.

nephrite, n. [1. néfrīt; 2. néfrait], fr. Germ. *nephrit*, fr. Lat. (*lapis*) *nephriticus*, fr. Gk. See next word. Scientific name of one of the two varieties of jade, so called from its earlier use as an amulet against disease of the kidneys; it is a calcium magnesium silicate.

nephritic, adj. [1. nefrítik; 2. nefrítik], fr. Gk. *nephrītikós*, 'of or belonging to the kidneys', fr. *nephrós*, 'kidney'; cogn. w. Lat. *nefrōnes*, 'kidneys'; O.H.G. *nioro*, Mod. Germ. *niere*, 'kidney'; all fr. *$neg^{wh}r$-. Cp. also Aryan base *$eneg^{w}$-, whence Lat. *inguen*, 'groin', see **inguinal.** Belonging to, affecting, the kidneys; renal: *nephritic stone*, renal calculus.

nephritis, n. [1. nefrítis; 2. nefráitis]. Gk. *nephrós*, see prec., & **-itis.** Inflammation of the kidneys; Bright's disease.

nephro-, pref. Form of Gk. *nephrós*, 'kidney', used in compounds. See **nephritic.**

ne plus ultra, n. [1. nē plus últra; 2. ni plas áltrə]. Lat., 'not further (more) beyond'. Point which one cannot surpass or go beyond; limit of excellence, acme.

nepotism, n. [1. népotizm; 2. népətizəm]. Fr. *népotisme*, Ital. *nepotismo*, fr. Lat. *nepōt-*, stem of *nepōs*, 'nephew', & **-ism**; cp. Scrt. *napāt*, 'grandson, descendant'; Lith. *nepùtis*, 'grandson'; O.E. *nefa*, 'grandson, nephew'. Cp. also Lat. *neptis*, 'niece', q.v. under **niece,** & see **nephew.** Favouritism shown to relatives, esp. in the matter of appointment to highly paid offices or sinecures; specif. (hist.) the lavish favours showered by some of the Mediaeval and Renaissance Popes upon their natural children, who were known euphemistically as their 'nephews'.

nepotist, n. [1. népotist; 2. népətist]. Prec. & **-ist.** One who practises nepotism.

Neptune, n. [1. népchōōn, -tūn; 2. néptʃən, -tjūn]. Lat. *Neptūnus*, 'the sea god; the sea'; perh. cogn. w. O. Pers. *napta-*, 'damp'; Scrt. (*a*)*naptaś*, 'not damp'. (astron.) Name of the most distant planet of the solar system, except Pluto, q.v.

Neptunian, adj. [1. neptū́nian; 2. neptjúniən]. Prec. & **-ian. 1.** Pertaining to Neptune. **2.** (geol.) **a** Formed by the agency of water; **b** pertaining to the views of the Neptunists.

Neptunist, n. [1. népchoonist; 2. néptʃunist]. **Neptune** & **-ist.** (geol.) Adherent of the view that the action of water has played a principal part in the formation of rocks.

Nereid, n. [1. nḗreid; 2. níəri-id], fr. Gk. *Nērēid-*, stem of *Nērēís*, name of a sea-nymph, 'daughter of Nereus', a sea-god; fr. *nērós*, *nārós*, 'wet', fr. same base, **sna-*, as in **naiad.** (zool.) A member of a genus of marine worms.

nero-antico, n. [1. nā́rō antḗkō; 2. néro antíko]. Ital., fr. *nero*, 'black', & *antico*, 'antique, ancient'. Name of a fine black marble found in ancient Roman buildings.

neroli, n. [1. nā́roli; 2. néərəli]. Ital., fr. name of discoverer. Oil obtained by distillation of orange flowers.

nervation, n. [1. nërvā́shun; 2. nʌvéiʃən]. See **nerve (I.)** & **-ation.** (bot. and zool.) System, arrangement, of the veins in a leaf, or in the wing of an insect.

nerve (I.), n. [1. nërv; 2. nʌv]. Lat. *nervus*, 'sinew, tendon; cord, string of bow', cp. Gk. *neûron* for **sneuro-*, 'sinew, string &c.; nerve'; possibly extended fr. base *nē-*. See **needle.** Alternatively, connexion w. O.E. *nearu* (see **narrow**) has been suggested, but is very doubtful. **1.** (only fig.) Sinew, tendon; in Phr. *to strain every nerve*, to make tremendous efforts. **2.** (anat. or physiol.) One of the cord-like fibres, or a bundle of fibres, composed of nerve-cells, which transmit sensations to the brain and volitional impulses from it to various parts of the body, forming, as a whole, the nervous system. **3.** State of the nervous system as exhibited in mental and physical condition; **a** healthy condition, hence self-command, firmness, energy, vigour; courage, assurance, self-confidence: *a man of nerve*; *nerves of iron, steel* &c.; *to have the nerve* (*to do*), (i.) be courageous enough (to do); (ii.) (colloq.) have assurance, impudence; **b** (usually pl.) unsound nervous condition, timidity, apprehension, excitability, jumpiness, irritability; depression: *to suffer from nerves*; *a fit of nerves*; *to get on one's nerves*, make one irritable or jumpy; *to have no nerves*, to be imperturbable in face of danger; *he doesn't know what nerves are*, is not troubled by timidity or fear. **4.** (bot. and zool.) Rib or vein in a leaf; vein in the wing of an insect.

nerve (II.), vb. trans., fr. prec. **a** To give, impart, physical or moral strength and vigour; to make strong; to embolden: *despair nerved his arm*; **b** *to nerve oneself*, to brace oneself, collect one's energies, summon up courage &c. for an effort.

nerve-cell, n. Cell of tissue of which a nerve is composed.

nerve centre, n. Collection of nerve-cells; ganglion.

nerveless, adj. [1. nërvles; 2. nʌ́vlis]. **nerve (I.)** & **-less. 1. a** Without energy, vigour, or courage; feeble, weak, slack: *his arm fell nerveless to his side*; **b** (fig.) *a nerveless style.* **2.** Without nerves; **a** (anat.) having no nervous system; **b** (bot.) having no veins on the leaf.

nervelessly, adv. Prec. & **-ly.** In a nerveless, weak manner.

nervelessness, n. See prec. & **-ness.** Condition or quality of being nerveless.

nerve strain, n. Excessive tension or stress laid upon the nervous system or a particular nerve.

nervine, adj. & n. [1. nërvēn; 2. nʌ́vīn], fr. **nerve (I.)** & **-ine.** (med.) **a** adj. Having an effect on the nerves; **b** n., drug affecting the nerves, esp. as a calming agent.

nervous, adj. [1. nërvus; 2. nʌ́vəs], fr. Lat. *nervōsus*, 'sinewy, vigorous, strong'. See **nerve (I.)** & **-ous. 1.** (anat. and physiol.) Concerned with, pertaining to, the nerves; affecting the nerves: *nervous system*, system, arrangement, of the nerves collectively; *nervous diseases*, those affecting the nerves; *a nervous breakdown*; *nervous excitement, irritability.* **2.** Having nerves in an unsound condition; **a** suffering from affections of the nervous system; **b** (in non-physical sense) (i.) apprehensive, timid; (ii.) excitable, highly strung, irritable. **3. a** Having strong sinews; vigorous, strong; well knit: *strong nervous arms, frame*; **b** (fig.) strongly, tersely, composed; vigorous: *a nervous style.*

nervously, adv. Prec. & **-ly.** In a nervous manner (in various senses).

nervousness, n. See prec. & **-ness.** State, condition, of being nervous; esp. apprehensiveness, timidity.

nervure, n. [1. nërvūr; 2. nʌ́vjə]. **nerve (I.)** & **-ure.** (bot. and zool.) A rib, line in a leaf, or in wing of an insect.

nervy, adj. [1. nërvi; 2. nʌ́vi]. **nerve (I.)** & **-y.** (colloq.) Nervous, full of nerves, easily excited, jumpy.

nescience, n. [1. nésiens; 2. nésiəns]. Next word & **-ce. a** Want of knowledge, ignorance; **b** specif., want of certainty of the existence or non-existence of God or a Divine creator; agnosticism.

nescient, adj. [1. nésient; 2. nésiənt], fr. Lat. *nescient-(em)*, Pres. Part. of *nescīre*, 'not to know'; *ne-*, 'not', *scīre*, 'to know'. See **science.** Not knowing, ignorant.

ness, n. [1. nes; 2. nɛs]. O.E. *næs*, 'headland, promontory'; prob. cogn. w. O.E. *nasu*, 'nose'. See **nasal & nose.** Headland, promontory; now chiefly surviving in Place-Names, as *Dungeness, Skegness, Holderness.*

-ness, suff. [1. nis; 2. nis]. O.E. *-nes(s), -nis, -nys*; O.S. *-nissi*; O.H.G. *-nissa, -nassi*; the suff. was orig. *-assi* &c., the *-n-* being part of the stem of preceding word; cp. Goth. *þiudinassus*, 'kingdom', fr. *þiudan-s*, 'king'. Suff. commonly used to form abstract ns., expressing **a** condition or quality, from adj.: *bitterness, coldness, goodness* &c.; also **b** something exhibiting a particular quality: *a brightness in the eye* &c. In *witness* the suff. forms a concrete n. The suff. is used with the utmost freedom, almost any adj. being capable of producing a n. by its use. It is constantly used to form ns. fr. adjs. of Fr. or Lat. origin: *horribleness, gentleness, dulcetness* &c.

nest (I.), n. [1. nest; 2. nɛst]. O.E. & M.E. *nest*; O.H.G. *nest*; cogn. w. Lat. *nīdus*, 'nest', fr. earlier **nizdo-*, the ultimate origin is fr. **ni*, 'down', cp. **nether**, & *-sd-*, vanishing grade of base **sed-*, 'to sit', see **sedate & sit. 1. a** Structure built by a bird in which it lays its eggs, and hatches out and rears its young; Phrs. *a stolen nest*, clutch of eggs laid by domestic hen elsewhere than in proper nesting box; *to feather one's nest*, to get rich in some way or other, usually with an implication of rather dishonest means; *to foul one's own nest*, to behave discreditably in one's own house; to disparage, belittle, criticize adversely one's own family, or an institution with which one is connected; **b** a breeding-place constructed by egg-laying animals, such as certain insects, as wasps, ants &c., by spiders and by certain fish, as sticklebacks, and reptiles, as turtles; **c** shelter made by female rat or mouse for rearing its young. **2.** The contents of nest, the eggs and young; swarm, brood: *to take a nest*, rob it of its eggs, or young birds; (also fig.) *a nest of vipers*; *nest of singing-birds*, of the lyric poets of the Elizabethan period. **3.** A warm, snug shelter or retreat: *a comfortable nest for one's old age.* **4.** (gen. in unfavourable sense) Place frequented by people of a certain class or character; haunt, den, breeding-place: *a nest of pirates*; *nest of crime and vice.* **5. a** Series of boxes &c. which fit into one another; **b** set of small drawers or shelves contained within a single frame.

nest (II.), vb. intrans. & trans., fr. prec. **1.** intrans. **a** (of birds) To build a nest, to lay eggs and begin hatching them; settle in, occupy, a nest: *the birds are beginning to nest*; **b** to hunt for birds' nests: *boys have gone nesting.* **2.** trans. (rare) To place, put, in a nest.

nest-egg, n. **1.** An egg, either real or a dummy, left in the nest of a fowl to encourage laying. **2.** Money saved and put by for emergencies, or to form basis of a fund.

nestle, vb. intrans. & trans. [1. nésl; 2. nésl]. O.E. *nestlian*, 'to build a nest'. See **nest** (I.) & **-le. 1.** intrans. To lie close in or against anything, as a bird does in its nest; to settle down snugly, cosily, in or among; to move, press, closely against: *nestle down in bed*; *nestle in the grass*; *child nestles against its mother's breast.* **2.** trans. To place, press, move against: *baby nestles its head against its mother.*

nestling, n. [1. nés(t)ling; 2. nés(t)liŋ]. **nest** (I.) & **-ling.** A young bird not fully fledged, and still unable to leave the nest.

Nestor, n. [1. néstor; 2. néstə]. Name of an old king in Homer's *Iliad* renowned for his wise counsel. **1.** One who is able to give wise advice by reason of his age and experience. **2.** (zool.) Genus of New Zealand parrots, including the kaka and kea.

Nestorian, adj. & n. [1. nestórian; 2. nɛstórian]. Lat. *Nestoriānus*, of *Nestorius.* **1.** adj. **a** Of or pertaining to Nestorius, Syrian patriarch of Constantinople in 5th cent. A.D., who gave his name to the heresy *Nestorianism*, that the divine and human natures were not merged in one person in Jesus Christ; **b** of or belonging to a religious community, the *Nestorian Church*, in Kurdistan and Persia, which preserves the name, but not the heresy. **2.** n. Member of the Nestorian Church.

net (I.), n. [1. net; 2. nɛt]. O.E. & M.E. *nett, net*; O.S. *net, netti*; O.H.G. *nezzi*; Goth. *nati*; possibly cogn. w. Gk. *nēdûs*, 'membrane containing the entrails; the paunch; the entrails'. **1.** An open-work fabric of knotted or woven twine, cotton, silk, or other thread, wire &c. with mesh of various sizes. **2.** A length of any material having a meshed structure, of whatever size, and for whatever purpose used, e.g. *fishing-net*; or one for snaring birds &c.; for enclosing or protecting anything, as *garden, hair, mosquito net*; one used in certain games, as *tennis net* &c. **3.** Fine, meshed, lace-like fabric. **4.** Network.

net (II.), vb. trans. & intrans., fr. prec. **A.** trans. **1. a** To catch by means of a net: *to net fish, birds* &c.; (fig., colloq.) **b** to catch, entrap: *to net a husband*; **c** to obtain as a result of efforts and devices: *to net a handsome profit* (see, however, **net** (III.), 2). **2.** To place, plant, nets in for purpose of catching something: *to net a river.* **3.** To cover, protect, surround, with a net or netting: *to net fruit trees, strawberries* &c.; *to net a tennis lawn.* **B.** intrans. To make a net or nets.

net (III.), adj. & vb. trans. Fr. *net*, 'neat, clean'. See **neat** (II.). **1.** adj. Clear, free, of all deductions; remaining over after all deductions have been made; opposite of 'gross': *net price*, real, not nominal, price, without discounts; *net profit*, profit after all costs, charges &c. have been deducted; *net tonnage* (of ship), registered tonnage giving cargo capacity. **2.** vb. To gain, produce, as a net profit: *to net a thousand a year.* (This sense may belong here originally, but is now usually felt as belonging to prec., **A. 1.**)

ne temere, n. [1. nē témere; 2. nī téməri]. Lat., 'not blindly, or rashly', as first words of the Bull. See **temerarious.** Title of a Papal Bull, 1907, declaring invalid all marriages of Roman Catholics unless celebrated by Roman Catholic priests, thus barring marriages between Protestants and Roman Catholics unless so celebrated.

nether, adj. [1. nédher; 2. néðə]. O.E. *neoþera, niþera*, 'lower', adj. formed fr. adv. *neoðor, niðer*, 'lower, downward'; O.S. *nithar*; O.H.G. *nidar*; fr. **ni-* &c., 'down', see also **beneath**; cp. Scrt. *ni*, 'downwards'; Gk. *neióthen*, 'from below'; the suff. *-þer* corresponds to the Gk. compar. *-teros*, cp. **inter** (II.). Lower, placed, situated, below, under; reverse of *upper*; (now either poet. or in specific combinations) *nether lip, nether millstone*; *nether garments*, trousers; *the nether man*, legs; *nether regions, nether world*, the world of the dead, hell; also used in Place-Names, e.g. *Netherby, Netherfield* &c.

nethermost, adj. [1. nédhermōst; 2. néðəmoust]. Prec. & **-most.** Lowest: *the nethermost hell.*

netsuke, n. [1. nétsuki; 2. nétsəki]. Jap. Small carved object consisting of a knob of ivory, bone, or wood, with holes pierced through it, through which a cord is passed for attaching a purse, pouch, medicine-box, or other small article to the girdle.

netting, n. [1. néting; 2. nétiŋ]. Vbl. n., fr. **net** (II.). **1.** Piece, length, of net or network: *wire-netting.* **2.** Act, process, of making nets, of fishing with nets &c.

nettle (I.), n. [1. nétl; 2. nétl]. O.E. *netele*; O.H.G. *nezzila*; apparently a dimin. fr. **nat-il*, cp. O.H.G. *nazza*, 'nettle'. **net** (I.) is fr. the same base. Plant, also called *stinging-nettle*, belonging to the genus *Urtica*, with stinging hairs on the leaves and stalks; it grows rampantly in waste or neglected patches of ground; also applied to a non-stinging but similar-looking plant, the 'dead-nettle', of a different botanical order. Phr. *to grasp the nettle*, to take hold and deal firmly and at once with a difficulty &c.

nettle (II.), vb. trans., fr. prec. To sting, irritate, vex, cause annoyance to, pique: *the criticism nettled him.*

nettle-creeper, n. Popular name of a small bird, which nests in nettle-beds, usually applied to the white-throat.

nettle-rash, n. A skin-eruption or rash, urticaria, the symptoms of which are red, inflamed patches, as if from the sting of a nettle.

network, n. [1. nétwërk; 2. nétwʌk]. **1.** Reticulated, meshed, structure or fabric of cord, wire &c. **2.** System of interlaced lines resembling a network, e.g. of canals, railway lines, wrinkles &c.

neum, neume, n. [1. nūm; 2. njūm]. L. Lat. *neuma*, fr. Gk. *pneûma*, 'breath'. See **pneumatic.** (Med. mus.) A symbol or system of notation indicating the notes to be sung to a single syllable in plain-song.

neural, adj. [1. nūral; 2. njúərəl]. Gk. *neûron*, 'nerve' &c. See **neur(o)- & -al.** Of or pertaining to the nerves.

neuralgia, n. [1. nūráljia; 2. njurǽldž(i)ə]. **neur(o)-** & *alg-*, stem of Gk. *álgos*, 'pain', & **-ia.** See **-algia & neglect.** Acute, intermittent pain, usually following the course of a nerve, esp. in the head or face.

neuralgic, adj. [1. nūráljik; 2. njurǽldžik]. Prec. & **-ic.** Pertaining to, resembling, neuralgia.

neurasthenia, n. [1. nūrasthḗnia; 2. njùərəsþínjə], fr. **neur(o)-** & Gk. *asthéneia*, 'weakness', fr. *asthenḗs*, 'weak', *a-*, priv. pref., & *sthénos*, 'strength'. See **sthenic.** Nervous debility or prostration; exhausted condition of the nerves.

neurasthenic, adj. & n. [1. nūrasthénik; 2. njùərəsþénik]. Prec. & **-ic. 1.** adj. Of, characterized by, suffering from, neurasthenia. **2.** n. A sufferer from neurasthenia.

neuration, n. [1. nūráshun; 2. njuəréiʃən]. Hybrid formation fr. Gk. **neur(o)-** & Lat. **-ation.** Arrangement, distribution, of nerves or veins in a leaf or insect's wing; nervation.

neurectomy, n. [1. nūréktumi; 2. njuəréktəmi], fr. **neur(o)-** & Gk. *ektomḗ*, 'cutting out, excision', fr. *ek*, 'out', & *tomḗ*, 'cutting', cp. *tém(nein)*, 'to cut', see **tome.** Excision of a nerve.

neuritis, n. [1. nūrítis; 2. njuəráitis]. **neur(o)-** & **-itis.** Inflammation of a nerve or group of nerves.

neur(o)-, pref., fr. Gk. *neûron*, fr. **snēuro-*, fr. base **snēu-*, 'to weave, bind', parallel w. **snēi-*, q.v. under **needle.** See also **nerve.** Used in compounds, indicating connexion with the nerves or nervous system.

neuroglia, n. [1. nūróglia; 2. njuərɔ́gliə], fr. **neur(o)-** & Gk. *gliā*, 'glue'. Cp. Gk. *gloiós*, 'gum', & see **gluten.** Interstitial tissue which acts as support to the essential nervous tissue, esp. of the brain and spinal cord.

neurologist, n. [1. nūrólojist; 2. nju(ə)rɔ́lədžist]. **neurology & -ist.** One skilled in the science of neurology; a nerve specialist.

neurology, n. [1. nūróloji; 2. nju(ə)rɔ́lədži]. **neuro- & -logy.** Scientific study of the nerves and nervous system.

neuroma, n. [1. nūrōma; 2. nju(ə)róumə]. **neur(o)- & -oma.** A tumour on, or connected with, a nerve.

neuropath, n. [1. nūropath; 2. njúərəpæþ]. Abbr. of next word. (med.) One who suffers from nervous disease or disorders; **a** neurasthenic.

neuropathic, adj. & n. [1. nūropáthik; 2. njùərəpǽþik]. **neuro- & -pathic. 1.** adj. **a** Of or pertaining to disease of the nerves; **b** having, suffering from, nervous disease. **2.** n. A sufferer from disease of the nerves.

neuropathist, n. [1. nūrópathist; 2. nju(ə)rɔ́pəþist]. Next word & **-ist.** Specialist in nervous diseases.

neuro-pathologist, n. [1. nūrō pathólojist; 2. njù(ə)rou pəþɔ́lədžist]. **neuro- & pathologist.** Student of neuro-pathology.

neuro-pathology, n. [1. nūrō pathóloji; 2. njù(ə)rou pəþɔ́lədži]. **neuro- & pathology.** Study of diseases of the nervous system.

neuropathy, n. [1. nūrópathi; 2. nju(ə)rɔ́pəþi]. **neuro- & -pathy.** Nervous disease; morbid affection or disease of a nerve or the nervous system.

neuro-physiology, n. [1. nūrō fizióloji; 2. njù(ə)rou fiziɔ́lədži]. **neuro- & physiology.** Physiology of the nervous system.

neuro-psychology, n. [1. nūrō sikóloji; 2. njù(ə)rou saikɔ́lədži]. **neuro- & psychology.** The special study of the connexion between the nervous system and the mental processes.

neurosis, n., pl. **neuroses** [1. nūrósis, -sēz; 2. nju(ə)róusis, -sīz]. **neuro- & -osis.** 1. (med.) A functional disorder of the nerves or nervous system without organic disease. 2. (psychol.) Physical activity in the nerve-cell which either causes, or accompanies, mental activity.

neurotic, adj. & n. [1. nūrótik; 2. nju(ə)rɔ́tik]. **neuro- & -otic.** 1. adj. a Of, belonging to, the nerves, affecting, acting on, the nerves; b suffering from, subject to, nerve disorder or disease; highly nervous: *neurotic person.* 2. n. a A neurotic person; b drug which acts on the nervous system, esp. as a poison.

neuter (I.), adj. [1. nūter; 2. njūtə]. Lat., 'neither of two, neither the one nor the other', also gram. 'of neither gender, neuter'; fr. *ne-*, neg. pref., & *uter*, 'either of two'. Cp. **neither & whether.** 1. (gram.) a Neither masculine nor feminine: *neuter gender, noun, pronoun, adjective*; b (of vbs.) neither active nor passive; intransitive. 2. a (bot.) Having neither pistils nor stamens; b (entom.) sexually undeveloped, as the worker bee or ant. 3. (rare) Taking neither side, part &c. in dispute; neutral.

neuter (II.), n., fr. prec. 1. (gram.) a A noun, pronoun, adjective, of the neuter gender; b an intransitive verb. 2. a A sexually undeveloped insect, such as a worker bee or ant; b castrated animal; esp. a cat so treated. 3. A neutral, one who takes no side in a dispute &c., one who takes a middle course and is neither one thing nor another.

neutral (I.), adj. [1. nūtral; 2. njūtrəl]. Lat. *neutrālis.* **neuter & -al.** 1. a Not taking either side in a dispute, argument, esp. in a war; indifferent, impartial, non-belligerent: *neutral attitude, opinion*; *a neutral state*; *to remain neutral*; b belonging to a state which remains neutral in a war, not exposed to or involved in hostilities: *neutral commerce, territory.* 2. Belonging to neither of two classes, things &c., having no marked characteristics: *neutral colour, tint, tone.* 3. (bot. and zool.) Not differentiated in sex, neither male nor female; undeveloped in sex; asexual. 4. a (chem.) Neither acid nor alkaline; b (elect.) neither positive nor negative.

neutral (II.), n., fr. prec. A state or subject of a state which takes neither side in a war: *rights and liabilities of neutrals.*

neutrality, n. [1. nūtráliti; 2. njūtrǽliti], fr. Fr. *neutralité.* See **neutral (I.) & -ity.** State of being neutral, esp. in a war; impartiality. Phr. *armed neutrality*, state of being ready, when necessary, to take part actively on one side or the other in a dispute, though not for the moment engaged.

neutralization, n. [1. nūtralīzáshun; 2. njūtrəlaizéiʃən]. Next word & **-ation.** 1. Act of neutralizing or making neutral; state of being neutralized. 2. Specif., agreement of states to treat a port, canal, stretch of territory &c. as neutral in time of war: *neutralization of the Suez Canal.* 3. Act or process of rendering ineffectual and useless: *neutralization of efforts, hopes* &c.

neutralize, vb. trans. [1. nūtralīz; 2. njūtrəlaiz], fr. L. Lat. *neutrālīzāre*, 'to make neutral'. See **neutral (I.) & -ize.** 1. To make neutral, treat as neutral, exempt from hostile acts in time of war. 2. To render ineffectual, remove or destroy special or distinguishing characteristics; to counteract by opposing something different: *neutralize efforts, work* &c.; *one colour neutralizes another.* 3. (chem.) To render inert: *an acid is neutralized by a base.*

neutralizer, n. [1. nūtralīzer; 2. njūtrəlaizə]. Prec. & **-er.** One who, substance or object which, neutralizes.

neutrally, adv. [1. nūtrali; 2. njūtrəli]. **neutral (I.) & -ly.** In a neutral manner.

neutrodyne, n. [1. nūtrōdīn; 2. njūtroudain]. See **neuter (I.) & dyne.** (wireless) An arrangement of a receiver where high frequency amplification is adapted for neutralizing the effects of capacity of the valve electrodes and the valve holder.

névé, n. [1. nā́vā; 2. néivei]. Fr., fr. Lat. *nivem*, acc. of *nix*, 'snow'; fr. **snigʷ-*, cp. Gk. *niphás*, 'snow-flake', see further under **snow**; *-é* is fr. Lat. *-ātum*, see **-ate.** Mass of hardened snow in process of becoming ice at the upper end of a glacier.

never, adv. [1. néver; 2. névə]. O.E. *nǣfre*, fr. *ne*, 'not', & *ǣfre*, 'ever'. See **ever.** 1. a Not ever; at no time, present, past, or future: *it is never used now*; *never has been used before or since*; *never will be used again*; b under no condition; not at all: *never refuse a good offer*; *never submit.* Phrs. *better late than never*, welcome, acceptable, however much delayed; *never too late to mend*, there's always time for repentance and reform; *now or never*, now is the last opportunity of acting. 2. a As emphatic negative, as *never fear*: *I'll do it, never fear!*, of course I will do it; *never mind*; b followed by indefinite or definite article: *he answered never a word*, not a single word; c followed by *so*: *never so much as spoke*, didn't even speak; *charm he never so wisely*, however wisely he may charm; d expressing surprise, incredulity &c.: *you were never such a fool as to lose your money!*, it is impossible that...; *well I never!*; *I never did!* (hear or see the like). 3. In free combination with participles &c.: *never-ending (watch)*, *never-failing (kindness* &c.).

nevermore, adv. [1. névermṓr; 2. névəmɔ̄́]. **never & more.** Never any more, never again.

Never Never Land, n. Northern Queensland, Australia, as being very remote and difficult of access.

nevertheless, adv. & conj. [1. nèverdhelés; 2. nèvəðəlés]. **never & the** (fr. O.E. *þȳ* = by that) & **-less.** None, not, the less; notwithstanding; all the same; yet: *he did it nevertheless*; *nevertheless, he did it.*

new (I.), adj. [1. nū; 2. njū]. O.E. *nīwe, nēowe*, M.E. *nēwe*; O.S. *niwi*; O.H.G. *niuwi*; Goth. *niujis*; cogn. w. Lat. *novus*, 'new'; Gk. *néos*, fr. **newos*, see **neo-**; Scrt. *navaš*; O. Slav. *novŭ*. 1. Not previously existing; appearing, produced, for the first time: *new book, play, building* &c.; *new discovery, idea.* Phr. *there's nothing new under the sun*, nothing is really original, everything has a predecessor. 2. Previously existing but only recently discovered or known: *new planet, element, plant* &c.; *new worlds*; *the New World*, the American continent; *this information is new to me.* 3. Reverse of *old*; a different from, taking place of, what has previously existed; recently acquired: *a new suit of clothes*; *to buy a new horse*; Phr. *new brooms sweep clean*, one entering on new employment is enthusiastic and vigorous; b marking fresh start or departure, characterized by conduct different from, and better than, that hitherto followed: *to lead a new life*; Phrs. *to turn over a new leaf*, behave better than in the past; *the new man*, regenerate man; *to make a new man of*, (i.) to improve his character and conduct; (ii.) to restore to good health; c recently appointed, just starting on activities: *the new Cabinet*; *the new bishop, curate* &c.; d (contemptuous) modern, freshly introduced, new-fangled: *the new diplomacy*; *the new styles of dancing*; *the new woman.* 4. Fresh, unspoiled, not worn out; recently repaired or restored: *the carpet looks nice and new*; *the fence must be made new*; *as good as new*; *the works of the watch are quite new, though the case is worn out.* 5. Fresh, newly grown or produced: *new milk, potatoes, wine* &c. 6. Beginning a fresh stage in a series, following that which has gone before, succeeding: *new moon*; *new chapter*; *begin a new game*; *a new year.* 7. a Inexperienced in, untried, unaccustomed to, not broken in to: *new to harness*; *new to the job, work*; b unfamiliar, strange, novel: *the work is new to me*; Phr. *an old dog can't learn new tricks.* 8. (in Place-Names) As recalling or named after or as replacing a former place: *New Zealand, New York.*

new (II.), adv., fr. prec. Newly, recently; afresh, anew, again; combined freely and usually hyphened with the qualified word following, also used to form verbs: *new-born, new-paved*; *new-build*, to rebuild; *new-fashion, new-form* &c.

New Art, n. Translating Fr. *l'art nouveau*, a new kind or style of decorative art, prevalent in Europe at end of 19th and beginning of 20th cent.

new-comer, n. One newly arrived; a recent arrival, stranger.

newel, n. [1. nūel; 2. njūil]. Earlier *nuell*, fr. O. Fr. *nuel, nouel*, Mod. Fr. *noyau*, 'kernel of a nut, stone of a fruit, also newel,' fr. Lat. *nucālis*, 'of, belonging to, a nut', fr. *nuc(em)*, 'nut'. See **nucleus & nux vomica.** (archit.) a The central shaft or pillar round which a winding stair turns; b the post supporting the rail of a straight staircase, at the foot or head; *hollow newel*, the open well of a staircase.

new-fangled, adj. [1. nū fànggled; 2. njū fǽŋgld]. Earlier *newfangel*, fr. **new** & *fangel*, obs. word meaning, 'eager to take, fond of taking', fr. stem *fang-*, 'to seize, take'. See **fang (I.).** 1. (obs.) Fond of what is new. 2. (contemptuous) Ultra-modern, strange, having no merit but novelty: *new-fangled ideas.*

Newfoundland dog, n. [1. nūfóundland dóg; 2. njūfáundlənd dɔ́g], fr. name of island off east coast of Canada. Large black or black and white dog, of spaniel breed, with great swimming and retrieving powers.

Newgate, n. [1. nūgit; 2. njūgit]. Famous old London prison, built where the West Gate of the City of London stood; *Newgate Calendar*, an old publication giving reports &c. of criminal trials at the Old Bailey, the criminal court next to the prison; *Newgate frill* or *fringe*, beard and whiskers framing or fringing the face, the cheeks, upper lip, and chin being shaved.

newish, adj. [1. nūish; 2. njūiʃ]. **new & -ish.** Rather new; nearly new.

new-laid, adj. (of eggs) Newly laid, just laid, quite fresh.

New Learning, n. The study of the Bible and of the Greek classics in their original languages at the time of the Renaissance and Reformation in England.

newly, adv. [1. nūli; 2. njūli]. **new & -ly.** 1. Recently: *newly wed* &c.; *newly come from the sea.* 2. Anew, afresh: *the gate has been newly painted.*

Newmarket, adj. & n. [1. nūmàrket; 2. njūmàkit]. Name of town in Cambridgeshire, famed for its racecourse. 1. A tightly-fitting coat with long skirts; also *Newmarket coat.* 2. A card game.

newness, n. [1. nūnes; 2. njūnis]. **new & -ness.** State or quality of being new (in various senses of this word).

news, n. pl. [1. nūz; 2. njūz], now treated as sing., formerly taking pl. vb. & pron., fr. **new**, as Fr. *nouvelles*, & L. Lat. *nova*, 'new things, news', neut. pl. of *novus*, 'new'. 1. a Intelligence, information, report of what has most recently happened : *foreign, home, news*; *the latest news*; *what's the news?*; *there is no news today*; Phrs. *no news is good news*, one is sure to hear the worst quickly; so *bad news travels quickly*; **b** that part of a newspaper containing recent intelligence, contrasted with leaders, special articles, reviews &c. **2.** Name of several newspapers : *Daily News* &c. **3.** Something of which one did not previously know; something which one has just learnt; tidings, fresh information : *what you say is news to me*; *I want to hear all your news*, i.e. recent doings of which I have not yet heard. Phr. *to break the news to*, to impart ill tidings.

news-agent, n. One who sells newspapers and other periodicals.

news editor, n. Person on staff of a daily newspaper in charge of reports of events coming in day by day.

news-letter, n. **1.** A circular weekly manuscript letter, containing the news of the day, sent to subscribers in the country by writers in London, in the 17th cent., an early predecessor of the newspaper. **2. a** Title of some old newspapers; **b** title of special section of some newspapers, giving special, local, or other news.

newsmonger, n. [1. nû́zmungger; 2. njúzmaŋgə]. **news** & **-monger.** One who deals in news; one who spends his time gathering and retelling news; (usually in depreciatory sense) a gossip, chatterer.

newspaper, n. [1. nû́zpàper; 2. njúzpèipə]. **news** & **paper.** A publication, printed and issued daily or weekly, containing all news of the day, comments thereon &c., and now usually advertisements, public notices &c. : *the newspaper world*, world of journalism.

news-print, n. **news** & **print.** Paper, esp. that made from wood pulp, used for the printing of newspapers.

news-room, n. Reading room in an institution &c. where newspapers and other periodicals are placed for perusal.

news-sheet, n. An early form of the printed newspaper; also a news-letter.

New Style, n. The rearrangement of the Calendar introduced by Pope Gregory XIII. in 1582, and adopted by England in 1752, by which time there was a difference of eleven days between the Old and New Styles, the latter being the later.

newsvendor, n. [1. nû́zvèndur; 2. njúzvèndə]. A seller of newspapers and other periodicals.

newsy, adj. [1. nû́zi; 2. njúzi]. **news** & **-y.** (colloq.) Full of news or gossip; gossipy.

newt, n. [1. nūt; 2. njūt]. O.E. *efeta*, M.E. *ewte*; *an ewte* later became *a newte*. See also **eft.** *Ewt* is still used in Engl. dialects. A small lizard-like amphibious batrachian, allied to the salamanders.

New Testament, n. Translation of the Greek *hē Kainḗ Diathḗkē*, the new, i.e. Christian, Covenant or Dispensation, Testament; that portion of the Bible which contains the books of the new Christian Covenant.

Newtonian, adj. & n. [1. nūtṓnian; 2. njūtóunian], fr. name of Sir Isaac Newton (1642–1727), & **-ian.** **1.** adj. Of or pertaining to Newton and his philosophy, theories, doctrines &c. : *Newtonian system, telescope* &c. **2.** n. Follower of Newton and his system.

New World, n. The North and South American Continent; the Western Hemisphere.

New Year, n. The first days after the end of an old year, beginning on *New Year's Day*, Jan. 1st.

next (I.), adj. & adv. [1. nekst; 2. nekst]. O.E. *nīext, nēxt*, fr. **nēah-ist*, superl. of *nēah*, 'nigh' M.E. *nest, next*. See **nigh** & cp. **near.** Nearest, adjoining without anything intervening; coming, standing, immediately before or after. **1.** (of position in space) *the next house*; *the house next to ours*; *the next chapter*; *take the next turning*; *in the next place*. Phrs. *next door* : **a** adj., *next-door neighbours*, living in adjoining or nearest house; **b** adv., *to live next door*, in next house; *next door to*, (fig.) nearly, almost amounting to : *next door to blasphemy* &c. **2.** (of occurrence in time) *Next day*; *on Tuesday next*; *next month*; *the Sunday next before Advent* (*Sunday*); *the next person I meet*; *next time I go out*. **3.** (of nearness in quality, value &c.) *The next kind, price*; *the next prize*; *to be next best*. Phr. *next best thing*, second best, that which is chosen if first choice fails. **4.** (specif. law) *Next friend*, person, not a guardian, who acts for a minor or one not legally able to act for himself in a suit at law; *next of kin*, nearest relatives by blood who take on an intestacy in order as laid down by statute.

next (II.), adv. See prec. In the next place, on the next occasion, in the next order of quality &c. : *the band came next*; *when I see him next*; *I like this best and that next*. Phr. *what next!*, expressing wonder at what extravagance, eccentricity, marvel, may follow : *dresses up to their knees! what next!*; *talking to New York! what next!*

next (III.), prep. See prec. In closest proximity to, nearest to; in immediate contact with &c. : *a seat next the window*; *the house next mine*; *sit next me*; *whom did you sit next at dinner?*

next (IV.), as n., fr. **next (I.)**, adj., a noun being omitted. *The next* (*person*) *to arrive*; *he will be the next* (*to go*); *look forward to his next* (*book*); *in my next* (*letter*); *to be concluded in our next* (*issue*).

nexus, n. [1. néksus; 2. néksəs]. Lat., 'that which binds together; bond, tie', fr. *nex-*, stem of *nectere*, 'to bind'. Relationships doubtful. **a** Link, bond, tie; connexion; **b** series, group, of objects or ideas connected by links.

nib (I.), n. & vb. trans. [1. nib; 2. nib]. Variant of **neb**, 'beak, nose, point'. **1.** n. **a** (obs.) Beak of a bird; **b** sharpened and split point of a quill-pen; the similar point of steel, gold &c. inserted in a penholder; **c** (pl.) crushed cocoa-beans. **2.** vb. (rare) **a** To sharpen a quill so as to form a nib; **b** to mend the nib of a quill-pen; to insert nib into a penholder.

nib (II.), n. Etymol. uncertain, but perh. same word as prec., w. the sense developed fr. the meaning 'face'. (slang, rare) Smart, grandly dressed person : *he's quite a nib*; (also in pl.) *his nibs*, of a self-important person.

nibble (I.), vb. intrans. & trans. [1. níbl; 2. níbl]. Etymol. doubtful; L.G. has *nibbelen*, also *knibbelen*, in same sense. **1.** intrans. **a** To bite at, gently or tentatively, as a fish at a bait; to bite at with small, close bites, as a rabbit at grass; **b** to show signs of being attracted by an offer, proposal &c.; also *nibble at*, to play, toy, with a suggestion, proposal, offer, without deciding to accept or reject it. **2.** trans. To bite (food &c.), as fish or rabbits &c.

nibble (II.), n., fr. prec. **a** Act of nibbling; tentative bite of a fish at a bait; **b** half-hearted, tentative motion of acceptance of suggestion &c.

niblick, n. [1. níblik; 2. níblik]. Etymol. unknown. (golf) A club with small, well-lofted and heavy head used for playing a ball out of sandy bunkers, hazards &c.

nice, adj. [1. nīs; 2. nais]. O. Fr. *nice*, 'stupid, dull', now obs.; fr. Lat. *nescius*, 'not knowing, ignorant', fr. *ne-*, neg. pref., & **sci-*, stem of *scīre*, 'to know'. See **science.** The original meanings (15th cent.) in English, 'foolish, not wise, senseless', and the later (16th and 17th cents.) 'wanton, luxurious, extravagant, strange', are now quite obs.; the meaning 'fastidious' (17th cent.) marks transition to present usages. **1. a** Fastidious, dainty, hard to please, refined, fanciful, in matters of choice, taste &c. : *nice in one's dress, appearance*; *nice in one's food*; **b** over-refined, finicky, too exacting, fussily fastidious : '*not exact, but nice*' (Pope). **2.** (in non-material things) Having an exquisite sense of honour and rectitude; having high standard of manners and conduct, precise, punctilious, scrupulous : *a nice sense of honour*; *not over nice in one's dealings*; *the nicest courtesy*; '*a nice marality, split my windpipe!*' (Lord Foppington in Vanbrugh's *Relapse*). **3.** Requiring, involving, exhibiting precision, exactness, delicacy, minuteness, discrimination of touch, treatment, judgement &c.; delicate, sensitive, discriminating : *a nice point* (*of law*); *a nice argument*; *negotiations needing nice handling*; *nice ear for sounds, eye for distances*; *nice taste in art, literature*; *nice shades of meaning, distinctions*. **4.** (gen., and of the widest application, often used as exact converse of *nasty*) **a** Pleasant, pleasing, agreeable; attractive, engaging; good, kind : *nice face, looks, smile*; *nice dress*; *nice day, weather*; *nice cooking*; *a nice cigar*; *nice manners, nice people* &c.; *nice people* has also sense of well-bred people; **b** not offensive, unpleasant, or in bad taste : *a nice book, play* &c.; **c** (ironical, colloq.) bad, awkward, nasty, cp. 'pretty' : *a nice muddle*; *a nice state of affairs, business* &c. Phr. *nice and*, emphasizing another adjective : *the place is nice and healthy*, quite healthy.

nicely, adv. Prec. & **-ly.** In a nice manner (in all senses); (colloq.) exactly : *that will suit me nicely*, will just suit me; *she's doing nicely*, is going on well, getting better.

Nicene, adj. [1. nīsḗn; 2. naisín]. Lat. *Nīcaenus*, later *Nīcēnus*, 'of or pertaining to Nicaea', Gk. *Nīkaia*, Nice, ancient city of Asia Minor. *Nicene Councils*, those held at Nicaea A.D. 325 and 787; *Nicene Creed*, the confession of faith drawn up at the first Council of Nicaea; said at the Communion Service.

niceness, n. [1. nísnes; 2. náisnis], fr. **nice** & **-ness.** State or quality of being nice; **a** delicacy of taste, judgement; **b** point of minute detail; nicety; **c** agreeableness, pleasantness.

nicety, n. [1. níseti; 2. náisiti]. See prec. & **-ty.** **a** Exactness, precision, accuracy : *nicety of his powers of observation*; **b** accuracy; careful, minute discrimination : *a matter, question, point, of extreme nicety*; **c** (usually pl.) minute, small points of difference, small details : *niceties of scale, gauge* &c.; *niceties of argument, evidence* &c.; Phr. *to a nicety*, exactly.

niche, n. & vb. trans. [1. nich; 2. nitʃ]. Fr., fr. Ital. *nicchia*, 'nook, niche'; etymol. doubtful; Ital. has also *nicchio*, 'shell', wh. may be an allied word; if so, origin may be found in Lat. **nītulum*, for *mītulum, mȳtilum*, 'a mussel'. **1.** n. **a** Small arched recess in a wall, to contain a statue, bust &c.; **b** (fig.) place, scope, suitable for person's capacity, work, occupation &c. : *to find a niche for oneself*. **2.** vb. (usually in P.P.) To place in a niche, furnish a niche for; settle (oneself) in a niche.

nick (I.), n. & vb. trans. & intrans. [1. nik; 2. nik]. Etymol. doubtful; possibly allied to **nock.** **1.** n. **a** A small cut, or slit, in wood &c., a notch, used as mark in a tally for reckoning accounts, marking time or as a sign; Phr. *in the nick of time*, at exactly the right moment; only just in time; **b** a throw, cast, in games of dice. **2.** vb. trans. **a** To cut a nick or notch in; specif., to make a cut across and under (a horse's tail to make it carry it higher); **b** (colloq., slang) to catch, steal, pinch : *to nick a handkerchief, watch* &c. **3.** vb. intrans. *Nick in*, same as *nip in*, q.v.

Nick (II.), n. Only in Phr. *Old Nick*, as appellation of the devil; short for 'Nicholas'.

nickel, n. [1. níkl; 2. níkl], fr. termination of Germ. *kupfernickel*, name given to the ore, wh. looked like copper, fr. wh. nickel was first extracted, leaving no copper behind; fr. *kupfer*, 'copper', q.v. & *nickel*, 'mischievous sprite, demon', cogn. w. **nix (I.)**, the word meaning 'vanishing, worthless copper'. **a** A metallic element, a very hard, malleable, and ductile metal, of whitish colour, taking a brilliant polish, used chiefly as an alloy in making *nickel-steel*, or *nickel-silver*, German silver; **b** (U.S.A. and Canada) a 5-cent piece.

nicker, vb. intrans. [1. níker; 2. níkə]. Imitative. To neigh, whinny, as does a horse.

nick-nack, n. See **knick-knack**.

nickname, n. & vb. trans. [1. níknām; 2. níkneim]. Earlier *nēke name*, for *an ēkenāme*, 'an additional name'; cp. O.N. *auknafn*. See **eke (II.)** & **name**. **1.** n. An additional name, a soubriquet, given in affection, or derision, or as a descriptive or familiar appellation to a person, place &c. **2.** vb. To give a nickname to.

Nicol prism, n. [1. níkl prìzm; 2. níkl prìzəm]. Named after William Nicol, d. 1851, Scottish physicist. A prism made of Iceland spar, used for experiments in the polarization of light.

nicotian, adj. [1. nikóshian; 2. nikóuʃiən]. See next word & **-ian**. Of, connected with, tobacco.

nicotine, n. [1. nìkotḗn; 2. nìkətín], fr. name of Jean Nicot, who introduced tobacco to France in 1560, & **-ine**. (chem.) An oily, colourless, highly poisonous alkaloid, found in tobacco.

nicotinism, n. [1. níkotinìzm; 2. níkətinìzəm]. Prec. & **-ism**. State of suffering from poisoning by nicotine or from excessive use of tobacco.

nictate. See next word.

nictitate, vb. trans. [1. níktitāt; 2. níktiteit], fr. L. Lat. *nictitāt-(um)*, P.P. type of *nictitāre*, freq. of Lat. *nictāre*, 'to wink, blink', fr. *nicere*, 'to beckon'; cp. Lat. *co-nīvēre*, 'to blink; to wink at', see **connive**; the base is **kneigʷ-*, wh. is found also in Goth. *hneiwan*, 'to bend towards, incline'; O.H.G. *(h)neigen*; O.E. *hnīgan*, 'to bend, bow, sink down' &c. To wink, open and close the eyes quickly, esp. of birds and animals possessing a third eyelid, at the side of the eye, the *nictitating membrane*, which can be drawn rapidly across the eyeball.

nidamental, adj. [1. nìdaméntl; 2. nàidəméntl], fr. Lat. *nīdāmentum*, 'that which forms a nest', Lat. *nīdus*, 'nest', & **-al**. See **nidus**. (zool.) Of or belonging to a covering for the eggs of certain molluscs, such as the octopus: *nidamental capsule, gland, sac* &c.

niddering, adj. [1. nídering; 2. nídəriŋ]. A spurious revival, used by Scott; based upon O.E. *niðing*, 'infamous person, coward, dastard', fr. Scand., cp. O.N. *niðingr*, fr. *nið*, 'malice, hatred'; cp. Goth. *neiþ*, O.H.G. *nīd*. Base, infamous, cowardly, faithless.

nide, n. [1. nīd; 2. naid], fr. Lat. *nīdus*, 'nest', cp. Fr. *nid*, & see **nidus**. A nest and its contents; specif., a brood of young pheasants.

nidificate, vb. intrans. [1. nídifikāt; 2. nídifikeit], fr. Lat. *nīdificāt-(um)*, P.P. type of *nīdificāre*, 'to build a nest', fr. *nīdus*, 'nest', see **nidus**, & **fic-*, see **-fy**, & **-ate**. To build, make a nest; to nidify.

nidification, n. [1. nìdifikā́shun; 2. nìdifikéiʃən]. Prec. & **-ion**. Act or process of forming nests; nesting.

nidify, vb. intrans. [1. nídifī; 2. nídifai]. See prec. & **-fy**. To make a nest, to nidificate.

nid-nod, vb. intrans. [1. níd nod; 2. níd nɔd]. Redupl. form of **nod**. To keep nodding.

nidus, n. [1. nīdus; 2. náidəs]. Lat. *nīdus*, 'nest', fr. **nisdos*. See under **nest**. A nest; breeding place; **a** (zool.) place, resembling a nest, in which certain insects and some spiders deposit their eggs; **b** a place where germs of disease &c., are harboured and developed; a site or source of infection.

niece, n. [1. nēs; 2. nīs]. M.E. *nēce*, *neyce*, fr. O. Fr. *niece*, fr. Lat. *neptis*, 'granddaughter', L. Lat. *neptia*, 'granddaughter, niece'; cp. *nepōt-*, 'nephew'. See **nepotism** & **nephew**. The daughter of one's brother or sister.

niello, n. [1. niélō; 2. niélou]. Ital., fr. L. Lat. *nigellum*, 'a kind of black or very dark enamel', fr. Lat. *nigellus*, 'blackish, somewhat black', dimin. of *niger*, 'black'. See **negro**. **1.** A deep-black, metallic amalgam of sulphur added to silver, copper, lead &c., used as an inlay for incised lines on silver or gold, as a form of decoration. **2.** Piece of silver &c., decorated with this black inlay; also used attrib., *niello-work*.

nielloed, adj. [1. niélōd; 2. niéloud]. Prec. & **-ed**. Decorated with niello.

Niersteiner, n. [1. nḗrstīner; 2. níəstainə]. Germ. adj., *Niersteiner(wein)*, fr. Nierstein, a village near Mainz, on the Rhine. A white, still Rhine wine or Hock.

Nietzschean, adj. [1. nḗchean; 2. nítʃiən], fr. F. W. Nietzsche, German philosopher, d. 1900. Connected with, based on, the philosophy of Nietzsche and his followers, of which the chief feature is a revulsion from Christian ethics as servile, the glorification of strength, the so-called 'will to power' of the 'superman'.

Nietzscheanism, n. [1. nḗcheanizm; 2. nítʃiənizəm]. Prec. & **-ism**. Nietzsche's philosophical doctrines.

nifty, adj. [1. nífti; 2. nífti]. Etymol. unknown. (Am. slang) Smart, stylish.

niggard, n. & adj. [1. nígard; 2. nígəd]. M.E. *nigard*; etymol. doubtful; the termination seems the same as in *laggard, drunkard* &c.; *nig* is prob. Scand., cp. O.N. *knöggr*, 'niggardly'. **1.** n. A miser; a stingy, covetous, avaricious person. **2.** adj. Covetous, avaricious, miserly, stingy.

niggardliness, n. [1. nígardlines; 2. nígədlinis], fr. **niggardly** & **-ness**. Avarice, meanness, stinginess.

niggardly, adj. & adv. [1. nígardli; 2. nígədli]. **niggard** & **-ly**. **1.** adj. Avaricious, covetous, stingy, mean, close-fisted, grudging. **2.** adv. Avariciously, stingily, grudgingly.

nigger, n. [1. níger; 2. nígə]. Earlier *neger*, fr. Fr. *nègre*, fr. Span. *negro*. See **negro**. **1.** (colloq.) A negro; also used loosely in contemptuous sense of dark-skinned natives of East Indies &c., and by Australians of the black aborigines. Phrs. (U.S.A.) *nigger in the woodpile*, some hidden fact, drawback, motive &c.; *to work like a nigger*, very hard, persistently, industriously. **2.** Also *nigger-minstrel*, person with blackened face and hands, often fantastically dressed, who sings and accompanies himself on a banjo or with the bones, esp. in the open air. **3.** A very dark chocolate brown coloured dye for dresses, stockings &c. **4.** (U.S.A.) Name of certain machines for doing very hard work, as for hauling logs &c. **5.** (attrib.) *Nigger-fish*, West Indian edible sea-fish, marked with black spots; *nigger melodies*, negro songs.

niggle, vb. intrans. [1. nígl; 2. nígl]. Etymol. doubtful; cp. Norw. dial. *nigla*, 'to save, scrape, to busy over trifles'. To fret, bother over petty details; to spend time working at trivial details or in a fussy, finicky way.

niggling, adj. [1. nígling; 2. nígliŋ]. Pres. Part. of prec. **a** (of persons) Fussy, finicky, worrying over trifles or petty details; **b** (of a task) demanding very careful, minute work at small details; **c** performed in an over-elaborated, minute way, not broad or free, cramped.

nigh, adv., prep. & adj. [1. nī; 2. nai]. O.E. *nēah*, 'near', adv. & adj., M.E. *neih, nēh, nīh*; O.H.G. & O.S. *nāh*, O.N. *nā*, Goth. *nēhwa*; not identified outside Gmc. See **near** (old comp.) & **next** (old superl.) (archaic and poet.) Near. **1.** adv. **a** Near to: *to come, draw, nigh*; **b** close to, in adjacent position: *to stand nigh*; **c** almost, nearly: *nigh worn out with fatigue*. **2.** prep. Close upon, near to: *stand nigh me*; *he is nigh death*. **3.** adj. Near, close: *the Lord is nigh unto them that fear Him*; *nigh unto death*.

night, n. [1. nīt; 2. nait]. O.E. & M.E. *niht*, fr. **nahti-*; O.S. & O.H.G. *naht*; Goth. *nahts*; O.Ir. *-nocht*; Scrt. *nakta-*, Lat. *noct-(em)* &c. See **noct(i)-**; Gk. *nukt-(ós)*, *núx*; O. Slav. *nošti*; Lith. *naktis* &c. **1. a** That period of the day when the sun has ceased to give light; period between sunset and sunrise, or, without reference to light, between 6 o'clock P.M. and 6 o'clock A.M.; **b** (popular usage) period of complete darkness, after twilight and before the dawn; **c** (law) from an hour after sunset until an hour before sunrise, in distinguishing burglary from house-breaking. Phrs. *all night, all night long*, throughout the whole night; *at night*, during the night, when night comes; *by night*, during the night; *to spend the night with*, to sleep at a person's house; *(to work &c.) night and day*, without ceasing, continually; *night after night, night by night*, every night; *o' (=on) nights*, (colloq. or dial.) by, at night, during the night, as a continual habit: *I can't sleep o' nights*. *To have, pass a good (bad) night*, to sleep well (badly); *to have a (the) night out, off*, to spend the evening (and night) in enjoyment away from the house or away from work or duty; *to make a night of it*, spend the night in gaiety, enjoyment &c.; sometimes with suggestion of disorder or indulgence in alcoholic refreshment; *to turn night into day*, to do at night what is usually done in the day. **2.** Darkness, **a** (lit.) the darkness of night: *under cover of night*; **b** the darkness of death: *the night of death* &c.; **c** of blindness: '*He saw; but blasted with excess of light, Closed his eyes in endless night*' (Gray, on Milton). **3.** (fig.) Darkness of ignorance, apprehension, adversity &c.: *during the night of paganism*; *the night of their affliction*. **4.** In combination, in sense of belonging to, used in, suitable for, the night: *night bell*, bell only for use at night, as for ringing up a doctor &c.; *night breeze*, breeze blowing off the land as the sun goes down; *night clothes, night attire*, dress worn in bed; *night fishing*; *night flower*, flower, such as that of the tobacco plant, evening primrose &c., which closes during the day and opens at nightfall; *night flying*, flying by night; *nightshift*, spell, shift, of work done at night; the gang of workmen employed on a nightshift.

night-bird, n. **1.** A bird that is about by night and sleeps during the day, nocturnal bird, as the owl; or sings by night, as the nightingale. **2.** Person, usually of doubtful character, who is much about at night and is not seen by day.

night-blindness, n. Inability to see at night; nyctalopia.

night-cap, n. **1.** Cap worn in bed at night. **2.** Drink, usually alcoholic, taken before going to bed.

night-commode, n. A movable covered-in pan for use at night in the bedroom by invalids; a night-stool.

nightdress, n. [1. nítdres; 2. náitdres]. Woman's nightgown.

nightfall, n. [1. nítfawl; 2. náitfōl]. The coming on of night and darkness; the end of daylight or the day; evening.

night glass, n. A binocular glass or telescope with special lenses and large field for concentrating rays of light for use at night.

nightgown, n. [1. nítgoun; 2. náitgaun]. Long robe of linen, cambric, or other material, worn by women in bed; nightdress.

night-hag, n. **a** A witch supposed to fly by night; **b** a nightmare.

night-hawk, n. **a** A North American bird, allied to the European nightjar or goat-sucker; **b** person whose habit it is to be about at night, usually for illicit purposes; a night-bird.

nightingale, n. [1. nítinggāl; 2. náitiŋgeil]. O.E. *nihtegale*, lit., 'the night-singer', fr. *niht(e)*, 'night', & *gale*, 'singer', fr. *galan*, 'to sing', cp. O.H.G. & O.S. *nahtigala*. See **night** & **yell**. **1.** A small migratory bird of Europe, Asia, & N. Africa, *Daulias luscinia*, of dark, reddish-brown colour with greyish underparts; the cock-bird is famous for its singularly powerful, sweet, and varied notes; the singing usually begins at dusk and continues far into the night. **2.** Name given to certain other singing birds, as the Indian, Japanese nightingales &c.

nightjar, n. [1. nítjar; 2. náitdžā], fr. **night** & **jar (I.)**, 'vibrating, discordant sound'. Popular name for the goat-sucker, from its harsh, jarring cry when hunting moths and other insects at dusk.

night-light, n. A light kept burning in a bedroom at night, consisting of a kind of short, stumpy candle, in cardboard case, or of a wick floating on oil.

night-line, n. Baited line, moored and buoyed, set to catch fish by night.

night-long, adj. Lasting the whole night.

nightly, adj. & adv. [1. nítli; 2. náitli]. **night** & **-ly.** **1.** adj. **a** Happening, performed, every night: *nightly watches, visits &c.*; **b** (poet.) occurring at, belonging to night; nocturnal. **2.** adv. Every night: *barking of dogs disturbs one nightly.*

nightmare, n. [1. nítmār; 2. náitmɛə], fr. **night** & *mare*, 'demon, incubus', O.E. *mara*, cp. O.H.G. & O.N. *mara*, 'ogress, nightmare'; ultimate derivation doubtful. **1.** (archaic) A demon, incubus, supposed to haunt sleepers with a sense of oppression and suffocation. **2.** A very bad, frightening dream; sometimes accompanied by a sense of weight on the chest and stomach, inability to move &c.; supposed to be due to indigestion. **3.** A horrible experience; something, or somebody, that one dreads, dislikes, or is obsessed by; a sense of approaching disaster, forebodings of evil; general feeling of horror and disgust: *life in prison must be a long nightmare to many*; *the memory of my first lecture is a regular nightmare.*

nightmarish, adj. [1. nítmārish; 2. náitmɛ̀əriʃ]. Prec. & **-ish.** Like a nightmare.

night-piece, n. **a** A painting representing a scene at night; **b** a literary composition dealing with the subject of night.

night-school, n. School held at night for workmen or others who are unable to attend during the day.

nightshade, n. [1. nítshād; 2. náitʃeid]. O.E. *nihtscada*, fr. *niht*, 'night', q.v., & *scada*, 'shade'; similar names for the plant are found in Mod. Germ. *nachtschatte*, Du. *nachtschada*; the meaning of the termination is not clear, & the identification of it w. **shade**, may be due to popular etymol. Name of various poisonous plants belonging to the family *Solanaceae*; the belladonna plant, the *deadly nightshade*; the bittersweet, or *woody nightshade* &c.

nightshirt, n. [1. nítshěrt; 2. náitʃɜ̄t]. Long shirt worn by men and boys in bed.

night-soil, n. Sewage from cesspools, earth-closets &c. removed at night.

night-stool, n. A night-commode.

night-time, n. Time of darkness from sunset to sunrise and from twilight to dawn; the period of night, as contrasted with *day-time.*

night-walker, n. **1.** One who walks in his sleep; somnambulist. **2.** A prostitute, night-bird, night-hawk.

night-walking, n. Somnambulism, walking in one's sleep.

night-watch, n. **1. a** A guard or watch kept through the night; **b** man or men performing this duty. **2. a** Period of time during the night in which watch is kept; (pl.) successive periods, usually three or four, at each of which the guard is changed; hence, **b** of wakeful, restless periods of night: *in the night-watches.*

night-watcher, n. One who keeps watch or guard at night.

night-watchman, n. One employed to keep watch at night in a factory, business premises &c.

nigrescence, n. [1. nīgrésens; 2. naigrésəns]. See next word & **-ce.** **a** Process of growing or becoming black; **b** blackness, esp. of complexion; black pigmentation of skin, eyes &c.

nigrescent, adj. [1. nīgrésent; 2. naigrésənt]. Lat. *nigrescent-(em)*, Pres. Part. of *nigrescere*, 'to become black'; inceptive vb., fr. *nigrere*, 'to be black', fr. *niger*, 'black'. See **negro.** **a** Growing, becoming, black; **b** rather black, tending to blackness.

nigritude, n. [1. nígritūd; 2. náigritjūd], fr. Lat. *nigritūdo*, 'blackness', fr. *niger*, 'black'. See **negro.** (poet. or rhet.) Blackness (of complexion &c.); (also fig.) *the nigritude of their crimes.*

nihil, n. [1. níhil; 2. náihil]. Lat., 'nothing', fr. *nehīlum*, *ne*, 'not', & *hīlum*, 'a little thing, a trifle'; cp. **hilum**; perh. fr. **ghēlum* & a variant of *fīlum*, 'a thread'. See **file (V.).** 'row, rank' &c. In Phrs. (chiefly legal) *nihil ad rem*, nothing to the point, nothing to do with the matter, irrelevant; *nihil dicit*, he says nothing, of prisoner or defendant who refuses to plead; *nihil habet*, he has nothing, as a return by a sheriff's officer when defendant has no goods on which to distrain; *ex nihilo nihil fit*, out of nothing, nothing can come, or be made.

Nihilism, n. [1. níilizm; 2. náiəlizəm], fr. Lat. *nihil*, 'nothing'. See prec. & **-ism.** **1.** (philos.) Doctrine of negation, the denial of all reality in phenomena; complete scepticism as to the real ground of truth or belief in religion, morals &c. **2.** Specif. **a** the doctrines and system of a revolutionary party in Russia during latter half of the 19th cent. and later, which aimed at the destruction of the existing social system and adopted terrorist methods of assassination &c.; **b** (in gen.) violent revolutionary beliefs, doctrines, propaganda &c.; terrorism, anarchism.

nihilist, n. [1. níilist; 2. náiəlist]. See prec. & **-ist.** Supporter of Nihilism; member of the Russian revolutionary party professing such doctrines and methods; terrorist, anarchist.

nihilistic, adj. [1. nī(h)ilístik; 2. nài(h)ilístik]. Prec. & **-ic.** Of or pertaining to Nihilism and its propaganda.

nihility, n. [1. nīhíliti; 2. naihíliti]. L. Lat. *nihilitas.* **nihil** & **-ity.** (rare) Nothingness; nullity.

nil, n. [1. nil; 2. nil]. Lat., contraction of *nihil*, 'nothing'. See **nihil.** Nothing, in amount or number: *the profits are nil*; (also fig.) *his influence is now nil.* Phrs. *nil admirari*, to be moved (to wonder or interest) at nothing; attitude of indifference; *nil desperandum*, nothing to be despaired of, never despair.

nilgai, nylghau, n. [1. nílgī, nílgou; 2. nílgai, nílgau]. Pers. & Hind. *nīlgāw*, lit. 'blue cow', fr. Pers. *nīl*, 'blue', & *gāw*, 'cow'. See **cow.** A large Indian antelope, the male of which is horned and of a bluish-grey colour.

nill, vb. [1. nil; 2. nil]. O.E. *nyllan*, 'to refuse, be unwilling', for *ne-*, 'not', & *willan*, 'to will', q.v. Obsolete, except in Phr. *will he, nill he*, whether he will or not, usually *willy-nilly.*

Nilometer, n. [1. nīlómeter; 2. nailɔ́mitə], fr. Gk. *Neilométrion*, fr. *Neilos*, 'the Nile', & *métron*, 'measure'. See **meter.** **a** Instrument in the form of a pillar and water chamber used for measuring the rise of the Nile; **b** an automatic gauge for measuring rise and fall of water in rivers.

Nilotic, adj. [1. nīlótik; 2. nailɔ́tik], fr. Gk. *Neilōtikós*, 'of or belonging to the Nile', & **-ic.** Belonging to the Nile and the regions which it waters: *Nilotic peoples, tribes &c.*

nimble, adj. [1. nímbl; 2. nímbl]. M.E. *nimel*, 'quick, nimble', O.E. *numol, numel*, 'capacious'; (of the mind) 'able to grasp'; fr. base seen in O.E. *niman*, 'to take, seize', q.v. under **numb**; the meaning being 'quick to take or grasp'. Quick, active, lively, agile: **a** (of physical activity) *very nimble on his feet*; '*O friends, I hear the tread of nimble feet*' (Milton, 'P. L.'). Phrs. *the nimble sixpence*, as circulating rapidly; *nimble fingered*, of a pickpocket; **b** (of mental activity) quick to grasp, alert, spry, clever; versatile, mentally agile: *nimble wits*; *a nimble mind.*

nimbly, adv. Prec. & **-ly.** In a nimble manner; actively, with agility.

nimbus, n. [1. nímbus; 2. nímbəs]. Lat., 'cloud, rain-storm, thunder-cloud; also, the bright vapour enveloping a god when appearing to mortals', fr. base **nembh-*, fr. a blending of **embh-* (cp. **imbricate**) & **nebh-*, both fr. **enebh-*, 'mist, rain'. See **nebula.** **1.** (art) A bright ring, disk, triangle, of gold or of rays of light depicted round or behind the head of a divinity, saint &c. in pictures or on statues; a glory, aureole, halo. **2.** (meteor.) A storm-cloud, rain-cloud.

nimiety, n. [1. nimíeti; 2. nimáiəti]. L. Lat. *nimietāt-(em)* 'excessiveness', fr. *nimius*, adj., *nimis*, adv., 'too much'; prob. fr. **ne mīs*, 'not a little', *mīs*, fr. **mi-is*, being an old compar. of **mejo-*, 'small'. See this base in **minus.** Excess, too-muchness, redundancy.

niminy-piminy, adj. [1. nímini pímini; 2. nímini pímini]. Prob. imitative of affected, mincing speech. Finicking, mincing, affected; old-maidish, paltry, lacking downrightness and virility.

Nimrod, n. [1. nímrod; 2. nímrɔd], fr. the name of the son of Cush, Gen. x. 8-10, 'a mighty hunter before the Lord'. Person much addicted to hunting and shooting.

nincompoop, n. [1. níngkumpōōp; 2. níŋkəmpūp]. Etymol. unknown; not a corrupt. of Lat. *non compos (mentis)*, 'not sound in mind'. Simpleton, booby, silly fool; a brainless, weak-minded person.

nine, adj. & n. [1. nīn; 2. nain]. O.E. *nigon, nigen*, M.E. *nyne, nīne*; O.S. *nigun*, O.H.G. & Goth. *niun*, O.N. *níu*; cp. Lat. *novem*; Gk. *ennéa* for **(en)newn*; Scrt. *náva*; cp. also Ir. & Gael. *naoi*, W. *naw*; O. Prussian *newīnts.* **1.** adj. One more than eight and less than ten; often used with omission of noun, as *nine*, for nine o'clock; *only nine (persons) appeared.* Phrs. *nine days' wonder*, piece of news, scandal &c. that causes a sensation for a short time only and is quickly forgotten; *a cat has nine lives*, is very difficult to kill; *nine men's morris*, an old English game resembling draughts played with counters, stones &c. on a board or on a marked space on the ground; also the board or space of ground on which it was played. **2.** n. **a** The figure or symbol representing the number nine; **b** a playing card having nine pips: *the nine of hearts*; **c** person, object, who holds the ninth place in a series, usually *number nine.* Phrs. *the Nine*, the nine Muses; *dressed up to the nines*, dressed elaborately, carefully, and smartly.

ninefold, adj. & adv. [1. nínfōld; 2. náinfould]. **nine** & **-fold.** Nine times repeated; nine times as many.

ninepins, n. [1. nínpinz; 2. náinpinz]. Game played with nine wooden pins arranged in a diamond pattern, at which a ball is bowled; skittles: *to fall, be knocked, over like a lot of ninepins*, of a number of persons or objects, falling right and left, in all directions.

nineteen, adj. & n. [1. nīntḗn; 2. nàintī́n]. O.E. *nigontȳne.* **nine** & **ten.** Nine plus ten; one less than twenty. Phr. *to talk nineteen to the dozen*, to talk continually, persistently; to keep on chattering.

nineteenth, adj. [1. nīntḗnth; 2. nàintī́nþ]. Prec. & **-th.** Following eighteen others in a series. Phr. *nineteenth hole*, (golf) facetious name for place in club-house where a drink is taken after playing a round of eighteen holes.

ninetieth, adj. [1. níntieth; 2. náintiiþ]. **ninety** & **-th.** Following eighty-nine in a series.

ninety, adj. & n. [1. nínti; 2. náinti]. O.E. *nigontiġ.* **nine** & **-ty.** **a** adj. Ten times nine; **b** n., number equal to ten times nine; symbol of this. Phrs. *the nineties*, the years ninety to ninety-nine, of a particular century, esp. of the 19th cent.; *ninety-nine times out of a hundred*, nearly always.

ninny, n. [1. níni; 2. níni]. Etymol. unknown; a corrupt. of *an innocent* has been suggested; also relation to or adaptation of Ital. *ninno, ninna*, 'baby, child'. Fool, simpleton.

ninth, adj. & n. [1. nīnth; 2. nainþ]. **nine** & **-th.** **1.** adj. Following eight others in a series. **2.** n. **a** One of nine equal parts; a ninth part; **b** (mus.) an interval, a semitone or tone greater than an octave.

ninthly, adv. Prec. & **-ly.** In the ninth place in a series.

Niobe, n. [1. níōbi; 2. náioubi]. Gk. *Nióbē.* **1. a** (class. mythol.) A daughter of Tantalus, all of whose children were slain because of her pride in them; she was turned into stone, and her tears formed a stream; **b** a disconsolate woman for ever weeping. **2.** (bot.) A genus of Japanese lilies; the *Funkia* or day-lily.

niobic, adj. [1. nīóbik; 2. naióubik]. See next word & **-ic.** Of or pertaining to niobium.

niobium, n. [1. nīóbium; 2. naióubiəm]. Coined fr. name of **Niobe**, daughter of Tantalus. (chem.) Metallic element, also called *columbium*; it resembles *tantalum*, whence the name.

nip (I.), vb. trans. & intrans. [1. nip; 2. nip]. M.E. *nippen*; etymol. doubtful; L.G. has *nipen*, 'to pinch', cp. Du. *nijpen*, 'to pinch', also *knippen*, 'to clip'; possibly allied to **nibble**; the word does not appear in O.E. **A.** trans. **1. a** To pinch sharply with the fingers, or with claws, as a crab; to bite suddenly with the teeth, as a horse, dog; **b** to pinch, cut, clip, with an implement. **2.** (of wind, frost) **a** To cut off, cut down, burn, check growth of, blight: *east wind nips the early blossom*; Phr. *to nip in the bud*, to put a stop to, at the start, from the beginning; **b** (fig.) to damp, depress: *a chilly reception nipped the first enthusiasm.* **3.** (colloq. and slang) **a** To steal, pinch; **b** to catch, seize, arrest. **4.** *Nip off*, to cut, pinch, off (the buds of flowers, dead leaves &c.). **B.** intrans. **1.** To perform the action of pinching, biting &c.: *a crab can nip quite severely.* **2.** To strike cold or keen: *the wind nips pretty hard today.* **C.** Followed by prepositions or adverbs, in general sense of to run, make a rapid movement. *Nip along*, to hurry. *Nip in*, cut in, move quickly in or before another; to interrupt, break in: *he nipped in just in front of me*; to intervene suddenly in conversation: *nip in with a smart question, retort* &c. *Nip off*, depart hurriedly, run away. *Nip on ahead*, run so as to get in front.

nip (II.), n., fr. prec. **a** A pinch, bite, of fingers or teeth; **b** a sharp, keen bite of cold, wind; tang: *a nasty nip in the air.*

nip (III.), n. & vb. trans. & intrans. Etymol. doubtful. L.G. & Du. have *nippen*, 'to sip'. **1.** n. A sip; a small quantity of drink: *to take a nip of whisky.* **2.** vb. To sip, take drink, in small quantities, esp. repeatedly: *to be always nipping* (*whisky*).

nipa, n. [1. nēpa, nípa; 2. nípə, náipə]. Malay. *nīpah.* **a** A species of East Indian palm, *Nypa*; **b** wine made from the fermented sap of the tree.

nipper, n. [1. níper; 2. nípə], fr. **nip (I.)** & **-er.** **1.** One who or that which nips, pinches, or bites. **2.** (slang or colloq.) Young boy, lad, originally a boy who helps a hawker or costermonger. **3.** (pl.) *A pair of nippers*; **a** small pincers for twisting, cutting, or breaking off wire; **b** small dentist's forceps; **c** horse's incisor teeth; **d** crab's or lobster's large pinching claws. **4.** (pl.) Eye-glasses, pince-nez.

nipping, adj. [1. níping; 2. nípiŋ], fr. Pres. Part. of **nip (I.)**. (chiefly of wind, air &c.) Keen, sharp, biting cold.

nippingly, adv. Prec. & **-ly.** Sharply, keenly, so as to nip.

nipple, n. [1. nípl; 2. nípl]. Etymol. unknown; an earlier form, *neble*, suggests dimin. of **neb**, 'projection, beak'. **1. a** Teat of female breast; **b** an artificial teat on a feeding-bottle. **2.** The projection on lock of a percussion musket on which the cap was placed. **3.** A small nipple-like projection on glass, sheet of metal &c.

nipple-wort, n. Prec. & **wort (I.)**, 'plant, herb'. A weed or herb with small yellow flowers.

nippy, adj. [1. nípi; 2. nípi]. **nip (I.)** & **-y.** (colloq.) Quick, active, nimble: *you'll have to be pretty nippy if you want to catch the train.*

nirvana, n. [1. nërváhna; 2. niəvánə]. Scrt. *nirvāṇa*, lit. 'a blowing out', fr. *nirva*, 'to blow'. (Buddhism) State of complete blessedness attained when the individual soul is absorbed into, and united with, the divine infinity, and all personality is extinguished.

nisi, conj. [1. nísī; 2. náisai]. Lat., 'unless, if not'. In legal Phrs.: *decree nisi*, decree of divorce, which, after a specified time, will be made 'absolute', unless reason against it is brought forward by the King's Proctor; also *order, rule, nisi*, of an order &c. of the Court, which will be valid unless before a certain date reasons are given for rescinding it. *Nisi prius* [1. nísī príus; 2. náisai práiəs], Lat., 'unless before'. Originally, a writ for summoning jurors to Westminster unless, before the date fixed, the case has been tried in the country by a Judge of Assize; now, the Court presided over by a Judge of Assize for trying civil cases in the country.

nit, n. [1. nit; 2. nit]. O.E. *hnitu*, M.E. *nite*, O.H.G. *hniz*; cogn. w. Gk. *konid-(os)*, stem of *konis*, 'egg of louse'; cp. also *knizein*, fr. **knid-jo-*, 'to scrape, scratch, irritate, itch'; & *knēn*, 'to scratch'. The egg of a louse or other verminous parasitic insect.

nitrate, n. & vb. trans. [1. nītrāt; 2. náitreit], fr. **nitre** & **-ate.** **1.** n. (chem.) A salt or compound of nitric acid with a base; potassium nitrate or saltpetre in its natural state; also sodium nitrate or Chile saltpetre; also these as obtained by the fixation of nitrogen in the air or by the action of bacteria in the soil &c. *Nitrate of silver*, lunar caustic. **2.** vb. To combine, treat, with nitric acid or a nitrate; convert, make, into a nitrate.

nitration, n. [1. nītrāshun; 2. naitréiʃən]. Prec. & **-ion.** Process of nitrating, esp. of action of nitric acid on hydrocarbons.

nitre, n. [1. nīter; 2. náitə]. Fr., fr. Lat. *nitrum*, fr. Gk. *nitron*, 'native carbonate of soda, natron'; prob. Semitic in origin, cp. Heb. *nether*, 'nitre', Arab. *niṭrūn.* (chem.) **a** Potassium nitrate, saltpetre; **b** sodium nitrate, Chile saltpetre; also called *cubic nitre.*

nitric, adj. [1. nītrik; 2. náitrik], fr. Fr. *nitrique.* Prec. & **-ic.** **1.** (obs.) Of or belonging to nitre. **2.** (chem.) Of, pertaining to, containing, nitrogen, esp. of compounds in which nitrogen has a higher valency than in *nitrous* compounds: *nitric acid*, a powerfully corrosive, oxidizing acid compound of hydrogen, nitrogen, and oxygen, *aqua fortis*; *nitric oxide*, colourless gas obtained by treating copper with nitric acid.

nitride, n. [1. nītrīd; 2. náitraid]. **nitro-** & **-ide.** (chem.) Compound of nitrogen with a metallic element.

nitrification, n. [1. nītrifikāshun; 2. naitrifikéiʃən], fr. Fr. See **nitrify.** Act, process, of nitrifying; specif., the formation of nitrates in soil or manures by the action of bacteria which form ammonia and change this into nitrites and nitrates.

nitrify, vb. trans. [1. nītrifī; 2. náitrifai], fr. Fr. *nitrifier.* **nitre** & **-fy.** To change into nitrous or nitric acid or into nitrates or nitrites by oxidation; to carry through the process of nitrification, as bacteria.

nitrite, n. [1. nītrīt; 2. náitrait]. **nitre** & **-ite.** (chem.) A salt or compound of nitrous acid.

nitro, adj. [1. nītrō; 2. náitrou], fr. next word. Containing nitrogen, or nitric or nitrous acid: *nitro compound*, compound made by the action of nitric acid on hydrocarbons.

nitro-, pref., fr. Gk. *nitron*, 'soda, natron'. See **nitre.** (chem.) A combining form indicating presence of, use of, nitrogen or nitric or nitrous acid, also to make names for compounds of nitrogen and of its acids: *nitro-bacteria*, bacteria found in the soil which have the power of combining the nitrogen of the atmosphere and forming fertilizing compounds; *nitro-benzene*, nitro-compound made from benzene, used in perfumery and in manufacture of aniline dyes; *nitro-cellulose*, an explosive, made by action of nitric acid on cellulose; *nitro-toluene*, high explosive, obtained by treating toluene with nitric acid.

nitrogen, n. [1. nītrojen; 2. náitrədžin], fr. Fr. *nitrogène.* **nitro-** & **-gen.** (chem.) A gaseous element, colourless and without taste or smell, forming about 78% of the atmosphere, formerly called 'azote', as incapable of supporting life by itself, but an essential to the life of animals and plants. *Nitrogen fixation*, the changing of the nitrogen in the air into forms useful for fertilizers, explosives &c.; *nitrogen-fixing*, adj., of certain bacteria, *nitro-bacteria*, see **nitro-.**

nitrogenous, adj. [1. nītrójenus; 2. naitródžinəs]. **nitrogen** & **-ous.** Of, belonging to, containing, nitrogen.

nitro-glycerine, n. [1. nītrō glíserin; 2. naitrou glísərin]. **nitro-** & **glycerine.** A colourless oily liquid, obtained by treatment of glycerine with nitric and sulphuric acids, extremely explosive and used in the manufacture of dynamite, gelignite, and other blasting explosives.

nitrous, adj. [1. nītrus; 2. náitrəs]. Lat. *nitrōsus*, 'full of nitre or natron'. **nitre** & **-ous.** **1.** (obs.) Of, belonging to, impregnated with, nitre. **2.** (chem.) Of, pertaining to, containing, nitrogen, esp. of compounds in which nitrogen has a lower valency than in *nitric* compounds: *nitrous acid*, acid which forms nitrite salts; *nitrous oxide*, gaseous oxide of nitrogen, nitrogen monoxide, used as an anaesthetic, the laughing-gas of dentists.

nitroxyl, n. [1. nītróksil; 2. naitróksil], fr. **nitro-** & **oxygen** & **-yl.** (chem.) A radical compounded of one atom of nitrogen with two of oxygen.

Nivôse, n. [1. nēvóz; 2. nivóuz], fr. Lat. *nivōsus*, 'snowy', fr. *nix, nivis*, 'snow'. See **snow** for cogn. words. Fourth month of the French Revolutionary calendar, Dec. 21st to Jan. 19th.

nix (I.), n. masc., **nixie**, fem. [1. niks, níksi; 2. niks, níksi]. Mod. Germ. *nix*, masc., *nixe*, fem.; O.H.G. *nichus*; cogn. w. O.E. *nicor*, 'water-sprite', cp. O.N. *nykr*, Du. *nikker*, of same meaning; possibly to be connected w. stem seen in Gk. *nizein*, 'to wash'. A water-sprite.

nix (II.), n. Dial. form of Mod. Germ. *nichts*, 'nothing'. (slang) Nothing.

nixie. See **nix (I.).**

Nizam, n. [1. nizáhm; 2. naizám]. Hind. & Pers., 'governor', fr. Arab. *niḍhām*, 'order, government'. **1.** Title of the ruler of Hyderabad, India; originally, *Nizām-al-Mulk*, 'Governor of the Empire'. **2.** A soldier of the Turkish army.

no (I.), adv. [1. nō; 2. nou]. O.E. *nā*, adv., fr. *ne*, 'not', & *ā*, 'ever', see **aye**; M.E. *na, ne*, adv., only before cons., see **none**; Common Gmc. & Aryan. **1.** (after *or*, as alternative) Not: *cold or no, you must go out today.* Phr. *whether or no*, in either case. **2.** (with compars.) In no respect, not any, not at all: *he's no better*; *it no longer exists* &c.; *no less than seven foot high*; *go no further.* Phrs. *no more*, **a** not any more: *no more war*; *no more of that!*; *I have no more to do*; **b** no longer: *Ilium is no more*, has ceased to exist; *to be no more*, be dead; **c** never again: *he will speak no more*; **d** (followed by *than*) in no greater degree than: *he's no more blind than you*; *can no more do it than fly*; **e** neither: *if you won't do it, no more will I*; *no sooner said than done*, done at once, immediately.

no (II.), adj. O.E. *nān*, M.E. *nōn*; fr. *ne ān*, 'not one', see **none**; *-n* was lost before cons. Not one, none, not any: **a** followed by noun: *there's no food in the house*; *he had no luck*; **b** implying the opposite of that expressed by the word that follows: *he's no fool*, is a clever fellow; *it is no distance from here*, quite close, hardly any distance; **c** followed by another adjective or verbal noun: *he showed no small skill*; *there's no getting over that*, one must acknowledge that; **d** as prohibition: *no Popery!*; *no surrender!*; *no compromise!* Phrs. (see also under separate headings as **nobody, nothing** &c.) *no doubt*, of course;

no end of money, friends &c., (colloq.) a great deal of, very many; *no end of a swell*, a very great one; *no go*, (colloq.) useless, hopeless, a failure: *it is no go, we're done for*; *nohow, no-how*, (colloq. & illit.) not anyhow: *I can't do it nohow*; *I feel nohow*, not up to the mark, rather unwell; *no man*, no one, nobody; *no man's land* (O.E. *nānes mannes land*): (i.) (hist.) a debatable land, borderland, which belongs to no one; (ii.) specif., ground between the most advanced trenches of two opposing forces in war; *by no means*, (i.) in no way, under no circumstance; (ii.) of course not; *no one*, nobody, no person, none; *no side*, (Rugby football) the end of the game, as called by the referee; *no thoroughfare*, (i.) (as notice), this road is closed; (ii.) (as n.) a closed road, a cul-de-sac; *at no time*, never; (*it was done &c.*) *in no time*, (colloq.) quickly, at once; *no wonder*, it is not surprising: *no wonder he ran away from her*, implying that he had every reason to do so.

no (III.), neg. particle. See **no** (I.). **1. a** A negative word; refusal, denial in word: *he answered No*; *will you do this? No*; **b** as a strong or emphasized negative with *nor* or *not*: *he could not persuade them, no, nor could an angel from heaven*; *no, not an inch farther*. **2.** n. pl. *The noes*, negative votes in House of Commons; in Phr. *the noes have it*.

Noachian, adj. [1. nōákian; 2. nouéikiən]. Heb. *Noach*, 'Noah'. Of or pertaining to the patriarch Noah or to the period in which he lived: *Noachian deluge*, the Flood.

Noah's Ark, n. [1. náwz árk; 2. nɔ́z ák]. Child's toy, consisting of a wooden receptacle shaped like the Ark according to the traditional conception, containing figures representing Noah and his family and the animals.

nob (I.), n. [1. nob; 2. nɔb]. Etymol. doubtful; prob. spelling variant of **knob**. **1.** (slang or colloq.) The head. **2.** (cribbage) The knave of the suit of the card turned up, counting one point to the holder: *one for his nob*.

nob (II.), vb. trans., fr. prec. (boxing) To hit on the head.

nob (III.), n. Prob. abbr. of *noble(man)* has been suggested. (vulg. or obs.) Person of rank or of high position; a personage.

no-ball, n. & vb. trans. **1.** n. (cricket) A ball improperly delivered by the bowler, counting one to the opposite side when so declared by the umpire. **2.** vb. (of the umpire) To attribute a no-ball; to declare (bowler) to have bowled such.

nobble, vb. trans. [1. nóbl; 2. nɔ́bl]. Etymol. unknown. (slang) **1.** To injure, or tamper with, a horse in training by drugging, laming &c., so as to prevent, or lessen, its chances of winning a race. **2.** To win over, by bribery or other inducement, for one's own purposes, esp. to induce a jockey to pull the horse he is riding, or otherwise prevent it from winning a race. **3.** To cheat, defraud, swindle. **4.** To obtain (money, prize &c.) by dishonest means.

nobbler, n. [1. nóbler; 2. nɔ́blə]. Prec. & **-er**. (slang) One who nobbles a horse, jockey &c.; swindler, cheat.

nobby, adj. [1. nóbi; 2. nɔ́bi], fr. **nob** (III.) & **-y**. (slang) Superior, smart, showy, stylish.

nobiliary, adj. [1. nōbíliari; 2. noubíliəri]. Fr. *nobiliaire*. See **noble** & **-ary**. Of or pertaining to nobility or to nobles: *nobiliary prefix*, prefix or particle preceding the surname, indicating rank, as the Germ. *von*, Fr. *de*, 'of'.

nobility, n. [1. nōbíliti; 2. noubíliti], fr. O. Fr. *nobilite*, Mod. Fr. *nobilité*, fr. Lat. *nōbilitāt-(em)*, *nōbilitas*, 'nobleness, nobility', fr. *nōbilis*. See **noble** & **-ity**. **1.** State, quality, of being noble; nobleness; **a** (of character, mind &c.) high-mindedness, magnanimity: *nobility of soul*; **b** (of outward appearance) grandeur, impressiveness, sublimity: *austere nobility of a Norman cathedral*. **2.** Condition of being noble by birth or rank. **3.** Body of noble persons collectively; specif. (in England) the members of the Upper House and their families; often contrasted with *gentry*.

noble (I.), adj. [1. nṓbl; 2. nóubl]. Fr. *noble*, fr. Lat. *nōbilis*, 'well-known, famous, of high birth or rank, noble'; for **gnōbilis*, fr. base **gnō-*, as in *(g)noscere*, 'to know'. See **notion, gnomon, know**. **1.** Famous, illustrious, renowned: *the noble names of chivalry*. **2. a** (of character and conduct) Lofty, magnanimous, directed by high ideals: *noble sentiments*; *noble life, actions* &c; **b** (of persons) animated by noble ideals, possessing noble qualities of character: *a noble soul*; **c** (of forms of expression) exhibiting noble qualities of mind: *a noble poem*; *Milton's noble lines*. **3.** Exciting admiration; grand, imposing, stately, impressive: *a noble countenance*; *planned on a noble scale*; *a noble horse, tree, mountain* &c.; Phrs. *the noble metals*, (as contrasted with the base metals) gold, silver, platinum, and other rare metals which do not quickly deteriorate or waste by oxidation; *the noble art*, boxing. **5.** Belonging to, sprung from, connected with, a family possessing hereditary nobility: *of noble birth*; *a noble line of ancestry*; *the noble Lord*, form of address or reference to another member in the House of Lords, or to one having the courtesy title of Lord in the House of Commons; *my noble friend*, referring to a peer, or person with courtesy title of Lord, in a public speech; also, now, *the noble lady*, to a peeress.

noble (II.), n., fr. prec. **1.** Person of noble birth; one who belongs to the ranks of the nobility; a peer, nobleman. **2.** (hist.) A gold coin and money of account, dating from the reign of Edward III., value about 6s. 8d.

noble fir, n. A giant fir, *Abies nobilis*, of Western United States.

nobleman, n. [1. nṓblman; 2. nóublmən]. A member of the nobility, a peer.

noble-minded, adj. Having a noble mind; magnanimous.

noble-mindedness, n. Prec. & **-ness**. Quality of being noble-minded.

nobleness, n. [1. nṓblnes; 2. nóublnis]. **noble** (I.) & **-ness**. Quality of being noble; in various senses.

noblesse, n. [1. nōblés; 2. noublés]. Fr., 'nobility, the nobility or peerage'. See **noble** (I.) & **-ess(e)**. The nobility; nobles as a class, esp. of a foreign country; high rank or position; in Phr. *noblesse oblige*, 'nobility obliges', high rank or position entails obligations of courage, generosity, magnanimity &c.

noblewoman, n. [1. nṓblwòoman; 2. nóublwùmən]. (rare) A woman of noble rank or birth; peeress.

nobly, adv. [1. nṓbli; 2. nóubli]. **noble** (I.) & **-ly**. In a noble manner; in a manner befitting a noble character; splendidly, magnificently, bravely: *sufferings nobly borne*.

nobody, n. [1. nṓbodi; 2. nóubədi]. **no** (II.) & **body**. **1.** No person, no one, not any one, not any body: *there was nobody present*. Phr. *everybody's business is nobody's business*, responsibility cannot be shared. **2.** A person of no account or importance; an insignificant, obscure individual: *she has married a nobody*; *a mere nobody*.

nock (I.), n. [1. nok; 2. nɔk]. Etymol. doubtful; Du. has *nok*, 'tip of a sail', & Swed. dial. *nokke*, 'notch'. **1.** A notch for holding the string at either end of a bow or at one end of an arrow. **2.** The upper fore-corner of a sail.

nock (II.), vb. trans., fr. prec. To make a notch on a bow or arrow for holding the string.

noct(i)-, pref. Lat., stem of *nox*, fr. *noct-s*, 'night'. See **night**. (chiefly zool.) Meaning 'of, by, at, night', as *noctambulant*, walking by night; *noctivagant, noctivagous*, wandering by night, as animals in search of prey &c.

noctule, n. [1. nóktūl; 2. nɔ́ktjūl]. Fr. See prec. & **-ule**. A large brown bat of British Isles and Europe.

nocturnal, adj. & n. [1. noktérnal; 2. nɔktánl]. L. Lat. *nocturnālis*, fr. Lat. *nocturnus*, 'of or by night'. See **noct(i)-** & **-al** & cp. **diurnal**. **1.** adj. Of, belonging to, the night; done or occurring in the night; *nocturnal sounds, habits, wanderings*; *nocturnal animals*, such as move about and become generally active at night. **2.** n. (astron.) Instrument for fixing the hour by relative position of the stars by night.

nocturnally, adv. Prec. & **-ly**. By night, during the night.

nocturne, nocturn, n. [1. nóktērn; 2. nɔ́ktān]. Fr., fr. Lat. *nocturnus*. See **nocturnal**. **1. a** (mus.) A composition of a pensive, melancholy character; **b** (paint.) a night-scene or night-piece. **2.** Evening service in church.

nocuous, adj. [1. nókūus; 2. nɔ́kjuəs]. Lat. *nocuus*, 'harmful', fr. *nocēre*, 'to harm, injure', & **-ous**; the base *noc-* is in gradational relation to *nec-* in *necāre*, 'to kill, destroy'; cp. also Gk. *nekrós*, 'corpse', q.v. under **necro-**. Harmful; poisonous, noxious.

nod (I.), vb. intrans. & trans. [1. nod; 2. nɔd]. M.E. *nodden*, vb.; not in O.E. nor, apparently, in other Gmc. languages; etymol. unknown. **A.** intrans. **1.** To make a short, sharp downward movement with the head, **a** as a sign of assent, comprehension, approval, acknowledgment; **b** as a greeting: *to nod to a person in the street*. Phr. *a nodding acquaintanceship with*, a casual, superficial knowledge of person, subject &c. **2. a** To allow the head to drop forward from time to time from drowsiness; to be overcome by drowsiness; to fall asleep: *to sit nodding in one's pew*; **b** (fig.) to be inattentive, careless; to make a slip or error, not to be always alert and wide awake: *to catch one nodding*. Phr. *Homer sometimes nods*, even the greatest make mistakes, are not always supreme. **3.** (of inanimate things) To bend, incline, sway, wave, as trees in the wind &c.; to dance, bob up and down, to toss as flowers on their stalks, and plumes in the breeze &c. **B.** trans. *To nod the head*, to jerk it forward with a nod, in sign of agreement, approbation &c.; '*Even mitred Rochester would nod the head*' (Pope, 'To Arbuthnot').

nod (II.), n., fr. prec. **a** A deliberate, sharp, short inclination of the head in token of assent or greeting; **b** involuntary movement forward of the head, from drowsiness, when seated. *The land of Nod*, sleep, dreams.

nodal, adj. [1. nṓdal; 2. nóudəl], fr. **node** & **-al**. Of or belonging to a node, esp. of the node or point of rest of a vibrating body.

noddle, n. [1. nódl; 2. nɔ́dl]. Etymol. dubious; possibly connected w. **nod** (I.). (colloq.) Head; esp. in Phr. *cannot get, drive, it (facts &c.) into his (one's) noddle*; *to wag one's noddle*, as in animated conversation &c.

noddy, n. [1. nódi; 2. nɔ́di]. Etymol. unknown. Cp. **noodle**. **1.** Simpleton, fool, booby. **2.** Popular sailor's name for a sea-bird, *Anous*, of the South Atlantic, so called from the easiness of its capture.

node, n. [1. nōd; 2. noud]. Fr., fr. Lat. *nōdus*, 'knot, knob'; perh. connected w. Lat. *nectere*, 'to bind'. See **nexus**. **1. a** Protuberance, knot, joint on a stem of a plant, from which the leaves spring; **b** hard swelling on a joint or muscle. **2. a** (astron.) Point where the orbit of a planet intersects the ecliptic or where two great circles cross each other; **b** (math.) point where a curve turns and crosses itself; **c** (phys.) point of rest of a vibrating body.

nodical, adj. [1. nṓdikl; 2. nóudikl]. Prec. & **-ic** & **-al**. (astron.) Pertaining to a node.

nodose, adj. [1. nṓdōs; 2. nóudous], fr. Lat. *nōdōsus*, 'full of knots'. See **node** & **-ous**. (bot., of plant stems) Full of knots or nodes.

nodosity, n. [1. nōdósiti; 2. noudɔ́siti]. Lat. *nōdōsitāt-(em)*. Prec. & **-ity**. (bot.) State of being full of knots or nodes; knottiness.

nodular, adj. [1. nódūlar; 2. nɔ́djulə]. **nodule** & **-ar**. Having nodules.

nodulated, adj. [1. nódūlāted; 2. nɔ́djuleitid]. **nodule** & **-ate** & **-ed**. Having nodules.

nodule, n. [1. nód-, nṓdūl; 2. nɔ́d-, nóudjūl]. Fr., fr. Lat. *nōdulus*, 'little knot', dimin. of *nōdus*, 'knot'. See **node**. **a** A small, rounded lump, as of a mineral; **b** knot on stem or root of plants &c.

nodulose, adj. [1. nódūlōs; 2. nɔ́djulous]. Prec. & **-ose**. Having nodules.

nodulous, adj. [1. nódūlus; 2. nɔ́djuləs]. See prec. & **-ous**. Having nodules.

nodus, n. [1. nṓdus; 2. nóudəs]. Lat. *nōdus*, 'knot'. See **node**. Knot, node; (chiefly fig.) knotty point, difficulty; complication in plot of a story.

Noel, n. [1. nṓel; 2. nóuel]. Earlier *nowel*, fr. Fr. *noël*, 'Christmas', fr. Lat. *nātālis*, n., 'birthday', adj., 'of birth'. See **natal**. **1.** Christmas. **2.** Cry of 'Noel', in joyous welcome of Christ's Nativity, and so as first word of well-known carol.

noesis, n. [1. nōḗsis; 2. nouísis]. Gk. *nóēsis*, 'perception of the mind, intelligence, thought', see next word. (psychol.) The working of the pure intellect or reason.

noetic, adj. [1. nōétik, -ḗtik; 2. nouétik, -ítik], fr. Gk. *noētikós*, 'of or belonging to perception or intelligence', fr. *noētós*, 'perceptible by the mind or intellect', fr. *noeîn*, 'to perceive by the mind, to think', fr. *noûs*, fr. *nóos*, 'mind'; the etymol. is quite uncertain. Cp. **nous**. (philos.) **1.** Of or pertaining to the intellect or reason, of the mind considered apart from sensation. **2.** (as n. pl.) *Noetics*, science of the mind or pure intellect.

nog (**I.**), n. & vb. trans. [1. nog; 2. nɔg]. Etymol. unknown. **1.** n. A wooden peg or pin, esp. a wooden brick-shaped block used as framing for brickwork. **2.** vb. To frame or fit brickwork with nogs or a wooden scantling, usually as vbl. n., *nogging*, brickwork framed in scantling.

nog (**II.**), n. Etymol. unknown. (obs.) **a** A drink, made of strong ale; **b** egg-nog.

noggin, n. [1. nógin; 2. nɔ́gin]. Etymol. unknown. (obs. or dial.) **a** Small cup or mug; **b** a measure of spirits equal to a gill.

nohow, adv. [1. nṓhou; 2. nóuhau]. See **no** (**II.**) & **how**. (vulg.) In no wise; by no means.

noil, n. [1. noil; 2. nɔil]. Etymol. unknown. Waste combings of wool, hair, or silk, cp. *top*.

noise (**I.**), n. [1. noiz; 2. nɔiz], fr. Fr. *noise*, 'quarrel, brawl'; O. Fr. has *nose* & Provenç. *nauza, nausa, noisa*, 'noise'; according to Meyer-Lübke, fr. Lat. *nausea*, 'sea-sickness'. See **nausea**. **1.** Clamour, uproar, disturbance, shouting; any loud, discordant, or unpleasant sound; din. Phr. *a big noise* (colloq., U.S.A.), a person of great importance, esp. in his own estimation. **2.** (obs. or archaic) Rumour, gossip: *the noise goes that . . .*

noise (**II.**), vb. trans., fr. prec. To proclaim, put about, spread rumour that; esp. *to noise abroad*.

noiseless, adj. [1. nóizles; 2. nɔ́izlis]. **noise** (**I.**) & **-less**. Without noise; silent, quiet.

noiselessly, adv. Prec. & **-ly**. Silently, quietly.

noiselessness, n. See prec. & **-ness**. State, quality, of being without noise; silence, quietness.

noisette (**I.**), n. [1. noizét, nwahzét; 2. nɔizét, nwāzét]. Fr. dimin. of *noix*, 'nut', fr. Lat. *nux, nūcis*, 'nut'. See **nux vomica**. Small piece of veal, mutton &c. cooked with special sauce.

noisette (**II.**), n., fr. name of grower, L. Noisette. A hybrid rose of the China and musk varieties.

noisily, adv. [1. nóizili; 2. nɔ́izili], fr. **noisy** & **-ly**. In a noisy manner.

noisiness, n. [1. nóizines; 2. nɔ́izinis]. See prec. & **-ness**. Clamour, noise, disturbance.

noisome, adj. [1. nóisum; 2. nɔ́isəm]. First element as in **annoy** & **nuisance**, & **-some**. (in both physical and moral sense) Harmful, unhealthy, hurtful; offensive, disgusting.

noisomeness, n. Prec. & **-ness**. Unwholesomeness, offensiveness.

noisy, adj. [1. nóizi; 2. nɔ́izi]. **noise** (**I.**) & **-y**. **a** Making a noise; loud, clamorous, rowdy, discordant: *a noisy engine, laugh, person, animal &c.*; **b** pervaded by noise: *noisy streets, a noisy house.*

nolens volens, adv. [1. nṓlenz vṓlenz; 2. nóulenz vóulenz]. Lat., Pres. Part. of *nōlo*, 'I will not', & *volo*, 'I will', lit. 'unwilling, willing'. See **voluntary**. Without or with consent, under compulsion, willy-nilly.

noli-me-tangere, n. [1. nṓlī mē tánjere; 2. nóulai mī tǽndžəri]. Lat., 'touch me not'. See prec. & **tangent**. **1.** Picture or other representation of Christ and Mary Magdalene at the sepulchre, John xx. 17. **2.** (bot.) A plant, genus *Impatiens*, whose seed-capsules burst at a touch when ripe. **3.** (med.) An ulcerous skin disease, such as lupus. **4.** Person of a repellent, forbidding manner or appearance; (also attrib.) *a noli-me-tangere look*.

nolle prosequi, n. [1. nóle prósekwī; 2. nɔ́li prɔ́sɛkwai]. Lat., 'to be unwilling to prosecute'. See **nolens volens** & **prosecute**. (law) A formal notice that a plaintiff will not continue a suit or that a prosecutor will not proceed with the charge.

nolo episcopari, n. [1. nṓlō episkopā́rī; 2. nóulou ɛpiskəpéərai]. Lat., 'I do not wish to become a bishop'. See prec. & **episcopal**. Form of words used in refusing an offer of a bishopric; (fig.) refusal to accept a position of responsibility.

nomad, n. & adj. [1. nómad; 2. nɔ́mæd]. Lat. *nomad-(em)*, acc. of *nomas*, 'wanderer, member of pastoral tribe', fr. Gk. *nomás, nomádos*, in same sense, fr. *nomós*, 'pasture, land allotted to tribe' &c., fr. *némein*, 'to distribute, allot'; also 'to pasture flocks &c. on', fr. base seen in **Nemesis** & **number**. **1.** n. Member of a wandering, pastoral tribe or people; a wanderer. **2.** adj. Wandering, pastoral, nomadic: *nomad tribes*.

nomadic, adj. [1. nōmádik; 2. noumǽdik]. Prec. & **-ic**. Wandering, pastoral, nomad.

nomadically, adv. [1. nōmádikali; 2. noumǽdikəli]. As prec. & **-al** & **-ly**. As a nomad, as nomads.

nomadism, n. [1. nómadizm; 2. nɔ́mædizəm]. **nomad** & **-ism**. State of being nomadic.

nomarch, n. [1. nómark; 2. nɔ́māk], fr. Gk. *nomárchēs, nómarchos*, 'ruler of an (Egyptian) *nomós*, or province', see **nome**, & **-arch**. Ruler, governor, of a nome, **a** in ancient Egypt, **b** in modern Greece.

nomarchy, n. [1. nómarki; 2. nɔ́māki]. Gk. *nomarchia*, as prec. & **-y**. Province, nome, in modern Greece, or in ancient Egypt, ruled by a nomarch.

nom de guerre, n. (partly Anglicized) [1. nòm de gā́r; 2. nɔ̃ də gέə]. Fr., lit. 'war-name'. Assumed name, pseudonym, sobriquet; originally as assumed name of a soldier enlisting for service not under his own name.

nom de plume, n. [1. nòm de plū́m; 2. nɔ̃ də plūm, plym]. Fr., 'pen name'; an English expression, not French. Assumed name, pseudonym, pen-name, of writer.

nome, n. [1. nōm; 2. noum]. Fr., fr. Gk. *nomós*, 'district, province', fr. *némein*, 'to distribute, allot'. See **nomad**, **Nemesis** &c. A district or province in ancient Egypt and modern Greece.

nomenclator, n. [1. nṓmenklā̀tōr; 2. nóumɛnklèitɔ]. Lat., 'caller of a name', fr. Lat. *nōmen*, 'name', & *calātor*, 'caller, crier', fr. *calāre*, 'to call'. See **nominal**, & the base of **clamant, claim** &c. **1.** A slave, or attendant, who supplied his master, when canvassing for office, with the names of clients, or of other people he met. **2.** An inventor, giver of names, esp. of new scientific names, with reference to classification.

nomenclature, n. [1. nṓmenklā̀cher, nōménklachur; 2. nóumɛnklèitʃə, nouménklətʃə], fr. Lat. *nōmenclātūra*, 'calling of names', as prec., but w. suff. **-ure**. System of naming or of names; terminology; esp. in the classification of the sciences and arts.

nomic, adj. [1. nómik; 2. nɔ́mik], fr. Gk. *nomikós*, 'legal, customary', fr. *nómos*, 'law, custom'. See **nomad**, **nome**, & suff. of **agronomy**. Customary, ordinary: *nomic spelling*, contrasted with *phonetic spelling*.

nominal, adj. [1. nóminal; 2. nɔ́minəl], fr. Lat. *nōminālis*, 'belonging to a name', fr. *nōmen, nōminis*, 'name', see **name**, & **-al**. The word was orig. distinct fr., but early associated w., the base *$*$g̑nō-*, 'to know', cp. **cognomen**; see **gnomon** & **know**. **1. a** Concerned with names: *a nominal error*; **b** (gram.) concerned with nouns: *nominal declension*; **c** containing names only: *a nominal index, register*. **2.** Existing in name only; **a** not actual or real; titular, merely so-called: *the nominal head of the State*; *only nominal power*; **b** inconsiderable, slight, light &c.: *a nominal price, damages*, very low; *duties that were only nominal*, very light.

nominalism, n. [1. nóminalizm; 2. nɔ́minəlizəm]. Fr. *nominalisme*. Prec. & **-ism**. (philos.) Doctrine of the scholastics (11th cent.) that universals or general abstract terms are names or words only, and have no realities or objective existences corresponding to them; contrasted with *realism*.

nominalist, n. [1. nóminalist; 2. nɔ́minəlist]. See prec. & **-ist**. One who holds the doctrine of nominalism; (also attrib.) *the nominalist school of philosophy*.

nominalistic, adj. [1. nòminalístik; 2. nɔ̀minəlístik]. Prec. & **-ic**. Of, pertaining to, nominalism or the nominalists.

nominate, vb. trans. [1. nóminā̆t; 2. nɔ́mineit], fr. Lat. *nōmināt-(um)*, P.P. of *nōmināre*, 'to name, make famous, nominate', fr. *nōmen*, 'name', see **nominal**, & **-ate**. To put down, and bring forward, the name of a person for appointment to an office, or as candidate for a post to be filled by election.

nomination, n. [1. nòminā́shun; 2. nɔ̀minéiʃən], fr. Lat. *nōminātiōn-(em)*, acc. of *nōminātio*, 'naming'. See prec. & **-ation**. **1. a** Act of nominating person for appointment to office, or as candidate for election &c.; **b** entry of name of a horse for a race. **2.** Right of nomination to office &c.: *to have the nomination of a candidate in one's hands*. **3.** Attributively, as *nomination day*, day fixed for nominating candidates for a parliamentary or other election.

nominatival, adj. [1. nòminatī́vl; 2. nɔ̀minətáivl]. Next word & **-al**. Nominative.

nominative (**I.**), adj., fr. Lat. *nōminātīvus*, 'of or belonging to a name'. See prec. & **-ive**. **1.** (gram.) [1. nóminativ; 2. nɔ́minətiv]. Of or belonging to that case of the noun, pronoun, or adjective which is that of the subject of a verb: *the nominative case*. **2.** [1. nóminā̆tiv; 2. nɔ́mineitiv] Nominated, named: *the nominative officials*, as contrasted with *elective*.

nominative (**II.**), n., fr. prec **a** The nominative case; **b** a word in that case.

nominator, n. [1. nóminā̆ter; 2. nɔ́minèitə]. **nominate** & **-or**. One who nominates.

nominee, n. [1. nòminḗ; 2. nɔ̀mini], fr. Lat. *nōmen*, 'name', see **nominal**, & **-ee**. Person nominated for office, appointment &c.

non, adv. [1. non; 2. nɔn]. Lat. *nōn*, fr. *ne*, 'not', & *ūnum*, 'one'. See **union**; cp. **none**. Not. The word is only used as negative prefix or combining form with nouns, verbal nouns, and adjectives; it has often a more neutral meaning than the parallel negative prefixes **in-** & **un-**, implying mere absence of qualities &c., rather than a positive or direct opposite. Only those compound words, which have some special or technical meaning and are usually hyphenated, are given under this heading. Others which are usually spelt as one word will be found in their proper place in alphabetical order, as will Latin phrases &c. *Non-access*, n., (law) impossibility of access of a husband to his wife, for the purpose of sexual intercourse. *Non-appearance*, n., (law) failure to appear in court as plaintiff or defendant in an action. *Non-attendance*, n., failure to attend at school, under the Compulsory Education Acts. *Non-committal*, adj., not committing oneself, not saying 'yes' or 'no', neutral: *gave a non-committal answer*. *Non-condensing*, adj., (of steam engines) allowing the steam to escape and be wasted in the air. *Non-conductor*, n., substance which does not conduct, transmit electricity, heat or sound; insulator. *Non-content*, n., vote or person voting in the negative in the House of Lords. *Non-co-operation*, n., state, act, of not co-operating or working with; specially of the policy pursued in India of not working with the Government, by boycotting British goods, refusing to pay taxes &c., or to take part in Government. *Non-effective*, adj. & n., (mil. and nav.) **a** adj., not liable for active service but still drawing pay; **b** n., one not liable for active service. *Non-essential*, adj. & n.; **a** adj., not essential, not absolutely necessary; **b** n., that which is not necessary, trifle: *do not trouble about non-essentials*. *Non-Euclidean*, adj. (of geometry) not based on the axioms and postulates of Euclid's geometry. *Non-feasance*, n., (law) omission to do what is legally obligatory. *Non-ferrous*, adj., (of metals) containing no iron, as copper, lead, nickel &c. *Non-intervention*, n., state, practice, of not intervening or interfering, esp. of one nation or state, in the policy &c., affairs or disputes of another. *Non-jury*, adj., (law) without a jury, of actions; see also **Nonjuror**. *Non-metallic*, adj. (chem.), not metallic, of those elements which are not metals. *Non-moral*, adj., not concerned with morals or ethics; neither moral nor immoral, having no standard of morality; wanting a moral sense. *Non-natural*, adj., not natural, not occurring according to ordinary natural law or in a natural sense or way. *Non-participating*, adj., (insurance) of policy which does not entitle holder to share in profits. *Non-party*, adj., without political party feeling or prejudices. *Non-professional*, adj., not done in the exercise or performance of a profession: *non-professional visit*, of a doctor's visit, of a friendly character, not entailing a fee (contrasted with *unprofessional*). *Non-resident*, adj. & n., **a** adj., not residing or living in or at the place where duties are performed, esp. of clergyman who does not live in his parish; **b** n., one who does not reside &c. *Non-resistance*, n., passive obedience to authority, law &c., without resisting by force. *Non-union*, adj., not belonging to a trades union; so *non-unionist*, n., one who is not a member of a union.

nonage, n. [1. nōnij; 2. nóunidž], fr. O. Fr. **non & age.** State, condition, of not being of age; minority; immaturity: *still in his nonage*.

nonagenarian, n. [1. nònajenárian; 2. nòunədžinéəriən], fr. Lat. *nōnāgēnārius*, adj., 'consisting of ninety'; n., 'commander of ninety men', L. Lat. 'person ninety years old', fr. *nōnāgēni*, 'ninety each', *nōnāginta*, 'ninety', fr. *nōnus*, 'ninth'. See **nine.** Person who has reached, or passed, the age of ninety, but has not yet reached a hundred years.

nonary, adj. [1. nónari; 2. nóunəri], fr. Lat. *nōnārius*, 'of the ninth', fr. *nōnus*, 'ninth'. See **nine.** (math.) Having the number nine as the basis in a system of notation.

nonce, n. [1. nons; 2. nɔns]. In M.E. *for then ōnes*, 'for the once, for the occasion'; *then* represents O.E. dat. case of def. art. after *for*; according to M.E. syll. division, the *-n* began the stressed syll. *fòrþe nōnes*. See **once. a** In Phr. *for the nonce*, lit. *for the once*, for a special occasion, for the time being, for the present, temporarily; **b** (attrib.) *a nonce-word*, a word invented for a special occasion and only used once.

nonchalance, n. [1. nónshalans; 2. nɔ́ʃaləns]; or as Fr. Fr. See next word & **-ce.** State of being nonchalant; indifference, want of enthusiasm or feeling; coolness, absence of excitability.

nonchalant, adj. [1. nónshalant; 2. nɔ́ʃalã]. Fr., Pres. Part. of O. Fr. *nonchaloir*, 'to neglect, be careless of', fr. *non*, 'not', & *chaloir*, 'to glow, be hot', fr. Lat. *calēre*, 'to be warm'. See **calescence.** Indifferent, not enthusiastic; cool, not excited · careless.

nonchalantly, adv. Prec. & **-ly.** In an indifferent, careless way or manner.

non-collegiate, adj. [1. nòn kolējiat; 2. nɔ̀n kəlídži-it]. **non & collegiate.** Not belonging to or attached to a college, specif., of students who are members of Oxford or Cambridge, but do not belong to any particular college; unattached.

non-combatant, n. & adj. [1. nòn kúmbatant; 2. nɔ̀n kámbətənt]. **non & combatant. 1.** n. **a** A member of the naval and military forces who does not belong to the fighting branches of the service; **b** a civilian. **2.** adj. Pertaining to, consisting of, non-combatants: *the non-combatant branches of the service*.

non-commissioned, adj. [1. nòn kumíshund; 2. nɔ̀n kəmíʃənd]. **non & commission & -ed.** Not having a commission: *non-commissioned officer*, abbr. N.C.O., a soldier holding the rank of sergeant or corporal, but not having a commission from the Crown.

non compos mentis, phr. [1. nón kòmpos méntis; 2. nɔ́n kɔ̀mpəs méntis]. Lat., 'not having mastery of the mind'. See **non & mental (I.).** Lat. *compos* is fr. **com-** & base seen in *potis*, 'able', *potens*, 'powerful'; see **potent (I.).** Not sound of mind, not having full mental powers.

nonconforming, adj. [1. nònkunfórming; 2. nɔ̀nkənfɔ́miŋ]. See next word & **-ing.** Refusing to conform; specif., belonging to a nonconformist body.

nonconformist, n. [1. nònkunfórmist; 2. nɔ̀nkənfɔ́mist]. **non & conform & -ist. 1.** One who does not conform; in specif. sense one not conforming to the doctrines, system of worship &c. of an Established Church, esp. of the Church of England; a dissenter, free-churchman. **2.** (attrib.) *Nonconformist Churches*, the Free Churches.

nonconformity, n. [1. nònkunfórmiti; 2. nɔ̀nkənfɔ́miti]. See prec. & **-ity. 1.** Act, state, practice of not conforming to doctrines &c. of an Established Church. **2.** Principles of nonconformists. **3.** Body of persons not conforming to an Established Church.

nondescript, adj. & n. [1. nóndeskript; 2. nɔ́ndiskript], fr. **non** & Lat. *descript-(um)*, P.P. of *describere*, see **describe. 1.** adj. Not easily described or classified; not belonging to any particular kind or class; lacking strongly-marked character; indefinite, vague. **2.** n. Person not readily assignable to any specific class.

none, pron. & n., adj. & adv. [1. nun; 2. nan]. O.E. *nān* for *ne*, 'not', & *ān*, see **one**; M.E. *nōn*, *noon*, as adj. formerly always used before vowels. See **no (II.). 1. a** pron. No one, not any one, not one: *there were none present*; *there is none (of it) left*. Phrs. *none but*, no one except: '*None but the brave deserves the fair*' (Dryden); *none so*, no one so, no persons so; *none so blind, deaf, as those who won't see, hear*; **b** n., not any (of), nothing: *none of it is worth having*; *I saw none of the people I wanted to see*; Phr. *he would have none of it*, refused absolutely to accept or consider it. **2.** adj. (archaic) Not any: *thou shalt have none other gods but Me*; *none other than the general himself*; *gold and silver have I none*; *to make of none effect* (archaic), to invalidate. **3.** adv. (with comparatives) None at all, to no account, not any; in no way: *none the better for seeing you*; *none the worse for a ducking*; *none the less*, nevertheless.

non-ego, n. [1. nón ēgō; 2. nɔ́n égou]. Lat., 'not I'. See **non & ego.** (philos.) That which is external to the ego or personality.

nonentity, n. [1. nonéntiti; 2. nɔnéntiti]. **non & entity. 1.** State of being non-existent; **a** non-existent thing or object. **2.** Person of no importance, a nobody; person of feeble personality.

nones, n. pl. [1. nōnz; 2. nounz], fr. Lat. *nōnae (diēs)*, 'ninth days', fem. pl. of *nōnus*, 'ninth', fr. **nowenos*. See **nine** & cp. **noon. 1.** (Rom. antiq.) The ninth day of the month before the Ides, counted inclusively; the 7th of March, May, July, and October, the 5th of other months. **2.** (eccles.) An Office to be said daily at the ninth hour, originally according to Roman time, 3 P.M., but now at midday or noon.

non est, phr. [1. nòn ést; 2. nɔ̀n ést]. Lat., 'he (it) is not', sc. *inventus*, 'found'. See **non & is.** Phr. *he (it) is non est*, he (it) is not to be found, has gone, disappeared.

nonesuch. See **nonsuch.**

non expedit, phr. [1. nòn ékspedit; 2. nɔ̀n ékspədit]. Lat., 'it is not expedient'. See **non & expedient.** First words of a Papal Bull forbidding Roman Catholics to take part in political elections in Italy.

nonillion, n. [1. nōnílliun; 2. nouníliən]. Formed fr. Lat. *nōnus*, 'ninth', on anal. of **billion. a** (Engl.) A million raised to the ninth power, 1 and 54 ciphers; **b** (Fr. and U.S.A.) the tenth power of a thousand, 1 with 30 ciphers.

nonjuring, adj. [1. nònjōōring; 2. nɔ̀ndžúəriŋ]. See next word. (Engl. hist.) Not taking the oath of allegiance &c. of the Nonjurors.

Nonjuror, n. [1. nònjōōrer; 2. nɔ̀ndžúərə], fr. **non & juror.** (Engl. hist.) One of those beneficed clergy of the English Established Church, who, after the Revolution of 1688, refused to take the oath of allegiance to William III. and Mary.

non obstante, phr. [1. nòn obstánte; 2. nɔ̀n əbstǽnti]. Lat. See **non & obstacle.** Notwithstanding; in spite of what has previously been enacted.

nonpareil (I.), adj. [1. nónparèl; 2. nɔ́npərèl]. Fr., 'unequalled', fr. *non*, 'not', & *pareil*, 'equal, similar', fr. L. Lat. *pariculus*, dimin. of *par*, 'equal'. See **parity.** Unequalled, without an equal; matchless; nonsuch.

nonpareil (II.), n., fr. prec. **1.** As name of various superior kinds of fruit &c. **2.** (typog.) 6 point size of type, twelve lines to the inch.

nonplus, n. & vb. trans. [1. nónplus; 2. nɔ́nplas]. Lat., 'not more, not further'. See **non & plus. 1.** n. State where nothing more can be done; state of difficulty or perplexity, baffling situation, quandary: *to reduce to, stand at, a nonplus*. **2.** vb. To reduce, bring to a nonplus, to place in a state of perplexity, baffle, disconcert, take aback: *to be completely nonplussed*.

non possumus, n. [1. nón pósūmus; 2. nɔ́n pɔ́sjuməs]. Lat., 'we cannot (do)'. See **non & potent (I.).** Statement, assertion, of the impossibility of doing some specified thing or of taking any action at all: *they met the request with a blank non possumus*.

nonsense, n. [1. nónsens; 2. nɔ́nsəns]. **non & sense. 1.** No sense; **a** absurd, unintelligible, meaningless group of words: *the sentence seems to me sheer nonsense*; **b** a statement which expresses some foolish idea; an illogical, badly thought-out proposal &c.: *to talk nonsense*; *the plan was all nonsense*; Phr. *a pack of nonsense*; **c** foolish conduct, senseless behaviour; unreasoning act; a stupid, affected manner: *none of your nonsense now*; *behave properly, and let's have no more nonsense*. **2.** (as interj.) What you say, propose, is absurd: *Oh, nonsense!*; *nonsense, nonsense!* **3.** (attrib.) *nonsense verses, rhymes*, absurd, comic verses, with apparently no sense in them.

nonsensical, adj. [1. nònsénsikl; 2. nɔnsénsikl]. Prec. & **-ical.** Full of nonsense; absurd, ridiculous.

nonsensically, adv. See prec. & **-ly.** In a nonsensical way or manner.

non sequitur, n. [1. nòn sékwitur; 2. nɔ̀n sékwitə]. Lat., 'it does not follow'. See **non & sequence.** A fallacy in reasoning, in which the conclusion or inference drawn does not logically follow from the premises.

nonsuch, nonesuch, adj. & n. [1. núnsuch; 2. nánsatʃ]. **none & such.** **1.** adj. (obs.) Unequalled, unrivalled. **2.** n. Person, thing, without an equal or parallel; nonpareil.

nonsuit, n. & vb. trans. [1. nònsū́t; 2. nɔ̀nsjū́t]. **non & suit.** **1.** n. (law) A decision of a judge stopping a plaintiff's suit at law for failure to show a *prima facie* case or for want of evidence. **2.** vb. To stop a plaintiff's suit: *to be nonsuited.*

non-user, n. [1. nòn ū́zer; 2. nɔ̀n jū́zə]. **non & user (II.).** (law) Failure to exercise a right or privilege, whereby it is liable to lapse.

noodle, n. [1. nōōdl; 2. núdl]. Etymol. unknown. A stupid person, fool, blockhead.

nook, n. [1. nook; 2. nuk]. Etymol. doubtful. M.E. *nōk*; prob. not connected w. Scots *neuk,* 'corner', & Gael. *nioc.* Corner, recess; a retreat, place of hiding.

noon, n. [1. nōōn; 2. nūn]. O.E. *nōn,* fr. Lat. *nōna (hōra),* 'the ninth hour'. See **nones 2.** **1.** **a** Midday, twelve o'clock of the day; **b** (poet.) midnight: *the noon of night.* **2.** (fig., rare) Period of greatest splendour, power &c.; prime, heyday: *at the noon of his career.*

noonday, n. [1. nōōndā; 2. núndei]. Prec. & **day.** Noon, midday, (also fig.).

noontide, n. [1. nōōntīd; 2. núntaid]. As prec. & **tide (I.).** Noon, noonday (esp. fig.).

noose, n. & vb. trans. [1. nōōz, nōōs; 2. nūz, nūs]. Prob. fr. O. Provenç. *nous,* 'slip-knot', fr. Lat. *nōdus,* 'knot', see **node.** **1.** n. A running knot, slip-knot, as in a halter, or lasso: *the hangman's noose;* (fig.) *the marriage noose.* Phr. *to put one's neck into the noose,* to allow oneself to be entrapped; to commit oneself to some line of action. **2.** vb. **a** To catch in a noose; to put a noose round; to form a noose or slip-knot in; **b** (fig.) to entrap, snare.

nopal, n. [1. nōpl; 2. nóupl]. Span., fr. Mexican *nopalli.* A Mexican cactus; used for the breeding of cochineal insects.

nor (I.), conj. [1. nōr; 2. nɔ̄]. In M.E.; contraction of obs. *nōther,* 'neither', see **neither;** influenced by the affirmative **or (II.).** **1.** Used to deny the second of two alternatives, the first of which is preceded by *neither*: *neither hot nor cold;* (archaic or poet.) without preceding *neither*: '*eye hath not seen nor ear heard*' (1 Cor. ii. 9); (also poet.) following another *nor*: '*Then star nor sun shall waken, Nor any change of light*' (Swinburne, 'Garden of Proserpine'). **2.** At beginning of a sentence, where no alternative is suggested, and . . . not: *nor will I deny that* &c.

nor' (II.), adj. Abbreviation of **north,** in compounds with other points of the compass: *nor'-east, nor'west* &c.

noraghe. See **nuraghe.**

Nordic, adj. [1. nórdik; 2. nɔ́dik], fr. Fr. or Germ. *nord,* 'north', see **north,** & **-ic.** Of or belonging to the Northern, Germanic races of Europe, to a type now most often represented among the Scandinavians, tall, fair-haired, blue-eyed, and long-headed.

Norfolk jacket, n. [1. nórfuk jáket; 2. nɔ́fək dʒǽkit]. Name of English county. Loose, pleated jacket, with a belt.

norm, n. [1. norm; 2. nōm], fr. Lat. *norma,* 'carpenter's square, rule, pattern', for **gnōrima,* cp. Gk. *gnṓrimos,* 'well-known', fr. base **g̑nō-.* See **know** & cp. **enormous.** A pattern, type, model; a recognized standard.

normal, adj. & n. [1. nórml; 2. nɔ́ml], fr. Lat. *normālis*; prec. & **-al.** **1.** adj. **a** Agreeing with an accepted standard, pattern, or form; not greater or less than what is usual or customary; regular, natural, usual; of mean or average value or quantity: *normal temperature,* 98·4° F., of human body; *Normal school,* school for the training of primary teachers; **b** (geom.) perpendicular, at right angles. **2.** n. **a** Average; ordinary usual standard, degree: *his temperature is not above the normal*; **b** (geom.) a perpendicular line.

normalcy, n. [1. nórmalsi; 2. nɔ́məlsi]. Prec. & **-cy**: an unnecessary, hybrid word, apparently an Americanism. Normality.

normality, n. [1. normáliti; 2. nōmǽliti]. **normal & -ity.** Normal state, condition, or quality.

normalization, n. [1. nòrmalīzā́shun; 2. nɔ̄məlaizéiʃən]. **normalize & -ation.** Act of normalizing; state, condition, of being normalized.

normalize, vb. trans. [1. nórmalīz; 2. nɔ́məlaiz], fr. **normal & -ize.** To make normal, to reduce to normality, cause to conform to a fixed standard, pattern, or rule.

normally, adv. [1. nórmali; 2. nɔ́məli]. **normal & -ly.** In a normal way; usually, ordinarily.

Norman, n. & adj. [1. nórman; 2. nɔ́mən]. O. Fr. *Normant,* Mod. Fr. *Normand,* 'Northman'. **north & man.** **1.** n. **a** Inhabitant of Normandy; one of the Scandinavian race, Northmen, which conquered and settled in Neustria (Normandy) in 10th cent.; **b** one of the Norman-French race which conquered England in 1066; **c** language of the Normans; Norman-French. **2.** adj. Of or belonging to the Normans: *Norman architecture,* name of an 11th cent. style of English architecture, adapted from the French Romanesque; *Norman-English,* English as modified by Norman-French after the Conquest; *Norman-French,* French as spoken by the Normans and used as the official language of England after the Conquest.

Norn, n. [1. norn; 2. nɔ̄n]. O.N. Etymol. doubtful. (Scand. mythol.) One of the three fates, represented as goddesses, giving good and ill to gods and men.

Norroy, n. [1. nóroi; 2. nɔ́rɔi], fr. **north &** O. Fr. *roy,* Mod. Fr. *roi,* 'king', see **royal.** The third English King-of-Arms, having jurisdiction north of the Trent.

Norse, n. & adj. [1. nors; 2. nɔ̄s]. Dan. & Norw. *Norsk,* Icel. *Norskr,* fr. *nord,* 'north', see **north.** **1.** n. The Norwegian language; *Old Norse,* the early, primitive Scandinavian language which modern Icelandic most closely resembles. **2.** adj. Scandinavian.

Norseman, n. [1. nórsman; 2. nɔ́smən], fr. prec. & **man.** Ancient inhabitant of Scandinavia.

north (I.), n. [1. north; 2. nɔ̄þ]. O.E. *norð*; O.N. *norðr*; cp. Du. *noord,* Germ., Dan., & Swed. *nord*; not found outside Gmc., whence Fr. *nord* is borrowed; origin unknown. **1.** One of the four cardinal points of the compass, the point which is on one's right hand when facing due west, opposite to the south. **2.** The northern hemisphere; the Arctic regions; northern parts of the earth generally: *the frozen north*; also the people living in northern regions: '*And dark and true and tender is the North*' (Tennyson). **3.** That part of a country, region, district &c., which is towards the north, or which lies north of a specified line or point: *the North of England,* north of the Humber; *North and South America (U.S.A.),* as divided by Mason and Dixon's line.

north (II.), adj. See prec. **1.** **a** Situated at, lying in or towards, the north; northern: *the North Country,* northern part of England; so *North countryman*; *north latitude*; *North Pole,* see **pole (III.)**; *North Star,* see **pole-star**; **b** directed towards the north; facing north: *the North Road,* from London towards the North of England; *north light,* window facing north; *north side,* (of church) that side which is on the left hand of one looking towards the Altar; the Gospel side; **c** coming from the north: *a north wind.* **2.** (in combination, cap.) As part of the name of the northern parts of a sea, region, country, district &c., or of peoples living in the north: *North Atlantic, North America*; *North Africans*; *North London*; *the North Sea,* the sea between Europe and the British Isles from the Channel to the Orkneys; formerly also called the German Ocean.

north (III.), adv. See prec. Towards the north, in a northerly direction: *to sail, go, north.*

north-east, northeast, also **nor'east,** n., adj., & adv. [1. nór(th) ḗst; 2. nɔ̄þ íst, nɔ̄r íst]. **north & east.** **1.** n. Point of the compass half-way between due north and east; region, district, towards this point: *north-east-by-east* or *by-north,* one point east or north of due north-east. **2.** adj. **a** Situated in or towards the north-east, facing the north-east: *north-east passage,* a navigable passage from the North Atlantic to the Pacific, lying north of Europe and Asia; **b** coming from the north-east: *north-east wind.* **3.** adv. Towards the north-east.

north-easter, n. [1. nór(th) ḗster; 2. nɔ̄þ ístə, nɔ̄r ístə]. Prec. & **-er.** A strong wind blowing from the north-east.

north-easterly, adj. & adv. Prec. & **-ly.** **1.** adj. **a** Situated in or toward, pertaining to, the north-east; **b** coming from the north-east: *north-easterly wind.* **2.** adv. In a north-easterly direction, towards the north-east.

north-eastern, adj. [1. nòr(th) ḗstern; 2. nɔ̄þ, nɔ̄r ístən]. **north & eastern.** Situated in, pertaining to, the north-east.

north-eastward, adv., adj., & n. [1. nòr(th) ḗstward; 2. nɔ̄þ ístwəd, nɔ̄r ístwəd]. See prec. & **eastward.** **a** adv. In a north-east direction; **b** adj., situated in or towards the north-east; **c** n., the north-east.

north-eastwardly, adv. & adj. Prec. & **-ly.** North-eastward.

norther, n. [1. nórther; 2. nɔ́þə]. **north (I.)** & **-er.** A very cold and strong north wind following a cyclone in Texas and the Gulf of Mexico.

northerly, adj. & adv. [1. nórdherli; 2. nɔ́ðəli]. Prec. & **-ly.** **1.** adj. **a** Toward the north: *a northerly course*; **b** coming from the north: *northerly wind.* **2.** adv. **a** Towards the north: *to progress northerly*; **b** from the north: *the wind blows northerly.*

northern, adj. [1. nórdhern; 2. nɔ́ðən]. O.E. *norðern,* M.E. *northren.* **north & -ern.** Situated in, pertaining or belonging to, the north; characteristic of the north: *Northern States* (of U.S.A.); *northern habits, customs* &c.; *northern hemisphere*; *(the) northern lights,* see **aurora borealis**; *Northern Territory,* (of Australia) semi-tropical district, administered by the Commonwealth government.

northerner, n. [1. nórdherner; 2. nɔ́ðənə]. Prec. & **-er.** Person belonging to the north; specif. (in U.S.A.) inhabitant of the Northern States of the U.S.

northernmost, adj. [1. nórdhernmōst; 2. nɔ́ðənmoust]. **northern & -most.** Most northern; farthest north.

northing, n. [1. nórdhing; 2. nɔ́ðiŋ], fr. **north & -ing.** (of ships) Difference in latitude north from the last point of reckoning.

Northman, n. [1. nórthman; 2. nɔ́þmən]. O.E. *norðman,* cp. **Norman.** One of the ancient Scandinavian race, esp. one of that sea-roving race invading Northern France and England; a viking.

north-north-east, n., adj., & adv. [1. nórth north ḗst, nór nōr ḗst; 2. nɔ̄þ nɔ̄þ íst, nɔ̄ nɔ̄r íst]. (In or towards) direction or point midway between north and north-east.

north-north-west, n., adj., & adv. [1. nórth north wést, nór nōr wést; 2. nɔ̄þ nɔ̄þ wést, nɔ̄ nɔ̄ wést]. (In or towards) direction or point midway between north and north-west.

north-polar, adj. **north & polar.** Arctic: *north-polar regions, expedition* &c.

northward, northwards, adv., adj., & n. [1. nórthward(z); 2. nɔ́þwəd(z)]. O.E. *norðweard,* fr. **north & -ward**; *-s* is adverbial. Toward the north: *sailing northward*; *take a northward direction*; *to the northward.*

northwardly, adv. Prec. & **-ly.** Northward, northwards, northerly.

northwards. Variant of **northward.**

north-west, northwest, also **nor'west,** n., adj., & adv. [1. nòr(th) wést; 2. nɔ̄(þ) wést]. **1.** n. Point of the compass half-way between due north and west; region, district, toward this point: *north-west-by-west* or *by-north,* one point west or north of due north-west. **2.** adj. Situated in or towards the north-west, facing or coming from the north-west: *the North-west Frontier* (of India); *North-West Mounted Police* (of Canada); *north-west passage*, a navigable passage to the Pacific from the North Atlantic lying to the north of America. **3.** adv. Towards the north-west.

north-wester, northwester, nor'wester, n. [1. nòr(th) wéster; 2. nɔ̄(þ) wéstə]. Prec. & **-er.** A strong north-west wind.

north-westerly, adv. & adj. Prec. & **-ly.** Towards or from the north-west.

north-western, adj. [1. nòr(th) wéstern; 2. nɔ̄(þ) wéstən]. Situated in, pertaining to, the north-west.

north-westward, adv., adj., & n. [1. nòr(th) wéstward; 2. nɔ̄(þ) wéstwəd]. **a** adv. In a north-west direction; **b** adj., situated in or toward the north-west; **c** n., the north-west.

north-westwardly, adv. Prec. & **-ly.** North-westward.

nose (I.), n. [1. nōz; 2. nouz]. O.E. *nosu*, M.E. *nōse*; O.H.G. *nasa*; O.N. *nōs*; cp. also Scrt. *nāsa*, O. Slav. *nosŭ*, 'nose'; Lith. *nasraĩ*, 'smell'; Lat. *nāsus, nāres* for **nāsis*. See also **nasal** & **nostril.** **1.** The external organ of smell in man and animals. Phrs. *cannot see beyond (the length of) one's nose*, (fig.) said of a person with no imagination, or insight; *to count noses*, count number of persons, esp. as representing votes &c.; *to cut off one's nose to spite one's face*, injure one's own cause or interests in a fit of temper or pique; *to follow one's nose*, to keep straight on; *to keep one's nose to the grindstone*, keep hard at work; *to lead by the nose*, to cause (person) to obey one's every wish; *to pay through the nose*, to pay an exorbitant price; *to poke one's nose into (another's business)*, to meddle, interfere with, what does not concern one; *to put one's nose out of joint*, (i.) to take one's place in another's affections or favour; (ii.) to upset, spoil, one's schemes; *to snap, bite, a person's nose off*, to speak sharply or snappishly to; *to turn up the nose at*, to look down on, despise, sneer at; *as plain as the nose on one's face*, as plain and clear as can be; *under one's very nose*, directly in front of one, in one's presence. **2. a** Keen sense of smell: *this hound has the best nose of the pack*; **b** flair, instinct for detecting and recognizing: *a good nose for a mystery, discovering first editions* &c. **3. a** Nozzle, spout, of a pipe, tube, or gun; **b** the end of the head of a golf-club; **c** foremost projecting part of a boat, aeroplane &c.; **d** the detachable part containing the primer of a torpedo. **4.** (slang) A police spy or informer.

nose (II.), vb. trans. & intrans., fr. prec. **A.** trans. **1.** Generally *nose out*, to smell, sniff, scent; to detect, find out, by smelling; esp. fig., to track down, run to earth, discover by instinct or by furtive inquiry: *he'll nose out a scandal anywhere.* **2.** To press the nose against, touch with the nose; to nuzzle: *the foal nosed its mother's flank.* **3.** To move cautiously forward: *the ship nosed her way through the winding channel.* **B.** intrans. **1.** To sniff, smell, at or about an object: *the dog kept nosing about the room.* **2.** To pry, interfere, meddle with: *he's always nosing into what doesn't concern him.*

nose-bag, n. A bag for holding a horse's feed, hung over its head.

nose-band, n. The lower band of a horse's bridle or headstall passing over the nose.

nose-bleeding, n. Effusion of blood from the nose; epistaxis.

nosed, adj. [1. nōzd; 2. nouzd], fr. **nose (II.)** & **-ed.** Having a nose of specified kind, shape &c.: *bottle-nosed, long-nosed, red-nosed.*

nose-dive, n. & vb. intrans. **a** n. A vertical, head-on descent of an aeroplane; **b** vb., to make such a descent.

nose-flute, n. A primitive kind of flute blown by the nostrils, used by certain Malay tribes.

nosegay, n. [1. nṓzgā; 2. nóuzgei], fr. **nose (I.)** & **gay,** obs. n., 'gay, bright object; pretty flower'. A bunch of bright, sweet-smelling flowers.

nose-leaf, n. Leaf-like projection of membrane on the nose of certain bats.

noseless, adj. [1. nṓzles; 2. nóuzlis]. **nose (I.)** & **-less.** Without a nose.

nose-piece, n. **a** A nose-band; nozzle; **b** specif., the lower end of a microscope tube to which the object glass is attached.

nose-ring, n. **a** Ring passed through the nose of a bull for leading, or of a pig to prevent grouting; **b** ornamented ring worn through the nostrils in the East by women, and also by various savage tribes.

nosey, nosy, adj. [1. nṓzi; 2. nóuzi]. **nose (I.)** & **-y.** (colloq.) **1.** Having a large nose. **2.** Given to prying; inquisitive, interfering, meddling. Phr. (vulg.) *nosey Parker*, a meddling, inquisitive person. **3.** Emitting a bad smell.

nosing, n. [1. nṓzing; 2. nóuziŋ]. **nose (I.)** & **-ing.** The projecting edge or rim of a step.

noso-, pref. Combining form fr. Gk. *nósos*, 'disease'; etymol. uncertain; possibly fr. base **(o)nodhto-*, whence O.S. *ando*, 'rage, anger'; O.E. *ande*, 'envy, malice, indignation, hostility'.

nosography, n. [1. nosógrafi; 2. nɔsɔ́grəfi]. Prec. & **-graphy.** Classification of diseases.

nosology, n. [1. nosóloji; 2. nɔsɔ́lədži]. See prec. & **-logy.** Science of diseases; the classification and nomenclature of diseases.

nostalgia, n. [1. nostáljia; 2. nɔstǽldžiə]. Coined Lat., fr. Gk. *nóstos*, 'return journey, return home', & **-algia,** fr. Gk. *álgos*, 'pain'. Gk. *nóstos* is cogn. w. Gk. *néomai* (fr. **nesomai*), 'to go, come, return', fr. base **nes-, *nos-*, 'to return, unite', whence also Scrt. *násatē*, 'to reunite'; Goth. *ga-nisan*, 'to heal', *nasjan*, 'to save'; O.E. *ġe-nesan*, 'to recover', *nerian* (fr. **nazjan*), 'to save'. Home-sickness; intense morbid longing for one's own home or country.

nostalgic, adj. [1. nostáljik; 2. nɔstǽldžik]. Prec. & **-ic.** Connected with, exhibiting symptoms of, nostalgia.

nostoc, n. [1. nóstok; 2. nɔ́stɔk]. Word coined by Paracelsus. A genus of jelly-like fresh-water and land algae.

Nostradamus, n. [1. nòstradámus; 2. nɔ̀strədéiməs]. Latinized form of *Nostredame*, name of French astrologer and soothsayer (d. 1566). A professional prophet, seer, soothsayer, esp. one who makes vague or ambiguous prophecies.

nostril, n. [1. nóstril; 2. nɔ́stril, -əl]. O.E. *nos(u)-þyrel*, M.E. *nosethirl, nostril*, fr. O.E. *nos(u)*, 'nose', & *þȳrel*, 'hole', fr. *þurh*, 'through', & dimin. suff. *-il.* See **nose** & **thrill.** One of the two external orifices of the nose, serving as passages for air to and from the lungs; also to convey odours to the olfactory nerves. Phrs. *to stink in the nostrils of*, (fig.) to be extremely offensive to; *the breath of one's nostrils*, something which one regards with great satisfaction, delight, and enthusiasm.

nostrum, n. [1. nóstrum; 2. nɔ́strəm]. Lat., neut. sing. of *noster*, 'ours', fr. *nōs*, 'we', cogn. w. Scrt. *naš*; O. Ir. *ni*, 'we'; O. Slav. *ny*, 'we', *nasŭ*, 'our'; Goth. *uns*, O.E. *ūs* (both fr. base **n̥s*), see **us**; cp. Gk. *nṓ*, 'we two'. **1.** An alleged remedy or cure for diseases, the secret of which is held by the manufacturer or seller; a quack medicine; patent medicine. **2.** A special, favourite, plan, scheme, or device put forward as a remedy for political or social evils; term applied by critics or opponents of a policy, with implication that it savours of charlatanism.

nosy. See **nosey.**

not, adv. [1. not; 2. nɔt]; unstressed [nt]. M.E. *nat, not*, contraction of **naught, nought.** Negative adverbial particle: **1.** Following auxiliary verbs: **a** '*Thou shalt not kill*'; '*All is not gold that glitters*'; colloq. abbr. to *n't*, as *isn't, aren't*; *can't, don't, won't* &c.; **b** *not* cannot now be placed immediately after a verb (other than an auxiliary or *can*) except in poetry or in rhetorical style: *I come not, go not, want not* &c. are archaic, and the sentences would become, normally, *I do not come, go, want* &c., with periphrastic construction. **2.** Preceding verbal nouns and infinitives: *not caring one way or another*; *tell them not to do that.* **3.** Following verbs other than auxiliaries: **a** (archaic) '*They toil not, neither do they spin*'; **b** (in elliptical Phr.) *I believe, think, suppose, not*, that it is not so, that such a thing will not happen, be done &c.; also *perhaps not.* In such cases *not* is always strongly stressed.

nota bene (abbr. N.B.), phr. [1. nṓta béne; 2. nóutə bíni]. Lat., 'note well'. See **notable** & **bene-.** Take notice; mark this; used in drawing particular attention to corrections, special clauses, important statements &c.

notabilia, n. pl. [1. nōtabília; 2. nòutəbíliə]. Lat., neut. pl. of *notābilis*, 'notable'. Things worth noting or worthy of notice.

notability, n. [1. nòtabíliti; 2. nòutəbíliti], fr. next word & **-ity**; cp. Fr. *notabilité.* **1.** Quality of being notable. **2.** A notable, remarkable, thing or person; a thing or person of note.

notable, adj. & n. [1. nṓtabl; 2. nóutəbl]. Fr., fr. Lat. *notābilis*, 'worthy of note', fr. *notāre*, 'to note'. See **note** & **-able.** **1.** adj. **a** Worthy of notice; **b** worth noticing; remarkable; distinguished; **c** easily noted or seen; conspicuous. **2.** n. A notable person; specif. (Fr. hist.) member of the *Assembly of Notables*, an assembly of prominent personages summoned for special purposes, as in 1787.

notably, adv. Prec. & **-ly.** In a notable manner; remarkably; plainly.

notarial, adj. [1. nōtárial; 2. noutéəriəl], fr. **notary** & **-al.** Of, pertaining to, performed, executed by, a notary: *notarial acts, attestation, seal* &c.

notarially, adv. See prec. & **-ly.** In due notarial form or manner.

notary, n. [1. nṓtari; 2. nóutəri]. A.-Fr. *notarie*, O. Fr. *notaire*, fr. Lat. *notārius*, 'shorthand writer, secretary', fr. *notāre*, 'to note, make a note of', fr. *nōta*, 'note'. See **note (I.).** A public official, in full *Notary Public*, whose duty it is to attest and certify certain documents, such as protested bills of exchange, deeds, depositions &c.

notation, n. [1. nōtáshun; 2. noutéiʃən]. Lat. *notātiōn-(em)*, acc. of *notātio*, 'a marking, designation; etymology, kind of shorthand', fr. *notāre*, 'to note'. See **note (I.)** & **-ation.** A system of symbols, characters, or marks used in science or art for representing numbers, quantities, as in arithmetic or algebra; musical notes, as in music: *musical notation*; speech-sounds: *phonetic notation*; the elements and their proportions: *chemical notation.*

notational, adj. [1. nōtáshunal; 2. noutéiʃənəl]. Prec. & **-al.** Pertaining to notation.

notch (I.), n. [1. noch; 2. nɔtʃ]. For *an otch*, cp. **newt**; fr. O. Fr. *oche*, Mod. Fr. *hoche*, 'notch, nick in a tally', fr. O. Fr. *ochier, oschier*, 'to cut'; perh. of Gmc. origin & connected w. **hack (I.),** 'to cut' &c. **1. a** A V-shaped cut or slit in wood &c.; a nock in an arrow or bow; a nick; specif. **b** the cut on a tally-stick for counting, as formerly in cricket; **c** (obs.) number, run, as in cricket. **2.** (U.S.A.) A narrow pass or defile.

notch (II.), vb. trans., fr. prec. To make a notch or cut on a stick &c. *Notch board*, board in a staircase, into notches in which the stairs are fitted; *notch wing*, name of various species of moths.

note (I.), n. [1. nōt; 2. nout]. Fr., fr. Lat. *nota*, 'mark, sign; character, letter'; etymol. doubtful; not fr. base **ĝnō-* &c., whence comes **know** &c. **1.** (mus.) A symbol, figure, or character used to show, by its place on the stave, the pitch of a tone, and, by its form or shape, the length and duration. **2.** One of the flat white plates, or black raised pieces of ebony, on keyboard of a piano or organ; a key: *to strike the notes.* Phrs. *to strike the right note*, (fig.) to express oneself in speaking or writing suitably and in harmony with one's audience; or in a way which commends itself as suitable to the prevailing sentiments; *to strike, sound, a false note* (of acts, speech &c.), not to ring true, to be out of tune with, or not suitable to, the context, conditions &c. accompanying the act &c. **3.** A musical sound or tone; characteristic acoustic quality of a bird's song, human voice, musical instrument &c.: *the blackbird's merry note*; *the crow's harsh note*; *the funeral note (of a bell)*; *a note of passion in his voice.* **4.** A distinctive graphic mark or sign: *note of exclamation (!)*; *note of interrogation (?).* **5.** Characteristic, distinguishing quality (often with a reference to or suggestion of **3** in a fig. or transf. sense): *frankness is the chief note in his character*; *the note of pessimism in his writings*; *a wide tolerance is the note of modern religion*; *to speak with a note of censure.* **6.** Distinction, pre-eminence, reputation: *a family of note*; *person, names, of great note.* **7.** Notice, attention: *worthy, deserving, of note.* Phr. *to take note of*, notice, pay attention to. **8.** A short record or abstract in writing; memoranda, **a** as for a speech, sermon; or **b** of this as heard; **c** of details of events, impressions &c.: *make a note of*; *to take notes of.* **9.** A short comment, annotation, explanation, added at the side or foot of a page (*footnote*), or at the end of a book. **10. a** Short, informal letter; **b** a formal, written, diplomatic communication from one state to another: *negotiations were conducted by an exchange of notes.* **11.** A written promise to pay a sum of money: *a promissory note*; *note of hand*; *a bank-note*; *circular note*; *currency, Treasury, note.*

note (II.), vb. trans. O. Fr. *noter*, fr. Lat. *notāre*, 'to make a *nota* or note'. See prec. **1.** To set down record of in writing, to make a note or notes of: *note down every word he says.* **2.** To notice, attend to, observe, mark: *note my warning*; *note his gestures.*

note-book, n. A book for taking notes; memorandum book.

noted, adj. [1. nṓted; 2. nóutid], fr. P.P. of **note (II.)**. Renowned, distinguished, famous, celebrated: *a noted writer*; *try our noted ales and stouts.*

notedly, adv. Prec. & **-ly**. In, to, a marked degree; conspicuously.

noteless, adj. [1. nṓtles; 2. nóutlis]. **note (I.)** & **-less**. **1.** Devoid of notes or sound. **2.** Unnoticed, inconspicuous.

note-paper, n. Writing paper for correspondence.

noteworthy, adj. [1. nṓtwĕrdhi; 2. nóutwə̄ði]. **note (I.)** & **worthy**. Worthy of note, deserving attention; remarkable.

nothing, n. [1. núthing; 2. náþiŋ]. **no (II.)** & **thing**. **1.** Not anything, nought; contrasted with *anything* or *something*: *there is nothing in the house*; *I can give you nothing. Next to nothing*, almost nothing, very little. *Nothing venture, nothing have*, one must risk something to gain any advantage. *To come to nothing*, to fail utterly. *To make nothing of*, (i.) to find no meaning in, be unable to understand: *I could make nothing of such an involved statement*; (ii.) to treat as negligible, treat lightly: *make nothing of one's illness*; (iii.) to fail to do, perform, use: *made nothing of the job*; *made nothing of his talents. Nothing doing* (colloq.), (i.) expression of failure, disappointment; (ii.) as refusal of request &c. *For nothing*, (i.) in vain, uselessly: *he has not travelled the world for nothing*; *to have all one's trouble for nothing*; (ii.) without payment or reward; gratis: *attended him for nothing*; *I got it for nothing*; (iii.) without any reason: *they quarrelled for nothing. Nothing but*, nothing else than, only: *nothing but peace can save the world. Nothing much*, very little, not a great deal, not much. *Nothing to*, (i.) of no interest to, does not concern: *my trouble is nothing to them*; (ii.) *she is nothing to me*, my affections are not set upon her; I have no intimate relations with her. *To be for nothing in*, to have no influence on, not to affect. **2. a** Something unimportant; negligible fact, circumstance that may be disregarded: *mere nothings*; **b** fact, circumstance, not equal to, not to be compared with, another: *my trouble is nothing to theirs.* **3.** (as adv.) In no wise or degree, not at all: *to differ nothing from.*

nothingness, n. [1. núthingnes; 2. náþiŋnis]. Prec. & **-ness**. **a** State, quality, of being nothing; non-existence, extinction: *to pass into nothingness*; **b** insignificance, nonentity, uselessness.

notice (I.), n. [1. nṓtis; 2. nóutis]. Fr., fr. Lat. *nōtitia*, 'information, knowledge', fr. *nōt-(um)*, P.P. of *nōscere*, 'to know'. See **gnostic, ignore**, & **know**. **1.** Observation, cognizance, attention: *to bring to one's notice*; *not worth, beneath, one's notice.* Phrs. *to take notice*, to observe, attend to, acknowledge; *the baby is beginning to take notice*, to show signs of intelligence; *sitting up and taking notice*, (facet. of an invalid) convalescent; *to take notice of (person)*, treat with particular consideration, show interest in; *to take no notice of*, to ignore. **2.** Information, intelligence; warning, announcement, of something to be done or to occur subsequently: specif. **a** *notice to terminate employment, lease, or other agreement* &c.; *to give a servant notice*, to dismiss him; *a month's, week's, notice*, warning of termination of engagement &c. at end of specified time; **b** *to have notice of a question*, be informed beforehand that it will be asked; **c** *I give you notice that——*, inform you (of something about to be done). **3. a** Brief announcement, paragraph giving specific information, e.g. in a newspaper: *obituary notice*, one announcing a death, or giving an account of career of deceased; *notice of an engagement*; **b** short reference to, review of, a new book; **c** written statement, announcement, warning: *to put up a notice on the door of the church.*

notice (II.), vb. trans., fr. prec. **1. a** To observe, pay attention to, take notice of: *baby notices everything now*; *police noticed a man leaving the house*; *I didn't notice how he was dressed*; **b** to give a sign of recognizing: *he didn't deign to notice me.* **2.** To refer to, make mention of: *to notice a person's services (in a speech &c.)*; *to notice a book (in a newspaper).*

noticeable, adj. [1. nṓtisabl; 2. nóutisəbl]. Prec. & **-able**. Attracting notice; remarkable, conspicuous.

noticeably, adv. Prec. & **-ly**. **a** In a noticeable manner, conspicuously: *noticeably dressed*; **b** to a noticeable degree: *not noticeably different.*

notifiable, adj. [1. nṓtifiabl; 2. nóutifaiəbl], fr. **notify** & **-able**. Required, needing, to be notified; specif. (of certain infectious diseases) to be notified to an authorized official, under various Public Health Acts.

notification, n. [1. nōtifikā́shun; 2. nòutifikéiʃən], fr. Lat. *nōtificāt-(um)*, P.P. type of *nōtificāre*, 'to make known', & **-ion**. See **notify**. **1. a** Act of making known or notifying, act of giving notice of; **b** notice so given. **2.** Specif., formal notice given to a registrar of a birth or death, or to a public health authority of any disease which is notifiable under various Acts of Parliament.

notify, vb. trans. [1. nṓtifī; 2. nóutifai], fr. Fr. *notifier*, fr. Lat. *nōtificāre*, 'to make known, notify', fr. *nōt-(um)*, 'known', see **notice**, & **-fy**. **a** To inform, give notice to: *to notify a person of one's address*; **b** to indicate, announce: *to notify one's intentions to the party concerned.*

notion, n. [1. nṓshun; 2. nóuʃən], fr. Lat. *nōtiōn-(em)*, acc. of *nōtio*, 'recognition, notice; idea, conception', fr. *nōt-(um)*, P.P. of *nōscere*, 'to know'. See **gnostic** & **know**. **1.** Apprehension by the mind; idea, conception; view, opinion: *everyone has a notion of what thirst means*; *have not the least notion of what you are talking about*; *have no notion of going there*, no idea of, no intention of. **2.** (Winchester College slang) **a** A special word, or phrase, current in the school and commonly used by all members of it; **b** a piece of information about the school, its life and traditions, which all members are supposed to possess; **c** a custom, mode of behaviour &c. commonly observed by all members of the school, and considered as *de rigueur.*

notional, adj. [1. nṓshunal; 2. nóuʃənəl]. L. Lat. *nōtiōnālis.* See prec. & **-al**. **a** Of or pertaining to a notion or idea; expressing an abstract concept; **b** speculative, imaginary, fanciful.

notionalist, n. [1. nṓshunalist; 2. nóuʃənəlist]. Prec. & **-ist**. One who indulges in intellectual speculation; theorist.

notionally, adv. **notional** & **-ly**. Speculatively, abstractly.

noto-, pref., fr. Gk. *nôton*, 'the back'; cogn. w. Lat. *natēs*, pl., 'the rump'. See **nates**.

notochord, n. [1. nṓtokord; 2. nóutəkɔ̄d]. Prec. & **chord**. Cartilaginous structure which, in certain types of animals, corresponds to, and takes the place of, the spinal column in vertebrates.

Notogaea, n. [1. nōtōjḗa; 2. nòutoudžíə]. Coinage fr. Gk. *nótos*, 'south wind; the south'; cp. Gk. *notís*, 'dampness', cogn. w. Lat. *nātāre*, 'to swim', see **natation**, & *gaîa*, 'earth', see **geo-**. (zoogeography) A primary division of the earth, including Australia and New Zealand, and, in some classifications, Polynesia and Hawaii.

notoriety, n. [1. nōtorī́eti; 2. nòutəráiəti], fr. Fr. *notoriété*, fr. Med. Lat. *nōtōrietas.* See next word & **-ity**. **1.** Quality, state, of being notorious, well known, chiefly in unfavourable sense. **2.** A well-known person.

notorious, adj. [1. nōtṓrius; 2. noutɔ́riəs], fr. Med. Lat. *nōtōrius*, 'well known', Class. Lat. *nōtāria*, n., 'information, advice', fr. *nōtor*, 'one who knows, witness', fr. *nōt-(um)*, P.P. type of *nōscere*, 'to know'. See **notice** & **know**. Well known; publicly or commonly known or recognized; usually in unfavourable sense: *it is notorious that*, is common knowledge that; *a place notorious for its luxury.*

notoriously, adv. Prec. & **-ly**. In a notorious manner; as everyone knows, in accordance with common knowledge: *notoriously unjust.*

notoriousness, n. See prec. & **-ness**. Notoriety.

notwithstanding, prep., adv., & conj. [1. nòtwidhstánding; 2. nɔ̀twiðstǽndiŋ]. **not** & **withstand** & **-ing**. **1.** prep. In spite of, despite: *he went notwithstanding your orders*; *my wishes notwithstanding, she accepted the invitation.* **2.** adv. Nevertheless, although, however, all the same: *whatever you say, I will go, notwithstanding.* **3.** conj. *Notwithstanding that*; also with omission of *that*: *he went notwithstanding (that) he was ordered not to.*

nougat, n. [1. nōōgah; 2. nū́gā]. Fr., fr. inflected type, *nucem* &c., of Lat. *nux*, 'nut'. See **nux vomica**. A sweetmeat of nuts and sugar-paste.

nought, n. [1. nawt; 2. nɔ̄t]. O.E. *nōwiht*, variant of *nāwiht*, **naught**. **1.** Nothing, naught: *to bring to, set at, nought.* **2.** The symbol 0, as a number, or in sense of zero, nothing &c.: *noughts and crosses*, child's game.

noumenal, adj. [1. nóumenal; 2. náuminəl]. See next word & **-al**. (philos.) Of or pertaining to noumena or the noumenon; contrasted with *phenomenal.*

noumenon, n., pl. **noumena** [1. nóumenon, -na; 2. náuminɔn, -nə], fr. Gk. *nooúmenon*, neut. sing., Pres. Part. Pass. of *noeîn*, 'to perceive'. See **nous** & **noetic**. (philos.) The object of pure reason, that which is apprehended by the intuition or understanding alone, without the aid of the senses; contrasted with *phenomenon.*

noun, n. [1. noun; 2. naun]. L.M.E. *nowne*, fr. O. Fr. *nun, non*, Mod. Fr. *nom*, 'name', fr. Lat. *nōmen*, 'a name'. See **nominal** & **name**. (gram.) A word used as the name of a person or thing; a substantive.

nourish, vb. trans. [1. núrish; 2. náriʃ]. M.E. *norischen* &c., O. Fr. *nurir, norir*, fr. Lat.

nūtrīre, 'to suckle, feed'. See **nutriment** & **nurse**. **1. a** To feed, supply nutriment to, sustain by providing necessary food; **b** to enrich (land) by adding manure; **c** (archaic) to foster, rear, bring up, train up: *to nourish animals and plants.* **2.** To have, bear, in the mind; to cherish, entertain: *to nourish feelings of hatred; to nourish illusions.*

nourishing, adj. [1. núrishing; 2. náriʃiŋ], fr. Pres. Part. of prec. Tending, serving, to nourish; providing nutriment; having the property of building up the body: *milk and eggs are very nourishing food.*

nourishment, n. [1. núrishment; 2. náriʃmənt]. **nourish** & **-ment.** That which nourishes; nourishing food, nutriment, sustenance.

nous, n. [1. nous; 2. naus]. Gk. *noûs*, 'mind, intellect'. Etymol. obscure; see **noetic.** (colloq.) Intelligence, mother-wit, common sense, gumption.

nouveau riche, n. [1. nōōvō rḗsh; 2. nū́vou riʃ], pl. *nouveaux riches.* Fr., 'new rich'; see **novel (I.)** & **rich.** A newly enriched person; a parvenu.

nova, n., pl. **novae** [1. nóva, nóvē; 2. nóvə, nóvī]. Lat., for *nova stella*, 'new star'. See **novel (I.)** & **new.** (astron.) A new star, appearing in or near a constellation: *nova Aurigae*, the new star in Auriga.

novation, n, [1. nōvā́shun; 2. nouvéiʃən]. Lat. *novātiōn-(em)*, 'renewal, making new', fr. *novāt-(um)*, P.P. type of *novāre*, 'to make new', fr. *novus*, 'new'. See **novel (I.)** & **new.** (civil law) The replacement of an old obligation or contract by a new one.

novel (I.), adj. [1. nóv(e)l; 2. nóv(ə)l]. O. Fr. *novel, nouvel*, Mod. Fr. *nouveau*, fem. *nouvelle*, fr. Lat. *novellus*, dimin. of *novus*, 'new'. See **new** & **neo-.** New, strange, of kind not known before; unfamiliar, unusual.

novel (II.), n., fr. Ital. *novella*, 'new things', applied to such tales as those of Boccaccio &c., fr. neut. pl. of Lat. *novellus*, see prec., & cp. Fr. *nouvelle*, 'short story'. **1.** A fictitious narrative (usually in prose) of some considerable length, representing human beings and their actions, adventures, and passions, and displaying varieties of human character in relation to life; distinguished in the last feature from the older Romance. **2.** (Roman law) One of the additional decrees added by Justinian to the Corpus of Civil Law.

novelette, n. [1. nòvelét; 2. nòvəlét]. Prec. & **-ette.** A short novel or story.

novelist, n. [1. nóvelist; 2. nóvəlist]. **novel (II.)** & **-ist.** A writer of novels.

novelty, n. [1. nóvelti; 2. nóvəlti], fr. O. Fr. *novelté*, Mod. Fr. *nouveauté.* See **novel (I.)** & **-ty. 1.** Quality of being novel; original, hitherto unknown; newness. **2.** A new or novel thing; something strange or unfamiliar; specif. (tradesmen's term) some attractive, ingeniously contrived object put on sale for the first time.

November, n. [1. nōvémber; 2. nouvémbə]. Lat. *Nōvembris (mensis)*, the ninth month of the Roman year which began in March, fr. *nōvem*, see **nine**; origin of termination unknown. Cp. **December.** The eleventh month of the year.

novercal, adj. [1. nōvérkl; 2. nouvə́kl], fr. Lat. *novercālis*, fr. *noverca*, 'stepmother'; fr. *novus*, 'new' (see **novel (I.)**), w. suff. on anal. of **māterca*, wh. may be assumed as the basis of *mātercula*, 'little mother'; cp. **mater.** Like a stepmother.

novice, n. [1. nóvis; 2. nóvis]. O. Fr., fr. Lat. *novīcius, novītius*, adj., 'new', esp. of one newly made a slave, fr. *novus*, 'new'. See **novel (I.). 1.** One who has been received on probation into a religious order and is waiting to take the full vows. **2.** A new convert; neophyte. **3.** A person who is new and inexperienced in a particular occupation, or business, or in some particular form of mental or bodily activity; an apprentice, new hand, tiro.

noviciate, novitiate, n. [1. nōvíshiāt; 2. nouvíʃieit]. Fr. *noviciat*, fr. Med. Lat. *novītiātus.* Prec. & **-ate. 1.** State of being a novice in a religious order; period during which this lasts. **2.** Apprenticeship; duration of this.

now, adv., conj., & n. [1. nou; 2. nau]. O.E. *nū*, M.E. *nou, nu*; Common Gmc. & Aryan; cp. O.H.G., O.S., Goth. *nu*, O.N. *nū*; Gk. *nūn*, Lat. *nunc*, Scrt. *nū.* **1.** adv. **a** At the present time, at this moment: *the bell is now ringing*; **b** under the circumstances: *I cannot go on now after what has happened*; **c** immediately, forthwith, at once: *do it now*; **d** a moment ago: (usually) *just now*; (archaic) *he is but now left*, has just left; **e** (in narrative) at time specified: *Hannibal was now crossing the Alps*; **f** from the moment that, seeing that: *now that I see your game*; *now that the weather is warmer*; Phrs. *now and again, now and then*, occasionally, from time to time; *now or never*, if ever, at the present moment; *now . . . now*, at one time . . ., at another . . .: *now hot, now cold*; *now now, now then*, in friendly protest or warning, e.g. *now now, a little less noise, please*; *now then, none of your nonsense!* **2.** conj. At beginning of a sentence, indicating a change or transition of thought or subject with no suggestion of particular time: *now while he was speaking I had my hand on the revolver in my pocket*; '*now Barabbas was a robber*'; *now that is pretty good, but there is more to come.* **3.** (following a prep., almost as n.) The present time: *by now*, by this time; *up to now*, up to the present.

nowadays, adv. [1. nóuadāz; 2. náuədeiz], for *now-on-days*, the last word being an advbl. genit. At the present time, in these days.

noway, noways, adv. [1. nṓwā(z); 2. nóuwei(z)]. In no way or manner, not at all, in no wise.

Nowel. See **Noel.**

nowhere, adv. [1. nṓwār; 2. nóuwɛə]. O.E. *nāhwǣr.* See **no** & **where.** In no place, not anywhere. Phr. *nowhere near*, far from, not nearly; *to be nowhere*, not to get a place in a race &c.; to be completely beaten: *Eclipse first and the rest nowhere.*

nowhither, adv. [1. nṓwidher; 2. nóuwiðə]. O.E. *nāhwiðer.* **no** & **whither.** (archaic, expressing motion towards) To, toward, no place, not in any direction, nowhere: '*Thy servant went nowhither*' (2 Kings v. 25).

nowise, adv. [1. nṓwīz; 2. nóuwaiz]. **no** & **-wise**, suff., 'way, manner'. In no way, by no means.

noxal, adj. [1. nóksal; 2. nóksəl]. Lat. *noxālis*, 'harmful, injurious', fr. *noxa*, 'injury'. See next word. (Roman law) Injurious, causing injury or damage.

noxious, adj. [1. nókshus; 2. nókʃəs], fr. Lat. *noxius*, 'harmful, injurious', fr. *noxa*, 'injury, harm', cogn. w. *nocēre*, 'to hurt, injure', fr. base **nek-, *nok-*, 'to destroy, be destroyed', cp. Lat. *necāre*, 'to kill', Gk. *nékus*, 'corpse', see **necro-**, & **-ous.** See also **nuisance, obnoxious, pernicious.** Physically or spiritually harmful, injurious, corrupting, offensive: *noxious weeds, doctrines, ideas* &c.

noxiously, adv. Prec. & **-ly.** In a noxious, harmful, injurious, way or manner.

noxiousness, n. See prec. & **-ness.** State or quality of being noxious.

noyade, n. [1. nwahyáhd; 2. nwǡjǡd]. Fr., 'a drowning', fr. *noyer*, 'to kill by drowning, to drown', fr. Lat. *necāre*, 'to kill'. See **noxious.** Execution by drowning; specif. (hist.) *the noyades*, the drowning of persons at Nantes during the Reign of Terror, 1794.

noyau, n. [1. nwáhyō; 2. nwǡjou]. Fr., fr. Lat. *nūcāle*, neut. of *nūcālis*, 'of, like a nut'. See **nux vomica.** A liqueur distilled from, or flavoured with, peach kernels.

nozzle, n. [1. nózl; 2. nózl]. Dimin. of **nose.** Cp. **nuzzle.** A projecting spout or vent: *the nozzle of a hose, of a pair of bellows* &c.

nuance, n. [1. nūáhns; 2. njūǡs]. Fr., fr. *nuer*, 'to shade', fr. *nue*, 'cloud', Lat. *nūbēs*, 'cloud'. See **nubiform.** A slight difference, delicate distinction, gradation; **a** in colour or tone; **b** in meaning of words &c.; **c** in feeling, emotion &c., and in modes of expressing these, as in manner.

nub, n. [1. nub; 2. nab]. Variant of **knob.** (very rare) A small round lump, esp. of coal.

nubble, n. [1. núbl; 2. nábl]. Prec. & **-le.** Nub.

nubbly, adj. [1. núbli; 2. nábli]. Prec. & **-ly.** Full of nubs or knobs; knobby, lumpy.

nubiform, adj. [1. nū́biform; 2. njū́bifōm], fr. Lat. *nūbēs*, 'cloud', & **-form.** Lat. *nūb-* is fr. base **(s)nudh-*, whence also W. *nudd*, 'mist', Avest. *snaoda-*, 'cloud'. See also **nystagmus.** Resembling a cloud in form.

nubile, adj. [1. nū́bil, nū́bīl; 2. njū́bil, njū́bail], fr. Lat. *nūbilis*, fr. *nūbere*, (of woman) 'to be married'. See **nuptial.** (of woman) Marriageable, old enough to marry.

nubility, n. [1. nūbíliti; 2. njūbíliti]. Prec. & **-ity.** State of being of marriageable age.

nuchal, adj. [1. nū́kl; 2. njū́kl], fr. L. Lat. *nūcha*, 'spinal marrow', cp. Fr. *nuque*, 'nape of the neck'; fr. Arab. *nūkhā*, 'spinal marrow'. (zool.) Of or pertaining to the back of the neck or pro-thorax in insects.

nuci-, pref., fr. Lat., stem of *nux*, 'nut'. See **nux.**

nuciferous, adj. [1. nūsíferus; 2. njūsífərəs]. Prec. & **-ferous.** Bearing nuts.

nucivorous, adj. [1. nūsívorus; 2. njūsívərəs]. **nuci-** & **-vorous.** Nut-eating.

nuclear, adj. [1. nū́klear; 2. njū́kliə]. **nucleus** & **-ar.** (biol.) Of or pertaining to a nucleus; forming a nucleus.

nucleate, vb. trans. & intrans. & adj. [1. nū́kleāt; 2. njū́klieit]. **nucleus** & **-ate. a** vb. To form or cause to form into or round a nucleus; **b** adj., having a nucleus.

nucleo-, pref., fr. **nucleus.** Connected with a nucleus.

nucleolar, adj. [1. nūklḗolar; 2. njūklíələ], fr. next word & **-ar.** Of or pertaining to a nucleolus or nucleoli.

nucleole, n. [1. nū́klēōl; 2. njū́klioul]. See next word. A nucleolus.

nucleolus, n., pl. **nucleoli** [1. nūklḗolus, -lī; 2. njūklíələs, -lai]. Lat., little nut', dimin. of **nucleus.** (biol.) A small nucleus within another nucleus of a cell.

nucleus, n. [1. nū́klēus; 2. njū́kliəs], learned (Lat.) pl. *nuclei* [1. nū́klēī; 2. njū́kliai], popular pl. *nucleuses.* Lat., 'kernel', dimin. fr. *nūc-*, 'nut'. See **nux vomica. 1.** A central core or kernel which gathers matter and increases by accretion; (fig.) starting-point, centre: *the nucleus of a library, of a collection*; *the nucleus of a plan.* **2.** (astron.) The bright dense part forming the head of a comet; the dark central part of a sun-spot. **3.** (biol.) The central part of a living animal or plant cell, and an essential factor in its growth, nutrition, and reproduction.

nude (I.), adj. [1. nūd; 2. njūd], fr. Lat. *nūdus*, 'naked, bare', for **nowedos*, fr. Aryan **nogʷedhos*; whence Goth. *naqaþs*, 'naked'; O.N. *nokkueðr*; O.E. *nacod*; O.H.G. *nakkot.* See **naked. 1. a** Naked, unclothed, bare: *a nude figure*; **b** (fig.) not concealed or dissembled, fully revealed: *a nude fact*; *a nude statement*, plain, unvarnished. **2.** (law) Bare, without consideration and therefore void: *a nude contract.*

nude (II.), n., fr. prec. A nude, undraped, figure in painting or sculpture. Phr. *the nude*, representation in painting or sculpture of the undraped human figure; *in the nude*, naked, undraped; manifest, with nothing concealed.

nudely, adv. **nude (I.)** & **-ly.** In a nude, naked, manner.

nudeness, n. See prec. & **-ness.** State of being nude; nudity.

nudge, vb. trans. & n. [1. nuj; 2. nadž]. Etymol. doubtful; possibly Scand., cp. Norw. *nugga, nyggja*, 'to push, jostle'. **1.** vb. To push gently and furtively with the elbow, esp. deliberately in order to attract attention. **2.** n. A slight push with the elbow &c.

nudity, n. [1. núditi; 2. njúditi], fr. Fr. *nudité*, fr. Lat. *nūditāt-(em)*, 'nakedness'; See **nude (I.)** & **-ity.** State, quality, of being naked; nakedness, nudeness.

nugae, n. pl. [1. núgē; 2. njúgī]. Lat., 'jests, idle speeches, trifles, nonsense'. Origin obscure. Light jests, trifles.

nugatory, adj. [1. núgaturi; 2. njúgətəri]. Lat. *nūgātōrius*, 'trifling, worthless, futile', fr. *nūgātor*, 'jester, chatterer', fr. *nūgae*, 'trifles'. See prec. **a** Trifling, valueless, useless; **b** of no force, ineffectual, futile; inoperative, invalid.

nuggar, n. [1. núgar; 2. nágə]. Native Egyptian name. A broad-bottomed boat or barge on the Nile.

nugget, n. [1. núget; 2. nágit]. Etymol. doubtful. A lump of metal, esp. of gold in its native state.

nuisance, n. [1. núsans; 2. njúsəns]. Fr., fr. *nuisant*, Pres. Part. of *nuire*, 'to harm, injure', fr. Lat. *nocēre*, 'to harm, hurt', & **-ce.** See **noxious.** **a** Act, object, state of affairs, which causes injury, damage, annoyance, or inconvenience, to another, or to the community; *to abate a nuisance*, to cause a nuisance, public or private, to cease; *Inspector of Nuisances*, public official whose duty it is to abate nuisances; *to make a nuisance of oneself*, to annoy, be troublesome. **b** an offensive, obnoxious, troublesome, disagreeable person: *you're a nuisance to yourself and everybody else.*

null, adj. [1. nul; 2. nal]. Cp. Fr. *nul*, fr. Lat. *nullus*, 'none, not any', fr. *ne*, 'not', & *ullus*, 'any'; fr. **oin-los*, dimin. of *oinos*, later *ūnus*, 'one'. See **union** & **one.** **a** Of no effect; not valid, having no legal force, void; Phr. *null and void*, of contracts &c. which have no validity or binding force; **b** of no value or significance; characterless, futile.

nullah, n. [1. núla; 2. nálə]. Anglo-Ind., fr. Hind. *nālā*. A watercourse, a gully; often, but not exclusively, applied to a dry watercourse.

nullification, n. [1. nùlifikáshun; 2. nàlifikéiʃən], fr. L. Lat. *nullificātiōn-(em)*, 'contempt', fr. *nullificāt-*, P.P. type of *nullificāre*, 'to despise'. See **null** & **-fication.** **a** Act of nullifying; **b** state of being nullified.

nullify, vb. trans. [1. núlifī; 2. nálifai], fr. Lat. *nullificāre*, 'to esteem lightly, count as nothing, despise'. See **null** & **-fy.** To make null and void; to render invalid or useless; to cancel, annul, destroy: *to nullify all one's efforts.*

nullity, n. [1. núliti; 2. náliti]. Cp. Fr. *nullité*. See **null** & **-ity.** **1. a** Quality or state of being null and void; invalidity; **b** act or proceeding which renders null and void: *nullity of marriage.* **2.** That which is null; a nobody, a nonentity.

numb, adj. & vb. trans. [1. num; 2. nam]. M.E. *nume(n)*, 'seized, taken'; hence 'overcome'; P.P. of M.E. *nimen*, 'to take', O.E. *niman*, P.P. *numen*, see **nimble**; prob. cogn. w. base **nem-*. See **nomad** & **number.** **1.** adj. Deprived of feeling and sensation, lacking power of movement; insensible, deadened; esp. *numb with cold*; also of the mind and feelings, deadened, insensible. **2.** vb. To render numb; deprive of sensation or sensibility, deaden, benumb.

number (I.), n. [1. númber; 2. námbə], fr. O. Fr. *nombre*, fr. Lat. *numerus*, 'number'; fr. base **nem-*, as in Gk. *némein*, 'to divide, distribute'. See prec., & also **Nemesis, nomad, numeral, numismatic** &c. **1.** A quantity, amount, sum, aggregate, of persons, objects, abstractions &c. Phrs. *by, in, number*, to the number of; *out of, without, number*, not to be counted or numbered, very many; *times without number*, over and over again; *to the number of*, amounting to. **2.** (math.) **a** An abstract unit or sum of units; the abstract ratio of one quantity to another of the same kind: *the science of numbers*, arithmetic; **b** the name of a mathematical number: *two, ten* &c.; **c** figure, symbol, representing such an abstract unit or sum, a numeral: 2, 10 &c. Specif. **3.** (usually abbr. *No.*; Lat. *numero*, 'in number') The figure or numeral which distinguishes one person or object from another belonging to the same numbered company, class, or series; particular person or object so distinguished: *policeman's, motor-car's, number*; *number of room in hotel, of house in a street* &c. Phrs. *to look after, take care of, number one*, look after oneself or one's own interests; *to lose the number of one's mess*, to die. **4.** Any single part of a magazine or other publication issued at intervals, or as a series; one of the numbered divisions of a literary or musical composition; a part. Phr. *a back number*, person, thing, which is out of date, old-fashioned, or forgotten. **5.** (gram.) The form of a word which denotes plurality or unity or, in some languages, as Greek, duality: *in the singular, plural, dual, number.* **6.** (poet., usually pl.) Verses: '*I lisped in numbers, for the numbers came*' (Pope). **7.** Specif. (cap. and pl.) *Numbers*, the title of fourth book of the Old Testament. See also **golden number.**

number (II.), vb. trans., fr. prec. **1.** To give a specific number to: *number the houses in a street, the pages in a book* &c. Phr. *to number off*, (of soldiers) to call out their numbers in rank, in drilling. **2.** To amount to: *they numbered fifty all told.* **3. a** (archaic) To count, reckon up, number of: *David numbered the people*; '*So teach us to number our days that we may apply our hearts unto wisdom*'; Phr. *his days are numbered*, are all told, his life is nearly at an end; **b** to count, reckon, regard as one of a company or class: *you can number me among the subscribers*; *to number a person among one's friends.*

numberless, adj. [1. númberles; 2. námbəlis]. **number (I.)** & **-less.** Without number; countless, innumerable.

numbness, n. [1. númnes; 2. námnis]. **numb** & **-ness.** Condition of being numb; insensibility.

numdah, n. [1. númdah; 2. námdā]. Hind. *namdā*. Kind of felt cloth; saddle cloth or blanket of this material.

numerable, adj. [1. númerabl; 2. njúmərəbl], fr. Lat. *numerābilis*. See next word & **number** & **-able.** (rare) Capable of being numbered or counted.

numeral, adj. & n. [1. númeral; 2. njúmərəl], fr. L. Lat. *numerālis*, 'of numbers', fr. *numerus*, see **number**, & **-al.** **1.** adj. Connected with, representing, expressing, a number or numbers: *numeral symbols.* **2.** n. **a** Graphic symbol, or character, representing a number or set of numbers: *the Arabic, Roman, numerals*; **b** the name of any such symbol.

numeration, n. [1. nùmeráshun; 2. njùməréiʃən], fr. Lat. *numerātiōn-(em)*, 'counting', fr. *numerāt-*, P.P. type of *numerāre*, 'to count', see **number**, & **-ion.** Counting by numbers; act or process of numbering; calculation; system of reading numbers or of expressing in or by numbers.

numerator, n. [1. númerātur; 2. njúməreitə]. L. Lat., 'one who numbers', fr. *numerāt-*, see prec., & **-or.** (arith.) The term or figure which in fractions denotes the number of units of the fraction; in vulgar fractions, the figure above the line; in decimal fractions, the figure following the decimal point.

numerical, adj. [1. nūmérikl; 2. njūmérikl], fr. Lat. *numer-(us)*, see **number**, & **-ic** & **-al.** **a** Of, pertaining to, denoting or expressing, a number or numbers; **b** expressed in or by numeral symbols.

numerically, adv. Prec. & **-ly.** In numbers, by means of numbers: *expressed numerically.*

numerous, adj. [1. númerus; 2. njúmərəs], fr. Lat. *numerōsus*, 'numerous', fr. *numerus*, see **number**, & **-ous.** **1.** Containing many units; of great number, very many: *a numerous company, acquaintance*; *a numerous collection of books* &c. **2.** (archaic or poet.) Written in poetic numbers; rhythmical, melodious: '*numerous verse*' (Milton).

numerously, adv. Prec. & **-ly.** In great numbers.

numismatic, adj. [1. nùmizmátik; 2. njùmizmǽtik], fr. Fr. *numismatique*, fr. Lat. *numisma*, 'coin', form prob. influenced by Lat. *nummus*, 'a coin'; fr. Gk. stem *nomismat-*, 'current coin', cp. *nómos*, 'custom'; cogn. w. *némein*, 'to assign, distribute'. See **Nemesis, nomad,** & **number.** Of or pertaining to coins and coinage: *a numismatic collection.*

numismatics, n. pl. Science, art, of coins and medals.

numismatist, n. [1. nūmízmatist; 2. njūmízmətist]. See prec. & **-ist.** Person skilled in the history, various styles &c. of coins and medals.

nummary, adj. [1. númari; 2. náməri], fr. Lat. *nummārius*, fr. *nummus*, 'coin'; cogn. w. Gk. *nómimos*, 'customary', fr. *nómos*, 'custom'. See **numismatic.** Pertaining to coins or money; in form of currency.

nummular, adj. [1. númūlar; 2. námjulə], fr. Lat. *nummulārius*, fr. *nummulus*, dimin. of *nummus*, 'coin'. See prec. Shaped like, resembling, a coin.

nummulite, n. [1. númūlīt; 2. námjulait], fr. Lat. *nummul-(us)*, as prec., & **-ite.** A fossil shell of one of the foraminifers, shaped rather like a coin.

nummulitic, adj. [1. nùmūlítik; 2. nàmjulítik]. Prec. & **-ic.** Formed of nummulites: *nummulitic limestone.*

numskull, n. [1. númskul; 2. námskal], fr. **numb** & **skull.** A dolt, blockhead.

nun, n. [1. nun; 2. nan]. O.E. *nunne*, also M.E. *nunne, nonne*, fr. Fr.; fr. L. Lat. *nonna, nunna*, 'old lady'; used as title of respect, as was *nonnus*, 'old man, father, monk'; Gk. has *nénnā, nánnē*, 'aunt', *nénnos*, 'uncle'; cp. also Scrt. *nanā*, 'mother', Russ. *njánja*, 'nurse', & W. *nain*, 'grandmother'. **1.** A member of a woman's religious order, living in a nunnery or convent under vows of chastity, poverty, and obedience. **2.** (zool.) Name of certain varieties of birds, such as pigeons, or of moths.

nun-buoy, n. First element fr. obs. *nun*, 'spinning top', of wh. etymol. is doubtful, & **buoy.** A type of buoy consisting of two cones placed base to base.

nunc dimittis, n. [1. núngk dīmítis; 2. náŋk daimítis]. Lat., 'now thou lettest depart'. Cp. **now** & **demission.** **1.** Name of Canticle beginning '*Lord, now lettest Thou Thy servant depart in peace*', taken from the Song of Simeon, Luke ii. 29, sq.; so called from the beginning in Latin version. **2.** A farewell, esp. one at the end of a life well lived, or a long task faithfully completed: *to sing one's nunc dimittis.*

nuncheon, n. [1. núnchun; 2. nántʃən]. In M.E. *noneschenche*, lit. 'a noon-drink', fr. *nōne*, see **noon**, & *schench(e)*, 'draught, drink poured out', fr. O.E. *sćenćan*, 'to pour', cp. Germ. *schenken*, 'to give, sell drink, to give as a present'; the word has no connexion w. **luncheon.** An old, now obsolete word for a midday or afternoon meal or draught.

nunciature, n. [1. núnshatūr; 2. nánʃətjə], fr. Ital. *nunciatura*, fr. Lat. *nuntiātūr-(us)*, Fut. Part. of *nuntiāre, nuntiāt-(um)*, 'to report, tell', fr. *nunti-(us)*, 'messenger'. See next word. **a** The office of a Papal Nuncio; **b** period, tenure, of such office.

nuncio, n. [1. núnshiō; 2. nánʃiou]. Ital., fr. Lat. *nuntius*, n., 'messenger, envoy', most prob. derived fr. *nuntium* (fr. **noventiom*), wh. may have meant orig. 'an augur's message, or statement', in wh. case cp. Scrt. *navatē*, 'he sounds, rejoices, praises'; & Lith. *nauju*, 'I call, cry out'. Another suggestion is **novi-ventius*, 'new-comer' (cp. **novel (I.)** & **venue**); cp. **announce, denounce, enunciate** &c. A diplomatic representative of the Pope at a foreign court; a Papal ambassador.

nuncle, n. [1. núngkl; 2. náŋkl], fr. 'an, or min(e), uncle', cp. **newt**. See **uncle**. (obs. and familiar) Uncle.

nuncupative, adj. [1. núngkūpåtiv; 2. náŋkjupèitiv], fr. Lat. *nuncupāt-(um)*, P.P. type of *nuncupāre*, 'to call by name, to name publicly as one's heir', fr. *nōmen*, 'name', see **nominal**, & *capere*, 'to take', see **captive**, & **-ive**. (chiefly of wills) Declared by word of mouth, instead of in writing; used of a will made when at the point of death, or by soldiers and sailors in battle.

nundinal, adj. [1. núndinal; 2. nándinəl]. Lat. *nundināl-(is)*, 'of or belonging to a market day'; cp. *nundinae*, 'ninth day, market day', & *nundinum*, 'market time', fr. *nōvem*, 'nine', & an old word **dino*, 'day' (markets being held every ninth (inclusive) day); cp. Scrt. *dínam*, 'day'; O. Slav. *dĭnĭ*, 'day'; seen also in Goth. *sin-teins*, 'daily, everlasting'; possibly also in O.E. *lenc-ten*, 'spring, Lent', see **Lent (I.)**. (Rom. antiq.) **1. a** Of, pertaining to, a fair or market; **b** pertaining to the *nundinae*, see above. **2.** *Nundinal letter*, any one of the first eight letters of the alphabet, used for each day of the week in succession.

nunhood, n. [1. núnhood; 2. nánhud]. **nun** & **-hood**. State of being a nun.

nunlike, adj. [1. núnlīk; 2. nánlaik]. **nun** & **-like**. Like a nun; meek, chaste, demure.

nunnation, n. [1. nunáshun; 2. nanéiʃən], fr. Arab. *nūn*, name of the letter *n*, & **-ation**. Addition of a final *n* in the declension of Arabic nouns.

nunnery, n. [1. núneri; 2. nánəri], fr. Fr. *nonnerie*, 'convent'. See **nun** & **-ery**. **a** The building in which a religious community of nuns reside; convent; **b** a community of nuns.

nun's veiling, n. [1. nùnz vāling; 2. nànz véiliŋ]. A soft, fine, woollen cloth for dresses &c.

nuphar. See **nenuphar**.

nuptial, adj. & n. [1. núpshal; 2. nápʃəl], fr. Lat. *nuptiāl-(is)*, 'of marriage or a wedding', fr. *nuptiae*, 'wedding', fr. *nupt-(um)*, P.P. of *nūbere*, 'to marry'; cogn. w. O. Slav. *snubiti*, 'to love', Czech. *snoubiti*, 'to seek in marriage'; also Gk. *númphē*, 'bride', see **nymph**. **1.** adj. Of or belonging to a wedding: *the nuptial bed, feast* &c. **2.** n. (usually pl.) *Nuptials*, wedding ceremonies; a wedding.

nuraghe, noraghe, n., pl. *-ghi* [1. nōōráhgā, -gē; 2. nūrágei, -gī]. Sardinian dial. word; possibly a corrupt. of Ital. *muraglia*, 'wall'. See **mural**. A prehistoric circular building or tower of a peculiar type found in Sardinia, believed to belong to the Bronze Age.

nurse (I.), n. [1. nērs; 2. nās]. M.E. *norice*, *nurice*, fr. O. Fr. *norice*, *norrice*, *nurrice*, *noursche*, sometimes *norrish* in 16th cent., by confusion w. *nourish*; Mod. Fr. *nourrice*; fr. L. Lat. *nūtrīcia*, 'nurse', fem. of *nūtrīcius*, adj., 'nursing', fr. *nūtrīc-(em)*, 'a nurse', cp. *nūtrīre*, 'to suckle, nurse, nourish'; prob. fr. base **sneu-*, **snāu-* &c., 'to trickle, allow to flow'; cp. also Scrt. *snauti*, 'she gives milk', & Gk. *néein*, 'to flow', for **snew-*; ultimately fr. base **snā-*, seen in Lat. *nāre*, 'to swim', see **natation**. Cp. **nourish**, **nurture**, **nutritious**. **1. a** A woman who suckles an infant from birth; also *wet nurse*; Phr. *to put out to nurse*, to send an infant from home to a foster mother or one who professes to take charge of infants; **b** woman who attends another at a birth and looks after the child and mother for a period; also *monthly nurse*; **c** woman attendant of a child; **d** worker bee, or ant, that attends to the young. **2.** Person of either sex, but generally a woman, specially trained to watch and attend upon the sick, wounded, or infirm, under the direction of a physician or surgeon: *hospital nurse*; *male nurse*; *Red Cross nurse*. **3.** (fig.) System or institution which fosters, protects, nourishes, encourages, moral and intellectual growth: *the college has been the nurse of many famous men*. **4.** (bot.) A tree, shrub &c., which acts as a shelter or protection for seedling plants.

nurse (II.), vb. trans. & intrans., fr. prec. **A.** trans. **1.** To suckle (an infant); to give the breast to: *mothers should always nurse their own babies*. **2.** To take charge of and attend to (a child). **3.** To fondle, embrace, support, in the arms, or on the lap: *to nurse a cat*. Phr. *to nurse the fire*, to sit very close, as though one would embrace it. **4.** To attend on, give skilled care to, a patient in illness: *to nurse a person through typhoid* &c. **5. a** To foster, cherish, encourage the growth of; to rear, bring up to maturity: *to nurse a plant, young tree* &c.; **b** to cherish in the mind, entertain: *to nurse hopes, ambitions, feelings of revenge, hatred* &c. **6.** To bestow particular care and solicitude upon; to manage carefully, husband, avoid waste of, in energy or expenditure: *to nurse an estate, one's resources, finances*; in various special Phrs. implying bestowal of care &c.: *to nurse a horse*, not ride or drive him too fast at first; *to nurse a constituency*, to give time and attention to the electorate before an election; *to nurse balls*, (billiards) to keep them close together for making 'nursery' cannons. **B.** intrans. To be, act as, a nurse to the sick.

nurse (III.), n. Etymol. doubtful; possibly fr. *an huss*, an obs. name of a dog-fish, of unknown origin, wh. might easily be assimilated to **nurse (I.)**, an old pronunciation of wh., now obs. or vulg., was '*nuss*' [nas]. The name of various species of dog-fish, also called *nurse-hound* and *nurse-shark*.

nurse child, n. A foster-child, child put out to nurse.

nurse-frog, n. The obstetric toad, also *nurse toad*.

nurseling, nursling, n. [1. nērsling; 2. nāsliŋ], fr. **nurse (I.)** & **-ling**. **a** An infant still being nursed at the breast; **b** a young tender plant.

nurse-maid, n. Young girl who helps a head nurse in a nursery; a nursery maid.

nursery, n. [1. nērseri; 2. nāsəri], fr. **nurse (I.)** & **-ry**. **1.** Room or rooms in a household, specially set apart, in which children live and play and take their meals during the daytime: *day nursery*; room in which they sleep: *night nursery*. **2.** Place where young plants, trees &c., are cultivated and reared for transplanting &c. **3.** (fig.) Place, sphere, of intellectual and moral training and influence: *universities are the nurseries of rising talent*.

nursery cannon, n. (billiards) Any of a series of cannons made by nursing or keeping the balls close together.

nursery garden, n. A garden where young plants are reared for sale.

nursery governess, n. A governess for quite young children still in the nursery, and needing nursing as well as teaching.

nursery maid, n. Girl whose business it is to clean and keep nurseries tidy, and to help the nurse in attending to the children.

nurseryman, n. [1. nērseriman; 2. nāsəriman]. Keeper of a nursery garden.

nursery rhyme, n. Verses, often embodying traditional songs and tales &c., sung to, and by, young children.

nursing (I.), adj. [1. nērsing; 2. nāsiŋ], fr. Pres. Part. of **nurse (II.)**. **a** Giving food to, supplying with food, as from the breast: *nursing mother*; **b** taking food from the breast: *nursing child*.

nursing (II.), n. **nurse (II.)** & **-ing**. **1. a** Occupation, profession, of a nurse, esp. of a skilled nurse for the sick; **b** care of young children. **2.** (attrib.) Connected with attendance upon the sick: *nursing profession, service* &c.

nurture, n. & vb. trans. [1. nērchur; 2. nātʃə]. M.E. *nortare*, fr. O. Fr. *norriture*, *nurriture*, Mod. Fr. *nourriture*, fr. L. Lat. *nūtrītūra*, 'nursling', fr. *nūtrīre*, 'to nurse'. See **nurse (I.)** & **nourish**. **1.** n. **a** Nourishment; **b** fostering care; education, training. **2.** vb. To nourish, foster; breed up, rear; educate, train up: *a delicately nurtured girl*.

nut (I.), n. [1. nut; 2. nat]. O.E. *hnutu*, M.E. *note*, *nute*; O.H.G. *nuz*, O.N. *hnut*; cp. W. *cneuen*; for relation w. Lat. *nux*, *nūcis*, see **nux vomica**. **1. a** The hard-shelled fruit of certain plants, containing an edible kernel; Phrs. (colloq. and slang) *for nuts*, at all or in any sort of fashion: *can't play golf for nuts*; *to be (dead) nuts on*, to be very keen on or fond of; *to be nuts to* or *for*, to be very attractive or fascinating to; to be a great treat or experience to or for; *a tough nut*, (i.) a strong, hardy, resolute person; (ii.) a violent person difficult to manage; *a hard nut to crack*, difficult problem to solve; **b** the kernel itself, usually distinguished by name of plant or place of origin &c.: *Brazil nut, hazel nut* &c., cp. also *chestnut*. **2.** (fig., slang) The head. **3. a** A small block of metal perforated with a female screw for securing or tightening a bolt &c.; **b** small knob forming projecting end of screw for tightening or loosening the hairs of a violin bow. **4.** (pl.) Small lumps or knobs of coal. **5.** (vulg. or facet.) A young swell, a dandy, a fop.

nut (II.), vb. intrans., fr. prec. To look for and gather nuts; chiefly in Phr. *to go nutting*.

nutate, vb. intrans. [1. nūtāt; 2. njūteit], fr. Lat. *nūtāt-(um)*, *nūtāre*, 'to nod', freq. form of *nuere*, 'to nod'; cogn. w. Lat. *nūmen*, 'nod, command, authority; hence, divinity', fr. base **(s)neu-*, **snū-* &c., 'to make a rapid movement'; cp. Scrt. *návatē*, 'turn'; Gk. *neúein*, 'to nod', *neûma*, 'a nod'; Lith. *snūsti*, 'to fall asleep'; perh. also Gk. *nússein*, 'to nudge'; Du. *nucken*, 'to shake the head'. Cp. **innuendo**. (bot.) To nod; droop the head; specif., of stem, to move in a circular direction during growth.

nutation, n. [1. nūtáshun; 2. njūtéiʃən]. Prec. & **-ion**. A nodding, drooping of the head, specif. **a** (astron.) small vibratory or oscillating movement of the earth's axis; **b** (bot.) a slight circular movement of the growing stem of a plant.

nut-brown, adj. Of a dark or reddish brown colour, as of ripe hazel-nut or chestnut: *nut-brown ale*; (of the complexion) *the Nut-brown Maid*.

nut-butter, n. A substitute for butter made from the kernels of various edible nuts.

nutcracker(s), n. **nut** & **cracker**. **1. a** Instrument, consisting of two narrow pieces of metal hinged together at one end, and squeezed together by the hand at the other, used for cracking nuts; **b** a type of face in which the nose and chin tend to meet, (usually attrib.) *a nutcracker face, jaws* &c. **2.** (zool.) A European bird, *Nucifraga*, of the crow family, feeding on nuts &c.

nut-gall, n. An oak-gall, used for dyeing, making ink &c.

nuthatch, n. [1. nút-hach; 2. náthætʃ], fr. **nut** & **hatch (IV.)**, 'to hack, engrave'; see **hack (I.)**. A small British bird, feeding largely on nuts, which it pierces and opens with its bill.

nutmeg, n. [1. nútmeg; 2. nátmεg]. M.E. *nutmuge*; first element **nut**; second element fr. O. Fr. *mugue*, 'musk', fr. **musgue*, fr. Lat. *muscus*, 'musk', q.v.; O. Fr. had *nois mugette*, 'nutmeg', of wh. the Engl. word is a hybrid translation. The pungent seed of a Malay tree, used as a spice in cooking, and as a flavouring in medicine.

nut-pine, n. Name of various pine trees, such as the stone-pine, which have edible seeds.

nutria, n. [1. nūtria; 2. njūtriə]. Span., 'otter'. The fur of the S. American coypu, a water rodent.

nutrient, adj. [1. nūtrient; 2. njūtriənt], fr. Lat. *nūtrient-(em)*, Pres. Part. of *nūtrīre*, 'to nourish'. See **nurse, nurture**. Nourishing, nutritious, nutritive.

nutriment, n. [1. nūtriment; 2. njūtrimənt], fr. Lat. *nūtriment-(um)*. See prec. & **-ment**. Nourishing food, nourishment; that which gives strength or power of growth.

nutrimental, adj. [1. nūtriméntl; 2. njūtriméntl]. Prec. & **-al**. Providing nutriment; nutritious, nourishing.

nutrition, n. [1. nūtríshun; 2. njūtríʃən], fr. Lat. *nūtrīt-(um)*, fr. *nūtrīre*, 'to nourish', see **nutrient**, & **-ion**. **1.** Process, or sum of processes, by which an organism is nourished by absorbing substances different from itself and assimilating them to substance identical with itself. **2.** That which nourishes; food.

nutritious, adj. [1. nūtríshus; 2. njūtríʃəs], fr. Lat. *nūtrītius*, fr. *nūtrix*, *nūtrīc-(is)*. See **nurse** & **-ious**. Nourishing, feeding, maintaining and increasing growth in an organism; nutritive.

nutritiously, adv. Prec. & **-ly**. In a nourishing way.

nutritiousness, n. See prec. & **-ness**. Property of being nutritious or nourishing.

nutritive, adj. & n. [1. nū́tritiv; 2. njū́tritiv]. Fr. *nutritif*, *-ve*, fr. Med. Lat. *nutritivus*. See **nutrient** & **-ive**. **1.** adj. Nourishing, nutritious; of or relating to nutrition. **2.** n. A nourishing substance.

nutritively, adv. Prec. & **-ly**. In a nutritive way; so as to nourish.

nutshell, n. [1. nútshel; 2. nátʃel]. **nut** & **shell**. The hard shell of a nut enclosing the kernel. Phr. *in a nutshell*, in the smallest space; in as few words as possible.

nutty, adj. [1. núti; 2. náti]. **nut** & **-y**. **1.** (rare) Full of, abounding in, nuts. **2.** Having the flavour of nuts (of ale, sherry &c.). **3.** (vulg. slang) **a** Very keen on, fond of; **b** like a nut (**I. 5**), smart, showy; **c** crack-brained, crazy, dotty.

nux vomica, n. [1. núks vómika; 2. náks vómikə], fr. Lat. *nux*, 'nut'; according to Walde fr. earlier **dnuk-*, itself, by transposition of consonants, fr. orig. **knud-*; fr. this the Gmc. **hnut-*, as in O.E. *hnutu*, 'nut', is a regular development, see **nut**. The form **vomica* is fr. *vomere*, see **vomit**. The seed of an East Indian tree, *Strychnos*, containing strychnine; medicinal substance extracted from this.

nuzzle, vb. intrans. & trans. [1. núzl; 2. názl]. Also earlier *nosyll*; fr. **nose** & **-le**. To push, press the nose against or in; to fondle in this way as a dog or a horse does.

nyctalopia, n. [1. nìktalṓpia; 2. nìktəlóupiə]. L. Lat., fr. Gk. *nuktálōps*, 'person who is blind at night', fr. *nukt-(ós)*, *núx*, 'night', see **nocti-**, *alaós*, 'blind', *ṓps*, 'eye', see **optic**. The etymol. of *alaós* is doubtful; it may be fr. **m̥lawós*, & thus fr. base **mĕl-*, **m̥il-*, **mōl-* &c., 'to be mistaken, uncertain; to deceive', seen in Gk. *méleos*, 'useless', *mōlus*, 'exhausted'; Lith. *mēlas*, 'deceit, lying'. A condition of the eyesight in which a person who can see quite well by day is nearly blind at night or on a very dark day; night-blindness.

nyctalopic, adj. [1. nìktalṓpik; 2. nìktəlóupik]. Prec. & **-ic**. Suffering from, affected by, nyctalopia or night-blindness.

nyctitropic, adj. [1. nìktitrópik; 2. nìktitrópik], fr. Gk. *nukt-(ós)*, *núx*, 'night', see prec., & *tróp-(ein)*, 'to turn', see **trope** & **tropic**, & **-ic**. (bot., of leaves &c.) Turning or changing position at night or in the dark.

nyctitropism, n. [1. nìktitrópizm; 2. nìktitrópizəm]. See prec. & **-ism**. (bot.) Habit, tendency, of parts of certain plants to turn or change position at night.

nyctophobia, n. [1. nìktofṓbia; 2. nìktəfóubiə], fr. Gk. *nukt-(ós)*, *núx*, 'night', see prec. words, & **-phobia**. Unreasoning, morbid fear, discomfort &c. experienced at night or in darkness.

nylghau, n. See **nilgai**.

nymph, n. [1. nimf; 2. nimf], fr. Lat. *nympha*, fr. Gk. *númphē*, 'bride, maiden, nymph', a nasalized form of the base seen in Lat. *nūbere*, 'to wed'; cp. also O. Slav. *snubiti*, 'to seek in marriage'; Aryan base **snu-(bh)*; other forms of the base **snu-* appear in Lat. *nurus*, Scrt. *snušā́*, O. Slav. *snŭcha*, O.E. *snoru*, 'daughter-in-law'. See **nubile** & **nuptial**. **1.** (class. antiq.) One of the many maiden deities supposed to haunt, and considered as the spirits of, woods, hills, springs, rivers, the sea &c. **2.** (poet.) A young woman. **3.** (entom.) An insect in a transitional or not fully developed stage; pupa, chrysalis.

nymphaeum, n. [1. nimfḗum; 2. nimfíəm]. Lat., fr. Gk. *númphaion*. See prec. A shrine, temple, of a nymph or the nymphs.

nymphal, adj. [1. nímfal; 2. nímfəl]. **nymph** & **-al**. **1.** Of or belonging to a nymph or the nymphs; nymphean. **2.** (entom.) Of or belonging to an undeveloped stage of an insect; pupal.

nymphean, adj. [1. nimfḗan; 2. nimfíən]. See prec. & **-an**. Nymphal, of or belonging to a nymph; nymph-like.

nympholepsy, n. [1. nímfōlèpsi; 2. nímfoulèpsi]. Formed on anal. of *epilepsy*, fr. Gk. *numphólēptos*, 'caught by the nymphs, in a state of rapture', fr. *númphē*, 'nymph', & **lab-*, stem of *lambánein*, 'to catch'. See **catalepsy**. (poet.) State of rapture or ecstatic emotion; frenzy caused by contemplation of, or furious desire for, an unrealizable ideal.

nympholept, n. [1. nímfōlept; 2. nímfoulept]. See prec. (poet.) Person in a state of nympholepsy.

nympholeptic, adj. [1. nìmfōléptik; 2. nìmfouléptik]. See prec. & **-ic**. In a state of nympholepsy.

nymphomania, n. [1. nìmfōmā́nia; 2. nìmfouméiniə], fr. **nymph** & **mania**. Extreme morbid sexual desire and excitement in women.

nymphomaniac, n. [1. nìmfōmā́niak; 2. nìmfouméiniæk]. Prec. & **-ac**. Woman suffering from nymphomania.

nypa, n. See **nipa**.

nystagmic, adj. [1. nistágmik; 2. nistǽgmik]. See next word & **-ic**. Of or pertaining to nystagmus.

nystagmus, n. [1. nistágmus; 2. nistǽgməs], fr. Gk. *nustagmós*, 'drowsiness', fr. *nustázein*, 'to be sleepy, drowsy'; cogn. w. Lith. *snudà*, 'sleeper', *snáudzu*, 'I sleep'; fr. base **sneudh-* &c., 'dullness, darkness', whence also Lat. *nūbēs*, 'cloud', q.v. under **nubiform**. (med.) An involuntary quivering or twitching of the eyelid.

O

O, o, [1. ō; 2. ou]. The fifteenth letter of the English alphabet; **a** a sign, mark, shaped like an O; **b** a cipher, nought &c. For use of letter in abbreviations and as symbol see list at end of Dictionary.

O, oh (**I.**), interj. [1. ō; 2. ou]. Common to many languages, cp. Germ., Du. *o*, Fr. *o*, Gk. *ō̆*, *ō* &c.; imitative; distinctions between *O!* & *Oh!* are arbitrary, but *O!* is now usually poet. or rhet. **1.** An exclamation expressing surprise, fear, admiration, wish &c.: *oh dear!*; *oh my!*; *oh, what a surprise!*; *O, for a real leader!* **2.** Used before name in addressing a person: *oh! Mrs. Jones.* **3.** (poet. or rhet.) As an invocation or appeal: *O all ye powers of the earth.*

O' (**II.**), pref. to certain Ir. surnames, as *O'Brien*, fr. Ir. *ō*, *ua*, 'descendant, grandson'.

o' (**III.**), prep. Abbr. of **of**, chiefly colloq., but still usual in *o'clock*, as *four o'clock*, and *man-o'-war* &c.

-o, suff. used as termination to the first element in compound words, properly for words of Gk. origin having this as stem vowel, but also extended to others; also now freely used in modern compounds fr. various sources: *Russo-Turkish (War)*, *Franco-British* &c.

oaf, n. [1. ōf; 2. ouf]. Earlier *awf*, *auf*; fr. O.N. *alfr*; variant of **elf**. **1.** A changeling; misshapen, deformed child. **2. a** Idiot, simpleton; **b** clumsy, awkward fellow, lout.

oafish, adj. [1. ṓfish; 2. óufiʃ]. Prec. & **-ish**. Clumsy, stupid, awkward.

oak, n. [1. ōk; 2. ouk]. O.E. *āc*, M.E. *ōke*, *ook*; O.H.G. *eih*, Mod. Germ. *eiche*; O.N. *eik*; Du. *eik*; anct. Aryan tree-name; cp. the cogn. Lat. *aesculus*, fr. **aigsculos*, 'the Italian oak'; Gk. *aigílōps*, a kind of oak with sweet fruit; also *krát-aigos*, tree of undetermined species; see **aegis**. **1.** (bot.) **a** Any tree of the genus *Quercus*; specif., *Q. robur*, the British oak, a forest tree yielding a fine-grained, hard, and lasting timber, with deeply indented leaves and wide-spreading branches, the fruit of which is the acorn; other species have usually an attributive prefixed, as *holm-oak*, the ilex; *cork-oak* &c.; Phr. *Hearts of Oak*, the ships and seamen of the British navy. *The Oaks*, the name of a race for three-year-old fillies, held at Epsom on the Friday following the Derby, named after an estate of the founder, Lord Derby, 1779; **b** a tree or shrub resembling the true oak in leaf or other characteristics, as the *poison-oak*, *ground-oak* &c. **2.** A heavy, stout, oaken outer door to a set of rooms in college at a university, or to chambers at an inn of court. Phr. *to sport one's oak*, to close the outer door, as a sign that callers will not be welcome. **3.** (attrib.) The more usual form instead of adj. *oaken*: *oak chest*, *door*, *oak tree* &c. *Oak-apple*, a large fleshy excrescence produced by gall-flies on oaks, an *oak-gall*, also called *oak-fig*, *potato* &c.; *Oak-apple Day*, May 29th, the date of Charles II.'s birthday and restoration; oak-apples and leaves used to be worn in memory of the king's hiding in an oak tree after the battle of Worcester; *oak bark*, the bark of the oak tree, used in tanning; *oak-fern*, a species of polypody fern, with delicate, triangular fronds; *oak-moth*, popular name of various moths whose caterpillars feed on the oak, such as the *oak-beauty*, *oak-egger* &c.

oaken, adj. [1. ṓken; 2. óukən]. O.E. *ācen*. **oak** & **-en**. Made of oak (now chiefly poet.).

oakum, n. [1. ṓkum; 2. óukəm], fr. O.E. *ācumba*, 'tow', fr. *ā*, 'off, away', & the base of *cemban*, 'to comb', see **comb**; cp. O.H.G. *āchambi*, 'tow'; assimilated in spelling to *oak*. The loose fibre or tow obtained from unpicking and teasing old hemp ropes, used for caulking the seams of ships &c. *Oakum picking*, the task formerly allotted to prisoners and casuals in a workhouse.

oar (**I.**), n. [1. ōr; 2. ɔ̄]. O.E. *ār*, M.E. *ōre*; O.N. (fr. O.E.) *ār*, cp. Dan. *aare*, Swed. *ara*; the O.E. form can only come fr. **air-*, & may be connected w. Lith. *ir-ti*, 'to row', but by no means w. Gk. *eréttein*, 'to row', *eretmón*, 'oar' &c. See these under **row** (**II.**). **1.** Implement used in rowing a boat, consisting of a long wooden shaft with a flat blade, which works in a rowlock that serves as a fulcrum, fixed to gunwale of the boat; distinguished by this last from a *paddle*, also, strictly, by its greater weight, needing two hands, from a *scull*, and from a *sweep*, which is pulled by more than one person: *pair oar*, *four oar*, *eight oar*, a boat with two, four, or eight oars. Phrs. *chained to the oar*, bound to a task, like a galley slave; *to pull a good oar*, to row well; *to put one's oar in*, to interfere, meddle, in other people's business; *to rest on one's oars*, to break off work, to suspend one's efforts, as though content with what has been done; *to ship*, *unship*, *oars*, to place them in, take them out of, the rowlocks; *to toss oars*, to raise oars straight up in salute. **2.** A rower, oarsman: *a good, poor, indifferent, oar.* **3.** Something resembling an oar in shape or function, paddle, as fin of a fish, a bird's wing &c.

oar (**II.**), vb., fr. prec. (poet.) To row, propel as with oars.

oarage, n. [1. ṓrij; 2. ɔ́ridž]. **oar** & **-age**. (poet.) **1.** Motion of oars or rowing. **2.** Set of oars.

oared, adj. [1. ord; 2. ɔd]. **oar** (**I.**) & **-ed**. Equipped with oars: *eight-oared boat.*

oar-fish, n. (zool.) A genus of ribbon-fishes, *Regalecus*, of large size and living at great depths of the sea; the ventral fins are long filaments with broad flattened tips like an oar blade.

oarsman, n. [1. órzman; 2. ɔ́zmən]. One who rows, a rower, esp. one who rows in a racing boat: *quite an oarsman*, a good rower.

oarsmanship, n. [1. órzmanship; 2. ɔ́zmənʃip]. Prec. & **-ship**. Skill in rowing or the use of oars, esp. in boat-racing.

oarswoman, n. [1. órzwòoman; 2. ɔ́zwùmən]. A woman rower.

oary, adj. [1. ṓri; 2. ɔ́ri]. **oar** (**I.**) & **-y**. (poet.) Resembling an oar in shape or use (of a bird's wing, foot of a swan &c.).

oasis, n., pl. **oases** [1. ōā́sis, -sēz; 2. ouéisis, -sīz]. Lat. *oasis*, Gk. *óasis*; of Egypt. origin, cp. Coptic *ouah*, 'to dwell', *ouahe*, 'dwelling-place'. **1.** A fertile, usually inhabited, place in a desert, where cultivation is possible owing to the presence of water. **2.** (fig.) Anything pleasing which comes as a refreshing contrast and relief after tedium or dreariness; a beautiful sight, or place, amid ugly surroundings.

oast, n. [1. ōst; 2. oust]. O.E. *āst*, 'kiln', M.E. *ōst*, cp. M. Du. *ast*, Mod. Du. *eest*; fr. Gmc. **aist-*, fr. **aidto-*; cogn. w. Lat. *aestus*, 'heat', *aestas*, 'summer', Gk. *aîthos*, 'burning heat'. See **aestivate** & **aedile**. Kiln for drying hops; *oast-house*, the building containing an oast or kiln.

oat, n. [1. ōt; 2. out]. O.E. *āt(e)*, M.E. *ōte*, pl. It is strange that no certain cognates of this common & familiar word are found in other languages. A connexion has been suggested w. O.H.G. *eitar*, 'poison', orig. perh. 'poisoned matter, pus, from a boil' &c., cp. O.E. *āttor*, 'poison', wh. is prob. cogn. w. Gk. *oîdos*, 'swelling'; cp. *oidáō*, 'I swell' (see **oedema**). This is not convincing, because oats are among the last of the cereals to suggest the idea of swelling. **1.** (bot., usually in pl.) A cereal grass, *Avena sativa*, or its grain, used as food for horses or as *oatmeal* for man; *wild oat*, the uncultivated species, *Avena fatua*, with small, useless grain and stiff, twisted awn. Phr. *to sow one's wild oats*, (of a young man) to indulge in a certain amount of dissipation before settling down. **2.** (poet.) **a** A pipe or flute made out of an oat stalk; **b** a pastoral poem: '*But now my oat proceeds*' (Milton, 'Lycidas', 88). **3.** (attrib.) Made of oats or oat straw, replacing obs. *oaten*.

oatcake, n. [1. ṓtkā̀k; 2. óutkèik]. A thin flat cake or biscuit of oatmeal, a kind of girdle cake.

oaten, adj. [1. ṓtn; 2. óutn]. **oat** & **-en**. (obs. or poet.) Made of oats or of oat straw; now replaced by (attrib.) *oat*: '*Tempered to the oaten flute*' (Milton, 'Lycidas', 33).

oath, n. [1. ōth; 2. ouþ]. O.E. *āð*, M.E. *ooth, ōthe*; O.S. *eð*; O.H.G. *eit*; Goth. *aiþs*; O.N. *eiðr*. See **enigma**. **1. a** A solemn asseveration with an appeal to God, or some specially sacred person or object, as a sanction and witness to the truth of the statement made or to be made; e.g. the oath of a witness in a court of law; Phr. *put* (person) *on oath*, cause him to take an oath; **b** a binding promise made in most solemn manner, with an appeal to God, or to sacred things, to perform faithfully some act or duty; e.g. the oath of a juror, or of a person entering on an office; **c** sacred promise of fidelity and loyalty to a person or cause: *to take the oath*; *to make oath*. Phr. *on oath, on my oath*, having been sworn. **2.** The form of words and the ceremony to be used and observed when taking an oath. **3.** The name of God or of sacred things profanely used or invoked; a curse, profanity, blasphemy.

oatmeal, n. [1. ṓtmēl; 2. óutmīəl]. **oat** & **meal** (**I.**). Meal made from oats.

ob-, pref. Occurs only in words of Lat. origin; fr. Lat. prep. *ob*, expressing **a** motion towards; **b** position before, against; **c** an object or cause, 'on account of, with regard to' &c.; **d** the consideration for wh. something is done, 'for'. In Lat. compounds, as pref., *ob* has various meanings, not all of wh. can be traced in its force as an independent word: (1) against, towards: *oppetere*, 'to go towards'; (2) 'in the way of', expressing hindrance: *opponere*, 'to be in the way of, oppose'; *obesse*, 'to be in the way of, injurious to'; (3) expressing hostility: *offendere*, 'to strike against'; (4) 'down': *opprimere*, 'to press down'; (5) expressing covering: *obtendere*, 'to stretch over'; (6) 'across', expressing motion: *obīre*, 'to travel over'. In Lat., when used as a pref., *ob* remains unchanged before vowels, & most consonants, but when the second element of the compound begins w. *p, f, c, g*, it becomes respectively *op-, of-, oc-, og-*. The earlier form of *ob* was *op-*, & *op, up* occur in Oscan; Lith. has *api-*, 'about'; Scrt. *ápi*, 'also, in addition', adv.; orig. form **opi-*, wh. is in gradational relation to Gk. *epi*, see **epi-**; cogn. w. Goth. *if-(tuma)*, 'the following'.

obbligato, adj. & n. [1. òbligáhtō; 2. ɔ̀bligā́tou]. Ital., 'obliged, bound', fr. Lat. *obligāt-(um)*, P.P. type of *obligāre*. See **oblige**. **1.** adj. (mus.) Required, necessary; of an additional but indispensable accompaniment by a single instrument to a musical composition for the voice or another instrument or both, to be performed as written and not left to the performer's discretion or improvisation, and so contrasted with *ad libitum*. **2.** n. An instrumental accompaniment to the voice and another instrument: *a violin obbligato*, to a song for the voice and pianoforte.

obduracy, n. [1. óbdūrasi; 2. ɔ́bdjurəsi]. See next word & **-cy**. Quality, condition, of being obdurate; stubbornness, inflexibility, hardness, (of heart or character).

obdurate, adj. [1. óbdūrit; 2. ɔ́bdjurit], fr. Lat. *obdūrāt-(um)*, P.P. type of *obdūrāre*, 'to harden', **ob-**, intens., & *dūrāre*, 'to make hard', *dūrus*, 'hard'. See **durable**. Hardened in feelings, hard-hearted; unyielding, stubborn, obstinate.

obdurately, adv. Prec. & **-ly**. In an obdurate manner; stubbornly.

obeah, obi, n. [1. ṓbea, ṓbi; 2. óubiə, óubi]. W. African negro word. **1.** A species of witchcraft or sorcery as practised by negroes in the West Indies. **2.** A fetish or magic object used in witchcraft: *obeah* (*obi*) *man, woman*, witch, sorcerer, sorceress.

obedience, n. [1. ōbḗdiens; 2. oubídiəns]. O. Fr., fr. Lat. *oboedientia*. See next word & **-ce**. **1. a** Act of obeying or submitting to authority; compliance with orders, law, rules &c.; submission to authority; **b** state, condition, of being obedient; *passive obedience*, non-resistance, unquestioning submission to authority. **2.** (eccles.) **a** The duty of obedience exacted from its members by a given church; jurisdiction, dominion, exercised by a church over its members; **b** the body of persons rendering obedience to the authority of a given church; esp. *the Roman obedience*.

obedient, adj. [1. ōbḗdient; 2. oubídiənt]. O. Fr., fr. Lat. *obēdient-(em)*, Pres. Part. of *obēdīre*, 'to obey'. See **obey**. Willing, ready, to obey; submissive to commands, to rule, or authority; yielding to another's will, or expressed desire. Phr. *your obedient servant*, the close of a formal or official letter.

obedientiary, n. [1. ōbēdiénshari; 2. oubìdiénʃəri], fr. Med. Lat. *obēdientiārius*. See prec. & **-ary**. A member of a monastic community subject to the authority of the Superior.

obediently, adv. [1. ōbḗdientli; 2. oubídiəntli]. **obedient** & **-ly**. In an obedient manner; with obedience; (formula) *yours obediently*, as close to a formal letter.

obeisance, n. [1. ōbā́sens; 2. oubéisəns], fr. O. Fr. *obeissance*, fr. *obeissant*, Pres. Part. of *obeir*. See **obey**. **a** A bow, inclination of the head, or other formal gesture of respect, reverence, or submission; **b** deference, homage: *to do obeisance to*, to do homage to; to obey, submit, respectfully.

obelisk, n. [1. óbelisk; 2. ɔ́bilisk], fr. Fr. *obélisque*, fr. Lat. *obeliscus*, fr. Gk. *obeliskos*, 'small spit, pointed implement, obelisk', dimin. of *obelós*, 'spit, obelisk'; apparently variant form of *obolós*, 'obol', see **obol**. **1.** An upright monolith or stone pillar, with four sides, tapering at the top into a pyramid or pointed cone. **2.** (also *obelus*) **a** (MSS.) A mark (– or ÷), to denote a spurious or doubtful passage; **b** (print.) a dagger (†), to mark a reference to a footnote.

obelize, vb. trans. [1. óbelīz; 2. ɔ́bɛlaiz]. Gk. *obelízein*. Prec. & **-ize**. To mark, in MSS. or in printing, with an obelisk or obelus.

obelus, n. [1. óbelus; 2. ɔ́bɛləs]. Gk. *obelós*. See **obelisk**. An obelisk, **2**.

obese, adj. [1. ōbḗs; 2. oubís], fr. Lat. *obēsus*, 'stout, plump', fr. **ob-** & P.P. type of *edere*, 'to eat'. See **edible**. Very fat; corpulent.

obesity, n. [1. ōbḗsiti; 2. oubísiti], fr. Fr. *obésité*. See prec. & **-ity**. Corpulence.

obey, vb. trans. & intrans. [1. ōbā́; 2. oubéi]. M.E. *obeyen*, fr. Fr. *obéir*, fr. Lat. *obēdīre*, 'to listen to, obey'; earlier *oboedīre*, fr. **ob-oizd-*, fr. **ob-awizd-*, fr. **ob-** & stem of *audīre*, 'to hear, listen to'. See **audible**. **1.** trans. **a** To carry out, perform, execute, the commands, or expressed desire of; to submit, be obedient, to; to act in accordance with: *obey orders, one's superiors*; **b** to submit to, act in accordance with: *to obey the laws of nature, the dictates of one's heart* &c. **2.** intrans. To do what one is ordered, to be obedient.

obfuscate, vb. trans. [1. óbfuskāt, obfúskāt; 2. ɔ́bfaskeit, ɔbfáskeit], fr. Lat. *obfuscāt-(um)*, P.P. type of *obfuscāre, offuscāre*, 'to make dark, darken, vilify, degrade', fr. **ob-** & *fuscāre*, 'to darken', fr. *fuscus*, 'dark, indistinct'. See **fuscous**. To obscure, darken, bewilder, confuse.

obfuscation, n. [1. òbfuskā́shun; 2. ɔ̀bfaskéiʃən]. Prec. & **-ion**. Act of obfuscating; state of being obfuscated; bewilderment.

obi (**I.**), n. See **obeah**.

obi (**II.**), n. [1. ṓbi; 2. óubi]. Jap. The broad sash worn by Japanese women and children.

obiit, vb. [1. óbiit; 2. ɔ́biit]. Lat., 'he died', 3rd sing. Pret. of *obīre*, see next word. Term used on tombstones, in documents &c. written in Lat.: *obiit sine prole*, died without issue.

obit, n. [1. ṓbit; 2. óubit]. O. Fr., fr. Lat. *obitus*, 'death', fr. *obitus*, P.P. of *obīre (mortem)*, 'to go towards, meet (death); to die'; **ob-** & *īre*, 'to go'. See **itinerant**. (obs.) Death; funeral; service, mass, requiem in memory of a dead person; cp. also **post-obit**.

obiter, adv. [1. ṓbiter, óbiter; 2. óubitə, ɔ́bitə]. Lat., 'by the way, in passing', fr. *ob*, 'on' &c., see **ob-**, & *iter*, 'road, way', see **iteration, itinerant**. In passing, by the way, incidentally; specif. (law) *obiter dictum*, pl. *dicta*, a passing remark or opinion expressed by a judge during the hearing of a case, which is incidental and does not form part of his decision or judgement and is not binding as a precedent or ruling.

obituary, adj. & n. [1. ōbíchooari; 2. oubítʃuəri], fr. Med. Eccles. Lat. *obituārius*, fr. Lat. *obitus*, 'death'. See **obit**. **1.** adj. Of, concerning, relating to, death, or to a particular death, or dead person: *obituary ceremony, notice* &c. **2.** n. **a** A notice in a newspaper &c. of a person's death, with a short biography; **b** (eccles.) a list of names of dead members of a religious community.

object (I.), n. [1. óbjekt; 2. ɔ́bdžikt], fr. Lat. *object-(um)*, P.P. of *objicere*, 'to throw against, put before, present', **ob-** & *jacere*, 'to throw'. See **jactitation** & **jet**. **1.** That which is presented to, or observed by, the senses; a material thing, anything visible or tangible: *a distant object; a minute object; common objects of the country-side.* **2. a** That which is presented to, and grasped by, the mind, that which can be apprehended or known: *an object of thought, for consideration* &c.; **b** that which arouses and attracts feelings and emotions: *an object of pity, contempt, admiration* &c. **3.** That on which the wishes and intentions are set; that to which the will is directed with desire of attainment; purpose, aim: *the object of one's life, efforts; to fail, succeed, in one's object; an object for a walk.* **4.** (gram.) A noun or clause which is governed by a transitive verb, or by a preposition. **5.** (colloq.) A person or thing of extraordinary or striking appearance, generally one which excites pity or disgust; a deplorable spectacle: *a pitiable object; disgusting object; a nice object he looked with two black eyes.* **6.** (attrib.) *Object ball* (billiards), the ball at which the player aims. *Object finder*, device for marking or registering the position of an object on a microscopic slide. *Object glass, lens*, the glass or lens in a microscope or telescope which is nearest the object. *Object lesson*, **a** a lesson, piece of instruction, in which the material object to be studied is exhibited by the teacher in concrete illustration of his remarks; **b** a practical and concrete illustration of a principle; often with the sense of a warning for the future. *Object staff*, surveyor's levelling staff.

object (II.), vb. intrans. & trans. [1. objékt; 2. əbdžékt], fr. Lat. *objectāre*, 'to oppose, object', freq. fr. *object-(um)*, P.P. type of *objicere*. See prec., cp. Fr. *objecter*. **A.** intrans. **1.** To feel dislike to, disapprove of, be definitely hostile and opposed to: *I object very much to a wet summer; do you object to smoking?*; (facet.) *I don't object to a good glass of wine*, I like it very much. **2.** To protest against; express disapproval of, and objection to: *I object to that question being asked; if you disliked the proposal you should have objected at the time; I object*, I protest, have and express an objection. **B.** trans. To say, state, as, or by way of, objection: *it was objected that the proposed clause might inflict hardship on deserving persons.*

objectification, n. [1. objèktifikā́shun; 2. əbdžèktifikéiʃən]. **objectify** & **-fication**. **1.** Act or process of objectifying; state of being objectified. **2.** That which is objectified.

objectify, vb. trans. [1. objéktifī; 2. əbdžéktifai]. **object** (I.) & **-fy**. To make, render, objective; to form objectively; to represent as an object, materialize.

objection, n. [1. objékshun; 2. əbdžékʃən]. Fr., fr. Lat. *objectiōn-(em)*. **object** (II.) & **-ion**. **1. a** Feeling of dislike, disapproval, reluctance, opposition: *to feel an objection to doing*; **b** statement, expression, of this; protest: *to take objection to; to make an objection to; to utter, lodge, a strong objection against.* **2. a** Circumstance or action which is, or might be, objected to; a drawback; defect: *the chief objection to the book is its great length*; **b** obstacle, hindrance, prohibition: *there is no objection to your leaving at once.*

objectionable, adj. [1. objékshunabl; 2. əbdžékʃənəbl]. Prec. & **-able**. **1.** Liable, open, to objection. **2.** Offensive, disagreeable, unpleasant.

objectionably, adv. Prec. & **-ly**. In an objectionable manner; offensively.

objective (I.), adj. [1. objéktiv; 2. əbdžéktiv]. **object** (I.) & **-ive**. Cp. Fr. *objectif*. **1.** Of, relating to, concerned with, external, material objects. **2.** (philos.) Having an independent existence in itself, and not existing merely in an individual mind; contrasted with *subjective*. **3.** Of, relating to, the object or purpose of action: *objective point*, the point to which military operations are directed. **4.** (gram.) Of, connected with, any case, other than the nominative, that is governed by a transitive verb or by a preposition.

objective (II.), n., fr. prec. **1. a** An objective point, the object or purpose aimed at in an action; **b** (mil.) position which it is desired to reach, to attainment or capture of which an operation is directed. **2.** (gram.) The objective case.

objectively, adv. **objective** (I.) & **-ly**. In an objective manner or way, contrasted with *subjectively*: *to consider something objectively*, as external to and apart from oneself.

objectiveness, n. See prec. & **-ness**. State, quality, of being objective; objectivity.

objectivism, n. [1. objéktivizm; 2. əbdžéktivizəm]. **objective** (I.) & **-ism**. (philos.) Doctrine that human knowledge is based on objective reality, and that our conception of the external world, derived from sensuous perceptions, has objective validity.

objectivity, n. [1. òbjektíviti; 2. ɔ̀bdžektíviti]. **objective** (I.) & **-ity**. Quality, state, of being objective; objectiveness; objective character, as contrasted with *subjectivity*.

objectless, adj. [1. óbjektles; 2. ɔ́bdžiktlis]. **object** (I.) & **-less**. Without an object, aim, or purpose; aimless.

objector, n. [1. objékter; 2. əbdžéktə]. **object** (II.) & **-or**. One who objects to, opposes, protests against, something.

objurgate, vb. trans. [1. óbjĕrgāt; 2. ɔ́bdžʌgeit], fr. Lat. *objurgāt-(um)*, P.P. type of *objurgāre*, 'to blame, reprove', fr. **ob-** & *jurgāre*, 'to quarrel, scold', for **jūrigāre*, fr. *jūr-*, stem of *jūs*, 'law, a suit', see **jury** & **justice**, & base **ag-* in *agere*, 'to drive', see **agent**. To blame, chide, reprove.

objurgation, n. [1. òbjĕrgā́shun; 2. ɔ̀bdžʌgéiʃən]. Fr., fr. Lat. *objurgātiōn-(em)*. See prec. & **-ion**. Reproof, blame, rebuke.

objurgatory, adj. [1. objĕ́rgaturi; 2. əbdžʌ́gətəri], fr. Lat. *objurgātōrius*. See prec. & **-ory**. Reproachful, rebuking.

oblate (I.), adj. [1. óblāt; 2. ɔ́bleit], fr. Lat. *oblāt-(um)*, P.P. type of *offerre*, 'to bring before, to offer' (see **offer**), fr. **ob-** & *lātum* for **tlātum*, cp. *tollere*, 'to lift, carry'. See **tolerate**. **1.** (eccles.) Offered, dedicated, to a monastic life; specif., *Oblate Fathers.* **2.** (geom., of spheroid bodies) Flattened at the poles.

oblate (II.), n., fr. prec. **a** One dedicated to a monastic life; **b** specif., a member of a Roman Catholic religious congregation of secular priests, *Oblates* or *Oblate Fathers.*

oblation, n. [1. ōblā́shun; 2. oubléiʃən]. Fr., fr. Lat. *oblātiōn-(em)*, *oblātio*, 'offering'. See prec. & **-ion**. **1.** An offering, dedication, presentation, to God, esp. of Christ in the consecrated elements in the Eucharist. **2.** A gift or donation for pious uses.

oblational, adj. [1. ōblā́shunal; 2. oubléiʃənəl]. Prec. & **-al**. Of the nature of an oblation.

oblatory, adj. [1. óblaturi; 2. ɔ́blətəri]. **oblate** (I.) & **-ory**. Of, relating to, an oblation.

obligate, vb. trans. [1. óbligāt; 2. ɔ́bligeit], fr. Lat. *obligāt-(um)*, P.P. type of *obligāre*. See **oblige**. (chiefly in P.P. *obligated*) To bind legally or morally; place under an obligation to do, or refrain from doing, something; to constrain, compel.

obligation, n. [1. òbligā́shun; 2. ɔ̀bligéiʃən]. Fr., fr. Lat. *obligātiōn-(em)*. **obligate** & **-ion**. **1.** That which binds or constrains a person to do or not to do; the binding power of a duty, law, moral feelings, promise, contract &c.: *obligations of conscience, humanity.* **2.** That which one is morally bound to do or not to do; a duty: *society lays obligations on everyone.* **3.** The state or position of being bound or indebted to another, by reason of benefits or favours received from him: *under an obligation to another.* **4.** (law) A written document or bond by which the *obligor* binds himself under a penalty to pay a certain sum to, or perform some act for, the benefit of another person, the *obligee.*

obligatory, adj. [1. oblígaturi, óbligaturi; 2. əblígətəri, ɔ́bligətəri]. L. Lat. *obligātōrius*, 'binding'. See **obligate** & **-ory**. Compulsory; imposed by law, rule, specific instructions, or by moral feeling, as necessary to be done; contrasted with *permissive*, or *discretionary.*

oblige, vb. trans. & intrans. [1. oblíj; 2. əbláidž], fr. Fr. *obliger*, fr. Lat. *obligāre*, 'to bind, to put under an obligation, oblige', fr. **ob-** & *ligāre*, 'to bind, tie'. See **ligament**. **A.** trans. **1.** To compel, constrain, by legal, moral, or physical force to do or not to do something. **2.** To put under an obligation; to meet the wishes of, do a favour to, accommodate, render grateful: *oblige me by closing the door; I am much obliged*, I thank you; Phr. *could you oblige me with half-a-crown?*, i.e. give or lend me one. **B.** intrans. (colloq.) To be so obliging, to do something as a favour: *to oblige with a song*, (be so amiable as to) sing one.

obliged, adj. [1. oblíjd; 2. əbláidžd]. P.P. of prec. (archaic) Chiefly in formula ending letters; grateful: *your obliged humble servant.*

obligee, n. [1. òblijḗ; 2. ɔ̀blidžī́]. Prec. & **-ee**. (law) The person in whose favour a legal obligation or bond is made (by the *obligor*).

obliging, adj. [1. oblíjing; 2. əbláidžiŋ]. Pres. Part. of **oblige**. **a** Ready and willing to oblige; disposed to do a kindness, and to be helpful; ungrudgingly serviceable: *I always found this servant good-tempered and obliging*; **b** (archaic) polite, gallant: *I declare you are very obliging.*

obligingly, adv. Prec. & **-ly**. In an obliging way or manner; courteously, politely.

obligingness, n. See prec. & **-ness**. Quality of being obliging; politeness, kindness.

obligor, n. [1. òbligór; 2. ɔ̀bligɔ́]. **oblige** & **-or**. (law) The person who binds himself by a bond to pay a sum to, or do something for, the benefit of another (the *obligee*).

oblique (I.), adj. [1. ōblḗk; 2. oublík]. Lat. *obliquus*, 'slanting, sidelong, indirect'; **ob-** & **liquis*, 'bent', cogn. w. *licinus*, 'curved, bent', fr. stem **lekʷ-*, **lek-*; the simplest form of the base is **lei-*, **li-*, 'to bend'. Cp. **limb**, **lithe**. **1. a** Slanting, sideways, inclining away from a straight line or direction: *oblique glance; 'and winds with ease, Through the pure marble air, his oblique way'* (Milton, 'P. L.' iii. 563-4); **b** (fig., in moral sense) not straightforward; indirect, allusive; tortuous: *an oblique reference; oblique methods.* **2.** Having a direction not perpendicular nor parallel to another line or axis: *oblique angle*, acute or obtuse angle; not a right angle; *oblique cone*, cone with axis not perpendicular to the base; *oblique muscle*, one that is placed diagonally to the main axis of the body. **3.** Indirect: *oblique narration, speech* (Lat. *oratio obliqua*), speech reported in the third person, as *he said that he was willing.* **4.** (gram.) Of cases of the noun other than nominative or vocative.

oblique (II.), vb. intrans., fr. prec. To move away, deviate, from the straight line; (of soldiers) to move forward half-right or left.

obliquely, adv. **oblique** (I.) & **-ly**. In an oblique direction, not horizontally nor perpendicularly; indirectly, in a sidelong way.

obliqueness, n. See prec. & **-ness**. State of being oblique; obliquity.

obliquity, n. [1. ōblíkwiti; 2. oublíkwiti], fr. Fr. *obliquité*, fr. Lat. *obliquitāt-(em)*, *obliquitas*. **oblique** (I.) & **-ity**. **1.** State, quality, of being oblique; deviation from a straight line or direction. **2.** Deviation from a straight course; departure **a** from moral rectitude: *obliquity of conduct*; **b** from sound judgement: *obliquity of mind, judgement* &c.

obliterate, vb. trans. [1. oblíterāt; 2. əblítəreit], fr. Lat. *obliterāt-(um)*, P.P. type of *obliterāre*, 'to blot out, conceal, something written'; also fig. 'to erase from remembrance, cause to be forgotten', fr. **ob-** & *litera*, 'letter', see **literate**, & **letter**; but prob. influenced in meaning by *oblitum*, P.P. of *oblinere*, 'to smear over, blot' (see **ob-** &

liniment), or *oblitum*, 'forgotten', P.P. of *oblīviscor*, 'forget', see **oblivion.** **1.** To blot, wipe, out, erase, render indecipherable, something written: *obliterate one's signature.* **2.** To efface, destroy, wipe out visible traces of anything: *obliterate one's footprints, tracks* &c.; *time has obliterated many monuments of former greatness.* **3.** To erase, banish, from the mind or memory: *all feelings of hatred had long been obliterated.*

obliteration, n. [1. oblìteráshun; 2. əblìtəréiʃən]. Lat. *obliterātiōn-(em).* See prec. & **-ion.** Act of obliterating; state of being obliterated; effacement, destruction.

oblivion, n. [1. oblívìun; 2. əblíviən]. Fr., fr. Lat. *oblīviōn-(em)*, 'a forgetting, oblivion', fr. stem of *oblīvisci*, 'to forget', fr. **ob-** &, according to Walde, prob. the base **lei-*, **lī-*, cp. Lat. *lēvis*, 'smooth', & *līma*, 'file'. See **levigate.** **1.** Act of forgetting; specif. **a** official act of forgetting or ignoring past offences; amnesty: *act of oblivion*; **b** fact of having forgotten; forgetfulness. **2.** State, fact, of being forgotten: *to sink into a well-deserved oblivion.*

oblivious, adj. [1. oblívius; 2. əblíviəs], fr. Lat. *oblīviōsus*, 'forgetful'. See prec. & **-ous.** **1.** Forgetful; unheeding; regardless; absent-minded; lost in abstraction: *oblivious of one's surroundings, duties, the consequences.* **2.** Inducing forgetfulness: '*(our faithful friends), Lie thus astonished on the oblivious pool*' (Milton, 'P. L.' i. 266).

obliviously, adv. Prec. & **-ly.** In an oblivious manner; forgetfully, absent-mindedly.

obliviousness, n. See prec. & **-ness.** State of being oblivious; forgetfulness, oblivion.

oblong (I.), adj. [1. óblong; 2. ɔ́blɔŋ], fr. Lat. *oblongus*, 'rather long, longish', fr. **ob-** & *longus*, see **long** (I.); the force of *ob-* is doubtful; possibly 'across, over'. **1.** Greater in length than breadth; elongated, prolonged, in one direction from a square or circular form. **2.** Of rectangular shape, having two sides greater than the other two.

oblong (II.), n. An oblong figure; object having this form.

obloquy, n. [1. óblokwi; 2. ɔ́blɔkwi], fr. Lat. *obloquium*, 'contradiction', fr. *obloqui*, 'to speak against, gainsay, contradict'. See **ob-** & **loquacious.** **1.** Calumny, defamation; blame, reproach; censorious language: *to heap obloquy upon.* **2.** State of being defamed or censored; disgrace.

obmutescence, n. [1. òbmūtésens; 2. ɔ̀bmjūtésəns], fr. Lat. *obmūtescent-(em)*, Pres. Part. of *obmūtescere*, 'to become dumb, to be speechless', fr. **ob-**, intens., & *mūtus*, 'dumb, mute'. See **mute** (I.). (archaic) Persistent silence; dumbness, speechlessness.

obmutescent, adj. [1. òbmūtésent; 2. ɔ̀bmjūtés(ə)nt]. See prec. (archaic) Dumb, silent, speechless.

obnoxious, adj. [1. obnókshus; 2. əbnɔ́kʃəs], fr. Lat. *obnoxius*, 'liable to harm or punishment, answerable, responsible; servile'. See **ob-** & **noxious.** **1.** Objectionable, offensive, disagreeable. **2. a** (archaic) Liable to, exposed to (harm, injury, censure): '*the parts . . . To shame obnoxious*' (Milton, 'P. L.' ix. 1094); **b** (law) subject to the authority of: *obnoxious to the law.*

obnoxiously, adv. Prec. & **-ly.** In an obnoxious manner; offensively.

obnoxiousness, n. See prec. & **-ness.** State, quality, of being obnoxious; offensiveness.

oboe, n. [1. ṓbō; 2. óubou]. Ital. spelling of Fr. *hautbois.* See **hautboy.** **1.** A musical wood-wind instrument played with a double reed, acting as soprano or treble to the bassoon. **2.** A reed stop in an organ.

obol, n. [1. óbl; 2. ɔ́bl], fr. Gk. *obolós*; apparently a variant of *obelós*, 'spit', whence **obelisk**; early Gk. money & weights were often in the form of metal nails or spikes; etymol. doubtful; cp. **drachma.** **a** A small ancient Greek silver coin, $\frac{1}{6}$ of a drachma; **b** a weight of same amount.

obscene, adj. [1. obsḗn; 2. əbsín], fr. Lat. *obscēnus, obscaenus*, 'ill-omened, inauspicious; repulsive, filthy, disgusting'; fr. *obs-*, fr. **ob-** & *caenum*, 'filth, mud'; cp. *cūnīre*, 'to defecate', also *in-quināre*, 'to defile, pollute'; cogn. w. O.E. *a-hwǣnan*, 'to grieve, tease', fr. **hwainjan.* **1.** Indecent, impure; offensive to morals or modesty: *obscene language, books* &c. **2.** (archaic or poet.) Disgusting, offensive, unclean: *obscene beasts, deities* &c.

obscenely, adv. Prec. & **-ly.** In an obscene manner or way; indecently, lewdly.

obsceneness, n. See prec. & **-ness.** State, quality, of being obscene; obscenity.

obscenity, n. [1. obséniti, obsḗniti; 2. əbséniti, əbsíniti]. **obscene** & **-ity**, cp. Fr. *obscénité*, fr. Lat. *obscēnitāt-(em)*, 'filthiness, lewdness'. State, quality, of being obscene; obscene language, actions &c.; lewdness, indecency.

obscurant, n. & adj. [1. obskū́rant; 2. əbskjúərənt], fr. Mod. Germ. *obskurant*, fr. Lat. *obscūrant-(em)*, Pres. Part. of *obscūrāre*, 'to hide, conceal, obscure'. See **obscure** (I.). **1.** n. An opponent of progress and advance in knowledge; opponent of enlightenment or instruction. **2.** adj. Tending to obscure; pertaining to an obscurant.

obscurantism, n. [1. òbskūrántizm; 2. ɔ̀bskjuərǽntizəm]. Prec. & **-ism.** Opposition to progress in knowledge or enlightenment.

obscurantist, n. & adj. [1. òbskūrántist; 2. ɔ̀bskjuərǽntist]. **obscurant** & **-ist.** **1.** n. One opposed to progress in knowledge, and to new ideas and methods; a reactionary. **2.** adj. Pertaining to, in accordance with, the prejudices of an obscurantist.

obscuration, n. [1. òbskūráshun; 2. ɔ̀bskjuəréiʃən]. Lat. *obscūrātiōn-(em)*, 'a hiding, concealment', fr. *obscūrāt-(um)*, P.P. of *obscūrāre*, see **obscure** (III.), & **-ion.** (astron.) Act of obscuring; state of being concealed or obscured; occultation.

obscure (I.), adj. [1. obskū́r; 2. əbskjɔ́, əbskjúə], fr. Fr. *obscur*, fr. Lat. *obscūrus*, 'dark, obscure', lit. 'covered over', fr. **ob-** & base **(s)kewa-*, 'to cover', cp. Lat. *scūtum*, 'shield', see **scutcheon.** See also under **shower** & **sky**, & further, **cutis.** **1.** (in physical sense, of visual impressions) **a** Dim, not clearly seen, indistinct; **b** not bright, not luminous or lighted up; **c** not giving out light; **d** not easy to find; remote, hidden away: *an obscure village, retreat.* **2.** (in moral or intellectual sense) **a** Not clearly expressed, difficult to understand, not clear in meaning: *an obscure style*; **b** not clearly understood, difficult to discover, not fully known; puzzling: *the part he played in the rebellion remains obscure*; **c** not clearly defined in the mind, vague, imperfectly realized: *obscure feelings, motives* &c. **3. a** (of persons, their way of life, talents &c.) Not distinguished, unimportant, not famous or renowned, not widely known: '*Their humble joys, and destiny obscure*' (Gray); *an obscure country squire*; **b** (also of actions, achievements &c.) hidden, unrevealed: *an obscure book by a forgotten author*; *many deeds of bravery remain obscure.*

obscure (II.), n., fr. prec. (poet.) Darkness, night; obscurity: '*And through the palpable obscure find out His uncouth way*' (Milton, 'P. L.' 406-7).

obscure (III.), vb. trans. Fr. *obscurer*, fr. Lat. *obscūrāre*, 'to make dark'. See **obscure** (I.). **1.** To make obscure; to dim, darken, hide, conceal: *windows obscured by curtains.* **2.** To make ambiguous in meaning; render less intelligible. **3.** To throw into the shade, render less conspicuous, cause to appear less brilliant, by contrast: *his fame was obscured by that of his greater father.*

obscurely, adv. [1. obskū́rli; 2. əbskjɔ́li, əbskjúəli]. **obscure** (I.) & **-ly.** In an obscure manner; **a** darkly; **b** unintelligibly; **c** without fame, inconspicuously; in a retired manner.

obscureness, n. See prec. & **-ness.** Obscurity.

obscurity, n. [1. obskū́riti; 2. əbskjɔ́riti, əbskjúəriti], fr. Fr. *obscurité*, fr. Lat. *obscūritāt-(em).* See **obscure** (I.) & **-ity.** State, quality, of being obscure; **a** darkness, gloom; **b** unintelligibility, ambiguity, vagueness; **c** humble, undistinguished, position in life.

obsecrate, vb. trans. [1. óbsekrāt; 2. ɔ́bsikreit]. Lat. *obsecrāt-(um)*, P.P. of *obsecrāre*, 'to entreat on religious grounds', fr. **ob-** & *sacrāre*, 'to make, treat as, sacred', fr. *sacer*, 'holy' &c. See **sacred.** (archaic) To entreat, beg earnestly, implore.

obsecration, n. [1. òbsekráshun; 2. ɔ̀bsikréiʃən]. Lat. *obsecrātiōn-(em)*, 'supplication, invocation, of the gods'. Prec. & **-ion.** A supplication, earnest prayer or entreaty; specif. of the prayers in the Litany beginning *By the mystery* &c. *we beseech Thee to hear us, Good Lord.*

obsequial, adj. [1. obsḗkwial; 2. əbsíkwiəl]. See **obsequy** & **-al.** Of, relating to, funeral rites and ceremonies.

obsequies, n. pl. [1. óbsekwiz; 2. ɔ́bsikwiz], fr. O. Fr. *obseque*, fr. L. Lat. *obsequiae*; meaning due to confusion of *exsequiae*, 'funeral rites', w. *obsequium*, 'compliance'. See next word. The sing., *obsequy*, is obsolete. Funeral ceremonies or rites; a funeral.

obsequious, adj. [1. obsḗkwius; 2. əbsíkwiəs], fr. Lat. *obsequiōsus*, 'complaisant, obedient', fr. *obsequium*, 'compliance, complaisance, obedience', fr. *obsequi*, 'to yield to the will of another, comply, obey'. See **ob-** & **sequela.** **1.** Excessively complaisant or submissive; cringing, servile, fawning. **2.** (in favourable sense) Obedient, compliant: '*she* (Eve) . . . *with obsequious majesty* . . .' (Milton, 'P. L.' viii. 508-9).

obsequiously, adv. Prec. & **-ly.** In an obsequious, cringing manner.

obsequiousness, n. See prec. & **-ness.** Servility; cringing, fawning compliance.

observable, adj. [1. obzḗrvabl; 2. əbzə́vəbl]. **observe** & **-able.** **1.** Capable of being observed; discernible. **2.** Noteworthy, remarkable.

observably, adv. Prec. & **-ly.** So as to be observable; noticeably.

observance, n. [1. obzḗrvans; 2. əbzə́vəns]. Fr., fr. Lat. *observantia*, 'attention, regard, observance'. See **observe** & **-ance.** **1. a** Act or habit of observing, keeping, paying attention to, a rule, law, custom &c.; **b** practice of regarding as sacred; commemoration: *the observance of Sundays and Feast days.* **2.** Something which is customarily observed; a rite, ceremony, custom, practice, esp. a religious rite or custom: *maintain the customary observances.* **3.** (archaic) Deference, attention: *to pay humble observance.*

observant (I.), adj. [1. obzḗrvant; 2. əbzə́vənt]. Fr., fr. Lat. *observant-(em)*, Pres. Part. of *observāre.* See **observe.** **1.** Attentive, strict in observance or the keeping of rules, orders &c.: *observant of God's laws.* **2.** Habitually exercising the faculties of observation, alert, given to observing closely; vigilant.

Observant (II.), n. Member of a strict branch of the Franciscans, Friars Observant.

observantly, adv. **observant** (I.) & **-ly.** In an observant manner; attentively.

observation, n. [1. òbzerváshun; 2. ɔ̀bzəvéiʃən], fr. Lat. *observātiōn-(em)*, 'a watching, observance; remark; care, exactness'; fr. *observāt-(um)*, P.P. type of *observāre.* See **observe** & **-ion.** **1. a** Act, practice, of observing, noticing, or watching; surveillance; Phr. *to keep under observation*, to watch; **b** specif., the act of observing and recording natural phenomena as they occur, for scientific or practical purposes; contrasted with *experiment.* **2.** Capacity, faculty, of observing or noticing: *a man of no observation.* **3.** Thing learnt, knowledge gained, as result of observation. **4. a** (pl.) Record of what is observed: *to publish one's observations of rainfall*; **b** remarks, excursus, by way of interpretation, and explanation, on what has been observed: *observations on primitive customs, the habits of ants* &c.; hence **c** an utterance, critical comment, on an action, event, statement &c.;

I have one or two observations to make on your conduct; **d** (colloq.) remark, conversational utterance: *he didn't make a single observation during the whole dinner.* **5.** (attrib.) *Observation-balloon,* (mil.) an anchored balloon used for observing an enemy's position and movements, directing gun-fire &c.; *observation car,* special carriage on a railway with wide windows for viewing scenery &c.; *observation post,* (mil.) an advanced post from which observations of the enemy can be made and reported.

observational, adj. [1. òbzervā́shunal; 2. òbzəvéiʃənəl]. Prec. & **-al.** Relating to observation; obtained by, based on, observation; contrasted with *experimental.*

observationally, adv. Prec. & **-ly.** By observation.

observatory, n. [1. obzẽrvaturi; 2. əbzʌ́vətəri]. See **observation** & **-ory.** A building with its instruments and apparatus for observing natural, esp. astronomical, phenomena.

observe, vb. trans. & intrans. [1. obzẽrv; 2. əbzʌ́v], fr. Fr. *observer,* fr. Lat. *observāre,* 'to watch, heed, notice, observe; to pay attention to, respect', fr. **ob-**, 'to', or as intens., & *servāre,* 'to save; to keep, protect; to maintain in a certain condition; to heed, pay attention to, watch'. See **serve. A.** trans. **1.** To keep, pay attention or respect to; be observant of: *to observe laws, rules, ceremonies, rites, customs*; *to observe the saints' days.* Phrs. *to observe the time,* to be punctual; *to observe silence,* not to speak; *to observe good manners, the nicest decorum,* to be scrupulously polite &c. **2. a** To consider carefully, and with concentrated attention, whether of eye or ear: *to observe the behaviour of birds*; *to observe a person's pronunciation*; **b** to notice, mark; to receive an impression of, become aware of, by observation: *did you observe his excellent manners?*; *I didn't observe the colour of her eyes*; **c** to notice, become conscious that: *he observed that it had suddenly grown much colder.* **3.** To utter by way of remark, observation, or comment, say that: *allow me to observe that you've been taken in*; *I have very little to observe on what has been said,* but few comments to make. **B.** intrans. To practise observation, be attentive, take notice: *he is a man who observes keenly but says very little.*

observer, n. [1. obzẽrver; 2. əbzʌ́və]. Prec. & **-er. 1.** One who observes, regards attentively, or watches: *an observer of the stars*; *patient observer of nature*; also as title of newspapers or periodicals: *The Observer.* **2.** One who keeps, adheres to, maintains: *an observer of his promises, of Sunday* &c.

observing, adj. [1. obzẽrving; 2. əbzʌ́viŋ], fr. Pres. Part. of **observe.** Observant, watchful, attentive; given to noticing.

observingly, adv. Prec. & **-ly.** Attentively, carefully.

obsess, vb. trans. [1. obsés; 2. əbsés], fr. Lat. *obsess-(um),* P.P. type of *obsidēre,* 'to haunt, frequent; besiege; to take possession of', fr. **ob-** & *sedēre,* 'to sit'. See **sedentary** & **sit. a** To possess, beset, haunt: *obsessed by a demon, by a delusion*; **b** to occupy the mind to the exclusion of other things; to preoccupy: *obsessed by the idea of one's own importance, by a fixed idea* &c.

obsession, n. [1. obséshun; 2. əbséʃən], fr. Lat. *obsessiōn-(em),* 'siege, blockade'. Prec. & **-ion. 1. a** Persistent possession and preoccupation of the mind, by an evil spirit; **b** exclusive preoccupation of the mind by a fixed idea, thought, desire &c. **2.** That which takes possession of the mind to the exclusion of all else; a fixed idea, crotchet, monomania.

obsidian, n. [1. obsídian; 2. əbsídiən], fr. Lat. *Obsidiānus lapis,* 'the stone of Obsidius', a false reading in Pliny for *Obsianus,* 'stone of Obsius', who discovered it in Ethiopia. A glassy, dark, extremely hard volcanic rock.

obsolescence, n. [1. òbsolésens; 2. òbsəlésəns]. See next word & **-ce.** State, process, of growing or becoming obsolete or obsolescent.

obsolescent, adj. [1. òbsolésent; 2. òbsəlésənt], fr. Lat. *obsolescent-(em),* Pres. Part. of *obsolescere,* 'to wear out, grow old'; freq. vb. of wh. the etymol. is doubtful; perh. fr. *obs-,* fr. **ob-** & variant of *alere,* 'to grow', prob. w. later influence of *solēre,* 'to be accustomed, be used to'; cp. also *exolescere,* 'to grow up; to grow out of use' &c., & *adolescere,* 'grow up'. See **adolescent.** Going, passing, gradually out of use, becoming obsolete or extinct.

obsolete, adj. [1. óbsolēt; 2. óbsəlīt], fr. Lat. *obsolēt-(um),* P.P. of *obsolescere.* See prec. **a** No longer in use; discarded, disused; **b** out-of-date, old-fashioned.

obsoletely, adv. Prec. & **-ly.** In an obsolete manner.

obsoleteness, n. See prec. & **-ness.** State, quality, of being obsolete.

obstacle, n. [1. óbstakl; 2. óbstikl, óbstəkl]. Fr., fr. Lat. *obstāculum,* 'hindrance, obstacle', for *obstāt-lom,* w. dimin. suff., fr. base of *obstāre,* 'to hinder, thwart, stand in the way of'. See **ob-, state,** & **stand.** A hindrance, obstruction, impediment (material or non-material); that which prevents advance: *a formidable obstacle to progress*; *obstacle race,* a foot-race in which various barriers, artificial or natural, have to be crossed.

obstetric, adj. [1. obstétrik; 2. əbstétrik], fr. Lat. *obstētricus,* 'of, pertaining to, a midwife or midwifery', fr. *obstētrīc-(em),* stem of *obstētrix,* 'midwife', lit. 'a woman who stands by or near one', fr. **ob-** & *stāre,* 'to stand'. See **state** & **stand.** Of, pertaining to, midwifery or obstetrics; *obstetric toad,* a toad, the male of which carries the eggs on its hind legs until they are hatched; the nurse toad.

obstetrical, adj. [1. obstétrikl; 2. əbstétrikl]. Prec. & **-al.** Obstetric.

obstetrician, n. [1. òbstetríshan; 2. òbstətríʃən]. See **obstetric** & **-ian.** One skilled in midwifery or obstetrics; a specialist accoucheur.

obstetrics, n. pl. [1. obstétriks; 2. əbstétriks]. Art and science of midwifery.

obstinacy, n. [1. óbstinasi; 2. óbstinəsi]. See **obstinate** & **-cy. 1.** Obstinate quality or habit, state of mind; unreasoning adherence to one's opinions, purpose, or programme; stubbornness, pigheadedness. **2.** (of disease) Resistance to remedy or cure.

obstinate, adj. [1. óbstinat; 2. óbstinit], fr. Lat. *obstināt-(um),* 'fixed, resolute, obstinate', P.P. of *obstināre,* 'to set one's mind on, persist in', fr. **ob-** & **stanāre,* fr. base of *stāre,* 'to stand'; cp. **destiny.** See **station, stand. 1. a** Unreasonably tenacious of one's opinions; adhering persistently to one's own purpose, line of action &c.; not to be moved by argument or persuasion; stubborn, pigheaded, mulish; pertinacious; **b** persistent, resolute: *obstinate resistance to attack.* **2.** (of disease &c.) Not yielding readily to remedy or cure; refractory, intractable.

obstinately, adv. Prec. & **-ly.** In an obstinate way or manner; stubbornly.

obstreperous, adj. [1. obstréperus; 2. əbstrépərəs], fr. L. Lat. *obstreperus,* 'clamorous, noisy', fr. *obstrepere,* 'to cry out, clamour against; to annoy, be troublesome to', fr. **ob-** & *strepere,* 'to make a noise, roar', prob. a remote connexion of *strīdere,* 'to hiss, buzz, rattle'. See **strident.** Noisy, clamorous; turbulent, unruly, ungovernable.

obstreperously, adv. Prec. & **-ly.** In an obstreperous, turbulent way or manner.

obstreperousness, n. See prec. & **-ness.** Obstreperous, turbulent conduct.

obstruct, vb. trans. & intrans. [1. obstrúkt; 2. əbstrákt], fr. Lat. *obstruct-(um),* P.P. of *obstruere,* 'to build, block, wall, up; to bar, render impassable', fr. **ob-** & *struere,* 'to build'. See **structure. A.** trans. **1. a** To block, bar, render impassable: *to obstruct a road, path, passage*; **b** to prevent, hinder (moving things) from passing: *to obstruct the traffic.* **2.** To hinder, prevent, interrupt, passage of light or sound, or of visual and auditive impressions: *obstruct the view*; *to obstruct a sound.* **3.** To oppose, hinder, impede, the progress of: *to obstruct reform, a bill in Parliament* &c. **4.** To hinder, thwart, impede, embarrass, hamper (persons in or from doing something): *to obstruct the police in the discharge of their duties.* **B.** intrans. To practise obstruction; to oppose progress: *he never lifts a finger to help us, he merely obstructs.*

obstruction, n. [1. obstrúkshun; 2. əbstrákʃən], fr. Lat. *obstructiōn-(em),* 'a building up, barrier, impediment'. Prec. & **-ion. 1.** Act of obstructing; the placing of a physical barrier which blocks, hinders, stops passage and movement. **2.** Act or conduct which prevents something being done; which impedes, hinders, retards progress: *a policy of obstruction*; specif., *Parliamentary obstruction,* process of deliberately delaying a measure. **3.** Something which obstructs; **a** material object which blocks a road, passage, or channel of any kind: *an obstruction on the railway, in a pipe, in the throat, intestines* &c.; **b** something which hinders the passage of light, air, sound &c., which prevents from seeing or hearing.

obstructionism, n. [1. obstrúkshunizm; 2. əbstrákʃənizəm]. Prec. & **-ism.** System of obstructing or impeding Parliamentary or other business.

obstructionist, n. [1. obstrúkshunist; 2. əbstrákʃənist]. See prec. & **-ist.** One who practises obstruction, esp. to hinder or impede Parliamentary or other business.

obstructive, adj. & n. [1. obstrúktiv; 2. əbstráktiv]. **obstruct** & **-ive. 1.** adj. Causing obstruction; tending to obstruct. **2.** n. An obstructive person or thing.

obstructively, adv. Prec. & **-ly.** So as to cause obstruction.

obstructiveness, n. Prec. & **-ness.** Obstructive action or conduct.

obtain, vb. trans. & intrans. [1. obtā́n; 2. əbtéin], fr. Fr. *obtenir,* fr. Lat. *obtinēre,* 'to hold, obtain', fr. **ob-** & *tenēre,* 'to hold'. See **tenable. A.** trans. To gain, get possession of; to acquire, win; to have conferred upon one: *to obtain a share of the plunder, a prize, a reward, salvation* &c. **B.** intrans. To be received in ordinary use; to prevail, be current or prevalent: *the custom has long obtained*; to hold good, to be accepted or recognized: *these views no longer obtain.*

obtainable, adj. [1. obtā́nabl; 2. əbtéinəbl]. Prec. & **-able.** Capable of being obtained; to be gained; procurable.

obtainment, n. [1. obtā́nment; 2. əbtéinmənt]. See prec. & **-ment.** (archaic) Act of obtaining; attainment.

obtected, adj. [1. obtékted; 2. əbtéktid], fr. Lat. *obtect-(um),* P.P. of *obtegere,* 'to cover up, or over', **ob-** & *tegere,* 'to cover', q.v. under **tegument,** & **-ed.** (zool.) Covered with a hard outer case or shell, as the pupae of certain insects.

obtest, vb. trans. & intrans. [1. obtést; 2. əbtést], fr. Lat. *obtestāri,* 'to beseech', **ob-** & *testāri,* 'to bear witness,' fr. *testis,* 'witness'. See **testimony. 1.** trans. (archaic) **a** To invoke as a witness, call to witness; **b** to beseech, supplicate; to beg for. **2.** intrans. To protest.

obtestation, n. [1. òbtestā́shun; 2. òbtestéiʃən]. Lat. *obtestātiōn-(em).* See prec. & **-ation.** Supplication; protestation.

obtrude, vb. trans. & intrans. [1. obtrṓōd; 2. əbtrū́d], fr. Lat. *obtrūdere,* 'to push, thrust against, push forward', **ob-** & *trūdere,* 'to thrust, push'; cogn. w. O. Slav. *trudīti,* 'to afflict'; cp. Goth. *us-þriutan,* 'to treat ill; threaten'; O.E. *þrēatian,* 'to threaten'. See **thrust** & **threat. 1.** trans. (not used of material action) To thrust, push, forward, force upon: *to obtrude one's opinions, oneself upon.* **2.** intrans. To intrude.

obtruncate, vb. trans. [1. obtrúngkāt; 2. əbtráŋkeit]. Lat. *obtruncāt-(um),* P.P. type of *obtruncāre*, 'to lop off'. See **ob-** & **truncate**. To lop off the head or top end of.

obtrusion, n. [1. obtrōōzhun; 2. əbtrúžən], fr. L. Lat. *obtrūsiōn-(em)*, fr. *obtrūs-(um)*, P.P. of *obtrūdere*, see **obtrude**, & **-ion**. Act of obtruding or thrusting upon: *obtrusion of opinions on others.*

obtrusive, adj. [1. obtrōōsiv; 2. əbtrúsiv]. See prec. & **-ive**. Disposed to obtrude, thrust, or push oneself forward; intrusive, pushing.

obtrusively, adv. Prec. & **-ly**. In an obtrusive manner.

obtrusiveness, n. See prec. & **-ness**. Obtrusive behaviour.

obtund, vb. trans. [1. obtúnd; 2. əbtánd], fr. Lat. *obtundere*, 'to beat against', fr. **ob-** & *tundere*, 'to beat'. See **obtuse**. (obs.) To blunt, take the edge off.

obturate, vb. trans. [1. óbtūrāt; 2. ɔ́btjureit], fr. Lat. *obtūrāt-(um)*, P.P. of *obtūrāre*, 'to stop, close up'; **ob-** & base **tu-*, 'lump, knob' &c., as in *tumēre*, 'to swell', see **tumid**. To stop, close, an opening, esp. to close the breech of a gun as prevention of the escape of gas on firing.

obturation, n. [1. òbtūrā́shun; 2. ɔ̀btjuréiʃən]. Lat. *obtūrātiōn-(em)*. Prec. & **-ion**. The closing, stopping, of an opening, esp. of a gun-breech.

obturator, n. [1. óbtūrāter; 2. ɔ́btjureitə]. **obturate** & **-or**. **1.** That which closes or stops an opening or passage; specif., a device for closing the breech of a gun to prevent escape of gas. **2.** *Obturator canal*, an opening in the hip-bone through which certain blood-vessels and nerves pass.

obtuse, adj. [1. obtū́s; 2. əbtjús], fr. Lat. *obtūsus*, 'blunted', fr. P.P. of *obtundere*, 'to beat against, blunt'. See **obtund**. The base has forms **tund-* & **tud-*; cp. Lat. *tudes*, 'a hammer'; Scrt. *tundatē, tudáti*, 'strikes, pricks'. **1.** Blunt, blunted; not having a sharp edge or point: *obtuse corner.* **2.** (of the senses, mental perceptions, also of persons) Dull, slow; stupid, dense: *obtuse mind*; *an obtuse person.* **3.** (geom.) *Obtuse angle*, one greater than a right angle; *obtuse angled triangle*, a triangle with an obtuse angle.

obtusely, adv. Prec. & **-ly**. In an obtuse manner; bluntly; stupidly.

obtuseness, n. See prec. & **-ness**. State, quality, of being obtuse; bluntness; stupidity.

obverse (I.), adj. [1. óbvērs; 2. ɔ́bvʌs], fr. Lat. *obvers-(um)*, P.P. of *obvertere*, 'to turn towards'; **ob-** & *vertere*, 'to turn'. See **version**. **1.** Turned towards, facing, fronting, the observer; contrasted with *reverse*. **2.** (bot.) Inverted, (of leaves &c.) having the attachment end narrow, as compared with the tip or apex. **3.** Forming a complement or counterpart.

obverse (II.), n., fr. prec. **1. a** That which faces or fronts the observer, contrasted with *reverse*; **b** specif. (numis.) that side of a coin or medal which bears the head of the sovereign or the principal device. **2.** A fact which answers to, serves as complement to, another fact, belief &c.

obversely, adv. [1. obvḗrsli; 2. əbvʌ́sli]. **obverse** (I.) & **-ly**. In an obverse form or manner.

obversion, n. [1. obvḗrshun; 2. əbvʌ́ʃən]. Lat. *obversiōn-(em)*, 'a turning towards, offering'. **obverse** & **-ion**. (log.) A process of conversion by immediate inference, in which the direct opposite of a proposition is at once inferred: *all men are mortal*, by obversion, *no men are immortal.*

obvert, vb. trans. [1. obvḗrt; 2. əbvʌ́t], fr. Lat. *obvertere*, 'to turn towards', fr. **ob-** & *vertere*, 'to turn'. See **version**. (log.) To infer by the process of obversion.

obviate, vb. trans. [1. óbviāt; 2. ɔ́bvieit], fr. Lat. *obviāt-(um)*, P.P. of *obviāre*, 'to meet in the way, go towards', fr. **ob-** & *via*, 'way, path'. See **viable** & **voyage**. To remove from the way, get rid of, clear away; make unnecessary: *to obviate a difficulty, a necessity.*

obvious, adj. [1. óbvius; 2. ɔ́bviəs], fr. Lat. *obvius*, 'lying in the way, meeting', hence, 'at hand, ready, obvious'. See prec. & **-ous**. **1. a** Readily, easily, perceived; plainly visible and apparent; not to be missed; unmistakable: *his embarrassment was obvious*; **b** (i.) too apparent; obtrusive; forcing itself upon the attention: *his correctness of speech, politeness, was perhaps a little obvious*; (ii.) (of colours) flaunting, garish: *dress that appeared too obvious amid the sombre surroundings.* **2. a** Clear, easily apparent to the mind and understanding, plainly manifest: *an obvious meaning, intention* &c.; **b** too simple, undisguised; lacking subtlety: *the sentiment, joke, was coarse and obvious.* **3.** (archaic) Open, exposed, to attack &c.: '*to the evil turn My obvious breast*' (Milton, 'P. L.' xi. 373-4).

obviously, adv. Prec. & **-ly**. Plainly, clearly, evidently, manifestly.

obviousness, n. See prec. & **-ness**. State, quality, of being obvious, plain, or evident; **a** obtrusiveness; **b** lack of subtlety.

oc-, pref., form of **ob-**, used in compounds in wh. the second element begins w. a *c*.

ocarina, n. [1. òkarḗna; 2. ɔ̀kərínə]. Ital., fr. *oca*, 'a goose', w. dimin. suff.; fr. Lat. *auca*, 'goose', fr. **avica*, fr. base of *avis*, 'bird', see **aviary**. A small musical instrument made of baked clay, with finger holes and mouthpiece, which gives out a low and flute-like note.

occasion (I.), n. [1. okā́zhun; 2. əkéižən], fr. Lat. *occāsiōn-(em)*, 'a falling out, happening, opportunity, occasion', fr. **oc-** & *cās-(um)*, P.P. type of *cadere*, 'to fall'. See **cadency** & **case** (I.). **1.** Point or moment of time at which some particular event occurs, or some action is performed: *on the occasion of one's marriage*; *this auspicious occasion.* **2.** A suitable, favourable moment, opportunity, for doing something: *to profit by the occasion*; *not the occasion for rejoicing*; *to choose one's occasion*, the right moment. Phrs. *to rise to the occasion*, to be equal to an emergency; *on occasion*, as opportunity arises; *to take occasion to do, say*, choose that moment. **3.** An event or incident which is the subsidiary cause of another: *the King's death was the occasion for risings on all sides.* **4.** A ground, reason, cause, for doing something: *no occasion to laugh, for anger*; *occasions of dispute.* **5.** (pl., archaic) Necessary business affairs; occupations: *going about their lawful occasions.*

occasion (II.), vb. trans., fr. prec. Cp. Fr. *occasionner*. To give occasion for, give rise to; to cause, bring about: *his conduct occasions me great anxiety.*

occasional, adj. [1. okā́zhunal; 2. əkéižənəl]. **occasion** (I.) & **-al**. **1. a** Occurring at irregular intervals; happening from time to time; not continuous: *occasional bouts of pain*; *occasional thunderstorms*; **b** coming, appearing, at rare intervals; seen on certain occasions only; infrequent: *an occasional visitor*; *an occasional reader in the library.* **2. a** Composed for, performed upon, some special occasion: *occasional verses, ode*, &c.; *occasional music*; **b** designed for, adapted to, some special purpose or requirement: *an occasional table, bookcase*, &c. **3.** *Occasional cause*: **a** a secondary, incidental cause, that which immediately precedes, but is not the efficient cause of anything; **b** in later Cartesian philosophy, the doctrine that, while mind and matter only act on each other as *occasional causes*, they are brought into mutual relation by God.

occasionalism, n. [1. okā́zhunalizm; 2. əkéižənəlizəm]. Prec. & **-ism**. The Cartesian doctrine of occasional causes.

occasionality, n. [1. okàzhunáliti; 2. əkèižənǽliti]. **occasional** & **-ity**. State, quality, of being occasional.

occasionally, adv. [1. okā́zhunali; 2. əkéižənəli]. See prec. & **-ly**. On occasions, at times, from time to time, now and then.

Occident, n. [1. óksident; 2. ɔ́ksidənt]. Fr., fr. Lat. *occident-(em)*, 'quarter of the setting sun, the west', n., fr. Pres. Part. of *occidere*, 'to fall down, set'. See **occasion**. (poet., cap.) **1.** The west; the western horizon or western part of the earth, as contrasted with *Orient*. **2.** The Western hemisphere; formerly Europe, as contrasted with Asia.

Occidental, adj. [1. òksidéntal; 2. ɔ̀ksidéntəl]. Prec. & **-al**. Of or pertaining to the Occident, to the West: *Occidental civilization, habits, climate* &c., as contrasted with *Oriental.*

occidentalism, n. [1. òksidéntalizm; 2. ɔ̀ksidéntəlizəm]. Prec. & **-ism**. Culture, customs, character, ideas &c., of Western or European peoples, as contrasted with those of Orientals.

occidentalist, n. [1. òksidéntalist; 2. ɔ̀ksidéntəlist]. **occidental** & **-ist**. One who prefers Occidental or Western to Oriental culture &c.

occidentalize, vb. trans. [1. òksidéntalīz; 2. ɔ̀ksidéntəlaiz]. **occidental** & **-ize**. To impart Western, European, culture and notions to.

occidentally, adv. [1. òksidéntali; 2. ɔ̀ksidéntəli]. See prec. & **-ly**. In an Occidental or Western manner.

occipital, adj. [1. oksípital; 2. ɔksípitəl], fr. Lat. *occipit-(em)*. See **occiput** & **-al**. (anat.) Of or belonging to the occiput or back of the head: *occipital bone, fracture* &c.

occiput, n., learned pl. **occipita** [1. óksiput, oksípita; 2. ɔ́ksipət, ɔksípitə]. Lat., fr. **oc-** & *caput*, 'head'. See **capital**. The back of the head.

occlude, vb. trans. [1. oklōōd; 2. əklúd], fr. Lat. *occlūdere*, 'to shut up', fr. **oc-** & *claudere*, to close, shut'. See **clause**, **close**, **cloister**. **1.** To close, shut in or shut out: *to occlude rays of light.* **2.** (chem.) To take up, and absorb, esp. of gases by certain substances.

occlusion, n. [1. oklōōzhun; 2. əklúžən], fr. Lat. *occlūsiōn-(em)*, fr. *occlūs-(um)*, P.P. of *occlūdere*. See prec. & **-ion**. **1.** Act or process of occluding; state of being occluded; specif. **a** closure of the eyes by drawing the eyelids over them; **b** momentary closure of vocal passage in speech, as in formation of stop consonants. **2.** (chem.) Absorption of gases by certain substances.

occlusive, adj. [1. oklōōsiv; 2. əklúsiv]. As in prec. & **-ive**. Tending to occlude, close, or shut up; tending to absorb; causing occlusion.

occult (I.), adj. [1. okúlt; 2. əkʌ́lt], fr. Lat. *occult-(um)*, P.P. of *occulere*, 'to cover up, conceal', **oc-** & base **kel-* &c., 'to hide', & seen in *cēlāre*, 'to hide', see **conceal**; also **clandestine** & **hell**. **1.** Hidden, secret, esoteric. **2.** Specif., supernatural, mystic, magical: *occult sciences*; also as noun, *the Occult.*

occult (II.), vb. trans. & intrans., fr. Fr. *occulter*, fr. Lat. *occultāre*, freq. form of *occulere*, 'to cover'. See prec. **A** trans. (astron.) To conceal from sight, to shut off light from by passing before, as the moon before a planet or star; to eclipse. **B.** intrans. To become concealed, as the intermittent light of a lighthouse: *an occulting light.*

occultation, n. [1. òkultā́shun; 2. ɔ̀kʌltéiʃən], fr. Lat. *occultātiōn-(em)*, 'concealment', as prec. & **-ation**. (astron.) The hiding, concealment, or eclipse of one heavenly body by another, usually a larger body, by passing between it and the earth, as *occultation of Venus*, by the moon.

occultism, n. [1. okúltizm; 2. əkʌ́ltizəm]. **occult-** (I.) & **-ism**. Theory of, and belief in supernatural, occult forces and powers; study or practice of occult sciences and arts.

occultist, n. [1. okúltist; 2. əkʌ́ltist]. **occult** (I.) & **-ist**. One who believes in or studies occultism.

occultly, adv. [1. okúltli; 2. əkʌ́ltli]. **occult** (I.) & **-ly**. By occult means.

occultness, n. [1. okúltnes; 2. əkʌ́ltnis]. See prec. & **-ness**. State, quality, of being occult.

occupancy, n. [1. ókūpansi; 2. ɔ́kjupənsi]. See **occupant** & **-cy**. **1. a** The act or fact of occupying, of taking and holding possession, esp. of a house, land &c.; **b** term during which a house &c. is occupied. **2.** (law) Acquirement of a title or right to something which does not belong to anybody, or which has been abandoned.

occupant, n. [1. ókūpant; 2. ɔ́kjupənt], fr. Lat. *occupant-(em)*, Pres. Part of *occupāre*, 'to take possession of'. See **occupy**. **a** An occupier; one occupying some particular place, dwelling, shelter &c. at a given moment; inhabitant, denizen, resident: *who is the occupant of the ruined cottage? At present its sole occupants are rats*; **b** one who holds a title to anything by occupancy.

occupation, n. [1. òkūpáshun; 2. ɔ̀kjupéiʃən]. Fr., fr. Lat. *occupātiōn-(em)*, 'a taking possession, seizing', fr. *occupāt-(um)*, P.P. type of *occupāre*, 'to take possession'. See **occupy** & **-ion**. **1.** Act of occupying or taking and keeping possession of: *occupation of a house*; *occupation of a town or country by the enemy* &c.: *occupation troops, army of occupation*, military forces in occupation of a defeated enemy's country during an armistice or till final terms of peace have been executed. **2.** Period during which a house &c. is occupied; occupancy, residence, tenure: *during the occupation of the farm*. **3.** State of being occupied; employment: *men out of occupation*. **4. a** That which engages or occupies one's time for the moment; specif. **b** that set of duties, tasks, operations, upon which one is regularly engaged or employed; business, trade, profession.

occupier, n. [1. ókūpīer; 2. ɔ́kjupaiə]. **occupy** & **-er**. One who is in occupation of house, or land, esp. temporarily as a tenant, not as owner.

occupy, vb. trans. [1. ókūpī; 2. ɔ́kjupai]. M.E. *occupien*, fr. Fr. *occuper*, fr. Lat. *occupāre*, 'to seize hold of, take possession of', fr. **oc-** & modified form of *capere*, 'to take', see **captive**. **1.** To take and keep possession of, to hold, as by military forces in war: *to occupy a country, a town* &c. **2.** To be in occupation or possession of; to reside in; to have for one's use: *to occupy a house, rooms, office* &c. **3. a** To fill, take up, a particular space: *to occupy a chair, a place, shelf* &c.; **b** to take up, use, spend (time): *the dinner and speeches occupied three hours*; **c** to fill the mind, thoughts &c.; engross attention: *many cares and anxieties occupied his mind*. **4. a** (pass.) *To be occupied in*, be employed on, be busied with, be engaged in: *workmen were occupied in pulling down the house*; **b** (reflex.) *occupy oneself (with)*, to spend one's time on, busy oneself with.

occur, vb. intrans. [1. okér; 2. əkə́], fr. Lat. *occurrere*, 'to run towards, to meet; to present itself, to happen', fr. **oc-** & *currere*, 'to run, go'. See **current** (I.) & **course**. **1.** (of objects, types &c.) To be met with, to be found to exist: *fossils do not occur in igneous rocks*; *black sheep occur in all families*. **2.** (of events, natural processes) To happen, take place: *several fires, storms &c. have occurred*; *this must not occur again*. **3.** (of thoughts and ideas &c.) To come into the mind, strike one; to suggest itself: *a fresh idea occurs to one*; *it occurs to me that* &c.

occurrence, n. [1. okúrens; 2. əkárəns]. Cp. Fr. *occurrence*. See **occur** & **-ence**. **1.** Fact or process of occurring: *the occurrence of thunder in winter is comparatively rare*. **2.** Something which occurs; an incident, event; a happening: *an occurrence of no importance*; *an everyday occurrence*; *strange occurrences*.

ocean, n. [1. óshan; 2. óuʃən]. O. Fr., fr. Lat. *Ocean-(um)*, *Oceanus*, 'the great outward sea', as contrasted w. the middle sea or Mediterranean, fr. Gk. *Ōkeanós*, in same sense; etymol. doubtful. **1.** The sea, as the whole body or expanse of salt water; esp. the deep or open sea, as contrasted with inland seas, channels, estuaries. **2.** (geog.) One of the great expanses of salt water into which the seas have been divided, as *Atlantic, Pacific, Indian, Arctic*, and *Antarctic Oceans*; *German Ocean*, the North Sea. **3.** A vast, unlimited number or quantity: *an ocean of difficulties*; also pl. (colloq.), plenty, sufficiency: *oceans of time, of money*.

Oceania, n. [1. òshiánia; 2. òuʃiéiniə]. Prec. & **-ia**; cp. Fr. *Océanie*. The Pacific Islands.

oceanic, adj. [1. ōs(h)eánik; 2. òuʃi-, òusiǽnik]. **ocean** & **-ic**. **a** Of, pertaining to, the ocean or deep seas; pelagic; **b** (cap.) of Oceania or the Pacific islands.

Oceanid, n. [1. ōséanid; 2. ousíənid], fr. Gk. *Ōkeanid-(os)*, *Ōkeanis*, daughter of *Ōkeanós*, 'the sea'. A nymph of the great sea or ocean, cp. *Nereid*.

oceanographer, n. [1. òshanógrafer; 2. òuʃənɔ́grəfə]. See **oceanography** & **-er**. A student of, specialist in, oceanography.

oceanographic(al), adj. [1. òshanōgráfik(l); 2. òuʃənougrǽfik(l)]. **oceanography** & **-ic** (& **-al**). Connected with, relating to, the science of oceanography: *oceanographical expedition, museum* &c.

oceanography, n. [1. òshanógrafi; 2. òuʃənɔ́grəfi]. **ocean** & **-graphy**. Branch of science concerned with the study of the ocean, its tides and temperatures &c., and with the forms of animal and plant life occurring in it.

ocellate(d), adj. [1. óselàt(ed); 2. ɔ́selèit(id)]. Lat. *ocellātus*, fr. *ocellus*, 'little eye'. See next word. (zool.) Provided, marked, with ocelli.

ocellus, n., pl. **ocelli** [1. ōsélus, -lī; 2. ouséləs, -lai]. Lat. dimin. of *oculus*, 'eye'. See **ocular**. (zool.) **1.** A simple, eye-like structure found in certain invertebrate animals, as contrasted with compound eyes of insects. **2.** An eye-like spot of colour, ringed with bands of another colour, as in the peacock, the ocellated turkey &c.

ocelot, n. [1. óselot; 2. óusilɔt]. Fr.; abbr. of Mexican *tlalocelotl*, 'field jaguar', fr. *tlalli*, 'field', *ocelotl*, 'jaguar'. A large wild cat, *Felis pardalis*, of Central and South America; the tiger-cat.

ochlocracy, n. [1. oklókrasi; 2. ɔklɔ́krəsi], fr. Fr. *ochlocratie*, fr. Gk. *okhlokratía*, fr. *ókhlos*, 'populace, the mob', the origin of wh. is doubtful, & *krátos*, 'strength, rule', cp. **-cracy**. Government by the mob; mobocracy, mob rule.

ochlocrat, n. [1. óklokrat; 2. ɔ́klɔkræt]. See prec. Leader, supporter, of mob rule.

ochlocratic, adj. [1. òklokrátik; 2. ɔ̀klɔkrǽtik]. Prec. & **-ic**. Of, pertaining to, mob rule.

ochre, n. [1. óker; 2. óukə]. O. Fr. *ocre*, fr. Lat. *ochra*, Gk. *ṓkhra*, 'yellow ochre', fr. *ōkhrós*, 'yellow, pale'; fr. **ō*, cogn. w. Scrt. *ā*, marking approximation, comparable to Engl. suff. *-ish*, & base **ghro-*, 'greyish yellow'; see **grey**. Cp. Scrt. *(vy-)āghraś*, 'tiger'. **1.** An earthy metallic oxide of iron, used for making yellow-brown pigments. **2.** The colours made from these pigments.

ochr(e)ous, adj. [1. ókr(e)us; 2. óukr(i)əs]. Prec. & **-ous**. Containing, resembling, ochre; of a yellow-brown colour.

-ock, suff. O.E. *-oc*, *-uc*, dimin. suff.; as in *hillock, bullock*.

o'clock [1. oklók; 2. əklɔ́k]. For *of the clock*. See **clock**.

oct-, octa-, octo-, pref. Forms used in compounds of Lat. *octo* or Gk. *oktṓ*, 'eight'; a name for the numeral common to most Aryan languages, see **eight**; O. Slav. has *osmi*, & Lith. *asztùm*, w. a different suff. on anal. of the ordinals, O. Slav. *osmŭ*, Lith. *āszmas*, 'eighth'.

octachord, n. [1. óktakord; 2. ɔ́ktəkɔ̄d], fr. Gk. *oktákhordos*, 'having eight strings'. **octa-** & **chord**. **1.** A musical instrument with eight strings. **2.** The diatonic octave.

octachordal, adj. [1. òktakórdal; 2. ɔ̀ktəkɔ́d(ə)l]. Prec. & **-al**. Eight-stringed; in a series of eight tones or notes.

octad, n. [1. óktad; 2. ɔ́ktæd], fr. Gk. *oktád-(os)*, *oktás*, 'the number eight', fr. *oktṓ*, 'eight', see **octa-**. **1.** (chem.) A radical atom which has a valency or combining power of eight. **2.** (math.) A group or series of eight numbers.

octagon, n. [1. óktagun; 2. ɔ́ktəgən], fr. Gk. *oktágōnos*, 'eight-angled', **octa-** & *gōnia*, 'angle', see **-gon**. **1.** (geom.) A plane polygonal figure with eight angles and eight sides. **2.** A building with eight sides.

octagonal, adj. [1. oktágunal; 2. ɔktǽgənəl]. Prec. & **-al**. Having eight angles and eight sides.

octagonally, adv. Prec. & **-ly**. With eight angles and sides.

octahedral, adj. [1. òktahédral; 2. ɔ̀ktəhídrəl]. See next word & **-al**. Having eight plane faces; formed of octahedrons.

octahedron, n. [1. òktahédrun; 2. ɔ̀ktəhídrən, -ɔn], pl. *octahedrons*, learned *octahedra* [1. òktahédra; 2. ɔ̀ktəhídrə]. Gk. *oktá(h)edron*, **octa-** & *hédra*, 'seat, base'. See **-hedron**. (geom.) A solid figure with eight plane faces, and, if regular, contained by eight equal equilateral triangles.

octant, n. [1. óktant; 2. ɔ́ktənt], fr. L. Lat. *octant-(em)*, fr. **oct-** & suff. on anal. of Lat. *quadrant-(em)*, 'fourth part'. See **quadrant**. **1.** An eighth part of circle; an arc of 45 degrees. **2.** (astron.) The position of the moon or other heavenly body, distant 45 degrees from another position, especially that of conjunction or opposition. **3.** (opt.) An instrument for measuring angles, with a graduated arc of 45 degrees.

octarchy, n. [1. óktarki; 2. ɔ́ktəki], fr. **oct-**, on anal. of **heptarchy**. (Engl. hist.) A government by eight rulers or kings; sometimes used for the so-called Heptarchy.

octaroon, n. See **octoroon**.

octastyle, adj. & n. [1. óktastīl; 2. ɔ́ktəstail], fr. Gk. *oktástūlos*, **oct-** & *stûlos*, 'pillar, column'; see **style** (**III.**). **1.** adj. Having eight columns. **2.** n. A building, such as a temple, with eight columns at either end.

Octateuch, n. [1. óktatūk; 2. ɔ́ktətjūk]. Gk. *oktáteukhos*. **octa-** & *teûkhos*, 'utensil; a book'. See second element in **Pentateuch**. The first eight books of the Old Testament.

octavalent, adj. [1. òktaválent; 2. ɔ̀ktəvéilənt]. Lat. **octa-** & *valent-(em)*, Pres. Part. of *valēre*, 'to be worth'. See **valency**. (chem.) Having a combining power or valency of eight.

octave, n. [1. óktāv, óktiv; 2. ɔ́kteiv, ɔ́ktiv]. Fr., fr. Lat. *octāva (diēs)*, 'eighth day', *octāvus*, 'eighth', *octo*, 'eight'. See **octa-**. **1.** (eccles.) The eighth day after a festival, including the day of the festival itself; the eight days after a festival; *in the octave*, during these eight days. **2.** (prosody) **a** A stanza containing eight lines; **b** the first eight lines of a sonnet. **3.** (mus.) **a** The eighth full tone above or below any note; **b** the interval between a note and its octave; **c** an open stop in an organ; **d** the piccolo, which is an **octave** higher in pitch than the flute.

octavo, n., written *8vo* [1. oktávō; 2. ɔktéivou], fr. Lat. *in octavo*. See prec. **1.** A book in which each of the sheets on which it is printed is folded into eight leaves or sixteen pages. **2.** The size of a book or page made up of sheets folded into eight, varying according to the size of the sheet used.

octennial, adj. [1. okténial; 2. ɔkténiəl], fr. Lat. *octenni-(um)*, 'period of eight years', **oct-** & *annus*, 'year'. See **annual** & **-al**. **a** Coming, happening, every eight years; **b** lasting eight years.

octet, octette, n. [1. óktet, oktét; 2. ɔ́ktet, ɔktét]. Formed w. **oct-** & on anal. of **duet**, **quartet** &c. **1.** A composition for eight instruments or eight voices. **2.** A group, set, of eight verses, esp. the first eight lines of a sonnet.

octillion, n. [1. oktíliun; 2. ɔktíliən]. **oct-** & **illion*, on anal. of **million**. **1.** (Engl. notation) One million raised to the 8th power, one followed by 48 ciphers. **2.** (Fr. and Am. notation) One thousand raised to the 9th power, one followed by 27 ciphers.

octo-, pref. See **oct-**.

October, n. [1. oktṓber; 2. ɔktóubə]. Lat., 'the eighth month of the year', the old Roman year beginning w. March. See **oct-**; the origin of the suff. is obscure. See **December**. **1.** The tenth month of the year. **2.** Beer or ale brewed in October.

Octobrist, n. [1. oktṓbrist; 2. ɔktóubrist]. Fr., fr. Russ. See prec. & **-ist**. The name of a moderate reforming party in pre-Soviet Russia whose measures for constitutional government were proclaimed in the Czar's manifesto of October 1905.

octocentenary, n. [1. òktōsentḗnari; 2. ɔ̀ktousentínəri]. **octo-** & **centenary**. An 800th anniversary.

octodecimo, n., written *18mo*. [1. òktōdésimō; 2. ɔ̀ktoudésimou]. Lat. *octōdecimus*, 'eighteenth', *octo*, 'eight', *decimus*, 'tenth'. See **oct-** & **decimal**. **1.** A book whose sheets are folded into 18 leaves. **2.** The size of book or page when sheets are so folded.

octogenarian, n. & adj. [1. òktōjenárian; 2. ɔ̀ktoudžinéəriən], fr. Lat. *octōgēnāri(us)*, & **-an**; fr. *octōgēni*, 'eighty each', *octōginta*, 'eighty'. See **oct-**. **1.** n. A person eighty years old. **2.** adj. Eighty years old, in the eightieth year of life.

octonal, adj. & n. [1. óktunal; 2. ɔ́ktənəl], fr. Lat. *octōni*, 'eight each'. See **oct-**. **1.** (of numbers, coins) Counted in groups of eight or by eight units. **2.** (of verse) Having eight feet.

octonarian, n. [1. òktonárian; 2. ɔ̀ktənéəriən], fr. Lat. *octōnārius* (*versus*). See prec. A verse in which each line has eight feet.

octopod, n. [1. óktopòd; 2. ɔ́ktəpɔ̀d], fr. Gk. *oktṓpod-(os)*, fr. **octo-**, 'eight', & *pod-*, 'foot'. See **-pod**. (zool.) Any animal belonging to the suborder, *Octopoda*, which includes the argonaut and octopus.

octopus, n., pl. **octopuses** [1. óktopus; 2. ɔ́ktəpəs]. L. Lat. *octōpus*, fr. Gk. *oktṓpous*, adj., 'eight feet long', also *oktápous*, 'having eight feet'. **octo-** & **-pod**. **1.** (zool.) A cephalopod mollusc with eight arms furnished with suckers; related to the cuttlefish. **2.** (fig.) Any powerful organization, influence &c. with wide-reaching branches or ramifications.

octoroon, octaroon, n. [1. òktorōōn; 2. ɔ̀ktərū́n]. Formed fr. **oct-**, on anal. of **quadroon**. A person of either sex with one-eighth negro blood; offspring of a white and a quadroon.

octosyllabic, adj. [1. òktōsilábik; 2. ɔ̀ktousilǽbik]. **octo-** & **syllabic**. (of verse) Having eight syllables in each line.

octosyllable, n. [1. òktōsílabl; 2. ɔ̀ktousíləbl]. **octo-** & **syllable**. **1.** A verse-line of eight syllables. **2.** Word of eight syllables.

octroi, n. [1. óktrwah; 2. ɔ́ktrwā]. Fr., orig. 'privilege, concession', fr. *octroyer*, 'to grant', fr. L. Lat. *auctorizāre*, formed fr. *auctor*, 'originator, founder; master, one having authority'. See **author** & **authorize**. **a** A tax or duty levied in some countries on all commodities entering a town or district; **b** the boundary or office where such duties are collected; **c** the officials in charge of such office.

octuple, adj. & vb. trans. [1. oktū́pl; 2. ɔktjū́pl], fr. Lat. *octūplus*, 'eightfold'; fr. *octo*, 'eight', see **octo-**, on anal. of *duplus*, 'twofold', see **double**. **1.** adj. Eightfold. **2.** vb. To make eightfold, multiply by eight.

ocular, adj. & n. [1. ókūlar; 2. ɔ́kjulə], fr. Lat. *oculāris*, fr. *oculus*, 'the eye', fr. base **okʷ-*, whence also Gk. *ósse*, dual, 'the two eyes'; *ópsomai*, 'I shall see'. Homeric *ṓps*, fr. **ōkʷ-*, 'face'; O. Slav. *oko*; Goth. *augō*, O.E. *ēage*, 'eye'. See also **optic** & **eye**. **1.** adj. Pertaining to, by means of, the eye or sight; visual: *ocular demonstration, proof* &c. **2.** n. The eye-piece of an optical instrument.

ocularly, adv. Prec. & **-ly**. By means of the eye.

oculate, adj. [1. ókūlāt; 2. ɔ́kjuleit]. Lat. *oculātus*, 'having eyes, seeing'. See **ocular**. (zool.) Having ocelli or eye-like spots; ocellate.

oculist, n. [1. ókūlist; 2. ɔ́kjulist], fr. Fr. *oculiste*, fr. Lat. *oculus*, 'eye'. See **ocular** & **-ist**. A medical practitioner who specializes in diseases of the eye.

oculo-motor, adj. [1. òkūlō mṓter; 2. ɔ̀kjulou móutə]. *Oculo-*, fr. Lat. *oculus*, 'eye', see **ocular**, & **motor (II.)**. (anat.) Moving the ball of the eye: *oculo-motor nerve*.

od (I.), n. [1. od; 2. ɔd]. Word coined by von Reichenbach (1788–1869). Hypothetical natural force or power, supposed by von Reichenbach to produce such phenomena as magnetism, chemical action, mesmerism &c.; also called *odyl* and *odylic force*.

od (II.), **'od**, also **odds**, interj. [1. od(z); 2. ɔd(z)]. Euphemism for *God*, as in 17th cent. oaths and expletives: as *odds fish* &c.

odal, n. See **udal**.

odalisque, n. [1. ṓdalisk; 2. óudəlisk]. Fr., fr. Turk. *odaliq*, 'maid-servant'. A female slave or concubine in an Oriental harem.

odd (I.), adj. [1. od; 2. ɔd]. M.E. *odde*, 'odd, unique, special; uneven (of numbers)'; fr. O.N. *oddi*, fr. **ord-*, 'triangle', whence the meaning 'odd number' is derived, fr. the uneven number of points; cp. also O.N. *odda-tala*, 'odd number', & *odda maðr*, 'odd man', the one who gives the casting vote. The orig. sense of the corresponding n. *oddr* is 'point, tip, of a spear, sword' &c.; it is also used for 'a point, spit, of land; a place, spot'. The n. is found in O.E. cogn. *ord*, 'point of a weapon; beginning, front; chief' &c.; & in O.H.G. & Mod. Germ. *ort*, 'place, spot'. Orig. form **uzdo-*, for wh. there seem to be no cognates outside Gmc. **1.** (of numbers) **a** Not even, not divisible by two: *an odd number*, as 3, 5 &c. Phr. *luck in odd numbers*; **b** (of persons or objects counted) called, identified, known by an odd number: *the odd houses*, in a street; *odd files*, in a rank of numbered soldiers; *odd months*, in the year, those having 31 days. **2.** Applied to one of a pair of objects, normally occurring or used together, when the other of the pair is missing: *an odd boot, glove*; also to one or more members of a set, series, or related group isolated from the remainder: *a few odd volumes of Gibbon*; *odd player, couple*, in a game, extra players, over and above the number actually required; *odd trick*, at whist &c., the seventh, the first that the winners count towards their score. Phr. *odd man out*, one left out when two or more have been paired off. **3.** Surplus, extra, not counted (of sums, numbers &c. of smaller denomination than the main sum or number): *three pounds odd*, not counting shillings and pence; *twenty odd years, pounds*, any number between 20 and 30; *the odd money*; *three hundred odd*, between 300 and 400. **4.** Outside what is habitual, regular, fixed; occasional, casual: *odd jobs*; *odd moments*, those not filled by regular occupations; spare time. **5.** Not ordinary; peculiar, strange; eccentric, queer; surprising: *odd people, manners*; *he looks very odd in uniform*; *odd way of speaking* &c.; *that's very odd*.

odd (II.), n. Always **odds**, except in Phr. *the odd*, the odd trick, as in whist, and in golf, **a** a handicap given by taking a stroke off from the score at a hole; **b** a stroke by which one player is above his opponent at a particular hole.

Odd Fellow, Oddfellow, n. [1. ód felō; 2. ɔ́d felou]. A member of a friendly society, *Order of Oddfellows*, which has certain secret rites and ceremonies resembling those of Freemasonry.

oddish, adj. [1. ódish; 2. ɔ́diʃ]. **odd (I.)** & **-ish**. Rather odd, queerish.

oddity, n. [1. óditi; 2. ɔ́diti]. **odd (I.)** & **-ity**. **1.** Quality of being odd, in appearance or character; queerness, strangeness, oddness: *the oddity of his dress and manners*. **2.** An odd, queer person or thing: *to look a regular oddity*.

oddly, adv. [1. ódli; 2. ɔ́dli]. **odd (I.)** & **-ly**. In an odd, queer, manner: *to behave oddly*. Phr. *oddly enough*, strange to say.

oddment, n. [1. ódment; 2. ɔ́dmənt]. **odd (I.)** & **-ment**. A remnant, odd piece; *oddments*, odds and ends.

oddness, n. [1. ódnes; 2. ɔ́dnis]. **odd (I.)** & **-ness**. Strangeness, queerness; oddity.

odds, n. pl. [1. odz; 2. ɔdz]. See **odd (II.)**. **1.** Things which are not even or equal, inequality: *to make odds even*. **2.** Difference, balance, chance in favour of one as against another: *the odds are against us*; *against fearful odds*; *it is odds that he will do this*. Phrs. *by long odds*, by a great difference; *to give, receive, odds*, to allow, receive, an equalizing amount, as of strokes in a game &c.; to be handicapped; *it makes no odds*, make no difference, it doesn't matter; *what's the odds?*, what difference does it make? **3.** Strife, quarrel, dispute, difference; usually in Phr. *to be at odds with*. **4.** (betting) The difference in amount between the money staked on a chance and that which will be paid if the chance comes off: *the odds are 10 to 1*. Phr. *to lay the odds*, of bookmaker &c. who bets that the other will not win.

odds and ends, n. pl. Remnants, oddments, miscellaneous articles.

ode, n. [1. ōd; 2. oud]. Fr., fr. Gk. *ōidḗ*, 'song', for *āoidḗ*, connected w. *āeidein*, 'to sing'; Lat. *ōda*, *ōdē*, is borrowed fr. Gk. Etymol. doubtful. **1.** A song, esp. one accompanied by music and dancing sung by the chorus in the ancient Greek drama: *a choral ode*. **2.** A poem, not of great length, whether in rhymed or unrhymed verse, of irregular or complicated lyrical form, usually composed for some special occasion, on a special theme, in honour of some special person &c., and often modelled on Greek or Latin poems of this kind: *Pindaric, heroic, ode*; *Sapphic, Horatian, ode* &c.

-ode (I.), suff. as in *geode*, fr. Gk. *-ṓdēs*, 'like', fr. *-o-* & *eîdēs*, 'having same shape or form'. See **-oid**.

-ode (II.), suff., fr. Gk. *hodós*, 'way, path', as in *cathode*. See first element in **hodometer**.

Odeum, n. [1. ōdḗum; 2. oudíəm]. Lat., fr. Gk. *ōideîon*, a public building at Athens designed for musical performances, but often used as a law court. See **ode**, cp. Fr. *odéon*. A hall or theatre for musical performances in ancient Greece and Rome; a concert hall.

odious, adj. [1. ṓdius; 2. óudiəs], fr. O. Fr. *odieus*, Mod. Fr. *odieux*, fr. Lat. *odiōsus*, 'hateful'. See **odium**. Arousing, inspiring, hatred or disgust; **a** hateful, detestable; **b** hideous, ugly.

odiously, adv. Prec. & **-ly**. In an odious manner.

odiousness, n. See prec. & **-ness**. State, quality, of being odious.

odium, n. [1. ṓdium; 2. óudiəm]. Lat. *odium*, 'hatred', cogn. w. *ōdī*, 'I hate', & also w. Lat. *āt-rox*, 'furious, fierce', see **atrocious**; also cp. Gk. *odússomai*, 'I am grieved, angry, at'; prob. also O.E. *atol*, 'dire; horrid, loathsome'. State, quality, of being odious or hated; property of arousing hatred or disgust; dislike, reprobation, disgust, aroused or incurred; opprobrium: *to bear the odium of*; *bring odium upon* &c.; *odium theologicum*, the enmity and bitterness caused by religious differences, or existing between different schools of theology.

odograph, odometer, ns. See **hodograph, hodometer**.

odont-, odonto-, pref., fr. Gk. *odónt-(os)*, genit. of *odoús*, 'tooth', for **odont-s*; see the cognates given under **dent-, denti-**.

odontalgia, n. [1. òdontáljia; 2. ɔ̀dɔntǽldžiə]. Gk. See prec. & **-algia**. (med.) Toothache.

odontalgic, adj. [1. òdontáljik; 2. ɔ̀dɔntǽldžik]. Prec. & **-ic**. Connected with, relating to, toothache.

odontic, adj. [1. odóntik; 2. ɔdɔ́ntik]. **odont-** & **-ic**. Of, pertaining to, the teeth; dental: *odontic nerve*.

odontoblast, n. [1. odóntōblàhst; 2. ədóntoublǽst]. **odont-** & first element in **blastoderm**. A cellular construction on the outside of a tooth which secretes the principal material or ivory composing the tooth.

odontoglossum, n. [1. odòntōglósum; 2. ədòntouglɔ́səm], fr. Mod. Lat. **odont-** & Gk. *glôssa*, 'tongue'. See **gloss (III.)**. (bot.) A genus of tropical American orchids, of various colours or forms, the lip being shaped like a tongue and not spurred.

odontoid, adj. [1. odóntoid; 2. ədóntɔid]. **odont-** & **-oid**. (anat.) Having the shape of, resembling, a tooth: *odontoid process*, a toothlike projection on the vertebra.

odontology, n. [1. òdontóloji; 2. òdəntɔ́lədži]. **odont-** & **-logy**. Systematic study of the teeth and their diseases.

odorant, adj. [1. ódurant; 2. óudərənt], fr. Lat. *odōrant-(em)*, Pres. Part. of *odōrāre*, 'to give a scent to, perfume', fr. *odor*. See **odour**. Bearing, carrying, odours or perfumes; fragrant, odoriferous.

odoriferous, adj. [1. òduríferus; 2. òudəríſərəs], fr. Lat. *odōrifer*, 'bearing, spreading, odours', fr. *odor*, see **odour**, & **-ferous**. Bearing, spreading, odours; fragrant; (facet.) smelly.

odoriferously, adv. Prec. & **-ly**. Odorously, fragrantly.

odoriferousness, n. As prec. & **-ness**. Odorousness, fragrance.

odorize, vb. trans. [1. ódurīz; 2. óudəraiz]. See **odour** & **-ize**. To impregnate with an odour, to perfume.

odorous, adj. [1. ódurus; 2. óudərəs]. See **odour** & **-ous**. **a** Scented, perfumed, fragrant, odoriferous; **b** whiffy, smelly.

odorously, adv. Prec. & **-ly**. Fragrantly, with an agreeable scent or smell.

odorousness, n. See prec. & **-ness**. State, quality, of being odorous; fragrance.

odour, n. [1. ódur; 2. óudə], fr. A.-Fr. *odour*, fr. Lat. *odōr-(em)*, *odōr*, 'scent, smell', cogn. w. Gk. *ózein*, 'to smell'; *odmḗ*, 'scent'; Lith. *údžiu*, 'I smell'. **1.** A smell, scent, whether pleasing or unpleasing; perfume, fragrance. **2.** (fig.) A suspicion, atmosphere, smack, savour: *an odour of trickery in the business.* **3.** Reputation: *to be in good, bad, odour.* Phrs. *the odour of sanctity*, a reputation for holiness: *to die in the odour of sanctity*, from the legend that the bodies of saints gave forth a fragrant perfume when dying, or on exhumation, as proof of their sanctity.

odourless, adj. [1. ódurles; 2. óudəlis]. **odour** & **-less**. Without odour, scentless.

odyl, n. [1. ódil; 2. ódil]. **od (I.)** & Gk. *hū́lē*, 'matter, material' (see **-yl**). Same as **od (I.)**.

Odyssey, n. [1. ódisi; 2. ɔ́disi], fr. Lat. *Odyssea*, fr. Gk. *Odússeia*, fr. *Odusseús*, 'Ulysses'. **1.** (Gk. liter., cap.) The second of the Homeric epics, treating of the adventurous wanderings and return home of Odysseus (Ulysses) after the siege of Troy. **2.** Any long, adventurous wanderings or travels.

oecist, n. [1. ésist; 2. ísist], fr. Gk. *oikistḗs*, 'settler', fr. *oikízein*, 'to settle', fr. *oîkos*, 'house, dwelling'. See first element of **economy**. (Gk. hist.) The founder of a colony.

oecology, ecology, n. [1. ēkóloji; 2. ikɔ́lədži], fr. Gk. *oiko(s)*, 'house', see **economy**, & **-logy**. (biol.) That branch of science which treats of plants and animals in relation to the environment in which they live.

oecumenical, adj. See **ecumenical**.

oedema, edema, n. [1. ēdḗma; 2. idímə]. Gk. *oidḗma, oidḗmat-(os)*, 'a swelling', fr. *oideín*, 'to swell', cogn. w. O.H.G. *eitar*, O.E. *ātor*, 'poison'; O.H.G. *eiz*, 'abscess'; Lat. *aemidus*, 'swelling'. (pathol.) A swelling in a portion of connective tissue caused by an excess of serous or watery fluid; a local dropsy.

oedematous, adj. [1. ēdḗmatus; 2. idímətəs]. See prec. & **-ous**. Of, pertaining to, an oedema; swollen, dropsical.

Oedipus complex, n. [1. édipus kòmpleks; 2. ídipəs kɔ̀mpleks], fr. Gk. *Oidípous*, lit. 'swollen foot', of the Greek myth, who solved the riddle of the Sphinx &, in ignorance, slew his father & married his mother, Jocasta. A term in psycho-analysis for a complex arising from the relations and conflict of a child with its parents.

oeil-de-boeuf, n. [1. ȳy de bḗf; 2. øj də bøf]. Fr., 'bull's eye'. (archit.) A round or oval window.

o'er, adv. & prep. [1. ōr; 2. ɔ̄]. Poet. abbr. of **over**.

oesophageal, adj. [1. ēsòfajḗal; 2. isɔ̀fədžíəl]. Next word & **-al**. Of, pertaining to, the oesophagus or gullet.

oesophagus, esophagus, n. [1. ēsófagus; 2. isɔ́fəgəs]. L. Lat., fr. Gk. *oisophágos*, 'the gullet'; etymol. of first element doubtful; for ending see **-phagous**. (anat.) That part of the alimentary canal which leads from the mouth to the stomach; the gullet.

oestrus, n. [1. éstrus; 2. ístrəs]. Lat., fr. Gk. *oîstros*, 'gadfly; sting; frenzy'; cogn. w. Lat. *īra*, 'anger'. See **ire**. A vehement, overwhelming desire; frenzy; sexual excitement in animals.

of, prep., stressed form [1. ov; 2. ɔv], unstressed [1. uv; 2. əv]. O.E. *of*, prob. unstressed form of **af*; cogn. w. O.S. *af*, O.H.G. *aba*, Mod. Germ. *ab*; O.N. *af*, cp. Lat. *ab*, Gk. *apó*, Scrt. *apa*, 'away'. O.E. *of* had various meanings: (1) motion away from: *of stōwe tō stōwe*, 'from place to place'; (2) from a given point of time: *of þissum forþ*, 'henceforth'; (3) expressing source, origin: *þā menn of Lundenbyriġ*, 'the men of (belonging to) London'; (4) indicating material 'out of which' something is made: *wyrċan mannan of eorþan*, 'to make man *out of* earth'; (5) expressing causal relation, 'on account of': *him stent eġe of þē*, 'he has fear *of* (on account of) thee'; (6) in partitive sense, 'some of': *of þæs trēowes wæstme*, 'of the fruit of the tree'; (7) expressing change: *of Lædene on Engliśc*, 'from, out of, Latin into English'; (8) expressing deprivation, 'out of': *of dēofles anwealde*, 'out of the power of the Devil'; (9) 'concerning, about': *sǣdon him fela spella of hira lande*, 'they told him many stories about their country'. See Sweet's Anglo-Saxon Dictionary. In Mod. Engl. *of* has very various shades of meaning, many of wh. may be deduced fr. ancient usage, as seen in the above examples. In many instances *from* has taken its place. Other mod. meanings are due to the influence of Fr. *de*, of wh. the chief instance is the use of *of* to express the possessive relation, e.g. *the house of my father*, as alternative to *my father's house*, w. the old genit. ending. It was further used to translate Lat. *ab* & *ex*. Generally speaking, *of* expressed relationship between a n. & another n. or adj., & in many cases has, in combination w. the following n., an attrib. or adjectival force; thus *the History of England* is English History; *a coat of many colours*, a many-coloured coat &c.; *man of sense*, sensible man. **1.** Expressing origin, source: *a man of royal descent, of humble origin; born of good stock.* **2.** Distance, position in space: *within ten miles of; south of.* **3.** Equivalent of adverbial genitive expressing time (now rather archaic): *a nap of an afternoon; can't sleep of a night.* **4.** Relief from: *rid of one's cold; cured of bronchitis.* **5.** Deprivation: *robbed of one's purse; loss of power* &c.; *to cheat a man of £5*, also after *deprive, defraud.* **6.** Possession, belonging to (equivalent of old genitive case in *-s*): *the Tower of London; end of the train; top of the house.* **7.** In respect of: *nimble of foot, quick of eye.* **8.** Forming adjectival phrase, indicating possession of certain attributes: *a man of ability*, able man; *a woman of no importance*, unimportant woman &c. **9.** Concerning, about: *tell me of your sorrows; a long story of adventures.* **10.** Expressing the material from, or out of which, a thing is made: *a dress of silk, wreath of flowers, houses of stone; a bowl of silver gilt; a cake of wheaten flour.* **11.** Expressing measure: *a foot of ground; a pint, a glass, of wine; a yard of cloth; ton of coal* &c. **12.** Expressing partitive sense: *some of that bread; none of the cake; a piece of meat.* **13.** Expressing causal relations: *to die of fright; afraid of dogs; sick of the palsy.* **14.** Expressing the agent: *the work of an enemy; tempted of the Devil; the deeds of Achilles.*

of-, pref. Form of Lat. *ob* in compounds whose second element begins w. *f-*. See **ob-**.

off (I.), adv. [1. awf, of; 2. ɔ̄f, ɔf]. Variant of **of**, orig. differentiated fr. it in pronunciation in stressed positions; not dist. fr. *of* in spelling before 14th cent., & then hardly in meaning. Away, away from, from. **1.** (with vbs.) **a** (with intrans. vbs. of movement, or w. *be*) Separation, departure, from, to, a distance: *run, fly, off; get off with you!; be off!; off you go!; I must be off; where are you off to?; off to the wars;* **b** as contrasted with *on*: *to get, fall, off (a horse* &c.); *keep off (the grass* &c.); **c** (with trans. vbs.) away, at a distance: *to ward off an attack; to put off*, postpone, delay; **d** contrasted with *on*: *to take off one's clothes, hat* &c.; **e** expressing separation from: *bite, cut, tear, off*; interruption from: *to cut, turn, off the gas, water* &c.; *to be cut off on the telephone*; **f** with various verbs in certain of their idiomatic senses for which see particular words; e.g. *buy, drop, go, palm, show, stand, take, off* &c. **2.** (of position in space or time) At a distance, away: *five miles off; only three months off.* **3.** Indicating completion of action: *to finish off, polish off.* Phr. *off and on*, now off and now on, now and again, occasionally, intermittently, irregularly.

off (II.), adj., fr. prec. **1.** Removed, separated, **a** from a main direction or line: *an off road;* **b** from a main or larger object: *his hat was off; the wheel is off.* **2.** Contrasted with *near*, on the right-hand side of the driver of a vehicle, rider or leader of a horse: *the off-hind wheel, leg; the off side of the road.* **3.** (cricket) Towards, from, on, that side of the field facing the batsman as he stands to play, contrasted with *on* or *leg side*: *an off break*, a ball that breaks back or in from the off side; *the off stump, an off drive* &c. **4.** Remote, distant, unlikely, improbable: *an off chance.* **5.** Implying postponement, intermission: *an off season; an off day*, one not occupied by business. **6.** Not fresh; not up to the mark: *the fish is a bit off*; not fit or well: *I am feeling rather off today.*

off (III.), prep., fr. **off (I.)**. From, away from; contrasted with *on*. (of position) *Off the road; off the roof; the wheel was off the car.* Phrs. *off one's head*, out of one's mind, crazy; *off one's feed*, having no appetite; *off duty*, free from duty; *off the mark*, (i.) (of a shot), not coming near object aimed at; (ii.) beside the point, irrelevant.

off (IV.), n., fr. **off (II.)**. (cricket) The offside.

offal, n. [1. ófal; 2. ɔ́fəl]. **off** & **fall**. Cp. Dan. *afval*, Germ. *abfall*. That which is discarded as useless; waste parts, refuse; specif. **a** the entrails of a slaughtered animal; **b** small fish, not large enough for food; **c** the bran, husks &c. of cereals, not suitable for flour &c.

offcast, adj. & n. [1. áwfkahst; 2. ɔ́fkāst]. **off** & **cast**. **1.** adj. Cast off, rejected, disowned. **2.** n. Person or thing cast off, disowned.

offence, n. [1. oféns; 2. əféns]. M.E., fr. O. Fr. *offens, offense*, fr. Lat. *offensus, offensum, offensa*, 'a striking against, shock; offence', fr. Lat. *offensa*, n., 'an offending, offence', fr. P.P. of *offendere*, 'to offend'. See **offend**. **1.** A wrong-doing, a breach of law, of rules, of good conduct &c.; misdemeanour, transgression: *an offence against good manners, decency* &c. **2.** **a** That which offends one's feelings; an affront, insult; **b** the feeling of being offended; wounded self-respect, resentment felt at a slight, real or supposed; umbrage: *to cause, give, offence; to take offence*, to be offended; *just cause of offence; without offence.* **3.** (mil.) Act of attacking; attack; the offensive; contrasted with *defence*: *weapons of offence*; *offence should be the rule in war.* **4.** (Bib.) That which causes another to offend, an occasion of transgression, stumbling-block: *rock of offence.*

offenceless, adj. [1. oféns*les*; 2. əfénsl*i*s]. Prec. & **-less.** Without offence; not offending or giving offence; inoffensive; innocent.

offend, vb. intrans. & trans. [1. ofénd; 2. əfénd]. M.E. *offenden*, fr. Lat. *offendere*, 'to strike against, to stumble; to hurt, injure', **of**, 'against', & **fendere*, 'to strike', only in composition. See **defend. A.** intrans. **1.** To commit an offence, be guilty of wrong-doing: *in what have I offended?* **2.** *Offend against*; **a** to transgress, infringe: *to offend against custom, law, good manners* &c.; **b** to transgress the laws of: *to offend against God.* **B.** trans. **1.** **a** (of physical effect) To be offensive to, annoy, displease, disgust: *these hideous houses offend the eye*; *some music offends, rather than pleases, the ear*; **b** (of moral effect) to outrage, do violence to: *to offend one's sense of justice, of propriety* &c. **2.** To wound the feelings of, give offence, cause resentment to: *I am deeply offended by his conduct.* **3.** (Bib.) To cause to offend, lead astray, be a stumbling-block to: '*if thy right eye offend thee*' (Matt. v. 29); '*whosoever shall offend one of these little ones*' (Mk. ix. 42).

offendedly, adv. [1. oféndedli; 2. əféndidl*i*]. *Offended*, P.P. of **offend**, & **-ly.** As though offended.

offender, n. [1. ofénder; 2. əféndə]. **offend** & **-er.** One who offends; specif., one who commits an offence against the law; a criminal, a delinquent: *first offender*; *juvenile offender.*

offending, adj. & vbl. n. [1. ofénding; 2. əfénd-iŋ]. **offend** & **-ing. 1.** adj. **a** Causing offence; **b** guilty of, committing, an offence. **2.** n. An offence.

offensive (I.), adj. [1. ofénsiv; 2. əfénsiv]. See **offence** & **-ive. 1.** **a** Causing offence, repulsion, disgust, to the senses; repellent, disgusting, loathsome: *an offensive sight, smell, sound* &c.; **b** provoking moral indignation, exciting resentment; insolent, insulting: *an offensive person, offensive manners, language* &c. **2.** Belonging to, used in, suitable for, attack; contrasted with *defensive*: *an offensive war, offensive weapons*; *offensive strategy, tactics.*

offensive (II.), n., fr. prec. Aggression, act of attacking, offensive action: *to act on, take, the offensive*; *the offensive is the safest defence in war.*

offensively, adv. **offensive** (I.) & **-ly.** In an offensive manner.

offensiveness, n. See prec. & **-ness.** State, quality, of being offensive.

offer (I.), vb. trans. & intrans. [1. ófer, áwfer; 2. ɔ́fə, ɔ̄fə]. O.E. *offrian*, 'to offer to God', M.E. *offren*, fr. Lat. *offerre*, 'to bring before, present, offer', fr. **of-** & *ferre*, 'to bring', see **-ferous** & **bear** (I.); the development of meaning has been influenced by Fr. *offrir.* **A.** trans. **1.** To present as an offering or sacrifice, in worship, honour, or supplication to God, to any deity, or to a revered person, or superior: *to offer prayers, homage*; also *offer up*, present (prayers, sacrifices) to God; *to offer up as a sacrifice.* **2.** To present for acceptance or refusal; to proffer, tender: *to offer assistance, help, a bribe*; *to offer an apology*; *to offer battle*; *to offer advice, an opinion*; *to offer to help*; Phr. *to offer one's hand*, (i.) to hold it out, as though to shake hands with a person; (ii.) to make a proposal of marriage to a lady. **3.** **a** To present for sale at a price: *to offer a house for £1000*; **b** to bid as a price for: *to offer £1000 for a house.* **4.** To make a show of, exhibit signs of intending to use: *to offer resistance, violence.* **B.** intrans. To present itself, to occur: *as occasion offers.*

offer (II.), n. See prec. **1.** Statement embodying a proposal, or expression of willingness, to do something; esp. an expression of willingness to afford help of some kind, to give something, or to confer a favour: *a kind offer*; *an offer of support, of food, of money*; also *an offer to help, to pay for* &c.; also *an offer of marriage*, proposal. **2.** Indication of willingness to pay a certain price for something, of readiness to purchase something for a specified sum; a bid: *an offer of £500 for a cottage*; *I am open to an offer*; *no reasonable offer refused*; also the actual sum offered: *you must make me a better, larger, offer.* **3.** Physical act of tendering, proffering, presenting, something for acceptance: *I ignored the offer of his hand.*

offering, n. [1. ófering, áw-; 2. ɔ́f(ə)riŋ, ɔ̄f-]. O.E. *offrung*, 'sacrifice, oblation to God'. **offer** (I.) & **-ing. 1.** Act of offering or presenting. **2.** Thing offered; **a** specif., something offered to God, dedicated to a cause &c.; a sacrifice, oblation: *a free-will, peace, thank-offering*; *Easter offering*, sum of money collected and presented to the incumbent of a parish at Easter; **b** something tendered for acceptance; a gift, a present: *I bring you a small offering for your birthday.*

offertory, n. [1. óferturi; 2. ɔ́fət(ə)ri], fr. L. Eccles. Lat. *offertōrium*, 'place at which offerings were made', fr. Low Lat. *offert-(um)*, P.P. of *offerre.* See **offer** (I.). **1.** Specif. (cap.) **a** that part of the Eucharistic service, during which a collection of alms is made, including sentences spoken by the priest, antiphon which is sung, and the prayer in which the alms and the unconsecrated elements are offered to God; **b** the alms taken on this occasion. **2.** Popularly, any collection of alms made during, or at the end of, a religious service in a church.

offhand, adj. [1. áwfhand; 2. ɔ̄fhænd], **offhand**, adv. [1. àwfhánd; 2. ɔ̄fhǽnd]. **off** & **-hand. 1.** adj. **a** Without preparation or previous study or thought; extempore, impromptu: *make a few offhand observations*; **b** rude, curt, casual, unceremonious: *an offhand manner.* **2.** adv. In an offhand way or manner: *to translate, speak, act &c. offhand.*

offhanded, adj. [1. àwfhánded; 2. ɔ̄fhǽndid]. Prec. & **-ed.** Offhand.

offhandedly, adv. Prec. & **-ly.** In an offhand manner.

offhandedness, n. See prec. & **-ness.** Offhand manner, behaviour.

office, n. [1. ófis; 2. ɔ́fis]. O. Fr., fr. Lat. *officium*, 'that which is done for another, performance of a service; ceremony; duty, function; business'; for the second element see **-fic**; origin of first element is doubtful; prob. = *opi-* fr. *opus*, 'work, labour, effort'. See **opus. 1.** That which is performed or done, that which it is necessary to do; a duty, service, task; function, purpose, assistance, services: *the eye ceases its office*; *the office of host* &c.; *good offices.* **2.** A position or appointment involving special duties or offices; position of authority or trust: *ministerial, judicial, office*; *office of Inspector of Nuisances* &c.; *to take, hold, resign, office.* Phr. *offices of profit*, technical term for certain paid ministerial appointments, acceptance of which by a member of Parliament entails resignation of his seat and re-election. **3.** **a** A public or state department, a ministry, including its collective powers and functions and all the members of its staff: *War Office, Foreign, Colonial*, and *Home Office, Office of Works* &c., but, in ordinary usage, *Admiralty, Board of Trade, Ministry of Health*; *the Holy Office*, the Inquisition; **b** house, set of apartments, building, in which the business of a state department is conducted. **4.** (often in pl.) The place, rooms &c. where the clerical, financial, and administrative work, as distinct from the productive side or the actual handling of goods, in a commercial business, is carried on: *a lawyer's, architect's, office*; *cashier's office*; *registered offices of a company*; *a post, telegraph, office*; *booking, lost property, office* &c.; Phr. (*my son is*) *in an office*, in business, esp. as a clerk; *the, one's, office*, place of business; the business itself. **5.** (pl.) *offices*, collection of rooms, buildings &c., where the domestic work of a house is carried on, together with lavatories &c.: *the usual domestic offices* &c. **6.** A business institution, company, now only regularly used of Insurance Companies: *Fire, Life, Office* &c. **7.** **a** A ceremony, rite, religious service: *to perform the last offices* (for a dead person); **b** a specific, prescribed religious service: *Divine Office*, as the Roman Breviary, or Matins, and Evensong &c. in Anglican Church: *to say one's Office*, to recite the Divine Office; *Office for the Dead*, the special funeral service; *the Office of the Mass.* **8.** (slang) Information, hint, tip: *to give one, take, the office.*

office-bearer, n. A holder, occupant, of an office or post.

office-boy, n. Boy or youth employed to do odd jobs in an office, esp. that of a commercial firm, to clean the rooms, take messages &c.

office-copy, n. An official, certified, copy of a document.

office-holder, n. An office-bearer.

officer (I.), n. [1. ófiser; 2. ɔ́fisə]. M.E. *officere*, fr. Fr. *officier*, fr. L. Lat. *officiārius*, 'one who holds an *officium* or office'. See **office. 1.** One who holds an office or position of authority, trust, or service: *the great officers of state*; *a police officer*, constable; *medical officer of health* &c.; *officer of the court*, a bailiff. **2.** Specif. **a** one who holds His Majesty's commission in the army or navy, as distinguished from *a private* (*soldier*) or from a *non-commissioned, petty*, or *warrant officer*; *officer of the day*, the commissioned officer in a battalion &c., who is on duty on a particular day and is responsible for supervision of the barracks, guard duties, prisoners &c.; *officer in waiting*, the officer of the day in a Guards' regiment; **b** the master or captain or any of the mates of a merchant vessel: *first, second &c. officer*, first, second, mate.

officer (II.), vb. trans., fr. prec. (usually in pass.) **1.** To provide with officers. **2.** To act as officer to, to command: *the regiment was well officered.*

official (I.), adj. [1. ofíshal; 2. əfíʃəl]. O. Fr., Mod. *officiel*, fr. Lat. *officiālis*, 'official'. See **office** & **-al. 1.** **a** Relating to, connected with, an office or position of trust or authority: *official duties, responsibilities* &c.; *official position*; **b** employed in a public office, holding official position: *official receiver, referee* &c. **2.** Issued by one holding an office, emanating from an official authority, authorized: *official statements*; *coming from an official source*; *that report is not official.* **3.** Suited to, befitting, a position of authority &c., characteristic of, usual to, holders of office; formal: *an official manner*; *official reply*; *official circumlocution.* **4.** (pharm.) Officinal, according to, accepted by, the medical profession, contained in the pharmacopoeia: *official drugs, prescriptions.*

official (II.), n., fr. prec. **1.** A person who holds a public office; person in authority or in a position of trust: *public officials.* **2.** (eccles.) Officer appointed to act as judge in an Ecclesiastical Court, usually styled *official principal.*

officialdom, n. [1. ofíshaldum; 2. əfíʃəldəm]. Prec. & **-dom. 1.** The body of public or state officials. **2.** (in unfavourable sense) Characteristic point of view and behaviour of officials; officialism.

officialism, n. [1. ofíshalizm; 2. əfíʃəlizəm]. **official** (I.) & **-ism.** Official system, formality; excessive attention to official routine and regulations; bumbledom, red-tape.

officialize, vb. trans. [1. ofíshalīz; 2. əfíʃəlaiz]. **official** (I.) & **-ize.** To make, render, official; to subject to official routine and control; to manage by officials.

officially, adv. [1. ofíshali; 2. əfíʃəli]. **official** (I.) & **-ly.** In an official manner; formally; with official authority.

officiant, n. [1. ofíshiant; 2. əfíʃiənt], fr. Med. Lat. *officiant-(em)*, Pres. Part. of *officiāre*. See **officiate**. An officiating priest or minister.

officiary, adj. [1. ofíshiari; 2. əfíʃiəri], fr. L. Lat. *officiārius*. See **officer**. Derived from an office or the tenure of an office: *officiary titles*, as *Your Worship* for a mayor &c.

officiate, vb. intrans. [1. ofíshiāt; 2. əfíʃieit]. Med. Lat. *officiāt-(um)*, P.P. type of *officiāre*, 'to perform the Divine office'. See **office**. **1.** To perform, discharge, duty of, to act (as), preside (at): *to officiate as chairman* (at a meeting), *as host* (at a dinner &c.). **2.** Specif., to conduct Divine service, discharge priestly duties: *to officiate at a marriage*.

officinal, adj. [1. ofísinəl, òfisínal; 2. əfísinəl, ɔ̀fisáinəl], fr. Med. Lat. *officīnālis*, 'of or belonging to a workshop', fr. Lat. *officīna*, 'workshop', for **opificīna*, fr. *opifex*, 'workman'. See **office** & **-ine** & **-al**. (pharm.) **1.** Kept in stock and sold by a chemist or druggist (of drugs, medicines &c.). **2.** Used in medicine. **3.** Authorized by the pharmacopoeia, now replaced by *official*.

officious, adj. [1. ofíshus; 2. əfíʃəs], fr. Lat. *officiōsus*, 'complaisant, obliging', fr. *officium*, 'service, favour'. See **office** & **-ous**. **1.** (archaic or obs.) Obliging, friendly. **2.** Interfering, meddlesome; offering services, advice &c. where they are neither invited nor required. **3.** (diplomacy) Unofficial, informal, not necessarily binding; as contrasted with *official*: *an officious statement*; *in an officious capacity*.

officiously, adv. Prec. & **-ly**. In an officious, meddlesome manner.

officiousness, n. See prec. & **-ness**. State, quality, of being officious; meddlesomeness, interference.

offing, n. [1. áwf-, ófing; 2. ɔ́f-, ɔ́fiŋ]. **off** & **-ing**. (naut.) The sea as far out as can be seen from land; chiefly in Phr. *in the offing*, (i.) not far from shore; (ii.) (fig.) near, in the neighbourhood; ready or likely to appear, or take part &c.

offish, adj. [1. áwfish; 2. ɔ́fiʃ]. **off** & **-ish**. (colloq.) Inclined to be distant or aloof in manner; stand-off.

offishness, n. Prec. & **-ness**. Distance, aloofness, frigidity, of manner.

off-licence, n. [1. áwf lìsens; 2. ɔ́f làisəns]. **off** & **licence**. A licence **a** to a publican to sell intoxicating liquor for consumption off, or away from, his premises; **b** to a shopkeeper to sell such liquor only for consumption off the premises.

offprint, n. [1. áwfprint; 2. ɔ́fprint]. **off** & **print**; translation of Mod. Germ. *abdruck* in same sense. A separately issued copy of an article published in a journal &c.; a pull.

offreckoning, n. [1. àwfrékuning; 2. ɔ̀frékəniŋ]. **off** & **reckon** & **-ing**. (pl.) A deduction from the pay of soldiers or sailors formerly made to meet certain expenses.

offscourings, n. pl. [1. áwfskòuringz; 2. ɔ́f-skàuəriŋz]. **off** & **scour** & **-ing**. **a** Dirt, filth, refuse, which is scoured or cleaned off anything; **b** (fig.) dregs, rabble, scum.

offset (I.), n. [1. áwfset; 2. ɔ́fset]. **off** & **set**, cp. **set-off**. **1.** That which springs from, or sets, starts off from something else; branch, offshoot, spur. **2.** That which sets off, balances, compensates for, something else; a set-off. **3.** (building) **a** A ledge in a wall formed by the wall above it being made thinner than the wall beneath; **b** a bend in a lead pipe or gutter to carry it round a corner or past a projection. **4.** (print.) An impression from newly printed sheet on to the back of one placed above it. **5.** (surv.) The measurement of a short distance at right angles from the main line taken in measuring an irregularly shaped area.

offset (II.), vb. trans. **1.** To set off, balance, compensate for. **2.** To make an offset, as in a wall, pipe, or in printing.

offshoot, n. [1. áwfshoot; 2. ɔ́fʃūt]. **off** & **shoot**. **1.** A small shoot or branch from the main stem of a plant; an offset. **2.** A lateral branch or spur of a mountain. **3.** A collateral descendant; branch of a family.

off-shore, adj. [1. áwf shōr; 2. ɔ́f ʃɔ̄]. **1.** Moving, coming, from or off the shore: *an off-shore breeze*. **2.** At a distance from the shore: *off-shore fishery*.

offside, adj. [1. àwfsíd; 2. ɔ̀fsáid]. (football or hockey) Of a player in a position on the field where, under penalty, he may not kick, handle, or hit the ball, because he is in front of the last player who touched it (Rugby), or, being in front, has only a certain number of opponents, two usually, between him and their goal (Association and hockey).

offspring, n. [1. áwfspring; 2. ɔ́fspriŋ]. O.E. *ofspring*, fr. *of*, 'off', & *springan*, 'to spring'. See **off** & **spring** (**I.**). **1.** A child or children; progeny, issue, descendants. **2.** (fig.) Product, result.

oft, adv. [1. awft, oft; 2. ɔ̄ft, ɔft]. O.E. *oft*, Common Gmc.; O.H.G. *ofto*, Goth. *ufta*, O.N. *oft*; ultimate origin unknown. **1.** (archaic or poet.) Often: *many a time and oft*. **2.** (in composition) *Oft told, oft recurring, oft repeated* &c.

often, adv. [1. áwf(e)n, óf(e)n; 2. ɔ̄f(ə)n, ɔ́f(ə)n]; sham-refined, vulg. [1. áwften, óften; 2. ɔ̄ftən, ɔ́ftən]. M.E. *ofte*; *often* before vowels. See prec. (N.B.—Queen Elizabeth spells *offen*.) **1.** Frequently, many times, repeatedly. **2.** (as adj., archaic) Frequent: *often times*, frequently, often.

ogam, n. See **ogham**.

ogee, n. [1. ōjḗ; 2. oudžī́]. Variant of **ogive**. **1.** A moulding having section in form of S, that is, with a double curvature, one part convex, the other concave. **2.** *Ogee arch*, pointed arch formed of two ogee curves meeting at the top.

ogham, ogam, n. [1. ógam; 2. ɔ́gəm]. O. Ir. *ogum*, Mod. Ir. *ogham*, supposed to have been invented by a legendary *Ogma*. **1.** Ancient British and Irish form of writing, having 20 letters, which are formed of strokes in groups of 1 to 5, drawn in relation to a transverse line, and made above, below, or passing right through it; these characters are also found cut on rectangular stones, the edge of which serves as the line. **2.** (attrib.) Written in, characteristic of, ogham.

og(h)amic, adj. [1. ogámik; 2. əgǽmik]. Prec. & **-ic**. Written in ogham characters.

ogival, adj. [1. ōjívl; 2. oudžáivl]. **ogive** & **-al**. Of, pertaining to, an ogive; characterized by having ogives.

ogive, n. [1. ṓjīv; 2. óudžaiv]. Fr.; O. Fr. *augive*, 'pointed arch, double-curved arch'; etymol. doubtful. (archit.) **a** The diagonal rib of a vault; **b** a pointed or Gothic arch (a French architectural term).

ogle, vb. intrans. & trans. & n. [1. ṓgl; 2. óugl]. Prob. fr. L.G. *oegeln*, *ogelen*, 'to ogle', freq. of *oegen*, 'to look at', fr. *oege*, 'eye'; cogn. w. **eye**. **1.** vb. **a** intrans. To keep looking about with intense, meaning glances, as though with longing, or coquettishness; to make eyes; **b** trans., to look at meaningly, and as though with amorous or coquettish intent; to make eyes at. **2.** n. A covert, amorous, coquettish glance.

ogler, n. [1. ṓgler; 2. óuglə]. Prec. & **-er**. One who ogles.

ogpu, n. [1. ógpōō; 2. ɔ́gpū]. Russ., fr. the initial letters of the phrase *Obedinennoe Gosudarstvennoe Politicheskoe Upravlenie* (Unified State Political Directorate). The secret bureau with its police agents which deals with political offences in Soviet Russia, formerly known as the Cheka, q.v.

ogre, n. [1. ṓger; 2. óugə]. Fr., etymol. doubtful; first used by Perrault in his fairy stories, 1697, & in Engl. in 1713, spelt *hogre*, in a translation of a Fr. version of the 'Arabian Nights'; possibly through Span. *huerco*, fr. Ital. *orco*, Lat. *Orcus*, the God of the dead, or of the underworld. **a** A monster, giant, in a fairy-tale who devours human flesh; **b** a hideous, coarse, or cruel man.

ogreish, adj. [1. ṓgerish; 2. óugəriʃ]. Prec. & **-ish**. Like an ogre.

ogress, n. [1. ṓgres; 2. óugris]. **ogre** & **-ess**. A female ogre.

Ogygian, adj. [1. ogíjian; 2. əgídžiən], fr. Gk. *Ogúgios*, 'of Ogyges'. **a** Of or belonging to Ogyges, an ancient, mythical king of Attica; **b** primeval, very ancient, prehistoric.

oh. See **O**.

ohm, n. [1. ōm; 2. oum], fr. G. S. Ohm, German physicist (d. 1854). (elect.) The unit of electrical resistance.

ohmic, adj. [1. ṓmik; 2. óumik]. Prec. & **-ic**. Of, relating to, an ohm; measured in ohms: *ohmic resistance*.

ohmmeter, n. [1. ṓmeter; 2. óumitə]. See prec. & **-meter**. An instrument for measuring electrical resistance.

oho, interj. [1. ōhṓ; 2. ouhóu]. **O** & **ho**!. An exclamation of surprise.

oh yes. See **oyez**.

-oid, suff. [1. oid; 2. ɔid], fr. Gk. suff. *-oeidēs*, *-o-* & *-eidēs*, 'like', fr. *eidos*, 'shape, form', fr. base **(e)id-*, as in *idein*, 'to see'. See **idea**, **idol**, & cp. **-ode** (**I.**). A suff. used to form ns. & adjs. indicating resemblance; like, in the form or shape of: *rhomboid*, *asteroid*; *anthropoid* &c.; fr. ns. in *-oid*, adjs. are formed with **-al**, as *rhomboidal*.

oil (**I.**), n. [1. oil; 2. ɔil], fr. O. Fr. *oile*, fr. Lat. *oleum*, fr. Gk. *élaion*, 'olive oil', fr. *elaia*, 'the olive tree'. See **olive**. **1. a** A general term applied to a large group of greasy, fatty, inflammable substances which are insoluble in water but soluble in ether or alcohol, and remain fluid at certain temperatures; classified according to their source of origin into *animal*, *vegetable*, or *mineral oils*, and, according to behaviour under heat, as *fixed*, or *volatile*, *oils*; of the former those that are solid at a temperature of 68° F. are fats or waxes; of the latter, the mineral oils are used as illuminants &c., and the vegetable (*essential*) oils in medicine, perfumery &c.; **b** any one of these substances, generally identified by the name of its source: *olive oil*, *palm oil*, *whale oil*, *oil of almonds* &c. *Holy oil*, the oil used in extreme unction for anointing the dying; *oil of consecration*, the oil used in the coronation service for anointing the sovereign. Phrs. *to burn the midnight oil*, to work late at night; *to pour oil on troubled waters*, to soothe, pacify, angry feelings, to arrange differences by tactful words &c.; *to strike oil*, (lit.) to discover a source of mineral oil; (fig.) to make a valuable discovery; to get rich suddenly or quickly; *to throw oil on the flames*, to make quarrels, anger, worse by incitement. **2. a** One of various substances having consistency of oil: *oil of vitriol*; **b** (usually pl.) oil-colours: *painted in oil(s)*; **c** (pl.) oilskins.

oil (**II.**), vb. trans., fr. prec. To cover, smear, impregnate, with oil; to lubricate with oil or other lubricants. Phrs. *to oil one's tongue*, speak flatteringly; *to oil a palm*, bribe; *to oil the wheels*, to make things work smoothly and easily by tactful handling.

oil-beetle, n. One of several beetles with a swollen body which emit an oily substance when alarmed.

oil-bird, n. A South American bird, allied to the nightjars, the guacharo, from which an oily fat is extracted, which the natives use as butter.

oil-box, n. A small receptacle attached to a wheel for holding lubricating oil.

oilcake, n. [1. óilkāk; 2. ɔ́ilkeik]. Food for cattle made from crushed linseed, cotton, rape, and other oil-containing seeds.

oil-can, n. A can for holding oil, esp. lubricating oil.

oilcloth, n. [1. óilklawth; 2. ɔ́ilklɔ̄þ]. For *oiled cloth*. A floor or table covering made of specially prepared tough, coarse canvas, thickly coated, usually on both sides, with oil-paint, and printed with a pattern; a special form is called linoleum.

oil-colour, n., usually pl. Paint in which oil is used as a medium for mixing the pigment.

oil engine, n. Internal-combustion engine driven by vaporized oil.

oiler, n. [1. óiler; 2. ɔ́ilə]. **oil (I.) & -er. a** An oil-can; **b** a greaser in an engine-room of a steamship; **c** a ship built for carrying oil.

oil-field, n. Area rich in mineral oil.

oil-fuel, n. Oil used to drive an oil engine.

oil-gauge, n. Instrument for measuring the density of oils.

oilily, adv. [1. óilili; 2. ɔ́ilili]. **oily & -ly. a** Like, resembling, oil; **b** in an oily manner; unctuously.

oiliness, n. [1. óilines; 2. ɔ́ilinis]. **oily & -ness. a** State, quality, of being oily; **b** (fig.) unctuousness of manner.

oilman, n. [1. óilman; 2. ɔ́ilmən]. One who deals in and sells oils and oil-colours.

oil-painting, n. **1.** The art of painting in oil-colours. **2.** Picture painted in oils.

oil-palm, n. A West African palm, the fruit and nuts of which yield palm-oil.

oil-press, n. A press or mill for extracting vegetable oils by pressure.

oil-silk, n. For *oiled silk*. Oiled silk, used as an air- and water-tight covering to maintain heat and moisture &c.

oilskin, n. [1. óilskin; 2. ɔ́ilskin]. **a** Cloth made waterproof by dressing with oil; **b** (pl.) coat and trousers made of oilskin.

oilstone, n. [1. óilstōn; 2. ɔ́ilstoun]. A whetstone dressed with oil.

oil-well, n. A shaft sunk in an oil-field for the extraction of mineral oils.

oily, adj. [1. óili; 2. ɔ́ili]. **oil (I.) & -y. 1.** a Having consistency or appearance of oil; **b** covered with, impregnated with, oil. **2.** (fig.) Unctuous, obsequious; plausible, insinuating.

ointment, n. [1. óintment; 2. ɔ́intmənt]. M.E. *oinement, oynement*, fr. O. Fr. *oignement*, fr. Lat. *unguentum*. See **unctuous & unguent & -ment.** An oily substance or compound, applied externally to heal wounds, soreness &c., or as a cosmetic; an unguent.

Oireachtas, n. [1. éraghthas; 2. íərəχþæs]. Ir. The Irish Free State legislature, consisting of the Crown and the two Houses, *Dail Eireann*, Chamber of Deputies, and *Seanad Eireann*, Senate.

okapi, n. [1. ōkáhpi; 2. oukápi]. Native African name. (zool.) A ruminant of Central Africa, allied to the giraffes, but with a short neck; the legs are strongly marked with black and white stripes, and the males have short horns.

okra, n. [1. ókra, ṓkra; 2. ɔ́krə, óukrə]. African native name. A plant cultivated in the Southern United States and in the West Indies for its seed-pods, which are used as a vegetable.

-ol, suff. [1. ol; 2. ɔl], **a** fr. *(alcoh)ol*, indicating substances belonging to the alcohol series, as *glycerol*; **b** fr. Lat. *ol(eum)*, 'oil', as *benzol*.

old (I.), adj. [1. ōld; 2. ould]. O.E. *āld* (W.S. *ēald*); M.E. *ōld*; O.S. *ald*; O.H.G. *alt*; Goth. *alþeis*; the base is found also in Goth. *alan*, 'to grow up'; O.N. *ala*, & Lat. *alere*, 'to nourish', & also in Lat. *adultus*; the ultimate meaning is 'nourished, grown up'. See **aliment, adolescence, adult. 1.** (of living things) **a** Having lived a long time; aged, advanced in years; not young nor middle-aged; elderly: *old people*; *an old horse, oak* &c.; *to grow old*; Phrs., *an old bachelor*; an unmarried man, often applied irrespective of age; *the old man*, (i.) (colloq.) one's father or husband, head of a household; (ii.) the skipper of a ship; (iii.) the head of a business; the master, boss; (iv.) (theol.) also *the old Adam*, human nature, as unregenerate; *old woman*, (i.) (colloq., slang) one's wife; (ii.) a fussy, nervous, elderly man; *old maid*, (i.) an elderly spinster; (ii.) a prim, nervous elderly man; (iii.) a simple, childish game of cards; *the Old Man of the Mountain*, the founder of the sect of the Assassins; *the Old Man of the Sea* (from Sindbad the Sailor in the 'Arabian Nights'), an incubus, some person or thing that one cannot get rid of; *the Old Lady of Threadneedle Street*, the Bank of England; **b** having the characteristics of one who has lived a long time; worn out, withered, exhausted, feeble &c.: *an old face, voice*; *a pair of old eyes*; *beginning to look old*; Phr. *(to have) an old head on young shoulders*, to be very wise for one's years; **c** having lived a certain number of years: *how old is he?*; *sixteen years old*; *three years old*; **d** (colloq.) as form of affectionate or familiar address: *my dear old fellow*; *good old So-and-so.* **2.** Belonging to a former age; connected with, dating from, a period before the present time; **a** having been a long time in existence, ancient: *old countries*; *an old house*; *an old family*; *an old wine*; **b** having existed in the past: *old civilizations*; *the old laws of our ancestors*; **c** created, composed, constructed, in a former age: *our old literature*; *old church music*; **d** having lived, flourished, been active, in a former age: *the old writers of drama*; *the old poets* &c.; Phr. *old masters*, (i.) painters of earlier times; (ii.) the pictures by these men; **e** (of mode of computing time) *Old Style, Old Calendar*, that given up in England and America in 1752 in favour of the *New Style*, the difference between the two being then eleven days, which we dropped; **f** connected with, based on, a dispensation and ordinance which has been superseded by a later or *new* dispensation: *Old Testament*, the first of the two main divisions of the canonical books of the Bible; **g** having been in use for a long time; worn out, becoming shabby: *an old hat*; *old boots, clothes* &c.; *old-clothes man*, dealer in second-hand clothes; **h** having formerly belonged as a member to a specified profession, body, institution &c., though now retired, occupying a different status &c.: *an old soldier*; *an old 52nd man*; *an old Wykehamist*, former member of Winchester College; *an old boy*, former pupil of a specified school; **i** familiar from time past, associated with what one has previously known: *old friends*; *the old familiar faces*; *one's old habits and customs*; *the old country*, the home or mother country; **j** experienced, long-practised: *an old offender*; *an old hand at the game*; *old in vice*; **k** (slang, colloq.) as an intensive expression: *a rare old time*; *kicked up a jolly old row.* **3.** Applied to the earliest recorded forms of languages; *Old English*, Anglo-Saxon, English down to about 1100; contrasted with Middle English; *Old High German*; *Old French* &c.

old (II.), n., fr. prec. Old people: *the old*; *old and young alike dance nowadays*. Phrs. *of old*, formerly, in times past: *in days of old*, belonging to past or former times: *our fathers of old*.

old age, n. The latter period, esp. of human life, during which all the natural powers gradually decline; reckoned as beginning at the age of sixty.

Old Catholic, n. **1.** One of a party in Church of Rome which repudiated allegiance to the Pope upon the promulgation of the doctrine of Papal Infallibility as *de fide* by the Vatican Council in 1870; it is now an independent church. **2.** (attrib.) *Old Catholic Party.*

olden (I.), adj. [1. ṓlden; 2. óuldən]. **old (I.) & -en.** Ancient, antique; of past times: *in the olden days*; *in olden times*.

olden (II.), vb. trans. & intrans. **old (I.) & -en**, vbl. suff. **a** trans. (very rare) To render old; **b** intrans., to grow old.

old-fashioned, adj. [1. ṓld fáshund; 2. òuld fǽʃənd]. Formed according to, following, adhering to, old fashions or customs; out of date, obsolete, antiquated.

Old Glory, n. The Stars and Stripes.

Old Guard, n. **1.** Napoleon I.'s Imperial Guard, raised in 1804, and so called in distinction from the *Young Guard*, raised in 1810. **2.** Any group of persons of fixed, conservative opinions; die-hards.

oldish, adj. [1. ṓldish; 2. óuldiʃ]. **old (I.) & -ish.** Rather, tending to be or become, old.

old-maidish, adj. [1. ṓld mádish; 2. òuld méidiʃ]. Like an old maid; characteristic of an old maid; fidgety, over-nice, pernickety, prudish.

old man's beard, n. The wild clematis.

oldster, n. [1. ṓldster; 2. óuldstə]. **old (I.) & -ster.** (colloq.) An old person, as contrasted with *youngster*.

old-time, adj. Belonging to the past or to the old times: *old-time customs*.

old-womanish, adj. [1. ṓld wóomanish; 2. òuld wúməniʃ]. (of men) Like an old woman in habits and temperament; fussy, nervous; tending to attach undue importance to trifles.

Old World (I.), n. The Eastern hemisphere, the European, Asiatic world and its civilization &c., as distinct from the *New World*, the Western hemisphere, the American world.

old-world (II.), adj. **1.** Old, ancient, belonging to former days: *an old-world garden*; *old-world courtesy.* **2.** Of or pertaining to the Western hemisphere, European or Asiatic.

oleaginous, adj. [1. ṑleájinus; 2. òuliǽdžinəs], fr. Lat. *oleāginus*, 'of, containing, olive oil', fr. *olea*, 'the olive'. See **olive**; cp. Fr. *oléagineux*. Oily, greasy; unctuous (in physical and fig. senses).

oleander, n. [1. ṑleánder; 2. òuliǽndə], fr. Fr. *oléandre*, 'the rose-bay', cp. Ital. *oleandro*; Med. Lat. *oleandrum*, also L. Lat. *lorandrum*; etymol. unknown. The rose-bay, an evergreen Mediterranean shrub with bright-red funnel-shaped, clustered flowers; the leaves and flowers are poisonous.

oleaster, n. [1. ṑleáster; 2. òuliǽstə]. Lat., 'the wild olive', fr. *olea*, 'olive tree', & **-aster. 1.** (bot.) A small S. European shrub with yellow flowers and olive-like fruit. **2.** The wild olive.

oleo-, pref. [1. ṓleō; 2. óuliou], fr. Lat. *oleum*, 'oil'. See **oil & olive.**

oleograph, n. [1. ṓleōgrahf; 2. óuliougrāf]. **oleo- & -graph.** A kind of chromolithograph made to look like an oil-painting.

oleo-margarine, n. **oleo- & margarine.** An artificial butter made by mixing oleo-oil with vegetable oils and milk.

oleometer, n. [1. ṑleómeter; 2. òuliɔ́mitə]. **oleo- & -meter.** An instrument for measuring the density of oils.

oleo-oil, n. Oil obtained from animal fats by pressure.

oleo-resin, n. **oleo- & resin.** A compound of an essential, volatile oil and a resin.

olfaction, n. [1. olfákshun; 2. ɔlfǽkʃən]. See next word & **-ion.** (rare) The sense of smell.

olfactory, adj. & n. [1. olfákturi; 2. ɔlfǽktəri], fr. Lat. *olfact-(um)*, P.P. type of *olfacere*, *olefacere*, 'to cause to smell; to smell', fr. *ol-ēre*, 'to smell', fr. **od-*, as in Lat. *odor*, see **odour**, & *fac-*, 'to make, do', see **fact**, & **-ory. 1.** adj. Pertaining to the sense of smell: *olfactory organs, nerve* &c. **2.** n. (usually pl.) Olfactory organs.

olibanum, n. [1. olíbanum; 2. ɔlíbənəm]. L. Lat., prob. as Gk. *líbanos*, fr. Arab. *al-luban*, 'frankincense'. A fragrant gum resin used in incense; frankincense.

olid, adj. [1. ólid; 2. ɔ́lid], fr. Lat. *olidus*, fr. *olēre*, 'to smell'. See **olfactory.** (archaic) Rank, stinking.

oligarch, n. [1. óligark; 2. ɔ́ligāk], fr. Gk. *oligárkhēs*. See **oligo- & arch-.** A member of an oligarchy.

oligarchic(al), adj. [1. òligárkik(l); 2. ɔ̀ligákik(l)]. Prec. & **-ic (& -al).** Of, pertaining to, an oligarch or oligarchy.

oligarchy, n. [1. óligarki; 2. ɔ́ligāki], fr. Gk. *oligarkhia*. See **oligarch & -y. a** Rule, government, by a few persons; state so governed or ruled; **b** persons ruling in such a state; the oligarchs.

oligo-, pref., fr. Gk. *olígos*, 'few, little, small'; the base is a reduced form of that seen in Gk. *loigós*, 'ruin, destruction, death; pestilence'; cp. also Lith. *ligà*, 'illness'; an extension of base **lei-*, **loi-*, **li-*, as in Lat. *lētum*, 'death, destruction' (see **lethal**); Gk. *loimós*, 'pest'; *līmós*, 'hunger'. See further under **left (I.)**, **delete, loathe.** The force of pref. is 'few' or 'small'.

oligocarpous, adj. [1. óligŏkárpus; 2. ɔ̀ligoukā́pəs]. See **oligo-**, **carpel**, & **-ous**. (bot.) Having few carpels or fruits.

oligocene, adj. [1. óligŏsēn; 2. ɔ́ligousīn]. See **oligo-** & second element of **eocene**. (geol.) Of, relating to, a Tertiary period between the Eocene and Miocene: *Oligocene period, system* &c.

olio, n. [1. ólio; 2. ɔ́liou]. For *olia*, Engl. spelling of native pronunciation of Span. *olla*, 'earthen pot', fr. Lat. *olla*, 'pot', as in **olla podrida**. **1.** An olla podrida. **2.** A medley, miscellany, hodge-podge, as of verses, literary pieces &c.

oliphant, n. [1. ólifant; 2. ɔ́lifənt]. O. Fr. *olifant*, 'ivory'. See **elephant**. (archaic) **1.** An elephant. **2.** A mediaeval hunting or battle horn, made of ivory.

olivaceous, adj. [1. òlivā́shus; 2. ɔ̀livéiʃəs]. See **olive** & **-aceous**. **a** Resembling the olive; **b** of the colour of the olive; olive-green.

olivary, adj. [1. ólivari; 2. ɔ́livəri]. Lat. *olīvār-(ius)*. See next word & **-ary**. (anat.) Shaped like an olive; oval; connected with, relating to, the *olivary body*, an oval protuberance on the *medulla oblongata* or lowest part of the brain.

olive (I.), n. [1. óliv; 2. ɔ́liv]. Fr., fr. Lat. *olīva*, 'olive tree, olive', also *olea*, fr. Gk. *elaía*, 'the olive tree'; the tree was introduced to Italy by the Greeks; connected w. *oleum*. See **oil**. **1. a** (bot.) An evergreen tree, belonging to the genus *Olea*, usually applied to *Olea europaea*, wild or cultivated, a native of the Mediterranean coast; the leaves are oblong, greyish green with silvery underside, the fruit is an oval drupe, and the flowers grow in small white panicles: *a crown, wreath, of wild olive*, given as a prize to the victors in the games in ancient Greece; **b** the fruit of the cultivated olive, yellowish green in colour when unripe and so pickled in brine as a relish, usually purplish black when ripe, and yielding by pressure *olive oil*; **c** the wood of the olive tree. **2.** Thin slice of meat rolled and stuffed with chopped olives and other seasoning: (usually in pl.) *beef, veal, olives*. **3.** An oval button or fastening. **4.** Olive colour.

olive (II.), adj., fr. prec. Of the colour of the unripe fruit of the olive, varying from a pale yellowish green to a brownish yellow: *olive brown*, greenish brown; *olive green*, brownish green.

olive branch, n. **1.** A branch of the olive with its leaves, the symbol of peace in ancient Greece. Phr. *to hold out the olive branch*, to make overtures for peace. **2.** (usually pl., fig., often facet.) Children, offspring; often in pl., fr. Ps. cxxviii. 4 (Prayer Book).

olive oil, n. A clear, pale yellow, non-drying oil obtained by pressure from the ripe fruit of the cultivated olive tree, used in cookery, salads, as a medicine, as a lubricant, and in the manufacture of toilet soap &c.

Oliver (I.), n. [1. óliver; 2. ɔ́livə], fr. Fr. *Olivier*. (cap.) One of Charlemagne's peers, a friend of **Roland**.

oliver (II.), n. Etymol. unknown. A small tilt-hammer used by blacksmiths or other metal workers, worked by a treadle.

olive shell, n. A gastropod mollusc of the tropics, with a highly polished oval shell.

olivet, n. [1. ólivet; 2. ɔ́livɛt]. Fr. *olivette*. **olive** & **-et**. A small oval-shaped imitation pearl.

olive wood, n. A hard, close-grained, yellowish-green wood, from the olive tree, delicately variegated and taking a high polish, used in ornamental carpentry.

olivine, n. [1. ólivēn; 2. ɔ́livīn]. Fr. **olive** & **-ine**. (mineral.) Chrysolite of an olive-green colour, a semi-precious stone, used in jewellery; also called *peridot*.

olla podrida, n. [1. ólya podrḗda; 2. ɔ́ljə pədrī́də]. Span., lit. 'rotten pot', cp. **olio**; second element cogn. w. **putrid**. **1.** A favourite Spanish dish consisting of various meats, cut up, mixed with vegetables, and stewed in an earthen pot. **2.** A miscellany, medley, hotchpotch; an olio, q.v.

ology, n. [1. óloji; 2. ɔ́lədži]. Abstracted fr. *geology, biology* &c. (humorous or colloq., usually pl.) The arts and sciences; branches of learning: *a smattering of all the ologies*.

Olympiad, n. [1. ōlímpiad; 2. oulímpiæd], fr. Lat. *Olympiad-(em), Olympias*, fr. Gk. *Olumpiád-(os), Olumpiás*. See **Olympic**. (Gk. antiq.) A period of four years, reckoned inclusively from one celebration of the Olympic games to another, and so used by Greek chronologists and historians in dating events, beginning from 776 B.C., the first year of the first Olympiad.

Olympian (I.), adj. [1. ōlímpian; 2. oulímpiən]. L. Lat. *Olympiān-(us)*, 'belonging to Olympus or Olympia'. **1.** Of, pertaining to, Olympus, the fabled dwelling-place of the greater ancient gods of Greece: *Olympian gods, Olympian Zeus* &c. **2. a** Befitting the Olympian gods; lofty, magnificent, stately: *an Olympian nod*; **b** (ironical) affecting magnificent aloofness of bearing; condescending as from an infinite height of superiority. **3.** Of, pertaining to, Olympia; Olympic, q.v.

Olympian (II.), n., fr. prec. **1.** A dweller on Olympus, one of the great gods of ancient Greece. **2.** A stately, awe-inspiring person; one himself famous and belonging to an august assembly.

Olympic, adj. [1. ōlímpik; 2. oulímpik]. Lat. *Olympicus*, fr. Gk. *Olumpikós*, 'of, pertaining to, Olympia'. Of, pertaining to, Olympia, a plain in Elis, ancient Greece, so called from the festival held there every four years in honour of Olympian Zeus, at which prizes in games, poetry, and music were awarded to competitors from the whole of Greece, a general peace being proclaimed. *Olympic Games*, **a** contests in various athletic exercises, chariot, horse-racing &c. held at the Olympic festival; **b** a modern revival of these for international competitors begun in 1900 at Athens.

Olympus, n. [1. ōlímpus; 2. oulímpəs]. Lat., fr. Gk. *Olumpos*. (cap.) **1.** The name of many mountains in ancient European and Asiatic Greece, esp. of a lofty mountain in Thessaly, which was fabled to be the dwelling-place of the greater gods. **2.** A celestial abode; heaven.

om, interj. [1. om; 2. ɔm]. Scrt. A mystic monosyllable equivalent to *Amen*, used in Hindu and Buddhist worship.

-oma, suff. [1. óma; 2. óumə], fr. Gk. *-ōma, -ōmatos*, as termination of neut. ns.; used in pathol. to indicate a diseased condition: *glaucoma* &c.

omadhaun, n. [1. ómadhawn; 2. ɔ́məðɔ̄n]. Ir. *amadán*. A fool, idiot, simpleton; a stupid, awkward lout, an oaf.

omasum, n. [1. ōmā́sum; 2. ouméisəm]. Lat. *omāsum*, 'bullock's tripe'; origin obscure. (anat., zool.) The third stomach of a ruminant animal.

ombre, n. [1. ómber; 2. ɔ́mbə]. Span., fr. *juego del hombre*, lit. 'the man's game', *hombre*, 'man', fr. Lat. *homin-i*, dat. of *homo*, 'man'. See **homage** & **human**. An old game of cards, played by three persons, fashionable in 17th and 18th cents.

ombro-, pref., fr. Gk. *ómbros*, 'rain'; cogn. w. Gk. *aphrós*, 'foam'; Lat. *imber*, 'shower of rain'; Scrt. *abhrám*, 'cloud, mist', see **imbricate**; the full form of the base was **enebh-*, whence Lat. *nebula*, see **nebula**.

ombrograph, n. [1. ómbrograhf; 2. ɔ́mbrəgrāf]. Prec. & **-graph**. A rain-gauge, which automatically records the amount of rain fallen.

ombrology, n. [1. ombróloji; 2. ɔmbrɔ́lədži]. **ombro-** & **-logy**. That branch of meteorology which deals with rain and rainfall.

ombrometer, n. [1. ombrómeter; 2. ɔmbrɔ́mitə]. See prec. & **-meter**. A rain-gauge.

omega, n. [1. ómega, ōméga; 2. óumegə, ouméga]. Gk. *ō méga*, 'the great, long *ō*'. The last letter of the Greek alphabet = *ō*; the end or conclusion: *alpha and omega*, the beginning and the end.

omelette, omelet, n. [1. ómlet; 2. ɔ́mlit]. Fr. *omelette*, earlier *aumelette, amelette*, for earlier *alemette*, fr. *alemelle*, 'thin knife blade, thin plate', prob. for *lamelle*, by wrong division of the article, fr. Lat. *lāmella*, 'thin plate of metal', dimin. of *lāmina*, 'plate'. See **laminate**. Eggs beaten up and fried, and served with various flavourings: *savoury omelette*, with chopped herbs; *sweet omelette*, with jam &c. Phr. *you cannot make omelettes without breaking eggs* (translation of a French phrase), you cannot do anything without taking trouble or making some sacrifice.

omen (I.), n. [1. ómen; 2. óumen]. Lat. *ōmen*, earlier *osmen*; etymol. doubtful; of the various suggestions Walde prefers that wh. assumes early **ovis-men*, & connects the word w. Gk. *oíomai*, fr. **owisjomai*, 'believe'. An occurrence which indicates that something is about to happen; a portent, warning, of things to come; augury: *of good, bad, omen*, foretelling good or bad news.

omen (II.), vb. trans., fr. prec. (poet. or rhet.) To foreshow, portend, to give warning of: *the clouds omen rain*; *ill-omened*, having bad omens, inauspicious.

omental, adj. [1. ōméntal; 2. ouméntəl]. See next word & **-al**. Of, relating to, the omentum.

omentum, n., pl. **omenta** [1. ōméntum, -ta; 2. ouméntəm, -tə]. Lat., 'membrane which encloses the bowels'; origin obscure. (anat.) The fatty fold of the peritoneum enclosing the intestines &c., and connecting them with other viscera.

ominous, adj. [1. óminus, ṓminus; 2. ɔ́minəs, óuminəs]. Lat. *ōminōsus*. See **omen** (I.) & **-ous**. Full of omens, or forebodings; portentous, significant, usually of evil tidings or events.

ominously, adv. Prec. & **-ly**. With evil omens; in a way which portends ill.

ominousness, n. See prec. & **-ness**. Quality, fact, of being ominous.

omissible, adj. [1. ōmísibl; 2. oumísibl], fr. Lat. *omiss-(um)*, P.P. type of *omittere*, 'to omit'. See **omit** & **-ible**. Capable of being omitted; to be left out if necessary or required.

omission, n. [1. ōmíshun; 2. oumíʃən], fr. Lat. *omissiōn-(em), omiss-*, as prec. See **omit** & **-ion**. The act of omitting, of leaving out, or undone; that which is omitted; neglect, failure to do something required; non-performance, non-inclusion or insertion.

omissive, adj. [1. ōmísiv; 2. oumísiv]. See prec. & **-ive**. Omitting, failing to perform or include.

omit, vb. trans. [1. ōmít; 2. oumít], fr. Lat. *omittere* for *ob mittere*, **ob-** & *mittere*, 'to let go, send', see **mission**. **1.** To neglect, fail, to do or perform; to leave undone: *to omit doing* or *to do*. **2.** To leave out, fail to include: *this part of the book may be omitted*.

omni-, pref. Combining form fr. Lat. *omnis*, 'all, every'; etymol. doubtful. A few unsatisfactory suggestions have been made; e.g. that *omnis* is for earlier **obnis*, fr. **ob-**, w. development of meaning unexplained; or that the word is cogn. w. Lat. *ops*, 'wealth' (see **opulent**), involving difficulties both in form & in meaning. As first element of a compound, indicates that the action, or existence expressed by the second, affects all things, everything; is present in all places; is performed for all.

omnibus, n. & adj. [1. ómnibus; 2. ɔ́mnibəs], pl. **omnibuses**; abbr. *bus*, q.v. Lat., 'for all people, for everyone', dat. pl. of Lat. *omnis* (see prec.); name first used in France for a public vehicle, c. 1828, & adopted by Shillibeer for the first London omnibus, 1829. **1.** n. **a** Large, wheeled, closed vehicle, with seats inside and often outside, licensed to ply for hire on specified routes for the conveyance of passengers; formerly drawn by horses, now usually driven by a motor engine; **b** somewhat similar, but smaller, vehicle belonging to a hotel, or to a private person, for the conveyance of passengers and luggage to and from a railway, hotel &c. **2.** adj. Used for, embracing, a variety of purposes, persons, items &c.; inclusive; *omnibus bar*, one of the principal bars or conductors carrying an electric current; *omnibus bill, clause, proposal*, one which includes various measures &c.; *omnibus box*, a box at an opera house or theatre which has room for a large number of persons.

omnicompetent, adj. [1. òmnikómpetent; 2. ɔmnikɔ́mpitənt]. **omni- & competent.** (law) Having competence or jurisdiction in every matter.

omnifarious, adj. [1. òmnifárius; 2. ɔmniféəriəs]. Lat. *omnifārius*, 'of all sorts and kinds', **omni-** & *-fārius*, cp. *fās*, 'utterance; law'; fr. base *fā-*, 'to speak'. See **fable, fame.** Treating of, concerned with, all sorts of subjects: *omnifarious knowledge, reading* &c.

omniparity, n. [1. òmnipáriti; 2. ɔmnipǽriti]. **omni- & parity.** Parity in everything; equality in all things or for all.

omnipotence, n. [1. omnípotens; 2. ɔmnípətəns]. Fr., fr. L. Lat. *omnipotentia*. See next word & **-ce.** **a** State, quality, of being omnipotent; universal, infinite power; **b** the Almighty God.

omnipotent, adj. [1. omnípotent; 2. ɔmnípətənt], fr. Lat. *omnipotent-(em)*. See **omni- & potent (I.).** **1.** Able to do, having power and authority over, all things; all-powerful, almighty. **2.** (as n.) *The Omnipotent*, Almighty God.

omnipotently, adv. Prec. & **-ly.** In an omnipotent manner; all-powerfully.

omnipresence, adj. [1. òmniprézens; 2. ɔmniprézəns]. **omni- & presence.** State, quality, of being omnipresent; ubiquity.

omnipresent, adj. [1. òmniprézent; 2. ɔmniprézənt]. **omni- & present.** Present everywhere; present in all places at the same time, as God; ubiquitous.

omniscience, n. [1. omnísiens; 2. ɔmnísiəns]. **omni- & science.** Quality of being omniscient; infinite knowledge, as of God; universal knowledge.

omniscient, adj. [1. omnísi-, omníshent; 2. ɔmnísi-, ɔmníʃənt]. See prec. & **-ent.** **1.** Possessing infinite knowledge, all-knowing, as God; possessing or claiming to possess, universal or vast knowledge or learning. **2.** (as n.) *The Omniscient*, God.

omnisciently, adv. Prec. & **-ly.** In an omniscient manner; all-knowingly; with universal or very vast learning.

omnium, n. [1. ómnium; 2. ɔ́mniəm]. Lat., 'of all', genit. pl. of *omnis*, 'all'; see **omni-.** Sum total; esp. the aggregate value of different stocks in which a loan is funded.

omnium gatherum, n. [1. ómnium gádherum; 2. ɔ́mniəm gǽðərəm]. Humorously coined fr. prec. & *gathering*. A miscellaneous, haphazard collection, assembly, of things or persons.

omnivorous, adj. [1. omnívorus; 2. ɔmnívərəs], fr. Lat. *omnivorus*, 'all-devouring', fr. **omni-** & *-vorous*. See **voracious.** **1.** Eating everything; of animals which eat both animal and vegetable food; both carnivorous and herbivorous. **2.** (fig.) Assimilating everything: *omnivorous reader*.

omnivorously, adv. Prec. & **-ly.** (chiefly fig.) In an omnivorous manner; voraciously.

omo- (I.), pref., fr. Gk. *ōmos*, 'the shoulder'; cogn. w. Scrt. *ámsa-*, 'shoulder'; Lat. *umerus* (see **humerus**); Goth. *ams*, 'shoulder'.

omo- (II.), pref., fr. Gk. *ōmós*, 'raw'; Scrt. *āmáś*, 'uncooked; unripe'; cp. Lat. *amārus*, 'bitter'.

omophagia, n. [1. òmōfájia; 2. òumoufeídžiə]. Gk. **omo- (II.)** & base of *phágein*, 'to eat'. See **-phagous.** Habit of eating raw flesh.

omophagic, omophagous, adj. [1. òmōfájik, ōmófagus; 2. òumoufǽdžik, oumɔ́fəgəs]. Prec. & **-ic** or **-ous.** Eating raw flesh.

omoplate, n. [1. ómōplāt; 2. óumoupleit]. Gk. *ōmoplátē*, fr. **omo- (I.)** & *plátē*, 'blade', cp. **plate.** The shoulder-blade, scapula.

omphal(o)-, pref. fr. Gk. *omphalós*, 'the navel'; cogn. w. Lat. *umbilīcus*, 'navel', see **umbilicus**; O.E. *nafela*, see **navel**; Scrt. *nā̆bhiś*; O. Prussian *nabis*, 'navel'; the Aryan base would be *onobh-, *nŏbh- &c. *Omphalic*, of, relating to, the umbilicus or umbilical cord; *omphalitis*, inflammation of the umbilicus; *omphalocele*, umbilical hernia.

omphalus, n. [1. ómfalus; 2. ɔ́mfələs]. Gk. *omphalós*, same word as prec., secondary meaning, 'boss on a shield', from its shape. **1.** (Gk. antiq.) A round, circular object, as the boss on a shield; specif., the circular or conical altar at Delphi which marked the supposed centre or hub of the earth. **2.** (by transf.) A centre, hub.

on (I.), prep. [1. on; 2. ɔn]. O.E. *an, on*, expressing **a** position: in, among; **b** motion: into, onto; **c** time: during, in; **d** instrumentality: by means of, by; **e** composition: of; **f** hostility: against; **g** change into; M.E. *on*, O.S. *an*, O.H.G. & Goth. *ana*, O.N. *á(n)*, cogn. w. Gk. *aná*, see **ana-**; see also **a-.** **1.** (expressing position) Supported by, placed, lying upon, covering, another object; upon: *a carpet on the floor*; *his hat on his head*; *on the roof of the house*; *on the surface of the water*; *to fall on one's feet, knees* &c.; *turn on a pivot*; *hang a picture on the wall.* **2.** (after vbs.) Expressing motion; towards, and resting at, upon, a particular position or object: *hit him on the head*; *to lay one's hands on his head*; *to put one's boots on one's feet*; *to jump on the top of*; *throw it on the table.* **3.** Connected with, employed in: *on the town council*; *on duty*; *go on an errand*; *to be on the Stock Exchange.* **4.** Near to, close to, in the direction of, towards: *a house on the river*; *on the near side of the road*; *on your right hand.* **5.** As expressing the ground or reason for: *on no account*; *on his authority, guarantee* &c.; *on purpose.* **6.** Expressing or specifying time, or occasion, when, or at which, something takes place: *on Tuesday week*; *on reaching home*; *on thinking the matter over.* **7.** Concerning, relating to, about: *talk on many subjects*; *have doubts on the subject*; *write a book on Chaucer*; *congratulate you on a success.* **8.** Expressing manner, state, or condition: *on sale*; *on fire*; *on the cheap*; *on the quiet.*

on (II.), adv. See prec. Defining action of verbs; in such a position as to be in contact with, covering, supported by or in any state expressed by the preposition *on.* **1.** As contrasted with *off*: *to keep one's hat on*; *put your coat on.* **2.** (after vbs. of motion) Forward: *to move, go, press on.* **3.** Expressing continuance of action: *go on talking*; *play on*; *sleep on*; *and so on*, as before, *et cetera.* **4.** In course of performance, in being, functioning: *the new play, the battle, is now on*; *breakfast is on from 8 to 10*; *the light is full on*, burning, illuminating, at full power. Phrs. *on and off*, now and then, not continually; *on and on*, without stopping, continuously.

on (III.), adj., fr. prec. **1.** (cricket, contrasted with *off*) Towards, from or on that side of the field behind the batsman as he stands to play; leg: *the on side.* **2.** (slang) Slightly intoxicated: *a bit on.*

on (IV.), n., fr. prec. (cricket) The on or leg side of the field.

onager, n. [1. ónager; 2. ɔ́nəgə], learned Lat. pl. **onagri**, Lat., fr. Gk. *ónagros*, fr. *ónos*, 'ass' (an eastern loan-word, cp. **asinine**), & *ágrios*, 'wild' (fr. *agrós*, 'field', q.v. under **acre**). The Asiatic wild ass of Persia, Baluchistan &c., with a broad brown white-edged stripe along the back.

onanism, n. [1. ṓnanizm; 2. óunənizəm], fr. *Onan*, in Gen. xxxviii. 9, & **-ism.** Sin of Onan; self-abuse.

once (I.), adv. [1. wuns; 2. wans]. O.E. *ānes*, M.E. *ōnes*; advbl. genit., fr. *ān*, 'one'. See **one.** **1.** On a single occasion, on one occasion only: *he did, he read &c. it once*; *but once a year*; *once every day* &c. Phrs. *more than once*, several times; *once and again, once or twice, once in a way*, now and again, occasionally; rarely; *once for all*, once and once only, finally; *once bitten twice shy*, one learns wisdom by experience; *not once* (*has he kept his promises*, &c.), never. **2. a** At one time, formerly; on a certain occasion in the past: *I once went round the world*; *there once lived a man*; *I was very fond of him once*; Phr. *once upon a time*, on a certain occasion in the past; formerly; **b** at some time or other in the future: *I should like to see him once before I go*; Phrs. *once again, once more*, again, on another occasion; *at once*, immediately, without delay: *do it at once*; at the same time: *at once cold and hot*; *all at once*, (i.) suddenly; (ii.) all together, all at the same time.

once (II.), conj., fr. prec. (with ellipse of *if, when*) As soon as, whenever: *once you give him a chance, he'll bolt*; *once you hesitate you are lost.*

once (III.), n., fr. **once** (I.). One occasion, one time: *do it this once*; *for once.*

oncer, n. [1. wúnser; 2. wánsə]. **once & -er.** (colloq., facet.) One who does a thing, esp. something obligatory, once; specif., a Scottish Presbyterian who goes to church only once a year.

on-coming, adj. & n. [1. ón kuming; 2. ɔ́n kamiŋ]. **1.** adj. Coming on, approaching. **2.** n. An approach.

on dit, n. [1. on dē; 2. ɔ̃ dī]. Fr., 'it is said, they say'. A report, rumour; piece of news or gossip: *merely an on dit.*

ondograph, n. [1. óndograhf; 2. ɔ́ndəgrāf], fr. Fr. *onde*, Lat. *unda*, 'wave', see **undulate,** & **-graph.** (elect.) Instrument for recording variations in waves in alternating currents.

ondometer, n. [1. ondómeter; 2. ɔndɔ́mitə]. See prec. & **-meter.** (elect.) Wave-meter.

ondoyant, adj. [1. ondwahyahn; 2. ɔ̃dwajā̃]. Fr., Pres. Part. of *ondoyer*, 'to wave', fr. *onde*, Lat. *unda*, 'wave', see **undulate.** Wavy, of surface of materials such as glass, silk.

one (I.), adj. [1. wun; 2. wan]. O.E. *ān*, 'one'; M.E. *oon, ōn*; O.H.G. *ein*, O.S. *ēn*; Goth. *ains*; O.N. *einn*; cogn. w. Lat. *ūnus* for earlier *oinos*; cp. Gk. *oínē*, 'the ace', on dice. See also **a, an.** Such a spelling as *won(e)* &c. appears as early as the 15th cent., & implies a type similar to our own. The other type [ōn] survived into 17th cent., & still exists in **only, alone, atone.** **1. a** (of numerals) Of, pertaining to, the cardinal number denoting unity; counted by the first integer; of the number less than two; single: *worth one pound*; *one pair of boots*; *one idea in his head*; **b** (after other numerals) *forty-one*; *one and forty* &c.; **c** as equivalent to the ordinal number *first*: *book one, chapter one.* **2. a** Forming a single whole or unity; undivided: *though of different races they formed one people*; *with one accord*; *'my Father and I are one'.* Phrs. *to be made one*, be married; *it is all one* (*to me what you do* &c.), is indifferent; **b** denoting a single, but not clearly defined, person or thing; some, a certain: *one day I will pay you*; **c** expressing contrast, difference, or opposition: *from one end of the street to the other*; *if A said one thing, B was sure to say another*; **d** single, only: *the one thing needful*; *there is but one way to do it*; *no one man could do it.*

one (II.), n. See prec. **1.** (of numerals) **a** The first whole number or integer; a single unit: *the number one*; *scored twenty all in ones*; **b** the symbol denoting this, 1; **c** house, room, so numbered: *lives at No. 1 in Black Street*; Phrs. *number one*, oneself: *he always thought first of number one.* **2.** A particular, single, individual person or thing: *he is the one I mean*; *the great ones of the earth*; *one of the best appointments which could have been made*; *will meet you at one*, one o'clock; *one and six*, one shilling and sixpence. Phrs. *one Brown*, a person so called; *one and all*, everyone; *one another*, mutually, reciprocally; *one with another*, on the whole, generally.

one (III.), indef. pron. See prec. **1.** A certain person or thing: *one came running*; also in combination *anyone, everyone, someone, no one.* **2.** Impersonal use, equivalent to Fr. *on*, Germ.

man; any body, any person indefinitely, including the speaker: *one must observe the rules*; *if one wants a thing done, one had best do it oneself*; *one must admit*, it must be admitted. **3.** (affected and precious) Referring to the speaker, I: *one is rather busy just now*; *one is glad to have seen you*; *one was only too pleased to help*.

one-, pref. representing **one (I.)**, in combination w. adjs.

-one, suff. [1. ōn; 2. oun], fr. Gk. adj. suff. *-ōnē*; used in chemistry to indicate that the substance belongs to the *ketone* group, e.g. *acetone*.

one-eyed, adj. Having a single eye.

one-horse(d), adj. [1. wún hors(t); 2. wán hōs(t)]. Drawn by, adapted for, a single horse; of a single horse-power; (colloq.) of poor, indifferent quality: *a one-horse kind of show*.

one-idea'd, adj. Having a single idea, obsessed by one object or purpose.

oneiromancy, n. [1. ōnírōmànsi; 2. ounáiərouмǽnsi], fr. Gk. *óneiro(s)*, 'a dream', cognates of wh. appear to exist only in Armenian & Albanian & throw no light on origin, & **-mancy**; cp. Gk. *oneirómantis*, 'interpreter of dreams'. Divination, prophecy, by interpretation of dreams.

oneiromantic, adj. [1. ōnìrōmántik; 2. oundàiərouмǽntik]. See prec. & **-ic.** Of, pertaining to, oneiromancy.

oneness, n. [1. wúnnes; 2. wánnis]. **one (I.)** & **-ness.** State, quality, of being one; unity, union; singleness, singularity.

oner, n. [1. wúner; 2. wánə]. **one** & **-er.** (slang) Some person or thing that is out of the way, or is to be singled out for size or other special quality: *he's a oner at pitching a yarn*; *caught him a oner on the head*; *told a oner*, thumping lie.

onerous, adj. [1. ónerus; 2. ɔ́nərəs], fr. O. Fr. *onereus*, Mod. Fr. *onéreux*, fr. Lat. *onerōsus*, fr. *oner-*, stem of *onus*, 'burden, load'; etymol. doubtful; possibly cogn. w. Scrt. *ánaš*, 'waggon'. See **onus. 1.** Burdensome, troublesome. **2. a** Specif. (law) entailing legal obligations; **b** (Scots law) given for valuable consideration, as contrasted with *gratuitous*.

onerously, adv. Prec. & **-ly.** In an onerous manner.

onerousness, n. See prec. & **-ness.** State, quality, of being onerous.

oneself, pron. [1. wunsélf; 2. wansélf]. **one (III.)** & **self. 1.** Reflexive form of indefinite pronoun **one**: *to see oneself as others see one*; *to hurt oneself*. **2.** Emphatic form of indefinite *one*: *there are some things one can't do for oneself*, implying that others should do them.

one-sided, adj. **1.** Having only one side. **2.** Leaning, inclining, to one side; unequally balanced; lop-sided. **3.** (fig.) **a** Seeing, understanding, admitting, only one side in an argument, dispute, proposition &c.; prejudiced; **b** having a narrow range of knowledge, intellectual interests, accomplishments &c. **4. a** Taking into account, derived from, only one group of facts, to the exclusion of others; biassed: *a one-sided judgement*; **b** based on insufficient data, ignoring certain factors and considerations: *a one-sided argument*.

oneyer, n. [1. wúnyer; 2. wánjə]. **one** & **-yer.** Archaic variant of *oner*.

onfall, n. [1. ónfawl; 2. ɔ́nfɔ̄l]. An attack, assault.

ongoing(s), n., usually pl. [1. óngōing(z); 2. ɔ́ngouiŋ(z)]. **a** Proceedings, events; **b** strange or uncalled-for behaviour.

onion, n. [1. úniun; 2. ánjən], fr. Fr. *oignon*, fr. Lat. *ūniōn-(em)*, 'oneness, unity; a large pearl; country name for an onion', fr. *ūnus*, 'one', q.v. under **one**, & **-ion. a** A hardy bulbous plant, *Allium*, having in all its parts a characteristic and pungent taste and smell, cultivated for its edible bulb; **b** bulb of the onion plant, used as a vegetable, for pickling and, above all, as a flavouring in cookery. *Onion couch, grass*, or *twitch*, a variety of wild oat; *onion fly*, an insect whose larvae feed on and destroy onion bulbs.

on-licence, n. [1. ón lìsens; 2. ɔ́n làisəns]. A licence to a publican to sell intoxicating liquor to be consumed only on the premises.

onlooker, n. [1. ónlòoker; 2. ɔ́nlùkə]. A looker on; spectator.

only, adj., adv., & conj. [1. ónli; 2. óunli]. O.E. *ānlīc*, 'unique, single', fr. *ān*, see **one**, & *līc*, see **-like** & **-ly. 1.** adj. **a** Single, sole; alone in its class: *an only child*; *the only book on the subject*; (also pl.) all the persons or things in particular category: *they were the only people present*; *the only things that matter*; Phr. *one and only*, unique; **b** the best of its class, pre-eminent: *our only statesman*; '*motley's the only wear*'. **2.** adv. In one manner; in no other way, at no other time; solely, merely; exclusively: *I only did it for his benefit*; *I can only speak of what I know*; *it is only right that you should know*; Phrs. *only just* (as intens.): *only just in time*, barely, with a narrow margin; *only just got out of bed*, but now, just this moment &c.; *am only too pleased to*, very pleased; *if only* (expressing a fervent wish): *if only he would stop talking!* **3.** conj. Except (that), were it not (that): *I would do it with pleasure, only I am too busy!*

onomatopoeia, n. [1. ónomàtopḗa; 2. ɔ̀nəмǽtəpíə]. Lat., fr. Gk. *onomatopoiía*, fr. *onómat-(os)*, *ónoma*, 'name' (cogn. w. Lat. *nōmen*, see **name**), & *poieîn*, 'to make', see **poesy** & **poet. a** (philol.) The formation of words by imitation of natural sounds associated with the object named, as *bowwow*, a dog; *cuckoo* &c.; *buzz*, of bees; **b** a word so formed.

onomatopoeic(al), adj. [1. ónomàtopḗik(l); 2. ɔ̀nəмǽtəpí-ik(l)]. Prec. & **-ic** & **-al.** Of, pertaining to, of the nature of, onomatopoeia; imitative, echoic.

onomatopoeically, adv. Prec. & **-ly.** In an imitative way or manner.

onrush, n. [1. ónrush; 2. ɔ́nraʃ]. A strong, forward rush (of troops &c.); onward flow (of water &c.).

onset, n. [1. ónset; 2. ɔ́nsɛt], fr. Phr. 'to set on'. **1.** Attack, assault. **2.** Beginning, start.

onslaught, n. [1. ónslawt; 2. ɔ́nslɔ̄t]. Etymol. doubtful; prob. ad. fr. Du. *aanslag*, 'an attempt', cp. Germ. *anschlag*, 'stroke', fr. *an*, 'on', *schlag*, 'blow, stroke'. See this base under **slay**; the termination has been influenced by *slaughter*. An assault, onset; a vehement, furious attack, whether by physical action or in words.

onto-, pref. Combining form, fr. Gk. *óntos*, *ón*, 'being', part. of *eînai*, 'to be', cp. **esse**, signifying relation either w. a being or individual, or w. being or existence.

ontogenesis, n. [1. òntōjénesis; 2. ɔ̀ntoudžɛ́nisis]. Prec. & **genesis.** (biol.) Origin, evolution, development, of an individual organism; ontogeny; as contrasted with *phylogenesis*, which is concerned with a class or group.

ontogenetic, adj. [1. òntōjenétik; 2. ɔ̀ntoudžɛnétik]. **onto-** & **-genetic.** Of, pertaining to, ontogenesis.

ontogenetically, adv. [1. òntōjenétikali; 2. ɔ̀ntoudžɛnétikəli]. Prec. & **-al** & **-ly.** According to ontogenesis.

ontogeny, n. [1. ontójeni; 2. ɔntɔ́džɛni]. See **ontogenesis** & **-y.** Ontogenesis.

ontological, adj. [1. òntōlójikl; 2. ɔ̀ntoulɔ́džikl]. **onto-** & **-logical.** (philos.) Of, pertaining to, ontology or the metaphysical nature of being, or existence, as such: *ontological speculations, theories* &c.

ontologically, adv. Prec. & **-ly.** (philos.) By way, means, of ontology; in reference to the nature of being.

ontologism, n. [1. ontólojizm; 2. ɔntɔ́lədžizəm]. See **ontology** & **-ism.** (philos.) A system of metaphysics based on the nature of being, or existence, regarded abstractly or as such.

ontology, n. [1. ontóloji; 2. ɔntɔ́lədži]. **onto-** & **-logy.** (philos.) That branch of metaphysics which treats of the nature of being, or existence, regarded abstractly or as such.

onus, n., only in sing. [1. ónus; 2. óunəs]. Lat., 'burden, weight'; Scrt. *ánaš*, 'cart for carrying heavy weights'; Gk. *ánios*, 'burdensome'; perh. also Goth. *ans*, 'beam'. Cp. **onerous.** A burden; obligation, responsibility, charge; esp. (law) *onus probandi*, the burden of proof, the responsibility of proving a statement, charge &c., which lies on the person who made it.

onward, adj. [1. ónward; 2. ɔ́nwəd]. **on** & **-ward.** Moving towards the front, or in direction of specified object or aim; going forward, advancing: *onward movement*; *onward progress*.

onward(s), adv. [1. ónward(z); 2. ɔ́nwəd(z)]. **on** & **-ward**; **-s**, advbl. genit. **a** Forward, forwards; to the front; in an advanced position: *to move onward*; *to lie farther onward*; **b** (as command) go forward, advance!

onwardly, adv. Prec. & **-ly.** (rare) With an onward or forward movement.

onyx, n. [1. óniks, óniks; 2. óuniks, ɔ́niks]. Lat., fr. Gk. *ónux*, *ónukhos*, 'nail, claw; the onyx', the latter meaning coming fr. the resemblance in appearance to the finger-nail; cogn. w. Lat. *unguis*. See **ungual** & cp. **nail.** A variety of chalcedony or agate, with black and white streaks, used as a gem stone, for cameos &c.

oo-, pref. Form used in compounds fr. Gk. *ōión*, 'egg', cogn. w. Lat. *ōvum*, cp. **ovi-** & **ovo-** & see **ovum** & **egg**; used in bot. & zool. terms.

ooecium, n. [1. ōḗsium; 2. ouísiəm]. **oo-** & Gk. *oîkos*, 'house'. See first element in **economy.** (zool.) A pouch or sac in certain polyzoa which contains the ova.

oof, n. [1. o͞of; 2. ūf]. Abbr. of Yiddish (Germ.-Jew.) *ooftisch*, for Germ. *auf dem tische*, 'on the table' = money down. (vulg. slang) Money; *the oof-bird*, a wealthy person.

oofy, adj. [1. o͞ofi; 2. ūfi]. Prec. & **-y.** (slang) Having lots of money; rich.

oogamous, adj. [1. ōógamus; 2. ouɔ́gəməs]. **oo-** & **-gamous.** (biol.) Having reproductive cells differentiated by sex; heterogamous.

oogenesis, n. [1. òojénesis; 2. òuədžénisis]. **oo-** & **genesis.** (biol.) Formation of the ovum, preparatory to fertilization and development.

oolite, n. [1. ōolīt; 2. óuəlait], fr. Fr. *oolithe*, fr. **oo-** & Gk. *líthos*, 'stone', see **-lite. 1.** A granular form of limestone, consisting of small grains of carbonate of lime, closely cemented together and resembling in appearance the roe of fish. **2.** (geol., cap.) A series of fossil-bearing oolitic rocks, lying above the Lias in the Jurassic system.

oolitic, adj. [1. òolítik; 2. òuəlítik]. Prec. & **-ic.** Formed of oolite; belonging to the Oolite.

oological, adj. [1. ōolójikl; 2. òuəlɔ́džikl]. **oo-** & **-logical.** Of, pertaining to oology or birds' eggs: *an oological collection*.

oologist, n. [1. ōólojist; 2. ouɔ́lədžist]. See next word & **-ist.** A student of oology; a collector of birds' eggs.

oology, n. [1. ōóloji; 2. ouɔ́lədži]. **oo-** & **-logy.** Study of birds' eggs.

oolong, oulong, n. [1. o͞olóng; 2. ūlɔ́ŋ]. Chin. *wu-lung*, 'black dragon'. A variety of China tea.

-oon, suff. (strongly stressed), used in Engl. for Fr. suff. *-on*, or Ital. *-one*, as *balloon*, *dragoon*, *saloon* &c.; this being orig. fr. Lat. acc. *-ōn-(em)*, of ns. in *-o*.

oont, n. [1. oont; 2. unt]. (Anglo-Indian slang) Camel.

oosperm, n. [1. óospërm; 2. óuəspɜ̄m]. **oo-** & **sperm (I.).** (zool.) A fertilized ovum.

oospore, n. [1. óospōr; 2. óuəspɔ̄]. **oo-** & **spore.** (bot.) A fertilized spore.

ooze (I.), n. [1. o͞oz; 2. ūz]. O.E. *wōs*, 'sap, juice'; first meaning influenced by the unrelated *wāse*, 'mire, mud, dirt'. **1.** Liquid mud, slime, esp. in sea- or river-bottom. **2.** The liquor used in tanning leather.

ooze (II.), vb. intrans. & trans., fr. prec. **A.** intrans. **1.** To flow slowly out; to drip, percolate; to issue from or through a substance: *the water is oozing through my shoes*; *blood oozes from a wound.* **2.** *Ooze with,* to exude: *boots ooze with water*; *wound oozes with blood.* **3.** (fig.) **a** To leak out: *secrets began to ooze out*; **b** to ebb away: *his courage was rapidly oozing away.* **B.** trans. To give out by oozing: *boots ooze water*; *wound oozes blood.*

oozily, adv. [1. ōōzili; 2. úzili]. **oozy** & **-ly.** In an oozy manner.

ooziness, n. [1. ōōzines; 2. úzinis]. See next word & **-ness.** State, quality, of being oozy; sliminess, muddiness.

oozy, adj. [1. ōōzi; 2. úzi]. **ooze** (I.) & **-y.** Slimy, muddy; dripping with, exuding, moisture.

op-, pref. Variant of **ob-**, used before *-p-*.

opacity, n. [1. ōpásiti; 2. oupǽsiti], fr. Fr. *opacité*, fr. Lat. *opācitāt-(em)*, 'darkness'. See **opaque** & **-ity.** State, quality, of being opaque; reverse of transparency or translucency; **a** obscurity, darkness; **b** (fig.) obscurity, dullness, of mind; obscurity of meaning.

opah, n. [1. ṓpah; 2. óupā]. Native W. Afr. name. A large marine fish of brilliant colours, *Lampris*, of the Atlantic Ocean; also called king-fish, moon- or sun-fish.

opal, n. [1. ṓpl; 2. óupl], fr. Fr. *opale*, fr. Lat. *opalus*, Gk. *opállios*, cogn. w. Scrt. *upala*, 'stone; gem stone'. **1.** A gem stone, consisting of silica containing a percentage of water; characterized by iridescent colours, the *common opal* having a pearly or milk-white appearance; the *fire opal* being darker and having flame-coloured iridescence. **2.** Opaline or opal-glass.

opalescence, n. [1. ōpalésens; 2. òupəlésəns]. Prec. & **-escence.** State, quality, of being opalescent; iridescence.

opalescent, adj. [1. ōpalésent; 2. òupəlésənt]. See prec. & **-escent.** Having the appearance of the opal; iridescent; reflecting a pearly light shot with different colours.

opaline, n. & adj. [1. ṓpalīn; 2. óupəlain]. **opal** & **-ine.** **1.** n. A kind of semi-translucent, opalescent glass; opal-glass. **2.** adj. Opalescent.

opalize, vb. trans. [1. ṓpalīz; 2. óupəlaiz]. **opal** & **-ize.** To make opalescent.

opaque, adj. [1. ōpā́k; 2. oupéik]. Earlier *opake*, also *opacous*, fr. Lat. *opācus*, 'shady, dark'; etymol. unknown; present form fr. Fr. **1.** Not allowing light to pass through, not transparent or translucent; impervious to rays of light. **2.** Dark, obscure; stupid, dense.

opaquely, adv. Prec. & **-ly.** In opaque fashion; obscurely, darkly.

opaqueness, n. See prec. & **-ness.** State, quality, of being opaque; opacity; darkness, obscurity.

ope, adj., vb. trans. & intrans. [1. ōp; 2. oup]. Shortened form of **open.** (poet.) **a** adj. Open: '*a casement ope at night*' (Keats, 'Ode to Psyche'); **b** vb., to open.

open (I.), adj. [1. ṓpen; 2. óupən]. O.E. & M.E. *open*; Common Gmc.; O.S. *opan*, O.H.G. *offan*, O.N. *opinn*; cp. Du. *aaben*, Germ. *offen*; cogn. w. **up**; the orig. sense is 'lifted, raised up', as the lid of a box or latch of a door. **1. a** Not shut or closed; in state which permits entrance or exit: *an open door, window*; *open box, drawer* &c.; *with open eyes, mouth*; *to throw, leave, a door &c. open*; Phrs. *to keep one's eyes or ears open,* to be watchful and alert; *to keep one's mouth open,* to be greedy; **b** specif. (phon.) *an open consonant,* one produced without complete closure of air-passage, e.g. [s, z, f, v, þ, ð] &c.; contrasted with *stop(ped) consonant*; **c** not enclosed or fenced in: *the open country*; *an open road*; *open fields*; *open-field system* (see below); **d** not barred or blocked: *the open sea,* not closed in by land, contrasted with a bay or harbour; *an open river,* not barred by ice; *the enemy had left this line of advance open*; **e** not covered in or over: *an open boat, carriage, motor-car*; *open drain, sewer*; *in the open air,* out of doors; *open string,* one of the strings of violin &c. when played without pressure by the finger; **f** unfolded, spread out, expanded, extended: *an open flower*; *with open wings*; *an open book*; (also fig.) *his mind was an open book,* to be read by all; *open order,* (of troops) extended order. Phrs. *with open hand,* generously, liberally; *(to welcome) with open arms,* cordially, affectionately, enthusiastically; **g** not healed over: *an open wound*; Phr. *an open sore,* (fig.) a standing abuse, disgrace &c. **2.** Not shut against; **a** accessible to all or to the public generally by right: *in open court*; *open spaces,* enjoyed by the public and not built on or enclosed; **b** not barred by tolls, taxes, or customs; free: *an open port, harbour*; Phr. *the open door,* policy of free trade or freedom from restrictive tariffs; **c** free to all, without qualifications or restrictions: *a career open to talent*; *open scholarship,* at a university, one not confined to boys from a particular school; *open competition, championship,* not confined to special clubs; either for amateurs or professionals. Phr. *open shop,* (U.S.A.) a trade or business in which both union and non-union workmen are employed. **3.** Free; **a** liberal, generous: *open hands*; *to keep open house,* offer hospitality freely to all comers; **b** not prejudiced or bigoted; not closed to argument; accessible to new ideas: *an open mind*; *open to persuasion*; **c** free to be argued and debated; not decided: *an open question*; *to leave the matter open*; Phr. *an open verdict,* that of a coroner's jury recording the fact and cause of a death, but not attributing it specifically to accident, suicide, or murder; **d** not settled, closed, or finished: *to keep one's account open at a bank*; *open chances*; *the match seems to be a very open one*; **e** (i.) free to be accepted or rejected: *to keep an offer open*; *to be open to an offer*; (ii.) not already occupied or engaged: *situation, post, is still open*; *to keep a day open for a meeting*; **f** not protected from attack; liable to be attacked, not defended: *an open town*; *open to injuries, abuse, temptation*; Phr. *to lay oneself open to (attack, insinuations &c.),* render oneself liable; **g** free from the restrictions implied by *close* or *closed*: *open season,* for shooting, fishing &c.; *open cheque,* one that is not crossed and can be cashed at the bank on which it is drawn. **4.** Not hidden or dissembled; **a** frank, not secretive: *an open character*; *to be frank and open about the matter*; *to be open with a person*; *an open countenance,* one expressing a frank, open character; **b** not secret, known to all, undisguised: *open quarrel, enmity*; *an open secret,* one known to everybody; *open scandal,* one that is flagrant and notorious. **5.** Ready for business, admission of the public; opened: *shop, theatre, exhibition, is now open.*

open (II.), n., fr. prec. Only in Phr. *the open,* the open air: *to come into the open,* not to keep secret or be secretive; to be quite frank, to disclose one's intentions &c.

open (III.), vb. trans. & intrans. O.E. *openian.* See **open** (I.). **A.** trans. **1.** To make, cause to be, open; to unclose, unfasten: *to open a door, gate, window* &c. Phrs. *to open one's eyes,* to express surprise; *to open the eyes of* (another) *to,* to undeceive, to inform him (of). **2.** To make, cut, an opening in, make a passage for egress or ingress: *to open an abscess*; *to open a mine, shaft, well* &c. **3.** To spread out; unfold; expand: *to open one's hand*; *open a book, letter* &c. Phr. *to open one's heart, mind, to,* to disclose one's feelings or thoughts to; to take into one's confidence. **4.** To render accessible for the public; to make ready, to throw, declare, open: *to open a park, Parliament, theatre* &c.; (special sense) *to open a shop* &c., set up, start, one. **5.** To begin, initiate: *to open an account at a bank*; *to open a debate, case in court*; *to open fire,* begin to shoot. **6.** (naut.) To obtain sight of by clearing an intervening object: *ship opens the harbour,* as by clearing a headland &c. **7.** To free from restrictions: *to open a cheque,* to leave it uncrossed. **8.** (followed by adv.) *Open out,* to expand, unfold: *to open out the wings*; *open out one's arms to,* to welcome heartily. *Open up,* to lay, throw, open; as a wound, mine &c. **B.** intrans. **1. a** To be opened, become open; allow of being opened: *the book opens at p. 20*; *the door opened at once*; *the door will only open inwards*; **b** (i.) to expand, unfold: *the buds are opening in the sun*; (ii.) (fig.) *the mind of youth opens with each new experience.* **2. a** To begin, start: *the story opens with a murder*; **b** to begin business, start, or renew, activities: *Parliament opens today.* **3.** To come into view, be disclosed, unfold itself: *a wide prospect opened below us*; (fig.) *a great career is opening for him.* **4.** (followed by adv. or prep.) *To open into, onto, out,* to have an opening, passage, into &c.: *the door opened into a smaller room*; *two rooms opening into each other,* communicating by a door.

openable, adj. [1. ṓpenabl; 2. óupənəbl]. **open** (I.) & **-able.** Able to be, capable of being, opened.

open-air, adj. **a** Taking place, carried on, in the open air or out of doors; outdoor: *an open-air life*; *open-air treatment,* for diseases such as consumption &c.; **b** accustomed to, fond of, the open-air: *an open-air person.*

open-armed, adj. With open arms; hearty, cordial: *an open-armed welcome, reception.*

open-eared, adj. Having the ears open; eager to listen, very attentive.

opener, n. [1. ṓpener; 2. óupənə]. **open** (II.) & **-er.** One who, thing which, opens: *pew-opener, tin-opener* &c.

open-eyed, adj. With open eyes, keeping the eyes wide open; watchful, vigilant; surprised: *open-eyed attention, astonishment.*

open-field, adj. (hist.) Of or characterized by a system (*open-field system*) of agriculture in which the arable land is not enclosed, but is cultivated by the several tenants or commoners in strips and then pastured in common after harvest.

open-handed, adj. With open hands; generous, liberal, lavish.

open-handedly, adv. Prec. & **-ly.** Generously, liberally.

open-handedness, n. See prec. & **-ness.** Generosity, liberality.

open-hearted, adj. With open heart; frank, candid; kindly, generous.

open-heartedly, adv. Prec. & **-ly.** Frankly, candidly.

open-heartedness, n. See prec. & **-ness.** Frankness, candour.

open hearth, adj. Of a system or process of steel-making in an open or unenclosed hearth or reverberatory furnace.

opening, n. [1. ṓpning; 2. óupniŋ]. **open** & **-ing.** **1.** An aperture, gap, passage, for egress or ingress: *opening in a wall, fence* &c. **2.** Beginning, commencement: *the opening of a speech, book, theatrical performance* &c.; *the opening of a career.* **3. a** A chance, favourable opportunity: *an opening for trade*; **b** chance of making a start in a career: *do you happen to know of a good opening for a reliable man?*

openly, adv. [1. ṓpnli; 2. óupnli]. **open** (I.) & **-ly.** In an open manner; **a** without secrecy or concealment; frankly: *to speak quite openly to a person*; **b** publicly, so as to be known to the world at large: *openly known for a scoundrel.*

open-minded, adj. Having an open mind; accessible to ideas; unprejudiced; liberal.

open-mindedly, adv. Prec. & **-ly.** In an open-minded way or manner.

open-mindedness, n. See prec. & **-ness.** State, quality, of being open-minded.

openness, n. [1. ṓpennes; 2. óupn(n)is]. **open** (I.) & **-ness.** State, quality, of being open; **a** spaciousness, freedom from enclosure; **b** frankness, candour; **c** liberality of mind, lack of prejudice.

open-work(ed), adj. [1. ṓpen wĕrk(t); 2. óupn wāk(t)]. Characterized by interstices or openings: *open-work lace, stockings.*

opera (I.), n. [1. ópera; 2. ɔ́pərə]. Ital., fr. Lat. *opera*, n. fem., 'service, labour, work; that which is done or produced, a work, composition'. See **opus**. A drama set to music, sung or recited to orchestral accompaniment; *comic opera*, one having a comic plot and characters, and spoken dialogue; *grand opera*, wholly sung, and usually having a tragic plot; *light opera*, of a lighter character than grand opera, but wholly sung or recited to music.

opera (II.), n. pl. See **opus**.

opera-bouffe, n. [1. ópera bṓōf; 2. ɔ́pərə búf]. Fr. *opéra-bouffe*, fr. Ital. *buffo*, 'farcical'. Cp. **buffoon**. Farcical, comic opera.

opera-cloak, n. A lady's long, loose cloak for wearing with evening-dress at the theatre &c.

opera-glass(es), n. Light binocular glasses, for use at the theatre.

opera-hat, n. A tall hat of plain black silk, worn by men with evening-dress, made to fold flat, so as to take up very little space; a gibus.

opera-house, n. Theatre built for opera.

operate, vb. intrans. & trans. [1. óperāt; 2. ɔ́pəreit], fr. Lat. *operāt-(um)*, P.P. of *operāri*, 'to work, labour, toil', fr. *oper-*, stem of *opus*, 'work, labour'. See **opus** & words there referred to. **A.** intrans. **1.** To carry out specific series of movements or processes, designed to achieve particular purpose; to work, to function: *machine operates by steam; the heart operates during sleep; his mind always operated slowly.* **2.** *To operate on, upon*, **a** to act, produce physical effect upon: *different drugs operate on different bodily organs*; **b** to exert an effect on the mind; to influence, persuade: *religious teaching operates powerfully on the young at an impressionable age.* **3.** (surg.) To perform a surgical operation: *we must operate at once; to operate on a limb* &c. **4.** To carry on military operations or movements: *the army operated over a wide area.* **B.** trans. **1.** To cause to work; set, keep, in operation: *to operate a machine.* **2.** (in non-material sense, rare or obs.) To direct, determine: *destiny operates our condition of life.*

operatic, adj. [1. òperátik; 2. ɔ̀pərǽtik]. Formed fr. **opera**, on anal. of *dramatic*. Connected with, of the nature of, taking part in, opera: *an operatic performance, singer.*

operatically, adv. [1. òperátikali; 2. ɔ̀pərǽtikəli]. Prec. & **-al** & **-ly**. In an operatic fashion; after the manner of an opera.

operating, adj. [1. óperāting; 2. ɔ́pərèitiŋ], fr. Pres. Part. of **operate**. (in various senses) *operating surgeon*, one who performs operations; *operating table*, one specially adapted for performance of surgical operations; *operating theatre*, room in a hospital, with tiers of seats for students, where surgical operations are performed.

operation, n. [1. òperáshun; 2. ɔ̀pəréiʃən]. M.E. *operacion*, fr. O. Fr. *operacion*, fr. Lat. *operātiōn-(em)*, 'a working, work, operation'; **operate** & **-ion**. **1. a** Action; process of operating or working; activity: *the operations of nature; in operation*, working, in action, effective, operative; *to come into operation*, to begin to be effective, to begin working; (also of mental processes); **b** effect, result, of a process: '*But that false fruit Far other operation first displayed*' (Milton, 'P.L.'). **2.** Act performed, transaction, in the way of business: *operations on the stock exchange; engaged in some mysterious operations.* **3.** (mil. and nav., often pl.) Series of movements of troops or ships in execution of tactical or strategical plans. **4.** (specif.) Act performed by a surgeon upon any part of the body, whether consisting merely of manipulation, or involving cutting or removing diseased or injured tissue. **5.** (math.) A change to be effected on quantities, such as multiplication, addition &c. indicated by symbols.

operative (I.), adj. [1. óperativ; 2. ɔ́pərətiv], fr. Fr. *opératif*, fr. L. Lat. *operātīvus*, 'formative, creative'. See **operate** & **-ive**. **1.** Operating, working; having force, acting; effective: *to become operative* (of a law); *operative words* (in a legal document); *operative dose of medicine.* **2.** Consisting of a surgical operation: *operative treatment.*

operative (II.), n., fr. prec. **1.** One who operates or works a machine. **2.** A worker in a factory where machinery is used; artisan, mill-hand: *cotton operatives.*

operatively, adv. Prec. & **-ly**. So as to be operative; effectively.

operatize, vb. trans. [1. óperatīz; 2. ɔ́pərətaiz]. **opera** & **-ize**, w. *-t-*, on anal. of *dramatize*. To make into an opera, to turn into operatic form.

operator, n. [1. óperāter; 2. ɔ́pərèitə]. **operate** & **-or**. **1.** One who operates or works a machine: *a telephone operator.* **2.** One who performs a surgical operation. **3.** One who engages in financial or commercial operations.

opercular, adj. [1. opĕrkūlar; 2. əpʌ́kjulə]. See **operculum** & **-ar**. (zool.) Pertaining to the operculum, or gill-cover of a fish: *opercular bones*, the bony plates of the operculum.

operculate(d), adj. [1. opĕrkulāt(ed); 2. əpʌ́kjuleit(id)]. See next word & **-ate** & **-ed**. (zool.) Furnished with an operculum, as fishes and certain molluscs.

operculum, n. [1. opĕrkūlum; 2. əpʌ́kjuləm]. Lat., 'cover, lid', for **opert-lom*, dimin. fr. *opert-*, P.P. type of *operire*, 'to cover, hide, conceal'; fr. **ob-** & *par-*, as in *parere*, 'to bear', & *parāre*, 'to get ready' &c. See **pare**. **1.** (zool.) **a** The long gill-cover of most fishes; **b** the lid-like process which closes the shell of certain gastropod molluscs when the animal withdraws inside the shell. **2.** (bot.) The lid of the seed-capsules in certain plants.

operetta, n. [1. òperéta; 2. ɔ̀pərétə]. Ital., dimin. of **opera**. A short light or comic opera.

operose, adj. [1. óperōs; 2. ɔ́pərous], fr. Lat. *operōsus*, 'laborious', fr. *oper-*, stem of *opus*, 'work' &c. See **opus** & **-ose**. (obs.) Laborious; attained by toil or labour; busy, hard-working.

ophicleide, n. [1. ófiklīd; 2. ɔ́fiklaid]. Fr. *ophicléide*, fr. Gk. *óphis*, 'serpent' (see next word), & *kleid-(ós)*, *kléis*, 'key', cogn. w. Lat. *clāvis*, 'key', *clāvus*, 'nail', see **claviform**. A brass musical wind instrument, consisting of a long tube doubled back on itself, with a cup mouthpiece and finger-keys.

ophidian, adj. [1. ofidian; 2. ɔfídiən]. Coined fr. Gk. *óphis*, 'snake', & **-ian**; the *d* is due to anal. of Gk. dimin. *ophídion*, 'a little snake'. Gk. *óphis* is fr. base **ogʷhis*; cp. the parallel base **eghi-* &c., whence Scrt. *áhiš*, 'serpent'. (zool.) Belonging to the division of reptiles, *Ophidia*, which includes the snakes or serpents.

ophiolatry, n. [1. òfiólatri; 2. ɔ̀fiɔ́lətri], fr. Gk. *óphi(s)*, 'snake', see prec., & **-olatry*, on anal. of **idolatry**. See **-latry**. Serpent worship.

ophiomancy, n. [1. ófiōmànsi; 2. ɔ́fioumæ̀nsi]. See prec. & **-mancy**. Divination by observation of movements &c. of serpents.

ophite (I.), n. [1. ófit; 2. ɔ́fait]. Gk. *ophítēs*, 'of, like, a snake', fr. *óphis*, 'snake' (see **ophidian**), esp. *ophítēs líthos*, 'a spotted kind of marble'. (mineral.) A rock resembling serpentine.

Ophite (II.), n. Gk. *óphis*, 'snake' (see prec.), & **-ite**. A sect of early Gnostic serpent worshippers.

ophthalmia, n. [1. of-thálmia; 2. ɔfþǽlmiə]. L. Lat., fr. Gk. *ophthalmía*, 'an inflammation of the eye', *ophthalmós*, 'the eye'. See **optic**. Inflammation of the eyes.

ophthalmic, adj. [1. of-thálmik; 2. ɔfþǽlmik], fr. Gk. *ophthalmikós*. Prec. & **-ic**. Pertaining to the eye: *ophthalmic arteries, disease, surgery* &c.

ophthalmitis, n. [1. òf-thalmítis; 2. ɔ̀fþælmáitis]. See prec. & **-itis**. Ophthalmia.

ophthalmologist, n. [1. òf-thalmólojist; 2. ɔ̀fþælmɔ́lədžist]. See prec. & **-logy** & **-ist**. One who studies ophthalmology.

ophthalmology, n. [1. òf-thalmóloji; 2. ɔ̀fþælmɔ́lədži]. See prec. & **-logy**. The science which deals with the eye, its anatomy, functions, and diseases.

ophthalmoscope, n. [1. of-thálmoskōp; 2. ɔfþǽlməskoup]. See prec. & **-scope**. An instrument, consisting of a reflecting mirror, pierced centrally, used by oculists for examining the interior structure of the eye.

ophthalmoscopist, n. [1. òf-thalmóskopist; 2. ɔ̀fþælmɔ́skəpist]. Prec. & **-ist**. An oculist skilled in use of the opthalmoscope.

ophthalmoscopy, n. [1. òf-thalmóskopi; 2. ɔ̀fþælmɔ́skəpi]. **ophthalmoscope** & **-y**. The art of using the ophthalmoscope; examination of the interior structure of the eye by this instrument.

-opia, suff., fr. Gk. *ōpós*, *ṓps*, 'eye', wh. is for **ōkʷ-*; cogn. w. Lat. *oculus*. See **ocular**. This suff. indicates a state, condition, of the sight: as *myopia, nyctalopia* &c.

opiate (I.), adj. [1. ṓpiat; 2. óupiət]. Fr., fr. Med. Lat. *opiātus*. See **opium**. (archaic or poet.) Containing opium or an opiate; narcotic, sleep-producing.

opiate (II.), n., fr. prec. **1.** A drug which contains opium or any of its derivatives; a narcotic. **2.** (fig.) Anything which soothes or induces calmness or lethargy; anodyne.

opiate (III.), vb. trans. [1. ṓpiāt; 2. óupieit], fr. prec. (rare) To mix with, put under the influence of, opium; to narcotize.

opine, vb. intrans. & trans. [1. ōpín; 2. oupáin], fr. Fr. *opiner*, fr. Lat. *opīnāri*, 'to suppose'; etymol. doubtful, but Walde compares O. Slav. *(ne-vŭz-)apĭnŭ*, 'unsuspected' &c. Cp. **opinion**. To hold and express an opinion; to take, hold, the view (that): *I opine that it will rain before night.*

opinion, n. [1. ōpíniun; 2. oupíniən]. Fr., fr. Lat. *opīniōn-(em)*, 'opinion, conjecture'; fr. base *opīn-*, as in *opīnāri*, 'to think, suppose'. See prec. & **-ion**. **1.** A belief or judgement which falls short of absolute conviction or certainty or positive knowledge; persuasion or view that certain facts, ideas &c. are probably true or likely to prove so: *political, religious, artistic, opinions; in my opinion* &c., as I judge; *public opinion*, the views of the general mass of people on any subject; *to have no settled opinions.* Phrs. *to be of opinion that*, to think, believe, suppose; *a matter of opinion*, a question on which more than one opinion is possible; *to have the courage of one's opinions*, to express one's beliefs and adhere to them; *to act up to one's opinions*, to act consistently with one's beliefs &c. **2.** Judgement, feeling, or sentiment concerning the character or qualities of persons or things; estimate, estimation: *to have a high, low, opinion of; to have no opinion of*, to think badly of; *to have a good opinion of oneself*, to be self-confident, to be conceited or vain. **3.** The expressed, professional, expert judgement on a particular subject or problem: *counsel's opinion*, that of a barrister on the law of a case; *to have, get, another opinion*, consult, call in, another expert.

opinionated, adj. [1. opíniunāted; 2. əpíniəneitid]. Prec. & **-ate** & **-ed**. Adhering firmly or obstinately to one's opinions; obstinate, stubborn, in beliefs or judgements; self-willed, dogmatic.

opinionatedly, adv. Prec. & **-ly**. In an opinionated, self-willed manner.

opinionatedness, n. See prec. & **-ness**. State, quality, of being opinionated.

opinionative, adj. [1. opíniunativ; 2. əpíniənətiv]. **opinion** & **-ate** & **-ive**. Opinionated; self-willed.

opisometer, n. [1. òpisómeter; 2. ɔ̀pisɔ́mitə], fr. Gk. *opisō*, 'backwards', cogn. w. Lat. **ob-**, & Lith. *api-*, 'around', & **-meter**. An instrument for measuring curved lines on a map.

opisthognathous, adj. [1. opís-thōgnàthus, òpis-thógnathus; 2. əpísþougnèiþəs, ɔ̀pisþɔ́gnəþəs], fr. Gk. *ópisthen*, 'behind', see prec., & **-gnathous.** Having retreating or receding jaws, contrasted with *orthognathous* and *prognathous*.

opium, n. [1. ṓpium; 2. óupiəm]. Lat., fr. Gk. *ópion*, 'the juice of the poppy, opium', fr. *opós*, 'juice'; prob. cogn. w. Scrt. *áp-*, 'water'; O. Prussian *ape*, 'river'; &, w. *-n* suff., Lat. *amnis* (fr. **abnis*), O. Ir. *abaun*, W. *afon*, 'river'. Drug obtained from the juice of the unripe seed-capsules of the white poppy *Papaver somniferum*, which contains the narcotic alkaloid morphine; and smoked or chewed as a narcotic intoxicant; also used medicinally as a sedative.

opium den, n. Low haunt where opium is provided for smoking.

opium-eater, n. One who habitually consumes opium in any form.

opiumism, n. [1. ṓpiumizm; 2. óupiəmizəm]. **opium** & **-ism.** The habitual use of opium; opium habit; morphinism.

opodeldoc, n. [1. òpodéldok; 2. òpədéldək]. Coined by Paracelsus for a kind of medical plaster. (med.) A camphorated or other soap liniment.

opopanax, n. [1. opópanaks; 2. əpɔ́pənæks]. Lat., fr. Gk. *opopánax*, the juice of the plant *pánax*, fr. *ópos*, 'juice', see **opium**, & *pánax*, 'a herb which heals all diseases'. See **panacea. a** A gum-resin obtained from the S. European plant *Opopanax*; formerly used in medicine, now chiefly in perfumery; **b** scent made from this.

opossum, n. [1. opósum; 2. əpɔ́səm]. N. Am. Indian. **1.** A small marsupial animal of the American continent, nocturnal and arboreal in habit, with long prehensile tail and dark grey fur. Phr. *to play 'possum*, (U.S. slang) to sham being dead. **2.** The phalanger of Australia.

oppidan, n. [1. ópidan; 2. ɔ́pidən], fr. Lat. *oppidānus*, 'living in, belonging to, a town', fr. *oppidum*, 'town', the orig. & essential meaning of wh. was 'enclosure', w. wh. Walde connects the adv. *oppido*, 'exceedingly, very', orig. 'inclusively', & M. Ir. *īdaim*, for **pīad-*, 'I close, encompass', & perh. Lat. *patrāre*, 'to accomplish, complete, compass'. **1.** (obs.) A townsman; dweller in a town. **2.** Specif., at Eton College, a member of the school who is not on the foundation and lives in a boarding-house outside the college proper; contrasted with *Colleger*.

oppilate, vb. trans. [1. ópilāt; 2. ɔ́pileit], fr. Lat. *oppīlāt-(um)*, P.P. type of *oppīlāre*, (*obpīlāre*), 'to block up', fr. **ob-** & *pīlāre*, 'to thrust, ram', fr. *pīlum*, 'pestle', for **pis(t)-lom*. See **pistil** & **pestle.** (med.) To obstruct, block, esp. the bowels.

oppilation, n. [1. òpiláshun; 2. ɔ̀piléiʃən], fr. Lat. *oppīlātiōn-(em)*. Prec. & **-ion.** Obstruction of the bowels.

opponency, n. [1. opṓnensi; 2. əpóunənsi]. Next word & **-cy.** State, quality, of being an opponent; antagonism.

opponent (I.), adj. [1. opṓnent; 2. əpóunənt], fr. Lat. *oppōnent-(em)*, Pres. Part. of *oppōnere*, 'to oppose', fr. **ob-**, 'to, against', and *pōnere*, 'to place'. See **deponent, opposite. 1. a** (rare or poet.) Situated opposite to, over against; **b** opposed to, antagonistic: *on the opponent bank*; *opponent to our thoughts.* **2.** Bringing into opposition: *an opponent muscle*, as of the fingers and thumb.

opponent (II.), n., fr. prec. **a** One who opposes; an antagonist, enemy; **b** adversary, rival, competitor, in a game or other competition.

opportune, adj. [1. óportūn; 2. ɔ́pətjūn], fr. Fr. *opportun*, fr. Lat. *opportūnus* (*obportūnus*), 'suitable, convenient, seasonable'; lit. 'before, at, the port or harbour', **ob-** & *portus*, 'harbour'. See **port** (I.). Happening, done, at a suitable, convenient, time; seasonable, timely, well-timed: *an opportune remark, act* &c.; *an opportune event*; *an opportune moment*, one suitable for something to be done or to happen.

opportunely, adv. Prec. & **-ly.** At a suitable time; seasonably.

opportuneness, n. See prec. & **-ness.** State, quality, of being opportune.

opportunism, n. [1. òportúnizm; 2. ɔ̀pətjúnizəm]. **opportune** & **-ism.** The habit, practice, or policy of adapting one's moral attitude and conduct to changing circumstances, instead of being guided by fixed principles; practice of taking advantage of events and opportunities to further one's own ends.

opportunist, n. [1. òportúnist; 2. ɔ̀pətjúnist]. See prec. & **-ist.** One who practises opportunism; a time-server.

opportunity, n. [1. òportúniti; 2. ɔ̀pətjúniti], fr. Fr. *opportunité*, fr. Lat. *opportūnitāt-(em)*, 'fitness, convenience; suitable time'. **opportune** & **-ity. 1.** Favourable conjunction of events and circumstances for doing something: *I am only waiting for an opportunity to take drastic action*; *to seize, take, the opportunity to do this or that.* **2.** Lucky, favourable, chance; occasion, time, propitious for realization of one's wishes &c.: *his life has been deficient in opportunities.*

opposability, n. [1. opòzabíliti; 2. əpòuzəbíliti]. See next word & **-ity.** State, quality, of being opposable or able to be resisted or opposed.

opposable, adj. [1. opṓzabl; 2. əpóuzəbl]. **oppose** & **-able.** Capable of being opposed or resisted.

oppose, vb. trans. [1. opṓz; 2. əpóuz]. M.E. *opposen*, cp. Fr. *opposer*. See **op-** & **pose** (I.), & cp. next word. **1. a** To set, place, opposite to or against, in position or by way of contrast or balance; pit against: *to oppose courage with courage, force with reason, one's will against another's, black with white* &c.; **b** (of physical movement, rare). **2.** To offer opposition to, to set oneself against as an adversary or opponent; to withstand, resist, contend against; to attempt to hinder or defeat: *to oppose the enemy with determination, one's rival with counter-measures*; *to oppose a bill in Parliament* &c.; Phr. *to be opposed to*, be hostile or adverse to. **2.** (absol.) To offer opposition: '*it is the duty of an Opposition to oppose*'.

opposite (I.), adj. [1. ópozit; 2. ɔ́pəzit]. Fr., fr. Lat. *opposit-(um)*, P.P. of *oppōnere*, fr. **op-** & *pōnere*, 'to place'. See **pose** (I.) & **position. 1.** Situated, placed, lying, over against; facing or fronting; situated on the other side of a dividing line: *his house is opposite to mine*; *the opposite sides of a street*; also adverbially: *the houses opposite*; or with omission of *to* (as prep.): *the house opposite (to) ours.* **2. a** Corresponding to, in relative position: *opposite number*; *opposite leaves on stem of a plant*, as contrasted with *alternate*; **b** contrary in character or nature: *the opposite sex.* **3. a** (of direction) Contrary, entirely different: *the opposite way, direction*; **b** (of ideas) in direct opposition or contrast; hence, antagonistic: *hold opposite opinions*; *opinions opposite to mine.*

opposite (II.), n., fr. prec. Person, or thing, which is the contrary of another: *black and white are opposites*; *my brother was thin and dark, I am just the opposite.* Phr. *opposite prompter* (abbr. O.P.), that side of the stage in a theatre which is opposite the prompt-side, that is, on the left hand of the actor.

oppositely, adv. **opposite** (I.) & **-ly.** In an opposite position, esp. of leaves of a plant on a stem, as contrasted with *alternately*.

oppositeness, n. See prec. & **-ness.** State, quality, of being opposite; opposition.

opposition, n. [1. òpozíshun; 2. ɔ̀pəzíʃən], fr. Lat. *oppositiōn-(em)*. See **opposite** (I.) & **-ion. 1. a** Situation or position opposite to or in contrast with another object or person: *in opposition*, opposite or contrasted; **b** specif. (astron.) the position of two heavenly bodies when diametrically opposite to each other: *when the moon is full, it is in opposition to the sun.* **2.** (log.) The relation between two propositions, which have the same subject and predicate but differ in quality, quantity, or both. **3. a** That which offers resistance; obstacle: *to meet with opposition*; **b** contrary, opposing, hostile action; antagonism, resistance: *the enemy offered opposition at every point.* **4.** Body of persons holding opinions adverse to a policy or proposal; specif. (cap.) the body of members of Parliament who are opposed to the party in office; the officially recognized party which is next in number to the party in office; called facet. *His Majesty's Opposition*; (also attrib.) *the Opposition benches, whips* &c.

oppositive, adj. [1. opózitiv; 2. əpɔ́zitiv]. See prec. & **-ive.** Tending to oppose; capable of being put in opposition; adversative.

oppress, vb. trans. [1. oprés; 2. əprés]. M.E. *oppressen*, fr. O. Fr. *oppresser*, fr. L. Lat. *oppressāre*, freq. vb. fr. *oppress-(um)*, P.P. type of *opprimere*, 'to press against or down, to suppress, overwhelm'; fr. **op-** & *premere*, 'to press'. See **press** (I.). **1.** (of human action) To crush, keep down, treat unjustly; use with cruelty and severity, behave as a tyrant to: *to oppress the poor and weak.* **2.** (of physical causes) To affect prejudicially the health and strength of; to prostrate: *to feel oppressed with the heat.* **3.** (of moral causes) To weigh heavily upon the mind and spirits of, to dishearten, depress: *oppressed with grief and anxiety.*

oppression, n. [1. opréshun; 2. əpréʃən]. Fr., fr. Lat. *oppressiōn-(em)*, 'weighing down, oppression'; Lat. *oppress-*, as prec., & **-ion. 1.** Act or process of oppressing; harshness, tyranny. **2.** Condition of being oppressed; **a** (physical) heaviness, languor; **b** (moral) sense of depression, heaviness of spirit.

oppressive, adj. [1. oprésiv; 2. əprésiv]. **oppress** & **-ive. 1.** Exerting, causing, oppression; tyrannical, severe, burdensome: *oppressive rule*; *oppressive system of taxation.* **2.** Causing a feeling of physical oppression: *oppressive weather, heat* &c.

oppressively, adv. Prec. & **-ly.** In an oppressive manner.

oppressiveness, n. See prec. & **-ness.** Quality of being oppressive.

oppressor, n. [1. opréser; 2. əprésə]. **oppress** & **-or.** One who oppresses; one who behaves oppressively.

opprobrious, adj. [1. oprṓbrius; 2. əpróubriəs], fr. O. Fr. *opprobrieus*, fr. L. Lat. *opprōbriōsus*; see **opprobrium** & **-ous. 1.** Casting opprobrium or reproach on; abusive, scurrilous; disgraceful: *opprobrious language.* **2.** Deserving, involving, opprobrium or reproach; disgraceful, infamous: *opprobrious conduct.*

opprobriously, adv. Prec. & **-ly.** In an opprobrious manner; abusively.

opprobriousness, n. See prec. & **-ness.** State, quality, of being opprobrious; opprobrium.

opprobrium, n. [1. oprṓbrium; 2. əpróubriəm]. Lat., 'reproach, taunt, disgrace'; fr. **op-** & *prōbrum*, 'disgraceful act; infamy, abuse'; etymol. doubtful. Reproach, abuse; infamy, disgrace.

oppugn, vb. trans. [1. opún; 2. əpjún], fr. Fr. *oppugner*, fr. Lat. *oppugnāre*, 'to attack, assault', fr. **op-** & *pugnāre*, 'to fight'. Cp. **pugnacious.** (archaic or rare) To fight against, to oppose; to oppose in argument, to controvert, reason against.

opsimath, n. [1. ópsimath; 2. ɔ́psimæþ], fr. Gk. *opsimathḗs*, fr. *opsé*, 'late', fr. same base as Gk. *opísō*, 'behind' (see **opisometer**), & *mathein*, 'to learn', see **mathematical.** (rare) One who acquires learning late in life.

opsonic, adj. [1. opsónik; 2. əpsɔ́nik]. See next word & **-ic.** (bacter.) Of, pertaining to, opsonin: specif. *opsonic index*, a ratio or standard between blood-serum before and after treatment with opsonin, or between the blood-serum of one person and that of another, in reference to the increase of white corpuscles in the blood.

opsonin, n. [1. ópsonin ; 2. ɔ́psənin]. Coined fr. Gk. *opsōneîn*, 'to buy food', fr. *ópson*, 'meat, fish; food other than bread', fr. pref. *o-*, 'with, together with', & **pson*, 'food, bread', connected w. *psōmós*, 'mouthful'; cogn. w. Gk. *psên*, 'to grate, reduce to powder, chew'. See **psoriasis.** (bacter.) A substance, obtained from dead bacteria, introduced into the blood-serum, the presence of which increases the power of the white corpuscles or phagocytes to destroy the bacteria of disease.

opt, vb. intrans. [1. opt ; 2. ɔpt], fr. Fr. *opter*, fr. Lat. *optāre*, 'to choose, wish'; fr. same base as that in **opine** & **opinion.** See further **option** & cp. **adopt.** To make a choice, to choose : *to opt for a particular candidate.*

optative, adj. & n. [1. optátiv ; 2. ɔptéitiv], fr. Fr. *optatif*, fr. L. Lat. *optātīvus*, fr. *optāt-(um)*, P.P. type of *optāre*, 'choose, wish', see prec. (gram.) **1.** adj. Designating a mood of the verb expressive of wish or desire, as in Greek and Sanscrit : *the optative mood*, distinct form of the verb so used. **2.** n. The optative mood.

optic, adj. & n. [1. óptik ; 2. ɔ́ptik], fr. Fr. *optique*, through Med. Lat., fr. Gk. *optikós*, 'of, pertaining to, the eyes or sight', fr. stem **op-*, fr. **okʷ-*, seen in *ópōpa*, 'I have seen', *ópsomai*, 'I shall see', *ópsis*, 'sight'. See **ocular** & **eye**, & cp. **ophthalmia. 1.** adj. Of, pertaining to, the eye or sight, chiefly used in anatomical terminology, as contrasted with *optical* : *the optic nerve*, the nerve connecting the eye with the special sight centres of the brain. **2.** n. (colloq. and facet.) An eye. See also **optics.**

optical, adj. [1. óptikl ; 2. ɔ́ptikl]. Prec. & **-al.** Connected with sight; ocular; *optical instrument*, one for assisting sight, increasing power of vision, such as the telescope &c.; *optical glass*, special kind from which lenses of optical instruments are made; *optical illusion*, a deceptive appearance, illusion due to misinterpretation of visual impressions.

optically, adv. Prec. & **-ly.** By sight or vision ; as appearing to the eye.

optician, n. [1. optíshan ; 2. ɔptíʃən], fr. Fr. *opticien* ; see **optic** & **-ian.** One who makes and sells optical instruments ; esp. a maker of spectacles.

optics, n. pl. [1. óptiks ; 2. ɔ́ptiks]. See **optic.** The branch of physical science which deals with the processes of vision, esp. in relation to light.

optimates, n. pl. [1. óptimāts ; 2. ɔ́ptimeits]. Lat., fr. *optimus*, 'best'. See **optimism** & **-ate.** (Roman hist.) The 'best men', the nobles or aristocracy.

optime, n. [1. óptimi ; 2. ɔ́ptimi]. Lat., 'excellently, very well', adv. fr. *optimus*, 'best'; fr. phr. *optime meruit*, 'has deserved excellently'. See next word. In the mathematical tripos at Cambridge University, one who is placed in the second class (*senior optime*) or third class (*junior optime*), contrasted with *wrangler.*

optimism, n. [1. óptimizm ; 2. ɔ́ptimizəm], fr. Fr. *optimisme*, fr. Lat. *optim-(us)*, *optumus*, 'best', fr. **opitumos*, used as superl. of *bonus*, 'good', prob. fr. base **opi-*, seen in *ops*, 'power, might; wealth', see **opulent**, & **-ism. 1.** (philos.) **a** The doctrine of Leibnitz that this world, as the work of God, is the best of all possible worlds ; **b** the doctrine that the good ultimately predominates or prevails over the evil, contrasted with *pessimism.* **2.** Tendency, inclination, disposition, to look on the bright or hopeful side of things ; sanguine temperament.

optimist, n. [1. óptimist ; 2. ɔ́ptimist]. See prec. & **-ist. a** Believer in optimism; **b** one who looks on the bright or more favourable side of things ; reverse of *pessimist.*

optimistic(al), adj. [1. òptimístik(l) ; 2. ɔ̀ptimístik(l)]. Prec. & **-ic** & **-al. 1. a** Adhering to, believing in, the doctrine of optimism ; **b** sanguine, hopeful. **2.** Based on, relating to, optimism.

optimistically, adv. Prec. & **-ly.** In an optimistic manner ; hopefully.

optimum, n. [1. óptimum ; 2. ɔ́ptiməm]. Lat., neut. sing. of *optimus*, 'best'. See **optimism.** The best or most favourable state, condition &c. ; (chiefly attrib.) *optimum temperature*, for growth of plants &c. ; *optimum capacity*, in electricity, of an induction coil.

option, n. [1. ópshun ; 2. ɔ́pʃən]. Fr., fr. Lat. *optiōn-(em)*, *optio*, 'choice', fr. stem of *optāre*, 'to wish'; etymol. doubtful ; possibly cogn. w. stem **op-*, as in Gk. *ópsomai*, 'I shall see', cp. **optic**, the sense being, 'to look out, pick out'. **1.** The right, liberty, or power of choosing ; exercise of the power of choosing ; choice : *if I had the option* ; *to have no option* ; *imprisonment without the option of a fine* ; *local option*, the right of electors in a municipality or district of deciding by their votes whether, to what extent, and under what conditions alcoholic beverages are to be sold in the particular district. **2.** (commerc.) A time-bargain ; a contract, on payment of a proportion of the price, to buy or sell something at a fixed price before a fixed date in the future : *to exercise, waive, an option* ; *to have an option on a house* &c.

optional, adj. [1. ópshunal ; 2. ɔ́pʃənəl]. Prec. & **-al.** At one's choice to accept or refuse, to do or not to do, allowing either for consent or refusal to act; not obligatory, not compulsory; voluntary : *purchase of tickets is, contributions are, purely optional.*

optionally, adv. Prec. & **-ly.** Of one's own option or choice ; voluntarily.

optometer, n. [1. optómeter ; 2. ɔptɔ́mitə], fr. base of **optic** & **-meter.** An instrument for measuring the power and range of vision, esp. the power of accommodating or focussing.

optometry, n. [1. optómetri ; 2. ɔptɔ́mitri]. See prec. & **-metry.** Measurement of the range of vision by mechanical methods.

optophone, n. [1. óptofōn ; 2. ɔ́ptəfoun]. See **optic** & **-phone.** Instrument converting visual effects or symbols into sounds.

opulence, n. [1. ópūlens ; 2. ɔ́pjuləns]. Next word & **-ce.** Wealth, riches ; abundance, luxuriance.

opulent, adj. [1. ópūlent ; 2. ɔ́pjulənt]. Fr., fr. Lat. *opulent-(us)*, *opulent-(em)*, fr. base of *ops*, 'power, might, wealth', cp. also *Ops*, 'goddess of plenty'; the origin of the suff. is doubtful. With *ops* cp. Scrt. *ā́pnaš*, 'profit, property'; Gk. *ómpnē*, 'food, crop, harvest'; Lith. *apstúmas*, 'plenty, richness'. The base is ultimately that in *opus*, 'work', see **opus**, the idea expressed being 'plenty, property &c.', considered as the product of labour. **a** Possessed of riches, wealthy : *an opulent banker* ; **b** abundant, luxuriant, plentiful : *opulent vegetation* ; *an opulent feast* ; **c** (of style &c.) copious, profuse, florid.

opulently, adv. Prec. & **-ly.** In an opulent manner ; profusely, abundantly.

opus, n. [1. ópus, ōpus ; 2. ɔ́pəs, óupəs]. Lat., 'work, labour'; cogn. w. Scrt. *ā́paš*, 'work', *ā́paš*, 'work ; religious act'; O.S. *ōbian*, 'to celebrate'; O.H.G. *uoben*, 'to start work; to practise; to honour'. See **opulent** ; cp. also **opera, operate.** A work or composition, esp. musical composition, usually abbreviated *op.*, followed by a number indicating its place in order of composition ; *magnum opus* (Lat., 'a great work'), the principal work, book, picture &c. of an author or artist ; the work of one's life.

opuscule, n. [1. ōpúskūl ; 2. oupáskjūl]. Fr., fr. Lat. *opusculum*, dimin. Prec. & **-cule. a** A lesser or minor work or composition ; **b** a small book or treatise.

or (**I.**), n. [1. ōr ; 2. ɔ̄]. Fr., fr. Lat. *aurum*, 'gold'. See **auriferous.** (her.) **a** The metal gold ; **b** the colour yellow in armorial bearings ; represented in black and white by small dots.

or (**II.**), conj. The O.E. word is *oþþe*, & *eþþa* (cogn. w. O.H.G. *eddo, odo* ; O.S. *eftho* ; Goth. *aiþþau*) ; in M.E. *oþþr, ōther, ouþer* are used for 'or', prob. on the anal. of *other, ǣiðer, eigþer* &c. (see **either**), & such words expressing alternatives ; cp. Mod. Germ. *oder*, 'or', for O.H.G. *odo* (*odar* is found, but is rare) ; the intervocalic [ð] in *other* has been lost (a process not unknown in Engl. of open cons. between vowels, cp. *e'er* for *ever*, & here perh. encouraged by the common occurrence of the word in unstressed positions), & *or* occurs in 14th cent. A disjunctive or co-ordinating particle ; **1. a** introducing an alternative : *sink or swim* ; *red or white* ; *stop in or go out* ; **b** offering a choice of a series : *will you take sherry* (*or*) *hock or claret?* ; **c** introducing an equivalent ; synonymous or explanatory word or phrase : *a stallion or entire horse* ; *the culinary art or art of cookery* ; **d** indicating some uncertainty or vagueness : *there or thereabouts* ; *about four or five miles off.* **2. a** Following *either* or *whether*, as emphasising a strict limitation of choice or result : *it must be either black or white* ; *you can either fight or run away* ; *whether he speaks or not, the result will be the same* ; **b** (poet.) instead of *either* or *whether* : '*Or in the heart or in the head*'. **3.** (archaic) Introducing a sentence, marking a change of thought &c. : '*Or what man is there of you*' &c. (Matt. vii. 9).

or (**III.**), prep. & conj. O.E. *ār*, variant of *ǣr*, 'ere', M.E. *ōr*. See **ere.** (poet. and archaic) Before, ere, esp. in Phr. *or ever, or e'er* : '*Or ever the silver cord be loosed, or the golden bowl be broken*' (Eccles. xii. 6).

-or, n. suffs. (1) fr. O. Fr. *-ur, -our, -or*, Mod. Fr. *-eur*, fr. Lat. ns. ending in *-or, -ōris*, as *terror, horror* &c. ; some words keep the O. Fr. form in *-our*, as *labour, honour* &c., except in America, where *-or* is used ; (2) for ns. expressing an agent or an instrument, derived through Fr. fr. Lat., or fr. Lat. direct : *donor, auditor, elevator, tractor* &c. The Engl. equiv. **-er**, wh. has now exactly the same pronunciation as **-or**, has ousted this in the spelling of some words fr. Fr. or Lat., cp. *barber*, O. Fr. & M.E. *barbour* ; in *sailor*, *-er* has been replaced by the Lat. suff., prob. on anal. of *tailor.*

orach, n. [1. órich ; 2. ɔ́ritʃ], fr. O. Fr. *arache*, Mod. Fr. *arroche*, fr. Lat. *atriplic-(em)*, *atriplex*, fr. Gk. *atráphaxus* ; etymol. unknown. The mountain spinach, red or green, cultivated as a vegetable.

oracle, n. [1. órakl ; 2. ɔ́rəkl], fr. Lat. *orāculum*, fr. **orāt-lom*, w. suff., fr. P.P. type of *orāre*, 'to speak, say'. See **oration. 1. a** The answer given by an ancient Greek priest or priestess, inspired by a god, to inquiries as to the future or as to the best way to set about an undertaking &c. ; **b** the place or shrine where such an answer was given, also the inspired answerer : *the ancient oracles were often vague and equivocal* ; *to consult the oracle of Apollo at Delphi* ; *to go to the oracle at Cumae* &c. Phr. *to work the oracle*, to pull the strings, to arrange matters beforehand so that a plan or stratagem is successful. **2.** (Bib.) The sanctuary containing the Ark in the Temple at Jerusalem ; the Urim and Thummim of the High Priest ; (pl.) the Scriptures. **3. a** A person who is considered as of great experience or knowledge, and whose opinion is taken as infallible ; often used ironically ; **b** the opinion, advice, of such a person ; an oracular statement.

oracular, adj. [1. orákūlar ; 2. ɔrǽkjulə]. Lat. *ōrāculārius.* See prec. & **-ar.** Pertaining to an oracle ; prophetic. **1.** (of statements) Resembling the answers of an oracle, in being equivocal or ambiguous. **2.** (of persons) Claiming to speak with the inspired authority of an oracle ; claiming to be infallible and authoritative.

oracularity, n. [1. orakūláriti ; 2. ɔrækjulǽriti]. Prec. & **-ity.** State, quality, of being oracular.

oracularly, adv. [1. orákūlarli ; 2. ɔrǽkjuləli]. See prec. & **-ly.** In an oracular manner.

oral, adj. [1. óral ; 2. ɔ́rəl], fr. Lat. *ōr-*, stem of *ōs*, 'the mouth, face', fr. **ōus-, *əus-*, cp. Scrt. *ā́š, ā́syam*, 'mouth'; O.E. *ōr*, 'front ; beginning'; O.N. *ōss*, 'mouth of a river'; cp. further Lat. *osculum*, 'little mouth; kiss'. See **osculate.** 1. Spoken; uttered in words, verbal; as contrasted with *written*: *oral evidence*; *oral traditions*; *oral examination*, one conducted by spoken question and answer. 2. (anat.) Pertaining to the mouth: *the oral cavity.*

orally, adv. Prec. & **-ly**. By word of mouth; verbally.

orange (I.), n. [1. órinj; 2. ɔ́rindž], fr. O. Fr. *arange*, later *orange*, for **narange*, w. loss of initial *n* & change to *o*, through association w. *or*, 'gold', fr. the colour; fr. M. Ital. *narancia*, Mod. Ital. *arancia*, cp. Span. *naranja*, fr. Pers. (Arab.) *nāranj*, cogn. w. Scrt. *nārañgas*, 'the orange tree'. 1. **a** One of several varieties of evergreen tree, *Citrus Aurantium*, with fragrant white flowers and deep golden-yellow, juicy, many-celled fruit; **b** fruit of this tree: *oranges and lemons*, an old-fashioned children's game; *Blenheim orange*, a large, finely flavoured dessert apple; *mock orange*, the syringa; **c** (attrib.) *orange blossom*, the flower of the orange tree, worn by a bride; *orange squash*, drink made from the juice of crushed orange pulp, usually sweetened. 2. Colour resembling that of the orange fruit; *orange-lily*, a variety of lily with deep-red or orange-coloured flowers; *orange-tip*, a small butterfly with deep orange tip on edge of the wings of the male.

orange (II.), adj., fr. prec. Having the colour of the rind of an orange; reddish, golden yellow.

Orange (III.), n. The name of a town and ancient principality in S.E. France (Lat. *Arausio*), from which the princes of the House of Orange-Nassau took their title, and hence used by the adherents of William III., Prince of Orange, and of the Protestant Succession in Ulster; hence transmitted to the later ultra-Protestant, anti-Catholic, and Unionist party in Northern Ireland, who wear orange-coloured favours, orange-lilies &c., on the anniversary of the battle of the Boyne; whence *Orange Lodges, Orangeman, Orangism, the Orange Drum* &c.

orangeade, n. [1. òrinjád; 2. ɔ̀rindžéid]. **orange** (I.) & *-ade*, on anal. of **lemonade**. A sweet drink, effervescent or still, made with orange juice.

orangery, n. [1. órinjeri; 2. ɔ́rindžəri], fr. Fr. *orangerie*. **orange** & **-ry**. A hot-house in which orange trees are cultivated.

orang-outang, **orang-utan**, n. [1. oráng ootáng; 2. ɔrǽŋ utǽŋ]. Malay. *orang*, 'man', *ūtan*, 'forest, wood; savage, wild'. A large, reddish-brown, anthropoid ape found in Borneo and Sumatra.

orate, vb. intrans. [1. orát; 2. ɔréit]. Secondary formation fr. *ōrāt-*, as in **oration.** (colloq. or humorous) To make long orations or speeches; to hold forth, harangue.

oration, n. [1. oráshun; 2. ɔréiʃən], fr. Lat. *ōrātiōn-(em)*, *ōrātio*, 'discourse, language; a speech; eloquence', P.P. type of *ōrāre*, 'to speak; to beseech; to pray', & **-ion.** Connexion w. Lat. *ōr-*, 'mouth', see **oral**, is now disputed; Walde prefers to relate to Scrt. *āryati*, 'he praises'; Gk. *ará* (Homer. *ārḗ*), 'prayer', cp. *aráomai*, 'I pray, supplicate'. The base was orig. imitative. 1. A set or formal speech or discourse delivered on a ceremonial occasion: *a funeral oration.* 2. (gram.) Manner of reporting speech; either in actual words of speaker, as *he said, 'I come to bury Caesar'* (direct oration), or *he said that he came to bury Caesar* (indirect oration).

orator, n. [1. órater; 2. ɔ́rətə], fr. O. Fr. *oratour*, Mod. Fr. *orateur*, fr. Lat. *ōrātor*, 'one who speaks', fr. *ōrāt-*, see prec., & **-or.** **a** An eloquent, public speaker: *he is no orator*; **b** one who delivers an oration; specif., *Public Orator*, the official speaker at Oxford or Cambridge University who delivers ceremonial Latin orations, presents candidates for honorary degrees &c.

Oratorian, adj. & n. [1. òratórian; 2. ɔ̀rətɔ́riən]. See **oratory** (II.) & **-an.** 1. adj. **a** Pertaining to an oratory; **b** belonging to the Society of the Oratory. 2. n. A member of the Society of the Oratory; an Oratorian father.

oratorical, adj. [1. òratórikl; 2. ɔ̀rətɔ́rikl]. **orator** & **-ic** & **-al.** **a** Characteristic of, pertaining to, oratory or an orator; **b** rhetorical.

oratorically, adv. Prec. & **-ly.** After the manner of an orator; rhetorically.

oratorio, n. [1. òratórió; 2. ɔ̀rətɔ́riou]. Ital., said to be taken from the oratory of St. Philip Neri at Rome, where such musical compositions were first performed, c. 1574. A musical semi-dramatic setting to a religious theme, usually adapted from Scriptural words or paraphrase, arranged for chorus, solo voices, and orchestra, and performed without costume, scenery, or dramatic gesture.

oratory (I.), n. [1. óraturi; 2. ɔ́rətəri], fr. Lat. (*ars*) *ōrātōria*, 'oratorical art'. **orator** & **-y.** **a** The art of the orator; **b** eloquence; **c** rhetoric.

oratory (II.), n. fr. Fr. *oratoire*, fr. Lat. *ōrātōrium*, 'place of prayer'. See prec. 1. **a** A small chapel for prayer, esp. for private prayer or devotion; one attached to a larger church, or to a private house; **b** church of the Oratorians. 2. (R.C. Ch.) A religious society of secular priests, the Fathers of the Oratory, founded in the 16th cent. for the purpose of providing preachers.

orb (I.), n. [1. orb; 2. ɔ̄b], fr. Lat. *orb-(em)*, *orbis*, 'ring, circle, orb', so *orbis terrārum*, 'the circuit of lands, the world'; cp. also *orbita*, 'track' &c., q.v. under **orbit**, cogn. w. Umbr. *urfeta*, 'a wheel-shaped object held in the hand as a symbol'. The orig. meaning of the base **orbh-*, **erbh-*, was 'to curve, arch over'; cp. Gk. *eréphein*, 'to cover, roof over'; also O.H.G. *rippa*, O.E. *ribb*, fr. earlier **rebjo-*. See **rib.** 1. **a** A sphere, globe; **b** specif., one of the heavenly bodies. 2. A golden globe, surmounted by a cross, symbolizing sovereignty, forming, with the sceptre, part of the regalia of a monarch. 3. (poet.) The eye, eyeball.

orb (II.), vb. trans., fr. prec. (poet.) To encircle, enclose, gather into, a globe or orb.

orbicular, adj. [1. orbíkūlar; 2. ɔ̄bíkjulə]. Lat. *orbiculār(is)*, adj., fr. *orbiculus*, dimin. of *orbis*, 'circle'. See **orb.** Having the shape of an orb or sphere; spherical: (chiefly in anat.) *orbicular ligament, muscle, process* &c.

orbiculate(d), adj. [1. orbíkūlāt(ed); 2. ɔ̄bíkjuleit(id)]. See prec. & **-ated** & **-e.** Orbicular: (chiefly bot.) *orbiculate leaf.*

orbit, n. [1. órbit; 2. ɔ́bit], fr. Lat. *orbita*, 'rut in the ground made by a wheel; track, course, path', fr. *orbis*, 'circle, ring, hoop'. See **orb.** 1. The eye-socket. 2. **a** Track, circuit, path, followed by a celestial body in its revolution round another body; also **b** (fig.) range, sphere, of action and experience; ordinary course of life and behaviour.

orbital, adj. [1. órbital; 2. ɔ́bitəl]. Prec. & **-al.** Of, pertaining to, an orbit, (chiefly anat.) pertaining to the eye-socket: *orbital nerve* &c.

orbito-, pref. Form of **orbit** used in compounds: *orbito-sphenoid*, of a bone or process in the skull.

orca, orc, n. [1. órk(a); 2. ɔ́k(ə)]. Lat. *orca*, 'grampus; large-bellied vessel, a butt or tun'; cp. also Lat. *urceus*, 'water-pot, pitcher'. See **urceolate.** (zool.) **a** *Orca*, the genus of killer-whales; **b** *orc*, a grampus; cp. Fr. *orque.*

Orcadian, adj. & n. [1. orkádian; 2. ɔ̄kéidiən], fr. Lat. *Orcades*, the Orkney Islands. 1. adj. Of, belonging to, the Orkney Islands. 2. n. An Orkney Islander.

orchard, n. [1. órchard; 2. ɔ́tʃəd]. O.E. *ortgeard*, *orceard*, 'orchard, garden'; Goth. *aurtigards*, 'garden'. Borrowing fr. Lat. *hortus*, 'garden', is unlikely. The first element is possibly connected w. Goth. *waurts*, 'root, plant', O.E. *wyrt*, 'vegetable, plant, herb; root'. See under **wort** (I.) & **root** & **radix.** The Gmc. stem is seen also in O.H.G. *orzōn*, 'to cultivate'. A plantation of fruit trees, esp. of apples, pears, cherries &c.

orchardman, n. [1. órchardman; 2. ɔ́tʃədmən]. One who keeps an orchard and sells the fruit.

orchestic, adj. [1. orkéstik; 2. ɔ̄késtik], fr. Gk. *orkhēstikós*, fr. *orkhēstḗs*, 'dancer'. See **orchestra.** Of, pertaining to, the art of dancing.

orchestics, n. pl., fr. prec. The art of dancing.

orchestra, n. [1. órkestra; 2. ɔ́kistrə]. Lat., fr. Gk. *orkhḗstra*, 'part of a theatre in which the chorus performed', lit. 'dancing place'; cp. *orkheisthai*, 'to dance'; cp. Scrt. *r̥gháyati*, 'tremble, be agitated'; the base **orgh-* is an extension of **or-*, **er-*, seen in Gk. *órnūmi*, & *ornúein*, 'rouse, stir up, start' &c.; cp. Scrt. *árnaš*, 'undulating, flowing'; fr. same base comes Lat. *orīri*, 'to rise', see **orient**, **origin**; for further derivatives fr. this base see **earl** & **run** (I.). 1. (class. antiq.) **a** The circular space in front of and below the proscenium or stage in a Greek theatre, where the chorus danced and sang; **b** semicircular space reserved for senatorial or official spectators in the Roman theatre. 2. Space in the modern theatre between the stage and the auditorium in which the band plays. 3. Group of musical performers, or band, in a theatre, concert-room &c., who play concerted music such as symphonies &c.; usually divided into four groups, strings, wood wind, brass wind, and percussion instruments.

orchestral, adj. [1. orkéstral; 2. ɔ̄késtrəl]. Prec. & **-al.** Of, pertaining to, an orchestra; composed for, performed by, an orchestra; *orchestral music*; *an orchestral accompaniment.*

orchestrate, vb. trans. [1. órkestrāt; 2. ɔ́kistreit]. **orchestra** & **-ate.** To write, arrange, (music) for performance by an orchestra.

orchestration, n. [1. òrkestráshun; 2. ɔ̀kistréiʃən]. Prec. & **-ion.** **a** The art of composing or arranging music suitably for performance by an orchestra; **b** mode, style, in which this is done.

orchestrion, n. [1. orkéstrion; 2. ɔ̄késtriən]. **orchestra** & **-ion.** A large, elaborate musical-box or barrel-organ, giving effects of various musical instruments.

orchid, n. [1. órkid; 2. ɔ́kid], fr. Lat., fr. Gk. *órkhis*, 'testicle; tuber, orchis' (fr. shape of bulb); cogn. w. Lith. *eržilas*, 'stallion'; an irreg. formation as if fr. a Lat. **orchid-(is).* (bot.) The name given to a large family, Orchidaceae, of monocotyledonous plants, some of which grow wild in Europe. The varieties of temperate regions are tuberous, with fleshy stems; the tropical kinds, much cultivated in hot-houses, are of various habit, many growing on trees, and have brilliant colours and fantastic shapes.

orchidaceous, adj. [1. òrkidáshus; 2. ɔ̀kidéiʃəs]. Prec. & **-aceous.** Of or belonging to the Orchidaceae or orchid family.

orchidist, n. [1. órkidist; 2. ɔ́kidist]. See prec. & **-ist.** A collector, cultivator, of orchids.

orchil. See **archil.**

orchis, n. [1. órkis; 2. ɔ́kis]. See **orchid.** (bot.) Any plant of the family Orchidaceae, esp. of the varieties growing wild in temperate regions: as *bee-orchis*, *fly-orchis* &c.

orchitis, n. [1. orkítis; 2. ɔ̄káitis], fr. Gk. *órkhis*, see **orchid**, & **-itis.** (med.) Inflammation of the testicles.

orcin, n. [1. órsin; 2. ɔ́sin], fr. *orcil*, variant of **archil.** (chem.) A substance obtained from lichens, aloes &c. and yielding a dark-red dye-stuff.

ordain, vb. trans. [1. ordán; 2. ɔ̄déin]. M.E. *ordeinen*, fr. O. Fr. *ordener*, Mod. Fr. *ordonner*, fr. Lat. *ordināre*, 'to order', fr. *ordin-(em)*, fr. *ordo*, 'order'. See **ordinal** & **order.** 1. To decree, enact, appoint, esp. of the decrees of God, or of fate. 2. (eccles.) To admit to holy orders, by the formal laying on of hands by a bishop, and the utterance of a prescribed form of words, giving authority to perform the functions of a minister: *to be ordained priest or deacon.*

ordainer, n. [1. ordáner; 2. ɔdéinə]. Prec. & **-er**. One who ordains or orders; specif. (Engl. hist.) one of a commission of nobles and bishops, *Lords Ordainers*, appointed in the reign of Edward II. to issue ordinances for the kingdom, manage the royal household &c.

ordeal, n. [1. ordḗl; 2. ɔdíəl]. O.E. *ordāl*, more rarely *ordēl*, for. W.S. *-dǣl*, M.E. *ordal*; O.S. *ordēli*, O.H.G. *urteili*, Mod. Germ. *urteil*, Du. *oordeel*, 'judgement, decision'; the old pref. *or-*, O.H.G. *ur-*, Goth. *uz-*, meant 'out, through', & hence came to imply 'thoroughness'; the second element is O.E. *dǣl*, 'division, share, portion', see **deal** (I.), or *dāl*, see **dole**. The orig. sense of the compound is 'something dealt out, adjudged'. **1.** (hist.) A primitive method of trial, whereby the guilt or innocence of accused was tested by the fall of lots, by his capacity to pass uninjured over fire or through water, or to defeat his accuser in battle: *ordeal by fire*; *ordeal of battle* &c. **2.** Any severe, searching, experience; something which is a test of courage, resolution, tenacity, and the like. **3.** (attrib.) *Ordeal bark, bean, tree*, W. African poisons used in trial by ordeal.

order (I.), n. [1. órder; 2. ɔ́də]. M.E. *ordre*, fr. O. Fr. *ordre*, earlier *ordene*, *ordine*, fr. Lat. *ordin-(em)*, fr. *ordo*, 'a straight row, regular series; methodical arrangement, order; a class or rank'; of doubtful etymol.; prob. connected w. base **or-*, seen in *orīri*, 'to rise up', & *ordīri*, 'to begin a web; to begin'. See **orient** & **origin**. **1. a** (of objects, names &c.) Mode of arrangement or placing; relative position in a series: *numerical, alphabetical order*; *in order of merit*; *not in the right order*; **b** (of events) mode of occurrence, relative place in time; succession: *the phases of the battle developed in the order anticipated*; **c** specif. (mil.) mode of disposition of troops: *battle order, order of battle*; *open order*, of ranks placed two paces behind each other; *close order*, one pace behind; Phr. *Parade Order*, full dress uniform. **2.** (of thoughts &c.) Logical sequence: *his thoughts occurred haphazard, and in no regular order*. **3. a** (of processes, phenomena of nature) Natural sequence or succession: *the order of the seasons*; **b** (of spiritual conditions) system, group of tendencies, ideals: *the old, new, order*. **4.** Careful, regular, systematic arrangement; disposal in the right place; **a** (of material objects) neatness, tidiness, orderliness: *cleanliness and order in a house, one's person* &c.; **b** (of non-material things) logical arrangement, coherence, system, right classification, plan: *to put one's ideas into order*; *in some learned books we find confusion instead of order, obscurity instead of clarity*; **c** (of business, affairs) *to leave one's affairs in perfect order*. **5. a** (of political and social conditions) Prevalence of law and discipline, law-abiding conduct; reasonable submission to law and government; absence of turbulence: *public order*; *perfect order reigned throughout the entire country*; *to restore peace and order*; *to keep order*; Phr. *quite in order*, regular, in accordance with rules; **b** specif., customary behaviour during Parliamentary debate, or public meeting, generally; established method and procedure in conduct of these: *out of order*; *to rise to a point of order*, indicate that a *breach of order* has been committed; this specific use tends to merge in that in No. 6, esp. in such a phrase as *breach of order*, which strictly is merely a departure from regular procedure, but may often mean, at the same time, noisy disorder; Phr. *Order! Order!*, called out in drawing attention to a formal departure from established rules of debate. **6.** Normal, healthy, sound condition; state in which the usual functions are carried on; **a** (of bodily condition) sound health, vigour, absence of disease: *to have one's eyes put in order*; *liver out of order*; **b** (of state of machinery or mechanical devices) working well, in good repair: *good working order*; *in thorough order*; *to get out of order*. **7.** Class, group, kind: **a** (zool., bot.) mode of classification, group of related animals or plants, below *class*, divided into families or genera; **b** (archit.) a specific mode or style of building and design, usually one of the classical styles: *Doric, Ionic, Corinthian, order*; **c** (math.) degree; **d** kind, sort, degree: *a different order of ideas*; *talents of a high order*. **8. a** Class, rank in society: *the lower orders*, the common people; *false to the traditions of his order*; **b** a group of persons belonging to a specific rank or class: *the Order of Knights Bachelor*; *Order of the Bath*; *Order of Merit*; **c** badge, insignia, worn by members of an order. **9.** (eccles.) **a** Specific spiritual grace, or office, conferred by the bishop by the imposition of his hands in ordination or consecration, giving the power to perform certain spiritual functions: *to confer orders*; *holy orders*; Phr. *to take (holy) orders*, to become a clergyman; **b** group of persons who have received any or all of the holy orders: *the order of Deacons, of Priests, of Bishops*. **10.** (eccles.) Group of persons bound by vows to a religious life: *the monastic orders*; *the order of Benedictines*. **11.** (eccles.) Prescribed form for performance of a ceremony, or administration of a rite: *the order of Holy Baptism*. **12.** A command, authoritative direction or instruction to do something: *to give, receive, orders*; *orders must be obeyed*; *under the orders of*, commanded by; special uses: *Order in Council*, one issued by the Sovereign on the advice of the Privy Council, which has the force of a statute, but comes into effect without requiring to be sanctioned by Parliament; *standing orders*, permanent rules of procedure adopted by Parliament or by any administrative or legislative body. **13.** Request or instruction to a commercial firm, or to a tradesman, to supply goods: *large orders for iron, coal*. Phr. *made to order*, according to special requirements, contrasted with *ready made*; *on order*, having been ordered, but not yet received (by dealer). **14.** Written authorization to a post office, or a banker, to pay money. **15.** A written or printed authorization permitting the holder to go somewhere, or do something: *an order to view (a house), to enter a building* &c.

order (II.) vb. trans., fr. prec. **1. a** To arrange, dispose, direct, regulate the course of: *God orders all things in heaven and earth*; *to order one's affairs, household* &c.; **b** specif. (mil.) *to order arms*, to bring the rifle down from the slope, place the butt on the ground, and hold it close to the right side. **2.** To give an authoritative order to; **a** to direct, command (a person) to do something or go somewhere: *to order a person to leave the room*; *to be ordered abroad*; **b** to command that something shall be done: *to order an advance*; **c** to prescribe something: *my doctor orders me a holiday*. **3. a** To direct (goods) to be supplied, give an order or commission for, esp. to a tradesman: *to order a leg of mutton, a new suit*; **b** to give orders for something to be brought: *to order luncheon for 1.30*; Phr. *to order dinner*, choose the courses of which it shall consist.

orderliness, n. [1. órderlines; 2. ɔ́dəlinis]. Next word & **-ness**. State, quality, of being orderly; **a** tidiness, neatness; **b** orderly behaviour; law-abiding conduct; good order.

orderly (I.), adj. [1. órderli; 2. ɔ́dəli]. **order** (I.) & **-ly**. **1.** Arranged, disposed, in order; systematically or methodically arranged; tidy, neat. **2. a** Observing, acting in accordance with, law; law-abiding, quiet, well-behaved: *an orderly crowd*; **b** exhibiting, inspired by, orderliness, and recognition of law; free from disorder or turbulence: *orderly behaviour, conduct*. **3.** (mil.) On duty; concerned with carrying out orders: *orderly officer*, the officer on duty for the day; *orderly book*, a book kept in the orderly room of a company for entering regimental and other orders &c.; *orderly room*, one set apart in barracks for administrative business of regiment or company.

orderly (II.), n., fr. prec. **a** A soldier in attendance on an officer to execute orders, take messages &c.; **b** an attendant at a military hospital.

ordinal (I.), adj. [1. órdinal; 2. ɔ́dinəl], fr. Lat. *ordinālis*, 'in order, of numerals', fr. *ordin-(em)*, 'row, series'. See **order** (I.). Indicating order or succession, esp. the position of a number in a series or order: *an ordinal number*, as *fourth, tenth* &c., as contrasted with *cardinal*.

ordinal (II.), n., fr. prec. **1.** An ordinal number. **2. a** Prescribed form of ceremony, words, and acts to be observed in the consecration of bishops, and in the ordination of priests and deacons; **b** book containing printed form of words, and directions as to acts, prescribed in consecration and ordination. **3.** Rubric of the Mass or Eucharist.

ordinance, n. [1. órdinans; 2. ɔ́dinəns], fr. O. Fr. *ordenance*. See **ordain** & **-ance**. **1. a** That which is ordained or ordered by authority: '*Thy blessed word and ordinance*' (Prayer Book); **b** specif., a decree, enactment, authoritative rule; formerly used of public enactments which were not statutes, now more generally styled *Orders in Council*. **2.** A prescribed and customary usage; specif., an ecclesiastical rite, esp. the Eucharist.

ordinand, n. [1. órdinand; 2. ɔ́dinænd], fr. Lat. *ordinandus*, gerundive of *ordināre*, 'to ordain', q.v. A candidate for ordination.

ordinarily, adv. [1. órdinarili; 2. ɔ́dinərili]. **ordinary** (I.) & **-ly**. **a** In an ordinary, normal, manner: *to behave quite ordinarily*; **b** according to custom; usually, commonly, as a rule: *I breakfast ordinarily at 8 o'clock*.

ordinariness, n. [1. órdinarines; 2. ɔ́dinərinis]. See prec. & **-ness**. State, quality, of being ordinary.

ordinary (I.), adj. [1. órdinari; 2. ɔ́din(ə)ri], colloq. [ɔ́dnri], fr. Lat. *ordinārius*, 'regular, in order, usual', fr. *ordin-(em)*, *ordo*, see **order** (I.) & *-ārius*, **-ary**, cp. Fr. *ordinaire*. **1.** According to regular or customary usage; normal, usual: *one's ordinary habits*; *an ordinary day's work*. Phrs. *out of the ordinary*, exceptional, rare; *in ordinary*, of permanent appointment, not special or extraordinary: as *Surgeon-in ordinary to the King*; *ordinary seaman*, O.S., one who has not the qualification of an *able seaman*, A.B. **2.** Of a kind usually met with; average *the ordinary man*. **3.** Of common or plain quality or appearance; not distinguished by particular merit; commonplace: *a man of very ordinary ability*.

ordinary (II.), n., fr. prec. **1.** An officer wielding direct authority in his own right, and not as the deputy of another; **a** (eccles.) (i.) an archbishop in his province, bishop in his diocese, incumbent in his parish; (ii.) formerly, specif., the chaplain of Newgate; **b** (Scots law) one of the five *Lords Ordinary*, or judges in the Outer Court of Session. **2.** (eccles.) Prescribed form of service or rite; order. **3. a** An inn or eating-house where meals can be obtained; **b** a set meal at an inn, served at a fixed price, as distinct from one specially ordered by a guest; **c** room where such meals are served. **4.** (her.) One of the simple charges first used as heraldic distinctions, also called *honourable ordinaries*; viz. *chief, pale, bend, fess, chevron, cross*, and *saltire*.

ordinate, n. [1. órdināt; 2. ɔ́dineit]. As *(co-)ordinate*; fr. Lat. use of *lineae ordinatae*, 'parallel lines'. See next word. (math.) A line drawn from a point to one of two coordinate axes.

ordination, n. [1. òrdináshun; 2. ɔ̀dinéiʃən], fr. Lat. *ordinātiōn-(em)*, 'a setting in order, arrangement', fr. *ordināt-*, P.P. type of *ordināre*, 'to set in order' &c. See **ordain** & **-ation**. Act of ordaining; specif., the conferring by the bishop of deacon's or priest's orders; formal admission to the ministry of the Church.

ordinee, n. [1. òrdinḗ; 2. ɔ̀dinī́]. **ordain** & **-ee**. Newly ordained deacon.

ordnance, n. [1. órdnans; 2. ɔ́dnəns]. Spelling variant of **ordinance**, cp. Fr. *ordonnance*, in phr. *engin de telle ordonnance*, 'of such size or bore' (Skeat). **1**. Artillery, cannon, or big guns of all sizes as distinguished fr. *small arms*. **2**. Military stores, equipment, and material: *the Ordnance Department*, of the War Office: *Army Ordnance Corps* &c. *Ordnance Survey*, the official geographical survey of the British Isles, formerly carried out by the Ordnance Department: so *ordnance map*.

Ordovician, adj. [1. òrdōvíkian; 2. ɔ̀douvíkiən], fr. the *Ordovices*, Lat. name of a Celtic-Welsh people or race. (geol.) Of a geological period or system following the Cambrian and preceding the Silurian.

ordure, n. [1. órdūr; 2. ɔ́djə]. Fr., fr. O. Fr. *ord*, 'filthy, foul', fr. Lat. *horridus*, 'horrid, wild, frightful', see **horrid**. Dung, manure, filth; also used in moral sense, obscenity.

ore, n. [1. ōr; 2. ɔ̄]. Formally representing O.E. *ār*, 'brass', but having the transferred meaning of O.E. *ōra*, 'ore, unwrought metal'. The latter is cogn. w. Du. *oer*; the former w. O.N. *eir*; O.H.G. *ēr*; Goth. *aiz*, 'brass'; cp. Lat. *aer-(is)*, *aes*, 'bronze'; Scrt. *ayaś*. See **aeruginous**. Native metal; metal in its unrefined state; any mineral compound from which valuable metal can be extracted; *ore-dressing*, the processes by which the waste is separated from the metal.

Oread, n. [1. ốread; 2. ɔ́riæd]. Lat. *Oread-(is)*, stem of *Oreas*, fr. Gk. *Oreiád-(os)*, stem of *Oreiás*, fr. *óros*, 'mountain'. The latter is fr. Gk. *órrhos*, 'rump, buttock', for **ors-os*, cogn. w. O.E. *ears*, see **arse**. (class. mythol.) A mountain nymph.

orectic, adj. [1. oréktik; 2. ɔréktik], fr. Gk. *orektikós*, fr. *orektós*, 'stretched out'; cp. also *órexis*, 'yearning desire for'; connected w. *orégein*, 'to reach, stretch out for', wh. is cogn. w. Lat. *regere*, 'to stretch; to guide, conduct'. See **regal, regulate**. (philos.) Of, relating to, the desires or appetites; appetitive.

oreïde, oroeide, n. [1. ốreïd; 2. ɔ́riīd]. Fr., fr. *or*, 'gold', fr. Lat. *aurum*, see **aureate**, & *-eide*, fr. Gk. *eîdos*, 'shape, form'. See **idol** & **-oid**. An alloy of copper and tin or zinc, used in making cheap imitation-gold jewellery.

organ, n. [1. órgan; 2. ɔ́gən]. M.E. *organe*, 'the musical instrument', fr. Lat. *organum*, 'implement, instrument, means', later specif. 'musical instrument'; borrowed fr. Gk. *órganon*, 'an instrument, tool; engine'; cogn. w. Gk. *érgon*, 'work'. See **ergon, energy, & work**. **1. a** A part of the bodily structure of an animal or plant which performs some particular function: *sense organ*; *organs of respiration, reproduction* &c.; *vocal organs, nasal organ* &c.; **b** specif., an individual human voice, thought of in relation to its range, power, quality: *he has a splendid organ, but is quite untrained in singing*. **2**. A means, instrument, or agency: *Parliament is the chief and final organ of government*. **3**. A medium, means, for influencing, or exchanging, opinion &c.; a newspaper: *the daily organs of the press*; *control of the party organs*. **4**. (mus., the earliest meaning of the word in Engl.) **a** The largest of musical wind-instruments, consisting of metal or wooden pipes of varying length and thickness, which produce the different notes, a bellows mechanically worked which supplies the air, manuals with keys like those of a pianoforte, by means of which the air is released from the pipes, and various pedals and stops which alter the quality or the volume of the sound; **b** the name of various other musical instruments, some resembling the organ in being operated by wind, as the *American organ* or harmonium; also the *barrel-organ*, resembling a large musical-box, worked by a handle, or the *piano-organ*, similarly worked.

organ-builder, n. The designer and maker of a musical organ.

organ-case, n. The wooden casing of an organ.

organdie, n. [1. órgandi; 2. ɔ́gəndi]. Fr. *organdi*; etymol. doubtful. A fine, transparent muslin, plain or figured.

organ-grinder, n. One who plays a barrel- or piano-organ in the street by turning a handle.

organic, adj. [1. orgánik; 2. ɔgǽnik], fr. Lat. *organicus*, fr. Gk. *organikós*. See **organ** & **-ic**. **1**. (of living things) Connected with, pertaining to, the bodily and vital organs of animals or plants: *organic structures*; *organic disease*, one which affects a bodily organ in its structure and not merely in its function; contrasted with *functional*. **2**. Possessing bodily organs variously specialized and differentiated to perform the several functions of a living animal or plant: *organic life*, contrasted with *inorganic*; *organic chemistry*, that dealing with the products of animal and vegetable organisms; now largely restricted to the study of carbon and hydrogen compounds. **3**. Having a definite, systematic, structural arrangement; organized: *an organic whole*, a complete unity.

organically, adv. [1. orgánikali; 2. ɔgǽnikəli]. Prec. & **-al** & **-ly**. In an organic manner; **a** structurally; **b** by means of bodily organs; **c** as an organic whole.

organism, n. [1. órganizm; 2. ɔ́gənizəm]. **organ** & **-ism**. **1**. (biol.) An individual possessing some degree of structural and functional differentiation and specialization, and capable of growth and reproduction. **2**. Something forming an independent unity, resembling a living organism in structure, possessing an orderly arrangement and specific differentiation of parts which have each their allotted function in the existence of the whole; applied to political and social entities.

organist, n. [1. órganist; 2. ɔ́gənist]. **organ** & **-ist**. One who plays on the organ.

organizable, adj. [1. órganīzabl; 2. ɔ́gənaizəbl]. **organize** & **-able**. Capable of being organized.

organization, n. [1. òrganīzáshun; 2. ɔ̀gənaizéiʃən]. **organize** & **-ation**. **1**. Act of organizing; state of being organized; mode in which something is organized; orderly, systematic arrangement, grouping of parts and assignment of functions. **2**. Something which is organized; specif., a system exhibiting organization; a body, association, of persons united by a common purpose, having various functions or lines of action allotted for carrying out the business and securing the objects of the whole.

organize, vb. trans. & intrans. [1. órganīz; 2. ɔ́gənaiz]. Med. Lat. *organizāre*, fr. *organum*, 'organ', cp. Fr. *organiser*. See **organ** & **-ize**. **A**. trans. **1**. (only in P.P.) To make organic; provide with structural and functional differentiation necessary to a living organism: *organized matter*. **2**. To give structural, systematic shape or form to; to arrange, group, the separate parts of, and allot to each a special function, so that all work together as a whole or unity: *to organize an army, government, party* &c. **3**. To arrange, make preparations for, and carry out (some undertaking): *to organize an entertainment*. **B**. intrans. **1**. To become organic. **2**. To carry on the process of organization.

organizer, n. [1. órganīzer; 2. ɔ́gənaizə]. Prec. & **-er**. One who organizes.

organ-loft, n. The gallery in which an organ is built and where the player sits.

organo-, pref. Form of **organon**, see **organ**, used in compounds; signifying relation, **a** with bodily organs, **b** with organisms.

organon, organum, n. [1. órganon, -um; 2. ɔ́gənən, -əm]. Gk., Lat., 'implement, tool, engine; means'. See **organ**. A system, means, method, whereby scientific and philosophic investigation may be carried on: *Aristotle's 'Organon'*; *Bacon's 'Novum Organum'*.

organotherapy, n. [1. òrganōthérapi; 2. ɔ̀gənouþérəpi]. See **organo-** & **-therapy**. Treatment of diseases by means of extracts from animal organs, such as the thyroid gland.

organ-pipe, n. Any one of the set of pipes of which the wind-organ is constructed.

organzine, n. [1. órganzēn; 2. ɔ́gənzīn], fr. Fr. *organsin*, fr. Ital. *organzino*. A fine kind of strong, silk thread with a double twist.

orgasm, n. [1. órgazm; 2. ɔ́gæzəm]. Fr. *orgasme*, fr. Gk. *orgasmós*, 'swelling', also 'softening, kneading', fr. *orgân*, 'to swell', cp. Gk. *orgḗ*, 'excitement, anger', cogn. w. Scrt. *ūrjā*, 'violence'; O. Ir. *ferg*, 'anger'. Violent excitement, paroxysm; specif., the height, culminating point, of excitement in the sexual act.

orgeat, n. [1. órjiat; 2. ɔ́džiæt]. Fr., fr. *orge*, 'barley', fr. Lat. *hordeum*, 'barley'; cogn. w. **groats**. A drink composed of barley-water flavoured with sweet almonds.

orgiastic, adj. [1. òrjiástik; 2. ɔ̀džiǽstik], fr. Gk. *orgiastikós*, 'performing orgies', fr. *orgiázein*, 'to celebrate by orgies'. See **orgy**. Of, pertaining to, orgies; revelling: *orgiastic rites*.

orgy, n. [1. órji; 2. ɔ́dži]. Earlier only in pl., Fr. *orgies*, fr. Lat. *orgia*, Gk. *órgia*, pl., prob. connected w. *érgon*, pl. *érga*, 'works, things done or performed; rites'. See **ergon** & **energy**. **1**. (Gk. and Rom. antiq.) The secret rites and ceremonies of the ancient mysteries, esp. those connected with the worship of Bacchus; Bacchic revelry. **2. a** Drunken carousals; lewd revelry; unrestrained practice of debauchery; also **b** in innocent sense, a continuous round of gaieties or entertainments: *a regular orgy of parties and concerts*.

oriel, n. [1. ốriel; 2. ɔ́riəl], fr. O. Fr. *oriol*, also in Med. Lat. *oriolum*, 'recess, gallery'; etymol. doubtful. A projecting bay or recessed window; usually on an upper storey, supported by corbels.

orient (I.), adj. & n. [1. ốrient; 2. ɔ́riənt]. Fr., fr. Lat. *orient-(em)*, *oriens*, 'the East', fr. Pres. Part. of *orīri*, 'to rise', cp. Lat. *ortus*, 'a rising'; cogn. w. Gk. *órthros*, 'early morning'; cp. also Gk. *érnos*, 'shoot, twig, sprout'. See **order** (I.) & cp. **orchestra**. **1**. adj. **a** (poet.) Rising in the East, oriental: *the orient sun*; **b** (of pearls) of the finest kind; lustrous. **2**. n. **a** (cap.) The East; Oriental countries; Asia; **b** superior quality or lustre of pearl, esp. of those coming from the Orient: *pearl of finest orient*.

orient (II.), vb. trans. [1. ốriènt; 2. ɔ́rient]. See prec. To orientate.

oriental, adj. & n. [1. òriéntl; 2. ɔ̀riéntl]. Fr., fr. Lat. *orientālis*. See **orient** (I.) & **-al**. **1**. adj. Of or pertaining to the Orient or East, esp. to Asia or the Far East; Asiatic: *oriental civilization, art, china* &c. **2**. n. (cap.) A native of the East or Asia; member of an Asiatic race; esp. of the Chinese & Japanese.

orientalism, n. [1. òriéntalizm; 2. ɔ̀riéntəlizəm]. Prec. & **-ism**. Custom, habit, method of thought &c. peculiar to the East or to Orientals.

orientalist, n. [1. òriéntalist; 2. ɔ̀riéntəlist]. **oriental** & **-ist**. One who makes a special study of oriental languages, art, civilization &c.

orientalize, vb. trans. [1. òriéntalīz; 2. ɔ̀riéntəlaiz]. **oriental** & **-ize**. To make oriental; to habituate to oriental ideas, customs, manners.

orientally, adv. [1. òriéntali; 2. ɔ̀riéntəli]. **oriental** & **-ly**. In an oriental manner; like an Oriental.

orientate, vb. trans. & intrans. [1. ốrientāt; 2. ɔ́rientèit]. **orient** & **-ate**. **A**. trans. **1**. (archit.) To plan, lay out, a building, esp. a church, so that the altar end of the main axis points to the east. **2**. To place a building, monument &c. so that the front, back, and sides shall correspond to the points of the compass. **3**. (fig.) **a** To place an object or oneself in definite relation to another object, situation &c.; to take one's bearings; **b** (usually reflex., fig.) to take one's intellectual bearings; ascertain moral relation, and significance of events and circumstances in relation to others; familiarize oneself with a subject or situation. **B.** intrans. **1.** To move, turn, towards the East. **2.** To take up a position in definite relation to another object or position.

orientation, n. [1. òrientáshun; 2. òrientéiʃən]. Prec. & **-ation.** **1.** Position of a body in relation with the points of the compass. **2.** (archit.) Placing of a church so that the altar is at the east end. **3.** Adjustment in relative position to another object, principle &c.

orifice, n. [1. órifis; 2. ɔ́rifis]. Fr., fr. L. Lat. *ōrificium*, 'an opening', lit. 'mouth-making', fr. *ōr-(is)*, 'the mouth', see **oral**, & *fic-*, stem of *facere*, 'to make', see **fact.** Mouth, outer opening, or aperture, of a tube or pipe &c.: *orifice of a wound, chimney* &c.

oriflamme, n. [1. óriflam; 2. ɔ́riflæm]. O. Fr. *oriflambe*, fr. Med. Lat. *auriflamma*, Lat. *aurum*, 'gold', see **aureate** & **aurora**, & *flamma*, see **flame.** **1.** The ancient battle standard of the kings of France, the banner of St. Denis, of red with streamers borne on a gilded lance. **2.** Anything which serves, actually or figuratively, as a focus for devotion and loyalty.

origan, origanum, n. [1. órigan, oríganum; 2. ɔ́rigən, ɔrígənəm]. Lat. *orīganum*, fr. Gk. *oríganon*, 'marjoram', fr. *óros*, 'mountain', see **Oread**, & *gános*, 'brightness, glory', fr. *gánumai*, 'to rejoice'. Sweet marjoram; also used of other plants of this genus or type.

origin, n. [1. órijin; 2. ɔ́ridžin], fr. Fr. *origine*, fr. Lat. *orīgin-(em)*, stem of *orīgo*, 'a beginning', fr. *orīri*, 'to arise, begin'; fr. base **or-*, 'to move'. See **orient** & **order.** **1.** That whence anything takes its rise; a source, starting-point; the earliest stages, beginnings of anything: *the origin(s) of civilization; insignificant origins*; **b** initial cause: *the origin of a quarrel.* **2.** Birth, parentage, ancestry: *a man of humble, lofty, origin.*

original (I.), adj. [1. oríjinal; 2. ərídžinəl, ərídžinl]. Fr., fr. Lat. *orīginālis*; see prec. & **-al**; much earlier in Engl. usage than the n. **1. a** Pertaining to the origin or beginning; existing from the first; earliest, most primitive: *the original inhabitants, language, of a country; translated from the original Latin; Stephenson's original locomotive; the original edition of a book*; specif. **b** *original sin*, the state of sin in which man is born into the world, as a result of the fall of Adam. **2.** (of persons and the human mind) Able to originate, initiate, create, new ideas, thoughts, or processes; constructive, inventive, creative: *an original writer, composer, genius.* **3.** (of products of the human mind) Created, made, invented, constructed, for the first time; not derived or copied from, not suggested by, something or someone else; first-hand; new: *few plots of plays are entirely original; an original plan, invention, idea.*

original (II.), n., fr. prec. **1.** (archaic) First cause, source; originator, author: '*The spacious firmament on high, With all the blue ethereal sky, And spangled heavens, a shining frame, Their great Original proclaim*' (Addison's Hymn). **2.** That from which other things are copied; the first pattern which serves as a model for subsequent reproductions; **a** *not the original, only a copy*, said of pictures and other works of art &c.; **b** the original or earliest edition of a book; **c** original language in which a work was composed: *to read Homer in the original*, not in translation. **3.** An eccentric person.

originality, n. [1. orìjináliti; 2. əridžinǽliti]. Prec. & **-ity.** Cp. Fr. *originalité.* **1.** (rare) Condition of being original; authenticity, genuineness; (of objects which are often copied) *the originality of a portrait.* **2.** State, quality, of being original; **a** (in human beings and the human mind) process of inventiveness; creative faculty; capacity to originate new ideas: *a man, a mind, of great originality*; **b** (of products of the human mind) quality of being spontaneous and newly-created; freshness, novelty: *a work of no great originality, plenty of originality in the idea.*

originally, adv. [1. oríjinali; 2. ərídžinəli]. **original** (I.) & **-ly.** In origin; from, in, the beginning, at first; primarily; formerly.

originate, vb. trans. & intrans. [1. oríjināt; 2. ɔrídžineit]. **origin** & **-ate. A.** trans. **1.** To be the prime cause of; to bring about, to cause to start: *what originated the Great War?; the use of steam originated many other changes.* **2.** To be the author or inventor of; to initiate; to create, produce for the first time: *to originate new ideas*, methods &c. **B.** intrans. **a** To start, have origin in: *the fire originated in a barn*; **b** to have as a cause, or source: *the quarrel originated in a misunderstanding. Originating summons*, a summons taken out, without a writ, for decision, order &c. before a judge or a master.

origination, n. [1. orìjináshun; 2. ɔridžinéiʃən]. Prec. & **-ion. a** Act, fact, mode of originating, or being produced; **b** power of originating.

originative, adj. [1. oríjinativ; 2. ɔrídžinətiv]. **originate** & **-ive.** Having the faculty of originating; original.

originatively, adv. Prec. & **-ly.** In such a manner as to originate.

originator, n. [1. oríjinàter; 2. ɔrídžineitə]. **originate** & **-or.** One who originates or initiates.

ori-nasal, adj. [1. òri názl; 2. òri néizl], fr. Lat. *ōr-(is)*, *ōs*, 'mouth'. See **oral** & **nasal.** (phon., a fancy term, best avoided) Of speech sounds, esp. vowels, formed or produced both in the mouth and nose, such as those in Fr. *bon, sang* &c.; best called simply *nasal vowels*, since all vowels, and most consonants, are formed in the mouth.

oriole, n. [1. óriōl; 2. ɔ́rioul], fr. O. Fr. *oriol*, fr. Med. Lat. *oriolus*, Lat. *aureolus*, dimin. of *aureus*, 'golden', fr. *aurum*, 'gold'. See **aureate** & **aurora.** Bird of which there are several species in all continents, mostly bright yellow in colour with black wings and tail.

Orion, n. [1. orían; 2. ɔráiən]. Lat., fr. Gk. *Oriōn*, a giant hunter of Greek mythology, slain by Artemis and made into a constellation. (astron.) A brilliant constellation, one of the signs of the zodiac; *Orion's belt*, three very bright stars across the centre of the constellation.

orison, n. [1. órizn; 2. ɔ́rizən]. O. Fr., later *oreison, oraison*, fr. Lat. *ōrātiōn-(em)*, 'speech, prayer'. See **oration.** (archaic or poet.) A prayer (oftenest used in pl.).

orle, n. [1. orl; 2. ɔ̄l]. Fr., fr. Med. Lat. *orla*, fr. *orula*, dimin. of Lat. *ōra*, 'margin, border', cogn. w. Lat. *ōs*, 'mouth', see **oral**; cp. O.E. *ōr*, 'rim, edge'. (her.) A narrow fillet or border, half the width of the bordure, going round the shield at some distance from the edge.

Orleans, n. [1. orléanz; 2. ɔ̄líənz]. Name of town in France. **a** A purple plum; **b** fabric of worsted and cotton.

orlop, n. [1. órlop; 2. ɔ́lɔp], fr. Du. *overloop*, 'deck of a ship, orlop', fr. *overloopen*, 'to run over'. See **over** & **leap.** The deck of a ship next above the hold, usually of ships with three decks or more.

ormer, n. [1. órmer; 2. ɔ́mə]. Channel Islands Fr., fr. Fr. *ormier*, corrupt. of *oreille de mer*, 'ear of the sea'. A univalve, edible mollusc, *Haliotis tuberculata*, the sea-ear; the shell is shaped like an ear with a row of holes.

ormolu, n. [1. órmoloo; 2. ɔ́məlū], fr. Fr. *or moulu*, 'gold ground or milled'. **1.** Preparation of gold used in gilding; bronze &c. gilded. **2.** Brass lacquered to resemble gold; furniture ornamented with this.

ornament (I.), n. [1. órnament; 2. ɔ́nəmənt], fr. O. Fr. *ornement*, fr. Lat. *ornāmentum*, 'equipment, trappings, decoration, ornament', fr. *ornāre*, 'to fit out, equip; decorate, adorn'; etymol. doubtful; possibly a contracted form of *ordināre*, 'to set in order'. See **ordain.** **1.** Decoration, embellishment; that which adorns or embellishes. **2. a** Decorative object, small figure, vase &c. used as part of the adornment of a room: *ornaments on the mantelpiece*; specif. **b** any kind of embellishment, such as lace &c., also jewels and trinkets, worn on the person; **c** an embellishment of style, figure. **3.** (fig.) A person or quality which brings credit or adds lustre to others &c.: *an ornament to his profession.* **4.** (usually pl.) Articles used in church for the purpose of the service, as vestments, communion plate &c., as enjoined, at least by implication, by the *Ornaments Rubric* in the Prayer Book: '*of the ornaments of the church and of the ministers thereof*'.

ornament (II.), vb. trans., fr. prec. [1. órnamènt; 2. ɔ́nəmènt]. To decorate, embellish.

ornamental, adj. [1. òrnaméntl; 2. ɔ̀nəméntl]. See **ornament** (I.) & **-al.** Decorative; of the nature of ornament.

ornamentalist, n. [1. òrnaméntalist; 2. ɔ̀nəméntəlist]. Prec. & **-ist.** A decorator; a decorative artist.

ornamentalize, vb. trans. [1. òrnaméntalīz; 2. ɔ̀nəméntəlaiz]. See prec. & **-ize.** To make ornamental; to supply with ornaments or decorations.

ornamentally, adv. [1. òrnaméntali; 2. ɔ̀nəméntəli]. **ornamental** & **-ly.** In an ornamental manner; as ornament.

ornamentation, n. [1. òrnamentáshun; 2. ɔ̀nəmentéiʃən]. **ornament** (II.) & **-ation.** **1.** Act of ornamenting or decorating; state of being ornamented. **2.** That which ornaments; decoration, embellishment.

ornate, adj. [1. ornát; 2. ɔ̄néit], fr. Lat. *ornāt-(um)*, 'adorned', P.P. of *ornāre*, 'to adorn'. See **ornament.** **1.** (of art) Excessively or extravagantly adorned; richly embellished. **2.** (of liter., or oratorical style) Highly elaborate in diction; characterized by a careful choice of rare and striking words, by the avoidance of simple and ordinary modes of expression, and often by rather fanciful figures of speech.

ornately, adv. Prec. & **-ly.** In an ornate manner.

ornateness, n. See prec. & **-ness.** State, quality, of being ornate.

ornitho-, pref., fr. Gk. *órnīth-(os)*, *órnis*, 'bird'; cogn. w. O.E. *earn*, O.H.G. *arn*, 'eagle', Lith. *erēlis*, O. Slav. *orĭlŭ*, 'eagle'; used in compounds.

ornithological, adj. [1. òrnithōlójikl; 2. ɔ̀niþoulɔ́džikl]. Prec. & **-logical.** Of, pertaining to, ornithology.

ornithologist, n. [1. òrnithólojist; 2. ɔ̀niþɔ́lədžist]. **ornitho-** & **-logy** & **-ist.** Student of birds and bird life.

ornithology, n. [1. òrnithóloji; 2. ɔ̀niþɔ́lədži]. **ornitho-** & **-logy.** Scientific study of birds, their varieties, structure, habits &c.

ornithomancy, n. [1. orníthomànsi; 2. ɔ̄nái-þomænsi]. **ornitho-** & **-mancy.** Divination by observation of the flight of birds.

ornithorhynchus, n. [1. òrnithōríngkus; 2. ɔ̀niþouríŋkəs]. **ornitho-** & Gk. *(h)rúngkhos*, 'snout, bill', etymol. doubtful. Australian pouched mammal with webbed feet and a duck's bill, which hatches out its young from eggs; also called *duck-billed platypus.*

ornithoscopy, n. [1. òrnithóskopi; 2. ɔ̀niþɔ́skəpi]. **ornitho-** & **-scopy.** Ornithomancy, augury.

oroeide. See **orëide.**

orographic(al), adj. [1. òrōgráfik(l); 2. ɔ̀rougrǽfik(l). Next word & **-ic** (& **-al**). Pertaining to orography.

orography, n. [1. ōrógrafi; 2. ɔ̄rɔ́grəfi], fr. Gk. *óros*, 'mountain', q.v. under **Oread**, & **-graphy.** The branch of physical geography which treats of mountains and mountain systems; orology.

orology, n. [1. ōróloji; 2. ɔ̄rɔ́lədži], fr. Gk. *óros*, 'mountain', see **Oread**, & **-logy.** Orography.

orometer, n. [1. ōrómeter; 2. ɔrɔ́mitə]. See prec. & **-meter**. An instrument for measuring the height of mountains or ascertaining the height above sea-level of the place where the measurement is made.

orotund, adj. [1. ṓrōtund; 2. ɔ́routand], fr. Lat. *ōr-(is)*, fr. *ōs*, 'mouth', see **oral**, & *rotundus*, 'round, rounded, smooth', as in Phr. *ore rotundo*. See **rotund** & **round (I.)**. **1.** (of the voice) Full, round, resonant, ringing. **2.** (of style in speaking or writing) Pompous, turgid, bombastic.

orotundity, n. [1. ōrōtúnditi; 2. ɔroutánditi]. Prec. & **-ity**. Quality of being orotund.

orphan (I.), n. [1. órfan; 2. ɔ́fən], fr. L. Lat. *orphanus*, fr. Gk. *orphanós*, 'destitute, fatherless, orphaned'; the earlier form in Engl. was *orphelin*, 'bereaved, parentless; childless; an orphan'; O. Fr. *orphelin*, earlier *orphenin*; the class. Lat. word was *orbus*, wh., together w. Gk. *orphanós*, goes back to a base **orbh-*. From this base come also Goth. *arbi*, 'inheritance', & *arbja*, 'heir'; cp. O.E. *ierfe*, 'inheritance; property'. A child who has lost one or both of its parents by death.

orphan (II.), adj., fr. prec. Bereft of both parents or of either parent: *an orphan child.*

orphan (III.), vb. trans., fr. **orphan (I.)** To deprive, bereave, (a child) of its parents.

orphanage, n. [1. órfanij; 2. ɔ́fənidž]. **orphan (I.)** & **-age**. **1.** State of being an orphan; orphanhood. **2.** An institution for the care and education of orphans.

orphanhood, n. [1. órfanhood; 2. ɔ́fənhud]. See prec. & **-hood**. State of being an orphan.

Orphean, adj. [1. orféan; 2. ɔfíən], fr. Lat. *Orphē-(us)*, 'of, pertaining to, Orpheus', & **-an**. (poet.) Of, pertaining to, Orpheus or the music with which he charmed the beasts; melodious: *Orphean lyre, strains* &c.

Orphic, adj. [1. órfik; 2. ɔ́fik], fr. Gk. *Orphikós*, 'of, pertaining to, Orpheus'. Of, connected with, pertaining to, the mysteries, rites, and ceremonies associated with Orpheus; mysterious, esoteric: *Orphic mysteries.*

Orphism, n. [1. órfizm; 2. ɔ́fizəm]. See prec. & **-ism**. The rites, ceremonies, and religious doctrine of the Orphic mysteries.

orphrey, n. [1. órfri; 2. ɔ́fri]. Earlier *orfray*, fr. O. Fr. *orfreis*, 'embroidery', fr. Lat. *auriphrygium*, 'gold Phrygian embroidery', fr. *aurum*, 'gold', see **aureate**, & *Phrygius*, 'Phrygian'. A gold-embroidered band or border on an ecclesiastical vestment.

orpiment, n. [1. órpiment; 2. ɔ́pimənt]. O. Fr., fr. Lat. *auripigmentum*, fr. *aurum*, 'gold', see **aureate**, & *pigmentum*, see **pigment**. Yellow sulphide of arsenic; used as a pigment.

orpine, n. [1. órpin; 2. ɔ́pin]. Fr. *orpin*, 'a plant with yellow flowers'; variant of prec. A stonecrop, *Sedum*, with fleshy leaves and purple-coloured flowers.

Orpington, n. [1. órpingtun; 2. ɔ́piŋtən]. Name of a village in Kent. A breed of domestic fowl: *buff, white, Orpington.*

orrery, n. [1. óreri; 2. ɔ́rəri], fr. title of Charles Boyle, 4th Earl of Orrery, who directed, and paid for the making of the first apparatus, c. 1713. An apparatus, moved by clockwork, showing the movements of the planets.

orris (I.), n. [1. óris; 2. ɔ́ris]. Prob. corrupt. of O. Fr. *orphreis*. See **orphrey**. Gold or silver lace or braid.

orris (II.), n. Prob. form of Med. Ital. *ireos*, 'orris-root', fr. Lat. *īris*, Gk. *îris*. See **iris**. The Florentine iris or flower-de-luce; specif., *orris-root*, the fragrant dried root of this or other species of iris, powdered, and used as dentifrice and in perfumery.

ort, n. [1. ort; 2. ɔt]. M.E. *ort*, & *ortys*, pl., 'refuse', cp. Du. *oor-aete*, 'remnants'; as fr. O.E. *or-*, 'not', & *ǣt*, 'food'. See **eat**. (provinc. or obs., usually in pl.) Remnants of food left after a meal.

ortho-, pref. Combining form fr. Gk. *orthós*, 'upright, straight', also in moral sense, 'right, true, exact; real, genuine; righteous, just'; cogn. w. Lat. *arduus*, steep, lofty; difficult', see **arduous**; Scrt. *ūrdhváś*, 'high'. Used in Engl., in old & new compounds fr. Gk. w. force of **a** straight; rectangular: *orthognathous*; *orthogonal*; **b** genuine, regular: *orthochromatic*; **c** true, right, correct: *orthodox* &c.

orthocephalic, orthocephalous, adj. [1. òrthōsefálik, -séfalus; 2. ɔ̀þousəfǽlik, -séfələs]. **ortho-** & **cephalic, (-ous)**. (of the skull) Having breadth of from ¾ to ⅘ of length; half-way between *dolicho-* and *brachycephalic.*

orthochromatic, adj. [1. òrthōkrōmátik; 2. ɔ̀þoukroumǽtik]. **ortho-** & **chromatic**. (photog.) Giving or producing true relative tones of light and shade.

orthoclase, n. [1. órthōklāz; 2. ɔ́þoukleiz]. **ortho-** & Gk. *kláein*, *klân*, 'to break, cleave'. See second element in **iconoclasm**. (mineral.) Common potash feldspar, a constituent of granite, gneiss &c.

orthoclastic, adj. [1. òrthōklástik; 2. ɔ̀þouklǽstik]. See prec. & **-ic**. (crystal.) Having a cleavage at right angles, as the common feldspars.

orthodox, adj. [1. órthodoks; 2. ɔ́þədɔks], fr. Gk. *orthódoxos*, 'having right opinions'; **ortho-** & *dóxa*, 'opinion'. See **dogma** & **doxology**. **1.** Correct, right in opinion or doctrine, esp. in theological or religious opinion; contrasted with *heterodox*. **2.** Specif. (cap.) belonging to the *Orthodox Eastern*, or *Greek Church*, of Greece, Bulgaria, Serbia, Roumania, and Russia; one of the ancient divisions of the Catholic Church, as contrasted with the *Roman* or *Western Church*. **3.** (gen. sense) Holding opinions which are conventionally regarded as true and correct or as being established by authority.

orthodoxy, n. [1. órthodòksi; 2. ɔ́þədɔ̀ksi], fr. Gk. *orthodoxía*, 'correct, right opinion'. Prec. & **-y**. State, quality, of being orthodox; correctness of religious or theological belief; also of scientific doctrine.

orthoepic, adj. [1. òrthōépik; 2. ɔ̀þouípik]. See **orthoepy** & **-ic**. Of, relating to, orthoepy or correct pronunciation.

orthoepist, n. [1. orthṓēpist; 2. ɔþóuipist]. See prec. & **-ist**. Teacher, student, of orthoepy.

orthoepy, n. [1. òrthṓēpi; 2. ɔþóuipi], fr. Gk. *orthoépeia*, fr. **ortho-** & *épos*, 'word', see **epic**, & **-y**. Correct pronunciation; study of, theory and teaching concerning, this.

orthogenesis, n. [1. òrthōjénesis; 2. ɔ̀þoudžénisis]. **ortho-** & **genesis**. (biol.) A consistent variation in successive generations resulting in a fresh type, independent of natural selection or other external factors.

orthognathous, adj. [1. òrthōgnā́thus; 2. ɔ̀þougnéiþəs]. **ortho-** & Gk. *gnáthos*, 'jaw', see **gnathic**, & **-ous**. Having a skull in which the forehead in profile is approximately in a straight line with the lower jaw, and not one in which one projects and the other recedes; contrasted with *opisthognathous* and *prognathous.*

orthogonal, adj. [1. orthógonal; 2. ɔþɔ́gənəl]. **ortho-** & Gk. *gōnía*, 'angle', see **-gon**. Right-angled, rectangular.

orthographer, n. [1. orthógrafer; 2. ɔþɔ́grəfə]. See **orthography** & **-er**. A correct speller; person skilled in orthography.

orthographic(al), adj. [1. òrthōgráfik(l); 2. ɔ̀þougrǽfik(l)]. See **ortho-** & **graphic** & **-al**. **1.** Of, pertaining to, orthography or correct spelling. **2.** (drawing) Pertaining to the orthography of a plan: *orthographic projection*, one in which the lines are perpendicular to the plane of projection, perspectively drawn as if seen from an infinite distance. **3.** (geom.) Pertaining to right lines or angles.

orthographically, adv. Prec. & **-ly**. According to the rules of orthography.

orthography, n. [1. orthógrafi; 2. ɔþɔ́grəfi], fr. O. Fr. *ortographie*, & so spelt in M.E., fr. Lat., fr. Gk. *orthographía*, 'correct writing'. **ortho-** & **-graphy**. **1.** Correct spelling; that is in accordance with the accepted standard of a given age. **2.** That part of grammar which treats of spelling and gives the accepted rules. **3.** (drawing) Art of drawing an elevation in correct projection.

orthopaedia. See **orthopaedy**.

orthopaedic, adj. [1. òrthōpḗdik; 2. ɔ̀þoupídik]. **orthopaedy** & **-ic**. Connected with, based on, orthopaedics: *orthopaedic surgery*; *orthopaedic hospital*, one where this branch of surgery is practised.

orthopaedics, n. pl. That branch of operative or manipulative surgery which deals with deformities of the bony structure of the body, esp. in young children.

orthopaedist, n. [1. òrthōpḗdist; 2. ɔ̀þoupídist]. See next word & **-ist**. One skilled in orthopaedics.

orthopaedy, n. [1. órthōpēdi; 2. ɔ́þoupìdi], fr. Fr. *orthopédie*, fr. **ortho-** & Gk. *paid-(ós)*, *paîs*, 'child'. See **paedo-**. Orthopaedics.

orthopedic &c. See **orthopaedic** &c.

orthopterous, adj. [1. orthópterus; 2. ɔþɔ́ptərəs]. **ortho-** & Gk. *pterón*, 'wing', see **ptero-**, & **-ous**. (entom.) Belonging to the order of insects, *Orthoptera*, including the locusts, grasshoppers, cockroaches &c. which have wings folding down the back.

orthoptic, adj. & n. [1. orthóptik; 2. ɔþɔ́ptik]. **ortho-** & **optic**. **1.** adj. Having normal, correct vision in both eyes. **2.** n. A perforated back-sight on a rifle.

ortolan, n. [1. órtolan; 2. ɔ́tələn]. Fr., fr. Ital. *ortolano*, 'gardener, garden bird', fr. Lat. *hortulānus*, 'belonging to a garden, gardener', fr. *hortulus*, dimin. of *hortus*, 'garden'. See **hortus siccus**. **1.** The garden bunting, *Emberiza hortulana*; netted and fattened as a table delicacy. **2.** The wheatear.

-ory, suff. [1. uri; 2. əri], fr. A.-Fr. *-ori*, masc., *-orie*, fem., Mod. Fr. *-oir*, *-oire*; fr. Lat. suff. *-ōrius, -a, -um*, adj. ending in *-ius* added to agent suff. **-or**; **a** for adjs.: *declamatory*; *preparatory* &c.; **b** for ns., fr. Lat. neuts. in *-orium*, or coined on anal.: *dormitory*, *laboratory*, so *factory.*

oryx, n. [1. óriks; 2. ɔ́riks]. Lat., fr. Gk. *órux*, 'a horned Egyptian antelope'. (zool.) A genus of African antelopes with long straight horns.

os, n., pl. **ossa** [1. os, ósa; 2. ɔs, ɔ́sə]. Lat. *ŏs, oss*, 'a bone'; cp. Gk. *ostéon*, 'bone', Lat. *osseum*; Scrt. *asthi*; cogn. w. Goth. *asts*, 'bough of a tree'; all fr. orig. type of base **od-thi*, wh. appears also in Gk. *ózos*, 'bough'. Cp. also O.E. *ōst*, 'knot in a tree'. Used in anatomical terminology in denominating bones: *os calcis* &c.

Oscan, adj. & n. [1. óskan; 2. ɔ́skən]. Lat. *Osci*, earlier *Opsci*, perh. fr. base seen in *ops*, 'power, wealth'; see **opulent**. **1.** adj. Of, pertaining to, the Osci, an ancient people of Campania, or to their language. **2.** n. The Italic dialect spoken by the Osci.

oscillate, vb. intrans. & trans. [1. ósilāt; 2. ɔ́sileit], fr. Lat. *oscillāt-(um)*, P.P. type of *oscillāre*, 'to swing, sway'. Etymol. doubtful; Walde suggests derivation fr. **obs-*, fr. **ob-**, & *clīnāre*, 'to bend, bow'. See **decline**. **A.** intrans. **1.** To swing backwards and forwards like a pendulum; to move, vibrate, between two fixed points. **2.** (fig.) To waver, vacillate, between two courses of action, opinions &c.; to act in a changeable, vacillating manner. **3.** (phys.) To exhibit the phenomenon of oscillation. **B.** trans. **1.** To cause to swing backwards and forwards. **2.** To cause oscillations in or to.

oscillation, n. [1. òsiláshun; 2. ɔ̀siléiʃən]. Lat. *oscillātiōn-(em)*, 'a swinging'. Prec. & **-ion**. **1. a** Act of oscillating, state of being in movement; **b** fluctuation, variation, vacillation, in action, opinions &c. **2.** (elect.) An irregular or intermittent discharge, electrical surging or disturbed movement of waves; as in wireless telegraphy and telephony.

oscillator, n. [1. ósilātur; 2. ɔ́sileitə]. **oscillate** & **-or**. Person who, thing which, oscillates; specif., electric system or apparatus which generates electro-magnetic waves, as in wireless telegraphy and telephony.

oscillatory, adj. [1. ósilàturi; 2. ɔ́siləitəri]. **oscillate** & **-ory**. Marked by oscillations, tending to oscillate; vibratory: *oscillatory circuit, current* &c.

oscillograph, n. [1. ósilograhf; 2. ɔ́siləgrāf]. Coined fr. **oscillate** & **-graph**. An instrument for registering oscillations or variations of electrical current.

oscine, adj. [1. ósīn; 2. ɔ́sain], fr. Lat. *oscin-is, oscen*, 'singing bird'; esp. a bird whose cry or song was used in augury', for **obscen*, fr. *ob(s)*, see **ob-**, & *canere*, 'to sing', see **chant**. (ornith.) Belonging to the *Oscines*, a group or suborder of Passerine birds, including the true singing birds.

oscitation, n. [1. òsitā́shun; 2. ɔ̀sitéiʃən]. Lat. *oscitātiōn-(em), oscitātio*, 'yawning', fr. *oscitāre*, 'to gape, yawn', fr. *ōs*, 'mouth', see **oral**, & *citāre*, 'to move', q.v. under **cite**. (rare) **a** Yawning, gaping, extreme drowsiness; **b** negligence, inattention.

osculant, adj. [1. óskūlant; 2. ɔ́skjulənt], fr. Lat. *osculant-(em)*, Pres. Part. of *osculāri*, 'to kiss'. See **osculate**. Kissing; hence, meeting, touching; specif. (biol.) forming a link between two groups or species.

oscular, adj. [1. óskūlar; 2. ɔ́skjulə], fr. Lat. *oscul-(um)*, 'mouth, kiss', dimin. of *ōs*, 'mouth', see **oral**, & **-ar**. **1.** Pertaining to the mouth; pertaining to a kiss. **2.** (biol.) Of, pertaining to, an *osculum*, opening or orifice as in sponges &c.

osculate, vb. trans. & intrans. [1. óskūlāt; 2. ɔ́skjuleit], fr. Lat. *osculāt-(um)*, P.P. type of *osculāri*, 'to kiss', fr. *osculum*, 'kiss'. See prec. & **osculum** & **-ate**. **1.** trans. To kiss. **2.** intrans. (biol., of different groups) To be nearly related, to have characteristics in common. **3.** (math.) To touch closely, as of curves at more than one point.

osculation, n. [1. òskūlā́shun; 2. ɔ̀skjuléiʃən], fr. Lat. *osculātiōn-(em), osculātio*, 'a kiss'. See prec. & **-ion**. **1.** A kiss. **2.** Specif. (math.) contact of a curve with another curve.

osculatory, adj. [1. óskūlaturi; 2. ɔ́skjulətəri]. **osculate** & **-ory**. **1.** Kissing. **2.** (math.) Osculating.

osculum, n. [1. óskūlum; 2. ɔ́skjuləm]. Lat., 'little mouth; a kiss', fr. *ōs*, 'mouth', see **oral**, & dimin. suff., q.v. under **-cule**. (zool.) **1.** One of the openings or holes in a sponge. **2.** A sucker whereby some lowly forms of life are able to attach themselves.

-ose, suff. (1) fr. Lat. suff. *-ōsus*, meaning 'full of, abounding in, having qualities of': *verbose, bellicose, jocose* &c; (2) (chem.) by anal., fr. *glucose*, taken fr. Fr., of carbohydrates: *cellulose, fructose* &c.

osier, n. [1. ózhier; 2. óužiə]. Fr., 'willow'; etymol. doubtful; L. Lat. has *ausāria, ōsāria*, 'bundle of willow twigs or shoots'. Any of several species of willow whose flexible twigs are used in basket-work.

osier-bed, n. Damp place abounding in osiers; clump of osiers.

-osis, suff., fr. Gk. *-ōsis*, suff. expressing state, condition, process: *metamorphosis* &c.; in modern medical usage it expresses a state of disease, as *necrosis* &c.

-osity, suff. See **-ose** & **-ity**.

Osmanli, n. [1. ozmánli; 2. ɔzmǽnli]. Turk. *Osmānli*. A Turk of European or Ottoman branch of empire founded by Osman I., 1301.

osmic, adj. [1. ós-, ózmik; 2. ɔ́s-, ɔ́zmik], fr. **osmium** & **-ic**. (chem.) Pertaining to osmium.

osmium, n. [1. ós-, ózmium; 2. ɔ́s-, ɔ́zmiəm]. Coined fr. Gk. *osmḗ*, 'a smell, odour', for **odsmā*; cogn. w. *ózein*, 'to smell', & Lat. *odor*, see **odour**. (chem.) A very hard white metallic element, associated with platinum, chiefly used for making filaments for electric lamps; its oxide gives off a powerfully smelling and poisonous vapour.

osmosis, n. [1. os-, ozmósis; 2. ɔs-, ɔzmóusis]. Modern coinage, formed fr. Gk. *ōsmós*, 'a pushing, impulse', fr. *ōthein*, 'to strike, push', & **-osis**. Cogn. w. Scrt. *vadh-*, 'to strike', *vādáya-*, 'to repulse'; fr. base **wŏdh-*, 'to strike'. (phys.) The interchange of place of two fluids separated by a permeable partition, each tending to pass through the latter at a rate determined by their respective densities.

osmotic, adj. [1. os-, ozmótik; 2. ɔs-, ɔzmɔ́tik]. Prec. & **-ic**. Of, pertaining to, osmosis.

osmund, osmunda, n. [1. ózmund, ozmúnda; 2. ɔ́zmənd, ɔzmʌ́ndə], fr. Fr. *osmonde*; etymol. doubtful. The royal or king fern, or flowering fern, *Osmunda regalis*.

osprey, n. [1. óspri, -ā; 2. ɔ́spri, -ei]. Fr. *orfraie*, fr. Lat. *ossifraga*. See **ossifrage**. **1.** A large fishing-hawk or sea-eagle, *Pandion haliaetus*. **2.** A milliner's term for an egret's plume; the osprey has no such plumes.

osseous, adj. [1. óseus; 2. ɔ́siəs], fr. Lat. *osseus*, 'bony', fr. *oss-(is), ōs*, 'bone'. See **os**. Bony; composed, consisting, of bone; having a bony, not cartilaginous, skeleton.

ossicle, n. [1. ósikl; 2. ɔ́sikl], fr. Lat. *ossiculum*, dimin. fr. *ōs*, 'bone'. See prec. (anat.) A small bone or bony structure, as in the ear.

ossification, n. [1. òsifikā́shun; 2. ɔ̀sifikéiʃən], fr. Lat. *ossi-*, 'bone', see **os**, & **-fication**; cp. **ossify**. **a** Process of changing into bone or becoming bony; **b** state of being ossified; **c** bony structure.

ossifrage, n. [1. ósifrij; 2. ɔ́sifridž], fr. Lat. *ossifraga*, 'bearded vulture', as if *ossifraga avis*, 'bone-breaking bird', *ossi-*, 'bone', see **os**, & *frag-*, a form of base in *frangere*, 'to break'. See **fracture, fragile**, & **break (I.)**. Cp. **osprey**. **a** The lammergeier; **b** osprey.

ossify, vb. trans. & intrans. [1. ósifī; 2. ɔ́sifai], fr. Lat. *ossi-*, 'bone', see **os**, & **-fy**. **1.** trans. To cause to become bony, or to assume the nature of bone. **2.** intrans. To change into bone or bony tissue; esp. of joints, to become filled with bony tissue and cease to be movable.

ossuary, n. [1. ósūari; 2. ɔ́sjuəri], fr. L. Lat. *ossuārium*, 'charnel-house'. See **os** & **-ary**. **a** A bone-vault or charnel-house; **b** an urn for holding the burnt bones of the dead.

osteal, adj. [1. ósteal; 2. ɔ́stiəl], fr. Gk. *ostéon*, 'bone'. See **osteo-** & **-al**. Osseous, bony.

osteitis, n. [1. òsteītis; 2. ɔ̀stiáitis]. See prec. & **-itis**. Inflammation of a bone or of bony tissue.

ostensibility, n. [1. ostènsibíliti; 2. ɔstènsibíliti]. **ostensible** & **-ity**. State, quality, of being ostensible.

ostensible, adj. [1. osténsibl; 2. ɔsténsibl]. Fr., fr. Lat. *ostens-(um)*, P.P. type of *ostendere*, fr. *obstendere*, 'to exhibit, show', **ob-**, 'before', & *tendere*, 'to stretch', see **tend (II.)**, & **-ible**. Shown, exhibited; apparent, pretended, professed; usually in contrast with *real* or *actual*: *ostensible motive, purpose* &c.

ostensibly, adv. Prec. & **-ly**. Apparently; so far as appearances go.

ostensive, adj. [1. osténsiv; 2. ɔsténsiv]. Lat. *ostens-*, see **ostensible**, & **-ive**. Ostensible.

ostensory, n. [1. osténsuri; 2. ɔsténsəri], fr. Med. Lat. *ostensōrium*, cp. Fr. *ostensoir*, fr. Lat. *ostens-(um)*, see **ostensible**, & **-ory**. A monstrance.

ostentation, n. [1. òstentā́shun; 2. ɔ̀stentéiʃən]. Fr., fr. Lat. *ostentātiōn-(em)*, fr. *ostentāt-(um)*, P.P. type of *ostentāre*, intens. form of *ostendere*, 'to show'. See **ostensible** & **-ion**. Act of making a deliberate display, or parade, of wealth, learning, or other possession or quality; pretentious, vulgar show, parade, or pomp; anything done merely to impress others, to draw public attention or applause.

ostentatious, adj. [1. òstentā́shus; 2. ɔ̀stentéiʃəs]. See prec. & **-ous**. Given to, marked by, exhibiting, ostentation; pretentious.

ostentatiously, adv. Prec. & **-ly**. In an ostentatious manner; so as to attract attention.

osteo-, pref., fr. Gk. *ostéon*, 'bone', cogn. w. Lat. **os**; chiefly used in forming medical and anatomical terms.

osteoblast, n. [1. ósteōblahst; 2. ɔ́stioublāst], fr. **osteo-** & Gk. *blastós*, 'bud, shoot'. See first element in **blastoderm**. Bone-forming cell.

osteogenesis, n. [1. òsteōjénesis; 2. ɔ̀stioudžénisis]. **osteo-** & **genesis**. (physiol.) Formation of bone.

osteoid, adj. [1. ósteoid; 2. ɔ́stiɔid]. **osteo-** & **-oid**. Resembling bone.

osteology, n. [1. òsteóloji; 2. ɔ̀stiɔ́lədži]. **osteo-** & **-logy**. Branch of anatomy dealing with bones, their development, structure, form, and arrangement.

osteoma, n. [1. òsteóma; 2. ɔ̀stióumə]. **osteo-** & **-oma**. (pathol.) A bony tumour; tumour on a bone.

osteomalacia, n. [1. òsteōmalásia; 2. ɔ̀stiouməléisiə]. **osteo-** & Gk. *malakía*, 'softness', fr. *malakós*, 'soft'. See **malaco-**. (pathol.) A disease marked by gradual softening of bones.

osteomyelitis, n. [1. òsteōmīelítis; 2. ɔ̀stioumaiəláitis]. **osteo-** & **myelitis**. (pathol.) Inflammation of the marrow of a bone, esp. in young children.

osteopath, n. [1. ósteōpath; 2. ɔ́stioupæþ]. **osteo-** & **-path**. One who practises osteopathy; bone-setter.

osteopathist, n. [1. òsteópathist; 2. ɔ̀stiɔ́pəþist]. Prec. & **-ist**. An osteopath.

osteopathy, n. [1. òsteópathi; 2. ɔ̀stiɔ́pəþi]. **osteo-** & **-pathy**. Treatment of diseases by manipulation of the bones, esp. of the spine; manipulative surgery, in English usage, esp. as performed by unqualified practitioners. Cp. *orthopaedics*.

osteoplastic, adj. [1. òsteōplástik; 2. ɔ̀stiouplǽstik]. **osteo-** & **plastic**. Of, pertaining to, the replacement of bone.

osteoplasty, n. [1. òsteōplásti; 2. ɔ̀stiouplǽsti]. See prec. & **-y**. Treatment of loss of bone or bony tissue by the transplanting of living bony tissue from another part of the body, or from some other animal.

ostiary, n. [1. óstiari; 2. ɔ́stiəri], fr. Lat. *ostiārius*, 'door-keeper', fr. *ostium*, 'entrance, door', formed fr. *ōs*, 'mouth'. See **oral** & cp. **usher**. A door-keeper of a church, the lowest of the minor orders in the Roman Catholic Church.

ostiole, n. [1. ósteōl; 2. ɔ́stioul]. L. Lat. *ostiolum*, dimin. of *ostium*, 'door'. See prec. (bot.) A small orifice or pore in various plants, such as sea-weeds or lichens.

ostitis, n. [1. ostítis; 2. ɔstáitis]. Osteitis.

ostler, n. [1. ósler; 2. ɔ́slə]. Earlier *hostler*, M.E. *hostiler*, fr. O. Fr. *hostelier*, 'inn-keeper', as **hostel** & **-er**. A groom or stableman at an inn.

ostracism, n. [1. óstrasizm; 2. ɔ́strəsizəm], fr. Gk. *ostrakismós*, fr. *ostrakízein*, 'to ostracize', fr. *óstrakon*, 'oyster shell, tile, potsherd; voting tablet', *óstreon*, 'oyster', cogn. w. *ostéon*, 'bone'. See **osteo-** & **oyster**. **1.** (Gk. hist.) A method of banishment for ten years of a person likely to disturb the peace of the State, practised at Athens; the citizens wrote on a scrap of broken pottery the name of the person they wished to be ostracized. **2.** (gen.) Exclusion, by popular feeling, from society, favour, or privileges: *to suffer political, social, ostracism*.

ostracize, vb. trans. [1. óstrasīz; 2. ɔ́strəsaiz], fr. Gk. *ostrakízein*, 'to banish by voting with potsherds'. See prec. **1.** (Gk. hist.) To banish by the method of ostracism. **2.** (gen.) To refuse to associate with, exclude, by popular feeling, from society; send to Coventry.

ostrei-, ostreo-, pref., fr. Gk. *óstreon*, 'oyster', see **oyster**.

ostreiculture, ostreoculture, n. [1. óstrei-, óstreōkùlchur; 2. ɔ́strii-, ɔ́strioukàltʃə]. See prec. & **culture**. The breeding or cultivation of oysters.

ostreophagous, adj. [1. òstreófagus; 2. ɔ̀striɔ́fəgəs]. **ostreo-** & **-phagous**. Feeding on oysters.

ostrich, n. [1. óstrij; 2. ɔ́stridž]. M.E. *ostrice, oystriche*, fr. O. Fr. *ostruce, ostruche*, Mod. Fr. *autruche*, cp. Port. *abestruz*, Span. *avestruz*, fr. Low Lat. *avis strūthio, avis*, 'bird', & *strūthio*, 'ostrich', fr. Gk. *strūthiōn*, 'ostrich', fr. *strouthós*, 'a bird, sparrow', *ho mégas strouthós*, 'the great bird, ostrich'; cp. **bustard** for another corrupt. of Lat. *avis*, & see **thrush** (I.). A large flightless bird, found in Africa, Arabia, and Syria, with short wings, long powerful legs which enable it to run very quickly, and a long straight neck; now domesticated on *ostrich-farms*, and bred for the beautiful black or white tail and wing feathers. Phrs. *a digestion like an ostrich*, from its habit of swallowing very hard objects to aid the working of the gizzard; *to bury one's head ostrich-like in the sand* (from the legend that when ostriches are hunted they hide their heads only, thinking they cannot be seen), to believe that one's manifest actions are not known, to be self-deluded.

otalgia, n. [1. ōtáljia; 2. outǽldžiə], fr. Gk. *ōtalgia*, fr. *ōt-*, stem of *oûs*, 'ear', fr. **ousos*, cogn. w. Lat. *auris*, fr. **ausis*, see **aural (II.)** & **audible**; & w. Goth. *ausō*; O.E. *ēare*, see **ear** (I.), & *álgos*, 'pain, grief', see **-algia**. (med.) Ear-ache.

other (I.), adj. [1. údher; 2. áðə]. O.E. *ōþer*, 'the second, following; other', fr. **anþar*; M.E. *ōther*; O.S. *ādar*, *ōđer*; O.H.G. *andar*; Goth. *anþar*; O.N. *annarr*; cogn. w. Scrt. *ántar-aš*, compar. of *ān*, 'that one', in the sense of 'second, beyond the one pointed out'; Lith. *ántras*, 'another'; the ending *-ther* is identical w. the compar. suff., e.g. Gk. *-teros*; cp. other Engl. words *either, neither, whether* &c. **1.** Different, distinct from, alternative to, that stated or pointed out: *give me the other coat, not this one*; *take it in your other hand*; *on the other side of the road*, that opposite; *needs other powers than mine*; *change into other clothes*. Phrs. *the other day*, some date, not specified, in the recent past; recently; *the other world*, the life to come. **2.** Additional, besides, over and above that or those in question: *to have other friends*; *is there no other use to be made of it?*; *I have my ordinary business and many other things to do besides*; *the truth is quite other than what you think*; '*Mary! I want a lyre with other strings*' (Cowper). **3.** Second; only in *every other day*, on alternate days, every second day.

other (II.), n. or pron. This might be considered an elliptical use of the adj. **1.** (always preceded by *the*) Other, different specified person or thing, the remainder: *this hand, not the other*; *I must consult the others*. **2.** Some person or thing unspecified or unknown: *some idiot or other was shouting all night*; *he must have eaten something or other which upset him*. Phr. *some day or other*, at some period in the future not defined.

other (III.), adv. See **other** (I.). Otherwise, differently: *if you think other than logically*; *I can't do other than accept*.

otherness, n. [1. údhernes; 2. áðənis]. **other** & **-ness**. (philos.) State, quality, of being other than, or separate and distinct from, that existing, experienced &c.: *conscious of a state of otherness*.

otherwhere, adv. [1. údherwār; 2. áðəwɛə]. **other** & **where**. (poet.) Elsewhere, in or to some other place.

otherwhile, adv. [1. údherwīl; 2. áðəwail]. **other** & **while**. (archaic) At some other time.

otherwise, adv. [1. údherwīz; 2. áðəwaiz]. See **other** & **wise** (II.). **1.** In another, different, manner: *this must be done quite otherwise*; *quite otherwise engaged*. **2.** Under circumstances other than those specified; if not: *do what you are told, otherwise you will be flogged*; *I was detained, otherwise I should have kept my appointment*. **3.** Apart from that, in other respects: *he has a squint, but is otherwise a handsome fellow*.

otherworldliness, n. [1. ùdherwérldlines; 2. àðəwáldlinis]. See next word & **-ness**. State, quality, of being otherworldly.

otherworldly, adj. [1. ùdherwérldli; 2. àðəwáldli]. **other** & **worldly**. Concerned with the future life, the other world, the world to come, to the exclusion of present worldly concerns or interests; spiritual; unworldly.

otic, adj. [1. ṓtik; 2. óutik], fr. Gk. *ōtikós*, fr. *ōtós*, *oûs*, 'ear'. See under **otalgia**. (anat.) Of, pertaining to, the ear or the organs of hearing: *otic ganglion*.

-otic, suff., fr. Gk. suff. *-ōtikos*, for forming adjs. fr. words ending in *-ōsis*, as *neurotic* fr. *neurosis* &c.; also in formations in Gk. fr. words ending in *-ōs*, as *erotic* fr. *érōs*. The force of the suff. is 'suffering from; resembling; conducing to'.

otiose, adj. [1. ṓtiōs, ṓshiōs, -z; 2. óutious, óuʃious, -z], fr. Lat. *ōtiōsus*, 'at leisure, disengaged, at ease, idle', fr. *ōtium*, 'leisure, idleness'; prob. fr. **au-tiom*; cp. Scrt. *ava-*, 'free from'; perh. also Goth. *auþeis*, 'desert, waste'. **1.** Superfluous, futile, without use or function: *his remarks were perfectly otiose*. **2.** (archaic or rare) At leisure, unemployed, idle.

otitis, n. [1. ōtítis; 2. outáitis], fr. *ōt-(ós)*, *oûs*, 'ear', see **otalgia**, & **-itis**. (med.) Inflammation of the ear.

otium cum dignitate [1. ṓshium kum dìgnitáte; 2. óuʃiəm kam dìgnitéiti]. See **otiose** & **dignity**. Lat. Phr., leisure with dignity; dignified retirement from office or business.

oto-, pref. Combining form, fr. Gk. *ōtós*, *oûs*, 'ear', in anatomical or medical terminology. See **otalgia**.

otolith, n. [1. ṓtōlith; 2. óutouliþ]. See prec. & **-lith**. Formation of chalky matter in the internal ear of some vertebrates, esp. fishes.

otology, n. [1. ōtóloji; 2. outóladži]. **oto-** & **-logy**. Special study of the ear and its diseases.

otoscope, n. [1. ṓtōskōp; 2. óutouskoup]. **oto-** & **-scope**. Instrument for examining the internal ear.

ottava rima, n. Anglicized to [1. òtava réma; 2. òtavə ríma]. Ital. See **octave** & **rhyme**. (prosody) A verse form or stanza of eight lines, the first six lines rhyming alternately, the last two forming a separate couplet; the Italian form has eleven, the English ten syllables, in each line.

otter, n. [1. óter; 2. ótə]. O.E. *oter*, *ottor*, M.E. *oter*; O.H.G. *ottar*; O.N. *otr*; fr. **utra-*; cogn. w. Lith. & Scrt. *udra*, 'otter'; all fr. base **wəd-* &c., 'water', as in Gk. *húdōr*, 'water', see **hydra**, **hydro-**. See further under **water** & **wet**. The otter is 'the water animal'. **1. a** An aquatic mammal with thick dark-brown fur, webbed feet, and long, flattened tail, genus *Lutra*; found in England and other parts of Europe; also the *sea-otter*, *Latax lutris*, of the N. Pacific; **b** the fur of the otter. **2.** (attrib.) *Otter-hound*, a breed of hound used for hunting otters; *otter trawl*, a fishing trawl in which the mouth is kept widely spread by boards on each side. **3.** Kind of fishing tackle, consisting of a plank weighted and moored some way from shore, with bait attached.

otto, n. Variant of **attar**.

Ottoman (I.), adj. & n. [1. ótoman; 2. ótəmən]. Fr., fr. Arab. *Othmān*, in Turk. *Osman*, name of the founder of the Turkish Osmanli dynasty, d. 1326. **a** adj. Turkish; **b** n., a Turk.

ottoman (II.), n., fr. prec. Kind of settee, of various shapes; usually low, thickly padded and upholstered, and sometimes consisting of three or more seats united at a central point, and so placed that the occupants all face different ways; another type consists of a circular continuous seat with a padded truncated pillar in the centre, which forms a back; a third is in the form of a low square sofa, the padded seat of which lifts up and discloses a box.

oubliette, n. [1. ōōbliét; 2. ùbliét]. Fr., fr. *oublier*, 'to forget', Lat. *oblīvisci*, q.v. under **oblivion**, & **-ette**. **a** A dungeon in a castle or prison, reached from a room above by a trap-door; also used of passage from the dungeon itself to the moat; **b** (loosely) a shaft leading from the upper chambers to the moat for disposal of drainage, and occasionally of unwanted or troublesome persons.

ouch, n. [1. ouch; 2. autʃ], fr. '*a nouch*', cp. *adder*, *apron* &c.; O. Fr. *nouche*, fr. L. Lat. *nusca*, 'brooch', prob. of Celt. origin, cp. Irish *nasc*, 'ring', *nasgain*, 'to fasten'. A jewelled brooch or clasp; morse.

ought (I.), n. [1. awt; 2. ɔt]. **1.** Obs. spelling of **aught**. **2.** Exists only in the vulgar *ought* for *nought*, a cipher: *oughts and crosses*.

ought (II.), auxil. vb. O.E. *āhte*, Pret. of *āgan*, 'to own, possess'; used early in M.E. w. present-day sense of obligation: *alðet he ahte to hauen*, 'ought to have' (Laud Chron., 1140). See **owe** & **own** (II.). Always followed by infin., the past tense being expressed by auxil. *to have* w. P.P. **1.** Expressing obligation, duty: **a** (pres.) *we ought all to love God*; *you ought to tell your mother at once*; **b** (past) *you ought to have done it long ago*. **2.** Expressing desirability: *you ought to come with us*; *you ought to have been there*, meaning it is a pity you were not there. **3.** Expressing probability: *I ought to be free by 4, with luck*; *we ought to win if all goes well*.

oui-ja, n. [1. wḗyah; 2. wíjā], fr. Fr. *oui* & Germ. *ja*, 'yes'. A board with an alphabet and figures on it, used in spiritualistic seances &c.

ounce (I.), n., abbr. *oz.* [1. ouns; 2. auns]. M.E. *ūnce*, fr. O. Fr.; fr. Lat. *uncia*, 'twelfth part of a pound or a foot'; lit. 'a unit', fr. *ūnus*, 'one'. See **unit**, also **inch** (I.). **1.** A unit of weight, $\frac{1}{16}$ of a pound avoirdupois, $\frac{1}{12}$ troy or apothecaries' weight: *fluid ounce*, eight (fluid) drachms; $\frac{1}{20}$ of imperial pint of water. **2.** A small quantity: *he hasn't got an ounce of sense*. Phr. *an ounce of practice is worth a pound of theory*.

ounce (II.), n., fr. Fr. *once*, cp. Span. *onza*, Ital. *onza* & *lonza*; etymol. doubtful; prob. Fr. *l'once*, for *lonce*, fr. a supposed L. Lat. **luncia* for *lyncea*, fem. of adj. fr. *lynx*. See **lynx**. **a** The snow-leopard of Tibet and Central Asia; **b** (loosely or poet.) a lynx or other medium-sized feline wild animal of the leopard or panther kind.

our, pronominal adj. [1. our; 2. áuə]. O.E. *ūre*, 'of us', possess. of *ūs*, pron. of 1st pers. pl.; used & declined as adj.; O.H.G. *unsar*; O.S. *ūser*; Goth. *unsara*. See **us** & **we**. **1.** Of or belonging to us; concerned with, relating to us: *our country, language* &c.; *our sovereign Lord, the King*; *this is our house*; *Our Father*, God as the Creator of the common humankind; *Our Lady*, the Virgin Mary; *in our midst*, in the middle of us, amongst us, that is, the people of this country. **2. a** (i.) Used by sovereigns speaking ceremonially, for *my*, as *we* for *I*: *our loyal subjects*; *our trusty and well-beloved X*; (ii.) by bishops: '*by the imposition of our hands*'; **b** as preserving anonymity, in expressing views of a paper, magazine &c.: *in our opinion* &c.

-our, suff. Variant of **-or**, the former being the O. Fr. & M.E. type, the latter fr. Lat. direct.

ours, pron. [1. ourz; 2. áuəz]. See **our**, an emphasized double possessive. **a** That or those that belong to us: *ours is a nice house*; *this country of ours*, our country; *don't go to their dance, come to ours*; **b** (absolutely) as pred. adjective: *those seats are ours*.

ourself, pron., pl. **ourselves** [1. oursélf, -sélvz; 2. auəsélf, -sélvz]. **our** & **-self**. **a** Emphatic *we*, or *us*: *for ourselves we want little*; *let us go ourselves*; *ourself* only when a sovereign speaks ceremonially: *we ourself*; **b** as reflexive pron.: *we must not deceive ourselves*.

-ous, suff. [1. us; 2. əs], fr. O. Fr. *-ous*, *-eus*, fr. Lat. *-ōsus*, cp. **-ose**, used to form adjs. meaning (1) 'abounding in, full of' &c.: *joyous*, O. Fr. *joyeus*, Mod. *joyeux*, Lat. *jocōsus*; also as regular adj. suff. for Lat. words in *-us* &c.: *stupendous, capacious* &c.; (2) (chem.) as contrasted w. *-ic*, having a lower valency than the equiv. in *-ic*: *nitrous, nitric, acid*.

ousel, n. See **ouzel.**

oust, vb. trans. [1. oust; 2. aust], fr. O. Fr. *oster*, 'to remove', cp. Mod. Fr. *ôter*; etymol. doubtful; the meaning seems against derivation fr. Lat. *obstāre*, 'to stand in the way of, hinder'; another possibility is L. Lat. *haustāre*, see **exhaust**, 'to draw off, drain away, carry away, remove', wh. is, however, objected to by Meyer-Lübke on phonological grounds. **a** To turn out, expel, drive out, esp. by underhand means; in material and non-material senses: *to oust a man from office, from the good graces of another*; **b** specif. (law) to dispossess, eject from a house or from other property, esp. by illegal process.

ouster, n. [1. óuster; 2. áustə], fr. prec., prob. a use of O. Fr. infin. *oster*, as vbl. n. (law) Dispossession, ejection from property, esp. by illegal process.

out (**I.**), adv. [1. out; 2. aut]. O.E. *ūt*, *ūte*, 'out, outside', expressing position & motion, M.E. *out(e)*; O.S. & Goth. *ūt*; O.H.G. *ūz* &c. Special uses of *out* after verbs are exhibited under the latter. **1.** (of relations in space) General sense, away from interior, from an enclosed space, towards, on, at, the exterior; **a** implying *motion* away from the inside, from interior, away from confinement, from a limited area, or specific place: *to go, run, pass, out*; *out of the bag, a box, out of the frying-pan*; *out of the house, the room*; *out of the village, the place, garden* &c.; also in fig. Phrs. (*the idea, hope* &c.) *comes out of one's own brain, heart* &c.; **b** expressing position, situation, rest, away from interior; beyond circumscribed limits, boundaries &c.: *to sit out of doors*; *remain out of the house*; *to stay out*; *to live out of town*; specif., of the ball in various games, not where it ought to be; in a spot beyond some prescribed limit; **c** expressing motion away from home and towards a given goal: *the journey out*, contrasted with *back*; *gone out to America*; *to start out*; **d** expressing distance from specified place: *five miles out of town.* **2.** Away from land, towards, on, the open sea: *out at sea*; *to row out.* **3.** Expressing various non-spatial relations: indicating absence of concealment; openness, publicity: *the secret is, has got, out*; *the new book is, has come, out*; *my daughter is not out yet*, not introduced to society as grown up. **4.** Expressing exclusion, **a** *out of office*; *locked out*; *the Whigs are out*; Phrs. *out of it*, not concerned with, not involved in, what is going on; *out of touch with*, isolated from (surrounding events, interests &c.); *out of the question*, not within sphere of discussion; impossible, impracticable; **b** (cricket) no longer batting, having been bowled, caught &c. **5.** Expressing a want, lack, insufficiency: *out of money*; *out of breath*; *out of work*; *the wine has run out.* **6.** Expressing exhaustion, extinction, disappearance; termination; completion: *the fire, the gas, is out*; *the fire has burnt out*; *my strength is out*; *the lease is out*; *hear me out.* **7.** Expressing deviation from some standard of good order; departure from what is correct, accurate, true, sound, harmonious: *out of tune, time*; *out in one's reckoning*; *out of (all) proportion*; *my eye is a bit out today*; *out of step*; *my watch is five minutes out*; *to be out with a person*, quarrel with him; *out of temper*; *out of one's mind*, insane; *out of repair.* **8.** Expressing liberation from confinement, freedom from restraint: *the floods are out*; *out of all bounds*; *to break out.* **9.** Expressing condition of being beyond power to control, influence, affect, attain &c.: *out of hand, control*; *out of one's reach*; *out of one's power to grant*; *the business is now quite out of my hands.* **10.** Expressing departure from what once was customary, deviation from formerly prevailing general usage: *frock-coats have gone out*; *out of fashion.* **11.** Expressing cause, reason, motive, consequence &c.: *he acted out of necessity, out of desire for improvement*; *out of fear*; *out of kindness*; *out of mischief*; *out of folly* &c. **12.** Expressing source, origin: *that's out of Shakespeare*; *a scene out of a play*; *an advertisement out of a newspaper*; *he came out of a wretched home, a slum* &c. **13.** Expressing thoroughness, completeness; in Phrs. *out-and-out, a scoundrel out-and-out*; as adj.: in *an out-and-out fool*; *out-and-away*, by far, beyond comparison: *out-and-away the handsomest woman there.*

out (**II.**), adj., fr. prec. Situated, being, on the exterior; specif. (games) reverse of *in*; cricket, not batting: *the out side.*

out (**III.**), n., fr. prec. That which is out; in games &c., *the outs*, the out side.

out (**IV.**) interj., fr. **out** (**I.**). (archaic or obs.) **1.** Expressing indignation, impatience; get out, be off, away with you &c. **2.** Expressing horror, protest &c.: *out upon you!*

out (**V.**), vb. trans., fr. **out** (**I.**). (colloq. or slang) To put or knock out: *out that man*, put him out of doors; *he was outed in the first round*, knocked out.

out-, pref., fr. **out** (**I.**). **1.** With nouns and adjectives; with chief stress; **a** situated outside; far-lying, remote; *outhouse*; *outbuilding*; *outpost*; *outwork*; *outlying*; **b** coming from without, living outside: *out-patient.* **2.** As prefix to verbs; with chief stress on verb; **a** (chiefly poet.), expressing same idea as the verb followed by *out*: *out-thrust*, to thrust out; *outflow*, to flow out; *outwear*, to wear out; **b** as intensive prefix to adjective, or P.P. used as adj.: *outspread, outworn.* **3.** (unstressed) Before verbs expressing **a** protracted, continued existence: *outlast, outlive*, to last, live, longer than, or beyond life or existence of; **b** enhanced action, greater intensity of action: *outsing, outshout*; *to out-Herod Herod*; often in facetious coinages, *to out-Jones Jones*, to beat J. at his own game; **c** superiority: *outshine, outfight, outnumber, outrun, outreach*; **d** expressing passing of a limit: *outgrow*; **e** excess: *outstay.* **4.** (with chief stress) As prefix to nouns; having the general sense of from within outwards: *outcrop*; *outcry*; *outfit*; *outgrowth*; *output* &c.; idea of excess: *out-size*; but often with specialized sense in the compound. See individual words.

outbalance, vb. trans. [1. outbálans; 2. autbǽləns]. To outweigh, to be of greater weight or balance than.

outbargain, vb. trans. [1. outbárgin; 2. autbágin]. To defeat in a bargain or deal.

outbid, vb. trans. [1. outbíd; 2. autbíd]. To bid higher than.

outboard, adj. & adv. [1. óutbord; 2. áutbɔ̄d]. (naut.) On, towards, the outer side of a ship; away from the centre; contrasted with *inboard.*

outbound, adj. [1. óutbound; 2. áutbaund]. Outward bound, on a voyage out or away from land.

outbrave, vb. trans. [1. outbrā́v; 2. autbréiv]. **1. a** To excel in daring or bravery; **b** to overcome by superior bravery. **2.** To defy.

outbreak, n. [1. óutbrāk; 2. áutbreik]. A breaking out, as of war, tumult, anger, disease.

outbuilding, n. [1. óutbìlding; 2. áutbìldiŋ]. Subsidiary building, such as stables, sheds &c., separate from the main building.

outburst, n. [1. óutbërst; 2. áutbʌ̄st]. A bursting out, outbreak; sudden forcible expression of emotion or passion: *an outburst of rage, tears* &c.; *an outburst of loyalty.*

outcast, adj., n. [1. óutkahst; 2. áutkāst]. **1.** n. Homeless, friendless person, one exiled from society; vagabond. **2.** adj. (rare) Cast out, driven away, exiled; homeless.

outcaste, adj., n., & vb. trans. See **caste.** Often confused w. prec. **1.** adj. Not having caste rights, not belonging to a caste; expelled from caste rights. **2.** n. Person who has no caste or has been expelled from his caste; pariah. **3.** vb. To expel from caste rights.

outclass, vb. trans. [1. outkláhs; 2. autklā́s]. To surpass; excel in merit; to belong to superior class to.

out-college, adj. [1. out kólej; 2. aut kɔ́lidž]. Residing out of college, not having rooms in college; not belonging to one's own college.

outcome, n. [1. outkum; 2. áutkam]. Result of an action, process, set of circumstances; issue, upshot.

outcrop, n. [1. óutkrop; 2. áutkrɔp]. Portion of rock or stratum which projects above, comes through, the surface of the ground.

outcry, n. [1. óutkrī; 2. áutkrai]. **a** A shout, noisy cry of alarm, indignation &c.; **b** (fig.) forcible, widespread protest; public expression of indignation, disapproval, or the like.

outdistance, vb. trans. [1. outdístans; 2. autdístəns]. To cover a greater distance in a given time than; travel faster than; to pass ahead of.

outdo, vb. trans. [1. outdóō; 2. autdū́]. To do something better than another; to surpass, excel in performance; to exhibit greater proficiency, zeal &c., than.

outdoor, adj. [1. óutdōr; 2. áutdɔ̄]. **1.** Used, performed, existing, living, out of doors, in the open air or away from a house &c.: *outdoor dress, games* &c.; *an outdoor life.* **2.** *Outdoor relief*, that given by the Relieving Officer outside the workhouse &c., to people in their own homes.

outdoors, adv. [1. òutdórz; 2. àutdɔ̄́z]. Out of doors, in the open air, out of the house.

outdweller, n. [1. óutdwèler; 2. áutdwèlə]. One who dwells outside the boundaries of a parish but holds land inside or has parochial rights &c.

outer, adj. & n. [1. óuter; 2. áutə]. New formation direct fr. **out** (**I.**) & **-er**, compar. suff.; the old form is seen in **utter**, w. specialized meaning. **1.** adj. **a** Farther out from; farther from the centre or inside; nearer to, on the outside; external; opposed to *inner*: *outer rooms*; *outer coverings*; *outer wall*; Phrs. *the outer man*, a man's external appearance, costume &c.; *the outer world*, (i.) the external, material world; (ii.) society in general with which one is not intimate or familiar; *Outer Bar*, also formerly *Utter Bar*, collective term for junior barristers not called within the bar as King's Counsel; *Outer House*, the hall in the Scottish Parliament House in which the Lords Ordinary of the Court of Session sit singly to hear cases; **b** (philos.) Objective, external, as opposed to *subjective* or *inner.* **2.** n. **a** That part of a target which is on the outside margin, next beyond the *inner*; **b** a shot on this part of a target.

outermost, adj. [1. óutermōst; 2. áutəmoust]. New formation fr. prec. & **-most.** See also **uttermost** & **utmost.** Superl. of *out.* Farthest outward; on the furthest or most extreme side; farthest from the inside.

outface, vb. trans. [1. outfā́s; 2. autféis]. To face boldly, stare down or out of countenance; to defy, browbeat.

outfall, n. [1. óutfawl; 2. áutfɔ̄l]. The place, point, where water falls out into a larger body of water &c., as the mouth of river, canal, drain &c.; outlet, point of discharge.

outfang(en)thief, n. [1. óutfang(en)thēf; 2. áutfæŋ(ən)þīf]. O.E. *ūtfangenþēof*, *ūt*, 'out', *fangen*, P.P. of *fōn*, 'to take, seize', see **fang** (**I.**), & *þēof*, **thief.** (Anglo-Saxon law) The right of the lord of a manor to try in his own court a dweller in his own manor who has been taken for felony committed outside; contrasted with *infangenthief.*

outfield, n. [1. óutfēld; 2. áutfīəld]. **1.** Farm-land lying away from the home farm. **2.** (fig.) An unexplored, unknown field of speculation or thought. **3.** (cricket) That portion of the field, or the fieldsmen placed there, which is farthest from the batsman; so *outfielding*, n., the fielding of the players in the outfield.

outfit, n. & vb. trans. [1. óutfit; 2. áutfit]. **1.** n. **a** That which fits out or equips a person completely for a specific purpose; equipment, kit: *military or naval outfit*; *outfit for a voyage*; *a carpenter's outfit*, his tools &c.; also (fig.) *mental outfit*; **b** (slang) organized group of persons. **2.** vb. (rare) Usually fit out; (chiefly in P.P.) *outfitted.*

outfitter, n. [1. óutfiter; 2. áutfitə]. Prec. & **-er**. One who supplies outfits or equipment: *gentleman's outfitter*, a hosier, shirtmaker &c.

outflank, vb. trans. [1. outflángk; 2. autflǽŋk]. **a** (mil.) To move to the outside of (an enemy's flank or wing); **b** (fig.) to outwit, circumvent (an opponent).

outflow, n. [1. óutflō; 2. áutflou]. A flowing or pouring out; outfall of a river &c.; outburst: *an outflow of water, of language* &c.

outfront, vb. trans. [1. outfrúnt; 2. autfránt]. To outface, confront; to stare out of countenance.

outgeneral, vb. trans. [1. outjéneral; 2. autdžén(ə)rəl]. To beat or excel in generalship; to outmanœuvre.

outgo, vb. trans. & n. **a** vb. [1. outgṓ; 2. autgóu]. To go beyond or faster than; to surpass, excel, outdo; (usually in Pret.) *outwent*; **b** n. [1. óutgō; 2. áutgou], that which goes out, esp. that which is expended; outlay, expenditure, outgoings; contrasted with *income*.

outgoing, adj. & n. [1. óutgōing; 2. áutgouiŋ]. **a** adj. Going out, departing: *an outgoing ship*; *outgoing tenant*, one who is giving up a tenancy; **b** n. (usually pl.), expenditure, outlay.

outgrow, vb. trans. [1. outgrṓ; 2. autgróu]. **1. a** To become too large for: *to outgrow one's clothes*; *my family has outgrown our house*; Phr. *to outgrow one's strength*, grow too rapidly, and become abnormally tall for one's age, so that health suffers; **b** to surpass in growth, grow taller than: *the younger has outgrown the elder brother*. **2.** To get rid of in course of time, to lose; cease to suffer from: *to outgrow a bad habit, shyness* &c.; *to outgrow the diseases of one's youth*.

outgrowth, n. [1. óutgrōth; 2. áutgrouþ]. **a** That which grows out of or proceeds from something: *an outgrowth from a tree*; **b** result, consequence, development from: *revolution is a frequent outgrowth of tyranny*.

out-Herod, vb. trans. [1. out hérud; 2. aut hérəd]. **a** To surpass Herod in cruelty &c., from 'Hamlet', iii. 2, '*it out-Herods Herod*', referring to the overacted part of Herod in the old mystery plays; **b** (fig.) to surpass, outdo, another in the very qualities by which he is characterized.

outhouse, n. [1. óut-hous; 2. áuthaus]. Building, shed &c. detached from the main house or building, such as a shed of any kind, cow-house &c.

outing, n. [1. óuting; 2. áutiŋ]. A pleasure trip, expedition, excursion, holiday spent out of doors or away from home.

outlander, n. [1. óutlander; 2. áutlændə]. S. Afr. Du. *uitlander*, 'person from an out or foreign land'. Foreigner, alien, esp. as applied to those not of Boer birth in the Transvaal.

outlandish, adj. [1. outlándish; 2. autlǽndiʃ]. Cp. O.E. *ūtlandisċ*, 'foreign; exiled'. **out-**, **land**, & **-ish**. **a** Foreign, strange, esp. of appearance or habits; **b** barbarous; queer, bizarre.

outlast, vb. trans. [1. outláhst; 2. autlást]. To last out longer than; to endure the longer; to outlive, survive.

outlaw, n. & vb. trans. [1. óutlaw; 2. áutlɔ̄]. O.E. *ūtlaga, ūtlah*, **out-** & **law**; prob. Scand. in origin, & borrowed fr. O.N. *ūtlagi*, 'outlaw'. **1.** n. **a** (hist.) A person placed outside, and deprived of the protection of, the law, by sentence of outlawry; **b** (i.) a lawless vagabond; (ii.) one banished or ostracized by society; a social outcast. **2.** vb. **a** To pronounce sentence of outlawry upon; **b** to banish, exile, ostracize, from society.

outlawry, n. [1. óutlawri; 2. áutlɔ̄ri]. Prec. & **-(e)ry**. **a** (hist.) A legal process whereby a person evading justice or refusing to come before a court of law was declared outside the law and considered civilly dead; **b** social ostracism.

outlay, n. [1. óutlā; 2. áutlei]. That which is laid out or expended; expenditure, expenses.

outleap, vb. trans. [1. outlḗp; 2. autlíp]. To leap farther than, surpass in leaping.

outlet, n. [1. óutlet; 2. áutlit]. **1.** A passage through which anything is let out; orifice, opening, safety-valve. **2.** (fig.) A means of, opportunity for, expression: *an outlet for one's energy, emotion* &c.

outlier, n. [1. óutlīer; 2. áutlaiə]. **a** That which lies out or away from a main body or mass, as a detached portion of rock &c.; **b** person or animal found living away from usual place of abode, or habitat.

outline (I.), n. [1. óutlīn; 2. áutlain]. **1. a** A line or lines indicating the boundary only of a figure; a contour line; **b** specif. (drawing) the representation of the imaginary line which bounds or contains the plane surface of a visible object, without direct indication of the modelling by shading. **2.** (fig.) **a** A general statement of main points in a scheme, plan, argument, &c. without indication of details; **b** a narrative of the main general features, and trend of events and actions, avoiding details; **c** (usually pl.) statement of general principles and main facts without minute detail. Phr. *in outline*, in summary form, without details.

outline (II.), vb. trans. fr. prec. **1. a** To draw the outline of; to draw in outline; **b** to indicate, reveal, outline of: *outlined against the light*. **2.** To sketch, summarize, give the main features of (place, narrative &c.).

outlive, vb. trans. [1. outlív; 2. autlív]. **1.** To live beyond, or longer than; to survive, outlast: *to outlive one's contemporaries*; *to outlive the century*. **2.** To outgrow, to live through or down: *to outlive disgrace, scandal* &c.

outlook, n. [1. óutlook; 2. áutluk]. **1. a** Act or fact of looking out, observing, watching; **b** place or position from which watch is kept, or observation is made. **2. a** That which is seen by looking out, or from a look-out; prospect, view: *a dreary outlook over waste ground and slums*; **b** vision presented to the mind by circumstances or events: *a bad outlook for trade*; *the political state of Europe presents a gloomy outlook*. **3.** Mode of considering events, ideas &c.; point of view, mental attitude: *a narrow, prejudiced, wide, humane, outlook*.

outlying, adj. [1. óutlīing; 2. áutlai-iŋ]. Lying, situated, far away, at some distance, detached from, a given point, or centre; remote.

outmanœuvre, vb. trans. [1. òutmanóóver; 2. àutmənúvə]. (lit. and fig.) To surpass in skill of manœuvre; to defeat by or in manœuvres, to outgeneral.

outmarch, vb. trans. [1. outmárch; 2. autmátʃ]. To march faster, or farther than; to surpass in marching power.

outmatch, vb. trans. [1. outmách; 2. autmǽtʃ]. To be more than a match for; to surpass, excel (in cunning, wit, audacity &c.).

outmost, adj. [1. óutmōst; 2. áutmoust]. (obs. or poet.) Outermost.

outness, n. [1. óutnes; 2. áutnis]. (philos.) State, quality, of being external to the mind or consciousness; objectivity.

outnumber, vb. trans. [1. outnúmber; 2. autnámbə]. To exceed in numbers, be more numerous than.

outpace, vb. trans. [1. outpā́s; 2. autpéis]. To take longer paces than; to walk faster than; to outstrip in pace.

out-patient, n. [1. óut pàshent; 2. áut pèiʃənt]. A patient at a hospital or institution who receives treatment, but is not a resident or inmate.

out-pension, n. [1. óut pènshun; 2. áut pènʃən]. A pension granted by an institution without the obligation of being an inmate.

out-pensioner, n. [1. óut pènshuner; 2. áut pènʃənə]. A person granted an out-pension.

outplay, vb. trans. [1. outplā́; 2. autpléi]. To play better than; to defeat in a game by superior skill.

outport, n. [1. óutport; 2. áutpɔ̄t]. A sea- or river-port outside or away from the chief port or seat of customs.

outpost, n. [1. óutpōst; 2. áutpoust]. **a** (mil.) One of a series of posts or stations set out at a distance in front of a main body of troops to observe the enemy and prevent surprise; (also attrib.) *outpost duty, outpost line of defence* &c.; **b** any distant settlement: *the outposts of the Empire*.

outpouring, n. [1. outpṓring; 2. autpɔ́riŋ]. A pouring out, overflow; (chiefly in non-material sense and pl.) fervid expression of feelings, in words or writing: *the outpourings of a sentimental mind*.

output, n. [1. óutpoot; 2. áutput]. **a** That which is put out or produced as a result of physical labour or work: *the output of a mine, factory* &c.; also **b** (of non-material things) any product of mental work: *the literary output of the year*.

outrage (I.), n. [1. óutrij; 2. áutridž], fr. O. Fr. *oultrage, ultrage, outrage*, fr. *oultre, oltre, outre*, fr. Lat. *ultrā*, 'beyond', see **ultra-**, & **-age**; cp. Ital. *oltraggio* & see **ulterior**; the meaning has been influenced by confusion w. *rage*. **1. a** A violent act of physical injury to another's property or person: *the mob committed many acts of outrage*; **b** specif., violation, rape. **2.** Gross, violent, transgression of law or decency; excessive violence done to sense of right, justice, propriety, judgement &c.

outrage (II.), vb. trans. [1. óutrāj; 2. áutreidž], fr. prec. **1.** To commit a physical outrage upon; to treat with violence; specif., to violate, rape. **2.** To set at nought, do violence to, offend against, flout (moral sense, reason, law, principles).

outrageous, adj. [1. outrā́jus; 2. autréidžəs], fr. O. Fr. *outrageus, outrageux*. **outrage** (I.) & **-ous**. Of the nature of, inflicting, constituting, an outrage; violent, excessive, flagrant; atrocious, monstrous.

outrageously, adv. Prec. & **-ly**. In an outrageous manner.

outrageousness, n. See prec. & **-ness**. State, quality, of being outrageous.

outrance, n. [1. óótrahns; 2. ūtrā̃s]. Fr., 'extremity, the end, limit'. See **outré** & **outrage**. Only in Phr. *à outrance*, q.v.

outrange, vb. trans. [1. outrā́nj; 2. autréindž]. To have a wider, longer, range than; **a** (of vision) to see farther than; **b** (of guns &c.) to carry farther than.

outré, adj. [1. óótrā; 2. útrei]. Fr., 'exaggerated', P.P. of *outrer*, 'to carry things, conduct &c. beyond reasonable limits'. See **outrage**. Exaggerated, overstepping the bounds of custom, decency, modesty, good sense: *outré conduct*; *dress that is outré*.

outreach, vb. trans. [1. outrḗch; 2. autrítʃ]. To reach out, extend, farther than; to surpass; to overreach.

outreign, vb. trans. [1. outrā́n; 2. autréin]. To reign longer than.

out-relief, n. [1. òut relḗf; 2. àut rilíf]. Relief, in money or kind, given by a Relieving Officer to poor persons not inmates of a workhouse or other poor-law institution; outdoor relief.

outride, vb. trans. [1. outríd; 2. autráid]. To ride faster, farther, or better, than; to get ahead of, arrive before, by riding.

outrider, n. [1. óutrīder; 2. áutraidə]. A mounted attendant or servant, accompanying a carriage.

outrigger, n. [1. óutrìger; 2. áutrìgə]. **1. a** A projecting spar or beam rigged out temporarily from a ship's side; mast with tackle for hoisting specially heavy weights &c.; **b** a similar structure from roof or side of a building. **2. a** A metal stay having a rowlock at the end projecting from the side of a light rowing or sculling boat to give extra leverage; **b** a boat with outriggers. **3.** A projecting beam fastened to native boats in the Pacific to prevent upsetting. **4.** A projection from the shafts or from the splinter bar of a carriage for holding the trace of an extra horse.

outright, adv. & adj. **1.** adv. [1. outrít; 2. autráit]. **a** Right out, openly: *told him outright what he thought of him*; **b** immediately, at once; once for all, entirely: *was killed outright*; *bought the house and contents outright.* **2.** adj. [1. óutrīt; 2. áutrait]. Direct, downright, positive, out and out; thorough: *gave an outright denial*; *an outright rogue and swindler.*

outrival, vb. trans. [1. outrívl; 2. autráivl]. To surpass, excel, a rival, competitor, or object compared: *outrivalled the stars in brilliance.*

outroot, vb. trans. [1. outro͞ot; 2. autrút]. (chiefly fig.) To root out, eradicate, destroy: *to outroot a passion from one's heart.*

outrun, vb. trans. [1. outrún; 2. autrán]. To run faster than; to outstrip, exceed, go beyond: '*the other disciple did outrun Peter*' (Gospel of St. John xx. 4); *let one's zeal outrun discretion.* Phr. *to outrun the constable*, spend more than one's means, to run into debt.

outrunner, n. [1. óutruner; 2. áutranə]. **1.** A running footman or attendant for a carriage. **2.** The leading dog of the team drawing a sleigh. **3.** An extra horse outside the shafts of a single-horsed, or outside the traces of a pair-horsed, vehicle.

outset, n. [1. óutset; 2. áutset]. A setting out, beginning, start, commencement, of a series of events: *at the outset of his career*; *from the outset the prospects were poor.*

outshine, vb. trans. [1. outshín; 2. autʃáin]. To shine more brightly than; to excel in splendour, brilliance &c.

outside (I.), adv. [1. outsíd; 2. autsáid]. **a** Externally; over, on, the surface: *to paint a house outside*; **b** on outward part, in the open air: *to ride outside* (on a coach &c.); *put these flowers outside* (of a room &c.)

outside (II.), prep. [1. óutsíd; 2. áutsáid]. **a** At, on, the exterior of; on outer side of: *outside the door*; **b** apart from, with the exception of: *no one knows outside one or two persons*; *outside one's own circle.*

outside (III.), adj. [1. óutsīd; 2. áutsaid]. **1.** External; **a** on, connected with, outer surface, or outer parts: *outside seats of a carriage*; **b** carried on out of doors, contrasted with *indoor*: *outside work, repairs* &c.; **c** coming from the outside: *outside labour.* **2.** Extreme, reaching to farthest limit: *an outside price.* **3.** Not connected with, not belonging to, or included in, a society, organization, or specific body: *outside broker*, one who is not a member of the Stock Exchange; *outside help, influence* &c.

outside (IV.), n. [1. óutsíd, óutsīd; 2. áutsáid, áutsaid]. **1.** **a** External part, surface, site of anything: *the outside of a house, of a head, of an omnibus*; specif., *outsides*, top and bottom quires of a ream of paper; **b** (of persons) personal appearance, exterior: *a rough outside but a good heart.* **2.** (in non-material sense) **a** That which is on the surface, the purely superficial appearance: *one should not judge too much by the outside*; **b** the external world of impressions, contrasted with the inner consciousness: *dreams come rather from within than from the outside.* **3.** Condition of being external to, not a member of, a body, a society, class, or of not sharing a set of ideas, beliefs &c.: *it is difficult for those on the outside to understand the inner life of a college.* **4.** The extreme limit or boundary, the utmost; chiefly in *at the (very) outside*, at the utmost.

outsider, n. [1. òutsíder; 2. àutsáidə]. **1.** One who is not a member of a social or other body, community, group &c., specified or previously referred to: *regiments are sometimes commanded by outsiders when suitable officers from within are lacking for the moment.* **2.** (racing) A horse which is not among those considered to have a chance of winning. **3.** (colloq.) One who is regarded as outside the pale of decent society; an ill-bred, impossible person; a vulgarian, a bounder.

outsit, vb. trans. [1. outsít; 2. autsít]. To sit longer than, to remain longer than others; to outstay.

outskirts, n. pl. [1. óutskērts; 2. áutskǝ̄ts]. The borders, margins, fringes, esp. of a town; suburbs, outlying areas.

outsoar, vb. trans. [1. outsór; 2. autsɔ́]. To soar, fly, pass, beyond: '*He has outsoared the shadow of our night*' (Shelley, 'Adonais', 40).

outspan, vb. trans. & intrans. [1. óutspan; 2. áutspæn]. S. Afr., fr. Du. *uitspannen*, fr. *uit*, 'out', cogn. w. **out**, & *spannen*, 'to span; to fasten', see **span (I.)**. **1.** trans. To unharness (oxen &c.) from waggon &c. **2.** intrans. To perform action of outspanning.

outspoken, adj. [1. outspóken; 2. autspóukən]. **a** (of persons) Given to frank, candid utterance; reverse of reticent; **b** (of utterances) candid, frank: *outspoken criticism, comments* &c.

outspokenly, adv. Prec. & **-ly**. In an outspoken manner; frankly, candidly.

outspokenness, n. See prec. & **-ness**. Quality of being outspoken; candour, frankness.

outspread, adj. [1. outspréd; 2. autspréd]. Spread out, expanded, extended: *with hands outspread.*

outstanding, adj. [1. outstánding; 2. autstǽndiŋ]. **1.** Standing out, prominent, conspicuous: *an outstanding figure.* **2.** **a** Standing over, left unsettled or unpaid: *outstanding liabilities*; **b** due to be done, but not completed; still to be done: *to leave a good deal of work outstanding.*

outstay, vb. trans. [1. outstá; 2. autstéi]. To stay longer than; Phr. *to outstay one's welcome*, stay so long that one ceases to be welcome.

outstretched, adj. [1. outstrécht; 2. autstrétʃt]. Stretched out, expanded, extended: *to lie outstretched on the ground*; *the outstretched hand.*

outstrip, vb. trans. [1. outstríp; 2. autstríp], fr. **out-** & **strip** in now obs. sense of 'to run'. To pass in running, exceed in pace; to leave behind; to surpass in excellence, be more successful than.

out-talk, vb. trans. [1. out táwk; 2. aut tɔ́k]. To talk quicker, longer, or louder than; to talk down.

out-top, vb. trans. [1. out tóp; 2. aut tɔ́p]. To exceed in height; (fig.) to be superior to, surpass, excel.

outvote, vb. trans. [1. outvót; 2. autvóut]. To vote in greater numbers than; to defeat by a majority of votes.

outvoter, n. [1. óutvòter; 2. áutvòutə]. One who has a vote in a constituency by property qualification, not by residence; a non-resident voter.

outward, adj. & n. [1. óutward; 2. áutwəd]. **out-** & **-ward**. **1.** adj. **a** Of, pertaining to, the outside or exterior; external: *outward appearance*; *the outward man*, a man's outward appearance; **b** of or pertaining to the bodily, material side: *outward, visible, sign.* **2.** n. (often pl.) The outside, exterior; outward parts or things, externals.

outward(s), adv. [1. óutward(z); 2. áutwəd(z)]. From within towards the outside; outwardly: *to thrust outward(s)*; *outward-bound*, of vessel on voyage out.

outwardly, adv. Prec. & **-ly**. **a** On, towards, the outside; outward; **b** externally, in respect of the outside.

outwardness, n. See prec. & **-ness**. State, condition, of being outward; externality, objectivity.

outwear, vb. trans. [1. outwár; 2. autwɛ́ə]. **1.** To wear or last longer than; to outlast: *old hand-made work will outwear new machine-made stuff.* **2.** To wear out, destroy, by constant use; (usually in P.P.) *outworn habits*, no longer practised, obsolete; '*A Pagan suckled in a creed outworn*' (Wordsworth); *outworn quotations* &c., no longer applicable; having lost force by constant reiteration; hackneyed, trite.

outweigh, vb. trans. [1. outwá; 2. autwéi]. (only in non-material sense) To weigh, count for, more than; to surpass in moral weight, value, importance, or quality: *the advantages outweigh the drawbacks.*

outwit, vb. trans. [1. outwít; 2. autwít]. To get the better of by stratagem, defeat by superior astuteness.

outwork (I.), n. [1. óutwērk; 2. áutwǝ̄k]. (fort.) An outlying, detached fort or defensive work some distance in advance of a main work.

outwork (II.), n. Work done away from a shop or workroom.

outworker, n. [1. óutwērker; 2. áutwǝ̄kə]. One who does outwork or work away from a shop or factory.

ouzel, ousel, n. [1. o͞ozl; 2. úzl]. O.E. *ōsle*, M.E. *ōsel*, fr. **amsal*; cp. O.H.G. *amsala*, 'a blackbird or thrush'. One of various kinds of thrush, as *ring-ouzel*, *water-ouzel* &c.; originally name of a blackbird or thrush.

ova, n. Pl. of **ovum**.

oval, adj. & n. [1. óvl; 2. óuvl], fr. Lat. *ōv-(um)*, 'egg', & **-al**, cp. Fr. *ovale*. See **ovum** & **egg**. **1.** adj. Egg-shaped; circular with lengthened sides and narrowed ends; elliptical. **2.** n. A figure having an oval or elliptical shape. *The Oval*, the Surrey County Cricket Ground at Kennington, London.

ovally, adv. Prec. & **-ly**. In an oval shape or figure; elliptically.

ovalness, n. See prec. & **-ness**. State, quality, of being oval or elliptical.

ovarian, adj. [1. ovárian; 2. ouvɛ́əriən]. **ovary** & **-ian**. Pertaining to, situated in, the ovaries.

ovari(o)-, pref., fr. prec. Used in compounds, to denote an ovary, q.v.

ovariotomy, n. [1. ōvāriótumi; 2. òuvɛəriɔ́təmi]. See prec. & **-tomy**. Excision of one or both of the ovaries.

ovaritis, n. [1. ōvarítis; 2. òuvəráitis]. See prec. & **-itis**. Inflammation of an ovary.

ovary, n. [1. óvari; 2. óuvəri], fr. Neo-Lat. *ōvārium*. See **ovum** & **-ary**. **1.** (anat.) One of the pair of organs of reproduction in female animals producing eggs or ova. **2.** (bot.) The lower part of a pistil which contains the ovules and develops into the fruit.

ovate, adj. [1. óvāt; 2. óuveit], fr. Lat. *ōvātus*. See **ovum** & **-ate**. Shaped like an egg, oval, elliptical, esp. (bot.) of surfaces, oval with a broader base or lower end.

ovation, n. [1. ováshun; 2. ouvéiʃən], fr. Lat. *ovātiōn-(em)*, *ovātio*, fr. *ovāre*, 'to rejoice, exult, triumph', cogn. w. Gk. *eudzein*, 'to utter cries of joy'. **1.** (Rom. antiq.) A lesser kind of triumph, granted to a general for a minor victory. **2.** An enthusiastic, popular reception, spontaneous expression of popular admiration; enthusiastic welcome or applause.

oven, n. [1. úven; 2. ávən]. O.E. *ofn, ofen*; cp. O.H.G. *ovan, ofan*, O.N. *ofn*; & perh. Goth. *aúhns*; possibly cogn. w. Gk. *ipnós*, 'oven'. **1.** An enclosed brick or metal receptacle in contact with fire, in which food is baked, or where things are dried. **2.** A small kiln or furnace for chemical or metallurgical processes.

oven-bird, n. The popular name of various S. American birds which build dome-shaped, oven-like nests.

over (I.), prep. [1. óver; 2. óuvə]. O.E. *ofer*, compar. form of *ufan*, adv., *be-ufan*, see **above**; O. Fris., M.Du., & L.G. *over*; O.S. *ovar*; O.H.G. *ubar*, prep., *ubiri*, adv., Germ. *über, ober*; O.N. *yfer*, Goth. *ufar*; Common Aryan; Scrt. *upari*, Gk. *hupér* (see **hyper-**), Lat. *super* (see **super-**). **1.** Expressing relations in space: **a** fixed position, above, resting upon, touching upper surface, closing, covering: *water standing over the road*; *a rug lying over a sofa*; *a piece of parchment tied over the top of a jam-pot*; **b** fixed across, arching, spanning from one side to the other: *a bridge over a river*; *a telegraph wire over a street*; *the clouds over one's head*; Phr. *over one's signature*, signed by; **c** expressing position on other side of something from speaker, or from that side first referred to: *the house over the way*; *the tree over the river.* **2.** Expressing movement, chiefly with or after verbs of movement:

a across, so as to pass or traverse : *to go over the mountains* ; *to fly over the river* ; *to travel overland* ; *to pass over the frontier* ; *to flow over the edge* ; the various idiomatic uses in combination with verbs are noted under these severally ; **b** expressing movement towards, and subsequent rest in, a given position : *pull a blanket over me* ; *to put one's hands over one's face.* **3.** Expressing physical superiority, excess : **a** more than, in extent : *over five miles long* ; **b** in amount, number, weight, bulk : *over a quart of wine* ; *over a hundred people there* ; *over three pounds in weight* ; *over forty inches round the waist* ; *over and above what is wanted.* **4.** Expressing superiority in rank, status, office, authority &c. : *a general is over a colonel* ; *these people want a strong man over them.* **5.** (of time) **a** Expressing duration : *to stay, last, over the week-end, over the night* ; **b** expressing excess beyond specified limit of time; more than : *to remain over a month in the same place.*

over (II.), adv. **1.** Expressing relations in space : **a** (stationary) above ; **b** expressing distance, remoteness, from speaker : *over in France for a week* ; **c** expressing movement from one place, direction, or side, to another ; above and across something : *come over and see us* ; *our friends were over yesterday* ; *to run over to America* ; *a flock of starlings have just flown over.* **2.** Expressing movement (N.B. the precise shade of meaning is determined by the verb of movement which precedes ; the various senses appear under these verbs) : **a** away from perpendicular, upright position : *to fall, be knocked, over* ; **b** from one side to another ; in opposite direction : *to turn, roll, over* ; **c** expressing motion upwards, outwards, and beyond some limit : *to boil over, foam, flow, over* &c. **3. a** (of events, circumstances, processes) Completed, finished, done with : *thank God, the War is over* ; *our life, troubles, sufferings will soon be over* ; Phr. *all over with* (*him*) &c., (i.) (he) is ruined, finished, (ii.) bound to die soon &c. ; **b** (of periods of time) past, passed away : *the good old times are over.* **4.** Expressing excess : **a** in addition to, more than, specified or required amount : *I paid my bill and have several pounds over* ; *I have five pounds and over* ; **b** used before adj. and adv. in sense of too (much), excessively : *to be over polite, over silent* ; such combinations are often hyphened ; (*to grieve &c.*) *over much,* too much, to an excessive degree. **5. a** In every part, covering, scattered at intervals over surface, throughout whole extent : *the earth in spring is sprinkled over with flowers* ; *covered over with paint* ; also (*covered*) *all over with* ; **b** (after certain vbs.) *go over,* visit, examine, thoroughly ; *look over* (*a house* &c.), inspect ; *think over,* ponder carefully in all its aspects &c. **6.** Expressing repetition, esp. in *over again,* once more.

over (III.), n., fr. prec. (cricket) Number of balls, originally four, now six, which a bowler delivers in succession from one end of the pitch, after which, at call ' over ' by umpire, the bowling begins at the other end and the field ' change over ' and alter their positions accordingly : *a maiden over,* an over from which no runs are scored.

over-, pref., fr. **over** (II.). **1.** (as adj.). Higher, upper, outer, superior, extra, as *overcoat, overlord, overtime.* **2.** (as prep.) **a** To form ns., adjs., & advs. (in all senses) : *overall, overboard, overland, overweight* ; **b** prefixed to vbs., esp. those often followed by *over* (in various senses), & governing an object otherwise governed by prep. : *overcome, overflow,* as flow over the banks, *overflow the banks* &c. ; *overlook, overrun* &c. **3.** (as adv.) **a** (with vb. or n.) Above, from above, down from, up to, beyond, in addition : *overbalance, overhaul, overtake, overthrow, overwhelm* &c. ; **b** (with vb. trans.) altogether, completely : *over-persuade.* **4.** (the main or most common sense, when prefixed to n., vb., adj., or adv.) In general sense of excess, exceeding, more than, normal, beyond what is good. This is so freely used and the sense so obvious in most cases that many words compounded thus are omitted : *overcharge,* n. and vb., *overpressure, overwork* &c.

overabundance, n. [1. ôverabúndans ; 2. òuvər-əbándəns]. An excess of abundance, superfluity ; superabundance.

overabundant, adj [1. ôverabúndant ; 2. òuvərəbándənt]. Exceeding in abundance ; superabundant, superfluous.

overabundantly, adv. Prec. & **-ly.** Superabundantly.

overact, vb. trans. & intrans. [1. ôverákt ; 2. òuvərǽkt]. (lit. and fig.) To act in an exaggerated manner ; to overdo, overplay : *to overact a part* ; *to overact in a part.*

overall (I.), adv. [1. ôveráwl ; 2. òuvərɔ́l]. Over the whole superficies : *measures 12 sq. ft. overall.*

overall (II.), n. [1. óverawl ; 2. óuvərɔl]. **a** A loose outer garment slipped on over other clothes to keep them clean and tidy, esp. for children, or women doing housework or in factories &c. ; **b** (pl.) loose trousers or leggings to be pulled over ordinary trousers for rough or dirty work &c. ; **c** (mil., pl.) officer's full-dress trousers.

over-anxious, adj. [1. ôver ángshus ; 2. òuvər-ǽŋʃəs]. Too anxious ; anxious to an excessive or unnecessary extent.

overarch, vb. trans. [1. ôverárch ; 2. òuvərɑ́tʃ]. To arch over ; to hang, spread, over like an arch.

overarm, adj. [1. óver àrm ; 2. óuvər ɑ̀m]. Delivered, struck, with the arm raised above the elbow ; overhand : *overarm bowling* (at cricket) ; *overarm service* (at lawn-tennis &c.).

overawe, vb. trans. [1. ôveráw ; 2. òuvərɔ́]. To keep in awe ; to daunt ; to strike fear into ; inspire with respect so as to reduce to subjection.

overbalance, vb. trans. & intrans. [1. ôverbálans ; 2. òuvəbǽləns]. **1.** trans. **a** To cause to lose balance or equilibrium, cause to fall over ; **b** to more than balance, exceed in weight or value ; to outweigh, preponderate over. **2.** intrans. To lose one's balance.

overbear, vb. trans. [1. ôverbấr ; 2. òuvəbɛ́ə]. (only in moral sense) **a** To break down the will of, to dominate, trample upon the wishes of, coerce into acquiescence ; **b** to bear down, persuade, by forcible argument and persuasion.

overbearing, adj. [1. ôverbấring ; 2. òuvəbɛ́əriŋ]. Domineering, dictatorial, masterful.

overbearingly, adv. In an overbearing manner.

overblown, adj. [1. ôverblṓn ; 2. òuvəblóun]. (chiefly of flowers) Past full bloom.

overboard, adv. [1. óverbord ; 2. óuvəbɔ̀d]. Over the board or side of a ship or boat, from the ship into the water : *to fall, throw, overboard* ; *man overboard !* Phr. *to throw overboard,* (fig.) to discard, desert, abandon.

overbold, adj. [1. ôverbṓld ; 2. òuvəbóuld]. Foolhardy, rash ; impudent, insolent.

overbrim, vb. trans. & intrans. [1. ôverbrím ; 2. òuvəbrím]. **1.** trans. To overflow, to cause to flow over the brim. **2.** intrans. To be too full : *overbrimming cup* ; *filled to overbrimming.*

overbuild, vb. trans. [1. ôverbíld ; 2. òuvəbíld]. To build too much, to crowd with buildings ; to build in excess of demand. Phr. *to overbuild oneself,* to build a house too large for one's means ; to build more houses than one can sell or let.

overburden, vb. trans. [1. ôverbérdn ; 2. òuvəbə́dn]. To lay too heavy burdens upon (lit. and fig.).

over-capitalize, vb. trans. [1. ôver kápitalīz ; 2. òuvə kǽpitəlaiz]. To raise and supply more capital for an undertaking than is required.

overcast (I.), vb. trans. [1. ôverkáhst ; 2. ouvəkɑ́st]. To stitch over the edge of a seam to prevent unravelling.

overcast (II.), adj. **a** (of sky) Cloudy ; **b** (fig.) sad, gloomy.

overcharge (I.), vb. trans. & intrans. [1. ôverchárj ; 2. òuvətʃɑ́dž]. **A.** trans. **1. a** To put too heavy a load upon ; **b** (fig.) to fill to excess with : *to overcharge a lecture with facts.* **2. a** To put too much loading in a gun ; **b** to charge too heavily with electricity. **3.** To demand too high a price from : *to be overcharged for a meal.* **B.** intrans. To be guilty of overcharging.

overcharge (II.), n. [1. óverchàrj ; 2. óuvətʃɑ̀dž]. **1.** Excessive charge, **a** of powder &c. in a gun ; **b** of electricity. **2.** Demand for payment which is excessive or inequitable.

overcloud, vb. trans. [1. ôverklóud ; 2. òuvəkláud]. **a** To cover with cloud(s) or shadows ; **b** (fig.) to cast an air, or feeling, of gloom.

overcoat, n. [1. óverkōt ; 2. óuvəkout]. A coat worn over another ; a greatcoat, top-coat.

overcolour, vb. trans. [1. ôverkúlur ; 2. òuvəkálə]. **a** To colour too highly ; **b** (fig.) to exaggerate the details of ; to overheighten, as in a descriptive narrative &c.

overcome, vb. trans. & intrans. [1. ôverkúm ; 2. òuvəkám]. In O.E. *ofercuman.* **A.** trans. **1.** To get the better of ; to prevail over, subdue, surmount : *to overcome difficulties, bad habits, temptations, one's opponents* &c. **2. a** To be too much for ; to master, deprive of self-control : *overcome by emotion, drink* &c. ; *his feelings overcame him* ; **b** to render weak, deprive of vigour, power of resistance &c. : *overcome by hunger, lack of sleep* &c. **B.** intrans. To conquer, win : *to him that overcometh.*

overcrop, vb. trans. [1. ôverkróp ; 2. òuvəkrɔ́p]. To reduce or exhaust the fertility of land by excessive cultivation and cropping.

overcrowd, vb. trans. [1. ôverkróud ; 2. òuvəkráud]. To crowd more people into a space than there is proper accommodation for : *to overcrowd a district, a house, an omnibus, theatre, train* &c.

overcrowding, n. [1. ôverkróuding ; 2. òuvəkráudiŋ]. Act, process, of overcrowding ; state of being overcrowded.

overdo, vb. trans. [1. ôverdṓ ; 2. òuvədū́]. **1.** To do to excess ; to exaggerate, overact : *he overdid his part.* Phr. *to overdo it,* (i.) be guilty of extravagance or excess in conduct ; (ii.) go too far in attempt to secure one's object ; (iii.) to tax one's strength too severely. **2.** To cook to excess.

overdose, n. [1. óverdōs ; 2. óuvədous] An excessive and harmful dose.

overdraft, n. [1. óverdrahft ; 2. óuvədrɑ̄ft]. An amount drawn on an account at a bank in excess of funds available to meet it.

overdraw, vb. trans. & intrans. [1. ôverdráw ; 2. òuvədrɔ́]. **a** trans. To draw out money in excess of : *to overdraw one's account* ; **b** intrans., to draw a cheque on an account at a bank in excess of the amount in credit.

overdrive, vb. trans. [1. ôverdrív ; 2. òuvədráiv]. To drive too hard, too fast, or too far ; to exhaust, wear out, by driving too hard &c. ; to overtax : *overdrive a horse, workmen* &c. ; *an overdriven horse* &c.

overdue, adj. [1. ôverdū́ ; 2. òuvədjū́]. Behind time fixed for performance, arrival &c. ; specif. (of payments, accounts) not paid when due.

overeat, vb. intrans. & reflex. [1. ôverḗt ; 2. òuvəríːt]. To eat more than is good for one, eat to excess ; (also reflex.) *overeat oneself.*

over-estimate, vb. trans. & n. **1.** vb. [1. ôver éstimāt ; 2. òuvər éstimeit]. **a** To put too high an estimate or value on ; to overvalue ; **b** to draw up estimates for proposed expenditure which prove to be excessive in amount and leave a balance unspent. **2.** n. [1. ôver éstimat ; 2. òuvər éstimit]. An excessive estimate or valuation.

overfall, n. [1. óverfawl ; 2. óuvəfɔ̄l]. **1.** A disturbed stretch of water, as in a river or sea, due to the meeting of cross-currents, shoals &c. **2.** An outlet to allow water to overflow at a lock gate &c. to keep water level.

over-fatigue, vb. trans. & n. [1. ôver fatḗg ; 2. òuvə fətíːg]. **a** vb. To fatigue to excess ; **b** n., excessive fatigue.

overflow (I.), vb. trans. & intrans. [1. ôverflố; 2. òuvəflóu]. O.E. *oferflōwan*. **A.** trans. **a** (of water, liquids) To flow over the brim, banks &c., to run over; to flood, inundate: *the river overflowed (its banks, the neighbouring land &c.)*; **b** to flow, run, pass, beyond limits of boundaries of, owing to excess of number or amount; to run over or out: *the crowd overflowed the barriers; the goods overflowed the warehouses.* **B.** intrans. *Overflow with*, to possess to an extreme degree, be filled superabundantly with: *to overflow with wealth, kindness; a land overflowing with resources of every kind.*

overflow (II.), n. [1. ôverflô; 2. óuvəflòu]. **1.** A flowing over, of water &c.; an inundation, flood. **2. a** That which overflows; amount in excess of space available or allotted: *an overflow of population* &c.; (attrib.) *an overflow meeting, audience* &c., a secondary meeting for the surplus people who have not found room at the principal meeting. **3.** Outlet, pipe, carrying off excess of water from a cistern &c.

overflowing, adj. [1. ôverflôing; 2. òuvəflóuiŋ]. So full as to overflow; brimming over; superabundant.

overfold, n. [1. ôverfōld; 2. óuvəfould]. (geol.) A fold of strata so complete that the lower part is inverted, and lies on the surface.

overground, adj. [1. ôvergróund; 2. òuvəgráund]. Situated, raised, above ground, as contrasted with *underground*: *still overground*, still alive.

overgrow, vb. trans. & reflex [1. ôvergrố; 2. òuvəgróu]. **1.** To grow over, cover with growth. **2.** To outgrow, grow larger than is normal or healthy for: *to overgrow one's strength.*

overgrown, adj. [1. ôvergrốn; 2. òuvəgróun]. **1.** (of human beings) Too much grown, too tall for age or strength; hence, gawky, ungainly; delicate: *an overgrown lad.* **2.** (of plants) Having grown too luxuriantly and wildly; hence, uncared for, untrimmed. **3.** Covered over with vegetable growth: *paths and alleys overgrown with weeds.*

overgrowth, n. [1. ôvergrốth; 2. òuvəgróuþ]. **1.** An excessive, over-luxuriant growth; abnormal, unhealthy growth. **2.** [1. ôvergrōth; 2. óuvəgrouþ] That which overgrows.

overhand, adj. & adv. [1. ôverhand; 2. óuvəhænd]. **1.** adj. Delivered, struck, propelled with the hand and arm above the shoulder; overarm: *overhand bowling* (cricket); *overhand service* (lawn tennis &c.); *overhand stroke*, (swimming) with propelling arm out of the water and above the head. **2.** adv. With the hand or arm raised above the shoulder: *to bowl, serve, overhand.*

overhang (I.), vb. trans. & intrans. [1. ôverháng; 2. òuvəhǽŋ]. P.P. & adj. *overhung*. **A.** trans. **1.** To hang, project, jut out, over: *the cliff overhangs the stream; overhung with creepers.* **2.** (fig.) To hang over threateningly; to impend over: *a danger overhangs us.* **B.** intrans. To hang, project, over; to impend over: *overhanging cliff, danger.*

overhang (II.), n. [1. ôverhang; 2. óuvəhæŋ]. A projecting part; projection: *the overhang of a roof or window; overhang at the bows or stern of a ship* &c.

overhaul (I.), vb. trans. [1. ôverháwl; 2. òuvəhṓl]. **1.** To examine thoroughly, originally of ships, for the purpose of repair, cleaning &c.; to take to pieces for examination; to make a thorough investigation of: *to overhaul a boat, motor-car* &c.; *to overhaul state of a business, accounts* &c.; *to be overhauled by a doctor.* **2.** To overtake and pass, originally of ships; to catch up with: *to overhaul a vessel, another runner* or *competitor.*

overhaul (II.), n. An overhauling; a thorough examination or investigation: *to undergo a thorough overhaul.*

overhead (I.), adv. [1. ôverhéd; 2. òuvəhéd]. Above one's head; a above: *the stars overhead; the people in the flat overhead*; **b** (rare) with one's head covered by or below something: *fall overhead into the water.*

overhead (II.), adj. **1.** Situated, placed, above one's head; raised above the ground: *overhead wires; an overhead railway.* **2.** (of a business) Permanent, standing, not subject to fluctuations of price, wages &c.: *overhead charges*, such as taxes, rent, insurance, directors' fees, managerial salaries &c.; also as noun: *the overhead*, overhead charges.

overhear, vb. trans. [1. ôverhḗr; 2. òuvəhíə]. To hear (people speaking, or what they say) without the speakers knowing, whether by listening deliberately or by accident.

overheat, vb. trans. & intrans. [1. ôverhḗt; 2. òuvəhít]. **a** trans. To make too hot; **b** intrans., to become too hot.

overhung, adj. [1. ôverhúng; 2. òuvəháŋ], fr. P.P. of **overhang**. **1.** Suspended from above: *overhung door*, one sliding on overhead rollers. **2.** Having the upper jaw and teeth projecting beyond, and closing over, the lower; reverse of *underhung*.

over-indulge, vb. trans. & intrans. [1. ôver indúlj; 2. òuvər indáldž]. **1.** trans. **a** To indulge (another) to excess; **b** (reflex.) to indulge oneself, pamper one's own tastes and appetites to excess. **2.** intrans. (with reflex. force) To practise self-indulgence; to indulge oneself excessively and habitually: *I fear he over-indulged in all sorts of ways, and has to pay for it.*

over-indulgence, n. [1. ôver indúljens; 2. òuvər indáldžəns]. **a** Excessive self-indulgence; **b** excess in indulging others.

over-indulgent, adj. [1. ôver indúljent; 2. òuvər indáldžənt]. Indulging (oneself or others) too much.

over-influence, vb. trans. [1. ôver ínflooens; 2. òuvər ínfluəns]. **a** To exert undue influence over; **b** to persuade (a person) against (his) better judgement.

overjoyed, adj. [1. ôverjóid; 2. òuvədžóid]. Extremely pleased, delighted, exultant.

overjump, vb. reflex. & trans. [1. ôverjúmp; 2. òuvədžámp]. **a** reflex. To jump too far, so as to strain oneself; **b** trans., to clear by jumping with such superfluous effort as to jump too high, or too far.

overladen, adj. [1. ôverládn; 2. òuvəléidn]. Overloaded, **a** having too heavy a cargo on board; **b** too profusely covered: *overladen with ornament* &c.

overland, adv. & adj. [1. ôverland; 2. óuvəlænd]. **1.** adv. By land, not by sea: *to travel overland.* **2.** adj. Passing by land; made across or by land: *overland mails, journey* &c.; *the overland route*, specif., the route to India and the East via Marseilles, thence to Egypt and from Suez by sea, as contrasted with the route round the Cape of Good Hope.

overlap (I.), vb., chiefly intrans. [1. ôverláp; 2. òuvəlǽp]. **1.** To lap or fold over; to project over, or beyond, edge of, so as partly to cover. **2.** (fig.) **a** To coincide with, e.g. in time: *your visit and mine will just overlap*; **b** to correspond, be partly identical, in scope, subject &c.: *the treatment in these two books largely overlaps.*

overlap (II.), n. [1. ôverlap; 2. óuvəlæp]. **a** Process or fact of overlapping; **b** that part of an object &c. which overlaps.

overlay, vb. trans. & n. **1.** vb. [1. ôverlā́; 2. òuvəléi]. **a** To cover with a layer or coating; to spread over; **b** incorrectly, to overlie. **2.** n. [1. ôverlā; 2. óuvəlei]. That which is overlaid; a covering, coating.

overlaying, n. [1. ôverlā́ing; 2. òuvəléi-iŋ]. **a** An overlay, covering; **b** (incorrectly) the act of overlying (babies).

overleaf, adv. [1. ôverlḗf; 2. òuvəlíf]. On the other side of a leaf or page of a book &c.

overleap, vb. trans. [1. ôverlḗp; 2. òuvəlíp]. To leap over, to jump over; to leap too far; to omit, pass over, skip: *to overleap oneself*, to go beyond one's capacity and miss what one aims at.

overlie, vb. trans. [1. ôverlī́; 2. òuvəlái]. To lie over or upon; to stifle, suffocate, by lying upon: *to overlie a baby; overlain infants.*

overload, vb. trans. & n. [1. ôverlṓd; 2. òuvəlóud]. **1.** vb. To load too much, to put too great a weight upon; to overcharge as with electric current. **2.** n. An excessive load or charge, as of electric current: *overload release* or *switch*, automatic device for breaking the circuit and so preventing this.

overlook, vb. trans. [1. ôverlóok; 2. òuvəlúk]. **1.** To look at, view from a higher position; to look out over and upon: *our neighbour's windows overlook the garden; a view overlooking the town.* **2.** To superintend, supervise, inspect: *to overlook men at work, the work in an office* &c. **3. a** To look at and fail to notice; to take no notice of: *to overlook a passage in a letter*; **b** to neglect, slight, fail to recognize merits of: *his services and claims to promotion have been overlooked for years*; **c** to take no cognizance of, fail to reckon with, or to take into account: *you seem to overlook the strong arguments brought against your views.* **4.** To omit to punish; to excuse; to bear with, make allowances for: *to overlook an offence, bad conduct* &c. **5.** To look at or over with the evil eye, to bewitch.

overlord, n. [1. ôverlord; 2. óuvəlōd]. A feudal superior; a lord paramount, suzerain.

overlordship, n. [1. ôverlòrdship; 2. óuvəlōdʃip]. Dignity, position, of an overlord.

overman, n. [1. ôverman; 2. óuvəmæn]. Translation of Germ. *übermensch*. The superman of Nietzschean philosophy; one born or formed to dominate others by his physical and intellectual superiority.

overmantel, n. [1. ôvermàntl; 2. óuvəmæntl]. An ornamental structure of carved wood, stone &c. over a mantelpiece.

overmaster, vb. trans. [1. ôvermáhster; 2. òuvəmástə]. To overcome, overpower; subdue, overwhelm, esp. *an overmastering passion, love, hate* &c.

overmeasure, n. [1. ôvermézhur; 2. òuvəméžə]. An amount or measure in excess of what is required or due; surplus.

overmuch, adv. [1. ōvermúch; 2. ouvəmátʃ]. Too much, in too great a degree.

overnight, adv. & adj. **1.** adv. [1. ōvernī́t; 2. ouvənáit]. **a** On, during, the previous evening or night; **b** through the night until next morning: *to stay overnight.* **2.** adj. [1. ôvernīt; 2. óuvənait]. Done, occurring, on or during the preceding evening or night: *an overnight conversation.*

overpass, vb. trans. [1. ôverpáhs; 2. òuvəpás]. To pass beyond; to exceed; to surpass.

overpast, adj. [1. ôverpáhst; 2. òuvəpást]. Past and gone, done away with.

overpay, vb. trans. [1. ôverpā́; 2. òuvəpéi]. To pay in excess of what is due or deserved.

overpayment, n. [1. ôverpā́ment; 2. òuvəpéimənt]. Excess payment.

over-persuade, vb. trans. [1. ôver perswā́d; 2. òuvə pəswéid]. To persuade against will or judgement of.

overpitch, vb. trans. [1. ôverpích; 2. òuvəpítʃ]. (cricket) To bowl so that the ball pitches so near the batsman that it is easy to hit; to pitch beyond a good length.

overplus, n. [1. ôverplus; 2. óuvəplas]. A surplus, excess; that which is above a necessary amount or supply.

overpower, vb. trans. [1. ôverpóur; 2. òuvəpáuə]. **1.** To overcome, get the better of, by superior strength, numbers &c.: *to overpower the enemy.* **2.** To be too intense for, to master, overwhelm: *the heat, my feelings, overpowered me.*

overpowering, adj. [1. ôverpóuring; 2. òuvəpáuəriŋ]. Extremely powerful; irresistible, overwhelming.

overpoweringly, adv. Prec. & **-ly**. To an overpowering degree; so as to overpower; with superior, overwhelming force.

overpraise, vb. trans. [1. ôverprā́z; 2. òuvəpréiz]. To praise too much or too highly; to give more praise than is deserved to.

overpressure, n. [1. ôverpréshur; 2. òuvəpréʃə]. **a** Excessive, undue, physical or mechanical pressure; **b** excessive intellectual or emotional strain.

overprint, vb. trans. [1. ōverprínt; 2. òuvəprínt]. **a** To print something on the top of a sheet already printed; **b** to print a photograph for too long a time.

over-produce, vb. trans. & intrans. [1. ōver prodū́s; 2. òuvə prədjū́s]. To produce too much of an article; to produce in excess of a possible demand.

over-production, n. [1. ōver prodúkshun; 2. òuvə prədákʃən]. Production in excess of demand; oversupply.

over-proof, adj. [1. ōver prṓōf; 2. òuvə prū́f]. Containing a larger proportion of alcohol than proof spirit.

overrate, vb. trans. [1. ōverā́t; 2. òuvəréit]. **1.** To rate too highly; to put too high a value on, to have too great an opinion of: *to overrate one's capacities; an overrated person.* **2.** To assess too highly for rates.

overreach (I.), vb. trans. & intrans. [1. ōverḗch; 2. òuvərītʃ]. **A.** trans. **1.** To reach or extend beyond. **2. a** To outwit, circumvent, get the better of; **b** *overreach oneself*, (i.) to fail through trying for something beyond one's powers of attainment; (ii.) defeat one's purpose by being too subtle in attempting to gain one's ends. **B.** intrans. **1.** To stretch oneself forward so as to strain oneself. **2.** Specif. (of a horse) to strike and cut a pastern of a hind leg against a front foot in jumping or galloping.

overreach (II.), n. [1. ṓverēch; 2. óuvərītʃ]. Act of overreaching in a horse; injury inflicted by this.

override, vb. trans. [1. ōverī́d; 2. òuvəráid]. **1.** To ride over or across; to ride upon, trample down; to ride over with hostile forces. **2.** (fig.) **a** To disregard, set aside; to overrule: *to override claims, another's authority or ruling;* **b** to domineer over (a person). **3.** To ride too much or to excess; to fatigue, wear out: *to override a horse; an overridden horse.* **4.** (med.) To slide, pass, over, overlap, esp. of fractured bones.

overripe, adj. [1. ōverī́p; 2. òuvəráip]. Past full ripeness; too ripe.

overrule, vb. trans. [1. ōverṓōl; 2. òuvərū́l]. **1.** To set aside a ruling, decision &c. of another by superior authority; to decide or rule against: *the House of Lords has overruled the judgements of the lower courts; the claims and proposals &c. were overruled.* **2.** To prevail over, to get the mastery of: *his greed overruled his caution; conscience may be overruled by passion.*

overrun, vb. trans. [1. ōverún; 2. òuvərán]. **1.** To run, spread, over; **a** to flood, overflow; **b** to swarm in, infest: *overrun with rabbits, mice &c.;* **c** to grow luxuriantly and rankly over: *weeds soon overrun a garden.* **2.** To spread over with hostile or destructive intent; to ravage, spoil: *enemy troops overran the country.* **3.** To exceed specified limits: *his speech overran the time allotted.* **4.** (print.) To adjust arrangement of (type) by shifting words, lines &c.

oversea, adv. & adj. **a** adv. [1. ōversḗ; 2. òuvəsī́]. Over, beyond, across the sea, abroad, in a foreign country: *to go oversea;* **b** adj. [1. ṓversē; 2. óuvəsī], foreign, to or from abroad; abroad: *oversea trade.*

overseas, adv. & adj. [1. ōversḗz; 2. òuvəsī́z]. Oversea.

oversee, vb. trans. [1. ōversḗ; 2. òuvəsī́]. To overlook, supervise, superintend.

overseer, n. [1. ṓversēr; 2. óuvəsīə]. One who oversees or superintends; superintendent, foreman; specif., *Overseer of the Poor*, formerly a parish officer or official of a Board of Guardians, with duties concerning the relief of the poor.

oversell, vb. trans. & intrans. [1. ōversél; 2. òuvəsél]. To sell more shares, stock, or commodities than one can deliver or supply: *an oversold market.*

overset, vb. trans. & intrans. [1. ōversét; 2. òuvəsét]. To turn over, upset; to overthrow, subvert: *to overset a boat; the boat overset; to overset the government; overset one's plans.*

oversew, vb. trans. [1. ōversṓ; 2. òuvəsóu]. To sew two edges of cloth together by passing needle through from one side only.

overshadow, vb. trans. [1. ōvershádō; 2. òuvəʃǽdou]. **1.** To throw a shadow or shade over. **2.** (fig.) **a** To put into the shade, to lessen the importance of by contrast; to outshine; **b** to cast a gloom over, render sad; detract from gaiety or enjoyment of: *our festivities were overshadowed by the recent calamities.*

overshoe, n. [1. ṓvershōō; 2. óuvəʃū]. A rubber shoe worn over another for protection from wet &c.; a golosh.

overshoot, vb. trans. [1. ōvershṓōt; 2. òuvəʃū́t]. **1.** To shoot over or beyond a mark; (also fig.) to go beyond, exceed, overstep, what is proper or right: *overshoot the mark or oneself*, to exaggerate, overdo something; to overreach oneself. **2.** To shoot over an area too frequently, so that the game diminishes. **3.** To shoot or flow over or from above.

overshot, adj. [1. ṓvershot; 2. óuvəʃɔt]. (of a water wheel) Turned by water flowing on to it from above.

overside, adv. [1. ōversī́d; 2. òuvəsáid]. Over the side: *the ship was discharging cargo overside.*

oversight, n. [1. ṓversīt; 2. óuvəsait]. **1.** Supervision, care: *to have the oversight of children.* **2.** Unintentional failure to notice; omission to do something; unperceived slip or mistake.

overslaugh (I.), n. [1. ṓverslaw; 2. óuvəslɔ̄], fr. Du. *overslag*, vb. *overslaan*, 'to omit', *over* & *slaan*, 'to strike'. **1.** (mil.) The omission of, passing over, a turn of duty, because detailed for a superior or more pressing duty. **2.** (U.S.A.) A bar or obstruction in a channel or river.

overslaugh (II.), vb. trans. See prec. **1.** (mil.) **a** To excuse, remit, from a particular duty as being detailed for another; to pass over or skip a turn of duty; **b** (U.S.A.) to pass over for an appointment or promotion. **2.** (U.S.A.) To obstruct, block, hinder, as a proposal, bill &c.

oversleep, vb. intrans. & reflex. [1. ōverslḗp; 2. òuvəslī́p]. **a** intrans. To sleep on beyond the normal time for waking; **b** (reflex.) *oversleep oneself* (in same sense).

overspend, vb. trans., intrans. & reflex. [1. ōverspénd; 2. òuvəspénd]. **a** trans. To spend more than: *to overspend one's allowance;* **b** intrans., to spend more than one's means; to spend extravagantly, to waste money; also *overspend oneself.*

overspread, vb. trans. [1. ōverspréd; 2. òuvəspréd]. To spread over, cover the surface of; to be scattered or diffused over.

overstate, vb. trans. [1. ōverstā́t; 2. òuvəstéit]. To state too strongly, to exaggerate: *to overstate one's case.*

overstatement, n. [1. ōverstā́tment; 2. òuvəstéitmənt]. An exaggerated statement.

overstay, vb. trans. [1. ōverstā́; 2. òuvəstéi]. To stay longer than, beyond, what is expected or desired: *to overstay one's welcome.*

overstep, vb. trans. [1. ōverstép; 2. òuvəstép]. To exceed, transgress, bounds and limits; to go beyond what is right or proper in conduct: *to overstep the modesty of nature.*

overstock, vb. trans. [1. ōverstók; 2. òuvəstɔ́k]. To stock too much; to supply with goods too great for demand; to furnish with too large a stock: *to overstock a shop, market &c.; to overstock a farm (with cattle).*

overstrain, vb. trans. & n. [1. ōverstrā́n; 2. òuvəstréin]. **1.** vb. To put too great a strain upon (bodily or mental powers); overexert; also *overstrain oneself.* **2.** n. Excessive strain or exertion.

overstride, vb. trans. [1. ōverstrī́d; 2. òuvəstráid]. To stride over or across; to stretch across or beyond.

overstrung, adj. [1. ōverstrúng; 2. òuvəstráŋ]. **1.** Overstrained, with nerves too highly strung; in a highly nervous condition. **2.** (of pianoforte) Having strings crossing diagonally.

over-subscribe, vb. trans. [1. ōver subskrī́b; 2. òuvə səbskráib]. (usually in pass.) To subscribe for more shares in a company, public loan &c. than have been offered on an issue: *the new loan has been over-subscribed.*

overt, adj. [1. ṓvërt; 2. óuvət]. O. Fr., fr. O. Fr. *ovrir*, 'to open'; ultimately fr. Lat. *aperīre*, 'to open', see **aperient**; the Fr. form wd. normally be *avrir, P.P. *avert, but has been influenced by anal. w. the converse *covrir, covert*, 'to cover', see **cover.** Openly, publicly done; open to view, plain, apparent: *in market overt*, in an open, public market; goods sold therein pass with a good title to the buyer against a rightful owner under certain conditions; *overt act*, an act committed openly in pursuance of some design.

overtake, vb. trans. [1. ōvertā́k; 2. òuvətéik]. **1.** To come up with, catch up with: *to overtake another on the road.* **2.** To come suddenly upon, to surprise: *overtaken by a storm; disaster overtook them.* **3.** To overcome, overwhelm: *to be overtaken with drink, with terror, surprise &c.*

overtax, vb. trans. [1. ōvertáks; 2. òuvətǽks]. **1.** To tax to excess; to lay too many or too heavy taxes on: *country is overtaxed.* **2.** To make too great demands on, overstrain: *to overtax one's patience, strength, capacities &c.*

overthrow, vb. trans. & n. **1.** vb. [1. ōverthrṓ; 2. òuvəþróu]. **a** To throw over, upset; overturn; **b** (fig.) to subvert, defeat. **2.** n. [1. ṓverthrō; 2. óuvəþrou]. **a** Defeat, ruin, destruction; **b** (cricket) (i.) a ball returned from the field and not gathered at the wicket, thus allowing extra runs to be made; (ii.) a run so made.

overthrust, n. [1. ṓverthrust; 2. óuvəþrast]. (geol.) A thrust of strata over other strata at the side of a fault.

overtime, adv. & n. **1.** adv. [1. ōvertī́m; 2. òuvətáim]. Beyond the ordinary or regular time, esp. of working hours: *to work overtime.* **2.** n. [1. ṓvertīm; 2. óuvətaim]. Time worked after regular working hours; work done after hours: *paid for overtime.*

overtly, adv. [1. ṓvërtli; 2. óuvətli]. **overt** & **-ly.** In an overt manner; publicly.

overtone, n. [1. ṓvertōn; 2. óuvətoun]. An harmonic.

overtop, vb. trans. [1. ōvertóp; 2. òuvətɔ́p]. To rise above or over the top of; to exceed in height, to be higher than.

overtrump, vb. trans. & intrans. [1. ōvertrúmp; 2. òuvətrámp]. (cards) **a** trans. To play a higher trump upon; **b** intrans., to take a trick by playing a higher trump.

overture, n. [1. ṓverchur; 2. óuvətʃə]. **O. Fr.**, cp. Mod. Fr. *ouverture*, 'opening'. See **overt** & **-ure.** **1.** (usually pl.) **a** Friendly approach to a person with a view to amicable relations; **b** formal approach by one party in a dispute, or in war, with view to arrange terms of peace &c. **2.** (mus.) An orchestral introduction or prelude to a considerable musical work; also applied to a separate composition, *a concert overture*, as Brahms's 'Tragic Overture'.

overturn, vb. trans. & intrans. [1. ōvertérn; 2. òuvətə́n]. To upset, to cause to fall down or be upset.

overweening, adj. [1. ōverwḗning; 2. òuvəwīniŋ]. *Ofer wēninde*, 'presumptuous', occurs in M.E.; for second element see **ween.** Arrogant, contemptuously proud or haughty; pretentious, presumptuous: *overweening pride, conceit &c.; overweening ambition.*

overweight, n. [1. ṓverwāt; 2. óuvəweit]. Weight over and above what is demanded or allowed.

overweighted, adj. [1. ōverwā́ted; 2. òuvəwéitid]. Carrying too much weight; overburdened.

overwhelm, vb. trans. [1. ōverwélm; 2. òuvəwélm]. **1. a** To flow over, pour down upon, descend upon, cover over (of waves, torrents &c.); **b** to render powerless or helpless by superior force or numbers (of troops &c.) **2. a** To produce powerful moral effect upon; to overpower, master: *overwhelmed by grief;*

b to stagger, astound, abash: *your kindness quite overwhelms me.*

overwhelming, adj. [1. ŏverwélming; 2. ŏuvəwélmiŋ]. Overpowering, irresistible: *overwhelming sorrows, disaster* &c.

overwind, vb. trans. [1. ŏverwínd; 2. ŏuvəwáind]. To wind up (a watch) too hard, so that the mainspring is unduly tightened and compressed.

overwork, vb. trans. & intrans. & n. [1. ŏverwérk; 2. ŏuvəwǻk]. **1.** vb. **a** trans. To cause, compel, to work too hard or too much: *to overwork a horse, oneself* &c.; **b** intrans., to work too hard. **2.** n. Excessive work.

overwrought, adj. [1. ŏveráwt; 2. ŏuvərɔ́t]. **1.** Overworked, exhausted by too much work. **2.** Having an overstrained nervous system; over-excited.

ovi- (I.), pref., fr. Lat. **ovum**, 'egg'.

ovi- (II.), pref., fr. Lat. *ovis*, 'sheep'. See **ovine**.

ovibovine, adj. [1. ŏvibóvīn; 2. ɔ̀vibóuvain]. **ovi-** (II.) & **bovine**. (zool.) Belonging to family of the musk-ox or *Ovibovidae*.

oviduct, n. [1. óvidukt; 2. óuvidakt]. **ovi-** (I.) & **duct**. (zool.) Duct through which the eggs pass from the ovary; in mammals the Fallopian tube.

oviform (I.), adj. [1. óviform; 2. óuvifɔ̄m]. **ovi-** (I.) & **form**. Egg-shaped.

oviform (II.), adj. [1. óvi-, óviform; 2. ɔ́vi-, óuvifɔ̄m]. **ovi-** (II.) & **form**. Resembling a sheep.

ovine, adj. [1. óvīn; 2. óuvain], fr. L. Lat. *ovīnus*, fr. *ovis*, 'sheep'; cogn. w. Gk. *óis* for **owis*; Scrt. *áviš*, Goth. *awis-tr*, 'sheep-fold'; O.H.G. *ouwi*, 'sheep'; O.E. *eowu*, 'ewe', see **ewe**. Connected with, belonging to, resembling, sheep.

oviparous, adj. [1. ŏvíparus; 2. ŏuvípərəs]. **ovi-** (I.) & *-parous*, fr. Lat. *parere*, 'to beget', & **-ous**. Cp. **parent**. (zool.) Producing eggs which hatch outside the body of the female, as birds, fish, insects &c.; contrasted with *viviparous*.

oviposit, vb. trans. [1. ŏvipòzit; 2. óuvipɔ̀zit]. **ovi-** (I.) & *posit-*, fr. Lat. *posit-(um)*, P.P. type of *pōnere*, 'to place'. See **position**. (of insects) To lay, deposit (eggs) with the ovipositor.

ovipositor, n. [1. ŏvipòzitur; 2. óuvipɔ̀zitə]. Prec. & **-or**. Apparatus or organ in insects and fish for depositing eggs in suitable position.

ovo-, pref., fr. Lat. *ōvum*, 'egg'. See **ovum**.

ovoid, adj. & n. [1. óvoid; 2. óuvɔid]. Prec. & **-oid**. **a** adj. Egg-shaped; **b** n., an ovoid body or figure.

ovolo, n. [1. óvōlō; 2. óuvoulou]. Ital., also *uovolo*, fr. *uovo*, fr. Lat. *ōvum*, 'egg'. See **ovum**. (archit.) A convex moulding, varying in section, the Roman ovolo being ¼ of a circle.

ovo-viviparous, adj. [1. óvō vīvíparus; 2. óuvou vaivípərəs]. **ovo-** & **viviparous**. (zool.) Partly oviparous, partly viviparous; said of animals producing fully developed eggs but hatching them out within the body, as many reptiles, some fishes &c.

ovular, adj. [1. óvūlar; 2. óuvjulə]. See next word & **-ar**. Of, pertaining to, an ovule or ovules: *ovular growths.*

ovule, n. [1. óvūl; 2. óuvjūl]. Fr., fr. Lat. *ōv-(um)*, 'egg', see **ovum**, & **-ule**. (bot.) A body in the ovary of a plant which on fertilization develops into the seed; (loosely) an unfertilized, rudimentary seed.

ovum, n., pl. **ova** [1. óvum, óva; 2. óuvəm, óuvə]. Lat.; cogn. w. Gk. *ōión* for **ṓwjon*; connected w. Lat. *avis*, 'bird'; it is doubtful whether 'egg' or 'bird' is the primary meaning of the base. See **aviary** & cp. **egg**. (biol.) The female germ-cell or egg, produced in the ovary, which on fertilization by the male sperm-cell develops into a new individual.

owe, vb. trans. & intrans. [1. ō; 2. ou]. O.E. *āgan*, 'to possess, own', M.E. *ōwen*, 'to own, have to do, be in debt to, owe'; **ought** (II.) is fr. old Pret. of this. Cogn. w. Goth. *aigan*, O.H.G. *eigen*, O.N. *eiga*, 'to possess, own'. See **own**. **A.** trans. **1.** To be indebted to (a person) for a certain sum; be under an obligation to pay (a person) so much: *I owe £50 to my tailor; I owe my tailor £50.* **2. a** To be, or feel that one is, under a moral obligation; to be indebted to, feel bound to express gratitude to, for services, kindness &c.: *I owe you my best thanks* &c.; *I owe it to you that I am still alive*; Phrs. *to owe a person a grudge*, to have a grievance against; *to owe no thanks to*, to have nothing to thank a person for; **b** to be in duty bound to render: *we all owe reverence and obedience to God; I owe no allegiance to a foreign king.* **3.** To be indebted to as the source, origin, cause of: *she owed her beauty to artificial assistance; owed his success to luck more than to capacity.* **B.** intrans. To be in debt: *to owe for one's board and lodging.*

owing, adj. [1. óing; 2. óuiŋ], fr. Pres. Part. of prec. **1.** (of debts) Due to be paid; unpaid, still owed: *how much is owing to you?; still £10 owing.* **2.** (with *to* as prep.) **a** Due to, resulting from, caused by, ascribable to: *there is scarcity of fruit owing to the rain; his death was owing to an accident*; **b** on account of, as a result of: *I could not come owing to another engagement; everything in the garden is late owing to the cold spring.* (In vulgar style *due to* is often incorrectly used in above (**2. b**) and similar constructions.)

owl, n. [1. oul; 2. aul]. O.E. *ūle*, M.E. *oule*; O.H.G. *ūwila*; Mod. Germ. *eule*; O.N. *ugla*; prob. imitative, cp. Lat. *ulula*, 'owl', & *ululāre*, 'to shriek' &c. See **ululation**. **1.** Any one of a large family, *Strigidae*, or group of birds of prey, mostly nocturnal, and notable for their characteristic cries, having large head and eyes, hooked beak, strong talons, and soft, mottled feathers. Phr. *as blind, as stupid, as an owl.* **2.** A fool, stupid person; as mild term of contempt or reproach: *don't be such a silly owl.*

owler, n. [1. óuler; 2. áulə]. Prec. & **-er**. (hist.) One who practises owling; smuggler.

owlet, n. [1. óulet; 2. áulit]. Dimin. of **owl**, also earlier **howlot**. A young owl; the small European owl.

owling, n. [1. óuling; 2. áuliŋ]. See **owl** & **-ing**, fr. the owl's nocturnal habits. (hist.) Smuggling, esp. of wool or sheep, out of the country.

owlish, adj. [1. óulish; 2. áuliʃ]. **owl** & **-ish**. Owl-like; foolish, stupid.

owlishly, adv. Prec. & **-ly**. In an owlish, stupid manner.

own (I.), adj. [1. ōn; 2. oun]. O.E. *āgen*, 'own, possessed by'; also as n., 'property'; orig. P.P. of *āgan*, 'to possess'. See **owe** & **own** (II.). **1.** Possessed by anyone; proper, peculiar, to oneself; with possessive pronoun or case, as a more emphatic indication of personal possession &c.: **a** possessed by no one else; exclusively individual or peculiar to specified person or thing: *my own house; his own idea; did it with their own hands; cricket is peculiarly the Englishman's own game; name your own price; the orange has a scent all its own*; **b** implying love and affection: *our own dear children; my own love.* **2.** Related directly to: *own brother, cousin, to the king*; having both parents in common, as contrasted with *step-* or *-in-law*: *own brother or sister; my own father*, not my stepfather &c. **3.** Expressing idea of personal activity rather than possession; done, produced &c. by oneself: *to build one's own house; make one's own clothes; be one's own doctor, architect* &c. **4.** (absol. as n.) **a** That which belongs to, or is produced by, oneself: '*a poor thing, but mine own*'; '*and his own* (kindred, people) *received him not*'; *the work, book &c. is entirely his own*, quite original; *one of my own; to do what one likes with one's own.* Phrs. *to come into one's own*, to come into what rightfully belongs to one; also, to obtain credit, fame &c. which one deserves; *to hold one's own*, (i.) to preserve one's dignity, self-possession, credit, in company, conversation, debate &c.; (ii.) to maintain one's ground against attack; (iii.) *the patient is holding his own*, is not losing strength; *on one's own*, (colloq.) independent: *to be on one's own; to do it on one's own*, on one's own initiative or responsibility, by oneself; **b** intensely and tenderly loved person; object of one's deepest affections: '*She is coming, my own, my sweet*' (Tennyson, 'Maud'); *farewell, my own.*

own (II.), vb. trans. & intrans. O.E. *āgnian*, fr. base of *āgan*. See **owe**. **A.** trans. **1.** To possess, hold in one's possession; to have a legal title to: *to own lands, property; to own stocks and shares* &c. **2. a** To acknowledge, recognize, as one's own: *to own a child*, admit paternity; *nobody will own the authorship of the book*; **b** to admit, recognize: *to own the force of an argument*; **c** to confess: *own one's faults, transgressions* &c. **B.** intrans. **a** To confess, admit: *own that one is wrong*; **b** *own to*, to admit: *to own to being wrong; own to the theft*; **c** *own up*, (colloq.) to confess frankly, make a clean breast of it: *you had better own up.*

owner, n. [1. óner; 2. óunə]. Prec. & **-er**. One who owns or possesses; proprietor; one who has a legal title to: *the owner of a house; owner of lost property. At owner's risk*, of goods carried by land or sea, where all loss falls on owner, not on the carrier.

ownerless, adj. [1. ónerles; 2. óunəlis]. Prec. & **-less**. Without an owner; unowned, unacknowledged or unknown as belonging to anyone: *an ownerless horse, child* &c.

ownership, n. [1. ónership; 2. óunəʃip]. See prec. & **-ship**. State, quality, fact, of being an owner, possessor, or proprietor; legal title to possession; proprietorship, possession.

ox, n., pl. **oxen** [1. oks(en); 2. ɔks(ən)]. O.E. *oxa*, pl. *oxan*; cp. O.H.G. *ohso*, Mod. Germ. *ochse*, Goth. *aúhsa*, O.N. *oxe* cogn. w. W. *ych* & Scrt. *ukšān*, pl., 'oxen, bulls'. **1.** A fully-grown castrated male of the domesticated genus *Bos taurus*, used for food or as a draught animal, as contrasted with *bull*, the uncastrated male, *cow*, the female, and *steer*, a young castrated ox. Phr. *as strong as an ox*, very strong. **2.** Any member of the bovine family; a ruminant cloven-footed quadruped, usually horned. **3.** (pl.) Bovine cattle in general.

oxal(o)-, pref., fr. **oxalic**.

oxalate, n. [1. óksalāt; 2. ɔ́ksəleit]. Prec. & **-ate**. (chem.) A salt of oxalic acid.

oxalic, adj. [1. oksálik; 2. ɔksǽlik], fr. Fr. *oxalique*, fr. next word & **-ic**. Of, derived from, the oxalis, q.v.; specif. (chem.) *oxalic acid*, an organic poisonous acid, originally prepared from the plant oxalis, or wood sorrel, but now from cellulose, and used in dyeing, bleaching, making of metal polish &c.

oxalis, n. [1. óksalis; 2. ɔ́ksəlis]. Lat., fr. Gk. *oxalis*, 'sour wine, the plant sorrel', fr. *oxús*, 'sharp, sour, acid', cogn. w. Lat. *ācer*, 'sharp, biting'. See **acrid** & **acerbity**. (bot.) A genus of plants, wood sorrel, with bright green clover-shaped acid-tasting leaves and delicately veined white or pink flowers; the leaves contain potassium oxalate, whence *oxalic acid* received its name.

oxbird, n. [1. óksbērd; 2. ɔ́ksbǝ̄d]. The popular name of several small birds, esp. the dunlin, allied to the sandpipers, found flying in flocks about pasture-land.

oxbow, n. [1. óksbō; 2. ɔ́ksbou]. **ox** & **bow** (I.), 'loop'. **1.** A U-shaped yoke or collar for a draught ox. **2.** A horse-shoe bend or loop in a river, leaving only a narrow strip of land at the neck; if this neck is cut through an *oxbow lake* is formed.

oxer, n. [1. ókser; 2. ɔ́ksə]. A fence for oxen, usually a thick-set hedge with ditch and a single rail.

ox-eye, n. **1.** Popular name for several plants resembling the daisy, as *the ox-eye daisy* or moon-daisy, *Chrysanthemum leucanthemum*; the *yellow ox-eye*, corn marigold. **2.** A round window or bull's-eye window, *œil-de-bœuf*.

ox-eyed, adj. Having large, round eyes like those of the ox.

Oxford, n. [1. óksferd; 2. ɔ́ksfəd]. University town of England, seat of the University of Oxford; specif. (attrib.) of, belonging to, the university town or district of Oxford: *Oxford accent*, a precise, pedantic, affected way of speaking, usually attributed, without any foundation, to members of Oxford University; *Oxford blue*, a dark blue colour; *Oxford clay*, (geol.) a thick bed of blue clay underlying the Middle Oolite in Oxfordshire and the midland counties; *Oxford frame*, a picture frame in which the ends of the sides project at the corners; *Oxford grey* or *Oxford mixture*, a dark grey cloth, speckled with white; a pepper-and-salt mixture; *Oxford movement*, the Tractarian, High Church, or Anglo-Catholic Movement of 1833–41, started by Keble, Pusey, J. H. Newman &c.; *Oxford shoe*, a low laced walking shoe.

oxgang, n. [1. óksgang; 2. ɔ́ksgæŋ], fr. **ox** & **gang**. Old measure of land, as much as an ox can plough in one day, also styled *bovate*.

oxhide, n. [1. óks-hīd; 2. ɔ́ks*haid*]. The hide of an ox; leather made from this.

oxidation, n. [1. òksidā́shun; 2. ɔ̀ks*aidéiʃən*]. Next word & **-ation**. (chem.) Process of oxidizing; state, condition, of being oxidized; oxidization.

oxide, n. [1. óksīd; 2. ɔ́ks*aid*]. Fr., also *oxyde*; fr. **oxy-**, combining form fr. *oxygen* & *(ac)ide*, 'acid'. (chem.) A compound of oxygen with another element or with a radical: *iron oxide*; *oxide of tin* &c.

oxidizability, n. [1. òksidīzabíliti; 2. ɔ̀ks*idaiz*əbíl*iti*]. See next word & **-ity**. State, quality, of being oxidizable.

oxidizable, adj. [1. óksidìzabl; 2. ɔ́ks*idàiz*əbl]. **oxidize** & **-able**. Capable of being oxidized.

oxidization, n. [1. òksidizā́shun; 2. ɔ̀ks*idaizéi*ʃən]. Next word & **-ation**. (chem.) The process or change which occurs when oxygen combines with another element or with a radical; process of oxidizing, state of being oxidized.

oxidize, vb. trans. & intrans. [1. óksidìz; 2. ɔ́ks*idàiz*]. **oxide** & **-ize**. **A.** trans. (chem.) To combine or cause to combine with oxygen; to convert into an oxide; to cover with a coating of oxide so as to make rusty; *oxidized silver*, silver coated with sulphide of silver so as to give a dull, dark sheen. **B.** intrans. To become oxidized; to combine with oxygen so as to become rusty.

oxidizer, n. [1. óksidìzer; 2. ɔ́ks*idàiz*ə]. Prec. & **-er**. (chem.) A substance acting as agent in oxidization.

oxlip, n. [1. ókslip; 2. ɔ́kslip]. O.E. *oxanslyppe*. **ox** & *-slip*, as in **cowslip**. **a** Primula with large clustered flowers; **b** (loosely) hybrid of the primrose and cowslip.

Oxonian, adj. & n. [1. okzṓnian; 2. ɔkzóuniən], fr. *Oxonia*, the Latinized form of **Oxford**, & **-an**. **1.** adj. Of or belonging to Oxford University. **2.** n. A member of the University of Oxford, past or present.

oxtail, n. [1. ókstāl; 2. ɔ́ksteil]. The tail of the ox, esp. as a dish; *oxtail soup*, made from this.

oxter, n. [1. ókster; 2. ɔ́kstə]. O.E. *ōhsta*, *ōxta*, cogn. w. Lat. *axilla*. See **axilla** & **aisle**. (Scots) The arm-pit.

ox-tongue, n. **1.** The tongue of an ox used as food. **2.** Popular name of plants with tongue-shaped leaves with rough surface, as the anchusa or bugloss, q.v.

oxy-, pref. **1.** From Gk. *oxús*, 'sharp', see **oxalis**, as *oxycarpous*, *oxytone* &c. **2.** Signifying **a** the presence of oxygen or an oxide; **b** the substitution of an atom of hydroxyl for one of hydrogen: *oxy-aldehyde* &c.

oxy-acetylene, n. [1. òksiasétilēn; 2. ɔ̀ks*iəsé*tilīn]. Prec. & **acetylene**. Of, pertaining to, consisting of, a mixture of oxygen and acetylene; esp. *oxy-acetylene blowpipe*, for producing a more intensely hot flame than the oxy-hydrogen blowpipe, q.v.

oxycarpous, adj. [1. òksikárpus; 2. ɔ̀ks*ik*ā́pəs]. See **oxy-** & **carpel**. (bot.) Having sharp-pointed fruits.

oxygen, n. [1. óksijen; 2. ɔ́ks*idžin*], fr. Fr. *oxygène*, formed fr. Gk. *oxús*, 'sharp, acid', see **oxy-**, **oxalis**, & base in **genesis**. Name given by Lavoisier, who regarded the gas as essential constituent of acids. A colourless, odourless, tasteless gas, essential to life, most widely distributed of the chemical, non-metallic elements, having symbol O; existing free in the atmosphere, forming nine-tenths of water, and, with other elements, found in most minerals and organic substances.

oxygenate, vb. trans. [1. óksijenāt; 2. ɔ́ks*i*džineit]. **oxygen** & **-ate**. **a** To combine, treat, with ogygen; **b** to impregnate with oxygen, as by respiration: *to oxygenate the blood*; *oxygenated water*, hydrogen dioxide.

oxygenation, n. [1. òksijenā́shun; 2. ɔ̀ks*i*džinéiʃən]. Next word & **-ion**. Process or state of being oxygenated.

oxygenize, vb. trans. [1. óksijenīz; 2 ɔ́ks*i*džinaiz]. **oxygen** & **-ize**. To oxygenate; to oxidize.

oxy-hydrogen, adj. [1. òksihídrojen; 2. ɔ̀ks*i*háidrədžin]. **oxy-** & **hydrogen**. Of, pertaining to, consisting of, a mixture of oxygen and hydrogen: *oxy-hydrogen gas*; *oxy-hydrogen blowpipe*, instrument for producing a flame, *oxy-hydrogen flame*, of intense heat, by mixing hydrogen and oxygen under pressure at the moment of combustion; *oxy-hydrogen light*, a brilliant light obtained by the incandescence of a substance such as lime in an oxy-hydrogen flame.

oxymoron, n. [1. òksimṓron; 2. ɔ̀ksimɔ́rɔn], fr. Gk. *oxúmōron*, *oxúmōros*, 'pointedly foolish', fr. *oxús*, 'sharp', see **oxalis**, & *mōrós*, 'foolish', see **moron**. Rhetorical figure, epigrammatic in form, in which what appear to be incongruous, contradictory, contrasted, ideas are associated; e.g. '*His honour rooted in dishonour stood*' (Tennyson, 'Lancelot and Elaine'); '*our final hope is flat despair*' (Milton, 'P. L.' ii. 142-3); '*loveliness . . . is, when unadorn'd, adorn'd the most*' (Thomson, 'Autumn', 204-206).

oxytone, adj. & n. [1. óksitōn; 2. ɔ́ks*itoun*], fr. Gk. *oxútonos*, fr. *oxús*, 'sharp', see **oxy-**, & *tónos*, 'tone', q.v. **1.** adj. (of syllables) In languages with musical accent, uttered on a high tone; this was denoted in Greek by the mark of so-called acute accent placed over the vowel. **2.** n. Syllable pronounced with this tone.

oyer, n. [1. óier; 2. ɔ́iə]. The first word in A.-Fr. law term *oyer et terminer*, 'to hear and determine', fr. *oyer*, Mod. Fr. *ouïr*, 'to hear', fr. Lat. *audīre*, 'to hear', see **audible**, & *terminer*, fr. Lat. *termināre*, 'to finish, determine', see **term**. A trial under the writ of *oyer et terminer*, a commission issued under royal seal to judges to try treasons, felonies, and misdemeanours; *a Court of Oyer and Terminer and Gaol Delivery*, the formal name of an Assize Court or Assizes.

oyez !, also **oyes !** & **O yes !**, interj. [1. ōyés; 2. oujés]. O. Fr., imperat. of *oir*, Mod. Fr. *ouïr*, 'to hear'. See prec. A call, repeated three times by court usher, or town-crier, to demand attention and silence.

oyster, n. [1. óister; 2. ɔ́istə]. M.E., fr. O. Fr. *oistre*, Mod. Fr. *huître*, fr. Lat. *ostrea*, fr. Gk. *óstreon*, 'oyster', so called fr. its bony, hard shell, fr. *ostéon*, 'bone'. See **osteo-** & cp. **os**; see also **ossify** & **ostracize**. O.E. *ostre*, 'oyster', was borrowed direct fr. Lat. **1.** A marine bivalve edible mollusc, belonging to the genus *Ostrea*, of which the European oyster, *O. edulis*, and American oyster, *O. virginica*, are distinct species and are cultivated. Phr. *as dumb as an oyster*, very silent. **2.** Any bivalve mollusc resembling the true oyster, as the pearl-oyster, *Meleagrina margaritifera*. **3.** A small, delicate piece of meat on each side of the back of a fowl.

oyster bar, n. A counter or bar in an inn or restaurant where oysters are sold.

oyster bed, n. A bed on the sea-bottom in an estuary or shallow bay where oysters breed and are cultivated.

oyster-catcher, n. A wading sea-bird with a wedge-shaped bill and black and white plumage of many species, belonging to the genus *Haematopus*.

oyster-knife, n. A broad-bladed knife for opening oysters.

oyster-patty, n. Small pie of light pastry containing oysters.

oyster-plant, n. Salsify, as having slight fishy flavour as of oysters when cooked.

oyster-sauce, n. A white sauce with oysters cooked in it.

ozocerit(e), n. [1. ōzṓkerīt,-it; 2. ouzóukərait, -it], fr. Gk. base *oz-*, 'to smell', fr. **odj-*, see under **odour**, & *kērós*, 'wax', see **cere**. Kind of wax-like mineral, yellowish, greenish, or brown in colour, and having, before being purified, a strong, unpleasant smell; used for making candles.

ozone, n. [1. ōzṓn; 2. ouzóun]. Fr., fr. Gk. *óz-(ein)*, 'to smell'. See under **odour**. **1.** A gaseous, concentrated form of oxygen, of a bluish colour and pungent smell, obtained by electric discharge in oxygen, highly explosive and a powerful oxidizing agent. **2.** (popularly) Invigorating, bracing air, esp. that of the sea-side.

ozonic, adj. [1. ōzṓnik; 2. ouzóunik]. Prec. & **-ic**. Pertaining to, containing, ozone.

ozoniferous, adj. [1. ōzōníferus; 2. òuzounífərəs]. See prec. & **-ferous**. Ozone-bearing, as of sea-breezes.

ozonize, vb. trans. [1. ṓzōnīz; 2. ouzóunaiz]. **ozone** & **-ize**. To convert (oxygen) into ozone; to impregnate with ozone.

P

P, p [1. pē; 2. pī]. The sixteenth letter of the English alphabet; for its use as symbol or in abbreviations see end of Dictionary. Phr. *to mind one's p's and q's*, to behave properly, be careful what one does or says.

pa, n. [1. pah; 2. pā]. Abbr. fr. **papa**. (colloq.) Father.

pabulum, n. [1. pábūlum; 2. pǽbjuləm]. Lat. *pābulum*, 'food'; cp. Lat. *pā-nis*, 'bread', see **panification**; *pā-scere*, 'to feed, pasture', see **pastor** & **pasture**; cogn. w. Goth. *fōdjan*, 'to feed'; O.E. *fōda*, 'food', see **food**; O.E. *fōstor*, 'feeding, food', see **foster**; Gk. *patéomai*, 'I eat'; *ápastos*, 'fasting'. Food, nourishment, sustenance; (often fig.) *mental pabulum*.

paca, n. [1. páka; 2. pǽkə]. Brazil. *pak*. Large spotted rodent of Central America.

pace (I.), n. [1. pās; 2. peis]. M.E. *pāce*, fr. O. Fr. *pas*, fr. Lat. *passus*, 'step, stride, pace', fr. P.P. type of *pandere*, 'to spread out', perh. connected w. *patēre*, 'to lie open'. See **patent** (I.). **1.** Single step in walking, running &c.; stride. **2. a** Space covered in single step; **b** distance between two successive points at which the same foot touches the ground in walking. **3.** Rate of, speed in, walking, running &c.; rate of progress: *to go at a good pace* (often fig.). Phr. *to keep pace with*, (lit. and fig.) to keep up with, advance at same rate as; *to go the pace*, (fig.) to live extravagantly or dissolutely. **4. a** Specific mode of walking, running &c., esp. of horse;

Phr. *to put a person through his paces*, test his abilities; **b** (specif., of horse) that manner of stepping in which both feet on same side are lifted together.

pace (II.), vb. intrans. & trans., fr. prec. **A.** intrans. **1.** To walk with measured tread. **2.** (of horse) To amble. **B.** trans. **1.** To cross, traverse, esp. repeatedly, with measured, rhythmical tread: *to pace a room.* **2.** Also *pace out*, to measure by pacing. **3.** To set pace for (runner in race &c.).

pace (III.), prep. [1. pāse; 2. péisi]. Lat. *pāce*, abl. of *pāx*, 'peace', see **pax**. (in expressing disagreement, opposed opinion) With all deference to opinion of (another): *pace Mr. Jones.*

-paced, adj. [1. pāst; 2. peist]. **pace** (I.) & **-ed.** Having pace of specified character: cp. *thorough-paced*, out-and-out.

pace-maker, n. One who sets the pace for another in race &c.

pacer, n. [1. pāser; 2. péisə]. **pace** (II.) & **-er.** One who, that which, paces, esp. horse whose usual gait is a pace.

pacha, n. See **pasha.**

pachisi, n. [1. pachēsi; 2. pətʃísi]. Hind., 'twenty-five', the highest number thrown. Indian game, played on a board with pieces moved according to throw of cowrie shells which are used as dice.

pachyderm, n. [1. pákidĕrm; 2. pǽkidʌm], fr. Fr. *pachyderme*, fr. Gk. *pakhú-(s)*, 'thick; strong; rich', fr. **bhṇghu-*; cogn. w. Scrt. *bahúś*, 'thick, abundant'; O.H.G. *bungo*, 'onion'; O.N. *bingr*, 'heap, mass'; Lith. *bisums*, 'thickness'; & *dérma, dérmat-os*, 'skin', see **-derm. 1.** Thick-skinned animal, esp. one of an obs. order of hoofed, non-ruminant mammals including the elephant, hippopotamus, and rhinoceros. **2.** Thick-skinned, stolid person.

pachydermatous, adj. [1. pàkidĕrmatus; 2. pækidʌ́mətəs]. See prec. & **-ous. 1.** Thick-skinned; of, of the nature of, a pachyderm. **2.** Stolid, insensible to impressions.

pacific, adj. & n. [1. pasífik; 2. pəsífik], fr. Lat. *pācific-(us)*, 'peace-making', fr. *pāci-*, stem of *pāx*, 'peace'. See **pax** & **-fic. 1.** adj. **a** Tending towards, promoting, peace; **b** of peaceful disposition or character; mild, tranquil; *Pacific Ocean*, between Asia and America. **2.** n. (cap.) *The Pacific*, Pacific Ocean.

pacifically, adv. [1. pasífikali; 2. pəsífikəli]. Prec. & **-al** & **-ly.** In a pacific manner.

pacification, n. [1. pàsifikā́shun; 2. pæsifikéiʃən], fr. Lat. *pācificātiōn-(em)*, 'establishing of peace'. See **pacify** & **-fication.** Act of pacifying; state of being pacified.

pacificatory, adj. [1. pàsifikāturi, pasífikāturi; 2. pæsifikéitəri, pəsífikeitəri], fr. Lat. *pācificātōri-(us)*, 'establishing peace', fr. *pācificāt-(um)*, P.P. type of *pācificāre*, 'to pacify'. See prec. & **-ory.** Tending to pacify.

pacificism, pacifism, n. [1. pasífisizm, pásifizm; 2. pəsífisizəm, pǽsifizəm]. **pacific** & **-ism**; the shortened form is now the commoner though, strictly, the less correct. Doctrine, theory, teaching, of the necessity for universal or international peace, and the abolition of war as means of settling disputes; systematic opposition to war and militarism.

pacificist, pacifist, n. [1. pasífisist, pásifist; 2. pəsífisist, pǽsifist]. See prec. & **-ist.** Adherent of, believer in, pacif(ic)ism.

pacifier, n. [1. pásifier; 2. pǽsifaiə]. See next word & **-er.** One who pacifies; peacemaker.

pacify, vb. trans. [1. pásifī; 2. pǽsifai], fr. Fr. *pacifier*, fr. Lat. *pācificāre*, 'to pacify', fr. *pāci-(s)*, genit. of *pāx*, 'peace', see **pax,** & **-fy. 1.** To make peaceful, quiet, calm; restore serenity to, appease: *to pacify a person, anger* &c. **2.** To establish peace in (a country, nation &c.).

pack (I.), n. [1. pak; 2. pæk]. M.E. *pakke*; orig. apparently a Flemish word wh. passed into High Germ. & into Engl., as well as into Fr. See **packet. 1.** Bundle of things put or fastened together, usually wrapped up or in bag, case &c., to be carried by person or beast of burden; specif. **a** pedlar's bundle of goods; **b** load for pack-animal. **2. a** Bale, bundle, of specific size or weight, as measure for certain goods, e.g. wool; **b** amount of fish &c. packed in a season. **3.** Number of animals or birds naturally herding together, or kept together for specific purpose, esp. **a** of hounds for hunting; **b** of wolves; **c** of grouse. **4.** (Rugby football) The forwards of a team. **5.** (implying contempt, anger &c.) Number, group, collection: *a pack of lies, nonsense, scoundrels* &c. **6.** Complete set of playing-cards. **7.** Extensive mass of broken, floating ice: usually *pack-ice.* **8.** (archaic or obs.) An impudent woman of light character: *a saucy pack.*

pack (II.), vb. trans. & intrans., fr. prec. **A.** trans. **1. a** To put or fit together closely in box, case, bag &c., esp. for transport or storing: *to pack clothes, furniture, goods* &c.; **b** to fit tightly together, cram, crowd: *to pack people into a room, railway-carriage* &c. **2.** To prepare and put into tins for preserving: *to pack meat, fruit* &c. **3. a** To put things into, fill with goods for transport &c.: *to pack a box, bag* &c.; **b** to fill tightly, cram, crowd: *the room was packed.* **4. a** To surround with tightly pressed substance for protection &c.: *to pack a joint* (of water-pipe &c.); **b** (med.) to wrap (patient) in wet sheet to reduce inflammation &c. **5.** To load (animal) with pack(s). **6.** To select members of (jury, committee &c.), to ensure desired verdict or decision. **B.** intrans. **1. a** To crowd together, press, throng, into small space: *the people packed into the carriages*; **b** (of animals) to form into a pack. **2.** To depart, go off, take oneself off; Phr. *to send a person packing*, dismiss summarily. **3.** (specif.) To bestow one's clothes and other belongings in trunks, travelling bags &c., ready for a journey: *as we start early tomorrow, we'd better pack today.* **C.** Followed by adverbs or prepositions. *Pack off*, **a** trans., to send off, cause to depart: *to pack a person off*; **b** intrans., to hurry off, depart hastily. *Pack up*, trans. and absol., to pack (goods, a parcel, a box &c.); specif., to put one's clothes and other effects into travelling trunks &c., preparatory to departure.

package, n. [1. pákij; 2. pǽkidž]. **pack** & **-age.** Bundle of things packed; bale, parcel.

pack-animal, n. Horse, mule, donkey &c. used for carrying packs.

packer, n. [1. páker; 2. pǽkə]. **pack** (II.) & **-er.** One who, that which, packs; esp. **a** (i.) a skilled workman who packs goods for transporting; (ii.) one who packs and preserves meat, fruit &c.; **b** machine for packing.

packet, n. [1. páket; 2. pǽkit], fr. A.-Fr. *pacquet*, M. Fr. *pacquet* & *paquet.* See **pack** (I.) & **-et. 1.** Small package, parcel, bundle. **2.** Mail-boat.

packet-boat, n. Mail-boat.

pack-horse, n. Horse used for carrying packs.

packing, n. [1. páking; 2. pǽkiŋ]. **pack** (II.) & **-ing. 1.** (specif.) Act of putting clothes and other personal belongings into trunks or bags, ready for a journey: *I must go and do my packing.* **2. a** Material used in packing, as protection for goods &c.; **b** tow, cotton-waste, or similar material, pressed between or round parts of machinery, exposed water-pipes, cisterns &c., to protect against jarring or cold.

packing-case, n. Box of rough boards in which goods are packed for transport.

packing-needle, n. Large needle for sewing up packages in canvas &c.

packing-sheet, n. **1.** Coarse canvas &c., for packing goods. **2.** Wet sheet applied to reduce inflammation &c.

packman, n. [1. pákman; 2. pǽkmən]. Pedlar.

pack-saddle, n. Saddle with straps for carrying packs.

pack-staff, n. Staff or stout stick on which a packman carried his pack; in the old saying *plain as a pack-staff*, the word has been changed to *pike-staff*, q.v.

pack-thread, n. Strong thread for stitching up packages in canvas.

pact, n. [1. pakt; 2. pækt], fr. O. Fr., fr. Lat. *pact-(um)*, 'contract, covenant, treaty', fr. P.P. type of *pacisci*, 'to make an agreement'; cp. Lat. *pāx*, 'peace'. See **pax,** & words there referred to. Agreement, covenant, compact, made between two or more persons, parties, or states.

pad (I.), n. [1. pad; 2. pæd], fr. Du. *pad*, 'path'; cp. O.E. *pæð*, see **path**; O. Fris. *path*, O.H.G. *pfad.* **1.** (slang) Road, esp. in Phr. *knight &c. of the pad*, highwayman. **2.** Also *pad-horse, pad-nag*, easy-paced horse: '*An abbot on an ambling pad*' (Tennyson, 'Lady of Shalott').

pad (II.), vb. trans. & intrans., fr. prec. **1.** trans. To trudge along, go on foot along (road &c.); Phr. (slang) *to pad it, pad the hoof*, to walk, tramp. **2.** intrans. To go on foot.

pad (III.), n. Etymol. doubtful; possibly a variant of **pod. 1.** Anything composed of or stuffed with soft material and used to prevent friction, pressure, or other injury, or to fill hollow, protect wound &c.; specif. **a** soft, stuffed saddle; **b** guard for leg, in cricket, for shin, in hockey or football. **2.** Number of sheets of paper fastened together one above the other for writing, drawing, painting &c.; (often in compounds) *writing-, blotting-pad.* **3. a** Thick-skinned, fleshy under-surface of foot of some quadrupeds; **b** paw of fox or hare. **4.** Large floating leaf of water-lily &c.

pad (IV.), vb. trans., fr. prec. To stuff or cover with soft material to prevent friction, jarring &c.; *padded cell*, room with padded walls in lunatic asylum. Phr. *to pad out a sentence, article, book*, to eke out poverty of ideas and matter with irrelevant material and prolix verbiage.

pad (V.), n. Etymol. uncertain. Small basket used as measure for fruit &c.

padding, n. [1. páding; 2. pǽdiŋ]. **pad** (III.) & **-ing. 1.** Soft material used for stuffing as protection &c. **2.** (fig.) Unnecessary verbiage in a speech or written composition, which adds nothing to the point or meaning, and is introduced in the absence of solid matter, in order to fill up the time, or cover more space.

paddle (I.), n. [1. padl; 2. pǽdl]. Origin unknown. **1. a** Short oar with rounded, spoon-shaped blade, used without rowlock, as in canoe &c.; *double paddle*, one with a blade at each end; **b** any tool or instrument shaped like a paddle. **2.** One of the boards fitted round circumference of paddle-wheel. **3.** A paddle-shaped limb, as of a turtle &c.; flipper, fin.

paddle (II.), vb. intrans. & trans., fr. prec. **1.** intrans. To move along the water, propel boat, esp. canoe, by means of paddle. **2.** trans. To propel (boat &c.) by means of paddle(s). Phr. *to paddle one's own canoe*, be independent of others.

paddle (III.), n., fr. prec. Act, spell, of paddling.

paddle (IV.), vb. intrans. & n. Perh. fr. **pad** (I.). **1.** vb. **a** To walk, dabble the feet, in shallow water; **b** to touch, toy, fidget with the fingers. **2.** n. Slush; liquid mud or filth.

paddle-box, n. Wooden case covering upper part of paddle-wheel.

paddle-wheel, n. Wheel propelling ship by means of a series of boards, placed round and at right angles to circumference, which press backwards against the water.

paddock (I.), n. [1. páduk; 2. pǽdək]. Prob. variant of M.E. *parrok*, fr. O.E. *pearroc*, q.v. under **park. 1.** Small field, esp. one near stables, in which horses are kept or exercised. **2.** Enclosure near racecourse, where horses assemble before race.

paddock (II.), n. M.E. *paddok*, dimin. of *padde*, 'toad', cp. O.N. *padde.* (archaic or provinc.) Toad.

Paddy (I.), n. [1. pádi; 2. pǽdi]. Pet-name fr. *Padraig*, Irish form of *Patrick.* (colloq.) An Irishman.

paddy (II.), n., fr. Malay. *padi.* Rice in the

husk; also growing rice; *paddy-field*, field of growing rice.

paddy (III.), **paddywhack**, n. [1. pádi(wak); 2. pǽdi(wæk)]. Prob. fr. **Paddy** (I.). (colloq.) A fit of temper.

pad(i)shah, n. [1. páhd(i)sha; 2. pád(i)ʃə], fr. Pers. *pati*, 'master', & *sah*, 'shah', see **shah**. Great king or ruler; specif. **a** (in Persia) the shah; **b** (in India) sovereign of Great Britain; **c** (in Europe) sultan of Turkey.

padlock, n. & vb. trans. [1. pádlok; 2. pǽdlɔk]. *Pad*, etymol. doubtful, & **lock** (II.). **1.** n. Detachable lock, with hinged or pivoted loop at the top to be hooked through staple &c. **2.** vb. To fasten by means of a padlock.

padre, n. [1. páhdrā; 2. pádrei]. Span. & Port. *padre*, 'father; priest', fr. Lat. *pater*, 'father'. See **pater**. (nav. and mil. slang) Chaplain; any clergyman.

padrone, n. [1. padrṓnā; 2. pædróunei]. Ital., same word as **patron**. **1.** Master of Mediterranean trading-ship. **2.** Italian who employs street-musicians, begging children &c. for his own profit. **3.** Italian inn-keeper.

paduasoy, n. [1. páhdesoi, pádūasoi; 2. pǽdəsɔi, pǽdjuəsɔi], fr. Fr. *pou-de-soie*; etymol. doubtful; apparent association w. Padua. Kind of corded silk, esp. as worn in 18th cent.

paean, n. [1. pḗan; 2. píən], fr. Lat. *Paean*, 'a name of Apollo; hymn to Apollo', fr. Gk. *Paiā́n*, orig. 'one who touches', hence, 'one who heals by a touch; the Healer, Deliverer, an epithet of Apollo', hence, 'hymn of praise to Apollo'; cp. Gk. *paíō*, 'I touch, strike'; Lat. *pavīre*, 'to strike, beat', see **pave**, Lith. *piauti*, 'to cut down, mow'. **1.** Song of thanksgiving for victory, originally addressed to Apollo. **2.** Song of praise, triumph, and joy.

paederasty, pederasty, n. [1. pḗd-, pḗderasti; 2. píd-, pédəræsti], fr. Gk. *paid-*, stem of *paîs*, 'boy', see **paedo-**, & *erast-(ḗs)*, 'lover', fr. *éramai*, 'I love', q.v. under **erotic**, & **-y**. Unnatural sexual offence between male persons; sodomy.

paedo-, pedo-, pref. representing Gk. *paidó-*, stem of *paîs*, 'child, boy, girl'; cp. Scrt. *pōtaś*, 'young animal', *putrá́ś*, 'child'; Lat. *puer*, 'child', see **puerile** & words there referred to. Pertaining to a child or children, e.g. *paedobaptism*, baptism of infants; *paedobaptist*, adherent of infant baptism.

paeon, n. [1. pḗon; 2. píən]. Lat. *paeōn*, 'paeon', fr. Gk. *paiṓn*, Attic form of *paiā́n*, 'hymn to Apollo'. See **paean**. Metrical foot consisting of three short syllables and one long, the latter occurring in any position in the group.

paeonic, adj. [1. pēónik; 2. piɔ́nik]. Prec. & **-ic**. Of, composed in, consisting of, paeons.

paeony, n. See **peony**.

pagan, n. & adj. [1. págan; 2. péigən], fr. Lat. *pāgān-(us)*, 'villager, countryman', fr. *pāg-(us)*, 'district; village', fr. base **pāk-*, **pāg-*, 'to join together', seen in *(com)pāges*, 'a joining, fastening; structure', see **compact** (I.); *pāx*, 'peace', see **pax**; see also **fair** (II.) & **fang** (I.). **1.** n. **a** A heathen, a Gentile; specif., a worshipper of false gods; one who is neither Christian, Jew, nor Moslem; **b** a barbarian, person, who from any point of view is unenlightened. **2.** adj. Having character or beliefs of a pagan.

pagandom, n. [1. págandum; 2. péigəndəm]. Prec. & **-dom**. **a** Heathen countries; **b** pagans collectively.

paganish, adj. [1. páganish; 2. péigəniʃ]. **pagan** & **-ish**. Resembling a pagan.

paganism, n. [1. páganizm; 2. péigənizəm]. **pagan** & **-ism**. State of being a pagan; beliefs and practices of pagans.

paganize, vb. trans. [1. páganīz; 2. péigənaiz]. **pagan** & **-ize**. To convert, reduce, to paganism; to heathenize.

page (I.), n. [1. pāj; 2. peidž]. In M.E., fr. O. Fr. *page*; Ital. *paggio*, fr. Gk. *paidion*, 'a young boy, or slave'. See **paedo-**. **1.** Boy in livery employed in household &c. to attend to door &c. **2.** Title of various officials of royal household: *page of the presence* &c. **3. a** Boy attending on person of high rank; **b** (hist.) young noble in training for knighthood, in service of knight.

page (II.), n., fr. Fr. *page*, fr. Lat. *pāgina*, 'strip of papyrus; leaf, page', fr. base **pāg-*, **pāk-*, 'to join together, fasten', seen in *(com)pāges*, 'fastening'; *pāx*, 'peace' &c. See **pax**. **1.** One side of leaf of book, sheet of writing-paper &c. **2.** (poet. or rhet.) Writings, records, annals: '*But Knowledge to their eyes her ample page, Rich with the spoils of time, did ne'er unroll*' (Gray's 'Elegy'); *the glowing pages of Scott*.

page (III.), vb. trans., fr. prec. To mark successive numbers on pages of: *to page a book* &c.

pageant, n. [1. pájent; 2. pǽdžənt]. M.E. *pagin*, *pagen(t)* was used of a movable stage or scaffold upon wh. mystery plays were performed, & also of the performance itself. The connexion in meaning between this & Lat. *pāgina*, 'page of a book' (see **page** (II.)), is hard to see, unless the primitive sense of 'putting together' survived, or the sense 'scaffold' developed fr. that of 'leaf, slab', a secondary meaning of *pāgina*, whence perh. 'platform'. **1.** A splendid, imposing, stately display, such as a procession of magnificently equipped persons, horses &c. **2.** Specif., a spectacular form of drama, illustrating various episodes in the history of a town or district, performed on or near the scene of such episodes, with costumed players, dialogue, music &c. **3.** (fig.) Empty pomp or display; a vain, specious show.

pageantry, n. [1. pájentri; 2. pǽdžəntri]. Prec. & **-ry**. **1.** Splendid display, grand and gorgeous spectacle. **2.** Vain show, empty pomp.

pagehood, n. [1. pájhood; 2. péidžhud]. **page** (I.) & **-hood**. Rank, status, of a page.

pageship, n. [1. pájship; 2. péidžʃip]. **page** (I.) & **-ship**. Pagehood.

paginal, adj. [1. pájinl; 2. pǽdžinl], fr. L. Lat. *pāginā̆l-(is)*, 'of a page', fr. *pāgina*, 'page', see **page** (II.), & **-al**. **a** Connected with, relating to, a page; **b** page for page, with pages corresponding: *a paginal transcription*.

paginary, adj. [1. pájinari; 2. pǽdžinəri], fr. Lat. *pāgina*, 'page', see **page** (II.), & **-ary**. (rare) Paginal.

paginate, vb. trans. [1. pájināt; 2. pǽdžineit], fr. Lat. *pāgin-(a)*, 'page', see **page** (II.), & **-ate**. To mark pages off with consecutive numbers; to page.

pagination, n. [1. pàjináshun; 2. pædžinéiʃən]. Prec. & **-ion**. **1.** Act of paging. **2.** State of being paged; arrangement and numbering of the pages of a book.

pagoda, n. [1. pagṓda; 2. pəgóudə], fr. Port. *pagode*; prob. of Hind. & Pers. origin; cp. Pers. *but-kadah*, 'house of idols'. **1. a** Eastern temple, esp. in India and China, circular in shape, built in several storeys, surmounted at the top by a slender, tapering pinnacle; each storey is slightly narrower than that below, so that the whole structure forms a tapering tower; each storey has a projecting ornamental roof; **b** model of this as ornament &c. **2.** Light, ornamented shed or booth where newspapers, tobacco &c. are sold in a public place. **3.** Gold coin formerly current in India.

pagoda tree, n. One of several kinds of Chinese and Japanese trees, whose habit of growth produces a pagoda-like form. Phr. *to shake the pagoda tree*, to go to India or Far East and amass wealth, used of the Nabobs of the 18th and early 19th cents., with reference to the gold coin called 'pagoda'.

pagurian, adj. & n. [1. pagū́rian; 2. pəgjṓriən], fr. Lat. *pagūr-(us)*, fr. Gk. *págour-(os)*, 'a kind of crab', fr. **pag-*, 'hard; firmly fixed', stem of *págos*, 'mountain peak, rocky hill'; cp. *pagetós*, 'frost'; *págē*, 'snare, trap'; *págios*, 'solid'; *pḗgnūmi*, 'I fix; construct; harden, freeze'; *pēktós*, 'fixed; constructed; congealed', see **pectin**, & words there referred to; for the second element, Gk. *ourá*, 'tail', see **uro-** (II.). **1.** adj. Of, pertaining to, the family *Paguridae*, which includes the hermit-crabs and purse-crabs. **2.** n. The hermit-crab.

pah (I.), interj. [1. pah; 2. pā]. Expressing disgust or contempt.

pah (II.), n., fr. Maori *pà*. Native Maori palisaded fort or village in New Zealand.

paid, Pret. & P.P. of **pay** (I.).

pail, n. [1. pāl; 2. peil]. O.E. *pægel*, 'wine vessel, gill'; M.E. *paile*, *payle*, 'milk pail'; cp. L.G. *pegel*, 'staff, post'. The original type of pail, wh. still survives, is made like a cask, of flat staves of wood shaped so as to fit round the wooden bottom and held together with hoops; this enables us to equate the word w. Lat. *baculum*, *-us*, 'a staff, walking-stick', see **bacillus**, also w. Lat. *imbēcillus*, 'weak', lit. 'unsupported', see **imbecile**. Both the O.E. & the Lat. words have the dimin. suff. See further under **peg**. **1.** Round open vessel or bucket for carrying liquid, usually somewhat conical in shape, standing upon its smaller end, and usually provided with a curved handle formed like the section of a hoop passing across the mouth from side to side; pails may be made from staves of wood hooped together: *milk pail*; from metal, such as galvanized iron, or from coarse porcelain: *bedroom pail*, *slop pail* &c. **2.** As much liquid as a pail will hold; a pailful: *a pail of water*.

pailful, n. [1. pálfool; 2. péilful]. Prec. & **-ful**. Amount of liquid contained in a pail.

paillasse, n. See **palliasse**.

paillette, n. [1. palyét; 2. pæljét]. Fr., dimin. of *paille*, 'straw'. See **palliasse**. **a** Piece of metal used in enamel-painting; **b** small disc of bright metal as ornament; spangle.

pain (I.), n. [1. pān; 2. pein], fr. O. Fr. *peine*, fr. Lat. *poena*, 'penalty'. See **penal**. **1. a** Bodily or mental suffering, distress, anguish: *to feel, be in, pain*; *he suffers no pain now*; *the pain of parting*; **b** an acute bodily smart, ache, soreness; a twinge, a shoot, a qualm, generally localized in some particular organ or part: *to have a pain*; *a pain in the stomach, head, knee* &c. **2.** Penalty, punishment; only in Phrs. *pains and penalties*; *under pain of death* &c., at the risk of incurring death &c. **3.** (pl.) Effort, care, trouble: *to take pains*; *to get little reward for one's pains*; *no pains were spared to ensure success*.

pain (II.), vb. trans. & intrans., fr. O. Fr. *pener*, fr. Med. Lat. *poenāre*, 'to penalize', fr. Lat. *poena*, 'penalty'. See prec. **1.** trans. **a** (chiefly in moral sense) To cause distress or suffering to, inflict mental or moral pain upon: *your disapproval pains me more than I can say*; also **b** (of physical suffering) *my tooth doesn't pain me now*. **2.** intrans. (colloq.) To give rise to, be a source of, pain; to ache, smart, be sore: *my wound is paining just for the moment*.

pained, adj. [1. pānd; 2. peind], fr. P.P. of prec. Feeling, evincing, pain, or distress of mind; having the feelings hurt; offended, wounded; showing this: *he looked pained*; *his face wore a pained expression*.

painful, adj. [1. pánfool; 2. péinful]. **pain** & **-ful**. **1.** Causing, involving, pain of body or mind: *a painful cut in the finger*; *a painful experience, task, piece of news* &c. **2.** (obs. or deliberately archaic) **a** (of persons) Painstaking, careful, taking trouble, industrious: *a painful preacher of the Gospel*; **b** (of actions) exacting, and showing results of, care and painstaking: *the painful labours of lexicographers*.

painfully, adv. Prec. & **-ly**. In a painful manner.

painfulness, n. See prec. & **-ness**. State or quality of being painful.

pain-killer, n. Medicine relieving pain.

painless, adj. [1. pánles; 2. péinlis]. **pain** (I.) & **-less**. **a** Without pain; **b** not causing or involving pain: *painless death, dentistry*.

painlessly, adv. Prec. & **-ly**. In a painless manner; **a** so as not to cause pain: *teeth painlessly extracted*; **b** without suffering pain: *he died painlessly*.

painlessness, n. See prec. & **-ness**. State or quality of being painless.

painstaking, adj. & n. [1. pánztāking; 2. péinzteikiŋ]. **1.** adj. Taking pains or trouble; careful, diligent, industrious. **2.** n. Care, diligence, act of taking pains.

paint (I.), n. [1. pānt; 2. peint]. See next word. **1.** Solid colouring-matter, pigment, mixed with oil or liquid and used to give colour to a surface. **2.** Cosmetic used to colour face &c.; rouge: *powder and paint*.

paint (II.), vb. trans. & intrans., fr. O. Fr. *peint*, P.P. of *peindre*, 'to paint', fr. Low Lat. **pinctum* for *pictum*, P.P. of *pingere*, 'to paint; to embroider', fr. base **pei-(g)-*, **pi-(g)-*, 'to adorn, deck'; cp. Scrt. *piñjáraš*, 'reddish'; *pišáti*, 'adorns, paints'; Gk. *poikilos*, 'gay'; Goth. *(filu)-faihs*, 'variegated'; O.E. *fāh*, 'coloured'. See **picture**. **A.** trans. **1. a** To cover surface of with paint; to spread paint on, cover with paint: *to paint a gate, house, wall* &c.; **b** to cover with paint of specified colour: *to paint a gate green*. Phr. (slang) *to paint the town red*, to create disturbance by a riotous jollification; to indulge in a rowdy spree, esp. one inspired by drink. **2.** To trace designs, patterns &c. on with paint, to adorn surface of with paint: *painted glass, china* &c. **3.** To represent in coloured picture, to portray in colours: *to paint a landscape, a design*; *to paint a person's portrait*. **4.** To add colour to by means of cosmetics: *to paint one's face*. **5.** (fig.) To describe vividly in words: *to paint a person's character, a scene, incident* &c.; *to paint one's experiences in glowing colours*. Phr. *not so black as he is painted*, of greater merit than would appear from his reputation. **B.** intrans. **1.** To practise painting as an art. **2.** To make use of cosmetics, rouge &c. to improve one's complexion: *she would look better if she didn't paint so much*. **C.** Followed by adverb. *Paint in*, to introduce, represent, in suitable place in a picture by means of paint: *to paint in the foreground*. *Paint out*, to conceal, efface, blot out, by means of paint.

paint-box, n. Box with compartments for cakes of paint.

paint-brush, n. Brush for applying paint to surface.

painted-lady, n. [1. pánted lādi; 2. péintidléidi]. Orange-red butterfly with black and white spots.

painter (I.), n. [1. pánter; 2. péintə]. **paint** (II.) & **-er**. **1.** One who paints pictures; one skilled in the art of painting. **2.** Person whose trade is to cover surfaces with paint, as a means of preservation, or decoration: *a house painter*; *painter and decorator*, one who undertakes the painting and decoration of houses; *painter's colic*, a form of lead poisoning, common among painters and plumbers who use white lead.

painter (II.), n. [1. pánter; 2. péintə]. M.E. *pantere*, 'noose, snare'; cp. Fr. *pantière*, fr. Lat. *panther*, 'hunting-net', fr. Gk. *panthéra*, fr. *pān*, 'all', see **pan-**, & *thḗr*, 'beast', see **theriac** & cp. **ferocious**. Rope fastened to bow of boat to moor it &c. Phr. *to cut the painter*, to set adrift; (fig.) to separate oneself finally from something.

painting, n. [1. pánting; 2. péintiŋ]. **paint** (II.) & **-ing**. **1. a** Act of colouring a surface by means of paint; **b** act of portraying objects &c. in colours. **2.** Occupation of painter: *to take up painting as a hobby*. **3.** Picture in colours, painted picture: *a collection of old but probably worthless paintings*.

paintress, n. [1. pántres; 2. péintris]. **painter** & **-ess**. (rare) Female painter.

painty, adj. [1. pánti; 2. péinti]. **paint** & **-y**. **1.** Of, covered with, smeared with, paint. **2.** (of picture) Overloaded with paint.

pair (I.), n. [1. pār; 2. pɛə], fr. Fr. *paire*, fr. Lat. *paria*, neut. pl. of *pār*, 'equal'. See **par**. **1.** Set of two similar or corresponding things, naturally existing, or normally used, together: *a pair of ears, shoes, gloves* &c. **2.** Object consisting of two equal or corresponding parts: *a pair of tongs, scissors, spectacles, scales* &c. Phr. *a pair of stairs*, a flight of stairs. **3.** Group of two persons or animals; specif. **a** married or engaged couple; *the happy pair*, esp. of couple just married; (**b** of animals) mated couple; **c** two horses harnessed together; **d** (Parliament) two members voting on opposite sides, who both agree to be absent from division.

pair (II.), vb. trans. & intrans., fr. prec. **A.** trans. To put together, arrange, group, in pairs, join in couples. **B.** intrans. **1.** To be arranged in, form into, couples. **2. a** To join, unite, in marriage; **b** (of animals) to mate. **3.** Of two persons belonging to opposite parties, in Parliament or any legislative or deliberative body, to agree that both shall abstain from voting on a particular occasion. **C.** Followed by adverb. *Pair off*, **1.** trans., to arrange in couples; **2.** intrans., **a** to form into pairs, be grouped in couples; **b** (colloq.) to marry.

pair-horse, adj. (of carriage &c.) For a pair of horses.

pair-oar, n. Boat to be rowed by pair of oars.

pajamas, n. See **pyjamas**.

pal, n. & vb. intrans. [1. pal; 2. pæl]. Gipsy, 'brother', for *prāl*, cp. Scrt. *bhrā́tar*, cogn. w. **brother**. **1.** n. (colloq., slang) Intimate friend; mate, companion. **2.** vb. intrans. (followed by *with*, usually *pal up*) To become friendly, intimate; to associate.

palace, n. [1. pálas; 2. pǽlis], fr. O. Fr. *palais*, fr. Lat. *Palātium*, 'Palatine Hill in Rome; house of Augustus on this hill'. **1.** Residence of sovereign or bishop. **2.** Large, splendid house. **3.** Large hall for entertainment &c.

palace-car, n. Luxurious railway-carriage.

paladin, n. [1. páladin; 2. pǽlədin], fr. O. Fr., fr. Lat. *palātīn-(us)*, 'of the Imperial Palace'. See **Palatine** (I.). **1.** Any one of the twelve peers of Charlemagne's household. **2. a** A knight-errant; a noble adventurer; **b** an heroic, chivalrous person.

palae(o)-, **pale(o)-**, pref., meaning 'ancient, old, primitive', representing Gk. *palaió-(s)*, 'ancient'; cp. Gk. *pálai*, 'formerly', fr. **kʷəl-*, cogn. w. Gk. *tēle*, 'far off', fr. **kʷel-*. See **tele-**.

palaeobotany, n. [1. pàl-, pàleobótani; 2. pæl-, pèilioubɔ́təni]. Prec. & **botany**. That branch of botanical science which deals with fossil or extinct plants.

palaeographer, n. [1. pàl-, pàleógrafer; 2. pæl-, pèiliɔ́grəfə]. **palaeo-** & **-graph** & **-er**. Student of, one learned in, palaeography.

palaeographic, adj. [1. pàl-, pàleōgráfik; 2. pæl-, pèiliougrǽfik]. **palaeo-** & **-graphic**. Of, relating to, palaeography.

palaeography, n. [1. pàl-, pàleógrafi; 2. pæl-, pèiliɔ́grəfi]. **palaeo-** & **-graphy**. Study of ancient handwriting, inscriptions, and manuscripts.

palaeolithic, adj. [1. pàl-, pàleolíthik; 2. pæl-, pèiliouliþik]. **palaeo-** & **-lith** & **-ic**. Belonging to the age of, characterized by the use of, rough stone implements; of the earlier stone age, as contrasted with *neolithic*.

palaeontology, n. [1. pàl-, pàleontóloji; 2. pæl-, pèiliɔntɔ́lədži]. **palaeo-** & **ontology**. Study of extinct forms of life; study of fossil remains.

palaeothere, n. [1. pál-, páleothēr; 2. pǽl-, péiliəþiə]. **palaeo-** & Gk. *thḗr*, 'wild beast'. See **theriac** & **ferocious**. Genus of extinct, primitive, hoofed mammals, somewhat resembling the tapir.

palaeotype, n. [1. paléotīp; 2. pælioutaip, péilioutaip]. **palaeo-** & **-type**. System of alphabetical phonetic notation invented by A. J. Ellis.

palaeozoic, adj. [1. pàl-, pàleōzóik; 2. pæl-, pèiliouzóuik]. **palaeo-** & **zoic**. (geol.) **a** (of rocks) Containing the earliest forms of life; **b** (of fossils) belonging to the first geological era.

palaestra, **palestra**, n. [1. paléstra, paléstra; 2. pælístrə, pæléstrə]. Lat. *palaestra*, fr. Gk. *palaistra*, 'gymnasium, wrestling-school'; cp. Gk. *palaiō*, 'I wrestle'; *pálē*, 'wrestling-match'. Etymol. doubtful. Wrestling-school, gymnasium.

palafitte, n. [1. pálafit; 2. pǽləfit]. Fr., fr. Ital. *palafitta*, 'fence', fr. *palo*, 'stake', fr. Lat. *pālus*, 'stake', see **pale** (I.), & *fitto*, 'fixed', see **fix**. Prehistoric Swiss or N. Italian lake-dwelling built on piles.

palanquin, n., also **palankeen** [1. pàlankḗn; 2. pælənkín], fr. Port. *palanquim*; cp. Malay. *palangki*, Hind. *palki*, 'litter'. Light, covered litter for one person, used in China and India, carried by four or six men.

palatable, adj. [1. pálatabl; 2. pǽlətəbl]. **palate** & **-able**. **1.** Pleasant to the taste; agreeable, savoury. **2.** (fig.) Pleasing, agreeable, to the mind.

palatably, adv. Prec. & **-ly**. In a palatable manner.

palatal, adj. & n. [1. pálatl; 2. pǽlətl], fr. Fr. *palatal*, fr. **palate** & **-al**. **1.** adj. **a** Pertaining to the palate; **b** specif. (phon., of speech sound) produced by approximation or contact of the tongue with the hard palate; better called *front* (*consonant* or *vowel*). **2.** n. Palatal or front consonant.

palatalize, vb. trans. [1. pálatalīz; 2. pǽlətəlaiz]. Prec. & **-ize**. To form (sound) with, or near, the front part, or middle, of the tongue; term applied to process of shifting area of articulation forward from the back to the front of the tongue, as when [k] gradually becomes [ṭ] and finally [tʃ]; to front.

palate, n. [1. pálat; 2. pǽlit], fr. Lat. *palātum*, 'palate; organ of taste; mental taste, critical judgement'; etymol. obscure. **1.** Roof of the mouth; *hard, soft, palate*, respectively the front and back portion of this; *cleft palate*, malformation of the mouth, consisting of a longitudinal fissure of the palate. **2. a** Sense of taste: *to suit one's palate*; *to have a delicate palate*; **b** (fig.) aesthetic taste.

palatial, adj. [1. paláshl; 2. pəléiʃl], fr. Lat. *Palāti-(um)*, 'Palatine Hill; palace on this hill', see **palace**, & **-al**. **a** Connected with, resembling, a palace; **b** splendid, sumptuous, spacious.

Palatinate, n. [1. palátinat; 2. pəlǽtinət]. See next word & **-ate**. Province of a Count Palatine; specif., *The* (*Rhine*) *Palatinate*, electoral state in former German Empire ruled by the Count Palatine of the Rhine.

Palatine (I.), adj. & n. [1. pálatīn; 2. pǽlətain], fr. Lat. *Palātīn-(us)*, 'of the Palatine Hill; of the imperial palace', fr. *Palāt-(ium)*, 'Palatine Hill; palace built on this', see **palace**, & **-ine**. **1.** adj. **a** *Count* (in Engl. *Earl*) *Palatine*, count (earl) having royal privileges and judicial rights within his territory, subject only to the emperor or king; **b** *County Palatine*, territory within his jurisdiction. **2.** n. (without cap.) Kind of fur tippet formerly worn by women.

palatine (II.), adj. & n. **palate** & **-ine**. **1.** adj. Pertaining to the palate; palatal. **2.** n. (pl.) *Palatines*, also *palatine bones*, two bones forming the hard palate.

palato-, pref. Form fr. **palate**, used in compounds, as *palato-dental*, of the palate and teeth &c.

palaver (I.), n. [1. paláhver; 2. pəlávə], fr. Port. *palavra*, 'word, talk', fr. Lat. *parabola*, 'discourse, parable'. See **parable**. **1.** Conference, talk, discussion, esp. between African natives and Europeans. **2.** Idle talk, chatter. **3.** Flattery, cajolery, blarney.

palaver (II.), vb. intrans. & trans., fr. prec. **1.** intrans. To talk idly and at length. **2.** trans. (rare) To flatter, wheedle.

pale (I.), n. [1. pāl; 2. peil], fr. Fr. *pal*, fr. Lat. *pālus*, 'stake', earlier **pakslos*, fr. stem **pāk-*, 'to fix, make firm', seen in *pācisci*, 'to make an agreement', *pāx*, 'peace'. See **pax** & words there referred to. **1.** Long narrow pointed piece of wood, or stake, fixed upright in the ground for fence &c. **2.** Boundary, limit, fence; obs. except in fig. Phr. *within, beyond, outside, the pale*, within, outside, the limits of what is recognized as decent behaviour; *the (English) Pale*, district in eastern Ireland under English rule after 12th cent. **3.** (her.) Vertical stripe on the shield, occupying one-third of the width of the shield.

pale (II.), adj., fr. O. Fr. *pal(l)e*, fr. Lat. *pallidus*, 'pale'; cp. Lat. *pallēre*, 'to grow pale', *pallor*, 'paleness'. See **pallid** & **pallor**. **1.** (of complexion) Whitish, wan, having little colour. **2.** (of colour) Faint, dimly coloured. **3.** (of light &c.) Dim, of faint lustre, not bright.

pale (III.), vb. intrans. & trans., fr. prec. **1.** intrans. **a** To grow pale; **b** (fig.) to become pale, appear less beautiful or important by comparison with something else: *lesser beauties paled beside the queen.* **2.** trans. To make pale.

palea, n., pl. **paleae** [1. pálea, -ē; 2. péiliə, -iī]. Lat., 'chaff'. See **palliasse**. (bot.) A chaffy bract or scale at the base of the florets of composite flowers; an inner scale of the flower of certain grasses &c.

paleaceous, adj. [1. pàleáshus; 2. pèiliéiʃəs]. Prec. & **-aceous**. (bot.) Consisting of, resembling, paleae.

pale-face, n. Name applied, in romances, by North American Indians to a white man.

palely, adv. [1. pálli; 2. péilli]. **pale** (II.) & **-ly**. In a pale manner; dimly, faintly.

paleness, n. [1. pálnes; 2. péilnis]. See prec. & **-ness**. State or quality of being pale.

paleo-. See **palaeo-**.

paletot, n. [1. páltō; 2. pǽlətou]. Fr., etymol. doubtful. (obsolesc.) An overcoat, esp. a child's coat.

palette, n. [1. pálet; 2. pǽlit]. Fr., orig. in gen. sense of 'a thin, flat piece of wood'; formed w. dimin. suff. fr. Lat. *pāla*, 'spade'; cp. also Lat. *pālus*, 'stake'. See **pale** (I.). **1.** Small oval board on which an artist mixes his colours. **2.** Colours used by specific artist or for specific picture.

palette-knife, n. Thin-bladed knife with round point and wooden handle for mixing colours on or cleaning palette.

palfrey, n. [1. páwlfri; 2. pɔ́lfri], fr. O. Fr. *palefrei*, fr. Low Lat. *palafredus, paraveredus*, fr. Gk. *pará*, 'beside, extra', & Lat. *verēdus*, 'light horse', fr. Gaulish **vorēdos*, fr. *rēda*, 'four-wheeled carriage'; cogn. w. O.H.G. *rītan*, O.E. *rīdan*, 'to ride', see **ride**. (archaic and poet.) Saddle-horse, esp. for a lady.

Pali, n. [1. páhli; 2. páli], fr. Scrt. *pāli-bhasa*, 'language of canonical books', fr. *pāli*, 'canon', & *bhasa*, 'language'. Language of the sacred books of the Buddhists.

palikar, n. [1. pálikar; 2. pǽlikā], fr. Mod. Gk. *palikári*, 'boy', fr. Gk. *pállax*, genit. *pállakos*, 'youth'; cp. *Pallás*, epithet of Athene. See **palladium** (I.). Follower of Greek or Albanian military chief, esp. in War of Independence, 1821–28.

palimpsest, n. & adj. [1. pálimpsest; 2. pǽlimpsest], fr. Lat., fr. Gk. *palimpsēston*, fr. *pálin*, 'again; backwards, in reverse direction'; cp. Gk. *pélomai*, 'I turn'; *pólos*, 'pivot', see **pole** (II.). The second element is fr. Gk. *psáiō*, 'I rub; crumble away'; cp. Scrt. *bábhasti*, 'to crush, crumble'; & Gk. *psêgma*, 'shavings, chips'; *psṓkhein*, 'to rub out'; O.H.G. *bar*; O.E. *bær*, 'bare', see **bare**. **1.** n. Parchment or other material upon which two or more writings are found, one superimposed upon the other; the earlier writing was supposed to be erased, but is often visible as well as the more recent. **2.** adj. (of parchment, manuscript &c.) Treated in this way.

palindrome, adj. & n. [1. pálindrōm; 2. pǽlindroum], fr. Gk. *palindromos*, 'running back again', fr. *pálin*, 'backwards; again', see prec., & *drom-*, 'running', stem seen in *drómos*, 'course, race', see **dromedary**; cp. Gk. *dédroma*, Perf. of *dramein*, 'to run'; Scrt. *drámati*, 'to run'. **1.** adj. (of word, verse &c.) Reading the same backwards and forwards. **2.** n. Word, line &c. reading the same backwards and forwards.

palindromic, adj. [1. pàlindrṓmik; 2. pælindróumik]. Prec. & **-ic**. Of, of the nature of, forming, a palindrome.

paling, n. [1. páling; 2. péiliŋ]. **pale** (I.) & **-ing**. Fence of pales or stakes.

palingenesis, n. [1. pàlinjénesis; 2. pælindžénisis], fr. Gk. *pálin*, 'again', see first element of **palimpsest**, & **genesis**. **1.** Rebirth, resuscitation. **2.** Doctrine of successive births by reincarnation. **3.** (biol.) The exact reproduction in offspring of ancestral characters.

palingenetic, adj. [1. pàlinjenétik; 2. pælindžinétik]. See prec. & **-genetic**. Pertaining to palingenesis.

palinode, n. [1. pálinōd; 2. pǽlinoud], fr. Gk. *palinōidia*, 'palinode', fr. *pálin*, 'again; backwards', see **palimpsest**, & *ōidḗ*, 'song', see **ode**. **a** Poem retracting what is said in a former one; **b** recantation.

palisade, n. & vb. trans. [1. pàlisád; 2. pæliséid], fr. Fr. *palissade*, fr. *palisser*, 'to fence with pales', fr. O. Fr. *pal*, 'stake'. See **pale** (I.) & **-ade**. **1.** n. **a** Fence of iron or wooden stakes for defensive purposes; **b** (mil.) strong, pointed stake. **2.** vb. trans. To surround, protect, with a palisade.

palish, adj. [1. pálish; 2. péiliʃ]. **pale** (II.) & **-ish**. Somewhat pale.

pall (I.), n. [1. pawl; 2. pɔ̄l]. O.E. *pæll*, M.E. *pall*, fr. Lat. *pallium*, 'cloak'; cp. Lat. *palla*, 'outer garment of Roman women'; prob. fr. **par(u)la*, fr. Gk. *phâr-(os)*, 'large piece of cloth; cloak'; cogn. w. Lith. *burva*, 'garment'; Lett. *burwes*, 'small sails'. **1.** Large cloth, usually of black or purple velvet, spread over a coffin. **2.** (fig.) Anything which serves as, or forms, a covering: *a pall of darkness, gloom, snow.* **3.** Pallium. **4.** (her.) Y-shaped bearing, representing a pallium, borne on the escutcheons of the Archbishops of Canterbury, Dublin, and Armagh.

pall (II.), vb. intrans. Perh. an aphetic form of **appal**, but cp. M.E. *pallen*, 'to become vapid, to lose spirit'; the basis is Lat. *pallescere*, 'to grow pale', but what is the intermediate O. Fr. form fr. wh. the M.E. vb. derives? Fr. *pâle* & *pâlir* offer difficulties in view of Lat. *pallidus*; Meyer-Lübke indicates, but does not clear up the difficulty. See **pale** (II.) & **pallor**. To satiate, become insipid, appear wearisome: *sensual pleasure soon palls*; also *pall (up)on*, to weary, disgust by custom, become tedious to: *modern music is apt to pall upon one in time.*

Palladian, adj. [1. paládian; 2. pəléidiən], fr. Andrea Palladio, Ital. architect, 1518–80. Of, in the style of, Italian Renaissance architecture, based on a revival of the classical Roman architecture of Vitruvius, as exhibited in the works of Palladio; the term is esp. applied to the style as introduced to England by Inigo Jones in the early 17th cent.

palladium (I.), n. [1. paládium; 2. pəléidiəm], fr. Lat., fr. Gk. *palládion*, 'statue of Pallas', fr. *Pallád-*, stem of *Pallás*, 'Greek goddess of wisdom'; etymol. doubtful; possibly simply 'maiden', cp. Gk. *pállax*, 'youth'; *pallakís*, 'concubine'. **1.** Wooden statue of Pallas Athene, on the preservation of which the safety of ancient Troy was believed to depend. **2.** Anything which affords protection and security; a safeguard.

palladium (II.), n., fr. Gk. *Pallád-*, stem of *Pallás*, name of one of the asteroids, see prec., & Lat. suff. *-ium*. Hard, silvery-white metal, belonging to the platinum group of metals.

pall-bearer, n. One of the persons appointed to hold edges of pall at a funeral, in token of respect to the dead.

pallet (I.), n. [1. pálet; 2. pǽlit], fr. O. Fr. *paillet*, dimin. of *paille*, 'straw'. See **palliasse**. Small hard mattress, esp. one made of straw.

pallet (II.), n., fr. **palette**. **1.** Artist's palette. **2.** Flat tool used by potters &c. **3.** Valve regulating admission of air to organ-pipe.

pallet (III.), n. **pale** (I.) & **-et**. (her.) Diminutive of the pale, q.v., one-half its width.

pallial, adj. [1. pálial; 2. pǽliəl], fr. Lat. *palli-(um)*, 'cloak', see **pall** (I.), & **-al**. Of, relating to, like, a pallium.

palliasse, paillasse, n. [1. páliàs, palyás; 2. pæliæs, pæljǽs], fr. Fr. *paillasse*, fr. *paille*, 'straw', fr. Lat. *palea*, 'chaff'; cogn. w. Scrt. *palāvaś*, 'chaff'; O. Prussian *pelwo*; Lith. *pelai*; Lett. *pelus*, 'chaff'. Prob. connected w. Lat. *pellis*, Gk. *pélas*, O.E. *fell*, 'skin'. See **fell** (I.), **pellicle**. Straw mattress.

palliate, vb. trans. [1. páliāt; 2. pǽlieit], fr. Lat. *palliāt-(um)*, P.P. type of *palliāre*, 'to cloak', fr. *palli-(um)*, 'cloak'. See **pall** (I.). **1.** To mitigate, alleviate, soften: *to palliate pain, disease* &c. **2.** To extenuate, excuse: *to palliate an offence* &c.

palliation, n. [1. pàliáshun; 2. pæliéiʃən]. Prec. & **-ion**. **1.** Act of palliating; state of being palliated. **2.** Something serving to palliate; excuse, extenuation.

palliative, adj. & n. [1. páliativ; 2. pǽliətiv]. **palliate** & **-ive**. **1.** adj. **a** Relieving, alleviating; **b** serving to palliate; extenuating. **2.** n. Remedy, fact, which serves to palliate.

pallid, adj. [1. pálid; 2. pǽlid], fr. Lat. *pallid-(us)*, 'pale'; cp. Lat. *pallēre*, 'to grow pale', *pallor*, 'paleness'. See **pallor**. Excessively pale (of complexion, sky &c.).

pallidly, adv. Prec. & **-ly**. In a pallid manner.

pallidness, n. See prec. & **-ness**. State or quality of being pallid.

pallium, n. [1. pálium; 2. pǽliəm]. Lat. *pallium*, 'bed coverlet; mantle, esp. long Greek mantle; coverlet'. See **pall** (I.). **1.** Large square mantle, esp. as worn by ancient Greeks. **2.** A white woollen band, with four purple crosses, worn by the Pope, and sent by him to R.C. archbishops and primates as a symbol that they share with him in the fullness of the episcopal office. The pallium is double, and Y-shaped, and is worn on the shoulders, falling in front and behind. **3.** (zool.) The mantle or fold of skin covering the gills of a mollusc.

pall-mall, n. [1. pél mél; 2. pélmél], fr. obs. Fr. *pallemaille*, fr. Ital. *pallamaglio*, fr. *palla*, 'ball', & *maglio*, 'mallet', fr. Lat. *malleus*, 'hammer'. See **malleus**. **1. a** An old game in which a ball was driven with a mallet through an iron ring hung at the end of an alley; **b** place, alley, where the game was played. Hence, **2** (caps.) **a** street in London, formerly a pall-mall alley; **b** the War Office (formerly situated in this street).

pallone, n. [1. palṓnā; 2. pælóunei]. Ital., 'large ball', fr. *palla*, 'ball'. An Italian game played between two sides of three players each, in a large court, with an inflated leather ball which is struck backwards and forwards over a white line, the player's arm being protected by a wooden guard over hand and wrist.

pallor, n. [1. pálor; 2. pǽlə]. Lat. *pallor*, 'paleness'; cp. Lat. *pallēre*, 'to be pale'; *pullus*, 'greyish'; *palumbes*, 'wood-pigeon'; cogn. w. Gk. *peliós*, 'livid'; *pellós*, 'blackish'; *poliós*, 'grey'; *peleiás*, 'wood-pigeon'; Scrt. *palitáś*, 'grey'; O. Slav. *pelesŭ*, 'grey'; Lith. *pelē*, 'mouse'; O.E. *fealo*, 'yellowish'. See **fallow** (IV.). State of being pale; extreme paleness, esp. of complexion.

palm (I.), n. [1. pahm; 2. pām]. M.E. *palme*, fr. O. Fr. *palme, paume*; fr. Lat. *palma*, 'palm of the hand, blade of an oar'; also 'palm branch, palm tree'; cogn. w. Gk. *palámē*, 'open hand, palm'; O. Slav. *palisi*, 'thumb', & Russ. *palets*, 'finger'; cp. also

O.E. *folm*, 'hand'; O.H.G. *folma*; O.E. *fēlan*, 'feel', O.H.G. *fuolen* are prob. fr. same base, see **feel**; & cp. also Lat. *palpāre*, 'to stroke, touch softly', see **palpable**. According to this etymol. the palm, or hand, wd. orig. be 'the toucher, feeler'; others derive *palm* &c. fr. a base **pelā-*, 'flat, spread out' &c., & compare Lat. *planta*, 'sole of the foot', see **plantar**, & Gk. *platús*, 'flat, broad', &, w. different medial consonant, O.N. *flatr*, see under **flat (I.)**. **1.** The inner surface of the hand between the wrist and the bases of the fingers. Phrs. *to grease a person's palm*, bribe him; *to have an itching palm*, to be corruptly avaricious, be eager to be bribed. **2.** (rare or obs.) The breadth of the palm, about 4 inches, as measure.

palm (II.), n. O.E. *palm*. Orig. the same word as prec., q.v.; so called fr. shape & flatness of its leaves; perh. partly suggested by Semitic *padmar*. **1.** Any member of a large order, *Palmaceae*, of trees, tropical and subtropical, having many genera and species, with a branchless trunk and a spreading mass of large leaves at the summit: *date palm, coco-nut palm* &c. **2.** Branch of palm as symbol of triumph, victory, pre-eminence; hence, victory, success. Phrs. *to bear the palm*, be acknowledged victor; *to yield the palm to*, acknowledge oneself vanquished by another. **3.** Branch of other trees (esp. willows) used as palm in colder countries in celebrating Palm Sunday.

palm (III.), vb. trans., fr. **palm (I.)**. **1.** To touch, stroke, with the palm. **2.** To conceal in the hand: *to palm a card* &c. **3.** *Palm off*, to impose by fraud, pass off, foist upon: *to palm something off upon a person.*

palmaceous, adj. [1. palmáshus; 2. pælméiʃəs]. **palm (II.)** & **-aceous**. Of, belonging to, the Palmaceae, or natural order of palms; of the nature of a palm.

Palma Christi, n. [1. pálma krísti; 2. pǽlmə krísti]. Lat., 'palm of Christ', fr. hand-like shape of leaf. Castor-oil plant.

palmar, adj. [1. pálmar; 2. pǽlmə]. **palm (I.)** & **-ar**. Relating to, in, the palm of the hand.

palmary, adj. [1. pálmari; 2. pǽlməri]. **palm (II.)** & **-ary**. Worthy of bearing the palm; triumphant, pre-eminent.

palmate, adj. [1. pálmāt; 2. pǽlmeit]. **palm (I. & II.)** & **-ate**. **1.** Shaped like the palm of the hand. **2.** (bot., of leaves) Having sections radiating from a common centre.

palmated, adj. [1. pálmāted; 2. pǽlmeitid]. Prec. & **-ed**. Palmate.

palm-civet, n. A civet-like arboreal animal of Asia and Malaysia, with dark striped or spotted fur and long tail; the paradoxure.

palmed, adj. [1. pahmd; 2. pāmd]. **palm (I.)** & **-ed**. Chiefly in compounds: *soft-palmed* &c.

palmer, n. [1. páhmer; 2. pāmə]. **palm (II.)** & **-er**. **1.** Pilgrim who had journeyed to the Holy Land and carried a palm-branch in commemoration of this. **2. a** Palmer-worm; **b** kind of artificial fly.

palmer-worm, n. Destructive, hairy caterpillar of various kinds: '*your fig trees and your olive trees . . . the palmer-worm devoured them*' (Amos iv. 9).

palmetto, n. [1. palmétō; 2. pælmétou]. Formed on anal. w. Ital. dimin. suff. *-etto*, fr. Span. *palmito*, dimin. of *palma*, fr. Lat. *palma*, 'palm'. See **palm (II.)**. Name of several varieties of small palm, esp. of the southern states of N. America.

palmiped, palmipede, adj. & n. [1. pálmiped, -pēd; 2. pǽlmipɛd, -pīd]. Lat. *palmipēs*, fr. **palm (I.)** & *-ped*, stem of Lat. *pēs*, 'foot'; see **pedal**. **1.** adj. Web-footed. **2.** n. Web-footed bird.

palmist, n. [1. páhmist; 2. pāmist]. **palm (I.)** & **-ist**. One who practises palmistry.

palmistry, n. [1. páhmistri; 2. pāmistri]. Prec. & **-ry**. Alleged delineation of a person's character and foretelling of his future from the lines on the palm of the hand.

palmitic, adj. [1. palmítik; 2. pælmítik], fr. Fr. *palmitique*. See **palm (II.)** & **-ite** & **-ic**. (chem.) Pertaining to an organic acid, *palmitic acid*, found uncombined in palm-oil and present in most animal and vegetable fats and oils.

palm-oil, n. **a** Oil obtained from various palms; **b** (fig. and facet.) a bribe.

Palm Sunday, n. The Sunday before Easter, commemorating Christ's entry into Jerusalem before His Passion, when palm branches were strewn in His path by the crowd.

palmy, adj. [1. páhmi; 2. pāmi]. **palm (II.)** & **-y**. **1.** Connected with, abounding in, palms. **2.** (fig.) Flourishing, successful, triumphant, esp. in Phr. (*one's*) *palmy days*, period of success and affluence; period of greatest beauty, vigour, perfection &c.

palmyra, n. [1. palmíra; 2. pælmáiərə], fr. Port. *palmeira*. Kind of palm of India, Ceylon &c. from which palm-wine is obtained, and which has broad leaves used for matting.

palp, palpus, n. [1. pálp(us); 2. pǽlp(əs)]. L. Lat. *palpus*, 'feeler', fr. Lat. *palpāre*, 'to stroke, touch gently'. See **palpable**. Jointed organ of sense in insects.

palpability, n. [1. pàlpabíliti; 2. pælpəbíliti], fr. L. Lat. *palpābil-(is)*, 'palpable', see next word, & **-ity**. Quality of being palpable.

palpable, adj. [1. pálpabl; 2. pǽlpəbl], fr. L. Lat. *palpābilis*, 'that may be touched', fr. *palp-(āre)*, 'to touch, stroke'. See **palm (I.)** & **feel**. **1.** Capable of being felt and perceived by sense of touch: *vapour is not palpable*. **2.** Easily perceived by the mind; obvious, evident, manifest: *a palpable absurdity*; '*the venison was palpable mutton*' (Pepys's Diary).

palpably, adv. Prec. & **-ly**. In a palpable manner.

palpal, adj. [1. pálpal; 2. pǽlpəl]. **palp** & **-al**. Of, relating to, the palp.

palpate, vb. trans. [1. pálpāt; 2. pǽlpeit], fr. Lat. *palpāt-(um)*, P.P. type of *palpāre*, 'to touch, stroke'. See **palpable**. To examine by touch, esp. of medical examination.

palpation, n. [1. palpáshun; 2. pælpéiʃən]. Prec. & **-ion**. Act of palpating; state of being palpated.

palpebral, adj. [1. pálpibral; 2. pǽlpibrəl], fr. Lat. *palpebra*, Mod. Fr. *paupière*, 'eyelid', i.e. 'that which moves quickly', cp. Lat. *palpitāre*, 'to tremble, vibrate, palpitate', see **palpitate**; *palpāre*, 'to touch', see **palpable**. Relating to the eyelids.

palpitate, vb. intrans. [1. pálpitāt; 2. pǽlpiteit], fr. Lat. *palpitāt-(um)*, P.P. type of *palpitāre*, 'to throb, tremble'; see **palpable**. To pulsate, throb; specif. (of the heart) **a** To beat irregularly, and too fast; to flutter; **b** (poet.) to beat, throb: *my heart palpitates for you alone*. Phr. *of palpitating interest*, intense, vibrant, thrilling.

palpitation, n. [1. pàlpitáshun; 2. pælpitéiʃən]. Prec. & **-ion**. Irregular, quickened action of the heart, due to functional derangement, or powerful emotion &c.

palsgrave, n. [1. páwlzgrāv; 2. pɔ́lzgreiv], fr. Du. *paltsgrave*; Germ. *pfalzgraf*. See **palatinate** & **reeve (II.)**. Count Palatine, esp. of the Rhine.

palstave, n. [1. páwlstāv; 2. pɔ́lsteiv], fr. Du. *paalstav*, fr. O.N. *pālstafr*, fr. *pāll*, 'hoe', & *stafr*, 'staff'. Prehistoric stone or bronze celt used as a tool or weapon.

palsy (I.), n. [1. páwlzi; 2. pɔ́lzi]. M.E. *palesie, parlesi*, fr. O. Fr. *paralisie*, fr. Lat. *paralysis*. See **paralysis**. Paralysis; a shivering, trembling, of the limbs.

palsy (II.), vb. trans., fr. prec. (lit. and fig.) To affect with palsy, paralyse.

palter, vb. intrans. [1. páwlter; 2. pɔ́ltə]. Origin obscure; apparently Scand., cp. Swed. dial. *pallta*, 'to hobble about'; prob. formed, as Skeat suggests, on anal. of *falter*. The base is prob. imitative in origin & seems to mean both 'irregular, fitful movement', & 'meaningless sound'; Kluge connects Germ. *poltern*, 'to bluster, make a noise', & Du. *bulderen*, in same sense, w. Russ. *boltati*, 'to shake', & Lith. *bildati*, 'to make a noise'. **1.** To trifle, shuffle, equivocate, refuse to face: *to palter with facts*. **2.** To bargain, chaffer.

paltriness, n. [1. páwltrines; 2. pɔ́ltrinis]. See next word & **-ness**. Quality of being paltry.

paltry, adj. [1. páwltri; 2. pɔ́ltri]. See **palter** & **-y**. Insignificant, trifling; petty, base.

paludal, adj. [1. palúdl; 2. pæljúdl], fr. Lat. *palūd-*, stem of *palūs*, 'marsh', & **-al**. Cp. Scrt. *palvalá-m*, 'pond'; *palvalyaš*, 'marshy'; O.H.G. *felawa*, 'willow'. **a** Of, pertaining to, a marsh; marshy; **b** (of fever) arising from marshes, malarial.

paly (I.), adj. [1. páli; 2. péili]. **pale (I.)** & **-y**. (her., of shield) Divided by pales.

paly (II.), adj. **pale (II.)** & **-y**. (poet.) Palish, wanting in colour.

pam, n. [1. pam; 2. pæm]. Said to be fr. Fr. *Pamphile*. (obs. or rare, cards) Knave of clubs at five-card loo.

pampas, n. [1. pámpas; 2. pǽmpəs]. Really pl. fr. Span., fr. Peruv. *pampa*, 'field, plain'. Large, treeless, grassy plains of S. America, south of the Amazon.

pampas-grass, n. Large ornamental grass with long, sharp-edged blades and thick, silvery-white plume-like flower.

pamper, vb. trans. [1. pámper; 2. pǽmpə]. Origin doubtful; perh. fr. Fr. *pampre*, 'young shoot or tendril of a vine', fr. Lat. *pampinus*, 'vine shoot' &c.; cp. Milton's '*pampered boughs*' (of fruit trees); this word is cogn. w. Lat. *papilla*, 'nipple', & *papula*, 'pustule'; the root idea is 'something swelling'; cp. the cogn. Lith. *pupûle*, 'a thick, fat bud', & see **papula**. To feed to excess, over-indulge; to cosset, coddle.

pampero, n. [1. pampárō; 2. pæmpéərou]. Span., fr. *pampa*, 'plain'. See **pampas**. Cold wind blowing from the Andes across the pampas.

pamphlet, n. [1. pámflet; 2. pǽmflit]. M.E., fr. O. Fr. *pamflet*; fr. a Med. Lat. dimin., fr. *Pamphilus*, a popular Lat. poem of 12th cent. Short, unbound treatise, usually controversial, on political or other subject of current interest.

pamphleteer, n. & vb. intrans. [1. pàmfletḗr; 2. pæmflitíə]. Prec. & **-eer**. **1.** n. Writer of pamphlets. **2.** vb. intrans. To write pamphlets.

pan (I.), n. [1. pan; 2. pæn]. O.E., M.E. *panne*, 'pan'; cp. O. Fris. *panne*; O.N. *panna*; Mod. Germ. *pfanne*; prob. fr. Low Lat. *panna*, fr. Lat. *patina*, 'dish'. See **patina**. **1. a** Broad, shallow vessel of metal or earthenware, for domestic use: *frying-pan, milk-pan*; **b** metal or earthenware vessel, usually deep and covered, for domestic use: *stew-pan, warming-pan* &c. **2.** Anything resembling a pan in shape; specif. **a** upper part of skull: *brain-pan*; **b** depression in ground, e.g. *salt-pan*; **c** a small floe of ice; **d** piece of hard subsoil impervious to water. **3.** Part of a firelock holding the priming. Phr. *a flash in the pan*, see **flash (II.)**.

pan (II.), vb. trans. & intrans., fr. prec. **1.** trans. *Pan off, out*, to wash (auriferous earth) in a pan to extract the gold. Phr. (colloq.) *to pan out*, produce money. **2.** intrans. *Pan out*, **a** to yield gold; **b** (fig.) to result, succeed, turn out: *to pan out well.*

Pan (III.), n. Gk. *Pán*; prob. the orig. meaning was 'feeder, pasturer', fr. root **pa-*, 'to feed'; see **panification, pastor**, & words there referred to; in later Gk. the name & word were associated w. pantheistic ideas & connected w. *pâs, pân*, 'all'. See **pan-**. The old Arcadian Greek god of the woods and fields, depicted usually with horns and legs of a goat.

pan-, pref. representing Gk. *pân*, neut. form of Gk. *pâs*, 'all'; cogn. w. Lat. *quantus*, 'how great', Umbr. *pant-*; Lat. *quantum*, 'so much as'; see **quantum**. All, universal;

e.g. *pan-African*, of, for, including, all Africans; *pan-American*, of, for, representing, all parts of America; *pan-Anglican*, pertaining to, including, all branches of the Anglican Church; *pan-cosmism*, theory that the material universe is all that exists; *pan-Hellenism*, union of all the Greeks in one political body; *pan-Islam*, union of all Mohammedan races.

panacea, n. [1. panaséa; 2. pænəsíə]. Lat. *panacēa*, fr. Gk. *panákeia*, 'plant healing all diseases', fr. **pan-** & *ák-(os)*, 'remedy'; cogn. w. Scrt. *yáčaš*, 'health, glory'; O. Ir. *icc*, 'healing'; W. *iach*, 'healthy'. Universal remedy; cure for all bodily, mental, and social ills.

panache, n. [1. panásh; 2. pænǽʃ]. Fr., fr. Ital. *pennacchio*, fr. *penna*, 'feather', fr. Lat. *penna*, 'feather'. See **pen (III.)**. **1.** Plume of feathers, as head-dress; military plume. **2.** (fig.) Display, pretension.

panada, n. [1. panáhda; 2. pænáda]. Span., fr. *pan*, 'bread', fr. Lat. *pānis*, 'bread'. See **panification & -ade.** Dish made of bread boiled and beaten to a pulp and flavoured.

Panama, n. [1. pànamáh; 2. pænəmá]. State of Central America. Also *Panama hat*, hat of fine, tough, flexible fibre, originally made in Panama, or elsewhere in Central and South America &c., from the leaves of the screw-pine.

pancake, n. [1. pánkāk; 2. pǽnkeik]. **1.** Thin, soft cake of batter fried in a pan. Phr. *flat as a pancake*, quite flat; *Pancake Day*, Shrove Tuesday, when, according to old custom, pancakes are eaten. **2.** A flattened-out, abrupt landing of an aeroplane; also as verb, *to pancake*, make such a landing. **3.** Thin flat piece of floating ice in Polar seas.

panchayat, n. [1. puncháhyat; 2. pantʃáʤət]. Tamil *panchāyattu*, fr. Scrt. *páñča*, 'five', see **penta-**. (India) Native village council of five or more members.

pancratiast, n. [1. pankráshiast; 2. pænkréiʃiæst], fr. Gk. *pagkratiastḗs*. Competitor in the pancratium, q.v.

pancratic, adj. [1. pankrátik; 2. pænkrǽtik]. See **pancratium & -ic.** Of, pertaining to, the pancratium.

pancratist, n. [1. pánkratist; 2. pǽnkrətist]. See prec. & **-ist.** Pancratiast.

pancratium, n. [1. pankráshium; 2. pænkréiʃiəm], fr. Lat., fr. Gk. *pagkrátion*, 'pancratium', fr. **pan-** & *krát-(os)*, 'strength', q.v. under **-cracy.** (anct. Greece) Athletic contest which combined boxing and wrestling.

pancreas, n. [1. pán-, pángkreas; 2. pǽn-, pǽŋkriæs], fr. Gk. *págkreas*, fr. **pan-** & *kréas*, 'flesh'. See **creatin(e) & crude.** Gland lying behind the stomach which discharges into the duodenum a juice possessing important digestive properties; the pancreas of the sheep is known as the sweetbread.

pancreatic, adj. [1. pàn-, pàngkreátik; 2. pæn-, pæŋkriǽtik], fr. Gk. *pagkréat-(os)*, genit. of *págkreas*. See prec. & **-ic.** Of, pertaining to, the pancreas: *pancreatic juice.*

pancreatin, n. [1. pán-, pángkreatin; 2. pǽn-, pǽŋkriətin]. See prec. & **-in.** The active principle of pancreatic juice.

panda, n. [1. pánda; 2. pǽndə]. Native. Small, carnivorous, bear- or cat-like mammal, *Aelurus fulgens*, of the Himalayas and Tibet, also called cat-bear, with reddish-brown stiff hair and ringed tail.

Pandean, Pandaean, adj. [1. pandéan; 2. pændíən]. Irregularly formed fr. Gk. *Pán*, Arcadian god of woods, pastures &c. See **Pan (III.) & -ean.** Of Pan; *Pandean pipe*, pan-pipe.

pandect, n. [1. pándekt; 2. pǽndekt], fr. Fr. *pandecte*, fr. Lat., fr. Gk. *pandéktēs*, 'receiver of all', fr. **pan-** & *déktēs*, 'receiver', fr. *dékhomai*, 'I receive'; cp. O. Slav. *desiti*, 'to find, obtain'; O.E. *tigðian*, 'to grant'. See **decent** & words there referred to. **1.** Chiefly *pandects*, digest of Roman civil law made by order of Justinian in 6th cent. **2.** Code of laws

pandemic, adj. & n. [1. pandémik; 2. pændémik], fr. Gk. *pándēm-(os)*, 'of the whole people', fr. **pan-** & **demos & -ic.** **1.** adj. (of disease) **a** Prevalent among a whole nation or over a whole country; **b** prevalent all over the world, contrasted with *endemic* and *epidemic*. **2.** n. Pandemic disease.

pandemonium, n. [1. pàndemónium; 2. pændimóuniəm]. Mod. Lat. See **pan- & demon.** **1. a** Abode or assembly of demons; **b** place or scene of wild disorder and uproar. **2.** Complete confusion.

pander (I.), n. [1. pánder; 2. pǽndə], fr. *Pandare*, character in Chaucer's 'Troilus and Cressida' & in Boccaccio, fr. Lat. *Pandarus*, fr. Gk. *Pándaros*. **1.** One who obtains for another the means of gratifying his sexual passions; a procurer, pimp. **2.** Tool, assistant, in evil designs.

pander (II.), vb. intrans., fr. prec. *Pander to*, to act as pander; to encourage, minister to: *to pander to a person's passions, folly, ambition* &c.

pandit, n. See **pundit.**

pandora, pandore, n. [1. pàndóra, pandór; 2. pændɔ́rə, pændɔ́]. Ital., fr. Lat. *pandūra*, 'three-stringed musical instrument', fr. Gk. *pandoûra*; etymol. unknown; cp. **mandola & mandoline.** Stringed instrument resembling a lute.

pandour, pandoor, n. [1. pándoor; 2. pǽnduə], fr. Fr., fr. Germ., fr. Croatian *pandur*; prob. fr. Med. Lat. *banderius*, 'follower of a banner'. See **banner.** One of a force of Croatian infantry soldiers raised by Austria against the Turks in 18th cent., celebrated for their brutality and want of discipline.

pane, n. [1. pān; 2. pein]. M.E. *pan(n)e*, 'pane of glass; patch, piece', fr. O. Fr. *pan(n)e*, fr. Lat. *pannus*, 'piece of cloth'; cogn. w. Goth. *fana*, 'piece of cloth'; O.E. *fana*, O.H.G. *fano*, 'cloth; banner'; O. Slav. *ponjava*, 'garment'. **1.** Single sheet of glass in division of window. **2.** Rectangular division in a design.

paned, adj., fr. prec. & **-ed.** Composed of strips of different materials.

panegyric, n. & adj. [1. pànejírik; 2. pænidžírik], fr. Fr. *panégyrique*, fr. Lat., fr. Gk. *panēgurik-(ós)*, adj., 'for a public festival', n. 'panegyric', fr. *panḗgur-(is)*, 'general assembly, national festival', fr. **pan-** & *agorá*, 'assembly; public place'; cp. *ageirein*, 'to assemble'; *gárgara*, 'swarm'; cogn. w. Lat. *grex*, 'flock', see under **gregarious.** Formal oration in praise of person or event; eulogy, laudation.

panegyrical, adj. [1. pànejírikl; 2. pænidžírikl]. Prec. & **-al.** Of, pertaining to, of the nature of, a panegyric.

panegyrist, n. [1. pànejírist; 2. pænidžírist]. See next word & **-ist.** Speaker, writer, of a panegyric.

panegyrize, vb. trans. & intrans. [1. pánejiriz; 2. pǽnidžiraiz]. See **panegyric & -ize.** **a** trans. To pronounce, write, a panegyric upon; to eulogize; **b** intrans., to make a panegyric.

panel (I.), n. [1. pánl; 2. pǽnl]. M.E. & O.Fr. *panel*, fr. Med. Lat. *pannellus*, dimin. of Lat. *pannus*, 'piece of cloth'. See **pane (I.).** **1.** Rectangular piece or slab of wood &c., forming part of surface of wall, door &c., but distinguished from rest of surface by being raised above or sunk below general level, by being surrounded by frame, moulding &c., or by being of different material. **2.** Sheet or strip of parchment; hence, a register, a list; specif. **a** list of persons summoned to serve on a jury; a jury; **b** (Scots law) person indicted for an offence; the accused in a criminal trial; **c** register of doctors in a district attending insured persons under Health Insurance Act, also attrib. *panel doctor* &c. **3.** Picture or photograph of a long, narrow shape. **4.** Strip of material, usually of different colour or fabric, inserted in woman's dress.

panel (II.), vb. trans., fr. prec. **1.** To fit, provide with, divide into, panel(s): *to panel a room* &c. **2.** To furnish, ornament, with panel(s): *to panel a dress* &c.

paneless, adj. [1. pánles; 2. péinlis]. **pane (I.) & -less.** Without panes.

panelling, n. [1. páneling; 2. pǽnəliŋ]. **panel (II.) & -ing.** Series of panels, in a wall &c.

panel-saw, n. A thin hand-saw with fine teeth, used to cut thin boards &c.

panful, n. [1. pánfool; 2. pǽnful]. **pan (I.) & -ful.** Amount contained in a pan.

pang, n. [1. pang; 2. pæŋ]. Etymol. uncertain. Sudden, sharp, mental or physical pain; twinge, spasm of anguish in body or mind.

pangolin, n. [1. panggólin; 2. pæŋgóulin], fr. Malay. *peng-gūling*, 'the roller', fr. *gūling*, 'to roll'. A scaly toothless mammal of S. Asia and Africa, resembling a lizard in shape, and having a long tongue like an ant-eater; it rolls itself into a ball when attacked or frightened.

panhandle, n. [1. pánhandl; 2. pǽnhændl], fr. **pan (I.) & handle.** A narrow, projecting tongue of land.

panic (I.), n. [1. pánik; 2. pǽnik], fr. Lat. *pānic-(um)*, 'Italian millet', fr. *pān-(us)*, 'a swelling; an ear of millet'; etymol. doubtful. Genus of grasses, including millet.

panic (II.), n. & adj., fr. Fr. *panique*, fr. Gk. *pānik-(ós)*, 'of Pan; (of fear) wild, unreasoning, believed to be due to the influence of Pan', fr. *Pan*, Greek god of woods and fields, see **Pan (III.), & -ic.** **1.** n. Sudden, excessive, unreasoning, uncontrollable and infectious terror: *a panic in a large crowd may lead to terrible disaster*; specif., a sudden, general alarm in commercial or financial circles caused by collapse of credit &c. **2.** adj. (much rarer than n.) Inspired by panic; sudden, wild, uncontrollable, unreasoning: *panic fear, haste.*

panicky, adj. [1. pániki; 2. pǽniki]. Prec. & **-y.** (colloq.) In a state of, liable to, affected by, panic.

panicle, n. [1. pánikl; 2. pǽnikl], fr. Lat. *pānicula*, 'tuft, panicle', fr. *pānic-(us)*, 'swelling, ear of millet'. See **panic (I.) & -ule.** (bot.) Irregularly branched flower-cluster.

panic-monger, n. **panic (II.) & monger.** One who creates, fosters, a panic.

panification, n. [1. pànifikáshun; 2. pænifikéiʃən], fr. Fr., fr. Lat. *pāni-(s)*, 'bread', fr. stem **pā-*, 'to feed', seen in Lat. *pāsci*, 'to graze', see **pastor**; *pābulum*, 'food', see **pabulum**; cogn. w. Gk. *patéomai*, 'to eat'; O.E. *fōda*, 'food', see **food.** Conversion into bread; the making of bread.

panjandrum, n. [1. pànjándrum; 2. pændžǽndrəm]. Invented word. Name, *the Great Panjandrum himself*, invented by Samuel Foote in piece of nonsense prose; used facetiously to designate a pompous, self-important, highly-placed official personage.

panmixia, n. [1. panmíksia; 2. pænmíksiə]. Neo-Lat., fr. **pan-** & Gk. *mixis*, 'a mingling', see **mix.** (biol.) Promiscuous interbreeding of animals or plants, without selection, resulting in degeneracy.

pannage, n. [1. pánij; 2. pǽnidž], fr. O. Fr. *pasnage*, fr. Med. Lat. *pāstiōnāticum*, fr. Lat. *pāstiōn-(em)*, 'pasture', fr. *pāst-(um)*, P.P. type of *pāsci*, 'to graze', see **pasture & -age.** **1. a** Pasturage of swine in woods &c.; **b** food picked up by swine in woods &c.; esp. fruit of forest trees, as beech-mast, acorns &c. **2. a** Right of pasturing swine in woods &c.; **b** payment for this.

panne, n. [1. pan; 2. pæn]. Fr., etymol. doubtful. A soft cloth dress material with long nap.

pannier (I.), n. [1. pánier; 2. pǽniə], fr. Fr. *panier*, fr. Lat. *pānārium*, 'bread-basket', fr. *pān-(is)*, 'bread', see **panification & -ary.** **1.** Basket, esp. **a** wicker basket for carrying loads on the back; **b** one of a pair of baskets carried by beast of burden. **2.** Covered basket for drugs and surgical instruments carried by an ambulance.

3. **a** Framework of whalebone &c., for extending a woman's dress at the hips; **b** drapery designed to produce the same effect.

pannier (II.), n. Lat. *pānārius*, see prec. (colloq.) Waiter in dining-hall of Inner Temple.

pannikin, n. [1. pánikin; 2. pǽnikin]. **pan** (I.) & **-kin**. **a** Small metal cup; **b** amount of liquid contained in such a vessel.

panoplied, adj. [1. pánoplid; 2. pǽnəplid]. See next word & **-ed**. Completely armed.

panoply, n. [1. pánopli; 2. pǽnəpli], fr. Gk. *panoplía*, 'full armour of a hoplite', fr. **pan-** & *hópla*, 'arms', q.v. under **hoplite**. (lit. and fig.) Complete equipment of armour.

panopticon, n. [1. panóptikon; 2. pænɔ́ptikən], fr. **pan-** & Gk. *optikón*, neut. form of *optikós*, 'of sight', see **optic**. Circular prison, as proposed by Jeremy Bentham, constructed so as to allow all the prisoners to be watched from a central point.

panorama, n. [1. panoráhma; 2. pænərámə], fr. **pan-** & Gk. *hórāma*, 'sight, spectacle', fr. *horáō*, 'I see', fr. **worā-*, 'attention'; cp. O.E. *waru*; O.H.G. *wara*, 'attention, care, precaution'; O.N. *varr*; O.E. *wær*, 'watchful, cautious', see **ware (II.)**; cp. further Lat. *verērī*, 'to observe anxiously; to revere', see **revere**. **1.** Continuous series of pictures representing a landscape, or an historical action or episode in its natural surroundings, painted on inside of cylindrical or other unbroken surface, or unrolled before spectator, so designed and arranged as to convey the impression of reality. **2.** Constantly changing scene. **3.** Wide, unbroken view (also fig.).

panoramic, adj. [1. panorámik; 2. pænərǽmik]. Prec. & **-ic**. Of, of the nature of, a panorama.

panoramically, adv. [1. panorámikali; 2. pænərǽmikəli]. Prec. & **-al** & **-ly**. As a panorama.

pan-pipe, n., fr. **Pan (III.)**, Gk. god of woods and fields. Wind-instrument consisting of a series of graduated reeds, bound together in a single row; a mouth-organ, also styled *Pandean pipe*.

pansy, n. [1. pánzi; 2. pǽnzi], fr. Fr. *pensée*, 'thought, pansy', fr. P.P. of *penser*, 'to think', fr. Lat. *pensāre*, 'to weigh carefully; to ponder, consider', see **pensive**. European wild and garden plant, *Viola tricolor*, of the violet family, having broad, flattish, variegated flowers, usually blue, purple, or yellow; heartsease.

pant (I.), vb. intrans. & trans. [1. pant; 2. pænt]. O. Fr. *panteisier*, 'to be breathless', through Low Lat. **phantasiāre*, 'to have nightmare', fr. *phantasia*, fr. Gk. *phantasía*, 'a making visible, display, parade'; see **fantasy**. **A.** intrans. **1.** To breathe quickly and convulsively, to labour in breathing as though out of breath, to gasp for breath. **2.** To speak in gasps, with short, laboured breaths. **3.** (fig.) To yearn, long intensely: *to pant for, after, something*. **B.** trans. To utter in a series of gasps; also *pant out*.

pant (II.), n., fr. prec. Short, laboured breath; gasp.

pant-, pref. representing **panto-** before vowels.

Pantagruelian, adj. [1. pàntagrooélian; 2. pæntəgruélian], fr. *Pantagruel*, character in Rabelais, & **-ian**. Of the nature of Pantagruelism.

Pantagruelism, n. [1. pàntagróoelizm; 2. pæntəgrúːilizəm]. See prec. & **-ism**. Rough, coarse satiric humour and buffoonery, resembling that of Pantagruel.

Pantagruelist, n. [1. pàntagróoelist; 2. pæntəgrúilist]. See **Pantagruelian** & **-ist**. Writer making use of Pantagruelism.

pantalet(te)s, n. [1. pantaléts; 2. pæntəléts]. See next word & **-ette**. Woman's drawers, esp. Early Victorian drawers reaching to the ankle, worn by women and children.

pantaloon, n. [1. pantalóon; 2. pæntəlúːn], fr. Fr. *pantalon*, fr. Ital. *pantalone*, Venetian character in Italian comedy, prob. fr. the Venetian saint, *St. Pantaleone*. **1.** (cap.) a Character in Italian comedy; now esp. **b** an elderly buffoon in pantomime, on whom the clown plays tricks. **2.** pl. (obsolesc. or facet.) Trousers.

pantechnicon, n. [1. pantéknikon; 2. pæntékniken]. Invented word, fr. **pan-**, 'all', & Gk. *tekhnikón*, neut. adj., 'pertaining to art', fr. *tékhnē*, 'art', see **technic**. **1.** Originally, a bazaar in London where specimens of every kind of art were sold. **2.** Warehouse where furniture is stored. **3.** Van for removing furniture; also *pantechnicon van*.

pantheism, n. [1. pánthēizm; 2. pǽnþiizəm]. **pan-**, 'all', & *theós*, 'God', & **-ism**, see **theism** (II.). **1.** Doctrine that the whole universe is God, or that every part of the universe is a manifestation of God. **2.** **a** Worship of all the pagan gods of whatever cult or race, as under the Roman Empire; **b** nature worship, animism.

pantheist, n. [1. pánthēist; 2. pǽnþiist]. See **prec.** & **-ist**. Believer in pantheism.

pantheistic(al), adj. [1. pànthēístik(l); 2. pænþiístik(l)]. Prec. & **-ic** & **-al**. Of, of the nature of, pantheism.

pantheon, n. [1. pánthion, panthéon; 2. pǽnþiən, pænþíən]. Lat. *Panthēon*, fr. Gk. *pánthe(i)on*, 'for all the gods', fr. **pan-** & *the-(ós)*, 'god', see **theo-** **1.** Temple for the worship of all the gods, esp. circular temple in Rome, built by Agrippa, now the church of Santa Maria Rotunda. **2.** Deities of a nation or country considered collectively: *the Egyptian, Scandinavian, pantheon*. **3.** Building, mausoleum, for commemorating the illustrious dead: *the Pantheon* (Church of Ste. Geneviève), Paris; *Westminster Abbey is the British Pantheon*. **4.** Building in London erected originally as a place of public amusement.

panther, n. [1. pánther; 2. pǽnþə], fr. O. Fr. *pantere*, fr. Lat. *panthēra*, fr. Gk. *pánthēr*, 'panther; leopard', possibly of Indian origin. **a** Carnivorous, spotted quadruped of cat tribe, found in Asia and Africa; leopard, esp. one of dark colour; **b** *American panther*, puma.

pantheress, n. [1. pántheres; 2. pǽnþəris]. Prec. & **-ess**. Female panther.

pantile, n. [1. pántīl; 2. pǽntail]. **pan** (I.) & **tile**. Roofing-tile showing a cross-section with one deep and one shallow curve.

pantisocracy, n. [1. pàntisókrasi; 2. pæntisɔ́krəsi]. **pant-** & **iso-** & **-cracy**. Ideal community or Utopia, planned by S. T. Coleridge, in which all were to have an equal voice in the government and equal rights.

panto-, pref. representing Gk. *pantó-(s)*, genit. of *pâs*, 'all', see **pan-**. All, universal; e.g. *pantology*, universal knowledge; book giving information on all subjects; *pantomorphic*, assuming any shape; *panto-pragmatic*, interfering with everything; *pantoscopic*, giving a wide field of vision.

pantograph, n. [1. pántograhf; 2. pǽntəgrāf]. **panto-** & **graph**. Instrument for reproducing a drawing, plan &c. on a larger or smaller scale.

pantographic, adj. [1. pantográfik; 2. pæntəgrǽfik]. Prec. & **-ic**. Of, produced by, a pantograph.

pantomime (I.), n. [1. pántomīm; 2. pǽntəmaim], fr. Lat. *pantomīm-(us)*, fr. Gk. *pantómīmos*, 'pantomimic actor', fr. **panto-** & **mime**. **1.** (class. drama) Actor performing in dumb-show. **2.** English dramatic performance of a burlesque character, embodying some well-known legend or fairy tale, usually given at Christmas, often concluding with a transformation-scene and harlequinade. **3.** Dumb-show; language of gestures: *to express oneself, present a scene, in pantomime*.

pantomime (II.), vb. intrans. & trans., fr. prec. **1.** intrans. To act in dumb-show. **2.** trans. To express in pantomime.

pantomimic, adj. [1. pantomímik; 2. pæntəmímik]. Prec. & **-ic**. Of, like, pantomime; representing, expressing, in action and gesture.

pantomimist, n. [1. pántomīmist; 2. pǽntəmaimist]. **pantomime** & **-ist**. Actor in pantomime.

pantoum, n. [1. pantóom; 2. pæntúm]. Fr., fr. Malay. *pantun*. A Malayan verse form of four-lined rhyming stanzas; also adapted by French poets.

pantry, n. [1. pántri; 2. pǽntri], fr. O. Fr. *paneterie*, fr. Med. Lat. *pānetāria*, 'bread-shop', fr. *pān-(is)*, 'bread'. See **panification**. **1.** Formerly, a room in a house where bread and other provisions were kept. **2.** In present day, room in which glass, china, plate &c., are kept, cleaned &c.; also *butler's pantry*.

pantryman, n. [1. pántriman; 2. pǽntrimən]. Man in charge of, or working in, pantry; butler or assistant.

pants, n. [1. pants; 2. pænts]. Abbr. fr. **pantaloon(s)**. **a** (archaic, or obs. colloquialism) Trousers; **b** (shop-word) men's drawers.

pap (I.), n. [1. pap; 2. pæp]. Imitative of infant feeding. **1.** Nipple of breast. **2.** (pl.) Rounded conical hills side by side.

pap (II.), n. Imitative, as prec. **1.** Soft, sloppy food given to infants and invalids. **2.** Mash, pulpy substance.

papa, n. [1. papáh; 2. pəpā́], fr. Fr., fr. Lat. *pāpa*, 'father'; perh. orig. imitative of child's cry. See **pope** (I.). (obsolesc. or old-fashioned) Father; esp. as mode of address.

Papacy, n. [1. pā́pasi; 2. péipəsi], fr. Med. Lat. *pāpātia*, 'papacy', fr. *pāpa*, 'pope', fr. Lat. *pāpa*, 'father'. See prec., & **-acy**, & cp. **pope** (I.). **1.** **a** Office of Pope; **b** Pope's tenure of office. **2.** Papal system.

Papal, adj. [1. pā́pl; 2. péipl], fr. Fr., fr. Eccles. Lat. *pāpāl-(is)*, 'of the pope', fr. *pāpa*, 'pope'. See prec. & **-al**. Of, pertaining to, the Papacy, or to the Pope.

Papalism, n. [1. pā́palizm; 2. péipəlizəm]. Prec. & **-ism**. Belief in, adherence to, the Papal system.

Papalist, n. [1. pā́palist; 2. péipəlist]. **Papal** & **-ist**. Adherent of the Papacy.

papalize, vb. trans. & intrans. [1. pā́palīz; 2. péipəlaiz]. **Papal** & **-ize**. **1.** trans. To convert to Papalism. **2.** intrans. To adopt the principles of Papalism.

papally, adv. [1. pā́pali; 2. péipəli]. **Papal** & **-ly**. In a Papal manner; by the Pope.

papaveraceous, adj. [1. papāverā́shus; 2. pəpèivəréiʃəs], fr. Lat. *papāver*, 'poppy'. See next word & **-aceous**. Papaverous.

papaverous, adj. [1. papā́verus; 2. pəpéivərəs], fr. Lat. *papāver*, 'poppy', prob. fr. stem **pap-*, 'to puff out, swell out', seen in Lat. *pampinus*, 'vine-shoot', *papula*, 'small swelling, pimple', see **papula**, & **-ous**. Of, like, having the properties of, the poppy.

papaw, n. [1. páwpaw, papáw; 2. pɔ́pɔ, pəpɔ́], fr. Span. *papaya*, fr. a Carib. word. **1.** **a** A tree, *Carica papaya*, growing in S. America, and in Africa, with large, dingy orange-coloured fruit, which is boiled and eaten, greenish flowers, and seven-lobed leaves; **b** the fruit of this tree. **2.** North American tree, *Asimina triloba*, with oblong pulpy fruit and dull, purple leaves.

paper (I.), n. [1. pā́per; 2. péipə], fr. O. Fr. *papier*, fr. Lat. *papȳrus*, 'papyrus'. See **papyrus**. **1.** Substance composed of pulp obtained from vegetable fibre or linen rags formed into thin sheets, and used for writing, printing, drawing on &c., for wrapping, lining walls &c. Phrs. *to commit to paper*, write down; *to put pen to paper*, begin to write; *paper war(fare)*, controversy carried on in newspapers, pamphlets, books &c.; *paper profits*, hypothetical profits, depending on transactions not yet completed; *on paper*, judging by statistics, documents &c. **2.** Written or printed document, deed, formal statement &c.; (in pl.) a group or collection of documents: *state papers*. Phr. *paper blockade*, one declared formally against a state but not enforced. **3.** (pl.) Documents establishing person's identity, standing, authority &c.; credentials. Phr. *to send in one's papers*, resign. **4.** **a** Written or printed pledges of payment which are negotiable, bills of exchange &c.; **b** also *paper money*, specially printed pieces of paper used as currency as substitute for coins. **5.** Journal, newspaper: *one's favourite paper*; *what do the papers say?* **6.** Set of printed questions for examination: *a difficult paper for such young candidates.* **7.** Essay, excursus, monograph, dissertation; esp. one read to a learned society. **8.** (slang) Free passes of admission to theatre &c.; member(s) of audience with such: *the house was filled, but largely with paper.*

paper (II.), vb. trans., fr. prec. **1.** To line, cover, decorate, with paper: *to paper a wall, room* &c. **2.** To enclose, fold, wrap, in paper; also *paper up*, cover (window, door &c.) by pasting paper over. **3.** (slang) To fill (theatre &c.) with 'paper'.

paper-chase, n. Sport, resembling *hare and hounds*, in which the 'pack', or majority of runners, pursue two others, 'hares', who are given a start and scatter a trail of paper.

paper-hanger, n. One whose occupation it is to hang or cover walls &c. with paper.

paper-hangings, n. pl. Paper, usually ornamental, for covering interior walls of rooms &c.

paper-knife, n. Flat, blunt blade of ivory, bone, wood &c., used for cutting folded paper, leaves of book &c.

paper-mill, n. Factory in which paper is made.

paper-stainer, n. One who prepares, prints, paints, wall-paper.

paper-weight, n. Small, heavy object laid upon loose papers to keep them from being scattered.

papery, adj. [1. páperi; 2. péipəri]. **paper** (I.) & **-y.** Like paper; having the appearance or consistency of paper.

papier mâché, n. [1. pápiā màshā; 2. pǽpiei mæ̀ʃei]. Fr., lit. 'chewed paper'; fr. Lat. *masticāre*, 'to chew'. See **masticate.** Paper pulp, moulded while soft into various objects, such as trays, boxes &c., and coated with variously coloured lacquer.

papilionaceous, adj. [1. papìlionáshus; 2. pæpìliənéiʃəs], fr. Lat. *pāpiliōn-(em)*, 'butterfly'; cogn. w. O.E. *fifealde*; O.H.G. *fīfaltra*, 'butterfly'. The base is prob. a redupl. form of **pal-*, 'to move rapidly, throb, vibrate', as in *palpitāre*, 'to throb'. See **palpitate.** (bot.) Having the corolla shaped like a butterfly, as in the pea.

papilla, n., pl. **papillae** [1. papíla, -lē; 2. pəpílə, -lī]. Lat. *papilla*, 'nipple', dimin. of *pap-(ula)*, 'a swelling'. See **papula** & cp. **pamper. 1.** (anat.) Small rounded protuberance in any part of the body, e.g. those on the surface of the tongue, in which the nerves terminate. **2.** (bot.) Small, fleshy, nipple-like protuberance.

papillary, adj. [1. papílari; 2. pæpíləri]. Prec. & **-ary.** Of, pertaining to, like, papillae.

papillate, adj. [1. papílāt; 2. pæpíleit]. **papilla** & **-ate.** Resembling, covered with, furnished with, papillae.

papillose, adj. [1. papílōs; 2. pæpílous]. **papilla** & **-ose.** Abounding in, covered with, papillae.

papist, n. [1. pápist; 2. péipist], fr. 16th cent. Lat. *pāpista*, fr. Lat. *pāp-(a)*, 'Pope', see **Papal** & **pope** (I.), & **-ist. 1.** Adherent of the Papacy, supporter of Papal supremacy. **2.** Roman Catholic; sometimes used, ignorantly, as term of disparagement.

papistic(al), adj. [1. papístik(l); 2. pəpístik(l)]. Prec. & **-ic** & **-al.** Pertaining to the Roman Catholic Church and its doctrines; usually in hostile, disparaging sense.

papistically, adv. Prec. & **-ly.** In a papistical manner.

papistry, n. [1. pápistri; 2. péipistri]. **papist** & **-ry.** (usually expressing hostility) The principles and practices of the Roman Catholic Church.

papoose, n. [1. papóōz; 2. pæpúz]. Native word. North-American Indian baby or young child.

papoosh, papouche, n. [1. papóōsh; 2. pæpúʃ], fr. Pers. *papósh*, 'shoe'. Babouche, q.v.

pappose, adj. [1. pápōs; 2. pǽpous]. See next word & **-ose.** Provided with, covered with, pappus.

pappus, n. [1. pápus; 2. pǽpəs]. Mod. Lat. fr. Gk. *páppos*, 'old man, grandfather'; childish formation; cp. Gk. *páppa*, 'father'; Lat. *pāpa*, 'father'. See **papa.** Downy tuft of hairs, supposed to resemble an old man's beard, forming an appendage to the seeds of some plants, such as thistle.

pappy, adj. [1. pápi; 2. pǽpi]. **pap** (II.) & **-y.** Like pap; soft, semi-liquid.

paprika, n. [1. papréka; 2. pæpríkə]. Hungarian. Red pepper, made from capsicum.

papula, papule, n. [1. pápūla, pápūl; 2. pǽpjulə, pǽpjūl], pl. *papulae, papules.* Lat. *papula*, 'a swelling; pimple'; cp., w. infixed nasal, Lat. *pampinus*, 'vine-shoot', cp. **pamper,** *papāver*, 'poppy', see **papaverous**; cogn. w. Scrt. *pippalaś*, 'berry'; Lett. *pampt*, 'to swell'; Lith. *pupùle*, 'bud'. A pimple.

papular, adj. [1. pápūlar; 2. pǽpjulə]. Prec. & **-ar.** Like, of the nature of, a papula.

papulose, adj. [1. pápūlōs; 2. pǽpjulous]. **papula** & **-ose.** Of, like, covered with, papulae.

papulous, adj. [1. pápūlus; 2. pǽpjuləs]. **papula** & **-ous.** Papulose.

papyraceous, adj. [1. pàpiráshus; 2. pæ̀piréiʃəs]. Next word & **-aceous.** Like paper in appearance, texture, consistency &c.

papyro-, pref. representing Gk. *pápūro-(s)*, 'papyrus', see **papyrus.**

papyrograph, n. [1. papírogràhf; 2. pæpáiərəgràf]. Instrument for multiplying copies of a document, esp. by the use of a paper stencil.

papyrologist, n. [1. pàpirólojist; 2. pæ̀pirɔ́lədžist]. **papyro-** & **-logy** & **-ist.** Student of papyrology.

papyrology, n. [1. pàpiróloji; 2. pæ̀pirɔ́lədži]. **papyro-** & **-logy.** Science, study, of papyri, i.e. of ancient MSS. written on papyrus.

papyrus, n. [1. papírus; 2. pəpáiərəs]. Lat. *papȳrus*, fr. Gk. *pápūros*, 'papyrus'. Etymol. unknown. See **paper. 1.** Sedge-like plant with smooth triangular stems, growing in marshy places, and formerly common in Egypt &c. **2.** Ancient writing material made by Egyptians, and later by Greeks and Romans, from strips of the pith of the papyrus. **3.** (pl. *papyri*) Manuscript written on papyrus.

par (I.), n. [1. par; 2. pā]. Lat. *pār*, 'equal; equality'; cp. Lat. *parāre*, 'to make, esteem, equal'; *comparāre*, 'to compare'; Avest. *pairyeinte*, 'they are compared'; perh. orig. w. reference to equal values in trade, & thus cogn. w. Lat. *pretium*, 'worth, price', see **price**; Gk. *pérnēmi*, 'sell'. **1.** Equality, equal value or footing, esp. in Phr. *on a par with.* **2.** (of stocks, shares &c.) *At par*, at face value; *above par*, at a premium, above face value; *below par*, at a discount. **3.** *Par of exchange*, recognized value of currency of one country, expressed in terms of that of another. **4.** Normal state, average condition of physical or mental health and vigour; *below par*, slightly out of health.

par (II.), n. Abbr. fr. **paragraph.** (colloq.) Paragraph.

para- (I.), pref. representing Gk. *pará*, 'from; beside; against, beyond; contrary to', cogn. w. Scrt. *pára*, 'beyond'; Goth. *faúr*, 'along'; O.E. *for-*, 'off, away', see **for-**; Lat. *prō-*, 'in front of', see **pro-**; see also **per-.** (in senses) **a** Beside, e.g. *parallel, paraphrase*; **b** beyond, e.g. *paralipsis*; **c** wrong, contrary to, e.g. *paralogism.*

para- (II.), pref. representing Ital. *para*, imperat. of *parare*, 'to ward off', fr. Lat. *parāre*, 'to prepare, furnish, get ready'. See **prepare.** Implying defence, shelter &c., e.g. *parasol, parapet.*

parabasis, n. [1. parábasis; 2. pərǽbəsis]. Gk. *parábasis*, 'a going aside; parabasis', fr. *parabainein*, 'to step aside', fr. **para-** (I.) & *bainein*, 'to step; to stand'. See **basis.** (in Gk. comedy) Principal choral part, addressed to the audience in the name of the poet.

parable, n. [1. párabl; 2. pǽrəbl], fr. Fr. *parabole*, fr. Lat. *parabola*, 'comparison; parable; speech'. See next word. **1.** Brief narrative or story, conveying a spiritual or moral lesson, or illustrating some spiritual condition or relation; an allegory. **2.** (archaic) Enigmatical speech, phrase with hidden meaning; proverb. **3.** (archaic) Speech, discourse; now chiefly in Phr. *to take up one's parable*, begin to speak.

parabola, n. [1. parábola; 2. pərǽbələ]. Lat. *parabola*, fr. Gk. *parabolḗ*, 'juxtaposition; comparison; illustration; parable', fr. *parabállein*, 'to throw or set beside', fr. **para-** (I.) & *bállein*, 'to throw', see **ballistics.** (math.) Plane curve such as is formed by the intersection of a cone by a plane parallel to its slope.

parabolic(al), adj. [1. pàrabólik(l); 2. pæ̀rəbɔ́lik(l)], fr. L. Lat. *parabolic-(us)*, 'parabolic', fr. *parabol-(a)*, 'comparison', see prec., & **-ic, -al. 1.** Of, of the nature of, under the form of, expressed by, a parable. **2.** Of, relating to, like, a parabola.

parabolically, adv. Prec. & **-ly.** In a parabolic manner; as a parable.

paraboloid, n. [1. paráboloid; 2. pərǽbələid]. **parabola** & **-oid.** (math.) Solid generated by rotation of a parabola about its axis.

parachronism, n. [1. parákronizm; 2. pərǽkrənizəm]. **para-** (I.) & Gk. *khrónos*, 'time', see **chronic,** & **-ism.** Chronological error in which a date is put too late.

parachute, n. [1. párashōōt; 2. pǽrəʃūt]. Fr., fr. **para-** (II.) & **chute,** 'fall'. **1.** Umbrella-like apparatus held by or fastened to one leaping from a height, which gradually opens as it passes through the air, and retards the speed of fall; used in case of accidents from balloons and aeroplanes. **2.** Natural provision or mechanical device enabling a body to float through the air, e.g. membrane of flying-fox, pappus of dandelion-seed &c.

parachutist, n. [1. párashōōtist; 2. pǽrəʃūtist]. Prec. & **-ist.** Person making a descent from a balloon &c. by means of a parachute.

Paraclete, n. [1. páraklēt; 2. pǽrəklīt], fr. Fr. *paraclet*, fr. Lat. *paraclētus*, fr. Gk. *paráklētos*, 'advocate, defender', fr. *parakaléō*, 'I call to aid', fr. **para-** (I.) & *kaléō*, 'I call'; cogn. w. Lat. *calāre*, 'to call', *clāmor*, 'cry'; see **clamour** & words there referred to. Advocate, intercessor, comforter; title given to the Holy Ghost (John xiv. 16; xvi. 7 &c.).

parade (I.), n. [1. parád; 2. pəréid], fr. Fr. *parade*, 'show, display', fr. Span. *parada*, fr. Lat. *parāta*, fem. P.P. of *parāre*, 'to prepare'. See **prepare** & **-ade. 1.** Ostentatious display, show: esp. *to make a parade* (*of one's knowledge, virtues, accomplishments* &c.). **2.** Muster and manœuvring of troops &c. for inspection; review. **3.** Ground on which military parade takes place. **4.** Public walk or street, promenade; specif., raised promenade and roadway skirting a sea coast.

parade (II.), vb. trans. & intrans., fr. prec. **A.** trans. **1.** To show off, display ostentatiously: *to parade one's wealth, knowledge* &c. **2.** To muster, assemble, marshal, for inspection: *to parade troops* &c. **3.** To march along, patrol, traverse ostentatiously, with display: *to parade the streets* &c. **B.** intrans. **1.** (of troops &c.) To assemble for inspection, review &c. **2.** To march in procession: *to parade before the General Officer commanding.*

parade-ground, n. Place in which parades are held.

paradigm, n. [1. páradīm; 2. pǽrədaim]. Fr. *paradigme*, fr. Lat., fr. Gk. *parádeigma*, 'pattern, model', fr. *paradeiknūmi*, 'I exhibit, represent', fr. **para-** (I.) & *deiknūmi*, 'I show'; cogn. w. Lat. *dīcere*, 'to say, tell'. See **diction** & words there referred to. Example, pattern, model, esp. (gram.) example serving as model for the inflexion of a group of words, declension of nouns, conjugation &c.

paradigmatic, adj. [1. pàradigmátik; 2. pæ̀rədigmǽtik], fr. *paradeigmat-(os)*, genit. of *parádeigma*, 'pattern', see prec., & **-ic.** Of the nature of, consisting of, a paradigm.

paradisaic(al), adj. [1. pàradisáik(l); 2. pæ̀rədiséiik(l)], fr. next word, on anal. of **Hebraic, Mosaic** &c. Paradisiac.

paradise, n. [1. páradīs; 2. pǽrədais], fr. Fr. *paradis*, fr. Lat. *paradīsus*, fr. Gk. *parádeisos*, 'a park; the Garden of Eden; paradise', a Persian loan-word; cp. Avest. *pairi-daēza*, 'enclose', cogn. w. Gk. *peri*, 'around', see **peri-**, & *toîkhos*, 'wall'; *teîkhos*, 'wall, fortification': Lat. *fingere*, 'to model', see **fiction**; O.E. *dāg*, 'paste, dough', see **dough. 1.** Garden of Eden, abode of Adam and Eve before the Fall. **2.** Abode of the blessed after death; heaven. **3.** Place of great beauty, state of bliss and perfection; anything suggesting this: *the woods are a paradise in spring; life would be a paradise but for sin, poverty, and disease.* **4.** An oriental pleasure garden, or park. **5.** Kind of apple largely used as a base upon which the finer sorts are grafted: *paradise stock.*

paradisean, adj. [1. paradísean; 2. pærədísiən]. Prec. & **-an.** Paradisiac.

paradise, bird of, n. See **bird of paradise.**

paradisiac, adj. [1. paradísiak; 2. pærədísiæk]. **paradise** & *-i-* & **-ac.** Of, pertaining to, like, paradise or a paradise.

paradisiacal, adj. [1. pàradisíakl; 2. pæ̀rədisáiəkl]. Paradisiac.

paradisial, adj. [1. paradísial; 2. pærədísiəl]. **paradise** & **-ial.** Paradisiac.

paradisian, adj. [1. paradísian; 2. pærədísiən]. **paradise** & **-ian.** Paradisiac.

paradisic(al), adj. [1. pàradísik(l); 2. pæ̀rədísik(l)]. **paradise** & **-ic** & **-al.** Paradisiac.

parados, n. [1. párados; 2. pǽrədɔs], fr. Fr. *parados*, fr. **para- (II.)** & *dos*, 'back', fr. Lat. *dorsum*, 'back'. See **dorso-.** Earthwork parapet thrown up behind a trench or other part of a fortified point to guard against attack or fire from the rear.

paradox, n. [1. páradoks; 2. pǽrədɔks], fr. Lat. *paradoxum*, fr. Gk. *parádoxon*, 'paradox', neut. form of *parádoxos*, 'contrary to opinion or expectation', fr. **para- (I.)** & *dóxa*, 'notion; opinion; expectation; reputation, credit, glory', see **doxology & dogma. 1.** Statement at first sight appearing absurd or self-contradictory but in reality containing a substratum of truth. **2.** Statement conflicting with received opinion or belief. **3.** Palpably incorrect, self-contradictory or absurd statement. **4.** Anything which appears inconsistent with known experience, or which seems to have certain qualities which are at variance with others possessed by it.

paradoxical, adj. [1. paradóksikl; 2. pærədɔ́ksikl]. Prec. & **-ic** & **-al.** Pertaining to, of the nature of, expressing, a paradox.

paradoxicality, n. [1. pàradòksikáliti; 2. pæ̀rədɔ̀ksikǽliti]. Prec. & **-ity.** Quality of being paradoxical.

paradoxically, adv. [1. pàradóksikali; 2. pæ̀rədɔ́ksikəli]. See prec. & **-ly.** In a paradoxical manner; as a paradox.

paradoxist, n. [1. páradòksist; 2. pǽrədɔ̀ksist]. **paradox** & **-ist.** One who utters paradoxes.

paradoxure, n. [1. paradóksūr, -dókshur; 2. pærədɔ́ksjə, -dɔ́kʃə], fr. Gk. *parádox-(os)*, 'contrary to expectation, incredible', see prec., & Gk. *ourá*, 'tail', see **uro-.** Civet-like, carnivorous mammal of Southern Asia, having a very long curving tail; palm-civet.

paradoxy, n. [1. páradoksi; 2. pǽrədɔksi]. **paradox** & **-y.** Paradox, paradoxicality.

paraffin, n. & vb. trans. [1. párafin, pàrafḗn; 2. pǽrəfin, pæ̀rəfīn]. Named by German chemist, K. von Reichenbach, fr. Lat. *par-(um)*, 'little', cp. *parvus*, 'small', prob. cogn. w. Gk. *paûros*, 'small', Lat. *paucus*, 'little', see **paucity**; the second element is fr. Lat. *affīn-(is)*, 'related', see **affinity**, fr. its lack of affinity w. other substances. **1.** n. **a** Tasteless, odourless, colourless, transparent, fatty, solid substance, obtained from petroleum, coal-tar, shale &c., and used in making candles &c.; **b** oil containing paraffin, used for lighting &c. **2.** vb. trans. To treat, coat, impregnate, with paraffin.

paraffin-oil, n. Oil containing paraffin.

paragoge, n. [1. paragóji; 2. pærəgóudži]. Lat. *paragōgē*, fr. Gk. *paragōgḗ*, 'a leading past; a variation, addition'; (gram.) 'paragoge', fr. **para- (I.)** & *agōgḗ*, 'the act of leading, bringing, carrying', n. formed w. reduplication fr. the stem **āg-, *ŏg-*, 'to lead; to carry; to perform', seen in Gk. *ágein*, 'to lead'; Lat. *agere*, 'to perform', see **agent**; Lat. *(amb)āges*, 'a going round; winding; digression', see **ambages.** Addition of sound at the end of a word; e.g. (vulg.) *gownd* for *gown.*

paragogic, adj. [1. pàragójik; 2. pæ̀rəgɔ́džik]. Prec. & **-ic.** Of, pertaining to, forming, a paragoge.

paragon (I.), n. [1. páragon; 2. pǽrəgən], fr. O. Fr., fr. Ital. *paragone*; fr. Gk. *pará*, 'against', see **para- (I.)**, & *akónē*, 'whetstone', cogn. w. Gall. *acaunum*, 'rock', Scrt. *áçan-*, 'stone for a sling'; fr. same base as Gk. *akís*, 'point', *ákaina*, 'pointed end'; see **acme. 1.** Model of excellence; person or thing exhibiting some extreme quality or excellence: *a paragon of beauty, virtue* &c. **2.** Perfect diamond of 100 carats or more.

paragon (II.), vb. trans., fr. prec. (poet.) To compare, place in comparison.

paragraph (I.), n. [1. páragrahf; 2. pǽrəgrāf], fr. Fr. *paragraphe*, fr. L. Lat., fr. Gk. *parágraphos*, 'line in margin indicating a break in the sense', fr. **para- (I.)** & **-graph. 1.** Distinct part or section of a document, book, chapter &c., begun on a new line, and having the first line more deeply indented than the remaining lines. **2.** Single brief item, article &c. in newspaper &c., printed without headline. **3.** Symbol (¶) formerly used to indicate beginning of new paragraph, now used to call attention to note &c.

paragraph (II.), vb. trans., fr. prec. **1.** To divide into paragraphs. **2.** To write a paragraph, news-item &c. about.

paragrapher, n. [1. páragrahfer; 2. pǽrəgrāfə]. Prec. & **-er.** Writer of newspaper paragraphs.

paragraphic, adj. [1. pàragráfik; 2. pæ̀rəgrǽfik]. **paragraph (I.)** & **-ic.** Of, pertaining to, forming, a paragraph.

paragraphically, adv. [1. pàragráfikali; 2. pæ̀rəgrǽfikəli]. Prec. & **-al** & **-ly.** In a paragraphic manner; in paragraphs.

paragraphist, n. [1. páragràhfist; 2. pǽrəgrāfist]. **paragraph (I.)** & **-ist.** Paragrapher.

paragraphy, n. [1. páragràhfi; 2. pǽrəgrāfi]. **paragraph (I.)** & **-y.** The writing of paragraphs.

Paraguay, n. [1. páragwī, -gwā; 2. pǽrəgwai, -gwei]. Name of S. American republic. *Paraguay tea*, maté.

paraheliotropic, adj. [1. pàrahēliotrópik; 2. pæ̀rəhīliətrɔ́pik]. See next word & **-ic.** Of, pertaining to, of the nature of, paraheliotropism.

paraheliotropism, n. [1. pàrahēliótropizm; 2. pæ̀rəhīliɔ́trəpizəm]. **para- (I.)** & **heliotropism.** Tendency of leaves in sunlight to take up a position parallel to the rays of light.

parakeet, paroquet, n. [1. párakēt, -ket; 2. pǽrəkīt, -ket], fr. O. Fr. *paroquet*; etymol. doubtful; prob. fr. Ital. *parrucchetto*, dimin. of *parrucca*, 'wig'. See **peruke.** Small variety of tropical and sub-tropical parrot, usually long-tailed.

parakite (I.), n. [1. párakīt; 2. pǽrəkait]. Formed fr. **parachute & kite.** Kite used as parachute.

parakite (II.), n. **para- (I.)** & **kite.** Special variety of tailless kite used in meteorological observations &c.

paraldehyde, n. [1. paráldehīd; 2. pærǽldinaid]. **para- (I.)** & **aldehyde.** A powerful hypnotic and sedative drug, with nauseous taste and smell.

paralipsis, paraleipsis, n. [1. paralípsis, -līpsis; 2. pærəlípsis, -láipsis], fr. Gk. *paráleipsis*, fr. *paraleipein*, 'to leave out, omit', fr. **para- (I.)** & *leípein*, 'to leave', q.v. under **lipo- & leave (II.).** Rhetorical device to fix the hearer's or reader's attention upon some point by the express statement that it is to be omitted; e.g. *I will not speak of Pope's filial piety, nor mention his noble tribute to his father and his loving care of his aged mother.*

parallactic, adj. [1. paraláktik; 2. pærəlǽktik], fr. Gk. *parallakt-*, fr. *parállaxis*, 'change', see next word, & **-ic.** Of, relating to, a parallax.

parallax, n. [1. páralaks; 2. pǽrəlæks], fr. Fr. *parallaxe*, fr. Gk. *parállaxis*, 'change', fr. *parallássein*, 'to change, transpose', fr. **para- (I.)** & *allássein*, 'to change', fr. *állos*, 'other'. See **allo-. 1. a** Apparent change in position of an object, due to change in position of observer; **b** amount of such apparent change. **2.** (astron.) Difference in the direction of a heavenly body viewed from a point on the earth's surface, and its direction calculated from the earth's centre.

parallel (I.), adj. [1. páralel; 2. pǽrəlel], fr. Fr. *parallèle*, fr. Lat. *parallēlus*, fr. Gk. *parállēlos*, 'parallel', fr. **para- (I.)** & *allḗlo-*, 'one another', fr. *állos*, 'other', see **allo-. 1.** (of lines &c.) Equidistant in all parts; lying in the same plane and never meeting, however far they may be produced; *parallel bars*, two horizontal bars supported on posts and used for gymnastic exercises; *parallel ruler*, two rulers joined by pivoted strips of metal, used for drawing parallel lines. **2.** (fig.) Similar, corresponding, having a close resemblance: *a parallel instance, case* &c.

parallel (II.), n., fr. prec. **1. a** Line equidistant from another in all parts; parallel line; specif. **b** also *parallel of latitude*, each of the parallel lines drawn round a globe or across a map, parallel to the equator, and showing degrees of latitude. **2.** (mil.) Trench running parallel to line of fortification. **3.** Person, thing, event, circumstance, analogous to, having close resemblance to, corresponding to, another: *the incident is without parallel.* **4.** Comparison: *to draw a parallel between two things.* **5.** (print.) Reference-mark, consisting of two upright, parallel lines (‖), drawing attention to a note &c.

parallel (III.), vb. trans., fr. prec. **1.** To produce an instance of something closely resembling, having same character as, being as remarkable as, something seen or referred to: *you won't easily parallel that.* **2.** (rare) To draw a comparison between (two things &c.).

parallelepiped, n. [1. páralèlepíped; 2. pǽrəlèləpáipəd], fr. **parallel (I.)** & Gk. *epípedon*, 'plane surface', neut. form of *epípedos*, 'level', fr. **epi-** & *pédon*, 'ground'; cp. Scrt. *padám*, 'step, track; place'; O.N. *fet*, 'step'; Lith. *pėdà*, 'track'; cogn. w. Lat. *pēs*, 'foot'. See **pedal (I.).** (geom.) Regular solid contained by parallelograms.

parallelism, n. [1. páralelizm; 2. pǽrəlelìzəm]. **parallel (I.)** & **-ism. 1.** State or quality of being parallel (in sense **1**). **2.** Resemblance, correspondence, in form or ideas.

parallelogram, n. [1. paralélogram; 2. pærəléləgræm], fr. Fr. *parallelogramme*, fr. Gk. *parállēlo-(s)*, 'parallel', see **parallel (I.)**, & **-gram.** Four-sided plane figure whose opposite sides are equal and parallel.

paralogism, n. [1. parálojìzm; 2. pərǽlədžìzəm], fr. Fr. *paralogisme*, fr. L. Lat., fr. Gk. *paralogismós*, 'false reasoning', fr. *paralogízomai*, 'I reason falsely'. See next word. False reasoning, bad logic.

paralogize, vb. trans. [1. parálojīz; 2. pərǽlədžaiz], fr. Gk. *paralogízomai*, 'I mislead by false reasoning', fr. *parálog-(os)*, 'beyond reason, calculation, or expectation', fr. **para-**

(I.) & *lógos*, 'word, speech, thought, reason', see **logos**, & **-ize**. To reason falsely.

paralysation, n. [1. pàralīzáshun; 2. pærəlaizéiʃən], fr. next word & **-ation**. **a** Act or process of paralysing; **b** state of being paralysed.

paralyse, vb. trans. [1. páralīz; 2. pǽrəlaiz]. Cp. Fr. *paralyser*. See next word. **1.** To affect with paralysis. **2.** (fig.) **a** To inhibit physical or intellectual capacity of: *paralyse with fear*; **b** to check, render useless or inoperative: *to paralyse one's efforts*.

paralysis, n. [1. parálisis; 2. pərǽlisis]. Lat. *paralysis*, fr. Gk. *parálusis*, 'paralysis', fr. *paralúein*, 'to loosen; to be paralysed', fr. **para-** (I.) & *lúein*, 'to loosen, release'; cogn. w. Lat. *luere*, 'to loose, pay'; Goth. *(fra)liusan*, O.E. *(for)lēosan*, 'to lose'. See **loose** & **lose**. **1.** Loss of sensation and motive power in any part of the body. **2.** (fig.) **a** Loss or absence of intellectual vigour and enterprise; **b** loss of will power; **c** blunting of sense of right and wrong: *moral paralysis*.

paralytic, adj. & n. [1. pàralítik; 2. pærəlítik], fr. Fr. *paralytique*, fr. Lat., fr. Gk. *paralutikós*, 'paralytic'. See prec. & **-ic**. **1.** adj. Of, pertaining to, affected with, paralysis (lit. and fig.). **2.** n. Person suffering from paralysis.

paralytically, adv. [1. pàralítikali; 2. pærəlítikəli]. Prec. & **-al** & **-ly**. In a paralytic manner.

paramagnetic, adj. [1. pàramagnétik; 2. pærəmægnétik]. **para-** (I.) & **magnetic**. Having the property of being attracted by the poles of a magnet.

paramagnetism, n. [1. pàramágnetizm; 2. pærəmǽgnitizəm]. See prec. & **-ism**. Property of paramagnetic substance.

paramatta, n. [1. pàramáta; 2. pærəmǽtə], fr. name of town in New South Wales. Light fabric like merino, made of wool and cotton.

parameter, n. [1. parámeter; 2. pərǽmitə]. **para-** (I.) & Gk. *métron*, 'measure', see **-meter**. (math.) A variable constant; e.g. in a series of circles, one within the other, having a common centre, a radius drawn from this, and passing through each circle in succession, is of constant length if confined to any given circle, but varies in length from circle to circle if conceived of as belonging to the whole system; this radius is a parameter.

paramo, n. [1. páramō; 2. pǽrəmou]. Span. *paramo*, prob. of native origin. High, bleak, treeless plain in tropical S. America.

paramount, adj. [1. páramòunt; 2. pǽrəmàunt), fr. O. Fr. *paramont*, fr. O. Fr. *par*, 'by', & *amont*, 'above, over', see **amount**. **1.** Having supreme authority or jurisdiction: *lord, lady, paramount*; *a paramount chief*. **2.** Predominant, superior to all others, pre-eminent: *a point of paramount interest*.

paramountcy, n. [1. páramòuntsi; 2. pǽrəmàuntsi]. Prec. & **-cy**. Quality of being paramount.

paramountly, adv. [1. páramòuntli; 2. pǽrəmàuntli]. See prec. & **-ly**. So as to be paramount.

paramour, n. [1. páramoor; 2. pǽrəmuə], fr. O. Fr. *par amour*, 'by love'; in M.E., with innocent meaning of 'wooer, lover'. See **amour**. Either of two persons between whom illicit sexual relations exist.

parang, n. [1. páhrang; 2. pάræŋ]. Malay. Heavy, straight-edged, Malay knife, used as weapon and tool.

paranoia, paranoea, n. [1. paranóia, -nḗa; 2. pærənóiə, -níə]. Gk. *paránoia*, 'madness', fr. *paráno-(os)*, 'distracted', fr. **para-** (I.) & *nóos*, 'mind', see **nous**, & **-ia**. Chronic disease of the mind, accompanied esp. by delusions of greatness, and by persecution mania.

parapet, n. [1. párapit, -pet; 2. pǽrəpit, -pɛt], fr. Ital. *parapetto*, fr. **para-** (II.) & *petto*, 'breast', fr. Lat. *pectus*, 'breast'; see **pectoral**. **1.** Low wall at the edge of a roof, terrace, bridge &c. **2.** (mil.) Wall or bank of stone, earth &c. to protect troops from hostile fire from in front; contrasted with *parados*.

parapeted, adj. [1. párapited; 2. pǽrəpitid]. Prec. & **-ed**. Furnished with a parapet.

paraph, n. [1. paráf; 2. pərǽf], fr. Fr. *paraphe*, fr. Med. Lat. *paraphus*, contracted fr. *paragraphus*, 'paragraph'. See **paragraph**. Mark or flourish after a signature.

paraphernalia, n. [1. pàrafernália; 2. pærəfənéiliə]. Lat., neut. pl. adj. fr. *parapherna*, 'separate possessions of a married woman', fr. **para-** (I.) & *phern-(ḗ)*, 'dower', fr. base **pher-*, 'to carry, bear', seen in Gk. *phérein*, Lat. *ferre*, 'to carry', see **-ferous**; O.E. *beran*, 'to carry', see **bear** (I.). **1.** (law) Formerly, articles of personal adornment &c. given to a wife by her husband for her use, but not becoming her absolute property. **2.** Miscellaneous articles of various kinds; trappings, appointments, accoutrements, mechanical accessories &c.

paraphrase, n. & vb. trans. [1. párafrāz; 2. pǽrəfrèiz], fr. Fr., fr. Lat., fr. Gk. *paráphrasis*, 'paraphrase', fr. **para-** & *phrásis*, 'speech', see **phrase**. **1.** n. **a** Rendering of the sense of a passage in other words; a free rendering of any work in prose or verse; **b** specif., one of several metrical versions of scriptural passages, used in the Church of Scotland. **2.** vb. To express in other words, give free rendering of.

paraphrastic, adj. [1. pàrafrástik; 2. pærəfrǽstik]. See prec. & **-ic**. Of, pertaining to, of the nature of, forming, a paraphrase.

paraphrastically, adv. [1. pàrafrástikali; 2. pærəfrǽstikəli]. Prec. & **-al** & **-ly**. In a paraphrastic manner; as a paraphrase.

paraplegia, n. [1. pàraplḗjia; 2. pærəplídʒiə], fr. **para-** (I.) & Gk. *plēg-(ḗ)*, 'a blow', fr. *plḗssein*, 'to strike', q.v. under **plectrum**. Paralysis affecting both sides of the body.

paraplegic, adj. [1. pàraplḗjik, -pléjik; 2. pærəplídʒik, -plédʒik]. Prec. & **-ic**. Of, of the nature of, affected by, paraplegia.

parasang, n. [1. párasàng; 2. pǽrəsæŋ], fr. Lat. *parasanga*, fr. Gk. *parasággēs*, 'parasang', fr. Pers. Ancient Persian measure of length, about 3¼ miles.

paraselene, n. [1. pàraselḗnē; 2. pærəsəlíni]. **para-** (I.) & Gk. *selḗnē*, 'moon', see **seleno-**. Luminous spot on lunar halo; mock moon, cp. *parhelion*.

parasite, n. [1. párasīt; 2. pǽrəsait], fr. Lat. *parasītus*, fr. Gk. *parásītos*, 'guest; parasite', fr. **para-** (I.) & *sitos*, 'food; corn, grain'; etymol. doubtful. **1.** (Gk. antiq.) A sycophant, toady, who paid for his entertainment at another's table by providing amusement for, and flattering, his host. **2.** A useless hanger-on who lives upon others, and contributes nothing by independent effort to the society which supports him. **3.** (biol.) An organism, plant or animal, which lives upon, or within, another organism, and derives its nourishment from its host; cp. *commensal*.

parasitic(al), adj. [1. pàrasítik(l); 2. pærəsítik(l)]. Prec. & **-ic** & **-al**. Of the nature of, caused by, a parasite; living as a parasite.

parasiticide, n. [1. pàrasítisīd; 2. pærəsítisaid]. **parasite** & **-cide**. Agent for destroying parasites.

parasitism, n. [1. párasītizm; 2. pǽrəsaitizəm]. **parasite** & **-ism**. State of being a parasite.

parasitize, vb. trans. [1. párasītīz; 2. pǽrəsaitaiz]. **parasite** & **-ize**. To infest as, or with, a parasite.

parasitology, n. [1. pàrasītóloji; 2. pærəsaitólədʒi]. **parasite** & **-logy**. The study of organic parasites.

parasol, n. [1. parasól, párasol, pàrasól; 2. pærəsól, pǽrəsol, pærəsóul]. Fr., fr. Ital. *parasole*, fr. **para-** (II.) & *sole*, 'sun', fr. Lat. *sōl*, 'sun', see **sol**. Sunshade; *parasol ant*, the umbrella ant.

parasynthesis, n. [1. pàrasínthesis; 2. pærəsínþəsis]. **para-** (I.) & **synthesis**. (gram.) Derivation of a word from a compound; formation of a word by derivation and composition.

parasynthetic, adj. [1. pàrasinthétik; 2. pærəsinþétik]. **para-** (I.) & **synthetic**. Of, formed by, parasynthesis.

paratactic, adj. [1. pàratáktik; 2. pærətǽktik], fr. Gk. *paratak-*, stem of *parátaxis*, 'arrangement'. See **parataxis** & **-ic**. Of, of the nature of, parataxis.

paratactically, adv. [1. pàratáktikali; 2. pærətǽktikəli]. Prec. & **-ly**. In a paratactic manner.

parataxis, n. [1. pàratáksis; 2. pærətǽksis], fr. Gk. *parátaxis*, 'arrangement, marshalling', fr. *paratássein*, 'to arrange, draw up in order', fr. **para-** (I.) & *tássein*, 'to draw up, array', see **taxis**. (gram.) Use or arrangement of successive clauses &c. without connecting words.

parathyroid, adj. [1. parathíroid; 2. pærəþáiroid]. **para-** (I.) & **thyroid**. (med.) Of, pertaining to, four small, ductless bodies, *parathyroid glands*, lying close to the thyroid gland, the function of which is obscure, but the removal of which results in coma &c. and death.

paratyphoid, n. [1. paratífoid; 2. pærətáifoid]. **para-** (I.) & **typhoid**. (pathol.) An infectious disease closely resembling in symptoms true typhoid fever, but caused by different infective bacilli.

paravane, n. [1. páravān; 2. pǽrəvein]. Invented word fr. **para-** (I.) & **vane**. An apparatus towed by a ship, in pairs, one on each side of the bows of a ship, with saw-edged jaws for cutting the moorings of submerged mines and bringing them to the surface; also similar device with charge of explosive for use against submarines.

parboil, vb. trans. [1. pàrbóil; 2. pàbóil], fr. O. Fr. *parboillir*, fr. L. Lat. *perbullīre*, 'to boil thoroughly', fr. **per-** & **boil** (II.); mod. usage due to confusion of first element w. **part**. **1.** To boil partially. **2.** (fig.) To make unpleasantly hot, overheat.

parbuckle, n. & vb. trans. [1. párbukl; 2. pábakl]. Origin unknown. **1.** n. Device for raising or lowering a heavy object, esp. a cask or log of wood, consisting of a long rope, one end of which is made fast at desired height, while the other is passed under and back over the object to be moved; this end is then hauled or paid out, and the object rolls up or down as required. **2.** vb. To raise by means of a parbuckle.

parcel (I.), n. & adv. [1. pársl; 2. pásl], fr. Fr. *parcelle*, fr. Lat. **particella*, dimin. of *part-(is)*, 'part'. See **part** (I.) & cp. **particle**. **1.** n. (archaic) **a** Part, portion; now only in Phr. *part and parcel*, essential part; or **b** *parcel of land*, piece, section, of land, esp. as forming part of a larger estate. **2.** n. Object or objects wrapped up to form single bundle or package: *to wrap up a parcel*; *to make things into a parcel*. **3.** adv. (archaic) Partly; now esp. in Phr. *parcel gilt*, partly gilded.

parcel (II.), vb. trans., fr. prec. **1.** (usually *parcel out*) To divide into portions, distribute. **2.** (naut.) To cover with canvas strips, wrap strips of canvas round: *to parcel a rope, a seam* &c.

parcelling, n. [1. párseling; 2. pásəliŋ]. Prec. & **-ing**. (naut.) Strips of canvas, usually tarred, for wrapping round rope &c.

parcel post, n. Post-office department dealing with transport of parcels.

parcenary, n. [1. pársenari; 2. pásinəri], fr. A.-Fr. *parcenarie*, fr. O. Fr. *parçonerie*, fr. *parçonier*, 'co-heir'. See next word & **-ery**. Co-heirship.

parcener, n. [1. pársener; 2. pásinə]. A.-Fr. *parcener*, fr. O. Fr. *parçonier*, fr. Med. Lat. *parti(ti)onārius*. See **partition** & **-er**. Co-heir.

parch, vb. trans. & intrans. [1. parch; 2. pātʃ]. Origin doubtful. **1.** trans. **a** (of heat, sun, thirst &c.) To make, cause to become, excessively dry; to scorch, burn up: *parched land*; *to be parched with thirst*; **b** to roast lightly, roast surface of: *parched peas.* **2.** intrans. To become very dry.

parchment, n. [1. párchment; 2. pā́tʃmənt]. M.E. *parchemin*, fr. O. Fr. *parchemin*, fr. Lat. *pergamēna* (*charta*), 'paper of Pergamum', city in Asia Minor. **1.** Skin of sheep, goat &c. prepared and smoothed for writing, painting &c. **2.** Manuscript, document, written on parchment; hence, a legal deed, charter &c. **3.** Parchment-like substance, esp. skin of coffee-bean.

parchmenty, adj. [1. párchmenti; 2. pā́tʃmənti]. Prec. & **-y.** Having the appearance or texture of parchment.

parcimonious, parcimony. See **parsimonious** &c.

parclose, n. [1. párklōz; 2. pā́klouz], fr. O. Fr. *parclos(e)*, properly P.P. of *parclore*, 'to close, shut in', fr. **per-** & *clore*, 'to close'; see **close (I.)**. (archit.) A screen, railing, in a church, enclosing a shrine, tomb &c., or shutting off a side chapel from the body of the building.

pard (I.), n. [1. pard; 2. pād]. O. Fr., fr. Lat. *pardus*, fr. Gk. *párdos*, 'panther'; prob. an eastern loan-word; cp. Scrt. *pṛdākuš*, 'panther; tiger'. (archaic) Leopard.

pard (II.), n. (slang) Abbr. fr. **partner.**

pardon (I.), n. [1. párdn; 2. pā́dn]. O. Fr. *perdun*, fr. *perdoner*, *pardoner*, 'to pardon'. See next word. **1.** Forgiveness; act of pardoning, state of being pardoned: *to have no hope of pardon*; *to ask for pardon*; *to ask pardon for one's sins.* **2.** (eccles.) **a** Papal indulgence; **b** festival at which indulgences are granted. **3.** (in making polite apology) Forbearance, forgiveness, indulgence (for slight offences, breaches of manners &c.); esp. in Phr. *I beg your pardon*; *to ask one's pardon.* **4.** (law) Esp. *free pardon*, legal action freeing a criminal or other offender from punishment for his crimes; *general pardon*, issued to number of persons concerned without specifying names &c.

pardon (II.), vb. trans., fr. O. Fr. *pardoner*, 'to forgive', fr. L. Lat. *perdōnāre*, 'to remit', fr. **per-** & *dōnāre*, 'to give'. See **donation.** **1.** (as affecting persons) **a** Specif. (law) to free a criminal, or other person, from the punishment to which he has been sentenced; grant a free pardon to; **b** to excuse, forgive; to remit punishment of, fail to punish, for crimes or sins committed: '*He pardoneth and absolveth all them that truly repent*'; *it is difficult to enforce the law when criminals are freely pardoned*; **c** to excuse, grant indulgence to (for committing breach of manners, or other trivial offence): *pardon me for interrupting you.* **2.** (as affecting the offences &c.) **a** *To pardon sins*; **b** *pardon my intrusion.*

pardonable, adj. [1. párdunabl; 2. pā́dənəbl]. Prec. & **-able.** Capable of being pardoned; excusable, forgivable.

pardonableness, n. See prec. & **-ness.** Quality of being pardonable.

pardonably, adv. See prec. & **-ly.** In a pardonable manner.

pardoner, n. [1. párduner; 2. pā́dənə]. **pardon (II.)** & **-er.** (hist.) One licensed to grant or sell papal indulgences.

pare, vb. trans. [1. pār; 2. pɛə], fr. Fr. *parer*, 'to adorn; prepare', fr. Lat. *parāre*, 'to prepare, make ready; to occupy oneself with'; fr. stem **per-*, **por-*, 'to bring, bring forward, give out, share', in Lat. *pārēre*, 'to appear', see **appear**, *portio*, 'share'; *pars*, 'part', see **part (I.)**. **1.** To cut, trim, shave, remove, slight irregularities from: *to pare one's nails.* **2.** To remove outer skin or rind from, peel: *to pare fruit*; also *pare off, away, down*, to remove, trim off, by cutting: *to pare skin, rind, edges &c.*; *to pare (down) one's expenses*, to reduce them little by little.

paregoric, n. [1. pàregórik; 2. pæ̀rigɔ́rik], fr. L. Lat. *parēgoric-(us)*, fr. Gk. *parēgorik-(ós)*, 'soothing, consoling', fr. *parḗgor-(os)*, 'consoling', fr. **para- (I.)** & *agor-(á)*, 'public speaking; public assembly'; cp. Gk. *ageirein*, 'to assemble'. See **gregarious** & cp. **panegyric.** Medicine which soothes pain; also *paregoric elixir*, camphorated aromatic tincture of opium.

pareira, n. [1. parára; 2. pərɛ́ərə], fr. Port. *parreira*, 'vine'. Drug obtained from the roots of various tropical American shrubs, and used in disorders of the urinary organs.

parenchyma, n. [1. paréngkima; 2. pəréŋkimə], fr. Gk. *parégkuma*, fr. **para- (I.)** & *égkhuma*, 'something poured in', fr. *egkhéō*, 'I pour in', fr. **en-** & *khéō*, 'I pour'; cp. Gk. *khūlós*, 'juice'. See **chyme** & **chyle.** **1.** (anat.) Soft cellular tissue forming chief substance of glands &c., as distinct from connective tissue &c. **2.** (bot.) Soft cellular tissue found in leaves, pulp of fruit &c.; contrasted w. *prosenchyma.*

parenchymal, adj. [1. paréngkimal; 2. pəréŋkiməl]. Prec. & **-al.** Of, like, composed of, parenchyma.

parenchymatous, adj. [1. pàrengkímatus; 2. pæ̀reŋkímətəs]. See **parenchyma** & **-ous.** Parenchymal.

parent, n. [1. pā́rent; 2. pɛ́ərənt]. O. Fr., fr. Lat. *parent-(em)*, 'parent', fr. *parere*, 'to beget; to bring forth'; cp. Lith. *periù*, 'brood'; Gk. *póris*, 'young animal, calf'; O.H.G. *far*; O.N. *farre*; O.E. *fearr*, 'bullock'; cp. **heifer**; the base **per-*, **por-*, 'to bring forth', is prob. identical w. the base **per-*, **por-*, 'to bring, carry; to distribute, give out'; cp. Gk. *poreîn*, 'to furnish, offer, present'; Lat. *pars*, 'part'; *portio*, 'share, portion'. See **part (I.), portion.** **1. a** Father or mother; **b** ancestor, forefather, esp. in Phr. *our first parents*, Adam and Eve. **2.** Organism, animal, plant, producing another; one from which others are derived; (often attrib.) *parent cell*; *parent bird, parent stem.* **3. a** Origin, source: *Latin is the parent of the modern Romance languages*; **b** cause, occasion: *ignorance is the parent of crime.*

parentage, n. [1. pā́rentij; 2. pɛ́ərəntidž]. Prec. & **-age.** **a** Condition of being a parent; **b** descent, derivation, from parents or ancestors; extraction, birth, origin.

parental, adj. [1. paréntl; 2. pəréntl], fr. Lat. *parentāl-(is)*, 'of parents', fr. *parent-(em)*, 'parent'. See **parent** & **-al.** Of, pertaining to, characteristic of, a parent.

parentally, adv. Prec. & **-ly.** In a parental manner.

parenthesis, n. [1. parénthesis; 2. pərénþisiz]. Med. Lat., fr. Gk., fr. **para- (I.)** & **en-** & **thesis (I.)**, lit. 'something placed within'. **1.** Word, phrase, clause, inserted into a sentence which is grammatically complete without it, usually distinguished in writing or printing by brackets, commas, or dashes. **2.** (usually pl.) *Parentheses*, round brackets ( ) used to mark off a parenthesis. **3.** Interval, interlude, independent episode, or incident.

parenthesize, vb. trans. [1. parénthesīz; 2. pərénþisaiz]. Prec. & **-ize.** **1.** To insert, introduce, as parenthesis. **2.** To put between brackets, mark as parenthesis.

parenthetic(al), adj. [1. pàrenthétik(l); 2. pæ̀rənþétik(l)], fr. Med. Lat. *parenthetic-(us)*. See **parenthesis** & **-ic** & **-al.** Of the nature of, pertaining to, forming, introduced as, indicating, a parenthesis.

parenthetically, adv. Prec. & **-ly.** In a parenthetic manner; as a parenthesis.

paresis, n. [1. páresis; 2. pǽrisis]. Gk. *páresis*, 'remission, relaxation', fr. *pariēmi*, 'I let go', fr. **para- (I.)** & *hiēmi*, 'I go; send', earlier **ji-jē-mi*; cogn. w. Lat. *ja-cere*, 'to throw'. See **jet (III.)**. Form of paralysis, affecting power of movement but not of sensation.

paretic, adj. [1. parétik; 2. pærétik], fr. prec. Pertaining to, of the nature of, affected by paresis.

par excellence, adv. [1. par ékselahns; 2. pār ékselā̃s]. Fr. Pre-eminently, in the highest degree.

pargana, n. See **pergunnah.**

parget, vb. trans. & n. [1. párjet; 2. pā́džit]. M.E. *pargeten*, fr. O. Fr. *pargeter*, fr. Lat. *projectāre*, 'to throw out, drive forth'. See **project.** **1.** vb. To plaster, cover (walls &c., esp. those of half-timbered houses) with smooth layer of plaster, usually decorated with impressed patterns. **2.** n. Plaster surface on wall.

pargetting, n. [1. párjeting; 2. pā́džitiŋ]. Prec. & **-ing.** **a** The layer of plaster covering a wall, often stamped with patterns; **b** surface of plaster thus applied.

parheliacal, adj. [1. pàrhēlíakl; 2. pā̀hīláiəkl]. See **parhelion** & **-ac** & **-al.** Of, pertaining to, of the nature of, a parhelion.

parhelic, adj. [1. parhélik; 2. pāhílik]. See next word & **-ic.** Parheliacal.

parhelion, n. [1. parhélion; 2. pāhílion], fr. Lat., fr. Gk. *parḗlion*, 'mock sun', fr. **para- (I.)** & *hḗlios*, 'sun'. See **helio-.** Spot of brilliant light appearing on solar halo, mock sun, cp. *paraselene.*

pariah, n. [1. paría, pā́ria, páhria; 2. pəráiə, péəriə, pā́riə], fr. Tamil *paṛaiyar*, pl. of *paṛaiyan*, 'drummer', hereditary beater of the *paṛai*, a large drum beaten at certain festivals. **1.** Member of a very low caste among the Hindus, which includes a large proportion of the population in Southern India; from this caste most domestic servants in Madras are drawn. The word has come to be applied by Europeans in India to the lowest castes generally, and to person without any caste. Hence, **2,** (in England) a social outcast, person ostracized by society.

pariah-dog, n. Vagabond, ownerless dog common in the East.

Parian, adj. & n. [1. pā́rian; 2. péəriən], fr. Lat. *Pari-(us)*, 'of the island of Paros', & **-an.** **1.** adj. Of, from, the island of Paros, one of the Cyclades, famous for its white marble. **2.** n. Kind of fine white porcelain used for statuettes &c.

parietal, adj. [1. paríetl; 2. pəráiətl], fr. Lat. *parietāl-(is)*, 'of walls', fr. *pariet-*, stem of *pariēs*, 'wall'; prob. for **twariet-*, & cogn. w. Lith. *tvcriù*, 'to fence in, hedge'; *tvártas*, 'hedge, hurdle'; O. Slav. *tvoriti*, 'to make, fashion'; cp. O.N. *þrūðr*, 'strong, firm'. **1.** Pertaining to, forming, the walls of any cavity in the body; specif., *parietal bones*, two bones forming part of the top and sides of the skull. **2.** (bot.) Developing from the side or wall of an organ.

pari mutuel, n. [1. pahrē mūtūel; 2. parī mytyɛl]. Fr., 'mutual wager'. System of betting, carried on by a mechanical apparatus, in which the winners divide the money staked by the losers, a tax on all takings being levied, cp. *totalizator.*

paring, n. [1. pā́ring; 2. péəriŋ]. **pare** & **-ing.** Part of anything removed by paring: *potato parings* &c.

pari passu, adv. [1. pā́ri pásū; 2. péəri pǽsjū]. Lat. *pari passu*, 'with equal pace', fr. *pār*, 'equal', see **par (I.)**, & *passus*, 'pace', see **pace (I.)**. With equal pace, together; at a corresponding rate or speed, degree.

Paris, n. [1. páris; 2. pǽris]. Name of capital of France. *Paris doll*, lay-figure used by dressmakers &c.; *Paris white*, fine whiting used in polishing; see also *plaster of Paris.*

parish, n. [1. párish; 2. pǽriʃ]. M.E. *paresche*, fr. O. Fr. *parosche*, fr. L. Lat. *parochia*, fr. Lat. *paroecia*, 'parish', fr. Gk. *paroikía*, 'ecclesiastical district, land round a church', fr. *pároik-(os)*, 'near by', fr. **para- (I.)** & *oikein*, 'to dwell', fr. *oikos*, 'dwelling'. See first element in **economy.** **1.** Ecclesiastical unit forming the smallest division within a diocese; area over which a single incumbent, whether rector or vicar, has jurisdiction: *parish clerk*, official performing certain duties connected with the church, and formerly leading the congregation in the responses. **2.** *Civil parish*, one of the districts into which a county is divided for the administration of the Poor Law &c.; *parish council*, local body administering Poor Law &c. Phr. *to go on the parish*, receive parochial relief.

parishioner, n. [1. paríshuner; 2. pəríʃənə], fr. O. Fr. *paroissen*, fr. *paroisse*, 'parish', fr. L. Lat. *parochia*, fr. Lat. *paroecia*, 'ecclesiastical district'. See prec. & **-an** & **-er**. Inhabitant of a specified parish.

parish-register, n. Book in which the christenings, marriages, and burials taking place within a parish are recorded.

Parisian, adj. & n. [1. parízian; 2. pərízìən], fr. Fr. *parisien*, fr. Lat. *Parisi-(i)*, 'Paris', & **-an**. **1.** adj. Of, pertaining to, characteristic of, originating in, Paris. **2.** n. Native, inhabitant, of Paris.

parisyllabic, adj. [1. pàrisilábik; 2. pæ̀risilǽbik], fr. Lat. *pār*, 'equal', see **par (I.)**, & **syllabic**. Having the same number of syllables; specif. (of Lat. and Gk. ns.) having this in all cases of the singular.

parity, n. [1. páriti; 2. pǽriti], fr. Lat. *paritāt-(em)*, 'equality', fr. *pār*, 'equal'. See **par (I.)** & **-ity**. **1.** Equality of rank, condition, degree &c.: *parity of exchange*; *to stand at parity*. **2.** Analogy, resemblance, similarity: *parity of reasoning*.

park (I.), n. [1. park; 2. pāk]. M.E. *park* (mid-13th cent.), fr. O. Fr. *parc*; fr. W. Gmc. **parrok-*; cp. M.H.G. *pferrich*; O.E. *pearruc*, 'enclosure'; the specif. sense of M.E. & present-day Engl. comes fr. Fr., the earlier O. & M.E. word being *friþ*. Skeat suggests that *par(r)-* is a variant of base **spar-*, 'to enclose', cp. O.E. *(ġe)spearrian*, 'to bar, shut'; the base orig. means 'a stake, piece of wood'. See **spar (I.)** & perhaps **spear**. **1. a** (law and hist.) Tract of land enclosed, stocked, and preserved for hunting, with the king's authority, but not subject to special laws; **b** tract of land containing pasture, lakes &c. planted with trees, surrounding a country house, often of recent origin, and formed by throwing a number of fields together and enclosing the whole; differing from **a** in not being made by royal authority. **2. a** Large tract of land preserved in its natural state for public benefit &c.; **b** enclosed, ornamental grounds in, or near, a town &c., reserved for public recreation; specif., *The Park*, Hyde Park. **3. a** (mil.) Space in encampment reserved for artillery, stores &c.; **b** space reserved for parking motor-cars.

park (II.), vb. trans., fr. prec. **1.** To enclose in or as a park. **2. a** (mil.) To arrange, bring together, in a park: *to park guns*; hence, **b** to place and arrange (vehicles) in a space or enclosure reserved for this purpose: *to park motor-cars*.

parkin, n. [1. párkin; 2. pākin]. Origin unknown; a Northern word. Kind of cake or biscuit made of oatmeal, ginger, and treacle.

parkish, adj. [1. párkish; 2. pākiʃ]. **park (I.)** & **-ish**. Like a park.

parky, adj. [1. párki; 2. pāki]. See prec. & **-y**. (slang, colloq.) Sharply cold, nipping (of wind or weather).

parlance, n. [1. párlans; 2. pāləns], fr. Fr. *parl-(er)*, 'to speak', fr. L. Lat. *parabolāre*, 'to talk', fr. *parabola*, 'comparison; parable; speech, discourse', see **parable**, & **-ance**. Manner of speaking, characteristic style, words, idiom: *in nautical, military, vulgar, legal &c., parlance*.

parlement, n. [1. párlemon; 2. parləmã]. Fr. See **Parliament**. (Fr. hist.) A judicial court of the old régime, with power to hear appeals, register decrees and other legislative enactments.

parley (I.), n. [1. párli; 2. pāli], fr. Fr. *parler*, 'to speak'. See **parlance**. Conference, discussion, on disputed point; esp. (mil.) discussion of terms by opponents. Phr. *to sound a parley*, to invite to a conference by trumpet-call.

parley (II.), vb. intrans & trans., fr. prec. **1.** intrans. To hold a conference, discuss terms: *to parley with an enemy*. **2.** trans. (colloq.) To speak, esp. a foreign language.

parleyvoo, n. & vb. intrans. [1. pàrlivóō; 2. pālivū], fr. Fr. *parlez-vous (français)?*, 'do you speak (French)?', fr. *parler*, 'to speak'. See **parlance**. (colloq.) **1.** n. **a** The French language; **b** a Frenchman. **2.** vb. To speak French.

Parliament, n. [1. párlament; 2. pāləmənt], fr. O. Fr. *parlement*, 'speaking', fr. *parler*, 'to speak', see **parlance**, & **-ment**. Deliberative and legislative assembly of a state or country, variously formed and constituted, either by popular election or by hereditary right; in England, consisting of two houses, the Lords (Spiritual and Temporal, the latter mostly hereditary) and the Commons (elected). Phr. *to enter, go into, Parliament*, become a member of the House of Commons.

parliamentarian, adj. & n. [1. pàrlimentárian; 2. pàlimənteəriən]. See next word & **-an**. **1.** adj. Pertaining to, connected with, Parliament. **2.** n. **a** Person experienced in the rules and methods of the English Parliament, or of other parliamentary bodies; specif. **b** adherent of parliamentary party as opposed to the king's party under Charles I.; a Roundhead.

parliamentary, adj. [1. pàrliméntari; 2. pàliméntəri]. **Parliament** & **-ary**. **1.** Of, pertaining to, enacted by, Parliament: *an old parliamentary hand*; specific uses: *parliamentary agent*, person, usually a solicitor, who manages the drafting and passing of private bills in Parliament; *parliamentary bar*, barristers specializing in private bills before Committees of Parliament; *parliamentary train*, one which, according to Act of Parliament, carries third-class passengers at rate not exceeding one penny a mile. **2.** *Parliamentary language*, such as is permitted in Parliament; hence polite, avoiding terms of abuse and other improprieties of speech.

parlour, n. [1. párlur; 2. pālə]. In M.E., fr. O. Fr. *parleor*, fr. Med. Lat. *parlatōrium*, fr. *parl-(āre)*, 'to talk'. See **parlance**. **1.** Sitting-room in private house; now old-fashioned or provincial. **2.** Room for reception of guests, as in a mayor's mansion house, a bank &c.; also in convent or monastery. **3.** Private room in an inn &c.; also (in U.S.A.) room for customers in a shop &c.: *a hairdresser's parlour*; *dental parlour* &c.

parlour-car, n. (in U.S.A.) Luxuriously furnished railway coach.

parlour-maid, n. Maid who waits at table &c.

parlous, adj. & adv. [1. párlus; 2. pāləs]. Variant of **perilous**. (archaic or facet.) **1.** adj. Perilous, dangerous, precarious, critical; perplexing; chiefly in Phr. *a parlous condition*. **2.** adv. Extremely, wonderfully: *parlous strange*.

Parmesan, adj. & n. [1. pàrmezán; 2. pàmizǽn]. Fr., fr. Ital. *Parmegiano*, 'of Parma'. Also *Parmesan cheese*, a dry, hard cheese, with delicate flavour, made originally at Parma, used chiefly grated as flavouring for other dishes.

Parnassian, adj. & n. [1. parnásian; 2. pānǽsiən]. See next word & **-ian**. **1.** adj. **a** Of Parnassus; **b** of, pertaining to, sacred to the Muses; **c** pertaining to a school of French poetry (1866–90), so called from title, *Parnasse contemporain*, of its first volume. **2.** n. A member of the Parnassian school of poetry.

Parnassus, n. [1. parnásus; 2. pānǽsəs]. Lat., fr. Gk. *Parnāsós*. Mountain in Greece, north of Gulf of Corinth, once sacred to Apollo and the Muses; (fig.) poetry; profession of poet; body of poets &c.

Parnellism, n. [1. párnelizm; 2. pānəlizəm], fr. name of C. S. Parnell (d. 1891) & **-ism**. Policy of Irish Home Rule, and the methods to attain it initiated by Parnell.

Parnellite, n. [1. párnelīt; 2. pānəlait]. See prec. & **-ite**. Adherent of Parnellism.

parochial, adj. [1. parókial; 2. pəróukiəl], fr. L. Lat. *parochiāl-(is)*, 'of a parish', fr. *parochia*, 'parish'. See **parish** & **-al**. **1.** Of, pertaining to, a parish. **2.** (fig., of interests, feelings, affairs &c., Having but a small range or scope; limited, confined, to a small area; hence, narrow, provincial.

parochialism, n. [1. parókializm: 2. pəróukiəlizəm]. Prec. & **-ism**. **1.** State or quality of being parochial. **2.** System of local government with parish as administrative unit.

parochiality, n. [1. paròkiáliti; 2. pəròukiǽliti]. **parochial** & **-ity**. Parochialism.

parochialize, vb. trans. [1. parókialīz; 2. pəróukiəlaiz]. **parochial** & **-ize**. **a** To form into a parish; to divide into parishes; **b** to make parochial.

parochially, adv. [1. parókiali; 2. pəróukiəli]. See prec. & **-ly**. In a parochial manner; as a parish.

parodist, n. [1. párodist; 2. pǽrədist]. **parody** & **-ist**. Writer, maker, of parodies.

parodos, n. [1. párodos; 2. pǽrədəs]. Gk. *párodos*, 'way past; passage, side-entry' &c., fr. **para- (I.)** & *hódos*, 'way, path'. See **hodometer**. (Gk. antiq.) **a** The gangway along the deck of a galley or ship, by the side of the rowers; **b** the side entrance to the orchestra in a theatre, by which the chorus entered; hence, the first entrance of the chorus in a Greek play.

parody (I.), n. [1. párodi; 2. pǽrədi], fr. Gk. *parōidia*, 'parody, burlesque', fr. **para- (I.)** & *ōid-(ḗ)*, 'song'. See **ode**. **1.** Deliberately ludicrous burlesque of an author's style and mannerisms. **2.** Incompetent attempt to imitate or reproduce another's work or style; a travesty.

parody (II.), vb. trans., fr. prec. To make a parody of; to imitate in such a manner as to secure a ludicrous effect: *to parody a poem, author, manner* &c.

parole (I.), n. [1. parṓl; 2. pəróul]. Fr. *parole*, 'word', fr. Lat. *parabola*. See **parable**. **1.** Word of honour, solemn pledge or promise to fulfil certain conditions: specif. that of a prisoner not to attempt escape. Phrs. *on parole*; *to break one's parole*, attempt escape after promising not to do so. **2.** Password used by officers of guard, as distinct from countersign.

parole (II.), vb. trans., fr. prec. (rare) To put (person) on parole.

paronomasia, n. [1. pàronomásia; 2. pæ̀rənəméisiə]. Lat. *paronomasia*, fr. Gk. *paronomasía*, 'a figure of speech', fr. **para- (I.)** & *onomasía*, 'naming'. See **onomatopoeia**. Play on words; pun: '*You catch the paronomasia, play 'po' words*' (Calverley, 'Cock and the Bull').

paronym, n. [1. páronim; 2. pǽrənim]. See next word. A paronymous word.

paronymous, adj. [1. parónimus; 2. pərónimәs], fr. Gk. *parṓnumos*, fr. **para-** & *ónuma*, 'name'. See **onomatopoeia**. (of words) **a** Having the same derivation; **b** having the same sound but differing in origin, spelling, and meaning, as *hare, hair* &c.

paroquet, n. See **parakeet**.

parotid, adj. & n. [1. parótid; 2. pərótid], fr. Fr. *parotide*, fr. Lat. *parōtid-(em)*, fr. Gk. *parōtís*, 'tumour near the ear', fr. **para- (I.)** & *ōt-*, stem of *oûs*, 'ear'. See **oto-**. **1.** adj. Situated near the ear; esp. *parotid gland*, the largest of the salivary glands situated between the lower jaw and the ear; *parotid duct*, leading from parotid gland to mouth. **2.** n. Parotid gland.

parotitis, n. [1. parotítis; 2. pærətáitis]. See prec. & **-itis**. (med.) Inflammation of the parotid gland; mumps.

paroxysm, n. [1. pároksizm; 2. pǽrəksizəm], fr. Fr., fr. Lat., fr. Gk. *paroxusmós*, 'irritation, exasperation', fr. *paroxúnein*, 'to provoke, exasperate', fr. **para- (I.)** & *oxúnein*, 'to sharpen', fr. *ox-(ús)*, 'sharp'. See **oxy-**. **1.** Periodic attack of disease &c.; sudden intensification of symptoms of disease &c. occurring at intervals. **2. a** Sudden spasm, attack, access, fit, of emotion, sensation &c.: *a paroxysm of pain, laughter, emotion, rage* &c.; **b** sudden activity, effort.

paroxysmal, adj. [1. paroksízmal; 2. pærəksízməl]. Prec. & **-al**. Of, relating to, of nature of, characterized by, paroxysms.

paroxytone, adj. & n. [1. paróksitōn; 2. pər-ǝ́ksitoun]. **para- (I.)** & **oxytone**. (Gk. gram.) **1.** adj. Having acute (rising or increasing) accent on penultimate syllable. **2.** n. Paroxytone word.

parpen, n. [1. párpen; 2. pā́pən], fr. O. Fr. *parpain*; origin doubtful. A binding stone extending through a wall from one side to another.

parquet, n. & vb. trans. [1. párket, parkét; 2. pā́kit, pākét], fr. Fr. *parquet*, 'enclosure; compartment; floor'; dimin. of *parc*, 'park'. See **park (I.)**. **1.** n. Flooring made of flat blocks of hard wood fitted together, and bedded in adhesive substance; the blocks may be of uniform kind and colour, or diversified, and arranged in geometrical patterns. **2.** vb. To floor with parquetry.

parquetry, n. [1. párketri; 2. pā́kitri]. Prec. & **-ry**. Parquet flooring.

par(r), n. [1. par; 2. pā]. Etymol. unknown. Young salmon, in its first year, marked with dark cross-bars, 'parr marks', on sides and tail.

parrakeet, n. See **parakeet**.

parricidal, adj. [1. pàrisídl; 2. pærisáidl]. See next word & **-al**. Of, pertaining to, guilty of, parricide.

parricide (I.), n. [1. párisīd; 2. pǽrisaid], fr. Fr., fr. Lat. *pāricīda, parricīda*, 'murderer of near relative', fr. **pār-*, 'relative', cogn. w. Gk. *pēós*, 'relation', earlier **pāsó-*; cp. Gk. *pēosúnē*, 'alliance'. The stem **pā-(r)-* is perh. connected w. **pā-*, 'father', in Lat. *pāter, pāpa*, 'father'. See **papa, pater**. For the second element see **-cide**. **a** One who murders a parent or near relative; **b** a traitor to his country.

parricide (II.), n., fr. Fr., fr. Lat. *pāricīdium*, 'crime of parricide', fr. **pār-*, 'relative', see prec., & **-cide**. Murder of a parent or near relative &c.

parrot (I.), n. [1. párut; 2. pǽrət]. Etymol. doubtful; only in Engl. about 1520; earlier name was 'popinjay', q.v.; perh. fr. Fr. *perrot*, a variant of **pierrot**. One of a large group or order, Psittaci, of climbing birds, usually tropical or sub-tropical, with short curved beak, fleshy tongue, often of brilliant plumage, including the true parrots, genus *Psittacus*, of which the African 'grey parrot' is typical, and also the parakeets, cockatoos, macaws &c.; many kinds possess the faculty of imitating human voice and speech; whence Phr. *to learn, repeat, like a parrot*, without attaching any meaning to the words uttered.

parrot (II.), vb. trans., fr. prec. To repeat mechanically, utter (words &c.), without understanding.

parrot-fish, n. One of several varieties of fish, named from the brilliance of their colouring or the shape of their jaws.

parrotry, n. [1. párotri; 2. pǽrətri]. **parrot** & **-ry**. Unintelligent imitation; parrot-like repetition.

parry, vb. trans. & n. [1. pári; 2. pǽri], fr. Fr. *parer*, fr. Ital., fr. Lat. *parāre*, 'to prepare'. See **pare**. **1.** vb. trans. To ward off, turn aside, avert: *to parry a blow, an inquisitive question* &c. **2.** n. The act of parrying; a defensive action or movement, esp. in fencing, boxing, wrestling.

parse, vb. trans. [1. parz; 2. pāz]. Prob. fr. Lat. *pars*, 'part'. See **part (I.)**. (gram.) **1.** To describe (a word) by classifying it as a part of speech, and indicating the grammatical reasons for its inflexion, its syntactic relation to rest of sentence &c. **2.** To analyse, resolve (a sentence) into its component parts, describing each of these in respect of its grammatical function, and indicating the syntactic relations of each to the other words.

Parsee, n. [1. parsḗ; 2. pāsī], fr. Pers. *Pārsī*, 'Persian', fr. *Pars*, 'Persia'. Member of a religious community descended from the Persian refugees who fled to India at the time of the Mohammedan persecutions in the 8th cent., practising a form of Zoroastrianism.

Parseeism, n. [1. parsḗizm; 2. pāsīizəm]. Prec. & **-ism**. Religion of the Parsees.

parsimonious, adj. [1. pàrsimṓnius; 2. pāsimóuniəs]. **parsimony** & **-ous**. Of, characterized by, given to, parsimony; mean, niggardly.

parsimoniously, adv. Prec. & **-ly**. In a parsimonious manner.

parsimoniousness, n. See prec. & **-ness**. Quality of being parsimonious.

parsimony, parcimony, n. [1. pársimuni; 2. pā́siməni], fr. Lat. *parsimōnia*, also *parcimōnia*, 'frugality', fr. *pars-(um)*, P.P. type of *parcere*, 'to spare, be sparing; to hold back, refrain'; cp. *(com)pescere*, 'to curb, hold in check', earlier **com-parc-sc-*; fr. stem **par-*, 'small; limited', seen in *parvus*, 'small'; *parum*, 'too little', see **paraffin**; for the second element see **-mony**. **a** Sparingness in use or expenditure of money &c.; undue economy; extreme frugality; also (fig.) *to exercise parsimony of phrase*; **b** meanness, stinginess.

parsley, n. [1. pársli; 2. pā́sli]. M.E. *perseli*, fr. O. Fr. *persil*, influenced by O.E. *petersilige*, both fr. L. Lat. *petroselīnum*, fr. Gk. *petrosélīnon*, 'rock-parsley', fr. *pétra*, 'rock', see **petro-**, & *sélīnon*, 'parsley', possibly fr. base *(*s*)*wel-*, 'to turn, twist', cp. Gk. *hélinos*, 'vine tendril'; *eiléō*, 'roll'; *elúein*, 'to wind', & see **volute, wallow**. Biennial, umbelliferous herb, with bright green, finely divided, crinkled, slightly aromatic leaves, used for flavouring, and for garnishing dishes &c.; *cow parsley*, wild chervil.

parsnip, n. [1. pársnip; 2. pā́snip]. M.E. *pa(r)snepe*, fr. O. Fr., fr. Lat. *pastināca*, 'parsnip; carrot', fr. *pastin-(um)*, 'two-pronged fork for digging and planting'; cp. Lat. *pāla*, 'spade'. Second element is O.E. *nǣp*, 'turnip', fr. Lat. *nāpus*. See **turnip**. **a** Biennial, umbelliferous, large-leaved plant with large, conical, cream-coloured root; **b** root of this, used as culinary vegetable &c.

parson, n. [1. pársn; 2. pā́sn]. M.E. *persone*, already used in specif. sense; cp. Chaucer's *Canterbury Tales*, Prologue and Persones Tale; variant of **person**, esp. in Med. Lat. phr. *ecclesiae persōna*, the person or representative of the church in a parish. **a** Specif., *the parson*, incumbent of a specified parish; rector, vicar; **b** *a parson*, a clergyman; (colloq.) *parson's nose*, rump of fowl &c.

parsonage, n. [1. pársunij; 2. pā́sənidž]. Prec. & **-age**. Residence of parish priest; rectory; vicarage.

parson-bird, n. New Zealand bird with black plumage and tufts of white feathers on the throat.

parsonic, adj. [1. parsónik; 2. pāsǝ́nik]. **parson** & **-ic**. Pertaining to, characteristic of, a parson.

part (I.), n. [1. part; 2. pāt], fr. Lat. *part-(em)*, *pars*, 'portion, part'; borrowed already in O.E. though not common; also in M.E., fr. O. Fr.; cogn. w. Lat. *portio*, see **portion**. **1.** One of several portions into which anything may be or is divided; **a** a portion actually detached, or severed from the whole; piece, fragment, slice &c.: *a piece of marble which was obviously a part of a statue*; **b** a portion, area, theoretical division of anything, thought of as distinct from the rest, but regarded as contributing to make up a larger whole: *the upper part of his face was hidden; the thick part of the hand; this part of the country is colder than the rest*. **2. a** Something less than the whole: *to lose part of one's money; only part of his story is true*; Phr. *in part*, partly, partially; **b** a certain number but not all: *part of the congregation slept throughout the sermon; the greater part of my apple trees have no fruit this year*. **3.** Each of several equal portions or divisions of a whole: *a minute is the sixtieth part of an hour; a quart is the fourth part of a gallon; three parts of vinegar to one of oil*. **4.** Essential constituent, element, component: *our experiences are parts of ourselves; the better part of a man's nature*. Phr. *to take* (something said or done) *in good part*, not to be offended by. **5. a** Organ, member, of a living organism; **b** distinct piece or portion of a machine, which fulfils a specific function in the working of the whole: *spare parts of a motor* &c. **6.** Division, section, of a literary work; single instalment of a work published periodically in sections. **7.** (pl.) Area, region, of the earth's surface: *how long are you staying in these parts?; to travel in foreign parts*. **8. a** Individual concern, interest, duty: *it is the part of a wise man to ignore such rumours*; Phrs. *to have neither part nor lot in*, no concern or share in; *for my part*, so far as I am concerned; *very queer conduct on the part of Brown*, Brown has behaved very queerly; **b** function, action, assigned to be performed, share in what is being, has been, or is to be, done: *to take an active part in; I took, had, but a small part in these events*. **9. a** Actor's rôle, character, in a play: *the part of Hamlet*; Phrs. *to play a part*, to act deceitfully, assume false character &c., be insincere; *to play a humble, important, worthy &c., part*; **b** the words spoken by a character in a play: *the actors didn't know their parts*. **10.** Party, side, in transaction, dispute, interest, cause &c. opposed to another: *agreement between Jones on the one part and Brown on the other part*. Phr. *to take the part of*, be on the side of, side with, support. **11.** (pl.) Intellectual quality, characteristic of mind, character &c.; ability: *a man of parts; of excellent parts*. **12.** (mus.) **a** One of the melodies combining to make a harmony; **b** melody, succession of notes, assigned to single voice or instrument. **13.** (gram.) *Part of speech*, one of the categories into which words are divided according to their functions; *the parts of speech*, all these collectively; Phr. *to be careful of, correct, one's parts of speech*, take care of, amend, one's grammar, or style generally.

part (II.), vb. trans. & intrans., fr. O. Fr. *partir*, fr. Lat. *partīre, partīri*, 'to divide', fr. *part-*, stem of *pars*, 'part'. See prec. **A.** trans. **1.** (archaic) To divide into shares, distribute: *to part the booty; 'They parted My garments among them'*. **2. a** (i.) To divide into parts, sections; (ii.) to sever: *the strain parted the rope*; **b** (i.) to cause to fork, branch; to divide; *an island parts the river into two branches; a smile parted her lips*; (ii.) specif., *to part one's hair*, to brush it in two different directions on either side of a line. **3.** To come between, separate, sunder: *a strait parts the island from the mainland*. **4.** To separate, intervene between: **a** to disunite, sever relationship or companionship of: *'Till death us do part'* (Marriage Service); *friends long parted*. Phr. *to part company*, (i.) sever companionship, relations; (ii.) to travel in different directions; (iii.) to disagree, hold different opinions; **b** to force, and keep, asunder: *to part the combatants*. **B.** intrans. **1. a** To separate, go in different directions; **b** to forsake one another's company, break off relations: *to part in anger; let us part friends*. **2. a** To divide into sections or branches: *the stream, road, parted*; **b** to open up, be divided by a rift: *the clouds parted*. **C.** Followed by preposition. *Part with*, (i.) give up, surrender, resign possession of: *to part with one's house, horses*; (ii.) to dispense with services of: *to part with one's butler*.

partake, vb. trans. & intrans. [1. partā́k; 2. pātéik]. Back-formation fr. *partaker*. **part** & **take** & **-er**. **A.** trans. To have a share of, take part in, share: *'Say, shall my little bark attendant sail, Pursue the triumph and partake the gale?'* (Pope). **B.** intrans. **1.** To consume food or drink: *won't you have something to eat? thank you, I'd rather not partake just now; he had partaken rather freely; partake of*, to eat, or drink, some or all of: *to partake of a meal, of some mutton* &c. **2.** *Partake of*, to have something of the quality, nature, characteristics, of: *his character partakes of charlatanism*.

partaker, n. [1. partáker; 2. pātéikə]. See prec. One who takes part, or partakes in; participant.

parterre, n. [1. partár; 2. pātéə]. Fr. *par terre*, 'on the ground'. **1.** Level piece of turf in a garden, diversified by flower-beds or paths. **2.** Ground-floor of theatre.

parthenogenesis, n. [1. pàrthenōjénesis; 2. pàþenoudžénisis], fr. Gk. *parthénos*, 'girl, virgin'; second element perh. fr. a stem **then-*, in the sense of 'physical development', fr. base **gʷhen-*, 'to increase, grow; to be enlarged, swell'; cp. Gk. *euthéneia*, 'abundance'; see also **genesis**. Reproduction without fertilization by male element.

parthenogenetic, adj. [1. pàrthenōjenétik; 2. pàþinoudžinétik]. See prec. & **-etic.** Of, reproducing by, produced by, parthenogenesis.

Parthian, adj. [1. párthian; 2. páþiən], fr. *Parthia*, ancient kingdom N.E. of Persia, & **-an.** Of Parthia; Phr. *Parthian shot, shaft* &c., parting shot, thrust; remark made at moment of departure, like arrows shot backwards by flying Parthian horsemen.

partial, adj. [1. párshl; 2. páʃl], fr. O. Fr., fr. L. Lat. *partiāl-(is)*, 'partial, incomplete', fr. *part-*, stem of *pars*, 'part', see **part (I.)**, & **-ial. 1.** Forming, involving, only part of the whole; incomplete: *partial knowledge*; *a partial success*; *partial eclipse*, in which only part of the sun &c. is obscured. **2.** Taking a side or part; biased, prejudiced, influenced by personal motives, views &c.; unfair: *a partial witness, judge, opinion* &c. Phr. *partial to*, having a liking for, fond of, addicted to.

partiality, n. [1. pàrshiáliti; 2. pàʃiǽliti], fr. Med. Lat. *partiālitāt-(em)*, 'partiality'. **partial** & **-ity. 1.** Biased judgement, prejudice. **2.** Special fondness, liking (followed by *to* or *for*).

partially, adv. [1. párshali; 2. páʃəli]. See prec. & **-ly. 1.** Not entirely; incompletely, partly. **2.** With bias in one direction, in a prejudiced manner.

participant, n. [1. partísipant; 2. pātísipənt], fr. Lat., fr. Pres. Part. of *particip-(āre)*, 'to partake of'. See next word & **-ant.** One who has a share, part; partaker.

participate, vb. intrans. & trans. [1. partísipāt; 2. pātísipeit], fr. Lat. *participāt-(um)*, P.P. type of *participāre*, 'to partake of, share in', fr. *parti-(s)*, genit. of *pars*, 'part', see **part (I.)**, & *-cip-*, fr. base of *capere*, 'to take', see **captive. 1.** intrans. **a** (i.) To have a share in, partake: *to participate in something with others*; *to participate in another's joy*; *to participate in a discussion, festivities* &c.; (ii.) to have a share in guilt of: *to participate in a crime*; **b** to partake of, have some of the qualities, nature, of. **2.** trans. (rare) To have a share in, have, experience, in common with others: *to participate something with others.*

participation, n. [1. pàrtisipáshun; 2. pàtisipéiʃən]. Prec. & **-ion.** Act of participating, act of sharing; act of taking part.

participial, adj. [1. pàrtisípial; 2. pàtisípiəl], fr. Lat. *particip-(ium)*, 'sharing; participle', see **participle**, & **-ial.** Of, pertaining to, based on, characterized by, of the nature of, a participle.

participially, adv. Prec. & **-ly.** In a participial manner; as a participle.

participle, n. [1. pártisipl; 2. pátisipl], fr. O. Fr. *participe*, fr. Lat. *participium*, 'a sharing, partaking; participle', fr. *particip-(āre)*, 'to participate'. See **participate.** Verbal adjective, part of a verb; often retaining some attributes of verb, such as tense and power of governing an object, but often having also the adjectival function of qualifying nouns.

particle, n. [1. pártikl; 2. pátikl], fr. Lat. *particula*, 'small part', fr. *part-*, stem of *pars*, 'part', see **part (I.)**, & **-cule. 1. a** Very small part, minute fragment; smallest amount: *a particle of dust* &c.; *not a particle of food*; **b** also of non-material things: *without a particle of feeling, truth* &c. **2.** One of the minor, indeclinable parts of speech.

parti-coloured, party-coloured, adj. [1. párti kùlurd; 2. páti kàləd]. Prob. fr. **party (II.).** Differently coloured in different parts; variegated.

particular (I.), adj. [1. partíkūlar; 2. pətíkjulə], fr. O. Fr. *particuler*, fr. Lat. *particulāris*, 'concerning a part', fr. *particula*, 'a small part'. See **particle** & **-ar. 1.** Distinct, separate, referring to one as distinguished from others: *to do something in a particular way*; *in a particular case*; *why did you choose that particular subject?* Phr. *in particular*, especially, as distinct from others. **2. a** Individual, peculiar, not general: *one's own particular weakness*; *Particular Baptists*, religious body holding the doctrine of *particular election* (see **particularism**); **b** (log.) affirmed or denied of part only, limited in application to a single class; contrasted with *universal* or *general*: *to reason from the general to the particular.* **3.** Special, noteworthy, remarkable: *of no particular importance*; *to take particular notice*; *nothing particular to do.* **4.** Minute, detailed, exact: *to give a full and particular account.* **5.** Fastidious, giving attention to details, not easily pleased: *very particular about one's food, in one's dress* &c.

particular (II.), n., fr. prec. **a** Detail, single item: *exact in every particular*; Phr. *to go into particulars*, to give details; **b** (pl.) detailed account, report, statement, specification: *to give particulars.*

particularism, n. [1. partíkūlarizm; 2. pətíkjulərizəm]. Prec. & **-izm. 1.** Doctrine that redemption is confined to particular individuals, and not extended to the human race as a whole. **2.** Exclusive devotion to a single interest, party &c. **3.** Policy of allowing individual states in a federation &c. to act independently.

particularist, n. [1. partíkūlarist; 2. pətíkjulərist]. See prec. & **-ist.** Adherent of particularism, in theology, politics &c.

particularity, n. [1. partikūláriti; 2. pətikjulǽriti]. **particular (I.)** & **-ity. 1.** Minuteness of detail, exactness. **2.** (rare) Quality of being particular; fastidiousness, niceness.

particularization, n. [1. partikūlarīzáshun; 2. pətikjuləraizéiʃən]. See next word & **-ation.** Act of particularizing; state of being particularized.

particularize, vb. trans. [1. partíkūlarīz; 2. pətíkjuləraiz]. **particular (II.)** & **-ize.** To enumerate, give particulars of, specify.

particularly, adv. [1. partíkūlarli; 2. pətíkjuləli]. **particular (I.)** & **-ly. 1.** Individually, specifically, distinctly: *that point was particularly mentioned.* **2.** Especially, remarkably: *not particularly difficult.* **3.** In detail; item by item.

parting (I.), n. [1. párting; 2. pátiŋ]. **part (II.)** & **-ing. 1.** Departure, leave-taking, separation. **2.** Point of division, separation, branching; esp. *the parting of the ways*, branching out of two roads; also (fig.) of choice between two opposed courses. **3.** Line of division made in combing the hair.

parting (II.), adj., fr. prec. (only attrib.) Spoken at, performed at, given at, time of departure: *parting words*; *a parting gift* &c.

partisan, partizan (I.), n. & adj. [1. pàrtizán, pártizan; 2. pàtizǽn, pátizæn], fr. Fr., fr. Ital. *partigiano*, fr. *parte*, 'part', see **part (I.)**, & **-an. 1.** n. **a** Adherent of party, cause &c., often used to imply blind and unreasoning devotion; **b** (hist.) Member of light-armed irregular troops employed on special service, in guerilla warfare &c. **2.** adj. Of, exhibiting, characterized by, blind devotion to a party &c.

partisan, partizan (II.), n. [1. pártizan; 2. pátizən], fr. Fr. *partizane*, fr. Ital. *partisana*; etymol. doubtful. (hist.) Long-handled pike, a kind of halberd.

partite, adj. [1. pártīt; 2. pátait], fr. Lat. *partīt-(um)*, P.P. type of *partīri*, 'to divide'. See **part (II.).** Divided, parted.

partition (I.), n. [1. partíshun; 2. pātíʃən], fr. Fr., fr. Lat. *partītiōn-(em)*, 'division', fr. *partīt-(um)*, P.P. type of *partīri*, 'to divide', see **part (II.)**, & **-ion. 1.** Act of dividing; state of being divided; division into parts or sections. **2.** Part divided from another; division, compartment. **3.** Something that divides; barrier, esp. interior wall between two rooms, cavities &c.

partition (II.), vb. trans., fr. prec. **1.** To divide into parts, sections, compartments &c. **2.** *Partition off*, to separate, cut off, by means of a partition: *to partition off part of a room* &c.

partitive, adj. & n. [1. pártitiv; 2. pátitiv], fr. Lat. *partītīv-(us)*, 'partitive'. See **partite** & **-ive. 1.** adj. **a** Having function of dividing; **b** (gram.) expressing a part, or relation of part to a whole: *partitive genitive.* **2.** n. A partitive word.

partitively, adv. Prec. & **-ly.** In a partitive manner; as a partitive.

partly, adv. [1. pártli; 2. pátli]. **part (I.)** & **-ly.** Affecting a part only; in part; to some extent; in some degree.

partner (I.), n. [1. pártner; 2. pátnə]. Prob. a variant of **parcener. 1.** One who shares, takes part, is associated, with another in action: *a partner in crime.* Various special uses: **2.** Person engaged, associated, with another in a commercial business, and taking a share in the profits or losses; *sleeping partner*, one taking no part in the management of the business. **3.** Either of two spouses. **4.** One of two persons playing on the same side in a game played by four people. **5. a** One of two persons dancing together; **b** either of two who go in to dinner, and sit, together. **6.** (naut., in pl.) Wooden framework helping to strengthen mast.

partner (II.), vb. trans., fr. prec. **1.** To join, bring together, associate, as partners. **2.** To act as the partner of, esp. in a game or dance.

partnerless, adj. [1. pártnerles; 2. pátnəlis]. **partner (I.)** & **-less.** Without a partner.

partnership, n. [1. pártnership; 2. pátnəʃip]. **partner (I.)** & **-ship. a** The state of being a partner or partners; **b** joint concern, interests, ownership.

part-owner, n. Person owning something jointly with another or others.

partridge, n. [1. pártrij; 2. pátridž]. M.E. *pertriche*, fr. Fr. *perdrix*, fr. Lat. *perdix*, fr. Gk. *pérdix*, 'partridge', perh. imitative, fr. the sound made by the bird on rising fr. the ground. **1.** A small bird related to the grouse family, abundant in cultivated areas in England, and prized for sporting purposes, and as food, esp. the common grey partridge, *Perdix cinerea*; and the red-legged partridge, *Caccabis rufa.* **2.** Name applied, in U.S.A. and Canada, where the true partridge is not found, to willow grouse and Virginian quail.

partridge-wood, n. **1.** Hard, variegated wood used in cabinet-work &c., obtained from tropical America. **2.** Thick, speckled crust formed on oak &c. by a kind of fungus.

part-song, n. Song, with or without instrumental accompaniment, the parts (bass, tenor, alto, and soprano) of which are sung by different persons or groups of persons, so as to form a harmony.

parturient, adj. [1. partúrient; 2. pātjúriənt], fr. Lat. *parturient-(em)*, Pres. Part. of *parturīre*, 'to be in labour', fr. *part-(um)*, P.P. type of *parere*, 'to bring forth'. See **parent.** About to give birth; in labour, travailing; also (fig.) of mind &c.

parturition, n. [1. pàrtūríshun; 2. pàtjuríʃən], fr. Lat. *parturītiōn-(em)*, 'a bringing forth', fr. *parturīt-(um)*, P.P. type of *parturīre*, 'to be in labour', see prec., & **-ion.** Act of giving birth; labour, travail.

party (I.), n. [1. párti; 2. páti], fr. Fr. *partie*, fr. fem. P.P. of *partir*, 'to divide'. See **part (II.). 1. a** Group or body of persons holding the same opinions, forming an opposing side, in a controversial, disputed, or political matter: persons united by common cause, interests, policy &c.; **b** political system based on organized parties: *to put public interest before party.* **2.** Group of persons assembled for some common purpose; specif. **a** social gathering; the guests who form this: *to give a party; a tea, dinner, party* &c.; **b** group of persons associated for the purpose of engaging in some common occupation or amusement: *a reading, sketching, fishing, party* &c. **3.** Small company, body, of soldiers &c. detailed for special service: *a firing-party, foraging party* &c. **4.** One of the persons or groups of persons engaging in a contract, transaction, legal action &c. **5.** Person taking part in, having full knowledge of, consenting to, supporting, an action; accessory: *to be a party to a conspiracy.* **6.** (vulg. or facet.) Person: *a cheery, dismal, old party.*

party (II.), adj., fr. Fr. *parti,* P.P. of *partir,* 'to divide'. See **part** (II.). (her., of shield) Divided into parts with different tinctures; *party per pale,* divided vertically through the centre.

party-coloured, adj. See **parti-coloured.**

party-spirit, n. Devotion to a party; partisanship.

party-spirited, adj. Showing, feeling, party-spirit.

party-wall, n. Common wall separating two houses.

parvenu, n. [1. párvenū; 2. pā́vənjū, pārvənȳ]. Fr., P.P. of *parvenir,* 'to arrive', fr. Lat. *pervenīre,* 'to come', fr. **per-** & *venīre,* 'to come'. See **venue.** Person who has rapidly or suddenly passed from obscurity to an important position in society, esp. one who has recently gained wealth or power; an upstart. Also attrib.: *a parvenu peer.*

parvis, n. [1. párvis; 2. pā́vis], fr. O. Fr. *parevis,* fr. Med. Lat. *paravīsus,* fr. Lat. *paradīsus,* 'paradise'; later, 'court in front of St. Peter's in Rome'. See **paradise.** Enclosed space in front of church.

pas, n. [1. pah; 2. pā]. Fr. *pas,* 'step'. See **pace** (I.). **1. a** A step, esp. in dancing; **b** dance; *pas seul, pas de deux,* dance for one person, for two persons. **2.** Right of preceding, precedence: *to have, give, take, the pas.*

Paschal, adj. [1. páskl; 2. pǽskl], fr. Fr. *pascal,* fr. L. Lat. *paschālis,* 'of the Passover; of Easter', fr. *pascha,* 'Passover; Easter', fr. Gk. *páskha,* fr. Heb. *pesakh,* 'Passover', & **-al. 1.** Connected with the Jewish Passover. **2.** Of, pertaining to, connected with, Easter.

pasha, pacha, n. [1. pasháh, pásha, páhsha; 2. pæʃā́, pǽʃə, pāʃa]. Turkish *pasha.* Title of Turkish military officers or civil officials of high rank; *pasha of three tails, two tails, one tail,* of first, second, third grade, from horse-tail ensigns formerly carried before them in war.

pashalic, pachalic, n. [1. pasháhlik, páshalik; 2. pæʃā́lik, pǽʃəlik]. Turkish *pashalik.* Jurisdiction, province, of a pasha.

pashm, n. [1. páshm; 2. pǽʃəm]. Pers. *pašm,* 'wool'; cp. Scrt. *pakšman,* 'hair, eye-brows'; Lith. *peszù,* 'to pull the hair of; to pluck, tear out'; Gk. *pékos,* 'fleece, wool'; *péktein,* 'to comb, shear'; Lat. *pecten,* 'comb', see **pecten**; *pexus,* 'woolly'; O.H.G. *fahs,* O.E. *feax,* 'hair'; O.N. *fax,* 'mane'. Fine wool obtained from goats in Tibet and North India, used for Cashmere shawls.

pasque-flower, n. [1. páhsk flòur; 2. pā́skflàuə]. Earlier *passe-flower,* fr. Fr. *passefleur,* fr. *passer,* 'to surpass', see **pass** (I.), assimilated to obs. *Pasque,* 'Easter', fr. Fr., fr. L. Lat. *pascha,* 'Easter'. See **Paschal.** One of several varieties of anemone, esp. one with purplish, bell-shaped flowers.

pasquinade, n. [1. paskwinā́d; 2. pæskwinéid], fr. Ital. *pasquinata,* fr. *Pasquino,* name given to a broken statue, found at Rome in 1501, on which lampoons &c. were posted. Lampoon, esp. one exhibited in public place.

pass (I.), vb. intrans. & trans. [1. pahs; 2. pās], fr. Fr. *passer,* fr. Lat. *pass-(us),* 'pace'. See **pace** (I.). **A.** intrans. **1.** To proceed, move, go forward, advance: *will you kindly allow me to pass?; pass along, by, on, out* &c. **2. a** To go by; to reach point of observation, or other specific point, and move beyond it: *to see a person pass; to notice a thing in passing;* **b** (of time, &c.) to elapse, be spent: *how quick time passes;* **c** (of speech &c.) be uttered: *the statement was allowed to pass unchallenged.* **3.** To become altered in character, circumstance &c.; **a** to change, be converted, transformed: *to pass from one state into another;* **b** to be transferred, fall naturally: *the estate passed to his heirs;* **c** (football, hockey, of player) to hand, kick, hit, ball to another player. **4. a** To be handed on, be transferred, given and received: *the goblet passed from hand to hand;* **b** to circulate, be current: *a Bank of England note used to pass anywhere.* **5. a** To be removed from sphere of one's observation, sensation &c.; to come to an end, cease, be exhausted: *the pain has now passed; his anger passed; all things must pass;* **b** specif., to die: (usually) *pass away.* **6.** (of events) To happen, take place, occur: *to observe what passes; did nothing pass between you?* **7. a** To be accepted, tolerated, as adequate, suitable, permissible: *it will pass;* **b** to be approved, accepted, agreed to, by legislative body &c.: *the bill, resolution, proposal &c., passed;* **c** (of candidate for examination) to reach required standard, satisfy examiner. **8.** To be known, generally recognized: *to pass by the name of.* **9.** (of judgement) To be pronounced: *judgement passed for the plaintiff* &c. **10.** (cards) To decline playing or declaring in a given round. **B.** trans. **1. a** To go by, go beyond, or away from: *to pass a person in the street; to pass a building* &c.; **b** (of mental action) to reach and get beyond, advance farther than: *we have passed that page; to have passed the early stages.* **2. a** To go through, across, over &c.; to traverse: *to pass an ocean, a desert, frontier, range of hills* &c.; **b** to go between, enter by way of: *to pass the gates; no food has passed my lips.* **3. a** To cause to go, move, direct motion of: *to pass one's hand over one's eyes;* **b** to place, put, guide, into position: *to pass a rope round an object;* **c** to cause to penetrate: *to pass a needle through a piece of material, a sword through a person's body* &c. **4.** To cause to go by, proceed past: *to pass troops in review;* also (fig.) *to pass (events &c.) in review,* contemplate, consider, successively. **5. a** To hand on, transfer, convey to another: *please pass the butter;* **b** to cause to circulate, give currency to: *to pass forged notes;* Phrs. *to pass the time of day,* exchange greetings; *to pass a remark,* speak, make an observation; **c** (football, hockey) to hand, kick, or hit (ball) to another player. **6. a** To surpass, excel: *the splendour of King Solomon passed anything before or since;* **b** to exceed, be greater than, go beyond: *to pass one's comprehension; 'the peace of God that passeth all understanding'.* **7. a** To approve, sanction, give consent to: *the Commons passed the Bill; to pass a resolution;* **b** to be approved, sanctioned, accepted by: *the Bill passed the Committee;* **c** to reach standard required by: *to pass an examination, examiner.* Phr. *to pass muster* (see **muster** (I.)). **8.** Specif. (law) *to pass sentence, judgement (upon),* to pronounce as judge the sentence of the Court, declare result of trial, and award penalty. **9.** To spend, consume: *to pass time, the winter* &c. **C.** Followed by adverbs and prepositions. *Pass away,* to come to an end; specif., to die. *Pass by,* **1.** intrans. & trans., to go past, pass; **2.** trans., to omit, ignore, disregard. *Pass for,* to be commonly regarded as, be accepted as, be taken for: *to pass for a rich man. Pass off,* **1.** intrans., **a** to decrease in activity or intensity: *the pain is passing off;* **b** (of events, proceedings &c.) to be carried through, take place; **2.** trans., to impose, palm off, represent falsely: *to pass oneself off as. Pass over,* to overlook, disregard. *Pass through,* **a** to traverse; **b** (fig.) to experience, go through.

pass (II.), n., fr. prec. Act, fact, process, of passing (in various senses). **1.** Standard which satisfies examiners without securing honours: *to miss a class and take,* or *get, a pass.* **2.** Juncture, critical condition or stage of events, or circumstances; crisis: *things have come to a strange pass.* Phr. *a pretty pass,* a deplorable, very exceptional, almost incredible, state of affairs. **3.** A stroking gesture of the hands; said esp. of those made by mesmerists. **4.** Authorization to go somewhere, occupy a seat &c.; small object, tally, or document &c. indicating possession of such permission; usually *free pass.*

pass (III.), n., fr. Fr. *pas,* 'step, passage'. See **pace** (I.). **1. a** Gap, defile, passage, leading through mountains; **b** (mil.) fortified place guarding pass forming entrance to country. Phrs. *to hold the pass,* to defend and maintain a cause or interest; *to sell the pass,* give away a position; betray a cause &c. **2.** Channel giving entrance to partially enclosed body of water at mouth of river &c. **3.** Narrow passage for fish over or at side of weir &c.

passable, adj. [1. páhsabl; 2. pā́səbl]. **pass** (I.) & **-able. 1.** Capable of being passed, traversed, crossed. **2.** Of a kind or quality that can be passed as adequate; fairly good, tolerable.

passably, adv. Prec. & **-ly.** In a passable manner, fairly well.

passage (I.), n. [1. pásij; 2. pǽsidž], fr. Fr. *passage.* **pass** (I.) & **-age. 1.** Act of passing, proceeding, crossing, traversing; transit, movement from one place to another. Phr. *bird of passage,* migratory bird; (fig.) person who stays in a place only for a time; temporary sojourner. Various special uses: **2.** Conveyance, transportation, by sea or air; voyage from point to point; crossing: *to have a rough passage.* **3. a** Right to be conveyed, place, accommodation, on ship: *to book one's passage;* **b** sum paid for this: *to pay one's passage.* **4.** Change, transition, from one physical or mental state to another. **5.** Means of access; **a** a path, way, road, clearing: *a passage through a thicket, between boulders;* **b** an opening, a channel: *a passage into a bay, through rocks* &c.; **c** an opening, way, clear of obstacles: *to force a passage through a crowd.* **6.** Possibility, right, of passing: *No passage this way!* **7.** Relatively narrow corridor in a building, running along the outside of a series of rooms and giving access to these; also such an internal corridor leading from one part of a building to another. **8.** Occurrence, episode, series of incidents; specif. **a** (pl.) what passes between two persons in conversation &c.: *to have stormy passages with;* **b** *passage of arms,* (lit. and fig.) fight, combat; dispute. **9.** Detached portion of book, speech &c. read, printed, quoted, or referred to separately: *to read a passage from Scripture.*

passage (II.), vb. intrans. & trans., fr. Fr. *passager,* fr. Ital. *passeggiare,* fr. *paseggio,* 'a walk', fr. Lat. *pass-(us),* 'pace'. See **pace** (I.). **1.** intrans. **a** (of rider) To cause horse to move sideways by pressure of the knee on its side; **b** (of horse) to move sideways, draw aside. **2.** trans. To cause to move aside or sideways.

passage-way, n. Corridor, gallery, passage.

passant, adj. [1. pásant; 2. pǽsənt], fr. Fr. *passant,* Pres. Part. of *passer,* 'to pass'. See **pass** (I.). (her., of animal) Represented as walking, having the dexter fore-paw raised; *passant guardant,* same, but with head turned so as to look out from the field, i.e. full face; *passant reguardant,* same, but with head turned to sinister side of shield, i.e. looking backwards.

pass-book, n. Book supplied by bank, showing sums deposited and withdrawn by customer.

passé, adj. [1. páhsā; 2. pasē]. Fr., P.P. of *passer,* 'to pass'. See **pass** (I.). **1.** Having lost the freshness and beauty of the prime; (esp. of a woman) *passée,* withered.

passementerie, n. [1. pahsmáhnterē; 2. pasmā́tərī]. Fr., fr. Fr. *passement,* 'trimming, gold lace' &c. See **pass (I.)** & **-ment** & **-ery.** Dress trimming of braid, beaded lace &c.

passenger, n. [1. pásenjer; 2. pǽsindžə]. M.E. & O. Fr. *passager*. **passage (I.)** & **-er**; for infixed *n* cp. **messenger. 1.** Person travelling in public conveyance by rail, road, or esp. sea; *foot-passenger*, one traversing the roads or streets on foot. **2.** (by transf., colloq.) Oarsman in boat who doesn't pull his weight; also (fig.) *the cabinet carries a few passengers.*

passenger-pigeon, n. Gregarious N. American pigeon, *Ectopistes migratorius*, with long, pointed wings, capable of long flight.

passe-partout, n. [1. pahs partōō; 2. pās pātū́]. Fr., 'pass everywhere'. **1.** Master-key. **2.** Kind of light picture-frame, usually of pasteboard and glass, with the picture held in position between these by means of strips of paper &c. pasted over the edges.

passer-by, n. [1. páhser bī́; 2. pā́sə bái]. Person who passes, walks past; a casually encountered stranger.

passerine, adj. & n. [1. páserīn; 2. pǽsərain]. Lat. *passer*, 'sparrow', etymol. doubtful, & **-ine. 1.** adj. **a** Belonging to the order of perchers; **b** of, pertaining to, like, a sparrow. **2.** n. Passerine bird, percher.

passibility, n. [1. pàhs-, pàsibíliti; 2. pā̀s-, pæ̀sibíliti], fr. L. Lat. *passibilitāt-(em)*, 'passibility', fr. *passibil-(is)*, 'passible', see next word, & **-ity.** Quality of being passible.

passible, adj. [1. pásibl; 2. pǽsibl], fr. L. Lat. *passibil-(is)*, 'capable of suffering', fr. *pass-(um)*, P.P. type of *pati*, 'to suffer', see **patient,** & **-ible.** (esp. theol.) Capable of feeling or suffering.

passim, adv. [1. pásim; 2. pǽsim]. Lat. *passim*, 'hither and thither; here and there; indiscriminately', fr. *pass-(um)*, P.P. type of *pandere*, 'to spread out, scatter about'; this is prob. fr. base *pat-*, seen in *patēre*, 'to lie open, be spread out', w. nasal infixed, & the medial consonant *t* voiced after the nasal. See **patent.** (in referring to word, phrase &c. in specified author, book, passage &c.) Here and there, throughout, in all parts.

passing (I.), adj. & adv. [1. páhsing; 2. pā́siŋ], fr. Pres. Part. of **pass (I.). 1.** adj. **a** Not lasting, transient: *the passing moment; passing joys;* **b** incidental, casual: *a passing reference.* **2.** adv. (archaic) Surpassingly, very, exceedingly: *passing strange, rich* &c.

passing (II.), vbl. n. See **pass (I.)** & **-ing.** Act of one who, process exhibited by that which, passes. In various senses. **1. a** Departure, disappearance: *the passing of the old régime;* **b** departure from life; death: *the passing of Arthur.* **2.** Process of moving past, passage onward: *to watch the passing of a procession.* **3.** Lapse, flight: *the passing of time.* **4.** Occurrence, enactment: *the passing of great events.*

passing-bell, n., fr. prec. Bell tolled immediately after a death.

passing-note, n. (mus.) Note introduced to secure smooth passage between two notes or chords, but not essential to the harmony.

passion (I.), n. [1. páshun; 2. pǽʃən], fr. O. Fr., fr. Lat. *passiōn-(em)*, 'suffering; affection, emotion', fr. *pass-(um)*, P.P. type of *pati*, 'to suffer', see **patient,** & **-ion. 1.** Strong feeling, intense emotion; specif. **a** violent rage, fury: *to fly into a passion;* **b** powerful enthusiasm: *a passion for gardening;* **c** sexual love or desire. Specif. **2.** (cap.) **a** sufferings of Christ, esp. on the Cross; **b** Gospel narrative of this; **c** musical setting of this narrative.

passion (II.), vb. intrans., fr. prec. (poet.) To feel and express passion.

passional (I.), n. [1. páshunal; 2. pǽʃənəl], fr. Med. Lat. *passiōnāle*, 'passional', fr. neut. form of Lat. adj. *passiōnālis*, 'passionate'. **passion (I.)** & **-al.** Book containing an account of the sufferings of saints and martyrs.

passional (II.), adj., fr. Lat. *passiōnāl-(is)*, 'passionate'. **passion** & **-al.** (rare, poet.) Pertaining to, characterized by, arising from, passion.

passionate, adj. [1. páshunat; 2. pǽʃənit], fr. Med. Lat. *passionāt-(us)*, 'passionate'. See **passion (I.)** & **-ate. 1.** Capable, susceptible, of passion; swayed, inspired, by passion. **2.** Readily inclined to anger; violent, quick-tempered. **3.** Expressing, exhibiting, passion. **4.** (of emotion &c.). Springing from, rooted in, passion; intense, ardent, fervid: *passionate love, hatred, desire; passionate loyalty.*

passionately, adv. Prec. & **-ly.** In a passionate manner.

passionateness, n. See prec. & **-ness.** Quality of being passionate.

passion-flower, n. Genus, *Passiflora*, of climbing plants with large flowers, named from the fancied resemblance of the flower to the instruments of Christ's Passion, the 'corona' representing the crown of thorns &c.

Passionist, n. [1. páshunist; 2. pǽʃənist]. **passion** & **-ist.** Member of a Roman Catholic order especially devoted to keeping in memory the Passion of Christ.

passionless, adj. [1. páshunles; 2. pǽʃənlis]. **passion** & **-less.** Not feeling, or expressing, not moved by, passion; free from passion, cold, unemotional.

passionlessly, adv. Prec. & **-ly.** In a passionless manner.

passionlessness, n. See prec. & **-ness.** Quality of being passionless.

Passion-music, n. Musical setting of Gospel narrative of the Passion.

Passion-play, n. Dramatic representation of the Passion of Christ.

Passion Sunday, n. Fifth Sunday in Lent.

Passion Week, n. Week before Easter; Holy Week.

passive (I.), adj. [1. pásiv; 2. pǽsiv], fr. Lat. *passīv-(us)*, 'capable of suffering'; (gram.) 'passive', fr. *pass-(um)*, P.P. type of *pati*, 'to suffer', see **patient,** & **-ive. 1.** (of persons, mental states &c.) Acted upon by external agency, receiving external impressions, but not acting: *to remain passive; to take a passive interest in events.* **2.** In a state of quiescence; inactive, inert; offering no active opposition. Phrs. *passive debt*, one on which no interest is paid; *passive resistance*, one unaccompanied by overt or active measures. **4.** (gram., of vbs. & vbl. forms) Designating that voice in which the grammatical subject is acted upon by the verb, and undergoes the action expressed by this, instead of performing it.

passive (II.), n., fr. prec. (gram.) Passive voice.

passively, adv. **passive (I.)** & **-ly.** In a passive manner.

passiveness, n. See prec. & **-ness.** State or quality of being passive; passivity.

passivity, n. [1. pasíviti; 2. pæsíviti]. **passive (I.)** & **-ity.** Passiveness.

pass-key, n. **a** Key which opens several locks; a master-key; **b** latch-key.

passman, n. [1. páhsman; 2. pā́smən]. One taking pass degree at University.

Passover, n. [1. páhsòver; 2. pā́sòuvə]. **pass (I.)** & **over**; translating Heb. *pesakh*, cp. **Paschal. 1. a** Jewish feast commemorating the night on which the destroying angel passed over the houses of the Israelites and smote the Egyptians (Exod. xii. 27); **b** lamb sacrificed at the Feast of the Passover (Exod. xii. 21): *to eat the Passover.* **2.** (fig.) Christ: '*Christ our Passover is sacrificed for us*' (1 Cor. v. 7).

passport, n. [1. páhsport; 2. pā́spɔ̄t], fr. Fr. *passeport*; **pass (I.)** & **port (I.),** 'harbour'. **1.** (rare) Official document granted by a State to ship, giving permission to leave port and requesting privilege of entry into a foreign port; usually styled 'sea letter'; it is carried by neutral vessel as certificate of neutrality. **2.** Official document granted to a native of country by his government, to enable him to travel abroad, certifying his identity, stating purpose of his visit to a specified country, and constituting the official sanction of his journey. **3.** Personal quality, endowment of mind or body, which serves to recommend its possessor to the favour and esteem of others, and to secure him wide acceptance: *good looks and good manners are a ready passport to society; a passport to one's affections, good graces* &c.

password, n. [1. páhswërd; 2. pā́swə̄d]. (mil.) Secret word identifying person using it as entitled to enter, pass sentries, through camp &c.; watchword.

past (I.), adj. [1. pahst; 2. pāst]. P.P. of **pass (I.). 1. a** (of time) Gone by, elapsed, ended: *the years that are past; one's past life;* **b** recently gone by: *during the past week;* **c** that has occurred in the past: *past danger, sins* &c. **2.** (gram.) Expressing action accomplished, or occurrence taking place in the past: *past participle; past tense.*

past (II.), n., fr. prec. **1.** Time that has gone by; time before the present, usually *the past.* **2. a** That which has happened, been done, in the past: *let us think of the future, we cannot undo the past;* **b** person's past life, actions, experiences &c.; specif., doubtful antecedents, questionable career: *a lady with a past.*

past (III.), prep., fr. **past (I.). 1. a** Beyond in time; after: *past ten o'clock; half-past one: past middle age;* **b** beyond in space; up to and further than: *to walk past the gate.* **2.** Beyond the limits, action, power of: *past cure; past endurance; past work; past comprehension;* Phr. *past praying for*, in a desperate condition or situation; beyond hope of amendment.

past (IV.), adv. See prec. So as to reach a point and go beyond it (in time or space); by: *to walk past; the years flew past.*

paste (I.), n. [1. pāst; 2. peist]. O. Fr., fr. L. Lat. *pasta*, fr. Gk. *pástē*, 'barley-mash', fr. *pássein*, 'to sprinkle'; etymol. doubtful. **1.** Soft, slightly moist, plastic compound; esp. mixture of flour with butter &c., formed into a dough and baked or boiled for meat pies or pudding or fruit tarts &c. **2.** Soft, thick, moist compound made by crushing and beating various ingredients together: *almond paste; anchovy paste* &c. **3.** Adhesive compound of flour or starch and water &c., used by paper-hangers, book-binders, bill-posters &c., or for pasting cuttings into a book &c. Phr. *scissors and paste*, of book or other publication, not an original composition but consisting of a patchwork of extracts from other books pieced and vamped together. **4. a** The vitreous compound used in making artificial gems; **b** the moistened, prepared clay used in making pottery and porcelain.

paste (II.), vb. trans., fr. prec. **1.** To fasten, stick, with paste; also *paste up*, (i.) to affix to wall &c. with paste: *to paste up a notice;* (ii.) close by pasting: *paste up a window; paste in*, fasten into a book with paste. **2.** To paste paper on to.

pasteboard, n. [1. pāstbord; 2. péistbɔ̄d]. **1.** Stiff sheet made of pieces of paper pasted together. **2.** Anything made of or remotely resembling pasteboard; small card, e.g. visiting-card &c.

pastel (I.), n. [1. pastél, pástel; 2. pæstél, pǽstel]. Fr., fr. Ital. *pastillo*, dimin. of Ital. & Lat. *pasta*. See **paste (I.). a** Compound of dry pigment and gum, used for making coloured crayons; **b** method of drawing with pastel on special paper; **c** drawing made in pastel.

pastel (II.), n. See prec. **a** Woad; **b** dye obtained from the plant.

pastel(l)ist, n. [1. pastélist, pástelist; 2. pæstélist, pǽstəlist]. **pastel (I.)** & **-ist.** Artist working in pastel.

pastern, n. [1. páhstern, pástern; 2. pā́stən, pǽstən], fr. O. Fr. *pasturon*, fr. O. Fr. *pasture*, 'tether for horse at pasture'. See **pasture** & **pastor.** Part of horse's foot between fetlock and hoof.

Pasteurism, n. [1. páhstêrizm; 2. pástàrizəm], fr. name of Fr. bacteriologist, Louis Pasteur (d. 1895), & **-ism.** Method of preventing or curing disease, esp. hydrophobia, by inoculations with the virus of the disease itself in attenuated form.

pasteurization, n. [1. pàhsterīzáshun; 2. pàstəraizéiʃən]. See next word & **-ation.** Prevention of deterioration of liquids, esp. milk, by sterilization produced by heating.

pasteurize, vb. trans. [1. páhstěrīz; 2. pástàraiz], fr. Pasteur. See **Pasteurism** & **-ize.** To sterilize (milk &c.) by Pasteur's methods.

pasticcio, n. [1. pastícho; 2. pæstítʃou]. Ital., fr. *pasta*, 'paste', see **paste (I.).** Pastiche.

pastiche, n. [1. pástēsh, pastḗsh; 2. pǽstiʃ, pæstíʃ]. Fr., fr. prec. **a** Musical or artistic composition consisting of a medley of passages or parts from various sources connected together; **b** a literary work written in imitation of the style of another author.

pastil(le), n. [1. pástil, pastḗl; 2. pǽstil, pæstíl], fr. Fr. *pastille*, fr. Lat. *pastillus*, 'small loaf, roll; lozenge', prob. dimin. of *pasta*, 'barley-mash' see **paste (I.)**, or perh. fr. *pāst-(um)*, P.P. type of *pāsci*, 'to graze, feed', see **pastor. 1.** Small mass, often cone-shaped, of aromatic substance mixed with charcoal, burnt as fumigator &c. **2.** Lozenge.

pastime, n. [1. páhstīm; 2. pástaim]. **pass (I.)** & **time. a** Recreation, amusement, diversion; **b** specific amusement; a game.

past-master, n. **1. a** (freemasonry) One who has passed the Chair, i.e. who has been Worshipful Master of a Lodge; **b** corresponding position in a guild, or in one of several benevolent societies. **2.** One who has thoroughly mastered, and become proficient in a science, art, or profession: *a past-master in diplomacy, in the art of writing* &c.

pastor, n. [1. páhster; 2. pástə], fr. O. Fr., fr. Lat. *pāstōr-(em)*, 'shepherd'; Eccles. Lat. 'minister, priest', fr. *pāsci*, 'to graze, feed'; fr. base **pā-*, 'to feed', as in Lat. *pābulum*, 'food'; *pānis*, 'bread'; cogn. w. O. Slav. *pasą*, 'graze'; Gk. *patéomai*, 'I eat'; Goth. *fōdjan*; O.E. *fēdan*, 'to feed', see **feed**; O.E. *fōd*, 'food', see **food**, also **pabulum, panification. 1. a** Priest, minister, in charge of church, or congregation; chiefly used in England of Protestant Nonconformist ministers; also of Lutherans and French Calvinists; **b** spiritual adviser, supervisor: '*My spiritual pastors and masters*' (Church Catechism). **2.** The crested or rosy starling of Western Asia and Southern Europe.

pastoral (I.), adj. [1. páhstoral; 2. pástərəl]. Prec. & **-al. 1. a** Connected with shepherds or shepherd life; **b** (of land) used for pasture. **2.** (liter.) Pertaining to, dealing with, a highly conventionalized form of rustic life, describing the loves of shepherds and shepherdesses. **3.** Treating of, connected with, the duties of spiritual pastors; *pastoral epistles*, those of St. Paul to Timothy and Titus, dealing with the pastoral office; *pastoral staff*, one symbolical of episcopal authority, usually shaped like shepherd's crook, carried before, or held by, a bishop on ceremonial occasions; *pastoral theology*, practical branch of teaching and study dealing with the duties of spiritual pastors.

pastoral (II.), n., fr. prec. **1.** A pastoral poem; conventional poem of rustic life. **2.** Letter, address, from minister to congregation, or from a bishop to his diocese.

pastorale, n. [1. pàhstoráhle; 2. pàstərάli]. Ital., fr. Lat. *pāstōrālis*, 'pastoral'. See **pastoral (I.).** Musical composition dealing with pastoral subject, portraying pastoral scene(s).

pastoralism, n. [1. páhstoralizm; 2. pástərəlizəm]. **pastoral (I.)** & **-ism.** Pastoral character.

pastorality, n. [1. pàhstoráliti; 2. pàstərǽliti]. See prec. & **-ity.** State, quality, of being pastoral.

pastorally, adv. [1. páhstorali; 2. pástərəli]. **pastoral (I.)** & **-ly.** In a pastoral manner; like a pastor.

pastorate, n. [1. páhstorāt; 2. pástəreit], fr. Med. Lat. *pāstōrāt-(us)*, 'pastorate'. **pastor** & **-ate. 1.** Office of pastor. **2.** Whole body of pastors.

pastorship, n. [1. páhstorship; 2. pástəʃip]. **pastor** & **-ship.** Office, rank, of pastor.

pastry, n. [1. pāstri; 2. péistri]. **paste (I.)** & **-ry. a** Paste of flour, butter &c. rolled into a sheet and baked; pie-crust; **b** pies &c. collectively.

pastry-cook, n. Confectioner or baker, who makes pastry, cakes, and sweet things generally.

pasturable, adj. [1. páhschurabl; 2. pástʃərəbl]. **pasture** & **-able.** (of land &c.) Fit for pasture.

pasturage, n. [1. páhschurij; 2. pástʃəridž]. O. Fr. See **pasture** & **-age. 1. a** Grass &c. as food for cattle; **b** land yielding such food. **2.** Cattle-grazing as occupation &c.

pasture (I.), n. [1. páhschur; 2. pástʃə], fr. Fr., fr. L. Lat. *pāstūra*, 'pasture', fr. *pāst-(um)*, P.P. type of *pāsci*, 'to graze'. See **pastor** & **-ure. a** Grass and other herbage, considered as food for cattle; **b** land on which cattle are grazed; **c** piece of ground, field, kept for grazing.

pasture (II.), vb. intrans. & trans., fr. prec. **1.** intrans. To feed on pasture, to graze. **2.** trans. **a** To put (sheep or cattle) to pasture: *to pasture cattle*; **b** (of cattle, sheep) to graze, feed on, eat down (grass on); to treat, use (land), as pasture.

pasty (I.), n. [1. pásti, páhsti, pāsti; 2. pǽsti, pásti, péisti], fr. O. Fr. *pastée*. See **paste (I.)** & **-ade.** Pie of meat &c. enclosed in pastry and baked without a dish.

pasty (II.), adj. [1. pāsti; 2. péisti]. **paste (I.)** & **-y.** Of, like, paste, in appearance or consistency; *pasty-faced*, having a pale, unhealthy complexion.

pat (I.), n. [1. pat; 2. pæt]. Prob. imitative. **1.** Light, quick blow or tap, esp. of one given with palm of hand, as caress &c. **2.** Sound made by light blow or tap, e.g. by the foot. **3.** Small lump of butter, shaped by patting.

pat (II.), vb. trans. & intrans. Imitative, as prec. **1.** trans. To touch lightly and quickly, strike gently, esp. with hand as mark of affection, approbation &c.; fig. Phr. *to pat a person, oneself, on the back*, to congratulate, express approval of. **2.** intrans. To carry out action, make sound, of patting.

pat (III.), adv. Prob. fr. **pat (I.). 1.** At the right time; fitly, appositely, aptly: *the anecdote came pat to the occasion*. **2.** Readily, fluently, as though well prepared: *to know a lesson off pat*. **3.** (of cards, as poker) In Phr. *to stand pat*, to keep and play the hand as first dealt, without drawing cards; also fig., to refuse to change, stick to one's decision, course of action &c.

Pat (IV.), n. Abbr. fr. *Patrick*. Irishman.

pat-a-cake, n. **a** First words of nursery rhyme; **b** child's game based on this.

patagium, n. [1. pàtagīum; 2. pætəgáiəm]. Lat. *patagīum*, fr. Gk. *patageîon*, 'border, edging, on gown &c.'; etymol. doubtful. (zool.) **a** Wing-membrane of bat; **b** membranous fold forming parachute of flying squirrel.

patavinity, n. [1. pàtavíniti; 2. pætəvíniti], fr. Lat. *patavīnitāt-(em)*, 'patavinity', fr. *Patavīn-(us)*, 'of Patavium', fr. *Patav-(ium)*, 'Padua', & **-ine** & **-ity. a** Characteristics of dialect of Patavium as seen in Livy's writings; hence **b** provincialism.

patch (I.), n. [1. pach; 2. pætʃ]. M.E. *pacche*; etymol. dubious. **1.** Piece of material used to cover, fill up, repair, a hole or tear in another article, garment &c. Phr. *not a patch on*, far inferior to, not comparable to. **2. a** Small piece of plaster placed over a cut or wound; **b** one of several small pieces of plaster, usually black, formerly, and sometimes still, worn by women to enhance the delicacy of the complexion by contrast. **3.** Pad or shield to protect injured eye. **4.** Area of a surface, visibly distinct, and differing from the rest, in colour, appearance &c.: *a patch of white on a horse's nose*; *a patch of sunlight on the floor, of moisture on a rock* &c. **5. a** Small piece of ground; plot; **b** plants &c. growing on this: *cabbage-patch*. **6.** Shred, fragment, remnant.

patch (II.), vb. trans., fr. prec. **1. a** To put a patch on, repair by means of a patch; **b** to serve as patch for. **2.** To make up of patches, piece together; to put together roughly and hastily; also *patch up*; (fig.) to make up, smooth over, settle: *to patch up a quarrel* &c. **3.** To ornament with a patch.

patchery, n. [1. pácheri; 2. pǽtʃəri]. **patch (I.)** & **-ery.** Work, material, composed of, repaired with, patches.

patchily, adv. [1. páchili; 2. pǽtʃili]. **patchy** & **-ly.** In a patchy manner; in patches.

patchiness, n. [1. páchines; 2. pǽtʃinis]. See prec. & **-ness.** State, quality, of being patchy.

patchouli, n. [1. páchooli; 2. pǽtʃuli]. Tamil *pachai*, 'green', & *ilai*, 'leaf'. **a** Indian shrub of the mint family; **b** perfume obtained from this.

patchwork, n. [1. páchwěrk; 2. pǽtʃwāk]. **a** Needlework, consisting of fastening patches together; esp. *patchwork quilt*, rug, or coverlet made up of fragments of various materials and of different colours; **b** (often fig.) work consisting of a heterogeneous collection of materials, roughly put together; medley, jumble.

patchy, adj. [1. páchi; 2. pǽtʃi]. **patch (I.)** & **-y. a** Composed of, giving the effect of, patches, not presenting a uniform surface, appearance, effect; **b** not of consistent and uniform quality.

pate, n. [1. pāt; 2. peit]. In M.E. Origin unknown. The head.

pâté, n. [1. pátā; 2. pǽtei]. Fr., fr. O. Fr. *pasté*. See **pasty (I.).** Small pie, patty.

-pated, adj. [1. pāted; 2. péitid]. **pate** & **-ed.** Having a head of a specified kind: *addle-pated, bald-pated, curly-pated* &c.

pâté de foie gras, n. [1. pátā de fwàh gráh; 2. pǽtei də fwà grá]. Fr., 'paste of fat liver'. Rich paste made of goose's liver with truffles.

patée, adj. See **pattée.**

patella, n. [1. patéla; 2. pətélə]. Lat., 'small dish; knee-cap', for **patinla*, dimin. of Lat. *patina*, 'pan'. See **paten. 1.** (Rom. antiq.) Small pan or dish. **2.** (anat.) Small flat bone in front of knee-cap.

patellar, adj. [1. patélar; 2. pətélə]. Prec. & **-ar.** Of, pertaining to, the knee-cap.

patellate, adj. [1. patélāt; 2. pətéleit]. **patella** & **-ate.** Like, having the form of, the patella.

paten, n. [1. páten; 2. pǽtən], fr. O. Fr. *patene*, fr. Lat. *patena, patina*, 'pan, shallow dish', fr. Gk. *patánē*, 'pan'; cp. Gk. *petánnūmi*, 'I lie open, spread out'; *pétalon*, 'leaf; thin plate', see **petal**; cogn. w. Lat. *patēre*, 'to lie open', see **patent (I.).** Plate, usually of gold or silver, used for holding the bread or wafer in the Eucharist.

patency, n. [1. pātnsi; 2. péitənsi], fr. Lat. *paten-(tem)*, 'lying open'. See next word & **-cy.** State, quality, of being patent; obviousness.

patent (I.), adj. [1. pāt(e)nt; 2. péit(ə)nt], fr. Lat. *patent-(em)*, Pres. Part. of *patēre*, 'to lie open'; cp. Lat. *patulus*, 'open, extended'; Gk. *petánnūmi*, 'I spread out'; *pétalon*, 'leaf, thin plate', see **petal**; O.S. *fathmos*, 'extended arms; fathom'; O.E. *fæþm*, 'embrace, fathom', see **fathom (I.)**; Lith. *petys*, 'shoulder'. **1.** Open, plain to see, obvious: *his annoyance was perfectly patent*; *a patent injury*. **2.** (legal pronunciation, [1. pátent; 2. pǽtənt]) **a** In Phr. *letters patent* (formerly *patents*), an open letter; one issued by a sovereign granting a privilege, conferring a title &c.; **b** specif., protected by letters patent and secured for the exclusive profit of a particular person: *patent medicines* &c.; **c** (colloq.) new, ingenious and practical; generally applied to a contrivance devised by oneself or some specified person: *I've got a patent dodge for cleaning pipes*; *a patent way of cording a box.*

patent (II.), n., fr. prec. **1. a** Royal or government grant of privileges; letters patent: *a patent of nobility*; **b** exclusive right, granted by official authority, to make or sell some mechanical device or apparatus, to use some process &c.: *to take out a patent for an invention* &c. **2. a** Article or process protected by a patent; **b** an ingenious device or method.

patent (III.), vb. trans., fr. prec. To secure by a patent, take out a patent for (invention &c.).

patentee, n. [1. pàtnté; 2. pèitntí]. **patent** (III.) & **-ee.** One to whom a patent is granted.

patently, adv. [1. pátntli; 2. péitntli]. **patent** (I.) & **-ly.** In a patent manner; obviously, manifestly.

pater, n. [1. páter; 2. péitə]. Lat. *pater*, 'father'; cp. Gk. *patḗr*; Goth. *fadar*; O.H.G. *fater*; O.E. *fæder*, see **father**; prob. fr. a child's word **pā-*, **pə-*, cp. **papa.** (schoolboy slang) Father.

paterfamilias, n. [1. páterfamílias; 2. péitəfəmíliæs]. Lat., 'head of a household'. See prec. & **family.** (Roman law, or facet.) Father of family, master of house.

paternal, adj. [1. patérnl; 2. pətə́nl], fr. Lat. *patern-(us)*, 'of a father', fr. *pater*, 'father'. See **pater** & **-al. 1.** Pertaining to, characteristic of, resembling, a father; fatherly. **2.** Related through one's father: *paternal grandfather.*

paternalism, n. [1. patérnalizm; 2. pətə́nəlizəm]. Prec. & **-ism.** System, habit, of being paternal, esp. of a government or employer in relation to citizens or employees; usually in derogatory sense of fussy interference in matters relating to social habits, morals, health &c.

paternally, adv. [1. patérnali; 2. pətə́nəli]. **paternal** & **-ly.** In a paternal manner; as a father.

paternity, n. [1. patérniti; 2. pətə́niti], fr. Lat. *paternitāt-(em)*, 'paternity', fr. *patern-(us)*, 'paternal', see prec. & **-ity. 1. a** State of being a father; fatherhood; **b** descent from father, paternal origin. **2.** (fig.) Authorship, origination.

paternoster, n. [1. páternòster; 2. pǽtənɔ̀stə]. Lat. *pater noster*, 'Our Father', see **pater** & **nostrum**, fr. opening words of Lord's Prayer. **1. a** The Lord's Prayer; **b** formula of words, used as a charm or incantation; *black, white, paternoster*, specific kinds of this. **2.** Bead of rosary indicating that the Lord's Prayer is to be repeated. **3.** Usually *paternoster-line*, a fishing-line with hooks and sinkers at regular intervals, like the beads on a rosary.

path, n. [1. pahth; 2. pāþ]. O.E. *pæþ*, M.E. *path*; cp. Du. *pad*; Germ. *pfad.* No cognates known outside Gmc. **1. a** Way, track, beaten by the feet, not specially constructed: *a path through a wood, across fields* &c.; **b** made track along the side of a road for foot-passengers only; footpath. **2.** Track specially constructed for cycle-racing &c. **3. a** Line along which anything moves; direction of progress; track, course: *the path of a comet, of a bird in the air*; **b** (fig.) (i.) line, direction, of development: *the path of progress, of civilization*; (ii.) way in which life or action proceeds; line of conduct: *the path of duty*; '*The paths of glory lead but to the grave*' (Gray's 'Elegy').

Pathan, n. [1. patáhn; 2. pətā́n]. Hind. *Paṭhān.* Afghan tribesman on N.W. frontier of India.

pathetic, adj. & n. [1. pathétik; 2. pəþétik], fr. L. Lat., fr. Gk. *pathētik-(ós)*, 'capable of feeling'. See **pathos. 1.** adj. **a** Evoking pity, sympathy, sorrow; pitiable; **b** affecting, relating to, the emotions; *the pathetic fallacy*, phrase used by Ruskin in 'Modern Painters', to denote the habit in poets of attributing human feelings, emotions &c. to inanimate nature. **2.** n. (pl.) *Pathetics*, study of human emotions; indulgence in emotional expression.

pathetically, adv. [1. pathétikali; 2. pəþétikəli]. Prec. & **-al** & **-ly.** In a pathetic manner.

pathless, adj. [1. páhthles; 2. pā́þlis]. **path** & **-less.** Without a path; trackless: *pathless wastes, woods* &c.

patho-, pref. representing Gk. *pátho-(s)*, 'experience; suffering, emotion'. See **pathos. a** Emotion, passion, e.g. *pathognomy*, study of expression of emotions; **b** suffering, disease, e.g. *pathogenic*, causing disease, as certain bacteria; *pathogenesis*, mode of production and development of a disease.

pathological, adj. [1. pàthológikl; 2. pæ̀þəlɔ́džikl]. **pathology** & **-ic** & **-al.** Caused by, of the nature of, disease; connected with pathology.

pathologist, n. [1. pathólojist; 2. pæþɔ́ledžist]. **pathology** & **-ist.** Student of pathology.

pathology, n. [1. pathóloji; 2. pəþɔ́lədži]. **patho-** & **-logy.** Systematic study of bodily diseases, their cause, symptoms, and treatment.

pathos, n. [1. páthos; 2. péiþɔs], fr. Gk. *páthos*, 'experience; suffering; emotion'; cp. Gk. *pénthos*, 'sorrow, affliction'; *páskhein*, 'to suffer'; cogn. w. Lith. *kenczù*, 'to suffer'; *pa-kanta*, 'patience'. That quality in human life and experience, or in external events and circumstances, which evokes sympathy and a sense of sorrow and pity.

pathway, n. [1. páhthwā; 2. pā́þwei]. **path** & **way.** Path, track, beaten by the feet; a way made for foot-passengers.

-pathy, suff. [1. pathi; 2. pəþi], representing Gk. *-pátheia*, in *homoiopátheia*, 'similar feeling, equal suffering', see **homoeopathy**, fr. Gk. *páth-(os)*, 'suffering', see **pathos.** Used to form ns., indicating methods of curative treatment, e.g. *allopathy, hydropathy.*

patience, n. [1. páshens; 2. péiʃəns], fr. O. Fr. *patience*, fr. Lat. *patientia*, 'patience, endurance; forbearance'; fr. *patient-(em)*, see **patient**, & **-ce. 1. a** Endurance of suffering, provocation &c. with fortitude, resignation, calmness, and courage; **b** capacity to endure in this manner. Phrs. *to be out of patience with*, provoked by, unable to tolerate calmly; *to have no patience with*, be exasperated by. **2.** Constant diligence in performance of a task; perseverance, pertinacity. **3.** Capacity for waiting without complaint, and bearing with calmness and without restlessness and over-eagerness, delay in the accomplishment of what one expects and desires to happen, or to be done: *if you will only have patience, everything you want will be done at last.* **4.** Game of cards, of many varieties, usually for one player.

patient (I.), adj. [1. páshent; 2. péiʃənt], fr. O. Fr., fr. Lat. *patient-(em)*, Pres. Part. type of *pati*, 'to suffer, endure, experience'; cp. Lat. *paenitet*, 'it grieves', *pēnūria*, 'want'; *paene, pēne*, 'nearly, almost'; the basal meaning appears to be 'want, lack'; cp. also Gk. *peina*, 'hunger', & perh. also *spánis*, 'lack, scarceness, rarity'. **1.** Having, exercising, showing, patience; specif. **a** enduring pain without murmuring; **b** enduring provocation, slow to anger; **c** tolerating delay without complaint; **d** laborious, diligent, in accomplishment of long, tedious task. **2.** Capable of bearing a specified meaning; in Phr. *patient of such and such a meaning, interpretation* &c.

patient (II.), n. See prec. **1.** Person undergoing medical treatment. **2.** Specif., sick person who is a client of a particular doctor.

patiently, adv. **patient** (I.) & **-ly.** In a patient manner; with patience.

patina, n. [1. pátina; 2. pǽtinə], fr. Fr. *patine*, 'patina', possibly w. an earlier sense 'cover', fr. Lat. *patina*, 'dish'. See **paten.** **a** Kind of greenish film formed on the surface of old copper or bronze through exposure to the atmosphere; **b** similar deposit upon the surface of ancient stone implements; **c** fine gloss acquired by age on the surface of old woodwork, furniture, panelling &c.

patinated, adj. [1. pátinàted; 2. pǽtinèitid]. Prec. & **-ate** & **-ed.** Having a patina.

patination, n. [1. pàtináshun; 2. pæ̀tinéiʃən]. **patina** & **-ation.** Condition of having a patina.

patinous, adj. [1. pátinus; 2. pǽtinəs]. **patina** & **-ous.** Pertaining to, resembling, patina.

patio, n. [1. páhtiō; 2. pā́tiou]. Span. Inner courtyard of Spanish or Spanish-American house.

patois, n. [1. pátwah; 2. pǽtwā]. Fr.; etymol. doubtful. Local, provincial, form of speech, esp. one confined to a small area; a sub-dialect; contrasted with one having a currency over a wider area.

patriarch, n. [1. pátriark; 2. péitriāk], fr. O. Fr., fr. Lat. *patriarcha*, fr. Gk. *patriárchēs*, 'father or chief of a race', fr. *patriá*, 'family, lineage', fr. *patr-*, stem of *patḗr*, 'father', q.v. under **pater** & **father**, & *-arkhós*, 'leader, ruler', see **arch-. 1.** Father or head of family, clan, tribe, which he rules by paternal right. **2.** (specif.) One of the early founders of Hebrew families, esp. Abraham, Isaac, or Jacob, and their sons. **3.** (eccles.) **a** Orig. a bishop in the ancient Church; esp. the holder of one of the great sees, Antioch, Rome, Jerusalem &c.; **b** in Eastern Church, a bishop of one of the four sees, Constantinople, Alexandria, Antioch, Jerusalem, and by extension applied to bishops of some other sees. **4.** Venerable old man; esp. one regarded as the founder, or head, of a family, the senior member of a society or community &c.: *a village patriarch.*

patriarchal, adj. [1. pàtriárkl; 2. pèitriā́kl]. Prec. & **-al. 1.** Connected with, ruled by, a patriarch; having the jurisdiction of a patriarch. **2.** Characteristic of a patriarch; venerable.

patriarchate, n. [1. pàtriárkāt; 2. pèitriā́keit]. **patriarch** & **-ate. 1.** Office, rank, of tribal patriarch; system of patriarchal government; patriarchy. **2.** Office, rank, jurisdiction, see, of an ecclesiastical patriarch.

patriarchism, n. [1. pátriarkizm; 2. péitriākizəm]. See prec. & **-ism.** System of government by patriarchs.

patriarchy, n. [1. pátriarki; 2. péitriāki]. **patriarch** & **-y. 1.** Primitive system of government in which the chief authority resides in the male head or chief of a family or clan; contrasted with *matriarchy.* **2.** Authority, jurisdiction, of a patriarch.

patrician, n. & adj. [1. patríshan; 2. pətríʃn], fr. Lat. *patrici-(us)*, 'of noble rank', fr. *patri-*, stem of *patḗr*, 'father'; *patres*, 'fathers of the city ruling class', see **pater**, & **-an. 1.** n. **a** Member of Ancient Roman nobility; contrasted with *plebeian*; hence, **b** an honorary title in later Roman Empire; **c** chief magistrate of Roman Empire in Italian and African provinces; **d** nobleman, esp. of mediaeval Italian republics and German Free Cities. **2.** adj. **a** Noble, aristocratic; specif. **b** belonging to the Ancient Roman nobility.

patricianship, n. [1. patríshanship; 2. pətríʃnʃip]. Prec. & **-ship.** State of being patrician; noble rank.

patriciate, n. [1. patríshiāt; 2. pətríʃieit], fr. Med. Lat. *patriciāt-(us)*, 'patriciate', fr. Lat. *patrici-(us)*, 'patrician', see **patrician**, & **-ate. 1.** Rank, position, of a patrician. **2.** Patrician class, nobility.

patrimonial, adj. [1. pàtrimṓnial; 2. pæ̀trimóuniəl]. See next word & **-al.** Of, pertaining to, patrimony; hereditary.

patrimony, n. [1. pátrimuni; 2. pǽtrimәni], M.E. *patrimonye*, fr. A.-Fr., fr. Lat. *pātrimōnium*, 'paternal estate', fr. *patri-*, stem of *patḗr*, 'father', see **pater**, & **-mony.**

1. a Property inherited from father or ancestors; b (fig.) heritage, inherited character or attribute. 2. (eccles.) Church property.

patriot, n. [1. pátriut, pā́triut; 2. pætriət, péitriət], fr. Fr., fr. L. Lat. *patriōta*, 'countryman', fr. Gk. *patriṓtēs*, 'fellow-countryman', fr. *pátri-(os)*, 'of one's fathers'; see **pater**. A loyal citizen of a state; one who has and shows love for his native land, and who devotes himself, even at sacrifice to himself, to promoting the welfare and glory of his country and its inhabitants.

patriotic, adj. [1. pàtriótik; 2. pætriɔ́tik]. Prec. & **-ic**. Having the sentiments and qualities of a patriot; exhibiting, inspired by, patriotism.

patriotically, adv. [1. pàtriótikali; 2. pætriɔ́tikəli]. Prec. & **-al** & **-ly**. In a patriotic manner; with patriotism.

patriotism, n. [1. pátriotizm; 2. pǽtriətizəm]. **patriot** & **-ism**. Patriotic sentiments and qualities; love for, loyalty to, one's own country.

patristic, adj. [1. patrístik; 2. pətrístik], fr. Lat. *patr-*, stem of *patĕr*, 'father', see **pater**, & **-ist** & **-ic**. 1. Connected with, derived from, the Fathers of the Church. 2. Of, relating to, the study of the writings and thought of the Early Fathers.

patrol (I.), n. [1. patrṓl; 2. pətróul], fr. Fr. *patrouille*, 'patrol', fr. *patrouiller*, 'to patrol'. See next word. 1. Perambulation by detachment of troops or police. 2. Detachment of troops, police &c. appointed to perambulate town, district &c., and maintain order.

patrol (II.), vb. intrans. & trans., fr. Fr. *patrouiller*, 'to patrol'; earlier *patouiller*, 'to dabble, paddle, with the feet, to trample, tramp about', fr. O. Fr. *pate*, 'paw, foot of animal', the origin of wh. is doubtful. 1. intrans. To go the rounds in camp &c. 2. trans. a To go round, traverse (camp, town &c.), for the purpose of guarding or inspecting: *police patrolling the streets*; b to march about, through: *bands of unemployed patrolled the town.*

patron, n. [1. pā́trun; 2. péitrən]. M.E. *patrōn*, 'patron, pattern', fr. O. Fr. *patron*, fr. Lat. *patrōnus*, 'protector', fr. *patr-*, stem of *patĕr*, 'father', see **pater**. 1. (Rom. antiq.) a Relation in which a citizen who had freed a slave stood to the latter; b patrician protector of plebeian client; correlative of *client*, q.v. 2. One who encourages, gives moral or financial support and countenance to, a cause, enterprise, or person: *a patron of the arts.* 3. (shopkeeper's word) Regular customer or employer. 4. Also *patron saint*, saint regarded as special protector of place, person, occupation &c. 5. Person having right of bestowing a benefice in the Church of England.

patronage, n. [1. pátrunij; 2. pǽtrənidž]. Prec. & **-age**. 1. Support, protection, encouragement, given by patron. 2. a Right of presentation to church benefice; b power of appointment to offices and positions in the state or elsewhere. 3. Patronizing manner, assumption of superiority in dealing with another. 4. (shop-word) Regular custom.

patronage secretary, n. Official title of the principal 'whip' of the Government in power.

patronal, adj. [1. patrṓnal; 2. pætrṓunəl]. **patron** & **-al**. Belonging to, in celebration of, patron saint: *patronal festival* (at, of, a Church), one held on the day of that saint to whom the church is dedicated.

patroness, n. [1. pā́trunes; 2. péitrənis]. **patron** & **-ess**. Female patron.

patronize, vb. trans. [1. pátrunīz; 2. pǽtrənaiz]. **patron** & **-ize**. 1. To act as patron towards; to give encouragement and countenance to; to support by being a customer. 2. To assume air of a patron towards; to treat with lofty condescension, as of a superior to an inferior.

patronizing, adj. [1. pátrunīzing; 2. pǽtrənaiziŋ], fr. Pres. Part. of prec. Exhibiting an assumption of patronage; condescending.

patronizingly, adv. Prec. & **-ly**. In a patronizing manner.

patronymic, adj. & n. [1. pàtrunímik; 2. pætrənímik], fr. Lat., fr. Gk. *patrōnúm-(ios)*, 'named after one's father', fr. *patr-*, stem of *patḗr*, 'father', q.v. under **pater**, & *ónoma*, 'name'. See first element in **onomatopoeia**, & **-ic**. 1. adj. (of name) Derived from father or ancestor. 2. n. Patronymic name.

patroon, n. [1. patrōōn; 2. pətrū́n]. Du. form of **patron**. (U.S. hist.) Person holding grant of land, with manorial rights (abolished c. 1850), from old Dutch government of New York and New Jersey.

pattée, patée, paty, adj. [1. pátā; 2. pǽtei]. Fr., fr. *patte*, 'paw, foot', see **patrol**. (her.) Of crosses, with arms expanding to a broad flattened end; also sometimes terminating in a trefoil or fleur-de-lis; the first type is sometimes wrongly named 'Maltese cross'; the flowered is styled 'cross fleury'.

patten, n. [1. pátn; 2. pǽtn]. M.E. *paten*, fr. O. Fr. *patine*, 'shoe', cp. Mod. Fr. *patin*, 'skate for the ice'; prob. fr. *patte*, 'foot' &c., q.v. under **patrol**. Kind of wooden over-shoe supported on an iron ring; formerly worn for walking short distances, to keep the feet out of the mud and wet; a clog.

patter (I.), n. [1. páter; 2. pǽtə]. See next word. 1. Dialect or jargon confined to a particular class: *thieves' patter.* 2. a *Patter song*, one with easy rhymes, set to a simple, catchy tune, occurring in a comic opera, and sung with the utmost rapidity; a good example is Gilbert's '*My name is John Wellington Wells*', in 'The Sorcerer'; b *conjuror's patter*, running remarks kept up in order to distract attention from acts which the audience is not meant to see.

patter (II.), vb. trans. & intrans., fr. first element of **paternoster**, so called fr. the habit of gabbling prayers. 1. trans. To utter, repeat, hurriedly and mechanically: *to patter prayers.* 2. intrans. To talk glibly, chatter.

patter (III.), vb. intrans., fr. **pat** & **-er**. a To make a succession of light, quick sounds: *rain-drops pattering on the glass*; b to run with short, light, quick steps.

patter (IV.), n., fr. prec. Succession of light taps.

pattern (I.), n. [1. pátern; 2. pǽtən], fr. M.E. *patron*, 'patron; person to be followed; pattern', see **patron**. 1. Person whose merits and qualities entitle him to be taken as example of conduct; one to be imitated, a model: *a pattern of propriety, virtue, industry* &c. 2. a Model or shape serving as a guide in constructing anything: *paper pattern for a dress*; b (in founding) full-sized model used for making the sand mould into which the metal is poured for castings. 3. Design embroidered, woven, carved, painted, or stamped as an ornament on any kind of material &c.: *pattern on carpet, wall-paper, china* &c. 4. Specif., figure formed by the marks on target as result of the shots successively fired at it by one person. 5. Small samples of cloth, wall-paper &c. from which choice can be made, supplied by tradesman.

pattern (II.), vb. trans., fr. prec. (rare) 1. To make, form, fashion, in accordance with a model: *to pattern a thing after, upon, a model, design* &c. 2. To put a pattern upon.

pattern-maker, n. One who makes patterns, specif., one who makes patterns for castings in a foundry.

pattern-shop, n. Place in factory, foundry, &c. where patterns are prepared.

patty, n. [1. páti; 2. pǽti], fr. Fr. *pâté*, 'pasty', see **pâté**. Little pie.

patty-pan, n. Small pan for baking a pie or cake.

patulous, adj. [1. pátūlus; 2. pǽtjuləs], fr. Lat. *patul-(us)*, 'spread out, extended', q.v. under **patent**, & **-ous**. Spread out, spreading, extended.

paty, adj. See **pattée**.

paucity, n. [1. páwsiti; 2. pɔ́siti], fr. Lat. *paucitāt-(em)*, 'fewness, scarcity', fr. *pauc-(us)*, 'few, little'; cp. Lat. *pauper*, 'poor'; cogn. w. Gk. *paûr-os*, 'little'; cogn. w. Goth. *fawai*, O.E. *fēawe*, 'few', see **few**. Smallness of number or amount; scarcity.

Pauline, adj. & n. [1. páwlīn; 2. pɔ́lain], fr. Saint Paul & **-ine**. 1. adj. Pertaining to, written by, St. Paul; esp. *Pauline epistles.* 2. n. Member of St. Paul's School, London.

paulo-post-future, n. [1. pàwlō pōst fū́chur; 2. pɔ́lou poust fjū́tʃə], fr. Lat. *paulō*, 'a little', fr. *paul(l)us*, 'little', prob. fr. **paur(o)l-os*, dimin. of **paur-(os)*, 'little', later *parv-us*, see **paucity**; for other elements see **post-**, **future**. 1. (Gk. gram.) Future perfect tense. 2. (facet.) Immediate future.

Paulownia, n. [1. pawlṓnia; 2. pōlóuniə], fr. Princess Anna Paulovna, of Russia. (bot.) Genus of shrubs and trees with showy, purple bell-shaped flowers; the flower is one of the national emblems of Japan.

Paul Pry, n. [1. páwl prí; 2. pɔ́l prái]. Character in comedy (1825) by John Poole, d. 1872. Inquisitive, meddling person.

paunch, n. [1. pawnch; 2. pɔntʃ], fr. A.-Fr. *panche*, fr. Lat. *pantex*, 'paunch'; etymol. doubtful. 1. Abdomen, belly; specif. a the first or largest stomach of ruminant; b (facet. or vulg.) human abdomen, esp. when large and prominent. 2. (naut.) Thick mat on mast or yards of a ship to prevent chafing.

paunchy, adj. [1. páwnchi; 2. pɔ́ntʃi]. Prec. & **-y**. Having a large, prominent abdomen.

pauper, n. [1. páwper; 2. pɔ́pə], fr. Lat. *pauper*, 'poor', fr. *pau-*, stem of *pau-cus*, 'little' &c., see **paucity**, & *par-*, stem of *parere*, 'to bring forth, produce; to gain, acquire', see **parent**. 1. a Destitute person supported by charity or public funds; b (law) person who, on account of poverty, is allowed to plead or defend a case without costs, i.e. *in forma pauperis.* 2. (colloq.) A person in straitened circumstances, one of small means; one who is regarded, or who regards himself, as poor.

pauperdom, n. [1. páwperdum; 2. pɔ́pədəm]. Prec. & **-dom**. 1. State of being a pauper. 2. Whole body of paupers.

pauperism, n. [1. páwperizm; 2. pɔ́pərizəm]. **pauper** & **-ism**. 1. State of being a pauper; destitution; dependence on charity or poor relief. 2. Paupers collectively; pauperdom.

pauperization, n. [1. pàwperīzā́shun; 2. pɔ̀pəraizéiʃən]. See next word & **-ation**. Act or process of pauperizing; state of being pauperized.

pauperize, vb. trans. [1. páwperīz; 2. pɔ́pəraiz]. **pauper** & **-ize**. To reduce to pauperism; to tend to make a technical pauper of, by encouraging dependence upon public aid for support, rather than upon personal exertion.

pause (I.), n. [1. pawz; 2. pɔz], fr. Fr., fr. Lat. *pausa*, 'stop, cessation', fr. Gk. *paûsis*, 'stopping', fr. *paúein*, 'to cause to cease'; etymol. doubtful. 1. Period of inaction; temporary cessation, brief intermission of activity; Phr. *to give pause to*, cause to hesitate. 2. a Momentary deliberate interruption in speaking, reading, singing &c., for the sake of expression, emphasis &c.; b cessation, check, in the flow of conversation during a brief, but appreciable period; a silence caused by embarrassment, lack of ideas &c.: *the unfortunate remark caused an awkward pause.* 3. (mus.) Graphic symbol in form of a curve, placed above note, indicating prolongation.

pause (II.), vb. intrans., fr. prec. 1. To make a pause; to intermit motion, or cease action, temporarily, from hesitation &c. 2. To linger, dwell upon: *to pause upon a note, word* &c.

pavage, n. [1. pā́vij; 2. péividž], fr. Fr. See **pave** & **-age**. a Process of laying pavements, or paving-stones; b tax paid towards paving of streets &c.

pavan, n. [1. paván; 2. pævǽn], fr. Fr. *pavane*, cp. Ital. & Span. *pavana*; etymol. doubtful.

a Slow, stately dance, in duple time, of 16th and 17th cents.; **b** music for such a dance.

pave, vb. trans. [1. pāv; 2. peiv], fr. Fr. *paver*, fr. Lat. *pavīre*, 'to beat, ram, tread down'; cp. Lith. *piáuti*, 'to mow, down'; cp. further Lat. *putāre*, 'to cut'. see **amputate**. To cover surface of, with flat stones, or other material, so as to form a pavement. Phr. *to pave the way for*, prepare the way for, facilitate the advance or introduction of.

pavé, n. [1. pávā; 2. pævei]. Fr., fr. P.P. of *paver*, 'to pave', see prec. **1. a** Pavement; **b** roadway, street, paved with stone setts or cobbles. **2.** Close setting of jewels.

pavement, n. [1. pávment; 2. péivmənt], fr. O. Fr., fr. Lat. *pavīmentum*, 'beaten floor'. **pave** & **-ment**. **1. a** Series of flat slabs, or blocks, of stone, wood &c., set close together on surface of ground, floor &c.; **b** specif., paved walk for pedestrians at side of street, contrasted with *road*. **2.** (zool.) Pavement-like arrangement of teeth, as in sharks &c.

pavement-artist, n. Man who draws pictures in coloured chalk, on the public pavement, and asks for money from passers-by, for doing so.

pavilion (I.), n. [1. pavílyun; 2. pəvíljən], fr. Fr. *pavillon*, fr. Lat. *pāpiliōn-(em)*, 'butterfly; tent'. See **papilionaceous**. **1.** Large tent. **2. a** Originally temporary shelter for spectators at a tournament; **b** a wooden building, with verandah, on cricket or football ground &c., for players and spectators. **3.** Ornamental projection, with tent-formed roof, from a large building.

pavilion (II.), vb. trans., fr. prec. To cover, shelter, surround, with, or as with, a pavilion.

paviour, n. [1. pávyur; 2. péivjə]. **pave** & **-our**. Person whose trade is to lay pavements.

pavonazzo, adj. & n. [1. pahvonátsō; 2. pāvənætsou]. Ital., fr. Lat. *pāvōn-(em)*, 'peacock'. See next word. **1.** adj. Having brightly coloured markings like colouring of peacock. **2.** n. Marble coloured in this way.

pavonine, adj. [1. pāvṓnīn; 2. peivóunain], fr. Lat. *pāvōnīn-(us)*, 'of, like, a peacock', fr. *pāvōn-*, stem of *pāvo*, 'peacock'; prob. of Eastern origin. Connected with, resembling, having the colouring of, a peacock.

paw (I.), n. [1. paw; 2. pɔ]. M.E. *pawe, powe*, fr. O. Fr. *poue, powe*; etymol. doubtful. **1.** Animal's foot, including nails or claws. **2.** (colloq.) Human hand.

paw (II.), vb. trans. & intrans., fr. prec. **1.** trans. **a** (of animals) To touch, feel, with the paw; **b** (of horse) to strike, scrape, with a front hoof: *to paw the ground*; **c** (of human beings) to touch, handle, coarsely, to maul; to stroke, touch unnecessarily with the hand; also *paw over*. **2.** intrans. (of horse) To strike and scrape the ground repeatedly and impatiently with one of the fore-hoofs.

pawkily, adv. [1. páwkili; 2. pɔ́kili]. **pawky** & **-ly**. In a pawky manner.

pawkiness, n. [1. páwkines; 2. pɔ́kinis]. See next word & **-ness**. Quality of being pawky.

pawky, adj. [1. páwki; 2. pɔ́ki]. Scots, cp. *pawk*, 'trick'; etymol. unknown. Arch and shrewd; having, exhibiting, a dry humour.

pawl, n. & vb. trans. [1. pawl; 2. pɔl]. W.; prob. same word as **pale** (I.). **1.** n. **a** Short, pivoted catch engaging with toothed wheel to prevent recoil; specif. **b** (naut.) bar used to prevent windlass &c. from recoiling. **2.** vb. trans. To secure (wheel, capstan &c.) with pawl.

pawn (I.), n. [1. pawn; 2. pɔn]. M.E. *poun*, fr. A.-Fr. *poun*; cp. Span. *peón*; Ital. *pedone*, 'foot soldier, pawn', fr. Lat. *pedōn-(em)*, 'foot soldier', fr. *ped-*, stem of *pēs*, 'foot'; see **pedal** (I.). **1.** Piece of lowest rank in chess. **2.** (fig.) **a** Unimportant person used by another as a cat's-paw or humble agent in accomplishing his designs; **b** a cause, principle, subject, disputed between political parties, and advocated or opposed without real conviction, in order to make party capital.

pawn (II.), n., fr. O. Fr. *pan*, 'piece of cloth, flap' &c.; fr. Lat. *pannus*, 'piece, flap &c. of cloth'; cogn. w. O.E. *fana*, 'banner', see **vane**; the sense of 'pledge' prob. comes fr. Du. *pand*, cp. Germ. *pfand*. **1.** (archaic) Something entrusted to another as a pledge, guarantee, or security, for a loan. **2.** State of being pledged, esp. in Phr. *in pawn*.

pawn (III.), vb. trans., fr. prec. **1.** To deposit with, surrender into the keeping of (a pawnbroker), as security for money advanced: *to pawn one's watch*. **2.** (fig., rare) To risk, stake, hazard: *to pawn one's good name*.

pawnbroker, n. [1. páwnbrōker; 2. pɔ́nbroukə]. Person who makes a business of lending money on interest, under licence, on the security of personal property, deposited with him as a pawn or pledge.

pawnbroking, n. [1. páwnbrōking; 2. pɔ́nbroukiŋ]. Pawnbroker's business.

pawnee (I.), n. [1. pawnḗ; 2. pɔní]. **pawn** (III.) & **-ee**. Person who accepts a pawn.

pawnee (II.), n. [1. páwni; 2. pɔ́ni]. Hind. *pāni*, 'water', fr. base seen in **bibulous**. Chiefly in *brandy pawnee*, brandy and water.

pawnshop, n. [1. páwnshop; 2. pɔ́nʃɔp]. Place where pawnbroking is carried on.

pax, n. [1. paks; 2. pæks]. Lat. *pāx*, 'peace'; cp. Lat. *pācisci*, 'to make a treaty or agreement'; *pangere*, 'to join, make firm'; *(com)pāges*, 'fastening'; *pālus*, 'post, stake'; *pāgus*, 'community; district; province'; *pāgina*, 'strips of papyrus fastened together; page'. Cogn. w. Gk. *pégnūmi*, 'I strengthen'; *pēgós*, 'firm, strong'; *págos*, 'something solid; hill; peak; frost'; Goth. *fāhan*; O.E. *fōn*, 'to seize, receive'; O.H.G. *fuoga*, 'joint'; O.E. *ġefēgan*, 'to join'; Goth. *-fāhjan*, 'to satisfy'; *fagrs*, 'fitting, suitable'; O.E. *fæġer*, 'beautiful'. Aryan base **pāḱ-, *pāḱ-*, 'to fix, join, unite'. See further **pacify**, **page** (II.), **pale** (I.), **fair** (II.). **1.** Small tablet of gold &c., bearing representation of Crucifixion, to which the priest gave the 'kiss of peace' at the Mass, and which was subsequently kissed by the congregation. **2.** (school slang, as interj.) Used to call for a truce. **3.** In Phr. *pax Romana*, peace maintained within the Roman Empire; *pax vobis(cum)*, peace be with you.

paxwax, n. [1. pákswaks; 2. pæ̀kswæks]. Earlier *fax-wax*, fr. O.E. *feax*, 'hair', & O.E. *weax-*, stem of *weaxan*, 'to grow', see **wax** (III.); for the first element cp. O.N. *fax*; O.S., O.H.G. *fahs*, 'hair'; O.N. *fǽr* (fr. **fāheza*), 'sheep'. Cp. further Lat. *pexus*, 'woolly'; *pecten*, 'comb', see **pecten**; *pékos*, 'fleece'. See also **pecuniary**. (provinc.) Strong tendon supporting neck in mammals.

pay (I.), vb. trans. & intrans. [1. pā; 2. pei]. M.E. *payen*, 'to satisfy, please, pay', fr. O. Fr. *payer*, fr. Lat. *pācāre*, 'to pacify, appease, satisfy', fr. *pāc-*, stem of *pāx*, 'peace', see **pax**. **A.** trans. **1. a** To give, hand over, to (a person) wages, salary, fee, due for services rendered or work done; to remunerate: *to pay one's servants, a teacher, the doctor*; **b** to give a satisfactory, or agreed, equivalent in money to, for goods supplied: *to pay the corn merchant, one's tailor* &c.; Phr. *to pay (a person) in kind*, hand over goods or material to, instead of money; *to pay the piper*, bear the expense of an undertaking &c. **2.** To discharge, extinguish, settle, by paying or handing over what is owing: *to pay one's debts, a bill*; Phrs. *to pay the penalty*, undergo punishment; *pay the debt of nature*, to die; also *to pay wages, a salary* &c.; equiv. to *pay for*, in Phr. *pay one's way*, keep out of debt by paying regularly; *pay (one's) expenses*, make payment for such as are incurred; *pay one's footing*, make such payments, perform such services, as are required of a new member of a society or the like; *poorly paid work*, ill remunerated. **3.** To hand over, transfer, make payment of: *to pay money into the Exchequer, into one's account*; *to pay a hundred guineas for a horse*. **4. a** To yield satisfactory returns to, produce profit for: *the enterprise will not pay you*; **b** to be to one's advantage: *submission will pay you better*. **5.** To bestow, render, offer, voluntarily, **a** (without implying obligation): *to pay attention to, court to*; *to pay a compliment to*; *to pay a call, visit*; **b** to render as a duty: *to pay homage, pay one's respects*. **B.** intrans. **1.** To make payment, discharge a debt &c.: *it's no good bargaining, we shall have to pay*. Phr. *to pay through the nose*, pay exorbitant price. **2. a** To yield adequate monetary returns, compensate for expense, effort: *it will never pay to work this mine*; *how to make farming pay*; **b** to be profitable, be to one's advantage or interest: *it always pays to buy really good clothes*; *it doesn't pay to make oneself unpopular*. **C.** Followed by adverbs or prepositions. *Pay away*, **a** to expend; **b** (naut.) to slacken and let out gradually: *to pay away a rope*. *Pay back*, **a** to return (money &c.) which has been borrowed; **b** to return money &c. to (a person); Phr. *to pay a man back in his own coin*, treat him as he has treated oneself, give him tit for tat. *Pay off*, **a** to pay wages of and discharge; **b** to settle (debt) by payment. *Pay out*, **a** to punish, take revenge on; **b** to give out, disburse (money); **c** (naut.) to pay away. *Pay up*, to pay amount owing in full.

pay (II.), n., fr. O. Fr. *paie*, fr. *paier*, 'to pay'. See prec. Remuneration, salary, sum paid in return for services; specif. **a** (in army and navy) remuneration paid to officers and men; **b** workmen's wages. Phr. *in the pay of*, paid, employed by, often with derogatory meaning.

pay (III.), vb. trans., Pret. & P.P. *payed*, fr. A.-Fr. *peier*, fr. Lat. *picāre*, 'to coat with pitch', fr. *pic-*, stem of *pix*, 'pitch'; cp. Gk. *pissa* (fr. **pikja*); O. Slav. *pĭklŭ*; Lith. *pìkis*, 'pitch', cp. further Lat. *opīmus*, 'fat, rich'; *pinguis*, 'fat', see **pinguid**; Gk. *píōn*, 'fat'; O.E. *fǣtt*, 'fat', see **fat**; O.N. *feitr*, 'fat'. (naut.) To coat, smear, with pitch, tar &c. to render waterproof.

payable, adj. [1. páabl; 2. péiəbl]. **pay** (I.) & **-able**. **1.** That must or may be paid; due. **2.** (of mine &c.) Likely to be profitable.

pay-day, n. Day on which payment is regularly made, esp. of debts and wages.

payee, n. [1. pāḗ; 2. peií]. **pay** (I.) & **-ee**. Person to whom payment is made.

payer, n. [1. páer; 2. péiə]. See prec. & **-er**. Person who pays.

paymaster, n. [1. pámahster; 2. péimāstə]. Officer, official, in army or navy, representative of employer &c. whose duty it is to pay troops, employees &c.

Paymaster-General, n. An unpaid member of the Ministry, through whom all payments, civil and military, are made.

payment, n. [1. páment; 2. péimənt]. **pay** (I.) & **-ment**. **1.** Act of paying; state of being paid. **2.** Amount paid. **3.** (fig.) Reward, recompense, compensation.

paynim, n. [1. pánim; 2. péinim]. M.E. *painim*, fr. O. Fr. *paienime*, fr. L. Lat. *pāgānismus*, 'heathenism'. See **pagan** & **-ism**. (archaic) Heathen, pagan, esp. applied to Moslems or Saracens during the Crusades.

paynize, vb. trans. [1. pánīz; 2. péinaiz], fr. Payne, inventor of process, & **-ize**. To harden and preserve (wood) by Payne's process of injections of various chemicals.

pay office, n. The office of the Paymaster-General.

pay-roll, n. (Am. usage) Pay-sheet.

paysage, n. [1. páizàhzh; 2. péiizāž]. Fr., fr. *pays*, 'country, country-side'. See **peasant** & **-age**. **a** Country scene, landscape; **b** landscape painting.

pay-sheet, n. List of names of employees, workmen &c. to be paid, with amount of wages &c. due to each.

pea, n. [1. pē; 2. pī]. Back-formation, fr. **pease**, wh. was regarded as pl. **1.** Leguminous, mostly annual, plant with climbing stems furnished with tendrils, bearing white or coloured flowers followed by seeds enclosed in pods; some varieties are cultivated for the seeds, which are edible, others for the sake of the bright, sweet-scented bloom. **2.** Seed of this plant, usually cooked for food while green; *split peas*, dried peas with outer skin removed, used for soup &c. Phr. *as like as two peas*, exactly alike.

peace, n. [1. pēs; 2. pīs]. M.E. *pes, pais*; fr. A.-Fr. *pēs*, O. Fr. *pais*, fr. Lat. *pācem*, nom. *pāx*, 'peace', see **pax**. **1.** Cessation of, freedom from, strife, warfare: *to decide between war and peace*; *to make peace*, bring about peace, to cease from war; *the piping times of peace*; *peace at any price*. **2.** (usually cap.) Treaty of peace between hostile nations. **3.** (of external conditions) **a** Freedom from civil disorder, disturbance, agitation; tranquillity: *the peace, the king's peace*, maintenance of order by laws of land: *to keep the peace*; *a breach of the peace*; **b** quiet, tranquillity, concord, freedom from strife, controversy or agitation: *an air of peace lay over the scene*; *to disturb the peace of the household*; Phrs. *at peace*, in a state of quiet; *to hold one's peace*, keep silent; *to make one's peace with*, be reconciled with; **c** freedom from interruption, disturbance, annoyance: *do let me have a little peace at last*. **4.** Mental calm, serenity of mind.

peaceable, adj. [1. pēsabl; 2. pīsəbl]. Prec. & **-able**. **1.** Quiet, tranquil, disposed for peace; not quarrelsome. **2.** At peace, not in a state of war or disorder.

peaceableness, n. See prec. & **-ness**. Quality, state, of being peaceable.

peaceably, adv. See prec. & **-ly**. In a peaceable manner.

peaceful, adj. [1. pēsfool; 2. pīsful]. **peace** & **-ful**. **a** Characterized by, characteristic of, in a state of, peace; calm, free from agitation or disorder: *a peaceful land, people*; *a peaceful death*; **b** exhibiting, suggesting, calm and quietness; serene, smiling: *a peaceful scene, landscape*.

peacefully, adv. Prec. & **-ly**. In a peaceful manner.

peacefulness, n. See prec. & **-ness**. Quality of being peaceful.

peacemaker, n. [1. pēsmāker; 2. pīsmeikə]. **1.** One who makes, brings about, peace, or effects reconciliation. **2.** (facet.) Instrument for keeping the peace, e.g. revolver, warship.

peace-offering, n. **a** Something offered as an overture to peace, or as a means of bringing about reconciliation; **b** (Bib.) thank-offering to God.

peace-pipe, n. More commonly *pipe of peace*; pipe smoked as sign of peace among N. American Indians; calumet.

peach (I.), n. [1. pēch; 2. pītʃ]. M.E. *pēche*, fr. O. Fr. *pesche*, fr. L. Lat. *persica*, 'peach', fr. Lat. *Persicum* (*mālum*), 'Persian (apple)', fr. *Pers-(ia)*, 'Persia'. See **Persian** & **-ic**. **1. a** Large roundish fruit, with velvety creamy or yellowish skin, tinged with red, with sweet, luscious, very juicy flesh, and a large rough stone; **b** tree bearing this fruit; also *peach tree*. **2.** (slang) A fresh, beautiful young girl.

peach (II.), vb. intrans. Earlier *appeach*, fr. O. Fr. *empechier*, 'to appeal against'. See **impeach**. (slang) To inform against an accomplice (followed by *against, upon*).

peach-bloom, peach-blow, n. Kind of pale pinkish glaze on pottery and porcelain.

peach-brandy, n. Spirit distilled from peaches, including the stones and kernels.

peach-colour, n. Soft, clear, pale red.

peachick, n. [1. pēchik; 2. pītʃik]. Young peacock or peahen.

peachiness, n. [1. pēchines; 2. pītʃinis]. See next word & **-ness**. Quality of being peachy.

peachy, adj. [1. pēchi; 2. pītʃi]. **peach** (I.) & **-y**. Of the colour or texture of a peach.

peacock (I.), n. [1. pēkok; 2. pīkɔk], fr. O.E. *pāwa, pēa*, fr. Lat. *pāvo*, 'peacock', see **pavonine**, & **cock**. Large, gallinaceous, crested bird, *Pavo cristatus*, the male of which has bright-coloured iridescent plumage, and a long tail the feathers of which are yellowish brown with large dark blue spots (eyes), and capable of being raised and spread out like a fan; the bird is often taken as a type of vanity and display. Phr. *proud as a peacock*.

peacock (II.), vb. intrans., fr. prec. To strut about, give oneself airs, show off; to make a display in personal adornment; assume airs of intellectual superiority.

peacock-blue, n. Bright, lustrous blue colour, similar to that in plumage of peacock's neck.

peacock-butterfly, n. Butterfly, *Vanessa Io*, with eye-like spots on its wings, resembling those on a peacock's tail.

peacock-coal, n. Iridescent variety of coal.

peacockery, n. [1. pēkokeri; 2. pīkɔkəri]. **peacock** & **-ery**. Ostentatious behaviour.

peacockish, adj. [1. pēkokish; 2. pīkɔkiʃ]. **peacock** & **-ish**. Like, characteristic of, a peacock; vain, ostentatious.

peacocklike, adj. [1. pēkoklīk; 2. pīkɔklaik]. See prec. & **-like**. Like a peacock, esp. in vanity.

peacocky, adj. [1. pēkoki; 2. pīkɔki]. **peacock** & **-y**. **a** Like a peacock in colour; **b** inclined to strut and swagger.

pea-flour, n. **pea** & **flour**. Meal made of dried peas.

peafowl, n. [1. pēfoul; 2. pīfaul], fr. O.E. *pēa*, 'peacock', see **peacock**, & **fowl**. Peacock or peahen.

pea-green, adj. See **pea** & **green**. Light, bright, green, of the colour of young pea-pods.

peahen, n. [1. pēhen; 2. pīhen]. See **peacock** & **hen**. Female of peacock.

pea-jacket, n., fr. earlier *pee*, fr. M. Du. *pie*, Mod. Du. *pij*, 'pea-jacket'. Sailor's short square-cut, double-breasted overcoat of thick, rough cloth.

peak (I.), n. [1. pēk; 2. pīk]. Variant of **pike** (I.). **1. a** Pointed top or end; esp. sharply tapering summit of mountain &c.; **b** highest point, degree, volume (of traffic &c.). **2.** Projecting point or edge; tapering projection: *the peak of a cap*. **3.** (naut.) **a** Narrowed part of hull or hold, at bow; **b** outer, upper corner of sail extended by gaff.

peak (II.), vb. intrans. Origin doubtful. To waste away, grow thin and weak, esp. in Phr. *to peak and pine*.

peak (III.), vb. trans. & intrans., fr. **apeak**. (naut.) **1.** trans. **a** To raise in vertical direction, tilt upwards; **b** to raise vertically, place apeak: *to peak oars*; **c** (of whale) to raise (tail) in the air. **2.** intrans. (of whale) To raise tail when diving perpendicularly.

peaked (I.), adj. [1. pēkt; 2. pīkt]. **peak** (I.) & **-ed**. Having, ending in, a peak.

peaked (II.), adj., fr. P.P. of **peak** (II.). Thin, pinched, emaciated.

peaky, adj. [1. pēki; 2. pīki]. **1. peak** (I.) & **-y**. Having, ending in, forming, a peak. **2. peak** (II.) & **-y**. Having a drawn, emaciated appearance.

peal (I.), n. [1. pēl; 2. pīəl]. Prob. fr. **appeal**. **1. a** Loud, prolonged ringing of bell(s); esp. **b** changes rung on a set of bells; Phr. *muffled peal*, with bells muffled. **2.** Set of bells tuned to each other; chime, carillon. **3.** Loud, prolonged, reverberant sound: *a peal of thunder, laughter* &c.

peal (II.), vb. intrans. & trans., fr. prec. **1.** intrans. To ring, resound, loudly, of bells; also *peal out*. **2.** trans. **a** To cause to ring loudly and clearly: *to peal a bell*; **b** also *peal out*, to utter sonorously, cause to resound.

peanut, n. [1. pēnut; 2. pīnat]. **pea** & **nut**. **1.** Trailing plant with yellow flowers, producing edible seeds ripened underground in very brittle pods. **2.** Oily, nut-like, edible seed of this plant.

pear, n. [1. pār; 2. pɛə]. O.E. *pere*, M.E. *pēre*, fr. L. Lat. *pira*, fr. Lat. *pirum*, 'pear', *pirus*, 'pear tree'. Etymol. doubtful. **a** Fruit, oval in shape, and tapering towards the stem, having a sweet and very juicy flesh; **b** tree of *Pyrus communis* producing this fruit.

pearl (I.), n. [1. pěrl; 2. pāl], fr. Fr. *perle*, fr. Med. Lat. *perla*; etymol. unknown. **1.** Lustrous calcareous concretion, usually white or pale bluish grey, formed in shell of various molluscs, esp. of the *pearl-oyster*; often possessing great value; *seed pearl*, small specimen. Phr. *to cast (one's) pearls before swine*, offer valuable thing to one who cannot appreciate it. **2. a** Anything resembling a pearl in size, shape, and lustre, e.g. tear, dewdrop; **b** small fragment, granule, globule, of various substances. **3.** (fig.) **a** Anything precious, highly valued; **b** person who possesses to a high degree the most admired qualities of a class &c.: *a pearl among women*. **4.** (typog.) *Pearl type*, smallest size of type but one, of those commonly made; about 15 lines of it go to the inch.

pearl (II.), vb. trans. & intrans., fr. prec. **1.** trans. **a** To cause to resemble pearls in shape, colour &c.; **b** to bespangle with pearl-like drops: *pearled with dew*. **2.** intrans. **a** To fish for pearls; **b** to form small, round drops.

pearl (III.), n. Prob. a variant of **purl** (I.). One of a series of loops forming edging for lace &c.

pearl-ash, n. Carbonate of potassium, crude potash of white, pearly appearance.

pearl-barley, n. Barley with outer coat removed, and reduced by rubbing to small round pearly grains.

pearl-button, n. Button made of mother-of-pearl.

pearl-diver, n. One who dives for pearl-oysters.

pearled, adj. [1. pěrld; 2. pāld]. **pearl** & **-ed**. Adorned, set, with pearls.

pearl-fisher, n. One who fishes for pearls.

pearl-fishery, n. **a** Occupation of pearl-fisher; **b** place where this is carried on.

pearliness, n. [1. pěrlines; 2. pālinis]. **pearly** & **-ness**. Quality of being pearly.

pearl-mussel, n. A fresh-water mussel, *Unio margaritiferus*, which produces small pearls.

pearl-oyster, n. Large marine oyster of tropical seas, genus *Avicula* or *Meleagrina*, yielding pearls.

pearl-powder, n. Cosmetic used to whiten the skin.

pearl-shell, n. Mother-of-pearl.

pearly, adj. [1. pěrli; 2. pāli]. **pearl** (I.) & **-y**. **1. a** Like a pearl in colour or lustre; **b** made of, lined with pearl. **2.** As n. pl. *pearlies*, (colloq.) large pearl-buttons, as formerly worn by costermongers.

pearmain, n. [1. pārmān, pěrmān; 2. pɛəmein, pāmein], fr. O. Fr. *permain*, prob. fr. Lat. **Parmānus*, 'of Parma'. Class of apple, the best known of which is the *Worcester Pearmain*, a medium-sized red apple ripening in September.

pear-shaped, adj. Shaped like a pear; i.e. of an elongated, rapidly tapering oval.

pear tree, n. Tree producing pears, esp. *Pyrus communis*.

peasant, n. [1. pézant; 2. péz(ə)nt], fr. A.-Fr. *paisant*, fr. O. Fr. *païs*, Mod. Fr. *pays*, 'country', fr. Lat. *pāgensis*, 'of a province or canton', fr. *pāgus*, 'district, canton, village', see **pagan** & cp. **paysage**. **a** Countryman, villager, rustic; specif. **b** one who cultivates a small piece of ground which he owns; *peasant proprietorship*, system of agriculture based on ownership and cultivation of small plots by peasants.

peasantry, n. [1. pézantri; 2. pézəntri]. Prec. & **-ry**. **a** Body or group of peasants; **b** peasants as a class.

pease, n. [1. pēz; 2. pīz]. O.E. *pise*, 'pea', M.E. *pese*, fr. L. Lat. *pisa*, fr. Lat. *pisum*, 'pea', fr. Gk. *pisos*, 'pea'; prob. a loan-word, of unknown origin. Peas; esp. in *pease-pudding*, mashed peas boiled.

peasecod, n. [1. pēzkod; 2. pīzkɔd]. M.E. *pēscodde*; prec. & O.E. *codd*, 'husk, shell', see **cod** (II.); cp. Du. *kodde*, O.N. *koddi*, 'bag'. (archaic) Pea-pod.

pea-shooter, n. Tube through which dried peas are blown as missiles.

pea-soup, n. Thick soup made from peas, esp. from dried peas; otherwise *green-pea soup*.

pea-souper, n. [1. pḗ sóoper; 2. pí súpə]. (colloq.) Thick yellow fog (esp. in London).

pea-soupy, adj. [1. pḗ sóopi; 2. pí súpi]. (of fog) Thick and yellow.

peat, n. [1. pēt; 2. pit]. M.E. *pēte*; etymol. doubtful. **1.** Spongy substance, from 20 to 40 feet in depth, chiefly formed by a partial carbonization of various kinds of mosses; found in certain moist areas in Great Britain, Ireland, and other temperate climates; peat is cut in turves or divots, and used as fuel, and as a fertilizer. **2.** Single rectangular block of this; a turf.

peat-bog, n. Bog in which peat is formed.

peatery, n. [1. pḗteri; 2. pítəri]. **peat** & **-ery**. Place where peat is dug.

peat-moss, n. **1.** Peat bog. **2.** Kind of moss which composes peat.

peat-reek, n. **1.** Smoke from peat fire. **2.** Flavour characteristic of whisky distilled over a peat fire.

peaty, adj. [1. pḗti; 2. píti]. **peat** & **-y**. Composed of, resembling, smelling of, peat.

pebble, n. [1. pébl; 2. pébl]. O.E. has *papol-(stān)*, the formal connexion between wh. & M.E. *pobbel* & *pibbil* is not clear; origin unknown. **1.** Small stone rounded by action of water, ice &c. **2. a** Rock-crystal used for lenses of spectacles &c.; **b** lens made from this. **3.** Kind of agate.

pebbly, adj. [1. pébli; 2. pébli]. Prec. & **-ly**. Abounding in pebbles: *pebbly beach.*

pébrine, n. [1. pebrḗn; 2. pεbrín]. Fr., fr. Provenç. *pebrino*, dimin. of *pebre*, 'pepper', fr. Lat. *piper*, 'pepper'. See **pepper**. Bacterial disease affecting silkworms.

pecan, n. [1. pekán; 2. pikǽn], fr. Fr. *pacane*, fr. native N. Am. Indian word. **a** A kind of hickory of the South and Central United States; **b** its olive-shaped edible fruit, *pecan-nut.*

peccability, n. [1. pekabíliti; 2. pεkəbíliti]. See next word & **-ity**. State of being peccable.

peccable, adj. [1. pékabl; 2. pékəbl], fr. Med. Lat. *peccābil-(is)*, 'peccable', fr. Lat. *pecc-(āre)*, 'to sin', see **peccavi**, & **-able**. Liable to sin.

peccadillo, n. [1. pekadílō; 2. pεkədílou], fr. Span. *pecadillo*, dimin. of *pecado*, 'sin', fr. Lat. *peccāt-um*, P.P. of *peccāre*, 'to sin'. See **peccavi**. Trivial irregularity of conduct; slight, unimportant offence; an indiscretion.

peccancy, n. [1. pékansi; 2. pékənsi], fr. Lat. *peccantia*, 'sin'. See **peccant** & **-cy**. **1.** Sinfulness. **2.** A sin, transgression. **3.** (med., of disease) Morbid condition.

peccant, adj. [1. pékant; 2. pékənt], fr. Lat. *peccant-(em)*, Pres. Part. of Lat. *pecc-(āre)*, 'to sin', see **peccavi**, & **-ant**. **1. a** Sinful, erring, criminal; **b** wrong, erroneous. **2.** (med.) Morbid; indicating or causing disease.

peccary, n. [1. pékari; 2. pékəri]. Native *pakira*, prob. fr. Port. *bacoro*, 'young pig'. Gregarious, pig-like quadruped of America, ranging from Texas to northern parts of S. America.

peccavi, vb. intrans. & n. [1. pekávī; 2. pεk-éivai]. Lat. *peccāvi*, 'I have sinned', Pret. of *peccāre*, 'to sin'; etymol. doubtful. **1.** vb. I have sinned, esp. in Phr. *to cry* '*peccavi*', to admit guilt. **2.** n. A confession of guilt.

peck (I.), n. [1. pek; 2. pεk]. M.E. *pekke*, fr. O. Fr. *pek*; etymol. doubtful. **1.** Measure of capacity for dry goods, two gallons, quarter of bushel. **2.** Vessel holding one peck. **3.** Large amount, quantity: *a peck of dirt, of troubles.*

peck (II.), vb. trans. & intrans.; prob. variant of **pick**. **A.** trans. **1. a** (of bird) To strike, prick, with beak; **b** (of persons) to kiss hurriedly and perfunctorily. **2.** To make by pecking: *to peck a hole.* **3.** To obtain, pluck out, by pecking: *to peck something out of a hole.* **4.** (slang) To eat rapidly and in small quantities. **B.** intrans. **1.** *Peck at*, to aim at, strike at, thing with beak. **2.** To strike, break, (esp. the ground) with a pointed instrument. **3.** *Peck at (one's food)*, to make a perfunctory meal.

peck (III.), n., fr. prec. **1. a** Stroke made with beak or pointed object; **b** a hurried kiss. **2.** Mark or wound made by pecking.

pecker, n. [1. péker; 2. pékə]. **peck (II.)** & **-er**. **1.** Bird that pecks holes in trees, usually in combination, as *woodpecker.* **2.** Pointed instrument, pick. **3.** (slang) The beak, the human nose. Phr. *to keep one's pecker up*, not to lose heart, keep up one's spirits.

peckish, adj. [1. pékish; 2. pékiʃ]. **peck (II.)** & **-ish**. (colloq.) Hungry.

Pecksniff, n. [1. péksnif; 2. péksnif]. Character in Dickens's *Martin Chuzzlewit.* A smug, pompous humbug; an unctuous, unprincipled hypocrite who affects airs of piety, and preaches morality and benevolence while practising the reverse.

Pecora, n. pl. [1. pékōra; 2. pékōrə]. Lat., 'cattle', pl. of *pecus.* See **pecten** & **pecuniary**. (zool.) Term used for the large group of ruminant, ungulate mammals, which includes oxen, sheep, goats, antelopes, deer &c.

pecten, n. [1. pékten; 2. péktən]. Lat. *pecten*, 'comb'; cp. *pectere*, 'to comb'; *pecus*, 'cattle, flock', lit. 'fleecy, hairy thing'; *pexus*, 'woolly'; cogn. w. Gk. *péktein, pékein*, 'to comb, to shear', *pókos*, 'uncombed wool, a fleece'; O.H.G. *fahs*; O.E. *feax*, 'hair'; O.N. *fax*, 'mane'; Lith. *pèszti*, 'to pull out one's hair'; Scrt. *pakšman*, 'eyebrows'; Pers. *pašm*, 'wool', cp. **pashm**. See further **pecuniary**. (zool.) **1.** Any organ or process which suggests the teeth of a comb in appearance; specif. one in the eye of birds and reptiles. **2.** Genus of marine bivalve molluscs, including the scallop.

pectic, adj. [1. péktik; 2. péktik]. See next word & **-ic**. Of, pertaining to, composed of, pectin.

pectin, n. [1. péktin; 2. péktin], fr. Gk. *pēkt-(ós)*, 'fixed; constructed, put together; congealed, curdled', fr. *pḗgnūmi*, 'I make fast; make solid'; cp. Scrt. *pajrás*, 'solid'; cogn. w. Lat. *(com)pāgēs*, 'fastening'; *pāx*, 'peace', see **pax** & words there referred to; for the suff. see **-in**. (chem.) A gelatinous substance found in some fruits, which causes jelly to form in jam.

pectinate, adj. [1. péktinat; 2. péktinət], fr. Lat. *pectin-*, see **pecten**, & **-ate**. Shaped like, having teeth like, a comb.

pectinated, adj. [1. péktināted; 2. péktineitid]. Prec. & **-ed**. Pectinate.

pectination, n. [1. pèktinā́shun; 2. pèktinéiʃən]. See prec. & **-ion**. **1.** State of being pectinated. **2.** Comb-like process.

pectoral, adj. & n. [1. péktural; 2. péktərəl], fr. Lat. *pectorāl-(is)*, 'pectoral', fr. *pector-*, stem of *pectus*, 'breast'; cogn. w. Scrt. *pákšas*, 'side, half, shoulder, wing'. **1.** adj. **a** Connected with, pertaining to, the breast: *pectoral muscles, arch* &c.; *pectoral fins*, the pair of fins of a fish just behind the gills, corresponding to the forelimbs of animals; **b** good for, designed to cure, diseases of the chest: *pectoral balsam*; **c** worn on the breast: *pectoral cross*, small gold cross, worn by bishops. **2.** n. **a** Ornament worn on the breast; specif., breast-plate of Jewish high priest; **b** (pl.) pectoral fins.

pectose, n. [1. péktōs; 2. péktous], fr. Gk. *pēkt-(ós)*, 'congealed', see **pectin**, & **-ose**. (chem.) Substance related to cellulose, easily changing into pectin.

peculate, vb. intrans. [1. pékūlāt; 2. pékjuleit], fr. Lat. *pecūlāt-(um)*, P.P. type of *pecūlāri*, 'to embezzle public money', fr. *pecūl-(ium)*, 'private property'. See **peculiar**. To appropriate to one's own use money held in trust for others.

peculation, n. [1. pèkūlā́shun; 2. pèkjuléiʃən]. Prec. & **-ion**. Act of peculating or embezzling; embezzlement.

peculiar (I.), adj. [1. pekū́liar; 2. pikjúliə], fr. Lat. *pecūliār-(is)*, 'of, relating to, private property; one's own; special, peculiar', fr. *pecūli-(um)*, 'private property', fr. *pecu(s)*, 'cattle; property'. See **pecuniary** & **pecten**. **1.** Belonging to no other, forming an exclusive possession, individual: *ideas peculiar to oneself; one's own peculiar temperament; to have peculiar privileges; peculiar people*, (i.) the Jews; (ii.) the elect of God; (iii.) (cap.) Protestant sect, founded 1838, relying in illness on prayer and anointing. **2.** Special, particular, of distinct character; marked: *to receive peculiar attention.* **3.** Unusual, odd, uncommon, singular: *a peculiar sort of man; peculiar behaviour; to look peculiar.*

peculiar (II.), n., fr. prec. **1.** Peculiar possession, property, privilege &c. **2.** (eccles.) Church or parish exempt from jurisdiction of the bishop in whose diocese it is situated.

peculiarity, n. [1. pekūliáriti; 2. pikjuliǽriti]. See prec. & **-ity**. **1.** Quality of being peculiar; distinctiveness. **2.** Something which is peculiar or distinctive; a characteristic property or quality; distinguishing feature of mind, body, character &c. **3.** Characteristic oddity, strangeness of appearance, habit &c.; eccentricity: *to affect peculiarity in dress; he has certain little peculiarities of manner which many resent.*

peculiarly, adv. [1. pekū́liarli; 2. pikjúliəli]. **peculiar (I.)** & **-ly**. **1.** Individually, personally, as far as one is oneself concerned: *to be peculiarly interested in an affair.* **2.** Specially, to a marked degree: *peculiarly sensitive to ridicule.* **3.** In a strange manner; oddly, queerly: *to behave peculiarly.*

pecuniarily, adv. [1. pekū́niarili; 2. pikjúniərili]. See next word & **-ly**. In a pecuniary manner; as regards, from point of view of, money.

pecuniary, adj. [1. pekū́niari; 2. pikjúniəri], fr. Lat. *pecūniāri-(us)*, 'of money', fr. *pecūnia*, 'property, riches; money', fr. *pecu-(s)*, 'cattle', hence 'property, possessions'; cp. O.H.G. *fihu*; O.E. *feoh*, 'cattle, property'; Goth. *faihu*, 'property; money', see **fee**; Scrt. *pášu*, 'cattle'. See further under **peculiar** & **pecten**. Connected with, pertaining to, consisting of, money: *pecuniary affairs; pecuniary assistance, losses, considerations* &c.; *pecuniary offence*, one involving a pecuniary penalty, entailing a fine.

pedagogic(al), adj. [1. pèdagógik(l), pèdagójik(l); 2. pèdəgógik(l), pèdəgódžik(l)]. **pedagogue** & **-ic** & **-al**. Of, pertaining to, pedagogy.

pedagogically, adv. Prec. & **-ly**. In a pedagogic manner; as a pedagogue.

pedagogics, n. [1. pèdagógiks, -gójiks; 2. pèdəgógiks, -gódžiks]. See prec. Science of teaching; pedagogy.

pedagog(u)ism, n. [1. pédagogizm, -gojizm; 2. pédəgəgizəm, -gədžizəm]. See next word & **-ism**. State of being a pedagogue; pedagogic character; usually with implication of pedantry.

pedagogue, n. [1. pédagog; 2. pédəgəg], fr. O. Fr., fr. Lat. *paedagōg-(us)*, 'slave in charge of children; governor, preceptor; pedant', fr. Gk. *paidagōgós*, 'slave who escorted children to school &c.; preceptor, tutor', fr. *paid-*, stem of *pais*, 'boy, child', see **paedo-**, & *agōgós*, 'guide, leader', fr. *ágein*, 'to lead, convey, bring; to carry out'; cogn. w. Lat. *agere*, 'to do, perform', see **agent**. **a** Teacher, schoolmaster; **b** a pedantic fellow who carries the manner of a schoolmaster into ordinary life and perpetually endeavours to instruct.

pedagogy, n. [1. pédagogi, -goji; 2. pédəgəgi, -gədži], fr. Lat., fr. Gk. *paidagōgía*, 'attendance on children; education', fr. *paidagōg-(ós)*, 'children's attendant'. See prec. & **-y**. Science of teaching.

pedal (I.), adj. [1. pḗdl; 2. pídl], fr. Lat. *pedāl-(is)*, 'of a foot', fr. *ped-*, stem of *pēs*, 'foot'; cp., w. different grade, Gk. *pod-(ós)*, genit. of *poús*, 'foot', see **-pod**; Scrt. *pāt*, acc. *pādam*, 'foot'; *padam*, 'footmark';

Goth. *fōtus*; O.E. *fōt*, 'foot', see **foot**. From **ped-* grade are Gk. *pedá*, 'after, i.e. on the track of'; *pédon*, 'ground'; Lith. *pėdà*, 'track'; O. Slav. *pěšŭ*, 'ground'; O.N. *fet*, 'step'; O.E. *fetian*, 'to fetch', see **fetch** (I.). Pertaining to a foot or feet; (chiefly zool.) *pedal extremities*, the feet; *pedal ganglia*, of molluscs &c.

pedal (II.), n. [1. pédl; 2. pédl], fr. Fr., fr. Ital. *pedale*, fr. Lat. See prec. A lever of various kinds worked by the foot, esp. the projecting part of such on which the foot rests. Specif. **1.** Lever or projecting part of such worked by the foot and used to transmit power or movement to a machine; treadle, as of bicycle, lathe, sewing-machine. **2.** (of organ &c.) **a** One of the wooden keys of the keyboard worked by the feet, contrasted with *manual*; **b** lever worked by the foot acting on a combination of stops and for other purposes; **c** foot lever for working the wind for harmonium &c. **3.** (of pianoforte) Either of two levers, one of which raises the dampers and increases and sustains the tone, *loud pedal*, the other muffling the hammers and strings, *soft pedal*. **4.** (mus.) Sustained note, usually in the bass, through several harmonies.

pedal (III.), vb. intrans. & trans., fr. prec. **1.** intrans. **a** To use the pedals, of organ, pianoforte &c.; **b** to progress by working pedals of bicycle; to ride a bicycle: *to pedal up a hill, along a road*. **2.** trans. To work, drive, by pedals: *to pedal a bicycle* &c.

pedant, n. [1. pédnt; 2. pédnt]. Fr., fr. Ital. *pedante*, the first element of wh. is seen in **pedagogue**. **1.** One who makes an inappropriate display of learning; one who, through defect in sense of proportion, attaches exaggerated importance to trifling or irrelevant details of scholarship and method; one who is inclined so to interpret formulae that the letter kills the spirit, and to sacrifice principles to verbal niceties and to interpretation of rules &c. **2.** Person obsessed by particular theory; a doctrinaire, a crank.

pedantic, adj. [1. pedántik; 2. pidǽntik]. Prec. & **-ic**. Pertaining to, like, characteristic of, a pedant, or of pedantry.

pedantically, adv. [1. pedántikali; 2. pidǽntikəli]. Prec. & **-al** & **-ly**. In a pedantic manner.

pedantry, n. [1. pédantri; 2. pédəntri]. **pedant** & **-ry**. **1.** Quality of being pedantic. **2.** Pedantic mode of thought and expression.

pedate, adj. [1. pédāt; 2. pédeit], fr. Lat. *pedāt-(us)*, fr. *ped-*, stem of *pēs*, 'foot', see **pedal**, & **-ate**. **1.** (zool.) **a** Having feet; **b** resembling, used as, foot. **2.** (bot., of leaf) Divided like foot.

peddle, vb. intrans. & trans. [1. pédl; 2. pédl]. Prob. back-formation fr. **pedlar**. **1.** intrans. **a** To carry on the business of a pedlar; **b** (fig.) to busy oneself about trifles, engage in petty, useless pursuits. **2.** trans. (lit. and fig.) To retail (goods or gossip) in a small way.

peddling, adj. [1. pédling; 2. pédliŋ], fr. Pres. Part. of prec. Small-minded, preoccupied by trifles; trumpery, unimportant, pettifogging: *peddling details*.

pederasty, n. See **paederasty**.

pedestal, n. & vb. trans. [1. pédestal; 2. pédistəl], fr. Fr. *piédestal*, fr. Ital. *piedestallo* for *piede di stallo*, 'foot of a seat'; fr. Lat. base *ped-*, 'foot', see **pedal**, & *stallo*, see **stall** (I.). **1.** n. **a** Base of a large column, statue &c.; **b** small column, or other support, e.g. for a bust, statue &c.; Phr. *to set (a person) upon a pedestal*, regard him as a superior being; **c** either of the two supports, often fitted with drawers, of a knee-hole desk or table; **d** support, foundation (lit. and fig.). **2.** vb. To set on a pedestal.

pedestrian (I.), adj. [1. pedéstrian; 2. pidéstriən], fr. Lat. *pedestri-(s)*, nom. *pedester*, 'on foot'; n., 'person on foot; foot-soldier', fr. *ped-*, 'foot', see **pedal**, & **-ian**. **1.** Connected with walking; performed on foot: *pedestrian exercise*. **2.** (of style and literary composition) Hasty, unpolished, not bearing evidence of special care; having appearance of being composed during the ordinary round of business; hence, mechanical, uninspired.

pedestrian (II.), n., fr. prec. Person on foot; a walker, foot-passenger.

pedestrianism, n. [1. pedéstrianizm; 2. pidéstriənizəm]. Prec. & **-ism**. Art or practice of walking.

pedestrianize, vb. intrans. [1. pedéstrianīz; 2. pidéstriənaiz]. See prec. & **-ize**. To go on foot.

pedicel, n. [1. pédisel; 2. pédisɛl], as fr. Lat. **pedīcell-(us)*, dimin.; usual form is *pedīcul-(us)*, 'a little foot'. See **pedicle**. **1.** (bot.) Small, secondary stalk supporting single flower in inflorescence. **2.** (zool.) Small stalk-like structure in animal.

pedicellate, adj. [1. pèdiselāt; 2. pèdiséleit]. Prec. & **-ate**. Having, supported by, like, a pedicel.

pedicle, n. [1. pédikl; 2. pédikl], fr. Lat. *pedīcul-(us)*, 'little foot; foot-stalk of flower or leaf', dimin. of *ped-*, 'foot'. See **pedal** & **-cule**. Pedicel.

pedicular, adj. [1. pedíkūlar; 2. pedíkjulə], fr. Lat. *pēdiculār-(is)*, 'pedicular', fr. *pēdīculus*, 'louse,' dimin. of *pēdis*, 'louse', perh. 'the runner', fr. base **pĕd-*, 'foot', see **pedal**. Pertaining to, infested with, lice.

pediculate, adj. [1. pedíkūlat; 2. pedíkjulət], fr. Lat. *pedīcul-(us)*, 'a little foot'. See **pedicle** & **-ate**. Pedicellate.

pediculosis, n. [1. pèdikūlósis; 2. pèdikjulóusis], fr. Lat. *pēdīcul-(us)*, 'louse'. See **pedicular** & **-osis**. (med.) Affection of the skin characterized by itching, caused by lice.

pediculous, adj. [1. pedíkūlus; 2. pedíkjuləs], fr. Lat. *pēdīculōs-(us)*, 'lousy', fr. *pēdīcul-(us)*, 'louse'. See **pedicular** & **-ous**. Pedicular.

pedigree, n. [1. pédigrē; 2. pédigrī]. Earlier *pedegru*, prob. fr. Fr. *pied de grue*, 'crane's foot', fr. shape of mark (⅄) indicating descent from ancestor, as used in genealogical tables; fr. Lat. *ped-*, 'foot', see **pedal**, & *de*, 'of', & *grue*, 'crane', fr. Lat. *grūs*, 'crane', q.v. under **crane** (I.). **1.** Genealogical table. **2.** (of person or animal) **a** Genealogy, ancestry, descent; specif. **b** ancient lineage: *a family of pedigree*. **3.** (of word) Derivation, etymology. **4.** (attrib.) Having a known pedigree: *pedigree herd, cattle* &c.

pedigreed, adj. [1. pédigrēd; 2. pédigrīd]. Prec. & **-ed**. Having a pedigree, having a known line of descent.

pediment, n. [1. pédiment; 2. pédimənt]. Supposed by Skeat to be for *periment*, a re-fashioning of **pyramid**, perh. influenced by *(im)pedīmentum*; the Lat. term is *fastigium*. (class. archit.) Triangular structure often richly sculptured, forming the gable or end of a two-pitched roof; any structure resembling this in form, in later architecture.

pedimental, adj. [1. pèdiméntl; 2. pèdiméntl]. Prec. & **-al**. Of, forming, shaped like, a pediment.

pedimented, adj. [1. pédimented; 2. pédimɛntid]. **pediment** & **-ed**. Having, crowned by, a pediment.

pedlar, n. [1. pédlar; 2. pédlə]. *Pedlere* in 14th cent.; evidently connected w. M.E. *pedder* &c., 'pedlar, a fish-hawker'; fr. *ped*, an old word for basket, esp. one for fish, the origin of wh. is unknown. **1.** Licensed itinerant vendor of miscellaneous small wares, which he carries about in a pack. **2.** (fig.) Retailer of gossip &c.

pedlary, n. [1. pédlari; 2. pédləri]. Prec. & **-ry**. **1.** Occupation of a pedlar. **2.** Pedlar's wares.

pedo-. See **paedo-**.

pedometer, n. [1. pedómeter; 2. pedɔ́mitə], fr. Lat. *ped-*, stem of *pēs*, 'foot'. See **pedal** & **-meter**. Instrument worn on the person which records the distance walked by the wearer.

peduncle, n. [1. pedúngkl; 2. pidáŋkl], fr. Lat. *ped-*, stem of *pēs*, 'foot', see **podal**, & **-uncle**. **1.** (bot.) Stem of a plant which supports the flower. **2.** (zool.) Stalk-like connexion or process.

peduncular, adj. [1. pedúngkūlar; 2. pidáŋkjulə]. Prec. & **-ar**. Of, pertaining to, like, a peduncle.

pedunculate, adj. [1. pedúngkūlat; 2. pidáŋkjulət]. **peduncle** & **-ate**. Having, supported by, a peduncle.

peek, vb. intrans. [1. pēk; 2. pīk]. Etymol. doubtful; M.E. has *pike*; cp. **peep** (III.). To peep, peer, esp. *peek in, out*.

peek-a-boo, n. [1. pék a bōō; 2. pík ə bú]. Children's game, bo-peep.

peel (I.), n. [1. pēl; 2. piəl]. M.E., fr. O. Fr. *pēl*, 'palisade, fort'; fr. Lat. *pālus*, 'a stake'. See **pale** (I.). Small, ancient, square tower, used as fortress and dwelling-house, built on Scottish borders.

peel (II.), n., fr. O. Fr. *pele*, fr. Lat. *pāla*, 'spade', see **palette**. Baker's thin, long-handled shovel for removing bread &c. from oven.

peel (III.), vb. trans. & intrans. O.E. *pilian*, M.E. *pēlen*, 'strip off', fr. Lat. *pilāre*, 'to take the hair off', see **pill** (III.). **A.** trans. **1.** To strip off skin or rind of: *to peel an apple, stick* &c. **2.** To strip off, remove: *to peel the bark off a tree* &c. **B.** intrans. **1.** Often *peel off*, to come off in strips; become detached from; said **a** of any thin outer covering: *the bark, plaster, paper &c. is peeling (off)*; also **b** of that which sheds its surface covering in strips: *the walls are peeling*, are losing their plaster or paper. **2.** (slang) To undress, strip.

peel (IV.), n., fr. prec. Outer skin, rind, of fruit; *candied peel*, of citron, orange, or lemon.

peeler, n. [1. pēler; 2. pílə], fr. Sir Robert Peel, d. 1850. **1.** (obs., colloq.) Policeman. **2.** (hist.) Member of Irish Constabulary founded by Peel, 1812–18.

Peelite, n. [1. pēlīt; 2. pílait], fr. Sir Robert Peel & **-ite**. Adherent of Peel at time of repeal of Corn laws in 1846.

peen, n. & vb. trans. [1. pēn; 2. pīn]. Cp. Norw. *pen*, Mod. Germ. *pinne*, in same sense; origin doubtful. **1.** n. That end of the head of a hammer which has a blunt wedge-shaped edge, opposite to the *face*, used in working stone &c. **2.** vb. To work on, bend, straighten, with the peen of a hammer.

peep (I.), vb. intrans. [1. pēp; 2. pīp]. Imitative of sound; perh. associated w. **pipe** (II.). To chirp, cheep, squeak; esp. of young birds or mice.

peep (II.), n., fr. prec. Thin, high-pitched sound as of young bird, mouse &c.; squeak, chirp.

peep (III.), vb. intrans.; etymol. doubtful, prob. variant of **peek**. **1.** To look hastily, to obtain a hurried glimpse, to peer secretly, furtively, cautiously: *to peep out of a window*; *to peep through a hedge*; *to peep over a wall*. **2.** **a** To come gradually into view, begin to appear: '*The little window where the sun Came peeping in at morn*' (Hood); *the stars were beginning to peep*; **b** (of character, qualities) become manifest, be revealed, emerge involuntarily: *the inherent meanness of the man was always peeping out*.

peep (IV.), n., fr. prec. **1.** Restricted view, glimpse; esp. something seen between, or over the top of intervening obstacles: *to get a peep of open country between the mountains*; *a peep of the sea over the house-roofs*. **2.** Furtive, cautious glance; hurried look of inspection: *let me have just one peep at the letter*. **3.** First appearance, esp. in Phr. *peep of day, dawn*. Phr. *Peep-of-Day Boys*, Irish Protestant society (1784) which visited houses of Roman Catholics at daybreak in search of arms.

peeper (I.), n. [1. pēper; 2. pīpə]. **peep** (I.) & **-er**. Bird, animal &c. that peeps, esp. a young bird.

peeper (II.), n. **peep** (III.) & **-er**. **1.** One who peeps. **2.** (slang) The eye.

peep-hole, n. Small opening, crevice, in a wall, door &c. through which one may peep at what is on the other side.

peep-show, n. Miniature exhibition of pictures &c. seen through small hole fitted with lens.

peepul, n. See **pipal**.

peer (**I.**), n. [1. pēr; 2. piə]. M.E. fr. O. Fr. *pēr(e)*, fr. Lat. *pār*, 'equal', see **par** (**I.**). **1.** Person or thing of equal merit, quality, rank &c. with another: '*Lycidas is dead . . . Young Lycidas, and hath not left his peer*' (Milton, Lyc. 8-9); *without a peer*, unequalled; *one's peers*, persons of same rank and standing as oneself. **2.** One entitled to sit in the House of Lords **a** by hereditary right, *peer of the realm*; **b** as a *peer of Parliament, life peer*, e.g. certain of the bishops, and the Lords of Appeal; **c** member of the Scottish peerage, who cannot sit in House of Lords unless elected as a representative peer; member of Irish peerage, who cannot now sit at all in House of Lords unless he is also in one of the other categories. *Temporal Peers*, all peers other than bishops; contrasted with *Spiritual Peer*, a bishop sitting in House of Lords.

peer (**II.**), vb. trans. & intrans., fr. M.E. *peren*, fr. O. Fr. *perer*, fr. Lat. *pariāre*, 'to make equal', fr. *pār*, 'equal', see **par** (**I.**). (rarely or never used) **1.** trans. **a** To equal, rank with, come up to; **b** to make a peer. **2.** intrans. To be equal in rank, quality &c. (followed by *with*).

peer (**III.**), vb. intrans. Origin unknown. To look closely, narrowly, stare, gaze fixedly and with attention: *to peer into a person's face*; *peering down a well*; (also fig.) *the sun peered through the clouds*.

peerage, n. [1. pērij; 2. píəridž]. **peer** (**I.**) & **-age**. **1.** Body of peers considered collectively. **2.** Rank of peer. **3.** Book containing list of peers and their lineage.

peeress, n. [1. pēres; 2. píəris]. **peer** (**I.**) & **-ess**. **a** Wife of peer; **b** woman holding a hereditary peerage.

peerless, adj. [1. pērles; 2. píəlis]. **peer** (**I.**) & **-less**. Without peer, unequalled, matchless, unique.

peerlessly, adv. Prec. & **-ly**. In a peerless manner.

peerlessness, n. See prec. & **-ness**. Quality of being peerless.

peeve, vb. trans. [1. pēv; 2. pīv]. Back-formation fr. next word. (slang) To annoy, make peevish; esp. in P.P. *peeved*.

peevish, adj. [1. pēvish; 2. pívıʃ]. M.E. *pevische* &c.; perh. variant of **perverse** (Weekley). **1.** (obs. or archaic) Malignant, perverse, churlish. **2.** Fretful, irritable, querulous, cantankerous.

peevishly, adv. Prec. & **-ly**. In a peevish manner.

peevishness, n. See prec. & **-ness**. State, quality, of being peevish.

peewit, n. See **pewit**.

peg (**I.**), n. [1. peg; 2 peg]. M.E. *pegge*; cp. L.G. *pigge*, 'spike', Du. dial. *peg*, 'nail'. **1.** Small, usually rounded, pin or bolt of wood or metal used to fasten pieces of framework together. Phr. *square peg in round hole*, person unfitted to his position. **2.** Wooden or metal pin driven into and projecting from a surface and used as a hold, or support; **a** one fastened into a wall: *hat peg* &c.; **b** one driven into the ground to hold something in position: *tent peg*; **c** *clothes-peg*, cleft stick clipped over a line, to support linen hung up to dry; **d** (fig.) subject, theme; pretext, upon which a discourse, argument &c. is based: *a good peg to hang a sermon on*. **3.** Wooden screw with flattened end, passing through holes in head of violin, or other instrument of this class, by means of which the strings are tightened. **4.** Small pointed piece of wood, ivory &c. for marking score at cribbage. **5.** A drink, esp. whisky or brandy, and soda; *king's peg*, brandy and champagne; probably from the small pegs formerly projecting from the internal sides of tankards to indicate the amount of liquor; from this fact also the Phr. *to take a person down a peg*, to drink more than he does; hence, to destroy his self-conceit, lower his pride.

peg (**II.**), vb. trans. & intrans., fr. prec. **A.** trans. **1.** To fasten with a peg. **2.** **a** (Stock Exchange) To keep price of stock steady by buying or selling freely at fixed price; **b** (financial) to fix prices, value (of currency) &c. by regulations &c. **3.** To indicate by means of pegs on cribbage-board. **B.** intrans & trans., followed by adverbs and prepositions. *Peg at*, to aim at, strike, with peg. *Peg away*, to keep working constantly, unremittingly. *Peg down*, **a** to fasten to the ground &c. by pegs; **b** (fig.) to restrict, bind down, pin down (to rule, statement, course of action &c.). *Peg out*, **1.** trans., **a** to mark with pegs, stake out (boundary &c.); **b** (croquet) to finish game by striking last peg; **2.** intrans., (colloq.) **a** to become exhausted, come to an end; **b** to die.

pegamoid, n. [1. pégamoid; 2. pégəmɔid]. Invented word. An artificial leather.

Pegasus, n. [1. pégasus; 2. pégəsəs]. Lat. *Pēgasus*, fr. Gk. *Pḗgasos*, fr. *pēgḗ*, 'fount, spring'; etymol. unknown, but see **beach** (**I.**). **1.** (Gk. mythol.) Winged horse of Bellerophon, sprung from the blood of Medusa, a blow from whose hoofs caused the fountain Hippocrene, sacred to the Muses, to flow on Mt. Helicon. **2.** Poetic genius or inspiration.

pegmatite, n. [1. pégmatīt; 2. pégmətait], fr. Gk. *pḗgmat-os, pēgma*, 'something fastened together, bond'. See **pax**. (geol.) A coarse crystalline rock, of quartz, feldspar &c., found in veins in granite.

peg-top, n. **peg** (**I.**) & **top**. Pear-shaped, wooden, spinning-top, with a spike at thin end; *peg-top trousers*, such as were cut broad at the thigh, and tapered rapidly to the ankles.

peignoir, n. [1. pānwar; 2. péinwā], fr. Fr., fr. *peigner*, 'to comb the hair', fr. *peigne*, 'comb', fr. Lat. *pectin-(em)*, 'comb', see **pecten**. Woman's loose robe; a dressing-gown.

peine forte et dure, n. [1. pān fórt ā dūr; 2. pèin fɔ̄t ei djúə]. Fr., 'severe and hard punishment'. (law) Punishment inflicted upon prisoners who refused to plead, which consisted of pressing them to death under heavy weights.

pejoration, n. [1. pējoráshun; 2. pīdžəréiʃən], fr. Lat. *pējōr-(āre)*, 'to make or grow worse', fr. *pējor*, 'worse', earlier **pedjōs*, fr. **petjōs*; cp. Lat. *pessimus*, 'worst', fr. *pessum*, 'downwards, to the ground', wh. is for **pot-to-*, fr. base **pet-*, 'to go, fall, fly'. See this under **pen** (**III.**) & **feather**. Depreciation in meaning of word.

pejorative, adj. & n. [1. pējorativ, pejórativ; 2. pīdžərətiv, pidžɔ́rətiv], fr. Lat. *pējōr-(āre)*, 'to make or grow worse'. See prec. & **-ative**. **1.** adj. Disparaging, giving a depreciatory sense: *a pejorative suffix*. **2.** n. Depreciatory word or suffix.

pekan, n. [1. pékan; 2. pékən]. Fr. *pékan*, fr. N. Am. Indian name, *pékané*. A large kind of marten, with valuable blackish-brown fur, of N. America.

pekin, n., fr. Fr. *pékin*, fr. Chinese *Pe-king*, 'northern capital'. **1.** [1. pēkín; 2. píkín] Kind of silk. **2.** (Fr. slang) [1. pékan; 2. pékæ̃] Civilian; used first by Napoleon's soldiers as term of contempt.

pekinese, pekingese, n. [1. pēkinēz; 2. pīkiníz]. See prec. & **-ese**. Small Chinese dog, allied to the pug, with long silky hair, large pendant ears, and bulging eyes.

Peking man, n. See **Sinanthropus**.

pekoe, n. [1. pékō, pēkō; 2. pékou, píkou], fr. Chinese *pek-ho*, fr. *pek*, 'white', & *ho*, 'down'. Superior kind of black tea, made from young, downy buds of leaves of tea-plant.

pelage, n. [1. pélij; 2. pélidž]. Fr., fr. O. Fr. *pel*, 'hair', fr. Lat. *pilus*, 'hair'. See **pill** (**III.**) & **-age**. Outer coat of quadruped.

Pelagian (**I.**), adj. & n. [1. peláјian; 2. peléidžən], fr. *Pelagi-(us)*, British monk of 4th cent., who denied doctrine of original sin, & **-an**. **1.** adj. Pertaining to Pelagius and his heresy. **2.** n. Follower of Pelagius.

pelagian (**II.**), adj. & n., fr. Lat. *pelagi-(us)*, 'of the sea', fr. *pelag-(us)*, 'the open sea', fr. Gk. *pélagos*, 'open sea; unbroken surface or expanse of sea'; fr. base **p(e)lāg-*, **p(e)ləg-*, 'to spread out flat'; cp. Lat. *plaga*, 'hunting-net; curtain; region'; Gk. *plágos*, 'side', see **plagal**; this base is an extension of **p(e)lā-*, **plə-*, 'extended', see **plain** (**I.**), **palm** (**I.**), & words there referred to. **1.** adj. Of, pertaining to, inhabiting, the open sea; oceanic. **2.** n. Deep-sea animal.

Pelagianism, n. [1. peláјanizm; 2. peléidžənizəm]. **Pelagian** (**I.**) & **-ism**. The heresy of Pelagius.

pelagic, adj. [1. pelájik; 2. pelǽdžik], fr. Lat. *pelagic-(us)*, 'of the open sea', fr. *pelag-(us)*, 'the open sea'. See **pelagian** (**II.**) & **-ic**. Connected with, inhabiting, the deep sea.

pelargonium, n. [1. pèlargōnium; 2. pèləgóuniəm]. Mod. Lat., fr. Gk. *pelārg-(ós)*, 'stork', fr. **pela-*, 'blackish'; cp. Lith. *palvas*; O. Slav. *plavŭ*; O.H.G. *falo*, 'pale'; O.E. *fealo*, 'dull-coloured', see **fallow** (**IV.**), & *argós*, 'white, clear, brilliant'. See **argil**. Genus of plants, with brightly coloured flowers, and strongly scented leaves, often cultivated under name of *geranium*.

Pelasgic, adj. [1. pelázjik; 2. pelǽzdžik], fr. Lat. *Pelasgic-(us)*, fr. *Pelasgi*, Gk. *Pelasgoí*, prehistoric race of the coasts of Greece and Asia Minor and the Aegean islands. Of, relating to, the Pelasgi; *Pelasgic architecture*, earliest existing form of Greek masonry, consisting of unhewn stones laid without cement.

pelerine, n. [1. pélerin, -ēn; 2. pélərin, -īn], fr. Fr. *pélerine*, 'tippet', fr. fem. of *pélerin*, 'pilgrim', fr. O. Fr. *pelegrin*, see **pilgrim**. Woman's long, narrow cape or tippet.

pelf, n. [1. pelf; 2. pelf]. M.E. *pelfer*, fr. O. Fr. *pelfre*; etymol. doubtful. See **pilfer**. Money, material wealth; usually in disparagement or contempt, and contrasted with more enduring spiritual riches; esp. of gains of avarice, supposed to bring no satisfaction to the possessor.

pelican, n. [1. pélikan; 2. pélikən], fr. L. Lat. *pelicān-(us)*, fr. Gk. *pelekán*, 'pelican'; cp. Gk. *pelekâs*, 'woodpecker'; fr. *pélek-(us)*, 'axe'; cp. Scrt. *paraśuš*, 'axe'; an eastern loan-word; cp. Babylonian-Assyrian *pilaqqu*, 'axe'. Large, fish-eating water-bird, genus *Pelecanus*, of many species, found in warm climates, having a long beak below which is a distensible pouch for storing food; formerly fabled to feed its young with blood from its own breast, whence, when represented in heraldry 'vulning' (wounding) itself, it is styled 'a pelican in her piety'.

pelisse, n. [1. pelḗs; 2. pelís]. Fr., fr. Lat. *pellicia* (*vestis*), '(garment) of skins, furs', fr. *pell-(is)*, 'skin'. See **pellicle**. **a** Long cloak, esp. one lined with fur; **b** child's outer coat or cloak; **c** cape or cloak worn as part of some military uniforms.

pell, n. [1. pel; 2. pel]. M.E., fr. O. Fr. *pel*, 'skin', fr. Lat. *pellis*. See **pellicle**. A skin or hide, specif. a vellum or parchment roll, now obs. or hist. as *Clerk of the Pells*, an official of the old Court of Exchequer.

pellagra, n. [1. pelágra, -ágra; 2. peléigrə, -ǽgrə]. Prob. fr. Ital. *pelle*, 'skin', & *agra*, 'rough'. A chronic disease, often endemic in certain parts of Italy and elsewhere, caused by a micro-organism communicated by the bite of sand-flies; the chief symptoms are severe eruptions leading to a drying or mummifying of the skin and severe disturbances of the digestive and nervous systems.

pellagrous, adj. [1. pelágrus, -ágrus; 2. peléigrəs, -ǽgrəs]. Prec. & **-ous**. Connected with, affected with, pellagra.

pellet (**I.**), n. [1. pélet; 2. pélit], fr. Fr. *pelote*, fr. Med. Lat. *pelota*, fr. Lat. *pila*, 'ball', perh. orig. 'ball of hair', fr. *pil-(us)*, 'hair'. See **pellicle**. **1.** Small ball rolled up from some soft substance, e.g. bread, wax, paper

&c. 2. Any small, round body, esp. **a** small pill; **b** small shot. 3. Small rounded boss on coin &c.

pellet (II.), vb. trans., fr. prec. To throw pellet at, hit with pellet.

pellicle, n. [1. pélikl; 2. pélikl], fr. Lat. *pellicula*, dimin. of *pelli-(s)*, 'skin, hide'; cp. O.N. *-fjall*; O.H.G. *fel*; O.E. *fell*, 'hide', see **fell**; Gk. *péllās*, 'skins'; *pélma*, 'sole'; O.E. *filmen*, 'thin skin', see **film**; Lith. *plėvė*, 'thin skin'. Thin skin or membrane.

pellicular, adj. [1. pelíkūlar; 2. pelíkjulə]. See prec. & **-ar**. Of, like, forming, a pellicle.

pellitory (I.), n. [1. péliturì; 2. pélitəri]. Earlier *pelleter*, fr. Lat. *pyrethrum*, fr. Gk. *púrethron*, 'fever-few', cp. *puretós*, 'fever'. See **pyretic** & **pyrethrum**. Also *pellitory of Spain*, perennial herb of the aster family, with pungent root, used as counter-irritant for toothache &c.; found in S. Europe and N. Africa.

pellitory (II.), n., fr. Lat. *parietāria*, 'pellitory', fr. fem. of *parietārius*, 'of walls', fr. *pariet-*, stem of *pariēs*, 'wall'. See **parietal** & **-ary**. Green-flowered plants growing often on old walls &c.

pell-mell, adv., adj., & n. [1. pél mél; 2. pél mél], fr. Fr. *pêle-mêle*; origin doubtful. 1. adv. **a** Confusedly, promiscuously; **b** headlong, precipitately. 2. adj. Confused, disorderly; headlong. 3. n. Medley, confusion.

pellucid, adj. [1. pelúsid; 2. peljúsid], fr. Lat. *pellūcid-(us)*, *perlūcid-(us)*, 'transparent', fr. *perlūc-(ēre)*, 'to shine through'. See **per-** & **lucid**. 1. Permitting the passage of light; clear, transparent, translucent. 2. (fig., of mind, style &c.) Extremely clear and lucid.

pellucidity, n. [1. pèlūsíditi; 2. pèljūsíditi]. Prec. & **-ity**. State or quality of being pellucid.

pellucidly, adv. [1. pelúsidli; 2. peljúsidli]. See prec. & **-ly**. In a pellucid manner; clearly, lucidly.

pelota, n. [1. pelóta; 2. pelóutə]. Span. *pelota*, 'ball', fr. *pella*, fr. Lat. *pila*, 'ball'. See **pellet**. Basque ball game somewhat resembling tennis, played in a walled court, with a long, curved, wicker, basket-shaped racket, fastened to the right wrist.

pelt (I.), n. [1. pelt; 2. pelt]. Cp. obs. *pell*, fr. O. Fr. *pel*, 'skin', fr. Lat. *pellis*, 'skin, hide'. See **pellicle**. 1. **a** Raw hide of ox, sheep, goat, with the hair or wool left on; **b** such skins prepared for tanning. 2. **a** Skin or coat of a living animal; **b** (facet.) human skin.

pelt (II.), vb. trans. & intrans. Cp. M.E. *pellen*, *pulten* &c., 'to push, thrust'; later 'to beat, strike'. Modern sense perh. fr. **pellet**. 1. trans. To attack, assail, with missiles; to throw things at: *to pelt one with stones*; also (fig.) *with incessant questions* &c. 2. intrans. (of rain, hail &c.) To fall, drive down, violently and continuously: *in pelting rain*.

pelt (III.), n., fr. prec. **a** Act of pelting; Phr. *full pelt*, at full speed; **b** blow from something falling or thrown.

pelta, n. [1. pélta; 2. péltə]. Lat. *pelta*, fr. Gk. *péltē*, 'small light shield'; prob. connected w. Gk. *péllās*, 'hides'; *pélma*, 'sole of the foot'; Lat. *pellis*, 'skin, hide' &c. See **pellicle**. 1. Small, light, leather-covered shield used by ancient Greek light-armed soldiers. 2. (bot.) Shield-shaped leaf &c.

peltast, n. [1. péltast; 2. péltæst], fr. Gk. *peltastḗs*. See prec. A Greek light-armed foot-soldier carrying a pelta.

peltate, adj. [1. péltat; 2. péltət]. **pelta** & **-ate**. (bot.) Shield-shaped.

peltry, n. [1. péltri; 2. péltri]. **pelt** (I.) & **-ry**. Pelts collectively, esp. fur-skins.

pelvic, adj. [1. pélvik; 2. pélvik]. See next word & **-ic**. Of, pertaining to, situated near, the pelvis.

pelvis, n. [1. pélvis; 2. pélvis]. Lat. *pēlvis* 'basin'; cp. Scrt. *pālāvī*, 'vessel'; Gk. *pelikā*, 'goblet', *pélla*, 'basin'; *pélēx*, 'helmet'; O. Slav. *polŭ*, 'bucket'; perh. orig. 'leather vessel'; cp. Lat. *pellis*, 'skin, hide'. See **pellicle**. 1. Bony girdle in vertebrates, formed by the hip-bones, which meet in front, and are joined behind by the sacrum. 2. Hollow interior part of kidney.

Pembroke table, n. [1. pémbrook tábl; 2. pémbruk téibl], fr. name of town in S. Wales. A kind of folding table.

pemmican, n. [1. pémikan; 2. pémikən]. Am. Indian *pimecan*, 'fat meat'. 1. Cake of pounded venison, or other meat, dried, smoked, and mixed with fat &c., first used by American Indians on journeys, and now by explorers, travellers &c., esp. in Arctic regions, as a concentrated and light food. 2. (fig.) Literary digest; highly condensed statement; summary.

pemphigoid, adj. [1. pémfigoid; 2. pémfigoid]. See **pemphigus** & **-oid**. Of, of the nature of, pemphigus.

pemphigous, adj. [1. pémfigus; 2. pémfigəs]. See prec. & **-ous**. Pemphigoid.

pemphigus, n. [1. pémfigus; 2. pémfigəs], fr. Gk. *pémphīgos*, genit. of *pémphix*, 'blister, bubble'; cp. Gk. *pomphós*, 'bubble; pimple; shield-boss'; prob. cogn. w. Lett. *pampt*, 'to swell'; Scrt. *pippalaś*, 'berry'; Lat. *pampinus*, 'vine-shoot'; *papilla*, 'breast'. See **papilla** & **pamper**. Skin disease characterized by formation of watery vesicles.

pen (I.), n. [1. pen; 2. pen]. O.E. *penn*; etymol. doubtful. 1. Small enclosure for domestic animals, fowls &c. 2. (W. Indian) Plantation, country estate.

pen (II.), vb. trans., fr. prec. 1. Usually *pen up*, *pen in*, to shut up in a pen. 2. To enclose, confine, shut up.

pen (III.), n., fr. O. Fr. *penne*, fr. Lat. *penna*, 'feather; wing', earlier **pet(s)nā*; cogn. w. Gk. *ptérux*, 'wing', see **ptero-**, & w. O.E. *feðer*, see **feather**; fr. base **pet-*, 'to go, fly' &c., as in Gk. *pétomai*, 'I fly', *potḗ*, 'flight'; Lat. *petere*, 'to go towards; to seek, demand', see **petition**; also **pejoration** & **impetus**. 1. Quill-feather, with end of shaft pointed and split, used for writing with ink. 2. Writing instrument, consisting of a metal point or nib fitted into a wooden handle: *fountain pen*, one with reservoir for ink; *pen and ink*, material, instruments, for writing. Phrs. *the pen is mightier than the sword*; *to live by one's pen*, by writing. 3. A female swan.

pen (IV.), vb. trans., fr. prec. To write, compose and put on paper, indite.

penal, adj. [1. pénl; 2. pínl], fr. Fr. *pénal*, fr. Lat. *poenāl-(is)*, 'of punishment', fr. *poena*, 'punishment', fr. Gk. *poinḗ*, 'punishment', fr. **kʷoinā*, 'vengeance, punishment; penalty, fine; hence price, value'; cp. Zend *kaēnā*, 'punishment'; O. Slav. *cěna*, 'honour'; Lith. *kainė*, 'value, price'; cp. also Scrt. *čáyatē*, 'to avenge, punish'. See also **pain** (I.) & **pine** (I.). 1. Connected with, pertaining to, punishment, esp. legal punishment: *penal code*. 2. Liable, rendering one liable, to punishment: *a penal offence*; *penal servitude*, imprisonment for three years or longer with hard labour; *a penal settlement*, convict settlement.

penalization, n. [1. pēnalīzáshun; 2. pìnəlaizéiʃən]. See next word & **-ation**. **a** Act of penalizing; **b** state of being penalized.

penalize, vb. trans. [1. pénalīz; 2. pínəlaiz]. **penal** & **-ize**. 1. To lay under a penalty, to punish; make, pronounce, penal. 2. To place at a disadvantage, inflict a hardship upon: *rich men often regard taxation as penalizing them unduly for the possession of wealth*.

penally, adv. [1. pénali; 2. pínəli]. **penal** & **-ly**. In a penal manner; with the consequence of punishment.

penalty, n. [1. pénlti; 2. pénlti]. **penal** & **-ty**; cp. Fr. *pénalité*. 1. **a** Punishment imposed for breaking a law, or committing legal offence; Phr. *(forbidden &c.) under penalty of £5* &c., subject to the punishment of; **b** suffering, loss &c. which results from sin or folly. 2. (sport) Disadvantage imposed on competitor in a contest for breaking a rule; also attrib., as *penalty kick*, *goal*, at football; or a handicap imposed on account of his known superiority to other competitors.

penance, n. [1. pénans; 2. pénəns], fr. O. Fr. *peneance*, fr. Lat. *paenitentia*, 'repentance', fr. *paenit-(ēre)*, 'to repent'. **penitent** & **-ce**. 1. One of the sacraments of the Catholic Church involving contrition, confession, satisfaction, followed by absolution. 2. Act of mortification voluntarily undertaken, or imposed by priest, as expression of penitence. Phr. *to do penance*, perform such an act.

pen-and-ink, adj. [1. pén an(d) íngk; 2. pén ən(d) íŋk]. Written, executed, with pen and ink: *a pen-and-ink drawing*.

penates, n. pl. [1. penátēz; 2. penéitīz]. Lat. *dī penātes*, 'household gods, deities of the inside of the dwelling'; cp. Lat. *penitus*, 'within'; *penus*, 'inner part of temple of Vesta, sanctuary; store-room'; *penes*, 'near'; *penetrāre*, 'to enter', see **penetrate**; prob. fr. a stem **pen-*, 'within', contracted fr. **(e)p'in*, 'towards the inside', fr. **ep-*, 'to, towards, on', cp. **epi-**, & **in**. 1. (Rom. mythol.) Household gods; primarily gods of the store-room; venerated in close association with the *lares*, q.v. 2. *Lares and penates*, personal, household, possessions, esp. such as have acquired a value from familiar association.

pence, n. [1. pens; 2. pens]. Pl. of **penny**.

penchant, n. [1. pónshon; 2. pãʃã]. Fr., fr. Pres. Part. of *pencher*, 'to slope', fr. Lat. **pendicāre*, fr. *pendēre*, 'to hang', see **pendant**. Inclination, taste, partiality, liking: *to have a penchant for oysters, eighteenth-century poetry* &c.

pencil (I.), n. [1. pénsl; 2. pénsl], fr. O. Fr. *pincel*, fr. Lat. *pēnicillum*, 'painter's brush', dimin. of *pēni-(s)*, 'tail', see **penis**. 1. (archaic) **a** Brush used by artist; hence, **b** (fig.) art or style of painter: *the masterly pencil of Rembrandt*. 2. **a** Instrument for writing, drawing &c., consisting of a thin stick of graphite, coloured chalk, slate &c., usually enclosed in a hollow cylinder of wood, metal &c., and sharpened to a point before use; hence, **b** one of various objects of similar shape, e.g. stick of caustic substance used by medical men. 3. **a** (geom.) Figure formed by set of lines meeting in a point; **b** rays of light meeting in a point; a thin ray of light.

pencil (II.), vb. trans., fr. prec. 1. To draw, write, mark, with a pencil: *to pencil a note*; *a pencilled line*. 2. (racing) To enter (horse's name &c.) in betting-book.

pencil-case, n. Case, holder, for pencil or lead.

pencilled, adj. [1. pénsild; 2. pénsild], fr. P.P. of **pencil** (II.). **a** Well marked, shapely: *pencilled eyebrows*; **b** delicately marked, tinted, with graceful design.

pencraft, n. [1. pénkrahft; 2. pénkrāft]. **pen** (III.) & **craft**. **a** Art, skill, of a writer; penmanship, calligraphy; **b** literary skill, style of an author.

pendant, **pendent**, n. [1. péndant; 2. péndənt]. Fr. *pendant*, fr. Pres. Part. of *pendre*, 'to hang'; or w. suff. *-ent* if straight fr. Lat. *pendēre*, 'to hang'; perh. orig. 'to hang and sway as a pendulum', & cogn. w. Scrt. *spandatē*, 'strikes, beats, swings'; Gk. *sphendónē*, 'sling', *sphadázein*, 'to struggle'. 1. Hanging ornament, esp. one composed of gems, made to hang from necklace &c. 2. (archit.) Moulded ornament in stone, hanging from ceiling or roof. 3. (naut.; also *pennant*) **a** Short line attached to block &c.; **b** long tapering flag flown at mast-head of vessel in commission; **c** tapering flag used for signalling &c. 4. (rare; also [pãdã]) **a** Match, companion; **b** (fig.) parallel, consequence, accompanying fact or circumstance.

pendant-post, n. (archit.) Short post placed against the wall and supported by a corbel, the upper end fixed to the tie-beam in mediaeval open-work timber roofs.

pendency, n. [1. péndensi; 2. péndənsi]. See next word & **-ency**. State of being pendent or pending.

pendent, -ant, adj. [1. péndent; 2. péndənt]. See **pendant**. **1. a** Hanging, suspended: *a pendent lamp; tree with pendent branches*; **b** overhanging, projecting: *roof with pendent eaves*. **2.** (fig.) Not decided, undetermined, pending: *lawsuit remains pendent*. **3.** (gram.) Having incomplete construction: *pendent clause*.

pendente lite, adv. [1. pendénti līti; 2. pendénti láiti]. Lat. abl. absol. See **pendant** & **litigate**. Pending the suit, while litigation is in progress.

pendentive, n. [1. pendéntiv; 2. pendéntiv]. **pendent** & **-ive**. (archit.) Portion of a dome or groined ceiling supported by a single pillar or impost.

pending, adj. & prep. [1. pénding; 2. péndiŋ]. As fr. vb. *to pend*, fr. Fr. *pendre*. See **pendant**. **1.** adj. Not decided, unfinished, awaiting settlement: *a suit, settlement, was pending*. **2.** prep. **a** During: *pending the discussion* &c.; **b** until, during the time intervening before; awaiting: *pending his return, decision* &c.

pendragon, n. [1. pendrágun; 2. pendrǽgən], fr. W. *penn*, 'head', & **dragon** (as chief's standard); w. the first element, cp. O. Ir. *cenn*, 'head'. (often cap.) Ancient British or Welsh chief, esp. supreme leader.

pendulate, vb. intrans. [1. péndūlāt; 2. péndjuleit], fr. Lat. *pendul-(us)*, 'hanging down; hesitating, doubtful', see **pendulous**, & **-ate**. **1.** To swing as a pendulum. **2.** (fig.) To hesitate, be doubtful, undecided.

penduline, adj. [1. péndūlīn; 2. péndjulain], fr. Fr., fr. Lat. *pendul-(us)*, 'hanging'. See next word & **-ine**. **1.** (of nest) Hanging, suspended. **2.** (of bird) Building penduline nest.

pendulous, adj. [1. péndūlus; 2. péndjuləs], fr. Lat. *pendul-(us)*, 'hanging', fr. *pend-(ēre)*, 'to hang', see **pendant**, & **-ous**. Hanging down loosely and freely, and swinging or swaying.

pendulum, n. [1. péndūlum; 2. péndjuləm]. Lat. *pendulum*, neut. of *pendulus*, 'hanging'. See prec. Body suspended from a point so as to be able to swing freely; esp. swinging weight regulating movement of clock; *compensation pendulum*, one constructed so as to adjust itself to changes of temperature. Phr. *swing of the pendulum*, tendency, movement, of popular passion, opinion &c., in opposite direction from that formerly prevailing.

Penelope, n. [1. penélupi; 2. penéləpi], fr. Gk. *Pēnelópē*, wife of Ulysses. Type of wifely constancy.

penetrability, n. [1. pènetrabíliti; 2. pènitrəbíliti]. **penetrable** & **-ity**. Quality, state, of being penetrable.

penetrable, adj. [1. pénetrabl; 2. pénitrəbl], fr. Lat. *penetrābil-(is)*, 'penetrable'. See **penetrate** & **-able**. Capable of being penetrated.

penetralia, n. [1. pènetrália; 2. pènitréiliə]. Lat. *penetrālia*, pl. of *penetral*, 'inner part, interior, esp. of building', fr. *penetr-(āre)*, 'to enter'. See **penetrate**. Innermost part; inner sanctuary or shrine.

penetrate, vb. trans. & intrans. [1. pénetrāt; 2. pénitreit]. Lat. *penetrāt-(um)*, P.P. type of *penetrāre*, 'to go into, enter, pierce'; formed fr. *penitus*, 'within, inside', on anal. of *intrāre*, 'enter'. Cp. **penates**. **A.** trans. **1. a** (of sharp point, cutting edge, missile) To pierce, cut through and enter: *the arrow penetrated the eyeball; no knife or bullet could penetrate such a thick hide*; **b** to force one's way through and into: *to penetrate a forest, a crowd* &c. **2. a** (of light and sound) To get through, be, or become, visible or audible through or beyond: *no ray can penetrate the gloom; his voice could not penetrate the walls*, i.e. was not heard inside &c.; **b** (of the eyesight, power of vision) to plumb, pierce, be able to see through or beyond: *no human eye can penetrate such darkness*. **3. a** (of the understanding) To fathom, comprehend, make sense of, unravel, find intelligible: *the human mind cannot penetrate the mystery of the infinite*; **b** (of ideas, meaning, mental problems &c.) to become intelligible, reach the understanding, be grasped: *my meaning did not penetrate his thick skull; new ideas penetrate the minds of most men but slowly*. **4.** (of non-material process) To imbue, saturate, permeate, be diffused through: (chiefly in pass. constructions) *thoroughly penetrated with heresy, discontent; penetrated with love and charity, with patriotic feeling* &c. **B.** intrans. To perform the action of penetrating, getting through, piercing; to go through process of diffusion &c.: (in physical and non-material senses) *if you fire enough bullets some are sure to penetrate; revolutionary ideas penetrate very slowly in this country*.

penetrating, adj. [1. pénetrāting; 2. pénitreitiŋ], fr. Pres. Part. of prec. Having the quality or power of penetrating in various senses: **a** (of the mind) discerning, perspicacious, acute, trenchant; **b** (of the eye, power of vision &c.) piercing, acute, searching: *a penetrating glance*; **c** (of sound) carrying far, easily audible; arresting; piercing, shrill: *a penetrating voice, cry, shriek, note* &c.

penetratingly, adv. Prec. & **-ly**. In a penetrating manner.

penetration, n. [1. pènetráshun; 2. pènitréiʃən], fr. Lat. *penetrātiōn-(em)*, 'a piercing'. See **penetrate** & **-ion**. **1.** Act or process of penetrating; state of being penetrated. Phr. *peaceful penetration*, method, fact, of acquiring influence and adherence to one's ideas, political, religious &c., by quiet, persistent, secret working, without arousing hostility or suspicion. **2.** Intellectual acuteness, comprehension, subtlety of mind; discernment, good judgement: *a man of great penetration*.

penetrative, adj. [1. pénetrativ; 2. pénitrətiv]. **penetrate** & **-ive**. Having the power to penetrate, physically or mentally.

penetratively, adv. Prec. & **-ly**. In a penetrative manner.

pen feather, n. **pen (III.)** & **feather**. Quill-feather of wing.

penguin, n. [1. pén-gwin; 2. péngwin]. Etymol. doubtful; since 16th cent.; prob. as early writers assert, a name given to certain sea-birds by W. or Bret. seamen; fr. W. *penn*, 'head', & *gwyn*, 'white', or fr. Bret. *pen gouin*; cp. Fr. variant *pingouin*. One of several varieties of short-legged, flightless, sea-birds, order *Impennes*, found in great numbers in Antarctic regions; they have dark-coloured backs and white throats and bellies, live chiefly on shell-fish, and the largest, *emperor* and *king penguins*, stand three feet high; the wings are covered with small scale-like feathers and act as paddles when the bird is diving and swimming.

pen-holder, n. Handle of wood &c. for holding pen-nib.

penial, adj. [1. pēnial; 2. píniəl], fr. Lat. *pēni-(s)*, 'tail; penis'. See **penis** & **-al**. Relating to the penis.

penicillate, adj. [1. pènisílāt; 2. pènisíleit], fr. Lat. *pēnicill-(um)*, 'brush'. See **pencil** & **-ate**. (bot. and zool.) **1.** Bordered or tipped with fine hairs or tuft(s) of hair; forming a hairy tuft. **2.** Marked with fine lines.

peninsula, n. [1. penínsūla; 2. penínsjulə], fr. Lat. *paeninsula*, 'peninsula', fr. *paene*, 'almost', & *insula*, 'island', see **insular**; for the first element cp. Lat. *pēnūria*, 'want, lack; poverty', see **penury**; *paenitet*, 'it grieves', see **penitent**. **a** Piece of land nearly surrounded by water; specif. **b** *the Peninsula*, Spain and Portugal.

peninsular, adj. & n. [1. penínsūlar; 2. penínsjulə]. Prec. & **-ar**. **1.** adj. **a** Of, like, forming, a peninsular; **b** of, pertaining to, *the Peninsula* (of Spain and Portugal); **c** of the war fought in the Peninsula between English and French, 1808-14. **2.** n. **a** Inhabitant of a peninsula; **b** (cap.) soldier who fought in Peninsular War.

peninsularity, n. [1. penìnsuláriti; 2. penìnsjulǽriti]. Prec. & **-ity**. State of being peninsular.

peninsulate, vb. trans. [1. penínsūlāt; 2. penínsjuleit]. **peninsula** & **-ate**. To make into a peninsula.

penis, n. [1. pēnis; 2. pínis]. Lat. *pēnis*, 'tail; penis'; prob. fr. **pes-nis*; cp. Gk. *péos* for **pes-os*, in same sense, & Scrt. *pásas*, 'pubic parts'; M.H.G. *visel*, 'penis'; O.E. *fæsl*, 'offspring, descendants'. Male organ of generation.

penitence, n. [1. pénitens; 2. pénitəns], fr. Lat. *paenitentia*, 'penitence'. **penitent** & **-ce**. State of being penitent; feeling of contrition and sorrow for offences committed.

penitent (I.), adj. [1. pénitent; 2. pénitənt], fr. Pres. Part. of Lat. *paenit-(ēre)*, 'to repent, be sorry; to displease, grieve'; cp. Lat. *pa-ti*, 'to suffer', see **patient**; *pēnūria*, 'want', see **penury**; *paene*, 'nearly'. Cogn. w. Gk. *peînā*, 'hunger'. Feeling, exhibiting, penitence; having a sense of sin or misdoing and a determination not to sin again; contrite.

penitent (II.), n., fr. prec. **1. a** One who is penitent; repentant sinner; esp. **b** person who has confessed to a priest and is undergoing penance. **2.** Member of one of several Roman Catholic orders subject to discipline, and devoted to good works.

penitential, adj. [1. pèniténshal; 2. pèniténʃəl], fr. Lat. *paenitentia*, 'penitence', see **penitence**, & **-al**. Connected with, pertaining to, expressing, of the nature of, penitence: *penitential psalms*, Nos. 6, 32, 38, 51, 102, 130, 143.

penitentially, adv. Prec. & **-ly**. In a penitential manner.

penitentiary (I.), n. [1. pèniténshari; 2. pèniténʃəri], fr. Lat. *paenitenti-(a)*, 'penitence', see **penitence**, & **-ary**. **1.** Central office in Rome which deals with punishments inflicted on those guilty of grave sins; *Grand Penitentiary*, cardinal presiding over this. **2. a** Reformatory; **b** institution, house of correction, for reformed prostitutes; **c** (in U.S.A.) a state prison.

penitentiary (II.), adj., fr. prec. **1.** Of, pertaining to, penance. **2.** Connected with the punishment and reform of criminals.

penitently, adv. [1. pénitentli; 2. pénitəntli]. **penitent** & **-ly**. In a penitent manner.

penknife, n. [1. pénnīf; 2. pénnaif]. Small pocket-knife; originally small knife for mending quill-pens.

penman, n. [1. pénman; 2. pénmən]. **1.** One who writes; usually one writing in specified manner: *a good penman*. **2.** Author, writer.

penmanship, n. [1. pénmanship; 2. pénmənʃip]. Prec. & **-ship**. **1. a** Art of, skill in, handwriting; **b** style of handwriting. **2.** (rare) Literary composition.

pen-name, n. Writer's assumed name; literary pseudonym, nom de plume.

pennant, n. [1. pénant; 2. pénənt]. Amalgamation of **pennon** & **pendant**. **1.** (naut.) Pendant, **3**. **2.** Pennon.

penniferous, adj. [1. peníferus; 2. penífərəs], fr. Lat. *penn-(a)*, 'feather', see **pen (III.)**, & *-i-* & **-ferous**. Having, bearing, feathers.

penniform, adj. [1. péniform; 2. pénifɔ̄m]. See prec. & **-form**. Like a feather in form or appearance.

penniless, adj. [1. péniles; 2. pénilis]. **penny** & **-less**. Without money; poverty-stricken, poor, destitute.

pennilessness, n. [1. pénilesnes; 2. pénilisnis]. Prec. & **-ness**. State of being penniless; poverty.

pennill, n. [1. pénil; 2. pénil]; or in W. [pénil]. W., fr. *penn*, 'head'. See **pendragon**. **a** (in pl. *pennillion*) Verse improvised to suit varying measure of harp, as sung at Welsh eisteddfod &c.; **b** single stanza of such verse.

pennon, n. [1. pénun; 2. pénən], fr. O. Fr. *penon*, prob. fr. Lat. *penn-(a)*, 'feather'. See **pen** (III.). **a** Long, narrow, pointed or swallow-tailed flag, esp. military flag of mediaeval knight or of modern regiment of lancers; hence, **b** (in general) flag, ensign.

pennoned, adj. [1. pénund; 2. pénənd]. Prec. & **-ed**. Having, displaying, a pennon.

penn'orth, n. [1. pénurth; 2. pénəþ]. Abbr. of **pennyworth**.

penny, n. [1. péni; 2. péni]. O.E. *pening*, *penig*; M.E. *peni*; cp. O.N. *peningr*; O. Fris. *penning*; O.H.G. *phenning*, *phenting*, Mod. Germ. *pfennig*. **1.** British bronze coin worth $\frac{1}{12}$ of shilling; after numerals abbreviated *d.* (see **denarius**). Phrs. *not to have a penny (to bless oneself with)*, to be very poor, penniless; *a pretty penny*, a large sum of money; *to turn an honest penny*, earn money; *in for a penny, in for a pound*, thing once undertaken or begun must be completed at whatever cost; (pl.) **a** *pennies*, number of single coins; **b** *pence*, collective pl.; always used for sum of money, *sixpence* &c.; *Peter's pence*, see **Peter**.

penny-a-liner, n. [1. pèni a líner; 2. pèni ə láinə]. One paid so much a line for literary work; a writer of cheap, illiterate stuff, esp. an inferior journalist who is supposed to pad out his paragraphs with redundancies in order to increase his emoluments.

penny-a-lining, n. [1. pèni a líning; 2. pèni ə láiniŋ]. Cheap, turgid style of writing, padded out with unnecessary verbiage.

penny post, n. Conveyance of letters at charge of 1d.

pennyroyal, n. [1. pèniróial; 2. pèniróiəl]. Prob. fr. earlier *pulyol ryal*, fr. O. Fr. *puliol*, 'thyme', fr. Lat. *pūlegiol-(um)*, dimin. of *pūlēgium*, 'flea-bane, pennyroyal'; prob. fr. Gk. *blḗkhōn*, 'pennyroyal', etymol. unknown, & **royal**. Aromatic herb of the mint family, with small clustered purple flowers, yielding an essential oil, formerly much used in medicine.

pennyweight, n. [1. péniwāt; 2. péniweit]. Twentieth part of an ounce troy, 24 grains troy, originally the weight of an old silver penny; abbr. *dwt.*

penny-wise, adj. Saving in small matters, esp. in Phr. *penny-wise and pound-foolish*, economical in little things, lavish in large matters.

pennywort, n. [1. péniwērt; 2. péniwʌt]. **penny** & **wort** (I.). **a** *Wall pennywort*, small round-leaved herb of the sedum family, growing on walls &c.; **b** *water pennywort*, kind of round-leaved herb growing in damp places.

pennyworth, n. [1. péniwērth; 2. péniwʌþ]. Amount that may be bought for a penny. Phr. *a good, bad, pennyworth*, a good, bad, bargain.

penological, adj. [1. pēnolójikl; 2. pīnəlɔ́dʒikl]. **penology** & **-ic** & **-al**. Of, pertaining to, penology.

penologist, n. [1. pēnólojist; 2. pīnɔ́lədʒist]. See next word & **-ist**. Student of, one learned in, penology.

penology, n. [1. pēnóloji; 2. pīnɔ́lədʒi], fr. Lat. *poena*, 'punishment'. See **penal** & **-logy**. Study of methods of punishment and their bearing on the prevention of crime; study of the management of prisons &c.

pensile, adj. [1. pénsil, -sil; 2. péns(a)il], fr. Lat. *pensil-(is)*, 'hanging down', fr. *pens-(um)*, P.P. type of *pendēre*, 'to hang', see **pendant**, & **-il(e)**. **1.** Hanging down, suspended, pendulous. **2.** (of bird) Building a hanging nest.

pension (I.), n. [1. pénshun; 2. pénʃən], fr. Fr., fr. Lat. *pensiōn-(em)*, 'payment', fr. *pens-(um)*, P.P. type of *pendere*, 'to pay', orig. 'to hang on the scales, to weigh', hence 'to value, estimate; to give value of'; cp. *pendēre*, 'to hang', & see **pendant**. **a** Periodic payment made to public servants, officers in army or navy, or to members of any branch of the civil service &c., who have completed their service, or who have resigned office and have relinquished their rights to receive the full payment of their ranks or appointments; **b** similar payment paid to soldiers and sailors on completion of service, or disablement through wounds &c.; **c** similar payment made by a company, or by private individuals, to persons who have been in their employ for a certain number of years and have retired; **d** *old age pension*, weekly payment made to the aged poor by the State.

pension (II.), vb. trans., fr. prec. To grant, pay, pension to. Phr. *pension off*, permit to retire from service with a pension.

pension (III.), n. [1. pónsyon; 2. pɑ̃sjɔ̃]. Fr., fr. Lat. *pensiōn-(em)*, 'payment'. See **pension** (I.). Boarding-house, especially one abroad. Phr. *en pension*, as boarder paying fixed rate for lodging and meals.

pensionable, adj. [1. pénshunabl; 2. pénʃənəbl]. **pension** (I.) & **-able**. Entitled to, entitling one to, a pension.

pensionary (I.), n. [1. pénshunari; 2. pénʃənəri], fr. Med. Lat. *pensiōnāri-(us)*. See **pension** (I.) & **-ary**. **1.** Recipient of pension; pensioner. **2.** Hireling, tool, mercenary. **3.** (hist.) Chief magistrate of a Dutch city &c.; *Grand Pensionary*, title of the president of the council of the Dutch Republic in 17th and 18th cents.

pensionary (II.), adj. **pension** (I.) & **-ary**. Of, relating to, a pension.

pensioner, n. [1. pénshuner; 2. pénʃənə], fr. O. Fr. *pensionnier*, fr. Med. Lat. *pensiōnārius*, 'pensionary'. See **pensionary**. **1.** One who receives a pension. **2.** (obsolesc.) Hireling, paid tool. **3.** (Cambridge Univ.) Undergraduate paying for his own commons &c., as distinct from a scholar, sizar &c.

pensionless, adj. [1. pénshunles; 2. pénʃənlis]. **pension** (I.) & **-less**. Receiving no pension; not entitling one to a pension.

pensive, adj. [1. pénsiv; 2. pénsiv], fr. Fr., *pensif*, *-ive*, fr. *penser*, 'to think', fr. Lat. *pensāre*, 'to weigh out; to ponder', fr. *pens-(um)*, P.P. type of *pendere*, 'to weigh, pay'. See **pension** (I.) & **-ive**. **1.** Immersed in thought; occupied with sad thoughts; wistful. **2.** Expressing thoughtful sadness: *a pensive lay*.

pensively, adv. Prec. & **-ly**. In a pensive manner.

pensiveness, n. See prec. & **-ness**. State, quality, of being pensive.

penstemon, n. Erroneous variant of **pentstemon**.

penstock, n. [1. pénstok; 2. pénstɔk]. **pen** (I.) & **stock**. **1.** Sluice, flood-gate. **2.** Trough conveying water to water-wheel.

pent, adj. [1. pent; 2. pent]. Variant of *penned*, P.P. of **pen** (II.). Shut up, shut in, confined, cooped up: '*Here in the body pent*'; '*To one who has been long in city pent*' (Keats); (gen.) *pent up*: *pent up in an office all day*.

penta-, pref. representing Gk. *pénte*, 'five'; cp. Scrt. *pañča*; Lat. *quinque*, see **quinque-**; Lith. *penkì*; Goth. *fimf*; O.E. *fīf*, see **five**. Five; e.g. *pentachord*, a five-stringed musical instrument; **b** scale of five tones; *pentadactyl*, having five digits on each limb; *pentahedron*, solid figure bounded by five plane faces; *pentamerous*, composed of five similar parts, esp. (bot.) having the corolla divided into five parts; *pentapody*, verse measure of five feet; *pentastich*, five-lined stanza; *pentatonic*, consisting of five notes &c.

pentacle, n. [1. péntakl; 2. péntəkl], fr. Med. Lat. *pentaculum*, prob. for **penta-** & **-cule**. Symbolic figure used in magic, esp. a pentagram.

pentad, n. [1. péntad; 2. péntæd], fr. Gk. *pentád-*, stem of *pentás*, 'group of five', fr. *pénte*, 'five', see **penta-**. **1. a** The number five; **b** group or series of five things. **2.** Period of five years.

pentagon, n. [1. péntagun; 2. péntəgən]. **penta-** & **-gon**. Plane figure with five sides and angles.

pentagonal, adj. [1. pentágunal; 2. pentǽgənəl]. Prec. & **-al**. Of, having the form of, a pentagon.

pentagram, n. [1. péntagram; 2. péntəgræm]. **penta-** & **-gram**. Five-pointed star formed by producing the sides of a pentagon until they meet, used as magic symbol.

pentameter, n. [1. pentámeter; 2. pentǽmitə]. Lat. *pentameter*, fr. Gk. *pentámetros*. **penta-** & **-meter**. (Lat. and Gk. prosody) Line of five feet, divided into two halves, of which the first may be dactylic or spondaic, while the second must contain two dactyls; used alternatively with the hexameter in elegiac verse.

pentane, n. [1. péntān; 2. péntein]. **penta-** & **-ane**. Hydrocarbon, as gas or volatile liquid, of paraffin series, found in petroleum.

Pentateuch, n. [1. péntatūk; 2. péntətjūk], fr. Lat., fr. Gk. *pentáteukh-(os)*, 'consisting of five books', fr. **penta-** & *teûkhos*, 'tool; vessel; book'; cp. *teúkhein*, 'to fashion, make, construct'; cogn. w. Goth. Pret. Pres. *daug*, O.E. *dēag*, 'it is suitable; it avails'. First five books of Old Testament.

pentateuchal, adj. [1. pèntatūkl; 2. pèntətjūkl]. Prec. & **-al**. Of, pertaining to, forming, the Pentateuch.

pentathlon, n. [1. pentáthlon; 2. pentǽþlən]. Gk., fr. **penta-** & *âthlon*, 'contest', see **athletic**. **a** (Gk. antiq.) An athletic contest, at the Olympic and other games, in which each competitor took part in five events, leaping, foot-race, wrestling, and throwing the discus and javelin; **b** similar contest in the modern Olympic games.

Pentecost, n. [1. péntekost; 2. péntikɔst], fr. Eccles. Lat., fr. Gk. *Pentecostḗ*, Pentecost, fr. *pentekostós*, 'fiftieth', fr. *pentḗkonta*, 'fifty', fr. **penta-** & *-konta*, 'ten', in numerals; cp. Lat. (*vīginti*), 'twenty', fr. **vī-kn̥t-*; Aryan base **k̂omt-*, **k̂m̥t-*, 'ten', q.v. under **hundred**, **cent**. **1.** Jewish harvest festival, fifty days after the Passover. **2.** Whitsunday.

pentecostal, adj. [1. pèntekóstl; 2. pèntikɔ́stl]. Prec. & **-al**. Of, relating to, occurring at, Pentecost.

penthouse, n. [1. pént-hòus; 2. pénthaus]. Popularly formed variant of next word. **1.** Sloping roof attached to wall of building &c. and forming a shelter. **2.** Any projecting shelter, canopy &c.

pentice, n. [1. péntis; 2. péntis]. M.E. *pentis*, fr. O. Fr. *apentis*, fr. L. Lat. *appendicium*, 'appendage', fr. *appendic-*, stem of *appendix*, 'appendage, addition', see **appendix**. (archaic) Penthouse.

pentstemon, n. [1. pentstḗmun; 2. pentstímən]. **penta-** & Gk. *stḗmōn*, 'warp in upright loom; thread', q.v. under **stamen**. (bot.) Genus of hardy herbaceous plants with pendulous, red, blue, or pink flowers.

penult, adj. & n. [1. penúlt; 2. penʌ́lt]. Abbr. fr. next word. Penultimate.

penultimate, adj. & n. [1. penúltimat; 2. penʌ́ltimət], fr. Lat. *paene*, 'almost', see **peninsula**, & **ultimate**. **a** adj. Last but one; **b** n., last syllable but one in a word.

penumbra, n. [1. penúmbra; 2. penʌ́mbrə], fr. Lat. *paene*, 'almost', see **peninsula**, & **umbra**. **1.** Partially shaded region bordering on completely shadowed area, esp. round region of total eclipse of sun or moon. **2.** Border round dark central part of sunspot. **3.** (in paint.) Border-line between light and shade.

penumbral, adj. [1. penúmbral; 2. penʌ́mbrəl]. Prec. & **-al**. Of, pertaining to, a penumbra.

penurious, adj. [1. penúrius; 2. penjɔ́riəs]. **penury** & **-ous**. **1.** Poor, yielding little, scanty. **2.** Parsimonious, mean, stingy.

penuriously, adv. Prec. & **-ly**. In a penurious manner.

penuriousness, n. See prec. & **-ness**. State or quality of being penurious.

penury, n. [1. pénūri; 2. pénjəri], fr. Lat. *pēnūria*, 'want, scarcity', cp. Gk. *penía*, 'poverty, want', *peîna*, 'hunger'. See **penitent** & **patient**. **a** State of extreme poverty; want, destitution; **b** scarcity, scantiness, lack.

pen-wiper, n. [1. pén wīper; 2. pén waipə]. Small object for wiping ink from pens; usually consisting of a bundle of small pieces of cloth and wash-leather.

peon, n. [1. pḗon; 2. píən]. Span., 'labourer'; a variant of **pawn (I.)**. **1.** (Span. S. Am. and Mexico) **a** Agricultural labourer; specif. **b** debtor working for creditor; criminal hired out and employed as labourer. **2.** (India, obs.) **a** Foot-soldier; **b** native policeman; **c** native orderly, footman &c.

peonage, n. [1. pḗonij; 2. píənidž]. Prec. & **-age**. **1.** Service, occupation, of peons. **2.** Employment of peons, as labourers; system under which this form of forced labour is carried on.

peony, n. [1. pḗuni; 2. píəni], fr. O. Fr. *peonie*, fr. Lat. *paeōnia*, fr. Gk. *paiōnia*, 'peony', fr. *Paiṓn*, physician of the gods. See **paean**. Genus of shrubby plants with large, single or double, crimson, pink, or white flowers.

people (I.), n. [1. pḗpl; 2. pípl], fr. O. Fr. *poeple, pople*, fr. Lat. *populus*, 'nation; crowd'; fr. earlier **po-pel-os*, w. reduplication, fr. base **p(e)lē*, **p(e)lə-* &c., 'to fill', as in Lat. *plēnus*, 'full', see **plenum**; cp. *plēbēs*, 'common people', see **plebeian**; cogn. w. *folc*, 'nation', see **folk**. **1.** Whole body of persons inhabiting one country, and forming a race, nation, community: *the English people; the peoples of Europe*. Phr. *the chosen people*, Jews. **2.** Whole body of persons forming a community or state, and regarded as the foundation, source of power, of the State: *the voice of the people; Parliament is elected by the people*. **3.** Lower classes, commonalty, populace: *a man of the people*. **4.** Body of individuals belonging to specific district, place, class, occupation &c.: *the village people; the people of Somerset; literary people*. Phr. *the good people*, fairies. **5.** (usually preceded by possessive) Group of persons bound together by common cause, under direction or rule of specific person; esp. **a** subjects of king &c.: *His Majesty's faithful people*; **b** band of retainers, followers, workers &c., subject to a specified leader, chief, employer &c.; **c** congregation, body of parishioners of a specified clergyman. **6. a** One's near relations, esp. parents, brothers, and sisters: *gone to stay with his wife's people*; **b** one's family in general; one's forbears: *my people have lived here for centuries*. **7. a** Human beings in general, society at large: *I see very few people here in the country; large crowds of people rush to the seaside in summer*; **b** (as indef. pron.) equivalent to *they, folks*, or Fr. *on*: *people tell me I speak indistinctly; do what you think right, and never mind what people say*.

people (II.), vb. trans., fr. prec. To fill with people, to plant inhabitants in, to populate; (often in P.P. as adj.) *a thickly, sparsely, peopled area*.

pep, n. See **pepper (I.) 4**.

peperino, n. [1. pèperḗnō; 2. pèpərínou]. Ital., fr. *pepere*, 'pepper', fr. Lat. *piper*, 'pepper', see **pepper**. A light, porous, brown or greyish volcanic rock or tufa with darker fragments, of basalt &c., embedded in it, much used by the Romans as a building material.

pepper (I.), n. [1. péper; 2. pépə]. O.E. *pipor*; M.E. *piper, peper*; fr. Lat. *piper*, 'pepper', fr. Gk. *péperi*; an Eastern loan-word; cp. Scrt. *pippalī*, 'pepper-corn'; *pippalaš*, 'berry'; cogn. w. Lat. *papula*, 'swelling', see **papula**. **1.** Pungent aromatic condiment, with hot taste, consisting of the dried berries of the pepper-plant, used whole or powdered; *black pepper*, made from the whole berry; *white pepper*, made from the berry with the skin removed by soaking and rubbing. **2.** Also *pepper-plant*, tropical climbing shrub from which pepper is obtained; esp. *black pepper*, kind chiefly cultivated for the condiment. **3. a** Any kind of capsicum; **b** its reddish berry, which has a pungent pepper-like taste and gives *red pepper*, see **cayenne**. **4.** (fig.) Pungency; keen, vigorous criticism; energetic action or treatment; abbr. (slang) as *pep*.

pepper (II.), vb. trans., fr. prec. **1.** To sprinkle, flavour, with pepper. **2.** To sprinkle, as with pepper from castor. **3.** (lit. and fig.) To pelt, hit with a series of missiles &c.: *to be peppered in the leg by a careless shooter; the speaker was peppered with awkward questions*.

pepper-and-salt, n. [1. péper an(d) sáwlt; 2. pépər ən(d) sɔ̄lt]. Cloth made of black and grey or black and white threads woven together.

pepper-box, n. **1.** Small, usually cylindrical, box of china, metal &c., with perforated conical top used for sprinkling pepper. **2.** Buttress projecting from wall into fives-court.

pepper-castor, -caster, n. Pepper-box.

peppercorn, n. [1. péperkorn; 2. pépəkɔ̄n]. Dried black, round berry of black pepper; *peppercorn rent*, nominal rent for premises held on long lease.

peppermint, n. [1. pépermint; 2. pépəmint, -mənt]. **pepper & mint (I.)**. **1. a** Pungent aromatic herb of mint family, used in medicine and confectionery; **b** oil obtained from this plant. **2.** Lozenge, confection, flavoured with peppermint.

pepper-pot, n. **1.** Pepper-box. **2.** West Indian stew of meat &c., flavoured with red peppers, juice of the cassava &c.

pepper tree, n. **a** A S. American tropical tree, the *Mulli*, the leaves of which yield a pungent resinous oil; **b** popular name of a tree, *Melia Azedarach*, grown on the coast of the Mediterranean.

peppery, adj. [1. péperi; 2. pépəri]. **pepper & -y**. **a** Of, like, abounding in, tasting of, pepper; **b** (fig.) hot-tempered, irascible, fiery, testy.

pepsin, n. [1. pépsin; 2. pépsin], fr. Gk. *péps-(is)*, 'cooking; digestion', & **-in**; cp. Gk. *peptós*, 'cooked'; *pépōn*, 'cooked by the sun, ripe'; Lat. *coquere*, 'to cook', see **cook**; Scrt. *páčyatē*, 'to cook; ripen'; *páčati*, 'to cook, roast'; O. Slav. *peką*, 'I roast'; O.E. *ā-figen*, 'roasted'. **a** Digestive ferment in gastric juice of the stomach, converting proteids into peptones; **b** extract of this, from gastric juice of calves &c., used to assist weak digestions in peptonizing the food.

peptic, adj. & n. [1. péptik; 2. péptik], fr. Gk. *pept-(ós)*, 'cooked'. See prec. & **-ic**. **1.** adj. Of, promoting, producing, digestion; *peptic glands*, those secreting pepsin; also in compounds as *dyspeptic, eupeptic*. **2.** n. (pl.) *Peptics*, (facet.) Digestive organs.

peptone, n. [1. péptōn; 2. péptoun], fr. Gk. *peptón*, 'cooked; digested'. See **pepsin**. Substance formed from proteids by the action of pepsin in the stomach.

peptonize, vb. trans. [1. péptunīz; 2. péptənaiz]. Prec. & **-ize**. **a** To convert (proteids) into peptones; **b** to subject to action of pepsin &c.

per, prep. [1. pĕr; 2. pā̆]. Lat. *per*, 'through, across, over; along; beyond; by means of'; cp. Scrt. *pári*, 'around; through'; Gk. *peri*, 'around; over', see **peri-**; Lith. *per̃*, 'through'; O. Slav. *pariy*, 'around'; stem **per-*, **por-*, denoting the completion of a forward movement. Cogn., though w. different vowel grades, are Gk. *pará*, 'beyond'; Goth. *faúr*, 'along'; Lat. *prō*, 'for; before', see **pro-**; *porta*, 'door'; *portus*, 'haven', see **port (I.)**; O.E. *faran*, 'to go', see **fare (III.)**, & words there referred to. **1.** (in Lat. phrs.) *Per annum, per procurationem* &c., qq.v. below. **2.** (in Engl. phrs.) **a** By means of, through: *per post, rail* &c.; **b** through the agency of, by the action of: (of a letter) *per J. Jones*, by the hand of; **c** for each: *per man; per pound; per cent*.

per-, pref. representing Lat. *per*, 'through, across, over; beyond; by means of'. See prec. **1.** In old Latin compounds, a expressing penetration; through, throughout, all over: *permeate, percolate*; **b** expressing intensity, thoroughness, completeness: *perfect, perdurable, persecute* &c.; **c** expressing loss, injury, destruction: *pervert, perjure* &c. **2.** Also, with the same force, in later compounds from words of Latin origin: *perfoliate, perfervid, peruse* &c. **3.** (chem.) Denoting largest proportion of some element in a compound compared with similar compounds: *perchloride, peroxide, persulphide* &c.; (also in adj.) *perchloric* &c.

peradventure, adv. & n. [1. pèradvénchur; 2. pèrədvéntʃə]. O. Fr. *par aventure*, 'by chance'. **per & adventure**. (archaic) **1.** adv. **a** Perhaps, perchance; **b** after *if, lest*, by any means or chance. **2.** n. (rare) Doubt, uncertainty: *beyond, without, peradventure*.

perai, n. [1. peráh-i, perī́; 2. pərái, pərái], fr. native name *piraya*. A S. American freshwater fish.

perambulate, vb. trans. [1. perámbūlāt; 2. pərǽmbjuleit], fr. Lat. *perambulāt-(um)*, P.P. type of *perambulāre*, 'to go through, traverse', fr. **per-** & *ambulāre*, 'to go, walk', see **amble**. **1.** To walk up and down (streets, a town); walk through or over, traverse (a district or area), esp. for the purpose of preserving order, surveying or inspecting; to walk. **2.** To walk round the confines or boundaries of, esp. to establish or maintain a boundary: *to perambulate a parish, estate* &c.

perambulation, n. [1. peràmbūláshun; 2. pərǽmbjuléiʃən]. Prec. & **-ion**. **a** Act of perambulating; esp. periodical survey of boundaries &c.; **b** official record of this.

perambulator, n. [1. perámbūlàtur; 2. pərǽmbjulèitə]. **perambulate & -or**. Light carriage for young children, usually with four wheels, pushed by hand; colloquially abbreviated to *pram* [præm].

perambulatory, adj. [1. peràmbūlā́turi; 2. pərǽmbjuléitəri]. **perambulate & -ory**. Of, pertaining to, perambulation.

per annum, adv. [1. pĕr ánum; 2. pər ǽnəm]. Lat. **per** & *annum*, acc. of *annus*, 'year', see **annual**. By the year; annually, yearly.

percale, n. [1. perkā́l, -káhl; 2. pəkéil, -kā́l]. Fr. *percale*; etymol. unknown. Kind of closely woven cambric.

per capita, adv. [1. pĕr kápita; 2. pā̆ kǽpitə]. Lat., 'by heads'. (So much) a head.

perceive, vb. trans. [1. persḗv; 2. pəsī́v]. M.E. *perceiven*, fr. O. Fr. **perceivre*, fr. Lat. *percipere*, 'to take possession of, seize; to perceive, observe; to comprehend', fr. **per-** & *capere*, 'to take', see **captive**. **1.** To take into the mind, apprehend, grasp. **2.** To become aware of by means of one of the senses; to discern.

per cent(um), adv. [1. per sént, pĕr séntum; 2. pə sént, pā̆ séntəm]. Lat., (so much) per hundred.

percentage, n. [1. perséntij; 2. pəséntidž]. **per & cent & -age**. **1.** Rate, proportion, per hundred. **2.** Allowance, interest &c., paid per cent. **3.** Proportion, part in relation to the whole: *a small percentage of water*.

percept, n. [1. pérsept; 2. pā́sept], fr. Lat. *percept-(um)*, P.P. type of *percipere*, 'to grasp, comprehend', see **perceive**. (philos.) Object of perception, thing perceived, as contrasted with the process of perceiving.

perceptibility, n. [1. persèptibíliti; 2. pəsèptibíliti]. See next word & **-ity**. Quality, state, of being perceptible.

perceptible, adj. [1. perséptibl; 2. pəséptibl], fr. Lat. *perceptibilis*, 'perceptible', fr. *percept-(um)*, P.P. type of *percipere*, 'to comprehend'. See **perceive & -ible**. Capable of being perceived by mind or senses.

perceptibly, adv. Prec. & **-ly**. In a perceptible manner; to a perceptible extent.

perception, n. [1. persépshun; 2. pəsépʃən], fr. O. Fr., fr. Lat. *perceptiōn-(em)*, 'a gathering in, collection; comprehension, perception', fr. *percept-(um)*, P.P. type of *percipere*, 'to take, seize; to comprehend', see **perceive**, & **-ion**. **1.** (philos.) Name given to the mental process which refers sensations to an object which is recognized as identical with one which has previously aroused similar sensations. **2.** Faculty of perceiving or recognizing such abstract qualities as truth, beauty &c.: *a man of the keenest perceptions.*

perceptional, adj. [1. persépshunl; 2. pəsépʃənl]. Prec. & **-al**. Of, pertaining to, of the nature of, perception.

perceptive, adj. [1. perséptiv; 2. pəséptiv]. **percept** & **-ive**. Of, pertaining to, having the power of, perception.

perceptively, adv. Prec. & **-ly**. In a perceptive manner.

perceptiveness, n. See prec. & **-ness**. State of being perceptive.

perceptivity, n. [1. pĕrseptíviti; 2. pʌseptíviti]. **perceptive** & **-ity**. State of being perceptive; readiness of perception.

perch (**I.**), n. [1. pĕrch; 2. pʌtʃ], fr. Fr. *perche*, fr. Lat. *perca*, fr. Gk. *pérkē*, also *perkis*, 'perch'. Apparently cogn. w. Scrt. *pṛśniś*, 'spotted', Gk. *perknós*, 'spotted, variegated'; cp. further O.H.G. *forhana*, 'trout'. Edible freshwater fish of Europe and N. America, greyish green in colour, with dark brown stripes, having a humped back, and broad, spiny fins.

perch (**II.**), n., fr. Fr. *perche*, fr. Lat. *pertica*, 'pole, staff; measuring rod'; etymol. doubtful. Original sense, rod, pole; used in various specific senses. **1. a** Piece of wood fixed horizontally as resting-place for birds; **b** branch of a tree or other object upon which a wild bird temporarily rests. Phrs. (colloq.) *come off your perch*, drop your assumed airs of superiority; *to hop the perch*, to die. **2.** (colloq.) **a** Comfortable, secure seat, esp. one higher than others; **b** (fig.) established position. **3.** Measure of length, 5½ yds.; also called *rod*, or *pole*.

perch (**III.**), vb. intrans. & trans., fr. prec. **1.** intrans. **a** (of bird &c.) To alight, come to rest after flight: *to perch on a twig* &c.; hence, **b** (of person) to stand or sit upon, balance oneself upon: *to perch on the arm of a chair.* **2.** trans. To place in a position which appears to be, or is, precarious or insecure; to set, fix, plant, in an elevated or inaccessible position: *to perch one's hat on the side of one's head*; *to perch a church on the top of a mountain.*

perchance, adv. [1. percháhns; 2. pətʃáns], fr. A.-Fr. *par chance*, 'by chance'. **per** & **chance**. (archaic) Perhaps.

percher, n. [1. pĕrcher; 2. pʌ́tʃə]. **perch** (**III.**) & **-er**. One who, that which, perches, esp. applied to the large group or order of perching or passerine birds with four toes, the one behind being flexed independently of the others; the order includes all the song-birds; see also **passerine**.

Percheron, n. [1. pársheron; 2. pérʃərɔ̃]. Fr., fr. (La) Perche, district of northern France. Breed of large, strong, quick-trotting, draught horses, originally from the district of La Perche.

percipience, n. [1. persípiens; 2. pəsípiəns]. See next word & **-ence**. State of being percipient; faculty of perceiving.

percipient, adj. & n. [1. persípient; 2. pəsípiənt], fr. Lat. *percipient-(em)*, Pres. Part. of *percipere*, 'to perceive', see **perceive**. **1.** adj. Capable of perceiving; having the power of perception. **2.** n. Percipient person; specif. (telepathy) person capable of receiving communications otherwise than by the senses.

percolate, vb. intrans. & trans. [1. pĕrkolāt; 2. pʌ́kəleit], fr. Lat. *percōlāt-(um)*, P.P. type of *percōlāre*, 'to filter', fr. **per-** & *cōlāre*, 'to strain', fr. *cōl-(um)*, 'strainer; net; wicker trap for fish'; etymol. doubtful. **1.** intrans. (lit. and fig.) To filter, ooze, drip gradually through. **2.** trans. To cause to percolate; to filter, strain.

percolation, n. [1. pĕrkoláshun; 2. pʌkəléiʃən], fr. Lat. *percōlātiōn-(em)*, 'a filtering'. Prec. & **-ion**. Act or process of percolating.

percolator, n. [1. pĕrkolātur; 2. pʌ́kəleitə]. **percolate** & **-or**. **a** One who, that which, percolates; specif. **b** an apparatus, vessel, with perforations for filtering liquid through, e.g. for making coffee &c.

per contra, adv. [1. pĕr kóntra; 2. pʌ kɔ́ntrə]. Lat. On the contrary; on the other or opposite side; often as adj. *per contra account.*

percuss, vb. trans. [1. pĕrkús; 2. pʌkás], fr. Lat. *percuss-(um)*, P.P. type of *percutere*, 'to strike through, pierce; to smite, beat', fr. **per-** & *quatere*, 'to shake, strike'; see **quash**; prob. cogn. w. O.S. *skuddjan*; O.H.G. *scutten*, 'to shake'; Lith. *kutéti*, 'to shake, rouse up'. To strike; specif. (med.) to tap with specially made rubber mallet, or with the knuckles, some hollow part of the body cavity in order to judge of internal condition from the quality of the sound which results.

percussion, n. [1. perkúshun; 2. pəkáʃən], fr. Lat. *percussiōn-(em)*, 'a beating, striking'. Prec. & **-ion**. **1.** Impact of one body against another; (mus.) *instruments of percussion*, played by striking, e.g. drums. **2.** Impression, shock, vibration, produced by such an impact. **3.** (med.) Act of percussing.

percussion cap, n. Small metal cap coated inside with a fulminating powder, which was used formerly in fire-arms; when struck by the hammer it exploded and fired the charge.

percussive, adj. [1. perkúsiv; 2. pəkásiv], fr. Lat. *percuss-(um)*, P.P. type of *percutere*, 'to beat, strike'. See **percuss** & **-ive**. Of, pertaining to, producing, produced by, percussion.

percutaneous, adj. [1. pĕrkūtáneus; 2. pʌkjūtéiniəs]. **per-** & **cutaneous**. Effected, performed, acting, through the skin.

perdition, n. [1. perdíshun; 2. pədíʃən], fr. O. Fr. *perdiciun*, fr. Lat. *perditiōn-(em)*, 'ruin', fr. *perdit-(um)*, P.P. of *perdere*, 'to lose, throw away, waste, ruin', fr. **per-** & *dare*, 'to give', see **date** (**I.**). Complete loss of salvation in the future state; eternal death, damnation.

perdu(e), adj. [1. perdú; 2. pʌdjú, perdȳ]. Fr. *perdu(e)*, P.P. of *perdere*, 'to lose'. See prec. **1.** (mil.) Acting as concealed outpost. **2.** Concealed, hidden, esp. in Phr. *to lie perdu*, to disappear deliberately from public ken, keep one's whereabouts unknown; to shirk publicity.

perdurability, n. [1. pĕrdūrabíliti; 2. pʌdjuərəbíliti]. See next word & **-ity**. State, quality, of being perdurable.

perdurable, adj. [1. perdúrabl; 2. pədjúərəbl]. **per-** & **durable**. **a** Very durable, remaining unchanged; **b** everlasting, eternal.

perdurably, adv. Prec. & **-ly**. In a perdurable manner.

père, n. [1. pār; 2. pɛə], fr. Fr. *père*, fr. Lat. *pater*, 'father'. See **pater**. **a** Father; added after name to distinguish a man from his son; as *Dumas père*; contrasted with *Dumas fils*; or of commercial firms or partnerships of father and son: *Legendre père et fils*; **b** title given to a priest as father confessor &c., e.g. *Père Hyacinthe.*

peregrinate, vb. intrans. [1. péregrināt; 2. périgrineit], fr. Lat. *peregrīnāt-(um)*, P.P. type of *peregrīnāri*, 'to travel about', fr. *peregrīn-(us)*, 'foreign, strange'. See **peregrine**. (archaic or facet.) To travel, roam about, journey.

peregrination, n. [1. pĕregrináshun; 2. pĕrigrinéiʃən]. Lat. *peregrīnātiōn-(em)*, 'travel'. Prec. & **-ion**. Act of peregrinating; travel, journeying.

peregrine, adj. & n. [1. péregrin; 2. périgrin], fr. Lat. *peregrīn-(us)*, 'foreign', fr. *peregrē*, 'abroad, away from home', orig. 'outside, beyond, the Roman territory', fr. **per-** & locative of *ager*, 'district, territory', & **-ine**. See **agrarian**, **acre**, & cp. **pilgrim**. (archaic) Foreign, from abroad; now only specif., *peregrine falcon*, type of British falcon formerly much used in hawking; the young birds migrate in the autumn, hence the name.

peremptorily, adv. [1. péremptŭrili, perémpturili; 2. pérəmptərili, pərémptərili]. **peremptory** & **-ly**. In a peremptory manner.

peremptoriness, n. [1. pérempturines, perémpturines; 2. pérəmptərinis, pərémptərinis]. See next word & **-ness**. Quality of being peremptory.

peremptory, adj. [1. péremptŭri, perémpturi; 2. pérəmptəri, pərémptəri], fr. Lat. *peremptōri-(us)*, 'destructive; decisive, final', fr. *perempt-(um)*, P.P. type of *perimere*, 'to prevent; destroy', fr. **per-** & *emere*, 'to take, buy, procure'. See second element of **exempt**. **1.** (esp. legal) Final, absolute, decisive: *peremptory writ*, *mandamus* &c. **2.** (of command &c.) Not admitting any refusal; precluding opposition, appeal, or denial. **3.** (of person, manner &c.) Imperious, dictatorial.

perennial (**I.**), adj. [1. perénial; 2. pəréniəl], fr. Lat. *perenni-(s)*, 'lasting through the year; unfailing, everlasting', fr. **per-** & *ann-(us)*, 'year', see **annual**, & **-al**. **1. a** Lasting through the year; **b** specif. (of stream, spring &c.) flowing at all seasons of the year. **2.** Perpetual, never-failing: *perennial youth.* **3.** (bot., of plant) Lasting more than two years; contrasted with *annual* and *biennial.*

perennial (**II.**), n., fr. prec. (bot.) Perennial plant.

pereniality, n. [1. pereniáliti; 2. pərèniǽliti]. Prec. & **-ity**. Quality of being perennial.

perennially, adv. [1. peréniali; 2. pəréniəli]. See prec. & **-ly**. Perpetually; from year to year.

perfect (**I.**), adj. [1. pĕrfekt; 2. pʌ́fikt], fr. Lat. *perfect-(um)*, P.P. type of *perficere*, 'to bring to an end, finish, complete', fr. **per-** & *facere*, 'to make, do', see **fact**. **1.** Reaching highest possible level of excellence; faultless, supremely excellent. **2.** Complete, finished, satisfactory, in all details; conforming to a standard; without defect, blemish, error: *a perfect specimen*; *a perfect circle.* **3.** Absolutely accurate, exact, precise: *a perfect copy*; *perfect reproduction*, *imitation.* **4.** Thoroughly competent; having attained highest possible degree of excellence, skill &c. of specified kind: *a perfect tennis player*, *actor*, *servant* &c.; *perfect in every branch of one's duties.* **5.** Thorough, complete, utter: *in perfect silence*; *a perfect fool*, *stranger* &c.; *a perfect humbug.* **6.** (gram.) Perfect tense, that expressing completed action; as '*I have finished my course*'.

perfect (**II.**), vb. trans. [1. perfékt, pĕrfekt; 2. pəfékt, pʌ́fikt], fr. prec. **1.** To improve, complete, make perfect, bring to state of perfection, or to required standard: *to perfect one's plans*, *a picture*, *an invention* &c. **2.** To train thoroughly, make highly skilled and competent: *to perfect oneself in an art.*

perfectibility, n. [1. perfèktibíliti; 2. pəfèktibíliti]. See next word & **-ity**. Quality or state of being perfectible.

perfectible, adj. [1. perféktibl; 2. pəféktibl]. **perfect** & **-ible**. Capable of being perfected.

perfection, n. [1. perfékshun; 2. pəfékʃən], fr. O. Fr., fr. Lat. *perfectiōn-(em)*, 'perfection'. **perfect** (**I.**) & **-ion**. **1. a** Act of perfecting; **b** state of being perfected (in all senses). **2. a** Highest attainable or conceivable degree of absolute excellence in condition, quality, or achievement; faultlessness; **b** (loosely) any high degree or standard of excellence. Phr. *done to perfection*, perfectly. **3.** Completeness, fullness of development; final stage in development. **4.** Anything which has reached, and exhibits, perfection; perfect person, thing, state.

perfectionism, n. [1. perfékshunizm; 2. pəfékʃənizəm]. Prec. & **-ism**. Doctrine that religious, moral perfection may be attained in this life.

perfectionist, n. [1. perfékshunist; 2. pəfékʃənist]. **perfection** & **-ist**. **1.** Adherent of perfectionism. **2.** (cap.) Member of a small community founded at Oneida Creek, N.Y., in 1848, on communistic lines.

perfectly, adv. [1. pẽrfektli; 2. pə̄fiktli]. **perfect (I.)** & **-ly**. **1.** In a perfect manner; to perfection. **2.** Thoroughly, completely.

perfectness, n. [1. pẽrfektnes; 2. pə̄fiktnis]. See prec. & **-ness**. State or quality of being perfect.

perfervid, adj. [1. pẽrfẽrvid; 2. pə̄fə̄vid]. **per-** & **fervid**. Very fervid; ardent, intense.

perfidious, adj. [1. perfídius; 2. pəfídiəs], fr. Lat. *perfidiōs-(us)*, 'treacherous'. See **perfidy** & **-ous**. Treacherous, faithless, not to be trusted.

perfidiously, adv. Prec. & **-ly**. In a perfidious manner.

perfidiousness, n. See prec. & **-ness**. Quality of being perfidious; perfidy.

perfidy, n. [1. pẽrfidi; 2. pə̄fidi], fr. Fr., fr. Lat. *perfidia*, 'faithlessness, treachery', fr. *perfid-(us)*, 'faithless', fr. **per-** & *fid-(ēs)*, 'faith'. See **fidelity**. Violation of faith; faithlessness, treachery.

perfoliate, adj. [1. pẽrfóliat; 2. pə̄fóuliət]. **per-** & Lat. *foli-(um)*, 'leaf', see **folio**, & **-ate**. (bot.) **a** Having the stem apparently passing through the leaf; **b** (of leaf) growing in such a way that the stem seems to pass through it.

perforate, vb. trans. & intrans. [1. pẽrfurāt; 2. pə̄fəreit], fr. Lat. *perforāt-(um)*, P.P. type of *perforāre*, 'to bore, pierce through', fr. **per-** & *forāre*, 'to bore'. See **foramen**. **1.** trans. **a** To pierce, penetrate into or through; make hole(s) in; **b** specif., to make a row of holes in paper around or at end of section, slip &c., to facilitate detachment: *perforated stamps, cheques* &c. **2.** intrans. To pierce, penetrate.

perforation, n. [1. pẽrfuráshun; 2. pə̄fəréiʃən]. Prec. & **-ion**. **1.** Act or process of perforating; state of being perforated. **2.** Result of perforating; hole bored, pierced, or stamped through or into something; specif., series of small holes made to facilitate tearing, e.g. round postage stamps.

perforative, adj. [1. pẽrfurātiv; 2. pə̄fəreitiv]. **perforate** & **-ive**. Tending, having the power, to perforate.

perforce, adv. [1. perfórs; 2. pəfɔ́s], fr. O. Fr. *par force*, 'by force'. See **per** & **force (I.)**. Of necessity, under compulsion.

perform, vb. trans. & intrans. [1. perfórm; 2. pəfɔ́m]. O. Fr. *parformer*, the second element being orig. *fournir*, 'furnish' &c. See **per-** & **furnish**. **A.** trans. **1.** To act in such a way as to get (something) completed; to accomplish, execute, carry out or through: *to perform a task, one's duties, what one has promised, a piece of work*; *to perform one's part*; *to perform Divine Service*; *to perform a surgical operation.* **2.** To go through, put into action, enact, in public: *to perform a play, a part in a play*; *to perform a conjuring trick.* **B.** intrans. **1.** To give an exhibition of artistic skill; to act, play an instrument, sing, &c.: *to perform before the king.* **2.** (of trained animals) To go through series of systematic movements, exhibit various tricks, as public entertainment.

performable, adj. [1. pẽrfórmabl; 2. pəfɔ́məbl]. Prec. & **-able**. Capable of being performed.

performance, n. [1. perfórmans; 2. pəfɔ́məns]. **perform** & **-ance**. **1.** Act of performing; fact, process, of being performed: *a discrepancy between promise and performance.* **2. a** Action performed; an intellectual or physical achievement; a feat: *to hold a large audience during a long speech is a fine performance*; *Hobbs's notable performance at the wicket*; *the address for the defence was a wretched performance*; **b** organized exhibition of artistic skill; rendering of a play, piece of music, song &c.; a show, entertainment.

performer, n. [1. perfórmer; 2. pəfɔ́mə]. **perform** & **-er**. One who performs; specif. **a** one who carries out some artistic or physical exercise with skill; an executant: *a performer on the banjo*; *a good performer at the wicket*; *quite a performer with the knife and fork*; **b** one who takes part in a theatrical or other organized performance.

performing, adj. [1. perfórming; 2. pəfɔ́miŋ], fr. Pres. Part. of **perform**. (of animals) Trained to do tricks &c. in public.

perfume (I.), n. [1. pẽrfūm; 2. pə̄fjūm], fr. O. Fr. *parfum*, fr. *parfumer*, 'to perfume'. See next word. **1. a** Smell, odour, generally; **b** pleasant smell, fragrant odour. **2.** Liquid consisting of spirit, containing pungent, sweet-smelling essence, used on the clothes and person.

perfume (II.), vb. trans. [1. perfúm; 2. pəfjúm], fr. Fr. *parfumer*, 'to perfume', fr. **per-** & *fūmāre*, 'to smoke, steam'. See **fume**. **a** To impregnate, fill, saturate, with sweet odours: *flowers perfume the room, the air*; specif. **b** to impregnate with fragrant, manufactured essence or scent: *to perfume one's handkerchief with eau-de-Cologne.*

perfumeless, adj. [1. pẽrfūmles; 2. pə̄fjūmlis]. **perfume (I.)** & **-less**. Having no perfume.

perfumer, n. [1. perfúmer; 2. pəfjúmə]. **perfume** & **-er**. One who makes or sells perfumes.

perfumery, n. [1. perfúmeri; 2. pəfjúməri]. **perfume** & **-ery**. **1.** Perfumes collectively. **2. a** Business of perfumer; **b** place where perfumes are made or sold.

perfunctorily, adv. [1. perfúngkturili; 2. pəfáŋktərili]. **perfunctory** & **-ly**. In a perfunctory manner.

perfunctoriness, n. [1. perfúngkturines; 2. pəfáŋktərinis]. See prec. & **-ness**. Quality of being perfunctory.

perfunctory, adj. [1. perfúngkturi; 2. pəfáŋktəri], fr. Lat. *perfunctōri-(us)*, 'done in a superficial manner', fr. *perfunct-(um)*, P.P. type of *perfungi*, 'to perform', fr. **per-** & *fungi*, 'to busy oneself with', see **function**. **a** Performed merely as a form or a duty: *a perfunctory piece of work*; *a perfunctory rendering of the Church Service*; **b** hasty, superficial: *a perfunctory examination, glance* &c.

perfuse, vb. trans. [1. perfúz; 2. pəfjúz], fr. Lat. *perfūs-(um)*, P.P. type of *perfundere*, 'to bedew, besprinkle', fr. **per-** & *fundere*, 'to pour', see **fuse (I.)**. **1.** To sprinkle, pour, over: *to perfuse a thing with water* &c.; *to perfuse water over something.* **2.** To shed, cast, over, suffuse: *to perfuse with light* &c.

perfusion, n. [1. perfúzhun; 2. pəfjúžən], fr. Lat. *perfūsiōn-(em)*, 'a pouring over'. Prec. & **-ion**. Act, process, of perfusing; condition of being perfused.

perfusive, adj. [1. perfúsiv; 2. pəfjúsiv]. **perfuse** & **-ive**. Tending to, able to, perfuse.

pergameneous, adj. [1. pẽrgaméneus; 2. pə̄gəmíniəs], fr. Lat. *pergamēn-(a)*, 'parchment', see **parchment**, & **-eous**. Consisting of, resembling, parchment.

pergola, n. [1. pẽrgola; 2. pə̄gələ]. Ital., fr. Lat. *pergula*, 'projecting roof; shed; vine-arbour', fr. *perg-(ere)*, 'to go forward, proceed', fr. **per-** & *regere*, 'to guide, direct', see **regent**. Structure of stone or wood bordering a path on either side, with arches going across at intervals, along and over which climbing and flowering plants are trained.

pergunnah, pergana, pargana, n. [1. pẽrgúna; 2. pə̄gánə], fr. Hind. *pargunah*, 'district'. Group of Indian villages forming a subdivision of a district, esp. for fiscal purposes.

perhaps, adv. [1. perháps; 2. pəhǽps]; colloq. [1. praps; 2. præps]. **per-** & **hap (I.)** & advbl. *-s*. It may be that; possibly, haply, perchance; expressing a complete uncertainty and indecision, bare possibility: *perhaps we shall just catch the train after all*; *perhaps I'll come, perhaps I won't*; **b** inclination in one direction, probability: *I feel that perhaps you ought not to go*, I'm fairly sure that you ought not; *if you are good boys, perhaps you shall have a half-holiday*, you almost certainly will.

peri, n. [1. pẽri; 2. píəri]. Pers. **1.** (Pers. mythol.) **a** One of the supernatural beings descended from fallen angels; hence, **b** fairy, sprite, elf. **2.** Lovely, graceful, attractive being.

peri-, pref. representing Gk. *perí*, 'around; about; towards'; connected w. Scrt. *pári*, 'round'; Lat. *per*, 'through, across', see **per**. Round, about; enclosing; e.g. *perichondrium*, membrane covering cartilage, except at joints; *periclinal*, (geol.) sloping from a common centre; *peripteral*, (of temple) surrounded by row of columns; *peristome*, fringe of teeth round mouth of capsule in some mosses. See below for other compounds.

perianth, n. [1. périanth; 2. périænþ]. **peri-** & Gk. *ánth-(os)*, 'flower', see **anther**. (bot.) Calyx and corolla combined so as to be indistinguishable.

periapt, n. [1. périapt; 2. périæpt], fr. Fr., fr. Gk. *periapton*, 'something hung on', fr. **peri-** & *háptein*, 'to fasten'; cp. Gk. *haphé*, 'sense of touch', *aphássein*, 'to touch'; etymol. doubtful. Object worn as charm; amulet.

pericarditis, n. [1. pèrikardítis; 2. pèrikādáitis]. Next word & **-itis**. Inflammation of the pericardium.

pericardium, n. [1. pèrikárdium; 2. pèrikādiəm]. Lat., fr. Gk. *perikárdion*, fr. **peri-** & *kardiā*, 'heart'. See **cardiac**. Membrane which surrounds and encloses the heart.

pericarp, n. [1. périkarp; 2. périkāp]. Gk. *perikárpion*, fr. **peri-** & *karpós*, see **carpel**. (bot.) Wall of ripened ovary; covering of fruit, seed-vessel.

periclase, n. [1. périklāz; 2. périkleiz], fr. **peri-** & Gk. *klásis*, 'breaking', fr. *kláein*, 'to break'; cp. *klásma*, 'fragment', see **cataclasm**; *kladarós*, 'fragile'; Lat. *clādēs*, 'destruction, disaster'; O. Slav. *kladivo*, 'hammer'. Green or colourless mineral containing magnesium and iron protoxide.

pericope, n. [1. perikopi; 2. pəríkəpi]. L. Lat. *pericopē*, fr. Gk. *perikopé*, 'a cutting; section of book', fr. **peri-** & *kopé*, 'cutting'; cp. *kóptein*, 'to strike, cut'; *kopís*, 'knife'; *kómma*, 'slice, piece; clause', see **comma**. **a** Passage, extract, from book; esp. **b** selection of passages from Gospels and Epistles to be read in public worship.

pericranium, n. [1. pèrikrānium; 2. pèrikréiniəm], fr. L. Lat., fr. Gk. *perikránion*, 'around the skull'. **peri-** & **cranium**. **a** Membrane surrounding the skull; hence, **b** (facet.) skull, cranium.

peridot, n. [1. péridot; 2. péridət], fr. Fr. *péridot*; etymol. doubtful. A gem stone, a yellowish-green variety of chrysolite; also called olivine.

perigean, adj. [1. pèrijéan; 2. pèridžíən]. See next word & **-an**. Of, pertaining to, perigee; occurring when moon is in perigee.

perigee, n. [1. périjē; 2. péridžī], fr. Fr. *périgée*, fr. Med. Lat., fr. Late Gk. *perigeion*, fr. **peri-** & *gê*, 'earth', see **geo-**. Point in orbit of moon or, more rarely, of planet, when it is nearest to the earth; reverse of *apogee.*

perihelion, n. [1. pèrihélium; 2. pèrihíliən], fr. **peri-** & Gk. *hélio-(s)*, 'sun'. See **helio-**. Point in orbit of planet or comet when it is nearest the sun; reverse of *aphelion.*

peril (I.), n. [1. péril; 2. péril], fr. Fr. *péril*, fr. Lat. *periculum*, 'trial, experiment; risk, hazard; danger'; cp. Lat. *peritus*, 'experienced'; *experīri*, 'to try, test', cp. **experience**; cp. Gk. *peîra*, 'experience'; fr. base **perē-*, 'to penetrate, examine, mentally', expanded fr. base **per-* &c., 'through, over, across', see **per**; cp. further Goth. *fraisan*, 'to tempt'; O.H.G. *freisōn*, 'to be in danger'; O.H.G. *fāra*, 'danger'; O.E. *fǣr*, 'danger, fear', see **fear**. Risk of injury, loss, destruction; danger, hazard. Phrs. *in peril of*, running risk of; *in peril of one's life*, in danger of death; *at one's peril*, taking risk on oneself, at one's own risk.

peril (II.), vb. trans., fr. prec. To expose to danger; to risk, imperil.

perilous, adj. [1. périlus; 2. périləs]. See prec. & **-ous**. Involving peril; dangerous, risky.

perilously, adv. Prec. & **-ly**. In a perilous manner; dangerously.

perilousness, n. See prec. & **-ness**. Quality of being perilous; danger, risk.

perimeter, n. [1. perímeter; 2. pərímitə], fr. Lat., fr. Gk. *perímetros*, 'perimeter'. **peri-** & **-meter**. **1. a** Line bounding closed figure; outline, circumference; **b** length of this line. **2.** Instrument for measuring field of vision.

perineal, adj. [1. pèrinéal; 2. pèriníəl]. See next word & **-al**. Of, pertaining to, the perineum.

perineum, n. [1. pèrinéum; 2. pèriníəm]. L. Lat., fr. Gk. *perínaion*, 'perineum', fr. **peri-** & *ináein*, 'to evacuate'; cp. Scrt. *iṣṇāti*, 'to put in motion'. Region of body between rectum and genital organs.

period, n. [1. périod; 2. píəriəd], fr. Fr. *période*, fr. Lat., fr. Gk. *períodos*, 'circuit, compass; cycle; period of time; sentence', fr. **peri-** & *hodós*, 'way, path'. See **hodometer**. Portion of time. In various specific uses: **1.** Portion of time marked by recurrence of astronomical phenomena. **2.** Specific portion of time; space of time during which some specific event happens; **a** course of a disease; stage in the course of a disease; **b** pl., *periods*, women's monthly courses; **c** *the period*, some specified time or age; **d** stage in history, or in career of individual; time elapsing between stages of development, or such as are marked by some notable event: *the period of Queen Elizabeth*; *the Restoration period*; *the period of adolescence*; **e** stage in art, literature &c.: *period of the Renaissance*; (also attrib.) *period furniture*. **3. a** Indefinite stretch of time: *long periods in the world's history when civilization appears to stand still*; **b** any portion of time: *I lived in Ireland for a period in my youth*. **4. a** Portion of a speech or piece of writing, generally one composed of several clauses or sentences; **b** pl., *periods*, rhetorical passages; flowery style; **c** pause at end of a sentence; punctuation expressing this, i.e. a full stop (.). **5. a** (elect.) Time required for one alternation of an alternating current or for one oscillation in a train of electro-magnetic waves; **b** (phys.) of waves, interval in time between the repetitions of a periodic disturbance, see **wave** (II.).

periodic, adj. [1. pèriódik; 2. pìəriódik]. Prec. & **-ic**. **1.** Recurring at intervals, esp. at regular intervals; cyclic. **2.** Of, pertaining to, revolutions of a heavenly body. **3.** Expressed in periods.

periodical, adj. & n. [1. pèriódikl; 2. pìəriódikl]. Prec. & **-al**. **1.** adj. **a** Recurring at intervals, esp. at regular intervals; **b** (of magazine &c.) published at regular intervals. **2.** n. A periodical publication; a magazine, learned journal &c.

periodically, adv. Prec. & **-ly**. In a periodical manner; at intervals of time.

periodicity, n. [1. pèriodísiti; 2. pìəriədísiti]. **periodic** & **-ity**. Quality of being periodic.

perioeci, n. pl. [1. pèriésī; 2. pèrìsai]. Lat. pl., fr. Gk. *perioikos*, *-oi*, fr. **peri-** & *oikos*, 'house, dwelling'. See first element in **economy**. In ancient Sparta, citizens without political rights who came between the Spartiates (full citizens) and helots.

periosteal, adj. [1. pèriósteal; 2. pèriɔ́stiəl]. See next word & **-al**. Pertaining to the periosteum; surrounding a bone.

periosteum, n. [1. pèriósteum; 2. pèriɔ́stiəm]. Lat., fr. Gk. *perióstεos*, 'round the bones'. **peri-** & *ostéon*, 'bone'. See **osteo-**. Membrane covering the bones.

periostitis, n. [1. pèriostítis; 2. pèriɔstáitis]. Prec. & **-itis**. Inflammation of the periosteum.

peripatetic (I.), adj. [1. pèripatétik; 2. pèripətétik], fr. Lat., fr. Gk. *peripatētik-(ós)*, 'walking about', esp. of Aristotle, when teaching, fr. *peripatéō*, 'I walk about', fr. **peri-** & *patéō*, 'I walk, tread'; cp. *pátos*, 'beaten track'; earlier **pn̥to-s*. Cp. further Scrt. *pánthāš*, 'path'; Lat. *pons*, 'bridge', see **pons**; O. Slav. *pǫti*, 'road'. See also **find** (I.). **1.** (cap.) Of, pertaining to, Aristotle or his teaching (referring to his custom of walking in the Lyceum while teaching). **2.** Walking about, moving from place to place, itinerant: *a peripatetic preacher*.

peripatetic (II.), n., fr. prec. **1.** (cap.) Follower of Aristotle. **2.** (usually facet.) Itinerant vendor.

peripatetically, adv. [1. pèripatétikali; 2. pèripətétikəli]. **peripatetic** (I.) & **-al** & **-ly**. In a peripatetic manner.

peripateticism, n. [1. pèripatétisizm; 2. pèripətétisizəm]. **peripatetic** & **-ism**. **1.** Habit, practice, of walking about, going from place to place. **2.** (cap.) Philosophical system of Aristotle and his followers.

Peripatus, n. [1. perípatus; 2. pərípətəs]. Lat., fr. Gk. *perípatos*, 'a walking about'. See **peripatetic**. (zool.) A genus of primitive land arthropods of tropical America and Africa &c., resembling a caterpillar or earthworm, supposed to form a link between the worm and the insect.

peripet(e)ia, n. [1. pèripetía; 2. pèripətáiə], fr. Gk. *peripéteia*, 'sudden change', fr. **peri-** & stem **pet-*, 'to fall'; cp. *pí-pt-ein*, 'to fall'; *eupetḗs*, 'favourable; easy'; *ptôsis*, 'falling'. See **ptosis** & **ptero-**. Sudden dénouement in drama; hence, sudden turn of fortune; vicissitude.

peripheral, adj. [1. períferal; 2. pərífərəl]. See **periphery** & **-al**. Of, pertaining to, a periphery.

peripherally, adv. Prec. & **-ly**. As a periphery.

periphery, n. [1. períferi; 2. pərífəri], fr. O. Fr. *periferie*; fr. L. Lat. *peripherīa*, fr. Gk. *periphéreia*, 'periphery, circumference', fr. **peri-** & *phérein*, 'to carry'; see **-ferous, ferry, bear** (I.). **1.** Line bounding figure, esp. circle; circumference. **2.** Outside, outer surface.

periphrase, n. [1. périfrāz; 2. périfreiz], fr. Lat., fr. Gk. *períphrasis*. See next word. Periphrasis.

periphrasis, n. [1. perífrasis; 2. pərífrəsis], fr. L. Lat., fr. Gk. *períphrasis*, 'circumlocution'. **peri-** & *phrázein*, 'to speak', see **phrase**. **1.** Circumlocution; roundabout way of speaking. **2.** Circumlocutory phrase.

periphrastic, adj. [1. pèrifrástik; 2. pèrifrǽstik]. **peri-** & *phrast-*, participial stem of *phrázein*, 'to speak', see **phrase**. Of, like, employing, periphrasis; expressed in a roundabout manner; (gram.) *periphrastic conjugation*, formed with auxiliary verb, *periphrastic genitive*, formed with preposition, not by inflexion.

periphrastically, adv. [1. pèrifrástikali; 2. pèrifrǽstikəli]. Prec. & **-al** & **-ly**. In a periphrastic manner.

perique, n. [1. perḗk; 2. pərík]. Fr.; origin doubtful. A very strong grade of tobacco, with dark, shiny, curled small leaves, used in blending to make a strong smoking mixture.

periscope, n. [1. périskōp; 2. périskoup]. **peri-** & **-scope**. Apparatus consisting of a tube containing mirrors and lenses which enable an observer to see over an obstruction, the image being transmitted to the eye at right angles to the direction from which it is first received through the far end of the tube; also similar, more elaborate, apparatus for use in submarines when submerged.

periscopic, adj. [1. pèriskópik; 2. pèriskɔ́pik]. **peri-** & **-scopic**. Connected with, received, transmitted by, a periscope.

perish, vb. intrans. [1. pérish; 2. périʃ], fr. M.E. *perissen*, *perischen*, fr. O. Fr. *periss-*, Pres. Part. stem of *per-(ir)*, 'to perish', fr. Lat. *perīre*, 'to be lost, pass away; to die, perish', fr. **per-** & *īre*, 'to go'. See **itinerate**. To come to an end, pass away; to be completely destroyed or ruined (lit. or fig.).

perishable, adj. & n. [1. périshabl; 2. périʃəbl]. Prec. & **-able**. **1.** adj. Liable to perish; liable to decay swiftly, be easily destroyed; fragile. **2.** n. (pl.) Goods liable to speedy decay, esp. foodstuffs in process of being conveyed from place to place.

perishableness, n. Prec. & **-ness**. Quality of being perishable.

perished, adj. [1. périsht; 2. périʃt], fr. P.P. of **perish**. Brought to state of extreme discomfort, exhaustion, or to point of death, by cold, hunger &c.: *to be perished with cold*.

perishing, adj. [1. périshing; 2. périʃiŋ], fr. Pres. Part. of **perish**. (of cold &c.) Causing extreme discomfort, exhaustion &c.

perishingly, adv. Prec. & **-ly**. To a perishing degree.

perispomenon, adj. & n. [1. pèrispómenon; 2. pèrispóuminən]. Gk. *perispṓmenon*, neut. P.P. of *perispáein*, 'I draw round', fr. **peri-** & *spáein*, 'to draw'. See **spasm**. **1.** adj. (of word) Having circumflex accent on last syllable. **2.** n. Word accented thus.

perissodactylate, adj. [1. perìsōdáktilāt; 2. pərìsoudǽktileit], fr. Gk. *perissós*, 'beyond the regular number, odd; extraordinary', fr. **peri-**, *ísos* 'even', see **iso-**, & *dáktulos*, 'finger, toe', see **dactyl**, & **-ate**. (zool.) Having odd or unevenly developed toes; specif., belonging to the suborder, *Perissodactyla*, of ungulate mammals, which includes the horse, rhinoceros, tapir &c.

peristalith, n. [1. perístalith; 2. perístəliþ], fr. Gk. *perístatos*, 'standing round', fr. *peri-istēmi*, 'I stand round, encircle'; fr. **peri-** & *hístēmi*, 'I stand'. See **state** & words there referred to; for the second element see **-lith**. (archaeol.) Ring of upright stones round burial-mound &c.

peristalsis, n. [1. pèristálsis; 2. pèristǽlsis]. **peri-** & Gk. *stálsis*, 'constriction', fr. *stéllein*, 'to put in order; to equip; to dress, array; to draw together, gather up'; cp. Gk. *stolḗ*, 'garment', & see **stole** (I.). Rhythmic involuntary contractions of the muscular fibres of the intestinal canal, whereby the contents are mixed with the digestive juices, and forced along the canal.

peristaltic, adj. [1. pèristáltik; 2. pèristǽltik], fr. **peri-** & Gk. *staltik-(ós)*, 'astringent, contracting', fr. *stéllein*, 'to draw together'. See prec. Of the nature of, resembling, exhibiting, peristalsis.

peristeronic, adj. [1. pèristerónik; 2. pèristərɔ́nik], fr. Gk. *peristerṓn*, 'dovecote', fr. *peristerá*, 'dove'; prob. fr. Semitic *perach-Istar*, 'bird of Istar'. (zool.) Connected with, pertaining to, pigeons.

peristyle, n. [1. péristīl; 2. péristail], fr. Fr., fr. Lat. *peristȳlum*, 'part of building surrounding inner court', fr. Gk. *perístūlon*, 'colonnade round temple or inner court', fr. **peri-** & *stûlo-(s)*, 'pillar', see **style** (III.). **a** Series of columns supporting a roof, surrounding a court; **b** court or other space thus surrounded by a colonnade, esp. the large, inner court of ancient Roman house.

peritoneal, adj. [1. pèrituneal; 2. pèritəníəl]. See next word & **-al**. Of, pertaining to, the peritoneum.

periton(a)eum, n. [1. pèrituneum; 2. pèritəníəm]. Lat. *peritonaeum*, fr. Gk. *peritónaion*, 'peritoneum', fr. **peri-** & stem **ton-*, 'stretching'; cp. Gk. *teinein*, 'to stretch'; *tónos*, 'something stretched; cord', see **tone**, & words there referred to. Serous membrane lining the abdomen and enclosing the viscera.

peritonitis, n. [1. pèritunītis; 2. pèritənáitis]. See prec. & **-itis**. Inflammation of peritoneum.

perityphlitis, n. [1. pèritiflítis; 2. pèritifláitis]. **peri-** & **typhlitis**. (med.) Inflammation of the caecum and the tissues surrounding it.

periwig, n. [1. périwig; 2. périwig]. Earlier *perwyke*, fr. Fr. *perruque*, see **peruke**. Head-dress of false hair; wig.

periwigged, adj. [1. périwigd; 2. péríwigd]. Prec. & **-ed.** Wearing a periwig.

periwinkle (**I.**), n. [1. périwingkl; 2. périwiŋkl]. O.E. *peruince*; M.E. *pervinke*; fr. Lat. *pervinca*, also *vinca pervinca*, 'periwinkle', fr. (*per*)*vincīre*, 'to bind, twist round'; cp. Lat. *vicia*, 'vetch', see **vetch**; Lat. *viēre*, 'to twist, weave'; O.E. *wiðig*, 'willow', see **withy.** Genus of plants, esp. *greater and lesser periwinkle*, trailing evergreen shrubs with flat blue flowers.

periwinkle (**II.**), n. Etymol. uncertain; O.E. has *pinewincle*, *winewincle*; first element possibly fr. Lat. *pinna*, 'mussel'; for second element see **winkle**; the word has been influenced by prec. An edible gastropod marine mollusc, with shell like that of a snail.

perjure, vb. reflex. [1. pěrjur; 2. pʌ́dʒə], fr. O. Fr. *parjurer*, fr. Lat. *perjūrāre*, 'to forswear oneself', fr. **per-** & *jūrāre*, 'to swear', see **juror.** To swear falsely, forswear oneself.

perjured, adj. [1. pěrjurd; 2. pʌ́dʒəd], fr. P.P. of prec. Forsworn, guilty of perjury: *a perjured witness, villain* &c.

perjurious, adj. [1. pěrjóorius; 2. pʌdʒúəriəs, pʌdʒɔ́riəs]. **perjury** & **-ous.** (rare) Of, guilty of, involving, perjury.

perjuriously, adv. Prec. & **-ly.** In a perjurious manner.

perjury, n. [1. pěrjuri; 2. pʌ́dʒəri], fr. A.-Fr. *perjurie*, fr. Lat. *perjūrium*, 'perjury', fr. *perjūr-*(*āre*), 'to swear falsely'. See **perjure.** **1.** (law) **a** False statement made deliberately in a court of justice, by a witness upon his oath; **b** act of false swearing under oath. **2.** Any deliberately uttered lie.

perk (**I.**), vb. intrans. & trans. [1. pěrk; 2. pʌk]. Etymol. uncertain. Usually *perk up.* **1.** intrans. **a** To lift up one's head jauntily, assume a perky air; **b** to be forward and impudent; **c** to regain one's spirits, become gayer, more cheerful. **2.** trans. **a** (reflex.) To make smart, jaunty, gay: *to perk oneself up*; **b** to raise, poise, in a jaunty manner: *to perk up one's head.*

perk (**II.**), adj., fr. prec. (rare) Smart, jaunty, perky.

perkily, adv. [1. pěrkili; 2. pʌ́kili]. **perky** & **-ly.** In a perky manner.

perkiness, n. [1. pěrkines; 2. pʌ́kinis]. See prec. & **-ness.** Quality of being perky.

perks, n. Vulgar slang abbr. of **perquisite(s).**

perky, adj. [1. pěrki; 2. pʌ́ki]. **perk** & **-y.** **a** In good spirits; lively, jaunty, gay; **b** jaunty, saucy, in manner.

perlite, n. [1. pěrlīt; 2. pʌ́lait]. Fr. *perle.* See **pearl** (**I.**) & **-ite.** Igneous, glassy rock like obsidian, composed of small enamel-like spherical bodies.

permanence, n. [1. pěrmanens; 2. pʌ́mənəns]. See **permanent** & **-ence.** State of being permanent.

permanency, n. [1. pěrmanensi; 2. pʌ́mənənsi]. See next word & **-ency.** **1.** State of being permanent. **2.** Something that is permanent, as a permanent employment, office &c.

permanent, adj. [1. pěrmanent; 2. pʌ́mənənt], fr. Lat. *permanent-*(*em*), Pres. Part. of *permanēre*, 'to endure, remain, continue', fr. **per-** & *manēre*, 'to remain'. See second element in **remain** & words there referred to. Continuing without change, lasting; intended to last, or remain, for an indefinite time; not to be changed or removed; contrasted with *temporary*; *permanent way*, railway line and prepared bed on which it is laid.

permanently, adv. Prec. & **-ly.** In a permanent manner; as a permanency.

permanganate, n. [1. pěrmángganāt; 2. pʌmǽŋgəneit]. **per-** & **manganese** & **-ate.** (chem.) A salt of permanganic acid, specif., *permanganate of potassium*, in red, purplish crystals, which when dissolved in water form a strong disinfectant and antiseptic.

permanganic, adj. [1. pěrmangánik; 2. pʌmæŋgǽnik]. **per-** & **manganese** & **-ic.** Of, pertaining to, an acid of manganese.

permeability, n. [1. pěrmeabíliti; 2. pʌmiəbíliti]. See next word & **-ity.** Quality of being permeable.

permeable, adj. [1. pěrmeabl; 2. pʌ́miəbl], fr. Lat. *permeābilis*, 'permeable', fr. *perme-*(*āre*), 'to pass through'. See **permeate** & **-able.** Capable of being permeated; allowing the free passage and interfusion of fluids.

permeance, n. [1. pěrmeans; 2. pʌ́miəns]. See **permeate** & **-ance.** Quality of being permeable.

permeant, adj. [1. pěrmeant; 2. pʌ́miənt]. See prec. & **-ant.** Capable of permeating; tending to permeate.

permeate, vb. trans. & intrans. [1. pěrmeāt; 2. pʌ́mieit], fr. Lat. *permeāt-*(*um*), P.P. type of *permeāre*, 'to pass through; to penetrate, pervade', fr. **per-** & *meāre*, 'to go, pass', see **meatus.** **1.** trans. **a** (in physical sense) To pass through all parts of, fill the interstices of, penetrate thoroughly, saturate: *water permeates the soil*; *a powerful scent permeates a room*; **b** (fig., of doctrine, influence, principles &c.) to pervade, be diffused through: *a spirit of indiscipline had permeated the enemy's army.* **2.** intrans. To penetrate, diffuse itself (followed by *among, through*).

permeation, n. [1. pěrmeáshun; 2. pʌmiéiʃən]. Prec. & **-ion.** Act or process of permeating; state of being permeated.

per mensem, adv. [1. pěr ménsem; 2. pʌ ménsem]. **per** & Lat. *mensem*, acc. of *mensis*, 'month'. See **meno-** & **month.** By the month.

Permian, adj. [1. pěrmian; 2. pʌ́miən], fr. Perm, province of East Russia, & **-ian.** (geol.) Of, forming, the uppermost group of strata of the Palaeozoic series, lying above the coal measures, and consisting of red sandstones, limestones &c.

permissible, adj. [1. permísibl; 2. pəmísibl], fr. O. Fr., fr. Lat. *permiss-*(*um*), P.P. type of *permitt-*(*ere*), 'to allow to pass; to let go, let loose; to suffer, allow'. See **permit** & **-ible.** Permitted, allowable.

permissibly, adv. Prec. & **-ly.** In a permissible manner.

permission, n. [1. permíshun; 2. pəmíʃən], fr. Lat. *permissiōn-*(*em*), 'a giving up, yielding; leave, permission', fr. *permiss-*(*um*). See **permissible** & **-ion.** Licence, leave, consent, sanction.

permissive, adj. [1. permísiv; 2. pəmísiv], fr. Lat. *permiss-*(*um*). See **permissible** & **-ive.** Allowing, permitting; conveying permission: *permissive clause* (in a bill), one which allows, but does not enforce, a certain line of action.

permissively, adv. Prec. & **-ly.** In a permissive manner.

permissiveness, n. See prec. & **-ness.** State of being permissive.

permit (**I.**), vb. trans. & intrans. [1. permít; 2. pəmít], fr. Lat. *permitt-*(*ere*), 'to allow to pass; to let loose; to give up; to suffer, allow', fr. **per-** & *mittere*, 'to send', see **mission.** **A.** trans. **1.** **a** To allow, give leave or permission to (a person to do something): *will you permit me to smoke?*; *permit me to remind you* &c.; **b** to suffer, tolerate, not to oppose (action or conduct): *I do not permit noise in my house*; *smoking is permitted everywhere nowadays.* **2.** To make possible, be capable of bearing; to admit, be patient of: *the words hardly permit doubt.* **B.** intrans. *Permit of*, **a** to allow, give permission; **b** to admit, make possible &c.: *so far as health permits.*

permit (**II.**), n. [1. pěrmit; 2. pʌ́mit], fr. prec. Document giving official, or other authoritative permission for something to be done; warrant.

permutation, n. [1. pěrmūtáshun; 2. pʌmjutéiʃən], fr. Lat. *permūtātiōn-*(*em*), 'changing, alteration', fr. *permūt-*(*āre*), 'to change'. See next word & **-ation.** **1.** Change, alteration. **2.** (math.) Any one of the possible orders in which a series of objects can be arranged.

permute, vb. trans. [1. pěrmút; 2. pʌmjút], fr. Lat. *permūt-*(*āre*), 'to change', fr. **per-** & *mūtāre*, 'to change', see **mutable.** To put in different order, change sequence of (objects &c.).

pern, n. [1. pěrn; 2. pʌn], fr. Mod. Lat. *pernis*, wrongly ad. fr. Gk. *pternis*, 'a kind of hawk'. The honey-buzzard.

pernicious, adj. [1. perníshus; 2. pəníʃəs], fr. Lat. *perniciōs-*(*us*), 'destructive', fr. *pernic-*(*ies*), 'destruction', fr. **per-** & *nec-*, stem of *nex*, 'death', & **-ous**; cp. Lat. *necāre*, 'to kill'; *nocēre*, 'to harm'; see **noxious**; Gk. *nekrós*, 'corpse', see **necro-.** (lit. and fig.) Highly injurious, very harmful: *a climate pernicious to health*; *pernicious examples, doctrines* &c.; *pernicious anaemia*, a progressive and usually fatal type of anaemia.

perniciously, adv. Prec. & **-ly.** In a pernicious manner.

perniciousness, n. See prec. & **-ness.** Quality of being pernicious.

pernickety, adj. [1. perníketi; 2. pəníkəti]. Origin unknown. (colloq.) Fussy, fidgety, fastidious; hard to please; pedantically meticulous and punctilious.

pernoctation, n. [1. pěrnoktáshun; 2. pʌnɔktéiʃən], fr. L. Lat. *pernoctātiōn-*(*em*), 'passing the night', fr. *pernoct-*(*āre*), 'to pass the night', fr. **per-** & *noct-*, stem of *nox*, 'night', see **nocti-**, & **-ation.** **a** Act of spending the night; **b** specif. (eccles.) all-night vigil.

perorate, vb. intrans. [1. pérorāt; 2. pérəreit], fr. Lat. *perōrāt-*(*um*), P.P. type of *perōrāre*, 'to conclude a speech; to speak at length', fr. **per-** & *ōrāre*, 'to speak', see **oration.** **a** To bring a speech to an end, sum up and conclude a speech; **b** to speak at length, deliver a harangue.

peroration, n. [1. pèroráshun; 2. pèrəréiʃən]. Prec. & **-ion.** **a** Act of concluding a speech; **b** concluding part of speech.

peroxide, n. [1. pěróksīd; 2. pʌrɔ́ksaid]. **per-** & **oxide.** (chem.) An oxide with larger proportion of oxygen than other oxides of same series; specif., *peroxide of hydrogen*, used in bleaching &c. and as an antiseptic.

perpend (**I.**), vb. trans. & intrans. [1. pěrpénd; 2. pʌpénd], fr. Lat. *perpend-*(*ere*), 'to weigh carefully; to ponder, consider', fr. **per-** & *pendere*, 'to weigh; to pay', see **pension.** **1.** trans. To consider carefully, reflect upon, ponder. **2.** intrans. To deliberate.

perpend (**II.**). n. See **parpen.**

perpendicular (**I.**), adj. [1. pěrpendíkūlar; 2. pʌpəndíkjulə], fr. O. Fr. *perpendiculer*, fr. Lat. *perpendiculāris*, 'perpendicular', fr. *perpendicul-*(*um*), 'weighted line, plumb-line', fr. *perpend-*(*ere*), 'to weigh carefully'. See **perpend** (**I.**) & **-ar.** **1.** At right angles to plane of horizon; exactly upright, erect, vertical. **2.** (of hill, ascent &c.) Very steep, almost vertical. **3.** (archit., cap.) Otherwise, late English Gothic style, in vogue from c. 1380 to 1520, following the Decorated period and characterized by long vertical lines, esp. in the mullions of the large windows, and in vertical panelling in buttresses &c.

perpendicular (**II.**), n., fr. prec. **1.** Perpendicular line. **2.** Perpendicular position: *out of the perpendicular.* **3.** Instrument for showing perpendicular line from a given point; plumb-rule &c. **4.** Perpendicular style of architecture.

perpendicularity, n. [1. pěrpendikūláriti; 2. pʌ́pəndìkjulǽriti]. Prec. & **-ity.** Quality or state of being perpendicular.

perpendicularly, adv. [1. pěrpendíkūlarli; 2. pʌpəndíkjuləli]. **perpendicular** (**I.**) & **-ly.** In a perpendicular position; vertically.

perpent, n. See **parpen.**

perpetrate, vb. trans. [1. pěrpetrāt; 2. pʌ́pitreit], fr. Lat. *perpetrāt-*(*um*), P.P. type of *perpetr-*(*āre*), 'to accomplish', fr. **per-** & *patrāre*, 'to effect'; cp. Lat. *impetrāre*, 'to obtain by request', see **impetrate**; prob.

cogn. w. O.H.G. *fazzōn*, 'to seize'; O.E. *fæt*, 'vessel', see **vat** & words there referred to. To commit, be guilty of: *to perpetrate a crime, blunder.* Phr. *to perpetrate a joke, pun.*

perpetration, n. [1. pĕrpetrâshun; 2. pə̄pitréiʃən]. Prec. & **-ion**. Act of perpetrating.

perpetual, adj. [1. perpéchooal, perpétūal; 2. pəpétʃuəl, pəpétjuəl], fr. Lat. *perpetuāl-(is)*, 'universal, general', fr. *perpetu-(us)*, 'unbroken, uninterrupted, permanent', fr. **per-** & **pet-*, stem of *pet-(ere)*, 'to go; to make for; to seek', see **petition. 1.** Everlasting, eternal: *heaven's perpetual bliss*; *perpetual damnation.* **2. a** Unceasing, constant, never-ending; continuing for an indefinite time: *the perpetual ebb and flow of the tide*; *land of perpetual night*; *perpetual motion*, that of a hypothetical machine, mechanically impossible, which, once set going, will go on continually by producing its own energy until worn out; **b** continuing for the whole of one's life: *perpetual imprisonment.* **3.** Constantly renewed or repeated; frequent: *perpetual chatter, questions, quarrelling* &c.

perpetually, adv. Prec. & **-ly. 1.** Continuously, uninterruptedly, unceasingly, for ever: *the sea perpetually ebbs and flows.* **2.** Constantly, frequently: *to quarrel perpetually.*

perpetuance, n. [1. perpétūans; 2. pəpétjuəns]. See next word & **-ance.** Perpetuation.

perpetuate, vb. trans. [1. perpétūāt; 2. pəpétjueit], fr. Lat. *perpetuāt-(um)*, P.P. type of *perpetuāre*, 'to make perpetual', fr. *perpetu-(us)*, 'continuous', see **perpetual. a** To make perpetual, cause to continue or last indefinitely; **b** to preserve from extinction or oblivion: *to perpetuate one's name and race.*

perpetuation, n. [1. perpètūâshun; 2. pəpètjuéiʃən]. Prec. & **-ion.** Act of perpetuating; state of being perpetuated.

perpetuity, n. [1. pĕrpetûiti; 2. pə̄pitjûiti], fr. Lat. *perpetuitāt-(em)*, 'perpetuity', fr. *perpetuus*, 'constant'. See **perpetual** & **-ity. 1.** Quality of being perpetual. Phr. *in perpetuity*, for ever. **2. a** Perpetual possession, inheritance &c.; esp. (law) the tying up of property so that it is inalienable for ever or for a long period; this is limited by *the rule against perpetuities*, restricting such to a life or lives in being and twenty-one years afterwards; **b** perpetual annuity.

perplex, vb. trans. [1. perpléks; 2. pəpléks], fr. obs. adj. *perplex*, fr. Lat. *perplexus*, 'involved, intricate', fr. **per-** & *plexus*, P.P. of *plectere*, 'to plait, weave', see **plexus** & words there referred to. **1.** To embarrass, puzzle, bewilder, cause doubt or hesitation to: *to perplex a person, one's mind* &c. **2.** To make involved, intricate, confused, to complicate; used chiefly in P.P. as adj., see next word.

perplexed, adj. [1. perplékst; 2. pəplékst], fr. P.P. of prec. **1.** Feeling perplexity; puzzled, bewildered: *to feel, be, perplexed about anything*; *a troubled and perplexed mind.* **2.** Confused, entangled, complicated: *a perplexed question.*

perplexedly, adv. [1. perpléksedli; 2. pəpléksidli]. Prec. & **-ly.** In a perplexed manner.

perplexing, adj. [1. perpléksing; 2. pəpléksiŋ], fr. Pres. Part. of **perplex.** Causing perplexity; bewildering, embarrassing, intricate.

perplexingly, adv. Prec. & **-ly.** In a perplexing manner.

perplexity, n. [1. perpléksiti; 2. pəpléksiti], fr. L. Lat. *perplexitāt-(em)*, fr. *perplex-(us)*, 'involved, intricate', see **perplex,** & **-ity. 1.** State or quality of being perplexed. **2.** Perplexing thing, circumstance &c.

per procurationem, adv. [1. pĕr prókūrâshiónem; 2. pə̄ próukjureiʃióunem]. Lat., 'through the administration of'. See **per, procuration.** By proxy, deputy; through the agency, by the hand of; abbr. *per pro., p.p.*

perquisite, n. [1. pĕrkwizit; 2. pə̄kwizit], fr. Lat. *perquisīt-(um)*, P.P. type of Lat. *perquīrere*, 'to search diligently for', fr. **per-** & *quaerere*, 'to seek, inquire, ask', see **query. 1.** (law) Casual profit accruing to lord of a manor. **2.** Profit additional to a regular wage or salary, which arises from pursuit, and in the course, of one's employment, and which is recognized as legitimate.

perron, n. [1. pérun; 2. pérən], fr. Fr., fr. Lat. *petr-(a)*, 'stone', see **petro-.** (rare) Broad flight of steps leading up to a terrace or platform before the entrance-door of large building.

perry, n. [1. péri; 2. péri], fr. O. Fr. *peré*, fr. L. Lat. *pera*, variant of *pira*, 'pear'. See **pear.** Fermented drink made from juice of pears.

per saltum, adv. [1. pĕr sáltum; 2. pə̄ sǽltəm]. Lat., 'by a bound'. See **per, saltation.** Without intermediate degrees; all at once.

per se, adv. [1. pĕr sē; 2. pə̄ sí]. Lat., 'in itself'. In itself, intrinsically, of its own nature.

perse, adj. & n. [1. pĕrs; 2. pə̄s]. M.E. *pers*, fr. O. Fr. *perse*, fr. L. Lat. *persus*; etymol. doubtful. **1.** adj. Greyish-blue. **2.** n. This colour.

persecute, vb. trans. [1. pĕrsekūt; 2. pə̄sikjūt], fr. Lat. *persecūt-(um)*, P.P. type of *persequi*, 'to follow, pursue', fr. **per-** & *sequi*, 'to follow', see **sequence. 1.** To harass continually with malignant and injurious attack; to treat with cruelty and oppression, esp. on account of religious beliefs. **2.** To worry, annoy persistently, importune.

persecution, n. [1. pĕrsekūshun; 2. pə̄sikjūʃən], fr. Lat. *persecūtiōn-(em)*, 'pursuit, persecution'. Prec. & **-ion. 1.** Act of persecuting; state of being persecuted. **2.** Specific case of systematic oppression and attack on account of religious beliefs: *the Marian persecution.*

perseverance, n. [1. pĕrsevérans; 2. pə̄siviərəns], fr. Fr., fr. Lat. *persevērantia*, 'steadfastness, constancy', fr. *persevēr-(āre)*, 'to continue steadfastly, to persist, persevere'. See **persevere. 1.** Act of persevering; capacity to persevere; steadfast and long-continued application; steady persistence in attempt to secure an aim, achieve a purpose &c. **2.** (theol.) Perpetual continuance of the elect in a state of grace.

perseverant, adj. [1. pĕrsevérant; 2. pə̄siviərənt]. See next word & **-ant.** (rare) Persevering, persistent.

persevere, vb. intrans. [1. pĕrsevḗr; 2. pə̄sivíə], fr. Fr. *persévérer*, fr. Lat. *persevērāre*, 'to persist, persevere', fr. *persevēr-(us)*, 'very strict'. **per-** & **severe.** To persist doggedly and with determination, diligence, and patience; with the object **a** of completing a task; **b** of overcoming difficulty or opposition; **c** of attaining a purpose, securing an aim &c.

persevering, adj. [1. pĕrsevéring; 2. pə̄siviəriŋ], fr. Pres. Part. of prec. Tenacious of purpose, maintaining constant diligence in pursuit of an object; persistent, unremitting.

perseveringly, adv. Prec. & **-ly.** In a persevering manner.

Persian, adj. & n. [1. pĕrshan; 2. pə̄ʃən]. Persia & **-an. 1.** adj. Pertaining to, made in, originating in, Persia: *Persian carpet*; *Persian cat*, one with long silky hair. **2.** n. **a** Native of Persia; **b** Persian language; **c** a Persian cat.

persiennes, n. pl. [1. pĕrsiénz; 2. pə̄siénz], fr. Fr., fem. pl. of *persien*, 'Persian'. See prec. Shutters for keeping out sun, fixed outside a window, and opening like casement windows.

persiflage, n. [1. pĕrsiflàhzh; 2. pə̄siflâž]. Fr., fr. *persifler*, 'to banter', fr. **per-** & Lat. *sibilāre*, 'to hiss, whistle', see **sibilant,** & **-age.** Light flippant chaff, banter, raillery; light, airy, frivolous treatment of a subject.

persimmon, n. [1. persímun; 2. pəsímən], fr. native N. Am. Indian name. **a** Tree yielding fine, hard wood, and bearing small white flowers and a fruit resembling a plum; **b** the fruit of this tree.

persist, vb. intrans. [1. persíst; 2. pəsíst], fr. Lat. *persist-(ere)*, 'to remain, persist', fr. **per-** & *sistere*, 'to stand', fr. *stāre*, 'to stand', see **state** & **stand. 1.** To continue steadfastly, adhere firmly or obstinately to a course of action &c., in spite of opposition or remonstrance: *to persist in a belief, statement* &c.; *to persist in one's folly*; *he will persist in talking when one wants to be quiet.* **2.** To remain, survive; to continue to exist, to endure: *the tendency still persists.*

persistence, n. [1. persístens; 2. pəsístəns]. Prec. & **-ence.** Act of persisting, quality of being persistent; **a** tenacity of purpose; **b** continuance.

persistency, n. [1. persístensi; 2. pəsístənsi]. Prec. & **-y.** Quality of being persistent; generally in unfavourable sense, obstinacy, inconvenient pertinacity; importunity.

persistent, adj. [1. persístent; 2. pəsístənt]. **persist** & **-ent. 1.** (of persons) Pertinacious; continuing on a course in spite of opposition &c.; obstinate or persevering, adhering to a purpose. **2.** (of processes, tendencies &c.) Remaining unchanged, tending to survive unchanged; tending to recur.

persistently, adv. Prec. & **-ly.** In a persistent manner.

person, n. [1. pĕrsn; 2. pə̄sn], fr. O. Fr. *persone*, fr. Lat. *persōna*, 'character, part, rôle; actor's mask; human being, person'; prob. of Etruscan origin; cp. Etruscan *phersu*, 'masked figures'. **1. a** A human being considered as possessing reason, a distinct personality and individuality: *we soon realize that a baby of a year old is a person*; **b** a personage; **c** personality. **2.** A human being in the most general and indefinite sense: *I noticed that two or three persons were there*; *I thought him a pleasant person.* **3. a** The bodily form of a man or woman, the outer man: *a young woman of an agreeable person*; Phr. *in person*, oneself, in actual bodily presence; **b** the body: *offences against the person*, bodily assaults &c. **4.** (theol.) One of the three modes of being of the Deity: *the First Person of the Trinity*, God the Father; *the Second Person*, God the Son; *the Third Person*, God the Holy Ghost. **5.** (gram.) One of the three relations involved in speech; that of the speaker himself, *first person, I, we*; the one spoken to, *second person, you*; the one spoken of, *third person, he, she, it, they.* **6.** (law) Human being, corporation or body regarded as having rights and duties.

persona, n. [1. pĕrsōna; 2. pə̄sóunə]. Lat. *persōna*, 'character, rôle; person'. See prec. Person. Phrs. *(to be) persona grata (to, with)*, person that is acceptable, well liked by; *in propria persona*, in one's own person.

personable, adj. [1. pĕrsunabl; 2. pə̄sənəbl]. **person** & **-able.** Of attractive appearance; good-looking, handsome.

personage, n. [1. pĕrsunij; 2. pə̄sənidž], fr. O. Fr., fr. Med. Lat. *persōnāticum.* **person** & **-age. 1.** Person, individual; esp. person of importance; **a** one of high rank; **b** one of distinction and eminence. **2.** Character in drama. **3.** Bodily form, person (Spenser, 'F. Q.' iii. 2. 26).

personal, adj. [1. pĕrsunal; 2. pə̄sənəl], fr. O. Fr., fr. Lat. *persōnāl-(is)*, 'personal'. **person** & **-al. 1.** Pertaining to, peculiar to, one person; individual, private: *to give one's personal opinion*; *personal tastes*; *a purely personal matter.* **2.** Directed towards or performed by an individual; carried on in one's own person, without intervention of others; individual, and not general or public: *a personal appeal, interview* &c.; *personal service.* **3. a** Directed against a particular individual: *personal remarks*; **b** directing an attack, insinuation, insult &c. against an individual: *try not to be personal.* **4.** Of, pertaining to, the person, to the human body: *personal beauty, appearance* &c. **5.** (gram.) Denoting, indicating, one of the three persons: *personal pronouns*; *the personal endings of the verb.* **6.** (law) **a** *Personal property, estate,* property consisting of movables, chattels, cash, and other belongings which are not *real property*, i.e. in land; **b** *personal action*, one brought for recovery of goods and chattels, for damages for injury &c., as distinguished from *real action*, for recovery of lands &c.

personality, n. [1. pĕrsunáliti; 2. pʌ̀sənǽliti]. Prec. & **-ity**. **1**. The state of being a person; individual existence as a self-conscious being; personal identity. **2**. Sum of mental and moral qualities which make up the distinctive character of an individual; characteristic combination of such qualities found in a single individual. **3**. Person, individual, personage. **4**. (gen. pl.) *Personalities*, expressions, remarks, esp. of an offensive character, aimed at an individual and referring to some specific quality of his character, mind, or person. **5**. (law, rare) Personal estate; personalty.

personalization, n. [1. pĕrsunalīzáshun; 2. pʌ̀sənəlaizéiʃən]. See next word & **-ation**. Act of personalizing; state of being personalized.

personalize, vb. trans. [1. pĕrsunalīz; 2. pʌ́sənəlaiz]. **personal** & **-ize**. **1**. To make personal. **2**. To attribute personal nature to; to personify.

personally, adv. [1. pĕrsunali; 2. pʌ́sənəli]. **personal** & **-ly**. **1**. As, in the form of, a person. **2**. In one's own person, in person: *to be personally responsible*. **3**. As far as one is oneself concerned, for one's own part: *personally, I think you are right*.

personalty, n. [1. pĕrsunalti; 2. pʌ́sənəlti], fr. A.-Fr. *personaltie*. **personal** & **-ty**. Personal estate; contrasted with *realty*.

personate (I.), vb. trans. [1. pĕrsunāt; 2. pʌ́səneit], fr. L. Lat. *persōnāt-(um)*, P.P. type of *persōnāre*, 'to take the part of, play', fr. Lat. *persōna*, 'mask; character in play'. See **person**. **1**. To play the part of, assume the rôle of, in a play. **2**. To assume the identity of, impersonate, pretend to be, esp. for fraudulent purpose.

personate (II.), adj. [1. pĕrsunat; 2. pʌ́sənət], fr. Lat. *persōnāt-(us)*, 'masked'. **person** & **-ate**. (bot.) Having a two-lipped corolla, the opening in which is covered by a projection of the lower lip, as a snapdragon.

personation, n. [1. pĕrsunáshun; 2. pʌ̀sənéiʃən]. Prec. & **-ation**. Act of personating; state of being personated.

personification, n. [1. persònifikáshun; 2. pəsɔ̀nifikéiʃən]. See next word & **-fication**. **1**. Act of personifying; state of being personified. **2**. Person or thing regarded as typical example, or embodiment, of a quality, attribute &c.: *the personification of youth, joy, evil* &c.

personify, vb. trans. [1. persónifī; 2. pəsɔ́nifai], fr. Fr. *personnifier*. **person** & **-fy**. **1**. **a** To conceive of and represent as a person; to endow with, regard as possessing, personal attributes: *primitive peoples personify natural phenomena*; **b** to represent symbolically by a human figure: *to personify a quality, virtue* &c. **2**. To typify, embody, be a striking example of, represent in one's own person: *the writer personifies the aspirations of his period*.

personnel, n. [1. pĕrsonél; 2. pʌ̀sənél]. Fr. *personnel*; fr. adj., fr. Lat. *persōnāl-(is)*, 'personal', see **personal**. **a** All the persons collectively engaged in a common undertaking; the staff of all grades concerned in carrying on the work of an institution &c.; specif. **b** the man power or human beings composing an army or navy; contrasted with *matériel*.

perspective (I.), n. [1. perspéktiv; 2. pəspéktiv], fr. Med. Lat. *perspectiva (ars)*, fr. Lat. *perspect-(um)*, P.P. type of *perspicere*, 'to look at', fr. **per-** & *specere*, 'to look', see **spectrum, specimen**, & **-ive**. **1**. **a** Art of representing, in drawing, various natural objects, on a plane surface, so as to produce upon the eye the impression of depth, roundness, relative distance, size &c. produced by the objects themselves; Phrs. *in perspective*, in accordance with the rules of this art; (fig.) *to see things in perspective*, to have a true view of events and circumstances, to see them in proper relative proportion &c.; **b** a picture drawn in perspective. **2**. Apparent relation between form, position &c. of objects visible simultaneously. **3**. (lit. and fig.) Distant view, prospect.

perspective (II.), adj., fr. prec. Of, pertaining to, perspective; in perspective; according to rules of perspective: *perspective drawing*.

perspectively, adv. Prec. & **-ly**. In a perspective manner; in perspective.

perspicacious, adj. [1. pĕrspikáshus; 2. pʌ̀spikéiʃəs], fr. Lat. *perspicāc-*, 'sharp-sighted, acute', fr. *perspicere*, 'to look closely at', see **perspective**, & **-ious**. **a** Having a clear and penetrating mind; acute, mentally alert, shrewd, far-seeing; **b** exhibiting these qualities: *a perspicacious mind, judgement* &c.

perspicaciously, adv. Prec. & **-ness**. In a perspicacious manner.

perspicacity, n. [1. pĕrspikásiti; 2. pʌ̀spikǽsiti], fr. Lat. *perspicācitāt-(em)*, 'discernment', fr. *perspicāc-*, stem of *perspicax*, 'acute', see **perspicacious**, & **-ity**. Quality of being perspicacious; acuteness, discernment.

perspicuity, n. [1. pĕrspikúiti; 2. pʌ̀spikjúiti], fr. Lat. *perspicuitāt-(em)*, 'transparency; clearness', see **perspicuous**, & **-ity**. Quality of being perspicuous; clearness, lucidity.

perspicuous, adj. [1. perspíkūus; 2. pəspíkjuəs], fr. Lat. *perspicu-(us)*, 'transparent, clear; evident, manifest', fr. *perspicere*, 'to look at', see **perspective**, & **-ous**. **1**. Clearly expressed, easily grasped by the understanding; lucid. **2**. (of persons &c.) Having the power of clear expression.

perspicuously, adv. Prec. & **-ly**. In a perspicuous manner.

perspicuousness, n. See prec. & **-ness**. Perspicuity.

perspirable, adj. [1. perspírabl; 2. pəspáiərəbl]. **perspire** & **-able**. **1**. Capable of being thrown off in perspiration. **2**. Allowing of perspiration.

perspiration, n. [1. pĕrspiráshun; 2. pʌ̀spiréiʃən]. **perspire** & **-ation**. **1**. Act or process of perspiring. **2**. Fluid given off in perspiring; sweat.

perspiratory, adj. [1. perspíraturi; 2. pəspáiərətəri], fr. Lat. *perspīrāt-(um)*, P.P. type of *perspīrāre*, 'to breathe', see next word, & **-ory**. Of, pertaining to, causing, perspiration.

perspire, vb. intrans. & trans. [1. perspír; 2. pəspáiə], fr. Lat. *perspīr-(āre)*, 'to breathe', fr. **per-** & *spīrāre*, 'to breathe', see **spirant**. **1**. intrans. To exude moisture from the pores of the skin; to sweat. **2**. trans. (rare) To give off in the form of sweat.

persuadable, adj. [1. perswádabl; 2. pəswéidəbl]. See next word & **-able**. Capable of being persuaded.

persuade, vb. trans. [1. perswád; 2. pəswéid], fr. Lat. *persuād-(ēre)*, 'to persuade, convince', fr. **per-** & *suādēre*, 'to advise', see **suasion, suave**. **1**. To induce to think, believe, or feel, something; to convince the judgement, or reason of (a person), by argument: *to persuade a person that something is true*; also *to persuade oneself that one ought to do something*. **2**. To induce, succeed in causing, to do something, a course of action: *to persuade a person to go*; *to persuade one into believing*.

persuaded, adj. [1. perswáded; 2. pəswéidid], fr. P.P. of prec. Convinced, sure, certain: *to be thoroughly persuaded of the truth of the matter*.

persuasibility, n. [1. perswàsibíliti; 2. pəswèisibíliti]. **persuasible** & **-ity**. Capacity for being persuaded.

persuasible, adj. [1. perswásibl; 2. pəswéisibl], fr. Lat. *persuās-(um)*, P.P. type of *persuādēre*, 'to persuade', see **persuade**, & **-ible**. Capable of being persuaded; open to, yielding to, persuasion.

persuasion, n. [1. perswázhun; 2. pəswéižn], fr. Lat. *persuāsiōn-(em)*, 'a convincing; belief, opinion', fr. *persuās-(um)*, P.P. type of *persuādēre*, 'to persuade'. See **persuade** & **-ion**. **1**. Act or process of persuading; state of being persuaded. **2**. Power of persuading; persuasiveness. **3**. **a** Settled belief, conviction, opinion; **b** specif., religious belief. **4**. **a** Religious sect or party holding specific belief: *of the Jewish persuasion*; **b** (facet.) sort, kind, class.

persuasive, adj. & n. [1. perswásiv; 2. pəswéisiv]. See prec. & **-ive**. **1**. adj. Intended to, having the power to, persuade. **2**. n. Something that persuades; motive, inducement.

persuasively, adv. Prec. & **-ly**. In a persuasive manner.

persuasiveness, n. See prec. & **-ness**. Quality of being persuasive.

pert, adj. [1. pĕrt; 2. pʌt]. M.E. *pert*, 'bold', fr. O. Fr. *apert*, 'open', fr. Lat. *apert-(us)*, P.P. of *aperīre*, 'to open', see **aperture**. Impudent, saucy, in speech or manner.

pertain, vb. intrans. [1. pertán; 2. pətéin], fr. O. Fr. *partenir*, 'to belong', fr. Lat. *pertinēre*, 'to belong, have reference to', see **pertinent**. **1**. **a** To belong to, be closely and necessarily associated with, to have natural connexion with: *the dignity which pertains to high office*; *the infirmities pertaining to old age*; **b** to be suitable, or appropriate to; to be becoming in: *it does not pertain to the young to instruct their elders*. **2**. To be relevant to, have reference to; to have logical connexion with: *that remark hardly pertains to the matter in hand*.

pertinacious, adj. [1. pĕrtináshus; 2. pʌ̀tinéiʃəs], fr. Lat. *pertināc-*, *pertinax*, 'holding firmly; steadfast; obstinate', fr. **per-** & *tenax*, 'holding fast', see **tenacious**. Adhering firmly to, tenacious of, one's point or purpose; stubbornly persevering and persistent.

pertinaciously, adv. Prec. & **-ly**. In a pertinacious manner.

pertinaciousness, n. See prec. & **-ness**. Quality of being pertinacious; pertinacity.

pertinacity, n. [1. pĕrtinásiti; 2. pʌ̀tinǽsiti]. See **pertinacious** & **-ity**. Quality of being pertinacious; persistency; stubborn perseverance.

pertinence, **-cy**, n. [1. pĕrtinens(i); 2. pʌ́tinəns(i)]. Next word & **-ce, -cy**. Quality of being pertinent; relevancy.

pertinent, adj. & n. [1. pĕrtinent; 2. pʌ́tinənt], fr. Lat. *pertinent-(em)*, Pres. Part. type of *pertinēre*, 'to reach; to belong, pertain to; to apply to', fr. **per-** & *tenēre*, 'to hold', see **tenable**. **1**. adj. Relevant, apposite; to the point: *a pertinent question, remark* &c.; *the point is not pertinent to the matter in hand*. **2**. n. (usually pl.) Appurtenance, accessory.

pertinently, adv. Prec. & **-ly**. In a pertinent manner.

pertly, adv. [1. pĕrtli; 2. pʌ́tli]. **pert** & **-ly**. In a pert manner.

pertness, n. [1. pĕrtnes; 2. pʌ́tnis]. See prec. & **-ness**. Quality of being pert; sauciness; trivial, superficial smartness and cleverness.

perturb, vb. trans. [1. pertĕrb; 2. pətʌ́b], fr. Lat. *perturb-(āre)*, 'to confuse, disturb', fr. **per-** & *turbāre*, 'to disturb', fr. *turb-(a)*, 'crowd; tumult', see **turbid**. To throw into disorder or confusion; esp. to cause agitation of mind to; to disturb, disconcert.

perturbable, adj. [1. pertĕrbabl; 2. pətʌ́bəbl]. Prec. & **-able**. Capable of being perturbed.

perturbation, n. [1. pĕrterbáshun; 2. pʌ̀təbéiʃən], fr. Lat. *perturbātiōn-(em)*, 'confusion'. See **perturb** & **-ation**. State of being perturbed; disquietude, agitation, of mind.

perturbative, adj. [1. pertĕrbativ; 2. pətʌ́bətiv], fr. Lat. *perturbāt-(um)*, P.P. type of *perturbāre*, see prec. & **-ive**. Tending to perturb.

perturbed, adj. [1. pertérbd; 2. pətə́bd], fr. P.P. of **perturb**. Agitated, disturbed in mind; anxious; embarrassed.

peruke, n. [1. pérūk, perōōk; 2. pérjūk, pərū́k], fr. Fr. *perruque*, 'wig', fr. Ital. *perruca*; origin obscure; Span. has *peluca*, wh. may be same word; this, if the *l* is orig., might be connected w. Lat. *pilus*, 'hair', see **pile (VII.)**. Cap, head-dress, of false hair; wig, periwig.

perusal, n. [1. perōōzl; 2. pərū́zl]. See next word & **-al**. Act of perusing or reading through.

peruse, vb. trans. [1. perōōz; 2. pi-, pərū́z]. **per-** & **use**; orig. sense, now obs., was 'to use up, wear out'. To read through, examine, look over.

Peruvian, adj. [1. perōōvian; 2. pə-, pirū́viən], fr. Mod. Lat. *Peruvia*, 'Peru', & **-an**. Of, pertaining to, found in, Peru; *Peruvian bark*, that of cinchona tree, used medicinally.

pervade, vb. trans. [1. pervā́d; 2. pəvéid], fr. Lat. *pervād-(ere)*, 'to spread through, go through', fr. **per-** & *vādere*, 'to go', see **vade-mecum**. **a** To pass into all parts of, permeate, penetrate thoroughly; also **b** (in moral sense) of influences, feelings &c.

pervasion, n. [1. pervā́zhun; 2. pəvéižn], fr. L. Lat. *pervāsiōn-(em)*, 'invasion', fr. *pervās-(um)*, P.P. type of *pervādere*, 'to go through'. See prec. & **-ion**. Act of pervading; state of being pervaded.

pervasive, adj. [1. pervā́siv; 2. pəvéisiv]. See prec. & **-ive**. Tending to pervade; penetrating, permeating.

pervasively, adv. Prec. & **-ly**. In such a manner as to pervade.

pervasiveness, n. See prec. & **-ness**. Quality of being pervasive.

perverse, adj. [1. pervérs; 2. pəvə́s], fr. Fr., fr. Lat. *pervers-(um)*, P.P. type of Lat. *pervertere*, 'to overthrow'. See **pervert**. **1.** (of persons) **a** Deliberately persisting in error or wickedness, remaining wilfully in the wrong; **b** intractable, unreasonably obstinate. **2.** (of circumstances &c.) Going wrong from point of view of a specific individual; developing in such a way as to defeat one's purposes; *a perverse verdict*, one contrary to the evidence or the judge's direction.

perversely, adv. Prec. & **-ly**. In a perverse manner.

perverseness, n. See prec. & **-ness**. Quality or state of being perverse.

perversion, n. [1. pervérshun; 2. pəvə́ʃən], fr. Lat. *perversiōn-(em)*, 'a turning about, perversion'. **perverse** & **-ion**. Act of perverting; state of being perverted.

perversity, n. [1. pervérsiti; 2. pəvə́siti], fr. Lat. *perversitāt-(em)*, 'perversity'. **perverse** & **-ity**. Quality of being perverse.

perversive, adj. [1. pervérsiv; 2. pəvə́siv], fr. Lat. *pervers-(um)*, P.P. type of *pervertere*, 'to overthrow'. See next word & **-ive**. Tending to pervert.

pervert (I.), vb. trans. [1. pervért; 2. pəvə́t], fr. Lat. *pervert-(ere)*, 'to turn round, overturn, overthrow', fr. **per-** & *vert-(ere)*, 'to turn', see **version**. **1.** To turn, divert, from proper use or function; to misdirect, misapply. **2.** To twist from proper meaning, give wrong significance to, misconstrue: *to pervert a person's words* &c. **3.** To turn from true belief, allegiance, morality &c.; give a wrong or distorted view to: *to pervert a person, mind, judgement* &c.

pervert (II.), n. [1. pérvert; 2. pə́vət], fr. prec. **a** A renegade, apostate, person who changes his religion; **b** one morally or physically abnormal and perverted; a degenerate.

pervious, adj. [1. pérvius; 2. pə́viəs], fr. Lat. *pervi-(us)*, 'pervious', fr. **per-** & *vi-(a)*, 'way', see **via**, & **-ous**. **1.** Capable of being passed through; giving passage, penetrable, permeable: *glass is pervious to light.* **2.** (in moral sense) Open to ideas; capable of being affected by rational argument, moral appeal &c.

perviousness, n. Prec. & **-ness**. Quality of being pervious.

peseta, n. [1. pesā́ta; 2. peséitə]. Span., fr. *pesa*, 'weight'. Spanish silver coin, nominally worth about 10d., the equivalent of the franc, lira &c. in the Latin monetary union.

Peshito, n. [1. peshḗtō; 2. peʃítou], fr. Syriac *p'shīt(t)ō*, 'simple'. Chief Syriac version of Old and New Testaments.

peshwa, n. [1. pā́shwah; 2. péiʃwa]. Pers. *peshwa*, 'chief'. Hereditary ruler of Mahrattas, formerly, the chief minister of Mahratta state.

pesky, adj. [1. péski; 2. péski]. Etymol. uncertain. (provinc. & Am.) Tiresome, troublesome, annoying.

peso, n. [1. pā́sō; 2. péisou]. Span., cp. **peseta**. A former Spanish silver coin equivalent to 5 pesetas, worth about 4s., still forming monetary unit in Spanish-American countries, equivalent to the dollar.

pessary, n. [1. pésari; 2. pésəri], fr. L. Lat. *pessāri-(um)*, fr. Gk. *pess-(ós)*, 'oval stone used in a game like draughts'; etymol. doubtful. Instrument worn in the vagina to correct uterine displacement.

pessimism, n. [1. pésimizm; 2. pésimizəm], fr. Lat. *pessim-(us)*, 'worst', prob. fr. *pet-s-; cp. *pēj-or*, 'worse', fr. *ped-j-, fr. *pet-j-. See **pejoration** & **-ism**. **1.** Doctrine that the world and its inhabitants are essentially and increasingly evil. **2.** Tendency to look at the dark side of things, to take a gloomy view of life; the habit of anticipating misfortune &c.

pessimist, n. [1. pésimist; 2. pésimist]. See prec. & **-ist**. One who takes a desponding view of life; adherent of the doctrine of pessimism.

pessimistic, adj. [1. pèsimístik; 2. pèsimístik]. Prec. & **-ic**. Pertaining to, characterized by, pessimism; tending to take a gloomy view of things, and to expect the worst.

pessimistically, adv. [1. pèsimístikali; 2. pèsimístikəli]. Prec. & **-al** & **-ly**. In a pessimistic manner.

pest, n. [1. pest; 2. pest], fr. Fr. *peste*, fr. Lat. *pest-(is)*, 'destruction, pestilence'; etymol. doubtful. **1.** Troublesome, vexatious, or destructive person, animal, or thing; *garden pest*, any kind of insect or vegetable parasite, blight, mildew &c. which destroys flowers or fruit &c. **2.** (archaic) Pestilence, plague.

pester, vb. trans. [1. péster; 2. péstə]. Cp. O. Fr. *empaistrier*, Mod. Fr. *empêtrer*, 'to entangle the feet'; Low Lat. *pastorium*, 'fetter, hobble', to prevent horses fr. straying when out at pasture. See **pasture**. To worry, plague, harass; especially to vex with petty, trivial annoyances: *to pester one with questions, with unwelcome attentions* &c.; *pestered with midges.*

pest-house, n. **pest** & **house**. (hist.) Hospital for plague and other infectious diseases.

pestiferous, adj. [1. pestíferus; 2. pestífərəs], fr. Lat. *pesti-(s)*, 'pestilence', see **pest**, & **-ferous**. **1.** Conveying pestilence; noisome, noxious, pestilential; specif., having a horrible, nauseous odour. **2.** Morally harmful, conveying moral evil; noxious, dangerous.

pestilence, n. [1. péstilens; 2. péstiləns], fr. Lat. *pestilentia*, 'infectious disease, plague'. **pestilent** & **-ce**. **a** Fatal infectious or contagious disease, a plague, esp. widespread epidemic; specif. **b** bubonic plague.

pestilent, adj. [1. péstilent; 2. péstilənt], fr. Lat. *pestilent-(em)*, 'infectious, unhealthy', fr. *pesti-(s)*, 'plague'. See **pest**. **1.** Hurtful or fatal to health or life; noxious, destructive. **2.** Injurious to morals &c., pernicious, having malign influence: *pestilent doctrines.* **3.** (colloq.) Troublesome, annoying, vexatious: *a pestilent fellow, scoundrel.*

pestilential, adj. [1. pèstilénshal; 2. pèstilénʃəl]. Prec. & **-ial**. **1.** Infested by, of the nature of, producing, pestilence. **2.** Pernicious, baneful, morally harmful. **3.** (colloq.) Highly objectionable; exciting disgust, extreme annoyance; detestable, outrageous: *he's a most pestilential bore, nuisance* &c.

pestilently, adv. [1. péstilentli; 2. péstiləntli]. **pestilent** & **-ly**. In a pestilent manner.

pestle (I.), n. [1. pésl; 2. pésl], fr. O. Fr. *pestel*, fr. Lat. *pistillum*, 'pestle'; cp. **pistil**; fr. *pins-tlo-, fr. *pins-, stem of *pinsere*, 'to beat, pound'; cp. Scrt. *pináṣṭi*, 'pounds, crushes'; *piṣṭá-m*, 'meal'; Gk. *ptíssein*, 'to winnow'; O. Slav. *pišeno*, 'meal'. Instrument with a shortish handle, and a rounded, heavy head, of stone, metal &c. used for crushing or pounding substances in a mortar.

pestle (II.), vb. trans. & intrans., fr. prec. **1.** trans. To pound with or as with pestle. **2.** intrans. To use a pestle.

pet (I.), n. [1. pet; 2. pet]. Origin obscure. **1.** Tame animal kept as companion and object of affection. **2.** Favourite, darling, cherished person, child &c.; esp. one that is indulged and unduly favoured; often used **a** as term of endearment; **b** (attrib.) *pet name*, one familiarly used as expressing affection; *one's pet aversion*, something especially disliked; bête noire.

pet (II.), vb. trans., fr. prec. To treat as a pet; to fondle, caress, soothe with caresses.

pet (III.), n. Origin doubtful; perh. fr. **pet (I.)**. Ill humour, peevishness, esp. in Phr. *to be in a pet.*

petal, n. [1. pétl; 2. pétl], fr. Gk. *pétal-(on)*, 'thin metal plate; leaf'. See **petalon**. Single section of the corolla of a flower.

petaline, adj. [1. pétalin, -in; 2. pétəl(a)in]. Prec. & **-ine**. Of, like, a petal.

petal(l)ed, adj. [1. pétld; 2. pétld]. **petal** & **-ed**. Having petals.

petaloid, adj. [1. pétaloid; 2. pétəloid]. **petal** & **-oid**. Like, consisting of, petals.

petalon, n. [1. pétalon; 2. pétələn]. Gk. *pétalon*, 'thin sheet of metal, metal plate; leaf'; cp. Gk. *pétalos*, 'spread out flat'; *pétasos*, 'wide-brimmed hat'; *petánnūmi*, 'I spread out, extend', all fr. stem *pet-, 'to spread out, extend, open out'; cp. Lat. *patēre*, 'to lie open', see **patent**; O.E. *fæðm*, 'extended arms; measure, fathom', see **fathom**. Gold plate on Jewish high priest's mitre.

petard, n. [1. petárd; 2. pitā́d], fr. Fr. *pétard*, fr. O. Fr. *péter*, 'to break wind', fr. Lat. *pēdit-(um)*, P.P. type of *pēdere*, 'to break wind', fr. *pezd-; cp. Lith. *bezdéti*; Gk. *bdéein*, 'to break wind'. **1.** Small, obsolete military engine used to break down doors, walls &c. Phr. *hoist with his own petard*, (from Hamlet', iii. 4) of person caught and injured by his own devices or plots against another. **2.** Kind of fire-cracker.

petasus, n. [1. pétasus; 2. pétəsəs]. Lat. *petasus*, fr. Gk. *pétasos*, 'broad-brimmed hat', fr. stem *pet-, 'to spread out'. See **petalon** & words there referred to. **1.** Ancient Greek low-crowned, broad-brimmed felt hat, esp. as worn by travellers, heralds &c., and characteristic of Hermes. **2.** Winged hat of Hermes.

petaurist, n. [1. petórist; 2. pitɔ́rist], fr. Gk. *petaurist-(ḗs)*, 'tumbler, rope-dancer', fr. *pétaur-(on)*, 'perch, roost; spring-board used by acrobats' &c., prob. fr. stem *pet-, 'to fly', seen in Gk. *pétomai*, 'I fly'; *pterón*, 'wing' &c. See **ptero-**. Genus of marsupials, including those having a membranous process connecting the fore and hind limbs, which enables them to take flying leaps, as the flying phalanger of Australia.

Peter (I.), n. [1. péter; 2. pítə]. Male Christian name, that of the Prince of the Apostles; fr. Lat., fr. Gk. *Pétros*, fr. *pétros*, 'stone'; cp Gk. *pétrā*, 'rock', & see **petro-**. In Phrs. *blue Peter*, blue flag with white square in centre, flown by ship about to sail; *to rob Peter to pay Paul*, to take or borrow from one person to pay another; *Peter's fish*, haddock, John Dory, or other fish with markings at each side of its mouth, supposed to have been made by St. Peter's thumb and finger; *Peter's penny* or *pence*, **a** (hist.) annual tax formerly paid to papal treasury; **b** voluntary contribution by Roman Catholics paid annually to Papal treasury for religious and charitable purposes.

peter (**II.**), vb. intrans. Etymol. uncertain; prob. fr. Fr. *péter*, 'to crackle, fizzle' &c. See **petard**. *Peter out*, (esp. of seam of ore &c., and fig.) to disappear gradually, be exhausted, give out.

petersham, n. [1. pĕtersham; 2. pítəʃəm], fr. Viscount Petersham (1780–1851, 4th Earl of Harrington). **1. a** Overcoat or breeches made of rough, heavy, woollen material; **b** this material. **2.** Strong corded silk or cotton ribbon.

petiolar, adj. [1. pétiōlar; 2. pétioulə]. **petiole** & **-ar.** Of, like, supported on, a petiole.

petiolate, adj. [1. pétiōlāt; 2. pétiouleit]. Next word & **-ate.** Having, supported on, a petiole.

petiole, n. [1. pétiōl; 2. pétioul], fr. Lat. *petiol-(us)*, 'little foot, fruit stalk'; etymol. doubtful. (bot.) Leaf-stalk.

petit, adj. [1. petḗ; 2. pətí]. Fr. *petit*, 'little'; etymol. doubtful. Phrs. *petits-chevaux*, kind of gambling game; *petit-maître*, coxcomb, dandy; *petit mal*, mild form of epilepsy without convulsions; *petit point*, a form of embroidery in which wool or silk is worked into an open-meshed material; *petits soins*, small attentions. For legal use see **petty.**

petite, adj. [1. petḗt; 2. pətít]. Fr. *petite*, fem. of prec. (of women) Small-made; usually implying also neatness, trimness, shapeliness of figure.

petition (**I.**), n. [1. petíshun; 2. pitíʃən], fr. Fr., fr. Lat. *petītiōn-(em)*, nom. *petītio*, 'attack, thrust; request; application', fr. *petīt-(um)*, P.P. type of *petere*, 'to rush at, let fly at, attack, assail; to fetch, seek for; to request, entreat'; cp. Lat. *impetus*, 'attack', see **impetus**; identical w. base **pet-* &c., 'to fly', seen in Gk. *pétomai*, 'I fly'; *ptéron*, 'wing', see **ptero-, feather**; Lat. *penna*, 'feather', see **pen** (**III.**). Humble, earnest supplication; an entreaty, urgent request; **a** formal request to the sovereign, or to some person or persons in authority, entreating him or them to do, or to refrain from doing, something; **b** a prayer, humble entreaty, addressed to God; **c** (law) formal application made to a court: *a petition in bankruptcy*; *to file one's petition* &c. *Petition of Right*, **a** (hist.) declaration of constitutional rights presented to Charles I. by Parliament and agreed to by him in June 1628; **b** (law) form of procedure in making claim against the Crown.

petition (**II.**), vb. trans. & intrans., fr. prec. **1.** trans. To address a petition to; **a** to entreat, beg, request urgently: *to petition the King, Parliament*; **b** to make an application to: *to petition a court of law*. **2.** intrans. To make a humble or urgent request, entreaty.

petitionary, adj. [1. petíshunari; 2. pitíʃənəri]. Prec. & **-ary.** Making, presenting, conveying, a petition.

petitioner, n. [1. petíshuner; 2. pitíʃənə]. **petition** (**II.**) & **-er.** One who makes, addresses, signs, a petition. Phr. *and your petitioners will ever pray*, formula used at the end of a formal petition.

petitio principii, n. [1. petíshiō prinsípiī; 2. pitíʃiou prinsípiai]. Begging the question.

petrel, n. [1. pétrel, pĕtrel; 2. pétrəl, pítrəl], fr. Fr. *pétrel*, *pétérel*, 'St. Peter's bird', dimin. fr. L. Lat. *Petr-(us)*, 'Peter', see **Peter** (**I.**), & **-el**; the name arose because the birds appear to walk upon the surface of the water. **a** Small black-and-grey sea-bird, *Procellaria pelagica*, with long pointed wings, found in the high seas; Mother Carey's chicken; *stormy petrel*, *storm-petrel*; also **b** (fig.) *stormy petrel*, a person whose advent is the cause of excitement, dispute, and unrest.

petrifaction, n. [1. pètrifákshun; 2. pètrifǽkʃən], fr. *petri-*; see **petro-**, & **faction. 1. a** Process of petrifying; state of being petrified; **b** (fig.) stupefaction. **2.** Petrified substance or organism.

petrify, vb. trans. & intrans. [1. pétrifī; 2. pétrifai], fr. Fr. *pétrifier*, fr. Lat. *petr-(a)*, 'rock', fr. Gk. *pétrā*, 'rock', see **petro-**, & **-fy. 1.** trans. **a** To turn into stone or stone-like substance by a chemical process, often produced by the long-continued action of water &c.; **b** (fig.) to stupefy, stun, bewilder, paralyse &c., as with amazement, horror, or the like. **2.** intrans. To become petrified.

petro-, also **petri-**, pref. representing Gk. *pétr-(a)*, 'rock'; etymol. doubtful; e.g. *petroglyph*, a carving on rock; *petrograph*, inscription on rock; *petrography*, study or description of formation, composition &c. of rocks.

petrol, n. [1. pétrol; 2. pétrəl, pétrɔl], fr. Fr. *pétrole*, abbr. fr. **petroleum.** Spirit made from refined petroleum, used in internal combustion engines, for motor-cars, aeroplanes &c.

petroleum, n. [1. petrṓleum; 2. pitróuliəm]. Lit. 'rock oil'; fr. Lat. *petr-(a)*, 'rock', fr. Gk. *pétra*, see **petro-**, & Lat. *oleum*, 'oil', see **oil.** Inflammable mineral oil found in the crust of the earth in certain regions, used for illumination and for driving certain types of engines.

pétroleur, n. [1. pètrōlḗr; 2. pètroulə́]. Fr., fr. *pétrole*, see **petrol**, & **-er.** Person using petroleum for purposes of incendiarism.

pétroleuse, n. [1. pètrōlḗz; 2. pètroulə́z]. Fr., fem. of prec. Woman incendiarist using petroleum.

petrolic, adj. [1. petrólik; 2. pətrɔ́lik]. **petrol** & **-ic.** Of, pertaining to, petrol or petroleum.

petrolin, n. [1. pétrolin; 2. pétrəlin]. **petrol** & **-in(e).** Paraffin obtained from Rangoon petroleum.

petrological, adj. [1. petrolójikl; 2. petrəlɔ́dʒikl]. **petrology** & **-ic-** & **-al.** Pertaining to petrology.

petrologist, n. [1. petrólojist; 2. pətrɔ́lədʒist]. See next word & **-ist.** Student of petrology.

petrology, n. [1. petróloji; 2. pətrɔ́lədʒi]. **petro-** & **-logy.** The study of the origin, structure &c. of rocks.

petronel, n. [1. pètrunél; 2. pètrənél], fr. Fr. *petrinal*, fr. O. Fr. *peitrine*, 'chest', fr. Lat. *pector-*, stem of *pectus*, 'breast, chest', see **pectoral,** & **-al.** Carbine of large calibre used by mounted men in 16th and 17th cents.; so called from being rested against the chest.

petrous, adj. [1. pétrus; 2. pétrəs], fr. Lat. *petrōs-(us)*, 'rocky', fr. *petr-(a)*, 'rock', see **petro-**, & **-ous. a** Of, consisting of, like, rock; **b** specif. (anat.) applied to part of the temporal bone.

petticoat, n. [1. pétikōt; 2. pétikout]. **petty** & **coat. 1.** Skirt, usually hanging from waist, worn as underskirt by women and children. **2.** (slang) A woman. **3.** (attrib.) Feminine; connected with, carried on by, women: *petticoat government*, control of woman in domestic affairs or in politics.

petticoated, adj. [1. pétikōted; 2. pétikoutid]. Prec. & **-ed.** Wearing petticoat(s).

petticoatless, adj. [1. pétikōtles; 2. pétikoutlis]. **petticoat** & **-less.** Without a petticoat.

pettifogger, n. [1. pétifoger; 2. pétifɔgə]. For first element see **petty**; origin of second element unknown. **1.** Inferior lawyer; specif., one who quibbles and uses means of doubtful honesty to secure his end. **2.** Person who splits hairs, raises small, insignificant points and logical quibbles.

pettifoggery, n. [1. pétifògeri; 2. pétifɔ̀gəri]. Prec. & **-ery.** Pettifogging.

pettifogging, adj. & n. [1. pétifoging; 2. pétifɔgiŋ]. **1.** adj. (prec. and suff. of Pres. Part.) **a** (of persons) Given to petty, often dishonest, quibbles and trumpery expedients; **b** paltry, trifling, unimportant, twopenny-halfpenny. **2.** vbl. n. Practice of mean, contemptible dodges, low tricks and quibbles.

pettily, adv. [1. pétili; 2. pétili]. **petty** & **-ly.** In a petty manner.

pettiness, n. [1. pétines; 2. pétinis]. **petty** & **-ness.** Quality of being petty.

pettish, adj. [1. pétish; 2. pétiʃ]. **pet** (**III.**) & **-ish.** Peevish, fretful, petulant.

pettishly, adv. Prec. & **-ly.** In a pettish manner.

pettishness, n. See prec. & **-ness.** Quality or state of being pettish.

pettitoes, n. [1. pétitōz; 2. pétitouz]. Origin uncertain; M. Fr. has *petitose*, 'giblets of fowl'; popular etymol. is **petty** & **toe.** Pig's feet used as food; trotters.

petto, n. [1. pétō; 2. pétou]. Ital. [pétto], fr. Lat. *pectus*, 'breast'. See **pectoral.** *In petto*, in secret, in one's own breast or heart; reserved; esp. of Cardinal, whose appointment has been determined by the Pope but not yet announced.

petty, adj. [1. péti; 2. péti]. M.E. *petit*, *peti*, fr. Fr. *petit*, 'small'. See **petit. 1.** Comparatively unimportant, trivial, of small worth, inferior, insignificant. Various special uses: *petty cash*, small items of expenditure &c.; *petty officer*, non-commissioned officer in navy; *petty jury*, common jury, as distinct from a grand or special jury; *petty larceny*, stealing of goods under a certain specified value; *petty sessions*, court of summary jurisdiction of justices of the peace. **2.** Working on small scale: *petty farmer*, *dealer* &c. **3.** (of non-material things) **a** Mean, trifling, contemptible, trivial: *petty quarrels*; **b** (of conduct &c.) ungenerous: *a petty grudge*; *petty malice* &c.

petulance, n. [1. pétūlans; 2. pétjuləns], fr. Lat. *petulantia*, 'impudence; petulance'. See next word & **-ce.** State or quality of being petulant; peevishness, irritability.

petulant, adj. [1. pétūlant; 2. pétjulənt], fr. Lat. *petulant-(em)*, 'saucy, impudent; petulant', fr. **petul-(āre)*, 'to attack in jest', fr. *pet-(ere)*, 'to attack', see **petition,** & **-ant.** Peevish, fretful, irritable, capricious.

petulantly, adv. Prec. & **-ly.** In a petulant manner.

petunia, n. [1. petūnia; 2. pitjū́niə], fr. Fr. *petun*, fr. Brazil. *pety*, 'tobacco plant'. **1.** Genus of herbs of nightshade family, with showy, funnel-shaped, white or purple flowers. **2.** Purple, deep violet colour.

petuntse, n. [1. petóontse, petúntse; 2. pitúntsi, pitántsi], fr. Chin. *pai-tun-tze*, fr. *pai*, 'white', & *tun*, 'stone'. Fine white clay used in making Chinese porcelain.

pew, n. [1. pū; 2. pjū]. M.E. *pūe*, 'pew', fr. O. Fr. *puie*, 'raised seat, balcony', fr. Lat. *podia*, pl. of *podium*, 'balcony, projection', fr. Gk. *pódion*; cp. Gk. *poús*, 'foot', q.v. under **pedal** & **-pod. 1. a** Long fixed bench, used as seat in church; sometimes furnished with a low door fastened with a catch; **b** specif., seat in church allotted to a family or individual. **2.** (familiar and colloq.) A seat of any kind; a chair: *can't you find a pew somewhere?*; *take a pew*, sit down (to a guest).

pewage, n. [1. pū́ij; 2. pjū́idʒ]. Prec. & **-age.** Rent paid for pew.

pewit, peewit, n. [1. pḗwìt; 2. píwìt]. Imitative. **1.** Bird of plover family, the lapwing or green plover. **2.** Cry of this bird.

pe(e)wit-gull, n. Black-headed gull.

pewless, adj. [1. pū́les; 2. pjū́lis]. **pew** & **-less.** Without pews.

pew-opener, n. Attendant who escorts persons to their places in church.

pew-rent, n. Money paid for seat or pew in church.

pewter, n. [1. pū́ter; 2. pjū́tə]. M.E. *peutre*, fr. O. Fr. *peutre*, fr. Ital. *peltro*; etymol. doubtful. **1.** Alloy of tin and lead &c., resembling lead in appearance when dull, but capable of receiving a high polish; used for making vessels, esp. tankards. **2. a** Vessel made of this alloy; **b** such vessels or utensils collectively. **3.** (slang) Prize-money.

pfennig, n. [1. pfénig; 2. pféniχ]. Germ., cogn. w. **penny.** Small German copper coin, one-hundredth of mark.

phaeton, n. [1. fā́(i)tn; 2. féi(i)tn], fr. Gk. *Phaéthōn*, son of Helios, the sun-god; by his unskilful driving of his father's chariot he set the heavens on fire; fr. *phaéthōn*, 'shining', fr. *pháein*, 'to gleam'; cp. Gk. *pháos*, 'light'; see **phantasm**, cogn. w. Scrt. *bhā́s*, 'light'; *bhā́ti*, 'to shine'; O. Ir. *bān*, 'white'; O.E. *bōnian*, 'to polish'. The Aryan base **bhā-*, **bhə-*, 'to shine', is prob. identical w. the base **bhā-* &c., 'to speak, to express in words', seen in Lat. *fāri*, 'to speak'. See **fate** & words there referred to. Light, four-wheeled open carriage for single horse or pair.

phaged(a)ena, n. [1. fàj-, fàgidḗna; 2. fædž-, fægidínə]. Lat. *phagedaena*, fr. Gk. *phagédaina*, 'voracity; a spreading ulcer', fr. *phag-(eîn)*, 'to eat'. See **-phagous**. (med.) Spreading ulcer; cancer, gangrene.

phaged(a)enic, adj. [1. fàj-, fàgidḗnik, -dénik; 2. fædž-, fægidínik, -dénik]. Prec. & **-ic.** Of, of the nature of, a phagedaena; cancerous.

phagocyte, n. [1. fágosīt; 2. fǽgəsait], fr. Gk. *phag-(eîn)*, 'to eat', see **-phagous**, & **-cyte**. (physiol.) One of the white corpuscles of the blood which have the property of digesting and eliminating, from the blood and bodily tissues, harmful bacteria which cause disease.

phagocytosis, n. [1. fàgosītṓsis; 2. fægousaitóusis]. Prec. & **-osis**. Process of destroying bacteria by the phagocytes.

-phagous, suff. representing Gk. *phag-(eîn)*, 'to eat', & **-ous**; cp. Scrt. *bhájati*, 'to share, partake'; *bhákṣati*, 'to enjoy, consume'; *bhágas*, 'happiness, wealth'; O. Slav. *bogatŭ*, 'rich'. Eating, feeding on; e.g. *anthropophagous*, feeding on human flesh.

-phagy, suff. representing Gk. *phag-(eîn)*, 'to eat', see prec., & **-y**. Habit of eating, feeding on, specified substance.

phalange, n. [1. fálanj; 2. fǽlændž], fr. *phalanges*, pl. of **phalanx**. **1.** (anat., zool., usually in pl.) Single bone of finger or toe. **2.** (bot.) Bundle of stamens joined by their filaments.

phalangeal, adj. [1. falánjeal; 2. fəlǽndžiəl]. Prec. & **-al**. (anat.) Of, pertaining to, a phalange.

phalanger, n. [1. falánjer; 2. fəlǽndžə]. **phalange** & **-er**. Genus of arboreal marsupials of Australia, with webbed toes on hind feet, and a long, thick, prehensile tail; some species have flying membranes, as the petaurist, q.v., or flying squirrel.

phalansterian, adj. & n. [1. fàlanstḗrian; 2. fælænstíəriən]. Next word & **-an**. **1.** adj. Of, pertaining to, a phalanstery. **2.** n. Member of a phalanstery.

phalanstery, n. [1. fálansteri; 2. fǽlənstəri], fr. Fr. *phalanstère*, fr. Gk. *phálag(g)-*, stem of *phálagx*, 'line of battle', see **phalanx**, on anal. of **monastery**. **1.** Socialistic community such as that proposed by Fourier (d. 1837) as an ideal social system. **2.** Buildings in which such a community lives.

phalanx, n. [1. fálangks, fálangks; 2. fǽlæŋks, féilæŋks]; pl. *phalanxes* or *phalanges* [1. falánjēz; 2. fəlǽndžīz]. Lat. *phalanx*, fr. Gk. *phálagx*, 'large round block of wood; troops in battle array, line of battle'; cp. Gk. *phálagges*, 'round rafters'; Lat. *(suf)flāmen*, 'drag for wheel'; O.H.G. *balcho*; O.E. *bealca*, 'beam', see **balk**. **1. a** (in anct. Greece) Heavy infantry in order of battle; specif., battalion of Macedonian troops drawn up in close order; **b** serried rank of battle offering an unbroken front; **c** (fig.) resolute group of persons banded together to support, and fight for, a common cause. **2.** (zool. and bot., usually in pl., *phalanges*) Phalange.

phalanxed, adj. [1. fálangkst; 2. fǽlæŋkst]. Prec. & **-ed**. Arrayed in a serried rank or phalanx.

phalarope, n. [1. fálarōp; 2. fǽləroup]. Fr., fr. Gk. *phalār-(is)*, 'coot, with white head', fr. *phal-(ós)*, 'white, shining'; cp. Scrt. *phāla-m*, 'brilliancy; forehead'; Lith. *báltas*, 'white'; Lat. *fulica*, 'coot'; O.H.G. *belihha*, 'coot'; O.N. *bāl*; O.E. *bǣl*, 'flame'; M.E. *balled*, 'bald', see **bald**; cp. further Gk. *pháein*, 'to shine', see **phaeton**; & see **blue** (I.), **blithe**. Genus of small wading birds allied to snipe.

phallic, adj. [1. fálik; 2. fǽlik]. **phallus** & **-ic**. Pertaining to the phallus or to phallicism.

phallicism, n. [1. fálisizm; 2. fǽlisizəm]. Prec. & **-ism**. Worship of the generative power in nature as symbolized by the phallus.

phallism, n. [1. fálizm; 2. fǽlizəm]. See next word & **-ism**. Phallicism.

phallus, n. [1. fálus; 2. fǽləs]. Lat. *phallus*, fr. Gk. *phallós*, 'phallus'; cogn. w. O.L.G. *bulle*; O.N. *bole*, 'bull'; O.E. *bulloc*, 'young bull', see **bullock**; O. Swed. *bulin*, 'swollen'; fr. Aryan base **bh(e)l-* &c., 'to swell'; cp. Gk. *phálagx*, 'large block'; *phálaina*, 'whale'; see **phalanx** & cp. **phyllo-**. Image of the male organ of generation, as symbolizing the generative power of nature, reproductiveness, and fertility, as worshipped in some primitive systems of religion.

phanariot, n. [1. fanáriot; 2. fənǽriət], fr. Mod. Gk. *phanariṓt-(ēs)*, fr. *phanári*, 'lighthouse', fr. Gk. *phanerós*, 'visible, conspicuous'; cp. Gk. *phainein*, 'to make visible, show'; *phanḗ*, 'torch'; *phantasiā*, 'apparition', see **phantasm**. Greek resident in Phanar quarter of Constantinople, esp. member of official class under Turks.

phanerogam, n. [1. fánerogàm; 2. fǽnərəgæ̀m], fr. Fr. *phanérogame*, fr. Gk. *phaneró-(s)*, 'visible', see **phantasm**, & Gk. *-gam-(os)*, 'married', see **gamo-**. (bot.) Plant bearing flowers and seeds; contrasted with the flowerless plants or *cryptogams*.

phanerogamic, adj. [1. fànerogámik; 2. fænərəgǽmik]. Prec. & **-ic**. Of, pertaining to, a phanerogam.

phanerogamous, adj. [1. fanerógamus; 2. fænərɔ́gəməs]. **phanerogam** & **-ous**. Having stamens and pistils.

phansigar, n. [1. fánsigar; 2. fǽnsigā], fr. Hind. *phansi*, 'noose', & *-gar*, suff. denoting the agent. A Thug.

phantasm, n. [1. fántazm; 2. fǽntæzəm], fr. Fr. *fantasme*, fr. Lat., fr. Gk. *phántasma*, 'apparition', fr. *phantázein*, 'to make visible', fr. *phan-*, stem of *phainein*, 'to show'; cp. *phanerós*, 'visible'; *phanḗ*, 'torch'; Scrt. *bhāna-m*, 'brilliance'; O.E. *bōnian*, 'to polish'; Lat. *fenestra*, 'opening, window'; cp. further, without formative element *-n-*, Scrt. *bhā*, 'light'; Gk. *pháein*, 'to shine', see **phaeton**; O.E. *bǣl*, 'flame'; the stem is prob. identical w. **bhā-*, **bhə-*, 'to speak'; cp. Lat. *fāri*, 'to speak'; *fābula*, 'speech', see **fable** & **fate**. **1.** Illusion, deceptive appearance, phantom, illusive vision. **2.** Apparition, ghost, spectre: *a phantasm of the dead, of the living.*

phantasmagoria, n. [1. fàntazmagória, -gória; 2. fæntæzməgɔ́riə, -góriə]. Prec. & Gk. *agorá*, 'assembly', see **paregoric** & **gregarious**. **1.** Series of images as optical illusion. **2.** Fantastic series of moving figures, real or illusory.

phantasmagoric, adj. [1. fàntazmagórik; 2. fæntæzməgɔ́rik]. Prec. & **-ic**. Of, like, a phantasmagoria.

phantasmal, adj. [1. fantázmal; 2. fæntǽzməl]. **phantasm** & **-al**. Of, like, of the nature of, a phantasm.

phantasmally, adv. Prec. & **-ly**. In a phantasmal manner; as a phantasm.

phantasmic, adj. [1. fantázmik; 2. fæntǽzmik]. **phantasm** & **-ic**. Of, pertaining to, of the nature of, a phantasm.

phantasy, n. Variant of **fantasy**.

phantom, n. [1. fántum; 2. fǽntəm]. M.E. *fantome*, fr. O. Fr. *fantosme*, fr. Lat. *phantasma*, 'apparition'; variant of **phantasm**. **1. a** A shadowy, immaterial form; apparition, spectre, ghost; **b** an appearance, manifestation, a vision: '*A phantom of delight*' (Wordsworth). **2.** An illusion, **a** of the organs of sight; **b** of the mind; a delusion; something existing only in the imagination.

Pharaoh, n. [1. fárō; 2. féərou], fr. Lat. *Pharao*, fr. Gk. *Pharaó*, fr. Heb. *paraōh*, fr. Egypt. *per'o*, lit. 'great house'. Title of kings of ancient Egypt.

Pharaoh's serpent, n. A chemical toy made of sulphocyanate of mercury in shape of a small egg or cone which on being lighted throws off a long serpent-like coil of residue.

Pharisaic(al), adj. [1. fàrisā́ik(l); 2. færiséiik(l)], fr. Lat. *Pharisaic-(us)*, fr. Gk. *Pharisaik-(ós)*, 'Pharisaic', fr. *Pharisai-(os)*, 'Pharisee', see **Pharisee**, & **-al**. Of, pertaining to, behaving like, characteristic of, a Pharisee; specif., hypocritical, self-righteous.

Pharisaically, adv. Prec. & **-ly**. In a Pharisaic manner.

Pharisaism, n. [1. fárisāizm; 2. fǽriseiizəm], fr. Gk. *Pharisai-(os)*, 'Pharisee'. See next word & **-ism**. Principles, practices, or character, of a Pharisee.

Pharisee, n. [1. fárisē; 2. fǽrisī], fr. Lat. *Pharisae-(us)*, fr. Gk. *Pharisai-(os)*, fr. Heb. *Perūshīm*, pl., 'the separated', fr. *pārash*, 'to separate'. **a** Member of ancient religious sect among the Jews, characterized by strict observance of all forms and ceremonies of the law, and priding themselves on their sanctity; hence **b** (i.) one pedantically attached to outward forms as the chief element of religion and morality; (ii.) a self-righteous person, a hypocrite.

pharmaceutical, adj. [1. fàrmasū́tikl; 2. fāməsjū́tikl], fr. Lat., fr. Gk. *pharmakeutik-(ós)*, 'of drugs', fr. *pharmakeut-(ḗs)*, 'druggist', fr. *pharmakeúein*, 'to give drugs', fr. *phármak-(on)*, 'drug', see **pharmacology**. **1.** Connected with, pertaining to, engaged in, pharmacy: *pharmaceutical chemist, society* &c. **2.** Pertaining to the use of medicinal drugs: *pharmaceutical treatment.*

pharmaceutically, adv. Prec. & **-ly**. In a pharmaceutical manner, as a pharmaceutist; by means of drugs.

pharmaceutics, n. [1. farmasū́tiks; 2. fāməsjū́tiks]. See **pharmaceutical**. Science of pharmacy; pharmacology.

pharmaceutist, n. [1. farmasū́tist; 2. fāməsjū́tist]. See **pharmaceutical** & **-ist**. Person skilled in, engaged in, pharmacy; pharmaceutical chemist.

pharmacologist, n. [1. farmakólojist; 2. fāməkɔ́lədžist]. See next word & **-ist**. Student of, person learned in, pharmacology.

pharmacology, n. [1. farmakóloji; 2. fāməkɔ́lədži], fr. Gk. *phármako-(n)*, 'charm, philtre, drug, remedy'; cp. Gk. *pharmássein*, 'to cast a spell on'; cogn. w. Lith. *burìù*, 'to charm', & **-logy**. The science of the nature, preparation, and use of medicinal drugs.

pharmacopoeia, n. [1. fàrmakopḗa; 2. fāməkəpíə], fr. Gk. *pharmakopoiía*, fr. *phármako-(n)*, 'drug', see prec., & *-poiia*, 'making', fr. *poieîn*, 'to make', see **poet**. **1.** Book, usually published by authority, containing a list of drugs and directions for their use. **2.** Collection or stock of drugs.

pharmacopoeial, adj. [1. fàrmakopḗal; 2. fāməkəpíəl]. Prec. & **-al**. Pertaining to a pharmacopoeia.

pharmacy, n. [1. fármasi; 2. fáməsi], fr. O. Fr. *farmacie*, fr. Gk. *pharmakeiā*, 'use of drugs', fr. *pharmak-(eúein)*, 'to administer a drug', fr. *phármak-(on)*, 'drug', see **pharmacology**. **1.** Art or practice of collecting, preparing, mixing, and dispensing drugs. **2.** Dispensary; chemist's shop.

pharos, n. [1. fā́ros; 2. féərɔs], fr. Lat., fr. Gk. *Pháros*, island near Alexandria, on which a lighthouse stood. Lighthouse; beacon to guide sailors, travellers &c.

pharyngal, adj. [1. farínggal; 2. færíŋgəl], fr. Gk. *phárugg-*, stem of *phárugx*, 'throat', see **pharynx** & **-al**. Pharyngeal.

pharyngeal, adj. [1. fàrinjḗal; 2. færindžíəl]. See prec. Pertaining to, situated in, the pharynx.

pharyngitis, n. [1. fàrinjítis; 2. færindžáitis]. See **pharynx** & **-itis**. Inflammation of the membranes of the pharynx.

pharyngo-, pref. representing Gk. *phárugg-*, stem of *phárugx*, 'throat, pharynx'. See next word. Pharynx; e.g. *pharyngoscope*, instrument for inspecting the throat; *pharyn-*

gotomy, operation of making an incision into the pharynx.

pharynx, n. [1. fáringks, fāringks; 2. fǽriŋks, féəriŋks], fr. Gk. *phárugx*, 'throat, gullet, pharynx'; cp. Lat. *frūmen*, 'throat, gullet'; O.N. *bárke*, 'neck'; cp. further Gk. *phárein*, 'split open'; Lat. *forāre*, 'to pierce', see **foramen**; O.E. *borian*, 'to bore', see **bore (I.)**. Cavity, lined with mucous membrane, lying behind nose, mouth, and larynx, communicating with these and with the oesophagus; in popular language, the back of the throat.

phase, n. [1. fāz; 2. feiz], fr. Gk. *phásis*, 'appearance, aspect', fr. *pha-*, stem of *phaínein*, 'to show, make visible', see **phantasm**. **1.** Aspect of illuminated heavenly body, of the moon or certain planets, at given time, according to amount of illumination, as at new moon, first quarter, full moon and last quarter. **2.** Aspect or character of person or thing at a single stage of development: *a marked contrast in the phases of this man's life*; *the war now entered on its last phase*; *but a passing phase of fashion*. **3.** (elect.) Relation in time between alternating currents of the same frequency, cp. **lag (IV.)**.

-phasia, suff. Form meaning 'speech', used in compounds as *aphasia*, fr. Gk. stem *pha-*, in *phánai*, infin. of *phēmí*, 'I speak' &c., see **fame**.

phasic, adj. [1. fāzik; 2. féizik]. **phase & -ic.** Of, pertaining to, of the nature of, a phase.

pheasant, n. [1. féznt; 2. féznt]. M.E. *fesant*, fr. A.-Fr. *fesant*, fr. Lat. *phāsiānus*, 'pheasant', fr. Gk. *Phāsiānós (órnis)*, 'Phasian bird', fr. *Phâsi-(s)*, river in Colchis, on the Black Sea. Game-bird, native of Asia, but naturalized and preserved in Europe; the males of most species have brilliant plumage and long tail-feathers.

pheasant-eyed, adj. (of flower) With marking like pheasant's eye.

pheasantry, n. [1. fézantri; 2. fézəntri]. **pheasant & -ry.** Place where pheasants are reared or preserved.

pheasants' eye, n. (bot.) **a** A plant, *Adonis*, belonging to the ranunculus order, with crimson flower and dark spot; **b** popular name of *Narcissus poeticus*, and also of the garden pink.

phen(o)-, pref. representing Gk. *phaín-ein*, 'to make visible; to shine', q.v. under **phantasm**; found in names of chemical substances derived from coal-tar.

phenacetin, n. [1. fenásetin; 2. finǽsitin]. Prec. & **acetic & -in(e)**. Crystalline compound used as antipyretic &c.

phenol, n. [1. fénol; 2. fínəl]. See prec. & **-ol.** Chemical name for carbolic acid.

phenological, adj. [1. fènolójikl; 2. fènəlódžikl]. Next word & **-ic & -al.** Of, pertaining to, phenology.

phenology, n. [1. fenóloji; 2. fenólədži]. See first element in **phenomenon, & -logy.** Systematic scientific study of the relation of the forms of organisms to their environment; esp. in matters of climate.

phenomenal, adj. [1. fenómenl; 2. finómінl]. See **phenomenon & -al.** **1.** Of, pertaining to, of the nature of, a phenomenon or outward manifestation; esp. in metaphysical sense, presented to, perceptible by, the senses, as contrasted with *real* or *noumenal*. **2.** Pertaining to natural phenomena. **3.** (colloq., journalese &c.) Remarkable, extraordinary, marvellous: *a phenomenal harvest*; *phenomenal weather for the time of year* &c.

phenomenalism, n. [1. fenómenalizm; 2. finóminəlizəm]. Prec. & **-ism.** Doctrine that phenomena are the only objects of positive knowledge.

phenomenalist, n. [1. fenómenalist; 2. finóminəlist]. **phenomenal & -ist.** One who believes in phenomenalism.

phenomenalistic, adj. [1. fenòmenalístik; 2. finòminəlístik]. Prec. & **-ic.** Pertaining to, of the nature of, phenomenalism.

phenomenalize, vb. trans. [1. fenómenalīz; 2. finóminəlaiz]. **phenomenal & -ize.** To represent, produce, as a phenomenon.

phenomenally, adv. [1. fenómenali; 2. finóminəli]. See prec. & **-ly.** **1.** In a phenomenal manner; as a phenomenon. **2.** (colloq.) Remarkably, extraordinarily: *phenomenally ugly*.

phenomenism, n. [1. fenómenizm; 2. finóminizəm]. See next word & **-ism.** Phenomenalism.

phenomenon, n., pl. **phenomena.** [1. fenómenun, -a; 2. finóminən, -ə]. Gk. *phainómenon*, neut. sing. of Pres. Part. of *phaínesthai*, 'to appear'; fr. same base as *phaínein*, 'to show', see **phantasm.** **1.** (Gk. philos.) A fact connected with the external forms of things as perceived by the senses, and liable to change, contrasted with the underlying, true, permanent reality. **2.** (common modern usage) Any event or occurrence known by observation or experience; also a thing, thought of chiefly as the result of a process: *the phenomena of nature*; *social and political phenomena*. **3.** An uncommon, rare, remarkable event, thing, or person; *infant phenomenon*, a child showing some precocious aptitude, skill &c.

phenyl, n. [1. fénil, fénil; 2. fínil, fénil]. **phen(o)- & -yl.** (chem.) Radical basis of phenol, benzine &c.

pheon, n. [1. féon; 2. fíən]. Origin uncertain. (her.) A bearing representing an arrowhead or spearhead pointing downwards.

phew, interj. Imitative. Conventional graphic rendering of exclamatory utterance expressing relief or astonishment.

phial, n. [1. fíal; 2. fáiəl]. M.E. & O. Fr. *fiole*, fr. L. Lat. *phiala*, fr. Gk. *phiálē*, 'broad, flat drinking-vessel', etymol. doubtful. Small glass bottle, esp. *medicine phial*.

phil-, pref. for **philo-**, before vowel or *h*.

-phil, -phile, suff. representing Gk. pref. *philo-*, 'loving', see **philo-**; forming ns. w. sense 'lover of', e.g. *bibliophil(e)*, lover, collector, of books; *Francophile*, one who admires the French and their civilization.

philander, vb. intrans. [1. filánder; 2. filǽndə], fr. obs. n. *philander*, 'philanderer', fr. Gk. *phílandr-(os)*, 'lover of men; woman who loves her husband', fr. **philo-** & *andr-*, stem of *anḗr*, 'man', see **andro-**. To make love, esp. in a trifling and insincere manner.

philanderer, n. [1. filánderer; 2. filǽndərə]. Prec. & **-er.** One who philanders; man or woman who engages, as a form of emotional excitement, in love affairs which are not intended to be serious, and who trifles with the affections of person of the opposite sex.

philanthrope, n. [1. fílanthrōp; 2. fílənþròup], fr. Gk. *philánthrōpos*, 'loving mankind, benevolent', fr. **philo-** & *ánthrōpos*, 'man', see **anthropo-**. Philanthropist.

philanthropic, adj. [1. filanthrópik; 2. filənþrópik]. Prec. & **-ic.** Pertaining to, characterized by, showing, love for one's fellow-men; humane, benevolent, given disinterestedly to works of charity.

philanthropically, adv. [1. filanthrópikali; 2. filənþrópikəli]. Prec. & **-al & -ly.** In a philanthropic manner.

philanthropism, n. [1. filánthropizm; 2. filǽnþrəpizəm]. **philanthropy & -ism.** Theory or practice of a philanthropist.

philanthropist, n. [1. filánthropist; 2. filǽnþrəpist]. **philanthropy & -ist.** One who practises philanthropy; promoter or supporter of schemes for the betterment of his fellow-men, and for the relief of suffering.

philanthropize, vb. intrans. & trans. [1. filánthropīz; 2. filǽnþrəpaiz]. See next word & **-ize.** **1.** intrans. To practise philanthropy. **2.** trans. **a** To make the object of philanthropy; **b** to make philanthropic.

philanthropy, n. [1. filánthropi; 2. filǽnþrəpi], fr. Gk. *philanthrōpía*, 'benevolence, acts of kindness', fr. *philánthrōp-(os)*, 'kindly', see **philanthrope.** Love of, sympathy with, mankind, esp. as shown in efforts for the improvement of social conditions, and in works of charity and benevolence.

philatelic, adj. [1. filatélik; 2. filətélik]. **philately & -ic.** Of, pertaining to, philately.

philatelist, n. [1. filátelist; 2. filǽtilist]. Next word & **-ist.** Collector of postage-stamps &c.

philately, n. [1. filáteli; 2. filǽtəli], fr. Fr. *philatélie*, fr. **philo-**, 'lover', & Gk. *atéleia*, 'exemption from taxation', fr. *a-*, neg. pref., see **a-**, & *tél-(os)*, 'end, completion; result; supreme authority; government; tax, duty', see **teleology.** The study and collection of postage-stamps.

philharmonic, adj. & n. [1. filharmónik; 2. filhāmónik]. **philo- & harmonic.** **1.** adj. Fond of music; chiefly used in names of musical societies. **2.** n. **a** (rare) Person fond of music; **b** a concert by a philharmonic society.

Philhellene, n. & adj. [1. filhélēn; 2. filhélīn], fr. Gk. *philéllēn*, fr. **philo-** & *Héllēn*, 'Hellene', see **Hellenic.** **1.** n. One loving the Greeks; specif., one who sympathized with the effort of modern Greece to regain her independence from Turkish rule. **2.** adj. Connected with, sympathizing with, Philhellenes and Philhellenism.

Philhellenic, adj. [1. filhelénik, -helénik; 2. filhelínik, -helénik]. Prec. & **-ic.** Of, pertaining to, Philhellenism.

Philhellenism, n. [1. filhélenizm; 2. filhélinizəm]. **Philhellene & -ism.** Policy of promoting freedom of the modern Greeks from Turkish rule.

Philhellenist, n. [1. filhélenist; 2. filhélinist]. See prec. & **-ist.** Lover of, supporter of, the Greeks.

philibeg, n. See **filibeg.**

philippic, n. [1. filípik; 2. filípik], fr. Lat., fr. Gk. *philippik-(ós)*, 'of, relating to, Philip', fr. *Phílipp-(os)* & **-ic.** **1.** (cap.) Specif. (pl.) **a** orations of Demosthenes against Philip of Macedon; **b** Cicero's orations against Antony. **2.** (gen.) Passionate invective, furious denunciation.

philippine, also **philippina, philopoena**, n. [1. filipēn, filipḗna; 2. filipīn, filipínə]. Fr., apparently fr. Germ. *viel-liebchen*, fr. *viel*, 'much', & *liebchen*, dimin. of *lieb*, 'dear', see **lief.** **1. a** Nut with twin kernels; **b** game, or agreement, whereby when such a nut is shared with another person, the reception of a present is involved by the one who first greets the other as *Philippine* at next meeting. **2.** Present given under these circumstances.

Philistine (I.), n. [1. filistīn, filistin; 2. filist(a)in], fr. L. Lat. *Philistīn-(us)*, fr. Gk. *Philistinos*, fr. Assyrian *Pilistu*. **1.** One of an ancient warlike non-Semitic tribe or race of Southern Palestine that for many years disputed with the Israelites the possession of the country. **2.** (facet.) Ruthless enemy. **3.** Term applied by Matthew Arnold to denote a person with middle-class tastes and outlook, largely selfish in his pursuits, and untouched by art or literature; still used by persons who regard themselves as arbiters of taste to denote those whose tastes are different from their own.

Philistine (II.), adj., fr. prec. Characteristic of the Philistine ((I.) 3).

Philistinism, n. [1. filistinizm; 2. filistinizəm]. Prec. & **-ism.** The point of view, tastes, and habits of the Philistine ((I.) 3).

philo-, pref. representing Gk. *philo-(s)*, 'loving, attached to'; cp. *philein*, 'to love'; etymol. doubtful. Loving, fond of, interested in; e.g. *philogynist*, lover of women; *philomath*, one who loves learning, esp. mathematics.

philologian, n. [1. filolṓjian; 2. filəlóudžiən]. **philology & -ian.** Student of philology; now more commonly *philologist*.

philological, adj. [1. filolójikl; 2. filələ́džikl]. **philology & -ic & -al.** Pertaining to, based on, dealing with, philology.

philologically, adv. Prec. & **-ly.** In a philological manner; in accordance with the methods and principles of philology.

philologist, n. [1. filólojist; 2. filɔ́lədžist]. **philology** & **-ist**. Student of, one learned in, philology.

philologize, vb. intrans. [1. filólojīz; 2. filɔ́lədžaiz]. **philology** & **-ize**. To study philology.

philology, n. [1. filóloji; 2. filɔ́lədži], fr. Lat. *philologia*, 'study of literature', fr. Gk. *philologia*, 'love of learning', fr. **philo-** & **-logy**. **1.** (now rare and archaic) The love and pursuit of learning and literature; study of polite literature. **2.** Linguistic science; study of the nature and development of language, or of a given language, and of the principles which determine this.

Philomel, n. [1. filomel; 2. filəmel], fr. Fr. *philomèle*, fr. Lat. *Philomēla*. See next word. (poet.) The nightingale.

Philomela, n. [1. filomḗlə; 2. filəmīlə]. Lat. *Philomēla*, fr. Gk. *philomḗlā*, 'nightingale'; etymol. doubtful; perh. fr. **philo-** & lengthened form of *mélos*, 'song', see **melody**. (poet.) Nightingale, esp. with reference to myth of Pandion's daughter, Philomela, who was said to have been changed into a nightingale.

philosopher, n. [1. filósofer; 2. filɔ́səfə], fr. Lat. *philosoph-(us)*, fr. Gk. *philósoph-(os)*, 'philosopher', see **philosophy**, & **-er**. **1.** Student of, one versed in, philosophy. **2. a** One whose life, thoughts, and conduct are supposed to be governed by philosophical principles; one who pretends to be moved purely by rational considerations, without allowing his feelings and emotions to assert themselves; **b** one who faces events and fate calmly and rationally, and is not unduly elated or depressed by good or evil fortune.

philosophers' stone, n. **a** Substance formerly sought for by alchemists, believed by them to have the property of turning base metals into gold; **b** (fig.) some ideal, but never realized, method of settling and smoothing out difficulties.

philosophic(al), adj. [1. filosófik(l); 2. filəsɔ́fik(l)], fr. L. Lat., fr. Gk. *philosophik-(ós)*, 'philosophic', fr. *philósoph-(os)*, 'philosophic', see **philosophy**, & **-ic** & **-al**. **1.** Pertaining to, in accordance with principles of, philosophy. **2.** Characteristic of a philosopher; serene, temperate, controlled, resigned. **3.** Devoted to, dealing with, philosophy or learning &c.; used to denote societies &c. having these aims.

philosophically, adv. Prec. & **-ly**. In a philosophical manner.

philosophism, n. [1. filósofizm; 2. filɔ́səfizəm], fr. Fr., fr. *philosophe*, 'philosopher', fr. Lat. *philosophus*, see **philosophy**, & **-ism**. Bogus philosophy; sophistry.

philosophist, n. [1. filósofist; 2. filɔ́səfist]. See prec. & **-ist**. Person addicted to philosophism.

philosophize, vb. intrans. & trans. [1. filósofīz; 2. filɔ́səfaiz]. See **philosopher** & **-ize**. **1.** intrans. **a** To indulge in philosophical theories or speculations; **b** to assume the character of a philosopher. **2.** trans. To make philosophic; to treat and regard from the point of view of a philosopher.

philosophy, n. [1. filósofi; 2. filɔ́səfi], fr. O. Fr. *filosofie*, fr. Lat., fr. Gk. *philosophia*, 'love of wisdom and knowledge; scientific investigation; philosophy', fr. *philósoph-(os)*, 'lover of wisdom, philosopher', fr. **philo-** & *sophós*, 'skilled; wise, learned', see **sophist**. **1.** The theory of knowledge; study of the mind and its processes; metaphysics; as a branch of learning, the term includes an inquiry into, and discrimination between, all the processes involved in perceiving, thinking, knowing; formerly divided into *Moral Philosophy*, the study just defined, and *Natural Philosophy*, now usually known as *Physics*. **2.** Wisdom in the conduct of affairs; mental balance, calmness, equanimity in dealing with and envisaging the events and experiences of human life.

-philous, suff. [1. filus; 2. filəs] forming adjs. based on ns. in *-phil(e)*. See **philo-** & **-ous**. Denoting fondness, predilection, for.

philtre, philter, n. [1. filter; 2. filtə], fr. Fr. *philtre*, fr. Lat. *philtrum*, fr. Gk. *philtron*, 'love-potion', fr. *phil-(os)*, 'loving', see **philo-**, & suff. expressing instrument. Love-potion; charm, drug, supposed to excite affection, and concentrate it upon a specific person.

phiz, n. [1. fiz; 2. fiz]. Abbr. of **physiognomy**. (colloq.) a Face; **b** expression.

phlebitic, adj. [1. flēbítik; 2. flībítik]. See next word & **-ic**. Of, pertaining to, phlebitis.

phlebitis, n. [1. flēbītis; 2. flībáitis]. See next word & **-itis**. Inflammation of membranous lining of vein.

phlebo-, pref. representing Gk. *phleb-*, stem of *phléps*, 'vein'; Gk. *phlúktaina*, 'blister'; cp. O.H.G. *bolca*, 'bubble'; possibly cogn. w. Lat. *fluere*, 'to flow', see **fluid**; fr. base **bh(e)l-* &c., 'to swell up, expand, overflow, flow'. See also **belly (I.)**. Pertaining to veins; e.g. *phlebography*, instrument recording pulsations of a vein; *phlebology*, science of veins; *phlebolith*, concretion formed in a vein.

phlebotomist, n. [1. flebótomist; 2. flibɔ́təmist]. See next word & **-ist**. Person practising or believing in phlebotomy.

phlebotomize, vb. intrans. & trans. [1. flebótomīz; 2. flibɔ́təmaiz]. See next word & **-ize**. **1.** intrans. To practise phlebotomy; to open a vein and draw blood. **2.** trans. To bleed (a person).

phlebotomy, n. [1. flebótomi; 2. flibɔ́təmi], fr. O. Fr. *flebotomie*, fr. Lat., fr. Gk. *phlebotomía*, 'blood-letting', fr. **phlebo-** & *-tomia*, 'cutting', see **-tomy**. Operation of blood-letting by opening a vein; used as a remedy; bleeding.

phlegm, n. [1. flem; 2. flεm]. M.E. & O. Fr. *fleume*, fr. L. Lat. *phlegma*, fr. Gk. *phlégma*, 'inflammation; a morbid humour', fr. *phlégein*, 'to burn', & **-ma**; cp. Gk. *phlóx*, 'flame'; cogn. w. Lat. *flagrāre*, 'to burn', see **flagrant**; *fulgor*, 'lightning', see **fulgent**. **1.** Viscid fluid secreted by mucous membranes, esp. as abnormally increased in volume by disease &c., and discharged by coughing &c. **2. a** (archaic) One of the four humours of the body; hence, **b** apathy, inertness; coolness, indifference; formerly supposed to be caused by excess of this humour.

phlegmatic, adj. [1. flegmátik; 2. flegmǽtik], fr. Gk. *phlégmat-*, stem of *phlégma*, see prec., & **-ic**. Not easily roused to emotion or activity; torpid, heavy, sluggish, in mind and body.

phlegmatically, adv. [1. flegmátikali; 2. flεgmǽtikəli]. Prec. & **-al** & **-ly**. In a phlegmatic manner.

phlegmon, n. [1. flégmon; 2. flégmən], fr. Lat. *phlegmon*, fr. Gk. *phlégmōn*, 'inflammation'. See **phlegm**. Inflammatory tumour in connective tissue.

phlegmonic, adj. [1. flegmónik; 2. flegmɔ́nik]. Prec. & **-ic**. Of, of the nature of, a phlegmon.

phlegmonous, adj. [1. flégmonus; 2. flégmənəs]. **phlegmon** & **-ic**. Phlegmonic.

phlegmy, adj. [1. flémi; 2. flémi]. **phlegm** & **-y**. Of, like, containing, phlegm.

phloem, n. [1. flṓem; 2. flóuεm], fr. Gk. *phló-(os)*, 'bark', & n. suff. *-ēma*. Cp. Gk. *phloûs*, 'reed'; *phloíein*, 'to be distended; to blossom'; *phléō*, 'I bubble up, overflow'; fr. base **bhel-*, 'to swell'. See **phlebo-**. Vascular bast-like tissue immediately below epidermis in plants.

phlogistic, adj. [1. flojístik; 2. flədžístik]. See **phlogiston** & **-ic**. **1.** Of, pertaining to, phlogiston. **2.** (med.) Inflammatory.

phlogisticated, adj. [1. flojístikāted; 2. flədžístikeitid]. Prec. & **-ate** & **-ed**. *Phlogisticated air*, old name for nitrogen.

phlogiston, n. [1. flojíston; 2. flədžístən], fr. Gk. *phlogistón*, fr. *phlogízein*, 'to set on fire', fr. *phlog-*, stem of *phlóx*, 'flame', see **phlox** & **phlegm**. Inflammatory principle formerly supposed to exist in all combustible bodies.

phlorizin, n. [1. florízin, flórizin; 2. flɔráizin, flɔ́rizin], fr. Gk. *phló-(os)*, 'bark', see **phloem**, & *rhíza*, 'root', see **rhizo-**, & **-in**. (chem.) Bitter crystalline substance found in bark of roots of apple and other fruit trees.

phlox, n. [1. floks; 2. flɔ́ks]. Lat. *phlox*, fr. Gk. *phlóx*, 'flame; a kind of flower'. See **phlegm**. Genus of cultivated plants with clusters of small, five-lobed, white, crimson, pink, or blue flowers.

-phobe, suff. [1. fōb; 2. foub] representing Gk. adj. suff. *-phobos*, fr. *phóbos*, 'fear, flight'; cp. Gk. *phébomai*, 'I fear; I flee from'; Lith. *bégu*, 'to flee'; cp. O. Slav. *běgŭ*, 'flight'; forming **a** ns. w. sense 'one who fears', **b** adjs. w. sense 'fearing'; e.g. *Anglophobe*, *hydrophobe*.

-phobia, suff. [1. fṓbia; 2. fóubiə] meaning 'fear, dislike', representing Gk. *-phobia*, forming abstract ns. fr. adjs. in **-phobe**; e.g. *hydrophobia*, *photo-phobia*, *Russo-phobia*.

Phoenician, adj. & n. [1. fēníshan; 2. finíʃən], fr. Lat. *Phoenīcia*, fr. Gk. *Phoiníkē*, district on Syrian coast, & **-an**. **1.** adj. Of, pertaining to, Phoenicia, its inhabitants and colonies; specif., *Carthaginian*. **2.** n. **a** Inhabitant of Phoenicia; **b** Phoenician language.

phoenix, phenix, n. [1. fḗniks; 2. fíniks]. Lat. *phoenix*, fr. Gk. *phoînix*, 'purple; the phoenix'; perh. of Eastern origin. **1.** (mythol.) Fabulous bird of brilliant plumage, supposed to have lived in the Arabian desert in cycles of 500 years; at the end of each cycle it burned itself on a funeral pyre and rose again from its own ashes with renewed youth and beauty. **2.** Person or thing of supreme excellence; paragon.

phonate, vb. intrans. [1. fṓnāt; 2. fóuneit]. **phone (II.)** & **-ate**. To produce vocal sounds.

phonation, n. [1. fōnā́shun; 2. founéiʃən]. Prec. & **-ion**. Act of phonating.

phonatory, adj. [1. fṓnaturi; 2. fóunətəri]. **phonate** & **-ory**. Of, producing, capable of producing, vocal sounds.

phonautograph, n. [1. fōnáwtograhf; 2. founɔ́təgrāf]. **phone (II.)** & **auto-** & **-graph**. Apparatus for recording visibly the vibrations set up by sound.

phone (I.), n. [1. fōn; 2. foun], fr. Gk. *phōnḗ*, 'voice, speech'; cp. Gk. *phēmí*, 'I speak'; *phḗmē*, 'rumour'; *phátis*, 'report'; cogn. w. Lat. *fāri*, 'to speak'; *fābula*, 'speech', see **fable**; *fāma*, 'report', see **fame**; Scrt. *bhánati*, 'to speak'; O. Slav. *basnĭ*, 'fable'; Lith. *bóju*, 'to ask after'; O.E. *bannan*, 'to summon', see **ban**; O.E. *bōn*, 'prayer', see **boon**. (rare) Single speech-sound; vowel or consonant.

phone (II.), vb. & n. Colloq. abbr. of **telephone**.

-phone, suff. representing Gk. *phōnḗ*, 'voice, speech', see **phone (I.)**; forming names of instruments for reproducing or transmitting sounds, esp. the human voice in specific way; e.g. *telephone*, *gramophone*, *microphone* &c.

phonendoscope, n. [1. fōnéndoskōp; 2. founéndəskoup]. **phone (II.)** & Gk. *éndon*, 'within', see **endo-**, & **-scope**. Instrument for testing the condition of the organs of the body by transmitting and intensifying the sounds produced by their movements &c.

phonetic (I.), adj. [1. fōnétik; 2. founétik], fr. Gk. *phōnētikós*, fr. *phōnētós*, 'to be spoken', fr. *phōnḗ*, 'sound'. See **phone (I.)**. Connected with, relating to, the sounds of human speech; *phonetic law*, statement of the way in which, and conditions under which, speech-sounds change or have changed in a given language; *phonetic notation*, method of recording and distinguishing exactly the various sounds of speech by graphic symbols; *phonetic spelling*, method of spelling representing, or supposed to represent, the facts of pronunciation.

phonetic (II.), n., fr. prec. (gen. pl. *phonetics*) Branch of linguistic science which deals with speech-sounds, their character, quality, and the way in which they are severally formed by the organs of speech.

phonetically, adv. [1. fōnétikali; 2. founétikəli]. **phonetic (I.) & -al & -ly.** From point of view of phonetics; according to phonetic principles.

phonetician, n. [1. fōnetíshan; 2. founitíʃən]. **phonetic (I.) & -ian.** Student of, one skilled in, phonetics.

phoneticism, n. [1. fōnétisizm; 2. founétisizəm]. See prec. & **-ism.** (word to be avoided) Phonetic representation of speech-sounds.

phoneticist, n. [1. fōnétisist; 2. founétisist]. **phonetic & -ist. 1.** Phonetician. **2.** Phonetist.

phoneticize, vb. trans. [1. fōnétisīz; 2. founétisaiz]. **phonetic & -ize.** To represent, express, phonetically.

phonetist, n. [1. fónetist; 2. fóunitist]. See **phonetic & -ist. 1.** Phonetician. **2.** Person who advocates phonetic spelling.

phonic, adj. [1. fónik, fónik; 2. fóunik, fónik], fr. Gk. *phōn-(é)*, 'voice, speech', see **phone (I.)**, & **-ic. a** Pertaining to sound; acoustic; **b** specif., connected with speech-sounds.

phono-, pref. representing Gk. *phōné*, 'voice, speech'. See **phone (I.)**. Sound, esp. vocal sound; e.g. *phonolite*, kind of volcanic rock giving out a metallic clang when struck; *phonometer*, instrument recording vibrations of sound; *phonoscope*, instrument for testing musical strings; *phonotype*, alphabetical system of phonetic representation.

phonogram, n. [1. fónogram; 2. fóunəgræm]. **phono- & -gram. 1.** Written or printed symbol representing spoken sound. **2.** Speech record made by phonograph.

phonograph, n. [1. fónograhf; 2. fóunəgrāf]. **phono- & -graph.** Instrument, predecessor of the gramophone, invented by Edison, which, by means of a sharp point fixed to a vibrating membrane, or layer of talc, and acting upon a rotating wax cylinder, records the vibrations set up by speech, musical instruments, or other sound-producing agents, and reproduces the sounds so transmitted by reversing the process, i.e. by allowing a rounded point to traverse the record previously made of the sounds, whereupon audible vibrations are set up by the sensitive body to which the reproducing point is fixed, exactly corresponding with the sounds originally uttered.

phonographer, n. [1. fōnógrafer; 2. founógrəfə]. **phonography & -er.** Old name for a shorthand writer.

phonographic, adj. [1. fōnográfik; 2. founəgrǽfik]. See prec. & **-ic.** Connected with a phonograph, or with sounds reproduced by its means.

phonographically, adv. [1. fōnográfikali; 2. founəgrǽfikəli]. Prec. & **-al & -ly.** By means of a phonograph.

phonographist, n. [1. fōnógrafist; 2. founógrəfist]. See next word & **-ist.** Phonographer.

phonography, n. [1. fōnógrafi; 2. founógrəfi]. **phono- & -graphy. 1.** Name given by Pitman to his system of shorthand, indicating that it was partly phonetic. **2.** The use of a phonograph for recording and reproducing sounds.

phonological, adj. [1. fōnolójikl; 2. founəlódžikl]. See next word & **-ic & -al.** Of, pertaining to, concerned with, phonology.

phonology, n. [1. fōnóloji; 2. founólədži]. **phono- & -logy. 1.** Study of the sounds of speech; now generally applied to the study of the facts and laws of the changes which overtake the sounds of a language in course of time; thus distinguished from *Phonetics*, which is concerned with the sounds of language as they are at a given time or with the general theory of the description and classification of speech-sounds. **2. a** System or group of speech-sounds existing in specific language, at specified period; **b** an account of this, generally involving a discussion of their earlier forms, and an account of the changes which have come about.

phonophore, n. [1. fónofōr; 2. fóunəfɔ̄]. **phono- & -phore.** A device attached to a telegraph wire by means of which telephonic messages can be sent simultaneously with its use for telegrams.

phonopore, n. [1. fónopōr; 2. fóunəpɔ̄]. **phono-** & Gk. *póros*, 'passage'. See **pore (I.)**. Phonophore.

-phore, suff. [1. fōr; 2. fɔ̄] representing Gk. *-phoros*, 'carrying', fr. *phérein*, 'to bear', q.v. under **-ferous**; see also **bear (I.)**; forming ns., denoting instruments or systems for transmitting signals, messages &c.; e.g. *semaphore*.

phormium, n. [1. fórmium; 2. fɔ́miəm], fr. Gk. *phormíon*, 'a woven or plaited mat'; also name of a plant, fr. *phormós*, 'basket', fr. *phérein*, 'to bear'. See prec. A genus of liliaceous plants, whose fibre is used for making cordage, paper &c.; the New Zealand flax.

-phorous, suff. [1. ferus; 2. fərəs] representing Gk. *-phor-(os)*, 'bearing, producing', & **-ous**, forming adjs., fr. Gk. stems, w. same sense as **-ferous**, of wh. it is a gradational variant; e.g. *phyllophorous*.

phosgene, n. [1. fósjēn; 2. fósdžīn]. Fr. *phosgène*, fr. Gk. *phôs*, 'light'. See first element in **phosphorus & -gen.** A very poisonous, odourless gas produced by compounding carbon monoxide and chlorine in sunlight; used in chemical warfare.

phosphate, n. [1. fósfit, -āt; 2. fɔ́sfit, -eit]. **phospho- & -ate.** A salt of phosphoric acid; (esp. pl.) various salts of this kind, either occurring in mineral or guano-beds or artificially produced, used as fertilizers.

phosphatic, adj. [1. fosfátik; 2. fɔsfǽtik]. Prec. & **-ic.** Of, pertaining to, containing, phosphates: *phosphatic deposits, beds* &c.

phosphene, n. [1. fósfēn; 2. fɔ́sfīn], fr. Gk. *phôs*, 'light', see **phosphorus**, & *phainein*, 'to show', see **phantasm.** Luminous spectrum seen when pressure is applied to the eyeball.

phosphide, n. [1. fósfīd; 2. fɔ́sfaid]. **phospho- & -ide.** Compound of phosphorus and some other element.

phosphite, n. [1. fósfīt; 2. fɔ́sfait]. See prec. & **-ite.** Salt of phosphorous acid.

phosph(o)-, pref. representing **phosphorus.**

Phosphor, n. [1. fósfōr; 2. fɔ́sfɔ̄]. See **phosphorus.** (poet.) The morning star.

phosphorate, vb. trans. [1. fósforāt; 2. fɔ́sfəreit]. See **phosphorus & -ate.** To combine, impregnate, with phosphorus; to make phosphorescent.

phosphor-bronze, n. A hard, tough, elastic kind of bronze alloy, the tin or copper of which contains a certain amount of phosphorus.

phosphoresce, vb. intrans. [1. fosforés; 2. fɔsfərés]. **phosphorus & -esce.** To emit faint light with very slow combustion and no sensible heat; to exhibit phosphorescence; to shine in the dark.

phosphorescence, n. [1. fosforésens; 2. fɔsfərésəns]. Prec. & **-ence.** State of being phosphorescent or luminous in the dark, esp. as exhibited by phosphorus and also by certain fishes, insects, such as fire-flies &c.

phosphorescent, adj. [1. fosforésent; 2. fɔsfərésənt]. **phosphorus & -escent.** Emitting, having the property of emitting, a faint light without sensible heat; luminous in the dark.

phosphoric, adj. [1. fosfórik; 2. fɔsfɔ́rik]. See **phosphorus & -ic.** Of, containing, phosphorus in its highest valency.

phosphorism, n. [1. fósforizm; 2. fɔ́sfərizəm]. See **phosphorus & -ism.** Necrosis of the jaw caused by phosphorus poisoning; also called *phossy-jaw*.

phosphorite, n. [1. fósforīt; 2. fɔ́sfərait]. See **phosphorus & -ite.** Kind of phosphate of lime.

phosphoro-, pref. Form of Lat. *phosphorus*, used in compounds; e.g. *phosphorogenic*, exciting phosphorescence; *phosphorograph*, impression made by luminous image on phosphorescent surface; *phosphoroscope*, a instrument for measuring duration of phosphorescence; **b** toy containing various phosphorescent substances, giving out light of different colours.

phosphorous, adj. [1. fósforus; 2. fɔ́sfərəs]. See next word & **-ous.** Of, containing, phosphorus in its lowest valency.

phosphorus, n. [1. fósforus; 2. fɔ́sfərəs]. Lat. *phosphorus*, 'morning star', fr. Gk. *phōsphóros*, 'light-bringing'; n., 'the morning star', fr. Gk. *phôs*, 'light', & *-phoros*, 'carrying', see **-phorous**; for the first element, *phôs*, contracted fr. **pháos*, cp. Gk. *phaéthōn*, 'shining', see **phaeton**; Scrt. *bhā́s*, 'light'. See also **phantasm.** Yellowish-white waxy inflammable and poisonous substance, emitting a faint glow at normal temperatures; one of the non-metallic elements, not occurring in the free state, but found in all animal bodies and plants and occurring in the mineral phosphate rocks &c.; red or amorphous phosphorus, obtained by chemical treatment of yellow phosphorus, is non-poisonous, and inflammable at high temperatures only.

phosphuret(t)ed, adj. [1. fósfurèted; 2. fɔ́sfərètid], fr. obs. *phosphuret*, 'phosphide', fr. **phospho-** & Mod. Lat. suff. *-uret(um)*, formed fr. ns. in *-ure*, & **-et.** Combined with phosphorus.

phossy-jaw, n. [1. fósi jàw; 2. fɔ́si džɔ̀]. Necrosis of the jaw-bone, phosphorism, prevalent among workers in yellow phosphorus, as in match-factories where red or amorphous phosphorus is not used.

photism, n. [1. fótizm; 2. fóutizəm], fr. Gk. *phōtismós*, 'illumination', fr. *phōtízein*, 'to illuminate', fr. *phōt-*, stem of *phôs*, 'light', see **phosphorus, & -ism.** Illusory sensation of light, usually accompanying some other sensation.

photo, n. & vb. trans. [1. fótō; 2. fóutou]. Abbr. fr. **photograph.**

photo-, pref. representing Gk. *phōt-*, stem of *phôs*, 'light', see **phosphorus. 1.** Light; e.g. *photogen*, kind of paraffin; *photogenic*, producing light; produced by the action of light; *photoglyph*, plate engraved by the action of light; *photometer*, instrument for measuring intensity of light; *photophobia*, morbid aversion to light; *photophone*, (i.) instrument transmitting sound by means of light rays; (ii.) luminous envelope round sun, emitting light and heat. **2.** Photography; e.g. *photochromy*, colour-photography; *photolithography*, art or process of producing a printing-surface on stone by photographic means; *phototype*, plate in relief, for printing from, made from photograph; print made by such a plate.

photograph, n. & vb. trans. [1. fótograhf; 2. fóutəgrāf]. **photo- & -graph. 1.** n. Picture, image, produced by chemical action of light on a sensitized film superimposed upon glass, paper, celluloid &c. **2.** vb. To take a photograph of.

photographer, n. [1. fotógrafer; 2. fətógrəfə]. Prec. & **-er.** Person who takes photographs; specif., one who does this professionally as a business.

photographic, adj. [1. fòtográfik; 2. fòutəgrǽfik]. **photo- & -graphic.** Of, pertaining to, produced by, photography; of, like, characteristic of, a photograph.

photographically, adv. [1. fòtográfikali; 2. fòutəgrǽfikəli]. Prec. & **-al & -ly.** By means of a photograph or of photographs.

photography, n. [1. fotógrafi; 2. fətógrəfi]. **photo- & -graphy.** Process whereby images are imprinted upon a sensitized plate or film by the chemical action of light.

photogravure, n. [1. fòtogravúr; 2. fòutougrævjɔ́]. Fr., fr. **photo-** & *gravure*, 'engraving', fr. *grav-(er)*, 'engrave', fr. Germ., see **grave (I.)**, & **-ure. a** Reproduction of an engraving by photographic process; **b** picture so produced.

photomicrograph, n. [1. fòtōmíkrograhf; 2. fòutoumáikrəgrāf]. **photo- & micro-**

graph. An enlarged photograph of an object viewed under a microscope.

photophore, n. [1. fṓtofōr; 2. fóutəfɔ]. **photo-** & **-phore.** A luminous or phosphorescent organ, as in certain deep-sea fishes.

photosphere, n. [1. fṓtosfēr; 2. fóutəsfiə]. **photo-** & **sphere.** The luminous, incandescent envelope surrounding the sun or other star.

photostat, n. [1. fṓtostat; 2. fóutəstæt]. Invented word fr. **photo-** & **static. a** An automatic device for taking photographic facsimiles of documents &c. direct from the object upon specially prepared paper without a reversal of the object as in the ordinary negative; **b** facsimile so produced.

photo-telescope, n. [1. fṓtō téleskōp; 2. fòutou téliskoup]. **photo-** & **telescope.** A telescope fitted with a photographic camera, used for photographing stars &c.

phrase (I.), n. [1. frāz; 2. freiz], fr. L. Lat. *phrasis*, 'diction', fr. Gk. *phrásis*, 'speech', fr. *phrázein*, 'to speak; to cause to understand'; cp. Gk. *phradḗs*, 'wise'; etymol. doubtful. **1. a** Group of words which forms a part of a sentence, but does not constitute a complete sentence; **b** a combination of words which taken together constitute or correspond to a single part of speech; e.g. *in a noble manner* = *nobly*, an adverbial phrase. **2. a** An idiomatic expression; **b** a striking, pregnant, pointed saying: *Disraeli was a great maker of phrases.* **3.** (mus.) Short rhythmical division of musical passage.

phrase (II.), vb. trans., fr. prec. To express in words; to put into a specific form of words: *I shouldn't phrase it quite like that.*

phrase-book, n. Book giving phrases and idioms of a foreign language.

phrase-monger, n. Person given to the invention and use of phrases, esp. of such as have a specious appearance of profundity but in reality amount to nothing; a lover of catch-words and slogans.

phraseogram, n. [1. frā́zeogram; 2. fréiziəgræm]. **phrase** & **-gram.** Graphic symbol representing a phrase, esp. in shorthand.

phraseograph, n. [1. frā́zeograhf; 2. fréiziəgrāf]. **phrase** & **-graph.** (shorthand) Phrase that may be represented by a phraseogram.

phraseological, adj. [1. frāzeolójikl; 2. frèiziəlɔ́džikl]. **phrase** & **-logical.** Of, pertaining to, phraseology.

phraseology, n. [1. frāzeóloji; 2. frèiziɔ́lədži]. **phrase** & **-logy.** Selection made of words and expressions in speech or writing; diction; way of expressing oneself.

phratry, n. [1. frā́tri; 2. fréitri], fr. Gk. *phrātria*, 'brotherhood, clan', fr. *phrā́tēr*, 'brother', cogn. w. Lat. *frāter*, O.E. *brōðor*, see **brother. 1.** (Gk. antiq.) Subdivision of tribe. **2.** Group of clans forming subdivision of tribe among primitive peoples.

phrenetic, adj. [1. frenétik; 2. frenétik], fr. O. Fr. *frenetike*, fr. Lat. *phrenēticus*-(*us*), fr. L. Gk. *phrenētik*-(*ós*), 'mad, delirious', fr. *phren*-(*itis*), 'delirium', fr. *phren*-, cogn. w. *phrḗn*, 'mind', see next word, & **-itis**; cp. **frantic** & **frenzy.** Wild, delirious, frantic; filled with frenzy.

phrenic, adj. [1. frénik; 2. frénik], fr. Gk. *phren*-, *phrḗn*, 'diaphragm; heart; mind'; etymol. doubtful, & **-ic.** (anat.) Of, pertaining to, the diaphragm.

phrenological, adj. [1. frenolójikl; 2. frenəlɔ́džikl]. **phrenology** & **-ic** & **-al.** Connected with, pertaining to, phrenology.

phrenologically, adv. Prec. & **-ly.** By means of, from point of view of, according to the methods of, phrenology.

phrenologist, n. [1. frenólojist; 2. frenɔ́lədžist]. See next word & **-ist.** One who practises phrenology.

phrenology, n. [1. frenóloji; 2. frenɔ́lədži], fr. Gk. *phren*-, 'mind' &c., see **phrenic**, & **-logy.** Pseudo-science, now practically obsolete, which professed to find a relation between the bumps on a person's skull and his intellectual, emotional, and moral aptitudes, capacities, and tendencies.

Phrygian, adj. [1. fríjian; 2. frídžiən], fr. Lat. *Phrygiān*-(*us*), fr. *Phrygia*, country in Asia Minor, & **-an.** Connected with, belonging to, Phrygia; *Phrygian cap*, round conical cap with drooping top; cap of liberty; *Phrygian mode*, (mus.) one of the ancient Greek modes.

phthisis, n. [1. thísis; 2. þáisis]. Gk. *phthísis*, 'a wasting, perishing', fr. *phthínein*, 'to decay, wane'; cp. Gk. *phthóē*, 'consumption'; Scrt. *kṣiṇā́ti*, 'to perish'; *kṣayaś*, 'loss, ruin'; Lat. *sitis*, 'thirst'. Wasting disease; specif., tuberculosis of the lungs, consumption.

phylactery, n. [1. filákteri; 2. filǽktəri], fr. Lat., fr. Gk. *phulaktḗri*-(*on*), 'amulet'; cp. Gk. *phúlak*-(*os*), 'guard'; *phulássein*, 'to watch over'; cp. Lat. (*bu*)*bulcus*, 'ox-driver, herdsman'. **1. a** Vellum strips inscribed with passages from the Scriptures, enclosed in leather case, and worn by the ancient Jews, fastened to forehead or arm with leather thongs, to remind them to keep the law; **b** (fig.) display of outer forms of religious observance. **2.** (rare) Charm, amulet, talisman.

phyletic, adj. [1. filétik; 2. failétik], fr. Gk. *phūletik*-(*ós*), 'tribal', fr. *phū̂l*-(*on*), 'tribe', see **phylo-**, & **-etic.** Pertaining to a phylum, race, or tribe; racial.

phyllo-, pref. representing Gk. *phúllo*-(*n*), 'leaf'; cp. Lat. *folium*, 'leaf', see **folio**; fr. base **bh*(*e*)*lē*-, **bh*(*e*)*lō*-, 'to swell'; cp. Lat. *flōs*, 'flower', see **floral**; O.E. *blōstma*, 'flower', see **blossom**; *blōwan*, 'to bloom', see **blow** (IV.); further, Lat. *flēmina*, 'swelling'; O.E. *blǣdre*, 'bladder', see **bladder**; O.E. *blāwan*, 'to blow', see **blow** (I.). Leaf; e.g. *phyllophagous*, leaf-eating; *phyllophorous*, leaf-bearing; *phyllopod*, having leaf-like feet; *phyllotaxis*, arrangement of leaves on stem.

phylloxera, n. [1. filoksḗra; 2. filɔksíərə]. Prec. & Gk. *xērós*, 'dry', see **xer(o)-.** Genus of plant lice or aphides very destructive to grape-vines.

phylo-, pref. representing Gk. *phū̂lo*-(*n*), 'race, tribe; kind'; perh. related to Gk. *phōleós*, 'lair'; O.N. *bōl*, 'lodging'; perh. cp. O.E., O.H.G. *būr*, 'room' &c., see **bower** (I.) & words there referred to; O.N. *būr*, 'shop; women's apartment'. See also **physio-.** Race.

phylogenesis, n. [1. filōjénesis; 2. fàiloudžénisis]. Prec. & **genesis.** Evolution of a species or type.

phylum, n. [1. fílum; 2. fáiləm]. Mod. Lat. fr. Gk. *phū̂lon*, 'race', see **phylo-.** (biol.) One of the divisions of plant or animal kingdom.

physic (I.), n. [1. fízik; 2. fízik], fr. O. Fr. *fisique*, fr. Lat. *physic*-(*us*), fr. Gk. *phusik*-(*ós*), 'of nature', fr. *phús*-(*is*), 'nature', see **physio-**, & **-ic. 1.** Medical profession. **2.** Remedial substance; medicine. **3.** See **physics.**

physic (II.), vb. trans., fr. prec. To administer physic to, to dose; specif., to dose with purgatives.

physical, adj. [1. fízikl; 2. fízikəl], fr. Med. Lat. *physicāl*-(*is*), fr. Lat. *physic*-(*us*), 'natural'. See **physic** (I.) & **-al. 1. a** Connected with, pertaining to, matter or the material universe; contrasted with *mental, moral, spiritual*: *physical process*; specif. **b** connected with the animal or human body: *physical strength, exercise* &c. **2.** Pertaining to nature and the natural features of the universe: *physical geography.* **3.** Of, relating to, physics and the forces and properties treated of in this science. **4.** In accordance with the laws of nature or natural philosophy: *a physical impossibility.*

physically, adv. Prec. & **-ly. a** In respect of external nature; **b** in respect of the body: *a fine man physically, but a fool.*

physician, n. [1. fizíshan; 2. fizíʃən], fr. O. Fr. *fisician*. See **physic** & **-ician.** Person trained in, and practising the medical profession; specif., one who diagnoses disease, and treats it by means of drugs, but does not operate; contrasted with a *surgeon.*

physicism, n. [1. fízisizm; 2. fízisizəm]. See **physics** & **-ism. 1.** Study of natural sciences. **2.** Doctrine of physicist.

physicist, n. [1. fízisist; 2. fízisist]. See **physics** & **-ist. 1.** Student of physics. **2.** One who believes that the phenomena of life are purely physical in origin, and due to the working of natural forces, without requiring the intervention of the conscious mind of a Creator.

physicky, adj. [1. fíziki; 2. fíziki]. **physic** (I.) & **-y.** Like physic.

physico-, pref. representing Gk. *phusikó*-(*s*), 'of nature'. See **physic** (I.). Physical; e.g. *physico-chemical*, having both physical and chemical features.

physics, n. [1. fíziks; 2. fíziks]. See **physic** (I.). **1.** Formerly the various branches of science dealing with the material world; also called *Natural Philosophy*, which is still used in the Scottish universities for physics in the modern and restricted sense. **2.** That group of sciences dealing with various phases and forms of inanimate matter, e.g. the theory of heat, light, sound, and mechanics; until recently, specifically excluding the consideration of chemical action.

physio-, pref. representing Gk. *phúsi*-(*s*), 'nature'; cp. *phúein*, 'to grow, develop'; *phutón*, 'plant, growth'; *phū̂lon*, 'tribe', see **phylo-**; the base is **bhewā*-, **bhū̆*- &c., 'to exist'; cp. further Scrt. *bhávati*, 'to exist'; *bhūtiš*, 'being; welfare'; O. Slav. *bhūma*, 'world'; O.N. *buð*, 'dwelling'; Scrt. *bhūtáš*, 'been; being'; Lith. *búta*, 'been'; Lat. *fui*, 'I have been'; *futūrus*, future Part. of 'to be', see **future**; O.E. *bēon*, 'to be', see **be**; *būan*, 'to dwell', see **boor.**

physiocracy, n. [1. fiziókrasi; 2. fìziɔ́krəsi]. Prec. & **-cracy.** The social and political system advocated by Quesnay and other French economists and philosophers of the 18th cent., embodying the doctrine that political economy is based on natural laws, with which government should interfere as little as possible.

physiocrat, n. [1. fíziōkrat; 2. fízioukræt]. Fr. *physiocrate.* See prec. Member of the school of French economists and philosophers who advocated physiocracy.

physiognomic(al), adj. [1. fiziōnómik(l); 2. fìziounɔ́mik(l)]. **physiognomy** & **-ic** & **-al.** Pertaining to physiognomy.

physiognomically, adv. Prec. & **-ly.** In respect of the physiognomy.

physiognomist, n. [1. fiziónomist; 2. fìziɔ́nəmist]. See next word & **-ist.** Observer of the human face, its forms and expressions, especially one who draws inferences as to race, character, capacity &c. from such observation.

physiognomy, n. [1. fiziónomi; 2. fìziɔ́nəmi]. M.E. *fis*(*e*)*nomie*, fr. Med. Lat. *phisonomia*, fr. Gk. *phusiognōmía*, 'art of judging a man's character from his face', fr. **physio-** & *gnṓmōn*, 'judge; indicator', see **gnomon. 1.** Art of judging character from outward bodily appearance, esp. features, expression &c. **2. a** General appearance of features, cast of countenance, type of face; hence, **b** (vulg.) face. **3.** (rare) General outward appearance, natural features: *physiognomy of a country, building* &c.

physiographer, n. [1. fiziógrafer; 2. fìziɔ́grəfə]. See **physiography** & **-er.** Student of, writer on, physiography.

physiographic(al), adj. [1. fiziográfik(l); 2. fìziəgrǽfik(l)]. See **physiography** & **-ic** & **-al.** Pertaining to physiography.

physiographically, adv. Prec. & **-ly.** From the point of, in accordance with the methods and facts of, physiography.

physiography, n. [1. fiziógrafi; 2. fìziɔ́grəfi]. **physio-** & **-graphy.** Description of nature, natural features, and processes; specif., physical geography.

physiologic(al), adj. [1. fiziolójik(l); 2. fìziəlɔ́džik(l)]. **physiology** & **-ic** & **-al.** Pertaining to, concerned with, physiology.

physiologically, adv. Prec. & **-ly**. From the point of view of, in accordance with the methods and facts of, physiology.

physiologist, n. [1. fiziólojist; 2. fìziɔ́lədžist]. See next word & **-ist**. Student of, one learned in, physiology.

physiology, n. [1. fizióloji; 2. fìziɔ́lədži], fr. Lat. *physiologia*, fr. Gk. *phusiología*, 'knowledge of nature'. **physio-** & **-logy**. Branch of biology dealing with the vital processes, and functions of the various parts of living organisms; contrasted with anatomy, which deals only with structure.

physique, n. [1. fizḗk; 2. fizík]. Fr., fr. adj., fr. Lat. *physic-(us)*. See **physic (I.)**. Physical form, structure; constitution.

-phyte, suff. [1. fīt; 2. fait] representing Gk. *phut-(ón)*, 'plant'; cp. Gk. *phúein*, 'to grow', cp. **physio-**; forming ns., w. sense **a** plant, vegetable organism; e.g. *saprophyte*; **b** plant-like organism; e.g. *zoophyte*.

phyto-, pref. representing Gk. *phutó-(n)*, 'plant'. See prec. Plant; e.g. *phytogenesis*, origin and evolution of plants; *phytography*, description of plants; *phytophagous*, plant-eating; *phytotomy*, dissection of plants; *phytozoon*, plant-like animal, zoophyte.

pi (I.), n. [1. pī; 2. pai]. Name of Gk. letter (π), representing P. (math.) Symbol used to denote the ratio of the circumference of a circle to its diameter.

pi (II.), adj. Abbr. of **pious**. (school slang) Pious; religious.

pi (III.), n. & vb. Printer's term. See **pie (III.)**.

piacular, adj. [1. piákūlar; 2. paiǽkjulə]. Lat. *piāculāris*, 'expiatory', fr. stem of *piāculum*, 'propitiatory sacrifice', wh. is for **piāt-lom*, fr. P.P. type of *piāre*, 'to appease, propitiate', see **pious**. **1.** Expiatory. **2.** Requiring expiation; very wicked, atrocious.

piaffe, vb. intrans. [1. piáf; 2. piǽf], fr. Fr. *piaffer*, 'to paw the ground'; etymol. doubtful. (of horse, rare) To move at a slow trot.

piaffer, n. [1. piáfer; 2. piǽfə], fr. Fr. *piaffer*. See prec. Slow movement of horse &c., with feet placed as in trotting.

pia mater, n. [1. pía māter; 2. páiə méitə]. Med. Lat. trans. of Arab. *umm raqiqah*, 'tender mother'. See **pious** & **mater**. Inmost of the three membranes enclosing the brain and spinal cord. See **meninx**.

pianette, n. [1. pianét; 2. piənét]. See **piano (II.)** & **-ette**. Small variety of the small upright piano.

pianissimo, adv. & n. [1. pìanísimō; 2. piənísimou]. Ital., superl. of **piano (I.)**. (mus. direction) **1.** Very softly. **2.** Passage played thus.

pianist, n. [1. pḗanist; 2. píənist]. See **piano (II.)** & **-ist**. Person who plays the piano, esp. skilled performer.

piano (I.), adv. & n. [1. pyáhnō; 2. pjánou]. Ital., fr. Lat. *plāno*, dat. of *plānus*, 'flat, smooth', later 'soft'; see **plain (I.)**. (mus. direction) **1.** Softly. **2.** Passage played thus.

piano (II.), n. [1. piánō, pḗanō; 2. piǽnou, píənou]. Abbr. of **pianoforte**. Musical instrument in which the sound is produced by small hammers striking on metal strings, and worked by levers attached to a keyboard; *cottage piano*, small upright piano; *grand piano*, large piano, the strings and frame of which resemble, roughly, a harp placed horizontally, the strings being struck by hammers from below; *upright piano*, one with strings placed vertically.

pianoforte, n. [1. pìanōfórte; 2. piǽnoufɔ́ti]. Ital., earlier *piano e forte*, 'soft and loud'. See **piano (I.)** & **forte (II.)**. Piano.

pianola, n. [1. pìanóla; 2. piənóulə]. Trade-name, dimin. of **piano (II.)**. Apparatus attached to a piano, containing a mechanism by means of which the keys are struck by small hammers instead of by the player's fingers.

piano-organ, n. Musical instrument, used by itinerant musicians, having strings and a hammer action like those of a piano, actuated by a revolving barrel with pins, as in a musical box.

piano-player, n. Instrument for playing piano mechanically.

piano-stool, n. Seat without back or arms, the height of which is adjustable, used by a player sitting at a piano.

piastre, piaster, n. [1. piáster; 2. piǽstə]. Fr. *piastre*, fr. Ital. *piastra*, 'thin metal plate, dollar, a plaster', fr. Low Lat. *plastrum*, see **plaster**. **a** Small silver coin used in Turkey, Egypt &c., worth 2d. to 6d.; **b** Spanish silver coin worth about 4s. 2d.; Spanish dollar.

piazza, n. [1. piátsa; 2. piǽtsə]. Ital., fr. Lat. *platēa*, 'broad street, open space', fr. Gk. *plateîa*, 'street', fr. *plat-(ús)*, 'broad, flat', see **platy-**. **1.** (esp. in Italy) Open space in town, public square. **2.** (U.S.A.) Veranda.

pibroch, n. [1. pḗbrogh, -ok; 2. píbrɔχ, -ɔk], fr. Gael. *piobaireachd*, fr. *piobar*, 'piper', fr. *piob*, 'pipe', see **pipe (I.)**. Form of bagpipe music of the Scottish Highlands, usually martial, consisting of an air with variations.

pica, n. [1. píka; 2. páikə]. Med. Lat., fr. *pīca*, 'woodpecker', see **pie (I.)**, fr. supposed resemblance to black and white plumage of the bird. **1.** (eccles., obs.) A collection of rules; ordinal of Latin Church. **2.** (typog.) A standard of size, i.e. one-sixth of an inch; *pica type*, the largest ordinarily used in books, six lines to the inch; so called because commonly used for printing ordinals and service books.

picador, n. [1. píkadòr; 2. píkədɔ̀]. Span., fr. *picár*, 'to prick', fr. *pica*, **pike (I.)**. Bull-fighter on horseback, armed with lance or pike.

picamar, n. [1. píkamar; 2. píkəmā], fr. Lat. *pic-*, stem of *pix*, 'pitch', see **pitch (I.)** & *amār-(us)*, 'bitter', cogn. w. Du. *amper*, 'sharp, sour'; O.N. *apr*, 'acid'; O.H.G. *ampfaro*, O.E. *ompre*, 'dock'; Scrt. *amláś*, 'sour'. Bitter oil distilled from wood-tar.

picaresque, adj. & n. [1. pikarésk; 2. pìkərésk], fr. Span. *picaresco*, fr. *picaro*, 'rogue', see next word, & **-esque**. **1.** adj. (of type of literature) Dealing with the adventures of wandering rogues and persons living by their wits: *the picaresque novel*; 'Gil Blas' is a famous example. **2.** n. *The picaresque*, a style of literature, which originated in Spain in 16th cent., and rapidly spread to England and other countries, representing a reaction against the older romances of chivalry.

picaroon, n. & vb. intrans. [1. pikarṓōn; 2. pìkərū́n], fr. Span. *picaron*, fr. *picar-(o)*, 'rogue'; etymol. doubtful. **1.** n. **a** A cheat, adventurer, a swindling rogue; a corsair; **b** a pirate's ship. **2.** vb. To live by one's wits, to sharp and swindle; to live by piracy.

picayune, n. [1. pikayṓōn; 2. pìkəjū́n]. Etymol. doubtful; prob. through Fr. *picaillon*, fr. Provenç. *picaioun*, 'a small copper coin'. **1.** Name in Louisiana for an old small silver coin, $\frac{1}{16}$ of the dollar, or $\frac{1}{2}$ the Spanish real. **2.** (colloq., U.S.A.) Anything of trifling value; (also attrib.) petty, mean, paltry.

piccalilli, n. [1. píkalili; 2. píkəlìli]. Etymol. unknown. Highly seasoned pickle of chopped vegetables, steeped in mustard and vinegar.

piccaninny, pickaninny, n. & adj. [1. píkanìni; 2. píkənìni]. Prob. fr. dimin. of Span. *pequeño*, 'child'. **1.** n. Small child, esp. an African negro baby. **2.** adj. Very small.

piccolo, n. [1. píkolō; 2. píkəlou]. Ital. *piccolo*, 'small; a small flute'. **a** Small shrill flute, pitched an octave above ordinary flute; **b** organ stop producing a high flute-like note.

pice, n. [1. pīs; 2. pais], fr. Hind. *paisa*. Copper coin of British India, $\frac{1}{4}$ of anna.

pichiciago, n. [1. pìchisiágō; 2. pitʃisiéigou], fr. S. Am. Span. *pichiciego*, the second element is perh. Span. *ciego*, 'blind', fr. Lat. *caecus*, see **caecum**. Small animal like the armadillo, found in Southern S. America.

pick (I.), n. [1. pik; 2. pik]. Prob. fr. **pike (I.)**. **1.** Tool with wooden handle fitted at right angles into the middle of a long, narrow, slightly curved head usually with a point at one end and a chisel-edge at the other, used for breaking stone, hard ground &c. **2.** Any pointed instrument for picking &c., as *tooth-pick*.

pick (II.), vb. trans. & intrans., fr. prec. **A.** trans. **1.** To break up, break surface of, make hole in, with pick &c.: *to pick ground, face of rock* &c. **2.** To make with or as with pick; to form by repeated blows of pointed instrument: *to pick a hole* &c. Phr. *to pick holes in*, to find fault with, criticize adversely. **3.** To poke, probe, with pointed instrument to remove extraneous matter: *to pick one's teeth*. **4.** To remove flesh &c., from, with teeth, beak, or other pointed tool: *to pick a bone* &c. Phr. *to have a bone to pick with*, to have a cause of complaint against. **5.** To take hold of, take up, esp. **a** to remove with fingers &c.: *to pick a thorn out of one's finger, a thread off one's dress* &c.; **b** to gather, pluck: *to pick a flower, fruit* &c.; **c** (of bird &c.) to take up in beak. **6.** To pull apart, tear asunder, with fingers &c.: *to pick oakum*; *to pick to pieces* (often fig.), to analyse and criticize adversely. **7.** (colloq.) To eat in small mouthfuls or fragments: *I could manage to pick a bit of food*. **8.** To open by means of some pointed instrument other than that normally used: *to pick a lock*. **9.** To select with care, choose carefully: *to pick and choose*; *to pick one's way, one's words* &c. **10.** (lit. and fig.) To remove some or all of contents of, with stealth or cunning, to obtain something from by stealth: *to pick one's pocket, brains* &c. **11.** (fig.) To seek occasion for, contrive: *to pick a quarrel*. **B.** intrans. **1.** To steal, pilfer; esp. in Phr. *pick and steal*. **2.** To eat slowly and in small quantities, nibble. **C.** Followed by adverbs. *Pick off*, **a** to remove by picking, pluck; **b** to shoot at with deliberate aim. *Pick out*, **1.** to choose, select: *to pick out a few things to purchase*; **2. a** to distinguish, recognize: *to pick out one's friends in an audience*; **b** to make out (meaning) by careful scrutiny: *to pick out the sense of a passage*; **3.** to play by ear: *to pick out a tune on the piano*; **4.** to relieve, variegate, with touches of different colour. *Pick up*, **1.** to break (the ground &c.) with pick; **2.** to take hold of and lift, snatch up: *to pick up one's hat and go*; **3. a** to gain, acquire: *to pick up information, a living* &c.; **b** to call for, find, overtake, and take along: *the train picks up passengers*; *I'll pick you up at your house*; **c** to make the acquaintance of casually: *to pick up some new friends in a hotel*; **4. a** trans., to regain, recover: *to pick up strength* &c.; **b** intrans., to regain one's health, spirits &c.

pick (III.), n., fr. prec. **1. a** Act of picking; selection, choice; **b** that which is selected, choice: *to have one's pick of*. **2.** Best part of, finest specimen of its kind. Phr. *the pick of the bunch*, best of the lot.

pick-a-back, pickaback, adv. [1. píkabak; 2. píkəbæk]. Origin doubtful; possibly fr. *pack on back?* On the back of another person: *to ride pick-a-back*.

pickax(e), n. & vb. trans. & intrans. [1. píkaks; 2. píkæks]. M.E. *pikeis, picois*, fr. O. Fr. *picois*; cp. O. Fr. *pic*, 'pike', see **pike (I.)**. The ending has been assimilated to **axe**. **1.** n. Tool for breaking ground &c., pick. **2.** vb. **a** trans. To break with pickaxe; **b** intrans., to use a pickaxe.

picker, n. [1. píker; 2. píkə]. **pick (II.)** & **-er**. **1. a** One who picks, gathers: *hop-picker*; **b** one who picks rags, oakum &c.: *rag-picker* &c. **2.** Instrument for picking, tearing &c.

pickerel, n. [1. píkerel; 2. píkərəl]. **pike (II.)** w. dimin. suff. *-rel*. Young pike.

picket (I.), n. [1. píket; 2. píkit], fr. Fr. *piquet*, 'stake', fr. *piqu-(er)*, 'to prick', see **pike (I.)**. **1.** Pointed stake, peg, post, used for forming palisade, for tethering horse &c. **2.** (hist.) Military punishment in which offender was forced to stand on one foot on pointed stake. **3.** (mil., also *picquet*) Small body of men used as outpost, on patrol duty, or kept in readiness for special service. **4.** Man or group of men placed on duty by trade union during a strike, nominally supposed to endeavour to prevent men from returning to work by moral suasion, but often employing more forcible means.

picket (**II.**), vb. trans. & intrans., fr. prec. **A.** trans. **1.** To secure, fasten, with picket(s). **2. a** To post as pickets; **b** (fig.) to station at intervals: *detectives were picketed here and there among the crowd*; **c** to intercept, guard, beset, with pickets: *to picket workers, factories* &c. **B.** intrans. To act as picket.

picking, n. [1. píking; 2. píkiŋ]. **pick** (**II.**) & **-ing**. **1.** Act of one who picks; pilfering, esp. in Phr. *picking and stealing*. **2.** That which is picked; esp. **a** (pl.) things acquired by petty thefts; **b** (pl.) that which is left to be picked up; scraps, remnants, gleanings (in material and non-material senses).

pickle (**I.**), n. [1. píkl; 2. píkl]. Prob. fr. M. Du. *pekel*; etymol. unknown. **1.** Solution of salt, brine, or vinegar &c. used to preserve meat, vegetables &c. Phr. *to have a rod in pickle for*, have a punishment, or something unpleasant in store for. **2.** Specif. (pl. *pickles*) vegetables chopped up, or young onions or cucumbers whole, preserved in vinegar, seasoned, and used as a condiment with meat. **3.** Diluted acid used for cleaning metal &c. **4.** Plight; awkward, unpleasant, situation or condition: *in a pretty pickle*, in a mess (lit. or fig.). **5.** (colloq.) Mischievous child: *a regular young pickle*.

pickle (**II.**), vb. trans., fr. prec. **1.** To preserve in, by means of, pickle. **2.** To clean with pickle. **3.** (naut.) To rub with salt or vinegar after flogging.

picklock, n. [1. píklok; 2. píklɔk]. **1.** Person who picks locks, esp. for dishonest purposes. **2.** Instrument used for this.

pick-me-up, n. [1. pík mē up; 2. pík mi ap]. **a** Stimulating drink, tonic &c.; also **b** anything stimulating to the mind or spirits.

pickpocket, n. [1. píkpòket; 2. píkpɔkit]. Person who steals things from the pockets of others as a means of livelihood.

picksome, adj. [1. píksum; 2. píksəm]. **pick** (**II.**) & **-some**. (rare) Careful in choosing, fastidious.

pickthank, n. [1. píkthangk; 2. píkþæŋk]. (archaic or provinc.) Flatterer, sycophant.

Pickwick, n. [1. píkwik; 2. píkwik], fr. *Mr. Pickwick*, character invented by Dickens in *Pickwick Papers*. Kind of cheap cigar.

Pickwickian, adj. & n. [1. pikwíkian; 2. pikwíkiən], fr. prec. & **-ian**. **1.** adj. (of a situation, a jest &c.) Resembling those represented in the *Pickwick Papers*. Phr. *in a Pickwickian sense*, not to be taken too literally or seriously. **2.** n. **a** Member of the Pickwick Club, founded by *Mr. Pickwick*, which combined conviviality with pseudo-intellectual discussion, and criticism of things observed in excursions &c.; **b** person deeply read in the *Pickwick Papers*, and well versed in the characters, their adventures, and remarks.

picnic, n. & vb. intrans. [1. píknik; 2. píknik], fr. Fr. *pique-nique*, said to have come into use c. 1692; etymol. doubtful. **1.** n. Outdoor pleasure party; an outing during which a meal is consumed in the open air. **2.** vb. intrans. **a** To have a picnic; **b** to live and feed in a muddled way as though on a picnic, making a shift to put up with inconveniences.

picnicker, n. [1. pikniker; 2. píknikə]. Prec. & **-er**. Person who takes part in a picnic.

picnicky, adj. [1. píkniki; 2. pikniki]. **picnic** & **-y**. Like, characteristic of, a picnic.

picot, n. [1. pikō; 2. píkou]. Fr., dimin. of *pic*, 'peak, pike', see **pike** (**I.**). Small loop of thread at edge of lace &c.

picotee, n. [1. pìkotḗ; 2. pìkətí], fr. Fr. *picoté*, 'with ornamental edging', fr. prec. Kind of small carnation with bright-coloured petals, sometimes marked at the edges with deeper colour.

picquet, n. See **picket** (**I.**), **3**.

picric, adj. [1. píkrik; 2. píkrik], fr. Gk. *pikr-(ós)*, 'sharp, bitter'; cp. Scrt. *piśáti*, 'to cut, carve'; O. Slav. *pĭstrŭ*, 'variegated'; fr. base **poik̑-*, **pik̑-* &c., 'to adorn by carving or colouring', whence Gk. *poikílos*, 'variegated; embroidered, chiselled'; O.E. *fāh*, 'variegated'; Lat. *pict-(um)*, 'coloured', see **picture** (**I.**). *Picric acid*, bitter yellow substance obtained from phenol &c. by action of nitric acid, used in explosives and in dyeing.

Pict, n. [1. pikt; 2. pikt], fr. L. Lat. *Picti*, prob. fr. Lat. *pict-(um)*, P.P. of *pingere*, 'to paint', see **picture**. Member of a race, possibly Iberian, formerly inhabiting Eastern and Northern Scotland.

Pictish, adj. [1. píktish; 2. píktiʃ]. Prec. & **-ish**. Of, pertaining to, the Picts.

pictograph, n. [1. píktograhf; 2. píktəgrāf], fr. Lat. *pict-(um)*, 'painted', see **picture** (**I.**), & *-o-* & **graph**. **a** Pictorial symbol representing an object or an idea; **b** primitive form of writing consisting of pictographs.

pictographic, adj. [1. pìktográfik; 2. pìktəgrǽfik]. Prec. & **-ic**. Of, composed of, pictographs.

pictographically, adv. [1. pìktográfikali; 2. pìktəgrǽfikəli]. Prec. & **-al** & **-ly**. By means of pictographs.

pictography, n. [1. piktógrafi; 2. piktɔ́grəfi]. **pictograph** & **-y**. Art or study of picture-writing.

pictorial, adj. & n. [1. piktórial; 2. piktɔ́riəl], fr. L. Lat. *pictōri-(us)*, 'of painters', fr. *pictor*, 'painter', fr. Lat. *pict-(um)*, P.P. of *pingere*, 'to paint', see **picture** (**I.**), & **-or** & **-ial**. **1.** adj. **a** Pertaining to, consisting of, expressed in, pictures: *pictorial art*; *a pictorial record*; **b** suitable for, like, a picture; picturesque. **2.** n. Journal in which pictures are the leading feature.

pictorially, adv. Prec. & **-ly**. By means of pictures.

picture (**I.**), n. [1. píkchur; 2. píktʃə], fr. Lat. *pictūra*, 'painting', fr. *pict-(um)*, P.P. type of *pingere*, 'to paint; to embroider'; cp. Scrt. *piŋgaláś*, 'reddish brown'; also, w. different formative element, Scrt. *piśáti*, 'adorns; carves out'; *péśaś*, 'form, colour'; Gk. *poikílos*, 'variegated'; O.E. *fāh*, 'variegated'; Lith. *pëszìù*, 'to write'. Cp. also Gk. *pikrós*, 'cutting, sharp', see **picric**. The orig. meaning of the base **pig̑-*, *pik̑-* &c., was prob. 'to adorn, diversify', either by colouring or by engraving, carving &c. See **paint**. **1.** Representation of an object in painting or drawing. **2.** Picture of specific person; portrait. **3.** View, scene, general impression of landscape &c. **4.** Pl., *the pictures*, also *moving pictures*, cinematograph film. **5. a** Typical embodiment: *to look the picture of health, despair* &c.; **b** person closely resembling and recalling another: *he is the picture of his father*. **6.** Beautiful person, object, or scene; something suitable for, or suggesting, pictorial treatment. **7.** Vivid verbal description: *Rudyard Kipling has given us realistic pictures of Indian life*. **8.** Mental impression, or image, conception; something imprinted on the memory: *it is hard to form a true picture of conditions in Russia*.

picture (**II.**), vb. trans., fr. prec. **1. a** To make a picture of in lines or colours; to draw, paint; **b** to give a vivid description of in words. **2.** To adorn with pictures. **3.** To form a mental image of; to imagine, conceive: *I can't quite picture him as a family man*; *picture to yourself what it must be to have no money and no friends*.

picture-book, n. Children's book consisting mainly of pictures, with little or no reading matter.

picture-card, n. King, queen, or knave in pack of cards; court-card.

picture-gallery, n. **a** Building or apartment in which a collection of pictures is exhibited; **b** a collection of pictures.

picture-hat, n. Woman's large-brimmed hat, esp. one trimmed with ostrich feathers &c., as in Gainsborough's portraits.

picture palace, n. A cinema.

picture post card, n. Post card with picture on one side.

picturesque, adj. [1. pìkchurésk; 2. pìktʃərésk], w. assimilation to **picture**, fr. Fr. *pittoresque*, fr. Ital. *pittoresco*, fr. *pittore*, 'painter', fr. Lat. *pictor*, see **pictorial**, & **-esque**. **1.** Like, suitable to, forming, a striking picture. **2.** (of language) Vivid, graphic; forcible, lurid. **3.** (of personality, character &c.) Strong, original, interesting; abounding in unexpected, individual features and aspects.

picturesquely, adv. Prec. & **-ly**. In a picturesque manner.

picturesqueness, n. See prec. & **-ness**. Quality of being picturesque.

picture-writing, n. Representation, expression, of ideas and conceptions by pictures; hieroglyphics, pictography.

picul, **pikul**, n. [1. píkul; 2. píkəl]. Malay. *pikul*. A Chinese weight, 133⅓ lb. avoirdupois.

piddle, vb. intrans. [1. pídl; 2. pídl]. Etymol. unknown. (archaic) To trifle, busy oneself with trifles: '*I can piddle here, On broccoli and mutton round the year*' (Pope, 'To Mr. Bethel').

piddock, n. [1. pídnk; 2. pídək]. Origin (?). Burrowing bivalve mollusc, used for bait.

pidgin, **pigeon**, n. [1. píjin; 2. pídžin]. Corrupt. fr. **business**. *Pidgin English*, jargon, or lingua franca, consisting chiefly of English words, used by English-speaking traders and natives in China and other parts of the East.

pie (**I.**), n. [1. pī; 2. pai]. O. Fr. *pie*, fr. Lat. *pīca*, 'magpie'; cp. *pīcus*, 'woodpecker'; Scrt. *pikaś*, 'cuckoo'; O.H.G. *speh(t)*, 'woodpecker'; perh. cogn. w. Gk. *poikílos*, 'variegated', q.v. under **picric**, **picture** (**I.**). **1.** Magpie. **2. a** Kind of woodpecker: (esp. in compounds) *French pie* &c.; **b** *sea-pie*, oyster-catcher. **3.** (eccles.) Pica.

pie (**II.**), n. M.E. *pīe*; perh. fr. prec. in sense of a mixed dish. Cp. **pica**. Meat, fruit &c. baked in a dish with cover, or with complete envelope of pastry. Phr. *to have a finger in the pie*, to be concerned in, take an active part in; often in compounds as *apple-pie*, *bran-pie*.

pie (**III.**), n. & vb. trans. See **pica** & cp. prec. **1.** n. **a** (also *printer's pie*) Indiscriminately mixed, disarranged, type; hence, **b** (fig.) disorder, confusion, chaos: *to make pie of anything*. **2.** vb. trans. To mix, disarrange, confuse (type).

pie (**IV.**), n., fr. Hind. *pa'i*, fr. Scrt. *pad*, 'quarter'. (Anglo-Indian) Small copper coin, $\frac{1}{3}$ of a pice.

piebald, n. [1. píbawld; 2. páibɔ̄ld]. **pie** (**I.**) & **bald**, in old meaning 'white'. **1.** (esp. of horse) Of two colours arranged in irregular spots or patches, usually black, or brown, and white. **2.** (fig.) Motley, varied in character or appearance.

piece (**I.**), n. [1. pēs; 2. pīs]. M.E. *pēce*, fr. O. Fr. *pece*, fr. Low Lat. *pecia*; perh. of Celt. origin; cp. W. *peth*, 'a little; a portion'. **1.** Object regarded as definite part or component of a whole; a bit, part: *to tear a piece off a newspaper*; *there's one piece missing*; *to break to pieces*; *in pieces*, broken, in fragments. **2.** Part, portion, detached from, or separated, marked off from: *a piece of bread, wood, coal, cloth* &c.; *a piece of paper*, a bit of paper torn from larger portion; also specif., a sheet, e.g. *a pen and a piece of paper*; *a piece of ground*, specific area of land fenced or marked off from surrounding areas. **3.** *A piece of news*, an item; *piece of advice, luck* &c., some. Phr. *to give a person a piece of one's mind*, to scold or criticize with frankness. **4.** Specific single object; esp. **a** example, specimen: *a fine piece of work, sculpture* &c.; **b** fire-arm: *field piece,* field gun; **c** coin: *a penny piece* &c.; *piece of eight,* Spanish dollar, equal to eight reals; **d** one of a set of chessmen, or draughtsmen; **e** literary, artistic, or musical composition: *to play a piece*; *a sea piece*; specif., drama, play. **5.** Specific quantity, esp. **a** (of wall-paper &c.), 12 yd.; **b** (of cloth, muslin &c.) 10 yd.; **c** cask of wine &c. Phrs. *by the piece,* according to amount; *of a piece,* (fig.) consistent, of the same character. **6.** Slang for *piece of flesh,* a girl or woman: *a pretty, saucy, piece.*

piece (**II.**), vb. trans., fr. prec. **A.** trans. **1.** To put together piece by piece, join up, make into a whole. **2.** Specif., to join threads in spinning. **B.** Followed by adverbs and prepositions. *Piece on,* to add, fit, or join on. *Piece out,* to eke out, complete by adding piece(s). *Piece together,* to join, fit, together, piece by piece: *to piece fragments of cloth together*; (also fig.) *to piece together evidence* &c. *Piece up,* to patch up, repair by adding piece(s).

pièce de résistance, n. [1. pyās de rāzistáhns; 2. pjēs də rezistā̃s]. Fr. Principal or most substantial dish at a meal; also figurative.

piece-goods, n. Textile fabrics, silk, cotton &c. made in standard lengths.

piecemeal, adv. & adj. [1. pḗsmēl; 2. písmīl]. **piece** & O.E. *mǣlum,* dat. pl. of *mǣl,* 'measure' (see **meal (II.)**), used adverbially, cp. O.E. *styččemǣlum,* 'piecemeal'. **1.** adv. Piece by piece, a bit at a time. **2.** adj. Coming, done, piece by piece.

piece-work, n. Work paid for by the piece, or amount done.

piecrust, n. [1. píkrust; 2. páikrast]. Baked pastry covering pie.

pied, adj. [1. pīd; 2. paid]. **pie (I.)** & **-ed.** Mottled, variegated, parti-coloured.

pied à terre, n., anglicized [1. pyād ah tár; 2. pjeid ā téə]. Fr., lit. 'foot on the ground'. Temporary lodging; place where one can stay from time to time.

pieman, n. [1. píman; 2. páimən]. One who sells pies, esp. one who hawks them in the streets.

pie powder, n. O. Fr. *pie pouldre,* 'dusty foot', name for a pedlar. *Court of pie powder,* a court formerly attached to every fair or market in England, presided over by the steward of the lord of the manor or of the owner of tolls, who settled all disputes and claims arising in the fair.

pier, n. [1. pēr; 2. piə]. M.E. *pēr,* Low Lat. *pera*; etymol. uncertain; perh. through Lat., fr. Gk. *pétra,* 'rock'. See **petro-.** **1.** Column or mass of stone, masonry &c.; esp. **a** support for span of bridge; **b** pillar supporting arch, roof &c.; **c** masonry between openings in wall, windows &c. **2.** Breakwater, mole. **3. a** Structure of stone, iron, wood &c. built out into the sea and used as landing-stage; a jetty; **b** ornamental structure supported by iron pillars and girders, built out into the sea at a watering-place, used partly as a landing-place for steamers, but chiefly regarded as a place of amusement, where entertainments are given, and as a promenade.

pierage, n. [1. pḗrij; 2. píəridž]. Prec. & **-age.** Dues payable for using pier.

pierce, vb. trans. & intrans. [1. pērs; 2. piəs]. M.E. *percen,* fr. O. Fr. *percer*; etymol. uncertain. **A.** trans. **1. a** (of a sharp point or a missile) To pass through surface of; to go, come, through, perforate; to penetrate, enter: *the arrow pierced the knight's armour*; *he was so thin that his bones seemed almost to pierce the skin*; *no ordinary bullet can pierce an elephant's hide*; **b** (of action of a person) to cause (a point &c.) to enter, to thrust through, make a hole in: *a soldier pierced the Saviour's side with a spear*; specif., *to have the ears pierced,* have holes made in the lobes for insertion of earrings. **2. a** (of light, sound, cold) To get, filter, through; to be visible, audible, to make itself felt, through, or in spite of intervention of: *no ray can pierce such darkness*; *a shrill cry suddenly pierced the stillness*; *pierced by the bitter cold*; **b** (of sight, hearing) to look through, discern, perceive through an obstacle; **c** (of the mind) to comprehend. **3.** (of emotion) To wound, afflict, affect deeply: *sorrow pierced her heart,* or *pierced her to the heart.* **B.** intrans. To effect a passage (in material and non-material applications): *a point as blunt as this will never pierce*; *here no light, sound, can pierce.*

piercing, adj. [1. pḗrsing; 2. píəsiŋ]. Prec. & **-ing.** Keen, sharp, penetrating: *a piercing glance*; *piercing cold, wind* &c.

piercingly, adv. Prec. & **-ly.** So as to pierce.

pier-glass, n. **pier** & **glass.** Long mirror, in which the whole person can be seen at once; originally used to fill space between windows &c.

Pierian, adj. [1. pīḗrian; 2. paiíəriən], fr. Lat. *Pīeri-(us),* 'of Pieria', mountain in N. Thessaly, sacred to the Muses, & **-an.** Pertaining to Pieria, hence, connected with knowledge or with poetry.

pierrette, n. [1. pērét, pyerét; 2. piərét, pjerét], fr. Fr. *Pierre,* see next word, & **-ette.** Female pierrot.

pierrot, n. [1. pḗro, pyérō; 2. píərou, pjérou]. Fr., dimin. of *Pierre,* 'Peter', fr. Lat. *Petrus,* see **Peter (I.).** **1.** A stock male character in French pantomime, having the face whitened and loose white overalls. **2.** One of a troupe of singers performing publicly, who affect baggy white linen garments with black spots, and white conical caps.

pietà, n. [1. pietáh; 2. pietá]. Ital., fr. Lat. *pietāt-(em),* see **piety.** Picture, carving &c., representing the Blessed Virgin Mary supporting, and lamenting over, the lifeless body of the Saviour.

pietism, n. [1. píetizm; 2. páiətizəm], fr. Germ. *pietismus.* **piety** & **-ism.** **1.** Religious revival in Lutheran Church in 17th cent. **2. a** System which emphasizes the devotional rather than the rational and intellectual aspects of religion; **b** a snuffling, insincere affectation of piety.

pietist, n. [1. píetist; 2. páiətist]. Prec. & **-ist.** Adherent of pietism.

pietistic(al), adj. [1. pietístik(l); 2. paiətístik(l)]. Prec. & **-ic** & **-al.** Pertaining to, connected with, pietism or pietists.

piety, n. [1. píeti; 2. páiəti, páiiti], fr. O. Fr. *piete,* fr. Lat. *pietātem, pietas,* 'dutiful conduct towards the gods, filial respect and affection shown to one's parents, or one's country; duty, loyalty'; fr. *pi-(us),* 'dutiful,' see **pious,** & **-ty.** **1. a** Reverence felt for God and religion; **b** conduct inspired by these feelings and principles. **2. a** Loving reverence shown to parents and benefactors, or to their memory; dutiful, loyal, feelings towards one's country; **b** dutiful, filial, service inspired by such feelings.

piezo-, form used in combination indicating pressure, see next word; as *piezo-electricity,* electrical charges or currents produced by subjecting crystals or other substances to pressure; *piezo-crystals,* used for experimental wireless transmission and for standardization of wireless wave-lengths.

piezometer, n. [1. piezómeter; 2. paiezómitə], fr. Gk. *piézein,* 'to press', & **-meter.** Cp. Scrt. *pīḍáyati,* 'to press, oppress'; fr. stem *(e)pi- &c., 'on', see **epi-,** & *sed- &c., 'to sit', whence Gk. *hézomai,* 'I sit', see **sit, sedate.** Instrument for measuring compressibility of, or the pressure exerted by, liquids and gases; also one for measuring sensitiveness of the skin to pressure.

piffle, vb. intrans. & n. [1. pífl; 2. pifl]. Perh. freq. formed fr. O.E. *pyffan,* see **puff,** w. suff. *-le,* fr. O.E. *-lian.* **1.** vb. To talk or act in a feeble, inconsequent, trifling, manner. **2.** n. Rubbish, nonsense, twaddle.

pig (**I.**), n. [1. pig; 2. pig]. M.E. *pigge*; origin doubtful. **1. a** Swine, hog; **b** a young animal of the species; Phrs. *in pig,* of a sow, pregnant; *to buy a pig in a poke,* agree to, or buy something without full information about it; **c** flesh of the pig as food: *roast pig.* **2.** (colloq.) Person regarded as showing characteristics of a pig; a greedy, dirty, selfish, or otherwise objectionable person. Phr. *to make a pig of oneself,* to be gluttonous, eat too much. **3.** Oblong mass of metal, esp. iron, taken from smelting-furnace and cooled in a rough mould.

pig (**II.**), vb. trans. & intrans., fr. prec. **1.** trans. (of a sow) To bring forth young. **2.** intrans. To live, herd together, like pigs; also *pig it, pig together.*

pig-bucket, n. Pail into which are thrown scraps of food, potato parings, dish-water &c., the contents being given to the pigs.

pigeon (**I.**), n. [1. píjin, -un; 2. pídžin, -ən]. M.E., fr. O. Fr. *pijon,* fr. Lat. *pīpiōn-(em),* 'chirping bird', fr. *pīp-(īre),* 'to chirp'; imitative. See **pipe.** **1.** Wild or domesticated bird of dove species; *homing pigeon,* one trained to return home, often carrying messages. **2.** Saucer-shaped clay disk thrown into air as target for shooting; also called *clay pigeon.* **3.** Person easily duped; a greenhorn, a cully.

pigeon (**II.**), vb. trans., fr. prec. To cheat, swindle.

pigeon-breasted, adj. [1. píj(i)n brèsted; 2. pídž(i)n-brèstid]. Having a bulging, convex, chest.

pigeon-English, n. See **pidgin.**

pigeongram, n. [1. píj(i)ngram; 2. pídž(i)ngræm]. **pigeon** & **-gram.** Message carried by pigeon.

pigeon-hole, n. & vb. trans. **1.** n. **a** Hole in wall of dovecote; nesting compartment; **b** small compartment in a desk or bureau, resembling this in shape, for keeping or filing papers &c. **2.** vb. trans. **a** To classify and place (paper &c.) in pigeon-hole; **b** to put aside for later attention or consideration: *to pigeon-hole for future reference.*

pigeonry, n. [1. píj(i)nri; 2. pídž(i)nri]. **pigeon (I.)** & **-ry.** Place where pigeons are kept.

pigeon's blood, n. A very deep ruby red.

pigeon-shooting, n. Shooting at live, or clay, pigeons released from a trap.

pigeon's milk, n. Half-digested food on which pigeons feed their young.

pigeon-toed, adj. Having the toes turned inwards.

piggery, n. [1. pígeri; 2. pígəri]. **pig** & **-ery.** **1. a** Place where pigs are kept or bred; **b a** pigsty. **2.** Untidy, dirty, room or house.

piggish, adj. [1. pígish; 2. pígiʃ]. **pig** & **-ish.** Resembling a pig in character or habits; dirty, untidy; greedy, selfish.

piggishly, adv. Prec. & **-ly.** In a piggish manner.

piggishness, n. See prec. & **-ness.** **a** Piggish character and behaviour; **b** piggish state, untidiness, filthiness.

piggy, n. [1. pígi; 2. pígi]. **pig** & **-y.** Child's word for pig.

piggy-wig, n. [1. pígi wig; 2. pígi wig]. (child's word) Little pig.

pigheaded, adj. [1. pig-héded; 2. pighédid]. Stupidly obstinate, like a pig.

pigheadedly, adv. Prec. & **-ly.** In a pigheaded manner.

pigheadedness, n. See prec. & **-ness.** Quality of being pigheaded; obstinacy.

pig-iron, n. Iron in oblong masses. See **pig (I.),** 3.

pig-jump, vb. intrans. (of horse) To jump with all four feet off ground at once.

piglet, n. [1. píglet; 2. píglit]. **pig** & **-let.** Young pig.

pig-like, adj. **pig** & **-like.** **a** Resembling a pig in appearance; **b** resembling a pig in character or behaviour; piggish.

pigling, n. [1. pígling; 2. pígliŋ]. **pig** & **-ling.** Young pig.

pigment, n. [1. pígment; 2. pígmənt], fr. Lat. *pigment-(um)*, 'colouring-matter', fr. **pig^-*, stem seen in *pingere*, 'to paint', see **picture (I.)**. **1.** Substance used for colouring; paint; dye. **2.** Substance which gives its colour to animal or vegetable tissue.

pigmental, adj. [1. pigméntl; 2. pigméntl]. Prec. & **-al.** Of, consisting of, yielding, secreting, pigment.

pigmentary, n. [1. pígmentari; 2. pígməntəri]. **pigment** & **-ary.** Pigmental.

pigmentation, n. [1. pìgmentáshun; 2. pìgmentéiʃən]. **pigment** & **-ation.** Natural coloration of the skin by the presence of pigment in the cellular tissue.

pigmy, n. See **pygmy.**

pignut, n. [1. pígnut; 2. pígnat]. Earthnut.

pigskin, n. [1. pígskin; 2. pígskin]. **1.** Leather made from skin of pig. **2.** (slang) Saddle.

pig-sticker, n. Person who takes part in pig-sticking.

pig-sticking, n. Sport of spearing wild boars.

pigsty, n. [1. pígstī; 2. pígstai]. **1.** Sty for pigs. **2.** Dirty room or dwelling.

pigtail, n. [1. pígtāl; 2. pígteil]. **pig** & **tail. 1.** Plait of hair, hanging down behind, as worn by young girls, by the Chinese till forbidden after the revolution, and formerly by sailors and soldiers. **2.** Roll of twisted tobacco.

pigtailed, adj. [1. pígtāld; 2. pígteild]. Prec. & **-ed.** Wearing a pigtail.

pigwash, n. [1. pígwosh; 2. pígwɔʃ]. **a** Kitchen refuse, contents of pig-bucket, used as food for pigs &c.; **b** abusive term for thin, tasteless soup or coffee.

pigweed, n. [1. pígwēd; 2. pígwīd]. Any variety of the herb chenopodium.

pike (I.), n. & vb. trans. [1. pīk; 2. paik]. Fr. *pique*, fr. vb. *piquer*, 'to prick'. Origin doubtful. **1.** n. Long slender shaft with iron or steel head; a short spear, used in warfare as weapon for infantry, till end of 17th cent. **2.** vb. To kill, pierce, with pike.

pike (II.), n. Prob. same as prec.; so called fr. shape of its snout. Large, long-snouted, voracious, fresh-water fish, genus *Esox*.

pike (III.), n. Prob. same as **pike (I.)**. Mountain-peak, esp. in northern English hill-names, as *Langdale Pikes*.

pike (IV.), n. Abbr. fr. **turnpike. 1.** Toll bar or gate. **2.** Turnpike road.

pikelet, n. [1. píklet; 2. páiklit]. Etymol. doubtful. A small round kind of tea cake with small holes in it, eaten toasted and buttered.

pikeman, n. [1. píkman; 2. páikmən]. **1.** Keeper of turnpike. **2.** Soldier armed with a pike.

pikestaff, n. [1. píkstahf; 2. páikstāf]. **pike (I.)** & **staff (I.)**. Shaft of a pike. Phr. *plain as a pikestaff*, perfectly plain to be seen; clear, plain, to the understanding; the term was originally *packstaff*.

pikul, n. See **picul.**

pilaster, n. [1. piláster; 2. pilǽstə], fr. Fr. *pilastre*, fr. Ital. *pilastro*, fr. Med. Lat. *pilastrum*, fr. Lat. *pīla*, 'pillar', see **pillar**, & **-aster.** A pier in form of a column, with shaft, capital, and base, but rectangular and projecting about a third of its width from a wall.

pilau, pilaw, pilaf(f), n., usually [1. piláf; 2. pilǽf], but also [1. pilóu; 2. piláu], fr. Pers. *pilaw*. Oriental dish of rice boiled with meat, spices &c.

pilch, n. [1. pilch; 2. piltʃ]. O.E. *pyl(e)ċe*, 'robe of skin', M.E. *pilche*; fr. Lat. *pellicia*, 'fur garment', see **pellicle.** Infant's triangular wrapper of flannel &c.

pilchard, n. [1. pílchard; 2. píltʃəd]. Earliest form *pilcher*; etymol. uncertain; Ir. *pilseir* is fr. Engl. Large-scaled fish of herring family, found in the English Channel and off the coasts of Spain and Portugal.

pile (I.), n. [1. pīl; 2. pail]. O.E. *pīl*, 'pointed stake, spike', fr. Lat. *pīlum*, 'javelin', perh. fr. **pigslom*, fr. base **pig^-* or *pik^-*, 'to prick', as in Lat. *pictum*, P.P. of *pingere*, 'to paint; to stitch, embroider', see **picture (I.)**. **1.** Pointed stake. **2. a** Strong, pointed, vertical beam driven into ground, bed of river &c., as support for building, bridge &c.; **b** similar structure of iron, concrete &c.

pile (II.), vb. trans., fr. prec. **1.** To furnish, support, with piles. **2.** To drive piles into.

pile (III.), n., fr. O. Fr. *pile*, fr. Lat. *pīla*, 'pillar', see **pillar. 1. a** Quantity of things placed one upon another; heap: *a pile of logs, stones*; **b** specif., wood and other combustibles heaped up for burning a corpse; also *funeral pile*. **2.** Large building or mass of buildings. **3.** (colloq., fr. U.S.A.) Large quantity of money; fortune: *to make one's pile*. **4.** (elect.) Apparatus for generating electric current; a dry battery.

pile (IV.), vb. trans., fr. prec. **1. a** To form a pile from, of, out of: *to pile stones*; (mil.) *to pile arms*, to stack rifles; **b** also *pile on*, place upon, in, a pile: *to pile on coal*. Phrs. *to pile it on*, to exaggerate, intensify; *pile up*, trans. & intrans., to heap up; accumulate. **2.** To cover with a heap or pile; to load: *to pile a cart with straw* &c.

pile (V.), n. Same word as **pile (III.)**; used as name of part of machine used in minting. (archaic) Reverse side of coin; esp. in Phr. *cross or pile*, heads or tails.

pile (VI.), n. Prob. fr. **pile (I.)**. (her.) Representation of point of a pile.

pile (VII.), n., fr. Lat. *pil-(us)*, 'hair'; cp. Lat. *pilleus*, 'felt cap'; Gk. *pilos*; O. Slav. *plŭstĭ*, 'felt', cp. **plush. 1.** Hair, down, wool. **2.** Soft, hair-like surface on cloth, velvet, carpet &c.; nap.

pile-driver, n. **pile (I.)**. Machine for driving piles.

pile-dwelling, n. A lake-dwelling, resting on piles.

piles, n. [1. pīlz; 2. pailz], fr. Lat. *pila*, 'ball', prob. orig. 'ball or twist of hair', fr. *pil-(us)*, 'hair'. See **pile (VII.)**. (always pl.) Haemorrhoids.

pileus, n. [1. píleus; 2. páiliəs]. Lat. *pīleus*, *pilleus*, 'felt cap', see **pile (VII.)**. **a** (bot.) The umbrella-shaped cap of a mushroom; **b** (zool.) umbrella of a jelly-fish.

pilewort, n. [1. pílwërt; 2. páilwɜ̄t]. **piles** & **wort (I.)**. Lesser celandine.

pilfer, vb. trans. [1. pílfer; 2. pílfə]. Etymol. doubtful; perh. conn. w. **pelf.** To steal in small quantities, be guilty of petty thefts.

pilferage, n. [1. pílferij; 2. pílfəridž]. Prec. & **-age.** Act of pilfering.

pilgrim, n. [1. pílgrim; 2. pílgrim]. M.E. *pelegrim*, fr. O. Fr. **pelegrin*, fr. Lat. *peregrīnus*, 'foreign', see **peregrine. 1.** One who journeys far from place to place; a wayfarer, esp. one who wanders in a strange country; archaic, except in such Biblical Phr. as *pilgrims on earth* &c. **2.** One who visits a shrine or object of religious veneration. *Pilgrim Fathers*, band of Puritans, schismatic from the Church of England, who landed in America in 1620, and founded the colony of Plymouth; *pilgrim signs*, small badges, such as a cockle-shell, small lead or pewter figure &c., worn, usually fastened to the hat, by pilgrims on their return from a pilgrimage as proof of their having been at a particular shrine.

pilgrimage (I.), n. [1. pílgrimij; 2. pílgrimidž]. Prec. & **-age. 1. a** Visit, journey, to a shrine or other object of religious veneration; **b** journey undertaken to any place or object of historic, literary, or sentimental interest. **2.** (fig.) Man's life on earth, conceived of as a series of wanderings: *life's pilgrimage* &c.

pilgrimage (II.), vb. intrans., fr. prec. To go on a pilgrimage.

pilgrimize, vb. intrans. [1. pílgrimīz; 2. pílgrimaiz]. **pilgrim** & **-ize.** To travel as a pilgrim.

piliferous, adj. [1. pīlíferus; 2. pailífərəs], fr. Lat. *pil-(us)*, 'hair', see **pile (VII.)**, & *-i-* & **-ferous.** (bot.) Bearing hairs.

piliform, adj. [1. píliform; 2. páilifɔ̄m]. See prec. & **-form.** Resembling a hair; hair-like.

pill (I.), n. [1. pil; 2. pil], fr. Lat. *pilula*, dimin. of *pila*. See **piles. 1.** Small ball composed of medicinal drugs, intended to be swallowed whole on account of the nauseous taste; Phrs. *a bitter pill*, something disagreeable and unavoidable; *to gild the pill*, put favourable gloss upon, make amends for, a disagreeable fact. **2.** (slang) **a** (pl.) *Pills*, balls used in games, esp. billiard balls; billiards: *a game of pills*; **b** small ball used in balloting.

pill (II.), vb. trans., fr. prec. (slang) To vote against in a ballot, reject, by dropping a black ball into the ballot-box, esp. for membership of a club; to blackball.

pill (III.), vb. trans. M.E. *pilien*, 'to peel; to rob', prob. fr. Lat. *pilāre*, 'to deprive of hair'; fr. *pil-(us)*, 'hair'. See **pile (VII.)**. **1.** (archaic) To plunder, rob, pillage. **2.** (dialectal) To peel, strip off bark &c., from.

pillage, n. & vb. trans. [1. pílij; 2. pílidž], fr. Fr. *pillage*, n., fr. *pill-(er)*, 'to rob'. See prec. & **-age. 1.** n. **a** Act of plundering and robbing; **b** fruits of robbery, plunder. **2.** vb. To rob openly and with violence, esp. of hostile force &c.; to plunder, sack.

pillar (I.), n. [1. pílar; 2. pílə]. M.E. *piler*, *pelare*, fr. O. Fr. *pilĕr*, fr. L. Lat. *pīlāre*, fr. Lat. *pīla*, 'pillar', fr. earlier **peilā*; cp. Oscan *eh-peilatasset*, 'are set up'; etymol. doubtful. **1.** Column, of varying thickness and height, usually comparatively slender, used in architecture to support a superstructure, as pedestal for a statue, or standing alone as a monument. Phrs. *from pillar to post*, from one place to another, from one predicament to another; *a pillar of the state, of society*, person of strong character or important position. **2.** Something shaped like a pillar; **a** column of air, water, smoke, fire, cloud &c.; **b** column of coal &c. left as a support for roof of mine.

pillar (II.), vb. trans., fr. prec. To adorn, support, with, or as with, pillars (lit. and fig.).

pillar-box, n. Low stout hollow pillar in street, with slit near the top, for posting letters in.

pillaret, n. [1. pilarét; 2. pilərét]. **pillar** & **-et.** Small pillar.

pill-box, n. **1.** Small round box for holding pills. **2.** (facet.) **a** Small closed vehicle; **b** (mil.) small, round, concrete shelter for machine-gun &c.

pillion, n. [1. píliun; 2. píliən]. Perh. Celt., cp. Ir. *pillean*; prob. ultimately fr. Lat. *pell-(is)*, 'skin'. See **pellicle.** Seat for a second person, usually a woman, on a horse's back, placed behind the saddle of the principal rider, also applied to similar seat on a motor-bicycle. Phr. *to ride pillion*, to occupy, ride on, this seat or in this way.

pilliwinks, n. [1. píliwingks; 2. píliwiŋks]. Etymol. doubtful. An old Scottish instrument of torture for crushing the fingers.

pillory (I.), n. [1. pílori; 2. píləri], fr. O. Fr. *pellori*; etymol. doubtful. **1.** Apparatus formerly used for punishing malefactors, consisting of a wooden framework, part of which was a movable board with semicircular holes which was shut down so as to confine the neck and wrists; persons thus imprisoned were exposed to public obloquy. **2.** (fig.) Public obloquy, derision, ridicule.

pillory (II.), vb. trans., fr. prec. **a** To place in the pillory; **b** (fig.) to hold up to contempt and ridicule; to criticize savagely and publicly.

pillow (I.), n. [1. pílō; 2. pílou]. M.E. *pil(e)we*, fr. inflected form of O.E. *pyle*; cp. Du. *peluw*; Mod. Germ. *pfühl*, 'pillow', fr. Lat. *pulvi-(nus)*, 'cushion, bolster'; etymol. doubtful. **1. a** Oblong cushion stuffed with down, or feathers, or horsehair, used as support for head in bed; Phr. *to take counsel of one's pillow*, think over a matter during the night; **b** any object used as a pillow or support for the head when lying down. **2.** Any pillow-shaped object, esp. one used as support for part of machine &c.

pillow (**II.**), vb. trans. & intrans., fr. prec. **1.** trans. **a** To lay, rest, upon, to support as on a pillow: *to pillow one's head on one's arm*; **b** to serve as a pillow for: *the earth shall pillow my head tonight*. **2.** intrans. (rare) To recline upon, or as upon a pillow.

pillow-case, n. Removable cover of linen or lawn for a pillow.

pillow-slip, n. (shop word) Pillow-case.

pillowy, adj. [1. pílōi; 2. píloui]. **pillow** (**I.**) & **-y**. Looking or feeling like a pillow, esp. soft and yielding.

pillwort, n. [1. pílwĕrt; 2. pílwʌt]. **pill** (**I.**) & **wort** (**I.**). A water fern with globular spore-capsules, having a close superficial resemblance to delicate grass; it grows on the margin of ponds and lakes.

pilose, adj. [1. pílōs; 2. páilous], fr. Lat. *pilōs-(us)*, 'hairy', fr. *pil-(us)*, 'hair', see **pile** (**VII.**), & **-ose**. (bot. and zool.) Covered with hair; pilous.

pilosity, n. [1. pīlósiti; 2. pailɔ́siti]. Prec. & **-ity**. State of being hairy.

pilot (**I.**), n. [1. pílut; 2. páilət], fr. Fr. *pillotte*, fr. Ital. *pilota*; perh. fr. earlier *pedotta*, fr. Gk. *pēdón*, 'the blade of an oar'; cp. Gk. *pēdân*, 'to bound', *pēdēma*, 'bound; pulsation'; cp., w. different vowel-grade, Lat. *ped-*, base of *pēs*, 'foot'; see **pedal** & **-pod**. **1.** (naut.) One who directs the course of vessels; specif., *a licensed pilot*, person taken on board a ship to conduct it through a difficult channel or river, or to direct its course into or out from a port. **2.** (aeronautics) Person qualified to control aircraft in flight. **3.** Person who acts as guide, whether in physical, moral, or intellectual sense.

pilot (**II.**), vb. trans., fr. prec. (lit. and fig.) To act as pilot or guide to, direct course of: *to pilot a boat through a channel*; *pilot person through a forest, through spiritual difficulties*.

pilotage, n. [1. pílutij; 2. páilətidž]. **pilot** & **-age**. **1.** Act of piloting. **2.** Fee payable to pilot.

pilot-cloth, n. Thick, blue, woollen material used for seamen's overcoats.

pilot-engine, n. Locomotive engine going on ahead of a train to clear the way.

pilot-fish, n. Small sea-fish closely related to the horse-mackerel; from its habit of accompanying ships, the notion arose that it acted as a pilot, and indicated the proximity of land; it is often found in the company of sharks.

pilot-jacket, n. Pea-jacket.

pilotless, adj. [1. pílutles; 2. páilətlis]. **pilot** & **-less**. Without a pilot.

pilous, adj. [1. pílus; 2. páiləs], fr. O. Fr., fr. Lat. *pilōs-(us)*, 'hairy', see **pilose**. (bot. and zool.) Covered with hairs; pilose.

pilular, adj. [1. pílūlar; 2. píljulə]. See next word & **-ar**. Resembling a pilule in shape; globular.

pilule, pillule, n. [1. pílūl; 2. píljūl], fr. Fr., fr. Lat. *pilula*, dimin., 'globule'. See **pill** (**I.**). Small pill; globule.

pilulous, adj. [1. pílūlus; 2. píljuləs]. Prec. & **-ous**. Like a pill.

pily, adj. [1. píli; 2. páili]. **pile** (**VII.**) & **-y**. Resembling pile; downy.

pimelode, n. [1. pímelōd; 2. pímiloud], fr. Gk. *pīmelód-(ēs)*, 'fatty, like fat', fr. *pīmel-(ḗ)*, 'fat'; cp. Gk. *piar*, 'fat, grease'; *piainein*, 'to fatten'; cogn. w. Lat. *pinguis*, 'fat', see **pinguid**; Scrt. *pívā*, 'fat, swollen'; O.N. *feitr*; O.H.G. *veiz*, 'fat'; O.E. *fǣtte*, see **fat**. Cat-fish.

pimento, n. [1. piméntō; 2. piméntou], fr. Span. *pimienta*, fr. Lat. *pigment-(um)*, 'paint; (later) spice'. See **pigment**. **a** Dried aromatic berries of a West Indian tree; allspice, Jamaica pepper; **b** tree from which these berries are obtained.

pimp, n. & vb. intrans. [1. pimp; 2. pimp]. Etymol. doubtful. **1.** n. Pander, procurer. **2.** vb. To play the pimp; to pander.

pimpernel, n. [1. pímpernel; 2. pímpənɛl], fr. O. Fr. *pimprenelle*, fr. Med. Lat. *pipinella*, perh. earlier **bipinella*, dimin. of Lat. *bipenn-(is)*, 'two-winged', fr. **bi-** & *penna*, 'wing', see **pen** (**III.**). Small annual plant belonging to the order of *Primulaceae*, with heart-shaped, stalkless leaves, and scarlet, blue, or white flowers.

pimping, adj. [1. pímping; 2. pímpiŋ]. Etymol. doubtful. **a** Small, puny, sickly; **b** mean, petty.

pimple, n. [1. pímpl; 2. pímpl]. Perh. ultimately fr. Lat. *papula*, 'pimple'. See **papula**. Small superficial, inflammatory tumour or boil on the skin.

pimpled, adj. [1. pímpld; 2. pímpld]. Prec. & **-ed**. Having, covered with, pimples.

pimply, adj. [1. pímpli; 2. pímpli]. **pimple** & **-y**. Pimpled.

pin (**I.**), n. [1. pin; 2. pin]. O.E. *pinn*; cp. Du. *pin*; perh. fr. Lat. *pinna*, 'point, pinnacle'. See **pinna**. **1.** Short, stiff, pointed piece of wire with flattened head, used for fastening clothing, sheets of paper &c. Phrs. *don't care a pin*, not at all; *pins and needles*, tingling sensation in limb recovering from numbness; *neat as a new pin*, perfectly neat; *in a merry pin*, jolly mood. **2.** Large pin with ornamental head, sometimes used as a personal ornament, decoration &c.; (often in compounds) *hat-pin*, *tie-pin* &c. **3. a** Peg, short bar, of wood, metal &c., used for fastening objects together; also, **b** (in various specific compounds) *belaying-pin*, *drawing-pin*, *rolling-pin* &c., q.v. **4.** Cask holding $4\frac{1}{2}$ gallons. **5.** (pl., colloq.) Legs: *quick on one's pins*.

pin (**II.**), vb. trans. & intrans., fr. prec. **A.** trans. **1.** To fasten, support, secure, attach, with pin: *to pin things together*; *to pin a flower to one's coat*; *to pin up a notice*. Phr. *to pin one's faith to, on*, rely implicitly on. **2.** To pierce, transfix, with pin or other pointed instrument. **3. a** To hold fast, prevent from moving, keep firmly held in one place or position: *the fallen branch pinned him to the ground*; **b** also *pin down* (in above sense, and fig.): *to pin a person down (to an admission, promise* &c.), to insist on acknowledgement, fulfilment &c., refuse to release from, bind down. **B.** intrans. To be fastened by a pin or by pins; to be capable of being pinned.

pin (**III.**), vb. trans. Prob. fr. M.E. *pinde*, fr. O.E. *pyndan*, 'to shut up', fr. **pund*, 'enclosure'. See **pound** (**III.**). To enclose in a pen.

pinafore, n. [1. pínafōr; 2. pínəfɔ̄]. **pin** (**II.**), & **afore**. Loose, sleeveless covering, esp. one worn by child over a dress to keep it clean.

pinafored, adj. [1. pínaford; 2. pínəfɔ̄d]. Prec. & **-ed**. Wearing a pinafore.

pinaster, n. [1. pīnáster; 2. painǽstə]. Lat. *pīnaster*, 'wild pine', fr. *pīn-(us)*, 'pine', see **pine** (**II.**), & **-aster**. Cluster pine from Mediterranean coast.

pince-nez, n. [1. pans nā; 2. pæ̃s nei]. Fr., fr. *pincer*, 'to pinch', etymol. doubtful, & *nez*, 'nose', fr. Lat. *nās-(us)*, 'nose', see **nasal**. Eye-glasses fastening on to the nose with a spring.

pincers, n. [1. pínserz; 2. pínsəz]. M.E. *pinsours*, fr. O. Fr. *pinc-(er)*, 'to pinch', see **pinch**, & **-or**. **1.** Also *pair of pincers*, instrument for gripping, having two handles acting as levers for two jaws working on a pivot. **2.** Pincer-like organ in crustaceans &c. for seizing prey.

pincette, n. [1. pansét; 2. pæ̃sét]. Fr., fr. *pinc-(er)*, 'to pinch', see next word, & **-ette**. Small pincers.

pinch (**I.**), vb. trans. & intrans. [1. pinsh; 2. pinʃ], fr. A.-Fr. **pinchier*; cp. Fr. *pincer*; etymol. doubtful. **A.** trans. **1. a** To squeeze, nip painfully, compress between two objects, esp. thumb and first finger; **b** to squeeze, crush: *to pinch one's fingers in the door*; **c** specif., to nip off young buds of plants in order to induce growth elsewhere; also *pinch out*. **2.** (fig.) **a** To distress, cause to become thin, haggard &c.: *pinched with cold, hunger* &c.; **b** (chiefly pass.) to be short of, be in need of: *to be pinched for money*. **3.** (slang) **a** To steal; **b** to arrest. **B.** intrans. **1.** To compress painfully, squeeze. Phr. *where the shoe pinches*, the source of difficulty or trouble. **2.** To be niggardly, parsimonious, enforce strict economy.

pinch (**II.**), n., fr. prec. **1.** Sudden sharp, painful compression; nip, squeeze, esp. of a portion of skin between finger and thumb, or between any two hard objects. **2.** As much of anything as can be taken up between finger and thumb: *a pinch of salt, snuff* &c. **3.** (fig.) Stringency, stress, esp. *the pinch of poverty*. Phrs. *at a pinch*, in an emergency; *when it comes to the pinch*, at the critical moment.

pinchbeck, n. & adj. [1. pínchbek; 2. píntʃbɛk], fr. name of the alleged inventor, a London watchmaker, C. Pinchbeck, d. 1732. **1.** n. Cheap alloy of copper, zinc, and tin, made to imitate gold. **2.** adj. Sham, meretricious, not genuine: *pinchbeck manners*; *a pinchbeck hero*.

pincushion, n. [1. pínkòoshun; 2. pínkuʃən]. Small hard cushion stuffed with bran or the like, into which pins are stuck to be ready for use.

Pindari, n. [1. pindáhri; 2. pindárī], fr. Hind. *pindari*. One of a horde of mounted freebooters in India in 18th and early 19th cents.

Pindaric, adj. & n. [1. pindárik; 2. pindǽrik], fr. Lat., fr. Gk. *Pindarik-(ós)*, 'Pindaric', fr. Pindar, Greek lyric poet, c. 522–443 B.C., & **-ic**. **1.** adj. Belonging to, in the manner of, Pindar; formerly used to denote an irregular ode. **2.** n. (usually pl.) **a** Pindaric metre; **b** Pindaric odes.

pine (**I.**), vb. intrans. [1. pīn; 2. pain]. O.E. *pīnian*, 'to torture, afflict', M.E. *pīnen*; fr. O.E. *pīn*, 'pain', fr. Lat. *poena*, 'pain, penalty', see **penal**; a variant of **pain**, wh. is derived through the Fr. **1.** To languish, droop; to waste away through sorrow, illness &c.; also *pine away*. **2. a** To be intensely anxious, eager, to do something: *he is pining to go into the army*; **b** *pine for*, to desire, long ardently for, be set upon: *he pines for a sight of his home*; *pining for one's dinner*.

pine (**II.**), n. O.E. *pīn*, fr. Lat. *pīnus*, 'pine; fir', prob. fr. the same base as *pītuīta*, 'slime, viscous moisture', see **pituitary**, *opīmus*, 'fat, rich'; Gk. *pīmelḗ*, 'fat'; Scrt. *pīvaš*, 'fat'; see further **pinguid** & **fat**. **1. a** Genus, *Pinus*, of evergreen coniferous trees of the northern hemisphere, bearing sheathed clusters of needle-shaped leaves; valuable for its timber and yielding tar, resin, turpentine &c.; cp. *fir*; the typical British pine is *Pinus sylvestris*, commonly known as *Scotch fir*; **b** the timber of the pine. **2.** Pine-apple.

pineal, adj. [1. pinēal, píneal; 2. painíəl, páiniəl], fr. Fr., fr. Lat. *pīnea*, 'pine-cone', fr. *pīn-(us)*, 'pine'. See **pine** (**II.**) & **-al**. Shaped like a pine-cone; (anat.) *pineal gland*, small conical gland behind third ventricle of brain; believed to be, morphologically, a remnant of a third eye.

pine-apple, n. So named from resemblance to pine-cone. Large, deep yellow coloured multiple fruit, native to S. America and W. Indies, shaped like a pine-cone, and surmounted by a tuft of spiky leaves, having a sweet, juicy, highly flavoured flesh; also, the plant *Ananas*, which bears this fruit.

pine-barren, n. Sandy tract on which pine trees grow.

pine-beauty, n. North European moth, destructive to pine trees.

pine-cone, n. Fruit of pine, conical in shape, and bearing the seeds at the ends of the scales of which it is composed.

pine marten, n. A species of marten, q.v., found in the pine forests of Northern Europe.

pinery, n. [1. píneri; 2. páinəri]. **pine** (**II.**) & **-ery**. **1.** Forest or plantation of pines. **2.** Hothouse or plantation where pine-apples are grown.

pinetum, n. [1. pinḗtum; 2. painítəm]. **pine (II.)** & Lat. *-ētum*, 'collection of trees', as in *arboretum*. Plantation, collection, of pine trees.

pin-feather, n. **pin (I.)** & **feather.** Small undeveloped feather.

pin-fire, adj. Referring to obsolete *pin-fire cartridge*, which was exploded by means of a movable pin which struck a cap enclosed in the cartridge.

pinfold, n. [1. pínfōld; 2. pínfould]. O.E. *pundfald*; M.E. *pun(d)fald, pinfald*; fr. O.E. **pund*, 'pound', see **pound (III.)**, & *fald*, 'fold', see **fold (III.)**. Pound for straying cattle.

ping, n. & vb. intrans. [1. ping; 2. piŋ]. Imitative. **1.** n. Sharp, short, shrill, ringing sound, as of a bullet or hailstones, striking a hard substance. **2.** vb. To strike, and make this sound.

ping-pong, n. [1. píng pong; 2. píŋ pɔŋ]. Imitative, fr. sound of bat striking ball. Game resembling lawn-tennis on small scale, played on a table, with small light, celluloid balls and parchment or wooden bats.

pinguid, adj. [1. pínggwid; 2. píŋgwid], fr. Lat. *pingu-(is)*, 'fat', fr. **pīm-gwo-*, & **-id**; cp. Lat. *(o)pīmus*, 'fat, rich'; Gk. *pīmelé, píar*, 'fat'; O.N. *feitr*, 'fat'; O.E. *fǣtte*, 'fatted', see **fat**; cp. also **pine (II.)** & **pay (III.)**. Fat, greasy, oily; (of soil) rich.

pinguin, n. [1. pínggwin; 2. píŋgwin]. Native name. West Indian plant of pine-apple family.

pin-head, n., more usually *pin's head*. **1.** Round or flattened top of pin. **2.** Minute object.

pin-hole, n. Small hole made by, or as though by, a pin.

pinion (I.), n. [1. pínyun; 2. pínjən], fr. O. Fr. *pignon*, fr. Lat. *penn-(a)*, 'feather', see **pen (III.)**. **1.** **a** Distal or terminal segment of bird's wing, comprising the flight-feathers; **b** one of the wing-feathers; **c** (carving of poultry) that part of the wing corresponding to forearm. **2.** (poet.) Wing.

pinion (II.), vb. trans., fr. prec. **1.** To cut off one pinion of a bird, to prevent it flying. **2.** To bind, strap, the arms of a person tightly to his sides; to tie up, fasten, bind firmly: *to pinion a prisoner to a tree.*

pinion (III.), n., fr. Fr. *pignon*, 'gable', fr. O. Fr. *penon*, 'battlement', fr. Lat. *pinna*, 'pinnacle; fin', see **pinna**. Small cogged wheel which gears with a larger wheel, or with a toothed rack.

pink (I.), n. [1. pingk; 2. piŋk]. Origin unknown. **1.** Any plant of the genus *Dianthus*, having single or double blooms, of which carnations are double-flowered varieties; also the flower itself, which occurs in pink, crimson, and white varieties. **2.** Highest, finest type or specimen; acme: *the pink of perfection, politeness*; *in the pink of condition*, thoroughly healthy and strong; (also vulg., colloq.) *in the pink.* **3.** **a** Any of numerous shades of pale, delicate, red colour; **b** specif., the colour of scarlet coats worn by fox-hunters; **c** coat of this colour.

pink (II.), adj., fr. prec. Of a pink colour; (also in compounds with qualifying first element) *rose-pink, salmon-pink* &c.

pink (III.), n., fr. M. Du. *pincke*; etymol. doubtful. Sailing-vessel with narrow, pointed stern.

pink (IV.), vb. trans. M.E. *pinken*; prob. a variant of **pick (II.)**; cp. L.G. *pinken*, 'to peck'. **1.** To decorate the edge of by cutting out perforations, or scallops. **2.** To strike through, stab; pierce with a shot or a pointed instrument: *to pink a man through the arm.*

pink (V.), n. Etymol. doubtful. A young salmon.

pink-eye, n. **pink (II.)** & **eye.** (med.) Kind of contagious conjunctivitis, occurring in men and horses.

pinking, n. [1. píngking; 2. píŋkiŋ], fr. **pink (IV.)** **a** Operation of decorating fabrics with scallops, indentations &c.; **b** decoration of this kind.

pinkish, adj. [1. píngkish; 2. píŋkiʃ]. **pink (II.)** & **-ish.** Tending towards a shade of pink.

pinkness, n. [1. píngknes; 2. píŋknis]. **pink (II.)** & **-ness.** Quality or state of being pink.

Pinkster, n. [1. píngkster; 2. píŋkstə]. Du. *pinkster, pinksteren*, ultimately fr. Gk. *pentēkosté*, see **Pentecost.** (U.S.A.) Whitsuntide. *Pinkster flower*, the pink azalea.

pinky, adj. [1. píngki; 2. píŋki]. See prec. & **-y.** Pink, pinkish.

pin-money, n. Woman's allowance for small personal expenses; pocket-money.

pinna, n. [1. pína; 2. pínə]. Lat. *pinna*, 'pinnacle; paddle or bucket of water-wheel; fin'; cp. O.E. *finn*, 'fin', see **fin**; fr. a base **(s)pĭ-d-*, **(s)pĭ-t-*, 'point'; cp. Lith. *spitnà*, 'tongue of buckle'; Lat. *spīna*, 'thorn', see **spine**; *spīca*, 'ear of corn, spike'; O.N. *spīk*, 'spike', see **spike.** **1.** (zool.) Fin or fin-like object. **2.** (bot.) Single division of pinnate leaf. **3.** (anat.) Upper part of external ear.

pinnace, n. [1. pínas; 2. pínis, pínəs], fr. O. Fr. *pinasse*, fr. Ital., prob. fr. Lat. *pīn-(us)*, 'pine', see **pine (II.)**, meaning orig. 'thing made of pine wood'. **a** Light vessel, formerly with sails, but also having oars, now usually driven by steam or petrol, used as a tender for a larger vessel, or for a warship; **b** a ship's boat.

pinnacle (I.), n. [1. pínakl; 2. pínəkl], fr. Low Lat. *pinnācul-(um)*, 'peak, pinnacle'; dimin. of **pinna** & **-cule.** **1.** Graceful, slender, tapering turret; pointed ornamental structure crowning roof, tower, or buttress. **2.** Slender mountain peak: '*Three silent pinnacles of aged snow*' (Tennyson, 'Lotus-eaters'). **3.** Highest point, summit, culminating point: *the pinnacle of earthly greatness.*

pinnacle (II.), vb. trans., fr. prec. **1.** To elevate, place, on, or as on a pinnacle: '*Pinnacled dim in the intense inane*' (Shelley, 'Prometheus Unbound'). **2.** To ornament, supply, with pinnacles. **3.** (fig., rare) To form the culminating point, climax, of.

pinnate, adj. [1. pínāt; 2. píneit], fr. Lat. *pinnāt-(us)*, 'feathered, winged', fr. Lat. *pinna*, 'wing, feather', variant of *penna*, see **pen (III.)**. **1.** (bot.) Having leaflets arranged on either side of a common petiole. **2.** (zool.) Having the form, arrangement, of a feather.

pinnated, adj. [1. pínāted; 2. píneitid]. Prec. & **-ed.** Having pinnate leaves &c.

pinnately, adv. [1. pínātli; 2. píneitli]. See prec. & **-ly.** According to the arrangement of pinnate leaves.

pinner, n. [1. píner; 2. pínə]. **pin (II.)** & **-er.** **1.** 18th-cent. head-dress with long flaps pinned on at each side of tight-fitting cap. **2.** Apron, pinafore.

pinni-, pref. representing Lat. *pinna*, 'fin', see **pinna.** Fin; e.g. *pinniferous*, having fins; *pinnigrade, pinniped*, having fin-like feet, flippers.

pinnothere, -tere, n. [1. pínothēr, -tēr; 2. pínəþiə, -tiə], fr. Lat. *pīnot(h)ēres*, fr. Gk. *pinnot(h)ḗrēs*, 'kind of crab', found in the shell of the *pina*, a kind of mussel; fr. Gk. *pínna*, wh. is prob. a loan-word, & *tēré-(ō)*, 'to guard'; cp. Gk. *tērós*, 'warden'. Cogn. w. Scrt. *čāyati*, 'to observe'; O. Slav. *čają*, 'I wait for'. Genus of small crabs living commensally in the shells of bivalve molluscs.

pinnular, adj. [1. pínūlar; 2. pínjulə]. See next word & **-ar.** Of, like, a pinnule.

pinnule, n. [1. pínūl; 2. pínjūl], fr. Lat. *pinnula*, 'small feather', see **pinna** & **-ule.** **1.** (bot.) Division of leaflet of pinnate leaf. **2.** (zool.) Small fin or fin-like organ. **3.** Small perforated metal plate used as sight at end of quadrant, astrolabe &c.

pinny, n. [1. píni; 2. píni]. Abbr. of **pinafore.** (nursery word) Pinafore.

pinocle, pinockle, n. [1. pínokl; 2. pínəkl]. Origin unknown. A game of cards resembling bézique.

pinole, n. [1. pinóle; 2. pinóuli]. Span., fr. Mexican (Aztec) *pinolli*. Parched grain, of maize &c., also meal of mesquite beans, mixed with sugar and spices, much used as food in Mexico and S.W. States of U.S.A.

pin-prick, n. **1.** Prick, puncture, made by pin. **2.** (fig.) Petty annoyance, trifling cause of irritation.

pint, n. [1. pīnt; 2. paint]. M.E., fr. O. Fr. *pinte*; etymol. doubtful. Measure of capacity for liquids &c.; half a quart, $\frac{1}{8}$ of gallon.

pintado, n. [1. pintáhdō; 2. pintádou], fr. Port. *pintado*, P.P. of *pintar*, 'to paint', fr. Lat. **pinct-(um)*, nasalized form of *pict-(um)*, P.P. type of *pingere*, 'to paint', see **paint** & **picture.** Usually *pintado bird, petrel*, a kind of petrel; **b** guinea-fowl.

pintail, n. [1. píntāl; 2. pínteil]. **1.** Kind of duck with central tail-feathers much elongated. **2.** Kind of sand grouse with similar tail.

pintle, n. [1. píntl; 2. píntl]. O.E. *pintel*, 'penis'; etymol. doubtful. **1.** (archaic) Membrum virile. **2.** Pin, bolt, esp. one on which something pivots or turns, e.g. pin of hinge &c.

pin-wheel, n. Kind of small Catherine-wheel.

pinxit, vb. trans. [1. píngksit; 2. píŋksit]. Lat. *pinxit*, 3rd sing. perfect of *pingere*, 'to paint', see **picture.** In signature of artist, e.g. *Velazquez pinxit*, Velazquez painted this; abbreviated *pinx.*

piny, adj. [1. píni; 2. páini]. **pine (II.)** & **-y.** Of, like, abounding in, pines.

piolet, n. [1. píolā; 2. píoulei]. Fr. Ice-axe used by mountain climbers.

pioneer (I.), n. [1. pīonḗr; 2. paiəníə], fr. Fr. *pionnier*, 'foot-soldier; pioneer', fr. *pion*, fr. Lat. *pedōnem*, 'foot-soldier'. See **pawn (I.)** & **-eer.** **1.** (mil.) One of a party of troops preceding an army on the march, in order to prepare the road &c. **2.** One who prepares the way for others, **a** in exploring unknown country; **b** in trying new enterprise, of any kind; **c** in investigating new fields of knowledge &c.

pioneer (II.), vb. intrans. & trans., fr. prec. **1.** intrans. To act as, do work of, pioneer. **2.** trans. **a** To open up (a road &c.); **b** to take the lead in, show possibilities of (an enterprise &c.); **c** to guide, conduct.

piou-piou, n. [1. pyōō pyōō; 2. pjū pjū]. Fr.; prob. corrupt. of *pion*, 'foot-soldier', see **pioneer (I.)**. (Fr. army slang) Foot-soldier; cp. *poilu.*

pious, adj. [1. píus; 2. páiəs], fr. Lat. *pius*, 'dutiful'; etymol. obscure; suggested connexion w. Lat. *pūrus*, 'pure', is highly speculative. **1.** Showing, characterized by, religious devotion and piety. Phr. *pious fraud*, deception practised from an unselfish motive in the interests of a cause, or of person deceived. **2.** (archaic) Dutiful, showing filial duty.

piously, adv. Prec. & **-ly.** In a pious manner.

pip (I.), n. [1. pip; 2. pip]. Prob. fr. M. Du. *pippe*, fr. Low Lat. *pīpīta*, fr. Lat. *pītuīta*, 'mucus', see **pituitary.** **a** *The pip*, disease of fowls, characterized by accumulation of mucus in the throat; **b** (slang) sullen depression of spirits, peevishness, ill-humour: *to get, give one, the pip.*

pip (II.), n. Abbr. of **pippin.** Seed of apple, pear, orange &c.

pip (III.), n. Earlier *peep*; etymol. doubtful; perh. same as prec. **1.** Single spot on playing-card, dice &c., star on army officer's shoulder. **2.** Single diamond-shaped division on rind of pine-apple. **3.** Flowering crown of single root-stock, esp. of lily of the valley.

pip (IV.), vb. trans. Prob. fr. **pip (II.)** **1.** To hit slightly with shot, or other missile. **2.** **a** To put an end to, stop, nip in the bud (an enterprise, hostile action &c.); **b** to get the better of, circumvent, thwart action of (a person).

pipal, peepul, n. [1. pḗpal; 2. pípəl]. Hind. The bo tree.

pipe (I.), n. [1. pīp; 2. paip]. O.E. & M.E. *pīpe*, 'musical pipe; tube', fr. L. Lat. *pīpa*, formed fr. vb. *pīpāre*, 'to chirp'; an imitative word; the n. denoted a musical instrument in the form of a tube, & thence came to mean a tube in general; the word is common in many other languages, cp. Germ. *pfeife*, Du. *pijp*; Gael. *piob*, cp. *pibroch* &c. See **fife**. **1. a** One of several musical wind instruments in form of a tube, in which the notes are formed by the fingers, placed upon different holes; the earliest form was made of a reed; specif. **b** *the pipes*, Scotch bagpipes; **c** whistle used by a ship's boatswain. **2.** Sound made **a** by a pipe or flute-like instrument; **b** by a bird: '*The earliest pipe of half-awaken'd birds*' (Tennyson, 'Princess', iv.); **c** by a child or other human being with a shrill, reedy voice. **3.** A hollow tube of any length and thickness, and of whatsoever material—metal, earthenware &c., whether consisting of a single length, or in a continuous series joined endwise; applied to such tubes as employed for various specific purposes; **a** for carrying water or other liquids: *water-pipe, drain-pipe* &c.; **b** for gas; **c** for steam; **d** for conveying air to an organ: *organ pipe*; **e** tube used for blowing through upon a flame to increase the heat: *blow-pipe*; **f** long tube used in glass-blowing. **4.** Canal conveying air from mouth to the lungs: *wind-pipe*. **5.** Object used in smoking tobacco, consisting of a shortish tube, one end of which is placed in the mouth, while the other broadens into a hollow bowl in which the tobacco is placed: *to smoke, have, a pipe*, i.e. smoke tobacco in a pipe; specif., to smoke as much tobacco as can be contained in the bowl of a pipe. Phrs. *put that in your pipe and smoke it*, think that well over, ponder it, esp. of some idea which is disagreeable to hearer; *pipe of peace*, see *peace-pipe*. **6.** Measure of wine, cask holding 105 gallons; this amount of wine. **7.** (Engl. hist.) *Pipe Roll* or *Great Roll of the Pipe*, annual record of accounts, and matters relating to the Exchequer and the king's revenue, started 1131, continued to 1832; so called, it is supposed, because these documents were rolled round pipes, or from their tubular form when rolled.

pipe (II.), vb. intrans. & trans. O.E. *pīpian*, 'to chirp'. See prec. **A.** intrans. **1.** To play on a pipe. Phr. *pipe up*, begin to pipe. **2. a** (of person) To speak or sing in a thin, reedy voice; Phr. (slang) *to pipe up*, begin to sing, or to speak; **b** to whistle; **c** (of bird) to sing, chirp. **B.** trans. **1.** To play (a tune) on a pipe; to utter in a reedy voice: *to pipe a tune*; *to pipe a song*; also of a bird. **2.** (naut.) To summon, give signal to, by means of boatswain's pipe: *to pipe all hands to work* &c. **3. a** To supply with pipes; **b** to convey (water) through pipes. Phr. *to pipe one's eye*, to weep. **4.** To propagate (plants) by means of cuttings. **5.** To trim with piping: *to pipe a dress with red*. **6.** To ornament with icing forced through a pipe.

pipe-clay, n. & vb. trans. **1.** n. **a** Fine white clay used for making tobacco-pipes and for whitening military accoutrements; **b** (fig.) exaggerated attention to details of uniform &c. in a regiment. **2.** vb. To whiten with pipe-clay.

pipe-fish, n. Genus of fishes of Atlantic and eastern Pacific, having a long slender body, bony scales, and straight tube-like snout.

pipeful, n. [1. pīpfool; 2. páipful]. **pipe** (I.) & **-ful**. Amount (esp. of tobacco) which a pipe will contain at a time.

piper, n. [1. pīper; 2. páipə]. **pipe** (II.) & **-er**. **1.** One who plays on a pipe, specif., a performer on the bagpipes. Phrs. *to pay the piper*, to bear expense or consequences of proceeding; *he who pays the piper calls the tune*, he who bears the expenses of an undertaking &c., has the right to control it. **2.** Kind of fish, esp. the gurnard. **3.** Broken-winded horse. **4.** Dog trained to decoy wild-fowl into trap.

pipe-rack, n. Rack to hold tobacco-pipes.

pipe-roll, n. See under **pipe** (I.), 7.

pipe-stone, n. Red clay used by American Indians for tobacco-pipes.

pipette, n. [1. pipét; 2. pipét]. Fr., dimin. of **pipe** (I.). Small, usually graduated, tube used in chemistry for removing or transferring small quantities of liquid.

piping (I.), n. [1. pīping; 2. páipiŋ]. **pipe** (II.) & **-ing**. **1.** Action of one who plays a pipe; sound so produced. **2. a** Thin, high-pitched human voice; sound of this; **b** song of a bird. **3.** Series or system of pipes for water-supply &c. **4.** Tube-like ornament, specif. **a** covered cord for trimming dress &c.; **b** slender, cord-like lines of icing on cake &c.

piping (II.), adj. **pipe** (II.) & **-ing**. Producing sound of, as of, pipe; characterized by use of pipe. Phrs. *the piping times of peace*, i.e. when the pastoral pipe is heard instead of martial music; *piping hot*, thoroughly hot.

pipistrel(le), n. [1. pipistrél; 2. pipistrél]. Fr. *pipistrelle*, fr. Ital. *pipistrello, vipistrello*, fr. Lat. *vespertīlio*, 'bat'; prob. fr. **vespertil-(is)*, 'belonging to the evening', see **vesper**. Small reddish-brown bat, a common British bat, *Vesperugo pipistrellus*.

pipit, n. [1. pípit; 2. pípit]. Imitative. One of a group of small passerine singing birds of the wagtail family, or *Motacillidae*; they are often mistaken for larks; as the *meadow pipit*, titlark, *Anthus pratensis*, and *tree pipit*, *A. trivialis* &c.

pipkin, n. [1. pípkin; 2. pípkin]. Etymol. doubtful; prob. fr. **pipe** (I.), in sense of 'cask', w. dimin. suff. **-kin**. Small earthenware pot, usually having a horizontally set handle.

pippin, n. [1. pípin; 2. pípin]. M.E. *pepin, pipin*, 'kernel; pippin', fr. O. Fr. *pepin*, 'seed'; etymol. uncertain. Name for several varieties of apple: *Cox's Orange Pippin*; *Ribston Pippin*; originally applied to an apple raised from seed instead of being propagated by grafting.

pippy, adj. [1. pípi; 2. pípi]. **pip** (II.) & **-y**. Full of pips.

pipy, adj. [1. pīpi; 2. páipi]. **pipe** (I.) & **-y**. Consisting of, resembling, a pipe or pipes.

piquancy, n. [1. pékansi; 2. píkənsi]. **piquant** & **-cy**. Quality of being piquant.

piquant, adj. [1. pékant; 2. píkānt]. Fr., Pres. Part. of *piquer*, 'to prick', see **pique** (I.). (in Engl. chiefly in moral sense) **1.** Startling to the mind, racy, often with suggestion of slight impropriety; lively, full-flavoured: *a piquant anecdote* &c. **2.** (of flavours, sauces &c.) Having a sharp, hot, biting taste.

piquante, adj. [1. pēkáhnt; 2. pīkāt, pīkánt]. Fr., fem. of prec. Only in *sauce piquante* on bills of fare.

piquantly, adv. [1. pékantli; 2. píkāntli]. **piquant** & **-ly**. In a piquant manner.

pique (I.), vb. trans. & reflex. [1. pēk; 2. pīk], fr. Fr. *piquer*, 'to prick', see **pick**. **1.** trans. (rare, except in P.P. used as adj.) To wound the pride of, to nettle. **2.** reflex. *To pique oneself (up)on*, to pride oneself on.

pique (II.), n. Fr., fr. prec. Sense of being slighted, feeling of wounded pride; resentment at supposed humiliation.

pique (III.), n. & vb. trans. & intrans., fr. Fr. *pic*; etymol. doubtful. **1.** n. (in piquet) Scoring of 30 points by one side before the other has scored at all. **2.** vb. **a** trans. To score a pique against; **b** intrans., to score a pique.

piqué, n. [1. pékā; 2. píkei]. Fr., P.P. of *piquer*, 'to prick', see **pique** (I.). Heavy, corded, cotton fabric.

piquet, n. [1. pikét; 2. pikét], fr. Fr. *piquet*; etymol. doubtful. Card game for two players with 32 cards.

piracy, n. [1. pírasi; 2. páiərəsi], fr. Lat., fr. Gk. *peirāteia*, 'piracy', fr. *peirāt-(és)*, 'pirate'. See **pirate**. **1.** Action, occupation, of a pirate; robbery under arms on the high seas. **2.** Infringement of copyright of a published work.

piragua, periagua, n. [1. pirágwa, periágwa; 2. pirǽgwə, periǽgwə]. Span., fr. a Caribbean word. **a** Canoe made of hollowed tree-trunk; dug-out; **b** flat-bottomed, two-masted sailing-vessel.

pirate (I.), n. [1. pírat; 2. páiərət], fr. Lat. *pīrāta*, fr. Gk. *peirātés*, 'pirate, corsair', fr. *peiráein*, 'to attempt, attack', fr. *peîra*, 'trial, attempt, experience'; cp. Lat. *perītus*, 'experienced'; *perīculum*, 'test, attempt; danger', see **peril**, **experience**; another cogn. is O.E. *fǣr*, 'danger, attack', see **fear**. **1.** Person illegally attacking and plundering vessels on the high seas; sea-robber, corsair; a marauder. **2.** Armed ship used by pirates. **3.** Person who reproduces for his own profit, and without leave or payment, the literary, artistic &c. productions of another. **4.** Privately owned omnibus running on the recognized routes of other regular omnibuses, esp. one that charges other than customary fares.

pirate (II.), vb. trans., fr. prec. **1.** (rare) To rob, plunder (ship &c.). **2.** To publish, for profit (a copyright book, print &c.), without owner's permission or payment of compensation.

piratic(al), adj. [1. pirátik(l); 2. pirǽtik(l)]. **pirate** (I.) & **-ic** & **-al**. Of, pertaining to, characteristic of, a pirate; engaged in, given to, piracy.

piratically, adv. Prec. & **-ly**. After the manner of a pirate.

piraya, n. See **perai**.

pirogue, n. [1. pirṓg; 2. piróug]. Fr., fr. Span. *piragua*, see **piragua**.

pirouette, n. & vb. intrans. [1. pirooét; 2. piruét]. Fr., 'spinning top; pirouette'; cp. Ital. *piruolo*, 'peg top'. **1.** n. Rapid whirl or spin round on tiptoe in dancing. **2.** vb. To spin round on tiptoe; to turn and whirl round, as in dancing.

pis aller, n. [1. pēz alā; 2. pīz aléi]. Fr., fr. *pis*, 'worse', fr. Lat. *pējus*, 'worse', see **pejoration**, & *aller*, 'to go', see **alley** (I.). Last resource; makeshift.

piscary, n. [1. pískari; 2. pískəri], fr. Med. Lat. *piscaria*, neut. pl. of Lat. *piscārius*, 'of fish or fishing', fr. *pisc-(is)*, 'fish', see **Pisces**, & **-ary**. (law) Right, attached to the holding of land, of fishing in waters belonging to another, usually those of the lord of the manor; only in Phr. *common of piscary*.

piscatology, n. [1. piskatóloji; 2. piskətɔ́lədži], fr. Lat. *piscāt-(um)*, P.P. type of *piscāri*, 'to fish', fr. *piscis*, 'fish', see **Pisces**, & **-logy**. Science and art, the love, of fishing.

piscatorial, adj. [1. piskatṓrial; 2. piskətɔ́rial]. Next word & **-al**. Connected with, pertaining to, fishermen or to fishing.

piscatory, adj. [1. pískaturi; 2. pískətəri], fr. Lat. *piscātōri-(us)*, 'of fishermen', fr. *piscātor*, 'fisherman', fr. *piscāt-*, P.P. type of *piscāri*, 'to fish', q.v. under **Pisces**. **a** Connected with, pertaining to, fishermen or to fishing; **b** addicted to fishing.

Pisces, n. [1. písēz; 2. písīz]. Lat. *pisces*, pl. of *piscis*, 'fish'; cogn. w. Goth. *fisks*, O.E. *fisc*, 'fish', see **fish**, O. Ir. *iasc*, 'fish'; other cognates are doubtful. The twelfth sign of the zodiac.

piscicultural, adj. [1. pisikúlchural; 2. pisikáltʃərəl]. Next word & **-al**. Of, pertaining to, pisciculture.

pisciculture, n. [1. písikùlchur; 2. písikàltʃə], fr. Lat. *pisci-(s)*, 'fish', see **Pisces**, & **culture**. Rearing of fish artificially as an industry.

pisciculturist, n. [1. pisikúlchurist; 2. pisikáltʃərist]. Prec. & **-ist**. Person engaged in pisciculture.

piscina, n. [1. piséna, pisína; 2. pisínə, pisáinə]. Lat. *piscīna*, 'fish-pond; tank, cistern', fr. *pisc-(is)*, 'fish', see **Pisces**. **1.** Fish-pond. **2.** Open-air swimming-bath of ancient Roman villa &c. **3.** (eccles.) Stone basin with a drain, in wall of a church, near the altar, used by the priest for washing his hands before, or during, Mass, and for cleansing the chalice after use.

piscine (I.), n. [1. písin, pisēn; 2. písin, písin]. Fr., fr. Lat. *piscīna*, 'pond'. See prec. Bathing-pool.

piscine (II.), adj. [1. písīn; 2. písain], fr. Lat. *pisc-(is)*, 'fish', see **Pisces**, & **-ine**. Of, pertaining to, fish.

piscivorous, adj. [1. pisívorus; 2. pisívərəs], fr. Lat. *pisci-(s)*, 'fish', see **Pisces**, & **-vorous**. Fish-eating.

pisé, n. [1. pēzā; 2. pīzéi]. Fr., P.P. of *piser*, 'to pound, ram', fr. Lat. *pinsere*, 'to beat, pound', q.v. under **pestle**. Stiff clay rammed down to make walls or floors, usually between boards, which are removed when the clay hardens.

Pisgah, n. [1. pízgah, pízga; 2. pízgā, pízgə]. Heb.; range of mountains east of Jordan. Mountain from which Moses saw the Promised Land (Deut. xxxiv. 1-4); in Phr. *Pisgah sight*, glimpse of something longed for, but never attained.

pish, interj. Imitative. Used to express disgust, contempt.

pishogue, n. [1. pishṓg; 2. piʃóug], fr. Ir. *pis(r)eog*. Witchcraft, sorcery; a charm, incantation.

pisiform, adj. [1. písiform; 2. páisifɔ̄m], fr. Lat. *pīs-(um)*, 'pea', see **pea**, & **-form**. Shaped like a pea; *pisiform bone*, small bone of the carpus.

pismire, n. [1. pismīr; 2. pismaiə]. Next word & obs. *mire*, 'ant'; cp. Du. *mier*, Dan. *mȳre*; O.N. *maurr*; cp. O. Slav. *mraviji*, 'ant'; Scrt. *vamraś*, 'ant-hill'; Lat. *formīca*, 'ant'; Gk. *múrmēx*. Ant.

piss, vb. intrans. & trans. & n. [1. pis; 2. pis], fr. O. Fr. *pissier*; etymol. doubtful. (vulg.) **1.** vb. intrans. To discharge urine, make water. **2.** vb. trans. **a** To discharge as, or with, urine; **b** to drench with urine. **3.** n. Urine.

pistachio, n. [1. pistáshiō, pistáhshiō; 2. pistǽʃiou, pistáʃ(i)ou], fr. Ital. *pistacchio*, fr. Lat. *pistācium*, fr. Gk. *pistákion*, 'pistachio', perh. of Eastern origin. **1.** Nut of a small tree of Western Asia, with greenish shell, and almond-flavoured, edible kernel. **2.** Tree producing this nut. **3.** Green colour of this nut.

pistil, n. [1. pístil; 2. pístil], fr. Lat. *pistill-(um)*, 'pounder, pestle'; fr. same base as Lat. *pīlum*, 'pestle; heavy javelin'. See **pile** (I.) & **pestle**. Ovary of a seed plant, with its appendages; so called from its shape.

pistillary, adj. [1. pístilari; 2. pístiləri]. Prec. & **-ary**. Of, pertaining to, a pistil.

pistillate, adj. [1. pístilāt; 2. pístileit]. **pistil** & **-ate**. **a** Having a pistil; **b** specif., having a pistil and no stamens.

pistilliferous, adj. [1. pistilíferus; 2. pistilífərəs]. **pistil** & **-ferous**. Having a pistil.

pistilline, adj. [1. pístilin; 2. pístilin]. **pistil** & **-ine**. Of, like, having, a pistil.

pistol, n. & vb. trans. [1. pístl; 2. pístl], fr. obs. Fr. *pistole*, prob. abbr. of *pistolet*, 'weapon, dagger, pistol', fr. Ital. *pistolese*, 'dagger made at Pistoia'. **1.** n. Small fire-arm with curved butt, held in one hand for firing. **2.** vb. To shoot with a pistol.

pistole, n. [1. pistṓl; 2. pistóul]. Fr., etymol. doubtful; possibly same as prec. (hist.) European gold coin, esp. Spanish coin worth about 18s.

pistolgraph, n. [1. pístlgrahf; 2. pístlgrāf]. **pistol** & **-graph**. Apparatus for taking instantaneous photograph.

pistol-shot, n. **a** Shot fired from pistol; **b** distance pistol-shot will carry, range of pistol: *within pistol-shot*.

piston, n. [1. pistun; 2. pístən], fr. Fr., fr. Ital. *pistone*, variant of *pestone*, 'pestle', fr. *pesto*, 'to pound', fr. Lat. *pist-(um)*, P.P. type of *pinsere*, 'to pound', see **pestle**. **1.** (mechan.) Movable part of a machine, a sliding body moved by, or moving against, fluid pressure, consisting of a short cylinder within a cylindrical vessel, along which it moves to and fro. **2.** (mus.) A valve applied to wind instruments for the purpose of obtaining a chromatic scale, as in the *cornet à piston*.

piston-rod, n. Rod attached to piston to which it imparts, or from which it receives, motion.

pit (I.), n. [1. pit; 2. pit]. O.E. *pytt*, M.E. *pitt* &c.; early loan-word fr. Lat. *puteus*, 'well'; cp. Lat. *putāre*, 'to cut'; Lith. *piáuti*, 'to cut'; see **putamen** & words there referred to. **1.** Natural or artificial cavity or hole in the ground. Various specific uses: **a** hole made in digging for minerals &c.; e.g. *chalk-pit, coal-pit, gravel-pit*; **b** excavation made for specific purpose of carrying on some occupation: *saw-pit* &c.; **c** cavity glassed over for rearing plants; **d** concealed hole in ground designed to entrap wild beasts, enemies &c.; pitfall; **e** wide, shallow excavation used for cock-fighting; cockpit; **f** covered cavity in the ground in which potatoes are stored. **2.** (fig.) In Phrs. *the pit; the pit of hell; the bottomless pit*, hell. **3. a** Ground floor of auditorium of theatre, esp. part behind the stalls, under dress-circle; **b** part of audience occupying this. **4.** (U.S.A.) Part of exchange devoted to dealing in a special commodity, e.g. *wheat-pit*. **5. a** Natural hollow, depression, on surface of plant or animal body: *pit of the stomach*, depression in human body between false ribs; *armpit*; **b** indentation or scar left by disease such as smallpox &c.

pit (II.), vb. trans., fr. prec. **1.** To put, store, in pit. **2.** To mark with small hollows, depressions: *pitted with smallpox*. **3. a** *Pit against*, originally of cock-fighting, to match one cock against another; **b** (fig., in material and non-material senses) to oppose, confront, match with, put in the field against: *whole nations were pitted against each other in the Great War; to pit oneself against heavy odds; to pit one's strength, brains, skill &c. against that of another*.

pit-a-pat, adv. & n. [1. pít a pat; 2. pít ə pæt]. Imitative. **1.** adv. With a succession of light beats; palpitatingly; of the heart, *to go pit-a-pat*. **2.** n. Rapid succession of light taps or beats.

pitch (I.), n. & vb. trans. [1. pich; 2. pitʃ]. O.E. *pic*; M.E. *pich*; fr. Lat. *pic-*, stem of *pix*, 'pitch'; cp. Gk. *pissa*; Lith. *pìkis*, 'pitch'; prob. cogn. w. Gk. *piar*, 'fat'; *pitus*, 'fir'; Scrt. *pitúś*, 'sap'; Lat. *pīnus*, 'pine', see **pine** (II.). **1.** n. Thick, tenacious, resinous, black or dark-brown substance obtained by distillation of coal-tar, turpentine &c.; used for caulking seams of ships, as a preservative for wood exposed to the weather, and in making varnish &c. Phr. *as dark as pitch*, very, quite, dark. **2.** vb. To coat, smear, caulk, with pitch.

pitch (II.), vb. trans. & intrans. M.E. *pichen*; origin uncertain. **A.** trans. **1.** To set up, fix in position, erect; specif. **a** *to pitch a tent, camp, a stall in a market* &c.; Phr. *to pitch one's tent*, take up one's abode, settle; **b** (cricket) *to pitch wickets*, place stumps and bails in position. **2.** To pave with flat, thinnish stones, bedded endwise, so as to leave the narrow edge uppermost. **3. a** To hurl, throw, fling, cast, toss; often expressing impatience, disgust &c.: *to pitch a book out of window; to pitch a letter into the fire, the waste-paper basket* &c.; specif. **b** (cricket, baseball) to deliver (ball) to batsman &c.: *to pitch a ball up, short* &c.; **c** (fig., colloq.) to relate: *to pitch a yarn*. **4. a** (mus.) To set the pitch, key, of: *pitch the song in a lower key*; **b** (fig.) to express with specified degree or kind of feeling: *to pitch a story in a sentimental strain*. **B.** intrans. **1.** To encamp. **2.** To fall heavily, plunge downward; esp. *to pitch on one's head*. **3.** (of ship) To seesaw up and down lengthwise; to toss, plunge; contrasted with *roll*. **C.** Followed by adverb and preposition. *Pitch into*, (colloq.) **a** (i.) to make a vigorous physical attack upon; (ii.) to scold vehemently; **b** to eat hungrily, tuck into, eat a good deal of. *Pitch upon*, **a** to allow one's choice to light upon, decide upon: *he pitched upon the wrong man for his purpose*; **b** to come upon, as by chance: *I pitched upon the very house that suited me*.

pitch (III.), n., fr. prec. **1.** Place at which person or thing is habitually stationed or fixed; customary or appointed position: *to take up one's pitch; at one's usual pitch*. Phr. (colloq.) *to queer the pitch*, to thwart one's purpose, upset one's plans or arrangements. **2. a** Act of pitching or throwing; **b** distance to which an object is pitched. **3.** (cricket) **a** Specially levelled and rolled space between the wickets, over which the ball is bowled; **b** length, method of delivery, of bowler. **4. a** Degree of slope, degree of inclination to horizon &c.; **b** specif. (archit.) amount of slope of roof, arch &c. **5. a** (mus. and acoustics) Musical tone of a note, relative degree of acuteness or gravity, due to difference in rates of vibration; **b** (fig.) degree of intensity to which a quality exists; stage of development, esp. an extreme: *the highest pitch of excellence; to fall to a low pitch*. **6.** Height to which a falcon rises before swooping on its prey; often fig. **7.** Pitching, plunging, motion of a ship. **8.** Distance between the centres of two teeth of a cog-wheel, threads of screw &c.

pitch-and-toss, n. [1. pich an(d) tós; 2. pitʃ ən(d) tɔ́s]. Game in which coins are pitched at a mark.

pitch-black, adj. **pitch** (I.) & **black**. Intensely black.

pitch-blende, n. **pitch** (I.) & **blende**. Oxide of uranium; one of the chief sources of radium; found in Bohemia, Hungary, Cornwall, and parts of N. America &c.

pitch-dark, n. & adj. **pitch** (I.) & **dark**. **a** n. Total darkness; **b** adj., totally dark.

pitched, adj. [1. picht; 2. pitʃt], fr. P.P. of **pitch** (II.). Only in Phr. *pitched battle*, one arranged beforehand, undertaken deliberately.

pitcher (I.), n. [1. picher; 2. pitʃə]. **pitch** (II.) & **-er**. **1.** One who pitches; specif. (baseball) player who delivers ball to batsman. **2.** Granite block &c. for paving.

pitcher (II.), n., fr. O. Fr. *pichier*, fr. Med. Lat. *picārium*, variant of *bicārium*, 'vessel', see **beaker**. **1.** Large vessel, usually of earthenware, with handle and spout, for holding liquids; a jug. Phr. *little pitchers have long ears*, the gist of private discussions is apt to become widely known. **2.** (bot.) Modified leaf taking form of pitcher.

pitcherful, n. [1. picherfool; 2. pitʃəful]. Prec. & **-ful**. Amount contained in pitcher.

pitcher-plant, n. One of several East Indian and American plants, whose leaves are enlarged into pitcher-shaped organs which secrete a sweet viscous liquid that attracts insects; this liquid has digestive properties enabling the plant to assimilate insects, white of egg, and even raw meat.

pitch-farthing, n. Chuck-farthing, q.v.

pitchfork, n. & vb. trans. [1. píchfork; 2. pítʃfɔ̄k]. Earlier *pickfork*; **pick** & **fork**, w. assimilation to **pitch** (II.). **1.** n. Long-handled fork with two prongs set far apart, for lifting hay &c. **2.** vb. **a** To lift, shift, with a pitchfork; **b** (fig.) to place (person) suddenly and unexpectedly into a post or position without due consideration of his fitness and preparedness for it: *the minister pitchforked the queerest people into bishoprics*.

pitchiness, n. [1. píchines; 2. pítʃinis]. **pitchy** & **-ness**. Quality of resembling pitch; specif., blackness, inky darkness.

pitching, n. [1. píching, -in; 2. pitʃiŋ, -in]. **pitch** (II.) & **-ing**. Pavement made of stones closely packed together, and bedded edgewise in the ground.

pitch-pine, n. **pitch** (I.) & **pine** (II.). One of several highly resinous pine trees, used as timber for building.

pitch-pipe, n. **pitch** (III.) & **pipe**. Small pipe giving note of required pitch; used to start singers who are performing without instrumental accompaniment.

pitchstone, n. [1. píchstōn; 2. pítʃstoun]. **pitch (I.)** & **stone**. Volcanic rock with pitch-like lustre.

pitch-wheel, n. **pitch (III.)** & **wheel**. Gear-wheel.

pitchy, adj. [1. píchi; 2. pítʃi]. **pitch (I.)** & **-y**. Like pitch; specif., intensely black or dark.

pit coal, n. Coal obtained from pit, as distinct from *charcoal*.

piteous, adj. [1. píteus; 2. pítiəs]. M.E. *pitous*, fr. O. Fr. *pitos*, fr. Lat. **pietōs-(us)*, 'dutiful; pitiful', fr. *piet-(as)*, 'piety; considerateness, compassion', see **piety**, & **-ous**. **1. a** Exciting pity; heart-rending; **b** expressing suffering and misery; lamentable, woeful. **2.** (archaic) Feeling and showing pity.

piteously, adv. Prec. & **-ly**. In a piteous manner.

piteousness, n. See prec. & **-ness**. Quality of being piteous.

pitfall, n. [1. pítfawl; 2. pítfɔ̄l]. **pit (I.)** & **fall**. **1.** Concealed pit as trap for animal, man &c. **2.** (fig., in material and non-material sense) Unexpected difficulty or obstacle, hidden snare; an error into which it is easy to fall.

pith (I.), n. [1. pith; 2. piþ]. O.E. *piþa*; M.E. *pithe*; cp. M. Du. *pitte*; Dan. *pit*, 'marrow'. **1. a** Soft, spongy, cellular tissue forming centre of stems and branches of monocotyledonous plants; **b** soft cellular lining of rind of orange &c. **2.** Spinal cord. **3.** (fig.) Essential part, quintessence, condensed substance. **4. a** Physical or mental strength, force, vigour, concentrated energy; **b** importance, weight, esp. in Phr. *pith and moment* (Shakespeare, 'Hamlet', III. i. 86).

pith (II.), vb. trans., fr. prec. To kill by piercing spinal cord.

pithecanthropus, n. [1. pìthekanthrópus; 2. piþikænþróupəs], fr. Gk. *pithēk-(os)*, 'ape', see next word, & *ánthrōp-(os)*, 'man', see **anthropo-**. Literally, monkey-man; Pliocene animal from Java, *Pithecanthropus erectus*, intermediate between the higher apes and man.

pithecoid, adj. [1. pithékoid; 2. piþíkɔid], fr. Gk. *píthēk-(os)*, 'ape', & **-oid**; cp. Gk. *píthōn*, 'monkey'; Lat. *foedus*, 'ugly'; Lith. *baisùs*, 'terrifying'; O. Slav. *běsu*, 'devil'. Like an ape.

pithily, adv. [1. píthili; 2. píþili]. **pithy** & **-ly**. In a pithy manner.

pithiness, n. [1. píthines; 2. píþinis]. See prec. & **-ness**. Quality of being pithy.

pithless, adj. [1. píthles; 2. píþlis]. **pith (I.)** & **-less**. **a** Without pith; **b** (fig.) lacking force, vigour, stamina.

pithy, adj. [1. píthi; 2. píþi]. **pith (I.)** & **-y**. **1.** Of, pertaining to, full of, pith. **2.** (fig.) (of utterance and expression) Forcible, containing much concentrated vigour; pregnant, pointed.

pitiable, adj. [1. pítiabl; 2. pítiəbl]. O. Fr. *pitiable*. **pity** & **-able**. **1.** Arousing pity; lamentable. **2.** Exciting contempt; wretched, paltry.

pitiableness, n. Prec. & **-ness**. Quality or state of being pitiable.

pitiably, adv. See prec. & **-ly**. In a pitiable manner.

pitiful, adj. [1. pítifool; 2. pítiful]. **pity** & **-ful**. **1.** Feeling and showing pity; compassionate. **2.** Exciting pity; touching. **3.** Exciting contempt; mean, contemptible.

pitifully, adv. Prec. & **-ly**. In a pitiful manner.

pitifulness, n. See prec. & **-ness**. Quality or state of being pitiful.

pitiless, adj. [1. pítiles; 2. pítilis]. **pity** & **-less**. Showing no pity; ruthless, implacable, remorseless.

pitilessly, adv. Prec. & **-ly**. In a pitiless manner.

pitilessness, n. See prec. & **-ness**. Quality of being pitiless.

pitman, n. [1. pítman; 2. pítmən]. Man working in pit, esp. collier.

pitpan, n. [1. pítpan; 2. pítpæn]. Native. Central American dugout.

pittance, n. [1. pítans; 2. pítəns], fr. O. Fr. & M.E. *pitance*, 'pity; pious dole', fr. Lat. *piet-(as)*, 'piety; pity', see **piety**, & **-ance**. **1.** (hist.) **a** Allowance of food in monastery; **b** bequest to religious house for extra food &c. **2.** A meagre, scanty, inadequate amount or allowance of money; esp. in Phr. *a mere pittance*.

pittite (I.), n. [1. pítīt; 2. pítait]. **pit (I.)** & **-ite**. Member of audience sitting in pit of theatre.

Pittite (II.), n., fr. name of William Pitt (1759–1806). Follower, supporter, of Pitt and his policy.

pituitary, adj. [1. pitúitari; 2. pitjúitəri], fr. Lat. *pītuītāri-(us)*, fr. *pītuīta*, 'slime; phlegm', fr. stem **pī-*, 'sap, juice', seen in Lat. *pīnus*, 'pine', see **pine (II.)** & **pinguid**; *opīmus*, 'rich' &c. Of, secreting, mucus or phlegm; *pituitary membrane*, mucous membrane of the nose; *pituitary gland, body*, ductless gland attached to base of brain, having important functions in the metabolism of the body, growth &c.

pituitous, adj. [1. pitúitus; 2. pitjúitəs], fr. Lat. *pītuīt-(a)*, 'phlegm', see prec., & **-ous**. Pituitary.

pit-viper, n. A very venomous American snake, belonging to same group as the rattlesnake, so named from the pit or depression near the eye and nostril.

pity (I.), n. [1. píti; 2. píti], fr. O. Fr. *pitet*, fr. Lat. *pietāt-(em)*, 'piety; compassion'. See **piety**. **1.** Grief, sorrow, sympathy, felt for the sufferings or misfortunes of another; compassion: *to have a feeling of pity for one*; *to have no pity on one*. Phrs. *to have, take, pity (up)on*, to show mercy to, compassionate; feel regret for sufferings of; *for pity's sake*, form of entreaty. **2.** Source or ground of regret, disappointment, discontent &c.: *what a pity!*; *more's the pity*, so much the worse; *the pity is*, what is to be regretted is.

pity (II.), vb. trans., fr. prec. To feel pity for; often expressing regret mixed with tolerant contempt, felt by a superior for the misfortunes of a weaker, inferior being.

pitying, adj. [1. pítiing; 2. pítiiŋ]. Prec. & **-ing**. Feeling, expressing, pity.

pityingly, adv. Prec. & **-ly**. In a pitying manner.

pityriasis, n. [1. pìtiríasis; 2. pìtiráiəsis], fr. Gk. *pitūron*, 'bran', & **-iasis**. (med.) Name given to various skin diseases, characterized by scaly patches of skin, as *P. alba*, dandruff; *P. rubra*, exfoliating dermatitis.

pivot (I.), n. [1. pívut; 2. pívət], fr. Fr. *pivot*; origin unknown. **1. a** Fixed point, generally a short shaft or pin, upon the upper end of which something turns; **b** (mil.) unit, or position, round which a body of troops wheels when changing front. **2.** (fig.) Circumstance, fact, argument, upon which others depend.

pivot (II.), vb. intrans., fr. prec. (lit. or fig.) To turn on, or as on, a pivot; to hinge.

pivotal, adj. [1. pívutal; 2. pívətəl]. See prec. & **-al**. **1.** Of, forming, a pivot. **2.** (fig.) Of the nature of a pivot; of cardinal importance, having other events &c. depending upon it.

pixy, pixie, n. [1. píksi; 2. píksi]. Earlier *pisky*; cp. Swed. *pysk*, 'a little fairy'. Origin unknown. Small fairy, elf, esp. in S.W. England.

pizzicato, adv., adj., & n. [1. pìtsikáhtō; 2. pìtsikátou]. Ital., fr. *pizzicare*, 'to twitch, pluck'. (mus. direction) **1.** adv. (to be played) By plucking string (of violin) with a finger instead of with the bow; abbreviation *pizz.* **2.** adj. (of note, passage) Played in this way. **3.** n. Note, phrase &c., played thus.

pizzle, n. [1. pízl; 2. pízl]. Cp. Du. *pees*. Penis of animal, esp. of a bull.

placability, n. [1. plākabíliti; 2. pleikəbíliti], fr. Lat. *plācābilitāt-(em)*, 'placability'. See next word & **-ity**. Quality of being placable.

placable, adj. [1. plákabl, plákabl; 2. pléikəbl, plǽkəbl], fr. Lat. *plācābil-(is)*, 'easily appeased,' fr. *plāc-(āre)*, 'to appease', see **placate**, & **-able**. Easily appeased, capable of being pacified; willing to forgive.

placably, adv. Prec. & **-ly**. After the manner of one who is placable.

placard, n. & vb. trans. [1. plákard; 2. plǽkād], fr. O. Fr. *placard*, fr. *plaquier*, 'to plaster', fr. Du. *plakken*, 'to glue', & **-ard**. **1.** n. Single sheet of paper with written or printed notice on one side, for display on wall &c. as public notice, advertisement &c.; poster. **2.** vb. also [1. plakárd; 2. plækád]. **a** To fix, paste, a placard on; **b** to display as a placard; **c** to advertise, give notice of, by means of a placard.

placate, vb. trans. [1. plākát; 2. pleikéit], fr. Lat. *plācāt-(um)*, P.P. type of *plācāre*, to appease'; cogn. w. Lat. *plācēre*, 'to please', q.v. under **placet**. To appease, pacify, allay resentment of; to conciliate.

place (I.), n. [1. plās; 2. pleis], fr. Fr., fr. Lat. *platēa*, 'street; open space', fr. Gk. *plateia (hodós)*, 'broad road, street', fr. fem. of *platús*, 'wide, broad', cp. **platy-** & see **plain (I.)** & words there referred to. **1. a** Specific part of, or position in, space; a definite locality: *one cannot be in two places at once*; **b** inhabited area of a country, a unit of population, having specific boundaries, **a** distinct social, political, administrative, identity, a distinguishing name; village, town &c.: *Bath is a very hot place in the summer*. **2.** Position, portion of space, in recognized relation to certain objects, allotted for particular purpose, to serve as accommodation for particular objects or persons: *to take one's place at table &c.*; *a place for everything*; *the members of the Government were all in their places* (in House of Commons). Phrs. *in place of*, as substitute for, instead of; *in, out of, place*, appropriate, inappropriate; *to give place to*, yield to, give way to, make way for: *to take place*, happen; *to take the place of*, act as substitute for. **3.** Open space, a square, or short street in town (esp. in proper names): *Gloucester Place*. **4.** (i.) Building, apartment &c.; also (ii.) an open space, adapted or used for a specific purpose: *place of business*; *place of worship, amusement &c.*; *bathing-place*; *market-place*. **5. a** Private house, residence, dwelling: *come down to my place tonight*; **b** country house and estate; seat: *to have a nice little place in the country*; *we saw quite a number of gentlemen's places*; **c** also in names of country mansions, e.g. *Penshurst Place*. **6.** Spot, specific part of surface of the body, or some other object: *a sore, tender, place on the leg*; *a rough place in the road*. **7.** Section, part of, or passage in, a book &c.: *put something to mark the place*; *to find one's place*; *the author repeats that in another place*. **8. a** Rank, station, in life, position in the world, degree; esp. in Phr. *to know one's place*; *to keep people in their proper places*; **b** (i.) relative position held in respect of intellectual or moral worth or eminence, or in the estimation of mankind: *Hardy must always occupy a high place as an English novelist*; *the place of Pope among poets has been much disputed*; **c** relative merit as tested by examination: *a high place in the final schools*. **9. a** Official position, political office: *politicians are apt to become greedy of place*; **b** situation of a domestic servant: *ten years in his last place*; *as much as my place is worth to do &c.*, I shall lose my place if I do &c.; **c** position, membership of an athletic team, crew &c.: *a place in the Oxford boat &c.* **10.** Duty proper to position, office &c.: *it's not my place to correct his errors*. **11.** Single step, stage, in argument &c.: *in the first place*. **12.** (racing) Position among first three at end of race: *the mare was beaten for a place by a short head*. **13.** (math.) Relative position of figure in number or group; specif., of figures after decimal point: *to calculate a result to four places of decimals*.

place (II.), vb. trans., fr. prec. **1. a** To put, set, in specified place, condition, position; to arrange in, assign to, proper places: *to place a cake in the oven*; *to place sentries*; **b** to put, cause to go, into a specific place or spot within a definite area: *to place one's balls skilfully in tennis* &c. **2. a** To arrange for employment of, secure appointment for, in a position, occupation, office &c.: *to place a boy in a good situation*; **b** to appoint to, select for, a post, office &c.: *he has been placed at the head of his department.* **3.** To put into appropriate hands, arrange for carrying out, performance or production of: *to place an order with a firm, a book with a publisher* &c. **4.** To invest, transfer as investment: *to place one's money to the best advantage.* **5.** To recognize, identify, connect with past experience, remember circumstances which connect one with: *I knew his face, but I couldn't quite place him.* **6.** To size up, estimate the true character or class of; to fit into true and proper sphere: *he was very rich, yet vulgar and uneducated, a very difficult person to place.* **7.** To fix, rest, repose: *to place confidence in, reliance upon.* **8.** (racing) To indicate final relative position of horse &c. in race, esp. of first three. Phr. *to be placed*, finish among first three.

place-card, n. Card indicating place of guest at formal dinner.

place-kick, n. (Rugby football) A kick at goal, after a try, the ball being taken out in a straight line from the place where it was touched down, and placed on the ground by one player and kicked by another.

placeman, n. [1. plásman; 2. pléisman]. Person occupying an official position; (usually contemptuous) a jack-in-office.

placenta, n. [1. plasénta; 2. pləséntə]. Lat. *placenta*, 'cake', fr. Gk. *plakoûnt-*, stem of *plakoûs*, 'flat cake'; cp. Gk. *pláx*, 'anything flat', see **plank. 1.** (anat.) Mass of tissue adherent to inside of the womb, connected, for nutritive purposes, to the foetus by the umbilical cord, and ejected, as afterbirth, after delivery. **2.** (bot.) Part of a seed-vessel to which the ovules are attached.

placental, adj. [1. plaséntl; 2. pləséntl]. Prec. & **-al**. Of, pertaining to, the placenta.

placer, n. [1. pláser, pláser; 2. pléisə, plǽsə], fr. Am. Span. *placer*, fr. *plaza*, 'place', fr. Lat. *platēa*, 'broad street'. See **place** (I.). Surface alluvial or glacial deposit containing gold or other valuable minerals in particles, which are obtainable by washing; *placer-mining*, method of washing out gold &c. from alluvial deposits.

placet, vb. & n. [1. pláset; 2. pléiset], also [1. pláket; 2. plǽkit]. Lat. *placet*, 3rd sing. pres. indic. of *placēre*, 'to please'; the orig. meaning was 'to smooth, make even'; cogn. w. Lat. *plānus*, fr. *placnos, 'level, flat, even'. See **plane** (II.) & **plain** (I.) & cp. **please. 1.** vb. *Placet, non placet*, it pleases, it does not please me; formulae used in voting for, or against a motion in congregation and convocation at Oxford and Cambridge. **2.** n. Vote given in favour of a motion: *the placets were in the majority.*

placid, adj. [1. plásid; 2. plǽsid], fr. Lat. *placid-(us)*, 'smooth, level, calm'; cp. *placēre*, 'to please', & see prec. (lit. and fig.) Calm, serene, peaceful, unruffled: *a placid stream*; *a placid mind, temper*; *placid smile* &c.

placidity, n. [1. plasíditi; 2. plæsíditi], fr. Lat. *placiditāt-(em)*, 'mildness, serenity', fr. *placid-(us)*. See prec. & **-ity**. State or quality of being placid.

placidly, adv. [1. plásidli; 2. plǽsidli]. **placid** & **-ly**. In a placid manner.

placket, n. [1. pláket; 2. plǽkit]. Origin doubtful. **1.** Pocket in woman's skirt. **2.** Also *placket-hole*, opening in skirt at back, for ease in putting it on, and to give access to the pocket.

placoid, adj. [1. plákoid; 2. plǽkoid], fr. Gk. *plak-*, stem of *pláx*, 'level surface; plate', q.v. under **plank**, & **-oid. 1.** (of fish-scale) Plate-like. **2.** (of fish) Having placoid scales.

plafond, n. [1. pláfon; 2. plǽfɔ̃]. Fr., 'ceiling'. **1.** Ceiling; esp. one carved or painted on the under side of a floor. **2.** Design painted or carved on ceiling.

plagal, adj. [1. plágl; 2. pléigl], fr. Med. Lat. *plagalis*, fr. *plaga*, 'plagal mode', prob. fr. Med. Gk. *plágios*, 'oblique; plagal', fr. Gk. *plágios*, 'oblique, slanting'; cp. Gk. *plágia*, 'sides'; *pélagos*, 'flat surface of sea, open sea' (see **pelagian** (II.)); Lat. *plaga*, 'hunting-net, curtain'; O.H.G. *flah*, 'flat'; fr. base *p(e)lā-, *p(e)lə- &c., 'flat, extended'. See **plane** (I.), **plain** (I.), **plank**, & words there referred to. Of a musical mode, having its key-note in the middle of its compass.

plagiarism, n. [1. pláj(i)arizm; 2. pléidž(i)ərizəm]. **plagiary** & **-ism. 1.** Act of plagiarizing. **2.** The product of plagiarism.

plagiarist, n. [1. pláj(i)arist; 2. pléidž(i)ərist]. **plagiary** & **-ist**. Person practising plagiarism.

plagiarize, vb. trans. [1. pláj(i)arīz; 2. pléidž(i)əraiz]. Next word & **-ize**. To adopt and reproduce as one's own, to appropriate to one's own use, and incorporate in one's own work, without acknowledgement, the ideas of others, passages from their writings &c.

plagiary, n. [1. pláj(i)ari; 2. pléidž(i)əri], fr. Lat. *plagiāri-(us)*, 'plunderer; kidnapper; plagiarist', fr. *plagi-(āre)*, 'to kidnap', fr. *plagi-(um)*, 'kidnapping', fr. Gk. *plági-(os)*, 'oblique; crooked; treacherous'. See **plagal** & **-ary**. (rare) **1.** Plagiarism. **2.** Plagiarist.

plagio-, pref. representing Gk. *plágio-(s)*, 'oblique, slanting, sideways', see **plagal**. Oblique; e.g. *plagiocephalic*, having the skull differently developed at either side, asymmetric; *plagioclastic*, (of rock) tending to break along oblique planes; *plagiodont*, having oblique teeth; *plagiostome*, genus of fishes, including sharks and rays, having mouth placed horizontally below snout.

plague (I.), n. [1. plāg; 2. pleig] M.E. & O. Fr. *plage*, fr. Lat. *plāga*, 'stroke; injury; affliction; pestilence', prob. fr. Gk. (Doric) *plāgā*, 'blow'; cp. Lat. *plangere*, 'to strike; to beat the breast'; Gk. *plḗssein*, 'to strike'; O.E. *flōcan*, 'to clap'; Goth. *flōkan*, 'to lament'; Lith. *plakù*, 'I strike'; O. Slav. *plakati*, 'to weep, lament'; orig. meaning of the base, prob. 'to beat flat', in wh. case it is cogn. w. that in Lat. *plānus*, 'level, flat'. See **plain** (I.) & **plane** (II.). **1. a** Affliction, calamity; **b** (colloq.) any vexatious or troublesome person or thing; annoyance: *that child is the plague of my life*; *the midges are a regular plague this year.* **2.** Pestilence, malignant epidemic disease, specif., *the plague*, bubonic or oriental plague.

plague (II.), vb. trans., fr. prec. **1.** To vex, harass, annoy, trouble; to worry, pester. **2.** To afflict with plague.

plaguesome, adj. [1. plágsum; 2. pléigsəm]. **plague** & **-some**. (colloq.) Troublesome, annoying.

plague-spot, n. **1.** Spot or swelling characteristic of plague. **2. a** Place where plague is prevalent; **b** (fig.) a centre of moral evil and contagion.

plaguily, adv. [1. plágili; 2. pléigili]. See next word & **-ly**. (colloq.) In a plaguy manner; so as to annoy.

plaguy, adj. & adv. [1. plági; 2. pléigi]. **plague** & **-y. 1.** adj. (colloq.) Annoying, vexatious. **2.** adv. **a** Exasperatingly, vexatiously; **b** thoroughly, exceedingly.

plaice, n. [1. plās; 2. pleis]. M.E. *plais*, fr. O. Fr. *plaiz*, fr. L. Lat. *platessa*, 'plaice', prob. fr. a Gk. word, fr. Gk. *plat-(ús)*, 'flat', see **platy-**. Edible flat-fish of Northern Europe, *Pleuronectes platessa*, with chestnut-coloured orange-spotted uppermost side.

plaid, n. [1. plad, plād; 2. plæd, pleid]. A Celt. word; cp. Gael. *plaide*, Ir. *plaid*, 'blanket'; etymol. doubtful; perh. contracted fr. Gael. *peallaid*, 'sheep skin', cogn. w. Lat. *pellis*, 'skin, hide', see **fell** (I.). **1.** Long rectangular piece of woollen cloth, often with tartan pattern, worn folded over shoulder, back, and breast as outer garment by Scottish Highlanders. **2.** Cloth from which a plaid is made; cloth with a chequered pattern; *shepherd's plaid*, cloth with a chequer of black on white ground.

plaided, adj. [1. pláded, pláded; 2. plǽdid, pléidid]. Prec. & **-ed. 1.** Wearing a plaid. **2.** Made of the cloth of which plaids are usually made.

plain (I.), adj. [1. plān; 2. plein], fr. O. Fr. *plein*, fr. Lat. *plān-(us)*, 'level, flat; clear, distinct; lowly, humble'; the base *p(e)lā-, *p(e)lə-, 'flat, spread out', also 'to strike or press flat', appears in many words in all the Aryan languages; cp. **a** w. senses, 'level, even, flat, broad', Gk. *platús*, 'wide', see **platy-**; O.N. *flatr*, 'level', see **flat**; Lith. *platùs*, 'broad'; O. Slav. *ploskŭ*, 'broad'; **b** w. sense 'flat surface or object', Lat. *palma*, 'palm of hand', see **palm**; *planta*, 'sole of foot', see **plantar**; Gk. *pélanos*, 'sacrificial cake'; *pláx*, 'surface of sea &c., flat plate', see **place, plate, plank**, *pélagos*, 'level surface of sea; high seas,' see **pelagian** (II.); related to O.E. *flōr*, 'floor', see **floor**; **c** w. sense 'to strike or press flat', Scrt. *práthati*, 'spreads out'; Lett. *plāt*, 'spread thinly'; Lith. *plóninti*, 'flatten, make thin'; **d** w. sense 'to strike', Lat. *plaudere*, 'to clap', see **plaudit**; *plangere*, 'to strike; to beat the breast', see **plain** (IV.), vb.; *plāga*, 'stroke', see **plague. 1. a** Easy to perceive by the sight or hearing; clear, distinct; clearly visible or audible; reverse of indistinct, blurred, dim, vague: *plain writing, print*; *the figures in the picture are quite plain*; *a plain articulation*; **b** easy to understand, clear to the intelligence, unambiguous: *the meaning is plain*; *plain English*; *a plain statement.* Phr. *plain sailing*, for nautical sense see **plane** (IV.); (chiefly fig.) conditions, circumstances, unattended by difficulty, obstacles to progress, or complexities of any kind. **2. a** Not elaborate or highly wrought; simple: *a perfectly plain dress*; Phr. *plain clothes*, mufti, contrasted with uniform, or official dress; **b** (of material) without ornamentation, not figured or variegated: *plain silk*; *a plain wall-paper*; **c** *plain cooking, food, diet*, simple, not rich; *plain cook*, one who can roast and boil, and make simple dishes. **3.** (of persons) **a** Simple, unsophisticated; straightforward, blunt, downright; not subtle: *the plain man*; hence **b** (of thoughts, character, expression) frank, sincere, ingenuous, candid: *a plain unvarnished tale*; *a plain statement*; *plain speaking*, outspokenness; *plain dealing*, honesty, straightforwardness. **4.** (of persons) Lacking beauty; not handsome; unprepossessing in appearance; rather ugly.

plain (II.), adv., fr. prec. Clearly and distinctly visible, audible, or comprehensible: *to write, speak, plain.*

plain (III.), n., fr. O. Fr. *plain*, fr. Lat. *plānum*, 'level ground, plain', fr. neut. form of *plānus*, 'flat, level'. See **plain** (I.). Large tract of flat, level, open country.

plain (IV.), vb. intrans. M.E. *plainen*, fr. O. Fr. *plaign-*, Pres. stem of *plaindre*, 'to mourn', fr. Lat. *plangere*, 'to strike; to beat the breast, to lament'; see **plague** & cp. **plaint** & **complain**. (archaic and poet.) **1.** To complain; mourn, lament, sorrow. **2.** To sing or cry plaintively, with melancholy.

plain-chant, n. Plain-song.

plainly, adv. [1. plánli; 2. pléinli]. **plain** (I.) & **-ly**. In a plain manner (in all senses).

plainness, n. [1. plánnes; 2. pléinnis]. See prec. & **-ness**. State or quality of being plain (in all senses).

plainsman, n. [1. plánzman; 2. pléinzmən]. Inhabitant of a plain.

plain-song, n. Ancient system of Gregorian church music, proceeding in a movement known as the first species of counterpoint;

still used in Roman Catholic and some English churches.

plain-spoken, adj. Outspoken, frank, candid.

plaint, n. [1. plānt; 2. pleint], fr. O. Fr. *plaint*, fr. Lat. *planctus*, 'lamentation', fr. Lat. *planct-(um)*, P.P. type of *plangere*, 'to lament'. See **plain (IV.)**, **plague**, & cp. **complain**. **1.** (archaic and poet.) Lamentation, mourning, complaint. **2.** (legal) Written accusation, formal statement of grievance and request for redress; suit.

plaintiff, n. [1. plāntif; 2. pléintif], fr. O. Fr. *plaintif*, 'complaining'. See next word. Person who brings an action in a court of law; opposed to *defendant*.

plaintive, adj. [1. plāntiv; 2. pléintiv], fr. O. Fr. *plaintive*, fem. of *plaintif*, 'mournful, complaining', fr. *plainte*, 'complaint'. See **plaint**. **a** Expressing mild, pensive sorrow, and gentle melancholy; mournful, sad; **b** complaining, inclined to recite personal woes and worries as though to excite compassion of hearers.

plaintively, adv. Prec. & **-ly**. In a plaintive manner.

plaintiveness, n. See prec. & **-ness**. Quality of being plaintive.

plait (I.), n. [1. plat; 2. plæt]. M.E. *plait*, fr. O. Fr. *pleit*, fr. Lat. *plicit-(um)*, P.P. type of *plicāre*, 'to fold or wind together', see **plicate**. **1.** Also (rarely) *plat*, braid, length of three or more interlaced strands of hair, ribbon &c. **2.** Flattened fold, more usually *pleat*, q.v.

plait (II.), vb. trans., fr. prec. **1.** To braid, weave into a plait. **2.** To pleat.

plan (I.), n. [1. plan; 2. plæn], fr. Fr. *plan*, fr. Lat. *plānus*, 'flat'. See **plain (I.)**. **1.** Drawing, made by projection, on flat surface, of designed or completed structure, showing dimensions, relative positions &c. of different parts. **2.** Map of small district, town &c. **3. a** Methodical and considered arrangement of the various means and steps necessary to carry out a project: *I have a plan for overcoming our difficulties*; **b** method of procedure, mode of action: *it would be a good plan to break the journey in Paris*; **c** something planned; a scheme, project, design: *his plan was brought to naught.*

plan (II.), vb. trans., fr. prec. **1.** To make a plan of, represent section of, on flat surface. **2.** To draw up plans for, design in detail: *to plan a house* &c. **3.** To think out plans for, determine on and devise methods of carrying out (a project &c.); also *plan out*: *to plan out a continental tour, a book* &c.

planarian, adj. & n. [1. planárian; 2. plənέərian], fr. L. Lat. *plānārius*, 'flat, level', fr. Lat. *plānus*. See **plain (I.)** & **-arian**. (zool.) **a** adj. Of, belonging, related to a class *Turbellaria*, of very lowly organized flat, worm-like animals, found in fresh- and sea-water; **b** n., an animal of this class.

planch, n. [1. plahnsh; 2. plān(t)ʃ], fr. Fr. *planche*, 'plank', fr. Lat. *planca*, 'board, plank', see **plank**. Slab or plate of metal, stone &c.; specif., supporting slab of fire-brick &c., used in an enamelling oven.

planchet, n. [1. pláhnshet; 2. plán(t)ʃit]. Prec. & **-et**. Plain metal disk out of which a coin is to be made, before stamping.

planchette, n. [1. plàhnshét; 2. plànʃét, plɑ̃ʃét]. Fr., dimin. of *planche*, 'plank'. See **planch** & **-ette**. Small heart-shaped board supported by two small wheels and having a pencil-point attached, which on being lightly touched by the hands of two persons appears to write automatically; used, sometimes in combination with a oui-ja board, by mediums and those interested in psychical phenomena &c.

plane (I.), n. [1. plān; 2. plein], fr. Fr. *plane*, fr. Lat. *platanus*, fr. Gk. *plátanos*, 'plane-tree'; i.e. the tree with wide-spreading branches', fr. Gk. *plat-(ús)*, 'wide, broad', see **platy-** & **plain (I.)**. Also *plane tree*, one of genus, *Platanus*, of wide-spreading trees with broad, palmate leaves, which periodically shed large portions of the old outer bark, esp. *Platanus orientalis*, native of Greece and W. Asia; *P. occidentalis*, of N. America, is known as button-wood or sycamore.

plane (II.), n. & vb. trans., fr. Fr. *plane*, fr. L. Lat. *plāna*, 'plane', fr. *plān-(āre)*, 'to level, make flat', fr. *plān-(us)*, 'flat'. See **plain (I.)**. **1.** n. **a** Tool for smoothing surface of wood, usually consisting of a block of wood or a metal frame with a handle on upper side, having a steel blade slightly projecting beneath lower surface which pares off a shaving from the surface across which it is pushed; also several compounds: *jack-plane, rabbet-plane, moulding-plane, smoothing-plane* &c.; **b** machine tool, usually *planing machine*, for smoothing metal surfaces. **2.** vb. **a** To smooth with, or as with, a plane; **b** to remove (inequalities &c.) with a plane: *to plane away irregularities.*

plane (III.), n., fr. Lat. *plānum*, 'level ground'. See **plain (III.)**. **1. a** A perfectly level surface, without curve, elevation, or depression on any part; *inclined plane*, a slope, incline, one of the simple mechanical powers; **b** specif. (geom.) surface such that a straight line drawn between any two points in it lies wholly in that surface. **2.** Level, pitch, stage, of development or attainment: *a high plane of civilization, excellence, virtue* &c.

plane (IV.), adj., fr. Lat. *plān-(us)*, 'flat, level'. See **plain (I.)**. Having neither elevations nor depressions; completely flat, level: *a plane figure, surface*; *plane sailing*, navigating a ship as if the earth's surface were flat; in fig. sense usually *plain sailing*. See **plain (I.) b.**

plane (V.), n. & vb. intrans. Abbreviated fr. **aeroplane**. **1.** n. **a** One of the ailerons of an aeroplane; **b** an aeroplane. **2.** vb. (of aircraft) To move through the air, drift downwards &c. by means of the planes, without using engines.

planet, n. [1. plánet; 2. plǽnit]. M.E., O. Fr. *planete*, fr. Lat. *planēta*, 'wandering star', fr. Gk. *planḗtes (astéres)*, 'wandering (stars)', fr. *planē-(s)*, 'wandering'; cp. Gk. *plános*, 'wandering course'; *plázein*, 'to strike; to move out of the right road; to wander'; cogn. w. Lat. *plangere*, 'to strike', q.v. under **plague**. Any one of the chief opaque heavenly bodies which revolve around the sun; contrasted with *fixed stars* or *suns*; they were formerly supposed to exert an influence upon human destiny.

planeta, n. [1. planēta; 2. plænítə], fr. Med. Lat. *planēta*, perh. same as prec., but connexion obscure. Folded chasuble worn in some churches during Advent and Lent.

plane-table, n. & vb. trans. **1.** n. Instrument used for plotting lines of a survey direct from observation, consisting of a drawing board on a tripod, and a ruler for pointing at the object observed. **2.** vb. To survey by means of a plane-table.

planetarium, n. [1. plànetárium; 2. plænitέəriəm], fr. L. Lat. *planētārium*, neut. form of *planētārius*, 'of planets', **planet** & **-ary**. Model of the solar system; an orrery.

planetary, adj. [1. plánetari; 2. plǽnitəri], fr. L. Lat. *planētāri-(us)*, 'of planets', **planet** & **-ary**. **1. a** Of, pertaining to, the planets; *planetary hour*, twelfth part of planet's natural day or night; *planetary system*, solar system; specif. **b** pertaining to the earth considered as a planet; mundane. **2.** Having the nature of a planet; wandering, erratic.

planetoid, n. [1. plánetoid; 2. plǽnitɔid]. **planet** & **-oid**. Minor planet, asteroid.

planet-stricken, -struck, adj. Affected by the supposed influence of the planets; bewildered.

plangency, n. [1. plánjensi; 2. plǽndžənsi]. See next word & **-cy**. State of being plangent.

plangent, adj. [1. plánjent; 2. plǽndžənt], fr. Lat. *plangent-(em)*, Pres. Part. of Lat. *plangere*, 'to beat, strike; to lament', q.v. under **plague**. Resounding, esp. of sound of breaking waves, beating, dashing, noisy.

plani-, pref. representing Lat. *plān-(us)*, 'level, flat'. See **plane (II.)**. Level, flat, plane; e.g. *planigraph*, instrument for reproducing drawings on a different scale; *planimeter*, instrument for measuring area of irregular plane figure &c.; *planisphere*, plane projection of the whole or part of a sphere.

planish, vb. trans. [1. plánish; 2. plǽniʃ], fr. O. Fr. *planiss-*, stem of obs. *planir*, 'to smooth', fr. *plan*, 'smooth, level'. See **plane (IV.)** & **-ish**. **1. a** To beat smooth, polish, or toughen (metal) by hammering or by rolling; also **b** to polish photographs with a roller.

plank (I.), n. [1. plangk; 2. plæŋk], fr. A.-Fr. *planke*, fr. L. Lat. *planca*, 'board, slab', prob. a loan-word fr. a nasalized form of the Gk. stem **plak-*, 'flat; broad', seen in Gk. *pláx*, 'flat surface; flat plate'. See **plain (I.)**. **1. a** Specif., long, flat, broad piece of sawed timber, thicker than a board, being usually 2 to 6 in. thick and at least 6 in. wide; **b** a wooden board of any width and thickness. Phr. *to walk the plank*, to be compelled to walk blindfold along a plank projecting over sea from ship's side, esp. as pirates' method of disposing of victims. **2.** (fig.) A basal principle upon which one stands, as upon a plank; used esp. of a principle adopted by a political party; cp. use of *platform.*

plank (II.), vb. trans., fr. prec. **1.** To cover, floor, with planks. **2.** (slang) *Plank down*, to put, place, lay, down, esp. *to plank down one's money, five shillings* &c.; to pay out readily; to advance.

plank-bed, n. Bed made of boards, esp. one without mattress, in a prison.

planking, n. [1. plángking; 2. plǽŋkiŋ]. **plank** & **-ing**. Series of planks forming floor &c.

plankton, n. [1. plángkton; 2. plǽŋktən], fr. Gk. *plagktón*, neut. form of *plagktós*, 'wandering', fr. perf. stem of *plázein*, 'to wander'. See **planet**. Collective term for the minute plant and animal organisms floating, feebly swimming, or drifting on or just below the surface of lakes, rivers and seas, cp. *benthos* and *nekton.*

planless, adj. [1. plánles; 2. plǽnlis]. **plan (I.)** & **-less**. Without a plan; showing no design or purpose in construction.

plano-, pref. representing Lat. *plān-(us)*, 'level, flat'. See **plain (I.)** & **plane (II.)**. Level, flat; e.g. *planoconcave, -convex*, flat on one side and concave, convex, on the other &c.

plant (I.), n. [1. plahnt; 2. plānt]. O.E. *plante*, fr. Lat. *planta*, 'sprout, shoot', prob. fr. **plantāre*, 'to prepare, smooth, the ground for sowing' &c., related to Lat. *planta*, 'sole of the foot', fr. base meaning 'flat, level'. See **plain (I.)**. **1.** Any vegetable organism as distinguished from an animal. **2.** (popular) **a** An individual specimen of one of the smaller plants, as contrasted with trees, with all its parts, in the earth; **b** (trade term) a young plant, cutting, sapling, ready for planting. **3. a** Complete mechanical equipment, or apparatus, machines, implements &c., necessary for carrying on some specific industrial operation: *lighting plant, farming plant*; (by extension) **b** equipment, books, scientific apparatus &c. for carrying out piece of intellectual work, research &c. **4.** (slang) Hoax, take-in, swindle; put-up job.

plant (II.), vb. trans., fr. O.E. *plantian*, fr. Lat. *plantāre*, 'to plant, transplant', fr. *planta*, 'slip, shoot'. See prec. **1.** To place, set, in the ground with intention that it shall grow: *to plant seeds, cabbages, a tree, corn, crops* &c.; *plant out*: **a** to set (seedlings &c.) in ground at intervals; **b** to transfer from pot, frame &c. to ground. **2.** To furnish, supply, with plants &c. for growth in: *to plant a garden* &c. **3.** To introduce, deposit, in river &c.: *to plant fish* &c. **4.** To fix firmly, thrust in, insert, place firmly in position: *to plant a stake in the ground*; *plant a dagger in one's heart.* **5.** To place in position, allot position to, station : *to plant oneself*, take up a position. **6.** To aim and strike, to deliver, place (a blow). **7. a** To place permanently, establish, give home to : *to plant people as settlers in a colony* ; **b** to supply (colony &c.) with settlers. **8.** (fig.) To inculcate, introduce, instil, into the mind; implant: *to plant ideas.* **9.** (slang) **a** To conceal : *to plant one's plunder* ; **b** *plant on*, to palm off on : *to plant worthless shares on the public.*

plantable, adj. [1. pláhntabl; 2. pl*á*ntəbl]. Prec. & **-able.** Capable of being planted.

plantain (**I.**), n. [1. pláhntin, plántin ; 2. pl*á*ntin, plǽntin]. M.E. *plantein*, fr. O. Fr. *plantain*, fr. Lat. *plantāginem*, 'plantain', fr. *planta*, 'sole of foot', fr. the flat leaves, see **plantar.** Genus of wild plants, growing as weeds, esp. *Greater Plantain*, perennial herb with low-growing, tough, ribbed, flat leaves, and a spike of inconspicuous flowers.

plantain (**II.**), n., fr. Span. *pla(n)tano*, fr. Lat. *platanus*, 'plane tree'. See **plane** (**I.**). Species of banana, both the tree and the fruit.

plantar, adj. [1. plántar ; 2. plǽntə], fr. Lat. *plantār-(is)*, 'of the sole', fr. *planta*, 'sole of foot'; cp. Gk. *platús*, 'broad'. See **platy-** ; & cp. **plain** (**I.**). (anat.) Belonging to, connected with, the sole of the foot.

plantation, n. [1. plahntáshun ; 2. plāntéiʃən]. **plant** (**II.**) & **-ation. 1.** Collection, group, of growing trees; recently planted wood, grove. **2.** Area devoted to planting and cultivating certain crops, esp. cotton, tobacco, tea, coffee ; *plantation song, melody*, one sung by negroes on the cotton plantations of N. America. **3. a** (hist.) Act of colonizing; state of being colonized, settled ; **b** colony.

planter, n. [1. pláhnter; 2. pl*á*ntə]. **plant** (**II.**) & **-er. 1. a** One who plants and cultivates certain crops as a business ; specif., one engaged in cultivation of cotton, tobacco, tea, coffee, rubber ; **b** owner of a cotton or other plantation. **2.** Instrument for planting. **3.** (Ir. hist.) English or Scottish settler to whom forfeited lands in north of Ireland were granted in 17th cent.

plantigrade, adj. & n. [1. plántigrād ; 2. plǽntigreid], fr. Lat. *plant-(a)*, 'sole', see **plantar**, & *-grad-(us)*, 'walking', fr. *gradus*, 'step', see **grade. 1.** adj. (zool.) Walking on the flat foot, with whole of sole and the heel touching the ground ; contrasted with *digitigrade.* **2.** n. Plantigrade animal, as the bear, badger &c.

plantlet, n. [1. pláhntlet; 2. pl*á*ntlit]. **plant** (**I.**) & **-let.** Little plant.

plantlike, adj. [1. pláhntlīk ; 2. pl*á*ntlaik]. Resembling, of the nature of, a plant.

plant-louse, n. Small insect infesting plants, esp. aphis.

plantocracy, n. [1. plahntókrasi ; 2. plāntókrəsi], fr. **planter** & **-cracy**, on anal. of *aristocracy.* (hist.) Planters of W. Indies as a dominant class.

planxty, n. [1. plángksti ; 2. plǽŋksti]. Ir.; etymol. doubtful. Irish dance tune ; the dance itself.

plaque, n. [1. plahk, plak ; 2. plāk, plæk]. Fr., fr. Flemish *placke*, 'small coin'. **1. a** Disk or slab of metal, porcelain, ivory &c., plain or ornamented ; such a disk enamelled ; **b** the enamels themselves. **2.** (pathol.) Small patch.

plaquette, n. [1. plakét ; 2. plækét]. Fr. Prec. & **-ette.** A small plaque ; **a** rectangular plaque used for portraiture ; **b** delicate design engraved or struck upon a plaquette.

plash (**I.**), n. [1. plash ; 2. plæʃ]. O.E. *plæsċ*, M.E. *plasch*, 'pool'; cp. M. Du. *plasch* ; prob. imitative. Shallow pool or puddle.

plash (**II.**), vb. trans. & intrans. Cp. Germ. *platschen.* Prob. imitative. **1.** trans. **a** To strike (water) gently, strike surface of ; **b** to splash lightly. **2.** intrans. (of water) To splash, break in ripples.

plash (**III.**), n., fr. prec. Light sound of water breaking gently on shore ; sound of water being struck : *the plash of oars.*

plash (**IV.**), vb. trans., fr. O. Fr. *plaissier*, fr. Lat. *plectere*, 'to plait, interlace' ; cp. O.H.G. *flehtan* ; O.N. *flētta*, 'to plait' ; Gk. *plektḗ*, 'net' ; *plékein*, 'to plait' ; Lat. *plicāre*, 'to fold', see **plexus, plicate, ply** (**I.**), & **pleach** ; prob. fr. same base as Goth. *falþan*, O.E. *faldan*, 'to fold', see **fold. 1.** To interweave ; bend and twist together : *to plash branches &c. into a hedge.* **2.** To make, repair, by plashing : *to plash a hedge.*

plashy (**I.**), adj. [1. pláshi ; 2. plǽʃi]. **plash** (**I.**) & **-y.** Abounding in shallow, muddy, pools ; damp, marshy, or muddy.

plashy (**II.**), adj. **plash** (**III.**) & **-y.** Like the sound of plashing water.

plasm, n. [1. plazm ; 2. plæzəm], fr. Gk. *plásma*, 'something moulded'. See next word. (biol.) Living matter of which a cell is composed.

plasma, n. [1. plázma ; 2. plǽzmə]. Lat. *plasma*, fr. Gk. *plásma*, 'something moulded', fr. *plássein*, 'to mould, model'; cp. Gk. *-pláthos*, 'modeller'; etymol. doubtful. Cp. **plastron. 1.** Green, transparent kind of quartz. **2.** Protoplasm. **3.** Colourless liquid forming chief part of blood, milk, lymph &c., contrasted with the corpuscles or the fat globules.

plasmatic, adj. [1. plazmátik ; 2. plæzmǽtik], fr. Gk. *plasmat-*, stem of *plásma*, see prec., & **-ic.** Of, pertaining to, plasma.

plasmic, adj. [1. plázmik ; 2. plǽzmik]. **plasm** & **-ic.** Pertaining to, consisting of, plasm or plasma.

plasmin, n. [1. plázmin ; 2. plǽzmin]. **plasma** & **-in(e).** (chem.) Proteid contained in blood plasma, to which coagulation is due.

plasmo-, pref. Form of **plasm** or **plasma** used in compounds. Protoplasm ; e.g. *plasmogen*, true, formative, protoplasm ; *plasmogeny, -gony*, spontaneous generation of organisms ; *plasmology*, science of the ultimate elements of living matter ; *plasmolysis*, contraction of the protoplasm of a living cell through the action of certain reagents.

plasmodium, n. [1. plazmṓdium ; 2. plæzmóudiəm]. Mod. Lat. fr. **plasma.** Mass of protoplasm formed by the union of a number of single cell organisms or protozoans.

plaster (**I.**), n. [1. pláhster ; 2. pl*á*stə]. O.E. *plaster*, fr. L. Lat. *plastrum*, fr. Lat. *emplastrum*, fr. Gk. *émplastron*, 'plaster'. See **en-** & **plastron** ; cp. also **plasm** & **plastic. 1.** Plastic composition of lime, sand, and water, rendered cohesive by admixture of hair, hardening when dry ; used to coat and give smooth surface to walls of house &c. **2. a** External, local remedy, consisting of a layer of medicinal drugs, or of curative or irritant substances with a backing of some fabric, e.g. *diachylon-, mustard-, corn-plaster* &c. ; **b** adhesive fabric used to protect a cut, abrasion of the skin &c., to strap the edges of a wound together, or to keep bandages in position &c. : *sticking-plaster.*

plaster (**II.**), vb. trans., fr. prec. **1. a** To cover, coat (wall &c.), with plaster ; **b** to smear, bedaub, with : *plastered with mud.* **2. a** To cover, stick all over, plentifully : *plastered with jewels* ; **b** to affix in abundance, give large supply of : *to plaster labels all over a parcel.* **3.** To apply a medicated or adhesive plaster to. **4.** To mix, doctor, with plaster of Paris or gypsum : *to plaster wine.*

plasterer, n. [1. pláhsterer ; 2. pl*á*stərə]. **plaster** (**II.**) & **-er.** One who, that which, plasters ; specif., man engaged in the trade of plastering walls &c.

plaster of Paris, n. So called from large deposits near Paris. Gypsum ground fine and mixed with water, used as a fine, hard plaster and as a cement for bedding dressed ashlars ; also mixed with ordinary plaster to give extra hardness.

plastery, adj. [1. pláhsteri ; 2. pl*á*stəri]. **plaster** (**I.**) & **-y.** Like plaster.

plastic, adj. [1. plástik ; 2. plǽstik], fr. Lat., fr. Gk. *plastik-(ós)*, 'of moulding', fr. *plássein*, 'to mould, model'. See **plasma. 1.** Capable of moulding, shaping, giving form ; formative, creative : '*plastic Nature*' (Pope). **2.** Connected with the art or process of moulding, modelling in clay &c., or of producing various forms and shapes by chiselling and carving : *the plastic arts*, modelling and sculpture. **3. a** (of clay or other similar substance) Capable of being moulded and shaped by pressing and squeezing ; **b** (biol., of organic matter) capable of undergoing, manifesting, metabolic changes ; **c** (fig., of the character, mind) capable of being formed, guided, moulded; pliable, impressionable. **4.** (med.) **a** Concerned with the restoration of injured, lost, or diseased parts of the body, by transference of fresh tissue, artificial modelling &c. : *plastic surgery* ; **b** fibrinous : *plastic pleurisy.*

plastically, adv. [1. plástikali ; 2. plǽstikəli]. Prec. & **-al** & **-ly.** In a plastic manner.

plasticine, n. [1. plástisēn ; 2. plǽstisīn]. **plastic** & **-ine.** Proprietary composition of specially treated clay which does not quickly dry and harden ; used for modelling.

plasticity, n. [1. plastísiti ; 2. plæstísiti]. **plastic** & **-ity.** State or quality of being plastic.

plastron, n. [1. plástrun ; 2. plǽstrən]. Fr., fr. Ital. *piastrone*, fr. *piastr-(a)*, 'breastplate', fr. L. Lat. *plastrum*, fr. Gk. *(ém)-plastron*, fr. *plássein*, 'to model'; etymol. doubtful. Cp. **plasma. 1.** Steel breast-plate worn under a coat of mail. **2.** Leather guard to protect the breast in fencing. **3. a** Ornamental, detachable front on woman's dress from throat to waist ; **b** (rare or obs.) man's shirt-front. **4.** Part of shell of turtle or tortoise covering the belly.

plat (**I.**), n. [1. plat ; 2. plæt]. Variant of **plot** (**I.**). Small piece of ground ; patch, plot : '*take and cast him into the plat of ground*' (2 Kings, ix. 26).

plat (**II.**), n. & vb. trans. Variant of **plait.**

plat (**III.**), n. [1. plah ; 2. plā]. Fr., 'dish', fr. adj. *plat*, 'broad'. See **plate** (**I.**) & cp. **platter.** Course of food at a meal.

platan, n. [1. plátan ; 2. plǽtən], also **platanus** [1. plátanus ; 2. plǽtənəs], fr. Lat. *platanus*, 'plane tree'. See **plane** (**I.**). Oriental plane tree.

plate (**I.**), n. [1. plāt ; 2. pleit]. M.E. *plāte*, fr. O. Fr., fem. of *plat*, 'flat' ; ultimately fr. Gk. *platús*, 'flat, broad'. See **platy-** & words there referred to. **1.** Relatively thin sheet or lamina of metal. Various specific uses : **a** such a piece of metal used to protect and strengthen : *the iron or steel plates on a warship* ; **b** thin sheet of metal or other material, kind of girder laid horizontally upon a wall to carry rafters of roof. **2. a** Thin sheet of copper or steel upon which designs or pictures &c. are engraved, and from which impressions are taken ; **b** impression printed from such a plate ; **c** specif., such an impression used as an illustration in a book ; (by extension) any full-page illustration in a book, esp. when separate from the text, no matter by what process produced ; **d** small thin strip of copper with name, address &c. engraved upon it, from whence visiting cards are printed. **3. a** Thin rectangular sheet of brass upon which name is engraved, fastened to the front door of physician, surgeon, dentist &c. ; Phr. (of a doctor) *to put up his plate in Harley Street* &c., to start practice at specified address ; **b** smaller, oblong sheet of brass, bearing name and date of birth and death, fastened to a coffin. **4.** Electrotype or stereotype mould of page of a book taken from the original type. **5.** (coll.) Various articles of gold, silver, pewter, or electroplate used at table ; cups, dishes, candlesticks, forks, spoons &c. : *piece of plate*, any one of such articles ; *church plate*, patens, chalices &c. **6.** Specif., articles similar to above made of *electroplate* ; contrasted with *silver.* **7. a** (i.) Flat, shallow utensil, usually made of porcelain or earthenware, upon which food is placed before persons sitting at meals; (ii.) amount of food contained on a plate: *a plate of soup, of ham* &c. **b** object in form of a plate in which the collection is taken in church: *to put a shilling in(to) the plate.* **8. a** A cup &c. of silver or the like given as a prize to winner of horse race; hence, **b** a race for such a prize; (loosely) a race for a prize; *selling plate,* horse-race for a prize, the winner of which must be sold at a specified price. **9.** (dentistry) Thin piece of hardened vulcanite, modelled to exact shape of roof of mouth and upper gums, to which artificial teeth are fixed; also *dental plate.* **10.** Sheet of glass covered with a film sensitive to light, upon which photographs are taken. **11.** Specific uses: **a** (baseball) the home base beside which the batter stands; **b** (wireless) the anode, formerly a flat plate, now a metal cup or cylinder, of a thermionic valve.

plate (**II.**), vb. trans., fr. prec. **1.** To cover, sheathe, overlay (ships &c.), with metal plates as protection. **2.** To overlay with a thin layer of gold, silver &c., on a foundation of other metal: *plated spoons* &c. **3.** (print.) To make electrotype or stereotype from.

plate-armour, n. **a** Defensive armour of small, overlapping metal plates; **b** plates of metal used as protective covering for ships of war.

plateau, n. [1. plahtṓ; 2. platóu]. Fr. *plateau,* fr. O. Fr. *platel,* dimin. of *plat,* 'dish', see **plat** (**III.**). **1.** Elevated plain, tableland. **2.** Decorative plaque. **3.** (obs.) Woman's flat-topped hat.

plate-basket, n. Baize-lined basket in which spoons and forks &c. are kept.

plateful, n. [1. plā́tfool; 2. pléitful]. **plate** (**I.**) & **-ful.** Amount (of food) that fills a plate; as much as a plate will contain.

plate-glass, n. Fine quality glass made in large thick sheets, used for large, esp. shop, windows.

plate-layer, n. Workman employed in laying and repairing railway lines, so called from the now obsolete type of rails, called 'plates' or plate-rails.

plate-mark, n. **a** One of several official marks on gold, silver, or pewter plate, e.g. in England (on silver) a lion, or leopard's head, letter indicating date of manufacture, initials of maker; **b** impression left on the paper of an engraving &c. by the plate.

platen, platten, n. [1. plátn; 2. plǽtn], fr. O. Fr. *platine,* fr. *plat,* 'flat', see **plate** (**I.**), & **-ine.** (print.) Iron plate which presses paper upon the inked type to receive impression; corresponding part in a typewriter.

plate-powder, n. Powder used for polishing gold and silver plate &c.

plater, n. [1. plā́ter; 2. pléitə]. **plate** (**II.**) & **-er.** **1.** Person engaged in plating with gold or silver. **2.** One engaged in making or attaching metal plates to ships &c. **3.** (racing) Horse that runs chiefly in selling races.

plate-rack, n. Rack in which dinner-plates &c. are put to drain after washing.

plateresque, adj. [1. plateresk; 2. plætərésk], fr. Span. *plateresco,* fr. *plata,* 'silver plate'. The name given to a highly ornate style of decoration in Spanish Renaissance architecture of the 16th cent. from its resemblance to the work of silversmiths.

platform, n. [1. plátform; 2. plǽtfɔ̄m], fr. O. Fr. *plateforme,* 'ground-plan', fr. *plate,* 'flat', see **plate** (**I.**), & **form.** **1.** Natural or artificial surface, terrace, flooring &c. raised slightly above adjoining level; esp. **a** raised floor or stage for public speaking &c., hence, (by transf.) the principal supporters of a public speaker who have seats on this; **b** raised stage of wood, stone &c. built parallel with the line at railway station, from which passengers enter the carriages, and upon which they alight on leaving train; **c** open stage at entrance to tram-car or omnibus, upon which the conductor or ticket-collector stands. **2.** Main principles which, for the moment, underlie the policy of a political party; declaration of these principles; cp. use of *plank.*

plating, n. [1. plā́ting; 2. pléitiŋ]. **plate** (**II.**) & **-ing.** **1. a** Art or process of coating with gold or silver; **b** coat of metal used in this process. **2.** (horse-racing) Competing for plates.

platinic, adj. [1. platínik; 2. plætínik]. See **platinum** & **-ic.** Of, like, containing, platinum.

platiniferous, adj. [1. plàtiníferus; 2. plætiníferəs]. See **platinum** & **-ferous.** Containing, yielding, platinum.

platinize, vb. trans. [1. plátinīz; 2. plǽtinaiz]. See **platinum** & **-ize.** To coat with platinum.

platinoid, n. [1. plátinoid; 2. plǽtinɔid]. See **platinum** & **-oid.** **1.** Alloy of nickel, zinc &c., somewhat resembling platinum. **2.** One of the platinum metals.

platinotype, n. [1. plátinotīp; 2. plǽtinətaip]. See **platinum** & **-type.** **1.** Method of producing photographs by the use of platinum-coated plates. **2.** Picture produced by this process.

platinous, adj. [1. plátinus; 2. plǽtinəs]. See next word & **-ous.** Belonging to, containing, platinum.

platinum, n. [1. plátinum; 2. plǽtinəm]. Earlier *platina,* fr. Span. *platina,* dimin. of *plata,* 'silver', ultimately fr. Gk. *plat-(ús),* 'broad', see **plate** (**I.**). A rare metallic element, tin white or steel grey in colour, of great weight, very ductile and malleable, having a melting-point 3,227 Fahrenheit, and showing great resistance to acids.

platinum-black, n. Black powder made from platinum.

platinum metals, n. pl. Name given to certain metals, found with and allied to platinum, as iridium, osmium, palladium &c.

platitude, n. [1. plátitūd; 2. plǽtitjūd]. Fr., fr. *plat,* 'flat', see **plate** (**I.**) on anal. of *latitude.* **1.** Dullness, commonplaceness, insipidity. **2.** Commonplace remark, pompous enunciation of an obvious and familiar principle or fact; a truism dully expressed.

platitudinarian, n. & adj. [1. plàtitūdinárian; 2. plætitjūdinéəriən]. See prec. & **-arian.** **1.** n. Person addicted to platitudes. **2.** adj. Of the nature of, consisting of, platitudes.

platitudinize, vb. intrans. [1. plàtitū́dinīz; 2. plætitjū́dinaiz], fr. **platitude** & **-ize.** To utter platitudes.

platitudinous, adj. [1. plàtitū́dinus; 2. plætitjū́dinəs]. See prec. & **-ous.** Pertaining to, of the nature of, a platitude.

platitudinously, adv. Prec. & **-ly.** In a platitudinous manner.

Platonic, adj. & n. [1. platónik; 2. plətɔ́nik], fr. Lat. *Platōnic-(us),* fr. Gk. *Platōnik-(ós),* 'of Plato', fr. *Plátōn,* 'Plato, Greek philosopher' (d. circa 347 B.C.), & **-ic.** **1.** adj. Of, pertaining to, Plato or Platonism; *Platonic love, affection,* one between persons of the opposite sex into which passion, or desire, does not enter. **2.** n. Follower of Plato; one learned in the philosophy or doctrines of Plato.

Platonically, adv. [1. platónikali; 2. plətɔ́nikəli]. Prec. & **-al** & **-ly.** In a Platonic manner.

Platonism, n. [1. plā́tunizm; 2. pléitənizəm]. See **Platonic** & **-ism.** The philosophical system of Plato.

Platonist, n. [1. plā́tunist; 2. pléitənist]. See prec. & **-ist.** Follower of Plato; student of his philosophical doctrines.

Platonize, vb. trans. & intrans. [1. plā́tunīz; 2. pléitənaiz]. **Platonic** & **-ize.** **1.** trans. To convert, transform, to Platonism. **2.** intrans. To follow the philosophical principles of Plato.

platoon, n. [1. platóon; 2. plətū́n], fr. Fr. *peloton,* 'ball, cluster, platoon', fr. *pelote,* 'ball', see **pellet.** Military unit formerly consisting of half a company, now one of the four divisions, of about 60 men each, of a company in an infantry battalion, commanded by a lieutenant or second lieutenant.

platter, n. [1. pláter; 2. plǽtə]. M.E. & O. Fr. *plater,* fr. *plat,* 'dish'. See **plat** (**III.**) & cp. **plate** (**I.**) **a** Specif., large, flat, thick slab of wood formerly used as a dish, or as a plate for food; **b** a large dish or plate; **c** round wooden slab, often decorated at edges, upon which a loaf is placed for cutting; also *bread platter.*

platy-, pref. representing Gk. *platú-(s),* 'broad; flat, level'. See cognates under **plain** (**I.**), **plane** (**I.**) & **plantar,** & cp. **plate** (**I.**). Broad; flat; e.g. *platycephalous,* flat-skulled; *platyphyllous,* broad-leaved &c.

platypus, n. [1. plátipus; 2. plǽtipəs]. See prec. & *poûs,* 'foot', see **pedal.** The ornithorhynchus or *duck-billed platypus.*

platyrrhine, adj. & n. [1. plátirīn; 2. plǽtirain], fr. **platy-** & Gk. *rhīn-(ós), rhīs,* 'nose', see **rhino-.** **1.** adj. Having a broad, flat nose with nostrils set widely apart, esp. applied to the American division of tropical monkeys and marmosets, *Platyrrhina.* **2.** n. A platyrrhine monkey.

plaudit, n. [1. pláwdit; 2. plɔ́dit], fr. Lat. *plaudit-(e),* imperat. pl. of *plaudere,* 'to applaud, clap', earlier **plōdere,* cp. **explode;** cp. also Lith. *plóti, plóju,* 'to clap, strike', see **plague, plain** (**IV.**). **a** Clapping of hands or other expression of public approbation; **b** any expression of approbation, praise.

plausibility, n. [1. plàwzibíliti; 2. plɔ̀zibíliti]. See next word & **-ity.** State or quality of being plausible.

plausible, adj. [1. pláwzibl; 2. plɔ́zibl], fr. Lat. *plausibil-(is),* 'praiseworthy', fr. *plaus-(um),* P.P. type of *plaudere,* 'to applaud', see **plaudit,** & **-ible.** **1.** (of statements, arguments &c.) Pleasing or reasonable on the surface; apparently sound; generally with suggestion of fundamental unsoundness; specious. **2.** (of person &c.) Inviting confidence, employing specious arts or arguments, fair-spoken, but not trustworthy or sound.

plausibly, adv. Prec. & **-ly.** In a plausible manner.

play (**I.**), vb. intrans. & trans. [1. plā; 2. plei]. O.E. *pleġ(i)an,* 'to play' (in various senses); M.E. *pleien;* prob. cogn. w. O.H.G. *pflegan;* Mod. Germ. *pflegen,* 'to take care of, look after; to perform, carry out; to have the habit of' &c.; cp. also O.E. *pleoh,* 'danger, risk', & *pliht,* 'danger, damage', see **pledge** (**I.**), & **plight** (**I.**). The O.E. n. *plega* has the various senses of 'quick movement; game, athletic sport, fighting; applause' &c.; the O.S. vb. *plegan* means 'to promise; to guarantee, be answerable for'. The word is clearly a very anct. W. Gmc. vocable, but it cannot at present be traced further back. **A.** intrans. **1.** To move about lightly, irregularly, fitfully, or capriciously; to dance, frolic, flutter, flicker: *the wind plays in the trees, through one's hair; butterflies play among flowers; a smile played on his lips; leaves play in the breeze; sunlight plays on the water; lightning plays in the sky.* **2.** (Of part of machine &c.) To move freely, to be capable of a limited amount of free movement. **3.** To be aimed and discharged at in regular or irregular succession: *guns play on a fort; a hose plays on flames* &c. **4. a** To amuse, divert, oneself, engage in any form of occupation, or activity, the object of which is recreation; contrasted with *to work;* **b** (of animals and young children) to gambol, frolic, caper about, frisk. **5.** **a** To take part in a specific game: *to play in a set of tennis;* Phrs. *to play fair,* (lit. and fig.) act fairly; *to play fast and loose,* behave irresponsibly and unreliably; *to play false,* betray, break a promise &c.; *to play into the hands of,* contrive to give advantage to; **b** to strike ball, as at cricket, in particular way: *to play back, forward; to play on,* to hit ball on to one's wicket. **6.** To gamble: *to play for money.* Phr.

played out, exhausted, with no more vitality or energy; worn out, of no further use; out of date. **7.** To be suitable for a game, be in good condition: *the lawn plays well.* **8. a** To perform on a musical instrument; **b** (of instrument) to produce characteristic musical sounds. **9.** To act, take part, perform rôle, in dramatic piece. Phrs. *to play up to*, support by sympathetic acting; (fig.) to support, back up by one's actions; *to play to the gallery*, so as to please the least cultivated part of the audience; hence, (fig.) to seek popular applause by undignified or unworthy action, behaviour, utterance &c. **B.** trans. **1.** To cause to move lightly and freely; make to hover, flutter, flash, flicker, upon or round about an object: *to play a searchlight upon an object.* **2.** (obs. or rare) To use, wield, ply: *to play a good knife and fork*, eat plentifully. **3.** To aim and discharge, direct, with rapid succession of missiles &c.: *to play a stream of water, bullets, upon.* **4.** To wear out, tire out (a fish), by alternately allowing it to take out the line, and then pulling it in. **5.** To amuse oneself with, perform, execute, engage in, as recreation &c.: *to play a game, cricket, tennis* &c. Phrs. *to play the game*, play, act, in accordance with rules; (fig.) behave fairly and honestly; *to play a deep game*, have a covert scheme on hand; *to play ducks and drakes with*, to squander; *to play it* (*rather*) *low down*, behave meanly, unscrupulously, dishonourably. **6.** To carry out, execute, put into effect, without serious intent: *to play a practical joke, trick, on one*; *to play one a trick.* Phr. *to play tricks with*, to meddle with, use, unskilfully. **7. a** To move, use, bring into operation in a game: *to play a card*; Phr. *to play one's cards well*, manage one's affairs to one's own advantage; **b** (cricket) to strike (ball) in specified manner or direction. **8.** To contend against, have as opponent, in game: *will you play me for half a crown?* **9. a** To perform on, produce music from: *to play the piano*; Phr. (fig.) *to play second fiddle* (*to*), occupy subordinate position (to); **b** to perform (music) on instrument(s): *to play a concerto*; **c** to accompany with music: *the band played them out of town.* **10.** To act part, assume rôle of, on the stage: *to play Hamlet.* Phrs. (fig.) *to play the man, the fool* &c., act, behave, like; *to play one's part well* &c.; *to play truant*, be truant; *to play a part*, assume a character other than one's own. **C.** Followed by adverbs and prepositions. *Play at*, **a** to engage in, take part in: *to play at cricket* &c.; **b** (of children &c.) to make a pretence of being or doing: *to play at robbers, keeping shop* &c.; **c** (fig.) to perform casually, without devoting serious attention to; to work at half-heartedly, as though part of a game: *merely playing at business, at being a solicitor* &c. *Play off*, **a** to use (a person, circumstances &c.) as a foil against or to counteract others: *to play off one person against another*; **b** to pass off in assumed character, display under false colours. *Play on, upon*, **a** to perform on: *to play on the flute*; **b** to work upon, excite, make unscrupulous use of: *to play upon a person's fears, emotions*; **c** *to play upon words*, (i.) to quibble; (ii.) distort ingeniously, make a pun. *Play with*, **a** to use in play, amuse oneself with: *to play with one's dolls* &c.; **b** (fig.) to trifle with, to deceive, use for one's own gratification, or unscrupulous purposes: *to play with a person's affections*; **c** to toy, dally with, allow the mind to dwell lightly upon: *to play with the idea of going to Australia.*

play (**II.**), n. O.E. *plega*; M.E. *plei.* See prec. **1.** Light, rapid, transitory, fleeting, intermittent, flickering, movement: *the play of light and shadow upon the grass*; *the play of expression in a face.* **2. a** Free, unfettered, vigorous, easy motion: *the play of one's muscles* &c.; **b** limited, permissible movement of a mechanical part in one or more directions, additional to those in which it is primarily intended to move; **c** limit and extent of such movement: *to give a wheel more play on the axle*; **d** (fig.) unfettered activity, scope: *to give free play to one's thoughts, emotion, imagination* &c. **3.** Any action of body or mind undertaken and performed for amusement, diversion, recreation: *fond of play*; *at play*; *all work and no play.* Phr. *to do, say, something in play*, without serious intent, as a joke, for fun; *a play upon words*, verbal quip, pun. **4.** Gambling: *to lose money at play*; *high play*, for high stakes. **5. a** Manner of playing style, in playing a game &c.: *pretty play*; *rough play* &c.; **b** (fig.) conduct, way of behaving in relation to others; *fair play*, honest dealing; *foul play*, treachery. **6.** State of mental or physical activity; operation: *the play of forces.* Phrs. *to come into play*, begin to operate; *bring into play*, make use of. **7. a** A literary composition in dramatic form; a drama; **b** performance of such a composition: *to see the new play.* Phrs. *to go to the play*, the theatre; *as good as a play*, highly diverting and interesting.

playable, adj. [1. plấabl; 2. pléiəbl]. Prec. & **-able**. **a** (of a ball in a game) Capable of being played; **b** (of ground, billiard table &c.) capable of being played on.

play-actor, n. Actor, as contemptuous term.

playbill, n. [1. plấbil; 2. pléibil]. Poster or handbill giving notice of performance of a play.

play-book, n. Printed words of a play.

play-box, n. Wooden box in which boys and girls take cakes, sweets, books, and private belongings other than clothes back to a boarding school.

play-boy, n. A festive, convivial, rollicking fellow; one fond of pleasure and gaiety.

play-day, n. Holiday at a school; day in which no work is done.

play-debt, n. Debt incurred in gambling.

player, n. [1. plấer; 2. pléiə]. **play** (**I.**) & **-er**. One who plays; specif. **a** person proficient in a game; one taking part in specified game; **b** (cricket, cap.) person paid to play for a team; professional; contrasted with *Gentleman*, one who plays merely for sport; amateur; **c** actor.

playfellow, n. [1. plấfèlō; 2. pléifèlou]. Friend who shares one's amusements; companion in childish games.

playful, adj. [1. plấfool; 2. pléiful]. **play** (**II.**) & **-ful**. **1.** Frolicsome, gay, sportive; frisky, skittish. **2.** Expressing a merry humour; exhibiting a frolicsome, humorous spirit or mood.

playfully, adv. Prec. & **-ly**. In a playful manner.

playfulness, n. See prec. & **-ness**. State or quality of being playful.

playgoer, n. [1. plấgōer; 2. pléigouə]. **play** & **go** & **-er**. One who goes frequently and habitually to the theatre.

playground, n. [1. plấground; 2. pléigraund]. Ground used for games, esp. one attached to school.

playhouse, n. [1. plấhous; 2. pléihaus]. Theatre.

playing-cards, n. [1. plấing kàrdz; 2. pléiiŋ kādz]. Those used in card games.

playing-field, n. [1. plấing fèld; 2. pléiiŋ fīəld]. Field or open space where games may be played.

playlet, n. [1. plấlet; 2. pléilit]. **play** (**II.**) & **-let**. Short play.

playmate, n. [1. plấmāt; 2. pléimeit]. Playfellow.

plaything, n. [1. plấthing; 2. pléiþiŋ]. **a** Something to play with; a child's toy; **b** (fig.) person regarded merely as something to play and toy with, not as a serious companion.

playtime, n. [1. plấtīm; 2. pléitaim]. Time devoted to recreation, amusement.

playwright, n. [1. plấrīt; 2. pléirait]. Dramatist.

plaza, n. [1. pláhza; 2. plāzə]. Span., 'place', cp. Ital. **piazza**. A public square or open place in a Spanish town.

plea, n. [1. plē; 2. plī]. M.E. *plaid, plei, ple*, fr. O. Fr. *plaid, plait*, fr. Lat. *placitum*, 'that which is pleasing', Low Lat., 'opinion; decree; principle', neut. P.P. of *placēre*, 'to please', see **placet**, & cp. **please**. **1.** (law) **a** Statement made by a party in an action in support of his case; a pleading; **b** answer made by defendant to allegation of plaintiff, or to the accusation brought in a criminal charge; *Court of Common Pleas*, an old Superior Court, having jurisdiction in civil matters only, now merged in the King's Bench Division of the High Court. **2.** An excuse, pretext. **3.** Urgent demand, entreaty.

pleach, vb. trans. [1. plēch; 2. plītʃ]. M.E. *pleche*, variant of **plash** (**IV.**). To plash, lay, and interlace branches &c. of a hedge, now rare except in P.P. *pleached.*

plead, vb. intrans. & trans. [1. plēd; 2. plīd]. M.E. *plaiden*, fr. O. Fr. *plaidier*, fr. *plaid*, 'plea', see **plea**. **A.** intrans. **1.** (law) (i.) To make a plea; (ii.) to conduct the pleadings in a court; (iii.) to present an answer to an indictment, or accusation: *to plead guilty*; *the prisoner was held to be insane and therefore unable to plead.* Phr. (fig.) *to plead guilty to*, to admit responsibility for. **2.** To urge an argument or demand with insistence; to entreat, supplicate: *to plead for mercy, for consideration* &c.; *to plead with a person for mercy.* **B.** trans. **1.** To argue, bring forward on behalf of another, in court or generally: *to plead a* (*prisoner's*) *cause.* **2.** To adduce, bring forward in defence, or as apology or excuse: *to plead one's ignorance, old age* &c.

pleadable, adj. [1. plḗdabl; 2. plīdəbl]. **plead** & **-able**. Capable of being pleaded.

pleader, n. [1. plḗder; 2. plīdə]. **plead** & **-er**. An advocate, in legal and general sense.

pleading (**I.**), n. [1. plḗding; 2. plīdiŋ]. **plead** & **-ing**. **1.** Action of one who pleads: *all his pleading was in vain.* **2.** (law) **a** Act of performing the part of an advocate; **b** act, art, of drawing pleas as an advocate. Phr. *special pleading*, see **special**. **3.** (pl. *pleadings*) The sum of the statements made by plaintiff and defendant in a legal action in support of their several cases, and in answer to each other, as drawn up in writing before the action is tried.

pleading (**II.**), adj. **plead** & **-ing**. Making a plea; imploring, entreating.

pleadingly, adv. Prec. & **-ly**. In a pleading manner.

pleasance, n. [1. plézans; 2. plézəns], fr. O. Fr. *plaisance*, fr. *plais-(ant)*, 'pleasant'. See next word & **-ance**. (archaic) **1.** Pleasure, delight, entertainment. **2.** Pleasure garden.

pleasant, adj. [1. pléznt; 2. pléznt], fr. O. Fr. *plaisant*, Pres. Part. of *plaisir*, 'to please', see **please**. **1. a** Agreeable, gratifying, producing pleasure to mind or senses &c.: *a pleasant voice, face*; *a pleasant walk* &c.; **b** (of persons) agreeable, affable, amiable, easy in manner and temper: *a pleasant companion*; *to make oneself pleasant.* **2.** (archaic) Humorous, facetious.

pleasantly, adv. Prec. & **-ly**. In a pleasant manner.

pleasantness, n. See prec. & **-ness**. State or quality of being pleasant.

pleasantry, n. [1. plézntri; 2. plézntri], fr. Fr. *plaisanterie*; **pleasant** & **-ery**. **1.** Jocularity, humour, playfulness. **2.** Jocular remark, jest.

please, vb. intrans. & trans. [1. plēz; 2. plīz]. M.E. *plaisen*, fr. O. Fr. *plaisir*, fr. Lat. *placēre*, 'to be pleasing, to please', orig. 'to be smooth, level', see **placet** & words there referred to. **A.** intrans. **1.** To afford pleasure, be agreeable, be a source of satisfaction, delight, gratification: '*Intent to reason, or polite to please*' (Pope); *such beauty cannot fail to please.* **2.** To be willing, to be minded, to choose, to be pleased to: *I shall do exactly as I please*; *will you please to come at once?*; (colloq.) *you can do it if you please*; *well, I don't please*; (ironic.) *he wanted me to finish the work that night, if you please!*; *if you* *please*, polite form of request, abbreviated to *please*: *will you have some more pudding? Yes, please.* This construction is derived from the older, impersonal one, *if it please you* &c.; cp. **like** (**III.**); *to do what one pleases*, is for *to do as it pleases one* (*to do*). Phrs. *please God*, if it be pleasing to God, if it be possible; cp. also (official formulae) *may it please your Majesty*, mode of beginning a petition to the King; *may it please your lordship*, barrister's opening of a speech in court. **B.** trans. **a** (i.) To give pleasure to, to delight, charm, gratify: *everything that could please the senses or the heart*; (ii.) to satisfy, give satisfaction to: *one can't please everybody.* Phrs. *be pleased to* (*pay at once*), form of peremptory demand; (colloq.) *to be very* (*much*) *pleased with* (*one's new house*) &c.; *to look pleased*, wear an expression of satisfaction; (official formula) *H.M. the King has been graciously pleased to* &c.; **b** to satisfy requirements of, give satisfaction to, impress favourably, conciliate: *a difficult master to please*; *if we do our duty we shall please God.*

pleased, adj. [1. plēzd; 2. plīzd], fr. P.P. of prec. **a** Feeling pleasure, satisfaction: *quite pleased to be leaving*; **b** showing satisfaction: *a pleased expression of countenance*; **c** contented, satisfied: *I hope you are pleased with what I've done for you.*

pleasing, adj. [1. plēzing; 2. plīziŋ]. **please** & **-ing**. Affording pleasure; agreeable.

pleasingly, adv. Prec. & **-ly**. In a pleasing manner.

pleasurable, adj. [1. plézhurabl; 2. pléžərəbl]. **pleasure** & **-able**. Of a kind or quality to afford pleasure; enjoyable.

pleasurableness, n. Prec. & **-ness**. Quality of being pleasurable.

pleasurably, adv. See prec. & **-ly**. In a pleasurable manner.

pleasure (**I.**), n. [1. plézhur; 2. pléžə], fr. O. Fr. *plesir*, *plaisir*, infin. used as n. See **please** & **-ure**. **1. a** Enjoyment, delight, pleasing emotion, satisfaction, derived from ideas, intellectual pursuits, or from higher kinds of sensuous or moral experience: *it gave me great pleasure to make his acquaintance*; *I read of your success with much pleasure*; *it is a pleasure, not a duty, to work for a man like that*; *the pleasures of friendship, of art, of philosophy*; Phrs. *to take* (*a*) *pleasure in*, to like, enjoy; (archaic) *to take one's pleasure*, enjoy oneself; *with pleasure*, willingly; (polite formulae) *may I have the pleasure of a dance* &c.?; *will you do me the pleasure of* (*coming to dine* &c.)?; *during one's pleasure*, for as long as one pleases; **b** (in formal uses, with *our*, *his* &c.) desire, will: *it is our royal pleasure that* &c.; *during His Majesty's pleasure.* **2.** Specif., gratification of the senses; self-indulgence: *the pleasures of sin*; *given up to pleasure*; *to get pleasure from a good dinner.* Phr. *man of pleasure*, sensualist, dissipated man. **3.** Source of pleasure: *to some men sport and dissipation are their chief pleasures, to others, study and reflection.*

pleasure (**II.**), vb. trans. & intrans., fr. prec. (archaic) **1.** trans. To give pleasure to, please, gratify: *I will do anything to pleasure you.* **2.** intrans. To take pleasure, enjoy oneself.

pleasure-boat, n. One used for pleasure trips.

pleasure-ground, n. Recreation ground.

pleat, n. & vb. trans. [1. plēt; 2. plīt]. Variant of **plait**. **1.** n. A fold in cloth. **2.** vb. To make a pleat in.

pleb, n. [1. pleb; 2. plɛb]. Abbr. of **plebeian**. Plebeian.

plebeian, n. & adj. [1. plēbéan; 2. plībíən], fr. Lat. *plēbēi-*(*us*), 'of the common people', fr. *plēb-*, stem of *plēbs*, 'crowd; lower classes', & **-an**. Cp. Gk. *plēthos*, 'crowd', see **plethora**, fr. base seen in **plenum** & **full** (**I.**). **1.** n. Member of the lower orders, proletarian; specif., of ancient Rome. **2.** adj. Characteristic of a plebeian; low born; undistinguished, common.

plebeianize, vb. trans. [1. plēbéanīz; 2. plībíənaiz]. Prec. & **-ize**. To make plebeian.

plebiscitary, adj. [1. plebísitari; 2. plɛbísitəri]. Next word & **-ary**. Of, pertaining to, a plebiscite.

plebiscite, n. [1. plébisit; 2. plébisit], fr. Lat. *plēbiscīt-*(*um*), 'decree of the people', fr. *plēbi-*, stem of *plēbs*, 'populace', see **plebeian**, & *scītum*, P.P. type of *scīscere*, 'to inquire into; to assent to; to decree', see **science**. **1.** Expression of the will of the people on a single important constitutional or other political issue, ascertained by general direct ballot of all electors. **2.** General expression of public opinion.

plebs, n. [1. plebz; 2. plɛbz]. Lat. See **plebeian**. **a** Common people of ancient Rome, collectively; **b** the proletariat generally.

plectrum, n. [1. plékrum; 2. pléktrəm]. Lat., fr. Gk. *plēktron*, 'instrument to strike with; specif., one for striking the lyre'; cp. Gk. *pléssein*, 'to strike'; *plēktēs*, 'warrior'; *plēgma*, 'blow'; *plēgé*, 'stroke'; see this base under **plague**. Small object of metal, horn &c., worn on the finger when playing the harp or other musical instrument with wire strings played by plucking, such as the mandolin, zither &c.

pledge (**I.**), n. [1. plej; 2. plɛdž]. M.E., fr. O. Fr. *plege*, *pleige*, 'security'; prob. of Gmc. origin, cp. O.H.G. *pflegan*, Germ. *pflegen*, 'to take care of, to care for, protect' &c.; later, 'to promise, give security for'; O.S. *plegan*, in same senses, & O.E. *pleġ*(*i*)*an*, 'to play, frolic'. The O.E. n. *plega*, besides the sense of 'play', has also those of 'quick movement, game', & specif., 'fighting', see **play** (**I.**), & cp. **plight** (**I.**). **1. a** Object given as security for performance of act, contract, obligation, payment of debt &c.; a gage; **b** specif., thing put in pawn; **c** state of being pledged: *to put in, take out of, pledge*; *to hold in pledge.* **2.** Token, sign, earnest of something else: *a pledge of fidelity, friendship* &c.; popular for *pledge of* (*conjugal*) *affection*, i.e. child, offspring: *two fair pledges* (*of our love*). **3. a** Promise, binding engagement: *under pledge of secrecy*; specif. **b** undertaking to abstain from intoxicating liquor: *to take, sign, the pledge.* **4.** Expression of good-will, wishes for success &c., in form of a health proposed; a toast.

pledge (**II.**), vb. trans., fr. prec. **1.** To put in pledge, give as security; to pawn. **2.** (fig.) To give, engage, plight: *to pledge one's word* &c. **3.** To drink the health of, toast: *to pledge a person's health.*

pledgeable, adj. [1. pléjabl; 2. plédžəbl]. Prec. & **-able**. Capable of being pledged.

pledgee, n. [1. plejḗ; 2. plɛdží]. **pledge** (**II.**) & **-ee**. Person with whom a pledge is deposited.

pledget, n. [1. pléjet; 2. plédžit]. Etymol. unknown. Small pad of lint, cotton &c., applied to wound &c.

pledgor, n. [1. plèjór; 2. plèdžɔ́]. **pledge** (**II.**) & **-or**. Person who pledges.

Pleiad, n. [1. plīad; 2. pláiæd], fr. Lat., fr. Gk. *Plēiád-*(*es*), (pl.) the seven daughters of Atlas, placed by Zeus among the stars, hence, 'a group of stars'; prob. related to Gk. *pálē*, Lat. *pulvis*, 'dust'; *pollen*, 'meal', see **pollen**, & **pulverize**; the form of Gk. *Pleiádes*, has, however, prob. been influenced by Gk. *pléō*, 'I sail', cogn. w. Gk. *plóein*, 'to flow', see **flow** (**I.**). **1.** (pl.) *Pleiad*(*e*)*s* [1. plīadz, plīadēz; 2. pláiædz, pláiədīz], one of a large group of stars in constellation Taurus, formerly supposed to be seven in number; the whole group. **2.** [1. plāad; 2. pléiæd] fr. Fr. *Pléiade.* Group, galaxy of exceptionally talented, brilliant, famous, or magnificent persons; specif., group of seven 16th-cent. French poets of whom Ronsard and Du Bellay are the best known.

pleistocene, n. [1. plīstosēn; 2. pláistəsīn]. Invented word fr. Gk. *pleīsto-*(*s*), 'most'; cp. Gk. compar. *pléōn*, 'more', see **pleonasm**; cogn. w. O.N. *flestr*, 'most'; fr. base seen in **plenum** & **full** (**I.**). The second element is fr. Gk. *kain-*(*ós*), 'new', see **kainite**, & cp. **recent**. (geol.) Denoting that period between the end of the Tertiary period and the beginning of history; also called, *Post-tertiary*, or *Glacial Period*, and the *Ice Age.*

plenarily, adv. [1. plénarili; 2. plīnərili]. See next word & **-ly**. In a plenary manner.

plenary, adj. [1. plénari; 2. plīnəri], fr. L. Lat. *plēnāri-*(*us*), 'full', fr. *plēn-*(*us*), 'full'. See **plenum** & **-ary**. **1.** Full, absolute, unlimited: *plenary powers, authority, indulgence* &c.; *plenary inspiration* (of writers of scripture), including all subjects, historical as well as religious &c. **2.** (of meeting, assembly &c.) **a** Attended by all those entitled to be present; forming a plenum; **b** representing all sections.

plenipotentiary, adj. & n. [1. plènipoténshari; 2. plènipəténʃəri], fr. Med. Lat. *plēnipotenti-āri-*(*us*), fr. L. Lat. *plēnipotent-*(*em*), 'having full power', fr. *plēn-*(*us*), 'full', see **plenum**, & *potent-*(*em*), 'powerful', see **potent** (**I.**), & **-ary**. **1.** adj. **a** (of person) Possessing full powers; **b** (of power, authority) absolute, complete. **2.** n. Ambassador, envoy, to whom is deputed full authority to act at his own discretion in the name of the state or body which he represents.

plenish, vb. trans. [1. plénish; 2. pléniʃ], fr. Pres. Part. type, *pleniss-*, of O. Fr. *plenir*, 'to fill', see **plenum**. (archaic) To supply, equip with; to replenish.

plenishing, n. [1. plénishing; 2. pléniʃiŋ]. Prec. & **-ing**. (Scots, usually pl.) Household furniture or stock.

plenitude, n. [1. plénitūd; 2. plénitjūd], fr. Lat. *plēnitūdo*, 'plenitude', fr. *plēn-*(*us*), 'full', see **plenum** & **-tude**. **1.** State of being full, copious, abundant; fullness, completeness, luxuriance. **2.** (med.) Repletion: *a feeling of plenitude after meals.*

plenteous, adj. [1. pléntyus; 2. plént∫əs, pléntiəs]. M.E. *plentevous*, *plentēus*, fr. O. Fr. *plentivous*. **plenty** & **-ive** & **-ous**. (chiefly poetical) Plentiful, abundant, copious.

plenteously, adv. Prec. & **-ly**. In a plenteous manner.

plenteousness, n. See prec. & **-ness**. State of being plenteous; abundance, plenty.

plentiful, adj. [1. pléntifool; 2. pléntiful]. **plenty** (**I.**) & **-ful**. Abundant, copious, ample; present or existing in large quantities.

plentifully, adv. Prec. & **-ly**. In a plentiful manner; abundantly.

plentifulness, n. See prec. & **-ness**. State of being plentiful.

plenty (**I.**), n. [1. plénti; 2. plénti], fr. O. Fr. *plentet*, fr. Lat. *plēnitāt-*(*em*), 'fullness, abundance', fr. *plēn-*(*us*) 'full', see **plenum**, & **-ity**. **1.** State of abundance, or of possessing abundance of material necessities; prosperity, opulence: *to live in peace and plenty.* **2.** An ample supply, sufficiency, for one's purpose; unstinted amount, abundance for all needs: *plenty of food, of money* &c.; *to have plenty of time*, to run no risk of being late.

plenty (**II.**), adv., fr. prec. (colloq. and vulg.) Quite enough, to a sufficient degree: *your coat is plenty long enough.*

plenum, n. [1. plḗnum; 2. plīnəm]. Lat. *plēnum*, fr. neut. form of *plēnus*, 'full'; cp. Lat. *plēre*, 'to fill'; cogn. w. Goth. *fulls*, O.E. *full*, 'full', see **full** (**I.**); Gk. (*pim*)*plēmi*, 'I fill'; *plēthein*, 'to be full', see **plethora**; *pléōs*, 'full; abundant; more', see **pleonasm**; *polús*, 'many', see **poly-**; O.E. *folc*, 'people', see **folk**. See also **people**, **plural**. **1.** A space completely filled with some form of matter; contrasted with *vacuum.* **2.** A full meeting of a legislative or administrative body in all its sections.

pleonasm, n. [1. plḗunazm; 2. plīənæzəm], fr. Lat., fr. Gk. *pleonasm-*(*ós*), 'pleonasm', fr. *pleonázein*, 'to be more than enough, be superfluous', fr. *pléon*, neut. form of *pléōn*, 'more'. See prec. & words there referred to for cognates. (rhet.) Redundancy of style; use of superfluous words, esp. of words expressing over again what has already been expressed in the sentence; e.g. *he was struck on the head and received a blow on the skull*; *he is dumb and cannot speak.*

pleonastic, adj. [1. plēunástik; 2. plīənǽstik], fr. Gk. *pleonast-*, fr. *pleonázein*, 'to be superfluous'. See prec. & **-ic**. Of the nature of a pleonasm; redundant, superfluous in expression.

pleonastically, adv. [1. plēunástikali; 2. plīənǽstikəli]. Prec. & **-al** & **-ly**. In a pleonastic manner; by the use of pleonasm.

plesiosaurus, n. [1. plēsiōsórus; 2. plísiousɔ́rəs], fr. Gk. *plēsi-(os)*, 'near'; cp. Gk. *pélas*, 'near'; *pelázein*, 'to approach'; for the second element see **saurian**. Extinct marine lizard-like reptile, found as a fossil, which had a small head, a long neck and tail, and all four limbs furnished with paddles for swimming; these reptiles varied from 10 to 40 ft. in length.

plessor, n. [1. plésor; 2. plésə], fr. Gk. *plḗssein*, 'to strike', q.v. under **plague**, & **-or**. Plexor, q.v.

plethora, n. [1. pléthora; 2. pléþərə]. Med. Lat., fr. Gk. *plēthṓrē*, 'fullness', fr. *plḗthein*, 'to become full'. See base under **plenum**. **1.** Excessive fullness, over-satiety, superabundance. **2.** (med.) Pathological condition due to excess of red corpuscles in the blood; repletion.

plethoric, adj. [1. plethórik; 2. pleþɔ́rik]. Prec. & **-ic**. Of, of the nature of, characterized by, plethora; full-blooded.

pleura, n. [1. plōōra; 2. plúərə]. Gk. *pleurá*, 'side; rib'; etymol. doubtful. Membrane which lines the thorax of mammals, and is turned back so as to cover the lungs themselves.

pleural, adj. [1. plōōral; 2. plúərel]. Prec. & **-al**. Pertaining to, connected with, the pleura.

pleurisy, n. [1. plōōrisi; 2. plúərisi], fr. L. Lat. *pleurisis*, variant of *pleurītis*, fr. Gk. *pleurîtis*, 'pleurisy', fr. *pleur-(á)*, 'side'. See **pleura** & **-itis**. Inflammation of the pleural membrane, of which there are three types, dry, effusive, and plastic, in which the membrane is covered with a thick granular, fibrinous substance.

pleuritic, adj. [1. plōōrítik; 2. pluərítik], fr. Gk. *pleurīt-(is)*, 'pleurisy', see prec. & **-ic**. Of, pertaining to, of the nature of, pleurisy.

pleur(o)-, pref. Form of Gk. *pleur-(á)*, 'side, rib', see **pleura**; used to form compounds in scientific terminology referring to the side of an animal or plant body, or to the pleura.

pleurocarpous, adj. [1. plōōrōkárpus; 2. pluəroukā́pəs]. Prec. & Gk. *karpós*, 'fruit', see **carpel**, & **-ous**. (bot.) Having the fruit on the side and not at the extremity of the stem, of certain mosses.

pleurodynia, n. [1. plōōrōdínia; 2. pluəroudíniə]. **pleuro-** & Gk. *odúnē*, 'pain'; see **anodyne**. (med.) Affection, accompanied by severe pain, of the muscles of the chest.

pleuronectid, adj. & n. [1. plōōrōnéktid; 2. pluərounéktid]. See prec. & Gk. *nḗktēs*, 'swimmer', fr. *nḗkhein*, 'to swim', q.v. under **natation**. (zool.) **a** adj. Belonging to the *Pleuronectidae*, family which includes the flat fishes, as sole, plaice, flounder &c.; **b** n., a flat fish of this family.

pleuro-pneumonia, n. [1. plōōrō nūmónia; 2. pluərou njūmóuniə]. **pleuro-** & **pneumonia**. Inflammation of both the pleura and the lungs, now chiefly used of a highly contagious disease of this nature attacking horses and cattle.

plexal, adj. [1. pléksal; 2. pléksəl]. **plexus** & **-al**. Connected with, pertaining to, a plexus.

plexiform, adj. [1. pléksiform; 2. pléksifɔ̄m]. See **plexus** & **-form**. Resembling a plexus.

pleximeter, n. [1. pleksímeter; 2. pleksímitə], fr. Gk. *plēxi-(s)*, 'a striking', fr. *plēk-, stem of *plḗssein*, 'to strike', q.v. under **plectrum**, **plague**. (med.) Small, thin plate placed over that part of the body which is to be percussed with a plexor.

plexor, n. [1. pléksor; 2. pléksə], fr. Gk. *plēx-(is)*, 'a striking', see prec., & **-or**. (med.) Small hammer used in percussion; also plessor.

plexus, n. [1. pléksus; 2. pléksəs]. Lat. *plexus*, 'braid, network', fr. *plex-(um)*, P.P. type of *plectere*, 'to plait'. See **plash (IV.)**. **1.** Intricately interwoven combination, **a** of material objects; **b** of ideas, interests, passions, events &c. **2.** (anat.) Intricate assemblage of intercrossing nerves or blood-vessels, e.g. *the solar plexus*, in the abdomen.

pliability, n. [1. pliabíliti; 2. plaiəbíliti]. See next word & **-ity**. State or quality of being pliable.

pliable, adj. [1. plíabl; 2. pláiəbl], fr. Fr. *pli-(er)*, 'to bend', fr. Lat. *plicāre*, 'to bend, fold'. See **plicate** & **-able**. **1.** Capable of being bent; flexible, supple. **2.** (of mind, character &c.) Capable of being influenced, and inclined in this or that direction; flexible, yielding; capable of adaptation to new ideas or conditions &c.

pliancy, n. [1. plíansi; 2. pláiənsi]. **pliant** & **-cy**. State or quality of being pliant.

pliant, adj. [1. plíant; 2. pláiənt], fr. Fr. *pliant*, Pres. Part. of *plier*, 'to bend'. See **pliable**. (of material objects, and of the mind &c.) Pliable, flexible, yielding.

pliantly, adv. Prec. & **-ly**. In a pliant manner.

plica, n. [1. plíka; 2. pláikə], pl. *plicae* [1. plísē; 2. pláisī]. Med. Lat. *plica*, 'a fold'. See next word. A fold; specif. **a** a fold in the skin; **b** (med.) matted, filthy condition of the hair due to disease, often called *plica Polonica*, Polish plait, as being endemic in Poland and Eastern Europe.

plicate, adj. [1. plīkāt; 2. plaikéit], fr. Lat. *plicāt-(um)*, P.P. type of *plicāre*, 'to fold, bend', fr. earlier **plecāre*, on anal. of compounds such as *explicāre*, 'to unfold', see **explicate**; cp. Lat. *plectere*, 'to plait', see **plash (IV.)** & **plait**; Gk. *plékein*, 'to plait'; *ploké*, 'network'; *plókos*, 'tress'; prob. cogn. w. Goth. *falþan*; O.E. *faldan*, to fold', see **fold (I.)**. Having folds or ridges; specif. (bot. and zool.) *plicate leaf, shell* &c.

plicated, adj. [1. plikāted; 2. plaikéitid]. Prec. & **-ed**. Plicate.

plication, n. [1. plīkāshun; 2. plaikéiʃən]. **plicate** & **-ion**. **1.** Act of folding; state of being folded. **2.** Fold; that which is folded.

pliers, n. [1. plíerz; 2. pláiəz], fr. M.E. *pli-(en)*, 'to bend', fr. O. Fr. *plier*, 'to bend'. See **pliable** & **plicate**. Small pincers for holding small objects; also for bending and cutting wire &c.

plight (I.), vb. trans. & n. [1. plīt; 2. plait]. O.E. *plihtan*, 'to pledge', fr. *pliht*, 'risk, danger'; cp. Du. *pligt*; M.H.G. *pflicht*, 'responsibility'; O.H.G. *pflegan*, 'to take care of'; cogn. w. O.E. *plēon*, 'to risk, expose to danger'; *pleoh*, 'risk, responsibility; danger'. See **play (I.)** & **pledge (I.)**. **1.** vb. trans. **a** To promise formally, engage, pledge: *to plight one's word, honour, troth*; **b** to engage, betroth: *plighted lovers*. **2.** n. Engagement, pledge.

plight (II.), n. M.E. *plīt*, *plīht*, 'condition', O. Fr. *ploit*, *pleit*; variant of **pleat**; influenced by prec., w. the older meaning of wh. it was associated. State, condition, circumstances; chiefly unfavourable circumstances; an awkward fix &c.: *in a sorry, evil, plight*.

Plimsoll, n. [1. plímsol; 2. plímsəl], fr. name of Samuel Plimsoll, d. 1898, advocate of load-line reforms. *Plimsoll's line, mark*, line on hull showing to what depth a vessel may be legally submerged when loaded.

plinth, n. [1. plinth; 2. plinþ], fr. Lat. *plinthus*, 'plinth', fr. Gk. *plínthos*, 'brick'; etymol. doubtful; possibly cogn. w. **flint**. (archit.) Plain surface below the base moulding of a column; in classical buildings it consisted of a low square block of stone.

plinthite, n. [1. plínthīt; 2. plínþait]. Prec. & **-ite**. Kind of red clay.

pliocene, adj. & n. [1. plíosēn; 2. pláiəsīn]. Invented word, fr. Gk. *pleíōn*, 'more', fr. earlier *pléōn*, see **pleonasm**, on anal. of *pleîstos*, 'most', see **pleistocene**; the second element is fr. Gk. *kainós*, 'new', see **kainite**. **1.** adj. (geol.) Denoting the uppermost strata of the Tertiary period. **2.** n. This period.

plod (I.), vb. intrans. & trans. [1. plod; 2. plɔd]. Prob. imitative. **1.** intrans. **a** To walk along or through, slowly and heavily, to walk laboriously, with dragging, painful steps; **b** (fig.) to work steadily, conscientiously, and laboriously, esp. at a tedious task: *to plod through a task*. **2.** trans. Only *to plod one's way*: '*The ploughman homeward plods his weary way*' (Gray's 'Elegy').

plod (II.), n., fr. prec. Heavy, laborious walk; steady, unremitting toil.

plodder, n. [1. plóder; 2. plɔ́də]. **plod (I.)** & **-er**. One who plods; esp. a slow, steady, conscientious worker.

plodding, adj. [1. plóding; 2. plɔ́diŋ]. **plod (I.)** & **-ing**. **a** (of walk) Slow and laborious; **b** (of work or worker) slow and steady, laborious.

ploddingly, adv. Prec. & **-ly**. In a plodding manner.

plop (I.), n. & adv. [1. plop; 2. plɔp]. Imitative. **1.** n. **a** Sound resembling that made by something bulky striking the surface of water, or like that of a cork coming suddenly out of a bottle; **b** act of plopping. **2.** adv. With a plop: *to fall plop into the river*; *the cork came out plop!*

plop (II.), vb. intrans. See prec. To make a plop; to jump or fall suddenly and clumsily into water; to pop, as of a cork flying out of a bottle.

plosive, adj. & n. See **implosive**.

plot (I.), n. [1. plot; 2. plɔt]. O.E. *plot(t)*, 'small piece of ground'; origin unknown; cp. **plat (I.)**. **a** Moderate-sized area of ground; a patch; **b** crop growing on a plot: *a plot of barley*.

plot (II.), vb. trans., fr. prec. **a** Generally *plot out*, to divide up into plots; **b** (fig.) to divide up, draw up scheme for division of: *to plot out one's time*. See also **plot (IV.)**.

plot (III.), n. Cp. Fr. *complot*, 'conspiracy'; also influenced by & associated w. **plot (I.)**, in sense of something divided up, mapped, or plotted out. **1.** **a** A conspiracy; secret scheme or intrigue to effect something, esp. a coup d'état, usually by violent and unlawful means, and by a sudden surprise: *the Gunpowder Plot*; *a plot to destroy orderly government*; **b** an innocent scheme to do something of a perfectly harmless character, agreed upon by several persons, the steps toward which are taken without the knowledge of some other person or persons: *we have a plot to present the headmaster with a new gown*. **2.** The series of incidents, situations &c., invented by a writer, upon which play or story is built, esp. series of complications in such a work solved or explained by a dénouement.

plot (IV.), vb. intrans. & trans., fr. prec. **1.** intrans. **a** To take part in a plot or conspiracy; to conspire; also *plot against*; **b** to scheme, form plans, devise: *we are plotting how we shall spend our holidays*. **2.** trans. **a** To devise, plan out secretly; to aim at accomplishing by conspiracy: *to plot the destruction of the empire*; **b** to plan surreptitiously and in an underhand way; to seek to secure by intrigue and dishonourable means: *his enemies are plotting his downfall*; **c** to plan, mark out: *to plot a curve on a chart*.

plotless, adj. [1. plótles; 2. plɔ́tlis]. **plot (III.)** & **-less**. (of story &c.) Without plot.

plotter, n. [1. plóter; 2. plɔ́tə]. **plot (IV.)** & **-er**. One who takes part in a plot; a conspirator; an intriguer.

plough, plow (I.), n. [1. plou; 2. plau]. Late O.E. *plōh*, perh. fr. O.N. *plōgr*; M.E. *plou(h)*; M. Du. *ploeg*; O.H.G. *pfluog*; the origin of this familiar word is obscure; attempts to relate it to other Aryan words (see Walde, under *dolo*) are not convincing; it is prob. not an orig. Gmc. word. **1.** Agricultural implement drawn by horses or oxen, or in recent times often driven by steam or petrol, having a blade which cuts furrows in the ground, turns up the slices and exposes the soil to the action of the weather. Phr. *to put one's hand to the plough,* (fig.) begin an undertaking (see Luke ix. 62). **2.** One of various implements somewhat resembling a plough in shape and action, e.g. *snow-plough,* device for driving a track through thick snow. **3.** Ploughed land: *fifty acres of plough.* **4.** (cap.) A constellation, called also *Great Bear, Charles's Wain, Dipper* &c. **5.** Failure to pass examination: *to take a plough.*

plough (II.), vb. trans. & intrans., fr. prec. **A.** trans. **1. a** To use a plough upon, break up with a plough: *to plough the fields;* Phr. *to plough the sand(s),* engage upon a futile, fruitless enterprise; **b** (fig., of a ship) to make a track through, cleave: *to plough (the face of) the ocean;* Phrs. *to plough one's, its, &c. way,* to force a passage; *the bullet ploughed its way through his flesh; to plough up,* turn up with a plough: *to plough up roots;* (fig.) *the engine left the rails and ploughed up the track for several yards.* **2.** To form, produce, by ploughing: *to plough a furrow.* **3.** (colloq.) To reject, refuse to pass (a candidate) in an examination. **B.** intrans. **1. a** To engage in tillage, to perform the act of ploughing: *to plough and sow;* **b** *plough through,* work, read, plod, laboriously through (a book &c.). **2.** (of land) To be suitable, in a fit state, for ploughing: the *land ploughs hard after the drought.* **3.** (colloq.) To fail in an examination.

plough-beam, n. Central shaft of plough.

ploughboy, n. [1. plóuboi; 2. pláubɔi]. Boy leading horses in plough; (gen.) a yokel, a clodhopper.

plougher, n. [1. plóuer; 2. pláuə]. **plough (II.)** & **-er.** (archaic) A ploughman.

plough-land, n. (hist.) As much land as could be ploughed by one team in a year; carucate.

ploughman, n. [1. plóuman; 2. pláumən]. Man who drives plough.

Plough Monday, n. (hist.) Monday after Epiphany, on which ploughing &c. began again after the Christmas holiday.

ploughshare, n. [1. plóushār; 2. pláuʃεə]. **plough (I.)** & **share.** Blade or part of a plough which cuts the furrow.

plough-staff, n. Tool with a long handle, ending in a kind of spade, for clearing ploughshare of earth, roots &c.

plough-tail, n. Back of plough. Phr. *at the plough-tail,* working as farm-labourer.

plover, n. [1. plúver; 2. plávə], fr. O. Fr. *plovier,* fr. L. Lat. **plovāri-(us),* fr. *pluvia,* 'rain', see **pluvial (I.)**. The general name of a large group of allied long-legged wading birds, of which the *golden plover, Charadrius pluvialis,* and the *grey plover, Squatarola helvetica,* are true plovers; allied kinds are the *green plover,* the lapwing or pewit (whose eggs are the 'plover's eggs' of commerce), and the sandpiper, stilt &c.

plover's page, n. The dunlin, which sometimes accompanies the golden plover.

plow. Variant (chiefly U.S.A.) of **plough.**

pluck (I.), vb. trans. & intrans. [1. pluk; 2. plak]. O.E. *pluccian;* M.E. *plukken;* cp. M. Du. *plucken;* M.H.G. *pflücken;* O.N. *plokka.* **A.** trans. **1. a** To nip, break, off; to gather: *to pluck flowers, fruit;* **b** to pull out with jerking movement; specif., *to pluck a fowl, goose* &c., remove feathers by pulling, before cooking; Phr. *to have a crow to pluck with,* have a ground of complaint against, have a bone of contention; **c** (fig.) to strip (a person) of money; to swindle, trick, out of property, esp. by cheating at play; Phr. *to pluck a pigeon,* swindle a green, inexperienced youth. **2.** *Pluck up,* only in Phr. *to pluck up courage (to do something),* make an effort of boldness. **3.** To twitch with finger and thumb; **a** (archaic university phr.) to pull the proctor's gown as a sign of protest against something proposed to be done, esp. against conferring a degree; hence, **b** to fail, plough (a candidate) in an examination; specif. **c** to twitch (the strings of a harp, zither, or similar instrument) in playing. **B.** intrans. Usually *pluck at,* to pull or twitch at.

pluck (II.), n., fr. prec. **1.** Act of plucking; a tug, twitch. **2.** Something plucked out; specif., heart, liver, and lungs of an animal. **3.** (fig.) Courage, bravery, spirit; endurance under danger and difficulty. **4.** (rare) Failure in examination.

plucked, adj. [1. plukt; 2. plakt], fr. P.P. of **pluck (I.)**. Having or showing courage and spirit, esp. in Phr. *a well-plucked one.*

pluckily, adv. [1. plúkili; 2. plákili]. **plucky** & **-ly.** In a plucky manner.

pluckiness, n. [1. plúkines; 2. plákinis]. See prec. & **-ness.** Quality of being plucky.

pluckless, adj. [1. plúkles; 2. pláklis]. **pluck (II.)** & **-less.** Wanting in pluck.

plucky, adj. [1. plúki; 2. pláki]. **pluck (II.)** & **-y.** Having, showing, courage, spirit, fortitude.

plug (I.), n. [1. plug; 2. plag]. Prob. fr. M. Du. *plugge;* etymol. doubtful. **1. a** Any small, solid object used to stop a hole, fill a gap or cavity, or to act as wedge &c.; peg, bung, stopper; specif., **b** the mechanism, including trap, handle &c., used in flushing and clearing water-closet after use. **2. a** Cake or stick of compressed tobacco; **b** piece of this cut off for chewing.

plug (II.), vb. trans. & intrans., fr. prec. **A.** trans. **1.** To put a plug into: *to plug a wall;* to stop, fill up, with plug: *to plug a hole;* also *plug up.* **2.** (slang) **a** To shoot, put, a bullet into; **b** to strike with the fist. **3.** (colloq. and vulg., U.S.A.) To force, compel, attention of public to by constant repetition &c.: *to plug a song, dance &c. on the audience.* **B.** intrans. (colloq.) To work laboriously, plod: *to plug away at a task.*

plug-ugly, n. (Am. slang) A street rowdy or ruffian, member of a gang of ruffians.

plum, n. [1. plum; 2. plam]. O.E., M.E. *plūme;* cp. O.N. *plōma;* O.S. *prūme;* fr. L. Lat. *prūnum,* fr. Gk. *proû(m)non,* 'plum'. See **prune. 1.** Any of many varieties of tree of Prunus family, bearing a roundish fruit with sweet juicy flesh, smooth skin, and flattish stone; also the fruit of such a tree. *French plum,* superior kind of dried plum or prune. Phr. *plum-ripe,* absolutely ripe. **2.** Raisin as used in a pudding or cake. **3.** (fig.) Coveted object; prize, choicest of its kind, the pick. **4.** (slang) £100,000.

plumage, n. [1. plo͞omij; 2. plúmidž], fr. O. Fr. *plumage.* See **plume (I.)** & **-age.** Bird's feathers collectively.

plumaged, adj. [1. plo͞omijd; 2. plúmidžd]. Prec. & **-ed.** Having plumage of specified kind: *gay-plumaged.*

plumassier, n. [1. plo͞omásier, -iā; 2. plūmǽsiə, -iei]. Fr. See **plume (I.)** & **-ier.** (rare) Dealer or worker in ornamental feathers.

plumb (I.), n., adj., & adv. [1. plum; 2. plam], fr. Fr. *plomb,* fr. Lat. *plumbum,* 'lead'; loan-word, possibly fr. Iberian; cp. perh. Gk. *mólubdos,* 'lead', see **molybdenum. 1.** n. **a** Weight, lump of lead &c., attached to line, esp. plumb-line, q.v.; Phr. *out of plumb,* not perpendicular; **b** sounding-lead. **2.** adj. **a** Vertical; absolutely level; true; **b** (fig.) absolute, complete, utter. **3.** adv. **a** Vertically; **b** exactly: *plumb in the middle.*

plumb (II.), vb. trans., fr. prec. **1.** To test verticality of, with a plumb-line. **2. a** To sound with, or as with, a plumb-line and plummet, to test depth of; (fig.) **b** (of the eye) to pierce, see to bottom of: *no eye can plumb those depths;* **c** (of the intelligence) to fathom, get to the bottom of, understand fully: *few men could plumb the depths of that subtle and profound mind.*

plumb (III.), vb. intrans. Prob. new formation fr. **plumber.** To work as a plumber.

plumbaginous, adj. [1. plumbájinus; 2. plambǽidžinəs], fr. Lat. *plumbāgin-(em),* stem of next word, & **-ous.** Connected with, resembling, composed of, containing, plumbago.

plumbago, n. [1. plumbágō; 2. plambéigou]. Lat. *plumbāgo,* 'plumbago', fr. *plumb-(um),* 'lead', see **plumb (I.)**. **1.** Mineral composed of carbon, iron &c., used for pencils, crucibles &c.; graphite, black-lead. **2.** Genus of herbs with greyish-blue or violet flowers; leadwort.

plumbeous, adj. [1. plúmbeus; 2. plámbiəs], fr. Lat. *plumbe-(us),* 'of lead', fr. *plumb-(um),* 'lead', see **plumb (I.)**, & **-ous. 1.** Connected with, resembling, containing, lead. **2.** Lead-coloured. **3.** Lead-glazed.

plumber, n. [1. plúmer; 2. plámə], fr. O. Fr. *plummier,* fr. Lat. *plumbāri-(us),* 'lead-work', fr. *plumb-(um),* 'lead', see **plumb (I.)**. **a** (obs.) Originally, a worker in lead; **b** skilled tradesman who fits and adjusts and repairs metal pipes of all kinds, for water, gas, drains &c.

plumbery, n. [1. plúmeri; 2. pláməri]. See prec. & **-ery.** Plumber's work.

plumbic, adj. [1. plúmbik; 2. plámbik]. See **plumb (I.)** & **-ic. 1.** (chem.) Of, containing, lead. **2.** (pathol.) Containing, caused by, lead.

plumbiferous, adj. [1. plumbíferus; 2. plambífərəs]. See **plumb (I.)** & *-i-* & **-ferous.** Containing, yielding, lead.

plumbing, n. [1. plúming; 2. plámiŋ]. **plumb (III.)** & **-ing. 1.** Work, trade, of a plumber. **2.** Plumber's work; (coll.) all the plumber's work of laying and fitting of pipes &c. connected with a building.

plumbism, n. [1. plúmbizm; 2. plámbizəm]. See **plumb (I.)** & **-ism.** Lead-poisoning.

plumbless, adj. [1. plúmles; 2. plámlis]. **plumb (II.)** & **-less.** Not capable of being sounded; (poet.) measureless in depth; unfathomable.

plumb-line, n. Line with one end fastened to a board, and having a weight attached to the other end, used by masons for ascertaining the perpendicular.

plumb-rule, n. Mason's or carpenter's rule fitted with plumb-line.

plum-cake, n. Cake containing raisins, currants &c.

plum-duff, n. Pudding of flour, raisins &c.

plume (I.), n. [1. plo͞om; 2. plūm], fr. O. Fr. *plume,* fr. Lat. *plūma,* 'down, feather'; perh. fr. **plusma,* & cogn. w. O.E. *flīes* &c., see **fleece (I.)**. **1.** Bird's feather, esp. a long, important, conspicuous feather, or group of such: *a cock's, eagle's, plumes;* Phr. *borrowed plumes,* dress or attributes not one's own; referring to fable of jackdaw in peacock's feathers. **2.** Large feather, tuft or bunch of feathers, worn as ornament, esp. on a helmet or hat, or in the hair: '*Press where ye see my white plume shine, amidst the ranks of war*' (Macaulay, 'Ivry'). **3.** Tuft of hair, leaves &c. resembling plume.

plume (II.), vb. trans., fr. prec. **1. a** To furnish with plume(s); **b** (fig.) *to plume oneself on,* to pride oneself on, take credit for. **2.** (of bird) To dress, preen, its feathers. **3.** To pull feathers out of.

plumeless, adj. [1. plo͞omles; 2. plúmlis]. **plume (I.)** & **-less.** Without plumes.

plumelet, n. [1. plo͞omlet; 2. plúmlit]. **plume (I.)** & **-let.** Small plume; small tassel-like tuft of young leaves: '*When rosy plumelets tuft the larch*' (Tennyson, 'In Memoriam').

plumelike, adj. [1. plo͞omlīk; 2. plúmlaik]. **plume (I.)** & **-like.** Resembling a plume.

plummer-block, n. [1. plúmer blok; 2. pláməblɔk]. Origin doubtful. Metal frame or case supporting end of revolving shaft.

plummet, n. [1. plúmet; 2. plámit]. M.E., fr. O. Fr. *plommet,* dimin. of *plomb,* 'lead'. See **plumb (I.)**. **1.** Sounding-lead. **2. a** Weight attached to plumb-line; **b** plumb-line. **3.** Weight attached to fishing-line to keep float in position.

plummy, adj. [1. plúmi; 2. plámi]. **plum** & **-y. 1.** Full of plums; resembling a plum in taste or odour. **2.** (colloq.) Rich, desirable.

plumose, adj. [1. plōōmōs; 2. plúmous], fr. Lat. *plūmōs-(us)*, 'downy, feathered', fr. *plūm-(a)*, 'feather, down', see **plume (I.)**, & **-ose**. a Bearing, covered with, feathers; **b** resembling a feather.

plump (I.), adj., & vb. trans. & intrans. [1. plump; 2. plamp]. M.E. *plump*; cp. Du. *plomp*. **1.** adj. (of bodily condition) Well covered with flesh; rounded, well filled out: *plump cheeks* &c. **2.** vb. trans. & intrans. Usually *plump up*, to make or become plump; to cause (fruits &c.) to swell as with ripeness: '*To swell the gourd, and plump the hazel shells With a sweet kernel*' (Keats, 'To Autumn').

plump (II.), vb. intrans. & trans. M.E. *plumpen*; cp. Du. *plompen*; prob. imitative. **A.** intrans. **1.** To fall abruptly and heavily. **2.** *Plump for*, to give all one's support in voting to a single candidate in an election where several are to be elected. **B.** trans. To cause to fall abruptly and heavily.

plump (III.), n., adv., & adj., fr. prec. **1.** n. **a** Heavy, abrupt, drop or plunge; **b** a sudden heavy fall of rain. **2.** adv. **a** With sudden, heavy fall: *to fall plump*; **b** bluntly, downright, without mincing matters: *I told him plump what I thought of him*. **3.** adj. Flat, downright: *a plump refusal*.

plump (IV.), n. Origin unknown. (archaic) Cluster, group, company; esp. in Phr. *plump of spears*, troop of spearmen.

plumper (I.), n. [1. plúmper; 2. plámpə]. **plump (I.)** & **-er**. Pad carried in the mouth to plump out hollow cheeks.

plumper (II.), n. **plump (II.)** & **-er**. **1.** **a** One who plumps for particular candidate; **b** vote given in this way. **2.** Downright, unqualified lie.

plumply, adv. [1. plúmpli; 2. plámpli]. **plump (I.)** & **-ly**. In a plump manner.

plumpness, n. [1. plúmpnes; 2. plámpnis]. See prec. & **-ness**. State or quality of being plump.

plum-pudding, n. **1.** Rich boiled or steamed pudding made with flour, raisins, eggs, suet, spices, peel &c.; esp. that eaten at Christmas. **2.** Plain boiled suet pudding with raisins &c.

plum-pudding dog, n. A Dalmatian, so called from its dark spots.

plum-pudding stone, n. Conglomerate of pebbles &c.

plumulaceous, adj. [1. plōōmūláshus; 2. plùmjuléiʃəs]. **plumule** & **-aceous**. Resembling a plumule; downy.

plumular, adj. [1. plōōmūlar; 2. plúmjulə]. See prec. & **-ar**. (bot.) Of, pertaining to, a plumule.

plumule, n. [1. plōōmūl; 2. plúmjūl], fr. Lat. *plūmula*, dimin. of *plūma*, 'feather, down'. See **plume (I.)**. **1.** Down-feather; little feather. **2.** (bot.) Rudimentary stem of young plant.

plumy, adj. [1. plōōmi; 2. plúmi]. **plume (I.)** & **-y**. **1.** Plume-like, feathery. **2.** Adorned with plumes.

plunder (I.), vb. trans. [1. plúnder; 2. plándə], fr. Germ. *plündern*, 'to plunder, pillage', fr. *plunder*, 'lumber, baggage, furniture; trash'; etymol. uncertain; it was introduced in 17th cent., first 1632, prob. by soldiers who had served in Thirty Years' War. **1.** **a** (specif., of invading army) To seize property by force from (a city); to sack, loot, despoil; **b** to deprive (person) of property or belongings of any kind. **2.** To take another's property by violence, force, or fraud; to steal, embezzle.

plunder (II.), n., fr. prec. **1.** Act of plundering. **2.** Property obtained by force or fraud; loot, booty. **3.** Gain, profit.

plunderage, n. [1. plúnderij; 2. plándəridž]. Prec. & **-age**. **1.** Robbery, esp. embezzlement of goods on board ship. **2.** Property obtained by plundering.

plunge (I.), vb. trans. & intrans. [1. plunj; 2. plandž], fr. O. Fr. *plunjer*, fr. Low Lat. **plumbicāre*, 'to heave the lead', fr. *plumb-(um)*, 'lead', see **plumb (I.)**. **A.** trans. **1.** **a** To immerse suddenly, and with rapid action, into any kind of liquid: *to plunge one's head into a bucket of water*; **b** to thrust forcibly into a cavity or receptacle: *to plunge one's hand into an ant-hill, into a bag* &c.; **c** to stick, strike, jab (a pointed instrument) into: *to plunge a knife into a pie, a sword into another's breast*. **2.** **a** To drive, force, into, involve suddenly in, specified condition or situation: *to plunge a country into war*; *to plunge one's family into poverty*; (fig.) **b** *to plunge the room in darkness*. **3.** (gardening) To sink (flower-pot) into ground up to rim. **B.** intrans. **1.** (lit. and fig.) To hurl oneself into the midst of; dive, rush into, enter suddenly: *to plunge into the river, into a discussion, fight* &c. **2.** To move hastily and violently, rush: *to plunge down the slope*. **3.** **a** (of horse) To throw itself suddenly forward upon its fore-feet; **b** (of ship) to pitch. **4.** To gamble, speculate irresponsibly & recklessly.

plunge (II.), n., fr. prec. Act of plunging, dive; sudden, violent movement. Phr. *to take the plunge*, decide to embark upon a new and doubtful course of action, to take a step concerning which one has hesitation or misgiving.

plunger, n. [1. plúnjer; 2. plándžə]. **plunge (I.)** & **-er**. **1.** One who, that which, plunges; specif., part of machine having plunging motion, as the ram of hydraulic press, part of pump which enters the water &c. **2.** (slang) **a** A rash, foolish, ignorant gambler; **b** (obs.) cavalry-man.

plunk, vb. trans. & intrans. & n. [1. plungk; 2. plaŋk]. Imitative, cp. **plump (II.)**. (colloq.) **1.** vb. **a** trans. To push, throw, heavily or abruptly; **b** intrans., to fall heavily. **2.** n. (U.S.A., slang) A dollar.

pluperfect, adj. & n. [1. plōōpérfekt; 2. plūpə́fikt], fr. Lat. *plūs quam perfectum*, 'more than perfect'. See **plus & perfect**. **1.** adj. *The pluperfect tense*, denoting action already completed, or an event which had already come about before some specified point of time in the past; e.g. *he had made his will a few days before he died*. **2.** n. Pluperfect tense.

plural, adj. & n. [1. plōōral; 2. plɔ́r(ə)l, plúər(ə)l], fr. Lat. *plūrāl-(is)*, 'of more than one; plural', fr. *plūr-*, stem of *plūs*, 'more', see **plus**, & **-al**. **1.** adj. **a** (gram.) Denoting more than one, or, in languages having a dual number, more than two; **b** containing, consisting of, more than one. **2.** n. **a** Plural number; **b** form of noun, verb &c. denoting plural number.

pluralism, n. [1. plōōralizm; 2. plɔ́rəlizəm]. Prec. & **-ism**. **1.** System or fact of holding more than one office (esp. more than one ecclesiastical benefice) at the same time. **2.** (philos.) Doctrine that there is more than one ultimate principle of existence and causality.

pluralist, n. [1. plōōralist; 2. plɔ́rəlist]. **plural** & **-ist**. **1.** Person holding more than one official position, or ecclesiastical benefice, at the same time. **2.** Adherent of the doctrine of pluralism.

pluralistic, adj. [1. plōōralístik; 2. plɔrəlístik]. Prec. & **-ic**. Of, pertaining to, pluralism or pluralists.

plurality, n. [1. plōōráliti; 2. plɔrǽliti], fr. Lat. *plūrālitāt-(em)*, 'plurality'. See **plural** & **-ity**. **1.** State of being plural; number greater than one. **2.** **a** Holding of more than one benefice at the same time; **b** one of the benefices held by a pluralist. **3.** Majority, greater number.

pluralize, vb. trans. & intrans. [1. plōōralīz; 2. plɔ́rəlaiz]. **plural** & **-ize**. **1.** trans. To make plural, express in the plural, give a plural form to. **2.** intrans. To hold more than one benefice at the same time.

plurally, adv. [1. plōōrali; 2. plɔ́rəli]. **plural** & **-ly**. In a plural sense.

pluri-, pref. representing Lat. *plūr-*, stem of *plūs*, 'more'. See next word. More; e.g. *pluriliteral*, (Heb. gram.) containing more than three letters; *pluripresence*, presence in more than one place.

plus, prep., adj., & n. [1. plus; 2. plas]. Lat. *plūs*, 'more'; cp. Lat. *plūrimus*, 'most'; cogn. w. Gk. *polús*, 'many', see **poly-**, *pléon*, 'more', see **pleonasm**, fr. base **plē-*, **p(e)lə-* &c., 'full; to fill, be full', see **plenum** & **full (I.)**. **1.** prep. Increased by, with addition of, opposite of *minus*: *the salary is £500, plus commissions*; (in math.) written +; specif., in handicapping, as in golf, denoting number of strokes the player has to give, as *plus 2, 4*, thus starting so many behind scratch player. **2.** adj. **a** Forming an addition, extra; **b** (math.) positive; indicating a positive quantity; **c** (elect.) electrified positively. **3.** n. **a** The symbol +; **b** extra quantity, addition; **c** (math.) positive quantity.

plus fours, n. pl. [1. plús fórz; 2. plás fɔ̄z]. Very loose knickerbockers, reaching well below the knee, adopted by golfers; so called not ironically, as suited only to experts on the plus 4 mark, but as a tailor's term, indicating an additional four inches over-lap below the knee.

plush, n. [1. plush; 2. plaʃ], fr. Fr. *pluche*, earlier *peluche*, fr. Low Lat. **piluceus*, fr. Lat. *pilus*, 'hair'. See **pile (VII.)**. **1.** Kind of silk or cotton cloth like velvet, but with longer and more open pile. **2.** (pl.) Footman's plush breeches.

plushy, adj. [1. plúshi; 2. pláʃi]. Prec. & **-y**. Of, like, plush.

plutarchy, n. [1. plōōtarki; 2. plútāki], fr. Gk. *ploût-(os)*, 'wealth', see **plutocracy**, & *-arkhia*, 'rule', fr. *árkh-(ein)*, 'to rule', q.v. under **arch-**. Plutocracy.

Pluto, n. [1. plōōtō; 2. plútou]. Gk. *Ploútōn*. **1.** (class. mythol.) God of infernal regions. **2.** (astron.) Name given to the planet most remote from the sun, beyond Neptune, discovered 1930.

plutocracy, n. [1. plōōtókrasi; 2. plūtɔ́krəsi], fr. Gk. *ploutokratía*, 'plutocracy', fr. *ploûto-(s)*, 'wealth', cogn. w. Gk. *polús*, 'many'; Scrt. *puruš*, 'numerous, rich'; see **plenum**, & **-cracy**. **1.** Government by wealth, or by the wealthy. **2.** (contempt.) Any body of persons who wield (undue) influence in the State, or in affairs generally, by reason of their wealth.

plutocrat, n. [1. plōōtokrat; 2. plútəkræt], fr. Gk. *ploutokrat-(ía)*, 'plutocracy'. See prec. Person who rules, or is influential, primarily by virtue of his wealth.

plutocratic, adj. [1. plōōtokrátik; 2. plūtəkrǽtik]. Prec. & **-ic**. Pertaining to a plutocracy or a plutocrat.

plutolatry, n. [1. plōōtólatri; 2. plūtɔ́lətri], fr. Gk. *ploûto-(s)*, 'wealth', see **plutocracy**, & **-latry**. Worship of wealth.

pluto monkey, n. See **Pluto**. A West African, long-tailed monkey, *Cercopithecus leucampyx*, allied to the guenon, of grizzled colour with white frontal band.

Plutonian, adj. [1. plōōtónian; 2. plūtóuniən]. See **Pluto** & **-ian**. Plutonic.

Plutonic, adj. [1. plōōtónik; 2. plūtɔ́nik], See prec. & **-ic**. (cap.) **1.** Of, pertaining to, Pluto or the infernal regions. **2.** (geol.) *Plutonic rocks*, igneous rocks originally formed at considerable depths below the surface of the earth; *Plutonic theory*, that which regarded heat as the main agency in causing geological phenomena.

Plutonism, n. [1. plōōtunizm; 2. plútənizəm]. See prec. & **-ism**. Plutonic theory.

Plutonist, n. [1. plōōtunist; 2. plútənist]. See prec. & **-ist**. Adherent of the Plutonic theory.

plutonomic, adj. [1. plōōtunómik; 2. plūtənɔ́mik]. **plutonomy** & **-ic**. Of, pertaining to, plutonomy.

plutonomist, n. [1. plōōtónumist; 2. plūtɔ́nəmist]. See next word & **-ist**. Student of plutonomy.

plutonomy, n. [1. plōōtónumi; 2. plūtɔ́nəmi], fr. Gk. *ploûto-(s)*, 'wealth'. See **plutocracy**. The second element is fr. Gk. *-nomia*, 'arrangement', see **nomad** & words there referred to. (rare) Political economy.

pluvial (I.), adj. [1. plōōvial; 2. plúviəl], fr. Lat. *pluviāl-(is)*, 'of rain, rainy', fr. *pluvia*, 'rain'; cp. Lat. *pluere*, 'to rain', Gk. *pléein*, fr. *plewein, 'to swim, sail', Scrt. *plávatē*, 'swims'; Gk. *plóos*, 'sailing'; O.E. *flēotan*, 'to float, sail', see **fleet** (I.). **1.** Pertaining to, characterized by, rain; rainy. **2.** (geol.) Caused by rain.

pluvial (II.), n., fr. Med. Lat. *pluviāle*, 'rain-cloak', fr. neut. form of Lat. *pluviāl-(is)*, 'rainy'. See prec. (eccles.) Another name for the cope.

pluviometer, n. [1. plōōviómeter; 2. plùviómitə], fr. Lat. *pluvi-(a)*, 'rain', see **pluvial** (I.), & *-o-* & **-meter**. Rain-gauge.

pluviometric(al), adj. [1. plōōviométrik(l); 2. plùviəmétrik(l)]. Prec. & **-ic** & **-al**. Of, pertaining to, a rain-gauge or the measuring of rain.

Pluviôse, n. [1. plūvióz; 2. plyvioz], fr. Lat. *pluvi-(us)*, 'rainy', fr. *pluvi-(a)*, 'rain', see **pluvial** (I.). Fifth month of the French Revolutionary calendar, from Jan. 20th to Feb. 18th.

pluvious, adj. [1. plōōvius; 2. plúviəs], fr. Lat. *pluvi-(us)*, 'rainy', fr. *pluvi-(a)*, 'rain', see **pluvial** (I.) & **-ous**. Pertaining to, liable to, rain; rainy.

ply (I.), n. [1. plī; 2. plai], fr. Fr. *pli*, 'fold', fr. O. Fr. *ploi*, fr. *ployer*, 'to fold', fr. Lat. *plicāre*, 'to fold, twist', see **plicate**. **a** Fold, layer, thickness, of cloth, wood &c.; **b** strand, thread, single twist, of rope, wood &c.; *2-, 3-, 4-ply*, having 2, 3, 4, strands, layers &c.

ply (II.), vb. trans. & intrans., fr. **apply**. **A.** trans. **1.** To wield, use vigorously, work with: *to ply a tool, one's needle* &c. **2.** To follow diligently, work at: *to ply a trade*. **3. a** To offer repeatedly to, supply persistently: *to ply a person with food, drink* &c.; **b** to importune, pursue constantly, repeatedly, assail: *to ply a person with questions* &c. **B.** intrans. **1.** To go regularly, take a regular course, esp. (of public conveyance) travel to and fro: *to ply for hire*. **2.** To attend regularly, wait for custom, usually at specific place. **3.** (naut.) To work against the wind.

Plymouth Brethren, n. [1. plímuth brédhren; 2. plíməþ bréðrin], fr. Plymouth, port in Devonshire. Small religious sect of Calvinistic views founded by John Darby about 1830 in Plymouth and in Dublin.

Plymouthism, n. [1. plímuthizm; 2. plíməþizəm]. Doctrines of Plymouth Brethren.

Plymouthist, n. [1. plímuthist; 2. plíməþist]. Member of Plymouth Brethren.

Plymouthite, n. [1. plímuthīt; 2. plíməþait]. Plymouthist.

Plymouth Rock, n. [1. plímuth rók; 2. plíməþ rɔ́k], fr. the famous rock at Plymouth, Mass. Breed of domestic fowls with blue-grey plumage uniformly barred with black; originally raised in U.S.A.

plywood, n. [1. plíwood; 2. pláiwud]. **ply** (I.) & **wood**. A tough material made of two or three layers or plies of wood glued together, the grain of each layer being placed crossways.

pneuma, n. [1. nūma; 2. njúmə]. Gk. *pneûma*, 'wind, air, breath'; cogn. w. *pnéein*, 'to blow', *pneûsai*, 'to breathe'; prob. also cogn. w. O.H.G. *fnehan*, 'to breathe', & O.E. *fnǣst*, 'breath, blast'. (anct. philos. and also theol.) The vital spirit, the breath of life; the soul or spiritual part of man; specif., the Holy Spirit.

pneumatic (I.), adj. [1. nūmátik; 2. njūmǽtik], fr. Gk. *pneúmat-*, stem of prec. & **-ic**. **1. a** Of, pertaining to, air, gases; **b** containing, made to contain, inflated by, air: *pneumatic tire*; **c** worked by compressed air: *pneumatic drill, lift, organ* &c.; *pneumatic despatch* or *post*, transmission of letters &c. by compressed air through tubes. **2.** (theol., rare) Pertaining to the pneuma or spirit; spiritual. **3.** (zool.) Containing, having, cavities filled with air; (used of certain bones in a bird).

pneumatic (II.), n., fr. prec. **1.** A pneumatic tire. **2.** A bellows or tube in an organ blown by compressed air.

pneumatically, adv. [1. nūmátikali; 2. njūmǽtikəli]. See prec. & **-al** & **-ly**. Driven, worked, by compressed air.

pneumatics, n. pl. The science of the mechanical properties of air, and other elastic bodies such as gases.

pneumato-, pref. Form of **pneuma**, 'air', used in compounds.

pneumatocyst, n. [1. nūmatōsist; 2. njúmətousist]. See prec. & **cyst**. Air cavity or sac in the body of certain marine animals &c.

pneumatology, n. [1. nùmatóloji; 2. njùmətɔ́lədži]. **pneumato-** & **-logy**. **1.** Pneumatics. **2.** (philos. or theol.) Doctrine concerning spiritual beings, esp. the Holy Spirit.

pneumatolytic, adj. [1. nùmatōlítik; 2. njùmətoulítik]. **pneumato-** & **-lytic**. (geol.) Formed by the pressure of heated air, of ores &c. found near volcanic or igneous rocks.

pneumatometer, n. [1. nùmatómeter; 2. njùmətɔ́mitə]. **pneumato-** & **-meter**. Instrument for measuring the force of respiration.

pneumatophore, n. [1. nūmatōfōr; 2. njúmətoufɔ̄]. **pneumato-** & **-phore**. **a** (bot.) A breathing organ on the roots of marsh-plants; **b** (zool.) a sac or air-cavity in various marine animals, such as jelly-fish &c.

pneumo-, pref. Combining form, fr. Gk. *pneúmon-(os)*, *pneúmōn*, 'the lung', see **pneuma**.

pneumococcus, n. [1. nùmōkókus; 2. njùmoukɔ́kəs]. See prec. & **coccus**. The infective micro-organism which causes acute lobar pneumonia or inflammation of the lungs.

pneumogastric, adj. [1. nùmōgástrik; 2. njùmougǽstrik]. **pneumo-** & **gastric**. Of, pertaining to, the regions of the lungs and stomach; *pneumogastric nerves*, those running through the neck and thorax to the stomach.

pneumonia, n. [1. nūmṓnia; 2. njūmóuniə]. Gk. *pneumonía*, 'a disease of the lungs'. See **pneumo-** & **pneuma**. Inflammation of a lung or of both lungs.

pneumonic, adj. [1. nūmónik; 2. njūmɔ́nik]. Prec. & **-ic**. Pertaining to the lungs or to pneumonia.

poa, n. [1. pṓa; 2. póuə]. Gk. *póā*, 'grass', prob. fr. **poiwa*, & cogn. w. Lith. *pëva*, 'meadow'. (bot.) The genus of grasses which includes the meadow grasses.

poach (I.), vb. intrans. & trans. [1. pōch; 2. poutʃ], fr. O. Fr. *pochier*, later *pocher*, also spelt *poucher*, 'to poke, thrust one's fingers into'; in Phr. *pocher le labeur d'autruy* (Cotgrave), 'to encroach on, interfere with another's work'; etymol. doubtful; prob. conn. w. **poke** (I.) & **pouch**. **A.** intrans. **1.** To trespass on land belonging to another in search of game or fish; to search for game or fish illegally: *to poach upon another's preserves*; (also fig.) to infringe another's rights, privileges, functions &c.: *to poach for pheasants, salmon* &c. **2.** (by transf.) **a** To encroach on what is another's sphere of action; to take an unfair advantage or start of: *to poach in other people's business*; *to poach for fresh ideas* &c.; **b** to take a ball, as in lawn tennis &c., which one's partner should take. **3.** To become sodden, trampled into wet holes, by cattle &c. (of land or turf). **B.** trans. **1.** To take, catch, game or fish on another's property illegally; to trespass on land in search of game or fish: *to poach pheasants, salmon* &c.; *to poach preserves, a river* &c. **2.** (by transf.) To take from, unfairly or by encroachment: *to poach ideas from another*; *to poach a start in a race, a ball in one's partner's court* &c. **3.** To trample into wet, muddy holes, as land or turf: *the cattle have poached the meadow*; *the lawn is poached and spoiled*.

poach (II.), vb. trans. Earlier *poche*; fr. O. Fr. *pochier*, later *pocher*, 'to poach eggs', *œufs pochés*; fr. *poche*, 'a pocket', see **pouch** & **poke** (I.); accepted as distinct word fr. prec. To boil eggs without their shells, breaking them into boiling water.

poacher, n. [1. pṓcher; 2. póutʃə]. **poach** (I.) & **-er**. **1.** One who trespasses on another's land in search of game or fish; one who catches game or fish illegally. **2.** One who encroaches on another's sphere of action, or who takes an unfair start or advantage.

poaching, n. [1. pṓching; 2. póutʃiŋ]. **poach** (I.) & **-ing**. Action of a poacher.

pochard, n. [1. pṓchard; 2. póutʃəd]. Etymol. uncertain. The male of various species of diving sea-ducks, the female of which is called the *dunbird*, with bright coppery red head, blue at the base of the broad bill, and black breast; American species are the red-head and canvas-back duck.

pock, n. [1. pok; 2. pɔk]. O.E. *pocc*, 'pustule', M.E. *pokke*; also Du. *pok*, cp. pl. form **pox**. (usually pl.) A pustule on the skin; as in various eruptive diseases, as small-pox and chicken-pox; pit or scar left by such pustule; chiefly in the compounds *pock-mark*, scar from small-pox &c.; *pock-marked*, having such scars.

pocket (I), n. [1. póket; 2. pɔ́kit]. M.E. *poket*, fr. A.-Fr. *pokete*, O. North. Fr. *poquette*, dimin. of *poque*; dialectal variant of Fr. *poche*, 'pouch'. See **pouch** & **poke** (I.). **1.** A bag or sack, now chiefly used as a measure of hops, wool, ginger &c. **2.** Small bag or pouch inserted in or forming part of one's clothing, for carrying money or other small articles. Phrs. *to pick a pocket*, to steal from the pocket of anyone; *to put one's pride in one's pocket*, to put, lay, aside one's pride; *to put one's hand in one's pocket*, to spend money; *to have a person in one's pocket*, to have him entirely under one's influence. **3.** (by transf.) Pecuniary means, money, cash. Phrs. *a deep pocket*, ample means; *to be in, out of, pocket*, to have gained, lost, money: *in, out of, pocket by so much*. **4.** Various special uses: **a** a small string bag or pouch at corners and centre of sides of a billiard table; **b** a small cavity or hole in the earth or rock containing gold, silver, or other ore; **c** a small sac or swelling in the body containing serous fluid or pus; **d** an area in the air in which, owing to atmospheric conditions, there exists a partial vacuum and which therefore does not afford support for an aeroplane; also *air-pocket*.

pocket (II.), vb. trans., fr. prec. **1.** To put into one's pocket. Phrs. *to pocket an insult*, accept it without protest; *to pocket one's pride*, to suppress it, humble oneself. **2.** Specif., to make a profit, enrich oneself: *he pocketed a nice sum over the transaction*. **3.** To put (a ball) into a pocket at billiards.

pocket-book, n. A small case for carrying letters, currency notes &c. in one's pocket; a small note-book.

pocket-borough, n. Type of parliamentary borough constituency existing before the Reform Act of 1832, election to which was in the control of a particular person or family.

pocketful, n. [1. póketfool; 2. pɔ́kitful]. **pocket** (I.) & **-ful**. As much as a pocket will hold; amount to fill a pocket. Phr. *a pocketful of money*, a considerable quantity; a fortune.

pocket-gopher, n. A small, rat-like, burrowing rodent, *Geomys bursarius*, of N. America, with large cheek-pouches opening from the outside, used for carrying food.

pocket-handkerchief, n. One carried in the pocket.

pocket-knife, n. A small knife with hinged, folding blade, to be carried in the pocket when closed.

pocket-money, n. Money for small personal current expenses; weekly or other allowance to children &c.

pock-marked, adj. See **pock**.

pocky, adj. [1. póki; 2. pɔ́ki]. **pock** & **-y**. Scarred by, covered with, pock-marks.

poco, adv. [1. pṓkō; 2. pṓko]. Ital., 'little, slightly'. (in musical direction) A little, somewhat: *poco più allegro*, a little more lively, rather quicker; *poco largo*, somewhat slowly &c.

pococurante, adj. & n. [1. pṓkōkōōráhntā, pṓkōkūránte; 2. pókokūrǽnte, póukoukjurǽnti]. Ital., fr. *poco*, 'little', & *curante*, 'caring'. **1.** adj. Caring little, indifferent, not enthusiastic, apathetic. **2.** n. An indifferent, unenthusiastic, apathetic person; trifler.

pococurantism, n. [1. pòkōkūrántizm; 2. pòukoukjurǽntizəm]. Prec. & **-ism.** Attitude of a pococurante; apathy, indifference.

pod (I.), n. & vb. trans. & intrans. [1. pod; 2. pɔd]. Etymol. unknown. **1.** n. **a** The long, narrow, seed-vessel of leguminous plants such as beans or peas; **b** a receptacle or case resembling a bean pod, as a silkworm cocoon, egg-case of a locust, narrow-necked eel-net &c.; **c** (vulg.) the belly. **2.** vb. **a** trans. To remove pod from, to shell (peas or beans); **b** intrans., to produce, swell into, pods; to swell out as the seeds ripen: *beans are podding early this year*; also *pod up*.

pod (II.), n. Etymol. unknown. A small cluster of seals or whales.

-pod, suff., fr. Gk. *pod-*, 'foot', fr. base seen in *poús*, fr. **pod-s*, see **pedal** & **foot**; used in sense of having specified number or kind of feet &c., e.g. *cephalopod*, *gastropod* &c.

podagra, n. [1. podágra; 2. pɔdǽgrə]. Lat., fr. Gk. *podágra*, fr. *pod-(ós)*, *poús*, 'foot', see prec., & *ágra*, 'a catching, seizure', cogn. w. Gk. *agréein*, 'to take, catch'; Avestan *azra*, 'chase'; W. *aer* (fr. **agro-*), 'battle'. Gout, especially in the feet.

podagric, podagrous, adj. [1. podágrik, -us; 2. pɔdǽgrik, -əs]. Prec. & **-ic, -ous.** Gouty.

podesta, n. [1. podestáh; 2. pɔdestǽ]. Ital., *podestà*, 'governor', fr. Lat. *potestāt-(em)*, *potestas*, 'power', fr. *potis*, 'able, capable', see **potent** (I.). **a** A chief magistrate or public official in an Italian municipality; **b** (hist.) originally, magistrate appointed in Lombardy as representative of the Holy Roman Empire, later the chief magistrate of the free, republican cities of Italy.

podgy, adj. [1. póji; 2. pɔ́dži]. Origin unknown. Fat, thick, pursy, stumpy and short: *a podgy person, fingers* &c.

podium, n. [1. pṓdium; 2. póudiəm]. Lat., fr. Gk. *pódion*, see **-pod.** **1.** (archit.) **a** The low wall round the arena of an amphitheatre; **b** the projecting lowest part of the stylobate or platform of a temple or other columned building; **c** a low projecting bench of stone round a hall or large room. **2.** (zool.) The footlike attachment or tube on the underside of a star-fish, sea-urchin &c.

podo-, pref. meaning 'foot'; fr. Gk. See **-pod**; e.g. *podophthalmate*, stalk-eyed, of certain crustaceans.

podocarpous, adj. [1. pòdokárpus; 2. pɔ̀dɔkáːpəs]. See prec. & **-carpous.** (bot.) Belonging to a genus, *Podocarpus*, of Asiatic and New Zealand conifers, the black pines, with curiously shaped, pulpy, one-seeded fruit.

podophyllin, n. [1. pòdofílin, podófilin; 2. pɔ̀dɔfílin, pɔdɔ́filin]. See **podo-** & **phyllo-** & **-in.** A bitter, purgative resin obtained from the wild mandrake or May apple, *Podophyllum peltatum*.

-podous, suff. [1. podus; 2. pədəs], forming adjs. fr. ns. ending in **-pod**; see **-ous**; e.g. *gasteropodous*.

poë, or **poë-bird**, n. [1. pṓe; 2. póui]. Tahiti native word for 'ear-ring, pearl bead'; given to the bird by Captain Cook. A New Zealand bird, with very dark metallic plumage and white tufts at the neck; also called *parson-bird*.

poem, n. [1. pṓim; 2. póuim], fr. Fr. *poème*, fr. Lat. *poēma*, fr. Gk. *poiēma*, 'something made, done; a composition, poem', fr. base seen in *poieîn*, 'to make', see **poet.** **1. a** A literary composition forming a unity in itself, written in a metrical form, rhymed or unrhymed; the word usually implies also a certain emotional, imaginative, or romantic treatment of the subject-matter, and a style and diction which are marked by appropriateness to the emotions and ideas expressed, together with beauty of sound, and the quality of evoking images; **b** a prose composition which, though lacking metre, has the other qualities of a poem. **2.** Any expression of human passion and emotion and the interplay of these, as revealed in a series of events and actions, and the situations arising from these.

poesy, n. [1. pṓ̇zi; 2. póuizi]. M.E. *poesie*, fr. O. Fr. *poesie*, Mod. *poésie*, fr. Lat. *poēsis*, fr. Gk. *poíēsis*, 'a making, creating, shaping; poetic power, poetry'. See **poet.** (archaic or poet.) Poetry; poems.

poet, n. [1. pṓ̇t; 2. póuit], fr. O. Fr. *poete*, Mod. *poète*, fr. Lat. *poēta*, fr. Gk. *poiētḗs*, 'one who makes, a maker, an artificer; a poet'; cp. Gk. *poieîn*; the base is **kʷei-*, **kʷoi-* &c., seen also in Scrt. *činṓti*, 'to bring together, arrange, pile up; construct', cogn. w. O. Slav. *činŭ*, 'order, command'. **a** A writer of poems or poetry, whether good or bad: *a poor poet*; specif. **b** one whose work is marked by high powers of imagination and great beauty of language; a good, or great, poet: *it seems absurd to deny that Pope was a poet*.

poetaster, n. [1. pṓitàster; 2. póuitǽstə]. **poet** & **-aster.** An inferior poet, a scribbler of verse.

poetess, n. [1. pṓites; 2. póuitis]. Prec. & **-ess.** A woman poet.

poetic, poetical, adj. [1. pōétik(l); 2. pouétik(l)], fr. Fr. *poétique*, fr. Lat. *poēticus*, fr. Gk. *poiētikós*. **poet** & **-ic** & **-al.** No very hard and fast distinction can be made between the usages of these two words; on the whole *poetical* refers more often to the form, and *poetic* to the inner and spiritual quality and essence of poetry. **1.** Pertaining to poetry; **a** having the form, or quality of poetry: *a poetical romance*; *poetical treatment*; **b** suitable to, characteristic of, used in, poetry: *poetic diction, language, style* &c.; **c** appropriate for poetry: *a poetic(al) subject, theme.* Phrs. *poetic(al) justice*, ideal, romantic justice as in a poem, play &c., where vice is punished and virtue rewarded; *poetic licence*, latitude permissible in poetry or other imaginative writing, in regard to absolute regularity of metre, to grammatical strictness, and adherence to literal facts, consistency of plot &c. **2. a** Marked by high, creative, and imaginative force or by other qualities essential to poetry: *poetic genius, faculty, imagination*; **b** like a poet or poetry; imaginative, full of imagination, romantic: *a poetical person*; *poetical fancies*.

poetically, adv. [1. pōétikali; 2. pouétikəli]. Prec. & **-ly.** In a poetic(al) form or spirit.

poeticize, vb. trans. [1. pōétisīz; 2. pouétisaiz]. **poetic** & **-ize.** To make poetic; to turn into poetry, put into poetical form; to treat poetically.

poetics, n. pl. [1. pōétiks; 2. pouétiks]. The theory, aesthetics, of poetry; *The Poetics*, treatise by Aristotle on poetry, dealing, in its extant form, with dramatic poetry.

poetize, vb. intrans. & trans. [1. pṓitīz; 2. póuitaiz]. **poet** & **-ize.** **1.** intrans. To play the poet; to compose, write poetry. **2.** trans. To treat in a poetical way; to make poetic.

Poet Laureate, n. See **laureate.**

poetry, n. [1. pṓitri; 2. póuitri], fr. O. Fr. *poeterie*, *poetrie*, fr. Low Lat. *poetria*; in Class. Lat. this word, as the Gk. orig. *poiḗtria*, has the sense of 'poetess'. See **poet** & **-ry.** **1.** The art of poets or of a poet; the work of a poet; **a** the expression of thought and emotion in verse, with an appropriate diction, which, according to Milton, must be 'simple, sensuous, and passionate'; poetry is classified according to its form as *dramatic, epic, lyric* &c., or according to the subject or motive, as *didactic, erotic, satiric* &c.; **b** (loosely) any composition in verse or what is intended as such, irrespective of whether it possesses any true poetic quality or not: *most young men write some poetry sooner or later.* **2.** (cap.) The inspiring Goddess or Muse of poetry and poets; the Muse, *par excellence.* **3.** Poems, poetical works: *Byron's poetry*; *Elizabethan poetry.* **4.** Emotional poetic quality; something which affects the mind as poetry does: *the poetry of nature, of motion* &c. **5.** Thoughts, ideas, in themselves possessing some poetic quality, expressed not in verse but in prose: *prose poetry.*

Poets' Corner, n. Place in the south transept of Westminster Abbey, where many great poets are buried or have monuments erected to their memory.

pogrom, n., Engl. pronunciation [1. pṓgrom; 2. póugrɔm], Russ. [1. pugróm; 2. pagrɔ́m], 'devastation, pillage'. An organized massacre and plunder, esp. of Jews, in Russia; any organized persecution of a class or sect.

poi, n. [1. pṓē, poi; 2. póuī, pɔi]. Hawaiian name. Paste made of pounded taro root and allowed to ferment, used as food.

poignancy, n. [1. póinansi; 2. pɔ́inənsi]. See next word & **-cy.** State, quality, of being poignant (in material as well as spiritual sense).

poignant, adj. [1. póinant; 2. pɔ́inənt]. O. Fr. Pres. Part. of *poindre*, 'to prick, sting', fr. Lat. *pungere*, 'to prick', see **point** (I.). (rarely used in other than spiritual sense) **a** Gripping, and affecting the feelings powerfully with a sense of unhappiness, pathos &c.: *poignant grief, sorrow*; *a poignant situation*; **b** pointed, biting, corrosive: *poignant wit, sarcasm*; *a poignant retort.*

poignantly, adv. Prec. & **-ly.** In a poignant manner.

poikilo-, pref. Gk. *poikílos*, 'of many colours, variegated'; cogn. w. **paint** (II.), **picture** (I.); as *poikilitic*, adj., of rocks &c., mottled; *poikilocytosis*, n., an advanced stage of anaemia, in which the blood corpuscles assume irregular shapes.

poilu, n. [1. pwahlū; 2. pwaly]. Fr., 'hairy; private soldier, a tommy'; fr. *poil*, 'hair', fr. Lat. *pilus*, see **pile** (VII.). A French private soldier.

poinding, n. [1. póinding; 2. pɔ́indiŋ], fr. O.E. *pyndan*, 'to impound', see **pound** (III.). (Scots law) Distraint; seizure of a debtor's chattels in satisfaction of a debt.

poinsettia, n. [1. pòinsétia; 2. pɔ̀insétiə], fr. J. R. Poinsett, American diplomatist, d. 1851. (bot.) A South American plant, genus *Euphorbia*, with brilliant red bracts to the small yellowish true flower.

point (I.), n. [1. point; 2. pɔint], fr. Fr. *point*, 'a pricking, piercing, mark, dot'; also *pointe*, 'piercing thing, sharp end', also directly, fr. Lat. *punct-(um)*, P.P. of *pungere*, 'to prick, pierce'; secondary meaning fr. L. Lat. *puncta*, 'point of a weapon, puncture'; in Class. Lat. *punctum* is used in sense 'a mark, dot, point in line or space'; cp. **pungent** & **puncture**, & fr. type **pug-*, **pugilist** & **pugnacious.** The various meanings may for convenience be grouped as **A**, that which is pricked or pierced; a mark, dot, and **B**, that which pricks or pierces; a pointed instrument; the uses shade into one another and cannot always be sharply differentiated. **A.** A mark, dot, actual or imaginary, as if made by a pricking or piercing instrument. **1.** A small mark or dot; **a** (in punct.) a mark, esp. the period or full stop; **b** (in Semitic languages) a dot or other mark used to indicate vowel and other sounds: *a vowel, diacritical, point*; **c** (in decimals) the dot marking off the fractional parts from the integral numbers: 4·7; *a four-point-seven gun*; **d** (in mus.) (i.) (archaic) a single short phrase, a call on a trumpet &c.: *a point of war*; (ii.) a mark to indicate a break in chanting; **e** (in print. of

Braille type) a raised dot which the fingers of the blind can feel in reading. **2.** A mark, material or non-material, indicating position in space or time; **a** (material) a particular, special place, spot, without reference to space occupied: *a point in a landscape, on a road, map*; *to move from point to point*; *a point of direction, departure* &c.; **b** (non-material) of mental attitude: *a point of conscience, honour*; *this is the point on which he refused to yield.* Phrs. *a point of view,* mental standpoint; position from which, way in which, anything may be thought of, or conceived; *at all points,* in every particular, perfectly, completely: *armed, prepared, at all points*; **c** (of time) actual, precise, or particular moment: *at this point he got up.* Phrs. *at, on, the point of,* at the moment of, on the verge, brink of: *at the point of death*; *on the point of going, doing* &c., just about to go, do &c.; *on the point of war*; *when it came to the point,* the moment when something has to be done. **3.** Specific uses of prec.: **a** (astron. and math.) an imaginary spot or place, without reference to space occupied, as at end or intersection of lines or circles: *solstitial, equinoctial points*; (in Euclid's geom.) that which has no parts and no magnitude but only position; **b** (cricket) the position of a fielder; the fielder occupying this position on off-side of and facing the batsman, and close in; cp. *cover-point*; and *silly point,* under **silly (I.)**; **c** (her.) one of the several parts or divisions of a shield or escutcheon on which a charge may be borne: *dexter, sinister, point*; *chief point* &c.; **d** (mach.) position in reference to movements &c. of various parts: *fixed, dead, point of a crank* &c.; **e** (perspective) that to which or from which lines are drawn: *point of sight, vanishing point* &c.; **f** (racing) landmark, formerly a steeple, to which a horse-race across country was run; *point-to-point race,* one ridden across country, by members of a local hunt, over a course in which the successive points are marked by flags. **4.** That which serves to mark off or divide; a division, head; individual, particular, important item or detail: *points in a speech, argument, sermon* &c.; *to follow an argument point by point*; **a** particular detail or item which is meant to strike home, or on which special stress is laid; that which is striking, essential, pungent, or pointed: *the point of a joke, story*; *the special points to be remarked in the picture, play* &c.; Phrs. *to make, score, a point,* render some point in an argument telling, convincing, and effective; *to catch, miss, the point,* to appreciate or fail to appreciate the point of a story &c.; *to make a point of,* to insist, lay stress on; *off, from, the point, to the point, in point,* straying from, adhering to, the main issue or point; *to come to the point,* to reach the essential detail; *in point of fact,* as a matter of fact; *just the point,* the essential fact; *to stretch a point,* make considerable concessions; **b** a particular characteristic feature, distinctive mark: *the best, weakest, strongest, point in his character* &c.; *the horse has some good points*; **c** objective, object, purpose, use: *what is the point of getting angry?*; *there's no point in doing that.* **5.** That which serves to mark off a degree or unit; a degree, unit, stage; **a** (in cards or other games) a unit of standard or scale by which gain or loss is counted: *to play for penny points*; *to give so many points to,* as handicap; *A is points better than B* &c.; **b** (naut. &c.) one of the thirty-two marks by which the compass is divided; the angular space, 11° 15′, between any two consecutive points, each point being subdivided into half and quarter points; **c** (of physical units) degree, as of temperature &c.: *boiling, freezing, melting point*; *to fall three points below zero* &c.; *temperature has gone up two points*; **d** (print.) a unit for measuring the body of type: *Didot point,* ·0148 of inch; *12 point* &c.; **e** (of prices &c.) a single unit of value: *cotton, shares, cost of living &c. has gone up, down, several points.* **B.** That which pricks or pierces. **1.** A sharpened or tapering end; **a** the sharpened end of a weapon, tool &c.: *the point of a sword, bayonet, spear* &c.; *point of a knife, needle, pin* &c.; Phr. *at the point of the sword,* under threat of direct violence or force, under duress; **b** a projecting, tapering end, tip: *on the point of one's toes, at the point of one's fingers*; *the point of the nose*; specif., *the point,* of the chin, in boxing, the place where a direct blow has a concussing, deadly effect, cp. *mark*; **c** a small projection of land into the sea &c., a small promontory or cape, frequent in Place-Names: *Start Point*; *Battery Point* &c.; **d** a sharp corner or edge &c.: *a blue-point,* variety of oyster; *point steak,* a cut from the corner of a rump steak. **2.** In various specific uses: **a** (anct. costume) a lace with an ornamental metal tag, used for fastening the hose to the doublet, lacing a stomacher, fastening together the slashes in a sleeve &c.; **b** (engraving) an engraving needle: *dry point*; *silver point,* a silver pencil for drawing on specially prepared paper; **c** (of horses) any extremity, esp. at the hoof: *a bay with black points*; **d** (lace-making) a needle used in lace-making, thus lace made only with the needle: *point lace*; *Brussels point*; *point d'Alençon* &c.; **e** (rlys., usually *points*) a tapered rail moved by a switch for changing a train from one set of rails to another. **3.** (fig.) That which is pointed, pungent, or which reaches its mark: *a joke, epigram, or story without any point,* see **A. 4,** prec.

point (II.), vb. trans. & intrans., fr. O. Fr. *pointer.* See prec. **A.** trans. **1.** To give a point to: **a** (of material things) to cut to a point; to sharpen: *to point a stake, a pencil* &c.; **b** (of non-material things) to give point, force, pungency, to: '*To point a moral, or adorn a tale*'. **2.** *Point at,* to direct, aim, at or towards: *to point a gun at a person, his head* &c.; *to point one's finger at.* **3.** *Point out,* to direct the eye, attention, to; to indicate by gesture or word: *to point out an object to another*; *point me out the thing you want*; *to point out errors.* **4.** To mark out by points, signs, or marks; specif. **a** to mark with punctuation marks: *to point a sentence*; **b** with diacritical or vowel points, as in Semitic languages; **c** (masonry) to fill the joints between stones or bricks with mortar pressed in by the point of a trowel; **d** (mus.) to mark off a chant with points to show the breaks. **B.** intrans. **1.** To direct, aim, a finger, stick &c. at or towards an object, so as to indicate, or draw attention to: *to point at a person, thing*; *to point with the finger* &c.; *it is rude to point*; *the hand of the clock points to five o'clock*; *point out,* to intimate, indicate, call attention to the fact that: *let me point out that it is getting late* &c. **2.** Specif. (of dogs, esp. pointers) to indicate presence of game by standing steady and pointing the nose at the bird.

point-blank, adj. & adv. Prob. fr. **point (I.)** & **blank,** fr. the centre of the old archery target wh. was a blank or white circle, cp. O. Fr. Phr. *de pointe en blanc.* **1.** adj. **a** (of gun &c.) Aimed, fired, directly at a mark, without allowing for any curve in trajectory; aimed horizontally: *point-blank shot*; *point-blank range,* distance within which a shot aimed horizontally will hit the object; **b** (fig.) direct, unqualified; plain, blunt, downright, flat: *a point-blank assertion, denial* &c. **2.** adv. In a point-blank manner or way; **a** at point-blank range; directly: *the gun was aimed point-blank at his head*; **b** without qualification, bluntly: *he denied the accusation point-blank*; *refused the offer point-blank.*

point d'appui, n., anglicized to [1. pwàn dapwé; 2. pwǣdæpwí]. Fr. Point of support, base; specif. (mil.) basis of operations, fixed point on which troops are formed, or rest, for manœuvre.

point-device, adj. & adv., for earlier M.E. *at point device,* fr. O. Fr. *à point devis,* 'to the point devised or arranged'. **point (I.)** & **device.** (archaic) **1.** adj. Perfectly arranged and correct; precise, exact, perfectly neat in dress, manner &c. **2.** adv. Correctly, exactly; neatly.

point-duty, n. A policeman's duty at a fixed, stationary point, as for regulating traffic &c.; contrasted with *beat.*

pointed, adj. [1. póinted; 2. póintid]. **point (II.)** & **-ed.** **1.** **a** Sharpened to a point, furnished with a point: *a pointed stake, pencil* &c.; **b** coming to a point, like a point in shape: *pointed fingers*; *a pointed nose*; **c** (archit.) *pointed arch*; *the pointed style,* Gothic. **2.** (in moral sense) Trenchant, incisive, pungent: *a pointed remark, retort, allusion* &c.

pointedly, adv. Prec. & **-ly.** In a pointed manner; incisively; explicitly.

pointedness, n. See prec. & **-ness.** State, quality, of being pointed; incisiveness.

pointer, n. [1. póinter; 2. póintə]. **point (II.)** & **-er.** One who, thing which, points. Specif. **1.** The hand of a clock, the index of a weighing-machine; a rod or wand for indicating places, words &c. on a map or blackboard. **2.** (astron.) *Pointers,* the two stars in the Great Bear, a line through which points in the direction of the pole-star. **3.** A special breed of smooth-haired sporting dogs, which stop at the scent of game, and stand rigid with muzzle pointing towards the bird &c., with one paw raised.

pointillisme, n. [1. pwantēyésm; 2. pwǣti-jīsm]. Fr. Name given to the method of a modern school of painting, in which effect of light and atmosphere is obtained by small dots or points of pure colour, which, viewed at a distance, are blended into a unity by the eye.

pointilliste, n. [1. pwantēyést; 2. pwǣtijīst]. Artist practising pointillisme.

pointing, n. [1. póinting; 2. póintiŋ]. **point (II.)** & **-ing.** Process of filling in the joints between the edges of bricks or stones in wall with mortar or plaster, so as to make them level with the surface of the wall.

point lace, n. Lace made entirely with the needle; contrasted with *pillow lace.*

pointless, adj. [1. póintles; 2. póintlis]. **point (I.)** & **-less.** **a** (rare) Without a point, blunt, blunted; **b** without intellectual point or relevancy; purposeless; ineffective: *a pointless remark, retort* &c.; (of games) **c** without scoring a point.

pointlessly, adv. Prec. & **-ly.** In a pointless manner.

pointlessness, n. See prec. & **-ness.** Quality of being pointless.

pointsman, n. [1. póintsman; 2. póintsmən]. **1.** A man on a railway who is in charge of the points for transferring trains from one set of rails to another. **2.** Policeman on point-duty.

poise (I.), vb. trans. & intrans. [1. poiz; 2. poiz]. M.E. *peisen, poisen,* fr. O. Fr. *poiser,* Mod. Fr. *peser,* fr. L. Lat. *pesāre,* for Lat. *pensāre,* 'to weigh carefully'; freq. fr. *pens-(um),* P.P. type of *pendere,* 'to weigh, balance; ponder, consider'. See **pension** & **pensive.** **A.** trans. **1.** To balance, to keep in equilibrium: *to poise a basket on one's head.* **2.** To hold, carry, in a particular manner: *the head is poised very much forward.* **B.** intrans. **1.** To be balanced, to hang, remain, in equilibrium: *a bird poised on a bough.* **2.** To hover: *dragonflies poise and dart above the surface of the water.*

poise (II.), n., fr. O. Fr. *pois,* 'weight', Mod. Fr. *poids.* See prec. **1.** Balance, equilibrium, **a** in physical sense, **b** in moral sense; mental balance; serenity, imperturbability, of mind. **2.** Mode of carrying oneself, physical bearing.

poison (I.), n. [1. póizn; 2. póizn]. M.E. *puison, poyson,* fr. O. Fr. *puison, poison,* fr. Lat. *pōtiōn-(em), pōtio,* 'a drink, draught, potion; a deadly poisonous draught', see **potion**. **1.** Any substance, organic or inorganic, which when absorbed into the system injures the health or destroys the life of an organism, esp. of a higher animal; a toxic agency; venom. Phr. (slang) *what's your poison?*, what will you drink? **2.** Any substance which is injurious, pernicious, to the health; something which disagrees powerfully with one: *roast pork is poison to some people.* **3.** Any system, principle, doctrine, example, influence, which is harmful to, subversive of, good morality, religion, the welfare of the State or of any beneficent institution or organization: *moral, political, poison; the poison of infidelity, Bolshevism, disloyalty.* **4.** Any action, conduct, passion, which has a destructive effect upon human happiness or which embitters human relations: *the poison of jealousy, envy, suspicion* &c.

poison (II.), vb. trans. See prec. **1.** To administer poison to; to kill, injure, by means of poison. **2. a** To put, smear, a poisonous substance upon: *a poisoned arrow*; **b** to put a poisonous substance into: *to poison a person's food; to poison the wells*; **c** to infect with septic substance, cause to become inflamed, septic, gathered: *to poison one's finger.* **3.** (fig.) To infect, corrupt, pervert (ideas, principles &c. of) by evil, poisonous suggestions: *to poison another's mind; to poison the wells of truth.* Phr. *to poison a person's mind against*, to prejudice, inspire animosity in.

poisoner, n. [1. póizner; 2. póiznə]. Prec. & **-er.** One who poisons, esp. one who murders another by poison.

poison gas, n. Gas used in modern warfare for destroying life, or for crippling and incapacitating, by its effect upon the heart, organs of respiration, or nervous system, when absorbed by the lungs.

poisoning, n. [1. póizning; 2. póizniŋ]. **poison** (II.) & **-ing.** Act, process, of poisoning or being poisoned; state of being poisoned.

poisonous, adj. [1. póiznus; 2. póiznəs]. **poison** (I.) & **-ous. 1. a** Having the properties, producing the effects, of a poison; tending to cause injury to the health or to destroy life by poisoning: *many toadstools are poisonous*; Phr. *a poisonous dose*, one sufficiently strong to cause death by poisoning; **b** pestilential, noxious, filthy; disgusting to the senses and injurious to health: *a poisonous smell*; **c** venomous: *a poisonous reptile, snake.* **2.** (in moral or fig. sense) **a** Pernicious, baneful, corrupting: *poisonous propaganda, influence*; **b** (colloq., of persons, things, conditions) unpleasing, disagreeable, disgusting, detestable: *a perfectly poisonous fellow; the heat is simply poisonous; I was riding an absolutely poisonous horse.*

poisonously, adv. Prec. & **-ly.** In a poisonous manner; so as to poison.

poitrel, poitrail, n. [1. póitrel; 2. póitrəl]. Fr. *poitrail*, fr. Lat. *pectorāle*, 'breast-plate', see **pectoral.** (anct. armour) Metal breastplate worn by a horse.

poke (I.), n. [1. pōk; 2. pouk]. Etymol. uncertain; prob. Scand., cp. O.N. *poki*, also M. Du. *poke*, & O. Fr. *poque*, Mod. Fr. *poche*, see **pouch** & cp. **poach** (I.); O.E. *pohha*, 'pouch, bag', is possibly related. A small bag or sack, obs. except in Phr. *to buy a pig in a poke*, to make a blind bargain, to buy something without seeing it first.

poke (II.), vb. trans. & intrans. Not in O.E.; M.E. *poken*; cogn. w. L.G. & Du. *poken*, 'to thrust, push, into', L.G. *pok*, 'dagger'; origin uncertain. **A.** trans. **1.** To push, thrust, against, in or into, as with a stick &c.: *to poke someone in the ribs; to poke a hole in the ground*; specif., *to poke the fire*, to smash up smouldering coal on a fire with thrusting, jabbing strokes with a poker. **2.** To push: *to poke one's head*, to thrust it forward, to stoop; *to poke a thing away*, to put it in some out-of-the-way place &c. Phrs. *to poke one's nose into*, to interfere in what does not concern one, in other people's affairs; *to poke fun at*, make fun of, ridicule. **B.** intrans. **1.** In vague senses: **a** To grope about, feel one's way, to look for as if in the dark: *to poke about for*; **b** *to poke into other people's business*, to thrust oneself where one is not wanted. **2.** (cricket) To play very slowly and cautiously, making only gentle strokes without lifting the bat.

poke (III.), n., fr. prec. A poking; a thrust, dig, nudge: *a poke in the ribs, in the eye.*

poke-bonnet, n. A woman's bonnet with a deep projecting brim; coal-scuttle bonnet, such as is worn by women of the Salvation Army.

poker (I.), n. [1. póker; 2. póukə]. **poke** (II.) & **-er. 1.** A stout metal rod or bar used for poking a fire. Phr. *as stiff as a poker*, specif. (of person) very stiff in carriage or bearing. *Red-hot poker*, a plant, genus *Tritoma*, with spikes of brilliant orange-red flowers; also called flame flower or poker plant. **2.** (univ. slang) The vice-chancellor's mace, also the university bedell who carries it before the vice-chancellor. **3.** Instrument used in poker work.

poker (II.), n. Etymol. doubtful; possibly fr. Fr. *poque*, an old card game. A card game, of American origin, usually played by more than two people with five cards each, and, in *draw poker*, with a chance to discard and draw other cards, the players betting on the value of what they hold.

poker (III.), n. Etymol. doubtful, cp. Dan. *pokker*, 'devil', & **puck** (I.). A hobgoblin, bogy; the devil; obs. except in Phr. *by the holy poker.*

poker work, n. **a** Process of tracing designs on a wooden surface with a red-hot poker or similar instrument; **b** design traced in this way.

poky, adj. [1. póki; 2. póuki]. **poke** (II.) & **-y.** Cramped, confined; stuffy; mean, petty: *a poky little house, room; poky hole of a place.*

polacca, n. [1. pōláka; 2. pouláekə]. Ital.; Fr. *polacre* also used, apparently meaning *Polish*; origin of name not known. A Mediterranean three-masted sailing-vessel with square-rigged, single-sparred, or lateen sails, and masts of one piece of timber.

polar, adj. [1. pólar; 2. póulə], fr. Med. Lat. *polāris*, fr. Lat. *polus*, Gk. *pólos*, 'pivot, axis, pole'. See **pole** (III.) and cp. Fr. *polaire*. **1.** (geog.) Of, belonging to, the North or South Pole of the earth: *polar circles, regions, expeditions* &c., Arctic or Antarctic circles, regions &c. **2.** (phys.) **a** Pertaining to a magnetic pole; magnetic; **b** having polarity, having two opposite properties or characters; having positive and negative electricity; **c** exactly, directly, opposite or opposed in character &c.

polar bear, n. Large white bear, *Ursus maritimus*, of the north polar regions.

polarimeter, n. [1. pōlarímeter; 2. poulərímitə]. **polar** & **meter.** (opt.) An instrument for determining the amount of polarization of light.

polarimetric, adj. [1. pòlarimétrik; 2. pòulərimétrik]. See prec. & **-ic.** Of, pertaining to, the polarimeter or its use.

polarimetry, n. [1. pōlarímetri; 2. poulərímitri]. As prec. & **-ry.** Art of using, use of, the polarimeter.

Polaris, n. [1. pōláris; 2. pouléəris]. See **polar.** (astron.) The pole-star.

polariscope, n. [1. pōláriskōp; 2. pouláeriskoup]. **polar** & **-scope.** (opt.) Instrument for examining the phenomena of polarization of light.

polarity, n. [1. pōláriti; 2. pouláeriti]. **polar** & **-ity. 1.** The quality, disposition, tendency, of a body to exhibit opposite or contrasted properties in opposite directions; possession of two poles, with opposite characters as of attraction or repulsion; quality of being negative and positive, e.g. the magnet. **2.** (biol.) Tendency of stems and roots of plants to develop root tissue at one end and buds at the other. **3.** Tendency of the axis of a body to incline in a particular direction. **4.** (fig.) Possession of attracting or repulsing powers; a feeling of attraction for, or repulsion from, another person, idea, object &c.

polarizable, adj. [1. pólarīzabl; 2. póuləraizəbl]. **polarize** & **-able.** Capable of being polarized.

polarization, n. [1. pòlarīzáshun; 2. pòuləraizéiʃən]. **polarize** & **-ation.** Act or process of polarizing; state, condition, of being polarized or having polarity or poles. Specif. **1.** *Polarization of light*, (opt.) the modification of light waves so that the transverse vibrations are given a definite direction by collecting them into one or more planes, obtained by reflection, *plane polarization*, or by transmission or refraction through prisms &c. of certain substances, such as spar, quartz, sugar-solutions &c., which give *rotatory* (to the right, *dextro-*, or left, *laevulo-*) *polarization.* **2.** *Electrical polarization*, **a** in primary batteries, deposit of hydrogen molecules on the positive plate checking the flow of current; **b** of an electro-magnet with coil permanently magnetized in one direction.

polarize, vb. trans. [1. pólarīz; 2. póuləraiz]. **polar** & **-ize. a** To alter, modify, the direction of the vibrations of light or radiant heat waves by passing it through a certain medium &c.; **b** (fig.) *to polarize thought, ideas* &c., to give specific direction and aim to.

polarizer, n. [1. pólarīzer; 2. póuləraizə]. Prec. & **-er.** A polarizing agent, esp. a prism, as a Nicol prism, for exhibiting polarization of light.

polar lights, n. pl. The Aurora Borealis.

polatouche, n. [1. pólatōōch; 2. pólətūtʃ]. Fr., fr. Russ. *poletutcha*, 'the flying animal', (*po*)*lĕtat*, 'to fly'. A small flying squirrel of north-eastern Russia and Siberia.

polder, n. [1. pólder; 2. póuldə]. Du. A tract of reclaimed land in Holland, lying below sea-level.

pole (I.), n. [1. pōl; 2. poul]. O.E. *pāl*, fr. Lat. *pālus*, 'stake'. See **pale** (I.). **1.** A long, tapering, rounded piece of wood, consisting usually of a whole tree stripped of its boughs and smoothed. Phr. *up the pole*, (slang) (i.) off one's head, mad; (ii.) in difficulties, in a predicament; in various specific senses: **a** a support for a tent, for telegraph or telephone wires, flags &c.; **b** long, light, slender spar for propelling a punt, *punt pole*; **c** similar piece of wood used in leaping across or over obstacles, esp. in the athletic sport of *pole-jumping*; **d** a single shaft on a carriage for a pair of horses; **e** a striped, coloured staff, used as a sign for a barber or hairdresser, *barber's pole*; **f** the decorated mast or staff used in the old celebrations on May Day, a *maypole.* **2.** A measure of length, a rod or perch, $5\frac{1}{2}$ yd.; in square measure $30\frac{1}{4}$ sq. yd.

pole (II.), vb. trans., fr. prec. To propel (a punt or boat) by means of a pole.

pole (III.), n. M.E. *pol*, fr. Lat. *pol-(um)*, *polus*, fr. Gk. *pólos*, 'pivot, axis, pole', fr. base **kʷol-*, **kʷel-* &c., 'to turn', cp. *pélein*, 'to move, be in motion', cogn. w. **cylinder, cycle,** & **wheel. 1.** (astron. and physical geog.) **a** Either of the two extremities of the axis of a sphere; specif., either of the two extremities, North and South, of the celestial sphere or of the earth; (loosely) the region in or near the North or South Pole; *magnetic poles*, points, N. and S., of the earth where the magnetic needle drops vertically; **b** (fig.) an opposite extreme; either of two contrasted or opposed characters, principles &c.: *to be poles asunder*, to be widely separated, to be in extreme opposition to one another. **2.** In various sciences: **a** (biol.) Either end of the axis of the nucleus of a cell; **b** (elect.) a terminal, positive or negative, of an electric battery, cell &c.; an electrode; **c** (magnetism) either of the two ends of a magnetic bar, the

North or positive, and South or negative poles; **d** (math.) a fixed point of reference.

Pole (**IV.**), n. Germ., fr. Pol. *pole*, 'field, flat plain'; cp. Pol. *poljane*, 'plain-dwellers, Poles, people of Poland'; cogn. w. **field.** A native of Poland.

pole-ax(**e**), n. & vb. trans. M.E. *pollax*, fr. **poll** (**I.**), 'head', & **axe**, cp. L.G. *pollexe*, 'pole-axe'; spelling due to idea of an axe fastened to end of a pole. **1.** n. **a** (hist.) A battle-axe with a spike on side of head opposite to the blade; **b** a sailor's boarding weapon with a hook on one side; **c** a butcher's slaughtering axe, with a hammer on side opposite to the blade. **2.** vb. To strike, specif. to slaughter cattle, with a pole-axe.

polecat, n. [1. pốlkat; 2. póulkæt]. M.E. *polcat*, *pulcat*; the second element is **cat**; etymol. of first element is doubtful; Fr. *poule*, 'hen, chicken', has been suggested, the animal being a notorious poultry thief; also O. Fr. *pulent*, 'stinking', fr. Lat. *purulent-*(*us*). A European carnivorous mammal, *Putorius foetidus*, belonging to the weasel family, with blackish-brown fur and yellowish-brown underfur and short bushy tail; characterized by its offensive smell; the American congener is the skunk, q.v.

polemarch, n. [1. pólimark; 2. pɔ́limāk], fr. Gk. *polémarkhos*, fr. *pólemos*, 'war', see **polemic**, & *arkhós*, 'ruler', see **arch-**. (Gk. hist.) Commander of an army; at Athens, the third archon, who originally had military functions.

polemic, adj. & n. [1. polémik; 2. pəlémik], fr. Gk. *polemikós*, 'of, pertaining to, war; warlike', fr. *pólemos*, 'war', fr. base **pol-*, **pel*, as in *pelemízein*, 'to shake', & prob. Lat. *pellere*, 'to drive', for wh. see **pulse** (**I.**). Cp. also **sympalmograph. 1.** adj. Of, pertaining to, controversy or dispute; controversial: *polemic theology.* **2.** n. **a** Controversy, dispute; (esp. in pl.) *theological polemics*; **b** controversialist, disputant.

polemical, adj. [1. polémikl; 2. pəlémikl]. Prec. & **-al.** Polemic, controversial.

polemically, adv. Prec. & **-ly.** In a polemical manner; controversially.

polemize, vb. intrans. [1. pólemīz; 2. pɔ́limaiz]. See **polemic** & **-ize.** To argue polemically, engage in controversy or polemics.

polenta, n. [1. polénta; 2. pəléntə]. Ital.; also in Lat., 'pearl barley'. See **pollen.** Porridge made of maize, barley, or chestnut meal.

pole-star, n. **1.** A star, Polaris Alpha, in the constellation of Ursa Minor, or the Little Bear, within $1\frac{1}{4}°$ of the true North of the celestial sphere; the North Star, the guiding star for sailors in the Northern hemisphere. **2.** (fig.) A guide, guiding principle, lodestar.

police (**I.**), n. [1. polḗs; 2. pəlís]. Fr., fr. Low Lat. *polītia*, 'the commonwealth, or its administration', fr. Gk. *politeía*, 'citizenship, the state, its condition and welfare'. See **policy** (**I.**). **1.** The internal civil administration of a state, for the protection of life and property, prevention of crimes and offences, and preservation of law and order. **2. a** Body of men organized to maintain civil law and order &c.; **b** (as pl.) the members of this force collectively.

police (**II.**), vb. trans., fr. prec. **1.** To administer and control the internal civil condition of a state, to maintain law and order by means of police. **2.** To furnish, provide, with police. **3.** (fig.) To control, discipline, regulate.

police constable, n. Policeman, member of a police force of the ordinary rank, below those of *police sergeant*, *police inspector* &c.

police court, n. Court of summary jurisdiction dealing with charges brought by the police, presided over by a *police magistrate* or stipendiary sitting permanently, as in London and other large towns.

policeman, n. [1. polḗsman; 2. pəlísmən]. A constable, a member of a police force.

police office, n. Chief office or headquarters of the police force of a town.

police officer, n. Member of the police force; policeman.

police station, n. The local or district headquarters of a police force, to which arrested persons are brought and at which they are first charged.

polichinelle, n. [1. polèshinél; 2. pɔlìʃinél]. Fr., 'Punch'. Punchinello, Punch: *secret de Polichinelle*, a secret that everyone knows, an open secret.

policlinic, n. [1. pòliklínik; 2. pɔ̀liklínik], fr. Gk. *pólis*, 'city, town'. See **policy** (**I.**) & **clinic. a** Originally, a clinic or training institution for medical students who attend patients in private houses in a town; **b** outpatients' department at a hospital.

policy (**I.**), n. [1. pólisi; 2. pɔ́lisi], fr. O. Fr. *policie*, fr. Lat. *polītia*, fr. Gk. *politeía*, citizenship, constitution, welfare of a city or state; statesmanship, policy', fr. *pólis*, fortified city, city; state; whole country', cogn. w. Gk. *púlē*, 'city-gate'; in pl. 'the gates of a town'; cp. Scrt. *pūr*, 'fortified town'; Lith. *pilìs*, 'fortress, castle'; etymol. doubtful. **1.** Government; the art of government, statecraft. **2.** Method of governing; **a** (i.) specific plan, scheme, measure, of government proposed by rulers of a state in the management of its affairs; (ii.) scheme put forward by a party; **b** (i.) general methods and ideals pursued by the government of a state, or governing body of any kind, in carrying out its duties; (ii.) political ideals of a party. **3. a** General conduct of an individual pursued in furtherance of his aims and desires; **b** plan, scheme, directed to attain certain ends; **c** a plan or course of action likely to achieve the desired ends; **d** wisdom, sagacity in conduct of affairs. **4.** (Scots, often pl.) Grounds of a country-house.

policy (**II.**), n., fr. Fr. *police*, 'a warrant in writing for money' &c., esp. *police d'assurance*, 'a contract for insurance', cp. Ital. *polizza*, 'invoice, ticket', Span. *poliza*, esp. *poliza de seguro*, 'insurance policy'; of doubtful etymol., but distinct fr. **policy** (**I.**); prob. a corrupt. of Med. Lat. *apodissa*, *apodixa*, 'a warrant or bond for money spent or received', fr. further Gk. *apódeixis*, 'a showing forth, demonstration, proof', fr. *apodeiknūmi*, 'to demonstrate, show', see **apo-** & **diction. 1.** A document, in full, *policy of assurance* or *insurance*, embodying a contract to insure a life, or to insure property against fire, accident, or loss generally, as *life, fire, policy* &c.; *policy of marine insurance* &c.; *to take out a policy on one's life*, to insure one's life. *Policy-holder*, one who holds a policy of insurance or to whom such a policy has been issued. **2.** (U.S.A.) A form of gambling on numbers drawn in a lottery. *Policy shop*, (U.S.A.) a place where policy gambling is carried on.

poligar, n. [1. póligar; 2. pɔ́ligā], fr. Marathi *pālegār*, fr. Tamil *pālaiyakhāran.* **a** A feudal chief in Madras Presidency of India; **b** one of his followers.

poliomyelitis, n. [1. póliōmīelítis; 2. póioumàiəláitis]. Formed fr. Gk. *poliós*, 'grey', & **myelitis.** The first element is cogn. w. Gk. *peliós*, 'leaden', *pelitnós*, 'livid', *peleiás*, 'dove'; cp. further Scrt. *palitáš*, 'grey'; Lat. *palumbus*, 'dove', *pallēre*, 'to be pale'. See **pale** (**II.**). (med.) Inflammation of the grey matter of the spinal cord; also called infantile paralysis.

polish (**I.**), vb. trans. & intrans. [1. pólish; 2. pɔ́liʃ]. M.E. *polischen*, fr. Fr. *poliss-*(*ant*), Pres. Part. of *polir*, fr. Lat. *polīre*, 'to make smooth, polish'; etymol. doubtful; cp. **polite. A.** trans. **1.** To make smooth and glossy, esp. by rubbing; to put a smooth, glossy surface upon: *to polish silver, glass* &c. **2.** (fig.) To give refinement to, to remove moral coarseness, smooth out intellectual crudities, to correct vulgarity of speech, manners &c.; generally bring to a finished, perfect condition: *to polish a set of verses*; *to polish the manners, appearance* &c.; *to have polished manners*; *polish off*, (colloq.) **a** to finish quickly, to bring to a speedy conclusion: *to polish off work, a job* &c.; **b** to kill, be the end or death of. **B.** intrans. To become smooth; to take a polish, receive a smooth, shiny surface: *mahogany polishes beautifully.*

polish (**II.**), n., fr. prec. **1.** Smoothness, glossiness, lustre, of surface obtained by rubbing; a polished surface: *the brilliant polish of silver, old mahogany* &c. **2.** Substance used for polishing surfaces: *boot-polish, metal-polish* &c.; *french polish*, q.v. **3.** (fig.) Refinement, urbanity, finished perfection; esp. of manners, bearing &c.; also finish in literary style: *the polish of cultivated society*; *the exquisite polish of Pope's couplets.*

Polish (**III.**), adj. [1. pṓlish; 2. póuliʃ]. **Pole** (**IV.**) & **-ish.** Of Poland or the Poles.

polisher, n. [1. pólisher; 2. pɔ́liʃə]. **polish** (**I.**) & **-er. a** One who polishes; specif., skilled workman who polishes wood or metal; **b** substance used in polishing.

polite, adj. [1. polít; 2. pəláit], fr. Lat. *polīt-*(*um*), P.P. of *polīre*, 'to polish'; etymol. doubtful; cp. **polish** (**I.**). **1.** Having polished, refined manners; well-bred, courteous, urbane. **2.** Refined, elegant: *polite letters, literature.* Phr. *to do the polite*, (colloq.) to take pains to behave politely; *the polite thing*, polite behaviour, that required by standards of politeness.

politely, adv. Prec. & **-ly.** In a polite manner; courteously.

politeness, n. See prec. & **-ness. 1.** State of high refinement in manners, mind, civilization. **2. a** Quality of being polite; urbanity, good manners; **b** specific act of courtesy; a polite compliment.

politic, adj. [1. pólitik; 2. pɔ́litik], fr. Fr. *politique*, fr. Lat. *politicus*, 'political', fr. Gk. *polītikós*, 'of, pertaining to, a citizen; statesmanlike, political'. See **policy** (**I.**) & **politics. 1.** Of, pertaining to, civil government or to the polity; political, rare except in *body politic*, the state as the organized body of its citizens. **2.** (of persons) **a** Prudent, wise, sagacious; acting in such a way as to achieve a specific aim or policy; **b** (in derogatory sense) cunning, crafty. **3.** (of actions, utterances &c.) Judicious, prudently calculated for specific purpose; adapted to gain a particular end; opportune, expedient: *a politic move, speech, retort* &c.

political, adj. [1. polítikl; 2. pəlítikl]. Prec. & **-al. 1.** Of, pertaining to, the science or philosophy of the state, or of government: *political geography*, geography which deals with state boundaries, frontiers &c., international rivers and communications &c.; *political science*, that which deals with the philosophic theories of the state or government. **2.** Pertaining to, connected with, the government or administration of a state or nation, or to its structure, constitution, functions, control &c.; also to relations between states and governments: *political liberties, rights* &c.; *political agent, officer*, civil official acting on behalf of, or representing a government, often contrasted with *civil, municipal, or social*; *a political prisoner*; *political reasons*, reasons of state. **3.** Of, pertaining to, politics: *political parties*; *a political career*; *political writer*; *political news.*

political economy, n. The science concerned with the production, distribution, and consumption of wealth, and with the theory of exchange; economics.

politically, adv. [1. polítikali; 2. pəlítikəli]. **political** & **-ly. 1.** In a political manner; **a** in regard, with reference to, the government of a state; **b** from the point of view of politics. **2.** In a politic manner.

politician, n. [1. pòlitíshan; 2. pɔ̀litíʃən]. Cp. Fr. *politicien.* **politic** & **-ian. a** One engaged in, experienced in, devoted to, skilled in, politics; **b** (in derogatory sense) one engaged in purely party politics, esp. as a career and means of advancement.

politicize, vb. intrans. & trans. [1. polítisīz; 2. pəlitisaiz]. **politic** & **-ize**. **a** To deal with, treat of, politics; **b** to discuss from the political point of view; to make the subject of party or general politics.

politicly, adv. [1. pólitikli; 2. pɔ́litikli]. **politic** & **-ly**. (rare) In a politic manner; prudently.

politico-, pref. [1. polítikō; 2. pəlitikou]. Representing **politic**; used in compound adjs.; e.g. *politico-economical, -commercial*, dealing with economics or commerce from a political point of view, of the relations between the state and economic or commercial problems &c.; *politico-ethical, -religious*, of politics as affected by or as affecting morals or religion.

politics, n. pl. [1. pólitiks; 2. pɔ́litiks]. **1.** The science or art of government or of the administration and management of public or state affairs: *a matter of high politics.* **2.** Political affairs, principles, practice, opinions, aims, schemes &c.: *party politics; the politics of a newspaper; to be engaged in politics; to object to a man's politics* &c. **3. a** The management, conduct, of private affairs: *the politics of a business*; **b** motives, aims, interests &c. which inspire public or private action.

polity, n. [1. póliti; 2. pɔ́liti], fr. Lat. *polītia*, fr. Gk. *polīteía*. See **policy (I.)**. The organized system of state government; the constitution of a state; an organized state or institution, a body politic.

polk, vb. intrans. [1. pōlk, polk; 2. poulk, pɔlk], fr. Fr. *polker*. See next word. (colloq.) To dance the polka.

polka, n. [1. pólka, pólka; 2. póulkə, pɔ́lkə]. Fr. & Germ.; prob. fr. Polish *polka*, 'a Polish woman'. **1.** A lively round dance for two persons, in 2-4 time, apparently of Czech origin; originally danced in Prague. **2.** Music composed for this dance.

poll (I.), n. [1. pōl; 2. poul]. M.E. *pol, polle*; of Low Germ. origin; cp. M. Du. *polle*, 'head, pate', Swed. dial. *pull*, Dan. *puld*, 'crown, top of the head'. **1. a** (archaic) The head, pate, esp. the back and crown as covered with hair: *a grey, snow-white poll*; '*blessings on your frosty pow*' (Scots variant); **b** an individual person among others; a head; *a challenge to the polls* (law), objection made by defendant to any particular juror. **2. a** A register or list of persons on whom a poll-tax is to be levied or who have the right to vote at parliamentary or other elections: *to have, put, one's name on the poll*; **b** the voting of those on the poll at an election; the place where the voting takes place: *the opening, close, of the poll; to keep people from, drive them to the poll* &c.; **c** the counting of votes at an election; number of votes cast or counted: *a heavy, poor, poll.*

poll (II.), vb. trans. & intrans., fr. prec. **A.** trans. **1.** To cut, trim, **a** (archaic) to cut, clip, crop, the hair short: '*Absalom polled his head*' (2 Sam. xiv.); **b** to cut off, to clip, the top of a tree; to pollard; to remove the horns of cattle; *polled tree, cattle*; **c** (law) to cut (document) even, as contrasted with *indenture*; only in *deed poll*, i.e. a polled deed. **2.** To register the votes of electors; to receive, as a candidate, the votes of electors: *the constituency was polled to the last man; the party only polled a quarter of the votes cast.* **B.** intrans. To register one's vote; to vote: *to poll early; to poll for a particular candidate* &c.

poll (III.), adj. For *polled*, P.P. of prec. Cropped, shorn, cut straight, esp. (law) *deed poll*, as contrasted with an *indenture*.

poll (IV.), n. [1. pol; 2. pɔl]. Prob. fr. Gk. (*hoi*) *polloi*, q.v. (Camb. Univ. slang) *The poll*, the undergraduates, collectively, who only take a pass degree and do not go in for honours; the passmen; *a poll degree*, a pass degree.

Poll (V.), n. Short for *Polly*, variant of *Molly*, familiar name for *Mary*. **a** A parrot, also *poll-parrot*; b (colloq.) a courtesan.

pollable, adj. [1. pólabl; 2. póuləbl]. **poll (II.)** & **-able**. Of votes, able to be polled or brought to the poll.

pollack, pollock, n. [1. póluk; 2. pɔ́lək]. Etymol. unknown. An edible sea-fish of the North Atlantic, esp. on the European coasts, genus *Pollachius*, of the cod family, lythe; the *black pollock* is the coal-fish.

pollan, n. [1. pólan; 2. pɔ́lən]. Etymol. doubtful; possibly fr. Gael. *poll*, 'small lake, pool'. A fresh-water fish of Irish lakes &c.; a whitefish.

pollard (I.), n. [1. pólard; 2. pɔ́ləd], fr. **poll (II.)** & **-ard**. **1.** A tree, such as a willow, oak &c., with its top branches polled or cut back, so that it throws out a thick, bushy head of new growth. **2.** A polled animal, such as a hornless ox, ram &c.; a stag that has shed its antlers. **3.** Bran with some of the flour still remaining, used as a feeding stuff for cattle.

pollard (II.), vb. trans., fr. prec. To make a pollard of; to lop the top branches of a tree, usually right back to the trunk, so as to reduce size or induce the tree to put up a new head.

Polled Angus, n. [1. pōld ánggus; 2. pould ǽŋgəs]. See **poll (II.)**. Breed of Aberdeenshire hornless cattle.

pollen, n. & vb. trans. [1. pólen; 2. pɔ́lin]. Lat., also *pollis*, fr. *poln-, 'fine flour, the dust of a mill', cogn. w. Lat. *palea*, 'chaff', Gk. *pálē*, 'sifted meal', also w. Lat. *pulvis*, 'dust' see **pulverize**; also Lat. *puls*, 'porridge made of meal', see **pulse**; prob. ultimately fr. *spel-, cp. **spelt**. **1.** n. The fine, powdery substance discharged from the anthers of flowers, being the male fertilizing element of flowering plants and grasses, which is either brought to the ovules directly, or carried to them by bees, and other insects. **2.** vb. To pollinate.

poll-evil, n. **poll (I.)** & **evil**. (veter.) A suppurating inflammation about the head of a horse.

pollex, n. [1. póleks; 2. pɔ́lɛks]. Lat.; perh. cogn. w. O. Slav. *palĭtsĭ*, 'thumb', & w. Lat. *palma*, see **palm (I)**. (anat.) The thumb. Phr. (Roman antiq.) *Pollice verso*, thumb extended, *pollice presso*, thumb down or under, symbolic gestures made by spectators, signifying death or mercy to the gladiator.

pollicitation, n. [1. polìsitáshun; 2. pəlisitéiʃən], fr. Lat. *pollicitātiōn-(em), pollicitātio*, 'a promise', fr. *pollicitāri*, freq. form of *pollicēri*, 'to promise'; for *per*, see **per-**, & *licēre*, see **licence**. **a** (law) An offer, promise, or engagement to do something without consideration; a voluntary offer; **b** (in Roman law) an unaccepted offer or promise.

pollinate, vb. trans. [1. pólināt; 2. pɔ́lineit], fr. Lat. *pollin-(em)*. **pollen** & **-ate**. (bot.) To fertilize the ovules of a plant with pollen.

pollination, n. [1. pòlinā́shun; 2. pɔ̀linéiʃən]. Prec. & **-ation**. (bot.) Fertilization of the ovules of plants with pollen.

pollinic, adj. [1. polínik; 2. pəlínik]. **pollen** & **-ic**. Of, pertaining to, pollen.

polliniferous, adj. [1. pòliníferus; 2. pɔ̀linífərəs]. *Pollini-*, stem of **pollen**, & **-ferous**. **a** (of plants) Bearing, producing pollen or male fertilizing spores; **b** (of bees &c.) carrying pollen from one flower to another.

pollock, n. See **pollack**.

polloi. See **hoi polloi**.

poll-tax, n. **poll (I.)** & **tax**. A tax of so much per head or person, levied on every male inhabitant of a country.

pollute, vb. trans. [1. polū́t; 2. pəljū́t], fr. Lat. *pollūtum*, P.P. of *polluere*, 'to pollute', fr. *pol-*, pref., a form of *per* or *pro*, & *luere*, 'to wash', a form of *lavāre*, 'to wash', see **lave**. **1.** To render foul or filthy: *to pollute water, air* &c. **2.** To defile, profane the sanctity of: *to pollute a temple.* **3.** To corrupt, contaminate the morals, and purity of: *to pollute the mind* &c.

pollution, n. [1. polū́shun; 2. pəljū́ʃən], fr. Lat. *pollūtiōn-(em)*. Prec. & **-ion**. Defilement, contamination, corruption (in physical or moral sense).

Polly, n. [1. póli; 2. pɔ́li]. Variant of *Molly*, familiar form of *Mary*. A girl's familiar name; a poll-parrot.

polo, n. [1. pōlō; 2. póulou]. Native Indian name, properly of the ball used, cp. Tibetan *pulu*, 'ball'. A ball game, of very ancient Indian or Persian origin, somewhat resembling hockey in character, but played on ponies; the players, four a side, use mallets with long cane handles for striking the ball, which is of hard wood. *Polo pony*, a pony, usually not over 14½ hands, bred and trained for playing polo; *water polo*, a game played by swimmers, with an inflated leather ball struck or thrown by hand.

polonaise, n. [1. pòlonā́z; 2. pɔ̀lənéiz]. Fr., fr. fem. adj., 'Polish'. **1.** A stately, ceremonial dance, in 3-4 time, of Polish origin; music composed for such or as an independent composition. **2.** A full-skirted bodice, open at the waist, as part of women's costume at various times since the 18th cent.

polonium, n. [1. polṓnium; 2. pəlóuniəm], fr. *Polonia*, Latinized name of Poland. A radio-active substance, or element, discovered in 1898 by Pierre and Marie Curie.

polony, n. [1. polṓni; 2. pəlóuni]. Prob. fr. Bologna, town in Italy, where such sausages were made. A kind of pork sausage.

poltergeist, n. [1. póltergīst; 2. pɔ́ltəgaist]. Mod. Germ., fr. *polter*, 'noise, racket, hubbub', & *geist*, 'ghost'. A noisy ghost or hobgoblin, the name given by modern spiritualists to the supposed agent of certain manifestations, such as the overturning or moving of furniture, breaking of crockery, or other noisy disturbances.

poltroon, n. [1. poltrṓōn; 2. pəltrū́n], fr. Fr. *poltron*, 'rascal, sluggard, coward', fr. Ital. *poltrone*, in same senses; fr. *poltro*, 'lazy', also as n., 'a bed'; etymol. doubtful; possibly cogn. w. O.H.G. *polstar*, 'cushion' &c., see **bolster**. A coward, a mean-spirited person.

poltroonery, n. [1. poltrṓōneri; 2. pəltrū́nəri], fr. Fr. *poltronnerie*. Prec. & **-ery**. Cowardice; want of courage or fighting spirit.

poly-, pref. Form of Gk. *polú(s)*, 'much, many', cogn. w. Lat. *plēnum*, 'full', see **plenum** & **full (I.)**.

polyadelphous, adj. [1. pòliadélfus; 2. pɔ̀liədélfəs], fr. Gk. *poluádelphos*, 'having many brothers', **poly-**, & *ádelphos*, 'brother'; lit. 'one born from same womb', cp. *delphús*, 'womb', fr. *g^welbh-, q.v. under **calf (I.)**. (bot.) Having the stamens united in more than two groups or bundles.

polyandrist, n. [1. pòliándrist; 2. pɔ̀liǽndrist]. **polyandry** & **-ist**. One who practises polyandry, a woman with several husbands.

polyandrous, adj. [1. pòliándrus; 2. pɔ̀liǽndrəs]. See next word & **-ous**. **1.** Pertaining to polyandry; practising polyandry, having several husbands. **2.** (bot.) Having large number of stamens, usually more than twenty.

polyandry, n. [1. pòliándri; 2. pɔ̀liǽndri]. **poly-** & Gk. *andr-(ós)*, stem of *anḗr*, 'a man, husband', see **androgenous**, & **-y**. Custom among uncivilized tribes for women to have more than one husband.

polyanthus, n. [1. pòliánthus; 2. pɔ̀liǽnþəs]. **poly-** & Gk. *ánthos*, 'flower', see **anther**. A cultivated garden plant, originally a hybrid of the cowslip and primrose, now a cultivated form of primula, with clusters of bright-coloured flowers springing from a single main stalk.

polyarchy, n. [1. póliarki; 2. pɔ́liāki]. **poly-** & **-archy**. Rule, government, by many persons, contrasted with *oligarchy*.

polycarpous, adj. [1. pòlikárpus; 2. pɔ̀likā́pəs]. See **poly-**, **carpel**, & **-ous**. (bot.) Having several carpels.

polychrestic, adj. [1. pòlikréstik; 2. pɔ̀likrístik], fr. Gk. *polúkhrēstos*. **poly-** & *khrēstós*, 'useful', q.v. under **chrestomathy**. **a** (of drugs &c.) Having many uses; **b** (of words) having many meanings.

polychromate, n. [1. pòlikrṓmāt; 2. pòlikróumeit]. **polychrome** & **-ate.** (chem.) A substance which shows or yields a variety of colours.

polychromatic, adj. [1. pòlikrōmátik; 2. pòlikroumǽtik]. **poly-** & **chromatic.** Having, exhibiting, many colours; changing colours.

polychrome, adj. & n. [1. pólikrōm; 2. pólikroum]. **poly-** & Gk. *khrôma*, 'colour', see **chromatic. 1.** adj. Having many colours; painted in several colours, esp. of ancient Greek statues or vases. **2.** n. A statue or vase painted in several colours.

polychromic, polychromous, adjs. [1. pòlikrṓmik, -us; 2. pòlikróumik, -əs]. Prec. & **-ic, (-ous).** Many-coloured.

polychromy, n. [1. pólikrōmi; 2. pólikroumi]. **polychrome** & **-y**, cp. Fr. *polychromie*. Painting in several colours, as of ancient Greek statues, vases &c.

polyclinic, n. [1. pòliklínik; 2. pòliklínik]. **poly-** & **clinic.** A general clinic, hospital, or other institution where various diseases are treated.

polycyclic, adj. [1. pòlisíklik; 2. pòlisáiklik]. **poly-** & **cyclic.** Having many circles or whorls; specif. (elect.) having many cycles, used of distributing system of a current of different frequencies and voltages.

polydactyl, adj. & n. [1. pòlidáktil; 2. pòlidǽktil]. **poly-** & **dactyl.** (zool.) **1.** adj. Having more than the normal number of fingers or toes. **2.** n. An animal, person, with number of fingers or toes in excess of the normal.

polygamist, n. [1. polígamist; 2. pəlígəmist]. **polygamy** & **-ist.** One who practises polygamy; a man who has several wives at the same time.

polygamous, adj. [1. polígamus; 2. pəlígəməs], fr. L. Gk. *polúgamos*, see **poly-** & **-gamous. 1.** Having more than one wife at the same time. **2.** (bot.) Having bisexual (hermaphrodite) or unisexual flowers on the same plant. **3.** (zool.) Having more than one mate.

polygamy, n. [1. polígami; 2. pəlígəmi], fr. Fr. *polygamie*, fr. Lat. *polygamia*, fr. Gk. *polugamía*. See prec. The custom and practice of having several wives at the same time; contrasted with *monogamy*.

polygenesis, n. [1. pòlijénesis; 2. pòlidžénisis]. **poly-** & **genesis.** Variety, plurality of origin; the theory that the different races of men, and the different species of the lower animals originated from several different pairs of ancestors; polygeny.

polygenetic, adj. [1. pòlijenétik; 2. pòlidžinétik]. **poly-** & **-genetic.** Having many different sources of origin.

polygenic, adj. [1. pòlijénik; 2. pòlidžénik]. **poly-** & **-genic.** (chem.) Forming several compounds with hydrogen or other monovalent elements.

polygenous, adj. [1. políjenus; 2. pəlídžənəs]. **poly-** & **-genous.** Having many kinds or varieties, esp. of geological formations.

polygeny, n. [1. políjeni; 2. pəlídžəni]. **poly-** & **-geny.** Descent from more than a single pair of ancestors; polygenesis.

polyglot, adj. & n. [1. póliglot; 2. pòliglɔt], fr. L. Gk. *polúglōttos*, 'many-tongued'; fr. **poly-**, & Gk. *glōtta, glôssa*, 'tongue, language', see **glottis** & **gloss (III.). 1.** adj. **a** Containing, consisting of, written in, various languages: *a polyglot Bible* &c.; **b** knowing and speaking several languages: *a polyglot speaker* &c. **2.** n. **a** A book, esp. the Bible, containing versions of the text in various languages; **b** one who knows, speaks, several languages.

polyglottal, -glottic, -glottous, adjs. [1. pòliglótl, -ik, -us; 2. pòliglɔ́təl, -ik, -əs]. See prec. & **-al, -ic,** or **-ous.** Speaking, written, in many languages; comprising versions in various languages.

polygon, n. [1. póligun; 2. póligən], fr. Gk. *polúgōnos*, 'many-angled', fr. **poly-** & *-gōnos*, 'angled', see **-gon.** (geom.) A plane rectilineal figure with more than four angles and sides; *polygon of forces*, (mechan.) a polygonal figure representing the direction &c. of a system of forces.

polygonal, adj. [1. polígunal; 2. pəlígənəl]. Prec. & **-al.** Of figures, geometrical or otherwise, having many angles or sides.

polygonally, adv. Prec. & **-ly.** With many angles and sides.

Polygonum, n. [1. polígunum; 2. pəlígənəm], fr. Gk. *polúgonon*, 'a plant'; **poly-** & **-gon**, here used in sense of 'joint'. (bot.) A genus of plants with jointed stems, which includes knotgrass, bistort &c.

polygynous, adj. [1. políginus, -jinus; 2. pəlíginəs, -džinəs]. See next word & **-ous. 1.** Practising polygyny; having several wives. **2.** (bot.) having many pistils.

polygyny, n. [1. polígini, -jini; 2. pəlígini, -džini]. **poly-** & Gk. *guné*, 'woman'. See **gyno-, gynaecology.** The custom of having several wives at the same time; polygamy.

polyhedral, adj. [1. pòlihédral; 2. pòlihídrəl]. See next word & **-al.** (geom.) Having many plane faces or sides, as of solid figures.

polyhedron, n. [1. pòlihédron; 2. pòlihídrən], fr. Gk. *polúhedron*; **poly-** & *hédra*, 'base, seat, side'. See **-hedron.** (geom.) A solid figure with many, usually more than six, plane faces or sides.

polyhistor, n. [1. pòlihístōr; 2. pòlihístɔ̄], Gk. *poluhístōr*, see **poly-**, & *hístōr*, 'learned, wise', see **history.** (obs.) A very learned man; a profound scholar on many subjects.

polymath, n. [1. pólimath; 2. pólimæþ], fr. Gk. *polumathḗs*, fr. **poly-** & *math-*, stem of *manthánein*, 'to learn', see **mathematical.** (obs.) One learned in many subjects.

polymorphic, adj. [1. pòlimórfik; 2. pòlimɔ́fik]. See **poly-** & first element in **morphology.** Polymorphous.

polymorphism, n. [1. pòlimórfizm; 2. pòlimɔ́fizəm]. See prec. & **-ism.** State, quality, of being polymorphous, or having various forms.

polymorphous, adj. [1. pòlimórfus; 2. pòlimɔ́fəs], fr. Gk. *polúmorphos*, 'of many forms, multiform', see **polymorphic** & **-ous.** Having, occurring in, capable of assuming, many shapes.

Polynesian, adj. & n. [1. pòlinḗzian; 2. pòliníziən], fr. Polynesia, wh. is fr. **poly-** & Gk. *nêsos*, 'island', etymol. doubtful, but possibly conn. w. Gk. *nḗkhein*, 'to swim', q.v. under **natation. 1.** adj. Of, pertaining to, Polynesia, the groups of islands in the Pacific, east of Fiji and the Gilberts. **2.** n. Native or inhabitant of Polynesia.

polynia, n. [1. polínia; 2. pəlíniə]. Russ. *polýnia*, fr. Russ. *pole*, 'open space, plain, field', cp. **Pole (IV.).** Open water in an ice-field, which is usually frozen over.

polynomial, adj. [1. pòlinṓmial; 2. pòlinóumiəl]. **poly-** & *-nomial*, as in **binomial.** (math.) Having many terms; multinomial.

polyonymous, adj. [1. pòliónimus; 2. pòliɔ́niməs]. Gk. *poluṓnumos*, fr. **poly-**, & *ónom(a)*, 'name', see **onomatopoeic,** & **-ous.** Having, known by, several names.

polyonymy, n. [1. pòliónimi; 2. pòliɔ́nimi]. Prec. w. suff. **-y.** The use of several names for the same object.

polyopia, n. [1. pòliópia; 2. pòlióupiə]. **poly-** & **-opia.** (pathol.) A disease of the eyes, marked by double or multiple vision.

polyp, n. [1. pólip; 2. pólip], fr. Fr. *polype*, fr. Lat. *polypus*, Gk. *polúpous*, 'cuttle-fish, polypus (in nose)'; fr. **poly-** & *poús, podós*, 'foot'; see **-pod.** (zool.) **1.** (now obs.) A cuttle-fish. **2.** Any one of various kinds of aquatic invertebrates, having a tube-like body and a single opening surrounded by tentacles; the pond hydra, sea-anemone, corals, are examples of different types.

polypary, n. [1. polípari; 2. pəlípəri]. Prec. & **-ary.** (zool.) The hard, calcareous structure in which a colony of polyps, as corals, are embedded.

polypetalous, adj. [1. pòlipétalus; 2. pòlipétələs]. **poly-** & **petal** & **-ous.** (bot.) Having the petals separate.

polyphagous, adj. [1. polífagus; 2. pəlífəgəs]. **poly-** & **-phagous.** (zool.) Feeding, living, on various kinds of food.

polyphase, adj. [1. pólifāz; 2. pólifeiz]. **poly-** & **phase.** (elect.) Of alternating currents with two or more currents of the same frequency but differing in phase.

polyphone, n. [1. pólifōn; 2. pólifoun]. Gk. See **poly-** & **phone (I.), phono-.** Graphic symbol representing or expressing more than one sound.

polyphonic, adj. [1. pòlifónik; 2. pòlifɔ́nik]. Prec. & **-ic. 1.** Having many sounds or voices. **2.** (mus.) Pertaining to, marked by, polyphony; contrapuntal. **3.** (philol.) Of graphic symbols, used to express more than one speech-sound.

polyphonist, n. [1. pólifònist; 2. pólifòunist]. See prec. & **-ist.** (mus.) One skilled in polyphony; a contrapuntist.

polyphonous, adj. [1. polífunus; 2. pəlífənəs]. **polyphone** & **-ous.** Polyphonic.

polyphony, n. [1. polífuni; 2. pəlífəni], fr. Gk. *poluphōnía*, 'variety of tones or sounds'. See **polyphone** & **-y. 1.** Multiplicity, multiplication, of sounds, as in an echo. **2.** (mus.) Composition in parts, each having its own melodic interest, as in a fugue, counterpoint, or canon; contrasted with *homophony*.

polyphyletic, adj. [1. pòlifilétik; 2. pòlifailétik]. **poly-** & Gk. *phūlḗ*, 'clan, tribe', see **phylo-,** & **-etic.** (biol.) Having more than one ancestral type or origin; descended from more than one ancestor; polygenetic.

polyphyllous, adj. [1. pòlifílus; 2. pòlifíləs], fr. Gk. *polúphullos*, 'many leaved'; **poly-** & *phúllon*, 'leaf', fr. base **bhel-* &c., 'to swell'. See **phyllo-** & cp. **blade** & **flower.** (bot.) Having many leaves.

polypite, n. [1. pólipīt; 2 pólipait]. **polyp** & **-ite.** (zool.) An individual polyp in a coral.

polypod, n. [1. pólipod; 2. pólipɔd]. Fr. *polypode*. See **polyp** & **polypus. a** An animal having many feet; **b** a polypodium fern.

polypodium, n. [1. pòlipṓdium; 2. pòlipóudiəm]. Latinized fr. Gk. *polupódion*, dimin. of *polúpous*, see **polypus.** (bot.) One of a genus of ferns containing 500 species.

polypody, n. [1. pólipōdi; 2. pólipoudi]. Engl. form of prec.

polypoid(al), adj. [1. pólipoid, pòlipóidl; 2. pólipɔid, pòlipɔ́idl]. **polyp** & **-oid** & **-al.** (zool.) Like a polyp, resembling a polyp in shape or form.

polypore, polyporus, n. [1. pólipōr, pòlipórus; 2. pólipɔ̄, pòlipɔ́rəs]. See **poly-** & **pore (I.).** (bot.) A fungus which grows on living or dead wood; it becomes woody or corky when old; also called *shelf-fungus* from its mode of growth.

polypous, adj. [1. pólipus; 2. pólipəs]. See next word & **-ous.** (pathol.) Of, like, a polypus; affected with a polypus.

polypus, n., pl. **polypi** [1. pólipus, -pī; 2. pólipəs, -pai]. Lat., fr. Gk. *polúpous*, 'cuttle-fish', also 'tumour, polypus'. See **polyp. 1.** (pathol.) A soft tumour, with branching roots, growing on the mucous membrane, esp. of the nose. **2.** (zool.) A polyp.

polystomatous, adj. [1. pòlistṓmatus; 2. pòlistóumətəs]. **poly-** & Gk. *stómat-(os), stóma*, 'mouth', see **stomach.** (zool.) Having many mouths, openings, or suckers; referring esp. to certain parasitic worms, belonging to the family Polystomatidae.

polystyle, adj. [1. pólistīl; 2. pólistail], fr. Gk. *polústulos*, **poly-** & *stûlos*, 'pillar, column', see **style (III.).** (arch.) Having many columns, esp. in the interior of a building.

polysyllabic, adj. [1. pòlisilábik; 2. pòlisilǽbik]. See **poly-** & **syllabic.** Having many or several syllables; applied to words with more than three syllables.

polysyllabically, adv. [1. pòlisilábikali; 2. pòlisilǽbikəli]. Prec. & **-al** & **-ly.** With many syllables.

polysyllable, n. [1. pòlisílabl; 2. pòlisíləbl]. **poly-** & **syllable**. A word of several, usually of more than three, syllables.

polysynthetic, adj. [1. pòlisinthétik; 2. pòlisinþétik]. **poly-** & **synthetic**. Fusing several distinct elements into a unity; consisting of such a fusion; (of languages, and their structure) characterized by polysynthetism.

polysynthetism, n. [1. pòlisínthetizm; 2. pòlisínþətizəm]. See prec. & **-ism**. System of linguistic structure exhibited by the native American languages, of combining into a single unity, nearly corresponding to a sentence, a number of word-elements.

polytechnic, adj. & n. [1. pòlitéknik; 2. pòlitéknik], fr. Fr. *polytechnique*, Gk., fr. **poly-** & *tekhnikós*, 'of, belonging to, the arts or skill', see **technical**. **1.** adj. Pertaining to many arts, crafts, and technical sciences; used to denote schools or institutions where practical instruction is given in arts, crafts, and technical sciences: *a polytechnic institution.* **2.** n. A polytechnic school or institution; also a place where machinery and practical applications of science are exhibited.

polytheism, n. [1. pólithēizm; 2. pólipīizəm], fr. Fr. *polythéisme*. **poly-** & **theism (II.)**. The belief in, and worship of, many or several gods; contrasted with *monotheism*.

polytheist, n. [1. pólithēist; 2. pólipīist]. **poly-** & **theist**. Believer in polytheism.

polytheistic, adj. [1. pòlithēístik; 2. pòlipīístik]. Prec. & **-ic**. Connected with, pertaining to, believing in, based on, of the nature of, polytheism.

Polyzoa, n. pl. [1. pòlizóa; 2. pòlizóuə]. Gk., **poly-** & Gk. *zôa*, pl. of *zôon*, 'an animal', see **zoo-**. (zool.) A group of minute marine organisms, usually occurring in colonies, which reproduce by budding.

polyzoan, adj. & n. [1. pòlizóan; 2. pòlizóuən]. Prec. & **-an**. **a** adj. Pertaining to Polyzoa; **b** n., one of the Polyzoa.

pomace, n. [1. púmis; 2. pámis]. Low Lat. *pomacium*, 'cider', fr. Lat. *pōmum*, 'fruit of a tree, apple', cp. O. Fr. *pomache*. Walde suggests that *pōmum* means 'the juicy fruit', fr. base **pōi-*, 'sap, juice', whence also *pīnus*, 'fir tree', see **pine (II.)**, cp. also Scrt. *pituš*, 'sap, nourishment'. **1.** The pulp of apples pressed into a solid mass, after the juice has been squeezed out to make cider. **2.** Any refuse or pulp left after oil &c. has been extracted, e.g. that of castor-oil beans, fish &c.

pomade, n. & vb. trans. [1. pomáhd; 2. pəmád], fr. Fr. *pommade*, fr. Ital. *pomata*, 'pomatum', fr. *pomme*, 'apple', as orig. made fr., or scented w., apples, fr. Lat. *pōmum*, 'fruit, apple'. See prec. **1.** n. A scented ointment for the hair; pomatum. **2.** vb. To put pomade on (the hair).

pomander, n. [1. pōmánder; 2. poumǽndə], for *pomamber*, fr. O. Fr. *pomme d'ambre*, lit. 'an apple of amber', fr. *pomme*, 'apple', see **pomace**, fr. the shape, and *ambre*, see **amber**. **a** (hist.) A ball made of various perfumes, esp. ambergris, musk &c., and other aromatic substances, used as a protection against fevers, plague &c., and bad smells, and contained in a perforated globe of gold, silver, or other metal; **b** the box in which a pomander was carried.

Pomard. See **Pommard**.

pomatum, n. [1. pomátum; 2. pəméitəm]. Latinized variant of **pomade**.

pombe, n. [1. pómbe; 2. pómbi]. Swahili. A native African beer made from grain.

pome, n. [1. pōm; 2. poum]. O. Fr., Mod. Fr. *pomme*, 'apple', fr. Lat. *pōmum*, 'fruit of a tree', in L. Lat. 'apple'. See **pomace**. **a** (bot.) A fruit, such as the apple, pear, or quince, with hard carpels forming a core round the seeds or pips; **b** a metal ball, filled with hot water and used for warming the hands.

pomegranate, n. [1. póm-, pómgrànat; 2. póm-, póumgrænit]. M.E. *pomegarnet*, *pomgarnet*, fr. O. Fr. *pome grenate*, *pome*, 'apple, fruit', fr. Lat. *pōmum*, see **pomace**, & *grānātum*, 'having many seeds', also as n., 'the pomegranate', *grānum*, 'grain, seed', see **grain (I.)**. **a** The fruit of a N. African and W. Asiatic tree, *Punica granatum*, of the shape and size of an orange, with hard, golden reddish rind, double carpels containing large numbers of seeds surrounded by a juicy, slightly acid, red pulp; **b** the tree bearing this fruit.

pomelo, n. [1. pómelō; 2. pómilou]. Etymol. uncertain; prob. a modification of Du. *pompelmoes*, Fr. *pampelmousse*, 'a shaddock'. The grape fruit or shaddock.

Pomeranian, adj. & n. [1. pòmeránian; 2. pòmərèiniən]. **1.** adj. **a** Of, pertaining to, Pomerania, in Prussia, on south coast of the Baltic; specif. **b** *Pomeranian dog*, a breed of medium-sized, also small-sized, dogs, with long silky hair, coming into a ruff at the neck, bushy tail curving over the back, sharp-pointed muzzle and ears; also called Spitz, the German name for the breed. **2.** n. A Pomeranian dog.

pomfret (I.), n. [1. pómfret; 2. pómfrit]. Etymol. doubtful; possibly corrup. of Port. *pampo*, 'a kind of fish'. The name of an edible marine fish found in the Pacific and Indian Oceans.

pomfret (II.), n. [1. pómfret; 2. pómfrɛt]. Phonetic spelling representing traditional pronunciation of the name *Pontefract* (Yorks.). Small round sweetmeat or lozenge of liquorice.

pomiculture, n. [1. pómikùlchur; 2. póumikàltʃə]. See **pome** & **culture**. Fruit-growing.

pomiferous, adj. [1. pōmíferus; 2. poumífərəs]. **pome** & **-ferous**. Fruit-bearing; bearing apples, pears &c.

Pommard, n. [1. pómar; 2. pómā]. Name of a commune in Burgundy, France, south of Beaune. A fine red Burgundy wine, produced from the vineyards of Pommard.

pommel (I.), n. [1. púml; 2. páml], fr. O. Fr. *pomel*, later & Mod. Fr. *pommeau*, dimin. of *pome*, *pomme*, 'apple', see **pomace**. **1.** The knob or rounded end of the hilt of a sword. **2.** The rounded projection at the front part of a saddle.

pommel (II.), vb. trans., fr. prec. Originally to thump, belabour, with the pommel of a sword; now, to thump soundly and repeatedly, to pound, with the fists.

pommelling, n. [1. púmeling; 2. páməliŋ]. Prec. & **-ing**. A thumping inflicted with the fists.

pomologist, n. [1. pōmólojist; 2. poumólədžist]. Next word & **-ist**. One skilled in the art of fruit-growing.

pomology, n. [1. pōmóloji; 2. poumólədži]. See **pome** & **-logy**. The science and art of fruit-growing.

Pomona, n. [1. pomóna; 2. pəmóunə]. Lat., fr. *pōmum*, 'fruit', see **pomace**. (Rom. mythol.) The goddess of fruits.

pomp, n. [1. pomp; 2. pəmp], fr. Fr. *pompe*, fr. Lat. *pompa*, fr. Gk. *pompḗ*, 'solemn procession, parade, pomp'; *pémpein*, 'to send, send off; to convoy, escort, conduct'; etymol. doubtful; possibly cogn. w. Lith. *kankù*, 'to reach, achieve', in wh. case the orig. form was **kʷenkʷ-*, **kʷonkʷ-*. Splendid display, parade; splendour: '*pomp and circumstance of glorious war*' (Shakespeare); (also in derogatory sense) ostentatious display, vain show: '*the pomps and vanity of this wicked world*'.

Pompadour, n. [1. pómpadōōr; 2. pómpəduə], fr. the Marquise de Pompadour, mistress of Louis XV. of France (d. 1764). The name of various objects named after Mme. de Pompadour, as **a** a style of dressing the hair swept back from the forehead over a pad or roll; **b** a rose-pink colour; **c** a low, square-cut bodice &c.

pompano, n. [1. pómpanō; 2. pómpənou], fr. Span. *pámpano*. An edible marine fish, *Trachinotus*, of the West Indies and the southern coasts of N. America.

pompier, n. [1. pómpiā; 2. pɔ̃pje]. Fr., 'fireman', fr. *pompe*, see **pump (I.)**. A fireman's scaling ladder, consisting of a single pole with cross-bars and a grappling hook at one end.

pom-pom, n. [1. póm pom; 2. póm pəm]. Imitative. An automatic, quick-firing gun firing one-pound shells.

pompon, n. [1. pómpon; 2. pɔ̃pɔ̃]. Fr.; etymol. doubtful. A small, rounded tuft of feathers, ribbons, wool &c. worn as a decoration on shoes, front of a soldier's shako &c.

pomposity, n. [1. pompósiti; 2. pəmpósiti]. See **pompous** & **-ity**. **1.** Quality of being pompous; **a** (of bearing) pretentious self-importance, combined with arrogance and solemnity; **b** (of language) floridness, bombast, turgidity, misplaced and exaggerated stateliness. **2.** Pompous person.

pompous, adj. [1. pómpus; 2. pómpəs], fr. Fr. *pompeux*, fr. L. Lat. *pompōsus*, 'stately, dignified'. See **pomp** & **-ous**. **1.** (rare and archaic) Displaying pomp; stately, dignified, magnificent, splendid: '*A pompous bride*' (Spenser, 'F. Q.' ii. 12. 50); '*These massy columns in a circle rise, O'er which a pompous dome invades the skies*' (Pope, 'Temple of Fame,' 244-5). **2.** (chiefly derogatory) **a** (of persons and manner) Pretentiously dignified, unduly self-important, affecting an unnatural stateliness expressive of conceit and arrogance; **b** (of speech and diction) expressing above qualities; florid, turgid, high-flown, declamatory, bombastic.

pompously, adv. Prec. & **-ly**. In a pompous manner.

pompousness, n. See prec. & **-ness**. Quality of being pompous; pomposity.

ponce, n. [1. pons; 2. pəns]. Etymol. doubtful; possibly fr. **pounce (I.)**. (slang) A prostitute's bully; souteneur.

ponceau, n. [1. ponsō; 2. pɔ̃so]. Fr. **1.** The corn poppy. **2.** A bright-red dye or colour.

poncho, n. [1. pónchō; 2. póntʃou]. S. Am. Span., fr. a native word. A S. American blanket-shaped cloak with an opening in the middle for the head; similar mackintosh cape for slipping on quickly.

pond (I.), n. [1. pond; 2. pənd]. Prob. a variant of **pound (III.)**, 'enclosure'. A small lake or pool of stagnant water; esp. one formed artificially.

pond (II.), vb. trans. & intrans., fr. prec. **a** trans. To form into a pond by damming; **b** intrans., to collect, as water, into a pond.

pondage, n. [1. póndij; 2. póndidž]. **pond** & **-age**. Amount of water contained in a pond; capacity of a pond or reservoir.

ponder, vb. trans. & intrans. [1. pónder; 2. póndə], fr. O. Fr. *ponderer*, fr. Lat. *ponderāre*, 'to weigh', fr. *ponder-*, stem of *pondus*, 'a weight', see **pound (I.)**; connected w. *pendere*, 'to weigh', see **pension (I.)**, & *pendēre*, 'to hang', see **pendant**. **A.** trans. To weigh, balance, in the mind; to consider, think over, examine with care or deliberation: *to ponder a question, problem, difficulty* &c. **B.** intrans. To engage in deep thought and meditation; to muse, cogitate: *to sit and ponder*; also *ponder over*, to dwell thoughtfully and pensively upon.

ponderability, n. [1. pònderabíliti; 2. pòndərəbíliti]. Next word & **-ity**. The capacity of being ponderable, weighed, or estimated.

ponderable, adj. [1. pónderabl; 2. póndərəbl], fr. L. Lat. *ponderābilis*. **ponder** & **-able**. **1.** **a** Capable of being weighed, actually and physically; **b** capable of being appraised by the mind; able to be calculated, foreseen, and estimated. **2.** (as n., usually pl., *the ponderables*) Things, events &c. which can be estimated in advance and taken into consideration.

ponderance, n. [1. pónderans; 2. póndərəns], fr. Lat. *ponderant-(em)*, Pres. Part. of *ponderāre*. See **ponder** & **-ance**. (rare) Weight, gravity.

ponderation, n. [1. pònderáshun; 2. pòndəréiʃən]. L. Lat. *ponderātiōn-(em)*, fr. *ponderāt-(um)*, P.P. type fr. *ponderāre*, 'to weigh', see **ponder**, & **-ion**. (rare) A weighing, balancing, esp. in the mind.

ponderosity, n. [1. pònderósiti; 2. pɔndərɔ́siti], fr. Fr. *pondérosité*. See **ponderous** & **-ity**. State, quality, of being ponderous; weightiness, gravity; (chiefly in moral sense) a dull, boring style, manner &c.

ponderous, adj. [1. pónderus; 2. pɔ́ndərəs], fr. Fr. *pondéreux*, fr. Lat. *ponderōsus*, 'heavy, weighty'. See **ponder** & **-ous**. **1.** (of material things) **a** Heavy, weighty, unwieldy: *a ponderous axe*; **b** giving an impression of weight; oppressive, massive: *a ponderous building, figure* &c. **2.** (of manner, style) Dull, heavy, lumbering; reverse of light, gay: *a ponderous joke, speech* &c.

ponderously, adv. Prec. & **-ly**. In a ponderous manner.

ponderousness, n. See prec. & **-ness**. Quality of being ponderous (in various senses).

pone (I.), n. [1. póni; 2. póuni]. Lat. imperat. of *pōnere*, 'to place', see **position**. **1.** (law) An obsolete writ, for removing a case from one court to another, or for enforcing an appearance in a court. **2.** The player who cuts the cards in various card games.

pone (II.), n. [1. pōn; 2. poun]. Am. Indian word. A cake, loaf, of maize flour: *corn pone*.

pongee, n. [1. pònjḗ; 2. pɔndzī́]. Etymol. doubtful; prob. a corrupt. of Chinese *punchi*, 'a domestic, home loom'. A fine soft unbleached Chinese or Indian silk fabric.

pongo, n. [1. pónggō; 2. pɔ́ŋgou]. Native name. An African anthropoid ape; the name is sometimes wrongly applied to the orang-outang.

poniard, n. & vb. trans. [1. póniard; 2. pɔ́niəd], fr. Fr. *poignard*, fr. *poing*, 'fist', as being grasped in the fist, fr. Lat. *pugnus*, 'fist'. See **pugnacious** & **-ard**. **1.** n. A dagger. **2.** vb. To stab with a poniard or dagger.

pons, n. [1. ponz; 2. pɔnz]. Lat. stem *pont-*, 'bridge'; cogn. w. Gk. *pátos*, fr. **pn̥t-*, 'beaten way, path'; Scrt. *panthāś*, 'path, road'; O. Slav. *pǫtĭ*, 'way'; fr. same base comes also O.E. *findan*, 'to come upon; to find'; see **find**. (anat.) A bridge or connecting part, esp. *Pons Varolii* (fr. *Varoli*, Italian anatomist), a band of nerve-fibres in the brain. *Pons asinorum*, Lat., the 'asses' bridge', the 5th proposition of Book I. of Euclid, as a difficult problem for beginners.

pontifex, n. [1. póntifeks; 2. pɔ́ntifeks]. Lat., 'high priest'; etymol. uncertain, but prob. fr. Umbrian *puntes* (pl.), the precise meaning of wh. is doubtful, but wh. refers to some religious ritual, & is rendered by some as 'sacrifices'; a connexion w. O. Slav. *světŭ*, & Lith. *szventas*, 'holy', has been suggested; in this case the orig. form was **k went-*, & we may connect Goth. *hunsl*, 'sacrifice', O.E. *hūsl*, 'Eucharist', see **housel**; *-fex* means 'agent, doer', fr. base *fac-*, 'to do' &c., see **fact**, also **-fy** & **-fic**. (Rom. antiq.) A member of a college of priests in ancient Rome which included also the flamens and Vestal virgins, and was presided over by the *Pontifex maximus*, the chief pontiff, which title was borne by the Roman Emperors and then by the Pope; see **pontiff**.

pontiff, n. [1. póntif; 2. pɔ́ntif], fr. Fr. *pontife*. As prec. **1.** (Rom. antiq.) A pontifex, esp. the *Pontifex maximus*. **2.** A high priest of the Jews. **3.** (R.C. Ch.) A bishop, esp. the Pope, as Bishop of Rome, the *Sovereign Pontiff*.

pontifical, adj. & n. [1. pontífikl; 2. pɔntífikl], fr. Lat. *pontificālis*, fr. *pontific-*, stem of **pontifex**, & **-al**. **1.** adj. **a** Of, pertaining to, a pontifex: *pontifical college*; or **b** to a pontiff, to a bishop, esp. to the Sovereign Pontiff, the Pope; Papal: *pontifical authority* &c. **2.** n. **a** (R.C. Ch.) A book containing the offices, services &c. as performed by a bishop; **b** (pl.) a bishop's vestments.

pontifically, adv. Prec. & **-ly**. In a pontifical manner; as, in the capacity of, a pontiff.

pontificate, n. & vb. intrans. [1. pontífikāt; 2. pɔntífikeit], fr. Lat. *pontificātus*, fr. stem of **pontifex**, & **-ate**. **1.** n. The office and dignity of a pontifex or pontiff, esp. of the Pope; period of time during which a pontiff holds the office. **2.** vb. **a** To officiate with episcopal ritual and insignia at an ecclesiastical function, especially the Mass; **b** to pontify.

pontify, vb. intrans. [1. póntifī; 2. pɔ́ntifai], fr. Fr. *pontifier*, fr. L. or Med. Lat. *pontificāre*, 'to hold the office of pontiff'. See **pontiff** & **-fy**. To play the pontiff; to act, speak, with airs of great authority or infallibility; to pontificate.

pontius, n. [1. pónshus; 2. pɔ́nʃəs]. Prob. fr. *Spongio-pilin*, a trade name for a thick waterproofed fabric made of felted hair and small pieces of sponge. (univ. rowing slang) A small mat tied on the fixed seat of a boat, to prevent blisters &c.

pont-levis, n. [1. pònt lévis; 2. pɔ̀nt lévis], or as Fr. [pɔ̃ləvī]. Fr. *pont*, 'bridge', see **pons**, & *lever*, 'to raise, lift', see **lever**. A drawbridge.

pontoneer, n. [1. pòntonḗr; 2. pɔ̀ntəníə], fr. Fr. *pontonnier*. See **pontoon** (I.). An engineer who builds pontoon-bridges or is in charge of pontoons; esp. a military engineer.

pontoon (I.), n. [1. pòntṓōn; 2. pɔ̀ntū́n], fr. Fr. *ponton*, fr. Lat. *pontōn-(em)*, *ponto*, 'a punt', later 'floating bridge'. See **pons**. **1.** A flat-bottomed boat, esp. one of a set of such moored in a river to carry a quickly built temporary bridge; *pontoon-bridge*, one built for the passage of troops. **2.** A metal cylinder, able to float and to act as a pontoon, for supporting a bridge. **3.** A caisson.

pontoon (II.), vb. trans. & intrans., fr. prec. **1.** trans. To bridge with pontoons. **2.** intrans. To cross by a pontoon-bridge.

pontoon (III.), n. Etymol. doubtful. A gambling game played with cards, resembling vingt-et-un.

pony, n. [1. pṓni; 2. póuni], through Lowland Scots *powney*, fr. O. Fr. *poulenet*, dimin. of *poulain*, 'colt', fr. L. Lat. *pullānus*, variant of Lat. *pullus*, 'a young animal, foal'. See **foal** & **pullet**. **1.** **a** A small stocky horse, esp. one of various special breeds, usually under 13 to 14 hands high, as *Shetland, Exmoor, New Forest pony* &c.; **b** (colloq.) any small horse, esp. for riding. *Pony-cart, -chaise*, a light cart or carriage drawn by a pony. **2.** (betting slang) Twenty-five pounds. **3.** (applied to various small objects) A small beer-glass; a small locomotive used for shunting trains &c.

pood, poud, n. [1. pōōd; 2. pūd]. Russ. *pud*, fr. L.G. *pund*. See **pound** (I.). A Russian weight of 40 Russian lb., equivalent to 36 lb. avoirdupois.

poodle, n. [1. pōōdl; 2. pū́dl], fr. Germ. *pudelhund*, 'poodle-dog', fr. L.G. *pudeln*, 'to splash, paddle, in water', cogn. w. **puddle**. A breed of dog kept as a pet because of its extreme intelligence, probably in origin a spaniel; of medium size, with thick, curly, usually black, hair, often clipped into patterns.

poogye, n. [1. pōōgē; 2. pū́gi]. Hind. Indian nose-flute.

pooh, interj. Imitative. Expression of contempt, impatience &c.

Pooh Bah, n. [1. pōō báh; 2. pū bá]. Name of a character in Gilbert & Sullivan's comic opera 'The Mikado'. A person who holds a variety of offices.

pooh-pooh, vb. trans. [1. pōō pōō; 2. pù pú]. To treat with contempt; to dismiss as of no importance, as not worth discussion: *to pooh-pooh suggestions, signs of danger, risk* &c.

pooja, n. See **puja**.

pookoo, n. See **puku**.

pool (I.), n. & vb. trans. [1. pōōl; 2. pūl]. O.E. *pōl*, also a variant *pul*; O.H.G. *pfuol*, Mod. Germ. *pfuhl*, L.G. *pohl*, & Du. *poel*; perh. one of the few genuine Gmc. *p-* words; cp. Lith. *balà*, 'swamp'. **A.** n. **1.** Place in a stream or river where the water is much deeper than elsewhere, and more or less still: *a salmon pool*. *The Pool* (*of London*), that part of the Thames which lies below London Bridge, reaching to Limehouse. **2.** **a** Any small quantity of still or stagnant water, a pond or puddle; **b** quantity of spilled liquid collected together: *a pool of blood*. **3.** (coal min.) A hole made to take a wedge for splitting coal. **B.** vb. (min.) To cut a hole for a wedge in splitting coal and in quarrying; to undermine or undercut a seam for extraction of coal &c.

pool (II.), n. & vb. trans. Apparently fr. Fr. *poule*, 'a hen, chicken'; also (slang) 'stakes in a game', see **pullet**; origin of the secondary meaning is unknown; 'plunder, booty', also 'eggs', have been suggested; the term came into use in Engl. in 17th cent., & was early identified w. **pool** (I.). **A.** n. **1.** **a** The stakes and penalties played for in various card and other games; **b** a receptacle for holding the stakes. **2.** A game played on a billiard-table, by several players, each having a different-coloured ball, to which three 'lives' are given, the object being to pocket and take a 'life' from an opponent's ball in order of colour; the winner takes the entrance stakes and the penalties paid on each 'life'. **3.** **a** A combination for gambling, speculating in stocks and shares &c., the various interests being 'pooled' or united and the members sharing profits and losses; **b** a combining of stocks of goods &c. for equal distribution. *Pool room* (U.S.A.), a public gambling place. **4.** A form of commercial combination or trust, formed to regulate prices and share profits on an agreed basis, thus avoiding competition. **B.** vb. To form into a pool, esp. a trade or commercial combination: *to pool interests* &c.; (also fig.) *to pool resources*, put money or other property, from several sources, into a common fund for the benefit of all the contributors.

poon, n. [1. pōōn; 2. pūn], fr. Sinhalese & Telugu *pūna*. An East Indian tree, *Calophyllum*, with hard timber; *poon oil*, oil from the seeds of this, used in medicine and as an illuminant.

poop (I.), n. & vb. trans. [1. pōōp; 2. pūp], fr. O. Fr. *pupe*, later *poupe*, fr. L. Lat. *puppa*, variant of Lat. *puppis*, 'stern of a ship, ship'; etymol. uncertain. **1.** n. The stern or after-part of a ship, esp. the highest deck at the stern of a ship. **2.** vb. **a** (of wave on sea) To break over (a vessel) from the stern; **b** (of vessel) to receive a wave over the stern: *the ship was pooped*.

poop (II.), n. See **pope** (III.). Place, spot, on the thigh.

poop (III.), n. Prob. imitative as **pooh**, & cp. Am. equiv. slang word *boob*. (obs. or obsolesc. slang) A silly, stupid, feeble sort of person.

poor, adj. [1. pōōr, pōr; 2. puə, pɔ̄]. M.E. *poure* & *povre*, fr. O. Fr. *povre*, Mod. Fr. *pauvre*, fr. Lat. *pauper*, 'poor, scanty, feeble', see **pauper**. **1.** Having small means, or means insufficient to support life in ease or comfort; needy, indigent. *The poor*, poor people, specif. those who receive relief from the parish, relieving officer &c., or from charity; specif., *poor prisoner*, person on trial who has no means to engage counsel for his defence. **2.** Worthy of pity or sympathy; unfortunate; usually as expression of sympathy: *how is your poor father?*; *got run over, poor fellow*; often used in referring to a person who is dead or has died, without any implication of other misfortune: *my poor brother died last night*; *my poor old mother used often to say . . .* **3.** Humble, insignificant (usually ironical): *to the best of my poor abilities* &c. **4.** **a** Scanty, deficient in quantity, not abundant: *a poor crop of apples*; **b** not yielding much, unproductive, barren: *poor soil*; *a poor farm*. **5.** Of inferior quality: **a** (of material objects) *poor wine*; *poor food, clothes* &c.; **b** (of mental or other capacities) *a poor speaker*; *a poor player*; **c** (of persons and character &c.) mean, contemptible, lacking elevation or nobility; not high-minded or courageous: *a poor creature*; *to show a poor spirit*; *poor* *sort of conduct.* **6.** Thin, meagre; not sound or healthy; weak, feeble: *a horse in poor condition*; *poor health.*

poor-box, n. Box in a church in which offerings for the poor of the parish may be placed.

poorhouse, n. [1. pŏŏrhous; 2. púəhaus]. Institution where paupers are maintained; a workhouse.

poor-law, n. That body of law relating to the relief and maintenance of paupers.

poorly, adv. & adj. [1. pŏŏrli; 2. púə-, pɔ̄li]. **poor** & **-ly.** **1.** adv. In a poor, weak, feeble manner or way; not well, not good; defectively: *a poorly built house*; *he spoke very poorly*; *to think poorly of*, not to have a good or high opinion of. **2.** adj. Not well in health, unwell, seedy: *I feel rather poorly this morning.*

poorness, n. [1. pŏŏrnes; 2. púənis]. See prec. & **-ness.** Quality, state, of being poor: **a** inadequacy, insufficiency, scantiness, paucity: *poorness of supply*; **b** unproductiveness, barrenness: *poorness of the soil*; **c** incompetence, shortcoming: *poorness of workmanship*; **d** sickliness, feebleness: *poorness of health, constitution* &c.; **e** moral deficiency, meanness: *poorness of character.*

poor-rate, n. Assessment, rate, made for the relief of the poor of a parish, district &c.

poor-spirited, adj. Poor in spirit, having no spirit or energy; timorous, pusillanimous.

pop (I.), n. [1. pop; 2. pɔp]. Imitative. **1.** A sudden, short, explosive sound: *the pop of a cork, pistol* &c. **2.** An effervescing drink: *ginger-pop*, ginger-beer. **3.** (colloq.) A shot: *to have a pop at a rabbit.*

pop (II.), adv. See prec. With the sound of a pop: *the cork, pistol &c. went pop*; also Phr. *to go pop*, to die, break, be ruined, suddenly.

pop (III.), vb. intrans. & trans., fr. **pop (I.).** **A.** intrans. To make a sound of a pop; to go off, break open, with a pop. **B.** trans. **1.** To cause to make a pop, to fire off (a gun &c.), draw (a cork), with a pop: *to pop a pistol off*; *to pop a cork out of a bottle.* **2.** To put on to, into, with a sudden, light, rapid action: *to pop something into one's mouth, pocket* &c.; *to pop a cake into the oven*; *to pop a hat on.* **3.** To perform (some action) with suddenness; only in Phr. *to pop the question*, to make a proposal of marriage (orig. implying that this was made suddenly and unexpectedly). **4.** (slang) To pawn: *to pop one's watch.* **5.** (U.S.A.) To heat, parch (Indian corn), so that the outside bursts open and the kernel exudes in a fluffy white expanded mass. **C.** Followed by prepositions. *Pop at*, intrans., to fire at. *Pop in*, intrans., **a** to call, pay a visit, casually and unexpectedly; to drop in: *I shall often pop in and see you*; **b** to enter a room suddenly: *he kept popping in and out the whole time I was there.* *Pop into*, intrans., to visit (a place), esp. on the spur of the moment: *he was always popping into Oxford for the day.* *Pop out*, intrans., **a** to rush, burst, suddenly and rapidly, from a room, house &c.: *he kept popping out all day to see the foal*; **b** to be extinguished suddenly: *a gust of wind made the candle pop out*; **c** (colloq.) to die (suddenly). *Pop off*, intrans., **a** (of a gun) to be fired, to detonate; **b** to depart suddenly and hurriedly; **c** (colloq.) to die.

pop (IV.), n. Abbr. fr. *popular.* A popular concert: *the Monday, Saturday, Pops.*

pop-corn, n. (U.S.A.) Parched, burst, or popped Indian corn or maize, eaten as a sweetmeat.

pope (I.), n. [1. pōp; 2. poup]. O.E. *pāpa*, M.E. *pōpe*, fr. Lat. *pāpa*, 'father', in Eccles. Lat. 'bishop', fr. late Eccles. Gk. *pápas*, 'father, bishop', for earlier Class. Gk. *páppas*, 'father', imitative in origin. See **papa** & **Papal.** **1.** (cap.) The Bishop of Rome, the head and spiritual father of the Roman Catholic Church. *Pope's head*, a long-handled feathered brush for brushing ceilings; *pope's nose*, the tail-end of a cooked goose or duck. **2.** One who assumes to speak with supreme authority and claims infallibility.

pope (II.), n., fr. Russ. *pop*, borrowed fr. Lat.; see prec. A parish priest of the Orthodox Greek Church in Russia.

pope (III.), n. & vb. trans. Also *poop*; etymol. unknown. **1.** n. A place or spot on the front part of the thigh, where a blow is especially painful and disabling. **2.** vb. To strike another on the pope; esp. in P.P., usually *pooped*, struck on the pope or poop of the thigh and temporarily disabled.

popedom, n. [1. pṓpdum; 2. póupdəm]. **pope (I.)** & **-dom.** **a** The rule, dominion, jurisdiction of the Pope; the Papacy; **b** (in hostile sense) popery.

pope-Joan, n. [1. pōp jṓn; 2. póup džóun]. **a** A mythical female Pope; **b** an old-fashioned card game.

popery, n. [1. pṓperi; 2. póupəri]. **pope (I.)** & **-ery.** The doctrines, practices &c. of the Roman Catholic Church; chiefly in derogatory or hostile sense: *No Popery!*

pop-gun, n. Child's toy, an imitation fire-arm which makes a loud pop by means of a sudden outburst of compressed air.

popinjay, n. [1. pópinjā; 2. pɔ́pindžei]. M.E. *popingay, papegay* &c., fr. O. Fr. *papegai*; cp. Ital. *papagallo*, fr. Med. Gk. *papagás*, all in sense of 'parrot'; the second element, *-gay* or *-jay*, is to be referred to the colours or chattering of the parrot, see **gay** & **jay**; the Ital. form is fr. Lat. *gallus*, 'cock'; the first element is doubtful; the Arab. *babaghai*, 'parrot', may be fr. Span. *papagayo*; prob. it is imitative, fr. the chatter of the bird. **1.** (obs.) A parrot. **2.** (hist.) A wooden, painted figure of a parrot or other bird, hung on a pole, as a target for archery contests. **3.** A dandy, fop; gaily dressed, showy, conceited swaggerer.

popish, adj. [1. pṓpish; 2. póupiʃ]. **pope (I.)** & **-ish.** Pertaining to, characteristic of, resembling, something in vogue in the Roman Catholic Church; usually in derogatory and hostile sense: *popish doctrines, practices, ceremonies &c.* *The Popish Plot*, bogus conspiracy falsely alleged by the perjuror Titus Oates in 1678 to have as its objects the murder of Charles II. and the restoration in this country of Roman Catholic rule.

popishly, adv. Prec. & **-ly.** In a popish manner; towards popery: *popishly inclined.*

poplar, n. [1. póplar; 2. pɔ́plə]. M.E. *popler, poplere*, fr. O. Fr. *poplier*, Mod. Fr. *peuplier*, fr. Lat. *pōpulus*, 'the poplar' (w. ō to distinguish it fr. *pŏpulus*, 'the people'); the word shows a redupl. form, **pō-pol*, the origin of wh. is uncertain. Walde, however, suggests connexion w. *palus*, 'swamp', see **paludal**, & O.H.G. *felawa*, 'meadow'; others compare Gk. *pelemizein*, 'to shiver', & Lat. *palpitāre*, 'to tremble', see **palpitate.** Any tree belonging to the genus *Populus*, of straight, tall, and rapid growth, soft wood, and trembling, vibrating leaves; the commonest species are the Black and White poplar, and the Lombardy poplar, the last resembling the cypress in growth. *Poplar moth*, **a** goat moth whose larvae burrow in and destroy poplars.

poplin, n. [1. póplin; 2. pɔ́plin], fr. Fr. *popeline*; etymol. doubtful; prob. fr. *papaline*, fr. Ital. *papalina*, 'papal', as made orig. at Avignon when it was a papal residence. Ribbed fabric made of silk and wool.

popliteal, adj. [1. pòplitḗal; 2. pɔ̀plitíəl], fr. Lat. *poplit-(em)*, *poplēs*, 'the ham', & **-al.** The etymol. of *poplēs* is dubious. Pertaining to, near, the hollow part of the leg behind the knee-joint, the ham: *popliteal artery, nerve* &c.

poppet, n. [1. pópet; 2. pɔ́pit]. Variant of **puppet.** **1.** **a** (obs. or dial.) A doll, a puppet; **b** term of endearment for a child &c. **2.** Of various small mechanical objects, as the *poppet head* of a lathe, a *poppet valve* &c.

popping, n. [1. póping; 2. pɔ́piŋ], fr. **pop (III.).** Act of going off with a pop: *the popping of corks &c.*; *popping crease*, (cricket) the striking crease or white line in front of the wicket at which the batsman stands when in play and over which his bat must be grounded to avoid his being stumped or run out.

popple, vb. intrans. & n. [1. pópl; 2. pɔ́pl]. M.E. *poplen*; prob. imitative as **pop.** **1.** vb. To bubble, ripple, heave, toss, as water in a choppy sea or of a river over shallows &c. **2.** n. A ripple, swell, heave, of a river or the sea.

poppy, n. [1. pópi; 2. pɔ́pi]. O.E. *popæġ, -iġ*, M.E. *popy*, fr. Lat. *papāver*, etymol. doubtful; Walde sees in the word the base **pap-*, 'to swell, blow', as in Lat. *papula*, 'pustule', see **papula.** **1.** (bot.) Any plant of the genus *Papaver*, of many species and varieties, esp. the opium poppy, *P. somniferum*, with white or purple flowers; the scarlet poppy of the cornfields, and various cultivated garden varieties, as the *Oriental poppy*, with deep red or pink flowers; *Shirley poppy*, a dwarf variety of many different colours; *poppy head*, **a** the seed capsule of the poppy, esp. of the species from which opium is extracted; **b** the ornamental finial or flower-like top to a stall or pew end in Gothic churches. **2.** Opium as extracted from poppies. **3.** A vivid scarlet colour, as of the cornfield poppy.

poppycock, n. [1. pópikok; 2. pɔ́pikɔk]. (slang) Nonsense, rubbish.

populace, n. [1. pópūlas; 2. pɔ́pjuləs]. Fr., fr. Ital. *popolaccio, popolazzo*, fr. *popolo*, 'the people', fr. Lat. *populus*, see **people** & **popular.** The common people; the multitude; the ordinary, general mass of the population undistinguished by rank, wealth &c.

popular, adj. [1. pópūlar; 2. pɔ́pjulə], fr. Lat. *populāris*, 'of, pertaining to, the people', fr. *populus*, 'the people', & **-ar.** The word shows reduplication of the base **pel-* &c., 'to fill', see **plenum, plebs, full (I.).** **1.** Of, pertaining to, the people or the populace, the general body of ordinary citizens without distinction of class &c.: *the popular voice, opinion* &c.; *popular government*, government by the votes of the majority of the citizens enjoying a wide franchise, as contrasted with *autocratic, oligarchic, government.* **2.** Suited to, adapted for, the needs of the people: *popular education*; *in popular language*; *at popular prices* &c. **3.** **a** Pleasing to, enjoying the favour of, admired by, the people: *a popular hero, singer, politician*; *a popular song, sport* &c.; **b** generally admired and liked: *to be popular*, to be generally liked.

popularity, n. [1. pòpūlárɪti; 2. pɔ̀pjulǽriti], fr. Lat. *populāritāt-(em).* Prec. & **-ity.** State, quality, of being popular, esp. of being generally liked and admired or esteemed by the people: *a politician's, actor's popularity*; *the popularity of a sport, proposal, measure* &c.; *to enjoy general popularity*, to be a general favourite.

popularization, n. [1. pòpūlarīzā́shun; 2. pɔ̀pjuləraizéiʃən]. Next word & **-ation.** Act, process, of popularizing; state, condition, of being popularized.

popularize, vb. trans. [1. pópūlarīz; 2. pɔ́pjuləraiz]. **popular** & **-ize.** To make, render popular; to spread among, make familiar and acceptable to or understandable by the people: *to popularize methods of hygiene, good art* &c.; *to popularize science.*

popularly, adv. [1. pópūlarli; 2. pɔ́pjuləli]. **popular** & **-ly.** In a popular manner; **a** by the people generally or as a whole: *as popularly understood or accepted*; **b** so as to be generally accepted, understood; in popular language: *an encyclopedia that is popularly written.*

populate, vb. trans. [1. pópūlāt; 2. pɔ́pjuleit], fr. L. Lat. *populāt-(um)*, P.P. type of *populāre*, fr. *populus*, 'the people'. See **popular.** To furnish a population to, supply with people; to people: *to populate a new country*; *a thickly populated area.*

population, n. [1. pòpūlā́shun; 2. pɔ̀pjuléiʃən]. L. Lat. *populātiōn-(em).* Prec. & **-ion.**

1. (rare) Act or process of populating. 2. The total number of the inhabitants of a country, town, district &c.

populism, n. [1. pópūlizm; 2. pɔ́pjulizəm]. Lat. *popul-*, as in prec. words, & **-ism.** The political theories, system &c., **a** of the 'People's Party', in U.S.A., aiming at public control of railways &c.; **b** of a Russian Communistic party before the Revolution of 1917.

populist, n. [1. pópūlist; 2. pɔ́pjulist]. *Popul-*, as in prec., & **-ist.** One who holds the doctrines of populism; a member of the 'People's Party', in U.S.A.

populous, adj. [1. pópūlus; 2. pɔ́pjuləs], fr. Lat. *populōsus*, fr. *populus*, 'the people'. See **popular & -ous.** Having many inhabitants, esp. as relative to the size, area &c. of the country, town, district &c. specified; thickly inhabited.

populously, adv. Prec. & **-ly.** With many inhabitants relatively to the size or area.

populousness, n. See prec. & **-ness.** State, condition, of being populous or thickly inhabited.

porbeagle, n. [1. pórbēgl; 2. pɔ̄bīgl]. Etymol. unknown; apparently a local Corn. name. A kind of shark of the N. Atlantic and Pacific Oceans, the mackerel-shark, *Lamna cornubica.*

porcelain, n. [1. pórslin; 2. pɔ̄slin], fr. Fr. *porcelaine*, fr. Ital. *porcellana*, adj., orig. applied to a shell w. polished lining; so called on account of its shape, like that of a small pig; fr. Lat. *porcellus*, 'little pig', dimin. of *porcus*, 'pig', see **pork.** A fine, translucent, white earthenware, with transparent hard or soft glaze; china ware, china; *porcelain clay*, kaolin.

porcelain(e)ous, adj. [1. pòrselán(e)us; 2. pɔ̄səléin(j)əs]. Prec. & **-(e)ous.** Made of porcelain; resembling porcelain, as having a hard transparent smooth surface.

porcelainize, vb. trans. [1. pórselanīz; 2. pɔ̄səlinaiz]. **porcelain & -ize.** To make into porcelain.

porch, n. [1. porch; 2. pɔ̄tʃ], fr. Fr. *porche*, fr. Lat. *porticus*, see **portico.** The projecting, covered entrance to a house, church, or other building. *The Porch*, colonnade at Athens where Stoic philosophy was taught; Stoic philosophy. See **stoic.**

porcine, adj. [1. pórsīn; 2. pɔ̄sain]. Fr. *porcin, porcine*, fr. Lat. *porcīnus*, 'belonging to a pig', fr. *porcus*, 'pig', see **pork.** Of, pertaining to, resembling, a pig or pigs.

porcupine, n. [1. pórkūpīn; 2. pɔ̄kjupain]. M.E. *porcepyn*, also *portepyn* & other variants, fr. O. Fr. *porc-espin*, 'spiny pig', see **pork,** & *spīna*, 'prickle, thorn', see **spine.** 1. A rodent mammal, genus *Hystrix*, of a family which is found in all the continents, covered with long, sharp-pointed erectile quills or spines; *porcupine ant-eater*, the echidna; *porcupine grass*, a long, coarse grass of S. Asia and Australia. 2. The name of a machine with sharp teeth or spikes used for heckling flax or mashing in brewing &c.

pore (I.), n. [1. pōr; 2. pɔ̄]. Fr., fr. Lat. *porus*, fr. Gk. *póros*, 'passage; a pore', cogn. w. Lat. *porta*, 'gate' &c., see **port (I. & III.)**; see also **fare (III.), ford.** 1. A minute opening in the skin of animals, or in the membrane of plants, serving as an outlet for perspiration, also as a means of absorption. Phr. *to sweat from every pore*, (i.) be extremely hot; (ii.) be frightened, or greatly excited. 2. A minute interstice between the particles of any body, e.g. of rocks.

pore (II.), vb. intrans. M.E. *puren, pouren*; etymol. uncertain. Usually *pore over, upon*; to gaze at with fixed attention; to become absorbed in: *poring over books*; '*And pore upon the brook that babbles by*' (Gray's 'Elegy').

porge, vb. trans. [1. porj; 2. pɔ̄dž]. Prob. a variant of **purge.** (Jewish word) To make (slaughtered beasts) ceremonially clean.

poriferous, adj. [1. pōríferus; 2. pɔ̄rífərəs]. See **pore (I.) & -ferous.** Having, provided with, pores; specif. (zool.) belonging to the division *Porifera*, which includes the sponges.

porism, n. [1. pórizm; 2. pɔ̄rizəm], fr. Gk. *pórisma, porismatos*, 'deduction', fr. *porizein*, 'to find, provide a way, to deduce', fr. *póros*, 'way, passage', see **pore (I.).** (ancient geom.) A type of proposition, contrasted with *theorem*, or *problem*, in which it was required to find something, e.g. the centre of a given circle.

pork, n. [1. pork; 2. pɔ̄k], fr. Fr. *porc*, 'pig, pig's flesh', fr. Lat. *porcus*, 'pig', cogn. w. O.E. *fearh*, 'pig', see **farrow.** The fresh, uncured flesh of the pig, considered as food.

pork-butcher, n. One who butchers and dresses pigs for sale, and deals in pork, sausages &c.

porker, n. [1. pórker; 2. pɔ̄kə]. **pork & -er.** A fattened pig, esp. a young pig ready for killing and turning into pork.

pork pie, n. Receptacle of pastry, completely closed, containing chopped pork well-seasoned, usually eaten cold.

pork-pie hat, n. **a** Small flat round hat formerly worn by women, supposed to resemble a pork pie in shape; **b** similarly shaped hat or cap, formerly worn in undress by officers and men in the British Army, now worn only by gentlemen cadets at Sandhurst.

porky, adj. [1. pórki; 2. pɔ̄ki]. **pork & -y.** Like pork, esp. of personal appearance, fat, over-fed, paunchy.

pornographer, n. [1. pornógrafer; 2. pɔ̄nɔ́grəfə]. See **pornography & -er.** One who deals in pornography; a writer of pornographic books &c.

pornographic, adj. [1. pòrnōgráfik; 2. pɔ̄nougrǽfik]. See next word & **-ic.** Pertaining to, of the nature of, pornography; obscene.

pornography, n. [1. pornógrafi; 2. pɔ̄nɔ́grəfi], fr. Gk. *pórnē*, 'harlot', cp. Hom. Gk. *pérnēmi*, 'I sell', & O. Ir. *renim*, fr. **prenim*, 'I sell'; & **-graphy.** **a** Treatise on prostitution; **b** licentious, indecent, obscene writing; obscenity generally.

porosity, n. [1. pōrósiti; 2. pɔ̄rɔ́siti]. Fr. *porosité*. See **porous & -ity.** State, quality, of being porous or permeable by liquids.

porous, adj. [1. pórus; 2. pɔ̄rəs]. **pore (I.) & -ous.** Full of pores; allowing liquids to pass through, permeable by liquids; not watertight.

porousness, n. [1. pórusnes; 2. pɔ̄rəsnis]. Prec. & **-ness.** Porosity.

porphyritic, adj. [1. pòrfirítik; 2. pɔ̄firítik]. See **porphyry & -ic.** (geol.) Resembling porphyry in structure.

porphyrogenite, n. [1. pórfirōjènīt; 2. pɔ̄firoudžènait], fr. L. Lat. *porphyrogenitus*, 'born in the purple', fr. Late, Byzantine, Gk. *porphurogénnētos*, as **porphyry & genesis.** (hist.) A member of the Imperial family of the Roman Empire of the East, born in the porphyry-lined chamber in the palace at Byzantium, in which empresses gave birth to their children.

porphyry, n. [1. pórfiri; 2. pɔ̄firi], fr. Lat. (Gk.) *porphyrītes*, fr. Gk. *porphúreos, pórphuros*, 'purple', fr. *porphúrā*, 'the purple shell-fish, purple'; prob. of Semitic origin. See also **purple.** A rock of red and white crystalline structure; specif. (geol.) a rock with red and white crystals of feldspar embedded in a red or purplish ground mass.

porpoise, n. [1. pórpus; 2. pɔ̄pəs], fr. O. Fr. *porpeis*, fr. *porc-peis*, 'pig-fish', Lat. *porcus*, 'pig', see **pork,** & *piscis*, 'fish'. See **Pisces.** A small cetacean mammal, genus *Phocaena*, of the N. Atlantic and Pacific, swimming in schools and preying on fish; distinguished from its congener, the dolphin, by blunt, rounded snout.

porpoise hide, n. Stout, very waterproof leather made from the skin of the porpoise.

porrect (I.), adj. [1. porékt; 2. pərékt], fr. Lat. *porrect-(um)*, P.P. of *porrigere*, 'to extend, put forth', fr. *por-*, **pro-,** 'forward', & *regere*, 'to rule, direct'. See **rectum.** Extended, stretched out.

porrect (II.), vb. trans. See prec. (eccles. law) To tender, present, submit.

porrection, n. [1. porékshun; 2. pərékʃən]. See **porrect (I.) & -ion.** (eccles.) in Phr. *porrection of the instruments*, act of tendering a Bible to a bishop at his consecration, or a chalice and Bible to a priest at his ordination.

porridge, n. [1. pórij; 2. pɔ́ridž]. Etymol. doubtful; prob. a form of **pottage.** Oatmeal boiled in water or milk.

porriginous, adj. [1. poríjinus; 2. pərídžinəs], fr. Lat. *porrīgin-*, stem of *porrigo*, see next word & **-ous.** Of, pertaining to, porrigo or scaly eruptions on the scalp.

porrigo, n. [1. porígō; 2. pərάigou]. Lat., 'dandruff'. Etymol. uncertain. (pathol.) A scaly eruption on the scalp.

porringer, n. [1. pórinjer; 2. pɔ́rindžə]. Earlier *pottanger, pottager*, fr. Fr. *potager*, 'a bowl for soup'; for intrusive *n* cp. *passenger*; see **porridge & pottage.** A porridge bowl, esp. a shallow bowl or cup of silver &c., for gruel, porridge &c.

port (I.), n. [1. port; 2. pɔ̄t]. O.E. already had *port*, 'gate, entrance; harbour; town', fr. Lat. *portus*, 'entrance, passage-way, harbour'; cogn. w. *porta*, 'gate', see **port (III.).** See also **per, fare (III.), & ford.** 1. A harbour, haven, esp. a place where merchant vessels may discharge and take in cargo: *port of call, destination, entry* &c. 2. A town on the sea or river which has a harbour, usually a *seaport* or *seaport town*, esp. one which has a custom house. 3. (fig.) A refuge, haven: *come safe to port.* Phr. *any port in a storm*, any way out (of difficulty &c.) must be accepted.

port (II.), n., fr. *Oporto*, 'the port', see prec.; name of a town in Portugal, the centre of the wine-shipping trade fr. Portugal. A strong, sweet, red wine of Portugal, properly applied to that produced in the Alto Douro district, near Oporto, and shipped from there; also *port wine.*

port (III.), n., fr. Fr. *porte*, fr. Lat. *porta*, 'gate', cogn. w. *portus*, 'harbour'. See **port (I.)** & cp. **porter (I.).** 1. A gate, gateway (obs., except in Scots usage); cp. *sally-port* and *portcullis.* 2. An opening in the side of a ship for loading and discharging cargo &c.; also for admission of light and air, and formerly as a gun-embrasure; a porthole. 3. A curved tongue-piece in a bridle-bit. 4. (mach.) An opening, passage-way for steam, air, water &c.

port (IV.), vb. trans., fr. Fr. *porter*, fr. Lat. *portāre*, 'to carry'; cogn. w. Scrt. *pārdyati*, 'leads through'; Goth. *farjan*, 'to carry, transport', see **ferry**; ultimately connected w. **port (I.) & (III.).** 1. (obs.) To bear, carry. 2. (mil.) To carry a rifle or sword across the body sloping from right upwards to the left, for inspection of arms &c.: *port arms!*, word of command.

port (V.), n., fr. prec. 1. Manner, style, in which a person bears or carries himself; carriage, bearing, mien: '*of regal port, But faded splendour wan*' (Milton, 'P. L.' iv. 869-70). 2. (mil.) Position of arms when ported: *at the port.*

port (VI.), vb. trans. & intrans. & n. Etymol. uncertain; vb. is earlier than n.; possibly fr. **port (I.),** the ship unloading lying, on entry, w. left side against a quay, when steering gear was on the starboard side; or fr. **port (III.),** opening for unloading cargo &c.; it supplanted the older *larboard* owing to the latter too closely resembling the sound of 'starboard'. 1. vb. **a** trans. To turn the helm of a ship to the left or port side: *to port the helm*; **b** intrans., to turn to the port side. 2. n. The left-hand side of a ship looking forward from the stern; (also attrib.) *on the port bow*; *the port watch* &c.

portability, n. [1. pòrtabíliti; 2. pɔ̄təbíliti]. See next word & **-ity.** State, quality, of being portable or easily carried or moved.

portable, adj. [1. pórtabl; 2. pɔ̄təbl]. Fr., fr. Lat. *portābilis*, fr. *portāre*, 'to carry', as **port (IV.) & -able.** **a** Capable of being, made to be, moved about or carried: not fixed: *a portable telephone*; **b** easily carried or transported; movable: *portable property, luggage.*

port-admiral, n. Chief naval officer in command of a harbour.

portage, n. & vb. trans. [1. pórtij; 2. pɔ̄tidž]. Fr. See **port (IV.)** & **-age**. **1.** n. **a** Act of carrying; carriage; transport; also cost of this: *portage of goods*; **b** (hist.) space allotted in lieu of wages for goods belonging to a sailor who has joined in a mercantile adventure; **c** specif., the carrying or hauling a boat, canoe &c. overland from one river or lake or other waterway to another. **2.** vb. To carry (a boat) overland from one waterway to another.

portal (I.), n. [1. pórtl; 2. pɔ̄tl]. O. Fr., Mod. Fr. *portail*, fr. Med. Lat. *portāle*, neut. sing. of Lat. *portālis*, fr. *porta*, 'gate'. See **port (III.)**. **a** A gate, doorway, esp. one of architectural pretensions or having a grand, splendid appearance; **b** (poet.) the entrance to any place; (also fig.) *death's dark portal.*

portal (II.), adj. Same as prec. (anat.) Of a fissure or entrance, *porta*, below the liver through which the vessels, as the *portal vein*, enter.

portamento, n. [1. pòrtaméntō; 2. pɔ̄təméntou]. Ital., fr. Lat. *portāre*, 'to carry', see **port (IV.)**. (mus.) A gradual glide from one note to another, passing through all the intervening tones; used in singing, and in playing instruments of the fiddle class.

portative, adj. [1. pórtativ; 2. pɔ̄tətiv]. Fr. *portatif*, fr. Lat. *portāt-*, P.P. type of *portāre*, 'to carry', see **port (IV.)**, & **-ive**. **1.** Capable of carrying a load or charge. **2.** (obs.) Portable: *portative organ*, a mediaeval, portable organ.

portcrayon, n. [1. pórtkrāon; 2. pɔ̄tkrèiən]. fr. Fr. *portcrayon*, fr. *porter*, 'to carry'. See **port (IV.)** & **crayon**. A metal tube or holder for crayons.

portcullis, n. [1. pórtkúlis; 2. pɔ̄tkális]. M.E. *porte-colys*, fr. O. Fr. *porte-coleïce*, lit. 'a sliding, gliding door or gate', fr. *porte*, 'door, gate', fr. Lat. *porta*, see **port (III.)**, & *coleïce*, Mod. Fr. *coulisse*, 'a groove, sliding, gliding', fr. *couler*, 'to flow', see **coulisse** & second element in **percolate**. **1.** A strong, heavy grating of iron, or of timber and iron, sliding in grooves, and capable of being raised and lowered, so as to open or close the main gateway of a castle or fortified place. **2.** (her.) A charge, representing a portcullis, on a coat of arms; a favourite Tudor badge, occurring also in arms of the City of Westminster &c. **3.** (cap.) One of the pursuivants of the College of Heralds.

Porte, n. [1. port; 2. pɔ̄t], fr. Fr. *la Sublime Porte*, transl. of Arab. *Babi Ali*, 'the High Gate', to the principal government office in Constantinople. (hist., in full) *The Sublime Porte*, the official name for the former seat of the Turkish Government, before it was removed to Angora; used of Turkey as a political power.

porte-cochère, n. [1. pórt koshár; 2. pɔ̄t kɔʃéə]. Fr., *porte*, 'gate', see **port (III.)**, & *cochère*, 'for a carriage', cp. **coach**. A carriage-way or large entrance-gate to a house.

porte-monnaie, n. [1. pórt mùni; 2. pɔ̄t màni]. Fr. See **port (IV.)** & **money**. A purse or pocket-book.

portend, vb. trans. [1. porténd; 2. pɔ̄ténd], fr. Lat. *portendere* for *prōtendere*, 'to point out, foretell, portend', fr. *prō*, 'in front of, forward', & *tendere*, 'to stretch'. See **pro-** & **tend (II.)**. To foretell, foreshadow, presage; to give warning of, serve as an omen of.

portent, n. [1. pórtent; 2. pɔ̄tent], fr. Lat. *portentum*, 'sign, omen', fr. P.P. of *portendere*. See prec. **1.** An omen, sign, warning: *portents of war, storm* &c. **2.** A portentous thing; marvel, prodigy: *the portents of modern science.* **3.** Significance, meaning, esp. as regards the future: *omens of evil portent.*

portentous, adj. [1. porténtus; 2. pɔ̄téntəs], fr. Lat. *portentōsus*, 'monstrous, hideous; marvellous, wonderful'. See prec. & **-ous**. **1.** Of the nature of a portent; ominous, presaging: *portentous events, occurrences*; *the portentous days before the outbreak of war.* **2. a** Marvellous, prodigious, imposing: *of portentous size*; *portentous abilities*; **b** (in derogatory sense) self-important, pompous: *a portentous manner.*

portentously, adv. Prec. & **-ly**. In a portentous manner; ominously; marvellously.

porter (I.), n. [1. pórter; 2. pɔ̄tə], fr. O. Fr. *portier*, fr. L. Lat. *portārius*, 'a door-keeper', fr. Lat. *porta*, 'gate, door', see **port (III.)**, & **-er**. A door-keeper or gate-keeper, at an institution such as a college, university, club, hospital &c.; similar functionary or concierge, at an hotel.

porter (II.), n. M.E. *portour*, fr. O. Fr. *porteour*, *portour*, Mod. Fr. *porteur*, fr. Lat. *portātōr-(em)*, fr. *portāre*, 'to carry', see **port (IV.)**. One who carries a burden or load, esp. a servant, **a** of a railway, who carries and handles passengers' luggage; or **b** of an hotel &c.; also **c** anyone employed at a meat, fish, or other market in carrying loads to and from the stalls &c. *Porter's knot*, a shoulder pad kept in place by a band round the head, used by market porters.

porter (III.), n., fr. prec. An inferior kind of stout, as formerly drunk by market or street porters in London &c.; hence originally called *porter's ale, beer* &c., a dark-brown or blackish beer made with charred malt.

porterage, n. [1. pórterij; 2. pɔ̄təridž]. **porter (II.)** & **age**. **a** The carriage of luggage &c. by a porter; **b** sum paid for this service.

porter-house, n. A chop-house, an eating house, where chops, steaks &c. are served with porter or other alcoholic liquors; *porter-house steak*, the choicest kind of beef-steak cut next to the sirloin.

portfire, n. [1. pórtfīr; 2. pɔ̄tfaiə]. Adaptation of Fr. *portefeu*, fr. *porter*, 'to carry', see **port (IV.)**, & *feu*, 'fire', see **focus**. Apparatus consisting of a case filled with an explosive for discharging rockets, or used as a slow-burning fuse in mining, quarrying &c.

portfolio, n. [1. portfṓliō; 2. pɔ̄tfóuliou], fr. Ital. *portafoglio*. See **port (IV.)** & **folio**, cp. Fr. *portefeuille*. **1.** A flat, portable case, usually of leather, for carrying loose sheets of music, drawings, prints &c. **2.** A case for carrying official documents, state papers &c.; hence a ministerial office of state; chiefly used of foreign ministries: *the portfolio of the Interior*, the ministry of the Interior or for Home Affairs; *minister without portfolio*, member of a ministry but without a specific department in his charge.

porthole, n. [1. pórt-hōl; 2. pɔ̄thoul]. **port (III.)** & **hole**. An opening in a ship's side for admission of light and air; formerly used as an embrasure for a gun.

portico, n. [1. pórtikō; 2. pɔ̄tikou]. Ital., fr. Lat. *porticus*, 'colonnade, covered gallery'; prob. fr. *portus*, 'entrance, harbour'. See **port (I.)** & cp. **porch**. A pillared arcade or piazza; a covered colonnade forming the entry or porch to a building.

portière, n. [1. pórtiār; 2. pɔ̄tiɛə]. Fr., fr. *porte*, 'gate, door'. See **port (III.)**. A heavy curtain hung over a doorway.

portion (I.), n. [1. pórshun; 2. pɔ̄ʃ(ə)n]. M.E. *porcioun*, fr. O. Fr. *porcion*, fr. Lat. *portiōn-(em)*, 'share, portion', cogn. w. Lat. *part-(em)*, 'part'. See **part (I.)**. **1.** A part, something less than the whole, a limited, small amount: *a small portion of the whole*; *a portion of land* &c. **2.** An allotted part, **a** a share, esp. of property &c.; *a wife's, widow's, younger son's, portion*; **b** specif., such an amount of any kind of food as is supplied to a hotel guest &c. at specified price. **3.** What is allotted to one by providence; one's fate, destiny: *our portion in life.*

portion (II.), vb. trans., fr. O. Fr. *porcionner*, *portionner*; fr. prec. **1.** Generally *portion out*, to divide into portions or shares: *to portion out food, land, property* &c. **2.** To give, allot, a portion or share to: *to portion a daughter*, give a dowry to.

portioner, n. [1. pórshuner; 2. pɔ̄ʃənə]. Prec. & **-er**. **1.** One who portions, gives a portion to. **2.** One who takes a portion; specif. (eccles.) a minister serving a benefice with others and receiving only a portion of the profits or tithe.

portionist, n. [1. pórshunist; 2. pɔ̄ʃənist]. See prec. & **-ist**. Portioner, **2**.

portionless, adj. [1. pórshunles; 2. pɔ̄ʃənlis]. **portion (I.)** & **-less**. Without a portion or share of an estate; specif., without a dowry: *portionless daughters.*

Portland, adj. [1. pórtland; 2. pɔ̄tlənd], fr. Portland, peninsula, Dorsetshire. *Portland cement*, a form of cement so called from its resemblance in colour to Portland stone; *Portland stone*, a yellowish-white limestone, used in building, obtained from quarries in Portland.

portliness, n. [1. pórtlines; 2. pɔ̄tlinis]. **portly** & **-ness**. Bodily condition of being portly; stoutness, embonpoint.

portly, adj. [1. pórtli; 2. pɔ̄tli]. **port (V.)** & **-ly**. **1.** (orig.) Having a fine port or carriage, demeanour, esp. used of a dignified or pompous bearing: *portly prelates.* **2.** Corpulent, stout: *portly aldermen.* The latter meaning is that now usually conveyed by the word.

portmanteau, n. & vb. trans. [1. portmántō; 2. pɔ̄tmǽntou]. Fr., fr. *porter*, 'to carry'. See **port (IV.)** & **mantle**. **1.** n. **a** Originally a light, flexible case for carrying extra clothes on horseback; **b** a large, leather travelling case or trunk for clothes, hinged at the back so as to form two separate compartments. **2.** vb. To combine two words &c. to form one; see next word.

portmanteau word, n. Term applied by 'Lewis Carroll', in 'Alice through the Looking-glass', to his invented words composed of two words run together and having a combined meaning, as *mimsy*, flimsy and miserable.

portolano, n. [1. portoláhnō; 2. pɔ̄təlánou]. Ital., fr. *porto*, 'harbour'. See **port (I.)**. A mariner's book of sailing directions, with charts, maps, and descriptions of harbours &c.

portrait, n. [1. pórtrit; 2. pɔ̄trit]. Fr., fr. P.P. of *portrayer*, 'to portray'. See **portray** & **protract**. **1.** A pictorial representation of a specific human being, esp. of a representation of his face, more rarely used of such a picture of an animal. *Portrait-bust*, a portrait in sculpture. **2.** A vivid or graphic description in words of a person's appearance and character. **3.** An image, resemblance, type.

portraitist, n. [1. pórtritist; 2. pɔ̄tritist]. Prec. & **-ist**. A portrait painter.

portraiture, n. [1. pórtrichur; 2. pɔ̄tritʃə]. **portrait** & **-ure**. **1.** Art of painting portraits; a portrait or collection of portraits: *English portraiture of the 18th cent.* **2.** Art of giving a vivid verbal description of a person in appearance and character.

portray, vb. trans. [1. portrā́; 2. pɔ̄tréi], fr. O. Fr. *pourtraire*, *portraire*, fr. Lat. *prōtrahere*, 'to draw out or forth', see **pro-**; the etymol. of Lat. *trahere*, 'to draw' is disputed & connexions have been suggested, **a** w. the base of **draw**; **b** w. that of **throe** & **thrall**. See **tract (I.)**. **1.** To paint, draw, the portrait of, to depict. **2.** To describe vividly in words.

portrayal, n. [1. portrā́al; 2. pɔ̄tréiəl]. Prec. & **-al**. **1.** Act, process, of portraying. **2.** Result of this; **a** in pictorial form; **b** in form of a description.

portreeve, n. [1. pórtrēv; 2. pɔ̄trīv]. O.E. *portgerēfa*, 'mayor of a town'; *port* in O.E. means 'town'; see **port (I.)**, & **reeve (II.)**, & cp. Germ. *graf*, 'count'. (obs.) The chief officer of a town; a bailiff.

portress, n. [1. pórtres; 2. pɔ̄tris]. **porter (I.)** & **-ess.** A woman door-keeper.

Portuguese, adj. & n. [1. pòrchoogéz; 2. pɔ̄tʃugíz], fr. Port. *Portuguez.* **1.** adj. Of, pertaining to, Portugal, its inhabitants, language &c. **2.** n. **a** A native of Portugal; **b** the language of Portugal. *Portuguese man-of-war,* the popular name of a genus, *Physalia,* of beautifully coloured jelly-fish, which have an air-filled float which allows them to sail before a wind.

pose (I.), vb. trans. & intrans. [1. pōz; 2. pouz], fr. Fr. *poser,* 'to place, put', fr. Lat. *pausāre,* 'to halt, rest, pause', in L. Lat. also, 'to put, place', fr. *pausa,* 'pause', see **pause**; influenced in meaning by Lat. base *pos-(itum),* P.P. of *pōnere,* 'to place', see **position,** & cp. **depose. A.** trans. **1.** To place, set, arrange, in position, or attitude, esp. for effect or for making a representation or painting of &c.: *to pose a model for a picture, statue; to pose a group of actors* &c. **2.** To lay down, assert, propound: *to pose a claim, argument; to pose a question.* **B.** intrans. **1.** To assume an attitude of body, to take up a particular position, as for an artist: *to pose for one's portrait.* **2.** To assume an attitude of mind, or character &c., for effect or for a studied purpose; to give oneself out as, pretend to be: *to pose as a model of all the virtues; pose as a hero* &c.

pose (II.), n., fr. prec. **1.** A position, attitude of the body, assumed for effect or for representation or as represented by an artist: *the pose in the portrait is dignified; he adopted a watchful, careful, pose.* **2.** An assumed attitude of mind, character &c.; a pretence: *his piety is a mere pose.*

pose (III.), vb. trans. Abbr. fr. **oppose.** To embarrass, disconcert, puzzle, baffle, by asking a question which the person asked cannot answer.

poser, n. [1. pṓzer; 2. póuzə]. Prec. & **-er.** A puzzling, difficult, awkward, question or problem.

poseur, n. [1. pōzę̄r; 2. pouzʌ́]. Fr. See **pose (I.).** An affected, attitudinizing person; one who is always posing and assuming for effect a character which is not his natural one.

posit, vb. trans. [1. pózit; 2. pɔ́zit], fr. Lat. *posit-(um),* P.P. of *pōnere,* 'to place'. See next word. To lay down as a fact, assert; to assume, postulate, as actual.

position (I.), n. [1. pozíshun; 2. pəzíʃən]. Fr., fr. Lat. *positiōn-(em),* 'a placing, sitting in place; posture, situation, position', fr. *posit-(um),* P.P. type of *pōnere,* 'to place, set', & **-ion.** Etymol. of *pōnere* quite doubtful. See **site. 1.** (physically) **a** The state of being placed in a certain relation to other objects; place, spot, where an object or person is or stands; locality, situation: *position of a place on a map; position of a house on a hill* &c.; *position of players on the field* &c.; **b** a place, locality, occupied by an object or person: *a commanding (military) position.* Phr. *in, out of, position,* placed rightly or wrongly; **c** the manner, way, in which an object or person is placed or acts, stands or lies &c.; attitude, posture: *an uncomfortable position; horizontal, vertical, position.* **2.** A situation, place of employment; status, rank; office: *a position as cashier; a position in the Ministry; a high, low, position in society.* **3. a** State, condition; situation in relation to other conditions: *the position of political affairs; the position is very critical; to be placed in a false position;* **b** a mental attitude; point of view: *to take up the position that,* to be of, maintain, the opinion that; *to define one's position.* Phr. *in a position to do something,* so situated that one can do it. **4.** In technical senses: **a** (log.) a proposition, affirmation, laid down as a fixed principle; **b** (mus.) relationship of the notes of a chord to each other in pitch &c.; **c** (prosody, Lat., Gk.) the lengthening of a short vowel by its preceding two consonants, when it is said to be long *by position.* (The fact is that any syllable ending in two consonants is 'long'; the vowel which precedes them may or may not be lengthened 'by position'.)

position (II.), vb. trans., fr. prec. To place, put, in the proper position; to determine the position of; to localize.

positional, adj. [1. pozíshunal; 2. pəzíʃənəl]. **position (I.)** & **-al.** Of, pertaining to, position; fixed by position.

positive (I.), adj. [1. pózitiv; 2. pɔ́zitiv]. Fr. *positive,* fem. of *positif,* fr. Lat. *positīvus,* 'settled by agreement or by arbitrary decision', opposed to *naturālis;* Lat. *posit-(um),* P.P. of *pōnere.* See **position** & **-ive. 1.** Definite, defined; contrasted with *qualified, implied,* or *inferential;* **a** definitely laid down, expressed without qualification; admitting of no choice or alternative; express, specific: *positive orders, instructions* &c.; *quite positive promises, statements* &c.; **b** directly expressed, stated as a fact: *positive evidence; proof positive; a positive fact;* **c** settled by agreement or drawn up arbitrarily, artificial: *positive laws,* as opposed to natural laws. **2.** (of persons, the mind &c.) **a** Fully assured, convinced, confident of the truth of: *are you sure? yes, I'm positive;* **b** over-confident, dogmatic: *a positive sort of person.* **3.** Having certain specified qualities which are absent in a correlative; contrasted with *negative* and *relative;* **a** existing in fact, actual, real; absolute, not speculative or relative: *positive philosophy; a positive good;* **b** (colloq.) complete, absolute: *a positive fool, humbug* &c. **4.** Specific uses: **a** (elect.) *positive charge,* that electrical state of a body from which one or more electrons have been removed; *positive current,* that current in a conductor which moves in reverse direction to electrons; *positive pole,* the anode; (of magnet) the north-seeking pole; **b** (gram.) expressing an unqualified, simple degree or state, as contrasted with *comparative* or *superlative: positive adjective;* **c** (math.) in number greater than zero; plus: *positive sign,* the symbol +; **d** (photog.) exhibiting the lights and shades as in nature and not reversed.

positive (II.), n., fr. prec. That which is positive and not negative: **a** (in gram.) the positive degree; **b** (elect.) the positive pole, plate &c.; **c** (photog.) a positive plate, film; a positive picture.

positively, adv. **positive (I.)** & **-ly.** In a positive way or manner; explicitly, actually; as an actual fact; not negatively.

positiveness, n. See prec. & **-ness.** State, quality, of being positive; reality, actuality; quality of being dogmatic.

positivism, n. [1. pózitivizm; 2. pɔ́zitivizəm], fr. Fr. *positivisme,* used by Comte for his philosophy. **positive (I.)** & **-ism. 1.** (philos.) **a** Any system of philosophy which is not based on metaphysical, *a priori* speculation, but is based solely on experience; **b** specif., (cap.) the philosophical system of Auguste Comte, 1798–1857, according to which all knowledge is based on positive facts, the phenomena observed in a universe governed by necessary laws to be discovered by scientific methods only; Comtism; **c** an ethical religion, based on Comte's philosophy, a religion of humanity. **2.** (gen.) State, quality, of being positive or dogmatic; dogmatism.

positivist, n. [1. pózitivist; 2. pɔ́zitivist]. See prec. & **-ist.** A believer in positivism, follower of the philosophy of Comte; a Comtist.

positivistic, adj. [1. pòzitivístik; 2. pɔ̀zitivístik]. Prec. & **-ic.** Of, pertaining to, positivism.

posology, n. [1. posóloji; 2. pɔsɔ́lədži], fr. Fr. *posologie,* fr. Gk. *pósos,* 'how much', & **-logy;** *pósos* is fr. a base *k^{wo}- &c., wh. gave rise to a large group of interrog. & rel. prons. & advs. See such words as **who, what** &c., & **quod (I.).** (med.) Science of doses; knowledge of exact amount of a drug, size of dose &c. which should be administered to a patient.

posse, n. [1. pósi; 2. pɔ́si]. Med. Lat., 'power', fr. Lat. *posse,* 'to be able', infin. of *possum,* 'I am able, can'. See **possible. 1.** (law) In full, *posse comitatus,* lit., the power of the county, the force which the sheriff can call out to suppress a riot, arrest malefactors &c.: *the sheriff's posse.* **2.** A crowd of people, rabble: *the whole posse of his partisans and hirelings.* **3.** In Lat. Phr. *in posse,* potentially, as contrasted with *in esse,* in being.

possess, vb. trans. [1. pozés; 2. pəzés], fr. O. Fr. *possessier, possesser,* fr. Lat. *possess-(um),* P.P. type of *possidēre;* 'to occupy, own, possess'; fr. *sedēre,* 'to sit'. See **sedentary** & words there referred to; origin of *pos-,* doubtful. **1. a** To hold as one's own, to own; to occupy and keep: *to possess property, a house, wealth* &c.; *to possess good qualities, character* &c.; specif. **b** *to possess a woman,* have sexual intercourse with her. **2.** To exercise control over, preserve, maintain, hold: *to possess one's mind, soul &c. in peace, patience.* Phr. *to possess oneself of,* to get possession of, to take and hold; *to be possessed of,* to be in possession of; *to be possessed by,* dominated. **3.** To influence strongly, to dominate, to occupy entirely: *a demon possesses him; to be possessed by a spirit, devil, idea* &c. Phr. *what possessed (him) to do it?,* for what reason did he do it?

possession, n. [1. pozéshun; 2. pəzéʃən]. Fr., fr. Lat. *possessiōn-(em),* 'a possessing, holding, possession'. See prec. & **-ion. 1. a** The act, or fact, condition, of possessing, or being the owner of; ownership, occupancy: *the possession of property.* Phr. *possession is nine points,* or *tenths, of the law,* possession or occupancy gives every advantage short of actual lawful ownership. *In possession,* possessed, owned: *the keys are in his possession; to be in possession of,* possessing, holding, keeping, owning: *in possession of all one's faculties, of one's senses; the man in possession,* a bailiff after serving a distraint &c.; **b** specif. in Phr. *to have, gain, possession of a woman,* have sexual intercourse with her. **2.** A thing, object, possessed, (often in pl.) property, wealth; territory subject to another country: *a few personal possessions; a man of great possessions; the French possessions in N. Africa.* **3.** (rare) Fact of obsessing, dominating spiritually: *possession by evil spirits.*

possessive, adj. & n. [1. pozésiv; 2. pəzésiv], fr. Lat. *possessīvus,* 'of, relating to, possession, possessive'. **possess** & **-ive. 1.** adj. **a** Of, pertaining to, possession or ownership: *possessive rights;* **b** (gram.) denoting, indicating, possession: *possessive case,* the case of the noun expressing this relationship by *'s,* the true English form, as *St. Paul's Cathedral, William's boots* &c., or by *of* (transl. Fr. *de*), *the King of England; possessive pronoun,* as *my, mine, our, ours, his, hers, their, theirs* &c. **2.** n. A possessive case or pronoun.

possessively, adv. Prec. & **-ly.** In a manner indicating possession or ownership.

possessor, n. [1. pozésur; 2. pəzésə]. **possess** & **-or.** One who possesses; an owner, proprietor; holder, occupant.

possessory, adj. [1. pozésuri; 2. pəzésəri], fr. Lat. *possessōrius.* Prec. & **-y.** Of, pertaining to, possession or a possessor: *a possessory title to land,* a title based on possession or occupancy.

posset, n. [1. póset; 2. pɔ́sit]. M.E. *poshote, pushote,* later *possyt.* Etymol. unknown. A drink of hot milk, thickened or curdled with wine or ale and spiced.

possibilist, n. [1. pósibilist; 2. pɔ́sibəlist], fr. Fr. *possibiliste.* See **possible (I.)** & **-ist.** A member of a political party which believes that proposals for reform should be limited to measures which are practicable or immediately capable of being carried out, esp. of a republican party in Spain, and Socialist party in France.

possibility, n. [1. pòsibíliti; 2. pòsibíliti], fr. Fr. *possibilité*, fr. Lat. *possibilitāt-(em)*, *possibilitas*. **possible** (I.) & **-ity**. **1.** State, quality, of being possible; power of happening or existing in fact or thought; feasibility: *the possibility of ghosts, miracles* &c.; *the possibility of flying-machines, wireless telephony* &c. *was long denied*; *a degree of possibility*; *within the range of possibility*. **2.** Something which is possible, which may exist or happen; usually implying remote or uncertain contingency, which is not likely: *just a possibility of success*; *no possibility of recovery*. **3.** (usually pl.) Power of, capacity for, use or development; prospects, future results, potentiality: *my garden is quite new, but has great possibilities*; *the new invention contains wonderful possibilities*.

possible (I.), adj. [1. pósibl; 2. pósibl, pósəbl]. Fr., fr. Lat. *possibilis*, 'possible', fr. *posse*, 'to be able', infin. of *possum*, 'I am able, can'; for **potisse, *potissum, *potis esse, *potis sum*, 'to be, I am powerful, able', fr. *potis*, 'powerful, able', see **potent** (I.), **power**; cogn. w. Gk. *pósis*, 'husband, i.e. master', see under **despot**. **1.** Capable of happening or existing; not contrary to nature, or the laws of thought, or to experience: *it is not possible that 2 and 2 can make 5*; *a possible event, accident* &c. **2.** Capable of being done; practicable, feasible: *it is not possible to prevent every form of disease*; *a possible task*; *a possible source of revenue*; *he will do it if it is possible*. **3.** That may or may not happen: *rain is possible today*; *a possible winner*; *a possible team to choose*; contrasted with *probable*, or *likely*. **4.** (colloq.) Capable of being tolerated; tolerable, endurable: *he is not a possible person*; *a possible house*, one that does not fulfil all requirements, but which can be put up with.

possible (II.), n., fr. prec. Something that is possible; possibility: *it is hard to see the limits of the possible in modern invention*.

possibly, adv. [1. pósibli; 2. pósibli]. **possible** (I.) & **-ly**. **1.** According to what is possible, within the limits of possibility; by any possible means: *as soon as I possibly can*; *cannot possibly do it*. **2.** Perhaps, by a remote chance: *it may possibly be fine today*; *he may possibly recover*; *the story is true, possibly*.

'possum, n. [1. pósum; 2. pósəm]. Colloq. abbr. of **opossum**. Phr. *to play 'possum*, to remain hidden; to exercise the greatest caution.

post (I.), n. [1. pōst; 2. poust]. In O.E., fr. Lat. *postis*, 'door-post'; etymol. uncertain, but possibly fr. base **twost-*, cp. Goth. *þwastiþa*, 'firmness; sureness'. **1.** A stout upright stake, pillar, or pole, round or square, of timber or metal, set firmly in the ground, in the flooring of a building &c., to act as a support, usually qualified according to its use or purpose: as *bed-post, door-post, lamp-post, sign-post* &c.; cp. *goal-post, winning-post, king-, queen-post* &c.; *post and rails*, as system of fencing, a fence made of posts supporting rails. Phr. (*to be driven*) *from pillar to post*, orig. a term of the tennis-court, to be driven hither and thither, hence, fig., from one corner to another, from one position, extremity, resource &c. to another. **2.** Specif., a block or pillar of coal, stone &c. left unhewn or quarried as a support for the roof of a gallery in a mine or quarry.

post (II.), vb. trans., fr. prec. **1.** To put up, affix, a notice, bill &c. (on) to a post, on a wall or other conspicuous place; also *post up*; to placard: *to post* (*up*) *an advertisement*; *to post a wall with notices* &c. **2.** To publish, announce, advertise, by posting a notice up in a public place &c.: *to post a ship as missing*; *to post a man as a defaulter*. Phr. (of persons) *well posted*, well informed; *to keep* (*a person*) *posted* (*with what goes on* &c.), send him regular news, information &c.; but cp. **post** (VI.) **3.**

post (III.), n., fr. Fr. *poste*, fr. Ital. *posto*, fr. Lat. *positum*, P.P. of *pōnere*, 'to place'. See **position**. **1. a** The place at which a soldier is stationed for duty; the ground which a soldier covers or guards when on duty: *the sentry at his post*; **b** position, place, taken by or occupied by troops; an outpost, small detached fort and its garrison: *a chain of posts along a frontier*; **c** a settlement, or occupied place, esp. in a foreign or uncivilized country, for commercial purposes &c.: *a trading post*; **d** any position or duty to which one is appointed or assigned: *a post of danger*; *to remain at one's post*; **e** a position, employment, appointment: *to obtain a post in the civil service*. **2.** Specif. **a** (mil.) one of two bugle-calls at night sounded at tattoo; *first, last, post*, also the latter as sounded at a military funeral; **b** (nav.) commission as full captain, *post captain*, formerly as commanding a ship of at least 20 gun rate.

post (IV.), vb. trans., fr. prec.; often confused w., & indistinguishable fr., **post** (II.). **a** To place a soldier or other person at a post; **b** to appoint to a specific duty.

post (V.), n. Fr. *poste*, fem., fr. Ital. *posta*; special use of **post** (I.). **1.** Any one of a series of posts or groups of men and horses stationed on a road at stages or intervals for the transmission of messages, letters &c., or for providing horses for riders or vehicles to the next stage, hence: *post-horse, post-chaise* &c., as below. **2.** The official conveyance, dispatch, and delivery of letters, parcels &c., at first by a series of posts or stages; then, with later development of methods of transport, by rail &c. direct; now under state management and control: *to send, transmit by the post* or *by post*; *to catch, miss, the post*, to be in time, too late, for dispatch by post. **3.** An office (post office), pillar or other box where letters &c. are taken, or placed, for conveyance and transmission: *to take letters to the post*. **4.** Letters &c. dispatched to or delivered by the post: *the post has been cleared* or *collected*; *the post came late this morning*; *no post today*. **5.** Various special uses: **a** a size of writing-paper, originally with a watermark of a postman's horn; **b** an old-fashioned children's game, 'general post', in which the players change places at call.

post (VI.), vb. intrans. & trans., fr. prec. **A.** intrans. **1. a** To travel by stages or posts: *to post from London to York*; **b** *post off*, to go, start, immediately, usually implying hurry: *post off at once and waste no time*. **B.** trans. **1.** To consign (letters &c.) to the post for conveyance by post; to drop (letters &c.) in a pillar-box, hand them in at a post office &c. **2.** (book-keeping, a special meaning usually grouped under this heading) To carry, transfer, from a day-book or journal to a ledger; also *post up*, to make a ledger complete and up to date by posting all the items from the day-book &c. **3.** (gen.) To inform, keep informed (usually in P.P.): *to keep a person well posted in the latest news*; but cp. **post** (II.) **2.**

post (VII.), adv., fr. **post** (V.). In Phr. *to ride post*, to ride with post-horses, changing them at various stages or posts; hence, to ride, travel &c. with the utmost speed to a specific place.

post-, fr. Lat. pref. **a** (of time) After, later than: *post-conquest*; *post-war* &c.; **b** (of position) behind: *post-orbital*. *Post* is fr. earlier **pos-*, w. *-t* fr. initial of the next element in old compounds, e.g. *postīcus*, adj., 'hinder', formed on anal. of *antīcus*, 'former, old', see **antique** &c.; **pos*, fr. **po*, is ultimately fr. *apo*, see **ab-** & **apo-**.

postage, n. [1. pṓstij; 2. póustidž]. **post** (VI.) & **-age**. The charge made by the post office for the carriage and delivery of letters, parcels &c.

postage-stamp, n. Stamp affixed to letters and parcels sent through the post, varying in value according to the destination and weight of the letter or article sent.

postal, adj. [1. pṓstl; 2. póustl]. See **post** (V.) & **-al**. Of, pertaining to, the post or post office; now, in most usages, displaced by *post* or *post office*, used attributively: *a postal package*; *postal service* &c.

postal order, n. A money order issued by a post office on payment, and payable to another person at another post office.

postal union, n. A union of various State Governments for regulating international post-office business.

post-boy, n. **post** (V.) & **boy**. A postilion; a letter-carrier.

post captain, n. **post** (III.). (nav.) A full captain, one who was formerly 'posted' to command a ship of at least 20 gun rate, now as title of the actual rank of captain, as distinguished from the courtesy title granted to a Commander when in command of a ship.

post card, n. Piece of pasteboard, oblong in shape, stamped and addressed on one side, and having a communication written or printed on the other, sent through the post as a letter.

post-chaise, n. **post** (V.) & **chaise**. A covered four-wheeled carriage for travelling post, drawn by two or more horses with postilions, and horsed afresh t each stage or post.

post-communion, n. That part of the Eucharistic service which follows the Communion; specif., the Collect said after this.

post-date, vb. trans. **1.** To assign a later date to an event than that on which it actually occurred: *earlier historians have post-dated the invention of writing*. **2.** To affix to a document, esp. to a cheque, a date for payment subsequent to that on which the document is actually signed.

postdiluvial, adj. [1. pṓstdilū́vial; 2. póustdiljū́viəl]. (geol. &c.) After, subsequent to, the diluvial epoch; later than the Flood.

posteen, n. [1. postḗn; 2. pəstín]. Pers. *pōstīn*, 'leathern'. Leather coat worn in Afghanistan.

post-entry, n. **1.** An entry inserted subsequently to the proper posting in a ledger. **2.** A late entry, as of the name of a horse, for a race.

poster, n. & vb. trans. [1. pṓster; 2. póustə]. **post** (II.) & **-er**. **A.** n. **1.** One who posts or placards advertisements, notices &c.: *a bill-poster*. **2.** A bill or placard, usually of a striking or decorative design, posted on walls or hoardings for advertising purposes &c. **B.** vb. **a** To affix a poster to: *to poster the walls*; **b** to advertise by means of posters: *the campaign was well-postered*.

poste restante, n. [1. pṓst réstahnt; 2. póust réstɑ̄nt]. Fr., 'remaining, resting, post'. A department in a post office where letters so addressed are kept till called for.

posterior (I.), adj. [1. postḗriur; 2. pəstíəriə]. Lat., compar. of *posterus*, 'coming after, succeeding'. See **post-**. **1.** Later in time or order; following after, subsequent, succeeding, contrasted with *prior*: *these events happened posterior to the armistice*. **2.** Situated behind, hinder, contrasted with *anterior*: *the posterior parts of the body*.

posterior (II.), n., fr. prec. The hinder parts, buttocks.

posteriority, n. [1. postèrióriti; 2. pəstìərióriti]. See prec. & **-ity**. State of being posterior, later or subsequent; contrasted with *priority*.

posteriorly, adv. [1. postḗriorli; 2. pəstíəriəli]. See prec. & **-ly**. At the back, behind, towards the hinder or posterior parts of the body.

posterity, n. [1. postériti; 2. pəstériti], fr. Fr. *postérité*, fr. Lat. *posteritāt-(em)*. See **posterior** & **-ity**. **1.** Descendants, children; the progeny of a common ancestor: *Abraham and his posterity*. **2.** Those who come after us, future generations: *to write for posterity*.

postern, n. [1. pṓstern; 2. póustən], fr. O. Fr. *posterne*, earlier *posterle*, fr. Low Lat. *posterula*, 'a small door or gate, back door', fr. *posterus*. See **posterior**. A back door or gate, esp. a concealed gate or exit from the walls of a castle or fort; a sally-port.

postero-, pref. Form fr. Lat. *posterus*, 'behind, hinder', used in compounds. See **posterior.** *Postero-lateral*, situated at the back and sides; *postero-ventral*, situated in the region of the back and abdomen.

post-fix, n. **post-** & **fix.** (rare) A suffix, as contrasted with *prefix*.

post-free, adj. & adv. Carried free of charge by the post office; franked; with postage prepaid or included in price.

post-frontal, adj. (anat.) Situated behind the frontal bone.

post-glacial, adj. (geol.) Subsequent to the glacial or pleistocene period.

postgraduate, adj. & n. [1. pòstgrádūit; 2. pòustgrǽdjuit]. **1.** adj. Of studies, research &c. carried on after graduation or the taking of a degree at a university: *a postgraduate course.* **2.** n. A graduate taking a postgraduate course.

post-haste, adv. & n., fr. 'haste, post! haste', addressed to a post or messenger; cp. **post (VII.).** a adv. With all speed, at the utmost speed: *to ride post-haste*; **b** n., great haste or speed: '*In haste, post-haste*' (Shakespeare).

post-horn, n. A long, straight, valveless metal horn, used by the guard of the old mail or post coach; now used on four-in-hands.

post-horse, n. A horse kept at a post or stage for horsing the mail-coaches and post-chaises.

posthumous, adj. [1. póstūmus; 2. pɔ́stjuməs]. Lat. *postumus*, 'last, last born', superl. formed fr. *post*, 'after, later than', see **post-**; also in Lat. *posthumus*, as if fr. *post* & *humus*, 'ground, earth', & w. meaning 'born after the father is in the ground'. **a** (of child) Born after the father's death; **b** (of liter. work) published after the author's death; **c** surviving, arising, after one's death: *posthumous fame, reputation* &c.

posthumously, adv. Prec. & **-ly.** After the death of a father or author: *born, published, posthumously.*

postiche, n. [1. póstēsh; 2. pɔ́stīʃ]. Fr., fr. Ital. *posticcio*, fr. Lat. *posticus*, 'hinder, after'. See **post-.** **1.** (liter.) Something added afterwards; an artificial, superfluous decoration; an imitation, counterfeit, sham decoration. **2.** Hairdresser's euphemism for wig, false front, curls &c.

posticous, adj. [1. póstikus; 2. pɔ́stikəs]. Lat. See prec. (bot.) Situated behind, turned away from, the axis.

postil, n. [1. póstil; 2. pɔ́stil], fr. Fr. *postille*, fr. Med. Lat. *postilla*, etymol. uncertain, prob. for *post illa* (*verba*), 'after those words'. (archaic) A marginal explanatory note or short commentary, esp. on a text of the Bible.

postilion, postillion, n. [1. postíliun; 2. pəstíliən], fr. Fr. *postillon*, fr. Ital. *postiglione*, fr. *posta*; see **post (V.).** One who rides on the near horse of the pair of leaders in a four-horsed carriage, or on the near horse of a pair-horsed carriage, when there is no driver; a post-boy.

post-impressionism, n. See next word & **-ism.** Art, school, of post-impressionist painting and painters, sculpture and sculptors.

post-impressionist, adj. & n. **post-** & **impressionist.** **1.** adj. Of an advanced school of painting and sculpture originating in France, based on expressionism and design rather than representation, and so called as following in time and being more advanced in aim than the impressionist school. **2.** n. A post-impressionist painter or sculptor.

postliminary, adj. [1. pōstlíminari; 2. pòustlíminəri]. Next word & **-ary.** **1.** Connected with, pertaining to, postliminy. **2.** (rare) Subsequent; reverse of *preliminary*.

postliminy, n. [1. pōstlímini; 2. poustlímini]. Lat. *postlīminium*. See **post-** & **limen.** **1.** (Rom. law) The right of a prisoner of war, or an exile on return to his own country to resume the full status of citizenship of which he had been deprived. **2.** (internat. law) The right of persons and things captured in war to revert to their original status and ownership or return to the state to which they belonged prior to capture.

postman, n. [1. pṓs(t)man; 2. póus(t)mən]. Man who collects letters from pillar-boxes &c. for the post, and who also distributes and delivers letters &c. sent out by the post office to the addressees.

postmark, n. & vb. trans. [1. pṓs(t)mark; 2. póus(t)māk]. **1.** n. A mark, impressed on or about the postage-stamp on a letter, parcel &c. by a post office, cancelling the stamp and giving name of place whence it starts, and the date and hour of dispatch, or time of arrival at place to which it is addressed. **2.** vb. To mark, stamp (a letter &c.) with a postmark.

postmaster (I.), n. [1. pṓstmahster; 2. póustmāstə]. Official in charge of a post office. *Postmaster-General*, the Minister in charge of the postal department of a state, including mails, telegraphs, telephones &c.; *Postmaster-Generalship*, office of the Postmaster-General.

postmaster (II.), n. Origin uncertain. One of the scholars on the foundation of Merton College, Oxford; also formerly called *portioner*.

postmastership, n. [1. pṓstmahstership; 2. póustmāstəʃip]. Prec. & **-ship.** **1.** The office of the head of a post office. **2.** A foundation scholarship held by a postmaster at Merton College, Oxford.

postmeridian, adj. [1. pōstmerídian; 2. póustmərídiən]. Lat. *postmeridiānus*. See **post-** & **meridian.** After the sun has passed the meridian; belonging, pertaining, to the afternoon.

post meridiem, adv. [1. pṓst merídiem; 2. póust mərídiəm]. Lat. *post*, 'after', & *meridiem*, acc. of *meridies*, 'mid-day', for *medi-. See prec. From 12 noon to 12 midnight: usually abbr. P.M. or p.m. [pí ém].

post-millennialism, n. [1. pṓst milényalizm; 2. póust milénjəlizəm]. **post-** & **millennialism.** Doctrine that the second coming of Christ will take place after and not at the time of the millennium.

post-millennialist, n. [1. pṓst milényalist; 2. póust milénjəlist]. **post-** & **millennialist.** Believer in post-millennialism.

postmistress, n. [1. pṓstmistres; 2. póustmistris]. A woman in charge of a post office.

post-mortem, adj. & n. Lat., 'after death'. **post-** & acc. sing. of *mors*, 'death', see **mortal.** **1.** adj. [1. pòst mórtem; 2. pòust mɔ́təm]. Made, occurring, done, after death: *post-mortem changes, examination.* **2.** n. [1. pṓst mórtem; 2. póust mɔ́təm]. An examination held upon a dead body to ascertain causes of death; an autopsy.

post-natal, adj. Occurring after birth.

post-natus, n., pl. **post-nati** [1. pṓst nấtus, -tī; 2. póust néitəs, -tai]. L. Lat., 'born after'. **post-** & P.P. of *nascor*, 'to be born', see **natal.** (legal hist.) One born after an event which changes the national status of the inhabitants of a country, as of one born in Scotland after the accession of James I. to the English throne, or of one born in America after the Revolution.

post-nuptial, adj. **post-** & **nuptial.** After marriage: *post-nuptial settlement*, a marriage settlement made after, and therefore not in consideration of, a marriage but for the benefit of the wife only.

post-obit, adj. & n. [1. pòst ṓbit; 2. pòust óubit]. **post-**, 'after', & Lat. *obit-(um)*, *obitus*, 'death', fr. *obīre*, 'to go to meet (death), to die', cp. **obituary.** **1.** adj. (law) To take effect after the death of a specified person; effective only after a death: *a post-obit bond*, a bond to pay money lent, only after the death of a specified person, when a reversion will vest in the person signing the bond. **2.** n. A post-obit bond.

post office, n. **1.** The department of State which deals with the conveyance by post of letters and parcels; also with telegraphs and telephones. **2.** An office or shop which handles postal matter &c. for a district. *Post office order*, a money order issued by a post office; *Post Office Savings Bank*, a savings bank controlled by the department of State in charge of the postal service.

postpone, vb. trans. [1. pōs(t)pṓn; 2. pous(t)póun], fr. Lat. *postpōnere*, 'to put, place, after, postpone', see **post-**, & *pōnere*, 'to place', see **position.** To put off to a later time; defer, delay.

postponement, n. [1. pōs(t)pṓnment; 2. pous(t)póunmənt]. Prec. & **-ment.** Act of postponing, of putting off to a later date; adjournment, delay.

postposition, n. [1. pòstpozíshun; 2. pòustpəzíʃən]. See **post-** & **position.** Word or particle placed after another; contrasted with *preposition*.

postpositional, adj. [1. pòstpozíshunal; 2. pòustpəzíʃənəl]. Prec. & **-al.** Of the nature of a postposition.

postpositive, adj. [1. pōstpózitiv; 2. pòustpɔ́zitiv]. **post-** & **positive.** Postpositional; placed after another word.

postprandial, adj. [1. pòstprándial; 2. pòustprǽndiəl]. **post-** & Lat. *prandium*, 'midday meal'; wh. is for **prām-*, 'former, early', cp. Lith. *pirmas*, 'first', O.E. *forma*, 'first', see **former**, & **edjom*, fr. base **ed-*, 'to eat', see under **edible**, & **-al.** Cp. **prandial.** After dinner: *a postprandial nap*; *postprandial oratory* &c.

postscript, n. [1. pṓs(t)skript; 2. póus(t)skript]. Lat. *postscriptum*, 'written afterwards, later'. See **post-** & **script.** An addition to a letter, written after and below the signature, abbr. P.S. [pí és].

post-town, n. A town in which the head post office of a district is situated, and where letters &c. are distributed over a specific area.

postulant, n. [1. póstūlant; 2. pɔ́stjulənt]. Fr., fr. Lat. *postulant-(em)*, Pres. Part. of *postulāre*. See **postulate.** One who postulates or requests; specif., one seeking admission to holy orders, or to a religious community; a candidate.

postulate (I.), vb. trans. & intrans. [1. póstūlāt; 2. pɔ́stjuleit], fr. Lat. *postulāt-(um)*, P.P. of *postulāre*, 'to demand, request'; for **porstlāre*, cogn. w. Lat. *poscere*, 'to ask', wh. is for **pr̥k̑-sko-*; the full base is **perek̑-*; cp. Lat. *precāri*, 'to pray', see **imprecate** & **pray**; further cogn. w. O.E. *frignan*, 'to ask' &c. **A.** trans. **1.** To demand, request, require (rare except as P.P.): *the claims postulated.* **2.** To assume, take for granted; esp. as a basis for argument. **3.** (eccles.) To nominate, admit, to a benefice, subject to sanction of a higher authority. **B.** intrans. To request, demand; to make a stipulation; to stipulate for: *to postulate for certain conditions.*

postulate (II.), n. [1. póstūlat; 2. pɔ́stjulit]. See prec. **1.** An assumption on which future reasoning may be based; supposition; a necessary, preliminary condition. **2.** (geom.) The assumption of the truth of a proposition without proof; the assumption of the possibility of doing something.

posture (I.), n. [1. póschur; 2. pɔ́stʃə]. Fr., fr. Lat. *positūra*, 'position', fr. *positum*, P.P. of *pōnere*, 'to place'. See **position** & **-ure.** **1.** Position, carriage of the body, assumed or arranged as by an artist for modelling and representing &c. **2.** Attitude of the body or mind, esp. an affected attitude. **3.** State, condition (of affairs).

posture (II.), vb. trans. & intrans., fr. prec. **1.** trans. To put, set, arrange, in a posture or attitude. **2.** intrans. To assume, adopt, a posture; to attitudinize; **a** to assume an affected position, or carriage of the body; **b** to affect a point of view, or a character which is not natural to one.

posy, n. [1. pṓzi; 2. póuzi]. A contraction of **poesy.** **1.** A line of verse, motto in verse or prose, inscribed inside a ring, on a knife &c. as accompanying a gift; *posy-ring*, a ring inscribed with a posy or motto. **2.** A nosegay, bouquet of flowers, probably from the use of the language of flowers to form posies or mottoes.

pot (I.), n. [1. pot; 2. pɔt]. O.E. *pott*, Du. *pot*; O.N. *potr*; in Med. Lat. *pottus*, whence Fr. *pot*; Celt. forms, such as Ir. *potadh* &c. are fr. Engl. **1.** A round vessel of any material, used for various purposes, which are often indicated by a defining word; **a** a drinking vessel: *a pint, quart pot.* Phr. *to put a quart into a pint pot*, to try to do what is impossible, to imagine that a person of weak capacity is able to do what is beyond him; **b** a metal or earthenware vessel for boiling or stewing food: *a cooking pot, stew-pot*; *pots and pans*, cooking utensils collectively; Phrs. *to keep the pot boiling*, to do work of any kind in order to make a living for oneself or others; to keep things going and lively; *the pot calling the kettle black*, of two persons accusing each other when both are equally to blame; **c** a metal vessel in which scrap metal is melted, also *melting-pot*, q.v. Phr. *to go to pot*, (slang) to become useless, to go to ruin, to be destroyed; probably from idea of a melting-pot for waste metal; **d** any of various circular vessels or receptacles, e.g. *jam-pot, glue-pot*; *coffee-, tea-pot*; *flower-pot*; basket-work trap for lobsters, *lobster-pot*; *chimney-pot* &c.; (colloq. and vulg.) chamber utensil. **2. a** A plain, round steel cap for the head; **b** a round hat, also *pot hat*. **3. a** The contents of a pot: *a pot of ale, of soup* &c.; **b** a measure of capacity, esp.used for plums. Phr. *pots of money*, a large sum. **4.** Deep hole in the ground containing water. **5.** (in various colloq. and specific senses) **a** A large sum of money; **b** a person of some consequence or importance: *a big pot*; **c** (vulg.) a bulging protuberant belly; **d** a prize for athletic or other sports, often consisting of a silver cup &c.; (fig.) a prize of any kind; **e** a shot aimed at a short distance; a pot-shot: *to take a pot at a bird.*

pot (II.), vb. trans. & intrans., fr. prec. **A.** trans. **1.** To place in a pot or pots; **a** to preserve food in a sealed receptacle: *to pot fruit*; *potted meat*; *to pot eggs*, preserve them in a jar with water-glass; **b** to plant in a pot: *to pot geraniums.* **2.** (billiards) To put down (a ball) into a pocket by striking it with one's own ball; to pocket. **3.** To shoot (game &c.) for the pot; to hit (a bird or any other object) within easy range; hit with a *pot-shot*. **B.** intrans. To take a pot-shot at.

potability, n. [1. pòtabíliti; 2. pòutəbíliti]. Next word & **-ity.** State, quality, of being drinkable.

potable, adj. & n. [1. pótabl; 2. póutəbl]. Fr., fr. Lat. *pōtābilis*, fr. *pōtāre*, 'to drink'. See **potion** & **-able.** **1.** adj. Drinkable. **2.** n. *Potables*, drinkables, beverages.

potage, n. [1. pótahzh; 2. pɔ́tāž]. Fr. **pot** (I.) & **-age.** Soup, broth.

pot ale, n. **pot** & **ale.** The waste grain residue or 'spent wash' left after distillation of whisky.

potamic, adj. [1. potámik; 2. pətǽmik]. See next word & **-ic.** Of, pertaining to, rivers.

potamo-, pref. Combining form fr. Gk. *potamós*, 'river'; lit. 'the flowing, moving thing'; the base is cogn. w. *pet-, 'to fly, go', q.v. under **pen** (III.), **ptero-**, **petition**, **feather.** Chiefly used in scientific terminology: *potamobius*, a kind of crayfish; *potamogale*, an insect-eating African otter; *potamogeton*, pond-weed &c.

potamology, n. [1. pòtamóloji; 2. pɔ̀təmɔ́lədži]. See prec. & **-logy.** That branch of geography which treats of rivers, their description, formation &c.

potash, n. [1. pótash; 2. pɔ́tæʃ]. **pot** (I.) & **ash** (I.); found earliest as a pl., *potashes*, formed as or borrowed fr. Du. *potasschen*, cp. Germ. *pottasche*. **1.** Crude potassium carbonate obtained from wood or other vegetable ashes by lixiviation and evaporation of the resulting lye, or alkaline solution, at one time in iron pots. **2.** Any of the many chemical compounds of potassium, esp. of those used in commerce as manures &c.: *caustic potash*, potassium hydrate; *sulphate, chlorate, of potash*, potassium chlorate, sulphate &c. **3.** An aerated water containing potassium bicarbonate: *a whisky and potash.*

potassium, n. [1. potásium; 2. pətǽsiəm]. Neo-Lat., fr. Med. Lat. *potassa*, Latinized form of **potash.** (chem.) One of the metallic alkaline elements, symbol K (see *kalium*), found only in various compounds widely spread as in plants, granite rocks, sea-water and in certain places in beds, *potash beds*, as at Stassfurt, Germany; when isolated it is soft, of brilliant silvery colour tinged with white, of great affinity with oxygen, oxidizing rapidly and exploding the hydrogen in water; many of its compounds, as *potassium bromide, chlorate, cyanide, iodide, permanganate, sulphate* &c., are of great value as drugs, fertilizers, and in various industrial processes.

potation, n. [1. pōtáshun; 2. poutéiʃən], fr. Lat. *pōtātiōn-(em)*, 'a draught', fr. *pōtāt-(um)*, P.P. of *pōtāre*, 'to drink'. See **potion** & **-ion.** Drinking; a draught, esp. a copious draught; (often in pl.) *deep potations* &c., drinking bout.

potato, n. pl. *potatoes* [1. potátō; 2. pətéitou], fr. Span. *patata*, fr. native Am. word. *batata*, 'the sweet potato'. **1.** Originally, the sweet potato, the edible, farinaceous, sweet root of a tropical climbing plant, *Ipomaea* or *Convolvulus batatas.* **2. a** The edible tuber of a cultivated plant, originally grown in Central America, later of Southern N. America, *Solanum tuberosum*, imported to Europe in 16th cent.; **b** the plant itself. *Potato blight*, a fungoid disease of potatoes; *potato beetle*, the Colorado beetle, highly destructive of the potato plant; *potato ring*, large ornamental silver ring, supporting a bowl in which potatoes were brought to table in Ireland, or used to keep potatoes together in a dish.

pot-barley, n. The grain of barley with the husk not completely stripped, used in distilling, contrasted with *pearl-barley.*

pot-bellied, adj. [1. pót bèlid; 2. pɔ́t bèlid]. Having a pot-belly.

pot-belly, n. **1.** A protuberant stomach. **2.** A person with a pot-belly.

pot-boiler, n. That which serves to keep the pot boiling, to provide a living. See Phrs. under **pot** (I.); specif., a piece of literary or other work, undertaken chiefly to make money.

pot-boiling, n. The performance of artistic work merely to earn a living.

pot-boy, n. A servant employed in a public-house for cleaning pots &c., drawing beer, and for other menial jobs; a potman.

poteen, potheen, n. [1. potyḗn; 2. pɔtjín], fr. Ir. *poitin*, 'a little pot', as **pot** (I.) w. dimin. suff. Whisky made (in Ireland) illicitly, and clandestinely, to escape the duties, in a small pot-still, by a private person not authorized or licensed to manufacture spirits.

potence, n. [1. pṓtens; 2. póutəns]. See **potency**, & cp. **potent** (II.). (obs.) **a** T-shaped crutch-handle, esp. in heraldry, of this form of cross; **b** a gallows.

potency, n. [1. pṓtensi; 2. póutənsi], fr. Lat. *potentia*, 'power'. **potent** (I.) & **-cy.** Capacity of exercising or displaying power or strength; potentiality; efficiency, power, strength: *the potency of his reason, of a drug* &c.

potent (I.), adj. [1. pṓtent; 2. póutənt], fr. Lat. *potent-(em)*, *potens*, 'powerful, able', Pres. Part. of *posse*, 'to be able', fr. *potis esse*, 'to be powerful'; the base *pot- occurs also in Scrt. *pátiš*, 'lord, master'; Gk. *pósis*, 'husband, lord', see **despot**; cp. also Lat. *hos-pit-*, stem of *hospes*, 'guest', see **host** (II.) & **hospital.** **1. a** Powerful, mighty; exerting power and influence: *a potent prince*; **b** convincing, cogent: *potent reasoning.* **2.** Strong, exerting powerful effects: *potent drug, drinks* &c.

potent (II.), n., fr. prec. (her.) **1.** A form of vair, one of the heraldic furs, where the patches of blue on silver ground take the form of a potence or T-shaped cross. **2.** (attrib.) *Cross-potent*, a potence or T-shaped cross with the staff end pointing down.

potentate, n. [1. pṓtentāt; 2. póutənteit], fr. Lat. *potentātus*, 'power, rule, dominion'. See **potent** (I.) & **-ate.** One who possesses great power; a king, great prince, ruler.

potential (I.), adj. [1. pōténshl; 2. pouténʃl], fr. L. Lat. *potentiālis*, 'having power', fr. Lat. *potentia*, 'power'. See **potent, potency**, & **-al.** **1.** (archaic or obs.) Having power; powerful, potent. **2. a** Latent, undeveloped, but capable of developing and becoming effective; existing in the germ; inherent; (of rights, powers &c.) existing in theory or fact, but not exercised; contrasted with *actual, active, effective*: *a potential genius*; *the seed is the potential flower and fruit*; *potential capacity*; **b** specif. (phys.) capable of energy, or of being exerted, though not acting or exerted at the moment. **3.** (gram.) Expressing possibility: *potential mood*, the subjunctive mood as expressing possibility, obligation, or liberty to act.

potential (II.), n., fr. prec. **1.** That which has a potential or latent power; that which may happen; potentiality: *all the industrial resources of a country may be regarded as potentials of war.* **2.** (gram.) The potential mood. **3. a** (phys.) Potential energy; **b** (elect.) electrical pressure; power to do work; force which, when there is a difference of potential between two poles of an electrical apparatus, causes a current to flow from the higher to the lower; cp. **electromotive.**

potentiality, n. [1. pōtènshiáliti; 2. poutènʃiǽliti]. **potential** (I.) & **-ity.** **1.** Inherent, latent, capacity to exert energy. **2.** (pl.) Hidden, unexerted powers of intellectual or spiritual action. **3.** Possibility, promise, of development; *the potentialities of a political situation.*

potentialization, n. [1. pōtènshalīzáshun; 2. poutènʃəlaizéiʃən]. See next word & **-ation.** Act of potentializing; state of being potentialized.

potentialize, vb. trans. & intrans. [1. pōténshalīz; 2. pouténʃəlaiz]. **potential** (I.) & **-ize.** (phys., of energy) To make or become potential.

potentiate, vb. trans. [1. pōténshiāt; 2. pouténʃieit], fr. Lat. *potentia*, 'power'. See **potency** & **-ate.** To render possible, to give power to.

Potentilla, n. [1. pòtentíla; 2. pòutəntílə]. Neo-Lat., dimin. of **potent.** (bot.) A genus of rosaceous flowering plants and shrubs including the cinquefoil.

potentiometer, n. [1. pōtènshiómeter; 2. poutènʃiɔ́mitə]. **potential** & **-meter.** Instrument for measuring or regulating differences of electrical potential, as voltmeter.

potently, adv. [1. pṓtentli; 2. póutəntli]. **potent** (I.) & **-ly.** In a potent manner; powerfully.

pother, n. [1. pódher, púdher; 2. pɔ́ðə, pʌ́ðə]. Etymol. unknown; not connected w. **bother.** (rare or obs.) A commotion, noise, turmoil; fuss.

pot-herb, n. Any cultivated herb, such as thyme, sage &c., used for the pot, that is, for cooking.

pot-hole, n. **1.** (geol.) A deep hole in a river-bed, in limestone or other rocks, formed by the action of loose stones or gravel agitated by water. **2.** Any hole in the surface of a road, caused by wear &c.

pothook, n. [1. pót-hòok, pótook; 2. pɔ́thuk, pɔ́tuk]. **a** An S-shaped hook for hanging a pot over a fire; **b** curved figure somewhat resembling this, used as a model for children to copy when learning to write; *pothooks and hangers*, the elements of writing.

pothouse, n. [1. pót-hous; 2. pɔ́thaus]. (always in pejorative sense) A public-house, a beer-house, esp. a small and disreputable one. Phr. *the manners of a pothouse*, low manners; *pothouse club*, low club whose real purpose is to facilitate excessive drinking.

pot-hunter, n. **a** A person who enters for competitions in all kinds of sports merely for the chance of winning a prize; **b** a person who is set on winning prizes of all kinds.

potiche, n. [1. pótēsh; 2. pɔ́tīʃ]. Fr., 'a porcelain vase', esp. one of Oriental design with cover. **pot** (I.) & dimin. suff. Chinese vase with a narrowed neck and a lid.

potion, n. [1. póshun; 2. póuʃən], fr. Lat. *pōtiōn-(em)*, 'a draught, drink'; fr. base *pōt-* as in *pōtāre*, 'to drink'; orig. **pōi-*, **pī-* &c.; cp. Gk. *pínō*, 'I drink', *pôma*, 'a drink'; Scrt. *pā́ti*, 'he drinks'; O. Slav. *piti*, 'to drink', *pivo*, 'a drink'; Mod. Russ. *pivo*, 'beer'; Lat. *bibere* for **pibere*, 'to drink', is fr. same base, see **bibulous, imbibe**; **poison** is a variant. A draught or dose of medicine or poison.

pot-luck, n. Whatever may be going at an ordinary family meal: *to take pot-luck with a person*, to accept an invitation to a meal given on the spur of the moment, and take one's chance as to the amount and quality of the food provided; cp. Fr. *la chance du pot.*

potman, n. [1. pótman; 2. pɔ́tmən]. Pot-boy, q.v.

pot-metal, n. **1.** Any alloy of scrap metal of various kinds. **2.** Specif., stained glass, for which the metal is mixed with the colours in the pot before melting.

potpourri, n. [1. pōpōōrē; 2. póupūri]. Fr., lit. 'rotten pot'; cp. **olla podrida. 1.** Dried rose-petals, lavender and other leaves, mixed with spices, kept in a jar as a perfume. **2.** Musical, literary medley; miscellany.

potsherd, n. [1. pótshērd; 2. pɔ́tʃə̄d]. A broken piece of pottery or earthenware.

pot-shot, n. **1.** (rare) A shot aimed at game to provide meat for the pot, that is, for a meal. **2.** An easy shot or range for shooting that requires little skill. **3.** A random, not specially aimed shot, a hit or miss shot: *to take a pot-shot at a rabbit*; fig., a haphazard, chancy attempt.

pot-still, n. A form of still, for the making of whisky, in which the heat comes directly against the container or 'pot', contrasted with *patent-still.*

potstone, n. [1. pótstōn; 2. pɔ́tstoun]. A form of steatite, or soapstone, used by prehistoric workers of stone implements &c. to make into pots.

pottage, n. [1. pótij; 2. pɔ́tidž]. Engl. variant of **potage**. (archaic) Soup, broth; meat stewed or boiled with gravy and vegetables. Phr. (fig.) *a mess of pottage*, some immediate material advantage, for the sake of which higher considerations are lost sight of; from story of Esau and Jacob in Gen. xxv. 29-34.

potter (I.), n. [1. póter; 2. pɔ́tə]. O.E. *potere*. **pot** (II.) & **-er**; cp. O. Fr. *potier*. One who makes earthenware pots and vessels; *potter's clay*, a fine clay free from impurities, such as iron &c.; *potter's disease*, a form of asthma and bronchitis induced by the dust in a pottery-making factory; *potter's wheel*, a circular, flat, horizontal disk, revolving on a spindle, worked by the foot of the potter or by other means, on which the clay is thrown and moulded.

potter (II.), vb. intrans. & trans. Etymol. unknown. **1.** intrans. To dawdle, to lounge, loaf; to set about a business in an irresolute, trifling, desultory manner; also *potter about*. **2.** trans. To waste, fritter; only in such Phr. as *to potter away one's time.*

pottery, n. [1. póteri; 2. pɔ́təri]. Fr. *poterie*. **pot** (I.) & **-ery. 1. a** Earthenware; **b** objects of earthenware collectively; **c** the making of earthenware. **2.** Workshop, factory, where earthenware is made; *the Potteries*, district in Staffordshire, lying round Stoke-on-Trent, the principal seat of earthenware and china manufacture.

potting, n. [1. póting; 2. pɔ́tiŋ]. **1.** The act of making pots. **2.** Process of preserving (food &c.) in a pot. **3.** Act of planting and propagating (plants) in pots.

pottle, n. [1. pótl; 2. pɔ́tl]. M.E. *potel*, fr. O. Fr. *potel*, dimin. of **pot** (I.). **1.** (obs.) An old liquid measure of two quarts; a tankard or pot containing that amount of liquor. **2.** A small chip basket for holding strawberries or other fruit.

potto, n. [1. pótō; 2. pɔ́tou]. W. Afr. native name. (zool.) **1.** A West African lemur, the 'slow-lemur', *Perodicticus potto*, small and reddish-grey in colour with rudimentary tail and index finger. **2.** The kinkajou.

Pott's fracture, n. [1. póts frákchur; 2. pɔ́ts frǽktʃə], fr. Percivall Pott, a famous surgeon (d. 1788). Fracture of lower end of tibia accompanied by dislocation of ankle joint.

potty, adj. [1. póti; 2. pɔ́ti]. Etymol. uncertain; perh. fr. **pot** (I.), in Phr. 'go to pot'. (slang) **1. a** Trivial, petty, insignificant: *a potty little town*; **b** easy, to be accomplished without effort: *a potty sort of game*; *potty set of questions*. **2.** Slightly mad, weak in the upper storey, cracked.

pot-valiance, n. The courage, valiance, valour given by drink; pot-valour.

pot-valiant, adj. Having the sort of courage inspired by strong drink.

pot-valour, n. Pot-valiance.

potwalloper, also **potwaller**, n. [1. pótwòl(op)er; 2. pɔ́twɔ̀l(əp)ə]. For second element cp. M.E. *wallopen*, 'to boil'; etymol. doubtful; cp. O.E. *w(e)allan*, intrans., 'to boil'. (hist.) One who boils his own pot, and is therefore a householder; name, in certain English boroughs, before the Reform Act, 1832, for a holder of a household franchise.

pouch (I.), n. [1. pouch; 2. pautʃ]. M.E. *pouche*, a Norm. Fr. variant of *poche*, 'pouch, pocket', see **poach** (I.) & **poke** (I.). **1.** A small bag or sack; a leather pocket or bag for carrying cartridges &c.; (archaic) a purse. **2.** Any small sac, resembling a pouch in shape; e.g. under the eyes. **3.** (zool.) **a** The sack-like receptacle in which a marsupial animal carries its young; **b** a small, pouch-like cavity in the cheeks of monkeys &c.

pouch (II.), vb. trans. & intrans., fr. prec. **1.** trans. **a** To put into a pouch; to pocket (money &c.); **b** to make into a pouch. **2.** intrans. To protrude as, form, a pouch.

pouched, adj. [1. poucht; 2. pautʃt]. **pouch** (I.) & **-ed. 1.** Provided with a pouch or pouches. **2.** In form of a pouch.

pouf, n. [1. pōōf; 2. pūf]. Fr. Imitative. **1.** A puffed way of dressing the hair; a high pad or roll of hair or puffed head-dress as worn by women at end of the 18th cent. **2.** A small circular, stuffed seat in the form of a thick, solid cushion, or hassock.

poulp(e), n. [1. pōōlp; 2. pūlp]. Fr., form of **polyp.** An octopus.

poult, n. [1. pōlt; 2. poult]. M.E. *pulte*, contr. of *pulet*. See **pullet. a** A young chicken; **b** a young turkey, pheasant &c.

poult-de-soie, n. [1. pōō de swáh; 2. pú də swā́]. Fr., also *pou-de-soie*; etymol. doubtful. Cp. **paduasoy.** A heavy, corded silk.

poulterer, n. [1. pólterer; 2. póultərə]. Earlier *poulter*, w. redundant **-er**; cp. O. Fr. *pouletier*; as **poult & pullet.** A dealer in poultry and game.

poultice, n. & vb. trans. [1. póltis; 2. póultis]. Found earliest as pl. *pultises*, prob. direct fr. Lat. *pult-(em)*, *puls*, 'pap, porridge'; see **pulse** (III.). **1.** n. Hot, moist mass of meal &c. applied to an inflamed or painful part of the body. **2.** vb. To apply a poultice to.

poultry, n. [1. póltri; 2. póultri], fr. O. Fr. *pouleterie*. See **poult & -ry.** Domestic fowls of all sorts, cocks and hens, ducks, geese and turkeys &c., kept for supplying the table with meat or eggs; contrasted with *game.*

pounce (I.), n. [1. pouns; 2. pauns]. Etymol. unknown; doubtfully referred to a supposed Low Lat. **punctiāre*, formed fr. Lat. *punct-(um)*, *pungere*, 'to prick, pierce'. See **puncture. 1.** (falconry) Any one of the three front toes of a hawk's claws, as contrasted with *talon*, the hind toe; the claw or talon of any bird of prey: *an eagle's pounces.* **2.** A sudden swoop down upon, and attempt to seize an object; an eager, sudden movement towards anything.

pounce (II.), vb. intrans., fr. prec. **1. a** To make a pounce, leap upon, or at, suddenly: *a cat ready to pounce*; **b** (fig.) to make an attack suddenly and eagerly with words, of reprimand, correction &c.; **c** to intervene suddenly and incisively in a conversation. **2.** *Pounce upon*, **a** to leap upon suddenly, as a bird or cat upon its prey; **b** (fig.) to assail suddenly with words, to come down upon (a person); **c** to detect, fasten upon, suddenly and swiftly, be quick to seize upon: *to pounce upon a mistake.*

pounce (III.), vb. trans. Etymol. doubtful; prob. a variant of **punch** (IV.), 'to drive a hole through'. **1.** To decorate a metal surface by driving or punching a design or pattern on to from the back or underside. **2.** To decorate leather or cloth by pricking or punching holes in it; to pink.

pounce (IV.), n. & vb. trans., fr. Fr. *ponce*, n., & *poncer*, vb., fr. Lat. *pumic-(em)*, see **pumice. 1.** n. **a** A fine powder, of cuttle-fish bone &c., dusted on unsized paper to prevent ink from spreading; or to prepare vellum for writing on; **b** powdered charcoal dusted through a stencil to form patterns &c. **2.** vb. **a** To smooth paper or other surface with pumice; to prepare vellum with pounce; **b** to imprint a pattern on cloth &c. through a stencil with pounce.

pounce(t)-box, n. [1. póuns(et) boks; 2. páuns(it) bɔ̀ks]. Prob. fr. Fr. *poncette*, 'a box for sprinkling pounce'. See prec. A box with a perforated under-lid for holding perfumes.

pound (I.), n. [1. pound; 2. paund]. O.E. *pūnd*, fr. Gmc. **pund*, fr. Lat. *pondō*, adv., 'by weight', properly an abl. sing. of *pondus*, 'weight' (2nd declens.), variant of *pondus, ponderis*, 'weight'; used adverbially in *lībra pondō*, 'pound by weight; a pound', or as an indeclinable n., w. a numeral as *quindecim* (sc. *lībrae*) *pondō*, 'fifteen pounds'; fr. stem *ponder-* comes *ponderāre*, 'to weigh', see **ponder. 1.** (abbr. *lb.*=Lat. *lībra*) A measure of weight; the standard unit of weight: *pound avoirdupois*=16 ounces, 7000 grains; *pound troy*=12 ounces, 5760 grains. Phr. (*to exact one's*) *pound of flesh*, the exact terms of a bargain, payment to the uttermost farthing, from 'The Merchant of Venice'. **2.** (abbr. £ or *l.*) A money of account, and the standard monetary unit, of twenty shillings, represented by the gold sovereign: *the pound sterling*; a note of the value of a pound of twenty shillings: *£1 Treasury note*; *five-pound* (*bank*) *note* &c.; *pound Scots*, obsolete money of account=20 English pence; *Egyptian* and *Turkish pound*, written £E, £T, =£1:0:6 and 18s. 2d. respectively. Phrs. *in for a penny, in for a pound*, when once started, a course of action must be pursued to the end at all costs; *penny-wise and pound-foolish*, grudging trifling expenditure, attentive to trivial points, thereby involving ultimate loss or failure; *take care of the pence and the pounds will take care of themselves*, converse of prec.; be as careful as possible of the trifling amounts and details and the savings will amount to much in the end, while in larger sums ordinary prudence will be sufficient.

pound (II.), vb. intrans., fr. prec. To test the variation of coins from the standard, mint weight by weighing the number that should weigh a pound.

pound (III.), n. O.E. *pund*, 'enclosure, fold'; etymol. uncertain, possibly connected w. **pond.** See also **pinfold.** A walled enclosure, either roofed or open, maintained by a local authority, in which straying or trespassing cattle were kept till the owner paid a fine, or in which cattle distrained for debt were kept till this was paid.

pound (IV.), vb. trans., fr. prec. Also **impound.** To place straying, trespassing cattle in the local pound.

pound (V.), vb. trans. & intrans. O.E. *pūnian*, M.E. *pounen*, 'to bruise, pound in a mortar'; final *d* a later development as in *sound*; cp. L.G. *pūn*, 'chips, fragments'. **A.** trans. **1.** To beat, break, up into small pieces or powder, as with a hammer: *to pound stones for road-making*; or with a pestle in a mortar: *to pound sugar* &c.; also *pound up*. **2. a** To beat, batter upon, continuously and violently as with heavy guns &c.: *to pound the walls of a fort*; **b** to thump, pummel, with the fist; to strike violently and heavily, in playing, to thump noisily: *to pound the piano*; *pound (out) a tune on the piano*. **B.** intrans. *Pound about, along*, to ride, run, walk along, with heavy, noisy steps: *to pound along a road*.

pound (VI.), n., fr. prec. A thump, heavy blow, noise.

poundage, n. [1. póundij; 2. páundidž]. **pound** (I.) & **-age**. **1.** A percentage of so much in the pound sterling, charged by way of commission &c., on amount obtained by sale of distrained goods. **2.** (hist.) A subsidy of one shilling in the pound levied on all goods imported and exported: *tonnage and poundage*.

pound cake, n. A rich kind of plum cake containing a pound in weight of each of its ingredients.

pounder, n. [1. póunder; 2. páundə]. **pound** (I.) & **-er**. **1.** A thing that weighs specified number of pounds (esp. of fish): *a 20-pounder*. **2.** Gun firing a shot of so many pounds. **3.** Person paying so many pounds' rates, rent &c.: *a ten-pounder (householder)*.

pour (I.), vb. trans. & intrans. [1. pōr; 2. pɔ̄]. M.E. *pouren*; etymol. unknown. **A** trans. **1.** To allow, cause, to flow in a stream, to discharge, empty out (liquids and, more rarely, sand, grain &c.): *to pour water out of a jug, wine from a bottle* &c.; *to pour out tea*. Phr. *to pour cold water on*, to dishearten, discourage, damp, as an enterprise, proposal &c. **2.** To endow with copiously; to confer freely, shower upon: '*pour upon us the grace of Thy Holy Spirit*'; *to pour gifts upon one*. **3. a** To emit, shed (light, heat &c.): *the sun poured forth its rays*; **b** to utter, give vent to, express freely and copiously: *to pour out words, song*; *to pour out one's troubles, woes*. **B.** intrans. **1. a** (of liquids) To flow out freely, impetuously; to issue in a flood, torrent, continuous stream; to fall persistently: *the rain is pouring down*; *the water came pouring down the stairs*; Phrs. *(in the) pouring rain*, coming down in a deluge; *a pouring wet day*; *it is pouring wet, pouring with rain*; **b** (of tears, sweat) to stream, run down, flow copiously: *tears pouring from her eyes, down her cheeks*; *perspiration pouring from him*; **c** (also of smoke, gas &c.) *dense smoke, fumes, vapours &c. pouring into the street*. **2.** (fig., of various things in impetuous, continuous movement) **a** (of a crowd of persons, a flock, troop of animals &c.) To move along steadily one after the other, to move in continuous streams: *crowds poured into the churches*; *the congregation poured out*; *the flock of sheep poured through the gate*; **b** (of uttered words) to issue in torrents, be spoken rapidly, impetuously: *entreaties, imprecations, poured from his lips*.

pour (II.), n., fr. prec. **1.** A heavy fall as of rain &c., usually *downpour*. **2. a** The opening from which molten metal pours into a mould; **b** amount of molten metal poured into a mould.

pourboire, n. [1. pōōrbwàr; 2. púəbwɑ̄]. Fr. *pour*, 'for', *boire*, 'to drink'. A gratuity, tip.

pourparler, n. [1. pōōrpárlā; 2. púəpɑ̄lei]. Fr. (lit.), *pour*, 'for', & *parler*, 'to speak; a discussion'. (usually pl.) A preliminary conversation, discussion &c., at beginning of diplomatic negotiations &c.

pourpoint, n. [1. pōōrpoint; 2. púəpɔint]. O. Fr., fr. *pour* for *par*, fr. Lat. *per*, 'through', & *point*, 'pricked', see **point**. A quilted doublet, worn by men in 14th and 15th cents.

pousse-café, n. [1. pōōs kafā; 2. pús kafe]. Fr., fr. *pousser*, 'to push', & *café*, 'coffee'. A liqueur taken with or after coffee following a meal, a chasse.

pou sto, n. [1. póu stō; 2. páu stóu]. Gk., 'where I may stand'. Something to stand on; point from which to work; basis, foundation, from which to operate.

pout (I.), n. [1. pout; 2. paut]. Etymol. unknown. The name of certain marine fishes, as the *eel-pout*, a kind of sea blenny, and *whiting-pout*; also (U.S.A.) a kind of catfish.

pout (II.), vb. intrans. & trans. & n. Etymol. unknown. **1.** intrans. **a** To thrust out the lips; **b** to do this as instinctive expression of displeasure, or sulkiness; **c** to be sulky, displeased. **2.** trans. Only in *pout (out) the lips*.

pout (III.), n., fr. prec. **a** A protrusion of the lips; **b** this as instinctive expression of displeasure; **c** sulkiness.

pouter, n. [1. póuter; 2. páutə]. **pout** (II.) & **-er**. One who pouts; specif., a *pouter-pigeon*, a breed of fancy pigeons, which dilates the crop in a marked degree.

poutingly, adv. [1. póutingli; 2. páutiŋli]. As prec. & **-ing** & **-ly**. In a pouting, sulky manner.

poverty, n. [1. póverti; 2. pɔ́vəti]. M.E. *poverte*, fr. O. Fr. *povorté, povreté*, Mod. Fr. *pauvreté*; fr. Lat. *paupertāt-(em)*, fr. *pauper*, 'poor'. See **pauper** & **-ty**. **1.** State, fact, of being poor; want, indigence; lack of means. **2.** Absence, deficiency, of qualities necessary or desirable: *poverty of ideas* &c.; *poverty of the land*, unproductiveness, barrenness.

poverty-stricken, adj. **a** Reduced to poverty; impoverished, poor: *a poverty-stricken people*; **b** conveying the impression of poverty; poor, mean (of a country &c.); shabby (of a house, personal appearance &c.).

powan, n. [1. póuan; 2. páuən], fr. Celt. The gwyniad.

powder (I.), n. [1. póuder; 2. páudə]. M.E., fr. Fr. *poudre*, earlier Fr. *poldre, puldre*, earlier *polre*, fr. Lat. *pulver-(em)*, 'dust; powder', see **pulverize** & cp. **pollen**. **1.** Fine, loose, uncompacted particles, derived from the breaking down of any dry, solid substance; dust. **2.** Specif., gunpowder; loosely, any dry explosive: *a powder factory*. Phrs. *not worth powder and shot*, not worth the trouble or cost of getting, of fighting about; *to smell powder*, to have experience of war. **3.** A drug, medicine, in the form of powder: *Gregory's powder*. **4. a** White, finely powdered flour or starch used for dressing the hair or wig in the 18th cent.: *to wear powder*; **b** a cosmetic powder, sometimes scented or tinted, applied to the face, arms &c.: *a face-powder*.

powder (II.), vb. trans. & intrans., fr. prec. **1.** trans. To sprinkle, cover, dust, with powder; specif. (hist.) to sprinkle meat with salt, spices, for preservation: *powdered beef*. **2.** intrans. To wear powder on the hair; to use powder on the face &c.

powder blue, n. Powdered smalt used as a pigment; a deep-blue colour obtained from this.

powder-closet, n. A small closet or room in 18th-cent. houses, usually opening out of a bed- or dressing-room, where the hair and wig were powdered.

powder-flask, -horn, n. A flask, cow's horn, used for carrying gunpowder, for the old muzzle-loading pistols and muskets.

powderiness, n. [1. póuderines; 2. páudərinis]. See **powdery** & **-ness**. State, quality, of being powdery.

powder-magazine, n. The magazine on board a ship of war in which the gunpowder or other explosive is stored.

powder-mill, n. Gunpowder factory.

powder-monkey, n. Boy on board an old ship of war who carried the gunpowder to the gunners.

powder-puff, n. A small puff used for apply ing powder to the face &c.

powdery, adj. [1. póuderi; 2. páudəri]. **powder** (I.) & **-y**. **1.** Resembling powder, in consistency and texture: *powdery snow*. **2.** Covered with powder or with what resembles powder: *powdery bloom on a leaf* &c. **3.** Easily friable or reducible to powder: *a powdery stone, rock* &c.

power, n. [1. póur; 2. páuə]. M.E. *poër, pouer*, fr. O. Fr. *poër*, fr. earlier *poter*, infin. as n.; new formation fr. Lat. *pot-*, 'to be able' &c., as in **potent**. **1.** (in living things) Capacity to do something; **a** (in human beings) capacity, ability, capability of mental or bodily action: *power of movement*; *power of thought*; *power of resistance*; Phrs. *to lose one's powers*; *his powers are failing* &c., faculties, senses, and intelligence; *beyond one's powers*, too much for one's abilities, for one's strength; more than one can perform; *to put it out of one's power to do* &c., make it impossible; *not in, out of, one's power (to help* &c.), beyond one's capacity, ability &c.; **b** (in other living things) ability, freedom, of movement. **2.** (in inanimate things) Capacity to exert physical influence, to carry out certain processes: *the power of nature*; *the power of heat, light* &c. **3. a** Conscious exertion of power, whether physical or mental; strength, vigour, competence, effectiveness: *to solve a difficulty by sheer power of intellect*; *to hold on by power of muscle*; Phr. *more power to your elbow*, may you have success in what you undertake; **b** effect of natural processes; energy, force: *the pool was dried up by the power of the sun's rays*; *the power of the waves battered down the wall*. **4.** (colloq.) **a** A large number: *a power of big-wigs*; **b** a large amount: *it's done me a power of good*; *a power of help* &c. **5.** Capacity to control, and to impose one's will; authority; government, dominion, rule: *the power of the law*; *power of the Crown, of the Cabinet* &c.; *to have power over*, to control, direct. Phrs. *to have* (a person &c.) *in one's power*, to be able to work one's will on him, have him at one's mercy; *to be in power*, to be in office, of a ministry, political party &c.; *to be in the power of*, under the control of, at another's mercy; *the power of the keys*, the authority to grant or withhold absolution, held, by the Church, to have been given to St. Peter and to his successors, the Christian priests and bishops. **6.** (often in pl.) *The powers*: **a** a body of persons, esp. a state, invested with authority, control, or influence: *the great world powers*; *a concert of powers*; Phr. *the powers that be*, persons in authority; **b** spiritual or other influences personified; **a** deity, deities, demons &c.: *the powers above*; *powers of darkness or evil*; **c** one of the nine grades or orders of angels: *dominations, principalities and powers* &c. **7.** Specific usages: **a** (law) an authority granted by one person, *appointer* or *donor*, to another to act on his behalf: *a power of appointment*; *power of attorney*; **b** (math.) the sum or product obtained by the multiplication of a number or quantity into itself: *a cube is the third power, a square is the second power* &c.; **c** (mechan.) mechanical energy or work or the source of it, as *water power, electric power* &c.; the rate at which mechanical energy or work is exerted or performed: *watt-power, horse-power* &c.; *power transmission*, the transference of energy produced by any prime mover, hydraulic, electrical &c., to a machine made to use it, as transmission of electric power from the generator to the motor by cables; **d** (opt.) the magnifying capacity of a lens of a telescope, microscope &c.

powered, adj. [1. póuerd; 2. páuəd]. Prec. & **-ed**. Equipped with the means of generating mechanical power, having the capacity of generating so much mechanical power: *a high-powered engine*.

powerful, adj. [1. póurfool; 2. páuəful]. **power** & **-ful**. Possessing great power; **a** capable of exercising great mental or bodily strength: *a powerful hand, grip, mind* &c.; **b** capable of performing well the appropriate functions: *powerful sight*; *a powerful battery*; c capable of imposing one's will; authoritative, exercising rule &c.: *a powerful king, government* &c.; d capable of affecting the mind strongly; cogent: *a powerful argument*; capable of producing considerable effects on the body: *a powerful drug*; e generating, producing, great physical energy: *a powerful light, heat, ray* &c.

powerfully, adv. Prec. & **-ly**. With great power, force, or energy; in a powerful manner: *the arguments affected him powerfully.*

power-gas, n. A gas made to drive an engine for the production of power.

power-house, -station, n. The building in which mechanical power, esp. electrical power, is generated.

power-lathe, -loom, n. A lathe, loom &c. worked by mechanical power or energy.

powerless, adj. [1. póurles; 2. páuəlis]. **power & -less**. 1. Lacking strength; impotent, feeble, weak: *the reins of government slipped from his powerless grasp.* 2. a Incapable, helpless; b lacking ability of a specific kind: *powerless to help.*

powerlessly, adv. Prec. & **-ly**. In a powerless manner.

pow-wow, n. & vb. intrans. [1. pòu wóu; 2. pàu wáu]. N. Am. Indian, 'medicine-man, sorcerer'. 1. n. a A conference with Indians; b (colloq.) any friendly conference or discussion. 2. vb. To discuss, confer about; to have a friendly conversation, to chat.

pox, n. [1. poks; 2. pɔks]. Pl. of **pock**. a Any of various diseases characterized by an eruption of pocks or small pustules on the skin, as *chicken-pox, small-pox*; b specif. (colloq. and vulg.; also *the pox*) syphilis, formerly the *great* or *French pox*; c (expletive, obs.) *a pox on you!*, plague take you!

pozzolana, pozzuolana, n. [1. pòts(u)oláhna; 2. pɔ̀ts(u)əlánə]. Ital., adj., fr. Pozzuoli, near Naples. A volcanic tufa or rock ground to powder and used for making hydraulic cement.

praam, n. See **pram (II.)**.

practicability, n. [1. pràktikabíliti; 2. prӕktikəbíliti]. **practicable & -ity**. Quality of being practicable; feasibility.

practicable, adj. [1. práktikabl; 2. prǽktikəbl]. See **practical & -able**. 1. Able to be done, feasible, capable of being put into practice: *a practicable scheme, plan* &c. 2. Capable of being used: *a practicable road*; *a practicable window, door.*

practicableness, n. Prec. & **-ness**. State, quality, of being practicable; practicability.

practicably, adv. See prec. & **-ly**. In a practicable manner.

practical, adj. [1. práktikl; 2. prǽktikl], fr. obs. *practic* & **-al**; fr. obs. Fr. *practique*, later *pratique*, fr. Low Lat. *practicus*, fr. Gk. *praktikós*, 'fit for action, business-like', cp. *praktós*, 'done, accomplished', vbl. adjs. fr. base **prak-* of *prássein, práttein*, 'to do, effect, perform', fr. same base as Gk. *pérā*, 'beyond', q.v. under **far**. 1. Concerned with, of the nature of, action and practice; contrasted with *theoretical*: *to adopt practical measures*; *a very practical difficulty.* Phr. *practical joke*, grotesque hoax or prank in the form of action. 2. a Trained, experienced, in the actual practice of some specific art, craft, trade &c.: *a practical gardener, farmer, engineer*; b good at practical affairs and applications, able to carry things out; efficient, capable: *not a very practical young man*; *a good, practical housewife*; *a practical mind*, one confined to matters of practical and concrete action, not given to abstract speculation. 3. a (of methods, plans &c.) Capable of being put into effect, workable: *a practical scheme*; b (of objects) designed for use; capable of being used; adapted for required purpose: *a really practical trouser-press.* 4. Virtual; being so in actual fact: *the practical ruler of the country.*

practically, adv. Prec. & **-ly** 1 In a practical manner; from a practical point of view; not theoretically or speculatively: *to look at a question practically*; *to know a language practically.* 2. In practice, in effect, virtually, to all intents and purposes: *the Prime Minister of England is practically the ruler of the country*; *practically speaking, there is no more to be done.*

practicalness, n. See prec. & **-ness**. Quality, state, of being practical.

practice, n. [1. práktis; 2. prǽktis]. Earlier *practize, practyze*, spelling variant of vb. **practise**; the earlier M.E. form was *practike*, fr. Fr. *practique*, obs. form of *pratique*; see **practical**. 1. a Action repeatedly or habitually performed; habit, custom: *a matter of common, daily, practice*; *to make a practice of daily exercise*; *the practice of going to bed late*; *a bad, good, practice*; b the carrying out or performance of what has been laid down in theory or been acquired by mere learning or knowledge: *a plausible idea, but will it work in practice?*; *to put into practice*; c specif., customary action performed in carrying out religious or other ceremony; ceremonial observance, habitual ritual: *Christian practices*; *Popish practices*; d systematic, repeated exercise in some art, craft, game &c., carried out with a view to acquiring proficiency: *two hours' practice at the piano*; *daily practice at the (cricket) nets*; *(to be) in, out of, practice*, to be in good or bad training for the exercise of some skill in art, games &c. Phr. *practice makes perfect*, a complete mastery of and skill in any art &c. can only be obtained by repeated performance; e the carrying on, exercise, of a profession; the scope, field, of such profession; the clients, patients &c. collectively dealt with by the person carrying on the profession: *a barrister's, doctor's, solicitor's practice*; *to give up, sell, a practice*; *in full practice*; *a large and increasing practice at the criminal bar*; f (usually in pl.) underhand dealing, artifice, stratagem; trickery: *artful practices.* 2. Specif. (arith.) a concise way of reckoning the prices and quantities of a number of commodities when each varies in price or quantity. 3. a (law) The rules, orders of procedure generally, of a court of law: *the practice of the High Court*; b customary routine, method habitually followed: *we cannot depart from our regular practice in such cases.*

practician, n. [1. praktíshan; 2. prӕktíʃən], fr. O. Fr. *practicien*; see **practical & -ian**. One skilled or experienced by practice; a practitioner.

practise, vb. trans. & intrans. [1. práktis; 2. prǽktis]. M.E. *practisen*, fr. O. Fr. *practiser, pratiser*, altered form of *pratiquer*, fr. Low & Med. Lat. *practicāre*, fr. *practicus*. See **practical**. A. trans. 1. a To do, perform, habitually or as a custom: *to practise early rising*; b to carry out in action what has been laid down in theory or acquired by learning; to put into practice: *to practise philosophy*; *to practise what one preaches.* 2. To follow, work at, a profession, art &c.: *to practise medicine, painting* &c. 3. To exercise oneself in an art, game &c. by constant practice with a view to gaining proficiency: *to practise lawn tennis, music, the violin, shooting* &c. 4. To train, exercise, (another) in some habit, action, skill &c.; to accustom: *to practise children in habits of obedience.* B. intrans. 1. (archaic) a To act habitually in a certain way, make a custom of particular mode of conduct: *if only you practise, you can form any habits*; b to set oneself to, make a practice of: *to practise to deceive.* 2. To work at, pursue, some profession: *to practise at the bar.* 3. To exercise oneself at some art, game &c.: *to practise at the piano.* 4. *Practise upon*, to try, scheme to influence, or impose upon, take advantage of: *to practise on another's weaknesses, feelings* &c.

practised, adj. [1. práktist; 2. prǽktist], fr. P.P. of prec. Experienced, skilled, expert: *a practised orator, liar* &c.

practitioner, n. [1. praktíshuner; 2. prӕktíʃənə]. Irregular formation fr. **practician.** One who practises or carries on a profession, esp. the medical profession: *general practitioner*, one who has a general, medical practice, and does not specialize in particular diseases &c.

prae-, pref. Lat., 'before', usually Englished as **pre-**.

praecipe, n. [1. présipi; 2. prísipi]. Lat., 'order', imperat. of *praecipere*, 'to give orders to, to make rules for'. See **precept.** (law) Any of various writs ordering a person to appear and show cause, or to do something; a precept.

praecocial, adj. [1. prēkóshal; 2. prīkóuʃəl]. See **precocious & -al**. (zool.) Of the young of birds, such as chickens, ducklings &c., which hatch out with downy feathers and are able to run about and feed themselves at once.

praedial, adj. See **predial.**

praemunire, n. [1. prèmūníre; 2. prīmjūnáiəri]. Med. Lat. for Lat. *praemonēre*, 'to warn', *prae*, 'before', see **pre-**, & *monēre*, 'to advise, warn', see **monition**; the words *praemunire facias*, 'see that you warn', being the first words of the writ. A special form of writ ordering the sheriff to summon a person to appear to answer a charge for a particular kind of offence, esp. under a *Statute of Praemunire*, of the reign of Richard II., that of asserting the authority and jurisdiction of the Pope in England; also this offence and the penalty incurred for it.

praenomen, n. [1. prènómen; 2. prīnóumən]. Lat., 'first name'. See **pre- & nominal**, cp. **cognomen.** (Rom. antiq.) The first, personal, name, as *Caius*, of *Caius Julius Caesar*, distinguishing individuals of the same family.

praepostor, n. [1. prèpóster; 2. prīpɔ́stə], fr. Med. Lat. *praepositor*, 'one who places another in authority', fr. *praeposit-(um), praepōnere*, 'to place, set, before or over'. See **preposition.** A monitor or prefect at a public school.

praetor, n. [1. prḗtōr; 2. prítɔ̄]. Lat., for **praeitor*, 'one who goes before'. See **pre- & itinerate.** (Rom. antiq. hist.) A Roman elected magistrate, originally a consul at the head of an army, later one ranking next to a consul, having civil, military, and esp. judicial functions, and governing provinces of the second rank.

praetorian, adj. & n. [1. prētórian; 2. prītɔ́riən]. Prec. & **-an**. 1. adj. Of, pertaining to, a praetor: *praetorian cohort*, the picked troops acting as the escort of a military praetor; *praetorian gate*, the gate of a Roman military camp, facing towards the enemy and opposite the praetor's headquarters or *praetorium*; *praetorian guard*, the bodyguard of the Roman Emperors. 2. n. a One who has held the office of praetor; b a soldier of the praetorian cohort or guard.

pragmatic, adj. [1. pragmátik; 2. prӕgmǽtik], fr. Fr. *pragmatique*, fr. Lat. *pragmaticus*, fr. Gk. *pragmatikós*, 'skilled in business or practical affairs, business-like', fr. *prág-mat-(os), prāgma*, 'thing done, business, affair of state', fr. stem **prak-* of *prássein, práttein*, 'to do, perform'. Cp. **practical.** 1. Connected with, relating to, affairs of state; only hist.: *Pragmatic Sanction*, in the later Roman Empire, an imperial rescript or decision relating to matters of more than private or personal concern; in European countries following Roman law, an ordinance of a sovereign defining powers and esp. regulating the succession to the throne, as, specif., that of the Emperor Charles VI., 1724, settling the Austrian succession, which led to the war of that name. 2. Pragmatical. 3. Relating to pragmatism, as concerned with the practical facts of life: *pragmatic lines of thought* &c.

pragmatical, adj. [1. pragmátikl; 2. prӕgmǽtikl]. Prec. & **-al**. a Officious, meddlesome, interfering; arbitrary, dogmatic: *pragmatical piety*; *a pragmatical kind of person*; b pragmatic.

pragmatically, adv. Prec. & **-ly.** In a pragmatical manner; officiously; dogmatically.

pragmatism, n. [1. prágmatizm; 2. prǽgmətizəm], fr. Gk. *prágmat-(os)*, stem of *prâgma*, 'thing done, act, business', & **-ism.** See **pragmatic.** (philos.) A system which takes as the criterion of the truth of a conception, assertion &c. the practical value of this as tested by the effect on human interests and activities, and does not base its metaphysics, logic, psychology, or ethics, on speculation or abstract thought.

pragmatist, n. [1. prágmatist; 2. prǽgmətist]. See prec. & **-ist.** One who adheres to the philosophic doctrine of pragmatism.

pragmatize, vb. trans. [1. prágmatīz; 2. prǽgmətaiz]. See prec. & **-ize.** To materialize, rationalize, to treat (a metaphor, myth &c.) as real.

Prairial, n. [1. prắriahl; 2. préəriāl], fr. Fr. *prairie*, 'meadow-land', fr. Med. Lat. *prātāria*, fr. Lat. *prātum*, 'meadow'. See next word. Ninth month of the French Revolutionary calendar, from May 20th to June 18th.

prairie, n. [1. prắri; 2. préəri]. Fr., 'meadow-land', fr. L., Med., Lat. *prātāria*, fr. Lat. *prātum*, 'meadow'; see **pravity.** A wide tract or area of level, treeless grass-land, first used of the grassy plains of central N. America; *prairie-schooner*, a long covered waggon used by the early immigrants to the Far West of N. America. Phr. *prairie value*, bare, natural value of land, apart from the labour and money expended on its cultivation and improvement.

prairie-chicken, -hen, n. The pinnated grouse.

prairie-dog, n. A squirrel-like, burrowing rodent, now more properly termed *prairie-marmot*.

prairie-wolf, n. The coyote.

praisable, adj. [1. prắzabl; 2. préizəbl]. See next word & **-able.** Capable of being praised; praiseworthy.

praise (I.), vb. trans. [1. prāz; 2. preiz]. M.E. *preisen*, fr. O. Fr. *preisier*, fr. L. Lat. *pretiāre*, 'to put a price on, to value', fr. *pretium*, 'price'. See **price & prize. 1.** To express approval, approbation of, give commendation to; to commend highly, eulogize, extol. **2.** To glorify and magnify (God) by worship or by recital, esp. in song, of His greatness and goodness; to laud; contrasted with *pray*.

praise (II.), n., fr. prec. **1. a** Act of praising; **b** expression of approval &c.; high commendation, eulogy. **2. a** Act of glorifying God; **b** worship, veneration, accorded to God.

praiseful, adj. [1. prắzfool; 2. préizful]. Prec. & **-ful.** Full of praise or commendation; giving praise.

praiseworthily, adv. [1. prắzwĕrdhili; 2. préizwāðili]. See **praiseworthy & -ly.** In a praiseworthy manner; so as to deserve praise, laudably.

praiseworthiness, n. [1. prắzwĕrdhines; 2. préizwāðinis]. See next word & **-ness.** Quality of being praiseworthy.

praiseworthy, adj. [1. prắzwĕrdhi; 2. préizwāði]. **praise (II.) & -worthy.** Worthy, deserving, of praise; commendable, laudable; often used with a note of condescension: *most praiseworthy efforts*; *very praiseworthy people.*

Prakrit, n. [1. práhkrit; 2. prákrit]. Scrt. *prakrt*, 'natural, original, unrefined, vulgar'. Cp. **Sanscrit.** Any of the Aryan vernacular dialects of India, including some recorded c. 250 B.C., and modern vernacular, as distinct from Sanskrit, the classical literary language.

praline, n. [1. prálēn; 2. prǽlin]. Fr. A sweetmeat of almonds or other nuts covered with sugar, and baked crisp and brown.

pram (I.), n. [1. pram; 2. præm]. Colloq. abbr. of **perambulator.**

pram (II.), praam, n. [1. prahm; 2. prām]. Du. *praam*; of Slav. origin, cp. Pol. *pram*, 'boat'. A flat-bottomed barge or lighter used in the Baltic for discharging and loading cargo.

prance (I.), vb. intrans. [1. prahns; 2. prāns]. M.E. *praunce(n)*; etymol. doubtful. **1. a** (of a horse) To spring, move forward from the hind legs, with the forefeet raised; also *prance along*; **b** (of a person) generally *prance about*, to move about energetically and excitedly, esp. with considerable action, or with a strutting, swaggering, pompous gait and bearing; to walk, carry oneself, in a pompous way: *prancing proconsuls.*

prance (II.), n., fr. prec. A prancing movement (of a horse &c.).

prandial, adj. [1. prándial; 2. prǽndiəl], fr. Lat. *prandium*, 'the midday meal, luncheon'. See **postprandial.** (facet.) Of or belonging to dinner.

prank (I.), n. [1. prangk; 2. præŋk]. Etymol. doubtful; possibly a derived meaning of **prank (II.).** A mischievous trick, an irresponsible action; a mad, merry frolic; practical joke: *they are up to their old pranks*; *to play pranks* (used by Polonius of Hamlet's actions and by Goneril of Lear's).

prank (II.), vb. trans. & intrans. M.E. *pranken*; cp. Du. *pronken*, Germ. *prunken*, 'to make a show, show off'. Cp. **prink. 1.** trans. To adorn, dress, deck: *meadows pranked with flowers*; *to prank oneself out with fine clothes.* **2.** intrans. To dress up for show, deck oneself: *pranked with the best.*

prankish, adj. [1. prángkish; 2. prǽŋkiʃ]. **prank (I.) & -ish.** Full of pranks; mischievous, freakish.

prase, n. [1. prāz; 2. preiz], fr. Lat. *prasius*, 'a green precious stone', fr. Gk. *prásios*, 'leek-green', fr. *práson*, 'a leek', a variant of **párson*; cogn. w. Lat. *porrum*, 'leek'; further etymol. unknown. (mineral.) A translucent, green variety of quartz; cp. also *chrysoprase.*

prate, vb. intrans. & trans. & n. [1. prāt; 2. preit]. M.E. *prāten*, cp. L.G. *praten*, 'to chatter'; O.N. *prata*, 'to talk'. Cp. **prattle. 1.** vb. **a** intrans. To chatter, talk idly or volubly; to prattle; **b** trans., to speak, tell, blab; *to prate the news all over the town.* **2.** n. Idle talk, chatter.

praties, n. [1. prắtiz; 2. préitiz]. Anglo-Irish. Potatoes.

pratincole, n. [1. prátingkōl; 2. prǽtiŋkoul]. Neo-Lat. *prātincola*, fr. Lat. *prātum*, 'meadow' (see **prairie**), & *incola*, 'inhabitant' (see **colony**). Genus of small slender birds allied to the sand-pipers, the various species of which are said to run like plovers and fly like swallows; found in S. Europe, W. Asia, and N. Africa, and occasionally visiting Britain; also called 'swallow plover'.

pratique, n. [1. prátēk; 2. prǽtīk]. Fr., 'practice, communication, dealings with'. See **practice.** Leave or permission granted to a vessel to land passengers, goods, and have general communication with the shore on showing a clean bill of health, or after remaining the due period in quarantine.

prattle, vb. intrans. & n. [1. prátl; 2. prǽtl]. Freq. of **prate. 1.** vb. **a** To chatter, gossip, babble; **b** to talk like a baby or child. **2.** n. Idle, childish chatter or talk.

prattler, n. [1. prátler; 2. prǽtlə]. Prec. & **-er. a** One who prattles; a babbler, continuous talker, persistent gossip; **b** (in playful sense, of a child) *a pretty prattler.*

pravity, n. [1. práviti; 2. prǽviti], fr. Lat. *prāvitāt-(em), prāvitas*, 'crookedness, perverseness, depravity', fr. *prāvus*, 'crooked, distorted, morally perverse, vicious'; Walde derives fr. a base **pra-*, 'to curve, to bend', wh. he finds also in Lat. *prātum*, 'meadow', see **prairie**, & compares w. O. Ir. *raith*, now called a *rath*, a space, often a mound, surrounded by a wall of earth, see **rath (I.).** (rare) Badness, corruption, depravity.

prawn, n. & vb. intrans. [1. prawn; 2. prōn]. M.E. *prayne, prane*; etymol. unknown; no cogn. word in other languages. **1.** n. An edible marine crustacean, resembling, but much larger than, a shrimp; of many varieties; the common prawn is *Leander serratus*; *Dublin prawn*, a small, brightly coloured species of lobster, also called the Norway lobster. **2.** vb. To catch, fish for, prawns.

praxis, n. [1. práksis; 2. prǽksis]. Gk. *prâxis*, fr. *prássein*, 'to do, perform'. See base in **practical. 1. a** The exercise, practice, of an art or science; contrasted with *theory*; **b** the usual practice or custom. **2.** (gram.) A set of examples or exercises.

pray, vb. trans. & intrans. [1. prā; 2. prei]. M.E. *preien, preyen*, fr. O. Fr. *preier*, later *prier*, fr. *precāre*, L. Lat. form of *precāri*, 'to ask, beg, pray', cp. *prec-(em)*, *prex*, 'prayer', cogn. w. Goth. *fraih-nan*, O.E. *friġ-nan*, Germ. *fragen*, 'to ask'. Cp. **postulate. A.** trans. **1.** (rare or obs.) To entreat, beg of, make supplication to: *we pray you take mercy on us.* **2.** To beg for, ask for, earnestly: *to pray God's forgiveness and mercy*; *we pray your attention.* Phr. (archaic) *to pray in aid*, to ask, call for the aid or help of. **B.** intrans. The usual construction is *to pray to* (God &c.) *for* (something) or *that* (such and such may happen). **1.** To utter prayers, engage in prayer to God: *we go to church to pray*; *watch and pray.* **2.** To utter prayers in order to obtain, to beg for earnestly; **a** to God: *to pray for strength and guidance*; **b** to another human being, to address earnest entreaties to, make supplication: *to pray for pardon*; *to pray that one may not be noticed.* **3.** Elliptically, as form of request: *pray* (for *I pray you*) *help yourself to anything you want*; *tell me the reason, pray!*

prayer (I.), n. [1. prār; 2. prɛə]. M.E. *preiere, preyere*, fr. O. Fr. *preiere*, later *prière*, fr. L. & Med. Lat. *precāria*, 'prayer', fr. Lat. *precārius*, 'obtained by prayer'. See prec. & **precarious. 1.** The act of praying to God: '*More things are wrought by prayer Than this world dreams of*' (Tennyson, 'Passing of Arthur'). **2.** Words uttered, or aspiration felt, and addressed to God as an act of worship, or as a petition; **a** in private devotions: *to say one's prayers*; **b** prescribed form of words used in public worship: *the Lord's Prayer*; *morning, evening, prayer*, the service of matins and evensong. **3.** A formal petition or request made to a superior authority: *a humble petition and prayer.* **4.** A fervent wish or request, expressed or unexpressed: *the unspoken prayer.*

prayer (II.), n. [1. prắer; 2. préiə], fr. **pray & -er.** One who prays.

Prayer Book, n. **a** Book containing prayers for public or private use; specif. **b** the Book of Common Prayer, containing the liturgy of the English Church.

prayerful, adj. [1. prārfool; 2. prɛ́əful]. **prayer (I.) & -ful.** Habitually and frequently using prayer; devotional, devout.

prayerfully, adv. Prec. & **-ly.** With much, frequent, prayer.

prayerfulness, n. See prec. & **-ness.** Practice of regular and frequent prayer; regular and habitual use of prayers.

prayerless, adj. [1. prārles; 2. prɛ́əlis]. **prayer (I.) & -less.** Without prayer; not using prayer.

prayer-meeting, n. A public meeting in which the members join in prayer or offer up prayers, esp. *extempore* prayers.

prayer-rug, n. A small kneeling mat used by Moslems at prayer.

prayer-wheel, n. A revolving metal drum or case containing written prayers used by Tibetan Buddhists.

praying, n. & adj. [1. prắing; 2. préi-iŋ]. **a** n. The act of uttering prayers; (also attrib.) *praying shawl*, a shawl or scarf with tassels worn over the head or shoulders by Jews when at prayer; the tallith; **b** adj., *praying insect*, the mantis.

pre-, pref., fr. later Lat. form of *prae*, adv. & prep., 'before, forwards, in front (of)'; earlier *prai*; connected w. Gk. *pará, parai*, 'beside, alongside of, proceeding from', see **para-**; Goth. *faur, faura*, 'before', O.E. *for, foran, fore*, see **for & fore. A.** *Prae-* has the following main senses in Lat. in composition:

(1) 'before, in advance of': *praemittere*, 'to send on in advance'; (2) before, previously: *praedīcere*, 'to tell beforehand, foretell'; (3) 'at the head of': *praepōnere*, 'to put at the head of, give command of'; (4) publicly, in front of everyone: *praedicātor*, 'one who makes a thing publicly known, proclaimer, crier'; (5) w. adj., 'very high, in a superior degree, before, beyond others': *praedūrus*, 'very hard'. **B.** In Engl. words borrowed direct fr. Lat., or through Fr., the pref. retains the force it had in the Lat. word, though later differentiations & amplifications of meaning may naturally occur in Engl. usage. **C.** The pref. is a living one, & is freely used to form compounds such as *pre-war* (*conditions* &c.), 'before the war'; *pre-Dreadnought*, 'ship built prior to the Dreadnought type', & so on. Such compounds as these are practically endless in number, & it is unnecessary to record them, as every educated speaker forms them constantly for himself as required.

preaccustom, vb. trans. [1. prèakústum; 2. prìəkástəm]. To accustom, habituate, beforehand.

preach, vb. trans. & intrans. [1. prēch; 2. prītʃ]. M.E. *prechen*, fr. O. Fr. *prechier*, Mod. Fr. *prêcher*, fr. Lat. *praedicāre*, 'to proclaim, make known to the public, announce'; in Eccles. Lat., 'to preach; to announce', formed fr. *dīcere*, 'to speak, say'. See **pre-** & **diction**. **A.** trans. **1.** To announce, expound, proclaim; to spread the message or tidings of: *to preach the Gospel*; *to preach Christ crucified* &c. **2.** To pronounce, deliver (a sermon or discourse), on a religious subject, usually from a text of Scripture: *to preach a good, long, poor, sermon.* **3.** To advocate strongly, support persistently, in speaking or writing; to urge a course of action on others: *to preach economy, patience, international peace* &c.; Phr. *to practise what one preaches*, make one's conduct conform to one's teaching &c. **B.** intrans. **1. a** To proclaim, announce publicly, the Gospel: *to preach to the heathen*; **b** to give moral or religious advice to; to admonish, lecture; esp. where such is not asked for and is resented: *too fond of preaching*; also *preach at.* **2.** To deliver a sermon: *to preach in Westminster Abbey*; *to preach on the Epistles.*

preacher, n. [1. préchėr; 2. prītʃə]. Prec. & **-er**. **1.** One who preaches a sermon; or advocates earnestly a course of action, doctrine &c. **2.** One who gives earnest, moral advice, esp. when unasked. **3.** (cap.) **a** The author of the book of Ecclesiastes; **b** the book itself.

preachership, n. [1. préchership; 2. prītʃəʃip]. Prec. & **-ship**. Appointment to preach a course of sermons.

preachify, vb. intrans. [1. préchifī; 2. prītʃifai]. **preach** & *-i-* & **-fy**. To preach in a tedious, wearisome, manner.

preaching, vbl. n. & adj. [1. préching; 2. prītʃiŋ]. **preach** & **-ing**. **1.** n. Act, art, of delivering a sermon; a sermon: *good, poor, preaching.* **2.** adj., fr. Pres. Part. *Preaching friar*, a Dominican friar.

preachment, n. [1. préchment; 2. prītʃmənt]. **preach** & **-ment**. A long, wearisome sermon or exhortation.

preachy, adj. [1. préchi; 2. prītʃi]. **preach** & **-y**. Fond of preaching and admonishing; inclined to give moral advice in and out of season.

pre-Adamite, adj. & n. [1. prē ádamīt; 2. prī ǽdəmait]. **a** adj. Existing on earth before Adam; **b** n., inhabitant of the earth before Adam.

preamble, n. & vb. intrans. [1. prēámbl; 2. prīǽmbl], fr. Fr. *préambule*, fr. Med. Lat. *praeambulum*, n., fr. Lat. *praeambulus*, adj., 'going before, preceding', fr. *praeambulāre*. See **pre-** & **amble**. **1.** n. **a** Introductory part of statute, legal document &c., beginning *Whereas*; **b** a preface; **c** the opening part of a speech, story &c. **2.** vb. To make a preamble; to open with a few remarks.

pre-announcement, n. [1. prè anóunsment; 2. prì ənáunsmənt]. A previous and preliminary announcement or notification.

pre-arrangement, n. [1. prè arānjment; 2. prì əréindžmənt]. An arrangement made beforehand.

pre-audience, n. [1. prē áwdiens; 2. prī ɔ́diəns]. Right of prior audience or hearing, as that of one barrister to address the Court before another.

prebend, n. [1. prébend; 2. prébənd], fr. O. Fr. *prebende*, fr. Med. Eccles. Lat. *praebenda*, 'allowance, stipend, pension paid from a public source', neut. pl., as n. sing. of Lat. *praebendus*, gerundive of *praebēre*, 'to supply, grant, allow', for *prae-hibēre*, 'to hold forth, offer', fr. *habēre*, 'to have, hold', see **pre-** & **habit**. **1.** An endowment in land, or a pension in money, given to a cathedral church for the maintenance of a priest being a member of the chapter. Since 1840 all members of the chapter, exclusive of the dean, are called *canons*, and many prebends have been disendowed. **2.** A benefice or living in the gift of the chapter serving as a prebend.

prebendal, adj. [1. prebéndl; 2. pribéndl]. Prec. & **-al**. Connected with, pertaining to, a prebend: *prebendal stall*, the stall in a cathedral or collegiate church allotted to the prebendary as holder of a particular prebend; by transference, a prebend.

prebendary, n. [1. prébendari; 2. prébəndəri], fr. Med. Eccles. Lat. *prebendārius*. **prebend** & **-ary**. Title given to the holder of a disendowed prebend in some ancient cathedral or collegiate churches; equivalent to an honorary canon.

pre-Cambrian, adj. [1. prē kámbrian; 2. prī kǽmbriən]. (geol.) Pertaining to the geological period and its rocks anterior to the Cambrian period.

precarious, adj. [1. prekārius; 2. prikɛ́əriəs], fr. Lat. *precārius*, 'gained by begging or prayer; doubtful', fr. *prec-(em)*, 'prayer', see **pray**. **1.** Depending on, held during the will, pleasure, or life of another: *precarious privileges, tenure*; *a precarious pension, allowance* &c. **2. a** Dependent on circumstances or chances, unknown, or outside one's control; uncertain, insecure, risky: *precarious livelihood, means of existence*; **b** (also in physical sense) insecure, dangerous: *a precarious foothold*; *a precarious state of health.* **3.** Based on uncertain or merely assumed premises: *a precarious argument.*

precariously, adv. Prec. & **-ly**. In a precarious manner; uncertainly; from hand to mouth: *to live precariously.*

precariousness, n. See prec. & **-ness**. State, quality, of being precarious; uncertainty, insecurity.

precatory, adj. [1. prékaturi; 2. prékətəri], fr. L. Lat. *precātōrius*, 'petitioning, precatory', fr. *precātor*, 'one who prays, an intercessor', fr. *precāt-(um)*, *precāri*, 'to pray'. See **pray** & **-ory**. Expressive of prayer or entreaty, supplicatory; specif. **a** (gram.) of word or form expressing an entreaty or request; **b** (law) expressing a wish or recommendation that certain things should be done without a distinct direction or order: *precatory words*, in a will; *precatory trust*, a trust created by such words as addressed to a trustee.

precaution, n. [1. prekáwshun; 2. prikɔ́ʃ(ə)n]. Fr., fr. L. Lat. *praecautiōn-(em)*. See **pre-** & **caution**. **1.** Caution, care taken beforehand; careful foresight: *precaution might have saved him.* **2.** A measure, act &c., taken to guard against danger, risk &c., or to secure success: *to take precautions against infection.*

precautionary, adj. [1. prekáwshunari; 2. prikɔ́ʃənəri]. Prec. & **-ary**. Pertaining to, of the nature of, (a) precaution: *precautionary measures.*

precautious, adj. [1. prekáwshus; 2. prikɔ́ʃəs]. **pre-** & **cautious**. (rare) Using precaution; very careful.

precede, vb. trans. & intrans. [1. prēséd; 2. prīsíd], fr. Fr. *précéder*, fr. Lat. *praecēdere*, 'to go before, precede'. **pre-** & **cede**. **A.** trans. **1.** To come, be, before in time: *lightning precedes the thunder*; *during the days preceding the outbreak of war.* **2.** To go, move, before or in front of, in place or order: *the regiment was preceded by its band*; *the book is preceded by a short biography of the author.* **3.** To come before, be superior to in rank, position, dignity; to take precedence of: *the Archbishop of Canterbury precedes the Lord Chancellor.* **4.** To be more important than, have greater urgency: *economy just now precedes every other problem.* **5.** (rare) To place before, anticipate: *to precede hostilities by a formal declaration of war.* **B.** intrans. To go or come before or first, in time, space, rank &c.; to have precedence of: *the preceding years*; *on a march the band precedes.*

precedence, n. [1. prēsédens, prés-, présidens; 2. prīsídəns, prís-, présidəns], fr. **precedent (I.)** & **-ce**. **1.** Act, state, of preceding or going before in time, space, importance &c.; priority: *the events can be taken in order of precedence*; *national defence must take precedence of other questions.* **2.** The right, derived from birth, or from official status &c., to a specific position or order in relation to other persons or classes, in a public ceremony, social function, or in the classification of ranks, orders &c.: *the order of, rules for, precedence*; *the Prime Minister has now a definite precedence by virtue of his office.*

precedency, n. [1. prēsédensi, prés-, présidensi; 2. prīsídənsi, prís-, présidənsi]. Prec. & **-y**. (rare or obs.) Precedence.

precedent (I.), adj. [1. prēsédent; 2. prīsídənt], fr. Fr. *précédent*, fr. Lat. *praecēdent-(em)*, Pres. Part. of *praecēdere*. See **precede**. Preceding, going before, anterior, previous to: *precedent events*; *conditions precedent*, terms or conditions necessary to be observed before another thing can be effected.

precedent (II.), n. [1. présedent, présedent; 2. présidənt, présidənt]. See prec. **1.** Something that has happened before, analogous to a present occurrence, which may serve as an example or model for future conduct &c.: *there is no precedent for this action.* **2.** Specif. (law) a previous judicial decision, a case which may be cited as authoritative in determining subsequent cases.

precedented, adj. [1. présedented, présedented; 2. présidentid, prísidentid]. Prec. & **-ed**. (rare) Based on, supported, justified, by precedent, by previous examples, authoritative decisions &c.; the negative *unprecedented* is far more frequent.

precedently, adv. [1. prēsédentli; 2. prīsídəntli]. **precedent (I.)** & **-ly**. Beforehand; antecedently.

precentor, n. [1. prēséntur; 2. prīséntə], fr. L. Lat. *praecentor*, 'one who leads the singing'. See **pre-** & **cantoris**. The title of the director of the singing and music of a cathedral or collegiate church; in cathedrals of the Old Foundation he is a member of the chapter and ranks next to the dean, the duties being performed by one of the vicars-choral, who is styled *Succentor*; in cathedrals of the New Foundation the precentor is the principal minor canon.

precentorship, n. [1. prēsénturship; 2. prīséntəʃip]. Prec. & **-ship**. Office of a precentor.

precept, n. [1. présept; 2. prísept], fr. Lat. *praeceptum*, 'maxim, rule' &c., fr. P.P. of *praecipere*, 'to give rules or instructions, to instruct', fr. *prae*, see **pre-**, & *capere*, 'to take', q.v. under **captive**. **1.** A rule, of action or conduct; a commandment, esp. a moral injunction or maxim: *divine precepts*; *to teach by example rather than by precept*; '*precept upon precept, line upon line*'. **2.** (law) **a** An order for payment under a rate, as issued by a local authority; **b** the writ giving the authority for holding an election.

preceptive, adj. [1. prēséptiv; 2. prīséptiv]. Prec. & **-ive**. Of the nature of a precept; using precepts for instruction; didactic.

preceptor, n. [1. prēséptur; 2. prīséptə]. Lat. *praeceptor*, 'teacher'. **precept & -or.** An instructor, teacher; a tutor: *College of Preceptors*, a chartered educational society, granting diplomas, after examination, for teaching.

preceptorial, adj. [1. prèseptórial; 2. prìseptṓriəl]. Prec. & **-ial.** Of, pertaining to, a preceptor or teacher.

preceptory, n. [1. prēsépturi; 2. prīséptəri], fr. Med. Lat. *praeceptoria.* See prec. & **-y.** (hist.) **a** A subordinate, provincial community of Knights Templars, under a *preceptor*, settled on estates belonging to the community, corresponding to the *Commandery* of the Knights Hospitallers; **b** estates, property of a preceptory.

preceptress, n. [1. prēséptres; 2. prīséptris]. **preceptor & -ess.** A female preceptor or teacher; a governess.

precession, n. [1. prēséshun; 2. prīséʃən], fr. L. Lat. *praecessiōn-(em)*, 'a going forward', fr. *praecess-(um)*, P.P. of *praecēdere*, **precede.** A going forward, advancing movement; specif. (astron.) *precession of the equinoxes*, a slow movement from east to west of the equinoctial points, where the equator intersects the ecliptic.

precessional, adj. [1. prēséshunal; 2. prīséʃənəl]. Prec. & **-al.** Of, pertaining to, the precession of the equinoxes: *precessional movement.*

précieuse, n. [1. prāsiëz; 2. presiǿz]. Fr., fem. of *précieux*, see **precious. a** One of a coterie of women in the literary salon of the Hôtel de Rambouillet in France during the 17th cent.; **b** a pedantic woman; a bluestocking.

precinct, n. [1. présingkt; 2. prísiŋkt], fr. L. Lat. *praecinctum*, 'a boundary', fr. P.P. of *praecingere*, 'to gird about, encircle, surround'. See **pre- & cincture. 1.** A space or enclosure within the boundaries or outer walls of a building or group of buildings, esp. of a cathedral or church. **2.** *Precincts*, (loosely) neighbourhood or environs of a town &c., esp. area in immediate vicinity of a cathedral or other important building. **3.** (U.S.A.) A subdivision of a county or other district for electoral purposes.

preciosity, n. [1. prèsiósiti; 2. prèsiɔ́siti], fr. Fr. *préciosité.* Next word & **-ity.** Affected, finicky, pedantic, over-refinement of pronunciation, diction, taste, manners &c.

precious, adj. [1. préshus; 2. préʃəs], fr. O. Fr. *precios, precieus*, Mod. Fr. *précieux*, fr. Lat. *pretiōsus*, 'valuable, having a high price', fr. *pretium*, 'price, value'. See **price & -ous. 1.** Of great intrinsic price or value, very costly or valuable: specif., *precious metals*, gold and silver, as used as a standard of value and medium of exchange; now also applied to platinum; *precious stones*, gem stones, jewels, strictly applied only to the diamond, ruby, emerald, and sapphire, as distinct from the *semi-precious* stones. **2.** (of non-material value) Highly esteemed or valued, beloved, held very dear: *precious memories; his devotion is very precious to me; my precious darlings*; (also elliptically as n.) *my precious !*, my beloved one. **3.** Affected, over-refined, fastidious, pedantic, nice, over-precise, in taste, utterance, and expression: *a precious style, pronunciation* &c. **4.** (colloq., as an ironical intens.) Perfect, complete, out-and-out: *a precious rogue, rascal, liar* &c.; *to leave things in a precious muddle*; (also adverbially): *I precious nearly missed the last train; they took precious little notice.*

preciously, adv. Prec. & **-ly.** Rare, except as adverb of **precious 3**: *to speak, write, rather preciously.*

preciousness, n. See prec. & **-ness.** Quality, state, of being precious; **a** extreme, high value or price; **b** pedantry, precision, preciosity.

precipice, n. [1. présipis; 2. présipis]. Fr., fr. Lat. *praecipitium*, 'steep place, precipice; a falling down headlong'; formed fr. *praecipitāre*, 'to throw down headlong', fr. *praecipit-(em), praeceps*, 'head foremost, headlong'; fr. *prae*, 'in front, before', see **pre-,** & *capit-(is), caput*, 'head', see **capital (I.). a** A high, sheer, perpendicular face of a cliff, mountain, or rock; a steep, abrupt declivity; **b** (fig.) a dangerous, threatening condition, situation, or crisis: *for years before 1914 Europe stood on the brink of a precipice.*

precipitable, adj. [1. presípitabl; 2. prisípitəbl]. See **precipitate (I.) & -able.** (chem.) Able to be precipitated or deposited from a solution.

precipitance, -cy, n. [1. presípitans(i); 2. prisípitəns(i)]. **precipitant & -ce, -cy.** Quality of being precipitate; **a** (in physical sense) haste, swiftness, speed; more usually, **b** (in moral sense) undue hastiness, rashness; hasty, ill-considered action.

precipitant, n. [1. presípitant; 2. prisípitənt], fr. Lat. *praecipitant-(em)*, Pres. Part. of *praecipitāre.* See **precipitate (I.).** (chem.) A substance which when added to a liquid causes the solid matter held in solution to precipitate.

precipitate (I.), vb. trans. & intrans. [1. presípitāt; 2. prisípiteit], fr. Lat. *praecipitāt-(um)*, P.P. type of *praecipitāre*, 'to throw, cast down headlong', fr. *praeceps*, 'headforemost, headlong'. See **precipice. A.** trans. **1.** To throw, hurl down, esp. from height or over a precipice. **2.** To cause to occur or to be done sooner than was necessary, fit, convenient, desired; to bring on, hasten on: *to precipitate a crisis, failure* &c. **3.** Specif. **a** (chem.) To cause to fall down and be deposited, as solid matter or particles held in solution in a liquid; **b** (meteor.) to condense and cause (vapour) to fall as dew, rain, hail, or snow. **B.** intrans. (chem.) To be precipitated.

precipitate (II.), n. [1. presípitat; 2. prisípitət]. See prec. That which is precipitated; **a** as solid matter from a solution; **b** as moisture from vapour.

precipitate (III.), adj. See prec. (in physical and moral senses) Hasty, violent, impetuous: **a** *precipitate movement, rush*; **b** *a precipitate action.*

precipitately, adv. Prec. & **-ly.** Hastily, rashly.

precipitateness, n. See prec. & **-ness.** Precipitancy.

precipitation, n. [1. presìpitáshun; 2. prisìpitéiʃən], fr. Lat. *praecipitātiōn-(em).* **precipitate (I.) & -ion. 1.** Hurried, impetuous, precipitate action. **2.** (chem. or meteor.) **a** Process, fact, of precipitating, or of being precipitated; **b** that which is precipitated.

precipitous, adj. [1. presípitus; 2. prisípitəs], fr. O. Fr. *precipiteux*, fr. Lat. *precipit-* as in **precipitate, & -ous. a** Resembling a precipice; sheer, vertically steep: *a precipitous height*; **b** (rare) precipitate, headlong, rash: *precipitous decision, rashness.*

precipitously, adv. Prec. & **-ly. a** Steeply, sheer down; **b** (rare) hastily, precipitately.

précis, n., sing. & pl., & vb. trans. [1. prāsē; 2. préisī]. Fr. See **precise. 1.** n. An abstract or summary of a document &c. **2.** vb. To make a précis of; to abstract, summarize.

precise, adj. [1. presís; 2. prisáis], fr. Fr. *précise*, fem. of *précis*, adj. fr. Lat. *praecīs-(um)*, P.P. type of *praecīdere*, 'to cut off in front, to cut off short'; fr. *prae*, see **pre-,** & *caedere*, 'to cut'. See **caesura & cement. 1.** Exactly, clearly, defined; accurately expressed; definite, distinct, exact: *precise boundaries; precise statement, interpretation of the law* &c.; *to strike the precise note*; *to arrive at the precise moment.* **2. a** (of persons) Strictly accurate in mind &c., punctilious and exact in following rules, performing duties &c.; **b** (of the mind) exact, clear-cut; working on prescribed lines, literal, rigid; **c** (of conduct and behaviour) strictly in accordance with custom, rule, convention; correct; **d** (of speech) (i.) clearly articulated, fastidiously clear; (ii.) pedantically exact, finicky.

precisely, adv. Prec. & **-ly. 1.** In a precise manner; clearly and accurately, plainly, without ambiguity; exactly: *tell me precisely what you want.* **2.** Expressing agreement with what another has said, just so.

preciseness, n. See prec. & **-ness.** Quality of being precise.

precisian, n. [1. presízhun; 2. prisížən]. **precise & -ian.** One who is exactly or rigidly precise in observance of rules and ceremonies, esp. those of religion; a formalist; a pedant.

precisianism, n. [1. presízhanizm; 2. prisížənizəm]. Prec. & **-ism.** Habits of thought, methods, of a precisian.

precision, n. [1. presízhun; 2. prisížən], fr. Lat. *praecīsiōn-(em).* See **precise & -ion. a** (in intellectual or moral sense) Accuracy, exactness, strict attention to detail; quality of being precise; preciseness: *precision of mind*; **b** material preciseness, justness: *precision in calculation, in movement, aim of a rifle* &c.

precisionist, n. [1. presízhunist; 2. prisížənist]. Prec. & **-ist.** One who attaches great importance to precision in details, of language, manner &c.

preclude, vb. trans. [1. prēklōōd; 2. prīklúd], fr. Lat. *praeclūdere*, 'to shut off, close, bar', fr. *prae*, 'in front of', & *claudere*, 'to shut'. See **pre- & close (I.). a** (only in non-material sense) To shut out, exclude, make impossible, in advance: *to preclude any chance of failure*; **b** to prevent, debar: *a prior engagement will preclude me from coming.*

preclusion, n. [1. prēklōōzhun; 2. prīklúžən], fr. Lat. *praeclūsiōn-(em), praeclūsio*, fr. *praeclūs-(um)*, P.P. type of *praeclūdere.* See prec. & **-ion.** Prevention by anticipation; hindrance, exclusion.

preclusive, adj. [1. prēklōōsiv; 2. prīklúsiv]. See prec. & **-ive.** Preventive; exclusive.

precocial, adj. See **praecocial.**

precocious, adj. [1. prekóshus; 2. prikóuʃəs], fr. Lat. *praecōc-(em), praecox*, 'ripe before its time, premature', fr. *prae*, 'before', & base of *coquere*, 'to cook, ripen'. See **pre- & cook**; also cp. **apricot. 1.** Having certain physical or mental faculties developed prematurely, before the usual age. **2.** Prematurely developed: *precocious talents, growth* &c.; *precocious dementia*, mental decay exhibited in adolescents, *dementia praecox.*

precociously, adv. Prec. & **-ly.** Prematurely; too early.

precociousness, n. See prec. & **-ness.** State, quality, of being precocious; precocity.

precocity, n. [1. prekósiti; 2. prikɔ́siti]. See **precocious, & -ity**; cp. Fr. *précocité.* Premature development; precociousness.

precognition, n. [1. prēkognishun; 2. prìkɔgníʃən], fr. L. Lat. *praecognitiōn-(em).* See **pre- & cognition. 1.** Antecedent cognition; previous knowledge, foreknowledge. **2.** (Scots law) **a** In criminal cases, the preliminary examination of witnesses conducted by the Procurator-fiscal before a judge or sheriff to decide whether there is a prima facie case for trial; **b** in civil cases, the written proof of evidence to be used for the examination of the witness at the trial.

preconceive, vb. trans. [1. prēkunsḗv; 2. prìkənsív]. **pre- & conceive.** To conceive, form a conception, opinion, or judgement beforehand.

preconception, n. [1. prèkunsépshun; 2. prìkənsépʃən]. **pre- & conception.** A conception, opinion, judgement formed beforehand; a prejudgement, prejudice.

preconcerted, adj. [1. prèkonsérted; 2. prìkənsə́tid]. **pre- & concert (II.) & -ed.** Arranged, planned, beforehand by agreement.

preconization, n. [1. prèkonizáshun; 2. prìkənizéiʃən]. Next word & **-ation.** (R.C.Ch.) The solemn announcement by the Pope to the cardinals of the names of new bishops and their sees.

preconize, vb. trans. [1. prékonīz; 2. prīkənaiz], fr. L. Lat. *praecōnizāre*, 'to proclaim, announce, publicly', fr. Lat. *praecōn-(em)*, stem of *praeco*, 'herald, public crier', for **praidicō*; etymol. doubtful. (eccles.) **a** To announce publicly; specif. (of the Pope) to approve and announce names of (new bishops); **b** to summon by name; esp. of an ecclesiastical court.

pre-conquest, adj. [1. prē kóngkwest; 2. prī kɔ́ŋkwest]. **pre- & conquest.** Before the Norman Conquest of 1066.

pre-contract, n. [1. prē kóntrakt; 2. prī kɔ́ntrækt]. **pre- & contract.** (legal hist.) An agreement to marry forming a canonical impediment to any marriage to another subsequently; any such marriage might formerly be treated as void by the ecclesiastical courts.

precursor, n. [1. prēkérsur; 2. prīkə́sə], fr. Lat. *praecursor*, fr. **pre-** & *curs-(um)*, P.P. type of *currere*, 'to run'. See **course (I.)**. **a** A forerunner, harbinger; **b** a predecessor.

precursory, adj. [1. prēkérsuri; 2. prīkə́səri]. Prec. & **-y.** Preliminary, introductory; preceding, anticipatory.

predacious, adj. [1. prēdáshus; 2. prīdéiʃəs]. See **predatory & -acious.** **a** Living by preying on others; predatory; **b** of, pertaining to, predatoriness: *predacious nature, instinct* &c.

predaciousness, n. Prec. & **-ness.** Quality of being predacious.

pre-date, vb. trans. [1. prē dát; 2. prī déit]. **pre- & date (II.).** To date before, to antedate, as letter, document &c.

predatory, adj. [1. prédaturi; 2. prédətəri], fr. Lat. *praedātōrius*, 'of, pertaining to, a *praedātor*, a plunderer, freebooter', fr. *praedāt-(um)*, *praedāri*, 'to plunder, pillage', fr. *praeda*, 'plunder, booty, prey'. See **prey.** **1. a** Living by plunder or robbery: *predatory bands*; **b** having plunder as an object: *a predatory war, expedition*; **c** (of persons and character) *a predatory ruffian*; *predatory nature*. **2.** (of animals) Living by preying on others; predacious: *predatory birds*, birds of prey.

pre-decease, vb. trans. & n. [1. prē disés; 2. prī disís]. **pre- & decease.** **a** vb. To die before another: *to pre-decease one's father*; **b** n., a death prior to that of another: *owing to the pre-decease of his father, he succeeded his grandfather directly in his estates.*

predecessor, n. [1. prédesèsur, prèdesésur; 2. prídisèsə, prìdisésə]. L. Lat., fr. *prae*, & Lat. *dēcessor*, 'one who retires from an office, a retiring official', fr. *dēcess-(um)*, *decēdere*, 'to leave, depart'. See **pre- & decease & -or.** **a** One who precedes another in office, state, position &c.: *predecessors in office*; **b** an ancestor: *buried with his predecessors*; **c** something which is replaced by another used for same purpose: *my present car is far superior to its predecessors.*

predella, n. [1. predéla; 2. pridélə]. Ital., 'a foot-stool, kneeling-stool'; etymol. uncertain, perh. fr. Germ. *pret*, 'board', & dimin. Ital. suff. **-ella.** **a** The step or platform on which an altar rests; also the raised shelf or super-altar at the back of the altar; **b** specif., a painting or sculpture on the face of the step or shelf; and, by extension, a painting at the foot of another larger painting.

predestinarian, n. & adj. [1. prèdestinárian; 2. prìdestinéəriən]. **predestine & -arian.** **a** n. One who holds the doctrine of predestination; **b** adj., of, pertaining to, predestination.

predestinarianism, n. [1. prèdestinárianizm; 2. prìdestinéəriənizəm]. Prec. & **-ism.** The doctrine, principles, of the predestinarians.

predestinate (I.), vb. trans. [1. prèdéstināt; 2. prìdéstineit], fr. Lat. *praedēstināt-(um)*, *praedēstināre*, 'to determine beforehand, to predestine'. See **pre- & destine.** **1.** To destine, determine, beforehand; to predestine. **2.** Specif. (theol., of God) to foreordain, as the expression of His unchangeable and eternal will: *to predestinate to election or reprobation.*

predestinate (II.), adj. [1. prèdéstinat; 2. prìdéstinət]. As prec. Predestinated, foreordained, predestined.

predestination, n. [1. prèdestináshun; 2. prìdestinéiʃən], fr. L., Eccles., Lat. *praedēstinātiōn-(em)*. See **predestinate (I.) & -ion.** **1.** Destiny, fate. **2.** Specif. (theol.) the act of God in determining the destiny of man; **a** the eternal purpose of God, as determined before the creation; **b** Calvinist doctrine that every human soul is predestined from all time either to perdition or to salvation.

predestine, vb. trans. [1. prēdéstin; 2. prīdéstin], fr. Lat. *praedēstināre*. See **pre- & destine.** **a** To destine, decree, settle, beforehand; **b** specif. (theol.) to predestinate.

predeterminate, adj. [1. prèdetérminat; 2. prìditə́minət]. **pre- & determinate.** Predetermined, preordained: (esp. theol.) *the predeterminate will of God.*

predetermination, n. [1. prèdetèrmináshun; 2. prìditə̀minéiʃən]. Prec. & **-ation.** **a** A determination, purpose, decision, formed beforehand; **b** (theol.) predestination.

predetermine, vb. trans. [1. prèdetérmin; 2. prìditə́min], fr. L., Eccles., Lat. *praedetermināre*, 'to fix, determine, beforehand'. See **pre- & determine.** **a** To determine, decide, beforehand; to predestine; **b** to influence, persuade, another to adopt a course of conduct &c.

predial, praedial, adj. [1. prédial; 2. prídiəl], fr. Med. Lat. *praediālis*, fr. Lat. *praedium*, 'farm, estate'; *praedi-*, base of *praes*, 'security, bail', & **-al**; *praes* is apparently fr. *prae-* (see **pre-**), & *vas*, 'security', q.v. under **wed.** (law) Of, pertaining to, land or landed property; real.

predicability, n. [1. prèd-, prèdikabíliti; 2. prèd-, prìdikəbíliti]. **predicable & -ity.** Quality of being predicable; capability of being predicated or affirmed of anything.

predicable, adj. & n. [1. préd-, prédikabl; 2. préd-, prídikəbl]. Fr. *prédicable*, fr. *prédic-*, as in **predicate, & -able.** **1.** adj. That may be predicated or affirmed; affirmable. **2.** n. Anything which can be predicated or affirmed of another, a general attribute, esp. one of (Aristotle's) five general classes of attributes, *the predicables*, regarded in relation to their subject.

predicament, n. [1. predíkament; 2. pridíkəmənt], fr. L. Lat. *praedicāmentum*, only in logical meanings; fr. *praedicāre*. See **predicate.** **1.** (log.) That which is predicated; a predicable; (in pl.) categories. **2.** A dangerous, awkward fix; unpleasant, painful situation.

predicamental, adj. [1. prèdikaméntl; 2. prìdikəméntl]. Prec. & **-al.** Of, pertaining to, a predicament.

predicant, adj. & n. [1. prédikant; 2. prédikənt]. Lat. *praedicant-(em)*, Pres. Part. of *praedicāre*, 'to publish, proclaim' &c. See next word. **1.** adj. Preaching, devoted to preaching: *predicant orders (of friars)*. **2.** n. A preacher, esp. a preaching friar, a Dominican.

predicate (I.), vb. trans. [1. prédikāt, prédikāt; 2. prédikeit, prídikeit], fr. Lat. *praedicāt-(um)*, P.P. type of *praedicāre*, 'to proclaim, announce'; fr. *praedīcere*. See **pre- & diction,** & cp. **preach.** **1.** To declare, assert. **2.** Specif. (log.) to assert (something) of a person or thing; to assert to be an attribute, quality, of person &c.

predicate (II.), n. [1. prédikat, prédikat; 2. prédikit, prídikit]. See prec. **1.** (log.) That which is asserted or denied of anything. **2.** (gram.) The word or words in a sentence which express what is stated concerning the subject.

predication, n. [1. prèd-, prèdikáshun; 2. prèd-, prìdikéiʃən], fr. Lat. *praedicātiōn-(em)*. Prec. & **-ion.** **a** Act of predicating or affirming; **b** that which is predicated or affirmed; a predicate.

predicative, adj. [1. prēdíkativ; 2. prīdíkətiv]. **predicate (I.) & -ive.** Expressing predication; predicating, affirming.

predicatively, adv. Prec. & **-ly.** As a predicate.

predicatory, adj. [1. prédikat(u)ri; 2. prédikət(ə)ri], fr. L. Lat. *praedicātōrius*, 'praising, laudatory', *praedicāre*, 'to proclaim, announce, extol, praise'; (later) 'to preach'. **predicate (I.) & -ory**; cp. **preach.** Of, relating to, preaching; preaching.

predict, vb. trans. [1. predíkt; 2. pridíkt], fr. *praedict-(um)*, P.P. type of *praedīcere*, 'to say, speak, beforehand; to foretell, predict'. See **pre- & diction.** To declare beforehand; to foretell, prophesy: *to predict the future*; *predict that rain is coming.*

predictable, adj. [1. predíktabl; 2. pridíktəbl]. Prec. & **-able.** Capable of being predicted or foretold.

prediction, n. [1. predíkshun; 2. pridíkʃən], fr. Lat. *praedictiōn-(em)*, *praedictio*. See prec. & **-ion.** **a** Act of predicting; **b** that which is predicted; prophecy.

predictive, adj. [1. predíktiv; 2. pridíktiv]. **predict & -ive.** Predicting, foretelling, prophetic.

predictively, adv. Prec. & **-ly.** By way of prediction; prophetically.

predictor, n. [1. predíktur; 2. pridíktə]. **predict & -or.** One who predicts or foretells; a prophet.

predikant, n. [1. prȧdikáhnt; 2. prèidikánt]. Du. See **predicant.** A preacher of the Dutch Reformed Church, esp. a Boer preacher of S. Africa.

predilection, n. [1. prèdilékshun; 2. prìdilékʃən]. Fr., fr. L. Lat. *praedīlectiōn-(em)*. **pre- & dīlectiōn-(em)**, 'choice, love', fr. *dīlect-(um)*, P.P. type of *dīligere*, 'to choose out, to love', see **diligent.** A previous liking or disposition towards; a partiality, prepossession, preference, for.

predispose, vb. trans. [1. prèdispóz; 2. prìdispóuz]. See **pre- & dispose.** **1.** To render liable to, make susceptible to: *both heredity and environment may predispose an organism to disease.* **2.** To cause the mind to be inclined to, to give a favourable bias to, to inspire a tendency in favour of: *both my training and my natural inclinations predispose me to conservatism.*

predisposition, n. [1. prèdispozíshun; 2. prìdispəzíʃən]. See **pre- & disposition.** Condition of being physically or mentally predisposed; tendency, liability, susceptibility to: *a predisposition to tuberculosis, towards piety* &c.

predominance, n. [1. prēdóminans; 2. prīdɔ́minəns]. **pre- & dominance.** Quality, condition, of being predominant, of predominating; supremacy, superiority, ascendancy, preponderance.

predominant, adj. [1. prēdóminant; 2. prīdɔ́minənt]. See **pre- & dominant.** Predominating, superior, having ascendancy over; prevailing: *predominant partner*, applied by the 5th Lord Rosebery to England in relation to Ireland.

predominantly, adv. [1. prēdóminantli; 2. prīdɔ́minəntli]. Prec. & **-ly.** In a predominant manner; so as to predominate.

predominate, vb. intrans. [1. prēdóminàt; 2. prīdɔ́mineit]. See **pre- & dominate.** **1.** To be superior; to exceed, preponderate: **a** in number or amount; **b** in physical, moral, or intellectual strength, power, influence; also *predominate over*, to be greater, more numerous, than; to be superior to; to preponderate over. **2.** To hold sway, be the chief element or factor in; have ascendancy: *dislike of another is often a mixed feeling in which jealousy predominates.*

predominatingly, adv. [1. prēdóminàtingli; 2. prīdɔ́mineitiŋli], fr. Pres. Part. of prec. & **-ly.** In a predominant manner; to a predominating degree.

pre-doom, vb. trans. [1. prē dōōm; 2. pri dûm]. **pre-** & **doom** (II.). To doom, condemn, beforehand, in anticipation: *pre-doomed to destruction.*

pre-election, n. [1. prè elékshun; 2. pri ilékʃən]. **pre-** & **election**. Election beforehand.

pre-eminence, n. [1. prē éminens; 2. pri éminəns]. See **pre-** & **eminence**. State, quality, of being pre-eminent; superior or supreme excellence; high superiority or distinction.

pre-eminent, adj. [1. prē éminent; 2. pri éminənt]. See **pre-** & **eminent**. Eminent above others; surpassing, excelling, others in some quality, in position &c.; distinguished from others by superiority of any kind.

pre-eminently, adv. Prec. & **-ly**. To a pre-eminent degree; in a pre-eminent manner; surpassingly.

pre-empt, vb. trans. [1. prē émpt; 2. pri émpt]. Back-formation fr. **pre-emption**. **a** To take up (public land) with the right of pre-emption; **b** (by transf.) to acquire, appropriate, by anticipation or before others.

pre-emption, n. [1. prē émpshun; 2. pri émpʃən], fr. Med. Lat. *prae-empt-(um)*, P.P. type of *praeimere*, 'to buy beforehand, in advance of another'. See **pre-**, & second element in **exempt**, & **-ion**. Usually in Phr. *right of pre-emption*, the right of purchase before others; specif. (internat. law) right of a belligerent to seize and buy at a fixed price contraband goods on their way to an enemy, belonging to neutrals.

pre-emptive, adj. [1. prē émptiv; 2. pri émptiv]. **pre-empt** & **-ive**. Of, pertaining to, pre-emption: *pre-emptive right.*

preen, vb. trans. [1. prēn; 2. prīn]. Apparently fr. M.E. *proyne* &c., see **prune** (III.), assimilated to M.E. *preonen, prenen*, 'to stitch, fasten together', fr. O.E. *prēon*, 'a pin, brooch', cp. M. Du. *priem*, M.L.G. *prēn*, 'spike, pin'. **a** (of birds) To go over and dress (the plumage) with the beak; (also reflex.) *to preen itself*; **b** (of persons, chiefly reflex.) to plume oneself, to show signs of self-complacency, satisfaction, pride.

pre-exilic, adj. [1. prè egzílik; 2. pri egzáilik]. **pre-** & **exile** & **-ic**. Prior to the Jewish exile in Babylonia.

pre-exist, vb. intrans. [1. prè egzíst; 2. pri igzíst]. **pre-** & **exist**. To exist in a previous state; to exist beforehand.

pre-existence, n. [1. prè egzístens; 2. pri igzístəns]. **pre-** & **existence**. Existence in a previous state; esp. that of the soul before birth in this world.

pre-existent, adj. [1. prè egzístent; 2. pri igzístənt]. **pre-** & **existent**. Existing prior to a specific time; existing previously in another state.

preface (I.), n. [1. préfas; 2. préfis], fr. Fr. *préface*, Med. Lat. *prefātia*, for Lat. *praefātio*, 'a saying beforehand; an introduction', fr. *praefāt-(um)*, P.P. of *praefāri*, 'to utter beforehand, premise'. See **pre-** & **fate**. Introductory remarks whether spoken or written. Specif. **1.** opening statement at the beginning of a book explaining the reason for writing it, excusing its defects, setting forth the writer's general views on the subject of the book or other matters &c.; called also, in pseudo-archaic English, *a foreword*; actually this is an affected pedantry modelled on German. **2.** (liturgical) First part of the Eucharistic service, leading up to the central part which is known as the *Canon of the Mass.* **3.** Initial and introductory part of a speech, leading up to, and preparing the way for, the main portion which deals with some specific subject or argument.

preface (II.), vb. trans., fr. prec. To begin (a speech or book), to utter or write by way of a beginning or introduction to: *to preface one's remarks by an apology*; *to preface a book by* (or *with*) *a life of the author.* The word is rarely or never used in the sense of to furnish (a book) with a preface in specific sense.

prefatory, adj. [1. préfaturi; 2. préfətəri], fr. Lat. *praefāt-(um)*. See prec. & **-ory**. **1.** Of the nature of, serving as, an introduction: *prefatory remarks in a speech.* **2.** Of the nature of, relating to, the preface of a book.

prefect, n. [1. prēfekt; 2. prífekt]. O. Fr., Mod. Fr. *préfet*, fr. Lat. *praefectus*, n. & P.P. of *praeficere*, 'to set over'. See **pre-** & **factor**, **fact**. **1.** (Rom. antiq.) Any of several magistrates or officials of high rank with civil or military functions. **2.** The administrative head of a department in France; also the head of the police, *Prefect of Police*, in Paris. **3.** Name given in some of the great public schools, e.g. Winchester, to a boy of senior standing, to whom certain minor disciplinary powers are delegated by the authorities; corresponding to a *monitor* in other schools.

prefectorial, adj. [1. prèfektórial; 2. prifektórial]. See prec. & **-ory** & **-al**. Of, pertaining to, a prefect or his command or office.

prefectural, adj. [1. prēfékchural; 2. prifékʧərəl]. Next word & **-al**. Of, pertaining to, a prefecture.

prefecture, n. [1. préfekchur; 2. prífektʃə]. Fr. See **prefect** & **-ure**. **1.** The place or office in which a French prefect conducts his business; generally also his official residence. **2. a** The jurisdiction, office, of a prefect; **b** tenure of this.

prefer, vb. trans. [1. prefér; 2. prifə́], fr. Fr. *préférer*, fr. Lat. *praeferre*, 'to carry, bear, set in front; to prefer'. See **pre-** & **-ferous**. **1. a** To like better: *to prefer the town to the country*; *to prefer to receive strike pay rather than work*; **b** in elliptical constructions without comparison expressed: *to prefer to wait* (i.e. rather than to go, act &c., at once). **2.** To bring forward, lay before, submit for consideration, decision &c.: *to prefer a charge against a person.* **3.** To raise, to appoint, to a higher position, office &c.; to promote: *to prefer a man to a bishopric.*

preferability, n. [1. prèferabíliti; 2. prèfərəbíliti]. See next word & **-ity**. Quality, state, of being preferable; preferableness.

preferable, adj. [1. préferabl; 2. préfərəbl]. Fr. See **prefer** & **-able**. More to be desired than, of a kind to be preferred to, something else: *poverty is preferable to ill-health.*

preferableness, n. Prec. & **-ness**. State, quality, of being preferable; preferability.

preferably, adv. See prec. & **-ly**. By preference; rather.

preference, n. [1. préferens; 2. préfərəns], fr. Fr., fr. Med. Lat. *praeferentia*, 'preference, preferment'. See **prefer** & **-ence**. **1. a** Act of preferring or choosing one thing rather than another; **b** the liking of one thing better than another: *to have a preference for.* **2.** Thing preferred or chosen: *this is my preference.* **3. a** Right, opportunity, power of preferring or of choice: *to offer, afford a preference*; specif. **b** (polit. econ.) the favouring of one country by discrimination in tariffs, allowing its goods to enter under lower customs duties than those from other countries; esp. *Imperial Preference*, as between Great Britain and the Dominions. **4.** Right of priority in payment: *to give a creditor an illegal preference*; *preference shares*, those on which a dividend is payable by a trading concern to the holders, before that on ordinary shares.

preferential, adj. [1. prèferénshl; 2. prèfərénʃl]. Prec. & **-al**. Pertaining to, enjoying, a preference; having, giving, a preference; favourable: *preferential duties, preferential treatment.*

preferentialism, n. [1. prèferénshalizm; 2. prèfərénʃəlizəm]. Prec. & **-ism**. System, practice, of giving preferences or advantages in arranging commercial tariffs.

preferentialist, n. [1. prèferénshalist; 2. prèfərénʃəlist]. **preferential** & **-ist**. A supporter of preferentialism.

preferentially, adv. [1. prèferénshali; 2. prèfərénʃəli]. **preferential** & **-ly**. By way of preference.

preferment, n. [1. preférment; 2. prifə́mənt]. **prefer** & **-ment**. **a** Act of preferring; **b** result of such an act; advancement, promotion to a higher position or office; esp. in the Church: '*A zealous High Churchman was I, And so I got preferment*' ('Vicar of Bray').

preferred shares, n. pl. [1. preférd shârz; 2. prifə́d ʃéəz]. Preference shares. See under **preference**.

prefiguration, n. [1. prèfigūráshun; 2. prìfigjəréiʃn]. **prefigure** & **-ation**. **a** The representation by a previous figure or type of what is to come; **b** the figure or type which foreshadows what is to come; a prototype.

prefigurative, adj. [1. prèfígūrativ; 2. prìfígjərətiv]. **prefigure** & **-ate** & **-ive**. Of the nature of prefiguration; anticipating by figure or type; prefiguring.

prefiguratively, adv. Prec. & **-ly**. By prefiguration.

prefigure, vb. trans. [1. prēfíger; 2. prifígə], fr. L., Eccles., Lat. *praefigūrāre*, fr. Lat. *prae*, 'before', & *figūrāre*, 'to form a figure, type, picture of, to imagine'. See **pre-** & **figure**. **1.** To represent in advance, to be a figure or type of; to foreshadow. **2.** To figure to oneself, imagine, beforehand.

prefix (I.), vb. trans. [1. prēfíks; 2. prifíks]. See **pre-** & **fix**. **a** To fix, set, place, in front of or at the beginning; **b** specif., to place before (a word) as a prefix.

prefix (II.), n. [1. préfiks; 2. prífiks]. See prec. **1.** Word, title &c. prefixed to, put in front of, another word or name. **2.** (gram.) A particle placed before a word in composition, which forms with this a new unity, with a modification of meaning.

preformation, n. [1. prèformáshun; 2. prìfōméiʃən]. **pre-** & **formation**. Previous formation; specif. (biol.) *theory of preformation*, the view formerly held that every part found in a fully developed organism exists in little in the germ cell, and merely increases in size as the organism grows.

preformative, adj. & n. [1. prèfórmativ; 2. prìfɔ́mətiv]. **pre-** & **formative**. **1.** adj. Prefixed as a formative element in a word. **2.** n. A word, syllable, so prefixed.

pre-glacial, adj. [1. prègláshial; 2. prigléiʃiəl]. **pre-** & **glacial**. (geol.) Before the glacial period.

pregnability, n. [1. prègnabíliti; 2. prègnəbíliti]. See next word & **-ity**. State, quality, of being pregnable.

pregnable, adj. [1. prégnabl; 2. prégnəbl]. M.E. & M. Fr. *prenable*, fr. *prendre*, 'to take, seize', fr. Lat. *prehendere*, 'to take hold of', see **prehensile**. The *g* in the spelling, which has also affected the pronunciation, has no historical warrant. Capable of being captured; not impregnable.

pregnancy, n. [1. prégnansi; 2. prégnənsi]. **pregnant** & **-cy**. **1.** Condition of being pregnant. **2.** (fig.) Condition of being pregnant in meaning.

pregnant, adj. [1. prégnant; 2. prégnənt], fr. Lat. *praegnant-(em)*, 'with child'; formed as though a Pres. Part. fr. **praegnāre*, 'to be about to give birth, to be before giving birth to', fr. *prae*, 'before', & base in *(g)nāsci*, 'to be born', see **agnate** & **genesis**, **nature**; the secondary meanings may have been influenced by O. Fr. *pregnant, preignant*, 'cogent, weighty, pressing', fr. O. Fr. *preindre*, earlier *preimbre*, fr. Lat. *premere*, 'to press', see **press** (I.). **1.** With child, with young; gravid; having conceived; about to give birth to a child or young. **2.** (archaic or poet.) Fertile, prolific: *the pregnant fields, year* &c. **3.** Full of imagination, fancy, inventiveness: *a pregnant wit.* **4.** Full of weight, significance, importance or hidden meaning: *pregnant words*; *a speech weighty and pregnant*; *events pregnant with dangerous consequences. Pregnant construction*, (gram.) a form of words, sentence &c. which implies more than is expressed.

pregnantly, adv. Prec. & **-ly**. With pregnancy, weight, or significance; significantly.

prehensile, adj. [1. prehénsīl; 2. prihénsail]. Fr., fr. Lat. *prehens-(um)*, P.P. type of *prehendere, praehendere*, 'to grasp, take hold of, seize, catch', fr. **pre-** & **hendere*; cogn. w. Gk. *khandánein*, 'to hold, contain', Goth. *be-git-an*, 'to find', O.E. *-ĝietan*, see **get**, & cp. **apprehend, predatory**, & **prize**, & **-ile**. Capable of grasping, enfolding, and holding on to: *the prehensile trunk of an elephant, tail of a monkey* &c.; *prehensile fingers, toes*.

prehensility, n. [1. prèhensíliti; 2. prihensíliti]. Prec. & **-ity**. Quality, state, of being prehensile.

prehension, n. [1. prehénshun; 2. prihénʃən], fr. Lat. *prehensiōn-(em)*; *prehens-* as in **prehensile** & **-ion**. **1.** (zool.) Act of grasping, holding, as with the tail or other prehensile organ. **2.** (psychol.) Simple, immediate apprehension.

prehistoric, adj. [1. prèhistórik; 2. prì-(h)istórik]. **pre-** & **historic**. **1.** Connected with, pertaining to, periods before recorded history. **2.** (colloq.) Very ancient, old-fashioned, worn-out: *a prehistoric joke*.

prehistorically, adv. [1. prèhistórikali; 2. prìhistórikəli]. Prec. & **-al** & **-ly**. At, in, a prehistoric period.

prehistory, n. [1. prèhístori; 2. prìhístəri]. **pre-** & **history**. An account of the civilization of prehistoric ages; prehistoric archaeology.

pre-human, adj. [1. prè húman; 2. prì hjūmən]. **pre-** & **human**. **a** Belonging to a period before the appearance of man on the earth; **b** pertaining to the ancestors of man before these had reached the human stage.

prejudge, vb. trans. [1. prèjúj; 2. prìdžádž], fr. Fr. *préjuger*, fr. Lat. *praejūdicāre*, 'to prejudge'. See **pre-** & **judge**. To form a judgement or opinion of, decide on, the merits of a case &c. before examining and inquiring into it.

prejudgement, n. [1. prèjújment; 2. prìdžádžmənt]. Prec. & **-ment**. Act of prejudging; a decision, opinion, formed before inquiry &c.

prejudication, n. [1. prèjoodikáshun; 2. prìdžūdikéiʃən], fr. Lat. *praejūdicāt-(um)*, P.P. type of *praejūdicāre*. See prec. & **-ion**. Act of prejudging; prejudgement; a previous legal decision serving as a precedent.

prejudice (I.), n. [1. préjoodis; 2. prédžudis]. Fr., fr. Lat. *praejūdicium*, 'a preceding judgement, precedent; disadvantage, prejudice'. See **prejudge**. **1.** An opinion or judgement formed without due consideration or impartiality; a preconceived unreasonable opinion; bias whether in favour of, or against, a person, course of action, thing &c.; a prepossession, predilection, partiality: *swayed by prejudice; to have a prejudice against Jews*. **2.** (law) Injury, damage, loss: *to the prejudice of*, so as to injure &c. Phr. *without prejudice*, without detraction from any claims or rights; used to imply a stipulation that any admissions, statements &c. made during negotiations shall not at a trial be used as evidence against the person making them.

prejudice (II.), vb. trans. See prec. **1.** To inspire a prejudice in; to bias, influence, a person in favour of or against some person, thing &c.: *his voice and manner prejudiced his audience against him; to be prejudiced in favour of, against; counsel should never attempt to prejudice the Court or the jury*. **2.** To cause damage or injury to; to impair, to detract from, weaken: *to prejudice one's chances of success; to prejudice one's case*.

prejudicial, adj. [1. prèjoodíshl; 2. prèdžudíʃl]. Prec. & **-al**. Causing, arousing, prejudice, danger, or injury; detrimental: *a course of action prejudicial to one's interests*.

prejudicially, adv. Prec. & **-ly**. So as to prejudice; in such a way as to injure.

prelacy, n. [1. prélasi; 2. préləsi], fr. L. Lat. *praelātia*. See **prelate** & **-cy**. **1.** The office, rank, of a prelate. **2.** The body of prelates collectively. **3.** System of church government by prelates; usually an opprobrious term for episcopacy.

prelate, n. [1. prélat; 2. prélit]. M.E. & O. Fr. *prelat*, fr. Lat. *praelātus*, 'set above, preferred, set in authority', fr. *prae*, see **pre-**, & *lātus* for **tlāt-*, fr. base **tel-*, **tol-* &c., q.v. under **tolerate**. A dignitary of the church, an ecclesiastic of high rank, esp. an archbishop or bishop; formerly applied also to an abbot or prior.

prelatic(al), adj. [1. prelátik(l); 2. prelǽtik(l)]. Prec. & **-ic** (& **-al**). Of, pertaining to, prelates or prelacy, usually opprobriously.

prelatically, adv. Prec. & **-ly**. In the manner of a prelate.

prelatism, n. [1. prélatizm; 2. prélətizəm]. **prelate** & **-ism**. Prelacy; government of the church by prelates.

prelatist, n. [1. prélatist; 2. prélətist]. See prec. & **-ist**. Supporter, adherent, of prelatism.

prelatize, vb. trans. [1. prélatīz; 2. prélətaiz]. **prelate** & **-ize**. To make prelatical; to bring under the rule of prelates.

prelature, n. [1. prélachur; 2. prélətʃə]. Fr., fr. L. Lat. *praelātūra*. As **prelate** & **-ure**. (archaic) Prelacy.

prelect, vb. intrans. [1. prēlékt; 2. prīlékt], fr. Lat. *praelect-(um)*, P.P. type of *praelegere*, 'to read before, aloud, to lecture', fr. *prae-* & *legere*, 'to read'. See **pre-** & **lecture**. To lecture publicly, esp. at a university as a prelector.

prelection, n. [1. prēlékshun; 2. prīlékʃən], fr. L. Lat. *praelectiōn-(em)*, 'lecture'. See prec. & **-ion**. A public lecture or set discourse; esp. one delivered at a university by a prelector.

prelector, n. [1. prēléktōr; 2. prīléktō]. Lat. *praelector*, 'reader, lecturer'. **prelect** & **-or**. A reader or lecturer at a University.

prelibation, n. [1. prèlībáshun; 2. prìlaibéiʃən], fr. L. Lat. *praelībātiōn-(em)*, 'tasting, taking away, beforehand; offering of first-fruits'. See **pre-** & **libation**. (rare) A foretaste.

prelim, n. [1. prelím; 2. prilím]. (colloq.) Abbreviation of *preliminary examination*.

preliminarily, adv. [1. prelíminarili; 2. prilíminərili]. See next word & **-ly**. As a preliminary; serving as an introduction or opening.

preliminary, adj. & n. [1. prelíminari; 2. prilíminəri], fr. **pre-** & Lat. *līmināris*, 'of, belonging to, a threshold or boundary'. See **limen** & **-ary**. **1.** adj. Coming before the main action, statement &c.; introductory, preceding, prefatory; preparatory: *preliminary remarks, negotiations* &c.; *a preliminary examination*, an entrance examination. **2.** n. **a** (pl. *preliminaries*) Preliminary, preparatory arrangements, steps, measures &c.: *the preliminaries of a business* &c.; **b** (sing.) a preliminary examination.

prelude (I.), n. [1. prélūd; 2. préljūd]. Fr., as though fr. a L., popular, Lat. *praelūdium*, of somewhat doubtful authenticity, fr. Lat. *praelūdere*, 'to play beforehand, to prelude'; see **pre-** & *lūdere*, 'to play', see **ludicrous**. **1.** That which serves as an introduction to a principal subject or more important matter; an introductory, preliminary, act, performance, event; an opening, preface. **2.** (mus.) A movement, passage, introducing the principal theme, the opening movement of a fugue or suite &c.

prelude (II.), vb. trans. & intrans. [1. prélūd, prelūd; 2. préljūd, prìljūd], fr. Lat. *praelūdere*, 'to play beforehand'. See prec. **A.** trans. To serve, act, as prelude to; to usher in, introduce; to precede; to foreshadow, forebode: '*Dan Chaucer, the first warbler, whose sweet breath Preluded those melodious bursts that fill The spacious times of great Elizabeth*' &c. (Tennyson, 'Dream of Fair Women', verse 2). **B.** intrans. To make, give, use, as a prelude or introduction: *he preluded with some banal remarks; preluding with a few masterly chords*.

prelusive, adj. [1. prēlūsiv; 2. prīljūsiv], fr. Lat. *praelūs-(um)*, P.P. of *praelūdere*. See prec. & **-ive**. Preluding, introductory; serving as a prelude.

premature, adj. [1. prématūr, prēmatūr; 2. prémətjō, prímətjō], fr. Lat. *praemātūrus*, 'very early; untimely'. See **pre-** & **mature**. Happening, done, before the normal time; earlier than is expected or usual; too soon, too early; before its time, untimely: *a premature birth, frost, decay, death* &c.

prematurely, adv. Prec. & **-ly**. Before the proper, usual, or expected time; hastily, hurriedly.

prematureness, n. See prec. & **-ness**. State, quality, of being premature; untimeliness; precocity.

prematurity, n. [1. prèmatúriti; 2. prèmətjóriti]. See **premature** & **-ity**. State, quality, of being premature; too early ripening or flowering; too early development or maturity; precocity.

premeditate, vb. trans. [1. prēméditāt; 2. prīméditeit], fr. Lat. *praemeditāt-(um)*, P.P. of *praemeditāri*. See **pre-** & **meditate**. To meditate beforehand; to plan, contrive, scheme, design, beforehand; chiefly in P.P.: *a premeditated crime, insult* &c.

premeditatedly, adv. [1. prēméditātedli; 2. prīméditeitidli]. P.P. of prec. & **-ly**. With premeditation.

premeditation, n. [1. prèmeditáshun; 2. prìmeditéiʃən], fr. Lat. *praemeditātiōn-(em)*. **premeditate** & **-ion**. Act of premeditating; deliberate planning or contriving in advance.

premeditative, adj. [1. prēméditātiv; 2. prīméditeitiv]. **premeditate** & **-ive**. Resulting from, exhibiting, premeditation.

premier (I.), adj. [1. prémier; 2. prémiə]. Fr., fr. Lat. *prīmārius*, 'of the first rank, primary', fr. *prīmus*, 'first'. See **primary**. First in rank, degree, importance &c.; leading, principal: *to take, hold, the premier place* &c.; *the premier duke, baronet*.

premier (II.), n., fr. prec. Prime minister, formerly *premier minister*; used especially of the chief minister of Great Britain or of one of the Dominions.

première, n. [1. prémiār; 2. prémiɛə]. Fr., fem. See **premier** (I.). The first performance of a play.

premiership, n. [1. prémiership; 2. prémiəʃip]. **premier** (II.) & **-ship**. **a** The office of premier; **b** time during which this office is held.

pre-millennialism, n. [1. prè milénjalizm; 2. prì milénjəlizəm]. See **pre-** & **millennialism**. Doctrine that the Second Coming or Advent of Christ will take place before the Millennium, contrasted with *post-millennialism*.

premise (I.), n. [1. prémis; 2. prémis]. Also *premiss*, the earlier but now obsolesc. form, still often used in logical sense, fr. O. Fr. *premisse*, fr. L. Lat. *praemissa*, sc. *propositio* or *sententia*, 'a premise', lit. '(the proposition) set, put out, before'. See **pre-** & the base discussed under **mission**. **1. a** Anything previously stated or assumed to be true, on which an argument can be based; specif. **b** (log.) one of the two propositions in a syllogism, *the major* or *minor premise*, containing the major and minor and common or middle term, from which is deduced the conclusion. **2.** (law, in pl.) The introductory part of a lease, setting forth in detail the property to be leased, afterwards referred to as *the premises*, i.e. the aforesaid property. **3.** (gen.) A building, house, residence, including the land immediately surrounding, and belonging to it: *warned off the premises; found on the premises; to be consumed on the premises*, of liquor sold by on-licence.

premise (II.), vb. intrans. [1. prēmíz; 2. prīmáiz], fr. prec. To set forth as premises on which a conclusion can be based; to make a statement as introduction, to assume that.

premium, n. [1. prēmium; 2. prímiəm], fr. Lat. *praemium*, 'reward, payment, bounty', for *prae-emium*; cp. **pre-emption.** **1.** A recompense, reward, prize: *a premium for good conduct.* **2.** Something paid in addition, as a bonus: *to pay a premium for the lease of a house.* **3.** A sum paid as a fee by a pupil for being taught a profession or business; (also attrib.) *a premium pupil.* **4.** The sum paid periodically for a policy of insurance. **5.** (of stocks and shares) The value above the par value or that at which the shares were issued, contrasted with *discount.* Phr. *to stand at a premium,* (of shares) to be of higher than par or issue value; (by transf.) to be of high value, to be difficult to buy, be in high esteem; *to put a premium on (lying* &c.), offer inducements or temptation to (lie &c.).

premonition, n. [1. prèmuníshun; 2. prìməníʃən], fr. Lat. *praemonitiōn-(em),* 'a warning beforehand'. See **pre-** & **monition.** **a** A warning given in advance of an occurrence; **b** foreboding, presentiment: *to have a premonition of disaster* &c.

premonitory, adj. [1. prēmónituri; 2. prīmɔ́nitəri]. See **pre-** & **monitory.** Of the nature of, serving as, a premonition: *premonitory symptoms of disease.*

Premonstratensian, adj. & n. [1. prèmonstraténshan; 2. prìmɔnstrətɛ́nʃən]. Med. Lat. *Praemonstrātensis,* 'of, belonging to, *Praemonstrātus*', Lat. name of *Prémontré,* near Laon, France. **a** adj. Of, belonging to, an order of canons regular founded at Prémontré in the 12th cent.; **b** n., a member of this order.

premorse, adj. [1. premórs; 2. primɔ́s]. Lat. *praemors-(um),* P.P. of *praemordēre,* 'to bite off in front'. See **pre-** & base of **morsel** & **mordant.** (bot. and zool.) Having the end cut off short, abruptly truncated; of roots of plants, antennae of insects &c.

pre-natal, adj. [1. prè nátl; 2. prì néitl]. **pre-** & **natal.** Occurring, existing, before birth: *pre-natal infection* &c.

prentice, n. [1. préntis; 2. préntis]. (archaic) Apprentice. Attrib. in Phr. *a, his, prentice hand,* an unskilled hand; clumsy effort or attempt resulting from lack of training and experience.

preoccupancy, n. [1. prēókūpansi; 2. prīɔ́kjupənsi]. **pre-** & **occupancy.** Act of preoccupying or taking possession of before another; as of wild, unpossessed land &c.: *by right of preoccupancy.*

preoccupation, n. [1. prèokupáshun; 2. prìɔkjupéiʃən]. Lat. *praeoccupātiōn-(em).* **pre-** & **occupation.** Act of preoccupying; state of being preoccupied. **1.** Occupation of, settlement on, land, property &c. previous to others: *on the site of the excavations there is no evidence of preoccupation.* **2.** State in which the mind is occupied, and absorbed by thoughts, interests, cares, unrelated to the immediate concerns and business before one; hence, absent-mindedness, obliviousness of the matter in hand.

preoccupiedly, adv. [1. prèókūpīdli; 2. prìɔ́kjupaidli]. See next word & **-ly.** In a preoccupied manner; absent-mindedly.

preoccupy, vb. trans. [1. prèókūpī; 2. prìɔ́kjupai]. Lat. *praeoccupāre.* See **pre-** & **occupy.** **1.** To take possession, of land &c., before another. **2.** **a** To occupy and engross the thoughts and interests of: *the future of his sons had preoccupied him greatly of late*; **b** to engross and fill (the mind) to the exclusion of other things: *my mind is preoccupied with private cares.* **3.** (Pass.) in Phr. such as *anxious and preoccupied,* inattentive to what is being said or done in one's presence; absent-minded, distraught, distrait.

prep., n. [1. prep; 2. prep]. Schoolboy abbreviation for **a** *preparation* **2**; **b** *preparatory school.*

preparation, n. [1. prèpar**á**shun; 2. prèpəréiʃən]. Through Fr., fr. Lat. *praeparātiōn-(em),* fr. *praeparāt-(um),* P.P. of *praeparāre,* see **prepare,** & **-ation.** **1.** Act of preparing; state, condition, of being prepared; readiness: *to make preparations for,* to prepare, make ready for; *in preparation,* in the course of being prepared or made ready. **2.** **a** Act of preparing school lessons for class; **b** time spent over this work. **3.** (trade phr.) A medicine, cosmetic, food &c. specially prepared for a definite purpose: *this invaluable preparation for baldness.* **4.** (mus.) The notes, chord &c. which lead up to a discord.

preparative, adj. & n. [1. prepárativ; 2. pripǽrətiv]. Lat. *praeparāt-(um),* P.P. type of *praeparāre,* see **prepare,** & **-ive.** **1.** adj. Serving to prepare or get ready; preparatory. **2.** n. That which serves to prepare, or as a preparation.

preparatively, adv. Prec. & **-ly.** As a preparation; in a preparative way.

preparatorily, adv. [1. prepáraturili; 2. pripǽrətərili]. See next word & **-ly.** By way of preparation; in preparation for.

preparatory (I.), adj. [1. prepáraturi; 2. pripǽrətəri]. Lat. *praeparāt-,* see **preparation,** & **-ory.** Serving to prepare or make ready; serving as a preparation; introductory: *a preparatory stage, training; preparatory school,* one in which boys or girls are prepared for a public or higher school. Phrs. *preparatory to,* (adverbially) previous to, in anticipation of: *he made his will preparatory to his voyage round the world.*

preparatory (II.), n., fr. prec. Preparatory school.

prepare, vb. trans. & intrans. [1. prepár; 2. pripέə]. Fr. *préparer,* fr. Lat. *praeparāre,* 'to make ready beforehand; to equip, prepare'. See **pre-** & **pare** & words there referred to. (gen. sense) To make ready; widely used of physical and intellectual action, and of action exerted upon both material objects and circumstances, and upon non-material things and conditions. **A.** trans. **1.** (of physical action) **a** To make ready, render available, for use; to take necessary steps to bring to a condition suitable for specific purpose: *to prepare a house for habitation, a net for fishing; to prepare the ground for crops; to prepare one's muscles for hard exercise* &c.; **b** to construct, make, put together, by blending, and otherwise treating, various elements and ingredients, or by arranging the constituent parts in desired order; to produce, provide, furnish: *to prepare a medicine, a lotion, a drink; to prepare (a) dinner, a meal; to prepare some fishing tackle; to prepare a means of communication;* **c** to fit out, equip, furnish, with necessary appliances, accoutrements &c.: *to prepare an expedition of exploration; to prepare a military force;* **d** to draft, plan out, draw up: *to prepare a scheme of action, plans for a battle, plans for building* &c. **2.** (of intellectual or moral action) **a** To dispose, direct (the thoughts, attention &c.) in particular direction; to accustom to particular kind of ideas, way of thinking &c.: *to prepare a person to receive bad news; to prepare the mind to receive new impressions* &c.; Phr. *to be prepared to accept, admit, say* &c., able and willing to; *quite prepared to be friendly,* disposed to be; **b** to instruct, give mental or moral training and equipment to, to exercise on particular lines of intellectual work: *to prepare a boy for examination; to prepare a youth for the battle of life;* Phr. *to prepare one's lessons,* to learn them. **3.** (reflex.) *Prepare oneself,* to put oneself in, bring oneself to, such a physical, mental, or moral condition as is necessary for particular action, or to meet particular circumstances: *to prepare oneself for a race, for a battle of wits, for death, for bad news, to meet one's enemies* &c. **B.** intrans. To get ready, be equipped, physically or mentally; to take necessary steps and measures, material or non-material; make preparations: *to prepare for action, for battle; to prepare for an examination; my son is preparing for the Army; prepare for a bad season, for death, for the worst; to prepare for a large party; prepare for a surprise.*

preparedly, adv. [1. prepáredli; 2. pripέəridli]. P.P. of prec. & **-ly.** In such a manner as to be prepared.

preparedness, n. [1. prepárednes; 2. pripέəridnis]. See prec. & **-ness.** State of being prepared; readiness.

prepay, vb. trans. [1. prēpá; 2. prìpéi]. **pre-** & **pay.** To pay for goods before they are received, or for services before they are rendered; specif., *to prepay a reply to a telegram,* pay for the answer when sending off the first message.

prepayable, adj. [1. prēpáabl; 2. prìpéiəbl]. **pre-** & **payable.** Requiring, admitting of, prepayment.

prepayment, n. [1. prèpáment; 2. prìpéimənt]. **pre-** & **payment.** Payment in advance.

prepense, adj. [1. prēpéns; 2. prīpéns], fr. earlier *prepensed,* fr. obs. vb. *prepense, purpense,* 'to premeditate'; fr. O. Fr. *purpenser,* fr. *pur, pour,* fr. Lat. *pro-,* cp. **purpose,** & *penser,* 'to think'. See **pro-** & **pensive.** Deliberate, aforethought, planned beforehand; chiefly in Phr. *of malice prepense,* of malice aforethought, with malicious intent or purpose.

preponderance, -cy, n. [1. prepónderans(i); 2. pripɔ́ndərəns(i)]. **preponderant** & **-ce** or **-cy.** State, quality, of being preponderant; superiority of weight or influence: *to have the preponderance over,* to be superior to in weight or influence.

preponderant, adj. [1. prepónderant; 2. pripɔ́ndərənt], fr. Lat. *praeponderant-(em),* Pres. Part. of *praeponderāre.* See **preponderate.** Preponderating, outweighing, superior to in amount, weight, importance, influence: *preponderant claims; a preponderant influence, position* &c.

preponderantly, adv. Prec. & **-ly.** In a preponderant degree.

preponderate, vb. intrans. [1. prepónderāt; 2. pripɔ́ndəreit], fr. Lat. *praeponderāt-(um),* P.P. type of *praeponderāre,* 'to outweigh'. See **pre-,** & **ponder** & words there referred to. (lit.) To outweigh; (chiefly in fig. senses) to exceed in number, amount, influence, importance; to predominate; also *preponderate over,* be more numerous, more important &c. than.

preposition, n. [1. prèpozíshun; 2. prèpəzíʃən], fr. Lat. *praepositiōn-(em),* 'a putting before, a preposition'. See **pre-** & **position.** (gram.) A word placed before a noun or pronoun, expressing various abstract relations, those of case, and of time and space; e.g. *to, for, with* &c.

prepositional, adj. [1. prèpozíshunal; 2. prèpəzíʃənəl]. Prec. & **-al.** Pertaining to, of the nature of, a preposition.

prepositionally, adv. Prec. & **-ly.** By means of a preposition; with the functions of a preposition.

prepositive, adj. [1. prēpózitiv; 2. prīpɔ́zitiv], fr. Lat. *praepositivus.* See **pre-** & **positive.** (gram.) Placed before, prefixed; said of words or particles capable of being prefixed to others, such as modified forms of words used as first elements of compounds.

prepositor, n. See **praepostor.**

prepossess, vb. trans. [1. prèpozés; 2. prìpəzés]. **pre-** & **possess.** **1.** (usually pass.) To produce favourable impression upon: *prepossessed by one's appearance, manners* &c. **2.** To influence, esp. favourably; to prejudice, create bias, usually in favour of: *his early training prepossessed him towards religion;* also, more rarely, *to prepossess against.*

prepossessing, adj. [1. prèpozésing; 2. prìpəzésiŋ], fr. Pres. Part. of prec. Attractive, charming: *prepossessing manners.*

prepossessingly, adv. Prec. & **-ly.** Charmingly, attractively.

prepossession, n. [1. prèpozéshun; 2. prìpəzéʃən]. **pre-** & **possession.** Prior possession; preoccupation of the mind by an idea, notion, impression; inclination, bias; usually in favourable sense, but also in sense of hostile prejudice: *foolish prepossessions against organized society.*

preposter, n. See **praepostor**.

preposterous, adj. [1. prepósterus; 2. pripóstərəs], fr. Lat. *praeposter-(us)*, 'the last first; inverted, reversed'. See **pre-** & **posterior** & **-ous**. (lit.) Putting that first which should be last; hence, contrary to common sense, unreasonable, absurd.

preposterously, adv. Prec. & **-ly**. In a preposterous manner.

preposterousness, n. See prec. & **-ness**. State, quality, of being preposterous or ridiculous.

prepotency, n. [1. prèpótensi; 2. pripóutənsi]. Next word & **-cy**. State, quality, of being prepotent; specif. (biol.) superior power of one parent to transmit characteristics to offspring.

prepotent, adj. [1. prèpótent; 2. pripóutənt]. Lat. *praepotent-(um)*, 'very powerful'. See **pre-** & **potent**. Superior in power or influence; specif. (biol.) having prepotency.

prepotently, adv. Prec. & **-ly**. In a prepotent manner.

prepuce, n. [1. prépūs; 2. prípjūs], fr. Lat. *praepūtium*, see **pre-**, & for second element, wh. here has sense of 'penis', see **puberty** & **puerile**. The foreskin.

preputial, adj. [1. prèpúshal; 2. pripjúʃəl]. Prec. & **-ial**. Of, pertaining to, the prepuce.

Pre-Raphaelite, adj. & n. [1. prè ráfaelīt; 2. prī ræ̃fiəlait]. **pre-** & Raphael, name of Ital. painter, fl. late 15th & early 16th cent., & **-ite**. **1.** adj. Of, belonging to, a group or society of painters, *the Pre-Raphaelite Brotherhood*, formed in England in 1848, the leading members of which were Holman Hunt and Dante Gabriel Rossetti, and for a time Millais, who aimed in their art at the close fidelity to nature characteristic of Italian painting before Raphael and the great schools of Italian art. **2.** n. A member of the Pre-Raphaelite Brotherhood, a Pre-Raphaelite painter.

prerequisite, adj. & n. [1. prèrékwizit; 2. prīrékwizit]. **pre-** & **requisite**. **1.** adj. Required, necessary, as a preliminary or previous condition. **2.** n. Something required or necessary as a condition for a future act, or to secure a purpose &c.: *diligence and intelligence are prerequisites to scholarship.*

prerogative, n. & adj. [1. prerógativ; 2. pirógətiv], fr. Fr. *prérogative*, fr. Lat. *praerogātīva*, 'a right or privilege of voting first, precedence in voting', fem. sing. fr. *praerogātīvus*, 'asked for an opinion or vote before others', fr. *praerogātus, praerogāre*. See **pre-** & **rogation**. **1.** n. **a** An exclusive or peculiar right or privilege; esp. *the royal prerogative*, the theoretically unlimited, discretionary right of the sovereign to act without accountability to Parliament; *the prerogative of mercy*; **b** any peculiar, particular, privilege, attaching to position, office &c.: *the prerogatives of their sex; within one's prerogative to do* &c. **2.** adj. Privileged, enjoyed by prerogative or privilege: *a prerogative right.*

presage, n. & vb. trans., fr. O. Fr. *presage*, fr. Lat. *praesāgium*, 'omen', fr. *praesāgīre*, 'to perceive beforehand', fr. *prae*, 'before', see **pre-**, & *sāgīre*, 'to be aware of', also *praesāgus*, 'foretelling, predicting', fr. stem *sag-*, as in **sagacious**; vb. fr. O. Fr. *presager*, as prec. **1.** n. [1. présij; 2. présidž]. An omen, portent; forewarning, foreboding: *a presage of a storm; presage of coming disaster.* **2.** vb. [1. presáj; 2. preséidž]. **a** To foretell, portend, give warning of: *the lowering clouds presage the storm*; **b** to have a foreboding, presentiment of: *in dreams one presages the future.*

presby-, pref., fr. Gk. *présbus*, 'old; venerable, beloved'; also 'an old man', primitive compound fr. *pres-, 'before, in advance', cogn. w. Gk. *pará*, 'near, along' &c., see **para-**, & Lat. *prae*, 'in front of' &c., see **pre-**; & base *gʷēu- &c., 'ox', whence Gk. *boûs, bôs*, see **bovine**; the compound occurs in Scrt. *purō-garáš*, 'guide'; orig., 'conductor, leader, of a band'. The development of meaning in Gk. was 'leader, guide; venerable person, an old man' &c.

presbyopia, n. [1. prèzbiópia; 2. prèzbióupiə]. Prec. & *-opia*, fr. Gk. *óps*, 'eye', see **optic**. (med.) That form of defective sight arising from, and characteristic of, old age.

presbyter, n. [1. prézbiter; 2. prézbitə]. Eccles. Lat., fr. Gk. *presbúteros*, 'elder', compar. of *présbus*, 'old', see **presby-**. **1.** (in the early Christian Church) An elder or superior in a local church or community; an overseer. **2.** (in Episcopal Churches) A priest. **3.** (in Presbyterian Churches) An elder.

presbyteral, adj. [1. prezbíteral; 2. prezbítərəl]. Prec. & **-al**. Of, pertaining to, a presbyter, a presbytery, or government by the latter.

presbyterate, n. [1. prezbíterāt; 2. prezbítəreit], fr. Eccles. Lat. *presbyterātus*. **presbyter** & **-ate**. **a** Office, rank, of a presbyter; **b** a presbytery.

presbyterial, adj. [1. prèzbitérial; 2. prèzbitíəriəl]. **presbyter** & **-ial**. Presbyterial.

Presbyterian, adj. & n. [1. prèzbitérian; 2. prèzbitíəriən]. **presbyter** & **-ian**. **1.** adj. Of, pertaining to, the form of ecclesiastical government by presbyters: *Presbyterian Church*, that which recognizes only one order in the ministry and is governed by a presbytery; contrasted with *Episcopal*. **2.** n. A member of a Presbyterian Church; adherent of Presbyterianism.

Presbyterianism, n. [1. prèzbitérianizm; 2. prèzbitíəriənizəm]. Prec. & **-ism**. Presbyterian system of Holy Orders and of Church government.

presbytery, n. [1. prézbiteri; 2. prézbit(ə)ri], fr. O. Fr. *presbiterie*, fr. Eccles. Lat. *presbytērium*, fr. L. Gk. *presbutérion*, 'place of the presbyter, assembly of presbyters'; see **presbyter** & **-y**. **1.** The sanctuary or eastern end of the chancel of a church. **2.** (R.C. Ch.) The house in which the priest of a parish &c. resides. **3.** (Presbyterian Ch.) **a** Body of presbyters forming a court within a district, consisting of the ministers and pastors and one elder from each church, ranking between a church session and a synod; **b** the district so represented.

prescience, n. [1. présiens; 2. prísiəns]. Fr., fr. Lat. *praescientia*, 'foreknowledge'. See **pre-** & **science**. Knowledge of what is going to happen; foresight, foreknowledge.

prescient, adj. [1. présient; 2. prísiənt]. Fr., fr. Lat. *praescient-(em)*, Pres. Part. of *praescīre*, 'to know beforehand'. See **pre-** & **science**. Foreseeing, seeing ahead, farsighted.

presciently, adv. Prec. & **-ly**. With foreknowledge or foresight.

prescind, vb. trans. & intrans. [1. prēsínd; 2. prīsínd], fr. Lat. *praescindere*, 'to cut off short or before'. See **pre-** & **scissors**. **1.** trans. (only in non-material sense) To cut off, separate; to abstract. **2.** intrans. To abstract, separate oneself from, by act of volition.

prescission, n. [1. prēsíshun; 2. prīsíʃən], fr. Lat. *praesciss-(um)*, P.P. of *praescindere*, see prec., & **-ion**. Act of prescinding; abstraction by disregarding all unimportant and non-essential details.

prescribe, vb. trans. & intrans. [1. preskríb; 2. priskráib], fr. Lat. *praescrībere*, 'to write beforehand; appoint, prescribe'. See **pre-** & **scribe**. **A.** trans. **1.** To lay down with authority, as a direction, or command; to order; ordain, dictate: *to prescribe his duties to a person; the law prescribes what should be done and the penalties for neglect.* **2.** (med.) To order, recommend, advise, a course of treatment, or a particular medicine for a patient: *to prescribe radio-therapy, massage, a holiday, a strong tonic &c. for.* **B.** intrans. **1.** To give, lay down, rules, orders &c.: *the law does not prescribe for such offences.* **2.** (law) To claim by prescription. **3.** (med.) **a** To give medical advice to, to attend as a medical adviser: *to prescribe for a person*; **b** to order, suggest, treatment and remedies for relief of: *to prescribe for the gout.*

prescript, n. [1. préskript; 2. prískript]. Lat. *praescript-(um)*, P.P. of *praescribere*. See prec. A rule, ordinance.

prescription, n. [1. preskrípshun; 2. priskrípʃən], fr. Lat. *praescriptiōn-(em)*. See prec. & **-ion**. **1.** **a** Act of prescribing (in various senses); **b** that which is prescribed; rule. Specif. **2.** (law) the enjoyment, possession, occupation, without disturbance, of interest or profits from time immemorial, or during period as laid down by statute which gives a right or title to such interests and profits. **3.** **a** Written recipe or directions of a physician for the preparation and use of a medicine; **b** the medicine itself.

prescriptive, adj. [1. preskríptiv; 2. priskríptiv], fr. L. Lat. *praescriptīvus*, as **prescript** & **-ive**. **a** Prescribed, by law or custom; **b** owned, claimed, by prescription: *a prescriptive right.*

prescriptively, adv. Prec. & **-ly**. By prescription; by prescribed law or custom.

presence, n. [1. prézens; 2. prézəns]. O. Fr., fr. Lat. *praesentia*. See **present (I.)** & **-ce**. **1.** State, quality, of being present, of being at a certain place at a certain time or of being within sight or hearing of; contrasted with *absence*: *the presence of strangers; to demand the presence of a witness* &c.; *Real Presence*, doctrine of the objective, true, substantial Presence of the Body and Blood of Christ in the eucharistic elements after consecration; contrasted with doctrines of a subjective, or figurative Presence; *presence of mind*, readiness, steadiness, control of mental faculties, in dangerous or critical circumstances; coolness. **2.** **a** The company, society, neighbourhood, of another; nearness, approach, to another: *to be admitted to, excluded from, the presence of another; in the presence of ladies; the presence of danger*; specif. **b** nearness, close vicinity, of the person of the sovereign when present at a ceremonial reception: *to approach, withdraw from, the presence*; **c** nearness, immanence, of certain conditions, circumstances, material, or existing in the mind: *the presence of danger, of fear, of joy* &c. **3.** **a** General bearing, carriage, mien; personality, demeanour: *of dignified, handsome, poor, presence*; **b** dignified bearing, deportment, appearance: *a man of no presence.* **4.** An invisible, intangible, ghostly, influence, as from some mysterious personality: *an evil presence in a house; comforted by some spiritual presence.*

presence chamber, n. The audience chamber of the sovereign.

present (I.), adj. [1. prézent; 2. prézənt]. O. Fr., fr. Lat. *praesent-(em), praesens*, 'being in front of or at hand', Pres. Part. of *praeesse*, 'to be at hand'. See **pre-** & **esse**. **1.** (of spatial conditions) **a** Being here or at a specified place at a specified time, being within sight or hearing, contrasted with *absent*: *very few people were present at the lecture; I ask those who are present, those here present*; Phr. *present company*, those now here; **b** (also of mental phenomena) *present in one's recollection, to one's mind*, actually remembered, existing and vivid in the consciousness. **2.** (of conditions in time) **a** Existing, occurring, now, not in the past or future; now under consideration, in process of being done, felt &c.: *the present Cabinet; my present sentiments; the present lawlessness; the present day, time* &c.; **b** (gram.) *present tense*, the tense of the verb denoting existence or action now, at the present time, as *I speak, am speaking; live, am living; present value* or *worth*, the value or worth of a sum which, with interest, will amount to a specified amount at a specified future. **3.** (archaic) Ready, efficacious, operative: *a present wit; 'a very present help in trouble* (Psalm 46.1)'.

present (II.), n., fr. prec. **1.** The present time, the present day: *the past, the present, and the future*; *no time like the present*, to do what you have to do at once. Phrs. *at present*, now, at the present time: *the work is not being continued, as nothing is wanted at present*; *for the present*, for the moment, for the time, temporarily: *I am staying in town for the present.* **2.** (gram.) A present tense. **3.** (law) In Phr. *by these presents*, present letters, the present document or that referred to.

present (III.), vb. trans. & intrans. [1. prezént; 2. prizént], fr. O. Fr. *presenter*, fr. Lat. *praesentāre*, 'to set, place, before, exhibit, present', formed fr. *praesent-(em)*. See **present** (I.). **A.** trans. **1.** To bring (a person) to the presence or notice of, to introduce formally to another: *to present a person to the king*; *to be presented at Court*; *allow me to present Mr. X to you*; Phr. *she was presented last year*, formally presented at Court. **2.** (reflex.) **a** To offer oneself for: *to present oneself for an examination*; **b** to call at, go to; appear: *to present oneself at another's house, on appointment*; *to present oneself at a meeting* &c. **3. a** To introduce, lay before, submit, offer for consideration; to state, set forth: *to present a petition*; *to present a case, subject, for discussion*; Phr. *to present a cheque, bill* &c. (for payment); **b** to exhibit to view, to show, to display; to organize public performance of: *to present a new play, an unknown actor* &c. **4. a** To exhibit, to turn or be placed in such a way as to face and be seen by the spectator: *to present a smiling face to the world*; *the mountain here presents an inaccessible wall of rock*; Phr. *to present an appearance of*, to appear as, make impression of; **b** (of non-material circumstances) to offer, be fraught with, give rise to: *the question, situation, presents great difficulties.* **5.** To offer for acceptance, bestow as a gift: *to present a person with five pounds*, or *present five pounds to a person.* Phr. *present one's compliments, best respects, humble apologies, to.* **6.** To nominate for an appointment, esp. to name to a bishop the person for institution to an incumbency or benefice: *the Rev. H. G. has been presented by his college to the living of W.* **7. a** To direct, point at, as a weapon: *to present a pistol at one's head*; **b** (mil.) to hold the rifle, sword, perpendicularly in front of the body as a salute to a superior officer: *to present arms*; also as noun in Phr. *at the present*, with arms presented as a salute. **B.** intrans. To exercise the right of presentation to a benefice: *it is the turn of the Crown to present.*

present (IV.), n. [1. prézent; 2. prézənt]. Not fr. **present** (III.), but fr. O. Fr. *present*, 'in the presence of, before', as in Phr. *mettre en present*, 'to present, offer', hence 'a gift'. Something given to another without payment in return; a gift: *to make, give, a present to (a person)*; *to make a present of (a thing) to (a person).*

presentability, n. [1. prezèntabíliti; 2. prizèntəbíliti]. See next word & **-ity.** State, quality, of being presentable.

presentable, adj. [1. prezéntabl; 2. prizéntəbl]. **present** (III.) & **-able.** **1.** Fit to be presented, suitable for presentation: *a presentable play*; *in presentable language*; *a presentable gift.* **2.** Suitable for presentation in society; **a** (of external appearance) decent, respectable, seemly, sufficiently smart &c.: *presentable clothes*; *to look quite presentable*; specif. **b** (of persons) having the manners and bearing of good society; well-bred.

presentably, adv. Prec. & **-ly.** In a presentable manner or fashion: *quite presentably dressed.*

presentation, n. [1. prèzentáshun; 2. prèzəntéiʃən]. Lat. *praesentātiōn-(em)*, fr. *praesentāt-(um)*, P.P. type of *praesentāre*, see **present** (III.), & **-ion.** **1.** Act of presenting (in various senses); **a** act of formally introducing (a person): *a presentation at Court*; **b** act of giving, tendering for acceptance, bestowal: *the presentation of an address of welcome*; *presentation copy* (of a book), one presented free, esp. by the author; **c** act and mode of setting forth, of stating; exposition: *the subject gains from the attractive presentation of the matter*; **d** act of presenting to an ecclesiastical benefice; **e** (med.) particular way or position in which a child about to be born presents itself at the mouth of the uterus. **2.** Something presented; **a** a gift, donation: *a handsome presentation was made to the retiring rector*; **b** (psychol.) anything present in the consciousness, as it exists or appears to exist at a given moment.

presentational, adj. [1. prèzentáshunal; 2. prèzəntéiʃənəl]. Prec. & **-al.** (psychol.) Connected with, of the nature of, a presentation.

presentationism, n. [1. prèzentáshunizm; 2. prèzəntéiʃənizəm]. **presentation** & **-ism.** (philos.) The doctrine 'that all the elements of psychical life are primarily and ultimately cognitive elements' (Prof. James Ward).

presentative, adj. [1. prezéntativ; 2. prizéntətiv]. Lat. *presentāt-*, as in **presentation**, & **-ive.** **1.** (eccles.) Having the right of presentation to a benefice. **2.** (philos.) Capable of being directly presented to, or cognized by, the mind.

present-day, adj. Belonging to, characteristic of, occurring in or at, the present time in which we live: *present-day manners, speech, events* &c.

presentee, n. [1. prèzenté; 2. prèzəntí]. **present** (III.) & **-ee.** **a** One to whom something is presented; recipient; specif. **b** one who is presented to an ecclesiastical benefice.

presentient, adj. [1. prèsénshient; 2. prìsénʃiənt]. See **pre-** & **sentient.** Feeling, perceiving, beforehand; having a presentiment of.

presentiment, n. [1. prezéntiment; 2. prizéntimənt]. See **pre-** & **sentiment.** A feeling, conviction, of something about to happen, esp. of something disastrous or unfortunate; a foreboding, apprehension: *a presentiment of danger.*

presentive, adj. [1. prezéntiv; 2. prizéntiv]. **present** (III.) & **-ive.** Presenting an object, idea &c. directly to the mind; contrasted with *representative* or *symbolical.*

presently, adv. [1. prézentli; 2. prézəntli]. **present** (I.) & **-ly.** **1.** (archaic or obs.) At this present time, now, at once, immediately. **2.** Not now, later on, at some later time; soon, before long.

presentment, n. [1. prezéntment; 2. prizéntmənt]. **present** (III.) & **-ment.** **1.** Presentation, exhibition, statement, delineation: *the presentment of a case*; *a careful presentment of character.* **2.** (eccles.) A formal complaint made at the visitation of a bishop or archdeacon by parish authorities, as the churchwardens. **3.** (law) The presenting of an indictment by a grand jury; specif., the notice by a grand jury of an offence, such as a nuisance &c., from their own knowledge and statement of such on oath, upon which a proper indictment is framed.

preservability, n. [1. prezèrvabíliti; 2. prizə̀vəbíliti]. See next word & **-ity.** State, quality, of being preservable.

preservable, adj. [1. prezérvabl; 2. prizə́vəbl]. **preserve** (I.) & **-able.** Capable of being preserved or saved from injury, decay &c.

preservation, n. [1. prèzerváshun; 2. prèzəvéiʃən]. **preserve** (I.) & **-ation.** **1.** Act or process of preserving: *engaged in the preservation of ancient buildings*; *to labour for the preservation of one's health* &c. **2.** Condition of being preserved: *eggs in a good state of preservation*; *an ancient manuscript in good preservation.*

preservative, adj. & n. [1. prezérvativ; 2. prizə́vətiv], fr. Fr. *préservatif, -ive*, fr. Med. Lat. *praeservātīvus.* See **preserve** (I.) & **-ative.** **1.** adj. Having the property of preserving, protecting, from decay, injury &c. **2.** n. Substance which tends to preserve.

preserve (I.), vb. trans. [1. prezérv; 2. prizə́v], fr. Fr. *préserver*, fr. Lat. *prae*, 'before', & *servāre, servāt-(um)*, 'to save, preserve'; Lat. has *praeservāre*, 'to observe beforehand'. See **pre-** & **serve.** **1.** To maintain in safety, protect, save from injury, harm, danger &c.: *may God keep and preserve you.* **2.** To keep, save, from decay by use of preservatives: *to preserve eggs in water-glass*; specif., to treat (foodstuffs) by boiling in sugar, curing, pickling &c., so as to retard decay or fermentation; esp. of fruit and vegetables. **3. a** To maintain, keep up, retain unaltered: *to preserve the memory of another*; *to preserve one's looks, strength*; *to preserve appearances*; **b** to keep from being lost; to save up, hoard: *he preserves all nails and pins which he picks up.* **4.** To rear, protect, and reserve (game &c.) for one's own use; to protect coverts, a forest, or river, also game or fish in these, for one's own shooting and fishing: *these woods are preserved*; *to preserve pheasants*; (also absol.) *the squire doesn't preserve now.*

preserve (II.), n., fr. prec. That which is preserved; (usually pl.) specif. **a** fruit preserved by boiling with sugar; jam; bottled fruit; **b** game coverts preserved for shooting; a part of a river or stream preserved for fishing. Phr. *to poach on another's preserves*, to encroach on subjects, or activities, which another claims a special right to pursue.

preserver, n. [1. prezérver; 2. prizə́və]. **preserve** (I.) & **-er.** **1.** One who preserves; protector, guardian, saviour. **2.** One who preserves game.

preside, vb. intrans. [1. prezíd; 2. prizáid], fr. Fr. *présider*, fr. Lat. *praesidēre*, 'to sit in front of, to guard, protect; to preside over, direct'. See **pre-** & **sedentary** & **sit.** (followed by *at* or *over*) To take, occupy, the place of authority, control, or chief importance, esp. at meetings of a deliberative assembly of any kind; to take the chair: *to preside at, over, a meeting, public dinner* &c.; (playfully) *to preside at a family dinner*, sit, as host, at head of the table.

presidency, n. [1. prézidensi; 2. prézidənsi]. **president** & **-cy.** **1. a** The office of a president: *the Presidency of the United States*; **b** period of office of a president: *he died during his presidency.* **2.** The name of each of three of the administrative provinces of the Indian Empire, of Madras, Bombay, and originally of Bengal; under the old East India Company the chief administrator was formerly styled President, later Governor; the term is no longer officially used.

president, n. [1. prézident; 2. prézidənt]. Fr. *président*, fr. Lat. *praesident-(em)*, used as n. in L. Lat.; Pres. Part. of *praesidēre.* See **preside.** The title of various persons holding an official position of authority or control; **a** the chief, elected, executive officer of a modern republic, the *President of the French Republic* &c.; **b** the title of certain ministers or heads of departments in Great Britain: *the Lord President of the Council*; *President of the Board of Trade, Agriculture, Education* &c., these being committees of the Privy Council whose chief was styled President as Lieutenant of the King; **c** of certain judges: *President of the Court of Session* (in Scotland); *of the Admiralty, Probate, and Divorce Division*; **d** the title of one elected to preside at the meetings of a learned, artistic, or other society: *the President of the Royal Society, Academy, College of Surgeons* &c.; **e** the title of the heads of certain colleges, Trinity, Magdalen, Corpus, and St. John's, at Oxford; of Queen's College at Cambridge; also of the heads of universities in the U.S.A.: *President of Harvard*; **f** (U.S.A.) the title of the chairman of a financial, industrial or other public corporation or company; **g** (in France) the presiding, elected, member of the Chamber of Deputies and of the Senate.

presidential, adj. [1. prèzidénshal; 2. prèzidénʃəl]. Prec. & **-ial.** Of, pertaining to, a president, esp. of a president of a republic: *a presidential election.*

presidentially, adv. [1. prèzidénshali; 2. prèzidénʃəli]. Prec. & **-ly.** As president: *he spoke not presidentially but in his private capacity.*

presidentship, n. [1. prézidentship; 2. prézidəntʃip]. **president** & **-ship.** Office, period of office, of a president.

presidiary, adj, [1. presídiari; 2. prisídiəri], fr. Lat. *praesidiārius*, fr. *praesidium*, 'a presiding over; a defence, guard'. See **preside** & **-ary.** Of, pertaining to, a guard or garrison.

presidio, n. [1. presídiō; 2. prisídiou]. Span., fr. Lat. *praesidium.* See prec. A fort, fortified station, in Spanish America.

press (I.), vb. trans. & intrans. [1. pres; 2. prɛs]. Fr. *presser*, Lat. *pressāre*, 'to press, clasp', formed fr. *press-(um)*, P.P. type of *premere*, 'to press', the origin and relations of wh. are doubtful. **A.** trans. (gen. senses) To apply weight gradually to from above; to squeeze between two masses or bodies; used in various specific and more definite senses, literally, and metaphorically. **1.** To apply weight from above for various purposes: **a** to squeeze juice, oil &c. out of: *to press grapes, nut kernels* &c.; **b** to render compact, dense; to compress into smaller space by pressing: *to press beef, hay* &c.; **c** to apply pressure to so as to flatten, smooth, remove creases: *to press clothes.* **2.** To thrust, push, so as to cause to move away from point at which the force is exerted: *to press the knob of an electric bell, a lever* &c. **3.** To cause pain or discomfort by bearing upon from above or from the side: *my shoe presses my toe.* **4.** To embrace and hold fast to, to clasp and draw towards one: *to press a person to one's breast.* **5.** To grasp with the hand with gentle pressure; to clasp, squeeze: *to press a person's hand*, in token of affection, sympathy &c. **6.** To apply, place, imprint upon with pressure: *to press a stamp on paper, a kiss on a person's lips.* **7. a** To follow up closely, close in upon; to harry, hustle: *to press one's opponent* (*in a game*); *to press the enemy hard*; Phr. *to press an attack*, carry it out with vigour and insistence; **b** to throng, crowd, upon, come up against in close contact: *the mob pressed me pretty close.* **8.** To urge, insist upon, emphasize: *to press a point, a question, an argument.* Phr. *to press home* (*an argument*), to urge it with force and cogency. **9.** To try persistently to persuade; to request insistently; to bring compulsion to bear upon: *to press a person to do something*; *to press a man for money* &c. Phr. *to press a gift, favour, drink &c. upon* (a person), offer insistently, insist upon acceptance. **10.** To oppress, weigh upon, cause distress and hardship to: *debts pressed heavily upon him*; also commonly in P.P.: *hard pressed* (in physical and moral sense). Phr. *to be pressed for time, money*, to be short of, have hardly enough. **B.** intrans. **1.** To exert pressure, apply a steady downward weight. **2.** To be urgent, to require immediate action: *have you any business that presses?* Phr. *time presses*, is running short. **C.** Followed by preposition or adverb. *Press back*, trans., **a** to bend backwards; **b** to cause to retreat by exerting force. *Press down*, trans., to thrust down, squeeze into smaller space by exerting pressure from above. *Press forward*, intrans., to hasten, go, forward; (of a crowd) to throng, sweep forward. *Press on*, intrans., to hasten onwards; to continue one's journey, or task, with determination. *Press for*, intrans., to demand urgently, make efforts to obtain: *to press for larger grants for education.*

press (II.), n., fr. Fr. *presse.* See prec. **1. a** Act of pressing, pressure: *a press of the hand*; **b** something which is pressed; specif., part of a machine which functions by pressure: *a bell-press.* **2.** Something exerting pressure; specif., a throng, crowd, of persons or things: *to make one's way through the press*; *in the press of battle*; *a press of sail*; (fig.) *press of business.* **3.** Any apparatus, machine, contrivance, for pressing, squeezing, enclosing, or holding &c.; specif. **a** machine for extracting juice &c.: *a wine-, cider-, olive-press*; **b** device for compressing, compacting, smoothing &c.: *a clothes-press*; *cheese-press*; **c** machine consisting of flat plates brought together by a lever or screw, between which letters to be multiplied are pressed upon a negative in copying ink; also *copying-press*; **d** a shelved cupboard, set of shelves for holding clothes, books &c., as a permanent fixture in a room or library. **4. a** Machine for printing; also *printing-press*; **b** the art, business, practice, of printing; printing: *to prepare, get ready, for press*; *to send to the press*; *in the press*, being printed; **c** a printing and publishing establishment: *the Clarendon Press*; *the University Press*; **d** printed publications generally, esp. newspapers and periodicals: *the power of the press*; *to write for, advertise in, the daily press*; *freedom, liberty, of the press*, freedom, liberty, to print and publish without a censorship, esp. a political censorship.

press (III.), vb. trans. & n. A back-formation fr. *pressed*, 'forced, compelled', wh. was confused w., & substituted for, *prest*, properly the earnest money paid to a sailor or soldier on enlistment before the time of compulsory recruiting for the fleet; *prest* or *prest-money* was also commonly used for money advanced or on loan. This is the O. Fr. *prest*, 'loan, advance', fr. *prester*, Mod. Fr. *prêter*, 'to lend', fr. Lat. *praestāre*, 'to stand before, to stand security for, to guarantee, furnish money for', fr. *prae-*, 'before', see **pre-**, & *stāre*, 'to stand', see **stand** (I.); cp. **impress** & **impressment.** **1.** vb. **a** To compel to serve, to enlist forcibly for service, in the royal navy, less usually in the army, esp. during the 18th cent. and until 1815; **b** to force into one's service, take for one's use: *to press into one's service.* **2.** n. Impressment; organized use of compulsion for enlisting recruits for the army or navy; commonly referred to as *the press.*

press-agent, n. A person who manages the newspaper advertising and publicity generally for a theatre, actor, musician &c.

press-box, n. A place reserved for reporters for the press on a cricket, football, ground &c.

press-copy, n. Copy of a letter &c. obtained by use of a copying press.

press-cutting, n. A paragraph, short notice &c. clipped from a newspaper; also press-clipping.

presser, n. [1. préser; 2. présə]. **press** (I.) & **-er.** **a** One who presses or uses a press, e.g. in glass-making, making of plates, flat dishes &c. of pottery, in the dressing and finishing of cloth &c.; **b** that part of a mechanical press &c. which exerts the pressure.

press - gallery, n. Gallery assigned to reporters and members of the press in the House of Commons.

press-gang, n. A body of men under an officer who 'pressed' or enlisted men by force for the fleet.

pressing, adj. [1. présing; 2. présiŋ], fr. Pres. Part. of **press** (I.). **1.** (of business, requests, needs &c.) Requiring immediate performance, compliance, satisfaction; urgent, exacting, important: *pressing business duties*; *a pressing invitation*, one strongly urging acceptance, cordial. **2.** (of persons) Urging requests, invitations &c. with insistence; importunate.

pressingly, adv. Prec. & **-ly.** In a pressing manner; urgently, importunately.

press-law, n. (usually pl.) Any law or body of laws governing the liberty of the press and the licensing and censorship of publications &c.

pressman, n. [1. présman; 2. présmən]. **a** Man in charge of a printing-press; **b** a journalist, a newspaper reporter.

press-mark, n. Mark, number &c. in a book or catalogue showing the press or shelf in a library where it is to be found.

press proof, n. The last revised proof of printed matter before it is sent to be printed off.

press-room, n. Room in a printing establishment in which the actual printing is carried on.

pressure, n. [1. préshur; 2. préʃə]. O. Fr., fr. Lat. *pressūra*, 'pressure, burden'. See **press** (I.) & **-ure.** **1. a** Act or process of pressing; force, constriction, bearing downwards, or exerted laterally: *the pressure of a weight*; *the pressure of a boot on one's foot*; *the pressure of a crowd*; **b** (fig.) *the pressure of business* &c. **2. a** (fig.) A state of difficulty or embarrassment; distress: *the pressure of old debts, of taxation, business*; **b** compelling force, constraint, compulsion: *the pressure of circumstances*; *to act under pressure*; *put pressure upon*; *bring pressure to bear upon* (a person). Phr. *at high pressure*, at great speed, with great vigour and energy. **3. a** (phys.) The sum of the forces exerted on its surroundings by a solid, a liquid, or a gas, expressed in pounds to the square inch or by kilogrammes to the square centimetre: *atmospheric pressure*; *a high-, low-pressure area*; **b** (mechan. &c.) the force exerted by one body on another by weight; the force, thrust, of one body against another.

pressure gauge, n. Instrument for measuring the pressure of fluids.

press-work, n. The operation of a printing press or machine, work done by the printing press &c.

prester, n. [1. préster; 2. préstə]. O. Fr. *prestre.* See **presbyter** & **priest.** A priest: *Prester John*, a legendary Christian priest and king of the Middle Ages, supposed to have reigned in Abyssinia or in various places in Asia.

prestidigitation, n. [1. prèstidijitáshun; 2. prèstidídžitéiʃən], Fr., fr. Lat. *praestō*, 'ready, quick', & *digitus*, 'finger'. See **presto** & **digit** & **-ation.** Sleight-of-hand, juggling, conjuring, legerdemain.

prestidigitator, n. [1. prèstidíjitāter; 2. prèstidídžiteitə], fr. Fr. *prestidigitateur.* See prec. & **-or.** Juggler, conjurer.

prestige, n. [1. prestḗzh; 2. prestíž]. Fr., orig. 'illusion produced by witchcraft', also formerly so used in Engl.; fr. Lat. *praestigia*, 'a juggler's trick, illusion, spell', fr. *praestringuere*, 'to bind fast, tie up; to dull the eyesight; to dazzle'. See **pre-** & **stringent.** Credit, good repute, fact of being held in high estimation, on account of recognized achievements, sterling character &c.: *the great prestige enjoyed by the Duke of Wellington made him one of the most powerful personages in Europe.*

prestissimo, adv. [1. prèstísimō; 2. prèstísimou]. Ital., superl. of **presto.** (mus.) Very quickly, as rapidly as possible.

presto, adv. & n. [1. préstō; 2. préstou]. Ital., fr. Lat. *praestō*, 'ready, at hand', dat. sing. of L. Lat. *praestus*, fr. *prae-*, see **pre-**, & base *sta-*, 'stand', as in **state, stand.** **1.** adv. (musical direction) Quickly. **2.** n. A passage to be played *presto.* Phr. *Hey presto!*, a conjurer's phrase at moment of performing a trick.

presumable, adj. [1. prezúmabl; 2. prizjúməbl]. **presume** & **-able.** To be presumed or assumed to be true without further or more direct evidence: *a presumable death, failure* or *success of plans* &c.

presumably, adv. Prec. & **-ly.** As may be presumed: *he knows, presumably, what is best for him.*

presume, vb. trans. & intrans. [1. prezúm; 2. prizjúm], fr. O. Fr. *presumer*, or direct fr. Lat. *praesūmere*, 'to take first; to presuppose, take for granted'. See **pre-** & second element in **assume, consume.** **A.** trans. **1.** To take for granted, assume something, for which there is no direct evidence, to be true, or a fact, failing proof to the contrary; to believe, infer as probable: *to presume the innocence of a prisoner, the death of a missing person*; *I am presuming what you say to be true.* **2.** To raise a (legal) presumption that: *a receipt for* *the premium on a policy presumes preceding payments.* **3.** To assume as a fact something not proved, but appearing likely to be true; hence (colloq.) to suppose, believe, imagine: *I presume from your speech that you are a foreigner.* **B.** intrans. To take too much for granted in respect of one's relations to others; to misjudge, overrate, the tolerance of another; hence, to show arrogance, or undue familiarity: *a man inclined to presume*; also *presume upon* (in various shades of meaning): *to presume upon a person's good nature, kindness,* make unreasonable, excessive claims, upon it; *to presume upon a short acquaintance,* to become unduly familiar, or impudent.

presumedly, adv. [1. prezū́medli; 2. prizjū́midli]. P.P. of prec. & **-ly**. Presumably.

presuming, adj. [1. prezū́ming; 2. prizjū́miŋ], fr. Pres. Part. of **presume**. Inclined to presume; presumptuous; pushing.

presumingly, adv. Prec. & **-ly**. In a presuming manner.

presumption, n. [1. prezúmpshun; 2. prizámpʃən]. Lat. *praesumpt-*, P.P. type of *praesūmere*. See **presume** & **-ion**. **1.** Act of presuming, or taking for granted, on evidence which makes a thing highly probable, but not absolutely certain: *presumption of death, of innocence.* **2. a** That which is presumed, or assumed, to be true, without conclusive proof: *what you say amounts to a mere presumption*; **b** grounds for presuming; likelihood, probability: *the presumption is that he will refuse*; *there is a strong presumption that he will succeed.* **3.** Act of overstepping bounds of respect, courtesy &c.; arrogant, forward behaviour, effrontery: *that he should address me at all is a great piece of presumption.*

presumptive, adj. [1. prezúmptiv; 2. prizámptiv], fr. Fr. *présomptif, -ive*, fr. L. Lat. *praesumptīvus*, fr. stem *presumpt-*, as in prec., & **-ive**. Founded on presumption or probability, not on direct proof; probable: *presumptive evidence, proof* &c. See also **heir presumptive**.

presumptively, adv. Prec. & **-ly**. By, according to, presumption; presumably.

presumptuous, adj. [1. prezúmpchoous; 2. prizámptʃuəs], fr. O. Fr. *presumtueux*, fr. L. Lat. *praesumptiōsus*, *praesumpt-*, as in **presumption**, & **-ous**. **1.** Exhibiting presumption and effrontery in behaviour; presuming. **2.** Over-confident, inclined to assume too much: *it would be presumptuous to take success for granted.*

presumptuously, adv. Prec. & **-ly**. In a presumptuous manner.

presumptuousness, n. See prec. & **-ness**. State, quality, of being presumptuous.

presuppose, vb. trans. [1. prèsupṓz; 2. prìsəpóuz], fr. Fr. *présupposer*. See **pre-** & **suppose**. **1.** To assume, suppose beforehand: *I must presuppose that you know the principal facts of the case.* **2.** To demand, require as a necessary preliminary or antecedent: *success in any career presupposes diligence and previous training.*

presupposition, n. [1. prèsupozíshun; 2. prìsapəzíʃən]. See **pre-** & **supposition**. Act of presupposing; thing, fact, presupposed or assumed beforehand; a presumption, conjecture.

pretence, n. [1. preténs; 2. priténs]. Fr., fr. L. Lat. *praetens-(um)*, for Lat. *praetent-(um)*, P.P. of *praetendere*. See **pretend**. **1.** A claim, pretension to: *to make no pretence to profound learning*; *to be full of pretences*; *there are no pretences about him.* **2.** A false, feigned, assumption of character &c.; simulation, a hypocritical show: *to make a pretence of affection*; *pretence of humility.* Phr. *under the pretence of religion,* using false show of religion as a cloak. **3. a** Act of pretending; thing done with intent to deceive or defraud; specif. (law) *false pretences,* acts of misrepresentation &c. calculated to deceive; **b** a fraud, sham, make-believe: *his illness was all a pretence.*

pretend, vb. trans. & intrans. [1. pretĕ́nd; 2. pritĕ́nd]. M.E. *pretenden*, fr. O. Fr. *pretendre*, fr. Lat. *praetendere*, 'to hold, spread out before; to allege as an excuse, pretend'. See **pre-** & **tend (II.)**. (Used by Spenser in etymological sense 'hold in front of'; '*Who . . . his target always over her pretended*' ('F. Q.' vi. 11. 19)). **A.** trans. **1.** To put forward, assert, allege, as excuse or pretext: *to pretend illness as a reason for his absence.* **2.** To feign falsely, to simulate: *he is merely pretending affection*; *to pretend that one is ill.* **B.** intrans. **1.** To make, put forward, a claim to, cherish pretensions to: *to pretend to the Crown*; *to pretend to great learning*; *to pretend to the hand of a lady in marriage.* **2. a** To feign, profess falsely: to assume, put on, a false appearance of being: *to pretend to be asleep*; *to pretend to be better than one is*; **b** (in innocent sense) to play at being, to make believe: *let's pretend to be robbers.*

pretended, adj. [1. pretĕ́nded; 2. pritĕ́ndid]. P.P. of prec. False, feigned, unreal: *pretended piety*; *a pretended admirer.*

pretendedly, adv. Prec. & **-ly**. With pretence, by false representations; falsely.

pretender, n. [1. pretĕ́nder; 2. pritĕ́ndə]. **pretend** & **-er**. One who pretends, or makes a claim to; a claimant; esp. a *Pretender to a throne*; specif., *the Old Pretender*, the Chevalier de St. George, the eldest son of James II.; *the Young Pretender*, Prince Charles Edward, his son.

pretension, n. [1. preténshun; 2. priténʃən]. As if fr. a Lat. **praetensiōn-(em)*, cp. Fr. *prétention*. See **pretence** & **pretend** & **-ion**. **1.** A claim, assertion of a claim to: *no pretensions to be a gentleman*; *to have pretensions to a lady's hand.* **2.** False representation, show, pretence: *pretensions of religion.*

pretentious, adj. [1. preténshus; 2. priténʃəs], fr. Fr. *prétentieux*. See prec. & **-ous**. Making great pretensions, assuming great merit or importance; ostentatious: *a pretentious person, manner, book, house* &c.

pretentiously, adv. Prec. & **-ly**. In a pretentious way or manner; ostentatiously.

pretentiousness, n. See prec. & **-ness**. State, quality, of being pretentious.

preter-, pref., fr. Lat. *praeter*, 'beyond, before, above, more than' &c.; in compounds, 'past, by, beyond, besides'; e.g. *praeterdūcere*, 'to lead past'; *praeterīre*, 'to go beyond'; *praetermittere*, 'to let go by; overlook'.

preterhuman, adj. [1. prḗterhū́man; 2. prītəhjū́mən]. **preter-** & **human**. Beyond what is human; superhuman.

preterite, adj. & n. [1. prḗterit; 2. prétərit]. Lat. *praeteritus*, 'past', P.P. of *praeterīre*, 'to go past, beyond'. See prec. & **iteration**, **itinerate** &c. (gram.) **1.** adj. (of the sense of a vb.) Expressing past action. *Preterite Present verb,* any one of group of Gmc. strong verbs, whose Pres. tenses were lost in the Prim. Gmc. period, the Pret. then acquiring a Pres. sense, and a new weak Pret. being formed; e.g. *can, may, shall.* **2.** n. The preterite tense.

preterition, n. [1. prèteríshun; 2. prìtəríʃən], fr. L. Lat. *praeteritiōn-(em)*, 'a passing over'. See prec. & **-ion**. A passing over, omission, disregard; esp. (theol.) the passing over, or disregarding by God, of those who are not of the elect, and are therefore left to eternal perdition.

pretermission, n. [1. prètermíshun; 2. prìtəmíʃən], fr. Lat. *praetermissiōn-(em)*, 'omission, passing over'. See **preter-** & **mission**; also **pretermit**. A passing by; omission, neglect: *pretermission of duty.*

pretermit, vb. trans. [1. prètermít; 2. prìtəmít]. Lat. *praetermittere*, 'to let go by; omit'. See **preter-** & the base of **mission**. To omit, neglect to do; to cease doing, to break off, interrupt: *to pretermit a course of studies.*

preternatural, adj. [1. prḗternáchural; 2. prītənǽtʃərəl]. See **preter-** & **natural**. Beyond what is natural; supernatural.

pretext, n. [1. prḗtekst; 2. prítekst], fr. Fr. *prétexte*, fr. Lat. *praetext-(um)*, P.P. of *praetexere*, 'to weave in front, to put a fringe or border to; to allege as an excuse or pretext'. See **pre-** & **text**. Something alleged as a reason for the performance, or non-performance of an action; a reason, motive, put forward to conceal the real one; an excuse.

pretonic, adj. [1. prḗtónik; 2. prìtónik]. **pre-** & **tonic (I.)**. (philol., of a sound, syllable) Occurring immediately before a stressed vowel or syllable.

pretor, n. See **praetor**.

prettify, vb. trans. [1. prítifī; 2. prítifai]. **pretty** & **-fy**. To render pretty; to adorn, trick out, in a trifling, superficially attractive way.

prettily, adv. [1. prítili; 2. prítili]. **pretty** & **-ly**. In a pretty manner; attractively; so as to please the mind or senses; charmingly: *to dress, speak, sing, behave prettily.*

prettiness, n. [1. prítines; 2. prítinis]. **pretty** & **-ness**. **a** State, quality, of being pretty; a charming, if slightly trivial, personal beauty; **b** attractiveness, facile charm appealing to the eye or ear: *his painting, verses, have a certain prettiness, but not the majesty of the great masters.*

pretty (I.), adj. [1. príti; 2. príti, prúti]. M.E. *prati, praty*, 'clever, attractive', O.E. *præt(t)ig*, 'tricky, cunning', fr. *prætt*, 'trick', cogn. w. E. Fris. *prettig*, 'droll, pleasant', *pret*, 'a trick', O.N. *prettugr*, 'tricky', *prettr*, 'trick'; M. Du. *pratte*, Mod. Du. *prettig*, 'sportive', *part*, 'trick, joke'; ultimate origin uncertain. **1.** Daintily, but somewhat superficially and trivially, attractive, or charming, in appearance, manner, style &c.; esp. applied to small things; as contrasted with *beautiful* or *handsome*: *a pretty house, face, girl, child, voice, song, view* &c.; *pretty ways,* engaging airs. **2.** Affectedly charming, effeminate, foppish: *pretty young gentleman*; *a pretty boy.* **3.** Fine, good, neat, stylish; excellent of its kind: *a pretty wit*; *a pretty stroke,* at cricket, golf &c.; (often ironical) *a pretty muddle, state of affairs* &c.; *a pretty way to behave*; Phr. *a pretty kettle of fish,* a muddle, confused state of affairs. **4.** (colloq.) Large, considerable in amount or extent: *made a pretty pot of money*; *it costs a pretty penny.* **5.** (ellipt. as n.) **a** *My pretty (one),* my darling, pet; **b** (pl.) pretty things, dresses &c.: *she has put on all her pretties.*

pretty (II.), adv., fr. prec. **1.** To some extent; moderately, fairly, not very: *to feel only pretty well, only pretty good.* **2.** As litotes, with an intensive force, to a considerable extent, to a high degree, considerably, very: *to speak pretty strongly*; *to feel pretty sick*; *I hope you are feeling pretty well*; *to be pretty sick about it,* extremely disgusted. Phr. *pretty much,* very much, to a great extent: *to do pretty much as one likes.*

pretty (III.), n., fr. **pretty (I.)**. The engraved or fluted part of a tumbler. Phr. *up to the pretty,* to the top of the pretty, about one third up.

prettyish, adj. [1. prítiish; 2. prítiiʃ]. **pretty (I.)** & **-ish**. Rather pretty.

pretty-pretty, adj. & n. [1. príti prìti; 2. príti prìti]. **a** adj. Merely pretty or superficially charming; affectedly charming; finicking, namby-pamby: *her affected, pretty-pretty ways*; *just a pretty-pretty face*; **b** n., knick-knacks, trifling ornaments, fluffy, fussy articles of dress &c.: *wearing all her pretty-pretties.*

preux chevalier, n. [1. prḗ shevȧ́hliā; 2. prø ʃəvalje]. Fr. A brave, gallant knight.

prevail, vb. intrans. [1. prevā́l; 2. privéil]. O. Fr., fr. *prevaloir*, fr. Lat. *praevalēre*, 'to have greater power or value, to prevail'. See **pre-** & **valiant**. **1.** To gain the mastery, victory, or advantage; to triumph, be victorious: *truth is great and will prevail*; *it is to be hoped that wiser counsels will prevail*; also *prevail over,* to get the upper hand of, triumph over: *skill often prevails over brute strength.* **2.** To exist, be current, to be prevalent; to be in use, be habitual: *excessive drinking no longer prevails as a common practice; regular attendance at the parish church still prevails in many country places.* **3.** *Prevail on, upon,* to persuade, overcome reluctance of, succeed in inducing: *can't I prevail upon you to have another helping of pie?*

prevailing, vbl. adj. [1. prevāling; 2. privéiliŋ], fr. Pres. Part. of prec. Prevalent, most usual, customary or general: *the prevailing fashions; a prevailing opinion, epidemic &c.; the prevailing wind at this time of year is south.*

prevailingly, adv. Prec. & **-ly.** To a prevailing degree; prevalently.

prevalence, n. [1. prévalens; 2. prévələns]. **prevalent & -ce.** **a** Condition, fact, of being prevalent; common occurrence; widespread existence: *prevalence of disease, of rumours;* **b** frequency, currency, as a habit: *the prevalence of short hair among women.*

prevalent, adj. [1. prévalent; 2. prévələnt], fr. Lat. *praevalent-(em),* Pres. Part. of *praevalēre.* See **prevail.** **a** Commonly received, in vogue: *prevalent fashions, phrase;* **b** widely practised: *prevalent habits;* **c** existing as common fact; **d** widely current, rife: *measles and whooping-cough are very prevalent just now; disorder is prevalent in many parts of the country.*

prevalently, adv. Prec. & **-ly.** In a prevalent manner (in all senses of prec.).

prevaricate, vb. intrans. [1. prevárikāt; 2. privǽrikeit], fr. Lat. *praevāricāt-(um),* P.P. of *praevāricāri,* 'to walk with the legs apart, straddle, to walk crookedly, not to be upright in dealings, act in collusion with'. See **pre-** & **varix.** To make an evasive, equivocal answer or statement; to attempt to disguise, or conceal the truth; to shuffle, quibble.

prevarication, n. [1. prevàrikáshun; 2. privæ̀rikéiʃən], fr. Lat. *praevāricātiōn-(em),* 'crooked going; departure from duty'. Prec. & **-ion.** An evasive, equivocal answer or statement; quibble, shuffle, equivocation.

prevaricator, n. [1. prevárikāter; 2. privǽrikeitə], fr. Lat. *praevāricātor,* 'one who walks crookedly; one who departs from duty'. **prevaricate & -or.** A quibbler, shuffler.

prevenient, adj. [1. prevḗnient; 2. privíniənt], fr. Lat. *praevenient-(em),* Pres. Part. of *praevenire.* See **prevent.** Going before, preceding; preventive; esp. (theol.) *prevenient grace,* the Grace of God which operates on the soul and predisposes it to repentance; cp. Milton, 'P. L.' xi. 3.

prevent, vb. trans. [1. prevént; 2. privént], fr. Lat. *praevent-(um),* P.P. of *praevenire,* 'to go, come before, get the start of, anticipate'; see **pre-** & base **gʷem-* under **come,** cp. **venue.** **1.** (archaic and rare) To go before, precede, esp. as a guide, provider, or guard: *'Prevent us, O Lord, in all our doings'* (Book of Common Prayer). **2.** To go before and block the way, stop; hence, **a** (in favourable sense) to guard against, preserve, keep safe from: *to prevent a disaster, a row; to prevent a man from injuring himself; to prevent the spread of disease;* **b** (in unfavourable sense) to hinder, thwart, put out of one's power to do; to impede: *to prevent a child from playing; to prevent progress; my cold prevents me from going out; nothing shall prevent me from doing my duty.*

preventability, n. [1. prevèntabíliti; 2. privèntəbíliti]. Next word & **-ity.** State, quality, of being preventable; capability of being prevented: *the preventability of disease.*

preventable, preventible, adj. [1. preventabl; 2. privéntəbl]. **prevent & -able, -ible.** Capable of being prevented.

preventative, adj. & n. [1. preventativ; 2. privéntətiv]. Variant of **preventive.** **a** adj. Tending to prevent, serving to guard against; **b** n., something, circumstance, or substance, which preserves from harm, disease, decay &c.

preventer, n. [1. prevénter; 2. privéntə]. **prevent & -er.** **a** One who, thing which, prevents or hinders; **b** specif. (naut.) an additional, temporary stay, rope, bolt &c.

prevention, n. [1. prevénshun; 2. privénʃən]. **prevent & -ion.** **a** Act or process of preventing, of preserving against, checking &c.: *the prevention of crime;* Phr. *prevention is better than cure;* **b** something which prevents; a preventive, preservative: *education often serves as a prevention against crime.*

preventive, adj. & n. [1. prevéntiv; 2. privéntiv]. **prevent & -ive.** **1.** adj. Serving to prevent, to keep off, ward off: *preventive medicine,* branch of medicine directed towards preventing the occurrence of disease, contrasted with the attempt to cure disease which has already developed; prophylaxis, prophylactic medicine; *preventive service, preventive officer* &c., coast-guard service, officer &c., as used for prevention of smuggling. **2.** n. **a** Medicinal substance, mode of treatment, which prevents the incidence of disease, crime &c.; **b** a coast-guard.

preventively, adv. Prec. & **-ly.** By way of prevention; as a preventive.

previous (I.), adj. [1. prḗvius; 2. príviəs], fr. Lat. *praevius,* 'going before, leading the way, on the way before'. See **pre-** & **via (I.).** **1.** Occurring earlier in time or order; prior, preceding, antecedent: *a previous illness; a previous marriage; on the previous page. Previous examination,* at Cambridge University, the first public examination for the B.A. degree, *Little-go.* Phr. *to move the previous question,* (parl. procedure) device for stopping a debate, amounting to a motion that the main question be not voted on. **2.** (colloq.) Too hasty, anticipating: *to be rather previous; to be a bit too previous for one.*

previous (II.), adv., fr. prec. *Previous to,* before: *he died previous to my arrival.*

previously, adv. [1. prḗviusli; 2. príviəsli]. **previous (I.) & -ly.** In time previous; before, beforehand.

previousness, n. [1. prḗviusnes; 2. príviəsnis]. See prec. & **-ness.** Quality of being previous; untimeliness, over-hasty action.

previse, vb. trans. [1. prēvíz; 2. priváiz], fr. Lat. *praevīs-(um),* P.P. of *praevidēre,* 'to foresee'. See **pre-** & **vision.** (rare) To forecast, foretell; warn.

prevision, n. [1. prēvízhun; 2. privížən]. As **pre-** & **vision.** Foresight, foreknowledge, prescience.

previsional, adj. [1. prēvízhunal; 2. privížənəl]. Prec. & **-al.** Foreseeing, prescient, anticipating; foreseen, anticipated.

previsionally, adv. Prec. & **-ly.** With foresight, prescience.

prey (I.), n. [1. prā; 2. prei]. M.E. *preie, preye,* fr. O. Fr. *praie, preie,* fr. Lat. *praeda,* 'booty, plunder'; prob. fr. **praeheda,* see **pre-** & form of base **hend-,* 'to seize', see **prehensile.** **1.** (archaic and Bib.) Booty, spoil, plunder: *'They brought the captives, and the prey, and the spoil, unto Moses'* (Num. xxxi. 12). **2.** **a** An animal hunted and seized for food by another animal: *the lion roaring after his prey; a bird, beast, of prey,* a predatory, carnivorous bird or beast; **b** (fig.) a person who becomes the victim of another, or to illness, misfortune &c.: *he fell an easy prey to sharks and swindlers, a prey to circumstances, passion &c.; a prey to disease, malaria, to misery, despondency, fears &c.*

prey (II.), vb. intrans., fr. O. Fr. *preer, preier,* fr. L. Lat. *praedāre,* class. Lat. *praedāri,* 'to plunder, spoil, prey upon'. See prec. Generally *prey upon:* **1.** (of animals) to take as a natural prey: *cats prey upon mice;* **b** (fig.) to swindle, fleece, rook: *there are plenty of rogues ready to prey upon the credulous.* **2.** **a** To plunder, mulct, despoil: *bands of armed robbers preyed upon the defenceless villages;* **b** to sponge upon, batten on, live on: *a despicable fellow who lives by preying on his relations.* **3.** (of sorrow, care &c.) To depress, damp; weigh upon, wear out: *remorse preyed upon his mind.*

priapism, n. [1. príapizm; 2. práiəpizəm], fr. L. Lat. *priāpismus,* fr. Gk. *priāpismós,* fr. *Príāpos,* the country god of gardens, flocks &c., and of fertility and procreation, & **-ism.** **a** Lewdness, lustfulness; **b** (med.) persistent, morbid, and excessive sexual excitement.

price (I.), n. [1. prīs; 2. prais]. M.E., fr. O. Fr. *pris,* fr. Lat. *pretium;* formed fr. adj. **pretios,* fr. prep. **preti,* 'over, against, opposite to, towards', cogn. w. Gk. *proti, prós,* 'towards, against'; also Scrt. *práti,* 'towards'; Lett. *prett,* 'against'. The starting-point of meaning is 'one thing put against another', hence 'equivalent'. Cp. also **precious.** **1.** **a** Amount of money demanded or paid for anything; cost; Phrs. *to put a price on the head of,* to offer a reward for the death or capture of; *every man has his price,* every man can be bought or bribed by some inducement or other; **b** (fig.) cost in other than monetary values; sacrifice, expenditure of labour, life, thought &c., necessary in order to obtain something: *such losses were too high a price to pay for victory; a life of ceaseless toil is generally the price of fame and success.* **2.** Value, worth: *a pearl of great price.* Phr. *beyond, above, price,* not to be valued, invaluable, priceless. **3.** (betting) Odds; *starting-price,* the final odds offered by the bookmakers at the start of a race; *a long, short, price,* rate of odds laid. Phr. *what price (the favourite)?,* at what odds is the favourite (horse)?; so (colloq.) what chance is there for?: *what price fine weather tomorrow?*

price (II.), vb. trans., fr. prec. To ask, fix, the price of anything; to set a price on, to value.

priced, adj. [1. prīst; 2. praist], fr. prec. **1.** Having the price fixed and indicated: *every article is plainly priced.* **2.** Valued at, costing, a specified price; in compounds: *low-priced, high-priced &c.*

priceless, adj. [1. prísles; 2. práislis]. **price (I.) & -less.** **1.** Without, beyond, price; invaluable, inestimable: *priceless jewels; priceless services to his country.* **2.** (slang) A vague intensive, either expressing satisfaction: *a perfectly priceless evening; a priceless person;* or derisive: *the cut of his clothes is simply priceless; it's absolutely priceless to hear them abusing each other.*

pricelessness, n. Prec. & **-ness.** State, quality, of being priceless.

price list, n. List of current prices; catalogue of goods offered for sale, with prices set out.

prick (I.), n. [1. prik; 2. prik]. O.E. *prica, pricu,* 'point, dot', M.E. *pricke* &c.; cp. L.G. *prik,* 'dot', M. Du. *prick,* 'prickle' &c. **1.** Any fine, sharp-pointed object capable of piercing, e.g. a goad, prickle of a thorn: *roses are full of pricks.* Phr. *to kick against the pricks,* to offer useless resistance and cause oneself the maximum of trouble or injury. **2.** **a** Wound, puncture, inflicted by a point or prick: *a prick in the finger;* also slight wound from a sword &c.; **b** sensation of pain caused by or resembling that caused by a prick: *to feel a slight prick* (from a needle &c.); **c** (fig.) a moral uneasiness or qualm: *the prick of conscience.* **3.** (obs.) A dot, mark, as of a prick or puncture (in various senses); e.g. **a** the mark on the face of a clock or watch indicating the time; **b** a musical note as written in *prick-song,* q.v.

prick (II.), vb. trans. & intrans. O.E. *prician,* fr. prec. **A.** trans. **1.** **a** To pierce, stab, slightly with a sharp, fine instrument or object, as a pin, thorn &c.: *to prick one's finger;* **b** (fig.) to cause a sharp, mental pain to, as from remorse: *my conscience pricked me.* **2.** **a** To make by use of pointed instrument: *to prick holes in the ground* (for young plants); **b** *to prick out, in,* to plant out young plants in holes which have been pricked. **3.** (archaic) To urge on (horse) by use of spur. **4.** *To prick the ears,* to raise them, cause them to become erect and point upwards, as dogs do when listening. Phr. *to prick up one's ears,* to become suddenly attentive to what is said. **B.** intrans. **1. a** To cause a wound by pricking; to cause the sharp, slight pain of a prick: *the thorns of roses prick rather badly*; **b** to cause sensation of pain resembling pricking: *my toe is pricking with the gout.* **2.** (archaic) To urge on horse with the spur, hence to ride, ride forward: '*They spyed a knight fair pricking on the plain*' (Spenser, 'F. Q.' iii. 8. 44); also *to prick on, forward.* **3.** (of dog's ears) To assume an erect position.

prick-eared, adj. **a** Having ears constantly erect, or pricked; **b** applied by the Cavaliers as term of contempt for the Roundheads, because of their cropped hair which exposed their ears and caused them to appear prominently.

pricker, n. [1. príker; 2. príkə]. **prick (II.)** & **-er.** Person who, thing which, pricks; specif. **a** a pricking implement, as a bodkin, bradawl &c.; **b** (obs.) a horseman who 'pricks on', rides in front &c.

pricket, n. [1. príket; 2. príkit]. **prick (I.)** & **-et. 1.** A buck, male of the fallow deer, in his second year, having straight antlers without tines or branches, cp. *brocket*, of similar stag. **2.** A primitive, early form of candlestick, with small spike on which the candle was fixed.

pricking, n. [1. príking; 2. príkiŋ]. Vbl. n., fr. **prick (II.)**. Act, process, of pricking; puncture or sensation caused by this.

prickle, n. & vb. trans. & intrans. [1. príkl; 2. príkl]. O.E. *pricel, pricle*, M.E. *prikil*, fr. **prick (I.)** & dimin. **-le. A.** n. **1.** A small, sharply pointed process or growth on the outer skin of a plant or tree, as of thistles, gorse, the acacia tree &c.; a small thorn; a spine of a hedgehog, stickleback, or other animal. **2.** A prickling or pricking sensation of the skin. **3.** (possibly a different word, etymol. unknown) A small basket made of willow twigs, used as a measure of weight. **B.** vb. **a** trans. To prick, as with a prickle: *prickling thorns*; **b** intrans., to feel the sensation of being prickled; to feel prickly: *the skin prickles.*

prickly, adj. [1. príkli; 2. príkli]. Prec. & **-y. 1.** Full of, covered with, prickles; inclined to prick: *a prickly nettle, gorse bush* &c.; also in name of many plants, *prickly ash, elder* &c. **2.** Tingling as though from being pricked: *a prickly feeling, sensation* &c.

prickly heat, n. Slight skin eruption caused by the inflammation of the sweat glands in intense heat, accompanied by great itching and prickling.

prickly pear, n. The edible fruit of a cactus of genus *Opuntia*.

prick-song, n. (archaic or obs.) **a** Music written down by means of pricks or dots; **b** specif., early counterpoint as pricked or noted above the plain-song.

pride (I.), n. [1. prīd; 2. praid], fr. O.E. type *prȳde*, M.E. *prīde*, formed fr. base *prūd*. See **proud. 1. a** Overweening sense of one's own moral or intellectual merit and worth; exaggerated self-esteem, and consciousness of, and satisfaction in, any quality or possession belonging to, or associated with, oneself; vainglory, haughtiness, arrogance; self-righteousness: *by pride the angels fell*; *the pride that apes humility*; *pride of birth, of position, of intellect* &c.; Phr. *pride goes before a fall*; **b** exhibition of these qualities in bearing and behaviour &c.: '*Pride in their port, defiance in their eye*' (Goldsmith, 'Traveller', 357). **2.** Legitimate sense of one's own personal worth and dignity, and of what becomes one's position in life; a high sense of self-respect; loftiness of character and sentiment which is repelled by what is base and mean: *a proper pride*; *a noble pride which scorns to cringe to power.* **3. a** Sentiment of satisfaction and complacency inspired by consciousness of one's own success and achievements, or by whatever is the result of one's own efforts, skill, talents &c.; feeling of pleasure arising from the merits and achievements of others, esp. of those closely related to one: *to feel pride at one's promotion*; *to take a pride in one's work*; *to take a pride in one's appearance, in being neat*; *to feel a natural pride in one's son's fine record*; *to feel pride in one's country's victory*; *no Englishman can read the life of Nelson without a glow of pride*; **b** the object of such a feeling of pride: *he was the joy and pride of his parents.* **4. a** Splendour, pomp, bravery; beauty, radiance: '*like to Flora in her morning pride*' (Marlowe, 1. Tamb. v. 1); *the summer's pride*; **b** exuberance of health and vigour; prime, flower: *in the pride of one's youth*; *in the full pride of harvest.* **5.** *Pride of a peacock*, fully spread tail; specif. (her.) *a peacock in his pride*, with wings and tail expanded. **6. a** Band, troop, of certain animals: *a pride of lions*; **b** a flock: *a pride of peacocks.*

pride (II.), vb., fr. prec. (only reflex.) *Pride oneself (on)*; **a** to be proud of, to take a pride in: *to pride oneself on one's good looks, on one's horsemanship, on one's garden* &c.; **b** to claim to be or to have, to take credit for: *to pride oneself on being the best shot in the county, on being able to grow roses, on being always punctual, on having a good seat on a horse.*

prideful, adj. [1. prídfool; 2. práidful]. **pride (I.)** & **-ful.** (provinc. or poet.) Haughty, disdainful.

prie-dieu, n. [1. prḗ dyë; 2. prí djø]. Fr., lit. 'pray God'. A low desk with a shelf for a book, at which to kneel at prayers.

priest (I.), n. [1. prēst; 2. prīst]. O.E. *prēost*, M.E. *prēst*; O.S. *prēstar*, O.H.G. *priestar*; early loan-word fr. Lat. **presbyter. 1.** (in pre-Christian and non-Christian religions) One who, by virtue of his office, performs sacred rites, ceremonies, and sacrifices, and acts as the representative of the people in their relation to the God whom they worship; used to translate Gk. *hiereús*, see **hierarch**, Lat. *sacerdos*, see **sacerdotal** & Heb. *kōhēn*. **2.** (in Christianity) **a** (Primitive Church) An elder or presbyter; **b** (in Episcopal churches) one who has been ordained to the second of the Holy Orders, next below a bishop and above a deacon, and authorized to administer the Sacraments, esp. the Eucharist and Absolution; **c** (in Ireland) the word usually means specifically a Roman Catholic priest, in current usage. **3.** A small club or mallet used to kill large fish when caught and before landing.

priest (II.), vb. trans., fr. prec. To ordain as priest; to make a deacon a priest; chiefly in Pass. in Phr. *to be priested.*

priestcraft, n. [1. prḗstkrahft; 2. prístkrāft]. **priest (I.)** & **craft.** Policy of a priest or of a priesthood, esp. when regarded as designed to get control of, and authority over, matters outside the proper sphere of religion; priestly interference in worldly affairs.

priestess, n. [1. prḗstes; 2. prístis, -ɛs]. **priest** & **-ess.** A woman priest, a woman hierophant.

priest-fish, n. Popular name of a black Californian rock-fish.

priesthood, n. [1. prḗst-hood; 2. prísthud]. **priest (I.)** & **-hood. 1.** The second Holy Order, that to which priests belong; the status, rank, of a priest. **2.** Priests collectively.

priestlike, adj. **priest (I.)** & **-like.** **a** Resembling a priest in character; priestly; **b** pertaining, suitable, to a priest: '*The moving waters at their priestlike task Of pure ablution*' &c. (Keats, last sonnet).

priestliness, n. [1. prḗstlines; 2. prístlinis]. See next word & **-ness.** State, quality, of being priestly; character or conduct of a priest.

priestly, adj. [1. prḗstli; 2. prístli]. **priest (I.)** & **-ly.** Pertaining to, befitting the character of, a priest: *a priestly blessing*; *priestly vestments*; *priestly behaviour*; *the Priestly Code*, certain parts of the first four books of the Pentateuch and of Joshua, which contain ceremonial rites, legal regulations, statistical details &c.; it is marked by a formal style.

priest-ridden, adj. Ruled, controlled, by priests.

priest's chamber, hole, n. A secret chamber in a house where Roman Catholic priests hid during times of persecution.

priest's hood, n. Popular name of the wild arum.

priest vicar, n. Title of minor canon in certain cathedrals.

prig (I.), n. [1. prig; 2. prig]. Etymol. doubtful. One who is very prim and precise, in manner, voice &c.; a conceited pedant or precisian; a person who is perfectly satisfied with his own mental or moral superiority and anxious to impress it on others.

prig (II.), vb. trans. & n. Etymol. uncertain; perh. a variant of **prick (II.)** 'to ride away hastily', used first of horse-stealers. **a** vb. (slang) To steal; to pinch; **b** n., a thief, pickpocket.

priggery, n. [1. prígeri; 2. prígəri]. **prig (I.)** & **-ery.** Priggishness.

priggish, adj. [1. prígish; 2. prígiʃ]. **prig (I.)** & **-ish. a** Like a prig; having the manner and characteristics of a prig; **b** characteristic of a prig.

priggishly, adv. Prec. & **-ly.** In a priggish manner.

priggishness, n. See prec. & **-ness. a** Character, manner, behaviour, of a prig; **b** priggish action or conduct.

prill, n. [1. pril; 2. pril]. Etymol. unknown. (min. and metal.) The better portion of ore after the dross has been removed; the button of metal from an assay.

prim, adj. & vb. trans. [1. prim; 2. prim]. Etymol. dubious; orig. a slang word; possibly fr. O. Fr. *prim, prime*, 'fine, delicate, thin', lit. 'first', fr. Lat. *primus*, 'first'. See **prime (I.). 1.** adj. **a** Neat and precise; stiffly formal; pedantically correct; **b** easily shocked. Phr. *prim and proper.* **2.** vb. To purse, arrange, form into a prim shape: *to prim one's lips.*

primacy, n. [1. prímasi; 2. práiməsi], fr. O. Fr. *primacie*, fr. Med. Lat. *prīmatia*. See **primate** & **-cy. 1.** The state, quality, of being the first; supremacy, pre-eminence; the prime or first position or rank. **2.** The office, rank, dignity, of a primate.

prima donna, n. [1. prḗma dóna; 2. prímə dónə]. Ital., 'first lady'. The principal, leading, woman singer in an opera.

prim(a)eval, adj. [1. prīmḗval; 2. praimív(ə)l], fr. Lat. *prīmaevus*, fr. *prīmus*, 'first', see **prime (I.)** & *aevum*, 'age', see **age**, & **-al.** Belonging to the early, first, ages of the world; prehistoric, primitive; very ancient.

prim(a)evally, adv. Prec. & **-ly.** In a primaeval time or period; prehistorically.

prima facie, adv. & adj. [1. prīma fáshiē; 2. práimə féiʃiī]. Lat., abl. sing. of *prīmus*, 'first', & *facies*, 'appearance'. See **prime (I.)** & **face.** On the face of it, on the first appearance, at first sight, on the first impression: *a prima facie case*, a case which at first sight seems to be true; or (in law) one which is sufficiently clear to be sent to the jury; *prima facie evidence*, evidence which until proved to be untrue is not inconsistent with the presumptions or probabilities of the case.

primage (I.), n. [1. prímij; 2. práimidž]. Fr., fr. Med. Lat. *primāgium*, etymol. doubtful; possibly connected w. Lat. *praemium*. See **premium.** A small additional percentage added to, included in, the freight paid to the owner by shippers, formerly a gratuity paid by shippers to the master for his care on the voyage.

primage (II.), n. **prime (III.)** & **-age.** The water from a steam-boiler carried off in steam.

primal, adj. [1. prímal; 2. práiməl], fr. Med. Lat. *prīmālis*. See **prime (I.)** & **-al.** Primary, first in time, original, chief in importance; primaeval, primitive.

primarily, adv. [1. prímarili; 2. práimərili]. **primary** & **-ly.** In the first place; originally.

primary (I.), adj. [1. prímari; 2. práimәri], fr. Lat. *prīmārius*, 'of the first rank, principal, chief'. See **prime** (I.) & **-ary**. **1.** First in order of time; **a** (geol.) primitive, primaeval: *primary rocks*, the lowest, palaeozoic rocks; **b** *primary organization, institutions* (of society &c.); *primary instincts* &c. **2.** Not derived; original, elemental: *primary colours*, such as red, blue, yellow, from which other colours can be derived by mixture; *primary meaning* (of words); *primary vocal sounds*; *primary tenses*, present, future, and perfect or preterite tenses. **3.** Preparatory, elementary, as contrasted with *secondary*: *primary school, primary education*, in or by which children are taught the elements of knowledge; esp. of schools and education at which attendance is compulsory; *a primary meeting, assembly*, see **primary**, n. **4.** (elect.) Producing electrical current: *primary battery*, as distinguished from a secondary or storage battery. **5.** First in importance, chief, principal: *a matter of primary importance*; *the primary planets*, those that revolve round the sun, as distinguished from satellites, as the moon &c.

primary (II.), n., fr. prec. **1.** That which stands first in importance, quality. Specific uses: **2.** (U.S.A.) a primary meeting or assembly, the meeting of electors before an election to choose and nominate candidates. **3.** (astron.) A primary planet; the brighter star of a double star. **4.** (zool., pl.) The largest quill feathers of a bird's wing, attached to the part corresponding to the hand.

primate, n. [1. prímit; 2. práimit], fr. Fr. *primat*, fr. L. Lat. *prīmāt-(em)*, adj., 'one of the first, chief, principal', fr. *prīmus*, 'first'. See **prime** (I.) & cp. **primus**. An archbishop: *Primate of all England*, the Archbishop of Canterbury; *Primate of England*, the Archbishop of York; *Primate of Ireland*, Archbishop of Armagh.

primates, n. pl. [1. prīmā́tēz; 2. praiméitīz]. Lat. Same as prec. (zool.) The highest order of mammals, including man and the apes, monkeys and lemurs.

primateship, n. [1. prímitship; 2. práimitʃip]. **primate** & **-ship**. The office, rank, of a primate or archbishop; the primacy.

primatial, adj. [1. prīmā́shal; 2. praiméiʃәl]. **primate** & **-ial**. Of, pertaining to, a primate.

prime (I.), adj. [1. prīm; 2. praim], fr. Lat. *prīmus*, 'first', for earlier **prismus*, see **pristine**, or old superl. of *prior*, 'former, previous', see **prior** (I.); ultimately connected w. Lat. *prae*, 'before', see **pre-**. **1.** First in order of time: *the prime cause.* **2.** First in rank, chief, most important: *of prime importance*; *the prime factor*, motive &c.; *a prime favourite.* **3.** Of the finest quality, of highest excellence; first-rate: *in prime condition*; *prime beef*; *a prime joint, cut of meat*; *to feel prime.* **4.** Primary, principal, elemental, fundamental; initial; specific uses: **a** (astron.) *prime meridian*, a meridian from which longitude is measured, as that of Greenwich; *prime vertical*, the vertical circle which cuts the E. and W. points of the horizon; **b** (commerc.) *prime cost*, the initial cost of production of a commodity without calculating overhead charges or margin for profit; **c** (math.) *prime number*, a number, such as 1, 2, 3, 5, 7, 11, which is only divisible by itself; **d** (mechan.) *prime mover*, a primary source of motive power, natural or mechanical, as wind, water, human or animal muscles, electricity &c., or an engine which applies and transmits the force of a natural mover by means of other machinery.

prime (II.), n. See prec. In O.E. *prīm*, 'prime, a canonical hour', fr. Eccles. Lat. *prīma (hora)*, 'first hour'. **1. a** The beginning, earliest and best period; the blooming time: *in the prime of the year*; **b** the period of greatest strength and vigour, full maturity, before the decline of life: *the prime of life, manhood* &c.; *cut off in his prime.* **2.** (eccles.) **a** The first of the canonical hours, 6 A.M., following lauds; **b** service said at this hour. **3.** (in various applications) That which is primary, initial &c., as **a** a prime number; **b** the first guard in fencing; **c** a mark (′) indicating a primary unit of measure, as an inch or a minute.

prime (III.), vb. trans. & intrans. As **prime** (I.); the connexion in meaning is not clear. **A.** trans. **1.** To charge, fill, equip, furnish; **a** to supply a fire-arm, mine &c. with an explosive charge or priming; **b** (fig., colloq.) to supply, fill up, with food or drink: *well primed with a hearty meal*; Phr. *well primed*, intoxicated; **c** to lay the first coat of colour or a preparatory coating of size &c. on. **2.** (of mental process) To furnish with information in advance, instruct, post up: *to prime a witness*; *fully primed with the latest news.* **3.** (in various mechan. uses) **a** To charge, impregnate, the steam in a cylinder with water by spraying; **b** to pour a small quantity of petrol into the cylinder of an internal combustion engine, to clear clogging from thickened oil and let the piston move easily. **B.** intrans. **a** To serve as priming for a fire-arm &c.; **b** (of water) to be carried over as spray and mixed with steam in the cylinder of a boiler.

primely, adv. [1. prímli; 2. práimli]. **prime** (I.) & **-ly**. In a prime, first-rate, way or manner; excellently.

prime minister, n. Chief executive minister of state; chief minister of the Crown; premier.

primeness, n. [1. prímnes; 2. práimnis]. **prime** (I.) & **-ness**. First-rate condition.

primer (I.), n. [1. prímer, prímer; 2. práimә, prímә]. Lat. *prīmārius*, adj., 'primary, first'. See **primary**. **1.** A book of hours, containing also Psalms, the Litany &c., for the use of laymen, before the Reformation; later a book containing the Catechism, Commandments, Lord's Prayer &c. for instructional purposes, containing also the Calendar &c., and often the alphabet. **2.** An elementary manual, a first teaching or reading book: *a Latin Primer.* **3** (typog.) [1. prímer; 2. prímә]. One of two sizes of type: *great primer*, large type about four and a quarter lines to the inch; *long primer*, seven and a half lines to the inch; between *small pica* and *bourgeois.*

primer (II.), n. [1. prímer; 2. práimә]. **prime** (III.) & **-er**. Contrivance, such as a cap or tube, containing a small charge of explosive ignited by percussion, friction, or electricity, used to ignite and explode the main charge of a gun, bomb, mine &c.

primero, n. [1. primḗrō; 2. primíәrou], fr. Span. *primera*, fem. of *primero*. See **primary**. An old 16th and 17th cent. game of cards.

primeur, n. [1. prēmër; 2. primā̃]. Fr. See **primary**. (usually pl.) Early vegetables, fruit, flowers &c., grown or forced specially for sale in advance of the ordinary season; (by transf.) early news.

primeval, adj. See **prim(a)eval**.

priming, n. [1. príming; 2. práimiŋ], fr. **prime** (III.) & **-ing**. **1.** Act of priming; that which primes; specif. **a** the powder &c. which explodes the charge of a gun, mine, bomb &c.; **b** the first coat of paint, size &c. **2.** *Priming of the tide*, the acceleration of the time of high water in advance of mean time between neap and spring tide, contrasted with *lag.*

primiparous, adj. [1. prīmíparus; 2. praimípәrәs], fr. Lat. *prīmipara*, 'animal that has given birth to young for the first time'. See **prime** (I.) & **parent**. Bearing a child or young for the first time.

primitive (I.), adj. [1. prímitiv; 2. prímitiv], fr. Lat. *prīmitīvus*, 'first, earliest, of its kind', fr. *prīmus*, 'first'. See **prime** (I.). **1.** Pertaining to, existing in, characteristic of, the earliest ages or periods; prehistoric: *primitive man*; *primitive customs, religion, culture* &c. **2.** Of, belonging to, the first, earliest, original period of anything: *the primitive Church*, the early, original, Christian Church; *the primitive form of a language* &c.; *primitive type of art* &c. *Primitive Methodist Connexion*, a body of Methodists who seceded from the parent body in 1810 for the purpose of reviving the early, primitive, fervour of Wesley and his followers. **3.** Characterized by the rudeness and simplicity of early or primitive times; not elaborate, highly developed, or refined; old-fashioned: *primitive tools, methods, habits*; *a primitive mode of dressing, cooking* &c.; *primitive in one's ways.*

primitive (II.), n., fr. prec. A person or thing belonging to a primitive period or found in a primitive form; specif. (paint.) a painter or sculptor belonging to a period before its fullest development, usually applied to artists antecedent to the Renaissance; a painting, sculpture, of a primitive period: *the Italian, French, Primitives.*

primitively, adv. [1. prímitivli; 2. prímitivli]. **primitive** (I.) & **-ly**. **a** In a primitive manner; **b** in, or at the beginning, originally.

primitiveness, n. [1. prímitivnes; 2. prímitivnis]. See prec. & **-ness**. State, quality, of being primitive.

primly, adv. [1. prímli; 2. prímli]. **prim** & **-ly**. In a prim, precise manner.

primness, n. [1. prímnes; 2. prímnis]. See prec. & **-ness**. State, quality, of being prim; preciseness.

primo, n. [1. prḗmō; 2. prímou]. Ital., fr. Lat. See **prime** (I.). (mus.) The first, leading, part in a duet, trio &c.

primo-, pref. Form of Lat. *prīmus*, used in compounds. See **prime** (I.). First.

primogenital, adj. [1. prīmōjénital; 2. praimoudžénitәl]. See **primo-** & **genital**. Primogenitary.

primogenitary, adj. [1. prīmōjénituri; 2. praimoudžénitәri]. See prec. & suff. **-ary**. Pertaining to, based on, primogeniture.

primogenitor, n. [1. prīmōjénitōr; 2. praimoudžénitō, -ә]. Med. Lat., fr. **primo-** & *genitor*, 'begetter, father', fr. stem *genit-(um)*, P.P. of *gignere*, 'to beget', see **genital** & words there referred to, & **-or**. An ancestor, forefather, progenitor; the earliest recorded ancestor of a race, stock &c.

primogeniture, n. [1. prīmōjénichur; 2. praimoudžénitʃә]. Med. Lat. *prīmogenitūra*. See stem of prec. & **-ure**. **1.** State, fact, of being the first or eldest born of the same father and mother. **2.** (law) System whereby the eldest son, or his eldest son &c., or descendant in direct line succeeds to a father or ancestor in real estate; system by which the whole of an intestate real estate passes to eldest son.

primordial, adj. [1. prīmórdial; 2. praimṓdiәl], fr. L. Eccles. Lat. *prīmordiālis*, fr. Lat. *primordius*, 'original, beginning', *prīmordium*, 'the beginning, commencement'. See **prime** (I.) & **order** & **-ial**. **1.** Of earliest origin, dating from the earliest beginnings; original, primaeval: *primordial customs, rocks* &c. **2.** (biol.) Earliest formed in the development of an organ or an individual.

primordialism, n. [1. prīmórdializm; 2. praimṓdiәlizәm]. Prec. & **-ism**. (biol.) Adherence to, persistence in, primordial state or conditions of existence.

primordiality, n. [1. prīmordiáliti; 2. praimōdiǽliti]. **primordial** & **-ity**. State, condition, of being primordial or original; not derivative.

primordially, adv. [1. prīmórdiali; 2. praimṓdiәli]. See prec. & **-ly**. In a primordial manner or condition; originally.

primrose, n. [1. prímrōz; 2. prímrouz]. Late M.E., fr. O. Fr. *prime rose*, fr. Med. Lat. *prīma rosa*, 'the first rose' (see **prime** (I.) & **rose** (I.)), applied apparently to various early spring flowers; the earlier M.E. is *primerole*, O. Fr., fr. a corrupt. of L. Lat. *prīmula*, 'the primrose' (see **primula**), used as the mod. botanical name for the genus. **1.** (bot.) **a** A plant belonging to the genus *Primula*, esp. the common wild herbaceous perennial plant, *P. vulgaris*, of early spring, with pale-yellow flowers, allied to the cowslip &c., and of which there are many cultivated varieties, and hybrids, as the polyanthus; **b** a flower of this plant. **2.** The evening primrose, a distinct plant, genus *Oenothera*, native of America, with large yellow flowers opening at sunset. **3.** A pale-yellow colour as of the primrose. **4.** (attrib.) Flowery, gay, full of pleasure: '*The primrose path of dalliance*' ('Hamlet', I. iii. 50); '*The primrose way to the everlasting bonfire*' ('Macbeth', II. iii. 21).

Primrose Day, n. April 19th, the date of the death of Lord Beaconsfield, 1881, on anniversary of which primroses are worn by Conservatives in his memory.

Primrose League, n. A political Conservative society founded, 1883, to spread the principles for which Lord Beaconsfield is remembered.

primrose yellow, n. & adj. **a** n. The colour of the primrose; **b** adj., of this colour.

primula, n. [1. prímūla; 2. prímjulə]. Med. Lat., fr. Lat. *prīmulus*, 'first', a dimin. of *prīmus*, 'first', as **prime (I.)** & cp. **primrose.** (bot.) A genus of perennial herbaceous plants, with variously coloured flowers, of which the common primrose is the type, esp. used of the cultivated garden species, such as the polyanthus, auricula &c.

primuline, n. [1. prímūlin, -ēn; 2. prímjulin, -in]. Invented name. See prec. & **-ine.** A yellow, aniline dye.

primum mobile, n. [1. prímum móbile; 2. práiməm móubili]. Lat., 'first movable thing'. See **prime (I.)** & **mobile (II.)**. (anct. astron.) The first, prime, source of motion, the tenth or outer sphere of the universe, bearing in its revolution the fixed stars and representing circular motion, the most perfect and divine of all movements.

primus, adj. & n. [1. prīmus; 2. práiməs]. Lat. See **prime (I.)**. **1.** adj. **a** First; Phr. *primus inter pares*, first amongst his equals or peers; **b** the eldest or senior of two or more boys bearing the same name, *Smith primus*, cp. *major.* **2.** n. The title of the bishop elected to preside over the Convocation of the Episcopal Church of Scotland.

prince, n. [1. prins; 2. prins]. Fr., fr. Lat. *princeps*, adj. & n., 'first, chief, principal; the most eminent, most distinguished, noble; (*princeps senatus*, head of Roman Senate, see **principate**); a ruler, a sovereign'; fr. **prīmiceps*, lit. 'one occupying the first, principal, place'; fr. *primus*, 'first', see **prime (I.)**, & base of *capere*, 'to take', see under **captive.** **1. a** A sovereign ruler of certain states whose head has not the rank and title of king: *the princes of the* (German or Holy Roman) *Empire*; *the Prince of Monaco*; **b** in referring to kings: *Charles I. was a gentle and pious prince.* **2.** Son of a sovereign, or other male member of royal or sovereign family: *their Majesties were gratified by the birth of a prince.* Phrs. *prince of the blood*, member of a reigning or royal house; *the manners of a prince*, courtly, distinguished, manners; *as happy as a prince*, extremely happy; *to live like a prince*, live luxuriously, maintain a splendid household. **3. a** Title given in official documents to English dukes and marquises: *the most high and puissant prince John Duke of* &c.; **b** high or highest title of nobility in several European countries, e.g. in France under the Empire; in Germany, Russia, the Papal States: *Prince of the Church*, a Roman Cardinal; *Prince of the Apostles*, St. Peter; *a prince among men*, person of lofty character and striking personality. **4.** A ruler, chief, in a spiritual sphere: *the Prince of Peace*, the Saviour; *prince of darkness, of this world*, Satan. **5. a** One distinguished among his fellows for his success in some particular sphere, or for the magnitude of his operations and activities: *a merchant prince*; *the prince of poets, of bankers, soap-boilers* &c.; also **b** (in derogatory sense) *the prince of swindlers, rogues* &c.

Prince Consort, n. Title borne by the husband of a Queen regnant of England.

princedom, n. [1. prinsdum; 2. prínsdəm]. **prince & -dom.** **a** Rank, dignity, of a prince; **b** principality.

princelet, n. [1. prínslet; 2. prínslit]. **prince & -let.** A petty prince, a princeling.

princelike, adj. [1. prínslik; 2. prínslaik]. See prec. & **-like.** Resembling, worthy of, a prince; lofty, dignified; generous.

princeliness, n. [1. prínslines; 2. prínslinis]. **princely & -ness.** State, quality, of being princely.

princeling, n. [1. prínsling; 2. prínsliŋ]. **prince & -ling.** A petty prince, princelet.

princely, adj. [1. prínsli; 2. prínsli]. See prec. & **-ly.** **1.** Of, pertaining to, a prince: *princely birth, rank* &c. **2. a** Possessing, exhibiting, the bearing or qualities befitting a prince; prince-like; **b** resembling that which a prince would possess or give; magnificent, sumptuous, lavish: *a princely house*; *a princely gift, entertainment* &c.

Prince of Wales, n. [1. prìns uv wālz; 2. prìns əv wéilz]. Title regularly conferred, since 1301, upon the eldest son and heir apparent of an English sovereign; first borne by Edward, eldest surviving son of Edward I. *Prince of Wales's Feathers*, the badge of the heir apparent of England, consisting of a plume of three ostrich feathers enfiled by a coronet of alternate fleurs-de-lis and crosses patée or.

princeps, adj. [1. prínseps; 2. prínseps]. Lat., adj. See under **prince.** **1.** First, original: *editio princeps*, the first edition of a book. Phr. *facile princeps*, easily first, or the best. **2.** (anat.) Principal; specif., of two branches of arteries, of the thumb (*p. pollicis*), and of the neck (*p. cervicis*).

Prince Regent, n. Royal person temporarily exercising the constitutional functions of the king.

Prince Rupert's drops, n. [1. prìns ro͝operts drŏps; 2. prìns rūpəts drɔ́ps]. From the inventor, Prince Rupert, nephew of Charles I. Small pear-shaped glass bubbles formed by dropping molten glass into cold water; when scratched they explode into powder.

Prince Rupert's metal, also **prince's metal**, n. An alloy of copper, used for imitation gold in making cheap jewellery.

prince's feather, n. A plant, *Amaranthus hypochondriacus*, with tall feathery spikes of red flowers.

princess, n. [1. prinsés; 2. prinsés]; when followed by a name [1. prínses; 2. prínses]. **prince & -ess**, cp. Fr. *princesse*, Ital. *principessa* &c. **1.** Woman ruler of a state in her own right. **2.** Female member of a royal family; used as a title before Christian name: *Princess Elizabeth*; *princess of the blood.* *Princess Royal*, courtesy title conferred on the eldest daughter of reigning sovereign of England. **3.** Wife of any kind of prince. **4.** (attrib.) *Princess robe, dress*, former style of woman's close-fitting dress with bodice and skirt in one piece, so called after Queen Alexandra, when Princess of Wales.

principal (I.), adj. [1. prínsipl; 2. prínsipl], fr. Lat. *principālis*, 'chief, principal', fr. *princip-*, stem of *princeps*, see **prince**, & **-al.** **1.** First in rank, importance, authority, degree &c.; chief; leading, main: *the principal people, towns, rivers* &c., in a country or district; *principal articles of commerce, food* &c.; *principal reason, cause.* **2.** (gram.) *Principal clause, sentence*, that to which other clauses or sentences are subordinate; *principal parts* (of a vb.), those representing the various types, from one or other of which the rest are derived.

principal (II.), n., fr. prec. **1. a** A chief, head, superior; one who takes a lead or principal part in anything, as distinguished from *a subordinate, second* &c.: *the principal of a business*; *the principals in a political or other movement*; *principals in a war*, the chief parties, belligerents, *in a duel*, the combatants; **b** the title of the head of some colleges at Oxford, of *Brasenose, Jesus, Hertford Colleges*; of the head, *Lady Principal*, of the various women's colleges at Oxford and Cambridge &c.; of the newly established theological colleges; of the heads of the universities of Scotland and of some of the newer provincial English universities; (in U.S.A.) only of the head of a school or academy. **2. a** (archit.) A main rafter or girder in a roof; **b** (commerc.) the sum originally invested or lent, the capital, as distinguished from the income or dividend or the interest; **c** (law) the person who employs another to act for him, and is responsible and liable for his actions &c., as contrasted with *agent*; the person primarily responsible for a debt or obligation, as contrasted with *surety*; the actual perpetrator of a crime, the chief person responsible for a crime, as contrasted with *abettor* or *accessory*; **d** (mus.) the chief open metallic stop of an organ.

principality, n. [1. prìnsipáliti; 2. prìnsipǽliti], fr. O. Fr. *principalite*, fr. L. Lat. *principālitāt-(em)*, *principālitas.* See **principal (I.)** & **-ity.** **1.** The state, rank, dignity, of a prince. **2.** The territory ruled by a prince, or which gives him his title; specif., *the Principality*, Wales. **3.** (pl.) One of the nine orders of angels: *principalities and powers.*

principally, adv. [1. prínsipali; 2. prínsip(ə)li]. **principal (I.) & -ly.** In the chief place, for the most part, mainly, chiefly.

principate, n. [1. prínsipāt; 2. prínsipeit], fr. Lat. *principātus*, 'the first place, pre-eminence; the rule, reign, power of the princeps, esp. of the emperors', fr. *princip-(em)*, *princeps*, see **prince.** **a** Principality; **b** (Rom. hist.) the rule of the early Roman emperors when they still preserved *princeps senatus* as their sole title of authority, together with some of the older republican constitution.

principia, n. pl. [1. prinsípia; 2. prinsípiə]. Pl. of Lat. *principium*, 'a beginning, origin; (in pl.) foundations, elements, principles', fr. *princeps*, see **prince.** First, fundamental, principles, elements: *Newton's* '*Principia*'.

principle, n. [1. prínsipl; 2. prínsipl], fr. Fr. *principe*, w. intrusive *l* (cp. *syllable*, fr. Fr. *syllabe*), fr. Lat. *principium.* See prec. & **prince.** **1.** The ultimate source or origin of anything; primary element, that from which all other things are derived: *earth, air, fire, water were to the ancients the principles of life and matter*; *the principles of existence.* **2.** A general, comprehensive law, doctrine, or truth, accepted as the basis or fundamental ground for other laws and doctrines deduced from it; general basal proposition or axiom: *the principles of biology, banking* &c.; *the principle of gravitation*; *to argue from false principles*; *a sound legal principle.* **3.** A moral, political, or other rule, tenet, or conviction, which serves as a guide for conduct or action, esp. for right conduct: *a man of principle, of no principles*; *to stick to one's principles*; *the principles of a political party*; *religious principles* &c. Phrs. *on principle*, from settled conviction, from settled motive; *in principle*, generally, as a general rule. **4.** A constituent, elementary substance from which special qualities are derived: *the emetic, carminative, sweet, bitter &c. principle of a drug* &c.

principled, adj. [1. prínsipld; 2. prínsipld]. Prec. & **-ed.** Having certain principles; usually with qualification, as *high-principled* &c., cp. **unprincipled.**

prink, vb. trans. & intrans. [1. pringk; 2. priŋk]. Variant of, or cogn. w., **prank.** (obs. or provinc.) To prank, dress oneself up; to preen, as a bird.

print (I.), n. [1. print; 2. print]. M.E. *prente, preynte, printe*, 'impression, stamp, mark', as on coin &c., fr. O. Fr. *preinte, priente*, fem. of P.P. of O. Fr. *preindre*, 'to stamp, impress'; also in compound form, *empreinte, empreindre*, fr. L. Lat. *imprimere*, fr. *in-*, 'on', & *premere*, 'to press'; cp. **imprint & press (I.)**. **1. a** A mark, shape, form, or pattern left upon a surface by the impression of another body; stamp, impression: *print* *of a foot upon the sand*; *print of one's fingers on a glass* &c.; **b** a stamp or die for making a print or impression on another object: *a print for butter.* **2.** (fig.) Impression, effect of some experience or influence: *sorrow's print upon his face*; *character which bore the print of early influences.* **3. a** That which is printed or produced by the art and process of printing or the printing press; printed letters or lettering: *small, large, clear print*; Phrs. *in print*, printed and published; *to see one's name in print*, to have one's views, opinions &c. printed and published in a newspaper, book &c.; *in print*, printed, published, and for sale; *out of print*, of book printed of which no more copies are on sale; **b** (chiefly U.S.A.) printed matter, such as newspapers, periodicals &c.; *newsprint*, paper specially made for use in printing newspapers. **4. a** Engraved, etched, picture, portrait &c. reproduced on paper &c. from a metal plate: *collection of prints*; **b** (photog.) a positive picture obtained from a negative plate or film by exposure of sensitized paper beneath the negative to light. **5.** Specif. **a** (in foundry work) a metal mould or pattern; **b** (textiles) calico or cotton fabric printed with coloured pattern: *calico, cotton, print*; *a print dress*; *made of print.*

print (II.), vb. trans. & intrans. M.E. *prenten, preenten*, later *printe*, fr. prec. **A.** trans. **1. a** To mark by pressure, to impress a surface with a mark: *to print wax with a seal*; *the mark of a foot printed on the sand*; *to print a kiss upon the cheek*; **b** (fig.) to leave a mental or moral impression on; to fix, impress on; to imprint, instil: *to print upon the memory, on the mind* &c.; *the name was printed on her heart.* **2. a** To transfer the impression of letters &c. from inked type to paper &c. by means of a printing machine: *to print a book, newspapers* &c.; **b** to get, cause to be, printed; to issue from a press; to publish in printed form: *to print one's essays and lectures*; **c** to reproduce a picture, design &c. from inked or coloured plates, blocks, stones &c.: *to print an etching*; *to print calico or cotton cloth.* **3.** To form letters in writing like printed characters: *please print all proper names in block capitals.* **4.** (photog.) To obtain a positive or print from a negative by exposure to light. **B.** intrans. **1.** To practise the art or business of a printer: *Caxton printed from 1476 to 1491.* **2.** To come out, be produced as result of a printing process: *the etching, photograph &c. has printed well, clearly* &c.

printable, adj. [1. príntabl; 2. príntəbl]. Prec. & **-able.** **1.** (usually in neg.) Able to be printed; able to be printed from: *the MS. is not in a printable state*; *the original plates are no longer printable.* **2. a** Worth printing; **b** proper, fit, for printing or reproducing: *the evidence, language &c. is not printable.*

printer, n. [1. prínter; 2. príntə]. **print** (II.) & **-er.** **1.** One who prints; specif. **a** person who works a printing press, or carries out any of the various processes involved in producing matter from a printing press; **b** person who owns, directs, manages, a printing establishment. **2.** Person engaged in any of the various processes of printing; e.g. *calico printer.*

printer's devil, n. An apprentice in a printing office; a messenger or errand boy who calls for copy for the press.

printer's ink, n. Special kind of ink used in printing. Phr. *to spill printer's ink*, to have one's writings printed.

printer's mark, n. The trade-mark, distinctive device &c. used by a particular printer or press: *the Aldine printer's mark.*

printer's pie, n. A mixed-up, confused set of type; confusion, chaos, muddle: *to make printer's pie of anything.*

printing, vbl. n. [1. prínting; 2. príntiŋ]. **1.** Act or process carried out by any kind of printer; specif. **a** the process of producing printed matter from a press; **b** of reproducing a photograph from a negative; **c** of impressing or stamping patterns on fabrics. **2.** The process considered as an art; style of printing, typography.

printing press, n. **1.** Machine for printing. **2.** Establishment, business premises, where printing is carried on.

prior (I.), adj. & adv. [1. prí̄or; 2. práiə]. Lat., 'previous, former, superior, better', a compar. fr. base **pri-* as in *prīmus*, 'first', see **prime** (I.); cogn. w. *prō*, 'in front of'. Cp. **pre-.** **1.** adj. **a** Earlier in time, antecedent: *a prior engagement*; **b** superior in importance, stronger: *a prior claim.* **2.** adv. *Prior to*, before: *prior to my arrival.*

prior (II.), n. O.E., fr. Lat., M.E. *priour*, fr. O. Fr., fr. Lat. *prior.* See prec. **1.** The head or superior of a priory of monks, ranking next below an abbot. **2.** The head or superior of one of the military orders of monks: *the Grand Prior of the Knights of St. John of Jerusalem.* **3.** One of the magistrates of the Republic of Florence in 13th cent.

priorate, n. [1. príorāt; 2. práiəreit], fr. Med. Lat. *priorātus.* See prec. & **-ate.** The office of a prior; priorship.

prioress, n. [1. príores; 2. práiərεs]. **prior** (II.) & **-ess.** The lady superior of a priory of nuns, ranking next to an abbess.

priority, n. [1. prīóriti; 2. praiɔ́riti]. **prior** (I.) & **-ity.** State, quality, of being prior or before in time, order, importance &c.; superiority, precedence: *priority of birth, claim, position* &c.; *to take priority of*, to take precedence of, to precede.

priorship, n. [1. príorship; 2. práiəʃip]. **prior** (II.) & **-ship.** **a** Office, dignity, of a prior; **b** period of office of a prior.

priory, n. [1. príori; 2. práiəri], fr. O. Fr. *priorie*, Mod. Fr. *prieuré*, fr. Med. Lat. *priōria*, as **prior** (II.) & **-y.** **1.** A monastery of monks or nuns, subordinate to, and a branch of, an abbey. **2.** A house or monastery of regular canons, independent of an abbey: *an Augustinian priory.* **3.** A community of military monks, as of the Order of St. John of Jerusalem.

prise, vb. See **prize** (IV.).

prism, n. [1. prízm; 2. prízəm], fr. Low Lat. *prisma*, fr. Gk. *prîsma*, 'something sawn off; prism', connected w. *prízein*, 'to saw', prob. orig., 'to divide into pieces'; cogn. w. Gk. *peírein*, 'to pierce', *póros*, 'way, passage', q.v. under **pore** (I.), **port** (I.). **1.** (geom.) A solid figure whose bases are equal, parallel planes, and whose sides are parallelograms. **2.** (opt.) A transparent body of glass, crystal &c., with parallel, usually triangular, bases and three or more rectangular plane sides or faces, used for refracting or dispersing light. **3. a** Any crystalline body, the sides or faces of which are parallel; **b** any refracting body such as a raindrop &c.

prismatic, adj. [1. prizmátik; 2. prizmǽtik], fr. Gk. *prismat-*, stem of *prisma*, see prec., & **-ic.** **a** Connected with, related to, a prism; **b** having shape of a prism; **c** having the refracting properties of a prism; *prismatic colours*, those existing blended in sunlight, and broken up by a prism; hence, any group of similar bright colours; **d** containing a prism: *prismatic compass*, a hand compass furnished with a prism enabling the dial to be read while taking a bearing or sight.

prismatically, adv. [1. prizmátikali; 2. prizmǽtikəli]. Prec. & **-al** & **-ly.** **a** By means of, as if through, a prism; **b** with prismatic colours.

prismoid, n. [1. prízmoid; 2. prízmɔid]. **prism** & **-oid.** A body, figure, resembling a prism but having the bases similar but not equal.

prismoidal, adj. [1. prizmóidl; 2. prizmɔ́idl]. Prec. & **-al.** Of, pertaining to, a prismoid.

prison (I.), n. [1. prízn; 2. prízn]. M.E., fr. O. Fr. *prisun, prisoun*, fr. Low Lat. **presiōn-(em)*, fr. Lat. *prensiōn-(em)*, 'a taking, capture', fr. *prens-(um)*, P.P. type of *prendere*, fr. *prehendere*, 'to take, seize, capture', see **prehensile.** **1.** A place of captivity; specif., a state building where convicted criminals are kept to undergo punishment or where those charged with a crime or offence are kept while awaiting trial; a gaol. **2.** Any place, position, of confinement or restraint, physical or mental.

prison (II.), vb. trans., fr. prec. (usually fig., poet.) To confine, restrain; to enfold, hold close: *prisoned in the arms of her lover.*

prison-breaking, n. Act, offence, of escaping by force from a prison.

prisoner, n. [1. prízuner; 2. príz(ə)nə], fr. O. Fr. *prisonier*; see **prison** (II.) & **-er**; in obs. & orig. sense, 'a gaoler'. **1. a** A captive, one taken and held in confinement: *prisoner of war*; *to keep a bird or other animal a prisoner in a cage* &c.; **b** (fig.) person detained in a given place; one whose action and movements are hampered for any reason: *my work will keep me a prisoner all summer*; *gout kept him a prisoner to his room.* **2.** Specif. **a** a person under arrest and in custody, charged with a crime or offence: *prisoner at the bar*; *prisoner on remand, on bail* &c.; **b** a person convicted of a crime or offence and undergoing punishment in a prison, penal settlement &c.

prisoner's base, n. Game, played by boys, in which each side has a base or home, to which anyone caught from the other side is brought, and which is a refuge for the home side.

prison-house, n. (rhet.) Prison, place of confinement; chiefly figurative.

pristine, adj. [1. prístin; 2. prístain]. O. Fr., fr. Lat. *pristinus*, 'belonging to former times, early'; cp. also Lat. *priscus*, 'ancient'; fr. **pri-*, 'former, before', see **prior** (I.) & **prime** (I.). The origin of suff. *-tinus* (cp. also Lat. *diutinus*, 'long, lasting') is not clear. Belonging to the earliest, or to an early time or period; primitive, original: *pristine innocence, vigour, strength* &c.

pri'thee, interj. [1. prídhi; 2. príði]. For 'I pray thee'. (archaic or poet.) Pray, I beg of you, please (followed by vb.): *pri'thee tell me.*

privacy, n. [1. prívasi; 2. práivəsi]. **private** & **-cy.** An English formation; the O. Fr. is *privaute.* Quality, state, of being private; **a** seclusion, retirement; freedom from observation, interruption &c.: *to live in privacy*; *in the privacy of one's thoughts*; *my walls and hedges secure me complete privacy in my garden*; **b** secrecy: *I tell you this in strict privacy.*

privat-docent, n. [1. priváht dōtsént; 2. privát dotsént]. Germ., 'private teacher'. See **private** & **docile.** At German and other European universities a lecturer in a special subject, or branch of a wider subject, officially recognized but not paid by the university.

private (I.), adj. [1. prívit; 2. práivit], fr. Lat. *prīvāt-(um)*, 'apart, belonging not to the State but to an individual', P.P. of *prīvāre*, 'to set apart, separate, deprive', fr. *prīvus*, 'single, alone, each, every individual; one's own, private', etymol. uncertain, prob. cogn. w. *prae*, 'before', in sense of 'sent forward, apart from the rest, alone' (see **pre-**); but this is conjectural, & the development of meaning is not clear. **1.** Belonging, pertaining, to, concerning, individual or personal affairs, interests &c., or an individual person; contrasted with *public, general*, or *common*: *private property, affairs, business* &c. *Private school*, one owned and managed by an individual, not vested in a public body and governed by them; a preparatory school; contrasted with a *public school.* **2.** Not open to the public in general: *a private road*; *private performance, exhibition*; *a private company*; *private offices, rooms* &c. **3.** Not in public employment, not occupied with public or state affairs: *to speak, act, in one's private capacity, as a private person.* Phrs. *private life*, one free from public or professional business; *private means*, not derived from profession; distinct from professional salary. **4.** Not holding a special, official, position, rank &c.: *a private member of Parliament, private soldier, private citizen. Private bill*, in Parliament, one brought forward by a private member, or one affecting private not general interests, as of a railway company, municipality &c. **5.** Belonging to oneself, as an individual; owned personally; employed by oneself: *one's private house, secretary.* **6.** Confidential, secret, for oneself alone: *private information, news; keep the matter private.* Phr. *for one's private ear; in private*, in secret, confidentially.

private (II.), n., fr. prec. **1.** A private soldier, one not holding commissioned or non-commissioned rank. **2.** (pl.) Private or secret parts, external genital organs.

privateer, n. & vb. intrans. [1. privitér; 2. praivitíə]. Prec. & **-eer.** **1.** n. **a** An armed ship, privately owned but authorized by the State, by letters of marque &c., to attack and capture merchant ships of the enemy in time of war; a commerce-destroyer, corsair; **b** commander or member of the crew of a privateer. **2.** vb. To cruise as a privateer; to attack and capture the enemy's mercantile commerce in a privateer.

privateering, n. & adj. [1. privitéring; 2. praivitíəriŋ]. Prec. & **-ing.** **1.** n. Act, occupation, of cruising as a privateer; act of raiding an enemy's commerce in a privateer. **2.** adj. Of, pertaining to, a privateer or privateering: *a privateering expedition, voyage.*

privateersman, n. [1. privitérzman; 2. praivitíəzmən]. A commander, member, of the crew of a privateer.

privation, n. [1. privấshun; 2. praivéiʃən]. Lat. *prīvātiōn-(em)*, fr. *prīvāt-(um)*, P.P. type of *prīvāre*, 'to separate from, deprive of', see **private**, & **-ion.** **a** Act of depriving or taking from; **b** state of being deprived of, absence of, loss of; want, need, destitution: *the privations of life; to suffer many privations; to die of privation.*

privative, adj. & n. [1. prívativ; 2. prívətiv], fr. Lat. *prīvātīvus.* See **private** & **-ive.** **1.** adj. **a** Indicating the absence, loss, or want of a special quality, character &c.; consisting in the absence or loss of a quality; negative, contrasted with *positive*: *pale, black, cold are privative words*, as only definable in negative terms; **b** (gram., of particles, pref., suff.) indicating absence of qualities, as *a-, un-, -less* &c. **2.** n. (gram.) A privative prefix or suffix.

privatively, adv. Prec. & **-ly.** In a privative manner; as a privative.

privet, n. [1. prívet; 2. prívit]. Etymol. dubious; earlier forms are *primprint, primeprint, primet.* An evergreen shrub, with small white flowers and dark, shiny green leaves, *Ligustrum vulgare*, generally kept closely trimmed, in garden hedges; *golden privet*, a variety with yellowish leaves.

privet hawk-moth, n. A large moth whose larvae feed on the privet.

privilege (I.), n. [1. prívilij; 2. prívilidž]. O. Fr., fr. Lat. *prīvilēgium*, 'a private law, law or ordinance against, or in favour of, a private person or individual'; fr. *prīvus*, 'private, single', see **private**, & *lēg-*, base of *lēx*, 'law', see **legal.** **1.** A special, individual right, advantage, benefit &c.; an immunity, exemption, or franchise granted to, and enjoyed by, some and not by others; esp. one enjoyed by a particular class, rank, holders of office &c.: *the privilege of clergy*, benefit of clergy; *the special privileges of high rank, wealth* &c. **2.** **a** A general, accepted right, guaranteed by the State as natural to all its citizens; prerogative: *the privilege of citizenship, of private property* &c.; **b** some right or advantage enjoyed by common consent and tolerance; *it is a privilege of age to be prosy.* **3.** A special, personal favour, advantage: *to enjoy the privilege of another's friendship, advice &c.; to listen to his conversation was a high privilege.*

privilege (II.), vb. trans., fr. prec. To grant a person a privilege or special advantage or favour; to exempt a person from a duty, burden; esp. as P.P.

privileged, adj. [1. prívilijd; 2. prívilidžd]. P.P. of prec. Endowed with, enjoying, a privilege: *a privileged person, class* &c.; specif. (law) *privileged communication*, a communication between two persons who stand in a special relation to each other, e.g. of doctor and patient, lawyer and client &c., treated as confidential and not to be disclosed legally in evidence.

privily, adv. [1. prívili; 2. prívili]. **privy** (I.) & **-ly.** In a privy manner, privately; secretly, stealthily.

privity, n. [1. príviti; 2. príviti], fr. O. Fr. *privité*, fr. Lat. *prīvus.* See **privy** (I.) & **-ty.** **1.** (archaic) State, condition, of being privy to, having private knowledge; knowledge shared between persons: *with, without, the privity of others.* **2.** (law) A special relation between two parties to a transaction, property &c., recognized by law, as between lessor and first lessee, ancestor and heir &c.: *privity of estate or tenure, of contract* &c.

privy (I.), adj. [1. prívi; 2. prívi], fr. Fr. *privé*, fr. Lat. *prīvatus.* See **private** (I.). **1.** **a** Having private knowledge of; secretly, privately knowing: *privy to the plot*; **b** (law) having privity of, being with privity: *privy to a contract* &c. **2.** Belonging to some person individually or exclusively for private, not for public, uses &c., esp. of certain offices &c., private to the sovereign: *Privy Council*, originally the King's Council, chosen and appointed by him and subject to his personal control, its main functions being now performed by the Cabinet, and chiefly formal for such matters as Orders in Council, affixing the Privy Seal &c.; technically, various ministries, e.g. Board of Trade, Education &c., are Committees of the Privy Council, and the *Judicial Committee of the Privy Council* is the Supreme Court of Appeal for the Dominions. *Privy Councillor, Counsellor* (abbr. *P.C.*), a member of the Privy Council, entitled to be styled *Right Honourable*; *Privy Purse*, the amount of money set apart in the Civil List for the personal use of the sovereign; *Privy Seal*, a Seal of Great Britain for documents that do not require the Great Seal or for grants &c. which have subsequently to pass the Great Seal; *Lord Privy Seal*, keeper of this seal, one of the Great Officers of State. **3.** Secret, private, secluded, hidden: *privy chambers, room &c.; privy parts*, external genital organs.

privy (II.), n., fr. prec. **1.** (law) A person having some special relationship or privity with another as recognized by law: *ancestor and heir are privies by estate, lessor and lessee by tenure* &c. **2.** A private place; specif., a latrine.

prize (I.), n. [1. prīz; 2. praiz]. M.E. *prīse*, fr. O. Fr. *pris*, Mod. Fr. *prix*, 'price, prize', fr. Lat. *pretium*, 'price, reward'; a variant of **price**, influenced by form of **prize** (III.). **1.** **a** That which is offered as a reward for merit, or to be contested for and given to the winner: *a prize for good conduct, a prize at an exhibition, show* &c.; *won the history prize*; **b** that which can be won in a game of chance, lottery &c.: *won a big prize in the Calcutta sweep*; **c** (by transf.) any valuable or envied possession, anything worth striving for: *to pick up a prize at a sale &c.; to gain the prizes of a profession; to scorn the prizes of life; good health is an inestimable prize.* **2.** (attrib.) **a** Awarded, given, as a prize: *prize fellowship, scholarship* &c.; **b** rewarded by a prize: *prize cattle, prize poem*; **c** contesting for a prize: *prize fight*, a fight with bare fists for a prize of money, as distinct from a boxing match with gloves; *prize-fighter, prize-fighting*; the *prize-ring*, prize fighters and their supporters; **d** (colloq.) deserving a prize, hence, a remarkable specimen of its kind; also ironic: *a prize idiot*, a complete fool.

prize (II.), vb. trans., fr. O. Fr. *preisier, prisier*, fr. Lat. *pretiāre*, 'to put a prize, value, on, to value, prize', fr. *pretium*, 'price'. See prec. & cp. **praise.** To value, rate, esteem, highly: *to prize the affection of one's friends; to prize a gift; one's most prized possessions.*

prize (III.), n., fr. Fr. *prise*, 'a taking, seizing, capture, thing taken, booty', fem. of *pris*, P.P. of *prendre*, 'to take, seize', fr. Lat. *prens-(um), prehendere*, 'to take, seize, grasp'. See **prehensile.** Act of seizing or capturing by force; that which is taken by force; specif. (in full) 'prize of war', a vessel and goods, property &c. in such vessel captured at sea by a belligerent according to the rules of war: *to make (a) prize of, to become (the) prize of, to*, to capture, be captured as a prize. *Prize Court*, a court of Admiralty having jurisdiction over prizes of war; *prize money, bounty*, the proceeds of the sale of enemy property captured at sea in war, formerly divided *pro rata* among officers and crew of the vessel taking the prize, now paid into a common pool and paid to all officers and crews of the Navy.

prize (IV.), vb. trans. See prec. Usually *prize open, prize up*, to force, lift up, by leverage: *to prize open a door; prize up the lid of a box* &c.

prizeman, n. [1. prīzman; 2. práizmən]. **prize** (I.) & **man.** A winner of a prize, prize scholarship, fellowship &c.: *Porson's prizeman; the Nobel prizeman* &c.

pro- (I.), pref. Lat. prep. *prō*; has various meanings as an independent word: (1) 'before, in front of' (of place); (2) 'for, in favour of, for the benefit of'; (3) 'in the place of, instead of'; (4) 'according to, by virtue of'. As pref. in compounds, *pro-* has the following force: (1) of place: in front of, forwards, forth; hence it expresses also, **a** prolongation, as in *prōdūcere*, see **produce** (I.); **b** projection to a distance, e.g. *prospicere*, see **prospect** (I.); **c** publicity; openly, aloud, e.g. *prōmulgāre*, 'to put up public notice of, to publish', see **promulgate**; **d** forwards, at full length; down, e.g. *prōclīvis*, 'sloping forwards, steep, going downwards'; (2) of time: before; before words denoting relationship = 'great', e.g. *pro-avus*, 'great-grandfather'; (3) expressing various relations: **a** in defence of, for the benefit of, e.g. *prō-pugnāre*, 'to fight in defence of'; **b** for, instead of; *prō-consul*; (4) in modern formations, as a living prefix *pro-* expresses a substitution: *pro-Chancellor*; **b** partisanship (contrasted with *anti-*): *pro-Bolshevik, pro-reformation* &c. Before words beginning w. a vowel, the form *prōd-* is sometimes used, e.g. *prōdesse.* The orig. form was *prōd*, the *-d* being prob. the old suff. of the abl., the case governed by this prep. The word is widespread in the Aryan languages, cp. Gk. *pró*, 'before', in place or time; Scrt. *prá*, Goth. *fra-* inseparable particle, also *faúra*, 'before, for'; O.E. *for*, see **for.**

pro- (II.), pref. fr. Gk. *pró*, 'before', in place & time; cogn. w. prec. In compounds this pref. has force of (1) before, forth, forward; before the eyes of; (2) beforehand, earlier; (3) intensive. The pref. occurs in many words of Gk. origin, e.g. *programme*, fr. Gk. *pró-gramma*, 'public proclamation' &c.; *propaideutic*, cp. Gk. *propaideúein*, 'to teach beforehand'.

pro, n. [1. prō; 2. prou]. Abbr. of **professional.** Chiefly used of professional players of some game: *a golf, cricket, pro.*

proa, n. [1. próa; 2. próuə]. Malay. *prāhū, prāū.* An outrigged double-ended sailing-boat with one flat side and lateen sails, of the Malay Archipelago.

pro and con, adv. & n. [1. pró an(d) kón; 2. próu ən(d) kón], fr. Lat. *prō*, 'for', & *contrā*, 'against'. **a** adv. For and against; on the supporting and opposing side; **b** n. (usually *pros and cons*), the arguments for and against: *to consider, weigh, the pros and cons.*

probabiliorism, n. [1. pròbabíliorizm; 2. pròbəbíliərizəm], fr. Lat. *probābilior*, compar. of *probābilis*. See **probable** & **-ism.** (R.C. theol.) The doctrine that in a controversy the side on which the evidence appears to be the strongest is to be presumed to be the right one.

probabilism, n. [1. próbabilizm; 2. prɔ́bəbilizəm], fr. Lat. *probābilis*. See **probable** & **-ism.** **1.** (casuistry) Doctrine that in the absence of certain knowledge, probability is the best test of truth or rightness, and that in difficult questions of conscience the opinion of a learned doctor of the Church is a safe guide. **2.** (philos.) The sceptical doctrine that real knowledge is impossible, but that in practical matters a man may believe what is generally held to be true.

probabilist, n. [1. próbabilist; 2. prɔ́bəbilist]. See prec. & **-ist.** A believer in probabilism.

probability, n. [1. pròbabíliti; 2. pròbəbíliti], fr. Fr. *probabilité*, fr. Lat. *probābilitāt-(em)*, *probābilitas*, 'credibility, probability', **probable** & **-ity.** **1.** State, quality, of being probable or likely; likelihood, a state between *certainty* and *doubt* or *possibility*; *there is every probability, no probability, of success.* Phr. *in all probability*, most probably, almost certainly. **2.** Something which is or appears to be probable; a probable event: *the probabilities are against us, in our favour.* **3.** (math.) The chance of occurrence of any one of a number of possible events, some one of which is bound to occur: *the probability of throwing an ace first with an unloaded dice is one in six.*

probable (**I.**), adj. [1. próbabl; 2. prɔ́bəbl], fr. Lat. *probābilis*, 'that may be assumed, believed, or proved credible, probable', fr. *probāre*, 'to prove'. See **probate. 1.** Likely to happen, likely to prove true; having more evidence for than against; not actually certain, but stronger than *possible* or *doubtful*: *probable issues, results, of an action*; *victory is now probable*; *success is possible but hardly probable.* **2.** In various elliptical constructions: *a probable candidate*, one likely to stand; *a probable winner*, one likely to win.

probable (**II.**), n., fr. prec. Person likely to do something &c.; event likely to happen; thing likely to be done &c.

probably, adv. **probable (I.)** & **-ly.** In a probable, likely, manner or degree; in all probability or likelihood: *it will probably rain*; *shall we win? Probably.*

probang, n. [1. próbang; 2. próubæŋ]. Earlier *provang*, an invented word; etymol. uncertain; present form fr. **probe.** (surg.) A slender, flexible rod, of whalebone &c., with a sponge fixed at one end, used for clearing obstructions from oesophagus.

probate, n. [1. próbat; 2. próubit], fr. Lat. *probāt-(um)*, 'thing proved', neut. sing. of P.P. of *probāre*, 'to try, test, show to be good; to manifest, prove'; fr. *probus*, 'good, serviceable', fr. **pro-**, & a second element, either fr. base **bho-* &c., 'brightness, light', see **balefire**, or fr. base **bhū-* &c., 'to be, exist', see **future** & **be**; see also **prove** & **probity. 1.** The official proving and the proof of the legality and validity of a will, granted after examination by an official of the *Probate Court*, a division of the High Court of Justice. **2.** The certified approved copy of a will, the original of which is filed. *Probate duty*, duty payable on the personal property of a deceased testator, now part of Estate duty.

probation, n. [1. prōbáshun; 2. proubéiʃən]. Fr., fr. Lat. *probātiōn-(em)*, 'trial, examination; approval; proof'. See prec. & **-ion. 1. a** Trial, test, examination, to prove the character, capacities of a person for any duty, position &c.; **b** time, period, of such trial or examination, novitiate: *to pass a probation*; *on probation*; *during probation*; specif., system of releasing first offenders or young criminals during good behaviour with supervision by a *probation officer.* **2.** Any testing or disciplinary time in this world or in any after life which tries or proves the moral character.

probational, adj. [1. prōbáshunal; 2. proubéiʃənəl]. Prec. & **-al.** Probationary.

probationary, adj. [1. prōbáshunari; 2. proubéiʃənəri]. **probation** & **-ary.** Of, pertaining to, probation or to a period of probation: *probationary system, sentence*; *probationary prisoner*, probationer.

probationer, n. [1. prōbáshuner; 2. proubéiʃənə]. **probation** & **-er. 1.** One serving on probation, undergoing probation; specif. **a** a novice in a monastery; **b** a young nurse at a hospital during the first period of training &c.; **c** one waiting for a call to a pastorate or ministry. **2.** A prisoner released on probation.

probative, adj. [1. próbativ; 2. próubətiv], fr. Lat. *probātīvus*, 'of, belonging to, proof'. See **probate** & **-ive.** Serving as, affording, proof; evidential.

probe, n. & vb. trans. [1. prōb; 2. proub], fr. L. Lat. *proba*, 'a proof'. See **probate. 1.** n. (med.) A slender, blunt-ended instrument used for exploring and ascertaining the depth of a wound, searching for pieces of a bullet &c., or examining deep-seated abscesses, internal cavities &c. **2.** vb. **a** To explore, examine, with a probe; **b** (in non-material sense) to search, examine thoroughly: *to probe a matter, accusation, motives, rumours &c. to the bottom.*

probity, n. [1. próbiti; 2. próubiti], fr. Lat. *probitāt-(em)*, 'honesty', fr. *probus*, 'good, upright, honest'; fr. same base as that discussed under **probate.** Honesty, integrity, uprightness of conduct or character.

problem, n. [1. próblem; 2. prɔ́blem]. M.E. & O. Fr. *probleme*, fr. Lat. *problēma*, fr. Gk. *próblēma*, 'something thrown or put forward for discussion, problem'; see **pro- (II.)** & *blēma*, 'a casting, throwing, thing cast', fr. **blē*, form of base of *bállein*, 'to throw', cp. **ballistics. 1. a** A question, proposition, put forward for discussion or solution; **b** anything required to be solved by calculation or skill: *a chess problem*; *a geometrical, mathematical, problem*, as to bisect a line, find an unknown quantity, contrasted with *theorem.* **2.** Perplexing circumstances, difficult situation; perplexities that have to be faced and dealt with; doubtful case; situation in which more than one line of action seems intellectually and morally defensible: *the problems of existence*; *it is a problem how to make both ends meet*; *the problem of London traffic*; *the truth of the case will always remain a problem. Problem novel, play*, novel or play of which the so-called 'problem' is usually how best to gloss over, or escape results of an immoral action.

problematic(al), adj. [1. pròblemátik(l); 2. pròblimǽtik(l)], fr. L. Lat. *problēmaticus*, fr. Gk. *problēmatikós*, fr. *problēmat-*, stem of *próblēma*. See prec. & **-ic** (& **-al**). Of the nature of a problem; doubtful; questionable: *whether the Government can carry on or not is problematical*; *a problematic question*; *conviction of the prisoner is problematic.*

problematically, adv. Prec. & **-ly.** In the manner of a problem; doubtfully, questionably.

pro bono publico [1. prō bónō públikō; 2. prou bóunou páblikou]. (Lat. Phr.) For the public good.

proboscis, n. [1. probósis; 2. prəbɔ́sis]. Lat., fr. Gk. *proboskis*, 'the trunk of an elephant, proboscis of a fly', see **pro- (II.)**; the second element is fr. *bóskein*, 'to feed', *bóskesthai*, 'to graze', fr. base **bot-*, as in *botḗr*, 'herdsman', *botánē*, 'grass, fodder'. See under **botany. 1.** (zool.) **a** The trunk of an elephant and of its extinct allies, such as the mammoth &c.; **b** the elongated, flexible snout resembling an elephant's trunk of tapir and other animals; **c** a prolongation of the parts about the mouth of various insects, as in moths and butterflies, flies &c., used as a sucking or boring instrument; also a protrusile, tubular organ in certain worms. **2.** (colloq., facet.) The nose of a human being.

proboscis monkey, n. Monkey with a long prominent nose, a native of Borneo.

pro-cathedral, n. [1. prō kathédral; 2. prou kəþídrəl]. **pro- (I.)** & **cathedral.** A church, usually a large parish church, used as a substitute for a cathedral; esp. **a** in a newly formed diocese in which a cathedral church has not yet been built; **b** name given to a large church built in England by the Roman Catholic Church and used as a cathedral.

procedure, n. [1. prōsédyer; 2. prousídʒə]. Fr. *procédure*, fr. *procéder.* See **proceed** & **-ure. 1.** (rare) Process, manner, of proceeding or making progress, advancement: *for the better procedure of religion*; *to make further procedure impossible.* **2.** Manner or method of proceeding or acting, method of conducting affairs or business; esp. *legal procedure*, the method in, rules under, which a case is brought before a court and conducted; legal practice; *parliamentary procedure*, the methods, rules, standing orders &c. according to which all parliamentary business, and that of public meetings generally, is conducted.

proceed, vb. intrans. [1. prōséd; 2. prousíd], fr. Fr. *procéder*, fr. Lat. *prōcēdere, prōcessum*, 'to go forward, advance, continue, proceed'. See **pro- (II.)** & **cede. 1.** To go on, advance, move forward or to: *the prisoner, the policeman said, then proceeded to the nearest public-house.* **2.** To move along, make progress, develop: *the play proceeds very slowly from this point.* **3. a** (i.) To go on doing, start and continue with a course of action: *to proceed to go to bed*; *he proceeded to give me a good scolding*; (ii.) to pass on to (something different): *we will now proceed to the next business*; **b** to continue speaking, go on to say: *my husband, she proceeded, used often to beat me*; *pray proceed*, go on with what you have to say (after interruption); **c** in Phr. *proceed against*, to take legal action against. **4.** To issue, come forth, result from, to arise from: *sounds of quarrelling proceeded from the house*; *clouds of smoke proceeded from the chimney*; *from what direction did the shots proceed?* **5.** Specif., to go on from a lower to a higher degree at a university: *to proceed D.D.*; *to proceed to (the degree of) D.D.*

proceeding, n. [1. prōséding; 2. prousídiŋ]. Prec. & **-ing. 1.** Act of going forward, continuing &c.; hence **a** a course, line, of action; behaviour, conduct; a transaction; steps taken in a business: *a doubtful sort of proceeding*; *a strange proceeding on his part*; specif. **b** *legal proceedings*, action in a court of law: *to take proceedings against*, to bring an action at law against. **2.** (in pl.) *Proceedings*, the published records, reports &c. of the transactions of a learned society &c.

proceeds, n. pl. [1. prṓsēds; 2. próusīdz], fr. **proceed**; the sing. is obs. That which proceeds, or results, from a transaction, from exploitation of property &c.; specif., product, realized profit: *to sell one's house and live on the proceeds*; *the proceeds of a business, sale, of one's estate* &c.

proceleusmatic, adj. [1. pròselūsmátik; 2. pròseljūsmǽtik], fr. Gk. *prokeleusmatikós*, fr. *prokeleúein*, 'to incite, rouse', fr. *pro-*, see **pro- (II.)**, & *keleúein*, 'to urge on', see **celebrate** & **celerity. 1.** (rare) Rousing, animating. **2.** (pros.) Containing four short syllables: *proceleusmatic foot*, a metrical foot of four short syllables.

procellarian, adj. & n. [1. pròsclárian; 2. prousəléəriən]. Neo-Lat. *procellaria* & **-an**, fr. Lat. *procella*, 'storm, tempest'; see **pro- (I.)**, & the base discussed under **celebrate** & **celerity. 1.** adj. (zool.) Belonging to the genus *Procellaria*, or the family *Procellaridae*, of sea-birds including the fulmars, albatrosses &c., and the typical species, the stormy petrel. **2.** n. A sea-bird belonging to this family; a stormy petrel, fulmar &c.

process (I.), n. [1. próses, próses; 2. próuses, prǝ́ses]. Fr. *procès*, fr. Lat. *processus*, 'advance, progress', fr. *prōcess-(um)*, P.P. type of *prōcēdĕre*. See **proceed**. **1**. The whole series and succession of movements or changes in position of the constituent parts of material objects, or of changes in the character of the substance of which these are composed, which occur in the operations of nature; esp. a series of such movements and changes as occur in inanimate substance, or if in animate, such as are involuntary, automatic, and unconscious; contrasted with *act, action*, which usually imply something consciously and deliberately done, as the result of volition, or at least something done by an animate or living organism: *a natural process; the process of development, decay, of reproduction, of digestion, of thawing; the process of water becoming ice; the process of petrifaction; a chemical process; in process of disintegrating*. **2**. Mode, method, according to which, manner in which, a series of deliberate material operations, directed to a given purpose, is carried out: *to invent a new process of dyeing; the processes of manufacture* &c.; *to cure deep-seated disease is generally a long process*. **3**. Series of mental operations; action of the mind in thought or volition: *psychological processes; the process(es) of reasoning* &c. **4**. Course; time during which something is being done before it is completed; fact of something being carried out: *in process of completion*, being done, but not finished. **5**. (legal) **a** Whole series of steps taken in legal proceedings; **b** specif., the writ, in full, *final process*, which brings a defendant to a court to answer to a civil or criminal action; *process server*, server of writ; sheriff's officer, bailiff. **6**. (print.) Any photo-mechanical method of reproducing pictures, illustrations &c., other than engraving by hand: *three-colour process* &c. **7**. (zool. and bot.) Any prominent, projecting part of an organism.

process (II.), vb. trans., fr. prec. To submit to, cause to undergo, some process of treatment: *to process meat*, i.e. in order to preserve it.

process (III.), vb. intrans. [1. prōsés; 2. prousés], fr. **procession**. (colloq.) To go, walk, in procession.

process-block, n. Block made by photo-mechanical process for reproducing pictures, illustrations &c.

procession (I.), n. [1. proséshun; 2. prǝséʃǝn]. Lat. *prōcessiōn-(em)*, 'a marching onwards, advance'; fr. *prōcess-(um)*, P.P. type of *prōcēdere*, see **proceed**. **1**. Act of proceeding; specif. (theol.) *procession of the Holy Ghost*, act and fact of proceeding, emanating, from the Father and the Son; Church's doctrine concerning this. **2**. That which proceeds, advances; specif., a continuous series, train &c. of persons, horses, carriages, or other objects, advancing in order, as part of a ceremony, to a given place: *funeral procession; procession of clergy; procession of boats* &c.

procession (II.), vb. trans. & intrans., fr. prec. **1**. trans. To march in procession along or through: *to procession the street, a town*. **2**. intrans. To form a procession &c.; go, march, in procession.

processional, adj. & n. [1. proséshunal; 2. prǝséʃǝnǝl]. See prec. & **-al**. **1**. adj. Connected with, pertaining to, of the nature of, used in, a procession: *a processional march, chant, cross* &c. **2**. n. **a** A book containing the service for use in ecclesiastical processions; **b** a processional chant or hymn.

processionally, adv. Prec. & **-ly**. In procession.

processionary, adj. [1. proséshunari; 2. prǝséʃǝnǝri]. **procession** (I.) & **-ary**. Processional, moving in procession: esp. *processionary caterpillar*, a hairy caterpillar of a moth, *Cnethocampa processionea*, and other species which marches when in search of food &c. in a long procession, and weaves large nests in oak trees, firs &c.

proces verbal, n., pl. *procès verbaux* [1. prósā várbahl; 2. prǝ́sei vérbal]. Fr., 'verbal process'. An official minute or record of transactions or proceedings, esp. the written deposition as to facts in relation to a criminal charge.

prochronism, n. [1. prôkronizm; 2. próukrǝnizǝm], fr. Gk. *prókhronos*, 'preceding in time', fr. **pro-** (II.) & *khrónos*, 'time' (on anal. of *anachronism*), see under **chronic**, & **-ism**. The dating of an event before it actually happened; ante-dating.

proclaim, vb. trans. [1. prōklám; 2. proukléim]. M.E. *proclamen*, fr. O. Fr. *proclamer*, fr. Lat. *prōclāmāre*, 'to call out, cry aloud, in defence or appeal', see **pro-** (I.) & **claim**. **1**. **a** To announce officially; to make known by proclamation: *to proclaim the king's accession, proclaim him king; proclaim war or peace; proclaim a man a traitor, outlaw* &c.; **b** to make known publicly, to publish abroad, to state openly and widely: *to proclaim the good news; to proclaim one's disgrace from the housetops*; **c** to reveal as, show to be: *his manners proclaimed him a gentleman*. **2**. To place under a ban, under restrictions: *to proclaim a district, country, meeting* &c.

proclamation, n. [1. pròklamáshun; 2. prǝ̀klǝméiʃǝn]. Lat. *prōclāmātiōn-(em)*, 'outcry, appeal', fr. *prōclāmāt-(um)*, P.P. of *prōclāmāre*. See prec. & **-ion**. **a** Act of proclaiming; **b** something proclaimed; especially an official, formal announcement; notice given of what is about to happen, of an order, of news &c.

proclamatory, adj. [1. proklámaturi; 2. prǝklǽmǝtǝri]. Prec. & **-ory**. Pertaining to, of the nature of, a proclamation.

proclitic, adj. & n. [1. prōklítik; 2. prouklítik]. Formed on anal. of **enclitic**; cp. Gk. *proklínein*, 'to lean forward'. **1**. adj. Losing its independent accent and, in popular phrase, 'throwing it forward' on to the next word; said of certain monosyllabic words in English such as articles, prepositions, auxiliaries, e.g. *the, to, am*, in such combinations as [1. dhe dóg; to gō; nō īm nót; 2. ðǝ dǝ́g; tǝ góu; nóu aim nǝ́t]. **2**. n. A proclitic word.

proclivity, n. [1. prōklíviti; 2. prouklíviti], fr. Lat. *prōclīvitāt-(em)*, lit. 'a sloping, leaning forward', hence, 'steep descent, declivity; tendency, propensity'. See **pro-** (I.) & the second element in **acclivity, declivity**. (only in moral sense) Tendency, inclination, propensity: *vicious proclivities; warlike proclivities; a proclivity to idleness*.

proconsul, n. [1. pròkónsl; 2. pròukǝ́nsl]. Lat., **pro-** (I.) & **consul**. **1**. Roman magistrate who performed the functions of a consul, a governor of a province, usually an ex-consul. **2**. (by transf.) A Governor of a colony or dominion.

proconsular, adj. [1. pròkónsūlar; 2. pròukǝ́nsjulǝ]. Prec. & **-ar**. Pertaining to, connected with, a proconsul: *proconsular powers; a proconsular province*.

proconsulate, n. [1. pròkónsūlat, -āt; 2. pròukǝ́nsjulit, -leit]. **proconsul** & **-ate**. Office of, period of office of, a proconsul.

proconsulship, n. [1. pròkónslship; 2. pròukǝ́nslʃip]. **proconsul** & **-ship**. Proconsulate.

procrastinate, vb. intrans. [1. prōkrástināt; 2. proukrǽstineit], fr. Lat. *prōcrāstināt-(um)*, P.P. type of *prōcrāstināre*, **pro-** (I.) & *crāstinus*, 'of, belonging to, tomorrow', fr. *crās*, 'tomorrow'; the etymol. of the latter is doubtful; possibly for **kᵃwṛs* & cogn. w. Scrt. *śvaś*, 'tomorrow'. To put off till tomorrow; to delay, defer, postpone; to be dilatory and hesitating in starting an action.

procrastination, n. [1. pròkrastináshun; 2. pròukræstinéiʃǝn], fr. Lat. *prōcrāstinātiōn-(em)*. Prec. & **-ion**. Act, habit, of procrastinating or putting off till tomorrow; dilatoriness.

procrastinator, n. [1. prōkrástināter; 2. proukrǽstineitǝ]. **procrastinate** & **-or**. One who procrastinates; a dilatory, unpunctual person.

procrastinatory, adj. [1. prōkrástinaturi; 2. proukrǽstinǝtǝri]. See prec. & **-ory**. Procrastinating, dilatory.

procreant, adj. [1. prôkreant; 2. próukriǝnt], fr. Lat. *prōcreant-(em)*, Pres. Part. of *prōcreāre*. See **procreate**. (poet.) Begetting, procreating, generating; fruitful, productive.

procreate, vb. trans. [1. pròkreāt; 2. pròukriéit], fr. Lat. *prōcreāt-(um)*, P.P. of *prōcreāre*, 'to beget'; **pro-** (I.) & **create**. To beget, engender, generate: *to procreate children, offspring*.

procreation, n. [1. pròkreáshun; 2. pròukriéiʃǝn], fr. Lat. *prōcreātiōn-(em)*. Prec. & **-ion**. Act of procreating; begetting and reproduction of offspring.

procreative, adj. [1. prókreātiv; 2. próukrieitiv]. **procreate** & **-ive**. Capable of procreating; productive.

Procrustean, adj. [1. prōkrústean; 2. proukrástiǝn], fr. *Procrustes*, Gk. *Prokroústēs*, a mythical robber who made his victims fit an iron bed by either stretching their limbs or cutting them off, fr. *prokroúein*, 'to beat, stretch out'; used primarily of the bed of Procrustes, fr. **pro-** (II.) & *kroúein*, 'to beat, strike'; fr. **krousein*; cogn. w. Lith. *kruszù*, 'to smash'; O. Slav. *kruchŭ*, 'piece, morsel'; O.N. *hreysar*, 'heap of stones'. Rendering adaptable, compelling conformity, by violent, rigorous means: *Procrustean methods* &c.

proctor, n. [1. prókter; 2. prǝ́ktǝ]. M.E. *proketour*, abbr. form of Lat. *prōcūrātor*. See **procurator**. One who acts on behalf of another; an agent; attorney, representative. Specif. **1**. (eccles.) a person elected to represent the clergy of a diocese, or the chapter of a cathedral in Convocation. **2**. (law) Formerly, one entitled to practise as an attorney in ecclesiastical and probate courts; now, a term of no special meaning, as all solicitors can so practise; the term survives in *King's Proctor (the Procurator General)*, an official representing the Crown with duty of watching matrimonial and probate causes with power of intervening in cases of collusion in divorce cases, suppression of material facts &c. **3**. (univ.) One of two university officials, *Senior and Junior Proctor*, appointed each year by colleges in rotation from among the Masters of Arts. The Proctors at Oxford and Cambridge represent the Masters of Arts, and the important administrative and disciplinary functions which they exercise are theoretically inherent in all Masters, and delegated to the Proctors for the time being.

proctorial, adj. [1. proktórial; 2. prǝktɔ́riǝl]. Prec. & **-ial**. Pertaining to, connected with, a proctor, esp. a University proctor: *proctorial duties, year, fine* &c.

proctorize, vb. intrans. & trans. [1. prókturīz; 2. prǝ́ktǝraiz]. **proctor** & **-ize**. **1**. intrans. To exercise the functions of a proctor. **2**. trans. (of a Univ. proctor) To exercise disciplinary functions, inflict penalties, upon (a member of the University): *to be proctorized for making a noise in the streets*.

proctorship, n. [1. próktership; 2. prǝ́ktǝʃip]. **proctor** & **-ship**. **a** Office of a proctor; **b** period of office of a proctor.

procumbent, adj. [1. prōkúmbent; 2. proukámbǝnt], fr. Lat. *prōcumbent-(em)*, *prōcumbens*, Pres. Part. of *prōcumbere*, 'to fall forward, to lie face downwards', see **pro-** (I.), & the base of second element of **incumbent**, & see **cubicle**. **1**. Lying face downwards; prone, prostrate. **2**. (bot.) Trailing on the ground, of creeping plants, stems &c.

procurable, adj. [1. prōkūrabl; 2. proukjɔ́rǝbl]. **procure** & **-able**. Able to be procured; obtainable.

procuration, n. [1. pròkūráshun; 2. prǝ̀kjuréiʃǝn]. Fr., fr. Lat. *prōcūrātiōn-(em)*, *prōcūrātio*, 'management, a taking care of'. See **procurator** & **-ion**. **1**. The management of another's legal affairs, the function of an ecclesiastical attorney or proctor; power of attorney, proxy. Phr. *per pro(c).* abbr. of *per procurationem*, by procuration, signature of one acting as agent for another. **2.** A sum paid in commutation for entertainment to a bishop or archdeacon on his visitation &c. by the incumbent of a parish. **3.** Act of procuring; procurement, agency; fee paid for such as for a loan &c. **4.** The procuring of women for immoral purposes.

procurator, n. [1. prókūrāter; 2. prɔ́kjureitə]. Lat., fr. *prōcūrāt-(um)*, P.P. type of *prōcūrāre*, 'to act, take care of, for another'. See **procure & -or. 1.** (Rom. hist.) An official in charge of the treasury or *fiscus*, the payment of troops &c. in certain provinces under the Empire; administration of an Imperial territory not advanced to the status of a province: *the procurator of Judaea.* **2.** (law) An attorney, proctor; specif. **a** *Procurator Fiscal* (Scots law), a public prosecutor; **b** *Procurator General*, the Treasury Solicitor, who is also *King's Proctor.*

procuratorial, adj. [1. pròkūratórial; 2. prɔ̀kjurətɔ́riəl]. Prec. & **-ial.** Of, pertaining to, a procurator or proctor.

procuratorship, n. [1. prókūrātership; 2. prɔ́kjureitəʃip]. **procurator & -ship.** Office, period of office, of a procurator or proctor.

procuratory, n. [1. prókūraturi; 2. prɔ́kjurət(ə)ri]. L. Med. Lat. *prōcūrātōrium.* **procurator & -y.** A mandate or authorization to act as procurator or proctor.

procuratrix, n. [1. prókūrātriks; 2. prɔ́kjurèitriks]. Lat., fem. of *prōcūrātor.* A nun in charge of the financial, administrative side of a nunnery.

procure, vb. trans. [1. prōkûr; 2. proukjɔ́], fr. Fr. *procurer*, fr. Lat. *prōcūrāre*, 'to take care of, look after, manage'. See **pro- (I.)** & **cure (II.). 1.** To gain, acquire, obtain by any means, by personal efforts, purchase, merit &c.: *to procure the earliest edition of a book*; *money may procure pleasures but not happiness*; *to procure an appointment, situation* &c. **2.** (archaic, poet.) To effect, bring about, cause: *his pride procured his downfall.* **3.** (also absol.) To get, obtain for unlawful, esp. sexual purposes; to act as a procurer or procuress.

procurement, n. [1. prōkûrment; 2. proukjɔ́mənt]. Prec. & **-ment.** The act of procuring (in all senses).

procurer, n. [1. prōkûrer; 2. proukjɔ́rə]. M.E. *procurour*, fr. O. Fr. *procureor*, Mod. Fr. *procureur*, fr. Lat. *prōcūrātor.* See **procurator.** One who procures for another, an agent; specif., one who procures a woman for the unlawful sexual purposes of another; a pander, a pimp.

procuress, n. [1. prōkûres; 2. proukjɔ́ris], fr. O. Fr. *procureresse.* Prec. & **-ess.** A woman procurer; female pander or pimp.

prod, n. & vb. trans. [1. prod; 2. prɔd]. Etymol. doubtful. **1.** n. **a** (obs. or provinc.) A sharp-pointed implement or stick; a goad, skewer; **b** a dig, poke, thrust; a jog, sharp, sudden jolt: *give him a prod in the ribs*; *a prod with a bayonet*; **c** (fig.) the action of rousing the attention, mental faculties, emotions &c. **2.** vb. **a** To poke, thrust, dig at, as with the end of a stick or pointed instrument; **b** (fig.) to rouse, stir up, incite: *to prod one's memory*; *to have one's energies prodded by another's example.*

prodigal, adj. & n. [1. pródigl; 2. prɔ́digəl]. O. Fr. *prodigal*, Mod. Fr. *prodigue*, fr. Lat. *prōdigus*, 'wasteful, lavish', also as n., 'a spendthrift, prodigal', fr. *prōdigere*, 'to drive forth, get rid of, to consume, waste', fr. *prōd-*, see **pro- (I.)**, & *agere*, 'to drive' &c. See under **agent. 1.** adj. **a** Lavish, bountiful, generous, open-handed: *prodigal of good things, of benefactions, favours*; **b** over-lavish, extravagant; wasteful, improvident: *prodigal expenditure*; *the prodigal son.* **2.** n. A prodigal person; spendthrift, wastrel, squanderer: *the return of the prodigal.*

prodigality, n. [1. pròdigáliti; 2. prɔ̀digǽliti], fr. Fr. *prodigalité*, prob. formed w. suff. **-ity**, fr. prec. & not fr. the rare Lat. *prōdigālitāt-(em).* **a** (in good sense) (i.) Plenty, abundance, profusion, copiousness: '*The pomp and prodigality of heaven*' (Gray, To Bentley); *the prodigality of nature*; (ii.) open-handedness; **b** (in unfavourable sense) undue lavishness, wastefulness, extravagance, over-profusion: *ruined by his prodigality.*

prodigalize, vb. trans. [1. pródigalīz; 2. prɔ́digəlaiz]. **prodigal & -ize.** (rare or obs.) To spend lavishly or wastefully; to spend like a prodigal.

prodigally, adv. [1. pródigali; 2. prɔ́dig(ə)li]. See prec. & **-ly.** In a prodigal fashion; wastefully, extravagantly.

prodigious, adj. [1. prodíjus; 2. prədídʒəs], fr. Lat. *prōdigiōsus*, 'marvellous, wonderful, monstrous', see **prodigy & -ous. a** Marvellous, amazing, wonderful; specif. **b** extraordinary in size, quantity &c.; immense, vast, enormous, abnormally large: *a prodigious waste of money*; *a prodigious building, display of learning* &c.

prodigiously, adv. Prec. & **-ly.** Marvellously, enormously, vastly.

prodigiousness, n. See prec. & **-ness.** State, quality, of being prodigious.

prodigy, n. [1. pródiji; 2. prɔ́didʒi], fr. Lat. *prōdigium*, 'prophetic sign, omen, portent', fr. *prōd*, see **pro- (I.)**, & **agion*, 'something said, proclaimed', fr. base of *aiō*, 'I say, relate', fr. **agjō*; prob. cogn. w. Gk. *ē*, 'he said' (fr. **ēkt-*); O. Ir. *ai, ae*, 'legend, saga'; cp. **adage.** An extraordinary, marvellous thing, person, event, esp. one out of the normal course of nature; a wonder, marvel, monster, formerly also a portent or omen: *prodigies or freaks of nature*; *a prodigy of learning*; *the nightly prodigy of the stars.* Phr. *infant prodigy*, a very talented or precocious child.

prodromal, adj. [1. prodrṓmal; 2. prodróuməl]. **prodrome & -al.** (med.) Of, pertaining to, prodromes; prodromic, premonitory: *prodromal symptoms of a disease.*

prodrome, n. [1. prṓdrōm; 2. próudroum], fr. Neo-Lat. *prodromus*, also irregular *prodroma*, pl. *prodromata*, fr. Gk. *pródromos*, adj., 'running before, going in advance'. See **pro- (II.)** & base discussed under **dromedary. 1.** (obs.) An elementary, preliminary, book of instruction; a primer. **2.** (med.) A warning, premonitory symptom of a disease.

prodromic, adj. [1. prōdrómik; 2. proudrɔ́mik]. Prec. & **-ic.** (med.) Prodromal.

produce (I.), vb. trans. & intrans. [1. prodûs; 2. prədjûs], fr. Lat. *prōdūcere*, 'to lead forward, bring forth; to bring into the world, beget, bear; produce; to draw out, lengthen'. See **pro- (I.)** & base in **duct, duke. A.** trans. **1.** To bring forward; to have at hand and exhibit for inspection &c.: *to produce one's passport, railway ticket* &c.; *to produce five pounds from one's pocket*; specif. (in law) *to produce a witness, evidence.* Phr. *to produce a play*, stage it, organize the introduction of it to the public. **2.** To bring forth, bear, yield: *the soil produces corn*; *the tree produces fruit*; *the flock produced many lambs*; *the investment produces a small income.* **3.** To be the cause of, to bring about; give rise to: *extravagance has produced heavy taxation*; *pleasures do not produce happiness*; *the war produced no Napoleon*; *their efforts produced no results.* **4.** To manufacture, make; **a** to turn raw material into economically useful and marketable goods: *to produce steel, cotton goods* &c.; specif., *to produce a book*, to print, bind, and publish it; **b** to create by intellectual effort, to be the author of: *to produce scientific works*; *to produce poetry, pictures* &c. **5.** To continue, extend: *to produce a line from one point to another*; *a produced side*, extended side. **B.** intrans. **1.** To yield, bear: *the mines no longer produced in paying quantities.* **2. a** To manufacture, to turn out, goods: *the salvation of trade is to produce*; **b** to be the author of literary, scientific, or artistic work: *he is supposed to be a very learned man, but he seems unable to produce.*

produce (II.), n. [1. pródūs; 2. prɔ́djūs], fr. prec. That which is produced; product, yield, the outcome of labour or of natural growth: *produce of the fields*; *the produce of the factories and mills.*

producer, n. [1. prodûser; 2. prədjúsə]. **produce (I.) & -er. 1.** Person who produces; specif. **a** one who grows natural produce, or who manufactures commodities out of raw material; contrasted with *consumer*; **b** person who produces, stages, a play. **2.** A special form of furnace for the making of *producer gas*, a cheap gas, principally carbon-monoxide, obtained from a special type of furnace with fuel on the top, steam and air being forced through it, the resulting gas being used for gas-engines &c.

producibility, n. [1. prodúsibíliti; 2. prədjûsibíliti]. See next word & **-ity.** State, quality, of being producible.

producible, adj. [1. prodúsibl; 2. prədjûsibl]. **produce (I.) & -ible.** Capable of being produced.

product, n. [1. pródukt; 2. prɔ́dəkt, -akt], fr. Lat. *prōduct-(um)*, P.P. type of *prōdūcere.* See **produce (I.). 1.** That which is produced; specif. **a** result of natural growth: *the products of the soil*; *natural products*; **b** anything produced by industry and manufacture: *the products of the loom and forge*; **c** something produced by intellectual activity: *the products of Shakespeare's genius.* **2.** (gen.) Result, outcome: *restlessness and discontent are among the products of modern social conditions.* **3.** (chem.) Any substance produced by, or as the result of, chemical change, as contrasted with *educt*, a substance merely separated from material. **4.** (math.) The result obtained by multiplying two or more numbers: *the product of 6 and 3 is 18.*

production, n. [1. prodúkshun; 2. prədákʃən]. Fr., fr. Lat. *prōductiōn-(em)*, 'a prolongation, extension'; in L. Lat., 'a bringing forward'; in present senses a new formation fr. **product & -ion. 1.** Act of producing; **a** a prolongation, extension: *production of a line*; **b** act of making, manufacturing: *production is falling off*; *the production of textiles*; **c** act of creating by intellectual effort: *the production of scientific research, of literature* &c.; **d** act of producing or staging a play. **2. a** Something produced, as a result of material or intellectual effort and labour, skill &c.: *the newest production of the factories*; *a production of genius*; **b** specif. (polit. econ.) the creation of wealth: *production and consumption.*

productional, adj. [1. prodúkshunal; 2. prədákʃənəl]. Prec. & **-al.** Pertaining to, concerned with, resulting from, production: *productional values.*

productive, adj. [1. prodúktiv; 2. prədáktiv], fr. L. Lat. *prōductīvus*, 'fit for production or elongation', in Med. Lat., 'productive', cp. Fr. *productif.* See **product & -ive. 1.** Having the power or quality of producing; (in various senses) producing in great quantity; fertile, yielding in abundance; creative: *productive soil*; *a productive vineyard, mine, oil-field* &c.; *a productive writer, poet, scholar* &c. **2.** Causing, tending to cause or produce: *productive of error, of evil*; *the age was productive of men of genius.* **3.** (polit. econ.) Producing that which is of exchangeable value; producing economic wealth: *productive and unproductive labour.*

productively, adv. Prec. & **-ly.** In a productive manner; by production; abundantly.

productiveness, n. See prec. & **-ness.** State, quality, of being productive; productivity.

productivity, n. [1. pròduktíviti; 2. prɔ̀daktíviti]. **productive & -ity.** State, quality, of being productive; fertility, productiveness.

proem, n. [1. próem; 2. próuɛm], fr. O. Fr. *proëme*, fr. Lat. *prooemium*, fr. Gk. *prooímion*, 'introduction, prelude', fr. **pro- (II.)** & *oimos*, 'path, way', cp. *oímē*, 'the way of song, a lay', fr. **oi-*, grade of base **ei*, 'to go', as in *eîmi*, 'I will go'. See this base under **itinerate**. A prelude, introduction, preface to a book, speech &c.

proemial, adj. [1. prōḗmial; 2. prouímiəl]. Prec. & **-ial**. (poet.) Of, pertaining to, a proem or prelude; prefatory, introductory.

profanation, n. [1. prŏfanā́shun; 2. prɔ̀fənéiʃən], fr. L., Eccles., Lat. *profānātiōn-(em)*, *profānāt-(um)*, P.P. type of *profānāre*. See **profane**. Act of profaning; desecration; treating of sacred things with irreverence or contempt: *profanation of a temple, of the name of God* &c.

profane (I.), adj. [1. prōfā́n; 2. prouféin]. Fr., fr. Lat. *profānus*, prob. orig. 'outside the temple', hence 'not sacred, unholy; common'. See **pro- (I.)** & **fane**. **1.** Not sacred or holy; concerned with, relating to, matters other than religious; secular: *profane history, writers, art* &c. **2.** Not admitted to the temple or shrine; uninitiated; hence common, vulgar: *the profane crowd*; (also ellipt. as n.) *the profane*; *esoteric mysteries are not for the profane*. **3.** Heathen, pagan: *profane rites and ceremonies*. **4.** Irreverent, blasphemous, sacrilegious: *profane language* &c.

profane (II.), vb. trans., fr. Lat. *profānāre*, 'to make profane'. See prec. **1.** To treat (sacred objects) with irreverence, violence, or contempt; to desecrate, pollute: *to profane a shrine, temple* &c. **2.** To treat with disrespect, to dishonour, put to a base or unworthy use: *to profane the Sabbath, the name of God, the national flag* &c.

profanely, adv. [1. prōfā́nli; 2. prouféinli]. **profane** (I.) & **-ly**. In a profane manner; with profanity; irreverently, blasphemously.

profaneness, n. [1. prōfā́nnes; 2. prouféinnis]. See prec. & **-ness**. State, quality, of being profane; profanity.

profanity, n. [1. prōfániti; 2. proufǽniti], fr. L., Eccles., Lat. *profānitāt-(em)*. **profane** & **-ity**. State, quality, of being profane; profaneness; a profane act, irreverence; specif., profane language &c.; blasphemy.

profess, vb. trans. & intrans. [1. profés; 2. prəfés]. In M.E. first as *professed*, P.P., 'bound by a vow' (of a monk or nun), fr. O. Fr. *profes*, masc., *professe*, fem., fr. Lat. *prōfessus*, 'avowed, confessed', P.P. of *prōfitēri*, 'to avow, declare in public'. See **pro- (I.)**, & for second element **fate, confess**. **A.** trans. **1. a** To assert, affirm, declare, avow: *to profess one's dislike of long speeches*; also **b** (reflex.) *profess oneself*: *to profess oneself glad to be home again, a lover of the country* &c., to state, assert, that one is . . .; represent oneself as being &c. **2.** To confess, avow, one's belief in; to follow precepts, accept doctrines of: *to profess no religion*; *to profess Christianity*. Such reflexive constructions as *to profess oneself a Christian* belong to **1, b**. **3. a** To feign, assert falsely, pretend: *to profess a love which one does not feel*; *to profess admiration for*; **b** to claim falsely, pretend, to be: *to profess to be a learned man*; **c** (reflex.) *to profess oneself fond of hard work*. **4.** To practise as a profession: *to profess law, medicine* &c. **5.** To teach as a professor: *to profess Greek, physics, chemistry* &c. **B.** intrans. **1.** To practise a religion. **2.** To take religious vows as a monk or nun. **3.** (colloq., back-formation fr. *professor*) To act as, be, a professor of a subject at a university: *he professes in Glasgow*.

professed, adj. [1. profést; 2. prəfést]. P.P. of prec. **1.** Avowed, declared, self-acknowledged: *a professed Jew*; *professed enemy of reform*. **2.** Having taken vows as a monk or nun: *a professed nun*. **3.** Falsely alleged to be, pretended: *a professed saint, but really a scoundrel*; *his professed piety was mere hypocrisy*.

professedly, adv. [1. profésedli; 2. prəfésidli]. Prec. & **-ly**. By profession, avowedly; ostensibly; according to one's own professions and claims.

professing, adj. [1. profésing; 2. prəfésiŋ], fr. Pres. Part. of **profess**. Making profession of, and obeying precepts of, a specified religion: *a professing Christian, Jew* &c.

profession, n. [1. proféshun; 2. prəféʃən]. Fr., fr. Lat. *prōfessiōn-(em)*, 'avowal, declaration'. See **profess** & **-ion**. **1. a** Confession (of faith); affirmation (of loyalty, affection &c.): *profession of faith, loyalty*; **b** untrue, insincere, expression of feeling, belief &c. **2.** That which one professes or practises as a calling, specif., one of the learned or liberal vocations, formerly sharply contrasted with *trade* or *business*, though the distinction is rapidly breaking down: *the learned, scientific, professions*; *the profession of a barrister*; *a doctor by profession*. **3.** The body of persons professing or practising a particular calling: *the etiquette of the profession*; *the profession as a whole condemned him*. **4.** Act of taking vows as a monk or nun and entering a religious community.

professional (I.), adj. [1. proféshunal; 2. prəféʃənəl]. Prec. & **-al**. **1.** (of persons) **a** Belonging to and practising one of the liberal professions: *a professional man*; *the professional classes*, contrasted with *tradesman, shopkeeping classes* on the one hand, and with *independent gentleman, landed classes* on the other; **b** engaged in, practising, a specified profession as a permanent occupation or as a means of livelihood: *a professional painter, actor, singer* &c., contrasted with *amateur*; **c** behaving, acting, in accordance with the accepted habits of a profession; trained, skilled, in the methods of a profession; pedantically observant of the mannerisms in vogue in a profession; specif. **d** playing a game for pay or gain; making a game one's profession or business; engaged in by professionals, contrasted with *amateur*, as playing merely for sport: *a professional cricketer, golfer, sculler* &c.; *professional match, tournament, race* &c. **2.** (of manners, behaviour, knowledge, traditions &c.) Current in, suitable to, characteristic of, a specific profession: *professional skill*; *professional etiquette*; *professional appearance*.

professional (II.), n., fr. prec. Contrasted w. *amateur*. **1.** A person engaged in practising an art or science as a profession or means of livelihood; specif., a professional painter, actor, musician, singer &c. Specif. **2**, one playing a game as a business or livelihood or for money prizes (abbr. *pro*); in cricket often styled *player*: *Gentlemen* v. *Professionals* or *Players*.

professionalism, n. [1. proféshunalizm; 2. prəféʃənəlizəm]. Prec. & **-ism**. **1.** The pursuit of a profession as a means of livelihood; status, manner, rules, practice, of a profession. **2.** The practice of employing professionals in a game; contrasted with *amateurism*: *some think that British sport is suffering badly from professionalism*.

professionalize, vb. trans. [1. proféshunalīz; 2. prəféʃənəlaiz]. **professional** (I.) & **-ize**. **a** To give a professional character or status to; **b** to employ professional players in.

professionally, adv. [1. proféshunali; 2. prəféʃənəli]. **professional** (I.) & **-ly**. In a professional manner; as a professional: *to consult a doctor, lawyer, professionally*, to seek medical, legal, advice; contrasted with consulting as a friend, on matter outside their professions.

professor, n. [1. proféser; 2. prəfésə]. Lat., 'a public teacher, one who makes teaching his profession or business'; see **profess** & **-or**. **1.** One who professes or declares publicly his religious belief: *a professor of Calvinism* &c. **2.** One who teaches publicly a branch of learning, science or art; specif., a teacher of the highest rank, holding an endowed chair at a university: *a Professor of Greek, of Astronomy* &c. **3.** (as pretentious title) One who teaches or claims to teach, or to be skilled in any art, game &c.: *professor of conjuring, dancing, golf, chiropody* &c.

professorate, n. [1. profésurāt; 2. prəfésəreit]. Prec. & **-ate**. Office of a professor; professorship.

professorial, adj. [1. pròfesórial; 2. prɔ̀fesɔ́riəl]. **professor** & **-ial**. Pertaining to, characteristic of, befitting, suitable to, a professor: *a professorial manner, dictum*.

professorially, adv. Prec. & **-ly**. In a professorial manner; as a professor.

professoriate, n. [1. pròfesóriat; 2. prɔ̀fesɔ́ri·it]. **professor** & **-ate**. The body of professors at a university.

professorship, n. [1. profésership; 2. prəfésəʃip]. **professor** & **-ship**. Post of professor at a university.

proffer, vb. trans. & n. [1. prófer; 2. prɔ́fə]. M.E. *profren, proferen*, fr. A.-Fr. *profrer*, O. Fr. *profrir, porfrir*. See **pro- (I.)** & **offer**. **1.** vb. **a** To offer for acceptance, to propose as a gift: *to proffer one's services, a gift, friendship* &c.; *refuse his proffered assistance*; **b** to propose: *he proffered to help*. **2.** n. (rare) **a** An offer; **b** something proffered, or offered, for acceptance.

proficiency, n. [1. profíshensi; 2. prəfíʃənsi]. See next word & **-cy**. State, quality, of being proficient; skill, efficiency, expertness, in an art, craft, game &c.

proficient, adj. & n. [1. profíshent; 2. prəfíʃənt], fr. Lat. *prōficient-(em)*, Pres. Part. of *prōficere*, 'to go forward, advance; to make progress; to accomplish'; **pro- (I.)** & **-fic**, form of base of *facere*, 'to make, do', see **fact**. **1.** adj. Skilled, expert, adept, competent. **2.** n. An expert, adept.

proficiently, adv. Prec. & **-ly**. In a proficient manner; with proficiency.

profile (I.), n. [1. prṓfēl; 2. próufīl], fr. Ital. *profilo*, Mod. Ital. *proffilo*, 'border, drawing in outline', fr. *prof(f)ilare*, 'to draw in outline'; **pro- (I.)** & *filo*, 'thread, line', fr. Lat. *fīlum*, 'a thread, string', see **file (III.)**. **1.** A drawing in outline, silhouette, the drawing in line of the side view of an object, esp. of the face: *drawn in profile*. **2.** The side view of the human face: *he has a fine profile, but is not so good looking full face*. **3.** (archit. and fort.) A contour drawing, an outline of the vertical section of a building, moulding &c., an outline of a transverse section of an earthwork showing the thickness at various heights.

profile (II.), vb. trans., fr. prec. To draw in profile or outline from a side view. *Profiling machine*, a machine tool for cutting plates of metal into irregular shapes according to patterns.

profilist, n. [1. prṓfēlist; 2. próufīlist]. Prec. & **-ist**. An artist who draws portraits in profile or silhouette.

profit (I.), n. [1. prófit; 2. prɔ́fit]. O. Fr., fr. Lat. *prōfectum*, n., 'advance, progress', & P.P. of *prōficere*, 'to advance, make progress, be profitable'. See **proficient**. **1.** Material or spiritual benefit, gain; advantage; a valuable result or consequence of action, work &c.: *to derive great profit from instruction*; *to do something with profit to one's health*; *what's the profit of doing that?*; *there is no profit in . . .* **2.** Specif. (often pl.) pecuniary gain; the excess, in money value, of receipts or returns over outlay or cost in a business, trade, occupation &c.: *to make a profit on*; *to work for profit*; *gross profits*, the excess difference of total receipts over expenditure without deductions of insurance, overhead charges &c.; *net profit*, with all deductions made; *profit and loss account*, an account showing side by side the profit and the loss during a single year of trade; *an office of profit*, an office, position, which brings pecuniary or material gain, the acceptance of which, if 'under the Crown' or Government, as defined by law, compels the resignation of a member of Parliament and another election.

profit (II.), vb. trans. & intrans. M.E. *profiten*, fr. Fr. *profiter*. See prec. **A.** trans. To yield profit or advantage to, to benefit;

to be of service, of use, or of profit to: '*what shall it profit a man if he . . . lose his own soul?*' (Mk. viii. 36); *this course of conduct won't profit you; all his wealth didn't profit him.* **B.** intrans. **a** To derive advantage, benefit; to profit by advice: *my health has profited greatly from my stay abroad*; **b** to make a pecuniary profit: *to profit by, over, a transaction.*

profitable, adj. [1. prófitabl; 2. prɔ́fitəbl]. Fr. See **profit (I.)** & **-able**. **1.** Advantageous, useful, beneficial: *profitable instruction, advice* &c. **2.** Yielding a pecuniary profit; lucrative: *a profitable business; profitable work.*

profitableness, n. See prec. & **-ness**. State, quality, of being profitable.

profitably, adv. Prec. & **-ly**. In a profitable manner; to a profitable degree; with profit or advantage.

profit à prendre, n. [1. prófit ah prahndr; 2. prɔ́fit *a* prɑ̃dr]. Fr., lit. 'profit to take'. (law) The right of the owner of a tenement, of land &c., to take a profit from the tenement of another by prescription or grant; a form of easement.

profiteer, n. & vb. intrans. [1. pròfitḗr; 2. prɔ̀fitíə]. **profit (II.)** & **-eer**. **1.** n. One who makes an exorbitant or unjustifiable profit out of a business or trade by taking advantage of a shortage of supply or of the necessities of consumers: *a war-profiteer.* **2.** vb. To make an exorbitant, unjustifiable profit by business or trade.

profiteering, n. & adj. [1. pròfitḗring; 2. prɔ̀fit*íəriŋ*]. Prec. & **-ing**. **1.** vbl. n. Act or fact of making an exorbitant profit: *profiteering of tradesmen.* **2.** vbl. adj. Inclined to profiteer; practising profiteering: *a profiteering scoundrel.*

profitless, adj. [1. prófitles; 2. prɔ́fitlis]. **profit (I.)** & **-less**. Having, yielding, no profit; fruitless, futile, vain; giving no result: *a profitless business; a profitless journey, effort, task.*

profitlessly, adv. Prec. & **-ly**. Without profit or gain; uselessly.

profit-sharing, n. [1. prófit shàring; 2. prɔ́fit ʃèəriŋ]. System of giving some share in the profits of a business to the workmen employed in it, as an addition to their regular wages.

profligacy, n. [1. prófligasi; 2. prɔ́fligəsi]. **profligate** & **-cy**. State, quality, of being profligate; profligate conduct, extravagance, dissipation.

profligate, adj. & n. [1. prófligat; 2. prɔ́fligit], fr. Lat. *prōflīgātus*, 'wretched, miserable, abandoned, dissolute', P.P. of *prōflīgāre*, 'to strike, cast down, overwhelm, destroy'. See **pro- (I.)** & second element of **afflict** & cp. **conflict**. **1.** adj. Dissolute, depraved, immoral. **2.** n. A profligate person.

profligately, adv. Prec. & **-ly**. In a profligate manner.

pro formâ, adv. & adj. [1. prṓ fórma; 2. próu fɔ́mə]. Lat. **a** adv. For form's sake, as a matter of form, as a sample or form; **b** adj., designating a form as a sample: *a pro formâ invoice*, invoice showing price &c. of goods to be sold.

profound (I.), adj. [1. profóund; 2. prəfáund], fr. O. Fr. *profund*, fr. Lat. *profundus*, 'deep, bottomless', fr. **pro- (I.)** & *fundus*, 'bottom', q.v. under **fund**. **1.** Very deep, reaching to a great depth: (in material sense, chiefly poet.) *depths profound; the profoundest depths of the ocean*; also *a profound slumber.* **2.** Mentally deep; going to the bottom of a subject; thorough, searching, subtle, contrasted with *superficial*: *a profound scholar, profound knowledge; a work which is not very profound; profound statesmanship.* **3.** Intense, deeply felt: *profound melancholy; profound contempt; profound regrets, apologies; profound respect for.* Phr. *to make a profound curtsy, reverence*, low bow &c. expressive of reverence and humility.

profound (II.), n., fr. prec. (poet. or rhet., with *the*) The deep, the sea or ocean; an abyss; infinite space.

profoundly, adv. [1. profóundli; 2. prəfáundli]. **profound (I.)** & **-ly**. In a profound manner; with deep and genuine feeling: *profoundly grateful, moved; to apologize, regret, profoundly.*

profoundness, n. [1. profóundnes; 2. prəfáundnis]. See prec. & **-ness**. State, quality, of being profound; depth, thoroughness, profundity: *to doubt the profoundness of his knowledge, statesmanship* &c.

profundity, n. [1. profúnditi; 2. prəfánditi], fr. Lat. *profunditāt-(em)*, 'depth, intensity'. See **profound** & **-ity**. (chiefly in nonmaterial sense; lit. and material sense rare except as poet. or rhet. usage) **a** State, quality, of being profound; depth: *profundity of feeling, of sorrow, of thought* &c.; **b** (poet.) *no eye could fathom the profundity of those depths.*

profuse, adj. [1. profū́s; 2. prəfjū́s], fr. Lat. *profūs-(um)*, 'spread out, extended, extravagant, lavish', P.P. of *profundere*, 'to pour out, shed; to stretch out, extend'. See **pro- (I.)** & **fuse (I.)**. **1.** Abundant, copious, plentiful: *profuse hospitality, generosity; profuse perspiration; profuse apologies, thanks.* **2.** (of persons) **a** Liberal, open-handed, generous, prodigal: *profuse in his hospitality; profuse in his thanks, expressions of goodwill* &c.; **b** over-lavish, extravagant: *profuse in expenditure.*

profusely, adv. Prec. & **-ly**. In a profuse manner; copiously, extravagantly.

profuseness, n. See prec. & **-ness**. Quality, state, of being profuse; lavishness, copiousness, profusion.

profusion, n. [1. profū́zhun; 2. prəfjū́ʒən], fr. Lat. *profūsiōn-(em)*. See **profuse** & **-ion**. **a** Profuseness, abundance, lavish supply, copious plenty: *a profusion of gifts; a profusion of fruit and blossom*; **b** excessive, extravagant, luxury: *a house furnished with profusion.*

prog (I.), n. [1. prog; 2. prɔg]. Etymol. doubtful. (vulg. slang) Food, grub.

prog (II.), n. & vb. trans. Facetious form of **proctor**. (slang) **a** n. A proctor at a university; **b** vb., to proctorize.

progenitive, adj. [1. prōjénitiv; 2. proudʒéni*tiv*]. See next word & **-ive**. Capable of begetting offspring, propagating, productive.

progenitor, n. [1. prōjéniter; 2. proudʒénitə], fr. **pro- (I.)** & *genitor*, 'parent, begetter', see base in **genital** & **-or**. An ancestor, forefather; the founder of a family.

progenitorial, adj. [1. prōjenitṓrial; 2. proudʒenitɔ́riəl]. Prec. & **-ial**. Of, pertaining to, a progenitor or progenitors.

progenitress, -trix, n. [1. prōjénitres, -triks; 2. proudʒénitris, -triks]. See **progenitor** & **-ess**, or fr. Lat. w. fem. suff. *-ix*. A female progenitor.

progeniture, n. [1. prōjénichur; 2. proudʒéni*tʃə*]. See **progenitor**, & **-ure**. **1.** Act of begetting offspring. **2.** Birth, ancestry.

progeny, n. [1. prójeni; 2. prɔ́dʒini], fr. obs. Fr. *progenie*, fr. Lat. *prōgenies*, 'descent, lineage; offspring, descendants'; **pro-** & base **ĝen-*, 'birth' &c. See **genesis, genus** &c. Offspring, children; descendants.

proggins, n. [1. próginz; 2. prɔ́ginz], fr. **prog (II.)**. (slang) A proctor at a university.

proglottis, n. [1. prōglótis; 2. prouglɔ́tis]. Neo-Lat., cp. Gk. *proglōssis*, 'the tip of the tongue'. See **pro- (II.)** & **glottis**. (zool.) Segment of a tapeworm, containing sexually mature male and female organs and so capable of reproduction when broken off from the main body.

prognathic, adj. [1. prōgnáthik; 2. prougnǽþik]. **pro- (II.)** & **gnathic**. Prognathous.

prognathism, n. [1. prōgnáthizm; 2. prougnǽþizəm]. See prec. & **-ism**. State, condition, of being prognathous; tendency to be prognathous.

prognathous, adj. [1. prōgnā́thus; 2. prougnéiþəs]. **pro- (II.)** & base *gnath-*, 'jaw', as in **gnathic**, & **-ous**. Having jaws projecting beyond the upper part of the face.

prognosis, n. [1. prognṓsis; 2. prɔgnóusis]. Lat., fr. Gk. *prógnōsis*, 'a knowing beforehand, previous knowledge'. See **pro- (I.)** & **gnosis**. **1. a** Act of foretelling or prognosticating; **b** specif. (med.) the opinion formed as to the probable future course of an illness, disease &c.; contrasted with *diagnosis.* **2. a** An indication, omen, prognostication; **b** specif. (med.) a symptom on which a prognosis may be formed.

prognostic, adj. & n. [1. prognóstik; 2. prɔgnɔ́stik], fr. Med. Lat. *prognosticus*, fr. Gk. *prognōstikós*. See **pro- (II.)** & **gnostic**. **1.** adj. Prognosticating, foretelling, forecasting: *prognostic symptoms; symptoms prognostic of a fatal issue.* **2.** n. A sign, indication, symptom; prediction, warning, prognostication: *a prognostic of success, failure; all the prognostics are favourable.*

prognosticable, adj. [1. prognóstikabl; 2. prɔgnɔ́stikəbl]. Prec. & **-able**. Capable of being prognosticated or foretold.

prognosticate, vb. trans. [1. prognóstikāt; 2. prɔgnɔ́stikeit], fr. Med. Lat. *prognosticāt-(um)*, P.P. type of *prognosticāre*, as **prognostic** & **-ate**. To foretell, forecast; to predict, presage, warn: *to prognosticate success or failure; the clouds prognosticate a storm.*

prognostication, n. [1. prognòstikā́shun; 2. prɔgnɔ̀stikéiʃən]. O. Fr., fr. Med. Lat. *prognosticātiōn-(em)*. See prec. & **-ion**. **1.** Act of prognosticating. **2.** Something which prognosticates; a warning symptom or indication; a prognostic.

prognosticative, adj. [1. prognóstikativ; 2. prɔgnɔ́stikətiv]. **prognosticate** & **-ive**. Having the quality, character, of a prognostication; prognosticating, predictive.

prognosticator, n. [1. prognóstikāter; 2. prɔgnɔ́stikeitə]. See prec. & **-or**. One who prognosticates.

programme, program (I.), n. [1. prṓgram; 2. próugræm]. Fr. *programme*, fr. Lat. *programma*, fr. Gk. *prógramma, prográmmatos*, 'public notice, edict'. See **pro- (II.)** & **-gram**. **1. a** Printed slip giving details in order of a public entertainment, concert, play &c., and the names of the performers; **b** the performance itself; the items rendered: *a poor programme*; **c** card containing list of dances at a ball with spaces for partners' names. Phr. *to fill up one's programme*, to have many partners. **2. a** An outline, schedule, of a course of study, of proceedings; list of engagements or of things intended to be done: *to draw up a programme of work for next term; the programme for tomorrow; a full programme*, numerous occupations, engagements &c.; **b** an outline of policy, contemplated legislation, promised reforms &c., of a political party with which it appeals to the electorate.

programme (II.), vb. trans., fr. prec. (rare) To draw up a programme for; to plan, design.

programme music, n. Orchestral or instrumental music composed with the purpose of describing by sound, and not by words or action, scenes, events, emotions &c.; the scenes &c. to be described being indicated in the programme or by the title.

progress (I.), n. [1. prṓgres; 2. próugres], fr. O. Fr. *progrez*, Mod. Fr. *progrès*, fr. Lat. *prōgressus*, n., 'a going forward, advance; growth, increase', fr. *prōgress-*, P.P. type of *prōgredi*, 'to go, move, forward'. See **pro- (I.)** & **gradus**. **1.** Forward movement or motion; locomotion, journey forward, or in any desired direction, away from starting-point: *further progress was delayed by deep snow; progress was greatly impeded by bad roads.* **2.** Advance, improvement, betterment, upward trend: **a** (in physical, material sense) *to make progress towards health; progress in the art of agriculture; progress in aviation*; **b** (in intellectual, moral, spiritual development) *progress in, of, education, knowledge; to make progress in one's education, in learning to write, in speaking French; the progress of* *mankind*; *the progress of medicine, surgery.* **3.** Expansion, increase, dissemination: *the progress of the Christian spirit*; *the progress of Bolshevism among the foolish and ignorant.* **4.** Forward movement, forward trend or natural course; development: *the progress of events*; *the disease makes rapid progress*; *the war seems to make no progress.* Phrs. *in progress*, going forward, continuing, in process of being carried out: *building is now in progress*; *to report progress*, (British Parliament) to wind up for the day all further debate or business on a bill before the House and defer further debate till a future date to be fixed; hence, to postpone anything to a more suitable or convenient time. **5.** An official journey, tour, or visitation, conducted with a certain pomp or ceremony, undertaken by a sovereign or other important person: *Queen Elizabeth's progresses.*

progress (II.), vb. intrans. [1. prōgrés; 2. prougrés], fr. prec. **1. a** To move forward, to move in direction desired, towards object aimed at: *in three hours we hardly progressed at all*; **b** to improve: *is your health progressing?*; *my knowledge of French progresses steadily*; **c** to develop into something better: *it must be admitted that mankind has progressed considerably during the historical period.* **2.** To continue to be carried out, to go forward towards completion: *the work of bringing in the harvest is progressing slowly but satisfactorily.* **3.** To go on a progress.

progression, n. [1. prōgréshun; 2. prougréʃən]. Fr., fr. Lat. *prōgressiōn-(em)*, *prōgressio.* See prec. & **-ion. 1.** Act of moving forward; movement forward, advance, progress (see various senses of the last): *means of progression.* **2.** (math.) A series of numbers in which the terms increase or decrease by a regular law: *arithmetical progression*, a series in which each number increases or decreases in consecutive order by the same quantity, as 2, 4, 6, 8 &c.; *geometrical progression*, where the increase or decrease is by a common ratio or proportion, as 4, 12, 36; *harmonic progression*, a series of quantities whose reciprocals are in arithmetical progression, as $\frac{1}{3}$, $\frac{1}{4}$, $\frac{1}{5}$. **3.** (mus.) A succession of notes or chords: *melodic* or *harmonic progression.*

progressional, adj. [1. prōgréshunal; 2. prougréʃənəl]. Prec. & **-al.** (poet. or rare) Of, pertaining to, a forward movement, progress, or advance: *the progressional march of events.*

progressionist, n. [1. prōgréshunist; 2. prougréʃənist]. **progression** & **-ist.** One who believes in the constant progression or progress of mankind to better things; believer in ultimate perfection.

progressist, n. [1. prógresist; 2. próugresist]. **progress (I.)** & **-ist.** One who believes in political progress; a member of any political party which styles itself 'progressive'.

progressive (I.), adj. [1. prōgrésiv; 2. prougrésiv]. **progress (I.)** & **-ive. 1.** Moving forward, advancing, going forward gradually, by regular stages: *progressive movement, course*; *to make a progressive advance.* **2.** Improving, tending to progress or advance materially or morally; tending to promote political or social reform: *a progressive party*; *a progressive mind, ideals* &c. **3.** Tending to continue and increase by gradual stages; **a** (med.) *progressive paralysis*; **b** (econ.) *progressive taxation*, the rate of which increases in proportion to income; **c** *progressive whist*, that in which some of the players change tables and partners after each game.

progressive (II.), n., fr. prec. Person of progressive mind, believer in reform; specif., member of a political party styling itself progressive.

progressively, adv. Prec. & **-ly.** In a progressive manner; by regular or gradual advancing stages or steps.

progressiveness, n. See prec. & **-ness.** State, quality, of being progressive; state of progression or improvement.

pro hac vice, adv. [1. prō hàk vísi; 2. próu hæ̀k váisi]. Lat., 'for this turn'. For this occasion only.

prohibit, vb. trans. [1. prōhíbit; 2. prouhíbit], fr. Lat. *prohibit-(um)*, P.P. of *prohibēre*, 'to hold back, hinder, restrain, prevent; to forbid'. See **pro- (I.)** & **habit. 1.** To forbid, refuse to allow; esp. by law or authority: *to prohibit betting in the streets*; *to prohibit one from driving on a particular road*; *smoking strictly prohibited.* **2. a** To prevent, render impossible: *his state of weakness prohibits much exercise*; **b** to prevent, debar (person) from doing: *I fear that a prior engagement will prohibit me from joining you at dinner.*

prohibiter, -or, n. [1. prōhíbiter; 2. prouhíbitə]. Prec. & **-er, -or.** One who prohibits.

prohibition, n. [1. prò(h)ibíshun; 2. pròu(h)ibíʃən]. Fr., fr. Lat. *prohibitiōn-(em).* See **prohibit** & **-ion. 1. a** Act of prohibiting, of forbidding; an enactment or authorized announcement forbidding something to be done; specif. **b** the forbidding by law of the consumption, sale or, in special cases, the manufacture of alcoholic beverages. **2.** (law) A writ issuing from the High Court forbidding an inferior Court to concern itself with a matter which is outside its jurisdiction.

prohibitionary, adj. [1. prò(h)ibíshunari; 2. pròu(h)ibíʃənəri]. **prohibition** & **-ary.** Pertaining to, connected with, prohibition: *prohibitionary measures, notices* &c.

prohibitionist, n. [1. prò(h)ibíshunist; 2. pròu(h)ibíʃənist]. See prec. & **-ist.** A supporter of the prohibition of trade in, and consumption of, alcoholic drink.

prohibitive, adj. [1. prōhíbitiv; 2. prouhíbitiv]. Fr. **prohibit** & **-ive. a** Prohibiting, forbidding, prohibitory; tending to check or prevent the use or misuse of anything: *a prohibitive tax, duties*; **b** (of price, charges &c.) so high, or so exorbitant, as to prohibit purchase, use &c.

prohibitively, adv. Prec. & **-ly.** In a prohibitive way; to a prohibitive degree; exorbitantly, excessively.

prohibitiveness, n. See prec. & **-ness.** Quality of being prohibitive.

prohibitory, adj. [1. prōhíbituri; 2. prouhíbitəri]. **prohibit** & **-ory.** Prohibitive; containing, implying, a prohibition: *prohibitory laws*; *the prohibitory words in a document* &c.

project (I.), vb. trans. & intrans. [1. prōjékt; 2. proudžékt], fr. Lat. *prōject-(um)*, P.P. type of *prōjicere*, 'to throw forth or before, to throw away or out; to stretch, extend outwards; to cause to jut out or protrude', fr. **pro- (I.)** & *jacere*, 'to throw, cast', see **jet (III.) A.** trans. **1. a** To throw, hurl, propel: *big guns can now project shells for many miles*; **b** to cast, cause to shine, in a given direction or upon a particular object: *to project a ray of light*; **c** (fig.) to cast the mind forward in time; to conjure up, imagine, something which has not yet happened: *let us project our thoughts forward a few centuries and imagine* &c. **2.** To plan in the mind, contrive, scheme out: *to project a new plan of campaign*; *to project the rebuilding of a street.* **3.** (fig.) To form in the mind the external shape or sensible image of an idea or thought; to externalize. **4. a** (geom.) To represent on a plane surface a solid or other figure by drawing lines through every point of it from a centre; **b** (map-drawing &c.) to make a projection of. **B.** intrans. To jut out, stick out, protrude: *the upper storey projects over the street*; *her upper teeth project in what foreigners call the English manner.*

project (II.), n. [1. prójekt; 2. pródžikt]. O. Fr. *project*, Mod. Fr. *projet.* See prec. A plan, scheme, design: *a hare-brained project*; *a mind full of projects.*

projectile, adj. & n. [1. prōjéktīl; 2. proudžéktail]. Fr. See **project (I.)** & **-ile. 1.** adj. **a** Projecting, throwing forward: *projectile force, movement*; **b** intended, suitable, for throwing: *a projectile weapon.* **2.** n. Something thrown, projected; a projectile missile; esp. a shell or bullet projected from a gun.

projection, n. [1. prōjékshun; 2. proudžékʃən]. Fr., fr. Lat. *prōjectiōn-(em)*, 'a throwing out, extension, protrusion'. See **project (I.)** & **-ion. 1.** Act of projecting; **a** act of hurling, propelling &c.; **b** act of casting, directing a ray of light; **c** act of projecting the mind; **d** act of planning, scheming out &c. **2.** That which is projected; **a** image, ray of light, projected upon a surface; **b** (map-making) the representation on a plane surface of any portion of the earth's surface, as Mercator's projection, in which the lines of latitude and longitude are parallel and at right angles to each other; **c** mental image which is externalized so as to appear an objective reality. **3. a** Fact of jutting out, projecting beyond; protrusion: *a projection of the lower lip*; **b** something which projects, which juts out or extends beyond something else: *the porch formed an ugly projection from the house.*

projective, adj. [1. prōjéktiv; 2. proudžéktiv]. See **project (I.)** & **-ive.** Pertaining to, formed by, derived from, projection (in various senses): *the projective quality, property, of a geometrical figure*; *the projective power of the mind.*

projectively, adv. Prec. & **-ly.** By projection.

projector, n. [1. prōjékter; 2. proudžéktə]. **project (I.)** & **-or. 1.** A person who forms projects; esp. of the framer of impracticable, rash, or fraudulent schemes. **2.** An optical instrument for projecting rays of light, as from a lighthouse lantern, or for throwing a picture on to a screen, as in the cinematograph.

prolapse, n. & vb. intrans. [1. prōláps; 2. prouléps], fr. Lat. *prōlapsus*, fr. P.P. type of *prōlābi*, 'to slide forward'. **pro-** & **lapse. 1.** n. (med.) The act or process of falling, slipping down or out of place; esp. of the rectum, and of the uterus; often in Lat. form: *prolapsus uteri.* **2.** vb. To fall down, slip out of place: *a prolapsed rectum.*

prolate, adj. [1. prólāt; 2. próuleit], fr. Lat. *prōlātus*, 'extended, stretched out', P.P. of *prōferre*, 'to carry forward, extend', fr. **pro- (I.)** & *ferre*, 'to bear', the P.P. *lātus* being for **tlātus*, fr. stem **tel-* of *tollere*, 'to lift, bear', cp. **tolerate. a** Elongated, stretched out, extended in the direction of the larger axis or of the polar diameter, contrasted with *oblate*; **b** (fig.) spread out, extended; **c** (gram.) prolative.

prolative, adj. [1. prólativ; 2. próulətiv]. Prec. & **-ive.** (gram.) Extending, filling out or completing a predicate: as in *you must do this, do is a prolative infinitive.*

proleg, n. [1. próleg; 2. próuleg]. **pro- (I.)** & **leg.** (entomol.) A foot-like fleshy organ on the underside of caterpillars or other larvae of insects, such as sawflies &c.

prolegomenary, adj. [1. pròlegómenari; 2. pròulegóminəri]. See next word & **-ary.** Serving as prolegomena or introduction; introductory.

prolegomenon, pl. **prolegomena**, n. [1. pròlegómenon, -a; 2. pròulegóminən, -ə]. Gk., neut. pass. of Pres. Part. of *prolégein*, 'to say in advance or beforehand, to preface', fr. **pro- (II.)** & *légein*, 'to say, speak, tell'. See **lecture, legend.** (gen. in pl.) An introduction, preface; specif., an introductory treatise on some special subject: *Green's 'Prolegomena to Ethics'.*

prolegomenous, adj. [1. pròlegómenus; 2. pròulegóminəs]. See **prolegomenon** & **-ous.** Prolegomenary; esp. taking too long over the introduction to a subject.

prolepsis, n. [1. pròlépsis; 2. pròulípsis]. Gk. *prólēpsis*, 'a taking beforehand, anticipation', fr. **pro- (II.)** & *lēpsis*, 'a taking, seizing', fr. *léps-(esthai)*, fut. of *lambánein*, 'to take, catch, seize'. See second element in **catalepsy.** Anticipation; rhetorical figure whereby future conditions or events, or certain expected results, are represented, or referred to, as though they had already come about, or been realized; thus: '. . . *the fairest of her daughters, Eve*' (Milton, 'P. L.', iv. 324).

proleptic, adj. [1. prōlḗptik; 2. proulíptik], fr. Gk. *prolēptikós*. See prec. & **-ic**. Of the nature of, pertaining to, prolepsis; anticipatory: *a proleptic use, expression, phrase* &c.

proleptically, adv. [1. prōlḗptikali; 2. proulíptikəli]. Prec. & **-al** & **-ly**. In a proleptic manner; by prolepsis.

proles, n. [1. prṓlēz; 2. próuliz]. Lat., 'offspring, children'; for **pro-oles*, see **pro- (I.)**, & the base **al-*, 'to nourish, rear,' discussed under **aliment** & **adolescence**. (law) In phr. *sine prole*, without issue.

proletarian, adj. & n. [1. prṑletárian; 2. pròulitéəriən], fr. Lat. *prōlētārius*, 'belonging to the non-propertied class of citizens', fr. *prōles*, 'offspring, children', see prec., & **-arian**. **1.** adj. **a** (Rom. hist.) Of, pertaining to, the general mass of citizens who were not graded by property qualifications, and served the State merely as begetters of children; **b** of, belonging to, the proletariat: *proletarian rule, dictatorship; proletarian classes of society*. **2.** n. A member of the proletariat.

proletarianism, n. [1. prṑletárianizm; 2. pròulitéəriənizəm]. Prec. & **-ism**. State, condition, of the proletariat; system of government by the proletariat.

proletariat(e), n. [1. prṑletáriat; 2. pròulitéəriət], fr. Fr. *prolétariat*. See **proletarian** & **-ate**. The lowest classes of society; the people, the common herd. Term used by modern socialists and communists for the whole body of wage-earning workers, regarded as exploited by capitalist employers and the 'bourgeoisie'; *the dictatorship of the proletariat*, the term used by the Russian Bolsheviks of their system of government by Soviets.

proletary, adj. & n. [1. prṓletari; 2. próulitəri]. See prec. & **-y**. Proletarian.

prolicide, n. [1. prṓlisīd; 2. próulisaid]. See **proles** & **-cide**. Killing of one's children; infanticide.

proliferate, vb. trans. & intrans. [1. prōliferāt; 2. proulífəreit]. See base in **proliferous** & **-ate**. (biol.) **a** trans. To reproduce; **b** intrans., to grow in quick succession by proliferation.

proliferation, n. [1. prōliferā́shun; 2. proulìfəréiʃən]. Fr. *prolifération*. See next word & **-ation**. Process of proliferating; (biol. and med.) rapid growth of cells by budding; reproduction of new parts; specif., rapid, pathological growth of cells in malignant disease.

proliferous, adj. [1. prōliferus; 2. proulífərəs], fr. Med. Lat. *prōlifer*, 'bearing offspring'. See **proles** & **-ferous**. (bot., zool., pathol.) Reproducing, increasing, extending, by proliferation.

prolific, adj. [1. prōlífik; 2. proulífik], fr. Low Lat. *prōlificus*. See **proles** & **-fic**. **1. a** (of men and animals) Producing many offspring; **b** (of land &c.) fertile, yielding abundant crops; **c** (of crops &c.) abundant. **2.** Intellectually productive, fruitful: *a prolific writer*; *a prolific intellect*. **3. a** Causing, resulting in, serving to produce: *Bolshevism has been prolific of crime and misery*; **b** abounding in: *a period prolific in great poets*.

prolificacy, n. [1. prōlífikasi; 2. proulífikəsi]. Prec. & **-acy**. Quality of being prolific; fruitfulness, fertility, copiousness.

prolifically, adv. [1. prōlífikali; 2. proulífikəli]. **prolific** & **-al** & **-ly**. In a prolific manner; abundantly, copiously.

prolificness, n. [1. prōlífiknes; 2. proulífiknis]. See prec. & **-ness**. State, quality, of being prolific; fruitfulness.

proligerous, adj. [1. prōlíjerus; 2. proulídžərəs]. See **proles** & **-gerous**. (rare) Producing, bearing, offspring; productive.

prolix, adj. [1. prṓliks; 2. próuliks], fr. Fr. *prolixe*, fr. Lat. *prōlixus*, 'extended, stretched out, prolix', fr. **pro- (I.)** & **lixus*, fr. *liquēre*, 'to flow, be liquid', the sense being that of 'overflowing, stretching beyond banks or limits'. See **liquid**. Lengthy, over-prolonged, tedious, verbose, diffuse: *a prolix speech, writer* &c.

prolixity, n. [1. prōlíksiti; 2. proulíksiti]. Prec. & **-ity**. State, quality, of being prolix; verbosity, diffuseness, tediousness.

prolixly, adv. [1. prṓliksli; 2. próulíksli]. **prolix** & **-ly**. In a prolix manner; tediously, diffusely.

prolocutor, n. [1. prōlókūter; 2. proulɔ́kjutə]. Lat., 'one who speaks for or on behalf of another; advocate', fr. **pro- (I.)** & *locūt-*, P.P. type of *loqui*, 'to speak'. See **locution** & **loquacious**. The presiding chairman or speaker of the Lower House of Convocation.

prolocutorship, n. [1. prōlókūtership; 2. proulɔ́kjutəʃip]. Prec. & **-ship**. Office, rank, of prolocutor.

prologue (I.), n. [1. prṓlog; 2. próulɔg]. Fr., fr. Lat. *prologus*, fr. Gk. *prólogos*, 'a speech beforehand, prologue'. See **pro- (II.)** & **logos**. **1.** An introduction, preface, to a poem, play &c.; opposite of *epilogue*: *the Prologue to the 'Canterbury Tales'*; *Dryden's Dramatic Prologues*. **2.** (by transf.) An event or act which precedes and leads up to some greater event &c.: *the murder at Serajevo was the prologue to the war*.

prologue (II.), vb. trans., fr. prec. To provide with a prologue; to introduce, usher in.

prolog(u)ize, vb. intrans. [1. prṓlogīz, -jīz; 2. próuləgaiz, -džaiz]. To make a prologue.

prolong, vb. trans. [1. prōlóng; 2. proulɔ́ŋ]. O. Fr. *prolonguer, prolonguier*, fr. L. Lat. *prolongāre*, 'to prolong'. See **pro- (I.)** & **long (I.)**. **1.** To make longer, extend, lengthen in space: *to prolong a line, road* &c. **2.** To lengthen in time, cause to last long or longer, increase the duration of, spin out: *to prolong one's life*; *prolong the agony*.

prolongable, adj. [1. prōlóngabl; 2. proulɔ́ŋəbl]. Prec. & **-able**. Capable of being prolonged.

prolongation, n. [1. prṑlonggā́shun; 2. pròulɔŋgéiʃən]. **prolong** & **-ation**. **1. a** Act or process of prolonging; **b** state of being prolonged. **2.** That which is prolonged.

prolusion, n. [1. prōlū́zhun; 2. prouljúžən]. Lat. *prōlūsiōn-(em)*, 'a prelude, trial, preliminary essay'; fr. **pro- (I.)** & *lūs-(um)*, P.P. type of *lūdere*, 'to play', see **ludicrous**, & **-ion**. A rehearsal; a prelude; introductory essay, preface.

prolusory, adj. [1. prōlū́suri; 2. prouljúsəri]. See prec. & **-ory**. Serving as a prelude or introduction; introductory, prefatory.

promenade (I.), n. [1. prṑmenáhd; 2. pròminɑ́d]. Fr., fr. *promener*, 'to lead, take out for a walk', *se promener*, 'to go out for a walk', fr. Lat. *prōmināre*, 'to drive (cattle &c.) forward or out to pasture' &c.; fr. **pro- (I.)** & *mināre*, 'to drive (cattle)', cp. *minārī*, 'to threaten'. See **minatory** & **-ade**. **1.** An expedition on foot or on horseback &c., undertaken for exercise or pleasure; a formal, ceremonial walk or drive for purposes of parade or display: *the Sunday morning promenade in Hyde Park*; *the campaign proved to be a mere military promenade*, i.e. with no serious fighting. **2.** A place in which people may promenade, such as an esplanade at a seaside resort &c., a foyer in a theatre &c. *Promenade Concert*, a concert where the audience may move about freely during the performance; *promenade deck*, an upper deck on a liner, on which the passengers may walk about.

promenade (II.), vb. intrans. & trans., fr. prec. **A.** intrans. To walk, ride, drive out for exercise, amusement, or parade: *to promenade in the streets, on the sea front*; *to promenade about*, to walk, stroll about, to strut, swagger, gallivant about. **B.** trans. To walk in, on, or through: *to promenade the streets, the decks* &c.

promenader, n. [1. prṑmenáhder; 2. pròminɑ́də]. Prec. & **-er**. One who promenades.

promerops, n. [1. prómerops; 2. prɔ́mərɔps]. Invented name, fr. **pro- (II.)** & Gk. *mérops*, 'bee-eater', etymol. unknown. A genus of small S. African birds, allied to the sunbirds; the typical species is the Cape promerops, with long tail and curved beak.

Promethean, adj. [1. promḗthean; 2. prəmíþiən], fr. Gk. *Promētheús*, the Titan who stole fire from heaven for men's use and was punished by being chained to a rock while a vulture preyed on his liver; fr. **pro- (II.)** & stem **math-*, of *manthánein*, 'to learn', cp. **mathematics**. Pertaining to Prometheus, his gifts to mankind, or his sufferings: *the Promethean spark from heaven*; *Promethean agonies*.

prominence, n. [1. próminens; 2. prɔ́minəns]. **prominent** & **-ence**. **1.** Fact, quality, of being prominent; **a** fact of protruding, sticking out: *the prominence of a man's nose*; **b** fact of being eminent, remarkable, important: *a person of considerable prominence*. **2.** Something which is prominent, something sticking, jutting, out; an eminence, protuberance: *a prominence on the landscape*.

prominency, n. [1. próminensi; 2. prɔ́minənsi]. See prec. & **-cy**. Quality of being prominent; prominence.

prominent, adj. [1. próminent; 2. prɔ́minənt], fr. Lat. *prōminent-(em)*, Pres. Part. of *prōminēre*, 'to jut out, project'. See **pro- (I.)** & base in **minatory**. **1.** Standing, jutting, out, projecting; conspicuous: *a prominent feature of the landscape*; *prominent teeth*. **2.** Distinguished, eminent; in the public eye: *a prominent politician, writer* &c.

prominently, adv. Prec. & **-ly**. In a prominent manner; conspicuously, with distinction.

promiscuity, n. [1. prṑmiskúiti; 2. prɔ̀miskjúiti]. See **promiscuous** & **-ity**. State, quality, of being promiscuous; indiscriminate confusion or intermingling of various kinds, classes: *promiscuity in social and racial relations*; *to dislike, enjoy, the promiscuity of crowds*.

promiscuous, adj. [1. promískūus; 2. prəmískjuəs], fr. Lat. *prōmiscuus*, 'mixed, confused', fr. **pro- (I.)**, in intens. sense, & base of *miscēre*, 'to mix, mingle', see **mix**, & **-ous**. Composed of various kinds or classes; confused, mingled together; haphazard, with no special regard to relationship, order &c.; indiscriminate: *a promiscuous crowd of people*; *promiscuous charity*; *promiscuous sexual connexions*.

promiscuously, adv. Prec. & **-ly**. In a promiscuous manner; confusedly, indiscriminately, haphazard.

promiscuousness, n. See prec. & **-ness**. State, quality, of being promiscuous; promiscuity.

promise (I.), n. [1. prómis; 2. prɔ́mis]. Earlier *promes*, fr. Fr. *promesse*, fr. Lat. *prōmiss-(um)*, P.P. type of *prōmittere*, 'to send, put forward; to foretell, promise'. See **pro- (I.)** & **mission**. **1.** An undertaking, engagement, assurance, by one person to another or others, to do or not to do something, or to give something, bestow some benefit or the like: *to make, break, a promise, one's promises*; *a promise to help, of help*; *a promise to keep away, of abstention*; *a promise of a brace of pheasants*; *breach of promise*, failure to carry out a promise or engagement to marry. Phr. *the land of promise*, the promised land (see below). **2.** Likelihood of success, of good; hope that appears well grounded: *the promise of spring*; *the crops are full of promise*; *no promise of a settlement yet*; *a young man, author, of promise*, likely to achieve something.

promise (II.), vb. trans. & intrans. See prec. **A.** trans. **1. a** To undertake, engage, make a promise to do or not to do something: *to promise immediate action*; *to promise secrecy, silence, attention* &c.; *promise not to tell*; *I promise faithfully that I'll be up to time*; **b** to undertake to give or procure something: *I promise you a pony for your birthday*; *to* *promise one's son an allowance; to promise help; to promise oneself a holiday*; **c** (colloq.) to assure, warrant: *I'll give him a good talking to, I'll promise you.* **2.** To give cause for, excite, expectation or hope of; to point to: *the apple trees don't promise much of a crop this year; everything now promises an early settlement.* **B.** intrans. **1.** To make a promise, to give an assurance: *I will try to do what you want, but I can't promise.* **2.** To give good prospect of; to afford ground for hope, for fulfilment of one's expectations &c.: *the crops promise well.*

Promised Land, n. [1. prómist lánd; 2. prɔ́mɪst lǽnd]. **a** The land of promise, Canaan, as promised to Abraham and his descendants; **b** (fig.) place or condition to which one looks forward as better than the present; future happiness, a better world, heaven.

promisee, n. [1. pròmisḗ; 2. prɔ̀misí]. **promise (II.) & -ee**, cp. *legatee* &c. (law) One to whom a promise is made; specif., the person to whom a promissory note is made payable.

promising, adj. [1. prómising; 2. prɔ́misiŋ], fr. Pres. Part. of **promise (II.)**. Exhibiting promise; likely to develop well, to achieve success, to improve, to yield satisfactory results, and so on: *a promising colt; a promising pupil; the weather, the wheat crop &c. looks promising.*

promisingly, adv. Prec. & **-ly**. In a promising manner; in a manner likely to turn out well.

promisor, n. [1. pròmisór; 2. prɔ̀misɔ́]. **promise (II.) & -or.** (law) One who makes a promise; the drawer of a promissory note.

promissory, adj. [1. prómisuri; 2. prɔ́misəri], fr. Med. Lat. *promissōrius.* As **promise (I.) & -ory.** Containing a promise or assurance; specif., *promissory note*, a written, signed promise to pay to a specified person or order a stated sum on demand or at a future specified date.

promontory, n. [1. prómunturi; 2. prɔ́məntəri], fr. L. Lat. *prōmonturium*, in Class. Lat. *prōmunturium*, 'headland, promontory', fr. *prōminēre*, 'to project, jut out, be prominent', see **prominent**; later influenced by association w. *mont-(em)*, 'mountain'. **1.** Portion of land jutting out so as to be distinguished from surrounding country; esp. piece of land jutting into the sea, headland; also portion of higher ground from neighbouring hills or mountains projecting into a plain. **2.** (anat.) A natural prominence, or protuberance, on some part of the body.

promote, vb. trans. [1. promót; 2. prəmóut], fr. Lat. *prōmōt-(um)*, P.P. of *prōmovēre*, 'to move forward; to promote'. See **pro- (I.) & move. 1.** To cause to go forward; to forward, further; **a** to assist in the start, incipience, or formation of: *to promote a scheme, undertaking, company*; **b** to excite, arouse: *to promote disorder, ill-will*; **c** to bring forward, propose, and support: *to promote a bill in Parliament*; **d** to aid, encourage, assist in the growth or advancement of: *to promote the love of learning*; **e** specif. (law) to institute a prosecution or action, as a common informer. **2.** To raise, advance, in station, give higher rank to; to prefer, exalt: *to promote an officer to the rank of general; to be promoted to Cabinet rank; to promote a subordinate over the heads of others.*

promoter, n. [1. promóter; 2. prəmóutə]. Prec. & **-er.** One who promotes; **a** one who encourages; supporter; patron: *a promoter of learning, charity*; **b** an inciter, one who stirs up: *promoter of disorder, treason, crime* &c.; **c** specif., one who promotes a trading company, by organization of the scheme, floating the shares &c.

promotion, n. [1. promóshun; 2. prəmóuʃən]. M.E. *promocion*, fr. Fr., fr. Lat. *prōmōtiōn-(em)*. See **promote & -ion. 1.** Act of promoting (in various senses): *promotion of a company, a scheme &c.; the promotion of learning; promotion of sedition, disorder* &c. **2.** Act or fact of preferring or advancing in rank; preferment, advancement in rank or status; specif. (in army and navy) *to get one's promotion*, to next higher rank; *to obtain promotion; promotion to Cabinet rank.*

promotive, adj. [1. promótiv; 2. prəmóutiv]. **promote & -ive.** Tending, serving, to promote.

prompt (I.), adj. [1. prompt; 2. prɔmpt]. Lat. *promptus, promtus*, 'brought forward to light; ready, quick, prompt', P.P. of *prōmere*, 'to bring forward to view', fr. *prō-*, 'forward', & *emere*, 'to take'. See **pro- (I.)** & second element of **exempt. 1.** (of persons) Ready, quick, in action, ready to do or act quickly; not dilatory: *a prompt and punctual supporter* &c.; *to be prompt in one's duty, payments* &c.; *to be prompt to obey, carry out an order.* **2.** (of actions) Done, made, at once; performed readily, or quickly: *prompt action, assistance; to make prompt payments; give a prompt answer; come to a prompt decision.* **3.** (commerc.) Paid, delivered, at once: *for prompt cash; prompt goods.*

prompt (II.), vb. trans., fr. prec. **1.** To move to action; to instigate, incite: *what motives prompted this rash act? the person who prompted the premature publication of the letters.* **2.** To suggest, inspire, dictate: *conscience prompts us to do right; memories of past injuries prompted revenge.* **3.** Specif. (theatr.) **a** to supply (an actor) with words of his part when he forgets them on the stage; also intrans., *will you prompt?*; **b** to mention a word, name &c. to (a speaker), which he has forgotten.

prompt (III.), n., fr. prec. Action of prompting (an actor or speaker &c.); the words spoken by the prompter to an actor: *to want, wait for, a prompt.*

prompt (IV.), n., fr. **prompt (I.)**. (commerc.) A time limit; note embodying this for payment of an account for goods ordered &c.; a prompt note.

prompt book, n. Book of the words of a play &c. used by the prompter in a theatre.

prompt box, n. The place in a theatre in which the prompter sits.

prompter, n. [1. prómpter; 2. prɔ́mptə]. **prompt (II.) & -er.** One who prompts; specif., a person who assists the memory of actors on the stage by reading the words of the play from the prompt box.

promptitude, n. [1. prómptitūd; 2. prɔ́mptitjūd]. Fr., fr. Med., Eccles., Lat. *promptitūdo.* See **prompt (I.)**. Fact, quality, of being prompt; readiness, quickness, alacrity, promptness, in action or decision.

promptly, adv. [1. prómptli; 2. prɔ́mptli]. **prompt (I.) & -ly.** In a prompt manner; at once, immediately, without delay or hesitation.

promptness, n. [1. prómptnes; 2. prɔ́mptnis]. See prec. & **-ness.** State, quality, of being prompt; readiness, quickness, promptitude.

prompt note, n. See **prompt (IV.)**. (commerc.) A note or memorandum stating the time limit for the payment of an account.

prompt side, n. The side of the stage to the actor's right hand; the side at which the prompter formerly stood (abbr. P.S., cp. O.P. for 'opposite prompter', actor's left hand).

promulgate, vb. trans. [1. prómulgāt; 2. prɔ́məlgeit], fr. Lat. *prōmulgāt-(um)*, P.P. of *prōmulgāre*, 'publish abroad', the etymol. of wh. is doubtful. **1.** To publish, announce publicly; to proclaim: *to promulgate a decree, laws, news.* **2.** To spread abroad, disseminate: *to promulgate official secrets, doctrines of socialism, a new form of religion* &c.

promulgation, n. [1. pròmulgáshun; 2. prɔ̀məlgéiʃən], fr. Lat. *prōmulgātiōn-(em).* See prec. & **-ion.** Act of promulgating; publication, public declaration: *promulgation of a decree, news, of doctrines, opinions* &c.

promulgator, n. [1. prómulgāter; 2. prɔ́məlgeitə]. Lat.; **promulgate & -or.** One who promulgates or publishes.

pronaos, n. [1. prōnáos; 2. prounéiɔs]. Gk. *prónāos*, fr. **pro- (II.)** & *nāós*, 'temple, cella of a temple', cogn. w. Gk. *naíō* (fr. **nasjō*), 'I inhabit; I build'. (archit.) The vestibule of a Greek temple leading to the cella or shrine.

pronate, vb. trans. & adj. [1. prṓnāt; 2. próuneit], fr. L. Lat. *prōnāt-(um)*, P.P. of *prōnāre*, 'to bend forward, bow', fr. *prōnus.* See **prone. 1.** vb. (anat.) To cause to assume position of pronation. **2.** adj. (of hand) Pronated; turned so that palm faces downwards; contrasted with *supine.*

pronation, n. [1. prōnáshun; 2. prounéiʃən]. Prec. & **-ion.** (anat.) A turning of the hand or forelimb so that the palm or under side is downward; contrasted with *supination.*

pronator, n. [1. prōnáter; 2. prounéitə]. **pronate & -or.** (anat.) Name of the muscle which pronates the hand or forelimb.

prone, adj. [1. prōn; 2. proun], fr. Lat. *prōnus*, 'tending, leaning forward, inclined, prone', fr. **pro- (I.)**. **1.** Face downward, flat on one's face, prostrate: *to fall, lie, prone.* **2.** Sloping, inclining, downward steeply; not level: *a prone stretch of ground.* **3.** Inclined, disposed, liable: *prone to anger, to jump to hasty conclusions, to rash acts* &c.

proneness, n. [1. prṓnnes; 2. próunnis]. Prec. & **-ness. 1.** State, condition, of being prone or prostrate. **2.** Disposition, tendency, inclination, towards.

prong, n. & vb. trans. [1. prong; 2. prɔŋ]. Etymol. uncertain; possibly cogn. w. L.G. *prange*, 'stick', cp. Du. *prangen*, 'to press, pinch'; M.E. has *pronge*, 'pang, pain'. **1.** n. **a** A fork for lifting dung, hay &c.; a stable fork, pitch-fork; **b** the point or tine of a table fork; **c** point of the antler of a stag. **2.** vb. To lift, pierce, with a prong.

pronged, adj. [1. prongd; 2. prɔŋd]. Prec. & **ed.** Having specified number of prongs or points or tines: *a three-pronged fork.*

prong horn, also **prong buck**, n. A horned ruminant of the western parts of N. America, *Antilocapra americana*, resembling an antelope, but forming a distinct family of which only one species is known.

pronominal, adj. [1. prōnóminal; 2. prounɔ́minəl], fr. L. Lat. *pronominālis*, fr. *pronōmen.* See **pro- (I.) & nominal**, & cp. **pronoun.** Belonging to, of the nature of, a pronoun: *a pronominal adjective.*

pronominally, adv. Prec. & **-ly.** As a pronoun, with the force, effect, of a pronoun.

prononcé, adj. [1. pronónsā; 2. prounɔ̃sei]. Fr. See **pronounce.** Pronounced, strongly marked; exaggerated, over-emphasized: *his nose was rather too prononcé; his political opinions are very prononcé.*

pronoun, n. [1. prṓnoun; 2. próunaun]. See **pro- & noun**, cp. Fr. *pronom*, fr. Lat. *prōnōmen*; see **pronominal.** (gram.) One of several classes of words used instead of a noun or proper name to denote or refer to the person or thing already mentioned, implied by the context &c. *Personal pronouns*, as *I, thou, you, he* &c.

pronounce, vb. trans. & intrans. [1. pronóuns; 2. prənáuns], fr. O. Fr. *pronuncier*, Mod. Fr. *prononcer*, fr. L. Lat. *prōnuntiāre.* See **pro- (I.) & nunciature**, & cp. **announce. A.** trans. **1.** To declare, announce, utter, solemnly and publicly; to deliver: *to pronounce sentence of death; to pronounce a curse upon; to pronounce absolution, the Blessing* &c. **2.** To declare (a thing to be) as the result of consideration; state it as one's opinion that (something) is: *the expert pronounced the picture to be a forgery.* **3.** To articulate; utter with the organs of speech: *to pronounce English badly, vulgarly &c.; a difficult word to pronounce; how do the Welsh pronounce ll?* **B.** intrans. **1.** To declare as one's opinion: *to pronounce on, for, against.* **2.** To articulate, utter speech sounds in a particular way; to have a specified style of pronunciation: *to pronounce clearly, abominably.*

pronounceable, adj. [1. pronóunsabl; 2. prənáunsəbl]. Prec. & **-able.** Capable of being pronounced with the vocal organs.

pronounced, adj. [1. pronóunst; 2. prənáunst], fr. P.P. of **pronounce**. Emphasized; strongly marked, well defined; decided: *a pronounced Yorkshire accent*; *a pronounced smell of onions*; *a pronounced taste for drink*; *pronounced opinions*; *pronounced features.*

pronouncedly, adv. [1. pronóunsedli; 2. prənáunsidli]. Prec. & **-ly**. In a pronounced manner; to a pronounced degree; with emphasis, strongly, markedly.

pronouncement, n. [1. pronóunsment; 2. prənáunsmənt]. **pronounce** & **-ment**. Act of pronouncing; declaration, formal, solemn announcement, of principles, opinions, policy &c.

pronunciamento, n. [1. pronùnsiaméntō; 2. prənànsiəméntou]. Modification of *pronunciamiento*, Span. form of prec. A manifesto, proclamation, esp. of political manifesto issued by a revolutionary party or its leader in Spanish-speaking countries.

pronunciation, n. [1. pronùnsiáshun; 2. prənànsiéiʃən], fr. Lat. *prōnuntiātiōn-(em), prōnuntiātio*. See **pronounce**. **1.** Act, process, of pronouncing speech-sounds: *language is changed in the very moment of pronunciation.* **2.** Habitual mode of pronouncing, customary style of articulation of individuals in speaking a given language: *a vulgar pronunciation*; *to teach English pronunciation*; *a provincial pronunciation is unpleasant in public speakers.* **3.** The received way in which a word, syllable, sound, is actually pronounced: *what is the pronunciation of the name Czech?*; *some people believe that English spelling should be altered to suit the pronunciation.*

proof (I.), n. [1. prōōf; 2. prūf]. M.E. *prōfe*, fr. O. Fr. *prueve*, fr. Lat. *proba*, 'proof', fr. *probāre*, 'to prove'. See **probate** & cp. **prove**. **1.** Demonstration; **a** the act of proving or demonstrating the truth of a fact, statement, charge &c., or of confirming belief in its truth: *much has to be taken for granted by most of us without actual proof*; **b** convincing evidence of the truth or falsity of a fact, statement, or charge: *the police have very strong grounds for suspicion, but no proofs*; *to have sufficient proof to satisfy a court of law*; *we must wait for better proof before we believe*; *to give a proof of one's loyalty, affection* &c.; **c** specif. (law) a written copy of what a witness is prepared to swear to in court; the record of evidence given in court; any document sufficiently attested to be accepted in court: *the witness was not up to his proof*, did not, under cross-examination, stand by what he had stated in his proof; **d** (Scots law) a trial by a judge alone without a jury. **2.** Test, trial, examination; **a** test of quality, truth &c.: *to put something to the proof*; **b** test, standard, of hardness, resistance, impenetrability or strength: *above, under, proof,* (of spirit) above or below the standard of proof-spirit (see **proof (II.), 2**). Phr. *the proof of the pudding is in the eating*, the only test of the quality of anything is not theory but experience and practical use. **3.** (engraving, etching &c.) A trial impression taken from a plate originally for the artist's approval or correction, now any one of such taken before the general issue is printed and the imprint is added: *an artist's proof*; *proof before letters.* **4.** (print.) A sample, trial impression from type, for correction by the author &c.; also *proof sheet*: *to make corrections in proof, on the proof.* **5.** (bookbinding) Any one of a number of smaller leaves which are left 'uncropped' or with rough edges to prove the margins have not been cut.

proof (II.), adj., fr. prec. **1. a** Having a standard quality of resistance, hardness, or impenetrability: *proof armour*; *to be proof against bullets, water* &c.; (also in combination) *bullet-proof, sound-proof*; *water-proof*; (facet.) *fool-proof*, made, stated, so that the stupidest person cannot misunderstand or go wrong; **b** (fig.) unshaken by, inaccessible to: *to be proof against all temptations, appeals for mercy* &c.; *the witness was proof against the fiercest cross-examination.* **2.** Having a certain standard of alcoholic strength: *proof-spirit*, a mixture of alcohol and water containing not less than 49·3% of pure alcohol.

proof (III.), vb. trans., fr. prec. To make proof against; specif., to make a fabric impenetrable against water: *to proof cloth* &c.

proof-reader, n. A professional corrector of printer's proofs.

proof-reading, n. Correction of printer's proofs.

prop (I.), n. [1. prop; 2. prɔp]. M.E. *proppe*; etymol. doubtful; not in O.E.; cogn. w. L.G. & Du. *proppe*, 'supporting branch', cp. also perh. Germ. *pfropf*, 'cork, stopper'. **1.** Something used to support a leaning weight, e.g. of a building, the branches of an old tree &c.; a support, stay, strut. **2.** (fig.) A moral or spiritual support; a supporter, upholder: *a good son is a prop for one's old age*; *the squirearchy is a great prop of the Church.*

prop (II.), vb. trans., fr. prec. (lit. and fig.) **a** To act as a prop; **b** to furnish with props; also *prop up*, maintain in position by props.

propaedeutic(al), adj. [1. prṑpēdū́tik(l); 2. pròupīdjū́tik(l)], fr. Gk. *propaideúein*, 'to give preliminary training or education to', fr. **pro- (II.)** & *paideúein*, 'to train, educate', fr. base *paid-(ós)*, 'boy, child', see first element of **pedagogue**, also under **puerile** & **foal**, & **-ic**. Giving preliminary training or education; serving as an introductory, preparatory, course of education.

propaedeutics, n. pl. [1. prṑpēdū́tiks; 2. pròupīdjū́tiks]. See prec. Introductory, preliminary, education or training.

propaganda, n. [1. propagánda; 2. prɔpəgǽndə]. Fem. abl. sing. of Lat. *prōpāgandus*, 'to be propagated', gerund. of *prōpāgāre*. See **propagate**. **1.** (R.C. Ch.) **a** *The Propaganda*, the Congregation or Committee of Cardinals, in full *congregatio de propaganda fide*, 'congregation for the propagation of the faith', in charge of foreign missions; **b** *Propaganda*, a training college at Rome for missionary priests. **2.** An association or organization for the propagating or dissemination of views, doctrines &c.: *to set up a propaganda for*; *a capable head of the propaganda.* **3. a** Organized method and system of propagating or disseminating principles and doctrines; **b** doctrines &c. thus spread.

propagandism, n. [1. pròpagándizm; 2. prɔ̀pəgǽndizəm]. Prec. & **-ism**. System, practice, of propagating opinions, principles &c.; proselytism.

propagandist, n. [1. pròpagándist; 2. prɔ̀pəgǽndist]. See prec. & **-ist**. **a** A member of the Propaganda, or of any association for propaganda work; **b** a zealous supporter of a cause or of propagandism; a proselytizer.

propagandize, vb. trans. & intrans. [1. pròpagándiz; 2. prɔ̀pəgǽndaiz]. **propaganda** & **-ize**. **1.** trans. To make propaganda among, throughout; to proselytize: *to propagandize a community, country* &c. **2.** intrans. To conduct a propaganda.

propagate, vb. trans. & intrans. [1. própagāt; 2. prɔ́pəgeit], fr. Lat. *prōpāgāt-(um)*, P.P. of *prōpāgāre*, 'to fasten, peg, down slips of plants for growth, to multiply plants by layering, to propagate'; fr. **pro- (I.)** & base **pāg-*, cp. *pēgi*, perf., & *pac-tum*, P.P. of *pangere*, 'to fasten; to set, plant with', &c. See **pax** & **page (II.)**. **A.** trans. **1.** To multiply by successive generation; to cause to multiply by reproduction: *to propagate a new variety of plant, breed of cattle* &c.; *the weeds propagate themselves rapidly*; *to propagate one's species.* **2.** To spread, extend; to spread from person to person, to disseminate; to propagandize: *to propagate disease, infection*; *to propagate doctrines, opinions* &c. **3.** To carry forward through a medium, to transmit: *to propagate sound, heat, light* &c. **B.** intrans. To have offspring; to multiply by reproduction: *animal and vegetable pests propagate with extreme rapidity.*

propagation, n. [1. pròpagáshun; 2. prɔ̀pəgéiʃən], fr. Lat. *prōpāgātiōn-(em)*, 'propagation, extension, enlargement'. See prec. & **-ion**. **1.** Act or process of propagating, or reproducing offspring. **2.** Act or process of spreading, disseminating: **a** (in physical sense) *propagation of disease, infection* &c.; **b** (in non-material sense) *propagation of the Gospel, of ideas, of peace* &c. **3.** Act or process of transmitting: *propagation of heat* &c.

propagative, adj. [1. própagātiv; 2. prɔ́pəgeitiv]. **propagate** & **-ive**. Pertaining to, connected with, propagation; having the power of propagating.

propagator, n. [1. própagāter; 2. prɔ́pəgeitə]. See prec. & **-or**. One who propagates; a promoter; propagandist.

proparoxytone, adj. & n. [1. prṑparóksitōn; 2. pròupərɔ́ksitoun]. Gk. *proparoxútonos.* See **pro- (II.)** & **paroxytone**. **a** adj. (Gk. gram.) Having the accent on the syllable next before the penultimate, as in Greek word above; **b** n., a word with such an accent.

propel, vb. trans. [1. propél; 2. prəpél], fr. Lat. *prōpellere*, 'to drive forward, propel', fr. **pro- (I.)** & base **pel-*, 'strike, thrust', q.v. under **pulse (I.)**. To drive, impel, forward; to cause to move forward by force; to urge, press, forward: *to propel a boat by rowing*; *the wind propelled the ship*; *a motor-car is propelled by a series of explosions in the engine.*

propellant, n. [1. propélant; 2. prəpélənt]. Prec. & **-ant**. See next word for regular form. A propelling agent; esp. one which serves to propel a projectile from a fire-arm of any kind, a propelling as distinguished from a bursting charge of a shell &c.

propellent, adj. & n. [1. propélent; 2. prəpélənt], fr. Lat. *prōpellent-(em), prōpellens*, Pres. Part. of *prōpellere*. See **propel**. **a** adj. Propelling, driving forward; **b** n., a propelling agent, a propellant.

propeller, n. [1. propéler; 2. prəpélə]. **propel** & **-er**. That which propels, which drives anything forward; specif., the driving portion, screw &c., of a ship or aircraft, acting in the water, or in the air.

propensity, n. [1. propénsiti; 2. prəpénsiti], fr. rare or obs. adj. *propense*, 'inclined, disposed, addicted', fr. Lat. *prōpensus*, in same sense, P.P. of *prōpendere*, 'to hang down; to weigh more; to be inclined, disposed', fr. **pro- (I.)** & *pendere*, 'to hang'. See **pendant**. Inclination, disposition, addiction, tendency: *a propensity to extravagance, for gambling*; *propensity to contradict.*

proper, adj. & n. [1. próper; 2. prɔ́pə], fr. Fr. *propre*, fr. Lat. *proprius*, 'one's own, particular, special; characteristic, personal'; etymol. uncertain; Walde suggests derivation fr. **pro-p(a)trios*, 'inherited from one's forefathers'. See **pro- (I.)** & **pater**. **A** adj. **1.** (obsolesc. or obs.) One's own, belonging to oneself: *one's own proper possessions*; *he became his proper self again*; '*to go to his proper place*'; '*our proper son*' (Shakespeare, 'Othello'). Specific uses: **a** (astron.) of that part of the apparent motion of a star formerly regarded as due, not to the motion of the solar system, but as peculiar to itself; **b** (gram.) *proper name, noun*, a name used as the designation of a single person, place, animal &c.: *William, Mary, Jones, Liverpool, Thames, Eclipse, Iron Duke* &c. **2.** Belonging especially to, characteristic of, normally occurring in or among a particular group of individuals, or under specified conditions or combination of circumstances: *ferocity is proper to tigers*; *instincts, feelings, proper to mankind*; *temperature proper to August.* **3. a** Fit, suitable, befitting: *with dignity proper to his high rank*; *his remarks and behaviour were only proper under the circumstances*; **b** correct according to rule and accepted custom, commonly regarded as right: *what is the proper dress to wear at a levee?*; *that's not the proper form of words to use*; *the proper psalms for today*; *everything in its proper place.* **4. a** Decent, decorous, circumspect, immaculate; chaste, modest: *not at all a proper person* *for you to know*; *quite a proper book, play* &c.; **b** exaggeratedly sedate in speech, behaviour &c.; prim: *I dislike proper children.* **5.** Rightly, properly, so termed; actual, real: *the book hardly belongs to literature proper.* **6.** **a** (archaic) Handsome, fine: *a proper young man*; **b** complete, thorough-paced: *a proper rascal.* **7.** (her.) Represented in natural, not heraldic, colours: *a tiger proper.* **B** n. (eccles.) Service, or part, for a special occasion: *proper of the Mass.*

properispomenon, adj. & n. [1. pròperispómenon; 2. pròuperispóumenən]. Gk. *properispómenon.* **pro- (II.)** & **perispomenon.** (Gk. gram.) **a** adj. Having a circumflex accent on the last syllable but one, as *eînai*, 'to be'; **b** n., a word so accented.

properly, adv. [1. próperli; 2. prɔ́pəli]. See **proper** & **-ly.** In a proper manner (in various senses); **a** decently, in a becoming, seemly, fashion: *to behave properly*; **b** appropriately, suitably: *properly dressed*; **c** correctly, accurately; according to reason or to rule: *to speak English properly*; *to play a game properly*; *properly speaking, you ought to go.*

propertied, adj. [1. própertid; 2. prɔ́pətid]. Next word & **-ed.** Owning, possessing, property, esp. landed property: *the propertied classes.*

property, n. [1. próperti; 2. prɔ́pəti]. M.E. *proprete, properte*, fr. O. Fr. *propreté*, Mod. Fr. *propriété*, 'property', *propreté*, 'propriety', fr. Lat. *proprietāt-(em)*, 'ownership, property; proper meaning, propriety', fr. *proprius*, 'one's own, proper'. See **proper** & **-(e)ty.** **1.** That which is proper to anything; a characteristic, and peculiar quality, power, attribute, inherent in a thing, or naturally associated with it: *elasticity is a marked property of indiarubber, porosity of a sponge.* **2.** (law) Right to possess, enjoy, and dispose of, anything; ownership: *the rights and duties of property*; *there is no property in wild animals*; *property in copyright*; *a war against property.* **3.** Thing owned or possessed; belongings, goods, and chattels: *the house and furniture are my property*; *a nice bit of property*; specif. **a** *personal property*, chattels, movables; **b** *real property*, real estate, land; *property owner*, owner of land or houses. Phr. (*the news &c.*) *is common property*, known to everyone. **4.** Specific use: *a property*, a landed estate. **5.** Things of value generally, assumed to belong to somebody, although the owner is not specified: *much property was destroyed by the floods*; *the preservation of life and property*; *a fine piece of property in the shape of an ancient silver tankard was found buried in a field.* **6.** (theatr., usually pl.) *Properties*, things used on the stage, as adjuncts to a play, such as dresses, furniture, armour &c.; *a property man*, person in charge of stage properties.

prophecy, n. [1. prófesi, -i; 2. prɔ́fisai, -i], fr. O. Fr. *profecie*, Mod. Fr. *prophétie*, fr. L. Lat. *prophetia*, fr. Gk. *prophēteía.* See **prophet** & **-cy.** **1.** The power, faculty, of prophesying: *the gift of prophecy.* **2.** Something prophesied; a prediction, a foretelling of the future; a prophetic utterance.

prophesier, n. [1. prófesīer; 2. prɔ́fisaiə]. See next word & **-er.** One who prophesies; a prophet, soothsayer.

prophesy, vb. intrans. & trans. [1. prófesī; 2. prɔ́fisai], fr. O. Fr. *profecier*; see next word. **A.** intrans. To speak, teach, as a prophet; to utter prophecies; to foretell the future, make predictions. **B.** trans. To foretell, predict: *to prophesy disaster, good tidings* &c.

prophet, n. [1. prófet; 2. prɔ́fit], fr. Fr. *prophète*, fr. L. Lat. *prophēta*, fr. Gk. *prophḗtēs*, 'one who speaks for and interprets the will of a god', lit. 'one who speaks for another, spokesman, interpreter'; fr. **pro- (II.)** & *phē-*, base of *phēmi*, 'I say, speak', q.v. under **fame, fate,** & agent-suff. *-tēs*; the word was used in the Septuagint to transl. Heb. *nábi*, 'announcer', and *roéh*, 'a seer'. **1.** An interpreter, teacher, of the will of a god; specif., a person inspired and directed by God to announce His will to men, to reveal and interpret religious truth concerning God, and to proclaim His judgements, especially in reference to the age in which he lived; such was the function of a prophet in the Old Testament: *the schools of the prophets*; *the major prophets*, Isaiah, Jeremiah, Ezekiel, and Daniel, *the twelve minor prophets*, from Hosea to Malachi; *the Prophets*, the prophetical books of the Old Testament. **2.** **a** (i.) One of the great non-Christian religious teachers and leaders: *Mohammed the prophet*; (ii.) also used of claimants of more dubious character: *Smith, the prophet of the Mormons*; **b** an inspiring, fervent and enlightened leader in a cause; one who proclaims ideals and principles with conviction and cogency. **3.** One who foretells the future and makes predictions regarding future events; a soothsayer: *a prophet of woe*; *a weather-prophet*; *a racing prophet*, tipster.

prophetess, n. [1. prófetes; 2. prɔ́fitɛs]. Prec. & **-ess.** A woman prophet.

prophethood, n. [1. prófit-hood; 2. prɔ́fithud]. **prophet** & **-hood.** Standing, condition, quality, of a prophet; the person, personality, of a prophet.

prophetic, adj. [1. profétik; 2. prəfétik], fr. L., Eccles., Lat. *prophēticus*, fr. Gk. *prophētikós.* See **prophet** & **-ic.** **1.** Pertaining to, connected with, of the nature of, a prophet or of prophecy: *prophetic mantle.* **2.** Predicting, foretelling; containing a prediction: *prophetic utterances, writings* &c.; *a prophetic dream.*

prophetical, adj. [1. profétikl; 2. prəfétikl]. Prec. & **-al.** Prophetic: *the Prophetical Books of the Old Testament.*

prophetically, adv. Prec. & **-ly.** In a prophetic manner; **a** after the manner of a prophet; **b** in the form of a prophecy, so as to predict.

prophylactic, adj. & n. [1. pròfiláktik; 2. prɔ̀filǽktik], fr. Gk. *prophulaktikós*, fr. Gk. *prophulássein*, 'to keep guard before, guard against, ward off'; fr. **pro- (II.)** & *phulássein*, 'to guard, protect'. See **phylactery.** **1.** adj. Serving to prevent, to preserve from, disease; preventive; as distinguished from *curative*: *prophylactic medicine, treatment* &c. **2.** n. A prophylactic, preventive medicine or treatment.

prophylaxis, n. [1. pròfiláksis; 2. prɔ̀filǽksis]. Invented word, fr. Gk. *prophúlax*, 'an advanced guard, outpost'. See prec. Preventive, preservative treatment; contrasted with *cure.*

propinquity, n. [1. prōpíngkwiti; 2. proupíŋkwiti], fr. O. Fr. *propinquité*, fr. Lat. *propinquitāt-(em)*, fr. *propinquus*, 'near', fr. *prope*, 'near', the origin of wh. is doubtful. State of being near; nearness, proximity, in time, space, relationship &c.

propitiate, vb. trans. [1. prōpíshiāt; 2. proupíʃieit], fr. Lat. *propitiāt-(um)*, P.P. type of *propitiāre*, 'to make favourable or propitious'. See **propitious.** To render favourable, win the goodwill of; to appease, conciliate.

propitiation, n. [1. prŏpishiáshun; 2. pròupiʃiéiʃən], fr. L. Lat. *propitiātiōn-(em).* Prec. & **-ion.** **1.** Act of propitiating; state of being propitiated. **2.** That which propitiates; atoning sacrifice: '*He is the propitiation for our sins*' (1 John ii. 2.)

propitiator, n. [1. prōpíshiāter; 2. proupíʃieitə]. L., Eccles., Lat. See **propitiate** & **-or.** One who propitiates; an appeaser, reconciler.

propitiatorily, adv. [1. prōpíshiāturili; 2. proupíʃieitərili]. Next word & **-ly.** By propitiation.

propitiatory, adj. [1. prōpíshiāturi; 2. proupíʃieitəri]. Eccles. Lat. *propitiātōrius.* See **propitiate** & **-ory.** Serving, having the power to, intended to, propitiate, appease, or reconcile: *propitiatory gifts, sacrifice* &c.

propitious, adj. [1. prōpíshus; 2. proupíʃəs], fr. O. Fr. *propicius, propice*, fr. Lat. *propitius*, 'favourable, kind', used esp. of the gods; prob. fr. **pro- (I.)** & base **pet-*, 'to go, fall', also 'to seek'. See **pen (III.)** & **petition** & **-ous**; if this etymol. is correct the word meant orig. 'falling forwards, towards one', & was perh. a term of augury. **1.** Favourable, gracious, kind: *may the gods be propitious.* **2.** Auspicious, fortunate: *propitious omens, season, weather.*

propitiously, adv. Prec. & **-ly.** In a propitious manner; auspiciously, favourably.

propitiousness, n. See prec. & **-ness.** State, quality, fact, of being propitious; favourable conditions.

propolis, n. [1. própolis; 2. prɔ́pəlis]. Gk. *própolis*, 'suburb of a town; bee-glue'; **pro- (II.)**, & *pólis*, 'city'. See **policy.** A reddish-brown resinous, waxy substance extracted from the buds of trees by bees, and used by them as a cement for stopping up holes in their hives.

proportion (I.), n. [1. propórshun; 2. prəpɔ́ʃən], fr. O. Fr. *proporcion*, fr. Lat. *prōportiōn-(em)*, 'proportion, symmetry'. See **pro- (I.)** & **portion.** **1.** The comparative relation of one thing to another, in size, quantity, degree &c.; ratio; relative size, number, quality &c.: *certain substances will mix freely in any proportion*; *the proportion of deaths from a particular disease.* **2.** Relative size or arrangement of the parts of a thing to each other or to the whole, esp. a due and just relation in these respects: *to appreciate the proportions of a building, a body* &c.; *of fine proportions*; *in perfect proportion*; *in proportion, out of proportion*, conforming, not conforming, to the laws of just proportion. **3.** A comparative, relative, part or share: *to take, occupy, a large proportion of the space available*; *a small proportion of the divisible profits.* **4.** Specif. **a** (arith.) the rule of three: *to do a sum in, by, proportion*; **b** (math.) equality of ratios.

proportion (II.), vb. trans., fr. prec. **1.** To adjust, adapt, to a proper or suitable proportion; to make proportionate: *to proportion the various parts of a building*; *to proportion one's work to the object aimed at, one's expenditure to income* &c. **2.** To share out, distribute, apportion, allot: *to proportion praise and blame to each according to their due.*

proportionable, adj. [1. propórshunabl; 2. prəpɔ́ʃənəbl]. Prec. & **-able.** Being in proportion; proportional; capable of being proportioned.

proportionably, adv. Prec. & **-ly.** According to proportion; proportionally.

proportional, adj. & n. [1. propórshunal; 2. prəpɔ́ʃənəl], fr. L. Lat. *prōportiōnālis*, as **proportion (I.)** & **-al.** **1.** adj. Having proportion; being in proportion, symmetrical, proportionate; *Proportional Representation*, abbr. P.R., a system of parliamentary or other election by which some due representation of minority votes is secured. **2.** n. (math.) A number or quantity in a proportion or equality of ratios.

proportionality, n. [1. propòrshunáliti; 2. prəpɔ̀ʃənǽliti]. Prec. & **-ity.** State, quality, of being proportional or in proportion.

proportionally, adv. [1. propórshunali; 2. prəpɔ́ʃənəli]. See prec. & **-ly.** In proportion; in due comparative relationship; comparatively.

proportionate, adj. & vb. trans., fr. L. Lat. *prōportiōnātus.* See **proportion** & **-ate**; vb. fr. adj. **1.** adj. [1. propórshunit; 2. prəpɔ́ʃənit] Adjusted, adapted, according to proportions or scale; proportional. **2.** vb. [1. propórshunāt; 2. prəpɔ́ʃəneit] To adjust, adapt to proportion, or scale; to make proportional.

proportionately, adv. Prec. & **-ly.** Proportionally.

proportioned, adj. [1. propórshund; 2. prəpɔ́ʃənd]. **proportion (II.)** & **-ed.** Having specified kind of proportion: *a well-, ill-proportioned body, building* &c.; *an evenly proportioned share.*

proportionment, n. [1. propórshunment; 2. prəpɔ́ʃənmənt]. **proportion** & **-ment.** **a** Act of proportioning; **b** state of being proportioned.

proposal, n. [1. propṓzl; 2. prəpóuzəl]. **propose** & **-al.** **1. a** Act of proposing; **b** that which is proposed; scheme, plan, design: *to make, offer, proposals of, for peace* &c. **2.** An offer, esp. an offer of marriage.

propose, vb. trans. & intrans. [1. propṓz; 2. prəpóuz], fr. Fr. *proposer*, fr. *pro-* & *poser*, 'to place'. See **pro- (I.)**, **pose (I.)**, & **pause.** **A.** trans. **1. a** To bring forward, submit, offer, as a suggestion for consideration or adoption; to suggest: *to propose a scheme*; *to propose drastic measures*; *to have nothing to propose*; Phr. *to propose marriage*, make offer of marriage; **b** specif., to bring forward formally, to submit for discussion, to move as a resolution: *to propose a motion, resolution.* Phr. *to propose a toast, a person's health.* **B.** intrans. **1.** To form plans; to scheme, to design: *man proposes, God disposes.* **2.** To intend, have the intention (to do, of doing): *I propose to take my holiday in June this year*; *do you propose to dine out tonight?* **3.** To offer marriage: *he is in no hurry to propose*; *he wants to propose to every girl he meets.*

proposition, n. [1. pròpozíshun; 2. prɔ̀pəzíʃən]. Fr., fr. Lat. *prōpositiōn-(em)*, fr. *prōposit-(um)*, P.P. type of *prōpōnere*, 'to put forward, set forth; to propound, propose'. See **pro- (I.)**, **position**, & cp. **propound.** **1.** The expression of a judgement; expression in which something is predicated; a statement, assertion. **a** (log.) sentence containing a subject and predicate connected by a copula, one in which some quality is affirmed or denied of the subject; specif. **b** (math.) a theorem, problem, formally stated or propounded, with or without the demonstration or proof. **2.** A proposal, plan, scheme; a project; (colloq. and vulg.) *an awkward, queer &c., proposition*, affair, business, state of affairs &c.; *he's a tough proposition*, a difficult person to deal with.

propositional, adj. [1. pròpozíshunal; 2. prɔ̀pəzíʃənəl]. Prec. & **-al.** Pertaining to, of the nature of, a proposition.

propound, vb. trans. [1. propóund; 2. prəpáund]. Earlier form *propone*, fr. Lat. *prōpōnere*, 'to place, set, put forward, to propound, propose'. See **propose.** **1.** To put, set forward, offer for consideration; to propose as a question for discussion: *to propound a question, problem* &c. **2.** (law) To bring forward, produce (a will) for the proper authority to certify as genuine, and valid.

propounder, n. [1. propóunder; 2. prəpáundə]. Prec. & **-er.** One who propounds; specif., one who propounds a will.

propraetor, n. [1. prṑprḗtŏr; 2. prɔ̀uprítɔ̄]. Lat. **pro- (I.)** & **praetor.** (Rom. hist.) A magistrate who after his year of office as praetor governed a province which did not require military rule or an army.

proprietary, adj. & n. [1. proprī́etari; 2. prəpráiətəri], fr. L. Lat. *prōprietārius*, adj. & n., fr. *prōprietas.* See **propriety** & **-ary.** **1.** adj. Belonging to a proprietor; owned, belonging as property: *proprietary rights*; *proprietary articles*, articles of manufacture, which by trade mark, patent, brand, or name can only be made and sold by a special person or body of persons owning such rights; *proprietary chapel*, a chapel in private ownership licensed for worship, the incumbent of which is largely paid by the pew rents charged; *proprietary company*, a company owning shares &c. in other companies or owning property in land &c. leased out to other companies. **2.** n. (archaic) A proprietor, body of proprietors; ownership, property.

proprietor, n. [1. prōprī́eter; 2. prouprái̇ətə]. See **propriety** & **-or.** Substituted in common usage for the earlier **proprietary**, n. An owner; one who holds and enjoys the use of property, esp. of land; used also in general and widest sense of owner, e.g. *cab proprietor.*

proprietorial, adj. [1. proprīetṓrial; 2. prəpràiətɔ́riəl]. Prec. & **-ial.** Of, pertaining to, ownership; proprietary: *proprietorial rights.*

proprietorially, adv. Prec. & **-ly.** As a proprietor; by right of ownership.

proprietorship, n. [1. proprī́etur̄ship; 2. prəpráiətəʃip]. **proprietor** & **-ship.** Ownership.

proprietress, n. [1. prōprī́etres; 2. prouprái̇ətrəs, -is]. See prec. & **-ess.** A woman proprietor or owner.

propriety, n. [1. prō-, proprī́eti; 2. prou-, prəpráiəti], fr. Fr. *propriété*, fr. Lat. *proprietāt-(em)*, 'property, peculiar nature or quality'; a doublet of **property**, w. specialization of meaning. (earlier, now obs. meanings) **1.** Individual right of property. **2.** Something proper or peculiar; inherent quality or peculiarity. **3.** (present usage) That which is suitable, which is in accordance with accepted standards; a conformity with correct standards of morality, conduct or behaviour; decency, modesty of bearing, demeanour &c.; **b** conformity with good standards of taste and correctness: *propriety of style, language, versification* &c.; **c** conformity with what is suitable and appropriate at the moment; expediency: *the propriety of his intervention at that point in the debate may be questioned.*

proprio motu, advbl. phr. [1. prṓpriō mṓtū; 2. próupriou móutjū]. Lat. See **proper** & **motion.** Of one's own motion; on one's own initiative; that is, without compulsion or suggestion from others.

proproctor, n. [1. prṓprókter; 2. próuprɔ́ktə]. **pro- (I.)** & **proctor.** A deputy or assistant proctor at a university.

props, n. pl. [1. props; 2. prɔps]. (slang) Stage properties.

proptosis, n. [1. proptṓsis; 2. prɔptóusis]. Gk. *próptōsis*, 'a falling forward', fr. **pro- (II.)** & *ptôsis*, 'a fall', of wh. **pt-* is a reduced grade of base **pet-*, 'to go, fly, fall'. See **ptero-**, & **petition**, & **-osis.** (med.) A protrusion, prolapse, esp. of the eye.

propulsion, n. [1. propúlshun; 2. prəpálʃən]. Fr., fr. Lat. *prōpuls-(um)*, P.P. type of *prōpellere.* See **propel** & **pulse (I.)**. & **-ion.** **a** Act of propelling or driving forward; **b** means of propelling; that which moves, impels, or urges one to act.

propulsive, adj. & n. [1. propúlsiv; 2. prəpálsiv]. See prec. & **-ive.** **a** adj. Having the power of propelling: *propulsive force* &c.; **b** n., a propulsive agent.

propylaeum, n., pl. **propylaea** [1. pròpiléum, -éa; 2. prɔ̀pilíəm, -íə]. Lat., fr. Gk. *propúlaion*, 'entrance', neut. sing. of *propúlaios*, 'before the gate', often as pl. *-aia* in Gk., fr. **pro- (II.)** & *púlē*, 'gate', the origin of wh. is doubtful. Cp. **pylon.** (class. archit.) Entrance, vestibule, portico in front of any important building; specif., *the Propylaea*, the group of buildings forming the entrance of the Acropolis at Athens.

propylite, n. [1. própilīt; 2. prɔ́pilait]. See next word & **-ite.** (geol.) A volcanic rock, a form of andesite, found in ore-deposits, formerly considered as marking the beginning of a volcanic epoch.

propylon, n. [1. própilon; 2. prɔ́pilɔn]. Gk. *própulon*, 'portico, vestibule'. See **propylaeum.** (Egyptol.) A gateway standing before the pylon or principal entrance to a temple.

pro rata, adv. [1. prṑ rā́ta; 2. pròu réitə]. Lat., for *pro rata parte*, 'according to the reckoned share'. See **pro- (I.)** & **rate (I.)**. In proportion, proportionately, according to the proper share, scale &c.

pro re nata, adv. [1. prṑ rē nā́ta; 2. pròu rī néitə]. Lat. (law) For an occasion as it arises.

prorogation, n. [1. prṑrōgā́shun; 2. pròurougéiʃən], fr. Lat. *prōrogātiōn-(em)*, 'extension of term of office, adjournment', fr. *prōrogāt-(um)*, P.P. type of *prōrogāre.* See **pro- (I.)** & **rogation.** Act of proroguing, or terminating, a session of Parliament, without a dissolution; the formal termination by the King or by Commission of a session.

prorogue, vb. trans. [1. prōrṓg; 2. prouróug] fr. O. Fr. *proroger, -guer*, fr. Lat. *prōrogāre*, 'to prolong; to put off, defer'; fr. **pro- (I.)** & *rogāre*, 'to ask'. See **rogation.** To terminate, bring to an end (session of both Houses of Parliament) without a dissolution, all business not finished having to be begun afresh, contrasted with *adjourn* and *dissolve*: *the King prorogued Parliament*; *Parliament stands prorogued.*

pros-, pref. Form used in compounds; Gk. *prós*, also Homeric *proti*, 'towards; to, in addition'; cp. Scrt. *práti*, 'towards, in the direction of'; prob. connected ultimately w. **peri-**.

prosaic, adj. [1. prōzā́ik; 2. prouzéiik], fr. L. Lat. *prōsaicus*, 'of, relating to, prose'. See **prose** & **-ic.** Like prose; lacking the beauty or imagination of poetry; dull, tedious, commonplace, monotonous, matter-of-fact, uninteresting; prosy: *prosaic details of everyday life*; *a very prosaic speaker.*

prosaically, adv. [1. prōzā́ikali; 2. prouzéiikəli]. Prec. & **-al** & **-ly.** In a prosaic, dull, commonplace manner.

prosaicness, n. [1. prōzā́iknes; 2. prouzéiiknis]. See prec. & **-ness.** State, quality, of being prosaic; dullness, tediousness, monotony.

prosaism, n. [1. prṓzāizm; 2. próuzeiizəm]. See **prose** & **-ism.** A prosaic word, phrase, expression; prosaic style, esp. when occurring in poetry.

prosaist, n. [1. prṓzāist; 2. próuzeiist]. See prec. & **-ist.** **a** A prosaic, commonplace writer; **b** a writer of prose.

proscenium, n. [1. prōsḗnium; 2. prousíniəm], learned pl. *proscenia.* Lat., fr. Gk. *proskḗnion*, 'stage'. See **pro- (II.)** & **scene.** **1.** (class. antiq.) The stage of a Greek or Roman theatre on which the actors stood, between the orchestra and the back wall. **2.** (mod. theatr.) The front part of the stage between the curtain and the orchestra, also the curtain and arch containing it which divides the stage from the auditorium. *Proscenium box*, a stage-box at a theatre.

proscribe, vb. trans. [1. proskrī́b; 2. prɔskráib], fr. Lat. *prōscribere*, 'to publish in writing, esp. a notice of confiscation of property, sentence of outlawry and banishment or death'. See **pro- (I.)** & **scribe.** **1.** To put outside the protection of the law; to outlaw. **2.** To denounce and forbid.

proscription, n. [1. proskrípshun; 2. prɔskrípʃən], fr. Lat. *prōscriptiōn-(em)*, fr. *prōscrip-(tum)*, P.P. type of *prōscribere.* See prec. Act of proscribing; outlawry; **a** (Rom. hist.) the publication of the names of persons condemned to banishment, death, or confiscation of property; **b** state of being proscribed; interdiction, prohibition.

proscriptive, adj. [1. proskríptiv; 2. prɔskríptiv]. See prec. & **-ive.** Of, pertaining to, proscription; proscribing: *proscriptive measures, notice* &c.

proscriptively, adv. Prec. & **-ly.** By proscription.

prose (I.), n. [1. prōz; 2. prouz]. Fr., fr. Lat. *prōsa*, in Phr. *prōsa ōrātio*, 'straight, direct, unadorned speech', fem. of *prōsus*, fr. *prōrsus*, 'straightforward, direct', for *prōversus*, 'turned, directed forward'. See **pro- (I.)** & **version.** **1.** Language, spoken or written, as in ordinary usage, without metre or rhyme, contrasted with *verse.* **2. a** Dull, commonplace, unimaginative style; **b** tediousness, monotony in experience; contrasted with *poetry*: *the drab prose of ordinary, everyday existence.*

prose (II.), vb. intrans. & trans., fr. prec. **1.** intrans. To talk (more rarely, to write) in a dull, unimaginative, uninspiring, tedious, prosy way: *to sit prosing about their experiences.* **2.** trans. (rare) To turn into prose; to render prosy.

prosector, n. [1. prōsékter; 2. prouséktə]. L., Eccles., Lat., 'anatomist', fr. *prōsect-(um)*, P.P. type of *prōsecāre*, 'to cut off from, to cut up'. See **pro- (I.)**, **sect**, & **-or**. One who makes and prepares dissections for demonstrations in anatomy; an assistant to a professor of or lecturer on anatomy.

prosectorship, n. [1. prōséktership; 2. prousέktəʃip]. Prec. & **-ship**. Office of a prosector.

prosecute, vb. trans. & intrans. [1. prósekūt; 2. prɔ́sikjūt], fr. Lat. *prōsecūt-(um)*, P.P. type of *prōsequi*, 'to follow after, pursue, to follow up; continue'. See **pro- (I.)** & **sequela** & **sociable**. **A.** trans. **1.** To follow, pursue, carry on or out, carry further: *to prosecute one's studies, inquiry* &c.; *to prosecute one's business, occupation.* **2. a** To start legal proceedings against: *to prosecute a person for theft*; **b** to try to enforce a right, claim, at law: *to prosecute a claim for damages.* **B.** intrans. To start and carry on a suit or prosecution: *he refused to prosecute; the right, power, to prosecute.*

prosecution, n. [1. pròsekúshun; 2. prɔ̀sikjúʃən], fr. L. Lat. *prōsecūtiōn-(em)*. See prec. & **-ion**. **1.** Act of prosecuting; pursuit, performance: *the prosecution of a trade* &c.; *in the prosecution of one's duties* &c. **2.** (law) **a** The setting in motion and carrying on of a suit against another to establish a claim or right; **b** the institution and carrying on of a criminal charge against a person or persons before a court of law; **c** the party prosecuting a suit or charge; contrasted with *defence*: *to conduct a prosecution; to appear for the prosecution; a prosecution for criminal libel*; *Director of Public Prosecutions*, the official who institutes criminal prosecutions on behalf of the Crown; public prosecutor.

prosecutor, n. [1. prósekūter; 2. prɔ́sikjūtə]. L. Lat., 'attendant, follower'; in Med. Lat., 'prosecutor', **prosecute** & **-or**. One who prosecutes a suit, or esp. a criminal charge, against another in a court of law: *Public Prosecutor*, official instituting criminal proceedings on behalf of the Crown.

proselyte, n. & vb. trans. [1. próselīt; 2. prɔ́silait], fr. O. Fr. *proselite*, fr. L. Lat. *proselytus*, fr. Gk. *prosḗlutos*, 'one who has come, a new-comer', hence, in Hellenic Gk., 'a Gentile convert to Judaism', fr. **pros-** & base **ēl(e)uth-* &c., 'to come', cp. Gk. *eleúthein*, 'to come', etymol. doubtful. **1.** n. **a** A newly made convert to a religion; freshly joined member of a religious party or sect; **b** a convert from one set of opinions or beliefs to another: *a proselyte to Christianity* &c. **2.** vb. (rare) To make a proselyte of, convert; to proselytize.

proselytism, n. [1. prósilītizm, -itizm; 2. prɔ́silaitizəm, -itizəm]. Prec. & **-ism**. Act, system, of making proselytes; conversion to a religion, set of opinions, party &c.

proselytize, vb. trans. or absol. [1. próselitīz; 2. prɔ́silitaiz]. **proselyte** & **-ize**. To make, attempt to make, proselytes for a religion or a cause.

proselytizer, n. [1. prósilitīzer; 2. prɔ́silitaizə]. Prec. & **-er**. One who proselytizes; propagandist.

prosenchyma, n. [1. prosèngkima; 2. prəsέŋkimə]. Mod. concoction fr. Gk., **pros-** & *en*, 'in', & *khūmós*, 'juice', see **chyme** & **chyle**. (bot.) That class of the cellular tissue of plants which consists of masses of long, pointed cells joined together continuously without intervening spaces, contrasted with *parenchyma.*

prosenchymatous, adj. [1. pròsenkímatus; 2. prɔ̀senkáimətəs], fr. stem *-chymat-* of prec., & **-ous**. Consisting of prosenchyma.

proser, n. [1. prōzer; 2. próuzə]. **prose (II.)** & **-er**. One who proses, talks in a dull, tedious, prosy way, without imagination or sparkle.

prosify, vb. trans. [1. prōzifī; 2. próuzifai]. See **prose** & **-fy**. To turn into prose, make prosy or tedious.

prosily, adv. [1. prōzili; 2. próuzili]. **prosy** & **-ly**. In a prosy manner.

prosiness, n. [1. prōzines; 2. próuzinis]. See prec. & **-ness**. State, quality, of being prosy.

prosit, interj. [1. prōzit; 2. próuzit]. Lat., 'may it do good to, be profitable', 3rd pers. sing. pres. subj. of *prōdesse*, 'to do good', see *prod-* under **pro- (I.)** & **esse**. Form expressive of good wishes, used in drinking a person's health, esp. by Germans.

prosodial, adj. [1. prosōdial; 2. prəsóudiəl]. **prosody** & **-al**. Of, pertaining to, prosody; prosodical.

prosodic(al), adj. [1. prosódik(l); 2. prəsɔ́dik(l)]. **prosody** & **-ic** (& **-al**.) Of, pertaining to, prosody, according to the rules of prosody; prosodial.

prosodically, adv. Prec. & **-ly**. In regard to, from the point of view of, prosody.

prosodist, n. [1. prósodist; 2. prɔ́sədist]. **prosody** & **-ist**. A person skilled in, or learned in, the theory of prosody.

prosody, n. [1. prósodi; 2. prɔ́sədi], fr. Fr. *prosodie*, fr. Lat. *prosōdia*, fr. Gk. *prosōidía*, 'a song sung to an instrumental or vocal accompaniment, accent, prosody'. See **pros-** & **ode**. The science or art of versification; theory and principles of rhythm and metre.

prosopopoeia, n. [1. pròsōpopḗa; 2. prɔ̀soupəpíə]. Lat., fr. Gk. *prosōpopoiía*, fr. *prósōpon*, 'a face, person', fr. **pros-** & *ōp-*, fr. *ṓps*, 'eye, sight, face', see **-opia**, & *poiein*, 'to make', see **poet**. Rhetorical figure by which **a** past events are described as though actually taking place, as by use of the historical present; or **b** dead persons are represented as present and speaking, and inanimate objects as though they had life and feeling; **b** introduction of dead person as alive, or of an absent person as present and speaking.

prospect (I.), n. [1. próspekt; 2. prɔ́spεkt], fr. Lat. *prospectus*, n., cp. *prospect-(um)*, P.P. type of *prospicere*, 'to look out over, to look forward, to view'. See **pro- (I.)**, **spectacle**, & **spy**. **1.** A wide outlook; view, vista over a stretch of country or sea: *a beautiful prospect to the south.* **2. a** Something looked forward to in the future; that which is anticipated, expected, or considered likely: *a prospect of success, recovery* &c.; *I see no prospect of peace*; Phr. *in prospect*, expected, anticipated; in view: *some relief to the taxpayers is in prospect*; **b** a person's probable future fate, fortune, or chances of success: *his prospects at present are poor*; **c** specif., favourable prospects, likelihood of good fortune in the future: *a man of small talents and no prospects.* **3.** (min. &c.) A place likely to yield ore, oil &c.; a sample of ore &c.; prospective yield of ore &c.: *to strike a good (gold) prospect.*

prospect (II.), vb. intrans. & trans. [1. prospékt; 2. prəspέkt], fr. prec. **A.** intrans. **1. a** To explore, have a look round, make an inspection: *to go round the farm and prospect*; **b** specif., to search for a likely mining prospect: *to prospect for gold, oil* &c. **2.** To yield specified result, make certain impression as result of prospecting: *the mine prospects well.* **B.** trans. **a** To inspect, explore: *to prospect one's new property*; **b** to examine thoroughly, search, test: *to prospect a likely stretch of country for gold* &c.

prospective, adj. [1. prospéktiv; 2. prəspέktiv]. **prospect (I.)** & **-ive**. Relating to, operating in, coming into existence in, passing into new phase in, the future; opposite of *retrospective*: *prospective benefits, obligations*; *the measure, law &c. is purely prospective*; *my prospective son-in-law.*

prospectively, adv. Prec. & **-ly**. In the future; contingently.

prospectiveness, n. See prec. & **-ness**. State, quality, of being prospective; contingency.

prospector, n. [1. prospékter; 2. prəspέktə]. **prospect (II.)** & **-or**; cp. L. Lat. *prospector*, 'one who looks out, watchman'. (min. &c.) One who prospects or explores for gold, oil &c.

prospectus, n. [1. prospéktus; 2. prəspέktəs]. Lat., 'a look out, distant view' &c. See **prospect (I.)**. Outline account of the plan, design, cost, advantages &c. of an institution (e.g. a school), or of an undertaking about to be launched (e.g. of a new book, or of a company about to be floated &c.).

prosper, vb. intrans. & trans. [1. prósper; 2. prɔ́spə], fr. Fr. *prospérer*, fr. Lat. *prōsperāre*, 'to make, render, prosperous or happy', fr. *prosper, prosperus.* See **prosperous**. **A.** intrans. To be prosperous, to excel, to flourish; to develop well; to be fortunate; to succeed in one's career: *the country, our trade, is prospering under a strong government*; *the eldest brother went abroad and prospered*; *the child's health prospers at the sea*; *the schemes of the wicked often prosper.* **B.** trans. To make prosperous, cause to succeed; to be favourable to: *may Heaven prosper you*; *a prospering breeze*; '*prosper Thou our handiwork*'.

prosperity, n. [1. prospériti; 2. prəspέriti]. M.E., fr. O. Fr. *prosperite*, fr. Lat. *prōsperitāt-(em)*, fr. *prosperus.* See next word & **-ity**. State, quality, of being prosperous; success, welfare, good luck, fortune; wealth; contrasted with *adversity*: *to wish you all prosperity*; *the prosperity of an undertaking, business* &c.

prosperous, adj. [1. prósperus; 2. prɔ́spərəs], fr. A.-Fr. & obs. Fr. *prospereus*; earlier in Engl. *prosper*, Fr. *prospere*, fr. Lat. *prosperus*, also *prosper*, 'agreeing with, favourable, according to, one's hopes or wishes, prosperous'; prob. for **prōspēre*, 'according to expectation', w. shortening of vowel; fr. base of *spēs*, 'hope', *spērāre*, 'to hope'; this is prob. cogn. w. *spīrāre*, 'to breathe', *spīritus* &c., see **spirit**, & *-spire*, as in **respire** &c.; see **spirant**. Successful, fortunate, prospering; thriving, lucky, favourable: *a prosperous year, business, voyage*; *prosperous weather* &c.; *to bring a plan to a prosperous issue.*

prosperously, adv. Prec. & **-ly**. In a prosperous manner; successfully, with good fortune.

prosperousness, n. See prec. & **-ness**. State, quality, of being prosperous; success, prosperity.

prostate, n. [1. próstāt; 2. prɔ́st(e)it], fr. Med. Lat. *prostata*, fr. Gk. *prostátēs*, 'one who stands before, guardian'. See **pro- (II.)** & **static.** (anat.) A gland, also called *prostate gland*, situated at the neck of the bladder in male mammals with important functions in connexion with the generative organs.

prostatectomy, n. [1. pròstatéktumi; 2. prɔ̀stætέktəmi]. Prec. & *ec-*, see **ex-**, & **-tomy**. Excision of a diseased prostate.

prostatic, adj. [1. prostátik; 2. prəstǽtik]. **prostate** & **-ic**. Of, pertaining to, the prostate and its functions: *prostatic secretion.*

prostatitis, n. [1. pròstatítis; 2. prɔ̀stətáitis]. **prostate** & **-itis**. Inflammation of the prostate.

prosthesis, n. [1. prósthesis; 2. prɔ́sþisis], fr. Gk. *prósthesis*, 'addition'. See **pros-** & **thesis**. **1.** (gram.) The addition, as prefix, of a syllable to a word, as *be-* in *beloved*, *de-* in *defend* &c. **2.** (surg.) The addition of an artificial limb, tooth &c. to take the place of one that is missing.

prosthetic, adj. [1. prosthétik; 2. prəsþέtik], fr. Gk. *prosthetikós*, 'disposed to add'. See prec. & **-ic**. (gram.) Added, prefixed; by way of addition or prefix.

prostitute (I.), n. & adj. [1. próstitūt; 2. prɔ́stitjūt], fr. Lat. *prostitūta*, n., fem. of *prostitūtus*, P.P. of *prostituere.* See next word. **1.** n. A woman who sells her body for sexual intercourse; a harlot, a courtesan. **2.** adj. (archaic or rare) Prostituted, infamous, mercenary: *talents prostitute to ambition.*

prostitute (II.), vb. trans., fr. Lat. *prostitūt-(um)*, P.P. type of *prostituere*, 'to expose publicly for sale, esp. for prostitution, to dishonour'; fr. **pro- (I.)** & *statuere*, 'to place, set', cp. **statute**. **1.** (of a woman) To traffic in her favours, sell herself for an immoral purpose. **2.** (fig.) To put to base, dishonourable use: *to prostitute one's honour, talents* &c.

prostitution, n. [1. prŏstitūshun; 2. prɔstitjū́ʃən], fr. Lat. *prostitūtiōn-(em)*. See prec. & **-ion.** **1.** Promiscuous intercourse practised by women for gain. **2.** (fig.) The unworthy employment of one's capacities, power, influence &c., esp. from a venal, sordid motive: *the prostitution of one's genius, intellectual powers* &c.

prostrate (I.), adj. [1. próstrāt; 2. prɔ́streit], fr. Lat. *prōstrāt-(um)*, P.P. type of *prōsternere*, 'to lay, throw, down forward or flat'. See **pro-** (I.) & **stratum.** **1. a** Lying flat on the ground; prone, supine; **b** (bot., of plants) trailing on the ground. **2.** (fig.) **a** Completely crushed, reduced to complete submission; unable and unwilling to strike a blow in self-defence: *thrones and principalities lay prostrate before the invincible Bonaparte*; **b** morally abased, terrorized, abject, submissive: *prostrate beneath the tyranny of the oppressor.* **3. a** Worn out physically; spent, powerless: *prostrate with fatigue, illness* &c.; **b** morally and mentally cast down, utterly dejected, broken down, disconsolate: *prostrate with grief* &c.

prostrate (II.), vb. trans. [1. prostrā́t; 2. prɔstréit], fr. prec. **1.** To throw, cast down, lay flat on the ground: *the storm prostrated hundreds of trees.* **2.** (reflex.) *Prostrate oneself*; **a** to throw oneself down, bow to the earth, in token of submission, respect, humility &c.: *the priest prostrated himself before the altar*; **b** (fig.) to abase oneself, cringe, show servility: *to prostrate oneself before rank and wealth.* **3.** To overcome, exhaust: *to be prostrated with fatigue, sickness* &c.

prostration, n. [1. prostrā́shun; 2. prɔstréiʃən], fr. Lat. *prōstrātiōn-(em)*. See prec. & **-ion.** **1.** Act of prostrating oneself: *prostration before the altar.* **2.** State of being prostrated; **a** extreme bodily exhaustion: *a condition of complete prostration*, as after a severe illness; **b** extreme moral depression and distress: *prostration of mind and spirit.*

prostyle, n. & adj. [1. próstīl; 2. próustail], fr. Lat. *prostȳlos*, fr. Gk. *próstūlos*, 'having columns in front'. See **pro-** (II.) & **style** (III.). **1.** n. A portico in front of a temple with not more than four columns. **2.** adj. Having a prostyle.

prosy, adj. [1. prṓzi; 2. próuzi]. **prose** (I.) & **-y.** Heavy, flat, dull, uninspired, uninteresting; wordy, long-winded: *a prosy author, speaker*; *a prosy style, book, discourse* &c.

protagonist, n. [1. prōtágunist; 2. proutǽgənist], fr. Gk. *prōtagōnistḗs*, 'first actor in a drama', fr. *prôtos*, 'first', see **proto-**, & *agōnistḗs*, 'competitor in games, actor', fr. *agṓn*, 'contest', see **agony**, & **-ist.** **1.** The leading, first, actor in a Greek drama. **2.** The principal character in a play, plot of a novel &c.; one who plays the leading part in anything, regarded dramatically; the chief leader.

pro tanto, adv. [1. prṓ tántō; 2. próu tǽntou]. Lat. For so much; to that extent, so far.

protasis, n. [1. prótasis; 2. prɔ́təsis]. Gk., 'proposition, premise'. **pro-** (II.) & *tásis*, 'a stretching, tension', fr. base **ten-*, **tn̥-* &c., 'stretch', whence also Gk. *teinein*, fr. **tenjō-*, 'stretch'; also Lat. *tendere*, 'to stretch', see **tension, tense** &c.; Goth. *-þanjan*, 'stretch'; also O.H.G. *dunni*, 'thin', O.E. *þynne*, see **thin.** (gram.) The introductory clause of a conditional sentence; contrasted with *apodosis.*

protatic, adj. [1. prōtátik; 2. proutǽtik], fr. Gk. *prōtatikós*. Prec. & **-ic.** Pertaining to the protasis of a conditional sentence.

protean, adj. [1. prōtḗan; 2. proutíən], fr. **Proteus** & **-an.** Having, like Proteus, various changing shapes and forms; variable; able to play various parts; versatile: *the protean changes of nature*; *a protean performer.*

protect, vb. trans. [1. protékt; 2. prətékt], fr. Lat. *prōtect-(um)*, P.P. type of *prōtegere*, 'to cover over, protect', fr. **pro-** (I.) & base **teg-*, 'to cover', q.v. under **tegument, tectorial**; cogn. w. **thatch.** **1.** (in physical, material, and spiritual, non-material senses) To cover, guard, from injury; to keep safe, preserve, defend: *to protect one's head from the cold, one's eyes from the sun*; *to protect one's country, children*; *to protect one's own interests, claims* &c.; *to protect one's soul from evil* &c. **2.** (commerc.) To provide funds to meet charges on a bill &c. for payment on maturity. **3.** (econ.) To give or attempt to give an advantage to home manufactures in face of the competition of foreign, imported goods by putting a duty on the latter under a tariff.

protection, n. [1. protékshun; 2. prətékʃən], fr. Lat. *prōtectiōn-(em)*. See prec. & **-ion.** **1. a** Act, process, means, of protecting, guarding, defending &c.; shelter, defence: *a father's first duty is the proper protection of his children*; *a ruler must be deeply concerned with the protection of his country against her enemies*; Phr. (of a woman) *to live under the protection of*, to be the kept mistress of; specif. **b** act, system, of protecting national manufactures and produce against foreign competition by the imposition of duties on imports; **c** a document affording safety from molestation; passport, safe-conduct. **2.** Condition, fact, of being protected: **a** *a thatched roof provides an excellent protection against sun*; *the weak and imbecile need the protection of the State*; *to enjoy the protection afforded by furs against cold*; **b** cover, security, against financial risk or loss: *modern systems of insurance give complete protection against all imaginable accidents and contingencies.*

protectionism, n. [1. protékshunizm; 2. prətékʃənizəm]. **protection** & **-ism.** System, plan, for helping home industries by the imposition of tariffs on imported goods.

protectionist, n. [1. protékshunist; 2. prətékʃənist]. **protection** & **-ist.** Believer in the protection of home industries by means of tariffs.

protective, adj. [1. protéktiv; 2. prətéktiv]. **protect** & **-ive.** **1.** Serving to protect; giving protection or shelter to: *protective armour.* Specific uses: *protective colouring* (in animals), quality, arrangement, of colours on coat or skin acquired by certain animals, so closely resembling that of their natural environment that they are practically indistinguishable from this to the eye, and thus escape their enemies; *protective instinct*, instinct to afford protection to others, e.g. of a mother to defend her young. **2.** Affording protection against foreign competition: *protective duties, tariff.*

protectively, adv. Prec. & **-ly.** In a protective way; so as to give protection.

protectiveness, n. See prec. & **-ness.** **a** State, quality, of being protective, of affording protection; **b** instinct, tendency, to protect others.

protector, n. [1. protékter; 2. prətéktə]. **protect** & **-or.** **1.** One who protects or guards: *the protector of the house, his wife's honour* &c. **2.** Specif. **a** one appointed to act as governor or regent of the realm during the incapacity or minority of the sovereign: *the Protector Somerset*; or during a Commonwealth; title held by Oliver and Richard Cromwell. **3.** Name applied to various articles which give protection of some kind, e.g. *chest protector*, pad worn over the chest by persons with weak lungs &c.

protectoral, adj. [1. protéktural; 2. prətéktərəl]. Prec. & **-al.** Of, pertaining to, a protector: *protectoral power, authority.*

protectorate, n. [1. protékturat; 2. prətéktərit]. Prec. & **-ate.** **1.** Office of, rule by, a protector or regent; period of such rule: *during the protectorate of Cromwell.* **2. a** State governed by a protector; **b** administration of a weaker or less civilized state by one more powerful.

protectorship, n. [1. protéktership; 2. prətéktəʃip]. **protector** & **-ship.** Office, rule, of a protector; protectorate.

protectory, n. [1. protékturi; 2. prətéktəri]. **protect** & **-ory.** An institution for the protection and guardianship of deserted or criminal children.

protectress, n. [1. protéktres; 2. prətéktris]. **protector** & **-ess.** A woman protector or guardian.

protégé, n., fem. *protégée* [1. prótezhā; 2. prɔ́težei]. Fr., P.P. of *protéger*. See **protect.** One who is under the care, protection, or patronage of another.

proteid, n. [1. prṓtēid; 2. próutīd]. Scientific concoction fr. Gk. *prôtos*, 'first', see **proto-**, & *eîdos*, 'form', see **idol**, & **-oid.** (chem.) Nitrogenous compound occurring in animal and vegetable substance; now more usually protein, q.v.

proteiform, adj. [1. prṓtiform; 2. próutifɔ̄m]. See **Proteus** & **-form.** (zool.) Very unstable in form.

protein, n. [1. prṓtēn; 2. próutīn]. Germ., fr. Gk. *prōtei-(os)*, 'holding the first place', fr. *prôtos*, 'first', & **-in.** See **proteid.** (chem.) A complex organic compound containing carbon, oxygen, hydrogen, and nitrogen, with some sulphur, the essential nitrogenous constituent of food, as the albumen of eggs, blood, casein of milk, creatin of meat &c.

proteinic, adj. [1. prōtḗnik; 2. proutínik]. Prec. & **-ic.** Of the nature of protein.

proteinous, adj. [1. prṓtinus; 2. próutinəs]. **protein** & **-ous.** Proteinic.

pro tempore, adv. (abbr. *pro tem.*) [1. prṓ témpori; 2. próu témpəri]. Lat. See **pro-** (I.) & abl. sing. of *tempus*, 'time', see **temporal** (I.). For the time being; temporarily; as adj., temporary.

proter(o)-, pref. Combining form fr. Gk. *próteros*, 'before, earlier, former', see **pro-** (I.) & **proto-**; used in compounds w. sense 'earlier, anterior'.

proterandrous, adj. [1. prŏterándrus; 2. pròutərǽndrəs]. Prec. & **anther.** (bot.) Having the anthers or stamens ripe and their pollen shed before the corresponding stigmas or pistils are ready for fertilization.

proterogynous, adj. [1. prŏteróginus, -ójinus; 2. pròutərɔ́ginəs, -ɔ́džinəs]. **protero-** & **-gynous.** (bot.) Having the pistils matured and withered before the stamens are ripe.

protest (I.), vb. trans. & intrans. [1. protést; 2. prətést], fr. Fr. *protester*, fr. Lat. *prōtestāri*, 'to bear witness publicly, testify, aver'. See **pro-** (I.) & base of **testify.** **A.** trans. **1.** To declare, affirm, solemnly; to assert, asseverate: *to protest one's loyalty, innocence.* **2.** (law, of notary public) To declare in due form that a bill of exchange has been duly presented and dishonoured or acceptance refused. **B.** intrans. **1. a** To declare or affirm solemnly: *to protest that one is innocent*; *his loyalty, he protested, was undoubted*; **b** (archaic, 17th and 18th cents., colloq.) *I protest*, loosely used, much as we use *I declare, I must say* &c., with no special emphasis or force: *I protest 'tis a spirited rascal*; *I protest thou'rt an arch wag*; *I protest I'm sick of the whole business.* **2.** To make a protest, raise objection, express disagreement, sense of injury &c.: *the time has come to protest*; *I can't listen to such misleading statements without protesting*; also *protest against*, to offer objection to, resist, refuse to entertain.

protest (II.), n. [1. prṓtest; 2. próutest], fr. O. Fr. *proteste*. See prec. **1.** Expression of objection, dissent, disapproval; specif., a formal request or petition, generally in writing, asking that something be not done: *to make, lodge, a protest.* Phr. *under protest*, unwillingly. **2.** Declaration by a notary public that payment or acceptance of a bill has been refused.

protestant (I.), adj. & n. [1. protéstant; 2. prətéstənt]. Fr., fr. Lat. *prōtestant-(em)*, Pres. Part. of *prōtestāre*. See **protest** (I.). **1.** adj. Protesting. **2.** n. Person making a protest.

Protestant (II.), n. & adj. [1. prótestant; 2. prɔ́tistənt]. Same as prec. **1.** n. **a** Member of one of many Christian bodies which reject the claim of the Pope to be the head of the Church, dispute the Roman Catholic theory of the Papacy generally, and which further disagree profoundly with the doctrine of transubstantiation; Protestants of more extreme type reject also the episcopal system of Church government, and the doctrine of apostolical succession in the Christian ministry, while some deny the objective force of the Sacraments; **b** person holding distinctively anti-papal views on religious matters. **2.** adj. Connected with, pertaining to, characteristic of, Protestants and their doctrines.

Protestantism, n. [1. prótestantizm; 2. prɔ́tistəntizəm]. **Protestant (II.)** & **-ism.** Religious doctrines and principles of Protestants.

Protestantize, vb. trans. [1. prótestantīz; 2. prɔ́tistəntaiz]. **Protestant (II.)** & **-ize.** To convert to Protestantism; to assimilate to Protestant practice and doctrine: *to Protestantize the Church of England.*

protestation, n. [1. pròtestā́shun; 2. prɔ̀testéiʃən]. Fr., fr. L. Lat. *prōtestātiōn-(em).* See **protest (I.)** & **-ation.** Strong, solemn declaration, asseveration, affirmation: *a protestation of innocence, of love, loyalty, faith* &c.

Proteus, n. [1. prṓtūs; 2. próutjūs]. Gk. *Prōteús.* See below. **1.** (cap.) **a** (class. mythol.) A sea-god who, if captured, had to prophesy the future, and to escape doing so could change into all kinds of shapes. **2.** (fig.) A person who can change his opinions, principles, character &c. very rapidly. **3.** (bacter.) A bacillus found in decomposing meat. **4.** (zool.) A genus of eel-like amphibians, partly blind, possessing four weak legs, found in the water of some caves.

prothalamium, n. [1. pròthalā́mium; 2. pròuþæléimiəm]. A coined word on anal. of *epithalamium*, fr. **pro- (II.)** & Gk. *thálamos*, 'bridal chamber', see **thalamus.** A marriage song.

prothallium, n. [1. prōthálium; 2. prouþǽliəm]. Neo-Lat., fr. **pro- (I.)** & **thallus**, fr. Gk. *thallós*, 'green shoot, stalk, bough'. (bot.) The small, thalloid generating body in ferns.

prothesis, n. [1. próthesis; 2. prɔ́þisis]. Gk., 'a setting out; a placing before'. **pro- (II.)** & **thesis. 1.** (Gk. Orthodox Ch.) The preliminary oblation of the bread and wine at the Eucharist. **2.** (gram.) Process of developing an initial sound before a word, as in O. Fr. *estang*, Mod. Fr. *étang*, 'pond', fr. Lat. *stagnum.*

prothonotary, n. Variant of **protonotary.**

protista, n. pl. [1. protísta; 2. prətístə]. Neo-Lat., fr. neut. pl. of Gk. *prṓtistos*, a redupl. superl., fr. *prṓtos*, 'first', see **proto-.** (biol.) Collective name for organisms consisting of a single cell, whether animal or vegetable.

proto-, pref. Form of Gk. *prṓtos*, 'first', used in compounds; a superl. formed fr. *pro*, 'before', see **pro- (II.). a** First in time, hence, original, primitive, as *protomartyr, protoplasm* &c.; also, quite freely, as *proto-Amerindian*, of the primitive, original stock of American-Indian races; *proto-Celtic, Slavonic* &c., of the original forms of Celtic and Slavonic languages &c.; **b** (chem.) of compounds in which the naming element has only one atom or combines with the smallest amount or single atom of another element.

protocol (I.), n. [1. prṓtōkol; 2. próutoukəl], fr. O. Fr. *prothocole, protocole*, fr. Low & Med. Lat. *prōtocollum*, fr. Late, Byzantine, Gk. *prōtókollon*; fr. **proto-** & *kólla*, 'glue', see **colloid. 1.** (hist.) A small slip or tab glued to the top edge of a roll of MSS., esp. of an official document, giving date, name of writer &c. **2.** A document containing the results of negotiations preliminary to a treaty or agreement, signed by the negotiating parties. **3.** A formula at the beginning or end of a papal bull.

protocol (II.), vb. trans. & intrans, fr. prec. To draw up, record, in protocol form; to draw up protocols.

protogenic, -genetic, adj. [1. prṑtōjénik, -jenétik; 2. pròutoudʒénik, -dʒənétik]. **proto-** & **-genic, -genetic.** (biol.) Born, formed, at the beginning; belonging to earliest period of formation.

protogyny, n. [1. prōtógini, -jini; 2. proutɔ́gini, -dʒini]. **proto-** & Gk. *guné*, 'woman, wife'. See **gynaeco-** & **-gynous.** (bot.) Condition, process, in certain plants, in which the stigma withers before the anthers mature.

protomartyr, n. [1. prṑtōmárter; 2. pròutoumā́tə], fr. Gk. *prōtómartur.* See **proto-** & **martyr.** The first Christian martyr, St. Stephen.

proton, n. [1. prṓton; 2. próutən]. **proto-**, with ending formed on anal. of **electron.** Positive small mass or unit of electricity, corresponding to the electron or negative unit.

protonotary, prothonotary, n. [1. prṑtōnṓtari; 2. pròutounóutəri], fr. L. Lat. *prōtonōtārius.* See **proto-** & **notary. 1.** (law) Title of the chief official of the old Courts of Chancery, Common Pleas, and King's Bench; now superseded by *Master.* **2.** (R.C. Ch.) One of twelve prelates, *Apostolic Protonotaries*, forming a college which registers papal acts, such as beatification &c. **3.** (Gk. Orthodox Ch.) The chief secretary of the Patriarch of Constantinople.

Protophyta, n. pl. [1. prōtófita; 2. proutɔ́fitə]. Neo-Lat. See **proto-** & **-phyte.** (bot.) The division or phylum of plants, including the simplest unicellular plants; corresponding to the zoological *Protozoa.*

protoplasm, n. [1. prṓtōplàzm; 2. próutouplæ̀zəm]. Gk. See **proto-** & **plasm.** (biol.) Physical basis of organic life; essential material of which cells are composed.

protoplasmic, adj. [1. prṑtōplázmik; 2. pròutouplǽzmik]. Prec. & **-ic.** Pertaining to, consisting of, of the nature of, protoplasm.

protoplast, n. [1. prṓtōplast; 2. próutouplæst], fr. Gk. *prōtóplastos*, 'first formed'. See **proto-** & **plastic. 1.** That which was formed first, a prototype, model; original supposed ancestor. **2.** Specif. (biol.) a mass or unit of protoplasm.

protoplastic, adj. [1. prṑtōplástik; 2. pròutouplǽstik]. Prec. & **-ic. a** Of, pertaining to, a protoplast; constituting an original type or model; **b** protoplasmic.

prototheria, n. pl. [1. prṑtōthḗria; 2. pròutouþíəriə]. **proto-** & Gk. *thēría*, pl. of *thḗrion*, dimin. of *thḗr*, 'animal, beast', see **theriac.** (zool.) Term applied to the lowest and most primitive order of mammals, such as the echidna, duck-billed platypus &c.

prototypal, adj. [1. prṑtōtī́pl; 2. pròutoutáipl]. Prec. & **-al.** Of the nature of, serving as, a prototype.

prototype, n. [1. prṓtōtīp; 2. próutoutaip]. Gk. *prōtótupos*, adj., 'primitive, original'. See **proto-** & **-type.** An original, primary, type; model, pattern.

prototypical, adj. [1. prṑtōtípikl; 2. pròutoutípikl]. **proto-** & **typical.** Prototypal.

protoxide, n. [1. prōtóksīd; 2. proutɔ́ksaid]. **proto-** & **oxide.** (chem.) Any metallic oxide of a series which contains the smallest proportion of oxygen.

Protozoa, n. pl. [1. prṑtōzṓa; 2. pròutouzóuə]. Concocted fr. **proto-** & *zōia*, 'animals, living things', pl. of *zōion*, q.v. under **zoo-.** (zool.) Collective term designating organisms belonging to the simplest form of animal life, consisting of a single cell, and reproducing themselves by fission; corresponding to the botanical term *Protophyta.*

protozoan, adj. & n. [1. prṑtōzṓan; 2. pròutouzóuən]. Prec. & **-an. a** adj. Of, pertaining to, the Protozoa; **b** n., a member of the Protozoa.

protozoic, adj. [1. prṑtōzṓik; 2. pròutouzóuik]. **Protozoa** & **-ic.** (geol.) a Belonging to the earliest period at which organic life can be shown to have existed; **b** (of deposits) containing remains of earliest forms of organic life.

protract, vb. trans. [1. prōtrákt; 2. proutrǽkt], fr. Lat. *prōtract-(um)*, P.P. type of *prōtrahere*, 'to draw forward, protract'. See **pro- (I.)** & **tract (I.). 1.** To draw out, prolong, lengthen duration of; delay: *to protract a debate, argument, one's stay* &c.; *protracted negotiations.* **2.** (surv.) To draw to scale, to plot out. **3.** (zool.) To thrust out, extend; opposite of *retract.*

protractedly, adv. [1. prōtráktedli; 2. proutrǽktidli]. Prec. & **-ed** & **-ly.** In a protracted, drawn-out, manner; lengthily.

protractile, adj. [1. prōtráktīl; 2. proutrǽktail]. **protract** & **-ile.** (zool.) Capable of being protracted; extensile.

protraction, n. [1. prōtrákshun; 2. proutrǽkʃən]. L. Lat. *prōtractiōn-(em).* **protract** & **-ion. 1. a** Act of protracting, of lengthening duration of: *protraction of a debate* &c.; **b** act of extending, thrusting out, an organ &c. **2.** (surv.) The drawing of a plan &c. to scale.

protractor, n. [1. prōtrákter; 2. proutrǽktə]. **protract** & **-or. 1.** (surv.) Instrument, with graduated scales, for measuring angles. **2.** (attrib.) *Protractor muscle*, muscle which protracts or extends a limb &c.

protrude, vb. trans. & intrans. [1. prōtrṓōd; 2. proutrū́d], fr. Lat. *prōtrūdere*, 'to thrust forward', fr. **pro- (I.)** & *trūdere*, 'to thrust'; cp. **intrude** & see **thrust. 1.** trans. To thrust forward, put out, cause to project: *to protrude one's tongue.* **2.** intrans. To project, stick out: *their eyes protruded.*

protrusile, adj. [1. prōtrṓōsil; 2. proutrū́sail], fr. Lat. *prōtrūs-(um)*, P.P. of *prōtrūdere*, see prec., & **-ile.** Capable of being protruded or thrust forward; protractile: *protrusile eyes*, as of snails &c.

protrusion, n. [1. prōtrṓōzhun; 2. proutrū́ʒən]. See prec. & **-ion. a** Act of protruding; **b** state of being protruded: *protrusion of the eyeballs.*

protrusive, adj. [1. prōtrṓōsiv; 2. proutrū́siv]. See prec. & **-ive. 1.** Tending to cause to protrude, to impel forward. **2.** Protrusile.

protuberance, n. [1. prōtū́berans; 2. proutjū́bərəns]. Next word & **-ce. a** State of being protuberant or prominent; **b** a projection, swelling.

protuberant, adj. [1. prōtū́berant; 2. proutjū́bərənt], fr. Lat. *prōtūberant-(em)*, Pres. Part. of *prōtūberāre*, 'to swell out', fr. **pro- (I.)** & *tūber*, 'a hump, swelling'. See **tuber.** Swelling, bulging out, protruding, prominent: *protuberant eyes.*

protyle, n. [1. prṓtīl; 2. próutail]. **proto-** & Gk. *hū́lē*, 'stuff, substance', see **-yl.** (chem.) Hypothetical, primordial, undifferentiated chemical matter out of which the various elements may have been differentiated.

proud, adj. [1. proud; 2. praud]. O.E. *prūt*, M.E. *prūt, prout*; *prūd, proud*; etymol. doubtful; the form *prȳte* in O.E., see **pride**, shows that the word is older than *i*-mutation; O.N. *prūðe* is prob. borrowed fr. O.E.; the word appears to have been borrowed fr. a L. Lat. source, whence also O. Fr. *prou*, 'brave', q.v. under **prowess. 1. a** Feeling, showing, a proper pride, and due sense of one's personal dignity: *proud poverty; too proud to beg*; **b** evincing noble pride: *that proud head was humbled and bowed.* **2.** Having undue sense of one's own importance; exulting in one's fancied superiority, taking credit to oneself for one's wealth, position &c.; arrogant, haughty: *too proud to fight.* Phr. *as proud as a peacock*, very vain or conceited. **3.** Taking a natural and worthy pride in, exulting in: *proud of one's country, one's house, school, children* &c.; *proud to have known the man.* **4.** Giving cause for justifiable pride: *a proud period in the country's history*; *a proud occasion.* **5.** Splendid, stately, magnificent: *in proud array*; *a proud company.* **6.** as adv. (colloq.) Proudly: *to do one proud*, to treat one splendidly, proudly; *to do oneself proud*, to treat oneself splendidly; *it will do, does, me proud*, it will suit me very well; gives me great satisfaction.

proud flesh, n. A granulated growth of flesh round a wound in the early stages of healing.

proudly, adv. [1. próudli; 2. práudli]. **proud & -ly.** a In a proud manner; with pride; b splendidly, magnificently: *banners fluttering and plumes tossing proudly.*

provable, adj. [1. proovabl; 2. prûvəbl]. **prove & -able.** Capable of being proved.

provably, adv. Prec. & **-ly.** In a way which can be proved; so as to be proved.

prove, vb. trans. & intrans. [1. proov; 2. prūv]. Either direct fr. O.E. *prōfian*, 'to assume to be', borrowed fr. Lat. *probāre*, w. sense influenced by O. Fr. *prover*, fr. same source, or fr. O. Fr. itself. The senses of *probāre* are, 'to test the value of anything, to approve', fr. *probus*, 'excellent, good, upright'. See **probity & proof. A.** trans. **1.** a To essay, try, test the quality of by experiment &c.: *to prove a man's honesty, the genuineness of anything* &c.; *to prove a gun*, subject it to rigid tests; Phr. *the exception proves the rule*, i.e. it tests the soundness of it, but does not demonstrate its truth; b to experience, learn by experience; to suffer, undergo: *to prove the extreme depths of poverty and sorrow.* **2.** To demonstrate, logically and beyond question, the truth or falsity of a statement, theory &c.; to demonstrate something to be, or not to be, a fact: *to prove one's statements by the strongest evidence*; *to prove a man's guilt* or *innocence.* **3.** Specif. a (arith.) to verify the correctness of a calculation; b (law) to establish the validity of: *to prove a will.* **4.** (reflex.) To show that one is, oneself to be: *he proved himself (to be) a capable general*, &c. **B.** intrans. To be found on trial, turn out, to be: *the rumour proves true*; *the treatment proved successful.*

proven, adj. [1. próven, prooven; 2. próuvən, prûvən]. **prove** & *-en*, ending of a strong P.P. Proved; (esp. in Scots law) *not proven*, a verdict which secures the acquittal of a prisoner, implying that the jury are unable on the evidence to find him either *guilty* or *not guilty*, but which has the practical results of the latter.

provenance, n. [1. próvenans; 2. prɔ́vənəns]. Fr., fr. *provenir*, 'to come from', fr. Lat. *prōvenīre*, 'to come forth'. See **pro- (I.) & venue & -ance.** Place from which anything comes, place where a thing has been found; place of origin, source: *the provenance of a MS., of a picture.*

Provençal, adj. & n. [1. pròvonsáhl; 2. prɔ̀vāsál]. Fr., fr. *Provence*, fr. Lat. *provincia*. See **province. 1.** adj. Of, belonging to, Provence, an old kingdom and province of southern France: *Provençal literature* &c. **2.** n. a The Provençal language; b inhabitant of Provence.

provender, n. [1. próvender; 2. prɔ́vində], fr. O. Fr. *provende, provendre*, 'provisions', w. *pro-* instead of *prae-*, fr. L. Lat. *praebenda*, 'payment, daily allowance for provisions', see **prebend.** Fodder for cattle; (colloq.) provisions, food.

provenience, n. [1. provēniens; 2. prəvíniəns], fr. Lat. *prōvenient-(em)* & **-ce.** See the Fr. variant **provenance.** Source, origin, provenance.

proverb, n. [1. próverb; 2. prɔ́vəb]. Fr. *proverbe*, fr. Lat. *prōverbium*, 'proverb'. See **pro- (I.) & verb. 1.** a A traditional, usually a trite, saying, embodying commonplace experience or obvious truism, in a brief, often inelegant, form of words; an adage, saw; b specif. (pl., cap.) a book of the Old Testament, containing wise maxims and sayings, attributed to Solomon. **2.** Something so well known and familiar as to have become notorious; a byword.

proverbial, adj. [1. provérbial; 2. prəvə́biəl], fr. Lat. *prōverbiālis*. See prec. & **-ial. 1.** a Connected with, of the nature of, a proverb; b handed down, couched in the form of proverbs. **2.** Commonly and generally recognized, admitted, asserted; notorious: *his meanness has become proverbial.*

proverbially, adv. Prec. & **-ly.** a By means of, in the form of, proverbs; b notoriously.

provide, vb. trans. & intrans. [1. províd; 2. prəváid]. Lat. *prōvidēre*, 'to act with foresight; see to beforehand, make preparation for; to see, or know, beforehand; to see to beforehand, prepare, provide', fr. **pro- (I.)** & *vidēre*, 'to see', q.v. under **vision. A.** trans. **1.** To procure and make available; furnish, supply; a (in material sense) *to provide a horse for a friend*; *to provide a meal*; b (in non-material sense) *to provide an excuse, a reason, a means of escape*; *provide good ground for believing* &c. **2.** To furnish, supply with; to equip: (followed by *with*, of material and non-material things) *can you provide me with a room for the night, with a fishing-rod?*; *to provide a boy with a good education*; (also reflex.) *to provide oneself with food and weapons* &c. **3.** (eccles.) To promote to a benefice in advance, before it is vacant, thus taking the gift out of the patron's hand. **B.** intrans. **1.** (absol.) To perform the act of providing, make provision: *God will provide.* **2.** *Provide for*, a to make provision on behalf of, take care for support of, furnish with means of support: *a man is bound to provide for his children*; b to foresee and prepare for; to take steps to secure, facilitate, make possible, counteract &c.; allow for: *in my plans for the journey, I have provided for possible accidents, and for unexpected additions to our party*; c (legal) to allow, permit of, render legally feasible: *our statutes provide for a certain elasticity in dealing with such contingencies.* **3.** *Provide against*, a to make preparations to prevent; take steps to preserve oneself from: *to provide against the danger of attack*; *to provide against hunger by taking food with one*; b (legal) to prohibit, render legally impossible: *this clause provides quite definitely against any unauthorized absence from duty.* **4.** (legal) *Provide that*, to stipulate, enjoin, to lay down as a necessary condition: *the agreement provides that six months' notice shall be given on either side.*

provided, conj. [1. províded; 2. prəváidid], fr. P.P. of prec. On condition, on the understanding that: *I will subscribe £10 provided twenty others will do the same.*

providence, n. [1. próvidens; 2. prɔ́vidəns]. Fr., fr. Lat. *prōvidentia*. See **provident & -ce. 1.** (rare) Quality of being provident; care for the future; foresight, prudence, thrift: *lessons of providence and thrift should be instilled at an early age.* **2.** (cap.) a The benevolent provision of God for His creatures: *the Providence of God*; b Almighty God Himself, conceived of as an omnipotent but benevolent being, who foresees and orders the course of all things in the universe, both in external nature and in the affairs of men, and directs the destinies of human beings in such ways as are best for them: *the inscrutable decrees of Providence.* **3.** (l.c.) Personification of the powers of nature, esp. as their action affects human nature; fate: *a special providence seemed to watch over me in all my wanderings.*

provident, adj. [1. próvident; 2. prɔ́vidənt], fr. Lat. *prōvident-(em)*, Pres. Part. of *prōvidēre*. See **provide.** Looking ahead, having regard for the future; hence, far-seeing; inclined to provide for future needs; careful of one's possessions, economical, thrifty.

providential, adj. [1. pròvidénshal; 2. prɔ̀vidénʃəl], fr. Lat. *prōvidentia*. See **providence & -al.** Connected with, pertaining to, worked, planned, by, Divine Providence; hence, merciful, favourable; beneficial.

providentially, adv. Prec. & **-ly.** By an act of providence; fortunately, luckily.

providently, adv. [1. próvidentli; 2. prɔ́vidəntli]. **provident & -ly.** In a provident manner; prudently, with foresight, thriftily.

provider, n. [1. províder; 2. prəváidə]. **provide & -er.** One who provides.

providing, conj. [1. províding; 2. prəváidiŋ], fr. Pres. Part. of **provide.** Provided, on condition, on the understanding, that.

province, n. [1. próvins; 2. prɔ́vins]. Fr., fr. Lat. *prōvincia*, 'a territory outside Italy acquired by the Romans, and brought under their government; office, responsibility'; fr. the base **prōw-*, seen also in Goth. *frauja*, 'lord, master'; O.E. *frēa*, q.v. under **frau.** Walde assumes an early Lat. base, **prōwīn-*, the second syll. being a gradational modification of the suff. in *nātiōn-*, & the suff. *-co-*, see **com- & co-.** The meaning wd. thus be, orig., 'lordship, jurisdiction', then the territory over wh. this extended. **1.** a A part of a country, division of a larger empire, remote from, but administered by, a central authority; b an area forming an administrative unit. **2.** A tract of country, a region, geographical area, remote from the capital or centre of government; contrasted with *the capital*; in England the term *the provinces* applies to the whole country outside London; thus the contrast is *London and the provinces.* **3.** An ecclesiastical division of a country coming under the jurisdiction of an Archbishop: *the Provinces of Canterbury and York.* **4.** a Department, branch, region, domain, sphere of knowledge, thought &c.: *practical language-teaching hardly falls within the province of philology*; b sphere or range of action; particular business, allotted duties, special functions: *it is not in the province of a junior officer to instruct his superiors.*

provincial (I.), adj. [1. provínshal; 2. prəvínʃəl], fr. Lat. *prōvinciālis*. Prec. & **-al. 1.** Consisting of, pertaining to, a province or provinces: *the provincial system of Ancient Rome*; *a provincial governor, synod* &c. **2.** a Connected with, belonging to, characteristic of, the provinces as distinguished from the capital: *the provincial areas*; hence, b countrified, rustic; local, limited: *a provincial accent*; *provincial manners, point of view.*

provincial (II.), n., fr. prec. **1.** An inhabitant of the provinces; a countryman, countrified person, rustic. **2.** a The ecclesiastical superior of a territorial division of a religious or monastic order; b the head of an Ecclesiastical Province; an Archbishop.

provincialism, n. [1. provínshalizm; 2. prəvínʃəlizəm]. **provincial (I.) & -ism. 1.** Something characteristic of the provinces, or of provincials; esp. a trick or mode of speech, manners; or a limited intellectual outlook. **2.** The fact of being provincial; provincial speech, a provincial point of view; narrowness of outlook, failure to consider questions from a national point of view.

provinciality, n. [1. provinshiáliti; 2. prəvinʃiǽliti]. **provincial (I.) & -ity.** Provincialism.

provincialize, vb. trans. [1. provínshalīz; 2. prəvínʃəlaiz]. **provincial (I.) & -ize.** To make provincial.

provision (I.), n. [1. provízhun; 2. prəvížən]. Fr., fr. Lat. *prōvīsiōn-(em)*, fr. *prōvīs-(um)*, P.P. type of *prōvidēre*. See **provide. 1.** Act of providing or supplying: *government was primarily occupied with the provision of troops.* **2.** Something provided; specif. (pl.) *provisions*, supplies, esp. of food. **3.** a Something provided, brought together, laid up, available, for future needs; esp. means of livelihood: *to make ample provision for one's wife and family*; b *provision against*, measures, steps taken, to meet some contingency that may arise in the future: *to make provision against attack by air, shortage of coal, unforeseen expenses* &c. **4.** a (law) Stipulation, condition, proviso: *the provisions of a settlement, lease* &c.; b (hist., pl.) the title of various enactments or statutes of the 13th and 14th cents., e.g. *Provisions of Oxford.* **5.** (eccles.) Arbitrary suspension by the Pope of right of patronage, so that he himself might present, & make provision for foreign ecclesiastics.

provision (II.), vb. trans., fr. prec. To supply with stores or provisions : *to provision a town.*

provisional, adj. [1. provízhunal ; 2. prəvížənəl]. Prec. & **-al.** Of the nature of a provision, condition, or stipulation ; conditional ; temporary : *a provisional agreement, arrangement* ; specif., *provisional order*, an authority given by a government to a local authority to carry out certain measures, afterwards confirmed by Parliament.

provisionally, adv. Prec. & **-ly.** In a provisional way ; temporarily, conditionally.

provision merchant, n. Dealer in provisions ; usually one who sells groceries, and also bacon, hams, tongues, butter &c.

proviso, n. [1. provízō ; 2. prəváizou]. Lat., 'it being provided', abl. neut. sing. of *prōvīsum*, 'provided', P.P. of *prōvidēre*. See **provide.** A provision, condition, or stipulation ; originally, a clause in a document, statute &c. commencing with the word *provided that* : *I must make it a proviso that I am absolutely free to change my plans if I wish to do so.*

provisor, n. [1. provízōr ; 2. prəváizə], fr. O. Fr. *provisour, proviseur*, fr. Lat. *prōvīsor*. See **provision, provide.** (hist.) A person provided with a benefice or provision, by the Pope, in anticipation of a vacancy : *Statutes of Provisors*, Acts of 1351 and 1390 to limit the Pope's right to appoint such provisors.

provisorily, adv. [1. provízurili ; 2. prəváizərili]. See next word & **-ly.** By way of a proviso ; provisionally, conditionally.

provisory, adj. [1. provízuri ; 2. prəváizəri]. **proviso** & **-ory.** Of the nature of a proviso ; provisional, temporary, conditional.

provocation, n. [1. provokáshun ; 2. prɔvəkéiʃən]. Fr., fr. Lat. *prōvocātiōn-(em)*, fr. *prōvocāt-(um)*, P.P. type of *prōvocāre*, 'to challenge, appeal'. See **provoke. 1.** Act of provoking : *to be guilty of grave provocation.* **2.** State of being provoked ; feeling of resentment, vexation : *I think I have reasonable grounds for feeling provocation.* **3.** That which provokes, which causes provocation ; ground for resentment : *to give provocation.*

provocative, adj. [1. provókativ ; 2. prəvɔ́kətiv], fr. L. Lat. *prōvocātīvus* ; fr. *prōvocāt-*, as in prec., & **-ive. 1.** Provoking ; serving, tending, to provoke, excite, arouse to anger : *provocative language, laughter* &c. **2.** Causing, giving rise to : *provocative of good, sorrow, mirth* &c.

provocatively, adv. Prec. & **-ly.** In a provocative manner ; so as to provoke.

provoke, vb. trans. [1. provṓk ; 2. prəvóuk]. M.E. *provōken*, fr. Lat. *prōvocāre*, 'to call forth, challenge, appeal, provoke'. See **pro-** (I.) & **vocal** & **vox. 1.** To call forth, cause, give rise to (in favourable and unfavourable sense) : **a** *to provoke mirth, amusement* &c. ; **b** *to provoke anger, doubt, indignation* &c. **2.** To rouse, stir up, instigate, excite : *to provoke a riot.* **3.** To rouse the temper of, irritate, make angry ; to displease, annoy : *to provoke one to fury* ; *to be provoked by a person's impudence.* **4.** To urge, incite, persuade, strongly, rouse into action : *he was at last provoked to write some poetry* ; *I only wish I could provoke you to throw off your indolence.*

provoking, adj. [1. provṓking ; 2. prəvóukiŋ]. Pres. Part. of prec. Exasperating, irritating, annoying : *provoking behaviour, noises* &c. ; *most provoking children.*

provokingly, adv. Prec. & **-ly.** In a provoking manner.

provost, n. [1. próvost ; 2. prɔ́vəst]. O.E. *prāfost, prōfost*, fr. L. Lat. *prōpositus*, for Lat. *praepositus*, 'a presiding official, overseer'. See **praepostor.** Name or title given to various official persons of which the chief in Great Britain are : **1.** The heads of Queen's, Worcester, and Oriel Colleges at Oxford, of King's College, Cambridge, of Trinity College, Dublin ; also the head of the governing body of Eton College. **2.** The chief magistrate of a Scottish burgh, corresponding to a *mayor* in England, *Lord Provost* corresponding to *Lord Mayor.*

provost-marshal, n. [1. provṓ márshl ; 2. prəvóu mɑ́ʃl]. **a** (mil.) The chief of the military police in a camp, in a garrison town, or on active service ; **b** (nav.) the master-at-arms on board ship where a court-martial is held.

provost-sergeant, n. [1. provṓ sárjent ; 2. prəvóu sɑ́dʒənt]. A sergeant in charge of a detachment of military police or head of the police where there is no provost-marshal.

provostship, n. [1. próvostship ; 2. prɔ́vəstʃip]. **provost** & **-ship.** Office, rank &c. of a provost.

prow, n. [1. prou ; 2. prau], fr. O. Fr. *proue*, cp. Ital. *prua*, Span. *proa*, fr. Lat. *prōra*, fr. Gk. *prōira*, 'prow', fr. **pro-** (II.). **a** The forepart of a ship, the parts about the stem of a ship or boat ; **b** (poet.) the ship itself.

prowess, n. [1. próues ; 2. práuis]. O. Fr. *proesce*, 'bravery', fr. O. Fr. *prou*, 'brave ; gallant'. See **proud.** Bravery, courage, gallantry, valour ; skill, success.

prowl (I.), vb. intrans. & trans. [1. proul ; 2. praul]. M.E. *prollen*, 'to go about searching, to search'. Etymol. uncertain. **1.** intrans. To go, wander, about in a furtive, stealthy way, esp. in search of something, as prey, plunder &c. : *beasts prowling after their prey* ; also *prowl about.* **2.** trans. To pass, wander, through, perambulate stealthily, as though in search of prey, plunder &c. : *he prowled the streets for hours.*

prowl (II.), n., fr. prec. Act of prowling stealthily : *to go on the prowl* ; *take a prowl round the streets.*

proximal, adj. [1. próksimal ; 2. prɔ́ksiməl], fr. Lat. *proximus*, 'nearest', superl. of *prope*, wh. is prob. for **prokw-*, 'near', cp. **propinquity,** & **-al.** Next, nearest, esp. (anat.) situated nearest to the central axis of the body or to a point of attachment of a limb, contrasted with *distal.*

proximate, adj. [1. próksimat ; 2. prɔ́ksimit], fr. L. Lat. *proximāt-(um)*, P.P. type of *proximāre*, 'to draw near, approach'. See prec. Nearest, next preceding or following, in time, space, order &c. ; approximate : *the proximate cause*, that which directly causes result without intervening agencies.

proximately, adv. Prec. & **-ly.** In a proximate manner, to a proximate degree ; directly, immediately, without anything else intervening.

proxime, adv. [1. próksimi ; 2. prɔ́ksimi]. Lat. adv. of *proximus*, 'next', see **proximal.** *Proxime accessit* [1. próksimi aksésit ; 2. prɔ́ksimi æksésit], lit. 'he has come nearest', of candidate who comes next to the winner of a prize, scholarship &c.

proximity, n. [1. proksímiti ; 2. prɔksímiti], fr. Fr. *proximité*, fr. Lat. *proximitāt-(em)* ; fr. *proxim-*, as in **proximal,** & **-ity.** State, quality, of being next or nearest in time, space ; also in relationship ; nearness : *in close proximity* ; *proximity of relationship, kindred* &c.

proximo, adv. (abbr. *prox.*) [1. próksimō ; 2. prɔ́ksimou]. Lat., abl. sing. masc. of *proximus*, 'next'. See **proximal** &c. Of, in, the next month : *on the 10th proximo*, on the 10th of next month.

proxy, n. [1. próksi ; 2. prɔ́ksi]. M.E. *prokesie*, contracted fr. *procuracie, procuracy*, fr. Med. Lat. *procurātia.* See **procure** & **-acy. 1. a** Authority given to a person empowering him to act as agent or deputy, esp. one giving voting power, as from shareholders in a company &c. ; agency : *to vote by proxy* ; *to be married by proxy* ; **b** document giving such authority. **2.** Authorized person acting as agent or deputy for another : *to find a proxy.* Phr. *stand proxy for.*

prude, n. [1. prōōd ; 2. prūd], fr. Fr., adj., 'prudish', fr. O. Fr. *prude*, 'modest, discreet', fem. of *prud*, another form of *prou*, 'brave, gallant', cp. **prowess** & **proud.** A woman of exaggerated or affected modesty or propriety in behaviour, dress, speech &c. ; rarely used of a man.

prudence, n. [1. prōōdens ; 2. prū́dəns]. Fr., fr. Lat. *prūdentia*, fr. **prudent** & **-ce** ; a variant of **providence.** State, quality, of being prudent ; careful, foreseeing thought ; sagacity, caution.

prudent, adj. [1. prōōdent ; 2. prū́dənt]. Fr., fr. Lat. *prūdent-(em)*, variant of *prōvident-*, 'foreseeing'. See **provident.** Careful, cautious ; acting with foresight or forethought ; not taking risks ; wise, discreet ; circumspect, provident.

prudential, adj. [1. prōōdénshal ; 2. prūdénʃəl], fr. Lat. *prūdentia*, 'prudence', & **-al.** Marked by, arising from, prudence ; prudent, discreet.

prudentially, adv. Prec. & **-ly.** In a prudential manner ; prudently.

prudently, adv. [1. prōōdentli ; 2. prū́dəntli]. Prec. & **-ly.** With prudence ; carefully, cautiously ; discreetly.

prudery, n. [1. prōōderi ; 2. prū́dəri], fr. Fr. *pruderie.* See **prude** & **-ery.** Exaggerated, affected modesty or propriety of behaviour, speech &c.

prud'homme, n. [1. prūdóm ; 2. prydɔ́m]. Fr., 'wise, skilful man', fr. O. Fr. *preu d'homme.* A member of a local French council, *conseil des prud'hommes*, dealing with disputes in labour matters.

prudish, adj. [1. prōōdish ; 2. prū́diʃ]. **prude** & **-ish.** Like a prude ; affectedly proper, over-nice in conduct, speech &c., easily shocked, or affecting to be so.

prudishly, adv. Prec. & **-ly.** In a prudish manner.

prudishness, n. See prec. & **-ness.** State, quality, of being prudish.

pruinose, adj. [1. prōōinōs ; 2. prúinous], fr. Lat. *pruīnōsus*, 'frosty, frosted', fr. *pruīna*, 'hoar-frost' ; this word is fr. earlier **pruswīna*, fr. a base **preus-, *prus-* &c. ; whence also Scrt. *pruṣva*, 'hoar-frost, drops of frozen water' ; Goth. *friūs*, 'frost' ; O.E. *frēosan*, 'to freeze'. See **freeze** & **frost.** (bot. and zool.) Covered with a white powder or bloom like hoar-frost ; frosted.

prune (I.), n. [1. prōōn ; 2. prūn]. Fr., fr. Med. Lat. *prūna*, fr. Lat. *prūnum*, 'a plum', *prūnus*, 'plum tree', fr. Gk. *proûnon, proûmnon*, 'plum', *proúmnē*, 'plum tree'. **a** A dried, candied plum for stewing or eating as a dessert fruit ; **b** a deep purple colour like that of prunes. Phr. *prunes and prisms*, phrase supposed to be used formerly in order to adjust the lips in a becoming expression ; hence, an affected, mincing way of speaking.

prune (II.), vb. trans., earlier *proine*, fr. O. Fr. *proigner, proöingier*, 'to trim (vines)', etymol. doubtful. **1.** To cut out, shorten, stop, unwanted or too exuberant growths in trees, shrubs, bushes, so as to induce the formation of flower and fruit buds ; also to cut (trees &c.) into shape. **2.** (fig.) Also *prune away, prune down*, to cut away, get rid of superfluous parts, reduce length, of a speech, article &c.

prune (III.), vb. trans. M.E. *proin, pruin, proyne*, possibly fr. *prune*, 'to lop, trim' (see prec.), though recorded earlier. (archaic) To trim, adorn, trick out ; (of birds) to preen.

prunella, prunello (I.), n. [1. prōōnéla, -élō ; 2. prūnélə, -élou]. Fr. *prunelle*, dimin. of **prune** (I.), prob. fr. dark plum colour of the fabric. A stout textile of silk and worsted, of dark colour, formerly used for clerical and legal gowns, and for the uppers of women's boots.

prunella (II.), n., fr. Fr. *prunelle*, earlier *brunelle* ; etymol. doubtful, prob. fr. Med. Lat. *brūnus*, 'brown'. See **brown. 1.** (archaic) A feverish disease of the throat ; quinsy, thrush. **2.** (bot., cap.) A genus of plants, including the weed self-heal, *P. vulgaris*, used formerly to cure quinsy and thrush.

pruning, vbl. n. [1. prōōning ; 2. prūniŋ]. **prune** (II.) & **-ing.** Act of one who prunes trees &c.

Prunus, n. [1. prōōnus ; 2. prū́nəs]. **Lat.**, 'plum tree'. See **prune** (I.). (bot., cap.)

A genus of rosaceous trees, grown in gardens for the blossom and foliage, including the wild and cultivated plums and cherries.

prurience, **pruriency**, n. [1. proориens(i); 2. prúərians(i)]. See next word & **-ce**, **-cy**. State, quality, of being prurient.

prurient, adj. [1. proorient; 2. prúəriənt], fr. Lat. *prūrient-(em)*, Pres. Part. of *prūrīre*, 'to itch, burn; to long for, desire, lewdly'; fr. same base *prus- &c. as in Lat. *pruīna*, 'frost', see **pruinose**; the identification of the sensations of freezing & burning is not otherwise unknown; cp. Milton, 'The parching air burns frore, And cold performs the effect of fire', 'P. L.' ii. 594-5. Over-curious, restlessly inquisitive in, morbidly interested by, indecent, obscene, ideas, objects &c.

pruriently, adv. Prec. & **-ly**. In a prurient manner.

pruriginous, adj. [1. prooríjinus; 2. pruərídžinəs], fr. Lat. *prūrīginōsus*, fr. *prūrīgin-(em)*, stem of *prūrīgo*, 'the itch'. See next word. (med.) Suffering from, caused by, prurigo.

prurigo, n. [1. proorígō; 2. pruəráigou]. Lat., 'itching, the itch', fr. *prūrīre*, 'to itch'. See **prurient**. (med.) An inflammatory skin disease, marked by intense itching and papular eruption.

pruritus, n. [1. proorítus; 2. pruəráitəs]. Lat., 'itching, desire'; fr. same base as prec. (med.) An intense itching of the skin, without eruption or inflammation, usually the accompaniment of other diseases or of senile decay.

Prussian, adj. & n. [1. prúshan; 2. práʃən], fr. *Prussia*, fr. Fr. *Prusse*, Germ. *Preussen*. **1.** adj. Of, pertaining to, Prussia, its inhabitants &c.; *Prussian blue, green*, a deep blue, and green, pigment, the latter derived from the former, a ferrocyanide of iron, formerly called *Berlin blue*. **2.** n. **a** A native or inhabitant of Prussia; **b** *Old Prussian*, the ancient language, closely akin to Lithuanian, of the Baltic districts of Prussia.

prussic acid, n. [1. prúsik ásid; 2. prásik ǽsid]. So called as related to Prussian blue. Poisonous liquid with a characteristic smell of bitter almonds; hydro-cyanic acid.

pry (I.), vb. intrans. [1. prī; 2. prai]. M.E. *pryen, prien*; etymol. uncertain. To search, look into, peer, spy; esp. with impertinent, unnecessary curiosity: (lit. and fig.) *to pry about, into, the house, other people's affairs* &c.

pry (II.), vb. trans. A form of **prize (IV.)**, 'to lever, lift up'. To raise, lift up, break open as with a lever; to prize.

prying, adj. [1. príing; 2. práiiŋ]. **pry (I.)** & **-ing**. Searching, peering, spying, inquisitive: *prying eyes*.

pryingly, adv. Prec. & **-ly**. In a prying, inquisitive, manner.

prytaneum, n. [1. pritanḗum; 2. pritəníəm]. Lat., fr. Gk. *prutaneion*, fr. *prútanis*, 'a principal official, president'. See next word. (Gk. antiq.) A public building in a Greek city in which foreign embassies, distinguished citizens &c. were entertained officially; it contained the sacred hearth of the city, the fire of which was never allowed to go out.

prytany, n. [1. prítani; 2. prítəni], fr. Gk. *prutaneia*, fr. *prútanis*, 'president, a member of one of the ten sections into which the senate at Athens was divided, the presidency of which was allotted to each during a tenth of the year'; cp. *protaini*, 'before'; etymol. doubtful. The presidency of the senate; period during which the *prútanis* of one section held it.

psalm, n. [1. sahm; 2. sām]. In O.E. as *sealm, salm*, fr. Lat. *psalmus*, fr. Gk. *psalmós*, 'a plucking, twitching, of the strings of a harp; the sound of the harp; later, song, psalm', fr. *psállein*, 'to pluck, twitch, the strings of a harp'; possibly cogn. w. Lat. *palpāre*, 'to stroke, caress', see **palpable**, & w. **feel**. A sacred song or hymn; specif., one of the sacred songs contained in the *Book of Psalms* in the Old Testament, attributed to David. *Psalm book*, psalter.

psalmist, n. [1. sáhmist; 2. sámist], fr. L. Lat. *psalmista*. **psalm** & **-ist**. The author or composer of psalms or sacred songs; specif., *the Psalmist*, David, the traditional author of the Book of Psalms.

psalmodic, adj. [1. salmódik; 2. sælmɔ́dik]. **psalmody** & **-ic**. Of, pertaining to, psalmody.

psalmodist, n. [1. sáhmodist, sálmodist; 2. sámədist, sǽlmədist]. See next word & **-ist**. One who sings psalms, one skilled in psalmody; psalmist.

psalmody, n. [1. sáhmodi, sálmodi; 2. sámədi, sǽlmədi], fr. Lat. *psalmōdia*, fr. Gk. *psalmōidia*, fr. *psalmós*, see **psalm**, & *ōidé*, 'song', see **ode**. **a** Art, practice, of singing psalms and sacred songs; **b** a collection of psalms with their musical setting.

psalm-singing, n. **a** The singing of psalms; **b** (fig.) the hypocritical assumption of religious fervour, expressed by frequent praying aloud and the singing of religious hymns &c.; also (attrib.) *a psalm-singing humbug*, religious hypocrite.

psalter, n. [1. sáwlter; 2. sɔ́ltə]. M.E. *sauter, psauter*, fr. O. Fr. *sautier, psaltier*, fr. Lat. *psaltērium*. See **psaltery**. **1.** The Book of Psalms, esp. the Psalms arranged for use in daily service as in the Common Prayer Book. **2.** Any special version of the Psalms, as a *Latin, the English Psalter*. **3.** A metrical version as used in Presbyterian Churches.

psalterium, n. [1. sawltḗrium; 2. sɔltíəriəm]. Lat. as prec.; fr. resemblance to the leaves of a book. (zool.) The third stomach or omasum of ruminants.

psaltery, n. [1. sáwlteri; 2. sɔ́ltri], fr. O. Fr. *psalterie*, fr. Lat. *psaltērium*, fr. Gk. *psaltḗrion*. See **psalm**. An ancient musical stringed instrument with a sound-board, resembling a dulcimer, but played with the fingers or plectrum and not with hammers.

psammite, n. [1. sámīt; 2. sǽmait], fr. Gk. *psámmos*, 'sand', fr. *psaphmos; cogn. w. Lat. *sabulum*, 'coarse sand', fr. *bhsabhlom; prob. fr. base *bhesā-, *bhsā- &c., 'to smash up, break small', whence also Scrt. *bhas-*, 'to crush, pulverize', cp. next word, & **-ite**. (petrol.) Rock composed of sandy particles; sandstone.

psephism, n. [1. sḗfizm; 2. sífizəm], fr. Gk. *pséphisma*, 'proposition carried by a vote', fr. *psêph-(os)*, 'small stone ground down by action of water; pebble used in counting, or voting'; cogn. w. Gk. *psámmos*, 'sand'. See prec. (Gk. hist.) A measure passed by a vote in the popular assembly at Athens.

pseudepigrapha, n. pl. [1. (p)sūdepígrafa; 2. (p)sjūdepígrəfə]. Gk. See **pseudo-** & **epigraph**. Spurious Biblical writings, ascribed to the Old Testament period or to Old Testament characters.

pseudepigraphy, n. [1. (p)sūdepígrafi; 2. (p)sjūdepígrəfi]. Prec. & **-y**. The ascription of false names of authors to books.

pseudo-, pref.; in old compounds in wh. the second element begins w. a vowel, **pseud-**. Gk., used in many anct. compounds, meaning 'sham, false, lying', fr. *pseûdos*, 'a lie, falsehood, untruth'; cp. also *pseudés*, 'lying, false, untrue', & *pseúdein*, 'to impose upon by lies; to cheat, defraud'; the origin & relations of the word are uncertain, & though various suggestions have been made, e.g. connexion w. Lat. *spurius*, 'bastard', or w. O.H.G. *spottōn*, 'to taunt' &c., they are all rejected by Walde & by Boisacq. The pref. occurs in Engl. in old compounds of Gk. origin, in recently formed words, both elements of wh. are Gk., & as a living pref. often written as a separate word & without a hyphen; the force is 'sham, false, pretended, seeming' &c.

pseudocarp, n. [1. (p)sūdōkarp; 2. (p)sjūdoukàp]. **pseudo-** & Gk. *karpós*, 'fruit', see **carpel**. (bot.) A fruit, such as the strawberry, not entirely composed of the ripened ovary.

pseudocarpous, adj. [1. (p)sūdōkárpus; 2. (p)sjūdoukápəs]. Prec. & **-ous**. (bot.) Of the nature of, pertaining to, a pseudocarp.

pseudograph, n. [1. (p)sūdōgrahf; 2. (p)sjūdougrāf], fr. Gk. *pseudográphos*, adj. See **pseudo-** & **-graph**. A writing falsely ascribed to a particular writer; a literary forgery.

pseudomorph, n. [1. (p)sūdōmorf; 2. (p)sjūdoumɔ̄f]. Gk. **pseudo-** & *morphḗ*, 'form, shape'. See **morphology**. An irregular or false form; specif., a mineral having the crystalline form of another mineral.

pseudomorphic, adj. [1. (p)sūdōmórfik; 2. (p)sjūdoumɔ́fik]. Prec. & **-ic**. Pseudomorphous.

pseudomorphism, n. [1. (p)sūdōmórfizm; 2. (p)sjūdoumɔ́fizəm]. **pseudomorph** & **-ism**. State, quality, of being pseudomorphous.

pseudomorphous, adj. [1. (p)sūdōmórfus; 2. (p)sjūdoumɔ́fəs]. See prec. & **-ous**. Having the characteristics of a pseudomorph; resembling another mineral in outward structure only.

pseudonym, n. [1. (p)sūdunim; 2. (p)sjūdənim]. **pseudo-** & Gk. *ónoma, ónuma*, 'name', see first element in **onomatopoeia**. A fictitious name; esp. one assumed by an author to disguise his identity; a nom-de-plume.

pseudonymity, n. [1. (p)sūdunímiti; 2. (p)sjūdənímiti]. Prec. & **-ity**. The employment of, habit of passing under, a pseudonym.

pseudonymous, adj. [1. (p)sūdónimus; 2. (p)sjūdɔ́niməs], fr. Gk. *pseudṓnumos*. See **pseudonym** & **-ous**. Written under a false or assumed name.

pseudonymously, adv. Prec. & **-ly**. With a pseudonym or assumed name.

pseudopod, -podium, n. [1. (p)sūdōpod, (p)sjūdōpṓdium; 2. (p)sjūdoupɔd, (p)sjūdoupóudiəm]. **pseudo-** & Mod. Lat. *podium*, formed fr. Gk. *pod-*, 'foot', q.v. under **pedal**. Temporary protrusion in a one-celled organism, serving as a means of locomotion.

pseudoscope, n. [1. (p)sūdōskōp; 2. (p)sjūdouskoup]. **pseudo-** & **-scope**. An optical instrument, which makes convexity appear concave, and concavity convex.

pseudoscopic, adj. [1. (p)sūdōskópik; 2. (p)sjūdouskɔ́pik]. Prec. & **-ic**. Producing the optical effect of a pseudoscope.

pshaw, interj. Imitative. Conventional mode of representing an exclamatory utterance expressing contempt. It is difficult to say what exclamation in actual use the spelling is supposed to represent; certainly no one says [1. shaw; 2. ʃɔ] except when coming across the above in print.

psilanthropic, adj. [1. (p)sīlanthrópik; 2. (p)sailænþrɔ́pik]. **psilanthropy** & **-ic**. Pertaining to psilanthropism and its adherents.

psilanthropism, n. [1. (p)sīlánthropizm; 2. (p)sailǽnþrəpizəm]. **psilanthropy** & **-ism**. Theological heresy that Jesus Christ was merely man; psilanthropy.

psilanthropist, n. [1. (p)sīlánthropist; 2. (p)sailǽnþrəpist]. See prec. & **-ist**. An adherent of, believer in, psilanthropism.

psilanthropy, n. [1. (p)sīlánthropi; 2. (p)sailǽnþrəpi]. Gk. *psīlánthrōpos*, 'merely human'; fr. *psilós*, 'bare, naked; mere', fr. base *bhesēi-, w. elimination of first syll. & reduction of second, whence, in Gk., *psi-*; the base occurs also in Gk. *psên* for *bsēinein, 'to scratch, scrape'; further cognates are O. Slav. *bosŭ*, 'bare-footed', & O.E. *bær*, 'bare, naked', fr. *baza-, see **bare**. The second element is Gk. *ánthrōpos*, 'man', q.v. under **anthropo-**. The heresy that Jesus Christ was a mere man, and had no Divine nature.

psilosis, n. [1. (p)sīlósis; 2. (p)sailóusis]. Gk., 'stripping bare of hair'. See first element of prec. & **-osis**. Disease causing loss of the hair.

psittacine, adj. [1. (p)sítasīn, -in; 2. (p)sítəsain, -in], fr. Lat. *psittacīnus*, fr. *psittacus*, Gk. *psittakós*, 'parrot'; etymol. uncertain; also *bittakos* & *sittákē*, prob. a foreign word. Of, pertaining to, birds of the parrot tribe, which includes macaws and parakeets &c.

psittacosis, n. [1. (p)sitakṓsis; 2. (p)sitəkóusis]. See prec. & **-osis.** **a** An infectious disease of parrots; **b** a disease of human beings, often epidemic, having symptoms resembling those of typhoid fever and pneumonia; it is said to be due to a filter-passing virus transmitted by infected parrots.

psoas, n. [1. (p)sṓas; 2. (p)sóuæs]. Acc. pl., treated as a sing., of Gk. *psóa*, 'a hip muscle'; etymol. unknown. (anat.) One of two muscles, *psoas major* and *minor*, of the loin.

psora, n. [1. (p)sṓra; 2. (p)sṓrə]. Gk. *psṓra*, 'itch, mange, canker', fr. **bhōisra*, **bhōis-* being a different grade of the base in Gk. *psên*, 'to scratch'. See discussion of Gk. *psīlós* under **psilanthropy.** A parasitic, contagious, skin disease, scabies, itch.

psoriasis, n. [1. (p)sōríasis; 2. (p)sōráiəsis]. Gk. *psōríāsis*, 'itch'. See prec. & **-asis.** A chronic, non-contagious skin disease characterized by red scaly patches.

psyche, n. [1. (p)síki; 2. (p)sáiki]. Lat., fr. Gk. *psūkhḗ*, 'life, breath, soul', fr. *psū́khein*, 'to blow, breathe'; the etymol. of the base & formative elements is uncertain; cp. **psycho-. 1.** (class. mythol., cap.) The soul, personified as a young maiden with butterfly wings as emblem of immortality, beloved by Eros. **2.** The human soul or spirit; the mind, considered apart from the body. **3.** (entom.) A genus of moths.

psychiatric(al), adj. [1. (p)sìkiátrik(l); 2. (p)sàikiǽtrik(l)]. **psychiatry & -ic (& -al).** Of, pertaining to, psychiatry or the treatment and cure of mental disease.

psychiatrist, n. [1. (p)sīkíatrist; 2. (p)saikáiətrist]. See prec. & **-ist.** One who practises psychiatry; an expert in mental disease; alienist.

psychiatry, n. [1. (p)sīkíatri; 2. (p)saikáiətri], fr. Neo-Lat. *psychiātria*, fr. Gk. *psūkhḗ*, 'soul', see **psyche,** & *iātreia*, 'healing', fr. *iātrós*, 'healer, physician', fr. *iâsthai*, 'to heal, cure'; cp. also *iainō*, 'restore, reanimate', fr. **isanjō*; cp. Scrt. *isanyati*, 'causes to move, excites'; cogn. w. Lat. *īra*, 'anger', for **eisa*. See **ire.** The treatment and cure of mental diseases.

psychic, adj. & n. [1. (p)síkik; 2. (p)sáikik], fr. Gk. *psūkhikós*, 'of the soul or life'. See **psyche & -ic. 1.** adj. Connected with the soul or spirit; esp. in reference to spiritualistic phenomena: *psychic force*, the supposed force which produces such phenomena. **2.** n. A person with so-called psychic powers or susceptibility; a medium.

psychical, adj. [1. (p)síkikl; 2. (p)sáikikl]. Prec. & **-al. 1.** Of, pertaining to, the human spirit or mind, esp. in their relation to sense, and to the external world; contrasted with *spiritual* and *rational* on the one hand, and with *physical* on the other. **2.** Relating to, concerned with, various unexplained phenomena, such as telepathy, automatic writing &c., or to such matters as hauntings, ghosts, second sight &c.; spiritualistic: *psychical research*, the scientific study of such unexplained phenomena.

psychically, adv. Prec. & **-ly.** In a psychical manner.

psychics, n. [1. (p)síkiks; 2. (p)sáikiks]. Pl. of **psychic,** used as sing. **1.** Psychology. **2.** The study of psychical phenomena.

psychist, n. [1. (p)síkist; 2. (p)sáikist]. See prec. & **-ist.** One who studies psychical phenomena; a medium.

psycho-, pref. Form of Gk. *psūkhḗ*, 'soul', used as pref. in compounds. See **psyche.** In Gk. the word means 'breath as a sign of life, spirit; the soul or spirit of man as opposed to the body, the immortal part of man; the seat of the will, desires, passions; the heart; desire, appetite; mind, reason, understanding'. As a pref. in Gk. words used in Engl., the word means 'mind, consciousness, reason'.

psycho-analysis, n. [1. (p)sìkō análisis; 2. (p)sàikou ənǽlisis]. **psycho- & analysis.** Method of investigation of mental processes and the motives of conduct, devised principally by Freud and Jung, based on a supposed conflict between the conscious will and subconscious or unconscious impressions, desires &c., which results in various 'repressions' and 'complexes'.

psycho-analyst, n. [1. (p)sìkō ánalist; 2. (p)sàikou ǽnəlist]. **psycho- & analyst.** One who practises psycho-analysis.

psycho-analytic, adj. [1. (p)sìkō analítik; 2. (p)sàikou ænəlítik]. **psycho- & analytic.** Concerned with, pertaining to, psycho-analysis.

psychological, adj. [1. (p)sìkōlójikl; 2. (p)sàikoulɔ́dʒikl]. See **psychology & -ic & -al.** Of, pertaining to, psychology or the study of mental processes; mental; *psychological moment*, (properly) the effective force, or momentum, of a fact, event, sensation, thought &c., on the mind; (loosely) the moment of time, the occasion, when a fact &c. has the greatest effect on the mind, thus, in common usage, *at the psychological moment*, just at the right time, in the nick of time.

psychologically, adv. Prec. & **-ly.** From the point of view of psychology; mentally.

psychologist, n. [1. (p)sīkólojist; 2. (p)saikɔ́lədžist]. **psychology & -ist.** Student of, one skilled in, psychology.

psychologize, vb. trans. & intrans. [1. (p)sīkólojīz; 2. (p)saikɔ́lədžaiz]. **psychology & -ize. 1.** trans. To treat psychologically. **2.** intrans. To study psychology.

psychology, n. [1. (p)sīkóloji; 2. (p)saikɔ́lədži]. **psycho- & -logy.** That branch of philosophy which examines and treats of the growth, functions, and processes, conscious or subconscious, of the mind in relation to sensations, feelings, emotions, memories, will, and conduct, whether examined introspectively, or from the behaviour of others under specified conditions; usually contrasted with *logic* and *metaphysics*.

psychometric(al), adj. [1. (p)sìkōmétrik(l); 2. (p)sàikoumétrik(l)]. **psychometry & -ic & (-al).** Of, pertaining to, psychometry.

psychometry, n. [1. (p)sīkómetri; 2. (p)saikɔ́mitri]. **psycho- & -metry. 1.** The measurement of the relations in time of mental processes or phenomena. **2.** Specif. (spiritualism) the unexplained knowledge, exhibited by certain mediums or psychic persons, of absent or unknown persons when handling physical objects that have been in contact with them or belonged to them.

psychomotor, adj. [1. (p)sìkōmṓter; 2. (p)sàikoumóutə]. **psycho- & motor.** Of, relating to, physical movement or action, directly induced by a mental condition.

psychopath, n. [1. (p)síkōpath; 2. (p)sáikoupæþ]. **psycho- &** *-path*, see **pathos.** One suffering from mental disorder.

psychopathic, adj. [1. (p)sìkōpáthik; 2. (p)sàikoupǽþik]. See prec. & **-ic.** Suffering from mental disorder; subject to extreme mental excitement; abnormally susceptible to, & affected by, emotions; hysterical; neuropathic.

psychopathist, n. [1. (p)sīkópathist; 2. (p)saikɔ́pəþist]. **psychopath & -ist.** One who treats mental disorders; alienist.

psychopathology, n. [1. (p)sìkōpathóloji; 2. (p)sàikoupəþɔ́lədži]. **psycho- & pathology.** The pathology of the mind; study, science, of mental disease and disorders.

psychophysical, adj. [1. (p)sìkōfízikl; 2. (p)sàikoufízikl]. **psycho- & physical.** Of, pertaining to, psychophysics.

psychophysicist, n. [1. (p)sìkōfízisist; 2. (p)sàikoufízisist]. **psycho- & physicist.** Student of psychophysics.

psychophysics, n. pl. [1. (p)sìkōfíziks; 2. (p)sàikoufíziks]. **psycho- & physics.** Branch of psychology which studies the inter-relations and connexions between physiological and psychological phenomena.

psychophysiology, n. [1. (p)sìkōfizióloji; 2. (p)sàikoufiziɔ́lədži]. **psycho- & physiology.** That branch of science which treats of the relations between psychology and physiology.

psychosis, n., pl. **psychoses** [1. (p)sīkṓsis, -sēz; 2. (p)saikóusis, -sīz]. **psycho- & -osis.** Disease of the mind which is not associated with any actual injury to, or disease in, the tissues of the brain.

psychotherapeutics, psychotherapy, n. [1. (p)sìkōtherapū́tiks, -thérapi; 2. (p)sàikouþerəpjū́tiks, -þérəpi]. **psycho- & therapeutics, -therapy.** Treatment of disease by action upon the mind only, by hypnotism, suggestion, psycho-analysis &c.

psychrometer, n. [1. (p)sīkrómeter; 2. (p)saikrɔ́mitə], fr. Gk. *psūkhrós*, also *psūkós*, 'cold', fr. base **bhes(ā)-*, 'to blow, breathe', as in **psyche, & -meter.** Kind of thermometer used for measuring the amount of moisture in the atmosphere.

ptarmigan, n. [1. tármigan; 2. tāmigən], fr. Gael. *tarmachan*; the excrescent *p* appears in Fr., possibly due to Gk. *pterón*, 'wing', found frequently in zool. terminology. See **ptero-. 1.** A species of mountain grouse of Northern Europe, *Lagopus mutus*, of grey plumage, mottled and barred with black in summer, turning white in winter. **2.** The willow-grouse, *Lagopus lagopus*, of Northern Europe and America.

pteri-, pref., fr. Gk. *ptéris*, stem *pterid-*, 'fern'; connected w. *pterón*, 'feather', q.v. under **ptero-.**

pteridologist, n. [1. (p)tèridólojist; 2. (p)tèridɔ́lədžist]. See prec. & **-logy & -ist.** A student of pteridology.

pteridology, n. [1. (p)tèridóloji; 2. (p)tèridɔ́lədži]. See **pteri- & -logy.** The systematic study of ferns.

Pteridophyta, n. [1. (p)tèridófita; 2. (p)tèridɔ́fitə]. **pteri(d)- &** *-o-* **& phyto-.** The division of flowerless plants including the ferns, club-mosses, and horse-tails.

ptero-, pref., fr. Gk. *pterón*, 'wing, feather'; **pt-* represents the 'vanishing' grade of the base **pet-*, 'to go, fly; fall', wh. occurs in various forms in most Aryan languages; cp. Scrt. *petram*, 'feather'; Lat. *penna*, 'feather', fr. **pet-na*, see **pen (III.)**; O.E. *feđer*, see **feather**; for sense of 'fall', see **ptosis;** cp. further **petition.**

pterodactyl, n. [1. (p)tèrodáktil; 2. (p)tèrədǽktil]. Prec. & Gk. *dáktulos*, 'finger, toe'. See **dactyl.** An extinct flying reptile, with membranous wings extending from the side of the body to the last digit, which was of great length, the other fingers being separate from the wing.

pterography, n. [1. (p)terógrafi; 2. (p)tərɔ́grəfi]. **ptero- & -graphy.** Description of birds' feathers.

pteropod, n. [1. (p)téropod; 2. (p)térəpɔd]. **ptero-** & Gk. *pod-(ós)*, fr. *poús*, 'foot'. See **pedal.** (zool.) One of a group of molluscs having wing-like lobes on the foot, by means of which it floats on the sea.

pteropus, n. [1. (p)téropus; 2. (p)térəpəs]. Neo-Lat., fr. Gk. *pterópous*, 'wing-footed'. **ptero-** & *poús*, 'foot'. See **pedal.** (zool.) The genus comprising the fruit-bats or flying-foxes.

pterosaur, n. [1. (p)térosōr; 2. (p)térəsɔ̄]. **ptero-** & Gk. *saûr-(os)*, 'lizard'. See **saurian.** Member of the order of extinct flying reptiles *Pterosauria*; the pterodactyl.

pterygium, n. [1. (p)teríjium; 2. (p)terídžiəm]. Neo-Lat., fr. Gk. *pterúgion*, dimin. of *ptérug-*, stem of *ptérux*, 'wing', wh. is cogn. w. *pterón*. See **ptero-.** (med.) A triangular fold of conjunctiva growing on the inner side of the eyeball, due to exposure to dust, wind, or heat, or to old age.

pterygoid, adj. [1. (p)térigoid; 2. (p)térigɔid]. Gk. *ptérug-*, 'wing'. See prec. & **-oid. 1.** Wing-like. **2.** Specif. (anat.) *pterygoid process*, one of two processes descending from the sphenoid bone in mammals; *pterygoid artery*, branch of maxillary artery.

ptisan, n. [1. tizán; 2. tizǽn], fr. Fr. *ptisane*, *tisane*, fr. Lat. *ptisana*, fr. Gk. *ptisánē*, 'barley, gruel'; cp. *ptissein*, 'to crush, grind; to peel'; cogn. w. Lat. *pistillum*. See **pistil** & **pestle**. A farinaceous drink; decoction, or tea, e.g. of camomile &c.

Ptolemaic, adj. [1. tòlemáik; 2. tòlimḗi-ik], fr. Gk. *Ptolemaïkós*, fr. *Ptolemaios*, 'Ptolemy', lit. 'mighty in war', fr. *ptólemos, pólemos*, 'war', see **polemic**. **1.** Of, belonging to, the period and dynasty of the Ptolemies, Greek rulers of ancient Egypt; extending from the death of Alexander the Great to that of Cleopatra. **2.** (astron.) Of or belonging to the astronomical system of Ptolemy of Alexandria, fl. c. A.D. 130, according to which the earth is the stationary centre of the universe, round which the sun, planets, and stars revolve.

Ptolemaist, n. [1. tòlemáist; 2. tòlimḗi-ist]. See prec. & **-ist**. A supporter of the Ptolemaic system.

ptomaine, n. [1. (p)tṓmān; 2. (p)tóumein], fr. Ital. *ptomaina*, coined by the discoverer, fr. Gk. *ptôma*, 'corpse', fr. stem **pet-, *pt-*, 'to fall'. See **ptero-**. Poisonous alkaloid substance formed by the putrefaction of animal or vegetable matter; *ptomaine poisoning*, caused by this substance, usually through eating tainted food.

ptosis, n. [1. (p)tṓsis; 2. (p)tóusis]. Gk. *ptôsis*, 'a falling', fr. base **pet-, *pt-*, 'to fall'. See **ptero-**. (med.) A drooping of the upper eyelid caused by paralysis of the muscle.

ptyalin, n. [1. (p)tíalin; 2. (p)táiəlin]. Gk. *ptúalon*, 'spittle', cp. *ptúein*, 'I spit', for **spiu-jō*; cogn. w. Lat. *spuere*, & O.E. *spēowan* &c., 'to vomit; to spit'. See **spew** & **-in**. Chemical substance found in the saliva of man, and some other animals.

ptyalism, n. [1. (p)tíalizm; 2. (p)táiəlizəm], fr. Gk. *ptúalon*, 'spittle'. See prec. & **-ism**. (med.) Excessive flow of saliva; salivation.

pub, n. [1. pub; 2. pab], for *public-house*. **1.** A public-house in narrower sense: *in and out of the pub all day long*. **2.** (slang) A hotel of any kind: *the smart pubs on the sea-front are too dear for me*.

puberty, n. [1. pū́berti; 2. pjū́bəti], fr. Lat. *pūbertāt-(em)*, 'marriageable age; virility'; fr. *pūber*, also *pūbes*, 'grown up; adult', fr. stem **pu*, 'to beget', as in *pūer*, 'boy'. See **puerile** & **pupil**. The age at which a male is able to beget, and a female to bear, offspring.

pubes, n. [1. pū́bēz; 2. pjū́bīz]. Lat., 'hair which appears on the body at puberty; the genital organs'; see prec. & words referred to. **1.** Hair which appears upon the body at puberty. **2.** Region of the body where this develops; the pubic region.

pubescence, n. [1. pūbésens; 2. pjūbésəns]. See next word & **-ce**. **1.** The age of puberty, arrival at the age of puberty. **2.** A covering of soft down on the leaves and stems of plants or on the bodies of insects.

pubescent, adj. [1. pūbésent; 2. pjūbésənt], fr. Lat. *pūbescent-(em)*, Pres. Part. of *pūbescere*, 'to reach the age of puberty; to become hairy'. See **puberty** & **pubes** & words there referred to. **1.** Reaching the age of puberty. **2.** Covered with downy, soft hair, as leaves of plants or bodies of insects.

pubic, adj. [1. pū́bik; 2. pjū́bik]. See next word & **-ic**. (anat.) Of, pertaining to, the region about the pubes: *pubic arch, bone, region* &c.

pubis, n. [1. pū́bis; 2. pjū́bis]. Neo-Lat. See **pubes**. (anat.) For *os pubis*, one of the bones composing the arch of the pelvis.

public (I.), adj. [1. públik; 2. páblik]. Fr., masc., fem. *publique*, fr. Lat. *publicus*, earlier *poplicus*, fr. *poplus*, earlier form of *populus*, 'the people'. See **popular** & **people**. **1.** Pertaining to, affecting, the people at large; generally contrasted with *private*; **a** pertaining to the people as a community, nation, or state; national: *a public bill, Act of Parliament*; *the public debt*; *public ownership*; *public health*; *a public holiday*, one appointed by authority for the whole community; **b** done for, by, in the name of, or for the advantage of, the people: *a public prosecution*; *public benefactor*; *in the public service*; *public spirit*, patriotism; **c** open to, provided for, the people generally: *a public library, park, road, place* &c.; *for public use and enjoyment*; **d** open to the knowledge or observation of all; not concealed; common, notorious: *a public scandal*; *to make the news public*; *a public protest*; *a matter of public knowledge*; **e** national, of the nations; international: *public international law*; *to declare a person a public enemy*. **2.** Specific uses: *public nuisance* (law), any act not legally allowed, or any omission to perform a legal duty, which damages, or inconveniences, the public generally in the exercise of their common rights, and is punishable at common law or by statute, as contrasted with a *private nuisance*, one which affects a private person only and is remedied by an action at law; *public orator*, the official speaker of a university; *public prosecutor*, a legal official who, on behalf of the Government, undertakes the prosecution of persons charged with serious crimes; *public trustee*, an official who acts as executor or trustee for any person in England who appoints him as such.

public (II.), n., fr. prec. **1.** The general body of the people; the members of a nation, community &c.: *the British, American, public*; *the public must decide*; *to appeal to the public*. Phr. *in public*, publicly, openly; in the view, hearing, of the public generally. **2.** A specific, particular portion of the people: *the theatrical, musical, public*; *an author's, actor's, favourite public*.

public (III.), n. Short for *public-house* (colloq.).

publican, n. [1. públikan; 2. páblikən], fr. Lat. *publicānus*, n., fr. *publicānus*, adj., 'belonging to the public revenue', see **public (I.)**, cp. Fr. *publicain*. **1.** (Rom. hist.) One to whom the public taxes and revenues were farmed; a farmer of the taxes; a tax-gatherer, often oppressive and exacting: *publicans and sinners* (N.T.). **2.** A keeper of a public-house; licensed victualler; innkeeper.

publication, n. [1. pùblikā́shun; 2. pàblikéiʃən]. Fr., fr. Lat. *publicātiōn-(em)*, 'assignment to, confiscation by, the public treasury', for *publicāt-(um)*, P.P. type of *publicāre*; the Engl. word has practically no connexion in meaning w. the Lat.; its meanings are derived fr. the vb. **publish**. **1.** Act of publishing or bringing to the notice and knowledge of the public; public notification, announcement, proclamation: *the publication of a death, balance-sheet, statute* &c. **2.** Specif., the offering, issuing for sale or distribution to the public, of a book, newspaper, reproduction of a picture, musical composition &c. **3.** Something published; specif., a book, newspaper &c. so issued to the public by a publisher. **4.** (law) The act of exhibiting, communicating, to a third person libellous matter, or slanderous statements; the proof of such an act having been committed is essential to a conviction for defamation.

public-house, n. A house licensed for the sale and consumption of alcoholic liquor during specified hours; an inn or tavern.

publicist, n. [1. públisist; 2. páblisist], fr. Fr. *publiciste*. **public** & **-ist**. **1.** A writer on international law, science of government, public rights &c. **2.** A political journalist.

publicity, n. [1. publísiti; 2. pablísiti], fr. Fr. *publicité*, a coined word. See **public** & **-ity**. State, quality, of being public, or generally known; notoriety; advertisement: *to court, shun, publicity*; *the advantage, disgrace, of publicity*; *publicity agent*, an advertising agent.

publicly, adv. [1. públikli; 2. páblikli]. **public (I.)** & **-ly**. In public; in a public manner, openly; generally known by the public.

public-minded, adj., **public-mindedly**, adv., **public-mindedness**, n., same as **public-spirited** &c.

public school, n. **a** Any school maintained by public funds and managed by a local educational authority under the Board of Education: *a public elementary* or *secondary school*; **b** specif., any of various large schools, of ancient or modern foundation, chiefly taking resident or boarding pupils above a certain age and educating them for the universities, professions &c., controlled by a board of governors; not run for private profit, and maintaining discipline &c., partly by the senior pupils, called prefects or monitors; distinguished from *private* or *preparatory schools*.

public-spirited, adj. Having a public spirit; patriotic; devoted to, acting in the interests, welfare &c., of, the public at large; not selfishly or personally interested.

public-spiritedly, adv. Prec. & **-ly**. In a public-spirited way; with public spirit.

public-spiritedness, n. See prec. & **-ness**. Quality of being public-spirited; patriotism.

publish, vb. trans. [1. públish; 2. pábliʃ]. M.E. *publischen, publishen*; stem of Fr. *publier*, Lat. *publicāre*, 'to take to public use, to make known to the public', w. vbl. suff. **-ish**; see **public (I.)**. **1.** To make generally known; to make public announcement of; to spread abroad, to divulge: *to publish the news*; *to publish notice of a death, marriage*; *to publish secrets*. **2.** To announce formally, to proclaim: *to publish an edict, order in council* &c. **3.** To notify by reading in church: *to publish the banns of marriage*. **4.** Specif. **a** (action of a publisher) to issue and offer for sale to the public, a book or anything printed or engraved, produced by a printing press; **b** (action of an author) to write, and obtain printing and publication for (an article, book &c.): *he has a reputation based on personal impressions only*; *so far he has published nothing of importance*. **5.** (law) To exhibit or communicate to a third party a libel or slander.

publishable, adj. [1. públishabl; 2. pábliʃəbl]. Prec. & **-able**. Worth publishing; good enough, fit for publication.

publisher, n. [1. públisher; 2. pábliʃə]. **publish** & **-er**. One who publishes; specif., one who prints and issues for distribution and sale to the public (books and other literary matter).

puccoon, n. [1. pukóōn; 2. pakū́n]. N. Am. Indian name. A North American plant, the blood-root, yielding a red pigment or dye.

puce, n. [1. pūs; 2. pjūs]. Fr., 'flea; flea-colour'; fr. Lat. *pūlex*, 'flea'; cp. Gk. *psúlla*; O. Slav. *blŭcha*, 'flea'; origin doubtful. A brownish-purple colour.

pucelle, n. [1. pūsél; 2. pjūsél]. Fr., O. Fr. *pucele*, fr. L. Lat. *pullicella*, 'maid' (Meyer-Lübke); etymol. doubtful. **a** (obs.) A virgin, maid, damsel: **b** specif., *La Pucelle*, St. Joan of Arc.

puck (I.), n. [1. puk; 2. pak]. O.E. *pūca*, M.E. *pouke*, 'goblin', cp. O.N. *pūki*, 'imp'; W. *pwca*, 'goblin'. **1.** A mischievous sprite or goblin; specif. (cap.) Robin Goodfellow, a playful, mischievous fairy, of old stories and legends. **2.** An impish, mischievous child.

puck (II.), n. Prob. fr. prec. The flat disk of rubber used as the ball in playing hockey on the ice.

puck (III.), n. Etymol. doubtful; the Surrey and Sussex local name is *Puckeridge*. **a** The goatsucker or night-jar; **b** a disease of cattle supposed to be caused by this bird.

pucka, pukka, adj. [1. púka; 2. pákə]. Anglo-Indian, fr. Hind. *pakka*, 'of full weight, ripe'. **a** Good, first-class, of its kind; **b** genuine, real, solid: *a pukka general*, a full, permanent, not a temporary, general; *a pukka sahib*, a perfect, undoubted, gentleman.

pucker, vb. trans. & intrans. & n. [1. púker; 2. pákə]. Etymol. uncertain. **1.** vb. **a** trans. To knit, draw together in folds or creases; to wrinkle: *to pucker (up) one's brows, lips*, &c.; *to pucker a seam, piece of cloth* &c.; **b** intrans., to become wrinkled, fall into creases. **2.** n. A wrinkle, crease, or fold.

puckish, adj. [1. púkish; 2. pákiʃ]. **puck (I.)** & **-ish.** Like Puck; like a puck or mischievous sprite; impish, mischievous; irresponsible, fond of mischief for its own sake.

puddening, n. [1. póodening; 2. púdəniŋ], fr. *pudden,* dial. form of **pudding** & **-ing.** (naut.) A bunch of rope-yarn, tow &c. used as a fender, or to prevent chafing.

pudding, n. [1. póoding; 2. púdiŋ]. Earlier [púdin, púdn], also spelt *pudden*; M.E. *poding, pudinȝ,* etymol. doubtful; earliest sense 'sausage or black pudding'; cp. L.G. *pudde-wurst,* 'black pudding'; also Fr. *boudin,* fr. wh. Engl. may have been adapted. **1.** The intestine of a pig stuffed with chopped meat, blood &c. and seasoned and boiled: *a black pudding.* **2.** A mixture of flour, suet, milk, eggs &c. boiled, steamed, or baked; made with various ingredients, meat, fruit &c.: *a Yorkshire, plum, pudding; steak and kidney pudding; apple pudding* &c. **3.** Any sweet dish of pudding-like consistency or appearance: *a rice pudding; bread and butter pudding; meat, but no pudding today.* **4.** (naut.) Puddening. **5.** Anything resembling a pudding in shape, appearance, consistency &c.: (usually attrib.) *pudding face,* a large, flat, expressionless face; *pudding head,* a thick-headed, stupid person, dolt.

pudding-stone, n. A siliceous conglomerate in which the embedded pebbles resemble the plums in a pudding.

puddingy, adj. [1. póodingi; 2. púdiŋi]. **pudding** & **-y.** **a** Like pudding in consistency; **b** (fig.) heavy, dull, lacking lightness and sparkle.

puddle (I.), n. [1. púdl; 2. pádl]. M.E. *pudel, pidel,* prob. a dimin. of O.E. *pudd,* 'ditch'; also *pydel* in Pl.-Ns.; origin unknown. **1.** A small pool of stagnant water; a quantity of spilled water. **2.** A mixture of clay, sand, and water kneaded together to form a watertight lining for a pond &c.

puddle (II.), vb. trans. & intrans., fr. prec. **A.** trans. **1.** **a** To knead and work clay &c. with water so as to make a watertight mixture; **b** to apply such to the bottom of a pond, a wall, embankment, so as to render it watertight. **2.** To convert cast-iron into wrought-iron by stirring the molten metal, thus freeing it from carbon. **B.** intrans. (with *about, in*) To dabble, paddle, wallow in dirty or stagnant water.

puddler, n. [1. púdler; 2. pádlə]. Prec. & **-er.** One who puddles; specif., one who puddles clay, or molten iron.

puddling, n. [1. púdling; 2. pádliŋ]. **puddle** & **-ing.** Process carried out by one who puddles, **a** in clay; **b** in molten iron.

pudency, n. [1. pūdensi; 2. pjūdənsi], fr. L. Lat. *pudentia,* fr. *pudent-(em),* Pres. Part. of *pudēre,* 'to be ashamed', & **-cy.** The base of the vb. is said by Walde to be identical w. that in *repudium,* 'putting away, separation' &c., see **repudiate,** an extension of that in *pavīre,* 'to beat down, strike, tread down', see **pavement.** Modesty, bashfulness.

pudendum, n., pl. **pudenda**, n. [1. pūdéndum, -da; 2. pjūdéndəm, -də]. Lat., 'that of which one should be ashamed', neut. sing. of gerundive, *pudendus,* of *pudēre,* 'to be ashamed'. See prec. (usually pl.) The external organs of generation.

pudge, n. [1. puj; 2. padž]. Origin unknown. A short, thick-set, fat, lumpy person.

pudgy, adj. [1. púji; 2. pádži]. Prec. & **-y.** Short, thick, and fat.

pudic, adj. [1. pūdik; 2. pjūdik], fr. Lat. *pudīcus,* 'modest', fr. stem of *pudēre,* 'to be ashamed'. See **pudency.** **1.** (obs.) Modest, chaste. **2.** (anat.) Of, pertaining to, the external organs of generation: *pudic artery, veins* &c.

pudicity, n. [1. pūdísiti; 2. pjūdísiti], fr. Fr. *pudicité,* Lat. *pudīcitia.* See prec. & **-ity.** Modesty, bashfulness.

pudsy, adj. [1. púdzi; 2. pádzi]. Variant of **pudgy.** Pudgy; short and thick, stout, plump.

pudu, n. [1. pōōdōō; 2. pūdū]. S. Am. Indian name. A genus of S. American mountain deer.

pueblo, n. [1. pwéblō; 2. puéblo]. Span., fr. Lat. *populus,* 'people'. See **populace** & cp. **public.** **1.** A village or settlement of native Indians in Mexico and in Arizona, New Mexico, or Texas, consisting of terraced, flat-roofed houses of stone and adobe, with underground halls. **2.** An Indian inhabiting a pueblo; the *Pueblo Indians* form tribes with a special culture, and are distinct from the Indians of the plains.

puerile, adj. [1. pūeril; 2. pjūərail], fr. Lat. *puerīlis,* 'boyish, childish'; fr. *puer,* fr. **pover,* 'that which is begotten, child, more particularly male child, boy,' & **-il(e)**; *puer* is fr. base **powe-,* whence also, w. different formative elements, **puberty**; Scrt. *pōtaš,* 'young'; & *putráš,* 'son, child'; Gk. *pais,* 'child', fr. **pawis.* See **paedo-, pedagogue** &c. Childish; foolish, silly, trivial, weak.

puerilely, adv. Prec. & **-ly.** In a puerile manner; childishly, foolishly.

puerility, n. [1. pūeríliti; 2. pjūəríliti], fr. Lat. *puerīlitāt-(em).* See **puerile** & **-ity.** **1.** (rare) State of being puerile; i.e. specif., status of a child between infancy and puberty. **2.** **a** That which is puerile; foolishness; **b** a foolish, futile action, remark &c.

puerperal, adj. [1. pūérperal; 2. pjuápərəl], fr. Lat. *puerperus,* usually as n. *puerpera,* 'a woman in labour', fr. *puer,* 'child', see **puerile,** & *-parus,* fr. *parere,* 'to bring forth, bear', see **parent.** Connected with, pertaining to, caused by, childbirth, esp. *puerperal fever, insanity* &c.

puff (I.), vb. trans. & intrans. [1. puf; 2. paf]. O.E. *pyffan,* 'to blow with the mouth', M.E. *puffen,* 'to blow'; also in Germ. & Du., cp. Swed. *puffa*; imitative; the base prob. also in the O.E. men's names *Pybba,* fr. **pub-ja,* & *Peufa,* both prob. nicknames meaning 'the puffer, blower'. **A.** trans. **1.** To blow, propel with gusts of air, to expel in short puffs: *to puff smoke in one's face; engine puffs clouds of steam.* **2.** (colloq.) To cause to pant for breath, to put out of breath: *I was frightfully puffed by the run.* **3.** To advertise, flatter, praise, unduly. **B.** intrans. **1.** To blow in fitful, intermittent gusts; **a** (rarely) of the wind; **b** to breathe jerkily, to pant, often *puff and pant, puff and blow,* to breathe with difficulty, as when out of breath. **2.** **a** To emit steam &c. in a series of sudden puffs: *a traction-engine puffing along the road;* **b** (of steam, smoke &c.) to be driven, emitted, in sudden gusts or clouds: *the smoke puffed full in his face.* **C.** Followed by preposition and adverb. *Puff away,* **1.** trans., to drive away by blowing in puffs: *to puff away smoke* &c.; **2.** intrans., **a** to move off, emitting puffs: *the engine puffed slowly away;* **b** to continue to emit puffs: *puffing away at a pipe. Puff out,* **1.** trans., **a** to extinguish by puffing: *to puff out a candle;* **b** to distend, cause to swell out: *to puff out one's cheeks; sails puffed out with wind;* (also fig.) *puffed out with self-importance;* **c** to exhaust by violent exercise, cause to become short of breath: *quite puffed out after the climb;* **2.** intrans., **a** to swell out; **b** to become suddenly extinguished, to go out with a puff (of a candle &c.); **c** to burst out in puffs: *smoke puffing out at every crevice. Puff up,* **1.** trans., (chiefly fig.) to cause to swell with pride and conceit, esp. in P.P. *puffed up with one's own conceit;* **2.** intrans., to rise in a puff or puffs: *the powder ignited and suddenly puffed up.*

puff (II.), n., fr. prec. **1.** **a** A slight, short emission of air, breath, smoke, steam &c.; **a** sudden, short, soft gust of wind; **b** the sound of such emission or gust; **c** something which is suddenly blown or puffed: *a puff of smoke, steam, air* &c. **2.** One of several objects, either inflated, or stuffed with, or made of, some soft resilient material; **a** a small gathered loose fold in a dress &c.; **b** a small round pad of swansdown or similar material used to apply powder to the skin: *powder-puff;* **c** light pastry, *a cream, jam puff.* **3.** A fulsome, flattering, notice or advertisement, in praise of a person or thing: *mere tradesman's puff; to get a good puff of one's book.*

puff-adder, n. Large, very poisonous African viper; its name is derived from its habit of distending its body when irritated.

puff-ball, n. **1.** A fungus, *Lycoperdon,* with rounded head, which, when ripe, bursts at a touch and emits the spores in a cloud. **2.** The feathery head of a dandelion after flowering.

puffer, n. [1. púfer; 2. páfə]. **puff (I.)** & **-er.** **1.** One who puffs (in various senses), esp. one who proclaims widely the merits of a person or thing by way of flattery or advertisement. **2.** Popular name of varieties of fish, such as the globe-fish, which can inflate or puff out their bodies.

puffery, n. [1. púferi; 2. páfəri]. **puff (I.)** & **-ery.** Act of puffing or praising unduly; flattery, advertisement.

puffin, n. [1. púfin; 2. páfin]. Etymol. doubtful; prob. fr. **puff (I.),** w. a dimin. suff.; fr. the rounded belly of the bird. A seabird of the N. Atlantic and N. Pacific, allied to the auks; the common puffin, *Fratercula arctica,* has black and white plumage and a large grooved red and orange parrot-like bill.

puffiness, n. [1. púfines; 2. páfinis]. **puffy** & **-ness.** State, quality, of being puffy; slight inflation.

puffy, adj. [1. púfi; 2. páfi]. **puff (II.)** & **-y.** **1.** Coming in slight, short gusts or puffs: *a puffy wind.* **2.** Panting, short of breath: *rather puffy after the climb.* **3.** Inflated, swollen: *puffy under the eyes; ankles a bit puffy.*

pug (I.), n. [1. pug; 2. pag]. Etymol. uncertain; the earliest meaning of 'imp, sprite', points to **puck (I.)** as the origin. **1.** (dial.) A popular name of a fox, also of a monkey. **2.** A snub-nose, usually *pug-nose.* **3.** Specif., a breed of small dog, with broad, flat nose, smooth hair, wrinkled face, and closely curled tail, resembling a dwarf bull-dog.

pug (II.), vb. trans. & n. Origin unknown. **1.** vb. **a** To mix wet clay for making bricks, pottery &c.; **b** to pack walls, floors &c. with clay or other material such as sawdust to deaden sound. **2.** n. Clay mixed by pugging; packing material used for deadening sound.

pug (III.), n. & vb. trans. Anglo-Indian, fr. Hind. *pag,* 'foot'. **1.** n. The track, footprint of a wild beast, esp. of a tiger. **2.** vb. To track by the pugs.

pug (IV.), n. Abbr. of **pugilist.** (old slang) A boxer, prize-fighter.

puggaree, puggree, n. [1. púgari; 2. págəri]. Hind. *pagri,* 'turban'. Small veil of light thin cloth worn over the top of the hat and hanging down so as to protect the back of the neck from the sun; also, the end of a turban fulfilling the same purpose.

pugging, n. [1. púging; 2. págiŋ]. **pug (II.)** & **-ing.** **1.** The mixing and working of clay in a pug mill to make it plastic and malleable. **2.** Packing, stuffing, used to deaden sound in building.

puggree, n. See **puggaree.**

pugilism, n. [1. pūjilizm; 2. pjūdžilizəm], fr. Lat. *pugil,* 'boxer', & **-ism**; fr. base **pug-,* cp. *pugnus,* 'the fist', *pugnāre,* 'to fight' &c., q.v. under **pugnacious.** The art, practice, of fighting with the fists; boxing.

pugilist, n. [1. pūjilist; 2. pjūdžilist]. Lat. *pugil,* 'boxer'. See prec. & **-ist.** **a** A fighter with the fists, a boxer, esp. a professional boxer, prize-fighter; **b** (fig.) a keen, ruthless antagonist or opponent in argument &c.

pugilistic, adj. [1. pūjilístik; 2. pjūdžilístik]. Prec. & **-ic.** Connected with, pertaining to, pugilism or pugilists: *a pugilistic encounter.*

pugilistically, adv. [1. pūjilístikali; 2. pjūdžilístikəli]. Prec. & **-al** & **-ly.** In a pugilistic manner; with the fists.

pug-mill, n. See **pug (II.)** & **mill.** A mill for grinding and mixing clay.

pugnacious, adj. [1. pugnā́shus ; 2. pagnéiʃəs], fr. Lat. *pugnāci-*, stem of *pugnax*, 'fond of fighting', & **-ous.** Cp. also *pugna*, 'fight, battle', *pugnāre*, 'to fight', *pugnus*, 'fist' &c. ; cogn. w. Gk. *púx*, 'with clenched fist'; O.E. *feohtan*, 'to fight,' see **fight**, may be fr. this base, though the vowel offers difficulty ; Walde considers that the base **peuĝ-*, **puĝ-* (also **peuk̂-*, &c.), meant primarily 'to stick out, stab', the sense 'fist' being derived orig. fr. the hand doubled so as to allow the middle finger to protrude ; cp. also Gk. *peúkē*, 'fir tree' (fr. its prickles), also Lat. *pugio*, 'dagger', see **poniard** ; Lat. *pugnāre* is orig., 'to fight with fists'. See further a nasalized form of the same base under **pungent.** Fond of fighting, combative.

pugnaciously, adv. Prec. & **-ly.** In a pugnacious, combative manner.

pugnaciousness, n. See prec. & **-ness.** State, quality, of being pugnacious ; pugnacity.

pugnacity, n. [1. pugnásiti ; 2. pagnǽsiti], fr. Lat. *pugnācitāt-(em)*, fr. *pugnāci-*, as in **pugnacious**, & **-ity.** Inclination to fight, fondness for fighting ; combativeness.

pug-nosed, adj. See **pug (I.)** & **nosed.** Snub-nosed.

puisne, adj. & n. [1. pū́ni ; 2. pjū́ni]. O. Fr. *puisné*, 'junior'. See **puny. 1.** adj. (law) Junior, of lower rank ; in phr. *puisne judge*, applied to all judges of the High Court of Judicature other than the Lord Chancellor, Lord Chief Justice, Master of the Rolls and President of Admiralty, Probate, and Divorce Courts. **2.** n. A puisne judge.

puissance, n. [1. pwísans, pū́isans ; 2. pwísəns, pjū́isəns]. Fr. Next word & **-ce.** (poet. or archaic) Power, might, strength.

puissant, adj. [1. pwísant, pū́isant ; 2. pwísənt, pjū́isənt]. Fr., 'powerful', cp. Ital. *possente*, both fr. Lat. Pres. Part. **possent-(em)*, formed on anal. of infin. *posse*, 'to be able', instead of regular *potent-(em)*, see **potent (I.)**. (poet. or archaic) Powerful, mighty, strong : *most mighty and puissant prince.*

puissantly, adv. Prec. & **-ly.** With power, might, or strength ; powerfully, mightily.

puja, pooja, n. [1. pŏŏjah ; 2. pū́džā]. Hind. & Scrt. *pūjā*, 'worship'. Religious worship of Hindu idol ; any Hindu religious rite.

puke, vb. intrans. & trans. [1. pūk ; 2. pjūk]. Etymol. **uncertain ; prob. imitative.** To vomit.

pukeko, n. [1. póokekō ; 2. púkikou]. Maori. Australasian swamp-hen.

pukka, adj. See **pucka.**

puku, n. [1. pŏŏkōō ; 2. púkū]. Native name. A small, reddish-brown antelope of Central Africa, the African waterbuck.

pulchritude, n. [1. púlkritūd ; 2. pálkritjūd], fr. Lat. *pulchritūdo*, 'beauty', fr. *pulchri-*, stem of *pulcher*, 'beautiful', the origin of wh. is entirely uncertain. (rare) Beauty, loveliness.

pule, vb. intrans. [1. pūl ; 2. pjūl]. Imitative, cp. Fr. *piauler*, 'to cheep, as a young bird, howl, as a puppy'. To whine, whimper feebly, as does a fretful or sickly child.

Pulex, n. [1. pū́leks ; 2. pjū́lɛks]. Lat., 'flea', origin & relations doubtful, cp. **puce.** (zool.) The genus flea.

pull (I.), vb., trans. & intrans. [1. pool ; 2. pul]. O.E. *pullian*, 'to pluck, twitch'. Origin unknown. General sense, to draw towards, or after one ; reverse of *push.* Various special uses, often followed by an adverb or other word giving specific definition. **A.** trans. **1.** To draw, drag, tug ; to cause to move towards one ; to cause to come nearer to some object from the direction of which force is exerted : *to pull a door open, shut* ; *to pull one's collar up, one's hat over one's eyes* ; specif., *to pull an oar*, to row, *pull a boat*, row it. Phrs. *to pull a good oar*, be a good rower ; *to pull one's weight*, use one's weight properly when rowing ; (fig.) to exert oneself, do one's fair share of work ; *to pull a face, faces*, make a grimace, grimaces ; *to pull to, in, pieces*, to tear, reduce to fragments ; (also fig.) to criticize severely ; *to pull a horse*, prevent it from winning a race by unfair riding. **2.** **a** To remove, extract, by pulling : *to pull a cork, a tooth* ; also *pull out* ; **b** to cause to move from position occupied ; to remove, drag out, or away by pulling : *to pull a person off a chair, out of bed.* **3.** To pluck, gather : *to pull fruit, flowers.* **4.** To pluck, or remove entrails from (a bird for the table) ; the usual phr. is *to draw*, in this sense. **5.** (print.) To take impressions, print, formerly, by pulling a lever to work the press, now, in general sense, to print off, take proofs of. **6.** (cricket or golf) To strike (a ball) in such a way as to cause it to travel at a right angle from one's left. **7.** To pluck sharply, twitch, with a sharp downward, or outward movement : *to pull a person's hair, ears, nose* &c. Phr. *to pull a person's leg*, to make fun of him, to chaff, take him in. **8.** To move along, and exert force so as to cause (an object) to follow, or to move along after : *to pull a cart.* **9.** **a** (thieves' slang) To arrest : *to pull a pick-pocket* ; also *pull in* ; **b** to raid : *to pull a gambling-den.* **B.** intrans. **1.** **a** To perform the action of pulling : *the horse on the near side isn't pulling at all* ; *now then, pull all together* ; **b** to allow of pulling, be capable of movement when pulled : *the cord won't pull.* **2.** To allow (smoke) to pass through when suction is applied, to draw : *my pipe is pulling very badly tonight.* **C.** Followed by preposition or adverb. *Pull apart*, **a** trans., to pull, tear into pieces ; **b** intrans., to become separated, parted, by pulling ; to break in two. *Pull at*, to extract smoke &c. from by suction ; to suck : *to pull at a pipe. Pull back*, **a** trans., to draw away from, back towards one : *to pull a person back* from a danger, dangerous course of action ; **b** intrans., to draw back from, back out, retreat : *he pulled back in time. Pull down*, trans., **a** to demolish, destroy : *pull down a building* ; **b** to degrade, abase, humble : *pull down a person's pride* ; **c** to weaken, render sickly, deprive of health or strength : *a bout of fever soon pulls you down. Pull in*, **1.** trans., **a** to draw in : *to pull in a horse, boat* &c. ; **b** to reduce, curtail : *to pull in one's expenses* ; **2.** intrans., **a** to move in : *the boat pulls in to shore* ; **b** to retrench, reduce expenses : *you must pull in now or you'll be bankrupt. Pull off*, **1.** trans. **a** to take, draw off, remove : *pull off one's boots, coat* &c. ; Phr. *to pull off one's hat to*, salute ; **b** to succeed in doing, winning something, to bring off : *to pull off a good speculation, coup* &c. ; **2.** intrans., to move away, draw off : *the boat pulled off from the shore. Pull on*, **1.** trans., to draw on or over : *to pull on one's clothes, gloves* &c. ; **2.** intrans., to continue pulling or rowing : *to pull on harder. Pull out*, **1.** trans., **a** to extract, draw out : *to pull out a cork, tooth* ; *to pull out a knife, revolver*, display one suddenly and threaten with it ; **b** to lengthen, extend, stretch : *to pull out a tale, story, till it bores one* ; **2.** intrans., **a** to move out or away from : *to pull out from the bank* ; **b** to be made so as to be drawn out : *the drawer won't pull out. Pull over*, to draw over one's head, usually of a jersey without buttons, cp. **pull-over**, n. below. *Pull round*, **1.** trans., to cause a person to recover from illness, to bring round : *the doctors tried in vain to pull him round* ; **2.** intrans., to recover after an illness, shock &c. : *after a holiday you'll soon pull round. Pull through*, **1.** trans., to get, help, another through, over, an illness, danger, difficulty &c. : *good nursing pulled him through* ; **2.** intrans., to get through, succeed in recovering from or in overcoming illness, difficulty &c. : *we shall pull through somehow. Pull together*, **1.** trans., **a** to pull two things towards each other so that they meet ; **b** (reflex.) *pull oneself together*, to rally, rouse oneself, to recover and exert one's energies ; **2.** intrans., to work together harmoniously, to co-operate : *it was improbable that two such strong personalities could pull together. Pull up*, **1.** trans., **a** to rein in (horse) ; to stop, check (car) &c. ; **b** (fig.) to check, arrest action or speech of : *to be pulled up by the chairman at a meeting* ; *to pull oneself up*, to restrain oneself, check oneself suddenly ; **2.** intrans., **a** to stop one's horse, car &c. ; to make a halt, to halt, to interrupt one's journey : *let us pull up at the next village* ; to come to a halt : *the train pulled up at the station* ; **b** to check, restrain oneself in a course of action : *to pull up in time before a financial crash. Pull up to, with*, to overtake, catch up to, to get on even terms with, as in a race or competition of any kind.

pull (II.), n., fr. prec. **1.** Act of pulling (in various senses) ; **a** act of drawing, tugging : *would you mind giving a pull at the bell?* ; **b** act of rowing : *a short pull on the river* ; **c** act of imbibing : *a pull at a bottle* ; **d** act of drawing in by suction : *pull at a pipe* ; **e** act of pulling a horse ; **f** act of pulling a ball (at cricket &c.). **2.** **a** Force, strain, exerted by pulling : *keep a steady pull on a rope* ; **b** force tending to drag something towards object exerting it ; attraction : *the pull of the moon on the sea causes the tides* ; **c** (fig.) advantage : *a good education gives a man a great pull.* **3.** One of various objects by means of which force of some kind is brought to bear ; **a** handle, knob of a bell : *a bell pull* ; **b** lever of a beer-engine : *a beer-pull* ; also, quantity drawn at one time by a beer-pull. Phr. *the long pull*, amount in excess of what is paid for. **4.** (print.) A proof 'pulled' for the press.

pulled, adj. [1. poold ; 2. puld]. P.P. of **pull (I.)**. Various special senses : *Pulled bread*, the crumb of a loaf of new bread pulled out and baked crisp ; *pulled figs*, dried figs shaped by pulling and packed flat ; *pulled wool*, low-grade wool separated by chemical processes.

puller, n. [1. póoler ; 2. púlə]. **pull (I.)** & **-er.** One who, that which, pulls. **1.** An implement of various kinds for pulling or drawing nails, corks &c. **2.** A horse which habitually pulls, that is, which keeps constant strain upon the bit. **3.** A rower, oarsman.

pullet, n. [1. póolet ; 2. púlit], fr. Fr. *poulet*, dimin. of *poule*, 'fowl', fr. L. Lat. *pulla*, 'hen', fem. of Lat. *pullus*, 'young animal' ; cp. **poultry.** Cogn. w. **puerile.** A young hen, during the first year of laying and before mating or moulting.

pulley (I.), n. [1. pòoli ; 2. púli]. M.E. *polie*, fr. O. Fr. *polie*, Mod. Fr. *poulie*, apparently through a L. Lat. *polidia*, cp. Ital. *puleggia*, fr. Gk. **polídion*, dimin. of *pólos*, 'pivot, axis', see **pole (III.)**. M.E., however, has also *poleyn, pulleyn*, fr. Fr. *poulain*, 'rope and tackle for lowering and hoisting casks', wh. derives fr. L. Lat. *pullānus*, 'colt', a variant of *pullus*, 'foal', see **pullet**, & cp. *donkey-engine, crane* &c. for similar application of animal names : in any case, the word has been closely associated w. **pull (I.)**. **1.** A small grooved wheel, contained in a block or frame, over which a cord, chain &c. passes. **2.** (mechan.) One of the six simple mechanical powers or prime movers, consisting of a single pulley or system of pulleys, for lifting a weight, changing the direction of motion, or for the transmission of power from or to different parts of machinery.

pulley (II.), vb. trans., P.P. *pullied*, fr. prec. To lift, hoist, move, by a pulley or pulleys.

Pullman, n. [1. póolman ; 2. púlmən], fr. designer's name. A railway saloon or sleeping-car.

pull-over, n. See **pull (I.)**. A woollen, knitted jersey, without buttons, pulled over the head when put on.

pull-through, n. A cord with a small weight at one end and a loop to hold a piece of oiled rag at the other, used to clean the barrel of a rifle.

pullulate, vb. intrans. [1. púlūlāt; 2. páljuleit], fr. Lat. *pullulāt-(um)*, P.P. of *pullulāre*, 'to sprout, grow', fr. *pullulus*, dimin. of *pullus*, 'young animal', see **pullet**. To sprout, grow; to spread abroad, spring up; multiply quickly.

pully-hauly, adj. & n. [1. pòoli háwli; 2. pùli hɔ̄li]. **pull (I.)** & **haul**. (naut. and colloq.) Pulling and hauling.

pulmo-, pref., fr. Lat. *pulmōn-(em)*, 'lung'; origin doubtful; possibly fr. base **pleu-*, **plu-*, 'to flow; to float', see **pluvial (I.)** & **float**; influenced to some extent by Gk. *pneúmōn*, 'lung', see **pneumonia**.

pulmo-branchiate, adj. [1. pùlmō brángkiāt; 2. pàlmou brǽŋkieit]. See prec. & **branchiate**. (zool.) Having gills modified so as to breathe air.

pulmo-gastric, adj. [1. pùlmō gástrik; 2. pàlmou gǽstrik]. **pulmo-** & **gastric**. (anat.) Of, pertaining to, the lungs and the stomach.

pulmometer, n. [1. pulmómeter; 2. palmɔ́mitə]. **pulmo-** & **meter**. Instrument for measuring breathing capacity of the lungs.

pulmonary, adj. [1. púlmunari; 2. pálmənəri], fr. Lat. *pulmōnārius*, fr. *pulmōn-*, 'lung', see **pulmo-**, & **-ary**. **1.** Of, pertaining to, connected with, affecting, the lungs: *pulmonary artery, vein; pulmonary diseases*. **2.** (zool.) Having lungs or lung-like breathing organs; pulmonate.

pulmonate, adj. & n. [1. púlmunàt; 2. pálmənèit]. See **pulmo-** & **-ate**. **1.** adj. Having lungs or lung-like breathing organs; belonging to the order *Pulmonata*. **2.** n. (zool.) A member of the order *Pulmonata* of gastropod molluscs, including the land and fresh-water snails, slugs &c., which have an external lung-like respiratory sac.

pulmonic, adj. [1. pulmónik; 2. palmɔ́nik]. See **pulmo-** & **-ic**. Pulmonary, affecting the lungs.

pulp (I.), n. [1. pulp; 2. palp]. Fr. *pulpe*, fr. Lat. *pulpa*, 'pulp of fruit, pith, flesh'; etymol. doubtful. **1.** Interior, fleshy and juicy part of fruit. **2.** The soft, nervous, vascular tissue filling the cavity of a tooth. **3. a** Any soft, coherent mass of crushed substance; specif. **b** any of various kinds of crushed vegetable tissue in process of being made into paper; e.g. *wood-pulp*. Phrs. *to beat (a person) to a pulp*, thump, pound, bruise badly; (fig.) *to be reduced to a pulp*, to be overcome with fatigue, tired out, or rendered helpless by emotional shock. **4.** Wet, crushed ore.

pulp (II.), vb. trans. & intrans., fr. prec. **1.** trans. To convert into pulp. **2.** intrans. To become pulp.

pulper, n. [1. púlper; 2. pálpə]. Prec. & **-er**. One who, that which, pulps; machine used in the making of paper.

pulpify, vb. trans. [1. púlpifī; 2. pálpifai]. **pulp (I.)** & **-fy**. To make pulp of, reduce to pulp, esp. for making paper.

pulpiness, n. [1. púlpines; 2. pálpinis]. **pulpy** & **-ness**. State, quality, of being pulpy.

pulpit, n. [1. póolpit; 2. púlpit], fr. O. Fr. *pulpite*, fr. Lat. *pulpitum*, 'platform, stage, scaffold', fr. **pl̥-plut-*, redupl. form of base **plut-*, as in *pluteus*, 'movable shed', the origin of wh. is unknown. **1.** Raised structure in a place of worship, consisting of a small stage with surrounding sides or parapet, in which the preacher stands while delivering the sermon. **2.** Public religious and moral teaching; also, the body of preachers; often contrasted with *platform* = political rhetoric: *denounced alike by pulpit and platform*.

pulpiteer, n. & vb. intrans. [1. pòolpitḗr; 2. pùlpitíə]. Prec. & **-eer**. **1.** n. A preacher (usually in disparaging sense); one who preaches in and out of season. **2.** vb. **a** To make a political use of the pulpit; **b** to hold forth in private life, as though preaching in public.

pulpless, adj. [1. púlples; 2. pálplis]. **pulp (I.)** & **-less**. Without pulp or pith; dry, desiccated.

pulpous, adj. [1. púlpus; 2. pálpəs], fr. Lat. *pulpōsus*. As **pulp (I.)** & **-ous**. Pulpy.

pulpy, adj. [1. púlpi; 2. pálpi]. **pulp (I.)** & **-y**. Of the consistency of, resembling, consisting of, pulp.

pulque, n. [1. póolki; 2. púlki]. Span.-Am., shortened form of *pulqueria* for *pulperia*, 'place for sale of drinks made from fruit' &c. See **pulp (I.)**. A Mexican intoxicating drink made from the fermented juice of the agave.

pulsate, vb. intrans. & trans. [1. púlsāt, pulsát; 2. pálseit, palséit], fr. Lat. *pulsāt-(um)*, P.P. of *pulsāre*, 'to beat, push', formed fr. *puls-(um)*, P.P. type of *pellere*, 'to drive, push', see **pulse (I.)**. **A.** intrans. **1.** To throb, beat, rhythmically, as the pulse or heart; to vibrate, quiver. **2.** (fig.) To throb, thrill, with excitement or emotion **3.** (elect.) To flow in one direction, with varying intensity: *pulsating current*. **B.** trans. To shake, agitate.

pulsatile, adj. [1. púlsatīl; 2. pálsətail]. Prec. & **-il(e)**. **1.** Pulsating, throbbing; capable of pulsation. **2.** (mus.) Played by beating or percussion.

pulsation, n. [1. pulsáshun; 2. palséiʃən], fr. Lat. *pulsātiōn-(em)*. See **pulsate** & **-ion**. **1.** A rhythmical beating, throbbing, as of the heart or pulse. **2.** A single beat or throb, as of sounds &c.; (esp. elect.) the variation of a pulsating current.

pulsator, n. [1. pulsáter; 2. palséitə]. **pulsate** & **-or**. Something which pulsates; specif., such a part in a machine.

pulsatory, adj. [1. púlsaturi; 2. pálsətəri]. **pulsate** & **-ory**. Pulsating, beating, throbbing rhythmically: *a pulsatory electric current*.

pulse (I.), n. [1. puls; 2. pals]. In M.E. *pous*; fr. O. Fr. *pous, pouls*, fr. Lat. *pulsus*, 'a beating, stamping'; also in phr. *pulsus venārum*, 'beat of blood in the veins', fr. *puls-(um)*, P.P. type of *pellere*, 'to push, strike, drive', see **compel** & **impel**; cogn. forms are second syll. in O.E. *anfilt*, see **anvil**, & **felt (I.)**. **1.** The throb, rhythmical beating, of the blood in the arteries and other blood-vessels, caused by the opening and shutting of the ventricles of the heart; specif., the beat felt in the wrist by which a doctor tests the character, strength &c. of the heart's action. Phr. *to feel the pulse*, to place the fingers on the pulse in the wrist as a means of testing a patient's state of health, degree of strength &c.; (also fig.) *to feel, have one's fingers on, the pulse of (the public* &c.), to judge, appraise, be in touch with the opinions, general feeling, of the public &c.; *to stir one's pulses*, excite the emotions, passions, enthusiasms &c.

pulse (II.), vb. intrans., fr. Lat. *pulsāre*. See prec. To beat, throb, pulsate.

pulse (III.), n. M.E. *puls*, fr. Lat. *puls, pultis*, 'a mess of meal pottage'; cp. Gk. *póltos*, 'porridge', & see **pollen** & **poultice**, & cp. **pulverize**. The edible seeds of leguminous plants, such as peas, beans, lentils &c.

pulseless, adj. [1. púlsles; 2. pálslis]. **pulse (I.)** & **-less**. Without pulse; without sign of life; inert, lifeless.

pulselessness, n. Prec. & **-ness**. State, quality, of being pulseless; lifelessness.

pulsimeter, n. [1. pulsímeter; 2. palsímitə]. **pulse (I.)** & **-meter**. An instrument for measuring the beat of the pulse; sphygmograph.

pulsometer, n. [1. pulsómeter; 2. palsɔ́mitə]. Variant of prec. A vacuum pump for raising water by the pulsatory action of steam.

pultaceous, adj. [1. pultáshus; 2. paltéiʃəs], fr. Lat. *pult-(is), puls*, 'pulse', see **pulse (III.)**, & **-aceous**. Like a mess of pulse or a poultice; pulpy, soft, semi-liquid.

pulverizable, adj. [1. púlverīzabl; 2. pálvəraizəbl]. **pulverize** & **-able**. Able to be pulverized or reduced to powder or dust.

pulverization, n. [1. pùlverīzáshun; 2. pàlvəraizéiʃən]. See next word & **-ation**. Act of pulverizing, state of being pulverized or reduced to powder; demolition, destruction.

pulverize, vb. trans. & intrans. [1. pulverīz; 2. pálvəraiz], fr. L. Lat. *pulverīzāre*, fr. Lat. *pulver-(em), pulvis*, 'dust'; fr. same base as Lat. *pollen*, see **pollen**, & *pultis*, 'porridge', see **pulse (III.)**; cp. also **powder**; for suff. see **-ize**. **1.** trans. **a** To reduce to fine powder, dust, or spray; **b** (fig.) to demolish (in argument &c.): *to pulverize an opponent, or his arguments*. **2.** intrans. To be reduced to dust.

pulverizer, n. [1. púlverīzer; 2. pálvəraizə]. Prec. & **-er**. One who, that which, pulverizes; **a** a machine for crushing and reducing soil, rubbish &c. to powder; **b** a spraying machine.

pulverulent, adj. [1. pulvérūlent; 2. palvérjulənt], fr. Lat. *pulverulentus*, fr. *pulver-(is), pulvis*, 'dust', q.v. under **pulverize**. Covered with powder or dust; tending to become powdery; crumbling.

pulvinate(d), adj. [1. púlvināt(ed); 2. pálvineit(id)], fr. Lat. *pulvīnātus*, fr. *pulvīnus*, 'cushion'; cogn. w. Lett. *spaliva*, 'animal hair; feathers'; further relations unknown. Cushion-shaped, like a cushion; **a** (archit., of a frieze or moulding) curved convexly; **b** (bot.) having a cushion-like swelling at the junction of a leaf with the stem; **c** (entom.) having a cushion-like pad or sucker on the foot.

pulwar, n. [1. pulwár; 2. palwā́]. Hind. *palwar*. Light native boat used on Indian rivers.

puma, n. [1. pū́ma; 2. pjū́mə]. S. Am. Peruvian native name. A large carnivorous feline mammal of S. America; also called the cougar, *Felis concolor*.

pumice, n. & vb. trans. [1. púmis; 2. pámis]. In O.E. *pumic-stān*, 'pumice-stone'; but M.E. *pomice, pumys*, whence present form, fr. O. Fr. *pomis*, fr. L. Lat. *pumic-(em)*, Lat. *pūmic-(em), pūmex*, cogn. w. *spūma*, 'foam', see **spume**. **1.** n. A light, porous volcanic stone, usually grey in colour, also called *pumice-stone*, used whole or powdered for polishing, also removing stains from the skin. **2.** vb. To polish with pumice-stone or powder.

pumiceous, adj. [1. pūmíseus; 2. pjūmíʃiəs]. Prec. & **-ous**. Consisting of, resembling, pumice-stone.

pummel, vb. trans. [1. púml; 2. páml]. Spelling variant of **pommel**, w. specialized meaning. To beat, strike, repeatedly with the fists.

pump (I.), n. [1. pump; 2. pamp]. M.E. *pumpe*, etymol. uncertain; cp. Du. *pomp*, Germ. *pumpe*, also *plumpen*, 'to pump'; Fr. *pompe* prob. borrowed fr. Gmc.; possibly imitative & variant of **plump**. **1. a** Any of various devices for raising water or other liquids by suction, also for transferring liquids, or for compressing air, gases &c.; the simplest form of pump is a tube containing a movable rod or piston, with a form of sucker, called a bucket, at the lower end; **b** applied to objects, such as the heart &c., which perform functions similar to those of a pump. **2.** (vulg. slang) A stupid, dull, pompous, and arid person, probably from the fact that he 'pumps up' his ideas and words with effort.

pump (II.), vb. trans. & intrans. See prec. **A.** trans. **1. a** To raise by means of a pump: *to pump water from a well*; **b** to use a pump on, extract water &c. from by means of a pump: *to pump a well dry*. **2. a** To drive, force, compress, by means of a pump: *to pump air, gas; to pump nourishment into a person*; **b** (fig.) to instil, inculcate, with effort: *to pump Latin grammar into a boy*. **3.** (fig.) To extract information from by questioning; to ply with questions directed to elicit particular kind of information: *I was very careful in what I said, as I knew he wanted to pump me*. **4.** To exhaust (a person) by violent effort which puts him out of breath: *I find running any distance pumps me rather badly*. **B.** intrans. **1. a** To perform the act of pumping, to use a pump; **b** to act like a pump: *the heart goes on pumping as long as life lasts.* **2.** To raise water or other liquid by means of a pump. **3.** To perform any movement resembling that of working a pump handle; to rise and fall by sudden movements or oscillations. **C.** Followed by adverbs &c. *Pump out,* trans., **a** to exhaust, empty, by pumping: *to pump out a well; to pump out water from a well;* **b** to render fatigued, to exhaust utterly: *to be fairly pumped out. Pump up,* trans., **a** to raise (water &c.) by pumping; **b** to fill with air, inflate, by pumping: *to pump up a bicycle tire.*

pump (**III.**), n. Etymol. doubtful; possibly fr. Fr. *pompe,* 'pomp', as in phrase *pied de pompe.* A light, low shoe, usually of patent leather with bow &c., ornamental buckle, and without fastening, worn by men with court or evening dress, esp. for dancing.

pumpernickel, n. [1. póompernikl; 2. púmpənikl]. Germ.; etymol. doubtful. A sweet, sticky malted bread of very dark colour.

pumpkin, n. [1. púmpkin; 2. pámpk*i*n]. Earlier *pompion, pumpion,* fr. Fr. *pompon,* fr. Lat. *pepōn-(em),* 'melon, pumpkin', fr. Gk. *pépōn,* adj., 'cooked by the sun, ripe', & n., 'melon', fr. same base as *péptein,* 'to cook', see **peptic**; also cp. **cook.** Edible fruit of any of several varieties of trailing plant, resembling a vegetable marrow &c.; in U.S.A. usually termed squash.

pun, n. & vb. intrans. [1. pun; 2. pan]. Etymol. unknown. **1.** n. A play upon words, a humorous use of words having the same or nearly the same sound with different meanings. **2.** vb. To make puns.

puna, n. [1. póona; 2. púnə]. Peruvian native name. **1. a** A dry, cold table-land in the Peruvian Andes; **b** a dry, cold wind blowing there. **2.** Mountain-sickness; difficulty of breathing experienced in dry altitudes.

Punch (**I.**), n. [1. punch; 2. pan(t)ʃ], abbr. of **Punchinello. 1.** (cap.) The hump-backed, long-nosed, grotesque hero of the puppet-play *Punch and Judy.* Phr. *pleased, proud, as Punch,* greatly delighted, very proud. **2.** The name of the humorous, satirical weekly paper, *Punch, or the London Charivari,* founded 1841.

punch (**II.**), n. Etymol. doubtful; earlier than prec. (in 'Pepys', Apr. 30th, 1669); possibly variant of **bunch.** A short, thick-set person or animal; esp. *Suffolk punch,* a short-backed, thick-set breed of draught horse.

punch (**III.**), n. Etymol. doubtful; possibly fr. Hind. *panch,* 'five', the orig. punch being composed of five ingredients. A drink, originally introduced from the East Indies, hot or cold, composed of spirits, water or milk, and lemons, spice, and sugar.

punch (**IV.**), n. & vb. trans. A shortened form of **puncheon** (**I.**); the vb. either fr. n. or a variant of **pounce** (**III.**), in either case ultimate origin is the same. **1.** n. **a** A tool usually in form of a short, stout piece of steel, one end of which is made flat for striking with a hammer, the other being shaped either to a blunt point, or hollow with a cutting edge; used for various purposes; e.g. for stamping round holes in leather, paper, metal plates &c.; for driving a rivet, broken screw &c., out of metal &c.; **b** small machine containing a punch, worked with a hand lever and a spring, for making holes in railway or tram tickets. **2.** vb. To perforate, make a hole in, stamp, by means of a punch: *to have one's ticket punched.*

punch (**V.**), vb. trans. & n. M.E. *punchen, punchyn*; etymol. doubtful, possibly a variant of **punish**; n., fr. vb. **1.** vb. To strike with a sharp, thrusting blow delivered with the fist: *to punch a person's head; punch a person about the body.* **2.** n. **a** A sharp, sudden, blow with the fist: *to get a punch on the nose;* **b** (colloq.) Vigour, pungency, effective meaning: *there was not much punch in his remarks.*

punch-bowl, n. **punch** (**III.**) & **bowl** (**I.**). **1.** Bowl in which punch is brewed and from which it is served. **2.** A deep, round hollow in the side of a hill or down.

puncheon (**I.**), n. [1. púnshun; 2. pánʃən]. M.E. *punchon,* fr. O. Nthn. Fr. *ponchon,* O. Fr. *poinçon,* 'awl, bodkin, stamp', fr. Lat. *punctiōn-(em),* 'a piercing, pricking'. See **puncture. 1.** A steel die, stamp, or punch used by workers in metals or by stone-cutters. **2.** (carpentry) A short, upright post or piece of timber used in framings; a stud post.

puncheon (**II.**), n. Etymol. doubtful; the word appears in O. Fr., as in Engl., in same forms as prec., & is prob. identical, the orig. meaning being the stamp marked on a cask w. a puncheon or punch. A large cask for wine, beer, or spirits, of varying capacity; the old beer puncheon contained 72 gallons, for wine 84 (wine) gallons; the puncheon for rum and spirits contains about 120 gallons.

Punchinello, n. [1. pùnchinélō; 2. pàntʃinélou]. A corrupt. of Ital. *Policinello, Pulcinello, Pulcinella*; the origin of the name is much disputed; the form in Engl. is due to connexion w. **punch** (**II.**), 'short, stout person'. **1.** The name of the buffoon in the Italian comedy of the early 17th cent., represented on the stage with white tunic and trousers, black mask and large beaky nose. **2.** A similar character in the puppet-shows of Italy; in the French adaptations represented as the dwarfish, hump-backed figure of *Punch and Judy,* brought to England towards the second half of the 17th cent.

punch-ladle, n. **punch** (**III.**) & **ladle.** Small silver or wooden ladle with long handle for filling glasses with punch.

punctate(d), adj. [1. pungktā́t(ed); 2. paŋktéit(*i*d)], fr. Lat. *punct-(um),* 'point', see **punctum,** & **-ate(d).** (bot. and zool.) Marked with dots or spots or small depressions.

punctation, n. [1. pungktā́shun; 2. paŋktéiʃən]. See prec. & **-ation. 1.** (bot. and zool.) A dot, spot, or depression. **2.** (legal hist.) A preliminary statement putting forward the points for negotiation in drawing up a contract, agreement &c.

punctilio, n. [1. pungktílio; 2. paŋktíliou], fr. Span. *puntillo* or Ital. *puntiglio,* dimin., fr. Lat. *punct-(um),* 'point', see **punctum. a** A nice point of behaviour, manners, or conduct; particularity, exactness in obeying the forms and rules of ceremony; **b** scrupulous attention to obligations or duties.

punctilious, adj. [1. pungktílius; 2. paŋktíliəs]. Prec. & **-ous.** Observant of punctilio, very nice, particular, and exact; **a** in obeying forms and ceremonies, points of deportment, manners &c.; **b** scrupulous in carrying out an obligation or duty.

punctiliously, adv. Prec. & **-ly.** In a punctilious manner; exactly, scrupulously.

punctiliousness, n. See prec. & **-ness.** State, quality, of being punctilious; exactness, scrupulousness.

punctual, adj. [1. púngkchooal; 2. páŋktʃuəl], fr. Fr. *ponctual*; fr. supposed Med. Lat. **punctuālis,* found in adv. *punctuāliter,* fr. Lat. *punctum,* 'point', see **punctum. 1.** (obs.) Punctilious. **2.** Exact to a point of time; observing regular or appointed times &c.; in good time, not late; prompt.

punctuality, n. [1. pùngkchooáliti; 2. pàŋktʃuǽliti]. Prec. & **-ity.** State, quality, of being punctual.

punctually, adv. [1. púngkchooali; 2. páŋktʃuəli]. See prec. & **-ly.** In a punctual manner; at the exact time appointed.

punctuate, vb. trans. [1. púngkchooāt; 2. páŋktʃueit], fr. Med. Lat. *punctuāt-(um),* P.P. type of *punctuāre,* 'to fix, define by points', fr. Lat. *punctum,* 'point'. See **punctum. 1.** To divide up written or printed words by stops, commas &c. **2.** To mark, distinguish (each one of a series) in some way; accompany with some distinguishing act &c.: *each word was punctuated by a blow; the audience punctuated the speech by outbursts of applause.*

punctuation, n. [1. pungkchooā́shun; 2. paŋktʃuéiʃən]. See prec. & **-ion. 1. a** Act of punctuating; **b** system according to which stops, commas &c., are distributed in a piece of writing. **2.** Insertion, use, of vowel points in writing a Semitic language; also called *pointing.*

punctuative, adj. [1. púngkchooātiv; 2. páŋktʃueitiv]. **punctuate** & **-ive.** Connected with, pertaining to, of the nature of, punctuation.

punctule, n. [1. púngktūl; 2. páŋktjūl], fr. L. Lat. *punctulum,* dimin. of *punctum,* 'point'. See **punctum.** A minute point, speck, dot, or spot.

punctum, n. [1. púngktum; 2. páŋktəm]. Lat., 'a point', fr. *punct-(um),* P.P. type of *pungere,* 'to prick'. See **pungent**; cp. **point.** (anat., bot., and zool.) A point, spot, depression, on the surface.

puncture, n. & vb. trans. & intrans. [1. púngkchur; 2. páŋktʃə], fr. Lat. *punctūra,* fr. *punctum,* see prec., & **-ure. 1.** n. Small prick, hole, perforation made by a sharp point: *a puncture in the skin, in the tire of a motor car* &c. **2.** vb. **a** trans. To pierce, prick, make a puncture in; **b** intrans., to be punctured, to receive a puncture: *the tire punctured a mile from home.*

pundit, n. [1. púndit; 2. pánd*i*t], fr. Hind. *pandit,* Scrt. *pandita,* 'learned man'. **1.** A Brahmin learned in Sanscrit and in Hindu law, religion, and philosophy. **2.** A very learned man; an authority on some subject; (often contemptuous) one whose alleged knowledge is of no practical value.

pungency, n. [1. púnjensi; 2. pándžəns*i*]. **pungent** & **-cy.** State, quality, of being pungent; sharpness, keenness.

pungent, adj. [1. púnjent; 2. pándžənt], fr. Lat. *pungent-(em),* Pres. Part. of *pungere,* 'to pierce, prick', P.P. *punctum*; nasalized form of base **peug̑-,* 'to stick, stab'; see **pugnacious** & **pugilist**; cp. *-pugn* in **impugn** &c. **1.** (in physical sense) Sharp, piercing; specially used of that which affects the senses of taste and smell; full-flavoured, high-seasoned; strong-scented, pervasively redolent. **2.** (in non-material sense, of the wit, mode of expression &c.) Biting, mordant; spicy, piquant, pointed.

pungently, adv. Prec. & **-ly.** In a pungent manner.

Punic, adj. [1. púnik; 2. pjúnik], fr. Lat. *Pūnicus,* earlier *Poenicus,* fr. *Pūnus, Poenus,* 'a Carthaginian', fr. Gk. *Phoînix,* 'a Phoenician'. See **phoenix.** (cap.) Belonging to, characteristic of, Carthage, or the Carthaginians; *Punic apple,* the pomegranate; *Punic faith,* the habitual treachery of the Carthaginians, from the Roman point of view.

punish, vb. trans. [1. púnish; 2. pániʃ]. M.E. *punischen,* fr. Fr. *puniss-(ant),* Pres. Part. of *punir,* see **-ish**; fr. Lat. *pūnīre,* 'to punish, exact, inflict, a penalty', for older *poenīre,* fr. *poena,* 'penalty, punishment', see **penalty** & cp. **pain. 1.** To inflict retribution upon, mete out retributive justice to, to chastise, either **a** for a private offence, such as breach of discipline or other objectionable conduct: *to punish a boy for impudence;* or **b** for a crime or offence against the law: *murder is punished by death.* **2.** To subject to severe treatment, to handle roughly, knock about, maul: *the champion was badly punished in the last round; the enemy was severely punished by our machine guns.* **3.** (pass. or reflex.) To suffer the natural results of one's folly, lack of judgement, misconduct &c.: *I have been sadly punished for my carelessness, rashness* &c. **4.** (facet.) To make a powerful onslaught on (food or drink), to pitch into: *we had punished the leg of mutton pretty well before we had done.*

punishability, n. [1. pùnishabíliti; 2. pàniʃəbíliti]. See next word & **-ity.** State, quality, of being punishable.

punishable, adj. [1. púnishabl; 2. pániʃəbl]. **punish** & **-able.** Liable, subject, to be punished by law: *a punishable offence.*

punishment, n. [1. púnishment; 2. pániʃmənt]. **punish & -ment. 1.** Act of punishing: *the punishment of wickedness and vice.* **2.** Penalty inflicted for offences or crimes. **3.** Unpleasant result, suffering of any kind, following naturally upon acts of folly or misconduct. **4.** Rough treatment, severe handling, mauling, e.g. received by a boxer or other combatant.

punitive, adj. [1. pū́nitiv; 2. pjū́nitiv], fr. Med. Lat. *pūnitīvus*; fr. Lat. *pūnīt-(um)*, P.P. type of *pūnīre*, **punish, & -ive. a** Of the nature of, inflicting, punishment: *punitive measures*; **b** designed, intended, to inflict punishment: *a punitive expedition.*

punitory, adj. [1. pū́nituri; 2. pjū́nitəri]. See prec. & **-ory.** Punitive.

punk (**I.**), n. [1. pungk; 2. paŋk]. Etymol. doubtful; prob. variant of **spunk**, 'tinder'. (dial. or U.S.A.) **a** Touchwood, decayed wood, dry fungus; hence **b** anything worthless.

punk (**II.**), n. Etymol. unknown. (obs. slang) Prostitute.

punka, punkah, n. [1. púngka; 2. páŋkə]. Hind. *pankhā*, 'fan', fr. *pankh*, 'feather, wing', fr. Scrt. *pákša-*, 'wing', q.v. under **pectoral.** Large kind of curtain, serving as a fan, worked by a cord and pulley, which swings to and fro; used in hot countries to keep rooms and verandahs cool.

punner, n. [1. púner; 2. pánə], fr. provinc. *pun*, origin unknown, 'to pound', & **-er.** A rammer for beating earth hard and firm.

punnet, n. [1. púnet; 2. pánit]. Etymol. unknown. A small, flat, round chip basket used especially for holding strawberries and other fruit when sold in small quantities.

punster, n. [1. púnster; 2. pánstə]. **pun & -ster.** One given to making puns.

punt (**I.**), n. & vb. trans. [1. punt; 2. pant]. In O.E., fr. Lat. *ponto, pontōnis*, 'a lighter, type of barge used by the Gauls'; fr. *pont-*, 'bridge'. See **pontoon** (**I.**). **1.** n. A long, rather narrow, flat-bottomed river boat with square ends, propelled by a pole. **2.** vb. **a** To propel a boat or punt by a pole pushed against the bottom of the river; **b** to carry in a punt; also **c** (absol.) to go, travel, in a punt.

punt (**II.**), vb. intrans. & n., fr. Fr. *ponter*, vb.; *ponte*, n.; etymol. doubtful; Ital. has *puntare*, Span. *punta*, all of games of cards; prob. fr. Lat. *punctum*, 'a point; an ace, pip, on the card'. See **punctum. 1.** vb. **a** At various card-games, originally of the obsolete game basset, to stake against the bank; **b** to bet, esp. heavily on a horse for a race. **2.** n. A stake or bet.

punt (**III.**), vb. trans. & n. Etymol. unknown. **1.** vb. To kick a football, after dropping it from the hands, before it has touched the ground. **2.** n. A volley kick at football. *Punt-about*, informal practice at kicking a football.

punter, n. [1. púnter; 2. pántə], fr. **punt**, in all three senses, & **-er.** One who punts in any sense of the word.

punty, n. [1. púnti; 2. pánti]. Etymol. doubtful; prob. fr. Fr. *pontil*, fr. Ital. *puntello*, dimin. of *punto*, 'point'. See **punctum.** A glass-blower's iron rod used for manipulating and twisting the molten material.

puny, adj. [1. pū́ni; 2. pjū́ni]. Variant of **puisne**; fr. Fr. *puis*, 'after', fr. Lat. *postea*, see **post-**, & *né*, 'born', fr. Lat. *nātus*, 'born', see **natal.** Weak, feeble, undersized.

pup (**I.**), n. & vb. intrans. [1. pup; 2. pap]. Abbr. of **puppy. 1.** n. **a** A puppy, young dog; also young seal or otter; Phrs. *in pup*, (of a bitch) to be pregnant; *to sell a man a pup*, (slang) to swindle him over a bargain; **b** a conceited, uppish boy or young man; a silly young ass. **2.** vb. (of bitch) To bring forth young.

pup (**II.**), n. Abbr. of **pupil.** (slang) Pupil.

pupa, n. [1. pū́pa; 2. pjū́pə]. Lat., 'girl, doll, puppet', fr. base **pu-* &c., 'to bring forth'. See **puberty & puerile,** & cp. **puppet & puppy.** (entom.) The form taken by insects, between the stages of the *larva* and *imago*; chrysalis.

pupal, adj. [1. pū́pl; 2. pjū́pl]. Prec. & **-al.** (entom.) Of, pertaining to, a pupa or chrysalis: *the pupal stage.*

pupate, vb. intrans. [1. pū́pāt; 2. pjū́peit]. **pupa & -ate.** (entom.) To become a pupa or chrysalis; to enter the pupal stage.

pupation, n. [1. pūpáshun; 2. pjūpéiʃən]. Prec. & **-ation.** (entom.) The stage between the larval form and that of the imago; the passing into the pupal stage.

pupil, n. [1. pū́pl, pū́pil; 2. pjū́pl, pjū́pil], fr. Fr. *pupille*, fr. Lat. *pūpillus*, 'pupil', *pūpilla*, 'pupil of the eye', dimin. of *pūpus*, 'boy', *pūpa*, 'girl'. See **pupa** & cp. **puerile & puberty. 1.** (Rom. and civil law) Young person under the age of puberty in charge of a guardian. **2. a** A person receiving instruction; **b** one being taught by a specified person: *my, his, pupil*, person being taught, or having been taught, by me, him &c. *Pupil teacher*, a young person finishing training as a state teacher, and being taught, but helping in the teaching of others in an elementary school. **3.** The expanding and contracting opening in the iris of the eye through which light rays reach the retina; (so-called originally, in Latin, from the little images or 'puppets' seen reflected in it).

pupilage, pupillage, n. [1. pū́pilij; 2. pjū́pilidž]. Prec. & **-age. 1.** State, condition, of being a pupil; of being under the age of puberty, or under the care of a tutor or teacher; state of being still under legal control; minority. **2.** (of races, and nations) Partially developed, half-civilized state.

pupilary, pupillary, adj. [1. pū́pilari; 2. pjū́piləri], fr. Lat. *pūpillāris.* See **pupil & -ary.** Being in the state, condition, of a pupil, esp. of a university student, being *in statu pupillari*, that is, being still subject to university discipline &c., lasting until the taking of a Master's degree.

pupiparous, adj. [1. pūpíparus; 2. pjūpípərəs], fr. **pupa** & *-parous*, fr. Lat. *parere*, 'to beget', & **-ous**; see **parent.** (entom.) Bringing forth the young in pupal or fully developed larval form, as do certain flies.

puppet, n. [1. púpet; 2. pápit]. M.E. *popet, popette*, fr. O. Fr. *poupette*, 'doll', dimin., fr. Lat. *puppa*, 'doll'. See **pupa. 1. a** A small jointed figure in human shape, moved in a lifelike manner by strings; a marionette; **b** figure, often life size, in form of a human being, the eyes, jaws, and head of which are made to move, so managed by ventriloquists as to appear to talk. **2.** A person with little will or character of his own, who becomes the mouthpiece and tool of another with a stronger personality. **3.** (mach.) A part of a lathe.

puppet show, n. Play acted by puppets or marionettes.

puppy, n. [1. púpi; 2. pápi], fr. Fr. *poupée*, 'doll, puppet'. See **pupa & puppet**; earliest sense in Engl. is 'lap dog'. **1.** The whelp or young of a dog. **2.** A conceited, ill-bred, impudent young man.

puppydom, n. [1. púpidum; 2. pápidəm]. Prec. & **-dom.** Condition, state, of a puppy.

puppyhood, n. [1. púpihood; 2. pápihud]. **puppy & -hood.** Condition, state, of a puppy; age of a puppy.

puppyish, adj. [1. púpiish; 2. pápiiʃ]. **puppy & -ish.** Like a puppy.

pur-, pref. O. Fr. *pur-, por-*, Mod. Fr. *pour*, fr. Lat. *por-*, variant of **pro-** (**I.**), as in *purchase, purvey* &c.; but note *purblind.*

Purana, n. [1. pooráhna; 2. purā́nə]. Scrt. *puraṇā*, 'belonging to former times, old', fr. *purā́*, 'formerly', cogn. w. Goth. *faúra*, O.E. *for*, Lat. *prae*, 'before', see **pre-.** One of a class of Sanscrit sacred, poetical books, dealing with the creation of the world, the history of the gods &c.

puranic, adj. [1. pooráhnik; 2. purā́nik]. Prec. & **-ic.** Of, pertaining to, the Puranas.

Purbeck, n. [1. pérbek; 2. pə́bɛk]. Also *Purbeck limestone*, limestone from Purbeck in Dorset; *Purbeck marble*, hard, fine, dark-grey or greenish variety of this.

purblind, adj. [1. pérblind; 2. pə́blaind]. Earlier also *pure-blind*, 'completely, purely blind'. **pure & blind** (**I.**). **1.** (archaic) Completely, entirely blind. **2.** Partly blind, short or near-sighted, dim-sighted. **3.** (fig.) Lacking spiritual, or imaginative, vision.

purblindly, adv. Prec. & **-ly.** In a purblind, near-sighted manner; short-sightedly (also fig.).

purblindness, n. See prec. & **-ness.** Condition of being purblind (lit. and fig.).

purchasable, adj. [1. pérchasabl; 2. pə́tʃəsəbl]. **purchase** (**I.**) & **-able. a** Capable of being purchased; to be bought; **b** (fig.) capable of being won over by bribery.

purchase (**I.**), vb. trans. [1. pérchas; 2. pə́tʃəs]. M.E. *purchasen, porchacen*, fr. O. Fr. *purchacer, porchacier*, later *pourchasser*, 'to pursue, acquire'. See **pur- & chase. 1. a** To acquire by payment of money, to buy: *to purchase a house, yacht* &c.; **b** (also fig.) to obtain as a result of effort, sacrifice, suffering: *his success was dearly purchased by years of toil.* **2.** (law) To acquire (land, houses &c.) by any other means than by inheritance. **3.** (naut. &c.) To apply a purchase or leverage to; to move, hoist, by mechanical power: *to purchase an anchor.*

purchase (**II.**), n. M.E., fr. O. Fr. *purchas, porchas.* See prec. **1. a** The acquisition of anything by the payment of money or its equivalent; the act or fact of buying: *to make a purchase; the purchase of food, coal* &c.; **b** specif. (law) the acquisition of land or houses by any means other than by inheritance. **2.** Something which has been purchased; property, belongings, just bought: *to leave the shop with one's purchases.* **3. a** Value, worth, esp. as reckoned in annual yield or return: *twenty years' purchase*, i.e. twenty times the annual rent; **b** (fig.) *the man's life is not worth a day's purchase*, he is not likely to live a day; he is in desperate danger. **4. a** Any mechanical means such as a lever, pulley, capstan &c. which will help to raise or move heavy weights; leverage: *to get a purchase on an anchor; to get a purchase with one's feet or hands when climbing* &c.; **b** (fig.) advantage, pull.

purchaser, n. [1. pérchaser; 2. pə́tʃəsə]. **purchase** (**I.**) & **-er. a** One who purchases, a buyer; **b** specif. (law) one who acquires property otherwise than by inheritance; usually contrasted with *vendor.*

purdah, n. [1. pérda; 2. pə́də], fr. Hind. & Pers. *pardah*, 'curtain'. **1.** The curtain or screen which guards Indian women from public view. **2.** The system of female seclusion as practised in India or elsewhere. **3.** A blue and white striped Indian cloth for curtains.

pure, adj. [1. pūr; 2. pjɔ̄, pjuə]. M.E. *pur, pure*, fr. Fr. *pur(e)*, fr. Lat. *pūrus*, wh. has practically all the meanings of the Engl. word; fr. base **pŭ-*, 'bright, shining; clear, pure', cp. Scrt. *pūtáś*, 'pure', *punā́ti*, 'purifier', cp. Gk. *pũr*, 'fire', see **pyro-**; also Lat. *putus*, 'clear, concise', whence *putāre*, 'to think', see **putative & purge. 1. a** Free from, not mixed with, anything which defiles; clean, uncontaminated: *pure air, water, food*; **b** unmixed with other substances: *a chemical, mineral, substance in a pure state*; **c** not crossed with another breed: *pure blood, descent* &c.; *a pure Hebrew, Englishman.* **2. a** Morally clean; chaste, in mind and thought; uncontaminated; **b** physically chaste, virgin. **3.** Free from low, sordid, interested motives; candid, disinterested, uncorrupted: *'blessed are the pure in heart'*; *pure motives*; *a pure, upright character.* **4.** Of a high, uncorrupted standard; not decadent or debased: *a pure style*; *a pure taste in literature* &c.; *pure English.* **5.** Regarded apart from practical application;

abstract: *pure science, mathematics*; as contrasted with *applied*. **6. a** Mere, sheer: *to do it out of pure necessity, kindness*; **b** complete, perfect: *all pure nonsense, pure imagination* &c.; *it was a pure accident*. **7. a** (of colour) Not mixed with any other colour or shade: *pure white, black, blue* &c.; **b** (of sound) not altered by the quality of another sound; in perfect tune.

pure-, pref., before adj., w. advbl. force; e.g. *pure-bred*, purely bred, of pure race, not of mixed blood: *a pure-bred Briton*, one of pure British blood, entirely free from alien admixture.

purée, n. [1. pūrā; 2. pjúərei]. Fr. **a** Any kind of soft material reduced to pulp, esp. a foodstuff so treated: *purée of potatoes*, mashed potatoes &c.; **b** specif., a soup made of a purée.

purely, adv. [1. pūrli; 2. pjúəli]. **pure & -ly. 1.** In a pure, clean, manner; in an unmixed condition: *to be purely English*. **2.** Chastely, virtuously: *to live purely*. **3.** Sheerly, merely: *purely accidental*.

pureness, n. [1. pūrnes; 2. pjúənis]. See prec. & **-ness**. State, quality, of being pure; purity (in various senses): **a** *the pureness of the water, gold* &c.; **b** *pureness of motives*; **c** *in pureness of living, life* &c.

purfle, vb. trans. & n. [1. pẽrfl; 2. pʌ́fl]. M.E. *purfilen*, fr. O. Fr. *porfiler, pourfiler*, fr. **pur-** & *filer*, 'to thread', fr. *fil*, 'thread', fr. Lat. *filum*, 'thread', see **file (III.)**; cp. **profile. 1.** vb. (archaic) **a** To decorate, ornament, embroider, with a flowered or patterned border; **b** (archit.) to decorate the parapet &c. of building with crockets; **c** (her.) to put a border of vair or fur round a shield. **2.** n. **a** An ornamented border, embroidered edge to a garment &c.; **b** crocketed parapet; **c** shield decorated with a border of vair or fur.

purfling, n. [1. pẽrfling; 2. pʌ́fliŋ]. Prec. & **-ing**. Ornamentation on a border or edge.

purgation, n. [1. pẽrgāshun; 2. pʌgéiʃən], fr. O. Fr. *purgacion*, fr. Lat. *purgātiōn-(em)*, fr. *purgāt-(um)*, P.P. type of *purgāre*. See **purge (I.) & -ion. 1.** Purification, cleansing, esp. of the soul, of worldly sin in purgatory. **2.** (legal hist.) The clearing of oneself from a charge, accusation, or suspicion, by oath or by ordeal, as by combat, cp. *compurgation*. **3.** Process of evacuating the bowels, by means of a purgative medicine.

purgative (I.), adj. [1. pẽrgativ; 2. pʌ́gətiv], fr. Fr. *purgatif, -ive*, fr. L. Lat. *purgātīvus*; see prec. & **-ive. 1.** Tending to purge, causing an evacuation of the bowels: *a purgative medicine*. **2.** Clearing of a charge; cleansing, purifying: *purgative evidence*; *purgative punishment*.

purgative (II.), n., fr. prec. A purgative medicine.

purgatorial, adj. [1. pẽrgatōrial; 2. pʌgətɔ́riəl]. See next word & **-al**. Pertaining to purgatory; expiatory: *purgatorial sufferings, masses, prayers* &c.

purgatory, n. [1. pẽrgaturi; 2. pʌ́gətəri], fr. L. Lat. *purgātōrius*, adj., 'cleansing, purging', Eccles. Lat. *purgātōrium*, n., 'purgatory'; see **purgation & -ory. 1.** (theol.) **a** State, condition, of those who have died in grace and faith, but still require a period of temporary punishment for the purging of such venial sins as do not merit eternal damnation; **b** the place where such are cleansed from their sins. **2.** Any place or state of temporary torment or torture, serving as an expiation or purification; often loosely, hell: *the purgatory of the trenches*; *during this period of mental distress he passed through a regular purgatory*.

purge (I.), vb. trans. [1. pẽrj; 2. pʌdž]. M.E. *purgen*, fr. O. Fr. *purger*, fr. Lat. *purgāre*, 'to cleanse, purify, purge'; for earlier *pūrigāre*, fr. *pūr-(us)*, 'pure, clean', see **pure**, & *-ig-*, a weakened form of base *ag-*, 'to do, act, cause', see **agent. 1.** To cleanse, purify, clean from impurities or contamination, physical or spiritual: '*purge me with hyssop and I shall be clean*'; *to purge the Augean stables*. **2.** (law) To clear oneself of an accusation, charge, or suspicion; to wipe out, expiate, an offence by suffering punishment: *the defendant has already purged his offence*, i.e. by undergoing punishment &c. **3.** To clear out, cause thorough evacuation of the bowels.

purge (II.), n., fr. prec. **1. a** A purgative medicine; **b** process of purging the bowels. **2.** (fig.) A method, means, of cleaning out, doing away with (abuses &c.); process of doing this.

purification, n. [1. pūrifikāshun; 2. pjɔrifikéiʃən], fr. Lat. *pūrificātiōn-(em)*, fr. *pūrificāt-(um)*, P.P. type of *pūrificāre*. See **purify & -ation**. Act of purifying in both physical and moral senses. Specif. (cap.) the ceremonial cleansing or purifying from various physical pollutions, according to the Jewish law: *the Purification of the B.V.M.*, a feast of the Church on Feb. 2nd.

purificator, n. [1. pūrifikāter; 2. pjɔrifikèitə]. Eccles. Lat. See **purification & -or.** (eccles.) A special cloth used after the Eucharist to cleanse the vessels.

purificatory, adj. [1. pūrifikāturi; 2. pjɔrifikéitəri]. See prec. & **-ory**. Tending, serving, to purify.

purify, vb. trans. [1. pūrifī; 2. pjɔ́rifai]. M.E. *purifien*, fr. Fr. *purifier*, fr. L. Lat. *pūrificāre*, 'to make pure, purify, cleanse'. See **pure & -fy**. To make pure (in all senses).

Purim, n. [1. pūrim, pōōrēm; 2. pjɔ́rim, pūrīm]. Heb., pl. 'lots'; origin doubtful; possibly fr. Assyrian *puru*, 'change of office by the casting of lots'. Jewish feast commemorating deliverance of the Jews from the plots of Haman. See Esther ix. 26.

purine, purin, n. [1. pūrin, -ēn; 2. pjɔ́rin, -īn]. Invented word, fr. Lat. words for **pure, uric, & -ine.** (chem.) The fundamental compound of the uric acid group of organic chemical substances.

purism, n. [1. pūrizm; 2. pjɔ́rizəm]. **pure & -ism**, cp. Fr. *purisme*. Strict adherence to correct usage or purity in language, style &c.

purist, n. [1. pūrist; 2. pjɔ́rist]. See prec. & **-ist**; cp. Fr. *puriste*. A strict adherent of, stickler for, correctness, or purity in language, style &c.

Puritan (I.), n. [1. pūritan; 2. pjɔ́rit(ə)n]. Formed fr. **purity & -an. 1. a** First applied, in Elizabeth's reign, to a member of the extreme Protestant party in the Church of England, who wished to abolish all forms and ceremonies as savouring of Popery and superstition; **b** a member of that party under Charles I., opposed to Episcopacy and Monarchy; contrasted with *Cavalier*, or *Royalist*. **2.** (gen. usage) **a** A person of unyielding Protestant views and principles in religion, and of rigid austerity in conduct and morals; **b** a rigid purist in non-religious matters.

puritan (II.), adj. See prec. Connected with, characteristic of, Puritans.

puritanic, adj. [1. pūritánik; 2. pjɔritǽnik]. Prec. & **-ic**. Rare, *puritanical* being generally used.

puritanical, adj. [1. pūritánikl; 2. pjɔritǽnikl]. Prec. & **-al**. (usually derogatory) Characteristic of, resembling, a Puritan or Puritanism; rigidly scrupulous and strict in religion and morals as understood by extreme Protestants.

puritanically, adv. Prec. & **-ly**. In a puritanical manner; in accordance with puritanical ideals and conduct.

Puritanism, n. [1. pūritanizm; 2. pjɔ́ritənizəm]. **Puritan (I.) & -ism**. The system of political and religious doctrines held by Puritans.

puritanize, vb intrans. & trans. [1. pūritanīz; 2. pjɔ́ritənaiz]. **puritan & -ize. 1.** intrans. (rare) To conform to Puritanism. **2.** trans. To convert to Puritanism.

purity, n. [1. pūriti; 2. pjɔ́riti]. M.E. *purte, purete*, fr. O. Fr. *purté, pureté*, fr. Lat. *pūritāt-(em)*. See **pure & -ity**. State, quality, of being pure (in all senses); **1.** (in physical sense) *Purity of air, water, gold* &c. **2.** (in moral senses) *Purity of life, motives* &c. **3.** Freedom from admixture: *purity of a language, tone, colour* &c.

purl (I.), n. & vb. trans. & intrans. [1. pẽrl; 2. pʌl]. Etymol. doubtful. **1.** n. **a** (obs.) A twisted cord or lace of gold or silver thread; **b** a loop forming an edging to lace, ribbon &c., also *pearl*; **c** (knitting) also *pearl*, an inverted or turned stitch producing a rib in the article knitted, contrasted with *plain*. **2.** vb. **a** To attach loops as a border to lace or ribbon &c.; **b** to knit with inverted stitches.

purl (II.), vb. intrans. & n. Etymol. doubtful. **1.** vb. Of a brook or stream, to flow with a murmuring, babbling sound; to babble. **2.** n. This sound.

purl (III.), n. Etymol. uncertain; possibly a spelling of **pearl (I.)**, in sense of 'bubble, bead', cp. Fr. *perlé*, of sugar boiled twice. An old drink of hot beer or ale flavoured with wormwood; later hot ale mixed with gin.

purl (IV.), vb. trans. & intrans. & n. Etymol. unknown. The word is rare among good speakers; prob. a provincialism. **1.** vb. (of horse) To throw, to upset, spill; (also obs.) to be thrown, to take a toss. **2.** n. A throw from a horse, spill; a toss.

purler, n. [1. pẽrler; 2. pʌ́lə]. Prec. & **-er**. Hardly in ordinary use; provinc. or vulg. slang. A spill, throw, from a horse, a cropper: *to come an awful purler*.

purlieu, n. [1. pẽrlū; 2. pʌ́ljū]. Anglo-Fr. law term, *puralee, puraley*, influenced by Fr. *lieu*, 'place', fr. O. Fr. *puraler, pouraler*, 'to go through, perambulate', in order to mark a boundary. See **perambulate & alley (I.)**. **1.** (legal hist.) An outlying part of a forest, disafforested and marked off from the forest after perambulation. **2.** The outlying parts of a district, outskirts; (often used in a derogatory sense) slums: *prowl about the purlieus of the town*. Phr. *the dusty purlieus of the law*, places frequented by lawyers; legal business.

purlin, n. [1. pẽrlin; 2. pʌ́lin]. Etymol. unknown. (archit.) A longitudinal beam of a roof, resting on the principal rafters, or principals, and carrying the common rafters.

purling, adj. & vbl. n. [1. pẽrling; 2. pʌ́liŋ], fr. **purl (II.)**. **1.** adj. (Pres. Part.) Murmuring, babbling, as a flowing stream: *the purling brook*. **2.** vbl. n. The sound of a babbling stream.

purloin, vb. trans. [1. pẽrlóin; 2. pʌlɔ́in]. M.E. *purlognen*, fr. O. Fr. *purloignier, porloigner*, 'to prolong, detain', fr. Lat. *prōlongāre*, 'to prolong', see **prolong**. To steal, filch.

purple (I.), n. [1. pẽrpl; 2. pʌ́pl]. O.E. *purpur*, direct fr. Lat.; M.E. *purpre*, later *purpel*, cp. *marble*, fr. O. Fr. *porpre, purpre*, later *pourpre*, fr. Lat. *purpura*, 'the purple-fish, the dye obtained from it, crimson', fr. Gk. *porphúrā*, 'purple-fish, dye', see **porphyry. 1.** A colour partaking of the qualities of blue and crimson, formerly obtained from the murex fish. **2.** This colour considered as characteristically belonging to emperors and kings and cardinals, robes of it being worn by them, and as symbolizing imperial, royal, or princely rank. Phrs. *raised to the purple*, (i.) made emperor; (ii.) made a cardinal; *born in the purple*, originally, (i.) born heir to the Holy Roman Empire, cp. **porphyrogenite**; later, (ii.) born in royal, or in very exalted, rank of life.

purple (II.), adj. See prec. Of the colour of purple; **a** used often of a reddish-blue tinge: *purple cheeks*; *a purple nose*; Phr. *to turn purple with rage*, to become furious; **b** (poet.) deep, bright red: *purple wine*; *purple blood*.

purple (III.), vb. trans. & intrans., fr. prec. **1.** trans. To make, dye, purple. **2.** intrans. To become purple.

purple emperor, n. A large butterfly with very rapid, powerful flight, and purple wings streaked with pale yellow; still occasionally found in some parts of England.

purple-fish, n. The murex. See **purpura**.

purple-heart, n. Also *purple-wood*, the hard, ornamental, purple-coloured wood of a Brazilian tree, *Copaifera*, used for inlay and other furniture work.

purple-wort, n. The marsh cinquefoil, a perennial rosaceous herb, with purple-brown stem and flowers.

purplish, adj. [1. pěrplish; 2. pʌ́pliʃ]. **purple (II.)** & **-ish.** Somewhat purple; inclined to a purple colour.

purply, adj. [1. pěrpli; 2. pʌ́pli]. **purple (II.)** & **-ly.** Purplish.

purport (I.), vb. trans. [1. pěrpurt; 2. pʌ́pət], more rarely [1. pěrpórt; 2. pʌpɔ́t], fr. A.-Fr. *purporter*, O. Fr. *porporter, pourporter*, 'to extend, to intend; to import, contain', fr. **pur-** & Lat. *portāre*, 'to carry', see **port (IV.).** **a** To convey, or be intended to convey, a certain meaning; to mean to be, or appear to mean or to be; to seem to signify: *a tract which purports to have been composed by Wycliffe; a cheque purporting to bear my signature*; **b** to have as a purport, to import, imply, involve, indicate: *his speech may purport his early resignation*, or, *that he will soon resign*.

purport (II.), n. [1. pěrpurt; 2. pʌ́pət]. See prec. **1.** That which appears to be the meaning, significance; import, bearing: *the main purport of his speech; the purport of a document, message* &c. **2.** Purpose, object: *what was the purport of his visit?*

purpose (I.), n. [1. pěrpus; 2. pʌ́pəs]. M.E. *purpos*, fr. O. Fr. *porpos, purpos, pourpos*, 'design, plan, proposal', cp. Fr. *propos*, ultimately fr. Lat. *prōposit-(um)*, 'that which is propounded or placed before one', see **propose**. Something intended or proposed to be done; an intention, determination; something set before one as an object, aim, design: *the purpose of his visit; to stick to, gain, one's purpose; to pursue a purpose steadily; to be weak of purpose; what is your purpose in doing this?; we cannot always read the purposes of God in His acts.* Phrs. *on purpose*, with a purpose, intentionally, designedly, not by accident, purposely; *to little or no purpose*, uselessly, fruitlessly, vainly; *to some purpose*, with considerable result; *of set purpose*, with intention, designedly.

purpose (II.), vb. intrans. & trans., fr. O. Fr. *purposer, pourposer*. See prec. **1.** intrans. To have as a purpose, to intend, propose, to do something; **2.** trans. To have as a purpose; to intend, propose, design: *to purpose a visit to America; I purpose coming next week; I do not purpose that he shall have his own way.*

purposed, adj. [1. pěrpust; 2. pʌ́pəst]. **purpose (I.)** & **-ed.** Resolved, determined, having purpose: (usually preceded by an adv.) *fully purposed* &c.

purposeful, adj. [1. pěrpusfool; 2. pʌ́pəsful]. **purpose (I.)** & **-ful.** **1.** Full of purpose; determined, resolute: *a purposeful character.* **2.** Full of meaning, pregnant, important: *a purposeful narrative, account* &c.

purposefulness, n. See prec. & **-ness.** State, quality, of being purposeful; resoluteness, determination.

purposeless, adj. [1. pěrpusles; 2. pʌ́pəslis]. **purpose (I.)** & **-less.** **a** (of persons) Lacking, devoid of, purpose and resolution of character; having no aims; **b** (of actions) done without a specific object in view; aimless, meaningless, futile.

purposelessly, adv. Prec. & **-ly.** Without a purpose or definite object in view; aimlessly.

purposelessness, n. See prec. & **-ness.** State, quality, of being purposeless.

purposely, adv. [1. pěrpusli; 2. pʌ́pəsli]. **purpose** & **-ly.** With purpose, on purpose, with design; intentionally; not accidentally: *he came all the way purposely to see me; they seem to run down people purposely.*

purposive, adj. [1. pěrpusiv; 2. pʌ́pəsiv]. See **purpose (I.)** & **-ive.** **1.** Done with a purpose; intended to achieve an end or object: *purposive actions; purposive adaptations* &c. **2.** Indicating purpose: *the purposive character of nature* &c.

purpresture, n. [1. pěrpréschur; 2. pʌpréstʃə]. Also *pourpresture*, Law Fr., fr. O. Fr. *porpresure, pourprissure*, fr. *purprise, pourprise*, P.P. of *pourprendre*, 'to occupy, seize, to the detriment of another'. See **pur-, prize (III.)**, & **-ure.** (law) Appropriation of another's land; encroachment on public or Crown lands, forests &c.; appropriation of public rights in property to private use.

purpura, n. [1. pěrpūra; 2. pʌ́pjurə]. Lat., 'purple-fish, dye'. See **purple.** **1.** (pathol.) **a** Eruption of purple or livid patches upon the skin or mucous membranes; **b** swine-fever. **2.** (cap.) Genus of molluscs, including the murex or purple-fish.

purpure, n. [1. pěrpūr; 2. pʌ́pjɔ]. O. Fr. See **purple.** (her.) The colour purple, one of the tinctures; expressed in engravings by thin diagonal lines drawn from the sinister to the dexter side of the shield.

purpuric, adj. [1. pěrpúrik; 2. pʌpjɔ́rik]. **purpura** & **-ic.** **1.** Of, pertaining to, purpura: *purpuric eruptions, patches* &c.; *purpuric symptoms.* **2.** (chem.) *Purpuric acid*, a nitrogenous acid, akin to uric acid, found only in purple-red compounds.

purpurin, n. [1. pěrpūrin; 2. pʌ́pjurin]. **purpura** & **-in.** (chem.) A red or orange-coloured dyestuff obtained from madder root.

purr (I.), vb. intrans. [1. pěr; 2. pʌ]. Imitative. **a** To make the characteristic low, continuous, rumbling, vibratory sound in the throat, whereby cats and other feline animals express satisfaction; **b** (of persons) *to purr with pleasure, content, satisfaction* &c., to express these feelings in a manner which suggests the purring of a cat.

purr (II.), n., fr. prec. The sound made by a cat &c. when purring.

purree, n. [1. púrē; 2. pári]. Hind. *pōōri.* A yellow pigment, used in India and China for colouring walls of houses.

purse (I.), n. [1. pěrs; 2. pʌs]. O.E. & M.E. *purs*; fr. Low Lat. *bursa*, 'pouch, leather purse'. See **bourse** & **bursar.** **1.** A small bag, pouch, or case, usually of leather, in which money is carried. **2.** Money, wealth, funds: *the power of the purse; who holds the purse rules the house; a long, fat, heavy, purse*, wealth; *slender, lean, light, purse*, poverty; *the public purse*, the treasury, public revenue and expenditure; so *privy purse*, the sum allotted in the Civil List for the private expenses of the sovereign. **3.** A sum of money subscribed as a prize for a contest or as a gift or reward: *to make up a purse*, collect, subscribe, a sum of money. **4.** Anything resembling a purse, a bag, pouch: *purses under the eyes.*

purse (II.), vb. trans., fr. prec. **1.** (archaic) To put into a purse, to pouch. **2.** To pucker, wrinkle up (the lips), like the mouth of a purse drawn together by a string: *to purse up one's mouth.*

purse-bearer, n. The bearer of a purse, esp. the official who carries the Great Seal in the train of the Lord Chancellor on ceremonial occasions.

purse-crab, n. A large tropical fruit-eating land crab of the islands of the Indian Ocean, with pouch or purse-like abdomen.

purseful, n. [1. pěrsfool; 2. pʌ́sful]. **purse (I.)** & **-ful.** That which a purse can hold; contents of a purse: *a purseful of money*, a good sum of money.

purse-net, n. A net for catching fish or rabbits, with a mouth that can be closed like a purse.

purse-proud, adj. Arrogant, valuing oneself, giving oneself airs, on the strength of one's wealth.

purser, n. [1. pěrser; 2. pʌ́sə], fr. **purse (I.)** & **-er**; cp. **bursar.** A ship's officer, esp. of a passenger vessel, who keeps accounts and acts as cashier &c.; formerly used also of a paymaster in the navy.

pursership, n. [1. pěrsership; 2. pʌ́səʃip]. Prec. & **-ship.** Office, position, of a purser.

purse-seine, n. Purse-net.

purse-strings, n. pl. The strings or cords closing a purse; only (fig.) in Phr. *to tighten, loosen, the purse-strings*, to reduce, increase, expenditure, to be miserly or generous of money; *to hold the purse-strings*, to have control of expenditure.

pursiness, n. [1. pěrsines; 2. pʌ́sinis]. **pursy (I.)** & **-ness.** State, quality, of being pursy, or stout and short of breath.

purslane, n. [1. pěrslin; 2. pʌ́slin], fr. O. Fr. *porcelaine*, fr. Low Lat. *porcilaca*, for Lat. *portulāca*, the name of the plant. (bot.) A plant belonging to the genus *Portulaca*, esp. *P. oleracea*, a fleshy annual herb, with leaves used for salads &c.; *P. grandiflora* is a cultivated garden species.

pursuable, adj. [1. persúabl; 2. pəsjúəbl]. **pursue** & **-able.** (Scots law) Capable of being prosecuted.

pursuance, n. [1. persúans; 2. pəsjúəns]. See next word & **-ce.** Act of pursuing, following out, carrying out; performance, prosecution, esp. in Phrs. *in pursuance of one's duties, one's intentions; in pursuance of your orders* &c.

pursuant, adj. & adv. [1. persúant; 2. pəsjúənt], fr. O. Fr. *porsuiant*, Pres. Part. See **pursue** & cp. **pursuivant.** **1.** adj. (with *to*) Following, according, conforming, conformable: *pursuant to the rules.* **2.** adv. Conformably, pursuantly.

pursuantly, adv. Prec. & **-ly.** Conformably, pursuant, accordingly.

pursue, vb. trans. & intrans. [1. persú; 2. pəsjú]. M.E. *pursuen*, O. Fr. *porsuir, porsivre*, see **pro- (I.)** & **sue**; fr. L. Lat. *prosequere* for Lat. *prōsequi*, 'to follow', see **prosecute.** **A.** trans. **1.** To follow after with the object of overtaking and capturing; to chase, track out: *to pursue a runaway.* Phr. *to pursue a subject* (of conversation), continue to discuss it further, more fully. **2.** (of non-material things) To follow, attend closely and persistently upon; to accompany continually, to dog: *ill-luck and ill-health pursued him till his death.* **3.** To adopt certain measures with a view of attaining an end or object; to prosecute: *to pursue pleasure; to pursue the proper legal remedies.* **4. a** To proceed with, follow out: *to pursue a line of inquiry, a foolish policy*; **b** to conduct; to follow, practise, carry on or out, perform duties of: *to pursue one's business, occupation, profession* &c. **B.** intrans. **1.** To follow in pursuit: *why flee, when no one pursues?* **2.** (rare) To proceed, go on, continue (in speaking): *and so, he pursued, we must* &c.

pursuer, n. [1. persúer; 2. pəsjúə]. Prec. & **-er.** **1.** One who pursues another: *to outdistance one's pursuers.* **2.** (Scots law) Prosecutor, plaintiff.

pursuit, n. [1. persút; 2. pəsjút]. Earlier *poursuit, pursuyt*, fr. O. Fr. *poursecute, pursute*; P.P. fem. of *poursuivre*, used as n. See **pursue.** **1.** Act of pursuing; endeavour to catch; **a** chase, hunt: *pursuit of the enemy; in hot pursuit; in pursuit of game*; **b** act of searching after, of trying to obtain: *the pursuit of health, wealth, happiness, pleasure* &c. **2.** Act of following up or out; course of action undertaken to secure a purpose; a quest: *in pursuit of one's aims.* **3. a** That upon which one is engaged; employment, occupation: *daily pursuits; literary pursuits*; **b** act of performing, of carrying on or out; performance: *the pursuit of one's business, profession.*

pursuivant, n. [1. pěrswivant; 2. pʌ́swivənt]. Fr. *poursuivant*; O. Fr. *porsivant, poursivant*; Pres. Part. of *poursuivre*, 'to follow'. See **pursue** & **pursuant.** **1.** (lit.) A follower, attendant; specif., a member of the third or lowest rank of officers of the College of

Heralds, originally an attendant of a herald, as *Rouge Croix Pursuivant at arms.* **2.** (poet.) A follower, attendant.

pursy (**I.**), adj. [1. pĕrsi; 2. pȧ́si]. M.E. *purcyfe, purseyf,* fr. M. Fr. *poursif* for O. Fr. *polsif,* fr. O. Fr. *polser,* 'to heave, push'; also 'to breathe with difficulty', fr. Lat. *pulsāre,* 'to beat, throb, pant'. See **pulsate** & **pulse** (**I.**) & cp. **push.** Short-winded and stout; corpulent and puffy: *a pursy little man.*

pursy (**II.**), adj. **purse** (**II.**) & **-y.** Pursed, puckered: *with pursy lips.*

purtenance, n. [1. pĕrtenans; 2. pȧ́tinəns]. M.E. *purtenaunce*; variant spelling of **pertinence.** See also **appurtenance.** (obs.) That which pertains to something; an appurtenance; esp. the heart, liver, and lungs of a slaughtered beast: '*roast with fire; his head with his legs, and with the purtenance thereof*' (Exodus xii. 9).

purulence, purulency, n. [1. pū́rūlens(i); 2. pjúərjuləns(i)]. **purulent** & **-ce, -cy.** State, quality, of being purulent; formation of pus or purulent matter.

purulent, adj. [1. pū́rūlent; 2. pjúərjulənt], fr. Lat. *pūrulentus,* fr. *pūr-,* stem of *pūs,* see **pus,** & suff. *-lentus,* 'full of', cp. *turbulent, violent.* Full of, discharging, pus; suppurating, septic.

purvey, vb. trans. & intrans. [1. pervā́; 2. pəvéi]. M.E. *purveien, porveien,* fr. A.-Fr. *purveier,* fr. O. Fr. *porvoir,* 'to provide', see **provide.** **1.** trans. To provide, supply, furnish (articles) to or for, esp. provisions: *to purvey meat, fish &c. to a household* &c. **2.** intrans. To act as purveyor: *to purvey for the army, royal household* &c.

purveyance, n. [1. pervā́ans; 2. pəvéiəns]. M.E., fr. A.-Fr. *porveance,* 'foresight, provision'. Prec. & **-ance**; cp. **providence.** **1. a** Act of purveying or providing provisions or supplies; **b** thing purveyed; supplies, provisions: *purveyance for the army.* **2.** (hist.) The forced supply of provisions &c. for the king and his retinue on a journey through his realms, at a valuation fixed by the Crown's appraisers and purveyors, abolished 1660.

purveyor, n. [1. pervā́or; 2. pəvéiə]. M.E. & A.-Fr. *purveour.* See **purvey** & **-or.** **1.** One who purveys or supplies provisions &c., esp. for a large number, or for a royal or other large household: *purveyor to H.R.H.* **2.** (hist.) One of the royal officials who exacted purveyance for the Crown.

purview, n. [1. pĕrvū; 2. pȧ́vjū], fr. A.-Fr. *purveu,* Mod. Fr. *pourvu,* 'provided', P.P. of *pourvoir.* See **purvey** & **provide.** **1.** A proviso, enactment, esp. used of that part of a statute following the preamble, commencing with the words, *it is provided that, be it enacted that,* in old law French *purveu est*; the scope, limit, intention, of a statute: *the matter is not within the purview of the statute.* **2.** Range, scope, extent, limit, sphere: *outside the purview of practical politics*; *within the purview of one's studies.*

pus, n. [1. pus; 2. pas]. Lat. *pūs,* 'matter produced by inflammation'; cogn. w. Gk. *púon,* 'matter'; Scrt. *pūya-,* 'matter, pus', *pūyati,* 'it stinks'; fr. base **pu-,* 'to stink'. See also **putrid** & **foul.** Yellowish-white matter produced by suppuration.

Puseyism, n. [1. pū́zi-izm; 2. pjū́zi-izəm], fr. name of one of the leaders of the movement, Dr. E. Bouverie Pusey (1800–1882), & **-ism.** Name given formerly to the Oxford Tractarian Movement; generally contemptuous.

Puseyite, n. [1. pū́ziīt; 2. pjū́ziait]. See prec. & **-ite.** (obsolesc.) Name given to a Tractarian in the earlier days of the movement.

push (**I.**), vb. trans. & intrans. [1. poosh; 2. puʃ]. M.E. *pussen,* fr. Fr. *pousser,* earlier *poulser,* fr. Lat. *pulsāre,* 'to beat, strike', freq. formed fr. *puls-,* P.P. type of *pellere,* 'to drive, beat' &c. See **pulse** (**I.**) & **pulsate.** (general sense) To cause to move along, roll, or slide, away from oneself, or from point at which force is exerted, by a steady, gradual thrusting or pressing against; to propel forward, shove; reverse of *pull,* and contrasted with *lift, carry, throw.* The word is used in innumerable ways to express varying actions, all of which are covered by the general definition. It is usually unnecessary to attempt detailed definition as examples are generally sufficient to make the precise sense clear in each case. **A.** trans. **1.** *I would rather push a wheelbarrow in front of me than pull it after me*; *the crowd pushed me off the pavement*; *to push a dish to the centre of the table*; *to push a ramrod through a gun-barrel, a cork into a bottle*; *to push a door to*; *to push a boat into the water, away from shore* &c.; *to push one's way through a crowd.* Phr. *to push one's way,* (fig.) to make one's way in life, to get on. **2.** (fig., or special uses) *To push aside all obstacles and difficulties*; *the city is gradually pushing its arms out into the country*; *to push out a new wing of a building*; *a plant pushes out new shoots in spring*; *a snail pushes out its horns*; *to push a person,* bring him forward, urge his claims to advancement, exert influence on his behalf; *to push one's business,* make zealous efforts to advance it; *to push one's claims*; *to push a person to the limits of his patience,* try his patience too hard; *to push a horse to the limits of his endurance,* put too much strain on, overdrive him, overtax his strength; *to be pushed for time, money* &c., to be hard pressed, harassed &c. **B.** intrans. To carry out the action of pushing: *you push while I pull.* **C.** Special uses when followed by prepositions or adverbs. *Push by,* intrans., to pass by pushing or thrusting. *Push in,* intrans., **a** (of boat &c.) to move in to shore; **b** (of person) to thrust oneself in. *Push off,* intrans., (of boat &c.) to move off from shore; (colloq., slang) to go away, clear off: *it's time for us to push off now.* *Push out,* intrans., to move out to sea. *Push through,* **1.** trans., to get something done, to complete: *to push the matter, business &c., through*; **2.** intrans., **a** to make a passage by pushing: *the crowd is so thick that I shan't be able to push through*; **b** to emerge, make an appearance: *the crocus buds are just pushing through.*

push (**II.**), n., fr. prec. **1.** Act of pushing or thrusting; steady pressure exerted against anything; a thrust, shove: *give him a good push.* Phrs. *to make a push,* to do something with an energetic effort; *to get the push,* (slang) to be dismissed; *at a push,* in an emergency, with an effort; *to be in the push,* (vulg. slang) in the swim. **2.** Self-assertive energy: *push generally succeeds in business*; *a man of push and go.*

pushable, adj. [1. pooshabl; 2. púʃəbl]. **push** (**I.**) & **-able.** Capable of being pushed.

push-ball, n. A game played by 11 players a side with a ball resembling an enormous football, which is pushed, not kicked, towards and through the goal-posts.

push-bicycle, n. An ordinary pedal bicycle, as distinguished from a *motor bicycle.*

push-cart, n. **a** A small barrow or cart, pushed by hand; **b** a small cart for a baby to sit in, pushed by hand; a go-cart.

pusher, n. [1. póosher; 2. púʃə]. **push** (**I.**) & **-er.** **1.** One who pushes; esp. one who pushes himself forward in hope of rising in the world; a self-assertive person. **2.** Anything used for pushing; specif., child's word for small piece of bread used for pushing food on to a fork, at an age before a knife is allowed; also, device for this purpose.

pushful, adj. [1. pooshfool; 2. púʃfəl]. **push** (**II.**) & **-ful.** Full of push, enterprising, pushing.

push-halfpenny, n. Shove-halfpenny.

pushing, adj. [1. pooshing; 2. púʃiŋ]. Pres. Part. of **push** (**I.**). **a** Self-assertive; active, go-ahead, energetic; esp. in one's own interests, advancement &c.; **b** tending to thrust oneself where one is not wanted; presuming, presumptuous.

pushingly, adv. Prec. & **-ly.** In a pushing manner; self-assertively.

push-pin, n. An old child's game played with pins.

Pushtu, Pushtoo, n. [1. pùshtōō; 2. pàʃtū́]. Pers. *Pashto.* The language of Afghanistan.

pusillanimity, n. [1. pūsilanímiti; 2. pjùsilənímiti], fr. L. Lat. *pusillanimitāt-(em)*; used in Vulgate. See **pusillanimous** & **-ity.** Quality of being pusillanimous; faint-heartedness, timidity, cowardice.

pusillanimous, adj. [1. pùsilánimus; 2. pjùsilǽniməs], fr. L., post-class., Lat. *pusillanimis,* 'faint-hearted', as in Vulgate; fr. Lat. *pusillus,* 'very small, insignificant', dimin. fr. *pullus,* 'young animal' &c., wh. is for **put-slos*; cp. *put-* in Scrt. *putraś,* 'son', cp. also **puerile**; for second element see **animus** & **-ous.** Feeble, weak of spirit or soul; faint-hearted; timid, cowardly.

pusillanimously, adv. Prec. & **-ly.** In a pusillanimous manner.

puss, n. [1. poos; 2. pus]. Prob. imitative, fr. the spitting of a cat; cp. Du. *poes,* Norw. *puse,* & similar words in non-European languages; Skeat quotes Tamil *pusie,* Afghan *pusha,* as names for the cat. **1.** A cat; esp. used to call one; also name for a hare. **2.** (playfully affectionate) A merry, mischievous, young girl.

puss-in-the-corner, n. A children's nursery game.

puss-moth, n. A large, light-coloured moth, with thick body, *Cerura vinula*; the larvae feed chiefly on poplar leaves.

pussy, n. [1. póosi; 2. púsi]. **puss** & **-y.** **a** A child's name, a pet name, for a cat: *pussy-cat*; **b** catkin of the willow or hazel.

pussyfoot, vb. intrans. & n. [1. póosifoot; 2. púsifut]. (U.S.A. slang) **1.** vb. To go quietly and cautiously in forming and carrying out a plan or campaign; specif., of the Prohibition Campaign in America, in its early stages when conducted by 'Pussyfoot' Johnson. **2.** n. One who 'pussyfoots', esp. a plausible supporter of prohibition.

pustular, adj. [1. pústūlar; 2. pástjulə]. **pustule** & **-ar.** Of the nature of, characterized by, covered with, pustules.

pustulate (**I.**), vb. trans. & intrans. [1. pústūlāt; 2. pástjuleit], fr. L. Lat. *pustulāt-(um),* P.P. of *pustulāre,* 'to form pustules'. See **pustule.** To form into pustules or blisters.

pustulate (**II.**), adj. See prec. **a** Covered with pustules; **b** (bot.) having warts or excrescences resembling pustules.

pustulation, n. [1. pùstulā́shun; 2. pàstjuléiʃən]. **pustulate** (**I.**) & **-ion.** The formation of pustules.

pustule, n. [1. pústūl; 2. pástjūl], fr. Lat. *pustula,* 'blister, pimple', also *pūsula,* fr. *pūs,* 'matter'. See **pus.** **1.** An inflamed vesicle or pimple on the skin containing pus as in small-pox &c. **2.** (bot.) A small excrescence or wart on a leaf &c. due to a parasite.

pustulous, adj. [1. pústūlus; 2. pástjuləs]. Prec. & **-ous.** Pustular, pustulate.

put (**I.**), vb. trans. & intrans. [1. poot; 2. put]. M.E. *putten.* The etymol. is very doubtful; there may be a connexion w. O.E. *potian,* 'to throw', & *putung,* 'instigation'. The modern senses may be fr. Scand. sources, cp. Dan. *putte,* 'to place', & Swed. dial. *putta,* 'to push'. One of the most general words in the language, *put* is widely used to express various actions of placing, laying, setting, directing &c., in both a physical and non-physical sense. The various uses are all derived from the following basal meanings: (1) (physical action) to cast, thrust; to set in a given and specified place; to bring into a specified position; to cause to move from one place to another; to bring to a certain physical condition; to use for a particular purpose; (2) (non-physical action) to bring into, cause to enter, a certain set of conditions, circumstances, a given situation, or predicament; to impose conditions or obligations upon; to cause, set, to perform a certain task, or series of actions; to direct the mind, attention, thoughts, in a given direction; to propound, give exposition of, lay before &c. The precise sense is usually determined by the following preposition, adverb, or adverbial phrase &c. Special idioms are here usually included under the various nouns, adverbs &c., or in section **C** below. **A.** trans. (implying physical action) **1.** To place, lay, set, in a specified place: *to put a thing in its right place, a dish on the table, a saddle on a horse*; *to put some water in a jug, some money in one's purse, some coal on the fire*; *to put a man in jail*; *to put a child to bed.* Phr. *to put a play on the stage*, produce, exhibit it, get it acted. **2. a** To move something in a given way, direction; to place something near or against, move it towards, a certain object; bring into contact: *to put one's hand on a man's shoulder, put one's lips to a person's ear, put one's head on the pillow, put one's eye to a telescope*; *to put a glass to one's lips, a handkerchief to one's nose*; *to put the hands of a clock forward*; *to put a stick &c. across a person*; Phr. *to put it across* (*him*), censure severely; **b** special use: *to put a cow to a bull*, to bring them together for breeding purposes. **3.** To cast, throw, specifically, by propelling with the arm shot out from the shoulder: *to put the weight.* **4.** To reduce to a specific order or the reverse; arrange in particular way; bring to a certain state or condition: *to put a room, one's dress &c., in order*; *to put names in alphabetical order*; *to put a machine out of gear*; *to put a watch wrong.* Phrs. *to put an end to*, cause to cease; *put a stop to*, to stop, make further continuance of impossible. **5.** To steer, direct, course of; turn in particular direction: *to put the rudder to port*; *to put a ship about*; *to put a horse's head towards home.* Phr. *to put a horse at a fence*, ride him at with a view to making him jump it. **6.** To bring into, cause to enter, a specific bodily or physical condition: *to put to death*, kill; *put to sleep*; *put to torture*; *put to flight.* Phr. (fig.) *put to the blush*, cause to blush for shame, to shame; *put out of countenance*, disconcert. **7.** To furnish, supply, with: *to put a new handle to a knife*; *put a ferule to a walking-stick.* **8.** To write, express in written form: *to put something on paper*; *to put one's name to a document.* Phr. (fig.) *to put one's name to*, to support, endorse. (expressing action other than bodily and physical) **9.** To bring into a particular set of circumstances, into certain predicament; cause to enter a certain state or mode of existence: *to put things right*; *put everything wrong*; *put one's affairs in order*; *to put a person in an unpleasant position, in a fix.* Phrs. *to put to the test*, to try, test; *hard put to it*, in an arduous, difficult position; embarrassed. **10.** To cause, set, to carry out a particular series of actions; set to perform a certain group of duties: *to put a boy out in service, to a trade, as apprentice to a joiner*; *to put a youth to business* &c. **11.** To direct the intelligence, thoughts &c., in a particular channel: *to put one's brain, mind,* (*on*) *to a problem.* **12.** To bring into a particular state of mind or emotion: *to put a man into a rage, into a fright*; *to put a man into a state of anxiety.* Phrs. *to put a man wise* (*about, on*), (slang) to inform him; *put a person in the wrong*, make him feel and appear wrong. **13. a** To state, expound, give an exposition of, lay before: *to put a case*; *to put a matter before a tribunal*; Phr. (archaic) *put case* (*that*), assuming, supposing; **b** to state, express, in a particular way: *the case was cleverly put*; *to put one's ideas into words*; *the compliment was clumsily put*; *I don't know how to put it*; *it is gracefully put by Virgil*; *let me put it in another way.* **14.** To submit, propose, ask: *to put a question*; *to put a resolution.* Phr. *I put it to you that*, I suggest that. **15. a** To estimate, calculate: *I put his income at £5000 a year*; **b** to assign, attribute (relative position to) as result of an intellectual or moral judgement; to rate: *to put Keats above Byron as a poet*; *I put Bagehot very high among sane critics.* **B.** intrans. Most intrans. usages are associated with particular prepositions or adverbs, and are included under **C** below. (rare) To carry out the action of putting a weight &c. **C.** Uses in combination with adverbs and prepositions. *Put about*, **1. a** trans., to change course or direction of movement: *to put the ship about*, to direct her on another tack, to change her course; **b** intrans., to move, go back or in another direction: *at this point we, the ship, put about*; **2.** to spread abroad, publish: *to put about a rumour*; **3.** (provinc. and chiefly in P.P.) to worry, disturb, put out: *to be much put about.* *Put aside*, to move away, remove, set aside, to put away, by; **a** of physical things: *to put aside the book one is reading*; **b** to discard: *to put aside one's old clothes*; **c** of non-physical action: *to put aside one's difficulties, one's work, another's question.* *Put away*, **A.** trans., **1.** (of physical action and objects) **a** to move, take away, remove, set aside or in its proper place: *to put away the tea things*; *to put away one's clothes* &c.; **b** to lay by for future use, to save: *a nice sum of money put away*; **c** (Bib., archaic) to divorce: *to put away a wife*; **2.** (colloq.) **a** to eat, drink; consume: *to put away a pound of steak, gallon of beer*; **b** to place in prison or asylum, to get rid of: *he's safely put away*; **3.** of non-physical actions: *to put away childish things*; **B.** intrans., (of ships) to move away: *to put away from harbour, to sea.* *Put back*, **A.** trans., **1.** to replace, restore, to former place or position: *put back the book where you found it*; **2.** to move backwards: (of physical action) *to put back* (*the hands of*) *the clock*, (fig.) to retard, check, to try to go back to former condition, to be reactionary; **B.** intrans., to return: *to put back to shore*; *put back to where we started from.* *Put by*, trans., to set, lay, aside for use at a future time, to save: *to put money by.* *Put down*, trans., **1.** to place, lay, set, down: *to put down a knife*; *to put down a cellar of wine*; Phr. (fig.) *to put one's foot down*, to be determined, fixed, in one's purpose; **2.** to suppress, quell by force &c.; to stop: *to put down a rebellion, riot* &c.; *to put down gambling*; **3.** to repress, silence: *to put a heckler down*; *the interrupter refused to be put down*; **4.** to degrade, deprive of power: *to put down the mighty*; **5.** to diminish, lower, cut down: *to put prices down*; *to put down one's expenditure*; **6. a** to write, put on paper: *everything he said was at once put down*; specif. **b** to enter one's name as a subscriber for so much: *put me down for £5*; **c** to enter on one's account, book (a sum owing): *ask the butcher to put the chops down to me*; **7.** to reckon, estimate, as: *I put him down as an imbecile*; **8.** to assign, attribute, the cause of: *to put the accident down to negligence*; *put the mistake down to me.* *Put forth*, **A.** trans., **1.** to extrude, put out, extend, push out: *plants put forth their leaves, sun its rays*; **2.** to make public, publish: *to put forth a new book*; **3.** to exert, show: *to put forth all one's energies, powers of argument, persuasion* &c.; **B.** intrans. (poet.), to go, venture, out, embark: *to put forth to sea, upon the sea.* *Put forward*, trans., **1.** to propose, suggest: *to put forward a new plan, theory*; **2.** to advance, to hasten progress of: *to put the business forward.* *Put in*, **A.** trans., **1.** to place in, to install: *the government was put in to do certain things which they have not done*; *to put the bailiffs in*; *to put in an execution*; *put a man in possession* (of a debtor's house &c.), for distraint; **2.** to interpose with, to get in: *to put in a blow, a word*; **3.** to insert, introduce as an addition or alternative: *to put in a word for a friend*; **4.** to enter, set forward, present, submit: *to put in a claim*; *to put in a document as evidence*; Phr. *to put in an appearance*, **a** to appear, show oneself; **b** (law) to enter an appearance, so as not to allow the case to go by default; *to put* (person or statement) *in evidence*, to submit as a witness or as evidence; **5.** to place, set in, cause to be in, certain condition &c.: *to put in force*, to enforce; *put in motion*, set going; *put in practice*, to practise; Phr. *to put in hand*, to begin, start on; *to put in a hole*, place in difficulties, in awkward position; *to put in mind*, to recall, remind: *to put in possession of*, to provide, furnish with; **6.** to do, perform: *to put in an hour's extra work*; (colloq.) to pass, spend; **B** intrans., **1.** *put in for*, to enter for, be a candidate or aspirant: *to put in for an appointment, job* &c.; **2.** to enter, visit, make a halt at: *when we reach the harbour we'll put in there for a bit*; *here's a good inn, let's put in here for luncheon.* *Put into*, **A.** trans., (non-material) instil, suggest: *put ideas into a person's head*; **B.** intrans., (of ship &c.) to enter, move towards: *to put into port.* *Put off*, **A.** trans., **1.** to lay aside, take off, divest oneself of, discard; **a** (of clothes &c.) *to put off one's hat, overcoat, winter things, armour* &c.; **b** (of non-material things) *to put off doubts, fears*; *put off the old man, mortality* &c; **2.** to pass off, dispose of, palm off: *to put off bad money on the public*; **3.** to postpone, delay: **a** (of things, actions) *to put off an appointment*; *put off the production of a play*; **b** (of persons) from an engagement &c.: *we are sorry to put you off today*; **4.** to evade, get rid of, with excuses &c.: *I will not be put off any longer, you must pay up*; *put-off*, n., (colloq.) a postponement, evasion; **5.** to hinder, baffle, balk, discommode: *to put a person off his game, stroke*; **6.** to dissuade, discourage; repel, revolt: *to be put off doing something*; *to be put off one's meals*; *I'm sorry to say it, but her face quite puts me off*; **B.** intrans., to start away, set out: *to put off on a long journey.* *Put on*, **1.** to place on or over any part of the body, to clothe oneself with: *to put on one's shirt, hat, boots* &c; **2.** to assume, affect, pretend to: *to put on airs and graces*, to act pretentiously or affectedly: *his modesty is all put on*; **3.** to bring into action or play, to set to, to exert: *to put more men on the work*; *to put another man on to bowl*; *to put on more trains*; **4.** to place on the stage: *to put on a new play*; **5.** to add to, increase: *to put on flesh, weight*; *to put £10 on the price*; *to put on the pace*, to hasten, hurry; Phr. (colloq.) *to put it on*, to charge exorbitantly; **6.** to score (as in games): *to put on 100 runs for the first wicket*; *to put on two goals before time*; **7.** to stake, bet: *to put a fiver on a horse*; *have you put on the winner?*; **8.** to put, move, forward, to advance: *to put on* (*the hands of*) *the clock*; **9.** to introduce to: *to put a person on the track of anything*; *I can put you on to a good speculation, a certain winner in the next race.* *Put out*, **A.** trans., **1.** to turn, drive, out, eject: *to put out of doors*; *to put disorderly people out of a meeting*; **2.** to hold, stretch, out, to extend: *to put out one's hand, foot* &c.; *to put one's head out of the window*; **3.** to put forth, shoot out: *a snail puts out its horns*; *plants put out their leaves*; **4.** to exert, show, manifest: *to put out one's strength, energies*; **5.** to dislocate: *to put out one's knee-joint, shoulder*; **6.** to extinguish, quench: *to put out the lights, a fire*; also *to put out the eyes of*; **7.** to place out or away from its ordinary, natural, or proper place: *to put out a horse to grass*; *put a baby out to nurse*; *to put work out*, to be done at worker's house, not in a factory or workshop; **8.** to turn out, finish, work: *to put out so much work, goods* &c., cp. *output*; **9.** to lend, place at interest: *so much money put out at 6 per cent*; **10. a** to confuse, disconcert; to worry: *noise always puts one out*; **b** to make angry: *she was evidently quite put out with me, and spoke crossly*; **B.** intrans., (of ship &c.) to set sail, to move out, away from: *to put out to sea.* *Put over*, intrans. (of ships &c.), to move, go across: *to put over to the other side of a river.* *Put through*, **1.** to carry out, perform thoroughly: *to put a job through*; **2.** to make to go or pass through; to push, thrust, through; **a** (of physical action &c.) *to put one's fist through a pane of glass*; **b** (of non-physical action) to subject to, cause to undergo: *to put a witness through a stiff cross-examination*; Phr. *to put through his paces,* (orig., of a horse) to test, examine the skill, ability, endurance &c.; **3.** (of telephone) to put into communication with: *put me through to X. Put together,* (of physical and mental action) to form a unity out of separate elements, to construct: *to put together a good dinner, a short account of one's travels, a novel, a dictionary* &c.; Phrs. *to put a large number of runs together*; *put two and two together,* to draw a conclusion, to base a judgement upon facts. *Put up,* **A.** trans., **1.** to hold up, lift up, raise: *to put up the sails, a flag*; *to put up one's hands,* **a** as token of surrender or as sign of being unarmed &c.; **b** to double one's fists and assume attitude of defence in readiness to fight; Phrs. *to put up the back of*; *put a person's back up,* to offend, anger, provoke; **2.** to offer, present: *to put up a prayer to God*; **3.** to select and propose as candidate for election, to parliament, to a club &c.: *X will be put up for B. at the next election*; *I will put you up for the A.B.C. club, if you like*; **4.** to rouse, start (game): *to put up a covey of partridges*; **5.** to offer for sale: *to put up to auction, for sale*; **6.** to raise: *to put up the price*; **7.** to prepare, mix: *to put up a prescription*; **8.** to pack: **a** (food &c. for preservation &c.) *to put up meat in barrels*; **b** (of things for carriage &c.) *to put up goods in a parcel* &c.; **9.** to replace, place in its proper position, to put away: *put up your sword,* sheathe it; Phr. *to put up the shutters,* **a** to close a business, shop &c. for the day; **b** (fig.) to retire from, close down, one's business &c.; **10.** to lodge, provide with food, lodging, or shelter: *to put up a horse at a livery stable*; *put your car up in our garage*; (of persons) *to put a man up for the week-end*; **11.** (colloq.) to arrange, plan, usually surreptitiously; to concoct: *to put up a swindle*; *a regular put-up job*; **B.** intrans., to lodge, shelter at: *to put up for the night at an inn. Put upon,* (usually in pass.) to impose on; to oppress: *I will not be put upon. Put up to,* **1.** to incite, instigate: *to put a person up to (do) some mischief, to (commit) a crime* &c.; **2.** to inform, give hints about: *to put one up to the ways of a place, to the latest tips. Put up with,* to endure, tolerate, stand: *to put up with the best one can get, with hardships, insults.*

put (II.), n., fr. prec. **a** Act of putting a weight &c.; **b** the distance a weight &c. is put.

putamen, n. [1. pūtámen; 2. pjutéimen]. Lat. *putāmen,* 'that which is trimmed or pruned off; clippings; shell, peel, bark', fr. *putāre,* 'to cut, trim, prune; to clean; adjust, fix; to reckon, count; to consider, think over', fr. base **pŭ,* 'to cleanse', cp. **pure**; cp. also second syll. in **compute, impute,** &c., & **putative.** **1.** (bot.) The hard endocarp or stone of a soft-fleshed fruit, such as peach, plum, apricot &c. **2.** (zool.) The membranous lining of the egg of a bird; also the outer grey layer of the lenticular nucleus of the brain.

put and call, n. [1. póot an(d) káwl; 2. pút ən(d) kɔ̄l]. (commerc.) An agreement between two parties whereby one has the option to 'put' or deliver and the other the option to 'call' or demand certain stocks, shares &c. at a certain price at or within a certain time.

putative, adj. [1. pûtativ; 2. pjûtətiv], fr. L. Lat. *putātīvus,* fr. *putāt-(um),* P.P. of *putāre,* 'to ponder, consider, think, reflect upon'; the same word as that meaning 'to cut' &c. See **putamen.** The differentiation of meaning is rather strange; it is suggested that the word came through the speech of gardeners, and meant first 'to cut, prune, dress, clean, vines &c.', then 'to adjust, set in order' &c., then 'to arrange one's thoughts, to consider' &c. See **compute, dispute, impute.** Generally thought or presumed; considered, reputed: esp. *putative father, marriage.*

putatively, adv. Prec. & **-ly.** Reputedly, presumably; by reputation or general assumption.

puteal, n. [1. pûteal; 2. pjûtiəl]. Lat., fr. *puteus,* 'well'; lit. 'something cut, dug, out', fr. same base, meaning 'to cut, cleanse' &c., as in **putamen,** & **-al.** (archit.) A stone parapet or curb round mouth of a well.

putlog, also **putlock**, n. [1. pútlog, -lok; 2. pátlɔg, -lɔk]. Etymol. uncertain; the first syll. may be a Western form of O.E. *pytt,* 'well, hole' &c., see **pit** (I.), & the second simply **log** (I.), the whole word meaning orig. 'a log stuck in a pit or hole'. A short piece of timber on which scaffolding boards are laid, one end resting in a hole left, or made, in the wall of the building: *a putlog-hole.*

putrefacient, adj. & n. [1. pùtrefáshient; 2. pjùtrifǽʃiənt], fr. Lat. *putrefacient-(em),* Pres. Part. of *putrefacere,* 'to make rotten'. See **putrid** & **fact.** **a** adj. Putrefactive; **b** n., a putrefactive substance.

putrefaction, n. [1. pùtrefákshun; 2. pjùtrifǽkʃən], fr. Lat. *putrefactiōn-(em),* formed fr. *putrefact-(um),* P.P. of *putrefacere.* See prec. & **-ion.** **a** Process of putrefying or becoming putrid; foul-smelling decomposition of organic matter; **b** something which has putrefied; rotten substance, putrescence.

putrefactive, adj. [1. pùtrefáktiv; 2. pjùtrifǽktiv]. See prec. & **-ive.** Causing putrefaction; putrefying: *putrefactive bacteria, agents* &c.

putrefy, vb. trans. & intrans. [1. pûtrefī; 2. pjûtrifai], fr. Fr. *putréfier,* fr. Lat. *putrefacere,* 'to make rotten', *putrēre,* 'to be rotten', see prec., & **putrid** & **-fy.** **1.** trans. To cause to decompose or to become putrid; to make rotten, cause putrefaction in. **2.** intrans. To become putrid; to decompose.

putrescence, n. [1. pūtrésens; 2. pjūtrésəns]. **putrescent** & **-ce.** **a** State of being putrescent; **b** putrescent matter.

putrescent, adj. [1. pūtrésent; 2. pjūtrésənt], fr. Lat. *putrescent-(em),* Pres. Part. of *putrescere,* 'to become putrid', inceptive of *putrēre,* 'to be putrid'. See **putrid.** Becoming putrid; in process of putrefying, stinking.

putrid, adj. [1. pûtrid; 2. pjûtrid], fr. Lat. *putridus,* 'rotten, stinking', fr. *putr-(is),* or *puter,* 'rotten', fr. base **pū,* 'to stink', see **pus,** & cp. **foul** & **filth.** **1.** Putrefied, putrefying; rotten, decayed and stinking. *Putrid fever,* old name of typhus fever or gaol fever; *putrid sore throat,* malignant, gangrenous sore throat. **2.** (colloq., slang) Applied to anything which excites dislike or disapproval; extremely unpleasant; bad: *a perfectly putrid book, party, dinner, lecture* &c.; *putrid conduct, manners* &c.

putridity, n. [1. pūtríditi; 2. pjūtríditi]. Prec. & **-ity,** cp. Fr. *putridité.* **a** A putrid condition; **b** putrid matter.

putridly, adv. [1. pûtridli; 2. pjûtridli]. **putrid** & **-ly.** In a putrid manner.

putridness, n. [1. pûtridnes; 2. pjûtridnis]. See prec. & **-ness.** Putridity.

putt, vb. intrans. & trans. & n. [1. put; 2. pat]. Variant of **put** (I.). (golf) **1.** vb. **a** intrans. To get the ball into a hole by striking with a special club or putter, and causing it to roll across the green; **b** trans., *to putt the ball.* **2.** n. Act of putting; stroke made in putting.

puttee, puttie, n. [1. púti; 2. páti]. Hind. *paṭṭi,* 'bandage', Scrt. *paṭṭa,* 'strip of cloth'. A narrow strip of cloth wound spirally round the leg from the ankle to below the knee; worn instead of a gaiter.

putter, n. [1. púter; 2. pátə]. **putt** & **-er.** (golf) A club with short stiff shaft and flat-faced metal or wooden head used for putting.

putti, n. pl. [1. póoti; 2. púti]. Ital. pl. of *putto,* 'small boy', fr. Lat. *pūtus,* 'boy'; cp. **puberty** & **puerile.** Small figures of naked Cupids, used as a decorative feature in pictures or sculpture; also called *Amorini,* 'loves'

puttier, n. [1. pútier; 2. pátiə], fr. **putty** & **-er.** One who applies putty; a glazier.

putting (I.), vbl. n. [1. póoting; 2. pútiŋ]. **put** (I.) & **-ing.** Act of one who puts; specif., *putting the weight* or *shot,* an athletic sport in which a round weight or shot, 16 lb., is 'put', not thrown, with a straight push from the shoulder, the putter standing within a 7 ft. square or circle.

putting (II.), vbl. n. [1. púting; 2. pátiŋ]. **putt** & **-ing.** (golf) Act of striking the ball into the hole; *putting green,* the piece of smooth, level turf surrounding a hole.

putty, n. & vb. trans. [1. púti; 2. páti], fr. Fr. *potée,* orig. of polisher's putty powder, see below; the lit. meaning is 'potful', of calcined tin or lead. See **pot.** **1.** n. **a** Jewellers' polishing powder made of tin and lead; **b** builders' cement mixed with lime and water; **c** soft plastic material made of linseed oil and whiting, used for fixing glass. **2.** vb. To apply putty to; to fix with putty.

puzzle (I.), vb. trans. & intrans. [1. púzl; 2. pázl]. Etymol. unknown; according to the O.E.D. the vb. is recorded earlier than the n.; if the n. was formed fr. the vb., the suggested derivation fr. obs. M.E. *opposaile, apposayle,* 'a question opposed, or put for solution', cannot be accepted. **A.** trans. **1.** To perplex, embarrass, confuse, bewilder; to baffle, nonplus: *the question puzzles me*; *to puzzle one's brains*; *to be puzzled what to do.* **2.** *Puzzle out,* **a** to ponder over, think out, try to solve; **b** to reach a solution by dint of reflection, cogitation &c. **B.** intrans. Chiefly *puzzle over,* to cogitate, think deeply about; to be puzzled by.

puzzle (II.), n. See prec. **1.** Something, the reason for, explanation of, which one does not know; something one cannot understand; **a** difficult question, conundrum, problem &c.: *the perpetual puzzle of existence*; *it is a puzzle to me how he managed to do it.* **2.** Specif., a verbal or mechanical problem or contrivance which requires some mental dexterity and ingenuity to solve: *a cross-word puzzle*; *jig-saw puzzle* &c.; *puzzle-ring* &c. **3.** State of being puzzled; perplexity: *to be in a puzzle about anything.*

puzzledom, n. [1. púzldum; 2. pázldəm]. Prec. & **-dom.** **1.** A state of bewilderment or of being puzzled. **2.** The world of puzzles generally.

puzzle-headed, adj. Confused in mind and ideas; muddle-headed.

puzzle-headedness, n. Prec. & **-ness.** State, quality, of being puzzle-headed.

puzzlement, n. [1. púzlment; 2. pázlmənt]. **puzzle** & **-ment.** Perplexity, bewilderment.

puzzle-peg, n. Piece of wood fastened to a dog's lower jaw to keep its head off the ground.

puzzler, n. [1. púzler; 2. pázlə]. **puzzle** (I.) & **-er.** **a** Person who puzzles; **b** a puzzling, baffling question.

puzzolana, n. See **pozzolana.**

pyaemia, n. [1. pīḗmia; 2. paiímiə]. Neo-Lat., fr. Gk. *púon,* 'pus', see **pus, putrid** &c., & *haíma,* 'blood', see **haema-, haemo-.** A form of blood-poisoning due to the introduction of pus-forming micro-organisms into the blood, resulting in the formation of abscesses in various parts of the body.

pyaemic, adj. [1. pīḗmik; 2. paiímik]. Prec. & **-ic.** Of, pertaining to, pyaemia; characteristic of pyaemia.

pycno-, pref. Combining form fr. Gk. *puknós,* 'close, thick, dense, crowded together', connected w. *púx,* adv., 'with the clenched fist', cp. **pugnacious.**

pycnometer, n. [1. piknómeter; 2. piknɔ́mitə]. **pycno-** & **-meter.** An instrument for measuring the density of liquids or solids.

pycnostyle, n. [1. píknostīl; 2. píknəstail]. Gk. *puknóstūlos,* fr. **pycno-** & *stûlos,* 'pillar'. See **style** (III.). Building with the columns arranged close together, with intervals of one and a half diameter.

pyelitis, n. [1. pīelítis; 2. pàiiláitis]. Neo-Lat., fr. Gk. *púelos*, 'bath, basin', for **plúelos*, fr. base **pleu-*, 'float' &c., cp. Gk. *pléō*, 'I sail, float' &c. See this base under **pluvial (I.)** & **float**, & **-itis**. (pathol.) Inflammation of the inner part, or pelvis, of the kidney.

pygal, adj. [1. pígal; 2. páigəl], fr. Gk. *pūgḗ*, 'rump'; cp. Scrt. *puñjaš*, 'ball, mass'; & **-al**. (zool.) Pertaining to the region of the buttocks, or to the lower part of the back.

pygmaean, adj. [1. pigmḗan; 2. pigmíən], fr. Lat. *pygmae-(us)* & **-an**. See next word. Dwarfish, pygmy.

pygmy, also, more rarely, **pigmy**, n. & adj. [1. pígmi; 2. pígmi]. fr. Lat. *pygmaeus*, n. & adj., fr. Gk. *pugmaîos*, 'of the height of a *pugmḗ*, the length of the arm from the elbow to the knuckles of the clenched fist; the fist'; cogn. w. *púx*, 'with clenched fist', q.v. under **pugilism** & **pugnacious**. **A.** n. **1.** (Gk. mythol. and hist.) The name given to the supposed fabulous race of dwarfs of the Nile region who fought with the cranes. **2.** A dwarf negrillo race of Central, Equatorial Africa. **3.** A dwarf; any diminutive person, animal, or thing; an insignificant, trifling person or thing. **B.** adj. **a** Dwarfish; very small, insignificant: *what are the pygmy efforts of man, when opposed to some great cataclysm of nature?*; **b** often used in zool., of very small varieties of animals: *pygmy elephant, hippopotamus* &c.

pyjamas, also **pajamas**, n. pl. [1. pī-, pijáhmaz, pajáhmaz; 2. pai-, pidžámaz, pədžáməz]. Hind. *pājāma*, 'drawers', fr. *pāe*, 'leg', *pā*, 'foot', & *jāma*, 'garment', also Pers. *paijāmah*. **1.** The loose silk or cotton trousers or drawers tied by a cord round the waist worn by Moslem men and women. **2.** A sleeping suit of jacket and trousers, first introduced into England by English residents in India.

pylon, n. [1. pílon; 2. páilɔn], fr. Gk. *pulṓn*, 'gateway to a temple or building', cp. also *púlē*, 'gate, one wing of a double gate or door'; etymol. unknown. Cp. **propylaeum.** **1.** The gateway to an ancient Egyptian temple, usually formed of a monolithic lintel supported by jambs and flanked by two truncated pyramids or towers. **2. a** A tower, of pylon form, used to mark the course in an aerodrome; **b** also of various struts or bracings in the structure of an aeroplane or airship; **c** structure, of various forms, used to carry electric cables across country.

pyloric, adj. [1. pīlórik; 2. pailɔ́rik]. See next word & **-ic**. Of, pertaining to, the pylorus.

pylorus, n. [1. pīlórus; 2. pailɔ́rəs]. L. Lat., fr. Gk. *pulōrós*, 'a gate-keeper, porter, the pylorus', fr. *púlē*, 'gate', see **pylon**, & *oûros*, 'watcher, guard', cogn. w. *ourá*, 'hinder part, tail; rearguard', see **uro- (II.)**. (anat.) The opening of the stomach into the intestine.

pyo-, pref. Combining form fr. Gk. *púon*, 'pus', see **pus**.

pyogenic, adj. [1. pīōjénik; 2. pàioudžénik]. Prec. & **-genic**. Producing, forming, pus: *pyogenic bacteria*.

pyoid, adj. [1. píoid; 2. páiɔid]. See prec. & **-oid**. Of the nature of pus, resembling pus.

pyorrhoea, n. [1. pīoréa; 2. pàiouríə]. Neo-Lat., fr. **pyo-** & Gk. *rhoía*, 'a flowing', connected w. *rhein*, 'to flow'. See under **rheo-** & cp. **stream**. (pathol.) A discharge of pus; specif., *P. alveolaris*, a disease of the part of the gums surrounding the necks of the teeth, accompanied by a discharge of pus.

pyracanth, n. [1. pírakanth; 2. páirəkænþ], fr. Gk. *purácantha*, fr. *pûr*, 'fire', see **pyre**, & *ákantha*, 'thorny tree, thorn', see **acanthus**. A S. European evergreen thorny shrub with white flowers and scarlet berries, the fire-thorn, *Crataegus pyracantha*.

pyramid, n. [1. píramid; 2. pírəmid], fr. Lat. *pȳramid-(em)*, *pȳramis*, fr. Gk. *pūramid(os)*, *pūramis*; etymol. unknown, prob. fr. an ancient Egyptian word. **1.** (archit.) A structure of stone with square base and four triangular faces or sides sloping to an apex; the typical pyramids are those of ancient Egypt, built as royal tombs. **2.** (geom.) A polyhedron, the base of which is a figure of three or more sides and the other faces triangles. **3.** Anything shaped like a pyramid; specif., fruit tree grown approximately in this shape; *inverted pyramid*, anything so shaped resting upon its apex; (fig.) an elaborate argument, and far-reaching conclusions, built up on a slender basis of fact. **4.** *Pyramids*, game played on a billiard table with fifteen red and one white ball, so called from arrangement of the balls at the outset of the game, usually played by two persons, the object being to pocket the greatest number of red balls.

pyramidal, adj. [1. pirámidal; 2. pirǽmidəl]. Prec. & **-al**. Pertaining to, in the shape of, a pyramid.

pyramidally, adv. Prec. & **-ly**. In form of a pyramid.

pyramidwise, adv. [1. píramidwīz; 2. pírəmidwaiz]. Pyramidally.

pyre, n. [1. pīr; 2. páiə], fr. Lat. *pyra*, fr. Gk. *purá*, 'funeral fire', fr. Gk. *pûr*, 'fire'; cogn. w. O.E. *fȳr*, see **fire**; the base is ultimately **pū-*, 'to cleanse', as in **pure**. Pile of wood upon which a corpse was ceremonially burnt; a funeral fire.

pyrethrum, n. [1. pīréthrum; 2. pairíþrəm]. Lat., fr. Gk. *púrethron*, 'the feverfew', fr. *pûr*, 'fire', see prec. **1.** (bot.) Genus of herbaceous perennial plants; feverfew. **2.** (hort.) Name usually applied to varieties of *bachelor's button*, and *ox-eye daisy*.

pyretic, adj. [1. pīrétik; 2. pairétik], fr. Gk. *puretós*, 'burning heat, fever', fr. *pûr*, 'fire'. See prec. & **-ic**. (med.) **a** Pertaining to fever; feverish, febrile; **b** used to reduce fever or feverish symptoms.

pyrexia, n. [1. pīréksia; 2. pairéksiə]. Neo-Lat., fr. Gk. *puréssein*, 'to be feverish', fr. *pûr*, 'fire'. See **pyre**. (med.) Feverish condition of body; fever.

pyrexic(al), adj. [1. pīréksik(l); 2. pairéksik(l)]. Prec. & **-ic** (& **-al**). Feverish.

pyrheliometer, n. [1. pìrhēliómeter; 2. pàiəhìliɔ́mitə]. Coined word, fr. Gk. *pûr*, 'fire', see **pyre**, & *hḗlios*, 'sun', see **helio-**, & **-meter**. Instrument for measuring the healing power of the sun's rays.

pyridine, n. [1. píridīn; 2. páiəridain]. Coined fr. Gk. *pûr*, 'fire', see **pyre**, & *-idine*, suff. used in chem. (chem.) Substance obtained by distillation from coal-tar and bone oil; used in various chemical processes, and medicinally.

pyriform, adj. [1. píriform; 2. pírifɔ̄m], fr. Lat. *pyrum, pirum*, 'pear'; see **Pyrus** & **-form**. Pear-shaped.

pyrites, n. [1. pīrítēz; 2. pairáitīz]. Lat., fr. Gk. *purítēs*, 'a fire-stone, flint, also iron pyrites', properly an adj., 'belonging to, emitting fire', fr. *pûr*, 'fire'. See **pyre** & **-ite**. A mineral compound of sulphur with various metals, having usually a bright, yellow metallic lustre; esp. the common sulphide of iron, *iron pyrites*, also called *pyrite*, or 'fool's gold'; *copper pyrites*, chalcopyrite; *tin pyrites*, stannite.

pyritic(al), adj. [1. pīrítik(l); 2. pairítik(l)]. Prec. & **-ic** & (**-al**). Of, pertaining to, like, pyrites.

pyritiferous, adj. [1. pìritíferus; 2. páiəritífərəs]. See prec. & **-ferous**. Bearing, yielding, pyrites.

pyro-, pref., fr. Gk. *pûr*, *purós*, 'fire', see **pyre**, chiefly used in chemical terminology.

pyrochemical, adj. [1. pìrōkémikl; 2. pàiəroukémikl]. Prec. & **chemical**. Pertaining to the chemical condition of substances at high temperature.

pyrogenetic, **pyrogenic**, adjs. [1. pìrōjenétik, -jénik; 2. pàiəroudženétik, -dženik]. **pyro-** & **-genetic**, **-genic**. Productive of heat or fever.

pyrogenous, adj. [1. pīrójenus; 2. pairɔ́džinəs]. **pyro-** & **-genous**. (geol.) Produced by the action of fire; igneous.

pyrography, n. [1. pīrógrafi; 2. pairɔ́grəfi]. **pyro-** & **-graphy**. The process of reproducing designs on wood with a hot iron; poker-work.

pyrolatry, n. [1. pīrólatri; 2. pairɔ́lətri]. **pyro-** & **-latry**, cp. **idolatry**. Fire worship.

pyroligneous, adj. [1. pìrōlígneus; 2. pàiərouligniəs]. **pyro-** & Lat. *ligneus*, 'of wood', see **lignum (vitae)**, & **-ous**. (chem.) Obtained by distillation of wood; *pyroligneous acid*, a reddish form of acetic acid with characteristic smell; *pyroligneous alcohol*, wood-alcohol.

pyrolysis, n. [1. pīrólisis; 2. pairɔ́lisis]. **pyro-** & **-lysis**. (chem.) Decomposition by heat.

pyromancy, n. [1. pírōmànsi; 2. páiərou mænsi]. **pyro-** & **-mancy**. Divination by fire.

pyromania, n. [1. pìrōmánia; 2. pàiərouméiniə]. **pyro-** & **-mania**. A morbid tendency to set fire to things; incendiary insanity.

pyrometer, n. [1. pīrómeter; 2. pairɔ́mitə]. **pyro-** & **-meter**. An instrument for measuring such high temperatures as cannot be registered by the ordinary mercury thermometer.

pyrope, n. [1. pírōp; 2. páiəroup]. Fr., fr. Lat. *pyrōpus*, fr. Gk. *purōpós*, lit. 'fiery eye; a bronze of a deep red colour', fr. **pyro-** & *ṓps*, 'eye', see **optic**. A garnet of a deep, fiery red colour.

pyrophobia, n. [1. pìrōfóbia; 2. pàiəroufóubiə]. **pyro-** & **-phobia**. A morbid fear of fire.

pyrophorous, adj. [1. pīróferus; 2. pairɔ́fərəs], fr. Gk. *purophóros*, 'fire-bearing'. See **pyro-** & **-phorous**. Producing fire or light; igniting, taking fire, spontaneously.

pyrophorus, n. [1. pīróferus; 2. pairɔ́fərəs]. Gk., see prec., w. Latinized ending. A substance which ignites spontaneously when exposed to air.

pyrophotometer, n. [1. pìrōfōtómeter; 2. pàiəroufoutɔ́mitə]. **pyro-** & **photo-** & **meter**. An optical instrument for the measurement, and comparison, of very high temperatures.

pyrotechnic(al), adj. [1. pìrōtéknik(l); 2. pàiərouteknik(l)]. Gk., fr. **pyro-**, 'fire', & *tekhnikós*, fr. *tékhnē*, 'art, craft', see **technic**, & **-al**. Of, pertaining to, fireworks or pyrotechnics.

pyrotechnics, n. pl. [1. pìrōtékniks; 2. pàiəroutékniks]. See prec. **1.** The art of making fireworks. **2. a** A display of fireworks; pyrotechny; **b** (fig.) a display of brilliant, dazzling oratory &c., usually ironical.

pyrotechny, n. [1. pírōtèkni; 2. páiəroutèkni]. Gk. **pyro-** & *tékhnē*, 'art' &c. See **pyrotechnic**. Pyrotechnics.

pyrotoxin, n. [1. pìrōtóksin; 2. pàiəroutɔ́ksin]. **pyro-** & **toxin**. (bacter.) A toxin causing fever.

pyroxene, n. [1. píroksēn; 2. páiərɔksīn]. Fr., fr. **pyro-** & Gk. *xénos*, 'stranger, foreigner', see **xenelasia**; so called fr. the mistaken notion that the mineral is foreign to the igneous rocks in wh. it is found. A black, crystalline mineral very common in igneous rocks.

pyroxylin, n. [1. pīróksilin; 2. pairɔ́ksilin], fr. **pyro-** & Gk. *xúlon*, 'wood', see **xylo-**, & **-in**. Gun-cotton, obtained by treating cellulose with nitric acid.

pyrrhic (I.), n. & adj. [1. pírik; 2. pírik], n., fr. Gk. *purrhikhḗ*; adj., fr. Lat. *pyrrichius*, fr. Gk. *purríkhios*, supposed to refer to the inventor, *Púrrhikhos*, of the measure and dance. (Gk. antiq.) **1.** n. **a** An old Greek war-dance, accompanied by the flute; **b** (prosody) a measure or foot of two short syllables. **2.** adj. Of, pertaining, **a** to this dance: *a pyrrhic dance*; **b** to the foot of two short syllables: *pyrrhic verse*.

Pyrrhic (II.), adj., fr. Gk. *Púrrhikos*, fr. *Púrrhos*, Pyrrhus. (Gk. and Roman hist.) Of, pertaining to, Pyrrhus, king of Epirus, and esp. of his victory, won at enormous and ruinous cost, over the Romans at Heraclea, 280 B.C.: *a Pyrrhic victory*, one that is so costly that it is equivalent to a defeat.

Pyrrhonic, adj. [1. pirónik; 2. pirɔ́nik], fr. Gk. *Púrrhōn*, 'Pyrrho', & **-ic**. Of, pertaining to, Pyrrhonism.

Pyrrhonism, n. [1. pírunizm; 2. pírənizəm]. See prec. & **-ism**. The sceptical system of philosophy founded by Pyrrho, of Elis, floruit c. 300 B.C.; scepticism.

Pyrrhonist, n. [1. pírunist; 2. pírənist]. See prec. & **-ist**. An adherent of Pyrrhonism; a sceptic.

Pyrus, n. [1. pírus; 2. páiərəs]. L. Lat. *pyrus*; Lat. *pirus*, 'pear tree'. See **pear**. (bot.) Genus of trees and shrubs, which includes the pear; formerly held to include also the apple and quince; *Pyrus japonica*, a red flowering garden shrub, the Japanese pear, with small, unimportant, red fruit.

Pythagorean, adj. & n. [1. pīthagoréan; 2. paiþægɔríən], fr. Lat. *Pȳthagorēus*, fr. Gk. *Pūthagóreios*, fr. *Pūthagóras* & **-an**. **1.** adj. Of, pertaining to, Pythagoras, of Samos, a Greek philosopher, floruit 6th cent. B.C., who founded a school of mystical, ascetic philosophy in S. Italy: *Pythagorean bean*, the seed of the Indian lotus; *Pythagorean proposition*, Proposition 47, of Euclid, Bk. I. **2.** n. Member of the philosophical school of *Pythagoras*.

Pythagoreanism, n. [1. pīthagoréanizm; 2. paiþægɔríənizəm]. Prec. & **-ism**. The philosophical system of Pythagoras.

Pythagorism, n. [1. pīthágorizm; 2. paiþǽgɔrizəm]. See prec. Pythagoreanism.

Pythian, adj. & n. [1. píthian; 2. píþiən], fr. Lat. *Pȳthi-(us)* & **-an**, fr. Gk. *Pūthios*, fr. *Pūthō*, old name of Delphi, also name of Apollo, the god of Delphi, cp. **python**. (Gk. antiq.) **1.** adj. **a** Of, pertaining to, the shrine and oracle of Apollo at Delphi: *the Pythian oracle*; *the Pythian priestess*; **b** of, pertaining to, the Panhellenic games held at Delphi every four years: *the Pythian games*; *the Pythian palm, laurel*, prize given for victory at the games. **2.** n. **a** The priestess of the oracle at Delphi; **b** Apollo, as the god and patron of Delphi.

python, n. [1. píthon; 2. páiþɔn, -ən], fr. Gk. *pūthōn*. See prec. **1.** (Gk. mythol.) The legendary gigantic serpent which Apollo slew at Delphi or Pytho. **2.** (zool.) A genus of large, non-venomous snakes found in Africa and the East Indies; allied to the boa. **3.** A person possessed by a familiar spirit; a soothsayer, diviner, sorceress, pythoness.

pythoness, n. [1. píthunes; 2. páiþənes], fr. Lat. *Pȳthōnissa*, cp. M.E. & O. Fr. *phitonesse, phitonise*, 'sorceress'. Prec. & **-ess**. **a** (Gk. antiq.) The priestess of Apollo at Delphi who, under the inspiration of the god, gave the answers of the oracle; **b** a woman soothsayer; sorceress, witch.

pyuria, n. [1. pīúria; 2. paijúəriə]. See **pyo-** & **-uria**. (pathol.) Discharge of pus with the urine; a symptom of unhealthy condition of the bladder or kidneys.

pyx (I.), n. [1. piks; 2. piks], fr. Lat. *pyxis*, fr. Gk. *puxis*, 'a box', fr. *púxos*, 'the box-tree, boxwood', see **box** (I.). **1.** Vessel, case, often of precious metal, and richly ornamented, in which the Host is reserved in churches; ciborium. **2.** Case used at the Royal Mint, in which coins of gold and silver are kept for the yearly trial of fineness and quality, called *the trial of the pyx*.

pyx (II.), vb. trans., fr. prec. To test (coins) for weight and fineness at the yearly trial of the pyx.

pyxidium, n. [1. piksídium; 2. piksídiəm]. Neo-Lat., fr. Gk. *puxídion*, dimin. of *puxis*, 'box'. See **pyx** (I.). (bot.) A seed-capsule, as in the plantain &c., which divides into two parts, the top falling off like the lid of a box.

pyxis, n. [1. piksis; 2. píksis]. Gk., 'a box'. See **pyx** (I.). (class. archaeol.) A vase with a cover, used in the toilet; a small box.

Q

Q, q [1. kū; 2. kjū]. Seventeenth letter of the English alphabet; for abbreviations &c. see list at end of Dictionary.

qua, conj. [1. kwā; 2. kwei]. Lat., abl. fem. sing. of *quī*, rel. pron., 'who'; the Lat. prons. in *qu-* are cogn. w. Engl. **which, who**. As, as relating to, in the character or capacity of: *qua literature the work is negligible, as a storehouse of facts it is valuable*; *Professor Jones said he spoke as a private person, and not qua professor*.

quack (I.), vb. intrans. & n. [1. kwak; 2. kwæk]. Imitative, cp. Du. *kwakken*; Mod. Germ. *quacken*; cp. also Gk. *koáx*, 'the croaking of frogs'. **1.** vb. **a** To make a noise like a duck; **b** to talk ceaselessly, idly; to gabble, chatter. **2.** n. **a** The noise or cry made by ducks, so *quack-quack*, baby name for a duck; **b** idle talk, chatter.

quack (II.), n. Abbr. of **quacksalver**. **1. a** One who pretends falsely to knowledge or skill in the art and practice of medicine or surgery, esp. one who recommends secret remedies or medical treatment which he claims as miraculous but knows to be worthless; a charlatan or impostor; **b** a plausible person who claims to be a man of learning or science while possessing in reality but very superficial knowledge. **2.** (attrib.) *Quack doctor*, an untrained, ignorant fellow claiming to effect miraculous cures with drugs &c. unknown to science; *quack medicines, remedies*, such as are recommended by quacks, and claimed to contain new and mysterious properties; *a quack politician*, one who recommends ill-considered measures as cures for social or political ills.

quackery, n. [1. kwákeri; 2. kwǽkəri]. Prec. & **-ery**. Methods, arts, treatment, practised and recommended by quacks; charlatanry.

quackish, adj. [1. kwákish; 2. kwǽkiʃ]. **quack** (II.) & **-ish**. Resembling, using the methods of, a quack; of the nature of quackery.

quacksalver, n. [1. kwáksalver; 2. kwǽksælvə]. Borrowed fr. Du. *kwakzalver*, 'one who quacks, puffs, or boasts about his salves and secret remedies, a charlatan', fr. *kwakzalven*, fr. *kwakken*, 'to quack like a duck', & *zalf*, see **salve** (I.). (most often in abbr. form *quack*) An itinerant vendor of salves, drugs, and remedies; a quack, a charlatan.

quad, n. [1. kwod; 2. kwɔd]. Abbr. of **a quadrangle**, commonly used in colleges and universities; **b quadrat**.

quadrable, adj. [1. kwódrabl; 2. kwɔ́drəbl]. Stem of **quadrate** & **-able**. (math.) Capable of being squared, or represented by a square of equivalent area.

quadragenarian, adj. & n. [1. kwòdrajenárian; 2. kwɔ̀drədžinéəriən], fr. Lat. *quadrāgēnārius*, fr. *quadrāgēni*, 'forty each', fr. *quadrāginta*, 'forty'; fr. *quadrus*, 'square, fourfold', cogn. w. *quatuor*, 'four'. See **quadri-** & cp. **four**. **a** adj. Forty years old; **b** n., a person forty years old.

Quadragesima, n. [1. kwòdrajésima; 2. kwɔ̀drədžésimə]. Fem. sing. of Lat. *quadrāgēsimus*, for earlier *quadrāgensimus*, 'fortieth', fr. *quadrāginta*, 'forty', see prec. word; in L., Eccles., Lat. used of the forty days' fast of Lent. Usually *Quadragesima Sunday*, the first Sunday in Lent.

quadragesimal, adj. [1. kwòdrajésimal; 2. kwɔ̀drədžésiməl], fr. L., Eccles., Lat. *quadrāgēsimālis*. Prec. & **-al**. Of, pertaining to, the forty days' fast of Lent; of, pertaining to, Lent; Lenten.

quadrangle, n. [1. kwódrànggl; 2. kwɔ́dræ̀ŋgl]. Fr., fr. L. Lat. *quadrangulum*, fr. *quadr(i-)*, 'four', & *angulum*. See **quadri-** & **angle** (I.). **1.** A four-angled and, therefore, four-sided plane figure, a square or rectangle. **2.** Familiarly *quad*, specif., a square or other rectangular court enclosed by buildings on all four sides; also used loosely of an enclosed court which has a fence on one or more sides, the others being formed by buildings; esp. used of such courts in colleges or universities.

quadrangular, adj. [1. kwodránggūlar; 2. kwɔdrǽŋgjulə]. See prec. & **-ar**; cp. Fr. *quadrangulaire*, L. Lat. *quadrangulāris*. **a** Having four angles and, therefore, four sides; **b** resembling, in the form of, a quadrangle (in specific sense).

quadrangularly, adv. Prec. & **-ly**. With four angles and sides.

quadrant, n. [1. kwódrant; 2. kwɔ́drənt], fr. Lat. *quadrant-(em)*, *quadrans*, 'a fourth part', as Pres. Part. of *quadrāre*, 'to make square'. See **quadrate**. **1.** (geom.) The fourth part of a circle or sphere; the arc of a circle containing 90°; the space included between such arc and two radii drawn from the centre of the circle to the extremities of such arc. **2.** An instrument used for measuring angles and altitudes, in astronomy, navigation, land surveying &c., consisting of a graduated metal arc of 90° with a movable index and an eye-piece; now superseded by the sextant.

quadrantal, adj. [1. kwodrántl; 2. kwɔdrǽnt(ə)l]. Prec. & **-al**. Of, pertaining to, a quadrant; contained in the fourth part of a circle; shaped like a quadrant.

quadrat, n. [1. kwódrat; 2. kwɔ́dræt]. See next word. (print.) Small piece of type-metal lower than type, used for filling out lines &c.; abbr. *quad*.

quadrate (I.), adj. & n. [1. kwódrat; 2. kwɔ́drit], fr. Lat. *quadrāt-(um)*, 'squared', P.P. type of *quadrāre*, 'to make square'; formed fr. *quadrus*, 'square', a variant of *quatr-*, as in Lat. *quātuor*, 'four', wh. occurs as *quadri-* in compounds. See **quadri-** & **-ate**. **1.** adj. Four-sided, squared, rectangular; (now rare except anat.) as *quadrate bone*, in birds, reptiles, and fishes, the bony part on each side of the skull to which the lower jaw is articulated; *quadrate lobe*, of the brain &c. **2.** n. A square, rectangular space; the quadrate bone.

quadrate (II.), vb. trans. & intrans. [1. kwódrāt; 2. kwɔ́dreit]. See prec. **A.** trans. **1.** To make square; to square, as the circle. **2.** (with *to* and *with*) To make to conform to or agree with. **B.** intrans. (with *with* or *to*) To square, correspond, conform.

quadratic, adj. & n. [1. kwodrátik; 2. kwɔdrǽtik]. **quadrate** (I.) & **-ic**. **1.** adj. **a** Of, resembling, a square or quadrate; square; **b** (alg.) of an equation, *quadratic equation*, in which *x*, the unknown quantity, is of the second power or squared. **2.** n. (pl.) The branch of algebra dealing with quadratic equations.

quadrature, n. [1. kwódrachur; 2. kwɔ́drətʃə]. Lat., 'squaring, esp. of the circle'. **quadrate** (II.) & **-ure**. **1.** (astron.) The relative position of two heavenly bodies when their difference of longitude is 90°. **2.** (math.) The finding of an area equal to a given area; specif., the finding of a square equal in area to a given area, as in the famous problem, *the quadrature* or *squaring of a circle*.

quadrennial, adj. [1. kwodrénial; 2. kwɔdréniəl], fr. Lat. *quadriennium*, 'period of four years'; **quadri-** & *annus*, 'year', see **annual**. Lasting four years; occurring every four years.

quadri-, quadru-, pref. Forms of **Lat.**

qua(t)tuor, 'four', used in compounds; the orig. form of the numeral is **kʷətwōr*, **kʷetwər* &c., cogn. w. Scrt. *čatur*; Gk. *téssares, téttares*, see **tessera** & **tetra-**; Goth. *fidwor*; O.E. *fēower*, see **four.**

quadricentennial, n. & adj. [1. kwòdrisenténial; 2. kwɔ̀drisenténiəl]. Prec. & **centennial.** **1.** n. **a** The four-hundredth anniversary of an event; **b** celebration of this. **2.** adj. Pertaining to a quadricentennial.

quadrifid, adj. [1. kwódrifid; 2. kwɔ́drifid], fr. Lat. *quadrifidus*; **quadri-** & non-nasalized stem **fid-*, of *findere*, 'to cleave, split', cp. **fissure.** (bot. and zool.) Divided into four lobes or parts: *quadrifid leaf, petal.*

quadriga, n. [1. kwodríga; 2. kwɔdráigə]. Lat., for *quadrijuga*; **quadri-** & *jugum*, 'yoke', see **jugate.** (class. antiq.) A four-horsed triumphal chariot.

quadrilateral, adj. & n. [1. kwòdrilláteral; 2. kwɔ̀drilǽtərəl]. See **quadri-** & **lateral (I.).** **1.** adj. Four-sided. **2.** n. **a** Four-sided figure; area of this form; specif. **b** an area defended by four fortresses: *the Venetian Quadrilateral.*

quadrilingual, adj. [1. kwòdrilínggwal; 2. kwɔ̀drilíŋgwəl]. **quadri-** & **lingual.** Knowing, speaking, composed in, four languages.

quadrille (I.), n. [1. ka-, kwadríl; 2. kə-, kwədríl]. Fr., fr. Ital. *quadriglio*, perh. fr. Span. *cuartillo*, 'meeting of four persons', fr. Lat. *quartus*, 'fourth'. See next word. An old game of cards, played by four people with a pack of 40 cards.

quadrille (II.), n. Fr., fr. Span. *cuadrilla*, cp. Ital. *quadriglia*, 'a squadron, square or band of horsemen', fr. Lat. See **quadrate** & **quadri-.** **1.** Old-fashioned square dance with five figures, for a number of groups of two couples each, placed facing each other. **2.** Music for a set of quadrilles.

quadrillion, n. [1. kwadríliun; 2. kwədríliən]. **quadri-** & **-illion,** on anal. of *million.* Number expressed in Great Britain by a unit followed by twenty-four zeros, in America and France by a unit followed by fifteen zeros.

quadrinomial, adj. [1. kwòdrinómial; 2. kwɔ̀drinóumiəl]. See **quadri-** & **nominal** & cp. **binomial.** (alg.) Consisting of four terms.

quadripartite, adj. [1. kwòdripártīt; 2. kwɔ̀dripátait], fr. Lat. *quadripartītus*; **quadri-** & P.P. of *partīre*, 'to divide into parts', see **part.** Consisting of, divided into, four parts; shared in, drawn up by, four persons or parties: *quadripartite vaulting*; *a quadripartite contract.*

quadrireme, n. [1. kwódrirēm; 2. kwɔ́drirīm]. Lat. *quadrirēmis*; **quadri-** & *rēmus*, 'oar', cp. **trireme.** (Rom. antiq.) A war-galley propelled by four banks of oars.

quadrisyllabic, adj. [1. kwòdrisilábik; 2. kwɔ̀drisilǽbik]. **quadri-** & **syllabic.** Having four syllables.

quadrisyllable, n. [1. kwódrisìlabl; 2. kwɔ́drisìləbl]. See prec. & **syllable.** A word of four syllables.

quadrivalence, -cy, n. [1. kwòdriválens(i); 2. kwɔ̀drivéiləns(i)]. **quadri-** & **valency.** (chem.) State, quality, of being quadrivalent.

quadrivalent, adj. [1. kwòdriválent; 2. kwɔ̀drivéilənt]. **quadri-** & **-valent.** (chem.) Having a valence of four.

quadrivium, n. [1. kwodrívium; 2. kwɔdríviəm]. Lat.; **quadri-** & *via*, 'road, path', see **via (I.).** The group of the four mathematical sciences, arithmetic, music, geometry, and astronomy, forming the higher course of study in the mediaeval universities. Cp. **trivium.**

quadroon, n. [1. kwodrōōn; 2. kwɔdrún]. Earlier *quarteron*, fr. Span. *cuarteron*, fr. *cuarto*, 'a fourth part', fr. Lat. *quartus*, 'fourth'. See **quadrate** & **quarter.** The offspring of a mulatto and a white person; one having only a fourth part of negro blood.

quadru-, pref. See **quadri-.**

quadrumanous, adj. [1. kwodrōōmanus; 2. kwɔdrúmənəs]. **quadri-,** altered to **quadru-** on anal. of next word, & Lat. *manus*, 'hand', & **-ous.** See **manual.** (zool.) Having four hands, belonging to obs. mammalian order *Quadrumana*, in which all four limbs end like hands with an opposable digit or thumb, including all the primates except man; contrasted with *bimanous.*

quadruped, n. & adj. [1. kwódrooped; 2. kwɔ́druped], fr. Lat. *quadruped-(em)* &c., 'having, going on, four feet', adj. & n., fr. **quadru-** & *ped-(em)*, 'foot', see **pedal.** **1.** n. (zool.) An animal having four feet; usually applied to mammals, far more rarely to reptiles. **2.** adj. Four-footed, quadrupedal.

quadrupedal, adj. [1. kwodrōōpedl; 2. kwɔdrúpidl]. Prec. & **-al.** Four-footed.

quadruple, adj., n., & vb. trans. [1. kwódroopl; 2. kwɔ́drupl]. Fr., fr. Lat. *quadruplus*, 'fourfold'; **quadru-** & base *plic-*, 'to fold', see under **plicate.** **1.** adj. **a** Fourfold; having four times the amount of: *to have a quadruple share*; *a rate quadruple of, to, that of another*; *a size quadruple of that of the earth*; **b** consisting of four parts or units: *quadruple time*, with four beats to the bar. **2.** n. Amount four times as large; a fourfold amount. **3.** vb. To multiply by four.

quadruplet, n. [1. kwódrooplet; 2. kwɔ́druplet]. **quadruple (I.)** & **-et,** on anal. of **triplet.** **1.** A group of four things of the same kind; esp. four children born at one birth. **2.** A bicycle for four riders.

quadruplicate (I.), adj. & n. [1. kwodrōōplikat; 2. kwɔdrúplikit], fr. Lat. *quadruplicāt-(um)*, P.P. type of *quadruplicāre*. **quadru-** & **plicate.** **1.** adj. Fourfold, repeated or copied four times. **2.** n. One of four exactly similar copies or examples: *to make a document in quadruplicate*; *quadruplicates*, four exactly similar copies or transcriptions.

quadruplicate (II.), vb. trans. [1. kwodrōōplikāt; 2. kwɔdrúplikeit], fr. prec. To multiply by four; to make in quadruplicate; to make four exactly similar copies or transcriptions.

quadruplication, n. [1. kwodrōōplikáshun; 2. kwɔdrùplikéiʃən]. Lat. Prec. & **-ion.** **1.** Multiplication by four; act of quadruplicating or making in quadruplicate. **2.** Something existing in quadruplicate.

quaere, vb. imperat. & n. [1. kwḗri; 2. kwíəri]. Lat. imperat. of *quaerere*, 'to ask, seek'; origin uncertain; connexion w. *quae*, interrog. pron., has been tentatively suggested, but is very doubtful. See **question.** (lit.) Inquire, make inquiry; equivalent to, it is a question, I should like to know; used as expression of doubt or wish for information or inquiry: *the object is most desirable, but quaere, is it practicable?*; *he says he is going to retire; quaere?*

quaestor, n. [1. kwḗstor; 2. kwístɔ]. Lat., contracted fr. *quaesītor*, fr. base *quaes-*, as in *quaerere* for *quaesere*, 'to ask, seek, inquire'. See prec. & **question.** (Rom. hist.) One of the lowest order of Roman magistrates, having originally powers of inquisition into criminal cases, later also administrative functions.

quaestorial, adj. [1. kwēstórial; 2. kwistɔ́riəl]. Prec. & **-ial.** Of, pertaining to, a quaestor or his office.

quaestorship, n. [1. kwḗstorship; 2. kwístɔʃip]. See prec. & **-ship.** **a** Office, rank, of a quaestor; **b** period of office of a quaestor.

quaff, vb. trans. & intrans. [1. kwahf; 2. kwāf]. Etymol. uncertain. (poet.) **a** trans. To take large gulps or draughts of, drink at a draught; **b** intrans., to drink copiously: *to sit quaffing all day.*

quag, n. [1. kwag; 2. kwæg]. Imitative, cp. **quake** & **wag.** A bog, marshy piece of land; quagmire, quaking bog.

quagga, n. [1. kwága; 2. kwǽgə]. Bantu (Zulu) name, prob. fr. *quag*, 'striped, mottled'; or Hottentot *ouagga*, imitative of its short, barking neigh. **1.** A South African quadruped, *Equus quagga*, now extinct, allied to the wild ass and the zebra; reddish brown with dark stripes on head and shoulders and forepart of the body, legs and back parts greyish white with no stripes. **2.** A species of the zebra, also and more properly styled Burchell's zebra, *Equus Burchelli.*

quaggy, adj. [1. kwági; 2. kwǽgi]. **quag** & **-y.** Boggy, marshy.

quagmire, n. [1. kwágmīr; 2. kwǽgmaiə]. Earlier *quake-mire.* See **quake, quag,** & **mire.** **1.** A bog, marsh, swamp, piece of quaking, marshy, or muddy ground. **2.** (fig.) A dangerous, difficult position from which it is hard to extricate oneself.

quahaug, quahog, n. [1. kwáw-hog, kwahóg; 2. kwɔ́hɔg, kwəhɔ́g], fr. N. Am. Indian *poquauhock.* The N. American clam, much used in stews and soups.

quaich, quaigh, n. [1. kwāgh; 2. kweiχ], fr. Gael. *cuach*, 'cup', cp. W. *cawg*; cogn. w. Lat. *caucus*, Gk. *kaûka*, 'bowl', prob. also of Celt. origin. A flattish drinking-cup or bowl, with two flat, projecting handles, made of horn or of wood, sometimes formed of staves with a silver hoop fastening them together like a cask.

Quai d'Orsay, n. [1. kā dorsā; 2. ke dorse]. Fr. **1.** The name of a quay on the south bank of the Seine in Paris, on which are situated the French Foreign Office and other Government buildings. **2.** **a** The French Foreign Office; **b** French diplomacy or foreign policy generally, cp. use of *Downing Street.*

quail (I.), n. [1. kwāl; 2. kweil], fr. O. Fr. *quaille*, Mod. Fr. *caille*, fr. L. Lat. *quacule*, cp. Ital. *quaglia*; O.H.G. *quahtela*, 'quail', is presumably borrowed fr. the Lat. On the other hand, the L. Lat. form itself may be of Gmc. origin, cp. O.H.G. *wahtala*, & the corresponding (rare) O.E. *wihtel*, fr. **wahtil-*, wh. appear to be cogn. w. Scrt. *vártikā*, & Gk. *órtux* for **wortuk-*. The O.H.G. & O.E. forms show an early (Gmc.) assimilation to the base **wak-*, 'to watch, wake' (see **wake (I.)**); the Lat. form was prob. felt as imitative of the bird's cry. **1.** A small, migratory, gallinaceous bird of Europe, Asia, and Africa, *Coturnix coturnix*; allied to the partridge, and much esteemed for its delicate flavour. **2.** (U.S.A.) The popular name of the Virginia partridge, *Colinus*, and of the crested *Lophortyx*, the California quail. *Quail call*, a call, imitating the cry of a quail, made by a *quail pipe*, a pipe or whistle used as a lure or decoy for quails when migrating.

quail (II.), vb. intrans. & trans. Apparently fr. O.E. *cwelan*, 'to die', cogn. w. O.E. *cwalu*, 'destruction', q.v. under **quell**; influenced in form & meaning by provinc. *quail*, 'to curdle', fr. O. Fr. *coailler, cailler*, fr. Lat. *coagulāre*, see **coagulate.** The word occurs frequently in 16th cent., in Spenser & Shakespeare, & was revived by the Romantic school in early 19th cent. **1.** intrans. To lose heart or spirit, to cower, flinch; to shrink back, give before: *his heart, courage, quailed*; *to quail before another's wrath, in the presence of danger* &c. **2.** trans. (obs.) To cause to quail.

quaint, adj. [1. kwānt; 2. kweint]. M.E. *cointe, queynte, queint*, 'famous, well known; clever, skilful; neat, elegant', fr. O. Fr. *coint*, 'skilful, neat, spruce', fr. Lat. *cognitus*, 'well known', P.P. of *cognoscere*, 'to know, learn', cp. **cognoscible.** **1.** Pleasing and attractive because of its strangeness and unfamiliarity; revealing intricacy and curious skill in workmanship; esp. of such qualities when associated or supposed to be associated with antiquity: *a quaint old house, piece of furniture* &c.; *quaint, old-fashioned customs, manners* &c.; often used by the vulgar as a term of undiscriminating approval of something which they do not appreciate but consider it wise to praise. **2.** Odd, eccentric: *a quaint person*; *quaint way of speaking, walking* &c.; *she wears quaint dresses.*

quaintly, adv. Prec. & **-ly.** In a quaint manner; oddly.

quaintness, n. See prec. & **-ness.** State, quality, of being quaint.

quair, n. See **quire (I.).**

quake, vb. intrans. & n. [1. kwāk ; 2. kweik]. O.E. *cwacian*, 'to tremble', M.E. *quāken*; origin unknown; connexion w. **quick** very improbable. **1.** vb. **a** (of inanimate things) To shake, tremble, rock, move convulsively to and fro, as the earth during an earthquake, a quicksand, a bog; **b** (of living things) to shake, shiver, shudder, tremble, esp. with fear: *to quake with fear, fright*; (more rarely) *to quake with cold* &c. **2.** n. A shake, tremor, an earthquake.

Quaker, n. [1. kwāker; 2. kwéikə]. **quake** & **-er.** **1. a** (cap.) The name given, about 1650, in derision, but now used with no offensive intention, to a member of the religious body calling themselves the Society of Friends, founded by George Fox, 1648–50; either because the members shook or quaked in their religious enthusiasm, or, more probably, from the warning of Fox, to those to whom he preached, 'to quake at the Word of the Lord'; **b** a person supposed to resemble a Quaker in the sobriety of his manners, dress, speech &c. **2.** Popular name for various plain-coloured birds and moths: (usually attrib.) *quaker-bird, quaker-moth*.

Quakerdom, n. [1. kwākədum; 2. kwéikədəm]. Prec. & **-dom.** **1.** The community of Quakers; the Society of Friends. **2.** The principles, customs &c. of Quakers.

Quakeress, n. [1. kwākeres; 2. kwéikəris]. See prec. & **-ess.** A woman Quaker.

Quakerish, adj. [1. kwākerish; 2. kwéikəriʃ]. See prec. & **-ish.** Like a Quaker; sober in manner, speech, dress; strict in principles; strait-laced.

Quakerism, n. [1. kwākerizm; 2. kwéikərizəm]. **Quaker** & **-ism.** Quakerdom.

Quakers' meeting, n. **a** The silent religious assembly of the Society of Friends in which only those speak whom the Spirit moves; **b** any very silent meeting or company.

quaking, adj. [1. kwāking; 2. kwéikiŋ]. Pres. Part of **quake.** Shaking, trembling; esp. *quaking ash*, the aspen; *quaking grass*, a grass, genus *Briza*, of several varieties with small oval spikelets on slender stalks which shake continually at the least breath of wind.

quakingly, adv. Prec. & **-ly.** Tremblingly.

qualification, n. [1. kwòlifikāshun; 2. kwòlifikéiʃən], fr. Med. Lat. *quālificātiōn-(em)*. See **qualify** & **-fication.** **1.** Act of qualifying or modifying; that which qualifies or modifies; a restriction, modification, reservation, abatement, or limitation: *to assert without any qualification*; *such a sweeping generalization requires qualification*; *we can praise the play, but with certain qualifications.* **2. a** Act of qualifying, of making, or becoming fit or suitable for; **b** that which qualifies; adaptation, fitness, or quality, capacity, natural or acquired, which fits a person for, or entitles him to, a position, right, privilege &c.: *qualification precedes the right to exercise the franchise*; *he has no qualifications for his office*; specif., official and authoritative recognition, statement &c., that one is properly trained and instructed, official sanction, for the practice of a profession: *medical, dental, qualifications.*

qualificatory, adj. [1. kwòlifikāturi; 2. kwòlifikéitəri]. Stem of prec. & **-ory.** Qualifying, modifying, limiting.

qualified, adj. [1. kwólifid; kwólifaid]. P.P. of **qualify.** **1.** Having a qualification or qualifications for anything; fitted by the possession of qualities for a position, function, privilege &c.; competent, fit: *a person well qualified for his position*; specif., possessing official qualifications: *a fully qualified medical practitioner.* **2.** Limited, modified: *a qualified statement.*

qualify, vb. trans. & intrans. [1. kwólifī; 2. kwólifai], fr. Fr. *qualifier*, fr. Med. Lat. *quālificāre*, 'to make of a certain quality, to give a certain quality to', fr. Lat. *quālis*, 'of what kind'. See **quality** & **-fy.** **A.** trans. **1. a** (often reflex.) To give the necessary qualities or qualifications to; to train and prepare, furnish with the necessary skill, knowledge &c. for a particular purpose, employment &c.: *to qualify oneself for one's life work, for the bar*; **b** to make legally qualified, to furnish with legal capacity &c.: *to qualify a person as voter by placing the name on the register*; *to qualify a juror by administering the oath.* **2.** To attribute specific qualities to, to describe as: *to qualify a person as a notorious liar*; *to qualify the policy of the Government as dangerous.* **3. a** To put qualifications or modifications upon, to modify, limit, by exceptions or reservations; to make less wide or extended, to restrict: *to qualify a statement*; *such sweeping generalizations should be much qualified*; **b** to moderate, lessen, temper, make weaker: *to qualify one's anger*; *to qualify the beauty, ugliness, of a building* &c.; *to qualify spirits with water*; **c** (gram.) to modify, limit, the meaning of: *adjectives qualify nouns, adverbs verbs.* **B.** intrans. **1. a** Specif., to obtain official qualifications, by study, training, and passing necessary examinations &c., for the legal exercise of a recognized profession or the like: *to qualify as a doctor, solicitor*; *to qualify for the rank of captain*; **b** to prepare oneself, become competent, by practice, acquisition of knowledge &c., to perform certain acts, or operations, functions &c.: *to qualify as a typist, a butler, a referee* &c. **2.** To take the necessary legal steps for obtaining the power to act in particular capacity: *to qualify as a juror*; *to qualify for the vote.*

qualitative, adj. [1. kwólitativ; 2. kwólitətiv], fr. Med. Lat. *quālitātīvus*, cp. Fr. *qualitatif.* See next word & **-ative.** Of, pertaining to, concerned with, affecting, quality, as contrasted with *quantitative*: *qualitative analysis*, that designed to discover the nature and properties of a substance; specif. (philol.) *qualitative sound changes*, those resulting in a sound gradually becoming a different sound; e.g. the change of O.E. *ā* to *ō* in M.E.: *hām, hōm*, 'home'.

quality, n. [1. kwóliti; 2. kwóliti]. M.E., fr. O. Fr. *qualite*, fr. Lat. *quālitāt-(em)*, 'quality, property, nature', fr. *quālis*, 'of what kind or sort'; the word *quālitas* was formed by Cicero to translate the Gk. philosophical term *poiótēs*, itself coined by Plato fr. *poîos*, 'of what kind'; the pref. *quā-* is connected w. the interrog. prons. *quis*, 'who?', *quod*, 'what?' &c.; see further under **what, who, which**; cp. also the cogn. Gk. *pēlikós*, 'how big?', for **kwālik-*, & O. Slav. *kolu*, 'how much?', both of wh. also contain the *-l-* suff. **1. a** That which marks out, identifies, or which distinguishes one thing from another; the essential nature of anything in its relation to other things; kind, sort; contrasted with *quantity*: *the quality of mercy*; *is laughter a quality of man only?*; *to test another's qualities*; **b** specif., good quality, excellence: *to aim at quality rather than quantity.* **2.** An attribute, property, or characteristic; condition, value: *of good, poor, high, low, quality*; *to admire the quality of*; *of various qualities*; *the quality of a voice, of colour* &c. **3.** High rank, gentle birth, distinguished social position: *a lady of quality.* Phr. *the quality*, persons possessing rank, good birth &c., the gentry; contrasted with *the common people.* **4.** (log.) Affirmation or negation of a proposition.

qualm, n. [1. kwahm; 2. kwām]; more rarely now [1. kwawm; 2. kwɔm]. O.E. *cwealm*, M.E. *qualm*, 'pestilence, plague, evil', cp. O.S. *qualm*, 'destruction, death'; cogn. w. O.E. *quellan*, 'to put an end to'. See **quell**, & cp. **quail (II.).** **1.** A feeling of faintness or sickness, queasiness, nausea: *qualms of sea-sickness.* **2.** A misgiving, doubt, a feeling of faint-heartedness, a compunction, scruple: *qualms of conscience.*

qualmish, adj. [1. kwáhmish; 2. kwámiʃ]. Prec. & **-ish.** (rare) Having qualms; squeamish.

quandary, n. [1. kwòndári, kwóndari; 2. kwɔndéəri, kwɔ́ndəri]. Only in Engl.; first c. 1580 when described as a Lat. form; possibly a corrupt. of some Med. scholastic Lat. phr.; Skeat suggests *quantum dare*, 'how much to give'. A state of perplexity, a difficult, perplexing situation; a dilemma: *to be put in a great, in rather a, quandary.*

quand même, adv. [1. kon mām; 2. kã mɛ̄m]. Fr. Even though, all the same, whatever may happen.

quant, n. & vb. trans. [1. kwont; 2. kwɔnt]. Etymol. doubtful; Kentish & East Anglian dial.; possibly through Lat. *contus*, fr. Gk. *kontós*, 'pole, boat-hook, punt-pole'. **1.** n. A punt-pole with a flange or disk to prevent sinking in muddy bottoms, used on barges on the East coast. **2.** vb. To propel (a boat or barge) with a quant.

quantic, n. [1. kwóntik; 2. kwɔ́ntik], fr. Lat. *quant-(us)*, 'how much'. See **quantum** & **-ic.** (math.) A rational, integral homogeneous function of two or more variables.

quantifiable, adj. [1. kwóntifiabl; 2. kwɔ́ntifaiəbl]. **quantify** & **-able.** Capable of being quantified.

quantification, n. [1. kwòntifikāshun; 2. kwɔ̀ntifikéiʃən]. See **quantify** & **-fication.** The act, process, by which anything is quantified; the expression of the quantity of; esp. (log.) the determination of the quantity or amount of the terms of a proposition: *the quantification of the predicate.*

quantify, vb. trans. [1. kwóntifī; 2. kwɔ́ntifai]. See **quantum** & **-fy.** **1.** To determine, express, the quantity or amount of; to measure in respect of quantity. **2.** (log.) To express explicitly the logical quantity, by use of *all, some, none.*

quantitative, adj. [1. kwóntitativ; 2. kwɔ́ntitətiv], fr. Med. Lat. *quantitātīvus*, cp. Fr. *quantitatif.* See **quantity** & **-ative.** Of, pertaining to, concerned with, quantity, as contrasted with *qualitative*: *quantitative analysis*, one undertaken in order to determine precise quantity and weight of a substance present; *quantitative sound change*, one involving an alteration in the length of sounds, e.g. O.E. *blĭnd*, fr. earlier *blīnd.*

quantity, n. [1. kwóntiti; 2. kwɔ́ntiti]. M.E. *quantite*, fr. Fr. *quantité*, fr. L. Lat. *quantitāt-(em)*, 'greatness, amount, quantity', fr. *quantus*, 'how great, how much, how many'. See **quantum** & **-ity.** **1.** The property in virtue of which anything can be measured; an attribute of size, weight, number, amount or extent, as correlative of or contrasted with *quality*: *to prefer quantity to quality.* **2.** A specified amount, sum, or number: *what quantity can be supplied?*; *a certain quantity of material, books* &c.; *to measure the quantity of rain which falls*; *a large, small, quantity.* *Quantity surveyor*, (building) the person whose duty it is to measure the work done, the amount of material used or required and prices &c. **3.** (often pl.) A large amount; profusion, abundance: *he collected a quantity of curious information, old pictures* &c.; *to eat a quantity of strawberries*; *flowers in quantities.* Specif. **4.** (log.) the extension of a term, esp. the extension of the subject of a proposition, as whether it is universal or particular, as indicated by *all* or *some.* Specif. **5.** (math.) **a** that on which mathematical processes may operate; **b** a symbol or figure representing a mathematical quantity; Phrs. *an unknown quantity*, **a** (math.) the symbol x in an equation; **b** (fig.) a person, influence, force, that cannot be foretold or estimated; *negligible quantity*, **a** (math.) that quantity which can be disregarded in statistics, mathematical processes &c.; **b** (fig.) a person, thing, of no importance. Specif. **6. a** (phon.) relative length or duration of vowels, consonants, or syllables; **b** (prosody) relative length of syllables in verse; **c** graphic symbol used to express this.

quantum, n. [1. kwóntum; 2. kwóntəm]. Lat., neut. sing. of *quantus*, 'how great, how much'; either fr. Lat. *quam*, 'how', & suff. *-to*, or possibly a primitive formation, cp. Gk. *pántes*, pl., 'all', q.v. under **pan-**. Quantity, amount; a certain, specified quantity or amount; share, portion: *each man receives his proper quantum*. Phrs. *quantum libet* (abbr. *quant. lib.* or *q.l.*), Lat., 'as much as you please, freely', in medical prescriptions &c.; *quantum meruit*, Lat., 'as much as he has deserved or earned', (law) the value of work done which can be sued for on a breach of contract; *quantum sufficit* (abbr. *quant. suff.*, *q.s.*), Lat., 'as much as suffices', in medical prescriptions &c., a sufficient quantity, that which is enough for the purpose.

quantum theory, n. The theory that radiation is propagated through space in discrete units of uniform value called 'quanta'. A 'quantum' is the unit of a concept known as 'action' based on the product of time and energy in a four-dimensional space when time is the fourth dimension.

quaquaversal, adj. [1. kwåkwavérsl; 2. kwèikwəvǽsl], fr. L. Lat. *quāquāversus* & **-al**, fr. Lat. *quāquā*, 'wheresoever', reduplication of *quā*, 'in what direction, where?', & *versus*, 'turned', see **version.** (geol., of strata) Turning, running, dipping in all directions.

quaquaversally, adv. Prec. & **-ly**. In every direction, as of strata from an axis.

quarantine (I.), n. [1. kwóranten; 2. kwórəntīn], fr. O. Fr. *quarantaine*, also more rarely *quarantine*, 'period of forty days', as of Lent; Med. Lat. *quarantānum*, fr. Low Lat. **quaranta*, shortened form of Lat. *quadrāginta*, 'forty', see **Quadragesima**; the present usage prob. derives fr. Ital. *quarantina*, of same origin. **1. a** The period, originally of forty days, during which a vessel, together with everybody and everything upon it, coming from an infected or suspected port, is isolated and kept under observation at the port of arrival in order to prevent spread of infectious or contagious disease; **b** any similar restriction placed on travellers, goods &c. where state of infection is suspected: *in quarantine*, isolated under observation. **2.** (legal hist.) Period of forty days' free and undisturbed occupation of a residence enjoyed by a widow after the death of her husband.

quarantine (II.), vb. trans., fr. prec. To put, keep, in quarantine; to impose quarantine regulations on, as ship, passengers &c.

quare impedit, n. [1. kwåre ímpedit; 2. kwéəri ímpedit]. Lat., 'for what reason does he hinder'. (eccles. law) Writ in an action where a refusal has been made to institute a particular person to a benefice, usually brought by a patron against bishop refusing to institute.

quar(r)enden, n. [1. kwórenden; 2. kwórəndən]. Etymol. unknown. An early dessert apple of a dark crimson colour; also called *Devonshire quar(r)enden*.

quarrel (I.), n. [1. kwórel; 2. kwórəl]. M.E. *querele*, fr. O. Fr. *querele*, fr. Lat. *querēla*, also *querella*, 'a complaining, complaint', cp. *querimōnia*, 'complaint', fr. *queri*, 'to complain'; cogn. w. Scrt. *śvas-*, 'to sigh'. Cp. **querulous.** **1.** A dispute, disagreement, contention, with another, esp. an angry, heated dispute, altercation, brawl. **2. a** Cause of dispute; ground, reason, for quarrelling: *to seek, pick, a quarrel with*; **b** a cause involving a dispute: *to espouse another's quarrel*.

quarrel (II.), vb. intrans., fr. prec. Cp. O. Fr. *quereler*. **1.** (absol.) **a** To engage in a quarrel; to fall out, have an angry dispute: *an ill-tempered man who is always quarrelling*; **b** (of two or more persons) to fall out with each other, become estranged: *he used to be a great friend of mine, but unfortunately we quarrelled*. **2.** *Quarrel with*, **a** to engage in a quarrel with, fall out with (a person); **b** to find fault with, complain of, take exception to (a thing, circumstance, conduct &c.): *I don't quarrel with the way the house is built, but with the extortions of the builder*. Phr. *to quarrel with one's bread and butter*, to act against one's own interests, behave like a spoilt child; to throw up one's employment in pique; to cut off one's nose to spite one's face.

quarrel (III.), n. M.E. *quarel*, fr. O. Fr. *quarrel*, *quarreau*, Mod. Fr. *carreau*, fr. Med. Lat. *quadrellus*, dimin. of Lat. *quadrus*, *quadra*, 'a square', cp. **quadrate.** **1.** (hist.) A short, heavy, square-headed iron bolt or arrow as shot from a crossbow or arbalest; also *quarry*. **2. a** A small, square or lozenge-shaped pane of glass, fitted in lead, for casement windows &c.; **b** a quatrefoil opening in Perpendicular tracery.

quarrelsome, adj. [1. kwórelsum; 2. kwórəlsəm]. **quarrel** (I.) & **-some**. Inclined to quarrel; cantankerous, disputatious.

quarrelsomely, adv. Prec. & **-ly**. In a quarrelsome manner.

quarrelsomeness, n. See prec. & **-ness**. Quality of being quarrelsome.

quarry (I.), n. [1. kwóri; 2. kwóri]. M.E. *querre*, fr. O. Fr. *cuiree*, Mod. Fr. *curée*, 'the spoil', fr. *cuir*, 'skin, hide', fr. Lat. *corium*, 'skin'. See **corium** & **cortex.** **1.** (hist.) A portion of the flesh of a hunted deer or beast of the chase placed on its hide and given to the hounds as a reward. **2.** Any animal being hunted by men, or by beasts or birds of prey: *the quarry was in sight*; *birds in search of quarry*. **3.** (fig.) An object pursued or sought with eagerness; object of vengeance.

quarry (II.), n. Variant of **quarrel** (III.). A small square or lozenge-shaped pane of leaded glass; a quarrel.

quarry (III.), n. M.E. *quarey*, fr. Med. Lat. *quareia*; also M.E. *quarrere*, fr. O. Fr. *quariere*, Mod. Fr. *carrière*, fr. Low Lat. *quadrāria*, 'place where stone is squared and dressed for use in building', fr. Lat. *quadrāre*, 'to make square', see **quadrate.** **1.** A place from which stone or slate is excavated for use in building &c.; used only of such a place where the working is visible and carried on in the open, as contrasted with *mine*. **2.** (fig.) Source from which information can be derived: *family papers are often a regular quarry of information for historians*.

quarry (IV.), vb. trans. & intrans., fr. prec. **A.** trans. **1. a** To fetch out, excavate (stone &c.) from a quarry; **b** to make a quarry in (land). **2.** (fig.) To dig out information from; to search (records &c.) for information. **B.** intrans. To carry out the operation of quarrying.

quarrying, n. [1. kwóri-ing; 2. kwóri-iŋ]. Act of making a quarry or of fetching stone out of it.

quarryman, n. [1. kwóriman; 2. kwórimən]. Worker in a quarry.

quart (I.), n. [1. kwort; 2. kwɔ̄t], fr. Fr. *quarte*, 'fourth part', fr. Lat. *quarta* (*pars*), 'fourth part', fr. *quartus*, 'fourth', ordinal fr. **kʷətwr̥tós*, fr. **kʷotwr̥*, Lat. *quattuor*, 'four', see **quadri-**; cp. also **four** & **tetra-**. **1. a** A measure of liquid capacity, a fourth part of a gallon, two pints; Phr. *to try to put a quart into a pint pot*, to try to make the less hold the greater, to try to do the impossible; **b** measure of dry capacity, the eighth part of a peck, two pints, used of beans or peas. **2. a** A quart measure; bottle, tankard, pot containing a quart; **b** a quantity of beer, cider &c., sufficient to fill a quart measure.

quart (II.), n. [1. kart; 2. kāt], fr. Fr. *quarte*, 'fourth movement'. Same as prec. **1.** A position in fencing; carte. **2.** (cards) A sequence of four cards of a suit, esp. in *piquet*; *a quart major*, ace, king, queen, and knave; *quart to the king*, king to ten.

quartan, adj. & n. [1. kwórtan; 2. kwɔ̄tən], fr. Fr. *quartaine*=*fièvre quartaine*, fr. Lat. *febris quartānus*, 'fever of, belonging to, the fourth (day)'; also *quartāna*, n., 'a quartan ague', fr. *quartus*, 'fourth'. See **quart** (I.) & **-an.** **1.** adj. (of fever, agues) Occurring with intervals of two days between attacks, i.e. on every fourth day reckoning from the first attack. **2.** n. Fever which recurs every fourth day.

quartation, n. [1. kwortáshun; 2. kwɔ̄téiʃən]. See **quart** (I.) & **-ation.** (assaying) Process of mixing three parts of silver to one of gold as first step in purification of the latter.

quarter (I.), n. [1. kwórter; 2. kwɔ̄tə]. O. Fr., Mod. *quartier*, fr. Lat. *quartārius*, 'a fourth part', fr. *quartus*, 'fourth'. See **quart** (I.). **1.** A fourth part of anything; one of four equal or corresponding parts or portions into which anything material or non-material may be divided or regarded as being divided. Phr. *not a quarter*, not nearly, nothing like, e.g. *not a quarter so, as, good as* &c.; *a bad quarter of an hour* (transl. of Fr. phr.), an unpleasant experience, a brief interval during which one passes through an ordeal of some sort; (athletic slang) *the quarter*, race of a quarter of a mile, 440 yds. **2.** One of the four legs of an animal, **a** considered as a joint for the table; **b** as part of the living animal. **3. a** One fourth part of the legal year, three calendar months, esp. as considered as period for which rent, rates &c. are payable; **b** rent &c. due for this period: *to be several quarters in arrear*; **c** (in some public schools) a school term. **4.** (in reckoning time) A quarter of an hour: *a quarter to, past, the hour*; *some clocks strike the quarters*. **5. a** Any one of the four cardinal points of the compass, North, South, East, West: *from what quarter does the wind blow?*; Phr. *lies the wind in that quarter?*, is that the situation, state of things &c.?; **b** a part, area, region, of the earth: *in every quarter of the globe*; Phr. *from every quarter, from all quarters*, from all directions; **c** a part, subdivision, of a district or area; specific part of a city set apart for or occupied by some particular section of the population; one in which some particular form of life or activity is carried on: *the native, Chinese, Jewish, quarter*; *industrial, residential, quarter*; **d** part of the population living in a particular quarter, hence, a section of society, group of persons, particular individuals &c.: *we learn from the highest quarters that* &c.; *his uncle helped him, though he had expected no sympathy from that quarter*. **6.** (pl.) *Quarters*, **a** (mil.) place allotted for troops as lodgings; house, building, where troops are lodged; barracks, station, billets; **b** (nav.) station, post, assigned to each officer and man when on duty, in action, for inspection &c.; **c** (gen.) place where one lodges or lives; habitation, abode; place to live in, accommodation: *excellent quarters at a hotel, farmhouse* &c.; Phrs. *close quarters*, narrow, poor, accommodation, a small house lacking space; *at close quarters*, in close proximity, near by; close together. **7. a** Clemency, esp. in sparing life, shown to a beaten enemy who surrenders in battle (possibly from the fact that shelter or 'quarters' had to be provided for prisoners): *to give quarter*; *quarter was neither given nor expected by either side*; **b** indulgence, moderation, forbearance shown to an opponent in a contest of any kind or to one to whom one stands in position of superior or in judicial capacity. **8.** (her.) **a** One of the four parts into which a shield is divided by a vertical crossing a horizontal line; **b** a bearing or ordinary occupying the dexter chief of a shield; a canton; **c** a quartering. **9. a** (naut.) Either side of the after-part of a ship from the main-chains to the stern; **b** (shoemaking) either of the side pieces of leather between the heel and the vamp. **10.** (of weight) **a** A fourth part of a hundredweight, 28 lb.; **b** specif. (of corn &c.) fourth part of a ton, 8 bushels.

quarter (II.), vb. trans. & intrans., fr. prec. **A.** trans. **1.** To divide into four parts or quarters; **a** to divide an animal's body into four parts, each with a limb; **b** to cut (traitor's body) into four parts after hanging and drawing. **2. a** To provide quarters or lodgings (for troops); **b** (reflex.) *to quarter oneself on*, or *with*, to billet oneself. **3.** (of hounds &c.) To traverse, pass over, cover, an area of ground in various directions in search of a fox or game &c.: *to quarter a* *covert, field of turnips* &c. **4.** (her.) **a** To divide a shield into four parts or quarters by horizontal and vertical lines crossing at the fess point; **b** to bear different coats of arms on the same shield, arranged quarterly, or in quarters; **c** to add another family's coat of arms to one's own in different quarters. **B.** intrans. (of troops) *Quarter at*, to occupy quarters, be stationed, lodged, at or with.

quarterage, n. [1. kwórterij; 2. kwɔ̃təridž]. **quarter (I.)** & **-age**. **1.** A quarterly allowance or payment; payment of a pension, wages &c., every quarter of the year. **2.** Provision of quarters or lodgings for troops &c.

quarter-back, n. (Am. football) The back who plays directly behind the line of forwards.

quarter-bell, n. The bell which sounds the quarter hours in a clock tower.

quarter-bill, n. (nav.) A list giving the stations of every officer and man when summoned to quarters, in action &c.

quarter-binding, n. Leather or cloth binding of a book on the back only and not at the corners; *quarter-bound*, adj., of book with such binding.

quarter-bred, adj. (of cattle, horses &c.) Having only one quarter of pure blood or breeding.

quarter-butt, n. (billiards) A long cue, shorter than the half-butt.

quarter-day, n. The day which begins each quarter of the legal year, for payment of rent &c., for the beginning and ending of tenancies of land or houses; **a** (Engl. law) *Lady Day*, Mar. 25th; *Midsummer*, June 24th; *Michaelmas*, Sept. 29th; *Christmas*, Dec. 25th; **b** (Scots law) *Candlemas*, Feb. 2nd; *Whitsunday*, May 15th; *Lammas*, Aug. 1st; *Martinmas*, Nov. 11th; **c** (U.S.A.) the 1st of Jan., April, July, and Oct.

quarter-deck, n. **1. a** The after-part of a ship's upper deck, extending in the days of sailing ships from the stern to the mainmast and including the poop; **b** the after-deck of a warship, reserved for officers, and, according to ancient custom, saluted by all who come upon it. **2.** The officers of a ship, contrasted with *the forecastle*, i.e. the crew.

quarter-evil, -ill, n. An infective disease, attacking young cattle and sheep, with purulent swellings in the hind-quarters, also called *blackleg* and *black-quarter*, and formerly thought to be allied to anthrax.

quartering, n. [1. kwórtering; 2. kwɔ̃təriŋ]. **quarter (II.)** & **-ing**. **1.** Act of dividing into quarters; specif., as punishment of a traitor: *hanging, drawing, and quartering*. **2.** (her.) **a** A method of marshalling two or more coats of arms on the same shield, as indicating alliances with or descent from different families; **b** a coat of arms so marshalled. **3.** (woodwork) A small strip or post of wood, forming a framework, intended to be plastered or boarded over.

quarterly, adj., adv., & n. [1. kwórterli; 2. kwɔ̃təli]. **quarter (I.)** & **-ly**. **1.** adj. **a** Occurring, recurring, each quarter of the year: *a quarterly meeting; quarterly payments*; **b** (her.) divided into quarters, marshalled in quarterings. **2.** adv. **a** Once every quarter of the year: *meetings are held, payments made, quarterly*; **b** (her.) in quarters or quarterings: *the Royal arms bore quarterly England and France, till 1603; quarterly quartered*, with one or more of the quarters on a shield also divided into quarters. **3.** n. A periodical which is published once every three months during the year.

quartermaster, n. [1. kwórtermàhster; 2. kwɔ̃təmàstə]. **1.** (mil., abbr. Q.M.) An officer in a regiment or battalion with the honorary rank of lieutenant, whose duties are to assign quarters, to receive, issue, and account for stores, rations, clothing, equipment &c. **2.** (nav.) A petty official attending to the steering, binnacle, signals &c.

quartermaster-general, n. (abbr. Q.M.G.) The general officer at the War Office, at the head of the supply departments of the army.

quartermaster-sergeant, n. A non-commissioned officer, of the rank of sergeant, attached to each company of a battalion to assist the quartermaster in his duties.

quarter-mile, n. A quarter of a mile, 440 yds., esp. considered as distance for a foot-race.

quarter-miler, n. Runner who excels especially in a quarter-mile race.

quartern, n. [1. kwórtern; 2. kwɔ̃tən]. M.E. *quartroun, quarteroun*, fr. O. Fr. *quarteron*, 'quarter (of pound &c.)', fr. Low Lat. *quarterōn-(em)*, 'quarter', fr. *quarterus*, form of Lat. *quartus*, 'fourth'. See **quart (I.)**. **1.** A liquid measure, the fourth part of a pint; a gill: *a quartern of gin, rum* &c. **2.** A dry measure, properly a quarter of a peck or stone, about 3½ lb. now usually as a standard measure for bread; *quartern loaf*, a 4-lb. loaf, as made from a quarter of a stone of flour.

quarter-plate, n. **a** A photographic plate or film, measuring 4¼ × 3¼ in.; **b** photograph produced from this.

quarter-saw, vb. trans. To saw (a log of timber) first into quarters from the circumference and then to saw each quarter into planks.

quarter-sessions, n. A court of the justices of the peace or magistrates of a county or part thereof, as of a riding in Yorkshire and of a city or borough, held four times a year, to hear appeals from petty sessions, and also appeals as to rates and from brewster sessions, and to try indictable offences other than treason, criminal libel, and homicide; in certain cities and boroughs the presiding judge is a Recorder, in the others a Chairman elected from and by the body of justices.

quarter-staff, n. A stout wooden staff, from 6 ft. to 8 ft. long, formerly used as a weapon of offence and defence, and in a rude, country sport of fencing, down to the 17th cent.; it was grasped by the left hand in the centre, and by the right hand at about a quarter way of its length at top or bottom.

quarter-tone, n. (mus.) An interval of half a semitone.

quarter-wind, n. A wind blowing on the quarter or after-side of a ship.

quartet, quartette, n. [1. kwortét; 2. kwɔ̄tét]. Fr. *quartette*, fr. Ital. *quartetto*, dimin. of *quarto*, 'fourth, a fourth part', fr. Lat. *quartus*, 'fourth'. See **quart (I.)**. **1.** Set, group, of four persons or things. **2.** Specif. **a** four singers, or four instrumentalists, who sing or play together; **b** a song, or piece of music, arranged for four voices, or four instruments; **c** a performance of such a song or piece of music.

quartile, adj. [1. kwórtīl; 2. kwɔ̃tail]. Fr. See **quart (I.)** & **-ile**. **1.** (astrol.) *Quartile aspect*, that of the planets when they are distant from each other 90° or a quarter of the circle. **2.** (statistics) *Quartile point*, point of comparison, one quarter above or below a median line.

quarto, n. [1. kwórtō; 2. kwɔ̃tou], fr. Lat. *in quarto*, 'in one fourth or quarter of original size', abl. sing. of *quartus*, 'fourth'. See **quart (I.)**. (abbr. *4to*, *4°*) **a** A size of paper, made by folding a sheet twice into four leaves; **b** a book having four leaves or eight pages to the sheet; (loosely) a volume of square or squarish form of about 9 × 12 inches.

quartz, n. [1. kworts; 2. kwɔ̄ts]. Mod. Germ.; etymol. unknown. A form of crystalline silica, found abundantly in granite, gneiss, sandstone, and other rocks; the hexagonal crystals are clear and transparent as in rock crystal or coloured as in amethyst, chalcedony, jasper &c.; it is the most common mineral found in association with gold.

quartzite, n. [1. kwórtsīt; 2. kwɔ̃tsait]. Prec. & **-ite**. A sandstone rock composed of quartz.

quash, vb. trans. [1. kwosh; 2. kwɔʃ]. M.E. *quaschen*, fr. O. Fr. *quasser*, Mod. Fr. *casser*, 'to break, annul', fr. Lat. *quassāre*, freq. of *quatere, quassum*, 'to shake', cogn. w. suff. *-cuss* in vbs. such as **concuss, discuss** &c.; cp. also **squash (I.)**. **1.** (law) To annul, make void, put an end to: *to quash an indictment; to quash further proceedings, a former verdict* &c. **2.** (colloq.) To suppress, put down, quell, extinguish: *to quash a row at a meeting* &c.

Quashee, Quashie, n. [1. kwóshi; 2. kwɔ́ʃi], fr. Ashantee *Kwasi*, a boy's name. A West African negro.

quasi, adj., adv., & pref. [1. kwā́sī; 2. kwéisai]. Lat., 'as if', fr. **qua**, & *si*, 'if, whether', wh. is perh. ultimately related to Engl. **so**. In a certain sense or degree, in a manner, almost, apparently, though not really; usually hyphened to nouns, adjectives, and adverbs: *a quasi-contract; quasi-proof* or *argument; quasi-sovereign, state* &c.

quass, n. See **kvass**.

quassia, n. [1. kwóshia; 2. kwɔ́ʃiə], fr. name of a negro *Quassi, Kwasi*, see **Quashee**, who discovered the value of the drug in the 18th cent. A bitter, medicinal tonic drug, obtained from the wood and bark of a S. American tree; also called Surinam tree, *Quassia amara*; used also for spraying rose-trees and other garden plants to get rid of green-fly.

quater-, pref. Lat., 'four times', formed fr. *quattuor*, 'four'. See **quadrate, quart (I.)**.

quater-centenary, n. [1. kwáter sentḗnari; 2. kwǽtə sentínəri]. A four-hundredth anniversary.

quaternary, adj. & n. [1. kwotḗrnari; 2. kwɔtə́nəri], fr. Lat. *quaternārius*, 'consisting of four each', fr. *quaterni*, 'four each'. See **quater-** & **-ary**. **1.** adj. **a** Consisting of four elements; by fours; in sets of four, having four parts: *quaternary compounds; quaternary number*, the mystical number 10, as composed, according to Pythagoras, of the numbers 1 + 2 + 3 + 4; **b** (geol., cap.) of, pertaining to, the period of geological time subsequent to the Tertiary period, and lasting to the present geological period: *Quaternary period; Quaternary rocks* &c. **2.** n. **a** The number four; a set of four things or parts; the Pythagorean number 10; **b** (geol.) the Quaternary period.

quaternion, n. [1. kwotérnion; 2. kwɔtə́niən], fr. L. Lat. *quaterniōn-(em)*, 'sum of four numbers', fr. Lat. *quaterni*, 'four each'. See prec. **1.** A set, or group, of four numbers, things, parts, or persons. **2.** (math.) *Quaternions*, a method or calculus, propounded by Rowan Hamilton, for dealing algebraically with operations with vectors.

quaternity, n. [1. kwotḗrniti; 2. kwɔtə́niti], fr. L. Lat. *quaternitāt-(em)*. See **quater-** & **-ity**. A group of four persons regarded as one; contrasted with *trinity* &c.

quatorzain, n. [1. katórzān; 2. kætɔ̃zein], fr. Fr. *quatorzaine*, fr. *quatorze*, 'fourteen', fr. Lat. *quattuordecim*, 'fourteen', see **quart (I.)** & **deci-**. Poem of fourteen lines with rhymes arranged *abab, cdcd, efef*, ending with a couplet *gg*; sometimes called a sonnet, but irregular as a form of this; all Shakespeare's sonnets are in this form.

quatrain, n. [1. kwótrān; 2. kwɔ́trein]. Fr., fr. *quatre*, 'four', fr. Lat. *quattuor*, 'four'. See **quarter (I.)** & **quater-**. A four-line stanza, usually rhyming *abab*.

quatrefoil, n. [1. kátrefoil; 2. kǽtrəfɔil]. O. Fr., 'four leaves', fr. *quatre*, 'four', see prec., & **foil (I.)**. **a** (archit.) An ornamental figure, used esp. in tracery, representing a flower with four petals; **b** (her.) similar device as a charge on a shield.

quattrocentist, n. [1. kwàtrōchéntist; 2. kwæ̀troutʃéntist]. See next word & **-ist**. An artist or writer of the quattrocento or 15th cent.

quattrocento, n. [1. kwàtrōchéntō; 2. kwæ̀troutʃéntou]. Ital., lit. 400, applied to the period beginning in 1400; hence the 15th cent. The 15th cent. as a period of Italian art and literature.

quaver (I.), vb. intrans. & trans. [1. kwā́ver; 2. kwéivə]. Cp. M.E. *quāven*, 'to shake'; prob. a variant of **quiver (I.)**. **1.** intrans. **a** To tremble, be tremulous, to shake, vibrate; used esp. of the voice under the influence of strong emotion, or through weakness; also of a musical instrument; **b** to make shakes, to trill, in singing. **2.** trans. To utter with a quavering voice: *to quaver a few words, notes.*

quaver (II.), n., fr. prec. **1.** A quavering, tremulous sound or note; esp. such a sound made by the voice. **2.** (mus.) A note of the time value of half a crotchet or one-eighth of a semibreve.

quaveringly, adv. [1. kwā́veringli; 2. kwéivəriŋli]. Pres. Part. of **quaver (I.)** & **-ly.** With a quavering, tremulous sound or utterance.

quavery, adj. [1. kwā́veri; 2. kwéivəri]. Full of quavers; shaky, tremulous.

quay, n. [1. kē; 2. kī]. M.E. *kay, key* &c., fr. O. Fr. *kai*, Mod. Fr. *quai*, cp. Span. *cayo*, 'a shoal, sand-bank'; of Celt. origin, cp. W. *cae*, 'an enclosure, field, hedge', Bret. *kai*, 'enclosure', as in many Place-Names; the Mod. Engl. spelling is due to Fr. *quai*. A pier, jetty, or wharf; a place for landing passengers and cargo from a ship; usually a kind of wall or mole of stone built along the edge of, or jutting out into, the water of the sea, a river, or a large lake.

quayage, n. [1. kḗ-ij; 2. kí-idž]. Prec. & **-age.** Quay dues, wharfage; room for vessels at a quay-wall.

quean, n. [1. kwēn; 2. kwīn]. O.E. *cwene*, 'woman', M.E. *quēne*; O.S. & O.H.G. *quena*; Goth. *qinō*, fr. **kwenō*; cogn. w. O. Slav. *žena*, 'woman', all fr. Aryan **gʷenā-*; **queen** is fr. a primitive variant of same base. (archaic and obsolesc.) A woman; the word quite early acquired a derogatory sense; a flaunting, brazen woman, a shameless jade, a hussy.

queasily, adv. [1. kwḗzili; 2. kwízili]. **queasy** & **-ly.** In a queasy manner.

queasiness, n. [1. kwḗzines; 2. kwízinis]. See next word & **-ness.** State, quality, of being queasy.

queasy, adj. [1. kwḗzi; 2. kwízi]. Etymol. uncertain; earlier form *coisy*, cp. O. Fr. *coisier, coissier*, 'to hurt'; also *quaysy*, cp. O.N. *kweisa*, 'a whitlow, boil', & Mod. Nor. *kveis*, 'crapulence'. **1. a** (of the stomach) Irritable, inclined to nausea, easily upset; **b** (of persons) feeling sick and unwell, inclined to vomit, having strong feeling of nausea; **c** (of food) producing nausea, nauseating. **2.** (in moral sense) **a** Fastidious, pernickety, hard to please; **b** having an over-delicate conscience; too scrupulous, squeamish.

queen (I.), n. [1. kwēn; 2. kwīn]. O.E. *cwēn*, fr. **cwōni-*, fr. **kwāni-*, 'wife, queen'; O.S. *quān*, Goth. *qēns*, stem *qēni-*, 'wife, queen'; cogn. w. Scrt. *jāni-*, 'woman', fr. **gʷēni-*, &, w. different vowel grade, Gk. *gunḗ*, fr. **gʷənā́*; see **gynaeco-** & also the variant **quean. 1. a** A woman reigning in her own right as sovereign over a kingdom, a *queen regnant*; correlative of *king*: *Victoria became Queen of England on the death of William IV.*; used as title before the name: *Queen Elizabeth*; **b** the wife of a king; in this case, strictly, *Queen Consort*; also as title before the name: *Queen Philippa*; **c** *queen dowager*, widow of a king; *queen mother*, a queen dowager who is mother of a reigning sovereign; **d** (in possessive) used in many titles, names of offices &c. when the reigning sovereign is a queen: *Queen's Colour, Counsel, Remembrancer; the Queen's Navy.* **2. a** A female deity, mythological or legendary figure, regarded as an object of veneration: *queen of night*, Diana; also the moon; **b** a woman who rules or is pre-eminent by beauty, charm, or other qualities: *queen of all hearts*; *queen of beauty, society* &c.; **c** a town, place, country, or other thing regarded as female and as ruling or pre-eminent: *Venice, Queen of the Adriatic*; *queen of the air, of the seas* &c. **3. a** (cards) A court card, representing a queen, ranking next below the king and above the knave: *queen of clubs, hearts* &c.; **b** (chess) the principal scoring and moving piece, placed at the start on her own colour; *queen's knight, bishop, pawn* &c., the knight, bishop, pawn &c. on that side and the pawn in front. **4. a** Female of certain animals, e.g. the cat; **b** a fully developed, fertile female of certain insects living in communities: *queen bee, wasp*; *queen ant* &c.

queen (II.), vb. trans., fr. prec. **1.** (rare) **a** To make a queen of; **b** to rule over (a country) as queen. **2.** (chess) To move a pawn into a square on the opposite end of the board and convert it into a queen or other piece. **3.** *Queen it*, to behave like a queen, play the queen; to take a pre-eminent position, dominate: **a** by virtue of natural qualities of charm, beauty, leadership &c.; **b** by forcing oneself arrogantly forward in a domineering manner.

Queen Anne, adj. [1. kwēn án; 2. kwīn ǽn]. Belonging to a style of architecture, furniture &c. dating from the first part of the 18th cent.

Queen Anne's Bounty, n. A fund, originally granted in 1703 by Queen Anne from the first-fruits, for increasing the stipends of poor clergy of the Church of England.

queendom, n. [1. kwḗndum; 2. kwíndəm]. **queen** & **-dom,** on anal. of *kingdom*. (rare) Rule, realm, of a queen; the kingdom of a queen.

queenhood, n. [1. kwḗnhood; 2. kwínhud]. **queen** & **-hood. a** State, condition, of a queen; **b** period of rule of a queen.

queening, n. [1. kwḗning; 2. kwíniŋ]. Origin uncertain. Kind of apple.

queenless, adj. [1. kwḗnles; 2. kwínlis]. **queen** & **-less.** Without a queen; esp. of swarm of bees.

queenlike, adj. [1. kwḗnlīk; 2. kwínlaik]. **queen** & **-like.** Queenly.

queenliness, n. [1. kwḗnlines; 2. kwínlinis]. **queenly** & **-ness.** Quality of being queenly.

queenly, adj. [1. kwḗnli; 2. kwínli]. **queen (I.)** & **-ly. 1.** Like a queen; stately, majestic. **2. a** Belonging, appertaining to, a queen: *the queenly office*; *her queenly word*; **b** fit, suitable, appropriate for, a queen: *they built a queenly palace*; *to live in queenly splendour.*

queen post, n. One of two short vertical posts of a truss in a roof, fixed in the tie-beam, and supporting the principal rafters.

queer (I.), adj. [1. kwēr; 2. kwiə]. Etymol. doubtful; orig. a slang word, prob. fr. Germ. *quer*, 'crosswise, across', wh. is a variant of earlier (O.H.G.) *zwerah*, 'crooked, crosswise', cogn. w. O.E. *þweorh*, see **thwart (I.)**; related to Lat. *torquēre*, 'to twist' &c., see **torque. 1.** Odd, strange, eccentric: *a queer sort of fellow*; *a queer dress*; *to speak a queer language.* **2.** Doubtful, suspicious, shady, questionable: *a queer sort of story*; *something queer about him.* Phr. *in Queer Street*, in difficulties, esp. shady financial ones. **3. a** Not in normal health, indisposed, out of sorts, poorly: *feeling a little queer*; **b** slightly mad: *he has become quite queer*; *queer in the head*; *gone queer.*

queer (II.), vb. trans., fr. prec. (colloq. or slang) To cause to go wrong; to spoil, put out of order. Phr. *to queer the pitch*, to spoil the chances of success of another, esp. by shady or doubtful means.

queerish, adj. [1. kwḗrish; 2. kwíəriʃ]. **queer (I.)** & **-ish.** Rather queer, somewhat odd.

queerly, adv. [1. kwḗrli; 2. kwíəli]. **queer (I.)** & **-ly.** In a queer manner.

queerness, n. [1. kwḗrnes; 2. kwíənis]. **queer (I.)** & **-ness.** State, quality, of being queer; a slight indisposition.

quell, vb. trans. [1. kwel; 2. kwɛl]. O.E. *cwellan*, M.E. *quellen*, 'to kill, strike'; O.S. *quellian*, 'to torture'; O.N. *kvelja*, 'to torment'; all fr. Gmc. **kwalljan*, fr. base seen in O.E. *cwalu*, 'death', & perh. in *cwealm*, see **qualm**; cp. further O.E. *cwelan*, 'to die' (strong vb.), fr. base **gʷel-*, **gʷol-* &c., whence Lat. *vallescit*, 'he perished', fr. **gʷəl-*; Lith. *gelà*, 'agony' &c.; see **quail (II.). 1.** To put down, suppress, subdue; to daunt, quench, stifle: *to quell a rebellion, mutiny, a hubbub.* **2.** (in moral sense) **a** To repress, restrain: *to quell one's passions*; **b** to allay, cause to abate and die down: *to quell fears* &c.

queller, n. [1. kwéler; 2. kwélə]. Prec. & **-er.** One who quells.

quench, vb. trans. [1. kwensh; 2. kwenʃ]. O.E. *cwencan*, 'to extinguish', M.E. *quenchen*, fr. **cwanc-jan*; cp. O.E. *cwincan*, Pret. *cwanc*, 'to die out, be extinguished'. **1. a** To put out, extinguish, damp down (fire, heat, light); **b** (in non-material sense) *to quench hope, desire, hatred* &c. **2.** To allay, slake (thirst).

quenchable, adj. [1. kwénshabl; 2. kwénʃəbl]. Prec. & **-able.** Capable of being quenched (in all senses).

quencher, n. [1. kwénsher; 2. kwénʃə]. See prec. & **-er.** One who, that which, quenches; esp. (colloq.) that which quenches thirst; drink.

quenelle, n. [1. kenél; 2. kənél]. Fr.; etymol. doubtful. A ball of finely minced chicken or veal, seasoned and fried quickly in boiling fat.

Quercus, n. [1. kwḗrkus; 2. kwʌ́kəs]. Lat., 'oak tree'; for **perkʷos*; cogn. w. O.H.G. *forha*, 'fir tree' &c.; O.E. *furh*, see **fir.** (bot.) The genus of trees which includes all the oaks.

querimonious, adj. [1. kwèrimṓnius; 2. kwiərimóuniəs], fr. Lat. *querimōnia*, 'complaint', & **-ous.** See **quarrel (I.).** Complaining, querulous.

querist, n. [1. kwḗrist; 2. kwíərist]. See **query** & **-ist.** One who inquires, makes queries or asks questions.

quern, n. [1. kwērn; 2. kwʌ̄n]. O.E. *cweorn*, 'hand-mill', O.N. *kvern*, Goth. *qairnus*; according to Walde, possibly cogn. w. Lat. *glārea*, 'gravel', for **grārea*, fr. base **gʷerā*, 'to grind'; cp. also Lith. *gírnos*; O. Slav. *žrŭny*, 'mill'; Scrt. *grāvan-*, 'stone for pressing out soma juice'. A hand-mill for grinding corn, spices, pepper &c.

querulous, adj. [1. kwérūlus; 2. kwérjuləs], fr. L. Lat. *querulōsus*, Lat. *querulus*, 'complaining, full of complaints', fr. *queri*, 'to complain'. See **quarrel (I.).** Complaining, full of complaints; habitually fault-finding; fretful, peevish.

querulously, adv. Prec. & **-ly.** In a querulous manner.

querulousness, n. See prec. & **-ness.** State, quality, of being querulous.

query (I.), n. [1. kwḗri; 2. kwíəri]. Anglicized form of Lat. *quaere*, imperat. of *quaerere*, 'to seek, ask', used as n. See **quaere** & cp. **question. 1.** A question, esp. one implying a doubt, suspicion, or objection. **2.** A mark of interrogation (?).

query (II.), vb. trans. & intrans., fr. prec. **A.** trans. **1. a** To express doubts concerning, to call in question (a statement, truth, accuracy of a statement, alleged facts &c.): *I query very much whether it is wise to act so hastily*; **b** to require further explanation concerning; to question. **2.** To place a mark of interrogation after (a written or printed word, sentence &c.). **B.** intrans. To question; to express doubt.

quest (I.), n. [1. kwest; 2. kwest], fr. O. Fr. *queste*, Mod. Fr. *quête*, fr. Low Lat. *questa*, fem., 'thing sought for', fr. Lat. *quaesīta*, fem. sing. of P.P. of *quaerere*, 'to seek'. See **question. 1.** A search, seeking, pursuit: *in quest of adventure*; *a knightly quest*; *the quest for the Grail.* **2.** (archaic and provinc.) Inquest; e.g. *crowner's quest.*

quest (II.), vb. intrans. & trans., fr. O. Fr. *quester*, Mod. Fr. *quêter*. See prec. **1.** intrans. To search, follow on a trail or track, as a hound: *to quest out, about, for game.* 2. trans. (rare) To seek, search for, pursue.

question (**I.**), n. [1. kwéschun; 2. kwéstʃən]. O. Fr., fr. Lat. *quaestiōn-(em)*, 'a seeking, inquiry, matter of investigation; case, question', fr. *quaesīt-(um)*, P.P. type of *quaerere*, 'to seek, inquire, ask', & **-ion.** Cp. **quaestor** & **quaere.** **1.** A demand, inquiry, for information; an interrogation which expects or demands an answer: *please give a civil answer to a civil question.* Phr. *without question*, without dispute; undoubtedly, unquestionably. See also **leading question.** **2.** A sentence in interrogative form, an interrogative sentence, which consists in English of (i.) one beginning with an interrogative pronoun or adverb: *who did this?*; *why did you do it?*; (ii.) one in which the verb is put before its subject: *are you coming?* Sentences of type (ii.) are uttered with a rising tone, the highest pitch being at the end; all interrogative sentences are followed by (?) when written. **3. a** Subject of uncertainty; point of discussion; speculation, inquiry, investigation: *how far Chaucer was acquainted with Dante is an interesting question*; *there are several questions I want to talk to you about*; *he raised the question of leaving the army*; *the question is*, the matter under discussion is; Phrs. *out of the question*, not to be discussed or considered at all; quite impossible; *to call in question*, challenge, express doubt concerning, demand proof of (a statement, alleged fact, &c.); **b** specif., matter, subject, under debate by a deliberative or legislative body; Phr. *to put the question*, submit (resolution) to the votes of the meeting; (for the *previous question*, see **previous**); *Question!*, exclamation at public meeting &c., (i.) calling attention to irrelevancy on part of a speaker; (ii.) expressing doubt or disagreement with a statement; **c** problem, group of problems, arising out of a set of facts; connected with social or other conditions, or with some special branch of study or investigation: *questions of the day*; *political, economic, questions*; *philological, grammatical, questions*; **d** in greatly weakened, generalized sense, matter, affair, situation, state of affairs: *it is a question of acting instantly or not at all*; *the question is whether we can arrive in time.* **4.** (hist.) Torture, employed as a method of extracting answers from an unwilling witness: *to put to the question.*

question (**II.**), vb. trans. & intrans. O. Fr. *questionner.* See prec. **A.** trans. **1.** To ask questions of, put questions to; to inquire of, interrogate, to examine by question and answer: *to question a witness.* **2.** To study natural phenomena, books &c., in order to gain information: *to question the stars*; *to question the Scriptures.* **3.** To call in question; to express doubts concerning, dissatisfaction with; to dispute: *to question the chairman's ruling*; *to question a person's honesty* &c.; *to question a person's right, power, to do* &c.; *I question whether daylight-saving is an unmixed blessing.* **B.** intrans. To ask questions; to inquire.

questionable, adj. [1. kwéschunabl; 2. kwéstʃənəbl]. Prec. & **-able.** Open to questioning, liable to be questioned, disputed, challenged; **a** of doubtful reliability, or veracity: *a questionable statement*; **b** of doubtful honesty, propriety, decency: *questionable conduct*; *questionable respectability.*

questionableness, n. Prec. & **-ness.** State, quality, of being questionable.

questionably, adv. See prec. & **-ly.** In a questionable manner.

questionary, adj. & n. [1. kwéschunari; 2. kwéstʃənəri]. See **question** (**I.**) & **-ary.** **1.** adj. Asking questions, interrogative. **2.** n. (rare) Questionnaire.

questioner, n. [1. kwéschuner; 2. kwéstʃənə]. **question** (**II.**) & **-er.** One who questions; an inquirer.

questioningly, adv. [1. kwéschuningli; 2. kwéstʃəniŋli]. Pres. Part. of **question** (**II.**) & **-ly.** In a questioning manner; interrogatively, inquiringly.

question-mark, n. The symbol (?) indicating that the sentence which precedes it is interrogative.

questionnaire, n. [1. kèstionár, kwèschunár; 2. kèstiənéə, kwèstʃənéə]. Fr. See **questionary.** Series of formal questions, usually printed with spaces left for the answers, devised to obtain statistics, opinions, and information generally on some specific subject.

quetzal, n. [1. kwétsal; 2. kwétsəl]. Span.-Am. *quetzale*, fr. anct. Mexican, *quetzalli*, the long green tail feather of the sacred bird. **a** A large, brilliantly coloured bird of Central America, the male of which has tail feathers of great length; **b** national emblem and unit of coinage of Guatemala.

queue (**I.**), n. [1. kū; 2. kjū]. Fr., fr. Lat. *cauda*, 'tail', cp. **caudal** & **cue** (**II.**). **1.** A twisted tail or plait of the natural hair or of a wig, as formerly worn by men, tied with ribbon, and allowed to hang down behind. **2.** A long line of people, one behind another, waiting their turn to be admitted to a theatre, enclosure, booking office &c.; line of vehicles waiting for their owners.

queue (**II.**), vb. intrans., fr. prec. (usually *queue up*) To form a queue; to take one's place, and wait, in a queue.

quia emptores, n. [1. kwía emptṓrēz; 2. kwáiə ɛmptṓriz]. Lat., 'because purchasers'. (hist.) The name of a Statute, 1290, in reign of Edward I., also called *Statute of Westminster*, which laid down that purchasers of land should hold from the chief lord.

quibble, n. & vb. intrans. [1. kwíbl; 2. kwíbl]. Etymol. doubtful; possibly a variant (dimin.) of **quip**; or a corrupt. of Lat. *quibus*, abl. pl. of *quī*, 'who', as part of legal jargon; cp. **quiddity.** **1.** n. An evasive, shifty answer, or statement; a questionable device for getting out of a difficulty in an argument &c.; an equivocation; a trivial, verbal, or metaphysical distinction made to score a point; a piece of chicanery. **2.** vb. To use quibbles; to equivocate; to practise chicanery.

quick (**I.**), adj. [1. kwik; 2. kwik]. O.E. *cwicu*, 'living', M.E. *quik* &c., 'alive, lively'; the Engl. form, together w. O.S. *quik*, O.H.G. *quek*, O.N. *kvikr*, 'living', all go back to a redupl. form **kwikwa-*, of Gmc. **kwiwa-*, or **kwiwu-*; this type survives in Goth. *qius*, 'living'. The Aryan form was **gʷiwo-*, **gʷeiwo-* &c., whence Lat. *vīvere*, 'to be alive'; see **vivacious**; *vīta*, 'life', fr. **vivita*, see **vital**; also Gk. *bíos*, 'life', see **bio-**, & perh. Gk. *zōós*, 'living', *zṓon*, 'living creature', see **zoo-**. **1.** (archaic, Bib., liturg.) Living, having life; esp. in Phr. *the quick and the dead.* **2.** (archaic, of woman) Pregnant with a child that has given signs of life, that has quickened. **3. a** (i.) Lively and vigorous in intellect; ready in understanding: *quick to understand, to learn*; *some children are very quick*; *quick to sympathize* &c.; (ii.) (of the mind), working rapidly; promptly responsive to instruction, to emotional appeal &c.: *a quick mind, wit*; *a quick temper*, one easily aroused, fiery; **b** responding readily to external, physical stimuli; sensitive, acute: *a quick eye, ear.* In modern usage the idea of speed and rapidity is usually more or less present in the mind in the above and similar sentences. **4.** (of action and movement) **a** Performed with speed; rapid, swift, speedy: *quick work*; *a quick gallop, walk* &c.; **b** brusque and sudden; hasty, hurried: *a quick thrust*; *a quick glance* &c. **5. a** (of actions and events thought of in relation to time) Carried out, done, taking place within, occupying, a brief space of time; not lasting long: *a quick luncheon*; *quick writing*; *a quick journey*; *only time for a quick walk round*; **b** (of persons and living things, gen.) acting, moving, rapidly; performing action and movements within a short space of time: *to be quick about one's work*; *a quick worker*; *this rose is a quick grower*; *do be quick and get your job done.*

quick (**II.**), adv. O.E. *cwice*, 'quickly'. See prec. (colloq.) Quickly; **a** rapidly: *don't talk too quick*; *run as quick as you can*; **b** within a brief space of time: *please come quick*; *now then, quick! you are too slow*; *you'll find the term will pass very quick*; also before adj. fr. Pres. Part.: *quick-flying, quick-growing* &c.

quick (**III.**), n., fr. prec. **1.** (obs.) A living creature. **2.** Living, growing, sensitive flesh; specif. **a** the sensitive part of the finger or toe below nail or from which the nail grows: *to cut the finger-nail to the quick*; **b** the very tender, innermost part of a wound, esp. where healthy flesh is beginning to grow: *to probe a wound to the quick*; **c** (fig.) the centre of feeling or emotion; place, spot, most sensitive of being touched or stirred: *the mere suspicion stung him to the quick*; *your coldness cuts me to the quick.*

quick-change, adj. Chiefly, *quick-change artist*, actor who changes his costume and appearance with great rapidity, in order to act a different part.

quicken, vb. trans. & intrans. [1. kwíken; 2. kwíkən]. **quick** (**I.**) & **-en.** **A.** trans. **1.** To make alive, give life to; to stir, stimulate, arouse: *to quicken the imagination.* **2.** To cause to move more rapidly; to hasten, accelerate: *to quicken one's steps*; *to quicken the time.* **B.** intrans. **1.** To revive; to become more alive, vigorous, or lively: *his anger quickened*; *imagination quickens at the thought.* **2. a** (of the child in the womb) To move, stir, show signs of life; **b** (of pregnant woman) to feel the stirring, and signs of life in the child. **3.** To move more rapidly; to be accelerated: *the pulse quickens* (also fig.); *his steps quickened*; *the rhythm of the music quickens.*

quick-fence, n. A quickset hedge.

quick-firer, n. [1. kwík fírer; 2. kwík fáiərə]. Gun with a single barrel fitted with special mechanism for loading and firing rapidly.

quicklime, n. [1. kwíklīm; 2. kwíklaim]. Unslaked lime.

quickly, adv. [1. kwíkli; 2. kwíkli]. **quick** (**I.**) & **-ly.** **a** Rapidly; **b** within a brief space of time.

quick march, n. (mil.) **a** A march in quick time, the usual rate of marching; **b** command to march in this way.

quick-match, n. A quickly burning match or fuse used for exploding a charge, made of cotton-thread saturated with a mixture of gunpowder, alcohol &c.

quickness, n. [1. kwíknes; 2. kwíknis]. **quick** (**I.**) & **-ness.** State, quality, of being quick: **a** alertness, readiness, promptness, of mind or body; *quickness of temper*, hastiness, proneness to become angry; **b** rapidity of movement &c.

quicksand, n. [1. kwíksand; 2. kwíksænd]. **1.** Loose, wet sand, in a mass, yielding easily to pressure and weight, liable to engulf those who attempt to cross it. **2.** Any intricate, dangerous, treacherous state of affairs.

quickset, adj. & n. [1. kwiksét; 2. kwiksét]. **1.** adj. Formed of quick or living plants, esp. of a hedge made of hawthorn. **2.** n. A quickset or hawthorn hedge.

quick-sighted, adj. Having a quick eye or sight; quick to see and understand.

quick-sightedness, n. Prec. & **-ness.** Quality of being quick-sighted; rapid, acute, vision.

quicksilver, n. & vb. trans. [1. kwíksilver; 2. kwíksilvə]. **quick**, 'living, lively, moving', & **silver**, fr. the silvery appearance, cp. Germ. *quecksilber*, & Lat. *argentum vivum.* **1.** n. **a** The metal mercury; **b** a mercurial, lively, temperament or character; person with such a temperament. **2.** vb. To cover with quicksilver.

quick step, n. **1.** The step used in marching at quick time. **2.** A march or dance tune in quick time.

quick time, n. (mil.) The ordinary marching step or rate of marching, of 128 steps, 33 inches in length, per minute.

quick-witted, adj. Having a quick or nimble wit.

quicunque vult, n. [1. kwikúngkwi vúlt; 2. kwaikáŋkwi vált]. The Athanasian Creed, from the two words, Lat., 'Whosoever will (be saved)', with which it begins.

quid (I.), n. [1. kwid; 2. kwid]. A dialectal variant of **cud**. A piece of hard, compressed tobacco leaf, used for chewing.

quid (II.), n. Etymol. doubtful; possibly abbr. of *quid pro quo.* (slang) A sovereign; the sum of a pound in money; not inflected in pl.: *half a quid*; *a couple of, five, quid.*

quiddity, n. [1. kwíditi; 2. kwíditi], fr. Med. Lat. *quidditas,* a term of the Schoolmen, on anal. of *quālitas,* 'quality', fr. Lat. *quid,* 'what' (cp. **what**), & **-ity.** **1.** (lit.) 'Whatness'; the essence, essential quality of anything. **2.** A quibble, captious question.

quidnunc, n. [1. kwídnùngk; 2. kwídnàŋk]. Lat. *quid,* 'what?', *nunc,* 'now'. An idle gossip and busybody; a person always eager to learn, and impart, information of a trivial character, esp. about the affairs of other people.

quid pro quo, n. [1. kwid prō kwṓ; 2. kwid prou kwóu]. Lat., 'something for something'. Something in return for, or as equivalent to something else: *to do nothing without a quid pro quo.*

quiesce, vb. intrans. [1. kwiés; 2. kwaiés], fr. Lat. *quiescere,* 'to rest, keep quiet; to cease, desist from'; formed fr. Lat. *quiēs,* n., 'rest, repose; peace, calm' &c. See **quiet** (II.). (rare) To become silent, quiet, or still.

quiescence, -cy, n. [1. kwiésens(i); 2. kwaiésəns(i)]. See next word & **-ce** or **-cy.** State, quality, of being quiescent; inactivity, passivity.

quiescent, adj. [1. kwiésent; 2. kwaiésənt], fr. Lat. *quiescent-(em),* Pres. Part. of *quiescere.* See **quiesce** & **quiet** (II.). Not moving, in a state of repose; quiet, motionless; inactive, dormant, passive.

quiescently, adv. Prec. & **-ly.** Passively, dormantly; without activity.

quiet (I.), adj. [1. kwíet; 2. kwáiət]. Lat. *quiētus,* 'calm, resting, keeping quiet', see **quietus,** fr. P.P. of *quiescere,* 'to rest, keep quiet, be still' &c., see **quiesce.** For etymol. see next word. General meaning, calm, still, peaceful; (various special applications). **1. a** (of inanimate objects) Free from movement, esp. from violent movement; not violently agitated or shaken; not stirring rapidly or violently: *a quiet sea*; *the winds are quiet now*; **b** (of living things) (i.) still, at rest; not moving: *I want to be quiet after my journey*; *now, children, keep quiet for a while after dinner*; (ii.) not restless: *the patient at last is quieter*; *that fiery heart is quiet now.* **2. a** Not noisy; causing, making, little or no sound; silent: *my car is a very quiet one*; *we have such quiet neighbours that we never hear them*; *he was very quiet all the evening, and hardly spoke*; Phr. *to keep something quiet,* not to talk about, or publish it abroad; **b** not boisterous or rowdy: *quiet fun*; *nice quiet people*; **c** having become silent and hushed: *everything is quiet after 10 o'clock*; **d** remote from, not disturbed by, noise: *a quiet street, neighbourhood.* **3.** (of the mind, conscience &c.) Free from excitement, serene; untroubled, unruffled; at peace with itself. **4. a** (of manner, bearing &c.) (i.) Restrained, placid, calm; (ii.) reticent, reserved; **b** (of movements, way of moving &c.) easy, smooth; not jerky, brusque, or spasmodic; graceful, well poised. **5. a** (of social or political conditions) Free from disturbance, peaceful: *the country was now quiet after the recent riots*; **b** (of surroundings, mode of life &c.) monotonous, uneventful, lacking variety; devoid of gaiety and excitement: *he finds life in the country too quiet*; *a quiet wedding,* one without ostentation and display; *a quiet dinner party,* informal, one with few guests. **6.** (of effect produced on the eye) Unobtrusive, not glaring or flamboyant: *quiet colours, decorations*; *a quiet style of dress.*

quiet (II.), n., fr. Lat. *quiēt-(em),* 'rest, repose, quiet, freedom from toil, sleep'. Cp. prec. & **quietus**; fr. base *k^weijē-, 'to lie at rest'; whence also Zend *šāitiš,* 'joy', O. Slav. *(po-)čiti,* 'to rest', *(po-)koji,* 'rest'; O.E. *hwīl,* 'time', O.N. *hvīla,* 'place of rest', see **while** (I.); possibly ultimately conn. w. Lat. *cīvis,* 'citizen', see **civil,** & cogns. there given. Cp. also **coy. 1.** Freedom from, absence of, noise, bustle, or fuss; stillness, silence: *the quiet of the country, of the sky, of open spaces.* **2.** Freedom from action, movement, toil; repose: *to enjoy a few hours of quiet after exertion.* **3.** Peace of mind, freedom from mental agitation; serenity, placidity: *the quiet of a contented mind.* **4.** Freedom from social and political agitation; absence of disturbance; peace, peacefulness: *the country enjoyed many years of quiet after the war.*

quiet (III.), vb. trans. & intrans. Cp. Low or Med. Lat. *quiētāre.* See prec. **1.** trans. To make, cause to become, quiet (in various senses); **a** to soothe, console, give peace of mind to: '*nothing but well and fair, And what may quiet us in a death so noble*' (Milton, 'Samson Agonistes', ll. 1723-4); **b** to mollify, pacify, silence &c. **2.** intrans. Chiefly *quiet down,* to become quiet; to abate, die down.

quieten, vb. trans. & intrans. [1. kwíeten; 2. kwáiətən]. Prec. & **-en.** (popular or vulg.) To quiet; also intrans., *quieten down.*

quietism, n. [1. kwíetizm; 2. kwáiətizəm]. Span. & Ital. *quietismo,* Fr. *quiétisme.* See **quiet** (I.) & **-ism. 1.** (cap.) A religious movement begun by Molinos in Rome, also in France by Madame Guyon and Fénelon, before the end of the 17th cent.; characterized by a passive mysticism, the contemplation of the perfection of God, and aiming at entire subordination of the will. **2.** Peace, quiet, tranquillity of mind and spirit.

quietist, n. [1. kwíetist; 2. kwáiətist]. Prec. & **-ist,** cp. Fr. *quiétiste.* One who advocates and practises quietism.

quietistic, adj. [1. kwietístik; 2. kwaiətístik]. Prec. & **-ic.** Pertaining to quietism or the quietists.

quietly, adv. [1. kwíetli; 2. kwáiətli]. **quiet** (I.) & **-ly.** In a quiet manner (in all senses of the adj.).

quietness, n. [1. kwíetnes; 2. kwáiətnis]. See prec. & **-ness.** State, quality, of being quiet (in all senses).

quietude, n. [1. kwíetūd; 2. kwáiətjūd]. Fr. See **quiet** (II.) & **-tude.** (chiefly in non-material sense) Rest, quietness; tranquillity.

quietus, n. [1. kwiḗtus; 2. kwaiítəs]. Lat., adj., P.P. of *quiescere,* see **quiesce** & **quiet** (I.); in Med. Lat. phr. *quiētus est,* 'he is finished with'. **1.** (archaic) Quittance, final discharge, as of an obligation or debt. **2.** Riddance, final discharge from life &c.: *to give a man his quietus*; *to get one's quietus.*

quill (I.), n. [1. kwil; 2. kwil]. Etymol. uncertain. **1. a** The hollow stem of the larger (tail) feathers of birds; the large feathers themselves; **b** any of various objects made from quills, esp. a pen for writing (made from a goose's quill), a small fishing float &c. **2.** One of the long, sharp spines of a porcupine. **3.** One of several things resembling a bird's quill in shape, e.g. the reed of a wooden wind instrument; a small roll of cinchona bark &c.

quill (II.), vb. trans. Prob. fr. prec. **1.** To fold, gather (lawn, lace &c.), into circular, quill-shaped rolls. **2.** To wind thread round a quill or bobbin.

quill-driver, n. Jocular and derisive name for a person who uses his pen continuously; esp. a clerk in a subordinate position.

quillet, n. [1. kwílet; 2. kwílit]. Etymol. doubtful; prob. a variant of **quiddity.** Skeat notes that 17th cent. Ital. has *quidita* & *quilita.* (archaic) A quibble; sublety, nicety: '*his quiddities . . . his quillets*' (Shakespeare, 'Hamlet', v. 1): *the quillets of the law.*

quilling, n. [1. kwíling; 2. kwíliŋ]. **quill** (II.) & **-ing.** Lace ruffles, ribbons &c. gathered into quills or rolls.

quilt, n. & vb. trans. [1. kwilt; 2. kwilt], fr. O. Fr. *cuilte,* fr. Lat. *culcita,* 'mattress, bolster', fr. base *k^wel-, 'to bend, roll'; cogn. w. Scrt. *kūrčáš,* 'bundle, ball'; prob. also w. Gk. *kólpos,* 'vault, curve', O.E. *hwealf,* O.N. *hvalf,* 'curve, arch', & O.H.G. *(h)welben,* 'to vault, arch'. **1.** n. **a** Coverlet made by placing some soft, thick substance, wadding &c., between two layers of material and cross-stitching it into place; **b** any material so treated. **2.** vb. **a** To form into a quilt or quilted material; **b** to line with quilting.

quilting, n. [1. kwílting; 2. kwíltiŋ]. Prec. & **-ing.** Quilted material.

quinary, adj. [1. kwínari; 2. kwáinəri], fr. Lat. *quīnārius,* 'containing five, consisting of five', fr. *quīni,* 'five each'. See **quinque.** Arranged in fives, consisting of five numbers; based on the number five.

quinate (I.), adj. [1. kwínāt; 2. kwáineit], fr. Lat. *quīni.* See prec. & **-ate.** (bot.) Of a compound leaf, made up of five leaflets.

quinate (II.), n. See **quinic** & **-ate.** (chem.) A salt of quinic acid.

quince, n. [1. kwins; 2. kwins]. Earlier *quins, quines,* pl. of obs. *quine,* also earlier *coin, coine,* fr. O. Fr. *coin, coing,* fr. Lat. *cotōnia,* a corrupt. or variant of *Cydōnia,* 'a quince, the Cydonian apple', fr. Gk. *kudōnia,* 'quince tree', *kudōnion mēlon,* 'quince', i.e. of Cydonia, town of ancient Crete. Pear-shaped fruit, deep yellow when ripe, very acid, and having a characteristic flavour; only eaten cooked, and then only mixed with apples in tarts &c., or made into a stiff conserve.

quincentenary, n. [1. kwìnsentḗnari; 2. kwìnsentínəri]. New formation, see **quinque-,** w. more familiar **centenary,** instead of **quingentenary.** A five-hundredth anniversary.

quincuncial, adj. [1. kwìnkúnshial; 2. kwìnkánʃiəl], fr. Lat. *quincunciālis.* See **quincunx** & **-al.** Of the form of a quincunx.

quincunx, n. [1. kwínkungks; 2. kwínkaŋks]. Lat., 'five dots marking $\frac{5}{12}$ of an ounce, also $\frac{5}{12}$ of a pound &c., the number five on dice, also of arrangement of trees', see **quinque,** 'five', & **uncia. 1.** Group of five objects so arranged that one is at each corner of a square and one in the middle. **2.** Specif., arrangement of fruit trees or shrubs in such groups: '*And he, whose lightning pierced the Iberian lines, Now forms my quincunx, and now ranks my vines*' (Pope, 'Epist. to Mr. Fortescue', 129-30).

quingentenary, adj. & n. [1. kwìnjentḗnari; 2. kwìndʒentínəri], fr. Lat. *quingenti,* '500', fr. **quinque-,** '5', & *centum,* '100' (see **cent**), & suff. as in **centenary. 1.** adj. Of, in, the 500th year. **2.** n. A five-hundredth anniversary.

quinia, n. [1. kwínia; 2. kwíniə]. Neo-Lat. See **quinine.** Quinine.

quinic, adj. [1. kwínik; 2. kwínik]. See next word & **-ic.** (chem.) A crystalline, white acid, obtained from cinchona bark: *quinic acid.*

quinine, n. [1. kwinḗn; 2. kwinín]. Fr., fr. Span. *quinquina,* also *quina, quina-quina,* fr. Peruv. *kina,* 'bark of the cinchona tree'. **1.** Alkaloid with very bitter taste, obtained from the bark of the cinchona. **2.** Preparation of this, esp. the sulphate, used medicinally, esp. as a specific against malaria.

quininism, quinism, n. [1. kwinḗnizm, kwínizm; 2. kwinínizəm, kwáinizəm]. Prec. & **-ism.** (rare) Condition of being overdosed with quinine.

quininize, quinize, vb. trans. [1. kwinḗnīz, kwínīz; 2. kwinínaiz, kwáinaiz]. See prec. & **-ize.** (rare) To overdose, saturate, with quinine.

quinquagenarian, adj. & n. [1. kwìngkwajenárian; 2. kwìŋkwədʒinéəriən], fr. Lat. *quinquāgēnārius,* adj., fr. *quinquāgēni,* 'fifty each', formed fr. *quinquāginta,* 'fifty', fr.

quinque, 'five', see **quinque-**. **1.** adj. Fifty years old. **2.** n. A person of fifty years of age.

quinquagenary, n. [1. kwìngkwajḗnari; 2. kwìŋkwədžīnəri]. See prec. & **-ary**. A fiftieth anniversary.

quinquagesima, n. [1. kwìngkwajésima; 2. kwiŋkwədžésimə]. Lat., 'fiftieth', as prec. word; in Med., Eccles., Lat. *quinquagesima dies*, 'fiftieth day'. (cap.) The Sunday before Lent, as the fiftieth day, reckoned inclusively, before Easter, or as the Sunday before Quadragesima Sunday, the first Sunday in Lent; also *Quinquagesima Sunday*.

quinquangular, adj. [1. kwìngkwánggūlar; 2. kwiŋkwǽŋgjulə]. **quinqua-** & **angular**. Having five angles.

quinque-, **quinqui-**, also, in some compounds, **quinqua-**, pref. Lat. *quinque*, 'five'; fr. earlier **penkʷe*, w. Lat. *q-* on anal. of *quattuor*, 'four', see **quater-** &c.; cogn. w. Scrt. *pañča*; Gk. *pénte*, see **penta-**; Lith. *penki*; Goth. *fimf*, 'five', see also **five** (**I.**) & **finger**.

quinquennial, adj. [1. kwìngkwénial; 2. kwìŋkwéniəl]. Formed on anal. of *biennial*, fr. Lat. *quinquennālis*, fr. *quinquennis*. See **quinque-** & **annual**. Occurring once in or at end of every five years; lasting five years; esp. *quinquennial valuation*, valuation of property for purpose of assessment for rating.

quinquennially, adv. Prec. & **-ly**. Once every five years: *to be valued quinquennially*.

quinquennium, n. [1. kwingkwénium; 2. kwiŋkwéniəm]. Lat. See **quinquennial**. A period of five years.

quinquereme, n. [1. kwíngkwerēm; 2. kwíŋkwərīm]. Lat. *quinquerēmis*, fr. *quinque*, 'five', & *rēmus*, 'oar'. See **quinque-** & **trireme**. Ancient vessel with five banks of oars.

quinquina, n. [1. kwinkwḗna; 2. kwinkwínə]. Sp., fr. Peruv. *kinkina*. See **quinine**. Peruvian bark, cinchona.

quinquivalent, adj. [1. kwingkwívalent; 2. kwiŋkwívələnt]. **quinque-** & **-valent**. (chem.) Having a valency of five.

quinsy, n. [1. kwínzi; 2. kwínzi]. M.E. *squinancy, quinancy*, fr. O. Fr. *squinancie*, later *esquinancie*, fr. Med. Lat. *quinancia*, fr. Gk. *kunágkhē*, 'a form of sore throat', lit. 'dog-throttling', fr. *kunós, kúōn*, 'dog', cogn. w. Lat. *canis*, see **canine**, & base of *ágkhein*, 'to throttle, choke', see **anguish**. Suppurative inflammation of the tonsils. *Quinsy-berry*, dialect name for the black-currant; *quinsy-wort*, a perennial borage; also called squinancy.

quint, n. [1. kwint; 2. kwint], fr. Fr. *quinte*, fr. Lat. *quinta*, fem. of *quintus*, 'fifth'; for **quinq-tus*, see **quinque-**. **1.** (mus.) **a** The interval of a fifth; **b** an organ-stop giving a tone one-fifth higher than the normal; **c** the E string of a violin. **2.** (piquet, usually [1. kint; 2. kint]) A sequence of five cards of the same suit: *a quint major*, from ace to ten.

quintain, n. [1. kwíntin; 2. kwíntin], fr. O. Fr. *quintaine*, in Med. Lat. *quintana*; prob. identical w. Lat. *quintāna via*, a street or road in a camp, where the market was situated, so called as separating the fifth from the sixth maniple; *quintānus*, 'fifth'. See prec. (hist.) A post used for tilting at, with a revolving cross-piece on one end of which was a bag of sand which swung round and struck the tilter who did not get away quickly.

quintal, n. [1. kwíntl; 2. kwíntl]. O. Fr. & Span., fr. Arab. *qinṭar*, weight of 100 lb., prob. derived ultimately fr. Lat. *centum*, 'one hundred'. See **cent**. A measure of weight used in Spain, 100 libras, or 101·4 lb.; the French quintal is 100 kilogrammes or nearly 2 cwts.

quintan, adj. & n. [1. kwíntan; 2. kwíntən], fr. Lat. *quintānus*, 'belonging to the fifth', esp. *quintāna* (*febris*), fr. *quintus*, 'fifth'. See **quinque-**. **1.** adj. Occurring every fifth day, occurring with three-day intervals and reckoning the days inclusively, of attacks of malarial or other periodic fevers: *a quintan fever, ague*. **2.** n. A quintan fever.

quinte, n. [1. kant; 2. kæ̃t]. Fr. See **quint**. A fencing thrust or parry, coming fifth in the old method of instruction.

quintessence, n. [1. kwintésens, kwíntesens; 2. kwintésəns, kwíntisəns]. Fr., fr. Med. Lat. *quinta essentia*, 'the fifth essence or element'. See **quint** & **essence**. **1.** (anct. and Med. philos.) The fifth, non-material substance distinct from the four elements of which the heavenly bodies were supposed to be composed, and which was believed to permeate everything. **2. a** Highly concentrated extract of a substance, containing its essential properties; essence; **b** (in non-material sense) embodiment, purest possible type or example of a quality.

quintessential, adj. [1. kwìntesénshal; 2. kwìntisénʃəl]. Prec. & **-al**. **1.** Of the nature of, consisting of, quintessence. **2.** Most concentrated; purest; most typical.

quintessentially, adv. Prec. & **-ly**. In a quintessential state or manner.

quintet, **quintette**, n. [1. kwìntét; 2. kwìntét]. Fr. *quintette*, fr. Ital. *quintetto*, dimin. of *quinto*, 'a fifth part', fr. Lat. *quintus*, 'fifth'. See **quint**. **a** A musical composition for five instruments or voices; **b** the five performers of such a composition.

quintillion, n. [1. kwintílion; 2. kwintíliən], fr. Lat. *quintus*, 'fifth', w. ending as in **million**. **a** A million raised to the fifth power; a unit followed by 30 ciphers; **b** in French and American numeration by 18 ciphers.

quintuple (**I.**), adj. & n. [1. kwíntūpl; 2. kwíntjupl]. Fr., fr. Lat. *quintus*, 'fifth', see **quint**, w. ending on pattern of **quadruple**. **1.** adj. Multiplied by five, of five times the amount; fivefold. **2.** n. **a** A fivefold amount; **b** set of five things.

quintuple (**II.**), vb. trans. & intrans., fr. prec. **1.** trans. To multiply by five. **2.** intrans. To become five times as great or as many.

quintuplet, n. [1. kwíntūplet; 2. kwíntjuplit]. **quintuple** (**I.**) & **-et**. A collection, group, of five things or persons.

quintuplicate, adj. & n. [1. kwintúplikit; 2. kwintjúplikit]. Formed fr. **quintuple**, on anal. of *duplicate*. **1.** adj. Multiplied by five; fivefold. **2.** n. A number, sum, amount, multiplied by five.

quintuplication, n. [1. kwìntūplikáshun; 2. kwìntjūplikéiʃən]. Prec. & **-ion**. Multiplication by five; act of increasing of an amount fivefold.

quip, n. & vb. intrans. [1. kwip; 2. kwip]. Earlier *quippy*; etymol. doubtful, prob. fr. Lat. *quippe*, 'forsooth, indeed', for **quid-pe*, 'what, indeed'. **1.** n. A fanciful jest, a waggish, whimsical remark, a lively sally, a merry conceit. **2.** vb. To make, utter, quips.

quipu, n. [1. kḗpōō; 2. kípu]. Native Peruv., 'knot'. Method of expressing and conveying meaning in use among ancient Peruvians, by an arrangement of cords and knots.

quire (**I.**), n. [1. kwīr; 2. kwaiə]. M.E. *quaer, quayer, quair*, fr. O. Fr. *quayer, quaer, cayer*, Mod. Fr. *cahier*, fr. L. Lat. *quaternum*, 'four sheets of paper together', fr. Lat. *quaterni*, 'four each', see **quaternary**. **1.** (hist.) Four sheets of paper folded so as to form eight leaves. **2.** (obs.) A small MS. book; a small work of literature; e.g. the 'Kingis Quair', poem by James I. of Scotland. **3.** Twenty-four sheets of writing-paper of the same size and quality. Phr. *in quires*, of printed book, folded in sheets, but not bound.

quire (**II.**), n. & vb. Archaic spelling for **choir**.

quirinal, n. [1. kwírinal; 2. kwírinəl], fr. Lat. *Mons Quirinālis*, now *Monte Quirinale*, one of the seven hills of Rome. (cap.) The Italian royal palace in Rome; hence, the Italian monarchical government, as contrasted with *the Vatican*.

quirk, n. [1. kwërk; 2. kwə̄k]. Etymol. unknown. **1.** A quip; a quibble. **2.** (archit.) A deep groove in a moulding. **3.** A twist or flourish in writing or drawing. **4.** (mus.) A sudden burst or flourish.

quirt, n. & vb. trans. [1. kwërt; 2. kwə̄t]. Prob. fr. Mex. Span. *cuarta*, 'rope', Span. *cuerda*, 'rope, cord', see **cord**. **a** n. A riding whip of twisted hide, with short stock; **b** vb., to flog, beat with a quirt.

quit (**I.**), adj. [1. kwit; 2. kwit], fr. O. Fr. *quite*, fr. Low Lat. *quĭtus, quītus*, for *quiētus*, 'at rest, free from labour &c.; free, satisfied', see **quiet** (**I.**); the adj. is earlier than the vb. in Fr. as in Engl. Discharged, released from an obligation or charge; free, clear, rid: *to get quit of one's debts*; *well quit of a bad bargain, of a rogue*.

quit (**II.**), vb. trans. & intrans., fr. O. Fr. *quiter*, formed fr. *quite*. See prec. **1.** trans. **a** To leave, go away from, abandon: *to quit a house*; Phr. *to quit hold*, leave, let, go, release one's hold; **b** to give up, retire from: *to quit the army, office, work* &c. **2.** (reflex.) To acquit, behave: *quit you like men*. **3.** intrans. **a** To depart: *notice to quit*; **b** (slang) give up something undertaken.

qui tam, n. [1. kwī tám; 2. kwái tǽm]. Lat., 'who as well'. (law) An action brought by an informer who sues for the Crown as well as in his own name.

quitch, n. [1. kwich; 2. kwitʃ]. O.E. *cwiċe*, 'couch-grass'; prob. fr. its tenacity & the difficulty of eradicating it. Cp. **quick** (**I.**) & the variant **couch** (**III.**). A coarse kind of grass with creeping, spreading roots; couch-grass; also *quitch-grass*.

quitclaim, n. & vb. trans. [1. kwítklām; 2. kwítkleim]. **quit** (**I.**) & **claim**. (law) **1.** n. **a** Release or relinquishment of a claim or right to land &c. granted to another; deed by which such a release is made. **2.** vb. To release, relinquish, a claim to.

quite, adv. [1. kwīt; 2. kwait]. M.E. *quȳte*, adj., 'paid, freed; satisfied', see **quit** (**I.**). **1.** Entirely, completely, altogether; absolutely: *to feel quite well*; *the work is quite finished*; *not quite satisfactory*; *not quite so good as I hoped*; *not quite a gentleman*; *quite delightful*; *I quite agree with you*; *I quite understand*; (various idiomatic usages) *not quite* . . ., unsatisfactory, not up to the mark, in some particular way indicated by context; *not quite proper*, rather improper; *not quite the thing to do*, bad form, dishonourable &c.; as an answer expressing agreement with what is said, understanding of a situation &c.: *I will do my best, but there are all sorts of complications!*; *oh quite*; also *quite so*, I entirely agree. **2.** To all intents and purposes; almost, very nearly, practically; in a manner of speaking, as one might say: *you are getting quite a big boy now*; *he looks quite grown-up*; *why, you are quite rich*; *quite crazy about golf*. **3.** Expressing reluctant consent to, acquiescence with, something which is more or less taken for granted; rather more or less, up to a point, to a certain extent: *she's quite pretty, but her face is uninteresting*; *he was quite polite, of course, but somehow I didn't like his manner*; also in understatement, as litotes: *quite a pretty girl, quite a nice fellow*, very pretty, very nice &c.; *he's quite a good amateur actor*, very good; *he gave us quite a good dinner*, an excellent one.

quitrent, n. [1. kwítrent; 2. kwítrənt]. **quit** (**I.**) & **rent** (**III.**). (law) A small, usually nominal rent, paid by a copyholder in commutation of the services formerly paid to the lord of the manor.

quits, adj. or adv. [1. kwits; 2. kwits]. Formed fr. **quit** (**I.**). (only pred.) On even or equal terms with, as being quit or discharged of an obligation or claim, by repaying or being repaid, or by getting some equivalent: *I will be quits with him some day*; *if you pay me another 15s. we shall be quits*. Phr. *to call, cry, 'quits'*, to agree to settle all differences, not to go on with a quarrel &c.; *double or quits*, method of settling a debt by casting lots, tossing a coin, throwing dice &c., it being understood that the debtor, if he loses, will pay twice what he originally owed, and that if he wins, the debt is cancelled.

quittance, n. [1. kwítans; 2. kwítəns]. M.E. *quitaunce*, fr. O. Fr. *quitance*, fr. *quiter*, 'to quit', see **quit** (II.). Release, repayment of an obligation or charge; receipt, acknowledgement of such payment.

quitter, n. [1. kwíter; 2. kwítə]. **quit** (II.) & **-er**. (colloq., slang) One who quits or gives up, abandons, a contest, undertaking, enterprise, duty &c.; a shirker; a faint-hearted person.

quittor, n. [1. kwíter; 2. kwítə]. M.E. *quetour*, *quiture*, fr. O. Fr. *coiture*, fr. L. Lat. *coctūra*, 'a cooking, boiling', fr. *coct-(um)*, P.P. of *coquī*, 'to cook'; see **cook** & **-ure**. An inflammatory disease of the hoof in horses, mules, and asses.

quiver (I.), vb. intrans. & trans. [1. kwíver; 2. kwívə]. Cp. **quaver**; both prob. imit. in origin. **1.** intrans. To tremble, shake, with tremulous motion, oscillate rapidly, vibrate; (variously used): *the leaves quivered in the breeze*; *his lips were quivering with emotion*; *to quiver with fear*; *the wings of insects quiver*; *the firelight quivers.* **2.** trans. To cause to quiver: *the butterfly quivers its wings over the flower.*

quiver (II.), n., fr. prec. A light, quick tremulous motion; a vibration: *not a quiver of an eyelid*; *the quiver of windswept grass.*

quiver (III.), n. In M.E., fr. O. Fr. *cuivre*, *coivre*, *quivre*; of Gmc. origin, cp. O.H.G. *kochar*, 'case for arrows'; cogn. w. O.E. *cocur*, the origin of wh. is obscure. A case for holding arrows.

quiverful, n. [1. kwíverfool; 2. kwívəful]. Prec. & **-ful**. **a** A collection of arrows which fill a quiver; **b** (jocular) a large family, cp. Ps. cxxvii. 5.

quivering, adj. [1. kwívering; 2. kwívəriŋ], fr. Pres. Part. of **quiver** (I.). Shaking, trembling; tremulous.

qui vive, n. [1. kē vēv; 2. kī vív]. Fr. The challenge of a French sentry, lit. 'for whom do you call *vive* (long life to)', *i.e.* 'to what side do you belong?', as pass-word, so equivalent to 'who goes there?' Only in Phr. *on the qui vive*, on the look out, on the alert.

quixotic, adj. [1. kwiksótik; 2. kwiksótik], fr. *Don Quixote*, name of the central figure of Cervantes' romance, a burlesque of chivalry and knight-errantry. Highly, even extravagantly, generous and chivalrous.

quixotically, adv. [1. kwiksótikali; 2. kwiksótikəli]. Prec. & **-al** & **-ly**. In a quixotic manner.

quixotism, n. [1. kwíksotizm; 2. kwíksətizəm]. See prec. & **-ism**. Chivalrous feeling or action; unnecessarily, or extravagantly, generous and chivalrous action.

quixotry, n. [1. kwíksotri; 2. kwíksətri]. See **quixotic** & **-ry**. Extravagant generosity and chivalry of conduct; the ideals and actions of a visionary.

quiz (I.), n. [1. kwiz; 2. kwiz]. Fashionable 18th-cent. slang; origin unknown. **1. a** (obs.) An odd, eccentric person, a 'queer fish': '*to make a quiz of yourself*' (Fanny Burney); **b** (archaic) a mild practical joker; one given to chaffing; a tease. **2.** (archaic) A mild hoax or practical joke.

quiz (II.), vb. trans. & intrans., fr. prec. **1.** trans. **a** To hoax, tease, play pranks on; **b** to stare at impudently, or inquisitively. **2.** intrans. To play the tease or quiz.

quizzical, adj. [1. kwízikl; 2. kwízikl]. **quiz** (I.) & **-ic** & **-al**. **1.** Addicted to quizzing, bantering, chaffing. **2.** Comical, eccentric, queer.

quizzically, adv. Prec. & **-ly**. In a quizzical manner.

quizzing-glass, n. [1. kwízing glahs; 2. kwíziŋ glās]. A single eye-glass used for staring at people.

quoad, prep. [1. kwóad; 2. kwóuæd]. Lat. *quō*, 'whither', *ad*, 'to'. So far as; as regards, as to: *quoad hoc*, so far as this, to this extent.

quod (I.), [1. kwod; 2. kwɔd]. Lat., 'which', neut. sing. of *quī*, 'who'. Cogn. w. **what**. *Quod erat demonstrandum*, Q.E.D., which was to be demonstrated; *Quod erat faciendum*, Q.E.F., which was to be done, formulae placed at end of geometrical propositions and problems; *quod vide*, q.v., which see, as a reference in a book.

quod (II.), n. & vb. trans. Etymol. uncertain; doubtfully referred to *quad*, abbr. of **quadrangle**. (slang) **a** n. Prison; **b** vb., to put in prison.

quodlibet, n. [1. kwódlibet; 2. kwɔ́dlibet]. Lat., 'what you please'. A nicety, subtlety; a debatable, nice point.

quoif, n. See **coif**.

quoin, n. & vb. trans. [1. koin, kwoin; 2. kɔin, kwɔin]. Variant of **coign**. **1.** n. **a** A wedge-shaped stone or brick used as an angle or corner-stone; the external or internal angle of a building, room &c.; **b** a wedge of metal or wood, used for locking type in a forme, for preventing barrels rolling &c. **2.** vb. To provide with quoins or wedges; to fix, wedge up, with a quoin.

quoit, n. [1. koit, kwoit; 2. kɔit, kwɔit]. M.E. *coyte*, later *coit*; etymol. unknown. **1.** An iron ring or disk with flattened, sharp edge used in the game of quoits. **2.** (pl.) A game in which the players fling a quoit on to or near a peg; *deck quoits*, a game played on board ship with rings made of rope.

quondam, adj. [1. kwóndam; 2. kwɔ́ndæm]. Lat., 'formerly', fr. *quom*, 'whenever', & pronominal stem **dē-*, cp. **to**. Having been formerly, or for a time; former, previous, sometime: *a quondam actor*; *quondam friends.*

quorum, n. [1. kwórum; 2. kwɔ́rəm]. Lat., 'of whom', genit. pl. of *quī*, 'who', cogn. w. **who**. **1.** (hist.) The number of justices of the peace who must be present to form a Court, the opening words of the Commission being *Quorum vestrum . . . duos, tres &c. esse volumus*, of whom we wish two, three &c. of you, . . . to be. **2.** Minimum number of persons, usually fixed by statute, required to be present at a meeting of a legislative or deliberative body, before business can be validly transacted.

quota, n., pl. *quotas* [1. kwóta; 2. kwóutə]. Lat. *quota* (*pars*), 'how great a part, how much', fem. sing. of *quotus*, 'in what number, how many', fr. *quot*, 'how many', fr. pronominal stem **kʷo-*; see **who**. A due proportion; proportional share, a part or share assigned to each member of a company &c.: *each town had to provide its quota of troops, food* &c.

quotability, n. [1. kwōtabíliti; 2. kwòutəbíliti]. See next word & **-ity**. State, quality, of being quotable; suitability for quotation.

quotable, adj. [1. kwótabl; 2. kwóutəbl]. **quote** (I.) & **-able**. **a** So apt as to be worthy of quotation; *not many quotable passages in the book*; *difficult to choose among so many quotable lines*; **b** fit to be quoted: *his language was not quotable*, was too bad to repeat.

quotation, n. [1. kwōtáshun; 2. kwoutéiʃən]. See **quote** (I.) & **-ation**. **1. a** Act of quoting or citing; **b** a passage quoted from a book, verse from a poem; utterance, saying, cited from another person. **2.** Statement of a price demanded for a commodity: *the daily market quotations*; estimate of cost of specified work: *send me a quotation for painting my house.* **3.** (print.) A piece of type metal used for filling blanks.

quotation mark(**s**), n. Mark(s) (' ') used to indicate the beginning and end of a quotation.

quotative, adj. [1. kwótativ; 2. kwóutətiv]. Lat. *quotāt-um*, P.P. type of *quotāre*. See **quote** (I.) & **-ive**. **a** Of, pertaining to, quotations; **b** making use of quotations.

quote (I.), vb. trans. & intrans. [1. kwōt; 2. kwout]. M.E., fr. O. Fr. *quoter*, fr. Med. Lat. *quotāre*, 'to mark off chapters and verses by numbers', fr. Lat. *quotus*, 'how many'. See **quota**. **1.** trans. **a** To reproduce, repeat, cite, in speech or writing (something written or uttered by another); **b** to refer to, recall, appeal to (an event, circumstance &c.) as an example or precedent; **c** to mention, state, estimate (a price). **2.** intrans. **a** To make use of quotations; **b** to name a price, give an estimate: *to quote for putting on a new roof.*

quote (II.), n., fr. prec. (printer's slang) Quotation mark.

quoth, vb. trans. [1. kwōth; 2. kwouþ]. O.E. *cwæþ*, Pret. sing. of *cweðan*, 'to speak, say'; M.E. *cwaþ*, *quath*; rounded form arose prob. in phr. *quaþhē*, the vb. being unstressed; perh. influenced by **quote** (I.), or by *spoke*; the vb. is found in O.S. *kwethan*, O.H.G. *queden*, O.N. *kveða*. Other cognates are doubtful. (sham archaic) Said: *quoth I, she, he*; '*quoth the raven*, '*Never more*'.'

quotha, adv. & interjec. [1. kwótha, kwótha; 2. kwóuþə, kwɔ́þə]. M.E. *quoth ha*, 'said he', the latter being unstressed form of *hē*, 'he'. See prec.

quotidian, adj. & n. [1. kwotídian; 2. kwətídiən]. Lat. *quotidiānus*, fr. *quotidie*, 'every day, daily', fr. *quoti-*, *quotus*, 'how many', see **quota**, & *dies*, 'day', see **diurnal**. **1.** adj. Occurring every day, daily; recurring every day: *a quotidian fever.* **2.** n. A quotidian fever.

quotient, n. [1. kwóshent; 2. kwóuʃənt]. Fr. *quotient*, fr. Lat. *quotiens*, adv., 'how many times'. See **quota**; formed as if fr. **quotient-(em)*. The number resulting from the division of one number by another, giving how many times a less number is contained in a greater: *the quotient of 15 divided by 5 is 3.*

quo warranto, n. [1. kwō wórantō; 2. kwóu wɔ́rəntou]. Law Lat., 'by what warrant or authority'. (law) **a** The name of writ issued against a person usurping or misusing an office, franchise, or privilege belonging to the Crown; **b** a public writ calling upon a person to show 'by what warrant' he is holding the office &c.

R

R, r [1. ar; 2. ā]. The eighteenth letter of the English alphabet. Phr. *the three R's*, reading, (w)riting, (a)rithmetic, as the foundation of elementary education. For use in abbreviations &c. see list at end of Dictionary.

rabbet (I.), n. [1. rábet; 2. ræbit], fr. O. Fr. *rabat*, 'a beating down or back, recess', fr. *rabattre*, 'to beat back or down'. See **rebate** (II.). (carpentry) A groove or slot cut longitudinally on the edge or surface of wood in which another piece of wood can fit or slide; *rabbet-joint*, a joint made by fastening two pieces of wood in a rabbet; *rabbet-plane*, plane used by carpenters for making rabbets.

rabbet (II.), vb. trans., fr. prec. To make a rabbet in; to join, fix together, by a rabbet-joint.

rabbi, n. [1. rábī; 2. ræbai]. Lat. & Gk., fr. Heb., 'my master', w. pronom. suff. *i*, 'my', added to *rab*, adj. 'great', n. 'master'; Heb. also has *rab*, of a lower, & *rabban*, of a higher, grade of teachers. **a** The title of and form of address to a Jewish doctor and teacher of the law and ritual; **b** one of the Jewish clergy.

rabbinic(al), adj. [1. rabínik(l); 2. ræbínik(l)], fr. Fr. *rabbin*, 'rabbi', see prec., & **-ic** (& **-al**). Of, pertaining to, the rabbis, their rules, teaching, and form of language: *rabbinic Hebrew*, later Hebrew; *rabbinical literature*, Jewish literature later than Talmudic.

rabbinically, adv. [1. rabínikali; 2. ræbínikəli]. Prec. & **-ly**. According to the rabbis.

rabbinism, n. [1. rábinizm; 2. rǽbinizəm]. See prec. & **-ism**. **a** The teaching, principles, traditions of the rabbis; **b** a special idiom, phrase &c. of rabbinic language.

rabbinist, n. [1. rábinist; 2. rǽbinist]. See prec. & **-ist**. One who follows and obeys the teaching and traditions of the rabbis, contrasted with *Karaite*.

rabbit (I.), n. [1. rábit; 2. rǽbit]. M.E. *rabet*, etymol. uncertain; cp. O.Du. & Flem. *robbe* & Walloon, *robbett*; the older Engl. word is **cony**. **1.** A burrowing, rodent, gregarious mammal, *Lepus cuniculus*, allied to the hare, but with shorter legs and smaller ears, usually of lightish brown colour in the wild state; humorously in *Welsh rabbit*, toasted cheese. Phr. *to breed like rabbits*, to be very prolific. **2.** (by transf.) **a** A timorous, weak, feeble creature: *to run like a rabbit*; *as scared as a rabbit*; **b** (colloq., slang) a poor, feeble, but enthusiastic player of a game.

rabbit (II.), vb. intrans., fr. prec. To hunt rabbits with ferrets; to shoot rabbits: *to go rabbiting*.

rabbit (III.), vb. trans. Etymol. doubtful; possibly on anal. of obs. *rat* in *'od rat 'em*, wh. is prob. really a variant of *rot*. (provinc. or slang) In Phr. *'od-rabbit 'em* &c., as a mild form of cursing.

rabbit-burrow, n. Hole dug by wild rabbits for breeding &c.

rabbit-hutch, n. Wooden cage for domesticated rabbits.

rabbit-warren, n. **1.** Tract of land honeycombed with rabbit-burrows. **2.** (fig.) **a** Building with complicated passages; district in town with many alleys and side streets; **b** overcrowded house or district.

rabbity, adj. [1 rábiti; 2. rǽbiti]. **rabbit** (I.) & **-y**. **a** Like, having the character of, a rabbit; **b** infested with, tainted by, rabbits.

rabble (I.), n. [1. rábl; 2. rǽbl]. M.E. *rabel*, 'a pack, swarm, of animals, insects' &c.; etymol. doubtful. **1.** A disorderly, riotous crowd or mob. **2.** *The rabble*, the lowest classes of the population; the mob, the scum of the populace.

rabble (II.), n., fr. Fr. *râble*, O. Fr. *roable*, fr. Med. Lat. *rotabulum*, Lat. *rutābulum*, 'a rake or shovel for use in a furnace', dimin. of *rut-(um)*, P.P. of *ruere*, 'to rake, scrape'; cogn. w. O.H.G. *rod*, 'a clearing', cp. Engl. *royd* in Pl.-Ns. A puddling iron, for stirring the molten metal in making iron and steel.

Rabelaisian, adj. & n. [1. ràbelázian; 2. ræbəléiziən], fr. François Rabelais (c. 1490–1553) & **-ian**. **1.** adj. (of humour, style) Resembling the broad, coarse, but humane spirit of Rabelais; outspokenly and coarsely humorous. **2.** n. An admirer or student of Rabelais and his works.

rabid, adj. [1. rábid; 2. rǽbid], fr. Lat. *rabidus*, 'raving, furious, mad', *rabere*, 'to rave, rage'; prob. connected w. Gk. *lábros*, 'furious, vehement', dissimilated fr. **rábhros*; cp. also Scrt. *rábhaš*, 'vehemence'. Cp. **syllable**. **1.** Affected with rabies; mad; of, pertaining to, rabies: *a rabid dog*; *rabid virus*. **2.** Furious; vehement; violently fanatical: *a rabid teetotaller, Communist* &c.

rabidity, n. [1. rabíditi; 2. ræbíditi]. Prec. & **-ity**. State, quality, of being rabid; rabidness, madness.

rabidly, adv. [1. rábidli; 2. rǽbidli]. **rabid** & **-ly**. In a rabid manner; madly, furiously.

rabidness, n. [1. rábidnes; 2. rǽbidnis]. See prec. & **-ness**. Rabidity.

rabies, n. [1. rấb(i)ēz; 2. réib(i)īz]. Lat., 'madness'. See base under **rabid**. Hydrophobia, disease suffered by dogs, wolves &c., canine madness; usually communicated to man through a bite from dog &c. suffering from it.

raca, adj. [1. ráhkah; 2. rấka]. Gk. *rhaké*, fr. Chaldee *rēkā*, 'worthless'. Term of reproach and abuse among the Jews (Matt. v. 22).

raccoon, n. See **racoon**.

race (I.), n. [1. rās; 2. reis]. M.E. (North.) fr. O.N. *rās*, 'a race, running'; cp. *rāsa*, 'to rush, run headlong'; cogn. w. O.E. *rǣs*, 'a rush, swift movement'; cogn. w. Lat. *rōrārii*, 'light-armed, swiftly moving troops'; the orig. sense was 'runners'; cp. *rōrāre*, 'to drip, distil, run', & *rōs*, 'dew', see **rosemary**. **1. a** A competition in running; a contest of speed in running, riding, rowing, sailing &c.: *a three-mile race*; *hurdle-race*; *a horse-race*; *boat-*, *yacht-race* &c.; *a pigeon-*, *whippet-race*. *The races*, a series of horse-races held at a stated time on a special course; a race-meeting: *to go to the races*; Phr. *his race is nearly run*, life almost over; **b** any contest of speed to finish some work before another, to do something, or get somewhere, in time or in a hurry: *a race for life*; *race for supremacy, wealth, power* &c. **2. a** A swiftly moving current in a tidal estuary or in the sea, often caused by the junction of two currents or tides: *a tide-race*; *the Race of Portland, of Alderney*; **b** narrow channel conveying a stream of water on to a water-wheel: *a mill-race*; *the head and tail race*, the stream above and below the point where it turns the wheel. **3.** A groove, slot, channel, in which a shuttle slides, or in which ball-bearings run.

race (II.), vb. intrans. & trans., fr. prec. **A.** intrans. **1. a** To run, compete, in a race; **b** to move hurriedly; to run or walk at high rate of speed. **2. a** To keep and run horses in races; **b** to attend race-meetings. **3.** (of mach.) To move, revolve, at too high a speed owing to a diminished load or want of resistance, as when the propeller of a steamer is raised out of the water. **B.** trans. **1.** To run a race with, to compete with in a race: *to race a person a mile*. **2.** To cause to run in, enter (horse &c.) for, a race: *to race a horse, yacht* &c.

race (III.), n. Fr., fr. Ital. *razza*, cp. also Span. *raza*, Port. *raça*; etymol. doubtful. **1.** A group of individuals possessing certain physical characteristics in common and regarded as being of one blood and sprung from the same original stock; specif. **a** (ethnol.) a variety or division of mankind, the members of which possess certain distinctive, permanent physical characteristics in common, marking them off from others: *the Negro, Mongolian, Jewish, race*; Phr. *the human race*, mankind in general; **b** (bot.) a special, permanent variety which will reproduce true to type: *to produce a new race of potatoes*; **c** a special breed or variety of domesticated animal: *the race of Alderney cows*; *the bloodhound race*. **2. a** Lineage, family, descent, stock, breed: *a man of ancient race*; **b** specif., distinguished, ancient and noble birth: *his features and bearing betokened race*. **3.** A class or group of persons having some spiritual, intellectual, or other characteristic in common: *the race of artists, gamblers* &c. **4.** A special or characteristic flavour, style, nature, or strength; raciness, piquancy: *the wine has a certain race*; *there is a race peculiar to this collection of letters*.

race (IV.), n., fr. O. Fr. *rais, raiz*, fr. Lat. *rādīc-(em)*, *rādix*, 'root'. See **radix**. (obs.) A root, esp. of ginger.

race-card, n. A programme containing a list of races and the names of horses, jockeys &c. at a race-meeting.

racecourse, n. [1. rấskors; 2. réiskōs]. The ground on which horse-races are run.

racehorse, n. [1. rấs-hors; 2. réishōs]. A horse specially bred and trained for racing.

raceme, n. [1. rásēm; 2. rǽsīm], fr. Lat. *racēmus*, 'stalk of a cluster of grapes; cluster of grapes'; according to some authorities, cogn. w. Scrt. *rāšiš*, 'crowd, heap, mass'; according to others, a pre-Aryan word. (bot.) Form of blossom consisting of a number of small separate flowers on equal lateral stalks springing from a main central stalk.

race-meeting, n. Group of horse-races held publicly on a day, or on several successive days, at a fixed date and on a specified course.

racemic, adj. [1. rasēmik; 2. ræsímik]. See prec. & **-ic**. (chem.) Obtained from grapes; esp. *racemic acid*, a variety of tartaric acid found in grapes.

racemose, adj. [1. rásemōs; 2. rǽsimous], fr. Lat. *racēmōsus*, 'clustering, in clusters'. **raceme** & **-ose**. **a** (bot.) Growing in the form of a raceme; **b** (anat.) resembling a cluster in form: *the pancreas is a racemose gland*.

racer, n. [1. rấser; 2. réisə]. **race** (II.) & **-er**. **a** A racehorse; **b** a vehicle or vessel, e.g. a motor-car, a yacht &c., used for racing.

rachis, n. [1. rấkis; 2. réikis]. Gk. *rhákhis*, genit. *rhákhios*, 'the spine', cogn. w. O. Ir. *fracc*, 'needle', Lith. *rãžas*, 'dry branch'. **1.** (anat.) The spine. **2.** (zool.) The part of a feather from which the barbs spring. **3.** (bot.) Prolongation of the stalk in compound leaves, whence the leaflets spring.

rachitic, adj. [1. rakítik; 2. rækítik]. See next word & **-ic**. Cp. Fr. *rachitique*. Of, pertaining to, characteristic of, rachitis or rickets.

rachitis, n. [1. rakítis; 2. rækáitis]. Neo-Lat., fr. Gk. *rhakhîtis*, sc. *nósos*, 'disease'. See **rachis** & **-itis**. (med.) Inflammatory disease of the rachis or spine; rickets.

racial, adj. [1. rấshial, rấsial; 2. réiʃiəl, réisiəl]. **race** (III.) & **-ial**. Of, pertaining to, a race, family, stock, or breed: *racial characteristics, feature* &c.

racially, adv. Prec. & **-ly**. As a race; from a racial aspect.

racily, adv. [1. rấsili; 2. réisili]. **racy** & **-ly**. In a racy manner; piquantly; with spirit, especial character &c.

raciness, n. [1. rấsines; 2. réisinis]. **racy** & **-ness**. Quality of being racy.

racing (I.), vbl. n. [1. rấsing; 2. réisiŋ]. **race** (II.) & **-ing**. **a** Act of running in races; **b** act of promoting, attending, horse-races, or of running horses in races as a sport.

racing (II.), adj., fr. Pres. Part. of **race** (II.). **a** Suitable, adapted for, used in, races: *a racing car*; *racing colours*, those worn by jockey in a race; *racing saddle*, for rider in horse-race; **b** addicted to the sport of horse-racing: *a racing man*.

rack (I.), n. [1. rak; 2. ræk]. M.E. *rakke* & *rekke*, prob. fr. M. Du. *recke*, 'framework', cp. L.G. *rakk*, 'framework, rack'; apparently the orig. meaning is 'something stretched out, or straight'; O.E. cogn. is *reccan*, 'to stretch'; cp. also Goth. *(uf)rakjan*, 'to stretch out'; the base **reg-* is seen in Lat. *regere*, 'to stretch, extend; to control, rule' &c., see **regent** & **rex**, perh. also in Lat. *rigēre*, 'to be stiff', see **rigid**. **1. a** A receptacle for hay &c. made of wooden or iron bars placed above a manger, and so arranged that the animal can pull out what it wants at the time, but cannot get at the main bundle; **b** one of various objects consisting of an arrangement of wooden or metal bars, pegs &c. for holding or hanging things: *plate-rack, hat-rack, toast-rack* &c.; **c** kind of shelf for light articles in a railway carriage, made of stout netting supported by a light horizontal bar with brackets placed at intervals beneath. **2.** Specif., a mediaeval instrument of torture used to extort confessions, consisting of framework of wood on which a person was bound, and gradually stretched by means of pulleys until the joints were dislocated. Phrs. *to put on, to, the rack*, to torture with the rack; *on the rack*, tortured, in torture, in great mental distress or anxiety. **3.** (various techn. senses) **a** Bar or rail with cogs gearing with a pinion or cog-wheel; a ratchet; **b** a set of sheaves through which the rigging of a sailing vessel runs.

rack (**II.**), vb. trans. See prec. **1.** (rare) To place in, furnish with, a rack or framework: *to rack hay* or *fodder*; *to rack a horse, sheep* &c.; *to rack plates.* **2. a** To torture by placing on the rack; **b** to torture, torment, afflict, physically or mentally: *racked with gout, by a cough*; *doubt and despair racked him*; Phr. *to rack one's brains,* exert one's powers of thought to the utmost, esp. to make a great effort to remember something, or to devise an expedient. **3.** To oppress, harass, put severe strain on resources of; (esp. of a landlord) to be very exacting, demand exorbitant rent for land. **4.** (rare) To wrench, strain, pervert, meaning of: *to rack a text to suit one's purposes.*

rack (**III.**), n. Etymol. doubtful; either borrowed fr. O.N. *rek,* 'drifting wreckage', *reka,* 'to drive, drift', or a variant of **wrack** & **wreck**. **1.** Drifting vapour or cloud. **2.** Wreckage, destruction, esp. in Phr. *to go to rack and ruin.*

rack (**IV.**), n. Abbr. of **arrack**. Arrack, as in *rack punch,* a punch or beverage made of arrack spirit.

rack (**V.**), vb. trans. Derived fr. the wine trade w. Gascony; fr. Provenç. *arracar,* fr. *raca,* 'skins, stems &c. of grapes left after wine-pressing'. Cp. **raceme** & **raisin**. To pour off (wine) from the dregs or lees: *to rack off wine.*

rack (**VI.**), n. & vb. intrans. Etymol. doubtful; possibly a variant of **rock** (**II.**). **1.** n. A particular gait or pace of a horse, with both feet on one side off the ground at a time. **2.** vb. To move, as a horse, with a rack.

racket, racquet (**I.**), n. [1. ráket; 2. rǽkit]. M.E. *rakket,* fr. Fr. *raquette,* etymol. uncertain; Span. has *raqueta,* Ital. *racchetta*; possibly fr. Arab. *rāḥa(t),* 'the palm of the hand'. Court or real tennis developed fr. a ball-game like 'fives', cp. Fr. *jeu de paume.* **1.** A kind of bat used in real tennis, lawn tennis, and rackets, shaped something like a guitar, having a long handle and an oval part for striking consisting of a strong wooden frame across which strings of catgut are tightly stretched. **2.** (pl.) A game of the tennis type for two or four players, played in a closed four-walled court.

racket (**II.**), n. & vb. intrans. Etymol. doubtful; prob. imitative; cp. dial. *rattick,* 'to racket', & **rattle**; vb. later than n. **1.** n. **a** A noise, din, clamour, disturbance: *to kick up, make, a racket*; Phr. *to stand the racket of,* (i.) be answerable, take responsibility, for; (ii.) pay the expenses of; **b** excitement, bustle, hurry: *to live in a constant racket of enjoyment*; Phr. *to go on the racket,* to indulge in dissipation. **2.** vb. To live an exciting, dissipated life; to make a, go on the, racket: *to racket about*; *a racketing life.*

racketeer, n. [1. ràketḗr; 2. rækitíə]. See next word. (slang, U.S.A.) One who practises racketeering.

racketeering, n. [1. ràketḗring; 2. rækitíəriŋ], fr. **racket** (**II.**). (slang, U.S.A.) Practice of blackmailing shops, trades, or businesses in a city or district by threats of violence and damage &c.

racket-tail, n. A kind of humming-bird with long tail feathers with two ends shaped like a racket.

rackety, adj. [1. ráketi; 2. rǽkiti]. **racket** (**II.**) & **-y**. Making, causing, a racket; noisy; living a life of racket, dissipated.

rack-rail, n. A central rack or cogged rail used in mountain railways.

rack-rent, n. & vb. trans., fr. **rack** (**II.**). **1.** n. **a** (legal) A rent of land, or house &c. equal or nearly equal to its full annual value; **b** an extortionate or excessively high rent. **2** vb. **a** To exact the highest possible rent for (land, houses); **b** to demand extortionate rent from.

rack-renter, n. [1. rák rènter; 2. rǽk rèntə]. Landlord who demands extortionate rents.

raconteur, n. [1. rákontėr; 2. rækɔ̃tǿ]. Fr. See **recount**. One skilled in telling stories and anecdotes; a clever, humorous storyteller.

racoon, raccoon, n. [1. rakóon; 2. rəkún], ad. fr. native Algonquin, N. Am. Indian name. Cp. popular abbr. *coon.* A small carnivorous mammal, *Procyon,* of N. America, with ringed, bushy tail and greyish-brown fur, arboreal and nocturnal in habit.

racquet, n. See **racket** (**I.**).

racy, adj. [1. rási; 2. réisi], fr. **race** (**III.**) & **-y**. **a** Having the full flavour or spirit of the race or kind to which it belongs; having special distinctive qualities or characteristics strongly marked; **b** spirited, vigorous; piquant, spicy. Phr. *racy of the soil,* having rustic simplicity and vigour; displaying characteristics of its origin.

rad, n. [1. rad; 2. ræd]. Vulg. abbr. of **radical** (**II.**) **4**.

raddle, n. & vb. trans. Variant of **ruddle**. **1.** n. Ruddle. **2.** vb. Esp. in P.P. *raddled,* with complexion painted, rouged &c.

radial (**I.**), adj. [1. rádial; 2. réidiəl]. See **radius** & **-al**. **1.** Of, pertaining to, a ray or radius; arranged in rays or radii, radiated; branching out from a centre; having spokes or radiations. **2.** Pertaining to the radius or bone of the forearm: *radial artery, nerve* &c.

radial (**II.**), n., fr. prec. Radial nerve or artery.

radialization, n. [1. ràdializáshun; 2. rèidiəlaizéiʃən]. See next word & **-ation**. The act of radializing; state of being radialized.

radialize, vb. trans. [1. rádialīz; 2. réidiəlaiz]. **radial** (**I.**) & **-ize**. To arrange in a radial pattern or radiately.

radially, adv. [1. rádiali; 2. réidiəli]. **radial** (**I.**) & **-ly**. In a radial arrangement; in form of a radius or of radii.

radian, n. [1. rádian; 2. réidiən]. **radius** & **-an**. **1.** Arc of a circle whose length is equal to the radius. **2.** Angle at centre of a circle subtending such an arc.

radiance, less commonly **radiancy**, n. [1. rádians(i); 2. réidiəns(i)]. **radiant** & **-ce, -cy**. Quality of being radiant (in both physical and spiritual sense).

radiant (**I.**), adj. [1. rádiant; 2. réidiənt], fr. Lat. *radiant-(em),* Pres. Part. of *radiāre,* 'to make beaming, irradiate', usually in pass., *radiātus,* 'irradiated, beaming'. See **radius**. **1. a** Emitting rays of light; shining: *the radiant sun, stars*; *radiant gems*; **b** luminous, brilliant, flooded with light: *the radiant morn.* **2. a** Displaying, expressing, great pleasure or delight; sparkling, beaming, gay: *radiant with joy*; *a radiant face*; **b** intellectually brilliant, illuminating, pellucid: *a radiant intelligence.* **3.** (astron.) Radiating, extending, from a central or focal point: *radiant point,* the point from which rays proceed; (cp. n. below). **4.** (phys.) Transmitted by radiation; operating radially: *radiant energy,* radiation; *radiant heat,* heat emitted by radiation direct from the heated body and not transmitted through other media.

radiant (**II.**), n., fr. prec. **1.** (astron.) A radiant point, the point or focus from which a shower of meteorites or shooting-stars seems to proceed. **2.** (geom.) A straight line proceeding from a pole or point round which it is assumed to revolve.

radiantly, adv. **radiant** (**I.**) & **-ly**. In a radiant manner; so as to give out or shed radiance; luminously, brightly, lucently; also in moral senses.

radiate (**I.**), vb. intrans. & trans. [1. rádiāt; 2. réidieit], fr. Lat. *radiāt-(um),* P.P. of *radiāre,* 'to shine with rays, to emit rays, to shine'. See **radiant** & **radius**. **A.** intrans. **1.** To emit rays of light or heat. **2. a** (of light and heat) To issue in rays, to spread, penetrate; **b** (of moral influence &c.) to spread abroad, make itself felt, be effective. **3.** To branch out as radii from a centre. **B.** trans. **1. a** To emit (light or heat) in form of rays; **b** (fig.) to give impression, show appearance of: *her eyes radiated love and joy.* **2.** (in moral sense) To exert influence, produce effect of, cause to be felt; to shed, diffuse: *to radiate happiness around one.*

radiate (**II.**), also **radiated**, adj. [1. rádiāt(ed); 2. réidieit(id)]. See prec. Having rays; arranged in rays or radially; radial.

radiately, adv. [1. rádiatli; 2. réidiətli]. Prec. & **-ly**. With rays or radii; with radiations from a centre.

radiation, n. [1. ràdiáshun; 2. rèidiéiʃən], fr. Lat. *radiātiōn-(em),* 'a shining; radiance, radiation'. See **radiate** & **-ion**. **1.** Act or process of radiating; **a** transmission of energy in form of rays; **b** diffusion of moral influence &c. **2.** Something radiated: **a** a ray of light, heat, or other form of energy; **b** (in moral sense) *a radiation of content, happiness* &c. **3. a** The branching out of a radius from a centre; **b** distribution, diffusion, from a central point or area.

radiative, adj. [1. rádiativ; 2. réidiətiv]. **radiate** (**I.**) & **-ive**. Having the property or quality of radiating or of being radiated.

radiator, n. [1. rádiāter; 2. réidieitə]. **radiate** (**I.**) & **-or**. That which radiates; specif. **a** apparatus of pipes and tubes for radiating heat derived from hot air, water &c. in a room &c.; **b** device for dissipating superfluous heat in a machine, esp. one for cooling engine of motor-car.

radical (**I.**), adj. [1. rádikl; 2. rǽdikl], fr. L. Lat. *rādīcālis,* 'having, pertaining to, roots', fr. *rādīc-(em), rādix,* 'root', & **-al**. See **radix**. **1. a** Of, pertaining to, going to, the root or origin, proceeding from the root; basal, fundamental; thorough, complete: *a radical error, principle* &c.; *a radical change*; hence, **b** (cap., politics &c.) going or supposed to go to the root of matters; inclined for, tending to reform of all kinds; advanced, progressive: *the Radical party*; *a Radical programme.* **2.** Specific uses: **a** (bot.) proceeding from the root or root stem; not rising above the ground; basal: *radical tubers, growths, leaves* &c.; **b** (math.) of, pertaining to, a root or radix of a number or quantity: *radical sign* √; **c** (obs., philol.) belonging, proceeding from, the root of a word: *radical form* &c.

radical (**II.**), n., fr. prec. A radical part, a root; that which is fundamental, primary, or original. Specif. **1.** (chem.) an element or group (*compound radical*) of such atoms capable of passing unaltered from compound to compound. **2.** (math.) The radical sign; a quantity expressed as the root of another. **3.** (philol., obs.) A root. **4.** (politics, usually cap.) One who holds radical political views or belongs to the Radical party.

Radicalism, n. [1. rádikalizm; 2. rǽdikəlizəm]. Prec. & **-ism**. The political principles and theories of Radicals, or of the Radical party.

radicalization, n. [1. ràdikalīzáshun; 2. rædikəlaizéiʃən]. Next word & **-ation**. Act of radicalizing; state of being radicalized.

radicalize, vb. trans. [1. rádikalīz; 2. rǽdikəlaiz]. **radical** (**I.**) & **-ize**. **a** To make radical; **b** to imbue with Radical principles, convert to Radicalism.

radically, adv. [1. rádikali; 2. rǽdikəli]. **radical** (**I.**) & **-ly**. **1.** In a radical way or manner; from the bottom, fundamentally, completely: *radically different, sound, wrong* &c. **2.** (cap.) After the manner of the Radicals: *to think Radically.*

radicle, n. [1. rádikl; 2. rǽdikl], fr. Lat. *rādīcula,* dimin. of *rādix,* 'root'. See **radix**. **1.** (anat.) The minute, root-like beginning of a nerve or vein. **2.** (bot.) Minute root of an embryo plant.

radicular, adj. [1. radíkūlar; 2. rædíkjulə]. Prec. & **-ar**. Of, pertaining to, roots or radicles.

radio-, pref. Form used in compounds, fr. Lat. *radius*, w. two general meanings, referring **a** to rays, radiation, or radium: *radioactive, radiography*; **b** to the radius or forearm: *radio-ulnar*.

radio, n. [1. rādiō; 2. réidiou]. Abbr. of *radio-telegraphy* or *telephony*. (colloq.) **a** Wireless telegraphy or telephony: *to send a message by radio*; **b** a wireless message: *to receive a radio*.

radioactive, adj. [1. rādiōáktiv; 2. réidiouǽktiv]. **radio- & active.** Possessing certain qualities found in radium, uranium, thorium, actinium &c., and their compounds, which emit spontaneously and continuously energy in the form of electrons.

radioactivity, n. [1. rādiōaktíviti; 2. réidiouæktíviti]. **radio- & activity.** Property of radioactive substances.

radiocarpal, adj. [1. rādiōkárpl; 2. réidioukárpl]. **radio- & carpal.** (anat.) Pertaining to the radius (forearm) and to the carpus (wrist-bone).

radiochemistry, n. [1. rādiōkémistri; 2. réidioukémistri]. Branch of chemistry concerned with radioactive substances and radioactivity.

radiofrequency, n. [1. rādiōfrékwensi; 2. réidioufríkwənsi]. The frequency of the electric waves in wireless telegraphy and telephony.

radiogoniometer, n. [1. rādiōgòniómeter; 2. réidiougòniómitə]. **radio- & goniometer.** A direction-finder, used on ships &c. for finding the direction and origin of wireless signals.

radiogram, n. [1. rādiōgram; 2. réidiougræm]. **radio- & -gram**, on anal. of *telegram*. **a** A radiograph; **b** a wireless telegram.

radiograph, n. & vb. trans. [1. rādiōgrahf; 2. réidiougrāf]. **radio- & -graph.** **1.** n. **a** An instrument for measuring and recording the sun's radiation or radiant energy; **b** a picture produced on a sensitized photographic plate by Röntgen or other rays, esp. of internal structures or objects. **2.** vb. To make a radiograph of an object.

radiographer, n. [1. rādiógrafer; 2. rèidiógrəfə]. Prec. & **-er.** Maker of radiographs; student of radiography.

radiographic(al), adj. [1. rādiōgráfik(l); 2. rèidiougrǽfik(l)]. Prec. & **-ic** (& **-al**). Of, pertaining to, a radiograph or radiography.

radiographically, adv. Prec. & **-ly.** By a radiograph or radiography.

radiography, n. [1. rādiógrafi; 2. rèidiógrəfi]. **radio- & -graphy.** Art, science, process, of making radiographs.

Radiolaria, n. [1. rādiōlária; 2. rèidiouléəriə]. Neo-Lat. pl., fr. L. Lat. *radiolus*, 'little ray', dimin. of **radius.** Order of microscopic marine animals living near the surface of tropical oceans.

radiolarian, adj. & n., [1. rādiōlárian; 2. rèidiouléəriən]. Prec. & **-an.** **a** adj. Pertaining to the Radiolaria; **b** n., member of this order.

radiologist, n. [1. rādiólojist; 2. rèidiólədžist]. See next word & **-ist.** One skilled in, a student of, radiology.

radiology, n. [1. rādióloji; 2. rèidiólədži]. **radio- & -logy.** That branch of physics which deals with radioactivity and radioactive substances, properties &c.

radiometer, n. [1. rādiómeter; 2. rèidiómitə]. **radio- & -meter.** An instrument for showing motion caused by the action of light, and for measuring the effect of radiation or radiant energy.

radiometry, n. [1. rādiómetri; 2. rèidiómitri]. **radio- & -metry.** Art of using the radiometer; measurement of radiant energy by this instrument.

radiophone, n. [1. rādiōfōn; 2. réidioufòun]. **radio- & -phone.** **a** Instrument for producing sound by means of radiant energy; **b** a wireless telephone.

radioscopy, n. [1. rādióskopi; 2. rèidióskəpi]. **radio- & -scopy.** **1.** Examination of the internal structure &c. of opaque objects by means of the Röntgen or other rays. **2.** Investigation of radioactive substances.

radiotelegram, n. [1. rādiōtélegram; 2. rèidioutéligræm]. **radio- & telegram.** A wireless telegram.

radiotelegraphy, n. [1. rādiōtelégrafi; 2. rèidioutelégrəfi]. **radio- & telegraphy.** Wireless telegraphy.

radiotelephone, n. [1. rādiōtélefōn; 2. rèidioutélifoun]. **radio- & telephone.** Wireless telephone.

radiotelephony, n. [1. rādiōteléfuni; 2. rèidiouteléfəni]. **radio- & telephony.** Wireless telephony.

radiotherapeutics, n. [1. rādiōthèrapūtiks; 2. réidioupèrəpjūtiks]. **radio- & therapeutics.** Treatment of disease by means of various rays.

radiotherapy, n. [1. rādiōthérapi; 2. rèidioupérəpi]. **radio- & -therapy.** Radiotherapeutics.

radish, n. [1. rádish; 2. rǽdiʃ], fr. Fr. *radis*, fr. Lat. *rādic-(em), rādix*, 'root'. See **radix.** Plant with coarse leaves, resembling, but much smaller than, the turnip, possessing an edible root with a pungent, hot taste.

radium, n. [1. rādium; 2. réidiəm], fr. Lat. *radius*, 'ray', fr. its radioactive properties. See next word. A scarce metallic element, with intense radioactive properties, discovered by the Curies in Paris in 1898.

radius, n., pl. **radii** [1. rādius, rādii; 2. réidiəs, réidiai]. Lat., 'staff, rod, spoke of a wheel, radius of a circle; bone of the forearm; a beam or ray of light'; the basal meaning is 'shoot of a plant, twig'; the base occurs also in Lat. *rāmus*, 'bough' &c., for **radmos*, see **ramose**, & in *rādix*, 'root', see **radix.** **1.** (anat.) The shorter and thicker of the two bones of the forearm in man or forelimb of vertebrate animals, as the foreleg of quadrupeds and the wing of birds. **2.** (geom.) A straight line drawn from the centre of a circle to the circumference. **3.** Something resembling the radius of a circle; movable part of a machine describing a circle from a central point; a spoke of a wheel. **4.** **a** A distance in any direction measured from a given centre; circular area within such a limit: *there are ten churches within a radius of three miles of my house*; **b** (fig.) sphere, range, of activity, field: *outside, within, the radius of knowledge, of one's capacity* &c.

radix, n. [1. rādiks; 2. réidiks]. Lat. *rādix*, 'root of a plant; lower part, foot, of an object; basis, foundation'; cogn. w. Gk. *rhádix* 'shoot, twig'; the base occurs in various forms, * *wrəd-*, **wr̥d-*, **urd-* &c.; cp. Goth. *aurti-gards*, 'garden', lit. 'plant enclosure'; O.E. *ort-ġeard*, see **orchard**; O.E. *wyrt*, 'plant, herb, root', see **wort (I.)**; also O.N. *rōt*, 'root', see **root.** **1.** (math.) A quantity or number taken as the base of a system of numeration: *the number 10 is the radix of the decimal system.* **2.** (obsolesc., philol.) A root, radical. **3.** (statistics) The number of persons or objects taken as the basis for making calculations of percentages &c., as 1000 in calculating death- and birth-rate &c. **4.** (rare) Source, origin.

raff, n. See **riff-raff.**

raffia, n. [1. ráfia; 2. rǽfiə]. A Malagasy word. The fibre obtained from the leaves of a Madagascar tree, *Raphia ruffia*, the *raffia-palm*; used by gardeners for tying up plants; also used for plaiting baskets &c.

raffish, adj. [1. ráfish; 2. rǽfiʃ], fr. **raff** in **riff-raff**, & **-ish.** Rakish, dissipated, disreputable.

raffle, n. & vb. intrans. & trans. [1. ráfl; 2. rǽfl]. M.E. *rafle*, 'a game of dice', fr. O. Fr.; origin dubious. **1.** n. A sale of an article by means of a lottery; numbered entrance tickets or shares are issued amounting in total value to the price placed on the article, and the person holding the winning number as determined by drawing lots becomes the possessor of the article. **2.** vb. **a** trans. To sell by means of a raffle: *to raffle a picture*; **b** intrans., to go in for a raffle: *to raffle for a picture.*

raft (I.), n. [1. rahft; 2. rāft]. M.E. *raft*, 'a beam', fr. O.N. *raptr*, 'a rafter'. See **rafter (II.).** **1.** A flat, buoyant structure of logs, planks, barrels &c., usually hastily and roughly put together, used instead of a boat in a shipwreck or other emergency. **2.** A floating structure of timber used as a landing-place for boats on a river, moored to the shore or to a boat-house, house-boat &c. **3.** A mass of felled timber or logs floated down a river from place of felling to that where it is required for use.

raft (II.), vb. trans. & intrans., fr. prec. (rare). **1.** trans. **a** To convey by means of a raft: *to raft goods, timber &c. from one point to another*; **b** to cross, traverse, on a raft: *to raft a river, stream.* **2** intrans. To go on a raft; to use a raft as a boat.

rafter (I.), n. [1. ráhfter; 2. rāftə]. Prec. & **-er.** A man who works a raft; a raftsman, esp. one who rafts timber or logs down a river.

rafter (II.), n. O.E. *ræfter*; cp. O.N. *raptr*, 'beam, rafter'; perh. cogn. w. Gk. *rhóptron*, 'a club, cudgel'. One of the sloping timbers of a roof, usually 2 in. wide and from $3\frac{1}{2}$ to 5 in. deep, supported by purlins, and supporting the framework to which the outer covering of stone, slate, tiles &c. is fixed. Phr. *from cellar to rafter*, throughout the entire house, from top to bottom.

raftered, adj. [1. ráhfterd; 2. rāftəd]. Prec. & **-er.** Furnished with rafters; *a raftered ceiling*, one having rafters exposed from inside.

raftsman, n. [1. ráhftsman; 2. rāftsmən]. Same as **rafter (I.).**

rag (I.), n. [1. rag; 2. ræg]. M.E. *ragge*, of Scand. origin, cp. O.N. *rögg*, 'tuft of fur or rough hair'. Etymol. uncertain. **1.** **a** Shred or wisp, tatter of cloth, of irregular shape, torn from a larger piece or from a garment; Phr. *like a red rag to a bull*, cause of extreme agitation and indignation; **b** discarded, useless, remnant of old linen, cotton, or woollen cloth; Phrs. *not a rag to one's back*, (i.) no clothes fit to wear; (ii.) no clothes at all; *to cram on every rag*, hoist all sails; **c** (in pl.) *rags*, tattered, torn, worn-out, clothes: *to go about in rags*; **d** (facet.) old, shabby garments: *I have nothing but my old rags to wear*; **e** a disreputable, worthless newspaper. **2.** Refuse, waste of cotton or linen cloth, from which the best class of paper is made. **3.** Something of irregular and indefinite outline; a wisp: *a rag of cloud, smoke.* **4.** (in non-material sense) Slight amount, trifling remnant, of some moral quality: *he has still a few rags of decency, reputation, virtue, left.*

rag (II.), n. Etymol. uncertain. **a** A hard limestone used for building, breaking in thick layers: *Kentish rag*, ragstone; **b** a rough kind of slate.

rag (III.), vb. trans. & intrans. Prob. fr. **rag (I.).** (colloq.) **1.** trans. **a** To subject to rough horse-play, to handle roughly; **b** to play rough practical jokes upon; **c** to tease good-naturedly, to chaff; **d** to scold, rate soundly, find fault with. **2.** intrans. To indulge, **a** in rough, boisterous horse-play; **b** in practical jokes; **c** in chaff; **d** in scolding.

rag (IV.), n., fr. prec. **a** A good-natured row; a series of boisterous, noisy, mischievous, but usually harmless pranks, practical jokes &c., esp. when carried out by a body of persons; **b** a rowdy scrimmage; **c** a joke; good-natured teasing or chaff: *I only said it for a rag.*

ragamuffin, n. [1. rágamùfin; 2. rǽgəmàfin]. In 15th cent. *Ragamoffyn* was the name of one of the bad characters or demons in mystery plays; fr. **rag (I.)** & some fanciful termination, cp. **muff (I.)**, a stupid, clumsy person. A ragged, ruffianly, disreputable person; a street-arab, gutter-snipe.

rag-and-bone-man, n. [1. rāg an(d) bōn man; 2. ræg ən(d) bóun mæn]. Itinerant dealer in household refuse such as old rags, bones, bottles &c.

rag-bolt, n. Wooden bolt furnished with barbs, or one of metal with jags or barbs to prevent withdrawal; the latter kind is made secure by having molten metal poured into the hole in which it lies.

rage (I.), n. [1. rāj; 2. reidž]. Fr., fr. Lat. *rabia*, a form of *rabies*, 'rage, madness'. See **rabid & rabies**. **1. a** Violent, furious, anger; a fit of violent anger, fury: *to fly into a sudden rage*; *to kill a man in a rage*; **b** violent fury, extreme boisterousness of forces of nature: *the rage of the waves, of the wind* &c. **2.** (archaic or poet.) a The inspired frenzy of the poet: '*And your true rights be term'd a poet's rage, And stretched metre of an antique song*' (Shakespeare, Sonnet xvii.); **b** strong emotion of any kind; ardour, enthusiasm: '*Chill penury repressed their noble rage*' (Gray's 'Elegy'). **3.** (rare) Violent outburst of emotion: *burst into a rage of tears, of grief*. **4. a** Something or somebody temporarily exciting general enthusiasm and interest: *bicycles were (all) the rage in the nineties of last century*; **b** unreasoning desire for, craze, mania: *to have a rage for horses and dogs*.

rage (II.), vb. intrans. See prec. **1.** (of persons) **a** To be violently angry, to be inflamed with rage: *he was simply raging at their stupidity*; **b** to act violently and furiously: '*why do the heathen so furiously rage together*'; *he raged about the room in his agony*; **c** *rage against, at*, to inveigh against, denounce furiously, to blame bitterly: *to rage against fate* &c. **2.** (of animals) To behave with violence and fury so as to exhibit angry excitement: *a raging lion*. **3.** (of natural forces &c.) **a** (of the weather and elements) To be in a state of violent agitation; to be extremely boisterous: *the storm, wind, waves, fire, raged for hours*; **b** (of diseases &c.) to be widely prevalent and severe: *plague, small-pox, is raging*. **4.** (of human feelings &c.) To be intensely violent: *a raging fever, pain, toothache* &c. **5.** (of human action) To be very prevalent, intense: *murder and every kind of social disorder appear to rage in China*.

ragged, adj. [1. ráged; 2. rǽgid]. **rag** (I.) & **-ed**. **1. a** (of edges or objects with edges) Jagged, uneven, having projecting points, wisps, threads &c.; presenting an irregular line: *a ragged cloud, piece of wood, knife blade*; often implying roughness caused by wear; frayed: *ragged collar, cuffs*; **b** (of hair, on head or face, of animal's coats &c., of grass, bushes &c.) rough, shaggy, unkempt, imperfectly trimmed or smoothed: *a ragged beard, whiskers* &c.; *a ragged lawn*; **c** (of the surface of solid masses) rough, having jags and irregular projections: *a ragged piece of rock*; *ragged staff*, a rough, stout cudgel with projections on either side; the badge of ancient Earls of Warwick. **2. a** (of wearing apparel and fabrics generally) Torn, tattered, hanging in shreds; shabby and full of slits and holes from long, hard wear; **b** (of persons) clad in ragged clothes: *a ragged urchin*. **3.** (of a piece of work, esp. of result of intellectual effort) Imperfectly finished, slipshod, lacking polish, not brought to a high pitch of perfection; loosely thought out or expressed: *his sentences have too many ragged edges*; *a ragged style in writing* &c.

raggedly, adv. Prec. & **-ly**. In a ragged manner (in various senses).

ragged robin, n. Kind of lychnis with pink flowers, the petals of which are deeply indented, giving it a ragged appearance.

ragged school, n. (obs.) Institution for destitute children in which they receive instruction and food.

ragger, n. [1. ráger; 2. rǽgə]. **rag** (III.) & **-er**. (colloq.) One who rags or plays rough, practical jokes.

ragging, n. [1. ráging; 2. rǽgiŋ]. See **rag** (III.). (colloq.) Act of one who rags; process of being ragged; **a** rough treatment, rude, practical jokes &c.; **b** chaff; **c** fault-finding, scolding: *he got a good ragging from his headmaster*.

ragman, n. [1. rágman; 2. rǽgmən]. M.E. *rageman*. Etymol. unknown; cp. **rigmarole**. (hist.) A document having many seals hanging from it: *Ragman rolls*, the set of rolls bearing the names of Scottish barons who swore allegiance to Edward I. in 1296.

ragout, n. [1. ragōō; 2. rægū́]. Fr. *ragoût*, fr. *ragoûter*, 'to bring back, revive, stimulate, the taste or appetite', see **re-**, 'back', *a(d)-*, 'to', see **ad-**, & *goût*, 'taste', see **gust** (II.). A highly seasoned stew, or hash, of meat and vegetables.

ragstone, n. [1. rágstōn; 2. rǽgstoun]. See **rag** (II.) & **stone**. A hard, bluish limestone, chiefly found in Kent, which splits into flat masses; used in building in the so-called 'random work'.

ragtag, n. [1. rágtag; 2. rǽgtæg]. **rag** (I.). Also *ragtag and bobtail*, the dregs of the populace; riff-raff.

ragtime, n. [1. rágtīm; 2. rǽgtaim], for 'ragged time'. **a** Strongly syncopated music, as in negro dances and songs; **b** a tune or dance in syncopated time, jazz.

raguly, adj. [1. rágūli; 2. rǽgjuli], fr. **rag** (I.). (her.) Notched, indented, used esp. of a cross, notched at equal distances on both sides of its arms and limbs.

ragweed, also **ragwort**, n. [1. rágwēd, -wërt; 2. rǽgwīd, -wʌ̄t]. **rag** (I.) & **weed, wort** (I.). The popular name for several common weeds with deeply indented, irregularly lobed leaves and clusters of bright-yellow, rayed flowers.

raid (I.), n. [1. rād; 2. reid]. A Nthn. Engl. variant of **road**; O.E. *rād*, cp. O.N. *reið*, 'a riding, raid'. Cp. **ride**. **1. a** A swift incursion or foray by armed, usually mounted, men into, descent upon, a country for purposes of plunder, or attack: *a border raid, moss-troopers' raid*; **b** (fig.) any sudden descent upon and appropriation of property: *a raid on a bank*; *Mr. Churchill was forced to make a raid on the Road Fund*. **2.** Any sudden or surprise attack, during a war, against the enemy: *a trench raid*; *an air raid*. **3.** (internat. law) A hostile invasion, by military or naval forces, of territory of a state at peace, undertaken without the recognition of the government of the state from which the raid comes: *the Fenian Raid*, into Canada from the United States, 1866; *the Jameson Raid*, into the Transvaal, 1895–1896. **4.** A sudden incursion by the police upon premises for making arrests, discovering crimes or offences, seizing stolen goods &c.: *a raid on a gaming-house, illicit night-club* &c.

raid (II.), vb. trans. & intrans., fr. prec. **a** trans. To make a raid into, or upon; to attack; to plunder; **b** intrans., to practise raiding.

raider, n. [1. rāder; 2. réidə]. Prec. & **-er**. One who makes a raid or sudden, violent incursion.

rail (I.), n. [1. rāl; 2. reil], fr. O. Fr. *raale, ralle*, Mod. Fr. *râle*; possibly an imitative word. Any of various kinds of small birds, with short tail and wings and rather long, curved beak, belonging to the family *Rallidae*, of which the *land-rail* or corncrake, *water-rail*, a wading bird, are members.

rail (II.), n. O.E. *hrægl*, 'a garment', M.E. *reil* &c. (obs.) *Night-rail*, referring to a woman's garment, still survives in the first third of the 18th cent.

rail (III.), vb. intrans., fr. Fr. *railler*; etymol. uncertain. Cp. **rally** (III.) & **raillery**. Usually *rail at*, or *rail against*, to inveigh against, utter complaints against; to reproach bitterly and violently.

rail (IV.), n., fr. O. Fr. *reille*, 'a bar, rail', fr. Lat. *rēgula*, 'a straight piece of wood, a ruler; rule'. See **rule**. **1. a** A horizontal bar of wood or metal, usually fixed to posts or resting on upright pillars to form a fence or barrier or to prevent falling from a raised platform, balcony &c.; **b** (in pl.) *rails*, a fence, railing. **2.** A bar supported by brackets, used for hanging clothes &c. **3.** A bar forming upper portion of banisters, used as support for the hand in ascending or descending stairs; also *hand-rail*. **4.** One of a pair of steel lines laid parallel to each other upon sleepers and continuing for long distances, forming a permanent track, esp. for locomotives and railway vehicles, or fixed into the roadway as a track for trams. Phr. *by rail*, by railway transport. **5.** Specif. (pl.) *rails*, a system of railway lines, more rarely tram lines; Phr. *off the rails*, (i.) (of railway engine &c.) having quitted the permanent track; (ii.) (fig.) having deviated from the right path, gone astray in thought or conduct; **b** (Stock Exchange) railway stock or shares.

rail (V.), vb. trans., fr. prec. **1. a** To furnish, fence, with rails; **b** also *rail in*, to shut in, fence, with rails; *rail off*, separate (piece of land &c.) by a railing; *rail out*, to exclude by means of a railing. **2.** To send by rail.

railage, n. [1. rālij; 2. réilidž]. **rail** (IV.) & **-age**. **a** Transport of goods by railway; **b** charge for this.

rail-chair, n. Metal clamp which keeps railway line firmly in its place.

railer, n. [1. rāler; 2. réilə]. **rail** (III.) & **-er**. One who rails; a reviler; a scoffer.

rail-head, n. The farthest point to which a railway in course of construction has been built.

railing (I.), adj. & n. [1. rāling; 2. réiliŋ]. Adj., fr. Pres. Part. of **rail** (III.), n. fr. this & **-ing**. **1.** adj. **a** Scoffing, derisive; **b** expressing violent censure or complaint; **c** jesting, bantering. **2.** n. **a** Jeers, expressions of contempt; **b** bitter complaint or denunciation; **c** banter.

railing (II.), n. **rail** (V.) & **-ing**. A fence of rails and posts.

raillery, n. [1. rāleri; 2. réiləri], fr. Fr. *raillerie*, fr. *railler*. See **rail** (III.). Banter, persiflage, light, satirical humour.

railroad, n. [1. rālrōd; 2. réilroud]. (Am.) A railway.

railway, n. [1. rālwā; 2. réilwei]. **rail** (IV.) & **way**. **1.** A permanent track of steel rails upon which trains run. **2. a** The whole system of lines belonging to a single company: *the Great Western Railway*; **b** the organization and working as a whole in all its departments. **3.** (often attrib.) *Railway carriage, line, company, station* &c.

raiment, n. [1. rāment; 2. réimənt]. Shortened form of *arrayment*, in sense of 'clothing'. See **array** & **-ment**. Dress, garments, clothing.

rain (I.), n. [1. rān; 2. rein]. O.E. *regn*, M.E. *rein*; O.S. & O.H.G. *regan*; Goth. *rign*, O.N. *regn*. Etymol. doubtful. **1. a** The moisture of the atmosphere condensed and falling in visible drops; **b** a fall or shower of such drops; also (fig.) *a rain of tears*. Phrs. *the rains*, (i.) the rainy season in a tropical country; (ii.) a rainy region in the N. Atlantic; *rain or shine*, whether it rains or shines, in foul or fair weather. **2. a** Fall, stream of something falling thickly in form of minute particles: *a rain of dust, ashes*; **b** fall or propulsion of something in a continuous shower or stream: *a rain of bullets, arrows*. Phrs. implying rapid succession or repetition, *a rain of blows*, series of blows following each other in rapid succession; *a rain of kisses*, kisses often repeated.

rain (II.), vb. intrans. & trans. O.E. *regnan*. See prec. **A.** intrans. **1. a** (impers.) *It rains, it is raining*, rain is falling; Phr. *it never rains but it pours*, things, events, never happen or come singly but always in numbers together; **b** (of moisture or water) to fall like rain; to fall in rapid drops: *hot tears rained down her cheeks*; *spray from the waterfall rained down upon us*; **c** (of minute particles of matter) to fall as thickly as rain: *dust, ashes, sand, rain(s) down upon us*. **2.** (of the sky, clouds) To send down, release, rain. **3. a** (of solid objects, falling or being thrown or sent) To arrive in large numbers, in continuous succession: *letters and telegrams kept raining upon me all day*; *bouquets rained from the boxes upon the singer*; *blows rained upon his* *devoted head*; **b** also used of *good wishes, congratulations, compliments* &c. **B.** trans. **1.** To send, pour, shower, down in rain: *the clouds rained huge drops upon us*; (also reflex.) *the storm, it, has rained itself out*, it has done raining for the present. Phr. *to rain cats and dogs*, to rain very heavily, pour with rain. **2.** To pour down, hurl (bullets, stones, bombs &c.) as thick as raindrops; also in Phr. *to rain blows, kisses*, bestow continuously in rapid succession. **3.** To bestow abundantly, give in great profusion, shower upon: *to rain gifts, blessings, compliments &c. upon a person.*

rain-bird, n. Popular name of various birds whose call is supposed to predict rain, as the green woodpecker; also in America, any of various birds of the cuckoo family.

rainbow, n. [1. rā́nbō; 2. réinbou]. O.E. *reġnboga, rēnboga*. See **rain (I.)** & **bow (I.)**. A bow or arc, showing the colours of the spectrum in concentric bands, formed in the sky opposite to the sun, or to the moon (*lunar rainbow*), by refraction and reflection of its light through falling drops of rain; identical effect produced by the spray of a waterfall &c. *secondary rainbow*, a larger, similar arc in the sky with reversed order of colours by double refraction and reflection. Phr. *all the colours of the rainbow*, every variety of colour.

rainbow trout, n. A variety of trout, *Salmo irideus*, native to the mountain rivers of California and Oregon &c., but introduced and cultivated elsewhere.

raincoat, n. [1. rā́nkōt; 2. réinkout]. Light overcoat supposed to keep out a shower of rain, but not calculated to give protection against a heavy downpour.

raindrop, n. [1. rā́ndrop; 2. réindrɔp]. A drop of rain.

rainfall, n. [1. rā́nfawl; 2. réinfɔ̄l]. A fall of rain; specif., the amount of water, in the form of rain, snow, mist, dew &c., that is precipitated from the atmosphere over a specified area, or at a particular place, during a given period, as measured by a rain-gauge.

rain-gauge, n. An instrument for measuring the depth in inches, of rainfall at a certain place during a given period.

rainless, adj. [1. rā́nles; 2. réinlis]. **rain (I.)** & **-less**. Devoid of rain, continuously dry: *a rainless season, district* &c.

rainlessness, n. Prec. & **-ness**. State, quality, of being rainless.

rain-maker, n. **a** A magician, or medicine-man, among savage races, who claims to be able to produce rain by his magic; **b** a magic instrument or charm, such as the bull-roarer, which is supposed to produce rain.

rainproof, adj. [1. rā́nprōōf; 2. réinprūf]. Resisting rain, proof against rain, but not necessarily absolutely waterproof.

rainstorm, n. [1. rā́nstorm; 2. réinstɔ̄m]. A heavy, violent, fall or storm of rain.

rainwater, n. [1. rā́nwàwter; 2. réinwɔ̄tə]. **a** Water falling as rain, snow &c. from the air, uncontaminated with soluble mineral or other matter from the earth; **b** such water collected and used for washing and cooking.

rainy, adj. [1. rā́ni; 2. réini]. **rain (I.)** & **-y**. Full of, abounding in, rain; wet with rain: *a rainy day, season, weather*; *a rainy district, place* &c. Phr. (fig.) *a rainy day*, an emergency, bad times.

raise, vb. trans. [1. rāz; 2. reiz]. M.E. *reisen*, fr. O.N. *reisa*; this is the exact cogn. of O.E. *rǣran*, 'to raise', fr. **raiz-jan*. See **rear (I.)**; the causative of **rise (I.)**. **1. a** To cause to rise; to lift, to move (something) from a lower to a higher level: *to raise a weight from the ground*; *to raise a dumb-bell above one's head*; *to raise the blind, the window*, pull, push, it up; **b** to lift, put up, hold up, elevate, some part or member of the body: *to raise one's arms, hands, eyebrows, head*; Phr. *to raise one's, its, head* (fig.), to give evidence of existence, appear; **c** to lift, hold up (something) with the hand(s): *to raise one's hat*, to take it off in bowing, greeting, or as sign of respect; *to raise one's glass to*, propose, drink, the health of; *raise one's hand to*, strike, or threaten to strike; **d** to cause to rise from recumbent position: *to raise a man from his knees, from a bed of sickness*; Phrs. *to raise from the dead*, bring to life again; *loud enough to raise the dead*, very loud; **e** specif., *to raise dough*, cause it to rise with yeast. **2.** To erect, cause to be built: *to raise a monument, a noble building* &c. **3. a** To stir up, cause to fly up: *to raise the, a cloud of, dust*; Phr. *to raise a dust*, make a fuss or commotion; **b** (fig.) to stir up, incite: *to raise a rebellion*; Phr. *to raise Cain, Hell*, create a violent disturbance &c. **4. a** (chiefly reflex.) To cause to rise in the world, improve fortunes of; bring to a higher social position: *he raised himself from a humble position to one of affluence, to a higher sphere*; **b** to advance to higher rank; to promote: *to raise a captain to the rank of major*; *to raise a man to the peerage*; Phr. *to raise (a private soldier) from the ranks*, give him a commission. **5. a** To increase amount, price, value, of: *to raise wages, a salary, the price* &c.; also *to raise one's claim by so much*; **b** (in non-material sense) to improve, enhance: *to raise one's reputation.* **6.** To increase in intensity; **a** *to raise the temperature*, make hotter; **b** *to raise one's voice*, speak loud, or louder; **c** *to raise the hopes, spirits of*, render more hopeful, more cheerful. **7. a** To evoke, cause, summon, to be present or to appear: *to raise the spirits, ghosts, of the departed*; **b** to call forth, cause to occur, or be made: *to raise a laugh, a storm of protests*; *to raise a blush on the cheek of innocence.* **8. a** To bring, recall, to the mind: *to raise old memories*; **b** to inspire, call, conjure, up in the mind: *to raise false hopes*; **c** to mention, submit for consideration, to moot: *to raise a point, a question, in argument.* **9. a** To produce, cause to grow; to breed, rear: *to raise cattle, wheat*; **b** to beget, bring up, nurture: *to raise a family*; Phr. (Am.) *where was he raised?*, where was he born and brought up? **10.** To collect together, call into being, recruit, enlist: *to raise an army, a regiment, a search-party.* **11.** To procure, obtain, get possession of, come by: *to raise money*; slang in such Phr. as *I can't raise a horse for the meet anywhere.* Phr. (colloq.) *to raise the wind*, obtain financial resources; **12.** To utter loudly, put up: *to raise a song of triumph, a shout, cheer* &c. Phr. *to raise one's voice*, speak, give utterance; *raise one's voice against*, utter a protest. **13.** To remove, inhibit, take off: *to raise a siege, a blockade*; *the ban on noxious drugs is not likely to be raised.* **14.** (naut.) in Phr. *to raise land*, come within, obtain, sight of (from the sea).

raisin, n. [1. rā́zn; 2. réizn], fr. O. Fr. *raizin*, 'grape', fr. Lat. *racēmus*, 'cluster of grapes'. See **raceme**. A grape of special variety dried in the sun or by artificial heat, so that the sugar crystallizes, and the fruit can be preserved for a considerable time.

raison d'état, n. [1. rā́zon dātáh; 2. rezɔ̄ detā]. Fr. Reason of State.

raison d'être, n. Anglicized to [1. rā́zon dā́tr; 2. réizɔn, -ɔ̄ déitr]. Fr., 'reason of being'. Reason for the existence of, the rational ground for, purpose of, justification for anything: *the raison d'être of the Income Tax is that we could not pay our way without it.*

raisonné, adj. [1. rā́zonā; 2. réizɔnei]. Fr., 'reasoned'. Arranged systematically or logically; arranged under subjects; esp. *a catalogue raisonné.*

rait, vb. See **ret**.

raj, n. [1. rahj; 2. rādž]. Hind. *rāj*, 'rule'; cogn. w. Lat. *rēx*, 'king'. See **rex** & **rajah**. Rule, reign, sway, supremacy; esp. *the British raj in India.*

rajah, n. [1. ráhja; 2. rā́džə]. Hind.; Scrt. *rājan-*, 'king', cogn. w. Lat. *rēx, rēgis*, 'king'. See **rex, regal, regent**. Indian king, native prince or ruler.

Rajput, Rajpoot, n. [1. ráhjpoot; 2. rā́džput]. Hind.; Scrt. *rājaputra*, 'king's son'. **a** Member of ruling caste claiming, in Rajputana, to be descendants of the old Hindu warrior caste; **b** term often applied elsewhere in Northern India to a substantial land-owner, irrespective of the purity of his descent.

rake (I.), n. [1. rāk; 2. reik]. O.E. *raca*, M.E. *rāke*; O.D. *rake*, O.H.G. *rehho*; O.N. *reka*, 'shovel'; Goth. *rikan*, 'to collect together, sweep up'. **1. a** An agricultural or garden tool of metal or wood consisting of a bar with teeth or prongs on lower surface, attached at right angles to a long handle, used for gathering together loose hay, leaves &c., and for scratching and smoothing over the surface of earth and gravel and for scratching moss from lawns &c.; **b** an implement of the same kind but much larger, and with longer, curved prongs, attached to wheels and drawn by a horse, used for gathering hay into rows in a large field or for scratching weeds out of grass meadows &c. **2. a** A pronged metal instrument for getting ashes &c. out of a furnace; **b** a small wooden implement used by a croupier for drawing in stakes won by the bank at a gaming table.

rake (II.), vb. trans. & intrans., fr. prec. **A.** trans. **1. a** To use a rake upon: *to rake a field, path, flower-bed* &c.; **b** *rake up, together* &c., to collect, gather together, with a rake: *to rake up hay in rows*; *to rake leaves off a lawn*; *to rake out (a fire)*, draw ashes and cinders from. **2. a** To collect, gather together, as with a rake; to scrape together or up, to collect from every source: *to rake recruits from every class*; **b** to ransack, scour: *to rake every source for rare pictures* &c.; **c** *rake out*, to ferret out, discover by searching or inquiry: *to rake out information*; **d** *rake up*, to stir up, revive: *to rake up old scandals.* **3. a** To sweep (ship or other target) with fire lengthways, to enfilade: *to rake a ship from stem to stern, a trench from right to left, end to end*; **b** to sweep with the eyes, to let the gaze travel along and scan carefully: *to rake the horizon with a telescope.* **B.** intrans. **a** To use, work with, a rake; **b** (fig.) to search, ferret about.

rake (III.), vb. intrans. & trans. Etymol. doubtful; Swed., dial., has *raka*, 'to reach'; *raka fram*, 'to reach forward'. **A.** intrans. **1.** To incline, project forward as the stem, stern, of a vessel beyond the line of the keel. **2.** To incline, lean from the perpendicular, either forward or more usually backward as a mast, funnel, forks of a bicycle &c. **B.** trans. To give a rake to; to cause to incline forward or backward or out of the perpendicular.

rake (IV.), n., fr. prec. **a** The projection of a ship's stem or stern beyond the line of the keel; **b** the inclination, slope of a mast, funnel &c.; also of stage in theatre.

rake (V.), n. Abbr. of earlier, now obs., **rake-hell**. A person, usually a male (formerly also applied to women), of dissolute and immoral character; a loose, raffish, dissipated person; a roué.

rakehell, n. [1. rā́khel; 2. réikhel]. Prob. popular refashioning on anal. of **rake (II.)** & **hell**; O.N. has *reikal*, 'vagrant, reckless'. Skeat quotes N. Udall, 'Apophthegms of Erasmus,' 1542, '*Such a feloe as a manne should rake helle for*'. (obs.) A rake, debauchee, roué.

rakehelly, adj. [1. rā́kheli; 2. réikheli]. Prec. & **-ly**. (obs.) Rakish, debauched, dissolute.

rakish (I.), adj. [1. rā́kish; 2. réikiʃ], fr. **rake (III.)** & **-ish**; also influenced by associations w. next word. **1.** (of ship) Smart, trim, having an appearance of speed, like the old pirate or corsair ships with their raking masts. **2.** Dashing, showy, extremely smart.

rakish (II.), adj., fr. **rake (V.)** & **-ish**. Like a rake; dissolute, dissipated; debauched, fast.

rakishly, adv. Prec. & **-ly**. **1.** (fr. **rakish (II.)**) In a rakish, dissolute way or manner. **2.** (fr. **rakish (I.)**) Smartly, dashingly: *his hat set rakishly on the side of his head.*

rakishness, n. See prec. & **-ness**. State, quality, of being rakish.

râle, n. [1. rahl; 2. rāl]. Fr., fr. *râler*, 'to rattle', etymol. doubtful. **1.** (pathol.) A rattling sound perceptible to the stethoscope, accompanying the normal sounds of breathing, usually symptomatic of lung disease. **2.** Sound made in the throat by a dying person; death-rattle.

rallentando, n. [1. ràlentándō; 2. rælɛntǽndou]. Ital., Pres. Part. of *rallentare*, 'to cause to go slower, hold back', fr. *re*, 'again', & *allentare*, 'to slow down, slacken', fr. Lat. *lentus*, 'slow', see **lentitude.** Musical direction indicating that the passage must be played gradually slower and slower.

ralli-cart, -car, n. [1. ráli kar(t); 2. rǽli kā(t)], fr. name of person who first made them fashionable. A light two-wheeled carriage of dog-cart type, holding four persons, sitting sideways.

ralline, adj. [1. rálīn; 2. rǽlain], fr. Neo-Lat. *rallus*. See **rail (I.)**. Belonging to the bird family *Rallidae*, which includes the rails, coots, moorhens &c.

rally (I.), vb. trans. & intrans. [1. ráli; 2. rǽli], fr. Fr. *rallier*, fr. Lat. *re*, 'again', *ad*, 'to', & *ligāre*, 'to bind'. See **re-** & **ally (I.)**. **A.** trans. **1.** To gather, collect together again; **a** to reassemble, re-form (troops, one's friends, party &c.), after a repulse, for a counter-attack, for a fresh effort, continued resistance &c.; **b** to gather together, concentrate (physical, intellectual powers, faculties), to rouse, revive for further effort. **B.** intrans. **1.** To collect together, assemble: *the clans are rallying for battle*; *rally round*, come to the help of. **2.** (of troops &c.) To reassemble, resume orderly formation after being scattered or defeated. **3. a** To recover, regain some signs of strength, to revive: *he seemed to be dying but suddenly rallied*; **b** (of markets, shares, merchandise) to rise in tone; to be more in demand, command higher prices: *lard started flat but later rallied in price.*

rally (II.), n., fr. prec. **1.** Act or process of rallying; **a** reassemblage, re-formation, reorganization, of troops, a political party &c., after being scattered and defeated; **b** recovery of strength, esp. after a disabling, prostrating attack of illness. **2.** (in games of tennis type) Continued rapid exchange of strokes between opposing players. **3.** An assembly, a gathering, a flocking together: *a rally of recruits to the colours, of the clans for battle.*

rally (III.), vb. trans., fr. Fr. *railler*, 'to rail'. See **rail (III.)** & cp. *raillery*. (archaic) To use raillery on; to banter, chaff, tease; to be mildly satirical to.

ram (I.), n. [1. ram; 2. ræm]. O.E. & M.E. *ram*, cogn. w. O.H.G. & Du. *ram*; O.N. *rammr*, 'strong', is prob. derivative. **1. a** A fully grown, uncastrated male sheep; a tup; **b** (astron., cap.) the sign of the zodiac and constellation *Aries*. **2.** Any of various mechanical devices for battering, or piercing; **a** ancient engine of war for battering down walls of forts &c., originally a heavy beam terminating in an iron ram's head; generally called *battering-ram*; **b** a metal spike, or other device for piercing, fixed to the prow of a vessel of war. **3.** Any of various devices for applying energy by thrusting, pressing &c.; **a** the plunger of a force-pump, hydraulic press, or lift; **b** the monkey or weight of a pile-driver; *hydraulic ram*; **c** machine for raising water by the energy of the water itself combined with the pressure of air caused by the movement.

ram (II.), vb. trans., fr. prec. **1. a** To crash, run into, collide forcibly with; **b** specif., deliberately to strike another ship with a ram with view to piercing it. **2.** To beat, batter, press down, or into place: *to ram a charge well home* (*in gun*); *to ram earth firmly round bottom of a post*; also *ram down*, to press into firm mass by beating: *to ram earth well down.* **3. a** To thrust, shove, roughly and hastily; to crush, jam, cram: *to ram one's clothes into a trunk*; *to ram one's hat on over one's ears*; *to ram food down a chicken's throat.* Phr. (fig.) *to ram something down a person's throat*, to assert something repeatedly, and with insistence, esp. to utter sentiments which listeners hear with reluctance; **b** (fig.) to convey to, to instil (knowledge, ideas &c.) into, the mind of another by persistent effort: *I tried to ram a little sense into him, a little Latin into his head* &c.

Ramadan, n. [1. rámadan; 2. rǽmədæn]. Arab. *Ramaḍān*, 'the hot month', fr. *ramaḍa*, 'to be hot'. The great Moslem fast, lasting throughout the ninth month of the Moslem year by lunar reckoning and thus shifting through the seasons; a complete fast is observed from sunrise to sunset.

ramble (I.), vb. intrans. [1. rámbl; 2. rǽmbl]. Etymol. doubtful; M.E. has *ramblyinge*, 'roaming'. **1. a** To wander, roam; to move about, walk, idly, and without any special object; to stroll about for pleasure; to saunter; **b** to read discursively, browse about among books, pass from one author to another as the fancy takes one. **2. a** To wander, be diffuse or incoherent, in thought or expression; to write or speak disconnectedly or discursively; to chatter, babble; *to ramble on*, to continue to speak in a vague, discursive manner for a long time; **b** specif., to be delirious, to be oblivious of one's surroundings, and babble meaninglessly, from fever &c. **3.** (of plants) To grow in long straggling shoots, to trail.

ramble (II.), n., fr. prec. **1.** A casual walk, a stroll without any specific object. **2.** Discursive study; a discursive, gossipy, treatise of a popular character: *a ramble among books.*

rambler, n. [1. rámbler; 2. rǽmblə]. Prec. & **-er.** **a** One who, that which, rambles; **b** a climbing, trailing plant; specif., a climbing rose with clustered flowers; *Crimson Rambler* is the best known variety.

rambling, adj. [1. rámbling; 2. rǽmbliŋ], fr. Pres. Part. of **ramble (I.)**. **a** Inclined to ramble; specific. of house &c., large, full of passages; spread out, reverse of *compact*; **b** climbing, trailing, straggling; **c** (of thought and expression) disconnected, discursive.

ramblingly, adv. Prec. & **-ly.** In a rambling manner; discursively.

ramekin, ramequin, n. [1. rámkin; 2. rǽmkin]. Fr. *ramequin*; etymol. uncertain. Dish consisting of a kind of savoury hash, covered with grated cheese and bread-crumbs, and baked in an earthenware casserole.

ramie, n. [1. rámē; 2. rǽmī], fr. Malay. *rami.* Fibre obtained from a stingless nettle of China, Malaya, and the Far East generally; also known as rhea and China grass; used in making incandescent gas-mantles, bank-note paper &c.

ramification, n. [1. ràmifikáshun; 2. ræmifikéiʃən]. See **ramify, -fic,** & **-ation. 1.** Process of ramifying or branching out. **2.** Something which is ramified; specif. **a** (bot.) the arrangement of branches on a tree, the system according to which a tree develops its branches; **b** the branching, bifurcation, subdivision, of a vein, nerve &c.; **c** bifurcation of a road, stream, channel &c. **3.** (in non-material sense) The spread, branching out, of a system, movement, scheme, influence &c. in several directions; a branch.

ramify, vb. intrans. & trans. [1. rámifī; 2. rǽmifai], fr. Fr. *ramifier*, fr. Med. Lat. *rāmificāre*, 'to form, send out branches, to branch', fr. *rāmus*, 'branch'. See **ramose** & **-fy. 1.** intrans. To form, have, ramifications (in various senses). **2.** trans. To produce ramifications in (usually in pass.).

Ramillies, n. [1. rámilēz; 2. rǽmilīz]. Name of village where Marlborough beat the French in 1706. (usually attrib.) *Ramillies hat*, a three-cornered cocked hat of the early 18th cent.; *Ramillies wig*, a wig tied at the back with a large bow at the top and smaller one at the bottom.

rammer, n. [1. rámer; 2. rǽmə], fr. **ram (II.)** & **-er.** An implement for ramming; e.g. **a** a heavy piece of wood, with a handle, for beating earth, stones &c. into a compact mass; **b** machine for driving home piles; **c** device for driving home the charge of a gun.

rammish, adj. [1. rámish; 2. rǽmiʃ]. **ram (I.)** & **-ish.** Like a ram; **a** rank-smelling; **b** lustful.

ramose, adj. [1. rámōs; 2. réimous], fr. Lat. *rāmōsus*, fr. *rāmus*, 'branch', for **wrādmos*; cogn. w. **radix.** (bot.) Branching, branched, of the stem or root of a plant.

ramp (I.), vb. intrans. & trans. [1. ramp; 2. ræmp]. Etymol. uncertain; apparently fr. O. Fr. *ramper*, 'to clamber, climb'; also in heraldic sense; later, 'to creep, crawl'; M.E. has *rampen*, 'to be rampant, to rage, to be furiously angry'. See **rampant** & **romp. A.** intrans. **1.** To rage, storm; to show fury like a wild beast; to rush violently about. **2.** (of plants) To grow and spread luxuriantly. **3.** (archit. and fort.) To slope upwards or downwards from one level to another. **B.** trans. **1.** (fort. &c.) To furnish with a ramp or sloping face. **2.** (slang) To swindle, to plant a ramp on a person.

ramp (II.), n., fr. Fr. *rampe*, 'slope', fr. *ramper*, 'to climb'. See prec. **1.** (archit.) **a** The slope between the levels of the abutments of a rampant arch; **b** the slope of a balustrade, stair-rail, or coping; a change of level or bend in these. **2.** (fort.) An inclined plane or slope on the interior face of a wall or rampart serving as connecting passage-way between two different levels. **3.** (her.) Position of a rampant heraldic beast. **4. a** (colloq.) Storm of anger; commotion, rampage; **b** (slang) a swindle, esp. of fraudulent company promoting or share-dealing.

rampage, n. & vb. intrans. [1. rampáj; 2. ræmpéidž]. Perh. fr. **ramp (I.)**. **a** n. A riot, an outbreak of excitement or turbulent behaviour, a ramp: *to go on the rampage*; **b** vb., to rage, riot, behave turbulently or excitedly.

rampageous, adj. [1. rampájus; 2. ræmpéidžəs]. Prec. & **-ous.** Violent, boisterous, uncontrolled, hard to restrain.

rampageously, adv. Prec. & **-ly.** In a rampageous manner; boisterously, violently.

rampageousness, n. See prec. & **-ness.** State, quality, of being rampageous.

rampancy, n. [1. rámpansi; 2. rǽmpənsi]. **rampant** & **-cy. 1.** Condition of being rampant; **a** luxuriancy of growth; **b** prevalence, frequency, of occurrence. **2.** (her.) Position of rampant beast.

rampant, adj. [1. rámpant; 2. rǽmpənt]. Fr., Pres. Part. of *ramper*. See **ramp (I.)**. **1. a** (of animals) Furious, violent, untamed; **b** (specif. her., esp. of lion) depicted in profile, reared up on hind legs, the fore paws being stretched out and held one higher than the other; **c** (of persons) angry, impatient, chafing, as under some annoyance: *he was simply rampant at the delay.* **2.** (of plants and their growth) Luxuriant, lush, flourishing, vigorous; unrestrained. **3.** (always in unfavourable sense) Dominant, rife, intensely prevalent: *disease and vice are rampant in the slums.*

rampantly, adv. Prec. & **-ly.** In a rampant manner; **a** (growing) freely, vigorously; **b** intensely and prevalently.

rampart, n. & vb. trans. [1. rámpart; 2. rǽmpāt, -ət], fr. Fr. *rempart*, O. Fr. *rempar*, fr. *remparer*, 'to fortify, put into a state of defence', fr. **re-**, 'again', & *emparer*, 'to take possession of beforehand', fr. *an-*, 'before', see **ante-**, & *parer*, 'to secure', fr. Lat. *parāre*, 'to prepare', see **pare. 1.** n. **a** A mound or embankment of earth thrown up from the ditch as a defensive wall, with broad flat top behind a stone or earthen parapet; **b** (fig.) protection, defence, of any kind. **2.** vb. To defend, fortify, with a rampart.

rampion, n. [1. rámpiun; 2. rǽmpiən], fr. Ital. *raponzolo*, cp. Fr. *raiponce*; etymol. unknown. (bot.) A kind of campanula or bell-flower, *Campanula Rapunculus*, with tuberous root, used as a salad.

rampire, n. [1. rámpīr; 2. rǽmpaiə]. Archaic form of **rampart**.

ramrod, n. [1. rámrod; 2. rǽmrɔd]. **ram (II.)** & **rod.** A metal rod used for ramming home the charge and shot of a muzzle-loading gun or small-arm. Phr. *as stiff as a ramrod*, stiff, upright, rigid in appearance, bearing, and demeanour.

ramshackle, adj. [1. rámshakl; 2. rǽmʃækl]. Earlier *ramshackled*; etymol. doubtful, possibly for *ransackle*, see **ransack.** Worn out, tumbledown, rickety: *a ramshackle old car; a ramshackle cottage.*

ramson, n. [1. rámsn; 2. rǽmsn]. O.E. *hramsa*, 'broad-leaved garlic', cogn. w. Gk. *krómuon*, 'onion', & Lith. *kermùszė*, 'garlic'. The broad-leaved garlic, *Allium ursinum*; root of this used in salads.

ran (I.), n. [1. ran; 2. ræn]. Etymol. unknown. A hank of twine 20 yards in length.

ran (II.), vb. Pret. of **run.** M.E. *ran*, fr. O.E. *ran*, Pret. of *rinnan*, 'to flow', or fr. O.N. *rann*, Pret. of *renna*, 'to run'. See **run.**

rance, n. [1. rans; 2. ræns]. Fr.; etymol. unknown. A variety of dark-red marble with blue and white veins, found in Belgium.

ranch, n. & vb. intrans. [1. rahnch; 2. rān(t)ʃ], fr. Span. Am. *rancho*, 'people feeding together, a mess, also mess-room', esp. of the huts in which the herdsmen and labourers of a farm live. **a** n. A cattle farm in U.S.A., Canada &c.; **b** vb., to keep, manage, a ranch.

rancher, n. [1. ráhncher; 2. rā́n(t)ʃə]. Prec. & **-er.** One who owns or runs a ranch; a ranchman.

ranchman, n. [1. ráhnchman; 2. rā́n(t)ʃmən]. **a** Rancher; **b** worker on a ranch.

rancid, adj. [1. ránsid; 2. rǽnsid], fr. Lat. *rancidus*, 'foul-smelling, stinking'; etymol. unexplained. Having an offensive, stale smell and taste; esp. of fats or oils, such as butter &c., which have gone bad.

rancidity, n. [1. rànsíditi; 2. rænsíditi]. Prec. & **-ity.** State, quality, of being rancid; a rancid smell or taste.

rancidly, adv. [1. ránsidli; 2. rǽnsidli]. **rancid** & **-ly.** In a rancid manner.

rancidness, n. [1. ránsidnes; 2. rǽnsidnis]. See prec. & **-ness.** Rancidity.

rancorous, adj. [1. rángkurus; 2. rǽŋkərəs]. **rancour** & **-ous.** Full of, evincing, rancour, spite, and malice; malicious, malignant.

rancorously, adv. See prec. & **-ly.** In a rancorous manner; malignantly.

rancour, n. [1. rángker; 2. rǽŋkə]. In O. Fr., fr. Lat. *rancōr-(em), rancor*, 'rancidity, rankness, stinking smell; a spite, old grudge'. Same base as **rancid.** Deep-rooted hatred or ill-will; inveterate spite or malice.

rand, n. [1. rand; 2. rænd]. O.E., 'margin, edge, rim'; prob. cogn. w. **rind.** **1.** (rare) **a** A border, margin, edge, as the strip of leather in the heel-piece of a shoe or boot; **b** the unploughed margin of an arable field. **2.** Specif., *The Rand*, a long gold-bearing reef or ridge near Johannesburg, in the Transvaal; the gold-mining district in or near this reef.

randan (I.), n. [1. ràndán; 2. rændǽn]. Etymol. unknown. A rowing-boat for three persons, stroke and bow each using an oar, the other a pair of sculls.

randan (II.), n. Prob. derived fr. **random.** (slang) Racket, spree, jollification: *to go on the randan.*

randem, n. & adv. [1. rándem; 2. rǽndəm]. Formed on anal. of **tandem**, prob. w. reference to **random.** **1.** n. A carriage with three horses driven one in front of the other, a tandem with additional leader; team of three driven one in front of the other. **2.** adv. With three horses thus harnessed and driven: *to drive randem.*

random, n. & adj. [1. rándum; 2. rǽndəm]. Earlier form *randon, randoun*, esp. in phr. *in a randon*, fr. O. Fr. *randon*, esp. in phr. *à randon*, 'at random, at great speed, impetuously, violently', fr. O. Fr. *randonner*, fr. *rander*, 'to move rapidly or violently, to gallop'; etymol. uncertain, possibly of Gmc. origin & cogn. w. *rand*, 'border, edge, as of a full stream or river rushing swiftly'. **1.** n. (obs.) Speed, haste, violence; rush of water, fire; a random course of action; only surviving in phr. *at random*, hastily, impetuously, without aim, thought, or premeditation; aimlessly, at haphazard: *to fire a shot at random.* **2.** adj. **a** Done, made, acting, at random; haphazard; without direction; without careful consideration, heedless: *a random shot, guess* &c.; **b** (masonry) *random work*, built of stones of irregular shape and size, esp. with use of ragstone in such building.

randy, adj. [1. rándi; 2. rǽndi], fr. obs. *rand*, variant of **rant**, & **-y.** Boisterous, rowdy, disorderly (chiefly in Northern or Scots vernacular).

ranee, rani, n. [1. ráhnē; 2. rā́nī]. Hind. *rānī*, fr. Scrt. *rajnī*, fem. of **rajah.** The wife of a rajah; a Hindu queen or princess.

rang, vb. [1. rang; 2. ræŋ]. Pret. of **ring (III.).** M.E. *rang.*

range (I.), vb. trans. & intrans. [1. rānj; 2. reindž], fr. O. Fr. *ranger*, earlier *rengier, rangier*, fr. *rang*, 'rank'. See **rank (I.).** **A.** trans. **1.** (poet.) Arrange: '*Oh, somewhere, meek, unconscious dove That sittest ranging golden hair*' (Tennyson, 'In Mem.' vi.). **2.** To set, place, in ranks or in rank; **a** to set out, arrange, in lines or rows or in line; to place in order; arrange: *to range troops in line; to range books on a shelf according to size*; **b** to arrange systematically, according to natural or conventional class or order; to classify: *to range plants, animals, according to genus and species; to range names of candidates in order of merit.* **3.** To set in line with; to level; to train: *to range a gun, telescope &c. on a particular object.* **4.** To get the range of, by firing beyond or short of: *to range the enemy's flagship.* **5.** (reflex. and pass.) To place oneself in a certain line, class, group &c.; to take sides with or against: *to range oneself on the side of law and order.* Phr. *to range oneself* (Fr. idiom), settle down to a regular, orderly life, esp. on marriage, after sowing one's wild oats. **6.** (archaic or poet.) To traverse, rove, roam over, wander through: *to range the whole world in search of new excitements; to range the woods in search of game* &c. **B.** intrans. **1.** To lie, run, in a line; **a** to lie in a particular direction; to correspond with a particular direction or line; to lie, move, alongside or parallel: *to range east and west, from north-east to south-west; to range along the coast; the line of cliffs ranges very closely with the river*; **b** to stretch, reach, extend: *the forest ranges from six miles north of A to five miles south.* **2.** (of animals, plants) *Range in*, to be found in, frequent, inhabit, to have as a habitat, be a denizen of: *the tiger ranges in the jungles of Bengal.* **3.** *To range in, over, through*, to move about in; **a** to wander, rove, about or through: *to range through woods or fields in search of game*; **b** (of the mind &c.) to be directed, pass, in succession, include in its grasp: *his fancy ranged over many subjects; his studies ranged over many languages.* **4.** To vary between specified extremes, within stated limits: *the temperature ranges from over 100 degrees to less than 60 in the course of the day; prices ranged from 25s. to 27s. per ton.* **5.** (of ordnance) To have a specific range; to traverse a certain range or distance: *the gun ranges five miles; the shell from the gun ranges five miles.*

range (II.), n., fr. prec. **1. a** Row, chain, continuous series, of objects: *a range of hills, buildings; a range of pictures*; **b** series, group, collection, of objects of the same kind or class: *a large range of motors for sale.* **2.** (rare) Direction. **3. a** Distance to which a gun will carry; **b** distance at which one can see or hear, or at which anything can be seen or heard: *beyond the range of the speaker's voice; outside my range of vision.* **4.** Stretch, extent, area: *the estate has a wide range.* **5.** Area ranged over, or inhabited, by specific animals: *the mammoth had a considerable range before the glacial epoch.* **6. a** Intellectual reach, grasp, power of comprehension: *a mind of extraordinary range*; **b** area, domain, of thought, knowledge, speculation, ranged or traversed by the mind; scope: *outside the range of human understanding; a task well within his range; a wide range of interests.* **7. a** Extreme limits within which variation takes place: *a wide range of prices*; **b** specif. (of the voice or of a musical instrument) extreme limits of pitch, compass. **8.** Specially prepared area, with targets, where shooting practice takes place. **9.** A cooking stove, fixed or movable, heated by coal, oil, gas, or electricity, fitted with all appliances for baking, boiling, and roasting food.

range-finder, n. An instrument for finding the distance of the target from the firing-point.

ranger, n. [1. rānjer; 2. réin(d)žə]. **range (I.)** & **-er.** **1.** One who ranges; **a** a rover, wanderer: *a bush-ranger*; **b** an official appointed as guardian or keeper of a royal forest or park, formerly one who ranged the forest in search of breakers of the forest laws &c. **2.** One of a body of mounted troops used to patrol and protect a certain district or area, esp. one on a frontier or over forest land belonging to the State, as in the U.S.A.

rangership, n. [1. rānjership; 2. réindžəʃip]. Prec. & **-ship.** **a** Office of a ranger of a royal park or forest; **b** period of his office.

rank (I.), n. [1. rangk; 2. ræŋk], fr. O. Fr. *ranc*, also *renc*, an obs. variant of *rang*, see **range (I.)**; perh. of Gmc. origin, & connected w. **ring (I.).** **1.** A row or line of persons or things; **a** a line, row, series, of persons or things arranged one behind the other or above one another; a queue, tier: *a rank of shelves* &c.; *to fall into rank*, to fall into line or into orderly arrangement; **b** a line of soldiers ranged side by side, as contrasted with *file*: *the front, rear, rank*; Phr. *to break ranks*, to fall out; to be thrown into confusion; (pl.) *the ranks*, the body of private soldiers; Phrs. *to reduce to the ranks*, to take away a non-commissioned officer's grade; *to rise from the ranks*, to obtain a commission as officer after enlisting as a private soldier; (also non-mil.) to rise in the world. **2.** A social class, division, order: *men of all ranks and classes; a person of high, of no, rank.* **3. a** A distinct grade in the army, navy, or peerage &c.: *the rank of major; the rank of marquis; brevet rank*, extra-regimental status in the army; **b** division, category, within a profession &c. based on general estimation or on actual status: *in the highest rank among scholars; the lower ranks of the clergy.* **4.** Degree of excellence, quality: *a writer of the first rank; a mind of the highest rank.*

rank (II.), vb. trans. & intrans., fr. prec. **A.** trans. **1.** To place in a rank or row; to range: *to rank books on a shelf.* **2. a** To assign a rank, class, position, to; to estimate value of: *I rank his abilities very high*; **b** *rank with*, to place among, consider as belonging to, esteem as equal in merit &c. to: *his name will be ranked with the great names of history.* **B.** intrans. **1. a** To take rank; to belong to a certain rank, class, category: *dukes rank above marquises; a brevet major ranks as a full major outside his regiment*; **b** *rank with*, (i.) to take place or rank with, be counted among: *archbishops rank with dukes*; (ii.) (also *rank among*) to be estimated as equal to, as belonging to the rank of, to hold rank among: *Keats will always rank with* (or *among*) *the greatest English poets.* **2.** (financial, of debts and assets) To count among sums which have to be paid, or as available funds; have a certain priority in respect of payment.

rank (III.), adj. O.E. *ranc*, 'strong, proud': L.G. & Du., Swed. & Dan. *rank*, 'thin, slender, erect', O.N. *rakkr*, 'straight, bold'; perh. a nasalized form of Gmc. base ***rak-,**

'to stretch out, extend', cp. **rack (I.)**; the late sense of 'foul-smelling' is due to influence of Fr. *rance*, 'stale, musty'. See **rancid**. **1. a** (of vegetation) Growing very vigorously; overgrown, coarse: *rank grass; a rank growth of weeds* &c.; **b** (of land &c.) producing vegetation in a rank, overluxuriant growth: *a garden rank with weeds; the soil is too rank for healthy crops.* **2.** Possessing specific qualities or character to a high or extreme degree; utter, complete, downright, flagrant; only in opprobrious sense: *rank traitor, treason; a rank atheist, outsider; rank cowardice.* **3. a** Strong and offensive in smell or taste; foul-smelling, rancid: *rank butter, fish &c.; lanes and alleys rank with filth; the rank smell of a goat*; **b** (fig.) corrupt, loathsome, repugnant: '*O my offence is rank, it smells to heaven*' (Shakespeare, 'Hamlet', iii. 3); **c** (colloq.) bad; also as intensive: *a rank stroke*, at golf &c.; *rank bad form.*

ranker, n. [1. rángker; 2. rǽŋkə]. **rank (I.)** & **-er.** A commissioned officer in the army who has been promoted from the ranks.

rankle, vb. intrans. [1. rángkl; 2. rǽŋkl], fr. O. Fr. *rancler*, earlier *raoncler, raancler*, fr. *rancle*, earlier *raancle, draoncle* &c., 'a fester, festering sore', fr. Med. Lat. *dracunculus*, 'sore, ulcer', lit. 'a little dragon', fr. Lat. *draco*, 'dragon', see **drake (II.)** & **dragon. 1.** (archaic or poet.) To fester, to become inflamed or sore; to be the cause of festering or inflammation: *the wound rankled; the arrow rankled in the wound; the poison still rankles in his veins.* **2.** (fig.) To be an abiding cause of pain, grief, bitterness, hatred &c.; *the frustration of his hopes rankled; the memory of the insult still rankles in his heart; rankling hatred, envy* &c.

rankly, adv. [1. rángkli; 2. rǽŋkli]. **rank (III.)** & **-ly.** In a rank manner; in various senses: *to grow, produce, rankly; to smell rankly.*

rankness, n. [1. rángknes; 2. rǽŋknis]. See prec. & **-ness. a** State, quality, of being rank; **b** a rank smell.

ransack, vb. trans. [1. ránsak; 2. rǽnsæk]. M.E. *ransaken*, fr. O.N. *rannsaka*, 'to ransack', lit. 'to search a house, as for plunder', fr. *rann*, 'house, dwelling, for **rasn*, cp. Goth. *razn*, O.E. *ærn*, 'house, chamber' &c., see **barn**, & *sækja*, 'to seek', see **seek. 1. a** To rummage, to search thoroughly, to hunt in for something; to turn everything upside down in order to find: *to ransack a room, box, cupboard &c. for plunder, lost articles* &c.; *ransack your pockets for some more money*; **b** (fig.) to search the mind thoroughly: *to ransack one's memory for forgotten things.* **2.** To plunder, pillage: *the house has been completely ransacked by burglars.*

ransom (I.), n. [1. ránsum; 2. rǽnsəm]. M.E. *raunson, ransoun*, fr. O. Fr. *ranson*, Mod. Fr. *rançon*; fr. Lat. *redemptiōn-(em)*, 'a buying back, ransoming, redemption'. See **redemption** & **redeem. 1.** The money, price, or value paid for the release of a prisoner of war, of one captured by brigands &c.; also for the redemption of property seized in war. Phr. *a king's ransom*, the very large sum that was demanded for the release of a king captured in war; (fig.) an enormous sum of money. **2.** The release, liberation, deliverance of a prisoner or captive or the redemption of seized property by payment of money: *to hold a prisoner to, for, ransom.* **3. a** Price paid as taxation &c., regarded as a ransom or redemption, for privileges, right, wealth &c.: *the doctrine of ransom*; **b** (theol., specif.) the offering or sacrifice of Christ, regarded as the price paid for the redemption of sinners: '*even as the Son of Man came to give His life a ransom for many*' (Matt. xx. 28).

ransom (II.), vb. trans., fr. O. Fr. *ransonner.* See prec. **1. a** To secure the release of a prisoner, to redeem captured property, by payment of ransom; **b** to exact ransom for or from; release on payment of ransom. **2.** Specif. (theol.) to redeem by sacrifice: '*the ransomed of the Lord shall return*' (Isaiah xxxv. 10).

ransom bill, bond, n. (hist.) A bill or bond given by the master of a vessel captured at sea in return for which the vessel was given a safe conduct, and a 'ransomer' or hostage handed over to the captors, the owner being later sued on the bond in the prize court.

ransomer, n. [1. ránsumer; 2. rǽnsəmə]. **ransom (II.)** & **-er. 1.** One who ransoms or redeems prisoners and captives; a redeemer. **2.** A hostage handed over from a vessel captured at sea as a pledge for the redemption of a ransom bill.

ransomless, adj. [1. ránsumles; 2. rǽnsəmlis]. **ransom (I.)** & **-less.** Without ransom; free from ransom.

rant (I.), vb. intrans. & trans. [1. rant; 2. rænt], fr. M. Du. *ranten, randen*, 'to be enraged, to rave'; cp. L.G. dial. *rantern*, 'to talk wildly, rant', & Mod. Germ. *ranzen*, 'to make a noise, frolic'. **A.** intrans. **1.** To use violent, extravagant language; to speak wildly, or with more noise than sense; to declaim in an extravagantly theatrical manner: *to rant and rave.* **2.** To preach, pray, in an unrestrained, enthusiastic style. **B.** trans. To utter, declaim, in a ranting manner: *to rant out a speech; to rant a scene on the stage.*

rant (II.), n., fr. prec. **1.** A ranting, wild, extravagant speech or piece of noisy, violently rhetorical, senseless declamation: *the common rant of tub-thumpers at street corners.* **2.** (Scots) A rowdy frolic or spree; a noisy jollification.

ranter, n. [1. ránter; 2. rǽntə]. **rant (I.)** & **-er. 1.** One who rants; **a** specif. (cap.) one of a fanatical religious sect in England during the Commonwealth who rejected all churches, ministers, and organized religious services; **b** in the 19th cent. applied opprobriously to the Primitive Methodists from their 'ranting' method of preaching and praying. **2.** (Scots) A noisy musician or singer.

ranula, n. [1. ránūla; 2. rǽnjulə]. Lat., 'a little frog; a swelling on the tongue of cattle', fr. *rāna*, 'frog'. See next word. (med.) A swelling or cyst under the tongue, caused by the obstruction of a salivary gland.

ranunculus, n. [1. ranúngkūlus; 2. rənáŋkjuləs]. Lat., 'a little frog'; also name of a medicinal plant, prob. a variety of the ranunculus; dimin. of *rāna*, 'frog', wh. is for **racsna*, 'the croaker, roarer', cp. Lat. *raccāre*, 'to roar like the tiger'; cogn. w. O.H.G. *ruohhōn*, 'to roar'. (bot.) One of a genus of plants, including the common buttercup or crowfoot and many garden varieties.

ranz-des-vaches, n. [1. ráhn dā váhsh; 2. rɑ̃ de vɑʃ]. Swiss-Fr., 'the calling of the cows', in Swiss-Germ. *kuhreigen.* A melody sung, or played on the horn, by herdsmen in the Swiss Alps.

rap (I.), n. [1. rap; 2. ræp]. Prob. imitative, cp. Dan. *rap*, 'tap, rap', Swed. *rapp*, 'stroke, blow'. **a** A light, smart, sharp blow, a tap; Phr. (fig.) *to get, give a person, a rap over the knuckles*, get, administer, a rebuke or snub; **b** a light knock or sound of knocking, as on a door &c.; or on the floor or table; specif., light knock heard at a spiritualistic séance, alleged to be made by spirits.

rap (II.), vb. trans. & intrans. See prec. **A.** trans. **1.** To administer a rap to, strike lightly and smartly, strike: *to rap a man over the knuckles*; (also fig.) to snub, rebuke; *to rap the ground with a stick; to rap the table to call a meeting to order* &c.; *to rap messages at a spiritualistic séance.* **2.** *Rap out*; **a** to elicit, express, by rapping: *to rap out a tune on the piano*, to strum; *to rap out a message*, at a séance; **b** to utter sharply: *to rap out an oath.* **B.** intrans. To perform the act of rapping: *to rap at, on, the door, the table* &c.; *some one is rapping.*

rap (III.), vb. trans. New formation fr. **rapt.** (obs.) To seize, snatch; esp. in Phr. *to rap and rend*, to seize and plunder.

rap (IV.), n. Etymol. uncertain; possibly fr. **rapparee. a** (hist.) A counterfeit Irish copper coin, nominally worth a halfpenny, current in reign of George I.; **b** something worthless or of trifling value; in Phr. *I don't care a rap*, not a straw; *I wouldn't give a rap for it*, wouldn't give anything.

rap (V.), n. Etymol. unknown. A skein of yarn of about 120 yds.

rapacious, adj. [1. rapā́shus; 2. rəpéiʃəs], fr. Lat. *rapāc-*, stem of *rapax*, 'grasping, rapacious'; fr. base in *rapere*, 'to seize'. See **rapid. a** Greedy, hungry, ravenous, voracious; **b** grasping, avaricious; extortionate.

rapaciously, adv. Prec. & **-ly.** In a rapacious manner.

rapacity, n. [1. rapásiti; 2. rəpǽsiti], fr. Fr. *rapacité*, fr. Lat. *rapācitāt-(em)*, fr. stem *rapāc-*, see prec., & **-ity.** Quality of being rapacious; greed, voracity; avarice.

rape (I.), vb. trans. [1. rāp; 2. reip]. M.E. *rāpen*; etymol. doubtful, prob. fr. Lat. *rapere*, 'to seize' (see **rapid**), but cp. next word. **1.** (archaic and poet.) To seize and carry off with violence. **2.** Specif., to violate, ravish (a woman).

rape (II.), n., fr. prec.; but cp. obs. M.E. *rape*, 'haste, hurry', cogn. w. or derived fr. O.N. *hrapa*, 'to hasten', Swed. *rapp*, Dan. *rap*, 'hurry'. **1.** (archaic or poet.) A seizure, carrying off by force: *the Rape of Helen; the Rape of the Lock.* **2.** Specif. (law) Unlawful carnal knowledge of a woman without her consent, by force, or fraud; violation.

rape (III.), n., fr. Lat. *rāpa*, also *rāpum*, cogn. w. Gk. *rhápus*, 'turnip', *rhaphanís*, 'radish', cp. Germ. *rübe*, 'turnip'. Plant, *Brassica napus*, resembling a cabbage, grown as food for sheep; *rape seed*, obtained from this, used as food for birds in captivity, and for making lubricating oil.

rape (IV.), n. Etymol. uncertain. Used already in Domesday; one of the six divisions of Sussex, corresponding to the wapentakes, tithings, or ridings &c. of other counties.

rape (V.), n., fr. Fr. *râpe*, fr. L. Lat. *raspa*, cp. Ital. *raspa*; etymol. doubtful. **1.** The refuse from grapes left after extraction of the juice for wine. **2.** A filter, filled with rape, used in making vinegar. *Rape wine*, a thin wine made from the rape of grapes.

Raphaelesque, Raffaelesque, adj. [1. ràfāelésk; 2. ræ̀feiəlésk], fr. painter's name & **-esque.** After, in the style of, the Italian painter Raphael, *Raffaello Sanzio*, 1483–1520.

raphe, n. [1. rā́fē; 2. réifī]. Gk. *rhaphé*, 'seam', fr. *rháptein*, 'to sew together'; perh. connected w. Lat. *verbēna* (plant name), see **verbena.** (anat. and bot.) A seam, suture, line of junction.

raphia, n. See **raffia.**

rapid (I.), adj. [1. rápid; 2. rǽpid], fr. Lat. *rapidus*, 'tearing, hurrying along, swift, rapid', fr. *rapere*, 'to seize, carry off', cogn. w. Gk. *harpázein*, 'to seize, carry off', cp. **harpy. 1.** Moving, acting, taking place, swiftly; swift, speedy, quick: *a rapid stream; rapid thinker, worker, speaker; rapid events.* **2.** (of action &c.) Done, performed, quickly or hastily: *rapid work; a rapid journey; to take a rapid glance.* **3.** Sudden, abrupt; steep: *a rapid ascent, descent; a rapid fall, descent, in a road* &c.

rapid (II.), n., fr. prec.; cp. Fr. *rapide.* (usually pl.) Part of a river where the current flows with peculiar speed and force, owing to a sudden, considerable fall in the bed, or to the water suddenly emerging from a narrowed or obstructed channel.

rapidity, n. [1. rapíditi; 2. rəpíditi], fr. Fr. *rapidité*, fr. Lat. *rapiditāt-(em).* See **rapid** & **-ity.** State, quality, of being rapid; swiftness, speed, quickness, velocity.

rapidly, adv. [1. rápidli; 2. rǽpidli]. **rapid (I.)** & **-ly.** In a rapid manner; with speed, swiftly, quickly.

rapidness, n. [1. rápidnes; 2. rǽpidnis]. See prec. & **-ness.** Rapidity.

rapier, n. [1. rā́pier; 2. réipiə], fr. Fr. *rapière*, in O. Fr. as adj. *espee rapiere*, 'rapier sword'; etymol. uncertain; possibly fr. *raspière*, 'rasper, poker', & first used as a derisive term. **1.** A light, thrusting sword with long narrow blade; used for fighting duels and fencing, dating from the 16th and 17th cents. **2.** (attrib.) Sharp, piercing, like a rapier: *a rapier glance, thrust.*

rapine, n. [1. rápin; 2. rǽpin]. Cp. Fr. *rapine*, fr. Lat. *rapīna*, 'plunder, rapine'; See base under **rapid**, and cp. **raven (II.)**. (poet. or rhet.) Plunder, pillage, violent robbery.

rapparee, n. [1. ràparḗ; 2. rǽpərí], fr. Ir. *rapaire*, 'short pike'. **1.** (hist.) An Irish irregular pike-man, employed in the war of the Revolution, 1688–91. **2.** An Irish free-booter.

rappee, n. [1. rapḗ; 2. ræpí], fr. Fr. *(tabac) râpé*, 'rasped, grated tobacco'; see **rasp (I.)**. A strong, coarse kind of snuff.

rapper, n. [1. ráper; 2. rǽpə]. **rap (I.)** & **-er**. **1. a** Person who raps; **b** device for rapping, door-knocker. **2.** (slang) An oath, lie, rapped out quickly; a thumping oath or lie, a whopper.

rapport, n. Anglicized as [1. rapṓr; 2. ræpɔ́]. Fr., fr. *rapporter*, 'to bring back to, refer to'. See **report**. Relation, communication, esp. in Phr. *to be in rapport*, or as Fr. *en rapport, with*, to have close reciprocal relations, to be in sympathy or close communication with; esp. used in spiritualistic terminology, of communication by means of a medium with an alleged spirit.

rapprochement, n. [1. rapróshmon; 2. ræprɔ́ʃmɑ̃]. Fr., fr. *rapprocher*, 'to bring together again, to cause to approach once more'. See **re-** & **approach**. Establishment, esp. re-establishment, renewal, of cordial relations between individuals, parties, states, where relations have not previously existed, or had become strained.

rapscallion, n. [1. ràpskáliun; 2. rǽpskǽliən]. Later form of obs. *rascallion*. See **rascal**. A rascal, ne'er-do-well, ragamuffin, scamp.

rapt, P.P. & adj. [1. rapt; 2. ræpt], fr. Lat. *raptum*, P.P. of *rapere*, 'to seize'. See **rapid** & **rape (I.)**. **1.** Seized, carried away, transported in body or mind from ordinary life or existence: *rapt to the seventh heaven.* **2.** Completely absorbed, engrossed; enraptured: *to be rapt in some absorbing task*; *rapt attention*; *a rapt expression of countenance.*

raptorial, adj. [1. raptṓrial; 2. ræptɔ́riəl]. Lat. *raptor*, 'one who seizes, a plunderer, preyer'. See prec. & **-or** & **-ial**. **1.** Preying, predatory, as of birds and animals: *raptorial beasts, birds*, beasts, birds, of prey. **2.** (zool.) Belonging to the order *Raptores* or birds of prey, characterized by the size and strength of their curved claws, hooked beaks, powers of sight and flight, and including the eagles, vultures, hawks &c., formerly the owls.

rapture, n. [1. rápchur; 2. rǽptʃə]. Formed fr. **rapt** & **-ure**. State, condition, of being rapt, transported, carried out of oneself by intense delight or powerful, pleasurable emotion; ecstasy, transport: *to recall childhood's raptures of delight.* Phr. *to go into raptures over*, to express extreme, vehement delight in, to be enraptured with.

raptured, adj. [1. rápchurd; 2. rǽptʃəd]. P.P. of obs. *rapture*, vb. trans. See prec. Enraptured.

rapturous, adj. [1. rápchurus; 2. rǽptʃərəs]. **rapture** & **-ous**. Inspiring, expressing, rapture; ecstatic: *rapturous enjoyment*; *rapturous applause.*

rapturously, adv. Prec. & **-ly**. With rapture, ecstatically.

rara avis, n. [1. rā́ra ā́vis; 2. rɛ́ərə éivis]. Lat., 'a rare bird'; see **rare (I.)** & **aviary**. Person or thing of a kind seldom met with.

rare (I.), adj. [1. rār; 2. rɛə]. Fr., fr. Lat. *rārus*, 'thin, loose, not dense in texture; scattered, scanty; infrequent; scarce, rare'; etymol. doubtful. **1.** Loosely compacted, of loose texture, thin, not dense; **a** (of atmosphere, gases &c.) rarefied, thin; **b** scattered; placed, growing, widely dispersed: *a few rare trees here and there.* **2.** Not frequent, not found commonly; seldom met with; **a** scarce, uncommon: *a rare bird, postage-stamp, book*; **b** exceptional, unusual: *a rare event*; *it is rare to find caution in the young.* **3.** Of exceptional quality; uniquely good, excellent: '*O rare Ben Jonson*'; '*rare and refreshing fruit*'; *a rare beauty*; (colloq.) *to have a rare time of it, rare fun* &c.

rare (II.), adv., fr. prec. (chiefly in colloq. phr.) *A rare good wine*; *a rare fine view* &c., exceptionally, extremely.

rare (III.), adj. O.E. *hrēr*; possibly connected w. Lat. *crūdus*, 'raw', see **crude**, but the vowel offers difficulties. (obs. or provinc. in England; used in Ireland and U.S.A.; of meat) Underdone; not thoroughly or well cooked.

rarebit, n. [1. rā́rbit; 2. rɛ́əbit]. Always *Welsh rarebit*, toasted cheese; bogus word for *Welsh rabbit.*

rare earths, n. pl. Certain metallic oxides found with rare or scarce minerals.

raree-show, n. [1. rā́rē shṓ; 2. rɛ́ərī ʃòu]. For 'rare show'. A portable peep-show, as seen at fairs &c.

rarefaction, n. [1. rā̀refákshun; 2. rɛ̀ərifǽkʃən]. Fr. See **rare (I.)** & **-faction**. Act, process, of rarefying; state of being rarefied, contrasted with *condensation.*

rarefactive, adj. [1. rā̀refáktiv; 2. rɛ̀ərifǽktiv]. See prec. & **-ive**. Producing rarefaction.

rarefiable, adj. [1. rā́refìabl; 2. rɛ́ərifaiəbl]. Next word & **-able**. Capable of being rarefied.

rarefy, vb. trans. & intrans. [1. rā́refī; 2. rɛ́ərifai], fr. Fr. *raréfier*. See **rare (I.)** & **-fy**. **A.** trans. **1.** To make rare or thin; to reduce the density of (air, gas &c.). **2.** (fig.) To refine, spiritualize; to attenuate: *to rarefy one's earthly desires*; *an argument which is too rarefied to be very cogent.* **B.** intrans. To become rarefied.

rarely, adv. [1. rā́rli; 2. rɛ́əli]. **rare (I.)** & **-ly**. **1.** Seldom, infrequently: *I come to London very rarely.* **2.** Uncommonly; in a manner so excellent as to be exceptional: *we dined rarely*; *rarely honest*; *rarely magnificent.*

rareness, n. [1. rā́rnes; 2. rɛ́ənis]. **rare** & **-ness**. State, quality, of being rare (in various senses).

rarity, n. [1. rā́riti; 2. rɛ́əriti], fr. Lat. *rāritātem*. See **rare (I.)** & **-ity**. **1.** State, quality, of being rare; **a** lack of density; **b** scarceness, uncommonness. **2.** A rare, scarce, object or quality.

rascal, n. & adj. [1. ráhskl; 2. rā́skl]. M.E. *raskaille*, 'the rabble', also of a beast of the chase, not full-grown, or out of condition, fr. O. Fr. *rascaille*, 'the rabble, dregs of the population'; etymol. doubtful; a connexion w. O. Fr. *rascler*, 'to scrape', has been suggested, in wh. case the orig. sense wd. be 'scrapings, refuse'. **1.** n. **a** A rogue, scamp, knave; a dishonest, disreputable fellow; **b** (affectionately) *you young rascal!*; *a merry rascal.* **2.** adj. (archaic) Of, pertaining to, the rabble or mob: *the rascal crowd.*

rascaldom, n. [1. ráhskldum; 2. rā́skldəm]. Prec. & **-dom**. Rascals collectively.

rascalism, n. [1. ráhskalizm; 2. rā́skəlizəm]. **rascal** & **-ism**. Rascality.

rascality, n. [1. rahskáliti; 2. rāskǽliti]. **rascal** & **-ity**. **a** Rascally conduct: *some fresh piece of rascality*; **b** a rascally action: *he is up to some new rascality.*

rascally, adj. [1. ráhskali; 2. rā́skəli]. **rascal** & **-ly**. Characteristic of a rascal; dishonest, mean, base: *a rascally trick*; *a rascally fellow.*

rase, vb. See **raze**.

rash (I.), adj. [1. rash; 2. ræʃ]. M.E. *rasch*, cogn. w. Du. & Germ. *rasch*, 'quick, hasty', cp. Dan. & Swed. *rask*, 'brisk, vigorous'. **1.** (of persons) Over-hasty, impetuous; incautious, imprudent, headstrong, reckless: *a rash general*; *rash politicians.* **2.** (of utterances &c.) Spoken, done, without caution or consideration; precipitate: *a rash act*; *rash promises.*

rash (II.), n. Not an early word; cp. O. Fr. *rasche, rache*, 'scurf', Ital. *raschia*, 'itch'; etymol. doubtful. An eruption; a series of patches or spots on the skin, a typical symptom of various fevers, e.g. measles, scarlet fever &c.

rasher, n. [1. rásher; 2. rǽʃə]. Etymol. doubtful; perh. fr. obs. *rash*, 'to cut, slice', a variant of **raze**. A thin slice of bacon or ham for grilling or frying.

rashly, adv. [1. ráshli; 2. rǽʃli]. **rash (I.)** & **-ly**. In a rash manner; hastily, recklessly, imprudently.

rashness, n. [1. ráshnes; 2. rǽʃnis]. See prec. & **-ness**. Quality of being rash; hastiness, incaution, recklessness, impetuosity.

rasorial, adj. [1. rāsṓrial; 2. reisɔ́riəl]. Lat. *rāsor*, 'scraper'. See **raze, razor,** & **-ial**. (of birds) Scraping, scratching the ground in search for food &c., formerly applied as a group name for all the kinds of domestic fowl; gallinaceous.

rasp (I.), vb. trans. & intrans. [1. rahsp; 2. rāsp]. O. Fr. *rasper*, Mod. Fr. *râper*; prob. of Gmc. origin; cp. O.H.G. *raspōn*. **A.** trans. **1. a** To file, scrape, smooth off roughnesses by scraping, filing &c.; **b** to produce a grating, harsh sound: *rasp out*, to utter in a rasping voice. **2.** To grate, scratch, act like a file, produce sensation of roughness upon; chiefly **a** to act as an astringent on (the tongue &c.); **b** to sound harshly, grate upon (the ear); **c** (fig.) to irritate, ruffle (the nerves or temper). **B.** intrans. To perform the action, carry out process, of rasping: (fig.) *a rasping voice*, one that is harsh and raucous.

rasp (II.), n. O. Fr. *raspe*, Mod. Fr. *râpe*. See prec. **1.** Kind of coarse file for smoothing rough surfaces, usually worked by grasping at either end and drawing smartly across the rough surface. **2.** A grating sound or sensation. **3.** (fig.) Irritation of mind.

rasp (III.), n. Colloq. form of **raspberry**.

raspatory, n. [1. ráhspaturi; 2. rā́spətəri], fr. Med. Lat. *raspātōrium*, fr. *raspāre*, 'to rasp'. See **rasp (I.)**. A surgical instrument for rasping or scraping diseased bones.

raspberry, n. [1. ráhzberi; 2. rā́zbəri]. Etymol. uncertain; earlier *raspis-berry*, fr. obs. & dial. *rasp*, 'the plant and fruit', & **berry**; *raspis*, the early form, may be the same as *raspice, raspise*, 'a thin, sweet wine', possibly 'raspberry wine'; O. Fr. has *vin raspé*, in Med. Lat. *raspecia*, 'wine produced from grapes after the first pressing', also *raspe*, 'pressed grapes', cp. Provenç. *raspa*, 'to glean, collect grapes', cp. **rape (V.)**. A juicy, bright-red or golden-yellow fruit consisting of a cluster of drupelets, with slightly acid characteristic flavour, growing from main stem or cane on slender stalks covered with sharp, fine spines.

raspberry-cane, n. New annual shoot of raspberry plant upon which the next year's fruit is produced.

raspberry vinegar, n. Syrup made from raspberries with addition of vinegar.

rasper, n. [1. ráhsper; 2. rā́spə]. **rasp (I.)** & **-er**. **1.** A large rasp or file; any instrument that is used for scraping or rasping. **2.** (hunting) A high, stiff fence.

rasping, adj. [1. ráhsping; 2. rā́spiŋ]. **rasp (I.)** & **-ing**. Scraping, grating; esp. producing a harsh, grating sound: *a rasping voice.*

raspingly, adv. Prec. & **-ly**. In a rasping, grating manner; harshly.

raspy, adj. [1. ráhspi; 2. rā́spi]. **rasp (I.)** & **-y**. Rasping.

rasse, n. [1. ras; 2. ræs]. Jav. *ranse* or *rase*. A tree-climbing civet-cat of Indo-China and Malay Archipelago.

rat (**I.**), n. [1. rat; 2. ræt]. O.E. *ræt*, M.E. *ratte, rat*; O.H.G. *rato, ratta*; cogn. w. Lat. *rādere, rōdere*, 'to gnaw', see **rodent**. **1.** Any of various long-tailed rodents resembling and allied to the mouse, but considerably larger, brown or grey in colour, and infesting houses, barns, stables, and ships; the name is loosely applied to other similar rodents of various species, such as the *water-rat* or water-vole &c. Phrs. *to smell a rat*, to perceive that something is afoot; to suspect a plot, conspiracy &c.; *like a drowned rat*, soaked to the skin, wet through; *oh rats!*, exclamation expressive of contempt, incredulity &c. **2.** A cowardly, mean, treacherous person; specif., one who deserts a cause or party, esp. when misfortune threatens.

rat (**II.**), vb. intrans., fr. prec. **1.** To hunt rats, gen. with ferrets, dogs. **2.** To behave like a rat; to change one's party from interested motives; desert a cause through weakness of purpose or cowardice.

rata, n. [1. ráhta; 2. rátə]. Maori. A New Zealand tree with hard, dark-red wood.

ratability, n. [1. rātabíliti; 2. rèitəbíliti]. **ratable** & **-ity**. Capacity for being, liability to be, rated.

ratable, adj. [1. rátabl; 2. réitəbl]. **rate** (**II.**) & **-able**. **1.** Capable of being rated, valued, estimated. **2.** Proportional, reckoned, counted according to a definite rate: *a ratable share in profits*. **3.** Specif., assessable, liable to pay rates for purposes of local taxation: *ratable value of property*, the yearly sum at which houses or land are assessed for rates, based on the rent, with deductions for repairs &c.

ratably, adv. Prec. & **-ly**. In proportion; by rate, proportionally.

ratafia, n. [1. ràtaféa; 2. rætəfíə]. Earlier *ratafee*; Fr. *ratafia*; etymol. doubtful. **1.** A liqueur or cordial distilled from almonds, peaches, apricots, or plums &c. and flavoured also with the crushed kernels of the fruit. **2.** A sweet biscuit similarly flavoured.

ratal, n. [1. rátal; 2. réitəl]. **rate** (**I.**) & **-al**. On anal. of **rental**. The amount at which property is assessed for the payment of rates; also attributively, as *ratal value*.

rataplan, n. & vb. intrans. & trans. [1. ràtaplán; 2. rætəplǽn]. Fr.; imitative. **1.** n. The sound of a drum being beaten. **2.** vb. To make such a sound by beating a drum.

rat-a-tat, n. [1. rát a tát; 2. ræt ə tǽt]. See **rat-tat**.

rat-catcher, n. [1. rát kàcher; 2. rǽt kætʃə]. **1.** One who makes it his business to catch and destroy rats. **2.** (pl., *rat-catchers*, slang) Man's dress of riding-breeches and gaiters, as opposed to regular hunting rig.

ratch, n. & vb. trans. [1. rach; 2. rætʃ]. See next word. **1.** n. A ratchet-wheel. **2.** vb. To fit with a ratchet; cut gear teeth in.

ratchet, n. & vb. trans. [1. ráchet; 2. rǽtʃit], fr. Fr. *rochet*, 'a bobbin, spindle', esp. in Phr. *roue à rochet*, 'a ratchet-wheel'; of Gmc. origin; cp. O.H.G. *roccho*, 'distaff'; see **rock** (**IV.**). **1.** n. (mechan.) A set of teeth on a bar or wheel, sloped in one direction, so that a catch or pawl working these allows motion in one direction, but checks it in the contrary sense. *Ratchet-bar, wheel*, bar, wheel, fitted with a ratchet and pawl; *ratchet-brace, drill*, brace and drill working with a ratchet and pawl. **2.** vb. To fit wheel, bar &c. with ratchets.

rate (**I.**), n. [1. rāt; 2. reit]. O. Fr., 'price, value', fr. L. Lat. *rāta* (sc. *pars*), 'settled, determined, part or thing', fr. Lat. *rata*, fem. sing. of P.P. *ratus*, 'reckoned, counted', of *rēri*, 'to think, count', see further under **ratio** & cp. **reason**; cp. also Lat. *rēs*, 'thing', lit. 'something thought of', see **re** (**II.**); cogn. w. Goth. (*ga*)*raþjan*, 'to count'; also O.E. *rǣd*, 'council', see **read** (**I.**). **1.** Amount, degree of something, measured in relation to something else; specif. **a** of distance in relation to time: *at a rate of forty miles an hour*; **b** of cost, charge, in relation to time: *wages at the rate of £3 per week*; **c** of number in relation to time: *birth, death, marriage rate*. **2.** Fixed relation, scale, proportion of amount, degree &c. between two things: *the rate of exchange*, sum in coinage of one country equivalent to a certain sum in that of another: *to buy at a high rate*, pay a large sum as price of something. **3.** Specif., speed, i.e. distance travelled, number of movements performed, in a given time: *to drive at a dangerous rate*. **4.** In various senses, arising fr. **1**, **2**, **3**, in specific Phr. *at any rate*, whatever happens, under all circumstances, in any case: *at any rate I will do nothing without further instructions*; *he has improved somewhat in manners at any rate*, i.e. whatever else may be unsatisfactory; *at this rate*, in this way: *you mustn't scold me at this rate*; *at that rate*, in that case, if what you say is true, that being so: *at that rate we shan't get any dinner today*; *he ought to be dismissed at that rate*; *if you go on at that rate you will injure your health*, if you continue to act or behave in such a way &c. **5.** **a** Class, category, based on estimated worth, quality, capacity &c.; obs. except in *first, second, third &c. rate*; used attributively, *a first-rate mind, a second-rate ability*; or pred., *this fruit, sermon, orchestra &c. is very second rate*; **b** specif. (naut.) (i.) class to which a ship belongs, fixed for warships according to its tonnage and armament; for merchant-men according to its relative value as an insurance risk; (ii.) relative standing and grade of a seaman. **6.** Amount levied for local purposes by municipal, district or county authorities on the assessment of the annual value of property: *poor-rate, water-rate* &c.; spoken of collectively as *the rates*.

rate (**II.**), vb. trans. & intrans., fr. prec. **A.** trans. **1.** To esteem, estimate, the value or qualities of, attribute certain degree of merit to; to appreciate; to assign to a certain class: *to rate the influence of religion very high*; *to rate a person high as a moral force*. **2.** To assess for rating; to fix the rate on property for local taxation: *the house is rated at £50 per annum*. **3.** Specific uses: **a** to fix in relation to variation from a standard: *to rate a coin, paper money*, above or below its real value; *to rate a chronometer*, to regulate according to standard mean-time; **b** (insurance) *rate up*, to fix a premium at a higher rate for special risks; **c** (naut.) to class a vessel according to size &c., or a sailor according to grading. **B.** intrans. To be classed in a certain rate or grade: *a ship rates as first, second* &c.

rate (**III.**), vb. trans. M.E. *raten*, cp. earlier form *araten* in same sense; etymol. uncertain; Swed. has *rata*, 'to find fault'. To scold, take to task, to chide, angrily or severely: *rate at*, to storm at, scold.

rate (**IV.**), vb. Variant of **ret**.

ratel, n. [1. rátel; 2. réitel]. S. Afr. Du. *ratelmuis*, 'ratel mouse'; possibly connected w. **rat**. A carnivorous mammal, somewhat resembling a badger, with grey upper and black under parts; also called *honey-badger*; the species *Mellivora ratel* is a native of S. Africa, the species *Mellivora indica* of India.

rate-payer, n. One who pays local rates on house or landed property.

rater (**I.**), n. [1. ráter; 2. réitə]. **rate** (**I.**) & **-er**. (only in compounds) One of a certain rate or class: *a first-, second-rater*.

rater (**II.**), n. **rate** (**III.**) & **-er**. One who rates or scolds: *a loud-voiced, bullying rater*.

rath (**I.**), n. [1. rahth; 2. rāþ]. Ir. *raith*. See **pravity** for possible cogn. words. (Ir. archaeol.) A prehistoric hill-fort or mound; often *Danish rath*.

rath (**II.**), also **rathe**, adj. [1. rādh, rahth; 2. reið, rāþ]. O.E. *hræð, hræd*, 'quick, agile, hasty', cp. O.E. *hraðian*, 'to hasten'; perh. connected w. the base of Lat. *cardo*, 'hinge', lit. 'that on which something swings', see **cardinal** (**I.**); cp. Gk. *kardáō*, 'I swing'; Scrt. *kúrdati*, 'springs, hops'. (archaic or poet.) **a** Coming early or before others, before the usual time, esp. of flowers, early blooming, of fruits, early ripening: '*Bring the rathe primrose that forsaken dies*' (Milton, 'Lyc.', 142); **b** (of persons): '*The men of rathe and riper years*' (Tennyson).

rather, adv. [1. ráhdher; 2. rā́ðə]. O.E. *hraðor*, 'more quickly', compar. of prec. The old meaning, 'more quickly', is obs., & only survives in the secondary sense of 'preferably'. **1.** Sooner, preferably, for choice; more willingly, more readily: *I would rather drink tea than coffee*; *they determined to die rather than surrender*; *I would rather not go to work today*; (also with archaic subj.) *I had rather never been born than have seen this day of shame*; (also inverted) *rather than submit to this, I would* &c. **2.** More, to a greater extent, in a greater degree; more accurately, truly, described as: *the colour seems green rather than blue*; *he relies on mere abuse rather than on argument*; *the building is a great success, or rather a triumph, for the designer*. **3.** Somewhat, to some extent, slightly: *I feel rather better today*; *rather good-looking*; *they rather expected to win*. **4.** (colloq., often [1. ráhdhĕr; 2. rā́ðǝ̄], as answer to a question, offer &c.) Certainly, assuredly, as an emphatic asseveration: *would you like a holiday? Rather!*

ratification, n. [1. ràtifikáshun; 2. rætifikéiʃən], fr. L. Med. Lat. *ratificātiōn-(em)*, fr. *ratificāt-(um)*, P.P. type of *ratificāre*. See **ratify**. Act of ratifying; state of being ratified; confirmation, sanction.

ratify, vb. trans. [1. rátifī; 2. rǽtifai], fr. Fr. *ratifier*, fr. L. Med. Lat. *ratificāre*, fr. Lat. *rat-(um)*, 'fixed, settled'. See **rate** (**I.**) & **-fy**. To confirm, make valid; to approve and sanction by formal consent and signature: *to ratify a treaty*; *to ratify the acts of an agent*.

rating (**I.**), n. [1. ráting; 2. réitiŋ]. **rate** (**II.**) & **-ing**. **1.** **a** Act of valuing, assessing; esp. act of fixing a rate on property &c.; **b** amount so fixed. **2.** **a** (naut.) The class or grade into which formerly ships of war were divided; **b** now, of yachts, motor-cars, or machinery, according to tonnage, horse-power &c. **3.** (naut.) The class, status, or grade as belonging to which a member of a ship's company is entered on the books: *the rating of a petty officer*; (pl.) *ratings*, the ship's crew according to their rating or grade.

rating (**II.**), n. **rate** (**III.**) & **-ing**. A scolding; an angry rebuke, reprimand.

ratio, n. [1. ráshiō; 2. réiʃiou]. Lat., 'reckoning, calculation, account; relation, method, plan; mental faculty, judgement, understanding, reason; reasonable cause, motive', fr. *rat-(um)*, P.P. type of *rēri*, 'to think, reckon'; cogn. w. Goth. *raþjō*, 'number, reckoning', q.v. under **read** (**I.**); Scrt. *rādhyati*, 'succeeds', *rādhaś*, 'generosity, favour'; O. Ir. (*imm*)-*rādim*, 'I consider'. Cp. **rate** (**I.**) & **reason**. **1.** The relation which one quantity or magnitude bears to another of the same kind, expressed by the quotient obtained by dividing one by the other. **2.** Fixed relation of number or degree; proportion.

ratiocinate, vb. intrans. [1. ràtiósināt; 2. rætiósineit], fr. Lat. *ratiōcināt-(um)*, P.P. type of *ratiōcināri*, 'to calculate, to deliberate, to reason, argue'; fr. *ratio*, perhaps with suffixes *-ci-, -ni-*. See prec. To reason formally, by means of syllogisms.

ratiocination, n. [1. ràtiosináshun; 2. rætiosinéiʃən], fr. Lat. *ratiōcinātiōn-(em)*. See prec. & **-ion**. Formal, syllogistic reasoning; the process of reasoning.

ratiocinative, adj. [1. ràtiósinātiv; 2. rætiósineitiv]. See **ratiocinate** & **-ive**. Pertaining to, characterized by, ratiocination or formal reasoning.

ration (**I.**), n. [1. ráshun; 2. rǽʃən], fr. Lat. *ratiōn-(em)*. See **ratio**. **1.** **a** A fixed amount or quantity of anything, esp. of provisions, allocated or dealt out; allowance: *a ration of bread*; *we have used our ration of coal for the week*; Phr. *to be put on rations*, to be rationed, be put on an allowance;

b (pl.) provisions, food: *on short rations*, on a limited allowance of food &c., on short commons. 2. (usually pl.) A fixed allowance of food &c. issued daily to a soldier or sailor; also of forage for horses. Phr. *the iron ration*, food in a very concentrated form issued to soldiers on active service, only to be used in the last emergency.

ration (II.), vb. trans., fr. prec. **1.** To allot a fixed amount of anything as a ration; specif., to assign by authority a restricted amount (of provisions, fuel &c.) per head of the population, in time of national shortage and stringency: *to ration sugar*. **2.** To supply with the daily ration of food &c.: *the army is well rationed*.

rational (I.), adj. [1. ráshunal; 2. rǽʃənəl], fr. Lat. *ratiōnālis*, 'reasonable'. See **ration** (I.) & **-al.** **1.** Pertaining to the reason or to reasoning. **2. a** Having the faculty of reasoning; endowed with reason or understanding: *man is a rational being*; **b** actually in possession of one's faculties: *the patient has moments when he is perfectly rational*. **3.** Based on, tested by, the reason only; derived from man's reasoning faculties; not derived from authority, revelation &c.: *rational theology*; *a rational explanation*; *a rational belief*. **4. a** Acting in accordance with reason; reasonable, sensible: *a rational man*; **b** done, performed, made, in accordance with principles of reason: *rational behaviour*; *a rational act*; *rational dress*, specif., one of many kinds so called, designed to secure comfort, freedom of movement, and health. **5.** (math.) Expressed without a radical sign; expressible by whole quantities; contrasted with *surd*.

rational (II.), n., fr. prec. **1.** A rational being. **2.** (math.) A rational quantity.

rationale, n. [1. ràshunáhli; 2. ræʃiənáli]. Lat., 'the rational thing', neut. sing. of *ratiōnālis*, adj. See prec. **a** Fundamental logical principle; reasoned theory or hypothesis of the why and how of an action or process; **b** exposition of this.

rationalism, n. [1. ráshunalizm; 2. rǽʃənəlizəm]. **rational** (I.) & **-ism.** **1.** (philos.) **a** Doctrine that reason is the principal, if not the only, source of certain knowledge; opposed to *sensationalism* and *empiricism*; **b** system of philosophy based on this. **2.** (theol.) Doctrine which makes reason the sole source of knowledge of religion and which rejects revelation.

rationalist, n. & adj. [1. ráshunalist; 2. rǽʃənəlist]. Prec. & **-ist.** **1.** n. An adherent of rationalism in philosophy or theology. **2.** adj. Pertaining to rationalists or to rationalism; rationalistic.

rationalistic, adj. [1. ràshunalístik; 2. rǽʃənəlístik]. Prec. & **-ic.** Rationalist.

rationalistically, adv. [1. ràshunalístikali; 2. rǽʃənəlístikəli]. Prec. & **-al** & **-ly.** In a rationalistic manner; after the manner of a rationalist.

rationality, n. [1. ràshunáliti; 2. rǽʃənǽliti], fr. Fr. *rationalité*. See **rational** (I.) & **-ity.** State, quality, of being rational; possession, exercise, of reason; reasonableness.

rationalization, n. [1. ràshunalīzáshun; 2. rǽʃənəlaizéiʃən]. See next word & **-ation.** Act of rationalizing; state of being rationalized; specif., reorganization of an industry or group of related industries, on a rational basis, by means of amalgamations, common selling agencies, price-fixing agreements, control of output &c. &c.

rationalize, vb. trans. & intrans. [1. ráshunalīz; 2. rǽʃənəlaiz]. **rational** (I.) & **-ize.** **A.** trans. **1. a** To explain entirely by reason; to bring into agreement with reason; to give a rational interpretation of; **b** to explain away rationalistically: *to rationalize the doctrine of the Resurrection*; *to rationalize theology, a myth, legend &c.* **2.** (math.) To clear, as an equation, from radical or irrational quantities. **B.** intrans. To carry out the process of rationalizing; to practise rationalization.

rationally, adv. [1. ráshunali; 2. rǽʃənəli]. **rational** (I.) & **-ly.** In a rational manner; in accordance with reason; reasonably, sensibly.

ratite, adj. [1. rátīt; 2. rǽtait], fr. Lat. *ratis*, 'raft', prob. cogn. w. Lith. *rèklès*, 'rack for drying', & perh. also w. O.H.G. *ruota*, 'rod,' O.E. *rōd*, 'rood, cross', see **rood**, & **-ite.** (ornith.) Belonging to the division of the *Ratitae*, or group of flightless birds, with keelless breast-bone, including the ostrich, emu, and cassowary &c.

ratlin, ratline, ratling, n. [1. rátlin; 2. rǽtlin]. Etymol. uncertain. (usually in pl.) Pieces of rope fastened across the shrouds of a ship, forming rungs of a rope ladder.

ratoon, n. [1. ratōōn; 2. rætūn], fr. Span. *retoño*, 'sprout, shoot'. A second and subsequent year's shoot from a sugar-cane after it has been cut down.

ratsbane, n. [1. rátsbān; 2. rǽtsbein]. **rat** (I.) & **bane.** **1.** Rat poison. **2.** Popular name for various poisonous plants.

rat-tailed, adj. **rat** (I.) & **-tailed.** **1.** (of horse) Having a thin hairless tail resembling that of a rat. **2.** (of spoon) Of a 17th or early 18th cent. type, having a tapering raised strip of silver shaped like the end of a rat's tail, forming a prolongation of the handle, and extending along the back of the bowl.

rattan, n. [1. ratán; 2. rætǽn], fr. Malay. *rōtān*, fr. *rāut*, 'to peel, pare'. **1.** A species of climbing palm, of the genus *Calamus*, of the East Indies, with a slender, many-jointed, flexible, hard stem; when peeled it is used for walking-sticks, basket-making &c. **2.** A walking-stick or cane made of this.

rat-tat, rat-a-tat-tat, n. [1. rát tát, ráta tàt tát; 2. rǽt tǽt, rǽtə tæ̀t tǽt]. Imitative. The sound of a loud and prolonged knocking on a door.

ratteen, n. [1. ratḗn; 2. rætīn], fr. Fr. *ratine*, fr. *ratiner*, 'to nap cloth'. A thick, twilled, woollen, lining fabric.

ratten, vb. trans. [1. ráten; 2. rǽtən]. Etymol. uncertain; possibly connected w. *ratten, ratton*, dial. forms of **rat** (II.). To remove, or cause injury to, tools, machinery &c. during a labour dispute so as to prevent continuation or resumption of work.

ratter, n. [1. ráter; 2. rǽtə]. **rat** (II.) & **-er.** One who hunts rats, esp. a dog that catches rats.

rattle (I.), vb. intrans. & trans. [1. rátl; 2. rǽtl]. M.E. *ratelen*, cp. Du. *ratelen*, Germ. *rasseln*; prob. imitative. **A.** intrans. **1. a** To emit a rapid succession of short, sharp sounds, as when hard objects knock against each other, or are shaken together in an empty vessel; to clatter: *these cheap cars rattle so*; *do try and stop the window rattling*; *the hail rattled on the roof*; **b** to make such a noise by knocking, shaking &c.: *someone rattled at the door*; *these snakes rattle when alarmed*; **c** to make such a sound through difficulty of breathing: *the dying man rattled in his throat*. **2.** (usually with advs. or preps.) **a** To move, fall, go, with a rattling noise: *the train rattled over the points*; *a shower of stones rattled down on our heads*; **b** to ride, drive, rapidly or briskly: *we rattled along the road at a great rate*. **3.** (usually with advs. or preps.) To talk, speak, quickly, noisily, and in a brisk, lively manner, usually with an idea of thoughtlessness: *she rattled on gaily about her travels*; *he rattled through his speech*. **B.** trans. **1. a** To cause objects to make short, sharp sounds by shaking them against each other, knocking them against others &c.: *to rattle the handle of a door*; *to rattle the dice in a box*; *the wind rattles the window*; **b** to cause to move with much jolting or shaking: *the train rattled us about*; *'rattle his bones over the stones'*. **2. a** To say, repeat, go through, rapidly, briskly, and in a lively manner: *to rattle off one's lessons*; **b** to get done hastily and rapidly: *to rattle a piece of business through*. **3.** (colloq.) To disconcert, confuse, upset nerve of, disturb, put off: *the constant interruptions rather rattled the speaker*; *the players were rattled by their opponents' tactics*; *nothing rattled the general*.

rattle (II.), n., fr. prec. **1.** A rattling sound; **a** sound produced by a number of loose objects being shaken against each other; **b** intermittent sound caused, e.g., by a window or door being shaken in its frame by the wind; **c** specif., *a rattle in the throat, death-rattle*, sound produced by the breath passing through the throat when this is partially constricted, or choked with phlegm &c.; often heard from dying persons; **d** sound produced by rattlesnake. **2.** One of various objects producing a rattling sound; specif. **a** a child's toy consisting of a number of peas or other small hard objects enclosed in a box, which rattle when shaken; **b** *watchman's rattle*, device formerly used by the watch for summoning help, which made a loud clatter when swung round; **c** *rattlesnake's rattle*, series of horny processes on the tail which the creature causes to rattle when aroused; **d** (bot.) plant whose seeds rattle in the pod: *the yellow* or *red rattle*. **3. a** Continuous sound of noisy, voluble conversation; clatter, noisy chatter; **b** person who indulges in such noisy talk.

rattle-box, n. **1.** A baby's rattle. **2.** (bot.) The yellow or red rattle.

rattle-brain, n. A person who has a shallow, empty brain.

rattle-brained, adj. Having an empty brain; feather-headed.

rattle-head, n. A rattle-brain.

rattle-headed, adj. Rattle-brained.

rattle-pate, n. A shallow, empty head; person with such a head.

rattle-pated, adj. Having a rattle-pate; feather-headed.

rattler, n. [1. rátler; 2. rǽtlə]. **rattle** (I.) & **-er.** **1.** One who, that which, rattles; specif. (colloq.) a rattlesnake. **2.** (slang, colloq.) A rattling person or thing; a very good specimen of its kind: *he's a rattler to hounds*.

rattlesnake, n. [1. rátlsnāk; 2. rǽtlsneik]. **rattle** (II.) & **snake.** A very venomous American snake, of the genus *Crotalus*, having a series of loosely interlocking joints at the end of its tail, which make a rattling sound when shaken.

rattle-trap, n. **rattle** (I.) & **trap.** **1.** A shaky, rattling, worn-out vehicle; a cheap, noisy motor-car. **2.** (pl.) Rubbishy curios, antiques; odds and ends of bric-à-brac &c.

rattling, adj. [1. rátling; 2. rǽtliŋ]. **rattle** (I.) & **-ing.** **1.** (in vbl. senses) Producing the sound of a rattle: *a rattling window* &c. **2.** (colloq., slang) **a** Brisk, vigorous, spanking: *a rattling breeze*; *at a rattling pace*; **b** first-rate, splendid: *had a rattling dinner, time* &c.; also as adv.: *a rattling good fellow*.

rattly, adj. [1. rátli; 2. rǽtli]. **rattle** (II.) & **-y.** Inclined to rattle; shaky, ill-fitting.

rat-trap, n. **rat** (I.) & **trap.** **1.** A trap to catch rats. **2.** Something which resembles a rat-trap: *a rat-trap pedal*, for a bicycle, with teeth on the upper side to prevent the foot slipping. **3.** (vulg. slang) The mouth.

ratty, adj. [1. ráti; 2. rǽti]. **rat** (I.) & **-y.** **1.** Infested with, characteristic of, rats: *a ratty house, smell* &c. **2.** (slang) Angry, ill-tempered, irritated: *he got quite ratty with me*.

raucous, adj. [1. ráwkus; 2. rɔ̄kəs], fr. Lat. *raucus*, 'hoarse', fr. **ravicus*, cogn. w. *ravus*, 'hoarse'; cp. *ravīre*, 'to talk oneself hoarse'; prob. fr. an imitative base **rē-*, seen also in Lith. *rěju*, 'to shout', O. Slav. *rarŭ*, 'echo'; O.N. *rāmr*, 'hoarse'; cp. a similar base **rēu-*, **rāu-* &c., in **rumour**; see also **roar.** Harsh-sounding, hoarse: *a raucous voice*.

raucously, adv. Prec. & **-ly.** With a raucous voice or sound; harshly, hoarsely.

raucousness, n. See prec. & **-ness.** Quality of being raucous; hoarseness.

raughty, rorty, adj. [1. ráwti; 2. rɔ̄ti]. Origin unknown. (slang) Jolly, pleasant, cheerful.

ravage (I.), n. [1. rávij; 2. rǽvidž]. Fr., fr. *ravir*, 'to carry off by force'; fr. base of **ravish** & **-age**. **a** Destructive violence; devastation, ruin, waste: *signs of ravage and havoc*; **b** (pl.) effects of these: *the ravages wrought by age and disease.*

ravage (II.), vb. trans. & intrans., fr. Fr. *ravager*, fr. prec. **A.** trans. **1.** To plunder and lay waste (a tract of country &c.); to devastate by violence, to despoil: *the victors ravaged the countryside*; *a population ravaged by plague and famine.* **2.** To ruin, to destroy, to spoil: *a countenance ravaged by time, disease, vice, grief* &c. **B.** intrans. To commit ravages; to engage in plunder and devastation: *the troops were let loose to ravage and plunder.*

ravager, n. [1. rávijer; 2. rǽvidžə]. Prec. & **-er.** One who ravages; plunderer, looter.

rave (I.), vb. intrans. [1. rāv; 2. reiv]. M.E. *raven*; etymol. doubtful; possibly fr. O. Fr., provinc. *raver*, also *ravasser*, 'to talk idly, to rave', wh. may be another form of O. Fr. *resver, rever*, Mod. Fr. *rêver*, 'to dream', see **reverie**; on the other hand, Span. *rabiar*, 'to rave', suggests a possible connexion w. Lat. *rabere*, 'to rage'. See **rabies** & **rage.** **1. a** To speak wildly, or incoherently, like a madman, or as one in delirium: to wander in one's speech: *the patient was conscious for a while and then began to rave*; Phr. *he must be raving (to talk like that)*, off his head; **b** to talk, declaim furiously or passionately: *to rave against one's fate*; *to rave about, of, one's misfortunes* &c.; *raving with fury*, madly angry; **c** (reflex.) *to rave oneself hoarse* &c. **2.** *Rave about*, to talk rapturously, enthusiastically, about; to go into raptures over; to express extravagant enthusiasm or delight at: *to rave about a new author*; *everyone is raving of the latest craze.* **3.** (of the elements) To howl, roar; to storm, rage: *the wind raves through the mountains*; *the sea raves against the cliffs*; also (reflex.) *the storm has raved itself out.*

rave (II.), n. Etymol. doubtful; a dial. variant is *rathe.* (usually pl.) Wooden framework placed inside a cart and projecting above the sides, for increasing the carrying capacity.

ravel (I.), vb. trans. & intrans. [1. rávl; 2. rǽvl], fr. M. Du. *ravelen*, Mod. Du. *rafelen*, 'to fray out, to unweave', cp. L.G. *rabbeln.* **A.** trans. **1.** To unweave, untwist the ends of: *to ravel a skein of wool, rope's end* &c. **2. a** To entangle, throw into a confused mass: *ravelled wool*; **b** (fig.) to make complicated, intricate, or involved to the mind: '*Knits up the ravelled sleave of care*' (Shakespeare, 'Macbeth'). **3.** *Ravel out*, to disentangle, separate the tangled ends of, to unravel; also (fig.) '*To ravel all this matter out*' (Shakespeare, 'Hamlet'). **B.** intrans. **1.** To fray out, to become unwoven, untwisted: *a selvedge prevents the cloth from ravelling.* **2.** *Ravel out*, **a** to be disentangled; to become free from intricacy; also **b** (fig.) *the difficulty will soon ravel out.*

ravel (II.), n., fr. prec. Loose, frayed end; entangled mass; entanglement, confusion, complication: *a ravel of wool, rope*; (also fig.).

ravelin, n. [1. rávelin; 2. rǽvəlin]. Fr., fr. Ital. *ravellino*, later *revellino, rivillino*; cp. also Span. *rebellin.* Etymol. unknown. (fort.) A triangular, detached work with an open base or gorge, placed in front of a curtain wall, between two bastions on the far side of the ditch, to give a sweeping, enfilading fire across the glacis and the bastions; in its earlier round form it was styled *half-moon* or *demi-lune.*

ravelling, n. [1. ráveling; 2. rǽvliŋ]. **ravel** (I.) & **-ing.** Thread or threads of wool, ends of rope &c. which have become frayed out, or ravelled.

raven (I.), n. & adj. [1. rāvn; 2. réivn]. O.E. *hræfn*; O.H.G. *hraban*; O.N. *hrafn*; cogn. w. Lat. *cornix*, 'crow', & *corvus*, 'raven'; cp. also Lat. *crōcīre*, 'to croak'; fr. a base imitative of the sound made by the bird. See further under **corvine.** **1.** n. A large bird, *Corvus corax*, closely related to, but larger than the crows, with glossy black plumage, black legs and bill, uttering loud, harsh, croaking cry; the bird is omnivorous, but preys on small or weakly animals, is intelligent and tamable, and can be taught to speak; commonly held to be a bird of ill-omen. **2.** adj. Black in colour like the raven; jet black: *raven locks, hair.*

raven (II.), vb. intrans. & trans. [1. rávin; 2. rǽvin], fr. O. Fr. *raviner.* See **ravin** & **rapine.** **1.** intrans. **a** To prey, go, prowl in search of prey; to plunder or search for plunder: *lions ravening for, after, their prey*; **b** to be rapacious, ravenous; to long for hungrily: *to raven for food*; '*Benjamin shall raven as a wolf*' (Gen. xlix. 27). **2.** trans. (rare) To devour ravenously.

ravening, adj. [1. ráveníng, rāv-; 2. rǽvəniŋ, réiv-], fr. Pres. Part. of prec. Fierce, savage, voracious: *ravening wolves.*

ravenous, adj. [1. rávenus; 2. rǽvənəs]. **raven** (II.) & **-ous.** **1.** (archaic) Eager to raven or prey; intent on prey; rapacious. **2.** Voracious, greedily hungry; famished with hunger: *ravenous wild beasts*; *ravenous for food*; *a ravenous appetite.*

ravenously, adv. Prec. & **-ly.** In a ravenous manner; hungrily, voraciously; greedily.

ravenousness, n. See prec. & **-ness.** A ravenous condition.

ravin, ravine, n. [1. rávin; 2. rǽvin]. Also earlier *ravine, raven*, O. Fr. *ravine*, 'robbery, rapine', not now used in this sense, see next word; fr. Lat. *rapīna*, 'plunder'. See **rape** (I.) & **rapine.** (archaic or poet.) Plunder, pillage, rapine; prey: '*Nature red in tooth and claw With ravine*' (Tennyson, 'In Mem.' lvi.).

ravine, n. [1. ravḗn; 2. rəvín]. Fr., 'violent rush of water; ravine'. See prec. A deep, narrow valley or gorge; deep cleft in a mountain or hill, esp. one formed by the action of a torrent.

raving, adj. & n. [1. rāving; 2. réiviŋ]. **1.** adj. (Pres. Part. of **rave** (I.)). **a** *A raving lunatic*; *a raving storm* &c.; **b** also as adv., *raving mad.* **2.** n. (**rave** (I.) & **-ing**). (often in pl.) Wild, incoherent speech; delirium: *the ravings of a lunatic.*

ravish, vb. trans. [1. rávish; 2. rǽviʃ]. M.E. *ravissen*, fr. Fr. *raviss-(ant)*, Pres. Part. type of *ravir*, 'to carry, snatch away, to ravish', fr. Lat. *rapere*, 'to seize'. See **rape** (I.). **1.** (archaic) To seize and carry off; to snatch, bear away: *death has ravished him from us*; *to ravish a kiss.* **2.** To take one out of one's senses; to transport, entrance, charm, delight, fill with rapture: *our ears were ravished by her voice*; *her glance ravished his susceptible heart.* **3.** To commit a rape upon, to violate.

ravishing, adj. [1. rávishing; 2. rǽviʃiŋ]. Pres. Part. of prec. Entrancing, bewitching, captivating; of a kind to transport one with delight.

ravishingly, adv. Prec. & **-ly.** In a ravishing manner; delightfully, charmingly.

ravishment, n. [1. rávishment; 2. rǽviʃmənt]. **ravish** & **-ment.** Act of ravishing; **a** (archaic) rape, violation; **b** rapture, delight.

raw (I.), adj. [1. raw; 2. rɔ̄]. O.E. *hrēaw*; O.H.G. *(h)rō*, O.N. *hrār*; cogn. w. Lat. *crūdus*, 'raw'. See **crude** & **cruel.** **1.** (of flesh or other food) **a** Uncooked, left in its natural state: *raw meat*; *to eat one's food raw*; *a raw potato, apple* &c.; **b** not sufficiently or thoroughly cooked; underdone: *this leg of mutton is quite raw.* **2.** (of various articles and substances) In the natural state; **a** *raw material*, some substance in crude state, unwrought and serving as the basis for some form of manufacture; **b** not burnt or subjected to heat: *raw brick*; *raw sienna*; **c** (of spirits) undiluted; **d** (of hides) untanned; **e** (of sugar) unrefined; **f** (of silk and cotton) not spun; left as it comes from the cocoon or the plant. **3.** Untrained, inexperienced: *a raw recruit*; *still somewhat raw to his work.* **4. a** (of wounds) Bloody, gaping so as to expose bleeding tissues below the skin; unhealed; Phr. *raw head and bloody bones*, used as object of terror; **b** (of surface of skin or mucous membrane) sore, galled, chafed, badly chapped, inflamed: *knees raw with riding*; *nose raw from rubbing*; *throat raw from shouting.* **5.** Damp and cold; penetrating and chilly: *a raw wind*; *a raw, foggy morning.*

raw (II.), n., fr. prec. A raw sore, galled place: *a raw on a horse's back.* Phr. *to touch one on the raw*, to wound in the most tender, sensitive spot (chiefly fig. of feelings).

raw (III.), vb. trans., fr. **raw** (I.). (rare) To make raw: *to raw a horse's back.*

raw-boned, adj. **raw** (I.) & **boned.** Insufficiently covered with flesh; thin, gaunt.

rawhide, adj. [1. ráwhīd; 2. rɔ̄haid]. See prec. & **hide** (I.). Made of untanned hide: *rawhide whip, boots.*

rawish, adj. [1. ráw-ish; 2. rɔ̄iʃ]. **raw** (I.) & **-ish.** Somewhat raw.

rawness, n. [1. ráwnes; 2. rɔ̄nis]. **raw** (I.) & **-ness.** **1.** Quality of being raw; **a** condition of being uncooked, or imperfectly cooked; **b** immaturity, inexperience; **c** penetrating cold and damp; **d** soreness, irritation, either bodily or mental.

ray (I.), n. [1. rā; 2. rei]. A.-Fr. *raye*, O. Fr. *raie*, fr. Lat. *rāia*; etymol. doubtful. Any of various marine fishes, having a flattened body, widely expanded pectoral fins, slender, whip-like tail and cartilaginous skeleton, forming, with the skates, the family Raiidae, or true rays.

ray (II.), n., fr. O. Fr. *raye*, also *rais*, fr. Lat. *radius*, 'spoke of a wheel; beam, ray'. See **radius, radix,** & cp. **radiation.** **1. a** A beam, shaft, gleam, of light, proceeding from a radiating or reflecting point: *rays of the sun, moon* &c.; *a ray of sunshine*; '*Full many a gem of purest ray serene*' (Gray's 'Elegy'); **b** (in non-material sense) a glimmer, a slight manifestation, faint trace: *not a ray of comfort, intelligence, hope* &c. **2.** (phys.) A line of radiant energy; the straight line in which the radiant energy which produces the sensation of light or heat is propagated to any given point: *actinic, infra-red, ultra-violet rays*; (attrib.) *Becquerel rays*, radiations emitted by radio-active bodies; *Röntgen* or *X-rays*, name given to the phenomena produced by discharge of cathode rays in a vacuum or Crookes-tube, rendering solid objects fluorescent, penetrating certain opaque materials otherwise impervious to light &c. **3.** Any one of a group of radiating lines; a radius. **4.** Pictorial representation of a ray of light: *a star with six rays.* **5.** Specif. uses: **a** (bot.) the radiating part of a flower, esp. the external whorl of florets in a composite flower, as a sunflower; **b** (zool.) any member of a radial arrangement or structure, as in the fin of a fish, arm of a starfish &c.

ray (III.), vb. intrans. & trans., fr. prec. (rare) **1.** intrans. To shine, issue in rays; to radiate. **2.** trans. **a** To send forth in rays; **b** to adorn with rays.

rayah, n. [1. ría; 2. ráiə]. Turk., fr. Arab. *ra'-iyah*, 'herd, flock', fr. *ra'-a*, 'to feed, pasture', cp. **ryot.** A non-Moslem taxpaying subject of a Moslem state, esp. one of the Christian subjects of Turkey.

rayed, adj. [1. rād; 2. reid]. **ray** (II.) & **-ed.** Having, furnished with, rays or radiations; (often in compounds) *a six-rayed star.*

rayless, adj. [1. rāles; 2. réilis]. **ray** (II.) & **-less.** Having no rays; destitute, deprived of, light; blind, dark.

raylet, n. [1. rālet; 2. réilit]. **ray** (II.) & **-let.** A diminutive ray.

Raynaud's disease, n. [1. rānōz dizḗz; 2. réinouz dizīz], fr. name of French doctor. (pathol.) A disease of the extremities, esp. the fingers and toes, which, owing to contraction of the blood-vessels, become pale, cold, and dead, and, in severe cases, gangrenous.

rayon, n. [1. rāon; 2. réiɔn]. Fr., 'ray', fr. O. Fr. *raye*, see **ray** (II.). Name for artificial silk made from cellulose, from its lustrous appearance.

rayonné, adj. [1. ráonā; 2. réiɔnei]. Fr. See prec. (her.) Depicted as decorated with rays of light or flame.

raze, rase, vb. trans. [1. rāz; 2. reiz], fr. Fr. *raser*, 'to scrape, shave', fr. Low Lat. *rāsāre*, freq. form fr. Lat. *rās-(um)*, P.P. type of *rādere*, 'to scrape', cogn. w. *rōdere*, 'to gnaw', see **rodent**. **1.** (rare) **a** To scrape, graze; **b** to erase, scratch out, (usually fig.) *to raze from the mind, memory.* **2.** To level to the ground, to destroy, overthrow completely: *to raze a house, town &c. to the ground.*

razee, n. & vb. trans. [1. rāzē; 2. reizí], fr. Fr. *rasée*, P.P. fem. of *raser*. See prec. (hist.) **1.** n. A ship, usually a ship of war, with the upper deck cut away, so as to reduce her rating. **2.** vb. To convert a ship into a lower rating by removing the upper deck.

razor, n. & vb. trans. [1. rázur; 2. réizə]. M.E. *rasour*, fr. O. Fr. *rasour*, *raser*. See **raze** & **-or**. **1.** n. Cutting instrument with a keen blade which folds into a handle, used for shaving; also an instrument for shaving consisting of a small oblong blade fixed at right angles to a short handle and furnished with a row of inward-curving teeth, designed to protect the skin of the face from being cut, called *safety razor*. Phrs. *to be on the (a) razor's edge*, to be on the verge of a great danger; to be in extreme difficulty, doubt &c.; *as sharp as a razor*, very sharp. **2.** vb. To use razor on; to shave; (rare, except in P.P.) *a well-razored chin.*

razor-back, n. The fin-backed whale or rorqual.

razor-backed, adj. Having a thin, lean back.

razor-bill, n. Any of several birds with a bill shaped like a razor; e.g. *the razor-billed auk.*

razor-edge, n. **1. a** The sharp, keen edge of a razor; **b** (fig.) a dividing line, critical point of division. **2. a** A steel bar with a fine edge used in delicate weighing machines; **b** a sharp ridge to a hill.

razor-fish, n. Razor-shell.

razor-grass, n. A West Indian sedge with sharp serrated edge.

razor-shell, n A bivalve, marine mussel, the solen or razor-fish, with long, narrow sharp-edged shell, shaped like the handle of a razor.

razzia, n. [1. rázia; 2. rǽziə]. Fr., fr. Algerian pronunciation of Arab. *ghāzīah*, 'raid', fr. *ghāsw*, 'to make war', cp. *Ghāzi*, 'leader in war'. A raid, a plundering expedition or foray carried out by Moslem tribes against non-Moslems to capture slaves &c.

razzle-dazzle, n. [1. rázl dázl; 2. rǽzl dǽzl] or [1. rázl dazl; 2. rǽzl dæzl]. Modified reduplication of **dazzle**. (slang) A rowdy spree, drunken, noisy frolic: *to go on the razzle-dazzle.*

re (I.), n. [1. rā; 2. rei]. (mus.) A syllable used in *solmization*, q.v.; the second tone of the diatonic scale.

re (II.), as prep. [1. rē; 2. rī]. Lat., abl. sing. of **res**, 'thing, matter'; cogn. w. Scrt. *rāś*, 'property, possessions, wealth', & *rātáś*, 'presented, rendered'. **1.** (law) In the matter of, properly *in re*: *Smith* v. *Jones*, (*in*) *re estate of Robinson.* **2.** (loosely, in popular, esp. commerc. jargon) Concerning, about, referring to: *re your esteemed favour of yesterday's date*; *I want to speak to you re your behaviour.*

re-, pref. (see note on stressing & pronunciation below). Lat. *re-*, *red-*, inseparable particle used as pref. The form *re-* is used in Lat. before consonants, *red-* before vowels & *h*. In later Lat. *re-* is used also before vowels & *h*. **A.** (etymol.) Brugmann and Walde consider that *red-* is the earlier form, and that this is from still earlier **wret-*, having the meaning 'turned back', the base being **wer-* as in Lat. *vertere*, 'to turn', see **version**. **B.** (force in Latin compounds) **1.** General and primary meaning, 'back'; *redūcere*, 'to lead back'; *respicere*, 'to look back'. **2.** Expressing repetition, again: *refingere*, 'to make again, rebuild'. **3.** Expressing opposition, against: *repugnāre*, 'to fight against, resist'; *resistere*, 'to withstand, resist'. **4.** Expressing reversal of action: *retexere*, 'to unweave, unravel'; *retegere*, 'to uncover, lay bare'. The greater number of compounds in English which have *re-* as a prefix are derived either straight from Latin words, or through the French from these. Of the latter, some are new formations in Low Latin, or in French itself. All these come under the Latin usage in respect of the force of *re-*, though in most cases the words are no longer felt as compounds at all, but have developed, often in Latin itself, independent meanings in which the old force of *re-* has been quite lost sight of. **C.** (as living pref. in English) Still used to form an almost indefinite number of words, some of which have a traditional existence from frequent use, while others are felt as individual creations even by those who use them. The force of the prefix in all such words is 'again', in the sense either **a** of repeated action, or **b** of a return to a former condition. Thus *retell*, 'tell again what has been told before', *rename*, 'name again, give new name to', *reappoint*, 'appoint again to a position formerly held', may be regarded as permanently established words. On the other hand, such words as *re-edit*, *re-copy*, *re-enter* have been, and are constantly being, formed afresh by independent acts on the part of different individual speakers or writers. **D.** (hyphenated spelling) It is the common practice to join *re-* to the following word by a hyphen when the compound thus made is felt as unusual or as a new coinage. It is often given as a rule that *re-* is hyphened before *-e-*, as in *re-emerge*, but most words in this group fall also under that of new formations, and would be hyphened in any case. **E.** (pronunciation and stressing) **1.** With strong stress =[rī]; **a** in all newly-formed compounds, or others in which the prefix is felt as merely modifying the sense of the main word, and where this preserves its independent meaning, the prefix is pronounced [rī]; it has also strong or secondary stress, while the main word also preserves its independent stress or emphasis; thus *re-count*, 'count over again' [rí káunt] compared with *recount*, 'to relate' &c. [rikáunt]; *re-formation*, 'new formation' [rí fōméiʃən], but *reformation*, 'process of reform' [rèfəméiʃən] &c.; *re-establish* [rì istǽbliʃ]; **b** *re-* is also pronounced [rī], even in old compounds, before words beginning with vowels or *h*, e.g. in *reappear* [rìəpíə], *reintegrate* [rìíntigreit], *rehabilitate* [ríhəbíliteit]; *rehearse* [rihə́s] is an exception; such words as *réflex*, *régress*, *réscript* [rī], may be regarded as new formations, or as due to the prefix retaining its independent sense, cp. *íngress*, *égress*. **2.** *re-* =[ri] in old compounds where the principal stress is on the syllable immediately following the prefix: *reserve*, *rebel*, vb., *return*, =[rizə́v, ribél, ritə́n] &c. **3.** *re-* =[rɛ] when it bears itself the principal stress, *recognize* [rékəgnaiz], *reference* [réfərəns], or when the principal stress is on some other syllable than the second of the compound, *re-* receiving a secondary stress, *recognition* [rèkəgníʃən], *reverential* [rèvərénʃəl], *reservation* [rèzəvéiʃən], *reformation* [rèfəméiʃən], *repetition* [rèpitíʃən].

reach (I.), vb. trans. & intrans. [1. rēch; 2. ritʃ]. O.E. *rǣcan*, 'to stretch out, extend'; M.E. *rēchen*, O.H.G. *reichen*, fr. Gmc. **raikjan*, Aryan **rēiĝ-*, 'to extend', occurring also in Lat. *rēx*, 'king', lit. 'one who extends, exerts power over', see **rex** & **regent**. **A.** trans. **1.** To stretch out, extend: '*reach hither thine hand*'; *to reach one's hand across the table*; more often *reach out*: *to reach out a hand, foot &c.*; *a tree reaches out its boughs towards the light.* **2. a** To obtain, get hold of, by stretching out a hand, and pass, hand over to: *would you reach me the mustard, please?*; **b** to deliver, deal, with outstretched arm, leg: *to reach a person a blow on the nose, a kick.* **3. a** To lay hold of by stretching up with extended arm: *to reach a book from the top shelf*; **b** to be able to touch by reaching, extend, be able to stretch far enough to touch, get at: *his sword was so short that he could not reach his opponent*; *by standing on tip-toe I can just reach the shelf.* **4. a** To attain to, get as far as, arrive at: *we shall never reach town before dusk*; *the train reaches Oxford at six*; **b** (in non-material sense) to attain to, achieve, realize: *to reach the object of one's desires*; *to reach perfection*; **c** to attain a certain condition, point of development &c.: *England reached a point of great prosperity and power under Elizabeth*; *the ancient Irish reached a stage of considerable skill in several arts*; *to reach adolescence, old age &c.* **5. a** To go, come, be thrown, to penetrate, carry, so far as to hit, touch, pass, affect &c.: *owing to the distance, none of our bullets reached the enemy*; *the water was too deep for light to reach the bottom*; *the heat from the fire doesn't reach the other side of the room*; *no sound reaches my ear*; **b** to come, pass, into the possession of, be received by: *your letter, message, request, never reached me.* **6. a** To extend as far as: *the new railway has not yet reached our village*; **b** be long enough to touch: *this ladder won't reach the window.* **B.** intrans. **1.** (usually followed by *out*, or *for*) **a** To stretch out an arm or leg so as to grasp or touch: *to reach out and take a person's hand*; *to reach for the bread, for one's hat, for a footstool*; **b** (of limb) to be thrust, stretched, out: *a hand reached out and held me*; **c** (of plants) to grow, be inclined: *boughs reach out towards the sun*; **d** *reach after*, (i.) to make an effort to grasp, touch, attain, by reaching: *to reach after something one has dropped*; (ii.) (of intellectual or moral effort) to aspire after, strive to gain, understand &c.: *the human heart reaches after happiness, affection &c.*; *to reach after fame, knowledge, an ideal.* **2.** To extend, stretch, be extended; to run: **a** (in space) *the rainbow reaches from heaven to earth*; *the park reaches down to the river*; **b** (in time) *an old man's memory reaches back over many years*; *Queen Victoria's reign reached into the 20th century*; **c** (in amount or number) *his income reached to a considerable figure*; *the congregation reached into many hundreds*; **d** (in moral influence &c.) *the authority of the law reaches over the whole of the king's dominions.* **3. a** To go, pass, be carried, be prolonged, as far as; to arrive at, attain to: *his beard reached to his waist*; **b** to carry, penetrate: *the sound of his voice reached easily to the back of the hall*; *the light of the sun does not reach to the bottom of the ocean*; Phr. *as far as the eye can reach*, to the utmost limits of vision, to the horizon.

reach (II.), n., fr. prec. **1.** Act of reaching or stretching out (the hand &c.): *to make a reach for anything.* **2. a** Power of reaching; possibility of grasping or touching (an object) by stretching out the hand or other part of the body: *the shelf is just out of, beyond, my reach*; *within reach of one's hand*; *to have a long reach with one's arm*; **b** power of arriving at, going to; possibility of being reached; accessibility: *within easy reach of London*; *a small village out of reach of the railway*; *out of reach of the guns.* **3. a** Power of attaining, of obtaining for one's use or benefit: *riches and fame are beyond the reach of most of us*; **b** power of grasping with the mind, mental range: *such philosophical subtleties are beyond my reach*; *he has a wonderful reach of imagination.* **4.** Possibility of affecting or of being affected by, extent to which influence can be exerted; sphere of influence: *beyond the reach of human aid*; *out of reach of danger, harm*; *few people are quite beyond the reach of an appeal to their better feelings.* **5.** (of light, sound, heat) Capacity for carrying, penetrating, being perceived, or of producing an effect. **6.** A level, uninterrupted stretch, extent, tract, of water, esp. on a river: *the upper reaches of the Thames.*

reach (III.), vb. intrans. See **retch**. To have sudden feeling of nausea; to strain violently and involuntarily as in vomiting.

reachable, adj. [1. réchabl; 2. rítʃəbl]. **reach (I.)** & **-able**. Capable of being reached; within reach.

reach-me-down, n. [1. réch mi dòun; 2. rítʃ mi dàun]. See **reach (I.)**. (colloq.) Ready-made garment; attrib., *reach-me-down suit*.

react, vb. intrans. [1. reákt; 2. riǽkt]. **re-** & **act**. **1.** To be affected by, act in response to, as result of, an external stimulus: **a** (of physical process) *if the knee be struck below the knee-cap, the leg reacts at once by jerking upwards; the eye reacts to light; a cold bath makes the skin react*; **b** (of moral or intellectual process) to respond to a suggestion, influence &c.; show signs of understanding or emotion as result of a mental stimulus: *I suggested that he might afford financial aid, but he did not react at all; an audience usually reacts readily to a good lecturer*. **2.** *React on, upon*, **a** (of several bodies, also of chemical substances, in contact) To exert reciprocal influence, have a reverse effect upon each other: *the wheel and the drag react upon each other*; **b** (of moral process) to affect, modify, reciprocally: *in a conflict of intellects, opinions, beliefs, each acts and reacts upon the other*; **c** *react against*, to exert opposing, contrary, influence or effect, physical or moral: *perhaps the people of Russia will one day react against Bolshevism*. **3.** (of opinions &c.) To show a reverse tendency, move in contrary direction: *in many directions the Church of England has reacted against the extreme Protestantism of the early Reformers*.

re-act, vb. trans. [1. ré ákt; 2. rí ǽkt]. **re-** & **act**. To act, do, perform, a second time; act over again.

reactance, n. [1. reáktans; 2. riǽktəns]. **react** & **-ance**. (elect.) Inductive resistance.

reaction, n. [1. reákshun; 2. riǽkʃən]. **re-** & **action**. **1.** Action in response to a stimulus; change taking place as a result of some physical or mental influence: *the reaction of the eye to light; of the skin to a cold bath; reactions to the war in the Far East; an artist's reaction to beauty*. **2.** Reciprocal action; the action of a body or mind upon another body or mind, influence &c. reacting upon it; return or reflex action: *action and reaction*; specif. **a** (chem.) the reciprocal action of on each other, changes in, substances when in contact, or when subjected to heat, light, electricity &c.; **b** (phys.) equal and opposite force exerted by a body on another body exerting force on it. **3.** Action, movement, as result of, in response to, a physical or mental stimulus. **4.** (med.) **a** Physical exhaustion, collapse of vital powers following upon overstrain through excessive exertion &c.; **b** extreme depression of spirits, loss of control &c., after prolonged and severe nervous tension, excitement &c. **5. a** Contrary action, reversed trend, revulsion of feeling, against a state of affairs, system of government, mode of thought, set of opinions &c., formerly existing or current; **b** specif., set of opinions, mode of thought strongly opposed to progress; unenlightened and prejudiced dislike of new ideas and methods: *the forces of reaction are often stronger than those of progress and reform*. **6.** (wireless) Process by which currents in adjacent inductive circuits react upon those already flowing, thus building up weak signals into powerful ones.

reactionary, adj. & n. [1. reákshunari; 2. riǽkʃənəri]. Prec. & **-ary**. **1.** adj. Pertaining to, characteristic of, reaction, esp. in politics, thought &c.; retrograde: *reactionary measures; reactionary tendencies in theology*. **2.** n. A reactionary person; one who opposes political or intellectual progress.

reactionist, n. [1. reákshunist; 2. riǽkʃənist]. **reaction** & **-ist**. A reactionary.

reactive, adj. [1. reáktiv; 2. riǽktiv]. **react** & **-ive**. Having power to react; tending to reaction.

reactively, adv. Prec. & **-ly**. In a reactive manner; so as to produce reaction.

reactivity, n. [1. rèaktíviti; 2. rìæktíviti]. See prec. & **-ity**. State, condition, of being reactive; property of reacting.

read (I.), vb. trans. & intrans. [1. rēd; 2. rīd], fr. O.E. *rǣdan*, 'to discuss, deliberate, decide; to interpret (documents &c.); to solve (a riddle); to peruse, read'; cp. also the O.E. n. *rǣd*, 'advice, discussion, council'; M.E. *rēden*, 'to explain, interpret'; also 'to read', in mod. sense. Cognates in other old Gmc. tongues are O.S. *rādan*; O.H.G. *rātan*; O.N. *rāða*, 'to advise' &c. In Goth. the vb. is found only in compounds, *(ga)rēdan*, 'to provide for oneself', &c. Outside Gmc. the base *rē-* &c. is found in Lat. *reor*, 'I think, suppose, imagine', the infin. of wh., *rē-ri*, shows a vowel corresponding to O.S., O.H.G. *ā*, O.E. *ǣ* (*rǣd* &c.); the P.P. *ratus* has the gradational type seen in Lat. *ratio*, 'process of thinking, a reckoning' &c., wh. is derived fr. it. Goth. *raþjō*, 'number, reckoning', whence *raþjan*, 'to count, reckon', appears to be an exact cogn. of this. See **ratio** & **reason**. The *-d-* in O.E. *rǣd* &c. must be regarded as an extension of the original base, as is *-t-* in *ratiō* &c. See also **riddle** & **rede**. **A.** trans. **1. a** To think out, and discover the explanation of; to solve, unravel, guess: *to read a riddle* (also, as archaism, spelt *rede*); **b** to receive information concerning, become aware of, understand true meaning of, form just estimate of, as a result of consideration and contemplation: *to read the signs of the times*; '*To scatter plenty o'er a smiling land, And read their hist'ry in a nation's eyes*' (Gray's 'Elegy'); **c** to find revealed, to interpret: *to read the story of Creation in the rocks*. **2. a** To look at, and obtain a visual perception of, to make out, the forms of graphic symbols written, printed, or engraved, whether alphabetic, in form of letters &c., and standing for speech sounds, words, sentences, or such symbols standing for musical notes: *I can't see to read the name without a light; the first letter on the coin is so rubbed that I can't read it*; **b** to understand the significance of graphic symbols when perceived, and interpret them in terms of the speech sounds, words, sentences, and associate them with the ideas or musical notes for which they stand: *to read a manuscript, a printed book, a piece of music*; Phrs. *to read aloud, read out, read out loud*, to pronounce what one is reading with an audible voice; *to read to oneself*, read silently; *to read French*, (i.) read something written in French &c.; (ii.) often implying power to understand from reading, but not to speak, the language; **c** *to read a thermometer, barometer*, to look at, examine, and note height of the mercury. **3. a** (chiefly Oxford usage) To make a study of: *to read Greats, Physics &c.*; also *to read an Honours School*, study the subjects prescribed for such; **b** *read up* (a subject), make a special study of it; refresh one's knowledge of it by renewed study. **4.** To derive knowledge of, become apprised of, learn, by reading: *that must be (can't be) true, for I read it in a newspaper; I have read somewhere that...* **5.** *Read into*, to invest (what is said or written) with some specified meaning, give a certain interpretation to; to assume as the meaning, bearing, content, of (a statement): *you are reading more into what I said than was intended or implied; we sometimes read our own thoughts into a poet's words; to read a compliment into what was meant as a rebuke*. **6.** To utter, deliver, in a specified way, giving a particular intellectual or emotional value to, and interpretation of, in reading aloud: *the bishop read the Burial Service most impressively*. **7.** Phr. *to read oneself in*, of a newly-appointed incumbent of an ecclesiastical benefice, to read the Thirty-nine Articles publicly in church in token of assent to the doctrines therein formulated. **8.** As instruction or correction in a text &c.: *read 'of' instead of 'for'* &c., i.e. alter text so that *for* may be read as *of*. **9.** (of recording instruments) To register, indicate: *the thermometer this morning reads 3 degrees above freezing-point*. **10.** (Parliamentary procedure, usually pass.) *The bill was read a third time*, was laid before the House and discussed. **B.** intrans. **1. a** To perform the act of reading printed or written characters: *to read in bed, at meals; to find time to read*; Phr. *to read between the lines*, to discover the real or hidden meaning of; **b** to master the art of reading printed or written characters: *to learn to read; you can't expect a child to read at 3 years old*; **c** to read aloud: *to read well*, clearly and with proper expression: *to read clearly, indistinctly, too rapidly; children like to be read to*. **2.** *Read of, about*, to ascertain, learn, become informed of by reading: *to read of a person's death; we read about the disaster*. **3.** To learn, study, by reading: *you must read harder next term*. Phr. *read for the Bar*, undergo the course of training and study necessary to be admitted a barrister; *to read for honours*, prepare oneself by study for an honours degree. **4. a** To convey a specific meaning, impression, when read: *the sentence reads oddly; the play acts better than it reads*; **b** to be couched, drawn up, in a specified way: *the passage quoted reads as follows; how does the sentence read now?*

read (II.), vb. [1. red; 2. red]. Pret. & P.P. of prec. O.E. *rǣdde, (ġe)rǣd(d)*; M.E. *redde, (ġe)red*.

read (III.), adj., fr. P.P. in intrans. sense of **read (I.)**. (preceded by adv.) Instructed, learned, versed, in a subject by reading or study: *a well-read man; not very deeply read in this subject; poorly read in history*.

read (IV.), n. [1. rēd; 2. rīd], fr. **read (I.)**. Act of reading; time spent in reading: *to enjoy a good read before the fire; to take a quick read at a book; time for a long read*.

readability, n. [1. rèdabíliti; 2. rìdəbíliti]. See next word & **-ity**. Quality, condition, of being readable; readableness.

readable, adj. [1. rídabl; 2. rídəbl]. **read (I.)** & **-able**. Capable of being, such as can be, read; **a** legible: *a readable handwriting*; **b** not tedious; written in an attractive style; interesting: *a readable book; an abstruse work yet presented in a readable form*.

readableness, n. Prec. & **-ness**. Readability.

readably, adv. See prec. & **-ly**. In a readable manner; interestingly.

readdress, vb. trans. [1. réadrés; 2. ríədrés]. **re-** & **address**. To address, direct, as a letter &c., a second time; to dispatch to a new address; to change the address, on a letter &c.

reader, n. [1. réder; 2. rídə]. **read (I.)** & **-er**. One who reads (in various senses of the vb.). Specif. **1.** a person who habitually reads books for instruction or amusement; a student, a lover of books: *a great reader; not much of a reader*. **2.** A person, not in orders, licensed to read aloud in church the lessons and certain portions of the liturgy: *a lay-reader*. **3. a** Person engaged by publishers to read MSS. and give advice as to their publication &c.: *a publisher's reader*; **b** person employed in correcting proofs for the press: *a printer's proof-reader*. **4.** An official lecturer of high status in certain faculties at a university: *Reader in Greek* &c. **5.** A reading-book, book containing passages from selected authors; often one to be used by those learning the language.

readily, adv. [1. rédili; 2. rédili]. **ready (I.)** & **-ly**. In a ready manner; **a** without objection, hesitation, or reluctance; cheerfully, willingly, promptly: *to give readily to charity; would readily die for a cause*; **b** without difficulty, easily: *it can readily be understood that* &c.

readiness, n. [1. rédines; 2. rédinis]. **ready (I.)** & **-ness**. Condition, quality, of being ready; **a** state of being prepared, preparation: *to get, put, everything in readiness for* &c.; **b** quickness, facility, ease: *readiness of wit*; **c** willingness, cheerful consent: *readiness to undertake a difficult task*.

reading (I.), n. [1. rḗding; 2. rídiŋ]. **read (I.)** & **-ing.** **1.** Act of one who reads (in various senses of the vb.); specif., ability to read: *to teach reading, writing, and arithmetic.* **2.** Knowledge, erudition, acquired by the study of books: *a man of wide reading.* **3. a** A public recital of passages from an author: *readings from Shakespeare*; **b** entertainment consisting of recitations &c.: *a penny reading.* **4.** Printed or written matter to be read: *not much reading in today's paper,* i.e. not much that is worth reading; *a good deal of tough reading in the book.* **5.** Record which can be read; specif., *the daily readings of a barometer, thermometer* &c. **6.** The form in which a word or words occur in different copies or editions of a MS., book &c.; a version: *to compare the different readings in the folios and quartos of Shakespeare*; *many new readings.* **7. a** Interpretation placed upon a document, law: *my reading of the rubric is different from yours*; **b** way in which a situation, event &c., is conceived: *one's reading of the political, military, situation* &c.; **c** conception, rendering, understanding, of a character. **8.** One of the three stages through which a Bill has to pass in either of the two Houses of Parliament, before it receives the royal assent; *first reading,* formal introduction without debate; *second reading,* debate on the principles preceding the committee stage; *third reading,* final debate on the Bill as amended in committee.

reading (II.), adj. Addicted to reading; studious: *a reading man.*

reading-desk, n. A desk with sloping top for holding an open book; esp. one supported by a tall pedestal in a church; a lectern.

reading-glass, n. A magnifying glass to be held in the hand used for reading small print or to help the short-sighted.

reading-lamp, n. A shaded, movable table-lamp which throws the light down on a book.

reading-room, n. A room set apart for reading or writing, in a public library, club, hotel &c.

readjust, vb. trans. [1. rḗajúst; 2. ríədžást]. **re-** & **adjust.** To adjust a second time; to make a fresh adjustment in; to change and correct the adjustment of.

readjustment, n. [1. rḗajústment; 2. ríədžástmənt]. Prec. & **-ment.** Act of readjusting; state of being readjusted.

ready (I.), adj. [1. rédi; 2. rédi]. M.E. *rēdi*; not in O.E., though *ġerǣde,* 'mounted, ready', occurs, wh. appears to be cogn. w. O.H.G. *reiti,* Mod. Germ. (*be*)*reit,* 'ready, prepared'; cp. also O.E. *ġerǣde,* 'trappings (of a horse), accoutrements', & O.N. *greiðr,* 'prepared', for *ga-reiðr.* If the orig. meanings were 'equipped, prepared, for riding', hence 'ready, prepared', in general, we might connect w. the base **raid-,* O.E. *rād,* as in Pret. of *rīdan,* see **ride** & **road.** It is possible that in the Engl. meanings, that of O.E. *rǣd,* 'counsel' &c. (cp. **read (I.),** has had an influence, see senses **2** & **3** below. **1. a** (of things) Prepared, arranged, in all particulars, in a state fit for use, prepared and waiting for use: *dinner is ready; the car is ready at the door; everything is ready, let us start at once; clothes all ready for wearing*; **b** (of persons) having made preparations; equipped, supplied with what is necessary, for some object or purpose; in fit condition for doing anything, going anywhere &c.: *are you ready to start on the journey?; she is never ready in time*; Phrs. *are you ready? go!,* in starting competitors for a race; *ready, present, fire!* (mil. command); *to get, make, ready,* to prepare, **a** trans., *get the children ready for a walk*; *make the room ready for dancing*; (also reflex.) *they made them ready for battle*; **b** intrans., *get ready quickly and we'll start at once*; *he made ready to cross the road.* **2. a** Prepared in mind, willing, determined, not reluctant: *ready for anything*; *ready to go anywhere and do anything*; *ready to conquer or die*; *he gave a ready assent*; **b** inclined, disposed to, likely; about to, on the point of: *only too ready to look at the worst side of things*; *she was ready to burst into tears*; *the sun is ready to break through the clouds.* **3.** Apt, prompt, quick; easy, nimble: *to have a ready hand, tongue, wit*; *the pen of a ready writer*; *a ready answer for any question.* **4.** Available immediately; handy, within reach: *help is ready at hand*; *a revolver ready in case of burglars*; *the readiest way, means, of escape, access, exit* &c. (see *ready money,* below). **5.** *Ready* (followed by P.P. with advbl. force), in a state of preparation, so as not to require anything further to be done: *food ready-cooked*; *ready-armed.*

ready (II.), n., fr. prec. **1.** (colloq. slang) *The ready,* ready money, hard cash. **2.** Position, condition, of rifle when ready for aiming and firing: *held at, come to, the ready.*

ready (III.), vb. trans., fr. **ready (I.).** To make, get, ready (rare, except in racing slang): *to ready a horse,* to pull or otherwise prevent a horse from winning a race in order to get a better handicap later on. Phr. *to ready up* (slang), to pay promptly, on the nail; to pay in hard cash.

ready-made, adj. [1. rédi mā́d; 2. rédi meid] predic.; [1. rédi mād; 2. rédi meid] attrib. Made ready for immediate use, esp. **a** *ready-made clothes,* made in stock sizes, as contrasted with those made to measure, or order; **b** (of ideas, opinions &c.) cut and dried, taken over from others, not original.

ready money, n. Money ready at hand, immediately available; hard cash. Phr. *to pay ready money, ready-money payment,* payment made on the spot when goods are bought, as distinguished from bought on credit and entered to the purchaser's account.

ready reckoner, n. A book containing tables of various calculations, for quick use in business &c.

reaffirm, vb. trans. [1. rḗafḗrm; 2. ríəfə́m]. **re-** & **affirm.** To affirm over again; to repeat an affirmation.

reaffirmation, n. [1. rḗàfermā́shun; 2. ríæfəméiʃən]. **re-** & **affirmation.** A repeated affirmation.

reafforest, vb. trans. [1. rḗafórest; 2. ríæfɔ́rist]. **re-** & **afforest.** To bring back (land) to a condition of afforestation, by planting timber.

reafforestation, n. [1. rèaforestā́shun; 2. rìæfɔristéiʃən]. **re-** & **afforestation.** Act or process of reafforesting; state of being reafforested.

reagency, n. [1. reā́jensi; 2. riéidžənsi]. **re-** & **agency.** Action, operation, of a reagent; reaction; power of reacting, function of being reactive.

reagent, n. [1. rēā́jent; 2. riéidžənt]. **re-** & **agent.** See **react (I.).** **1.** That which reacts or produces reaction; specif. (chem.) a substance used to produce a specific chemical change or reaction in another substance; esp. as thus establishing, detecting, the presence of that substance, or causing its separation from a compound. **2.** Person reacting to a physiological or psychological stimulus.

real (I.), adj. [1. rḗal; 2. ríəl], fr. L. Lat. *rēālis,* 'belonging to the thing itself', esp. as used in Med. philos., see **realism,** fr. Lat. *rē-,* stem of *rēs,* 'thing, object, fact', see **re-,** & *-ālis,* see **-al.** **1. a** Having material existence, existing in fact; substantial, actual, objective, usually with implication of contrast with what is subjective: *to have real existence*; specif. (theol.), *Real Presence,* that of Christ in the Eucharist; **b** not imaginary or the result of illusion &c.: *a real oasis, not a mirage*; *a real noise awakened me*; *it was a real man I saw, not a ghost*; *to distinguish between real things and their shadows*; **c** contrasted with *ideal*: *the real, hard facts of life.* **2.** Existing as in nature; authentic, genuine; contrasted with *artificial, spurious* or *imitated*: *real pearls, silk*; *to drink real wine on the stage*; *the real heir to the throne.* **3.** Not invented or fictitious; actual: *the tale is taken from real life*; *what is the man's real name?* **4.** Represented as actual or existing; vividly drawn: *the characters in the play, novel, seem quite real.* **5.** Corresponding to the facts, true in fact, not merely apparent, or ostensible; contrasted with *nominal, formal*: *the real ruler of the country*; *difficulties more apparent than real*; *the real reason*; *a man's real character, motives* &c.; *what is the real influence of the press?* **6. a** Sincere, genuine, not affected or put on: *to feel real sympathy, grief*; **b** worthy of the name, complete, not merely apparent and transitory: *to effect a real cure*; *an act of real charity*; *I want a real holiday.* **7.** (colloq., only in U.S.A., as quasi-adv.) Really: *to have a real good time*; *I am real pleased to meet you.* **8.** (law) Of, pertaining to, the thing itself or to things permanent and immovable, opposed to *personal*: *real action,* one of the two old kinds of action at law in which the plaintiff asks the court to award him the actual thing (*res*) sued for, *the personal action* being one in which a sum of money is sued for as a debt or as damages; *real property* (in U.S.A. and Canada usually *real estate*), freehold property in immovable things such as land or houses (formerly including copyholds), as contrasted with *chattels real,* leaseholds and *personal property,* such as money, shares, furniture &c.; *real assets,* assets of a company &c. consisting of real property; *real rights,* rights arising out of land, such as rights of way, fishery &c. **9. a** (philos.) Having an absolute and necessary existence, not contingent, nominal, or phenomenal; **b** (log., of propositions) giving information, significant, not merely formal or verbal.

real (II.), n., fr. prec. *The real,* something, that, which is real; a reality; contrasted with *the ideal.*

real (III.), n. [1. rāā́hl; 2. reiā́l]. Span., 'royal', adj. used as n., fr. Lat. *rēgālis,* see **regal (I.).** **a** An old Spanish silver coin, value about 6d.; the coin of 8 reals was the 'piece of eight', value 1 dollar; **b** a unit and money of account in use until 1868, value about 2½d.

realgar, n. [1. reálgar; 2. riǽlgā]. Med. Lat. & O. Fr., cp. Span. *rejalgar,* fr. Arab. *rahj-al-ghār,* lit. 'powder of the cave or mine, mineral powder', fr. *rahj,* 'powder', & *ghār,* 'cave, mine'. Native red sulphide of arsenic, red orpiment, used in tanning as a pigment and in making fireworks, such as Bengal lights &c.

realism, n. [1. rḗalizm; 2. ríəlizəm]. **real (I.)** & **-ism.** **1.** (philos.) **a** (scholasticism) Theory that general ideas or universals have an existence independent of the individual mind; contrasted with *nominalism*; **b** (later philos.) theory that the physical world has an existence independent of the mind's perception of it; contrasted with *idealism.* **2.** Habit of thought, tendency of the mind, to dwell upon, be preoccupied with, fact, with the actual and practical, rather than with what is imaginary or theoretical. **3.** (pictorial, plastic, arts and literature) Attempt to depict or express nature and life, often in minute details, as the artist conceives or sees them actually to exist, without either eliminating or concealing what is ugly or sordid, or idealizing and embellishing the subject in an effort to secure beauty; contrasted with *romanticism.*

realist, n. [1. rḗalist; 2. ríəlist]. **real (I.)** & **-ist.** An adherent, practitioner, of realism, **a** in philosophy; **b** in ordinary processes and habits of thought; **c** in any kind of art.

realistic, also, less usually, **realist,** adj. [1. rèalístik, rḗalist; 2. rìəlístik, ríəlist]. Prec. & **-ic.** **a** Pertaining to, characteristic of, realism or realists, in philosophy or art; **b** practical, attached to reality; concerned with actual fact, not visionary or idealistic.

reality, n. [1. reáliti; 2. riǽliti], fr. Med. Lat. *rēālitāt-em.* See **real (I.)** & **-ity.** **1.** State, quality, property, of being real, of existing in fact; actual as opposed to imaginary or apparent existence: *the reality of our* *experiences is sometimes disputed.* **2.** That which is real and not imaginary, fictitious, or pretended; actual fact or existence: *our expectations were as nothing to the reality; a description based on reality.* Phr. *in reality,* really, actually, in actual fact. **3.** Faithful, life-like, representation of, or correspondence with, a real, actual object or person; fidelity to fact or nature: *the reality of some of the prehistoric drawing is remarkable.*

realizable, adj. [1. rēalízabl, réalizabl; 2. riəldáizəbl, ríəlaizəbl]. **realize** & **-able.** Able to be realized.

realization, n. [1. rèalīzáshun; 2. rìəlaizéiʃən]. Next word & **-ation.** **1.** Act or process of bringing something vividly before one's mind in such a way that one apprehends it, and knows it to be real; act of making oneself conscious of something as a fact: *to have a true realization of one's danger, one's position* &c. **2.** Act or process of making real, of converting something hoped for, aimed at &c., into a reality; achievement, fulfilment: *the realization of one's hopes, dreams* &c. **3.** Act or process of converting any form of property into ready money available for use.

realize, vb. trans. [1. réalīz; 2. ríəlaiz]. **real (I.)** & **-ize.** **1.** To cause to appear real, actual, vivid, to the mind; to form a clear conception of, be fully conscious of: *I can hardly yet realize the full extent of my loss.* **2.** To cause to become real; to convert a hope, dream, aspiration &c., into an actual, accomplished fact; to achieve the fulfilment of: *to realize one's ambitions* &c. **3.** (rare) To give reality to, cause to appear as real: *Scott, more than any writer, can realize the events and personages of history for us.* **4.** **a** To convert (intangible right or property) into money, to sell for money: *to realize one's securities* &c.: (also absol.) *you had better realize at once;* **b** to be sold for a certain sum, to fetch certain price: *(the sale of) his pictures realized £10,000;* **c** to acquire, gain, amass: *he had been able to realize a large fortune before his death.*

really, adv. [1. réali; 2. ríəli]. **real (I.)** & **-ly.** **a** In a real manner; in reality; in fact; truly, actually, positively, in actual fact: *a really devout man; do you really mean it?; really and truly; he is really a very kind person; sixty is not really old; tell me what you really think; he does really know;* **b** as expression of slight doubt, surprise, or as a mild protest: *the strike is over. Really?; well, really, it is too bad of you.*

realm, n. [1. relm; 2. relm]. M.E. *reaume, realme, rēme,* fr. O. Fr. *reaume, realme, reialme,* Mod. Fr. *royaume;* fr. a hypothetical L. Lat. **rēgālimen,* formed fr. Lat. *rēgālis,* 'regal, royal', see **regal.** **1.** (chiefly poet., rhet., or legal) The whole of a continuous tract of country forming the dominions, and acknowledging the jurisdiction, of a single ruler; kingdom, country: *this noble realm of England; an order of the High Court that the person do not quit the realm; Defence of the Realm Acts,* various statutes, passed during the Great War, to meet emergencies, enforce necessary restrictions &c. (abbr. colloq. as D.O.R.A.). Phr. *the realm of Nature,* Nature and her products as a whole; the natural world. **2.** (fig.) Domain, sphere, region: *in the realm of fancy; the realm of science* &c. **3.** (bot. and zool.) A primary distributive division of flora and fauna, in accordance with geographical distribution or habitat; a region.

real-politik, n. [1. rāáhl pòlitḗk; 2. rēál pòlitīk]. Germ., 'real politics'. Policy of reality, as practised by Bismarck and his successors in Germany, embodying the doctrine that the material interests of the nation must be the sole consideration of its rulers and statesmen.

realschule, n. [1. rāáhlshōōla; 2. rēálʃùle]. Mod. Germ., 'real school'. One of a class of secondary schools in Germany, teaching science, modern languages, and technical subjects only, without classics; contrasted with a *gymnasium.*

realtor, n. [1. réaltor; 2. ríəltə]. Formed fr. **realty** & **-or.** (U.S.A.) A real estate agent or broker; one who deals in land for development.

realty, n. [1. réalti; 2. ríəlti]. Contracted form of **reality.** (law) Real property, real estate; property in land; a piece of real property.

ream (I.), n. [1. rēm; 2. rīm], fr. O. Fr. *rayme, raime,* Mod. Fr. *rame,* prob. through Span. *resma,* cp. Ital. *risma,* fr. Arab. *risma,* 'bundle'. A measure for paper, consisting of 480 sheets or 20 quires; the newspaper ream is 500 sheets, and the printer's or *long ream,* 516 sheets, allowing for waste.

ream (II.), vb. trans. O.E. *rēman,* S.E. dial. form = W.S. *rȳman,* 'to make room, widen', fr. *rūm,* 'room'; M.E. *rēmen, rīmen;* cp. provinc. or dial. *rime.* See **room.** **1.** To enlarge a hole in metal; to enlarge the bore of a gun. **2.** To bevel out, countersink. **3.** To open the seams of a vessel for caulking.

reamer, n. [1. rémer; 2. rímə]. Prec. & **-er.** A special tool with cutting edge for reaming or enlarging a hole in metal.

rean, n. See **rhine.**

reanimate, vb. trans. [1. rēánimāt; 2. rīǽnimeit]. **re-** & **animate.** To restore to animation; to bring back, give, new life, fresh spirit, courage, or strength to: *to re-animate the apparently drowned; to reanimate defeated and discouraged troops, depressed spirits, nerves* &c.; *with reanimated courage, energy, dash.*

reanimation, n. [1. rèanimáshun; 2. rìænimèiʃən]. See prec. & **-ion.** Act of reanimating; state of being reanimated.

reap, vb. trans. & intrans. [1. rēp; 2. rīp]. The usual O.E. word is *rīpan,* 'to reap', wh., however, cannot be the ancestor of *reap,* since it wd. give Mod. Engl. **ripe.* The forms *ripan, ripian,* are also found in O.E., derived from the type *rip-* and the variant *reopan* fr. *ripan,* wh. occurs, is quite normal. From this comes M.E. *rēpen,* whence *reap.* See further under **rip (I.).** **A.** trans. **1.** **a** To cut (corn), primarily, with a sickle or reaping-hook, but now also used of cutting crops with a reaping-machine; **b** to clear of grain, gather grain from (a field, etc.) by reaping: *to reap a field; to reap two acres of oats;* **c** to obtain by reaping: *to reap a splendid harvest of corn.* **2.** (fig.) To gather, obtain, receive, as the reward, or result, of an action or of conduct: *to reap the benefits of hard work, kindness* &c.; *to reap the consequences of one's folly; to reap a harvest of trouble.* Phr. (fig.) *to sow the wind and reap the whirlwind,* obtain punishment for folly, misconduct &c. **B.** intrans. To perform the act of reaping; to harvest; to cut, gather in, crops of grain &c.: *now is the time to reap;* (also fig.) '*They that sow in tears shall reap in joy*'. Phr. *to reap where one has not sown,* to gain for oneself what another has worked for.

reaper, n. [1. réper; 2. rípə]. Prec. & **-er.** **a** One who reaps; a harvester; **b** a reaping-machine; also called a *reaper and binder.*

reaping-hook, n. [1. réping hòok; 2. rípiŋ hùk]. A sickle.

reaping-machine, n. [1. réping mashḗn; 2. rípiŋ məʃīn]. A machine, usually horse-drawn, which reaps corn and binds it into sheaves.

reappear, vb. intrans. [1. rèapḗr; 2. rìəpíə]. **re-** & **appear.** To appear again, be seen once more, esp. after disappearance.

reappearance, n. [1. rèapḗrans; 2. rìəpíərəns]. **re-** & **appearance.** Renewed appearance; fact of being seen or perceived again after having disappeared.

reapplication, n. [1. rèaplikáshun; 2. rìæplikéiʃən]. **re-** & **application.** A renewed application.

reapply, vb. trans. [1. rèaplī; 2. rìəplái]. **re-** & **apply.** To apply again.

reappoint, vb. trans. [1. rèapóint; 2. rìəpóint]. **re-** & **appoint.** To appoint afresh to the same or another position.

reappointment, n. [1. rèapóintment; 2. rìəpóintmənt]. Prec. & **-ment.** Renewed appointment to the same or to another position.

rear (I.), vb. trans. & intrans. [1. rēr; 2. riə]. O.E. *rǣran,* 'to raise', M.E. *rēren;* fr. **rāz-jan,* fr. **rās-jan,* gradational form of **rise.** See also **raise.** **A.** trans. **1.** **a** To raise, lift, put up; (archaic, poet., or rhet., except in a few phrs.) raise on high: *to rear the (its, his) head;* (chiefly fig.) show itself or himself, appear, be found; become conspicuous: *vice could not rear its head;* also *the mountains reared their crests into the clouds* &c.; **b** to set up; erect, build: *to rear a monument to his memory;* (fig.) *to rear the standard of revolt.* **2.** **a** To produce, raise, breed, grow: *to rear cattle, pigs; to rear crops;* **b** to nourish, to bring up (to full age), to foster: *to rear a sturdy race of sons; a delicate child is difficult to rear; the hen rears her brood.* **B.** intrans. Also *rear up;* specif. (of horses &c.) to stand up on the hind legs.

rear (II.), n. Abbr. form of **arrear.** That which is behind: **a** that part of an army or fleet which comes last or is behind the van or centre or behind the front rank or line; place, position, behind an army or fleet: *to bring up the rear; to follow in the rear; go to the rear; to be at the rear;* Phr. (*to attack, take the enemy) in rear,* from behind; **b** the back, hindmost, of anything: *at the rear of the house;* **c** (colloq. or vulg.) buttocks, rump; **d** (colloq., slang, only among men) water-closet.

rear-admiral, n. An admiral next in rank to a vice-admiral; formerly commanding the rear squadron of a fleet.

rear-arch, also **rere-arch,** n. **rear (II.)** & **arch (I.).** (archit.) An inner, supporting arch of a deep-set window or door, usually of a simpler style or of different form from the arch in the front.

rear-guard, n. A special body of troops detached to protect the rear of an army on the march: *rear-guard action,* action fought by the rear-guard to protect a retreat.

rearise, vb. intrans. [1. rēarīz; 2. rīəráiz]. **re-** & **arise.** To arise, rise, again.

rearm, vb. trans. & intrans. [1. rèárm; 2. rìám]. **re-** & **arm.** **1.** trans. **a** To equip again with arms; **b** to equip (an army, troops) with new arms, esp. with arms of a new, improved pattern: *during the last quarter of the 19th century every country was rearmed with the magazine-rifle.* **2.** intrans. **a** To take up arms, arm oneself, again; **b** to equip oneself with a new type of arms: *the quick-firing gun forced the powers to rearm.*

rearmament, n. [1. rèármament; 2. rìáməmənt]. **re-** & **armament.** The equipment of armies or troops with new or improved arms.

rearmost, adj. [1. rérmōst; 2. ríəmoust]. **rear (II.),** attrib., & **-most.** Hindmost; farthest in the rear.

rearouse, vb. trans. [1. rèaróuz; 2. rìəráuz]. **re-** & **arouse.** To arouse, rouse, again, re-awaken, rekindle.

rearrange, vb. trans. [1. rèaránj; 2. rìəréindž]. **re-** & **arrange.** To arrange over again; **a** to put in order again after disturbance; **b** to arrange in a new and different way or order.

rearrangement, n. [1. rèaránjment; 2. rìəréindžmənt]. Prec. & **-ment.** **a** Act of rearranging; **b** condition of being re-arranged; **c** new arrangement.

rear-rank, n. The rank of troops drawn up in line behind the front rank.

rear-vault, n. **rear (II.)** & **vault (I.).** An inner vault of a deeply recessed window or entrance; cp. *rear-arch.*

rearward, adj. & n. [1. rérward; 2. ríəwəd]. **rear (II.)** & **-ward.** **1.** adj. Situated at or towards the rear. **2.** n. Rearward portion; position in the rear.

rearward(s), adv. [1. rérward(z); 2. ríəwəd(z)]. Towards the rear.

reason (I.), n. [1. rḗzun ; 2. rízən]. M.E., fr. O. Fr. *raisún* &c., fr. Lat. *ratiōn-(em)*. See **ratio,** & cp. **rate** (I.). **1.** Faculty of thinking logically, power of drawing conclusions from premises, of inferring ; capacity of forming judgements : *man alone of living creatures possesses reason.* **2. a** The normal, healthy human mind ; sanity : *to lose one's reason,* go mad ; **b** sane thought or argument ; common sense : *to refuse to listen to reason* ; **c** action, behaviour, which is reasonable, which accords with sanity or common sense : *it is not in reason to expect me to* &c. ; *I will do anything in reason.* Phrs. *neither rhyme nor reason,* neither sound sense nor clear expression ; *without rhyme or reason,* lacking common sense ; sheer nonsense ; *it stands to reason that,* it is obvious to the sane mind. **3. a** Logical sanction of, reasonable motive for, thought or action : *the reason why I dislike him is . . . ; I have good reasons for doing, saying, this ; I have good reason to fear that . . . ; give me your reasons for refusing* ; **b** logical necessity, compelling logical motive : *there can be no reason for your resignation.* **4.** Chain of events, conditions, circumstances leading up to and producing a result ; cause, predisposing facts : *what is the reason of the tides, storms, the dew ? ; the reasons of the German defeat were many and complex.*

reason (II.), vb. intrans. & trans. See prec. **A.** intrans. **1. a** To use the faculty of reason ; to think consecutively or coherently ; to draw conclusions from data or premises ; to form judgements : *the ability to reason distinguishes man from the lower animals* ; (note elliptical phr., *to reason why, how,* to excogitate causes, motives &c., where the vb. is apparently trans.) ; **b** to come to a conclusion as the result of reasoning : *I reason in this way on the matter* ; **c** *reason about,* to use the faculty of reason upon (a question &c.), to examine critically. **B.** trans. **1.** To think out, analyse logically, to arrange arguments concerning in logical sequence ; to expound clearly the train of reasoning involved ; (chiefly in P.P.) *his speech was admirably reasoned ; a reasoned statement* ; also *reason out* : *you must reason your case out a bit more.* **2. a** *Reason out of,* to persuade, induce (a person) to relinquish an opinion or intention and to think or act differently by reasoning and argument : *to reason a man out of his obstinacy* ; **b** *reason into,* to persuade (a person) by reasoning to adopt an opinion or line of conduct : *to reason a man into accepting a proposal.*

reasonable, adj. [1. rḗzunabl ; 2. rízənəbl]. M.E., fr. O. Fr. *raisonable.* See **reason** (I.) or (II.) & **-able. 1.** Able to reason, having the faculty of reason ; rational : *are the lower animals reasonable beings ?* **2.** Able to be reasoned with ; ruled by, susceptible to, reason, or reasoned argument ; exercising common sense and sane judgement : *you must really be reasonable, and prepared to make concessions.* **3.** Conformable to reason ; fair, just : *a reasonable excuse, cause.* **4.** Within the limits of reason ; not extravagant or exorbitant ; moderate : *a reasonable price, claim, demand* ; *a reasonable chance.*

reasonableness, n. Prec. & **-ness.** State, quality, of being reasonable.

reasonably, adv. See prec. & **-ly.** In a reasonable manner or degree ; moderately ; fairly.

reasoner, n. [1. rḗzuner ; 2. ríz(ə)nə]. **reason** (II.) & **-er.** One who reasons.

reasoning (I.), n. [1. rḗzuning ; 2. ríz(ə)niŋ]. **reason** (II.) & **-ing. 1.** Act, process, of using the faculty of reason ; consecutive thought ; reasoning power, ratiocination, intelligence. **2.** Reasons, arguments, proofs as used by one who reasons.

reasoning (II.) adj., fr. Pres. Part. of **reason** (II.). **a** Able to reason, exercising the faculty of reason ; rational : *man is a reasoning creature* ; **b** connected with reason : *the reasoning faculties.*

reasonless, adj. [1. rḗzunles ; 2. ríz(ə)nlis]. **reason** (I.) & **-less.** Lacking reason. In various senses : **a** lacking the faculty of reason ; **b** not directed by reasonable motive : *reasonless forces of nature ; reasonless conduct* ; **c** lacking common sense : *reasonless arguments.*

reassemblage, n. [1. rèasémblij ; 2. rìəsémblidž]. **re-** & **assemblage.** A new or renewed assemblage or gathering ; a reassembly.

reassemble, vb. trans. & intrans. [1. rèasémbl ; 2. rìəsémbl]. **re-** & **assemble. 1.** trans. To bring, put, together again. **2.** intrans. To come together again after dispersion.

reassembly, n. [1. rèasémbli ; 2. rìəsémbli]. **re-** & **assembly.** A reassemblage.

reassert, vb. trans. [1. rèasért ; 2. rìəsə́t]. **re-** & **assert.** To assert over again ; to repeat an assertion.

reassertion, n. [1. rèasérshun ; 2. rìəsə́ʃən]. **re-** & **assertion.** A repeated assertion.

reassume, vb. trans. [1. rèasū́m ; 2. rìəsjū́m]. **re-** & **assume.** To assume again ; to take up again or a second time, to resume.

reassumption, n. [1. rèasúmpshun ; 2. rìəsámpʃən]. **re-** & **assumption.** Act of reassuming ; a new, second, assumption.

reassurance, n. [1. rèashóorans ; 2. rìəʃɔ́rəns]. See next word & **-ance. 1.** Repeated assurance ; renewed assurance or confidence ; restored courage &c. **2.** Usually *re-assurance,* reinsurance.

reassure, vb. trans. [1. rèashóor ; 2. rìəʃɔ́]. **re-** & **assure. 1.** To inspire with fresh assurance, confidence ; to free from fear, anxiety &c., set mind of at rest. **2.** Usually *re-assure,* to reinsure.

reassuring, adj. [1. rèashóoring ; 2. rìəʃɔ́riŋ], fr. Pres. Part. of **reassure.** Affording reassurance to ; encouraging, comforting.

reassuringly, adv. Prec. & **-ly.** In a reassuring, encouraging, comforting manner.

Réaumur, adj. [1. rā́ōmûr ; 2. réioumjùə], fr. name of the French physicist R. A. F. de Réaumur, d. 1757. Pertaining to, based on, according to, the thermometer and thermometric scale invented by Réaumur, with freezing-point at zero and boiling-point at 80° ; abbr. R.

reave, reive, vb. intrans. & trans. [1. rēv ; 2. rīv]. O.E. *rēafian,* 'to rob, plunder, ravage ; seize' ; cp. O.H.G. *raubōn,* O.S. *rōbōn,* 'to rob', Goth. *(bi)raubōn,* 'to despoil' ; O.N. *raufa,* 'to rob' ; cogn. w. base in **rupture.** See also **rob** & **bereave. 1.** intrans. To plunder, rob ; to play the reiver : *the moss-troopers set out to reive along the Border.* **2.** trans. To deprive, carry off, bereave ; spoil, plunder : *to reive the countryside ; to reive their neighbours of their cattle* ; *reft of life, children* &c.

reaver, more usually **reiver,** n. [1. rḗver ; 2. rívə]. Prec. & **-er.** A plunderer, freebooter.

rebaptism, n. [1. rèbáptizm ; 2. rìbǽptizəm]. **re-** & **baptism.** A second, repeated, baptism ; the giving of a new name to anything.

rebaptize, vb. trans. [1. rèbaptíz ; 2. rìbæptáiz]. **re-** & **baptize.** To baptize a second time ; to rename.

rebate (I.), n. [1. rḗbāt ; 2. ríbeit], fr. O. Fr. *rabat.* See next word. **1.** A deduction, abatement ; a remission of a certain sum off that which is to be paid, a drawback, discount : *a rebate for prompt payment ; rebate of customs duties on re-export.* **2.** Usually [1. rábit ; 2. rǽbit]. See **rabbet.**

rebate (II.), vb. trans. [1. rábet ; 2. rǽbit], fr. O. Fr. *rabattre,* 'to beat, down, blunt'. See **re-** & **abate. 1.** To cut a rebate or rabbet in. **2.** (her.) To cut off one or more of the extremities of a charge in a shield : *a rebated cross.*

rebec, rebeck, n. [1. ríbek, rébek ; 2. ríbɛk, rébɛk]. O. Fr., also in variant form *rebebe, rabebe* ; cp. Ital. *ribeca, ribeba,* fr. Arab. *rabāb, rebāb,* name of the instrument. A three-stringed mediaeval musical instrument with a pear-shaped, round-backed body, played with a bow ; early form of viol.

rebel (I.), n. [1. rébel ; 2. réb(ə)l]. Fr. *rebelle,* adj., Lat. *rebellis,* 'rebellious', fr. **re-** & *bellum,* 'war', see **bellicose. 1. a** Person who openly opposes and flouts lawful authority, esp. one who offers forcible resistance to lawful government ; **b** (gen.) person impatient of, opposed to, control or constraint of specified kind. **2.** (attrib.) Rebellious ; pertaining to rebels.

rebel (II.), vb. intrans. [1. rebél ; 2. ribél], fr. Fr. *rebeller,* fr. Lat. *rebellāre,* 'to make war again, to revolt after being conquered, to rebel'. See prec. **1.** To revolt, to rise in arms against, resist, by arms or force, the constituted government or sovereign power of one's country ; to raise, join, a rebellion ; to act as a rebel ; also *rebel against.* **2. a** (absol. or followed by *against*) To feel, and exhibit, strong repugnance for, be repelled by, to complain of, resent, control, constraint, guidance &c., and to react against these : *his whole temperament rebelled against the conditions in which he lived* ; **b** (also of natural process or action) to be disordered by, be out of harmony with, react against : *the stomach rebels against too much food.*

rebeldom, n. [1. rébeldum ; 2. réb(ə)ldəm]. **rebel** (I.) & **-dom. a** Rebels collectively ; **b** sphere of action of, area occupied by, rebels ; rebellion.

rebellion, n. [1. rebélyun ; 2. ribéljən], fr. Fr. *rébellion,* fr. Lat. *rebelliōn-(em).* See **rebel** (I.) & **-ion.** The act of a rebel. **1.** A state of organized, armed, and open resistance against the authority and government or sovereign of the country to which one is in allegiance ; distinguished from *civil war,* usually by the smaller number of the rebels ; *the Great Rebellion,* the Civil War of 1642–52. Phr. *in rebellion,* in open revolt against authority, rebellious. **2.** Defiance of, resistance to, any authority or control.

rebellious, adj. [1. rebélyus ; 2. ribéljəs], fr. **rebellion** & **-ous,** or fr. **rebel** & *-i-* & **-ous. 1.** Taking part in, engaged in, a rebellion ; rebel : *rebellious subjects.* **2.** Of the nature or character of a rebellion : *a rebellious assembly ; rebellious acts.* **3.** Resisting, revolting against, any authority or control ; insubordinate, undisciplined : *a rebellious temperament.* **4.** (med.) Difficult to treat ; resisting treatment, refractory, stubborn : *a rebellious disease ; rebellious growths, lesions* &c.

rebelliously, adv. Prec. & **-ly.** In a rebellious manner ; by means of rebellion.

rebelliousness, n. See prec. & **-ness.** State, quality, of being rebellious.

rebellow, vb. trans. & intrans. [1. rèbélō ; 2. rìbélou]. **re-** & **bellow. a** trans. To bellow back ; **b** intrans., to re-echo loudly.

rebind, vb. trans. [1. rèbínd ; 2. rìbáind]. **re-** & **bind. a** To bind a second time or again ; **b** to put a new binding on (a book).

rebirth, n. [1. rèbérth ; 2. rìbə́þ]. **re-** & **birth. a** A second birth, as, spiritually, by baptism ; **b** a second form of existence, as by reincarnation, transmigration of soul &c.

rebite, vb. trans. [1. rèbít ; 2. rìbáit]. **re-** & **bite.** To apply acid to an etched plate so as to remedy defects or make corrections.

reboant, adj. [1. rébōant ; 2. rébouənt], fr. Lat. *reboant-(em),* Pres. Part. of *reboāre,* 'to rebellow, resound, re-echo', fr. **re-** & *boāre,* 'to bellow, cry aloud, roar', cogn. w. Gk. *boáein* ; imitative. (rare and poet.) Rebellowing, resounding, re-echoing loudly.

reborn, adj. [1. rèbórn ; 2. rìbɔ́n]. **re-** & **born.** Born again ; **a** by spiritual rebirth, by baptism ; or **b** by reincarnation.

rebound (I.), adj. [1. rèbóund ; 2. rìbáund]. P.P. of **rebind.** (of books &c.) Bound again, furnished with fresh binding.

rebound (II.), vb. intrans. [1. rebóund ; 2. ribáund], fr. O. Fr. *rebondir,* as **re-** & **bound** (III.), 'to spring'. **1.** (of elastic bodies) To bound, spring, back after striking another object, surface &c.; to bounce back: *a ball rebounds from a wall, opponent's racket* &c. 2. (of non-material process) a To have a reactive effect; to follow as a result of one's own action, to recoil: *his bitter attacks on his opponents rebounded upon him to his own discomfort*; b to spring back into life or vigour; to revive: *his spirits rebounded after the long depression.*

rebound (III.), n., fr. prec. Process of rebounding, bounce: *to take a ball on the rebound*; (also fig.) *his courageous words took his depressed supporters on the rebound.*

rebuff (I.), n. [1. rebúf; 2. ribáf]. Obs. Fr. *rebuffe*, fr. Ital. *ribuffo*, fr. *ri-*, **re-**, & *buffo*, 'puff'; but cp. **buffet** (I.), 'blow'. A repulse, abrupt rejection of offer of friendliness, help &c.; a snub, check; an unexpected defeat of plans, hope &c.

rebuff (II.), vb. trans. See prec. To give a rebuff to; to check, snub.

rebuild, vb. trans. [1. rèbíld; 2. rìbíld]. **re-** & **build.** To build again, afresh; to reconstruct; esp. from a ruin: *the house has been entirely rebuilt*; (also by transf.) *to rebuild his shattered fortunes.*

rebuke (I.), vb. trans. [1. rebúk; 2. ribjúk], fr. A.-Fr. & O. Norm. Fr. *rebuker*, 'to repel, beat back, defeat'; O. Fr. *rebuchier*; **re-** & O. Fr. *buschier, buchier*, Mod. Fr. *bûcher*, 'to strike, beat'; etymol. uncertain. To chide, reprove, reprimand; to censure for a fault.

rebuke (II.), n., fr. prec. A reproof, reprimand, censure: *to give, receive, a rebuke.* Phr. *without rebuke*, blameless, irreproachable.

rebukingly, adv. [1. rebúkingli; 2. ribjúkiŋli], fr. Pres. Part. of **rebuke** & **-ly.** With rebuke; reprovingly, chidingly.

rebus, n. [1. rébus; 2. ríbəs]. Fr. *rébus*, fr. Lat. *rēbus*, 'by things', abl. pl. of *rēs*, 'thing, object', see **re** (II.). a A kind of riddle, in which names, words or their syllables, mottoes &c. are represented by objects or by a combination of objects, letters, or words; b (her.) a device or charge representing thus the name or title of the bearer of the device &c.; canting charge or device.

rebus sic stantibus, phr. [1. rébus sìk stántibus; 2. ríbəs sìk stǽntibəs]. Lat., 'things standing so'. Under the circumstances; things being as they are.

rebut, vb. trans. [1. rebút; 2. ribát], fr. O. Fr. *rebouter*, 'to thrust, push back'; *re-*, 'back', & *bouter, buter*, 'to push, thrust'. See **butt** (IV.). 1. To thrust back, repel, check, esp. accusations, charges &c.; to refute: *to rebut an insinuation.* 2. (law) To contradict, refute, meet, reply to by opposing plea, evidence, argument &c.; *rebutting evidence*, evidence brought forward by one party to disprove or counteract the evidence brought forward by the other.

rebuttal, n. [1. rebútal; 2. ribát(ə)l]. Prec. & **-al.** (law) The giving of rebutting or countervailing evidence; evidence which rebuts.

rebutter, n. [1. rebúter; 2. ribátə]. **rebut** & **-er.** (law) The answer of a defendant to a plaintiff's surrejoinder, or answer to a rejoinder.

recalcitrance, -cy, n. [1. rekálsitrans(i); 2. rikǽlsitrəns(i)]. See next word & **-ce** or **-cy.** a State, quality, of being recalcitrant; b recalcitrant behaviour.

recalcitrant, adj. [1. rekálsitrant; 2. rikǽlsitrənt], fr. Lat. *recalcitrant-(em)*, Pres. Part. type of *recalcitrāre*, 'to kick back; to be disobedient, petulant', fr. **re-** & *calcitrāre*, 'to kick, to resist, be stubborn', fr. *calci-*, stem of *calx*, 'heel'. See discussion of first element in **calceolaria**, & cp. **inculcate.** Obstinately non-compliant; not amenable to discipline or persuasion; refusing to accept or conform to a system, convention &c.; refractory.

recalcitrate, vb. intrans. [1. rekálsitrāt; 2. rikǽlsitreit], fr. Lat. *recalcitrāt-(um)*, P.P. of *recalcitrāre.* See prec. a (rare) To kick backwards, or against something; b to be refractory, to refuse to comply with an order, rule &c.

recalesce, vb. intrans. [1. rèkalés; 2. rìkælés], fr. Lat. *recalescere*, 'to become hot or warm again, to grow hot or warm', fr. **re-** & *calescere*, 'to be hot', freq. of *calēre.* See **calescence.** (of metals) To exhibit recalescence.

recalescence, n. [1. rèkalésens; 2. rìkælésəns]. See next word & **-ce.** Sudden, temporary renewal in the glow of iron which has been made red-hot, and is cooling, when a certain degree of diminution of temperature is reached.

recalescent, adj. [1. rèkalésent; 2. rìkælésənt]. Lat. *recalescent-(em)*, Pres. Part. of *recalescere.* See **recalesce.** Exhibiting recalescence.

recall (I.), vb. trans. [1. rekáwl; 2. rikɔ́l]. **re-** & **call.** 1. To call, summon back, cause to come back by calling. 2. Specif., to summon, call back again; a to one's home or country: *to be recalled from abroad by urgent private affairs*; b (of troops, ships) to the base, original line of advance, port of departure &c.; c to an office or position which one has left: *an order to recall all officials now on leave*; d from an office, to order to leave or give it up: *to recall an ambassador* &c.; e (fig.) to remind, bring back to consciousness of: *to recall a person to a sense of his duties.* 3. a To call, bring back from death to life: *we would not, if we could, recall him from the grave to such a life of pain*; b to bring back to a state of activity from one of quiescence; to revive, renew: *to recall old quarrels from the past.* 4. To call, bring back, to one's mind or memory by an effort of will; to recollect: *to recall the words of a song*; *recall what was said*; *to recall old faces.* 5. To take back, revoke, cancel, annul: *to recall an order, decree* &c.; *to recall one's words.*

recall (II.), n., fr. prec. 1. A summons to return; specif., an order to relinquish a position, or the duties entrusted to one: *recall of an ambassador, of a general.* 2. Act or power of recalling or remembering, revoking &c.; esp. in Phr. *beyond, past, recall*, not to be recalled; a irrevocable; b forgotten. *Recall of judges and public officials*, or *of judicial decisions*, (U.S.A.) a right, proposed but not in force, that judges and public officials could be recalled or removed from office by popular vote before expiry of their term, and that judicial decisions could be similarly reversed. 3. (mil.) Signal given by drum or trumpet, to troops to return to camp, to a rallying-point &c.

recallable, adj. [1. rekáwlabl; 2. rikɔ́ləbl]. **recall** (I.) & **-able.** Capable of being recalled (in various senses).

recant, vb. trans. & intrans. [1. rekánt; 2. rikǽnt], fr. Lat. *recantāre*, 'to repeat in singing, sing over again, to revoke, recant', **re-** & *cantāre*, 'to sing', see **chant** & **cant** (I.). A. trans. To recall, take back, withdraw and repudiate; to disavow opinions, statements &c., formerly held or expressed; esp. to do this formally: *to recant a heresy*; *to recant one's vows.* B. intrans. To disavow, repudiate, retract publicly, an opinion, doctrine formerly held and avowed, by open confession of error: *heretics were formerly often brought to recant under torture.*

recantation, n. [1. rèkantáshun; 2. rìkæntéiʃən]. Prec. & **-ation.** Act of recanting; disavowal, repudiation, retractation.

recapitulate, vb. trans. [1. rèkapítulāt; 2. rìkəpítjuleit], fr. Lat. *recapitulāt-(um)*, P.P. type of *recapitulāre*, 'to summarize', fr. **re-** & *capitulāre*, 'to draw up under headings', fr. *capitulum*, 'heading, chapter'. See **re-** & **capitulate** & **chapter.** 1. To repeat, restate in a brief concise form, or in outline; to summarize, to give a summary of. 2. (absol.) To restate briefly or in outline or summary: *so much for the detailed argument*; *I will now recapitulate.*

recapitulation, n. [1. rèkapitūláshun; 2. rìkəpitjuléiʃən]. fr. Lat. *recapitulātiōn-(em).* See prec. & **-ion.** 1. A restatement or repetition in brief, concise form or in outline; a summary. 2. (biol.) *Recapitulation theory*, the theory that an individual organism in process of development from the ovum to the fully formed embryo, passes through a series of forms which resemble the stages through which the species has passed in its evolution.

recapitulative, adj. [1. rèkapítūlativ; 2. rìkəpítjulətiv]. See prec. & **-ive.** Of the nature of recapitulation: *in recapitulative form*; *the statement was merely recapitulative.*

recapitulatory, adj. [1. rèkapítūlaturi; 2. rìkəpítjulətəri]. See prec. & **-ory.** Recapitulating, summarizing: *a recapitulatory chapter.*

recaption, n. [1. rèkápshun; 2. rìkǽpʃən]. **re-** & **caption.** (law) The retaking by peaceable means of one's goods &c. which have been wrongfully taken or held by another.

recapture (I.), vb. trans. [1. rèkápchur; 2. rìkǽptʃə]. **re-** & **capture.** To retake, capture again; see various senses of *capture.*

recapture (II.), n. a Act of recapturing; b thing, person, recaptured.

recast (I.), vb. trans. [1. rèkáhst; 2. rìkɑ́st]. **re-** & **cast** (I.). To cast a second time or in a new form; a to cast or mould again: *to recast a gun, bell* &c.; b to give a new or improved form to, to reconstruct: *to recast one's plan*; *to recast a book, play* &c.; c to reckon up, count a second time, to make a second cast of: *to recast accounts*; d (usually with hyphen) to give a new cast to, to change the performers in: *to recast a play.*

recast (II.), n., fr. prec. Act of recasting; that which is recast; result, product, of recasting.

recede, vb. intrans. [1. resḗd; 2. risíd], fr. Lat. *recēdere*, 'to go back, withdraw, recede'; **re-** & **cede.** 1. To move backwards, to move farther away, withdraw; a (of physical action) *the ship recedes from the shore*; *the tide has receded from the rocks*; *the sea recedes at one point and encroaches at another along the coast*; Phr. *to recede into the background*; (i.) (of persons) to lose influence, to take less important position; (ii.) (of questions, rights) to become less important, bulk less largely, be of less interest; b to have the appearance of receding, to become dim and less visible as one goes farther away: *the mountain peaks recede into the distance as one leaves the shore.* 2. To slope, incline backwards: *the cliff recedes abruptly from its base upwards*; *a receding chin, forehead.* 3. (of non-material action) a To withdraw, get out of, retreat from: *to recede from an impossible position*; *to recede from a bargain, contract or agreement*; b to become lower, to fall below former level; to decline in value &c.: *prices have receded*; *his power, influence, capacities, seem to have receded.* 4. (of mental impressions) To become hazy, and less distinct in the mind, to fade from the memory: *the faces and personalities of the friends of our childhood, the events of early years, recede into the dim past.*

re-cede, vb. trans. [1. rè sḗd; 2. rì síd]. **re-** & **cede.** To cede, hand back, yield, return, to former owner: *to re-cede territory once or already ceded.*

receipt (I.), n. [1. resḗt; 2. risít]. M.E. *receit*, fr. O. Norm. Fr. or A.-Fr. *receite*, fr. Lat. *recept-(um)*, P.P. of *recipere*, q.v. under **receive**, & cp. **reception.** 1. a Act of receiving or getting; fact of being received; the coming into one's possession or keeping or knowledge: *the receipt of a letter, good* &c.; *receipt of a message, news.* Phrs. *to be in receipt of*, to receive; *on the receipt of*, when received; b that which is received; (esp. and often in pl.) amount received or paid in, as contrasted with what is paid out, takings: *the total receipts barely covered expenses.* 2. An acknowledgement in writing of goods received, or, esp., of money paid for services rendered, money lent &c.: *a stamped receipt*; *endorsement on the cheque will be sufficient* *receipt*; *please send receipt by return. Receipt book*, book with counterfoils and forms for giving receipts; *receipt stamp*, an adhesive or embossed stamp affixed to receipts for money above a certain amount and cancelled by signature of payee. **3.** See also under **recipe**; formula of directions for making something, esp. a dish for the table, setting forth the ingredients, the several proportions of these, mode of mixing and cooking &c.: *a receipt for a plum-pudding*; more generally, any set of instructions for making something or achieving something; a prescription: *a receipt for making weed-killer, for getting rid of rats*; (jocularly) *I wish you would give me the receipt for your rosy cheeks.*

receipt (**II.**), vb. trans., fr. prec. To affix a receipt or signed statement of having received payment to: *to receipt a bill.*

receivability, n. [1. resēvabíliti; 2. risīvəbíliti]. Next word & **-ity.** State, quality, of being receivable.

receivable, adj. [1. resévabl; 2. risívəbl]. Next word & **-able. a** Capable of being received; fit to be received; suitable for reception: *goods not in a receivable condition*; **b** (commerc.) of bills and other negotiable instruments held, on which payment is due, *bills receivable*, as contrasted with *bills payable.*

receive, vb. trans. & intrans. [1. resév; 2. risív]. M.E. *receiven*, fr. A.-Fr. *receivre*; fr. Lat. *recipere*, 'to take back, recover; to accept, take, receive', fr. **re-** & *capere*, 'to take', see **captive. A.** trans. **1.** To obtain, get, acquire, by having anything given, sent, offered &c.: *to receive a present, letter, payment* &c.; *to receive orders, an invitation*; *your letter will receive our immediate attention.* **2. a** To meet with, be the object of, to have bestowed upon one, encounter; be subjected to: *to receive sympathy from*; *we received a most hearty welcome*; **b** to have inflicted upon one: *to receive severe punishment, a heavy sentence, a mortal wound, a blow on the head.* **3.** To take, stand, bear, the impact of: to support, resist by opposing: *the weight of the dome is received by eight piers*; *the hot metal receives the stamp of the die*; *our garden receives the full force of the sun.* **4. a** To accept, come into possession of; to consent to presentation of: *to receive a confession, proposal, petition*; **b** specif., *to receive the Sacrament*, to take the consecrated elements, in Holy Communion, from the hands of the celebrant and consume them; **c** *to receive stolen goods*, to take from the thief and be in possession of goods, knowing them to be stolen. **5.** To take in, act as receptacle for; to hold, contain; to have room or capacity for: *the dustbin receives the household rubbish*; (also in non-material sense) *how much is his mind capable of receiving?* **6.** To admit, entertain; **a** to grant, allow, entrance to; to give admittance to; accept as member of a society &c.: *to be received into the Church*; *hotel now open to receive guests*; **b** (i.) to admit to one's presence, permit visit of: *the king received the new ambassador yesterday*; *to receive a deputation*; *if A calls, I will not receive him*; (ii.) to recognize as member of, give right of entry to: *she is no longer received in society*; '*He came unto His own, and His own received Him not*'; **c** to welcome, greet; to treat on entry, appearance, utterance &c., in a particular manner: *the speaker (speech) was received coldly, with shouts of derision, tumultuous applause*; **d** to admit into the mind, to acknowledge, accept, recognize as true: *beliefs and customs received by the whole world.* **B.** intrans. **1.** To accept, take; to be given, to be recipient of gifts, benefits: '*It is more blessed to give than to receive*'. **2.** To partake of the consecrated elements: *in the Roman Catholic Church the priest alone receives in both kinds.* **3.** To give a reception; to entertain company; to be at home to guests: *Lady X is not receiving today.*

received, adj. [1. resévd; 2. risívd]. P.P. of **prec. 1.** Accepted, commonly held to be true, authentic: *the received view, opinion*; *the received text* (of a book), version reputed to be the most authentic obtainable. **2.** Recognized as conforming to a standard, as being in accordance with common practice: *the received manner of addressing a bishop*; *a received mode of speech* &c.; specif., *Received Standard English.*

receiver, n. [1. resévor; 2. risívə]. **receive** & **-er.** Person who, or thing which, receives. Various specific meanings: **1.** (of persons) **a** (law) Any of several officials appointed by a court of law to collect and receive moneys, or administer property, which are forfeited, or the ownership of which is under dispute: *official receiver in bankruptcies* &c.; **b** a receiver of stolen goods, one who buys goods which he knows to be stolen property. **2.** Any of several objects of technical use; e.g. **a** an apparatus which receives electric or other waves, and transforms them, according to the nature of the instrument, into sound, light, heat &c.; as the ear-piece of a telephone, the valves, crystal, of a wireless set &c.; **b** vessel which receives liquor from the retort in distillation &c.

receivership, n. [1. resévership; 2. risívəʃip]. Prec. & **-ship. a** Office of a receiver, esp. of one appointed by the court to receive and administer the assets and estates of another; **b** period of his office.

receiving (**I.**), adj. [1. reséving; 2. risíviŋ], fr. Pres. Part. of **receive.** In various senses. Specif., *receiving order*, an order of a court in bankruptcy appointing a receiver; *receiving set*, apparatus for reception of wireless transmissions.

receiving (**II.**), n. **receive** & **-ing.** Act of one who receives; specif., the purchase from a thief of goods known to be stolen.

recency, n. [1. résensi; 2. rísənsi]. See **recent** & **-cy.** State, quality, of being recent; newness, lateness, freshness: *the recency of the news, event* &c.; *the recency of his sorrow, loss* &c.

recension, n. [1. resénshun; 2. risénʃən], fr. Lat. *recensiōn-(em)*, 'enumeration, a reviewing', fr. *recensēre*, 'to examine, review, survey'; **re-** & *censēre*, 'to rate, estimate' &c. See **censure. a** The critical examination and revision of the text of an author; **b** a text so revised.

recent, adj. [1. résent; 2. rísənt]. Lat. *recent-(em)*, 'fresh, young; new, recent'; prob. fr. **re-**, 'again, repeated', or as intensive, & base seen also in Gk. *kainós*, 'new, fresh'. See **kainite.** Having appeared, first existed, happened, been discovered, become known, used &c., in a time but shortly before the present; new, fresh, novel.

recently, adv. Prec. & **-ly.** In recent times; not long since; lately; freshly, newly.

recentness, n. See prec. & **-ness.** State, quality, of being recent; recency; newness, freshness; lateness of occurrence or origin.

recept, n. [1. résept; 2. rísɛpt]. Formed on anal. of **concept** & **percept**, w. **re-** & *-cept* as in these words. See **reception.** (psychol.) A mental image formed by a succession of sensuous impressions, or percepts, of the same object, thus differing from a concept, which has an intellectual basis.

receptacle, n. [1. reséptakl; 2. riséptəkl], fr. Lat. *receptāculum*, 'reservoir, magazine; receptacle; shelter, refuge', fr. *recept-(um)*, P.P. type of *recipere*. See **receive. a** That which receives, holds, or contains; a vessel, container; space, depository, in which things may be placed or stored; specif. **b** enlarged thickened part of a flower where it joins the stem, acting as a support and containing the sexual organs; the axis of a flower-cluster.

receptacular, adj. [1. rēseptákūlar; 2. risɛptǽkjulə]. Prec. & **-ar.** (bot.) Of, pertaining to, the receptacle of a flower.

receptibility, n. [1. resèptibíliti; 2. risèptibíliti]. Next word & **-ity.** State, quality, of being receptible.

receptible, adj. [1. reséptibl; 2. riséptibl], fr. L. Lat. *receptibilis*, fr. *recept-(um)*, P.P. type of *recipere*. See **receive. a** Capable of being received; **b** capable of receiving.

reception, n. [1. resépshun; 2. risépʃən], fr. Lat. *receptiōn-(em)*, fr. *recept-(um)*, P.P. of *recipere*. See **receive. 1.** Act of receiving, taking, getting; state of being received &c.: *the reception of air into the lungs, of food into the stomach*; *the reception of wireless signals*; *reception by wireless was good.* **2.** Act of allowing, admission, acceptance: *the reception of evidence by a court of law.* **3. a** The receiving, welcoming, entertaining &c. of persons, as visitors, guests &c., formally or ceremoniously: *to hold a reception*; *the reception of the new ambassador by the king*; **b** the formal receiving and incorporation of a new member into a learned society &c.: *the reception of doctors, of academicians*; **c** manner of welcoming, greeting, or receiving person, play, novel &c.: *to have, meet with, a warm reception*; *the play had a hearty, cold, reception.* **4.** Act or process of receiving into the body; consumption, assimilation; specif., *the reception of bread and wine in the Eucharist*, i.e. act of taking and consuming. **5.** Act, process, of receiving into, of taking in by, the mind; mental acceptance, recognition, admission: *the reception of new ideas, impressions* &c. **6.** (attrib.) *Reception clerk*, (U.S.A.) hotel booking-clerk; *reception room*, a room in a house used for reception; a house-agent's term for any room in a house other than bedroom, kitchen, and offices.

receptive, adj. [1. reséptiv; 2. riséptiv], fr. O. Fr. *receptif*, from Med. Lat. *receptīvus*; see prec. & **-ive.** Having the quality or capacity of receiving, taking in, absorbing, by the mind; apt to take in, esp. capable of taking in new ideas or impressions: *a receptive mind.*

receptively, adv. Prec. & **-ly.** In a receptive manner.

receptiveness, n. See prec. & **-ness.** State, quality, of being receptive.

receptivity, n. [1. rèseptíviti; 2. rìseptíviti]. Cp. Fr. *réceptivité.* **receptive** & **-ity.** Receptiveness.

recess (**I.**), n. [1. resés; 2. risés], fr. Lat. *recessus*, 'a going back, receding, withdrawal', fr. *recess-(um)*, P.P. of *recēdere*. See **recede. 1.** Withdrawal, cessation, from work; relief from duty; esp. **a** a suspension, intermission, of the sittings and business of a legislative body; period of such suspension: *Parliament is now in recess*; **b** (U.S.A.) vacation of a university or court of law; school holidays. **2.** A place of retirement or withdrawal; a secret, withdrawn place: **a** *the deepest recesses of the country*; **b** *the secret recesses of the heart.* **3.** A receding space, space set back; **a** indentation in a chain of mountains, in a coast-line &c.; a combe or small bay; **b** a niche, alcove, in a wall of a room &c.; **c** (anat., bot.) a sinus or cleft.

recess (**II.**), vb. trans., fr. prec. **a** To make a recess in: *to recess a wall*; **b** to set back from a line; to set in a recess: *to recess a hedge, house, from the line of a road*; *recessed arch*, one of a set of arches built one within the other, as in the porch of a cathedral &c.

recession, n. [1. reséshun; 2. riséʃən], fr. Lat. *recessiōn-(em)*. See **recess** (**II.**) & **-ion. 1.** Act of receding or withdrawing; withdrawal from a place or position: *the recession of clergy and choir after service*, contrasted with *procession.* **2.** A recess or receding part of a wall, line &c.

re-cession, n. [1. rè séshun; 2. rì séʃən], fr. **re-cede.** Act of re-ceding or restoring conquered territory to the original possessors or sovereign.

recessional, adj. & n. [1. reséshunal; 2. riséʃənəl]. Prec. & **-al. 1.** adj. **a** Of, pertaining to, a recession of clergy &c. after service: *recessional hymn*; **b** of, pertaining to, a parliamentary recess: *recessional activities of members in their constituencies.* **2.** n. A recessional hymn, or music for this.

recessive, adj. [1. resésiv; 2. risésiv]. See **recess** & **-ive**. Tending to recede or be thrown or go back; (biol.) *recessive character*, one possessed by one of the parents of a hybrid, which, though it may not appear in the hybrid, can be transmitted to its descendants; (phon.) *recessive accent*, tendency, as in English speech, to place the chief stress away from the final, and on or towards the first, syllable of a word.

Rechabite, n. [1. rékabīt; 2. rékəbait], fr. Rechab, father of Jehonadab (2 Kings x.), & **-ite**. **1.** One of the descendants of Jehonadab, son of Rechab (see Jer. xxxv.), who abstained from strong drink, and did not live in houses. **2.** A member of a benefit society for total abstainers, *Independent Order of Rechabites*, founded 1835.

recharge (I.), vb. trans. [1. rēchárj; 2. rītʃádž]. **re-** & **charge** (I.). **1.** To charge or load (a firearm) again; to reload. **2.** To make a second or repeated charge on: *to recharge the enemy.* **3.** To make a second charge or accusation against: *to recharge a man with a crime.*

recharge (II.), n., fr. prec. A second, repeated, charge; specif., the amount used in recharging or reloading a gun &c.

réchauffé, n. [1. rāshṓfā; 2. reiʃóufei]. Fr. P.P. of *réchauffer*, 'to heat, warm, up', used as n. See **re-** & **chauffeur**. **1.** A dish of cooked food warmed up and served again. **2.** (fig.) Something made up of old materials, esp. a rehash of one's own or other people's work, in slightly different form.

recherché, adj. [1. reshárshā; 2. rəʃéəʃei]. Fr., P.P. of *rechercher*, 'to search out with care'. See **research**. Carefully selected or thought out; choice, select; of rare or refined quality, excellence, or taste.

rechristen, vb. trans. [1. rēkrísn; 2. rīkrísn]. **re-** & **christen**. To christen again, rebaptize.

recidivism, n. [1. resídivizm; 2. risídivizəm], fr. Fr. *récidivisme*. See next word & **-ism**. State of a recidivist; relapse into crime.

recidivist, n. [1. resídivist; 2. risídivist], fr. Fr. *récidiviste*, fr. *récidiver*, 'to relapse', fr. Lat. *recidīvus*, 'falling back, recurring, relapsing', cp. *recidere*, 'to fall back, return'; fr. **re-** & *cadere*, 'to fall', see **cadence**. A relapsed criminal; a criminal who after punishment or temporary reform returns to his old criminal life; an habitual, professional, criminal.

recipe, n. [1. résipi; 2. résipi]. Lat., 'receive, take (this)', imperat. of *recipere*, 'to receive, take'. See **receive** & cp. **receipt**. A formula or set of directions for the making of something which is to be taken or received; a receipt; **a** directions for making and cooking a dish or a drink (also *receipt*): *the recipes in an old cookery book*; **b** formula for making medicines, compounding drugs, now usually styled *prescription*; **c** any action, method, thing proposed as a remedy or cure: *the latest recipe for our social failures.*

recipience, -cy, n. [1. resípiens(i); 2. risípiəns(i)]. See next word & **-ce, -cy**. **a** Act of receiving; reception; **b** (rare) state, quality, of being recipient; receptiveness.

recipient, adj. & n. [1. resípient; 2. risípiənt], fr. Lat. *recipient-(em)*, Pres. Part. of *recipere*, 'to receive'. See **receive**. **1.** adj. Receiving, receptive: *to have a recipient mind.* **2.** n. One who receives, to whom something is given: *the first recipient of the news.*

reciprocable, adj. [1. resíprokabl; 2. risíprəkəbl]. See **reciprocate** & **-able**, Capable of being reciprocated.

reciprocal (I.), adj. [1. resíprokl; 2. risíprəkl], fr. Lat. *reciprocus*, 'turning back the same way, returning; alternating, reciprocal'; fr. **re-** & a base the etymol. of wh. is doubtful. **1.** Done by each of two individuals or parties to the other; mutual; done by one in return for something received from or done by another: *whatever kindness he feels for us is reciprocal.* **2.** Complementary, inversely corresponding: *reciprocal functions of two corresponding parts of a machine or organ; the juxtaposition of two different colours has reciprocal effects on each.* **3.** Mutually interchangeable, as in logic: *reciprocal terms*, terms having exactly the same significance, and so able to be converted or interchanged without danger of a fallacy. **4.** Expressing mutual relation: **a** (gram.) *reciprocal pronoun*, as *one another, each other*; **b** (math.) *reciprocal proportion, ratio*, ratio between the reciprocals of two quantities.

reciprocal (II.), n. (math.) The quotient resulting from the division of unity by a quantity: *the reciprocal of a is* $\frac{1}{a}$, *of 6 is* $\frac{1}{6}$ &c.

reciprocally, adv. [1. resíprokali; 2. risíprəkəli]. **reciprocal** (I.) & **-ly**. Mutually, in return; (math.) inversely.

reciprocate, vb. intrans. & trans. [1. resíprokāt; 2. risíprəkeit], fr. Lat. *reciprocāt-(um)*, P.P. of *reciprocāre*, 'to move backwards and forwards, to come and go, reciprocate', fr. *reciprocus*; see **reciprocal** & **-ate**. **A.** intrans. **1.** To move alternately backwards and forwards; to alternate, to act reciprocally (chiefly of machinery): *reciprocating engine*, one in which the piston moves backwards and forwards in a straight line, thus reversing the motion at each stroke, necessitating conversion into circular motion, contrasted with *rotary engine*; *reciprocating motion*, a method for transmission of power in which parts on each side of a rigid axis or centre alternately take the positions of those on the other. **2.** To perform a reciprocal action, to give and take, mutually; to give in return: *to every attack he reciprocated with a blow; for the concession the other side should reciprocate.* **3.** (math.) To change or be changed reciprocally or by reciprocation. **B.** trans. **1.** To give reciprocating motion to. **2.** To give and return, exchange mutually or reciprocally: *to reciprocate sentiments, dislike, hostility, concessions, favours* &c.

reciprocation, n. [1. resìprokáshun; 2. risìprəkéiʃən]. Lat. *reciprocātiōn-(em)*. See prec. & **-ion**. Act of reciprocating, or of mutual exchange or return: *reciprocation of favours, ideas, motion* &c.

reciprocative, adj. [1. resíprokàtiv; 2. risíprəkèitiv]. See **reciprocate** & **-ive**. Tending to reciprocate, marked by reciprocation.

reciprocatory, adj. [1. resíprokaturi; 2. risíprəkətəri]. **reciprocate** & **-ory**. Reciprocating (of machines &c.).

reciprocity, n. [1. rèsiprósiti; 2. rèsiprósiti], fr. Fr. *réciprocité*. See **reciprocal** & **-ity**. State, condition, of being reciprocal; mutual action and reaction, give and take, esp. in relations of trade &c. between two countries, involving an arrangement of tariffs by a reciprocity treaty, to the benefit of both the exporting and the importing country.

recitable, adj. [1. resítabl; 2. risáitəbl]. **recite** & **-able**. Capable of being recited; suitable for recitation.

recital, n. [1. resítal; 2. risáit(ə)l]. **recite** & **-al**. **1.** **a** Act of reciting; **b** something recited; a detailed enumeration, narration, of facts, events &c.; a narrative, story. **2.** (law) Statement of facts, as to title, interests &c. in a legal document such as a conveyance. **3.** (mus.) **a** Performance by a single singer or instrumentalist; **b** performance of works by a single composer.

recitation, n. [1. rèsitáshun; 2. rèsitéiʃən], fr. Lat. *recitātiōn-(em)*, 'a reading aloud'. See **recite** & **-ation**. **1.** Act of reciting; recital, narration. **2.** **a** Delivery in public of a piece of prose or poetry committed to memory; **b** piece so delivered or selected for such delivery.

recitative, n. [1. rèsitatḗv; 2. rèsitətīv], fr. Ital. *recitativo*, cp. Fr. *récitatif*. See **recitation** & **-ive**. A species of declamatory singing in opera or oratorio, accompanied either by a few sustaining chords or with a full and continuous setting, used for the purely narrative or prose, as contrasted with the lyrical or melodic parts.

recite, vb. trans. & intrans. [1. resít; 2. risáit], fr. Lat. *recitāre*, 'to read out, recite'; **re-** & *citāre*, see **cite**. **A.** trans. **1.** To declaim, repeat aloud from memory: *to recite a poem, passage from a play* &c. **2.** To recount, narrate, enumerate: *to recite the history of one's adventures, trials* &c. **3.** (law) To set forth facts, as in the opening of a document such as a lease; to state in the recital to a deed or conveyance. **B.** intrans. To give a recitation. *Reciting note*, a note held or sustained in chanting.

reciter, n. [1. resíter; 2. risáitə]. **recite** & **-er**. **1.** One who recites; specif., one who gives recitations. **2.** A book containing a collection of short poems, or extracts in prose and verse, suitable for recitation.

reck, vb. intrans. & trans. [1. rek; 2. rek]. O.E. *rēċċan*, M.E. *recchen, rekken*; Common Gmc.; O.S. *rōkian*, O.H.G. *ruohēn*, O.N. *rækja*; cogn. w. **reckon**. (archaic, poet., or rhet.; in neg. and interrog. sentences only) **1.** intrans. To care about, take heed of, pay heed to; to take account of; **a** (followed by *of*) *he recked not of the danger*; **b** (with dependent clause) *what recked they if*, or *though, they were marching on death?*; *what reck they whether they live or die?* **2.** trans. To heed, to regard; to have a care or thought for. **3.** (impers.) It concerns: *it recks him not what others think or say.*

reckless, adj. [1. rékles; 2. réklis]. O.E. *reċċelēas*. See prec. & **-less**. Not recking; heedless, careless, regardless; rash: *reckless of danger*; *a reckless career*; *reckless expenditure.*

recklessly, adv. Prec. & **-ly**. In a reckless manner; heedlessly, rashly.

recklessness, n. See prec. & **-ness**. State, quality, of being reckless; heedlessness.

reckon, vb. trans. & intrans. [1. rékun; 2. rék(ə)n]. O.E. (*ġe*)*recenian* for **rekonōjan*, 'to explain'; cp. also O.E. *recon*, 'enumeration'; M.E. *rekenen, reknen*, 'to enumerate; reckon, compute'; cp. O.H.G. *rehhanōn*, 'to count'; prob. ultimately cogn. w. **reach** (I.) & **right** (I.). **A.** trans. **1.** To count, number; to calculate, enumerate: *to reckon money due*; *'reckon not our offences'*; also *reckon up*: *to reckon up one's debts.* **2.** To count, include: *you can reckon me among your supporters*; *they were reckoned in the company present.* **3.** To estimate, value, account; to regard as, consider: *he reckoned the work as one of his greatest successes*; *to be reckoned a clever person.* **4.** To attribute, impute: *to reckon something to a person for righteousness.* **5.** (followed by *that*, and objective clause) To suppose, conclude, think: *to reckon that something will not happen*; *to reckon it is going to rain.* **B.** intrans. **1.** To count, calculate, cast up accounts: *taught to read, write, and reckon.* **2.** (usually in parentheses) To consider, suppose: *he will come soon, I reckon.* Phr. *to reckon on, upon*, to count on, rely on. *To reckon with*, **a** to settle accounts with: *we will reckon with these defaulters later on*; **b** to take into account, treat seriously: *he is a doughty opponent and one to be reckoned with*; Phr. *reckon without one's host*, to take one's own point of view only, to overlook or neglect possible opposition or difficulties, perhaps from idea of a guest at an inn who estimates the likely charges before getting the bill from the host.

reckoner, n. [1. rékner; 2. réknə]. Prec. & **-er**. **a** One who reckons or counts; **b** book containing tables &c. as an aid in reckoning or calculating.

reckoning, n. [1. rékuning; 2. rék(ə)niŋ]. **reckon** & **-ing**. **1.** Act of one who reckons, act of calculating or counting: *to be good at reckoning.* **2.** **a** Statement of accounts, charges &c.; bill, esp. a score at a tavern: *to pay the reckoning*; **b** (fig.) payment for an offence, or for folly; retribution: *there will be a heavy reckoning to pay for his crimes.* **Phr.** *the day of reckoning*, **a** day when final accounts must be settled; **b** the Day of Judgement.

3. Calculation, determination, of a ship's position by means of astronomical observation or by *dead-reckoning*, q.v.; position of ship so determined. Phr. *to be out of* (or *in*) *one's reckoning*, to miscalculate one's position; to be mistaken in one's judgement.

reclaim (I.), vb. trans. & intrans. [1. reklā́m; 2. rikléim], fr. O. Fr. *reclamer*, 'to call often or earnestly on; to appeal to, to claim or call back', fr. Lat. *reclāmāre*, 'to call out against, to contradict loudly', fr. **re-** & *clāmāre*, 'to call', see **claim** (I.); the earliest use in Engl. is as a term in hawking of calling back a falcon to the wrist. **A.** trans. **1.** To bring back, recover (land), into cultivation from a wild, waste or uncultivated state, or from the sea. **2.** To tame, train (a hawk), from a wild state. **3.** To bring back (persons) from error, vice, barbarism &c. into good behaviour; to reform: *to reclaim a criminal, a drunkard, a fallen woman.* **4.** To claim back; to demand the restoration of: *to reclaim lost property, territory* &c. **B.** intrans. **1.** (obs. or very archaic) To cry out, protest, against. **2.** (Scots law) To appeal from the Lord Ordinary to the inner house of the Court of Session.

reclaim (II.), n., fr. prec. A reclaiming, reclamation; obsolete except in Phr. *beyond, past, reclaim*, past reform; irreclaimable.

reclaimable, adj. [1. reklā́mabl; 2. rikléimәbl]. **reclaim** (I.) & **-able.** Capable of being reclaimed (in all senses of vb.).

reclamation, n. [1. rèklamā́shun; 2. rèklәméiʃәn]. Fr. *réclamation*, fr. Lat. *reclāmātiōn-(em)*, 'a cry of disapproval or opposition'. See **reclaim** & **-ation.** **1.** Act of reclaiming or recovering from a wild, waste condition; the bringing back to cultivation: *the reclamation of land.* **2.** Act of reclaiming or reforming; reformation: *the reclamation of hardened offenders.*

réclame, n. [1. rāklàhm; 2. rèiklā́m]. Fr., fr. *réclamer*. See **reclaim** (I.). Notoriety, publicity, gained by advertisement; self-advertisement.

reclinate, adj. [1. réklināt; 2. réklineit], fr. Lat. *reclīnātus*, P.P. of *reclīnāre*. See next word & **-ate.** (bot.) Bent, curving, downwards.

recline, vb. trans. & intrans. [1. reklín; 2. rikláin], fr. Lat. *reclīnāre*, 'to bend back, to recline', as reflex., 'to lean back', **re-** & *clīnāre*, 'to lean, slope'. See under **clinical** & cp. **lean** (II.). **A.** trans. To lean, lay, back; to place in a recumbent position, as one's head, body &c.: *to recline one's head on the pillow; to recline the body on the bed; with head reclined upon his hand; they lay reclined upon the grass.* **B.** intrans. **1.** To rest, place oneself, in a recumbent position; to lie down; also *recline against*, lean back against. **2.** (fig.) To rely, depend, on for moral support: *to recline too much on flattering but doubtful supporters.*

reclothe, vb. trans. [1. rēklṓdh; 2. rìklóuð]. **re-** & **clothe.** **1.** To put clothes upon again: *reclothe oneself*, put on one's clothes again. **2.** To clothe afresh, provide new and different clothes or coverings for.

recluse, adj. & n. [1. reklóos; 2. riklús], fr. Fr. *reclus*, masc., *recluse*, fem., P.P. of **reclure*, 'to shut in, enclose', used first of cloistered monks or nuns; fr. Lat. *reclūs-(um)*, P.P. of *reclūdere*, 'to open, unclose, reveal', in L. Lat., 'to shut up, enclose'. See **re-** & **claustral** & **close** (I.). **1.** adj. (obs. or rare) Enclosed, shut up, or off; **a** (of persons) living apart from the world or social life; solitary: *a recluse monk or nun*; **b** (of state, condition) sequestered, secluded, isolated: *a recluse life.* **2.** n. **a** A solitary person, one who chooses to live apart from his fellows; one who lives a retired life and shuns society; **b** specif., a hermit, an anchoress.

reclusely, adv. Prec. & **-ly.** (rare) In a recluse, solitary manner.

recluseness, n. See prec. & **-ness.** (rare) Condition, quality, of being recluse; seclusion, solitariness.

reclusion, n. [1. reklóozhun; 2. riklúʒәn], fr. L. Lat. *reclūsiōn-(em)*. See **recluse** & **-ion.** (rare) Condition, quality, of being a recluse; the usual word is *seclusion.*

recoal, vb. intrans. & trans. [1. rèkṓl; 2. rìkóul]. **re-** & **coal.** **a** intrans. (of a ship) To take in a fresh supply of coal; **b** trans., to put fresh coal into (esp. into a ship).

recoat, vb. trans. [1. rēkṓt; 2. rìkóut]. **re-** & **coat.** To give a fresh coat (of paint &c.) to.

recognition, n. [1. rèkogníshun; 2. rèkәgníʃәn], fr. Lat. *recognitiōn-(em)*, fr. *recognit-(um)*, P.P. type of *recognoscere*, see **recognize**, & **-ion.** **1.** Act of recognizing; state of being recognized; **a** acknowledgement, acceptance, admission, of another's position, claims &c.: *recognition of a child as lawful heir; recognition by the people at the coronation of the sovereign*; **b** (i.) formal acknowledgement, acceptance, by foreign governments of the form of government set up in a State as a lawful government for purposes of diplomatic relations; (ii.) acceptance by foreign governments of the sovereignty and independence of a State. **2.** Consideration, notice, attention: *to receive, meet with, recognition in return for services* &c. **3.** **a** Act of identifying (person or thing) by means of one of the senses, as being known to one, as having been seen or heard &c. before, or as being a specific person or thing: *my recognition of him was immediate*; **b** acknowledgement of such an identification by noticing and greeting: *he only gave me a passing recognition.*

recognitory, adj. [1. rekógnitori; 2. rikógnitәri]. See prec. & **-ory.** (rare) Pertaining to, concerned with, recognition, acknowledgement, or acceptance.

recognizability, n. [1. rèkognīzabíliti; 2. rèkәgnaizәbíliti]. **recognizable** & **-ity.** Condition, quality, of being recognizable.

recognizable, adj. [1. rekognízabl; 2. rekәgnáizәbl]. **recognize** & **-able.** Capable of being recognized; identifiable.

recognizably, adv. Prec. & **-ly.** In a recognizable manner; so as to be recognized.

recognizance, n. [1. rekó(g)nizans; 2. rikó(g)nizәns]. M.E. *reconissaunce*, fr. O. Fr. *reconoissance*, later spelt *recognoissance*, through the influence of Lat. spelling. See **recognize** & **-ance.** (law) **a** An obligation undertaken by a person before a court of record to appear to answer or prosecute a charge and to be of good behaviour in the interim, at the same time acknowledging or recognizing that, on default, he owes a certain sum to the Crown: *to enter into recognizances*; **b** the sum to be forfeited if the party fails to appear &c.: *to forfeit one's recognizances.*

recognize, vb. trans. [1. rékognīz; 2. rékәgnaiz]. O. Fr. *reconiss-*, stem of *reconoistre*, fr. Lat. *recognoscere*, 'to know again, recall to mind; to authenticate, identify'; assimilated to **-ize** vbs. See **re-** & **cognition.** **1.** To know (person or thing) again, to recall to mind; to identify as previously known, seen, heard, or described: *he was so much changed that I hardly recognized him; it is easy to recognize the style of Milton.* **2.** To acknowledge as known, as an acquaintance or friend, by salutation or greeting: *to recognize a person in the street; I refuse to recognize him any longer.* **3.** **a** To acknowledge, admit, accept as authentic and genuine: *to recognize a person as one's son and heir; to recognize claims as justified*; **b** to accept as a fact, admit, be prepared to face: *to recognize one's position, one's duty, that one is beaten* &c. **4.** To acknowledge and show appreciation of by some mark of favour, by reward &c.: *to recognize services, loyalty, devotion* &c.; *his great learning has at last been recognized by his university.* **5.** To make formal acknowledgement of, to admit the status of: *to recognize rebels as belligerents; to recognize the independence of a new state or nation.*

recoil (I.), vb. intrans. [1. rekóil; 2. rikóil]. M.E. *recoilen*, trans., 'to drive back', *reculen*, intrans., 'to recoil', fr. Fr. *reculer*, 'to go back or backwards, retire', fr. **re-** & *cul*, 'the back, posterior', fr. Lat. *cūlus*, 'posterior, tail', cogn. w. O. Ir. *cūl*, 'back'. **1.** (of physical motion or action) To draw or fall back; **a** (of persons) to retire, withdraw, retreat: *the advancing troops recoiled before the counter-attack*; **b** (of things) to rebound, spring back, after impact or discharge; to kick: *the gun recoiled; vessel recoiled at the collision*; **c** (fig., of actions and conduct) to react upon, affect, him who is responsible: *his cruelty to others recoiled in the end upon himself.* **2.** (of moral action) To shrink from, feel repugnance or alarm at: *to recoil from a degrading action; recoiled in horror from the spectacle.*

recoil (II.), n., fr. prec. **1.** (in physical sense) **a** Process of recoiling; rebound, backward motion: *the recoil of a gun, spring* &c.; **b** (fig.) effect in contrary direction: *to feel the recoil of one's own folly.* **2.** (in moral sense) Feeling of shrinking, disgust, repugnance.

recoin, vb. trans. [1. rèkóin; 2. rìkóin]. **re-** & **coin** (II.). To coin anew; to melt used or defaced coins and mint them again.

recoinage, n. [1. rèkóinij; 2. rìkóinidž]. Prec. & **-age.** Act of recoining; a reminting; defaced, worn, coinage reminted.

recollect, vb. trans. [1. rékolèkt; 2. rékәlèkt], fr. Lat. *recollect-(um)*, P.P. of *recolligere*, 'to gather together again, to collect together; to regain'. **re-** & **collect** (II.). To recall to mind; to succeed in remembering: *I cannot recollect the exact words; to recollect one's childhood days*; (also absol.) *as no doubt you recollect, it was* &c.

re-collect, vb. trans. [1. rè kolékt; 2. rì kәlékt]. New formation w. **re-.** **a** To gather together again; to rally: *to re-collect what was scattered or dispersed*; **b** *re-collect oneself, one's thoughts*, to regain one's composure, normal state of mind, often [1. rékolèkt; 2. rékәlèkt].

recollection, n. [1. rèkolékshun; 2. rèkәlékʃәn]. L. & Med. Lat. *recollectiōn-(em)*. See prec. & **-ion.** **1.** Act of recollecting or recalling to the mind; act of remembering, remembrance: *some events are past recollection, too trivial for recollection.* **2.** **a** Power, faculty, of recollecting or remembering; memory: *outside my recollection*; **b** period over which one's memory extends: *the events did not happen within my recollection.* **3.** (often pl.) That which is recollected or recalled; reminiscence: *he is writing his recollections; the recollections of one's childhood.*

recollective, adj. [1. rèkoléktiv; 2. rèkәléktiv]. **recollect** & **-ive.** Pertaining to, having, the faculty of recollection.

recolonization, n. [1. rèkolonīzā́shun; 2. rìkәlәnaizéiʃәn]. See next word & **-ation.** **a** Act of recolonizing; **b** state, condition, of being recolonized.

recolonize, vb. trans. [1. rèkólonīz; 2. rìkólәnaiz]. **re-** & **colonize.** To colonize afresh or over again; to plant, establish, a second set of colonists or colonies upon or in.

recolour, vb. trans. [1. rèkúlur; 2. rìkálә]. **re-** & **colour.** To colour again; to give fresh colour or paint to; to repaint.

recommence, vb. trans. & intrans. [1. rèkoméns; 2. rìkәméns]. **re-** & **commence.** To commence, begin, over again; to start afresh.

recommencement, n. [1. rèkoménsment; 2. rìkәménsmәnt]. Prec. & **-ment.** A new beginning, fresh start (of an action or process).

recommend, vb. trans. [1. rèkoménd; 2. rèkәménd], fr. L. or Med. Lat. *recommendāre*. See **re-** & **commend.** **1.** **a** To single out and commend (persons or things) to the notice of another; to give a favourable account of, or opinion concerning; to represent as being suitable for a particular purpose or use: *to recommend a chauffeur, a good doctor, a cheap car, a dictionary* &c.; **b** to speak favourably of, advise use of : *to recommend light food and lots of exercise* ; *I cannot recommend this wine.* **2.** To advise (person) to do particular thing or to pursue specified line of conduct : *I recommend you to take a holiday* ; *I have been recommended to say nothing for the present.* **3.** To commit, entrust, to the charge of , to bespeak favourable consideration for : *to recommend one's soul to God* ; *he recommended his wife and children to the pity of his captors.* **4.** To give a favourable impression of, induce (others) to think well of ; to act as a recommendation for ; to cause to appear in a favourable light : *his good looks and agreeable manners recommended him to high and low alike* ; *your plan has very little to recommend it.*

recommendable, adj. [1. rèkoméndabl ; 2. rèkəméndəbl]. Prec. & **-able.** Fit, suitable, to be recommended ; worthy of recommendation.

recommendation, n. [1. rèkomendáshun ; 2. rèkəmendéiʃən]. **recommend** & **-ation. 1.** Act of recommending or bringing to the favourable notice of another. **2.** That which recommends ; **a** a letter, statement, favourable to the person, thing &c., recommended ; **b** qualities, capacities, which recommend, or which secure approbation : *his personal recommendations for the post appear to be of the slightest.*

recommendatory, adj. [1. rèkoméndaturi ; 2. rèkəméndətəri]. Lat. *recommendāt-(um)*, P.P. type of *recommendāre*, see prec., & **-ory.** Tending, serving, to recommend ; serving as a recommendation.

recommit, vb. trans. [1. rèkumít ; 2. rìkəmít]. **re-** & **commit.** To commit a second time ; specif., to refer a parliamentary Bill a second time or back to a committee.

recommitment, n. [1. rèkumítment ; 2. rìkəmítmənt]. Prec. & **-ment.** Recommittal.

recommittal, n. [1. rèkumítal ; 2. rìkəmítəl]. The referring back or a second time of a Bill to a committee ; recommitment.

recompense, vb. trans. & n. [1. rékumpèns ; 2. rékəmpèns], fr. O. Fr. *recompenser*, fr. L. Lat. *recompensāre.* See **re-** & **compensate. 1.** vb. **a** To make an equal return for ; to requite ; to reward or punish : *to recompense a person for his services, for his misdeeds* ; *to be recompensed for losses, damages* &c. ; **b** to give satisfaction, compensate, for loss, injury, disappointment &c. : *I was amply recompensed for my accident by the kindness I received.* **2.** n. (from vb.) **a** Something given or done, whether as reward or punishment, for acts performed, services rendered &c. ; requital ; reward ; retribution ; **b** something done or given to make good, afford satisfaction for loss or injury &c. suffered ; compensation, amends : *I should like to offer some slight recompense for your disappointment.*

recompose, vb. trans. [1. rèkumpṓz ; 2. rìkəmpóuz]. **re-** & **compose. 1.** To compose again ; to recombine, to rearrange : *the whole design should be recomposed* ; *the Prime Minister is engaged in recomposing the Cabinet.* **2.** To bring back to composure, order, or peace : *to recompose one's features, one's feelings, mind* &c. ; *to recompose the quarrels among the extremists in the party.*

recomposition, n. [1. rèkompozíshun ; 2. rìkəmpəzíʃən]. **re-** & **composition. 1.** Act of recomposing ; state of being recomposed. **2.** (print.) The resetting of matter composed in wrong type or in type which has been broken.

reconcentrate, vb. trans. [1. rèkónsentrāt ; 2. rìkɔ́nsəntreit]. **re-** & **concentrate.** To concentrate again or afresh.

reconcentration, n. [1. rékònsentráshun ; 2. ríkɔ̀nsəntréiʃən]. Prec. & **-ion. a** Act of reconcentrating ; **b** condition of being reconcentrated ; specif., the dispersal and resettlement of population.

reconcilability, n. [1. rèkonsīlabíliti ; 2. rèkənsailəbíliti]. Next word & **-ity.** Condition, quality, of being reconcilable.

reconcilable, adj. [1. rèkonsílabl ; 2. rèkənsáiləbl]. **reconcile** & **-able. a** Capable of being reconciled (in various senses) ; **b** capable of reconciliation.

reconcilably, adv. Prec. & **-ly.** In a reconcilable manner ; by reconciliation.

reconcile, vb. trans. [1. rékonsīl ; 2. rékənsail], fr. Lat. *reconciliāre*, 'to bring together again, to reconcile '. See **re-** & **conciliate. 1.** To restore (persons) to friendly relations after a quarrel or estrangement ; *to reconcile to God*, restore to favour and grace by repentance, after sin and estrangement. **2.** To adjust, smooth over, settle, compose (quarrels, disagreements, differences, disputes &c.). **3.** *Reconcile with*, to bring into logical agreement with each other or with other facts or arguments, to make compatible or apparently compatible (different statements, arguments, facts) : *to reconcile a statement with a fact* ; *to reconcile two opposite arguments* ; *a character difficult to reconcile with what is known of his life* ; *to reconcile duty and pleasure.* **4.** (reflex. or pass.) *Reconcile oneself* ; *become, be, reconciled to*, to become tolerant of, acquiescent in, to submit to, to acquiesce in, be resigned to : *to reconcile oneself to one's fate* ; *to be reconciled to a life of obscurity* ; *I am now quite reconciled to living in London.* **5.** Specific uses : **a** (eccles.) to purify (sacred building) after desecration or profanation, by ceremonial less than that of reconsecration ; **b** (shipbuilding) to join (one timber with another) smoothly, esp. at a curve.

reconcilement, n. [1. rèkonsílment ; 2. rèkənsáilmənt]. Prec. & **-ment.** (rare) Act of reconciling ; fact of being reconciled ; reconciliation : *the reconcilement of love with self-interest.*

reconciler, n. [1. rékonsīler ; 2. rékənsàilə]. **reconcile** & **-er.** One who, condition which, reconciles : *death is the great reconciler.*

reconciliation, n. [1. rèkunsiliáshun ; 2. rèkənsiliéiʃən], fr. Lat. *reconciliātiōn-(em)*, 're-establishment, renewal ; reconciliation ', fr. *reconciliāt-(um)*, P.P. of *reconciliāre.* See **reconcile** & **-ion. 1.** Act of reconciling ; state, condition, of being reconciled ; renewal, restoration, of friendship. **2.** Act of harmonizing, of making consistent and compatible, things, conditions &c. that are apparently inconsistent with each other : *a reconciliation of religion and science* ; condition of being so reconciled.

reconciliatory, adj. [1. rèkunsíliaturi ; 2. rèkənsíliətəri]. See prec. & **-ory.** Serving to reconcile ; reconciling, conciliatory.

recondite, adj. [1. rékundīt ; 2. rékəndait] or [1. rekóndit ; 2. rikɔ́ndit], fr. Lat. *recondit-(um)*, P.P. type of *recondere*, 'to put up again, put away, hide, conceal ', fr. **re-** & *condere*, 'to put together, to construct ; to put away ; to hide ' ; for the first element of *condere*, see **con-** ; the second is the base ***dhē-*, ***dhə-*, 'to place, put, set ' &c., wh. appears in Lat. *facere*, 'to make ' &c., see **fact** ; in Gk. *títhēmi*, 'to place ', see **thesis (I.)** ; & in **do. a** Hidden from ordinary knowledge ; secret, obscure : *the recondite motives of human action* ; **b** dealing, concerned, with abstruse subjects : *recondite learning, studies.*

reconditely, adv. Prec. & **-ly.** In a recondite manner.

reconditeness, n. See prec. & **-ness.** Condition, quality, of being recondite.

recondition, vb. trans. [1. rèkondíshun ; 2. rìkəndíʃən]. **re-** & **condition (II.).** To put into condition again ; to repair, refit.

reconduct, vb. trans. [1. rèkundúkt ; 2. rìkəndákt]. **re-** & **conduct.** To conduct back again ; to lead back to the place of starting.

reconnaissance, n. [1. rekónisans ; 2. rikɔ́nisəns]. Fr., earlier *reconnoissance.* See **recognizance** & cp. next word. (mil.) **1.** Act of reconnoitring ; an inspection, examination, carried out by single scouts or by a body of troops on land or, at sea, by one or several ships, for the purpose of ascertaining the position and strength of the enemy &c., generally, of picking up information ; *reconnaissance in force*, one carried out by a sufficiently large body of troops or of ships as to force the enemy to reply and disclose fully his position and strength or to retire. **2.** Body of troops or ships making a reconnaissance ; a reconnoitring party.

reconnoitre (I.), vb. trans. & intrans. [1. rè konóiter ; 2. rèkənɔ́itə], fr. Fr. *reconnoître*, earlier *reconnoistre*, Mod. Fr. *reconnaître*, fr. Lat. *recognoscere.* See **recognizance. A.** trans. **1.** To make a reconnaissance of ; to make a preliminary survey or exploration of (enemy's position). **2.** To explore, examine (area, position, state &c.). **B.** intrans. To make a reconnaissance, explore, look round ; to ascertain, by examination, the nature of an area, position, or the state of affairs.

reconnoitre (II.), n. A reconnaissance.

reconquer, vb. trans. [1. rèkóngker ; 2. rìkɔ́ŋkə]. **re-** & **conquer.** To conquer again ; to make a second conquest of ; regain by conquering again.

reconquest, n. [1. rèkóngkwest ; 2. rìkɔ́ŋkwest]. **re-** & **conquest.** A second, repeated, conquest.

reconsecrate, vb. trans. [1. rèkónsekrāt ; 2. rìkɔ́nsikreit]. **re-** & **consecrate.** To consecrate (sacred building) a second time, as after desecration or profanation, with full rites and ceremonial.

reconsecration, n. [1. rèkonsekráshun ; 2. rìkɔnsikréiʃən]. Prec. & **-ation. a** Act of reconsecrating ; **b** condition of being reconsecrated.

reconsider, vb. trans. [1. rèkonsíder ; 2. rìkənsídə]. **re-** & **consider. 1.** To consider, debate, in one's mind or openly a second time : *to reconsider a question.* **2.** To take into consideration again, with a view to change : *to reconsider one's position, decision.*

reconsideration, n. [1. rèkonsideráshun ; 2. rìkənsidəréiʃən]. **re-** & **consideration.** Act of reconsidering.

reconstituent, n. [1. rèkunstíchooent ; 2. rìkənstítʃuənt]. **re-** & **constituent.** That which reconstitutes or builds up anew or afresh ; a rebuilding medicine or food.

reconstruct, vb. trans. [1. rèkonstrúkt ; 2. rìkənstrákt]. **re-** & **construct. 1.** To construct over again, to rebuild ; esp. to rebuild in a new form, in one differing from the original. **2.** To build up something, parts of which are missing, into its supposed original form, supplying by conjecture the missing parts : *to reconstruct a mammoth from a few bones* ; *to reconstruct a defective line in a MS.* ; *to reconstruct a scene from a few data.*

reconstruction, n. [1. rèkonstrúkshun ; 2. rìkənstrákʃən]. Prec. & **-ion. a** Act of reconstructing ; **b** something reconstructed.

reconstructive, adj. [1. rèkunstrúktiv ; 2. rìkənstráktiv]. **reconstruct** & **-ive.** Tending to reconstruct ; aiding in reconstruction.

reconversion, n. [1. rèkonvérshun ; 2. rìkənvə́ʃən]. **re-** & **conversion.** Act of reconverting ; state of being reconverted.

reconvert, vb. trans. [1. rèkonvért ; 2. rìkənvə́t]. **re-** & **convert. a** To convert back again to original religion, set of opinions &c. ; **b** to change back into original form.

record (I.), vb. trans. & intrans. [1. rekórd ; 2. rikɔ́d]. M.E. *recorden*, 'to repeat, bring to mind ', fr. O. Fr. *recorder*, 'to repeat, report ', fr. Lat. *recordāri*, 'to think over, to call to mind, to remember ', fr. **re-** & **cord-**, stem of *cor*, 'heart, mind ', see **cordate. A.** trans. **1.** To set down in writing, inscribe, make a note of, keep a permanent record of : *to record a speech* ; *to record the date of a birth in the family Bible.* **2.** To give a written account of, write descriptive narrative of : *to record one's thoughts and experiences in a diary.* **3.** To preserve permanent record : **a** (of sounds) *the gramophone records the sounds of the human voice* ; **b** (of visual images) *the brush of the painter and the camera record the features of persons long dead.* **B.** intrans. To make, keep, a record, or records.

record (II.), n. [1. rékord; 2. rékɔ̄d]. O. Fr. See prec. **1.** A written note; fact recorded; account, narrative, of events: *the records of the past; a man's fame soon passes from record and recollection.* Phrs. *a matter of record,* a fact duly recorded and thus authenticated; *on record,* recorded, remembered and proved as having taken place: *to bear record to,* testify to the truth of (facts &c.); *to have a good, bad, record,* to have such and such a character and reputation based on known and recorded facts. **2. a** An authenticated, official document containing an account of acts, events, or proceedings, public or private, written down at the time they occurred; *Court of Record,* a court, the evidence of whose records duly enrolled cannot be disputed: *the High Court of Judicature is a superior, the County Court an inferior, Court of Record;* (more specif.) **b** a public, official document of State acts, proceedings &c. as preserved in the Record Office, in the charge of the Master of the Rolls or in various Government departments: *the Public Records; the records of the India, Foreign, Office* &c. **3.** Any pictorial or plastic representation of persons, objects, events &c., considered as illustrating and giving information about past history: *the records of mediaeval life in the British Museum; the records of the illustrious dead in the National Portrait Gallery.* **4. a** A series of indentations made upon a cylinder or disk of wax, vulcanite &c., by a needle or other point caused to vibrate by sound-waves produced by the voice, by a musical instrument &c., and capable of reproducing these sounds on the phonograph or gramophone; **b** such a cylinder, disk &c.

recorder, n. [1. rekórder; 2. rikɔ́də]. **record** (I.) & **-er**; cp. O. Fr. *recordeur.* **1. a** One who records or sets down, for purpose of remembrance; specif., **b** the principal judicial official, for civil and criminal matters, of certain cities or boroughs having a Court of Quarter Sessions; *the Recorder of London* is a Judge of the Central Criminal Court. **2.** Any of various mechanical devices for recording sounds, electric currents &c.; e.g. one attached to a phonograph for making records, or to a telephone for sending signals &c. **3.** (mus.) An ancient species of flageolet or pipe.

recordership, n. [1. rekórdership; 2. rikɔ́dəʃip]. Prec. & **-ship.** Office, rank, of a recorder; period of office of a recorder.

recording, adj. [1. rekórding; 2. rikɔ́diŋ], fr. Pres. Part. of **record** (I.). Keeping a record, registering: *recording telegraph, telephone* &c. *Recording angel,* angel who keeps a record of all the deeds, good and evil, of men while in this life.

recount, vb. trans. [1. rekóunt; 2. rikáunt], fr. O. Fr. *reconter,* 'to tell again, relate'. See **re-** & **count** (I.). To narrate, give an account of.

re-count, vb. trans. & n. [1. rē kóunt; 2. rī káunt]. **1.** vb. To count over again, count a second time; esp. to count over again the votes given, for both candidates, at an election, when the accuracy of the first counting is challenged. **2.** n. A second counting of votes at an election.

recoup, vb. trans. [1. rekóōp; 2. rikúp], fr. Fr. *recouper,* 'to cut again or back', in O. Fr. also 'to lessen, diminish'; fr. **re-** & *couper,* 'to cut', see **coup** & **coppice.** **1.** (law) To keep back part of something due; to deduct from what is claimed by a counterclaim. **2.** To compensate, indemnify, reimburse, recover: *to recoup a person for loss or damage; to recoup oneself at another's expense; to try to recoup losses by speculation.*

recoupment, n. [1. rekóōpment; 2. rikúpmənt]. Prec. & **-ment.** **a** Act of recouping; **b** that which is recouped.

recourse, n. [1. rekórs; 2. rikɔ́s]. Fr. *recours,* fr. Lat. *recursus,* 'a running back, return'. **re-** & **course** (I.). **1.** Resort, resorting to another person or to some object for assistance &c.; application for help: *to have recourse to money-lenders; his last recourse will be to join his old party.* **2.** (rare) Person to whom, object to which, recourse is had. Phr. *without recourse,* (commerc. law) translation of French *sans recours,* protecting words added by the indorser of a bill of exchange against liability to subsequent holders.

recover (I.), vb. trans. & intrans. [1. rekúver; 2. rikávə], fr. O. Fr. *recovrer, recuvrer,* Mod. Fr. *recouvrer,* fr. Lat. *recuperāre,* see **recuperate.** **A.** trans. **1.** To get, win back, regain what has been lost, damaged, or destroyed; **a** (of material things) *to recover stolen property, a lost umbrella;* **b** (of non-material things) *to recover the friendship, esteem &c. of another.* **2.** To regain possession, power, control, over, use of: **a** (material objects) *to recover a conquered town, a lost throne; to recover land from the encroachment of the sea* &c.; *to recover one's oar,* &c., after dropping it; **b** (of mental or bodily faculties) *to recover consciousness, one's senses; to recover one's health, sight, voice, power of walking, control of one's temper.* **3.** To discover again: *to recover a lost art or skill, forgotten knowledge* &c. **4.** To regain (a position, place &c.); **a** (in physical sense) *to recover one's seat on a horse; to recover oneself after a stumble or fall; to recover one's balance.* Phr. (fencing) *to recover a sword,* bring it back to defensive position after thrusting; **b** (in non-material sense) *he has recovered his old ascendancy with his party, his reputation as an artist* &c. **5.** (archaic) To bring back to life, strength, vigour, or health: '*From death to life thou might'st him yet recover*' (Drayton). **6. a** To retrieve, make up for, win back as compensation: *to recover one's losses by hard work; to recover time wasted or lost;* specif. **b** (law) to gain as compensation or return for injury, debt &c.: *to recover damages.* **B.** intrans. **1.** (absol. or with *from*) **a** To regain, get back to a condition, state, position &c. which has been lost, injured &c.: *to recover from a defeat, disaster, fall, or stumble;* **b** to get well again, to regain health, strength &c.: *to recover from sickness, a particular disease, accident* &c.; *the patient has recovered very quickly;* **c** (fencing) to come back to defensive position after thrusting. **2.** (law) To gain a judgement, obtain redress, damages, compensation in a law suit: *the client was advised that he could not recover.*

recover (II.), n., fr. prec. **a** Act of recovering or drawing back a sword or other weapon to its original position after a thrust or point; **b** position of sword &c. so recovered: *at the recover.*

re-cover, vb. trans. [1. rē kúver; 2. rī kávə]. **re-** & **cover** (I.). To put a new cover upon: *to re-cover an armchair with new cretonne* &c.; *to have an old umbrella re-covered.*

recoverable, adj. [1. rekúverabl; 2. rikávərəbl]. **recover** (I.) & **-able.** Capable of being recovered (in various senses of verb).

recovered, adj. [1. rekúverd; 2. rikávəd], fr. P.P. pass. of **recover** (I.). Restored to health after sickness &c.: *I am now completely recovered.*

recovery, n. [1. rekúveri; 2. rikávəri], cp. O. Fr. *recouvree.* See **recover** (I.) & **-y.** Act of recovering or regaining; **a** the regaining possession of what has been lost: *recovery of stolen property; recovery of land from the sea; recovery of lost influence* &c.; **b** regaining of balance of original position &c.: *recovery from a fall or stumble; recovery of a sword* (in fencing), *oar* (in rowing) &c.; **c** regaining of, restoration to, health, strength &c.: *recovery from an illness; to make a quick recovery;* **d** (law) the obtaining of a thing, right, damages &c., by verdict and judgement in court of law; *collusive or feigned recovery,* fictitious action, abolished 1833, by which a tenant in tail changed his estate into fee-simple and so barred the entail.

recreancy, n. [1. rékreansi; 2. rékriənsi]. See next word & **-cy.** State, quality, of being recreant; apostasy; cowardice.

recreant, adj. & n. [1. rékreant; 2. rékriənt]. O. Fr., Pres. Part. of *recroire,* 'to change one's faith; acknowledge one's self beaten in a duel', fr. L. Lat. *recrēdere,* in same sense, fr. **re-** & *crēdere,* 'to believe', see **creed.** **1.** adj. Forswearing, false to, one's principles, vows &c.; hence traitorous, apostate. **2.** n. An apostate.

recreate, vb. trans. & intrans. [1. rékreāt; 2. rékrieit], fr. Lat. *recreāt-(um),* P.P. type of *recreāre,* 'to create, make anew, to revive, refresh', fr. **re-** & *creāre,* see **create.** **1.** trans. **a** (unusual) To revive, refresh after exertion, work, anxiety &c.: *change of occupation recreates one; to recreate oneself with a hobby, by a holiday* &c.; **b** (rare) to amuse, entertain, divert, provide recreation, relaxation for. **2.** intrans. **a** (rare) To recreate oneself, to relax after work &c.; **b** to indulge in recreation, amuse, entertain oneself.

re-create, vb. trans. [1. rē kreāt; 2. rī kriéit]. **re-** & **create.** To create afresh.

recreation, n. [1. rèkreāshun; 2. rèkriéiʃən], fr. Lat. *recreātiōn-(em),* 'a recovery from illness'. See **recreate** & **-ion.** Act of recreating, reviving, or refreshing; specif., that which recreates, revives &c.; relaxation, amusement, entertainment; play, a game, sport, pastime, diversion. *Recreation ground,* an open space set apart for the playing of games &c.

re-creation, n. [1. rē kreāshun; 2. rī kriéiʃən]. **re-** & **creation.** Act of re-creating; a fresh, new, creation.

recreative, adj. [1. rékreātiv; 2. rékrieitiv]. **recreate** (I.) & **-ive.** Serving to recreate, revive, or refresh; serving to provide recreation; entertaining, enlivening.

recrement, n. [1. rékrement; 2. rékrimənt], fr. Lat. *recrēmentum,* 'refuse, dross', of ores, wheat &c.; **re-,** & see second element in **excrement** & words there referred to. (rare) **1.** Refuse, dross, waste, or superfluous matter of ore &c. **2.** (physiol.) A substance secreted by an organ from the blood, as saliva, bile &c., and absorbed again.

recriminate, vb. intrans. & trans. [1. rekríminǡt; 2. rikrímineit], fr. L. or Med. Lat. *recrīmināt-(um),* P.P. type of *recrīmināre,* 'to make counter accusations or charges against', fr. **re-** & Lat. *crīmināre,* 'to accuse, charge', fr. *crīmin-,* stem of *crīmen,* 'accusation, charge', see **crime.** **1.** intrans. To make counter-charges; to retort with an accusation or charge. **2.** trans. (obs. or rare) To accuse an accuser; to make a counter-charge against.

recrimination, n. [1. rekrìmināshun; 2. rikrìminéiʃən]. Prec. & **-ion.** Cp. Fr. *récrimination.* Act of recriminating; counter-charge, accusation brought by accused person against accuser.

recriminative, adj. [1. rekríminativ; 2. rikríminətiv]. See prec. & **-ive.** Recriminatory.

recriminatory, adj. [1. rekríminaturi; 2. rikríminət(ə)ri]. **recriminate** & **-ory.** Of the nature of, consisting of, characterized by, recrimination.

recross, vb. trans. [1. rèkráws; 2. rìkrɔ́s]. **re-** & **cross** (II.). To cross (over) again, to return across: *to recross a road; to cross and recross.*

recrudesce, vb. intrans. [1. rèkrōōdés; 2. rìkrūdés], fr. Lat. *recrūdescere,* 'to become raw again, to break out afresh', fr. **re-** & *crūdescere,* 'to grow, become, worse, violent', fr *crūdus,* 'raw, bleeding', see **crude.** **1.** (of wounds, sores, diseases &c.) To break out afresh, to renew itself with equal or greater violence after temporary healing or cessation. **2.** (fig., of violence, crime, vice &c.) To break out afresh, to become active again, to revive.

recrudescence, n. [1. rèkrōōdésens; 2. rìkrūdésəns]. See next word & **-ce.** Fresh outbreak, renewed severity, activity; **a** of wound, disease &c.; **b** of crime, violence, unrest, vice &c.

recrudescent, adj. [1. rèkroodésent; 2. rīkrūdésənt], fr. Lat. *recrūdescent-(em)*, Pres. Part. of *recrūdescere*. See **recrudesce**. Tending to recrudesce, in process of recrudescing.

recruit (I.), n. [1. rekrōōt; 2. rikrūt], fr. obs. Fr. *recrute*, 'levy, reinforcement'; a provinc. form of P.P. of *recroître*, 'to grow again, to increase' &c., used as n., fr. **re-** & *croître*; O. Fr. *creistre*, 'to grow', is fr. Lat. *crescere*, 'to grow', see **crescent**. **1.** A newly enlisted soldier or sailor, in the early stages of training. **2.** (fig.) **a** One who has recently joined a party, cause, corporate body &c.; a new member, a novice, tiro; esp. *new recruit*; **b** also with specific sense of additional member, adherent &c.; *to gain but few recruits to one's party*.

recruit (II.), vb. trans. & intrans., fr. Fr. *recruter*, 'to raise, levy troops', fr. obs. *recrute*. See prec. **A.** trans. **1. a** To enlist (persons) for the army or navy; **b** to obtain a supply of recruits for: *to recruit a regiment*. **2.** To enrol as supporters, members, for: *to recruit a party, society, cause* &c. **3. a** To repair, to supply the want, loss of; to restore, reinvigorate, refresh: *to recruit one's health, strength* &c.; **b** to add to, increase: *to recruit one's numbers*. **B.** intrans. **1. a** To enlist soldiers or sailors; to obtain recruits; **b** to enrol, gain, new supporters or members. **2.** To gain or seek to gain new health, strength &c.: *you must take a holiday and try to recruit*.

recruital, n. [1. rekrōōtal; 2. rikrūtəl]. Prec. & **-al**. **a** Recruiting, enlistment; **b** new supply of health and strength.

recruiting sergeant, n. [1. rekrōōting sàrjent; 2. rikrūtiŋ sádžənt]. Sergeant entrusted with the task of obtaining recruits for a particular regiment.

recruitment, n. [1. rekrōōtment; 2. rikrūtmənt]. **recruit (II.)** & **-ment**. **a** Act, process, of recruiting men for army or navy; **b** act, process, of recruiting, recovering health.

rectal, adj. [1. réktal; 2. réktəl]. See **rectum** & **-al**. Of, pertaining to, the rectum.

rectangle, n. [1. réktànggl; 2. réktæŋgl], fr. Lat. *rectus*, 'right', see **rectum**, & **angle (I.)**. L. Lat. has *rectiangulus*, 'right-angled'. A plane four-sided figure whose angles are all right angles; a right-angled parallelogram.

rectangled, adj. [1. réktanggld; 2. réktæŋgld]. Prec. & **-ed**. Having one or more right angles; rectangular.

rectangular, adj. [1. rektánggūlar; 2. rektǽŋgjulə]. See prec. & **-ar**, on anal. of **angular**. Right-angled, having one or more right angles; square.

rectangularity, n. [1. rèktanggūláriti; 2. rèktæŋgjulǽriti]. Prec. & **-ity**. Quality, state, of being rectangular.

rectangularly, adv. [1. rektánggūlarli; 2. rektǽŋgjuləli]. See prec. & **-ly**. In rectangular form; at right angles.

rectifiable, adj. [1. réktifīabl; 2. réktifaiəbl]. **rectify** & **-able**. Capable of being rectified.

rectification, n. [1. rèktifikáshun; 2. rèktifikéiʃən]. See **rectify** & **-fication**. **1. a** Act of rectifying or putting right or straight; correction; *rectification of errors, abuses, of an injustice* &c.; *rectification of a frontier or boundary line*; **b** something which has been rectified. **2.** (chem.) The purifying, refining, of spirits by repeated distillation. **3.** (geom.) The determination of a straight line equal to some portion of a curve.

rectifier, n. [1. réktifīer; 2. réktifaiə]. **rectify** & **-er**. One who, that which, rectifies; applied to various mechanical devices, as **a** (elect.) a commutator, valve, or other apparatus which converts an alternating into a direct current; **b** (naut.) instrument for determining and rectifying variations of the compass.

rectify, vb. trans. [1. réktifī; 2. réktifai], fr. Fr. *rectifier*, fr. L. Lat. *rectificāre*, 'to make straight, correct', fr. Lat. *rectus*, 'straight, right'. See **rectum** & **-fy**. **1. a** To make straight, put right, correct, amend: *to rectify errors, anomalies* &c.; *to rectify a miscarriage of justice*; *to rectify a frontier, boundary line* &c.; **b** to set right, remedy, cure: *to rectify abuses, state of disorder, complaints*. **2.** (chem.) To purify, refine, get rid of coarser elements by repeated distillation; esp. alcohol, spirits, ether, volatile oils &c. **3.** (elect.) To transform by a rectifier an alternating into a direct current. **4.** (geom.) To determine, find, a straight line equal to a part of a curve. **5.** (mechan.) To adjust movement, balance &c. of: *to rectify a chronometer, globe* &c.

rectilineal, adj. [1. rèktilíneal; 2. rèktilíniəl]. See next word & **-al**. Rectilinear.

rectilinear, adj. [1. rèktilínear; 2. rèktilíniə], fr. Low Lat. *rectiline-(us)*, fr. Lat. *rectus*, 'straight, right', see **rectum**, & *līnea*, see **line (II.)**, & **-ar**. In a straight line; forming a straight line; formed, bounded, by straight lines: *rectilinear angle*; *rectilinear plan, motion* &c.; *rectilinear figure*.

rectilinearity, n. [1. rèktilineáriti; 2. rèktiliniǽriti]. Prec. & **-ity**. State, quality, of being rectilinear.

rectilinearly, adv. [1. rèktilínearli; 2. rèktilíniəli]. See prec. & **-ly**. By straight lines, in a straight line.

rectitude, n. [1. réktitūd; 2. réktitjūd]. Fr., fr. L. Lat. *rectitūdo*, 'straightness, uprightness', fr. *rectus*, 'straight, right'. See **rectum** & **-tude**. Conformity with high moral principles in conduct and character; probity, integrity.

recto, n. [1. réktō; 2. réktou]. Lat., abl. sing. of *rectus*, 'right', in phr. *recto folio*, 'on the right leaf or page'. See **rectum**. The right-hand page of a book when opened; the front of a sheet or leaf of paper; opposed to *verso*.

rector, n. [1. rékter; 2. réktə]. Lat., 'ruler, leader, director', fr. *rect-(um)*, P.P. of *regere*, 'to rule, guide, direct', see **regent** & **-or**; in L. Eccles. Lat., 'a ruler of the church', applied to bishops, abbots, and priests. **1.** (eccles., Engl. Ch.) A parish priest, being the incumbent of a benefice, to whom the great tithes are paid; dist. from *vicar*. *Lay rector*, a layman holding the great tithes of a benefice, which at suppression of the monasteries were often granted by the Crown to laymen. **2.** (educ.) **a** Title of the head of a German university (*Rector Magnificus*); **b** title of headmaster, or principal, of various schools and colleges in Scotland; **c** title of the headmaster of various Roman Catholic schools and colleges in Great Britain, esp. of Jesuit and Benedictine schools: *Rector of Downside*; **d** title of the heads of Exeter and Lincoln Colleges at Oxford University; **e** *Lord Rector*, title of the elected president of a Scottish university, corresponding to the English *Chancellor*.

rectorate, n. [1. rékturit; 2. réktərit]. L. Eccles. Lat. *rectorātus*. See prec. & **-ate**. Office, status, position, of a rector; rectorship.

rectorial, adj. [1. rektórial; 2. rektɔ́riəl]. **rector** & **-ial**. Pertaining to a rector: *rectorial tithes*, the tithes payable to a rector.

rectorship, n. [1. réktership; 2. réktəʃip]. **rector** & **-ship**. **a** Office, status, position of a rector; **b** benefice held by a rector; rectorate; **c** period of the office of rector.

rectory, n. [1. rékturi; 2. réktəri], fr. Med. Eccles. Lat. *rectoria*. See **rector** & **-y**. **a** Benefice, incumbency, of a rector; **b** the clergyman's house in a parish, the incumbent of which is a rector; a rector's house, as contrasted with *vicarage*.

rectress, rectoress, n. [1. rékt(o)res; 2. rékt(ə)ris]. **rector** & **-ess**. **a** The woman head of a college or school; **b** (facet.) a rector's wife.

rectrix, n. [1. réktriks; 2. réktriks]. Lat., fem. of **rector**. (ornith.) One of the quill feathers in the tail of a bird.

rectum, n. [1. réktum; 2. réktəm]. Lat. *rectum intestīnum*, neut., 'the straight intestine', fr. *rectus*, 'straight, upright; correct, right, proper; good; virtuous'; fr. *rect-(um)*, P.P. type of *regere*, 'to stretch, lead in straight line; to conduct, direct, rule' &c.; for base **rĕg-*, see **regent, rex**; cogn. w. **right (I.)**. Lowest, terminal part of the large intestine; actually the last few inches of this forming the exit of the alimentary canal.

recumbency, n. [1. rekumbensi; 2. rikámbənsi]. **recumbent** & **-cy**. State of being recumbent; recumbent position.

recumbent, adj. [1. rekúmbent; 2. rikámbənt]. Lat. *recumbent-(em)*, Pres. Part. of *recumbere*, 'to lie back, down, to recline', fr. **re-** & a nasalized variant of base **cub-*, as in *cubāre*, 'to lie, recline', see **cubicle**. Lying, leaning back or down; reclining.

recumbently, adv. Prec. & **-ly**. In a recumbent manner or position.

recuperability, n. [1. rekûperabíliti; 2. rikjûpərəbíliti]. See next word & **-ity**. Capacity of recuperation, ability to recuperate.

recuperable, adj. [1. rekûperabl; 2. rikjûpərəbl]. See next word & **-able**. (obs.) Able to recuperate; recoverable.

recuperate, vb. trans. & intrans. [1. rekûperāt; 2. rikjûpəreit], fr. Lat. *recuperāt-(um)*, P.P. of *recuperāre*, 'to recover', prob. a variant of *recipere*. See **receive** & cp. **recover**. **A.** trans. **1. a** To recover, regain, restore (health &c.); **b** *to recuperate a person*, restore him to health. **2.** To recover, regain (financial loss). **B.** intrans. **1.** To recover one's health &c.: *to recuperate after illness*. **2.** To recover from financial losses.

recuperation, n. [1. rekûperáshun; 2. rikjûpəréiʃən], fr. Lat. *recuperātiōn-(em)*. See prec. & **-ion**. Act, process, of recuperating.

recuperative, adj. [1. rekûperativ; 2. rikjûpərətiv], fr. Lat. *recuperātīvus*. **recuperate** & **-ive**. Promoting recuperation.

recur, vb. intrans. [1. rekĕr; 2. riká́], fr. Lat. *recurrere*, 'to run back, return, recur', **re-** & *currere*, 'to run', see **current** & **courier**. **1. a** To return (to), in mind or expression; to advert again (to): *to recur to past experiences, memories* &c.; *I shall recur to the subject later on*; **b** (of a thought, idea) to return to one's mind: *his former mistake recurred to him in time*. **2. a** To come up once more, manifest itself again: *this question, difficulty, problem &c. is bound to recur*; **b** to occur, appear, again, to be repeated: *certain fevers recur at regular intervals*; *steps have been taken so that the accident can never recur*; **c** (math.) to repeat itself indefinitely in a fixed series of numbers: *recurring decimals*.

recurrence, n. [1. rekúrens; 2. rikárəns]. See next word & **-ce**. **1.** Act or process of recurring; state, condition, of being recurrent; a return: *recurrence of an epidemic*; *one of the characteristics of malaria is its recurrence*. **2.** (rare) Resort, recourse; in Phr. *to have recurrence to*.

recurrent, adj. [1. rekúrent; 2. rikárənt], fr. Lat. *recurrent-(em)*, Pres. Part. of *recurrere*. See **recur**. **1.** Recurring, returning, occurring again or repeatedly or periodically: *a recurrent fever*. **2.** (anat.) **a** Turning back in the opposite direction, having a reflex course: *recurrent nerve, artery, vein*; **b** (ellipt. as n.), one of the two recurrent nerves of the larynx.

recurrently, adv. Prec. & **-ly**. In a recurrent manner; repeatedly.

recursant, adj. [1. rekĕrsant; 2. rikásənt], fr. Lat. *recursant-(em)*, Pres. Part. of *recursāre*, freq., formed fr. *recurs-(um)*, P.P. type of *recurrere*. See **recur** & **recourse**. (her.) Of an eagle, represented with back towards the spectator as if flying away.

recurvate, adj. [1. rēkĕrvāt; 2. rīkáveit]. Lat. *recurvāt-(um)*, P.P. of *recurvāre*, see **recurve**, & **-ate**. (bot.) Bent backward, recurved, reflexed, of leaf or stem.

recurvature, n. [1. rēkĕrvachur; 2. rīkávətʃə]. Prec. & **-ure**. (bot.) A bending backwards.

recurve, vb. trans. & intrans. [1. rēkĕrv; 2. rīkáv]. **re-** & **curve**. **a** trans. To bend, curve, back; **b** intrans., to be curved, bent, back in an opposite direction.

recusancy, also obs. **recusance**, n. [1. rékūzans(i); 2. rékjuzəns(i)]. See next word & **-cy**. Act of refusing to obey; state of being a recusant; refusal to obey, esp. in matters of religion or religious conformity.

recusant, adj. & n. [1. rékūzant; 2. rékjuzənt]. Fr., fr. Lat. *recūsant-(em)*, Pres. Part. type of *recūsāre*, 'to object to, to decline, refuse', fr. **re-** & *causa*, see **cause** & second element of **accuse**. **1.** adj. Objecting, refusing, to obey, or to conform to laws, authority &c.; esp. in regard to matters of religion or religious conformity: *a recusant priest*. **2.** n. One who refuses to obey or conform to the religious ordinances of an Established Church; applied esp. to the Roman Catholics who refused to attend the services of the English (Reformed) Church in the 16th and 17th cents.

recuse, vb. trans. [1. rekúz; 2. rikjúz], fr. Lat. *recūsāre*. See prec. (obs.) To refuse to acknowledge, challenge authority of; esp. to refuse to recognize the authority or jurisdiction of an ecclesiastical judge or court.

red (I.), adj. [1. red; 2. red]. O.E. *rēad*, M.E. *rēd(e)*; O.S. *rōd*; O.H.G. *rōt*; Goth. *rauþs*; O.N. *rauðr*; cogn. w. Lat. *ruber* & *rūfus*, see **rubric** & **rufous**; Gk. *eruthrós*; Scrt. *rudhiraš*. See further **rouge, rudd, russet**. **1.** Having, being of, the colour red, see **red (II.)**; of a colour occurring in varying shades, in various objects and substances, such as rubies, raw beef, the sky at sunset, human lips, blood, iron rust, a full dress military tunic, a certain type of coppery, deep yellow hair, glowing embers &c. Phrs. *to see red*, go mad, be blinded, with rage; *to paint the town red*, indulge in drunken, rowdy, ruffianly conduct, esp. in public places; *paint the map red*, extend the British Empire; *red light*, signal of danger on railway &c., also fig. **2.** Specif. (polit.) **a** belonging, pertaining, to the revolutionary movement, connected with, in sympathy with, Communism, Anarchism, Bolshevism (this application is due to the colour chosen as distinguishing badge, e.g. the *red flag*): *the Red Army*, that of Soviet Russia; *the Labour Party appears to become more and more red as time goes on*; **b** (as n.) *the Reds*, revolutionaries, Communists. **3.** Various specific or idiomatic uses: *red eyes*, with red rims from inflammation &c., or having eyelids, or surrounding tissues, red, as from weeping &c.; *a red face, cheeks, complexion*, ruddy, sanguine, as from health or exposure to weather &c.; (*to become*) *red in the face*, inflamed, coloured by excessive flow of blood, as from exertion, violent emotion &c.; *red hands*, bloodstained; (fig.) blood-guiltiness; *red hair*, of a coppery or deep golden tinge. **4.** (as n.) A red object; specif. **a** the red ball in billiards: *to pot, play on to, the red*; **b** the red division, square &c. on roulette table or board: *to put one's stake on the red*; *the red wins*.

red (II.), n. See prec. **1.** A primary colour appearing at the lower end of the spectrum, varying in shade from vermilion through bluish crimson to the paler shades which are called *pink*. **2.** A pigment producing the colour red.

red-, pref. Variant of **re-**.

redact, vb. trans. [1. redákt; 2. ridékt], fr. Lat. *redact-(um)*, P.P. of *redigere*, 'to bring back, to collect, gather together, to reduce', fr. **red-** & *agere*, 'to bring, drive'; see **act** & **agent**. The current use is formed fr. **redaction**, rather than fr. Lat. To edit, arrange, reduce to proper form, for publication.

redaction, n. [1. redákshun; 2. ridékʃən]. Fr. *rédaction*; fr. Lat. *redact-(um)*, P.P. type of *redigere*, see prec., & **-ion**. **a** The arranging, editing, revision, of a work for publication; **b** a new or revised edition of a work.

redactor, n. [1. redákter; 2. ridéktə]. **redact** & **-or**, cp. Fr. *rédacteur*. Editor.

red admiral, n. A European and N. American butterfly, *Pyrameis Atalanta*, common in England, velvety, black and brown, with brilliant red bands and blue and white spots.

redan, n. [1. redán; 2. ridǽn]. Fr., for older *redent*, fr. **re-** & *dent*, 'tooth', see **dental**. (fort.) A field-work of two parapets forming a salient angle to the front with the gorge or rear open at the back, usually joined with other such works by a length of trenches &c.

red ant, n. Any ant of various species which are reddish in colour, as *Formica rufa*, the wood ant &c.

red-backed, adj. Having a red back; specif. in *red-backed shrike*, the butcher-bird, *Lanius collurio*.

red bark, n. Red Peruvian bark, a variety of cinchona.

red bird, n. Popular name of various birds, such as the cardinal bird, scarlet tanager &c.

red-blindness, n. Form of colour-blindness in which the colour red is confused with green.

red-book, n. Name of various books always or usually bound in red, as the official papers of the former Austro-Hungarian Empire, cp. *blue-book*; a directory or reference book, as a court guide, peerage &c. *The Red Book of the Exchequer, Liber ruber Scaccarii*, containing returns of the tenants in chief for the year 1166, compiled in the reign of Henry III.

red box, n. An official dispatch box used by members of the British Government for their papers.

redbreast, n. [1. rédbrest; 2. rédbrest]. The robin.

red button, n. The official button worn on the cap by Chinese mandarins of the first and second grade, the first wearing a transparent red stone, the second a red coral.

red cedar, n. A name used of various conifers with hard red wood, esp. the American or Virginian Juniper, *Juniperus virginiana*, used in fine carpentry or for the making of pencils; also the giant arbor vitae, *Thuja gigantea*, of California or N.-W. America; the Australian and Jamaican red cedars, *Cedrela Toona* and *C. odorata*, are allied to the mahoganies and are not conifers.

red cent, n. The old copper cent (coin) of the U.S.A.; only in colloq. Phrs. *not worth a red cent*; *don't care a red cent for* &c.

red-coat, n. A British soldier, so called from the scarlet tunic formerly worn on all occasions by most regiments of the army.

red corpuscles, n. pl. Those corpuscles in the blood-stream which contain haemoglobin and bring oxygen from the air into the system; singly they are yellowish in colour, being red only in mass; distinguished from the white corpuscles or leucocytes.

Red Crescent, n. The symbol used by Turkey as equivalent to the Christian *Red Cross* for medical organizations &c. for the sick and wounded in war.

Red Cross, n. **1.** A red cross on a white ground, St. George's Cross, the national emblem of England, the White Ensign of the Royal Navy, and embodied in the Union Jack. **2.** A similar cross as worn by Crusaders, granted by Pope Eugenius III. for the Second Crusade, and thus the special mark of Knights of the Order of the Temple. *The Red Cross Knight*, one of the principal characters in Spenser's 'Faërie Queene', hence a Crusader (hist. or fig.). **3.** **a** The similar emblem adopted at the Geneva Convention, 1864, for the International Societies organized for the treatment of the sick and wounded in war, and so borne by ambulances, hospitals, and all attached to such service; in origin it was the national Swiss flag with colours reversed as typical of neutrality; **b** any society organized for such service under the Geneva Convention: *the British, Belgian, Red Cross* (*Society*) &c.; *the Royal Red Cross*, British decoration for services in war granted to nurses.

red currant, n. A species of currant, *Ribes rubrum*, cultivated for its juicy, red, clustered fruit.

red deal, n. The wood, timber, sawn as 'deals', of the Scotch fir or Northern pine, *Pinus sylvestris*.

red deer, n. The largest species of British deer, *Cervus elaphus*, still surviving in its wild state in the Scottish highlands and on Exmoor.

redden, vb. trans. & intrans. [1. rédn; 2. rédn]. **red** & **-en**. **1.** trans. To make, cause to become, red. **2.** intrans. To become red; to blush, flush.

reddendum, n., pl. **reddenda** [1. redéndum, -da; 2. redéndəm, -də]. Lat., 'that which must be returned', neut. of *reddendus*, gerundive of *reddere*, 'to give back, return', fr. **red-** & *dare*, 'to give', see **date (I.)**. (law) The clause in a lease reserving the rent to the grantor.

reddish, adj. [1. rédish; 2. rédiʃ]. **red** & **-ish**. Rather, somewhat, red in colour; tinged with red.

reddle, n. & vb. trans. [1. rédl; 2. rédl]. Variant of **ruddle**.

rede (I.), n. [1. rēd; 2. rīd]. O.E. *rǣd*, 'counsel, advice'. See next word. (archaic) **a** Counsel, advice; **b** reason, judgement; **c** lot, fortune, destiny; **d** a tale, story; proverb, wise saying; **e** explanation, interpretation, as of dream &c.

rede (II.), vb. trans. O.E. *rǣdan*, 'to advise' &c. See **read (I.)**. (archaic) **a** To advise, counsel; **b** to interpret, explain.

Red Eagle, n. Title of the second order of knighthood of the former kingdom of Prussia.

redeem, vb. trans. [1. redém; 2. ridím], fr. Fr. *rédimer*, or direct fr. Lat. *redimere, redemptum*, 'to buy back, redeem', fr. **red-**, & *emere*, 'to buy, take'; see second element in **exempt**. **1.** To buy back, repurchase; **a** to regain possession by payment of a sum due or agreed: *to redeem a mortgage, mortgaged property*, after the mortgagee has come into possession; *to redeem pawned goods*; **b** to regain by physical or moral effort: *to redeem one's good name, honour* &c.; *to redeem one's ruined, conquered, country*. **2.** To clear, buy up or off, remove a charge or monetary obligation, esp. by a lump sum instead of making annual payments: *to redeem the tithes, a national debt*; *to redeem bonds, promissory notes* &c.; specif., *to redeem paper money, bank notes*, of the bank of issue or government, to pay for them in coin in order to take them out of circulation. **3.** To fulfil, perform: *to redeem a promise, obligation, duty*. **4.** **a** To make good; to atone for, make amends for: *to redeem an error, one's character*; **b** to counterbalance, make up for, a defect: *a charm of voice redeemed his uncouth appearance*. **5.** To ransom, to liberate, free from captivity &c.; to purchase the freedom of: *to redeem a prisoner, slave*; *to redeem oneself*; *to redeem a captured city, one's country from an indemnity*; specif. (theol., of God or Christ) to save, deliver, from the consequences of sin; to save from damnation.

redeemable, adj. [1. redémabl; 2. ridíməbl]. Prec. & **-able**. **1.** Able to be redeemed; capable of redemption or repurchase: *a redeemable pledge in pawn*; *redeemable paper currency, annuities, bonds* &c. **2.** (theol.) Capable of redemption from damnation by the agency of God or Christ.

redeemer, n. [1. redémer; 2. ridímə]. **redeem** & **-er**. One who redeems; specif. (cap.) *the Redeemer*, Jesus Christ; *Order of the Redeemer*, the highest order of knighthood of the kingdom of Greece.

redeless, adj. [1. rédles; 2. rídlis]. O.E. *rǣdlēas*. See **rede (I.)** & **-less**. (obs.) Without counsel, wisdom, prudence &c.; witless, helpless.

redeliver, vb. trans. [1. rèdelíver; 2. rìdilívə]. **re-** & **deliver**. To deliver (a letter, message &c.) again.

redemption, n. [1. redémpshun; 2. ridémpʃən], fr. Lat. *redemptiōn-(em)*, fr. *redempt-(um)*, P.P. type of *redimere*, see **redeem**, & **-ion**. **1.** Act of redeeming (in various senses of the vb.): *a redemption of an error, one's promise,* *of prisoners* &c.; *redemption of paper currency, bonds, tithes* &c.; **b** (law) *equity of redemption*, the right, by rules of equity, of a mortgagor to redeem his property from a mortgagee in possession; also the value of this right, being that of the property recovered less what has to be paid for redemption. **2.** Act of delivering, saving &c.; state of being saved; specif. **a** (theol., cap.) deliverance of mankind from sin and its consequences, by the atonement of Christ; salvation; **b** act of delivering, state of being emancipated, won, from evil courses; reformation, reclamation: *punishment should aim at the redemption of a prisoner*. Phr. *beyond, past, redemption*, beyond, past, hope of reform, or improvement, irreclaimable. **3.** That which redeems, a redeeming fact, feature &c.: *suffering proved his redemption*.

Redemptionist, n. [1. redémpshunist; 2. ridémpʃənist]. Prec. & **-ist**. A member of a religious order, called also *Trinitarians*, founded in the 12th cent. for the liberation of Christian captives from the Moslems.

redemptive, adj. [1. redémptiv; 2. ridémptiv]. Lat. *redempt-(um)*, P.P. of *redimere*, see **redeem**, & **-ive**. Redeeming; tending, serving, to redeem.

Redemptorist, n. [1. redémpturist; 2. ridémptərist], fr. Lat. *redemptor*, 'redeemer', & **-ist**. A member of a R.C. religious order, founded 1732 by St. Alfonso dei Liguori, for preaching to, and teaching, the poor and outcast.

red ensign, n. The red flag with the Union flag in the canton as flown by the British mercantile marine.

red-eye, n. The rudd (fish), also called *rock bass*.

red-eyed, adj. Having red eyes; having red rims to the eyes; having a red ring round eyes, as in popular names for certain birds, as *red-eyed fly-catcher, pochard*, or fishes, *red-eyed bass, perch* &c.

red fir, n. Popular name of various coniferous trees with reddish timber, as the Norway spruce, Douglas spruce, Scotch fir &c.

red-fish, n. Trade name for salmon, as contrasted with *white fish*.

red flag, n. A flag of a red colour. **1.** Flag used as a danger signal on railways, rifle-ranges &c. **2.** Specif., flag used as the symbol of revolution and as the international flag of Communists, Socialists &c. **3.** Name of a song, supposed to celebrate the future triumph of the proletariat in all countries, sung to the German tune, 'O Tannenbaum', and used by certain political parties instead of the National Anthem, or other patriotic songs.

red grouse, n. The chestnut-brown speckled grouse of the heather moors, *Lagopus scoticus*, only found in the British Isles, north of Derbyshire and Monmouth, and of a corresponding line in Ireland; it is the game bird usually referred to as 'grouse', without qualification, and does not turn white in winter.

red-gum, n. **1.** A rash which affects the gums of infants when teething. **2.** Any of various species of Australian eucalyptus from which a red-coloured resin or gum is extracted.

red hand, n. (her.) The device of a left hand displayed with the palm outwards, coloured red or gules, the arms of the Province of Ulster and granted by James I. as a badge to baronets of Great Britain and Ireland.

red-handed, adj. With hands red as if with blood, hence fresh from commission of a murder or other crime; having the stains, marks, of crime upon one. Phr. *to be caught red-handed*, in the act of crime.

red hat, n. A cardinal's hat, a broad-brimmed, low-crowned hat of cardinal red, with tassels, the symbol of a cardinal's office; presented by the Pope on appointment; represented in cardinal's coat of arms, and placed on his catafalque, and hung over his tomb at death.

red-head, n. **1.** Popular or local name for the widgeon. **2.** Person with red hair.

red-heat, n. The temperature at which iron &c. becomes red-hot.

red herring, n. A herring salted and smoke-cured to a reddish colour. Phrs. *neither fish, flesh, nor good red herring*, neither one thing nor the other; *to draw a red herring across the path*, to divert, distract attention from the main subject of discussion by introducing some irrelevant topic &c., from the use of a red herring in training foxhounds to follow a scent.

red-hot, adj. **1.** Heated to redness, red with heat. **2.** (fig.) Inflamed with passion, anger, enthusiasm; highly excited.

red-hot poker, n. Popular name of *Kniphofia*, or flame-flower, a garden liliaceous plant with tall, handsome spike of flame-coloured flowers.

redif, n. [1. rédif; 2. rédif]. Turk., fr. *radaf*, 'to follow'. A reservist of the Turkish army.

Red Indian, n. One of the copper-coloured aborigines of N. America; a redskin.

redingote, n. [1. rèdinggōt; 2. rèdiŋgóut]. Fr., corrupt. of Engl. *riding-coat*. A long, double-breasted, skirted overcoat; now used only of one worn by women.

redintegrate, vb. trans. [1. redíntegrāt; 2. redíntigreit], fr. Lat. *redintegrāt-(um)*, P.P. type of *redintegrāre*, 'to make whole again, restore', fr. **red-** & *integrāre*, 'to make whole', see **integrate** & **integer**. To make whole or united again; to restore to completeness or unity; to re-establish in perfect state.

redintegration, n. [1. rèdintegrāshun; 2. rèdintigréiʃən], fr. Lat. *redintegrātiōn-(em)*, 'renewal, restoration'. Prec. & **-ion**. Restoration to a whole, united, perfect state; renewal.

redirect, vb. trans. [1. rèdirékt; 2. rìdirékt]. **re-** & **direct**. To put a fresh address on a letter &c.; to readdress.

redirection, n. [1. rèdirékshun, rèdīrékshun; 2. rìdirékʃən, rìdairékʃən]. Prec. & **-ion**. **a** Act of redirecting; **b** new address written upon a letter &c.

red iron, n. Haematite.

rediscover, vb. trans. [1. rèdiskúver; 2. rìdiskávə]. **re-** & **discover**. To discover a second time; esp. to discover again something which has been forgotten or lost.

rediscovery, n. [1. rèdiskúveri; 2. rìdiskávəri]. Prec. & **-y**. A fresh discovery of something previously known, but subsequently lost or forgotten.

redistribute, vb. trans. [1. rèdistríbūt; 2. rìdistríbjūt]. **re-** & **distribute**. **1.** To distribute a second time, make a further distribution of. **2.** To distribute differently, to rearrange the distribution of, esp. in parliamentary sense, see below.

redistribution, n. [1. rèdistribúshun; 2. rìdistribjúʃən]. Prec. & **-ion**. **1.** A second or repeated distribution. **2.** A different distribution; specif., the rearrangement of the boundaries, areas, numbers of parliamentary constituencies, number of members &c. embodied in a *Redistribution Act*.

redistributive, adj. [1. rèdistríbūtiv; 2. rìdistríbjutiv]. See prec. & **-ive**. Tending to redistribute, having the power of redistributing.

redivide, vb. trans. & intrans. [1. rèdivíd; 2. rìdiváid]. **re-** & **divide**. **1.** trans. **a** To divide again; **b** to divide differently, to change the division of. **2.** intrans. To become redivided, to be split up repeatedly into several parts.

redivision, n. [1. rèdivízhun; 2. rìdivížən]. **re-** & **division**. **a** Act or process of re-dividing; **b** something redivided.

red lamp, n. The red light shown outside a doctor's house or chemist's shop at night; also as danger signal on railways at night.

red lane, n. Nursery Phr. *down the red lane*, (of something swallowed) down the throat.

red lead, n. Red oxide of lead, minium, used as a pigment, and, in plumbing, mixed with putty for making joints water-tight.

red-leg, n. Popular name of various birds with red legs.

red-legged, adj. Having red legs, of various birds, esp. *red-legged partridge, Caccabis rufa*, of Western Europe, the French partridge.

red-letter, adj. Marked by a red letter, as saint's day, and festival, in a calendar; *red-letter day*, **a** a saint's day, festival, so marked; **b** a day memorable for some joyful event, a day of happy memories or especially fortunate.

redly, adv. [1. rédli; 2. rédli]. **red (I.)** & **-ly**. With a red colour or appearance.

red man, n. A Red Indian, redskin.

Red Mass, n. (R.C. Ch.) A mass at which the liturgical vestments, appointed to be worn by the priest, are red; esp. a Mass held in England at the opening of a law term, attended by Roman Catholic judges and barristers.

red meat, n. Beef, mutton, as opposed to *white meat* such as pork, veal, or chicken.

red mullet, n. A marine fish, genus *Mullus*, with thin scales and of reddish colour, highly prized as a food fish, distinct from the grey mullet, *Mugil*.

red-necked, adj. [1. réd nekt; 2. réd nekt]. Having a red neck, esp. of various birds, as *red-necked grebe, phalarope* &c.

redness, n. [1. rédnes; 2. rédnis]. **red** & **-ness**. State, quality, of being red.

re-do, vb. trans. [1. rē dōō; 2. rì dū]. **re-** & **do**. To do over again.

red ochre, n. An earthy variety of haematite of a deep-red colour, used as a pigment; ruddle.

redolence, n. [1. rédolens; 2. rédələns]. Next word & **-ce**. Quality, state, of being redolent; fragrance, scent.

redolent, adj. [1. rédolent; 2. rédələnt], fr. Lat. *redolent-(em)*, Pres. Part. of *redolēre*, 'to emit a scent', **red-** & *olēre*, 'to smell'. See **olfactory** & **odour**. (usually followed by *of*) **1.** Having, emitting, a strong (pleasant) scent; fragrant: *spices redolent of the East*; *flowers redolent of springtime*. **2.** (fig.) Characterized by, strongly suggestive or reminiscent of; steeped in: *tales redolent of mystery, of ancient memories*.

redouble, vb. trans. & intrans. [1. redúbl; 2. ridábl], fr. Fr. *redoubler*. **re-** & **double**. **1.** trans. To increase in amount or intensity, intensify: *the crowd redoubled their applause*; *to redouble one's efforts*; *their fears were redoubled*. **2.** intrans. To become, grow, greater or more intense: *the noise, their fears, redoubled*.

re-double, vb. trans. [1. rē dúbl; 2. rì dábl], fr. prec. To double again; **a** to reduplicate, as of numbers, bets, in card-playing &c.; **b** to fold a second time, to refold.

redoubt, n. [1. redóut; 2. ridáut], fr. Fr. *redoute*, w. intrusive *b* fr. confusion w. next word; fr. Med. Lat. *reductus*, 'place to which to withdraw, a retreat', fr. *reduct-(um)*, P.P. of *redūcere*. See **reduce**. (fort.) A small, independent, enclosed outwork, used as a strong point in a chain of defensive works.

redoubtable, adj. [1. redóutabl; 2. ridáutəbl]. M.E. *redoutable*, fr. O. Fr. *redoutable*, in M. Fr. *redoubtable*, fr. Fr. *redouter*, 'to fear'. See **re-** & **doubt**. Formidable, dreaded; valiant: *a redoubtable antagonist*.

redoubted, adj. [1. redóuted; 2. ridáutid], fr. obs. vb. *redoubt*, 'to fear', see prec., & **-ed**. (archaic) Redoubtable.

redound, vb. intrans. [1. redóund; 2. ridáund], fr. Fr. *redonder*, 'to overflow, abound', fr. Lat. *redundāre*, in same sense. See **redundant**. (only in non-material senses) **1.** *Redound upon*, to react, recoil, upon: *these crimes will redound upon their authors*. **2.** *Redound to*, to result in, conduce, contribute to; to promote; esp. in such Phr. as, *to redound to a person's credit, advantage* &c.

red pepper, n. Cayenne pepper.

red pine, n. Name given to various conifers having reddish bark or timber, as *Pinus* *resinosa* of N. America, Australian cypress, the Douglas spruce &c.

redpoll, n. [1. rédpōl; 2. rédpòul]. **red** & **poll** (I.), 'head'. **1. a** A British song-bird, *Acanthis linaria*; closely related to the linnet, with reddish-brown plumage and crimson crown; **b** name given to the group to which this bird belongs. **2.** (pl.) A breed of red-haired, hornless cattle.

red rag, n. **1.** Anything which excites or inflames to fury, animosity; esp. in Phr. *a red rag to a bull.* **2.** Derisive name sometimes applied by loyalists to the *red flag* of the revolutionaries.

redress (I.), vb. trans. [1. redrés; 2. ridrés], fr. Fr. *redresser.* See **re-** & **dress**. **1.** To put straight again, to adjust, restore to former position, make good a deficiency in: *to redress the balance of.* **2.** To put, set, right; to remedy, rectify; repair; to make amends for: *to redress abuses, social evils*; *to redress a wrong, an injury.*

redress (II.), n., fr. prec. **1.** Act of redressing or remedying: *the redress of grievances is one of the chief functions of government.* **2.** Reparation, amends: *there should be no wrong without redress*; *for such injuries there is no adequate redress.*

re-dress, vb. trans. [1. rē drés; 2. rī drés]. **1.** To dress, clothe, oneself or others over again, or differently. **2.** To cleanse and bandage (a wound &c.) afresh; renew dressings on (wound &c.).

redresser, n. [1. redréser; 2. ridrésə]. **redress** & **-er**. One who redresses, remedies, repairs a wrong or injury.

red ribbon, n. **1. a** The ribbon of the Order of the Bath; **b** that of the Legion of Honour. **2. a** Membership of these orders; **b** the order itself.

red rot, n. A woody fungus infesting and very destructive to coniferous trees.

red rust, n. Fungoid disease of plants which appears in the form of reddish, rust-coloured patches on the leaves, causing them to dry up and fall off.

red sanders, n. [1. réd sáhnderz; 2. réd sándəz], fr. obs. *sanders*, fr. O. Fr. *sandre.* See **sandal-wood**. A dark red dye-wood obtained from an East Indian tree, also called red sandal-wood.

redshank, n. [1. rédshangk; 2. rédʃæŋk]. **red** & **shank**. An Old World shore bird, *Totanus calidris*, allied to the plovers, with brownish upper and white lower parts and bright orange-coloured legs and feet. Phr. *to run like a redshank*, run very fast.

red-short, adj. Of certain impure forms of iron, which become short, or brittle, when red-hot, opposed to *cold-short.*

redskin, n. [1. rédskin; 2. rédskin]. A North American Indian, red man.

red snow, n. Snow which is coloured bright red by masses of a minute alga, occurring in Arctic regions.

red spider, n. A minute web-spinning red mite, infesting greenhouses and gardens; esp. destructive to vines.

redstart, n. [1. rédstart; 2. rédstāt]. **red** & O.E. *steort*, 'tail'. See **stark-naked**. A migrating song-bird of Europe, Asia, and N. Africa, *Ruticilla phoenicurus*, allied to the thrushes; both sexes have a bright red tail, which is continually twitching or flirting; the cock bird has a black throat and chestnut breast and white patch on the forehead.

red tape, n. **1.** The red or pinkish tape with which documents, esp. in Government offices, are tied into bundles. Hence **2. a** Pedantic methods, excessive adherence to official rules and formalities and routine, involving unnecessary delays and difficulties in getting business done; **b** also attributively: *red-tape pedantry, system, habits* &c. *Red-tapery, red-tapism*, pedantic system or habits in performance of business; *red-tapist*, one who practices methods of red tape.

reduce, vb. trans. [1. redús; 2. ridjús], fr. Lat. *redūcere*, 'to bring, lead, back; to bring to some form or shape; to reduce', fr. **re-** & *dūcere*, 'to lead', see **duct** & **duke**. The original (Lat.) sense of bringing back to former state or position is almost lost; most of the senses now imply diminution, abbreviation, deprivation, inferiority &c. **1.** (med.) *To reduce a dislocation*, to replace dislocated joint in its normal position; *to reduce a swelling*, cause it to become smaller. **2.** To convert into another (simpler) form; to break up, break down: *to reduce a compound to its elements*; *to reduce to a pulp*; also in non-material sense, to simplify, to remove complexities: *to reduce a statement to plain terms*; *to reduce an argument to its simplest form.* Phr. *to reduce to an absurdity*, to render absurd, to leave nothing (in a sentence, plan, line of action) but absurdity. **3.** To bring (person) to a specified state, as of mind, of behaviour &c.: *to reduce to terror, to tears, silence*; *to reduce to submission.* **4.** To bring (ideas, objects, affairs) into a specified condition; to dispose, arrange, in a certain way: *to reduce to order, to an orderly arrangement*; *to reduce to chaos, to a system.* **5.** To cut down, diminish, lessen; **a** in quantity or amount, number, price, weight, bulk &c.: *to reduce one's expenditure, income* &c.; *to reduce prices, the price, value, of*; *to reduce supplies, production*; *to reduce the size of* &c.; **b** in duration: *to reduce the length of a lecture, term of imprisonment*; **c** in extent, length, height, space: *to reduce the distance between two points*; *to reduce the length of a skirt*; **d** in intensity: *to reduce the temperature*; *to reduce pain, pressure, speed* &c. **6. a** To lower in rank, position, worldly prosperity: *to reduce to the ranks, to the rank of private*; *to reduce to poverty*; Phr. *reduced circumstances*, poverty, impoverishment; *in reduced circumstances*, impoverished; **b** to bring to, place in, an inferior position, force to have recourse to makeshifts through deprivation, lack of resources &c.: *reduced to begging in the streets, to eating nothing but dry bread*; *reduced to reading by candlelight when the electric light goes wrong.* **7. a** To weaken, exhaust, impair bodily health or strength of; to render thin and emaciated: *greatly reduced by illness*; *to reduce the vitality of*; Phr. *reduced to nothing, to a skeleton*, become very thin; **b** to diminish power, effectiveness, of some bodily or mental faculty: *to reduce one's sight, power of vision, hearing, sense of smell, taste* &c.; *old age reduces one's power to remember names and figures.* **8.** In various technical and specific uses: **a** (arith.) to change the denomination or form of without alteration of value: *to reduce pounds to shillings and pence*; *to reduce fractions to a common denominator*; **b** (chem.) to remove the oxygen from, to deoxidize; to combine with or add hydrogen to; to convert to a metallic state by removing non-metallic elements; **c** (log.) to change the form (of a syllogism) from an imperfect to one of the perfect moods.

reducer, n. [1. redúser; 2. ridjúsə]. Prec. & **-er**. One who, that which, reduces, esp. applied to various contrivances, substances &c. used in metallurgy for reducing ores to metals &c., or in chemistry as reducing agents.

reducibility, n. [1. redùsibíliti; 2. ridjùsibíliti]. See next word & **-ity**. State, quality, of being reducible.

reducible, adj. [1. redúsibl; 2. ridjúsibl]. **reduce** & **-ible**. Capable of being reduced (in various senses of vb.); resolvable; capable of being diminished in number, size, weight, extent, intensity, strength &c.

reductio ad absurdum, n. [1. redúkshiō àd absérdum; 2. ridákʃiou æd æbsə́dəm]. Lat., fr. *reduct-(um)*, P.P. type of *redūcere*, see **reduce**, & **-ion**. Reduction to absurdity, a mathematical and logical method of proof and disproof; **a** the proof of a theory or proposition by assuming that the contrary is true and deducing an obviously absurd conclusion, a method often used in Euclid; **b** the disproof of a theory or proposition by deducing logically a conclusion which is obviously absurd, impossible, or contrary to truth and reason.

reduction, n. [1. redúkshun; 2. ridákʃən]. See prec. Act of reducing, state of being reduced; see senses of **reduce**; diminution, shortening, abbreviation.

reduit, n. [1. redwḗ; 2. redwí]. Fr. *réduit*, variant of *redoute*. See **redoubt**. (fort.) A small, enclosed work within a larger work, to be used as a keep or citadel for resistance and refuge when the main defences are carried.

redundance, -cy, n. [1. redúndans(i); 2. ridándəns(i)]. **redundant** & **-ce**, or **-cy**. **1.** State, quality, of being redundant, superfluous or in excess. **2.** That which is redundant; superfluity, excess.

redundant, adj. [1. redúndant; 2. ridándənt], fr. Lat. *redundant-(em)*, Pres. Part. of *redundāre*, 'to overflow'. See **re-** & **undulate**, & cp. **redound**. **1.** Exceeding what is necessary or useful; superfluous, excessive, unnecessary: *redundant words*, in a will, clause &c.; *a redundant style*, pleonastic. **2.** Superabundant, copious, plentiful, luxuriant: *redundant food, population* &c.

redundantly, adv. Prec. & **-ly**. In a redundant manner.

red underwing, n. [1. réd úndërwing; 2. réd ándəwiŋ]. Name of a British moth, having the lower wings scarlet bordered with black.

reduplicate, vb. trans. [1. redúplikāt; 2. ridjúplikeit], fr. L. Med. Lat. *reduplicāt-(um)*. See **re-** & **duplicate**. To redouble, to repeat; specif. (gram.) to repeat the first syllable in forming words, to form by reduplication, e.g. *ce-cī-di*, 'I struck, cut, killed', perf. of *caedere*. See also account of form **hight**.

reduplication, n. [1. redùplikáshun; 2. ridjùplikéiʃən]. Prec. & **-ion**. Act of reduplicating or repeating; something reduplicated; specif. (gram.) the repetition of the initial syllable, esp. in conjugation (see prec.).

reduplicative, adj. [1. redúplikativ; 2. ridjúplikətiv]. **reduplicate** & **-ive**. Tending to reduplicate; pertaining to, formed by, reduplication.

red-water fever, n. Texas fever, a disease of cattle caused by a blood parasite, *Piroplasma*, akin to the malaria parasite, conveyed by the cattle tick, a marked symptom of which is the red colour of the urine.

redwing, n. [1. rédwing; 2. rédwiŋ]. A species of thrush, a winter visitant of the British Isles, whose underwings are bright orange-red, and which has a conspicuous white streak above the eyes.

redwood, n. [1. rédwood; 2. rédwud]. A general term for various trees having reddish timber and yielding a red dye; specif., the Californian giant *Sequoia* or *Wellingtonia.*

re-dye, vb. trans. [1. rē dí; 2. rī dái]. **re-** & **dye**. To dye a second time.

ree, n. [1. rē; 2. rī]. Variant of **reeve**. The female of the ruff, sandpiper.

re-echo, vb. intrans. & trans. & n. [1. rē ékō; 2. rī ékou]. **re-** & **echo**. **1.** vb. To echo again, to resound, reverberate. **2.** n. A return echo, the echo of an echo.

reed (I.), n. [1. rēd; 2. rīd]. O.E. *hrēod*; O.S. *hriod*; O.H.G. *hriot*; apparently not found outside W. Gmc. **1. a** Any of various tall, jointed-stemmed grasses, growing in, or close to, the water, in marshes, or the borders of lakes, rivers &c.; esp. the common reed *Arundo phragmites*; **b** (coll.) a mass of growing reed, also dry reed or straw used for thatching; Phr. *a broken reed*, unreliable, untrustworthy person; something which fails one when relied on for support. **2.** A single hollowed stem of a reed; hence (poet.) **a** an arrow; **b** a shepherd's pipe made of a reed or straw with mouthpiece and finger-holes; **c** (by metonymy) pastoral poetry. **3.** Specific uses: **a** (archit., usually pl.) a small convex moulding generally grouped like a bundle of reeds; **b** (mus.) a vibrating tongue of split reed, cane, wood, or metal inserted in the mouthpiece of certain wind-instruments, known collectively as *reeds*, or *reed-wind*, in an orchestra, such as bassoon, oboe, clarinet, and saxophone; also a similar device in an organ-pipe, in the bag-pipes &c., where the wind is applied by pressure and not directly by the player's mouth; **c** (weaving) a part of a loom, formerly made of split reed or cane, now of wire, in the form of a comb, used to separate the warp threads and beat home the weft.

reed (II.), vb. trans., fr. prec. **1.** To thatch with reeds. **2.** To decorate with a reed moulding. **3.** To supply a musical instrument, as an organ, with reeds.

reed-babbler, n. The reed-warbler.

reed-buck, n. Cape Du. *riet bok*; **reed (I.)** & **buck (I.)**. A small South and Central African antelope of pale reddish colour, with bushy tail, and short horns.

reed-bunting, n. Also *reed sparrow*, **a** a small bird, nesting in reeds, with black head, white neck and under parts, and chestnut wings and upper parts; **b** the reedling or bearded titmouse.

reeded, adj. [1. rḗded; 2. rídid]. **reed (II.)** & **-ed.** Ornamented with reed moulding; having ridges and grooves.

re-edify, vb. trans. [1. rē édifī; 2. rī édifai]. **re-** & **edify.** **1.** (rare) To rebuild (house &c.). **2.** (rare) To restore, renew, revive (in spiritual sense).

reediness, n. [1. rḗdines; 2. rídinis]. **reedy** & **-ness.** Quality of being reedy.

re-edit, vb. trans. [1. rè édit; 2. rī édit]. **re-** & **edit.** To edit again; usually with modifications, corrections, additions &c.

re-edition, n. [1. rè edíshun; 2. rī edíʃən]. **a** Act of re-editing; **b** a new edition.

reedling, n. [1. rḗdling; 2. rídliŋ]. **reed (I.)** & **-ling.** The bearded titmouse.

reed-mace, n. A common tall marsh plant (*Typha latifolia*) with long flat leaves and flower growing in form of a thick round club or mace; it is one of the two different plants called bulrush.

reed-pipe, n. **a** A shepherd's pipe; **b** an organ-pipe provided with a reed.

reed-stop, n. A set of reed-pipes in an organ worked by a single stop.

reed-warbler, n. A small migratory bird, a warbler, *Acrocephalus streperus*, with brown plumage.

reedy, adj. [1. rḗdi; 2. rídi]. **reed (I.)** & **-y.** **1. a** Abounding in reeds: *a reedy marsh, lake* &c.; **b** (poet.) made of, consisting of, a reed: *the shepherd's reedy pipe*; **c** resembling a reed in shape, long and thin: *a reedy youth.* **2.** (of sound, voice) Thin, shrill, piping; lacking sonority.

reef (I.), n. [1. rēf; 2. rif]. Earlier form *riff*, borrowed in 17th cent. fr. Du. *ref*, *rif*; cp. Mod. Germ. *riff*, 'reef of rock', fr. same source; prob. cogn. w. O.N. *rīfa*, 'to split'; cp. **rive.** **1.** A ridge, shelf of rock or sand in an estuary, or off the seashore, near the surface of the water. **2.** (min.) A lode of gold-bearing quartz.

reef (II.), n. M.E. *riff*, prob. fr. O.N. *rif*, 'reef', cp. *rifa*, 'to fasten together'; cogn. w. Du. *reef*. Any one of the horizontal parts of a sail which can be taken in, rolled up, and made fast by short ropes, thus reducing the effective area of the sail. Phr. *to take in, shake out, a reef*, to shorten, increase, sail; also (fig.) allow oneself more, or less, freedom of action and latitude of conduct.

reef (III.), vb. trans., fr. prec. **1.** To reduce the area of (sail) by taking in one or more reefs. **2.** To lower part of a spar, as in a top-mast; to bring in-board part of the bow-sprit.

reef-band, n. A horizontal strip of canvas on a sail dividing the sail into reefs, giving it strength and furnished with eyelet holes for the reef-points.

reefer, n. [1. rḗfer; 2. rífə]. **reef (III.)** & **-er.** **1.** One who reefs, formerly a naval slang name for a midshipman. **2.** A double-breasted jacket of thick, usually blue cloth; also *reefer jacket.* **3.** A reef-knot.

reef-knot, n. A square double knot tied symmetrically, as used in tying the reef-points of a sail.

reef-point, n. One of the small pieces of rope arranged in rows across a sail at the reef-bands and passing through the eyelet holes when the sail is shortened.

reek (I.), n. [1. rēk; 2. rīk]. O.E. *rēc* fr. *rēac*, 'vapour', M.E. *rēke*; O.H.G. *rouh*; cogn. w. Lat. *ērūgere*, 'to eructate'; Gk. *ereúgomai*, 'I spit, vomit, out'. See **eructate.** **1.** (chiefly in liter. and Scots usage) Smoke, steam, vapour. **2.** Heavy, clinging, stale odour; fumes, stench: *the reek of a pothouse, of the slums*; *the reek of stale tobacco.*

reek (II.), vb. intrans. O.E. *rēocan*, 'to smoke, steam; to stink'; O.H.G. *riohhan*, 'to stink'; in gradational relation to O.E. *rēac*, 'smoke'. See prec. **1.** To emit smoke, vapour, steam; to smoke, steam: *reeking chimneys.* **2.** To emit vaporous fumes, as from a heated body &c.: *labourers reeking from their toil.* **3. a** To smell, stink: *his clothes reek of tobacco*; *the room reeks of stale beer*; also **b** (fig.) to be tainted, saturated: *to reek with snobbery, flattery*; *to reek of mystery.*

reeky, adj. [1. rḗki; 2. ríki]. **reek (I.)** & **-y.** Smoky, vaporous; cp. Scots *Auld Reekie*, colloquial name for Edinburgh.

reel (I.), n. [1. rēl; 2. rī(ə)l]. O.E. *hrēol*; only found in Engl., not cogn. w. O.N. *hræll*, 'a weaver's sley'. **1. a** A small wooden cylinder, spool or bobbin, round which cotton or silk thread is wound for use in sewing; **b** quantity of yarn, thread &c. wound on a reel; **c** larger cylinder upon which wire, rubber tubing, cables &c. are wound. **2. a** Small revolving cylinder with a short handle, fastened to a fishing-rod, upon which the line is wound, and by means of which the latter is controlled, being lengthened or shortened as required; Phr. *off the reel*, straight off, in quick, uninterrupted succession, without a break or hitch; **b** similar device for winding and unwinding the log line on board ship.

reel (II.), vb. trans., fr. prec. **1. a** To wind (silk, cotton &c.) on to a reel; **b** *reel in, reel up*, to wind in (line or fish) on a reel; **c** *reel off*, to allow to run off a reel by unwinding. Phr. *to reel off*, to rattle off, recite rapidly, volubly, fluently (a story, series of names). **2.** (of insects) To make a whirring, clicking sound like the reel of a fishing-rod.

reel (III.), vb. intrans. Prob. fr. **reel (I.)**. **1. a** To stagger in one's gait, to walk as though one had lost one's balance, and the control of one's limbs; to walk unsteadily, like a drunken man; also *reel about, go reeling about*, stagger about; **b** to stagger suddenly, lose one's equilibrium while standing, as from a sudden and violent blow. Phrs. *one's brain reels*; *enough to make one's brain reel*, (i.) in reference to result of a physical jar, or sudden blow; (ii.) in reference to feeling of giddiness experienced when looking down from great height &c.; (iii.) (fig.) in reference to result of a moral, or emotional shock, as of surprise, wonder, or the like. **2. a** (of solid, or firmly fixed objects) To be suddenly shaken, be made to rock, tremble, and oscillate: *the huge oak, the house, reeled as the hurricane struck it*; *both bodies of cavalry reeled from the shock of impact*; **b** (of a ship or other moving object) to go forward with an irregular motion suggestive of a staggering gait. **3.** (of subjective impression) To make the momentary impression on a person dizzy from a sudden physical shock, or having his mental balance upset by some sudden cause, of swaying and rocking: *everything reeled before his eyes.*

reel (IV.), n. & vb. intrans. Etymol. doubtful; cp. Gael. *righil*, but perh. a special sense of prec. The vb. is fr. the n. **1.** n. **a** A lively Scottish or Irish dance with elaborate figure steps, danced by couples who, however, for the most part, do not take hold of each other; *foursome reel*, one with two couples; *eightsome reel*, one with four couples; **b** music composed for such a dance. **2.** vb. To dance a reel.

re-elect, vb. trans. & intrans. [1. rḗ elékt; 2. rī ilékt]. **re-** & **elect.** **a** trans. To elect (the same person) again, to the same, or to another post; **b** intrans., to proceed to a re-election of either the same, or of another candidate.

re-election, n. [1. rḗ elékshun; 2. rī ilékʃən]. **re-** & **election.** A second, repeated election.

re-eligible, adj. [1. rè élijibl; 2. rī élidžibl]. **re-** & **eligible.** Eligible for re-election.

re-embark, vb. intrans. & trans. [1. rḗ embárk; 2. rī ɛmbák]. **re-** & **embark.** To embark again; **a** intrans., to go; **b** trans., to put, take (persons or goods) on board a second time.

re-embarkation, n. [1. rḗ embarkáshun; 2. rī ɛmbākéiʃən]. **re-** & **embarkation.** Act of re-embarking; process of being re-embarked.

re-emerge, vb. intrans. [1. rè emérj; 2. rī imə́dž]. **re-** & **emerge.** To emerge again.

re-emergence, n. [1. rè emérjens; 2. rī imə́džəns]. **re-** & **emergence.** Act of re-emerging; a second, repeated, emergence.

reen, n. See **rhine.**

re-enable, vb. trans. [1. rè enábl; 2. rī inéibl]. **re-** & **enable.** To enable again; to provide with means of, or capacity for, doing again.

re-enact, vb. trans. [1. rè enákt; 2. rī inǽkt]. **re-** & **enact.** To enact over again.

re-enactment, n. [1. rè enáktment; 2. rī inǽktmənt]. **re-** & **enactment.** A new, fresh, enactment.

re-endow, vb. trans. [1. rè endóu; 2. rī indáu]. **re-** & **endow.** To endow again; to grant a fresh endowment to.

re-endowment, n. [1. rè endóument; 2. rī indáumənt]. **re-** & **endowment.** A new, repeated, endowment.

re-enforce, vb. See **reinforce.**

re-engage, vb. trans. [1. rè engáj; 2. rī ingéidž]. **re-** & **engage.** To engage, employ (workman &c.) a second time.

re-engagement, n. [1. rè engájment; 2. rī ingéidžmənt]. **re-** & **engagement.** Engagement, employment, a second time.

re-enlist, vb. trans. & intrans. [1. rè enlíst; 2. rī inlíst]. **re-** & **enlist.** To enlist a second time.

re-enlistment, n. [1. rè enlístment; 2. rī inlístmənt]. **re-** & **enlistment.** Enlistment a second time.

re-enter, vb. trans. & intrans. [1. rè énter; 2. rī éntə]. **re-** & **enter.** **A.** trans. **1.** To enter again, to go or come into again; specif. (law, of lessor) to enter and take possession of (leased property &c.) under a proviso of re-entry. **2.** (techn. uses) **a** (calico-printing) to overlay with additional colours material already partly printed; **b** (engraving) to cut deeper engraved lines. **B.** intrans. **1.** (law) To enter again: *lessor has right to re-enter.* **2.** (fort., of line) To point inward and form a re-entrant: *a re-entering angle.*

re-entrance, n. [1. rè éntrans; 2. rī éntrəns]. **re-** & **entrance.** Act of re-entering; re-entry.

re-entrant, adj. & n. [1. rè éntrant; 2. rī éntrənt]. **re-enter** & **-ant.** **1.** adj. Re-entering, esp. (fort.) *a re-entrant angle*, one of which the apex is directed inwards, and away from the enemy's line, opposed to *salient.* **2.** n. A re-entrant angle.

re-entry, n. [1. rè éntri; 2. rī éntri]. **re-** & **entry.** Act of re-entering, re-entrance, esp. (law) act of a lessor or grantor of leasehold property in entering upon and resuming possession of the property on failure of the lessee to perform covenants, pay rent due &c., the right to do so being conferred by 'provisos of re-entry' in the lease.

re-establish, vb. trans. [1. rè estáblish; 2. rī istǽbliʃ]. **re-** & **establish.** To establish again; to restore: *peace has now been re-established.*

re-establishment, n. [1. rè estáblishment; 2. rì istǽbliʃmənt]. **re-** & **establishment.** Act of re-establishing; state of being re-established; restoration.

reeve (**I.**), n. [1. rēv; 2. rīv]. Also *ree*; etymol. uncertain; formal connexion w. **ruff** (the male bird) quite uncertain. The female of the ruff, a kind of sandpiper.

reeve (**II.**), n. O.E. *ġerēfa*, 'officer, governor'; prob. fr. *rōf-ja, cp. O.E. *rēfan*, 'to call out', & *rōf*, 'host, number of soldiers', thus meaning orig. 'master, commander of a troop'. The connexion w. Mod. Germ. *graf* is considered doubtful. Cp. also Scots **grieve** (**II.**). **1.** (hist.) **a** The name of an official who was the chief magistrate of a town or other district, usually with a prefix as *town-reeve, burg-reeve, port-reeve* &c., cp. **sheriff**; **b** a bailiff or steward of a manor. **2.** (Canada) The president of a village or town council. **3.** (min.) Foreman, overseer, in certain coal-mining districts.

reeve (**III.**), vb. trans. Prob. fr. Du. *reven*, 'to reef'. See **reef** (**II.**). (naut.) **1.** To pass (thread, a rope &c.), through a hole or opening in a block, ring-bolt &c.: *to reeve a rope through a block* &c. **2.** To pass a rope &c. through: *to reeve a ring-bolt* (*with a rope*). **3.** To fasten by reeving, *reeve on, in, over, round, to*: *to reeve a rope to a yard.* **4.** (of ship &c.) To pass carefully through (shoals &c.).

re-examination, n. [1. ré egzàminā́shun; 2. rí igzæ̀minéiʃən]. See next word & **-ation.** A second examination; specif. (law) examination of a witness by his own counsel after cross-examination, on this.

re-examine, vb. trans. [1. rē egzámin; 2. rì igzǽmin]. **re-** & **examine.** To examine a second time; specif. (law) to question a witness, after cross-examination, with view of getting rid of the effects of the cross-examination, explaining admissions &c.

re-export, vb. trans. & n. **re-** & **export.** **1.** vb. [1. ré eksport; 2. rí ɛkspɔ̄t]. To export goods which have been imported. **2.** n. [1. rè éksport; 2. rì ékspɔ̄t]. Re-exported goods.

reface, vb. trans. [1. rēfás; 2. rìféis]. **re-** & **face.** To put a new face or surface upon; to give a new facing to; esp. *to reface a building with stone* &c.; *to reface stone in a building*, to dress it afresh.

refashion, vb. trans. [1. rēfáshun; 2. rìfǽʃən]. **re-** & **fashion.** To fashion afresh; to give a new shape, pattern, or arrangement to.

refection, n. [1. refékshun; 2. rifékʃən]. Fr., fr. Lat. *refectiōn(-em)*, 'a remaking, restoration; refreshment', fr. *refect-(um)*, P.P. of *reficere*, 'to remake'; & **-ion.** See **re-** & **faction.** **a** Refreshment: *a light meal spread for our refection*; **b** light repast.

refectory, n. [1. réfékturi, réfektri; 2. riféktəri, réfəktri], fr. Med. Lat. *refectorium*, cp. Fr. *réfectoire.* See stem of prec. word & **-ory.** The dining-hall of a monastery, convent, or similar institution.

refer, vb. trans. & intrans. [1. refér; 2. rifə́], fr. Lat. *referre*, 'to carry, bring back, relate, refer'. See **re-** & **-ferous.** **A.** trans. **1.** To attribute, assign to as cause, origin &c.: *he referred his wealth to his own hard work.* **2.** To assign to, identify with, a date, place, class &c.: *to refer Stonehenge to the neolithic or bronze age*; *a tendency to refer all Irish glass to Waterford*; *minute organism which some refer to animals, others to plants.* **3.** To send, direct, hand over, commit to person or thing for information, consideration, decision &c.: *to refer a student to the best authorities*; *I was referred to the secretary for information*; *the dispute will be referred to an arbitrator.* **B.** intrans. Chiefly *refer to.* **1.** To appeal, have recourse to, for information, as an authority &c.: *to refer to the Bible, to a standard work* &c.; *to refer to one's notes for assisting one's memory*; *to refer to one's watch for correct time*; *to refer to a former employer for a character.* **2.** To speak of, allude to; to make an allusion or reference to: *the speaker referred to his past experiences*; *do you refer to me by that insinuation?* **3.** **a** To relate, be related, to; to concern, apply to, to have reference to: *the regulations refer only to children*; **b** to indicate, direct attention to, to point to: *an asterisk refers to a footnote.*

referable, adj. [1. réferabl; 2. réfərəbl]. Prec. & **-able.** Capable of being referred or related to something else as the cause &c.: *malaria is referable to a microbe conveyed by the bite of a mosquito.*

referee, n. & vb. intrans. [1. rèferḗ; 2. rèfərí]. **refer** & **-ee.** **1.** n. A person to whom anything is referred for decision; adjudicator, arbitrator: specif. **a** (law) one of four officials, *Official Referees*, of the High Court of Justice, to whom cases of complicated details, esp. of accounts, are referred; **b** (games &c.) an umpire, esp. in boxing contests and in football. **2.** vb. To act as referee; chiefly in connexion with games.

reference (**I.**), n. [1. réferens; 2. réfərəns]. **refer** & **-ence.** Act of referring, state of being referred. **1.** A referring, sending, handing over of a question, matter of dispute, inquiry &c. to some person or persons for consideration, investigation, and report: *a reference to a Royal Commission*; *a case of complicated accounts is one for reference*, i.e. to an Official Referee; *to keep to, within, the terms of, reference*, not to go beyond the scope of what is to be investigated and reported upon; *wide, limited, reference*, terms of free or narrow scope. **2.** Act of referring to, consulting, a person for information, esp. as to character, ability, financial stability &c.: *to make a reference to one's former employer, to one's banker.* **3.** **a** Statement, by one who knows him, as to a candidate's qualifications for a situation; testimonial, character; **b** statement in respect of a person's general honesty, financial stability &c.: *highest references given and required.* **4.** Person referred to or consulted in regard to another's character, qualifications for a post &c.: *who are your references?* **5.** Act of referring to, consulting, a book or other source of information: *to make reference to the guide-book, to a catalogue*; *work of reference, reference book*, a book of general or special information to be consulted on specific points but not read through, such as a dictionary, encyclopaedia, gazetteer &c. **6.** Indication, notice, statement of a passage, page of a book &c., where a quotation, information &c. may be found: *the writer gives no references to his authorities*; *verify your references*; *cross reference*, reference in a book to another page, statement &c. in the same book. **7.** Act of alluding to, that which refers or alludes to; allusion: *you make no reference to your plans in your letter*; *his memoirs contain many references to interesting people.* **8.** Correspondence, relation, respect, regard: *the various sections of the structure seem to have no reference to each other*; *the great sales of this book have little or no reference to its value.* Phrs. *in, with, reference to*, in regard to, concerning, about; *without reference to*, not concerning, irrespective of.

reference (**II.**), vb. trans., fr. prec. To provide, furnish (a book &c.) with references to other sources of information &c.

referendary, n. [1. rèferéndari; 2. rèfəréndəri], fr. Med. Lat. *referendārius.* See next word & **-ary.** **1.** (Med. hist.) A high official of imperial, papal, or other courts having the power of issuing and sealing diplomatic and other documents, receiving and answering petitions &c. **2.** (rare and archaic) A referee, arbitrator, adjudicator, assessor.

referendum, n. [1. rèferéndum; 2. rèfəréndəm]. Lat., 'that which is to be referred', gerundive of *referre.* See **refer.** Reference of a political measure direct to the people for acceptance or rejection, instead of deciding this by the votes of elected popular representatives, cp. *initiative.*

referential, adj. [1. rèferénshal; 2. rèfərénʃəl], fr. Lat. *referent-(em)*, Pres. Part. of *referre*, see **refer**, & **-ial.** Containing a reference; used, intended, for reference: *for referentia; use.*

refill, vb. trans. & n. [1. rēfíl; 2. rìfíl]. **re-** & **fill.** **1.** vb. To fill, charge again: *to refill a pipe, fountain-pen* &c. **2.** n. That which refills or is used to refill; a fresh fill recharge.

refine, vb. trans. & intrans. [1. refín; 2. rifáin]. **re-** & **fine** (**VII.**); influenced as to meaning by Fr. *raffiner*, fr. *re* & *affiner.* **A.** trans. **1.** (in material sense) To free, make clear, from impurities, sediment, dross; to purify, clarify; to reduce to a fine, pure state: *to refine sugar, gold, silver, iron*; *to refine wine, olive oil* &c. **2.** (in non-material sense) To clear, free from coarseness, vulgarity; to make cultured, elegant, polished; to give a polish to: *to refine manners, style, language, taste* &c.; *a person of refined manners and taste*; *a refining influence.* **B.** intrans. **1.** To become purified, clear of impurities; to become cultured, polished in manner, style &c. **2.** *Refine on, upon*, to improve upon, add delicacy or refinement to: *eighteenth-century poets thought they could refine upon, on, their predecessors.* **3.** To use niceties, subtleties in thought, language; to affect extreme subtlety or refinement; to elaborate details.

refined, adj. [1. refínd; 2. rifáind]. P.P. of prec. **1.** Purified, cleared from dross &c.; reduced to pure, fine state: *refined sugar, gold.* **2.** Free from vulgarity, coarseness in thought, speech, manners &c.; polished, cultured; exquisite: *a refined accent*; *refined society* &c.

refinedly, adv. [1. refínedli; 2. rifáinidli]. Prec. & **-ly.** In a refined manner.

refinement, n. [1. refínment; 2. rifáinmənt]. **refine** & **-ment.** **1.** Act, process, of refining; state of being refined, product of refining. **2.** Fineness, delicacy, of manners, style, language, taste &c.; polish, culture; example of such: *a person of refinement.* **3.** Subtlety, over-elaboration: *refinements of metaphysical thought*; *refinements of cruelty, torture* &c.

refiner, n. [1. refíner; 2. rifáinə]. **refine** & **-er.** One who refines; esp. **a** one engaged in refining metals, sugar &c.; **b** apparatus for refining such materials.

refinery, n. [1. refíneri; 2. rifáinəri]. Prec. & **-ery.** Place, building, plant, where materials are refined in process of manufacture.

refit, vb. trans. & intrans. & n. [1. rēfít; 2. rìfít]. **re-** & **fit** (**III.**). **1.** vb. **a** trans. To make fit, adapt, again for use; to repair; to supply with fresh stores &c.: *to refit a ship*; **b** intrans., (of ship &c.) to be refitted, re-equipped; to undergo repairs, get in new stores &c. **2.** n. Repairing, refurnishing with stores &c.; refitment.

refitment, n. [1. rēfítment; 2. rìfítmənt]. Prec. & **-ment.** Refit.

reflect, vb. trans. & intrans. [1. reflékt; 2. rifléкt], fr. Lat. *reflectere*, 'to bend, turn back', in phr. *animum reflectere*, 'to turn back the mind, to reflect', fr. **re-** & *flectere*, 'to bend', see **flex** (**I.**). **A.** trans. **1.** **a** (of physical process) To throw, cast back, radiate, give out or back (light, heat, sound); **b** (in non-material sense) to invest with, shed upon, cause to be attributed to: *his action reflected the greatest credit and glory upon him.* **2.** **a** To reproduce, yield a visual image of from polished surface: *a mirror reflects a face*; *clouds reflected in the water*; **b** (fig.) to give an exact, faithful impression of; to express, be expressive of: *his face reflected his emotions*; *many newspapers merely reflect the opinions of those who read them.* **3.** (followed by *that, how, what*, and dependent clause) To consider, remind oneself, have it in one's thoughts that: *to reflect that life will soon be over*; *to reflect how to get out of a difficulty*; *just reflect what misery dishonesty brings upon the guilty.* **B.** intrans. **1.** **a** To throw back light, sound &c.; **b** (of polished surfaces) to give, cast back, a visual image. 2. *Reflect on, upon,* to hint, insinuate, something discreditable concerning; to disparage, cast doubt, aspersions on: *to reflect (up)on a person's honesty, veracity.* 3. *Reflect upon,* to have an unfavourable effect upon, react upon unfavourably: *his conduct will reflect seriously upon his future career.* 4. a To ponder, think deeply, meditate: *I want time to reflect;* b *reflect on, upon,* to meditate upon, think over, consider, ponder deeply; to turn over in one's mind: *reflect upon all I have said to you; to reflect upon a problem, upon what one is going to say.*

reflectingly, adv. [1. refléktingli; 2. rifléktiŋli], fr. Pres. Part. of prec. & **-ly**. By reflection; in a reflecting manner; thoughtfully.

reflection, reflexion, n. [1. reflékshun; 2. riflékʃən]. As though fr. **reflect** & **-ion**; formerly & more correctly spelt *reflexion,* fr. Lat. *reflexiōn-(em),* formed fr. *reflex-(um),* P.P. type of *reflectere.* See **reflect**. 1. Process of reflecting; the process of reflecting or throwing back light, heat, sound, from a surface. 2. That which is reflected, e.g. a light, heat, sound, and esp. b a reflected, visual image: *a reflection on the water;* c (fig.) a person who imitates or resembles another; action, manner, utterance, mode of thought &c., inspired by, or imitated from, another: *he is simply a reflection of his father; his speech and gestures were faint reflections of those of his master.* 3. (anat. and physiol., usually *reflexion*) A bending, turning, back upon itself; part turned, bent back, or reflected; specif., stimulation of a nerve due to action on another nerve; reflex action. 4. a Act of intense, concentrated thinking; meditation, profound consideration, cogitation; Phr. *on reflection,* after thinking it over; b (in pl.) thoughts, ideas, resulting from reflection: *to leave a man to his own reflections;* c utterance, remark, comment made as a result of reflection: *I have just a few reflections to offer on what you have said.* 5. a Reproach, censure, blame: *to cast a reflection upon;* b a remark, utterance, expressive of censure; an aspersion, animadversion: *to say that he was credulous is a reflection, not on his integrity, but on his intelligence;* c action, conduct, which entails censure or reproach, or which brings discredit upon one: *his behaviour in this matter is a grave reflection upon his honesty.*

reflectionless, adj. [1. reflékshunles; 2. riflékʃənlis]. Prec. & **-less**. a Giving back, casting, no reflection (in physical sense); b incapable of reflecting, or of reflection (in psychol. sense).

reflective, adj. [1. refléktiv; 2. rifléktiv]. **reflect** & **-ive**. 1. a Reflecting light, heat &c.: *a reflective surface;* b (rare) reflected, caused by reflection: *reflective sound, light* &c. 2. Pertaining to, characterized by, reflection; cogitative; a (of the mind and its faculties) capable of, practising, reflection; b (of persons) given to reflection; thoughtful, meditative. 3. (rare) a (of mechan. or physiol. action) Reciprocal, reflex; b (gram.) reflexive.

reflectively, adv. Prec. & **-ly**. a By reflection; b in a reflective manner (in various senses of n. and adj.).

reflector, n. [1. reflékter; 2. rifléktə]. **reflect** & **-or**. 1. That which reflects; a a surface or body which reflects light, heat, sound &c.; b a polished surface, or mirror, of glass or metal which collects and reflects back rays of light in a specific direction, as in lanterns, astronomical and optical instruments. 2. a One who or thing which reflects, throws back, reproduces or mirrors mental impressions, feelings &c.: *where can one find a true reflector of public opinion?;* b (rare) one who reflects or meditates; a contemplative person.

reflet, n. [1. reflā; 2. rəfléi]. Fr., 'reflection'. See **reflect**. Brilliancy of surface; iridescence, lustre, esp. the metallic glaze on majolica and other lustred pottery.

reflex (I.), adj. [1. réfleks; 2. ríflɛks], fr. Lat. *reflex-(um),* P.P. type of *reflectere,* 'to bend, turn back'. See **re-** & **flex** (I.). 1. Turned, bent, back, of leaves or stems. 2. Reflected, of light in a picture depicted as coming from a window, mirror &c. 3. Retroactive, reactive, returning with effect upon the agent or origin: *reflex influence, effect* &c.; specif., *reflex action,* (physiol.) involuntary action of nerves and muscles induced by a stimulus from without, transmitted backwards to the nerve centre, and then, by efferent nerves, outwards again to the part at which stimulus is applied.

reflex (II.), n., fr. Lat. *reflexus.* See prec. 1. That which is reflected; reflection: a *the reflex of light, reflex of colour, sound;* b (fig.) outward manifestation or result of some essential fact or quality: *a man's behaviour is but a reflex of his character; revolutions are reflexes of past tyranny and repression.* 3. (physiol.) Involuntary, muscular, or nervous movement caused by reflex action; a reflex action.

reflexed, adj. [1. rèflékst; 2. rìflékst]. P.P. of obs. vb. *reflex,* **reflect**. (bot. and zool.) Bent, folded back, recurved.

reflexibility, n. [1. reflèksibíliti; 2. riflèksibíliti]. See next word & **-ity**. State, quality, of being reflexible.

reflexible, adj. [1. refléksibl; 2. rifléksibl]. **reflex** & **-ible**. Capable of being reflected: *reflexible rays of light.*

reflexion, n. See **reflection**.

reflexive, adj. & n. [1. refléksiv; 2. rifléksiv]. **reflex** (I.) & **-ive**. 1. adj. a *A reflexive verb* is one expressing an action which comes back upon the agent or subject; b *reflexive pronoun,* one referring to the subject of the sentence. 2. n. A reflexive word, reflexive verb or pronoun.

reflexively, adv. Prec. & **-ly**. In the manner of, by means of, a reflexive verb or pronoun.

refloat, vb. trans. & intrans. [1. rēflṓt; 2. rīflóut]. **re-** & **float**. 1. trans. To cause to float again, to set (something) afloat again after it has been sunk or stranded &c. 2. intrans. To float again.

reflorescence, n. [1. rèflorésens; 2. rìflɔrésəns]. **re-** & **florescence**. A second flowering.

refluence, n. [1. réflooens; 2. réfluəns]. Next word & **-ce**. Reflux, refluent action.

refluent, adj. [1. réflooent; 2. réfluənt], fr. Lat. *refluent-(em),* Pres. Part. of *refluere,* 'to flow back, flow away'. See **re-** & **fluent**. Flowing back, ebbing (of tide, blood &c.).

reflux, n. [1. réfluks; 2. ríflaks]. **re-** & **flux**. A flowing back, refluence; ebbing, contrasted with *flux: the flux and reflux.*

refoot, vb. trans. [1. rèfóot; 2. rìfút]. **re-** & **foot**. To put a new foot to (a stocking).

reform (I.), vb. trans. & intrans. [1. refórm; 2. rifɔ́m], fr. Lat. *reformāre,* 'to form, shape again, to remould, to change; to alter; to reform'. **re-** & **form**. 1. trans. a To improve condition of by removal of abuses &c.: *to reform a system of education;* b to improve character or conduct of (a person). 2. intrans. To become, behave, better; undergo an improvement in one's character or conduct.

reform (II.), n., fr. prec. Change for the better, removal of abuses; amendment, improvement; specif. a social and political improvement; *Reform Bill,* that of 1832, which extended parliamentary franchise; b improvement in a person's character and conduct.

re-form, vb. trans. & intrans. [1. rèfórm; 2. rìfɔ́m]. **re-** & **form**. To form over again, remake; specif. (of troops) to put into, take up again, a formation which has been altered or broken up.

reformation, n. [1. rèformáshun; 2. rèfəméiʃən]. See **re-** & **formation**. Act of reforming, state of being reformed. 1. A definite change for the better; amendment, correction of faults, errors, or abuses; improvement in habits, character &c.: *reformation of political, social life; reformation of a criminal; reformation in* or *of manners* &c. 2. Specif. (cap.) the religious movement, at the beginning of the 16th cent., directed against various abuses in the Church, which ended in the emancipation of many European countries from the papacy and the founding of Reformed or Protestant Churches.

re-formation, n. [1. rē formáshun; 2. rī fɔméiʃən]. A new, fresh, formation.

reformative, adj. [1. refórmativ; 2. rifɔ́mətiv]. See **reformation** & **-ive**. Tending, serving, intended, to reform.

reformatory, adj. & n. [1. refórmaturi; 2. rifɔ́mətəri]. See prec. & **-ory**. 1. adj. Tending to reform, to produce reformation. 2. n. Institution to which young criminals are sent to undergo mental and moral training and discipline, in order to rescue them from crime and make decent citizens of them.

reformed, adj. [1. refórmd; 2. rifɔ́md]. P.P. of **reform** (I.). 1. Amended, improved, corrected: *reformed criminal, drunkard* &c., one who has turned over a new leaf and ceased to be a criminal or a drunkard. 2. Specif. (referring to religion) *Reformed Churches,* those which have adopted Protestant principles and renounced the jurisdiction of the Pope; contrasted with *Roman; the Reformed Faith,* Protestantism.

reformer, n. [1. refórmer; 2. rifɔ́mə]. **reform** (I.) & **-er**. 1. One who reforms, or carries out a reform. 2. Specif. a one of the leaders of the religious Protestant Reformation of the 16th cent.; b a supporter of parliamentary reform, esp. that of the Reform Bill and Act of 1832.

reformist, n. [1. refórmist; 2. rifɔ́mist]. **reform** (I.) & **-ist**. One in favour of reform; a reformer.

refract, vb. trans. [1. refrákt; 2. rifrǽkt], fr. Lat. *refract-(um),* P.P. type of *refringere,* 'to break up, break to pieces; to break away, off or back'; fr. **re-** & *frangere,* 'to break', see under **fraction**. (of light, heat, sound) To deflect rays or waves from a straight path by passing them into a different medium, e.g. by passing light through a lens.

refractable, adj. [1. refráktabl; 2. rifrǽktəbl]. Prec. & **-able**. Capable of being refracted.

refracting, adj. [1. refrákting; 2. rifrǽktiŋ], fr. Pres. Part. of **refract**. (in senses of vb. *refract*) Specif. a *refracting angle,* the angle formed by the two faces of a triangular prism; b *refracting telescope,* one with an object-glass or concave mirror rendering the rays of light convergent, and forming an image magnified by the eye-piece.

refraction, n. [1. refrákshun; 2. rifrǽkʃən]. **refract** & **-ion**. a Process of refracting or deflecting a ray of light, heat, or a sound wave; b process of being refracted.

refractional, adj. [1. refrákshunal; 2. rifrǽkʃənəl]. Prec. & **-al**. Of, pertaining to, refraction; refractive.

refractive, adj. [1. refráktiv; 2. rifrǽktiv]. **refract** & **-ive**. Having the property of refracting.

refractometer, n. [1. rèfraktómeter; 2. rìfræktɔ́mitə]. **refract** & *-o-* & **-meter**. An instrument for measuring refraction.

refractor, n. [1. refrákter; 2. rifrǽktə]. **refract** & **-or**. That which refracts, a refractive medium; specif., a refracting telescope.

refractorily, adv. [1. refrákturili; 2. rifrǽktərili]. **refractory** & **-ly**. In a refractory way or manner.

refractoriness, n. [1. refrákturines; 2. rifrǽktərinis]. See prec. & **-ness**. State, quality, of being refractory.

refractory, adj. [1. refrákturi; 2. rifrǽktəri], fr. Lat. *refractārius,* 'stubborn, unyielding', cp. Fr. *réfractaire;* w. change fr. *-ary,* by assimilation. See **refract** & **-ory**. 1. (of persons, character &c.) Not amenable to discipline; unmanageable, stubborn, obstinate. 2. Difficult to deal with, resistent; a (of disease &c.) hard to treat, cure; b (of substances) difficult to reduce or disintegrate.

refrain (I.), vb. trans. & intrans. [1. refrán; 2. rifréin]. M.E. *refreinen*, fr. O. Fr. *refrener*, 'to bridle, curb', fr. Lat. *refrēnāre*, 'to curb, hold in with a bit'. See **re-** & **fraenum**. **1.** trans. (archaic or obs.) To restrain, curb, check, hold back: *to refrain oneself, one's desires or appetites, one's tears, grief* &c. **2.** intrans. To keep oneself from; to abstain, forbear: *to refrain from doing*; *to refrain from tears, emotion*; *to refrain from food*; (also absol.) *I might easily have answered but I refrained.*

refrain (II.), n. O. Fr., fr. *refraindre*, 'to restrain, check'; also 'to repeat', fr. Low Lat. **refrangere*, fr. *refringere*, 'to break back'. See **refract**. The burden of a song; the repeated, recurring words, or line, at the end of a verse or of a musical phrase.

refrangibility, n. [1. refrànjibíliti; 2. rifrændžibíliti]. See next word & **-ity**. State, quality, of being refrangible.

refrangible, adj. [1. refránjibl; 2. rifrǽndžibl]. New formation as fr. uncompounded Lat. type *frang-*, see **fraction**, instead of fr. compounded *refring-*. Able to be refracted.

refresh, vb. trans. & intrans. [1. refrésh; 2. rifréʃ]. M.E. *refreschen, refreshen*, fr. O. Fr. *refrescher, refreschier*, Mod. Fr. *rafraîchir*. See **re-** & **fresh**. **A.** trans. **1.** (of physical and material action) **a** (of food, drink, rest, sleep) To make fresh again; to give fresh strength and vigour to; to revive, reinvigorate; **b** to make cool, brace up, give feeling of renewed vigour after exposure to heat: *refreshing breezes*; **c** to give fresh strength and vigour to (another) by supplying with food, drink &c.; (also reflex.) *to refresh oneself.* **2.** (of action on the mind) To stimulate, quicken, cause to function more actively: *to refresh one's memory.* **3.** To give a fresh supply to: *to refresh a ship with stores, water* &c.; *to refresh a fire with more fuel.* **B.** intrans. **1.** (colloq.) To take refreshment, esp. drink. **2.** (of ship) To take in fresh stores, water &c.

refresher, n. [1. refrésher; 2. rifréʃə]. Prec. & **-er**. One who, that which, refreshes; specif. (colloq.) **a** a refreshing, cooling drink; **b** (law) a fee, additional to that marked on the brief, paid to counsel when a case is adjourned or unduly prolonged.

refreshing, adj. [1. refréshing; 2. rifréʃiŋ], fr. Pres. Part. of **refresh**. **1.** Affording material refreshment; reinvigorating, tending to revive and freshen. **2. a** Stimulating to the mind; spiritually bracing and satisfying; revivifying: *a refreshing sermon*; **b** unexpectedly fresh and engaging; affording pleasure by rarity and because so infrequently encountered: *a refreshing innocence, candour, frankness* &c.

refreshingly, adv. Prec. & **-ly**. In a refreshing manner; so as to refresh.

refreshment, n. [1. refréshment; 2. rifréʃmənt], fr. O. Fr. *refreschement*. See **refresh** & **-ment**. **1.** Act of refreshing; state of being refreshed; restoration to strength, vigour; reanimation: *refreshment of body or mind.* **2.** Something which refreshes; a restorative of the body or the mind: *a hot bath is a great refreshment after a long journey*; *many find refreshment in poetry amid life's worries.* **3.** Specif., food and drink; a meal: *let me offer you some refreshment, a little light refreshment*; (also pl.) *refreshments*, various kinds of food and drink: *refreshments can be obtained at the station, in the hotel lounge* &c.

refreshment-room, n. Room or place where refreshments are obtainable; esp. at a railway station, public exhibition, or at a large private or public party or entertainment.

refrigerant, adj. & n. [1. refríjerant; 2. rifrídžərənt], fr. Lat. *refrīgerant-(em)*, Pres. Part. of *refrīgerāre*. See **refrigerate**. **1.** adj. **a** Cooling, freezing, causing refrigeration; **b** reducing bodily heat or fever. **2.** n. **a** A substance which causes refrigeration; esp. any of the various chemical substances used in refrigerating machinery; **b** a cooling medicine or drink; any medical preparation for reducing fever.

refrigerate, vb. trans. & intrans. [1. refríjerāt; 2. rifrídžəreit], fr. Lat. *refrīgerāt-(um)*, P.P. of *refrīgerāre*, 'to make cool or cold again', fr. **re-** & *frīgerāre*, 'to cool', fr. *frīgus*, 'coldness', see **frigid**. **A.** trans. To make cool or cold; to freeze; specif. **a** to make into ice; **b** to preserve (meat, fish, fruit &c.), by freezing or partially freezing mechanically; to put into cold storage. **B.** intrans. To become cold or frozen.

refrigerating machine, n. [1. refríjeràting mashḗn; 2. rifrídžəreitiŋ məʃín]. Mechanical device for making ice, or for preserving food &c. by refrigeration.

refrigeration, n. [1. refrìjerā́shun; 2. rifrìdžəréiʃən], fr. Lat. *refrīgerātiōn-(em)*, 'a cooling, coolness'. **refrigerate** & **-ion**. Act or process of refrigerating; state of being refrigerated; specif., the process of preserving food by reducing mechanically to a very low temperature.

refrigerative, adj. [1. refríjerativ; 2. rifrídžərətiv]. **refrigerate** & **-ive**. Cooling, tending to cool; tending to refrigeration in specific sense.

refrigerator, n. [1. refríjeràter; 2. rifrídžərèitə]. **refrigerate** & **-or**. That which refrigerates, freezes, or keeps cool; specif., a box, or chamber, filled with ice, or otherwise kept artificially at a very low temperature, in which food can be kept and preserved.

refrigeratory, adj. & n. [1. refríjeraturi; 2. rifrídžərətəri], fr. Lat. *refrīgerātōrius*. See prec. & **-ory**. **1.** adj. Causing refrigeration; refrigerating, refrigerative, refrigerant. **2.** n. A refrigerator; **a** the chamber in a refrigerator in which the ice or other cooling substance is stored; **b** a water-filled vessel for condensing vapour in a still.

refringent, adj. [1. refrínjent; 2. rifríndžənt], fr. Lat. *refringent-(em)*, Pres. Part. of *refringere*. See **refract**. Refractive.

reft, adj. [1. reft; 2. reft]. P.P. of **reave**. (poet.) Deprived of, bereft.

refuge, n. [1. réfūj; 2. réfjūdž]. Fr., fr. Lat. *refugium*, 'a taking refuge; a place of refuge', fr. *refugere*, 'to run away; shrink from'. See **re-** & **fugacious**. **1.** Shelter, protection, from bodily or mental danger, pain, distress: *to seek, take, refuge from a storm, from one's worries.* **2. a** Place which affords shelter, protection, safety &c.; an asylum, retreat, sanctuary, hiding-place; (also in non-material sense) '*Lord, Thou hast been our refuge from one generation to another*' (Ps. 90.1); **b** specif., piece of raised pavement placed in the middle of a broad, crowded thoroughfare to facilitate crossing by pedestrians. **3.** Line of action resorted to, to escape dangers, difficulties, the results of wrongdoing and the like: *lying is a natural refuge for a criminal when cornered*; *suicide is the last refuge of misery and despair.*

refugee, n. [1. rèfūjḗ; 2. rèfjudží], fr. Fr. *réfugié*, P.P. of *réfugier*, fr. Lat. *refugere*, 'to flee away, escape'. **refuge** & **-ee**. A fugitive from his own country, seeking shelter in another, esp. from persecution on account of religious or political views.

refulgence, more rarely **refulgency**, n. [1. refúljens(i); 2. rifáldžəns(i)], fr. L. Lat. *refulgentia*. See next word & **-ce**, **-cy**. Quality, state, of being refulgent; splendour, brightness; a blaze of light.

refulgent, adj. [1. refúljent; 2. rifáldžənt], fr. Lat. *refulgent-(em)*, Pres. Part. of *refulgēre*, 'to flash back, reflect a blaze of light; to shine brightly'; fr. **re-** & *fulgēre*, 'to shine', see **fulgent**. Shining, bright; radiant, glowing, lucent.

refulgently, adv. Prec. & **-ly**. With refulgence; brightly, radiantly.

refund (I.), vb. trans. & intrans. [1. refúnd; 2. rifánd], fr. Lat. *refundere*, 'to pour back, to throw back, to restore'. See **re-** & **found** (II.) & **fuse** (I.); influenced by **fund**. **A.** trans. To repay, reimburse, make compensation for: *to refund out-of-pocket expenses*; *to refund what has been borrowed.* **B.** intrans. To make repayment.

refund (II.), n., fr. prec. Repayment.

re-fund, vb. trans. [1. rē fúnd; 2. rī fánd]. **re-** & **fund**. To fund again, to form a fresh fund for: *to re-fund a national debt* &c.

refundment, n. [1. refúndment; 2. rifándmənt]. **refund** (I.) & **-ment**. Repayment, reimbursement; a refund.

refurbish, vb. trans. [1. rēfĕ́rbish; 2. rīfə́biʃ]. **re-** & **furbish**. To furbish up again, to renovate.

refurnish, vb. trans. & intrans. [1. rēfĕ́rnish; 2. rīfə́niʃ]. **re-** & **furnish**. To furnish again; to equip with new furniture.

refusable, adj. [1. refū́zabl; 2. rifjū́zəbl]. **refuse** (I.) & **-able**. Capable of being refused; admitting of refusal.

refusal, n. [1. refū́zl; 2. rifjū́zəl]. **refuse** (I.) & **-al**. **1.** Act of refusing; denial or rejection of anything asked or offered: *a flat refusal to answer a question*; *refusal of an invitation*; *refusal of a good offer.* Phr. *to take no refusal*, to refuse to take 'no' for an answer. **2.** Choice of accepting or declining an offer; right or option before others to take or refuse: *to ask for, have, give, the (first) refusal of* (the lease of a house &c.).

refuse (I.), vb. trans. & intrans. [1. refū́z; 2. rifjū́z]. M.E. *refusen*, fr. Fr. *refuser*, fr. Low Lat. **refūsāre*, formed fr. Lat. *refūs-(um)*, P.P. of *refundere*, 'to pour back'. See **refund**. **A.** trans. **1.** To decline to give, or grant what is asked for; to withhold, deny: *to refuse a person money*; *to refuse leave of absence* &c.; *to refuse one's consent.* **2.** To decline to take, or receive (what is offered); to reject offer of: *to refuse an offer, a gift, a bribe, a peerage, cabinet rank* &c. Phr. *to refuse a suitor* (of a woman), to decline his offer of marriage. **3.** Special uses: **a** (cards) to be unable to follow a lead in a certain suit: *to refuse hearts*; **b** (of a horse) to decline to jump: *to refuse a fence.* **B.** intrans. **1.** To make, give, utter, a refusal; to decline: *he refuses to do what he is asked, to give anything to charity, to allow his name to be mentioned, to take money.* **2.** Specif. (of a horse) to decline to jump: *it refused at the first fence.*

refuse (II.), adj. & n. [1. réfūs; 2. réfjūs], fr. M. Fr. *refus*, 'thrown out, rejected, refused'. See prec., cp. O. Fr. *mettre en refus*, 'to cast, throw away, abandon'. **1.** adj. Rejected, thrown away as useless or worthless: *refuse matter.* **2.** n. That which is rejected; **a** waste matter left over from process of manufacture &c.: *cotton-refuse*; **b** rubbish, garbage: *house refuse.*

re-fuse, vb. trans. [1. rē fū́z; 2. rī fjū́z]. **re-** & **fuse** (I.). To fuse over again.

refuser, n. [1. refū́zer; 2. rifjū́zə]. **refuse** (I.) & **-er**. One that refuses, esp. a horse which refuses to jump a fence.

refutable, adj. [1. réfūtabl; 2. réfjutəbl]. **refute** & **-able**. Capable of being refuted; liable to refutation.

refutal, n. [1. refū́tl; 2. rifjū́tl]. See prec. & **-al**. Act of refuting; refutation.

refutation, n. [1. rèfūtā́shun; 2. rèfjutéiʃən], fr. Lat. *refūtātiōn-(em)*. See next word & **-ation**. Act of refuting; argument, statement, which refutes.

refute, vb. trans. [1. refū́t; 2. rifjū́t], fr. Lat. *refūtāre*, 'to repel, rebut, refute'. See **re-** & second element of **confute**, & cp. **fuse** (I.). **1.** To prove the falsity of (an argument, a statement &c.); to repel, rebut by argument. **2.** To prove (a person) wrong: *to refute an opponent.*

regain, vb. trans. [1. rēgā́n; 2. rīgéin], fr. M. Fr. *regaigner*, Mod. Fr. *regagner*. See **re-** & **gain**. **1.** To gain, get back, to recover possession of (material and non-material things): *to regain lost or stolen property*; *to regain one's health, senses, peace of mind*; *to regain a person's affections.* **2.** To get back to, to reach again (place, position, condition &c.): *to regain one's home, native country; to regain one's old place in a person's estimation.*

regal (I.), adj. [1. rḗgal; 2. ríg(ə)l], fr. Lat. *rēgālis*, 'belonging to a king', fr. **rēg-*, base of *rēx*, 'king'. See **rex, regent**, & cp. **royal.** **1.** Of, pertaining to, a king or to his office; royal: *the regal state, title, power.* **2.** Fit for, suitable to, a king; kingly; splendid, stately: *regal splendour, magnificence; regal courtesy, bearing.*

regal (II.), n. Fr. *régale.* See prec. An old form of portable organ with reed stops, used in the 16th and 17th cents.

regale (I.), vb. trans. & intrans. [1. rēgā́l; 2. rīgéil], fr. Fr. *régaler*, Ital. *regalare*, 'to lavish gifts on'. See next word. **A.** trans. **1.** To entertain, treat, feast, lavishly: *the guests were regaled with great profusion and magnificence.* **2.** To delight, gratify &c.: *delightful music regaled their ears; to regale oneself with a cigar, on a beautiful scene* &c. **B.** intrans. (rare) *To regale on, upon,* **a** to feast on; **b** to enjoy.

regale (II.), n. Obs. Fr. *régale*, cp. Ital. *regalo*, 'gift'; etymol. obscure. (obs.) **a** A feast, banquet, splendid repast; **b** a choice dish; fine flavour or taste: *a feast of great regale.*

regalement, n. [1. regā́lment; 2. rigéilmənt]. **regale** (I.) & **-ment.** Act of regaling; a sumptuous feast or entertainment.

regalia (I.), n. pl. [1. regā́lia; 2. rigéiliə]. Lat., 'royal things', neut. pl. of *rēgālis*, 'royal'. See **regal. 1.** (hist. and archaic) Royal privileges, rights, and prerogatives; regalities. **2.** The emblems or insignia of royalty used at the coronation of the sovereign or at other special ceremonies, consisting of the crown, sceptre, and orb, together with various swords of state &c. **3.** The insignia, jewels, emblems &c. of Freemasons, or other societies such as the Odd Fellows &c.

regalia (II.), n. Span., 'a royal privilege or right'. See prec. The name of a large Havana cigar of a special size and quality.

regalism, n. [1. rḗgalizm; 2. rígəlizəm]. **regal & -ism.** Theory, doctrine, of royal supremacy, esp. in Church matters.

regalist, n. [1. rḗgalist; 2. rígəlist]. **regal & -ist.** A supporter of regalism.

regality, n. [1. rēgáliti; 2. rīgǽliti], fr. O. Fr. *regalité.* See **regal & -ity. 1.** Sovereign right, privilege; sovereignty, royalty, status of a king. **2.** (pl.) Royal rights and privileges, regalia. **3.** (Scots law, obs.) Sovereign jurisdiction held by a subject by a grant from the Crown.

regard (I.), vb. trans. & intrans. [1. regárd; 2. rigā́d]. Fr. *regarder*, 'to look at; think of, have reference to'. See **re-** & **guard** (II.). **A.** trans. **1. a** To gaze at, observe, intently: *he regarded me with a stony stare;* **b** (fig.) to look upon: *to regard* (a person or thing) *with favour, with dislike.* **2.** (of mental action) To contemplate, look at, consider: *I wish you would regard the matter for a moment from my point of view.* **3. a** (rare, chiefly neg.) To esteem highly, have regard for: *I do not regard his opinion in such questions;* **b** (chiefly neg.) pay attention to, heed, have respect for: *he regards neither the laws of God, nor those of man;* **c** to think of in a specified way, hold specified opinion, or estimate concerning: *to regard a person as a fool, as a danger to society; I regard the situation as serious; the matter may be regarded as closed.* **4.** To concern, have relation to, have a bearing upon: *the matter does not regard you at all; it regards me vitally to know* &c. Phr. *as regards* (*that* &c.), so far as that is concerned, with reference to that; *regarding,* (i.) with regard to: *regarding what you say, I may tell you at once* &c.; (ii.) about, concerning: *he spoke to me regarding his future.* **B.** intrans. (rare) To look at; to heed: *he doesn't regard where he is going.*

regard (II.), n. Fr. See prec. **1.** Look, gaze, esp. a fixed, significant look: *he looked at him with a stern regard, with a reproachful regard.* **2.** Concern, heed, consideration, attention: *to pay no regard to one's duties; to act without regard to other people's feelings; to have regard for the laws of social conduct; regard must be had to his wishes.* **3. a** Respect, esteem, consideration: *to hold a person in high, low, regard; to have little regard for other people's opinions;* **b** (in pl.) compliments, expressions of kindly feeling &c.: *with kind regards; give our kindest regards to your mother.* **4.** Relation, respect, reference, bearing: *his remarks have special regard to the question at issue.* Phr. *in, with, regard to,* in reference, with respect to, about.

regardant, adj. [1. regárdant; 2. rigā́dənt]. Fr., Pres. Part. of *regarder.* See **regard** (I.). **1.** (archaic or poet.) Looking backwards, observant, watchful: *to turn, keep, a regardant eye upon.* **2.** (her.) Of heraldic animals, represented with the head turned, and looking backwards.

regardful, adj. [1. regárdfool; 2. rigā́dful]. **regard** (II.) & **-ful.** Showing regard and respect (for); mindful, heedful, attentive, observant of: *regardful of the needs of others, of one's promises, duties.*

regardfully, adv. Prec. & **-ly.** In a regardful manner; attentively, heedfully.

regardfulness, n. See prec. & **-ness.** State, quality, of being regardful; heedfulness, attentiveness.

regarding, prep. [1. regárding; 2. rigā́diŋ], fr. Pres. Part. of **regard** (I.). In regard to, as regards, concerning, about.

regardless, adj. [1. regárdles; 2. rigā́dlis]. **regard** (II.) & **-less. a** Not having regard or respect for; without regard, heedless, careless; negligent: *regardless of life, expense* &c.; *regardless of his duties;* **b** (slang) as adv., *got up, dressed, regardless,* i.e. of expense.

regardlessly, adv. Prec. & **-ly.** Without regard; in a regardless manner; heedlessly, carelessly.

regardlessness, n. See prec. & **-ness.** State, quality, of being regardless; heedlessness, carelessness.

regatta, n. [1. regáta; 2. rigǽtə]. Ital., also *rigatta*, 'a strife, contention for the mastery', orig. used of gondola races in Venice; etymol. uncertain. A rowing or sailing match, esp. a meeting for boat or yacht races: *Henley, Cowes, regatta.*

regelate, vb. intrans. [1. rḗjelāt; 2. rídžileit]. **re-** & Lat. *gelāt-(um)*, P.P. of *gelāre*, 'to freeze', fr. *gelu*, 'frost'. See **gelid.** To become fused into a solid mass again, after temporary thaw.

regelation, n. [1. rèjeláshun; 2. rìdžiléiʃən]. **re-** & Lat. *gelātiōn-(em)*; prec. & **-ion.** Process of being frozen and fused together again, or regelated, after thaw.

regency, n. [1. rḗjensi; 2. rídžənsi]. **regent & -cy. a** Office, position, authority, of a regent, or regents; deputed government; specif. (cap.) that of the Duke of Orleans in France (1715–23), or that of George, Prince of Wales, afterwards George IV., in England (1811–30); **b** period of duration of such government.

regenerable, adj. [1. rējénerabl; 2. rīdžénərəbl]. See **regenerate & -able.** Capable of being regenerated.

regeneracy, n. [1. rējénerasi; 2. rīdžénərəsi]. **regenerate & -cy.** State, quality, of being regenerate; regeneration.

regenerate (I.), vb. trans. & intrans. [1. rējénerāt; 2. rīdžénəreit], fr. Lat. *regenerāt-(um)*, P.P. of *regenerāre.* See **re- & generate. A.** trans. **1.** To generate, produce, again; to recreate, reproduce: *certain animals are able to regenerate lost parts of the body.* **2. a** (theol.) To cause, effect, regeneration in; to cause to be spiritually born again; **b** to produce reform in, cause to lead a new and amended life. **3.** To build up again on new and improved basis; reorganize after decay; inspire a new life and spirit in: *to regenerate a country, society, institutions* &c. **4.** Phr. *to regenerate a battery,* to recharge, generate more electricity in. **B.** intrans. **1.** To form again; to be reproduced as by new growth: *nails and hair are constantly regenerating.* **2. a** To become regenerated, to be born again spiritually; **b** to reform oneself morally.

regenerate (II.), adj. [1. rējénerat; 2. rīdžénərit], fr. Lat. *regenerātus.* See prec. **1.** (theol.) Born again spiritually; regenerated. **2.** Improved, restored; made better, reformed; contrasted with *degenerate.*

regeneration, n. [1. rèjeneráshun; 2. rìdženəréiʃən], fr. Lat. *regenerātiōn-(em), regenerātio.* See **regenerate** (I.) & **-ion. 1.** Process of regenerating; condition of being regenerated. **2.** Specif. (theol.) **a** process of being spiritually regenerated to a new life of grace; **b** state of being regenerate.

regenerative, adj. [1. rējénerativ; 2. rīdžénərətiv]. **regenerate** (I.) & **-ive.** (in various senses) Having power to regenerate; producing, characterized by, regeneration; specif., *regenerative furnace,* one in which the outgoing hot air or gas heats the incoming fresh air or gas, so as to prevent much waste of heat and fuel.

regenerator, n. [1. rējénerāter; 2. rīdžénəreitə]. **regenerate & -or.** One who, that which, regenerates; specif., a device for saving fuel by conserving heat in furnaces, a regenerative furnace.

regenesis, n. [1. rèjénesis; 2. rìdžénisis]. **re- & genesis.** Rebirth, recrudescence, renewal.

regent (I.), adj. [1. rḗjent; 2. rídžənt]. Lat. *regent-(em)*, Pres. Part. of *regere*, 'to rule'. See base **reg-* under **rex, regal;** also **rectum. 1. a** Exercising the functions of a ruler; ruling; **b** specif., exercising deputed functions of a ruler, acting as regent; (usually following the n.) *the Prince Regent.* **2.** (univ.) Exercising the functions of a member of the governing body: *regent masters.*

regent (II.), n. Same as prec. **1.** One who rules or governs in the place of another; specif., a person appointed as administrator of a kingdom during the minority or incapacity of the sovereign. **2.** (univ.) **a** (hist., at Oxford and Cambridge) One of the body of Masters of Arts, *regent masters,* who presided in the schools; **b** (U.S.A.) a member of the governing board of certain universities.

regentship, n. [1. rḗjentship; 2. rídžəntʃip]. **regent** (II.) & **-ship.** Regency.

regerminate, vb. intrans. [1. rējérmināt; 2. rīdžə́mineit]. **re- & germinate.** To germinate, sprout, bud, shoot afresh.

regicidal, adj. [1. réjisīdl; 2. rédžisaidl]. See next word & **-al. a** Connected with, pertaining to, a regicide; **b** connected with, of the nature of, the crime of regicide.

regicide, n. [1. réjisīd; 2. rédžisaid]. Formed on anal. of *parricide* &c., fr. Lat. *rēgi-*, stem of *rēx*, 'king', see **regal,** & **-cide. 1.** One who kills or takes part in the killing of a king or sovereign; specif., *the Regicides,* those who sat as judges on, condemned, and signed the death-warrant of Charles I. **2.** The crime of killing a king or other hereditary ruler. **3.** (attrib.) *A regicide peace,* peace with regicides or with the nation whose king has been killed.

régie, n. [1. rázhē; 2. réižī]. Fr., fem. of P.P. of *régir*, 'to rule, administer'. See **regent.** System of government monopoly of the sale of certain goods, esp. of tobacco and salt, used as means of revenue.

régime, regime, n. [1. rázhēm, rāzhḗm; 2. réižīm, reižī́m]. Fr. *régime.* See next word. **1.** System, method, of government or administration; social, political system: *a regime of patronage, privilege; we must work for a new regime;* specif. (hist.) *ancien régime,* the social system and polity of monarchical France before the French Revolution. **2.** Method, rule, course of treatment, esp. in matters of health; regimen: *to be put on a strict regime; a careful regime of diet and physical exercises.*

regimen, n. [1. réjimen; 2. rédžimen]. Lat., 'rule, guidance', fr. base *reg-, 'to rule, guide, as in *regere*, 'to rule'. See **regent** & **rex**. **1.** (archaic) Régime, administration, system, of government. **2.** System, course of treatment, esp. in matters of diet, exercise &c. laid down by a doctor. **3.** (gram.) Relation in syntax between words; government.

regiment (I.), n. [1. réjiment; 2. rédžimənt]. O. Fr., 'rule, government'; in mil. sense fr. Fr. *régiment*, fr. L. Lat. *regimentum*, later form of prec. **1.** (obs. or archaic) Rule, government: *The Monstrous Regiment of Women*, title of book by John Knox. **2.** A military unit; applied **a** to a battalion consisting of four companies, and commanded by a lieut.-colonel; and **b** to a larger unit of two (linked) battalions, commanded by a colonel; each of these battalions may have an independent name and history; e.g. the old 43rd Regiment of Foot is the 1st battalion of the Oxfordshire and Buckinghamshire Light Infantry, of which the old 52nd is the 2nd battalion; **c** a cavalry unit, of four squadrons. **3.** (by transf.) Any large number of persons or things; swarm, legion: *whole regiments of locusts*.

regiment (II.), vb. trans., fr. prec. **1.** (obs.) To form into a regiment or regiments. **2.** To arrange, systematize, group together and subject to discipline: *the Germans were accustomed to be regimented.*

regimental, adj. [1. rèjiméntl; 2. rèdžiméntəl]. **regiment** (I.) & **-al**. Of, belonging to, a regiment: *the regimental colour*; *regimental history* &c.

regimentally, adv. Prec. & **-ly**. According to regiments; according to the arrangement, customs &c. of a regiment.

regimentals, n. pl. [1. rèjiméntalz; 2. rèdžiméntəlz], fr. the adj. Uniform and accoutrements worn in a particular regiment.

regimentation, n. [1. rèjimentáshun; 2. rèdžimentéiʃən]. See **regiment** (II.) & **-ation**. Process of arranging, forming, in or into regiments; grouping, classification.

regina, n. [1. rejína; 2. ridžáinə]. Lat., 'queen', fr. base *reg-, as in **regent** & **rex**. The official title of a reigning queen, abbreviated R., as in signatures &c., V.R., *Victoria Regina*, or *Reg.*, as in title of law cases brought by the Crown: *Regina* v. *Cox*; *Reg.* v. *Cox*.

reginal, adj. [1. rejínal; 2. ridžáinəl]. Prec. & **-al**. (rare or archaic) Queenly, befitting a queen; correlative of *regal*.

region, n. [1. réjun; 2. rídžən]. M.E., fr. Fr. *regioun*, fr. Lat. *regiōn-(em)*, 'a making straight; a direction; a boundary, limit; quarter, tract of earth or sky'; fr. base *reg-, 'to guide, straighten; to rule' &c. See **rectum, rex, regent**. **1.** A quarter, tract, area, district, of earth, sea, sky, or of space generally, with rather undefined limits: *the Arctic regions*; *forest regions*; *the upper regions of air* &c.; *region of perpetual snow*. Phrs. *the lower, infernal, regions*, hell; also jocularly, the basement of a house; *in the region of*, in the approximate neighbourhood of. **2.** A tract or division of the body, usually designated with reference to some important organ or member: *the lumbar region*, that near the loins. **3.** Sphere, realm, domain, of thought and science: *the regions of philosophy, of psychology* &c.

regional, adj. [1. réjunal; 2. rídžənəl]. Prec. & **-al**. Connected with, belonging to, characteristic of, a region of the globe.

register (I.), n. [1. réjister; 2. rédžistə]. M.E., fr. Fr. *registre*, fr. Med. Lat. *registrum*, mistaken form of *registum*, 'roll, record, register', fr. Lat. *regestum*, usually in pl. *regesta*, 'catalogue, list', fr. *regest-(um)*, P.P. type of *regerere*, 'to bring, carry back, to record', fr. **re-** & *gerere*, 'to carry, bear', see **-gerous** & **gerent**. **1. a** A record of events, proceedings, names &c., esp. an official record kept for authoritative reference; **b** book &c. containing such lists or records: *register of births, marriages, and deaths*; *parish register*, of baptisms, marriages, and funerals kept by the minister of a parish; *register of shareholders, voters* &c.; specif. (naut.) (i.) *ship's register*, certificate issued by the customs, giving nationality, name of owners, names of master and crew, and description of the vessel; (ii.) *Lloyd's register*, of shipping. **2.** Mechanical device, usually a movable iron plate, for regulating the draught in a stove, furnace &c., or a valve for regulating passage of air in a ventilator. **3.** Mechanical device for registering or recording (numbers, speed &c.), e.g. *cash register*. **4. a** Range, compass, of a voice; **b** the series of notes in a voice having the same quality, that is, which can be sung in the same manner and without readjustment of the vocal chords. **5. a** (photog.) Correspondence of the focussing screen with the plate or film; **b** (print.) (i.) exact adjustment in line &c. of one page of printed matter with its reverse side; (ii.) adjustment of impression, as in colour printing, of the various series of blocks or plates.

register (II.), vb. trans. & intrans. See prec. **A.** trans. **1. a** To enter in a register, to record formally in writing: *to register a birth, death* &c.; *to register names of members*; *to register one's name as a voter*; **b** to record in one's mind, to form a mental impression of: *his face was registered in my memory*. **2.** To indicate, record, automatically: *the thermometer registered three degrees of frost*; *the heaviest rainfall of the year was registered yesterday*. **3.** (print. &c.) To make to correspond, to adjust exactly: *to register a page, colour print* &c. **4.** To insure against loss or damage and secure delivery of (letter, parcel) by payment of special fee, entry of name &c.: *to register a letter at the Post Office*; *to register luggage on a railway*. **B.** intrans. **1.** To enter one's name on a register (esp. at hotel &c.). **2.** (print. &c. of page &c.) To correspond exactly.

register (III.), n., fr. prec. (a Scots usage) **1.** One who registers; a registrar: *the Lord Clerk Register*, keeper of the Scottish records. **2.** A registry; also attrib. *Register House*, Edinburgh.

registrable, adj. [1. réjistrabl; 2. rédžistrəbl]. **register** (II.) & **-able**. Capable of being registered (in various senses of vb.).

registrar, n. [1. rèjistrár; 2. rèdžistrá]. Med. Lat. *registrārius*. See also **register** (III.). One who registers; the official in charge of a register; keeper of records: *Registrar of births, marriages, and deaths*; *the Registrar of a university* &c. *Registrar-General*, the chief official of the principal or central Registry office, in London, in charge of all vital statistics.

registrarship, n. [1. réjistràrship; 2. rédžistràʃip]. Prec. & **-ship**. Office, position, of a registrar; period of office of a registrar.

registrary, n. [1. réjistrari; 2. rédžistrəri]. See **registrar** & **-y**. A registrar, obsolete except as title of the registrar of Cambridge University.

registration, n. [1. rèjistráshun; 2. rèdžistréiʃən]. Med. Lat. *registrātiōn-(em)*, fr. *registrāt-(um)*, P.P. of *registrāre*, see **register** (II.), & **-ion**. **1. a** Act, fact, of registering or entering in a register; **b** an entry, a registry: *registration of voters, of births, marriages, or deaths* &c. **2.** (print. &c.) Exact correspondence or adjustment of two printed pages, impressions of series of colours in a print &c. **3.** (mus.) Act of combining the stops on an organ so as to produce desired effect.

registry, n. [1. réjistri; 2. rédžistri]. **register** & **-ry**. **1.** Place, office, in which a register is kept, or in which a registrar works: *a district, parish, registry*. **2.** Registration, entry in a register.

registry office, n. **a** Local registry for births, marriages, and deaths: *marriage at a registry office*, a civil marriage before a registrar; **b** office for the hiring of domestic servants.

Regius, adj. [1. réjius; 2. rídžiəs]. Lat., 'royal', fr. *rēgi-, stem of *rēx*, 'king'. See **rex** & **regal**. Royal; appointed, founded, by a king; used only in connexion with certain professors and chairs at the older English universities, founded by King Henry VIII., and with some in Scotland, appointments of, or to, which are made by the Crown: *a Regius Professor, Professorship*.

reglet, n. [1. réglet; 2. réglit]. Fr. *réglet*, dimin. of *règle*, 'rule', fr. Lat. *rēgula*. See **regular** & **rule**. **1.** (archit.) Small flat moulding used to separate panels, or interlaced as an ornament. **2.** (print.) Small strip of wood or metal, less than the height of type, for separating lines &c.

regnal, adj. [1. régnal; 2. régn(ə)l], fr. Med. Lat. *regnālis*, fr. Lat. *regnum*, 'kingdom, reign'; fr. *rēg-, as in **rex**, & **-al**. Of, belonging to, a sovereign's reign: specif., *regnal year*, the year in which a sovereign begins his reign; used in title of statutes: *regnal day*, day of a sovereign's accession.

regnant, adj. [1. régnant; 2. régnənt], fr. Lat. *regnant-(em)*, Pres. Part. of *regnāre*, 'to rule, reign'. See **regent** & **rex**, & cp. **reign**. **1.** Reigning, ruling; exercising sovereign power by hereditary right: *Queen Regnant*, as opposed to *Queen Consort*. **2.** Ruling, reigning, predominant, prevalent: *the regnant fashion*; *customs now regnant*; *the regnant qualities in his character*.

regorge, vb. trans. & intrans. [1. regórj; 2. rigɔ́dž], fr. Fr. *regorger*, fr. **re-** & *gorger*, see **gorge** (II.). **1.** trans. **a** To vomit, disgorge; **b** to swallow again. **2.** intrans. To flow back, be thrown back, as water from a hole &c.

regrant, vb. trans. & n. [1. regráhnt; 2. rīgránt]. **re-** & **grant**. **1.** vb. To grant again; to renew a grant. **2.** n. A renewed grant; renewal of a grant; a second grant.

regrate, vb. trans. [1. regrát; 2. rigréit], fr. O. Fr. *regrater*; etymol. uncertain; prob. fr. **re-** & *grater*, mod. *gratter*, 'to scrape', see **grate** (I.). (hist.) To buy commodities, esp. provisions, corn &c., in large quantities at markets or fairs, with a view to retailing at a high profit at the same market or within four miles therefrom; formerly a criminal offence; cp. **forestall** (II.), with which it is often coupled.

re-grate, vb. trans. [1. règrát; 2. rīgréit], fr. **re-** & **grate** (I.). (masonry) To grate or scrape the surface of a wall to give it a fresh appearance.

regrater, regrator, n. [1. regráter; 2. rigréitə]. **regrate** & **-er, -or**; cp. Fr. *regrattier*, 'huckster, middleman'. One who regrates, a middleman.

regress (I.), n. [1. régres; 2. rígres], fr. Lat. *regressus*, n., fr. *regress-(um)*, P.P. type of *regredi*, 'to go back, return', **re-** & *gredi*, 'to step, walk', see **gradus**. **1.** A going back, return; re-entry, passage back: *right of egress and regress*. **2.** (in spiritual sense) Retrogression, retrograde movement in moral development, civilization &c.; contrasted with *progress*. **3.** (law) **a** Right of recourse to another, as the person primarily responsible for a debt &c.; **b** right of re-entry to forfeited lands, a vacant benefice &c.

regress (II.), vb. intrans. [1. regrés; 2. rigrés]. See prec. To go, move, backward; to return to former place or state.

regression, n. [1. regréshun; 2. rigréʃən], fr. Lat. *regressiōn-(em)*. See prec. & **-ion**. **1.** Act of going or moving back or backwards; a backward movement; return. **2.** Moral retrogression, relapse; reversion to inferior state. **3. a** (astron.) The movement backwards of the nodes of the moon, the complete backward revolution taking some 18½ years; **b** (math.) the backward flexion of a curve from a cusp.

regressive, adj. [1. regrésiv; 2. rigrésiv]. See prec. & **-ive**. Moving backward, retrogressive (in material or moral senses).

regressively, adv. Prec. & **-ly**. In a regressive manner.

regret (I.), vb. trans. [1. regrét; 2. rigrét]. M.E. *regretten*, fr. O. Fr. *regreter*; *regrater*, Fr. *regretter*; etymol. uncertain; the second element prob. of Gmc. origin, cp. O.E. *grētan*, 'to weep, bewail', see **greet (II.)**. **1.** To feel and express sorrow for; to be sorry for; to deplore: *to regret a person's death, absence* &c.; *to regret the failure of plans*; *to regret to hear*; *regret to have to announce the death of*; *I regret to say that So-and-so has died*. Phr. *it is to be regretted that*, it is unfortunate, a pity, that. **2.** To be sorry for the loss of, to remember with regret; to think of with longing, to miss: *to regret one's happy youth, the old home* &c. **3.** To remember with sorrow or remorse, to lament; to repent of: *to regret the follies of one's youth*; *a mistake which he regretted all his life*; *to regret one's lost chances, wasted opportunities*; *have you nothing to regret in your life?*

regret (II.), n. Fr. See prec. **1.** Sorrow, grief, distress of mind, at an event, situation, loss or absence of: *to hear with regret of*; *to feel regret for*; *it is with great regret we have to announce the death of*; *an expression of regret and sympathy*. **2.** Feeling of distress and longing for what is past and lost beyond recall: '*Deep as first love and wild with all regret*' (Tennyson, 'Princess'). **3.** Repentance, sorrow, remorse, for what has been done: *to feel regret for past misdeeds*; *to have no regrets*.

regretful, adj. [1. regrétfool; 2. rigrétful]. Prec. & **-ful**. **a** Feeling regret: *I am most regretful for my apparent discourtesy*; **b** expressing, signifying, betokening, regret: *a regretful apology, refusal*; *a regretful glance, sigh* &c.

regretfully, adv. Prec. & -ly. With regret.

regrettable, adj. [1. regrétabl; 2. rigrétəbl]. **regret (I.)** & **-able**. To be regretted; causing regret: *a regrettable error*; *a most regrettable loss to the country*.

regrettably, adv. Prec. & **-ly**. In a regrettable manner; to a regrettable extent.

regroup, vb. trans. [1. rēgroōp; 2. rigrúp]. **re-** & **group**. To group again; to arrange into new groups.

regula, n. [1. régūla; 2. régjulə]. Lat. *rēgula*, 'a straight wooden staff, ruler; a rule'; fr. base **rĕg-*, 'to straighten; to guide; to direct, to rule'. See **rectum, regent, rex**; cp. **rule**. **1.** The rule of a monastic order. **2.** (archit.) A square block or small fillet below the taenia of a frieze on a Doric architrave.

regulable, adj. [1. régūlabl; 2. régjuləbl]. See prec. & **regulate** & **-able**. Capable of being regulated.

regular (I.), adj. [1. régūlar; 2. régjulə], fr. Lat. *rēgulāris*, 'of, belonging to, a ruler or bar; containing rules or regulations'. See **regula** & **-ar**. **1.** (eccles., the only sense in Engl. till 16th cent.) Subject to, bound by, living under, the *regula* or rule of a monastic order; belonging to a monastic order, contrasted with *secular*: *regular clergy*, monks, friars; *canons regular*. **2.** Arranged according to a rule, plan, system, or principle; following some definite order or arrangement; orderly, systematic; symmetrical, harmonious: *a regular plan for streets*; *a regular building, style of architecture*; *regular features*; *regular verse*; *a regular system* &c. **3.** Not varying or changing; done, operating, recurring, uniformly; not subject to change; constant, habitual; not capricious: *regular hours, work*; *a regular mind*; *regular habits, way of life* &c.; *the functions of the body in health are quite regular*; *a regular pulse*. **4.** **a** Conforming to a standard, to a generally accepted custom, order, or usage; correct, normal: *everything was quite regular when the fire broke out*; *what is the regular dress for such occasions?*; *the proceedings were regular*; **b** properly, duly, qualified or authorized; belonging to a recognized or established body: *a regular doctor, nurse* &c. **5.** Various specific senses: **a** *the regular army, regular soldiers*, originally applied to the *standing* or permanent army and its soldiers, contrasted with *irregulars*, levies disbanded after a war; hence to the army, with its soldiers, which is always in service, as distinct from militia and volunteers &c.; now from the Territorial army and its soldiers; **b** *regular marriage*, one which takes place in church after publication of banns or by licence, as distinct from one before a registrar; **c** (gram.) of words, formations &c., conforming to the usual, normal inflections; in English grammar, often applied to *weak verbs*, i.e. those of the largest class which form Pret. and P.P. in *-ed* &c. **6.** (of shape) Exact, symmetrical: **a** (bot.) having the whorls exactly symmetrical: *a regular flower*; **b** (crystal.) isometric; **c** (geom.) having all the sides and angles equal: *a regular polygon*; (of solid bodies) having faces exactly similar: *a regular polyhedron*. **7.** (colloq.) Thorough, downright; out-and-out, perfect: *a regular row, rogue*; *a regular brick*; *a regular holiday*.

regular (II.), n., fr. prec. **1.** (eccles.) A member of the regular clergy; a monk or friar, as distinct from a parish or secular priest. **2.** A regular or professional soldier; an officer or soldier belonging to the regular army.

regularity, n. [1. règūláriti; 2. règjuláeriti]. See **regular (I.)** & **-ity**, cp. Fr. *régularité*. State, quality, of being regular: *regularity of features*; *regularity in conduct, hours* &c.

regularization, n. [1. règūlarīzáshun; 2. règjuləraizéiʃən]. See next word & **-ation**. Act of regularizing; state of being regularized.

regularize, vb. trans. [1. régūlarīz; 2. régjuləraiz]. **regular (I.)** & **-ize**. To make regular; **a** to put in order, to arrange according to a plan, system &c.; **b** to bring under, put in accordance with, a law or rule; make lawful: *to regularize a marriage, one's position*.

regularly, adv. [1. régūlarli; 2. régjuləli]. **regular (I.)** & **-ly**. **1.** In a regular manner, according to rule, plan, custom &c.: *streets arranged regularly*; *to behave, to dress, regularly*; *proceedings regularly conducted*. **2.** At regular intervals or periods; constantly, duly: *he calls here regularly every week*; *he goes to church regularly*. **3.** (colloq.) Thoroughly, completely: *I was regularly taken in over that business*.

regulate, vb. trans. [1. régūlāt; 2. régjuleit], fr. L. Lat. *rēgulāt-(um)*, P.P. type of *rēgulāre*. See **regula**. **1.** To make to conform to a rule or standard; to control by, or adjust, direct, restrict, moderate, in accordance with, a principle or system &c.: *to regulate one's conduct according to others*; *to regulate expenditure*. **2.** To put in order, to make to work properly and accurately; to adjust: *to regulate a clock*. **3.** To control, adjust to a particular standard, rate &c.: *to regulate the temperature of a room, the speed of a machine, the flow of water through a pipe*.

regulation, n. [1. règūláshun; 2. règjuléiʃən]. Prec. & **-ion**. **1.** Act of regulating; state of being regulated: *the regulation of our habits*; *regulation of conduct, of the finances* &c. **2.** A rule, precept, ordinance; a prescribed, regulating, principle: *to keep to the regulations*; *the regulations of a university, club* &c. **3.** (attrib.) Ordered, prescribed; according to rule, order &c.; normal, ordinary: *regulation dress, pattern, uniform*; *at a regulation rate, speed* &c.

regulative, adj. [1. régūlativ; 2. régjulətiv]. **regulate** & **-ive**. Regulating; tending to, having the power to, regulate or adjust: *regulative principles, faculties* &c.

regulator, n. [1. régūlàter; 2. régjuleitə]. **regulate** & **-or**. One who or that which regulates or adjusts; esp. any part of a mechanism which keeps the movement regular or adjusts and controls it; e.g. device for regulating movement of a watch or clock, the pressure of steam in an engine &c.

reguline, adj. [1. régūlīn; 2. régjulain]. See next word & **-ine**. (chem. and metal.) Of, pertaining to, like, a regulus.

regulus, n., pl. **reguli** [1. régūlus, -lī; 2. régjuləs, -lai]. Lat., 'petty king or prince; a small bird', dimin. of *rēx*, 'king'. See **rex**. **1.** (astron., cap.) A star of the first magnitude in the constellation *Leo, alpha-Leonis*. **2.** (chem. and metal.) **a** (alchem.) Metallic antimony, combining readily with the royal metal, gold; **b** partially purified metal precipitated to the bottom of the crucible after smelting of ores; matte. **3.** A genus of birds, the kinglets, esp. the golden-crested wren, *Regulus cristatus*.

regurgitate, vb. intrans. & trans. [1. rēgérjitāt; 2. rīgə́džiteit], fr. L. Lat. *regurgitāt-(um)*, P.P. of *regurgitāre*, fr. **re-** & Lat. *gurgitāre*, 'to engulf', fr. *gurgit-(is)*, stem of *gurges*, 'whirlpool, gulf', see **gurgle**. **a** intrans. To flow, gush, back; **b** trans., to throw back, pour out, as from the stomach.

regurgitation, n. [1. rēgérjitáshun; 2. rīgədžitéiʃən]. Prec. & **-ation**. A flowing or pouring back; **a** the flowing back or rising into the throat or mouth of liquids or solids from the stomach; **b** the reverse flow of blood to the heart.

rehabilitate, vb. trans. [1. rèhabílitāt; 2. rìhəbíliteit], fr. L. Lat. *rehabilitāt-(um)*, **re-** & P.P. of *habilitāre*, 'to make fit or able', fr. *habilis*, 'handy, suitable, fit', see **able**. **1.** To restore to former estate, position, capacity; to reinvest with a forfeited privilege or right; to reinstate. **2.** To re-establish in good repute, restore to forfeited esteem and credit; to clear good name of by dispelling suspicion and removing aspersions; also (reflex.) *rehabilitate oneself*.

rehabilitation, n. [1. rèhabilitáshun; 2. rìhəbilitéiʃən]. Prec. & **-ion**. Act of rehabilitating; state of being rehabilitated; restoration to esteem, in reputation, to former rights &c.

rehandle, vb. trans. [1. rèhándl; 2. rìhǽndl]. **re-** & **handle (II.)**. To handle, deal with, over again, afresh; to recast, rearrange.

rehash, vb. trans. & n. [1. rèhásh; 2. rìhǽʃ]. **re-** & **hash**. **1.** vb. To hash again, afresh; to work up old, stale material into a new form, esp. to recast old literary material, and produce it under a different title. **2.** n. Anything made up of old, stale material.

rehear, vb. trans. [1. rèhḗr; 2. rìhíə]. **re-** & **hear**. To hear or try (case in law court) a second time.

rehearing, n. [1. rèhḗring; 2. rìhíəriŋ]. A second hearing, or trial, of a case.

rehearsal, n. [1. rehḗrsl; 2. rihə́sl]. Next word & **-al**. Act of rehearsing (a play &c.); trial performance, preparatory recital for practice.

rehearse, vb. trans. & intrans. [1. rehḗrs; 2. rihə́s]. M.E. *rehercen, rehersen*, fr. O. Fr. *rehercer, reherser*, 'to rake over again, reharrow; to repeat', fr. **re-**, & *herce, herse*, 'harrow', see **hearse (I.)**. **A.** trans. **1.** (poet. or rhet.) To repeat, tell over, narrate in detail; to give account of, enumerate: *to rehearse the tale of his crimes, one's sorrows, the glorious deeds of one's ancestors*. **2.** To go through, try over, perform (a play, piece of instrumental music, song &c.) in private, by way of practice, before public performance. **B.** intrans. To hold a rehearsal.

rehouse, vb. trans. [1. rèhóuz; 2. rìháuz]. **re-** & **house**. To provide (persons) with, lodge (them) in, new houses; esp. to put (people) into a new house in place of an old one destroyed as insanitary.

Reich, n. [1. rīgh; 2. raij]. Mod. Germ., 'empire, state, kingdom', fr. O.H.G. *rīhhi*; cogn. w. O.E. *rīce*, 'kingdom' &c., see **rich**, & suff. in **bishopric**; ultimately fr. base **rĕg-*, 'to rule, direct' &c. See **regent, rex**, & cognates there referred to. In Germany used of the Empire, now of the Republic, as a whole, as distinct from the subsidiary states which compose it.

Reichstag, n., properly, in Germ. [1. rígh-stahgh; 2. ráijstāʒ, -tāχ]. See prec. & **day**. The supreme legislature of the former German Empire and the present Republic.

reification, n. [1. rèifikáshun; 2. riifikéiʃən]. See **re** (II.) & **-fic** & **-ation**. Act of reifying or materializing; materialization.

reify, vb. trans. [1. réifī; 2. ríifai], fr. Lat. *rēs*, 'thing', see **re** (II.), & **-fy**. To materialize an abstraction, make concrete; to treat as real.

reign (I.), n. [1. rān; 2. rein], fr. O. Fr. *regne*, fr. Lat. *regnum*, 'rule, kingdom'. See **regnal** & words there referred to. **1. a** The rule, supreme power, sway, of a king or other sovereign; **b** period of duration of a ruler's reign: *the reign of Queen Victoria lasted more than sixty years.* **2.** Ruling power, sway, predominating influence: *the reign of fashion; reign of law, of peace, of anarchy* &c.; *Reign of Terror*, **a** (hist.) that period of the French Revolution, from May 1793 to July 1794, characterized by ruthless executions of opponents; **b** any period of political terrorism, anarchy, and bloodshed.

reign (II.), vb. intrans. M.E. *regnen*, fr. O. Fr. *regner*, fr. Lat. *regnāre*, 'to reign'. See prec. & **regnant**. **1.** To rule as sovereign; to be king or queen: '*And peace and plenty tell, a Stuart reigns*' (Pope, 'Windsor Forest', 42); *to reign over a vast domain.* **2.** To hold sway, to exert a predominant influence, be acknowledged as supreme: *a reigning opera star; a reigning beauty of the 'seventies.* **3.** To prevail, to be prevalent, to predominate: *peace and goodwill should reign in our hearts; silence reigned in the woods.*

reimburse, vb. trans. [1. rèimbérs; 2. riimbə́s]. **re-** & obs. *imburse*, fr. Low Lat. *imbursāre*, *in* & *bursa*, 'purse', cp. Fr. *rembourser*, & see **bursar**. To repay what has been expended; to refund; to compensate by payment: *to reimburse a person for his expenses; to reimburse the expenses of another.*

reimbursement, n. [1. rèimbérsment; 2. riimbə́smənt]. Prec. & **-ment**. Repayment of expenses.

reimport, vb. trans. & n. **re-** & **import**. **1.** vb. [1. rèimpórt; 2. riimpɔ́t]. To import again; to import goods after exporting them. **2.** n. [1. rèimport; 2. riimpɔt]. (usually pl.) Goods reimported; reimportation.

reimportation, n. [1. rèimportáshun; 2. riimpɔtéiʃən]. Prec. & **-ation**. Act of reimporting; that which is reimported; reimports.

reimpose, vb. trans. [1. rèimpóz; 2. riimpóuz]. **re-** & **impose**. To impose again, esp. of taxes which have been withdrawn or abolished.

reimposition, n. [1. rèimpozíshun; 2. riimpəzíʃən]. **re-** & **imposition**. A renewed imposition (of taxes &c.) after withdrawal.

rein (I.), n. [1. rān; 2. rein]. M.E. *reine*, *regne*, fr. O. Fr. *reine*, *resne*, Mod. Fr. *rêne*; A.-Fr. has also *redne*, cp. Ital. *redina*, & Span. *rienda*, fr. Low Lat. **retina*, 'rein, halter', fr. *retinēre*, 'to hold back'. See **retain**. **1. a** Leather strap fastened to a bit, or head-piece, for leading and holding a horse; **b** (pl.) *reins*, pair of straps having one end of each buckled into the rings at the side of a bit, by means of which a horse is controlled by rider or driver. **2.** (fig.) In various Phrs., with sense of restraining force or influence, means of control &c.: *to give the rein to* (one's passions, fancy &c.), allow full play to; *to keep a tight rein on* (a person), to discipline severely; *the reins of government*, power in the state; *a tight rein*, severe methods of discipline.

rein (II.), vb. trans., fr. prec. **1.** To put a rein or reins on to. **2.** To apply the rein to, to control, hold in with the rein; also *rein in*, to restrain, hold back, by applying the rein; commonly used figuratively: *to rein in one's temper, passions* &c.

reincarnate, vb. trans. & adj. **re-** & **incarnate**. **1.** vb. [1. rèinkárnāt; 2. riinkánet]. To incarnate again; to give bodily form to (a spirit) a second time; to cause to be reborn in other form. **2.** adj. [1. rèinkárnat; 2. riinkánit]. Reincarnated, born again in bodily form.

reincarnation, n. [1. rèinkarnáshun; 2. riinkānéiʃən]. **re-** & **incarnation**. **1. a** Act of reincarnating; **b** state of being reincarnated. **2.** The doctrine of metempsychosis, by which the soul after the death of the body appears again with a new body.

reindeer, n. [1. rándēr; 2. réindiə], fr. O.N. *hreinn*, 'reindeer', & Engl. **deer**; on model of O.N. *hreindýri*. See **rinderpest**. Large, domesticated deer, genus *Rangifer*, with long, branching antlers; kept in Lapland for drawing sledges, and for milking. *Reindeer moss*, a grey spreading lichen, *Cladonia rangiferina*, of arctic and subarctic regions, forming the pasturage of reindeer in winter.

reinforce (I.), vb. trans. [1. rèinfórs; 2. riinfɔ́s]. **re-** & **enforce**. **1. a** (mil. and nav.) To strengthen (body of troops or a fleet) by supplying additional troops or ships; **b** to add to numbers of (a body of persons). **2.** To strengthen (fabric, substance &c.) by increasing the thickness, and solidity, and durability of.

reinforce (II.), n., fr. prec. Any material added as a strengthening substance; specif., the stronger, thicker part of a gun near the breech.

reinforced concrete, n. [1. rèinfórst kóngkrēt; 2. riinfɔ́st kɔ́ŋkrit]. Mass of concrete used in building, strengthened by iron or steel bars embedded in it.

reinforcement, n. [1. rèinfórsment; 2. riinfɔ́smənt]. **reinforce** (I.) & **-ment**. **1.** Act of reinforcing; state of being reinforced. **2.** That which reinforces; specif. (usually pl.) new, additional, troops, ships &c. for the strengthening of an army or fleet.

reinless, adj. [1. ránles; 2. réinlis]. **rein** (I.) & **-less**. **a** Without a rein or reins; **b** uncurbed, unchecked, uncontrolled.

reins, n. pl. [1. rānz; 2. reinz]. O. Fr., fr. Lat. *rēnēs*, pl. of *rēn*, 'kidneys, reins', see **renal**. (archaic and Bib.) The kidneys; the region round the kidneys, the loins, esp. as regarded as the seat of the passions and affections: *the reins and the heart.*

reinstate, vb. trans. [1. rèinstát; 2. riinstéit]. **re-** & **in** & **state**. To replace in a former position; to restore to a former state: *to reinstate a person in his former office, to his lost privileges.*

reinstatement, n. [1. rèinstátment; 2. riinstéitmənt]. Prec. & **-ment**. Act of reinstating; state of being reinstated; restoration to former position, state &c.

reinsurance, n. [1. rèinshóorans; 2. riinʃɔ́rəns]. **re-** & **insurance**. Act of reinsuring; a contract by which an underwriter or insurance company agrees to indemnify one who has accepted a risk on an insurance policy in case of loss; third-party insurance.

reinsure, vb. trans. [1. rèinshóor; 2. riinʃɔ́]. **re-** & **insure**. To protect by a policy of reinsurance.

reintegrate, vb. trans. [1. rèintegrāt; 2. riintigreit]. **re-** & **integrate**. To integrate, restore to a whole or complete state again; to restore completely, re-establish.

reintegration, n. [1. rèintegráshun; 2. riintigréiʃən]. Prec. & **-ion**. Act of reintegrating; state of being reintegrated; restoration, re-establishment.

reinter, vb. trans. [1. rèintér; 2. riintə́]. **re-** & **inter** (I.). To inter, bury again; to rebury.

reinvest, vb. trans. [1. rèinvést; 2. riinvést]. **re-** & **invest**. **1. a** To invest, endow again, after loss or deprivation; to give back: *to reinvest a person with his former privileges, his old rank* &c.; **b** to lay siege to again: *to reinvest a fortress.* **2.** To invest (money) again; esp. to invest otherwise, in fresh securities.

reinvestiture, n. [1. rèinvéstìcher; 2. riinvéstitʃə]. **re-** & **investiture**. Act of reinvesting; state of being reinvested; a second investiture with old privileges &c.

reinvestment, n. [1. rèinvéstment; 2. riinvéstmənt]. **re-** & **investment**. A new investment (of money).

reinvigorate, vb. trans. [1. rèinvígurāt; 2. riinvígəreit]. **re-** & **invigorate**. To give fresh vigour, life, spirit to.

reis, n. pl. [1. rās; 2. reis]. Port., pl. of **real** (III.). A Portuguese and Brazilian money of account, 1000 reis = 1 milreis, now the chief monetary unit.

reissue, vb. trans. & n. [1. rèísū, -íshū; 2. riísju, -íʃju]. **re-** & **issue**. **1.** vb. To issue (currency, bills &c.) again, a second time; to republish (a book, article &c.). **2.** n. Something which is reissued; esp. reprint of a book, usually implying no change of, or addition to, the original matter; distinct from *new edition.*

reiterant, adj. [1. rēíterant; 2. riítərənt], fr. Lat. *reiterant-(em)*, Pres. Part. of *reiterāre*, 'to repeat'. See next word. Repeating, saying, doing, over and over again.

reiterate, vb. trans. [1. rēíterāt; 2. riítəreit], fr. Lat. *reiterāt-(um)*, P.P. of *reiterāre*, 'to repeat, reiterate', lit. 'to go over again'. As **re-** & **iterate**. To say, do, over and over again; to repeat (action or utterance) many times: *reiterated cries of dissent.*

reiteration, n. [1. rèiteráshun; 2. riitəréiʃən]. Prec. & **-ion**. **a** Act of reiterating or repeating; **b** that which is reiterated; repetition.

reiterative, adj. & n. [1. rēíterativ; 2. riítərətiv]. See prec. & **-ive**. **1.** adj. Reiterating, repeating; characterized by reiteration or repetition. **2.** n. (gram.) A word formed by the repetition of a word, sometimes with slight modification; as *tittle-tattle, dilly-dally* &c.

reive, reiver. See **reave, reaver.**

reject, vb. trans. [1. rejékt; 2. ridžékt]. O. Fr. *rejecter*, fr. Lat. *reject-(um)*, P.P. of *rejicere*, 'to throw, cast, back'; to cast off, repel; to reject, disdain, scorn', fr. **re-** & *jacere*, 'to throw'. See **jet** (III.). **1. a** To single out, and throw away, cast aside, to discard, as useless or valueless: *to reject weak, unhealthy plants, a poorly written article* &c.; **b** (of the stomach) to throw up, be unable to retain and digest. **2.** To refuse, decline, to accept or receive: *to reject an offer; to reject a suitor, a proposal of marriage.* **3.** To refuse to grant, refuse to assent to; to disallow: *to reject an appeal; to reject a bill in Parliament.* **4.** To be unable or unwilling to give intellectual assent to; to decline to believe: *to reject the doctrines of the Church.*

rejectable, adj. [1. rejéktabl; 2. ridžéktəbl]. Prec. & **-able**. Deserving, admitting of, rejection.

rejectamenta, n. pl. [1. rejèktaménta; 2. ridžèktəméntə]. Neo-Lat. See **reject** & **-ment**, w. Lat. pl. suff. Things thrown away or rejected as worthless or useless; rubbish; specif. **a** waste products of a living organism; **b** flotsam and jetsam.

rejection, n. [1. rejékshun; 2. ridžékʃən], fr. Lat. *rejectiōn-(em)*, *rejectio*. See **reject** & **-ion**. Act of rejecting; refusal to accept or grant.

rejoice, vb. trans. & intrans. [1. rejóis; 2. ridžɔ́is]. M.E. *rejoisen*, *rejoicen*, fr. O. Fr. *resjoiss-(ant)*, Pres. Part. stem of *resjouir*, Mod. Fr. *réjouir*, fr. **re-** & O. Fr. *esjoir*, Mod. Fr. *éjouir*, fr. Lat. *ex*, 'out', see **ex-**, & *gaudēre*, 'to be glad, rejoice', see **gaud** & **joy**. **A.** trans. **1.** To make glad, to cause joy to, to gladden; delight: *to rejoice a father's heart; a sight to rejoice one's eyes.* **2.** To feel delight and satisfaction; to be glad: *I rejoice to see you here; we should rejoice that he has been spared.* **B.** intrans. **1.** To make merry, to hold a joyful celebration: *let us rejoice together on this great occasion.* **2.** *Rejoice in, at*, to feel, take, delight in; to enjoy. Phr. *to rejoice in the name of*, to be named (facet.).

rejoicing, n. [1. rejóising; 2. ridžɔ́isiŋ]. Prec. & **-ing**. (often pl.) **a** Gladness, satisfaction; **b** outward expression of these; merry-making, festivities.

rejoin, vb. trans. & intrans. [1. rejóin; 2. ridžóin], fr. Fr. *rejoindre*. See **re-** & **join**. **A.** trans. To join again; to associate oneself again with; to take one's place again in or with: *to rejoin one's regiment, ship*; *you go on and I will rejoin you later.* **B.** intrans. **a** To reply, make answer; **b** specif. (law, of defendant's pleadings) to reply to plaintiff's replication.

re-join, vb. trans. & intrans. [1. rē jóin; 2. rī džóin]. **a** trans. To bring together again, cause to reunite; **b** intrans., to come together again, become reunited; esp. of something severed, or broken in two.

rejoinder, n. [1. rejóinder; 2. ridžóində], fr. Fr. *rejoindre*, infin. used as n. See **rejoin**. Answer, reply, retort; specif. (law) the reply in defendant's pleadings to plaintiff's replication.

rejuvenate, vb. trans. & intrans. [1. rējóōvenāt; 2. rīdžúvəneit]. **re-** & Lat. *juvenis*, 'young', see **juvenile**, & **-ate**. **1.** trans. To make young and vigorous again, to renew youth of. **2.** intrans. To become young and vigorous again; to rejuvenesce.

rejuvenation, n. [1. rejōōvenáshun; 2. ridžūvənéiʃən]. Prec. & **-ion**. Act of rejuvenating; state of being rejuvenated.

rejuvenator, n. [1. rejóōvenāter; 2. ridžúvənèitə]. See prec. & **-or**. One who, that which, rejuvenates.

rejuvenesce, vb. intrans. & trans. [1. rējōōvenés; 2. rīdžūvənés], fr. L. Lat. *rejuvenescere*, 'to grow young again'. See **rejuvenate**. **1.** intrans. To become, grow, young again; (biol.) to exhibit rejuvenescence. **2.** trans. (biol.) To cause rejuvenescence in.

rejuvenescence, n. [1. rèjōōvenésens; 2. rìdžūvənésəns]. Prec. & **-ence**. **1.** State of being or becoming young again; renewal of youth and vigour. **2.** Specif. (biol.) the formation of new cells in various lower organisms from the protoplasm of older cells.

rejuvenescent, adj. [1. rējōōvenésent; 2. rīdžūvənésənt]. **rejuvenesce** & **-ent**. Growing, becoming, young again.

rejuvenize, vb. trans. [1. rējóōvenīz; 2. rīdžúvənaiz]. Stem of **rejuvenate** & **-ize**. To cause to grow young again; to rejuvenate.

rekindle, vb. trans. & intrans. [1. rēkíndl; 2. rīkíndl]. **re-** & **kindle**. **1.** trans. **a** To kindle, set on fire again, relight; **b** (non-material) to arouse, inspire, again: *to rekindle hope, interest.* **2.** intrans. **a** To become rekindled, to blaze out again; **b** to become aroused, inflamed, again.

relabel, vb. trans. [1. rèlábl; 2. rìléibl]. **re-** & **label**. **a** To label again; put a fresh label on; **b** to give a fresh name, designation, to.

relapse (I.), vb. intrans. [1. reláps; 2. riláeps], fr. Lat. *relaps-(um)*, P.P. of *relābi*, 'to slip, fall back'. See **re-** & **lapse**. **1.** To slip, lapse, fall, back into a former, and inferior, state of mind, morals, belief &c.; to backslide: *to relapse into melancholia, into heresy, barbarism* &c. **2. a** To fall back into a lower, less active condition of body: *to relapse into coma, lethargy*; *to relapse into silence*; **b** to fall back into, resume, a former bad habit, line of conduct &c., after reform: *to relapse into vice, crime, drunkenness* &c.

relapse (II.), n., fr. prec. A slipping, falling, back into a former, bad condition (of bodily health, morals, belief, habits &c.): *the patient has had a serious relapse*; *a relapse into crime, vice, heresy* &c.

relapsing fever, n. [1. relápsing fḗver; 2. riláepsiŋ fīvə]. An intermittent, contagious fever, due to a bacillus, *Spirillum*, occurring epidemically during famines and in periods of scarcity in certain countries.

relate, vb. trans. & intrans. [1. relát; 2. riléit], fr. Lat. *relāt-(um)*, used as P.P. of *referre*, 'to bring back, trace back; to bring back word, to report', see **refer**; *lātum*, 'borne, carried', is for **tlātum*, fr. base **tel-*, **tol-*, 'to bear', cp. Lat. *tollere*, 'to carry, bear', see **tolerate**. **A.** trans. **1.** To tell, recount, narrate: *to relate one's adventures, one's grievances.* **2.** To bring into (logical or causal) relation or connexion with; to show, establish, such a relation between: *to relate facts to events*; *weather conditions can now be related to known causes.* **3.** (usually pass.) **a** To have, stand in, a genealogical connexion with, to belong to same genus, species, family &c.: *the domestic cat is distantly related to the tiger*; *Darnley was closely related to Mary Queen of Scots*; **b** to connect, associate, bring into relation with: *we are related by marriage and by ancient friendship.* **B.** intrans. **1.** To have connexion, be capable of being connected or associated with; to fit in with: *your statement does not relate well with the facts.* **2.** To refer, have reference to: *this paragraph relates to my father*; *to what event did your remarks relate?*

related, adj. [1. reláted; 2. riléitid]. Prec. & **-ed**. **a** Having causal or logical connexion, or relation: *a body of related facts, phenomena* &c.; **b** having genealogical or blood relationship: *all of us here are related*; *related languages.*

relatedness, n. [1. relátednes; 2. riléitidnis]. Prec. & **-ness**. State, fact, of being related.

relation, n. [1. reláshun; 2. riléiʃən]. Lat. *relātiōn-(em)*, 'a bringing back; a report, narrative'. See **relate** & **-ion**. **1.** Something related; **a** a tale, narrative; **b** a statement, a setting forth, exposition. **2.** Causal, logical, or grammatical, connexion: *the relation between wages and prices*; *the relation of weather conditions to the quality of harvests*; *the relation between cause and effect, between facts and the conclusions drawn from them*; *the relation of words in a sentence.* Phrs. *in relation to*, with reference to, in connexion with; *out of all relation to*, quite disproportionate. **3.** Way in which persons are connected with, related to, others; position in, footing on, which they stand to each other; mode of contact between persons; manner in which they touch and affect each other mutually in social or political connexions: *the relations between father and son, husband and wife, master and servant*; *I had the happiest relations with my colleagues*; *our relations were purely of a business character.* **4. a** Connexion in blood, genealogical descent from a common ancestor; blood relationship, family tie, kinship, relationship: *what was the relation between Elizabeth and James I.?*; **b** (i.) person related to another by ties of blood: *one's parents and one's children are one's nearest relations*; also (ii.) a person connected with another through marriage, though not by blood; a connexion, a relative: *a relation by marriage.* **5.** (law) The referring back, the coming into effect of, giving effect to, an act, by a fiction, to, or at, a date earlier than that at which it was actually completed or sanctioned: in such a case an act is said to come into effect *by relation.*

relational, adj. [1. reláshunal; 2. riléiʃənəl]. Prec. & **-al**. Pertaining to, indicating, a relation, esp. *relational parts of speech*, those which express grammatical relations.

relationally, adv. Prec. & **-ly**. In a relational manner; by relational parts of speech.

relationless, adj. [1. reláshunles; 2. riléiʃənlis]. See prec. & **-less**. **a** Without relation or connexion; **b** without family or kinsmen.

relationship, n. [1. reláshunship; 2. riléiʃənʃip]. **relation** & **-ship**. **a** State of being related by birth or marriage; kinship; also **b** connexion, relation, in wider sense.

relatival, adj. [1. rèlatíval; 2. rèlətáivəl]. **relative (II.)** & **-al**. (gram.) Pertaining to relative words, esp. to relative pronouns &c.

relativally, adv. Prec. & **-ly**. (gram.) By means of relative words, as pronouns &c.

relative (I.), adj. [1. rélativ; 2. rélətiv], fr. Lat. *relātīvus* 'having relation or reference, referring, relative', or through Fr. *relatif, -ive*. See **relate** & **-ive**. **1.** Relating to, referring to, having connexion with; relevant, pertinent: *all the details relative to the matter at issue*; *evidence hardly relative to what has to be proved.* **2.** Resulting from, dependent on, existing in relation to, or connexion with, something else; proportionate, comparative; not absolute: *the relative speed of two moving bodies*; *relative values of the dollar and the sovereign*; *quantity in language is purely relative*; *hot, cold, weak, strong are relative terms*; *happiness is a relative conception.* **3.** Having mutual relations; correlative, reciprocal, respective: *the relative duties of employer and employed.* **4.** (gram., of pron., adj., adv.) Relating, referring, to an antecedent word, sentence, or clause, expressed or implied.

relative (II.), n., fr. prec. **1.** A person connected with another by blood or marriage, kinsman, kinswoman, relation; sometimes used to designate a remoter connexion than the word *relation*. **2.** (gram.) A relative word, such as a pronoun.

relatively, adv. [1. rélativli; 2. rélətivli]. **relative (I.)** & **-ly**. In a relative manner; compared with something else; not absolutely: *he is relatively a wealthy man.*

relativeness, n. [1. rélativnes; 2. rélətivnis]. See prec. & **-ness**. State, quality, of being relative; relativity.

relativism, n. [1. rélativizm; 2. rélətivizəm]. **relative** & **-ism**. (philos.) Doctrine of those who maintain the relativity of knowledge.

relativist, n. [1. rélativist; 2. rélətivist]. See prec. & **-ist**. One who holds the doctrine of relativism.

relativity, n. [1. rèlatíviti; 2. rèlətíviti]. **relative (I.)** & **-ity**. **1.** State, quality, of being relative; relativeness. **2.** Specif. **a** (philos.) esp. in Phr. *relativity of knowledge*, the doctrine that knowledge is not absolute or positive, but depends on the relations in which things stand to each other, that it can be concerned only with such relations, and is limited by the changing conditions of our perceptive faculties; **b** (phys.) the theory that the uniformity of the phenomena of the universe is real or absolute to observers in the same 'framework' of space and time but may not hold good for observers in a different 'framework', and is therefore only 'relative'; by a generalization of this theory, Einstein worked out the geometry of the universe on a non-Euclidean basis.

relator, n. [1. reláter; 2. riléitə]. Lat. See **relate** & **-or**. (law) The person who makes a relation, i.e. lays such information before the Attorney-General as to enable him to take action, undertake a prosecution &c.

relax, vb. trans & intrans. [1. reláks; 2. riláeks], fr. Lat. *relaxāre*, 'to relax', fr. **re-** & *laxāre*, 'to loosen', fr. *laxus*, 'loose'. See **lax (I.)**. **A.** trans. **1.** (in physical senses) To make lax or loose; to cause to be loosened or slackened, to reduce tension or rigidity: *to relax a tight bearing-rein*; *to relax the muscles, one's grasp on anything*; specif., *to relax the bowels*, to relieve them from constipation; *a relaxed throat*, a form of sore or inflamed throat; *a relaxing climate, place*, one which is enervating; contrasted with *bracing.* **2.** (in non-physical senses) To loosen the strain of, to make less severe or rigorous, to slacken, ease off: *to relax discipline, a rule*; *to relax one's attention, efforts* &c. **B.** intrans. **1.** (in physical sense) To become lax, loose, slack, less tense or rigid: *muscles relax in sleep*; *his grip relaxed.* **2.** (in non-physical sense) To become less severe, or rigorous; to unbend: *to relax in manner*; *his stern demeanour relaxed*; *to relax in hard endeavour.*

relaxation, n. [1. rèlaksáshun; 2. rīlæksé iʃən], fr. Lat. *relaxātiōn-(em)*. See prec. & **-ation**. **1.** Act of relaxing; state of being relaxed (in physical and non-physical senses). **2.** (law) Remission of penalty in part if not in whole. **3.** Cessation from work; recreation, amusement: *his chief relaxations were hunting and shooting.*

relay (I.), n. [1. relā́ ; 2. rilḗi], fr. O.F. *relais*, 'set of fresh hunting dogs, or of horses'; etymol. doubtful; the Fr. vb. *relaier, relayer*, is apparently fr. the n. **1.** Specif., a set, supply, of fresh horses or hounds, kept ready at specified places to relieve the tired ones in hunting or on a journey. **2. a** A gang of men relieving others in shifts at a piece of work: *to work in, by, relays*; **b** supply of material similarly used. **3.** (elect.) Device by which a weaker current is enabled to control a heavier current on another circuit.

relay (II.), vb. trans. & intrans., fr. O. Fr. *relaier*. See prec. word. To supply by, arrange for, relays; to send or receive by relays.

re-lay, vb. trans. [1. rè lā́; 2. rī léi]. **re-** & **lay** (III.). To lay again: *to re-lay a cable, a railway line.*

relay race, n. A foot race in which two or more teams compete, each competitor running part of the distance only and handing over a baton to another on finishing his section, the winning team being that one whose last member comes in first with the baton.

relay station, n. Wireless station transmitting signals &c. received by telephone line from another station.

releasable, adj. [1. relḗsabl; 2. rilísəbl]. **release** & **-able**. Capable of being released or remitted.

release (I.), vb. trans. [1. relḗs; 2. rilís]. M.E. *relessen, relesen*, fr. O. Fr. *relesser*, M. Fr. *relaisser*, fr. Lat. *relaxāre*, see **relax**. **1.** To let go, discharge, allow to go forward, fall &c. (something held, contained, confined): *to release an arrow from a bow, a bomb from an aeroplane, gas from a cylinder.* **2.** To set free, let go from physical, corporeal, constraint or confinement, to set at large, give liberty to: *to release a prisoner*; *to release a person from slavery, from prison, from his handcuffs.* **3.** To free, relieve, from pain, suffering, distress of mind, distressing or oppressive circumstances: *to release from suffering*; *released from cares, anxieties* &c. **4.** To discharge, free, relieve, from an obligation: *to release a person from a promise, from a debt*; *released from a burdensome task.* **5.** (law) **a** To give up, surrender, remit (a right); to grant a release to: *to release a debt, claim*; **b** to surrender, convey, an estate or interest in property, real or personal, by a release. **6.** To set free, make available, for public use &c.

release (II.), n., fr. O. Fr. *reles*, see prec. **1.** Act of releasing: **a** loosing off, discharge: *release of a bomb* &c.; **b** act of setting at liberty, liberation, deliverance from captivity, confinement: *the release of a prisoner* &c. **2.** Liberation, relief, setting free from suffering, anxiety &c. Phr. *a happy release*, esp. by death, from prolonged suffering. **3.** Liberation from an obligation, duty &c.: *to obtain a release from a debt, promise* &c. **4.** (law) **a** A formal discharge or extinguishment in writing, of a debt, obligation &c.; **b** instrument by which such are extinguished: *a release to a trustee.* **5.** (mechan.) That which releases something held in position, a spring, catch, or other device which releases or unfastens some part of the machine &c.

re-lease, vb. trans. [1. rè lḗs; 2. rī lís]. **re-** & **lease** (I.). To grant a new lease of (house, property &c.).

releasee, n. [1. relḕsḗ; 2. rilīsí]. **release** (I.) & **-ee**. (law) One to whom a release is made.

releasor, n. [1. relḕsṓr; 2. rilīsɔ́]. See prec. & **-or**. (law) One who makes a release.

relegable, adj. [1. rélegabl; 2. réligəbl]. See **relegate** & **-able**. Capable of being, fit to be, relegated.

relegate, vb. trans. [1. rélegāt; 2. réligeit], fr. Lat. *relēgāt-(um)*, P.P. of *relēgāre*, 'to send out of the way, to banish, to reject', fr. **re-** & *lēgāre*, 'to send', esp. w. a charge or commission, see **legate**. **1.** (rare and obs.) To banish, send into exile. **2.** To consign, send, dismiss to some inferior or obscure position (lit. or fig.): *to relegate one's old clothes to a jumble sale*; *to relegate a question to the limbo of lost causes.* **3.** To transfer, hand over, submit, refer, for decision, performance, information: *to relegate a question to another authority.*

relegation, n. [1. règegā́shun; 2. rèligéiʃən], fr. Lat. *relēgātiōn-(em)*. See **relegate** & **-ion**. Act of relegating; state of being relegated; specif. (Rom. law) form of banishment less severe than deportation.

relent, vb. intrans. [1. relént; 2. rilént], fr. O. Fr. *ralentir*, 'to slacken, relent', fr. Lat. *relentescere*, 'to grow slack or soft', fr. **re-** & *lentus*, 'soft, slack, also pliant'. See **lentitude** & cp. **lithe**. To become less hard, severe, determined, in mind; to become less stern or obstinate; to yield to pity, entreaty &c.: *to relent at the sight of misery.*

relentingly, adv. [1. reléntingli; 2. riléntiŋli]. Pres. Part. of prec. & **-ly**. In a relenting manner; with feelings of compassion or mercy; yieldingly.

relentless, adj. [1. reléntles; 2. riléntlis]. See prec. & **-less**. Unmoved by pity or appeal; unrelenting, unyielding; pitiless; inflexible; unremitting.

relentlessly, adv. Prec. & **-ly**. In a relentless manner.

relentlessness, n. See prec. & **-ness**. Quality of being relentless.

re-let, vb. trans. [1. rè lét; 2. rī lét]. **re-** & **let** (II.). To let (house or land &c.) or lease again; to sublet.

relevance, -cy, n. [1. rélevans(i); 2. rélivəns(i)]. See next word & **-ce, -cy**. State, quality, of being relevant; pertinence, applicability, appositeness.

relevant, adj. [1. rélevant; 2. rélivənt]. Fr., Pres. Part. of *relever*, see **relieve**; orig. sense was 'assisting, helpful'. Bearing upon, applying strictly to, the matter in hand, or to the point at issue &c.; pertinent, apposite, applicable.

relevantly, adv. Prec. & **-ly**. In a relevant manner; pertinently.

relevé, n. [1. relevā; 2. rəlǝve]. Fr., P.P. of *relever*, see **relieve**. A course at dinner which relieves or succeeds another, esp. the principal dish; remove.

reliability, n. [1. relìabíliti; 2. rilàiəbíliti]. See next word & **-ity**. State, quality, of being reliable.

reliable, adj. [1. relíabl; 2. riláiəbl]. **rely** & **-able**. To be relied upon; dependable, trustworthy.

reliableness, n. Prec. & **-ness**. Reliability.

reliably, adv. See prec. & **-ly**. In a reliable manner.

reliance, n. [1. relíans; 2. riláiəns]. **rely** & **-ance**. **1.** Act of relying; state of being reliant; feeling of confidence, trust: *to put, place, reliance in, on, another person or thing*; *he acted in reliance upon loyal support*; *our reliance should be in our sense of right.* **2.** (rare) Object on which one relies or depends; ground of trust or confidence: *his chief reliance was his own courage.*

reliant, adj. [1. relíant; 2. riláiənt]. **rely** & **-ant**. Possessing, feeling, characterized by, reliance; confident.

relic, n. [1. rélik; 2. rélik]. M.E. *relyke*, later spelt *relique*, after the Fr., usually in pl., fr. Lat. *reliquiae*, 'remains', cp. *reliquus*, 'remains, what is left', fr. **re-** & base **likw-*, Lat. **liqu-*, 'to leave'. See **relinquish**. **1. a** A material object or part of one which survives from the past, esp. one which has survived the decay and disappearance of most other things belonging to the same period: *rusty armour, broken shields, and other relics of ancient days*; *stone implements, rude carvings, are precious relics of prehistoric times*; **b** a custom, belief, mode of thought &c. which has survived from a bygone age, from another, different, stage of society &c.: *a relic of barbarism, of a superstitious age*; *in the laws of the most civilized peoples we can often trace the relics of primitive custom.* **2. a** Some portion of the body of a saint, martyr, or other holy person, or some article associated with him or her, anything with very sacred associations, often regarded as possessing miraculous properties, preserved as an object of religious veneration: *the pilgrimage to the relics of St. Thomas at Canterbury*; '*The worshipping of reliques is a fond thing, vainly invented*' (Article xxii, P.B.); **b** any object preserved and treasured as a memento of the past: *a lock of hair, a ribbon, some faded flowers, pathetic relics of one's past.* **3.** (in pl., archaic or poet.) The remains of the dead: '*While angels with their silver wings o'ershade The ground now sacred by thy reliques made*' (Pope, 'Unfortunate Lady', 67-8).

relict, n. [1. rélikt; 2. rélikt], fr. Lat. *relicta*, fem. of P.P. of *relinquere*, 'to leave behind'. See prec. & **relinquish**. A widow, regarded as having been left behind on the death of her husband; rare and archaic, chiefly found on old tombstones: *Jane, relict of Thomas Smith.*

relief (I.), n. [1. relḗf; 2. rilíf]. Fr., in O. Fr. *relef*, fr. *relever*. See **relieve**. **1.** The relieving, state of being relieved; removal, alleviation, of pain, discomfort, distress, anxiety &c.; removal of circumstances or conditions which are oppressive: *to give a patient relief (from pain)*; *to give, get, relief from anxiety, from taxation* &c. **2. a** Aid, assistance in money or kind granted to the indigent poor by the administrators of the poor law: *outdoor relief*, at their own homes; *indoor relief*, in the workhouse; **b** help, succour, assistance, esp. for those in special need or danger, such as is supplied to people suffering from a great disaster, an epidemic, famine, during a strike &c.; hence (attrib.) *relief fund*, money collected for such purpose; *relief works*, works such as road-making &c. set going by public funds for the relief of sufferers or unemployed &c. **3. a** The raising of the siege of a beleaguered town or fort; **b** assistance sent to save a position in danger from the enemy, by troops, stores, ammunition &c.: *the relief of a town, outpost*; *reinforcements were sent to the relief of the army.* **4. a** Thing, substance, treatment, circumstance, which affords bodily or mental relief (from pain, fatigue, anxiety &c.): *a hot bath is a great relief after a long journey*; *it was an immense relief to find that my family were all safe*; **b** something which offers a pleasant contrast, something which breaks monotony, relaxes prolonged strain: *green, fertile country is a great relief after a huge stretch of desert*; *Shakespeare's comedy comes as a relief after the tragic scenes.* **5. a** Release from a post or duty; act of relieving of those on duty as sentries &c. by others who take their places; **b** persons detailed for this purpose. **6.** Redress by legal remedy; remission of, exemption from, penalties incurred: *a court may grant relief from a fine* &c. **7.** (feudal law) A payment, in money or kind, made to a lord by an heir on death of an ancestor for the right of succession to a fief.

relief (II.), n., fr. Ital. *rilievo*, fr. *rilevare*, 'to raise, lift up'; ultimately same as prec. **1. a** Mode of carving or moulding figures and designs so that they project or stand out from a flat surface which forms the background, either to about one-half of the supposed total depth of the figure &c. (*high relief*), or only to a very small extent (*low relief*); Phr. *in relief*, carved so as to project from a flat surface; **b** a figure or design cut and modelled in relief. **2. a** The apparent projection, on a plane surface as in painting, drawing &c., of figures or objects, produced by means of contrast of light and shade, or of colours, or lines, arranged so as to give the effect of solidity and depth; **b** (in map-making) the representation of varying levels, as of mountains, valleys &c., by hachures, shading, and mixture of colour and contour lines; *relief map*, one in which the elevations are thus given and not by contour lines alone. **3. a** Distinctness, sharpness of outline and contour by contrast with a background &c.: *a figure, object &c. seen in relief against the sky*; **b** contrast of ideas; emphasis, enhanced significance, of actions or events conveyed by contrast with others: *a competent historian knows how to place important and picturesque incidents in strong relief.*

relievable, adj. [1. relḗvabl; 2. rilívəbl]. **relieve** & **-able.** Capable of being relieved.

relieve, vb. trans. [1. relḗv; 2. rilív]. M.E. *releven*, fr. O. Fr. *relever*, fr. Lat. *relevāre*, 'to lift up, raise; to lighten, make light; to alleviate, mitigate, relieve', fr. **re-** & *levāre*, 'to lift up, make light; to free', fr. *levis*, 'light'. See **levity, Levant**, & cp. **light (IV.)**. **1. a** To mitigate, lighten, assuage, bodily or mental pain or distress: *to relieve the sufferings, the wants, of others*; **b** to free (sentient beings) from pain, suffering, distress, a burden, of body or mind: *to relieve a person of a headache, from fear and anxiety, of a load.* **2.** To lighten, ease, relax, reduce (pressure, strain, tension &c.; in physical and moral senses). Phr. *to relieve nature, the bowels, oneself*, to evacuate bowels or bladder; *to relieve one's feelings*, give vent to strong emotion by forcible speech or action, by tears &c. **3.** To bring assistance, succour, to; to minister to: *to relieve the poor and needy*; specif. (mil.) *to relieve a besieged town, garrison*, to raise the siege. **4. a** To free, release, from a duty or obligation, esp. by taking it on oneself: *I will relieve you of your attendance for the afternoon*; specif., *to relieve a guard, policeman, sentry*, to take over his (their) duties; **b** to deprive of, remove from, dismiss from: *to relieve a person of his rank, office, position*; Phr. *to relieve a person of his money, property* &c., to deprive him of them by stealing them. **5.** To break uniformity, or monotony of, by introducing variety and contrast: *to relieve the dullness of a street with bright window-boxes*; *a plain black dress relieved at the throat by white lace*; *no flash of wit or merriment relieved the dreariness of the party.*

relieving arch, n. [1. relḗving àrch; 2. rilíviŋ átʃ]. One built into a wall to take the pressure of the superstructure from the part below.

relieving officer, n. Official appointed by a local authority in charge of the relief of the poor.

relievo, n. [1. relḗvō; 2. rilívou]. Anglicized form of Ital. *rilievo*. See **relief (II.)**. (archit. and sculpt.) Relief: *alto relievo*, high relief; *basso relievo*, low relief, bas relief.

relight, vb. trans. & intrans. [1. rèlī́t; 2. rìláit]. **re-** & **light (II.)**. **1.** trans. To kindle, light, again. **2.** intrans. To take fire again, to rekindle.

religion, n. [1. relíjun; 2. rilídžən], fr. Lat. *religiōn-(em)*, 'reverence for the gods, fear of God, religious awe, consciousness of wrong, religious scruple'; only in L. Lat. of a religious system & esp. of Christianity, *Christiana religio*; the word is now thought to be connected w. *relegere*, 'to gather together, collect; to ponder over, to give heed to, observe, care for', fr. **re-** & a base found also in **diligent, negligent**, & Gk. *alégein*, 'to pay heed to', esp. w. neg., of paying no heed to the gods. Although orig. the word, if the above etymol. be correct, had nothing to do w. Lat. *religāre*, 'to bind', see **ligature**, there is no doubt that *religio* was connected in popular etymol. w. the idea of 'a binding, an obligation' &c., in fact some anct. Lat. writers suggest this origin, while others connect it, as above, w. the idea of 'taking heed, pondering over'. **1.** Belief in, acknowledgement of, a supernatural power which controls the universe and directs man's destiny; belief in the existence of some personal God or gods to whom some form of worship and obedience is due; often contrasted with *atheism*. **2.** Specific system of belief in God, including a group of doctrines concerning Him, and His relations to man and the universe, and customary rites to be observed in worship: *the Christian religion*; *the religion of the Hebrews* &c. Phr. (vulg.) *to get religion*, to become converted to a sense of sin, and to a feeling for the need of a closer relation with God. **3.** Religious state of mind; mode of life governed by religion; specif., monastic life; formal dedication of oneself to the service of God and religion by taking the vows of a monastic order: *the life of religion*; *to enter religion.* **4.** Object of great devotion; esp. a principle or practice regarded with the veneration paid to something sacred, and persistently observed: *the pursuit of success became a religion to him.*

religionary, n. [1. relíjunari; 2. rilídžənəri]. Prec. & **-ary.** (rare) One whose profession or vocation is religion, esp. a member of a religious order.

religioner, n. [1. relíjuner; 2. rilídžənə]. **religion** & **-er.** (rare) **1.** A religious enthusiast. **2.** Member of a religious order, religionary.

religionism, n. [1. relíjunizm; 2. rilídžənizəm]. **religion** & **-ism. 1.** Excessive, extravagant devotion to religious practices, or zeal for religion; religious enthusiasm. **2.** Affected, pretended, religious zeal.

religionist, n. [1. relíjunist; 2. rilídžənist]. See prec. & **-ist.** A religious zealot or enthusiast.

religionize, vb. trans. & intrans. [1. relíjunīz; 2. rilídžənaiz]. **religion** & **-ize. 1.** trans. To convert to religion, imbue with religious feeling, zeal. **2.** intrans. To display, profess, religion or religious zeal.

religionless, adj. [1. relíjunles; 2. rilídžənlis]. **religion** & **-less.** Destitute of, not professing, or believing in, religion; having no religious system.

religiose, adj. [1. relìjiṓs; 2. rilìdžióus], fr. Lat. *religiōsus*, fr. stem of **religion** & **-ose.** Morbidly, emotionally religious.

religiosity, n. [1. relìjiósiti; 2. rilìdžiósiti], fr. Lat. *religiōsitāt-(em)*. See prec. & **-ity.** State, quality, of being religiose; morbid, emotional zeal for religion.

religious (I.), adj. [1. relíjus; 2. rilídžəs]. M.E., fr. O. Fr., fr. Lat. *religiōsus*, see **religiose. 1.** Pertaining, relating to, concerned with, religion: *religious duties*; *a religious book, society*; *religious teaching*; *religious wars* &c. **2. a** Believing in, professing and practising religion; devoted to, imbued with, religion; pious, devout, godly: *a religious man*; *a religious country*; *the religious*, religious persons; **b** conforming to, characterized by, religion: *to lead a religious life*; **c** arising out of, caused by, religion: *a religious ecstasy*; *religious emotion.* **3.** Specif., bound by vows to religion and a monastic life; belonging to a monastic order: *religious orders*, monastic orders; *a religious house*, a monastery or nunnery. **4.** (by transf.) Scrupulous, conscientious, strict: *he kept his promise with religious care*; *his loyalty was religious in its devotion.*

religious (II.), n., fr. prec. One bound by vows of religion, member of a monastic order.

religiously, adv. [1. relíjusli; 2. rilídžəsli]. **religious (I.)** & **-ly.** In a religious manner: **a** in accordance with the principles and practices of religion; piously, devoutly: *to behave religiously*; **b** strictly, scrupulously, exactly: *to carry out instructions religiously.*

religiousness, n. See prec. & **-ness.** Quality, state, of being religious.

reline, vb. trans. [1. rèlī́n; 2. rìláin]. **re-** & **line (IV.)**. To put a new lining in.

relinquish, vb. trans. [1. relíngkwish; 2. rilíŋkwiʃ], fr. Fr. *relinquiss-*, Pres. Part. stem of *relinquir*, Lat. *relinquere*, 'to leave behind, forsake, abandon; to give up, resign, relinquish', fr. **re-** & *linquere*, 'to leave'; the base appears in both nasalized & unnasalized forms, in other Aryan languages; cp. Goth. *leihwan*, 'to lend, to borrow', fr. **liŋχw-*, whence also O.H.G. *līhan*, & O.E. *lēon*, fr. **līhan*, 'to grant, lend'; further Gk. *limpánein*, 'to leave', fr. **linkʷ-*; the unnasalized type is seen in Gk. *leípein*, 'to leave behind', *loipós*, 'remaining, surviving', & in the Lat. P.P. type *lictum* for **likʷ-tom.* See further under **lend** & **loan. 1. a** To leave, withdraw, retire from, to quit, to abandon, surrender: *to relinquish a position to the enemy*; *lands relinquished by their former owners*; **b** to loosen, let go (one's grip): *to relinquish one's hold of a rope.* **2.** To cease from, give up, to desist from, abandon: *to relinquish the pursuit, bad habits, a plan of reform.* **3.** To give up, renounce, forgo: *to relinquish a claim, one's rights* &c.

relinquishment, n. [1. relíngkwishment; 2. rilíŋkwiʃmənt]. Prec. & **-ment.** Act of relinquishing.

reliquary, n. [1. rélikwari; 2. rélikwəri]. Cp. Fr. *reliquaire*, fr. Low Lat. *reliquiārium.* See **relic** & next word & **-ary.** A casket, box, shrine, for the keeping of relics.

reliquiae, n. pl. [1. relíkwiē; 2. relíkwiī]. Lat., 'remains, relics', fr. *reliquus*, 'remaining, left over', fr. *reli(n)quere*, see **relinquish. 1. a** Remains, relics of the dead or of the past; **b** an author's literary remains. **2.** Specif. **a** (bot.) leaves which remain on the stem when withered; induviae; **b** (geol.) fossilized organic remains.

relish (I.), n. [1. rélish; 2. réliʃ]. M.E. *reles*, fr. O. Fr. *reles, relais*, 'after taste', fr. *relesser*, see **release. 1. a** That which affects the sense of taste or of taste and smell; smack, flavour, aroma: *a relish of garlic in cooking*; *there's a relish of the sea in the air*; **b** a distinctive, appetizing flavour, taste, quality in food &c.: *food, tobacco &c. loses its relish when one is ill.* **2.** (fig.) Any stimulating, attractive, enlivening quality; a spice: *the danger gives relish to climbing*; *without betting, racing would lack its relish for many*; *to find no relish in one's work.* **4. a** That which gives or adds an appetizing flavour to food &c.; a condiment; anything with an appetizing flavour: *hunger is the best relish for food after all*; **b** (by transf.) something which stimulates, adds zest, spice, or interest to: *emulation is a relish even to the most monotonous work.* **5. a** Pleasure, enjoyment in eating or drinking &c.; keen appetite: *to lose all relish for one's food*; *to eat with evident relish*; **b** (fig.) inclination, gusto, zest: *he has no relish for the fight*; *to recite poetry with relish and spirit.*

relish (II.), vb. trans. & intrans., fr. prec. **A.** trans. **1.** (rare) To give a relish or appetizing flavour to, to serve as a relish for: *hunger will relish the plainest fare.* **2. a** To partake of, with pleasure and appetite, to enjoy: *to relish one's food*; **b** (fig.) to like, appreciate; to enjoy, be pleased with: *I do not much relish the prospect of a long journey.* **B.** intrans. **1. a** To have a relish or flavour of, to taste of: *Greek wine relishes of resin*; **b** (fig.) to smack of, to have a trace or suggestion: *conversation which relishes of wit.* **2.** To affect the taste well or ill.

relive, vb. intrans. & trans. [1. rèlív; 2. rìlív]. **re-** & **live (I.)**. **1.** intrans. To live again; to come to life again, to revive. **2.** trans. To live through again, to experience again, esp. in imagination: *to relive one's life*; *to relive the past.*

reload, trans. & intrans. [1. rèlṓd; 2. rìlóud]. **re-** & **load (II.)**. **a** trans. To load again, put fresh load on, or in (a cart, a gun); **b** intrans., to load a gun &c. again: *they were ordered to fire and reload.*

relucent, adj. [1. rēlū́sent; 2. rìljúsənt], fr. Lat. *relūcent-(em)*, Pres. Part. of *relūcēre*, 'to shine forth'. See **re-** & **lucent.** (rare or poet.) Shining, bright, refulgent.

reluct, vb. intrans. [1. relúkt; 2. rilákt], fr. Lat. *reluctāri*, 'to struggle, fight against', fr. **re-** & *luctāri*, 'to wrestle, struggle', cogn. w. *lucta* for **lugta*, 'wrestling', *luctor*, 'wrestler'; cp. Gk. *lugízein*, 'to twist, bend, writhe, as in wrestling'. The primitive meaning of the base is 'to bend, twist'. See further under lock (III.). (rare or archaic) To struggle, strive against; to resist, show reluctance to or against.

reluctance, n. [1. relúktans; 2. rilʌ́ktəns]. Next word & **-ce**. State, quality, of being reluctant; unwillingness, repugnance, aversion, mental hesitation: *with reluctance*, reluctantly, unwillingly; *to show reluctance to do* &c.

reluctant, adj. [1. relúktant; 2. rilʌ́ktənt], fr. Lat. *reluctant-(em)*, Pres. Part. of *reluctāri*. See **reluct**. **1.** Offering resistance to treatment, difficult to treat: *a reluctant tooth, tumour*. **2. a** Unwilling, loath, doubtful, disinclined, showing reluctance: *to be reluctant to do anything*; *a reluctant witness*; **b** expressing, animated by reluctance: *reluctant consent, answer* &c.

reluctantly, adv. Prec. & **-ly**. In a reluctant manner; with reluctance, unwillingly, doubtfully.

relume, vb. trans. [1. rēlūm; 2. rīljūm], fr. **re-** & **illume**, cp. Fr. *rallumer*. (poet.) To relight, rekindle; to make bright, cause to lighten again.

rely, vb. intrans. [1. relí; 2. rilái]. Etymol. doubtful; earlier meanings 'to rally to, join, adhere to', point to Fr. *relier*, 'to fasten together', fr. Lat. *religāre*, see **re-** & *ligāre*, 'to bind', see **ligature**; the general sense suggests a hybrid formation fr. **re-** & **lie** (III.), 'to lie back upon, to rest, lean on'. *Rely on, upon*, to trust, depend, to rest with confidence in: *to rely upon a person or thing*, for support &c.; *I can rely on them to do what they are told*; *on that you may rely*; *his loyalty can be relied on*.

remain (I.), vb. intrans. [1. remán; 2. riméin], fr. O. Fr. *remaindre*, fr. Lat. *remanēre*, 'to stay, remain behind; to be left, to continue, endure', fr. **re-** & *manēre*, 'to stay, stop; to last, continue'; cogn. w. Gk. *ménein*, 'to abide, stay, linger', & *moné*, 'a staying, tarrying'; Scrt. *ámaman*, 'to hesitate, stand still'; the ultimate connexion of this base w. *men-, 'to think', see **memory**, **mental** (I.), **mind**, is very doubtful. **1.** To be left over after part has been used, destroyed, removed &c.; to survive; **a** (of physical objects, and persons) *of the crew only three remained to tell the tale*; *a few stones of the building remain*; **b** (of non-material things) *with his last remaining strength*; *no hope of safety remained*. **2.** To continue to exist, to last, endure, persist: *what will remain of our boasted civilization?*; *a doubt still remains in the mind*; *memories of happy days remain with us*. **3.** To stand over to be dealt with later, be left for future treatment, use &c.: *little now remains to be done, told*; (also impers.) *it remains to be seen whether, to be proved that*. **4.** To stay, continue in the same place; to be left behind in the same place: *we shall remain at home for the winter*; *he remained abroad for several years*; *to remain at one's post*; *remain where you are for the present*; *our luggage can remain here while we are away*. **5. a** To continue in the same condition, to continue to be: *the house remained empty for a long time*; *things remained much as they were*; *the mystery remains unsolved*; *weather remains unsettled*; **b** (as formulae at end of a letter) *I have the honour to remain your obedient servant*; *I remain yours affectionately*.

remain (II.), n., fr. prec. Always in pl. *remains*. **1. a** That which is left or survives; what remains over after use, loss &c.; remnant, remainder: *remains of one's dinner*; *the remains of a fortune, of an old building*; *the remains of beauty, strength*; **b** survivors, persons who are left: *remains of an army*. **2. a** Relics, surviving traces: *remains of a past civilization, a country's glory, history*; **b** specif., ruined buildings. **3.** A dead body, corpse: *his remains lie in Westminster Abbey*. **4.** Writings left unpublished by an author at his death.

remainder (I.), n. [1. remánder; 2. riméində], fr. A.-Fr. *remainder*, infin. See **remain** (I.). **1. a** Remaining persons; those who are left behind or remain; the rest: *the remainder of the company was lost*; **b** what is left, remaining things, residue, remnant: *the remainder of the feast*; *the remainder of his sentence is remitted*; *for the remainder of one's life*. **2.** Specif. (arith.) number, quantity, left after subtraction: *take 3 from 10 and the remainder is 7*. **3.** Copy, copies, of a work remaining unsold in publisher's stock when demand and sale have ceased, and generally offered at a greatly reduced price. **4.** (law) An estate in expectancy, usually in land, an interest depending on a particular prior estate which will come into effect and be in possession of the devisee on the determination of that estate; distinct from *reversion*.

remainder (II.), vb. trans., fr. prec. To treat copies of (book) as a remainder, and offer for sale at greatly reduced price.

remainder-man, n. The devisee of an estate in remainder.

remaindership, n. [1. remándership; 2. riméindəʃip]. **remainder** & **-ship**. Right of succession to an estate in remainder.

remake, vb. trans. [1. rēmák; 2. rīméik]. **re-** & **make**. To make again; to make differently.

remand (I.), vb. trans. [1. remáhnd; 2. rimánd], fr. O. Fr. *remander*, fr. L. Lat. *remandāre*, 'to send back word, notify; to repeat a command', fr. **re-** & *mandāre*, 'to order', see **mandamus**. **1.** (rare or obs.) To send, call back; to consign again, remit. **2.** Specif. (law) to send back, recommit to prison a person charged before a magistrate with an offence, in order to obtain further evidence or make further inquiries.

remand (II.), n., fr. prec. Act of remanding or recommitting; specif., recommittal of a prisoner: *on remand*, of prisoner so recommitted.

remanent, adj. [1. remánent; 2. riméinənt], fr. Lat. *remanent-(em)*, Pres. Part. of *remanēre*, see **remain** (I.). (archaic) Remaining, surviving; additional.

remanet, n. [1. rémanet; 2. rémənet]. Lat., 'it remains', 3rd sing. pres. of *remanēre*, 'to remain'. See **remain** (I.). That which remains or is left over, a remainder; specif. **a** (law) a case adjourned or postponed for another sitting of the court, as at Assizes &c.; **b** a parliamentary bill carried over to another session.

remark (I.), vb. trans. & intrans. [1. remárk; 2. rimák], fr. Fr. *remarquer*. See **re-** & **mark**. **A.** trans. To notice, take notice of; to observe, perceive; **a** (by one of the senses) *I remarked the heat as soon as I entered the room*; *to remark the resemblance between two things*; *to remark an unpleasant odour, taste*; **b** (by the mental faculties) *to remark the ambiguity of a statement* &c. **B.** intrans. **1.** To notice, observe, note, perceive, that; **a** (of physical act) *to remark that it had suddenly grown colder*; **b** (of mental process) *in the course of my reading, I have often remarked how rare is clearness of statement among writers*. **2. a** To utter a comment, say, or write, by way of comment; to say: *I should like to remark that . . .*; *many writers have remarked that . . .*; also **b** *remark on, upon*, to comment on, make an observation on: *the king remarked upon the loyalty of his reception by the public*.

remark (II.), n. Fr. *remarque*. See prec. **1. a** Act of remarking, perceiving; consideration, notice, observation: *buildings, pictures, deserving, worthy, of remark by visitors*; **b** act of commenting; a reflection: *a matter of general and unfavourable remark*. **2. a** Uttered comment, observation; Phrs. *to pass a remark*, make an observation; *to make no remark*, to say nothing; **b** written note or comment. **3.** (engraving) Remarque.

re-mark, vb. trans. [1. rē márk; 2. rī mák]. **re-** & **mark**. To mark, stamp, again or afresh.

remarkable, adj. [1. remárkabl; 2. rimákəbl]. **remark** (I.) & **-able**. Noticeable, noteworthy, conspicuous, striking, unusual, extraordinary: *a remarkable occurrence*; *to make oneself too remarkable*; *it is remarkable that I should not have been told*.

remarkableness, n. Prec. & **-ness**. State, quality, of being remarkable.

remarkably, adv. See prec. & **-ly**. In a remarkable way; to a remarkable degree.

remarque, n. [1. remárk; 2. rimák]. Fr. See **remark** (II.). **a** A miniature drawing or sketch on the margin of an engraved plate or print, often removed from later impressions; **b** a proof so marked, usually *remarque proof*.

remarriage, n. [1. rēmárij; 2. rīmǽridž]. **re-** & **marriage**. Act of marrying again; a marriage which takes place after widowhood or divorce.

remarry, vb. trans. & intrans. [1. rēmári; 2. rīmǽri]. **re-** & **marry**. **1.** trans. **a** (act of priest &c.) To perform marriage ceremony, unite in marriage, two persons, one or both of whom have been married before; to repeat the ceremony of marriage for; **b** (of party in marriage ceremony) to marry, be united to (husband or wife) a second time, after divorce, or annulment of former marriage. **2.** intrans. To marry, enter into the state of matrimony, a second time.

Rembrandtesque, adj. [1. rèmbrantésk; 2. rèmbræntésk], fr. name of Rembrandt, Dutch painter (1606–69), & **-esque**. After the manner of the painting, drawing, etching &c. of Rembrandt, usually with reference to the strong contrasts of light and shade.

remediable, adj. [1. remédiabl; 2. remídiəbl]. **remedy** (II.) & **-able**. Capable of being remedied; admitting of a remedy.

remediably, adv. Prec. & **-ly**. So as to be capable of being remedied.

remedial, adj. [1. remédial; 2. remídiəl]. Low Lat. *remediālis*, 'healing'. **remedy** (I.) & **-al**. Affording, providing, a remedy; intended, designed, to remedy: *remedial laws, treatment, punishment*.

remedially, adv. Prec. & **-ly**. So as to remedy; by way of remedy.

remediless, adj. [1. rémediles; 2. rémidilis]. See next word & **-less**. **1.** Without remedy; incapable of being remedied, incurable: *remediless evils, disease* &c. **2.** Irremediable, irreplaceable: *remediless loss*. **3.** Unable to find a remedy, hopeless: *against such disaster one is remediless*.

remedy (I.), n. [1. rémedi; 2. rémidi]. M.E. & A.-Fr. *remedie*, Mod. Fr. *remède*, fr. Lat. *remedium*, 'relief, remedy', fr. **re-** & *medēri*, 'to heal again, to remedy, cure', see **medical**. **1.** Substance or treatment which relieves, heals, a disease, pain &c.; a medicine. **2.** Action, method, which corrects, counteracts, tends to mitigate, an evil or wrong: *drastic action on the part of a government is the best remedy for sedition and rebellion*; *a remedy for social ills*. **3.** Allowance, redress, reparation for loss or injury: *there is no wrong without a remedy*; specif. **a** (law) legal means, as by suit, for recovery of a right, damages for injury &c.; **b** allowance at the mint for deviation in weight or fineness of a coin; tolerance.

remedy (II.), vb. trans., fr. Fr. *remédier*, fr. L. Lat. *remediāre*, 'to remedy'. See prec. **1.** (archaic) To cure by medical treatment. **2.** To provide a remedy for, improve bad condition of; **a** (of material things) to put, set right, mend; to remove defect in: *to remedy a leak in a pipe, knocking in machinery* &c.; **b** (of abstract or non-material things) to redress, alleviate, allay, check: *to remedy social ills, the evils of overcrowding*.

remember, vb. trans. & intrans. [1. remémber; 2. rimémbə]. M.E. *remembren*, fr. O. Fr. *remembrer*, 'to remember', fr. Low Lat. *rememorāri*, 'to call to mind again, remember'; **re-** & Lat. *memorāri*, 'to bring to mind, recall, remind', fr. *memor*, 'mindful, remembering'. See **memory**. **A.** trans. **1.** To call, recall, to mind; to recollect: *I* *know your face, but cannot remember your name*; *I shall never be able to remember the numbers on the spur of the moment*; *I often remember what my old father used to say.* **2.** To retain in the memory; to have, bear, in mind; not to forget: *to remember what one is told*; *I no longer remember the time*; *I'll give you something you'll remember all your life.* **3.** To recall to mind, bear, cherish, in the mind in association with some special feeling, favourable or unfavourable: *I shall always remember your kindness to my son*; *you may be sure I shall remember next time the atrocious way you have behaved*; *to remember something against a person*; '*Remember not, Lord, our offences, nor the offences of our forefathers*'. **4.** To signify one's remembrance by gift, reward &c.: *to remember a child on its birthday,* send it a present; *please remember the waiter,* don't forget to tip him; *to remember a person in one's will,* leave him a legacy. **5.** To put a person in mind of (another), recall to his memory; in polite formula: *remember me kindly to your father*; *he wishes to be remembered to you.* **B.** intrans. **1.** To recall things to mind; to exercise the faculty of memory in regard to past events &c.: *now just remember! I shan't pay you another penny*; *it is often happier to forget than to remember.* **2.** To possess the faculty of memory: *as one gets old one does not remember as one used to do.*

rememberable, adj. [1. remémberabl; 2. rimémbərəbl]. Prec. & **-able.** (rare) Of a kind that can be remembered; worth remembering, memorable.

remembrance, n. [1. remémbrans; 2. rimémbrəns]. O. Fr., 'memory'. See **remember** & **-ance.** **1. a** Act, process, of remembering; memory: '*the remembrance of our sins is grievous to us*'; **b** state of being remembered: *how soon the past fades from remembrance*; '*Take and eat this in remembrance that Christ died for thee*'. **2.** Faculty of remembering; individual memory or recollection: *that has long passed from my remembrance.* **3.** That which reminds, which keeps in mind, which serves as a memorial of; **a** a keepsake, souvenir: *I send a small remembrance,* a gift in memory of the donor, or of another; **b** (pl.) a message of goodwill, greeting: *to send kind remembrances to all.*

remembrancer, n. [1. remémbranser; 2. rimémbrənsə]. A.-Fr. See prec. & **-er.** **1.** One who reminds or calls to one's remembrance or memory; that which reminds or serves as a reminder. **2.** Specif. (cap.) **a** An official, *King's (Queen's) Remembrancer,* of the Supreme Court of Judicature, representing the Exchequer in the collection of debts due to the Crown by the Court; **b** *City Remembrancer,* a legal official of the City of London, representing the Corporation at Parliamentary Committees &c.

remigrate, vb. trans. [1. rèmígrāt; 2. rìmáigreit]. **re-** & **migrate.** To migrate again; to return to the place from which one migrated.

remigration, n. [1. rèmīgráshun; 2. rìmaigréiʃən]. Prec. & **-ion.** Act of remigrating.

remind, vb. trans. [1. remínd; 2. rimáind]. A late word of early 18th cent., fr. **re-** & **mind.** To put in mind of, to cause to remember, to recall to the memory: *please remind me to write tomorrow*; *that reminds me that I must go to London.* Phr. *you remind me of your father,* recall him to my mind through your resemblance to him.

reminder, n. [1. reminder; 2. rimáində]. Prec. & **-er.** Something which reminds: *my note will serve as a reminder of our appointment*; *a gentle reminder,* a hint.

remindful, adj. [1. remíndfool; 2. rimáindful]. **remind** & **-ful.** (rare) Serving, acting, as a reminder; keeping the memory alive; careful to remind.

reminisce, vb. intrans. [1. rèminís; 2. rèminís]. Back-formation fr. **reminiscent.** (colloq.) To tell one's reminiscences.

reminiscence, n. [1. rèminísens; 2. rèminísəns]. Fr., fr. L. Lat. *reminiscentia.* See next word & **-ce.** **1.** Act of remembering or recalling to mind; power, faculty, of recalling or recovering in the mind what is past; memory, recollection: *only a faint reminiscence of what happened.* **2.** Specif. (philos.) *the doctrine of reminiscence,* as translating Gk. *anámnēsis,* the doctrine of Plato that the soul merely recovers knowledge of what it has known directly and intuitively in a former existence; in modern phraseology, subconscious memory, race-memory. **3.** That which serves to remind; something which survives as a reminder of, or which suggests something else: *a reminiscence of Keats in this man's poetry.* **4. a** Something remembered, something that lingers in the memory: *I have a delightful reminiscence of the week I spent at the Lakes*; **b** (pl.) *reminiscences,* account, narrative, of one's memories and experiences; memoirs.

reminiscent, adj. [1. rèminísent; 2. rèminísənt], fr. Lat. *reminiscent-(em),* Pres. Part. of *reminisci,* see **re-,** & base ***men-,** 'to remember, think' &c., see under **mental (I.)** & **mind.** **1.** Serving to remind by reason of resemblance; suggestive of: *a villa built in a style reminiscent of a baronial castle*; *much of the minor poetry of the nineties was reminiscent of Swinburne.* **2.** (of persons, moods &c.) Tending to recall the past; dwelling on, narrating, one's memories: *old men tend to be reminiscent*; *in a reminiscent frame of mind.*

reminiscential, adj. [1. rèminisénshal; 2. rèminisénʃəl]. Prec. & **-ial.** (philos.) Characterized by reminiscence; reminiscent of a former existence: *knowledge according to Plato is purely reminiscential.*

reminiscently, adv. [1. rèminísentli; 2. rèminísəntli]. **reminiscent** & **-ly.** In a reminiscent manner; by way, means, of reminiscences.

remint, vb. trans. [1. rèmínt; 2. rìmínt]. **re-** & **mint (III.).** To mint (coin) over again; to strike new coinage from old.

remise (I.), n. & vb. trans. [1. rēmíz; 2. rīmáiz], fr. Fr. *remis, remise,* P.P. of *remettre.* See **remit.** (law) **1.** n. A surrender, release, or quittance, by deed, of a claim, right &c. **2.** vb. To make a remise of; to surrender, release, give up, by deed, as a claim or right.

remise (II.), n. [1. reméz; 2. rəmíz]. Fr., in both senses given below. See prec. **1.** (obs.) A coach-house; carriage kept at a livery stable or hired from one. **2.** (fencing) A second thrust, given in same lunge, without recovery, when opponent does not make a *riposte.*

remiss, adj. [1. remís; 2. rimís], fr. Lat. *remissum,* P.P. of *remittere,* 'to relax, slacken'. See **remit.** **1.** Lax, negligent, careless; slack: *remiss in one's payments, duties, fulfilment of promises.* **2.** (rare) Slow, languid, not energetic.

remissible, adj. [1. remísibl; 2. rimísibl], fr. Lat. *remissibilis,* fr. *remiss-(um),* P.P. of *remittere.* See **remit.** Capable of being remitted or forgiven: *a remissible fine, penalty.*

remission, n. [1. remíshun; 2. rimíʃən]. O. Fr., fr. Lat. *remissiōn-(em).* See **remiss** & **-ion.** **1.** Act of remitting or forgiving; state of being forgiven, pardon, forgiveness: *the remission of sins*; *to gain remission.* **2.** Act of remitting, forgoing, surrendering, or relinquishing in whole or part: *the remission of a debt, claim &c.*; *remission of taxation, penalty, punishment* &c. **3.** Process of abating, relaxing; abatement, diminution: *a remission of a fever, disease, paroxysms, excitement.* **4.** (rare) Remittal, remittance.

remissive, adj. [1. remísiv; 2. rimísiv], fr. Lat. *remissivus.* See **remiss, remit,** & **-ive.** Causing, allowing, remission, pardon, or abatement; abating, relaxing.

remissly, adv. [1. remísli; 2. rimísli]. **remiss** & **-ly.** In a remiss manner; negligently, laxly, carelessly.

remissness, n. [1. remísnes; 2. rimísnis]. **remiss** & **-ness.** **a** State, quality, of being remiss; negligence, carelessness; **b** (rare) want of energy, diligence, vigour; slackness.

remit, vb. trans. & intrans. [1. remít; 2. rimít], fr. Lat. *remittere, remissum,* 'to send back; to relax, abate', fr. **re-** & *mittere,* 'to send', see **mission.** **A.** trans. **1. a** To refrain from exacting, to forgo, relinquish, give up in whole or part: *to remit a punishment, fine*; *the sentence has been remitted*; *to remit taxes*; **b** specif. (theol.) to forgive, pardon, to relieve, excuse, from punishment: *Christ gave St. Peter authority to remit sins.* **2.** To abate, moderate, slacken: *to remit one's anger, an attempt, efforts* &c. **3. a** To refer, send back; (law) to send (case) to an inferior court; **b** to refer (case &c.) to an authority for decision. **4.** To adjourn, postpone, for further inquiry: *to remit a matter till a certain date, for further consideration* &c. **5.** To send, transmit: *to remit money by post*; *to remit goods by railway* &c. **B.** intrans. **1.** (archaic) To abate, moderate in violence, severity &c.: *the fever has remitted, is remitting*; *the drought begins to remit.* **2.** (tradesman's usage) To pay: *kindly remit,* pay up.

remittal, n. [1. remítl; 2. rimítəl]. Prec. & **-al.** Act of remitting or referring back, esp. the remitting or sending back of a case from one court to another.

remittance, n. [1. remítans; 2. rimítəns]. See prec. & **-ance.** **1.** The sending of money to a person in another place. **2.** Payment, sum of money sent as payment, allowance &c. *Remittance man,* person who lives abroad, esp. in the colonies, on remittances sent from his home.

remittent, adj. & n. [1. remítent; 2. rimítənt]. See **remit** & **-ent.** **1.** adj. Remitting, abating, at intervals, but not entirely ceasing, having relief or growing better from time to time, of fevers &c., contrasted with *intermittent,* when the fever recurs only at stated periods and ceases altogether during the interval. **2.** n. A remittent fever.

remitter, n. [1. remíter; 2. rimítə]. **remit** & **-er.** **1.** One who remits (money) to another. **2.** (law) **a** The remittal of a case from one court to another; **b** the shifting back or remitting to a better title to an estate in land in cases where the possessor has a defective title and obtains or is entitled to a more valid one.

remnant, n. [1. rémnant; 2. rémnənt], fr. O. Fr. *remanant,* 'remaining', fr. O. Fr. *remanoir, remaindre.* See **remain (I.).** **1. a** Something left over after use, remaining fragments &c.: *the remnants of a feast*; **b** specif., odds and ends, oddments; short pieces of fabric &c. left after the greater part has been sold; *remnant sale,* sale of such articles at reduced prices. **2.** Something which has survived destruction, decay &c.; relic, last trace: *the remnants of former grandeur*; *the last remnant of courage, strength* &c.; *a remnant of ancient custom, belief* &c.

remodel, vb. trans. [1. rèmódl; 2. rìmódl]. **re-** & **model.** To model, shape, form, fashion afresh; to recast: *to remodel a bust*; *to remodel one's conduct*; *to remodel the party programme, a play, novel* &c.; *a remodelled army.*

remonetization, n. [1. rèmunetīzáshun; 2. rìmanitaizéiʃən]. Next word & **-ation.** Act of remonetizing; restoration of currency &c. as legal tender.

remonetize, vb. trans. [1. rèmúnetīz; 2. rìmánitaiz]. **re-** & **monetize.** To restore a currency, metal, to its former position and value as legal tender.

remonstrance, n. [1. remónstrans; 2. rimónstrəns]. See next word & **-ce.** **1.** Act of remonstrating; expostulation, formal protest: *to make a remonstrance against*; *to say in remonstrance that.* **2.** A formal statement of grievances; specif., *the Grand Remonstrance,* of 1641, in which Parliament laid the public grievances before the Crown.

remonstrant, adj. & n. [1. remónstrant; 2. rimɔ́nstrənt], fr. Med. Lat. *remonstrant-(em)*, Pres. Part. of *remonstrāre*. See next word. **1.** adj. Remonstrating, expostulating; making remonstrances. **2.** n. One who remonstrates or joins in a remonstrance; specif. (cap.) one of a body of Dutch Protestants who seceded from the Calvinist Church in 1610, following the doctrines of Arminius.

remonstrate, vb. intrans. [1. remónstrāt; 2. rimɔ́nstreit], fr. L. Med. Lat. *remonstrāt-(um)*, P.P. of *remonstrāre*, fr. **re-** & *monstrāre*, 'to point out, show'. See **monstrance** & **monster.** **1.** To protest, expostulate; to set forth formally complaints or grievances; **a** *remonstrate against* (conduct, measures &c.), to act in opposition to; urge reasons, protest against; **b** *remonstrate with* (person), expostulate, plead, with. **2.** (absol.) To utter, make, a remonstrance: *if this goes on, we must remonstrate.*

remonstratingly, adv. [1. remónstrātingli; 2. rimɔ́nstrèitiŋli]. Pres. Part. of prec. & **-ly.** By way of remonstrance; by remonstrating.

remonstrative, adj. [1. remónstrativ; 2. rimɔ́nstrətiv]. **remonstrate** & **-ive.** **a** Uttering, making, remonstrance; **b** of the nature of a remonstrance.

remonstrator, n. [1. remónstrāter; 2. rimɔ́nstrèitə]. See prec. & **-or.** One who remonstrates.

remontant, adj. & n. [1. remóntant; 2. rimɔ́ntənt]. Fr., Pres. Part. of *remonter.* See **remount.** (bot.) **1.** adj. Blossoming a second time in a season. **2.** n. Plant which blossoms a second time.

remora, n. [1. remóra; 2. rimɔ́rə]. Lat., 'delay, hindrance', also, 'the delayer', name given to the fish, as believed to stop a ship or boat; fr. **re-** & *mora*, 'delay', see **moratory.** A small sea fish, *Echeneis*, with a sucking disk on the head by which it attaches itself to sharks and other large ocean fishes.

remorse, n. [1. remórs; 2. rimɔ́s], fr. O. Fr. *remors*, fr. L. Lat. *remorsum*, P.P. of *remordēre*, 'to bite again, to vex, torment', **re-** & *mordēre*, *morsum*, 'to bite', see **mordant.** Pangs, qualms, of conscience, sense of guilt; regret and repentance for sins committed, wrongs done, or duty not performed. Phr. (to act, do so-and-so) *without remorse*, without feeling or showing any compunction; callously, mercilessly.

remorseful, adj. [1. remórsfool; 2. rimɔ́sful]. Prec. & **-ful.** Feeling, exhibiting, remorse.

remorsefully, adv. Prec. & **-ly.** With remorse; with regret and compunction.

remorseless, adj. [1. remórsles; 2. rimɔ́slis]. **remorse** & **-less.** **a** (of persons and human action) Not feeling or exhibiting remorse or compunction; pitiless, ruthless; **b** (of forces and processes of nature; of events) acting, happening, blindly and inevitably, and without relation to human wishes and feelings; relentless.

remorselessly, adv. Prec. & **-ly.** Without remorse; pitilessly, mercilessly, relentlessly.

remorselessness, n. See prec. & **-ness.** Quality of being remorseless.

remote, adj. [1. remót; 2. rimóut], fr. Lat. *remōtum*, 'far-removed; retired; distant', P.P. of *removēre*, 'to move, put away', see **remove,** & cp. **motion, motive.** **1.** Removed to a distance; distant; **a** (of place or position) far away; sequestered, secluded, out of the way: *the remote regions of the earth*; *remote from any place of habitation*; *a remote village, dwelling*; **b** (of time) far distant from the present: *the remote past*; *the remote future.* **2.** Separated in spirit, feeling, sympathy, interests, from other men; aloof, distant: *to keep oneself, dwell, remote from human passions and affections*; '*Remote, unfriended, melancholy, slow*' (Goldsmith, 'Traveller', 1). **3.** Distant; **a** removed from by many descents in pedigree: *a remote ancestor*; **b** many degrees removed from a common ancestor: *a remote cousin, kinsman.* **4. a** Having but a slight logical relation: *your argument has a very remote bearing on the question*; **b** having but a slight causal connexion; indirect: *our actions often have but a remote effect on events*; *the influence we exert on the conduct of others is sometimes very remote*; Phr. (law) *remote damages*, those which do not directly result from the act of the party sued. **5.** Far removed from what is possible or probable; unlikely to happen: *a remote possibility*; *not the remotest chance of success.* **6.** Far from completeness, sameness, truth, fact &c; unsubstantial, shadowy, vague: *I have not the remotest idea what you mean*; *the portrait bears not the remotest resemblance to you.*

remotely, adv. Prec. & **-ly.** In a remote manner, distantly, at a distance; to a remote degree; in all senses of the adjective.

remoteness, n. See prec. & **-ness.** State, quality, of being remote; in all senses of adjective.

remould, vb. trans. [1. rēmṓld; 2. rīmóuld]. **re-** & **mould (IV.).** To remodel, recast.

remount (I.), vb. trans. & intrans. [1. rēmóunt; 2. rīmáunt], fr. Fr. *remonter.* See **re-** & **mount (II.).** **A.** trans. **1.** To mount (a horse) again. **2.** To go up, ascend, climb on to (a hill &c.) again. **3.** (mil.) To supply fresh horses or remounts to or for (army, regiment &c.). **4.** To put (a picture) on a new mount. **B.** intrans. **1.** To get up on horseback again. **2.** To climb up, on to, a hill, platform &c. again. **3. a** To go back to, be derived from: *the origin of these customs remounts to a primitive state of society*; **b** to reach, be traceable, extend, back in time: *royal pedigrees often remount to the remotest antiquity.*

remount (II.), n. [1. rḗmount; 2. rímaunt], fr. prec. One of a reserve supply of horses collected and held ready to make up losses in war time.

removability, n. [1. remōōvabíliti; 2. rimūvəbíliti]. See next word & **-ity.** State, quality, of being removable; capability of being removed or displaced.

removable, adj. [1. remṓōvabl; 2. rimúvəbl]. **remove (I.)** & **-able.** **1.** Capable of being removed: *removable partition*; *the fixtures are not removable*; *a removable evil* &c. **2.** Specif., subject to removal or dismissal from place or office: *judges are not removable at the pleasure of a Minister or the Crown.*

removal, n. [1. remṓōval; 2. rimúvəl]. **remove** & **-al.** **1.** Act of removing; taking away, shifting; specif., *removal of furniture*, act of shifting furniture from a house; *a removal to a new house*, act of moving oneself and belongings. **2.** Act of displacing from office; dismissal: *removal of a judge.* **3.** Act of doing away with; abolition: *removal of grievances.*

remove (I.), vb. trans. & intrans. [1. remṓōv; 2. rimúv]. O. Fr. *removoir*, Lat. *removēre*, 'to take away'. See **re-** & **move.** **A.** trans. **1. a** To lift, take, carry, shift (thing), away (usually from a place specified or implied): *kindly remove the dishes*; *to remove furniture from a house*; *thieves have removed the family plate*; Phr. *to remove oneself*, to go away; **b** to take, pull, off: *to remove one's coat, boots, spectacles* &c.; Phr. *to remove one's hat*, (i.) take it off for a moment, as in greeting; (ii.) to keep one's hat off, remain bare-headed, out of respect. **2. a** To withdraw, take, pull, away (part of body): *to remove one's hand*; *to remove one's glance, eyes*; *to remove one's head from the window, from the light*; **b** to withdraw, take away (person): *to remove one's son from school on account of ill-health.* **3. a** To wipe away, wipe, wash, out, do away with; to erase, obliterate: *to remove stains, traces of weeping*; *to remove an old coat of paint*; *to remove a name from a list*; **b** to get rid of, abolish: *to remove all grounds of complaint, causes of objection, doubts* &c. **4.** To oust (person); dismiss from, turn out of, relieve of an office, rank, post, position: *to remove an officer from his command, a teacher from his appointment, post* &c.; *to remove a boy from a school for misbehaviour.* **B.** intrans. To go away, depart, from one place to another; esp. to move one's place of abode to another place: *to remove to London.*

remove (II.), n., fr. prec. **1.** (rare) A move, moving, change, from one place to another. **2. a** Distance from, degree, grade, step, interval by which one thing &c. is distant or removed from another: *the scene changes at each remove*; *at many removes from*, at a great distance from; **b** degree of blood-relationship: *a first cousin at one remove*, child of a first cousin. **3. a** Promotion from one class or form at a school to a higher one: *to get a remove*; also **b** (in some schools, e.g. Charterhouse) a form between upper fourth and lower fifth. **4.** That which is removed; a dish or course which follows another, usually the principal dish, on the menu; relevé.

removed, adj. [1. remṓōvd; 2. rimúvd]. P.P. of **remove (I.).** In other than ordinary senses of verb. **1.** Distant, separated, distinct, not connected: *from motives entirely removed from self-interest*; *a character far removed from holiness.* **2.** (of kinship) Distant by one or more generations: *a first cousin once removed*, of child of a first cousin.

remover, n. [1. remṓōver; 2. rimúvə]. **remove (I.)** & **-er.** One who removes or takes away, changes position of &c.; specif., *household furniture remover*, one who makes it his business to convey furniture from one house to another for persons changing residence.

remunerable, adj. [1. remúnerabl; 2. rimjúnərəbl]. Next word & **-able.** Capable of being, fit to be, remunerated.

remunerate, vb. trans. [1. remúnerāt; 2. rimjúnəreit], fr. Lat. *remūnerāt-(um)*, P.P. stem of *remūnerāri*, later *remūnerāre*, 'to repay, reward, recompense', fr. **re-** & *mūnerāre*, 'to give, present', fr. *mūnus*, *mūneris*, 'gift, reward'. See **municipal** & cp. **munificence.** **1.** To pay, reward, compensate, give as equivalent for anything done, service rendered &c.: *to remunerate a person for his labour, work &c., services, sacrifices* &c. **2.** To serve as remuneration or recompense for: *his followers' loyalty amply remunerated him for all his labours.*

remuneration, n. [1. remūneráshun; 2. rimjūnəréiʃən], fr. Lat. *remūnerātiōn-(em).* Prec. & **-ion.** Act of remunerating; that which remunerates, repays, or compensates; payment, wages, salary.

remunerative, adj. [1. remúnerativ; 2. rimjúnərətiv]. **remunerate** & **-ive.** Affording remuneration; paying, profitable: *a remunerative position, business, salary.*

remuneratively, adj. Prec. & **-ly.** So as to be remunerative; profitably.

remunerativeness, n. See prec. & **-ness.** Quality of being remunerative.

renaissance, n. [1. renásans, renásahns; 2. rənéisəns, rənéisɑ̃s]. Fr., 're-birth', fr. *renaiss-(ant)*, Pres. Part. of *renaître*, 'to be born again'; cp. variant **renascence.** **1.** A rebirth, revival; specif., *the Renaissance*, revival of classical (anct. Greek) art, learning, and literature in Western Europe during 15th and 16th cents. **2.** Any similar revival in art, letters, religious activity &c.: *the renaissance of the Church in the 19th century*; *a renaissance of the theatre, of popular music* &c.

renal, adj. [1. rḗnl; 2. rínl], fr. Lat. *rēnālis*, 'of, belonging to, the kidneys', fr. Lat. *rēn*, 'kidney', the origin & connexions of wh. are unknown. Pertaining to, connected with, the kidneys; lying near, in the region of, the kidneys: *renal diseases*; *a renal calculus*; *renal arteries, veins*; *the renal region.*

rename, vb. trans. [1. rēnā́m; 2. rīnéim]. **re-** & **name.** To give a new name to.

renascence, n. [1. renásens, renā́sens; 2. rinǽsəns, rinéisəns]. See next word & **-ce**; **a** Latinized form of **renaissance.** **1.** Rebirth, revival, renewal: *the renascence of plants in spring*; *the renascence of crime* &c. **2.** Specif., the Renaissance.

renascent, adj. [1. renásent; 2. rinǽsənt], fr. Lat. *renascent-(em)*, Pres. Part. of *renasci*, 'to be born again'. See **re-** & **nascent.** Being born again; reviving, springing into fresh life and vigour: *renascent growth*; *renascent energies*; *a renascent enthusiasm* &c.

rencontre, n. [1. ronkontr; 2. rā̃kɔ̃tr̥]. Fr., fr. *rencontrer*, 'to meet, encounter', fr. **re-** & *encontrer*, 'to meet'. See **encounter. 1.** A hostile meeting or contest; a duel, collision, clash. **2.** A casual, haphazard meeting of two persons.

rencounter, n. & vb. trans. & intrans. [1. rènkóunter; 2. rènkáuntə]. Anglicized variant of prec. **1.** n. (rare or obs.) A rencontre. **2.** vb. To have a rencontre with; to meet hostilely or casually.

rend, vb. trans. & intrans. [1. rend; 2. rend]. L.O.E. *rendan*, 'to tear, cut', M.E. *renden*, cogn. w. O. Fris. *renda, randa*, 'to cut, break'; perh. fr. **randjan*, 'to cut, tear, the edge off', fr. O.E. *rand*, 'edge, border'; cp. O.H.G. *rant*, 'border', in gradational relation to **rind.** Cp. similar development of meaning in vbs. *bark* (*one's shins*), *skin*, *tear.* **A.** trans. **1. a** (archaic or poet.) To tear apart, asunder, in two, in pieces: '*the veil of the temple was rent in twain*'; *to rend one's clothes*; **b** (fig.) *to rend the feelings*; '*rend your heart and not your garments*'. **2. a** To split, shiver, blast, shatter, divide; **b** (fig.) *to rend the air with cries* &c.; **c** *a party rent by factions.* **3.** *Rend from*, tear away, separate forcibly: *infants were rent from their mothers' arms.* **B.** intrans. To be torn, shattered, split &c.

render, vb. trans. & intrans. [1. rénder; 2. réndə]. M.E. *rendren*, 'to restore'; to translate', fr. Fr. *rendre*, Low Lat. *rendere*, w. nasalized form of first syll. fr. Lat. *reddere*, 'to put back, give back, restore; to give up, deliver, pay; to translate from one language into another; to imitate, represent'; fr. *red-*, see **re-**, & *dare*, 'to give' &c., see **date** (**I.**) & **donation. A.** trans. **1. a** To give in exchange, by way of requital: *to render good for evil*; **b** to pay as a due: '*Render unto Caesar the things that are Caesar's*'; *to render obedience to one's lawful superior*; *to render thanks.* **2.** To present, tender, offer, submit, for consideration: *to render an account, bill &c. for payment.* Phr. *to render an account of*, give a description, present a narrative of; *to render an account of one's actions*, account for, accept responsibility for. **3.** To cause to become, to make: *climbing renders me giddy*; *to be rendered furious, speechless with rage* &c.; *the machine was rendered useless by unskilful handling*; *my efforts were rendered futile.* **4. a** To reproduce, express, depict, by means of art: *a portrait renders a personality*; *a good actor renders a character to the life*; *to render a piece of music*, to interpret it in performance; **b** to reproduce the meaning of by different words, or in a different language; to translate; to interpret: *you have rendered my meaning accurately, in very simple terms*; *to render a piece of English into Latin*; *to render the sense of the original in a translation.* **5.** To perform (an action) to the intention of, for the benefit or the reverse of a person or a cause: *to render help, a service, a favour, a disservice* &c. **6.** To clarify (fat, oil &c.) by melting. **7.** To put a coat of rendering on (a wall). **8.** To pay out, slacken (a rope) so that it will run through a block &c. **B.** intrans. (of a rope) To run easily and smoothly through a block &c.

render (**II.**), n., fr. prec. **1.** (rare or obs.) Return, payment, esp. of rent. **2.** (techn. uses) **a** Coat of plaster applied to a wall; **b** result obtained by the rendering of fats and oils.

rendering, vbl. n. [1. réndering; 2. réndəriŋ]. **render** (**I.**) &**-ing.** Act of one who renders; that which is rendered. Specif. **1. a** mode of translating from one language to another; **b** interpretation, reproduction, expression, of an emotion, character &c. by means of art. **2.** (techn. uses) **a** Act or process of purifying fats &c.; **b** act of putting first coat of plaster on brickwork; first coat of plaster applied to brickwork; **c** smooth running of a rope through a block.

rendezvous (**I.**), n. [1. róndāvōō; 2. rā́deivū]. Fr., 'render, assemble, betake yourselves', imperat. pl. of *se rendre.* See **render** (**I.**). **1.** A meeting of troops or ships as and where appointed; meeting of troops &c. **2. a** A meeting by appointment or agreement; place and time agreed on for such meeting; **b** a place of general resort, a popular place for meeting.

rendezvous (**II.**), vb. intrans., fr. prec. To meet by rendezvous or appointment; to meet at a rendezvous, of ships, troops &c.

rendition, n. [1. rendíshun; 2. rendíʃən]. Fr., fr. Low Lat. *renditiōn-(em)*, Lat. *redditiōn-(em)*, fr. *reddit-(um)*, P.P. of *reddere.* See **render. 1.** (obs. or rare) Act of surrendering or returning, esp. of escaped criminals, to a foreign government. **2.** (pedantic) A rendering, translation; representation.

renegade (**I.**), n. [1. rénegād; 2. rénigeid]. M.E. *renegate*, &, in corrupted form, *runagate*, later *renegado*, Span. P.P. of *renegar*, 'to deny one's faith'; fr. Med. Lat. *renegāre, renegātum*, 'to deny again, forswear'. See **re-** & **negation. 1.** One who forswears his faith; an apostate; originally of those who abjured Christianity for Islam in Spain at the conquest by the Moors. **2.** One who forsakes or deserts principles, a cause, or a party; a deserter, turncoat.

renegade (**II.**), vb. intrans., fr. prec. (rare) To become a renegade; to apostatize.

renegation, n. [1. rènegáshun; 2. rènigéiʃən]. See *renegāt-(um)*, under **renegade,** & **-ion.** Apostasy; desertion of party or principles.

renew, vb. trans. [1. renū́; 2. rinjū́]. **re-** & **new. 1.** To restore to original condition of freshness, to give, gain, back, the old vigour, vitality &c.: *to renew one's health, youth, enthusiasm.* **2.** To give a new spiritual nature to; to regenerate: *to renew the heart and mind.* **3. a** To replace (what is old, worn, faded, exhausted &c.) by something new, fresh, sound; to renovate, supply afresh: *to renew the paint in a house, the carpets* &c.; *to renew one's wardrobe*; *to renew one's store of petrol* &c.; **b** to replace by growing again: *a snake renews its skin*; *the trees renew their foliage every spring.* **4. a** To begin to utter again, to reiterate, repeat: *to renew one's application, one's entreaties, demands, complaints* &c.; **b** to begin to make, carry on, again; to engage in prosecution of anything; to resume: *to renew an attack*; *to renew an old quarrel*; *to renew a former practice.* **5.** To recall to existence, to revive, set going again in the mind: *to renew ancient jealousies, long-forgotten disappointments, sorrows* &c. **6.** To prolong, extend existence or validity of, to continue (conditions of): *to renew an agreement, a lease, an appointment* &c.

renewability, n. [1. renūabíliti; 2. rinjūəbíliti]. Next word & **-ity.** Quality of being renewable.

renewable, adj. [1. renū́abl; 2. rinjū́əbl]. **renew** & **-able.** Capable of being renewed; admitting renewal.

renewal, n. [1. renū́al; 2. rinjú́əl]. **renew** & **-al.** Act of renewing; state of being renewed in all senses.

reniform, adj. [1. réniform; 2. rínifɔ̄m]. Lat. *rēni-*, stem of *rēn*, 'kidney', see **renal,** & **-form.** Kidney-shaped.

rennet (**I.**), n. [1. rénet; 2. rénit]. Cp. M.E. *rennels*, 'rennet'; connected w. M.E. *rennen*, 'to cause to run'; cp. O.E. *rinnan*, 'to run', & *ġerinnan*, 'to run together, coagulate', see **run.** An extract from or preparation of the inner membrane of the stomach of a calf, used for curdling milk, in making cheese or junket.

rennet (**II.**), n., fr. Fr. *reinette*, 'little queen', see **regina.** A variety of eating apple.

rennin, n. [1. rénin; 2. rénin]. Coined fr. first syll. of **rennet** (**I.**) & **-in.** (chem.) A ferment with coagulating properties, found in the gastric juices of animals; the active principle of rennet.

renominate, vb. trans. [1. rènóminăt; 2. rinɔ́mineit]. **re-** & **nominate.** To nominate again for a position, office &c.

renomination, n. [1. rènominā́shun; 2. rinɔminéiʃən]. Prec. & **-ion.** Act of renominating.

renounce (**I.**), vb. trans. & intrans. [1. renóuns; 2. rináuns]. In M.E., fr. O. Fr. *renoncier*, fr. Lat. *renuntiāre*, 'to carry back word, to report; to retract, refuse; to renounce'; fr. **re-** & *nuntiāre*, fr. *nuntius*, 'messenger', see **nuncio. A.** trans. **1. a** To make a formal statement that one gives up, and will no longer prosecute (claim to); to resign, withdraw; **b** to cease to advance, to abandon (claim &c.): *to renounce one's rights to an inheritance, to the throne* &c. **2. a** To announce formally that one disowns, repudiates (an allegiance, faith, claim upon one &c.): '*Dost thou renounce the devil and all his works . . .? I renounce them all*'; **b** to disown, repudiate, disavow: *to renounce the authority of the law, one's former religion* &c. **3.** To give up the practice, enjoyment, use, of: *to renounce one's old bad habits*; *to renounce smoking and drinking, violent exercise* &c. **4.** (card playing) To admit having no card of (suit led), by playing from a different suit: *to renounce hearts.* **B.** intrans. **1.** (cards) To admit having no card of suit led, by playing from another suit. **2.** (law) To decline to act as executor, or trustee.

renounce (**II.**), n., fr. prec. (cards) Inability to follow suit and consequent playing of a card of different suit.

renouncement, n. [1. renóunsment; 2. rináunsmənt]. **renounce** (**I.**) & **-ment;** cp. Fr. *renoncement.* Act of renouncing; renunciation.

renovate, vb. trans. [1. rénovāt; 2. rénəveit], fr. Lat. *renovāt-(um)*, P.P. of *renovāre*, fr. **re-** & *novāre*, 'to make new', fr. *novus*, 'new', see **novel** (**I.**) & **new.** To do up; to make good dilapidations in, to restore to a former condition.

renovation, n. [1. rènovā́shun; 2. rènəvéiʃən], fr. Lat. *renovātiōn-(em)*, 'renewal'. See prec. & **-ion. a** Act of renovating, or renewing; **b** something which has been renovated.

renovator, n. [1. rénovāter; 2. rénəveitə]. **renovate** & **-or.** One who renovates.

renown, n. [1. renóun; 2. rináun]. M.E., fr. A.-Fr. *renoun*, fr. O. Fr. *renon*, later *renom*; fr. O. Fr. *renomer*, 'to make famous, to celebrate', fr. **re-** & O. Fr. *non*, Mod. Fr. *nom*, 'name', see **noun.** Fact of having a great or celebrated name; fame, celebrity, high or exalted reputation.

renowned, adj. [1. renóund; 2. rináund]. Prec. & **-ed.** Possessing renown; famous, celebrated.

rent (**I.**), adj. & P.P. [1. rent; 2. rent], fr. P.P. of **rend.** Torn, lacerated.

rent (**II.**), n., fr. prec. **1. a** Hole, slit, torn in a fabric or other thin substance; **b** a cleft, fissure, opening, in a solid, or apparently solid, and massive body: *a rent in a hill-side, in the clouds* &c. **2.** (fig.) Division of, difference in, opinions; schism, discord: *a rent in a party.*

rent (**III.**), n., fr. O. Fr. *rente*, fr. Low Lat. *rendita*, Lat. *reddita*, 'that which is rendered or given back', P.P. fem. as n., of *reddere.* See **render. 1.** Payment made by a tenant to the owner, or landlord, for the right to use land, houses &c. **2.** Payment made by a user to owner of other things, e.g. of machinery, for the right to use them temporarily.

rent (**IV.**), vb. trans. & intrans., fr. prec. **A.** trans. **1.** To occupy, use, hold (land, buildings &c.), with obligation to pay a specified rent for such: *to rent a farm, house, rooms &c. from an owner or landlord.* **2.** To let, hire, out for payment of a certain rent:

to rent a farm, house &c. to a person ; *a house rented at £60 a year.* **B.** intrans. To be let or rented : *the farm rents at so much.*

rentable, adj. [1. réntabl ; 2. réntəbl]. Prec. & **-able. 1.** Available for occupation or use, for hire, at a certain rent. **2.** Of a kind, in such a condition, that rent may be obtained for it.

rental, n. [1. réntl ; 2. réntl]. A.-Fr. ; also in L. & Med. Lat. *rentale*, 'rent roll'. See **rent (III.)** & **-al. 1.** Amount paid or received as rent. **2.** A rent-roll.

rent charge, n. **a** An income charged by will or settlement on the rents received from an estate, payable by the heir or other owner of the estate to persons named ; **b** an annuity charged on land, payable out of its income.

rente, n. [1. ront ; 2. rãt]. Fr. See **rent (III.). 1.** An annuity, rent charge. **2.** Specif. (usually pl. and in full *rentes d'état*) **a** the State securities for the Consolidated Debt of France, also of other countries in Europe, answering to the British *Consols* ; **b** interest paid on these.

rent-free, adj. & adv. **a** adj. Granted for occupation without payment of rent ; **b** adv., free of, without paying, rent : *to live rent-free.*

rentier, n. [1. róntiā ; 2. rãtiei]. Fr., fr. **rente** & **-ier. 1.** A holder of French *rentes*. **2.** One who lives on an income from investments &c. ; a person of independent means.

rent-roll, n. **1.** A list, originally a roll, of tenants and the rents payable by them on a landed estate. **2.** The total income derived from rents by the owner of a landed estate.

rent seck or **sec**, n. A.-Fr. *rente seque*, 'dry rent'. See **rent (III.)** & **sec (I.).** A rent granted without power of distress, now equivalent to a rent charge.

rent service, n. (legal hist.) **a** Service, as by labour, paid as, or in addition to, rent for the occupation of land ; **b** tenure of land by such service.

renumber, vb. trans. [1. rènúmber ; 2. rinámbə]. **re-** & **number (II.).** To number over again ; to change the numbers of (objects &c.) in a series : *to renumber the houses in a street.*

renunciation, n. [1. renùnsiáshun ; 2. rinànsiéiʃən], fr. Lat. *renunciātiōn-(em)*, fr. *renunciāt-(um)*, P.P. of *renunciāre*, see **renounce, & -ion.** Act of renouncing (in various senses) ; **a** act of announcing abandonment of, or of abandoning, a right, claim &c. ; **b** act of announcing intention to repudiate, or of repudiating, an obligation &c. ; **c** act of giving up practice, use, enjoyment of &c.

renunciatory, adj. [1. renúnsiaturi ; 2. rinánsiətəri]. See prec. & **-ory.** Expressing, of the nature of, a renunciation.

reo-, pref. in electrical terminology. See **rheo-.**

reoccupation, n. [1. rèokūpáshun ; 2. riɔkjupéiʃən]. **re-** & **occupation.** Act of reoccupying (premises &c.) ; state of being reoccupied.

reoccupy, vb. trans. [1. rèókūpī ; 2. riɔ́kjupai]. **re-** & **occupy.** To occupy again ; to take up again the occupation, settlement, of land, houses &c.

reopen, vb. trans. & intrans. [1. rèópen ; 2. rióupən]. **re-** & **open (III.). 1.** To open again after closing or being closed : *to reopen a window, door* ; *to reopen a theatre* ; *to reopen a wound.* **2.** To begin, open up, again ; to resume, renew, recommence (discussion, action), after temporary cessation : *to reopen an argument* ; *to reopen fire, the attack.*

reorganization, n. [1. rēorganīzáshun ; 2. riɔ̄gənaizéiʃən]. **re-** & **organization.** Act of reorganizing ; state of being reorganized.

reorganize, vb. trans. [1. rēórganīz ; 2. riɔ́gənaiz]. **re-** & **organize.** To organize again ; put on a new basis ; to give a new, fresh, organization to ; to change the system, administration, personnel of : *to reorganize an army, the country's finances &c.* ; *to reorganize a Ministry, staff of a business &c.*

rep (I.), also **repp, reps**, n. [1. rep ; 2. rep]. Fr. *reps* ; etymol. doubtful. A thick, corded, ribbed material of silk or wool or a mixture of both, used for curtains and upholstery.

rep (II.), n. Abbr. of **reprobate**, now more commonly **rip (III.)** ; but see **demi-rep.** A dissolute person, a rip.

rep (III.), n. Abbr. of **repetition.** (schoolboy's slang) Repetition.

repair (I.), vb. trans. [1. repár ; 2. ripéə], fr. O. Fr. *reparer*, fr. Lat. *reparāre*, 'to get again, to recover, to repair' ; **re-** & *parāre*, 'to get, to prepare', see **pare. 1. a** To restore to good condition ; to make good injury, damage, wear and tear, decay &c. ; to mend : *to repair a house, clothes, a worn road, ship, a watch &c.* ; *repairing lease*, lease of a house under which the tenant has to do the repairs ; **b** to restore, recruit, revive : *to repair one's exhausted energies &c.* **2. a** To amend, set right, to remedy : *to repair a loss, mistake, defeat* ; **b** to make amends for, to compensate for : *to repair a wrong, injury, injustice &c.*

repair (II.), n., fr. prec. **1. a** Act of repairing or restoring to good or sound condition ; process, operation, of repairing : *repair of a roof, watch, clothes* ; *the house is badly in need of repair* ; (often in pl.) actual processes carried out or requiring to be carried out, in order to repair : *the tenant has to do all the repairs* ; *certain repairs will be necessary before we can live in the house* ; *during repairs, under repair*, of building, in process of being repaired ; also **b** *repair of one's health, strength &c.* **2.** Condition in relation to the need for repairing or to soundness or working order : *to be in good, sound, bad, repair, out of repair.*

repair (III.), vb. intrans. M.E. *repairen*, fr. O. Fr. *repairer, repairier*, 'to frequent, to return to', fr. L. Lat. *repatriāre*, 'to return to one's own country', fr. **re-** & *patria*, 'one's native country', see **patriot** & cp. **repatriate.** Followed by *to, thither*, or other word of direction : **1.** To go to, to resort to, to frequent : *the birds repair to warmer climes in winter* ; *they repaired to their homes, homeward.* **2.** To have recourse to : *he repaired to his father for aid.*

repair (IV.), n. O. Fr. *repaire.* See prec. (archaic and rare) **1.** Resort, recourse : *to have repair to.* **2.** Place to which many people go ; haunt ; resort : *a place of repair, of great repair.*

repairable, adj. [1. repárabl ; 2. ripéərəbl]. **repair (I.)** & **-able.** Capable of being repaired, admitting of repair, worth repairing : *the boots are not repairable* ; *houses in a slum are not repairable.*

repand, adj. [1. repánd ; 2. ripǽnd], fr. Lat. *repandus*, 'bent back, turned up', fr. **re-** & *pandus*, 'bent', fr. *pandāre*, 'to bend, curve', connected w. *pandere*, 'to spread, stretch out', prob. ultimately fr. same base as *patēre*, 'to stand open', see **patent** & cp. **expand.** (bot., of leaves) Having a gently undulating margin, slightly wavy, contrasted with *serrated.*

repaper, vb. trans. [1. rèpáper ; 2. ripéipə]. **re-** & **paper.** To put fresh paper on (walls).

reparable, adj. [1. réparabl ; 2. répərəbl]. Fr., fr. Lat. *reparābilis.* See **repair (I.)** & **-able.** Capable of being repaired or made good : *a reparable loss, injury, mistake &c.*

reparation, n. [1. rèparáshun ; 2. rèpəréiʃən], fr. O. Fr. *reparacion*, Mod. Fr. *réparation*, fr. Lat. *reparātiōn-(em)*, fr. *reparāt-(um)*, P.P. of *reparāre.* See **repair (I.)** & **-ation.** Act of putting right, restoring, repairing &c. ; **a** something done by way of repairing, to material objects, now more usually *repair(s)* ; **b** amends for wrong done ; compensation : *German reparations for the war* ; **c** (in non-material sense) atonement ; redress, restitution : *to make reparation for one's neglect.*

reparative, adj. [1. réparativ ; 2. répərətiv]. See prec. & **-ive.** Tending to repair, restore, redress.

repartee, n. & vb. intrans. [1. rèparté ; 2. rèpātī]. Earlier *reparty*, fr. Fr. *repartie*, in same sense, fem. sing. of *reparti*, P.P. of *repartir*, 'to part, start again ; to reply', fr. **re-** & *partir*, 'to go, start', see **part (II.). 1.** n. **a** A witty reply or retort ; **b** readiness in making repartees : *famous for repartee.* **2.** vb. (rare) To make a repartee.

repartition, n. & vb. trans. [1. rèpartíshun ; 2. ripātíʃən]. **re-** & **partition. 1.** n. **a** Act of dividing up again, of redistributing, of making new division and apportionment ; **b** state of being redivided, reapportioned &c. **2.** vb. To partition, divide up again ; to redistribute, make a fresh partition of.

repast, n. [1. repáhst ; 2. ripā́st]. O. Fr., Mod. Fr. *repas*, fr. L. Lat. *repas-(tum)*, P.P. of *repascere*, 'to feed again', fr. **re-** & Lat. *pascere*, 'to feed'. See **pastor.** A meal, a feast : *a light, generous, rich repast.*

repatriate, vb. trans. [1. rēpátriāt, rēpátriāt ; 2. ripǽtrieit, ripéitrieit], fr. L. Lat. *repatriāt-(um)*, P.P. stem of *repatriāre*, fr. **re-** & Lat. *patria*, 'native country, fatherland'. See **patriot** & cp. **repair (III.).** To send back, return, to the native country : *to repatriate immigrants, slaves, indentured labourers, refugees &c.*

repatriation, n. [1. rèpatriáshun ; 2. ripætriéiʃən]. Prec. & **-ion.** Act of repatriating ; state of being repatriated.

repay, vb. trans. & intrans. [1. rēpá ; 2. rīpéi], fr. O. Fr. *repaier.* See **re-** & **pay. A.** trans. **1. a** To pay back, refund, to make repayment of (money) ; **b** to pay back (money) to (a person). **2. a** To make a return for ; to do or give something by way of requital or equivalent for what has been done for, or received by, one : *I can never repay all your kindness* ; **b** to reward, requite, make a return to (a person) for (something done or given) : *I know not how to repay you for your kindness.* **3.** (rare) In Phr. *to repay a visit*, pay one in return, to a person who has visited oneself ; more usually *to return a visit.* **B.** intrans. or absol. **1.** To make repayment : *you must repay as soon as you can.* **2.** To make requital : '*Vengeance is mine, I will repay*'.

repayable, adj. [1. rēpáabl ; 2. rīpéiəbl]. Prec. & **-able.** That may, must, or is to be repaid : *the debt is repayable in three months.*

repayment, n. [1. rēpáment ; 2. rīpéimənt]. **repay** & **-ment. a** Act of returning, remunerating, requiting ; a repaying ; **b** sum repaid.

repeal, vb. trans. & n. [1. repél ; 2. ripíl], fr. O. Fr. *rapeler*, Mod. Fr. *rappeler*, 'to call back, recall'. See **re-** & **appeal. 1.** vb. To rescind, revoke, abrogate ; to annul (a law or statute). **2.** n. Act of repealing ; rescission, revocation, abrogation, annulment (of a statute or law) ; specif., the repeal of the Act of Union, 1801, between Great Britain and Ireland, esp. as advocated by O'Connell, 1829-43.

repealer, n. [1. repéler ; 2. ripílə]. Prec. & **-er.** One who repeals or advocates repeal of a statute ; specif., O'Connell, *the Great Repealer.*

repeat (I.), vb. trans. & intrans. [1. repét ; 2. ripít]. Fr. *répéter*, fr. Lat. *repetere*, 'to go back to, to revisit ; to ask, to demand, again' ; **re-** & *petere*, 'to go ; to seek ; to ask', see **petition. A.** trans. **1.** To say again, to reiterate : *let me repeat what I have just said* ; *to repeat an order* ; esp. by way of emphasis : *I repeat that this is the last time such conduct will be tolerated.* Phr. *to repeat oneself*, to say the same thing, make same jokes &c., over and over again. **2. a** To say, utter, reproduce orally, what one has learnt by heart ; to recite : *to repeat a lesson, one's Catechism &c.* ; **b** (i.) specif., to spread abroad, give currency to, make known, by repeating, what one has heard, esp. something told one in confidence : *I'll tell you a secret if you'll promise not to repeat it* ; *these stories ought not to be repeated* ; (ii.) to reproduce in conversation, the ideas and sayings of others : *a man of no particular views who simply repeats what he hears said.* **3. a** To do over again : *such conduct must never be repeated* ; *to repeat a fine performance, an effort, an error, an attack*

&c.; **b** to cause to occur, to appear, again: *to repeat a colour in several parts of a picture; a design repeated at intervals along a surface; history repeats itself*; **c** to cause something to be undergone, taken, submitted to, again: *to repeat an experience, a punishment, a treatment; repeat the dose until relief is obtained.* **B.** intrans. **1.** (of a watch) To strike the last hour, quarter, and minutes. **2.** (of something taken into the stomach; coarse) To rise, continue to be tasted for some time after consumption. **3.** (of numbers, as decimals) To recur.

repeat (II.), n., fr. prec. **1.** (usually colloq.) Repetition, that which is repeated: *repeat of a song; the repeat of a design, pattern; repeat of an order, message* &c. **2.** (mus.) **a** A passage scored only once but intended to be repeated or played over again; **b** indication on musical score that a passage is to be played again.

repeatedly, adv. [1. repḗtedli; 2. ripítidli]. *Repeated*, P.P. of **repeat (I.)**, & **-ly**. Over and over again, at constantly recurring intervals.

repeater, n. [1. repḗter; 2. ripítə]. **repeat (I.)** & **-er**. Person who, thing which, repeats; specif. **a** a watch which, upon a spring being pressed, strikes the last hour, and the number of quarters and minutes; **b** a repeating rifle; **c** (polit. slang, U.S.A.) one who 'repeats' or votes illegally more than once at an election.

repeating rifle, n. [1. repḗting rīfl; 2. ripítiŋ ráifl]. Rifle with a chamber containing several cartridges, enabling it to be fired several times in rapid succession without reloading.

repeating watch, n. A repeater.

repel, vb. trans. [1. repél; 2. ripél], fr. Lat. *repellere, repulsum*, 'to drive back, repulse', fr. **re-** & *pellere, pulsum*, 'to drive, to beat'. See base under **compel** & **pulse (I.)**. **1.** To drive back, beat off, repulse; **a** (of bodily action) *to repel an enemy, an attack, assault, blow* &c.; **b** (of intellectual or moral action) (i.) to repudiate: *to repel an accusation*; (ii.) to resist, subdue, thrust aside, keep down: *to repel evil thoughts, temptations.* **2.** To reject, to refuse to admit or accept; to turn away, repulse, spurn: *to repel a suppliant, a request; to repel advances, attempts at reconciliation* &c. **3.** To provoke aversion, excite feelings of dislike in, to be highly unattractive to: *his manner, appearance &c. repels one; desert life repels some and attracts others; he was repelled by the thought of the drudgery of his task.* **4.** (phys.) To cause to move back, away, or apart; to cause repulsion to; to refuse to mix with: *two positive electric charges repel each other; water repels oil*; contrasted with *attract*.

repellent, adj. [1. repélent; 2. ripélənt], fr. Lat. *repellent-(em)*, Pres. Part. of *repellere*. See **repel**. Exciting dislike and aversion; disgusting, revolting: *a repellent appearance; repellent subject, character; to me he is a most repellent person.*

repellently, adv. Prec. & **-ly**. In a repellent manner; so as to repel.

repent (I.), adj. [1. rḗpent; 2. rīpənt], fr. Lat. *rēpent-(em)*, Pres. Part. of *rēpere*, 'to creep, crawl'; fr. **wrep-*; cp. Gk. *(h)répein*, 'to incline, fall, turn downwards'; *(h)ropḗ*, 'a sinking, falling'; Lith. *virpiù*, 'I heave, shudder'; *várpa*, 'ear of corn', lit. 'that which trembles'. (bot., of plants) Creeping, trailing.

repent (II.), vb. trans. & intrans. [1. repént; 2. ripánt], fr. Fr. reflex. *(se) repentir*, 'to repent of', fr. **re-** & Lat. *poenitēre*, 'to cause to feel sorry, make to repent'; usually in impers., *poenitet me*, 'it repents me, I repent', see **penitent**. **A.** trans. **1.** To feel penitence, sorrow, or regret for, to think of with penitence; to be sorry, penitent, for; to wish one had not done: *to repent one's sins; to repent the doing of, doing, the crime; he soon repented his generosity, rashness, folly; they will soon bitterly repent what they did.* **2.** (reflex. or impers., archaic) '*The Lord repenteth him of the evil*'; *I repent me; it repented me of my former sins.* **B.** intrans. To be penitent; to feel penitence, sorrow, or regret: *repent and be saved; unless ye truly repent*; also *repent of (one's sins)* &c.: *I have many things to repent of.*

repentance, n. [1. repéntans; 2. ripéntəns]. Fr. See prec. & **-ance**. **a** Act of repenting; penitence, sorrow, regret felt for something done amiss; **b** state of mind in which penitence is felt.

repentant, adj. [1. repéntant; 2. ripéntənt]. Fr., Pres. Part. of *repentir*. See prec. & **-ant**. **1.** Feeling repentance, repenting, penitent, regretful, sorrowful for past sins &c.: *a repentant sinner.* **2.** Feeling, expressing, repentance: *a repentant heart; repentant tears* &c.

repentantly, adv. Prec. & **-ly**. With repentance, penitence; in a repentant manner.

repeople, vb. trans. [1. rēpḗpl; 2. rīpípl]. **re-** & **people**. To people anew; to supply (country) with fresh inhabitants; to repopulate.

repercussion, n. [1. rèperkúshun; 2. rīpəkáʃən], fr. Lat. *repercussiōn-(em)*. See **re-** & **percussion**; the vb. *repercuss*, 'to drive back, reverberate', is obs. **1.** A beating back; the rebound, recoil, resulting from striking against anything; also (of sound) echo. **2.** (fig.) Influence, effect, resulting from an action or event exerted, often indirectly, upon human affairs apparently remote from the action or event: *an action of a British Cabinet may have repercussions all over Europe.*

repercussive, adj. [1. rèperkúsiv; 2. rīpəkásiv]. See prec. & **-ive**. Of the nature of, producing, resulting from, repercussion.

repertoire, n. [1. répertwar; 2. répətwā]. Fr., fr. Lat. See next word. A stock of plays, pieces, songs &c. which an actor, singer, musician, or a company of such has rehearsed and is familiar with, and which can be performed at any time as occasion arises; a repertory.

repertory, n. [1. réperturi; 2. répətəri], fr. Lat. *repertōrium*, 'catalogue, list, inventory, repertory', fr. *repert-(um)*, P.P. stem of *reperīre*, 'to procure, find again, to find out, discover, invent', fr. **re-** & *parīre*, older form of *parēre*, 'to produce, get', see **parent**. **1.** A storehouse, treasury; esp. a book in which facts of various kinds are brought together: *a repertory of useful information.* **2.** Specif., a repertoire; collection, stock of plays, pieces, songs &c. which can be performed without much rehearsal; (attrib.) *a repertory theatre*, one with a permanent company, depending on constant change of plays and not on a long run of a single piece.

repetend, n. [1. rèpeténd; 2. rèpiténd], fr. Lat. *repetend-(us)*, 'to be repeated', gerundive of *repetere*, see **repeat (I.)**. (math.) A repeating decimal; the number in a repeating decimal which is repeated.

repetition, n. [1. rèpetíshun; 2. rèpitíʃən], fr. Lat. *repetitiōn-(em)*, fr. *repetīt-(um)*, P.P. of *repetere*, see **repeat (I.)**, & **-ion**. **1.** **a** Act of repeating, of saying or doing something over again: *the repetition of a word or a phrase, of a mistake*; **b** something repeated, something said or done over again: *that is a mere repetition of what you said before, of your former action*; **c** a copy, imitation: *each of this author's books is but a repetition of the others with slight differences.* **2.** **a** Act of repeating or reciting what has been learnt: *repetition is a most useful exercise for the memory*; **b** piece so learnt for recitation: *repetition for tomorrow will be 'Lycidas'.* **3.** (mus.) The repeating or reiteration of a note rapidly by an instrument.

repetitional, adj. [1. rèpetíshunal; 2. rèpitíʃənəl]. Prec. & **-al**. (rare) Of the nature of, exhibiting, characterized by, repetition.

repetitionary, adj. [1. rèpetíshunari; 2. rèpitíʃənəri]. See prec. & **-ary**. (rare) Repetitional.

repetitious, adj. [1. rèpetíshus; 2. rèpitíʃəs]. See **repetition** & **-ous**. (rare) Repetitional.

repetitive, adj. [1. repétitiv; 2. ripétitiv]. See prec. & **-ive**. Tending to repeat; repeating; marked by repetition.

repine, vb. intrans. [1. repīn; 2. ripáin]. **re-** & **pine (I.)**, 'to grieve'. To fret, complain, murmur, be discontented; to grieve: *whatever trials overtake him, he never repines*; also *repine at* (one's fate &c.).

repiningly, adv. [1. repīningli; 2. ripáiniŋli]. Pres. Part. of prec. & **-ly**. In a repining, complaining manner; discontentedly.

repique, n. & vb. trans. & intrans. [1. repḗk; 2. ripík]. Fr. *repic*. See **re-** & **pique (III.)**. **1.** n. In the game of piquet, the scoring of 30 points by a player from his hand before a card is played, scoring an additional 60, making 90 points in all. **2.** vb. **a** trans. To score a repique against: *to repique your opponent*; **b** intrans., to score repique.

replace, vb. trans. [1. rēplás; 2. rīpléis]. **re-** & **place**. **1.** To put back in, restore to, former place or position; **a** to put back again: *all books must be replaced on the shelves*; **b** to restore, repay: *to replace money, stolen or borrowed*; **c** to restore to former rank, office &c.: *all the old gang are snugly replaced in their former offices.* Phr. *difficult, impossible, to replace*, of such a quality as to make it difficult to find another to fill place of. **2.** To take the place of, to supersede, succeed: *Mr. X replaces Mr. B as wicket-keeper, as Chancellor of the Exchequer; the telephone is rapidly replacing the telegraph.* **3.** *Replace by*, to fill the place of, to substitute for, put in the place of, to supply as equivalent to: *to replace Mr. A by Mr. B in an office* &c.; *to replace an original picture by a copy; to replace coal fires by gas.*

replaceable, adj. [1. rēplásabl; 2. rīpléisəbl]. Prec. & **-able**. Capable of being replaced.

replacement, n. [1. rēplásment; 2. rīpléismənt]. See prec. & **-ment**. Act of replacing; state of being replaced.

replant, vb. trans. [1. rèpláhnt; 2. rīplánt]. **re-** & **plant**. **1.** To plant again; **a** to plant (tree &c.) in the ground a second time; to lift (tree &c.) and plant in another place; **b** to plant (ground) with a different crop, with other trees &c.

replantation, n. [1. rèplahntáshun; 2. rīplāntéiʃən]. **re-** & **plantation**. **a** Act of replanting; **b** state of being replanted; **c** crops, trees &c. which have been replanted.

replenish, vb. trans. [1. replénish; 2. ripléniʃ]. M.E. *replenissen*, fr. O. Fr. *repleniss-(ant)*, Pres. Part. stem of *replenir*, 'to fill up'; fr. **re-** & Lat. *plēnus*, 'full', see **plenum**. **a** To fill up again; to restock: *to replenish one's coffers, one's larder, one's petrol-tank*; also *replenish with*, restock with, fill up with; **b** to stock with living creatures: '*replenish the earth*' (Gen. i. 28).

replenishment, n. [1. replénishment; 2. ripléniʃmənt]. Prec. & **-ment**, cp. O. Fr. *replenissement*. Act of replenishing; state of being replenished; a fresh supply; renewal of stores &c.

replete, adj. [1. replḗt; 2. riplít]. Fr. *replet, replète*, fr. Lat. *replēt-(um)*, P.P. stem of *replēre*, 'fill again; fill to the full', fr. *plēnus*, 'full', see **plenum**. **1.** Well filled; gorged, stuffed: *replete with food; profiteers replete with ill-gotten gains.* **2.** Completely furnished, well provided, thoroughly stocked: *replete with every comfort and luxury; a mind replete with learning.*

repletion, n. [1. replḗshun; 2. riplíʃən]. Fr. Prec. & **-ion**. **1.** State of being completely full: *a vessel filled to repletion.* **2.** Specif. (of bodily condition) a state of being replete (esp. with food), undue fullness; surfeit; **b** (med.) fullness of blood, plethora.

replevin, n. [1. replévin; 2. riplévin]. A.-Fr., fr. O. Fr. *plevin, plevine*, 'warranty'. See next word. (law) **1.** The recovery of the actual goods or chattels wrongfully taken or detained, esp. under a wrongful or excessive distraint, on a warranty that the case shall be tried in court and the goods recovered be returned to the holder or distrainer if the claim fails. **2. a** The action which decides whether the goods are wrongly detained or not; **b** the writ in such an action.

replevy, vb. trans. & intrans. & n. [1. replévi; 2. riplévi]. Earlier *replevie*, fr. O. Fr. *replevir*, fr. **re-** & *plevir*, 'to pledge, give a warranty'; of Gmc. origin; cogn. w. O. Fr. *plege*, see **pledge**. **1.** vb. To recover goods or chattels by replevin: *to replevy goods*; *goods replevied*; *to replevy on goods.* **2.** n. Replevin.

replica, n. [1. réplika; 2. réplikə]. Ital., fr. *replicare*, 'to duplicate'. See next word. A duplicate, copy, reproduction, of anything, esp. one of a work of art executed by the artist himself; generally, anything imitated from, or closely resembling, another.

replicate (I.), vb. trans. [1. réplikāt; 2. réplikeit], fr. Lat. *replicāt-(um)*, P.P. of *replicāre*, 'to fold over, bend back; to turn over in the mind; to repeat; to reply'; fr. **re-** & *plicāre*, 'to fold', see **plicate** & cp. **reply.** (rare) **1.** To fold, bend back, as a leaf. **2.** To repeat; to duplicate; to make a replica of.

replicate (II.), adj. & n. [1. réplikat; 2. réplikit], fr. prec. **1.** adj. (bot.) Folded, bent back on itself. **2.** n. (mus.) A tone repeated one or more octaves above a given tone.

replication, n. [1. rèplikā́shun; 2. rèplikéiʃən]. Lat. *replicātiōn-(em)*, 'reply'. **replicate** & **-ion.** **1.** A reply, rejoinder; answer; esp. (law) the plaintiff's reply in pleadings to the defendant's plea or answer. **2.** (bot.) A folding, bending back, as of a leaf. **3.** A copy, duplicate, replica.

reply (I.), vb. intrans. & trans. [1. replí; 2. ripldi]. M.E. *replier*, *replyer*, fr. O. Fr. *replier*, *reploier*, 'to fold, bend back', cp. Mod. Fr. *répliquer*, 'to reply', fr. Lat. *replicāre*. See **replicate.** **A.** intrans. **1. a** *Reply to*, to make a response to; to answer in speech or in writing: *to reply to a question, a letter*; **b** to give an answer; to say something in response when spoken to or addressed: *when asked her age she did not reply*; *I know not how to reply*; *I wrote to him several times, but he never had the decency to reply*; **c** *reply for*, (i.) to answer on behalf, instead of, as deputy for another: *the Home Secretary replied for the Prime Minister*; (ii.) to respond as representing (a person, institution &c.) in answer to a toast: *to reply for the Navy.* **2.** (law) To answer a defendant's plea; to make a replication. **3.** To perform an act in response to some other act or to something said; to answer by action: *to reply to a signal*; *when remonstrated with he replied by a violent blow*; *to reply to the enemy's fire.* **B.** trans. To return as an answer: *he did not know what to reply*; *to have nothing to reply*, to have no answer to make; to refuse to answer.

reply (II.), n., fr. prec. Act of replying, statement made, act done, in replying; answer, rejoinder, response: *a reply to a question, request, letter* &c.; *to make no reply*; *his reply was a rambling statement*; *the enemy's reply to our fire was weak*; *the reply of the Papacy to the loss of the Temporal power was the declaration of Infallibility.* Phr. *in reply*, in, as, answer: *in reply to your letter of May 15th*; *he neither said nor did anything in reply.*

repoint, vb. trans. [1. rèpóint; 2. ripóint]. **re-** & **point (II.).** To point (masonry &c.) afresh.

repolish, vb. trans. [1. rèpólish; 2. ripóliʃ]. **re-** & **polish.** To polish up again.

répondez s'il vous plaît [1. rāpondā sēl voo plā; 2. repɔ̃de sil vu plɛ]. Fr., 'reply, if you please'. Abbreviated to *R.S.V.P.*, as request for a reply accepting or declining an invitation.

repopulate, vb. trans. [1. rèpópūlāt; 2. ripópjuleit]. **re-** & **populate.** To repeople.

report (I.), vb. trans. & intrans. [1. repórt; 2. ripɔ́t], fr. O. Fr. *reporter*, fr. Lat. *reportāre*, 'to carry back', fr. **re-** & *portāre*, 'to carry, bear'. See **port (IV.).** **A.** trans. **1. a** To announce, give an account of something seen, ascertained, investigated; to state, to relate: *to report the condition of the crops, good weather in the Atlantic, the results of an expedition, a new discovery, the arrival of the cuckoo* &c.; *what the old travellers reported was often imaginary*; *it is reported that over a million died in the earthquake*; **b** to give an account of regularly, or at stated intervals: *to report the variations of rainfall*; *to report one's movements, address, to the police*; **c** to make a formal statement of; to give an official account of: *the Registrar-General reports a remarkable decline in infantile mortality*; *the Royal Commission will report its conclusions tomorrow*; *the Treasury reports the total receipts and expenditure for the year.* Phrs. *to report oneself*, give formal notice of one's presence or arrival; (parl.) *to report a Bill*, (of Chairman of Committees) to announce the end of the Committee stage of a Bill, between second and third reading; *to report progress* (see **progress**). **2.** To repeat, hand on, transmit, communicate (something uttered by another): *the speech, as reported to me by one who was there, was grossly insulting*; *reported speech*, indirect, oblique oration, e.g. *he said that he could not consent to the motion* &c. **3.** Specif. **a** to take, write, down, verbatim, or in summary, and transcribe for publication (what is said): *to report the proceedings of a law court, debates in Parliament* &c.; *to report a speech*; **b** to write a descriptive account of, to describe for publication in the Press: *to report a fire, a marriage or other ceremony.* **4. a** To give information, lodge a complaint, prefer a charge against (a person): *to report an employee for misconduct*; *to report a boy to the headmaster*; **b** to draw attention to and complain of (conduct &c.): *to report the incivility of officials to their superiors.* **B.** intrans. **1.** To make, give, a report, draw up and send or issue account or statement: *the Commission reports tomorrow*; *to report on the condition of the crops*; *to report badly of a person's health.* **2.** To take down a speech &c., describe an event &c., for publication; to act as a reporter: *to report for the Press.* **3.** To present oneself as available for service; to make known one's address, movements &c.; to report oneself: *to report for duty at Headquarters*; *to report to the police.*

report (II.), n. O. Fr., Mod. Fr. *rapport*, fr. prec. **1.** That which is reported, repeated, or related; **a** rumour, common popular talk; what people say: *as report has it, goes*; *to have only report to go on*; *mere, idle, reports*; **b** repute, estimation, what people say of a person, how he is spoken of: *to be of good, ill, report.* **2.** Statement made as the result of an inquiry, investigation &c.; as record of statistics &c.: *a report on a new discovery, on condition of the crops*; *the weather report*; specif. **a** the official statement issued at the conclusion of a Royal or other Commission of Inquiry, with summary of evidence, recommendations &c.: *the Coal Commission's Report*; **b** a statement as to a pupil's work, conduct &c. issued periodically by his schoolmasters: *the boy has a bad report this term.* **3.** A written account, description of proceedings, events &c.: *a newspaper report*; *a report of a disastrous earthquake*; specif. **a** *Law Reports*, the body of judicial decisions serving as precedents, as reported by an official law reporter, and collected now according to the court in which they were delivered, formerly also under the name of the reporter: as *King's Bench Reports*; *House of Lords' Reports*; *Coke's Reports*; **b** *Parliamentary Reports*, the official verbatim accounts of debates in the Houses of Parliament; *Report stage*, that stage in the passage of a Bill through Parliament after it has been 'reported' by the Chairman of Committees. **4.** The sound of an explosion; bang, loud explosive noise: *the report of a gun, rocket, burst tire of a motor-car*; *exploded with a loud report.*

reportable, adj. [1. repórtabl; 2. ripɔ́təbl]. **report (I.)** & **-able.** Capable of being, fit to be, reported.

reporter, n. [1. repórter; 2. ripɔ́tə]. **report (I.)** & **-er.** One who reports; specif. **a** one of the official law reporters of a court of law or of parliamentary proceedings; **b** one who reports for a newspaper.

reposal, n. [1. repózl; 2. ripóuzl]. Next word & **-al.** Act of reposing or placing trust, confidence &c. in: *the reposal of a trust on or in another.*

repose (I.), vb. trans. [1. repóz; 2. ripóuz], fr. Lat. *repos-(itum)*, P.P. stem of *repōnere*, 'to replace', fr. **re-** & *pōnere*, 'to place', as assimilated to **pose**, & cp. next word, & **compose, propose.** To place, set in or on: *to repose confidence, hope, trust &c. in or on another, in promises.*

repose (II.), vb. trans. & intrans., fr. Fr. *reposer*, fr. Low Lat. *repausāre*, 'to rest, repose', fr. **re-** & Lat. *pausāre*, 'to stop, rest, pause', see **pause**, & **pose (I.).** Confused w. prec. in meaning. **A.** trans. **1.** To rest, lay down in or to rest in: *to repose one's head on*; also *repose oneself.* **2.** (rare) To give rest to; to calm. **B.** intrans. **1. a** To lie at rest; to rest: *to repose upon a bed*; *his head reposing on a pillow*; *to repose in sleep, death*; **b** to pause, dwell (on): *his mind reposed upon the past.* **2. a** To rely (on), be confident (in), to trust (in); to be reposed (in): *his trust reposed in God*; **b** to be supported (by), to be based or founded (on): *the scheme reposes on a revival of trade.*

repose (III.), n., fr. Fr. *repos.* See prec. **1.** State of one who, that which, reposes; cessation from toil; relaxation of effort, rest, of body or mind: *one's night's repose*; *in the repose of death.* **2. a** State of inactivity, cessation of movement or agitation; stillness, immobility: *a face in repose*; **b** peace, quietude, of mind: *repose of conscience, of mind.* **3. a** Composure, ease, calmness, serenity of manner and deportment: *his behaviour lacked the repose of perfect breeding*; **b** similar quality in any form of artistic expression; dignified restraint, serenity, freedom from fussiness.

reposeful, adj. [1. repózfool; 2. ripóuzful]. **repose (III.)** & **-ful.** Producing sense of repose; restful, peaceful; quiet, serene, untroubled.

reposefully, adv. Prec. & **-ly.** Restfully, peacefully, quietly.

repository, n. [1. repózituri; 2. ripɔ́zitəri], fr. Lat. *repositōrium*, 'storehouse', fr. *reposit-(um)*, P.P. of *repōnere*, 'to replace', see **repose (I.)**, & **-ory.** **1.** Place where things may be deposited, stored, preserved; a storehouse; store, magazine, depository. **2.** That which, one who, contains a large amount or abundance of anything: *the earth is a vast repository of oil-bearing strata*; *the volumes form a repository of rare erudition, of all kinds of information*; *Bacon was a repository of the learning of his time.* **3.** A person in whom confidence, trust &c. is reposed; confidant: *he was the repository of all her secrets.*

repossess, vb. trans. [1. rèpozés; 2. ripəzés]. **re-** & **possess.** **1.** To possess again, to regain possession of, to recover: *to repossess property one has been deprived of*; *to repossess a title to land.* **2.** To restore (person) to possession: *to be repossessed in a title to land.*

repossession, n. [1. rèpozéshun; 2. ripəzéʃən]. Prec. & **-ion.** Act of repossessing; restoration to possession; recovery.

repost (I.), n. See **riposte.**

repost (II.), vb. trans. [1. rèpóst; 2. ripóust]. **re-** & **post (VI.).** To post (letter &c.) again; to deliver again to the post; to redirect and post: *to repost letters to a new address.*

repoussé, adj. & n. [1. repōōsā; 2. rəpúsei]. Fr., P.P. of *repousser*, 'to push, thrust back', fr. **re-** & *pousser*. See **push**. **1.** adj. Formed in relief, as patterns, figures &c., on thin plates of metal by hammering and pressure on the reverse side: *repoussé work*. **2.** n. Repoussé work.

repp, n. See **rep (I.)**.

repped, adj. [1. rept; 2. rɛpt]. See **rep (I.)**. Ribbed as rep.

reprehend, vb. trans. [1. rèprehénd; 2. rèprihénd], fr. Lat. *reprehendere*, 'to hold back, restrain; to retake, reprehend'; fr. **re-** & *prehendere*, 'to hold, seize'. See under **prehensile**. To rebuke, reprove, reprimand; to blame, censure, find fault with.

reprehensible, adj. [1. rèprehénsibl; 2. rèprihénsibl], fr. L. Lat. *reprehensibilis*, 'blamable'. See prec. & **-ible**. Deserving reprehension; blameworthy, blamable, censurable.

reprehensibly, adv. Prec. & **-ly**. In a reprehensible manner; so as to deserve reprehension.

reprehension, n. [1. rèprehénshun; 2. rèprihénʃən], fr. Lat. *reprehensiōn-(em)*, see **reprehensible** & **-ion**. Act of reprehending; censure, reproof, blame.

represent, vb. trans. [1. rèprezént; 2. rèprizént]. Fr. *représenter*, fr. Lat. *repraesentāre*, 'to bring back to, to bring before one; to display, show, represent; to portray'; also in L. Lat., 'to stand in the place of'. See **re-** & **present (III.)**. **1.** (rare) To bring before the mind, cause to be understood; to explain, bring home to the understanding: *the subject is so difficult that I know not how to represent it to you*; *to represent to oneself*, to conceive, imagine. **2.** To depict, portray, exhibit in specified way by means of painting or sculpture: *the painter has represented him in his robes of office*; *whom does this portrait represent?* **3.** **a** To exhibit in verbal description as, to describe as, delineate character as being of such and such a kind: *Macaulay represents King Charles as a faithless fanatic*; **b** *to represent oneself as, to be*, to claim to be, convey the impression that one is, describe oneself as. **4.** **a** To state, set forth, make clear, describe: *do represent forcibly the danger we are in!*; **b** to convey a particular impression of, describe as, allege to be: *he represented his father as stern and unjust*. **5.** To stand as embodiment of an idea; to have, convey, a meaning; to mean, signify: *statements of that kind represent very little to me*. **6.** To act the part of (in a play); to impersonate: *he is somewhat old to represent Romeo*. **7.** To be a type, image of, to typify, to symbolize: *the sceptre of a king represents his power and authority*; *mythological personages often represent the forces of nature*; *letters are graphic symbols which represent sounds*. **8.** **a** To serve as a specimen, example of; to be a representative of: *every class, party &c. was represented at the meeting*; *the British Army of 1914 represented the flower of the nation*; **b** to correspond to, be the counterpart of: *the civilization of the Bushman pretty nearly represents that of primitive man*. **9.** **a** To act for, act as agent, substitute, or deputy of; to take the place of; to speak, act, with the authority or on behalf of: *to be represented by counsel in a lawsuit*; *General X represented the king at the ceremony*; specif. **b** to be a deputy or a representative of in Parliament or other elective body: *to represent a constituency*. **10.** To state, affirm, convey the impression that: *he represented that he came with an introduction from you*; *I ought to represent to you that the matter is urgent*.

re-present, vb. trans. [1. rē prezént; 2. rī prizént]. **re-** & **present**. To present over again or a second time: *to re-present a cheque*; *re-present a play* &c.

representation, n. [1. rèprezentā́shun; 2. rèprizɛntéiʃən]. Fr., fr. Lat. *repraesentāt-(um)*, P.P. type of *repraesentāre*, see **represent**, & **-ion**. Act of representing; something represented (in various senses). **1.** **a** Act, fact, of representing, expressing, depicting, in painting &c.: *the representation of movement is a problem which painters are always trying to solve*; **b** something represented in painting &c.; a portrait, graphic reproduction &c.: *a life-like representation of a pig*; *a poor representation of a great scene*. **2.** A statement, assertion &c.: *you have listened to the representations of my enemies*. **3.** **a** Act of representing a party, constituency &c., on an elective body: *the representation of persons of varied opinions is no easy matter*; **b** fact of being represented on elective body &c.: *nearly every shade of opinion now finds representation*.

representational, adj. [1. rèprezentā́shunal; 2. rèprizɛntéiʃənəl]. Prec. & **-al**. Pertaining to representation.

representative (I.), adj. [1. rèprezéntativ; 2. rèprizéntətiv], fr. Low Lat. *repraesentātīvus*; see **representation**, & **-ive**. Serving, tending to represent; that represents; representing. **1.** **a** Portraying, depicting, describing: *illuminations representative of mediaeval life*; **b** based on representation or depiction of natural objects: *advanced painters deny the value of strictly representative art*. **2.** Serving as an example, pattern, type; reproducing the general characteristics of, typical: *John Bull and Uncle Sam are no longer the representative Briton and American*; *the exhibition is quite representative of modern French art*; *not truly representative of a class*. **3.** **a** Acting for, representing others, as delegate, agent &c.; esp. as parliamentary deputy: *a representative body, chamber* &c.; *he was sent in a representative capacity*; **b** based, founded on, constituted according to political representation of the electors by elected delegates: *representative government, institutions* &c. **4.** Specif. **a** (philos.) presenting ideas or images to the mind: *the representative faculty of imagination*; **b** (bot., zool. &c.) similar, corresponding, analogous to: *the Spanish fighting bulls are representative survivors of the extinct aurochs*.

representative (II.), n., fr. prec. One who, that which, represents, stands for, plays the part of: **1.** An example, specimen, typical instance, analogue, type of: *a representative of the national character*; *the last representative of his class*; *there are no longer any representatives of the mammoth*. **2.** One who acts as the agent, delegate, substitute, for another: *our representative*; *a representative of a trading firm*; *diplomatic representatives of a nation*, ambassadors, ministers, consuls &c. **3.** Specif., an elected deputy for a legislative body, as representing the electors of his constituency: *House of Representatives*, the lower house or chamber of Congress or of a State legislature in U.S.A.; also of Japan, Mexico &c. **4.** (law) One who represents or stands in the place of another; *real, natural, representative*, the heir as representing the ancestor; *legal, personal, representative*, executor, administrator of a will, also trustee, receiver in bankruptcy &c.

representatively, adv. [1. rèprezéntativli; 2. rèprizéntətivli]. **representative (I.)** & **-ly**. In a representative manner; by representation.

representativeness, n. [1. rèprezéntativnes; 2. rèprizéntətivnis]. See prec. & **-ness**. State, quality, of being representative.

repress, vb. trans. [1. représ; 2. riprés], fr. Lat. *repress-(um)*, P.P. stem of *reprimere*, 'to press back'. **re-** & **press (I.)**. **1.** To press, beat back or down; to suppress, put down: *to repress a riot, rebellion, riotous mob* &c. **2.** To keep down, restrain, curb, check, overcome: *to repress one's emotions, tears*.

represser, n. [1. represér; 2. riprésə]. Prec. & **-er**. One who represses, suppresses; a tyrant.

repression, n. [1. représhun; 2. ripréʃən]. See **repress** & **-ion**. Act of repressing, state of being repressed; suppression, restraint, check: *repression of rebellion*; *repression of one's feelings*.

repressive, adj. [1. représiv; 2. riprésiv]. See prec. & **-ive**. Tending, serving, to repress: *repressive acts, measures*.

repressively, adv. Prec. & **-ly**. In a repressive manner; by repression.

repressiveness, n. See prec. & **-ness**. State, quality, of being repressive.

reprieve (I.), vb. trans. [1. reprḗv; 2. riprív]. M.E. *reprēven*, 'to reprove', variant of *reprōven* (see **reprove**), is the formal ancestor, but the sense is derived fr. earlier *repry*, fr. Fr. *repris*, P.P. type of *reprendre*, 'to take back', see **reprehend**. The old sense of *repry* was 'to postpone, remand'; the later meaning was influenced by *reprove*, in sense of 'find fault with, disallow'. **1.** (law) To postpone, defer, the execution of sentence upon (a criminal), esp. of a death sentence. **2.** (gen.) To allow a temporary respite (to a person) from care, anxiety &c.

reprieve (II.), n., fr. prec. **1.** Specif. (law) postponement; remission of execution of a (death) sentence. **2.** A respite, interval of relief, ease.

reprimand (I.), n. [1. réprimahnd; 2. réprimānd], fr. Fr. *réprimande*, earlier *reprimende*, fr. Lat. *reprimenda*, fem. sing. of *reprimendus*, 'that is to be repressed, checked', gerundive of *reprimere*. See **repress**. A severe rebuke, censure, or reproof, esp. one administered officially by a superior.

reprimand (II.), vb. trans., fr. Fr. *réprimander*. See prec. To administer a reprimand to; to rebuke, censure, reprove severely.

reprint (I.), vb. trans. [1. rēprínt; 2. rīprínt]. **re-** & **print**. To print again; to make a new impression, or second edition of a book &c.

reprint (II.), n., fr. prec. [1. rḗprint; 2. ríprint]. A reprinted book, article &c.; a new impression, as distinct from a *new edition*, which usually implies more extensive alterations, enlargements &c.

reprisal, n. [1. reprízl; 2. ripráizl], fr. O. Fr. *reprisaille*, Mod. Fr. *représaille*. See next word & **-al**; cp. Ital. *rappresaglia*. **1.** Act levelled against another person by way of retort for injury, unfriendly action &c. suffered at his hands; retaliation. **2.** (internat. law) Retaliatory action undertaken by one State against another in return for insult to the national honour of the former, or to secure redress of grievances suffered by its nationals as the result of some action of the offending State. Reprisals are not necessarily of the nature of warlike action, though they may lead to it; they may also take the form of intensified severity of action during a war with a view to stopping breaches of the customs of civilized warfare by a belligerent.

reprise, n. [1. repríz; 2. ripráiz]. Fr., fem. of *repris*, P.P. of *reprendre*, 'to take back', fr. Lat. *reprehendere*. See **reprehend**. **1.** (archaic or obs.) **a** Renewal, resumption, of action; **b** reprisal; **c** (fencing) renewal, of an attack. **2.** (law, usually pl.) Yearly deductions from charges upon an estate, as by annuities, a rent charge &c. **3.** (mus.) Repetition of a theme.

reproach (I.), vb. trans. [1. reprṓch; 2. ripróutʃ], fr. O. Fr. *reprochier*; prob. fr. Low Lat. **repropiāre*, 'to bring near to, to cast at or in one's teeth', hence 'to reproach'. See **approach**. **a** To upbraid, censure, find fault with (a person): *I am not reproaching, but merely warning you*; **b** *reproach with*, to charge with, attribute (some fault) to (a person): *to reproach a person with carelessness* &c.

reproach (II.), n., fr. Fr. *reproche*. See prec. word. **1.** Act of reproaching or rebuking; censure, blame: *to cast reproaches upon*; *to meet with nothing but reproach and abuse*; *a look of reproach*. Phr. *term of reproach*, word implying disapproval, contempt &c.: '*bourgeois*' *has become in some quarters a term of reproach*. **2.** A cause, occasion, of shame, disgrace, or discredit; anything which brings discredit upon: '*I have rolled away the reproach of Egypt*' (Josh. v. 9); *the slums are a reproach to London*. 3. State, conduct, worthy of reproach; disgrace, infamy, shame, discredit: *a knight without fear and without reproach*; *to bring reproach upon*. 4. Object of censure, blame, or reproach: '*I will make thee a reproach among the nations*' (Ezek. v. 14). 5. (R.C. liturgy) *Reproaches*, service for Good Friday, consisting of set of antiphons and responses containing the words of Christ reproaching the people for their ingratitude &c.

reproachful, adj. [1. repróchfool; 2. riprόutʃful]. **reproach (II.) & -ful**. 1. Containing reproach, blame or censure; expressive of reproach; upbraiding, censorious, rebuking: *reproachful taunts*; *a reproachful speech, letter* &c.; *a reproachful look*. 2. Deserving of reproach; shameful, discreditable: *a reproachful life*.

reproachfully, adv. Prec. & **-ly**. 1. In a reproachful manner; so as to imply or express reproach. 2. (archaic) Shamefully, infamously: '*And shall I then be used reproachfully*' (Shakespeare, '2 Henry VI.').

reproachfulness, n. See prec. & **-ness**. State, quality, of being reproachful.

reproachingly, adv. [1. repróchingli; 2. riprόutʃiŋli], fr. Pres. Part. of **reproach (I.)** & **-ly**. So as to convey reproach; reproachfully.

reprobate (I.), vb. trans. [1. réprobàt; 2. réproubèit], fr. Lat. *reprobāt-(um)*, P.P. type of *reprobāre*, 'to reject, disapprove, condemn'. See **re-** & **probate** & **prove**. 1. To feel and express strong disapproval, disapprove of; to condemn, censure severely: *to reprobate plans, proposals* &c.; *they reprobated the cruelty and misdeeds of their countrymen*. 2. (theol., of God) To disown, abandon to damnation; to exclude from salvation. 3. (eccles. and Scots law) To take exception to, to exclude, set aside, disallow.

reprobate (II.), adj. & n. [1. réprobat; 2. réprəbit]. See prec. 1. adj. **a** Reprobated by God, excluded from salvation, damned as abandoned to sin: '*men . . . reprobate concerning the faith*' (2 Tim. iii. 8); **b** depraved, vicious, unprincipled, profligate: *a reprobate character, person* &c.; **c** (archaic) condemned, rejected, as not enduring proof or trial; not of standard purity: '*reprobate silver*' (Jer. vi. 30). 2. n. A reprobate person; person of depraved character; a profligate, scoundrel.

reprobation, n. [1. rèprōbáshun; 2. rèproubéiʃən], fr. Lat. *reprobātiōn-(em)*. See **reprobate (I.)** & **-ion**. Act of reprobating; state of being reprobated; **a** condemnation, rejection by God; **b** severe censure or disapproval: *such acts meet with general reprobation*.

reproduce, vb. trans. & intrans. [1. rèprodús; 2. rìprədjús]. **re-** & **produce**. **A.** trans. 1. To become the parent of, to generate: *to reproduce offspring, one's kind*. Phr. (reflex.) *reproduce oneself*, to generate, produce, offspring. 2. To produce afresh, by process of natural growth: *lobsters are able to reproduce claws when these are torn off*. 3. **a** To reproduce a copy or representation of: *to reproduce a figure on canvas, a voice on the gramophone, movement on a film* &c.; **b** to present, publish, again: *to reproduce a play, novel* &c.; **c** to make again: *artistic work which cannot be reproduced today*; *a design which will not be reproduced*. 4. To cause to appear again, to repeat, revive: *to reproduce the social conditions of pre-war days is impossible*. **B.** intrans. To reproduce offspring.

reproducer, n. [1. rèprodúser; 2. rìprədjúsə]. Prec. & **-er**. **a** One who reproduces; **b** that which reproduces, esp. any device for reproducing a sound, as in the phonograph &c.

reproducible, rarely **reproduceable**, adj. [1. rèprodúsibl; 2. rìprədjúsibl]. **reproduce** & **-ible**, **-able**. Capable of being reproduced.

reproduction, n. [1. rèprodúkshun; 2. rìprədákʃən]. **re-** & **production**. 1. Act or process of reproducing (in all senses); specif. (biol.) the process of producing fresh organisms from cells generated within the body of the parent, which develop into independent individuals. 2. That which is reproduced; a copy, representation.

reproductive, adj. [1. rèprodúktiv; 2. rìprədáktiv]. See prec. & **-ive**. 1. Pertaining to, employed, used in, reproduction: *reproductive organs*; *the reproductive functions, system* &c. 2. Tending to, causative of, reproduction; fertile: *a reproductive bud, stock, race* &c.

reproductively, adv. Prec. & **-ly**. In a reproductive manner; so as to reproduce; by reproduction.

reproductiveness, n. [1. rèprodúktivnes; 2. rìprədáktivnis]. **reproductive** & **-ness**. Quality of being reproductive.

reproductivity, n. [1. rèproduktíviti; 2. rìprədaktíviti]. See prec. & **-ity**. Reproductiveness.

reproof, n. [1. repróof; 2. riprúf]. M.E. *reprove, reproef*, fr. O. Fr. *reprove*. See **reprove** & cp. **proof**. 1. Censure, blame for wrongdoing, fault &c.: *he will not tolerate reproof of any kind*; *a word of reproof*. 2. Expression of censure; a rebuke, reprimand: *a stern reproof*.

reprovable, adj. [1. repróovabl; 2. riprúvəbl]. **reprove** & **-able**. (rare or archaic) Deserving reproof; blameworthy.

reprove, vb. trans. [1. repróov; 2. riprúv], fr. O. Fr. *reprover*, fr. Lat. *reprobāre*, 'to disapprove, reprobate; to reprove'. See **re-** & **prove** & cp. **approve**. To chide, rebuke: *to reprove a person*; *to reprove a person's conduct* &c.

reprovingly, adv. [1. repróovingli; 2. riprúviŋli]. Pres. Part. of prec. & **-ly**. In such a way as to imply, convey, express, reproof.

reprovision, vb. trans. [1. rèprōvízhun; 2. rìprouvižən]. **re-** & **provision (II.)**. To re-stock with provisions.

reps, n. See **rep (I.)**.

reptant, adj. [1. réptant; 2. réptənt], fr. Lat. *reptant-(em)*, Pres. Part. of *reptāre*, freq. of *rēpere*, 'to creep'. See **repent (I.)** & next word. (bot., zool.) Creeping, crawling.

reptile (I.), n. [1. réptīl; 2. réptail], fr. L. Lat. *reptile*, neut. sing., of *reptilis*, 'creeping, crawling', fr. *rept-(um)*, P.P. type of *rēpere*, 'to creep, crawl'. See **repent (I.)**. 1. A creeping, crawling animal, one that moves like a snake on its belly, or, like lizards &c. on short or rudimentary legs; specif. (zool.) one of the class *Reptilia*, of vertebrate, air-breathing animals, cold-blooded, oviparous or ovoviviparous, covered with scales or horny plates, including snakes, lizards, crocodiles, turtles, tortoises, and their extinct congeners and ancestors; the term was formerly used to include frogs, toads, newts &c., or *Batrachia*. 2. A mean, base, treacherous, malevolent person.

reptile (II.), adj. See prec. word. 1. (of animal) Like a reptile, creeping, crawling, reptilian: *the reptile race*; *a country teeming with reptile life*. 2. (by transf.) Malevolent, mean, despicable: *the reptile crew of libellers and blackmailers*; *the reptile press*.

reptilian, adj. & n. [1. reptílian; 2. reptíliən]. **reptile (II.)** & **-ian**. 1. adj. **a** Of, pertaining to, reptiles or to the *Reptilia*; **b** like a reptile: *a reptilian head*. 2. n. A reptile, any member of the *Reptilia*.

reptiliferous, adj. [1. rèptilíferus; 2. rèptilífərəs]. **reptile** & **-ferous**. (geol.) Bearing fossil remains of reptiles.

reptiliform, adj. [1. reptíliform; 2. reptáilifōm]. **reptile** & **-form**. (zool.) Reptile-like, reptilian.

reptilivorous, adj. [1. rèptilívorus; 2. rèptilívərəs]. **reptile** & **-vorous**. (zool.) Eating, living on, reptiles.

republic, n. [1. repúblik; 2. ripáblik]. Through Fr. *république*, or directly fr. Lat. *rēspublica*, 'the state, commonwealth, body politic'; fr. *rēs*, 'thing, concern, affair', see **re-**, & *publicus*, see **public** & **people**. 1. **a** Form of government in which the head of the state is elected by the citizens, and usually called President, contrasted with *Hereditary Monarchy*; **b** a state organized in this form: *the city republics of Mediaeval Italy*; *the French Republic*; *Union of Socialist Soviet Republics*. 2. (hist. or archaic) The State, Commonwealth; cp. Plato's '*Republic*', translating Greek *politeia*. Phr. *the republic is in danger*; *the republic of letters*, the body of men of letters and learning; the literary world considered as a society where all are equal.

republican (I.), adj. [1. repúblikan; 2. ripáblikən]. Prec. & **-an**, cp. Fr. *républicain*. 1. Of, pertaining to, a republic; consisting of, constituted as, a republic: *republican government*; *a republican system*. 2. Supporting, advocating, consonant with, the principles of a republic: *to hold republican opinions*. 3. (cap.) *Republican party*, one of the two chief political parties in the U.S.A., originally an anti-slavery party, upholding a strong centralized federal policy, a high tariff &c.; cp. *Democratic*. 4. (of birds) Social, living in communities.

republican (II.), n., fr. prec. 1. One who supports the principles of a republic; advocate of republicanism. 2. (cap.) Member of the Republican party, in U.S.A., opposed to *Democrat*.

republicanism, n. [1. repúblikanizm; 2. ripáblikənizəm]. See prec. & **-ism**. 1. A republican system of government; principles, theory, of republican government. 2. Feeling of attachment to, sympathy with, a republican form of government; republican opinions.

republicanize, vb. trans. [1. repúblikanīz; 2. ripáblikənaiz]. **republican (I.)** & **-ize**. 1. To make the government of a state republican. 2. To convert to republican opinions.

republication, n. [1. rèpublikáshun; 2. rìpablikéiʃən]. **re-** & **publication**. 1. Act of republishing. 2. Something (esp. a book) which has been republished; republished form of a book.

republish, vb. trans. [1. rèpúblish; 2. rìpábliʃ]. **re-** & **publish**. To publish again; **a** to publish, promulgate, again, as a decree, will &c.; **b** to publish, issue, a new edition of (a book &c.).

repudiate, vb. trans. & intrans. [1. repúdiāt; 2. ripjúdieit], fr. Lat. *repudiāt-(um)*, P.P. of *repudiāre*, 'to put away (a wife), to divorce; to disown, reject, repudiate', fr. *repudium*, 'dissolution of marriage, separation, repudiation'; fr. **re-** & stem **pud-*, seen in *pudet*, 'to feel shame, be ashamed of', *pudor*, 'shame' &c. See **pudency**. **A.** trans. 1. To put away, divorce, disown (a wife); usually of non-Christian divorces effected by mere disavowal of the tie and dismissal. 2. To disown, cast off, refuse to recognize or have dealings with: *to repudiate one's relations, any connexion with person or thing*. 3. To reject, refuse to accept or acknowledge; to disavow: *to repudiate a gift, benefice* &c.; *to repudiate a claim, authority*; *to repudiate one's creed or religion*. 4. To refuse to discharge or pay (a debt due); to refuse to acknowledge as due or binding: *to repudiate an obligation*; *the State repudiated debts incurred by a former government* &c. **B.** intrans. To repudiate a public debt: *Russia has repudiated*.

repudiation, n. [1. repūdiáshun; 2. ripjūdiéiʃən], fr. Lat. *repudiātiōn-(em)*. Prec. & **-ion**. Act of repudiating, state of being repudiated; specif. **a** a divorce, disownment of a wife; **b** (eccles.) refusal of a benefice; **c** refusal to acknowledge and pay a State debt.

repudiationist, n. [1. repūdiáshunist; 2. ripjūdiéiʃənist]. Prec. & **-ist**. One in favour of the repudiation of State debts.

repudiator, n. [1. repúdiāter; 2. ripjúdieitə]. **repudiate** & **-or**. One who repudiates; supporter of the repudiation of a State debt.

repugn, vb. intrans. & trans. [1. repŭn: 2. rĭpjŭn]. Cp. Fr. *répugner*, 'to disgust', fr. Lat. *repugnāre*, 'to fight against, resist, oppose', fr. **re-** & *pugnāre*, 'to fight', see **pugnacious.** (rare or archaic) **1.** intrans. (with *against*) To resist; offer resistance; to oppose, strive. **2.** trans. **a** To strive against, oppose violently; **b** to cause repugnance in; to repel.

repugnance, -cy, n. [1. repúgnans(i); 2. rĭpágnəns(*i*)]. See next word & **-ce, -cy. 1.** Feeling of strong aversion, disgust, dislike: *to feel, have, a repugnance for a person* &c.; *to be inspired with repugnance by.* **2.** Contradiction, inconsistency: *a repugnance between two theories.*

repugnant, adj. [1. repúgnant; 2. rĭpágnənt], fr. Lat. *repugnant-(em)*, Pres. Part. of *repugnāre*, see **repugn. 1.** Causing repugnance; distasteful, offensive, disgusting: *conduct repugnant to a man of honour; all food is repugnant to me just now; he is a most repugnant character.* **2.** Inconsistent, contradictory, contrary: *nothing in College Bye-laws must be repugnant to what is laid down in the Statutes; such conduct appears repugnant to his known character.* **3.** Opposing, resisting, refractory: *repugnant forces; chemical elements which are repugnant.*

repugnantly, adv. Prec. & **-ly.** In a repugnant manner; so as to be repugnant.

repulse (I.), vb. trans. [1. repúls; 2. rĭpáls], fr. Lat. *repuls-(um)*, P.P. type of *repellere*, 'to drive back', see **repel, & pulse** (I.). **1. a** To repel, to drive, beat back or off (an enemy, an attack) by force: *the enemy was repulsed with great loss;* **b** to rebut, repel (charges, accusations &c.), by argument or evidence. **2. a** To snub, rebuff, dash (a person), by treating with disdain, coldness, indifference; **b** to discourage, reject, repel (friendly advances, offers of friendship or affection &c.).

repulse (II.), n., fr. Lat. *repulsa*, 'a rejection'; fr. P.P. of *repellere*. See prec. **1.** Act of repelling or repulsing: **a** by bodily force; **b** by cold and disdainful treatment; a snub, a rebuff. **2.** State of being repulsed; **a** a defeat, check (to troops); **b** a snub, rebuff, administered to a person.

repulsion, n. [1. repúlshun; 2. rĭpálʃən], fr. L. Lat. *repulsiōn-(em)*. See **repulse** (I.) & **-ion. 1.** A feeling of aversion, repugnance, dislike, disgust. **2.** (phys.) Tendency of certain bodies to repel or be repelled by each other; contrasted with *attraction.*

repulsive, adj. [1. repúlsiv; 2. rĭpálsiv]. **repulse** (I.) & **-ive**, cp. Fr. *répulsif.* **1.** Inspiring physical or moral repulsion; loathsome, offensive, repellent, disgusting: *a repulsive sight, smell, taste* &c.; *repulsive manners; morally repulsive.* **2.** (phys.) Having repulsion: *repulsive forces.*

repulsively, adv. Prec. & **-ly.** In a repulsive manner.

repulsiveness, n. See prec. & **-ness.** Quality of being repulsive.

repurchase, vb. trans. & n. [1. rèpérchas; 2. rīpə́tʃəs]. **re-** & **purchase. 1.** vb. To buy back again; to regain by purchase. **2.** n. Act of buying back or regaining by purchase; that which is bought back or repurchased.

reputable, adj. [1. répūtabl; 2. répjutəbl]. **repute** (II.) & **-able.** Of good repute; held in esteem; honourable; respectable: *a man of reputable character; not a particularly reputable occupation; to lead a reputable life.*

reputably, adv. Prec. & **-ly.** In a reputable manner; honourably, respectably.

reputation, n. [1. rèpūtáshun; 2. rèpjutéiʃən]. Lat. *reputātiōn-(em)*, 'reckoning, computation; a thinking over, consideration', fr. *reputāt-(um)*, P.P. type of *reputāre*, see **repute** (I.), & **-ion. 1.** Estimation, opinion, commonly held concerning a person or thing; character, qualities, generally attributed to person or thing: *to enjoy, have, a good, poor, indifferent, reputation; to live up to one's reputation; the reputation of these razors stands very high.* **2.** Opinion (good or bad) commonly held of a person or thing as possessing specific qualities, as being, or doing, something specified: *to have a reputation for swindling, for being kind to the poor; to have the reputation of (being) a good landlord, of liking one's own way, of being difficult to get on with.* **3.** Good reputation; **a** high character, credit, good name for integrity: *it is impossible to suspect a man of his reputation of dishonesty; to lose one's reputation;* Phr. *a person of no reputation*, a bad character; **b** celebrity, fame, distinction, general esteem, esp. on account of intellect or achievements: *his recent discoveries have greatly added to his reputation; to enjoy a high reputation as a writer, a man of science, a soldier; a man of world-wide reputation.*

repute (I.), vb. trans. [1. repū́t; 2. rĭpjū́t], fr. Lat. *reputāre*, 'to count over, reckon; to think over, meditate, reflect', fr. **re-** & *putāre*, 'to count, think'. See **putamen. 1.** (archaic or poet.) To deem, consider, reckon: *men repute him (to be) brave.* **2.** (only in pass.) **a** To be commonly considered as, to have general reputation of being; to be thought of as (being): *he is reputed (to be) most generous, a perfect fool; his wealth is reputed (to be) enormous;* **b** to be generally thought or spoken of: *to be well, highly, doubtfully, ill, reputed.*

repute (II.), n. See prec. Reputation; **a** character generally attributed, whether good or bad: *to know a person, thing, by repute; of good, bad, evil, repute; through good and ill repute,* whatever people thought; **b** specif., good reputation, esteem, fame: *authors of repute.*

reputed, adj. [1. repū́ted; 2. rĭpjū́tĭd], fr. P.P. of **repute** (I.). **1.** Having a good reputation, noted, famous: *buy our reputed gin.* **2.** Having the reputation of, considered as being, to be generally regarded as, thought, supposed to be, usually with implication of doubt or uncertainty: *his reputed generosity; the reputed father of a child,* putative father; *the reputed owner of property,* (law) one who has ostensibly the right to, and actual possession of, property; *reputed pint,* a bottle (of beer, wine &c.), to be taken, and actually sold, as holding a full pint, but not guaranteed as an imperial pint.

reputedly, adv. Prec. & **-ly.** By repute, in common estimation or opinion.

request (I.), n. [1. rekwést; 2. rĭkwést], fr. O. Fr. *requeste*, fr. Low Lat. *requesta*, 'things asked for or required', fr. Lat. *requīsīta*, P.P. of *requīrere.* See **require** & cp. **quest. 1.** Act of requiring, demanding, asking, for something; expression of need or desire for something; petition, prayer, entreaty: *to make many requests for assistance; at the urgent request of his followers he consented to remain in office; he refused to yield to their request; the piece was played by request,* in response to an expressed demand. **2.** That which is demanded or asked for; the object of a demand or entreaty: *he refused to grant their requests; what is your request?* **3.** Demand, call for; state of being in demand: *there is great request for this author's books; his books are now much in request. Court of Requests,* (legal hist.) **a** an old court of equity for persons petitioning the sovereign; **b** an old court, also called 'court of conscience', for the recovery of small debts; *letter of request,* (eccles. law) a document used for transferring a case from a diocesan court to a higher one, such as the Court of Arches.

request (II.), vb. trans., fr. O. Fr. *requester.* See prec.; the word is less peremptory & more polite than *demand.* **1. a** To make a request for; to beg, ask for; to demand politely and with deference, to solicit: *subscriptions are requested for a deserving charity; your presence is requested immediately; we request attention to this letter; to request leave, permission, to do, see, go* &c.; also (absol.) *to request to be allowed to go* &c.; **b** (with subordinate clause) to ask that: *to request that something should be done about the matter; it is requested that a vote be taken.* **2.** To make a request to; to ask to do &c.: *we request the favour of a reply at your early convenience; gentlemen are requested not to smoke;* also expressing politely veiled peremptoriness: *I must request you to hold your tongue, to obey orders* &c.

requicken, vb. trans. & intrans. [1. rèkwíken; 2. rīkwíkən]. **re-** & **quicken. 1.** trans. To quicken again; to bring to life or vigour again, to reanimate. **2.** intrans. To become requickened, to come to life or vigour again.

requiem, n. [1. rékwiem; 2. rékwiɛm]. Lat., acc. sing. of *requies*, 'rest after labour, suffering' &c., fr. **re-** & *quies*, 'rest', see **quiet. 1.** A dirge, funeral hymn or poem. **2.** (R.C. Ch.) **a** A mass for the dead, so called from the first word of the Introit, *Requiem aeternam dona eis, Domine,* 'Grant unto them, O Lord, eternal rest'; **b** musical setting for this mass; **c** any musical service or hymn for the dead, or, generally, a memorial service, in churches other than Roman.

requiescat, n. [1. rèkwiéskat; 2. rèkwiéskæt]. Lat., 'may he (she) rest', subj. of *requiescere.* See **re-** & **quiescent.** A prayer or wish for the repose of the dead, first word of the common inscription upon graves &c., *requiescat in pace* (abbr. R.I.P.), 'may he (she) rest in peace'.

require, vb. trans. & intrans. [1. rekwír; 2. rĭkwáiə], fr. Lat. *requīrere*, 'to seek again; to search for; to inquire; to need, miss, be in want of, to require', fr. **re-** & *quaerere*, 'to seek, ask'. See **quaere. A.** trans. **1.** To ask, demand, claim as a right or by authority; to insist on having: *your presence is urgently required in London; 'His blood will I require at thine hand'* (Ezek. iii. 18). **2. a** To order, command, to do: *you are required to report to headquarters at once; I will do all that is required of me;* **b** to prescribe, lay down as obligatory: *the law requires strict observance in every detail.* **3.** To need, want; to call for, demand as necessary, indispensable; to depend on for completion, success &c.: *your services will not be required after next week; the house requires a new coat of paint; how much is required to ensure the building's safety? this requires careful consideration.* **B.** intrans. To be necessary; to need, be under the necessity of: *it only requires to be stated (for it) to be admitted at once.*

requirement, n. [1. rekwírment; 2. rĭkwáiəmənt]. Prec. & **-ment. 1.** Something required, desired, needed; a requisite, want, a need, necessity: *my requirements are few and reasonable.* **2.** Something enjoined, laid down, demanded; a condition, provision: *you have evidently not fulfilled the requirements of the law.*

requisite, adj. & n. [1. rékwizit; 2. rékwizit], fr. Lat. *requīsīt-(um)*, P.P. of *requīrere.* See **require** & cp. **quest. 1.** adj. Required, needed; necessary for some purpose, required by circumstances: *everything requisite for comfort; have you the requisite patience for such a task? visas for passports are no longer requisite.* **2.** n. Something required, needed; thing essential, for some specified purpose &c.: *the requisites for a long journey; hard work seems no longer a requisite for a living.*

requisiteness, n. Prec. & **-ness.** Quality of being requisite.

requisition (I.), n. [1. rèkwizíshun; 2. rèkwizíʃən], fr. Lat. *requīsītiōn-(em)*, 'examination, inquiry, a searching for', a rare word. See prec. & **-ion. 1.** Act of requiring or demanding; a formal demand or request made as of right or by authority; a formal application for something to be supplied or done; specif., such a demand on an individual, or on a community to assist the military authorities with labour or goods in time of war. **2.** (law) A formal request for answers to inquiries as to title made by a purchaser or mortgagee to the owner of the property: *requisitions on title.* **3.** State of being demanded, put into use or service. Phr. *in requisition*, in demand.

requisition (II.), vb. trans., fr. prec. **1.** To make a requisition for, to demand the supply of, esp. for military purposes: *to requisition all the horses in a district*; *to requisition stores from a town*. **2.** To make a requisition upon; to demand supply from: *to requisition a town for provisions* &c.

requital, n. [1. rekwítl; 2. rikwáitl]. Next word & **-al**. Act of requiting, action performed in order to requite; **a** act of retaliation, retribution; punishment; **b** act of rewarding; recompense, remuneration.

requite, vb. trans. [1. rekwít; 2. rikwáit], fr. **re-** & *quite*, obs. variant of **quit**. **1.** To repay, make a return for; **a** to avenge, make retaliation for (as injury &c.); **b** to reward, recompense, acknowledge (a service, benefit &c.). **2.** To repay (persons) in kind; **a** to punish, chastise (for an offence); **b** to reward (for services).

re-read, vb. trans. [1. rē réd; 2. rī ríd]. **re-** & **read** (I.). To read over again, or a second time.

rerebrace, n. [1. rḗrbrās; 2. ríəbreis], fr. Fr. *arrière-bras*. See **rear** (II.) & **brace** (I.). In mediaeval armour, a metal plate for protecting the upper part or back of the arm.

reredos, n. [1. rḗrdos; 2. ríədɔs], fr. A.-Fr. *areredos*, fr. O. Fr. *arere*, later *arrière*, 'at the back', see **rear** (II.), & *dos*, fr. Lat. *dorsum*, 'back', see **dorsal**. A screen, often richly ornamented with carving, at the back of an altar in a church.

res, n. [1. rēz; 2. rīz]. Lat., *rēs*; cogn. w. Scrt. *rāś*, 'possession, property'; *rātiś*, 'loan, favour'; *rāyiś*, 'gift'. In various Latin, usually legal, phrs.; **a** thing, matter, cause, action: *res (ad)judicata*, matter finally decided by a court of law, *chose jugée*; **b** *res gestae*, facts, events, relating or incident to a matter at issue before a court, usually as a term for such things as are admissible in evidence; **c** property: *res alienae*, things, property, belonging to another.

rescind, vb. trans. [1. resínd; 2. risínd], fr. Lat. *rescindere*, 'to cut, tear off, down, open; to annul, repeal, rescind, abolish', fr. **re-** & *scindere*, 'to cut, split'; the base appears also without a nasal in *scidi*, perf. of *scindere*, & in *scissum*, P.P., for **skid-tom*; cp. Gk. *skízein*, 'to split'. See the Gmc. forms under **shed** (I.) & words there referred to. To make void, abrogate, repeal, annul: *to rescind a law, resolution*; *to rescind a judgement, decree, contract* &c.

rescission, n. [1. resízhun; 2. risížən], fr. Lat. *rescissiōn-(em)*, fr. *resciss-(um)*, P.P. of *rescindere*, see prec., & **-ion**. Act of rescinding, annulling, or abrogating; annulment, abrogation.

rescissory, adj. [1. resísori; 2. risísəri], fr. Lat. *rescissōrius*, see prec., & **-ory**. Rescinding, annulling; having the power or effect of rescission: *a rescissory act*.

rescript, n. [1. rḗskript; 2. rískript], fr. Lat. *rescriptum*, 'an imperial rescript', fr. the P.P. of *rescrībere*, 'to write back in reply, to reply in writing', fr. **re-** & *scrībere*, *script-(um)*, 'to write', see **scribe**, & **script**. **1.** a (Roman law and hist.) A written reply of the Emperor to a petition for a ruling as to how the law was to be applied in a particular case; such interpretations had the force of law and formed a source of law; **b** (Church of Rome) a written answer of the Pope to a petition or to a question on matters of law or morals. **2.** Any official edict, decree, or order.

rescue (I.), vb. trans. [1. réskū; 2. réskjū]. M.E. *rescouen*, fr. O. Fr. *rescour(r)e*, fr. Med. Lat. *rescutere*, fr. **re-excutere*, fr. **re-** & Lat. *excutere*, 'to shake off, drive away, get rid of', fr. **ex-** & *quatere*, 'to shake', see **quash** & second element of **concussion**. **1.** To set free, deliver persons or things, **a** from confinement or restraint: *to rescue a prisoner, slave*; **b** from danger, physical or moral: *to rescue persons from shipwreck, fire, a woman from the streets, children from bad homes*; **c** to save, preserve from threatened injury or destruction &c.: *to rescue an old building from decay*. **2.** Specif. (law) **a** to remove (a prisoner) out of lawful custody by violence, or other unlawful means; **b** (internat. law) to recover by force a prize seized by the enemy.

rescue (II.), n. M.E. *rescous*, fr. O. Fr. *rescousse*, P.P. as n. of *rescour(r)e*. See prec. **1.** A rescuing, deliverance, liberation, from physical or moral danger, from captivity, from destruction, or from evil conditions generally. Phrs. *to go, come, to the rescue of*, make an effort to save; *to go, come, to the rescue*, to afford help of any kind; *rescue home*, establishment for the betterment of fallen women; *rescue work*, work of rescuing women or children from evil surroundings &c. **2.** Specif. (law) **a** the forcible removal of a prisoner from lawful custody; **b** the forcible recovery or recapture of property seized under a distraint, or captured by the enemy.

rescuer, n. [1. réskūer; 2. réskjuə]. **rescue** (I.) & **-er**. One who effects a rescue.

research (I.), n. [1. resérch; 2. risə́tʃ], fr. M. Fr. *recerche*, Mod. Fr. *recherche*. See **re-** & **search**. Diligent search and inquiry; specif., systematic investigation in some branch of science or learning; trained observation, and inquiry directed upon any department of knowledge with a view to the discovery of new information; *researches*, series of investigations, pieces of research, concerned with different problems, or with different aspects of a problem in learning or science.

research (II.), vb. intrans., fr. prec. To carry on research; often *research into*, to investigate minutely and thoroughly.

researcher, n. [1. resércher; 2. risə́tʃə]. Prec. & **-er**. One engaged in research.

reseat, vb. trans. [1. rēsḗt; 2. rīsít]. **re-** & **seat**. **1.** To seat, place in a seat, again: *to reseat (a deposed king) on the throne*. **2.** **a** To furnish with new seats: *to reseat a church, theatre* &c.; **b** to put a new seat to or on: *to reseat a chair* &c.

resect, vb. trans. [1. rēsékt; 2. rīsékt], fr. Lat. *resect-(um)*, P.P. type of *resecāre*, 'to cut off', fr. **re-** & *secāre*, 'to cut', see **sect**. (surg.) To cut, pare down, esp. the end of a bone at a joint.

resection, n. [1. rēsékshun; 2. rīsékʃən]. Prec. & **-ion**. (surg.) Operation of resecting.

reseda, n. [1. resḗda; 2. resídə]. Lat., name of a plant; etymol. doubtful, possibly fr. *resēdā*, imper. of *resēdāre*, 'to allay, arrange', fr. **re-** & *sēdāre*, 'to make calm, cause to settle down,' see **sedentary**, the word being used in an incantation for cure of diseases by the plant. **1.** (bot., cap.) A genus of plants, which includes the mignonette. **2.** (usually as Fr. *réséda*) [1. rázādah; 2. rezedā] A pale greyish-green colour as of mignonette flowers.

reseize, vb. trans. [1. rēsḗz; 2. rīsíz]. **re-** & **seize**. **1.** To seize, take hold of, again. **2.** (law) To take possession of disseized lands, to reinvest with the seizin of.

reseizure, n. [1. rēsḗzhur; 2. rīsížə]. **re-** & **seizure**. (law) Act of reseizing.

resell, vb. trans. [1. rēsél; 2. rīsél]. **re-** & **sell**. To sell (goods &c.) shortly after one has bought.

resemblance, n. [1. rezémblans; 2. rizémbləns]. O. Fr. See **resemble** & **-ance**. State, quality, of resembling or being like; likeness, similitude, similarity of appearance, form, or quality: *he has a strong resemblance to his father*; *there is no resemblance between his promise and performance*.

resemblant, adj. [1. rezémblant; 2. rizémblənt]. See prec. & **-ant**. (archaic or obs.) Resembling, similar, like.

resemble, vb. trans. [1. rezémbl; 2. rizémbl], fr. O. Fr. *resembler*, Mod. Fr. *ressembler*, fr. **re-** & *sembler*, 'to seem, be, like', fr. Lat. *similāre*, 'to make like, imitate', fr. *similis*, 'like'. See **similar**. To be like or similar to, in external shape or form or in quality; to have features or qualities in common with; to have a resemblance to.

resent, vb. trans. [1. rezént; 2. rizént], fr. Fr. *ressentir*, earlier *resentir*, esp. in phr. *se ressentir de*, 'to be fully sensible of, to feel affected by', fr. **re-** & *sentir*, 'to feel', fr. Lat. *sentīre*, see **sentient** & **sense**; the orig., now obs., meaning had no implication of indignation or grievance. To feel and evince indignation, displeasure, irritation at; to regard as offensive, insulting, or troublesome: *to resent a person's actions, remarks*; *I resent constant interruptions when I am working*.

resentful, adj. [1. rezéntfool; 2. rizéntful], fr. *resent*, obs. variation of **resentment**, & **-ful**. **a** Feeling resentment; **b** inclined to resent, apt to take offence.

resentfully, adv. Prec. & **-ly**. In a resentful manner; with resentment.

resentment, n. [1. rezéntment; 2. rizéntmənt]. **resent** & **-ment**, cp. Fr. *ressentiment*. The feeling of one who resents; **a** animosity, ill-feeling, a grudge: *to cherish resentment for days*; *to have no resentment against*; **b** feeling, condition, of indignation; umbrage, soreness, dudgeon: *he will soon get over his resentment*.

reservation, n. [1. rèzervā́shun; 2. rèzəvéiʃən], fr. Low Lat. *reservātiōn-(em)*, formed fr. *reservāt-(um)*, P.P. type of *reservāre*, 'to keep back'. See **reserve**. Act of reserving (in various specific senses). **1.** Act or practice of retaining and guarding one or both consecrated elements, but esp. the Host, after a celebration of the Eucharist, for use in communicating the sick, or others, on a later occasion, or for devotional purposes. **2.** Right, reserved to the Pope, of appointing to a benefice. **3.** (law) The retention in a conveyance or lease by the vendor or lessor of some right or interest, right or interest so retained. **4.** (U.S.A. and Canada) **a** The system, practice, of reserving certain tracts of land for the sole use of native Indian tribes; **b** tract of land so reserved. **5.** **a** Act of concealing, keeping back, refusing to state something which is in the mind; **b** thought, idea, qualifying condition, present in the mind, but not expressed; disingenuous suppression of, and failure to disclose, one's intentions; some particular in which one's complete assent is tacitly withheld in giving a pledge or the like; **c** limiting condition, qualifying proviso: *I can agree with certain reservations*; *without reservation*, frankly, completely, whole-heartedly.

reserve (I.), vb. trans. [1. rezérv; 2. rizə́v], fr. O. Fr. *reserver*, fr. Lat. *reservāre*, 'to keep back, save up, reserve', fr. **re-** & *servāre*, 'to keep', see **serve**. **1.** To keep, hold back, for future or other use, enjoyment &c.; to keep in store or in reserve: *to reserve money for emergencies*; *to reserve troops to meet a counter-attack, follow up an assault* &c.; *to reserve one's strength, energies*, not exhaust them all at once: *to reserve oneself for a greater effort to come*. Specif. **2.** (eccles.) *to reserve the Sacrament*, to set aside part of the consecrated elements for the sick or dying or for devotional purposes. **3.** To keep, set aside, for the use, enjoyment, benefit, of a particular person, or group of persons: *to reserve a seat at a theatre*; *all rights of translation and republication in this book are reserved*, i.e. for benefit of author and original publisher. **4.** (eccles., of the Pope) To retain the right of presentation to a benefice; (of Pope or Bishop &c.) to retain power of granting absolution in special cases of sin. **5.** (law) To retain by express proviso rights or interest in a conveyance or lease. **6.** To hold over, defer, postpone, till a future time, another occasion &c.: *this question must be reserved for further consideration*; *the court will reserve judgement*. **7.** To set apart, hold, keep in store for, destine: *fate reserved a severer punishment for him*; *a great future is reserved for you*, is in store for, awaits, you.

reserve (**II.**), n., fr. Fr. *réserve.* See prec. **1.** That which is reserved, something kept back for future use; extra supply, store, stock: *a reserve of food, ammunition* &c.; *a reserve of force, energy, strength*; specif. **a** (commerc.) cash or liquid assets easily available kept to meet all demands: *the reserve of a bank*; *the gold reserve* (of Bank of England), that kept to cover its note issue; Phr. *to place to reserve*, to allocate to the reserve fund; **b** (mil. and nav.) (i.) troops or ships, kept back in battle and held ready or 'in reserve' for support, reinforcement &c.; (ii.) *the Reserve*, body of men who have served a stated time with the colours, or at sea, and who are liable to be called up for active service in war or other special emergency; (also of ships) *to be placed to the reserve*, go out of commission but be kept by a nucleus crew ready for a full crew &c.; *Royal Naval Reserve*, force recruited from the Mercantile Marine, going through an annual training and liable for active service in war; **c** other specific uses: (i.) (in sports and games) a spare man ready to act as substitute if wanted; (ii.) award, at an exhibition &c., entitling the winner to a prize if another is disqualified. **2.** Tract of land reserved and protected for a special purpose: *a reserve for wild animals*; *a forest reserve.* **3.** State of being reserved, held back or kept for some purpose, later use &c.: *in reserve*, available, for use if needed. **4.** Limitation, qualification, exception, reservation; **a** (of mental condition) cautious withholding of complete approval or endorsement: *to accept* (*statement &c.*) *with, without, reserve*; *we make the announcement with great reserve*; **b** (of things) restriction, limitation, of price: *to place a reserve upon a house, picture* &c., price below which it is not to be sold; *to be sold without reserve*, without any restrictions as to price; *a reserve price*, price below which no bid will be accepted. **5. a** Cast of mind, peculiarity of temperament, which manifest themselves in a frigid manner and aloof bearing; absence of effusiveness and expansiveness; restraint, reticence: *the traditional reserve of the Englishman*; *he received my advances with considerable reserve*; **b** (of literary and artistic expression) disciplined control and restraint, absence of extravagance; **c** (casuistry) intentional suppression, withholding of facts, suppression of the truth or part of it.

reserved, adj. [1. rezẽrvd; 2. rizə́vd]. **reserve** (**I.**) & **-ed.** **1.** Kept, set, apart for use of particular person: *reserved seats*, those which can be booked in advance. **2.** (R.C. Ch.) *Reserved sins*, special sins, power of absolving which is reserved for a bishop or other superior. **3.** (of character, manner &c.) Possessing, exhibiting, reserve; reverse of forthcoming; reticent, not expansive; diffident. **4.** *Reserved list*, list of the naval officers on the Reserve.

reservedly, adv. [1. rezẽrvedli; 2. rizə́vidli]. Prec. & **-ly.** In a reserved, reticent, manner.

reservist, n. [1. rezẽrvist; 2. rizə́vist]. **reserve** (**II.**) & **-ist.** Soldier or sailor belonging to the Reserve.

reservoir, n. [1. rézervwar, -wōr; 2. rézəvwā, -wɔ̄], fr. Fr., fr. Low Lat. *reservātōrium*, fr. *reservāt-*(*um*), P.P. type of *reservāre.* See **reserve** (**I.**) & **-ory.** A place where anything is kept or stored for further use. **1.** Specif., a large receptacle, often forming an artificial lake, in which water for a town or district is collected and stored. **2.** Any receptacle for holding liquids: *the reservoir of a lamp, of a fountain pen* &c. **3.** A small sac or space in which fluid collects, as in plants, an animal body &c. **4.** (also in non-material sense) A reserve, store, supply: *a reservoir of knowledge, wealth, strength* &c.

reset, vb. trans. & intrans. & n. [1. rēsét; 2. rīsét], fr. O. Fr. *receter*, 'to receive', fr. L. Lat *receptāre*, freq. of Lat. *recipere.* See **receive.** **1.** vb. (archaic or Scots law) **a** trans. To receive, as stolen goods; **b** intrans., to act as a receiver of stolen goods. **2.** n. The receiving of stolen goods.

re-set, vb. trans. [1. rē sét; 2. rī sét]. **re-** & **set** (**I.**). **1.** To set, sharpen, again: *to re-set a saw, razor.* **2.** To refix in the setting: *to re-set jewellery* &c.

resettle, vb. trans. [1. rēsétl; 2. rīsétl]. **re-** & **settle** (**II.**). **1.** To arrange, settle (disputes, affairs), again. **2.** To plant (a country) with settlers again.

resettlement, n. [1. rēsétlment; 2. rīsétlmənt]. **re-** & **settlement.** **a** Act of resettling (in various senses); **b** state of being resettled.

reshape, vb. trans. & intrans. [1. rēsháp; 2. rīʃéip]. **re-** & **shape.** **1.** trans. To shape again, to give a new shape, plan, course, to. **2.** intrans. To assume a new, different, shape, condition &c.; to take a new line of development; (also reflex.) *affairs are gradually reshaping themselves.*

reship, vb. trans. [1. rēship; 2. rīʃíp]. **re-** & **ship.** To ship again, to put on board again; to change (goods) from one ship to another.

reshipment, n. [1. rēshípment; 2. rīʃípmənt]. Prec. & **-ment.** **a** Act of reshipping; **b** cargo which is reshipped.

reshuffle, vb. trans. & n. [1. rēshúfl; 2. rīʃáfl]. **re-** & **shuffle.** **1.** vb. To shuffle (cards) again; (also fig.) to rearrange, give new relation and tendency (to events &c.). **2.** n. Act of reshuffling.

reside, vb. intrans. [1. rezíd; 2. rizáid], fr. Lat. *residēre*, 'to sit back, remain sitting, to remain behind, to dwell, abide, reside', fr. **re-** & *sedēre*, 'to sit'. See **sedentary.** **1.** (of persons) **a** To have one's home or usual abode; to dwell in, inhabit permanently, or for a considerable space of time: *he resides at No. 11 High Street*; *he resides in London, but is now staying in the country*; **b** to live in a specified place during a specified period, as a condition imposed by an institution: *in order to keep a term at Oxford, one must reside for at least seven weeks.* **2.** (of rights &c.) to be vested, rest, lie, in: *sovereignty resides in Parliament*; *in whom does the full ownership reside?* **3.** (of qualities, properties) To inhere, to be present; to be found in: *it is in such actions that true courage resides.*

residence, n. [1. rézidens; 2. rézidəns]. Fr., fr. Low Lat. *residentia.* See **resident** & **-ce.** **1.** Act, fact, of residing; **a** fact of having an abode: *residence in London is extremely unpleasant to many*; **b** specif., act of residing in specified place for specified period as a qualification for some office, in discharge of duty &c.: *the University of Oxford demands residence from undergraduates and teachers alike.* Phr. *in residence*, (of persons in official position) actually living at the official residence; (of members of university) residing in a college, or other place within the university. **2. a** Place where one resides, abode, home, permanent or habitual dwelling: *he will be found at his residence*; *the official residence*; **b** (in auctioneer's jargon) a large house, usually of less pretension than 'mansion': *a delightful Georgian residence for sale or lease.*

residency, n. [1. rézidensi; 2. rézidənsi]. **resident** & **-cy.** **1.** The official residence in India of British representative or Resident at a native court. **2.** (hist.) An administrative area in certain protected states in the East Indies, as in Java, parts of India &c.

resident (**I.**), adj. [1. rézident; 2. rézidənt], fr. Lat. *resident-*(*em*), Pres. Part. of *residēre.* See **reside.** **1. a** Residing, dwelling, having one's home or abode permanently or regularly in a place: *resident abroad*; *resident aliens*; **b** (zool., of birds) non-migratory. **2.** Residing in, occupying, an official residence, having quarters in house &c., in fulfilment of official duties &c., opposed to *non-resident*: *the incumbent of a benefice must be resident*; *the resident physician of a hospital*; specif., *resident magistrate* (abbr. R.M.), a stipendiary magistrate in Ireland; *minister resident* or *resident minister*, a diplomatic agent of the third rank resident at a foreign court. **3.** Residing in, situated, present; inherent: *faculties identified as resident in a particular part of the brain*; *powers which are resident in the royal prerogative.*

resident (**II.**), n. See prec. **1. a** One who resides or lives permanently in a given town or district; an inhabitant, member of the resident population; **b** (zool.) a resident, non-migratory bird: *the winter, summer, residents.* **2.** Specif. **a** a political agent resident at a native court in India, representing the Viceroy and Government, and acting as a legislative and administrative adviser; also similar official at the courts of Protectorates and Dependencies in the East, as in Borneo, Sarawak &c.; **b** (diplomacy) a minister resident.

residential, adj. [1. rèzidénshl; 2. rèzidénʃl]. Lat. *resident-*, stem of Pres. Part. of *residēre.* See **resident** & **-ial.** **1.** Pertaining to, connected with, residence: *residential franchise, qualification.* **2.** Used for, occupied by, suitable for, private houses, esp. of a superior class: *a residential district, neighbourhood, quarter* (*of a town*) &c., usually as contrasted with business areas.

residentiary, adj. & n. [1. rèzidénshari; 2. rèzidénʃəri], fr. Med. Lat. *residentiārius*, n. See **resident** (**I.**) & **-ary.** **1.** adj. **a** Resident; bound to occupy and reside in, an official residence; esp. applied to canons: *a canon residentiary*; **b** carrying an obligation of official residence: *a residentiary canonry.* **2.** n. An ecclesiastic, esp. a canon, who is bound to be continuously in residence in the cathedral city for a regular period each year.

residentship, n. [1. rézidentship; 2. rézidəntʃip]. **resident** & **-ship.** Office, period of office, of an official resident.

residual (**I.**), adj. [1. rezíjooal; 2. rezídžuəl]. See **residuum** & **-al.** **1.** Pertaining to, connected with, a residuum or residue; remaining, left over after a part has been taken away or dealt with; residuary. **2.** (math.) **a** Left over after subtraction; **b** not eliminated, not accounted for, of errors or differences.

residual (**II.**), n., fr. prec. **1.** A residuum, residue. **2.** (math.) A residual quantity or difference.

residuary, adj. & n. [1. rezíjooari; 2. rezídžuəri]. **residue, residuum,** & **-ary.** **1.** adj. **a** Pertaining to, consisting of, a residuum or residue, remaining, left over, residual; specif. **b** (law) pertaining to, of the residue of an estate: *residuary clause*, the clause in a will which disposes of the residue of the estate and names *the residuary devisee* for the residue of the real property, and *the residuary legatee* for the personal property. **2.** n. (rare) A residuary legatee.

residue, n. [1. rézidū; 2. rézidjū], fr. Fr. *résidu*(*e*). See next word. **1. a** A remainder, rest, that which is left over after a part has been taken away, dealt with &c.; **b** (chem.) residuum. **2.** (law) That part of a testator's estate which remains over after all charges, administration expenses, debts, and specific devises or legacies have been discharged and paid.

residuum, n., pl. **residua** [1. rezíduum, -dūa; 2. rezídjuəm, -uə]. Lat., P.P. neut. sing. fr. *residēre*, 'to remain behind, be left over'. See **reside.** Remainder, residue; specif. **a** (chem.) that portion of a substance which remains over after separation, combustion, evaporation &c.; **b** (math.) a residual error, amount not accounted for; remainder left by subtraction; **c** (rare) the dregs of the populace.

resign, vb. trans. & intrans. [1. rezín; 2. rizáin]. M.E. *resignen*, fr. O. Fr. *resigner*, fr. Lat. *resignāre*, 'to break the seal of, to unseal, open; to annul, cancel; to transfer, assign; to give back, resign', fr. **re-** & *signāre*, see **sign.** **A.** trans. **1. a** To give up, surrender, relinquish: *to resign office, a position of trust*;

he resigned the Chancellorship, his seat in Parliament; **b** (*resign to*) to hand over, yield: *to resign one's duties to more capable hands*; **c** to abandon, renounce: *to resign a claim, property, rights*; *to resign all hope, one's expectations*. **2.** (reflex.) *To resign oneself*; **a** to yield, give up; to submit, entrust to: *resign yourselves to the will of God*; *I will readily resign myself to your protection, teaching* &c.; **b** to reconcile oneself to; to make up one's mind to do, to face &c.; to accept with resignation: *to resign oneself to the decrees of fate*; *to resign oneself to performing, the performance of, a disagreeable duty*; *I do not willingly resign my mind to the idea of failure*. **B.** intrans. To withdraw from, give up an office, surrender a post, appointment &c.; to retire: *the Ministry has resigned*; *he refused to resign from his living*.

re-sign, vb. trans. [1. rè sín; 2. rī sáin]. **re- & sign.** To sign (a document &c.) over again.

resignation, n. [1. rèzignáshun; 2. rèzignéiʃən]. Fr. See **resign** & **-ation.** **1. a** Act, fact, of resigning an office, post &c.: *the resignation of the ministry is expected hourly*; **b** document, statement, announcing resignation: *to send in one's resignation*; **c** offer, expression of wish, to resign: *his resignation was immediately accepted*. **2.** State of being resigned or reconciled (to an event, misfortune &c.); acceptance with patience and calm uncomplaining composure and fortitude, of something painful but inevitable; submission to the will of God: *he met his fate with resignation*.

resigned, adj. [1. rezínd; 2. rizáind]. **resign & -ed.** Feeling and showing resignation; submissive: *with a calm and resigned mind*; *resigned to one's fate*; *we grow resigned to old age*.

resignedly, adv. [1. rezínedli; 2. rizáinidli]. Prec. & **-ly.** In a resigned manner, with resignation; submissively, uncomplainingly.

resile, vb. intrans. [1. resíl, -zíl; 2. risáil, -záil], fr. Lat. *resilīre*, 'to jump, spring, back, rebound', fr. **re-** & *salīre*, 'to leap, spring'. See **salient. 1.** (of elastic bodies) To return to former position after displacement, to resume former shape after being submitted to pressure or deformation; to exhibit resilience. **2.** (in moral sense) **a** To show power of mental recuperation, to exhibit elasticity of mind or spirits; to recover rapidly from depression; **b** to react, respond, readily to a mental stimulus; to be responsive.

resilience, -cy, n. [1. resíliens(i), -zíliens(i); 2. risílians(i), -zílians(i)]. **resilient & -ce, -cy.** Act of resiling; property of being resilient; **a** (in physical sense) elasticity; **b** (moral sense) recuperation; recuperative power.

resilient, adj. [1. resílient, -zílient; 2. risíliənt, -zíliənt], fr. Lat. *resilient-(em)*, Pres. Part. of *resilīre*, 'to spring back' &c. See **resile.** Elastic; **a** in physical sense; **b** in moral sense, capable of recuperation; responsive.

resiliometer, n. [1. resiliómeter, -ziliómeter; 2. rεsilióm itə, -zilióm itə]. **resile & -o- & -meter.** Instrument for measuring and testing the resiliency of substances.

resin, n. & vb. trans. [1. rézin; 2. rézin], fr. Fr. *résine*, fr. Lat. *rēsina*, fr. Gk. *rhētínē*; cp. Lat. *rāsis*, 'a kind of rough, powdered pitch, used to mix with wine', prob. fr. Gk. **rhásis*, a gradation variant of *rhētínē*; fr. base **srē-*, **srə-*, prob. a variant of **ser-*, 'to flow', seen in **rheo-, stream** &c. **1.** n. A sticky substance, which hardens on exposure to the air, secreted by most plants, but especially by pines, firs, and other conifers; used **a** in making varnish, lacquer &c.; **b** in medicine; **c** (usually called *rosin*, q.v.) for enabling the bow of violins and similar instruments to grip the strings. **2.** vb. To apply resin (or rosin) to; to treat with resin.

resinaceous, adj. [1. rèzináshus; 2. rèzinéiʃəs]. **resin & -aceous.** Having the properties of resin; resinous.

resinate, n. [1. rézināt; 2. rézineit]. **resin & -ate.** (chem.) A salt of the resinic acids.

resinic, adj. [1. rezínik; 2. rεzínik]. **resin & -ic.** (chem.) Obtained from resin.

resiniferous, adj. [1. rèziníferus; 2. rèziníferəs]. **resin & -ferous.** Yielding resin.

resinification, n. [1. rèzinifikáshun; 2. rèzinifikéiʃən]. **resin & -fication.** Process of resinifying.

resiniform, adj. [1. réziniform; 2. réziniform]. **resin & -form.** Having the form of resin.

resinify, vb. trans. & intrans. [1. rezínifī; 2. rεzínifai]. **resin & -fy. a** trans. To convert into resin; to treat with resin; **b** intrans., to become resinous.

resinous, adj. [1. rézinus; 2. rézinəs]. **resin & -ous. a** Pertaining to resin; of the nature of, like, rosin; obtained from resin; **b** (elect.) negative, non-conductive.

resipiscence, n. [1. rèsipísens; 2. rèsipísəns], fr. Lat. *resipiscentia*. See next word & **-ce.** (rare) Change to a better or wiser state of mind; return to sense or wisdom; recognition of error.

resipiscent, adj. [1. rèsipísent; 2. rèsipísənt], fr. *resipiscent-(em)*, Pres. Part. of *resipiscere*, 'to become wise again', fr. **re-** & inceptive form of *sapere*, 'to be wise'. See **sapient.** (rare) Having, exhibiting, resipiscence.

resist (I.), vb. trans. & intrans. [1. rezíst; 2. rizíst]. Fr. *résister*, fr. Lat. *resistere*, 'to stand back, stay, remain; to withstand, oppose, resist', fr. **re-** & *sistere*, 'to cause to stand; to put, place'; cp. Gk. *hístēmi* for **sístēmi*, redupl. form of base *stā-*, 'to stand'. See **state, stand, station. A.** trans. Expressing various physical actions or processes: **1.** To stand up against, retain, remain in, position, without breaking or being moved aside by pressure, weight, or the like; to withstand: *the sea-wall cannot resist the force of the waves*; *the door resisted the blows rained upon it*. **2.** To obstruct, impede, bar: *non-conductors resist the passage of an electric current*. **3.** To throw off, drive back, repel, by exercise of physical force: *the enemy was everywhere satisfactorily resisted*; *our troops successfully resisted the attacks of the enemy*; *to resist a charge of cavalry*. **4.** To offer opposition to, show active hostility to; to hinder, thwart, impede: *to resist the police in the discharge of their duty*. **5.** To remain unaffected and uninjured by; to be proof against, to ward off, keep out; **a** (of living organisms) *to resist disease*; *his feeble frame was unable to resist the fatigues and hardships of the journey*; **b** (of lifeless objects) *a cement that will resist damp*; *thatch resists heat much better than tiles*; *gold and silver resist rust*; *some substances resist the action of acid*. Expressing moral action:—**6. a** To offer moral opposition to, to withhold assent to; to endeavour to prevent becoming effective: *I feel bound to resist the proposals by every constitutional means*; **b** to refuse to acknowledge and comply with; to disregard, disobey: *to resist the law, properly constituted authority* &c. **7. a** To refuse to allow oneself to be allured, or one's conduct to be influenced by; to repel the desire or impulse to be, to prevent oneself from being, attracted by: *to resist the wiles of an enchantress*; *to resist temptation, the temptation to do something*; *to resist strong drink*; **b** (chiefly with neg.) to prevent oneself by a moral effort from enjoying or doing; to deny oneself: *he never can resist making a joke*; *I can't resist your invitation to shoot*; *I never can resist strawberries and cream*. **B.** intrans. To offer resistance (in all senses).

resist (II.), n., fr. prec. Something which resists or prevents a specific action or result. Specif. (calico printing) a substance applied to certain parts of the cloth which resists the action of the dye and prevents it being imprinted on the part so protected.

resistance, n. [1. rezístans; 2. rizístəns]. Fr. *résistance*; **resist (I.)** & **-ance. 1. a** Act or process of resisting in physical senses; **b** act of resisting by moral effort. **2. a** Standing up, remaining firm and unshifted, against pressure &c.: *so frail a structure cannot offer adequate resistance to the wind*; **b** capacity, power, of resisting (pressure &c.): *such a building has practically no resistance*. **3.** (phys.) **a** Non-conductivity; specif. (elect.) measure of capacity in a conducting body to resist passage of a current; also applied to apparatus designed to resist passage of a current, cp. *rheostat*; **b** opposition offered by any form of matter to attempt to displace it: *the resistance of water or air*. Phr. *line of least resistance*, direction in which a force is most readily exerted; (also fig.) the easiest line of action to pursue. **4. a** Effort made to resist (attack &c.) by bodily force: *the enemy offered but slight resistance*; **b** capacity to make such an effort: *the enemy's resistance was completely destroyed*. **5.** Act of thwarting, impeding, hampering, preventing, by bodily action: *the mob offered no resistance to the police in their attempts to preserve order*. **6.** Natural opposition of an organism to, and its reaction against, unfavourable conditions and the like: *the resistance of plants to disease*. **7. a** Moral act of resisting, or withholding assent to, and of attempting to nullify; counteraction, antagonism: *the Opposition offered resistance to the bill at every stage*; **b** refusal to obey or to comply with: *resistance to established law is foreign to the habits of the English people*. Phr. *passive resistance*, mode of protesting against a law which is resented by refusal to pay rates or taxes when demanded, without however offering forcible resistance to consequent distraint of goods.

resistance coil, n. Coil of insulated wire which increases the resistance in an electric circuit.

resistant, adj. & n. [1. rezístant; 2. rizístənt]. **resist (I.) & -ant. 1.** adj. Offering, making, resistance; resisting. **2.** n. **a** Person who resists, a resister; **b** a resist.

resister, n. [1. rezíster; 2. rizístə]. **resist & -er.** On who resists. Phr. *passive resister*, one who adopts the plan of *passive resistance*, q.v. under **resistance.**

resistibility, n. [1. rezìstibíliti; 2. rizìstibíliti]. Next word & **-ity.** Quality of being resistible; capacity to offer resistance.

resistible, adj. [1. rezístibl; 2. rizístibl]. **resist (I.) & -ible.** Capable of being resisted.

resistive, adj. [1. rezístiv; 2. rizístiv]. **resist (I.) & -ive.** Tending to resist, having power of resistance.

resistless, adj. [1. rezístles; 2. rizístlis]. **resist (I.) & -less. 1.** Incapable of being, not to be, resisted, kept back, stayed, turned aside; inevitable, irresistible: *the resistless march of events*. **2.** (rare) Not offering resistance, lacking power to resist.

resistlessly, adv. Prec. & **-ly.** In a resistless manner.

resole, vb. trans. [1. résól; 2. rísóul]. **re- & sole (II.).** To put a new sole on (a boot or shoe).

resoluble, adj. [1. résolūbl; 2. résəljubl], fr. L. Lat. *resolūbil-(is)*, 'resoluble'. **re- & soluble.** Capable of being resolved; specif., capable of being broken up, analysed.

resolute, adj. [1. rézolūt; 2. rézəljūt], fr. Lat. *resolūt-(um)*, P.P. type of *resolvere*, 'to loosen, separate, lay open'. See **resolve.** Firm, unhesitating, unyielding; steadfast in purpose, unflinching.

resolutely, adv. Prec. & **-ly.** In a resolute manner.

resolution, n. [1. rèzolúshun; 2. rèzəljúʃən], fr. Lat. *resolūtiōn-(em)*, 'an untying, relaxing; solution', fr. *resolūt-(um)*, P.P. type of *resolvere*, 'to loosen'. See **re- & solution. 1. a** Act of resolving into component parts; **b** state of being resolved; analysis; disintegration. **2.** Act of converting, process of being transformed; conversion into something different, transformation, substitution; specif. **a** (prosody) use of two short syllables in place of one long one; **b** (mus.) passing of discord into concord; **c** (med.) disappearance or dispersion of tumour or of inflammation without suppuration. **3.** Act of solving; state of being solved, solution: *resolution of a doubt* &c. **4. a** Formal statement of opinion or expression of intention by legislative body, public meeting &c.; **b** form of proposal made to legislative body &c. for consideration and adoption. **5. a** Act of resolving, determining, deciding; **b** thing resolved upon, determined action; firm intention, determination: *to make resolutions to behave better in future.* **6.** Quality of being resolute; firmness of purpose, unwavering adherence to intended course of action: *a man of no resolution of character.*

resolutive, adj. & n. [1. rézolūtiv; 2. rézəljūtiv]. See **resolute** & **-ive**. **1.** adj. **a** (chiefly med.) Capable of dissolving, dispersing, disintegrating; **b** (legal) *resolutive condition,* one the fulfilment of which terminates a contract, obligation &c. **2.** n. (med.) Resolutive application, drug &c.

resolvable, adj. [1. rezólvabl; 2. rizólvəbl]. Next word & **-able**. Capable of being resolved.

resolve (I.), vb. trans. & intrans. [1. rezólv; 2. rizólv], fr. Lat. *resolvere,* 'to loosen, unfasten, relax; to disclose; to solve', **re-** & **solve**. **A.** trans. **1.** (in physical sense) **a** To break up, split, dissolve, into component parts; to analyse; **b** (reflex.) *resolve itself* &c., to disintegrate, melt. **2.** (of mental action; growing rare) **a** To determine, settle, clear up, solve: *to resolve a person's fears, doubts* &c.; **b** to break up (a problem &c.) into its constituent elements, make critical analysis of; to simplify by disentangling the various issues involved. Phr. *the question resolves itself into this,* comes down to, amounts to. **3. a** (rare) To cause (a person) to come to a decision, to determine, cause to make up one's mind: *the facts resolved him to act at once;* **b** (pass. usual construction) *I am resolved to do so and so,* I have made up my mind to &c. **B.** intrans. **1.** To make a resolution, to determine, decide (to act in a certain way): *I have resolved to . . .* **2.** (law) To become void, to lapse.

resolve (II.), n., fr. prec. **1.** Something resolved, fixed intention, determination, a resolution (to do something): *to make good resolves for the New Year.* **2.** Firmness of character and purpose; resolution: *a man of resolve.*

resolved, adj. [1. rezólvd; 2. rizólvd], fr. P.P. of **resolve** (I.). Resolute, firm.

resolvedly, adv. [1. rezólvedli; 2. rizólvidli]. Prec. & **-ly**. In a resolute manner.

resolvent, adj. & n. [1. rezólvent; 2. rizólvənt]. **resolve** (I.) & **-ent**. **a** adj. (chiefly med. and chem.) Having the power to dissolve, disintegrate, disperse; **b** n., drug &c. which has these properties.

resonance, n. [1. rézonans; 2. rézənəns], fr. Lat. *resonantia,* 'echo'. See **resonant** & **-ance**. Sonority, ring; vibrant, amplified effect produced by sound causing sympathetic vibration in surrounding bodies; specif. (elect.) state of an electric circuit when the frequency of the electromotive force applied equals the natural frequency of the circuit; the basis of all tuning of wireless apparatus.

resonant, adj. [1. rézonant; 2. rézənənt], fr. Lat. *reson-(āre),* 'to resound, echo', fr. **re-** & *sonāre,* 'to sound', see **sonant**, & **-ant**. **1.** (of sound, the voice &c.) Sonorous, ringing; producing full vibrant notes. **2.** (of body, wall, room &c.) Producing effect of resonance.

resonantly, adv. Prec. & **-ly**. In a resonant manner.

resonator, n. [1. rézonāter; 2. rézəneitə], fr. Lat. *resonāt-(um),* P.P. type of *resonāre,* 'to resound', see **resonant**, & **-or**. **1.** Device for increasing resonance of sounds. **2.** Instrument vibrating in response to a single musical note, and used to detect the presence of this in a complex sound.

resorb, vb. trans. [1. resórb; 2. risɔ́b], fr. Lat. *resorb-(ēre),* 'to suck back', fr. **re-** & *sorbēre,* 'to suck up, swallow'. See **absorb**. To absorb again.

resorbence, n. [1. resórbens; 2. risɔ́bəns]. Prec. & **-ence**. Quality of being resorbent.

resorbent, adj. [1. resórbent; 2. risɔ́bənt]. **resorb** & **-ent**. Having the power, tending, to reabsorb something already given out.

resorcin, n. [1. rezórsin; 2. rizɔ́sin]. Coined fr. first syll. of **resin** & **orcin**. Colourless crystalline compound obtained from resin &c. used in dyeing, medicine &c.

resorption, n. [1. resórpshun; 2. risɔ́pʃən], fr. Lat. *resorpt-(um), P.P. type of *resorbēre,* 'to reabsorb', see **resorb**, & **-ion**. Act of resorbing; state of being resorbed.

resort (I.), vb. intrans. [1. rezórt; 2. rizɔ́t], fr. O. Fr. *resortir,* fr. **re-** & *sortir,* 'to go out'; see **sortie**. **1.** To have recourse, turn for aid, adopt as means: *to resort to violence, bribery; to resort to new schemes* &c. **2.** To go, betake oneself to, to frequent: *a place to which many tourists resort.*

resort (II.), n., fr. O. Fr. *resort,* fr. *resortir.* See prec. **1.** Act of resorting; recourse: *without resort to force.* Phr. *in the last resort,* when everything else has failed. **2.** Thing adopted as aid or means; expedient; person or thing to whom recourse is made: *that is my only resort.* **3.** Act of visiting, resorting to (a place): *taverns and other places of resort.* **4.** Place to which many resort or which one frequently visits, esp. for specified reason or purpose: *health resort; seaside resort* &c.

re-sort, vb. trans. [1. rē sórt; 2. rī sɔ́t]. **re-** & **sort** (II.). To sort over again.

resound, vb. intrans. & trans. [1. rezóund; 2. rizáund]. **re-** & **sound** (II.). **A.** intrans. **1.** (of sound, instrument &c.) To be prolonged, be resonant, echo, reverberate. **2.** (of place) To be filled with sound, re-echo, ring with prolonged sound. **3.** (fig., of deed, event, fame &c.) To be celebrated, be widely known: *the fame of his deeds resounded through the country.* **B.** trans. **1.** (of place &c.) To re-echo, give out an echo, reverberate. **2.** (fig.) To celebrate, acclaim, make widely known: *to resound a person's fame, praise* &c.

resounding, adj. [1. rezóunding; 2. rizáundiŋ], fr. Pres. Part. of prec. Reverberating, resonant.

resoundingly, adv. Prec. & **-ly**. In a resounding manner.

resource, n. [1. resórs; 2. risɔ́s], fr. Fr. *ressource,* fr. O. Fr. *resourdre,* 'to rise again, recover', fr. Lat. *resurgere,* 'to rise again'. See **resurge**. **1.** (usually pl.) **a** Available supply, stock, of provisions, means of supplying needs; **b** whole available property, funds, pecuniary means; **c** actual and potential wealth, natural advantages; sources of potential wealth (of a country). **2. a** Something available as a help or support; resort, shift, expedient: *that is my last resource;* **b** form of activity or occupation to which one may turn for recreation, pastime, distraction: *some men find in games an unfailing resource; reading is a great resource in illness.* **3.** Inventiveness; readiness in adapting things and circumstances to one's purpose, skill in discovering means and methods of accomplishing this: *a man full of resource in any emergency.* **4.** (rare) Possibility of aid, rescue &c.: *lost without resource.*

resourceful, adj. [1. resórsfool; 2. risɔ́sful]. Prec. & **-ful**. Fertile, ingenious, in resource and expedients; skilful in finding means.

resourcefully, adv. Prec. & **-ly**. In a resourceful manner.

resourcefulness, n. See prec. & **-ness**. Quality of being resourceful.

resourceless, adj. [1. resórsles; 2. risɔ́slis]. **resource** & **-less**. Lacking in resource; more rarely, lacking resources.

resourcelessness, n. Prec. & **-ness**. Lack of resource.

respect (I.), n. [1. respékt; 2. rispékt], fr. Lat. *respect-(us),* 'a looking about; regard, consideration', fr. *respect-(um),* P.P. type of *respicere,* 'to look about'. See next word. **1.** Heed, regard, attention: *without respect to one's feelings; respect should be had to his wishes.* Phr. *without respect of persons,* without undue inclination, bias, partiality, esp. for persons of importance. **2. a** Deferential regard, esteem, due appreciation: *to have respect for old age; to be held in respect;* Phrs. *to pay one's respects to,* to visit, wait upon, greet, as sign of esteem and respect; *my best respects to,* greetings &c.; **b** due regard, serious consideration, faithful observance: *to have respect for one's promise* &c. **3.** Special aspect, particular detail or feature: *alike in some, all, respects.* **4.** Reference, regard, relation: *with respect of, to, what you say; in respect of, to, that there is nothing to be said.* Phr. *in respect that,* considering.

respect (II.), vb. trans., fr. Lat. *respect-(um),* P.P. type of *respicere,* 'to look about', fr. **re-** & *specere,* 'to look at', q.v. under **species**. **1.** To regard, pay heed to, pay attention to: *to respect a person's prejudices; we must respect his sorrow.* Phr. (archaic) *to respect persons,* to be influenced by personal or social considerations. **2.** To regard with deference, hold in esteem, look upon with respect: *to respect one's parents; a man generally respected; to respect oneself,* show self-respect. **3.** To have regard to, treat as binding, to refrain from violating: *to respect the law, one's word; I respect your confidence.*

respectability, n. [1. respèktabíliti; 2. rispèktəbíliti]. See next word & **-ity**. **1. a** Quality of being respectable; **b** (iron.) quality of being over scrupulous and careful in one's speech, conduct &c.; excessive and undiscriminating observance of the external proprieties; exaggerated, priggish conventionality. **2. a** One who or that which is respectable; person of good repute and fair social standing; **b** (iron.) slavish follower of convention, a prig.

respectable, adj. [1. respéktabl; 2. rispéktəbl]. **respect** (II.) & **-able**. **1.** Deserving, commanding, respect; estimable. **2. a** Decent and orderly in conduct; well-conducted; bearing a good character: *a most respectable man;* **b** (iron.) exaggeratedly observant of external propriety, slavishly and priggishly conventional in outward demeanour &c.: *he's altogether too respectable for my taste.* **3.** Decent, seemly, suitable for the occasion, conforming to current standards of propriety: *I must put on some more respectable clothes; that hat is hardly respectable.* **4. a** Moderate, passable, fair, mediocre: *his talents were respectable but no more;* **b** (as litotes) not inconsiderable, pretty good: *quite a respectable income, position* &c. **5.** *The respectable,* respectable persons.

respectably, adv. Prec. & **-ly**. In a respectable manner.

respecter, n. [1. respékter; 2. rispéktə]. **respect** (II.) & **-er**. One who respects; specif. in Phr. *no respecter of persons,* one who is not unduly biassed by social position &c.

respectful, adj. [1. respéktfool; 2. rispéktful]. **respect** (I.) & **-ful**. Showing, expressing, respect; deferential: *a valet must be obliging and respectful; a respectful bow.* Phr. *at a respectful distance,* not too near.

respectfully, adv. Prec. & **-ly**. In a respectful manner.

respectfulness, n. See prec. & **-ness**. State or quality of being respectful.

respecting, prep. [1. respékting; 2. rispéktiŋ], fr. Pres. Part. of **respect** (II.). Referring, in reference, to; with regard to, about: *he talked for a long time respecting his future; respecting our last conversation.*

respective, adj. [1. respéktiv; 2. rispéktiv]. **respect** (II.) & **-ive**. Of each in relation to each; pertaining severally to each of those considered: *tell me your opinion of the respective merits of the candidates.*

respectively, adv. Prec. & **-ly**. Referring to each severally; each of several, in their due relations: *we discussed the virtues of both men respectively.*

respell, vb. trans. [1. rèspél; 2. rīspél]. **re-** & **spell (II.)**. To spell over again; to spell in a different manner.

respirable, adj. [1. réspirabl, respírabl; 2. réspirəbl, rīspáiərəbl]. **respire** & **-able**. Capable of being, suitable to be, breathed.

respiration, n. [1. respiráshun; 2. respiréiʃən], fr. Lat. *respīrātiōn-(em)*, 'act of breathing; rest, respite'. **respire** & **-ation**. **1.** Act or process of respiring; breathing: *respiration is difficult in an attenuated atmosphere*; *artificial respiration*, breathing induced by artificial or mechanical means. **2.** Single breath, single inspiration and expiration. **3.** (bot.) Process by which a plant absorbs oxygen and gives off carbon dioxide.

respirator, n. [1. réspirāter; 2. réspireitə], fr. Lat. *respīrāt-(um)*, P.P. type of *respīrāre*, 'to breathe out; to breathe', see **respire** & **-or**. Appliance worn over mouth or nose to warm or filter the air which is breathed; specif., a device used to prevent the inhalation of gas-fumes.

respiratory, adj. [1. réspiràturi, respíraturi; 2. réspirèitəri, respáiərətəri]. See prec. & **-ory**. Of, pertaining to, concerned in, respiration.

respire, vb. intrans. & trans. [1. respír; 2. rispáiə], fr. Lat. *respīr-(āre)*, 'to breathe out; to breathe; to recover breath, be refreshed', fr. **re-** & *spīrāre*, 'to breathe'. See **spirant**. **A.** intrans. **1.** To breathe, carry out the process of inhaling and exhaling. **2.** (fig.) To enjoy relief, take rest, have a respite or breathing-space. **B.** trans. **1.** To breathe, take (air) into the lungs. **2.** (rare or poet.) To exhale, give off as exhalation.

respite (I.), n. [1. réspit, réspīt; 2. réspit, réspait], fr. O. Fr. *respit*, fr. Lat. *respect-(us)*, 'a looking about; regard, consideration; a refuge, retreat'. See **respect (I.)**. **1.** Temporary intermission of effort, obligation &c.; period of repose, of freedom from duty &c.: *a brief respite from one's labours, responsibility* &c. **2.** Temporary postponement of some event fixed for a certain time; specif., delay in execution of the capital sentence; reprieve.

respite (II.), vb. trans., fr. prec. **1.** To reprieve, grant temporary postponement of death-penalty on: *to respite a condemned man* &c. **2.** To relieve by temporary cessation of suffering &c.: *to respite a sufferer* &c. **3.** (mil.) **a** To withhold pay from; **b** to withhold, check, payment of: *to respite one's pay.*

resplendence, -cy, n. [1. resplénden s(i); 2. rispléndəns(i)], fr. L. Lat. *resplendentia*, 'splendour'. Next word & **-ce, -cy**. Dazzling brilliance, lustre, splendour.

resplendent, adj. [1. resplén dent; 2. rispléndənt], fr. Lat. *resplend-(ēre)*, 'to shine, glitter', fr. **re-** & *splendēre*, 'to shine', see **splendent**. **a** Gorgeously bright, dazzling, brilliant, refulgent; **b** magnificent, very splendid: *resplendent in full uniform.*

resplendently, adv. Prec. & **-ly**. In a resplendent manner.

respond (I.), vb. intrans. [1. respónd; 2. rispɔ́nd], fr. Lat. *respond-(ēre)*, 'to offer or give in return; to reply', fr. **re-** & *spondēre*, 'to promise, pledge', see **sponsion**. **1. a** To reply, make answer, speak in return; **b** specif. (eccles.) to make responses. **2.** To act in answer to, as result of, another's action; to perform corresponding or retaliatory action: *to respond with a blow.* **3.** To show the effect of an action, be responsive to, react to: *children generally respond to kindness*; *plants respond at once to proper treatment.* **4.** (rare) To correspond, suit.

respond (II.), n., fr. prec. **1.** (eccles.) Response. **2.** (archit.) Semi-column, pilaster &c., placed against a wall to support an arch.

respondence, -cy, n. [1. respónden s(i); 2. rispɔ́ndəns(i)]. **respond (I.)** & **-ence, -ency**. **1.** Act or process of responding. **2.** State of being respondent.

respondent, adj. & n. [1. respóndent; 2. rispɔ́ndənt]. **respond (I.)** & **-ent**. **1.** adj. **a** Giving answer, speaking or acting in return; responsive; **b** occupying position of defendant in lawsuit. **2.** n. **a** Person who defends thesis &c. in dispute; **b** (legal) defendant in lawsuit, esp. in one for divorce.

response, n. [1. respóns; 2. rispɔ́ns], fr. Lat. *respons-(um)*, 'answer, reply', fr. P.P. type of *rēspondēre*, 'to reply'. See **respond (I.)**. **1.** Act of responding: *in response to.* **2.** Word spoken, action performed, in reply to, as result of, another action; answer. **3.** Feeling, emotion, evoked by another's action or feeling; reaction to emotional or intellectual stimulus: *his oratorical efforts evoke no response in his audience.* **4.** (eccles.) Part of liturgy said or sung by choir and congregation in reply to officiating priest: *to say, answer, the responses.*

responsibility, n. [1. respònsibíliti; 2. rispɔ̀nsibíliti]. See next word & **-ity**. **1.** State, fact, of being responsible; moral obligation, liability: *a position of responsibility*; *to take, disclaim, responsibility (for)*; *(to act) on one's own responsibility*, on one's own initiative, without specific authorization. **2. a** Duty, charge, for the performance of which one is morally or legally liable and responsible: *the education of children is a grave responsibility*; **b** office involving responsibility: *I can't undertake fresh responsibilities.*

responsible, adj. [1. respónsibl; 2. rispɔ́nsibl], fr. O. Fr., fr. Lat. *respons-(um)*, P.P. type of *respond-(ēre)*, 'to answer'. See **respond** & **-ible**. **1.** Legally or morally answerable, personally accountable, for action, performance of a duty, fulfilment of an obligation &c.: *I am not responsible to you for my actions*; *to be responsible for a person's safety*; *responsible government*, answerable to the people for its actions, one whose power is limited by the will of the governed. **2.** Capable of assuming responsibility; having sufficient moral or mental capacity to be accountable for one's actions; capable of right or reasonable conduct. Hence, **3, a** involving responsibility, carrying with it certain obligations: *a responsible post*; **b** involving capacity for recognizing and accepting moral obligation: *a responsible act.*

responsibly, adv. Prec. & **-ly**. In a responsible manner.

responsions, n. [1. respónshunz; 2. rispɔ́nʃənz], fr. Lat. *responsiōn-(em)*, 'reply', fr. *respons-(um)*, P.P. type of Lat. *respondēre*, 'to answer'. See **respond** & **-ion**. (Oxford Univ.) First of three examinations to be passed by candidate for B.A. degree; familiarly known as *Smalls.*

responsive, adj. [1. respónsiv; 2. rispɔ́nsiv], fr. Lat. *respons-(um)*, P.P. type of *respond-(ēre)*, 'to reply'. See **respond** & **-ive**. **1.** Replying; specif., responding readily to an intellectual or emotional appeal; evincing interest; sympathetic: *a responsive audience*; *I didn't find him very responsive when I talked to him.* **2.** (of a liturgy) Having responses.

responsively, adv. Prec. & **-ly**. In a responsive manner.

responsiveness, n. See prec. & **-ness**. Quality of being responsive.

responsory, n. [1. respónsuri; 2. rispɔ́nsəri], fr. Lat. *responsōria*, 'responses', neut. pl. fr. *respons-(um)*, P.P. type of *respondere*, 'to reply', see **respond**, & **-ory**. **1.** Anthem sung by choir after lesson. **2.** Liturgical response.

ressaldar, n. [1. résaldar; 2. résəldā]. Hind. *risāladār*, fr. Arab.; fr. Hind. (Arab) *risāla*, 'a troop of native (Indian) cavalry'; the Arab. word means properly the office of a *rasūl*, 'civil officer employed to make arrests'. Formerly, in Upper India, the commander of a corps of Hindustani horse; in the south, applied to an infantry officer; now, a native officer who commands a *ressala*, or troop, in a British native regiment of irregular horse.

rest (I.), n. [1. rest; 2. rest]. O.E. *rest*, 'resting-place, bed; grave; sleep; rest'; O.S. *rasta*, 'resting-place; grave'; O.H.G. *rasta*, 'peace; rest'; Goth. *rasta*, 'stage of a journey'; O.N. *rost*, in same sense as Goth. word; prob. cogn. w. Goth. *razn*, 'dwelling-place, house'; O.E. *ærn*, 'place, chamber', see second element of O.E. *bere-ærn*, q.v. under **barn**; cp. further perh. Gk. *erōē* (fr. * *erōsu*) 'any quick violent motion; retreat from, rest from', w. wh. cp. O.E. *rǣs*, 'rush, attack'. If the Gk. word has really the same origin in both the above senses, we might suppose that the primary meaning of the base was 'movement', whether into action, or away from it, fr. wh. latter sense we later got the sense 'retreat, cessation from action, rest'. **1.** Cessation, intermission, of activity or movement; bodily or mental repose for the purpose of refreshment and recuperation after effort and fatigue: '*sleep on now and take your rest*'; *to need rest after a long journey* &c. Phrs. *to go to rest*, go to bed, to lie down and enjoy repose; *at rest*, quiet, still; *to set (a question, matter) at rest*, to settle, so as to obviate further discussion; *to set a person's mind at rest*, to reassure, relieve from anxiety. **2.** Spell of repose: *I need a long rest in the country.* **3. a** Place of rest; bed, grave: *he has gone to his rest*, is dead; Phr. *laid to rest*, buried; **b** specif., a rest-house, institution for repose and recreation: *seamen's rest.* **4.** That on which something rests; a support, prop: *a rest for a gun, for billiard cue*; *a rest for one's head.* **5. a** (mus.) A silence, a pause; **b** (prosody) pause, caesura.

rest (II.), vb. intrans. & trans. O.E. *restan*, 'to rest from; remain'. See prec. Often confused w. **rest (III.)** in some senses. **A.** intrans. **1.** To repose, be still; to take, enjoy, rest: *to lie down and rest.* **2.** To intermit, cease from, activity, or movement: *to rest from one's labours.* **3.** *Rest on*, to settle; to have, occupy, take up, a position, to be supported by: *his foot rested a moment on top of the bank, and then he leapt*; *his glance rested an instant on her face*; *clouds for ever rest upon the mountain-top.* Phr. *to rest on one's oars*, (i.) to stop rowing and lean slightly upon the oars while keeping them in the water; (ii.) (fig.) to enjoy a period of inactivity after great efforts. **4.** See also **rest (III.)**. To remain, abide, lie: *the next move rests with you*; Phr. *you may rest assured that (everything has been tried)*, you may feel sure, confident &c. **B.** trans. **1.** To give rest or repose to; allow to take repose: *to rest one's weary bones*; *to rest one's horse.* **2.** To support, prop up with, lean on, cause to be supported by: *to rest one's head on one's hands, one's elbow on the mantelpiece.*

rest (III.), vb. intrans., fr. Fr. *rester*, 'to remain', fr. Lat. *restāre*, 'to remain', fr. **re-** & *stāre*, 'to stand', see **state**. Confused with some senses of prec. **1.** (archaic) To remain, be left: *nothing rests but despair.* **2.** See prec. **4.** To remain in specified condition or state: *rest assured that I will do my best*; *to rest satisfied, content* &c.; *it rests with him*, is in his hands, to deal with &c.

rest (IV.), n., fr. Fr. *reste*, 'remainder', fr. *rester*, 'to remain'. See prec. **1.** *The rest*, what is left, remainder, remaining part or parts; remnant, residue; *eat some and give the rest away*; the others (of persons): *some of us are here, but we've missed the rest*; *the rest of us.* Phrs. *for the rest*, as regards what remains, as for the other matters, persons, things &c., not already mentioned; *and the rest, all the rest of it*, much more besides. **2.** (banking) Balance kept as reserve fund. **3.** (tennis &c.) Long succession of return strokes.

rest (V.), n., fr. **arrest**; but confused w. **rest (I.) 4.** (hist.) Projection on armour on which butt of lance is supported when couched for charging: '*Not like that Arthur who, with lance in rest, From spur to plume a star of tournament*' &c. (Tennyson, 'Morte d'Arthur').

restamp, vb. trans. [1. rēstámp; 2. ristǽmp]. **re-** & **stamp (I.)**. To stamp over again; put a fresh stamp on.

restart, vb. intrans. & trans. [1. rēstárt; 2. rīstát]. **re-** & **start (I.)**. To start again.

restate, vb. trans. [1. rēstát; 2. rīstéit]. **re-** & **state (III.)**. **a** To state over again; **b** to put into a different or amended form; formulate differently.

restatement, n. [1. rēstátment; 2. rīstéitmənt]. Prec. & **-ment**. **1. a** Act of restating; **b** repetition of a statement. **2. a** A repeated statement; **b** a new and different mode of stating; a re-defining, fresh formulation: *a restatement of one's religious position.*

restaurant, n. [1. réstoron; 2. réstərã]. Fr., fr. *restaurer*, 'to refresh, restore', fr. Lat. *restaurāre*, 'to restore, repair'. See **restore** & **-ant**. Place where meals and other refreshments may be obtained and consumed in a public room; public eating-house; public room for meals in a large hotel, shop, place of entertainment &c.

restaurateur, n. [1. rèstoratér; 2. rèstərətá]. Fr., fr. Lat. *restaurāt-(um)*, P.P. type of *restaurāre*, 'to restore'. See prec., & *-eur* under **-or**. Restaurant-keeper.

rest-balk, n. Ridge of land left unploughed.

rest-cure, n. Mode of treatment of nervous disorder, in which the patient avoids all exercise, and even unnecessary movement, is fed on nourishing food, and endeavours to occupy the mind as little as possible, refraining from reading, writing, and conversation.

rest-day, n. Day of rest.

rested, adj. [1. résted; 2. réstid], fr. P.P. of **rest (I.)**. Restored to energy &c., refreshed by repose: *to feel thoroughly rested.*

restful, adj. [1. réstfool; 2. réstful]. **rest (I.)** & **-ful**. (chiefly in moral sense) Producing a sense of peace, tranquillity and repose: *a restful life, scene* &c.; but not *a restful chair.*

restfully, adv. Prec. & **-ly**. In a restful manner.

restfulness, n. See prec. & **-ness**. Quality of being restful.

rest-harrow, n. fr. obs. *rest*, 'to check', fr. **arrest**, & **harrow (I.)**. Plant with tough, woody roots, *Ononis spinosa.*

rest-house, n. Hut, shed &c., in which travellers can obtain shelter, esp. in lonely regions remote from human habitations.

restiff, adj. [1. réstif; 2. réstif], fr. O. Fr. *restif.* See **restive.** (archaic) Restive.

resting-place, n. [1. résting plās; 2. réstiŋ plèis]. Place in which one may rest; *one's last resting-place*, the grave.

restitute, vb. intrans. & trans. [1. réstitūt; 2. réstitjūt], fr. Lat. *restitūt-(um)*, P.P. type of *restituere*, 'to replace, restore', fr. **re-** & *statuere*, 'to set up', see **statute.** (rare) **1.** intrans. To make restitution. **2.** trans. To restore.

restitution, n. [1. rèstitūshun; 2. rèstitjūʃən], fr. Lat. *restitūtiōn-(em)*, 'restoration', fr. *restitūt-(um)*. See prec. & **-ion**. **1.** Act of restoring; state of being restored; restoration of thing to rightful owner; indemnification, reparation for wrong &c.: *to make restitution.* **2.** (esp. theol.) Restoration to original state, esp. final return of all things to a state of goodness and happiness. **3.** (phys.) Tendency of elastic bodies to resume original shape.

restive, adj. [1. réstiv; 2. réstiv], fr. O. Fr. *restive*, fem. form of *restif*, 'inert', fr. **rest (III.)** & **-ive**. **1.** (of horse &c.) Inclined to jib, refusing to advance; difficult to control, making uneasy, nervous movements; refractory. **2.** (of persons) Out of control, impatient of discipline or restraint; fidgety.

restively, adv. Prec. & **-ly**. In a restive manner.

restiveness, n. See prec. & **-ness**. Quality or state of being restive.

restless, adj. [1. réstles; 2. réstlis]. **rest (I.)** & **-less**. **1.** Continually moving, never in a state of quiet and tranquillity: *restless waves.* **2.** (of persons) **a** Unable to obtain rest; tending to toss about from bodily discomfort; fidgety; *a restless night*, one during which one is restless; **b** disturbed, anxious in mind, unable to concentrate the mind, unsettled in purpose.

restlessly, adv. Prec. & **-ly**. In a restless manner.

restlessness, n. See prec. & **-ness**. State or quality of being restless.

restock, vb. trans. [1. rēstók; 2. rīstók]. **re-** & **stock (II.)**. To supply with fresh stock.

restorable, adj. [1. restórabl; 2. ristórəbl]. **restore** & **-able**. Capable of being restored.

restoration, n. [1. restoráshun; 2. restəréiʃən]. Earlier *restauration*, fr. Lat. *restaurātiōn-(em)*, 'restoration', fr. *restaurāre*, 'to restore'. See **restore**, to wh. modern spelling has been assimilated. **1.** Act of restoring; state of being restored. **2.** Specif., *the Restoration*; a return of Charles II. to his kingdom in 1660; **b** period following this event. **3. a** Act of bringing something which has become ruinous, dilapidated, worn, to approximately its original condition, by partial reconstruction and renovation &c.: *the restoration of ancient buildings, works of art* &c.; **b** an object thus reconstructed and renovated.

restorationism, n. [1. restoráshunizm; 2. restəréiʃənizəm]. Prec. & **-ism**. Doctrine of ultimate readmittance of every soul to happiness and divine favour.

restorationist, n. [1. restoráshunist; 2. restəréiʃənist]. **restoration** & **.-ist**. Adherent of the doctrine of restorationism.

restorative, adj. & n. [1. restórativ; 2. ristórətiv], fr. O. Fr. *restoratif*, fr. Lat. *restaurāt-(um)*, P.P. type of *restaurāre*, 'to restore, refresh'. See **restore** & **-ive**. **1.** adj. Having the property of restoring strength, bringing back lost vigour, consciousness &c.: nourishing, stimulating. **2.** n. Restorative food, drug &c.

restoratively, adv. Prec. & **-ly**. As a restorative.

restore, vb. trans. [1. restór; 2. ristó]. O. Fr. *restore*, fr. Lat. *restaurāre*, 'to repair, rebuild, renew'; **re-** & cp. Lat. *instaurāre*, 'to renew', fr. Low Lat. *staurum*, 'store'; cp. Gk. *staurós*, 'stake, pole'. See **stauroscope** & **steer (I.)** & words there referred to. **1.** To bring back to its former place, position, something which has faded, disappeared, been lost &c.: *to restore the colour to a person's face, and brightness to his eyes*; *to restore a book to its place in a shelf.* **2. a** To place (a person) once more in the position, rank &c., which he formerly held; to reinstate: *after his acquittal by court-martial, the captain was restored to his rank and honours*; **b** specif., to recall a dethroned monarch to his kingdom and royal power: *Charles II. was restored soon after Cromwell's death.* **3.** To call (a system, institution, practice, custom &c.) which has been temporarily discontinued, back again into active existence, usage; to reintroduce: *to restore a monarchy*; *to restore the good old ceremonies at Christmas.* **4.** To give back, make restitution of (a thing &c. to a person), cause (thing &c.) to pass again into his possession, put him again in possession of something formerly owned or enjoyed: *to restore money to him from whom it was stolen*; '*Restore my vanished mistress to my arms*'; *who can restore the lost years of our youth?* **5.** To bring back to its former condition; to reconstruct, renovate; repair, make good, the dilapidation, decay of: *to restore an old castle, a church, a faded picture* &c.; specif., *to restore a text*, make conjectural emendations of corrupt passages.

restorer, n. [1. restórer; 2. ristórə]. Prec. & **-er**. One who restores (esp. in sense **5**).

restrain, vb. trans. [1. restrán; 2. ristréin]. M.E. *restrei(g)ne*, fr. O. Fr. *restraign-*, Pres. Part. stem of *restraindre*, 'to restrain', fr. Lat. *restringere*, 'to bind back, tighten, restrict', fr. **re-** & *stringere*, 'to tie', see **stringent**. **1. a** To hold back, control, check, keep within proper limits, keep under: *to restrain one's temper*; **b** to prevent, hold back, from doing something: *to restrain a man from wasting his property.* **2.** Specif., to put, keep, under legal restraint; to incarcerate, put in an asylum: *mad people have to be restrained.*

re-strain, vb. trans. [1. rēstrán; 2. rīstréin]. **re-** & **strain (I.)**. To strain again.

restrainable, adj. [1. restránabl; 2. ristréinəbl]. **restrain** & **-able**. Capable of being restrained.

restrained, adj. [1. restránd; 2. ristréind], fr. P.P. of **restrain**. **1.** (of persons) Exhibiting restraint (**1, a**). **2.** (of modes of expression, esp. in art and literature) Executed with restraint (**1, b**); reverse of *flamboyant, exuberant, extravagant*: *his work was very austere and restrained.*

restrainedly, adv. [1. restránedli; 2. ristréinidli]. Prec. & **-ly**. With restraint, with moderation.

restraining, adj. [1. restráning; 2. ristréiniŋ], fr. Pres. Part. of **restrain**. Tending to, having the power to, restrain: *a restraining hand, influence* &c.

restraint, n. [1. restránt; 2. ristréint]. O. Fr. *restrainte*, P.P. of *restraindre*. See **restrain**. **1.** Act or process of restraining; **a** control, discipline, reining in, of one's emotions and passions; moderation: *the wise man exercises restraint in his behaviour and enjoyments*; specif. **b** that moderation, reticence, and judicious control of emotion which prevents excess and undue exuberance of expression: *a work of art should show just the right amount of restraint.* **2.** State of being restrained, condition of being under control; curtailment of complete liberty of action. Phr. (*to put*) *under restraint*, incarcerate, confine in lunatic asylum. **3.** Circumstance, state of affairs which imposes restraint, which limits, hampers one in, incapacitates one from, action; a curb, restriction: *the restraints of illness, poverty.* Phr. *without restraint*, freely.

restrict, vb. trans. [1. restríkt; 2. ristríkt], fr. Lat. *restrict-(um)*, P.P. type of *restringere*, 'to bind back'. See **restrain**, & cp. **strict**. To keep within, impose limits upon; to bound, confine, control by limitations: *to restrict one's activities, sphere of influence, freedom* &c.

restricted, adj. [1. restríkted; 2. ristríktid], fr. P.P. of prec. Limited, circumscribed, not far-reaching: *a restricted application, significance.*

restrictedly, adv. [1. restríktedli; 2. ristríktidli]. Prec. & **-ly**. In a restricted manner.

restriction, n. [1. restríkshun; 2. ristríkʃən], fr. Lat. *restrictiōn-(em)*, 'limitation', fr. *restrict-(um)*, P.P. type of *restringere*, 'to bind back', see **restrain**, & **-ion**. **1. a** Act of restricting; **b** fact of being restricted. **2.** Circumstance, condition, which restricts; limitation: *the restrictions of space*; *restrictions imposed by law.* **3.** Reserve, qualification: *a mental restriction.*

restrictive, adj. [1. restríktiv; 2. ristríktiv]. **restrict** & **-ive**. Tending, serving, to restrict; restraining.

restrictively, adv. Prec. & **-ly**. So as to restrict.

restuff, vb. trans. [1. rēstúf; 2. rīstáf]. **re-** & **stuff (III.)**. To stuff afresh.

result (I.), vb. intrans. [1. rezúlt; 2. rizált], fr. Lat. *result-(āre)*, 'to leap back; to resound', fr. **re-** & *saltāre*, 'to dance, bound'. See **saltant** & **salient**. **1.** (archaic and poet.) To spring up, grow: '*The golden grain resulting from the ground*' (Pope, 'Iliad', xiii.). **2.** To happen, follow, as actual, natural, or logical consequence; to arise from a cause, be the outcome of an action &c.: *nothing has resulted from my efforts*; *from what you say, it results that we have failed.* **3.** *Result in*, to have as natural effect or outcome, to develop naturally or logically into, produce as consequence, end in specific manner: *the defeat resulted in the overthrow of the monarchy*; *his efforts resulted in failure.*

result (II.), n., fr. prec. **1.** That which ensues as consequence of an action, or process, from conditions, causes, circumstances &c.; outcome, effect, conclusion: *the result was beyond expectation*; *what kind of results can you* *expect from such folly?*; *the result was that he had a fit*; *without result*, in vain, fruitlessly. **2.** Completed calculation, computed answer, quantity &c. obtained by calculation.

resultant, adj. & n. [1. rezúltant; 2. rizáltənt]. **result** & **-ant**. **1.** adj. Arising as a result; resulting, consequent, esp. as outcome of effect of two or more different forces in combination. **2.** n. **a** That which results; **b** (mechan.) a resultant force.

resultful, adj. [1. rezúltfool; 2. rizáltful]. **result** & **-ful**. Producing result(s), effective.

resultless, adj. [1. rezúltles; 2. rizáltlis]. **result** & **-less**. Without result.

resume, vb. trans. & intrans. [1. rezū́m; 2. rizjū́m], fr. Lat. *resūm-(ere)*, 'to take up again, take back', fr. **re-** & *sūmere*, 'to take up'; see second element in **consume**. **A.** trans. **1.** To take, assume, again, reoccupy, become once more possessed of: *to resume one's liberty, health*; *to resume dominion, command* &c. **2.** To continue (an action) after interruption, cessation &c.; begin again, go on with: *to resume work, a story, meal* &c. **3.** To summarize, sum up, recapitulate. **B.** intrans. (esp. of speaker) To continue, go on again after temporary pause, interruption &c.: *well, to resume* . . .

résumé, n. [1. rázūmā; 2. rézjumei]. Fr., fr. P.P. of *résumer*, 'to resume'. See **resume**. Summary, abstract.

resummons, n. [1. rēsúmunz; 2. rīsámənz]. **re-** & **summons**. Repeated summons.

resumption, n. [1. rezúmpshun; 2. rizámpʃən], fr. Lat. *resumptiōn-(em)*, 'recovery', fr. *resumpt-(um)*, P.P. type of *resūmere*, 'to take up again', see **resume**, & **-ion**. Act of resuming.

resumptive, adj. [1. rezúmptiv; 2. rizámptiv]. See prec. & **-ive**. Resuming, summarizing.

resupinate, adj. [1. resū́pinat; 2. risjū́pinət], fr. Lat. *resupīnāt-(um)*, P.P. type of *resupīnāre*, 'to bend back', fr. **re-** & *supīnāre*, 'to place on the back', fr. *supīn-(us)*, 'on the back, backward'. See **supine**. (bot., of flower, leaf &c.) Upside-down, inverted.

resupination, n. [1. resūpináshun; 2. risjūpinéiʃən]. Prec. & **-ion**. (bot.) Inverted position.

resurge, vb. intrans. [1. resérj; 2. risə́dž], fr. Lat. *resurg-(ere)*, 'to rise again', fr. **re-** & *surgere*, 'to rise'. See **surge (I.)**. (rare) To rise up anew, rise again, revive.

resurgence, n. [1. resérjens; 2. risə́džəns]. Next word & **-ce**. Revival, renewal, fresh uprising.

resurgent, adj. [1. resérjent; 2. risə́džənt]. **resurge** & **-ent**. Renewed, reviving: *resurgent hopes*.

resurrect, vb. trans. & intrans. [1. rèzurékt; 2. rèzərékt]. Back-formation fr. **resurrection**. **A.** trans. (colloq.) **1. a** To raise from the dead, restore to life; **b** to exhume, disinter. **2.** To bring back into practice, vogue, use &c.: *to resurrect an obsolete custom, last year's hat*. **B.** intrans. To rise from the dead, come back to life.

resurrection, n. [1. rezurékshun; 2. rezərékʃən], fr. Lat. *resurrectiōn-(em)*, 'rising from the dead', fr. *resurrect-(um)*, P.P. type of *resurgere*, 'to rise again', see **resurge**, & **-ion**. **1. a** Specif., *the Resurrection*, the rising of Christ from the grave; **b** festival commemorating this. **2.** (cap.) The rising of the human race from the dead at the last day. **3.** Act or process of reviving, and bringing, or coming, again into existence, activity, or use; state of being revived; resuscitation, renewal: *the resurrection of one's hopes*; *nature's resurrection in the spring*; (slang) *resurrection pie*, compounded of remnants from previous meals. **4.** Disinterment, exhumation; *resurrection man*, body-snatcher, one who exhumed corpses illegally for sale to schools of anatomy.

resurrectional, adj. [1. rèzurékshunal; 2. rèzərékʃənəl]. Prec. & **-al**. Of, pertaining to, of the nature of, resurrection.

resurrectionism, n. [1. rezurékshunizm; 2. rezərékʃənizəm]. See prec. & **-ism**. The stealing of bodies from graves; body-snatching.

resurrectionist, n. [1. rezurékshunist; 2. rezərékʃənist]. **resurrection** & **-ist**. Body-snatcher.

resurvey (I.), vb. trans. [1. rēsërvā́; 2. rīsəvéi]. **re-** & **survey**. To make a new survey of.

resurvey (II.), n. [1. rēsérvā; 2. rīsə́vei], fr. prec. New or repeated survey.

resuscitate, vb. trans. & intrans. [1. resúsitāt; 2. risásiteit], fr. Lat. *resuscitāt-(um)*, P.P. type of *resuscitāre*, 'to revive', fr. **re-** & *suscitāre*, 'to raise up, erect', fr. **sus-** for *sub-*, & *citāre*, 'to put into action; rouse, call', see **cite**. **1.** trans. **a** To restore to life, consciousness, activity; to revive, revivify, reanimate; **b** to bring back into use; rescue from oblivion. **2.** intrans. To return to life, activity &c.; be reanimated.

resuscitation, n. [1. resùsitáshun; 2. risàsitéiʃən]. Prec. & **-ion**. Act or process of resuscitating; state of being resuscitated; renewal, restoration.

resuscitative, adj. [1. resúsitativ; 2. risásitətiv]. See prec. & **-ive**. Tending to, serving to, resuscitate; revivifying, renewing.

ret, rait, rate, vb. trans. & intrans. [1. ret, rāt; 2. ret, reit]. M.E. *rēten*, 'to soak', cp. Du. *reten, roten*, Swed. *röta*. Cogn. w. **rot**. **1.** trans. To steep, soak, soften by exposure to moisture: *to ret flax* &c. **2.** intrans. (of hay &c.) To rot from moisture.

retable, n. [1. rētàbl; 2. rīteibl], fr. Fr. *rétable*. **re-** & **table**. Shelf, ledge, behind and above an altar, on which are placed the cross, lights, vases.

retail (I.), n. & adv. [1. rḗtāl; 2. rīteil], fr. O. Fr. *retail*, 'piece cut off, fragment', fr. *retaillier*, 'to cut off', fr. **re-** & *taillier*, 'to cut', see **tailor**. **1.** n. Sale of goods in small quantities for the personal use or consumption of purchaser, contrasted with *wholesale*; often attributively: *retail dealer*. **2.** adv. By retail: *to buy retail*.

retail (II.), vb. trans. & intrans. [1. rētā́l; 2. rītéil], fr. prec. **A.** trans. **1.** To sell (goods) in small quantities direct to consumers &c. **2.** To circulate, put about, hand on, repeat (news); esp. *to retail scandal, tittle-tattle, gossip*. **B.** intrans. To be sold by retail.

retailer, n. [1. rētā́ler; 2. rītéilə]. Prec. & **-er**. **a** Retail dealer; **b** one who circulates (gossip &c.).

retain, vb. trans. [1. retā́n; 2. ritéin], fr. O. Fr. *retenir*, 'to retain', fr. Lat. *retinēre*, 'to hold back, hold fast; to check, restrain; to retain, preserve', fr. **re-** & *tenēre*, 'to hold'. See **tenable** & words there referred to. **1.** To hold; to support, keep from falling, escaping: *the cistern retains water*; *the wall retains the bank* &c. **2.** (of material and non-material things) To keep in one's possession, keep control of, maintain in use or practice, preserve: *to retain one's rights, an old custom, a habit*; *to retain one's self-respect, one's patience, presence of mind*; *to retain the affection of one's friends*. **3.** To engage services of, esp. *to retain a barrister*; *retaining fee*, preliminary fee paid to barrister &c. to secure his services if required. **4.** To preserve in one's mind, remember: *to retain facts* &c.

retainable, adj. [1. retā́nabl; 2. ritéinəbl]. Prec. & **-able**. Capable of being retained.

retainer (I.), n. [1. retā́ner; 2. ritéinə], fr. O. Fr. *retenir*, infin. See **retain** & **-er**. (legal) **a** Act by which a client retains services of a barrister; **b** document embodying the engagement; **c** fee paid to a barrister &c. in order to secure his services.

retainer (II.), n. **retain** & **-er**. (hist.) Dependent of, one in service of, person of superior rank.

retaining fee, n. [1. retā́ning fē; 2. ritéiniŋ fī]. Fee paid, esp. to a barrister to secure his services; retainer.

retaining wall, n. One built against a bank of earth to prevent it from collapsing.

retake, vb. trans. [1. rētā́k; 2. rītéik]. **re-** & **take**. To take, capture, again; to take back.

retaliate, vb. trans. & intrans. [1. retáliāt; 2. ritǽlieit], fr. L. Lat. *retāliāt-(um)*, P.P. type of *retāliāre*, 'to retaliate', fr. **re-** & *tāl-(is)*, 'such, similar', q.v. under **talion**. **1.** trans. (rare) To reply to, repay (an injury, insult), by an action or utterance of the same kind; to requite. **2.** intrans. To pay back in kind; to reply to an action or utterance by a similar one; usually said of action taken, or words uttered, in reply to a hostile or unfriendly act or speech: *it is only human to retaliate when one is injured*.

retaliation, n. [1. retàliáshun; 2. ritæ̀liéiʃən]. Prec. & **-ion**. Act of retaliating; reprisal, requital; *law of retaliation*, system of inflicting punishment of the same nature as the offending act.

retaliative, adj. [1. retáliativ; 2. ritǽliətiv]. **retaliate** & **-ive**. Of the nature of retaliation; tending to retaliate, eager for retaliation.

retaliatory, adj. [1. retáliāturi; 2. ritǽlieitəri]. See prec. & **-ory**. Pertaining to, of the nature of, retaliation.

retard (I.), vb. trans. & intrans. [1. retárd; 2. ritā́d], fr. Fr. *retarder*, fr. Lat. *retardāre*, 'to keep back, hinder, delay', fr. **re-** & Lat. *tardus*, 'slow'. See **tardy**. **1.** trans. **a** To reduce speed, check progress of; to hinder, delay, make slow or late: *to retard one's arrival*; *I was retarded by a visitor at the last moment*; **b** to delay, postpone, put off: *his death was probably retarded by some years by the skill of the surgeons*. **2.** intrans. (rare) To delay, be late, be retarded.

retard (II.), n., fr. prec. State of being retarded; retardation, delay: specif., *retard of the tide*, interval between full moon and high water due to it.

retardation, n. [1. rētardáshun; 2. rītādéiʃən]. **retard (I.)** & **-ation**. Act or process of retarding; state of being retarded.

retardative, adj. [1. retárdativ; 2. ritā́dətiv]. See prec. & **-ative**. Tending to retard.

retardatory, adj. [1. retárdaturi; 2. ritā́dətəri], fr. Lat. *retardāt-(um)*, P.P. type of *retardāre*, 'to keep back'. See **retard (I.)** & **-ory**. Of, pertaining to, retardation.

retardment, n. [1. retárdment; 2. ritā́dmənt]. **retard (I.)** & **-ment**. Retardation.

retch, vb. intrans. & n. [1. rēch; 2. rītʃ]. O.E. *hrǣcan*, 'to spit'; cp. O.E. *hrāca*, O.N. *hrāki*, 'phlegm'. **1.** vb. To make an effort to vomit, strain as in vomiting. **2.** n. Act of retching.

retell, vb. trans. [1. rētél; 2. rītél]. **re-** & **tell**. To tell over again, repeat.

retention, n. [1. reténshun; 2. riténʃən], fr. Lat. *retentiōn-(em)*, 'holding back, retention, preservation', fr. *retent-(um)*, P.P. type of *retinēre*, 'to retain', see **retain**, & **-ion**. Act of retaining; state of being retained; specif. (med.) abnormal accumulation of, and failure to get rid of, any secretion: *retention of urine*, inability to discharge it.

retentive, adj. [1. reténtiv; 2. riténtiv], fr. Lat. *retent-(um)*, P.P. type of *retinēre*, 'to hold back'. See **retain** & **-ive**. **1.** (of substance) **a** Having the property of retaining, tending to retain: *retentive of moisture*; specif. **b** retaining moisture. **2.** (of mind, memory) Tenacious, not easily forgetting. **3.** (med.) Serving to keep some organ &c. in place.

retentively, adv. Prec. & **-ly**. In a retentive manner.

retentiveness, n. See prec. & **-ness**. Quality of being retentive.

retiary, adj. & n. [1. rḗshari; 2. rīʃəri], fr. Lat. *rētiāri-(us)*, 'gladiator who tried to entangle his adversary in a net', fr. *rēte*, 'net'; cogn. w. Gk. *erēmos*, 'lonely, apart', see **hermit**; Sert. *ṛté*, 'excluding, except'; O. Slav. *oriti*, 'to dissolve'; Lith. *rětis*, 'sieve'; fr. base *(e)rē-, *(e)rə-, 'loose, thin, easily separable'; cp. further Lat. *rārus*, 'thin, not dense'. See **rare (I.)**. **1.** adj. **a** (obs. and rare) Pertaining to nets, like a net; **b** (of certain spiders) constructing a net. **2.** n. A retiary spider.

reticence, n. [1. rétisens; 2. rétisəns], fr. Lat. *reticentia*, 'silence', fr. *retic-(ēre)*, 'to be silent', fr. **re-** & *tacēre*, 'to be silent', see **tacit**, & **-ence**. Reserve in expression; dislike and avoidance of expressing one's feelings, or of stating what one knows.

reticent, adj. [1. rétisent; 2. rétisənt]. See prec. & **-ent**. Reserved in speech; disinclined to give expression to one's feelings, or to impart information; uncommunicative: *reticent about one's hopes and fears, on what happened.*

reticently, adv. Prec. & **-ly**. In a reticent manner.

reticle, n. [1. rétikl; 2. rétikl], fr. Lat. *rēticulum*, 'small net'. See **reticulum**. Fine network of threads or ruled lines on object-glass of telescope &c., to assist in determining position of object to be observed.

reticular, adj. [1. retíkūlar; 2. ritíkjulə]. See **reticulum** & **-ar**. Of, forming, like, a network.

reticulate, adj. [1. retíkūlat; 2. ritíkjulit] & vb. trans. & intrans. [1. retíkūlāt; 2. ritíkjuleit], vb. formed fr. adj. See **reticulum** & **-ate**. 1. adj. Having form of, forming, a network. 2. vb. a trans. To divide, arrange, in, or as in, a network; to cover with, cause to appear as, a network; b intrans., to be arranged reticulately, form a network.

reticulated, adj. [1. retíkūlāted; 2. ritíkjuleitid]. Prec. & **-ed**. Reticulate.

reticulately, adv. [1. retíkūlatli; 2. ritíkjulətli]. **reticulate** & **-ly**. As though forming, so as to form, a network.

reticulation, n. [1. retìkūlā́shun; 2. ritìkjuléiʃən]. **reticulate** & **-ion**. Network; anything in form of, resembling, a network.

reticule, n. [1. rétikūl; 2. rétikjūl], fr. Fr. *réticule*, fr. Lat. *rēticulum*, 'small net, bag'. See **reticulum**. 1. Reticle. 2. Small bag, originally one of network, but applied to one of any material, used by women for carrying small articles, e.g. handkerchief, purse, scent bottle &c.

reticulose, adj. [1. retíkūlōs; 2. ritíkjulous]. See next word & **-ose**. Forming a network.

reticulum, n. [1. retíkūlum; 2. ritíkjuləm]. Lat. *rēticulum*, 'small net; network bag', fr. *rēti-*, stem of *rēte*, 'net', see **retiary**, & **-cule**. 1. Any network or net-like structure. 2. Second stomach of ruminant, in which the folds of lining membrane form a honeycomb structure.

retiform, adj. [1. rétiform; 2. rítifɔ̄m], fr. Lat. *rēti-*, stem of *rēte*, 'net', see **retiary**, & **-form**. In form of network; reticulate.

retina, n. [1. rétina; 2. rétinə]. Med. Lat., prob. fr. Lat. *rēte*, 'net'. See **retiary**. The sensitive membrane at the back of the eye which receives the impressions of light and communicates them to the brain through the optic nerve, with which the retina is directly connected.

retinal, adj. [1. rétinal; 2. rétinəl]. Prec. & **-al**. Of, pertaining to, the retina.

retinitis, n. [1. rètinítis; 2. rètináitis]. **retina** & **-itis**. Inflammation of the retina.

retinue, n. [1. rétinū; 2. rétinjū], fr. O. Fr. *retenue*, fr. P.P. of *retenir*, 'to retain', see **retain**. Suite, train of attendants, body of retainers.

retire (I.), vb. intrans. & trans. [1. retír; 2. ritáiə], fr. Fr. *retirer*, 'to withdraw' &c. (trans.); **re-** & *tirer*, 'to draw, pull'. Of Gmc. origin, fr. base of **tear** (I.), 'to rend'. A. intrans. 1. To withdraw, go away from a position; a to pass out of sight, withdraw from a company &c.: *to make one's speech, bow, and retire*; b to go to rest, go to bed: *to retire for the night*; *to retire at 11 o'clock.* 2. (mil., of troops) To evacuate a position, retreat: *heavy machine-gun fire caused the enemy to retire*; *to retire in good order.* 3. a To withdraw voluntarily from an office; cease to take an active part in, give up, one's business, profession, usual occupation &c.: *to retire from the army, from the civil service, from the chairmanship of a company* &c.; *professors are now generally compelled to retire at 65*; b to seek quiet and seclusion, withdraw from social activities: *to retire from the world, from the social whirl* &c. Phr. *to retire into oneself*, become a recluse, shun society, become extremely reserved. B. trans. 1. To cause to retire (from office &c.): *it was found necessary to retire several generals who lacked energy and enterprise.* 2. (mil.) To cause to retreat, to withdraw (troops) from a position. 3. (finance) *To retire a bill*, withdraw it from currency.

retire (II.), n., fr. prec. (mil.) Signal on trumpet to troops to retire: *to sound the retire.*

retired, adj. [1. retírd; 2. ritáiəd], fr. P.P. of **retire**. 1. Withdrawn from public view; remote, secluded: *a retired life*; *a retired spot, glade* &c. 2. Having withdrawn from active life, service, profession &c.: *a retired colonel.* 3. a Pertaining to, granted to, one who has retired: *retired pay*, pension; b of, consisting of, those who have retired: *retired list.*

retiredness, n. [1. retírdnes; 2. ritáiədnis]. Prec. & **-ness**. State of being retired; privacy, seclusion.

retirement, n. [1. retírment; 2. ritáiəmənt]. **retire** (I.) & **-ment**. 1. a Act of retiring; retreat, withdrawal; b state of being retired; solitude, privacy, seclusion: *to go into, live in, retirement.* 2. State of having retired from a post, profession.

retiring, adj. [1. retíring; 2. ritáiəriŋ]. **retire** (I.) & **-ing**. 1. (of person, character &c.) Disposed to withdraw from observation; unobtrusive, unassuming, diffident, reserved. 2. (of pay, pension &c.) Given on retirement from public service &c.

retiringly, adv. Prec. & **-ly**. In a retiring manner.

retiringness, n. See prec. & **-ness**. Quality of being retiring; diffidence, reserve.

retort (I.), vb. intrans. & trans. [1. retórt; 2. ritɔ̄t], fr. Lat. *retort-(um)*, P.P. type of *retorquēre*, 'to twist or bend back; to retort', fr. **re-** & *torquēre*, 'to twist'. See **tort, torque**. 1. intrans. a To reply to an argument, criticism, accusation, by making an answering remark of similar kind against him who makes it; give tit for tat; b to reply sharply, and with acerbity. 2. trans. To cast back, return (an accusation, censure &c.); to make a reply of similar nature in answer to criticism, censure &c.

retort (II.), n., fr. prec. a Sharp retaliatory reply, esp. to a criticism, accusation &c.; b a reply, answer: *the retort courteous.*

retort (III.), n., fr. Lat. *retort-(us)*, P.P. of *retorquēre*, 'to twist backwards'. See **retort** (I.). Vessel of glass, earthenware, iron &c., with a long neck bent at a different angle; used in chemical experiments, in distilling, manufacture of gas &c.

retortion, n. [1. retórshun; 2. ritɔ̄ʃən], fr. Lat. *retort-(um)*, P.P. type of *retorquēre*, 'to twist back', see **retort** (I.), & **-ion**. 1. Act of bending or twisting back; state of being bent backwards. 2. (internat. law) Retaliation in kind, practised as a reprisal against another nation.

retouch, vb. trans. [1. rètúch; 2. rìtátʃ]. **re-** & **touch**. To touch up, add finishing touches to (a picture or other work of art, a piece of writing &c.).

retrace, vb. trans. [1. rètrā́s; 2. rìtréis], fr. Fr. *retracer*. See **re-** & **trace** (II.). 1. To go over again; a to go over the same ground again; esp. *to retrace one's steps*, go back again over the same path by which one has come; b to repeat something which has been done or said before: *to retrace the story of man's fall.* 2. To go over again in memory, look back upon, recall to mind: *to retrace the events and experiences of one's youth.*

retract (I.), vb. trans. [1. retrákt; 2. ritrǽkt], fr. Lat. *retract-(um)*, P.P. type of *retrahere*, 'to draw back, withdraw'. See **re-** & **tract** (I.). To draw back, draw in, withdraw: *a cat can retract its claws at pleasure.*

retract (II.), vb. trans. & intrans. As prec. or w. sense fr. Lat. *retractāre*, 'to handle over again; to reconsider and revise; to refuse, decline, be reluctant; withdraw', freq. of *retrahere*. See prec. 1. trans. To take back, withdraw, disavow (a statement, promise &c.). 2. intrans. To withdraw an opinion, statement &c.; to recant.

retractable, adj. [1. retráktabl; 2. ritrǽktəbl]. 1. **retract** (I.) & **-able**. Capable of being drawn in, retracted; retractile. 2. **retract** (II.) & **-able**. Capable of being withdrawn.

retractation, n. [1. rētraktā́shun; 2. rìtræktéiʃən]. **retract** (II.) & **-ation**. Act of retracting, withdrawing, disavowing (statement, accusation &c.); a recantation.

retractile, adj. [1. rētráktīl; 2. rītrǽktail]. **retract** (I.) & **-ile**. Capable of being drawn back or inwards: *a cat's claws are retractile.*

retractility, n. [1. rètraktíliti; 2. rìtræktíliti]. Prec. & **-ity**. Quality of being retractile.

retraction, n. [1. retrákshun; 2. ritrǽkʃən], fr. Lat. *retractiōn-(em)*, 'a drawing back', fr. *retract-(um)*, P.P. type of *retrahere*, 'to draw back', see **retract** (I.), & **-ion**. 1. Act of retracting, drawing backwards or inwards; state of being retracted; opposed to *protrusion.* 2. (sense derived fr. **retract** (II.)) Act of withdrawing (a charge, statement &c.), recantation, retractation.

retractive, adj. [1. retráktiv; 2. ritrǽktiv]. **retract** (I.) & **-ive**. Capable of retracting; tending to retract.

retractor, n. [1. retráktur; 2. ritrǽktə]. **retract** (I.) & **-or**. 1. (anat. and zool.) Muscle which retracts a limb. 2. (med.) Instrument for drawing or holding back edges of wound &c.

retral, adj. [1. rētral; 2. rítrəl]. **retro-** & **-al**. Situated at or towards the back; backward.

retranslate, vb. trans. [1. rètrahnzlā́t; 2. rìtrānzléit]. **re-** & **translate**. To translate over again; a to translate back into original language or into a different language; b to make a new and different translation (into the same language).

retread, vb. trans. [1. rètréd; 2. rìtréd]. **re-** & **tread** (I.). To tread, walk, over or along again: *to retread a path* &c.

re-tread, vb. trans. [1. rē tréd; 2. rì tréd]. **re-** & **tread** (II.) To put a new tread on (tire &c.).

retreat (I.), vb. intrans. & trans. [1. retrḗt; 2. ritrít], fr. O. Fr. *retraiter*, fr. n., fr. Lat. *retract-(um)*. See **retract** (I.). A. intrans. 1. a To go back, withdraw, move away or backwards: *they watched his retreating figure*; esp. b (of troops) to retire, withdraw, move back, after advance and as result of threatened or actual attack, danger, defeat &c. 2. (fig.) To give up, withdraw from, a controversy, one's standpoint in an argument &c. B. trans. (chess) To move (a piece) backwards.

retreat (II.), n., fr. O. Fr. *retrait*, fr. P.P. of *retraire*, 'to retreat'. See prec. 1. Act of retreating, withdrawal, retirement; specif., of naval or military force &c. before enemy &c.: *the retreat from Mons.* 2. Signal to retreat, given to troops by drum, trumpet &c.: *to sound, beat, a retreat*; Phr. *to beat a retreat*, withdraw, retire, run away. 3. a Place of retirement; place to which one withdraws for safety, quiet, privacy, recreation: *a country retreat*; b (poet.) a quiet, sheltered, secluded spot in woodland or moorland country: '*The mossy fountains, and the green retreats*' (Pope, Second Pastoral, 72). 4. Temporary retirement, seclusion, esp. in a religious institution, for purposes of devotion and spiritual refreshment: *to go into retreat.*

retrench, vb. trans. & intrans. [1. retrénsh; 2. ritrénʃ], fr. O. Fr. *retrencher*. **re-** & **trench** (I.). 1. trans. To cut down, diminish amount of; a specif., to reduce expenditure; b to shorten, abridge, cut out: *several passages of the book might be retrenched.* 2. intrans. To practise retrenchment of expenses; to economize.

retrenchment, n. [1. retrénchment; 2. ritréntʃmənt]. Prec. & **-ment**. Act of retrenching; esp. act of cutting down expenses; economy.

retrial, n. [1. rètríal; 2. rītráiəl]. **re-** & **trial**. Act of trying over again in a court of law; a fresh trial.

retribution, n. [1. rètribúshun; 2. rètribjúʃən], fr. Lat. *retribūtiōn-(em)*, 'repayment', fr. *rĕtribūt-(um)*, P.P. type of *retribuere*, 'to repay, restore', fr. **re-** & *tribuere*, 'to allot, grant'. See **tribute**. **1.** Punishment which follows upon, or is inflicted for, wickedness or folly; Nemesis, requital. **2.** Penalty exacted for an injury; reprisal; satisfaction.

retributive, adj. [1. retríbūtiv; 2. ritríbjutiv]. See prec. & **-ive**. Occurring as, inflicted by way of, retribution.

retributively, adv. Prec. & **-ly**. By way of retribution.

retrievable, adj. [1. retrévabl; 2. ritrívəbl]. **retrieve** & **-able**. Capable of being retrieved.

retrieval, n. [1. retrévl; 2. ritrívl]. **retrieve** & **-al**. Act of retrieving.

retrieve (I.), vb. trans. & intrans. [1. retrév; 2. ritrív], fr. O. Fr. *retreuver, retrover, retrouver*, fr. **re-** & *trover*, 'to compose verse &c.; to invent, devise; to find'. See under **trover**. **A.** trans. **1.** (of dogs) To discover and bring in (game that has been shot). **2.** To regain something which has been mislaid or lost; to collect, pick up, take possession of: *to retrieve a book left at a friend's house.* **3.** To make good, repair, restore to former good condition; **a** *to retrieve one's fortunes*; **b** to rehabilitate, re-establish: *to retrieve one's character.* **4.** To atone, make amends for: *to retrieve one's errors.* **5.** To wean, rescue (from error, misfortune &c.): *to retrieve a person from bad ways, from ruin* &c. **B.** intrans. (of dogs) To retrieve game.

retrieve (II.), n. See prec. (archaic) Recovery; only in Phr. *beyond, past, retrieve.*

retriever, n. [1. retréver; 2. ritrívə]. **retrieve** (I.) & **-er**. One who, that which, retrieves; specif., dog trained to retrieve game; esp. of special breed with black or brown curly or wavy coat, allied to the setter and spaniel.

retrim, vb. trans. [1. rètrím; 2. rītrím]. **re-** & **trim**. **1.** To clean and put in order for relighting: *to retrim a lamp.* **2.** To put fresh or different trimming upon (a hat, garment).

retro-, pref. Lat. *retrō*, 'backwards, at the back, behind', fr. **re-** & *-trō*, on anal. of **intro-**. **1.** Backwards, in reverse direction; in return: *retroflexed, retroact, retrograde* &c. **2.** Behind, situated at the back: *retrocardiac*, behind the heart; *retrochoir* &c.

retroact, vb. intrans. [1. rètrōákt; 2. rītrouǽkt]. **retro-** & **act**. **1.** To act in a backward, opposite, direction. **2.** To act retrospectively, take effect on, have application to, past actions, circumstances &c.

retroaction, n. [1. rètrōákshun; 2. rītrouǽkʃən]. Prec. & **-ion**. **1.** Action in a backward or opposite direction, reverse action. **2.** Retrospective effect.

retroactive, adj. [1. rètrōáktiv; 2. rītrouǽktiv]. **retroact** & **-ive**. Tending to retroact; retrospective.

retroactively, adv. Prec. & **-ly**. In a retroactive manner.

retroactivity, n. [1. rètrōaktíviti; 2. rītrouæktíviti]. **retro-** & **activity**. Condition of being retroactive.

retrocede (I.), vb. trans. [1. rètrōséd; 2. rītrousíd]. **retro-** & **cede**. To give, cede (territory), back again; to restore after cession: *to retrocede territory* &c.

retrocede (II.), vb. intrans. [1. rétrōsēd; 2. rítrousīd], fr. Lat. *retrōcēdere*, 'to move back', fr. **retro-** & *cēdere*, 'to go back, retire'. See **cede**. **1.** To move back, move in reverse direction, recede, draw back. **2.** (med., of disease &c.) To pass, be transferred, to inner part of body; to strike inwards.

retrocedence, n. [1. rètrōsédens; 2. rītrousídəns]. Prec. & **-ence**. Act or process of retroceding.

retrocedent, adj. [1. rètrōsédent; 2. rītrousídənt]. **retrocede** (II.) & **-ent**. Tending to retrocede.

retrocession (I.), n. [1. rètrōséshun; 2. rītrouséʃən]. **retro-** & **cession**. The act of yielding, ceding, granting, back; state of being retroceded.

retrocession (II.), n., fr. Lat. *retrōcessiōn-(em)*, 'act of retiring', fr. *retrōcess-(um)*, P.P. type of *retrōcēdere*, 'to move back'. See **retrocede** (II.). **1.** Act of retroceding; movement backwards, movement in reverse direction. **2.** (med., of disease &c.) Process of striking inwards.

retrocessive, adj. [1. rètrōsésiv; 2. rītrousésiv], fr. Lat. *retrōcess-(um)*, P.P. type of *retrōcēdere*, 'to move back', see **retrocede** (II.), & **-ive**. **1.** Tending to move in backward direction. **2.** (med.) Tending to strike inwards, to affect inner part of body.

retrochoir, n. [1. rétrōkwīr; 2. rítroukwaiə]. **retro-** & **choir**. Space in a church behind high altar.

retroflected, adj. [1. rètrōflékted; 2. rītroufléktid], fr. Lat. *retrōflect-(ere)*, 'to bend back', fr. **retro-** & *flectere*, 'to bend', see **flex** (I.), & **-ed**. Bent or turned backwards, reflexed.

retroflex, adj. [1. rétrōfleks; 2. rítroufleks], fr. Lat. *retrōflex-(um)*, P.P. type of *retrōflectere*, 'to bend back'. See prec. Retroflected.

retroflexed, adj. [1. rétrōflekst; 2. rítrouflekst]. Prec. & **-ed**. Retroflected.

retroflexion, n. [1. rètrōflékshun; 2. rītroufléкʃən]. **retroflex** & **-ion**. State of being retroflex.

retrogradation, n. [1. rètrōgradáshun; 2. rètrougrædéiʃən], fr. L. Lat. *retrōgradātiōn-(em)*, 'a going back'. See **retro-** & **gradation**. **1.** Backward movement, movement in reverse direction, retrogression. **2.** Deterioration, decline in quality, retrograde development. **3.** (astron.) Apparent westward movement of planet &c. among fixed stars.

retrograde (I.), adj. [1. rétrogrăd; 2. rétrəgreid], fr. Lat. *retrōgrad-(us)*, 'going back'. See **retro-** & **grade**. **1. a** Moving, going, backwards, or in reverse direction: *a retrograde movement*; **b** (zool.) normally moving backwards, instead of, or as well as, forwards. **2.** Returning, tending to return, to a more primitive, simpler, less advanced, less highly organized stage of physical, intellectual, or moral development.

retrograde (II.), vb. intrans. See prec. **1.** To move backwards, in reverse direction. **2.** To deteriorate; go back to less advanced stage of physical, intellectual, or moral development; to degenerate. **3.** (astron., of planet &c.) To move apparently from east to west.

retrogress, vb. intrans. [1. rètrogrés; 2. rītrougrés], fr. Lat. *retrōgress-(um)*, P.P. type of *retrōgradi*, 'to go backwards'. See **retro-** & **grade**. **1.** To move backwards or downwards. **2.** To decline, deteriorate.

retrogression, n. [1. rètrogréshun; 2. rītrougréʃən]. Prec. & **-ion**. **1.** Backward motion; movement in reverse direction. **2.** Backward tendency in development; deterioration. **3.** (astron.) Retrogradation.

retrogressive, adj. [1. rètrogrésiv; 2. rītrəgrésiv]. See prec. & **-ive**. **1.** Moving backwards, retrograde. **2.** Tending to decline, deteriorate; having a backward tendency towards an inferior stage of development.

retrogressively, adv. Prec. & **-ly**. In a retrogressive manner.

retropulsion, n. [1. rètropúlshun; 2. rītrəpálʃən], fr. **retro-** & Lat. *puls-(um)*, P.P. type of *pellere*, 'to beat, drive', see **pulse** (I.) & **-ion**. **1.** Act of pushing or forcing backwards; state of being forced backwards; opposite of *propulsion.* **2.** (med.) Tendency of disease to extend from external to internal part of body.

retrorse, adj. [1. retrórs; 2. ritrós], fr. Lat. *retrōrs-(us)*, 'turned back', contracted fr. *retrōversus*. See **retro-** & **version**. (zool., bot.) Turned backwards or downwards.

retrorsely, adv. Prec. & **-ly**. In a retrorse direction.

retrospect, n. [1. ré-, rétrospekt; 2. rí-, rétrəspekt], fr. Lat. *retrōspect-(um)*, P.P. type of *retrōspicere*, 'to look back', fr. **retro-** & *specere*, 'to look', see **species**. A looking backward in memory; a contemplation of past events and experiences; a mental review or survey of the past.

retrospection, n. [1. rè-, rètrospékshun; 2. rī-, rètrəspékʃən]. Prec. & **-ion**. Act or power of recalling past events &c., contemplation of the past: *to indulge in retrospection.*

retrospective, adj. [1. rē-, rètrospéktiv; 2. rī-, rètrəspéktiv]. **retrospect** & **-ive**. **1.** Looking back upon, surveying, the past. **2.** (law) Having effect on, applying to, past action and events; referring to the past; retroactive.

retrospectively, adv. Prec. & **-ly**. In a retrospective manner.

retroussé, adj. [1. retrōōsā; 2. rətrúsei]. Fr., P.P. of *retrousser*, 'to turn up, tuck up', fr. **re-** & *trousser*, 'to pack up, fasten or heap together'. See **truss**. (of nose) Turned-up.

retroversion, n. [1. rētrovérshun; 2. rītrəvə́ʃən], fr. Lat. *retrōvers-(um)*, 'turned back'. See **retro-** & **version** & cp. **retrorse**. Act of retroverting, state of being retroverted; specif. (med.) *retroversion of the uterus*, backward displacement.

retrovert (I.), vb. trans. [1. rètrovért; 2. rītrəvə́t], fr. **retro-** & Lat. *vertere*, 'to turn', see **version**. **1.** To turn, bend, backwards; esp. P.P. *retroverted* (med., of uterus), displaced.

retrovert (II.), n., fr. prec. Person who is reconverted to his original religious belief.

retry, vb. trans. [1. rètrí; 2. rītrái]. **re-** & **try** (I.). Try (person or cause) judicially, over again.

rettery, n. [1. réteri; 2. rétəri]. **ret** & **-ery**. Establishment for retting flax &c.

retting, n. [1. réting; 2. rétiŋ]. **ret** & **-ing**. Process of steeping or retting flax &c.

returf, vb. trans. [1. rètérf; 2. rītə́f]. **re-** & **turf**. To lay fresh turf upon.

return (I.), vb. intrans. & trans. [1. retérn; 2. ritə́n], fr. O. Fr. *returner*. **re-** & **turn**. **A.** intrans. **1. a** To come or go back to starting-point, to place of departure, abode, or origin: *he left home early this morning and has not yet returned*; *to return in triumph*; *he will go by the cliffs and return along the shore*; **b** to pass, go back, revert, to former condition, habits &c.: *to return to a state of nature*; *the body shall return to dust*; *to return to the old way* &c. **2.** (of condition, emotion &c.) To come back, reappear, be renewed, manifest itself once more: *the longing, pain, fever &c. returned*; *the bad weather has returned.* **3.** To pass back into possession of, be transferred naturally, revert to: *the property will return to the other branch of the family.* **4.** To recur, hark back to, go back again to use, consider, treat of: *I now return to my former plan, line of argument*; *please return to the point.* **B.** trans. **1. a** To give, send, convey, hand, back; to restore to former owner &c.: *to return a book, a lost dog* &c.; *in case of non-delivery, return to the sender*; Phr. *to return a ball* (in tennis &c.), hit it back to opponent; **b** to put back, restore to former place or position: *to return a sword to its sheath.* **2. a** To give something as corresponding, equivalent, to, or of same nature as, that which one has received: *to return a kindness, hospitality, a blow* &c.; *to return the compliment*; *to return good for evil*; *to return a bow*, bow to person who bows to one; **b** to be responsive to, reciprocate: *to return another's affection*; **c** to give, send, utter, in reponse to something given, said &c.: *to return an answer*; *to return thanks.* **3.** (cards) *To return a lead*, lead from a suit already led by one's partner. **4.** To yield, produce as profit: *an investment which returns a good interest.* **5.** To render an account of, make a return of, report on, officially or formally: *to return a list of casualties*; *to return a soldier as killed*, report him killed.

6. To elect, make formal choice of, give majority of votes to: *to return a member to Parliament.*

return (**II.**), n., fr. prec. **1.** Act or process of returning; a coming or going back to place of starting or of origin: *to await one's return*; *a return home.* Phr. (*to answer a letter* &c.) *by return* (*of post*), by next post out. **2.** (attrib.) *Return journey, cargo* &c.; *return ticket*, also *return*, entitling traveller to go and return by given route; *return valve*, allowing liquid to flow back again in case of overflow. **3.** Act of returning; **a** act of restoring, sending, bringing back (thing) to owner: *I must request the return of the books I lent you*; **b** act of putting back in, of restoring to, former or rightful place or position: *I insist on the return of books to the shelves.* **4.** Reappearance, recurrence, repetition, renewal: *a return of the pain, symptoms* &c.; *the return of spring*; *many happy returns of the day*, as greeting on birthday &c. **5.** Requital, repayment; equivalent of something given or act performed, by another; recompense, compensation: *a poor return for your kindness*; *in return*, as repayment, as an equivalent: *nothing but ingratitude and blame in return for all one's trouble.* **6.** Profit, increase; proceeds of enterprise; interest from an investment &c.: *a good return on one's capital*; *small profits and quick returns.* **7.** Formal, official report, statement: *a return of all expenses incurred.* **8.** (archit.) Part of surface of building, moulding &c., forming an angle with main or adjoining surface. **9.** (tennis &c.) Act or manner of returning ball to opponent. **10.** (pl.) A kind of mild tobacco.

returnable, adj. [1. retérnabl; 2. ritánəbl]. **return** (**I.**) & **-able.** **1.** Capable of being returned; to be returned. **2.** (of writ &c.) Capable of being, to be, returned or delivered.

returned, adj. [1. retérnd; 2. ritánd], fr. P.P. of **return** (**I.**) **1.** Having returned: *a returned traveller, soldier* &c. **2.** Sent back to original sender: *returned letters*; *returned empties*, crates, packing-cases &c., sent back by consignee &c.

returning officer, n. [1. retérning ófiser; 2. ritániŋ ɔ́fisə]. Official presiding over and reporting on election &c.

returnless, adj. [1. retérnles; 2. ritánlis]. **return** (**II.**) & **-less.** Yielding no returns.

retuse, adj. [1. retū́s; 2. ritjū́s], fr. Lat. *re-tūs-(um)*, P.P. type of *retundere*, 'to beat down, blunt', fr. **re-** & *tundere*, 'to beat'; cp. Lat. *tudes*, 'hammer'; Scrt. *tundatē*, 'strikes'; O.E. *stunt*, 'dull, stupid'; *styntan*, 'to stupefy', see **stint.** (bot., zool. &c.) Having a rounded end with a slight depression at the centre.

reunion, n. [1. rēū́nyun; 2. rijū́njən], fr. Fr. *réunion.* **re-** & **union.** **1.** Act of reuniting; **a** act of bringing, coming together again after separation: *the reunion of a family*; **b** act or state of being in, coming into, agreement, harmony, friendly relations after differences, quarrels &c.: *the reunion of hearts, of former enemies* &c.; **c** *reunion of the Churches*, a reuniting of the various branches of Christianity separated by doctrinal and other differences. **2.** Social gathering, assembly, esp. of former associates: *a family reunion*; *a reunion of old Wykehamists* &c.

reunionism, n. [1. rēū́nyunizm; 2. rijū́njən-izəm]. Prec. & **-ism.** Policy of reunionist.

reunionist, n. [1. rēū́nyunist; 2. rijū́njənist]. **reunion** & **-ist.** Person advocating reunion of the branches of the Christian Church.

reunite, vb. trans. & intrans. [1. rèūnít; 2. rijūnáit]. **re-** & **unite.** **1.** trans. To bring together again, unite afresh, restore unity of. **2.** intrans. To join or come together again, become united again, whether by meeting again in the flesh, or by spiritual concord.

revaccinate, vb. trans. [1. rèváksināt; 2. rivǽksineit]. **re-** & **vaccinate.** To vaccinate a second time or again.

revalenta, n. [1. revalénta; 2. revəléntə]. Earlier *ervalenta*, fr. Lat. *erv-(um)*, 'vetch'; Gk. *órobos*, 'kind of pea'; O.H.G. *araweiz*, Mod. Germ. *erbse*, 'pea'; the second element is fr. Lat. *lent-*, stem of *lens*, 'lentil', see **lens.** Farinaceous food made from lentil-meal &c.

reveal (**I.**), vb. trans. [1. revḗl; 2. rivíəl], fr. Lat. *revēl-(āre)*, 'to uncover, disclose', fr. **re-** & *vēl-(um)*, 'veil'. See **velum** & cp. **veil.** **1.** To disclose, make visible, exhibit to the sight (what was formerly hidden): *daylight revealed a strange scene*; *he turned so that his face was revealed*; *the telescope reveals many distant stars to our sight.* **2. a** To disclose something not previously known; to divulge, betray: *to reveal a secret*; *to reveal one's identity*; **b** to explain, make intelligible: *to reveal a mystery.* **3.** (esp. of God) To make known, communicate (knowledge), make manifest, by supernatural agency: *God reveals the truths of religion through the inspired writings of the prophets and saints*; *revealed religion*, that taught by divine revelation.

reveal (**II.**), n., fr. prec. (archit.) Side of an opening of a window or door, between the surface of the wall and the window, or door frame.

revealable, adj. [1. revḗlabl; 2. rivíləbl]. **reveal** (**I.**) & **-able.** Capable of being revealed.

reveille, n. [1. revéli; 2. rəvéli]. Fr., imperat. of *réveiller*, 'to awake'; fr. **re-** & Lat. *vigilāre*, 'to watch', see **vigil.** (nav. and mil.) Signal sounded by bugle at sunrise.

revel (**I.**), vb. intrans. & trans. [1. révl; 2. révl], fr. O. Fr. *reveler*, 'to make an uproar', fr. Lat. *rebellāre*, 'to revolt', see **rebel** (**II.**). **A.** intrans. **1.** To engage in merrymaking; to feast, carouse. **2. a** To indulge freely in, take part in, enjoy, without restraint: *to revel in excess of every kind*; **b** to take great delight in, enjoy thoroughly: *to revel in the beauties of the country.* **B.** trans. (very rare) To spend in, devote to, revelry: *to revel one's time away.*

revel (**II.**), n., fr. prec. **a** Merrymaking, festivity; jollification, carousal; **b** (in pl.) rejoicing accompanied by organized entertainment, mumming, sports &c.: *let the revels begin.*

revelation, n. [1. rèveláshun; 2. rèviléiʃən], fr. Lat. *revēlātiōn-(em)*, 'an uncovering; revelation', fr. *revēl-(āre)*, 'to disclose', see **reveal**, & **-ation.** **1.** Act, process, of revealing: *God taught man in the past by direct revelation.* **2. a** Knowledge revealed direct by divine action; revealed religion: *we cannot question the teachings of revelation*; **b** a fact or experience which is new and comes as a surprise or an illumination: *it is a revelation to hear for the first time a great virtuoso play the violin*; *it was quite a revelation to me to learn what incomes are sometimes made at the Bar.* **3.** A disclosure; a making public of something hitherto kept hidden and secret: *strange revelations are expected during the trial.* **4.** The last book of the Scriptures —*the Revelation of St. John the Divine*; also called *Revelations.*

revelational, adj. [1. rèveláshunal; 2. rèviléiʃənəl]. Prec. & **-al.** Of, pertaining to, revelation.

revelationist, n. [1. rèveláshunist; 2. rèviléiʃənist]. **revelation** & **-ist.** **a** Person who believes in divine revelation; specif. **b** *The Revelationist*, author of the *Book of the Revelation.*

reveller, n. [1. réveler; 2. révələ]. **revel** (**I.**) & **-er.** Person taking part in a revel; a roisterer, junketer, riotous merrymaker.

revelry, n. [1. révelri; 2. révəlri]. **revel** (**II.**) & **-ry.** Noisy mirth and feasting; unrestrained jollification; junketing, carousal.

revenant, n. (partly Anglicized) [1. révenon; 2. révənã]. Fr., fr. Pres. Part. of *revenir*, 'to return', fr. **re-** & *venir*, 'to come', fr. Lat. *venīre*, 'to come', see **venue.** **a** Person returned after long absence; **b** one who has returned from the dead; ghost, apparition.

revendication, n. [1. revèndikáshun; 2. rivèndikéiʃən], fr. Fr., fr. **re-** & Lat. *vindicātiōn-(em)*, 'claiming of property, civil action; avenging'. See **vindication.** Recovery of property &c. by formal claim.

revenge (**I.**), vb. trans., reflex., & intrans. [1. revénj; 2. rivéndž], fr. O. Fr. *revenger*, fr. Lat. *revindicāre*, 'to exact retribution from', fr. **re-** & *vindicāre*, 'to lay claim to; to appropriate; to liberate; to avenge', see **vindicate.** **1.** trans. To exact vengeance for; to avenge, perform retaliatory action for, repay, requite by injurious action: *to revenge a wrong, insult, slight* &c. Phr. *to be revenged*, revenge oneself. **2.** reflex. *Revenge oneself upon* (a person), to take vengeance, to inflict punishment, injury &c. on another, in return for evil done to oneself. **3.** intrans. (archaic) To act revengefully.

revenge (**II.**), n., fr. prec. **1.** Act of inflicting injury, punishment &c. on another in return for injury &c. received, esp. implying spite, malice, vindictiveness. **2.** Vindictive, malicious feeling; desire to injure another in return for evil received. **3.** (sport, cards &c.) Return game &c. giving loser in previous game an opportunity to win: *to give a person his revenge*, to play such a match with him.

revengeful, adj. [1. revénjfool; 2. rivéndžful]. Prec. & **-ful.** **a** Characterized by, eager for, revenge; **b** said or done in revenge; vindictive.

revengefully, adv. Prec. & **-ly.** In a revengeful manner.

revengefulness, n. See prec. & **-ness.** Quality of being revengeful.

revenue, n. [1. révenū; 2. révənjū], fr. O. Fr., fr. P.P. of *revenir*, 'to return'. See **revenant.** **1.** Total income, receipts, funds accruing, from all sources; esp. total amount received by government for State purposes; *Inland Revenue*, State funds derived from income tax, death and succession duties, excise and customs duties, stamps &c.; *revenue cutter, officer*, employed by customs department to prevent smuggling. **2.** (pl.) Items of income considered collectively. **3.** Government department dealing with collection of national revenue.

reverberant, adj. [1. revérberant; 2. rivábərənt], fr. Lat. *reverberant-(em)*, Pres. Part. of *reverberāre*, 'to cause to rebound'. See next word. (chiefly poetical) Resounding, re-echoing, reverberating.

reverberate, vb. trans. & intrans. [1. revérberāt; 2. rivábəreit], fr. Lat. *reverberāt-(um)*, P.P. type of *reverberāre*, 'to strike back, cause to rebound', fr. **re-** & *verberāre*, 'to beat'; cp. Lat. *verbera*, 'rods, whips', & see **verbena.** **A.** trans. **1.** To throw back, cause to resound, re-echo: *to reverberate sound* &c. **2.** To throw back, reflect: *to reverberate light, heat* &c. **B.** intrans. **1.** (of sound) To resound, re-echo, be prolonged. **2.** (of light, heat) To be thrown back, reflected. **3.** (rare, fig.) To have an answering effect upon, react upon.

reverberating, adj. [1. revérberàting; 2. rivábəreitiŋ], fr. Pres. Part. of prec. **a** Echoing, resounding: *a reverberating peal of thunder*; **b** (of fame &c.) noised abroad, widespread.

reverberation, n. [1. revèrberáshun; 2. rivàbəréiʃən]. See prec. & **-ion.** Prolonged, echoing sound; a resounding.

reverberative, adj. [1. revérberativ; 2. rivábərətiv]. **reverberate** & **-ive.** Of, pertaining to, causing, reverberation; tending to reverberate.

reverberator, n. [1. revérberātur; 2. rivábəreitə]. **reverberate** & **-or.** Something that causes reverberation; specif. **a** reflector for lamp &c.; **b** reverberatory furnace.

reverberatory, adj. [1. revérberaturi; 2. rivábərətəri]. See prec. & **-ory.** Of, pertaining to, produced by, of the nature of, reverberation; *reverberatory furnace*, constructed so that heat is reflected from the inner surface on to the substance to be baked, fused &c.

revere, vb. trans. [1. revḗr; 2. rivíə], fr. Lat. *reverēri*, 'to respect', fr. **re-** & *verēri*, 'to observe with awe; to respect'; cp. Gk. *oûros*, 'watcher'; *horáein*, 'to see'; Goth. *war*, O.E. *wær*, 'watchful', see **ware (II.)**. To entertain deep respect for; to venerate, to reverence profoundly.

reverence (I.), n. [1. réverens; 2. révərəns], fr. Lat. *reverentia*, 'respect, awe', fr. *rever-(ēri)*, 'to revere'. **reverent** & **-ce**. **1.** a Feeling of deep respect, affection, and admiration, inspired by a holy person or thing, or by some lofty intellectual or spiritual quality; veneration; **b** quiet, decent behaviour expressive of respect, homage, deference. **2.** Bodily action or gesture expressing respect; specif., a deep bow or curtsey; an obeisance. **3.** Person deserving and receiving respect; *your, his, reverence* (archaic or facet., except in Ireland), mode of addressing, or referring to, a clergyman.

reverence (II.), vb. trans., fr. prec. To regard or treat with the deepest respect, love, and admiration; to feel profound veneration for; to revere, venerate: *to reverence the name of God*; *to reverence wisdom, a person's memory* &c.

reverend, adj. [1. réverend; 2. révərənd], fr. Lat. *reverend-(us)*, 'to be feared, inspiring awe', adj. fr. *reverēri*, 'to revere'. See **revere**. **1.** Worthy to be revered; entitled to respect and reverence; venerable. **2.** Mode of addressing a clergyman (on letters), or of referring to (esp. in written documents): *the Reverend (Rev., Revd.) X. Y.*; (in polite reference) *the reverend gentleman*, the clergyman referred to; (for Deans) *the Very Revd. the Dean of*; (for Bishops) *the Right Revd. the Lord Bishop of*; (for Archbishops) *the Most Revd. the (Lord) Archbishop of*. **3.** (archaic) Showing reverence; reverent.

reverent, adj. [1. réverent; 2. révərənt], fr. Lat. *reverent-(em)*, Pres. Part. of *reverēri*, 'to revere'. See **revere**. Inspired with, feeling, reverence; exhibiting reverence in behaviour.

reverential, adj. [1. reverénshal; 2. revərénʃəl]. Prec. & **-ial**. Of, pertaining to, caused by, proceeding from, a feeling of reverence.

reverentially, adv. Prec. & **-ly**. In a reverential manner.

reverently, adv. [1. réverentli; 2. révərəntli]. **reverent** & **-ly**. In a reverent manner.

reverie, n. [1. réveri, réverē; 2. révəri, révərī]. Fr., fr. *rêve*, 'a dream', *rêver*, 'to dream'; O. Fr. *resver*, 'to dream', the origin of wh. is very doubtful; the mod. forms show change of pref. **a** State of musing; dreamy contemplation, abstraction of mind; day-dream; **b** name given to a musical composition supposed to reflect such a state of mind.

revers, n. [1. revâr; 2. rəvéə]. Fr., fr. Lat. *revers-(us)*, 'turned back'. See **reverse (I.)**. (often pl.) Part of edge of garment turned back, sometimes with facing of different colour or material.

reversal, n. [1. revérsl; 2. rivə́sl]. **reverse (II.)** & **-al**. Act of reversing; state of being reversed: *a reversal of the natural order of things*.

reverse (I.), adj. [1. revérs; 2. rivə́s], fr. Lat. *reversum*, P.P. type of *revertere*, 'to turn back'. See **re-** & **version**. Turned round, turned backward or upside-down; having an opposite position or direction; contrary: *reverse movement*; *the reverse side*; *by the reverse method*.

reverse (II.), vb. trans. & intrans., fr. Fr., fr. L. Lat. *reversāre*, 'to turn round', fr. **re-** & *versāre*, 'to turn', formed fr. *vers-(um)*, P.P. type of *vertere*, 'to turn'. See **version**. **A.** trans. **1.** To turn over or round, turn backwards, place back to front or upside-down; cause to proceed in opposite direction: *to reverse an object*. Phr. (mil.) *to reverse arms*, carry rifle &c. pointing downwards. **2.** To exchange, transpose, put (things) in each other's places: *to reverse the normal order of precedence*; *positions are reversed*. **3.** To cause to work or run in backward direction: *to reverse an engine*. **4.** To destroy effect of, cancel, annul: *to reverse a sentence, decree* &c. **B.** intrans. To move along in a direction contrary to that usually or habitually followed; specif. (dancing) revolve in opposite direction.

reverse (III.), n., fr. O. Fr. *revers(e)*, fr. Lat. *revers-(us)*, 'turned back'. See **reverse (I.)**. **1.** Thing, quality, action, which is contrary to, or exact opposite of, another: *to believe the reverse of what one hears*; *his gait is the reverse of stately*; *is she pretty? no, quite* (or *very much*) *the reverse*. **2.** a Lower, under, side or surface; less important side; back; opposed to *obverse*; **b** design on reverse of coin &c.; **c** back of leaf of parchment, paper &c.; verso. **3.** a Change of course of events in contrary direction: *a reverse of fortune*; **b** a misfortune, a check, a set-back (in plans, affairs &c.): *to meet with a reverse*; Phr. *to have, experience, reverses*, specif., to have financial losses; **c** (mil.) a defeat; failure to achieve specified purpose of an operation.

reversely, adv. [1. revérsli; 2. rivə́sli]. **reverse (I.)** & **-ly**. In a reverse manner or direction.

reversi, n. [1. revérsi; 2. rivə́si]. Fr., fr. *revers-(er)*, 'to turn back'. See **reverse (II.)**. Obsolete game played on draught-board, with counters coloured differently above and beneath and reversed as they pass from one player to another.

reversibility, n. [1. revérsibíliti; 2. rivə̀sibíliti]. See next word & **-ity**. Quality of being reversible.

reversible, adj. [1. revérsibl; 2. rivə́sibl]. **reverse (II.)** & **-ible**. Capable of being reversed; specif. (of textile fabric &c.) carefully finished on both sides.

reversion, n. [1. revérshun; 2. rivə́ʃən], fr. O. Fr., fr. Lat. *reversiōn-(em)*, 'a turning back, return'. See **re-** & **version**. **1.** (law) **a** The passing back of an estate to the grantor or his heirs after expiry of grant; **b** right, expectation, of future enjoyment of property &c. **2.** Act, process, of reverting, or turning back; specif. (biol.) *reversion to type*, return of an individual organism to an ancestral type in form, or structure; atavism.

reversional, adj. [1. revérshunal; 2. rivə́ʃənəl]. Prec. & **-al**. (law) Of, pertaining to, reversion.

reversionally, adv. Prec. & **-ly**. By reversion.

reversionary, adj. [1. revérshunari; 2. rivə́ʃənəri]. **reversion** & **-ary**. (law) Of, pertaining to, arising from, involving, reversion: *reversionary interest in property*.

reversioner, n. [1. revérshuner; 2. rivə́ʃənə]. **reversion** & **-er**. Person to whom estate passes in reversion.

revert (I.), vb. intrans. & trans. [1. revért; 2. rivə́t], fr. Lat. *revert-(ere)*, 'to turn back'. See **reverse (II.)**. **A.** intrans. **1.** (obs.) To go back, move backwards, turn in backward direction: '*So two wild boars outstrip the following hounds*; *Then swift revert, and wounds return for wounds*' (Pope, 'Iliad'). **2.** (legal) To return, pass back legally, to original owner, or grantor: *the estate, office &c. will revert to the Crown*. **3.** To return, direct one's attention again to, recur, refer to, again: *to revert to the original topic of conversation*. **4.** To return to former state; **a** (of land) to become wild again, go out of cultivation; **b** (biol.) to go back to ancestral type; **c** (anthropol.) to return to more primitive state of civilization: *to revert to barbarism*. **B.** trans. (rare) To turn, direct, backwards.

revert (II.), n. [1. rēvért; 2. rívə̄t], fr. prec., on anal. of **convert** &c. Person who returns to original religious belief; retrovert.

revertible, adj. [1. revértibl; 2. rivə́tibl]. **revert (I.)** & **-ible**. Tending to revert; passing by reversion.

revet, vb. trans. [1. rēvét; 2. rivét], fr. Fr. *revêtir*, fr. L. Lat. *revestīre*, 'to clothe again', fr. **re-** & *vestīre*, 'to clothe'. See **vest (II.)**. To face, cover (surface), with a layer of stone, stone slabs &c., for greater strength, support &c.: *to revet the slope of an embankment, wall* &c.; *to revet a trench*, with sandbags, fascines &c.

revetment, n. [1. revétment; 2. rivétmənt]. Prec. & **-ment**. Layer of stone or other material covering the slope or face of a mound, embankment &c., to give greater strength and support.

revictual, vb. trans. & intrans. [1. revítl; 2. rìvítl]. **re-** & **victual**. **1.** trans. To supply with fresh provisions. **2.** intrans. To obtain, take in, a fresh supply of provisions.

review (I.), vb. trans. & intrans. [1. revū́; 2. rivjū́]. **re-** & **view**. **A.** trans. **1.** To recall and consider, call to mind in detail, contemplate, go over again in one's mind the details of: *to review the situation, one's past life*. **2.** To inspect formally and officially, esp. to hold an inspection of a display on a large scale: *to review troops* &c. **3.** To examine critically, go through in detail for the purpose of making additions, corrections &c., revise. **4.** To write a critical review of (a book &c.). **5.** (law) To consider (findings, decrees, of a lower court) for confirmation or revision. **B.** intrans. To write reviews.

review (II.), n., fr. O. Fr. *reveue*, P.P. of *revoir*, fr. Lat. *revidēre*, 'to see again', fr. **re-** & *vidēre*, 'to see'. See **vision**. **1.** Reflective survey, consideration in detail, contemplation, esp. in retrospect: *to pass one's life in review*. **2.** Critical examination, revision, critical scrutiny. **3.** Formal, official inspection, esp. of naval or military forces, or display by these. **4.** Critical consideration, estimate, appreciation, of a literary composition; written discussion and criticism. **5.** Periodical consisting of articles on general and special problems, and of criticisms of books &c. **6.** (legal) Examination by higher court of decrees &c. of lower court.

reviewable, adj. [1. revúabl; 2. rivjúəbl]. **review (I.)** & **-able**. Capable of being reviewed.

reviewal, n. [1. revúal; 2. rivjúəl]. **review (I.)** & **-al**. Act of reviewing.

reviewer, n. [1. revúer; 2. rivjúə]. **review (I.)** & **-er**. One who reviews; esp. writer of reviews of books &c.

revile, vb. trans. & intrans. [1. revíl; 2. riváil], fr. O. Fr. *reviler*. **re-** & **vile**. **1.** trans. To speak evil of, abuse, heap reproaches on. **2.** intrans. To utter abuse, speak opprobriously.

reviling, n. [1. revíling; 2. riváiliŋ]. Prec. & **-ing**. Abuse, bitter reproach.

revilingly, adv. Prec. & **-ly**. In a reviling manner; abusively.

revisable, adj. [1. revízabl; 2. riváizəbl]. **revise (I.)** & **-able**. Capable of being revised.

revisal, n. [1. revízl; 2. riváizl]. See next word & **-al**. **1.** Act of revising; state of being revised; revision. **2.** Something that has been revised.

revise (I.), vb. trans. [1. revíz; 2. riváiz], fr. Fr. *reviser*, fr. Lat. *revīsere*, 'to see again', formed fr. **re-** & *vīs-(um)*, P.P. type of *vidēre*, 'to see'. See **vision**. **1.** To go through for the purpose of correction, addition &c.; re-examine, consider critically, survey and amend: *to revise a document, book* &c. Phr. *Revised Version*, revised English translation of the Bible, made 1870-84. **2.** To change after consideration, amend, reform: *to revise one's opinions*.

revise (II.), n., fr. prec. **1.** (rare) Act of revising; revision. **2.** (print.) Proof printed from corrected first proof.

reviser, n. [1. revízer; 2. riváizə]. **revise (I.)** & **-er**. One who revises; proof-reader; specif., one of those who prepared the Revised Version of the Bible.

revising barrister, n. [1. revízing bàrister; 2. riváiziŋ bǽristə]. Barrister formerly appointed to revise the register of parliamentary voters in a constituency, hear claims and objections &c.

revision, n. [1. revízhun; 2. rivížən], fr. L. Lat. *revisiōn-(em)*, 'a seeing again'. **revise (I.)** & **-ion**. **1.** Act of revising; state of being revised. **2.** Something that has been revised; a revised version or copy.

revisional, adj. [1. revízhunal; 2. rivížənəl]. Prec. & **-al.** Of, pertaining to, involving, revision.

revisit, vb. trans. [1. rèvízit; 2. rìvízit]. **re-** & **visit.** a To visit again, return to, after absence; b to make another visit to.

revisory, adj. [1. revízori; 2. riváizəri]. **revise** (I.) & **-ory.** Of, pertaining to, for the purpose of, revision.

revitalize, vb. trans. [1. rèvítalīz; 2. rìváitəlaiz]. **re-** & **vitalize.** To put fresh life into, give fresh vigour to, reanimate.

revivable, adj. [1. revívabl; 2. riváivəbl]. **revive** & **-able.** Capable of being revived.

revival, n. [1. revíval; 2. riváivəl]. **revive** & **-al.** 1. Act or process of reviving; state of being revived; esp. a process of becoming active and vigorous again; rebirth, reawakening: *revival of the drama*; *a revival of interest*; *revival of learning* (specif. (cap.) the Renaissance); b process of bringing back into use; reintroduction, resuscitation: *the revival of ancient customs, of old words and expressions*; *Gothic revival*, reproduction of this type of architecture during 19th century. 2. An intensive campaign of prayer and preaching, a series of meetings at which rousing sermons are preached and extempore prayers are offered, designed to excite an emotional religious fervour.

revivalism, n. [1. revívalizm; 2. riváivəlizəm]. Prec. & **-ism.** Methods followed in religious revivals; state of religious enthusiasm engendered by these.

revivalist, n. [1. revívalist; 2. riváivəlist]. **revival** & **-ist.** Person who conducts religious revival meetings.

revive, vb. intrans. & trans. [1. revív; 2. riváiv], fr. L. Lat. *revīv-(ere)*, 'to live again', fr. **re-** & *vivere*, 'to live'. See **vital.** A. intrans. 1. To return, be restored to, recover, consciousness, animation, health: *to revive after a fainting-fit.* 2. To recover, be renewed; become lively and vigorous again: *his spirits, courage, hope(s), revived.* 3. To come back into use, become active or current again: *a tendency, fashion, that has revived.* B. trans. 1. To restore, bring back, to consciousness or animation, resuscitate. 2. To restore to fresh vigour; to reanimate, after period of depression &c.; to renew, refresh: *a run of success revived his hope and spirits.* 3. a (i.) To bring into operation again; put in practice again, restore to use or currency: *to revive an obsolete law, fashion* &c.; (ii.) to bring back to, cause to exist, or become active again in the mind: *to revive a memory*; *to revive interest in a subject*; *to revive a longing*; b specif., *to revive a play* &c., produce once more, after considerable interval. 4. (chem.) To restore to the natural state: *to revive a metal.*

reviver, n. [1. revíver; 2. riváivə]. Prec. & **-er.** One who, that which, revives; specif. a (slang) stimulant; b preparation for renovating cloth &c., restoring colour &c.

revivification, n. [1. revìvifikáshun; 2. rivìvifikéiʃən]. See next word & **-fication.** Act of revivifying; state of being revivified.

revivify, vb. trans. [1. revívifī; 2. rivívifai], fr. Fr., fr. L. Lat. *revivificāre*, 'to restore to life'. **re-** & **vivify.** 1. To restore to animation, vigour, activity; to revive, reanimate, give fresh life or spirit to. 2. (chem.) To restore to original, natural, or efficient state.

reviviscence, n. [1. rèvīvísens; 2. rìvaivísəns]. See next word & **-ce.** Revival, renewal, of life, vigour, activity.

reviviscent, adj. [1. rèvīvísent; 2. rìvaivísənt], fr. Lat. *revīviscent-(em)*, Pres. Part. of *revīviscere*, 'to come to life again, revive', fr. **re-** & *vīviscere*, 'to come to life', freq. of *vīvere*, 'to live'. See **revive.** Tending to revive; awakening or arousing after period of inactivity &c.

revocable, adj. [1. révokabl; 2. révəkəbl]. **revoke** (I.) & **-able.** Capable of being revoked, liable to revocation.

revocation, n. [1. rèvokáshun; 2. rèvəkéiʃən]. **revoke** (I.) & **-ation.** Act of revoking, state of being revoked; esp. (law) reversal, annulment, cancellation, of edict, decree, grant &c.

revocatory, adj. [1. revókaturi, révōkaturi; 2. rivɔ́kətəri, révoukətəri], fr. Lat. *revocātōri-(us)*, 'revocatory', fr. *revocāt-(um)*, P.P. type of *revocāre*, 'to call back', see **revoke** (I.) & **-ory.** Tending to revoke; expressing, conveying, revocation.

revoke (I.), vb. trans. & intrans. [1. revók; 2. rivóuk], fr. Lat. *revoc-(āre)*, 'to call back, withdraw, retract'; fr. **re-** & *vocāre*; 'to call'. See **re-** & **vocal.** A. trans. To withdraw, repeal, annul, reverse; cancel effect of: *to revoke a decree, edict, promise, one's sanction* &c. B. intrans. 1. To revoke a decree, rescind an order &c. 2. (cards) To play a card of a different suit from that led, when one has a card of this latter suit in one's hand.

revoke (II.), n., fr. prec. (cards) Act of revoking.

revolt (I.), vb. intrans. & trans. [1. revólt; 2. rivóult], fr. Fr. *révolter*, fr. **re-** & *volūtāre*, 'to turn about, revolve', fr. *volūt-(um)*, P.P. type of *volvere*, 'to roll'. See **volute.** A. intrans. 1. a *Revolt from, against*; to turn against, refuse to submit to, renounce allegiance to; to rebel: *to revolt from one's allegiance*; *to revolt against authority*; b (absol.) forcibly to resist established authority; to become a rebel: *unjust government often causes people to revolt.* 2. To be disgusted, nauseated by, feel repugnance and aversion to: *his whole nature revolted against, from, deceit.* B. trans. To inspire repugnance and aversion in; to disgust, to nauseate: *cruelty and meanness revolt decent people.*

revolt (II.), n., fr. prec. 1. Insurrection, popular rising, rebellion; active, concerted opposition to authority. 2. Feeling of aversion, repugnance, disgust.

revolted, adj. [1. revólted; 2. rivóultid]. **revolt** (I.) & **-ed.** Having renounced allegiance; rebellious.

revolting, adj. [1. revólting; 2. rivóultiŋ]. See prec. & **-ing.** Causing physical or moral disgust; loathsome, repulsive.

revoltingly, adv. Prec. & **-ly.** In a revolting manner.

revolute (I.), adj. [1. rèvolút; 2. rèvəljút], fr. Lat. *revolūt-(um)*, P.P. type of *revolvere*, 'to roll back, unroll, revolve'. See **revolve.** (bot., zool. &c.) With margins rolled backwards, towards under surface.

revolute (II.), vb. intrans. Back-formation fr. next word. (slang) To take part in a revolution.

revolution, n. [1. rèvolúshun; 2. rèvəljúʃən], fr. Lat. *revolūtiōn-(em)*, 'a revolving', fr. *revolūt-(um)*, P.P. type of *revolvere*, 'to roll back, revolve', see **revolve**, & **-ion.** 1. a Motion of body along a path forming a closed curve; movement in orbit; b motion of circle, globe &c. about a circle or axis so that every point on circumference or surface returns periodically to its original position; rotation; c single complete turn or passing of a body about a centre or axis; d time occupied by such complete turn. 2. Any motion or arrangement about an axis; spiral, whorl &c. 3. Series of events forming a cycle; recurrence of regular, periodic, changes or developments: *the revolution of the seasons.* 4. Complete subversion of established political authority, and establishment of new form of government; overthrow of existing political conditions; *The Revolution*, any of several important revolutions in history; that of 1688 in England, which brought William of Orange to the throne; that of 1789 in France &c. 5. Complete upheaval, radical change, in thought, belief, custom; such a change in scientific theory and method &c.

revolutionary (I.), adj. [1. revolúshunari; 2. revəl(j)úʃənəri]. Prec. & **-ary.** 1. Of, pertaining to, tending to, characteristic of, political revolution: *revolutionary ideas, speeches, leaders* &c. 2. Of, causing, involving, revolution in belief, method, custom &c.: *revolutionary discoveries* &c. 3. Revolving, tending to revolve.

revolutionary (II.), n., fr. prec. Person advocating, or taking part in, a revolution.

revolutionism, n. [1. rèvolúshunizm; 2. rèvəljúʃənizəm]. **revolution** & **-ism.** Principles, doctrines, of a revolutionist.

revolutionist, n. [1. rèvolúshunist; 2. rèvəljúʃənist]. **revolution** & **-ist.** Person advocating, supporting, taking part in, revolution.

revolutionize, vb. trans. [1. rèvolúshunīz; 2. rèvəljúʃənaiz]. **revolution** & **-ize.** 1. To make revolutionary, imbue with revolutionary principles &c. 2. a To make fundamental changes in, cause radical reform in (habits, practice, a system): *motors have largely revolutionized modern life*; b to upset and reverse, or gravely modify, existing theory and method &c.: *English philology has been revolutionized during the last half-century.*

revolve, vb. intrans. & trans. [1. revólv; 2. rivɔ́lv], fr. Lat. *revolv-(ere)*, 'to roll back; to revolve; to reflect upon', fr. **re-** & *volvere*, 'to turn, roll'. See **volute.** A. intrans. 1. To go round, move in circular path about a centre: *the earth revolves round the sun.* 2. To rotate, move constantly about an axis: *the earth revolves on its own axis.* 3. To move, occur, in cycles; to develop or return periodically: *the revolving year, seasons* &c. B. trans. 1. To cause to revolve. 2. To ponder, meditate upon, turn over in one's mind: *to revolve schemes for revenge.*

revolver, n. [1. revólver; 2. rivɔ́lvə]. Prec. & **-er.** Pistol with mechanically revolving cylinder containing cartridges, for firing several shots successively without reloading.

revue, n. [1. revū; 2. rəvy]. Fr. See **review** (II.). Kind of theatrical production or entertainment; a (orig. Fr. usage) a satirical, burlesque review of the political, social, or artistic topics of the year and of outstanding personalities in all walks of life, expressed and illustrated in dialogue, song, dance &c.; b a light, musical miscellaneous entertainment, with little or no construction.

revulsion, n. [1. revúlshun; 2. riválʃən], fr. Lat. *revulsiōn-(em)*, 'a tearing off', fr. *revuls-(um)*, P.P. type of *revellere*, 'to pluck off'. See **re-** & second element in **convulse.** 1. Sudden complete change in, reversal of, feeling, condition; violent reaction. 2. (rare) Sudden withdrawal or separation. 3. (med.) Attraction or diversion of pain, disease &c. from one part of the body to another, esp. by means of a counter-irritant.

revulsive, adj. & n. [1. revúlsiv; 2. riválsiv]. See prec. & **-ive.** 1. adj. (med.) Of, pertaining to, causing, revulsion. 2. n. (med.) Substance, apparatus, causing revulsion; counter-irritant.

reward (I.), n. [1. rewórd; 2. riwɔ́d], fr. A.-Fr. *reward*, fr. *rewarder*, variant of O. Fr. *regarder*, 'to look at', both of Gmc. origin. See **guard**, & cp. further **ward.** 1. Something given or done in return for good, or, more rarely, evil, received; recompense, requital: *the reward of valour*; *a reward for one's services.* 2. Sum of money offered for return of lost articles, for information regarding, or apprehension of, criminal &c.

reward (II.), vb. trans., fr. A.-Fr. *rewarder.* See prec. 1. a To give something in return for; to repay, recompense, requite: *to reward a service, bravery* &c.; b to accrue as result of: *success has rewarded my efforts.* 2. a To give a reward to, repay, compensate (person): *I rewarded him handsomely for his services*; b (chiefly pass.) to be compensated for, derive moral satisfaction from: *I am amply rewarded for all my trouble by the kind things people say.*

rewardless, adj. [1. rewórdles; 2. riwɔ́dlis]. **reward** (I.) & **-less.** Receiving no reward.

rewin, vb. trans. [1. rèwín; 2. rìwín]. **re-** & **win.** To win back, regain possession of.

reword, vb. trans. [1. rèwérd; 2. rìwə́d]. **re-** & **word.** To express, repeat, in other words; to word differently.

rewrite, vb. trans. [1. rērít; 2. rīráit]. **re-** & **write**. **a** To write out over again; recopy; **b** to compose (book &c.) afresh; to revise, recast, expand and modify.

rex, n. [1. reks; 2. reks]. Lat. *rēx*, 'ruler, king', for **rēg-s*; cp. Lat. *rēgīna*, 'queen', *regere*, 'to rule'; O. Ir. *rī*, 'king'; Goth. *rīks*, O.E. *rīc*, 'powerful', Scrt. *rāj-*, 'king'; *rājyáś*, 'royal'. See **regal, regent**. Reigning king, esp. **a** in signature, often abbreviated: *George R.* &c.; **b** used as title of plaintiff in criminal prosecution &c.: *Rex* v. *Robinson*.

Reynard, n. [1. rénard; 2. rénād, rénəd], fr. O. Fr. *Renart*, name of fox in popular epic *Roman de Renart*. Used as proper name for the fox.

rhabdomancy, n. [1. rábdomànsi; 2. rǽbdəmænsi], fr. L. Lat., fr. Gk. *rhabdomanteía*, 'divination by means of a rod', fr. *rhábdo-(s)*, 'rod, twig', for **wrabdo-*; cp. Lat. *verbera*, 'rods'. See **verbena, warp (I.)**, & **-mancy**. Divination by means of a rod, as in water-finding.

Rhadamanthine, adj. [1. radamánthīn; 2. rædəmǽnþain]. See next word & **-ine**. Of, pertaining to, like, characteristic of, Rhadamanthus.

Rhadamanthus, n. [1. ràdamánthus; 2. rædəmǽnþəs]. Lat., fr. Gk. *Rhadámanthos*, judge in infernal regions. A stern but just judge.

Rhaetian, adj. & n. [1. rēshan; 2. rīʃən], fr. Lat. *R(h)aetia*, country between the Danube, the Po, & the Rhine, & **-an**. **1.** adj. Of, belonging to, Rhaetia; esp. *Rhaetian Alps*, in south-eastern Switzerland. **2.** adj. & n. Rhaeto-Romance.

Rhaetic, adj. [1. rētik; 2. rītik], fr. Lat. *R(h)aetic-(us)*. See prec. & **-ic**. Of, pertaining to, the Rhaetian Alps, esp. (geol.) of a group of strata of the Triassic system.

Rhaeto-Romance, Rhaeto-Romanic, adj. & n. [1. rētō rōmáns, rōmánik; 2. rītou roumǽns, roumǽnik], fr. Lat. *Rhaet-(ia)*, see **Rhaetian**, & **Romance, Romanic**. **1.** adj. Of, pertaining to, **a** the people of south-eastern Switzerland; **b** the dialect of this area. **2.** n. Group of dialects spoken in south-eastern Switzerland and Tyrol.

rhapsode, n. [1. rápsōd; 2. rǽpsoud], fr. Gk. *rhapsōidós*. See **rhapsody**. Ancient Greek minstrel, travelling from place to place and reciting epic and heroic poems.

rhapsodic, adj. [1. rapsódik; 2. ræpsódik]. Prec. & **-ic**. **1.** Of, pertaining to, having the form of, a rhapsody. **2.** Rhapsodical.

rhapsodical, adj. [1. rapsódikl; 2. ræpsódikl]. Prec. & **-al**. Of, like, a rhapsody; emotionally enthusiastic; over-effusive and high-flown.

rhapsodically, adv. Prec. & **-ly**. In a rhapsodical manner.

rhapsodist, n. [1. rápsodist; 2. rǽpsədist]. See next word & **-ist**. **1.** Writer, composer, of rhapsodies. **2.** Rhapsode.

rhapsodize, vb. intrans. & trans. [1. rápsodīz; 2. rǽpsədaiz]. **rhapsody** & **-ize**. **1.** intrans. To write, utter, a rhapsody. **2.** trans. To sing, recite as, put into the form of, a rhapsody.

rhapsody, n. [1. rápsodi; 2. rǽpsədi], fr. Gk. *rhapsōidía*, 'recitation of epic poetry; epic poem; canto of epic'; fr. *rhapsōid-(ós)*, 'rhapsodist'; Gk. *rhap-* is for Aryan **wr̥p-*, reduced grade, fr. base **werp-* &c., 'bend, weave'; cp. Gk. *rháptein*, 'to sew, weave; to weave, contrive, plots; to compose songs'; cp. Lith. *verpti*, 'to spin'. **1. a** Ancient Greek epic poem; **b** section of epic recited at one time by rhapsode. **2.** Highly emotional, enthusiastic, and extravagant utterance, esp. one which is disjointed and rambling. **3.** (mus.) Composition of emotional character and irregular in form.

rhatany, n. [1. rátani; 2. rǽtəni], fr. Port. *ratanhia*, fr. S. Am. Indian *rataña*. **a** Peruvian shrub; **b** astringent root of this shrub, used in medicine and for adulterating and colouring wine.

rhea (I.), n. [1. rēa; 2. rīə], fr. name of Gk. goddess, *Rhéā*, mother of the gods. Small, three-toed ostrich of South America.

rhea (II.), n. Assamese word. Ramie.

Rhemish, adj. [1. rēmish; 2. rīmiʃ], fr. obs. *Rhemes*, Engl. form of *Rheims*, & **-ish**. Of, pertaining to, coming from, Rheims; esp. of English translation of New Testament made at Roman Catholic College of Rheims, published in 1582.

Rhenish, adj. & n. [1. rénish; 2. réniʃ], fr. M.H.G. *rīnisch*, 'of the Rhine', assimilated to Lat. *Rhēn-(us)*, 'Rhine'. (archaic) **1.** adj. Of, pertaining to, coming from, the Rhine or the country through which it flows. **2.** n. Rhine wine.

rheo-, pref. representing Gk. *rhéo-(s)*, 'stream'; cp. Gk. *rhéō*, 'I flow', for **srew-*; cp. Gk. *rhoûs*, 'current'; *rheûma*, 'stream, flow, discharge', see **rheum**; *rhúax*, 'torrent'; cogn. w. Scrt. *sravaś*, 'flow'; *srutiś*, 'flood'; Lith *s(t)rovē*, 'river'; O. Slav. *struja*, 'river'; O.N. *straumr*; O.E. *strēam*, 'river', see **stream**. Current, esp. **a** (elect.) electric current, e.g. *rheoscope*, instrument showing presence or direction of current; *rheostat*, a variable resistance regulating strength of current; **b** (biol.) current of a stream &c.; e.g. *rheotaxis*, tendency of certain organisms to move against the current.

rhesus, n. [1. rēsus; 2. rīsəs]. Invented name. A small long-tailed, greyish-brown North Indian monkey, *Macacus rhesus*.

rhetor, n. [1. rētōr; 2. rītɔ̄], fr. Gk. *rhḗtōr*, 'public speaker'; cp. Gk. *rhḗtrā*, 'covenant'; *rhêma*, 'word'; *rhêsis*, 'speech'; all fr. stem **wrē-*; cogn. w. Scrt. *vratám*, 'order'; Lat. *verbum*, 'word', see **verb**; Lith. *vardas*, 'name'; see also **word**. **1.** Ancient Greek teacher of rhetoric. **2.** Professional orator.

rhetoric, n. [1. rétorik; 2. rétərik], fr. Lat. *rhētoric-(a)*, fr. Gk. *rhētorikḗ (tékhnē)*, 'art of rhetoric'. See prec. & **-ic**. **1.** The art of oratory; theory and practice of elegant and persuasive speaking. **2.** (in derogatory sense) Flowery, showy, high-flown, highly decorated, or bombastic style in speaking and writing; style designed to appeal rather to the emotions than to the reason.

rhetorical, adj. [1. retórikl; 2. ritɔ́rikl]. Prec. & **-al**. **1.** Of, pertaining to, the art of rhetoric or eloquence: *a man of great rhetorical power*. **2. a** (of style, diction) Pertaining to, characteristic of, a high-flown, bombastic style; flowery but shallow, elaborate but artificial and insincere; *rhetorical question*, one put for effect and not requiring an answer; **b** (of speakers and writers) given to, indulging in, a flowery, highly ornamented style.

rhetorically, adv. Prec. & **-ly**. In a rhetorical manner.

rhetorician, n. [1. rètorishan; 2. rètəríʃən]. **rhetoric** & **-ian**. **a** Person skilled in the art of rhetoric; **b** one who indulges in a flowery, elaborate, over-decorated style.

rheum, n. [1. rōōm; 2. rūm], fr. Gk. *rheûm-(a)*, 'flow; discharge', fr. **sreu-*. See under **rheo-**. (archaic) **1.** Discharge from mucous membrane of mouth, throat, nose &c. **2.** Nasal catarrh.

rheumatic, adj. & n. [1. rōōmátik; 2. rūmǽtik], fr. Gk. *rheûmat-(os)*, stem of *rheûma*, 'a flow', see **rheum**, & **-ic**. **1.** adj. Of, pertaining to, caused by, affected with, rheumatism; *rheumatic fever*, one accompanied by severe rheumatic pains. **2.** n. **a** Person suffering from rheumatism; **b** *the rheumatics*, (colloq.) rheumatism.

rheumatism, n. [1. rōōmatizm; 2. rūmətizəm], fr. L. Lat. *rheumatism-(us)*, 'rheum, catarrh', fr. L. Gk. *rheumatismós*, fr. *rheumatizomai*, 'I am troubled with rheum', fr. *rheûmat-*, stem of *rheûma*, 'flow; discharge', see **rheum**, & **-ism**. Name given to various diseases or forms of a disease attended with pains and inflammation in the muscles and joints caused by a deposit of uric acid.

rheumatoid, adj. [1. rōōmatoid; 2. rūmətoid], fr. Gk. *rheûmat-*, stem of *rheûma*, 'rheum', see **rheum**, & **-oid**. Of, resembling, rheumatism.

rheumy, adj. [1. rōōmi; 2. rūmi]. **rheum** & **-y**. (archaic) **1.** Of, like, full of, consisting of, rheum. **2.** Causing, tending to cause, catarrh.

rhinal, adj. [1. rīnal; 2. ráinəl]. See **rhino-** & **-al**. (anat., zool.) Of, pertaining to, the nose.

rhine, rean, reen, n. [1. rēn; 2. rīn]. Etymol. uncertain. A large open drain or ditch in marshy, low-lying country.

rhinestone, n. [1. rīnstōn; 2. ráinstoun], fr. Rhine, river of Germany and Holland, & **stone**. **1.** Kind of rock-crystal. **2.** Colourless paste gem made in imitation of diamond.

Rhine wine, n. [1. rīn wīn; 2. ráin wáin]. Light white, also red, wine, grown in vineyards on and near the Rhine; hock.

rhino (I.), n. [1. rīnō; 2. ráinou]. Abbr. fr. **rhinoceros**. (slang) Rhinoceros.

rhino (II.), n. Etymol. unknown. (slang) Money.

rhino-, pref. representing Gk. *rhīn-*, stem of *rhī́s* for **rhin-s*, 'nose', fr. base **srī-*, **srēi-*, 'to flow'; ultimately connected w. **rheo-**. Nose; e.g. *rhinopharyngeal*, of the nose and pharynx; *rhinoplasty*, plastic surgery of the nose; *rhinoscope*, instrument for examining the nose.

rhinoceros, n., pl. *rhinoceroses* [1. rīnóserus; 2. rainɔ́sərəs], fr. L. Lat. *rhīnoceros*, fr. Gk. *rhīnókerōs*, 'rhinoceros', fr. **rhino-** & *kér-(as)*, 'horn'. See **keratin**. Large, heavily built, pachydermatous mammal of tropical Africa and Asia, with one or two horns projecting from the upper surface of the nose.

rhinocerotic, adj. [1. rīnoserótik; 2. ràinɔsərɔ́tik], fr. Gk. *rhīnokerōt-*, stem of *rhīnókerōs*, see prec., & **-ic**. Connected with, resembling, a rhinoceros.

rhizo-, pref. representing Gk. *rhíz-(a)*, 'root', fr. **wred-ja*; cp. Gk. *rhádamnos*, 'young branch, shoot'; *rhā́dix*, 'branch'; Lat. *rādix*, 'root', see **radical**; *rāmus*, 'branch'; Goth. *waurts*, O.E. *wyrt*, 'root, plant', see **wort (I.)**; O.N. *rōt*, 'root', see **root**. (bot.) Root; e.g. *rhizocarp*, plant with annual stem and perennial root; *rhizogen*, parasitic plant growing on root of another plant; *rhizotaxis*, arrangement of roots.

rhizome, n. [1. rízōm; 2. ráizoum], fr. Gk. *rhizōm-(a)*, 'root', fr. *rhizó-ein*, 'to take root', fr. *rhiza*, 'root'. See prec. (bot.) Underground stem which sends up shoots from upper surface and produces roots from the lower.

Rhodian, adj. & n. [1. rōdian; 2. róudiən], fr. Lat. *Rhodi-(us)*, 'of Rhodes', fr. Lat. *Rhodos*, fr. Gk. *Rhódos*, an island off the coast of Asia Minor, & **-an**. **1.** adj. Of, belonging to, Rhodes. **2.** n. Native of Rhodes.

rhodic, adj. [1. rōdik; 2. róudik]. See next word & **-ic**. Of, derived from, rhodium.

rhodium (I.), n. [1. rōdium; 2. róudiəm]. **rhodo-** & **-ium**. Hard, greyish-white metal resembling platinum, producing rose-coloured salts; it is very hard and heat-resisting, is used for tipping the nibs of gold pens and for incandescent gas mantles &c.

rhodium (II.), n., fr. Mod. Lat. *rhodium (lignum)*, neut. adj. formed fr. Gk. *rhód-(on)*, 'rose', see **rhodo-**. Also *rhodium-wood*, scented wood resembling rose-wood, obtained from shrub of Canary Islands.

rhodo-, pref. representing Gk. *rhódon*, 'rose' (Aeolic *hródon*), fr. **wródon*; according to Boisacq an early loan-word fr. Iranian **wr̥da-*, cp. Mod. Pers. *gul*, 'rose'; Aryan **wr̥dho-*, whence also Lat. *rubus*, 'bramble bush'. **a** Pertaining to, resembling, producing, roses; **b** rose-coloured, red.

rhododendron, n. [1. ròdodéndron; 2. ròudədéndrən], fr. L. Lat., fr. L. Gk. *rhodódendron*, fr. **rhodo-**, & *déndron*, 'tree', see **dendro-**. Genus of shrubs and small trees having showy, five-lobed flowers, and usually evergreen leaves.

rhodous, adj. [1. rōdus; 2. róudəs]. Formed fr. **rhodium (I.)** & **-ous**. Of, derived from, rhodium.

rhomb, n. [1. rom(b); 2. rɔm(b)], fr. Lat. *rhomb-(us)*, fr. Gk. *rhómbos*, 'spinning-top; wheel; rhomb'; cp. Gk. *rhémbomai*, 'I roll about'; nasalized form of base **wer-b-*, **wor-b-*, 'to turn, twist; something that can be twisted'. See **warp** (**I.**) & **verbena**. Equilateral parallelogram with two acute and two obtuse angles.

rhombic, adj. [1. rómbik; 2. rɔ́mbik]. Prec. & **-ic**. Of, like, having the form of, a rhomb.

rhombo-, pref. representing Gk. *rhómb-(os)*, 'wheel, rhomb'. See **rhomb**.

rhombohedral, adj. [1. ròmbōhḗdral, -hédral; 2. rɔ̀mbouhídrəl, -hédrəl]. See next word & **-al**. Of, in the form of, forming, a rhombohedron.

rhombohedron, n. [1. ròmbōhḗdron, -hédron; 2. rɔ̀mbouhídrən, -hédrən]. **rhombo-** & **-hedron**. **a** Solid bounded by six rhombic planes; specif. **b** crystal of this form.

rhomboid, adj. & n. [1. rómboid; 2. rɔ́mbɔid], fr. Lat. *rhomboīd-(es)*, fr. Gk. *rhomboeidḗs*, 'rhomboid', fr. **rhombo-** & **-oid**. **1.** adj. **a** Having the shape of a rhomb; **b** nearly resembling a rhomb in shape; *rhomboid muscle*, joining scapula to spine. **2.** n. **a** Parallelogram of which only the opposite sides and angles are equal; **b** rhomboid muscle.

rhomboidal, adj. [1. ròmbóidl; 2. rɔ̀mbɔ́idəl]. Prec. & **-al**. Rhomboid.

rhombus, n. [1. rómbus; 2. rɔ́mbəs]. Lat. *rhombus*, 'rhomb'. See **rhomb**. **1.** Rhomb. **2.** Kind of flat-fish.

rhotacism, n. [1. rṓtasizm; 2. róutəsizəm]. See next word & **-ism**. Act of rhotacizing, tendency to rhotacize.

rhotacize, vb. intrans. [1. rṓtasīz; 2. róutəsaiz], fr. Gk. *hrōtakizein*, fr. Gk. *hrō*, name of letter *r*. **1.** To mispronounce the sound [r]. **2.** To substitute [r] for another sound, or change another sound into [r]; e.g. in Lat. *z* between vowels becomes *r*: *soror*, 'sister', for **swezor*.

rhubarb, n. [1. rōōbarb; 2. rúbāb, rúbəb], fr. O. Fr. *rubarbe*, fr. Med. Lat. *rhabarbarum*; fr. Lat. *rhā barbarum*, 'foreign rhubarb', Gk. *rhēon*, *rhā*, 'rhubarb', apparently fr. *Rha*, name of the Volga River where the plant came from, & *barbarus*, 'foreign', see **barbarian**. **1. a** Perennial garden herb with broad leaves and small flowers; **b** thick, fleshy, acid leaf-stalks of this plant cooked and eaten as fruit. **2. a** Medicinal root of various Eastern varieties of rhubarb, esp. *Chinese rhubarb*; **b** purgative prepared from this root. **3.** Yellowish-brown colour.

rhubarby, adj. [1. rōōbarbi; 2. rúbābi]. Prec. & **-y**. Like, having the flavour of, rhubarb.

rhumb, n. [1. rum; 2. ram], fr. Fr., fr. Lat. *rhomb-(us)*, 'wheel; magic circle; rhomb'. See **rhomb**. **1. a** Any one of the thirty-two points of the compass; **b** angle subtended by arc separating two of these points, 11° 15'. **2.** Also *rhumb-line*, line, ship's course, cutting all meridians at the same angle.

rhyme (**I.**), n. [1. rīm; 2. raim]. M.E., fr. O. Fr. *rīme*, fr. Lat. *rhythmus*, 'rhythm', fr. Gk. *rhuthmós*, 'measured motion; time; symmetry, order, method'. See **rhythm**. **1.** Identity of sound or sounds between the latter part of two or more syllables occurring in separate words; **a** identity of final vowels in two or more words of one syllable, e.g. *day, play*, or in the stressed final vowels of words of more than one syllable, e.g. *supply, deny, rely*; **b** identity of vowel and final consonant of stressed syllables between two or more words, e.g. *dog, flog, agog*; **c** identity of sound between two or more groups of syllables; in this case the identity must include all the sounds which follow the last stress, e.g. *bétter, létter, gétter*. Phr. *without rhyme or reason*, without sense. **2.** Word or syllable which makes a rhyme with another: '*laugh*' *is a good rhyme to* '*chaff*'. **3. a** Rhymed verse: *nursery rhymes*; **b** poetry in general: '*And beauty making beautiful old rhyme In praise of ladies dead and lovely knights*' (Shakespeare, Sonnet 106).

rhyme (**II.**), vb. trans. & intrans., fr. prec. **A.** trans. **1.** To use as rhyme with: *to rhyme words together which do not sound alike*. **B.** intrans. **1. a** To compose rhymed verse; **b** to bring, string, together words or syllables that form rhymes. **2.** (of words or syllables) To constitute a rhyme or rhymes: '*mead*' *and* '*shade*' *do not rhyme in our present pronunciation, though formerly they were pronounced alike*.

rhymed, adj. [1. rīmd; 2. raimd], fr. P.P. of prec. Arranged so as to rhyme; rhyming together: *rhymed verse*; *rhymed couplets*.

rhymeless, adj. [1. rīmles; 2. ráimlis]. **rhyme** & **-less**. Having no rhyme, not rhyming.

rhymer, n. [1. rīmer; 2. ráimə]. **rhyme** (**II.**) & **-er**. Writer of verse; often specif. inferior poet.

rhyme-royal, n. [1. rīm róial; 2. ráim rɔ́iəl]. Stanza of seven ten-syllabled lines with rhymes in the order *ababbcc*; so called from its use by James I. of Scotland.

rhymester, n. [1. rīmster; 2. ráimstə]. **rhyme** & **-ster**. Writer of verse, esp. an inferior poet; a poetaster.

rhyming, adj. [1. rīming; 2. ráimiŋ]. **rhyme** (**II.**) & **-ing**. Exhibiting, connected by, rhyme: *rhyming words, lines* &c.; *rhyming dictionary*, one containing classified lists of rhyming words.

rhymist, n. [1. rīmist; 2. ráimist]. See prec. & **-ist**. One who uses rhyme in a specified way: *a poor, a careful, rhymist* &c.

rhythm, n. [1. rídhm; 2. ríðəm], fr. Lat. *rhythmus*, fr. Gk. *rhuthmós*, 'measured motion, time, rhythm; proportion, symmetry; temper, disposition', fr. base **sreu-*, **sru-* &c., 'to flow'; cp. Gk. *rhein*, 'to flow'. See **rheo-**. **1.** Movement characterized by regular recurrence and intermission, or by increase and decrease at regular intervals, of force, emphasis, stress, beat, loudness; cadence; the essential quality of rhythm is to produce a sense of symmetry and regularity; hence we speak of rhythm in music, dancing, verse, and occasionally also in prose. **2.** Particular kind of rhythm in music, verse &c. **3.** (more gen.) Regular recurrence of processes, events &c.: *the rhythm of the seasons, of nature*; *the rhythm of history*.

rhythmic(**al**), adj. [1. ríthmik(l); 2. ríþmik(l)]. Prec. & **-ic** (& **-al**). Characterized by, exhibiting, rhythm; **a** specif. (of verse, music &c.) cadenced; **b** recurring at regular periods: *the rhythmic(al) rise and fall of the tide*; *the rhythmic courses of nature* &c.

rhythmically, adv. Prec. & **-ly**. In a rhythmical manner.

rhythmist, n. [1. ríthmist; 2. ríþmist]. **rhythm** & **-ist**. One skilled in, practising, rhythm in verse or music.

rhythmless, adj. [1. rídhmles; 2. ríðəmlis]. **rhythm** & **-less**. Without rhythm.

riant, adj. [1. rīant; 2. ráiənt]. Fr., Pres. Part. of *rire*, 'to laugh', fr. Lat. *rīdēre*, 'to laugh, smile'. See **risible**. (chiefly of landscape, aspects of nature &c.) Gay, smiling.

rib (**I.**), n. [1. rib; 2. rib]. O.E. *ribb*; M.E. *ribbe*; cp. O.H.G. *ribbi*, *rippi*; M. Du. *ribbe*; O.N. *riff*; cp. further O.H.G. *rebo*, 'tendril'; O. Slav. *rebro*, 'rib'; orig. sense 'something bent'; possibly cogn. w. Lat. *orbis*, 'curve, circle'. See **orb**. **1.** One of the bones in vertebrates curving forward from either side of the spine and enclosing the thorax: *true, sternal, ribs*, attached to the sternum in front of the thorax; *floating ribs*, those attached only to the spine; *ribs of beef*, joint for the table. **2.** Any long, narrow ridge rising above surrounding surface; e.g. raised stripe or ridge on surface of knitted material &c. **3.** Various objects in form of a long, slender, raised ridge or strip; specif. **a** one of the curved timbers forming framework of ship; **b** (archit.) long, narrow, curved section of wood or stonework supporting an arch, vault &c.; **c** beam supporting part of bridge; **d** thin, flexible, jointed metal rod serving as framework of umbrella; **e** (bot.) vein of leaf; **f** (min.) narrow strip of ore &c. left to support roof of working. **4.** (facet.) Wife.

rib (**II.**), vb. trans., fr. prec. To furnish with, to mark off in, ribs.

ribald, n. & adj. [1. ríbald; 2. ríbəld]. M.E. *ribaud*, *ribald*, 'worthless creature', fr. O. Fr. *ribau(l)d*; etymol. doubtful. **1.** n. Coarse, irreverent, profane speaker. **2.** adj. (of speech, laughter &c.) Irreverent, scurrilous, loose.

ribaldry, n. [1. ríbaldri; 2. ríbəldri]. Prec. & **-ry**. Ribald speech.

riband, n. See **ribbon**.

ribanded, adj. See **ribboned**.

ribband, n. [1. ríband; 2. ríbənd]. **rib** & **band**. Narrow strip of wood or metal used to hold the ribs of a ship in position during construction.

ribbed, adj. [1. ribd; 2. ribd], fr. P.P. of **rib** (**II.**). Marked with, ornamented with, supported by, formed in, ribs.

ribbing, n. [1. ríbing; 2. ríbiŋ]. **rib** (**II.**) & **-ing**. **1.** Series of, arrangement in, ribs. **2.** Act of forming or arranging in ribs.

ribbon, riband, n. [1. ríbun; 2. ríbən]. M.E. *riban(d)*, fr. O. Fr. *riban*; etymol. doubtful; alternative spelling *riband* shows association w. *band*. **1. a** Silk or satin fabric, woven as a strip finished at both edges and usually less than ten inches in width; *baby ribbon*, narrowest variety; **b a** piece of ribbon. **2.** Specif., band of ribbon of distinctive colour used as symbol of an order of knighthood, of a military or other decoration: '*Just for a riband to stick in his coat*' (Browning, 'Lost Leader', I.); also of membership of club, team &c. **3.** Long, narrow strip or band; ribbon-shaped object: *to be torn to ribbons*, to tatters; *ribbons of mist*. **4.** (pl., colloq.) Driving-reins: *to take the ribbons*; *to handle the ribbons*, drive.

ribboned, adj. [1. ríbund; 2. ríbənd]. **ribbon** & **-ed**. Furnished, ornamented, fastened, with ribbons.

ribbon-fish, n. Any of several kinds of fish named from their shape or markings.

ribbon-grass, n. Ornamental grass with long leaves striped lengthwise with white.

ribbon-snake, n. Harmless, yellow-striped snake of U.S.A.

ribes, n. [1. rībēz; 2. ráibīz], fr. Med. Lat., fr. Arab. *ribās*, 'sorrel'. Genus of small, sometimes prickly, shrubs, including gooseberry and currant; specif., a variety of this, the so-called American currant, cultivated for its pendulous pink blossoms which appear in early spring.

rib-grass, n. Kind of plantain.

ribless, adj. [1. ríbles; 2. ríblis]. **rib** (**I.**) & **-less**. Without ribs.

Ribston(**e**) **pippin**, n. [1. ríbstun pípin; 2. ríbstən pípin], fr. Ribstone Hall in Yorkshire. Kind of sweet, juicy, dessert apple with strong and agreeable flavour.

rib-wort, n. Ribgrass.

Ricardian, adj. & n. [1. rikárdian; 2. rikā́diən], fr. name of political economist, David Ricardo, d. 1823. **1.** adj. Of, pertaining to, the economic theories of Ricardo. **2.** n. Adherent of Ricardo's economic theory.

rice, n. [1. rīs; 2. rais], fr. O. Fr. *ris*, fr. Ital. *riso*, fr. L. Lat. *orȳza*, fr. Gk. *óruza*, 'rice', prob. of Eastern origin. **1.** Annual cereal plant, *Oryza sativa*, grown in tropical and subtropical climates in marshy or flooded land, esp. in India, China &c. **2.** White seeds of this plant boiled or stewed and used as food.

rice-bird, n. **a** Small bird of U.S.A., bobolink; **b** Java sparrow.

rice-flour, n. Ground rice used for cakes &c.

rice-milk, n. Milk boiled and thickened with rice-flour.

rice-paper, n. Fine paper made in China from the pith of a tree grown in Formosa.

rice-pudding, n. Baked pudding of sweetened milk and rice.

rice-water, n. Invalid's drink made of water in which rice has been boiled.

rich, adj. [1. rich; 2. ritʃ]. M.E. *riche*, fr. O. Fr. *riche* (of Gmc. origin); cp. O.E. *rīce*, 'strong, powerful, rich'; cp. Goth. *reiks*; O.H.G. *rīhhi*; O.N. *rīkr*; Celt. loan-word; cp. M. Ir. *rīge*, 'kingdom'; *rī(g)*, 'king', see **rex**; M.E. *riche*, though primarily Fr., was no doubt felt to be connected w. the O.E. word. **1. a** Possessing abundant financial resources, wealthy, opulent, having much or plenty of money: *rich people*; *a rich community* &c.; *the rich*, rich people, the wealthy; **b** fortunate in the possession of, blessed: *rich in the affection of one's children.* **2.** (of land &c.) Yielding abundantly, fertile: *rich fields, soil*; producing in large quantities: *rich gold-fields* &c. **3.** (of objects) Fine, sumptuous, luxurious, costly, valuable: *rich silks, dresses, hangings, jewels* &c. **4.** (of food) **a** Containing much fat, or much fat and sugar: *rich milk, cakes* &c.; **b** highly seasoned: *rich dishes.* **5.** Plentiful, abundant, luxuriant: *rich foliage, harvest* &c. **6.** (of sound, colour &c.) Full, deep, intense. **7.** (of non-material things) Copious, ample, abundant: *a rich reward.* **8.** (colloq.) Full of humour or interest, highly entertaining.

riches, n. [1. richez; 2. rítʃiz]. Old sing.; now felt to be, & used as, a pl.; M.E. *richess*, fr. O. Fr. *richesse*, fr. *riche*, 'rich'. See **rich** & **-ess.** **1. a** Material possessions, wealth: *to heap up riches*; **b** potentiality of wealth: *the riches of the soil, of gold-mines.* **2.** Abundance, plenty, copious supply; **a** (material) *the riches of the harvest*; **b** (non-material) *the riches of divine grace.*

richly, adv. [1. richli; 2. rítʃli]. **rich** & **-ly.** **1.** In a rich manner. **2.** In a great degree, abundantly, thoroughly; esp. in Phr. *to deserve richly*: *he richly deserves punishment, to be punished.*

richness, n. [1. richnes; 2. rítʃnis]. See prec. & **-ness.** Quality of being rich: *richness of material, colour* &c.

rick (I.), n. [1. rik; 2. rík]. O.E. *hrēac*; M.E. *rēk*; cp. O.N. *-hraukr*, 'rick, mound'; *hrūga*, 'heap'; W. *crūg*, 'heap'; O.H.G. *hrukki*; O.E. *hryċġ*, 'ridge, back'; Scrt. *krúñcati*, 'curves, bends'. Perh. cogn. w. Lat. *crux*, 'cross', see **crux.** Large pile of hay, straw &c. packed and thatched for storing in the open; a stack.

rick (II.), vb. trans., fr. prec. To form into ricks.

rick (III.), vb. & n. See **wrick.**

rick-cloth, n. Canvas or tarpaulin cover for unthatched rick.

ricketiness, n. [1. rìkitines; 2. ríkitinis]. **rickety** & **-ness.** State of being rickety.

rickets, n. [1. ríkets; 2. ríkits]. Prob. fr. Fr. *rachite*, cp. **rachitis**, influenced by **wrick**, 'to twist, sprain', cp. Swed. *vricka*, 'to shake'. Disease of young children, characterized by softening of the bones and consequent deformity, usually caused by malnutrition, deficiency of vitamins, of sunlight &c.

rickety, adj. [1. ríketi; 2. ríkiti]. See prec. & **-y.** **1.** Affected by, showing effects of, like, rickets. **2.** Unstable, shaky, tottery, liable to fall: *a rickety table.*

ricksha(w), n. [1. ríkshaw; 2. ríkʃɔ̄]. Jinricksha.

rick-stand, n. Set of short wooden or stone pillars supporting rick above ground.

rick-yard, n. Enclosure in which ricks are built.

ricochet, n. & vb. [1. rìkoshét, rìkoshā́; 2. rìkəʃét, rìkəʃéi]. Fr. Etymol. doubtful. **1.** n. **a** The rebounding of a projectile or other object, from an object which it strikes; **b** glancing blow. **2.** vb. **a** intrans. To glance off, rebound; **b** trans., to cause (projectile &c.) to glance off an object.

rictus, n. [1. ríktus; 2. ríktəs]. Lat. *rictus*, 'aperture of the mouth, esp. in laughing', fr. Lat. *rict-(um)*, P.P. type of *ringi*, 'to open the mouth; to snarl'; cp. O. Slav. *ręgnęti*, 'to yawn'; Serb. *regnuti*, 'to snarl'; *režati*, 'to show the teeth'. Cp. **ringent.** **1.** Involuntary, spasmodic grin disclosing the teeth; caused by muscular contraction. **2. a** Extent of opening of mouth of animal or beak of bird; gape; **b** (bot.) amount of opening of labiate corolla.

rid, vb. trans. [1. rid; 2. rid]. M.E. *riden*, fr. O.N. *hryðja*, 'to clear, empty'. To free, disembarrass, deliver: *to rid a person, a country &c. of something harmful*; *to rid oneself of foolish notions.* Phr. *to get rid of*, free oneself, be freed, from; to expel, dismiss: *to get rid of a cold*; *I shall have to get rid of my butler.*

ridable, adj. [1. rídabl; 2. ráidəbl]. **ride** & **-able.** Capable of being ridden.

riddance, n. [1. rídans; 2. ridəns]. **rid** & **-ance.** Act of getting rid; state of being rid; *a good riddance*, a welcome relief, deliverance, from something harmful or unpleasant.

rid(d)el, n. [1. rídl; 2. rídl]. O.E. *ridel*; cp. Fr. *rider*, 'to wrinkle'; of Gmc. orig.; cp. O.H.G. *rīdan*, 'to turn, twist', cogn. w. **writhe.** A curtain, esp. altar curtain.

ridden, adj. [1. rídn; 2. rídn], fr. P.P. of **ride**; O.E. *(ġe)riden*; M.E. *riden.* Dominated, under subjection: *ridden by fears*; (often in compounds) *priest-ridden, fear-ridden* &c.

riddle (I.), n. [1. rídl; 2. rídl]. O.E. *rǣdels*, M.E. *redels, rideles*; fr. stem of *rǣd-(an)*, 'to take counsel, deliberate, to interpret, solve', see **read** (I.) & n. -suff. *-els.* **1.** An enigma, a puzzle, deliberately devised for others to exercise their ingenuity upon; generally in form of question *Why is x like y?* &c. **2.** Anything which puzzles, perplexes one; person, thing, situation, difficult to fathom, interpret.

riddle (II.), vb. intrans. & trans., fr. prec. **1.** intrans. To make obscure and puzzling statements &c.; to utter, speak in, riddles. **2.** trans. To solve, explain, supply answer or solution to.

riddle (III.), n. M.E. *rid(d)el*, fr. O.E. *hriddel*, w. dissimilation fr. earlier *hridder*, 'coarse sieve'; cp. O.H.G. *rītera*, 'sieve'; cogn. w. Lat. *crībrum*, 'sieve', see **cribriform**; *cernere*, Pret. *crēvi*, 'to sift, divide, discern', see **discern**; Gk. *krīnein*, 'to divide, distinguish', *krēséra*, 'fine sieve'. **1.** Coarse sieve for gravel, broken ore &c. **2.** Slab fitted with pins for straightening wire.

riddle (IV.), vb. trans., fr. prec. **1.** To sift, screen, by means of a riddle. **2.** To make many holes in, perforate in all directions; esp. *to riddle a person, ship &c. with shot*; *to riddle with holes.* **3.** (fig.) To subject to severe and searching criticism, to show weaknesses and inconsistencies in: *to riddle an argument, theory.*

ride (I.), vb. intrans. & trans. [1. rīd; 2. raid]. O.E. *rīdan*, M.E. *rīden*; cp. O.H.G. *rītan*, O. Fris. *rīda*, O.N. *rīða.* Cogn. w. Lat. *rēda, raeda*, 'four-wheeled carriage', Celt. loan-word; cp. M. Ir. *riadaim*, 'I drive'; W. *rhwyddan*, 'to advance', *(go)rhwydd*, 'horse', & see **road (I.).** **A.** intrans. **1. a** (i.) To bestride, sit upon back of, and be carried by, horse or other animal: *to ride well*; *to ride away*; *to ride far*; *to ride hard, full speed, full tilt* &c.; (ii.) to sit upon, bestride, and travel upon a bicycle. Phr. *to ride for a fall*; (i.) ride recklessly; (ii.) (fig.) behave in such a way as to court disaster; *to ride and tie* (of two persons with one horse), take alternate spells of riding and walking, the rider leaving horse tied up at end of his spell, to await the walker; *to ride to hounds*, in fox-hunting; *to ride rough-shod over*, see **rough-shod**; **b** to engage habitually in equestrian exercise, make a practice of riding a horse: *I used to ride in my youth, but I've ceased to ride for some years.* **2.** To sit, be, in, and be carried along by, a vehicle of any kind: *to ride in a carriage, a motor-car, a train, on a cart* &c. **3.** To sit upon as upon a horse &c.: *to let a child ride on one's back, foot* &c. **4.** To float, be supported, borne up, or appear to be supported, **a** (by water) *the ship rides at anchor*; **b** (in the air) *the moon rides above the clouds*; *the sun rides high in heaven*; *the bird rides on the wind.* **5.** To move, be carried, supported, while in action, or at work: *the wheel rides on the axle.* **6.** (med., of two parts of fractured bone) To overlap. **7.** To be suitable for riding; to produce specified impression upon rider: *the country rides well, stickily.* **B.** trans. **1.** To bestride, sit on back of, be carried by: *to ride a horse, donkey* &c.; *to ride one's horse to death*, kill by exhausting; hence, (fig.) *to ride a joke, theory, argument, &c., to death*, render tedious, or ineffective by over-emphasis, excessive repetition &c. **2.** To sit on seat of and propel or direct: *to ride a bicycle, motor-bicycle.* **3.** To be supported by, borne up by, float on: *the ship rides the waves*; *the bird rides the storm.* **4.** To take part in, on horseback, bicycle &c.: *to ride a race.* **5.** To give a ride to, allow to ride: *to ride a child on one's foot.* **6.** To weigh when dressed and accoutred for riding: *to ride 9 stone.* **C.** Followed by adverb or preposition. *Ride at*, **a** intrans., to direct one's horse &c., towards; **b** trans., to turn, direct, towards: *to ride one's horse at a fence.* *Ride down*, trans., **a** to pursue and overtake on horseback &c.; **b** to knock down and trample beneath hoofs of horse &c. *Ride out*, (of ship) to keep afloat, survive, endure force of: *to ride out a storm, gale* &c. *Ride up*, to work, slide, upward, out of proper position: *a bad tie, coat-collar &c. rides up.*

ride (II.), n., fr. prec. **1. a** Act, spell, of riding; journey &c., on horseback, bicycle &c.: *to have a long ride*; *to go for a ride*; *to give a child a ride on one's back*; **b** a journey in which one is conveyed in any sort of vehicle: *a ride in a bus, a train, a car, a carriage.* **2.** Road, track, esp. for riding through wood.

rider, n. [1. ríder; 2. ráidə]. **ride (I.)** & **-er.** **1. a** One who rides; specif. **b** one who rides well: *he'll never make a rider.* **2. a** Rope or part of rope lying above another; **b** part of machine, placed above and working upon another part; **c** (naut.) extra set or layer of plates or timbers strengthening frame of ship. **3. a** Supplementary clause added to a document after the completion of the latter; **b** clause added to jury's verdict, making some recommendation or expressing some further opinion with reference to the point at issue; **c** inference, proposition, deduced naturally from another proposition &c.; corollary. **4.** (math.) Geometrical problem depending for its solution on a specific proposition, to which it is usually attached. **5.** Gold coin, bearing the figure of a rider, formerly current in Holland.

riderless, adj. [1. ríderles; 2. ráidəlis]. Prec. & **-less.** (of a horse) Without, having lost, its rider.

ridge (I.), n. [1. rij; 2. ridž]. O.E. *hryċġ*, M.E. *riġġe*, 'back; ridge'; cp. O.N. *hryggr*, O.H.G. *hrucki*, O.S. *hruggi.* See also **rick (I.)**, **crux.** **1.** Long narrow elevation with sloping sides; line of highest elevation of hill or any structure, from which ground &c., slopes away at either side; specif. **a** elongated summit of mountain, hill, rock &c.; **b** line in which two slopes of roof &c. meet; **c** line of earth turned up by plough &c.; elevated part between furrows. **2.** Long, narrow hill, range of hills &c., esp. as watershed. **3.** Rib, raised part between grooves, e.g. on edge of a coin.

ridge (II.), vb. trans. & intrans., fr. prec. **1.** trans. To form into, mark with, ridges. **2.** intrans. To become marked with ridges; to wrinkle, break into ridges.

ridge-pole, n. **1.** Horizontal beam at ridge of roof. **2.** Horizontal pole supporting top of rectangular tent.

ridge-tile, n. Tile with curve or angle, forming part of covering for ridge of roof.

ridge-tree, n. Ridge-pole.

ridgeway, n. [1. ríjwā; 2. rídžwei]. Road along ridge of hill &c.

ridgy, adj. [1. ríji; 2. rídži]. **ridge** & **-y.** Forming, consisting of, a ridge; covered with ridges.

ridicule (I.), n. [1. rídikūl; 2. rídikjūl], fr. Lat. *rīdicul-(um)*, 'thing to be laughed at, jest', fr. neut. form of *ridiculus*, 'laughable, funny', fr. *rīd-(ēre)*, 'to laugh, smile', see **risible.** **1.** (archaic) Object of derision, person, or thing made game of. **2.** Act of ridiculing; state of being ridiculed; mockery, derision: *to hold (a person) up to ridicule.*

ridicule (II.), vb. trans., fr. prec. To make fun of, laugh at, make a mock of, make the object of amused contempt; to deride.

ridiculous, adj. [1. ridíkūlus; 2. ridíkjuləs], fr. Lat. *rīdiculōs-(us)*, 'laughable, ridiculous', fr. *rīdicul-(us)*, 'amusing'. See **ridicule** (I.) & **-ous.** **a** Exciting ridicule; absurd, grotesque; **b** exciting indignation; preposterous, outrageous: *it is ridiculous to expect me to believe such lies.*

ridiculously, adv. Prec. & **-ly**. In a ridiculous manner.

ridiculousness, n. See prec. & **-ness**. State or quality of being ridiculous.

riding (I.), n. [1. ríding; 2. ráidiŋ]. **ride** (I.) & **-ing**. **a** Act of one who rides, esp. on horseback; equestrian exercise: *riding is a very healthy exercise; riding came natural to him;* **b** road, track, for riders on horseback.

riding (II.), n., for *thriding*, cp. O.N. *thrithjungr*, 'third part'. See **third** & **-ing**. **a** One of three administrative districts of Yorkshire: *North, East, West, Riding;* **b** subdivision of county in New Zealand &c.

riding-habit, n. Costume with long skirt and tight-fitting coat worn by women riders.

riding-light, n. Light displayed at night in rigging of ship riding at anchor.

riding-master, n. One who teaches (soldiers and others) to ride.

riding-rhyme, n. Old name for decasyllabic couplet; so called, apparently, from its use by Chaucer in the Canterbury Tales, which are told by pilgrims 'riding' to Canterbury. (Saintsbury). Cp. 'a notable kind of ryme called ryding ryme . . . such as our Mayster & Father Chaucer used in his Canterburie Tales', Gascoigne, 'Concerning the making of verse or ryme in English', 1575.

rifacimento, n., Anglicized pronunciation [1. rēfahchiméntō; 2. rīfātʃiméntou]. Ital. Recasting, or readaptation of literary or musical work.

rife, adj. [1. rīf; 2. raif]. O.E., M.E. *rīf*, 'abundant, frequent'; cp. O.N. *rīfr*; Du. *rijf.* (only pred.) Current, prevalent; existing in large quantities, abundant: *superstition is rife among uncivilized people.*

rifeness, n. Prec. & **-ness**. State of being rife.

riffle, n. [1. rifl; 2. rífl]. Cp. Germ. *riefeln*, 'to groove'. See **rifle**. A channel or groove formed by some obstruction placed lengthways in the sluice or trough to catch the free gold particles washed out of the sand or ore.

riff-raff, n. [1. ríf raf; 2. ríf ræf]. In earliest form *riff and raff*, cp. **raffish.** Lower part of the populace, rabble.

rifle (I.), vb. trans. [1. rífl; 2. ráifl], fr. O. Fr. *rifler*, 'to scratch', of Gmc. origin; cp. Germ. *riefeln*; Swed. *reffla*, 'to rifle'. **1.** To go through, turn upside down, in hopes of finding something to steal; to plunder, to rob. **2.** To make spiral grooves in: *to rifle a gun, barrel of gun* &c.

rifle (II.), n., fr. prec. **1.** One of the spiral grooves in the bore of a rifled firearm. **2.** Earlier, *rifle-gun*; portable firearm, musket, with spiral grooves or rifling in the barrel to give a rotary motion to bullet &c., and increase accuracy of shot. **3.** (pl.) Infantry armed with rifles, esp. (cap.) in names of certain regiments.

rifle-bird, n. Kind of purple and green bird of paradise of Australia and New Guinea.

Rifle Brigade, n. Group of British infantry regiments, consisting of the 60th Rifles and the battalions of the King's Royal Rifles.

rifle-corps, n. Body of troops, armed with rifles.

rifled, adj. [1. rífld; 2. ráifld], fr. P.P. of **rifle** (I.). **1.** (of gun or barrel) Made with spiral grooves on inner surface. **2.** (of bullet) With projections fitting into grooves of barrel.

rifle-green, n. Dark green, colour of uniform of Rifle Brigade.

rifle-grenade, n. A grenade fixed to a metal rod fitting the barrel of a rifle from which it is fired.

rifleman, n. [1. rífllman; 2. ráiflmən]. **1.** Soldier armed with rifle, esp. one belonging to Rifle Brigade. **2.** Rifle-bird.

rifle-pit, n. Trench protecting riflemen in action.

rifle-range, n. **1.** Place with targets &c., for practice in rifle-shooting. **2.** Distance which rifle carries.

rifle-shot, n. **1.** Shot fired from rifle. **2.** Distance which rifle carries. **3.** Person who is a good shot with a rifle.

rifling, n. [1. rífling; 2. ráifliŋ]. **rifle** (I.) & **-ing**. **1.** Act of making spiral grooves in barrel of gun. **2.** Spiral grooves in barrel of gun.

rift (I.), n. [1. rift; 2. rift]. M.E. *rift*; Scand.; cp. O.N. *repta*, 'to break'. See **rive**. An opening, cleavage; a cleft, a rent. Phr. *a rift in the lute*, (fig.) some circumstance, apparently insignificant, which is sufficient to endanger or destroy happiness, satisfaction, concord &c.

rift (II.), vb. trans., fr. prec. To split, crack, rend, tear asunder.

riftless, adj. [1. ríftles; 2. ríftlis]. **rift** & **-less.** Without rifts.

rifty, adj. [1. rífti; 2. rífti]. **rift** & **-y**. Having, full of, rifts.

rig (I.), vb. trans. & intrans. [1. rig; 2. rig]. Etymol. doubtful; prob. fr. O.N. *rigga*, 'to wrap round'. (of a ship) To equip, be equipped, with rigging. *Rig out*, to equip, fit out, provide with clothes &c. Phr. *rigged out*, dressed up. *Rig up*, **a** to rig out; **b** to erect, construct, contrive, esp. as makeshift, with means at one's disposal.

rig (II.), n., fr. prec. **1.** Distinctive style of ship's rigging, masts, sails &c. **2.** (colloq.) **a** Clothing; a dress, a suit, a costume; **b** particular style of dressing; general personal appearance, including both dress and bearing.

rig (III.), vb. trans. & n. Etymol. unknown. **1.** vb. To manipulate dishonestly, influence, arrange by underhand means: *to rig an election, a committee; to rig the market*, arrange prices artificially so as to suit one's own transactions. **2.** n. Act of rigging; result of this; Phr. *to run a rig*, cut a caper, play pranks.

Riga, n. [1. rēga; 2. rígə]. Port on Baltic; capital of Latvia. *Riga hemp*, exported from Riga; *Riga balsam*, medicinal oil obtained from pine.

rigadoon, n. [1. rigadóon; 2. rigədún], fr. Fr. *rigaudon.* **a** Quick, lively dance for two people; **b** music accompanying or suitable for this dance.

rigescence, n. [1. rijésens; 2. ridžésəns]. Next word & **-ce**. State of being rigescent.

rigescent, adj. [1. rijésent; 2. ridžésənt], fr. Lat. *rigescent-(em)*, Pres. Part. of *rigescere*, 'to begin to stiffen', fr. *rigēre*, 'to be stiff; to stiffen', see **rigid**. Becoming stiff, growing numb or rigid.

rigged, adj. [1. rigd; 2. rigd], fr. P.P. of **rig** (I.). Having rig of specified kind; (usually in compounds) *barque-rigged* &c.

rigging, n. [1. ríging; 2. rígiŋ]. **rig** & **-ing**. Complete system of ship's ropes, sails, spars &c.

rigging-loft, n. **1.** Place where rigging is prepared, fitted &c. **2.** (theatr.) Part of theatre above stage, from which scenery is raised or lowered.

right (I.), adj. [1. rīt; 2. rait]. O.E. *riht*; M.E. *riht*, 'right, straight, erect'; cp. O.H.G. *reht*; O.N. *rēttr*; Goth. *raihts*; cogn. w. Lat. *rectus*, 'straight, right'; Gk. *orektós*, 'erect'; further, w. Lat. *regere*, 'to put straight, guide, rule'. See **rectum**, & words there referred to. **1.** Straight, direct, not curved or bent; obsolete, except in *right line; right sailing; right angle*, one of 90°. **2.** **a** Designed, likely, to achieve a desired end; appropriate to a particular purpose; proper, suitable, approved, correct; good or best in view of existing circumstances and conditions: *the right road, method, amount* &c.; *the right thing to do or say; the right way to do it; the right man in the right place; just the right colour;* Phr. *on the right side of thirty*, under thirty; **b** correct, true; accurately ascertained, calculated, given or stated: *the right answer; to get a sum right; is that the right address?; can you tell me the right time?;* Phr. *to get it right*, to understand thoroughly, be perfectly clear about: *just let's get this right before I go*, be under no misapprehension concerning it; **c** the one actually intended or referred to: *not the right Mr. Jones; be sure you bring the right book.* **3.** **a** Further from the main part of the heart: *the right side of the body*; towards the east when person or thing faces north; **b** situated on, towards, this side of body: *right hand, foot, eye* &c.; **c** corresponding to, on same side as, person's right hand, &c.: *the right side of the road; right wing of the army* &c.; *right bank of a river*, that on the right hand of person looking down stream, towards the mouth; **d** opposite to, situated nearest to, right side of spectator; **e** towards the right: *a right turn.* **4.** Knowing what is true, wise, expedient &c.; correct in one's opinion, judgement &c.: *he is always right; you are perfectly right*, what you think, or say, is true. Phr. (colloq.) *right you are!*, form of agreement with, acquiescence in, proposal &c. **5.** Morally advisable or obligatory; in accordance with justice; conforming to the highest moral standard; just, equitable: *to do what is right; it is not right to lie;* '*Whatever is, is right*' (Pope, 'Ess. on Man', i. 294). **6.** In good health, free from disease, discomfort &c.; sound, healthy: *to feel all right; not right in the head; in one's right mind.* Phr. *right as rain, as a trivet*, perfectly well, sound, comfortable &c. **7.** In Phr. *right side* (*of cloth* &c.), the best, most carefully finished, surface; that intended to be exposed and seen.

right (II.), adv. O.E. *rihte.* See prec. **1.** In a straight line; straight, directly, exactly: *right ahead, overhead; to go right on, right opposite.* **2.** On, towards, the right: *to turn right or left; right turn*, (as mil. command) turn to the right through an angle of 90°. Phr. *right and left*, in all directions, on every side. **3.** In the proper way, correctly, properly (in moral or practical sense): *to act right; to do a thing right; to guess right.* Phr. *to set, put, oneself right with* (another person), (i.) get on good terms with, into good graces of; (ii.) make up a disagreement with; *to come right*, improve, turn out well; *to put (a machine &c.) right*, repair it; *put (a person) right*, cure him of illness, restore him to health. **4.** **a** Completely, thoroughly, quite: *go right to the end; rotten right through;* **b** exactly, precisely: *right in the middle;* Phr. *right away*, immediately; (Am.) *come right in*, straight in; *right here*, here and now. **5.** **a** (archaic) In a high degree, very: *I know right well; a right cunning worker; to fight right nobly;* **b** in forms of address: *the Right Honourable John Jones* (of privy councillor); *the Rt. Honble. the Lord* &c. (of a peer); *Right Reverend* (of a bishop).

right (III.), n. O.E. *riht.* See **right** (I.). **1.** That which is accurate, correct, in accordance with facts. Phr. *in the right*, free from error; *the rights* (*of a question* &c.), the true facts. **2.** Action, conduct, in accordance with, conforming to, principles of truth, duty, justice; that which is right: *to distinguish between right and wrong; to defend the right.* Phr. *the rights and wrongs*, facts and the reverse; *by right(s)*, rightfully; *put something to rights*, into proper, working condition. **3.** Right side or hand of body or other object: *to turn, keep, look, to the right; to sit on the right of the host.* **4.** (polit.) *The Right*, the Conservative party, from its usual place in a legislative chamber in relation to the presiding officer. Cp. **left** (I.), 3.

right (IV.), n., fr. prec. **1.** Just claim, proper authority: *to have a right to one's own opinions; to have no right to speak; divine right of kings.* Phr. *by right of*, in virtue of, on account of;

in one's own right, as independent, personal claim. **2.** Thing claimed as justly due, privilege: *to demand one's rights*; *civil, natural, rights*; *it is your right to know*.

right (V.), vb. trans., fr. O.E. *rihtan*, fr. *riht*, adj. See **right (I.)**. **1. a** To put into erect position: *to right a fallen or falling object*; **b** (reflex.) *to right oneself*, (i.) to regain erect position, recover one's balance; (ii.) to recover from a moral lapse, rehabilitate oneself. **2.** To put right, to correct, reform, improve: *to right a wrong*. **3.** To secure rights for; relieve: *to right the oppressed*.

rightable, adj. [1. rítabl; 2. ráitəbl]. Prec. & **-able**. Capable of being righted.

right-about, adj. & n. **1.** adj. *Right-about turn*, through an angle of 180°, until reverse position is reached. **2.** n. Only in Phr. *to send a person to the right-about(s)*, to reject, dismiss, summarily.

right-and-left, adj. & n. [1. rít an(d) léft; 2. ráit ən(d) léft]. **1.** adj. **a** (of screw) Having threads cut in a different direction at each end; **b** (of shot) from both barrels. **2.** n. **a** Shots from both barrels in succession, *a right-and-left*; **b** (of boxer) two successive blows from different hands.

right-angled, adj. [1. rít anggld; 2. ráit æŋgld]. Forming, having, a right angle.

right-down, adj. & adv. (colloq.) **a** adj. Thorough, complete: *he's a right-down liar*; **b** adv., thoroughly, to a high degree.

righten, vb. trans. [1. ríten; 2. ráitən]. **right** & **-en**. (rare) To set right, reform, amend.

righteous, adj. [1. ríchus, ríteus; 2. ráitʃəs, ráitjəs]. O.E. *rihtwīs*, 'righteous'; **right (I.)** & **wise (II.)**; remodelled w. **-ous**, on anal. of **duteous** &c. **1.** (of person, character, action) Conforming to spiritual and moral principles; upright, virtuous. **2.** Justified by cause or motive: *righteous indignation*.

righteously, adv. Prec. & **-ly**. In a righteous manner.

righteousness, n. See prec. & **-ness**. State or quality of being righteous.

rightful, adj. [1. rítfool; 2. ráitful]. **right (I.)** & **-ful**. **1.** Based on justice, virtue: *a rightful cause, act* &c. **2.** Having a just or proved claim: *the rightful heir* &c. **3.** Belonging, assigned, by established and recognized right: *one's rightful position*.

rightfully, adv. Prec. & **-ly**. By right (in various legal and moral senses).

rightfulness, n. See prec. & **-ness**. State or quality of being rightful.

right hand, n. [1. rít hánd; 2. ráit hǽnd]. **1.** The hand further from the heart, on right side of the body. **2.** (fig.) A person who acts for and helps another to the point of being indispensable to him.

right-hand, adj. [1. rít hand; 2. ráit hænd]. Of, pertaining to, situated on, the right: *the right-hand side, edge* &c. Phr. *right-hand man*, (i.) person on one's right in a line &c.; (ii.) most reliable, indispensable, helper or supporter.

right-handed, adj. **1.** More dexterous with right hand than with left, naturally using right hand in preference to left. **2.** Delivered, done, made to be used, by the right hand: *right-handed blow, tool* &c. **3.** Turning from left to right; clockwise.

right-handedness, n. State of being, tendency to be, right-handed.

right-hander, n. [1. rít hánder; 2. ráit hǽndə]. (colloq.) Blow given with right hand.

rightless, adj. [1. rítles; 2. ráitlis]. **right (III.)** & **-less**. Without right.

rightly, adv. [1. rítli; 2. ráitli]. **right (I.)** & **-ly**. In accordance with right; justly, duly; correctly, properly.

right-minded, adj. Having a just, upright, mind.

right-mindedness, n. State of being right-minded.

rightness, n. [1. rítnes; 2. ráitnis]. **right (I.)** & **-ness**. State, character, quality, of being right; correctness; justness.

right-of-way, n. [1. rít uv wā; 2. ràit əv wéi]. **1.** Public right of free passage over road, path, &c., esp. one established by usage through private property. **2.** Road, path, subject to free passage.

rightward, adj. & adv. [1. rítward; 2. ráitwəd]. **right (I.)** & **-ward**. **1.** adj. Towards, directed to, the right. **2.** adv. Rightwards.

rightwards, adv. [1. rítwardz; 2. ráitwədz]. **right (I.)** & **-wards**. Towards, in the direction of, the right.

right-whale, n. One of the larger whales producing whalebone, esp. the Greenland whale, *Balaena mysticetus*.

rigid, adj. [1. ríjid; 2. rídžid], fr. Lat. *rigidus*, 'hard, stiff; inflexible, stern; rough, severe'; cp. *rigēre*, 'to be, become, stiff'; *rigor*, 'stiffness'; various etymols., none of wh. is at all certain, have been suggested; the base is possibly connected w. **reg-*, 'to guide, direct, rule &c.' See **regent, rex**, & words there referred to. **1. a** Stiff, not flexible, not to be bent; firm, not to be moved: *a rigid rod, bar* &c.; **b** (of the body and its members) having the muscles tense and hard; immobile. **2.** (in moral sense) **a** (of persons) Stern, severe, inflexible, unyielding, unaccommodating; morally austere, uncompromising: *a rigid disciplinarian*; *rigid in one's views*; **b** (of action and conduct) harsh, severe: *rigid discipline*; *rigid rules*, strict, such as are strictly enforced and must be observed, such as cannot be broken or avoided; *his mind has become rather rigid*, fixed, not open to new ideas.

rigidity, n. [1. rijíditi; 2. ridžíditi], fr. Lat. *rigiditāt-(em)*, 'stiffness'. See prec. & **-ity**. State or quality of being rigid (in physical and moral senses); stiffness; unadaptability, uncompromisingness.

rigidly, adv. [1. ríjidli; 2. rídžidli]. **rigid** & **-ly**. In a rigid manner.

rigmarole, n. [1. rígmarōl; 2. rígmərəul], fr. earlier *ragman-roll*, 'list, catalogue, register of names' &c.; etymol. of *ragman-* uncertain. See **ragman**. Long, rambling, incoherent, tedious narrative or discourse.

rigor, n. [1. rígōr; 2. ráigɔ]. Lat. 'stiffness, hardness; chilliness'; cp. Lat. *rigēre*, 'to stiffen'. See **rigid**. Fit of shivering, attended with sense of chill and convulsive trembling, such as usually precedes a fever; *rigor mortis* (Lat., 'stiffness of death'), rigidity of the muscles which sets in a few hours after death.

rigorism, n. [1. rígorizm; 2. rígərizəm]. **rigour** & **-ism**. **1.** Strictness of principles and conduct; austerity of life. **2.** Severity, insistence on great precision and chastity of style.

rigorist, n. [1. rígorist; 2. rígərist]. See prec. & **-ist**. One who practises rigorism.

rigorous, adj. [1. rígorus; 2. rígərəs]. **rigour** & **-ous**. **1.** Stern, inflexible, uncompromising, exacting, relentless: *rigorous enforcement of the law*; *rigorous discipline*. **2.** Strictly accurate, exact: *rigorous scientific method*. **3.** Severe, harsh, inclement: *a rigorous climate*.

rigorously, adv. Prec. & **-ly**. In a rigorous manner.

rigour, n. [1. ríger; 2. rígə], fr. O. Fr., fr. Lat. *rigōr-(em)*, nom. *rigor*, 'stiffness'. See **rigor**. **1.** Severity, sternness, inflexibility, austerity of disposition, character &c. **2.** Strictness; uncompromising, unqualified action; relentless enforcement: *the utmost rigour of the law*, the severest punishment which the law allows. **3.** Uncompromising, unrelieved strictness and simplicity in manner of life, thought, doctrine &c. **4.** Severity, harshness, inclemency of weather &c.: *the rigours of an English spring*.

Rigsdag, n. [1. régzdahg; 2. rígzdāg]. Dan., fr. *rige*, 'kingdom', cogn. w. **rich**, & *dag*, 'day', cogn. w. **day**; cp. *Reichstag*. The Danish Parliament.

Rig-veda, n. [1. rig vāda; 2. rig véidə]. Scrt., fr. *ric*, 'hymn of praise', & **Veda**. Oldest and most important of the Vedas.

Riksdag, n. [1. réksdahg; 2. ríksdāg]. Swed., cp. **Rigsdag**. The Swedish Parliament.

rile, vb. trans. [1. rīl; 2. rail]. Variant of obs. & dialectal *roil*, 'to stir up, make muddy, turbid'. (colloq.) To make angry, to vex, irritate, annoy with taunts &c.

rilievo, n. [1. rilyāvō; 2. riljéivou]. Ital., fr. Lat. *relev-(āre)*, 'to raise'. See **relieve**. **relief (II.)**.

rill, n. & vb. intrans. [1. ril; 2. ril]. Cp. Germ. *rille*, 'small furrow, channel'; Du. *ril*. **a** n. Small brook, streamlet, rivulet; **b** vb., to flow as a rill.

rille, n. [1. ril; 2. ril], fr. Germ. *rille*, 'furrow'. See prec. (astron.) Narrow trench or furrow on surface of moon.

rillet, n. [1. rílet; 2. ríl(l)it]. **rill** & **-et**. Small rill.

rillett(e)s, n. [1. rilḗts; 2. rilḗts], fr. Fr. *rillettes*. Tinned mixture of chicken, ham, truffles &c., highly spiced.

rill-mark, n. (esp. geol.) Slight furrow, channel, left in sand &c. by ripples of ebbing tide.

rim (I.), n. [1. rim; 2. rim]. O.E. *rima*, M.E. *rime*, 'edge, border'; cp. O.N. *rime*, 'ridge'. **1. a** Raised or projecting edge, border, esp. of circular or curved object: *the rim of an eyeglass* &c.; **b** hence, edge, margin, brim: *the rim of a cup*. **2.** Outer circle of wheel, excluding tire. **3.** (naut.) Surface of water.

rim (II.), vb. trans., fr. prec. To supply with a rim, form a rim for, surround with a rim.

rim (III.), n. O.E. *rēoma*, M.E. *rim, rēme*, 'membrane'; cp. Germ. *riemen*, 'thong, strap'. (archaic) Membrane lining abdomen; peritoneum.

rime (I.), n. & vb. trans. [1. rīm; 2. raim]. O.E. *hrīm*; M.E. *rīm*, 'hoar-frost'; cp. O.N. *hrīm*; O.H.G. *rīm*; Du. *rijm*. **1.** n. Hoar-frost. **2.** vb. To coat with hoar-frost.

rime (II.), n. & vb. trans. Earlier, obs., but lately revived spelling of **rhyme**, fr. O. Fr. *rime*.

rimer, n. [1. rímer; 2. ráimə]. Variant of **reamer**.

rimless, adj. [1. rímles; 2. rímlis]. **rim (I.)** & **-less**. Without a rim.

rimmed, adj. [1. rimd; 2. rimd], fr. P.P. of **rim (II.)**. Having a rim, usually of specified kind: *gold-rimmed spectacles*.

rimose, adj. [1. rímōs; 2. ráimous], fr. Lat. *rīmōs-(us)*, 'full of fissures', fr. *rīma*, 'chink, crack, fissure'; the origin of wh. is doubtful. Full of chinks, clefts, fissures.

rimous, adj. [1. rímus; 2. ráiməs]. Same as prec. w. suff. **-ous**. Rimose.

rimy, adj. [1. rími; 2. ráimi]. **rime (I.)** & **-y**. Covered with rime or hoar-frost.

rind, n. [1. rīnd; 2. raind]. O.E., M.E. *rīnd*; cp. M. Du. *rinde*; O.H.G. *rinda*. **1.** Outer skin or covering of part of plant or vegetable product; peel, bark, husk &c. **2. a** Tough, hard outer layer of cheese; **b** tough skin of bacon &c. **3.** (fig.) Outward aspect, apparent character.

rinderpest, n. [1. rínderpest; 2. ríndəpest]. Germ., fr. *rinder*, pl. of *rind*, 'ox'; O.H.G. *hrind*; cp. O.E. *hrȳðer*; O. Fris. *hrīther*, 'ox'; O.N. *hreinn*, 'reindeer', see **reindeer**. See further under **cervine, hart, keratin**. Cattle-plague.

ring (I.), n. [1. ring; 2. riŋ]. O.E. *hring*; M.E. *ring*; cp. O.S., O.H.G. *hring*; O.N *hringr*; cogn. w. O. Slav. *krągŭ*, 'circle' **1. a** Line enclosing round space, circle: *to draw a ring on the ground*; esp. **b** distinct circular mark or formation: *to have rings round one's eyes*; *fairy ring*, see **fairy-ring**; **c** specif. (pl.) series of rings visible on section of tree-trunk, of which each represents a layer of wood formed by a year's growth; **d** circular course or track: *to run round in a ring*. **2. a** Circular object with round, hollow centre large in proportion to thickness of sides: *a ring of iron, light* &c.; *smoke rings*; *to fasten a piece of wire through a ring*; specif. **b** small band, hoop, of gold &c., sometimes set with gem(s), worn on a finger; **c** similar ornament worn on some other part of the body, (often in compounds) *ear-ring, nose-ring, ankle-ring* &c.; **d** metal or wooden ring attached to an object as handle &c.; **e** short hollow cylinder, (often in compounds) *napkin-ring* &c. **3.** Group of objects, persons &c. standing, or arranged, in a circle: *a ring of stones; to dance in a ring.* **4.** More or less circular enclosure for specific purpose, **a** *the Ring*, in boxing, *Prize-ring*; **b** for circus performance; **c** for bookmakers &c. at race-meeting: *the ring*, bookmakers collectively; **d** in show-ground, for judging animals &c. **5.** Group of people combining to obtain control of commercial or political affairs.

ring (II.), vb. trans. & intrans., fr. prec. **A.** trans. **1.** To encircle, surround: '*Ringed round with a flame of fair faces*' (Swinburne, 'Dolores'). Phr. *to ring cattle*, round them up. **2.** To put a ring on to: *to ring a pig, bull* &c., put ring through its nose. **3.** (gardening) To cut a circular groove in bark of: *to ring a tree.* **B.** intrans. (of bird, esp. hawk) To rise in spirals.

ring (III.), vb. intrans. & trans. O.E. *hringan*; M.E. *ringen*; cp. O.N. *hringja*; M. Du. *ringhen*; Germ. *ringen*, 'to ring'; prob. imitative. **A.** intrans. **1.** (of metal, esp. bell) To produce a clear, vibrating, resonant, sound when struck. Phr. *to ring true, false*, (of coin) to produce distinctive sound of genuine or false coin; hence (fig.) of voice, statement &c. **2. a** To sound clearly, resound, re-echo: *a ringing voice; a shot, cheer, command, rang out; a voice ringing in one's ears, dreams* &c.; **b** (fig.) to resound, recur to, be preserved in: *words ringing in one's mind* &c. **3. a** To be filled, reverberate, resound: *the air, the hall, rang with shouts and laughter*; **b** (also fig.) *the world rang with his praises.* **4.** (of ears) To have the sensation of a constant humming or buzzing. **5.** To cause a bell to ring as warning, signal, summons &c.: *to ring for tea, for a servant* &c.; *to ring at the front door.* **B.** trans. **1. a** To cause to ring: *to ring a coin on the counter*; specif. **b** *to ring the bell* (as signal, summons &c.). **2.** To produce by means of bell(s): *to ring a chime, peal, alarm* &c.; *to ring changes; ring the changes on*, (i.) recur constantly to the same theme, set of ideas and so on, in slightly different words; (ii.) to exhibit, use, a limited number of objects, or repeat the same series of songs, musical compositions &c. in varying order: *to ring the changes on the same old songs.* Phr. *to ring the knell of*, indicate destruction, downfall, of. **3.** (of bell) To produce (sound) when rung for specific purpose, in specific way: *to ring a peal* &c. **C.** Followed by adverbs and prepositions. *Ring down*, to give signal for lowering: *to ring down the curtain at the end of a play* &c. *Ring in*, to salute, proclaim, by ringing bells: *to ring in the New Year, a new era* &c. *Ring off*, to signal conclusion of telephone call. *Ring out*, to salute, take leave of, by ringing bells: *to ring out the Old Year. Ring up*, **1.** to give signal for raising: *to ring up the curtain*; **2.** to summon, rouse, by ringing a bell; specif., to summon to telephone, get into communication with by telephone.

ring (IV.), n., fr. prec. **1.** Act of ringing. **2. a** Distinctive, resonant sound produced by metal when struck: *the ring of the hammer on the anvil; the ring of a coin*; specif. **b** sound of bell: *to hear the ring of the door-bell; to answer one's ring.* **3. a** Clear, resonant sound: *the ring of his laughter, voice* &c.; **b** (fig.) clear mental or moral effect: *his story has the ring of truth about it.*

ring-bark, vb. trans. To cut off a ring in the bark round the trunk of a tree, in order to kill it, limit its growth &c.

ring-bolt, n. Bolt with ring at one end.

ring-bone, n. Pathological bony growth on pastern-bone of horse.

ring-cartilage, n. Ring-shaped cartilage in larynx.

ring-dove, n. Wood-pigeon, from white band on neck.

ringed, adj. [1. ringd; 2. rĭŋd], fr. P.P. of **ring** (II.). **a** Wearing a ring; **b** encircled by, marked with, a ring.

ringent, adj. [1. rínjent; 2. ríndžənt], fr. Lat. *ringent-(em)*, Pres. Part. of *ringi*, 'to open the mouth'. See **rictus**. (bot., zool.) Gaping, opened wide.

ringer (I.), n. [1. rínger; 2. ríŋə]. **ring** (II.) & **-er**. **1.** Quoit falling so as to surround pin. **2.** Hunted fox which takes a circular course.

ringer (II.), n. **ring** (III.) & **-er**. **1.** Bell-ringer. **2.** Device for causing bell to ring.

ring-fence, n. **a** Fence entirely surrounding estate &c.; **b** (fig.) moral boundary, complete barrier.

ring-finger, n. Third finger, esp. of left hand.

ring-hunt, n. Hunt in which fires are started in a ring round the game.

ringing, adj. [1. rínging; 2. ríŋiŋ]. **ring** (III.) & **-ing**. Clear, loud, and resonant: *a ringing voice, laugh, cheer* &c.

ringleader, n. [1. rínglēder; 2. ríŋlīdə]. Leader, organizer, of riot &c.

ringless, adj. [1. ríngles; 2. ríŋlis]. **ring** (I.) & **-less**. Without ring(s).

ringlet, adj. [1. rínglet; 2. ríŋlit]. **ring** (I.) & **-let**. **1.** Small ring. **2.** Curling, spiral, lock of hair.

ringleted, adj. [1. ríngleted; 2. ríŋlitid]. Prec. & **-ed**. **1.** Marked with ringlets. **2.** Wearing, arranged in, ringlets.

ringlety, adj. [1. ríngleti; 2. ríŋliti]. See prec. & **-y**. Like ringlets; ringleted.

ring-mail, n. Mail made of rings interlocked or stitched to leather &c.; chain-mail.

ringman, n. [1.ríngman; 2. ríŋmən]. Bookmaker.

ring-master, n. Person directing public performance in circus-ring.

ring-money, n. Metal rings used as money, esp. in primitive communities.

ring-neck, n. **a** Kind of N. American plover; **b** ring-necked duck.

ring-necked, adj. [1. ríng nekt; 2. ríŋ nekt]. Having a band of distinct colour round neck.

ring-net, n. Bag-like net fastened to a small hoop, for catching butterflies &c.

ring-ouzel, n. Small bird like thrush with white band on neck.

ring-snake, n. Small, harmless snake of N. America, with yellow band round neck.

ring-stand, n. Small, branched structure of china &c. on which finger-rings are hung.

ring-straked, adj. [1. ríng strākt; 2. ríŋ streikt]. (Bib.) Striped in rings.

ring-tail, n. Female of hen-harrier.

ring-tailed, adj. Having the tail marked with ring(s).

ring-taw, n. Game played with marbles.

ring-wall, n. Wall entirely enclosing estate &c.

ringworm, n. [1. ríngwěrm; 2. ríŋwʌ̄m]. Skin disease, *Tinea tonsurans*, with circular eruptions, usually on the scalp; due to a fungoid parasite.

rink, n. & vb. intrans. [1. ringk; 2. riŋk]. Old word (14th cent.) for jousting-ground. Origin doubtful. **1.** n. **a** (i.) Smooth, flat, hard surface specially prepared for roller-skating; (ii.) artificially prepared sheet of ice for skating; **b** part of sheet of ice marked off for curling. **2.** vb. To skate on a rink.

rinse (I.), vb. trans. [1. rins; 2. rins], fr. Fr. *rincer*, fr. O. Fr. *raincer*; perh. variant of O. Fr. *recincier*, 'rinse', possibly fr. Med. Lat. *resincerāre*, 'to cleanse'. See **re-** & **sincere**. **1.** Often *rinse out*, **a** to wash, cleanse, (linen &c.) by dipping and shaking in clean water, or pouring clean water upon; specif. **b** to remove soap from by shaking out in clean water after washing. **2.** Often *rinse out*, to put clean water &c. into, shake round and empty out: *to rinse out one's mouth, a jug* &c. **3.** To remove by rinsing: *to rinse the soap out of washed clothes* &c.

rinse (II.), n., fr. prec. Act of rinsing.

rinsings, n. pl. [1. rínsingz; 2. rínsiŋz]. Water which has been used for rinsing out a vessel &c.; matter thus washed out; dregs.

riot (I.), n. [1. ríut; 2. ráiət], fr. O. Fr. *riot*, also in Ital. *riota*. Etymol. doubtful. **1.** Disturbance of public peace by three or more persons uniting in lawless, turbulent conduct; civil outbreak, tumult. *Riot Act*, statute of 1715, for prevention and dispersal of riotous assemblies. Phr. *to read the Riot Act* (of magistrate &c.), to read this act as warning to rioters to disperse or become guilty of felony, hence (colloq.) to utter warning to unruly persons, children &c. **2. a** Lawlessness of life, dissipation, profligacy; Phr. *to run riot*, behave in an unrestrained manner, to show lack of discipline and control; **b** (fig.) unrestrained luxuriance, profusion, superabundance: *a riot of colour* &c.

riot (II.), vb. intrans., fr. O. Fr. *rioter*, fr. **riot**, 'riot'. See prec. **1.** To take part in a riot. **2.** To live, conduct oneself, in a wanton, profligate manner; to indulge in dissipation and extravagance. **3.** To indulge in to excess, revel in: *to riot in emotion* &c.

rioter, n. [1. ríuter; 2. ráiətə]. **riot** (II.) & **-er**. One who takes part in a riot; one who breaks the public peace; profligate, debauched person.

riotous, adj. [1. ríutus; 2. ráiətəs]. **riot** (I.) & **-ous**. **1.** (of persons and conduct &c.) Tending to provoke riot, promoting a breach of the public peace; turbulent. **2. a** Pertaining to, of the nature of, profligacy and debauchery; **b** (of persons) profligate, roistering. **3.** (fig.) Unrestrained, tending to run wild, impatient of control: *a riotous fancy.*

riotously, adv. Prec. & **-ly**. In a riotous manner.

riotousness, n. See prec. & **-ness**. State of being riotous.

riotry, n. [1. ríutri; 2. ráiətri]. **riot** (I.) & **-ry**. (rare) **1.** Riotousness. **2.** Riotous behaviour, rioting.

rip (I.), vb. trans. & intrans. [1. rip; 2. rip]. M.E. *ripen*, 'to tear'; apparently Scand., cp. Swed. *repa upp*, 'to rip up'; prob. connected w. **ripe**; cp. *rip-*, gradational form of O.E. *rīpan*, 'to reap', P.P. *ripen*. **A.** trans. **1.** *Rip open, up*, to slit, tear, asunder, by a sudden violent cutting or rending action: *to rip a sack open; to rip open a bag* &c.; *a bull rips up a horse with his horns; to rip one's coat up the back.* **2. a** *Rip off*, to tear off, remove by violent tearing or cutting: *to rip trimming off a garment* &c.; **b** *to rip a garment, the seams of a garment*, take to pieces by cutting stitches. **3.** To split (wood) by sawing with the grain. **4.** To tear, cut (a hole) by a ripping movement. **5.** (fig.) In such Phr. as *to rip up forgotten scandals* &c., to revive them, tear them from oblivion and recall them to mind. **B.** intrans. **1.** To tear, be liable to tear or come asunder: *the sort of cloth that rips at once.* **2.** Phrs. (colloq.) *let her, it, rip*, don't check, impede, stop (a machine &c.); *to let things rip*, be careless of consequences, allow events to follow their course without trying to guide them.

rip (II.), n., fr. prec. Long rent, slash, tear, e.g. in cloth, skin &c.

rip (III.), n. Variant of **rep** (II.), **reprobate**. **1.** Worn-out, useless horse, a screw. **2.** Disreputable, profligate person; a reprobate.

riparian, adj. & n. [1. rīpárian; 2. raipéəriən], fr. Lat. *rīpāri-(us)*, 'of, frequenting, river-banks', fr. *rīpa*, 'bank of stream'; cp. Gk. *eripnē*, 'broken cliff, crag'; & *ereipein*, 'to tear down'; further connected w. Lat. *rīvus*, 'stream, brook'. See further under **river**. **1.** adj. **a** Of, pertaining to, a river-bank: *riparian proprietor*, owner of land along bank of a river; *riparian rights*, those of owner of land along one or both banks of a stream; **b** (bot., zool.) growing on, frequenting, river-banks. **2.** n. Riparian proprietor.

ripe (I.), adj. [1. rīp; 2. raip]. O.E. *rīpe*, M.E. *rīpe*; cp. O.H.G. *rīfi*; O.S. *rīpi*; primary meaning 'ready to be harvested', hence 'mature'; cp. O.E. *rīpan*, 'to reap'. See discussion under **reap**. **1.** Ready to harvest as food &c.; grown to full perfection;

mature: *ripe fruit, corn* &c.; (fig.) *ripe lips*, red as ripe fruit. **2. a** Fully matured, perfected by being stored or treated until in proper or best state for eating, drinking &c.: *ripe game, wine, cheese* &c.; **b** fully developed, having attained full degree of perfection; expanded: *ripe beauty*. **3.** Mature, fully developed: *ripe experience, learning, judgement* &c. Phrs. *of ripe age*, mature, old; (*men &c.*) *of riper years*, grown up. **4.** Ready; having reached, developed into, been brought to, stage suitable for specific purpose and use: *schemes ripe for execution*; *minds ripe for rebellion*; *ripe for action*.

ripe (II.), vb. trans. & intrans., fr. prec. Rare and chiefly poetical for **ripen**.

ripely, adv. [1. rípli; 2. ráipli]. **ripe (I.)** & **-ly**. In a ripe manner.

ripen, vb. intrans. & trans. [1. rípen; 2. ráipən]. **ripe (I.)** & **-en**. **1.** intrans. To become ripe, approach maturity. **2.** trans. To make ripe, bring to maturity or full development.

ripeness, n. [1. rípnes; 2. ráipnis]. **ripe (I.)** & **-ness**. State of being ripe; maturity.

riposte, n. & vb. intrans. [1. ripóst; 2. ripóust], fr. Fr. *riposte*, fr. Ital. *risposta*, fr. P.P. of *rispondere*, 'to reply', fr. Lat. *respondēre*, 'to reply'. See **respond**. **1.** n. **a** (fencing) Quick lunge after parry; hence, **b** retort, repartee. **2.** vb. To make a riposte.

ripper, n. [1. ríper; 2. rípə]. **rip (I.)** & **-er**. **1.** One who, that which, rips; specif. **a** instrument for removing or shaping roof-tiles; **b** machine for ripping cloth &c.; **c** rip-saw. **2.** (slang) Admirable person or thing; equivalent to *topper, brick* &c.

ripping, adj. & adv. [1. ríping; 2. rípiŋ], fr. Pres. Part. of **rip (I.)**. (slang) **1.** adj. Arousing admiration and approval; splendid, thoroughly satisfactory. **2.** adv. Splendidly, capitally: *a ripping good story*.

rippingly, adv. Prec. & **-ly**. (slang) In a ripping manner, to a ripping degree.

ripple (I.), n. & vb. trans. [1. ripl; 2. rípl]. Cp. Du. *repel*; Germ. *riffel*, 'comb for flax'. **1.** n. Long-toothed, metal comb for stripping seeds &c. from flax. **2.** vb. To clean (flax) by means of a ripple.

ripple (II.), n. Perh. connected w. **rumple**. **1.** Slight undulation on surface of water, small wave or series of waves, gentle disturbance of surface by breeze &c., or by passage over rough stones &c. **2.** Slight wave in hair or on surface of any soft material. **3.** Light sound rising and falling gently and repeatedly: *a ripple of talk, laughter* &c.

ripple (III.), vb. intrans. & trans., fr. prec. **A.** intrans. **1.** (of water, stream &c.) To move in slight waves, be gently ruffled or disturbed by breeze or by passing over rough surface. **2.** (of sound) To rise and fall lightly and gently. **B.** trans. To cause to ripple; to curl, ruffle, surface of slightly.

ripple-mark, n. Ridge produced on surface of sand by action of waves.

ripplet, n. [1. ríplet; 2. ríplit]. **ripple (II.)** & **-et**. Small ripple.

ripply, adj. [1. rípli; 2. rípli]. **ripple (II.)** & **-y**. Covered with small waves; rippling.

rip-saw, n. **rip (I.)** & **saw (III.)**. Saw with large teeth for cutting planks &c. lengthwise with the grain.

Ripuarian, adj. [1. ripūárian; 2. ripjuéəriən], fr. Med. Lat. *rīpuāri-(us)*, prob. fr. Lat. *rīp-(a)*, 'river-bank'. See **riparian**. Of, pertaining to, the Franks settled on the banks of the Rhine, near Cologne, in the 5th cent.

Rip van Winkle, n. [1. rip van wíngkl; 2. ríp væn wíŋkl]. Name of hero of Washington Irving's 'Sleepy Hollow', who slept for twenty years. Person who is very much behind the times in ideas &c., and represents the views, prejudices, and ideals of a former generation.

rise (I.), vb. intrans. [1. rīz; 2. raiz]. O.E. *(ā)rīsan*; M.E. *rīsen*; cp. O.S. *rīsan*; O. Fris., O.N. *rīsa*; Goth. *(ur)reisan*, 'to rise'; O.H.G. *rīsan*, 'to rise, flow, fall'; perh. cogn. w. Lat. *rīvus*, 'stream'. See **river**, & cp. **raise** & **rear (I.)**. **A.** intrans. **1. a** To ascend, pass, go up, be carried, to higher level: *the aeroplane rose in the air*; *the mist is rising*; *his hand rose in salute*; *the lift rose*; specif. **b** (i.) (of curtain) to be raised at beginning of dramatic performance &c.; (ii.) (fig.) *the curtain rises*, a new situation, set of circumstances, begin(s); events start to develop. **2. a** (of fish) Be attracted to, and thrust nose through, break, surface of water after a fly &c.; **b** (fig., of persons) *to rise at* or *to a bait*, (i.) to be tempted into action by hope of advantage, reward &c.; (ii.) *rise to it*, to be irritated into replying to a provocative remark. **3. a** To come to erect position after lying, sitting, or kneeling; to get up: *to rise when a person enters*; *to rise from table, from one's knees* &c.; specif. **b** to get out of bed in the morning: *to rise early, with the sun, lark* &c.; **c** (of assembly, committee, Parliament &c.) to close a session; **d** (of a speaker) to stand up to address a meeting &c.; **e** to be restored to life: *to rise again*; *to rise from the dead*. **4. a** To increase in volume, spread, swell: *the river, water, flood, rises*; *the rising tide*; specif. **b** (of dough, bread &c.) to swell through action of ferment; **c** to become swollen through inflammation &c.: *a blister's rising on my heel*. Phr. (fig.) *my gorge rises at the thought* &c., I am strongly disgusted. **5.** (of sun, moon &c.) To become visible above the horizon. **6.** (of sound) To reach a higher pitch: *his voice rose to a shriek*; *rising and falling tones*. Phr. *a rising diphthong*, one with greater stress on second element. **7. a** To reach higher rank or position in life: *to rise from nothing*; *to rise in the world*; **b** to come to stand higher, gain in respect, consideration, and so on: *to rise in a person's estimation*. Phrs. *to rise above*, show oneself superior to; *to rise to*, show oneself equal to: *to rise to an occasion, emergency* &c. **8.** To increase in intensity, amount, degree &c., reach a greater degree, be intensified: *the wind rises*; *the temperature, value &c. rises*; *prices rise*; *rising excitement, anger* &c.; *one's spirits rise*; *her colour rose*. **9. a** To slope upward: *a hill rises behind the house*; *the ground rises gradually*; **b** to be visible as an elevation; tower up: *the building rose before them*. **10.** To revolt, rebel; to start active opposition: *to rise in arms, in rebellion*; *to rise against a tyrant*. **11. a** To have origin, come into existence: *the river rises in the hills*; **b** to originate, become perceptible to mind or senses: *thoughts rise within one*; *a lovely vision rose before me*.

rise (II.), n., fr. prec. **1.** Act of rising, upward movement, specif., of fish to surface of water in search of food, after bait &c.: *to fish all day and not have a rise*. Phr. *to take, get, a rise out of* (a person), provoke into showing unnecessary annoyance, petulance &c. by good-natured chaff. **2. a** Increase in amount, quality, intensity, value, pitch, volume &c.: *a rise of prices, temperature, wages* &c.; *prices are on the rise*, going up; *the rise and fall of the voice*; **b** amount of increase: *a rise of a pound a week*. **3.** (of heavenly body) Appearance above horizon, fact, process, of becoming visible; (usually in compounds) *sunrise, moonrise* &c. **4.** Attainment of higher position or rank: *a rise in life, in the world*; *his rise to power*. **5. a** Upward slope, ascent: *to follow a gentle rise*; **b** amount of slope: *a rise of 2 in 30*; **c** elevation, high ground, hill: *to look down from the rise*. **6.** (of material and non-material things) Origin, source, starting-point; process of developing or beginning to develop: *the rise of industrialism*. Phrs. *to have, take, its rise in*, to originate in; *to give rise to*, be cause or starting-point of. **7.** (archit.) **a** Riser **2**; **b** height of step. **8.** (min.) Shaft constructed from below.

risen, vb. [1. ríz(e)n; 2. ríz(ə)n]. P.P. of **rise (I.)**; O.E. *(ġe)risen*, M.E. *risen*.

riser, n. [1. rízer; 2. ráizə]. **rise (I.)** & **-er**. **1.** One who, that which, rises; esp. *a late, an early, riser*, person who gets up late, early. **2.** Upright face of step, between two treads.

risibility, n. [1. rizibíliti; 2. rizibíliti]. Next word & **-ity**. **a** Inclination to laugh; **b** capacity for laughter.

risible, adj. [1. rízibl; 2. rízibl], fr. Lat. *rīsibil-(is)*, 'able to laugh', fr. *rīs-(um)*, P.P. type of *rīdēre*, 'to laugh'; etymol. doubtful. Possibly cogn. w. Scrt. *vrīḍyati*, 'is ashamed', earlier **wrizd-*; for the meaning cp. Scrt. *smayatē*, 'smiles, smiles shamefacedly, blushes'. **1.** Capable of laughing, tending to laugh. **2.** Connected with, pertaining to, used in, laughing: *risible muscles* &c. **3.** (rare) Causing laughter; laughable, ridiculous.

rising (I.), adj. [1. rízing; 2. ráiziŋ], fr. Pres. Part. of **rise (I.)**. **1.** Increasing in importance, value, knowledge, distinction, power &c.: *a rising man, barrister* &c. Phr. *the rising generation*, the younger people of the period. **2.** Sloping upward, ascending: *rising ground*. **3.** *Rising forty* &c., approaching the age of.

rising (II.), n. **rise (I.)** & **-ing**. Act, process, of that which rises (in various senses); specif. **a** *the rising of the sun*, appearance above horizon; **b** resurrection; also *rising-again*; **c** revolt, organized rebellion; **d** small swelling, pimple.

risk (I.), n. [1. risk; 2. risk], fr. Fr. *risque*, fr. Ital. *risco*, fr. *riscare*, 'to risk'; etymol. doubtful. **1.** Possibility or likelihood of danger, injury, loss &c.; hazard: *there is no risk of drowning in shallow water*; *to take, run, risks*; *I'll take the risk of that*, will face the chance or danger (of). Phr. *at one's own risk*, oneself being responsible for possible loss, injury, incurring of blame &c. **2.** (insurance) **a** amount covered by insurance, sum insured; **b** he who, that which, is insured.

risk (II.), vb. trans., fr. Fr. *risquer*, fr. *risque*. See prec. **1.** To expose to risk; incur the possibility of loss, injury &c.; to venture, hazard: *to risk one's life, fortune, health* &c. **2.** To take the chance of, be prepared for possibility of, face result of: *to risk a battle*; *to risk a person's anger*; *to risk losing one's train*.

riskful, adj. [1. rískfool; 2. rískful]. **risk (I.)** & **-ful**. Involving many risks.

riskily, adv. [1. rískili; 2. rískili]. **risky** & **-ly**. In a risky, hazardous, manner.

riskiness, n. [1. rískines; 2. rískinis]. See prec. & **-ness**. State or quality of being risky.

riskless, adj. [1. ri̇skles; 2. rísklis]. **risk (I.)** & **-less**. Without risk, involving no risk.

risky, adj. [1. ríski; 2. ríski]. **risk (I.)** & **-y**. **1.** Involving risk; dangerous, hazardous. **2.** Risqué.

risqué, adj. [1. réskā; 2. rískei], fr. Fr., P.P. of *risquer*, 'to risk', see **risk (I.)**. (of story, play &c.) Tending towards, verging on, impropriety.

rissole, n. [1. rísōl; 2. rísoul], fr. Fr.; etymol. doubtful. Ball, cake, or roll of minced meat or fish mixed with potato and yolk of egg, more or less highly flavoured, rolled in bread-crumbs and fried.

ritardando, adv., adj., & n. [1. rètardándō; 2. ritādǽndou], fr. Ital., fr. gerund of *ritardare*, 'to make slow, go slowly', fr. Lat. *retardāre*, 'to hinder', see **retard**. **1.** (mus.) **a** adv. To be played more slowly, decreasing speed; **b** adj. (of passage &c.) played slower, with gradually decreasing speed. **2.** n. Passage to be played with gradually decreasing speed.

rite, n. [1. rīt; 2. rait], fr. Lat. *rīt-(us)*, 'religious ceremony; custom, practice'; cp. Lat. *rīte*, 'with due ceremony, solemnly'; & Lat. *rēri*, 'to think', see **ratio**; Gk. *arithmós*, 'number', see **arithmetic**; O.E. *rīm*, 'number'; O.H.G. *rīm*, 'series, number'; the orig. meaning of base **rei-* was 'to put together', hence 'to arrange in a specific way; to carry out in appointed manner', & on the other hand, 'to arrange in a series, enumerate, count'. **1. a** Form, consisting of prescribed or customary symbolic bodily actions, **or**

gestures, and of words, used in performing religious and other ceremonies; **b** series, group, of such symbolic observances associated with some specific service: *the rite of baptism*; **c** liturgy and ceremonial prescribed in some specific branch of the Christian Church: *the Anglican rite*. **2.** Observance of customary forms and formalities associated with specific occasion: *the rites of hospitality*.

ritual, n. & adj. [1. rítūal, ríchooal; 2. rítjuəl, rítʃuəl]. Lat. *rituāle*, neut. of *rituālis*, 'pertaining to rites'. See prec. **1.** n. **a** Rites and ceremonies collectively; religious or other solemn ceremonial; **b** specific form of ritual; **c** a book setting forth ceremonies to be followed in religious or other solemn observance. **2.** adj. Pertaining to rites or to ritual.

ritualism, n. [1. rítūalizm; 2. rítjuəlizəm]. Prec. & **-ism**. **a** The practice of, and insistence on, ritual; esp. undue insistence on importance of ritual in religious worship; **b** specif. (in disparagement) the practice of and insistence upon elaborate ritual among the High Church party in the Church of England.

ritualist, n. [1. rítūalist; 2. rítjuəlist]. **ritual** & **-ist**. **a** Person who practises and attaches great importance to ritual in public religious worship; **b** specif., one of a party in the Church of England which does this, and desires to restore pre-Reformation ritual.

ritualistic, adj. [1. rìtūalístik; 2. rìtjuəlístik]. Prec. & **-ic**. **a** Pertaining to ritualists or ritualism; **b** insisting on, practising ritualism.

ritualistically, adv. [1. rìtūalístikali; 2. rìtjuəlístikəli]. Prec. & **-al** & **-ly**. In a ritualistic manner.

ritualize, vb. trans. & intrans. [1. rítūalīz; 2. rítjuəlaiz]. **ritual** & **-ize**. **1.** trans. To use ritual in (ceremonies), make ritualistic. **2.** intrans. To become ritualistic; practise ritualism.

ritually, adv. [1. rítūali; 2. rítjuəli]. **ritual** & **-ly**. In a ritual manner; according to ritual.

rivage, n. [1. rívij; 2. ráividž], fr. Fr. *rivage*, fr. O. Fr. *rive*, 'bank', fr. Lat. *rīpa*, 'bank of river', see **riparian**, & **-age**. (rare or poet.) Shore, bank, margin, of river or stream.

rival (I.), n. [1. rívl; 2. ráivl], fr. Lat. *rīvāl-(is)*, 'rival, competitor'; cp. also Lat. *rīvinus*, 'rival'; etymol. unknown. Person striving, or tending, to equal or excel another; person endeavouring to obtain some object for which another is also contending; a fellow-competitor; opponent: *to be jealous of one's rival*; *rivals in love*; *rivals for a woman's hand*, *in trade* &c. Phr. *without a rival*, unequalled.

rival (II.), adj., fr. prec. Playing the part of a rival; competing, emulating: *rival firms*.

rival (III.), vb. trans. & intrans., fr. **rival (I.)**. **1.** trans. To approach, or attain, equality with; to compete with, equal, vie with, be comparable to: *Donne cannot rival Milton in grandeur and beauty*; *her cheeks rival the rose in hue*. **2.** intrans. (rare) To be rivals.

rivalry, n. [1. rívlri; 2. ráivlri]. **rival (I.)** & **-ry**. Act of competing with another, state of being rivals; **a** act of competing for same object as another; **b** state of being equal with another in possession of some quality; close approach to equality in merit or other quality between two persons or things; *friendly rivalry*, reciprocal emulation between two persons.

rivalship, n. [1. rívlship; 2. ráivlʃip]. **rival (I.)** & **-ship**. (rare) Rivalry.

rive, vb. trans. & intrans. [1. rīv; 2. raiv]. M.E. *rīven*, fr. O.N. *rīfa*, 'to break'; cp. M. Du. *rijven*, Germ. *reiben*, 'to rub'; prob. cogn. w. Gk. *ereipein*, 'to throw down; to fall headlong'; *eripnē*, 'precipice'; Lat. *rīpa*, 'steep bank, river-bank'. See **riparian** & **river**. **A.** trans. **1.** To split, force asunder, rend, cleave. **2.** To tear forcibly, wrench, remove by force. **B.** intrans. To be torn or split asunder.

rivel, vb. intrans. & trans. [1. rívl; 2. rívl]. M.E. *rivelen*, perh. back-formation fr. O.E. *rifelede*, 'wrinkled', fr. O.E. **rifel*, M.E. *rivel*, 'wrinkle'; cp. O.E. *gerifod*, 'wrinkled'. (rare or archaic) **1.** intrans. To wrinkle, contract, shrivel up. **2.** trans. To draw together, cause to wrinkle.

riven, adj. [1. rívn; 2. rívən]. M.E. *riven*, fr. O.N. *rifinn*, P.P. of *rīfa*, 'to break', see **rive**. (chiefly poet. and archaic) Rent asunder by force; split, cleft.

river, n. [1. ríver; 2. rívə], fr. O. Fr. *rivere*, fr. Low Lat. **rīpāria*, fr. Lat. *rīpāri-(us)*, 'of a river-bank', fr. *rīpa*, 'steep bank, bank of river, shore'; cp. Gk. *ereipein*, 'to throw down; to fall headlong'; *eripnē*, 'precipice, slope'; prob. cogn. w. O.N. *rīfa*, 'to break', see **riparian** & **rive**, *rifna*, 'to split'. **1.** Large body of water flowing in a definite, natural channel and discharging into the sea, a lake, or another river. **2.** Plentiful flow, copious stream: *a river of lava*; *rivers of tears, of blood*.

riverain, adj. & n. [1. ríverān; 2. rívərein], fr. Fr. See **rivière** & **-an**. **1.** adj. Of, pertaining to, frequenting, dwelling near, a river or its banks. **2.** n. Person dwelling on bank of river.

river-basin, n. Land drained by river and its tributaries.

river-bed, n. Bottom of channel in which river flows.

rivered, adj. [1. ríverd; 2. rívəd]. **river** & **-ed**. Having rivers; (often in compounds) *well-rivered* &c.

river-god, n. Deity presiding over and haunting river.

river-horse, n. Hippopotamus.

riverine, adj. [1. ríverīn; 2. rívərain]. **river** & **-ine**. Of, pertaining to, frequenting, a river or its banks.

riverless, adj. [1. ríverles; 2. rívəlis]. **river** & **-less**. Without rivers.

river-meadow, n. Low-lying meadow on bank of river.

riverside, n. & adj. [1. ríversīd; 2. rívəsaid]. **1.** n. Ground on or near river-bank. **2.** adj. Situated on, found on, bank of river.

rivet (I.), n. [1. rívet; 2. rívit], fr. Fr., fr. *river*, 'to clench'; etymol. uncertain. Metal pin or bolt with head at one end, used for fastening plates of metal &c. together, the pin being passed through corresponding holes in the plates &c., and the end hammered out into a second head.

rivet (II.), vb. trans., fr. prec. **1.** To fasten with a rivet. **2.** To hammer down head of (rivet &c.) to make fastening secure. **3.** (fig.) **a** To attract and fix firmly, concentrate: *to rivet one's eyes, attention, on*; **b** to attract strongly, absorb: *the performance riveted his attention*.

rivière, n. [1. riviār; 2. rívjɛə], fr. Fr. *rivière*, fr. O. Fr. *rivere*, 'stream', see **river**. Necklace of diamonds &c., usually in several strings.

rivulet, n. [1. rívūlet; 2. rívjulit], fr. Lat. *rivul-(us)*, 'brook', dimin. fr. *riv-(us)*, 'brook', see **river**, & **-et**. **1.** Small stream, brook. **2.** Kind of geometer moth.

rix-dollar, n. [1. ríks dolar; 2. ríks dɔlə], fr. Du. *rijksdaler*, fr. *rijk*, 'kingdom'; cp. O.H.G. *rīhhi*, Goth. *reiks*, 'kingdom'; O.E. *rīce*, 'power; kingdom', see **rich**, & **dollar**. Silver coin formerly current in Holland, Sweden, Denmark, and Germany.

roach (I.), n. [1. rōch; 2. routʃ], fr. O. Fr. *roche*; etymol. doubtful. Small silvery, freshwater fish, *Leuciscus rutilus*, of the carp family; Phr. *as sound as a roach*, thoroughly healthy or robust.

roach (II.), n. Etymol. unknown. (naut.) Curve cut in foot of square-sail to clear sail immediately below.

road (I.), n. [1. rōd; 2. roud]. O.E. *rād*, 'a riding, a journey'; in gradational relation to O.E. *rīdan*, see **ride (I.)**; M.E. *rood*; cp. O.N. *reið*, M.H.G. *reite*, 'riding'; M. Du. *reede*, 'roadstead'. **1.** Track with artificially levelled and prepared hard, smooth surface, constructed upon a basis of stones tightly packed and rammed down, used as means of communication between one place and another. Phrs. *on the road*, travelling, passing from place to place; *rule of the road*, regulation controlling relative position of vehicles &c. meeting or overtaking on highway, of ships at sea &c.; (*to go, travel*) *by road*, travel on foot, horseback, or by a vehicle along the highway; contrasted with journey by rail; *to take the road*, start on journey by road, (also archaic) to become a highwayman. **2.** Way of approach, path, route, course by which a destination is reached: *to be uncertain of one's road*; *our road lies through the forest*. Phrs. *in the road*, in the way, hampering movement or action; acting as a hindrance (lit. & fig.); *to get in one's road*, hinder, obstruct progress; (also fig.) *get out of the road* &c. **3.** (fig.) Method, mode, means, line of action, by which an object, aim, is gained, or some desired condition attained to: *the road to fame, success, wealth*; *the road to ruin*, mode of conduct which will end in disaster; *no royal road to*, no easy method of gaining, no means of obtaining without personal effort. **4.** (naut., usually pl.) Roadstead.

road (II.), vb. trans., fr. prec. (of dog) To track by scent.

road-book, n. Book with maps, description of routes, roads &c. for use of travellers.

road-hog, n. Motorist &c. with no consideration for safety or comfort of others.

roadless, adj. [1. rṓdles; 2. róudlis]. **road (I.)** & **-less**. Without roads.

roadman, n. [1. rṓdman; 2. róudmæn]. Man employed in care and repair of roads.

roadmender, n. [1. rṓdmender; 2. róudmɛndə]. Man employed in mending, repairing, roads with fresh metal.

road-metal, n. Stones broken up for use in making or repairing roads.

roadside, n. & adj. [1. rṓdsīd; 2. róudsaid]. **1.** n. Edge, border, of, tract adjacent to, a road. **2.** adj. Found, situated, at or on the side of a road: *a roadside inn*.

roadstead, n. [1. rṓdsted; 2. róudsted]. **road** & **stead**. Piece of water near shore but outside harbour, where ships may ride in safety.

roadster, n. [1. rṓdster; 2. róudstə]. **road** & **-ster**. **1.** Horse, motor-car, bicycle, for long journeys by road. **2.** Ship at anchor in roadstead.

road-surveyor, n. Official supervising care and maintenance of highways &c.

roadway, n. [1. rṓdwā; 2. róudwei]. Part of road kept for traffic; esp. as distinct from footpath(s) at side.

roadworthy, adj. [1. rṓdwërdhi; 2. róudwɜ̄ði]. Fit to be used on the road.

roam (I.), vb. intrans. & trans. [1. rōm; 2. roum]. M.E. *rōmen*, 'to direct one's course, wander, roam'; etymol. doubtful. **1.** intrans. To wander; go or travel without fixed route or destination; to ramble: *to roam about the country, forest* &c. **2.** trans. To travel, voyage over, range: *to roam the world, the seas* &c.

roam (II.), n., fr. prec. (rare) Act of roaming; ramble.

roamer, n. [1. rṓmer; 2. róumə]. **roam (I.)** & **-er**. One who roams; a wanderer; one who seeks distractions away from home; a rolling stone.

roan (I.), adj. & n. [1. rōn; 2. roun], fr. O. Fr. *rouen*; cp. Provenç. *rouant*; Ital. *roano*; etymol. doubtful. **1.** adj. (of horses &c.) Of dark bay or chestnut colour mingled with grey or white. **2.** n. Roan horse.

roan (II.), n. Perh. fr. Pl.-N. Rouen, in France. Soft leather made of sheepskin and used in bookbinding.

roar (I.), vb. intrans. & trans. [1. rōr; 2. rɔ̄]. O.E. *rārian*; M.E. *rōren*; cp. O.H.G. *rēren*, 'to bellow'; cp. the remote cognates Lith. *rēt*, 'to bark', fr. *réju*, 'to cry aloud'; Lett. *rāt*, 'to scold'; O.N. *rōmr*, 'voice'; Lat. *rāvus*, 'hoarse'; *raucus*, 'hoarse'. See **raucous** & also **rumour**. **1.** intrans. **a** (i.) (of animals) To utter, produce, a deep, hoarse, loud, rumbling, or vibrant, inarticulate sound: *the lion roars*; (ii.) of inanimate things or forces: *the wind, sea, roars*; *the fire roars up the chimney*; **b** (of persons) to speak, cry out, laugh, with loud, deep, resonant sound; to speak with the voice much raised; to shout: *don't roar at me.* Phr. *to roar with laughter*, laugh loudly and heartily; **c** specif. (of horse) to produce a loud, hoarse sound in breathing, owing to inflammation of larynx &c. **2.** trans. To utter in a deep, loud, resonant voice: *to roar a command*; *to roar out a song.*

roar (II.), n., fr. prec. **1.** Loud, deep, hoarse, resonant sound: *the roar of a lion, of waves, of a torrent, of the wind in the trees, of traffic.* **2.** Loud, deep, prolonged sound of laughter, or of the voice in pain, anger &c.: *roars of laughter*; *a roar of anger.*

roarer, n. [1. rōrer; 2. rɔ́rə]. **roar** (I.) & **-er.** Horse suffering from roaring.

roaring (I.), adj. [1. rōring; 2. rɔ́riŋ]. **roar** (I.) & **-ing.** **1.** Noisy, boisterous, rough. Phr. *the roaring forties*, stormy tract in Atlantic between 40° and 50° N. lat. **2.** Brisk, active, flourishing: *in roaring health*; *doing a roaring trade.*

roaring (II.), n. **roar** (I.) & **-ing.** **a** Sound made by anything that roars: *the roaring of the wind* &c.; **b** specif., disease of horses characterized by loud breathing due to narrowing of windpipe through inflammation &c.

roast (I.), vb. trans. & intrans. [1. rōst; 2. roust]. M.E. *rōsten*, fr. O. Fr. *rostir*, of Gmc. origin; cp. O.H.G. *rōsten.* **A.** trans. **1. a** To cook, esp. (meat) before an open fire; Phr. *a fire big enough to roast an ox*, a very big, hot fire; **b** (now, usually) to cook in a hot oven, bake; **c** to cook by covering with hot ashes. **2. a** To expose to extreme heat: *to roast one's feet at the fire*; **b** to expose to excessive heat as form of torture: *to be roasted alive*; also fig., to feel very hot. **3.** To dry, parch, by exposure to heat: *to roast coffee.* **4.** To bring to state of extreme heat for the purpose of removing impurities &c.: *to roast metal.* **5.** (archaic slang) To banter, chaff. **B.** intrans. **1.** To be cooked by roasting: *the joint will never roast before such a small fire.* **2.** (chiefly in Pres. Part.) *I'm simply roasting*, am extremely hot.

roast (II.), n., fr. prec. Joint of roast meat. Phr. *to rule the roast*, to be master or leader.

roaster, n. [1. rōster; 2. róustə]. **roast** (I.) & **-er.** **1.** One who, that which, roasts; specif., machine, oven, device, for roasting meat, coffee &c. **2.** Furnace for roasting ore. **3.** Pig, chicken, &c. suitable for roasting.

roasting-jack, n. [1. rōsting jàk; 2. róustiŋ džǽk]. Apparatus placed before the fire, with a hook which revolves so as to expose to the heat in turn every side of a joint which is being roasted.

rob, vb. trans. [1. rob; 2. rɔb]. M.E. *robben*, fr. O. Fr. *rober*, of Gmc. origin; cp. O.H.G. *roubōn*, M. Du. *rōven*; the O.E. cognate is *rēafian*, 'to rob, plunder'. See **reave.** **1. a** To steal, carry off, property from (a person): *to rob a man of his money*: *to rob one's benefactor*; **b** to steal, take unlawfully, the contents of; to plunder, loot, rifle: *to rob a safe, a till, house.* **2.** To deprive of rightful property or what is due: *to rob a person of his inheritance, rights, of his fair name.*

robber, n. [1. rόber; 2. rɔ́bə]. Prec. & **-er.** One who robs.

robbery, n. [1. rόberi; 2. rɔ́bəri]. **rob** & **-ery.** **a** Act of robbing; theft, unlawful seizure of another's property by force or intimidation; **b** unfair extortion of money; exorbitant charge: *to ask such prices is sheer robbery.*

robe (I.), n. [1. rōb; 2. roub], fr. O. Fr. *robe*, 'dress', orig. 'booty'; of Gmc. origin, cogn. w. **rob.** **1.** Loose, flowing outer garment; specif. **a** (pl.) official, ceremonial, full dress, consisting of one or more long, flowing outer garments: *royal robes*; *peers', bishops', judges', robes*; *academic robes*; *Mistress of the Robes*, highest lady in royal household; Phr. *gentlemen of the long robe*, lawyers; **b** (archaic) a woman's dress. **2.** (poet.) Something which envelops, wraps, covers; a pall: *Nature wore a robe of snow.*

robe (II.), vb. trans. & intrans., fr. prec. **1.** trans. To cover, array, invest, with a robe or robes, esp. with official dress: *the bishop was robed by his chaplain.* **2.** intrans. To put on, array oneself in, official robes: *the peers had robed before arriving.*

robe-de-chambre, n. [1. rob de shombr; 2. rɔb də ʃɑ̃br]. Fr. Dressing-gown.

robin, n. [1. róbin; 2. rɔ́bin], fr. O. Fr. *Robin*, dimin. of personal name *Robert.* **1.** Also *robin-redbreast*, small, brown, English singing-bird, with a bright reddish-orange breast, fond of human society. **2.** Outside British Isles the name is applied to different birds, e.g. in U.S.A., to a red-breasted thrush; also called *American robin.*

Robin Goodfellow, n. [1. róbin góodfelō; 2. rɔ́bin gúdfelou]. A merry, mischievous elf or goblin.

Robinia, n. [1. rōbínia; 2. roubíniə], fr. J. & V. Robin, French botanists, 17th cent. The false acacia or locust tree.

roborant, adj. & n. [1. rόborant; 2. róubərənt], fr. Lat. *rōborant-(em)*, Pres. Part. of *rōborāre*, 'to strengthen', fr. *rōbor-*, stem of *rōbur*, 'strength'. See **robust.** (med.) **1.** adj. Strengthening, restorative. **2.** n. Strengthening medicine, tonic.

robot, n. [1. rόbot; 2. róubɔt], fr. Slav. *robotnik*, 'workman'; O. Slav. *robŭ*, 'servant', & Russ. *robóta*, 'work', are either old Gmc. loans, or cogn. w. Goth. *arbaiþs*, 'labour, hardship', O.E. *earfoð*, 'hardship', O.H.G. *arabeit*, Mod. Germ. *arbeit*, 'work'. A mechanical man, automaton, from the play, 'R.U.R.' (Rossum's Universal Robots), by Karel Capek.

Rob Roy canoe, n. [1. rób rói kanōō; 2. rɔ́b rɔ́i kənú]. Adopted by the inventor, J. Macgregor, fr. title of Scott's novel, used by him as a pen-name. A canoe, partly decked in and paddled by double-bladed paddles.

roburite, n. [1. rόburīt; 2. róubərait], fr. Lat. *rōbur*, 'strength', see **robust**, & **-ite.** Powerful kind of flameless explosive.

robust, adj. [1. rōbúst; 2. roubʌ́st], fr. Lat. *rōbustus*, 'oaken; solid, strong; robust'; fr. *rōbur* (for *rōbus*), 'hard, central part of oak; oak timber; hardness, solidity; strength, vigour', named fr. the colour of the wood, cp. Lat. *rōbus, ruber*, 'red'. See **rubric.** Strong, sound, healthy, vigorous, in body or mind; also *a robust intellect, intelligence* &c.

robustious, adj. [1. rōbúschus; 2. roubʌ́stʃəs]. Prec. & **-ious.** (obs.) Boisterous, assertive, blustering, noisy, hearty in manner.

robustly, adv. [1. rōbústli; 2. roubʌ́stli]. **robust** & **-ly.** In a robust manner.

robustness, n. [1. rōbústnes; 2. roubʌ́stnis]. See prec. & **-ness.** State or quality of being robust; vigour, capacity to endure strain and hardship &c.

roc, n. [1. rok; 2. rɔk], fr. Arab. *rokh.* Large, fabulous bird of Arabia and Persia.

rocambole, n. [1. rókambōl; 2. rɔ́kəmboul]. Fr. Etymol. doubtful. Tall, perennial herb resembling leek and with garlic-like flavour.

rochet, n. [1. róchet; 2. rɔ́tʃit], fr. O. Fr., of Gmc. origin; cp. Germ. *rock*, 'coat'; O.E. *rocc*; O.N. *rokkr*, 'tunic, upper garment'; cogn. w. M. Ir. *rucht*, 'tunic'. White surplice-like vestment of lawn, worn by bishops under the black chimere; with, in the Anglican Church, the loose sleeves showing; in the Roman Church the sleeves are tight and adorned with lace.

rock (I.), n. [1. rok; 2. rɔk]. M.E. *rokke* &c.; cp. O.E. *rocc*, & O. Fr. *rok* & *roke*; origin uncertain. **1. a** Mass of hard, stony matter, esp. an extensive formation of such matter; **b** an isolated portion of stony matter, projecting from surrounding soil, or from the sea; a crag; Phrs. *as firm as a rock*, very rigid, steady, immovable; *the Rock*, Gibraltar; **c** detached piece of such matter, of considerable size; a boulder. **2. a** Portion of rock in the sea, coming near to, or projecting above, the surface, considered as a source of danger to ships; Phr. (fig., of persons) *on the rocks*, in financial straits; **b** any circumstance causing, or likely to cause, disaster, failure, disagreement &c.: *religious prejudice was the rock upon which the measure was wrecked.* **3.** (geol.) Any solid mineral substance, of whatever character, naturally deposited, forming part of the surface or crust of the earth; from a geological point of view granite, chalk, gravel, sand, clay are all rocks. **4.** A hard sweetmeat made of sugar.

rock (II.), vb. trans. & intrans. O.E. *roccian*; M.E. *rocken*; cp. O.H.G. *rucchen*; Swed. *rucke, rocke*; M. Du. *rucken*; Germ. *rücken*, 'to pull, push, agitate'. **A.** trans. **1.** To cause to move, swing, sway, backwards and forwards on, or as on, an axis or point, esp. for the purpose of soothing or quieting: *to rock a cradle, a child in a cradle, a child in one's arms*; *to rock oneself to sleep*; *the waves rock the boat.* **2.** To cause to sway, shake, oscillate, violently; cause to reel from side to side, backwards and forwards: *the earthquake rocked the houses.* **3.** (min.) To shake, wash, in a cradle: *to rock gold-bearing sand.* **B.** intrans. **a** To sway from side to side on, or as on, an axis or point: *the cradle rocks*; *the boat rocks on the water*; *the trees rock in the wind*; **b** to shake, oscillate, with violence: *the earthquake made the houses rock.*

rock (III.), n., fr. prec. Act of rocking.

rock (IV.), n. M.E. *rok*; cp. O.N. *rokkr*; O.H.G. *roccho*; M. Du. *rocke.* Cp. **rocket** (I.). (hist.) Distaff.

rock-bird, n. Bird living or nesting in rock, esp. puffin.

rock-bottom, adj. Down to the rock (chiefly colloq. or fig.), very lowest: *rock-bottom prices* &c.; also as n., *down to rock-bottom.*

rock-bound, adj. Surrounded, hemmed in, by rocks.

rock-bun, rock-cake, n. Small currant cake with a rough, hard top.

rock-cork, n. Kind of light-coloured asbestos.

rock-crystal, n. Fine, transparent kind of quartz, esp. when found in hexagonal prisms.

rock-dove, n. Wild pigeon, *Columba livia.*

rock-drill, n. Instrument for boring into rock.

Rock English, n. Dialect of Gibraltar.

rocker, n. [1. róker; 2. rɔ́kə]. **rock** (II.) & **-er.** **1.** One of the curved supports of cradle, rocking-chair &c. **2.** Cradle used in mining. **3.** (skating) **a** Skate with curved blade; **b** rocking-turn.

rockery, n. [1. rókeri; 2. rɔ́kəri]. **rock** (I.) & **-ery.** Artificial mound of earth with rocks built in or embedded at irregular intervals, so as to leave pockets of earth; used in gardens for growing rock-plants.

rocket (I.), n. [1. róket; 2. rɔ́kit], fr. Ital. *rocchetta*, dimin. of *rocca*, 'distaff'. **rock** (IV.) & **-et.** Firework in the shape of a cylinder, usually fixed to a stick, propelled to considerable height by explosion of gas in interior, used as signal, to convey life-line, or for ornamental display.

rocket (II.), vb. trans. & intrans., fr. prec. **A.** trans. To fire rockets in the direction of. **B.** intrans. **1.** (of bird, esp. game) To rise straight upwards. **2.** (of horse, rider) **a** To dart swiftly forward; **b** to give a bounding plunge.

rocket (III.), n., fr. Fr. *roquette*, fr. Ital. *ruchetta*, dimin. of *ruca*, fr. Lat. *ērūca*, 'cole-wort'. Etymol. doubtful. Genus of garden herbs and flowering plants of many varieties, esp. (i.) *Eruca sativa*, with white flowers veined with purple, growing wild in some parts of Europe, the leaves being used for salad; and (ii.) *Hesperis matronalis*, the garden rocket, perennial plant with white, blue, or pink flowers, and sweet perfume.

rocketer, n. [1. róketer; 2. rɔ́kitə]. **rocket** (II.) & **-er.** Rocketing bird.

rock-fever, n. Kind of intermittent fever prevalent in Malta and Gibraltar.

rock-fish, n. Kind of wrasse or goby, found off rocky coasts.
rock-garden, n. Artificially arranged system of rocks built into banks or mounds for cultivation of rock-plants.
rock-goat, n. Wild goat, ibex.
rock-hewn, adj. Carved out of the rock.
rockily, adv. [1. rókili; 2. rɔ́kili]. **rocky** & **-ly.** In a rocky manner.
rockiness, n. [1. rókines; 2. rɔ́kinis]. See prec. & **-ness.** State or quality of being rocky.
rocking-chair, n. [1. róking chār; 2. rɔ́kiŋ tʃɛə]. Chair mounted on rockers.
rocking-horse, n. Wooden, painted horse, mounted on rockers for a child to ride.
rocking-stone, n. Large boulder poised so as to rock with slight impulse.
rocking-tool, n. Instrument for roughening copper plate in mezzotint engraving.
rocking-turn, n. (skating) Turn from an edge to same edge in opposite direction.
rock-leather, n. Rock-cork.
rockless, adj. [1. rókles; 2. rɔ́klis]. **rock (I.)** & **-less.** Without rock(s).
rocklet, n. [1. róklet; 2. rɔ́klit]. **rock (I.)** & **-let.** Small rock.
rock-like, adj. **rock (I.)** & **-like.** Resembling rock.
rockling, n. [1. rókling; 2. rɔ́kliŋ]. **rock (I.)** & **-ling.** Small sea-fish.
rock-oil, n. Petroleum.
rock-paper, n. Rock-cork.
rock-pigeon, n. Rock-dove.
rock-plant, n. Any small plant of Alpine habit, often grown in rockeries and rock-gardens.
rock-rabbit, n. Cony, hyrax.
rock-ribbed, adj. Containing, supported by, ridges or seams of rock.
rock-rose, n. Kind of Cistus or Helianthemum, with single yellow, pink, red, or white flowers.
rock-salt, n. Salt found in solidified state.
rock-shaft, n. Oscillating shaft in engine &c.
rock-silk, n. Kind of asbestos.
rock-snake, n. Python.
rock-sucker, n. Lamprey.
rock-tar, n. Petroleum.
rock-whistler, n. Marmot.
rock-wood, n. Kind of brown asbestos.
rock-work, n. Artificial bank, wall, or mound of rocks.
rocky (I.), adj. [1. róki; 2. rɔ́ki]. **rock (I.)** & **-y.** **1.** Full of, abounding in, composed of, resembling rock(s); *the Rocky Mountains*, great mountain range of N. America; (colloq.) *the Rockies.* **2.** (fig.) Hard, unyielding, or unfeeling.
rocky (II.), adj. **rock (II.)** & **-y.** (slang) Inclined to rock; shaky, unsteady, tottery.
Rocky Mountain sheep, n. The big-horn.
rococo, adj. & n. [1. rŏkṓkō; 2. ròukóukou]. Fr.; origin doubtful; possibly altered form of *rocaille*, 'rock work'. **1.** adj. (of archit., furniture; also of lit. style) Characterized by excess of ornament; florid, flamboyant. **2.** n. Architecture &c. of this kind; taste for the florid in art.
rod, n. [1. rod; 2. rɔd]. O.E. *rodd*, cp. O.N. *rudda*, 'club'; etymol. doubtful. **1.** Long, slender, straight sapling, twig, shoot, cut from a tree or bush; *ash rod*, young ash sapling; specif. **a** (usually in compounds) rod cut or used for specific purpose: *divining-rod, curtain-rod* &c.; **b** symbol of office or authority; also as name of official bearer of such: *Black Rod*; **c** switch, or bundle of switches used for punishment; Phrs. *to kiss the rod*, submit willingly to severe discipline; *to have a rod in pickle for*, have punishment waiting for; **d** (fig.) corporal punishment, discipline, correction. Phr. *to spare the rod and spoil the child.* **2.** Long, light, slender pole, usually in detachable sections, to which fishing-line and reel are attached; also *fishing-rod.* **3.** Slender metal bar forming connexion or support. **4.** Measure of length, 5½ yards; pole, perch. **5.** (anat.) One of the small rod-like bodies contained in the retina &c.

rode, vb. [1. rōd; 2. roud]. O.E. *rād*; M.E. *rood*; Pret. of **ride.**
rodent (I.), adj. [1. rṓdent; 2. róudənt], fr. Lat. *rōdent-(em)*, Pres. Part. of *rōdere*, 'to gnaw'; cp. Lat. *rādere*, 'to scrape, scratch'; cogn. w. Scrt. *rádati*, 'tears, scrapes, gnaws'; *radanaš*, 'tooth'; O.H.G. *rāzi*, 'sharp, acid'; O.E. *rætt*, 'rat'. See **rat. 1.** Of an order of vertebrates having two slightly curved lower incisors and no canine teeth; e.g. the mouse, rat, beaver, squirrel &c. **2.** Gnawing, eating away: *a rodent ulcer.*
rodent (II.), n., fr. prec. Rodent animal.
rodential, adj. [1. rōdénshal; 2. roudénʃəl]. Prec. & **-ial.** Of, pertaining to, of the nature of, a rodent.
rodeo, n. [1. rōdā́ō; 2. roudéiou]. Span., fr. *rodear*, 'to surround', fr. Lat. *rōtāre*, 'to revolve', see **rotate. a** Rounding up of cattle for branding &c.; **b** exhibition in which the skill of cowboys is displayed.
rodless, adj. [1. ródles; 2. rɔ́dlis]. **rod** & **-less.** Without a rod or rods.
rodlet, n. [1. ródlet; 2. rɔ́dlit]. **rod** & **-let.** Small rod.
rodomontade, n., adj., & vb. intrans. [1. ròdomontáhd; 2. rɔ̀dəmɔntā́d], fr. Fr., fr. Ital. *Rodomonte*, in *Orlando Furioso*, & **-ade. 1.** n. Boastful speech, bombast. **2.** adj. Boastful, bragging, blustering. **3.** vb. To boast, brag, swagger.
roe (I.), n. [1. rō; 2. rou]. O.E. *rā(h)*; M.E. *roo*; cp. O.N. *rā*; O.H.G. *rēh.* Also *roe-deer*, small reddish-brown deer, *Capreolus caprea*, of Europe and Western Asia.
roe (II.), n. M.E. *rown*; cp. O.N. *hrogn*; Germ. *rogen.* **1.** Also, *hard roe*, mass of eggs of fish or crustacea. **2.** *Soft roe*, milt of male fish.
roe-buck, n. Male of roe-deer.
roe-corn, n. Single egg in fish's roe.
roed, adj. [1. rōd; 2. roud]. **roe (II.)** & **-ed.** Having, containing, roe.
roe-deer, n. See **roe (I.).**
roe-stone, n. Kind of limestone, oolite.
rogation, n. [1. rōgā́shun; 2. rougéiʃən], fr. Lat. *rogātiōn-(em)*, 'proposal put before the people; question; request', fr. *rogāt-(um)*, P.P. type of *rogāre*, 'to ask; to beg, entreat', orig., 'to have a desire for, incline towards'; cp. *regere*, 'to direct towards, guide, lead'. See **regent, rex. 1.** (Roman hist.) Formal submission of proposed law &c., to people for acceptance. **2.** (pl.) Form of litany; *Rogation Days*, three days before Ascension Day, on which the litany is sung in procession, often with special petitions for a blessing on the crops; *rogation flower*, milkwort; *Rogation Week*, in which Rogation Days fall; *Rogation Sunday*, preceding Rogation Days.
rogational, adj. [1. rōgā́shunal; 2. rougéiʃənl]. Prec. & **-al.** Of, pertaining to, Rogation Days.
Roger, n. [1. rójer; 2. rɔ́dʒə]. Man's name, fr. Fr. *Roger*, of Gmc. origin; cp. O.E. *Hrōþgār.* **1.** *Jolly Roger*, pirates' flag with skull and crossbones on black field. **2.** *Sir Roger (de Coverley)*, an old-fashioned country-dance.
rogue (I.), n. [1. rōg; 2. roug]. Cp. Fr. *rogue*, 'haughty, disdainful'. Origin unknown. **1.** Vagabond, vagrant, wandering beggar, esp. in phrase, *rogue and vagabond*; *rogues' gallery*, collection of pictures of convicted criminals, made by the police for reference; *rogue's march*, music, noise, made in derision, when a disgraced soldier is drummed out of the service, as a rogue and vagabond was driven out of a town &c. **2. a** Dishonest person, scoundrel, rascal; **b** (in facet. and affectionate sense) a humorously mischievous, waggish person. **3.** Also, *rogue-elephant*, elephant which lives separate from the herd and has become savage and dangerous. **4.** Specimen of different kind among a collection of seedlings, bulbous plants &c.
rogue (II.), vb. trans., fr. prec. To pick out rogues from (plants &c.).
roguery, n. [1. rṓgeri; 2. róugəri]. **rogue (I.)** & **-ery. a** Knavish conduct, tricks, fraud; **b** mischief, waggishness.

roguish, adj. [1. rṓgish; 2. róugiʃ]. **rogue** & **-ish. a** Like, having the nature of, characteristic of, a rogue; **b** arch, waggish.
roguishly, adv. Prec. & **-ly.** In a roguish manner.
roguishness, n. See prec. & **-ness.** Quality of being roguish.
roil, vb. trans. [1. roil, rīl; 2. rɔil, rail]. Etymol. doubtful; cp. **rile.** (obs. and provinc.) **a** To stir up, trouble (water &c.); **b** to vex, rile.
roister, vb. intrans. [1. róister; 2. rɔ́istə], fr. obs. *roister*, 'roisterer,' fr. O. Fr. *rustre*, 'clown, boor', fr. *ruste*, fr. Lat. *rusticus*, 'rural'. See **rustic.** To act in a boisterous, turbulent, blustering manner; to indulge in loud, rough merry-making.
roisterer, n. [1. róisterer; 2. rɔ́istərə]. Prec. & **-er.** Noisy, boisterous reveller.
roistering, adj. [1. róistering; 2. rɔ́istəriŋ], fr. Pres. Part. of **roister.** Boisterous, blustering, turbulent.
Roland, n. [1. rṓland; 2. róulənd]. Fr. *Roland*, nephew of Charlemagne and one of the champions in the Charlemagne cycle. Bold and chivalrous hero; *(to give) a Roland for an Oliver*, retaliatory and equally effective action or speech; tit for tat.
rôle, n. [1. rōl; 2. roul]. Fr. *rôle*, fr. O. Fr. *rolle.* See next word. **1.** Part played by actor; *title-rôle*, character in play from whom the name of the play is taken. **2.** Part or function assumed by a person in any action or proceeding.
roll (I.), n., fr. O. Fr. *rolle*, fr. Lat. *rotul-(us)*, variant of *rotula*, 'small wheel', dimin. of *rota*, 'wheel'. See **rota. 1.** Packet or bundle formed by folding flexible material into a cylindrical shape: *a roll of oilcloth, paper, notes* &c. **2. a** Official document usually kept in form of a roll; Phr. *the Rolls*, place where public records were formerly kept; *Master of the Rolls*, the presiding judge of the English Court of Appeal and ex-officio keeper of the Public Records; **b** official register, list of persons, estates; specif., official list of solicitors; Phr. *to strike (a person) off the rolls*, disqualify solicitor from practising. **3.** Any mass or body more or less cylindrical in shape: *a roll of tobacco, paste* &c.; specif., small loaf or twist of fancy bread. **4.** Article of food made by folding or rolling dough, paste &c., into more or less cylindrical form, often with meat, jam &c., enclosed or folded inside: *sausage-roll*; *swiss-roll* &c. **5. a** Cylinder, roller, used in various mechanical processes, for crushing, flattening &c.; **b** (book-binding) small tool with wheel for marking pattern on leather. **6.** (archit.) Scroll, volute, in Ionian capital.
roll (II.), vb. intrans. & trans., fr. prec. **A.** intrans. **1. a** To move along by turning over and over: *to roll down hill*; **b** (of the eyes) to move round with a sweeping circular motion. **2. a** To perform a partially rotating, rocking, swaying movement, swinging backwards and forwards esp. on the back: *the horse fell and rolled on the ground, on its rider*; to turn from side to side or completely over; to flounder, wallow: *to roll in the mud*; Phr. *to be rolling in money*, be extremely rich; **b** (i.) (of a ship), to be swayed up and down from side to side by motion of the waves; contrasted with *pitch*; (ii.) to walk, run, along with swaying motion from side to side, suggestive of a rolling ship: *to roll in one's gait.* **3. a** (of river &c.) To move along smoothly, to flow; **b** (fig., of time) to pass; **c** to move cumbrously, heavily, along on wheels: *heavy coaches rolled past all day*; also **d** (of clouds) to drift slowly and heavily. **4. a** (of the sea) To be stirred into, have surface broken by, large, slow undulations; **b** (of wide tract of country) to stretch away, be marked with alternate rounded elevations and depressions, resembling the surface of a rolling sea; to undulate. **5. a** (of thunder) To produce, in rapid succession a continuous series of deep reverberating peals; **b** (of drums) to be so played

as to give out a continuous, unbroken, deep, rattling sound. **B.** trans. **1. a** To propel, cause to advance by turning over and over: *to roll a hoop; to roll a ball along the ground; to roll tree-trunks down a hill*; **b** to cause to move along upon wheels; to trundle. **2.** To cause to move round and round, give rotatory motion to: *to roll tobacco between one's fingers; to roll wine on one's tongue.* **3.** To impart a rotatory motion to, turn from side to side: *to roll one's eyes.* **4. a** To fold, wrap, wind (soft or pliable material) round a centre or axis, to form into a ball or cylinder; to wind: *to roll wool into a ball, cotton round a reel; the hedgehog, kitten, rolled itself into a ball*; **b** to form by rolling into a cylinder &c.: *to roll a cigarette*; Phr. (*two things*) *rolled into one*, combining two characters, filling two functions. **5.** To wrap round, enfold, envelop: *to roll something in a piece of paper; to roll oneself in a rug.* **6. a** To pass a roller over, so as to flatten or smooth surface of: *to roll a lawn, road*, &c.; **b** to spread out into a thin sheet with a rolling-pin: *to roll pastry, metal* &c. **7.** (of organ) To peel out with deep, resonant sound: *the organ rolled forth its stately welcome.* **8.** To utter with vibration of point of tongue or of uvula; to trill: *to roll one's r's.* **9.** To beat (a drum) with rapid succession of light blows. **C.** Followed by adverb or preposition. *Roll in*, to come in, come together, in large numbers or quantities: *recruits, subscriptions, offers of help &c., are rolling in. Roll on*, intrans., to move forward steadily and continuously. *Roll out*, to flatten, spread out into sheet, by pressing with a roller: *to roll out pastry. Roll over*, **1.** trans., to cause to turn completely over, cause to revolve: *to roll a person over*, upset, throw down; **2.** intrans., **a** to turn completely over; **b** to turn from one side to the other, turn partially over: *to roll over in bed. Roll up*, **1.** to cause to assume a cylindrical or spherical shape by rolling: *to roll up a picture, piece of cloth* &c.; *the hedgehog rolled itself up*; **2.** to envelop, enwrap, by rotatory motion: *to roll a person up in a blanket; to roll a thing up in paper.*

roll (III.), n., fr. prec. **1.** Action of rolling: *the slow roll of the ship; the dogs are having a roll on the lawn.* **2.** Rolling, swaying, action in walking or running: *a nautical roll.* **3.** Deep, continuous reverberating sound, caused, or appearing to be caused, by a rapid succession of blows: *the roll of a drum*, or by a series of explosions: *the roll of thunder.*

rollable, adj. [1. rṓlabl; 2. róulәbl]. **roll (II.)** & **-able.** Capable of being rolled.

roll-call, n. The reading out of roll, or list of names of a body of persons, in order to ascertain who is present.

roll-collar, n. Large collar of coat &c. rolled back.

roller, n. [1. rṓler; 2. róulә]. **roll (II.)** & **-er.** **1.** Heavy cylindrical object of metal, or wood, revolving on an axis, used for crushing, flattening, smoothing, pressing out &c. **2.** Cylinder of wood, metal &c. placed beneath heavy objects to facilitate their passage, or under any thin moving sheet of fabric (e.g. a blind) to reduce friction &c. **3.** Long, heavy wave of cylindrical shape. **4. a** Bright-coloured crow-like bird of Europe &c.; **b** tumbler-pigeon; **c** kind of canary. **5.** A roller-bandage.

roller-bandage, n. Long, narrow, surgical bandage lightly rolled up to facilitate handling.

roller-skate, n. Device consisting of small solid wheels with ball-bearings, fastened to the feet, for running upon a smooth, hard surface.

roller-towel, n. Long towel, with ends joined, running on a roller.

rollick, vb. intrans. & n. [1. rólik; 2. rólik]. Perh. a combination of **roll** & **frolic.** **1.** vb. To behave in a gay, careless, hilarious manner; chiefly in Pres. Part., *rollicking.* **2.** n. Careless revel, frolic.

rolling, adj. [1. rṓling; 2. róuliŋ], fr. Pres. Part. of **roll (II.)**. (of landscape, tract of country) Spacious, stretching far, and undulating; diversified by small rounded hills and valleys.

rolling-mill, n. Mill, factory, in which heated metal is rolled and pressed out into sheets, rails &c. between heavy rollers.

rolling-pin, n. Long cylinder of smooth, heavy wood, glass &c. for pressing out paste, dough &c.

rolling-press, n. Machine of various kinds with two or more rollers for smoothing printed pages, rolling cloth &c.

rolling-stock, n. Locomotives, carriages, and trucks, collectively, of a railway system.

roll-top desk, n. Desk with movable cover made of connected slats, sliding in a groove, and running back into a recess in the top.

roly-poly (I.), n. [1. rṓli pṓli; 2. róuli póuli], fr. **roll (I.)**. **1.** Pudding made of jam or fresh fruit rolled up in a sheet of paste, and then baked or boiled. **2.** Short, plump child or person.

rom, n. [1. rom; 2. rɔm]. Romany, *rom*, 'man'. Gipsy.

Romaic, n. & adj. [1. rōmā́ik; 2. rouméiik], fr. Gk. *Rhōmaïk-(ós)*, 'Roman; of the Eastern Empire', fr. Gk. *Rhṓm-(ē)*, 'Rome', fr. Lat. *Rōma*, see **Rome.** **1.** n. Language of Modern Greece. **2.** adj. Of, pertaining to, Romaic.

romaika, n. [1. rōmā́ika; 2. rouméiikә], fr. Gk. *Rhōmaïké*, fr. fem. form of *Rhōmaïkós*, 'Roman'. See prec. Modern Greek national dance.

Roman (I.), adj. [1. rṓman; 2. róumәn], fr. Lat. *Rōmān-(us)*, 'of Rome', fr. *Rōm-(a)*, 'Rome'. See **Rome** & **-an.** **1.** Connected with, pertaining to, derived from, characteristic of, Rome (esp. ancient Rome) and its empire, or to the (ancient) Romans; *Roman numerals*, capital letters (I, V, &c.) used as numerals, now chiefly for numbers of volumes, on clocks &c. **2.** Connected with, pertaining to, the Latin Church, whose head on earth is the Pope, and whose headquarters are in Rome; also *Roman Catholic.* **3.** (of type) Of ordinary style used in printing; contrasted with *italic*; abbreviation *rom.*

Roman (II.), n., fr. prec. **1.** Inhabitant, citizen of (ancient) Roman empire. **2.** A Roman Catholic, or Papist. **3.** (print.) Roman type.

Roman candle, n. Kind of firework.

Roman Catholic, adj. & n. **1.** adj. Of, pertaining to, characteristic of, that branch of the Catholic Church which regards the Pope as the head of the Church on earth. **2.** n. Member of Roman Catholic Church.

Roman Catholicism, n. The organization or doctrine of the Church of Rome.

Romance (I.), adj. [1. rōmáns; 2. roumǽns], fr. O. Fr. *romanz*, fr. Low Lat. **romanice*, 'in popular Latin', advbl. form fr. Lat. *Rōmānic-(us)*, 'Roman', fr. *Rōmān-(us)*, 'Roman', see **Roman,** & **-ic.** (cap.) **a** Of, pertaining to, the dialects developed from Latin; **b** of, in, Romance.

romance (II.), n. M.E. *roma(u)nce*, O. Fr. *romans* &c., see prec., 'something written in the popular tongue, not in Latin'; hence 'a tale (of chivalry &c.), a novel'. **1.** (cap.) Mediaeval tale in prose or verse, celebrating the exploits and adventures, in love and war, of some hero of chivalry. **2. a** Series of unusual adventures, esp. in which some particular person, or group of persons, are concerned, involving the actions and feelings of these, including as a rule a love episode: *his whole life was a romance*; **b** narrative of such adventures; a novel dealing with sentimental and adventurous episodes in the career of the principal character or hero; **c** literary genre dealing with such tales. **3.** Feeling, moral atmosphere, of the marvellous, mysterious, sentimental, picturesque: *a house with no suggestion of romance about it.*

romance (III.), vb. intrans., fr. prec. To invent fanciful stories, to tell highly coloured tales, to exaggerate, embroider, in one's accounts and descriptions of incidents and experiences.

romancer, n. [1. rōmánser; 2. roumǽnsә]. Prec. & **-er.** One who invents fanciful accounts of his experiences, who touches up and embroiders upon what he is told.

Romanes, n. [1. rómanes; 2. rɔ́mәnεs], fr. **Romany.** Romany language.

Romanesque (I.), n. [1. rṑmanésk; 2. rṑumәn ésk]. **Roman** & **-esque.** **1.** Style of architecture prevalent in Western Europe between 5th and 12th cents., developed from Roman, and characterized by round arches. **2.** (rare) Romance dialect(s).

Romanesque (II.), adj., fr. prec. **1.** Of, pertaining to, characteristic of, Romanesque. **2.** (rare) Of, pertaining to, Romance.

Romanic (I.), adj. [1. rōmánik; 2. roumǽnik], fr. Lat. *Rōmānic-(us)*, 'Roman'. See **Romance (I.)**. **1.** (of dial.) Derived from Latin; Romance. **2.** Of, pertaining to, characteristic of, originating in, the Roman Empire or its civilization.

Romanic (II.), n., fr. prec. Romance dialect.

Romanish, adj. [1. rṓmanish; 2. róumәniʃ]. **Roman** & **-ish.** (in depreciatory sense) Of, pertaining to, the Church of Rome.

Romanism, n. [1. rṓmanizm; 2. róumәnizәm]. **Roman** & **-ism.** System of discipline and doctrine of Roman Catholic Church.

Romanist, n. [1. rṓmanist; 2. róumәnist]. **Roman** & **-ist.** Member of Church of Rome.

Romanistic, adj. [1. rōmanístik; 2. roumәnístik]. Prec. & **-ic.** Roman Catholic.

Romanity, n. [1. rōmániti; 2. roumǽniti]. **Roman** & **-ity.** (rare) Civilization of, membership of, Roman Empire.

Romanization, n. [1. rṑmanīzā́shun; 2. rṑumәnaizéiʃәn]. Next word & **-ation.** Act of Romanizing, state of being Romanized.

Romanize, vb. trans. & intrans. [1. rṓmanīz; 2. róumәnaiz]. **Roman** & **-ize.** **A.** trans. **1.** To make Roman in character, bring under the influence of the civilization of the Roman Empire. **2.** To imbue with Roman Catholic doctrine, to convert to Roman Catholicism. **3.** (of Anglican clergy) To approximate teaching, doctrine, practice, to those of Roman Church. **B.** intrans. To become Romanized.

Romanizer, n. [1. rṓmanīzer; 2. róumәnaizә]. Prec. & **-er.** One who Romanizes.

roman letters, type, n. The kind of upright type ordinarily used in printing; contrasted with *italic type.*

Roman nose, n. Nose with high, arched bridge.

Romano-, pref. [1. rōmā́nō; 2. rouméinou], representing Lat. *Rōmān-(us)*, 'Roman', see **Roman.** Of Rome or the Roman Empire; *Romano-British*, pertaining to the Romanized inhabitants of Britain.

Roman pearl, n. Artificial pearl made in Rome.

Romansh, R(o)umansh, n. [1. rōmánsh, roománsh; 2. roumǽnʃ, rumǽnʃ], fr. Low Lat. *rōmānice*, 'in popular Latin'. See **Romance (I.)**. **1.** One of the Rhaeto-Romanic dialects. **2.** Rhaeto-Romanic.

romantic (I.), adj. [1. rōmántik; 2. roumǽntik], fr. Fr. *romantique*, fr. O. Fr. *romant*, 'romance', variant of *romanz.* See **romance (II.)**. **1.** Connected with romance; **a** addicted to, indulging in, fantastic, unreal, sentimental, picturesque, dreams and ideas: *a romantic person, mind, imagination*; **b** based on tales and legends of romance; incorporating, exhibiting, the sentiments and situations which form the subject of mediaeval romances; **c** possessing the elements of strangeness, mystery, heroic action, and sentimental temper, which characterize romance: *a romantic adventure, episode, situation* &c.; **d** inspiring romantic feelings; suggestive of, suitable for, romance: *a romantic spot, abode* &c. **2.** (of a literary school, class of writings) Characterized by freedom of style and treatment, and in choice of matter seeking not so much conventional correctness and restraint, as breadth, picturesqueness, and the vivid expression of sentiment, and the description of strange and moving actions and episodes; contrasted with *classical, antique*: *romantic poets*; *the romantic revival*; also applied to painting and sculpture and other arts.

romantic (II.), n., fr. prec. **1.** A romantic poet; adherent of romantic school of writers. **2.** (pl.) *Romantics*, high-flown sentiments or utterance: *to indulge in romantics.*

romantically, adv. [1. rōmántikali; 2. roumǽntikəli]. **romantic (I.) & -al & -ly.** In a romantic manner.

romanticism, n. [1. rōmántisizm; 2. roumǽntisizəm]. **romantic** (I.) & **-ism. 1.** Quality of being romantic; romantic character or style. **2.** Specif., revolt against classicism, and revival of mediaeval forms and spirit in 18th cent. literature, art &c.

romanticist, n. [1. rōmántisist; 2. roumǽntisist]. **romantic (I.) & -ist.** Adherent of romanticism; writer, painter &c. of romantic school.

romanticize, vb. intrans. & trans. [1. rōmántisīz; 2. roumǽntisaiz]. **romantic (I.) & -ize. 1.** intrans. To write &c. in romantic style. **2.** trans. To make, consider as, romantic; to treat (artistic theme) in romantic manner.

Romany (I.), n. [1. rómani; 2. rɔ́məni], fr. Gipsy, *romani*, pl. form of adj. fr. **rom**, 'man'. **1.** a Gipsy; **b** gipsies collectively. **2.** Gipsy language.

Romany (II.), adj., fr. prec. Pertaining to the gipsies or their language.

Rome, n. [1. rōm; 2. roum], fr. Fr., fr. Lat. *Rōma*, 'Rome', prob. of Etruscan origin. Capital of Italy, and centre of ancient Roman Republic and Empire, and of the Christian Church in the West; hence, **a** the Roman Empire; **b** the Church of Rome.

Romeward, adj. & adv. [1. rómward; 2. róumwəd]. **Rome & -ward. 1.** adj. Tending towards Roman Catholicism. **2.** adv. Romewards.

Romewards, adv. [1. rómwardz; 2. róumwədz]. **Rome & -wards.** With a tendency towards Roman Catholicism.

Romish, adj. [1. rómish; 2. róumiʃ]. **Rome & -ish.** (in depreciatory sense) Roman Catholic, Papistical.

romp (I.), vb. intrans. [1. romp; 2. rɔmp]. Perh. variant of **ramp** (I.). **1.** (of child &c.) To play about energetically, with violent movements and noisy, boisterous cries. **2.** (racing, of horse &c.) To move swiftly and easily: *to romp along, romp over the course* &c. Phr. *to romp home*, win a race easily.

romp (II.), n., fr. prec. **1.** Child, esp. girl, who plays roughly and noisily. **2.** Rough, noisy game, boisterous frolics.

rompy, adj. [1. rómpi; 2. rɔ́mpi]. **romp & -y.** Inclined to romp; resembling a romp.

rondeau, n. [1. róndō; 2. rɔ́ndou], fr. Fr., fr. earlier *rondel*. See next word. Metrical form consisting of ten or thirteen lines, with only two rhymes which are variously placed, the opening words, or part of first line, being repeated at the end of the eighth and of the final line, but not rhyming.

rondel, n. [1. róndel; 2. rɔ́ndəl], fr. Fr. *rondel*, fr. *rond*, 'round'. See **round** (II.), & **-le.** Variant of rondeau, consisting of fourteen lines, with two rhymes, the first two lines being repeated as sixth and seventh, and again as thirteenth and fourteenth lines.

rondo, n. [1. róndō; 2. rɔ́ndou]. Ital. *rondo*, 'round'. See **rondeau & round (II.).** Musical composition with a subject repeated after each of a series of subordinate themes in different keys.

rondure, n. [1. róndūr; 2. rɔ́ndjə], fr. Fr. *rondeur*. **round (I.) & -er.** (poetical) Circular, spherical, or curved form; roundness.

Röntgen ray(s), n. [1. rĕntyen rá(z); 2. røntjən réi(z)], fr. name of discoverer, W. K. Röntgen; also **X-ray(s).** Rays capable of penetrating in varying degrees several forms of solid and opaque matter, but stopped or partially stopped by others, esp. metals, so that the latter cast a deep shadow upon a white screen when the rays are directed at them.

rood, n. [1. rōōd; 2. rūd]. O.E., M.E. *rōd*, 'cross'; cp. O.S. *rōda*, 'cross'; O.H.G. *ruota*, 'rod'; cogn. w. Lat. *ratis*, 'raft'; Lith. *rēkles*, 'scaffolding'; *rēju*, 'to arrange in layers, pile up'; cp. also O.E. *rǣd*, 'plan, scheme; advice', see **rede** (I.). **1.** (archaic) **a** Cross of Christ; **b** crucifix, esp. one placed above entrance to chancel. **2.** Measure of extent; one-fourth of an acre.

rood-arch, n. Arch between nave and choir.

rood-beam, n. Beam across entrance to chancel and supporting a cross.

rood-cloth, n. Veil used to cover rood during Lent.

rood-loft, n. Gallery above rood-screen.

rood-screen, n. Screen separating nave from chancel &c., surmounted by the rood.

rood-tree, n. (archaic) Cross of Christ.

roof (I.), n. [1. rōōf; 2. rūf]. O.E. *hrōf*; M.E. *rōf*; cp. O. Fris. *hrōf*. **1.** Outer covering extending over the top of a building. Phr. *the roof of the world*, high tableland; *under one's roof*, in one's house. **2.** Something resembling a roof in position or function: *the trees met overhead to form a roof*; specif. **a** the top of a covered vehicle, used for passengers or luggage; **b** *roof of the mouth*, the hard palate.

roof (II.), vb. trans., fr. prec. **a** To provide with a roof: *to roof a house*; **b** to extend over, cover, as does a roof: *a road roofed with overhanging branches.*

roofage, n. [1. rōōfij; 2. rūfidž]. **roof & -age.** Material, style, whole extent, of roof.

roofed, adj. [1. rōōft; 2. rūft]. **roof & -ed.** Having, covered by, a roof; (usually in compounds) *flat-roofed, red-roofed* &c.

roof-garden, n. Garden made upon a roof; group of flowering or other plants growing upon roof of a building.

roofing, n. [1. rōōfing; 2. rūfiŋ]. **roof & -ing.** Material of which roof is composed.

roofing-slate, -tile, n. Slate, tile, used in constructing a roof.

roofless, adj. [1. rōōfles; 2. rūflis]. **roof & -less.** Without a roof; esp. having lost its roof.

roof-tree, n. **a** Principal beam in a roof, into which the rafters are fixed; the ridge-pole; **b** (by extension) the roof itself.

rook (I.), n. [1. rook; 2. ruk]. O.E. *hrōc*; M.E. *rōk*; cp. O.N. *hrōkr*; O.H.G. *hruoh*, 'crow'; one of a large class of related, imitative words; cp. O.E. *hræfn*, 'raven', see **raven** (I.); Lat. *cornix*, 'crow'; *corvus*, 'raven', see **corvine**; Gk. *kórax*, 'raven'; Lat. *crōcire*, 'to croak'; cp. Goth. *hrūkjan*, 'to crow'. **1.** Black, gregarious bird, *Corvus frugilegus*, of crow family. **2.** Swindler, card-sharper.

rook (II.), vb. trans., fr. prec. **1.** To cheat, defraud, swindle, esp. at cards. **2.** To charge (exorbitant prices): *I was rooked*, or *they rooked me, £10 for my berth.*

rook (III.), n., fr. O. Fr. *roc*, fr. Pers. *rukh.* (chess) Castle.

rookery, n. [1. rókeri; 2. rúkəri]. **rook (I.) & -ery. 1. a** Group of trees in which a colony of rooks build; **b** colony of rooks. **2.** Breeding-place of penguins, seals &c. **3.** Group of poor houses; a squalid, crowded dwelling-house, esp. a crowded tenement building.

rookie, n. [1. róoki; 2. rúki]. Corrupt. of **recruit.** (army slang) Recruit.

rooklet, n. [1. róoklet; 2. rúklit]. **rook (I.) & -let.** Young rook.

rookling, n. [1. róokling; 2. rúkliŋ]. **rook (I.) & -ling.** Young rook.

rook-rifle, n. Small-bored rifle for shooting rooks.

rooky, adj. [1. róoki; 2. rúki]. **rook (I.) & -y.** Inhabited by, full of, rooks.

room (I.), n. [1. room; 2. rum], provinc. [1. rōōm; 2. rūm]. O.E., M.E. *rūm*; cp. O.H.G., O.S., O.N. *rūm*; Goth. *rūms*, 'room, space'; cogn. w. Lat. *rūs*, 'open country', see **rustic & rural**; O. Pers. *ravah-*, 'space'; O. Slav. *ravinū*, 'level'. **1.** Separate apartment in a building, esp. in a dwelling-house, divided off from other apartments or passages by partitions or walls reaching from floor to ceiling; a chamber; (also in compounds) *dining-room, billiard-room, gun-room* &c. **2.** (pl.) *Rooms*, **a** set of private rooms assigned to, occupied by, a particular person or family in a large house: *rooms in college, in a boarding-house*; *come to my rooms*; **b** lodgings in another's house: *to take rooms at Eastbourne for the holidays.* **3.** People in a room; assembled company: *to keep the whole room laughing.* **4.** Space, esp. free, unoccupied, available or adequate space: *to have plenty of room*; *no room to move*; *the table takes up too much room*; *there is room on the shelf for another book.* Phrs. *no room to swing a cat*, very confined space; *to make room for*, withdraw so as to leave a space free for, to open a passage for. **5.** (lit. and fig.) Portion of space, position, occupied by person or thing, esp. in Phrs. *in the room of*, in place of, as substitute for; *to prefer a person's room to his company*, to prefer his absence. **6.** Opportunity, occasion, opening: *room for improvement, doubt* &c.

room (II.), vb. intrans., fr. prec. (American use) To lodge, have rooms (at, with &c.).

roomed, adj. [1. roomd; 2. rumd]. **room (I.) & -ed.** Having a room or rooms; (usually in compounds) *a two-roomed cottage* &c.

roomful, n. [1. róomfool; 2. rúmful]. **room (I.) & -ful.** Amount (of furniture) or number (of persons) occupying a room.

roomily, adv. [1. rōōmili, róomili; 2. rūmili, rúmili]. **roomy & -ly.** In a roomy manner.

roominess, n. [1. rōōmines, róomines; 2. rūminis, rúminis]. See next word & **-ness.** State of being roomy; spaciousness.

roomy, adj. [1. rōōmi, róomi; 2. rūmi, rúmi]. **room & -y.** Large, spacious, affording ample room.

roost (I.), n. [1. rōōst; 2. rūst]. O.E. *hrōst*; M.E. *rōst*, 'perch'; cp. O.S. *hrōst*, M. Du. *roest.* **1.** Perch, pole, bar, branch &c. on which a bird rests at night. Phr. *to rule the roost*, Mod. substitute for *roast*, q.v. **2. a** Part of chicken-house &c. for birds at night; **b** (colloq.) resting or sleeping place for person. Phrs. *at roost*, sleeping; *to go to roost*, retire to rest; *curses, misdeeds &c. come home to roost*, recoil upon originator.

roost (II.), vb. intrans., fr. prec. (of birds) To sit, go to rest, upon a perch; to go to roost.

rooster, n. [1. rōōster; 2. rūstə]. Prec. & **-er.** Cock.

root (I.), n. [1. rōōt; 2. rūt]. O.E. *rōt*, fr. O.N. *rōt*; cogn. w. O.E. *wrōt*, 'snout, trunk'; *wyrt*, 'plant'; Goth. *waurts*, 'root', see **wort (I.)**; cp. further Lat. *rādix*, 'root', see **radix. 1. a** Downward-growing part of plant which attaches it to ground &c. and by means of which it obtains nourishment from the soil; Phrs. *to take root*, (lit. and fig.) become established; *root and branch*, completely, thoroughly; **b** *roots*, specif., edible roots, root-crops. **2.** Single plant together with its root. **3.** That part of an object, body, or structure which is embedded in, or attached to, a larger body or mass: *the root of a tooth, hair* &c.; *the root of the tongue.* **4.** Source, origin, from which an action, circumstance &c. springs, arises, develops; germ, nucleus, point of growth: *the root of all evil*; (*to get at*) *the root of a matter.* Phr. *to strike at the root of*, attack fundamental principle, essential part, of. **5.** (archaic philol.) Theoretical, original form from which, by means of formative elements, suffixes &c., a word or group of cognate words is developed; the term *base* is now preferred. **6.** (math.) *Root of a number*, quantity which when multiplied by itself a specified number of times produces that number; *square root*, number to be multiplied by itself twice; *cube root*, to be multiplied three times to produce a given number: *3 is the square root of 9, the cube root of 27.* **7.** (mus.) Note on which a chord is built up.

root (II.), vb. trans. & intrans., fr. prec. **A.** trans. **1.** To fix firmly by the roots, implant roots of firmly in ground. **2.** (fig.) To cause to remain immovable, establish firmly: *terror rooted him to the spot.* **3.** (of non-material things) To implant, establish, firmly: *to root a principle in the mind; a deeply rooted prejudice; 'His honour rooted in dishonour stood'* (Tennyson, 'Lancelot and Elaine'). **4.** *Root out, up,* (lit. and fig.) to remove by the roots, eradicate, tear up. **B.** intrans. **1.** **a** (of plants) To take root; **b** (fig.) to be firmly established. **2.** **a** To dig, burrow, turn up or over: *a pig roots (about) for acorns with its snout;* **b** to turn things over, rout about in, esp. as though seeking some object among a number of other things: *to root about in a drawer.*

rootage, n. [1. rōōtij; 2. rūtidž]. **root (I.)** & **-age.** **1.** Act of taking root; state of being rooted. **2.** Complete system of roots of plant.

root-crop(s), n. Plants grown for their edible roots.

rooted, adj. [1. rōōted; 2. rūtid], fr. P.P. of **root** (II.). Firmly fixed, well established: *a rooted objection.*

rootedly, adv. Prec. & **-ly.** Fixedly, determinedly.

rootedness, n. See prec. & **-ness.** State of being rooted.

rootery, n. [1. rōōteri; 2. rūtəri]. **root (I.)** & **-ery.** Artificial mound of large roots &c. filled in with soil for cultivation of ferns &c.

rootle, vb. intrans. [1. rōōtl; 2. rūtl]. **root (II.)** & freq. **-le.** To fork, burrow, dig, about in.

rootless, adj. [1. rōōtles; 2. rūtlis]. **root (I.)** & **-less.** Having no root(s).

rootlet, n. [1. rōōtlet; 2. rūtlit]. **root (I.)** & **-let.** Small slender root or branch of root.

root-stock, n. **1.** Rhizome. **2.** (fig.) Origin, source, of development.

rooty, adj. [1. rōōti; 2. rūti]. **root (I.)** & **-y.** **1.** Full of, abounding in, roots. **2.** Like, characteristic of, a root.

rope (I.), n. [1. rōp; 2. roup]. O.E. *rāp;* M.E. *rōp;* cp. O.N. *reip;* O.H.G. *reif;* Goth. *raip.* **1.** **a** Thick, strong twist of intertwined fibres of flax, hemp, jute &c., usually from one to ten inches in circumference; thick cord; **b** single length of this. Phrs. *the rope,* (i.) cord used in hanging, hence punishment by hanging, (ii.) tight-rope, q.v.; *the ropes,* those enclosing boxing-ring &c.; *to know, show one, the ropes,* arrangements, customs, usual procedure &c. of a place, institution, business &c.; *on the rope* (of mountaineers &c.), roped together; *on the high ropes,* (i.) elated, strung up; (ii.) haughty, arrogant; *to give one rope, plenty of rope,* allow one a reasonable freedom of action; *give a fool rope enough, and he will hang himself,* a foolish, headstrong person who is allowed to have his own way will effect his own ruin; *rope of sand,* (fig.) frail, useless bond or support. **2.** Rope-like structure made by plaiting or twisting: *a rope of hair; a rope of pearls,* large string of pearls. **3.** Glutinous thread or thready structure, esp. in wine, dough &c.

rope (II.), vb. trans. & intrans., fr. prec. **A.** trans. **1.** **a** To attach, fasten, tether, tie up, with rope: *to rope a box;* **b** specif. (mountaineering) to fasten one (person) to another with a line of rope in order to give confidence and support to each and all, and to make it possible to hold up one who slips. **2.** *Rope in,* to enclose, delimit; rope off, mark off, by means of a rope. Phr. *to rope (a person) in,* enlist his services; persuade him to join a movement &c. **B.** intrans. To form sticky, glutinous threads.

rope-dancer, n. One who performs on a tight-rope.

rope-ladder, n. Ladder made of ropes.

rope-moulding, n. (archit.) Moulding having the appearance of twisted rope.

rope-quoit, n. Rope ring used in deck-quoits.

rope's end, rope-end, n. & vb. trans. **1.** n. Short length of rope used for flogging. **2.** vb. To flog with rope's end.

rope-walk, n. Long shed, alley &c. for spinning rope-yarn or twisting rope.

rope-walker, n. Performer on tight-rope.

rope-yard, n. Establishment for making ropes.

rope-yarn, n. **1.** Yarn spun from fibres and used in making rope. **2.** (fig.) Unimportant part, thing, or detail; trifle.

ropiness, n. [1. rōpines; 2. róupinis]. **ropy** & **-ness.** Quality, state, of being ropy.

roping, n. [1. rōping; 2. róupiŋ]. **rope (I.)** & **-ing.** System or arrangement of ropes; cordage.

ropy, adj. [1. rōpi; 2. róupi]. **rope (I.)** & **-y.** Forming, containing, glutinous, viscid threads.

Roquefort, n. [1. rókfōr; 2. rɔ́kfɔ̄(r)]. Town in Southern France. Kind of goat's milk cheese with strong scent and flavour.

roquelaure, n. [1. rókelōr; 2. rɔ́kəlɔ̄], fr. Fr., fr. name of Duke of Roquelaure. Kind of short cloak of early 18th cent.

roquet, vb. trans. & intrans. & n. [1. rókā; 2. róukei]. Form of **croquet.** **1.** vb. In croquet, to hit from a distance opponent's ball with one's own. **2.** n. Act of doing this.

roric, adj. [1. rórik; 2. rɔ́rik], fr. Lat. *rōr-(em),* &c., inflected type of *rōs,* 'dew'; cp. O. Slav. *rosa;* Lith. *rasà,* 'dew'; Scrt. *rásaš,* 'sap'; *áršati,* 'flows'. Pertaining to, resembling, dew.

rorqual, n. [1. rórkwal; 2. rɔ́kwəl], fr. Fr., fr. Norw. *rōyrkval,* fr. *raud,* 'red', q.v. under **red,** & *hval,* 'whale', see **whale.** Genus of large whales with dorsal fin; the fin-back.

rorty, adj. See **raughty.**

rosace, n. [1. rózās; 2. róuzeis], fr. Fr. *rosace,* 'rose-window', fr. Lat. *rosāceus,* 'of roses'. See **rose (I.).** **1.** Rose-like medallion, ornamental plaque &c. **2.** Rose-window.

rosacean, adj. [1. rōzāsean; 2. rouzéisiən]. Prec. & **-an.** Rosaceous.

rosaceous, adj. [1. rōzāshus; 2. rouzéiʃəs]. See **rosace** & **-ous.** Of, pertaining to, the rose family.

rosaniline, n. [1. rōzánilin; 2. rouzǽnilin]. **rose** & **aniline.** Crystalline compound obtained from aniline, producing red salts used as dye.

rosarian, n. [1. rōzárian; 2. rouzéəriən]. **rosary** & **-an.** **1.** Rose-grower. **2.** (eccles., cap.) Member of (R.C.) Fraternity of the Rosary.

rosarium, n. [1. rōzárium; 2. rouzéəriəm]. Lat. *rosārium,* 'rose-garden'. **rose (I.)** & **-arium.** Rose-garden.

rosary, n. [1. rózari; 2. róuzəri], fr. Lat. *rosāri-(um),* 'rose-garden'; L. Lat., 'garland, chaplet', fr. *rosa,* 'rose', see **rose (I.).** **1.** Rose-garden. **2.** (eccles., esp. R.C.) **a** String of beads used in devotions, consisting of groups of ten small beads, representing Ave Marias, divided by larger ones representing Paternosters; a Gloria is recited after each decade; **b** series of prayers recited according to rosary.

Roscian, adj. [1. róshian; 2. rɔ́ʃiən]. See next word & **-an.** Of, like, Roscius.

Roscius, n. [1. róshius; 2. rɔ́ʃiəs]. Name of celebrated Roman actor of 1st cent. B.C. A celebrated and accomplished actor; also one who imagines himself such.

rose (I.), n. [1. rōz; 2. rouz]. O.E. *rose,* fr. Lat. *rosa,* 'rose', fr. Gk. *rhódo(n),* 'rose', see **rhodo-.** **1.** **a** Genus of shrubs with prickly stems, pinnate leaves, and red, pink, white, or yellow flowers, usually scented: *Alpine, brier, cabbage, China, moss, tea rose* &c.; **b** flower of shrub of this genus; *the Wars of the Roses,* civil war in 15th cent. between Houses of York and Lancaster, the former taking a white rose as its badge, the latter a red rose; Phrs. *the rose of (the party* &c.), most beautiful woman in; *no rose without a thorn,* no favourable circumstance or condition without some drawback; *a bed of, path strewn with, roses,* position, condition, of complete ease and comfort; *not all roses,* not entirely devoid of discomfort or unpleasantness; *under the rose,* in secret; *to have roses in one's cheeks,* pink and white complexion, esp. as an indication of health; *to bring back the roses to (her) cheeks,* restore to health; **c** (her.) conventional representation of five-petalled rose, esp. as emblem of England. **2.** One of several plants resembling the rose, e.g. *Chinese rose,* kind of hibiscus; *Christmas rose,* kind of hellebore flowering in midwinter; *Rose of Jericho,* annual plant of Syria &c., with leaves withering in dry season and expanding again in wet. **3.** Object, structure, design, resembling a rose in shape or formation; specif. **a** (archit.) ornament, window &c. with lines radiating from centre; **b** round cluster, knot of ribbons &c. radiating from a point; rosette; **c** round, perforated nozzle of watering-can &c.; **d** (ornith.) ridge round eye in some birds. **4.** A colour; light crimson, pale or moderately deep pink; *old rose,* deep shade of this. **5.** Method of cutting precious stone, esp. diamond, with flat base and hemispherical upper part cut in small facets.

rose (II.), vb. O.E. *rās;* M.E. *roos;* Pret. of **rise.**

rose-apple, n. **a** East Indian tree cultivated for its flowers, foliage, and fruit; **b** edible fruit of this tree.

roseate, adj. [1. rózeat; 2. róuziət, -eit]. See **rose (I.)** & **-ate.** Rosy, rose-coloured (lit. and fig.).

roseately, adv. Prec. & **-ly.** With a roseate tint.

rose-bay, n. One of several varieties of plants, e.g. oleander, rhododendron, willow-herb.

rosebud, n. [1. rózbud; 2. róuzbad]. **1.** **a** Bud of rose; **b** a blooming young girl. **2.** (attrib.) Like a rosebud: *rosebud mouth.*

rose-bush, n. Rose plant; shrub bearing roses.

rose-chafer, n. Kind of destructive beetle.

rose-colour, n. **1.** Colour of deep pink rose. **2.** (fig.) Favourable, attractive, outlook or prospects.

rose-coloured, adj. **1.** Of rose-colour, roseate. **2.** (fig.) Attractive, favourable. Phr. *to see things, everything, through rose-coloured spectacles,* take an optimistic view of life.

rose-cut, adj. (of gem) Cut as a rose.

rose-diamond, n. Rose-cut diamond.

rose-drop, n. Skin-disease with red eruptions.

rose-engine, n. Instrument fitted to lathe for producing curved lines and designs.

rose-gall, n. Excrescence on stem of rose plant, produced by an insect.

rose-garden, n. Garden or part of garden where roses are grown.

rose-leaf, n. **1.** Leaf of rose. **2.** Petal of rose. Phr. *crumpled rose-leaf,* some trifling annoyance or inconvenience made a ground of excessive complaint.

rose-like, adj. Resembling a rose.

rose-lipped, adj. Having rosy lips.

rosemary, n. [1. rózmari; 2. róuzməri]. Earlier *rosmarine,* fr. Lat. *rōs marīnus,* 'rosemary', fr. *rōs,* 'dew', see **roric,** & **marine,** assimilated in Engl. to *Mary.* Evergreen shrub of Southern Europe and Western Asia, with blue flowers and greyish leaves, producing a pungent, refreshing perfume.

rose-noble, n. Obsolete English gold coin, worth 6s. 8d., bearing a rose as a device.

roseo-, pref. representing Lat. *rose-(us),* 'rosy', see **roseate,** & *-o-.* (chem., in names of salts) Reddish.

roseola, n. [1. rōzéola; 2. rouzíələ]. Mod. Lat., fr. Lat. *rose-(us),* 'rosy'. See **roseate.** **1.** Reddish rash. **2.** German measles.

roseolar, adj. [1. rōzéolar; 2. rouzíələ]. Prec. & **-ar.** Of, like, characteristic of, roseola.

roseolate, adj. [1. rōzéolat; 2. rouzíəleit]. **roseola** & **-ate.** Roseolar.

rose-pink, n. & adj. **1.** n. **a** Rose-colour; **b** pigment made of whiting coloured with Brazil-wood. **2.** adj. Rose-coloured (lit. and fig.).

rose-rash, n. Roseola.

rose-red, n. & adj. **1.** n. Colour of red rose. **2.** adj. Of this colour; as red as a rose.

rose-root, n. Kind of stonecrop with fragrant root.

rosery, n. [1. rṓzeri; 2. róuzəri]. **rose (I.)** & **-ery.** Rose-garden.

rose-tree, n. Rose plant, esp. standard.

rosette, n. [1. rōzét; 2. rouzét], fr. Fr. **rose (I.)** & **-ette.** Object somewhat resembling a small rose in shape, formation, or appearance; specif. **a** bunch of ribbon &c. usually arranged in concentric circles with lines, folds &c. radiating from centre, used as ornament, badge &c.; **b** (archit.) design with radiating lines; circular arrangement of leaves &c.; **c** (biol.) rose-like group or arrangement of organs, markings &c.; **d** rose-diamond.

rosetted, adj. [1. rōzéted; 2. rouzétid]. Prec. & **-ed.** Wearing, ornamented with, arranged as, a rosette.

rose-vinegar, n. Aromatic, refreshing infusion of rose-leaves in vinegar.

rose-water, n. **a** Perfume distilled from rose-leaves; **b** (fig.) affected sentiment or delicacy.

rose-window, n. Round window with tracery radiating from centre.

rose-wood, n. One of several varieties of hard, dark-coloured, fragrant wood used in cabinet-making; not the wood of the rose tree.

Rosicrucian, adj. & n. [1. rṑzikrṓōshan; 2. ròuzikrū́ʃən], fr. Lat. *ros-(a)*, 'rose', see **rose (I.)**, & *-i-* & *cruc-*, stem of *crux*, 'cross', see **crux**, & **-ian**; Latinized form of Rosenkreuz, name of alleged founder. **1.** adj. **a** Of, pertaining to, a secret society, supposed to have been founded in Germany by Rosenkreuz in 15th cent. for the study of occultism and magic arts; **b** connected with, pertaining to, one of the higher orders of Freemasonry. **2.** n. **a** Member of this society; **b** member of an order of Freemasonry.

Rosicrucianism, n. [1. rōzikrṓōshanizm; 2. rouzikrū́ʃənizəm]. Prec. & **-ism.** Methods or practices of Rosicrucian society.

rosily, adv. [1. rṓzili; 2. róuzili]. **rosy** & **-ly.** In a rosy manner.

rosin, n. & vb. trans. [1. rózin; 2. rɔ́zin]. Variant of **resin. 1.** n. Resin, esp. amber-coloured, solid resin left after distillation of oil of turpentine, used esp. on a violin-bow. **2.** vb. To rub, coat, with rosin, apply rosin to: *to rosin a violin-bow.*

Rosinante, Rozinante, n. [1. ròzinánte; 2. rɔ̀zinǽntɛ], fr. Span. *Rocinante*, Don Quixote's horse, fr. Span. *rocin*, 'worn-out horse'; cp. M.E. *rounci*, 'hack', fr. O. Fr. *roncin*. Old, broken-down riding-horse.

rosiness, n. [1. rṓzines; 2. róuzinis]. **rosy** & **-ness.** State or quality of being rosy.

rosiny, adj. [1. rózini; 2. rɔ́zini]. **rosin** & **-y.** Resembling, consisting of, covered with, rosin.

rosolio, n. [1. rozṓliō; 2. rɔzóuliou]. Ital., fr. Lat. *rōs*, 'dew', & *sōli-(s)*, genit. of *sōl*, 'sun', see **sol (I.)**, fr. former use of sundew in manufacture of this cordial. Sweet cordial made from raisins.

roster, n. [1. rṓster; 2. róustə], fr. Du. *rooster*, 'list', orig. 'gridiron', fr. lines dividing list into columns; cp. Du. *roosten*, 'to roast'. See **roast. a** (mil.) List giving rotation of duty of men, companies &c.; hence **b** any list or roll of names; a register.

rostral, adj. [1. róstral; 2. rɔ́strəl], fr. L. Lat. *rōstrāl-(is)*, 'of, belonging to, the rostra', fr. *rōstr-(um)*, 'beak, snout; ship's prow'; (pl.) 'platform in forum', see **rostrum**, & **-al. a** Of, pertaining to, a rostrum; **b** rostrate.

rostrate(d), adj. [1. róstrāt, rostrā́ted; 2. rɔ́streit, rɔstréitid], fr. Lat. *rōstrāt-(us)*, 'beaked; adorned with beaks of ships', fr. *rōstr-(um)*, 'beak, snout; ship's beak; rostrum', see **rostrum**, & **-ate** (& **-ed**). **1.** (of column, platform &c.) Adorned with beaks of ships or representations of these. **2.** (zool.) Having a rostrum.

rostriferous, adj. [1. rostríferus; 2. rɔstrífərəs]. See **rostrum** & **-ferous.** (zool.) Having a rostrum.

rostriform, adj. [1. róstriform; 2. rɔ́strifɔ̄m]. See prec. & **-form.** (zool.) Having the form of a rostrum.

rostro-, pref. representing Lat. *rōstr-(um)*, 'beak, snout'. See next word. (zool.) Beak, beak-like organ or part.

rostrum, n. [1. róstrum; 2. rɔ́strəm]. Lat. *rōstrum*, 'beak, snout, muzzle; curved end of ship's prow; (pl.) orators' platform in the forum, adorned with beaks of captured ships', earlier **rōd-tr*; for first element cp. *rōd-ere*, 'to gnaw', see **rodent**; *-tr* expresses the agent or instrument. **1.** (usually pl.) *Rostra*, orators' platform in Roman forum, adorned with curved beaks of ships captured at Antium, 338 B.C. Hence, **2.** Pulpit, stage, platform, of public speaker or orator. **3.** (zool., anat.) Beak or snout, beak-like projection, beak-shaped organ. **4.** Curved projection resembling a beak; specif., curved end of ship's prow.

rosulate, adj. [1. rózūlat; 2. rɔ́zjulət], fr. L. Lat. *rosul-(a)*, 'little rose', fr. *ros-(a)*, 'rose', see **rose**, & **-ule** & **-ate.** (bot.) Having the leaves arranged in clusters like rose-petals.

rosy, adj. [1. rṓzi; 2. róuzi]. **rose (I.)** & **-y. 1.** Having the colour of a pink rose; reddish, warmly pink; *rosy cross*, emblem of Rosicrucians, q.v. **2.** Made of, adorned with, hung with, roses. **3.** (fig.) Bright, propitious, favourable, promising success: *rosy prospects*; *the outlook is not very rosy.*

rot (I.), n. [1. rot; 2. rɔt]. M.E. *rot*, prob. fr. O.N. *rot*; cogn. w. O.E. *rotian*, 'to rot'. See next word & cp. **ret. 1.** Process of rotting, state of being rotten; decay, putrefaction. **2.** One of various kinds of destructive disease attacking plants, timber &c. caused by fungi; specif., dry-rot, q.v. **3.** Kind of wasting disease, esp., usually, *the rot*, liver disease of sheep &c. **4.** (slang) Rubbish, nonsense; applied to a foolish idea, expression, practice &c. (often as exclamation): *rot!, what rot!, don't talk rot!* &c. **5.** (cricket and other games) Sudden, unexpected collapse; e.g. the fall of several wickets in quick succession; esp. in Phr. *a rot set in.*

rot (II.), vb. intrans. & trans. O.E. *rotian*, M.E. *roten*; cp. O.N. *rota*; M. Du. *roten*; O.H.G. *rozzēn*, 'to rot'. **A.** intrans. **1.** (of organic substance) To become decomposed, to disintegrate, by natural process through exposure to air, moisture &c. **2.** (fig.) To become spoilt, useless, decay gradually from stagnation, neglect, lack of support or care &c. **3.** (slang) To talk nonsense, jest; talk ironically. **B.** trans. **1.** To cause to rot, decay, putrefy. **2.** (slang) To tease, chaff, make fun of.

rota, n. [1. rṓta; 2. róutə]. Lat. *rota*, 'wheel'; cp. Scrt. *rátha*, 'car, chariot'; O.H.G. *rad*, 'wheel'; Lith. *rãtas*, 'wheel'; *ritù*, 'I roll'. **1.** List or register of persons performing a duty in turn. **2.** Succession or round of duties. **3.** (R.C. Ch.) Supreme ecclesiastical court of appeal, consisting of twelve prelates, subject only to the authority of the Pope.

Rotarian, adj. & n. [1. rōtā́rian; 2. routéəriən]. See next word & **-an. 1.** adj. Pertaining to a Rotary Club or to the Rotary movement. **2.** n. Member of a Rotary Club.

rotary, adj. [1. rṓtari; 2. róutəri], fr. Lat. *rot-(a)*, 'wheel', see **rota**, & **-ary.** Turning like a wheel, moving in rotation. Specific uses: **a** *rotary engine*, type of steam engine, as the turbine, in which the necessary continuous rotary motion is obtained directly, instead of being converted, as in a *reciprocating engine*; **b** *Rotary Club*, club or society of business and professional men in a town or district, each representing a special business or profession, elected in rotation, and meeting to discuss and assist the trade and activities of the town, with the aim of general improvement and service; the movement, started in the U.S.A., has spread to Europe.

rotatable, adj. [1. rōtā́tabl; 2. routéitəbl]. **rotate (I.)** & **-able.** Capable of being rotated.

rotate (I.), adj. [1. rṓtāt; 2. róuteit], fr. Lat. *rot-(a)*, 'wheel', see **rota**, & **-ate.** (bot.) Wheel-shaped.

rotate (II.), vb. intrans. & trans. [1. rōtā́t; 2. routéit], fr. Lat. *rotāt-(um)*, P.P. type of *rotāre*, 'to turn like a wheel, go round in a circle, revolve', fr. *rota*, 'wheel'. See **rota. A.** intrans. **1.** (of an object) To go round about its own axis or centre. **2.** To follow in regular and repeated succession: *the seasons rotate.* **B.** trans. To cause to rotate, give rotary motion to.

rotation, n. [1. rōtā́shun; 2. routéiʃən], fr. Lat. *rotātiōn-(em)*, 'rotation', fr. *rotāt-(um)*, P.P. of *rotāre*, 'to go round in a circle', see **rotate (II.)** & **-ion. 1.** Act or process of rotating; state of being rotated. **2.** Regular succession or alternation; recurrence: *to hold office in rotation*; *rotation of crops*, planting, growing, of different crops in successive seasons in a specific area of land, to prevent exhaustion of the soil and encourage fertility.

rotational, adj. [1. rōtā́shunal; 2. routéiʃənəl]. Prec. & **-al.** Of, pertaining to, rotation.

rotative, adj. [1. rṓtativ; 2. róutətiv]. **rotate (II.)** & **-ive.** Of, pertaining to, causing, rotation.

rotator, n. [1. rōtā́ter; 2. routéitə]. **rotate (II.)** & **-or. a** That which rotates or causes rotation; specif. **b** (anat.) muscle producing rotary motion in some part of the body.

rotatory, adj. [1. rṓtaturi; 2. róutətəri]. **rotate (II.)** & **-ory.** Of, pertaining to, of the nature of; having, causing, rotation.

rotch(e), n. [1. roch; 2. rɔtʃ]. Earlier *rotge*; cp. Du. *rotje*, 'petrel'; Fris. *rotgies*, 'brent-goose'. Little auk.

rote, n. [1. rōt; 2. rout]. M.E. (Chaucer) as name of musical instrument; fr. O. Fr.; cp. also O.H.G. *rotta*; perh. fr. Low Lat. *crotta*, of Celt. origin, see **crowd (III.).** Originally the name of an instrument of the guitar or violin type; survives only in Phr. *to know, learn, get, by rote*, by heart, from memory.

rot-gut, n. (slang) Liquor of inferior quality which is injurious to the consumer; also (attrib.) *rot-gut liquor.*

rotifer, n. [1. rṓtifer; 2. róutifə], fr. Lat. *rot-(a)*, 'wheel', see **rota**, & *-i-* & **-ferous.** Minute freshwater organism furnished with rings of cilia which, when in motion, have the appearance of rotating wheels.

rotor, n. [1. rṓter; 2. róutə]. Abbr. or irregular form of **rotator.** Rotating part of a machine; a rotating, revolving cylinder; specif., one of the pair of such cylinders, used instead of sails to drive a vessel, *rotor ship*, by cross pressure of the wind.

rotten, adj. [1. rótn; 2. rɔ́tn], fr. O.N. *rotinn*, 'rotten, putrid'; cp. O.E. *rotian*, O.N. *rota*, 'to rot'. See **rot. 1.** (of organic substances) In process of natural decomposition; decaying, putrid. **2.** Falling, or liable to fall, to pieces from age, neglect, action of the weather &c.; in process of disintegration, liable to tear; brittle, frail, perished: *sails and rigging grown rotten.* **3.** (fig.) Morally debased, corrupt, unprincipled: *a rotten system of government, administration* &c. *Rotten borough*, one of the small parliamentary boroughs swept away by the Reform Act of 1832, where the electorate had become so small that the right to have a member was ridiculous and gave a scandalous opportunity for corruption. **4.** (slang) Of inferior quality; bad, unsatisfactory: *a rotten voice, player, book*; *rotten luck.*

rottenly, adv. Prec. & **-ly.** In a rotten manner.

rottenness, n. See prec. & **-ness.** State or quality of being rotten; decay, putrescence; inferiority.

Rotten Row, n. [1. rótn rṓ; 2. rɔ́tn róu]. Perh. fr. *rotten*, but etymol. doubtful; used as street-name in a number of towns. Broad track for use of riders in Hyde Park, London; also called simply *the Row.*

rotten-stone, n. Soft, friable limestone, used for polishing.

rotter, n. [1. róter; 2. rɔ́tə]. **rot (II.)** & **-er.** (slang) Worthless, unreliable, futile person.

rotund, adj. [1. rōtúnd; 2. routʌ́nd], fr. Lat. *rotund-(us)*, 'round', fr. *rot-(a)*, 'wheel'. See **rota** & **round (I.). 1.** (rare) Round, disk-shaped. **2.** Rounded, plump, nearly or completely spherical: *a rotund figure.* **3.** (of voice) Sonorous, deep, full-toned. **4.** (of style of writing &c.) Well-rounded, magniloquent, florid.

rotunda, n. [1. rōtúnda; 2. routándə]. Earlier *rotonda* (w. assimilation to prec.), fr. Ital. *rotonda*, fem. of *rotondo*, fr. Lat. *rotund-(us)*, 'round'. See prec. Building, chamber, of circular shape, with a domed roof.

rotundate, adj. [1. rōtúndat; 2. routándət]. **rotund** & **-ate**. Rounded, convex, specif., with the end(s) rounded.

rotundi-, pref. representing Lat. *rotund-(us)*, 'round'. See **rotund**. (chiefly bot.) Round; e.g. *rotundifolious*, round-leaved.

rotundity, n. [1. rōtúnditi; 2. routánditi], fr. Lat. *rotunditāt-(em)*, 'roundness', fr. *rotund-(us)*, 'round', see **rotund**, & **-ity**. **a** Roundness; round, spherical or globular shape; specif. **b** plumpness, corpulence (of person).

rotundly, adv. [1. rōtúndli; 2. routándli]. **rotund** & **-ly**. In a rotund shape.

rotundo-, pref. representing Lat. *rotund-(us)*, 'round'. See **rotund**. (chiefly bot.) Round; e.g. *rotundo-ovate*, egg-shaped.

roturier, n., Anglicized [1. rōtúriā; 2. routjóriei]. Fr., 'a plebeian', fr. *roture*, 'kind of feudal tenure; plebeian rank', prob. fr. Lat. *ruptūra*, 'fracture', see **rupture**, & **-ier**. Commoner, plebeian.

rouble, n. [1. ro͞obl; 2. rūbl]. Fr., fr. Russ. *rubl*; origin doubtful; perh. fr. Pers. *rūpīya*. See **rupee**. Unit of Russian monetary system; silver coin formerly worth about 2s. 1½d.

roucou, n. [1. ro͞oko͞o; 2. rūkū]. Fr., fr. Brazilian. Orange dye obtained from W. Indian tree.

roué, n. [1. ro͞oā; 2. rúei], fr. Fr., P.P. of *rouer*, 'to break on a wheel', fr. *roue*, 'wheel', fr. Lat. *rota*, 'wheel'. See **rota**. Dissolute, profligate person; a rake.

rouelle, n. [1. ro͞oél; 2. ruél]. Fr., dimin. fr. *roue*, 'wheel', fr. Lat. *rota*, 'wheel', see **rota**, & dimin. *-elle*. Gaulish disk-shaped amulet, symbolizing the sun.

rouge (I.), n., vb. intrans. & trans. [1. ro͞ozh; 2. rūž]. Fr., adj., 'red', fr. Lat. *rubeus*, see **rubric**. **1.** n. **a** Reddish powder used for improving the complexion; **b** red peroxide of iron used for polishing plate. **2.** vb. **a** intrans. To apply rouge to the cheeks &c.; **b** trans., to apply rouge to.

rouge (II.), n. [1. ro͞oj; 2. rūdž]. Origin unknown. Scrum; touching down in Eton football.

Rouge Croix, n. [1. ro͞ozh krwáh; 2. rúž krwá]. Fr., 'red cross'. **Rouge Dragon** [1. ro͞ozh drágun; 2. rúž drǽgən]. Names of two officers of the English College of Heralds, called Pursuivants at Arms.

rouge-et-noir, n. [1. ro͞ozh ā nwár; 2. rúž ei nwá]. Fr., 'red and black'. Gambling game in which the betting is on red or black, played with six packs of cards on a table marked with two red and two black diamonds.

rouge-royal, n. [1. ro͞ozh róial; 2. rúž róiəl]. Kind of reddish marble.

rough (I.), adj. [1. ruf; 2. raf]. O.E. *rūh*, M.E. *rouh, rough* &c.; O.H.G. *rūh*; cp. Goth. *in-rauhi-jan*, 'to grow fierce'; cogn. w. Scrt. *rūkšáš*, 'rough'; Lat. *rūga*, 'a wrinkle', see **rugose**. **1.** (of surfaces gen.) Reverse of smooth, even, or glossy; having irregularities and projections; shaggy, rugged; **a** prickly, hairy, unsmooth, unpolished, irregular, to the touch: *a rough skin, hands, paper, cloth, bark of tree, leaf* &c.; **b** (of appearance) corrugated, crinkled, spiky, hairy: *a rough brick, rock, wall, bark of tree; rough hair*, unkempt; *a rough edge*, having indentations, jagged. **2.** Reverse of level or smooth; **a** having alternate depressions and elevations: *rough country; a rough lawn, common*; **b** specif. (of surface of sea) having surface broken by waves, agitated: *rough water; a rough passage, crossing, voyage,* one across *a rough sea.* **3.** (of weather, climate, states of atmosphere &c.) Boisterous, stormy, squally, tempestuous: *rough wind; a rough night.* **4. a** (of motion and movement) Violent, immoderately vigorous; brusque, vehement: *rough games, play; a rough blow, push, pull, gesture; a rough boy*; Phr. (colloq.) *a rough house*, (i.) a disorderly, turbulent, unruly meeting or assembly; (ii.) a row, a fight; **b** (of mode of touching or handling) clumsy, unskilful, lacking gentleness, delicacy, or deftness: *rough surgery, rough usage; fragile glass is easily broken by rough handling.* **5. a** (of conduct) Rude, discourteous, inconsiderate; harsh, unkind, untender: *rough usage of children; a rough manner; a rough answer; to call a person rough names*; **b** (of manners and behaviour &c.), exhibiting ignorance of decent conventions; unpolished, coarse, ill-bred, boorish: *a rough bow; a rough fellow.* Phr. *a rough customer*, a violent, boorish fellow. **6.** (of sounds) Harsh, unmusical, discordant: *a rough voice, laugh; a rough clanging of bells.* **7.** (of tastes) Producing astringent effect upon the tongue; styptic, crude, acid: *claret is often a very rough wine; rough cider.* **8. a** Incomplete, not properly finished, unpolished, not brought to perfection, not fully elaborated: *work still in the rough state; a rough piece of carpentry; a rough draft, sketch, attempt*; specif. (of precious stones) uncut, unpolished; Phr. *a rough diamond*, vulgar, ill-bred, but honest and good-hearted fellow; **b** lacking refinements, attended by discomfort, involving physical hardship: *rough accommodation; a rough life in the jungle*; Phr. *rough and ready*, of the nature of a makeshift; **c** not fully thought out, not precise; approximate: *a rough estimate, guess* &c.

rough (II.), n., fr. prec. **1.** Something rough or unsmooth in appearance, or to the touch; rough part of something; e.g. part of horseshoe roughened to prevent slipping. Phr. *to take the rough with the smooth*, (fig.) accept facts as they are; be tolerant of vicissitudes of fortune. **2.** Unfinished, incomplete state of anything in process of being made: *a picture, sculpture, in the rough.* **3.** (specif. golf) *The rough*, rough, uncut ground outside the fairway between tee and the green. **4.** A rough person; specif., a low, turbulent blackguard, a violent rowdy, a hooligan.

rough (III.), vb. trans., fr. **rough** (I.). **1.** To make rough; specif. **a** to raise projecting points with a file on lower surface (of a horseshoe) to prevent slipping. **2.** Only in Phr. *to rough it*, to live under rough or hard conditions, do without comforts and conveniences. **3. a** *Rough in*, to draw, sketch, shape, in rough outline, make preliminary sketch of; **b** *rough out*, to plan, draft, in outline, make rough preliminary plan or design in outline. **4.** Specif., *to rough a diamond* &c., begin to cut it.

rough (IV.), adv., fr. **rough** (I.). Roughly. Phr. *to live rough*, live hard, without refinements and comforts; Phr. *to treat (person) rough*, use harshness and severity towards him.

rough and ready, adj. [1. rúf an(d) rédi; 2. ráf ən(d) rédi]. Done, made, hastily and roughly, without expenditure of great care or skill.

rough and tumble, adj. & n. [1. rúf an túmbl; 2. ráf ən támbl]. **1.** adj. (of fight, struggle &c.) Violent, boisterous, confused. **2.** n. A rough, confused, violent, disorderly struggle; a rough house.

rough-cast, n., adj., & vb. trans. **1. a** n. Coating of mortar mixed with pebbles, gravel &c. applied to outer walls of buildings; **b** adj., coated with this. **2.** vb. **a** To coat (walls) with rough-cast; **b** to plan out in the rough, arrange general form of.

rough-dry, vb. trans. To wash and dry (clothes &c.) without ironing.

roughen, vb. trans. & intrans. [1. rúfen; 2. ráfən]. **rough** (I.) & **-en**. **a** trans. To make rough; **b** intrans., to become rough.

rough-footed, adj. (of birds) Having feathered feet.

rough-grind, vb. trans. To grind coarsely.

rough-hew, vb. trans. (lit. and fig.) To shape, carve, hack out, roughly.

rough-hewn, adj. **a** Roughly carved or shaped; without proper finish; **b** (fig.) unpolished, without culture; uncouth.

rough-hound, n. Dogfish.

roughish, adj. [1. rúfish; 2. ráfiʃ]. **rough** (I.) & **-ish**. Fairly rough.

roughleg, n. [1. rúfleg; 2. ráfleg]. Kind of hawk of Europe and N. America.

rough-legged, adj. (of bird) Having thickly feathered legs.

roughly, adv. [1. rúfli; 2. ráfli]. **rough** (I.) & **-ly**. In a rough manner (in all senses).

rough-neck, n. (U.S.A. slang) Hooligan.

roughness, n. [1. rúfnes; 2. ráfnis]. See prec. & **-ness**. **1.** State or quality of being rough (in all senses). **2.** Something that is rough (in all senses).

rough-rider, n. Man who rides and breaks in rough, untamed horses.

rough-shod, adj. (of horse) Having shoes roughed to prevent slipping. Used as adv. in Phr. *to ride rough-shod over*, treat in an overbearing, arrogant, inconsiderate manner.

rough-spoken, adj. Given to, using, rough speech.

rough-wrought, adj. Having received preliminary treatment, cutting, dressing &c.

roulade, n. [1. ro͞oláhd; 2. rūlád]. Fr., fr. *roul-(er)*, 'to roll'. See **roll** (II.) & **-ade**. Musical passage consisting of a series of short notes which pass rapidly but smoothly one into the other; a run.

rouleau, n. [1. ro͞oló; 2. rūlóu], fr. Fr., dimin. of *rôle*, 'roll', see **roll** (I.). Roll, cylindrical coil; specif., pile of coins rolled up in paper.

roulette, n. [1. ro͞olét; 2. rūlét]. Fr., dimin. of *rouelle*, 'small wheel', itself a dimin. of *roue*, 'wheel', fr. Lat. *rota*, 'wheel', see **rota**. **1.** Gambling game played on a table marked with squares numbered from 1 to 36 and zero, and with spaces for red and black, odd and even &c., the winning number, colour &c. being decided by the fall of a small ball into one of the marked compartments of a revolving disk or wheel placed in the centre. **2.** Tool fitted with small revolving wheel, for engraving or cutting a perforation &c.

Rouman, n. & adj. [1. ro͞omáhn; 2. rūmán], fr. Fr. *Roumain*, fr. Roumanian *Român*, fr. Lat. *Rōmān-(us)*, 'Roman'. See **Roman**. Roumanian.

Roumanian, adj. & n. [1. ro͞ománian; 2. rūméiniən]. Prec. & **-ian**. **1.** adj. Of, pertaining to, Roumania. **2.** n. **a** Native of Roumania; **b** language of Roumania.

Roumeliote, n. [1. ro͞oméliot; 2. rūmíliət]. *Roumeli-(a)* & **-ot**. Native of Roumelia.

rouncival, n. [1. róunsival; 2. ráunsivəl], fr. Place-Name Roncesvalles. Kind of marrow-fat pea.

round (I.), adj. [1. round; 2. raund]. M.E. *round*, fr. O. Fr. *rund*, fr. Lat. *rotundus*, 'wheel-shaped, round'. See **rotund**. **1. a** (of flat surface) Having a circular outline; completely or nearly circular: *a round hoop; a round face; a round O; a round window; round eyes; a round hole*; **b** having the shape of a sphere, globe, or cylinder; globular &c.: *the round earth; a round ball; a round apple; a round bowl.* **2.** Special uses: **a** *round cheeks, arms*, plump, having curved contour; **b** *round back, shoulders*, curved, humped. **3. a** (i.) Moving in a circle, involving revolution: *round dance*, in which couples revolve; (ii.) *round game*, one in which all the players take part in turn; **b** involving motion, travel, in a circle or partial circle, and return to starting-point: *a round tour.* **4. a** (of voice) Rich, smooth, full-toned; **b** *a round wine*, one of rich, mellow quality, free from acidity or astringency of taste; **c** (of style) well-balanced and finished; cadenced, flowing. **5.** Considerable in amount, degree, intensity, vigour &c.: *a good, round sum; at a round pace.*

6. Blunt, downright, outspoken, unambiguous: *rated him in round terms*; *rapped out a round oath.* **7.** Stated approximately, without implying exactness and completeness in all details: *in round numbers*; *a round sum.* **8.** (archit.) **a** *A round arch,* semicircular; **b** (of style) employing round as distinct from pointed arches. **9.** (phon.) *Round* or *rounded vowels,* such as are uttered together with protrusion or advancing of the lips.

round (II.), n., fr. prec. **1.** Circle, ring; figure enclosed by circle or curve approximating to a circle: *to draw a round*; *to dance in a round.* **2.** Completely, or nearly, cylindrical or spherical object; specif., *round of beef,* joint cut from haunch as transverse slice; *round of toast,* slice cut right across loaf; *round of a ladder,* rung. **3.** Circular course, route, circuit; specif., **a** walk &c. following more or less circular course and ending at point of departure: *to go for a long round*; **b** fixed circuit, beat, esp. of patrol, for inspection &c.: *to go the rounds*; *to make one's round(s)*; Phr. *to go the round of,* (i.) to pass from one to another (of persons, places &c.) in succession; (ii.) to be passed on, circulate: *news goes the round of a village*; **c** (golf) single game, in which the whole succession of holes is played. **4.** Series, succession, of actions, duties &c.: *a round of visits, gaieties* &c.; *the daily round,* ordinary routine of activities. **5.** Single action or spell regarded as one of a series of actions; specif. **a** single bout or stage, e.g. in a prize fight; **b** single shot or volley: *40 rounds (of ammunition).* **6.** Unified burst of utterance by a number of persons at the same time: *a round of cheers, applause.* **7.** (mil.) Officer and guard making round of inspection &c. **8.** (mus.) Kind of song the parts or lines of which are devised to harmonize when sung at the same time by different persons who begin singing in succession, the second singing first line while the first singer is singing the second line, &c.; cp. *canon.* **9.** A dance performed in a circle. **10.** (sculp.) Method in which the object is shown complete on all sides, opposed to *relief.*

round (III.), vb. trans. & intrans., fr. **round** (I.). **A.** trans. **1. a** To make round, give round shape or finish to: *to round the corners of a table, room* &c.; *stones rounded by the action of water*; **b** (fig.) to complete, give satisfactory finish to: *to round one's career, character* &c. **2.** To go round, go about, follow curve or angle of: *to round a corner*; *the ship rounded the cape.* **3.** (phon.) To pronounce (a vowel) with the lips slightly advanced or brought towards each other. **B.** intrans. To become round, assume round or curved shape. **C.** Followed by adverb or preposition. *Round off,* **a** to give round shape to; **b** to bring to state of completion, give satisfactory or suitable finish to: *to round off the evening with a dance*; *to round off a sentence* &c. *Round out,* **a** trans., to fill out, cause to assume rounded contour(s); **b** intrans., to become rounded. *Round up,* to bring together, collect; specif., *to round up cattle,* by riding round them and driving them in; *round up a gang of criminals,* arrest them. *Round (up)on,* to turn upon, attack, esp. suddenly and unexpectedly and treacherously.

round (IV.), adv., fr. **round** (I.). **1. a** In a circular direction; so as to describe or indicate a circle or curve: *to turn round*; *walk, look, round*; *the wind has gone round to the north*; specif. **b** so as to complete a revolution with return to point of departure: *the wheel turns round*; forming a completed circuit or cycle: *Christmas soon comes round again*; Phrs. *all round, right round,* completely round; *round and round,* with repeated revolutions; *to sleep the clock round,* for at least 12 hours. **2.** So as to encircle: *a crowd gathered round.* **3.** Following a circuit, going from one to another in a series: *to go round to all the cottages*; *tea was carried round*; *the news was soon passed round.* Phr. (*not enough to go*) *all round,* for everyone; *taking it all round,* considering it from every point of view. **4.** Not by direct route, circuitously: *a long way round.* **5.** Of specified measure or distance in circumference: *his waist must be 4 ft. round.* **6. a** From a place unspecified to another place in which the speaker is or will be: *come round and see us this evening*; *bring my car round*; **b** to a specified place, or to that in which person addressed is, or will be: *I'll come round to your house*; *I'll come round and see you.*

round (V.), prep., fr. prec. **1.** (expressing position) Passing, lying, quite about so as to encircle: *a rope round a tree*; *a noose round one's neck.* **2.** (expressing movement) **a** Moving in a circle about, pursuing a path or course which passes on every side of and returns to starting-point: *to run round the house*; *to sail round the world*; **b** passing partly around, from one side to another of: *to go round the corner.* **3.** In all directions, all around: *to look round the room*; *to walk round the estate*; *snow falling round me.*

round (VI.), vb. trans. & intrans. O.E. *rūnian*; M.E. *rounen,* 'to whisper, talk', fr. O.E. *rūn,* 'secret, mystery; secret counsel or discussion'. See **rune.** (archaic or obs.) To speak low or mysteriously, to whisper; esp. in Phr. *to round one in the ear.*

roundabout, adj. & n. [1. róundabout; 2. ráundəbaut]. **1.** adj. **a** Circuitous, not following direct route; **b** (of speech &c.) circumlocutory, indirect; **c** (of the figure) portly, plump. **2.** n. Something which moves round; specif., a merry-go-round.

round and round, adv. & prep. Completely round, many times round: **a** adv., *to turn round and round*; **b** prep., *birds fly round and round a lighthouse.*

round-arm, adj. (cricket, of bowling) With arm swung through horizontal curve.

roundel, n. [1. róundl; 2. ráundl], fr. O. Fr. *rondel.* See **rondel. 1.** Small circle, ring, disk; specif. (her.) small disk-shaped charge. **2.** Rondel.

roundelay, n. [1. róundelā; 2. ráundilei], fr. O. Fr. *rondelet,* **rondel** & **-et,** w. Mod. Engl. form assimilated to **lay (I.).** Song with refrain set to simple music.

rounder, n. [1. róunder; 2. ráundə]. **round** (III.) & **-er. 1.** One who, that which, rounds; specif., tool of various kinds for giving curved or rounded shape. **2. a** (pl.) Game played with bat and soft ball, in which the player runs from one to another of a series of stumps placed in a circle; **b** complete circuit by single player of the whole series of stumps; the score in the game is reckoned by these.

round-fish, n. Common carp.

round-hand (I.), n. Style of handwriting with free and flowing curves.

round-hand (II.), adj. Round-arm.

Roundhead, n. [1. róund-hed; 2. ráundhed]. Member of Parliamentary party in Civil War of 1642–49; so called from his close-cropped hair contrasted with *Cavalier.*

round-headed, adj. Brachycephalic.

round-house, n. **1.** (naut.) Cabin on after part of quarter-deck. **2.** (hist.) Place for temporary detention of prisoners.

rounding, n. [1. róunding; 2. ráundiŋ]. **round** (III.) & **-ing. 1.** Act of giving a round or curved shape or appearance to; specif. (book-binding) process of giving rounded shape to back of book-cover. **2.** (phon.) Advancing of the lips in pronouncing a round vowel, such as [ū, ō, ɔ̄] &c.

round-iron, n. Tool with round head used in soldering.

roundish, adj. [1. róundish; 2. ráundiʃ]. **round** (I.) & **-ish.** Fairly round.

roundly, adv. [1. róundli; 2. ráundli]. **round** (I.) & **-ly. 1.** Vigorously, energetically, briskly. **2.** Without ambiguity or hesitation; in plain terms, without mincing words: *to abuse a person roundly.*

roundness, n. [1. róundnes; 2. ráundnis]. See prec. & **-ness.** State, quality, of being round; rotundity.

round robin, n. Series of signatures to a petition, protest &c., often written in a circle so that no single name heads the list.

round-shot, n. Spherical shot; ball; as distinct from shells &c.

round-shouldered, adj. Having curved, humped, stooping, shoulders.

Round Table, n. (caps.) a Table at which King Arthur and his knights sat; **b** name of Knightly Order, supposed to have been instituted by Arthur.

round-top, n. Small platform at top of mast.

round tower, n. Tall cylindrical tower, separate from neighbouring church &c., tapering towards the top; found in Ireland and believed to date from the early Christian period and to have been used primarily as belfries.

round-turn, n. Single hitch of rope round post &c. as temporary support &c.

round-up, n. **a** Driving together of cattle on a ranch; **b** the collection by the police of criminals or other persons for arrest.

round-worm, n. One of a class of parasitic worms.

roup (I.), vb. trans. & n. [1. roup; 2. raup]. The present pronunciation is difficult to explain. The O.E. n. & vb. are *hrōp, hrōpan,* 'to cry out, shout, call'; M.E. *rōp, rōpen*; cp. O.H.G. *hruof, hruofan* (Mod. Germ. *ruf* &c.); Goth. *hrōps, hrōpjan*; O.N. *hrop,* 'jest'. (chiefly Scots) **1.** vb. To sell by auction. **2.** n. Auction; usually *public roup.*

roup (II.), n. [1. ro͞op; 2. rūp]. Perh. imitative. Catarrhal disease of poultry.

roupy, adj. [1. ro͞opi; 2. rūpi]. Prec. & **-y.** Resembling, affected with, roup.

rouse (I.), n. [1. rouz; 2. rauz]. Prob. fr. **carouse,** in such a Phr. as *to drink carouse* [dríŋk əráuz]. **1.** Draught, cup, bumper, of liquor. **2.** Drinking of health, toast. Phr. *to give a rouse,* drink a toast. **3.** Carouse, revel, drinking-bout.

rouse (II.), vb. trans. & intrans. Orig. hunting term; etymol. uncertain. **A.** trans. **1.** To startle, start, put up (game from cover). **2. a** To awake, stir up, from sleep, physical torpor, lethargy, unconsciousness; **b** to stir up from mental torpor, stimulate to action; to bring from a state of inaction, indifference &c. to one of activity: *to rouse to action* &c.; *to rouse oneself.* **3.** To excite (feeling), to awaken, inflame: *to rouse evil passions, interest.* **4.** To stir, agitate: *to rouse liquid.* **B.** intrans. Generally *rouse up,* to awaken, be stirred into activity.

rouse (III.), n., fr. prec. (mil.) Reveille.

rouse (IV.), **roose,** vb. trans. [1. rouz, ro͞oz; 2. rauz, rūz], fr. O. Fr. *arrouser,* fr. Lat. *adrōrāre,* 'to bedew', fr. **ad-** & *rōrāre,* 'to distil dew, drip, drizzle', fr. *rōr-,* stem of *rōs,* 'dew', see **roric.** To roll, pickle, in salt: *to rouse herrings.*

rouser, n. [1. róuzer; 2. ráuzə]. **rouse** (II.) & **-er.** One who, that which, awakens, rouses, excites; specif. (slang) a startling, audacious, speech or action.

rousing, adj. [1. róuzing; 2. ráuziŋ]. See prec. & **-ing.** Tending to, having the power to, excite, inflame, stir up the feelings; stirring, moving: *a rousing welcome, chorus*; *rousing cheers*; *a rousing sermon.*

Rousseauan, adj. [1. ro͞osóan; 2. rūsóuən], fr. Jean Jacques Rousseau, French philosopher & writer, 1712–78, & **-an.** Pertaining to, based on, Rousseau or his teaching.

Rousseauesque, adj. [1. ro͞osōésk; 2. rūsouésk], fr. Rousseau, see prec., & **-esque.** Resembling, in the manner of, the writings or doctrines of Rousseau.

Rousseauian, adj. [1. ro͞osóian; 2. rūsóuiən], fr. Rousseau, see **Rousseauan** & **-ian.** Rousseauan.

Rousseauism, n. [1. ro͞osōizm; 2. rūsouizəm]. See **Rousseauan** & **-ism.** Opinions, doctrines, of Rousseau, esp. on education, economics, religion &c.

Rousseauist, n. [1. ro͞osōist; 2. rūsouist]. See **Rousseauan** & **-ist.** Adherent of Rousseauism.

Rousseauite, n. [1. rōōsōīt; 2. rūsouait]. See **Rousseauan** & **-ite**. Rousseauist.

Roussillon, n. [1. rōōsēyon; 2. rūsijɔ̃]. Fr., fr. name of old province in Southern France. Red wine from Roussillon, resembling burgundy.

rout (I.), n. [1. rout; 2. raut], fr. M.E. *route*, 'crowd, host', fr. O. Fr. Ultimately formally the same as **route**, but showing different development of meaning; perh. orig. 'broken, disorderly host'. **1. a** Confused, disorderly crowd or assembly; rabble, mob; **b** specif. (legal) group or assembly of three or more persons met with intent to commit an unlawful act. **3.** (archaic) Large social gathering; a party. **4.** Overwhelming defeat resulting in disorderly retreat or flight. Phr. *to put to rout*, defeat utterly.

rout (II.), vb. trans., fr. prec. To defeat, put to flight.

rout (III.), vb. intrans. & trans. Variant of **root** (III.). To root; also *rout out*, to drive, drag, or fetch out forcibly.

route, n. [1. rōōt; 2. rūt], borrowed fr. Fr., later than **rout** (I.) & therefore preserving Fr. sound of vowel; fr. Lat. *rupta* (*via*), 'broken-up path', fr. P.P. type of *rumpere*, 'to break', see **rupture**. **1.** The way taken in going from one place to another; esp. the way chosen on specific occasion; the customary or prescribed course, road, way, which is followed in travelling between two given places: *the shortest route; my route lay through a forest; a devious route.* Phr. *en route*, Fr., on the way. **2.** (mil.) also [1. rout; 2. raut]. Marching orders. Phr. *to get the route*, receive marching orders; *route step*, method of marching adopted on long marches; *column of route*, formation of troops when on the march; *route march*, long march of troops, when in training.

routine, n. [1. rōōtēn; 2. rūtīn], Fr., fr. **route** & **-ine**. **1.** Regularly recurring, prescribed, or customary series of actions: *the day's routine; the routine of business, of official duties* &c. **2.** Regular procedure followed in specific circumstances. **3.** (in unfavourable sense) Hidebound, inelastic system of procedure which destroys, or forbids initiative and adaptability.

routinism, n. [1. rōōtēnizm; 2. rūtīnizəm]. Prec. & **-ism**. Adherence to, belief in, routine; esp. in unfavourable sense.

routinist, n. [1. rōōtēnist; 2. rūtīnist]. See prec. & **-ist**. A stickler for routine at all costs.

rove (I.), vb. intrans. & trans. [1. rōv; 2. rouv]. Prob. fr. Du. *rooven*, 'to rob'; cogn. w. **reave**; see also **rob**, but the earliest use is as a term in archery. **A.** intrans. **1. a** To wander without fixed home or destination, move from place to place at random or without definite route; to roam: *to rove far afield; a band of roving bandits;* **b** (of affections, interests &c.) to be constantly transferred from one object to another. **2.** (of eyes) To be constantly changing direction, wander from point to point. **3.** (archery) To aim at a casual or indefinite mark. **4.** (fishing) To troll with live bait. **B.** trans. To wander over or through, traverse at random: *to rove the woods.*

rove (II.), n. & vb. trans. Etymol. doubtful. **1.** n. Slightly twisted strand of silk, wool, cotton &c. **2.** vb. To form into roves.

rover (I.), n. [1. rōver; 2. róuvə]. **rove** (I.) & **-er**. **1. a** Person given to roving; wanderer; **b** (archaic) specif., a wandering robber; a pirate: *Ralph the Rover.* **2.** (archery) Chance object chosen as mark for long-distance shooting &c. Phr. *to shoot at rovers*, **a** to shoot at random; **b** to shoot at distant mark or one with range undetermined. **3.** (croquet) Ball which has passed through all the hoops, but has not been pegged out and is free to move anywhere.

rover (II.), n. **rove** (II.) & **-er**. Frame &c. for twisting and drawing out strands of wool &c.

row (I.), n. [1. rō; 2. rou]. O.E. *rāw*; M.E. *rōwe*, 'row, succession'; O.H.G. *rīga*, 'row'; Du. *reesem*, 'row'; cogn. w. Lith. *rēkė*, 'slice of bread'; Scrt. *rēkhā*, 'rent, split, line'; Lat. *rīma*, 'tear, split'; Gk. *ereikein*, 'to rend'. **1. a** Series of objects arranged to form a straight line: *a row of trees, bottles, houses, soldiers* &c.; specif. **b** row of seats, places, in theatre &c. **2.** (in street-names &c.) Street with row of houses on one or both sides. **3.** *The Row*, Rotten Row, q.v.

row (II.), vb. intrans. & trans. O.E. *rōwan*, M.E. *rōwen*; cp. O.N. *rōa*; M.H.G. *rüejen*, 'to row'; O.E. *rōðer*, O.N. *rōðr*, 'oar', see **rudder**; cogn. w. Lat. *rēmus*, 'oar', cp. **bireme**; Gk. *erétēs*, 'rower'; Scrt. *arítraš*, 'oar'; Lith. *írti*, 'to row'. **A.** intrans. **a** To propel boat on surface of water by means of oars; specif. **b** to take part in rowing of boat, esp. in race &c.: *to row in the Oxford boat.* **B.** trans. **1.** To propel (boat) by means of oars: *to row a boat.* **2.** To convey in rowing-boat. **3.** To carry out actions of rowing for specified time or in specified way: *to row an uneven stroke.* **4.** To take part in, in rowing-boat: *to row a race.* **C.** Followed by adverb or preposition. *Row down*, to overtake by rowing. *Row over*, to gain easy victory in rowing race.

row (III.), n., fr. prec. Act of rowing; specif. **a** spell of rowing, turn at the oars; **b** trip in rowing-boat: *to go for a row;* **c** distance rowed: *it is a long row across the estuary.*

row (IV.), n. [1. rou; 2. rau]. First found in late 18th cent.; etymol. unknown. (colloq.) **1.** Noise, disturbance, uproar, harassing or unpleasant sound. Phr. *to kick up a row*, make a noise, create disturbance; (fig.) raise strong, persistent objections &c. **2. a** Violent dispute, noisy quarrel: *to have a row with;* **b** brawl, fray, fight: *a street row.* **3.** Act of scolding, reprimanding; state of being scolded: *to get into a row*, to incur censure, get a scolding; *to make a row about*, scold, find fault with (person) on account of.

row (V.), vb. trans., fr. prec. **1.** To create a noisy disturbance; to brawl. (colloq.) **2.** To scold, reprove forcibly, rate.

rowan, n. [1. rōan, róuan; 2. róuən, ráuən], fr. Scand.; cp. Swed. *rōn*; O.N. *reynir*. **a** Also *rowan-tree*, mountain-ash; **b** red berries of mountain-ash.

row-boat, n. [1. rō bōt; 2. róu bout]. Rowing-boat.

row-de-dow, rowdy-dow, n. [1. ròu de dóu; 2. ràu di dáu]. Imit. Disturbance, hubbub, uproar.

rowdily, adv. [1. róudili; 2. ráudili]. **rowdy** & **-ly**.

rowdiness, n. [1. róudines; 2. ráudinis]. See next word & **-ness**. State or quality of being rowdy.

rowdy, adj. & n. [1. róudi; 2. ráudi]. Am., orig. sense 'backwoodsman'; etymol. unknown. **1.** adj. Rough, turbulent, noisy; characterized by, creating, noisy violence. **2.** n. A rowdy person; one given to making disturbances; a rough, a hooligan.

rowdyish, adj. [1. róudiish; 2. ráudiiʃ]. Prec. & **-ish**. Given to rowdyism.

rowdyism, n. [1. róudiizm; 2. ráudiizəm]. **rowdy** & **-ism**. Rough, turbulent conduct.

rowel (I.), n. [1. róuel; 2. ráuil]. M.E. *rouelle*, 'rowel', fr. O. Fr. *rouel*, dimin. fr. *roue*, 'wheel', fr. Lat. *rota*, 'wheel', see **rota**, & **-le**. **1.** Small spiked revolving wheel at end of spur. **2.** Circular, perforated disk of rubber &c. inserted beneath horse's skin to assist discharge of pus.

rowel (II.), vb. trans., fr. prec. **1.** To strike with rowel of spur. **2.** (vet. surg.) To insert rowel in.

rowing-boat, n. [1. rōing bōt; 2. róuiŋ bòut]. Boat propelled by oars.

rowlock, n. [1. rúluk; 2. rálək]. Prob. fr. O.E. *ārloc*, 'oar lock', w. assimilation of first element to **row** (II.). U-shaped projection, pair of projecting wooden pins, pegs, or thole-pins, attached to gunwale of rowing-boat, in which oar works when in use.

Roxburghe, n. [1. róksburo; 2. rɔ́ksbərə]. Named after Duke of Roxburghe, 1740–1804. Style of book-binding, with cloth or paper sides, plain leather back, gilt top, and untrimmed edges.

royal (I.), adj. [1. róial; 2. rɔ́iəl]. In M.E., fr. O. Fr. *roial*, fr. Lat. *rēgāl-(is)*, 'royal', see **regal**. **1.** Of, pertaining to, belonging to, characteristic of, emanating from, granted by, a king or queen: *royal family, palace, crown, bounty* &c.; *a royal prince*, of royal family; *Princess Royal*, courtesy title, granted by the King of England to his eldest daughter; *Royal Highness; of royal blood; the blood royal; the royal signature; a royal charter; his royal master; Royal Standard*, with arms of United Kingdom; *rhyme royal*, see **rhyme-royal**. **2.** Under patronage of the King, having received authority, charter &c. from king or queen: *royal burgh, Royal Academy, Society, Royal Navy, Royal Artillery, Engineers, Army Medical Corps* &c.; also of corps and certain regiments, as *Royal West Surrey Regiment* &c. **3.** Suitable for, worthy of, a king; splendid, magnificent: *to live in royal state; a royal feast, welcome* &c. Phr. *royal road to*, see **road**. **4.** Of large or unusual size, of superior importance, position &c.; *Royal Arch*, degree in Freemasonry; *royal fern*, of genus Osmunda; *royal mast*, section of mast above topgallant mast; *royal octavo*, folded from royal paper; *royal paper*, size of paper, 20 × 25 or 19 × 24; *royal sail*, above topgallant sail; *royal stag*, of seventh year, with fully developed antlers. Phr. *a battle royal*, see **battle royal**.

royal (II.), n., fr. prec. **1.** (pl.) *The Royals*, first British regiment of foot, now the Royal Scots (Lothian) Regiment. **2.** Royal paper. **3.** Royal stag. **4.** (naut.) Royal sail.

royalism, n. [1. róializm; 2. rɔ́iəlizəm]. **royal** (I.) & **-ism**. Attachment to a monarchy; belief in monarchical principles and system of government.

royalist, n. [1. róialist; 2. rɔ́iəlist]. See prec. & **-ist**. Advocate of royalism; supporter of monarchy, or of a specific monarch; specif., adherent of Charles I. in the Civil War; cavalier.

royalistic, adj. [1. roialístik; 2. rɔiəlístik]. Prec. & **-ic**. Of, pertaining to, characteristic of, royalism or royalists.

royally, adv. [1. róiali; 2. rɔ́iəli]. **royal** (I.) & **-ly**. In a royal manner.

royalty, n. [1. róialti; 2. rɔ́iəlti]. **royal** (I.) & **-ty**. **1.** State of being royal; rank, office, character, of a king or queen. **2. a** Royal personage, member of royal family; **b** royal persons collectively. **3. a** Payment made to an owner for the right to exploit his property; e.g. by mining company to owner of land in which mine is situated; **b** percentage of money derived from sales of a book, song &c. paid to the author by the publisher; share of profits paid by theatrical producer to the author of a play.

Royston crow, n. [1. róiston krō; 2. rɔ́istən króu], fr. Royston, Herts. Hooded or grey crow.

rub (I.), vb. trans. & intrans. [1. rub; 2. rab]. In M.E., prob. of Scand. origin. **A.** trans. **1. a** To move (something) repeatedly backwards and forwards or up and down, over the surface of (something else); to apply friction to: *to rub one's chin with one's hand; to rub one's chest with oil;* often implying intention of drying, polishing, cleaning: *to rub silver, a glass, with a cloth; to rub one's hands on a towel;* Phr. *to rub one's hands*, to stroke one with the other, press palms together, squeeze the back of each with the other, as in washing; (fig.) to execute such gestures as expressing triumph, satisfaction &c.: *he was rubbing his hands over the result of the election; to rub the wrong way*, (i.) to stroke (cat &c.) in direction contrary to that in which its coat grows; (ii.) to offend, hurt feelings of, make angry; **b** to touch lightly and repeatedly on some part of surface: *a cat rubs his head against one*; **c** to brush against lightly, to graze in passing: *your coat has rubbed (against) the wet paint*; Phr. *to rub shoulders with*, brush against in passing; (fig.) to meet, come into social contact with, associate with. **2.** To cause an abrasion on, make sore, by friction: *the collar has rubbed the horse's neck*; *my shoe is rubbing my heel.* **3.** Specif., to take an impression (of something engraved) by rubbing paper &c. placed above, with black lead &c.: *to rub brasses*, to take a rubbing of. **B.** intrans. To perform the act or process of rubbing. **C.** Followed by adverb or preposition. *Rub along*, (colloq.) to contrive to exist or keep on one's course in spite of hardships or difficulties. *Rub down*, trans., **a** to rub thoroughly, with towel &c. for cleansing or drying: *to rub a horse down*; **b** to wear down, remove irregularities on surface of, by rubbing. *Rub in*, trans., **a** to force in by rubbing: *to rub ointment in*; **b** to emphasize pointedly (idea, fact &c.); to reiterate insistently and tediously. *Rub off*, **a** trans., to remove by friction; **b** intrans., to be liable to become detached, to come off. *Rub out*, **a** trans., to remove by friction, erase; **b** intrans., to be easily erased. *Rub together*, intrans., to be rubbed one against the other. *Rub up*, **a** To brighten, clean, by friction; to polish, burnish; **b** (fig.) to freshen, renew: *to rub up one's knowledge of a subject.*

rub (**II.**), n., fr. prec. **1.** Act, spell, of rubbing: *to give a thing a rub.* **2.** Something which causes friction, which hinders progress; an obstacle, obstruction; specif. **a** (bowls) irregularity in surface of ground, projection, or depression; **b** (golf) *rub of the green*, chance deflection of ball; **c** (fig.) hindrance, drawback: '*aye, there's the rub*' ('Hamlet' iii. 1).

rub-a-dub, n. [1. rúb a dub; 2. ráb ə dab]. Imitative. Sound of beaten drum.

rubato, adj. & n. [1. rōōbáhtō; 2. rūbátou]. Ital., lit. 'robbed'. (mus.) **1.** adj. (sc. *tempo*), Strongly marked or modified, by lengthening of one note at expense of another. **2.** n. Modification of time in this way.

rubber (**I.**), n. [1. rúber; 2. rábə]. **rub** (**II.**) & **-er. 1.** One who, that which, rubs; specif. **a** person practising massage; **b** cylindrical shaped stone for whetting a scythe &c. **2.** Object used for applying friction; specif. **a** part of machine with which friction is applied; **b** piece of india-rubber used for erasing. **3. a** India-rubber, caoutchouc; the elastic substance obtained from the rubber-plant &c.; **b** any of various articles made of this; a rubber garment; *rubbers*, rubber shoes, goloshes.

rubber (**II.**), vb. trans., fr. prec. To cover, coat, with india-rubber.

rubber (**III.**), n. Origin doubtful; earliest use as term, in pl. *rubbers*, in game of bowls. **1.** Group of three games in whist, bridge &c.: *a rubber of whist.* **2.** Decisive game in group of three: *to win the rubber.*

rubberneck, n. & vb. intrans. [1. rúbernek; 2. rábənek]. (American slang) **a** n. Person who goes about peering intently and inquisitively at everything, as though stretching his neck to get a nearer view; used esp. of tourists and sightseers; **b** vb., to look curiously, inquisitively, at everything.

rubber plant, tree, n. Any of various tropical plants or trees yielding a milky, elastic latex, caoutchouc, or india-rubber, esp. *Hevea braziliensis*, growing wild in S. America and now cultivated in the Far East, yielding 'para' rubber, and *Ficus elastica*, indigenous to Asia, the india-rubber tree.

rubbing, n. [1. rúbing; 2. rábiŋ]. **rub** (**I.**) & **-ing. 1.** Act of applying friction. **2.** Reproduction of design in relief, or incised, on paper placed above it and rubbed with heel-ball &c.

rubbish, n. [1. rúbish; 2. rábiʃ]. L.M.E. (15th cent.) *robous*, glosses Lat. *petrosa*; cp. Ital. *robaccia*, 'trash'; origin uncertain. **1.** Waste matter, anything rejected or thrown away, refuse: *household rubbish.* **2.** Anything worthless or useless, or of inferior quality; trash; **a** (in material sense) *the goods in this shop are just rubbish*; **b** (in non-material sense) worthless, futile, foolish ideas or talk; nonsense: *don't talk rubbish*; *to suppose that you are too ill to work is all rubbish.* **3.** (as interj.) *Oh, rubbish!*, implying contempt for, disbelief in, what is said.

rubbishing, adj. [1. rúbishing; 2. rábiʃiŋ]. Prec. & **-ing**. Rubbishy.

rubbishy, adj. [1. rúbishi; 2. rábiʃi]. **rubbish** & **-y.** Of the nature of rubbish; inferior, worthless, paltry, trashy.

rubble, n. [1. rúbl; 2. rábl]. Etymol. unknown. Cp. Icel. *rubbi*, 'refuse'. **1.** Small, broken, or crushed pieces of undressed stone, brick &c. used in rough masonry. **2.** (geol.) **a** Disintegrated layer on upper surface of rock; **b** layer or mass of water-worn stones.

rubbly, adj. [1. rúbli; 2. rábli]. Prec. & **-y.** Consisting of, containing, like, rubble.

rubefacient, adj. & n. [1. rōōbefáshient; 2. rūbiféiʃiənt]. See **rubefy** & **-facient. 1.** adj. Causing redness of the skin by irritation. **2.** n. Medicinal substance irritating and reddening the skin.

rubefaction, n. [1. rōōbefákshun; 2. rūbifækʃən]. **rubefy** & **-faction. 1.** Act of rubefying; state of being rubefied. **2.** Redness caused by irritation.

rubefy, rubify, vb. trans. [1. rōōbifī; 2. rūbifai], fr. Lat. *rubefacere*, 'to redden', fr. *rubē-(re)*, 'to redden', see **rubric**, & **-fy.** To redden, give reddish tinge to; specif. (med.) to redden through irritation.

rubicelle, n. [1. rōōbisel; 2. rūbisel]. Fr., prob. fr. O. Fr. *rubis*, see **ruby**, & **-elle.** Orange-coloured precious stone, kind of spinel.

Rubicon, n. [1. rōōbikun; 2. rūbikən]. River of Tuscany, which formed boundary between Italia proper and Julius Caesar's Gallic province, and which Caesar crossed as declaration of war against Pompey. **1.** (cap.) Chiefly in Phr. *to cross, pass, the Rubicon*, to take a decisive step, commit oneself to a definite course of action. **2.** (l.c.) The winning of a game of piquet before opponent has scored 100; also as vb., to defeat (opponent) in this way.

rubicund, adj. [1. rōōbikund; 2. rūbikand], fr. Lat. *rubicund-(us)*, 'red', fr. *rub-(ēre)*, 'to be red', see **rubric. a** Reddish, ruddy, healthily rosy: *a rubicund face, complexion*; **b** having a fresh, ruddy complexion.

rubicundity, n. [1. rōōbikúnditi; 2. rūbikánditi]. Prec. & **-ity.** State of being rubicund.

rubidium, n. [1. rōōbídium; 2. rūbídiəm], fr. Lat. *rubid-(us)*, 'reddish', fr. *rub-(ēre)*, 'to be red', see **rubric**, & **-ium**; named fr. the two red lines in the spectrum of the metal. Rare, soft, silvery-white metallic element belonging to the potassium group.

rubiginous, adj. [1. rōōbíjinus; 2. rūbídžinəs], fr. Lat. *rūbīgin-*, stem of *rūbīgo, rōbīgo*, 'rust'; cp. Lat. *robus*, 'red'; the vowel *ō* is prob. of dialectal origin; cp. Lat. *ruber*, 'red', see **rubric**, & **rust.** Brownish red, rusty.

rubigo, n. [1. rōōbígō; 2. rūbáigou]. See prec. A parasitic fungus causing rust or mildew on plants.

rubious, adj. [1. rōōbius; 2. rūbiəs]. **ruby** & **-ous.** Like, of the colour of, a ruby.

rubric, n. [1. rōōbrik; 2. rūbrik], fr. Lat. *rubrīc-(a)*, 'red earth, red pigment; title of law inscribed in red', hence 'law', fr. Lat. *rubr-*, stem of *ruber*, 'red'; cp. Lat. *rubēre*, 'to be red'; *rūfus*, 'light red'; *rōbīgo*, 'rust'; *russus*, 'red', fr. **rudh-*, **reudh-*, **roudh-*, q.v. under **red**, & cp. **rufous. 1.** Heading of chapter, paragraph &c. in MSS. illumined, later printed, in red. **2.** Line, section, passage, in written or printed document, distinguished by red colouring or other device; specif. **a** liturgical direction in prayer book &c. printed in red or special type; hence, **b** any instruction or direction in a liturgy or other document.

rubrical, adj. [1. rōōbrikl; 2. rūbrikl]. Prec. & **-al.** Connected with, of the nature of, according to, a rubric.

rubrically, adv. Prec. & **-ly.** In the manner of, according to, a rubric.

rubricate, vb. trans. [1. rōōbrikāt; 2. rūbrikeit], fr. Lat. *rubrīcāt-(um)*, P.P. type of *rubrīcāre*, 'to colour red', fr. *rubrīca*, 'red earth', see **rubric**, & **-ate. 1.** To colour, distinguish, illuminate, with red lettering. **2.** To provide with rubrics.

rubrication, n. [1. rōōbrikáshun; 2. rūbrikéiʃən]. Prec. & **-ion. 1. a** Act of rubricating; **b** rubricated heading &c.; rubricated document. **2.** Heading, passage &c. written or printed in red.

rubricator, n. [1. rōōbrikāter; 2. rūbrikeitə]. **rubricate** & **-or.** Person who inserts red lettering, headings &c. in manuscript &c.

rubrician, n. [1. rōōbríshan; 2. rūbríʃən]. **rubric** & **-ian. a** One versed in, a student of, rubrics; **b** person who adheres strictly to terms of rubric.

rubricism, n. [1. rōōbrisizm; 2. rūbrisizəm]. **rubric** & **-ism.** Strict adherence to the letter of a rubric.

rubricist, n. [1. rōōbrisist; 2. rūbrisist]. See prec. & **-ist.** Rubrician.

rub-stone, n. Whetstone.

ruby (**I.**), n. [1. rōōbi; 2. rūbi], fr. O. Fr. *rubi-(s)*, 'ruby', prob. fr. Lat. *rubeus*, 'red', fr. *rub-(ēre)*, 'to be red', q.v. under **rubric. 1. a** Hard, transparent, deep red precious stone, a variety of corundum; also *Oriental ruby*; **b** rose-coloured or crimson precious stone, a variety of spinel; also *spinel, balas, ruby.* Phr. *above rubies*, invaluable. **2.** Deep crimson or purplish-red colour; *ruby glass*, glass tinted with oxide of copper, iron &c. **3.** (print.) Small size of type, between pearl and nonpareil.

ruby (**II.**), adj., fr. prec. Of the colour of a ruby, deep glowing red.

ruby-throat, n. Kind of humming-bird.

ruche, n. [1. rōōsh; 2. rūʃ]. Fr., 'beehive'; prob. Celt., cp. Gael. *rusg*, 'bark, rind'. Strip of silk, lace, muslin &c. frilled or pleated along one edge.

ruched, adj. [1. rōōsht; 2. rūʃt]. Prec. & **-ed.** Formed into, adorned with, a ruche.

ruck (**I.**), n. [1. ruk; 2. rak]. M.E. *ruke*, 'heap'; cp. Swed. dial. *ruka*, 'little heap'. Crowd or number of unimportant, commonplace, more or less negligible persons or things; the common herd.

ruck (**II.**), n., fr. O.N. *hrukka*, 'wrinkle'. Irregular fold, crease, wrinkle.

ruck (**III.**), vb. trans. & intrans., fr. prec. Also *ruck up*, to wrinkle, rumple.

ruckle, n. & vb. trans. & intrans. [1. rúkl; 2. rákl]. See **ruck** (**II.**) & **-le. 1.** n. Wrinkle, ruck. **2.** vb. To ruck, wrinkle.

rucksack, n. [1. róoksak; 2. rúksæk], fr. Germ. *rücksack*; fr. *rück-(en)*, 'back', q.v. under **ridge**, & *sack*, 'bag', see **sack** (**I.**). Bag or wallet made to strap on the shoulders of walker or climber, for holding clothes, food &c.

ruction, n. [1. rúkshun; 2. rákʃən]. Etymol. unknown; only fr. early 19th cent. (slang, often pl.) Disturbance, outbreak, uproar, a row.

rudbeckia, n. [1. roodbékia; 2. rudbékiə]. After Swedish botanist, Olaus Rudbeck, d. 1702. Genus of composite plants of the aster family, cultivated in gardens.

rudd, n. [1. rud; 2. rad]. Prob. fr. M.E. *rudde*, 'redness', fr. O.E. *rudu*, 'red colour'; cp. O.N. *roði*, 'red'; cogn. w. Lat. *ruber*, 'red'; Gk. *eruthrós*, 'red'; O. Slav. *rūdru*, 'blood' &c.; cp. Goth. *rauþs*, O.E. *rēad*, 'red'. See **red, rubric.** Red-finned freshwater fish, red-eye, *Leuciscus erythrophthalmus*, allied to the roach.

rudder, n. [1. rúder; 2. rádə]. O.E., M.E. *rōðer*, 'rudder, oar'; cp. O.H.G. *ruodar*; O.N. *rōðr*. See **row** (**II.**). **1. a** Broad flat plate of wood or metal, placed vertically on hinges at stern of boat, ship, or aircraft, and capable of being moved from side to side to direct the course; **b** (fig.) guiding motive or principle. **2.** (brewing) Paddle-like instrument used to stir malt.

rudder-fish, n. Kind of fish that follows ships; pilot-fish.

rudderless, adj. [1. rúderles; 2. rádəlis]. **rudder** & **-less**. Without a rudder; lacking a guiding principle.

ruddily, adv. [1. rúdili; 2. rádili]. **ruddy** & **-ly**. With a reddish colour or glow; so as to look red.

ruddiness, n. [1. rúdines; 2. rádinis]. See prec. & **-ness**. State or quality of being ruddy.

ruddle, n. & vb. trans. [1. rúdl; 2. rádl], fr. M.E. *rudd-(e)*, 'red', see **rudd**, & **-le**; cp. M.E. *rodel-wort*. **1.** n. Kind of red pigment obtained from iron ore; used esp. for marking sheep; red ochre. **2.** vb. To mark, colour with, ruddle.

ruddock, n. [1. rúduk; 2. rádək]. O.E. *rudduc*, M.E. *ruddok*, 'robin', fr. O.E. *rud-(u)*, 'red', see **ruddy** & **-ock**. (provinc.) Robin.

ruddy (I.), adj. [1. rúdi; 2. rádi]. O.E. *rudig*, M.E. *rudi*; fr. O.E. *rud-(u)*, 'red', see **rudd**, & **-y**. **1. a** Red, reddish, rosy: *ruddy cheeks* &c.; **b** lit up by red glow: *ruddy sky* &c. **2.** Characterized by red complexion, with healthy glow: *ruddy health*. **3.** (vulg. slang) Used to qualify persons and things for which strong dislike or disapproval is felt; a euphemistic form of the more vulgar 'bloody'.

ruddy (II.), vb. trans. & intrans., fr. prec. To make or become ruddy, redden.

rude, adj. [1. rōōd; 2. rūd], fr. Lat. *rud-(is)*, 'unwrought, rough, raw; unskilled, ignorant', orig. of red colour of raw flesh; cp. Lat. *raudus*, 'shapeless piece of brass used as coin'; Scrt. *lōháš*, 'reddish metal, copper, iron'; O. Slav. *ruda*, 'brass'; O.N. *rauðe*, 'red iron'. See **red, rubric**. **1.** Rough, irregular, in shape; formless, unwrought: *a rude mass of stone*. **2. a** Uncultivated, in a primitive state of civilization: *a rude and barbarous people*; *rude mountain tribes*; **b** in Phr. *rude health*, vigorous, robust; reverse of *delicate*. **3.** Exhibiting but small skill, training, cultivation; rough, unpolished, crude: *rude stone huts*; *rude verses, drawings* &c.; *rude style, method* &c. Phr. *a rude awakening*, sudden, violent, distressing disillusionment. **4. a** (of manners, behaviour, utterance &c.) Characteristic of rough, uncultivated persons; hence, insulting, deliberately discourteous, uncivil, offensive; **b** (of persons) having such manners.

rudely, adv. Prec. & **-ly**. **1.** In a rough, uncultured, crude manner: *a rudely carved inscription*. **2.** Uncivilly, in an ill-bred, discourteous, manner; insolently. **3.** Violently, boisterously.

rudeness, n. See prec. & **-ness**. State or quality of being rude (in various senses).

Rudesheimer, n. [1. rōōdez-hīmer; 2. rūdəzhaimə], fr. Germ. Rüdesheim, on the Rhine, near Bingen. Kind of light hock or white Rhine wine.

rudiment, n. [1. rōōdiment; 2. rūdimənt], fr. Lat. *rudīment-(um)*, 'beginning, first attempt; first principles'; fr. *rudi-(s)*, 'unwrought', see **rude**, & **-ment**. **1.** Slight trace of something as yet undeveloped and in embryonic stage; vestige of something the development of which has been arrested; **a** *the rudiments of buds, organs*; **b** *the rudiments of civilization*; *some rudiments of common sense*. **2.** First elements or principles of some branch of knowledge: *the rudiments of Latin, of botany* &c.

rudimental, adj. [1. rōōdiméntl; 2. rūdiméntl]. Prec. & **-al**. Pertaining to, of the nature of, rudiments; undeveloped.

rudimentary, adj. [1. rōōdiméntari; 2. rūdiméntəri]. **rudiment** & **-ary**. Having the character of a rudiment; **a** incipient, vestigial, embryonic: *a rudimentary organ*; **b** elementary, characteristic of initial stage: *a rudimentary knowledge of mathematics*.

rue (I.), vb. trans. & intrans. [1. rōō; 2. rū]. O.E. *hrēowan*, M.E. *rēwen*, 'to grieve, be sorry, pity'; cp. O.H.G. *riuwan*; Du. *rouwen*; O.N. *hryggva*, 'to sadden'; cogn. w. Gk. *kroúein*, 'to strike, beat'. **1.** trans. **a** (archaic) To grieve for, regret; feel pity for; **b** now, to regret, be sorry for, repent of; chiefly in Phrs. *to rue the day*; *he will live to rue it* &c. **2.** intrans. (archaic) To repent, regret, be sorry.

rue (II.), n. O.E. *hrēow*; M.E. *rēwe*, 'grief, repentance'. See prec. (archaic) **1.** Regret, grief as result of action or event. **2.** Pity, mercy, compassion.

rue (III.), n., fr. Fr., fr. Lat. *rūta*, fr. Gk. *rhūtḗ*, 'bitter herb, rue'; etymol. doubtful; associated w. prec. Genus of small, shrubby, perennial herbs, esp. *Ruta graveolens*, with bitter leaves, formerly used in medicine as stimulant and irritant; in literary usage this herb typifies repentance and sorrow: *crowned with rue*.

rueful, adj. [1. rōōfool; 2. rūful]. **rue** (II.) & **-ful**. Feeling, expressing, displaying, regret or disappointment: *a rueful countenance*.

ruefully, adv. Prec. & **-ly**. In a rueful manner.

ruefulness, n. See prec. & **-ness**. State or quality of being rueful.

rufescent, adj. [1. rōōfésent; 2. rūfésənt], fr. Lat. *rūfescent-(em)*, Pres. Part. of *rūfescere*, 'to redden', fr. *rūf-(us)*, 'red', see **rufous**. (zool.) Reddish, tinged with red.

ruff (I.), n. [1. ruf; 2. raf]. See **ruffle** (II.). **1.** Full, pleated, stiffly starched frill or ruffle; esp. as worn round neck in 16th cent. **2.** Thick ring of projecting feathers &c. round bird's neck &c., of hair round animal's neck &c. **3. a** Kind of sandpiper, *Machetes pugnax*, the male of which has an erectile ruff at breeding season; the female is called *reeve*, q.v.; **b** kind of pigeon.

ruff (II.), n. M.E. *ruffe*, perh. fr. **rough** or prec. Kind of small, perch-like, greenish, brown-spotted, freshwater fish.

ruff (III.), vb. trans. & intrans. & n., fr. obs. *ruff*, 'card-game', fr. O. Fr. *roffle, ronfle*, perh. fr. *triomphe*. See **triumph**. **1.** vb. **a** trans. To take (a trick at whist &c.) with a trump when one has no cards of the suit led; to trump; **b** intrans., to take tricks by ruffing. **2.** n. Act of ruffing or trumping at cards.

ruffed, adj. [1. ruft; 2. raft]. **ruff** (I.) & **-ed**. Having a ruff round the neck: *ruffed grouse* (*Bonasa umbellus*), a game bird of N. America; called also *pheasant* and *partridge*.

ruffian, n. [1. rúfyan; 2. ráfjən], fr. O. Fr.; cp. Ital. *ruffiano*; etymol. doubtful. A violent, lawless, brutal person; a bully, a blackguard.

ruffianism, n. [1. rúfyanizm; 2. ráfjənizəm]. Prec. & **-ism**. Ruffianly conduct or character.

ruffianly, adj. [1. rúfyanli; 2. ráfjənli]. **ruffian** & **-ly**. Pertaining to, characteristic of, a ruffian.

ruffle (I.), vb. trans. & intrans. [1. rúfl; 2. ráfl]. M.E. *ruffelen*; cp. L.G. *ruffelen*, 'to rumple'. **A.** trans. **1.** To raise surface of in folds or lines; wrinkle, destroy flatness, evenness, or smoothness of: *the wind ruffles the water*; *to ruffle one's hair*; *the bird ruffles (up) its feathers*. **2.** To disturb serenity of, disconcert, upset temper of: *to ruffle a person's temper*; *a man impossible to ruffle*. **B.** intrans. (lit. and fig.) To be ruffled, lose smoothness or tranquillity.

ruffle (II.), n., fr. prec. **1.** Gathered or pleated frill as ornament of dress, worn at neck or wrist. **2.** Bird's ruff; frill of hair &c. about animal's neck. **3. a** Slight disturbance on surface of water; ripple; **b** disturbance, discomposure of temper &c., slight feeling of discord.

ruffle (III.), vb. intrans. & n. Possibly same as **ruffle** (I.). **1.** vb. To swagger, bluster; to act in a boisterous, turbulent manner. Also *to ruffle it*, to swagger, cut a dash; in harmless sense. **2.** n. (rare) Turbulence, discord.

ruffled, adj. [1. rúfld; 2. ráfld]. **ruffle** (II.) & **-ed**. (of animal &c.) Having a ruffle.

ruffler, n. [1. rúfler; 2. ráflə]. **ruffle** (III.) & **-er**. (archaic) Arrogant, swaggering fellow, bully.

rufi-, pref. representing Lat. *rūf-(us)*, 'red'. See next word. (in chemical terms &c.) Red, reddish.

rufous, adj. [1. rōōfus; 2. rūfəs], fr. Lat. *rūf-(us)*, 'red, light red', & **-ous**; cogn. w. Lat. *ruber*, 'red'; *rūbidus*, 'dark red'; see **rubric** & **red**. Dull or brownish red.

rug, n. [1. rug; 2. rag]. Scand., cp. Swed. *rugg*, 'matted hair'. **1.** Piece of heavy fabric, usually with long pile, used as floor-covering, esp. one covering part of a floor; strip placed in front of hearth &c. **2.** Piece of thick woollen fabric as covering for feet, knees, bed &c.

ruga, n., pl. **rugae** [1. rōōga, -gē; 2. rūgə, -gī]. Lat., 'wrinkle, fold'; cogn. w. O.E. *rūh*, see **rough** (I.). (med.) Fold, esp. in mucous membrane of the stomach.

rugate, adj. [1. rōōgāt; 2. rūgeit]. Prec. & **-ate**. (anat., zool.) Having folds or wrinkles.

Rugby, n. [1. rúgbi; 2. rágbi], fr. public school at Rugby, Warwickshire. Short for *Rugby football*, one of the two main types of the game, played by fifteen players a side, a full-back, four three-quarter-backs, two half-backs, and eight forwards, forming the 'scrummage', the ball being oval in shape and punted, dropped or passed from hand to hand, the object being to gain a 'try', or touch down behind opponents' line, and to kick over cross-bar and between side posts of the goal.

rugged, adj. [1. rúged; 2. rágid]. **rug** & **-ed**. **1. a** Having a rough, uneven surface, with sharp, irregular projections; not smooth: *a rugged elm*; *rugged crags*; *a rugged coast*; *rugged walls*; **b** (in moral sense) lacking sensitiveness, great refinement, or subtlety of feeling; rough and unpolished, but firm, strong, and stable: *a rugged character*; *rugged kindness*. **2. a** Coarsely though boldly shaped; having a rough, harsh outline, lacking in symmetry and fineness: *rugged features, form* &c.; **b** lacking refinement and perfection; unpolished, rough, ill-finished: *rugged verses*.

ruggedly, adv. Prec. & **-ly**. In a rugged manner.

ruggedness, n. See prec. & **-ness**. State or quality of being rugged.

rugger, n. [1. rúger; 2. rágə]. Abbr. form of **Rugby** & **-er**. (slang) Rugby football.

rugose, adj. [1. rōōgōs; 2. rūgous], fr. Lat. *rūgōs-(us)*, 'wrinkled', fr. *rūga*, 'wrinkle, crease'. See **ruga**. Covered with wrinkles; creased, furrowed, corrugated.

rugosely, adv. Prec. & **-ly**. In a rugose manner.

rugosity, n. [1. rōōgósiti; 2. rūgósiti], fr. Lat. *rūgōsitāt-(em)*, 'rugosity'. **rugose** & **-ity**. **a** State of being rugose; **b** a wrinkle, corrugation.

rugous, adj. [1. rōōgus; 2. rūgəs], fr. Lat. *rūgōs-(us)*, 'wrinkled', see **rugose**, & **-ous**. Rugose.

ruin (I.), n. [1. róoin, rōōin; 2. rúin, rūin], fr. Fr. *ruine*, fr. Lat. *ruīna*, 'fall; downfall, disaster; ruins', fr. *ru-(ere)*, 'to fall violently'; cogn. w. Gk. *ékhraon*, 'fell upon, overcame'; Lith. *griūvù*, 'to fall down, fall in ruins'. **1. a** State of decay, disintegration, destruction, collapse, which destroys physical or moral soundness, stability, strength, or efficiency: *the ruin of one's country, health, hopes, reputation, character*; specif. **b** financial disaster, total loss of property; bankruptcy: *face to face with ruin*. Phr. *to bring to ruin*, cause ruin of. **2.** Something which has fallen into complete decay and disintegration; specif., a dilapidated building, group of buildings (*ruins*) which have been shattered, dismantled, broken down by age, neglect, fire, destruction, or violence: *Pevensey Castle is a mere ruin*; *the ruins of one's home*, after a fire &c. Phr. *in ruins*. **3.** Cause of ruin, pernicious and destructive influence: *drink will be his ruin*, or *the ruin of him*.

ruin (II.), vb. trans. & intrans., fr. prec. **1.** trans. **a** To bring to ruin, cause disaster to fall upon; to damage or destroy, to spoil, irretrievably: *to ruin one's career*; *the rain will ruin the roses*; specif. **b** to bring to financial ruin, impoverish: *he was ruined by his own extravagance*; **c** to destroy chastity of, seduce (a woman). **2.** intrans. (chiefly poet.) **a** To fall in ruins, perish; **b** (archaic) to fall or rush headlong, plunge downwards.

ruination, n. [1. ro͞oināshun; 2. rùinéiʃən, rûinéiʃən]. **ruin** & **-ation**. **1.** Act of ruining; state of being ruined. **2.** Something that causes ruin.

ruined, adj. [1. ro͞oind; 2. rúind, rûind], fr. P.P. of **ruin (II.)**. (of buildings, more rarely of country, trees &c.) **a** In a state of ruin; dilapidated, falling into decay and disintegration: *a ruined castle, abbey* &c.; **b** blasted, devastated; ravaged: *a ruined heath*; *a ruined elm.*

ruinous, adj. [1. ro͞oinus; 2. rúinəs, rûinəs], fr. Lat. *ruīnōs-(us)*, 'going to ruin', fr. *ruīn-(a)*, 'ruin', see **ruin (I.)** & **-ous**. **1. a** Tending towards, likely to cause, financial ruin: *ruinous expenditure*; **b** tending to spoil or destroy: *heavy rain is ruinous to fine dresses.* **2.** Falling into ruin, dilapidated, in a state of disrepair: *the castle is completely ruinous.*

ruinously, adv. Prec. & **-ly**. In a ruinous manner, so as to cause ruin.

ruinousness, n. See prec. & **-ness**. Ruinous condition.

rule (I.), n. [1. ro͞ol; 2. rūl]. M.E. *riule, reule*; fr. O. Fr. *riule*, fr. Lat. *rēgula*, 'straight strip of wood, ruler; measuring-rod; stick, bar', fr. stem **rĕg-*, 'to guide', seen in Lat. *regere*, 'to rule', see **regent, rex**, & words there referred to. **1. a** Statement, formula, direction, serving, or intended, to guide, and control action, conduct, behaviour: *to make a rule that . . .*; *a rule of the institution*; *rules of conduct*; *to make, break, obey, rules*; Phrs. *rules of the road*, recognized conventions observed in meeting or passing traffic on the highway; *golden rule*, method that experience has shown to be good, specif., the maxim, 'do as you would be done by'; specif. **b** collection of precepts and orders laid down by founder of a religious order, regulating the conduct of the members: *the Rule of St. Benedict.* **2.** Habitual practice; line of conduct commonly observed; principle which regulates one's behaviour: *my rule is to breakfast at eight o'clock*; *I make it a rule not to give to beggars.* Phr. *as a rule*, usually. **3.** Act of ruling; government, sway, exercise of authority, administration of law: *the long rule of George III.*; *under the wise rule of the headmaster the school flourished.* **4.** Instruction, order, made by a court of justice: *Rules of the High Court.* **5.** Graduated strip of metal or wood for measuring: *with rule and line.* **6.** (print.) Thin strip of metal used for separating lines and columns.

rule (II.), vb. trans. & intrans. M.E. *riulen*, fr. O. Fr. *riuler*, fr. Lat. *rēgulāre*, 'to direct, regulate'. See prec. & **regulate**. **A.** trans. **1. a** To govern, control, direct, hold rule over: *to rule one's affections, actions* &c.; **b** specif., to hold rule over as a king or governor: *some kings rule their subjects by fear, others by love.* **2.** (of a judge, the chairman of a meeting &c.) To give a judicial decision: *to rule a person out of order*; *to rule that a certain resolution cannot be moved.* **3.** To draw (lines) with a ruler: *to rule lines on paper*; *to rule paper with lines.* Phr. *to rule out*, to exclude. **B.** intrans. **1.** To exercise the functions of a ruler: *kings ought to rule with justice, but with mildness.* **2.** (commerc., of prices) To have a specified prevalent level, at a given time: *prices for lard ruled high*; also *lard ruled high.*

ruleless, adj. [1. ro͞olles; 2. rûllis]. **rule (I.)** & **-less**. Without rule or ruler; uncontrolled.

ruler, n. [1. ro͞oler; 2. rûlə]. **rule (II.)** & **-er**. **1.** Person who rules, one who exercises authority, esp. in a State; governor, sovereign. **2.** Flat strip, or cylindrical bar, of wood, metal &c., for ruling lines on a page.

rulership, n. [1. ro͞olership; 2. rûləʃip]. Prec. & **-ship**. Office, term of office, authority, of a ruler.

ruling (I.), adj. [1. ro͞oling; 2. rûliŋ]. **rule (II.)** & **-ing**. Exercising, wielding, authority, influence, control; dominating: *the ruling race, class.* Phr. *ruling passion*, prevailing, strongest, motive of conduct.

ruling (II.), n. **rule (II.)** & **-ing**. **1.** Act of one who rules; government, domination. **2.** Judicial decision of judge, court, chairman &c.

rum (I.), n. [1. rum; 2. ram]. Earlier *rumbullion, rumbo*; origin dubious. **1.** Spirit distilled from fermented juice of sugar-cane. **2.** (U.S.A.) Any alcoholic, esp. spirituous, liquor; term used esp. by prohibitionists.

rum (II.), adj.; origin uncertain; first in 16th cent. as cant word meaning 'gallant, fine', said to be corrupt. of Gipsy *rom*, q.v. (slang) Odd, peculiar, queer. Phr. *to feel rum*, feel indisposed; feel nervous or queer.

rumble (I.), vb. intrans. & trans. [1. rúmbl; 2. rámbl]. M.E. *romblen*; cp. Mod. Germ. *rummeln*; Dan. *rumle*; Du. *rommelen*; prob. imitative of sound. **A.** intrans. **1.** To make a prolonged, dull, deep, vibrant sound; esp. of thunder, deep voice, laughter. **2.** (of vehicle &c.) To move, lumber, along with a rumbling sound. **B.** trans. To cause to make, move along with, a rumbling sound.

rumble (II.), n., fr. prec. **1.** Low, heavy, continuous, jarring sound, a pulsating roar: *the rumble of traffic, an earthquake, thunder, guns* &c. **2.** Seat, and receptacle for luggage, at back of old-fashioned horse vehicle.

rumble-tumble, n. Rough, jarring motion.

rumbustious, adj. [1. rumbúschus; 2. rambástʃəs]. Prob. variant of **robustious**, through influence of **rum (II.)**. Boisterous, blustering, turbulent.

rumen, n. [1. ro͞omen; 2. rûmen]. Lat. *rūmen*, 'throat, gullet'; cp. Scrt. *rōmanthaš*, 'chewing the cud'; Lith. *raumũ*, 'muscle'; the orig. meaning was prob. 'muscle', hence, specif., 'muscle of the throat'. First and largest stomach of ruminants.

ruminant (I.), adj. [1. ro͞ominant; 2. rûminənt], fr. Lat. *rūminant-(em)*, Pres. Part. of *rūminārī*, 'to chew the cud'. See prec. & **ruminate**. **1.** (of animals) Chewing the cud; belonging to the division *Ruminantia*. See next word. **2.** (of person, fig.) Thoughtful, meditative.

ruminant (II.), n., fr. prec. Ruminant animal, member of the division *Ruminantia*, of ungulate herbivorous mammals, which have stomachs with four or three chambers.

ruminate, vb. intrans. & trans. [1. ro͞omināt; 2. rûmineit], fr. Lat. *rūmināt-(um)*, P.P. type *rūminārī*, 'to chew the cud'; fig., 'to ponder, reflect', fr. *rūmin-*, stem of *rūmen*, 'throat, gullet', see **rumen**. **A.** intrans. **1.** (of animal) To regurgitate food to be ground by molar teeth, after it has been first swallowed and softened in the rumen; to chew the cud. **2.** To ponder deeply, turn things over in the mind, meditate, muse: *to ruminate upon, about, a project.* **B.** trans. To reflect upon, ponder, consider.

rumination, n. [1. ro͞omināshun; 2. rûminéiʃən]. Prec. & **-ion**. **1.** Act or process of chewing the cud. **2.** Mental reflection, meditation, consideration.

ruminative, adj. [1. ro͞ominativ; 2. rûminətiv]. **ruminate** & **-ive**. Thoughtful, contemplative; given to rumination.

ruminatively, adv. Prec. & **-ly**. In a ruminative manner.

ruminator, n. [1. ro͞omināter; 2. rûmineitə]. **ruminate** & **-or**. One who ruminates.

rumly, adv. [1. rúmli; 2. rámli]. **rum (II.)** & **-ly**. (slang) In a rum manner; oddly, queerly.

rummage, vb. intrans. & trans. & n. [1. rúmij; 2. rámidž], fr. obs. n., fr. O. Fr. *arrumage*, 'stowing of goods in hold' &c., fr. *arrum-(er)*, 'to stow, stow away'; etymol. doubtful. **1.** vb. **a** intrans. To grope about among, and turn over, a pile of miscellaneous objects, or among objects packed in a receptacle, in the endeavour to find something: *to rummage about*; also *rummage in (a drawer &c.)*; *rummage about*; **b** trans., *rummage out, up*, to find, turn up, rout out, by rummaging: *to rummage old clothes out of a cupboard.* **2.** n. **a** Act, process, of rummaging; **b** objects found in rummaging, miscellaneous collection of articles; rubbish, lumber.

rummage-sale, n. Sale, the proceeds of which are usually devoted to charity, of miscellaneous, discarded objects, rummaged out of boxes and lumber-rooms.

rummer, n. [1. rúmer; 2. rámə]. Cp. Du. *roemer*; Mod. Germ. *römer*; perh. = *Roman (glass)*. Tall, wide-mouthed drinking-glass.

rummily, adv. [1. rúmili; 2. rámili]. **rummy (I.)** & **-ly**. In a rummy, queer, manner.

rumminess, n. [1. rúmines; 2. ráminis]. Next word & **-ness**. Rumness.

rummy (I.), adj. [1. rúmi; 2. rámi]. **rum (II.)** & **-y**. (slang) Rum, queer.

rummy (II.), n.; perh. fr. prec. A simple card-game for two or more persons.

rumness, n. [1. rúmnes; 2. rámnis]. **rum (II.)** & **-ness**. Quality of being rum; queerness.

rumour, n. [1. ro͞omer; 2. rûmə], fr. O. Fr., fr. Lat. *rūmōr-(em)*, 'common talk, hearsay', earlier **rēum-*; cp. Scrt. *rāuti*, 'cries'; Gk. *ō-rūomai*, 'I howl'; O.E. *rȳn*, 'roar'. Cp. further Lat. *rāvus, raucus*, 'hoarse', see **raucous**; Lith. *rĕju*, 'to cry aloud'; O. Slav. *rarŭ*, 'sound'. Cp. also **roar**. Unverified or unauthenticated report or statement; story, report, not necessarily false, but circulated irresponsibly without full knowledge of facts: *the rumour ran that*; *rumour has it that* &c.; *a mere rumour.*

rumoured, adj. [1. ro͞omerd; 2. rûməd]. Prec. & **-ed**. Put about, made current, by rumours; stated and passed on as a fact without full knowledge of the truth.

rump, n. [1. rump; 2. ramp]. M.E. *rumpe*; cp. Dan. *rumpe*; Swed. *rumpa*. **1.** Fleshy part of the back at lower end of the backbone, above the thighs; the buttocks, hind-quarters. **2.** (fig.) Last or inferior remnant; specif., *the Rump*, remnant of Long Parliament after the expulsion by Pryde of Presbyterian royalists in 1648.

rumple, vb. trans. [1. rúmpl; 2. rámpl]. Cp. M. Du. *rompelen* and see **crambo**. To draw together in uneven folds; to destroy tidiness or smoothness of, to ruck up, wrinkle, tousle: *to rumple one's clothes, hair* &c.

rumpless, adj. [1. rúmples; 2. rámplis]. **rump** & **-less**. (of bird) Without a tail.

rump-steak, n. Beef-steak cut from rump.

rumpus, n. [1. rúmpus; 2. rámpəs]. Origin unknown. Disturbance, row, uproar; a fuss.

rumpy, n. [1. rúmpi; 2. rámpi]. **rump** & **-y**. The tailless Manx cat.

rum-runner, n. **rum (I.)** & **runner**. (U.S.A.) **a** Person who attempts to smuggle prohibited liquor into the United States, esp. by sea; **b** vessel employed in this traffic.

rum-shrub, n. **rum (I.)** & **shrub (II.)**. Drink made of rum, lemon-juice, sugar &c.

run (I.), vb. intrans. & trans. [1. run; 2. ran]. O.E. has usually *irnan*, intrans., & *ærnan*, trans., w. metathesis; *rinnan*, without metathesis, being rare until much later; O.S., O.H.G., & Goth. all have *rinnan*, & O.N. *rinna*. The P.P. in O.E. is usually *urnen*, the unmetathesized *runnen* being rare. Mod. Engl. *run*, instead of earlier *rin*, in infin. & pres., must be due to the P.P. type *runnen*, wh. was common in M.E. The Gmc. base **rinn-* is cogn. w. Scrt. *rinvati, rināti*, 'makes run or flow', & *rīnaš*, 'flowing'; O. Slav. *rinąti*, 'to flow'; Gk. *orínein*, 'to move'; cp. also Lat. *rīvus*, 'stream', see **river**; further connexion w. Lat. *orīrī*, 'to rise, spring from', see **origin**, is probable; see also **earl**. (gen. senses) To move rapidly, to flow. **A.** intrans. **1.** (of men and animals) **a** To move along swiftly by means of a rapid, alternate movement of the feet; to go forward rapidly, but smoothly in this way; contrasted with the slower progress of *walking*, *crawling*, and the jerky motion of *hopping*; *run* is not generally applied to the movement of birds along the ground, nor of the paces of a horse, see, however, No. 3 below; Phrs. *to run* *wild*, (i.) (of persons) live in unrestrained, undisciplined freedom; (ii.) (of plants) to grow rampantly in all directions; *to run the gauntlet*, between two rows of persons, each of whom inflicts a blow; also (fig.): *run the gauntlet of public criticism*; *to run riot*, behave riotously, without proper restraint and decency; *run counter to*, oppose, thwart; **b** to hasten, rush: *to run to a person's aid.* **2.** Specif., to escape by running, to take flight, run away: *after the third volley the enemy ran.* Phr. *to run for one's life*, flee, escape, with utmost speed. **3.** To take part in a race, or running contest; **a** (of men) *I used to run when I was at Oxford*; **b** (of horses) *this horse ran in the Derby*; *the following horses did not run*, did not take part in a given race; Phr. *also ran*, (i.) of horses which are not among the first three in a race; (ii.) as n., *an also ran*, an unsuccessful competitor for a prize or post; one who is unsuccessful in the race of life. **4.** To pass, traverse, lightly and rapidly: *fire ran along the ground*; *his fingers ran over the strings, keys.* **5.** (of vehicles, ships) To proceed on journey or voyage; to start, go, sail &c.; ply: *trains, buses, trams, run every five minutes*; *steamers run daily between France and England.* **6.** To flow (of liquids gen.); **a** (of rivers, tide &c.) *rivers run into the sea*; *the current is running strong*; Phr. *feeling ran high*, was much excited, was powerfully moved; **b** (of liquids in pipes, casks &c.) to flow freely out or along: *water runs from a tap, cistern* &c.; *beer runs from a cask*; **c** (of blood) (i.) to circulate: *good blood runs in his veins*; (ii.) to be shed: *blood was running from his wound*; *blood ran in torrents at Waterloo*; **d** (of tears) to trickle, be shed. **7.** To be drenched by a flow of liquid; to stream: *the streets ran with blood.* **8.** **a** To become diffused, to spread one into another: *the colours of dyed material are apt to run if exposed to wet*; **b** to become liquefied, melt from heat. **9.** To move along, slide, slip, be moved: *trains run on rails*; *curtains run on metal rods.* **10.** (of machines) **a** To be in working order, capable of performing proper functions and movements; to work: *I can't make the lawn-mower run properly*; **b** to be actually moving; to revolve, be in action: *to leave the engine (of motor-car) running*; **c** (fig.) to take effect, proceed in the way desired: *all my arrangements ran smoothly.* **11.** To pursue a course, go through period or stage of activity; (of books) appear, be published in: *to run through, into, several editions*; (of plays) be continuously performed: *to run for six months.* **12.** To pass, extend, be continued, for specified distance, or in specified position or direction: *the road runs some miles by the sea*; *a scar ran across his cheek.* **13.** (of time) To elapse: *how fast the years run by*; *his life had only a few hours to run.* **14.** **a** (of sensations) To be felt, to pass along sensitive nerves: *a cold shiver ran down his spine*; *a stab of pain ran up his arm*; **b** (of mental images, memories &c.) to traverse the mind, come into the consciousness, or memory; be constantly in, recur frequently to, the mind: *the tune was, his words were, running in my head all day.* **15.** To pass into, assume, attain to, a specified condition: *to run to fat*; *to run to seed*; *run amuck*; *run dry*; *run cold.* **16.** (of series of words, notes &c.) To have specified form and sequence: *this is how the verse, tune, runs.* **17.** **a** To have currency, be current, be circulated: *the rumour, story, runs that . . .*; **b** to have effective currency, be recognized as authoritative, have authority: *the King's law, writ, doesn't run among rebels.* **B.** trans. **1.** **a** To cause, compel, to run: *to run a horse out, up and down*; **b** to drive, direct: *to run a car into a garage*; in certain Phrs., *to run contraband, run liquor* &c., to smuggle, pass it into a country without paying duty. **2.** To compel to flee, or to attempt to escape; to chase: *to run a fox, hare* &c. Phr. *to run (a thing, or a person) close*, be a formidable competitor to; be almost equal to, as good or as bad as; *to run it fine*, barely allow oneself time for. **3.** To drive, push, thread (a thing) through, into, against: **a** *to run a knife into a person*; **b** *to run a string through a hem*; **c** *to run one's head against a wall*, also (fig.) to attempt the impossible, be stopped by insurmountable obstacles. **4.** To cause to flow, direct flow of: *to run water into casks, lead into moulds.* **5.** With cognate objective, or followed by adverbial phrase: *to run a race, a mile*; *a disease will run its course.* Phr. *to run a rig*, engage in an escapade, have a frolic. **6.** To manage, direct, keep going: *to run a hotel, a hat shop.* **7.** To incur, encounter, take chances of: *to run risks*; *to run the risk of*, render oneself liable to the danger, or likelihood of. **C.** Followed by adverb or preposition. *Run about*, to run hither and thither, move about quickly from one place to another; play about; bustle actively about over one's business. *Run across*, to meet accidentally, come across. *Run after*, **a** to pursue, chase, endeavour to catch or overtake; **b** to attempt to reach, or to gain. *Run against*, **a** to come into collision with; **b** to run across, meet by accident. *Run at*, intrans., to run towards, attack. *Run away*, intrans., **a** To flee, take to flight, escape; **b** to depart hurriedly. *Run away with*, **a** to carry off; to take away unlawfully, to steal; **b** specif., to elope with: *he ran away with the governess*; **c** (of the emotions) to overpower, cause to lose one's self-control: *his temper ran away with him.* Phr. *to run away with the idea that . . .*, to come to a hasty, ill-founded conclusion. *Run down*, **1.** intrans., **a** to descend by running, move quickly down; **b** (i.) (of machinery esp. of watch or clock) to cease to function through loss of motive power; become unwound; (ii.) (of electric battery) to become exhausted; **2.** trans., **a** to pursue and overtake, capture after pursuit: *to run down a fugitive*: **b** to run into, collide with: *to run down a pedestrian with a motor*; *to run down a ship*; **c** to disparage, speak ill of; **3.** in Phr. *to be run down*, be in weak health, be debilitated. *Run in*, trans., **a** to arrest, take into custody; **b** (print.) to insert a word, matter &c., without beginning new line or paragraph. *Run into*, intrans., **a** to collide with; **b** to become liable to, affected by, specified conditions: *to run into debt, danger* &c. *Run off*, **1.** intrans., to run away, depart swiftly; specif., *run off with*, elope with; **2.** trans., **a** to cause to flow from receptacle, drain; **b** to print, produce copies of. *Run on*, intrans., **a** to continue speaking without intermission, ramble on: *once started, he will run on for hours about his grievances*; **b** (print.) to continue without break in the same line or paragraph; **c** to be occupied with, have as subject, dwell on: *the talk, his thoughts, ran on recent events.* *Run out*, **1.** intrans., **a** to project, jut out: *a pier running out into the sea*; **b** to fail, become exhausted: *supplies have run out*; **2.** trans., (cricket) to cause the other batsman to be put out by his failure to reach wicket in time after a run. *Run out of*, intrans., to be depleted, not to have enough of. *Run over*, **1.** intrans., to overflow; **2.** trans., **a** (of vehicle &c.) to knock down and pass over; **b** to peruse, scan, go through hastily: *just run over these proofs for me as I'm in a hurry*; **c** to narrate hastily: *run over your story again while the points are fresh in your mind.* *Run through*, trans., **a** to pierce, transfix; **b** to exhaust, spend: *to run through a fortune*; **c** to go hastily through; peruse or recount quickly, run over. *Run up*, **1.** trans., **a** to raise, hoist, rapidly: *to run up a flag*; **b** to put together, erect, construct, hastily: *to run up a house, dress* &c.; **c** to increase continuously, cause to mount up: *to run up expenses, a bill*; **2.** intrans. (of expenses &c.) to mount up, increase.

run (II.), n., fr. prec. The O.E. n. is *ryne*. **1.** **a** Act of running on foot: *to go for, take, a run before breakfast*; specif., in fox-hunting, unbroken spell of galloping after hounds; Phr. *on the run*, (i.) in flight; (ii.) continuously active, busy: *on the run all day*; *to have the run of*, free access to, liberty to use, visit &c.; *to come down with a run*, fall rapidly, violently; **b** duration of run; the distance run: *a run of several hours*; *a run of a mile*; specif. (cricket) successful traversing of the distance between the wickets by both batsmen; point scored for this &c.; **c** strength, capacity to run: *no more run left in him.* **2.** Course, continuous action of a process, unbroken sequence, spell, bout, of events or activities: *a play has a run of so many nights*; *a run of luck.* Phrs. *to have a run for one's money*, to obtain something, however small, or unsatisfactory, as a result of one's actions; *in the long run*, on the whole. **3.** Rush, eager effort to obtain something, strong demand for: *a great run on the new novel*; *a run on a bank*, widespread action among customers to withdraw their money. **4.** **a** Area, stretch of open country used for grazing: *a sheep run*; **b** enclosed space for poultry, rabbits, &c.; **c** path, esp. round a building, marked off from surrounding ground. **5.** Common, average class, type, quality &c.: *above, outside, the ordinary run of mankind.* **6.** (mus.) Series of notes, sung or played in rapid, unbroken succession; a roulade.

run (III.), adj., fr. P.P. of **run** (I.). **1.** (of fish) Having run, having migrated, passed up river from sea &c.; usually preceded by adv.: *a clean, freshly, run salmon.* **2.** Extracted, drained off: *run honey*, extracted from the comb.

runabout, n. [1. rúnabout; 2. ránəbaut]. **run** (I.) & **about**. **a** One who wanders, a gadabout; **b** small, light motor-car.

runagate, n. [1. rúnagāt; 2. ránəgeit]. **run** (I.) & *agate* = **on** & **gait**, but partially assimilated in meaning to **renegade**. **1.** Fugitive, truant, vagabond. **2.** Renegade.

runaway, n. & adj. [1. rúnawā; 2. ránəwei]. **run** (I.) & **away**. **1.** n. **a** Fugitive; **b** horse whose rider or driver &c. has lost control. **2.** adj. (i.) Having run away: *a runaway horse*; (ii.) having eloped: *a runaway couple*; (iii.) involving flight; *runaway match*, that of couple who have eloped.

runcinate, adj. [1. rúnsinat; 2. ránsinət], fr. Lat. *runcīna*, 'plane', fr. Gk. *rhukáne*, 'plane', assimilated to the cogn. Lat. word *runcāre*, 'to root up; to weed out; to pluck out'; cp. Scrt. *luñčati*, 'plucks'. (bot.) Saw-toothed, with teeth pointing backwards.

rundale, n. [1. rúndāl; 2. rándeil]. Origin doubtful. (obs.) System of tenure and division of land (esp. in Ireland) in adjoining strips between those of other owners or tenants.

rune, n. [1. rōōn; 2. rūn], fr. O.N. *rūn*; cp. O.E. *rūn*, 'mystery, secret; counsel, discussion; secret conversation, whisper'; Goth. *rūna*, 'secret'; O.H.G. *rūnēn*, O.E. *rūnian*, 'to whisper', see **round** (VI.); cogn. w. Lett. *runāt*, 'to speak'; Gk. *éreuna*, 'examination'. **1.** One of the angular characters of the alphabet in use among Anglo-Saxons, Norse, or other ancient Germanic peoples; it was derived from the Greek alphabet with some additional symbols and adapted for cutting, or scratching, on stone, metal, ivory, or other hard material. **2.** Magic or mysterious symbol or letter.

rune staff, n. **1.** Runic calendar. **2.** Magic rod inscribed with runes.

rung (I.), n. [1. rung; 2. raŋ]. O.E. *hrung*, 'pole'; M.E. *ronge*, 'rung'; cp. M.H.G. *runge*; Goth. *hrugga*, 'rod'; perh. cogn. w. O.E. *hring*, see **ring** (I.). **a** Cross-piece, step, of a ladder; bar of similar shape tying legs of a chair &c.; **b** spoke of wheel.

rung (II.), vb. P.P. of **ring**. O.E. (*ġe*)*rungen* M.E. *runge*(*n*).

runged, adj. [1. rungd; 2. raŋd]. **rung** (I.) & **-ed**. Having rungs.

runic (I.), adj. [1. rōōnik; 2. rūnik]. **rune** & **-ic**. Connected with, pertaining to, written in, inscribed with, runes.

runic (II.), n., fr. prec. (print.) Kind of ornamental, slightly curving, thick type.

runlet (**I.**), n. [1. rúnlet; 2. ránlit]. See **runnel** & **-let**. Small stream, rill, runnel.

runlet (**II.**), n., fr. O. Fr. *rondelet*, dimin. of *rondel*, dimin. of *ronde*, 'round'. See **round** (**II.**). (archaic) Small wine-cask.

runnel, n. [1. rúnl; 2. ránl]. O.E. *rynel*; M.E. *runel*, 'stream', fr. O.E. *ryne*, 'stream', cogn. w. **run**, & **-le**. **1.** Rivulet, rill. **2.** Small channel, gutter.

runner, n. [1. rúner; 2. ránə]. **run** & **-er**. **1.** One who runs: *a poor, fast, runner*; specif. **a** one taking part in a race; **b** (archaic) police officer: *Bow Street runner*. **2.** Kind of duck. **3.** Smuggler, (in compounds) *gun-runner, rum-runner* &c. **4.** That on which an object moves or slides; specif. **a** blade of a sledge; **b** blade of skate; **c** roller on which part of machine moves. **5.** Rotating stone in grinding-mill. **6. a** Slender, prostrate stem of strawberry &c., which puts out roots at the nodes; **b** one of various kinds of twining plants, esp. *scarlet runner*, q.v.

runner-up, n. **1.** (coursing) Dog beaten by winner in final heat. **2.** Competitor next to winner of golf match &c.

running (**I.**), adj. [1. rúning; 2. rániŋ]. **run** (**I.**) & **-ing**. **1.** Performed while running: *running fight*, while one party is in retreat. **2.** Continuous, unbroken; (in various specif. senses) *a running commentary*; *running fire*, rapid series of shots; *running hand*, cursive writing; *running account*, current account. **3.** Coming one after the other, successive: *four days running*. **4.** Discharging, suppurating: *a running sore*.

running (**II.**), n. **run** (**I.**) & **-ing**. Act of one who runs; swift movement; esp. racing. Phrs. (lit. and fig.) *to make the running*, to set or force the pace; *to take up the running*, to take the lead, take the initiative; *in, out of, the running*, to have a chance, no chance, of success in a contest &c.

running-knot, n. Knot used to form noose which tightens up when the cord &c. is pulled.

running powers, n. pl. Right of one railway company to use the lines of another.

running title, n. (print.) Head-line at top of each page.

runrig, n. [1. rúnrig; 2. ránrig], fr. **run** & *rig*, northern form of **ridge**. (Scots) Rundale.

runt, n. [1. runt; 2. rant]. Origin unknown. (provinc.) **1.** Small ox, esp. of Welsh breed. **2.** Small, stunted, undersized person or animal. **3.** One of a breed of large domestic pigeons.

rupee, n. [1. ro͞opḗ; 2. rūpí], fr. Hind. *rūpīya*, fr. Scrt. *rūpya*, 'silver'. **a** Indian monetary unit, sixteen annas, now worth about 1s. 4d.; **b** Indian silver coin of this value.

rupture (**I.**), n. [1. rúpchur; 2. ráptʃə], fr. Lat. *ruptūra*, 'fracture, breach', fr. *rupt-(um)*, P.P. type of *rumpere*, 'to break, burst, tear'; cp. Lat. *rūpes*, 'rock; cliff, abyss'; cogn. w. Scrt. *rōpayati*, 'breaks off'; O.E. *rēofan*; O.N. *riúfa*, 'to break, tear'; O.E. *rēaf*, 'booty'; *rēafian*, 'to rob', see **reave**; Lith. *rūpéti*, 'to be troubled about'; *rupas*, 'rough'. **1.** Act of breaking, splitting, tearing apart; state of being torn or broken: *the rupture of a blood-vessel* &c. **2.** (med.) Swelling caused by protrusion of organ or part of organ; hernia, esp. abdominal hernia. **3.** (in non-material sense) **a** Breaking off, severance: *rupture of friendly relations*; **b** a quarrel: *a rupture between friends*.

rupture (**II.**), vb. trans. & intrans., fr. prec. **A.** trans. **1. a** (in material and non-material sense) To break, burst, separate violently; **b** specif. (med.) to produce rupture, or hernia in. **B.** intrans. To be broken, burst apart, ruptured.

rural, adj. [1. ro͞oral; 2. rúərəl, rɔ́rəl], fr. Lat. *rūrāl-(is)*, 'of the country, rustic', fr. *rūr-*, stem of *rūs*, 'country, as distinct from town', see **rustic**. **1.** Of, pertaining to, characteristic of, the country as distinct from the town: *rural scenes, dwellings*; *rural quiet*; *a rural life* &c.; *rural dean*, see **dean**. **2.** Of, pertaining to, agriculture: *rural economy*.

rurality, n. [1. ro͞oráliti; 2. ruər-, rɔrǽliti]. Prec. & **-ity**. State of being rural.

ruralization, n. [1. ro͞oralizā́shun; 2. rùər-, rɔ̀rəlaizéiʃən]. Next word & **-ation**. Act of ruralizing; state of being ruralized.

ruralize, vb. trans. & intrans. [1. ro͞oralīz; 2. rúərəl-, rɔ́rəlaiz]. **rural** & **-ize**. **1.** trans. To make rural, give a rural character to. **2.** intrans. To assume a rural character; to adopt a rural life.

rurally, adv. [1. ro͞orali; 2. rúərəli, rɔ́rəli]. See prec. & **-ly**. In a rural manner.

ruridecanal, adj. [1. ro͞oridekā́nl; 2. rùəri-, rɔ̀ridikéinl], fr. Lat. *rūr-*, stem of *rūs*, 'country'. See **rural** & **decanal**. Of, pertaining to, a rural dean or deanery.

rusa, n. [1. ro͞osa; 2. rúsə]. Malay. *rūsa*, 'deer'. Genus of East Indian deer.

ruse, n. [1. ro͞oz; 2. rūz], or as Fr. [ryz]. Fr., fr. *ruser*, 'to get out of the way; to drive back'. See **rush** (**II.**). Trick, stratagem, artifice; action designed to mislead others as to one's real intentions.

rusé, adj. [1. ro͞ozā; 2. rúzei, ryze]. Fr., 'cunning'. See prec. Cunning, wily.

rush (**I.**), n. [1. rush; 2. raʃ]. O.E. *risc, rysc*; M.E. *rusch*; cp. M.H.G. *rusche*; M.L.G. *riske*. One of various kinds of aquatic herb, genus *Juncus*, usually with slender, round, leafless stems, with a cluster of small green flowers at the top; often dried and used for making baskets, hats, mats, seats of chairs &c. Phrs. *not worth a rush*, worthless; *not give a rush for*, attach no value or importance to; *not to care a rush*, be indifferent.

rush (**II.**), vb. intrans. & trans. M.E. *russchen*, fr. A.-Fr. *russher*, fr. O. Fr. *rehusser, ruser*, 'to double on one's tracks; to get out of the way; to cause to retreat'. Cp. **ruse**; etymol. doubtful. **A.** intrans. **a** To hurl oneself, run, forward impetuously and violently; to move, flow, rapidly and with violence; be hurled forward; Phr. *to rush to a conclusion*, form one hastily; *to rush into an undertaking*, engage in it hurriedly; *to rush into print*, publish something without due consideration; **b** (of material action or process) *an idea rushed into my mind*, suddenly occurred to me; *words rushed to his lips*, came freely and rapidly. **B.** trans. **1. a** (i.) To cause to travel rapidly, to hurry, bustle along; *to rush a person round the countryside*; (ii.) to bring up at high speed: *to rush an ambulance to the scene of an accident*; **b** to compel to act hastily; to hustle, drive into precipitate action without giving time for consideration: *I won't be rushed*. **2. a** To overcome, capture, gain possession of, by rushing forward: *to rush a position*; **b** to pass, get over, by riding at high speed: *to rush a fence*. **3.** To carry out, perform, put into effect with great, esp. undue, haste: *to rush one's work*; *to rush a Bill through Parliament*.

rush (**III.**), n., fr. prec. **1.** Act of rushing; swift, impetuous, headlong, forward movement: **a** (of human, animate action) *a rush for the door*; *with one rush they were up the hill*; **b** (of processes of nature) a violent, irresistible, onward sweep, gush, flow: *a rush of water, wind* &c.; **c** excessive activity, bustle and fussiness; absence of repose: *the rush of modern life*. **2. a** Unusual amount, sudden increase, overwhelming pressure: *a rush of work, business* &c.; **b** sudden, rapid development; spurt, burst, of natural growth: *a rush of buds*; *flowers came out with a rush*. **3.** Abnormal demand for, sudden increase in calls for, a run on; general eagerness to obtain or reach: *a rush for gold, wealth*; *a rush to see the last fashionable actor*.

rush-bearing, n. Annual country festival on which the parish church is strewn and decorated with rushes.

rush-candle, n. Rushlight.

rushlight, n. [1. rúshlit; 2. ráʃlait]. **a** Candle made of the pith of a rush dipped in tallow or wax; also *farthing rushlight*, from original price; (fig.) **b** an unimportant, feeble, ineffective teacher, guide, or influence.

rushlike, adj. [1. rúshlīk; 2. ráʃlaik]. **rush** (**I.**) & **-like**. Resembling a rush.

rushy, adj. [1. rúshi; 2. ráʃi]. **rush** (**I.**) & **-y**. **a** Like, made of, rushes; **b** abounding in, full of, rushes.

rusk, n. [1. rusk; 2. rask], fr. Span. *rosca*, 'roll, twist of bread'. Kind of light bread or biscuit, baked crisp throughout.

Ruskinian, adj. & n. [1. ruskínian; 2. raskíniən], fr. John Ruskin, 1819–1900. **1.** adj. Of, pertaining to, Ruskin or his teaching. **2.** n. Follower of Ruskin.

Ruskinism, n. [1. rúskinizm; 2. ráskinizəm]. Ruskin & **-ism**. Doctrines or principles of Ruskin in art and economics.

Russ, n. & adj. [1. rus; 2. ras], fr. Russ. *Rus*, 'Russia; Russian'. **1.** n. **a** Native of Russia; **b** the Russian language. **2.** adj. Russian.

Russell, n. [1. rúsl; 2. rásl]. Origin uncertain. Also *Russell cord*, kind of twilled or corded fabric of wool or cotton and wool.

russet (**I.**), n. [1. rúset; 2. rásit]. M.E. *russet*, fr. O. Fr. *r(o)usset*, fr. Lat. *russ-(us)*, 'red'; cogn. w. O.H.G. *rosamo*, 'rust'; cp. also Lith. *rùsvas*, 'reddish brown'; O. Slav. *rusŭ*, 'fair'. See also **rust, rubric,** & **red**. **1.** Reddish or yellowish brown colour. **2.** Coarse homespun fabric of this colour. **3.** Kind of apple with rough, coarse skin of yellowish or reddish brown colour; also *russet apple*.

russet (**II.**), adj., fr. prec. **1.** Yellowish or reddish brown. **2.** Of, made of, russet; homespun. **3.** (archaic) Rustic, simple.

russety, adj. [1. rúseti; 2. rásiti]. **russet** (**I.**) & **-y**. Of the colour of russet.

Russia, n. [1. rúsha; 2. ráʃə], fr. name of country. Also *Russia leather*, fine leather, strongly scented with oil of birch-bark, used for bookbinding, making bags &c.

Russian, adj. & n. [1. rúshan; 2. ráʃən], fr. Fr., fr. Med. Lat. *Russiān-(us)*, fr. *Russia* & **-an**. **1.** adj. Belonging to, coming from, Russia. **2.** n. **a** Native of Russia; **b** language of Russia.

Russianize, vb. trans. [1. rúshanīz; 2. ráʃənaiz]. Prec. & **-ize**. To make Russian, give Russian character to.

Russification, n. [1. rùsifikā́shun; 2. ràsifikéiʃən]. **Russ** & **-fication**. Act or process of Russifying; state of being Russified.

Russify, vb. trans. [1. rúsifī; 2. rásifai]. **Russ** & **-i-** & **-fy**. To Russianize.

Russniak, n. [1. rúsnyak; 2. rásniæk], fr. Russ. *Rusnyak*. A Little Russian, Ruthenian.

Russo-, pref. Belonging to, connected with, Russia or the Russians; *Russo-Byzantine*, of the typical Russian type of architecture; *Russophile*, one who admires or favours Russian customs, policy &c.

rust (**I.**), n. [1. rust; 2. rast]. O.E. *rūst*; M.E. *rust*. See **russet** & words there referred to. **1.** Reddish or yellowish-brown coating produced on iron, steel, and other metals by oxidation, esp. through exposure to moisture. **2.** (fig.) Tendency to, condition of, feebleness, dullness, incapacity, inactivity, in mental powers and accomplishments. **3.** (bot.) **a** Kind of parasitic fungus developing on plant tissues; **b** disease caused by such a fungus.

rust (**II.**), vb. trans. & intrans., fr. prec. **A.** trans. **1.** To affect with rust, make rusty. **2.** (fig.) To weaken, destroy (mental faculties &c.) through inaction &c. **B.** intrans. **1.** To become rusty, be affected with rust. **2.** (fig., of mental faculties) To be weakened, become dull, lose vigour, through inaction or disuse. **3.** (bot.) To become affected with rust. **4.** To become rust-coloured.

rustic (**I.**), adj. [1. rústik; 2. rástik], fr. Lat. *rustic-(us)*, 'of the country', fr. *rūs*, 'country'; cogn. w. Scrt. *ravas-*, 'space'; base also in Goth. *rūms*, 'room, space', see **room**, & cp. **rural**. **1.** Connected with, pertaining to, characteristic of, suitable for, the country, for rural life or country people; contrasted with *urban*: *rustic dwellings, garments* &c. **2.** Characteristic of country folk; **a** (in favourable sense) simple, unsophisticated, homely: *rustic simplicity, courtesy* &c.; **b** (in derogatory sense) rough, boorish, unpolished; *his manners and speech were rustic in the extreme*. **3.** (of woodwork &c.) Made of rough, undressed branches. **4.** (of style of lettering) *Rustic capitals*, style of Latin MSS. before 5th cent., lighter and more roughly formed than square capitals.

rustic (II.), n., fr. prec. Countryman, peasant.

rustically, adv. [1. rústikali; 2. rástikəli]. **rustic (I.)** & **-al** & **-ly**. In a rustic manner.

rusticate, vb. trans. & intrans. [1. rústikāt; 2. rástikeit], fr. Lat. *rusticāt-(um)*, P.P. type of *rusticāri*, 'to live in the country; to be a farmer', fr. *rustic-(us)*, 'of the country', see **rustic**. **A.** trans. **1. a** To send into, banish to, the country; specif. **b** to send down temporarily from University, as a punishment. **2.** To make rustic, give a rustic character to. **3.** (masonry) To give strongly or deeply marked joints to. **B.** intrans. To live in the country; to adopt rural life, pursuits &c.

rustication, n. [1. rùstikáshun; 2. ràstikéiʃən]. Prec. & **-ion**. Act of rusticating; state of being rusticated.

rusticity, n. [1. rustísiti; 2. rastísiti], fr. Lat. *rusticitāt-(em)*, 'country life; rustic behaviour, character' &c.; fr. *rustic-(us)*, 'of the country', see **rustic (I.)**, & **-ity**. State or quality of being rustic; rustic character.

rusticly, adv. [1. rústikli; 2. rástikli]. **rustic (I.)** & **-ly**. (rare) In a rustic manner.

rustic-work, n. (archit.) Style of masonry with rough surface and deep grooves at the joints.

rustily, adv. [1. rústili; 2. rástili]. **rusty** & **-ly**. In a rusty manner.

rustiness, n. [1. rústines; 2. rástinis]. See prec. & **-ness**. (lit. and fig.) State of being rusty.

rustle (I.), vb. intrans. & trans. [1. rúsl; 2. rásl]. Imitative. **A.** intrans. **1.** (of light, dry objects or surfaces) To emit a soft, crisp, whispering sound when brought lightly into contact: *the leaves, straw, rustled underfoot; rustling silk*. **2.** To move with sound of rustling garments. **B.** trans. To cause to rustle: *the wind rustles the leaves*.

rustle (II.), n., fr. prec. Sound produced by rustling; sound made by light, dry surfaces rubbed together.

rustless, adj. [1. rústles; 2. rástlis]. **rust (I.)** & **-less**. Not liable to rust.

rustling, adj. & n. [1. rúsling; 2. rásliŋ], forming vbl. n. **1.** adj. Pres. Part. of **rustle (I.)**. Producing, resembling, a rustle. **2.** n. **rustle (I.)** & **-ing**. Sound produced by that which rustles.

rustlingly, adv. Prec. & **-ly**. So as to rustle.

rusty, adj. [1. rústi; 2. rásti]. **rust (I.)** & **-y**. **1. a** Coated with, affected by, rust, through exposure to air or moisture, disuse &c.: *rusty iron; a rusty sword*; **b** having the colour of rust. **2.** (fig.) **a** (of persons) Having lost former skill, knowledge, aptitude; out of practice: *a bit rusty in shooting, throwing a fly* &c.; *I've got rusty in my drill*; **b** (of bodily or mental aptitudes) grown unfamiliar by lack of practice: *my billiards, French &c. have got rather rusty*. **3.** (of fabrics) Grown dingy, discoloured, faded, by age and exposure: *a rusty old coat*. **4.** In Phr. *to turn rusty*, to take offence, become testy &c.

rut (I.), n. [1. rut; 2. rat]. Origin doubtful. **1.** Depression left in surface of ground by the wheel of a vehicle &c., or by succession of wheels; deep grove, wheel-track. **2.** (fig.) Habitual, conventional, mechanical course of action, mode of life, thought &c.; groove, beaten track: *to get into a rut*.

rut (II.), n. & vb. intrans., fr. O. Fr. *ruit*, fr. Lat. *rugītus*, 'roaring', fr. *rugīre*, 'to roar'; cp. Gk. *erugónta*, 'bellowing'; *rhúzein*, 'to snarl'; O.E. *rēoc*, 'fierce'; O.H.G. *rohōn*, 'to roar'; O. Slav. *rykati*, 'to roar'. **1.** n. Sexual excitement, appetence, of male animal, esp. of deer; period of heat. **2.** vb. To be affected with rut.

ruth, n. [1. rōōth; 2. rūþ]. M.E. *reuþe, ruþe*. **rue (I.)** & **-th**. (archaic) Pity, tenderness, compassion: '*Look homeward, Angel, now, and melt with ruth*' (Milton, 'Lyc.', 163).

Ruthenian, adj. & n. [1. rōōthḗnian; 2. rūþíniən]. Med. Lat. *Rut(h)eni*, 'Ruthenians', connected w. *Russi*, 'Russians'. **1.** adj. Of, pertaining to, the Little Russian race of Southern Russia, or to their language &c. **2.** n. **a** A member of this race; **b** the language of the Ruthenians.

ruthenium, n. [1. rōōthḗnium; 2. rūþíniəm]. fr. prec., as found in S. Russia. A rare metallic element, found in platinum ores.

ruthless, adj. [1. rōōthles; 2. rúþlis]. **ruth** & **-less**. Having, showing, no ruth; pitiless, merciless; cruel, relentless.

ruthlessly, adv. Prec. & **-ly**. In a ruthless manner; without compunction.

ruthlessness, n. See prec. & **-ness**. State or quality of being ruthless.

rutty, adj. [1. rúti; 2. ráti]. **rut (I.)** & **-y**. Marked with, full of, ruts.

-ry, suff. [1. ri; 2. ri] forming ns.; shortened form of **-ery**; e.g. *poultry, devilry, infantry, carpentry, pedantry* &c.

rye, n. [1. rī; 2. rai]. O.E. *ryge*; M.E. *rīe*; cp. O.N. *rugr*; M. Du. *rogge*; O.H.G. *rocko, roggo*. **a** Cereal plant, *Secale cereale*, of Northern Europe, used as fodder; **b** grain of this plant, used when ground to a coarse flour as food-stuff in N. Europe; **c** rye-whisky.

rye-grass, n. Kind of grass grown for pasture.

ryepeck, n. [1. rípek; 2. ráipek]. Etymol. doubtful. Mooring post driven into river-bed, esp. for punt.

rye-whisky, n. Whisky made from rye.

ryot, n. [1. rīut; 2. ráiət], fr. Hind. *raiyat*, fr. Arab. *ra'iyah*, 'herd, flock', see **rayah**. Indian farmer or peasant.

S

S, s [1. es; 2. ɛs]. The nineteenth letter of the English alphabet; for use in abbreviations &c. see list at end of Dictionary, and for *Collar of SS* see under **esses**.

Sabaean, Sabean, adj. & n. [1. sabḗan; 2. sæbíən], fr. Lat. *Sabaeus*, fr. Gk. *Sabaios*, of Saba, (Bib.) *Sheba*, fr. Arab. *Saba*, 'traders'. **1.** adj. Pertaining to Saba in S. Arabia, mod. Yemen: '*Sabean odours from the spicy shore Of Araby the blest*' (Milton, 'P. L.', iv. 162–3). **2.** n. A native of Saba.

Sabaoth, n. pl. [1. sábāoth, sabáoth; 2. sǽbeiɔþ, sæbéiɔþ]. Heb. *tsevāóth*, 'armies, hosts', sing. *sáva*. Only in Phr. *Lord God of Sabaoth*, the Lord of Hosts or armies.

sabbatarian, adj. & n. [1. sàbatárian; 2. sæ̀bətéəriən]. Lat. *sabbatārius*, fr. *sabbatum*, see **Sabbath**, & **-ary** & **-an**. **1.** adj. Concerned with, belonging to, the Sabbath and its observance. **2.** n. One who observes the Christian Sunday as though it were the Jewish Sabbath, esp. one who adheres rigidly to an interpretation of the fourth Commandment which regards it as forbidding enjoyment or amusement on Sunday.

sabbatarianism, n. [1. sàbatárianizm; 2. sæ̀bətéəriənizəm]. Prec. & **-ism**. Principles and practice of sabbatarians; insistence on strict observance of Sunday as a day of gloom and idleness.

Sabbath, n. [1. sábath; 2. sǽbəþ]. M.E. *sabbat*, fr. Fr., Lat. *sabbatum*, fr. Gk. *sábbaton*, fr. Heb. *shabbāth*, 'rest; day of rest'. Also (attrib.) *Sabbath day*. **1.** The seventh day of the Jewish week, on which the fourth Commandment enjoins abstention from work of all kinds. Phr. *Sabbath day's journey*, distance of 2000 cubits, about 5 furlongs, which a Jew was allowed to walk on the Sabbath. **2.** Name applied to Sunday by some Protestant religious bodies. **3.** A midnight meeting of a coven of witches.

sabbatical, adj. [1. sabátikl; 2. səbǽtikl], fr. Gk. *sabbatik-(ós)*, see **Sabbath**, & **-al**. Of, pertaining to, like, the Sabbath, as bringing cessation from work; *sabbatical year*, **a** every seventh year, during which, according to Mosaic law, the land was to lie fallow; **b** year off from routine duties, for recuperation and special study, allowed once every seven years to teachers in some universities &c.

sabbatize, vb. trans. [1. sábatīz; 2. sǽbətaiz], fr. Gk. *sabbatízein*. See prec. word & **-ize**. To turn into, treat as, a Jewish Sabbath.

Sabellian (I.), adj. & n. [1. sabélian; 2. səbéliən], fr. Lat. *Sabellus*, adj., & *Sabelli*, n. pl., 'Sabine, the Sabines'. (Rom. antiq.) **1.** adj. Belonging to a group of tribes in ancient Central Italy, including the Sabines and Samnites. **2.** n. A member of this group of tribes.

Sabellian (II.), n., fr. the name of the heretic Sabellius, 3rd cent. A.D., & **-an**. One who holds the heresy of Sabellius, that the three Persons of the Trinity are three aspects or manifestations of a single Person.

Sabellianism, n. [1. sabélianizm; 2. səbéliənizəm]. Prec. & **-ism**. The heretical doctrines of Sabellius.

Sabian, n. [1. sábian; 2. séibiən]. Arab. *as-Sābi'ūn*, prob. fr. Aramaic word meaning, 'to wash, be baptized'. One of a sect grouped in the Koran with Jews and Christians as 'people of a book', and therefore not to be condemned as pagan.

Sabine, n. & adj. [1. sábīn; 2. sǽbain]. Lat. *Sabīnus*. **1.** n. Member of a tribe in ancient Italy, closely allied to the Samnites. **2.** adj. Belonging to, connected with, this tribe.

sable (I.), n. [1. sábl; 2. séibl]. O. Fr., 'fur of the sable'; Med. Lat. has *sabelum*, n., *sabelīnus*, adj., whence Mod. Fr. *zibeline*, & M.E. *sabeline*, adj., wh. occurs earlier than the n.; of Slav. origin, Russ. & Pol. *sobol*, whence Swed. *sobel*, Gmc. *zobel* &c.; etymol. unknown. **1. a** A small carnivorous mammal, *Mustela zibellina*, allied to the martens of Northern, sub-arctic Europe and Asia, the most valuable of fur-bearing animals; the fur is very dark brown, approaching to black; **b** the allied pine-marten of N. America, *Mustela americana*, with lighter and less valuable fur. **2.** The fur of the sable; often in pl. of coat &c. made up of many sable skins: *priceless sables*.

sable (II.), adj. & n. Fr., first in her.; prob. fr. prec. **1.** adj. **a** (her.) Of the colour or tincture, black, represented in engraving &c. by crossed vertical and horizontal lines; **b** (poet.) black, dark: '*Afric's sable sons*', (Pope, 'R. of L.', iii. 82); '*sable-vested Night*' (Milton, 'P. L.', ii. 962); *the mourner's sable raiment*. **2.** n. **a** (her.) The tincture or colour black; **b** (poet.) black garments as sign of mourning.

sable antelope, n. A large antelope of S. and E. Africa, *Hippotragus niger*, with fine backward-curving horns and black coat.

sabot, n. [1. sábō; 2. sǽbou]. Fr.; etymol. unknown. **1.** A wooden shoe made out of a single piece of wood, as worn by French peasants &c.; also a wooden-soled shoe or clog. **2.** A wooden disk or soft piece of metal attached to the projectile formerly used in muzzle-loading cannon.

sabotage, n. [1. sábotahzh; 2. sǽbətaž]. **Fr.**,

fr. prec. & **-age**; prob. orig. the use of heavy wooden sabots in kicking and injuring persons and property. **a** Tampering with, infliction of damage upon, persons, machinery, or other property of employers, in connexion with trade disputes; **b** action, other than violence, intended to cause injury to a business.

sabre, n. & vb. trans. [1. sáber; 2. séibə]. Fr., also in early form *sabel*; an 18th cent. word, borrowed fr. Germ. *sabel, säbel*; words resembling the Germ. form occur in Slav. & Hungarian. Origin unknown. **1.** n. **a** Heavy, curved cavalry sword, used for cutting and thrusting; **b** cavalry soldier. **2.** vb. To use a sabre upon, cut down, kill, with a sabre.

sabretache, n. [1. sábertash; 2. sǽbətæʃ]. Fr., fr. Germ. *säbeltasche*, fr. *säbel*, 'sabre', & *tasche*, 'pocket'. Square, flat bag of leather, generally ornamented, slung from sword-belt by long straps; worn as part of full uniform by cavalry and artillery officers.

sabre-toothed, adj. [1. sáber tōōtht; 2. séibə tūþt]. Applied to lion and tiger, esp. to extinct genus *Machaerodus*, having upper canine teeth shaped like a sabre.

sabreur, n. [1. sabrér; 2. sæbrắ], or as Fr. [sabrør]. Fr., fr. **sabre**. In Phr. *beau sabreur*, a dashing, gallant cavalry officer.

sabulous, adj. [1. sábūlus; 2. sǽbjuləs]. Lat. *sabulum*, 'coarse sand, gravel', & **-ous**; *sabulum* is supposed to stand for **psaflom*, fr. **bhsabhlom*, whence also Gk. *psámmos*, 'sand', for **psáphmos*; Aryan **bhsā-* means 'to grind, rub down', as in Scrt. *bábhasti*, 'he chews up', cp. also Scrt. *bhasman*, 'ashes'; cp. Gk. *psaíō*, 'I grind'. See also **sand**. Sandy; chiefly (med.) of urine, containing sediment.

saburra, n. [1. sabúra; 2. sæbárə]. Lat., 'sand', connected w. prec. (pathol.) Granular sedimentary deposit in the stomach.

sac (I.), n. [1. sak; 2. sæk]. Fr., fr. Lat. *saccus*. See **sack** (I.). A small membranous bag, pouch, or cavity, usually containing fluid, in the body of animals or in plants; a cyst, vesicle.

sac (II.), n. O.E. *sacu*, 'dispute; jurisdiction'. See **sake**, & cp. **soc**. The right of the lord of a manor to try causes in his court and to impose fines.

saccate, adj. [1. sákāt; 2. sǽkeit]. See **sac** (I.) & **-ate**. (bot.) Formed into a sac or vesicle; contained in a sac.

sacchar-, sacchari-, saccharo-, pref. Forms used as first element in words indicating the presence &c. of sugar, fr. Lat. *saccharon*, fr. Gk. *sákkharon* or *sákkhar*, 'sugar'; orig. borrowed fr. an Indian dial., cp. Scrt. *śarkarā*, 'grit, gravel'. Cp. **crocodile**.

sacchariferous, adj. [1. sàkaríferus; 2. sæ̀kəríferəs]. **sacchari-** & **-ferous**. Sugar-bearing, producing sugar.

saccharify, vb. trans. [1. sakárifī; 2. sækǽrifai]. **sacchari-** & **-fy**. To convert into sugar, esp. applied to the conversion by chemical means of starch into sugar.

saccharimeter, saccharometer, n. [1. sakarímeter, -ómeter; 2. sækərímitə, -ómitə]. See **sacchar-** & **-meter**. An instrument, a form of hydrometer, used to test the quantity of sugar or saccharine matter in any solution.

saccharin, n. [1. sákarin; 2. sǽkərin]. See next word. A white, intensely sweet, crystalline substance obtained from coal-tar; used as a substitute for sugar.

saccharine, adj. [1. sákarīn; 2. sǽkərain]. **sacchar-** & **-ine**. **a** Of the nature of, resembling, connected with, sugar; sweet; **b** (fig., of mode of expression &c.) sugary.

saccharose, n. [1. sákarōs; 2. sǽkərous]. See prec. & **-ose**. (chem.) Cane or beet sugar, as contrasted with *glucose*.

sacciform, adj. [1. sáksiform; 2. sǽksifōm]. See **sac** (I.) & **-form**. (biol.) Sac-like, shaped like a sac or vesicle.

saccule, n. [1. sákūl; 2. sǽkjūl], fr. Lat. *sacculus*, dimin. of *saccus*, 'sack, sac'. See **sac** (I.). A small sac, vesicle, or cyst.

sacerdotal, adj. [1. sàserdṓtl; 2. sæ̀sədóutl], fr. Lat. *sacerdōtālis*, fr. *sacerdōt-(em)*, 'priest', lit. 'presenter of sacred offerings', fr. base seen in **sacred**, & a form of base **dā-* &c., 'to give', see **date** (I.) & **donation**. Pertaining to priests or the priesthood.

sacerdotalism, n. [1. sàserdṓtalizm; 2. sæ̀sədóutəlizəm]. Prec. & **-ism**. **a** System of religious polity in which the priest is assigned an important place; priestcraft; **b** rule, undue influence by priests; superstitious reverence for priests and their functions.

sacerdotalist, n. [1. sàserdṓtalist; 2. sæ̀sədóutəlist]. See prec. & **-ist**. A supporter of sacerdotalism.

sachem, n. [1. sáchem; 2. séitʃem]. N. Am. Indian, cp. **sagamore**. **a** A supreme chief among the N. American Indians; **b** an important personage, a bigwig.

sachet, n. [1. sáshā; 2. sǽʃei]. Fr., dimin. of **sac** (I.). **a** A small folding case of soft fabric for holding handkerchiefs &c.; **b** a small bag containing highly scented, aromatic powder, kept among clothes, on the person &c.

sack (I.), n. [1. sak; 2. sæk]. O.E. *sacc*, M.E. *sack*; fr. Lat. *saccus*, fr. Gk. *sákkos*, fr. Semitic, cp. Heb. *saq*, 'haircloth, sackcloth, sack, bag'. **1. a** A large narrow bag of some coarse textile, such as jute &c., styled 'sacking', used for holding and carrying heavy commodities, such as coals, potatoes &c.; **b** such a bag as a unit or dry measure of capacity for certain commodities, varying at different times and in different localities; *a sack of coal*, 2 cwt.; *of wheat, potatoes* &c., 3 bushels; *of wool*, $3\frac{1}{4}$ cwt. Phrs. *to give the sack to*, to dismiss; *get the sack*, be dismissed; the phrase is found in 17th cent. French, as shown by Cotgrave '*on luy a donné son sac et ses quilles*, he hath his passport given him', 'said of a servant whom his master hath put away', i.e. turned out bag and baggage. **2. a** A woman's loose dress of the 18th cent., also, as if a French word, written *sacque*; **b** a long folded or pleated piece of silk or other material fastened to the shoulders and forming a train to a dress; **c** a coat, for men or women, with straight, loosely fitting back: *a sack coat*.

sack (II.), vb. trans., fr. prec. **1.** To put, place, in a sack: *to sack potatoes* &c. **2.** (colloq.) To dismiss from employment, to give the sack to.

sack (III.), n. & vb. trans., fr. Fr. *sac*, 'plunder, pillage, spoil', prob. fr. *sac*, 'bag', see prec. word, as shown in phr. *mettre à sac*, 'to put to the sack, to plunder'; Ital. has *sacco*, in same sense, & L. Lat. *saccāre*, 'to put into a sack'; the vb. is fr. the n.; Fr. has *saccager*. **1.** n. Act of pillaging and plundering a captured town by troops; often accompanied by indiscriminate massacre of civilians. **2.** vb. To plunder, pillage, spoil; to loot.

sack (IV.), n. Early form also *seck*, n. or adj., as *sherris sack*, fr. Fr. *sec*, 'dry', *vin sec*, fr. Lat. *siccus*, 'dry'. See **siccative**. A white, dry wine of Southern Europe, of the 16th and 17th cents., esp. one from Spain, the Canary Islands, or Madeira: so *sherry sack*, 'sherry', *Canary sack* &c., usually mulled and spiced.

sackbut, n. [1. sákbut; 2. sǽkbat]. Etymol. doubtful; many fantastic suggestions; Fr. has *saquebute*, 'trombone'. **1.** An old musical wind instrument with bell mouth and a sliding tube, the precursor of the modern trombone. **2.** An old stringed instrument, in Dan. iii. used wrongly to translate the Aramaic *sabbekā*, Gk. *sambúkē*.

sackcloth, n. [1. sákklawth; 2. sǽkklōþ]. **sack** (I.) & **cloth**. Coarse textile fabric of hemp, jute &c. used for making sacks; sacking. Phr. *(to repent) in sackcloth and ashes*, cp. 2 Sam. iii.; from Eastern method of expressing sorrow, penitence, and humiliation &c.; the material referred to was probably made of goat's hair.

sack coat, n. **sack** (I.) & **coat**. A loosely fitting, straight-backed coat for men or women; a sack.

sacking, n. [1. sáking; 2. sǽkiŋ]. **sack** (I.) & **-ing**. Sackcloth; esp. as used for wrapping and packing large articles for transit.

sackless, adj. [1. sákles; 2. sǽklis]. O.E. *sæcclēas*, 'innocent', fr. *sacu*, 'dispute, contention' &c. See **sac** (II.), **sake**, & **-less**. (archaic or provinc.) **1.** Without blame, innocent. **2.** Harmless, shy, inoffensive. **3.** Weak in mind or body, helpless; moping, melancholy.

sack race, n. **sack** (I.) & **race**. A race in which competitors are tied in sacks up to their necks, and move along by a series of short jumps.

sacque, n. [1. sak; 2. sæk]. Frenchified spelling of **sack** (I.). A sack dress or coat.

sacral (I.), adj. [1. sákral; 2. séikrəl], fr. **sacrum** & **-al**. (anat.) Pertaining to, in region of, the sacrum.

sacral (II.), adj. Lat. *sacr-*, *sacer*, 'holy', see **sacred**, & **-al**. Pertaining to religious rites.

sacrament, n. [1. sákrament; 2. sǽkrəmənt]. M.E. *sacrement*, fr. Fr. *sacrement*; also *sacrament*, directly fr. Lat. *sacrāmentum*, 'oath, solemn obligation', formed fr. stem of *sacrāre*, 'to set apart as sacred, to dedicate', fr. *sacer*, see **sacred**; in eccles. Lat. the word means that which is to be kept sacred, a secret, & is used to translate the Gk. *mustḗrion*, 'mystery', with various applications, see **mystery**. **1.** 'An outward and visible sign of an inward and spiritual grace' (Ch. Catechism). **2. a** One of those 'ordained by Christ Himself as generally necessary to salvation' (Ch. Catechism), i.e. Baptism and the Lord's Supper; **b** one of certain other rites recognized as sacraments by the Catholic Church, i.e. Confirmation, Orders, Penance, Extreme Unction, Matrimony. **3. a** Specif., *The Sacrament*, the Eucharist, Holy Communion, the Mass; **b** the consecrated bread or wafer used in the Eucharist: *to reserve the Sacrament*; it is usual among members of the Church of England, and the Roman Church, to speak of *the Blessed Sacrament*. **4.** Something having a mysterious and sacred meaning; the spiritual benefit derived from this. **5.** Sacred and solemn oath, pledge, obligation.

sacramental (I.), adj. [1. sàkraméntal; 2. sæ̀krəméntəl]. Prec. & **-al**. **1.** Pertaining to, of the nature of, a sacrament; specif., connected with the *Sacrament*, or Sacraments: *sacramental rites, ceremonies, tests, symbols* &c.; **2.** Bound, binding by, a sacrament: *sacramental oath*; *the sacramental army of Christ*.

sacramental (II.), n., fr. prec. (R.C. Ch., usually pl.) Certain ceremonies, acts, observances, resembling the Sacraments, instituted, however, not by Christ, but by the Church, such as the consecration of a sacred building, exorcism, the use of holy water, of the sign of the cross &c.

sacramentalism, n. [1. sàkraméntalizm; 2. sæ̀krəméntəlizəm]. **sacramental** (I.) & **-ism**. The doctrine of the efficacy and necessity of the Sacraments; insistence upon the Sacraments as means of grace, and as necessary to salvation.

sacramentalist, n. [1. sàkraméntalist; 2. sæ̀krəméntəlist]. **sacramental** (I.) & **-ist**. A believer in sacramentalism.

sacramentally, adv. [1. sàkraméntali; 2. sæ̀krəméntəli]. **sacramental** (I.) & **-ly**. In, by, after the manner of, a sacrament.

sacramentarian, adj. & n. [1. sàkramentárian; 2. sæ̀krəmentéəriən], fr. Med. Lat. *sacrāmentārius*. See prec. & **-arian**. **1.** adj. **a** Pertaining to a sacrament or the Sacraments; sacramental; **b** of, pertaining to, the Sacramentarians: *the Sacramentarian controversy*. **2.** n. **a** (Ch. hist., cap.) The name given in the 16th cent. to Zwingli and his followers, who repudiated both the Lutheran doctrine of Consubstantiation as well as that of Transubstantiation, and denied the Real Presence altogether, holding that the bread and wine were only symbols of Christ's Body and Blood, and that the service of the Eucharist was merely commemorative: **b** (modern usage) one who holds definite and specific views on the efficacy of the Sacraments; **a** sacramentalist.

sacramentarianism, n. [1. sàkramentárianizm ; 2. sækrəmentɛ́əriənizəm]. Prec. & **-ism**. **a** Doctrine, principles, of the 16th cent. Sacramentarians ; **b** doctrine of a sacramentarian ; sacramentalism.

sacrarium, n. [1. sākrárium ; 2. seikrɛ́əriəm]. Lat., fr. *sacr-(um), sacer*, 'sacred', & *-ārium*. See **sacred** & **-ary**. **1.** Shrine for the household gods in an ancient Roman house. **2.** Part of the chancel within the altar rails in a Christian church.

sacred, adj. [1. sákred ; 2. séikrid], fr. M.E. *sacred*, P.P. of *sacren*, 'to consecrate, dedicate', fr. Fr. *sacrer*, fr. Lat. *sacrāre*, 'to set apart, consecrate', fr. *sacer*, 'dedicated to a divinity, holy' &c. The etymol. is not very clear ; Walde connects Lat. *sancīre*, 'to make sacred or inviolable ; to appoint, ordain, confirm' &c., whence, fr. P.P. type, *sanctus*, 'rendered sacred or inviolable ; pure, holy', **sanctity** & **saint**; outside Lat. cp. O.N. *sāttr*, 'reconciled, conciliated'. **1.** Set apart for, dedicated, consecrated, to a deity, person, purpose, or sentiment &c.: *groves sacred to the Muses ; sacred to the memory of . . . ; fields sacred to innocent pastimes* &c. **2. a** Associated with the religion, with the religious rites and practices, of a people ; embodying the laws and principles of a religion : *the sacred writings, books, of ancient India* ; **b** endowed with mystical, symbolical virtue, venerated from association with religious rites : *the sacred elephant, monkey &c. of the East.* **3.** Specif. **a** associated with the worship of, belief in, God, and with the Christian religion : *a sacred edifice* ; **b** connected with the Divine relations with man and the universe : *sacred history*, based on the events recorded in the Old and New Testaments ; *sacred music, songs*, having a religious motive, based on a theme from Scripture ; contrasted with *profane* or *secular.* **4.** Felt, regarded, observed, as sacrosanct ; hallowed, deserving of veneration, inviolate, on account of inherent qualities, or of association with some deeply rooted feeling, some solemn event &c. : *a sacred trust ; my oath is sacred ; whatever happens, the person of the ambassador is sacred* ; in the Phr. *his Sacred Majesty*, the word no doubt meant originally 'consecrated', having been 'sacred' (see M.E. meaning above), whence it acquired various other meanings arising from the fact.

Sacred College, n. The College of Cardinals.

Sacred Heart, n. Also *Sacred Heart of Jesus*, **a** festival held in Roman Church to commemorate the living, bodily heart of the Saviour as an object of special devotion ; **b** society founded in connexion with this.

sacredly, adv. [1. sákredli ; 2. séikridli]. **sacred** & **-ly**. **a** (rare) Reverently ; **b** strictly, inviolably : *an oath sacredly preserved.*

sacredness, n. [1. sákrednes ; 2. séikridnis]. See prec. & **-ness**. Quality of being sacred; **a** venerability, sanctity ; **b** inviolability.

sacrifice (I.), n. [1. sákrifis ; 2. sǽkrifais]. Fr., fr. Lat. *sacrificium*, 'a making holy or sacred, sacrifice', fr. stem *sacri-*, fr. *sacer*, see **sacred**, & *-ficium*, fr. a form of *facere*, 'to make', see **-fic** & **fact**. **1. a** Act of offering, dedicating, something to the use and service of a deity ; **b** material object so dedicated, or spiritual offering of prayer, thanksgiving, repentance, thus dedicated. **2.** Specif. **a** the offering of Christ upon the Cross as a propitiation for the sins of mankind ; **b** the representation of this in the Eucharist or Mass. **3. a** Act of giving up, surrendering, forgoing, something precious, something that one values, as for the benefit of a person or cause : *to make the sacrifice of one's holiday in order to finish one's work ; I cannot accept the sacrifice of your whole youth in my service ; to make a sacrifice of truth and honour for the sake of material reward* ; Phr. *to fall a sacrifice*, be sacrificed ; *to make sacrifices*, practise self-sacrifice, deny oneself ; **b** act of parting with, selling, disposing of, something at a price below its supposed value : *to sell at a sacrifice*, at a loss.

sacrifice (II.), vb. trans. & intrans., fr. prec., cp. Fr. *sacrifier*, fr. Lat. *sacrificāre*. **A.** trans. **1. a** To make an offering or sacrifice of ; to present, devote, to a deity ; esp. **b** to slaughter ceremonially (an animal or person) as an offering : *to sacrifice sheep, oxen* &c. ; *the Druids used to sacrifice children* ; '*Christ, our Passover, is sacrificed for us*' (1 Cor. v. 7). **2.** To give up, surrender, suffer to be injured, destroyed, or lost, in order that something else may be gained or improved, or for the sake of another person : *to sacrifice appearance to comfort, orderliness to convenience ; to sacrifice one's whole career for a passing whim ; to sacrifice oneself for the good of humanity ; beautiful old houses had to be sacrificed to make room for modern buildings.* **B.** intrans. To offer, make, a sacrifice : *Solomon went to Gibeon to sacrifice there.*

sacrificer, n. [1. sákrifiser ; 2. sǽkrifaisə]. Prec. & **-er**. One who sacrifices ; the officiating priest at a sacrifice.

sacrificial, adj. [1. sàkrifíshal ; 2. sæ̀krifíʃəl]. **sacrifice** (I.) & **-ial**. Pertaining to, connected with, of the nature of, sacrifice or a sacrifice.

sacrificially, adv. Prec. & **-ly**. In the manner, by way, of a sacrifice.

sacrilege, n. [1. sákrilij ; 2. sǽkrilidž]. O. Fr., fr. Lat. *sacrilegium*, 'robbing of a temple, stealing of sacred things' ; fr. *sacrilegus*, 'temple robber, sacrilegious person', fr. *sacri-*, stem of *sacer*, see **sacred**, & *leg-*, as in *legere*, 'to gather, pick up, steal', see **legend**. **1.** The profanation of sacred places or things ; outrage on, insult offered to, what is venerated and held sacred. **2.** Specif. (law) **a** Forcible entry into, theft from, malicious damage to, a consecrated building ; **b** alienation of ecclesiastical property for secular purposes ; appropriation of Church property by laymen.

sacrilegious, adj. [1. sàkrilíjus ; 2. sæ̀krilídžəs]. Prec. & **-ous** ; pronunciation of third syll. influenced by *religious.* **1.** (of persons) **a** Irreverent, showing no respect for sacred things ; **b** specif., guilty of the crime of sacrilege. **2.** (of acts) Of the nature of, involving, sacrilege ; **a** exhibiting irreverence, disrespectful, impious ; **b** specif., partaking of the crime of sacrilege.

sacrilegiously, adv. Prec. & **-ly**. In a sacrilegious manner ; profanely, impiously.

sacrilegist, n. [1. sàkrilējist ; 2. sæ̀krilídžist]. See prec. & **-ist**. (archaic or rare) One guilty of sacrilege ; a sacrilegious person.

sacring, n. [1. sákring ; 2. séikriŋ]. M.E., vbl. n., fr. *sācre(n)*, 'to consecrate', see **sacred**, & **-ing**. **1.** Consecration of the elements at the Eucharist ; *sacring-bell*, also *sanctus-bell*, rung at the elevation of the Host after consecration. **2.** Consecration of a bishop, or of a sovereign at his Coronation.

sacrist, n. [1. sákrist ; 2. sǽkrist], fr. O. Fr. *sacriste*, fr. L. Lat. *sacrista.* See stem of **sacred** & **-ist**. **1.** Official who keeps the sacred vessels and vestments of a church ; keeper of the sacristy ; sacristan. **2.** Official of a cathedral who copied out music for the use of the choir and kept the books.

sacristan, n. [1. sákristan ; 2. sǽkristən], fr. Med. Lat. *sacristānus*, more commonly *sacrista*, see prec., & **-an**. **1.** A sacrist, keeper of the sacristy. **2.** A sexton.

sacristy, n. [1. sákristi ; 2. sǽkristi], fr. Fr. *sacristie*, Med. Lat. *sacristia*. See **sacrist** & **-y**. The room or chamber in or adjoining a church, in which the sacred vessels and vestments are kept ; a vestry.

sacro-, pref. **1.** Form of Lat. *sacer*, 'consecrated, holy' &c., used in compounds. See **sacred**. **2.** Ultimately fr. same source, but derived immediately fr. **sacrum**, & referring to the region of the pelvis.

sacrosanct, adj. [1. sàkrōsangkt, sàkrōsángkt ; 2. sǽkrousæŋkt, sæ̀krousǽŋkt]. Lat. *sacrosanctus*, 'sanctified by a sacred rite', hence 'doubly sacred, inviolable'. See **sacro-** & **sanctus**. Sacred and inviolable ; secured against sacrilege, outrage, or violation ; hence, of especial sanctity, deserving and obtaining peculiar veneration and respect : *the sacrosanct person of the king ; a sacrosanct building, place, custom, usage, law* &c.

sacrum, n. [1. sákrum ; 2. séikrəm], fr. Lat. *os sacrum*, 'the sacred bone', see **sacred** ; so called fr. use made of the bone in sacrifices. Triangular bone formed by the fusion of five vertebrae at lower end of the spine, and forming the posterior part of the pelvis.

sad, adj. [1. sad ; 2. sæd]. O.E. *sæd*, 'satiated, wearied', M.E. *sad*, 'sated, full ; weary, tired ; sober, solid, dark-coloured' ; O.S. *sad*, O.H.G. *sat*, O.N. *saðr*, Goth. *saþs* ; cogn. w. Lat. *satis*, Gk. *hadēn*, 'enough', see **satis**. **1.** (of persons, the mind &c.) Sorrowful, melancholy, gloomy, dejected, mournful : *to feel sad ; it makes one sad ; a sad heart ; a sad expression in the eyes.* **2. a** (of events, circumstances) Causing sadness and sorrow ; mournful, lamentable, to be deplored : *a sad misfortune ; his early death is very sad ; it is sad that you failed in your exam.* ; *what you tell me is very sad ; how sad that he made such an unfortunate marriage!* ; **b** (of actions) attended with, provoking, sadness in the performer : *the sad task, duty, of burying one's mother.* **3.** (archaic) Sober, prudent, serious, not gay or frivolous : *sad and discreet persons* ; '*Never sad but when she sleeps*' (Shakespeare). **4.** (rare or obs.) Heavy, cohesive, hard to work or manipulate : *land with a sad, cold soil ; sad dough, bread* &c. **5.** Dark-coloured : *garments of sad hue.* **6.** (colloq.) As intensive, possessing qualities indicated to a high degree, terrible, shocking ; often humorously : *a sad rogue, puss, flirt* &c.

sadden, vb. trans. & intrans. [1. sádn ; 2. sǽdn]. Prec. & **-en**. **1.** trans. To make sad, cause grief to. **2.** intrans. To become sad.

saddle (I.), n. [1. sádl ; 2. sǽdl]. O.E. *sadol*, M.E. *sādel* ; O.H.G. *satal, -ul* ; O.N. *soðull* ; not directly cogn. w. **sit**. It is possible that Gmc. **sadula-*, 'seat' &c., may be a loan-word fr. another Aryan language, & may indeed be derived fr. some form of the base **sed-*, 'to sit'. See **sederunt**, **sedilia** &c. **1. a** Seat, usually of leather, padded and lined, for a rider on a horse &c., fastened with girths which pass round the animal's belly ; Phr. *in the saddle*, on horseback ; also (fig.) in position of authority ; *to put the saddle on the wrong horse*, attribute something to the wrong person ; **b** seat of rider on a bicycle, tricycle &c., made of leather, and somewhat resembling a saddle in shape ; **c** part of harness of a draught horse, which bears the weight of the shafts, furnished with straps to which the breeching is attached. **2.** That part of an animal's back, between the shoulder and the loins, upon which a saddle is placed : *a horse rather long in the saddle.* **3.** Joint of mutton served at table, consisting approximately of that part of the back described in **2**, and including the backbone and the ribs on either side ; usually *saddle of mutton.* **4.** Applied to various things supposed to resemble a saddle in shape ; **a** the top stone of a gable ; **b** a ridge in a hill or mountain between two peaks ; **c** one of various mechanical devices for supporting, keeping in place, e.g. support for cable of suspension bridge, a so-called 'chair' on a railway line which rests upon the sleepers and supports the rail.

saddle (II.), vb. trans. O.E. *sadelian*. See prec. **1.** To put a saddle on to : *to saddle a horse, mule* &c. **2.** To place a burden on ; to load, burden, encumber : *saddled with debts, impecunious dependants &c.* ; *I can't be saddled with any more responsibilities.*

saddleback, n. [1. sádlbak ; 2. sǽdlbæk]. One of various objects having a concave back, shape, or outline like a saddle. **1.** (archit.) A sloping roof between two gables. **2.** (geog.) A concave ridge between two heights ; a saddle or col. **3.** (zool.) Applied to several animals which have a distinctive saddle-shaped patch or marking on the back, e.g. the harp-seal, the black-backed gull, a New Zealand bird akin to the starling &c.

saddlebacked, adj. [1. sádlbakt; 2. sǽdlbækt]. Prec. & **-ed.** **1.** (of animals) **a** Having a back low and head and neck high, like a horse; **b** having markings on the back like a saddle. **2.** (of mountain, roof) Having a ridge, or outline, concave, like a saddle.

saddle-bag, n. **1.** One of a pair of bags, of leather or other stout fabric, joined by a strap, made to be carried on either side of saddle. **2.** A heavy, stout kind of coloured carpet or rug of Persian or oriental style, of which camels' pack saddles and bags are made; used also for upholstering easy chairs.

saddle-bar, n. **1.** The side bar of a saddle-tree joining the cantle to the pommel. **2.** (building) An iron cross-bar or stay joining, or passing through, the mullions of a window, to which the lead for the lights is fastened.

saddle-bow, n. The bow or arch forming the front of the framework of a saddle, the top of which is the pommel.

saddle-cloth, n. Cloth of thick felt, often shaped like the saddle, but larger, placed upon horse's back for the saddle to rest on.

saddle-horse, n. A horse broken in, and used, for riding.

saddle-joint, n. An overlapping joint used in roofing with sheet metal, the edge of one sheet being turned up and folded down over the upturned edge of the next sheet.

saddle-nail, n. A short nail with large, flat head used in nailing the leather to the framework of a saddle.

saddler, n. [1. sádler; 2. sǽdlə]. **saddle (II.)** & **-er.** **1.** One who makes or deals in saddlery and harness. **2.** A soldier in charge of the saddlery of a cavalry regiment: *saddler-corporal, sergeant.*

saddle-room, n. Room attached to a stable, in which harness of all kinds is kept.

saddlery, n. [1. sádleri; 2. sǽdləri]. Prec. & **-y.** **1.** The requisites for riding and driving, such as saddles, bridles, and harness generally as made and sold by a saddler. **2.** **a** The shop, place, where such articles are sold or made; **b** room attached to a stable where the saddlery and harness are kept; saddle-room. **3.** Occupation of a saddler and harness-maker.

saddle-tree, n. **1.** The framework, of wood, on which the saddle of a horse is built up. **2.** The N. American tulip tree; from the shape of its leaves.

Sadducean, adj. [1. sàdūsḗan; 2. sædjusíən]. See next word & **-an.** Pertaining to, connected with, the Sadducees and their doctrines.

Sadducee, n. [1. sádūsē; 2. sǽdjusī], fr. L. Lat. *Saddūcaeus*, Gk. *Saddoukaîos*, usually in pl. translating Heb. pl. *Tsedūqim*, 'the righteous', fr. *tsādaq*, 'to be just, righteous'. A member of an aristocratic, conservative, priestly party among the Jews, from about the 2nd cent. B.C. to the destruction of the Temple, A.D. 70.

sadism, n. [1. sáhdizm; 2. sádizəm]. Fr. *sadisme*, fr. the name of the insane Marquis de Sade, d. 1814, author of many obscene novels. A form of sexual perversion, characterized by a delight in inflicting suffering.

sadly, adv. [1. sádli; 2. sǽdli]. **sad** & **-ly.** **1.** Sorrowfully, with sadness. **2.** To a sad, deplorable, extent: *sadly changed since we last met* &c. **3.** (colloq.) *To feel, be, look, sadly*, ill, poorly.

sadness, n. [1. sádnes; 2. sǽdnis]. **sad** & **-ness.** **1.** Quality of being sad; melancholy, misery, wretchedness. **2.** Sad state of mind; unhappiness, depression of spirits, dejection.

safari, n. [1. safáhri; 2. səfári]. Arab. 'travel, journey'. A hunting or shooting expedition.

safe (I.), adj. [1. sāf; 2. seif]. M.E. *sauf, sāf*, fr. Fr. *sauf*, fr. Lat. *salvus*, 'whole, safe'. See **salvage.** **1.** Free from danger, not liable or exposed to risk or danger; protected, sheltered, secure: *to be safe from attack, one's enemies* &c.; *inoculation renders one safe from infection*; *a safe seat in Parliament*; *steeple-jacks at work do not look safe but they feel safe*; '*to make the world safe for democracy*'. **2.** Freed from, escaped from, out of, danger; having escaped damage, injury &c.; uninjured, unharmed, in good, sound condition: *to come home safe from the war*; *to bring something back safe*; *the ship is now safe in port*; *the crisis is over and the patient is now safe.* Phr. *safe and sound*, uninjured and in good health. **3.** Affording security, protection, shelter; secure against danger, injury &c.: *a safe place to live in*; *a safe anchorage.* **4.** **a** Not likely to be the cause of danger or disaster; involving no risk: *the rope is perfectly safe*, won't break; *is it safe to travel so fast?*; *the bridge is now safe for traffic*; *it is not safe to skate on thin ice*; Phr. (*better to be*) *on the safe side*, not to take any risks; **b** free from error, secured against risk of making mistakes; unlikely to be erroneous: *you are perfectly safe in believing what he tells you*; *it is safe to bet on what is certain.* **5.** **a** Securely confined, unable to break out, prevented from inflicting injury &c.: *safe in gaol*; **b** incapable of being broken through, escaped from &c.: *the Tower was considered the safest place for traitors*; *in safe custody.* **6.** (of persons) **a** Cautious, prudent, not taking rash risks, not reckless; inspiring confidence: *a very safe surgeon to consult*; *it is sometimes better to have a safe than a brilliant leader*; *my chauffeur is a very safe driver*; **b** (in unfavourable sense) possessing foregoing qualities to an exaggerated degree; hence, unenterprising, afraid to take any risk; taking always a conventional course; timid in action: *it is too often the safe men who get the important posts.* **7.** **a** Morally reliable, discreet; trustworthy, faithful to a trust or obligation: *a perfectly safe person to confide in*; **b** certain to be faithfully kept; inviolate: *your secret will be safe with me.* **8.** **a** Likely or certain to occur: *it is safe to get warmer as the day goes on*; **b** certain to do something, or to undergo something: *the Tory candidate is safe to get in*; *the favourite is safe to win*; Phr. *a safe* (parliamentary) *seat*, one always held, and therefore considered certain to be won, by a candidate of a particular party.

safe (II.), n. Earlier form is *save*, fr. vb. **1.** A specially strong receptacle, often made of steel and built into a wall, for keeping valuables of any kind. **2.** A receptacle, cooled and ventilated, for storing food; esp. *a meat-safe.*

safe-conduct, n. & vb. trans. **safe (I.)** & **conduct**, 'a leading, guidance', cp. Fr. *sauf conduit.* **1.** n. **a** A document, signed by the sovereign of a country or his representative, allowing safe passage through the country, given to an enemy in time of war, or to a traveller in districts of which the inhabitants are hostile to foreigners &c.; **b** a similar document or pass, signed by a military commander, giving permission to an enemy or neutral to pass through the lines &c. in time of war; **c** a guard or convoy accompanying the holder of a safe-conduct. **2.** vb. To grant a safe-conduct to; to escort safely through a dangerous or hostile country or district.

safe-deposit, n. A building containing a number of separate safes or strong-rooms, which can be hired by individuals for the deposit and safe-keeping of valuables &c.

safeguard, safe-guard, n. & vb. trans. [1. sáfgard; 2. séifgād]. O. Fr. *sauvegarde.* See **safe (I.)** & **guard.** **1.** n. That which serves to protect or guard; a defence, protection; specif., a condition, stipulation, proviso, which prevents or is intended to prevent loss, damage; that which protects from danger or injury: *a safeguard against accidents*; *to find safeguards against evasion*; *safeguards for one's interests* &c. **2.** vb. To ensure, secure, protect: *to safeguard one's interests*; *to safeguard industries*, impose a form of protection against undue foreign competition by means of a tariff on competing imported goods, granted, after official inquiry, to certain selected industries.

safe-keeping, n. Act of keeping in safety; safe custody: (of persons or things) *to be in safe-keeping*, to be kept safe; to be in custody.

safely, adv. [1. sáfli; 2. séifli]. **safe (I.)** & **-ly.** In a safe manner (in various senses of adj.); with safety.

safeness, n. [1. sáfnes; 2. séifnis]. See prec. & **-ness.** State, quality, of being safe.

safety, n. [1. sáfti; 2. séifti], fr. Fr. *sauveté*, O. Fr. *salveté*, fr. Med. Lat. *salvitāt-(em)*, fr. Lat. *salvus*, 'safe, whole'. See **safe (I.)** & **-ity.** **1.** Quality, state, of being safe (in various senses of adj.). Phrs. *safety in numbers*, victory is always with the majority; *to play for safety*, not to take any risk or chances of defeat or loss; *safety first*, slogan inculcating caution, esp. (i.) in national affairs; (ii.) in movement amid motor traffic. **2.** (rarely used) Abbreviation of compounds such as *safety-bicycle* &c.

safety-bicycle, n. Name given, when they were first invented, to the type of bicycle, now universal, which has two low wheels of equal size; contrasted with *high bicycle*, the name of the old type of machine.

safety-bolt, -catch, or **-lock**, n. A device in the breech mechanism of a fire-arm which prevents the accidental discharge.

safety-fuse, n. A fuse for discharging explosives made so as to burn at a given rate and explode at a fixed time.

safety-lamp, n. A miner's lamp so constructed as to prevent the flame coming into direct contact with fire-damp and causing explosion.

safety-lock, n. **1.** A lock on a door &c., which can only be opened by the proper key and cannot be picked. **2.** A safety-bolt or catch on a fire-arm.

safety-match, n. A match which can only be ignited on specially prepared surface.

safety-pin, n. A pin for fastening, made in the form of a brooch or clasp, with backpiece and a hinge or spring, the point fitting into a guard or loop so as not to prick the wearer.

safety-razor, n. A razor in which the blade fits into a holder fixed at right angles to the handle, with a comb-like guard supposed to allow shaving to be accomplished without much danger of cutting the skin.

safety-valve, n. **1.** A valve which automatically opens to relieve the excess pressure of steam, gas, or liquid, in a boiler, hydraulic machine &c. so as to prevent explosion. **2.** (fig.) Any outlet as a relief for excitement, violent emotion &c. Phr. *to sit on the safety-valve*, to prevent any relief from over-pressure, excitement &c.; to suppress, repress the exhibition of strong feelings and passions, thus risking a violent outburst sooner or later.

saffian, n. [1. sáfian; 2. sǽfiæn]. Germ., fr. Russ. *safyān*, prob. of Pers. origin, cp. *sakhtiān*, 'goat's skin'. A goat's or sheep's skin tanned with sumach and dyed bright yellow or red.

safflower, n. [1. sáflour; 2. sǽflauə]. Etymol. doubtful; Du. has *saffloer*, O. Fr. *saffleur*, & early Ital. *saffiore*; all having the second element equiv. to 'flower'; first element prob. Arab, *safra*, 'yellow'. **1.** An annual herb, resembling a thistle, *Carthamus tinctorius*, also called *bastard saffron*, native of the East Indies and cultivated in S. Europe &c., bearing orange-coloured flowers which, when dried, yield a red, orange, or pink dye; also ground fine, and made into rouge. **2.** **a** The dye or rouge made from the flowers; **b** a drug used in place of saffron.

saffron, n. [1. sáfrun; 2. sǽfrən]. M.E. *saffran*, fr. Fr. *safran*, cp. Ital. *zafferano*, Span. *azafran*, fr. Arab. *za'farān.* **1.** (bot.) A plant, variety of crocus, *Crocus sativus*, with light, purple flowers, long cultivated in the East and later introduced to Europe, the dried orange-red stigmas of which yield a dye, also an aromatic, pungent drug, and flavouring substance. **2.** The dye and flavouring substance from the saffron. **3.** (attrib.) Saffron-coloured; bright yellow; flavoured with **saffron**; *a saffron cloak*, formerly a royal robe in ancient Ireland; *saffron cake* &c. **4.** The safflower, *bastard saffron.*

safranin(e), n. [1. sáfranin; 2. sǽfrənin]. Fr., fr. *safran*, 'saffron', & **-ine.** (chem.) A synthetic orange-red dye-stuff obtained from coal-tar.

sag (I.), vb. intrans. & trans. [1. sag; 2. sæg]. M.E. *saggen*; of Scand. origin, cp. Norw. *sakka*, Dan. *sakke*, 'to sink, settle down', also Du. *zakken*, 'to sink, subside'; prob. cogn. w. **sink. A.** intrans. **1. a** To sink, droop, bend, curve, downwards at the middle, from a horizontal line, to bulge downwards beyond place where either end is supported under weight or pressure: *elm beams are apt to sag*; **b** to buckle, bend, droop forward, from the vertical: *candles sag in hot weather.* **2.** (naut.) To drift away from the course: *the ship sags to leeward*, makes leeway. **3.** (fig.) **a** (of prices &c.) To drop, decline in value; **b** (of mind, spirits &c.) to droop, flag. **B.** trans. (rare) To cause to sag.

sag (II.), n., fr. prec. Act or process of sagging (in various senses of vb.).

saga, n. [1. sáhga; 2. sā́gə]. O.N., 'thing told, tale, story', cogn. w. O.E. *sagu*, 'a saying', see **saw (III.)** & **say (I.)**. **1.** An ancient Norse prose epic, or narrative, written down and read or recited aloud, dealing with the fights and pedigrees of chiefs and kings of old days, with law, and custom &c. **2.** Any romantic tale of adventure and heroism.

sagacious, adj. [1. sagáshus; 2. səgéiʃəs], fr. Lat. *sagāci-*, stem of *sagax*, 'of quick, acute senses, keen-scented; mentally acute, shrewd', & **-ous**; the word is cogn. w. Lat. *sāgire*, 'to perceive quickly and keenly, to be mentally acute or shrewd', & w. Lat. *sagitta*, 'arrow', see **sagitta** & cp. **seek. 1.** Used by Milton in the special, archaic sense, 'perceiving keenly with the senses', hence, keenly aware of, scenting: (of Death) '*So scented the grim Feature, and upturn'd His nostril wide into the murky air, Sagacious of his quarry*' ('P. L.' x. 279-81). **2.** (of persons) Having keen, acute mental faculties; keenly intelligent, far-seeing, shrewd; of penetrating, practical judgement: *sagacious statesmen, counsellors.* **3.** (of actions, ideas, expression of these) Exhibiting, animated by, arising from, sagacity: *sagacious advice, course of action*; *a sagacious comment, remark.* **4.** (of lower animals) Intelligent, acting as if endowed with reasoning powers: *the sagacious elephant.*

sagaciously, adv. Prec. & **-ly.** In a sagacious manner; with sagacity.

sagacity, n. [1. sagásiti; 2. səgǽsiti]. Fr. *sagacité*, fr. Lat. *sagācitāt-(em)*, *sagācitas*, fr. *sagax.* See **sagacious** & **-ity. a** Quality of being sagacious; possession of keen mental faculties; sound judgement, practical wisdom; shrewdness: *the sagacity of age and experience*; *the cleverness of his speech was recognized, its sagacity was questioned*; **b** intelligence, quality resembling reason in lower animals.

sagamore, n. [1. ságamōr; 2. sǽgəmɔ̄], fr. N. Am. Indian, *sagamo.* Sachem, q.v.

sage (I.), n. [1. sāj; 2. seidž]. M.E. *sauge*, *sawge*, fr. O. Fr. *sauge*, fr. *saulge*, fr. Lat. *salvia*, fr. *salvus*, 'safe, whole', the herb having healing properties, see **salvage** & **Salvia.** A shrubby garden herb, *Salvia officinalis*, with bitter, aromatic taste; used in combination with onions for stuffing roast pork and duck.

sage (II.), adj. Fr., fr. Low Lat. **sabius*, form of **sapius*, wh. occurs in Lat. only in compound *nesapius*, 'foolish', fr. Lat. *sapere*, 'to be wise', see **sapient. 1.** (of persons) **a** Wise, having sound powers of judgement, based on experience; far-seeing, judicious, sagacious: *sage counsellors*; **b** (of appearance &c., often ironical) wise-looking, solemn, serious: *he looks as sage as an owl.* **2.** (of judgement, actions &c.) Characterized by wisdom and sagacity: *sage advice.*

sage (III.), n., fr. prec. **a** A sage, wise person; one venerable for his years, gravity, and wisdom; *the sage*, term often applied by Boswell to Dr. Johnson; *The Seven Sages*, seven early Greek philosophers, of the 6th cent. B.C., to each of whom was attributed a wise saying; e.g. to Solon, 'know thyself'; Cleobulus, 'the golden mean', Pittacus, 'take time by the forelock' &c.; also **b** (iron.) a learned pedant; pundit; person who takes himself too seriously.

sage-brush, n. **sage (I.)** & **brush (I.)**. A low-growing shrub, with aromatic, pungent leaves, genus *Artemisia*, growing profusely on the barren, alkaline plains of N. America.

sage-cock, also **sage-grouse**, n. A large N. American grouse, *Centrocercus urophasianus*, which feeds on the aromatic buds of the sage-brush.

sagely, adv. [1. sā́jli; 2. séidžli]. **sage (II.)** & **-ly.** In a sage manner; wisely, prudently, sagaciously; discreetly.

sageness, n. [1. sā́jnes; 2. séidžnis]. See prec. & **-ness.** Quality of being sage; wisdom, sagacity.

sage-tea, n. An infusion of the leaves of the herb sage, used by herbalists as a tonic and astringent drink.

sagger, saggar, n. [1. ságer; 2. sǽgə]. Etymol. doubtful; provinc. form is *saggard*; perh. a contraction of **safeguard. 1.** Vessel or case of fireclay in which fine pottery or porcelain is enclosed for baking. **2.** (metal.) Box or case in which cast-iron can be decarbonized and rendered malleable.

sagitta, n. [1. sajíta; 2. sædžítə]. Lat., 'arrow'; fr. a base **sāg-*, meaning 'sharp', though usually referring to mental acuteness; cp. Lat. *sāgus*, 'prophetic'; *sagax*, see **sagacious**; *sāgire*, 'to perceive quickly'; cogn. w. Goth. *sōkjan*, 'to seek', see **seek**, & w. O.E. *sacu*, 'dispute' &c. See **sake. 1.** (astron., cap.) A small constellation in northern hemisphere. **2.** Kind of marine worm; also called *arrow-worm.*

sagittal, adj. [1. sájital; 2. sǽdžitəl]. Prec. & **-al.** Arrow-shaped, esp. (anat.) of a suture in the skull.

Sagittarius, n. [1. sàjitárius; 2. sædžitéəriəs]. Lat., 'archer', **sagitta** & *-ārius*, see **-ary.** (astron.) A southern constellation and sign of the Zodiac, 'the Archer', representing the centaur Chiron as an archer.

sagittate(d), adj. [1. sájitāt(ed); 2. sǽdžiteit(id)]. **sagitta** & **-ate.** (bot., of leaves) Shaped like the head of an arrow.

sago, n. [1. sā́gō; 2. séigou]. Malay. *sāgu.* The starchy pith of certain palms of the Malay Archipelago; it is mixed with water and granulated and used for milk puddings; also for stiffening calico and other textiles.

Sahara, n. [1. sahháhra; 2. sāhā́rə], fr. Arab. *ṣaḥra*, 'desert'. **1.** The great desert of North Africa, stretching from the Atlantic almost to the Nile and from the Atlas Mts. almost to the Niger. **2.** (not cap.) **a** Any great, arid, sterile, or desert country or area: *a sahara of ice and snow*; **b** (fig.) something dreary, uninteresting or sterile: *the sahara of dead theological controversy.*

Saharan, Saharian, Saharic, adjs. [1. sahháhran, -ian, -ik; 2. sāhā́rən, -iən, -ik]. Prec. & **-an, -ian, -ic.** Pertaining to the Sahara; pertaining to desert life, conditions &c.; arid, dry, sterile.

sahib, n. [1. sah-ib; 2. sāib]. Hind. & Arab. *ṣāḥib*, 'companion, lord, master'; fem. *ṣahiba.* **1.** (cap.) The title used in India in addressing, or speaking of, men of rank and position, equivalent to sir, lord; following the name or rank: *Raja Sahib*; *the Colonel Sahib*; *Smith Sahib.* **2.** Specif., British or European gentleman or officer: *the rule of the sahibs.* Phr. *a pucka sahib*, a genuine European of ruling class; hence, a well-bred, honourable gentleman.

said (I.), adj. [1. sed; 2. sed]. P.P. of **say (I.)**; see next word. Before-mentioned, aforesaid, usually in legal documents: *the said A. B.*; *the said premises* &c.

said (II.), vb. Pret. & P.P. of **say (I.)**. O.E. Pret. *sæ̆gde*, *sǣde*; P.P. *(ġe)sæġd*, *(ġe)-sǣd*; M.E. *seid*, *sed(e).*

saiga, n. [1. sā́ga, síga; 2. séigə, sáigə]. Russ., fr. the native Tatar name. An **antelope**, *Saiga tatarica*, having spiral horns and a curious puffed nose, found on the steppes of Asiatic Russia.

sail (I.), n. [1. sāl; 2. seil]. O.E. *seġel*, *seġl*, M.E. *seil*, *seyl*; Common Gmc., O.H.G. *segal*, O.N. *segl*; Germ. & Swed. *segel*, Du. *zeil.* **1.** A piece of thick canvas or other cloth, forming part of a ship's rigging, so arranged as to catch the wind and to cause the vessel to move forward. Phrs. *in full sail*, with all sails set; *under sail*, with sails set, sailing; *to clap on sail*; *crowd sail*, to set every sail possible; *to hoist, set sail*, to spread, unfurl the sails; to start on a voyage; used both of the vessel and of persons carried: *the Majestic set sail yesterday*; *we set sail tomorrow*; *to lower, strike sails*, to furl, reef sails when voyage is over or when vessel is lying to; *to shorten, take in sail*, to reef and lessen the amount of sail spread; (also fig.) to restrain, moderate activities &c.; *to take the wind out of the sails of*, **a** to steer a ship between the wind and another ship so that the latter's sails are useless; **b** to surprise and defeat an opponent by anticipating his attack, confuting his arguments in advance and utilizing such material &c. as he was prepared to use. **2. a** A ship, esp. a sailing vessel: *not a sail in sight*; *a sail on the starboard bow*; *sail ho!*, call when a ship is sighted; **b** (coll.) ships, vessels: *a fleet of 30 sail.* **3.** One of various objects which resemble a sail in function or shape; **a** one of the revolving parts of a windmill which catch and are driven by the wind; **b** device used to catch the wind and ventilate a mine or a ship's hold &c.; **c** the dorsal fin of the sail-fish; the membranous tentacle of the nautilus.

sail (II.), vb. intrans. & trans., fr. prec. O.E. *seġelian*, *seġlian.* **A.** intrans. **1.** (of vessel) **a** Specif., to move along on the surface of the sea, a lake or river, by means of the driving power of the wind on the sails; **b** (of steamers &c.) to float along, travel, in the water: *the Aquitania is one of the largest ships that sail*; **c** (of swans &c.) to glide in a stately manner through the water. **2.** (of all vessels, however driven) **a** To start on a sea voyage: *the Armada sailed from Lisbon on May 20th, 1588*; *the Lusitania sailed on her last voyage in May 1915*; **b** to move, be handled, on the water: *the new yacht sails well, heavily, fast* &c. **3.** (of persons) To travel in, and more esp., to handle, manage, steer &c. a sailing vessel in the water; to practise the art of seamanship in a sailing vessel: *I used to sail on the Forth a good deal as a boy.* **4. a** To embark, begin a voyage, start on a sea trip (in a vessel of any kind): *I sail tomorrow by the Cunard line*; **b** (of cargo) to be despatched by sea: *the goods sailed yesterday from Bristol.* Phrs. *to sail near the wind*, (i.) to steer a sailing vessel as nearly against the wind as will allow way; (ii.) (fig.) to go as close as possible to incurring the charge of breaking a law, rule of conduct, moral principle &c. without actually doing so; (colloq. and fig.) *sail in*, to take decisive action, act, intervene, with confidence, and effect: *to sail in and settle the dispute at once.* **5.** (of birds and aircraft) To pass, float, fly, steadily and easily through the air: *a flock of herons sailed over our heads*; *the great airship sailed over London unharmed.* **6.** (of persons) To move, walk, in a stately, important manner, like a ship in full sail: *to sail into the room.* **B.** trans. **1. a** (of vessels or persons) To pass, move on, over, across, through: esp. *to sail the sea*; **b** (of birds, aeroplanes &c.) *to sail the air.* **2.** To handle, steer, navigate (a ship).

sail (III.), n., fr. prec. A trip in a sailing vessel, a cruise: *fine day for a sail, sir!*; *a few hours' sail.*

sailcloth, n. [1. sálklawth; 2. séilklɔ̄þ]. Canvas for making sails, of flax or cotton, or a mixture of both, or of hemp or ramie fibre.

sailed, adj. [1. sāld; 2. seild]. P.P. of **sail (II.)**. Having sails, of specified kind: *heavy-, light-sailed vessel.*

sailer, n. [1. sáler; 2. séilə]. **sail (II.)** & **-er.** A vessel propelled by sails; contrasted with *steamer*; or preceded by an adjective: *a good, fast, slow sailer.*

sail-fish, n. Name given to certain fishes which have a very large dorsal fin, esp. **a** a genus of sword-fish, *Histiophorus*, the fin being raised above the water, thus aiding movement; **b** the basking shark.

sailing (I.), adj. [1. sáling; 2. séiliŋ], fr. Pres. Part. of **sail (II.)**. **1.** Moved by sails and wind: *sailing ship, boat* &c. **2.** Dealing with, concerned with, sailing or other vessels: *sailing instructions, orders*, directions or orders issued to the master of a ship as to the voyage; also, orders to sail, to start on a voyage; *sailing master*, master, skipper, or navigating officer.

sailing (II.), vbl. n., fr. **sail (II.)**. **1.** Act of a person who sails; **a** act of one who navigates, handles a sailing vessel; **b** act of one who travels in sailing boat. Phr. *plain sailing*, (i.) originally, *plane sailing*, sailing by a plane chart, a simple form of navigation; (ii.) any task, undertaking &c.. that is simple and straightforward. **2. a** Progress made by a vessel under sail: *sailing was bad near the coast*; **b** departure, start, of a vessel on a voyage: *weekly sailings to the Cape*; *hours of sailing will be announced daily.*

sailmaker, n. [1. sálmàker; 2. séilmèikə]. One who makes and repairs ships' sails.

sailor, n. [1. sáler; 2. séilə]. **sail (II.)** & **-or** instead of **-er**, on anal. of *tailor*. **1. a** One who sails on a ship; one whose occupation is at sea on board a ship; a mariner, seaman; **b** specif., a common seaman, below the rank of petty officer: *a sailor before the mast*; *the sailor's life.* **2.** A person who travels on a ship, regarded as liable or not liable to sea-sickness: *a bad, a wretched, a good, sailor.*

sailor hat, n. **a** A hat only so called (formerly) when worn by women; one made of stiff straw, with flat top and brim; known simply as a straw hat when worn by men; also, **b** hat of straw with wide, pliable brim, formerly worn by sailors and also by children.

sailoring, n. [1. sálering; 2. séiləriŋ]. **sailor** & **-ing.** The life, business, of a sailor.

sailorlike, adj. [1. sálerlīk; 2. séiləlaik]. **sailor** & **-like.** In sailor fashion; after the manner of a sailor.

sailorly, adj. [1. sálerli; 2. séiləli]. **sailor** & **-ly.** (rare) Sailorlike.

sailorman, n. [1. sálerman; 2. séiləmæn]. (colloq.) Sailor, mariner.

sailors' home, n. An institution at a seaport where sailors may board and lodge more cheaply and in better and safer conditions than in the ordinary boarding-houses.

sailor's knot, n. A loose slip-knot used in tying a necktie.

sain, vb. trans. [1. sān; 2. sein]. O.E. *segnian*, 'to make sign of cross on, to bless'; fr. Lat. *signāre*, 'to sign, mark'; M.E. *seinen, sainen.* See **sign.** (archaic, Scots, and Nthn. dial.) To make the sign of the cross on or over; to bless, consecrate, esp. as protection against evil.

sainfoin, n. [1. sánfoin; 2. sǽnfɔin]. Fr., fr. *sain*, 'wholesome, healthy', fr. Lat. *sānus*, see **sane**, & *foin*, 'hay', fr. Lat. *faenum, fēnum*, 'hay', the etymol. of wh. is doubtful. A low-growing perennial leguminous plant, *Onobrychis sativa*, with long pinnate leaves and pink flowers, cultivated as fodder for sheep and cows.

saint (I.), n. [1. sānt; 2. seint]. M.E., fr. O. Fr. *seint* &c., fr. Lat. *sanctus*, 'holy'. See **sanctus** & **sacred. 1.** Specif. **a** a person recognized and venerated by the Christian Church as having gained Paradise, either from the known sanctity of his life, his services to religion, or by the manner of his death, if this was by martyrdom; among certain proofs of such sanctity is the working of miracles, revealed either during life, or after death at place of burial. Such persons after due inquiries by the authorities are canonized, and their aid and intercession was and is invoked by the faithful; **b** the Apostles, the ancient Bishops, and Fathers of the Christian Church; **c** (cap.) title, usually abbreviated to St. or S., placed before name of an apostle &c. or of a canonized person; such a title is pronounced without stress as [1. sn; 2. sən] before consonants, [1. snt; 2. sənt] before vowels, the stress falling on the name which follows: *St. Edmond, St. Peter, St. John, St. Thomas à Becket* &c.=[sənt édmənd, sən pítə, sən dʒɔ́n, sən tɔ́məs ə békit] &c.; **d** *St. Peter's, St. Paul's, St. Anne's* &c., as names of churches, colleges &c., referring to the saints to whom they are dedicated; **e** *St. Asaph, St. David's* &c., names of places named after saints. **2.** (pl.) *The saints, the blessed saints* &c., the faithful departed who died in a state of grace and are believed to be with God. **3.** A person of great purity and sanctity of life, who exhibits remarkable piety and meekness. Phr. *enough to try the patience of a saint*, exceedingly exasperating, aggravating, intolerable.

saint (II.), vb. trans., fr. prec. **1.** (obs. or rare) **a** To address as saint; **b** to call blessings of the saints upon. **2.** (rare, except in P.P. as adj., see **sainted**) To canonize; to regard as a saint.

St. Andrew's cross, n. [1. snt ándrōōz kráws; 2. sənt ǽndrūz krɔ́s]. A cross shaped like the letter X; as blazoned, **a** white cross on a blue ground.

St. Anthony's fire, n. [1. snt ántuniz fīr; 2. sənt ǽntəniz fáiə]. Erysipelas.

St. Bernard, n. [1. sn bérnard; 2. sən bə́nəd]. A breed of large and very intelligent dogs, of the mastiff type, usually a light reddish brown and white, or quite white in colour, and with curly hair; originally bred by the monks of the Hospice at the top of the Great St. Bernard Pass, Switzerland, and trained to search for and rescue travellers lost in the snow.

saintdom, n. [1. sántdum; 2. séintdəm]. **saint (I.)** & **-dom.** State of being a saint; canonization, sainthood.

sainted, adj. [1. sánted; 2. séintid], fr. obs. **saint (II.)**, & **-ed.** Venerated, regarded as a saint: *the sainted dead*; regarded as sacred: *a sainted place.*

St. Elmo's fire, n. [1. snt élmōz fīr; 2. sənt élmouz fáiə]. A discharge of electricity seen as a flame at the head of masts at sea; also called *corposant*; St. Elmo is the patron saint of sailors.

St. George's cross, n. [1. sn jórjiz kráws; 2. sən dʒɔ́dʒiz krɔ́s]. A red Greek cross on a white ground, as flown by the Royal Navy.

sainthood, n. [1. sánt-hood; 2. séinthud]. **saint (I.)** & **-hood.** Saintdom, saintship.

St. James's, n. [1. sn jámziz; 2. sən dʒéimziz]. Name of the old Tudor palace of the kings of England. *Court of St. James's*, official title of British Court to which ambassadors from foreign powers are accredited.

St. John of Jerusalem, n. [1. sn jón uv jerōōsalem; 2. sən dʒɔ́n əv dʒirúsələm]. Order of knighthood, one of the great crusading orders of military monks, the Hospitallers, also called Knights of Malta; the English branch survives as an organization for Red Cross work in war and for ambulance and hospital work generally.

St. John's wort, n. [1. sn jónz wért; 2. sən dʒɔ́nz wə̀t]. A low-growing, perennial, evergreen herb, *Hypericum perforatum*, with oval leaves and bright yellow flowers.

St. Leger, n. [1. sn léjer; 2. sən lédʒə]. A horse-race, run at Doncaster, Yorks, in September, named after the founder.

saintlike, adj. [1. sántlīk; 2. séintlaik]. Like a saint; saintly, holy.

saintliness, n. [1. sántlines; 2. séintlinis]. **saintly** & **-ness.** Quality, condition, of being saintly; piety, holiness of life.

saintly, adj. [1. sántli; 2. séintli]. **saint (I.)** & **-ly.** Like a saint; saintlike, holy.

St. Luke's summer, n. [1. sn lōōks súmer; 2. sən l(j)ūks sámə]. See **summer.**

St. Martin's summer, n. [1. mártinz súmer; 2. sən mátinz sámə]. See **summer.**

saintship, n. [1. sántship; 2. séintʃip]. **saint (I.)** & **-ship.** State, quality, of a saint; saintdom, sainthood.

Saint-Simonism, n. [1. sn símunizm; 2. sən sáimənizəm], fr. Comte de Saint-Simon, French economist (1760–1825). A socialist system of state management, and ownership of property, with division of the product among the workers according to value of the work they do.

St. Stephen's, n. [1. sn stévenz; 2. sən stívənz]. The House of Commons, so named from the ancient chapel of St. Stephen, attached to the Royal Palace of Westminster, in which the House used to sit.

St. Valentine's day, n. [1. sn válentīnz dā; 2. sən vǽləntainz dèi]. The 14th of February, on which it was formerly the custom to send letters, cards, and other love-tokens to one's lady-love.

St. Vitus's dance, n. [1. sn vítusiz dáhns; 2. sən váitəsiz dáns]. Popular name for chorea, a disease characterized by involuntary movements of the muscles.

sake, n. [1. sāk; 2. seik]. O.E. *sacu*, 'dispute, quarrel; fighting, strife; persecution, affliction; jurisdiction in lawsuits'; M.E. *sāke*; O.H.G. *sahha*, 'strife, cause of dispute; lawsuit; affair, thing'; cp. Mod. Germ. *sache*, 'thing, object, affair'; O.S. *saka*; Goth. *sakjō*, 'strife, quarrel'; cp. O.E. *sacan*, 'to quarrel; to accuse'; further related to Goth. *sōkjan*, 'to seek', O.E. *sēcan*, see **seek**; cp. also **sagacious. 1.** The old meaning, 'lawsuit, jurisdiction', is preserved in the word **sac (II.)**. **2.** Chiefly, *for my, his &c. sake*; or, *for the sake of* . . . In present usage the sense is extremely vague and general; the word survives only in a few phrases in which the meaning is: **a** cause, advantage, behalf: *do it for my sake*, because I need, desire, it; thus the phrase comes to mean for love of, out of consideration for, me; *for the sake of our old friendship*, because of, bearing in mind &c.; also *for God's sake* (*do it, don't do it*) &c., for the love of God do it, on no account do it; *for goodness', mercy's, sake*, in same sense; **b** aim, purpose, ground; in order to secure: *for the sake of money, of peace and quiet*; *for safety('s) sake*; in the interests of: *for the sake of order and decency.*

saké, n. [1. sáhkā; 2. sáki]. Jap. The national alcoholic drink of Japan, obtained by fermentation of rice.

saker, n. [1. sáker; 2. séikə], fr. Fr. *sacre*; Span. & Port. *sacre*, cp. Ital. *sagro*, fr. Arab. *çaqr*, 'hawk'. (archaic) **1.** A species of falcon, *Falco sacer*, used in hawking; chiefly of female bird, which is larger than the male. **2.** A small cannon of the 16th and 17th cents.

sakeret, n. [1. sàkerét; 2. sèikərét]. Prec. & dimin. **-et.** Name applied to the male of the saker, which was smaller than the female.

saki, n. [1. sáhki; 2. sáki]. Native name. A South American monkey, *Pithecia*, with non-prehensile tail, long dark hair, and yellowish-white face and neck-ruff.

sakia, n. [1. sáhkia; 2. sákiə], fr. Arab. *sāqiya.* An Oriental water-wheel, used for irrigation purposes.

sal (I.), n. [1. sal; 2. sæl]. Lat. *sāl*, genit. *sălis* 'salt'; perh. simplified fr. **salt-*, fr. **saldo-* cp. Gmc. cognates wh. end in *-t* &c. under **salt.** Chemical name for any of various salts.

sal (II.), **saul**, n. [1. sahl, sawl; 2. sāl, sɔ̄l]. Hind. *sāl.* An Eastern tree, producing tough, close-grained timber.

salaam, n. & vb. intrans. [1. saláhm; 2. səlám]. Arab. *salām*, 'saluting, salutation, peace', cp. **Islam** & **Moslem. 1.** n. **a** A salutation, mode of greeting used in the East, esp. among Moslems, which consists in uttering the word *salām*, 'peace', and bowing low with the palm of the right hand pressed against the forehead; hence, **b** the uttered greeting itself; **c** an obeisance. **2.** vb. To make a salaam; to bow and utter the word *salaam.*

salability, n. [1. sàlabíliti; 2. sèiləbíliti]. Next word & **-ity**. Quality, condition, of being salable; salableness.

salable, adj. [1. sálabl; 2. séiləbl]. **sale** & **-able**. **1. a** Of such a nature or quality, or in such a condition, as will attract purchasers; **b** actually in demand. **2.** (of price) In proportion to the value of the article, not extortionate, such as will find someone ready to pay it.

salableness, n. Prec. & **-ness**. Salability.

salacious, adj. [1. saláshus; 2. səléiʃəs], fr. Lat. *salāci-*, stem of *salax*, lit. 'leaping', hence, of goats and other animals, 'lustful', fr. *salīre*, 'to leap; of animals, to cover', see **salient**, & **-ious**. **a** (of persons) Lewd, lustful, lecherous; **b** (of speech, books, pictures &c.) expressing, dealing with, lewd thoughts and subjects.

salaciously, adv. Prec. & **-ly**. In a salacious manner.

salaciousness, n. See prec. & **-ness**. Quality of being salacious; salacity.

salacity, n. [1. salásiti; 2. səléisiti]. Lat. *salācitāt-(em)*, fr. stem of **salacious**, & **-ity**. Salaciousness.

salad, n. [1. sálad; 2. sǽləd], fr. Fr. *salade*, fr. O. Ital. *salata*, or Port. *salada*, 'something salted or pickled', fr. Lat. *sal*, **salt**. **a** Any of various cold dishes composed of lettuce or other vegetables, raw or cooked, flavoured with onion, and mixed with oil and vinegar; also lobster dressed with piquant sauce and garnished with lettuce &c.; **b** lettuce itself, as forming chief ingredient of a salad. Phr. *salad days*, age of youth and inexperience.

salad dressing, n. Sauce used in salads.

salade, n. See **sallet**.

salamander, n. [1. sálamànder; 2. sǽləmæ̀ndə], fr. Fr. *salamandre*, fr. Lat. *salamandra*, fr. Gk. *salamándra*, prob. of Pers. origin, cp. Pers. *samander*, *samandel*. **1. a** A kind of lizard which was supposed to exist in fire without being burnt; **b** (fig.) a person who can stand and who enjoys heat. **2.** Iron plate, with long handle, heated and held over food to brown it. **3.** (zool.) A genus, *Salamandra*, of tailed batrachians, of Europe, Africa, and West Asia; allied to the newts.

salamandrian, **salamandrine**, adj. [1. sàlamándrian, -drīn; 2. sæ̀ləmǽndriən, -drain]. Prec. & **-ian**, **-ine**. **a** Resembling, of the nature of, a salamander; **b** living in, resisting, fire.

salamandroid, adj. [1. sàlamándroid; 2. sæ̀ləmǽndrɔid]. **salamander** & **-oid**. (zool.) Resembling the genus of salamanders.

salame, n. [1. sálamā; 2. sǽləmei]. Ital., fr. **sal (I.)**. A highly seasoned and salted Italian sausage.

sal-ammoniac, n. [1. sál amóniak; 2. sǽl əmóuniæk]. **sal (I.)** & **ammoniac**. Chemical substance, colourless and odourless, having strong salt taste; used medicinally; known also as *ammonium chloride*.

salangane, n. [1. sálanggān; 2. sǽləŋgein]. Fr., fr. Malay. word. Any of various species of swifts of the Far East which build the edible birds' nests, prized by the Chinese.

salaried, adj. [1. sálarid; 2. sǽlərid], fr. P.P. of **salary (II.)**. (of person) Receiving a salary; (of post) having a salary attached to it.

salary (I.), n. [1. sálari; 2. sǽləri], fr. A.-Fr. *salarie*, fr. Lat. *salārium*, 'money paid to a soldier in lieu of his allowance of salt (Lat. *sal*), soldier's pay; stipend, salary'. See **sal (I.)** & **salt**. A payment made for a stipulated time and paid at stated periods, usually monthly, quarterly, half-yearly, or yearly, for services other than manual or mechanical labour, remunerated by daily or weekly *wages*.

salary (II.), vb. trans., fr. prec. To pay a salary to.

sale, n. [1. sāl; 2. seil]. O.E. *salu* occurs once; cogn. w. **sell**. **1.** Transfer of property of any kind from one person to another, who becomes the owner, on payment of a stipulated price: *goods for, on, sale*, to be sold. **2. a** Act, business, of selling: *no sale took place during the day*; specif. **b** act of offering goods for sale, esp. by auction; **c** the offering of goods for sale at reduced prices in order to clear off old stock: *July is the season of sales.*

Salem, n. [1. sálem; 2. séiləm]. Heb. **1.** A place mentioned in Gen. xiv. 18 as the seat of the kingdom of Melchizedek, very doubtfully identified with Jerusalem, but used as its name in hymns or religious poetry; also given to one of the earliest Puritan settlements in Massachusetts, U.S.A. **2.** A Nonconformist place of worship, a bethel.

salep, n. [1. sálep; 2. sǽlɛp]. Fr., fr. Arab. *sahleb*, *tha'leb*, 'fox', as name of an orchid. Meal obtained from the dried tubers of various kinds of orchid, used as a drug and also as a nutritious food.

saleratus, n. [1. salerātus; 2. sæləréitəs], fr. Neo-Lat. *sal aëratus*, 'aerated salt'. Bicarbonate of soda, used in baking powder.

salesman, n. [1. sálzman; 2. séilzmən]. **sale** & **man**. **a** Person engaged to sell goods either to a customer in a shop, or as a traveller or agent to a retailer; **b** one engaged on the selling side of a business, as advertiser, traveller &c.

salesmanship, n. [1. sálzmanship; 2. séilzmənʃip]. Prec. & **-ship**. **a** Business, art, skill, of a salesman; selling capacity or ability; **b** the marketing or selling of goods.

sale(s)room, n. [1. sál(z)room; 2. séil(z)rum]. Room in which goods are set forth for sale; auction room.

Salic, **-ique**, adj. [1. sálik, salḗk; 2. sǽlik, sælík], fr. Fr. *salique*; fr. *Salii*, name of a Frankish tribe, & **-ic**, **-ique**. Of, pertaining to, the Salian Franks or Merovingians; specif., *Salic law*, **a** an ancient (chiefly penal) code of law of the Salian Franks, which contained a clause prohibiting the inheritance of land by daughters; **b** a constitutional law, forbidding succession of women to the throne, supposed to be based on the ancient law, and so adopted by France and other European countries.

salicet, n. [1. sáliset; 2. sǽlisɛt]. Fr., fr. Lat. *salic-*, 'willow', see **salix**. A reed stop in an organ with delicate flute-like note.

salicin, n. [1. sálisin; 2. sǽlisin]. Fr. *salicine*, fr. Lat. *salic-(em)*, *salix*, 'willow'. See **salix** & **sallow (I.)**. (chem.) The bitter substance obtained in the form of white crystals from the bark and leaves of various species of willow, used medicinally.

salicional, n. [1. salíshunal; 2. sælíʃənəl]. See **salicet** & **-ion** & **-al**. Salicet.

salicyl, n. [1. sálisil; 2. sǽlisil]. Same base as **salicin** & **-yl**. (chem.) The radical of salicylic acid.

salicylate, n. [1. sàlisílāt; 2. sæ̀lisíleit]. Prec. & **-ate**. (chem.) A salt of salicylic acid; esp. *sodium salicylate*, salicylate of soda, used as a specific for acute rheumatism.

salicylic, adj. [1. sàlisílik; 2. sæ̀lisílik]. **salicyl** & **-ic**. (chem.) Of, pertaining to, salicyl or salicin; esp. *salicylic acid*, a crystalline, white acid, formerly obtained from salicin, now from phenol, a coal-tar product, and used medicinally as an antiseptic and antipyretic &c., and as the source of various salicylates, esp. sodium salicylate.

salicylism, n. [1. sàlisílizm; 2. sæ̀lisílizəm]. **salicyl** & **-ism**. Condition produced by excessive consumption of salicylates or salicylic acid.

salience, **-cy**, n. [1. sáliens(i); 2. séiliəns(i)]. **salient** & **-ce**, **-cy**. **1.** Quality of being salient; prominence (in concrete and abstract senses). **2.** Something which is salient; **a** (in physical sense) (i.) a projection, a prominence; (ii.) specif. (mil.) a position or area projecting into, and partly surrounded by, the enemy's lines, but not held by him; **b** (fig.) a characteristic feature, something remarkable, noteworthy &c.

salient (I.), adj. [1. sálient; 2. séiliənt]. Lat. *salient-(em)*, Pres. Part. of *salīre*, 'to leap'; cogn. w. Gk. *hállomai*, 'to spring, leap', & apparently w. Scrt. *ucchalati*, 'rises quickly'; other cognates doubtful. See also **resilient** & **sally (I.)**. **1. a** Jutting, projecting, pointing outwards, contrasted with *re-entering*: *a salient angle*, in a line of trenches; *a salient feature*, in a line of coast, face &c.; **b** (fig.) prominent, conspicuous, noteworthy: *a salient feature in one's character* &c. **2.** (archaic or poet., of water) Leaping, gushing, springing up; also fig., *salient spirits of youth*. **3.** (her., of animals) Depicted as leaping with fore-feet in the air and both hind-feet on the ground, as distinct from *rampant*.

salient (II.), n., fr. prec. A salient, projecting, angle; specif., projection in a line of trenches.

saliently, adv. **salient (I.)** & **-ly**. (chiefly fig.) Remarkably, noticeably.

saliferous, adj. [1. salíferus; 2. səlífərəs]. See **sal (I.)** & **-ferous**. (geol., of strata &c.) Salt-bearing; containing, producing, salt.

salifiable, adj. [1. sálifìabl; 2. sǽlifàiəbl]. **salify** & **-able**. Capable of being salified.

salification, n. [1. sàlifikáshun; 2. sæ̀lifikéiʃən]. Next word & **-fication**. Act, process, of salifying; state of being salified.

salify, vb. trans. [1. sálifì; 2. sǽlifai]. See **sal (I.)** & **-fy**. To make salty; **a** to impregnate with salt; **b** (chem.) to form a salt, convert into a salt.

saline (I.), adj. [1. sálīn; 2. séilain]. **sal (I.)** & **-ine**. Salty, impregnated with salt; containing common salt or any of the various chemical, metallic, alkaline, salts, as potassium, magnesium, salts &c.: *a saline marsh, draught*; *the water is saline, has a saline taste* &c.

saline (II.), n. [1. sálīn, salín; 2. séilain, səláin]. See prec., & cp. Lat. *salīnae*, 'salt marshes', *salīnum*, 'salt-cellar'. **1.** A salt-marsh, salt-pan. **2.** (chem.) A metallic, alkaline salt. **3.** A saline draught, used medicinally as aperient or febrifuge.

salinity, n. [1. salíniti; 2. sælíniti]. **saline (I.)** & **-ity**. Saltness; amount of salt in a solution.

salinometer, n. [1. sàlinómeter; 2. sæ̀linɔ́mitə]. See prec. & *-o-* & **-meter**. Device for ascertaining degree of salinity of a solution.

Salique, adj. See **Salic**.

saliva, n. [1. salíva; 2. səláivə]. Lat.; said to be cogn. w. O.E. *salo*, *salowig*, 'dark-coloured', wh. seems improbable. The fluid excreted by the salivary glands of the mouth, which aids in the digestion of starchy foods.

salivary, adj. [1. sálivari; 2. sǽlivəri]. Lat. *salīvārius*, 'slimy, clammy'. Prec. & **-ary**. Connected with, pertaining to, saliva; esp. *salivary glands*, those which secrete saliva.

salivate, vb. trans. & intrans. [1. sálivāt; 2. sǽliveit], fr. Lat. *salīvāt-(um)*, P.P. of *salīvāre*, 'to spit, discharge saliva; to salivate'. **1.** trans. To produce excessive flow of saliva in (a person). **2.** intrans. To secrete an excessive amount of saliva.

salivation, n. [1. sàliváshun; 2. sæ̀livéiʃən]. Prec. & **-ion**. **a** Act, process, of salivating; **b** condition of being salivated.

salix, n. [1. sáliks; 2. sǽliks]. Lat., 'willow'; cogn. w. O.E. *sealh*, 'willow'. See **sallow (I.)**. (bot.) A genus of trees and shrubs which includes the willow, osier, and sallow.

salle, n. [1. sal, sahl; 2. sæl, sāl]. Fr., fr. Ital. *sala*, 'hall'; of Gmc. origin; cp. O.H.G. *sal*, 'house, hall'; O.E. *sæl*, & *sele* (fr. **sæli*); cogn. w. Lat. *solum*, 'ground, soil; foundation; pavement', see **soil (I.)**. A large room. *Salle-à-manger*, partially anglicized [1. sál a monzhā; 2. sǽl ə mɑ̃žei], the public dining-room of a hotel, coffee-room. *Salle d'armes*, [1. sál dárm; 2. sǽl dɑ̄m], Fr., 'fencing-school'. *Salle d'attente* [1. sál datáhnt; 2. sæl dætɑ̃t], Fr., 'waiting-room'.

sallenders, n. pl. [1. sálenderz; 2. sǽlindəz]. Cp. Fr. *solandres*; etymol. unknown. A dry waxy eruption on a horse's hock.

sallet, **salade**, n. [1. sálet, saláhd; 2. sǽlit, səlā́d], fr. Fr. *salade*; etymol. doubtful; Ital. has *celata*, for this kind of helmet; prob. fr. Lat. *caelāt-(um)*, P.P. stem of *caelāre*, 'to engrave, chase', fr. *caelum*, 'chisel', for **caed-*

lom, fr. base of *caedere,* 'to strike, cut'. See **cement.** (anct. armour) A bowl-shaped, close-fitting helmet with projecting neck-guard and coming low down over the forehead; somewhat similar in shape to the modern English steel shrapnel helmet or 'tin-hat'.

sallow (I.), n. [1. sálō; 2. sǽlou]. O.E. *sealh,* M.E. *salwe, salewe;* O.H.G. *salaha,* O.N. *selja;* cogn. w. **salix;** Gk. *heliké,* 'willow'. A species of willow, *Salix caprea,* of low, shrubby growth and with broad leaves.

sallow (II.), adj. & n. O.E. *salu,* M.E. *salow,* cp. O.H.G. *salo,* 'dark coloured, dusky', M.H.G. *sal,* whence Fr. *sale,* 'dirty', O.N. *sölr,* 'yellowish'; cogn. w. O. Slav. *slavočije,* 'greyness'. **1.** adj. (of complexion) Yellowish in colour; contrasted with *ruddy.* **2.** n. (rare) A pale, sickly yellow colour.

sallowish, adj. [1. sálōish; 2. sǽlouiʃ]. Prec. & **-ish.** Rather sallow.

sallowness, n. [1. sálōnes; 2. sǽlounis]. See prec. & **-ness.** Yellow, sickly colour or complexion.

sally (I.), n. [1. sáli; 2. sǽli], fr. Fr. *saillie,* fem. of *sailli,* P.P., as n., of *saillir,* 'to come, issue, forth suddenly', earlier, 'to leap, dance', fr. Lat. *salīre,* 'to leap'. See **salient. 1.** (mil.) A sudden rush made by troops from a besieged town or fortress to attack the besieging forces; a sortie. **2.** (fig.) A lively flight of wit or fancy; a quip.

sally (II.), vb. intrans., fr. prec. *Sally forth, out;* **a** (mil.) to make a sally; **b** to set out on an excursion; to come, go, out of doors: *let us sally forth and look at the town.*

Sally (III.), n. Familiar for *Sarah.* See **Aunt Sally.**

Sally Lunn, n. [1. sáli lún; 2. sǽli lán], fr. the name of the itinerant vendor in Bath who first made these articles. (archaic) A kind of tea-cake.

sally-port, n. **sally** (I.) & **port** (III.). A small concealed postern gate in the walls of a fortress through which sallies can be made.

salmagundi, n. [1. sàlmagúndi; 2. sǽlməgándi]. Fr. *salmigondis;* etymol. doubtful. Dish consisting of chopped meat, eggs &c., seasoned with onions and anchovies.

salmi, n. [1. sálmi; 2. sǽlmi]. Fr.; prob. shortened form of prec. A stew of game, esp. of birds, with highly seasoned sauce.

salmon, n. [1. sámun; 2. sǽmən]. M.E. *saumoun,* fr. O. Fr. *saumon,* fr. Lat. *salmōn-(em),* prob. 'the leaping fish', fr. base of *salīre,* 'to leap', see **salient** (I.). **1. a** A large fish, of which there are several species, abounding in the N. Atlantic and adjacent waters and coasts; each breeding season it comes up from the sea into rivers and lakes to spawn, returning later to the sea; the salmon has silvery skin, and pale red or pink flesh, of firm consistency and delicate flavour; special names, as *parr, smolt, grilse,* are given to it in its various stages of development; **b** also *king salmon,* a fish belonging to the same family, of the N. Pacific; **c** *rock salmon,* fishmonger's name for a large sea blenny. **2.** Silvery pink, or pale red, the colour of the salmon's flesh.

salmon colour, n. & adj. **1.** n. The colour of the salmon's flesh; pink or pale red. **2.** adj. **a** (pred.) *The petals are salmon colour;* **b** also *salmon-coloured: a salmon-coloured rose.*

salmon trout, n. The sea-trout, *Salmo trutta.*

salon, n. [1. sálon; 2. salɔ̃]. Fr., 'reception room', see **salle;** the suff. is Lat. acc. *-ōnem,* see **-oon. 1.** A large hall, reception room; **a** public drawing-room in a hotel; **b** name given to drawing-room in private house in French-speaking countries. **2.** Reception, social gathering, held at regular intervals in private house of a great lady who is a recognized leader of society, esp. such an assembly whose regular guests are notable in the world of intellect, art, literature, politics &c. **3.** Annual exhibition of modern pictures held in Paris, corresponding to that held by the Royal Academy in London.

saloon, n. [1. salóon; 2. səlúːn]. Anglicized variant of prec. **1.** A large reception room; **a** in a hotel; **b** in a large private house; also *grand saloon.* **2.** Any large room set apart for specific public purposes; **a** *dancing saloon, billiard saloon, hair-dresser's saloon* &c.; **b** (U.S.A., before Prohibition) a public-house for sale of drink; **c** (in Engl. usage) usually *saloon bar,* one of the better-class bars in a public-house. **3. a** The main cabin on board a passenger steamer; **b** a large first-class cabin on a passenger steamer; also *saloon cabin;* **c** a large, specially luxurious railway carriage, not divided into compartments, and having separate armchairs instead of fixed seats; also such a compartment fitted with sleeping-berths, or one fitted with chairs and dining-tables; **d** closed motor-car without partition between driver and passengers.

saloop, n. [1. salóop; 2. səlúp]. Variant of **salep.** A hot drink of salep or sassafras.

Salopian, adj. & n. [1. salópian; 2. səlóupiən], fr. *Salop,* 'Shropshire', & **-ian;** M.E. *Saloppesberie, Sloppesberie,* was a Norm.-Fr. corrupt. of O.E. *Scrobbesbyriġ,* Shrewsbury. **1.** adj. **a** Belonging to Shropshire; **b** belonging to Shrewsbury; **c** belonging to Shrewsbury School. **2.** n. **a** Native of Shropshire or of Shrewsbury; **b** former, or present member of Shrewsbury School.

Salpiglossis, n. [1. sàlpiglósis; 2. sǽlpiglósis]. Neo-Lat., fr. Gk. *sálpigx,* 'trumpet', & *glôssa,* 'tongue', see **gloss** (I.). (bot.) A genus of annual plants with brightly coloured trumpet-shaped flowers and tongue-like stigmas.

salsify, salsafy, n. [1. sálsifi; 2. sǽlsifi], fr. Fr. *salsifis,* etymol. doubtful, cp. Ital. *sassefrica.* A biennial plant, cultivated for its long tubular fleshy root, which is used as a vegetable; popularly called *oyster-plant,* from the flavour; *wild salsify* is known as *purple goat's-beard.*

salt (I.), n. [1. sawlt; 2. sɔ̄lt]. O.E. *s(e)alt;* O.S., O.N. *salt;* Goth. *salta;* O.H.G. *salza;* cp. also Lat. *sal* & Gk. *hál-(os), háls,* see **halieutic. 1.** One of many chemical substances; specif., *common salt* or sodium chloride, a white, crystalline substance with sharp, characteristic taste, used as an essential seasoning for animal food, and as a preservative; obtained in natural state from beds, or by evaporation of sea-water. Phrs. *(to take a statement) with a grain of salt,* with qualification, with caution and reserve; *not, hardly, worth one's salt,* good for nothing; *to share a man's bread and salt,* partake of his hospitality; *to put a pinch of salt on his tail,* ironical suggestion how to catch a bird &c. **2.** In Phr. *an old salt,* experienced sailor. **3.** *Salts,* any of various mineral salts used in medicine &c.: *Epsom, Glauber's, salts;* also *smelling salts; a dose of salts,* purgative medicine in form of a salt. **4.** A salt-cellar. Phr. *to sit above, below, the salt,* in superior or inferior position, from old custom in placing guests and retainers at table. **5.** (fig.) **a** That which gives a zest, interest, spice: *adventure is the salt of life to many;* **b** wit, pungency, sharpness of humour; Phr. *Attic salt,* highly refined, pointed wit, expressed with restraint and elegance; **c** (of persons) purifying, ennobling influence; in Phr. *they are the salt of the earth,* cp. Matt. v. 13. **6.** (chem.) **a** Sodium chloride, common salt (see above); **b** any of various compounds formed by replacing the hydrogen of an acid by a metal, indicated by the suffix **-ate** or **-ite; c** the name of various compounds, as used in old chemistry: *salts of lemon,* acid potassium oxalate, used for removing ink or other stains from clothing &c.

salt (II.), adj., fr. prec. Containing, impregnated with, salt; **a** having salt in solution: *salt water, a salt spring;* **b** tasting of, having the flavour or smell of, salt: *the food, water, is too salt; salt breezes;* (fig.) *salt tears,* sorrowful, bitter, tears; **c** preserved in salt, salted: *salt beef, salt cod* &c.; **d** (of soil) flooded with, impregnated by, salt water: *a salt pasture, meadow;* **e** growing in salt soil or water: *salt grasses, salt weeds.*

salt (III.), vb. trans., fr. **salt** (I.), O.E. *sealtan,* cp. Germ. *salzen.* **1.** To flavour with salt. **2. a** To preserve in salt or brine; to pickle; also *salt down,* put in pickle; **b** (colloq., by transf.) to put away or by for safety, to save, especially secretly: *to salt down money, profits, illicit gains* &c. **3.** To sprinkle with salt. **4.** (commerc. slang) **a** *To salt books, receipts* &c., represent profits as greater than they are; **b** *to salt a mine,* to place ore rich in gold, silver &c. where it will be found by prospectors, so as to give false impression of the value of the mine; **c** *to salt prices,* to put fantastically high price on goods with intention of reducing them in order to delude purchasers.

saltant, adj. [1. sáltant, sáwltant; 2. sǽltənt, sɔ́ltənt], fr. Lat. *saltant-(em),* Pres. Part. of *saltāre,* 'to dance, leap', frequent. of *salīre,* 'to leap'. See **salient.** Leaping, dancing; esp. (her.) of animals depicted as leaping or jumping.

saltarello, n. [1. saltarélō; 2. sæltərélou]. Ital. See base of prec. word. **a** A lively Italian or Spanish dance for two people, with a hopping, skipping step; **b** music composed for this dance.

saltation, n. [1. sal-, sawltáshun; 2. sæl-, sɔltéiʃən]. Lat. *saltātiōn-(em),* fr. *saltāt-,* P.P. type of *saltāre.* See **saltant & salient. 1.** A leaping, jumping; dancing with leaping steps. **2.** A sudden change, movement, or development, as if skipping intervening stages: *evolutionary saltation.*

saltatorial, adj. [1. sal-, sawltatórial; 2. sæl-, sɔltətɔ́riəl], fr. next word & **-al.** Saltatory.

saltatory, adj. [1. sál-, sáwltaturi; 2. sǽl-, sɔ́ltətəri]. See **saltation & -ory. 1.** Leaping, jumping: *saltatory exercises, movements.* **2.** (biol.) Changing by sudden variation, not by regular stages of development: *saltatory variation, evolution.*

salt-box, n. Wooden box in which salt is kept for kitchen and other uses.

salt-cake, n. Unpurified sodium sulphate used in glass and soap making.

salt-cat, n. Second element unexplained. **a** A lump of salt from a salt works; **b** a mixture of salt with sand, meal, lime &c. used to attract pigeons.

salt-cellar, n. The first element is in fact tautological, since the second element was orig. *saler,* fr. O. Fr. *salier,* 'salt-box', fr. Lat. *salārium,* see **sal** (I.) & **salary;** this was assimilated to *cellar* in 16th & 17th cents., & the tautological *salt* was added. Small receptacle of silver, glass &c. placed on the table at meals for holding salt; formerly an imposing gold or silver vessel which marked the superior from the inferior guests according as they sat above or below it.

salter, n. [1. sáwlter; 2. sɔ́ltə], fr. **salt** (III.) & **-er. 1.** Dealer in, maker of, salt; workman in a salt works or mine. **2.** A drysalter, q.v.

saltern, n. [1. sáwltërn; 2. sɔ́ltən]. O.E. *sealtærn,* fr. *sealt,* see **salt** (I.), & *ærn,* 'place, chamber' &c., q.v. under **barn. a** A salt-works, where salt is obtained from brine or sea-water by evaporation; **b** a series of ponds filled by sea-water for this process.

salt-horse, salt-junk, n. (sailors' slang) Salt beef, salt meat.

saltier, n. See **saltire.**

saltigrade, adj. & n. [1. sáltigrād; 2. sǽltigreid], fr. Lat. *salt-(um),* P.P. type of *salīre,* 'to leap', see **salient, & grade. 1.** adj. (of spiders) Having legs fitted for jumping or leaping; belonging to the group *Saltigradae.* **2.** n. A jumping spider.

saltimbanco, n. [1. sáltimbángkō; 2. sǽltimbǽŋkou]. Ital., fr. *saltāre,* 'to dance, leap', see **saltant,** *im-,* 'in, on', *banco,* 'bench'; cp. **mountebank.** (obs.) Literally, one who leaps upon a bench; a mountebank.

saltiness, n. [1. sáwltines; 2. sɔ́ltinis]. **salty & -ness.** State, quality, of being salty; esp. the taste of salt.

salting, n. [1. sáwlting; 2. sɔ́ltiŋ]. **salt (I.)** & **-ing**, 'a meadow', a common suff. in Place-Names. A salt-marsh; a meadow or pasture rich in salt, and so good pasture for cattle.

saltire, saltier, n. [1. sál-, sáwltīr; 2. sǽl-, sɔ́ltaiə]. M.E. *sautyre, sautire*, fr. O. Fr. *sautoir*, 'an X-shaped stile, a stirrup; a saltire', fr. L. Lat. *saltārium*, 'stile', *saltātōrium*, 'stirrup', fr. *saltāre*, 'to leap'. See **saltation.** (her.) An ordinary on a shield consisting of a bend dexter and bend sinister crossing one another diagonally in shape of St. Andrew's cross.

saltirewise, adv. [1. sáltīrwīz; 2. sǽltaiəwaiz]. Prec. & **-wise.** In the manner of a saltire, crosswise diagonally.

saltish, adj. [1. sáwltish; 2. sɔ́ltiʃ]. **salt (II.)** & **-ish.** Rather, somewhat, salt.

saltless, adj. [1. sáwltles; 2. sɔ́ltlis]. **salt (I.)** & **-less.** Without salt; not tasting of salt; tasteless, insipid; also (fig.) lacking point and sharpness of wit.

salt-lick, n. **a** A place to which animals resort in order to lick an outcrop of rock-salt; **b** a lump of rock-salt placed for horses and cattle to lick.

salt-marsh, n. Low-lying, marshy ground flooded by the sea and impregnated with salt, yielding rich pasture for cattle; a salting.

saltness, n. [1. sáwltnes; 2. sɔ́ltnis]. **salt (II.)** & **-ness.** Quality, state, of being salt.

salt-pan, n. **a** A pan or other vessel used in obtaining salt by evaporation; **b** a shallow pond or basin filled with sea-water evaporated in salt-making.

saltpetre, n. [1. sawltpéter; 2. sɔltpítə], fr. O. Fr. *salpetre*, fr. L. Lat. *salpetra*, Lat. *sal petrae*, lit. 'salt of the rock or stone', prob. as first found exuding fr. rocks (see **1** below); see **sal (I.)** & *petra*, fr. Gk. *pétra*, 'rock, stone', see **petro-.** **1.** Colourless substance, potassium nitrate or nitre, with a bitter, salty taste, found as a superficial deposit in many hot climates, also obtained by chemical treatment of Chile saltpetre; used as a constituent of gunpowder, as a food preservative and in medicine. Phr. '*villainous saltpetre*', gunpowder (Shakespeare). **2.** Sodium nitrate, *Chile* or *cubic saltpetre*, found in beds in S. America, and known locally as *caliche*, used in making potassium nitrate and for manures &c.

salt-pit, n. Salt-pan.

salt-spoon, n. A very small spoon with deep round bowl for helping oneself to salt.

saltus, n. [1. sáltus; 2. sǽltəs]. Lat., 'a leap', fr. *salt-(um)*, P.P. type of *salīre*, 'to leap'. See **salient.** A sudden change or leap, a break in continuity; esp. **a** in development; **b** in an argument.

salt-water, adj. Belonging to, living in, sea-water, hence, marine: *salt-water fish.*

salt-well, n. A well sunk for the purpose of pumping brine from a salt-mine.

saltwort, n. [1. sáwltwërt; 2. sɔ́ltwʌt]. **salt (I.)** & **wort (I.).** A plant, genus *Salsola*, which grows in salt-marshes or near the sea.

salty, adj. [1. sáwlti; 2. sɔ́lti]. **salt (II.)** & **-y.** Having a salt taste.

salubrious, adj. [1. salúbrius; 2. səljúbriəs], fr. Lat. *salūbris*, 'healthy', fr. *salu-*, base of *salūs*, 'health'. See **salutary.** Promoting, giving, health; healthful, healthy: *salubrious climate, air, situation.*

salubriously, adv. Prec. & **-ly.** In a salubrious, health-giving manner; so as to produce or promote health.

salubriousness, n. See prec. & **-ness.** State, quality, of being salubrious; wholesomeness, healthfulness.

salubrity, n. [1. salúbriti; 2. səljúbriti], fr. Lat. *salūbritāt-(em)*; stem of **salubrious** & **-ity.** State, quality, of being salubrious; salubriousness.

Saluki, n. [1. salóoki; 2. səlúki]. A breed of hunting-dog or hound, of Persia and Arabia, with a silky coat; used for hunting gazelles.

salutary, adj. [1. sálūtari; 2. sǽljut(ə)ri]. Cp. Fr. *salutaire*, fr. Lat. *salūtāris*, fr. *salūt-(em)*, fr. *salūs*, 'health, safety'; cogn. w. *salvus*, 'safe', see **salvage** & **safe.** Health-giving, promoting health and well-being; beneficial, wholesome; used in physical sense, but more commonly in moral sense: *a salutary lesson, warning.*

salutation, n. [1. sàlūtáshun; 2. sæ̀ljutéiʃən]. In M.E. & O. Fr., fr. Lat. *salūtātiōn-(em)*, *salūtātio*, fr. *salūtāt-(um)*, P.P. type of *salūtāre*, 'to greet', see **salute.** **1.** Act of saluting, greeting, or welcoming, expressing goodwill, usually by spoken or written words: *a word of salutation; with many tokens of greeting and salutation;* now more usually replaced by *greeting, welcome.* **2.** Words uttered, gestures made, in greeting, welcoming, or addressing: *he gave a perfunctory salutation as he passed; to utter a cordial salutation; the Angelic Salutation*, Hail Mary, Ave Maria.

salutational, adj. [1. sàlūtáshunal; 2. sæ̀ljutéiʃənəl]. Prec. & **-al.** Of the nature of, pertaining to, a salutation.

salutatory, adj. [1. salútaturi; 2. səljútətəri], fr. Lat. *salūtātōrius*, stem as in **salutation**, & **-ory.** (rare) Containing, expressing, salutations; welcoming, greeting: *a salutatory oration.*

salute (I.), vb. trans. & intrans. [1. salút; 2. səljút], fr. Lat. *salūtāre*, 'to wish health to; to greet, hail; to salute', fr. *salūt-(em)*, stem of *salūs*, 'health, safety', cogn. w. *salvus*, 'whole, healthy, safe'. See **salvage** & **safe.** **A.** trans. **1.** To make a salutation to; to greet, welcome; acknowledge, recognize, by a customary or ceremonial gesture, as by a bow, the raising of the hat, a kiss &c.: '*salute the brethren with a holy kiss*'; *they saluted each other with a frigid bow.* **2.** (mil. and nav.) To make, perform, prescribed act or gesture in honour and acknowledgement of, out of respect for: *to salute one's superior officer, the king's colour as it passes in the street; one ship salutes another; the right to be saluted with 21 guns* &c. **3.** (archaic) To hail, acknowledge: *the people saluted him as king.* **4.** To receive, meet; **a** to accost, receive (persons), in a specified way: *to salute a person with a scowl, with a shower of stones, oaths, with cordiality, a smile* &c.; **b** (of external phenomena, circumstances &c.) to present itself to the senses; to meet, lie before; to assail, fall upon: *a gloomy view saluted us; our ears were saluted by hostile shouts.* **B.** intrans. To perform, make, a salute, esp. in military or naval sense: *soldiers must be taught to salute properly and smartly.*

salute (II.), n., fr. Fr. *salut.* See prec. **1.** Act of saluting or greeting; greeting; act done, gesture made, as expressing recognition, welcome, respect, honour &c.: *to give, return, a salute; he acknowledged their salutes with a bow and smile; a salute to the dead.* **2.** (archaic or humorous) A kiss on hand or cheek at meeting or parting: *to imprint a chaste salute upon her maiden cheek.* **3.** (mil. and nav.) One of various, customary, ceremonial acts; **a** a prescribed, formal, ceremonial gesture made with the hand by soldiers and sailors in meeting an officer of commissioned rank, or by an officer to his superior, and returned by the person saluted; **b** act of presenting arms, performed by a stationary body of troops in saluting an important personage, the colours &c.; **c** act of firing a number of guns, determined by rank of person saluted, from a ship or from a fortress &c.; **d** act of dipping flags, performed by ships in passing each other at sea. Phrs. *at the salute*, standing at attention and saluting with hand or arms; *to take the salute*, to receive, acknowledge, a salute; to be saluted, of person, officer, to whom the salute is made; *royal salute*, of 21 guns. **4.** (fencing) Formal engagement of foils or swords at commencement of a contest.

salvability, n. [1. sàlvabíliti; 2. sæ̀lvəbíliti]. **salvable** & **-ity.** State, quality, of being salvable.

salvable (I.), adj. [1. sálvabl; 2. sǽlvəbl]. **salve (II.)** & **-able.** Capable of being salved, soothed, remedied by a salve.

salvable (II.), adj. **salve (III.)** & **-able.** Capable of being salvaged or rescued from shipwreck or fire &c.

salvage (I.), n. [1. sálvij; 2. sǽlvidž]. O. Fr., fr. O. Fr. *salver*, Fr. *sauver*, 'to save', fr. Lat. *salvāre*, 'to save', fr. *salvus*, 'safe, unhurt, sound'; cogn. w. Lat. *salūt-*, stem of *salūs*, 'sound, safe condition, health; welfare' &c., see **salute** & **salutary**; cogn. w. Scrt. *sarvaś*, 'uninjured, whole'. See suff. **-age.** **1. a** The saving or rescue of a ship, her crew, and cargo by another vessel from wreck, fire, or other peril of the sea, such as disablement, abandonment &c.; also (in war) from capture or destruction by the enemy's forces: *a brave act of salvage; little hope of salvage;* **b** compensation, reward, paid by the owners or insurers of the vessel salved to the owner, master, and crew of the rescuing vessel (*the salvors*), either as agreed by the parties or on award by the Court of Admiralty; *salvage money*, money so paid as reward for saving a vessel. **2.** Ship, cargo &c. so saved or salvaged: *the ship is now in port and held as salvage by the insurers.* **3.** The raising, recovery, of a sunk or wrecked ship and her cargo by divers and various apparatus, specially built vessels &c.: *salvage company*, one that contracts to supply such vessels &c. for the salvage of wrecks. **4.** (of property or land) **a** Rescue of goods or other property, usually as insured, from damage or loss by fire; **b** property so rescued or preserved; **c** amount paid for such rescue, or deducted as their value from insurance to be paid. **5. a** The saving and utilization of waste material of all kinds: *some enterprising towns have now a department for salvage;* **b** (fig.) rescue (of persons) from crime, poverty &c.; persons so rescued: *devoted persons engaged in salvage in the slums; the salvage of the streets.*

salvage (II.), vb. trans., fr. prec. To save from wreck, fire, capture &c.; to make salvage of: *to salvage a ship, her cargo* &c.

salvage corps, n. A special corps, attached to a fire brigade, but paid by a Fire Insurance Company, whose duty it is to save goods insured from damage or destruction at a fire.

salvarsan, n. [1. sálvarsàn; 2. sǽlvəsæ̀n]. Coined word, fr. Lat. *salv-(us)*, 'safe, whole', see **salvage**, & **arsenic.** (med.) A compound of arsenic, invented by Ehrlich in 1907; cure for syphilis and anthrax; also known as 606; now superseded by neo-salvarsan and other preparations of arsenic &c.

salvation, n. [1. sàlváshun; 2. sælvéiʃən]. Direct fr. L. Lat. *salvātiōn-(em)*; formed fr. *salv-* as in *salvus*, 'safe' &c., see **salvage**, & **-ation.** **1.** Act of saving; **a** specif. (in spiritual sense) redemption, deliverance from sin and its effects, by the merits of Christ's death: *Christ's salvation of the world;* **b** (in material sense) *the salvation of his country was his only aim.* **2.** State of being saved; **a** specif. (in spiritual sense) redemption from sin: '*In Christ is our salvation*'; Phr. *to find salvation*, to be convinced of sin and of the efficacy of Christ's redeeming power of salvation; to be converted; **b** (in material sense) preservation, rescue, from danger, calamity &c.: *the people owed to him their salvation from slavery.* **3.** Person who, thing which, saves; **a** specif. (in spiritual sense) the Saviour: *Christ is my salvation;* **b** (in material sense) *by his unfailing courage he was the salvation of his country.*

Salvation Army, n. Religious, missionary, body founded by the Rev. William (afterwards known as 'General') Booth in 1877, organized on quasi military lines, inculcating a rather crude 'enthusiastic' form of doctrine, the central formula being that if a man believes in Christ he is at once 'saved'; the organization is engaged in evangelical and rescue work among the destitute and outcast poor throughout the world.

Salvationism, n. [1. salváshunizm; 2. sælvéiʃənizəm]. **salvation** & **-ism.** The doctrines, principles, methods, of the Salvation Army.

Salvationist, n. [1. salvā́shunist; 2. sælvéiʃənist]. **salvation** & **-ist.** Member of the Salvation Army.

salve (I.), n. [1. salv, sahv; 2. sælv, sāv]. O.E. *sealf*, 'ointment'; O.S. & O.H.G. *salba*; cogn. w. Scrt. *sarpis*, 'clarified butter', & prob. w. Gk. *ólpē*, 'oil-flask', & *élphos*, 'butter', a rare word. **1.** A healing ointment for wounds, sores &c.; a healing, soothing, remedy; chiefly poet. or obs. except in *lip-salve*, ointment for chapped, sore lips. **2.** (fig.) Something which soothes and heals spiritual wounds; a balm: *a salve for wounded honour, for a tender conscience.*

salve (II.), vb. trans. O.E. *sealfian*, 'to anoint', cogn. w. Goth. *salbōn*; see prec., sense **2** prob. fr. Lat. *salvāre*, 'to save', see **salvage. 1.** To apply a salve to; heal by use of a salve (in material and spiritual senses). **2.** To overcome, evade, gloss over, to reconcile, by some saving clause or reservation: *to salve a difficulty, discrepancy, doubt* &c.

salve (III.), vb. trans. [1. salv; 2. sælv]. Back-formation fr. **salvage.** To salvage; to save, rescue, a ship, her cargo &c., or other property from loss or damage.

salve (IV.), interj. & n. [1. sálvē; 2. sælvi]. Lat., 'be well!, good day!', as general form of greeting, orig. a vocative of *salvus*, but regarded as imperat. of *salvēre*, 'to be well, in good health', fr. *salvus*, 'whole, sound, healthy, well'. See **salvage** (I.). **1.** interj. Hail! God save you! **2.** n. (R.C. Ch.) **a** Antiphon, sung after lauds from Trinity Sunday to Advent, addressed to the B.V.M., beginning with the words *Salve, regina misericordiae*, Hail, queen of compassion; **b** music composed for this antiphon.

salver, n. [1. sálver; 2. sælvə]. Through Fr. *salve* or direct fr. Span. *salva*, 'the tasting of food before serving, as precaution against poisoning, the dish on which the food was served; a salver', fr. *salvar*, 'to save, preserve, to taste food as a precaution', fr. Lat. *salvāre*, see **salvage**, & **-er**, the common agent-suff. A flat tray of silver or other metal on which refreshments, letters &c. are handed by a servant.

Salvia, n. [1. sálvia; 2. sælviə]. Lat., 'the sage plant', fr. *salvus*, 'whole, sound, healthy', fr. its medicinal qualities. Cp. also **sage** (I.). **1.** (hort.) Flower of sage family, cultivated for its bright-blue or scarlet colour. **2.** Botanical name for sage.

salvo (I.), n. [1. sálvō; 2. sælvou]. Lat., fr. phr. *salvo jure*, 'the right being reserved or saved'; abl. sing. of *salvus*, 'whole, safe'. See **salvage.** (rare or legal) A reservation, saving clause; a nice distinction, quibble: *with a salvo as regards certain named rights* &c.; (also advbl.) without prejudice: *salvo the said rights.*

salvo (II.), n. Earlier *salva*, fr. Ital., 'a salute, volley', fr. Lat. *salve*, 'hail!' See **salve** (IV.). **1.** A discharge of guns fired simultaneously in war, esp. in naval actions, a broadside or as a salute; cp. **volley**, of small-arms: *three salvos from the after turrets*; *a salvo of 21 guns.* **2.** Shouts, cheers, collectively; a combined simultaneous shout as from a crowd: *salvos of applause, cheering* &c.

sal volatile, n. [1. sàl vōlátili; 2. sæl voulǽtili]. Neo.-Lat., 'volatile salt'. An alcoholic, aromatic solution of ammonium carbonate, used as a restorative in faintness &c.

salvor, n. [1. sálver, -ōr; 2. sælvə, -ɔ̄]. **salve** (III.) & **-or.** One who helps in the salvage of a vessel and her cargo, or of other property; also (pl.) the ship, her owner, master, and crew effecting the salvage of another vessel.

Sam, n. [1. sam; 2. sæm]. Short for Samuel; *Uncle Sam*, Brother Jonathan, the typical figure of the U.S.A., corresponding to *John Bull*; (in various colloq. and slang phrs.) *To stand Sam*, to pay the reckoning, to pay for everyone present, esp. to stand drinks; *upon my Sam*, on one's oath; *I'll take my Sam upon it.*

samara, n. [1. samáhra; 2. səmā́rə]. Lat., also *samera*, 'the seed of the elm'; etymol. unknown. (bot.) The dry, usually two-celled fruit, with wing-like extrusions, of certain trees, as the ash, maple, sycamore &c.

Samaritan, n. & adj. [1. samáritan; 2. səmǽritən], fr. Lat. *Samarītānus*; adj. & n., fr. Gk. *Samareitēs*, fr. *Samaría*, Gk. *Samareia*, 'Samaria'. **1.** n. **a** Inhabitant, language, of the ancient Samaria; **b** *a good Samaritan*, a person always ready to befriend the unfortunate and relieve distress; from the Parable, Luke x. **2.** adj. **a** Pertaining to the ancient Samaritans, their language, beliefs &c.; **b** *a Samaritan fund*, one for the assistance of the poor; *Samaritan home*, for destitute, homeless, children.

Samaritanism, n. [1. samáritanizm; 2. səmǽritənizəm]. Prec. & **-ism.** Principles of charity; charitableness, charity.

samblind, adj. See **sand-blind.**

Sambo, n. [1. sámbō; 2. sæmbou], fr. Span. *zambo*, 'bandy-legged'; etymol. doubtful. **1.** (in S. and Central Am.) A half-breed of Indian and negro descent. **2.** (colloq. and slang) A negro; usually as form of address.

Sam Browne, n. [1. sám bróun; 2. sæm bráun], fr. Gen. Sir Samuel Browne, d. 1901. Leather uniform belt worn by commissioned and warrant officers in the British Army, having two straps crossed behind, passing over the shoulders, and attached back and front by rings to the belt; designed to take the weight of the sword.

sambur, n. [1. sámbur; 2. sæmbə]. Hind. *sāmbar, sābar.* (zool.) A species of large, maned, and antlered deer, found in India, Ceylon, and the Malay Peninsula.

same, adj. [1. sām; 2. seim]. O.E. *same*, only as adv., in constructions *same swā*, 'similarly', & *swā same swā*, 'just as'; cp. O.N. *samr*, adv.; cp. Swed. & Dan. *samme*, adj.; O.S. *sama*; O.H.G. *sam*, adj.; Goth. *sama*, 'the same', *samana*, 'together'; further cognates are Scrt. *sama*; Gk. *homós*, 'the same', *homoîos*, 'like', see **homo-**; Lat. *similis*, 'like', see **similar**; *simul*, 'together, at the same time'. Cp. further Scrt. *saṃi*, 'together', see **Sanscrit.** See also under **some. 1.** Preceded by *the*: identical, of individual persons or things, also *one and the same, the very same*, as emphasizing the identity &c.: *was that the same man we saw here last week?*; *meet me tomorrow in the same place as yesterday*; *the family has lived in the same house for generations*; *she won't wear the same dress two days running*; *they both died on the same day.* Phr. *at the same time*, introducing some qualification to a previous statement which is admitted. **2.** Similar, alike in kind, degree, quality &c.; identical with, corresponding: *on the same day as this last year*; *are women and men to get the same wages for the same work?*; *one cannot eat the same food every day*; *give the patient the same medicine as last time*; *we must all say the same thing*; *hold the same opinions as those of the majority*; *the same causes produce the same effects*; *the same sort, kind, of thing*; *at the same price, in the same way.* **3.** Not different, unchanged: *my elder brother is not the same man since his illness*; *still the same queer old fellow*; *the patient is much (about) the same.* Phr. *it is all, just, the same to me*, it is a matter of indifference; it does not matter either way. **4.** Without *the*; (very rare) unchanged, unchanging, not varying, monotonous, marked by sameness: *a tendency to become somewhat same in this author's work*; *the fear of being too same.* **5.** With *that, this, these, those* (archaic and rare), usually expressing emphasis or marking contrast &c.: *these same boasted heroes were the first to run away*; *that same wealth once so carefully hoarded was now spent recklessly.* **6.** (as pron., used elliptically) The aforesaid person or thing; **a** '*The stone which the builders rejected, the same is become the head of the corner*' (Matt. xxi. 42); '*The same was in the beginning with God*' (John i. 2); *whatever A said or did, B felt obliged to say and do the same*; *to the same, from the same*, as heading to one of a series of letters, poems &c. written to or by the same person; *and the same* (i.e. petitioners) *will ever pray* &c.; **b** (legal and commerc. use, also, illiterately, without *the*) used for an ordinary personal or demonstrative pronoun as *he, they, it, this* &c.: *to erecting fence, £10, to painting same, £4*; *with reference to our letter of the 12th ult., and your answer to same*; *we have heard from Mr. Jones and have written to same.* **7.** (as adv.) In the same way: *Orientals do not look at things the same as we do*; *can you feel the same towards him as you used to?*; *we do not think the same of people after a long absence.* Phrs. *all the same, just the same*, nevertheless, notwithstanding what has been done, said &c., after all: *he is often rude, but I like him all the same.*

sameness, n. [1. sā́mnes; 2. séimnis]. **same** & **-ness. 1.** State, quality, of being the same; identity, exact likeness; exact correspondence, resemblance or similarity: *sameness of character, look* &c.; *sameness in taste.* **2.** Unvarying, uniform character; monotony, tedious want of variety: *a deadly sameness in life.*

Samian, adj. & n. [1. sā́mian; 2. séimiən], fr. Lat. *Sami-us*, fr. Gk. *Sámios*, fr. *Sámos.* 'Samos', island in the Aegean Sea, & **-ian. 1.** adj. Of, belonging to, coming from, produced in, Samos: *Samian wine*; esp. *Samian pottery* or *ware*, a fine glazed red or black pottery, originally made of potter's clay from Samos, often ornamented with decorations in relief, made by the Romans in Gaul, and imported to, and so constantly found on, Roman sites in Britain &c. **2.** n. Inhabitant of Samos.

samisen, n. [1. sámisen; 2. sæmisen]. Jap., fr. Chinese *san-hsien*, 'three strings'. A Japanese three-stringed musical instrument, played with a plectrum.

samite, n. [1. sámīt; 2. sæmait]. In M.E., fr. O. Fr. *samit*, fr. Med. Lat. *samitum, examitum*, fr. L. Med. Gk. *hexámiton*, 'cloth woven with six threads', fr. Gk. *héx*, 'six', & *mítos*, 'thread', cp. **dimity.** (archaic or poet.) A fine, thick silk material, often interwoven with gold or silver threads.

samlet, n. [1. sámlet; 2. sæmlit]. See **salmon** & **-let.** A young salmon; parr.

Samnite, n. [1. sámnīt; 2. sæmnait]. Lat. *Samnītes*, pl. A member of an ancient tribe of South Central Italy, inhabiting the district of Samnium.

Samoan, adj. & n. [1. samóan; 2. səmóuən]. Samoa & **-an. 1.** adj. Of, belonging to, Samoa, a group of islands of Polynesia. **2.** n. A native, the language, of Samoa.

samovar, n. [1. sámovar; 2. sæməvā]. Russ. *samovár*, 'self-boiler', fr. *samo-*, 'self', & *variti*, 'to boil'. A Russian tea-urn, with internal tube, through which heated air circulates.

Samoyed, n. [1. sámoyèd; 2. sæmɔjèd]. Russ. One of a Mongol race dwelling in Russian Siberia.

sampan, n. [1. sámpan; 2. sæmpæn], fr. Chinese *san-pan*, 'three boards'. A light boat of Chinese and Far Eastern rivers and coastal waters, rowed with a scull from the stern, and usually provided with a sail of matting and an awning.

samphire, n. [1. sámfīr; 2. sæmfaiə]. Early form *sampire, sainpere*; for Fr. *Saint Pierre*, in full, *l'herbe de St. Pierre*, 'St. Peter's herb'. **1.** A salty, fleshy plant, *Crithmum maritimum*, growing on rocks and cliffs near the sea; used in pickles. **2.** Glass-wort, the marsh-samphire, *Salicornia herbacea.*

sample (I.), n. [1. sáhmpl; 2. sā́mpl]. Variant of **example**; M.E. *assaumple*, divided as *a sample.* A portion of anything taken as a pattern, specimen or example to show quality or character of the whole; **1.** (commerc., of material things) a representative specimen of the quality, style, appearance &c., esp. of goods offered for sale: *to take a sample of wheat, cloth &c. sent on approval*; *to take a sample of something for* *examination and test*; *a sample bottle, package* &c., one containing sample; *a sample book*, book of patterns; *sample room*, room in a warehouse where goods may be examined and sampled. Phr. *up to sample*, equal in quality, weight, measure &c., to the sample offered for approval or examination. **2.** (fig., of non-material things) A representative illustration: *to give a sample of one's courage, skill* &c.; *that is a fair sample of his manners.*

sample (II.), vb. trans. & intrans., fr. prec. **A.** trans. **a** To take a sample or samples of; to test quality of, from a sample or specimen: *to sample wheat, wine* &c.; **b** to try, test quality of; taste, enjoy: *I think we might sample my new claret tonight.* **B.** intrans. (commerc. &c.) Usually *sample out*, to show results after being sampled: *the goods sample out quite satisfactorily*; *the ore so far produced samples out at 3 oz. per ton.*

sampler, n. [1. sáhmpler; 2. sámplə]. Prec. & **-er**; cp. O. Fr. *essemplaire* & **exemplar.** **1.** One who samples; one who arranges, or sets out samples for examination. **2.** Specif., a specimen of a young person's needlework or embroidery, esp. a square of canvas exhibiting a variety of designs, letters, figures of animals and often pious sentiments &c., in colours.

Samson, n. [1. sámsn; 2. sǽmsn], fr. name of O.T. hero & strong man; Fr., fr. Lat., fr. Gk. *Sampsṓn*, fr. Heb. *Shimshōn*, 'the splendid, shining one', cp. *shĕmesh*, 'the sun', as name of the Israelite hero of mighty strength. **1.** A man of abnormal strength; a Hercules. **2.** (without cap.) A samson-post.

samson-post, n. A strong, supporting pillar or post, esp. in a ship.

samurai, n., sing. & pl. [1. sámoorī; 2. sǽmurai]. Jap., 'guard'. **1.** (hist.) **a** The name of the now extinct class of ancient Japanese feudal military retainers of the daimios or nobles; **b** a member of this class. **2.** **a** The class of gentry, in present-day Japan, as distinguished from the trading, and the working class, frequently serving in the army and navy; **b** a Japanese gentleman.

sanable, adj. [1. sánabl; 2. sǽnəbl], fr. Lat. *sānābilis*, 'curable', fr. *sānāre*, 'to cure, make sound or whole'. See **sane** & **-able.** (rare or archaic) Curable.

sanative, adj. [1. sánativ; 2. sǽnətiv], fr. L. Med. Lat. *sānātivus*, 'tending to cure', fr. *sānāt-(um)*, P.P. type of *sānāre*, 'to cure, make sound or healthy', fr. *sānus*, 'sound, healthy', see **sane.** Curative, tending to cure, having the power of curing or healing, body or mind; sanatory.

sanatorium, n., pl. **sanatoria** [1. sanatṓrium, -ia; 2. sænətṓriəm, -iə]. Neut. sing. of Lat. *sānātōrius*, 'sanatory'. See prec. & **-ory.** **1.** An institution for the treatment of the sick or convalescent; specif., one for the special treatment of patients suffering from tuberculosis. **2.** A health resort, esp. in India or other hot countries, usually a hill-station. **3.** The hospital attached to a school.

sanatory, adj. [1. sánaturi; 2. sǽnətəri]. English form of prec. Curative, sanative, conducing to, tending to promote, health; to be distinguished from *sanitary.*

sanbenito, n. [1. sànbenḗtō; 2. sænbenítou], fr. Span. *sambenito*, fr. *San Benito*, 'Saint Benedict'. **1.** (hist.) The garment shaped like a Benedictine scapular worn by heretics under the Spanish Inquisition; that worn by penitents was yellow with a red St. Andrew's cross; that worn by impenitents, at the stake, was black painted with figures of devils and flames. **2.** A penitential garment of sackcloth.

sanctification, n. [1. sàngktifikā́shun; 2. sæŋktitikéiʃən], fr. Eccles. Lat. *sanctificātiōn-(em).* See **sanctify** & **-fication.** Act, process, of sanctifying or making holy; state of being sanctified.

sanctified, adj. & n. [1. sángktifīd; 2. sǽŋktifaid], fr. P.P. of next word. **1.** adj. **a** Dedicated, consecrated: *a sanctified building, nun, monk*; **b** sanctimonious, affectedly holy or saintly: *sanctified airs, manners* &c. **2.** n. *The sanctified*: holy persons; those who have been saved by the merits of Christ's death.

sanctify, vb. trans. [1. sángktifī; 2. sǽŋktifai], fr. Fr. *sanctifier*, in O. Fr. *saintifier*, fr. Eccles. Lat. *sanctificāre*, 'to make holy', fr. Lat. *sanctus*, 'sanctified, made holy, sacred', P.P. of *sancīre*, 'to consecrate, make holy'. See **sanctus** & **-fy.** To make holy, to hallow: **1.** (in religious senses) **a** To purify from sin: '*That He might sanctify the people with His own blood*' (Heb. xiii. 12); **b** to consecrate, hallow: '*God blessed the seventh day, and sanctified it*' (Gen. ii. 3); **c** to regard as holy: '*Sanctify the Lord of Hosts*' (Isaiah viii. 13). **2.** To give a sanction to; to sanction, justify; to cause to be reverenced or respected: *devotion to one's country sanctifies every act*; *the end sanctifies the means*; *the practice has long been sanctified by custom.*

sanctimonious, adj. [1. sàngktimṓnius; 2. sæŋktimóuniəs]. **sanctimony** & **-ous.** **1.** (obs.) Possessing sanctity; holy, religious, pious. **2.** Pretending to, making an outward show of, extreme piety; making play with pious formulae; hypocritical in expressing religious sentiments.

sanctimoniously, adv. Prec. & **-ly.** In a sanctimonious manner.

sanctimoniousness, n. See prec. & **-ness.** Quality of being sanctimonious; a sanctimonious manner, mode of speech &c.

sanctimony, n. [1. sángktimuni; 2. sǽŋktimәni], fr. O. Fr. *sanctimonie*, fr. Lat. *sanctimōnia*, 'sanctity, chastity, virtue'. See **sanctus** & **-mony.** **1.** (obs.) Holiness, piety. **2.** Affected piety, sanctimoniousness.

sanction (I.), n. [1. sángkshun; 2. sǽŋkʃən], fr. Lat. *sanctiōn-(em)*, 'the decreeing or ordaining of something as sacred or inviolable, decree, ordinance, sanction', fr. *sanct-(um)*, P.P. type of *sancīre*, 'to decree as sacred or inviolable'. See **sanctus** & **saint** & **-ion.** **1.** **a** Act of a superior and recognized authority confirming, ratifying, or permitting an act or action of others; authorization, express permission, or consent: *to obtain the sanction of the proper authorities*; *official sanction has not yet been given*; **b** support, general encouragement, permission, or countenance for acts or conduct: *the sanction of fashion, of polite society*; *custom gives sanction nowadays to what would have been regarded as bad form in the past.* **2.** Specif. **a** (jurisprudence) that which gives binding force to, or which provides for the enforcement of, a law; the penalty attached to the breaking of a law, or to the failure to carry out its provisions: *imprisonment is the sanction against theft*; *to execute, suffer, the last sanctions of the law*, of capital punishment; **b** (ethics) that which enforces or makes binding any rule of conduct: *moral, religious sanctions*; *the sanction of conscience*; *the lowest sanctions are the mere pleasure or pain experienced after an act*; **c** rational justification for an act, or for conduct.

sanction (II.), vb. trans., fr. prec. To give sanction to (in all senses of noun).

sanctitude, n. [1. sángktitūd; 2. sǽŋktitjūd], fr. Lat. *sanctitūdo*, see **sanctus** & **-ude.** (rare) Saintliness, sanctity: '*sanctitude severe and pure*' (Milton, 'P. L.' iv. 293).

sanctity, n. [1. sángktiti; 2. sǽŋktiti]. Lat. *sanctitāt-(em)*, *sanctitas*, 'state of holiness', fr. *sanctus.* See **sanctus** & **-ity.** **1.** Holiness, pureness of life, saintliness: *the sanctity of his life*; *to make no pretence of sanctity.* **2.** Sacredness, state of being consecrated or dedicated to God or deity: *the sanctity of a temple.* **3.** Binding force, inviolability: *the sanctity of an oath.* **4.** Thing held sacred; holy feelings, ties, duties &c.: *the sanctity of the family, home* &c. (also in pl.).

sanctuary, n. [1. sángkchooari; 2. sǽŋktʃuəri], fr. O. Fr. *saintuarie*, fr. Lat. *sanctuārium*, 'holy place, shrine', see **sanctus** & **-ary.** **1.** A holy place; a shrine; the most sacred part of a temple or place of worship; specif. **a** the sacrarium of a church, in which the altar stands; **b** any place sanctified and made venerable by tradition, association &c.: *Westminster Abbey is one of the most precious of our national sanctuaries.* **2.** A place of refuge, an asylum; specif. **a** (hist.) a sacred place where, under ecclesiastical law, fugitives from justice, criminals, or debtors, might take refuge and claim protection for a certain time and under certain conditions; Phrs. *right of sanctuary*, right to grant or claim protection or sanctuary; *to take sanctuary*, to take refuge in a sanctuary; *to break sanctuary*, to violate such right and take away a criminal in sanctuary; **b** (by transf.) a refuge or reservation for animals where they are protected from interference in the breeding season &c.; esp. *a bird sanctuary*; **c** (fig.) a place of retreat, a private, secret place not to be violated or profaned by others: *the sanctuary of one's thoughts*; *to find a sanctuary in sleep.*

sanctum, n. [1. sángktum; 2. sǽŋktəm]. Lat., neut. sing. of **sanctus**, 'holy'. A place of retreat; a private, reserved place; esp. a private room, study; *sanctum sanctorum*, **a** the Holy of Holies, the place in the Jewish tabernacle or temple where the ark of the Covenant is placed; the sanctuary; **b** (i.) any private or inviolate retreat; (ii.) a very sacred object.

sanctus, n. [1. sángktus; 2. sǽŋktəs]. Lat., 'holy', fr. P.P. of *sancīre*, 'to make holy or sacred; to appoint, ordain' &c.; fr. nasalized form of base in Lat. *sacer*, q.v. under **sacred.** **1.** The hymn in the Eucharistic service beginning with the words 'Holy, holy, holy'; also styled the *Tersanctus*, the threefold sanctus. **2.** Musical setting for the hymn.

sanctus bell, n. A bell, usually hung at the junction of the nave or transept and the chancel of a church, rung at that point of the Eucharistic service when the sanctus is sung.

sand (I.), n. [1. sand; 2. sænd]. In O.E. & M.E.; O.H.G. *sant*, O.N. *sandr*; Du. *zand*; it is suggested that the Aryan type was **bhsə̄m(ə)dh-*, whence also Gk. *psámathos*, 'sand', & also, w. a different development of **bhs-*, Gk. *ámathos* for **hámathos*, fr. **sámathos*; Lat. *sabulum*, 'sand', is also fr. same base **bhsā̆-*, w. a different suff., & may stand for **psaflom* (see **sabulous**). The base **bhsā̆-* means 'to rub down, grind, reduce to powder', cp. Scrt. *bhas-*, 'to grind'. **1.** Fine, dry, gritty substance consisting of minute particles of disintegrated rock, found esp. on shores of seas and estuaries, in river beds, or in beds of former rivers, and in deserts. Phrs. *to plough the sand(s)*, to undertake useless labour; *to make ropes of sand*, to try to do what is impossible; *to build on sand*, to build on insecure foundations (chiefly fig.); *to put sand in the wheels, in the machine*, to obstruct, prevent, render impossible, the smooth working of an institution, organization, or of an arrangement of any kind between persons, by deliberate adverse actions. **2.** (pl.) *Sands*, **a** stretch of sand by the shore of a sea or an estuary &c.: *the Sands of Dee*; *to play on the sands*; **b** of the accumulation of sand in a desert: *the sands of the desert*; **c** (fig., of sand in an hour-glass), moments of time: *the sands are running out*, time is passing. **3.** (colloq., U.S.A.) Grit, pluck: *a man with plenty of sand in him.*

sand (II.), vb. trans., fr. prec. **1.** To cover, sprinkle, with sand: *to sand a road* (in slippery weather); *a sanded floor.* **2.** To put sand into, mix with sand: *to sand the sugar.*

sandal, n. [1. sándl; 2. sǽndl], fr. Fr. *sandale*, fr. Lat. *sandalium*, fr. Gk. *sandálion*, dimin. of *sándalon*, *sámbalon*; etymol. doubtful. **a** Protection for the foot worn in ancient Greece and Rome, and still worn in many parts of the East, and by some religious orders in Europe, consisting of a leather sole, with thongs passing over instep; **b** somewhat similar object worn instead of shoes by young children.

sandalled, adj. [1. sándld; 2. sǽndld]. Prec. & **-ed.** Furnished with sandals: *with sandalled feet.*

sandal-wood, also **sandal**, n., fr. Fr. *sandal, santal*, L. Lat. *sandalum*, cp. Arab. *sandal*, Scrt. *çandana.* **1.** A hard, close-grained wood of yellowish colour and fragrant scent, obtained from an East Indian tree, *Santalum album*, or from other allied trees of the Pacific, Australia &c. **2.** The sandal-wood tree.

sandal-wood oil, n. Oil obtained from sandal-wood tree, used medicinally for internal inflammation.

sandarac, sandarach, n. [1. sándarak; 2. sǽndəræk], fr. Lat. *sandaraca*, fr. Gk. *sandarákē*, perh. of Pers. origin. **1.** A resin obtained from Moroccan tree, *Callitris*, the 'sandarac tree', used in making varnish. **2.** (obs.) Red arsenic, realgar.

sand-bag (I.), n. A bag filled with sand, used for various purposes: **a** as ballast for boats, balloons &c.; **b** in field fortifications, to make parapets, to line trenches &c.; **c** in slender, elongated shape, to keep out draughts from windows; **d** in similar form, as a stunning weapon, used by criminals.

sandbag (II.), vb. trans., fr. prec. **1. a** To place sand-bags upon; **b** to protect with sand-bags. **2.** To strike and disable with a sand-bag.

sand-bank, n. A bank or shoal of sand at mouth of a river, in an estuary or channel &c.

sand-bar, n. A bank or bar of sand at the mouth of a river, at the entrance of a harbour &c.

sand-bath, n. **1.** A bath taken by rolling, or being covered, in sand, as birds do in cleaning themselves. **2.** (chem.) A vessel filled with hot sand, in which retorts &c. can be kept at an even temperature.

sand-bed, n. (geol.) A bed or stratum of sand.

sand-blast, n. A jet or blast of sand forced by air or steam pressure against a hard material, as glass &c., for cutting, roughening &c., for scaling metal plates and other purposes.

sand-blind, adj. Prob. by popular etymol. for obs. *samblind*, 'half-blind', O.E. *sām-*, 'half', cogn. w. Lat. *sēmi-*, see **semi-**, & **blind** (I.). (dial. or archaic) Purblind; dim-sighted; weak-sighted.

sand-box, n. A box filled with sand, used for various purposes: **a** on a locomotive, for sprinkling the rails when wet or slippery, thus giving a grip to the wheels; **b** for use on golf-links, at each tee; **c** (archaic) small box, used before blotting-paper was invented, with perforated lid for sprinkling sand on wet ink on paper.

sand-boy, n. A boy who carted round sand for sale; now only in Phr. *as jolly, merry, as a sand-boy.*

sand-crack, n. **1.** A crack in the hoof of a horse, causing lameness if neglected. **2.** A flaw in a brick due to bad mixing.

sand-dab, n. Any of various small flounders found in the sand in shallow water.

sand-eel, n. A small eel-like marine fish, genus *Ammodytes*, frequenting sandy shores, burying itself in the sand when the tide is out; also called *sand-launce.*

sanderling, n. [1. sánderling; 2. sǽndəliŋ]. Etymol. doubtful, but prob. fr. **sand** (I.) & dimin. **-ling.** A small wading bird, *Calidris arenaria*, allied to the sandpipers; it frequents wet sandy beaches, where it finds its food.

sanders, saunders, n. [1. sáhnderz; 2. sɑ́ndəz], fr. O. Fr. *sandre*, a variant of *sandal.* (archaic) Sandal-wood.

sand-flea, n. **a** The jigger or chigoe; **b** the sand-hopper.

sand-fly, n. A small biting fly or midge. *Sand-fly fever*, disabling fever, of tropical or subtropical climates, caused by a germ conveyed by the bite of various species of sand-fly.

sand-glass, n. A device for measuring intervals of time, consisting of two pear-shaped glass bulbs joined together at their pointed ends by a narrow tube, through which sand slowly runs from the bulb which is uppermost at the moment, into the lower one, in a given space of time; the bulbs are protected and held in position by a stand in which they are fixed, so made as to be reversible and stand on either end. These instruments are practically obsolete now, except in a small size, for measuring the time required to boil an egg (3 to 5 minutes); the larger sizes were called *hour-glasses.*

sand-grouse, n. Name due to the supposed relationship of the bird to the grouse. A game-bird with grey, buff, and black plumage, allied to pigeons, of family *Pteroclidae*, found in Africa and Asia, and occasionally in Europe.

sand-hill, n. A sand dune.

sand-hopper, n. Popular name for a small marine crustacean, *Talitrus locusta*, found on sandy shores between tide-marks, having great leaping powers and acting as a useful scavenger of decaying matter.

sandiness, n. [1. sándines; 2. sǽndinis]. **sandy** (I.) & **-ness.** State, quality, of being sandy.

sand-iron, n. Special golf-club for lifting a ball lying in sand.

sandiver, n. [1. sándiver; 2. sǽndivə]. Earlier *sandever*; prob. a popular form of Fr. *suint de verre*, 'sweating of glass'. A salty scum which rises from fused glass in the making; skimmed off and pulverized, it is used for polishing &c.; also styled 'glass-gall'.

sand-launce, n. [1. sánd lahns; 2. sǽnd lɑ̄ns]. **sand** (I.) & *launce*, earlier form of **lance**; cp. Fr. *lançon.* Sand-eel.

sand-lizard, n. A species of lizard found on the continent of Europe and in Southern England &c., *Lacerta agilis*, laying eggs in the sand.

sand-man, n. The man who, according to the fairy-tale, throws sand in children's eyes to make them feel sleepy at bed-time; cp. *dustman.*

sand-martin, n. A species of martin which builds its nest in holes in sand-pits or sandy banks &c.

sand-paper, n. & vb. trans. **1. n.** A cotton fabric coated with fine sand, used for smoothing rough surfaces of wood &c.; coarser than glass-paper and finer than emery-paper. **2. vb.** To polish with sand-paper.

sand-pipe, n. Tubular formation, of varying depth, in chalk, caused by solvent action of rain water; usually filled with sand, gravel, or earth.

sandpiper, n. [1. sán(d)pīper; 2. sǽn(d)paipə]. So called from its note and habit. Popular name of several different species of migratory birds, genus *Totanus*, frequenting streams; it is allied to the plovers.

sandstone, n. [1. sán(d)stōn; 2. sǽn(d)stoun]. (geol.) A rock formation of compacted sand, usually of quartz, cemented by carbonate of lime, silica &c.; much used for building; *Old, New, Red Sandstone*, of such strata below or above the carboniferous system.

sandstorm, n. [1. sán(d)storm; 2. sǽn(d)stɔ̄m]. A storm of wind on a desert which carries with it clouds of sand.

sandwich (I.), n. [1. sán(d)wich, -wij; 2. sǽn(d)witʃ, -widž]. Said to be so called from John Montagu, 4th Earl of Sandwich, 1718–92, who used this form of food to allow him to continue gambling for long periods without interruption. Two slices of buttered bread with a thin slice of meat, egg, tomato, cucumber &c. placed between them. Phr. *to ride, sit, sandwich*, to sit between two other people, esp. of a thin person between two stout ones, or of a woman between two men.

sandwich (II.), vb. trans., fr. prec. To insert, introduce, squeeze, in between two others: *to sandwich a dangerous clause between harmless ones in a proposal, bill; to be sandwiched in between two other persons.*

sandwich-boat, n. In bumping races at Oxford and Cambridge, the boat rowing head of a lower division which has to row last in the division next above on the same night of the races.

sandwich-man, n. A man who walks the streets carrying two advertisement boards, one hung in front and one behind.

sand-worm, n. Thick worm which burrows in the sand and is found at low tide; used for bait in sea-fishing; a lug-worm.

sandwort, n. [1. sándwërt; 2. sǽndwʌ̄t]. A low, shrubby plant growing in sandy soil, genus *Arenaria.*

sandy (I.), adj. [1. sándi; 2. sǽndi]. **sand** (I.) & **-y.** **1. a** Consisting of, abounding in, containing, covered with, sand: *sandy soil; a sandy floor, path*; **b** gritty, feeling like sand: *a sandy taste, feel.* **2.** (of the hair) Palish brown in colour; (of persons) having such hair.

Sandy (II.), n. Short for *Alexander*, as common name in Scotland. A Scotsman.

sandyish, adj. [1. sándiish; 2. sǽndiiʃ]. **sandy** (I.) & **-ish.** Rather sandy in consistency, feel, colour &c.

sane, adj. [1. sān; 2. sein], fr. Lat. *sānus*, 'sound in body or mind, whole, healthy'; various proposed etymols. are cited by Walde, & dismissed by him as improbable; the origin is so far untraced. **1.** Sound in mind, mentally normal; in one's right mind. **2.** Sound, reasonable, sensible; moderate, not unreasonable or exaggerated: *a sane policy, proposal.*

sanely, adv. Prec. & **-ly.** In a sane, sensible manner.

saneness, n. See prec. & **-ness.** State, quality, of being sane.

sang, vb. [1. sang; 2. sæŋ]. O.E., M.E. *sang*; Pret. of **sing.**

sangar, n. [1. sánggar; 2. sǽŋgə]. Hind. *sunga.* A dry-stone wall used as a protection against rifle-fire, much used on N.-W. frontier of India.

sangaree, n. [1. sànggaré; 2. sæŋgərí], fr. Span. *sangria*, 'bleeding', fr. *sangre*, 'blood', see **sanguine**, as made of red wine. A West Indian drink made of wine, sweetened, spiced, and mixed with lime-juice, and sometimes with brandy.

sang-de-bœuf, n. & adj. [1. sàhn de bḗf; 2. sɑ̃ də bǿf]. Fr., 'bullock's blood'. **1. n. a** A deep blood-red colour, esp. as found in old Chinese porcelain; **b** Chinese porcelain of this colour. **2. adj.** Coloured deep blood-red.

sang-froid, n. [1. sáhn frwáh; 2. sɑ̃ frwɑ́]. Fr., lit. 'cool blood'. Coolness, presence of mind; freedom from excitement; composure, imperturbability in dangerous or trying circumstances.

sangrail, sangreal, n. [1. sán-grál; 2. sǽn-gréil]. See **grail.**

sanguification, n. [1. sànggwifikáshun; 2. sæŋgwifikéiʃən]. Formed fr. Lat. *sangui-* for *sanguis*, 'blood', see **sanguine**, & **-fication.** The conversion, by digestion &c., of food into blood.

sanguinarily, adv. [1. sánggwinarili; 2. sǽŋgwinərili]. **sanguinary** & **-ly.** In a sanguinary manner.

sanguinariness, n. [1. sánggwinarines; 2. sǽŋgwinərinis]. See prec. & **-ness.** State, quality, of being sanguinary.

sanguinary, adj. [1. sánggwinari; 2. sǽŋgwinəri], fr. Lat. *sanguinārius.* **sanguine** & **-ary.** **1.** Accompanied by bloodshed or slaughter; bloody, murderous: *a sanguinary battle.* **2.** Blood-stained, bloody; flowing with blood: *sanguinary hands, dagger.* **3.** Bloodthirsty, cruel, delighting in bloodshed: *a sanguinary tyrant, villain* &c.; *with sanguinary thoughts, purpose.* **4. a** As describing bad language, esp. that which includes the use of the common vulgar expletive 'bloody': *rather sanguinary language*; **b** as euphemism for 'bloody': *a sanguinary fool.*

sanguine (I.), adj. [1. sánggwin; 2. sǽŋgwin], fr. Fr. *sanguin*, fr. Lat. *sanguineus*, 'of blood, bloody, blood-red', fr. *sanguin-(em)*, nom.

sanguis, 'blood'; various etymols. have been suggested wh. are highly ingenious, but are perh. too elaborate & complicated to be very convincing; perh. the most probable is that wh. connects the base of *sanguin-* w. Goth. *sigqan*, O.E. *sincan*, see **sink** (I.), in wh. case the Lat. word meant orig. 'that which falls or flows'. An identical association of ideas is seen in O.S. *drōr*, 'blood', connected w. *driosan*, 'to fall'; cp. also O.E. *drēorig*, 'blood-stained', fr. base **dreus-*, as in O.E. *drēosan*, 'to fall', see **dreary**. **1.** Of the colour of blood; **a** (of complexion) ruddy, fresh-coloured, florid: *a sanguine face, lips*; **b** (poet.) blood-red in colour, flaming: *sanguine banners, flames* &c.; **c** (her.) of a dark purplish red, murrey coloured. **2. a** (from the ancient physiological doctrine concerning the humours) Having the cheerful, courageous, ardent, or passionate temperament of one in whom the blood is the strongest, most predominant humour, and having a ruddy complexion, and a full and rapid pulse; **b** hence, cheerful, hopeful, confident; always anticipating the best; optimistic: *a sanguine temperament, disposition*; *sanguine of success*; *a sanguine person*, an optimist; *sanguine hopes*; *he was too sanguine*; *a sanguine report.*

sanguine (II.), n., fr. prec. **a** A crayon dyed red with haematite or red oxide of iron; **b** a drawing in red crayon.

sanguinely, adv. [1. sánggwinli; 2. sǽŋgwinli]. **sanguine** (I.) & **-ly**. In a sanguine, confident, optimistic manner.

sanguineness, n. [1. sánggwinnes; 2. sǽŋgwinnis]. See prec. & **-ness**. State, quality, of being sanguine; confidence, optimism.

sanguineous, adj. [1. sanggwíneus; 2. sæŋgwíniəs], fr. Lat. *sanguineus*, 'consisting of blood, blood-stained'. See **sanguine** (I.) & **-ous**. **1.** (bot.) Blood-red in colour. **2.** (med.) Of, pertaining to, the blood. **3.** Full-blooded, sanguine.

sanhedrim, sanhedrin, n. [1. sánedrim, -in; 2. sǽnidrim, -in]. Late Heb. *sanhedrīm, sanhedrīn*, a transliteration of Gk. *sunhédrion*, 'a sitting together, council, assembly', fr. *sún*, 'with', see **syn-**, & *hédra*, 'a seat', fr. base **hed-* for **sed-*, 'sit', see under **sedentary** & **sit**. **1.** (Jewish antiq.) Ancient supreme council and court of justice of the Jews, sitting in Jerusalem, consisting of seventy-one members, presided over by the High Priest. **2.** (gen.) Any similar assembly; council of elders.

sanicle, n. [1. sánikl; 2. sǽnikl]. O. Fr., fr. Med. Lat. *sānicula*, prob. fr. *sānus*, 'whole, healthy', see **sane**, so called fr. its healing properties. An umbelliferous plant, genus *Sanicula*, esp. black snake-root.

sanify, vb. trans. [1. sánifī; 2. sǽnifai], fr. Lat. *sānus*, 'sound, healthy'. **sane** & **-fy**. (rare) To make clean, wholesome, or sanitary.

sanitarian, adj. & n. [1. sànitárian; 2. sæ̀nitέəriən]. **sanitary** & **-ian**. **1.** adj. Of, pertaining to, public health and hygiene, sanitary matters, or sanitation. **2.** n. An advocate of public health and sanitation.

sanitarily, adv. [1. sánitarili; 2. sǽnitərili]. **sanitary** & **-ly**. In a sanitary manner.

sanitariness, n. [1. sánitarines; 2. sǽnitərinis]. See prec. & **-ness**. State, quality, of being sanitary.

sanitary, adj. [1. sánitari; 2. sǽnitəri], fr. Fr. *sanitaire*, fr. Lat. *sanit-*, as in *sanitāt-*, q.v. under **sanity**, & **-ary**. **1.** Pertaining to health, or to the rules, conditions, connected with health, as drainage, and esp. to freedom from dirt, filth, or other agents of infection or disease: *sanitary laws, sanitary science*; *sanitary engineer*, one skilled in laying down, and keeping in order, the drainage of a town or house; a grandiloquent name for a plumber; *sanitary inspector*, official appointed by a local authority to inspect nuisance, report defective drains &c. **2.** Free from dirt, filth, or other matter deleterious to health; in a clean, healthy condition; hygienic; having good sanitation or drainage: *in a sanitary condition*; *a sanitary cottage.*

sanitate, vb. trans. [1. sánitāt; 2. sǽniteit]. Back-formation fr. next word. (rare) To introduce sanitation into; to adopt sanitary rules for; to cleanse, render sanitary.

sanitation, n. [1. sànitáshun; 2. sæ̀nitéiʃən], fr. Lat. stem *sanit-*, see **sanity**, coined in connexion w. the modern ideas associated w. **sanitary**, & **-ation**. **a** (in larger sense) All those measures which conduce to the preservation of public health, esp. efficient drainage, proper disposal of sewage, ventilation, a pure water supply; the system by which these are secured; **b** (in narrower but more usual sense) specif., drainage and disposal of sewage, both in individual dwellings, workshops &c., and in towns generally.

sanity, n. [1. sániti; 2. sǽniti], fr. Fr. *sanité*, fr. Lat. *sānitāt-(em)*, 'health, soundness of body or mind'. See **sane** & **-ity**. **1.** Condition of being sane; soundness of mind, mental health. **2.** Conduct of a sane person; soundness of judgement, prudence in action; levelheadedness.

sanjak, n. [1. sánjak; 2. sǽndžæk]. Turk., 'flag'. An administrative district of Turkey, a subdivision of the vilayet.

sank, vb. [1. sangk; 2. sæŋk]. O.E. *sanc*, M.E. *sank*; Pret. of **sink** (I.).

sans, prep. [1. sanz; 2. sænz], in Fr. phrs. [1. sahn; 2. sɑ̃]. Fr., 'without', ultimately fr. Lat. *sine*, see **sine die**. **1.** (obs.) Without; only used in quoting, or as echo of 'As You Like It', II. vii. 166, (of old age) '*sans teeth*..., *sans everything*'. **2.** In various French phrs. current in ordinary English usage: *sans cérémonie*, without ceremony or formality; e.g. *come and dine with us sans cérémonie*, in a friendly way; *sans doute*, without doubt, doubtless, certainly; *sans façon*, without ceremony, without fuss; *sans gêne*, n., a casual, offhand manner, lack of constraint; *sans phrase*, without circumlocutory or complimentary phrases, plainly, bluntly; in a word; *sans souci*, n., gay, irresponsible unconcern, thoughtless happiness.

Sanscrit, Sanskrit, n. & adj. [1. sánzkrit; 2. sǽnzkrit]. In the language itself, *saṃskṛta*, lit. 'made, fitted, together, symmetrically arranged', fr. *sam̥i*, 'together', cogn. w. **same**, & *kṛta*, 'made', cogn. w. Lat. *creāre*, see **create**; cp. *Prakrit*, 'the common language'. **1.** n. The ancient, classical, literary and sacred language of the Hindus, belonging to the Aryan family, preserved in documents far older than those of any other Aryan language. **2.** adj. Of, pertaining to, written in, Sanscrit.

Sanscritic, adj. [1. sanzkrítik; 2. sænzkrítik]. Prec. & **-ic**. Belonging to, allied to, Sanscrit; *the Sanscritic languages*, now usually called *Aryan languages.*

sansculotte, n. [1. sáhnkūlót; 2. sɑ̃kylɔt]. Fr., 'without breeches'. **1.** (hist.) The name given, originally in contempt, to the mob or lower classes; later to the more violent revolutionaries, or Jacobins, in the French Revolution, as wearing pantaloons or loose trousers and not the knee-breeches of the gentry. **2.** A violent republican or revolutionary, equivalent to the modern Bolshevik.

sansculottism, n. [1. sáhnkūlótizm; 2. sɑ̃kylɔ́tizəm]. Prec. & **-ism**. Principles, methods, of the sansculottes; violent republicanism or revolutionary principles; mob-rule.

sanserif, n. [1. sànsérif; 2. sæ̀nsérif], fr. Fr. *sans*, 'without', & **serif**. A form of type without serifs.

Santa Claus, n. [1. sánta kláwz; 2. sǽntə klɔ́z]. American adaptation of Du. *Sint Klaus*, 'Saint Nicholas'. Father Christmas.

santal, n. [1. sántal; 2. sǽntəl]. Fr., fr. Med. Lat. *santalum*. Sandalwood, q.v.

santalin, n. [1. sántalin; 2. sǽntəlin]. Prec. & **-in**. (chem.) The red colouring substance of sandalwood.

santon, n. [1. sántun; 2. sǽntən]. Span., fr. *santo*, fr. Lat. *sancto*, dat. or abl. of *sanctus*, 'holy'. See **sanctus**. A Turkish dervish or holy man.

santonin, n. [1. sántunin; 2. sǽntənin], fr. Lat. *santonica*, 'wormwood', fr. name of *Santones*, a Gaulish tribe of Aquitania, & **-in**. (chem.) A bitter substance obtained from various species of wormwood, *Santonica*, used as a drug for expelling intestinal worms.

Saorstat Eireann, n. [1. sárstath áran; 2. séərstəþ éərən]. Ir. The Irish Free State.

sap (I.), n. [1. sap; 2. sæp]. O.E. *sæp*; O.H.G. *saf* (Mod. Germ. *saft*); prob. borrowed fr. Lat. *sapa*, 'must, new wine', wh. is related to *sapor*, 'flavour', & *sapere*, 'to taste of'. See **sapid**. **1.** The juice or fluid which circulates in the tissues of plants, esp. in woody tissue. **2. a** Any fluid or essence regarded as giving life and vigour; e.g. (poet.) blood; **b** (fig.) vigour, spirit, richness of temperament.

sap (II.), vb. trans., fr. prec. (chiefly fig.) To drain away the life and strength of, to weaken, cause to dwindle or decline; overstrain: *to sap one's health, strength, energies* &c. Probably associated with next word.

sap (III.), n., fr. O.Fr. *sappe*, 'a digging implement', Fr. *sape*, 'entrenching, mining, tool'; cp. Ital. *zappa*; Med. Lat. has *sappa*, 'mattock, spade'; etymol. doubtful. **1.** (mil.) A covered trench, often having a parapet on one side, made by an attacking or besieging force as a means of approach towards the enemy's fortifications, usually constructed in zig-zag so as to prevent enfilade fire. **2.** (fig., rare) An insidious, secret attack or destructive agency. **3.** (schoolboy's slang, possibly a different word) **a** Hard work, a disagreeable task; swot, grind; **b a** hard-working, studious person.

sap (IV.), vb. trans. & intrans., fr. Fr. *saper*. See prec. word. **A** trans. **1.** (mil.) To attack, approach, by means of saps: *to sap a line of trenches*. **2.** See **sap** (II.). **B** intrans. **1.** (mil.) To dig a sap. **2.** (slang) To work hard, be studious: *to sap at a job.*

sapajou, n. [1. sápajōō; 2. sǽpədžū], fr. Fr. *sapajiou*, fr. a S. Am. native word. A small S. American monkey with prehensile tail, a capuchin monkey, genus *Cebus.*

sapan-wood, n. [1. sápan wood; 2. sǽpən wud], fr. Malay. *sapang*. A red dye-wood obtained from a tree, *Caesalpinia sapan*, of the Malay archipelago and elsewhere in the tropical East Indies.

sap green, n. **sap** (I.) & **green**. A dull green colouring matter obtained from the juice of buckthorn berries.

sap-head (I.), n. **sap** (III.) & **head**. (mil.) That end of a sap nearest to the line of trenches to be attacked.

saphead (II.) n. [1. sáp-hed; 2. sǽphed], fr. **sap** (I.) & **head**. (slang) Person with a head like sapwood; a foolish, dull, spiritless person.

sapid, adj. [1. sápid; 2. sǽpid], fr. Lat. *sapidus*, 'savoury, tasty', fr. *sapere*, 'to taste, discern, be wise', see **sapient**, & cp. **insipid**. **a** Having taste or flavour; **b** possessing point or interest.

sapidity, n. [1. sapíditi; 2. sæpíditi]. Prec. & **-ity**. Quality of being sapid; flavour, sapidness.

sapidness, n. [1. sápidnes; 2. sǽpidnis]. **sapid** & **-ness**. Sapidity.

sapience, n. [1. sápiens; 2. séipiəns]. Fr., fr. Lat. *sapientia*, 'wisdom', see next word, & **-ce**. Wisdom, real or assumed; often ironical for self-satisfied stupidity and ignorance.

sapient, adj. [1. sápient; 2. séipiənt], fr. Lat. *sapient-(em)*, Pres. Part. of *sapere*, 'to have a taste, to taste; to discern, to be wise, to know', cogn. w. O.H.G. (*ant-*)*seppen*, 'to take cognizance of', O.S. *ansebbjan*, 'to notice, perceive taste of'; O.E. *sefa*, 'mind, heart; thoughts'. **a** (rare) Wise, sagacious, shrewd, knowing; **b** (ironic) wise in one's own conceit, would-be knowing.

sapiential, adj. [1. sàpiénshal; 2. sèipiénʃəl], fr. Lat. *sapientiālis*. See prec. & **-ial.**

(rare) Having wisdom; expounding wisdom; *the Sapiential Books*, in Bible, *Proverbs, Wisdom, Ecclesiastes*, and *Ecclesiasticus*.

sapiently, adv. [1. sápientli; 2. séipiəntli]. **sapient & -ly.** Wisely, with an air or pretence of wisdom.

sapless, adj. [1. sáples; 2. sǽplis]. **sap (I.) & -less.** Lacking, having lost, sap; dry, withered; without vigour or life.

sapling, n. [1. sápling; 2. sǽpliŋ]. **sap (I.) & -ling. 1.** A young tree, esp. a young forest tree during first three or four years of growth. **2.** A youth just emerging from boyhood. **3.** (coursing) A young greyhound in first year of training: *sapling stakes*, coursing stakes for greyhound saplings.

sapodilla, n. [1. sàpodíla; 2. sæ̀pədílə], fr. Span. *zapotilla*, dimin. of *zapote*, fr. Mexican *tzapotl*, name of the tree. A South American and West Indian evergreen tree, *Achras sapota*, with hard wood, edible fruit, and yielding a gum, chicle, used in America in making chewing-gum.

saponaceous, adj. [1. sàponáshus; 2. sæ̀pənéiʃəs], fr. Lat. *sāpōn(-em)*, stem of *sāpo*, 'soap', & **-aceous**; Lat. *sāpō* is supposed to be a borrowing fr. Gmc. *saip-, cp. O.H.G. *seifa*, O.E. *sāpe*; this word is cogn. w. Lat. *sēbum*, 'tallow', see **sebaceous. 1.** Having the properties of soap, containing soap; soapy. **2.** (fig.) Unctuous in manner; oily, obsequiously flattering.

saponifiable, adj. [1. sapónifīabl; 2. sæpɔ́nifaiəbl]. **saponify & -able.** Capable of being converted into soap.

saponification, n. [1. sapònifikáshun; 2. sæpɔ̀nifikéiʃən]. See **saponify & -fication.** Chemical process of converting fats or oils into soap by hydrolysis with an acid; state of being saponified.

saponifier, n. [1. sapónifīer; 2. sæpɔ́nifaiə]. **saponify & -er.** Agent used in saponification.

saponify, vb. trans. [1. sapónifī; 2. sæpɔ́nifai]. Fr. *saponifier*; Lat. *sāpōn-(em)*, 'soap'. See **saponaceous & -fy.** To convert into soap by chemical process.

sapor, n. [1. sápōr; 2. séipɔ]. Lat., 'taste, savour'. See **sapid.** (rare) Taste, flavour, savour.

sapper, n. [1. sáper; 2. sǽpə]. **sap (IV.) & -er.** One who saps; specif. (mil.) a member of the Royal Engineers, formerly styled *Sappers and Miners*.

Sapphic, adj. & n. [1. sáfik; 2. sǽfik], fr. Lat. *Sapphicus*, fr. Gk. *Sapphikós*, 'of Sappho', Gk. *Sapphṓ*, name of lyric poetess of Lesbos, c. 600 B.C. **1.** adj. Connected with, pertaining to, Sappho; *Sapphic verse*, metre used by Sappho, also by Horace, and sometimes attempted in modern verse, consisting of a four-line stanza of three lines followed by a short one, the first three lines having five beats, the middle being of three syllables, the others of two each. **2.** n. (usually pl.) *Sapphics*, Sapphic verse, stanzas in Sapphic form and metre.

sapphire, n. & adj. [1. sáfīr; 2. sǽfaiə]. M.E. *saphir, safir*, fr. Fr. *saphir*, fr. Lat. *sapphīrus*, fr. Gk. *sáppheiros*, applied to a gem-stone which was prob. lapis lazuli; of Oriental origin, cp. Heb. *sapir*, 'lapis lazuli'. **1.** n. **a** A translucent precious stone, of varying shades of intense blue in colour; **b** (mineral.) a hard, translucent variety of corundum, of different colours, the constituent of the true sapphire and also of the ruby, with many intermediate stages, as *white sapphire*, often passed as a diamond; **c** a deep bright blue colour, as of the sapphire: *the sapphire of the skies, of eyes, of a butterfly's wings* &c. **2.** adj. **a** Pertaining to, composed of, set with, a sapphire or sapphires: *a sapphire ring*; **b** resembling a sapphire in colour, of a bright intense blue; azure: *a sapphire sea*; *sapphire eyes* &c.

sapphirine, adj. & n. [1. sáfirīn; 2. sǽfirain]. **sapphire & -ine. 1.** adj. **a** Resembling, consisting of, sapphire; **b** deep bright blue. **2.** n. (mineral.) A blue or green silicate of aluminium and magnesium.

sappiness, n. [1. sápines; 2. sǽpinis]. **sappy & -ness.** State, quality, of being sappy.

sappy, adj. [1. sápi; 2. sǽpi]. O.E. *sæpig*; **sap (I.) & -y. 1.** Full of sap, juicy; young, vigorous. **2.** (slang) Soft, weak, flabby.

sapr(o)-, pref. used to form compounds, fr. Gk. *saprós*, 'putrid, rotten', cogn. w. *sḗpein*, 'to rot', *sḗps*, 'ulcer'; etymol. doubtful.

sapraemia, n. [1. saprḗmia; 2. sæprímiə]. **sapro-** & Gk. *haima*, 'blood'. See **haemo-.** (med.) Septicaemia.

saprogenic, -genous, adj. [1. sàprōjénik, saprójenus; 2. sæ̀proudžénik, sæprɔ́džinəs]. **sapro- & -genic, -genous.** Producing, produced by, putrefaction: *saprogenic bacteria*.

saprolite, n. [1. sáprōlīt; 2. sǽproulait]. **sapro- & -lite**, fr. Gk. *líthos*, 'stone'. (geol.) Decomposed, disintegrated, rock.

saprophagous, adj. [1. saprófagus; 2. sæprɔ́fəgəs]. **sapro- & -phagous.** (zool.) Feeding, living, on decaying, putrifying organic matter.

saprophyte, n. [1. sáprōfīt; 2. sǽproufait]. **sapro- & -phyte**, fr. Gk. *phutón*, 'plant'. (bot.) A vegetable organism that lives on decaying organic matter, such as certain fungi.

saprophytic, adj. [1. sàprōfítik; 2. sæ̀proufítik]. Prec. & **-ic.** (bot.) Living on decaying organic matter; saprophagous.

sap-rot, n. **sap (I.) & rot.** Dry rot, in timber.

sapwood, n. [1. sápwood; 2. sǽpwud]. **sap (I.) & wood.** The newer, relatively soft, growing wood of a tree near the bark; also called *alburnum*; contrasted with the *heartwood*, the valuable part of timber.

sar, also **sargo**, n. [1. sar(gō); 2. sā(gou)]. Fr., fr. Lat. *sargus*, cp. Gk. *sargós*. A fish, sea-bream.

saraband, n. [1. sáraband; 2. sǽrəbænd], fr. Fr. *sarabande*, fr. Span. *zarabanda*; etymol. doubtful; prob. of Moorish origin; Pers. *sarband*, 'fillet for a woman's head-dress', has been suggested. **a** A slow, graceful Spanish dance, in triple time, with accented second beat in the bar; **b** music composed for this.

Saracen, n. [1. sárasen; 2. sǽrəsən], fr. L. Lat. *Saracēnus*, fr. L. Gk. *Sarakēnós*; etymol. doubtful, perh. of Arab. origin. Name applied, **a** to various tribes of Syrian and Arabian origin, esp. to the nomad tribes of the Syrian and Arabian desert; **b** to any Moslem; specif., those who opposed the Crusaders.

saracen corn, n. Buckwheat.

Saracenic, adj. [1. sàrasénik; 2. sæ̀rəsénik]. **Saracen & -ic.** Connected with, pertaining to, the Saracens, or Moslems: *Saracenic architecture*, Moslem, Arabian, architecture.

Saracen's head, n. A Turk's or Arab's head as heraldic charge, crest, or inn sign.

Saratoga trunk, n. [1. sàratóga trúngk; 2. sæ̀rətóugə trʌ́ŋk], fr. Saratoga Springs, fashionable resort, New York State. Travelling-trunk of great size, used by Americans.

sarcasm, n. [1. sárkazm; 2. sákæzəm]. Fr. *sarcasme*, fr. L. Lat. *sarcasmus*, fr. Gk. *sarkasmós*, 'mockery, sarcasm', fr. *sarkázein*, 'to tear, gnaw flesh like dogs, to bite the lips, to sneer, taunt', fr. *sark-(ós), sárx*, 'flesh', see **sarco-. 1. a** A mocking, sneering, taunt, intended to wound; an ironical jibe; **b** ironical mockery; satire. **2. a** Turn of mind inclined to irony, mocking bitterness, veiled sneers, and satirical taunts; **b** facility in uttering, proneness to utter these.

sarcastic, adj. [1. sarkástik; 2. sākǽstik], fr. Gk. *sarkastikós*. See **sarcasm & -ic. a** (of utterances) Expressing sarcasm; bitterly mocking; contemptuously ironical or satirical; **b** (of persons) given to using sarcasm.

sarcastically, adv. [1. sarkástikali; 2. sākǽstikəli]. Prec. & **-al, -ly.** In a sarcastic manner; with sarcasm.

sarcenet, sarsenet, sarsnet, n. [1. sárs(e)net; 2. sás(ə)nɛt]. O. Fr. *sarcenet*, also A.-Fr. *sazzinett*, fr. Low Med. Lat. *sarracēnicum*, 'stuff made by the Saracens, Saracen cloth'. See **Saracen.** A fine, thin, soft silk material used for ribbons, linings &c.

sarco-, pref. Used to form compounds fr. Gk. *sark-(ós), sárx*, 'flesh'; etymol. doubtful; perh. for Aryan *twrkʷ-, & connected w. Lat. *torquere*, 'to twist', see **torque.**

sarcocarp, n. [1. sárkōkàrp; 2. sákoukàp]. **sarco-** & Gk. *karpós*, 'fruit', see **carpel.** (bot.) The fleshy part of a fruit.

sarcode, n. [1. sárkōd; 2. sákoud]. **sarco- & -ode.** (biol.) Protoplasm of a unicellular organism.

sarcoma, n. [1. sarkṓma; 2. sākóumə]. Gk. *sárkōma*, 'fleshy substance'. See **sarco-.** Malignant growth formed from connective tissue, liable to occur in various parts of the body.

sarcophagus, n., pl. **sarcophagi** [1. sarkófagus, -gī, -jī; 2. sākɔ́fəgəs, -gai, -džai]. Lat., fr. Gk. *sarkophágos*, 'flesh-eating, flesh-consuming'. See **sarco- & -phagous**; from a kind of limestone of which coffins were made by the Greeks, said to disintegrate the soft parts of the body enclosed in them within a short period. **1. a** (specif. archaeol.) A large coffin, as used in Egypt, ancient Greece, and Rome &c., usually of stone, highly ornamented with carvings or paintings and monumental inscriptions; **b** a large stone structure, resembling a kind of chest in shape, placed over a grave, bearing inscriptions relative to those who lie beneath it. **2.** Eighteenth-century wine-bin of mahogany, made in form of a sarcophagus, often forming part of, or kept in a recess below, a large sideboard.

sarcous, adj. [1. sárkus; 2. sákəs], fr. **sarco- & -ous.** (anat.) Consisting of, pertaining to, soft tissue, muscle &c.

sard, n. [1. sard; 2. sād], fr. Fr. *sarde*, fr. Lat. *sarda*, fr. Gk. *sárdion*, also *sárdios líthos*, 'Sardian stone', fr. *Sárdeis*, 'Sardis', in anct. Asia Minor. Semi-precious, very hard, stone, orange or orange-red in colour, a variety of chalcedony, used for intaglios.

sardine (I.), n. [1. sàrdḗn; 2. sādín]. Fr., fr. Lat. *sardīna*, also *sarda*, fr. Gk. *sardḗnē*, 'small fish used for pickling', probably the pilchard or sardine, fr. Sardinia, off the coasts of which it was caught. Name given to an immature pilchard, and some other small fish, caught in the Mediterranean and off the West Coast of France; preserved in olive oil and tinned. Phr. *packed like sardines*, crowded very close together so that it is impossible to move.

sardine (II.), n. [1. sárdīn; 2. sádain], fr. Gk. *sárdion*. See **sard.** A precious stone, mentioned in Rev. iv. 3 (A.V.), '*like a jasper and a sardine stone*'; R.V. has *sardius*.

Sardinian, adj. & n. [1. sardínian; 2. sādíniən]. *Sardinia* & **-an. 1.** adj. Of, belonging to, the island, or former kingdom, of Sardinia. **2.** n. A native of the island; a subject of the kingdom, which included also Piedmont and Savoy, till the formation of the modern kingdom of Italy in 1861.

sardius, n. [1. sárdius; 2. sádiəs], fr. Gk. *sárdios, sárdion*, 'the Sardian stone'. See **sard.** Sard.

sardonic, adj. [1. sardónik; 2. sādɔ́nik], fr. Fr. *sardonique*, fr. Lat. *Sardonicus*; another form of *Sardonius*, fr. Gk. *sardánios, sardónios*, either 'Sardinian' in reference to 'Sardinian herb', wh. was supposed to contort the face of one eating it by its bitter taste; or related to Gk. *sairein*, 'to grin', etymol. doubtful. Cynical, bitter, malicious; *a sardonic laugh, chuckle, smile*, grim, not expressing real merriment.

sardonically, adv. [1. sardónikali; 2. sādɔ́nikəli]. Prec. & **-al & -ly.** In a sardonic manner; grimly, maliciously.

sardonyx, n. [1. sárduniks; 2. sádəniks]. Lat., fr. Gk. *sardónux*. See **sard & onyx.** A semi-precious stone consisting of alternate layers of red sard or carnelian and white chalcedony; used in cameos.

saree, sari, n. [1. sáhrē; 2. sárī]. Hind. *sāṛī*. Garment forming principal part of woman's dress in N. India, consisting of a cloth wound round the body with one end thrown over the head.

sargasso, n. [1. sargásō; 2. sāgǽsou], fr. Port. *sargaço*, fr. *sargo*, 'grape'. Species of sea-weed (*Sargassum*), with berry-like air-sacs, found floating in great masses, as in *the Sargasso Sea*, in the N. Atlantic, and in the S. Pacific &c.; also called gulf-weed.

sargo, n. See **sar.**

sari, *n.* See **saree.**

sark, n. [1. sark; 2. sāk]. M.E. *serke*; Scand., fr. O.N. *serkr*, 'shirt'; cogn. w. O.E. *serċe*, 'shirt, tunic'. (Scots or archaic) Shirt, shift.

Sarmatian, adj. & n. [1. sarmáshan; 2. sāméiʃən]. **1.** adj. Of, belonging to, ancient Sarmatia, region north of the Black Sea, part of modern Poland and Russia. **2.** n. Inhabitant of Sarmatia; (poet.) a Pole or Russian.

sarmentose, sarmentous, adj. [1. sármentōs, sarméntus; 2. sāmɛntous, sāméntəs]. Lat. *sarmentōsus*, 'full of twigs or branches'; *sarmentum* for **sarpmentum*, 'trimmed off brush-wood, faggot'; fr. *sarpere*, 'to lop, trim'; cogn. w. Gk. *hárpē*, 'sickle'; & O. Slav. *srŭpŭ*, 'sickle'. It has been suggested that the sense 'to cut', of the base **serp-* &c., is secondary, & comes fr. the sense, 'sickle, hook', & that this again was orig., 'the curved implement', fr. **serp-*, 'to wind, creep' &c., see **serpent.** (of plants) Producing prostrate, trailing, branches, or runners.

sarong, n. [1. sáhrong; 2. sárɔŋ]. Malay. *sārung*. The principal garment of Malay men and women, consisting of a rectangular piece of striped silk or cotton cloth worn round the waist, forming a kind of kilt or petticoat.

sarsaparilla, n. [1. sàrsaparíla; 2. sàsəpərílə], fr. Span. *zarzaparrilla*, fr. *zarza*, Basque *zartzia*, 'bramble'; the second element is doubtful; prob. a dimin. of *parra*, 'vine trained against a wall'; *Parillo*, name of supposed discoverer of medical use, has also been suggested. **1.** (bot.) Any species of the South or Central American smilax. **2.** (med.) A decoction made from the dried roots of the above, used as a tonic, blood purifier &c.

sarsenet, sarsnet, n. See **sarcenet.**

sarsen stones, n. [1. sársen stōnz; 2. sásən stòunz]. Prob. a variant of **Saracen** (stones), in sense of 'pagan, heathen'. The large blocks of very hard siliceous sandstone very common on the Wiltshire Downs, of same kind as those which are used in the prehistoric circles of Stonehenge and Avebury; also called 'grey wethers'.

sartorial, adj. [1. sartṓrial; 2. sātɔ́riəl]. Lat. *sartōri-*, stem of *sartor*, 'a tailor', & **-al**; the Lat. n. is derived fr. *sart-*, P.P. type of *sarcere*, 'to patch, botch, mend'; prob. cogn. w. Gk. *hérkos* for **serkos*, 'fence, protection', orig. 'a hurdle of wicker-work'. Cp. **exorcize.** Connected with, pertaining to, the trade and work of a tailor; pertaining to clothes made by a tailor; (chiefly jocular) *a sartorial triumph*, a well-made suit; *the sartorial art*, tailoring &c.

sartorius, n. [1. sartṓrius; 2. sātɔ́riəs]. Lat. adj., 'pertaining to a tailor', fr. *sartor*. See prec. (anat.) The long leg muscle which passes obliquely across the front of the thigh, used in crossing the legs when squatting, or sitting like a tailor at his work.

Sarum, n. [1. sárum; 2. séərəm]. Med. Lat., supposed to be due to a misreading of an abbr. form of Lat. *Sarisburia*, 'Salisbury'. Ecclesiastical name of Salisbury and its diocese; used in the signature of the bishop, e.g. *John Sarum*; *Sarum use*, form of liturgy used in the diocese of Salisbury until the Reformation.

sash (I.), n. [1. sash; 2. sæʃ], fr. Arab. *shāsh*, muslin used to make the turban, & so first used in Engl. as equiv. to 'turban'. **1. a** An ornamental scarf, strip, or band of silk worn over the shoulder, or round the waist by officers and certain non-commissioned officers as part of full-dress uniform; **b** the broad ribbon worn over the shoulder and carrying the badge worn by members of the higher classes of various orders of knighthood &c. **2.** An ornamental, coloured scarf, or broad piece of ribbon, worn round the waist by women and children.

sash (II.), n. Corrupted form of Fr. *châssis*, 'framework, framing', see **chassis.** One of the two, upper and lower, pieces of frame-work, made to slide up and down, for opening and shutting, in which the panes of glass in a window are fixed; *sash cord, line*, cord attached to either side of a sash, with the balancing weights at the other end enabling the window to be easily raised and lowered; *sash-weight*, one of these leaden weights; *sash window*, one constructed with sashes; as distinguished from a *casement window*.

sasin, n. [1. sásin; 2. séisin]. Nepalese. The Indian antelope, the males of which have long spiral horns.

sassafras, n. [1. sásafras; 2. sǽsəfræs]. Fr., fr. Span. *sasafras*, also *saxifras*; etymol. doubtful; prob. confused w. Lat. *saxifraga*, **saxifrage.** A laurel-like bush or tree of N. America, with an aromatic bark, from which a volatile oil is extracted, used as an astringent medicine, as a tonic, and as a flavouring substance.

Sassanian, adj. [1. sasánian; 2. sæséiniən]. *Sāsān*, see next word, & **-ian.** Of, belonging to, the Sassanid dynasty, or to the period during which they ruled; Sassanid.

Sassanid, n. & adj. [1. sásanid; 2. sǽsənid], fr. Sāsān, name of the founder of a dynasty of Persian kings who ruled fr. c. A.D. 226 to 641. **1.** n. A member of this dynasty. **2.** adj. Connected with, belonging to, the dynasty; Sassanian.

Sassenach, n. [1. sásenahgh; 2. sǽsənāχ]. Gael. & Ir. form of **Saxon.** An Englishman; also a Lowland Scot, as distinguished from a person of Highland, or Celtic Irish blood.

Sastra, Shastra, Shaster, n. [1. shástra; 2. ʃǽstrə]. Scrt. *śāstra*, 'sacred ordinance'. One of the sacred writings, or books of the law, of the Hindus.

sat, vb. [1. sat; 2. sæt]. Pret. & P.P. **of sit,** fr. O.E. Pret. *sæt*; M.E. *sat*. Cp. the O.E. P.P. (*ġe*)*seten*, M.E. *seten*.

satable, adj. [1. sátabl; 2. séitəbl]. **sate & -able.** Capable of being sated or satisfied.

Satan, n. [1. sátan; 2. séit(ə)n], fr. Lat. *Satanas* in the Vulgate, Gk. *Satanâs*, in Septuagint, for Hebrew *Sātān*, 'the enemy, the adversary'; fr. *sātan*, 'to oppose, persecute'; cogn. w. Arab. *shaitan*, fr. *shatana*, 'to oppose'. The Devil, the arch-enemy of mankind.

satanic(al), adj. [1. satánik(l); 2. sətǽnik(l)]. Prec. & **-ic & -al.** The shorter is now the commoner form. **a** (cap.) Connected with, emanating from, pertaining to, Satan: *Satanic influence*; hence **b** fiendish, devilish, diabolical; utterly malignant and wicked: *with satanic glee*; *satanic cruelties, blasphemies* &c.; *satanic energy*, so great as to be abnormal, daemonic. Phrs. *the Satanic host*, the fallen angels (Milton); *His Satanic Majesty*, humorous way of referring to the Devil; *Satanic school of poetry*, applied by Southey to the poetry of Byron and Shelley.

satanically, adv. Prec. & **-ly.** In a satanic manner.

Satanism, n. [1. sátanizm; 2. séitənizəm]. **Satan & -ism.** Infamous modern form of superstition or blasphemy, in which the Devil is invoked and worshipped with a travesty of Christian ceremonial, and with celebration of the so-called, Black Mass, attended with monstrous impieties; diabolism.

Satanist, n. [1. sátanist; 2. séitənist]. See prec. & **-ist.** One who practises Satanism.

Satanology, n. [1. sàtanóloji; 2. sèitənɔ́lədži]. **Satan & -o- & -logy.** Study of Satan in Christian theory and in legend; historical account of theories and legends concerning Satan.

satara, n. [1. satáhra; 2. sətárə], fr. name of town in India. A heavy, ribbed woollen broadcloth.

satchel, n. [1. sáchel; 2. sǽtʃəl], fr. O. Fr. *sachel*, fr. L. Lat. *sacellus*, dimin. of *saccus*, see **sack (I.).** A small sack or bag, of leather or canvas, furnished with a strap to pass over the shoulder, esp. one used by children for carrying books to and from school.

sate (I.), vb. trans. [1. sāt; 2. seit]. Possibly based on M.E. *sāde*, O.E. *sadian*, 'to make sated, to satiate', see **sad**, but assimilated to Lat. *sat, satis*, 'enough'; perh., more prob., merely a shortened form of **satiate.** (chiefly in pass.) To satisfy, gratify, appetite, desire, to the full, or to repletion; to glut, to satiate, surfeit: *to be sated with food, drink, pleasure*; also *to sate oneself with*, satisfy completely, beyond measure.

sate (II.), vb. [1. sat; 2. sæt]. Archaic Pret. of **sit**; now *sat*.

sateen, n. [1. satḗn; 2. sætín], fr. **satin**, w. suff. *-een*, variant of **-ine**, indicating a derivative or imitation. Cp. **velveteen.** A cotton or wool fabric with glossy surface made to imitate satin.

sateless, adj. [1. sátles; 2. séitlis]. **sate (I.) & -less.** (poet.) Not to be sated; insatiable.

satellite, n. [1. sátelīt; 2. sǽtilait]. Fr., fr. Lat. *satellit-(em)*, *satelles*, 'an attendant, guard', in pl., 'escort, retinue; partner, abettor of crime, accomplice'; etymol. doubtful. **1.** An attendant, dependent, follower of a superior; a member of the retinue or train of an important personage; an obsequious minion, hanger-on, jackal, of the great. **2.** (astron.) A secondary planet revolving round a greater planet, as the moon round the earth.

satellitic, adj. [1. sàtelítik; 2. sæ̀tilítik]. Prec. & **-ic.** Having the qualities and character of a satellite; revolving as a satellite round a greater body.

satelloid, n. [1. sáteloid; 2. sǽtilɔid]. **satellite & -oid.** A small body resembling a satellite, as the bodies that form the rings of the planet Saturn.

sati, n. See **suttee.**

satiable, adj. [1. sásh(i)abl; 2. séiʃ(i)əbl]. See **satiate (II.) & -able.** Capable of being satiated or sated.

satiate (I.), adj. [1. sáshiāt; 2. séiʃieit], fr. Lat. *satiāt-(um)*, P.P. type of *satiāre*, 'to fill full, to satisfy', fr. *sat, satis*, 'enough, sufficient', see **satis.** (archaic or poet., followed by *with* or *of*) Having enjoyed enough, or more than enough; sated, satiated; surfeited, glutted: *satiate with pleasure*; *'In life's cool evening, satiate of applause'* (Pope, 'Epistle to Bolingbroke', 9.).

satiate (II.), vb. trans., fr. prec. **a** To satisfy; to sate, fill to satiety (persons); **b** to appease, satisfy (desire, appetite &c.); to dull, cloy, by over-indulgence.

satiation, n. [1. sàshiáshun; 2. sèiʃiéiʃən]. Prec. & **-ion.** Act of satiating; state of being satiated.

satiety, n. [1. satíeti; 2. sətáiəti], fr. Fr. *satiété*, fr. Lat. *satietāt-(em)*, fr. *satis*, 'enough'. See **satiate (I.) & -ity.** State of being satiated or satisfied to repletion; feeling of having had enough or more than enough; surfeit.

satin (I.), n. [1. sátin; 2. sǽtin]. Fr., cp. Ital. *setino*, 'a thin silk stuff', Port. *setim*; etymol. doubtful; Low Lat. has *satinus*, *setinus*, 'a silk stuff, satin', apparently fr. Lat. *sēta*, 'bristle, hair', also, in Low Lat., 'silk'. See **seta & seton. 1.** A soft rich silk fabric with a smooth, lustrous, glossy surface. **2. a** Any soft, smooth, glossy, lustrous surface: *the satin of a fine skin, of the coat of a horse* &c.; **b** (slang) gin, also *white satin*. **3.** (attrib.) **a** Made of satin: *a satin dress*; **b** resembling satin in appearance and texture; smooth, silky, to the touch; bright and glossy: *a horse's satin coat*; *a satin polish.*

satin (II.), vb. trans., fr. prec. To make satiny or like satin; to give a satin-like surface to: *to satin paper.*

satinet, satinette, n. [1. sàtinét; 2. sætinét]. Fr. See **satin (I.)** & dimin. **-et, -ette**. A cotton and woollen fabric with glossy surface imitating satin.

satin-finish, n. A glossy polish given to silver by a brush with metal bristles.

satin-flower, n. (bot.) Honesty, also called *white satin*.

satin-paper, n. A fine writing-paper with glossy surface.

satin-spar, n. A fibrous form of calcium carbonate or gypsum, taking a pearly, glossy polish.

satin-wood, n. **1.** A fine, hard wood, of light colour, mottled and grained, taking a beautiful satin polish, and used for cabinet-work in inlays, or veneers. **2.** The name of two kinds of tree, of the E. and W. Indies, from which this wood is obtained.

satiny, adj. [1. sátini; 2. sætini]. **satin (I.)** & **-y.** Resembling satin in texture or glossiness.

satire, n. [1. sátīr; 2. sætaiə], fr. Lat. *satura*, later *satira*, properly the fem. sing. of *satur*, 'full, sated', fr. *satis*, 'enough, sufficient', see **satis** & **saturate**; orig. in Phr. *satura lanx*, 'a full dish', esp. of a dish filled with various kinds of firstfruits, presented to Ceres and Bacchus; hence, a medley such as the earliest satires were. **1.** (in anct. Rom. liter.) A dramatic medley in rude, Fescennine verse, full of coarse raillery, ridicule &c., later developing into the classical verse form as in the invective of Juvenal or the light raillery of Horace. **2.** The holding up of human follies, vices, and hypocrisies &c. to ridicule, reprobation, or bitter contempt directed against society in general, or individuals, in verse or prose; **a** literary art of this kind: *Voltaire, that master of satire*; *satire was perhaps at its highest in France and England in 17th and 18th cents.*; **b** a literary work of this kind: *the Satires of Horace, Dryden, Pope* &c.; '*Gulliver's Travels*' *is a political and social satire*. **3.** Use of ridicule, mockery, sarcasm, irony, in spoken or written words, to expose the follies, vices &c., of others, esp. of those unconscious of such failings: *on some people satire is wasted*. **4.** That which brings ridicule, scorn, or contempt; a mockery: *his actions are a satire on his boastful pretensions*; *what a satire on our wonderful civilization the war proved to be!*

satiric, adj. [1. satírik; 2. sətírik], fr. L. Lat. *satiricus*. See prec. & **-ic.** Pertaining to, containing, satire or satires; containing, writing, satires: *satiric verse*; *a satiric poem, poet*; *a satiric style*.

satirical, adj. [1. satírikl; 2. sətírikl]. Prec. & **-al.** Employing, addicted to, satire; sarcastic, cynical; characterized by satire: *satirical person, laughter* &c.

satirically, adv. Prec. & **-ly.** In a satirical manner.

satirist, n. [1. sátirist; 2. sætirist]. **satire** & **-ist.** **a** A writer of satires; **b** a satirical person.

satirize, vb. trans. [1. sátirīz; 2. sætiraiz]. **satire** & **-ize.** To make (person or thing) the object of satire; to attack by means of satire.

satis, adv. [1. sátis; 2. sætis]. Lat., 'enough, sufficient', adv. & indecl. adj.; cogn. w. Goth. *saþs*, O.S. *sad*, O.E. *sæd*, 'satiated, wearied', see **sad**; cp. Lat. *satiāre*, 'to fill, to satisfy'. Enough, sufficient; used in reports on conduct to show that this has been satisfactory, and on examination papers &c. to indicate that the candidate has obtained sufficient marks to pass; also in Phr. *jam satis*, 'already enough'.

satisfaction, n. [1. sàtisfákshun; 2. sætisfækʃən]. Fr., fr. Lat. *satisfactiōn-(em)*, 'security for a creditor, bail; apology, explanation; reparation, amends, satisfaction'. See **satis** & **-faction.** **1.** Act of satisfying; gratification (of material or spiritual desires, needs, appetites &c.). **2.** State of being satisfied, contentment: *a feeling of satisfaction*; *to find satisfaction in doing or not doing*, to be satisfied, pleased; *to give satisfaction to*, to satisfy; *to one's own satisfaction*, so that one is pleased with oneself: *to express one's satisfaction at, with, some work or result*. **3.** That which satisfies; cause of satisfaction &c.: *it is a satisfaction to know that . . .* &c.; specif. **a** (theol.) atonement; the suffering of Christ accepted as a substitute for the punishment of mankind for sin: '*a full, perfect, and sufficient sacrifice, oblation, and satisfaction for the sins of the whole world*' (Prayer of Consecration, Communion Service, in P.B.); **b** settlement (of debt &c.): *in full and complete satisfaction*; **c** reparation for injury or insult: *to demand, to give, satisfaction*.

satisfactorily, adv. [1. sàtisfákturili; 2. sætisfæktərili]. **satisfactory** & **-ly.** In a satisfactory manner.

satisfactoriness, n. [1. sàtisfákturines; 2. sætisfæktərinis]. See next word & **-ness.** State, quality, of being satisfactory.

satisfactory, adj. [1. sàtisfákturi; 2. sætisfæktəri]. See **satisfaction** & **-ory.** **1.** Fulfilling one's hopes, wishes, expectations; of such a nature as to relieve the mind from doubt, uncertainty, anxiety &c.: *the experiment has been quite satisfactory*; *his reply to my questions was not at all satisfactory*; *the patient's improvement continues to be satisfactory*; *his behaviour is anything but satisfactory*. **2.** Affording satisfaction; pleasing, agreeable, gratifying; in accordance with one's standards and requirements; hence, often simply good: *it is very satisfactory to hear of his success*; *the cooking here is very satisfactory*; *a satisfactory horse to ride* &c. **3.** (theol.) Atoning, giving satisfaction in full; making complete reparation and amends: *the sacrifice of Christ, once offered, was satisfactory for the sins of mankind*.

satisfiable, adj. [1. sátisfīabl; 2. sætisfaiəbl]. **satisfy** & **-able.** (rare) Capable of being satisfied.

satisfy, vb. trans. & intrans. [1. sátisfī; 2. sætisfai]. O. Fr. *satisfier*, Lat. *satisfacere*, 'to make content; to make amends, make reparation; to convince by proof'. See **satis** & **-fy.** **A.** trans. **1.** To give physical, intellectual, or spiritual contentment to; to gratify, satiate; to slake, quench; **a** *to satisfy appetite, desire, lust* &c.; *to satisfy one's ambitions, aspirations, needs of body and mind* &c.; **b** *to satisfy a person who wants something*. **2. a** To give enough to, be enough for, suffice for, render content: *however much I do, I can't satisfy him*; *he is so grasping that no reasonable sum will satisfy him*; **b** to come up to one's ideals, standard of excellence; to suffice to give one complete satisfaction: *this piece of work doesn't quite satisfy me, but it is the best I can do*. Phr. *to satisfy the examiners*, just to reach the lowest standard; hence, to pass an examination by the skin of one's teeth. **3.** To fulfil, discharge; to comply with, perform, observe fully (requirements; rules, conditions &c.). **4. a** To pay (i.) (a person) in full (for a debt): *to satisfy one's creditors*; (ii.) to discharge, meet: *to satisfy a claim, an obligation*; **b** to make reparation to, compensate, make amends to, indemnify (a person, for an injury). **5. a** To convince, persuade, by bringing proof or evidence; to set doubts, anxieties, at rest: *you must satisfy me that you are capable of fulfilling the duties, before I appoint you to the post*; *I had doubts, but your explanation satisfies me*; *I easily satisfied him that there was no danger*; also, *to satisfy oneself* (i.) *that a person is honest*; (ii.) *of a person's honesty*, to ascertain by inquiry &c. that he is honest; **b** to allay, set at rest, relieve: *you have completely satisfied my fears, anxiety, doubts* &c. **B.** intrans. **1.** To give satisfaction. **2.** (rare and archaic) To atone.

satisfying, adj. [1. sátisfīing; 2. sætisfai-iŋ], fr. Pres. Part. of prec. Affording bodily or spiritual satisfaction: *a satisfying meal*; *a satisfying performance*.

satisfyingly, adv. Prec. & **-ly.** So as to satisfy.

satrap, n. [1. sátrap, sátrap; 2. séitræp, sætræp]. Either fr. Fr. *satrape*, or direct fr. Lat. *satrapēs*, fr. Gk. *satrápēs*, a later form of *exaitrápēs*, borrowed fr. O. Pers. *khsatrapāvan*, 'protector, ruler, of a district or province', fr. *khsatra*, 'province', & *pā*, 'to protect, guard'. **1.** (anct. hist.) A viceroy or governor of a province in the ancient Persian Empire. **2.** A despotic ruler of a dependency; a subordinate tyrant living in luxury; sometimes applied by anti-imperialists to colonial or Indian governors.

satrapy, n. [1. sátrapi; 2. séitrəpi]. Fr. *satrapie*, fr. Lat. *satrapia*, Gk. *satrapeia*. Prec. & **-y.** **a** Province, government, ruled by a satrap; **b** jurisdiction, governorship, of a satrap.

Satsuma, n. [1. sátsooma; 2. sætsumə]. Name of group of islands & province of Japan. A special kind of Japanese glazed, enamelled ware with yellow ground.

saturable, adj. [1. sáchurabl; 2. sætʃərəbl]. Lat. *saturābilis*. See **saturate (I.)** & **-able.** Capable of being saturated; capable of saturation.

saturant, adj. & n. [1. sáchurant; 2. sætʃərənt], fr. Lat. *saturant-(em)*, Pres. Part. of *saturāre*. See **saturate (I.)**. **1.** adj. Saturating, impregnating fully. **2.** n. Substance which saturates; specif. (chem.) substance, such as magnesia, which neutralizes acidity.

saturate (I.), vb. trans. [1. sáchurāt; 2. sætʃəreit], fr. Lat. *saturāt-(um)*, P.P. type of *saturāre*, 'to fill, cloy, satiate; to saturate', fr. *satur*, 'full'. See **satis.** **1.** (of liquids) **a** To interpenetrate completely, become interfused in substance of: *the dew has saturated the grass*; **b** to soak thoroughly, drench: *you will be saturated if you go out in this rain*; **c** *saturate with*, to cause to absorb, to soak with, moisture: *saturate the begonia-bed thoroughly with water*; (fig.) *to saturate oneself with sunshine*. **2.** (chem.) To cause one substance to combine completely with another; to combine, amalgamate, with another substance: *water is often saturated with various salts*. **3.** (in non-material sense) **a** *To saturate oneself in* (a subject, study, an author), to study it deeply, become steeped in, make oneself thoroughly familiar with by prolonged concentration of mind upon it; **b** *to be saturated with* (learning, superstition, vice &c.), (i.) (of persons and the mind) to be steeped in, habituated to; (ii.) (of manners, style &c.) to be profoundly characterized, affected, pervaded, by: *a style saturated with the atmosphere of the classics, with affectation* &c.

saturate (II.), adj. See prec. **1.** (poet.) Saturated. **2.** (optics &c., of colours of the spectrum &c.) Free from admixture of white; full, deep in colour.

saturated, adj. [1. sáchurāted; 2. sætʃəreitid]. P.P. of **saturate (I.)**. (chem., phys.) Holding in combination or solution all of the substance, gas &c. that is possible: *saturated compound*, one in which all the units of affinity are engaged; *saturated steam*, wet steam.

saturation, n. [1. sàchuráshun; 2. sætʃəréiʃən], fr. Lat. *saturātiōn-(em)*. **saturate (I.)** & **-ion.** Act, process, of saturating; state of being saturated; specif. (chem. &c.) *saturation point*, stage at which a substance can absorb no more of another.

Saturday, n. [1. sáturdi; 2. sætədi]. O.E. *sætern(es)dæg*, *sæterdæg*; M.E. *Saterday*; translated fr. Lat. *Saturni dies*, 'Saturn's day'. The seventh or last day of the week, usually a half-holiday; the Jewish Sabbath.

Saturn, n. [1. sátĕrn; 2. sætən], fr. Lat. *Saturnus*, lit. 'the sower', fr. base ***sat-**, as in P.P. of *serere*, 'to sow', cogn. w. **semen** & **seed.** **1.** (Rom. mythol.) The ancient agricultural god of the Italic tribes, later identified by the Romans with the Greek Cronos, the Titan, father of Zeus (Jupiter), whose reign was a 'golden age'. **2. a** (astron.) A major planet, next in size to Jupiter and, until discovery of Neptune and Pluto, the farthest from the sun of the known planets, distinguished by its ten satellites or moons, and its rings composed of a dense mass of satelloids; **b** (alchem.) the metal lead; **c** (astrol.) the leaden planet, supposed to have a gloomy, depressing influence on those born beneath it.

saturnalia, n. pl. [1. sàturnā́lia; 2. sæ̀tənéiliə]. Lat., neut. pl. of *Saturnālis*, 'of, belonging to, Saturn'. See prec. & **-al**. **1.** (Rom. antiq., cap.) The yearly festival of Saturn, held about Dec. 17th, when slaves were liberated, all business ceased, and there was general feasting and revelry, the ancient predecessor of Christmas time, celebrating the winter solstice. **2.** (often as sing.) Bout, outbreak, of noisy riot and revelry; an orgy.

saturnalian, adj. [1. sàturnā́lian; 2. sæ̀tənéiliən]. Prec. & **-an**. **1.** Of, pertaining to, the Saturnalia. **2.** Licentious, riotous.

Saturnian, adj. & n. pl. [1. satérnian; 2. sætə́niən], fr. Lat. *Saturnius*, see **Saturn** & **-ian**. **1.** adj. **a** Belonging to, connected with, the old Roman deity Saturn; *Saturnian age*, the supposed golden age when Saturn reigned, marked by simplicity, purity, and happiness. *Saturnian metre*, the oldest Roman metre, used in primitive folk-songs, of a lively dancing measure; the typical verse has three iambic feet, and an extra syllable, followed after the break by three trochees; it has been compared by Macaulay to the nursery rhyme metre of '*The queen was in the parlour, eating bread and honey*'; **b** (astron.) of, belonging to, the planet Saturn: *Saturnian rings, satelloids* &c. **2.** n. pl. *Saturnians*, Saturnian verses.

saturnine, adj. [1. sáturnīn; 2. sǽtənain], fr. M. Fr., fr. *Saturn*, in astrol. sense, & **-ine**. **1. a** (astrol.) Born under the influence of Saturn, the leaden planet, hence, of a gloomy, morose, temperament; contrasted with *mercurial*; **b** (of expression, temper &c.) gloomy, glowering, frowning, morose: *a saturnine expression of face*; *a person of saturnine temper, appearance* &c. **2.** (old chem. & med.) Of, pertaining to, resembling, lead: *saturnine poisoning, colic* &c., lead-poisoning; *saturnine red*, minium.

satyr, n. [1. sátir; 2. sǽtə], fr. Lat. *satyrus*, fr. Gk. *sáturos*; etymol. unknown, the Doric form is *títuros*. **1.** (Gk. mythol., usually cap.) A woodland and mountain deity, half-beast, half-man, depicted with horse's ears and tail, or with goat's horns and tail; one of the followers of Dionysus or Bacchus in his revels; a wild lover of wine and women; the Romans identified the satyrs with the fauns, and depicted them with goat's legs and hoofs. **2.** A lecherous man. **3.** A butterfly belonging to the sub-family *Satyrinae*, or Argus butterflies.

satyriasis, n. [1. sàtirī́asis; 2. sæ̀tiráiəsis], Gk. **satyr** & **-iasis**. Sexual mania in males.

satyric, adj. [1. satírik; 2. sətírik], fr. Lat. *satyricus*, fr. Gk. *saturikós*. **satyr** & **-ic**. Pertaining to, consisting of, satyrs, especially as the attendants of Dionysus or Bacchus. *Satyric drama*, a form of ancient Greek, esp. Attic, drama, burlesquing the legends of the gods &c., and having a chorus of satyrs.

sauce (I.), n. [1. saws; 2. sɔ̄s]. Fr., fr. L., popular, Lat. *salsa*, fem. sing. of Lat. *salsus*, 'salted', see **sal** (I.). **1. a** One of numerous kinds of more or less highly flavoured and thickened gravies, or other liquids, used to add a relish to meat and fish &c. Phr. *what's sauce for the goose is sauce for the gander*, that which is applicable for one person or in one case should be applicable to all others in the same circumstances; **b** (fig.) something which adds zest and gusto: *any little excitement is a sauce to the monotony of a quiet life.* **2.** (colloq.) Sauciness, impudence, impertinence, pertness: *now then, none of your sauce.*

sauce (II.), vb. trans., fr. prec. **1.** To season with sauce. **2.** (colloq.) To be pert, impudent, impertinent, to.

sauce-boat, n. Small vessel or tureen of silver or china in which sauces are served at table.

sauce-box, n. A 16th-cent. term. A saucy, impudent young person.

saucepan, n. [1. sáwspan; 2. sɔ́spən, -pæn]. **sauce** (I.) & **pan** (I.). Kitchen utensil of copper, iron &c., with a cover and a long handle, in which food is boiled; originally a vessel for boiling sauces.

saucer, n. [1. sáwser; 2. sɔ́sə], fr. O. Fr. *saussier, saussiere*, Fr. *saucière*, 'a dish for holding salt or sauces'. See **sauce** (I.) & **-er**. **1. a** A small, flat, round dish placed below a tea-cup &c.; **b** a flat earthenware dish with a high rim placed below a flower-pot to catch water draining away from the plant. **2.** Round shallow depression in the ground.

saucer-eyed, adj. Having large and round eyes, or wide-open eyes as though startled.

saucerful, n. [1. sáwserfool; 2. sɔ́səful]. As much as would fill a saucer.

saucily, adv. [1. sáwsili; 2. sɔ́sili]. **saucy** & **-ly**. In a saucy manner; impertinently, pertly.

sauciness, n. [1. sáwsines; 2. sɔ́sinis]. See next word & **-ness**. Quality of being saucy; impertinence.

saucy, adj. [1. sáwsi; 2. sɔ́si]. **sauce** (I.) & **-y**. **1. a** Pert, impudent; **b** lively, vivacious, cheerful. **2.** (vulg. slang) Smart, coquettish; stylish, modish: *a coat of saucy cut*; *a saucy little hat.*

sauerkraut, n. [1. sóurkrout; 2. sáuəkraut]. Germ., fr. *sauer*, **sour**, & *kraut*, 'vegetable, cabbage'. A German dish of cabbage pickled in brine and allowed to ferment.

Saumur, n. [1. sṓmūr; 2. sóumjuə], or as Fr. [somyr]. Name of town, Maine-et-Loire, France. A white French wine, with an aromatic flavour, from the vineyards near Saumur.

saunders, n. See **sanders**.

saunter, vb. intrans. & n. [1. sáwnter; 2. sɔ́ntə]. Perh. fr. Low Lat. **exadventurāre*, 'to set out on adventures'. See **ex-** & **adventure**. **1.** vb. **a** To walk slowly, in a leisurely manner, to stroll; **b** to loiter, potter, linger; to walk too slowly and as if without purpose; hence, **c** to loiter, potter, over one's work. **2.** n. A quiet, leisurely walk, a stroll.

saunterer, n. [1. sáwnterer; 2. sɔ́ntərə]. Prec. & **-er**. One who saunters.

saunteringly, adv. [1. sáwnteringli; 2. sɔ́ntəriŋli]. Pres. Part. of **saunter** & **-ly**. With a saunter; slowly, leisurely; loiteringly.

Sauria, n. pl. [1. sáwria; 2. sɔ́riə]. Mod. Lat., fr. Gk. *saûros*, 'lizard', see **sauro-**. Family of reptiles, including the extinct dinosaurs &c., and lizards; crocodiles were also formerly grouped under this class.

saurian, adj. & n. [1. sáwrian; 2. sɔ́riən]. Prec. & **-an**. **1.** adj. Belonging to the Sauria. **2.** n. One of the Sauria.

sauro- pref., fr. Gk. *saûros*, 'lizard', cogn. w. Gk. *saûlos*, 'twisting, vacillating'; cognates in other languages not known; *saurognathous* (of birds, such as woodpeckers), having the bones of the head arranged like those of lizards.

-saurus, suff. Mod. Lat., fr. prec. Used in names of various extinct lizard-like monsters, *ichthyosaurus* &c.

saury, n. [1. sáwri; 2. sɔ́ri]. See **sauro-**. Popular name of various fishes with long slender beaks.

sausage, n. [1. sósij; 2. sɔ́sidž], fr. Fr. *saucisse*, fr. L. Lat. *salsitia*, 'salted, seasoned meat, sausage', fr. Lat. *salsus*, 'salted, seasoned', see **sauce** (I.). **a** Bag, relatively long and slender, of thin membranous tissue, having the ends tied or twisted, containing finely minced and highly seasoned pork, beef &c.; **b** object shaped like a sausage, esp. an observation balloon; also called *sausage-balloon.*

sausage-meat, n. Finely chopped, seasoned meat as used for sausages or for stuffing.

sausage-roll, n. Baked oblong pasty containing sausage-meat.

sauté, adj. & n. [1. sṓtā; 2. sóutei]. Fr., P.P. of *sauter*, 'to jump', fr. Lat. *saltāre*, see **saltant**. **a** adj. (of articles of food) Fried quickly and lightly in boiling fat, and frequently turned during process; **b** n., a dish cooked in this way.

Sauterne, n. [1. sōtérn; 2. soutə́n]. *Sauternes*, name of a district of Gironde, in France. A light, sweet, white wine from this district.

sauve qui peut, n., partly anglicized [1. sṓv kē pē; 2. sóuv kī pø]. Fr., 'save himself who can'. A hasty, precipitate flight; a complete rout, a general stampede.

savable, adj. [1. sā́vabl; 2. séivəbl]. **save** (I.) & **-able**. Capable of being saved or rescued (chiefly in moral sense).

savage (I.), adj. [1. sávij; 2. sǽvidž]. Earlier *salvage* (Spenser), fr. O. Fr. *salvage, savaige*, fr. Lat. *silvāticus*, 'of the woods, woodland', hence 'wild', in Low Lat. also *salvāticus*, fr. Lat. *silva*, 'wood', see **silvan**. **1. a** Wild, uncivilized, in a primitive, natural state: *savage races of mankind*; *a savage tribe*; **b** pertaining to, characteristic of, inhabited by, such races &c.: *savage customs, beliefs* &c.; *to explore savage countries*; *that purely savage state of mankind which some have regarded as ideal.* **2.** (of country, scenery &c.) Showing no trace of human influence or action; wild, rugged, impressively grand and stern. **3. a** (of animals) Fierce, untamed, ferocious: *a savage bull, dog*; **b** (of persons, actions &c.) fierce, cruel, merciless, brutal. **4.** (colloq.) Furious, very angry, with temper out of control: *to get savage with a person*; *the news made him really savage.* **5.** (her.) Often in archaic form, *salvage*, of figures as supporters, naked or clad in green leaves, skins &c.

savage (II.), n., fr. prec. **1.** A human being in the most primitive stage of civilization; a member of a savage tribe or race: *the savages of Central Africa*; *the noble savage*, 18th-cent. conception of primitive man, living in the state of nature, unspoilt by civilization. **2.** A cruel, fierce, merciless person; a brute; one of rude, uncivilized manners or behaviour: *the savages that form a riotous mob*; *the young savages of the slums.* **3.** (her.) A supporter representing a wild, naked man.

savage (III.), vb. trans., fr. prec. **1.** (rare) To make savage. **2. a** To treat brutally and cruelly and with physical violence; **b** (of horses &c.) to behave to in a savage, untamed manner, to seize in the jaws, bite, and worry ferociously: *the stallion savaged the groom's arm.*

savagedom, n. [1. sávijdum; 2. sǽvidždəm]. **savage** (II.) & **-dom**. The condition, mode of life, of savages; savages collectively.

savagely, adv. [1. sávijli; 2. sǽvidžli]. **savage** (I.) & **-ly**. In a savage manner; fiercely, wildly, cruelly.

savageness, n. [1. sávijnes; 2. sǽvidžnis]. See prec. & **-ness**. Condition of being savage, wild, or fierce.

savagery, n. [1. sávijri; 2. sǽvidžri]. **savage** (I.) & **-ry**, cp. Fr. *sauvagerie.* **1.** Condition of being savage, uncivilized, wild; a savage, primitive state: *to live in savagery*; *a gradual change from savagery to civilization.* **2.** Condition, quality, of being savage in temper and behaviour; savage disposition; cruelty, fierceness, brutality; violence &c.: *the savagery of a riotous mob*; *the savagery with which the revolt was suppressed.* **3.** (of scenery &c.; rare and archaic) Wildness; bleak, stern aspect: *awestruck by the savagery of the mountains.*

savannah, savanna, n. [1. savána; 2. səvǽnə], fr. Span. *zavana, cavana*, later *sabana*; prob. a native Carib. word. An open, treeless, level tract of country; used esp. of the wide, level tracts of grass-land in sub-tropical and tropical America; a prairie.

savant, n. [1. sávon; 2. sǽvɑ̃]. Fr., Pres. Part. of *savoir*, 'to know'. See **sapient**. A man of learning or of science, esp. one of eminence and distinction.

savate, n. [1. savát; 2. sævǽt]. Fr., 'a rough shoe', cp. **sabot**. A French form of rough boxing in which the feet are used.

save (I.), vb. trans. & intrans. [1. sāv; 2. seiv]. M.E. *sauven, sāven*; fr. O. Fr. *sauver*, fr. Lat. *salvāre*, fr. *salvus*, 'safe'. See **salvage & salvation**. **A.** trans. **1. a** To put into a condition of safety; to rescue or preserve from, prevent from incurring (danger, harm, injury, destruction, and evil of any kind, bodily or spiritual): *to save a person from drowning, from falling down, from bad ways, disgrace, humiliation* &c.; *to save one's country*; *if the ship can make the harbour it will be saved*; *fortunately the wind changed and the houses next to the burning building were saved*; *my life was saved by good nursing*; Phrs. *to save one's bacon*, manage to preserve one's property from loss; *to save one's skin*, to take no risk of personal injury; *to save one's face*, to escape discomfiture, humiliation; preserve one's reputation &c., esp. by some cunning device or pretence; *to save appearances*, preserve outward appearance of decency and decorum &c.; *to save the situation*, avert apparently inevitable disaster; *to save a person from himself*, protect him from results of his own folly; *save me from my friends*, prevent disastrous results from well-meant but injudicious intervention in one's affairs; **b** (archaic) to guard, keep, preserve, in health and well-being: *God save you, sir*; '*God save the King*'. **2.** Specif. (theol.) to preserve, liberate, deliver, from the results of sin; to redeem, to give salvation to: *Christ came into the world to save sinners*. Phr. *the saving grace of God*; also transf., as *he has the saving grace of modesty*, i.e. redeeming, compensating for, other defects &c. **3. a** To store, preserve untouched, unused, unspoilt, unimpaired, for future use: *to save what is left of the joint for tomorrow*; *to save one's best clothes for grand occasions*; *to save one's strength for a great effort*; **b** to preserve from waste, to economize; hoard up, put by: *to save money*; *one saves petrol by skilful management in driving*; also *save up* (money), to economize it. **4. a** To prevent the necessity, or occurrence of, make it possible to dispense with; guard against: *to save oneself trouble*; *wealth cannot save one from ill-health*; *I met the doctor in the street, which saved a journey to his house*; **b** to avoid the loss or expenditure of; to gain specified advantage &c.: *to save a mile* (*by taking the shortest road*), to reduce one's journey by, prevent necessity of travelling, an extra mile; *to save a post*, to secure earlier delivery of a letter &c. by posting by a given hour in a given place; *to save an hour by taking the express*. **B.** intrans. **1.** To exercise the power of saving and redeeming from sin and damnation; to perform the functions of the Saviour: *Christ alone has power to save*. **2.** To hoard up, save, put by, money; to make economies: *it is difficult for anyone to save with the income tax what it is*.

save (II.), n., fr. prec. (football, cricket &c.) Prevention of the opposing side scoring a goal, a run &c.

save (III.), prep., conj., & adv., fr. O. Fr. *sauf*, 'safe', used in abl. absol. construction as in *sauf mon droit*, 'saving, excepting my right'. Cp. legal use of **salvo** (I.). (archaic, poet., or rhet.) **1.** prep. Except, with the exception of, exception made of, saving: *all is lost save honour*; *all dead save him*, or *him alone*; *forty stripes save one*, all but one; in the construction *save thou there is none to help*, the word is practically an adjective = thou excepted. **2.** Conj. or adv. in such constructions as *all were drowned save he*, = but he, he alone excepted; *not a sound save that from time to time a bird called*, or, *save when a bird called*, or, *save for the call of a bird* (*save for* might be taken as a prep. or as an advbl. phr.).

save-all, n. **save** (I.) & **all**. (archaic) One of various things which save or prevent waste; e.g. a money-box; a small strip of extra canvas added to a sail to catch the slightest wind; device attached to a candlestick enabling candles to be consumed to the last fragment.

saveloy, n. [1. sàvelói; 2. sæ̀vəlɔ́i]. Popular form of Fr. *cervelas*, fr. Ital. *cervellata*, fr. *cervello*, 'the brain', see **cerebrum**. A highly seasoned, dried sausage; formerly made of pig's brains, now of young salted pork.

saver, n. [1. sáver; 2. séivə]. **save** (I.) & **-er**. **1.** (of persons) **a** One who saves or rescues; a saviour: *a saver of souls, lives* &c.; **b** one who saves, hoards, or economizes: *a saver of money, odds and ends* &c.; *a saver of time*. **2.** (of things) That which helps one to save, a means of saving: *machinery regarded merely as a saver of labour*; *new inventions devised as savers of time and money*. **3.** *-saver* (in compounds): *a life-saver*; *the device will prove a great labour-saver*.

savin, n. [1. sávin; 2. sǽvin]. O.E. *safine*, fr. Lat. *sabīna*, sc. *herba*, 'the Sabine herb'. An evergreen bushy shrub, a species of juniper, the shoots of which yield a bitter essential oil, used medicinally.

saving (I.), adj. [1. sáving; 2. séiviŋ], fr. Pres. Part. of **save** (I.). **1. a** Inclined to save (money); thrifty, economical, frugal: *the English are not a saving race*; **b** stingy, niggardly. **2.** Containing a stipulation, a reservation: *a saving clause*. **3.** *-saving* (in compounds): *labour-saving devices*.

saving (II.), n. **1.** Act of saving or rescuing. **2.** Action of economizing; example of this: *there is a saving of some millions to the revenue*; *rapid travel is a great saving of time*. **3.** (pl. *savings*) That which is saved; the result of economy, esp. in money, money saved or put by: *he has lost the savings of a lifetime*; *all my small savings are in Government securities*.

saving (III.), prep. & conj. **1.** prep. Except, excepting, save: *saving a few stones, nothing remains of the building*; *nothing wrong with him saving a slight deafness*. Phr. *saving your presence*, (as apology) without meaning any offence. **2.** conj. (followed by *that* or advbl. clause or phr.) *Saving that he is slightly deaf, he has preserved all his faculties*; *he was never idle, saving in his sleep, when asleep*. Such constructions as *none saving I, he*, I, he, alone, are now archaic.

savingly, adv. [1. sávingli; 2. séiviŋli]. **saving** (I.) & **-ly**. In a saving, economical, manner; frugally, thriftily.

savings bank, n. [1. sávingz bangk; 2. séiviŋz bæŋk]. Institution established for the promotion of thrift, which receives deposits of small amounts of money and devotes all profits to the benefit of the depositors.

saviour, n. [1. sávyur; 2. séivjə]. M.E., fr. O. Fr. *sauveur, sauveour*, fr. L. Lat. *salvātōr*, fr. *salvāt-(um)*, P.P. type of *salvāre*, see **salvage**, & **-or**. **1.** One who saves, delivers, from danger, destruction &c.: '*And the Lord gave Israel a saviour*' (2 Kings xiii. 5); *he proved the saviour of the nation*; *a saviour of society*. **2.** Specif. (cap.) the Redeemer, Jesus Christ: *the Saviour*; *our Blessed Saviour*.

savoir-faire, n. [1. sávwar fár; 2. sǽvwā féə]. Fr. phr., 'to know, knowledge, how to do or behave'. Social knowledge and experience; specif., knowledge of the ways of good society; good breeding and manners; social tact.

savoir-vivre, n. [1. sávwar vḗvr; 2. sǽvwā vívr]. Fr., 'knowledge how to live'. Savoir-faire.

savory, n. [1. sávuri; 2. séivəri], fr. O. Fr. *saverie*, fr. Lat. *saturēia*, name of the herb; associated w. & assimilated to **savoury**. An aromatic variety of mint, cultivated for its use in cookery.

savour (I.), n. [1. sávur; 2. séivə]. O. Fr., fr. Lat. *sapōr-(em)*, fr. *sapere*, 'to taste', see **sapid**. **1. a** Taste, flavour, relish; **b** (Bib.) sweet, pleasant odour, fragrance; **c** (of non-material quality) a stimulus, zest, spice: *danger adds a savour to adventures*. **2.** (fig.) A slight suggestion, perceptible trace, smack: *a savour of insolence in his manner*.

savour (II.), vb. intrans. & trans., fr. O. Fr. *savourir*. See prec. **A.** intrans. *Savour of*: **1.** (in physical sense, somewhat rare or archaic) To have a particular savour, to have a certain taste, or, more rarely, smell; to smack of: *those Southern dishes which seem always to savour of garlic*. **2.** (fig.) To show signs or traces, to suggest, have an appearance, smack of: *criticism that savours of pedantry*; *his remarks savour of insolence*. **B.** trans. **1.** (archaic and rare) To give a savour or taste to; to season, flavour: **a** (in physical sense) *meat savoured with salt*; **b** (in fig. senses) *a life well savoured with humour and adventure*. **2.** (rare or poet., usually in fig. sense) To taste of, smack of; to show signs or traces of, to suggest, indicate, presence of: *conduct savouring inordinate pride*. **3.** To perceive a savour or flavour in; to taste with pleasure, to relish, appreciate taste of: *smoking prevents one savouring the bouquet of wine*; (also fig.) to taste, appreciate critically: *no foreigner can savour the delicacy and precision of French verse*.

savourily, adv. [1. sávurili; 2. séivərili]. **savoury** (I.) & **-ly**. In a savoury manner; with plenty of flavour or seasoning; appetizingly.

savouriness, n. [1. sávurines; 2. séivərinis]. See prec. & **-ness**. Quality of being savoury.

savourless, adj. [1. sávurles; 2. séivəlis]. **savour** (I.) & **-less**. Without savour; tasteless, insipid.

savoury (I.), adj. [1. sávuri; 2. séivəri]. **savour** (I.) & **-y**. **1. a** Full of savour or taste; tasty, appetizing; **b** specif. (of a dish) made with herbs and salted, not sweet: *a savoury omelette*. **2.** (usually w. neg., = *unsavoury*) **a** (of places &c.) Having a pleasant smell; fragrant; agreeable, pleasant; clean: *to have to live in a not very savoury district*; **b** (in fig. sense) reputable, attractive: *he has not a very savoury reputation*.

savoury (II.), n., fr. prec. A small, light, savoury dish, usually highly flavoured, served after the sweets, and before dessert and the wine at dinner.

savoy, n. [1. savói; 2. səvɔ́i], fr. Fr. *chou de Savoie*, 'cabbage of Savoy', province of France. A hardy winter cabbage with closely curled, wrinkled leaves.

Savoyard, n. [1. sáv(w)oiard; 2. sǽv(w)ɔiǽd]. Fr. An inhabitant of Savoy, formerly a province of the old kingdom of Sardinia, ceded to France.

savvy, vb. & n. [1. sávi; 2. sǽvi]. Corrupt. of Span. *sabe*, 'he knows', fr. Lat. *sapere*. See **sapient & sapid**. (slang) **1.** vb. To know, understand, have one's wits about one. **2.** n. Understanding, knowingness, wits.

saw (I.), n. [1. saw; 2. sɔ]. O.E. *sagu*, 'a saying', M.E. *sawe*, cogn. w. O.E. *seċgan*, 'to say'. See **say** (I.). A traditional saying, maxim, proverb: '*Full of wise saws and modern instances*' (Shakespeare, 'As You Like It').

saw (II.), vb. Pret. of **see**; O.E. *sæh* (W.S. *seah*); M.E. *sauh*, Pret. sing.; the *w* is prob. due to the influence of the O.E. Pret. pl. *sāwon*.

saw (III.), n. O.E. *sage*, M.E. *sāwe*; O.H.G. *sega, saga*; cogn. w. O.E. *sigðe*, see **scythe**; further cp. Lat. *secāre*, 'to cut', see **section**. A tool made in various shapes and sizes, consisting of a thin strip of steel with a toothed edge, worked by hand or by machinery, used for cutting through wood, stone, and other hard substances; the action of a hand-saw is backwards and forwards; a circular saw, worked by machinery, is a flat round disk with a toothed edge and cuts by a revolving motion.

saw (IV.), vb. trans. & intrans., fr. prec., P.P. *sawn*. **A.** trans. **1. a** To cut with a saw: *to saw a log in half*; *to saw timber into planks*; *to saw through a bone*; also *saw up* (*a log* &c.), to cut in pieces with a saw; **b** to form, shape, by cutting with a saw: *to saw planks out of a log*; Phr. (fig.) *to saw a horse's mouth*, to work the bit against, from side to side, by pulling first one rein and then the other rapidly, as though sawing; *to saw the air*, to make movements in the air with the arms suggestive of sawing. **B.** intrans. **1.** To use a saw: *I would rather saw than chop any day.* **2.** (of a saw itself) To cut: *it (the saw) saws easily, will not saw at all.* **3.** (of material to be sawn) To admit of being sawn, to be cut with a saw: *this kind of wood does not saw easily.*

saw-back, n. A serrated ridge, as of a mountain or mountain range; a sierra.

sawbones, n. [1. sáwbōnz; 2. sɔ́bounz]. (jocular) A surgeon.

sawder, n. [1. sáwder; 2. sɔ́də]. Variant of **solder.** (colloq.) Only in Phr. *soft sawder*, flattery, insincere compliments, humbug, blarney.

sawdust, n. [1. sáwdust; 2. sɔ́dast]. Minute particles of wood which fall from timber as the saw cuts through it. Phr. *to let the sawdust out of a person*, to take the stuffing out, take the conceit out of; from the sawdust stuffing of a doll.

sawer, n., more usually **sawyer.**

saw-fish, n. Large fish, *Pristis*, allied to the skates, with a long, bony, flat, serrated projection from the snout resembling a saw.

saw-fly, n. One of a numerous family of flies which lays its eggs in the leaves and stems of plants by means of a saw-like ovipositor; they attack many kinds of plants from fir trees to roses and turnips, and their larvae are very destructive.

saw-frame, n. The frame which holds a frame-saw.

saw-gin, n. See **gin (II.).** A cotton gin used for separating the seed from the fibres of cotton, consisting of a set of revolving toothed saws which draw the fibres through a wire mesh.

sawing-horse, n. [1. sáwing hors; 2. sɔ́iŋ hɔ̄s]. Rack for holding logs which are being sawn, shaped like two figures of **X** facing one another, and joined in the middle, or where the legs cross, by a stout piece of timber.

saw-mill, n. Business premises, works, where timber is sawn up by machinery.

Sawney, n. [1. sáwni; 2. sɔ́ni]. Sense **1**, a variant of **Sandy (II.)**; sense **2** doubtful, possibly a variant of **zany. 1.** A Scotsman. **2.** (without cap.) A simpleton; a feeble, weak-minded person, a softy.

saw-pit, n. A pit across which timber is laid and sawn by two men with a long two-handled saw, one standing below in the pit, the other above.

saw-set, n. A tool for setting the teeth of a saw.

saw-tooth, n. **1.** The tooth of a saw, usually large inserted tooth of a circular saw. **2.** A saw-like tooth of an animal.

saw-toothed, adj. [1. sáw tōōtht; 2. sɔ́ tūþt]. **1.** Having saw-teeth. **2.** Serrated.

saw-wort, n. A perennial herb bearing serrated leaves and small thistle-like flowers with reddish-purple crowns, yielding a yellow dye.

saw-wrack, n. A sea-weed with serrated leaves.

sawyer, n. [1. sáwyer; 2. sɔ́jə]. **saw (II.)**, & a variant of **-ier.** Cp. **lawyer. 1. a** A man whose trade is to saw timber; **b** one of the two men in a saw-pit, called respectively *bottom-* and *top-sawyers.* **2.** A long horned beetle whose larvae bore into the wood of pines and firs.

sax, n. [1. saks; 2. sæks]. O.E. *seax, sæx*, 'knife', O.N. & O. Fris. *sax*, O.S. & O.H.G. *saks*, fr. same base as **Saxon & saw (III.)**; orig. perh. 'a stone implement', & cogn. w. Lat. *saxum*, 'stone, rock'. See next word & **saxifrage. 1.** (obs. or hist.) A cutting weapon, knife, short single-edged sword or dagger. **2.** A slate-cutter's tool, a sort of chopper with point at the back for piercing holes.

saxatile, adj. [1. sáksatīl; 2. sǽksətail], fr. Lat. *saxātilis*, fr. *saxum*, 'rock'; the base seems to be the same as that in Lat. *secāre*, 'to cut', see **section**, & *segmentum*, 'a slice', see **segment**, cp. also **saw (III.) & sax**; it is not clear wh. is the primitive meaning, whether *saxum* was regarded as a material which could be split, or whether the Gmc. *sax* was orig. a cutting implement of stone. (bot. and zool.) Growing or living among or on rocks.

saxe, adj. [1. saks; 2. sæks]. Fr., 'Saxony', Germ. *Sachsen.* Applied to various things coming from, or made in, Saxony; specif., *saxe blue*, a bright pale blue dye obtained from indigo; the colour of this dye; *saxe paper*, an albumenized photographic paper.

saxhorn, n. [1. sáks-horn; 2. sǽkshɔ̄n]. Named after the inventor Adolphe Sax (1814–94). A brass musical wind instrument of trumpet type.

saxicoline, adj. [1. sàkzíkolīn; 2. sæ̀kzíkəlain], fr. Lat. *saxum*, 'rock, stone', see **saxatile**, & *colere*, 'to dwell, inhabit', see **colony**, & **-ine. 1.** (bot.) Saxicolous. **2.** (zool.) **a** Inhabiting rocks; **b** pertaining to the *Saxicola*, a genus of birds which includes the stonechat, wheatear &c.

saxicolous, adj. [1. sàkzíkolus; 2. sæ̀kzíkələs]. See prec. & **-ous.** (bot.) Growing on rocks.

saxifrage, n. [1. sáksifrij, -frāj; 2. sǽksifridž, -freidž]. Fr., fr. Lat. *saxifraga (herba)*, 'the maiden-hair fern or *Adiantum*', fem. sing. of *saxifragus*, 'rock-breaking herb', possibly as being used medicinally for stone in the bladder &c., or more likely because it grows in crannies in rocks; fr. *saxum*, 'rock, stone', see **saxatile**, & base *frag-*, 'to break, split', see **fragment.** Any perennial herb of the genus *Saxifraga* or natural order *Saxifragaceae*, a rock plant with tufted foliage and panicles of white, yellow, or red flowers; London Pride is a common English species, and there are many Alpine varieties cultivated in rock gardens.

Saxon, n. & adj. [1. sáksun; 2. sǽks(ə)n]. L. Lat. *Saxōn-(em)*, pl. *Saxōnes*, W. Gmc. *Sax-*, cp. O.E. *Seaxe*; prob. fr. *seax*, 'knife, sword', as the typical weapon of these tribes. See **sax. 1.** n. **a** A member of a Nordic people of N.W. Germany, settled chiefly at the mouth of the Elbe, some of whom, with the Angles and Jutes, migrated to Britain in the 5th and 6th cents., the rest remaining in Germany; **b** ancient language of these tribes. **2.** adj. Connected with, pertaining to, the Saxons, their language or country.

Saxonism, n. [1. sáksunizm; 2. sǽksənizəm]. Prec. & **-ism.** A word, term, idiom, surviving in English, derived from Anglo-Saxon, or Old English; contrasted with *Latinism.*

saxony, n. [1. sáksuni; 2. sǽksəni], fr. L. Lat. *Saxonia.* See **Saxon & -y. a** A kind of fine woollen yarn produced in Saxony; **b** fine woollen cloth made from this.

saxophone, n. [1. sáksofōn; 2. sǽksəfoun], fr. *Sax*, as in **saxhorn**, & **-phone.** Wind instrument with keys, made of a metal tube with the reed mouthpiece end curved like a ram's horn, and the other end turned up and outwards.

say (I.), vb. trans. & intrans. [1. sā; 2. sei]. O.E. *seċġan*, 'to say, tell', M.E. *seġġen, seyen*; the latter, a new formation derived fr. the O.E. type of 2nd & 3rd pers. sing. pres. *seġ(e)st, seġ(e)þ*, is the ancestor of the Mod. form; the Gmc. starting-point is **saʒʷ-(ō)jan*, whence also O.S. *seggian*, O.H.G. *sagēn*; O.N. *seggja* &c.; see also **saw (I.)**; the Aryan base is **sekʷ-*, as in Goth. *saihwan*, 'to see', O.E. *sēon*, see **see (I.)**; the connexion in meaning is through the causative sense, 'make to see, make known, show, indicate', whence 'tell, say'. Further cognates are Lat. *inseque*, 'tell!', imperat.; Gk. *énnepe* for **ensekʷe*, 'say! tell!'; Lith. *sakýti*, 'to say'; O. Slav. *sočiti*, 'to indicate, show'; cp. also Lat. *signum*, 'mark, token', see **sign. A.** trans. **1.** To utter, express in words: *to say what one means*; *better to say too little than too much*; *who said that?*; followed by *to* before name of person addressed: *I am saying to you what I wouldn't say to everyone*; *say good morning to the gentleman.* Phrs. *what I say is* &c., my opinion is &c.; *I should say that (he's rather stupid* &c.), I am inclined to think, I should suppose that &c.; *if £50 is too much, shall we say £35*, make the suggestion of £35; *to have something to say to a person*, usually implies a complaint, censure &c.; *to have nothing to say to a person*, have no dealings with him; *what do you say to (a game of billiards* &c.)*?*, how would you like? **2.** (in pass. construction) *It is said in the Bible, it was said by Bacon* &c., *that* &c., the statement is made, the opinion is expressed, and in the following words; referring to a specified statement which is quoted. **3. a** To report, allege: *people say that*; *it is generally said*; *they say that* &c.; **b** (in pass.) it is reported concerning: *he is said to be a great artist*; *he is said to sing well.* **4.** To repeat, recite, utter aloud, by heart: *to say grace, a piece of poetry, one's lessons, one's prayers*; also *say over*, go through in recitation; **b** (in liturgical use) to recite or read without intoning: *to be said or sung*; *Matins will be said at 11 o'clock*; Phr. *to say Mass*, (of a priest) to celebrate the Eucharistic service. **B.** intrans. To assert, make a statement, utter an opinion, express ideas in speech: *no right to say so*, to make a specified statement; *so you say*, you make such and such a statement, but I rather doubt it; *who said so?*; *you may well say so*, what you say is perfectly correct, justified &c.; *it goes without saying*, is so obvious as not to need to be stated, cp. Fr. *cela va sans dire*; *it is just as you say*, in accordance with your statement; *say on*, (archaic), go on with what you have to say; *I say!*, interjection expressing surprise, satisfaction, protest &c., also to attract a person's attention; *that is to say*, expressing a statement more precisely in other words, giving explanation &c.: *in three weeks' time, that is to say, on January 12th.*

say (II.), n., fr. prec. Only in Phrs. *to have one's say*, (to be allowed) to say what one has to say; *to say one's say*, to say all one wishes to say; *to have a say in the matter*, to have some influence, weight, in decision of; *to have no say in the matter*, to have no right or standing to express an opinion, or to intervene in a particular discussion.

say (III.), n., fr. O. Fr. *saie*, fr. Lat. *saga*, pl. of *sagum*, 'a cloak, kind of cloth', loan-word fr. Celt.; cogn. w. Lett. *segene*, 'large cloth, cloak', *segt*, 'to cover'; O. Prussian *saxtris*, 'rind, husk'. L. Gk. *ságos*, 'cloth for pack-saddles', is borrowed fr. Lat. (obs.) A fine kind of serge cloth.

sayid, n. See **sayyid.**

saying, n. [1. sáing; 2. séiiŋ]. **say (I.) & -ing.** That which is said, a statement; esp. a proverb, adage, maxim, saw: *as the saying is, goes* &c.

sayyid, n., also **sayid, said** [1. sād; 2. seid]. Arab., 'lord'. A Moslem title of honour, borne by the descendants of Ali, husband of Mohammed's daughter Fatima.

sbirro, n., pl. **sbirri** [1. zbírō, zbírē; 2. zbírou, zbíri]. Ital. An Italian policeman.

'sblood, n. [1. zblud; 2. zblad]. (obs.) A euphemism for 'God's blood', used as an oath in late 16th to early 18th cents.

scab (I.), n. [1. skab; 2. skæb]. Scand., fr. O.N. **skabbr*, Mod. Swed. *skabb*, Dan. *skab*, cogn. w. O.E. *sċeabb*, see **shabby**, influenced in meaning by Lat. *scabies*, 'itch', see **scabies. 1. a** A dry crust which forms over a wound or sore in the course of healing; a cicatrice; **b** one of various diseases attacking the skin of animals, or the rind of fruit. **2.** A term of abuse applied by strikers to those in the trade who refuse to join, or by trade-unionists to workmen who do not belong to a union; a blackleg.

scab (II.), vb. intrans., fr. prec. To form a scab.

scabbard, n. [1. skábard; 2. skǽbəd]. Earlier M.E. forms *scauberk, scaubert, seaubert*, in A.-Fr. *escaubers*; etymol. doubtful. The leather, wooden, or metal sheath of a sword, dagger, or bayonet.

scabbard fish, n. A long, narrow, silvery eel-like sea fish, *Lepidopus caudatus.*

scabbed, adj. [1. skabd; 2. skæbd]. **scab** & **-ed.** **a** Covered with scabs; scabby; **b** affected by the disease known as scab.

scabbiness, n. [1. skábines; 2. skǽbinis]. **scabby** & **-ness.** State of being scabby.

scabby, adj. [1. skábi; 2. skǽbi]. **scab (I.)** & **-y.** Scabbed; **a** covered with scabs; **b** affected by scab.

scabies, n. [1. skábiēz; 2. skéibiīz]. Lat., 'roughness, scurf; the mange'; connected w. *scabere*, 'to scratch, scrape'; cogn. w. **shave.** (med.) The itch.

scabious (I.), adj. [1. skábius; 2. skéibiəs], fr. Lat. *scabiōsus*, 'affected by the itch'. See prec. & **-ous.** (obs.) Affected by scab; scabby; suffering from itch or mange.

scabious (II.), n., fr. Med. Lat. *Scabiōsa herba*, plant having healing properties for the itch. An herbaceous plant, genus *Scabiosa*, with small round cushion-like pink, red, or blue flowers.

scabrous, adj. [1. skábrus; 2. skéibrəs], fr. L. Lat. *scabrōsus*, fr. *scabr-(um)*, *scaber*, 'rough, affected by itch', fr. **scabies.** **1.** (of animals and plants &c.) Having a rough, uneven surface, covered with small scales or protuberances; scurfy. **2.** (of subjects &c.) Difficult to handle in writing &c., with delicacy; indecent, improper.

scabrously, adv. Prec. & **-ly.** In a scabrous manner.

scabrousness, n. See prec. & **-ness.** State of being scabrous; roughness, harshness &c.

scabwort, n. [1. skábwërt; 2. skǽbwʌt]. **scab (I.)** & **wort (I.).** Popular name of the plant elecampane.

scad, skad, n. [1. skad; 2. skæd]. Etymol. uncertain; perh. variant of **shad.** Popular name for the horse-mackerel, ***Trachurus saurus.***

scaffold (I.), n. [1. skáfōld, skáfold; 2. skǽfould, -əld], fr. O. Fr. *eschafault*, *escafaud*, earlier *escadafaut*, Mod. Fr. *échaufaud*; of doubtful etymol.; perh. orig. the same as **catafalque.** **1.** (also *scaffolding*) Temporary structure of poles and planks, put up for workmen to stand on while erecting, repairing, painting, or working upon, a building. **2.** **a** The raised platform, of wood, upon which criminals are executed; (in general) **b** the place of execution; **c** (by metonymy) capital punishment. Phrs. *to go to, mount, the scaffold*, to suffer capital punishment; *to send to the scaffold*, to condemn to be executed. **3.** (various techn. uses) **a** (anat.) A bony framework; **b** (metal.) an obstruction formed of layers of adherent, unfused material in a blast furnace; **c** (min.) a timber stage or platform used in the working of a coal mine.

scaffold (II.), vb. trans., fr. prec. To furnish, as a building &c., with a scaffold or scaffolding.

scaffolding, n. [1. skáfolding; 2. skǽfəldiŋ]. **scaffold (I.)** & **-ing.** Collective term for the poles and planks forming a scaffold; the scaffold itself.

scaglia, n., as Ital. [1. skáhlya; 2. skáljə], or w. Engl. spelling-pronunciation; Ital., 'scale, thin piece of stone' &c. See **scale (II.).** A kind of Italian limestone, of red or reddish colour.

scagliola, n. [1. skàhliόla; 2. skàliόlə]. Ital., dimin. of prec. An imitation ornamental stone made of plaster.

scalable, adj. [1. skálabl; 2. skéiləbl]. **scale (VI.)** & **-able.** Capable of being scaled (in various senses).

scalar, adj. & n. [1. skálar; 2. skéilə], fr. Lat. *scālāris*, 'of, belonging to, a *scāla*, or ladder'. See **scale (V.)** & **-ar.** **1.** adj. **a** (bot. and zool.) Resembling a ladder; scalariform; **b** (math.) of the nature of a scalar. **2.** n. (math.) A pure number in a quaternion.

scalariform, adj. [1. skàláriform; 2. skèilǽrifōm]. Prec. & **-form.** (bot. and zool.) Shaped like a ladder, as of the cells and vessels of plants, veins of insect wings &c.

scalawag, n. See **scallywag.**

scald (I.), vb. trans. [1. skawld; 2. skōld], fr. O. Norm. Fr. *escalder*, O. Fr. *eschalder*, Mod. Fr. *échauder*, fr. L. Lat. *excaldāre*, 'to steep, wash, in hot water', fr. *ex-*, 'out, very', & *cal(i)dus*, 'hot'. See **cauldron.** **1.** To injure or destroy the soft tissues of the body by the action of boiling liquid or steam. Phr. (fig.) *scalding tears*, tears of bitter sorrow, remorse &c. **2.** To bring (milk &c.) to a temperature just below boiling-point: *scalded cream*, cream gathered from milk scalded and allowed to stand. **3.** To treat with, subject to action of, boiling water; **a** to eliminate bristles of dead pigs by this means; **b** to clean, sterilize, vessels with boiling water.

scald (II.), n., fr. prec. An injury to the skin and soft tissues caused by boiling water or steam.

scald (III.), n. Scandinavian poet. See **skald.**

scald-head, n. [1. skáwld hed; 2. skōld hɛd], fr. *scalled head*. See **scall.** (archaic) Popular name for various diseases of the scalp, as ringworm, tinea &c.

scaldino, n., pl. **scaldini**, [1. skahldḗnō, -nē; 2. skaldínou, -nī]. Ital., fr. *scaldare*, 'to make hot or warm'. See **scald (I.).** A small earthenware brazier, used in Italy for warming one's hands or feet &c.

scale (I.), n. [1. skāl; 2. skeil]. M.E. *scāle*, fr. O. Fr. *escale*; of Gmc. origin. Cp. O.H.G. *skāla*, 'drinking-cup', cogn. w. O.E. *scalu*, 'shell, husk, dish; scale of a balance', & O.N. *skál* in same sense. See **scale (III.)** & **shell.** The ancient Teutons applied the word **skǣlō* only to drinking-cups made fr. skulls; the word **skull** is another cogn. **1.** **a** One of the two shallow dishes or pans of a simple weighing-machine; hence (usually in pl.), *the scales, pair of scales*, the weighing-machine or balance itself, consisting of a beam, pivoting in the centre, from which is hung a scale, pan, dish &c., at either end, in one of which the measured weights are placed and in the other the thing to be weighed; **b** (often fig.) esp. (in pl.) as the symbol of justice; Phrs. *to hold the scales even*, (fig.) to judge impartially; *to throw* (argument &c.) *into the scale*, to influence a decision one way or another; *to turn the scale*, to cause the balance to sink in one direction or scale or another; hence (fig.) to determine the result of an action or event; *to turn the scale at so many pounds*, to weigh so much. **2.** (caps., pl.) *The Scales*, the sign Libra, or the Balance, in the Zodiac. **3.** Specif. (racing) the weighing-machine in which jockeys are weighed before and after a race. Phrs. *to go to scale*, to be weighed before and after a race; *to go to scale at*, to weigh so much; also of boxers &c.; *Clerk of the Scales*, official in charge of the weighing-room at a race meeting.

scale (II.), vb. trans. & intrans., fr. prec. **1.** trans. **a** (rare) To weigh in scales, to find the weight of; **b** to weigh, have a weight of (so much): *he scaled 14 stone without his clothes*. **2.** intrans. To be weighed: *jockeys scale in and out before and after a race.*

scale (III.), n. M.E. *scāle*, fr. O. Fr. *escale*; borrowed fr. Gmc., see words given under **scale (I.)**; cp. O.H.G. *skala*, 'husk of fruit; egg-shell'; cogn. w. O.E. *scalu*, 'husk; drinking-cup'. There were two words in W. Gmc., **skǣl-*, see **scale (I.)**, & **skăl-*, fr. wh. the present word seems to be derived; the words are close cognates, representing different grades of the same base, & the meanings are also closely related & often hard to disentangle. Any thin, small flake or plate, a lamina, hard film. **1.** (zool.) **a** One of the thin, usually overlapping, horny plates or laminae forming a protective covering of the skin of most fishes and reptiles; **b** similar small hard plates on the legs of birds; **c** minute, downy, scale-like structure on the wings of moths, butterflies, and other insects. **2.** (bot.) A modified or rudimentary leaflet, as of a leaf-bud before bursting, a bract of a pine-cone, catkin &c. **3.** Any of various objects resembling the scales of fishes; **a** **a** thin flake of hardened, dead outer skin which becomes loose and separated from the healthy skin below, as in diseases and affections of the skin; **b** a flaky or furry encrustation on the inside of boilers, kettles &c., formed by deposits, usually of lime, from the water boiled in them; **c** the encrustation of tartar on the teeth; **d** flake or blister of oxide forming on iron &c. after heating or when rusted; **e** a friable, flaky encrustation on the surface of stone after exposure to weather or the chemical action of a smoky atmosphere. **4.** In various specific uses: **a** one of the two plates of bone, metal &c. which form the sheath or handle of a clasp knife, razor &c.; **b** one of the small overlapping metal plates in *scale-armour*, q.v.; **c** a plain form of epaulette without fringe. **5.** A film, as in cataract of the eye, esp. (fig.) physical or spiritual blindness. In Phr. *to remove the scales from one's eyes*; *the scales fell from his eyes* (see Acts ix. 18).

scale (IV.), vb. trans. & intrans., fr. prec. **A.** trans. **1.** **a** To strip, clear, scrape scales from: *to scale fish*; *to scale a boiler* &c.; **b** to remove from by scraping: *to scale tartar from teeth, decayed surface from stone* &c.; also, *scale off*. **2.** To cause scales to form on, to encrust with scales: *lime in the water scales a kettle*; *London smoke has scaled the stones of its buildings.* **B.** intrans. **1.** Also, *scale off*, to flake, peel off, to come away in scales, to shed scales: *some of the paint has scaled off*; *the skin scales after scarlet fever.* **2.** To become encrusted with scales: *stone which has scaled through weather* &c.

scale (V.), n. Through Ital. *scala*, or directly, fr. Lat. *scāla*, 'ladder, flight of steps'; for **scandla*, fr. base of *scandere*, 'to climb'. See **scan.** **1.** (archaic and obs.) Flight of steps; scaling-ladder; used in both senses by Milton. **2.** (mus.) The sounds which subdivide the interval of the octave, arranged in successive order. Phrs. *to learn one's scales*, to begin the study of music; *learning one's scales*; in the first stages of this study. **3.** **a** Scheme, system, of grouping, classifying, in an order graduated according to some accepted standard of relative rank, importance, perfection &c.: *the social scale*; *the scale of animal life*; *high, low, in the scale of civilization*; **b** system of grading according to relative size, amount, extent &c.: *a scale of charges, wages, pensions* &c. Phrs. (*to do something*) *on a large, grand, scale*, widely, extensively, lavishly, splendidly &c.; *on a small scale*, in a small way, meanly, moderately. **4.** (arith.) A system of numeration or numerical notations, in which the value of a figure depends on its place in the order according to the constant or radix chosen as the basis of the system: *the decimal scale*; *binary, duodecimal scale.* **5.** Proportion, ratio of size, relative dimensions, of the representation of an object to those of the object itself; system of exact proportional reduction or enlargement: *a map drawn to a scale of ten miles to the inch, or of one inch to ten miles*; *picture of an object reduced to a scale of one-twelfth the natural size*; *a large, small, scale map.* Phr. *drawn to scale*, according to the scale or proportions adopted. **6.** **a** A set of graduated marks as on a rule &c.; **b** a rule, line &c. so marked, used for measuring distances, indicating the scale used on a map &c.

scale (VI.), vb. trans., fr. prec. **1.** To climb up, or over, ascend, reach the top of by ladder or by clambering; to clamber up: *to scale a wall*; *to scale the highest peaks of a mountain*; (also fig.) *heights of philosophical abstraction which his intellect cannot scale.* **2.** **a** To regulate according to a scale; to fix the proportions, measurements, according to a scale; to ascertain the scale of: *to scale a building, map* &c.; **b** *scale up, down*, to increase, or reduce, according to a fixed scale or ratio: *to scale up prices, scale down wages.*

scale-armour, n. **scale (III.)** & **armour.** Armour formed of small, over-lapping, scale-shaped pieces of metal fastened to a backing of leather or cloth.

scale-beam, n. **scale (I.)** & **beam (I.)**. The beam or lever of a balance or weighing-machine.

scale-board, n. **scale (III.)** & **board (I.)**. A very thin slab of wood, used as backing for a framed picture, mirror &c.

scale-fern, n. A polypody fern, the fronds of which are covered with small scales.

scaleless, adj. [1. skā́lles; 2. skéillis]. **scale (III.)** & **-less**. (of fish, reptiles) Without scales.

scale-moss, n. A plant, the liverwort or hepatica, the leaves of which are formed of small scales like moss.

scalene, adj. & n. [1. skalḗn; 2. skælín], fr. L. Lat. *scalēnus*, fr. Gk. *skalēnós*, 'unequal, odd', perh. cogn. w. *skoliós*, 'crooked'. See **scolex**. **1.** adj. **a** (geom.) (i.) (of triangles) Having unequal sides; (ii.) (of cones, cylinders) having the axis not perpendicular to the base; **b** (anat.) of, pertaining to, a triangular series of muscles of the lower neck. **2.** n. **a** (geom.) A scalene triangle or cone; **b** (anat.) a scalene muscle, scalenus.

scalenus, n. [1. skalḗnus; 2. skælínəs]. See prec. (anat.) One of the triangular series of muscles of the lower neck.

scaler (I.), n. [1. skā́ler; 2. skéilə]. **scale (IV.)** & **-er**. **a** One who scales or strips or scrapes the scales of anything; **b** instrument for scaling the teeth, encrusted boilers &c.

scaler (II.), n. **scale (VI.)** & **-er**. **1.** One who scales or climbs. **2.** One who uses a graduated scale in measuring, surveying &c.

scaliness, n. [1. skā́lines; 2. skéilinis]. **scaly** & **-ness**. State of being scaly.

scaling (I.), n. [1. skā́ling; 2. skéiliŋ]. **scale (II.)** & **-ing**. Action of weighing in scales.

scaling (II.), n. **scale (IV.)** & **-ing**. **1.** Removal of the scales of fish &c. or of scale from teeth, iron &c. **2.** Formation, arrangement, of scales on fish, reptiles &c. **3.** Flaking, peeling off, of scale from stone &c.

scaling (III.), n. **scale (VI.)** & **-ing**. **1.** Act of climbing, ascending. **2.** Graduation, arrangement, in a scale.

scaling-ladder, n. **a** A ladder used for making an escalade on a fortified wall &c.; **b** a fireman's ladder.

scall, n. [1. skawl; 2. skōl], fr. O.N. *skalle*, 'a bald head', cp. Swed. *skallig*, 'bald', perh. fr. same base as **scale (III.)**, **skull**. (archaic) A scaly, scurf disease of the skin, esp. of the scalp; scald-head.

scallawag, n. See **scallywag**.

scallion, n. [1. skáliun; 2. skǽliən]. M.E. *scalyon*; fr. O. Fr. *escalone*, fr. Lat. *caepa Ascalōnia*, 'onion of Ascalon'. A kind of onion or shallot.

scallop (I.), n. [1. skólup, skálup; 2. skɔ́ləp, skǽləp], fr. O. Fr. *escalope*, Gmc. borrowing. See **scale (I.)** & **(III.)**. **1. a** A bivalve marine mollusc, genus *Pecten*, having fan-shaped shells deeply grooved and ridged with undulating edge; **b** single valve of the scallop-shell; representation of this, esp. as badge of pilgrims to Holy Land in Middle Ages, and esp. to shrine of St. James of Compostella in Spain; often borne on coat of arms by descendants of these pilgrims; usually *scallop-shell*. **2. a** One valve of a scallop-shell, or small porcelain dish in form of this, used to cook oysters, the scallop itself, or other fish; **b** dish of oysters &c. highly seasoned, and cooked in a scallop-shell: *scallop of oysters* &c. **3.** *Scallops*, series of pleats resembling edge of scallop-shell, used as ornament on edge of a dress, flounce &c.

scallop (II.), vb. trans., fr. prec. **1.** To cook (oysters &c.) in scallop-shells. **2.** To ornament (edge of dress &c.) with scallops.

scallop-shell, n. The shell or one valve of the shell of the scallop; representation of this as heraldic device.

scallywag, scal(l)awag, n. [1. skáliwag; 2. skǽliwæg]. Orig. Am. slang, said to be a corrupt. of *Scalloway*, in Shetland, in allusion to the ponies. **1.** A name for undersized, poor-conditioned cattle. **2.** (U.S.A.) Term of abuse applied by Southerners to those who accepted the Northern reconstruction policy after the Civil War. **3.** A scamp; idle, disreputable fellow.

scalp (I.), n. [1. skalp; 2. skælp]. Only in Engl. in specific sense, but borrowed by Fr. & Germ. in sense of a Red Indian's scalp; apparently of Scand. origin, cp. O.N. *skálpr*, 'sheath', M. Swed. *skalp*, Dan. dial. *skalp*, 'shell', & Du. *schelp*, 'shell', cogn. w. **scale (I.)** & **(III.)**, & cp. **scallop**. **1. a** The skin and hair covering the top of the head; **b** this part as stripped off by Red Indians from a defeated enemy, and preserved as a trophy. Phr. (fig.) *to take scalps*, to have a victory; *to have the scalp of*, to defeat, subdue, in argument or otherwise; to pay out for some injury. **2.** Upper part of a whale's head. **3.** Esp. in form *scaup*, a bare rounded rock or hill-top.

scalp (II.), vb. trans., fr. prec. To strip off the scalp of.

scalpel, n. [1. skálpel; 2. skǽlpɛl], fr. Lat. *scalpellum*, dimin. of *scalprum*, 'knife', fr. *scalpere*, 'to cut, carve, scrape', cogn. w. *sculpere*, 'to carve'. See **sculpture**. A small, straight, slender knife used by surgeons.

scalper (I.), n. [1. skálper; 2. skǽlpə]. **scalp (II.)** & **-er**. One who scalps, esp. of Red Indians.

scalper (II.), n., fr. Lat. *scalprum*. See **scalpel**. A surgical instrument used for scraping bone &c.; a surgical file or rasp.

scalping-iron, n. [1. skálping ī́ern; 2. skǽlpiŋ áiən]. See **scalper (II.)** & **iron**. A surgical scraping instrument; scalper.

scalpless, adj. [1. skálples; 2. skǽlplis]. **scalp (I.)** & **-less**. Lacking, having lost, one's scalp.

scalp-lock, n. The lock or tuft of hair left unshaven by Red Indian braves as a challenge to their enemies.

scalpriform, adj. [1. skálpriform; 2. skǽlprifōm], fr. Lat. *scalprum*. See **scalpel** & **-form**. (zool.) Chisel-shaped; of the incisor teeth of rodents.

scaly, adj. [1. skā́li; 2. skéili]. **scale (III.)** & **-ly**. **1.** Covered with scales, as fish, reptiles &c. **2. a** Resembling scales or flakes; **b** peeling, flaking off in scales.

scammony, n. [1. skámuni; 2. skǽməni], fr. O. Fr. *scammonie*, fr. Lat. *scammōnia*, fr. Gk. *skam(m)ōnia*, 'bind-weed'. A gum resin obtained from the fleshy root of a species of convolvulus from the Eastern Mediterranean, used medicinally.

scamp (I.), n. [1. skamp; 2. skæmp]. Prob. fr. **scamper**, an earlier word. **1.** (obs.) A highwayman. **2.** An idle rogue, rascal; worthless fellow; often used playfully in same way as *rogue*: *a handsome young scamp*, a gay, high-spirited, young man.

scamp (II.), vb. trans. Prob. variant of **scant**, & cp. **skimp**. **a** To do (work &c.) in a hurried, careless, perfunctory, inadequate, way; **b** to use insufficient or inferior materials in doing some particular work.

scamper (I.), vb. intrans. [1. skámper; 2. skǽmpə]. Prob. fr. O. Norm. Fr. *escamper*, 'to flee, decamp, escape', fr. Lat. *ex*, 'away, out', & *campus*, 'field', see **camp (I.)**; & cp. Ital. *scampare* of same origin, in present Engl. sense; the O.E.D. suggests that *scamper* was a military word of the late 17th cent. **1.** (obs.) To run away, flee, decamp; now *scamper off, away*. **2.** To run about gaily, to caper, skip about from place to place (esp. of children and young animals); also *scamper about*.

scamper (II.), n., fr. prec. A brisk run, a rapid gallop &c.

scan, vb. trans. & intrans. [1. skan; 2. skæn], fr. Lat. *scandere*, 'to climb, ascend, mount'; also by grammarians &c., in Phr. *scandere versus*, 'to measure verses by taking them foot by foot'; cogn. w. Gk. *skándalon*, 'a trap; a stumbling-block', see **scandal**; cp. also **scale (V.)** & second element in **ascend, descend** &c. **A.** trans. **1. a** To utter (verse) so as to bring out full metrical value, giving the proper importance to all the elements of metrical effect; **b** to analyse (verse) into its metrical elements. **2. a** (i.) To look at closely; to examine, scrutinize: *to scan the horizon, a person's face* &c.; (ii.) to study, analyse, minutely: '*presume not God to scan; The proper study of Mankind is Man*' (Pope, 'Essay on Man', ii. 1-2); **b** to consider, glance at, cursorily, and perfunctorily. **B.** intrans. (of verse) To be so constructed as to allow of proper scansion.

scandal, n. [1. skándl; 2. skǽndl], fr. Fr. *scandale*, fr. Eccles. Lat. *scandalum*, translating Hellenistic Gk. *skándalon*, 'snare, stumbling-block, offence', cp. in Class. Gk. *skandálēthron*, 'the spring of a baited trap or snare'; cogn. w. Lat. *scandere*, 'to climb', see **scan**, & Scrt. *skándati*, 'he hastens, leaps' &c.; & cp. **slander**. **1.** (Bib.) **a** For Greek *skándalon*, as in Gal. v. 11, 1 Cor. i. 23 &c., translated *offence* in A.V., *stumblingblock* in R.V., that which occasions difficulty of religious faith: *the scandal of the cross*; hence **b** that which brings discredit to the churches or causes offence to religious feelings: *to cause scandal to the brethren*. **2. a** Act, circumstance, person &c., that brings disgrace on and damage to reputation of, or arouses feelings of shame, indignation &c. in others: *the slums are a scandal to the town*; **b** feeling of disgrace, indignation, outrage, as expressed in common talk: *conduct which has caused great scandal in the neighbourhood*. **3.** Talk, gossip, damaging to the reputation of others; malicious, or merely idle, careless talk concerning the frailties and foibles of others: *to talk, listen to, scandal*; *people who dearly love a bit of scandal*. **4.** (law) Defamatory statement, or affront, esp. one in a court of law, irrelevant to the issue; defamation of character, slander, q.v.

scandalize (I.), vb. trans. [1. skándalīz; 2. skǽndəlaiz], fr. O. Fr. *scandaliser*, L. Lat. *scandalizāre*, fr. Hellenistic Gk. *skandalizein*, 'to cause offence to'. See prec. & **-ize**. **1.** (rare) To slander, to utter scandal about, to defame. **2.** To cause scandal to; to shock the moral feelings of, arouse horror or indignation in: *his elderly aunts were scandalized at his goings on*.

scandalize (II.), vb. trans., for *scantelize, 'form into small parts, divide; shorten sail', fr. obs. *scantle*, dimin. of **scant (II.)**. (naut.) In Phr. *to scandalize a sail*, to reduce its area.

scandalmonger, n. [1. skándlmungger; 2. skǽndlmaŋgə]. One who spreads scandal, one given to idle and malicious gossip about others.

scandalmongering, n. [1. skándlmùnggering; 2. skǽndlmàŋgəriŋ]. Prec. & **-ing**. Act of spreading scandal.

scandalous, adj. [1. skándalus; 2. skǽndələs], fr. Fr. *scandaleux*, L. Lat. *scandalōsus*. See **scandal** & **-ous**. **1.** Of such a nature as to offend and wound the sense of morality and decency; disgraceful, deserving condemnation: *the conditions in slum areas of some large towns are perfectly scandalous*. **2.** Bringing scandal and infamy; infamous: *scandalous conduct, crime* &c. **3. a** Defamatory, libellous: *scandalous reports*; **b** fond of scandal, given to spreading scandal: *a scandalous set*; *a scandalous tongue*.

scandalously, adv. Prec. & **-ly**. In a scandalous manner.

scandalousness, n. See prec. & **-ness**. State, quality, of being scandalous.

scandalum magnatum, n. [1. skándalum magnā́tum; 2. skǽndələm mægnéitəm]. Med. Lat., 'scandal of magnates'. (legal hist.) A special form of defamation or slander, being any words spoken in derogation of temporal or spiritual peers, judges, and other 'magnates' of the realm; an actionable offence punishable under an old statute now repealed.

Scandinavian, adj. & n. [1. skàndinā́vian; 2. skæ̀ndinéiviən]. **1.** adj. Pertaining to, connected with, Scandinavia, its people, language &c.: *Scandinavian languages*, Old Norse, Icelandic, Norwegian, Danish, and Swedish. **2.** n. **a** A native of Scandinavia; **b** a Scandinavian language.

scandium, n. [1. skándium ; 2. skǽndiəm]. So named by Nilson, who discovered it in Scandinavia. (chem.) One of the metallic elements, discovered in 1879.

scannable, adj. [1. skánabl ; 2. skǽnəbl]. **scan** & **-able**. (of verse) Capable of being scanned.

scanning, n. [1. skáning ; 2. skǽniŋ]. **scan** & **-ing**. **1.** Scansion. **2.** Close examination, scrutiny.

scansion, n. [1. skánshun ; 2. skǽnʃən], fr. Lat. *scansiōn-(em)*, fr. *scans-(um)*, P.P. type of *scandere*, see **scan**, & **-ion**. **a** Mode of scanning verse; metrical arrangement of a verse, way in which a verse scans ; **b** act of scanning.

scansorial, adj. [1. skansórial ; 2. skænsɔ́riəl], fr. Lat. *scansōri-(us)*, 'for climbing', fr. *scans-(um)*, see prec., & **-al**. (of birds) Adapted for climbing.

scant (I.), adj. [1. skant ; 2. skænt], fr. O.N. *skamt*, neut. of *skammr*, 'short, brief', cogn. w. O.H.G. *scamm*, 'short', see **scamp (II.)** & cp. **skimp**. Only in a few constructions and Phrs.: a small, spare : *a scant attendance* (at a meeting); **b** inadequate in amount : *a scant supply* (of food &c.) ; '*fat and scant of breath*', short of ; **c** grudging, not frank or ample : *to treat a person with scant courtesy*.

scant (II.), vb. trans., fr. prec. (archaic and rare) To skimp, stint.

scantily, adv. [1. skántili ; 2. skǽntili]. **scanty** & **-ly**. In a scanty manner; insufficiently.

scantiness, n. [1. skántines ; 2. skǽntinis]. **scanty** & **-ness**. State, quality, of being scanty.

scantling, n. [1. skántling ; 2. skǽntliŋ]. O. Fr. *escantillon*, 'pattern, sample'; etymol. doubtful. Rarely used in any sense. **1. a** A sample ; **b** a small amount. **2.** Dimensions of building materials. **3.** Timber frame to support a cask.

scantly, adv. [1. skántli; 2. skǽntli]. **scant (I.)** & **-ly**. **a** Scarcely, barely, hardly; **b** sparingly ; inadequately.

scantness, n. [1. skántnes ; 2. skǽntnis]. **scant (I.)** & **-ness**. State of being scant or deficient in number or quantity.

scanty, adj. [1. skánti ; 2. skǽnti]. **scant (I.)** & **-y**. **a** Insufficient : *scanty means, nourishment* ; **b** meagre, reverse of ample : *scanty garments* &c. ; **c** poor, thin, not abundant : *crops are very scanty this year*.

scape (I.), n. [1. skāp ; 2. skeip], fr. Lat. *scāpus*, fr. Gk. *skâpos*, cogn. w. *skêptron*, see **sceptre**. A shaft, stem, stalk ; **a** of a column ; **b** of a feather ; **c** of a flower.

scape (II.), n. Back-formation fr. **landscape**. A view of scenery ; scenery itself ; chiefly used in forming compounds: *sea-scape, cloud-scape* &c.

scape (III.), vb. & n. Poet. form of **escape**.

scapegoat, n. [1. skā́pgōt ; 2. skéipgout], for *escape goat*, used in Authorized Version, to translate Heb. word *Azazel* (Lev. xvi.), the meaning of wh. is doubtful, where Vulgate has *caper emissarius*, 'the goat sent out or allowed to go free'. **1.** A goat set free by the High Priest on Jewish Day of Atonement, and supposed to have the sins of the people transferred to it. **2.** One who bears the blame, or suffers the punishment, due to another : *to be made the scapegoat for other people's crimes*.

scapegrace, n. [1. skā́pgrās ; 2. skéipgreis], fr. *escape grace*, 'one who has escaped grace'. A graceless person, a rogue, a ne'er-do-well, a good-for-nothing fellow ; also semi-humorously.

scapement, n. See **escapement**.

scaph(o)-, pref. Form used in compounds, meaning 'boat-shaped', fr. Gk. *skáphē*, 'boat', orig. 'a dug-out', fr. base in *skáptein*, 'to dig out'; cp. **scapula** ; cogn. w. O. Slav. *kopati*, 'to dig'; Lett. *kapát*, 'to chop small', *kaps*, 'tomb'.

scaphocephalic, -ous, adj. [1. skàfōsefálik, -séfalus ; 2. skæ̀fousifǽlik, -séfələs]. **scapho-** & **cephalic, -ous**. (anat.) Having a 'boat-shaped' skull; the defect is due to premature union of the side bones.

scaphoid, adj. & n. [1. skáfoid ; 2. skǽfɔid]. **scapho-** & **-oid**. (anat.) **a** adj. Boat-shaped, of a bone ; **b** n., one of the scaphoid bones, one of which is in the wrist, and one in the ankle.

scapula, n. [1. skápūla ; 2. skǽpjulə]. L. Lat., 'shoulder-blade, shoulder'; earlier Lat. has only *scapulae*, pl., 'shoulder-blades, shoulders', the orig. meaning is 'shovel', fr. the use made of these bones by early man for digging & shovelling ; cp. Gk. *skáptein*, 'to dig', *skáphē*, 'something scooped out, hollow vessel ; a boat' &c. ; cp. **scapho-**. (anat.) Shoulder-blade.

scapular (I.), adj. [1. skápūlar ; 2. skǽpjulə], fr. L. Lat. *scapulāris*, fr. Lat. *scapulae*, 'shoulder-blade'. See prec. & **-ar**. (anat. and zool.) Of, pertaining to, the scapula, shoulder-blade, or shoulder : *scapular arch*, the pectoral arch ; *scapular feather*, one springing from the wing joint and lying along the back.

scapular (II.), n., in first sense, prec. used as n.; in second sense fr. Med. Lat. *scapulāre*, also *scapulārium*, fr. *scapula*, 'shoulder'. **1.** (anat. and zool.) A scapular feather. **2.** (eccles.) **a** (also *scapulary*) A short cloak worn over the shoulders by monks of certain religious orders ; **b** a vestment worn by monks and others under the garments as an act of devotion, consisting of two small squares of cloth joined by shoulder straps and hanging in front and behind.

scapulary. See **scapular (II.) 2**.

scapulo-, pref. See **scapula**, 'shoulder-blade', used to form compounds, as *scapulo-clavicular, -humeral* &c.

scapus, n. [1. skā́pus ; 2. skéipəs]. Lat., 'shaft, stem', cogn. w. **scopa** & cp. **sceptre**. (zool.) **a** The shaft of a bird's feather ; **b** the basal foot of a polyp.

scar (I.), n. [1. skar ; 2. skā], fr. O. Fr. *escare*, Mod. Fr. *escarre, eschare*, fr. L. Lat. *escara*, 'scar', fr. Gk. *eskhára*, 'hearth, brazier, scar left by a burn'; further etymol. unknown. **1. a** (i.) The mark left upon, and hardening of, the skin and underlying tissues, after the healing of a wound, from a cut, burn, or other injury ; a cicatrice ; (ii.) a disfiguring blemish; **b** similar mark left after injury to the bark of trees &c. ; mark left on inorganic matter, such as rock, earth &c. ; **c** specif. (bot.) the mark left on a plant where a leaf, branch, seed &c. has fallen off. **2.** (fig.) **a** Result left on the mind by a moral injury, mental suffering &c. ; **b** physical signs of mental suffering ; e.g. lines, furrows on the face.

scar (II.), vb. trans. & intrans., fr. prec. **1.** trans. To mark with a scar ; also fig. : *a face scarred with sorrow*. **2.** intrans. *Scar over*, (of wounds &c.) to heal, leaving a scar ; to cicatrize.

scar (III.), n. Rock. See **scaur**.

scarab, n. [1. skárab ; 2. skǽræb, -əb], fr. Fr. *scarabée*, fr. Lat. *scarabaeus*, cogn. w. Gk. *kárabos*, 'stag-beetle ; kind of prickly crab'; prob. not a true Gk. word. **1.** Any beetle belonging to the genus *Scarabaeus*, esp. *S. sacer*, the black, winged, dung-beetle of Egypt and the Mediterranean coasts, regarded by the ancient Egyptians as sacred to the sun-god and symbolical of life and creation &c. **2.** A representation of this beetle in stone, glazed pottery &c., with flat under side, inscribed with a name, title, sacred word &c., used as a seal, amulet &c. ; also as pectoral ornament of mummies.

scarabaeid, n. [1. skàrabéid ; 2. skæ̀rəbí-id]. Prec. & **-id**. Any beetle belonging to the family *Scarabaeidae*, including the sacred scarab or dung-beetles, the cockchafers &c.

scarabaeoid, adj. & n. [1. skàrabéoid ; 2. skæ̀rəbíɔid]. See **scarab** & **-oid**. **1.** adj. Resembling a scarab beetle ; or a scarab gem. **2.** n. A seal or gem having the shape of a true Egyptian scarab.

scaramouch, n. [1. skáramouch ; 2. skǽrəmautʃ], fr. Fr. *Scaramouche*, fr. Ital. *Scaramuccia*, name of a character in 17th Italian farces, lit. 'the skirmisher'. See **skirmish**. **1.** A stock buffoon character in old Italian farce, representing a boastful coward, beaten by Harlequin. **2.** A disreputable tatterdemalion, a rogue.

scarce, adj. [1. skārs ; 2. skɛəs]. M.E. *scars*, fr. O. Norm. Fr. *escars*, O. Fr. *eschars*, 'scanty, scarce', cp. Ital. *scarso* ; etymol. doubtful, prob. fr. Low Lat. **scarpsus* for *excarpsus*, form of Lat. *excerptus*, 'picked out, selected, select, rare', P.P. of *excerpere*, see **excerpt**. **1.** Deficient in quantity or number ; insufficient, scanty, not plentiful : *food, money &c. is scarce* ; *fruit will be scarce and dear this season*. **2.** Not often met with or found ; infrequent, rare ; difficult to find or collect : *a scarce book, portrait* &c. ; *coins of this period in a mint state are scarce*. Phr. *to make oneself scarce* (colloq.), (i.) to go away, make off, to steal off, depart quietly ; (ii.) to keep out of the way, to absent oneself. **3.** (as adv., poet. or liter.) Scarcely : *he scarce could speak*.

scarcely, adv. Prec. & **-ly**. **1.** Barely, hardly, not quite, only just : *he died when he had scarcely reached manhood* ; *scarcely thirty people were present* ; *it is scarcely time for dinner* ; *he had scarcely begun his speech when* &c. **2.** (in various qualified or restricted negative senses) **a** With difficulty : *I could scarcely drag one foot before another* ; **b** expressing sense of improbability, doubt, difficulty : *he can scarcely have said what is alleged* ; *I should scarcely pay twice as much as the thing is worth, should I?* ; *I can scarcely believe such a story as that* &c.

scarcement, n. [1. skā́rsment ; 2. skɛ́əsmənt]. Etymol. doubtful ; possibly fr. obs. vb. *scarce*, 'to make scarce, diminish', & **-ment**. A set-off or rebate in a wall ; small flat ledge formed by this ; any projecting, flat ledge.

scarceness, n. [1. skā́rsnes ; 2. skɛ́əsnis]. **scarce** & **-ness**. **1.** Deficiency, scarcity : *scarceness of money, food* &c. **2.** Rarity : *a marked scarceness of first-rate pictures, authors* &c.

scarcity, n. [1. skā́rsiti ; 2. skɛ́əsiti]. M.E. *scarsete*, fr. O. Norm. Fr. *escarceté*, O. Fr. *escharseté*. See **scarce** & **-ity**. Quality of being scarce. (in various senses) **1.** Deficiency of supply, smallness of quantity, number : *a scarcity of food, rain* &c. **2.** Dearth, famine ; a period of dearth : *a time of great scarcity* ; *a great war is followed always by a scarcity*. **3.** Rarity : *the price of an old edition of a book is determined by its scarcity*.

scare (I.), vb. trans. [1. skār ; 2. skɛə]. The formal connexion of M.E. *skēren*, 'to frighten', & *scar*, 'frightened', cp. O.N. *skjarr*, 'timid', w. the present-day form is not clear ; the spelling & pronunciation presuppose a M.E. *scāre*. The O.N. word may be connected w. **sheer (III.)**. **1. a** To startle, fill with unreasoning terror, as by some sudden, unexpected sight or sound ; to strike fear into : *a sudden noise in the dark is apt to scare children* ; *you scared me by coming in so quietly* ; **b** to fill with apprehension and dread, to oppress with sense of danger : *the nearness of the enemy scared the peaceful inhabitants* ; *the knowledge that a volcano may erupt at any moment is enough to scare people who live near it*. **2.** To drive off by frightening : *to scare birds from an orchard* ; also, *scare away, off* : *I keep a dog to scare away tramps*.

scare (II.), n. See prec. **a** A panic, overwhelming and widespread fear caused by a sudden calamity, or by rumour of a great disaster ; **b** an ill-founded alarm.

scarecrow, n. [1. skā́rkrō ; 2. skɛ́əkrou]. **scare (I.)** & **crow (I.)**. **1. a** A dummy figure used to scare birds from standing crops ; **b** a boy with a rattle employed for the same purpose. **2.** A statement, circumstance, fact, which fills people with needless alarm. **3.** A badly dressed, shabby, ugly, unkempt person ; a figure of fun, a guy.

scared, adj. [1. skārd; 2. skεəd], fr. P.P. of **scare (I.)**. **1.** Thoroughly frightened, filled with terror: *a scared child.* **2.** (of face and expression) Evincing terror.

scare-heading, -headline, n. A sensational headline in a newspaper, intended to startle and arouse interest, thus inducing people to buy the paper.

scaremonger, n. [1. skármùngger; 2. skέəmàŋgə]. **scare (II.)** & **-monger.** One who originates and circulates alarming reports which tend to produce a public scare.

scaremongering, n. [1. skármùnggering; 2. skέəmàŋgəriŋ]. Prec. & **-ing.** Act of inventing and circulating alarming reports.

scarf (I.), n. [1. skarf; 2. skāf]. 16th cent., not in M.E. The origin & history of the word are difficult. Connexion w. O. Fr. *escarpe*, said to be fr. *escreppe*, 'pilgrim's scrip', see **scrip**, is hard to explain, seeing the final *-f*; cp. also Du. *scherf*, 'officer's sash'. **1. a** A long piece of silk or other fabric worn about the neck; **b** one worn chiefly as an ornamental accessory by women; **c** a warm muffler, worn to protect the throat by either sex; **d** a loose necktie or cravat for men (a haberdasher's term). **2.** Long, broad piece of black silk worn by clergy of the Church of England over a surplice, somewhat resembling a stole in form; worn round the neck and hanging down in front on either side; also called a tippet. **3.** (mil.) A sash.

scarf (II.), n. & vb. trans. Scand; cp. Swed. *skarfva*, 'to join together'; perh. related to O.E. *sċeorfan*, 'to scrape, shred'. **1.** n. **a** End of a piece of wood, metal, leather &c. prepared for chamfering, welding &c.; **b** union of two pieces by chamfering, welding &c., a scarf-joint. **2.** vb. To fasten, join together, by a scarf-joint.

scarf-joint, n. **scarf (II.)** & **joint.** See prec., **1 b.**

scarf-pin, n. **scarf (I.)** & **pin (I.)**. Ornamental pin worn in a necktie; better called *tie-pin.*

scarf-ring, n. **scarf (I.)** & **ring (I.)**. Ring of gold &c., through which the ends of a scarf or tie are passed, the ring being drawn up close to the neck.

scarf-skin, n. Origin doubtful, cp. **scarf (II.)**. The outer skin or cuticle, esp. of the skin at the root of the nails.

scarification, n. [1. skàrifikáshun; 2. skæ̀rifikéiʃən], fr. L. Lat. *scarīficātiōn-(em)*, fr. *scarīficāt-(um)*, P.P. type of *scarīficāre*, see **scarify**, & **-ion.** Act of scarifying; mark left by scarifying.

scarificator, n. [1. skárifikàter; 2. skæ̀rifikèitə]. Lat. *scarīficāt-*, as in prec., & **-or.** **a** A surgical instrument used in scarifying; **b** an agricultural scarifier.

scarifier, n. [1. skárifier; 2. skæ̀rifaiə]. **scarify** & **-er.** **1.** One who scarifies, esp. in fig. sense. **2.** An agricultural implement for breaking up the soil.

scarify, vb. trans. [1. skárifī; 2. skæ̀rifai], fr. Fr. *scarifier*, fr. Lat. *scarīficāre*, lengthened form of *scarīfāre*, borrowed fr. Gk. *skarīphaésthai*, 'to sketch, draw, in outline', fr. *skárīphos*, 'pencil, stylus', cogn. w. Lat. *scrībere*, 'to write', see **scribe.** **1.** To tear, lacerate, scratch; specif. **a** (surg.) to puncture, make a number of superficial incisions in (the skin); **b** to break, loosen, the surface of (soil) with a scarifier. **2.** (fig.) To lacerate feelings of by severe censure or criticism; to tear (a work) to pieces in criticism.

scarious, adj. [1. skárius; 2. skέəriəs], fr. Fr. *scarieux*, fr. Neo-Lat. *scariōsus*, fr. Lat. *scaria*, 'a thorny shrub'; etymol. unknown. (bot.) Dry, shrivelled, membranous (of bracts or scales).

scarlatina, n. [1. skàrlatḗna; 2. skālətínə], fr. Ital. *scarlattina*, fr. *scarlatto*, see **scarlet (I.)**, & dimin. suff. Scarlet fever; popularly applied to what is supposed to be a milder disease than, or a mild form of, scarlet fever.

scarlet (I.), n. [1. skárlet; 2. skālit], fr. O. Fr. *escarlate*, cp. Ital. *scarlatto* &c., prob. fr. Pers. *saqalāt*, *siqlāt*, a kind of rich, heavy cloth, usually of a bright red colour. **1.** A brilliant, vivid red colour, slightly inclining to orange. **2.** Scarlet cloth, esp. as used for full-dress uniforms in the British Army, the robes of judges of the King's Bench division of the High Court, the robes and hat of a cardinal &c.; hence *to wear scarlet*, to wear scarlet uniform or robes. **3.** (fig.) The colour typical or symbolical of sin: '*Though your sins be as scarlet, they shall be as white as snow*' (Isaiah i. 18).

scarlet (II.), adj., fr. prec. Of the colour of scarlet. Phr. *to turn scarlet*, to blush deeply.

scarlet fever, n. An infectious disease, accompanied by high temperature, a scarlet rash, and sore throat.

scarlet hat, n. A cardinal's hat, esp. as symbol of the rank of cardinal.

scarlet oak, n. A North American oak, *Quercus coccinea*, the leaves of which turn scarlet in autumn.

scarlet runner, n. A variety of cultivated, climbing bean, *Phaseolus multiflorus*, with bright scarlet flowers.

scarlet woman, n. Term applied to the Papacy, and to Rome, as the seat of the Roman Catholic Church, by violent Protestant controversialists; in reference to the woman mentioned in Rev. xvii., 'sitting upon a scarlet-coloured beast . . . arrayed in purple and scarlet colour'.

scaroid, adj. & n. [1. skároid; 2. skέərɔid]. **Scarus** & **-oid.** **a** adj. Pertaining to, resembling, fish belonging to the genus *Scarus*; **b** n., a scaroid fish.

scarp (I.), n. [1. skarp; 2. skāp], fr. O. Fr. *escarpe*, fr. Ital. *scarpa*, fr. Gmc. See **sharp (I.)** & **escarp.** **1.** (fort.) The steep slope on the inner face of a ditch below the curtain wall or rampart. **2.** A steep slope or face of a hill, embankment &c.; an escarpment.

scarp (II.), vb. trans., fr. prec., cp. O. Fr. *escarper*. **1. a** To cut in a steep face or slope; **b** (fort.) to provide (a wall, rampart &c.) with a scarp. **2.** (slang) To steal, pinch (cp. *sharp*).

scarpment, n. See **escarpment.**

Scarus, n. [1. skárus; 2. skέərəs]. Lat., fr. Gk. *skáros*, 'a kind of fish'. (zool.) A genus of brightly coloured marine fishes, with jaws resembling a parrot's beak, belonging to the family Scaridae or parrot-wrasses; also called *parrot-fish.*

scary, adj. [1. skári; 2. skέəri]. **scare (II.)** & **-y.** (colloq.) **1.** Causing a scare; terrifying, frightening. **2.** Liable, subject, to scares, easily frightened, timorous.

scat (I.), n. [1. skat; 2. skæt], fr. O.N. *skattr*, 'tribute, tax', cogn. w. O.E. *sċeat*, 'property, treasure; tribute'. Cp. **scot.** The land-tax paid to the Crown by a udal tenant in Orkney and Shetland.

scat (II.), n. Etymol. doubtful, prob. imitative. Cp. **scatter.** **1.** (provinc., esp. Corn. colloq.) **a** A blow; sound, noise, of a blow; **b** sound of an explosion, as of gun &c. **2.** As adverb in colloq. Phr. *to go scat*, to go, fall, to pieces, esp. of business, trader &c., to go bankrupt, fail.

scathe, n. & vb. trans. [1. skādh; 2. skeið]. M.E. *skāthe*, fr. O.N. *skaði*, 'injury, harm', & vb. *skaða*, 'to hurt', cogn. w. O.E. *sċaðian*, 'to injure', *sċ(e)aða*, 'one who injures, enemy; criminal', O.S. *scaðo*, 'harm'; O.H.G. *scado*, 'harm' &c.; Goth. *skaþjan*, O.E. *sċeþþan*, 'to injure'; cogn. w. Gk. *(a)skēthés*, 'unharmed, unscathed'. **1.** n. **a** (poet. and archaic) Harm, injury (chiefly in neg. senses): *without scathe*, unharmed, unscathed; *to keep from scathe*, to protect, shield, from harm; **b** (Scots) injury for which compensation can be claimed; legal damages. **2.** vb. (practically obs. even in poet.) To injure; to blast (see **scathing**).

scatheless, adj. [1. skádhles; 2. skéiðlis]. **scathe** & **-less.** Without scathe; unharmed, unscathed.

scathing, adj. [1. skádhing; 2. skéiðiŋ], fr. Pres. Part. of *scathe*, vb., now obs. See **scathe.** Cutting, bitter, withering: *scathing comments, criticism, satire* &c.

scathingly, adv. Prec. & **-ly.** In a scathing manner, with scathing words &c.

scatological, adj. [1. skàtolójikl; 2. skæ̀təlɔ́dʒikl]. Next word & **-ic** & **-al.** Of, pertaining to, scatology.

scatology, n. [1. skatóloji; 2. skətɔ́lədʒi], fr Gk. *skatós*, genit. of *skôr*, 'dung', & **-logy**, *skôr* is cogn. w. O.E. *sċearn*, 'dung'. **1.** The study of coprolites or fossilized excrement of extinct animals. **2.** Obscene literature &c.; pornography.

scatophagous, adj. [1. skatófagus; 2. skætɔ́fəgəs]. See prec. & **-phagous.** (zool.) Dung-eating (of certain beetles and other insects).

scatter, vb. trans. & intrans. [1. skáter; 2. skǽtə]. Apparently a dial. variant of **shatter**, & influenced by obs. or provinc. **scat (II.)**, 'to fall to pieces, to break, burst'. **A.** trans. **1. a** To fling about in various directions; to sprinkle; to disperse: *to scatter seed*; *to scatter sand on the floor*; *to scatter paper bags and orange peel about*; *fragments of bursting shells are scattered far and wide*; **b** to diffuse: *to scatter fragrance, perfume* &c.; **c** to bestow (benefits &c.) in various directions; to shower widely and indiscriminately: *formerly, kings scattered wealth and titles among their favourites.* **2.** To spread, strew over with something, to sprinkle with: *to scatter the fields with seed*; *the public parks are scattered with rubbish after a bank holiday.* **3. a** To break up, separate, put to flight, drive off in disorder,; to disperse: '*Let God arise, let his enemies be scattered*' (Psalm lxviii. 1); *the police scattered the crowd*; *the sun, wind, soon scattered the clouds*; *this great collection of books has now been scattered to the four quarters of the globe*; **b** (fig.) to defeat, frustrate; to shatter, dissipate: *all our hopes and plans are scattered to the four winds.* **4.** To waste, dissipate, squander: *to scatter a fine estate, one's inheritance* &c. **B.** intrans. **1.** To be dispersed, to go off, run away, fly off, in all directions: *the crowd scattered at the approach of the police*; *a flock of birds scatters when a shot is fired*; *clouds scatter before the wind.* **2.** (of shot &c. from a gun) To spread, be distributed widely.

scatter-brain, n. One who cannot concentrate his powers of thinking; a flighty, thoughtless, careless, giddy person.

scatter-brained, adj. Lacking power of mental concentration; flighty, heedless, thoughtless, giddy.

scattered, adj. [1. skáterd; 2. skǽtəd], fr. P.P. of **scatter.** Lying, situated, in various directions, occurring at wide and irregular intervals; dispersed, straggling: *a few scattered houses, villages* &c.; *several scattered references to personal experiences in the book.*

scaup, n. [1. skawp; 2. skɔ̄p]. Variant of **scalp (I.)** & **(III.)**. **1.** A bare hill, rock, or ridge of sand. **2.** A mussel or oyster bed. **3.** A scaup-duck.

scaup-duck, n. A duck of the sea-coasts of the northern hemisphere, genus *Fuligula*, the male being glossy black with green head, so-called because it feeds on scaups or mussel beds.

scauper, n. [1. skáwper; 2. skɔ́pə]. Variant of **scalper (II.)**. A kind of engraving tool, shaped like a gouge.

scaur, scar, n. [1. skōr, skar; 2. skɔ̄, skā]. Scand.; connected w. O.N. *sker*, 'reef, rock in the sea'. Cp. **skerry.** **a** A precipitous rock, crag, or cliff; **b** a low-lying rock or reef in the sea.

scavage n. [1. skávij; 2. skǽvidʒ], fr. A.-Fr. *(e)scauvage*, fr. *escauwer*, 'to inspect', fr. O.L.G. (Flem.) *scauwen*, cogn. w. O.E. *sċēawian*, 'to look at, gaze on'. See **show.** (hist. and obs.) **a** The duty of inspecting imported foreign goods offered for sale in the city of London and other towns; **b** toll imposed on foreign merchants offering goods for sale.

scavager, n. [1. skávijer; 2. skǽvidžə]. Prec. & **-er.** (hist.) Official whose duty was to inspect foreign goods and collect the toll, also employed as superintending the cleaning of the streets &c.

scavenge, vb. trans. & intrans. [1. skávenj; 2. skǽvindž]. Back-formation fr. **scavenger (I.)** **1.** trans. To clean the streets, collect rubbish &c.; to scavenger. **2.** intrans. To act as, be, a scavenger.

scavenger (I.), n. [1. skávenjer; 2. skǽvindžə]. Form of **scavager**, w. intrusive n., cp. *messenger* & *passenger*. **1.** A person employed to clean the streets and collect house refuse and rubbish generally for destruction. **2.** An animal which feeds on and clears away carrion, garbage, or any decaying organic matter, e.g. vultures, certain beetles and other insects, shrimps, crabs &c.

scavenger (II.), vb. trans. & intrans., fr. prec. **1.** trans. To clean (the streets), collect rubbish from (houses) &c.; also fig. **2.** intrans. To act as, be, a scavenger.

scavengering, n. [1. skávenjering; 2. skǽvindžəriŋ]. Prec. & **-ing.** Action of a scavenger.

scavenger's daughter, n. Said to be a popular refashioning of *Skeffington* or *Skevington*, name of a lieutenant of the Tower of London, under Henry VIII. An instrument of torture under the Tudors, by means of which every part of the body was subjected to pressure gradually increasing in severity.

scavenging, n. [1. skávenjing; 2. skǽvindžiŋ]. **scavenge** & **-ing.** Scavengering, specif., expulsion of exhaust gases from an internal combustion engine, as in a motor-car &c.

scazon, n. [1. skázun; 2. skéizən]. Gk., fr. *skázō*, 'I limp', fr. **skn̥g-jō*; cogn. w. Scrt. *khanjati*, O.H.G. *hinkan*, 'to limp'. (Gk. and Lat. pros.) An irregular, 'limping', iambic verse, ending with a spondee; a choliambic verse.

scena, n. [1. shána; 2. ʃéina]. Ital. See **scene.** (mus.) **a** A scene of an opera; **b** dramatic, accompanied recitative interspersed with melody, often preceding an aria, either as part of an opera or as separate musical composition.

scenario, n. [1. shānáhriō; 2. ʃeinάriou]. Ital., fr. prec. & suff. equiv. to **-ary.** The complete outline of a play, opera, film &c., giving the names of the characters, different acts or scenes, situations, stage-directions &c. (cp. *synopsis*).

scene, n. [1. sēn; 2. sīn], fr. Fr. *scène*, fr. Lat. *scēna, scaena*, 'stage, scene', fr. Gk. *skēnḗ*, 'tent, booth; background of the stage; stage'; connected w. Gk. *skiá*, 'shade'; also w. **shade, shine,** & **sky.** **1. a** (class. antiq.) The stage of the ancient Greek or Roman theatre, strictly the stone or wooden background, representing a palace, house &c., the platform or stage proper being the *proscenium*, q.v.; **b** (archaic or rhet.) (i.) dramatic art, profession of acting: *a reigning figure of the tragic scene*; (ii.) a theatre, a stage, '*a sylvan scene . . . a woody theatre*' (Milton, 'P. L.', iv. 140-1); **c** (fig.) life, the world, regarded as a stage: *to enter on, quit, this scene of troubles*, to be born, die. Phr. *to come on the scene*, to appear, come into notice or prominence. **2. a** The place, locality, where the actions and events of a play, also of a novel, poem &c., are supposed to occur: *the scene is laid in France in the 18th century*; *the scene changes from London to a country inn*; *which Cathedral town is the scene of the Barchester novels?*; Phr. *change of scene*, change, variation, of place, surroundings &c., esp. as secured by travel; **b** place, locality, surroundings, where any event takes place: *the scene of his labours, exploits, adventures* &c. **3. a** Painted screen, or group of these representing the surroundings, rooms, buildings, landscape &c. in which the action of a play is supposed to take place; (coll. pl.) scenery: *to shift, change, the scenes*; *drop scene*, a painted curtain let down between the acts or scenes; Phrs. *behind the scenes*, (i.) (lit.) out of sight of the audience, among the actors and the stage machinery &c., so that one sees the reality behind the make-believe; (ii.) (fig.) not in the public eye, but in a position to observe and gauge the motives of public action, the causes of events &c.; also, (iii.) wielding influence privately: *a power behind the scenes*; *the scene changes* (in narration), the story now deals with new and different surroundings and events &c.; **b** a spectacle, vision, of real places, people, objects, with or without action, incidents &c., presented to the eye or called up by the mind: *a woodland scene*; *a scene of wild grandeur*; *scenes of merriment, sadness, squalor, luxury* &c.; *we shall meet again amid very different scenes*. **4. a** One of the smaller sections into which a play is divided, a subdivision of an act, often marked by the fall of the curtain and a change of locality, time &c., or by the close of a situation; **b** situation, incidents, dialogue occurring in such subdivision: *the balcony scene in 'Romeo and Juliet'*; **c** an incident, episode, situation, real or imaginary: *a painful, dramatic scene in Court*; **d** specif., an exhibition of excitement, temper, strong feeling; a row: *please don't make a scene*; *a scene in the House of Commons*.

scene-dock, n. The place in a theatre, near the stage, where the scenery is stored.

scene-painter, n. One who paints scenes or scenery for the theatre.

scene-painting, n. Art of painting scenery for the theatre.

scenery, n. [1. sḗneri; 2. sínəri]. Earlier *scenary*, fr. Lat. *scēnārius*, 'of, belonging to, the stage'. See **scene** & **-ery.** **1.** The painted scenes, used on the stage to represent the place and surroundings in which the action of a play is supposed to take place. **2.** The general aspect of external nature, esp. the relative disposition, grouping, and character of the larger features, such as sky, hills, woods, rivers, plains, and so on; landscape: *the wild scenery of the Highlands*; *most people nowadays have, or at least profess, a love of natural scenery*.

scene-shifter, n. A stage-hand employed in shifting or changing the scenes at a theatre.

scenic, adj. [1. sḗnik, sénik; 2. sínik, sénik]. Fr. *scénique*, fr. Lat. *scēnicus*, fr. Gk. *skēnikós*, 'of, pertaining to, the stage'. See **scene** & **-ic.** **1.** Of, pertaining to, the stage or theatre; **a** dramatic, theatrical: *scenic poets*, the poetic dramatists, esp. the Greek and Latin dramatists; *scenic conventions, actions*; **b** used on, suitable for, use or representation on the stage, or in stage scenery represented on the stage: *scenic effects, machinery*; *scenic magnificence*. **2.** Connected with, pertaining to, natural scenery, picturesque, affording views of landscape: *the scenic attractions of the place are few*.

scenical, adj. [1. sḗnikl, sénikl; 2. síníkl, séníkl]. Prec. & **-al.** (rare) Scenic, esp. in sense of theatrical, stagy.

scenically, adv. Prec. & **-ly.** In a scenic manner; by means of scenes or scenery; dramatically, theatrically.

scenograph, n. [1. sḗnōgrahf; 2. sínougrāf]. See **scenography.** **a** A perspective drawing or picture; **b** a scenographer.

scenographer, n. [1. sēnógrafer; 2. sinógrəfə]. Prec. & **-er.** A draftsman, painter in perspective, one who practises scenography; a scene-painter.

scenographic, adj. [1. sēnōgráfik; 2. sìnougrǽfik], fr. Gk. *skēnographikós*. See **scenography** & **-ic.** Of, pertaining to, scenography or drawing in perspective or scene-painting.

scenography, n. [1. sēnógrafi; 2. sinógrəfi], fr. Gk. *skēnographía*, 'scene-painting'. See **scene** & **-graphy.** Drawing, painting in perspective; scene-painting.

scent (I.), vb. trans. & intrans. [1. sent; 2. sent]. M.E. *senten*, fr. O. Fr. *sentir*, 'to feel; to smell', fr. Lat. *sentīre*, 'to perceive by the senses; to feel, hear, see &c.; to experience, undergo; to observe, perceive with the mind; to think, deem'; Walde's proposal to connect w. Goth. *sinþs*, 'time, occasion', O.E. *sīþ*, 'time; journey', Goth. *gasinþs*, O.E. *ġesīþ*, 'travelling companion', also w. Goth. *sandjan*, O.E. *sendan*, q.v. under **send,** is uninviting on account of the remoteness in meaning. The -*c*- in the present Engl. spelling has no significance or justification; it is a mere vagary of the 17th cent., as in **scythe.** **A.** trans. **1. a** To perceive by the organ of smell; to smell: *to scent spring in the air*; **b** to track by sense of smell: *hounds scent a fox*; also *scent out*; **c** (fig.) to perceive with the mind; to suspect: *to scent a mystery*; *to scent Popery in the new Prayer Book*; *to scent danger* &c. **2. a** To diffuse perfume through, impart fragrance, perfume, to, impregnate with perfume: *the clove pinks scent the whole garden*; *the air was scented with the odour of pinewoods*; **b** to apply perfume to, sprinkle perfume upon: *to scent one's person, one's handkerchief* &c. **B.** intrans. **1.** To track, hunt (game &c.), by the sense of smell. **2.** Milton uses the vb. in the sense of 'to sniff, to perceive, take in scent or smell', in comparing Death to birds of prey scenting carrion from afar: '*So scented the grim Feature, and upturn'd His nostril wide into the murky air* ('P. L.', x. 279-80).

scent (II.), n. See prec. **1.** That which gives rise to olfactory sensation, pleasant or the reverse; an odour, smell, effluvium, fragrance, perfume: *the sweet scent of roses*; *a nasty scent of stale tobacco*. **2.** An artificially manufactured liquid alcoholic essence, possessing a powerful, penetrating, and pleasant fragrance or odour, used to perfume the person, garments &c.: *to put scent on one's handkerchief*. **3.** The taint or odour left by an animal on the ground, or in the air, by means of which it is tracked by other animals; specif. (i.) odour left by the fox, hare, stag, which hounds follow *the scent was poor, cold*; *hounds lost the scent at the brook* &c.; also (ii.) trail of paper dropped by the 'hares' in a paper-chase. Phr. *on the scent*, in the act of following it; (also fig.) on the track, in course of pursuit or discovery: *hot on the scent of an important discovery* &c.; also, *to throw, put, one off the scent, on a wrong, false, scent*, all hunting phrases, used figuratively of the pursuit of an object of investigation &c. **4.** (esp. of hounds &c.) **a** Power of scenting out, or tracking by sense of smell: *to hunt by scent* &c.; also **b** (of persons) intuitive capacity, instinct, for perceiving, detecting, or discovering; flair: *a keen scent for a mystery, an error* &c.

scent-bag, n. **1.** Small, external pouch or sac, found in certain animals, e.g. the civet-cat, containing a strong-smelling substance, secreted esp. during the breeding season; a scent-gland. **2.** A bag of aniseed, used as an artificial scent, for hounds, as in a drag-hunt. **3.** A small bag or sachet, containing scented powder &c., for perfuming clothes, handkerchiefs &c.

scent-bottle, n. **1.** A bottle of scent or perfume. **2.** Ornamental bottle, usually of cut-glass, filled with scent, for the toilet-table, or for carrying on the person.

scented, adj. [1. sénted; 2. séntid]. **1. a** Impregnated with scent, perfumed: *a scented handkerchief*; *scented cigarettes are an abomination*; **b** possessing, giving out, fragrance: *a scented rose*, contrasted with *scentless*. **2.** -*scented* (prec. by adv.), **a** having a specified kind of scent: *strong-scented*; **b** having a power of scent, of specified quality: *keen-scented* &c.

scent-gland, n. Gland possessed by civet-cats, and such animals, which secretes a strong-smelling substance, esp. when the animal is being pursued.

scentless, adj. [1. séntles; 2. séntlis]. **scent (II.)** & **-less.** **1.** Having, yielding, no scent: *scentless flowers*. **2.** (hunting) Affording no scent for hounds; not carrying scent: *scentless ground, weather* &c.

scepsis, skepsis, n. [1. sképsis; 2. sképsis], fr. Gk. *sképsis*, 'inquiry, doubt'; for base see next word. (philos.) Scepticism, philosophic doubt.

sceptic (I.), adj. [1. sképtik ; 2. sképtik], fr. Fr. *sceptique*, adj. & n., fr. Lat. *scepticus*, fr. Gk. *skeptikós*, 'inquiring, thoughtful, reflective, doubting'; cp. also *sképtomai*, 'I look carefully, examine, consider', & w. different grade, Gk. *skopeîn*, 'to contemplate, survey' &c., see **scope** & **-scopy**. The type *skep(t)-* is peculiar to Gk., & is apparently for **spek(t)-*, cp. Lat. *spectāre*, 'to look at; to bear in mind; to judge, try, test' &c., see **spectator**; further *specere*, 'to look at, behold'; *species*, 'sight, outward appearance', see **species**. (rare) Sceptical; connected with the sceptics: *the sceptic school; sceptic philosophers* &c.

sceptic (II.), n. See prec. **1. a** (anct. philos., usually cap.) One of the school of Greek philosophy, founded by Pyrrho of Elis, c. 300 B.C., holding the doctrine that no real, certain knowledge of things is possible, even of the so-called facts of experience, and that universal mental doubt, undisturbed and calm, should be the attitude of all philosophers; **b** (mod. philos.) one who doubts or denies the validity of any judgement, and the competence of reason, outside the field of human experience. **2. a** One who refuses to accept dogmatic assertions at their face value, or any claims to knowledge not proved to his own reason; one who adopts a critical attitude in any sphere of knowledge, and prefers to suspend judgement; **b** (i.) specif. (in theology or religion) one who refuses to accept, or doubts, the truth of Christianity or other revealed religion; an agnostic; (ii.) popularly, an unbeliever, an atheist.

sceptical, adj. [1. sképtikl ; 2. sképtikl]. Prec. & **-al**. **1.** (philos.) Concerned with, pertaining to, the doctrines of the Sceptics; referring to an attitude of mind inclined to question all statements which are not absolutely proved, and to doubt the possibility of proving or of knowing anything. **2.** (popular use) Doubtful, inclined to call in question, not sanguine about the truth of, some specific statement, alleged fact, or event: *I am rather sceptical about, of, the genuineness of his pedigree, his vaunted wealth, your prospects of success* &c.

sceptically, adv. Prec. & **-ly**. In a sceptical manner.

scepticism, n. [1. sképtisizm ; 2. sképtisizəm]. **sceptic** & **-ism**. **1.** (philos.) The doctrines, principles, of the Sceptics; Pyrrhonism. **2. a** An attitude of mind inclined to doubt, criticize, demand absolute proof, before accepting anything as true, or likely; **b** the doubt, uncertainty, about the truth of facts and statements felt by a sceptical mind.

sceptre, n. [1. sépter ; 2. séptə]. M.E. *sceptre, septre*, fr. O. Fr. *septre*, later, on model of Lat., *sceptre*, Lat. *scēptrum*, fr. Gk. *skêptron*, 'staff, sceptre', fr. *sképtein*, 'to prop, support', *sképtesthai*, 'to prop oneself, to lean on (something)', cogn. w. Lat. *scāpus*, 'shaft, stalk, beam', cp. **scapus**, & w. O.E. *sceaft*, see **shaft**. **1.** A rod of gold, highly decorated and bejewelled, held in the hand by kings or reigning princes, on ceremonial occasions, as the symbol of sovereignty and royal sway. **2.** (fig.) Royal, or imperial office, rank and function; kingly power, authority; sovereignty: *to wield, lay down, the sceptre.*

sceptred, adj. [1. sépterd ; 2. séptəd]. Prec. & **-ed**. a Invested with the sceptre; (i.) wielding sovereign power: *a sceptred king*; (ii.) connected with, sprung from, kings or ruling princes: *'Ah, what avails the sceptred race?'* (Landor, 'Rose Aylmer'); **b** actually holding a sceptre: *a portrait of H.M. the King, sceptred and crowned.*

schedule, n. & vb. trans. [1. shédūl ; 2. ʃédjūl], but in U.S.A. [1. skédūl ; 2. skédjūl], M.E. *cedule, sedule*, fr. L. Lat. *scedula, schedula*, 'small sheet of paper', dimin. of *scheda, scida*, 'strip of papyrus bark', fr. Gk. *skhídē*, also *skhiza*, 'splinter of wood', fr. *skhízein*, 'to split, cleave', cp. **schism**. **1.** n. **a** A written or printed list, inventory, catalogue &c., often attached as an explanatory appendix to a longer or more formal document, giving details &c. in tabular form; **b** any tabular, detailed statement. **2.** vb. To set out, state, in, put into, the form of a schedule; to tabulate.

schema, n., pl. **schemata** [1. skḗma, skḗmata; 2. skímə, skímətə]. Lat. *schēma*, fr. Gk. *skhêma*, stem *skhḗmat-(os)*, 'appearance, form; bearing, mien; the manner of a thing; the nature of a thing; a figure in dancing'; fr. base **skhē-*, as in fut. *skhḗ-sō* of *ekhō*, 'I have, hold, possess', wh. is for **segh-*; cogn. w. Scrt. *sáhaš*, 'triumphant strength'; & Goth. *sigis*, 'victory', O.E. *sige*; O.H.G. *sigi*; cp. first element in Gmc. names such as *Sigismund, Siegfried* &c. See also **epoch**. An outline, figure, synopsis, systematic arrangement, scheme; specif. **a** (gram. and rhet.) a figure of speech; **b** (log.) a figure of the syllogism; **c** (Kantian philos.) the result of the use of the transcendental imagination in giving form or generality to sense-perceptions.

schematic, adj. [1. skēmátik ; 2. skīmǽtik]. Gk. *skhēmat-*, stem of prec., & **-ic**. Pertaining to, connected with, of the nature of, a scheme, or a schema; arranged in diagrammatic, synoptical form; arranged according to a scheme or system.

schematically, adv. [1. skēmátikali ; 2. skīmǽtikəli]. Prec. & **-al** & **-ly**. In a schematic manner.

scheme (I.), n. [1. skēm ; 2. skīm], fr. Gk. See **schema**. **1.** Orderly, systematic arrangement; an organized combination of things, events &c. on a definite plan or design: *a scheme of life; under the present scheme of society; a painter's scheme of colour; the scheme of a sonata, symphony.* **2.** A proposed method or design for doing something; a programme of action; a plan, project, undertaking, enterprise: *to lay down a scheme of education, of rebuilding a town; to prepare a scheme of imperial defence, political reform; a great literary scheme.* **3.** An underhand device, design, intrigue, plot: *I distrust his schemes and intrigues.* **4.** A classified tabular statement of a plan; synopsis, outline, summary: *the scheme of the work can be found in the detailed chapter headings.*

scheme (II.), vb. trans. & intrans., fr. prec. **A.** trans. **1.** To arrange, plan as a scheme; to formulate, plan a scheme or design for (also *scheme out*): *to scheme (out) a system of water supply; the new method of traffic control seems well schemed; scheme to (do something).* **2.** To plan in an underhand way, to plot for; devise dishonest and unscrupulous means to effect: *he began at once to scheme the downfall of his rivals.* **B.** intrans. **1.** To make schemes, to conceive, or execute plans; to design. **2.** To plot, intrigue; to act as a designing person; also *scheme for (power* &c.).

schemer, n. [1. skḗmer ; 2. skímə]. Prec. & **-er**. One who schemes, esp. in bad sense, a plotter, intriguer, a crafty designer.

scheming (I.), adj. [1. skḗming ; 2. skímiŋ], fr. Pres. Part. of **scheme** (II.). Given to hatching schemes; esp. in bad sense, crafty, plotting, designing, contriving, intriguing: *a scheming, plausible rogue.*

scheming (II.), n., fr. **scheme** (II.) & **-ing**. **1.** The formation of plans and schemes. **2.** Plotting, intrigue: *all their scheming was of no use.*

schemingly, adv. **scheming** (I.) & **-ly**. In a scheming manner; craftily, designingly.

scherzando, adv. [1. skārtsándō ; 2. skeətsǽndou]. Ital., gerund of *scherzare*, 'to play, sport'. See next word. (mus.) A direction to play in a playful, lively manner, as in a scherzo.

scherzo, n. [1. skártsō ; 2. skéətsou]. Ital., 'sport, play'; Gmc. in origin, cp. M.H.G. *scherz*, back-formation, fr. vb. *scherzen*, for **schernzen*, 'to sport, jest', cp. O.H.G. *skern*, 'jest, sport' &c.; cogn. w. Lat. *scurra*, 'buffoon, jester', see **scurrilous**. (mus.) A lively, sportive, playful passage or movement, esp. a movement in a sonata or symphony following one that is slow and solemn.

Schiedam, n. [1. skḗdam, shḗdam ; 2. skídæm, ʃídæm]. Name of town in Holland. Hollands gin.

schipperke, n. [1. skíperki, shíperki ; 2. skípəki, ʃípəki]. Du., dimin. of *schipper*, lit. 'little skipper'. A kind of small black dog, tailless, smooth-haired, and with prick ears and a ruff, bred in Holland and Flanders as a watch-dog for barges, whence its name.

schism, n. [1. sízm ; 2. sízəm]. M.E. *scisme, cisme*, fr. O. Fr. *scisme, cisme*, fr. Eccles. Lat. *schisma*, fr. Gk. *skhisma*, 'a split, tear, rent'; in N.T., in fig. sense, 'division, dissension', cp. 1 Cor. xii. 25; fr. *skhizein*, 'to split, cleave', fr. base **skheid-*, 'to cleave'; cogn. w. Lat. *scindere*, P.P. *scissum*, 'to cut, cleave'. Cp. **scissile**. **a** Division, dissension, cleavage, in an organized body or society, esp. in the Christian Church; deliberate separation of themselves by a group of Christians from communion with the rest of the Church; **b** the offence of separating oneself from the main body of the Church; **c** (rare) a schismatic body.

schismatic, adj. & n. [1. sizmátik ; 2. sizmǽtik], fr. Fr. *schismatique*, fr. Eccles. Lat. *schismaticus*, fr. Gk. *skhismatikós*, fr. *skhismat-*, stem of *skhisma*. See prec. & **-ic**. **1.** adj. Connected with, pertaining to, schism; guilty of the sin of schism; tending to secede from a Church and form a separate body. **2.** n. One who is guilty of schism; a member, promoter, supporter, of schism.

schismatically, adv. [1. sizmátikali ; 2. sizmǽtikəli]. Prec. & **-al** & **-ly**. So as to cause, by virtue of, a schism.

schist, n. [1. shist ; 2. ʃist]. Fr. *schiste*, through Lat., fr. Gk. *skhistós*, 'split, fissile', as n., sc. *lithos*, 'stone', fr. *skhízein*, 'to split', see base under **schism**. (geol.) A name applied to a crystalline, metamorphic rock formation, which splits easily into plates or laminae; there are many varieties, defined respectively by their chief mineral constituent, as *hornblende-schist, mica-schist* &c.; in English usage, the shales, slates &c. are not included in the term.

schistose, adj. [1. shístōs ; 2. ʃístous]. Prec. & **-ose**. Of, pertaining to, schist; resembling schist in formation, laminated, splitting readily into plates or laminae; schistous.

schistous, adj. [1. shístus ; 2. ʃístəs]. **schist** & **-ous**. Schistose.

schizanthus, n. [1. skīzánthus ; 2. skaizǽnþəs], **schizo-** & Gk. *ánthos*, 'flower', see **anther**. (bot.) A genus of S. American annual plants with bright-coloured flowers and deeply divided leaves.

schizo-, pref. Form used in compounds, fr. Gk. *skhízein*, 'to split'. See **schism**.

schizocarp, n. [1. skízōkarp ; 2. skáizoukāp]. **schizo-** & Gk. *karpós*, 'fruit', see **carpel**. (bot.) Fruit which splits into several single-seeded mericarps.

schizogenesis, n. [1. skīzōjénesis ; 2. skàizoudžénisis]. **schizo-** & **genesis**. (biol.) Reproduction by fission.

schizomycete, n. [1. skìzōmísēt ; 2. skàizoumáisit]. **schizo-** & Gk. *múkēs, múkēt-(os)*, 'fungus', see **myco-**. (bacter.) One of a group of unicellular vegetable micro-organisms reproducing by fission, the fission fungi, including the bacteria.

schnapper, n. [1. shnáper ; 2. ʃnǽpə]. Germ. See **snapper**. A sea-fish of Australia and New Zealand, valuable for food.

schnapps, n. [1. shnaps ; 2. ʃnæps]. Germ., orig. a small portion of drink consumed at a gulp. See **snap** (I.). Name applied to various kinds of strong spirits, esp. to a kind of Hollands gin.

schnorrer, n. [1. shnórer ; 2. ʃnórə]. Yiddish, fr. Germ. *schnurren*, 'to hum, whirr', hence slang, 'to beg', fr. the sound of a musical instrument carried by beggars. A Jewish beggar.

scholar, n. [1. skólar; 2. skɔ́lə]. M.E. *scoler*, fr. O.Fr. *escoler*, fr. L. Lat. *scholāris*, fr. *schola*. See **school** & **-ar.** **1.** (archaic, provinc., or vulg.) A pupil, esp. a boy, in a school: *the scholars were all out in the playground.* **2.** (archaic, now rare) A person regarded as acquiring experience or information; an apprentice, a learner: *he proved an apt scholar in the usages of good society, in the art of warfare.* **3.** A learned man; **a** one trained in accuracy and critical method, and who possesses a mastery of some subject, esp. of some branch of humane learning; often contrasted with *man of science*; **b** specif. (in narrower sense) one who has a minute knowledge and mastery of the refinements of the classical languages. **4.** (popular and illiterate) A person who has some slight education, esp. one who can read and write: *I'm a poor hand as, not much of, a scholar*, means in effect, I can hardly read or write. **5.** (colloq.) A person having a competent, or exceptional, knowledge of a specified (usually) modern language: *he is a good French scholar*, knows French well. **6.** Specif. **a** a member of a public school, or of a college at Oxford or Cambridge, who is on the foundation, that is, who has been elected, after examination, to a scholarship, and receives annually a sum of money for a certain number of years while he is at school or college: *a scholar of Winchester, of New College*; **b** a person who receives, usually after examination, a sum of money yearly from one of the newer universities, from a county council, or other public body, to enable him to prosecute his studies.

scholarlike, adj. [1. skólarlīk; 2. skɔ́ləlaik]. Prec. & **-like.** Scholarly.

scholarly, adj. [1. skólarli; 2. skɔ́ləli]. See prec. & **-ly.** Characteristic of a scholar; marked by, exhibiting, learning or scholarship; learned, erudite: *scholarly mind, habits; a scholarly edition, work of criticism.*

scholarship, n. [1. skólarship; 2. skɔ́ləʃip]. **scholar** & **-ship. 1.** Learning, erudition; specif. **a** (in wider sense) specialized, systematized knowledge, esp. in humane studies, characterized by a high standard of accuracy, by minuteness and thoroughness; **b** (in special and narrower sense) classical learning; in particular, minute and thorough knowledge of the classical languages, and a keen sense of the refinements and niceties of their style and idiom. **2.** Humane studies in general, systematic investigation of historical, linguistic, literary, and textual problems; often specifically distinguished from research in the natural sciences: *science and scholarship.* **3. a** A foundation for the furtherance of education, consisting of the grant of a recognized status, and an annual payment of money, to a boy at a school, or to an undergraduate at a college or university, made by the governing bodies of these institutions, for his maintenance while pursuing his studies; **b** yearly grant of money for the same purpose made by a county council or other public body, tenable at a school or university; election to a scholarship is usually made on the results of a competitive examination.

scholastic (I.), adj. [1. skolástik; 2. skəlǽstik], fr. Lat. *scholasticus*, 'of, belonging to, a school, esp. of rhetoric', fr. Gk. *skholastikós*, 'having, enjoying, leisure, using this for study or learning; studious, learned'. See **school (I.). 1. a** Pertaining to schools, universities, or to education: *the scholastic profession; a scholastic institution; scholastic dress*; **b** acquired at school or university; befitting a scholar or learned man: *scholastic attainments*; **c** (in unfavourable sense) academic, donnish, inelastic, pedantic, formal: *a purely scholastic training; a dead, scholastic style; a narrow, scholastic mind.* **2.** Specif. **a** pertaining to the mediaeval schoolmen, to their system teaching &c. (see **scholasticism**): *scholastic logic, theology, philosophy*; **b** characteristic of the schoolmen; over-subtle, laying stress on precise, logical arguments and hair-splitting definitions: *scholastic subtleties and niceties.*

scholastic (II.), n., fr. prec. **1. a** One of the mediaeval schoolmen or teachers in the universities, esp. in logic, philosophy, and theology, in Lat. *scholastici doctores*; a follower, adherent of scholastic philosophy and theology: *Thomas Aquinas, the great scholastic*; **b** a theological or philosophical precisian; one who delights in logical subtleties and quibbling arguments. **2.** (specif. in R.C. Ch.) A member of the third grade or novitiate in the Society of Jesus.

scholastically, adv. [1. skolástikali; 2. skəlǽstikəli]. **scholastic (I.)** & **-al** & **-ly.** In a scholastic manner.

scholasticism, n. [1. skolástisizm; 2. skəlǽstisizəm]. **scholastic (I.)** & **-ism. 1.** The theory and methods of teaching prevalent in the schools of the mediaeval universities of Europe from the 10th to the 15th cent., in logic, philosophy, and theology, based on Aristotle's logic and the early Christian fathers. **2.** Exaggerated, narrow insistence on dogma, tradition, and formal teaching.

scholiast, n. [1. skṓliast; 2. skóuliæst], fr. L. Lat. *scholiasta*, fr. Gk. *skholiastēs*, fr. *skoliázein*, 'to write scholia', see next word. One who writes scholia or marginal explanatory notes and comments on the works of an author; specif., one of the ancient grammarians and annotators of the texts of the Greek and Latin classics.

scholium, n. [1. skṓlium; 2. skóuliəm]. L. Med. Lat., fr. Gk. *skhólion*, fr. *skholḗ*, see **school (I.).** An explanatory comment or note, esp. one of the marginal notes written by the ancient grammarians and commentators on the text of a Greek or Latin writer.

school (I.), n. [1. sko͞ol; 2. skūl]. O.E. *scōl*, borrowed fr. Lat. *schola, scola*, fr. Gk. *skholḗ*, 'leisure, spare time, ease; employment of leisure; that in which leisure is employed, learned, philosophical discussion, disputation; a lecture, study, learning; place of discussion and learning; school'; cp. also *skholázein*, 'to be at leisure, to have a rest or respite from something'; fr. base *segh-, 'to have, hold', as in Gk. *ékhein*, 'to have' &c., see **schema. 1. a** An establishment or institution for education and instruction; specif., one for the young of either sex, through all stages up to a university; Phrs. *to keep a school*, to manage, be a head master or mistress of, a school, esp. of one privately owned; *to teach school* (now archaic), to be a schoolmaster &c.; **b** a main division of a large school, including smaller units such as forms or classes: *senior, junior, school; the upper, lower, school.* **2. a** The building or buildings of such an institution; *to build a new school*; **b** any one of the classrooms &c. at a school: *big school*, the main hall of a public school; *sixth form school* &c. **3.** The pupils of a school collectively: *the school was given a half-holiday; the whole school was punished.* **4.** Time during which teaching goes on in a school; period of instruction: *school begins at 8 o'clock; to be kept in after school.* Phr. *to tell tales out of school*, (lit., or more usually fig.) to repeat what was not meant to be generally known; to betray a confidence or secret. **5.** Training and instruction given in a school; education: *to go to school; to send, keep, a boy at school; he left school very young.* Phr. *to go to school to*, to be taught, trained by. **6.** A special institution, establishment, or organization for teaching, instruction, or research in a special subject, for adults as well as younger students: *a medical school*, attached to a hospital; *the London School of Economics; British School* (of Archaeology) *at Athens* &c.; *a dancing, riding, fencing, school* &c. **7.** (fig.) Circumstances, surroundings, general environment, or occupation &c., thought of as a means of discipline, of forming the character &c.: *in the hard school of daily life; the school of experience, adversity* &c. **8. a** A group of persons taught by, or following the teaching of, the same master; similar group trained in, or following, the principles and methods taught at a particular place, in a particular country &c.; any group holding the same principles, aiming at the same object &c.: *the Socratic, Hegelian, school of philosophy; a school of thought; Wagnerian school of music; French Impressionist school of painting; the Manchester school of economics* &c.; **b** a body of opinions, customs, manners &c. held by people in common; persons holding such opinions &c.; particular way of thinking: *a gentleman of the old school; he belongs to the new school of journalism.* **9. a** The body of teachers and students at a mediaeval university; such a body as teaching one of the faculties: *the logic school; school of theology* &c.; **b** (pl.) *the schools*, the teaching of a mediaeval university, as embodied in the doctrines of its various faculties. **10. a** Any one of the faculties or branches of learning in which examinations for a degree are held at a modern university; specif., at Oxford, one in which an 'honours' degree may be taken, equivalent to the Cambridge 'Tripos': *the Honour School of Literae Humaniores, or Greats; to be reading for the Law School, School of Theology, Natural Science* &c.; **b** (pl.) the examinations for a degree in such faculty: *to be in, sitting, for one's schools; in for schools.* **11. a** The building, lecture rooms &c., set apart at a mediaeval university, in which a particular faculty was taught, and disputations and examinations were held: *the Old Divinity School at Oxford*; **b** (pl.) *the Schools*, (Oxford) building in which university examinations are held, and where university lectures are given.

school (II.), vb. trans., fr. prec. **1.** (archaic and rare) To send to school; to get educated, provide education for; to teach in school: *he was sent to be schooled very young.* **2.** To train, educate, instruct: *to be schooled in war, by adversity.* **3. a** To discipline; to bring under control: *to school one's tongue, temper, feelings; to school oneself to fatigue, to undergo privations*; specif. **b** *to school a horse*, teach it to jump by taking it across country and making it jump the fences.

school (III.), n. & vb. intrans., fr. Du. *school*, 'troop, shoal of fish', see **shoal (I.). 1.** n. A shoal or large number of fish, or esp. porpoises and whales, swimming together. **2.** vb. To collect, swim together, in a school or shoal.

schoolable, adj. [1. sko͞olabl; 2. skúləbl]. **school (II.)** & **-able.** Capable of being schooled, trained, or taught; of an age to be sent to school.

school age, n. Age at which boys and girls are sent to school.

school attendance, n. Attendance at school, esp. at public elementary school, as compulsory under the Education Acts: *school attendance officer*, local official charged with duties of investigating, reporting &c. on cases of non-attendance at school.

school board, n. A body or board of persons elected by the rate-payers of a district to provide and maintain public elementary schools, hence called *board schools*, and to perform such functions as are, since 1902 in England and Wales, entrusted to the county and municipal education committee.

school-book, n. A book for use in schools; an elementary book.

schoolboy, n. [1. sko͞olboi; 2. skúlbɔi]. A boy attending a school.

school-day, n. **1.** A day on which a school is open for teaching. **2.** (pl.) Time, period of one's life, when one was at school: *were our school-days really as happy as they seem to us now?*

schoolfellow, n. [1. sko͞olfèlō; 2. skúlfèlou]. One educated at the same school and at the same time as another: *the boy is popular with his schoolfellows; an old schoolfellow of mine.*

schoolgirl, n. [1. sko͞olgẽrl; 2. skúlgʌ̄l]. A girl attending school.

school-house, n. **1.** A building used for a school; the house provided for a schoolmaster or mistress of an elementary school. **2.** *School*

House, the headmaster's house at some public schools; the boys belonging to this house.

schooling, n. [1. skōōling; 2. skūliŋ]. **school (II.)** & **-ing. 1.** Teaching, education, at a school: *he did not get much schooling; to pay for the schooling of one's children.* **2.** Specif., training of a horse and rider.

school-inspector, n. An inspector of schools; a government official under the Board of Education who inspects, examines, and reports on schools, esp. the public elementary schools.

school-ma'am, -marm, n. [1. skōōl mahm; 2. skūl mām]. A schoolmistress; (chiefly iron.) a prim, proper, rather pedantic, female.

schoolman, n. [1. skōōlman; 2. skūlmən]. (often cap.) One of the teachers of logic, philosophy, and theology in the schools of mediaeval universities; a writer on, or one versed in, these subjects; a scholastic theologian.

schoolmaster, n. [1. skōōlmàhster; 2. skūlmāstə]. **school (I.)** & **master. 1. a** The headmaster, or one of the assistant masters of a school; **b** person who follows the profession of teacher in a school: *to make one's son a schoolmaster.* Phr. '*the schoolmaster is abroad*', education is in the air (Lord Brougham, in a speech, 1828). **2.** (fig.) One who, that which, educates and trains: '*The law was our schoolmaster to bring us unto Christ*' (Gal. iii. 24).

schoolmastering, n. [1. skōōlmàhstering; 2. skūlmāst(ə)riŋ]. Prec. & **-ing.** Occupation, profession, of a schoolmaster; teaching in a school.

schoolmasterly, adj. [1. skōōlmàhsterli; 2. skūlmāstəli]. Prec. & **-ly.** Like, characteristic of, a schoolmaster, (usually in depreciatory sense) dictatorial, pedantic, concerned with petty questions of conduct and so on: *fond of laying down the law in true schoolmasterly fashion.*

schoolmate, n. [1. skōōlmāt; 2. skūlmeit]. (archaic) A schoolfellow; companion, friend, at school.

schoolmiss, n. [1. skōōlmis; 2. skūlmis]. A schoolgirl; (usually in unfavourable sense) a self-conscious, inexperienced, pert, silly girl.

schoolmistress, n. [1. skōōlmistres; 2. skūlmistris]. Woman who teaches in a school.

schoolroom, n. [1. skōōlroom; 2. skūlrum]. **a** A classroom in a school; **b** a room in a private house where the children are taught at home, or where they prepare their lessons for school.

school-teacher, n. Master or mistress in a school, usually in a public elementary school.

school-teaching, n. **1.** Teaching given in a school. **2.** Occupation of a school-teacher.

school-time, n. **a** Time during which school is held and teaching goes on; **b** school-days.

schooner, n. [1. skōōner; 2. skūnə]. Said to have been first borrowed fr. Engl. by Du. & readopted in U.S.A. in early 18th cent., w. present spelling; etymol. doubtful; perh. fr. provinc. *scoon, scun*, 'to skim, skip', as stones on water or ice. **1.** A fore-and-aft-rigged vessel, usually with two masts, but sometimes with three or more, and then styled *three-, four-masted schooner* &c.; if with topsails on one or both of the masts it is a *topsail schooner.* **2.** (U.S.A.) **a** A covered waggon: *a prairie schooner*; **b** a large beer glass.

schorl, n. [1. shorl; 2. ʃɔl]. Fr., fr. Germ. *schörl*, earlier *schurl, schrul* &c. Etymol. unknown. Black tourmaline.

schottische, n. [1. shotēsh; 2. ʃɔtiʃ]. Mod. Germ. *schottische tanz*, 'Scottish dance'. **a** A lively round dance for two persons, like a polka, in 2-4 time; not of Scottish origin; **b** music composed for such dance.

sciagram, skiagram, n. [1. sí-, skíagram; 2. sái-, skáiəgræm]. Sciagraph.

sciagraph, skiagraph, n. [1. sí-, skíagrahf; 2. sái-, skáiəgrāf]. Formed fr. **sciagraphy. 1.** (with *sc-*) A vertical, perspective section of the interior of a building. **2.** (with *sk-*) A photograph taken by the Röntgen or X-rays, a radiograph.

sciagrapher, skiagrapher, n. [1. sī-, skīágrafer; 2. sai-, skaiǽgrəfə]. Prec. & **-er.** One who makes sciagraphs or skiagraphs.

sciagraphic, skiagraphic, adj. [1. sī-, skī-agráfik; 2. sài-, skàiəgrǽfik]. **sciagraph** & **-ic.** Of, pertaining to, sciagraphy; reproduced in a sciagraph or skiagraph.

sciagraphy, skiagraphy, n. [1. sī-, skīágrafi; 2. sai-, skaiǽgrəfi]. L. Lat. *sciagraphia*, fr. Gk. *skiagraphía*, 'a drawing in light and shade, scene painting in perspective', fr. *skiá*, 'shade, shadow', cogn. w. **shine**, & **-graphy. 1.** (with *sc-*) **a** The art of drawing in light and shade; drawing in perspective; **b** a sciagraph. **2.** (with *sk-*) Photography by Röntgen or X ray, radiography.

sciamachy, n. [1. sīámaki; 2. saiǽməki], fr. Gk. *skiamakhía*, 'fighting in the shade, that is, in a school of exercise, fighting with a shadow, sham fighting', fr. *skiá*, 'shade', see first element of prec., & *mákhē*, 'battle', see **-machy. a** A sham fight; **b** (fig.) a fighting with shadows or with imaginary enemies.

sciametry, skiametry, n. [1. sī-, skīámetri; 2. sai-, skaiǽmitri], fr. Gk. *skiá*, 'shadow', see **sciagraphy**, & **-metry. 1.** (astron.) Mathematical theory of eclipses. **2.** (phys.) Mathematical study of radiography.

sciatic, adj. [1. sīátik; 2. saiǽtik], fr. Fr. *sciatique*, L. Med. Lat. *sciaticus*, fr. Lat. *ischiadicus*, fr. Gk. *iskhiadikós*, 'suffering from lumbago', fr. *iskhiad-*, stem of *iskhiás*, 'lumbago', fr. *iskhion*, 'the hip-joint, loins'; etymol. doubtful. **1.** (anat.) Pertaining to, connected with, the hip or hip-joint: *sciatic artery, nerve* &c. **2. a** Affecting the hip or sciatic nerve &c.: *sciatic pain*; **b** suffering from sciatica: *a sciatic patient.*

sciatica, n. [1. sīátika; 2. saiǽtikə]. Med. Lat., fem. sing. of adj. *sciaticus.* See prec. Neuralgia of the great sciatic nerve, causing acute pain down the back of the thigh.

science, n. [1. síens; 2. sáiəns]. Fr., fr. Lat. *scientia*, 'knowledge, experience, science', fr. *scient-(em)*, Pres. Part. type of *scīre*, 'to know'; the primitive sense was 'to separate (one thing from another) in the mind, to distinguish; hence, to recognize, know'; the base *ski- &c. is that in Lat. *scindere*, 'to split', see **scissile, schism,** & **schist**; for suff. see **-ce. 1.** (archaic or obs.) Knowledge in general; learning. **2. a** Systematized, co-ordinated knowledge based upon the accurate observation of facts, and the relation of these to general principles or laws; an inquiry into the causes and conditions which determine the character of the phenomena observed; **b** any collection of facts and principles, and methods bearing upon a particular group of phenomena; a branch of knowledge: *the science of history, of language; the classification of the sciences.* Phr. *the dismal science*, political economy. **3.** Specif., natural science; the study and investigation of the phenomena of external nature, and the laws and principles which determine these, as distinguished from, and in contrast to, those branches of knowledge which are concerned with man as an intellectual, ethical, or social being; in this narrower and definite sense the word is used when we speak of *Science and Learning, Science and Scholarship; to prefer Science to History and Literature* &c.; *Physics, Chemistry, and the other sciences*, and so on. **4.** Great proficiency, dexterity, skill, based on long experience and practice; rather than on mere natural aptitude in some bodily exercise, game, sport &c.: *of the two players, boxers &c., one had greater strength, the other more science.*

scienter, adv. & n. [1. siénter; 2. saiéntə]. Lat., 'knowingly'; formed fr. *scient-(em)*, Pres. Part. type of *scīre*, 'to know'. See prec. (law) **a** adv. Knowingly, with full knowledge, deliberately, wittingly: *the plaintiff was deceived, but was the act of the defendant done scienter?*; **b** n., knowledge: *to prove (a) scienter is necessary in cases of fraud.*

sciential, adj. [1. siénshal; 2. saiénʃəl], fr. Med. Lat. *scientiālis*, fr. *scientia*, see **science**, & **-al.** Of, pertaining to, science or knowledge, having efficient knowledge.

scientific, adj. [1. sientífik; 2. sàiəntífik]. Through Fr. *scientifique*, or directly fr. L. Med. Lat. *scientificus*, 'producing knowledge or science, pertaining to science'. See **science** & **-fic. 1.** Pertaining to science, its principles and methods; specif., connected with, referring to, natural science: *his studies were rather scientific than literary; scientific and learned circles.* **2. a** Regulated by, based on, in accordance with, the principles and methods of science; systematic, exact: *scientific method, principles, evidence, proof; a scientific classification, arrangement, of a subject*; **b** (of persons and mental processes) trained in, acting, working, in accordance with, the knowledge accumulated, and the methods practised, in science, or in some specified branch of it: *a scientific soldier, engineer; a truly scientific mind; a scientific reasoner.* **3. a** (of games and forms of sport) Played, carried out, according to the methods gained by experience and practice: *scientific cricket, boxing* &c.; **b** (of players &c.) acquainted with these methods, and putting them into practice; highly trained, experienced, skilled, expert: *a scientific boxer, cricketer.*

scientifically, adv. [1. sientífikali; 2. sàiəntífikəli]. Prec. & **-al** & **-ly.** In a scientific manner; in accordance with the principles of science.

scientism, n. [1. síentizm; 2. sáiəntizəm], fr. *scient-*, as in **scientific**, & **-ism.** (rare) Methods, principles, of science; mental attitude of scientists.

scientist, n. [1. síentist; 2. sáiəntist]. *Scient-*, as in prec., & **-ist.** A man of science; one learned, trained, in natural science; a scientific investigator, student; the word is disliked and avoided by many, who prefer *man of science.*

scilicet, adv. [1. síliset; 2. sáilisɛt]. Lat., abbr. of *scīre licet*, 'it is permitted to know, you may know, understand'. (abbr. *sc.* or *scil.*) That is to say, to wit, namely; cp. *viz.*

Scilla, n. [1. síla; 2. sílə]. Lat., fr. Gk. *skilla*; cp. also **squill.** (bot.) A genus of liliaceous, bulbous plants, including the squill, the wild hyacinth or bluebell &c.

scimitar, n. [1. símitar; 2. símitə]. Also *scimetar, scymitar*, & earlier *cimetar* &c.; adopted fr. late 16th cent. Fr. *cimeterre*, or fr. Ital. *scimitarra*; origin doubtful; perh. fr. Pers. *shamshīr, shimshīr*, 'scimitar, sabre', lit. 'lion's claw', fr. *sham*, 'nail, claw', *shīr*, 'lion'. A short, curved sabre, with single edge on the convex side, the typical sword of Turks, Persians, and Arabs.

scintilla, n. [1. sintíla; 2. sintílə]. Lat., 'spark, bright point of light'; possibly cogn. w. O.E. *scīnan.* See **shine.** Spark, gleam; (only in fig. uses) trace, particle, atom, as in Phr. *not a scintilla of evidence, truth* &c.

scintillant, adj. [1. síntilant; 2. síntilənt], fr. Lat. *scintillant-(em)*, Pres. Part. type of *scintillāre.* See **scintillate.** Sparkling, scintillating.

scintillate, vb. intrans. & trans. [1. síntilāt; 2. síntileit], fr. Lat. *scintillāt-(um)*, P.P. type of *scintillāre*, 'to emit sparks, to sparkle'. See **scintilla. A.** intrans. **1.** To sparkle, twinkle; to flash, gleam: *the stars, diamonds, bright eyes, scintillate.* **2.** To sparkle intellectually; to be witty and brilliant in conversation; to emit flashes of wit and humour. **B.** trans. To emit, send forth, to sparkle with: *stars scintillating their light; her eyes scintillated anger.*

scintillating, adj. [1. síntilāting; 2. síntileitiŋ]. Prec. & **-ing.** Sparkling, twinkling.

scintillation, n. [1. sintiláshun; 2. sintiléiʃən], fr. Lat. *scintillātiōn-(em).* **scintillate** & **-ion.** Act of scintillating; a sparkling, twinkling; a flash; (also fig.) *scintillations of wit.*

sciolism, n. [1. síōlizm; 2. sáioulizəm]. Lat. *sciolus*, 'one who doesn't know much', dimin. fr. base *sci-*, 'to know', see **science**, & **-ism**. A show of knowledge; pretentious, superficial knowledge, quackery; a smattering of knowledge.

sciolist, n. [1. síōlist; 2. sáioulist], fr. *sciolus*, 'smatterer', see prec., & **-ist**. A pretentious quack, a superficial pretender to knowledge.

sciomachy, n. See **sciamachy**.

sciomancy, n. [1. síōmànsi; 2. sáioumæ̀nsi], fr. Gk. *skio-*, *skia-*, 'shadow', & *manteia*, 'divination', see first element in **sciagraphy**, & **-mancy**. Divination by means of communication with the shades of the dead.

scion, n. [1. síun; 2. sáiən]. Earlier spelt *cion*, *sion*, *syon* &c., fr. O. Fr. *cion*, *sion*, Mod. Fr. *scion*, etymol. doubtful, possibly connected w. Fr. *scier*, 'to saw, cut', fr. Lat. *secāre*, 'to cut'. See **section**. **1.** A bud, shoot, slip, sucker, of a plant, esp. one suitable for propagation by grafting. **2.** An offshoot of a human stock or family, a descendant, esp. a young member of a family; a sprig: *scion of an ancient, noble, race.*

scioptic, scioptric, adj. [1. síópt(r)ik; 2. saiɔ́pt(r)ik], fr. Gk. *skiá*, 'shade, shadow', see **sciagraphy**, & *optikós*, 'of, pertaining to, sight or vision', see **optic**; the second form is formed on the anal. of *dioptric*. Of, pertaining to, the camera obscura or its use.

scire facias, n. [1. síri fásias; 2. sáiəri fǽsiæs]. Lat., 'cause, make (him), to know'. (law, abbr. *sci. fa.*) A judicial writ, now mainly obsolete, founded on a record, requiring the person against whom it is issued to appear and show cause why the record should not be either enforced or annulled.

scirocco, n. See **sirocco**.

scirrhoid, adj. [1. síroid; 2. sírɔid]. See **scirrhus** & **-oid**. Scirrhous; resembling, like, a scirrhus.

scirrhous, adj. [1. sírus; 2. sírəs]. **scirrhus** & **-ous**. **a** Of the nature of a scirrhus; scirrhoid; **b** proceeding from, caused by, a scirrhus.

scirrhus, n. [1. sírus; 2. sírəs]. Neo-Lat., fr. Gk. *skírros*, *skíros*, 'hard coat or shell', fr. *skirros*, 'hard'; origin obscure. (pathol.) A hardened organ, or part of an organ; esp. an indurated gland.

scissel, n. [1. sísl; 2. sísl], fr. O. Fr. *cisaille*, 'clipping, as of a coin', fr. *ciseler*. See **chisel**. Clippings of metal, made in the course of punching out disks, coins &c., from plates or sheets.

scissile, adj. [1. sísīl; 2. sísail], fr. Lat. *scissilis*, 'easily cut or split', fr. *sciss-(um)* for **scid-tum*, P.P. type of *scindere*, 'to cut, split'; cogn. w. Gk. *skhiza*, 'a chip', *skhízein*, 'to split'; also Scrt. *čináti*, 'he cuts, splits', & *čēdaš*, 'a slice', see **schism** & **schist**, & suff. **-ile**. Capable of being cut or split; splitting easily into plates or laminae.

scission, n. [1. síshun; 2. síʃən], fr. Lat. *scissiōn-(em)*, base as in prec., & **-ion**. **a** Act of cutting, splitting, or dividing; **b** state of being cut or split; division, separation.

scissor, vb. trans. [1. sízur; 2. sízə]. See **scissors**. (colloq.) **1.** To cut, clip, with scissors: *to scissor up a newspaper*, cut it up into pieces; *to scissor off a piece of cloth* &c. **2.** (with *out*) To cut, clip, from anything: *to scissor out a paragraph from a newspaper.*

scissor-bill, n. A sea-bird, the skimmer or shearwater.

scissor-bird, n. The scissor-tail.

scissoring, n. [1. sízuring; 2. sízəriŋ]. **scissor** & **-ing**. **a** Act of cutting or clipping with scissors; **b** (pl.) *scissorings*, clippings, cuttings, from cloth, newspapers &c.

scissors, n. pl. [1. sízerz; 2. sízəz]. M.E. *cysoures*, *sisours*, fr. O. Fr. *cisoires*, 'shears', cogn. w. *cisiaux*, 'scissors', pl. of O. Fr. *cisel*, 'chisel', fr. Lat. (form found only in compounds) *-ciss-(um)*, P.P. of *-cīdere*, 'to cut', fr. *caes-*, P.P. of *caedere*, 'to cut', see **caesura**; spelling *sciss-* is due to confusion w. Lat. *scissor-(es)*, 'carver, butcher', fr. *sciss-(um)*, *scindere*, 'to cleave, split', see **scissile**. Cutting instrument, like a small pair of shears, consisting of a pair of blades with overlapping edges and with a loop end of each for the finger and thumb, pivoted together on the middle and opening into the form of X. Usually, *a pair of scissors*, *three pairs of scissors*, &c., but *my scissors*, (pair of) *nail scissors* &c.

scissor-tail, n. An American bird, the fork-tailed fly-catcher; scissor-bird.

scissure, n. [1. síshur; 2. síʃə]. Fr., fr. Lat. *scissūra*. See **scissile** & **-ure**. A cleft, fissure, opening, natural or made by cutting.

sciurine, adj. & n. [1. sīūrin; 2. saijúrain], fr. Lat. *sciūrus*, 'squirrel'; the Lat. word is borrowed fr. Gk. *skíouros*, lit. 'shadow-tail'; see first element of **sciagraphy**; second element is Gk. *ourá*, 'tail', see **uro- (II.)**; cp. **squirrel**. **1.** adj. Connected with, belonging to, a squirrel, or the genus *Sciurus* or squirrels; squirrel-like. **2.** n. A squirrel.

sciuroid, adj. [1. síūroid; 2. saijúrɔid]. See prec. & **-oid**. Sciurine.

sclaff, vb. trans. [1. sklaf; 2. sklæf]. Scots, of imitative origin. (golf) To scrape or graze the ground before hitting the ball.

sclera, n. [1. sklḗra; 2. sklíərə]. See **scler(o)-**. The sclerotic or external membrane covering the white of the eyeball.

sclerenchyma, n. [1. sklerénkima; 2. skleréŋkimə]. **sclero-** & Gk. *égkhuma*, 'infusion'. Cp. **parenchyma**. **1.** (bot.) The thickened, woody cell-tissues of certain plants, as in the stems of palms, shells of nuts &c. **2.** (zool.) The hard skeletal tissue of corals; scleroderm.

scleriasis, n. [1. sklēríasis; 2. skliəráiəsis]. See **scler(o)-** & **-iasis**. Cp. **psoriasis**. (pathol.) A morbid hardening or induration of tissue.

scleritis, n. [1. sklērítis; 2. skliəráitis]. See **sclera** & **-itis**. Inflammation and hardening of the sclera or sclerotic membrane of the eyeball.

scler(o)-, pref. fr. Gk. *sklērós*, 'hard', reduced grade of base **skel-*, 'dry', &c. as in *skéllein*, 'to dry up, parch', cp. also *skeletós*, 'desiccated', see **skeleton**; cogn. w. L.G. *schal*, 'dry'; Swed. *skäll*, 'thin', Lett. *kals*, 'thin', *kalstu*, 'to become dry'; used chiefly to form scientific terms in anatomy, pathology, physiology &c.

scleroderm, n. [1. sklḗrōdėrm; 2. sklíəroudə̀m]. See **sclero-** & **-derm**. **1.** The hard, outer skeleton of corals. **2.** A hard-scaled fish or reptile.

scleroderma, n. [1. sklērōdérma; 2. skliəroudə́mə]. Formed fr. prec. (pathol.) A disease consisting of a chronic hardening or induration of the skin.

sclerodermatous, adj. [1. sklērōdérmatus; 2. skliəroudə́mətəs]. **sclero-** & Gk. *dérmat-(os)*, stem of *dérma*, 'skin', see **-derm**, & **-ous**. **a** Having a hard skin; sclerodermic; **b** (zool.) belonging to the group of fishes or reptiles known as sclerodermes; **c** (pathol.) suffering from scleroderma.

sclerodermic, adj. [1. sklērōdérmik; 2. skliəroudə́mik]. See **scleroderm** & **-ic**. Sclerodermatous.

sclerogen, n. [1. sklḗrōjen; 2. sklíəroudžen]. **sclero-** & **-gen**. (bot.) The hard woody substance in plant-cells which forms the sclerenchyma, as in shells of nuts, fruit stones &c.

sclerogenic, -genous, adj. [1. sklērojénik, sklērójinus; 2. skliərədžénik, skliərɔ́džinəs]. Prec. & **-ic**, **-ous**. (bot.) Producing, formed of, sclerogen.

scleroid, adj. [1. sklḗroid; 2. sklíərɔid]. **sclero-** & **-oid**. (bot.) Hard, indurated, formed of sclerogen.

scleroma, n. [1. sklērṓma; 2. skliəróumə]. Gk. *sklḗrōma*, 'hardening, induration'. See **sclero-** & **-oma**. (pathol.) An induration, hardening, of the tissues; a hard tumour, scleriasis.

sclerosis, n. [1. sklērṓsis; 2. skliəróusis]. Gk. *sklḗrōsis*, 'induration'. See **sclero-** & **-osis**. (path.) A morbid hardening and thickening or induration of the tissues: *sclerosis of the arteries.*

sclerotic, adj. & n. [1. sklērótik; 2. skliərɔ́tik]. **sclero-** & **-otic**. **1.** adj. Hard, indurated: **a** (anat.) connected with, pertaining to, the sclera: *sclerotic coat*, *membrane*, or *tunic*; **b** (bot.) formed of, hardened by, sclerogen. **2.** (pathol.) Suffering from, affected by, sclerosis. **3.** n. The sclerotic coat of the eye; sclera.

sclerotitis, n. [1. sklērōtítis; 2. skliəroutáitis]. Prec. & **-itis**. Inflammation of the sclerotic coat of the eye; scleritis.

sclerous, adj. [1. sklḗrus; 2. sklíərəs]. See **sclero-** & **-ous**. **a** Hard, indurated, bony; **b** affected by sclerosis.

scobs, n. [1. skobz; 2. skɔbz]. Lat., also *scobis*, 'scrapings, filings', cogn. w. *scabere*, 'to scrape', see **scabies**. Filings, scrapings, of wood, metal &c.; sawdust, shavings.

scoff (I.), n. [1. skof; 2. skɔf]. Prob. Scand., M.E. *scof*, *skof*; etymol. doubtful; M. Dan. has *skof*, *skuf*, 'jest, taunt', *skuffe*, 'to mock, deceive'; prob. cogn. w. O.N. *skop*, *skaup*, 'scoff, taunt'. Not common. **1.** Expression of contempt, derision, or ridicule; taunt, mocking gibe: *delighting in scoffs and jeers.* **2.** An object of derision, contempt, or mockery: *to be the scoff and jest of a heedless mob.*

scoff (II.), vb. intrans., fr. prec. To display contempt, to jeer, mock; esp. to show disrespect for, or hostility to, religion: '*And fools, who came to scoff, remained to pray*' (Goldsmith); also *scoff at*, to deride, jeer at, make a jest of, hold up to contempt, speak of slightingly and with disrespect: *to scoff at religion*; *new ideas are often scoffed at to begin with.*

scoffer, n. [1. skófer; 2. skɔ́fə]. Prec. & **-er**. One who scoffs, a mocker; specif., one who scoffs at religion and sacred things.

scoffing, adj. & n. [1. skófing; 2. skɔ́fiŋ]. **1.** adj. (from Pres. Part. of **scoff (II.)**) Using scoffs; mocking, contemptuous: *scoffing laughter* &c. **2.** vbl. n. (fr. **scoff (II.)** & **-ing**) Derision, mockery: *tired of this constant scoffing and railing.*

scoffingly, adv. Prec. & **-ly**. In a scoffing manner; contemptuously, derisively.

scold (I.), n. [1. skōld; 2. skould]. Etymol. doubtful; it appears earlier than vb.; prob. fr. O.N. *skáld*, 'poet', see **skald**, O.E. **skāld*. The secondary, intermediate meaning of the O.N. word, according to the O.E.D., being 'libeller, lampooner', it has been usually connected w. O. Fris. *skelda*, Du. *schelden*, Germ. *schelten*, 'to scold', the n. being derived fr. the vb.; this the O.E.D. rejects. A person, esp. a woman, who uses loud, abusive language; a shrewish, nagging, abusive woman; a virago; *a common scold*, a woman indictable at common law as a public nuisance because of her abusive tongue; *scold's bridle*, also *the branks*, a sort of gag formerly used as a punishment for common scolds.

scold (II.), vb. trans. & intrans., fr. prec. **1.** trans. To reprove angrily, to rate soundly, find fault with; take to task: *to scold a naughty child*; *she was always scolding her maidservants.* **2.** intrans. To find fault angrily; to use railing, abusive language: *more ready to laugh than to scold.*

scolder, n. [1. skṓlder; 2. skóuldə]. Prec. & **-er**. One who scolds.

scolding, n. [1. skṓlding; 2. skóuldiŋ]. **scold (II.)** & **-ing**. Angry reproof; fault-finding: *give the child a good scolding*; *constant scolding is worse than useless.*

scolex, n. [1. skṓleks; 2. skóulɛks], fr. Gk. *skṓlēx*, 'worm'; cp. Gk. *skōlúptomai*, 'to twist and turn'; fr. a different grade of **skel-*, 'crooked, bent', cp. Gk. *skélos*, 'leg', lit. 'curvature', cp. *skoliós*, 'twisted'; cogn. w. Lat. *scelus*, 'crime', lit. 'crooked conduct'; O.H.G. *scelah*, 'curved', O.E. *sceolh*, 'wry, oblique', see **scowl**, & cp. Mod. Germ. *scheel*, 'bent, crooked', & *schielen*, 'to look crooked, to squint', whence perh. the name *Schiller*='the squinter'; cp. the Fr. name *Loucheur* w. same meaning. The embryo stage of a tapeworm.

scoliosis, n. [1. skòliósis; 2. skòlióusis], fr. Gk. *skoliōsis*, fr. *skoliós*, 'bent, curved, crooked'. See prec. & **-osis.** (med.) A lateral curvature of the spine.

scoliotic, adj. [1. skòliótik; 2. skòliɔ́tik]. See base of prec. & **-otic.** Pertaining to, afflicted with, scoliosis.

scollop, n. & vb. See **scallop.**

scolopaceous, adj. [1. skòlopáshus; 2. skòləpéiʃəs], fr. Gk. *skolópax*, 'a woodcock or snipe', & **-aceous.** The Gk. name of the bird is prob. derived fr. *skólops*, 'pointed stake', on account of the long beak wh. it uses for burrowing out insects, fr. a base *skel-, *skol- &c., meaning 'to cut, scratch, dig, burrow', cp. Gk. *skálops*, 'mole, the digging, burrowing animal'; fr. same base comes Lat. *sculpere*, 'to carve, engrave', see **sculpture.** Belonging to, resembling, the genus, *Scolopax*, of birds which includes the woodcock, snipe, and redshank, or any member of it.

scolopendrine, adj. [1. skòlopéndrīn; 2. skòləpéndrain], fr. Gk. *skolópendra*, 'a millipede', & **-ine**; the word is prob. a foreign importation into Gk. (zool.) Of, related, belonging to, resembling, the larger centipedes.

Scolopendrium, n. [1. skòlopéndrium; 2. skòləpéndriəm]. Neo-Lat., fr. Gk. *skolopéndrion*, 'fern, resembling a millipede'. See prec. word. (bot.) A genus of ferns, including the hart's-tongue fern.

Scomber, n., pl. **Scombri** [1. skómber, -brī; 2. skɔ́mbə, -brai]. Lat., fr. Gk. *skómbros*, 'the tunny, mackerel'; etymol. doubtful. (zool.) The genus of fishes which includes the mackerel.

scombroid, adj. [1. skómbroid; 2. skɔ́mbrɔid]. Prec. & **-oid.** Resembling the mackerel; belonging to the genus *Scomber*.

scon, n. See **scone.**

sconce (I.), n. [1. skons; 2. skɔns], fr. O. Fr. *esconse*, 'hiding-place, a dark lantern', fr. L. Med. Lat. *absconsa*, fem. sing. as variant of Lat. *abscondita*, 'hidden, concealed', P.P. of *abscondere*, 'to hide', see **abscond. 1. a** A metal bracket, often of ornamental form, with a reflector behind, attached to a wall, for holding candles or a lamp; **b** the metal, tubular socket of a candlestick. **2.** (slang) The head, esp. the crown or top of the head: *get a crack over the sconce.* **3.** (Oxford Univ.) A fine (now usually consisting of a tankard of beer) imposed, for a breach of customs or manners, upon an undergraduate by the senior at his table in a college hall.

sconce (II.), vb. trans. See prec. (Oxford Univ.) To fine (an undergraduate) for breach of customs &c. at table in hall.

scone, scon, n. [1. skon, skōn; 2. skɔn, skoun]. Prob. a shortened form of L.G. *schonbrod*, 'fine bread'; cogn. w. O.H.G. *scōni*, 'bright, beautiful' &c., Germ. *schön*, 'fine, beautiful', O.E. *scēne*, 'bright, beautiful', whence Mod. Engl. **sheen.** A thin, flat cake, properly unsweetened, and made without butter, cooked quickly over a hot fire on a girdle; also called *girdle cake*.

scoop (I.), n. [1. skōōp; 2. skūp]. M.E. *scōp*, either fr. O. Fr. *escope*, itself of Gmc. origin, cp. Du. *schop*, 'shovel', or more prob. direct fr. Scand., cp. Swed. *skopa*; related to **shove & shovel. 1.** One of variously shaped shallow vessels with long or short handles, used for dipping, bailing, or ladling liquids, or for shovelling up dry substances such as flour, sugar, bran &c.; a kind of dipper, ladle, or small shovel. **2.** A kind of small gouge, for digging out small pieces from a cheese. **3.** Act of using a scoop; that which is lifted in a scoop at one operation: *to make a scoop*; *in one scoop.* **4.** (slang) Something obtained by good luck, in the way of profit; e.g. **a** a piece of interesting information, not generally accessible, obtained by a newspaper, and likely to sell the edition of the paper; **b** a considerable financial gain in a business transaction.

scoop (II.), vb. trans., fr. prec. **1.** To shovel or ladle (a substance) out, or up, with a scoop: *to scoop water out of, from, a boat, sand out of a barrel* &c.; also *to scoop up*: *to scoop up water by the gallon*; (fig.) *to scoop up money*, to make it copiously and rapidly. **2. a** To hollow out, dig, excavate, with a scoop, or by other means: *to scoop out a hole to lie in*; *to scoop a hole in the sand*; **b** to gouge, graze deeply, tear out; to furrow: *the mudguard of his car scooped a deep groove in the paint of my car as he passed.* **3.** (slang) **a** To make a scoop of; to get before another paper in making a scoop: *the paper scooped some wonderful news yesterday*; *the proprietors would pay anything to scoop a rival paper*; **b** to obtain as a profit &c. in advance of others: *he scooped all the shares he could lay hands on.*

scooper, n. [1. skōōper; 2. skūpə]. **scoop** (II.) & **-er. a** One who, that which, scoops; **b** an engraver's tool; **c** old name for the avocet.

scoop-net, n. A fishing-net made to sweep along the bottom of a river; a small long-handled dip-net.

scoop-wheel, n. A wheel with scoops or buckets, used for dredging, drawing water &c.

scoot, vb. intrans. [1. skōōt; 2. skūt]. Origin doubtful; possibly formed fr. **scuttle** (IV.). (slang, colloq.) **a** To run quickly; **b** to run away, to bolt.

scooter, n. [1. skōōter; 2. skūtə]. Prec. & **-er. a** A narrow wooden board, raised a few inches from the ground with a small wheel at either end, the front one attached to a steering-handle, and propelled by a series of pushes given by one foot on the ground; used by children as a toy runabout; **b** a similar but more elaborate apparatus driven by petrol, upon which the passenger stands and leans against a kind of seat: *motor scooter.*

scopa, n., pl. **scopae** [1. skópa, -pē; 2. skóupə, -pī]. Lat., 'bundle of twigs, a broom', cogn. w. **scapus**, 'shaft'; cp. also **sceptre.** A small tuft of hairs or bristles, as on the legs of bees, on which pollen is carried from flower to flower.

scopate, adj. [1. skópāt; 2. skóupeit]. Prec. & **-ate.** (entom.) Provided with scopae, as a bee's legs.

scope, n. [1. skōp; 2. skoup], fr. Ital. *scopo*, 'mark to shoot at, target, intent, aim, scope', fr. Gk. *skopós*, 'mark to shoot at; watcher, spy', fr. root *skep-, as in *sképtesthai*, 'to watch, spy, look out, examine', see **sceptic. 1.** (archaic and rare) Aim, purpose in view, intention: *the scope of a law.* **2.** Range, reach of mind or activity, extent of view, outlook, grasp: *a mind of wide, limited, scope*; *we wonder at the scope of the Greek intellect*; *subjects which lie beyond, within, one's scope.* **3.** Area, sphere, field, range, within which any form of activity takes place; field covered by observation or action: *the scope of a scientific, historical, work*; *scope of an inquiry, undertaking* &c. **4.** Room, opportunity, for liberty of action or activity; free vent, outlet: *to have free scope for one's activities*; *to give one full, abundant, scope for the exercise of one's powers*; *no scope for the imagination.* **5.** (naut.) Length, extent, of a cable at which a vessel rides when at anchor; usually *riding-scope.*

-scope, suff. fr. Gk. *skopós*, 'watcher; that on which one fixes the eye', cp. *skopein*, 'to look at, examine'; & see prec. Used as a second element in compound nouns denoting scientific instruments of visual observation, such as *telescope, ophthalmoscope, spectroscope* &c.

-scopic, suff. [1. skópik; 2. skɔ́pik]. Used to form adjs. fr. ns. in *-scope*, meaning 'of, pertaining to, examined by, such instruments'; also, capable only of observation by: *microscopic, telescopic, examination*; *microscopic objects* &c.

-scopy, suff. [1. skopi; 2. skəpi]. Used to form ns., meaning use of, examination by, instruments ending in **-scope**: *laryngoscopy* &c.

scorbutic, adj. & n. [1. skorbūtik; 2. skōbjūtik]. Fr. *scorbutique*, adj., fr. *scorbut*, disease itself. The word, like the disease, is late, & appears to be due to a Latinization of Du. *scheurbot* (now *-buik*); the first element means 'a tear, laceration, cut', cp. **shear** (I.). **1.** adj. Pertaining to, like, affected by, scurvy: *scorbutic disease, patient* &c. **2.** n. **a** A remedy for scurvy; **b** person suffering from scurvy.

scorch (I.), vb. trans. & intrans. [1. skorch; 2. skōtʃ]. M.E. *scorchen*, fr. O. Fr. *escorchier*, 'to flay, take the skin off', fr. Lat. *excorticāre*, 'to flay'. See **ex- & cortex.** It is possible that the sense has been influenced by a Scand. word meaning 'to parch, shrivel, wrinkle', cp. Norw. *skrokkna*, 'to shrivel'. **A.** trans. **1. a** (of action of fire) To burn slightly and superficially; to char and discolour the skin or surface of: *to scorch one's face*; *to scorch linen in ironing*; **b** (of action of sun, or of cold wind) to dry up, parch, wither, blast (young plants, buds &c.); also to render (the skin) sore. **2.** (fig., in moral sense) To affect injuriously, to sear, wither up, as by biting sarcasm &c. **B.** intrans. **1.** To become scorched. **2.** (colloq. slang, esp. of a bicyclist or motorist) To ride or drive too fast; go at breakneck speed; esp. to ride or drive thus without regard to the safety of others on the road.

scorch (II.), n., fr. prec. **1.** A superficial burn or mark caused by scorching; scorching effect. **2.** (colloq. slang) Driving, riding, at high or excessive speed; a turn, spell, of this.

scorcher, n. [1. skórcher; 2. skɔ́tʃə]. **scorch** (I.) & **-er. 1.** One who, that which, scorches; **a** anything very hot or burning: *the day was a scorcher*; **b** a person who motors or bicycles at excessive speed. **2.** (slang) Something excessive, startling, extravagant.

scorching (I.), adj. [1. skórching; 2. skɔ́tʃiŋ], fr. Pres. Part. of **scorch** (I.). **1. a** Very hot, burning, parching: *a scorching day*; **b** (as adv.) *scorching hot.* **2.** (fig.) *Scorching wit, sarcasm* &c.

scorching (II.), vbl. n. **1.** Action or process of that which scorches; effects of this, superficial burn &c. **2.** (slang) Act of riding bicycle or driving motor-car on the road at excessive speed.

scorchingly, adv. **scorching** (I.) & **-ly.** In a scorching manner; witheringly.

score (I.), n. [1. skōr; 2. skō]. O.E. *scoru*, 'number of twenty', fr. O.N. *skor*, 'notch, tally; twenty'; the word is a grade of *sceran*, 'to cut', see **shear** (I.); the orig. sense is 'a cut, a notch'; it is supposed that in using notches for counting, every twentieth one was distinguished by extra length & became *the* notch or score; hence, the secondary meaning 'twenty'. **1. a** A notch, incision, cut, scratch: *scores on rock made by ice*; **b** mark, line drawn or scratched: *make a score through the name with a pen*; *deep scores of pain and sorrow on his face.* Phr. *to start off from score, go off at full score*, to start off at full speed at once, from the line or score marked as the starting-point of a race. **2.** A reckoning at an inn, of drink &c., kept by marking in chalk on a board or the door; hence an account, sum due: *to run up a score*; *to pay, wipe off a score.* Phr. *to pay off old scores*, to get even with someone for past wrongs or injuries; *on the score of*, on account of: *on that score*, for that reason. **3.** A notch made on a piece of wood or tally used in old methods of counting; **a** (in cricket and other games) number of runs made, goals &c. scored, by a player, side or team; record of such points made in a game; *his best score this season*; *what's the score now?*; *to keep the score*, enter it as made on sheet of paper or score-book; Phr. *to make a score off one's own bat*, do anything without help from others; **b** point, hit at another's expense, any successful act, remark &c.; advantage gained for oneself by such act &c

or through good fortune: *quick at making a score off an awkward heckler*; *it would be a great score if someone would lend us a car for the journey*. **4.** Set of twenty persons or objects; **a** (uninflected after numerals) *threescore years and ten*, seventy years, (also elliptically) *he was nearly fourscore when he died*; **b** specif., in counting various things: *five score of herring*; or, with pounds understood, in weight of pigs, cattle &c.: *prime bullocks are fetching so much a, or per, score*; **c** (in pl.) an indefinite large number: *people came in scores*; *scores of times*, very often. **5.** (mus.) A copy written or printed, of a musical composition in which all the parts, vocal or instrumental, are shown on staves formerly scored through or joined by a line.

score (II.), vb. trans. & intrans., fr. prec. **A.** trans. **1. a** To mark with scores, cuts, incisions or notches; to make scores, marks on: *rocks scored by glacial action*; (also fig.) *a heart scored by sorrow and remorse*; **b** to mark with lines &c. as with the pen: *the page was scored with underlinings, erasures* &c.; also, *score out*, to erase, cancel by a line or score drawn through (words &c.): *the name and date have been scored out*. **2.** *Score up*, to make a score or record; **a** of what is owed: *score 5s. up against me*; **b** of points made in a game: *to score up runs as they are made*. **3. a** To make a score or points in a game: *to score 150 runs for one wicket*; Phr. *to score a point, an advantage*, to gain an advantage, to have a stroke of luck; **b** (of strokes, cards &c.) to count (so much) towards the score: *hazards off the red score three*. **4.** To arrange in score, to orchestrate, arrange (music) for instruments. **B.** intrans. **1.** To keep a score (at a game). **2. a** To make a score, accumulate points (at a game); **b** (fig.) to gain an advantage, be fortunate; to find circumstances profitable, favourable for one: *we found a good and cheap hotel at once, so we rather scored*. Phr. *to score off a person*, to get the better of him in argument &c.; turn a joke against him.

score-book, n. A book in which the score (at games) is recorded.

score-card, n. A card on which the names of the teams, scores, fall of wickets &c. are printed, for sale at a cricket match.

scorer, n. [1. skórer; 2. skɔ́rə]. **score** (II.) & **-er.** Person **a** who keeps the score; or **b** who makes a score, at cricket &c.

scoria, n., pl. **scoriae** [1. skória, -iē; 2. skɔ́riə, -ii]. Lat., fr. Gk. *skōria*, 'refuse, dross', fr. *skōr*, 'dung', see **scatology. 1.** Dross, slag, left after metal has been smelted from the ore. **2.** (usually pl.) The loose, cellular, light clinker found on the surface of molten lava after cooling and mixing with the air.

scoriaceous, adj. [1. skōriáshus; 2. skɔriéiʃəs]. Prec. & **-aceous.** Of the nature of scoria.

scoriated, adj. [1. skóriāted; 2. skɔ́rieitid]. **scoria** & **-ate** & **-ed.** Scorified, reduced to scoria.

scorification, n. [1. skōrifikáshun; 2. skɔrifikéiʃən]. **scorify** & **-fication. a** Process of scorifying or reducing to scoria; **b** product of this.

scorifier, n. [1. skórifīer; 2. skɔ́rifaiə]. **scorify** & **-er.** A fire-clay vessel used in the scorification of a metal.

scorify, vb. trans. [1. skórifī; 2. skɔ́rifai]. **scoria** & **-fy.** To reduce to dross, slag, or scoriae, specif., to assay (gold, silver &c.) by fusion of the ore with lead and borax in a fire-clay vessel.

scorn (I.), n. [1. skorn; 2. skɔn]. M.E. *scorn, skarn*, fr. O. Fr. *escarn*, of Gmc. origin, cp. O.H.G. *skern*, 'mockery', *skernōn*, 'to mock'; origin doubtful; popularly associated w. O. Fr. *escorner*, 'to disgrace', lit. 'to dishorn', L. Lat. *excornāre*, see **ex-** & **corn** (III.). **1. a** Loftily contemptuous, disdainful, state, attitude, of mind: *to feel, have, nothing but scorn for cowardice*; **b** outward expression of this in word, look, act; lofty, contemptuous treatment, disdainful utterance: *he was cowed by the scorn and invective of his opponent*. Phrs. *to hold in scorn*, to despise; *to laugh to scorn*, to treat with derision; *to think scorn of*, to despise; *to think, hold, it scorn to do*, to be too proud to do. **2.** An object of scorn, person held in, or up to contempt: *to become a scorn of (to) one's enemies*.

scorn (II.), vb. trans. See prec. **a** To feel scorn for; **b** to express scorn for; treat disdainfully, or contemptuously: *scorn to (do)*, to feel it beneath, or unworthy of, one to do, hence, to refuse to do, abstain from doing on this account: *to scorn to tell a lie*.

scorner, n. [1. skórner; 2. skɔ́nə]. **scorn** (II.) & **-er.** One who feels or expresses scorn.

scornful, adj. [1. skórnfool; 2. skɔ́nful]. **scorn** (I.) & **-ful.** Feeling, expressing, expressive of, scorn.

scornfully, adv. Prec. & **-ly.** In a scornful manner.

scornfulness, n. See prec. & **-ness.** State, quality, of being scornful.

Scorpio, n. [1. skórpiō; 2. skɔ́piou]. Lat., fr. Gk. *skorpios, skorpiōn*; cogn. w. O.E. *sċearfian*, 'to scrape', & *sċeorfan*, 'to gnaw, scrape, shred', see **scarf** (II.). The Scorpion, the zodiacal constellation and eighth sign of the Zodiac.

scorpioid, adj. & n. [1. skórpioid; 2. skɔ́pioid], fr. Gk. *skorpioeidḗs*. See prec. & **-oid. 1.** adj. **a** (bot., of inflorescence) Curled up like the end of a scorpion's tail and uncurling as the flower develops; **b** (zool.) like a scorpion; belonging to the family of scorpions. **2.** n. **a** (bot.) A scorpioid inflorescence; **b** (zool.) a member of the scorpion family; animal resembling a scorpion.

scorpion, n. [1. skórpiun; 2. skɔ́piən], fr. Lat. *scorpiōn-(em)*, stem of **Scorpio. 1. a** Any of various animals, known as arachnids, found in tropical countries, belonging to the genus *Scorpio*, or order *Scorpionidea*, which have a long, incurving, flexible tail armed with a poisonous sting, two large pincers or claws, resembling a lobster's, sharp mandibles, and four pairs of legs; **b** (army slang) *rock scorpion*, a native of Gibraltar. **2.** (cap.) The constellation and zodiacal sign *Scorpio*. **3.** A malicious, venomous person. **4.** An ancient form of ballista or catapult for hurling stones &c.

scorpion-broom, n. A kind of thorny, yellow-flowered broom, *Genista scorpius*, of S. Europe.

scorpion-fish, n. A spiny sea-fish, belonging to the genus *Scorpaena*, the sea-scorpion.

scorpion-fly, n. A black neuropterous insect, *Panorpa*, with incurving tail like that of a scorpion and beak-like mouth.

scorpion-grass, n. The wild forget-me-not, or myosotis.

scorpion-plant, n. **a** A Javanese orchid with large white or yellow flowers shaped like a spider; **b** scorpion-broom.

scorpion-shell, n. Shell inhabited by a mollusc, found in Indian Ocean, suggestive of a scorpion in shape.

scot (I.), n. [1. skot; 2. skɔt], fr. O. Fr. *escot*, 'payment to a common fund', fr. O.N. *skot*, 'payment, contribution', cogn. w. O.E. *sċeot*, 'shot, reckoning', fr. *sċēotan*, 'to shoot, pay in to a fund, contribute', see **shot** (IV.). (hist.) A sum of money assessed and paid; contribution to a sum assessed; a tax or rate; esp. *scot and lot*, an old parish or town tax, assessed according to ability to pay. Phr. *to pay (one's) scot and lot*, to take one's fair share of a collective burden.

Scot (II.), n. O.E. *Scottas*, pl., L. Lat. *Scōti, Scotti*, fr. *Scōtus, Scottus*; etymol. unknown. **1.** A native of Scotland, a Scotsman. **2.** Member of a Celtic race in ancient Ireland, many of whom migrated to Scotland in the 6th cent.

scotch (I.), vb. trans. [1. skoch; 2. skɔtʃ]. Origin unknown; suggested etymologies appear to be mere shots. **1.** (obs.) To cut, score, make a gash or incision in. **2. a** To crush, render harmless; to maim, kill: *to scotch a black beetle, a rat*; **b** to take vigorous action against, put down, thwart, stifle, stop, put an end to: *to scotch a mutiny*; *to scotch a plot, a nefarious scheme* &c.

scotch (II.), n., fr. prec. A cut, incision; mark scored or drawn on the ground &c., as in the game of *hop-scotch*.

scotch (III.), n. & vb. trans.; etymol. unknown. **1.** n. A block, wedge placed under a wheel, cask, or other round object to prevent movement or rolling. **2.** vb. To block wedge a wheel &c. with a scotch.

Scotch (IV.), adj. & n., contracted form of **Scottish. 1.** adj. Connected with, pertaining to, Scotland, its people, vernacular language &c. *Scottish* or *Scots* are the forms preferred by the people themselves, and now commonly used by English writers, except in such established collocations as *Scotch whisky, Scotch terrier* &c. **2.** n. **a** *The Scotch*, the Scottish people collectively; **b** the dialect of the Lowlands of Scotland; **c** (colloq., specif.) Scotch whisky: *a small Scotch*.

Scotch barley, n. Pot barley, with the husk ground off.

Scotch broth, n. Mutton broth thickened with pearl barley.

Scotch cap, n. Type of headdress worn with Highland dress; esp. the so-called glengarry.

Scotch collops, n. pl. Collops of beef, cut small and stewed; also called by some dictionary-makers, but apparently by no one else, *scotched collops*.

Scotch fir, n. The common N. European pine, *Pinus sylvestris*.

Scotchman, n. [1. skóchman; 2. skɔ́tʃmən]. A native of Scotland; a Scotsman, Scot.

Scotch mist, n. A thick wet mist, accompanied by a fine, thick drizzle.

Scotch pebble, n. A variety of crystalline quartz, as agate, chalcedony, cairngorm &c., cut and polished and used as an ornamental stone, in brooches, tops of snuff-boxes &c.

Scotch pine, n. Scotch fir.

Scotch terrier, n. A breed of short-legged, long-bodied terrier with a rough, wiry, iron-grey, or grizzled coat, pricked ears, and short tail carried erect.

Scotch whisky, n. Whisky, often having a smoky flavour of peat, as distilled in Scotland.

Scotchwoman, n. [1. skóchwòoman; 2. skɔ́tʃwùmən]. Female native of Scotland; Scotswoman.

Scotch woodcock, n. Scrambled egg with anchovies underneath, on a thin slice of hot buttered toast, served as a savoury.

scoter, n. [1. skóter; 2. skóutə]. Etymol. doubtful, possibly fr. O.N. *skoti*, fr. *skota*, 'to jut, shoot out'. A large black sea-duck of Northern and Arctic waters, genus *Oedemia*.

scot-free, adj. **scot** (I.) & **free. 1.** (rare) Free from payment of 'scot', not liable for payment to a fund, subscription, account &c. **2.** Unharmed, unpunished: *to go, get off, scot-free*, (i.) to escape punishment; (ii.) to get off uninjured.

scotia, n. [1. skótia; 2. skóutiə]. Lat., fr. Gk. *skotia*, fr. *skótos*, 'darkness, shadow', see **scoto-.** (archit.) A deep, concave moulding, esp. at the base of a column, having a dark shadow within the hollow.

Scotism, n. [1. skótizm; 2. skóutizəm], fr. Lat. *Duns Scōtus*, scholastic philosopher, d. 1308, & **-ism.** The scholastic philosophy of Duns Scotus and his followers; opposed to that of *Thomism*, of Thomas Aquinas.

Scotist, n. [1. skótist; 2. skóutist]. Prec. & **-ist.** Adherent of Scotism.

Scotland Yard, n. [1. skótland yárd; 2. skɔ́tlənd jád]. Name of London street where the police office once stood; formerly site of the palace kept for the reception of the Scottish sovereign. The headquarters of the Metropolitan Police; hence the London police force itself, and esp. the Criminal Investigation Department or detective branch, as distinguished from the provincial borough or county detective force.

scoto-, pref., fr. Gk. *skótos*, 'darkness'; cogn. w. **shade**; used to form words indicating darkness, impairment of vision &c.

scotodinia, n. [1. skótōdínia ; 2. skɔ̀toudáiniə]. Prec. & Gk. *dinos*, 'whirling', also, 'whirlwind'; fr. the base seen in *dienai*, 'to hasten', *díō*, 'I flee'; & further in Scrt. *dīyati*, 'to fly', Lett. *dīt*, 'to dance'. Giddiness, vertigo, accompanied by dimness of vision and headache.

scotograph, n. [1. skótōgrahf ; 2. skɔ́tougrāf]. **scoto-** & **-graph.** **1.** Instrument for writing in the dark or for use by the blind. **2.** Radiograph.

Scots, adj. & n. [1. skots ; 2. skɔts]. Nthn. M.E. *Scottis*. See **Scot (II.)** & **-ish** ; & cp. **Scottish. 1.** adj. Scottish, esp. in such collocations as **a** *Scots language*, the form of English spoken in the Lowlands of Scotland ; *Scots law*, an English usage, the form of law which prevails in Scotland and the Scottish Courts of law, differing from English law in many points from the strong infusion of the civil or Roman law from the 16th cent. until the 19th, and esp. in terminology ; **b** in coins, weights, and measures &c. formerly used in Scotland : *pounds Scots*, as contrasted with *sterling* ; *a Scots mile* &c. ; **c** in titles of regiments of the British army : *Scots Fusiliers, Scots Greys, Scots Guards.* **2.** n. The Scots, or Scottish language : *to speak broad Scots.*

Scotsman, Scotswoman, n. [1. skótsman, -wòoman ; 2. skɔ́tsmən, -wùmən]. Male, female, native of Scotland.

Scottice, adv. [1. skótisē ; 2. skɔ́tisī]. Med. Lat., adv. of *Scot(t)icus*, 'Scottish'. In the Scots language ; as a Scotsman would say or pronounce.

Scotticism, n. [1. skótisizm ; 2. skɔ́tisizəm]. See prec. & **-ism.** A Scots phrase, idiom, word, pronunciation &c.

Scotticize, vb. trans. & intrans. [1. skótisīz ; 2. skɔ́tisaiz]. See prec. & **-ize. 1.** trans. **a** To cause to be or become like the Scots ; to make Scottish ; to imbue with Scottish feeling, character, type &c. ; **b** to translate into the Scots tongue. **2.** intrans. To introduce Scottish pronunciation, words, idioms, when speaking, or writing English.

Scottish, adj. [1. skótish ; 2. skɔ́tiʃ]. In M.E., a new formation fr. **Scot (II.)** & **-ish** ; cp. **Scots** ; the O.E. form is *Scyttisc*, & means 'Irish'. Connected with, pertaining to, Scotland, its people, language &c., used now preferably for **Scotch** : *Scottish Church* ; *the Scottish Office* &c.

scoundrel, n. [1. skóundrel ; 2. skáundrəl]. Etymol. of first element unknown ; the suff. *-(e)rel* is a dimin., often w. a disparaging sense, as **mongrel** &c., & the *d* is developed between *n* & *r*, as in *thunder*. A dishonourable, unprincipled, person ; a blackguard, a rogue, a good-for-nothing rascal.

scoundrelism, n. [1. skóundrelizm ; 2. skáundrəlizəm]. Prec. & **-ism.** Conduct, acts, of a scoundrel ; rascality, blackguardism.

scoundrelly, adj. [1. skóundreli ; 2. skáundrəli]. **scoundrel** & **-ly.** Having the character of a scoundrel ; characteristic of a scoundrel ; rascally.

scour (I.), vb. trans. & intrans. [1. skour ; 2. skauə]. Etymol. obscure ; the O.E.D. rejects the usually accepted derivation fr. O. Fr. *escourre*, fr. Lat. *excurrere*, 'to run out, about', fr. *ex-*, 'out', & *currere*, 'to run', see **excursion** ; & is inclined to connect the vb. w. O.N. *skura*, 'to rush violently, to storm', *skúr*, 'a storm', cogn. w. **shower.** Cp. also **scurry. 1.** trans. To pass over, traverse, range, hasten over or along ; esp. in search or pursuit : *to scour the plain* ; *police scouring the streets.* **2.** intrans. To move, run about quickly, earnestly, with vigour, in search or pursuit of anything ; to range, rove : *to scour about in search of food* ; *dogs scouring through the woods after game.*

scour (II.), vb. trans. & intrans. Perh. through M. Du. & L.G. *schuren*, 'to polish, clean', fr. O. Fr. *escurer*, fr. L. or Med. Lat. *escūrāre, scūrāre*, 'to clean, scour', fr. **ex-**, 'out, away', & Lat. *cūrāre*, 'to take care of, to keep clean'. See **cure (II.). A.** trans. **1. a** To clean by hard rubbing, to clean and polish by friction with abrasives, such as sand, or with soap and water &c. : *to scour a rusty kettle* ; *to scour pots and pans* ; *to scour out a dirty cupboard, scour down the steps* ; **b** to get rid of, remove by rubbing : *to scour rust off a knife, grease from a pot* &c. ; **c** specif., to cleanse (wool, cloth) of grease and dirt by various chemical processes. **2.** (of running water) **a** To clean, wash clean, to flush and remove dirt, obstructions &c. from : *to scour (out) a ditch, drain-pipe* &c. ; *the river has scoured its bed of silt* ; **b** to remove from, clear, wash away, by the rapid flow of water : *the river has scoured the mud from the estuary, from the foundations of the bridge* ; *heavy rainfall scours the sewage out of the drains* ; **c** to dig out, form, by the rush of water : *the tide has scoured a channel through the sand.* **3.** To purge, clear the intestines : *to scour a horse, cow*, by drugs ; *to scour worms for bait*, by placing them in damp moss, bran &c. ; *eels scour themselves in fresh-running water.* **4.** (influenced by **scour (I.)**) To sweep clear of, get rid of, free from : *to scour the sea of pirates, slavers* &c. **B.** intrans. **1.** To clean, remove dirt, by scouring : *a hard worker who can scrub and scour* ; *sand and water are good to scour with.* **2.** To be purged ; to suffer from scours.

scour (III.), n., fr. prec. **1. a** Action of running water, as of a river, current &c., in washing away, or scouring, silt, mud &c., or of forming channels &c. : *the scour of the river has affected the foundations of the bridge* ; *the great scour of the tide* ; **b** place, bed, channel &c., formed by the flow of a river &c. : *there is a deep scour under the embankment at this point.* **2.** A kind of dysentery or diarrhoea affecting cattle &c. ; also *scours.* **3.** Chemical substance used in scouring wool, cloth &c.

scourge, vb. trans. & n. [1. skĕrj ; 2. skɜ̄dž]. M.E. *scourgen*, O. Fr. *escorgier*, fr. Lat. *excoriāre*, 'to take the bark or skin off'. See **excoriate. 1.** vb. **a** To chastise, flog, whip ; **b** (in moral sense) to afflict, oppress, punish with severity : *scourged by the memory of one's misdeeds.* **2.** n. **a** An instrument for flogging ; a whip, lash ; **b** some severe punishment, affliction ; anything which afflicts severely ; a pest : *epidemics of infectious disease were a constant scourge in the Middle Ages* ; *flies and wasps are a regular scourge in summer.*

scout (I.), n. [1. skout ; 2. skaut]. M.E. *scoute*, fr. O. Fr. *escoute*, 'spy, eavesdropper, scout', fr. *escouter*, earlier *escolter*, Mod. Fr. *écouter*, 'to listen', fr. Lat. *auscultāre*, 'to listen carefully to', see **auscultation** & cp. **audience** & **ear (I.). 1.** (mil. and nav.) Person, or ship, sent out to obtain information about position and movements of the enemy, and generally to reconnoitre. **2.** Member of the organization known as *Boy Scouts*, founded in 1908, by Sir Robert (afterwards Lord) Baden-Powell, for training boys in outdoor habits, self-reliance, discipline, comradeship, knowledge of nature, woodcraft, and, in general, 'individual efficiency for the service of others'. **3.** Man-servant in an Oxford college, who waits on, and attends to the rooms of, resident members.

scout (II.), vb. intrans. See prec. **a** To act as a scout, to reconnoitre ; **b** *scout about, scout round*, to go from place to place in search, or as though in search, of something ; to prowl.

scout (III.), vb. trans. Scand., cp. O.N. *skūta*, 'a taunt'. To refuse to consider or entertain (an idea, suggestion &c.) ; to treat as absurd ; to flout.

scout (IV.), n. Etymol. doubtful ; possibly a variant of **scout (I.)**, but more prob. of **scoter.** Popular name of various sea-birds of the auk family, esp. the guillemot and puffin.

scout-master, n. **scout (I.)** & **master.** Leader of a group of Boy Scouts.

scow, n. [1. skou ; 2. skau], fr. Du. *schouw*, 'ferry-boat'. A large, flat-bottomed, square-ended boat, used as a lighter or barge.

scowl (I.), vb. intrans. [1. skoul ; 2. skaul]. M.E. *scoulen* ; apparently Scand. Most dictionaries connect the word w. various others in Scand. & Du. meaning, 'to lurk, lie hid' &c. This is unlikely, & it seems better to relate the word to O.E. *sčeolh*, 'wry', & *sčēolēagede*, 'squint-eyed'. See words given under **scolex.** To assume, wear, a frowning, lowering, sullen expression, to stare with lowered and puckered brows ; to frown : *he made no reply, but simply scowled* ; *scowl at*, look at with angry, sullen glance ; *scowl down* (a person), reduce to silence, daunt him, by scowling.

scowl (II.), n., fr. prec. A sullen, angry frown ; sullen, lowering glance or aspect.

scowlingly, adv. [1. skóulingli ; 2. skáuliŋli], fr. Pres. Part. of **scowl (I.)** & **-ly.** In a scowling manner ; with a scowl or sullen look.

scrabble, vb. intrans. [1. skrábl ; 2. skrǽbl]. Variant of dial. *scrapple*, freq. of **scrape (I.).** (rare) **1.** To scrape, scratch, paw, with rapid movements of the hands, as if in search of something : *to scrabble about in the dirt for coppers.* **2.** (archaic or Bib.) To scrawl, scribble : '*David . . . scrabbled on the doors of the gate*' (1 Sam. xxi. 13) ; the marginal note says 'made marks'.

scrag (I.), n. [1. skrag ; 2. skræg]. Of Scand. origin ; cp. Norw. *skragg*, 'a lean, poor, feeble person', Dan. *skrog*, 'lean carcase' ; possibly connected w. **shrink. 1.** A lean, skinny, thin, spindly, poorly developed creature ; a stunted tree or plant. **2. a** The neck-bone of a sheep, esp. the leaner joint, usually *scrag-end*, of a neck of mutton ; used for making broth &c. ; **b** (slang or colloq.) the neck of a person.

scrag (II.), vb. trans., fr. prec. (colloq. or slang) **a** To twist the neck of, to hang, put to death by hanging ; **b** to throttle, to garotte ; **c** to tackle round the neck as in Rugby football.

scrag-end, n. The neck-end or scrag of a neck of mutton.

scraggily, adv. [1. skrágili ; 2. skrǽgili]. **scraggy** & **-ly.** In a scraggy shape or form.

scragginess, n. [1. skrágines ; 2. skrǽginis]. **Scraggy** & **-ness.** Scraggy condition.

scraggy, adj. [1. skrági ; 2. skrǽgi]. **scrag (I.)** & **-y.** Gaunt, lean, skinny, thin ; insufficiently covered with flesh.

scramble (I.), vb. intrans. & trans. [1. skrámbl ; 2. skrǽmbl]. Not in M.E. ; dial. Engl. has *scramp* & *scramb*, 'to snatch at, to rake, scrape together', prob. a nasalized form of **scrabble. A.** intrans. **1.** To clamber, climb, crawl, make one's way, along, up and down &c., as best one can, using hands and feet : *children love scrambling among rocks* ; also *scramble about, up, down, through.* **2.** *Scramble for*, **a** to struggle, roughly and eagerly with others, in order to obtain something which all want ; specif., to scuffle and fight in a crowd for small objects, esp. money, scattered broadcast ; **b** (fig.) *to scramble for office, promotion* &c. **B.** trans. **1.** To throw down, scatter (objects), to be scrambled for : *to scramble pennies for the children in the street.* **2.** To cook eggs by breaking them into a saucepan, mixing and beating with butter, and heating till partially solid.

scramble (II.), n., fr. prec. Act of scrambling ; **a** an irregular mode of progression, a climb, clamber, using both hands and feet, over rough, steep ground where regular progress is impossible ; **b** a rough-and-tumble, a struggle or scuffle for material or other objects : *a scramble for pennies* ; *the general scramble for wealth, place* &c.

scramblingly, adv. [1. skrámblingli ; 2. skrǽmbliŋli], fr. Pres. Part. of **scramble (I.)** & **-ly.** In a scrambling way ; by a scramble.

scran, n. [1. skran ; 2. skræn]. Etymol. doubtful ; O.N. has *skran*, 'rubbish', & cp. next word. Refuse, scraps. Phr. (Ir.) *bad scran to you*, bad luck to you.

scrannel, adj. [1. skránl; 2. skrǽnl]. Scand., cp. Norw. *skran*, 'lean, thin, scraggy'. Thin, poor, weak, wretched; chiefly known through Milton's lines: '*Their lean and flashy songs Grate on their scrannel pipes of wretched straw*' ('Lycidas').

scrap (I.), n. [1. skrap; 2. skræp]. Scand., cp. O.N. *skrap*, 'scrapings, trifles'. See **scrape** (I.). **1.** A small piece of anything: *a scrap of bread, meat, paper* &c.; Phr. *a mere scrap of paper*, a negligible, worthless, invalid document; (in pl.) *scraps*, broken meat, odds and ends of waste food; also, *a few scraps of news* &c. **2.** *Scraps*, collection of newspaper cuttings, illustrations &c., preserved and pasted in a book. **3.** *Scrap*, waste material, refuse of various kinds; **a** old iron &c.; **b** dry, crisp refuse of fat, fish &c., after the oil has been squeezed out, used as cattle-food. **4.** A very small portion of anything: *you have not eaten a scrap all day.* Phr. *I don't care a scrap*, not at all.

scrap (II.), vb. trans., fr. prec. **1.** To make into scrap: *to scrap metal, iron* &c. **2.** To discard, throw away, treat as waste, worn out, useless: *to scrap machinery, old ships* &c.; (also of non-material things) *I shall scrap that chapter of my book, and write it over afresh.*

scrap (III.), n. & vb. intrans.; prob. variant of **scrape** (II.). (slang) **1.** n. **a** An informal fight, a rough-and-tumble, a scrimmage, a scuffle: *always ready for a scrap*; *he had a bit of a scrap with the police*; **b** a boxing match. **2.** vb. To fight, engage in a scrap; also *scrap with*, to fight (with).

scrap-book, n. A book with blank sheets in which scraps, such as newspaper cuttings, various literary odds and ends, illustrations &c., cut out of books &c., can be pasted for preservation.

scrap-cake, n. Cake made of fat, fish scrap, used as a feeding-stuff for cattle.

scrape (I.), vb. trans. & intrans. [1. skrāp; 2. skreip]. M.E. *scrāpen*, *scrāpien*; of Scand. origin, cp. O.N. *skrapa*, cogn. w. O.E. *screpan*, 'to scrape, scratch', cp. M.H.G. *schrepfen*, 'to scratch', wh. Kluge derives tentatively fr. base seen in **sharp** (I.). **A.** trans. **1. a** To pass a sharp instrument or edge over the surface of anything so as to graze or abrade it or to render it smooth, or clear of something adhering: *to scrape a wall*, so as to remove paint, paper &c.; *to scrape a ship's bottom*, to remove barnacles &c.; *to scrape a dish, plate* &c., to remove and eat every scrap of food on it and leave it clean; *to scrape one's chin*, to shave; **b** to bring (something) into contact with a hard, rough, body, so as to cause grazing, scratching, or abrasion: *to scrape one's knee against a stone, on the ground*; *the car scraped its side against the wall*; **c** *to scrape away, off, out, down*, to remove, clear off, take away by scraping: *scrape paint off a wall, the dirt off one's boots*; *scrape away accretions from a ship's bottom*; *scrape out a mark, one's signature*; *to scrape down a wall*, remove paint, dirt &c. thoroughly from it. **2. a** To draw (something) roughly across, to draw along or over anything so as to cause a harsh, grating, scratchy sound: *to scrape one's nail over a slate, pen over paper*; *scrape a bow across a fiddle*; Phr. (obs.) *to scrape the foot*, draw back one foot, at the same time making an awkward bow, in greeting a superior; **b** to produce a grating sound by scraping: *to scrape out a tune from a fiddle*; *to scrape one's throat.* **3. a** (usually *scrape up, together*) To collect, gather, together by scraping: *to scrape up the dirt from the road*; *scrape together the litter left by picnickers*; **b** (also fig.) to collect, get, together with effort or great difficulty: *scrape a few pounds, a little money, together*; Phrs. *to scrape a living*, to eke out a livelihood by saving and scraping, to make a bare living; *to scrape acquaintance with*, to get to know a person by some means or other, usually with the implication of thrusting oneself upon him, without proper introduction; **c** *scrape out*, to dig, excavate; to draw or drag out: *to scrape out a hole in the ground*; *to scrape out a pipe*; *scrape out the ashes from a grate.* **B.** intrans. **1.** To scrape, rub, anything so as to smooth, remove dirt &c. **2.** (followed by *against, along, by, through*) To graze, rub against anything; to pass along, by, anything so as to touch lightly, or to avoid doing so by a narrow margin: *the car scraped against the wall*; *the two cars just managed to scrape by without touching.* Phrs. *to scrape through*, to pass, get through, extricate oneself from anything with difficulty or by a narrow margin: *to scrape through a hedge*; also fig., *we shall scrape through somehow*; *scrape through an examination*, just pass; *scrape along*, (i.) pass along or over so as to scrape; (ii.) to manage to exist in spite of difficulty, poverty &c. **3. a** To rub against, with a harsh, grating sound; to draw one thing across another; to rub, graze, against anything with a grating sound: *to scrape on a fiddle*; *don't scrape with your feet*; *there is something scraping against the window.* Phrs. *to bow and scrape*, make an awkward bow and scrape back one foot; usually fig., to behave obsequiously; **b** to collect, get money together, with difficulty, to save by great economy or with difficulty; to be miserly or penurious: *to scrape and screw*, to hoard, be niggardly and miserly.

scrape (II.), n., fr. prec. **1. a** The act of scraping (in various senses); Phr. *a bow and a scrape*, a rustic salute, referring to the movement of the foot at the moment of touching the forelock; **b** something thinly smeared or scraped on to something else. Phr. *bread and scrape*, thinly buttered bread. **2.** Effect of scraping; **a** an abrasion, scratch, on the surface of anything: *a scrape on the shin*; **b** sound made by scraping, a squeak, a grating: *the scrape of a pencil on a slate, of a bow on a fiddle, of a bough on the window-pane* &c. **3.** An unpleasant, awkward, predicament, esp. a situation brought about by the victim's own discreditable conduct; disgrace: *his son has been getting into a scrape again.*

scraper, n. [1. skrāper; 2. skréipə]. Prec. & **-er.** **1.** One who scrapes (in various senses); specif. **a** a bad fiddler; **b** miser, skinflint. **2.** One of various instruments used for scraping; **a** a device placed outside a hall-door for removing mud from one's boots; also called *door-*, *shoe-scraper*; **b** apparatus of various types for clearing mud &c. from roads: *road-scraper*; **c** any of various tools with sharp or roughened edges used for scraping and cleansing skins, leather &c.

scrap-heap, n. **a** Dust heap, pile of refuse; **b** a limbo of rejected and forgotten things; oblivion: *a book fit only for the scrap-heap.*

scraping, n. [1. skrāping; 2. skréipiŋ]. **scrape** (I.) & **-ing.** **1.** Act of scraping (in various senses, mostly idiomatic); **a** *screwing and scraping*, mean, petty, economy, miserliness; **b** *bowing and scraping*, originally a rustic greeting of respect made by pulling the forelock and scraping the ground with one foot, probably, in origin, an imperfect genuflexion, hence, (i.) obsequious demeanour towards superiors; (ii.) airs and graces, extreme formality and observance of etiquette &c. **2. a** Something scraped off: *give me a small scraping of butter*; (often pl.) *scrapings*: *the scrapings of plates and dishes*; **b** (fig.) *the scrapings and scourings of the streets*, the disreputable elements of a population; riff-raff.

scrapper, n. [1. skrāper; 2. skrǽpə]. **scrap** (III.) & **-er.** (slang) One who scraps or fights; one ready to have a scrap with anyone; a plucky, hard-fighting boxer.

scrappily, adv. [1. skrápili; 2. skrǽpili]. **scrappy** & **-ly.** In a scrappy, fragmentary manner.

scrappiness, n. [1. skrápines; 2. skrǽpinis]. See next word & **-ness.** State, quality, of being scrappy.

scrappy, adj. [1. skrápi; 2. skrǽpi]. **scrap** (I.) & **-y.** **1.** Consisting, made up, of scraps and oddments; fragmentary: *a scrappy dinner*; *furniture of the house rather scrappy.* **2.** (of mental action or its results) Disconnected, loose, full of gaps; inconsequent: *a scrappy mind*; *scrappy mode of thinking*; *a scrappy lecture*; *knowledge that is varied but scrappy.*

scratch (I.), vb. trans. & intrans. [1. skrach; 2. skrætʃ]. A purely Engl. word, the origin of wh. is obscure; the attempts to derive it fr. a blending of two words, M.E. *skratten* & *cracchen*, one of Scand., the other of L.G. origin, are not convincing & are best disregarded. **A.** trans. **1. a** To tear slightly and leave a mark on the skin or surface of, with a sharp point of any kind: *the cat has scratched me with its claws*; *don't scratch the paint*; **b** to break up the surface (of ground) by digging, raking, or harrowing superficially; **c** (fig.) to deal with, treat of, study, in a perfunctory manner: *you have so far only scratched the surface of the subject, there is still much more to learn.* **2.** To incur a slight tearing of the skin or surface; to be marked, scored: *I've scratched my hand with the thorns.* **3. a** To produce counter-irritation, to relieve itching, tickling &c. by rubbing lightly with the nails or tips of the fingers: *never scratch a mosquito bite*; Phrs. *scratch my back and I will scratch yours*, help, flatter me, do me a good turn, and I will do the same for you; *to scratch one's head*, hesitate, pause, as if in perplexity; *scratch one's head over*, ponder over in a puzzled manner, wonder what to do about a matter; **b** to tickle, give gentle friction to: *cats like to be scratched under the chin.* **4. a** To excavate by scratching: *to scratch a hole in the ground*; **b** to draw an outline, write by an action resembling scratching: *a drawing scratched on a wall*; *to scratch a few lines of a letter.* **5.** Specif., *to scratch a horse*, withdraw it from a race &c., from the action of scratching out and erasing the name. **6.** Followed by prepositions or adverbs: *scratch out*, to strike out (word &c.) with a pen &c.; to score out, delete, erase; *to scratch through*, to scratch out; *scratch up*, to collect, rake together (lit. and fig.). **B.** intrans. **1.** To perform the action of scratching (in various senses); **a** to use claws, wound with claws: *cats scratch, dogs bite*; **b** to produce counter-irritant by scratching: *itching makes one want to scratch*; **c** to produce a squeaking, scraping sound: *this pen scratches badly.* **2.** To scratch, scrape, the ground, esp. of animals, with claws, feet, paws: *hens ought to be made to scratch for their corn*; *the dog is scratching as if he smelt a rat.* **3.** To scratch out one's name from list of competitors in a race or other contest; hence, **a** to withdraw from competing; **b** (fig.) to back out of, abandon, give up an undertaking.

scratch (II.), n., fr. prec. **1.** Act of scratching: *dogs enjoy a good scratch.* **2. a** Mark, wound, superficial tear, made on skin or surface by scratching: *a scratch on the face, on fresh paint, on a silver tray* &c.; specif. **b** a very slight, trivial, wound: *my injury was nothing, merely a scratch.* Phr. *without a scratch*, without the slightest wound or injury. **3. a** Sound made by scratching; scraping, squeaking sound: *silence save for the scratch of his pen on the paper*; **b** slight hasty movement made in scratching; specif., *the scratch of a pen*, the writing of a few words: *the business could be settled by the scratch of a pen*, i.e. by a brief written order, or by the writing of a signature. **4. a** Mark made on the ground &c. to indicate starting-point of a race, the place for boxers to stand at beginning of a match &c.; hence, *to come up to scratch*, be ready to start race, match &c. at proper time; also (fig.) to be ready to embark on an enterprise, to fulfil one's engagements &c.; *to start from scratch*, to have no handicap, run the whole course of a race; **b** zero, par, in games scored by numerical points. **5. a** A scratch-wig; **b** (veter., pl.) *scratches*, a disease affecting horses' heels, accompanied by dry cracks or scabs, swelling and suppuration.

scratch (III.), adj., fr. **scratch** (I.). Hastily collected or scratched together; recruited as best one can or from any source: *a scratch crew, team; put up with a scratch dinner.*

Scratch (IV.), n. Etymol. doubtful, but cp. O.N. *skratta*, 'goblin'. (never used now) *Old Scratch*, the Devil.

scratch-back, n. An obsolete implement consisting of a small ivory or wooden hand on a long flexible handle, used for scratching one's back.

scratcher, n. [1. skrácher; 2. skrǽtʃə]. **scratch** (I.) & **-er**. One who, that which, scratches; specif. (zool.) an old name for the scratching or rasorial birds.

scratchily, adv. [1. skráchili; 2. skrǽtʃili]. **scratchy** & **-ly**. In a scratchy manner (various senses).

scratchiness, n. [1. skráchines; 2. skrǽtʃinis]. See prec. & **-ness**. Quality of being scratchy.

scratch man, n. Competitor in race or other game who starts from scratch or receives no handicap.

scratch-race, n. A race where all competitors start from scratch.

scratch-wig, n. A small 18th-cent. wig, covering only part of the head.

scratchy, adj. [1. skráchi; 2. skrǽtʃi]. **scratch** (II.) & **-y**. **1.** Having the appearance of being scratched or drawn rudely or roughly; depicted by scratches: *a scratchy drawing, writing.* **2.** Producing the sound of scratching: *a scratchy pen.* **3.** Scratch; collected, scratched together, haphazard: *a scratchy crew, team.* **4. a** Itching, irritating; causing irritation: *scratchy cloth*; **b** inclined to scratch oneself, scratching oneself: *the dog seems very scratchy today.*

scrawl (I.), vb. intrans. & trans. [1. skrawl; 2. skrōl]. Etymol. obscure, possibly a variant of **scroll**. **1.** intrans. **a** To write in a sprawling, straggly, shapeless hand; **b** to make sprawling, meaningless marks with a pencil, or pointed instrument: *someone has scrawled all over the wall.* **2.** trans. To write (a letter &c.) hastily and in a shapeless, unformed, sprawling handwriting.

scrawl (II.), n., fr. prec. **a** A shapeless, sprawling, untidy handwriting; **b** letter or other document written in such a handwriting.

scray, n. [1. skrā; 2. skrei], fr. W. *yscraen*, 'tern'. The common tern, the sea-swallow.

scream (I.), vb. intrans. & trans. [1. skrēm; 2. skrīm]. M.E. *scrēmen*, fr. O.N. *skræma*, 'to terrify, scare', cp. Swed. *scrāna*, 'to scream'. **A.** intrans. **1.** (of human beings, birds, beasts &c.) **a** To utter a shrill, piercing cry, esp. of fear or pain; to shriek: *the baby screamed all night*; Phr. *to scream with laughter*, to laugh heartily; hence, **b** to laugh heartily and uproariously: *he was so funny, he made us scream*; **c** *scream out*, call out loudly and shrilly. **2.** (of wind, machines &c.) To produce a shrill, piercing noise. **3.** (of colours) To produce the effect of violent discord, to be at once loud and inharmonious; to clash. **B.** trans. To utter (words &c.) with, in, a scream: *to scream curses and defiance*; also *scream out.*

scream (II.), n., fr. prec. **1.** A loud, piercing cry, esp. one expressing fear or pain; a shriek, high wail. Phr. *screams of laughter*, hearty burst of laughter. **2.** (vulg. slang) Person or thing that excites great amusement and entertainment: *a perfect scream*; also in unfavourable sense, object of derision.

screamer, n. [1. skrḗmer; 2. skrīmə]. **scream** (I.) & **-er**. **1.** One who, that which, screams; specif. (ornith.) **a** a S. American bird, *Palamedes*, of semi-aquatic habit, having a harsh, screaming cry; **b** popular name of the swift. **2.** (slang) Something evoking or likely to evoke a scream of laughter, wonder &c., a scream; a marvellous, incredible story or yarn.

screaming (I.), n. [1. skrḗming; 2. skrīmiŋ]. Act of making, sound of, a scream, or of screams.

screaming (II.), adj., fr. Pres. Part. of **scream** (I.) & **-ing**. **1.** Of the nature, producing effect, of a scream, like, uttered with, a scream: *a screaming cry, voice; a howling, screaming wind.* **2.** Evoking screams of laughter, very funny: *a screaming farce.*

screamingly, adv. Prec. & **-ly**. In a screaming manner; *screamingly funny*, so funny as to produce screams of laughter.

screamy, adj. [1. skrḗmi; 2. skrīmi]. **scream** (II.) & **-y**. Resembling a scream; screaming, screechy: *a screamy voice.*

scree, n. [1. skrē; 2. skrī]. Prob. for **scre(th)es* (cp. pronunciation of *clothes*); connected w. O.N. *skriða*, 'landslip', fr. *skriða*, 'to slide'; cp. O.E. *scrīþan*, 'to move, glide, go'. Accumulation of small or broken stones on a steep hill or mountain-side which slides away when trodden on; collection of similar material artificially brought together for growing alpine plants in gardens.

screech (I.), vb. intrans. & trans. [1. skrēch; 2. skrītʃ]. Variant of **shriek**. The formal connexion between these & the M.E. words meaning the same thing is obscure, & the origin still more so. **1.** intrans. To shriek with a shrill, harsh, disagreeable sound. **2.** trans. To utter with a screech; also *screech out.*

screech (II.), n., fr. prec. A shrill, piercing scream or cry; often, *to let out a screech.*

screech-owl, n. The barn-owl, from its note when hunting.

screed, n. [1. skrēd; 2. skrīd]. Northern variant of **shred**. A long, wearisome speech or recitation; a long passage from a book.

screen (I.), n. [1. skrēn; 2. skrīn]. M.E. *scrēn*, fr. O. Fr. *escrēn*, 'fire-screen, curtain', Mod. Fr. *écran*; etymol. uncertain. **1.** Any of various structures designed to afford shelter, protection, from wind, to cut off light, to separate or conceal one part of a room or building from another; curtain, partition; **a** portable piece of furniture, consisting usually of a framework with several panels of wood, covered with leather, cloth &c., each division of which is hinged so that it can be folded close or opened out; used to exclude draughts, or to secure privacy in part of a room &c.; **b** structure, often elaborately carved, of wood or stone, having traceries and arches, separating the nave from the choir in a large church; **c** portable framework filled with thick glass, or containing a wooden panel covered with fabric; or a structure of basket-work, used to protect the face or back from the direct heat of a fire in a room; **d** framework holding glass or talc used to protect passengers in a motor-car from rush of wind; device on railway engine protecting driver from wind. **2. a** Large sheet, or curtain with white surface, upon which pictures are thrown by a magic-lantern, or apparatus in a cinema; **b** large structure of boarding, painted white, used on cricket field as a background against which the batsman can see the ball better. **3. a** Any object serving to conceal, or affording shelter from wind, or from the heat of the sun, such as a hedge, row or belt of trees; specif. **b** (mil. and nav.) troops or ships sent forward in advance of the main body, esp. when on the move, to protect from sudden attack, to conceal its movements, numbers &c. from the enemy: *a screen of cavalry, of light cruisers &c.*; *smoke-screen*, a dense, low-lying cloud of smoke artificially produced for purposes of defensive or offensive concealment.

screen (II.), vb. trans., fr. prec. **1. a** To protect, conceal, with, or as with, a screen: *to screen one's eyes from the fire; to screen oneself from observation*; **b** to intercept, mask, cut off, by means of a screen: *to screen the fire from one's back.* **2.** *Screen off*, to divide, shut off (building, room), by a screen, partition, curtain &c.: *to screen off a bay window from the rest of the room.* **3.** (in non-material sense) To afford protection to, intervene between (person) and punishment, censure, disgrace &c.; to shelter from moral injury &c.: *it was felt that the accused was screening the real culprit; all her youth she was carefully screened from the slightest contact with the wickedness and cruelty of the world.*

screen (III.), n. Origin unknown; usually assumed to be identical w. **screen** (I.) & (II.), the origin of wh. is equally dubious. It is difficult to find any relation in meaning between a means of concealment or shelter & a sieve! **1.** A large coarse riddle or sieve, usually made with a mesh of thick wire, used to clean and grade coal, gravel &c., or sift earth, cinders, and the like. **2.** Specif. uses, probably derived from above: **a** (elect.) a body or substance which prevents or hinders the passage of high-frequency currents or magnetic induction effects; **b** (photog.) device used for controlling the passage of light through a lens, esp. piece of glass covered with a mesh of fine lines used in taking photographs for reproduction by the half-tone or other processes.

screen (IV.), vb. trans., fr. prec. To clean, grade, sift (coal, gravel &c.) by passing through a screen.

screenings, n. pl. [1. skrḗningz; 2. skrīniŋz]. Prec. & **-ing**. Whatever is left after passing matter through a screen; specif., rubbish of any sort left after screening corn.

screw (I.), n. [1. skrōō; 2. skrū]. M.E. *screu*, fr. O. Fr. *escroe*; etymol. doubtful; possibly connected w. **scroll** (I.). **1.** Object used for fastening two pieces of wood or metal together, in the form of a cylindrically shaped piece of metal, relatively thick in proportion to its length, having a flattened head projecting beyond the shaft, with a groove to facilitate turning; the shaft, which tapers slightly towards the point, has a deep spiral groove or thread, so that the screw can only penetrate into the wood &c. by being turned round and round, or be withdrawn by being turned in reverse direction. Phrs. *a screw loose*, something amiss, all is not in proper order or adjustment: *there is a screw loose somewhere*; *to have a screw loose*, to be off one's head, to be a little mad. **2.** One of various mechanical contrivances whereby the principles of a screw are utilized for lifting or pressing. Phrs. *to put the screw on, apply the screw to, give another turn to the screw*, (in fig. use) to put moral pressure on, coerce, exercise compulsion upon, oppress, compel to act in a manner desired. **3.** A screw propeller of a steamboat. The following appear to be new formations from the verb: **4. a** Action of screwing, turning, twisting: *to give a nut a good screw*; **b** twisting, sideways bias or direction, a spin imparted to a moving body which causes it to depart suddenly from, alter, its direction, or to depart from straight path: *to put a screw on a billiard or tennis ball.* **5.** Something screwed or twisted up: *a screw of tobacco*, small amount twisted up in paper. **6.** Person who screws and scrapes; a stingy person, a miser, a skinflint. **7.** (colloq.) Amount received as wages, salary, stipend: *a poor screw; a monthly, yearly, screw*, from idea that it is wrung, or screwed, out of employer. **8.** (perhaps a different word) A broken-down horse · one that has some defect, though not necessarily useless.

screw (II.), vb. trans. & intrans., fr. prec. **A.** trans. **1.** To fasten with a screw: *to screw a lock on to a door*; followed by prepositions or adverbs: **a** *screw up*, (i.) to turn (a bolt &c.) until it is tight; (ii.) to close completely, make perfectly secure, with screw or screws: *to screw up a coffin, box, door &c.*; **b** *screw in*, drive home (screw) by turning it; **c** *screw down*, to close down and make fast with screws; **d** *to screw on*, to fasten with a screw, tighten by screwing: *to screw on a knob*; Phr. *to have one's head screwed on tight, the right way*, to be shrewd and level-headed. **2. a** To turn, twist, with a movement similar to that of tightening a screw: *to screw a person's arm*; **b** to turn round as far as possible: *to screw one's head round*; also *screw up*, (i.) tighten by a screwing movement: *to screw up the strings of a* *fiddle*; (ii.) (fig.) to brace up, stimulate (a person, oneself, one's courage), to the point of performing some particular task; (iii.) *to screw up discipline*, make it more severe. **3.** To twist, pucker, contort: *to screw one's features into a grimace*; also *screw up*, contort, twist energetically: *to screw up one's face, eyes*; *to screw up a piece of paper into a ball*. **4.** To squeeze, press, by screwing, twisting movement; esp. *screw out*, **a** to extract, squeeze out, by screwing: *to screw water out of a sponge*; **b** (fig.) (i.) to extort from, compel to give, or pay, by compulsion: *to screw money, or promises, out of people*; (ii.) to give, pay out (money &c.), grudgingly and with reluctance: *at last he screwed out half a crown for a taxi fare*. **5.** To hit (a ball) in such a way as to put a screw on to it: *to screw the red into a pocket*. **B.** intrans. **1.** To be made to screw, to be capable of being screwed: *that bolt doesn't slide in, it screws*; *this handle won't screw*. **2. a** (of a player) To impart a screw to a ball: *if I knew how to screw, I could get my ball in off the red*; **b** (of a ball) to twist aside, or backwards, on striking the ground or another ball: *my ball screwed into a pocket off the red*. **3.** (of persons) To indulge in petty, mean economies; to stint, be miserly and stingy: *the old curmudgeon had screwed all his life*.

screw-bolt, n. A bolt with blunt end and external thread fitting into a nut with internal thread, used for fastening metal or other plates together.

screw-box, n. **a** Device for cutting wooden screws; **b** socket for screw.

screw-cap, n. Cap or cover made to screw on to a jar or bottle.

screw-coupling, n. A threaded joint or collar at end of rods or pipes, used to fasten two lengths together.

screw-cutter, n. Tool, machine, for cutting screws.

screw-driver, n. Tool shaped like a chisel with a blunt edge, used for turning, tightening, or loosening screws.

screwed, adj. [1. skrōōd; 2. skrūd]. Prob. P.P. of **screw** (**II.**), w. reference to twisting, turning, staggering. (slang) Intoxicated, drunk.

screw-eye, n. Screw with a loop at one end instead of a flattened, grooved head.

screw-gear, n. Endless screw working against a cogged wheel.

screw-hook, n. Metal hook with a shank in form of a screw.

screw-jack, n. A lifting jack, in which the leverage is worked by a screw; a jack-screw.

screw-key, n. A wrench or spanner the jaws of which are opened, closed, and held at the desired position by means of a screw.

screw-pile, n. One in the form of a large screw, usually having a ring at the upper end, through which a rod is passed for screwing into the ground.

screw-pine, n. A genus, *Pandanus*, of shrubs and trees found in the Malay Peninsula and tropical islands, with leaves arranged in spirals, and aerial roots.

screw-plate, n. A steel plate with threaded holes, used for cutting threads or screws.

screw-press, n. A press worked by means of a screw.

screw-propeller, n. Revolving shaft fitted with blades arranged in a spiral, whereby ships and aeroplanes are driven.

screw-steamer, n. A steamer driven by a screw-propeller.

screw-tap, n. **1.** An instrument used for cutting internal screws. **2.** Water-tap which closes with a screw movement.

screw-wheel, n. A cogged wheel or gearing fitting into the thread of an endless screw, for transmitting motion.

screw-wrench, n. Spanner working on a screw; a screw-key.

screwy, adj. [1. skrōōi; 2. skrúi]. **1.** Curving, twisty. **2.** Given to screwing and petty economies; stingy, mean.

scribal, adj. [1. skríbl; 2. skráibl]. **scribe** (**I.**) & **-al.** Connected with, pertaining to, due to, a scribe; arising in process of writing: *scribal traditions*; *a scribal error*.

scribble (**I.**), vb. trans. & intrans. [1. skríbl; 2. skríbl]. Freq. form of **scribe** (**II.**). **A.** trans. **1. a** To write hastily, carelessly, or illegibly: *to scribble a note, letter* &c.; **b** (rare) to make meaningless marks on, to scrawl upon: *to scribble a wall* &c. **2.** To compose, write, without regard to correctness or style: *to scribble verses, silly novels*; *I've only time to scribble a hasty note*. **B.** intrans. **1. a** To write in a hasty, illegible, careless way; to scrawl; **b** to compose in a careless hurried way &c. **2.** (usually self-depreciatingly) To be a writer, to make one's living by authorship: *one has to scribble for a bare existence*; *an eighteenth-century gentleman would admit that he scribbled for his own amusement*.

scribble (**II.**), n., fr. prec. **1.** Hasty, illegible handwriting, scrawl. **2.** Anything written in a hasty, careless way, without regard to composition or style.

scribble (**III.**), vb. trans., fr. Swed. *skrubbla*, 'to card wool', freq. of *skrubba*, see **scrub** (**II.**). To card wool or cotton roughly, as a first stage in the carding process; to pass through the scribbler or scribbling-machine.

scribbler (**I.**), n. [1. skríbler; 2. skríblə]. **scribble** (**I.**) & **-er.** One who scribbles; **a** one who writes hastily, illegibly &c.; **b** a bad, ignorant, inferior author: '*venal and licentious scribblers*' (Macaulay, On Milton).

scribbler (**II.**), n. **scribble** (**III.**) & **-er.** A machine for scribbling or roughly carding wool.

scribbling-machine, n. [1. skríbling mashēn; 2. skríbliŋ məʃīn]. A scribbler for carding wool.

scribbling-paper, n. Inferior kind of writing-paper for making rough notes &c.

scribe (**I.**), n. [1. skrīb; 2. skraib], fr. Lat. *scrība*, 'official writer, clerk, secretary', fr. *scrībere*, 'to write'; orig. 'to tear, scratch', fr. same base as Gk. *skaripháomai*, 'I scratch, tear', & *skariphismós*, 'a scratching, scraping'; O.E. *scrīfan*, 'to decree, allot, assign', see **shrive**, is a loan-word fr. Lat. **1.** Penman, writer; esp. a professional writer or copyist of MSS. before invention of printing. **2.** (Jewish hist.) One of a class of ecclesiastical lawyers who read and expounded the sacred law. **3.** A small pointed instrument used for marking a line to indicate where wood or stone is to be cut; also called *scribe-awl* or *scriber*.

scribe (**II.**), vb. trans., fr. prec. (carpentry) To mark (stone, wood &c.) with a scribe.

scribe-awl, scriber, n. [1. skrīb awl, skrīber; 2. skráib ɔ̄l, skráibə]. See **scribe** (**I.**), **3.**

scrim, n. [1. skrim; 2. skrim]. Etymol. unknown. Kind of thin, loosely woven canvas, used for linings in upholstery, bookbinding &c.; also of jute for packing &c.

scrimmage, scrummage, n. & vb. intrans. [1. skrímij, skrúmij; 2. skrímidž, skrámidž], variant of **skirmish. 1.** n. **a** (i.) A confused struggle or rough-and-tumble; a fight, a row, brawl, tussle; (ii.) a heated, noisy dispute; **b** (usually *scrummage*, abbr. *scrum*, in Rugby football) (i.) the pack of forwards; (ii.) the grouping of the forwards of both sides compactly together, with heads down, on each side of the ball, which is placed on the ground between them, after a man has been collared &c. **2.** vb. **a** To take part in a scrimmage, engage in a rough-and-tumble; to brawl; **b** (Rugby football, usually *scrummage* or *scrum*) to pack together, form one of a scrummage.

scrimmager, n., more usually **scrummager**, [1. skrímijer, skrúmijer; 2. skrímidžə, skrámidžə]. Prec. & **-er.** A Rugby forward.

scrimp, vb. trans. & intrans. [1. skrimp; 2. skrimp], fr. O.E. *scrimman*, see **shrimp**, & cp. **shrink**, cogn. w. Dan. *skrumpe*, Germ. *schrumpfen*. To skimp, q.v.

scrimpy, adj. [1. skrímpi; 2. skrímpi]. Prec. & **-y.** Skimpy.

scrimshank, vb. intrans. [1. skrímshangk; 2. skrímʃæŋk]. Origin doubtful; occurs first apparently in late 19th cent.; Nthn. dial. has *scrimp*, 'to stint', & *shankle*, 'to loiter, shirk work'. (army slang) To shirk duty, work, fatigues &c.

scrimshanker, n. [1. skrímshangker; 2. skrímʃæŋkə]. Prec. & **-er.** One who shirks duty &c.

scrimshaw, n. & vb. trans. & intrans. [1. skrímshaw; 2. skrímʃɔ̄]. A sailor's term; prob. a surname. **1. a** n. Decoration of shells, elephants' teeth, ivory &c. with incised and coloured designs; **b** any neat piece of work. **2.** vb. **a** trans. To decorate (shells &c.) in this way; **b** intrans., to do this kind of work.

scrinium, n. [1. skrínium; 2. skráiniəm]. Lat.; etymol. unknown. Persson compares Lith. *krēwas*, 'wound round, curved, oblique', fr. base **kʷere-*, 'to turn, bend'. See **curve, crown**, & words there referred to. A press or case for books or MSS. in old, mediaeval libraries; originally cylindrical in shape.

scrip (**I.**), n. [1. skrip; 2. skrip]. In O.E. *scripp*, M.E. *scrippe*, prob. Scand., cp. O.N. *skreppa*, 'bag, knapsack', possibly connected w. **scrap** (**I.**). A small bag, wallet, or satchel, esp. in Phr. *pilgrim's scrip*.

scrip (**II.**), n. Variant pronunciation of **script** in 17th & 18th cents. **a** Provisional document of allotment issued to holder of stocks or shares; **b** shares themselves.

script, n. [1. skript; 2. skript], fr. O. Fr. *escript*, 'a writing', fr. Lat. *scriptum*, 'thing written', P.P. of *scrībere*, 'to write', see **scribe** (**I.**). **1.** Handwriting, as opposed to print; handwriting like print; specif., a form of printer's cursive type imitating handwriting. **2.** A piece of writing, written document; specif. **a** (law) the original, as contrasted with the copy of a document; **b** paper of answers written by a candidate in an examination.

scriptorium, n. [1. skriptórium; 2. skriptɔ́riəm]. L. Lat. See prec. & **-ory.** A writing room; specif., room in a monastery set apart for the copying of MSS., and for writing and study generally.

scriptural, adj. [1. skrípchural; 2. skríptʃərəl]. **scripture** & **-al.** Pertaining to, based on, according to, the Holy Scriptures; Biblical.

scripturalism, n. [1. skrípchuralizm; 2. skríptʃərəlizəm]. Prec. & **-ism.** Rigid adherence to, and insistence upon, a literal, particularly one's own, interpretation of the text of a book, esp. of the Bible, as the only guide in faith and morals.

scripturalist, n. [1. skrípchuralist; 2. skríptʃərəlist]. **scriptural** & **-ist.** One who practises scripturalism.

scripturally, adv. [1. skrípchurali; 2. skríptʃərəli]. **scriptural** & **-ly.** In a scriptural manner; as contained in the Bible.

scripture, n. [1. skrípchur; 2. skríptʃə], fr. O. Fr. *escripture*, fr. Lat. *scriptūra*, 'a writing'. **script** & **-ure. 1.** (archaic and obs.) A writing, anything written; a manuscript, inscription. **2.** Specif. (cap.) **a** holy writ, the Bible, the books of the Old and New Testament, or either of them, sometimes including the Apocrypha; in either of the following forms: *Holy Scripture* or *Scripture teaches us*; also *the Scriptures*: *to read the Scriptures*; **b** (archaic) *a, the, Scripture*, a specific passage from, text of, the Bible as quoted or referred to: *there is a scripture which says*; '*that the scripture might be fulfilled*'; **c** *the Scriptures*, a copy of the Old or New Testament; a Bible. **3.** Sacred, religious books of a non-Christian religion: *the Scripture of Islam*; *Buddhist, Hindu, Scriptures*. **4.** (attrib.) Pertaining to, contained in, taken, quoted, from the Bible; scriptural: *a scripture lesson, text* &c.

scripture reader, n. A lay reader of the Bible, esp. one employed to read the Bible in people's homes to those unable to read for themselves &c.

scrivener, n. [1. skrívner; 2. skrívnə], fr. earlier obs. *scriven* & **-er**, fr. O. Fr. *escrivain*, fr. L. Lat. *scribānus*, fr. *scribere*, 'to write', see

scribe. (archaic or obs.) **1.** A professional writer; a legal draftsman or copyist, notary. **2.** A money-broker, one who received money from others on deposit and placed it out at interest; also *money-scrivener*.

scrivener's palsy, n. Writer's cramp.

scrobiculate, adj. [1. skrobíkūlāt; 2. skrɔbíkjuleit], fr. Lat. *scrobiculus*, 'a small pit or trench', dimin. of *scrobis*, 'ditch, trench', & **-ate**; *scrobis* is cogn. w. O.E. *scræf*, 'a cave', & more remotely w. **sharp** (I.). (anat. and bot.) Marked by small furrows or depressions; pitted.

scrofula, n. [1. skrófūla; 2. skrɔ́fjulə]. Lat., only found in pl. *scrōfulae*, lit. 'little pigs; glandular swellings', *scrōfula*, dimin. of *scrōfa*, 'a breeding sow'; the connexion is not very obvious, unless it be fr. the idea of something unclean. The etymol. is disputed. (pathol.) The old name of tuberculosis, esp. of that type which attacks the lymphatic glands, particularly of the neck; struma, the 'king's evil'.

scrofulous, adj. [1. skrófūlus; 2. skrɔ́fjuləs]. Prec. & **-ous**. **a** Pertaining to, of the nature of, scrofula: *scrofulous tumours*; *scrofulous diathesis*; **b** affected with scrofula: *scrofulous glands*; *a scrofulous person.*

scrofulousness, n. Prec. & **-ness**. Condition of being scrofulous.

scroll (I.), n. [1. skrōl; 2. skroul]. Earlier spelt *scrowl*, prob. dimin. of M.E. *scrowe*, *scroue*, fr. O. Fr. *escroue*, 'scroll', also 'screw'; etymol. doubtful. **1.** A roll of parchment or paper; hence, **a** an ancient manuscript book or volume, as being rolled; **b** a list, schedule: *on the scroll of fame*; **c** (her.) a ribbon bearing a motto placed beneath a coat of arms. **2.** Anything, esp. an ornamental design or feature, having the form of a partly unrolled scroll of parchment; a spiral or spiral tracery; specif. **a** a flourish, in writing, added to a signature, special words, or figures; **b** the curved head of a fiddle, arm of a chair &c.; **c** the volute of an Ionic capital.

scroll (II.), vb. intrans. & trans., fr. prec. (rare) **1.** intrans. To roll, curl, up, like a scroll. **2.** trans. (usually in P.P.) To decorate with a scroll or scrolls.

scroll-gear, n. A gearing fitted with a scroll-wheel.

scroll-head, n. A timber at a ship's bow carved into a scroll.

scroll-saw, n. A fret-saw for cutting scrolls.

scroll-wheel, n. A flat disk with cogs arranged spirally on one face, giving variation of speed when working in a gearing.

scroll-work, n. Ornamental carving, cut out with a scroll-saw; also similar work drawn or painted.

Scrophularia, n. [1. skròfūlária; 2. skrɔ̀fjuléəriə]. Neo-Lat., fr. **scrofula**, the figwort being formerly considered good for the disease. (bot.) A genus of plants, the figworts; the family includes the foxgloves, snapdragon, speedwell, mullein &c.

scrotal, adj. [1. skrṓtl; 2. skróutl]. **scrotum** & **-al**. Connected with, pertaining to, the scrotum.

scrotitis, n. [1. skrṑtítis; 2. skròutáitis], fr. **scrotum** & **-itis**. Inflammation of the scrotum.

scrotocele, n. [1. skrṓtōsēl; 2. skróutousīl]. **scrotum** & **-cele**. Hernia of the scrotum.

scrotum, n. [1. skrṓtum; 2. skróutəm]. Lat., ultimately cogn. w. Lat. *scortum*, 'skin, hide', wh. see under **cortex**. The bag of skin which contains the testicles.

scrounge, vb. intrans. & trans. [1. skrounj; 2. skraundž]. Etymol. uncertain; *scrunge*, *scrouge*, & other forms appear in dial., meaning 'to crush, squeeze, press', cp. slang use of *pinch*, 'to thieve, steal'. (army slang) **1.** intrans. To obtain anything one wants surreptitiously; to cadge, pilfer. **2.** trans. To obtain surreptitiously, pilfer from others: *scrounge firewood from the next trench*; *scrounge a meal somehow or other.*

scrounger, n. [1. skróunjer; 2. skráundžə]. Prec. & **-er**. One who scrounges; a pilferer, cadger.

scrub (I.), n. [1. skrub; 2. skrab]. Scand., cp. M. Dan. *skrubbe*, 'brushwood', see **shrub** (I.), of wh. it is a variant form. **1.** **a** Brushwood; small, stunted, dwarf trees or bushes, esp. when growing thickly together; **b** land covered with such growth. **2.** Stunted, undersized, dwarfish creature; mean, insignificant person: *a wretched little scrub.*

scrub (II.), vb. trans. & intrans. M.E. *scrobben*, 'to rub down a horse', fr. M. Dan. *skrubbe*, 'to rub hard, to scrub', prob. fr. prec., cp. use of **broom** & **brush**. **A.** trans. **1.** **a** To clean by hard rubbing, esp. with a brush, and soap and water: *to scrub the floor*; *to scrub a dirty child*; *to scrub one's hands, nails* &c.; **b** to remove by scrubbing: *to scrub dirt off the walls, paint off one's hands* &c. **2.** To rub hard, apply friction to with energy: *to scrub oneself with a towel.* **3.** (gas-making) To remove ammonia and other impurities from coal-gas by spraying with water. **B.** intrans. To use a brush, water, and soap for cleaning things; to clean things by hard rubbing: *girls should be taught how to cook and scrub.*

scrub (III.), n., fr. prec. Act of scrubbing; the being scrubbed; a hard rubbing and washing: *the floors need a good scrub.*

scrubber, n. [1. skrúber; 2. skrábə]. **scrub** (II.) & **-er**. **1.** One who scrubs; brush used for scrubbing. **2.** (specif., gas-making) Apparatus used in washing coal-gas &c. by spraying.

scrubbiness, n. [1. skrúbines; 2. skrábinis]. **scrubby** & **-ness**. Condition of being scrubby or stunted.

scrubbing-brush, n. [1. skrúbing brush; 2. skrábiŋ braʃ]. A hard, rough brush used for scrubbing.

scrub-bird, n. **scrub** (I.) & **bird**. A small Australian bird, living in thick scrub, of peculiar anatomical structure and forming a genus, *Atrichornis*, of passerine birds.

scrubby, adj. [1. skrúbi; 2. skrábi]. **scrub** (I.) & **-y**. **1.** **a** Of the nature of scrub or brushwood; stunted, dwarfed: *scrubby trees*; **b** (of persons) mean-looking, small, insignificant; dirty, untidy and ill-dressed. **2.** Full of scrub; overgrown with brushwood and stunted trees: *scrubby land.*

scrub-oak, n. **scrub** (I.) & **oak**. A dwarf oak of N. America.

scruff, n. [1. skruf; 2. skraf]. Earlier *scuft*, *scuff*, fr. O.N. *skopt*, 'hair of the head', cp. Goth. *skuft*, 'hair of the head, tuft of hair', perh. cogn. w. **sheaf**. The loose folds of skin at the back of the neck; the nape; usually in Phr. *scruff of the neck.*

scrummage, n., usually abbr. **scrum**. See **scrimmage**.

scrumptious, adj. [1. skrúmpshus; 2. skrámpʃəs]. Modern, coined word. (colloq.) Extremely pleasing to any of the senses; delicious.

scrunch, vb. trans. & intrans. & n. [1. skrunch; 2. skrantʃ]. Imitative. See **crunch**. **1.** vb. To crunch, crush, squeeze; to crunch up noisily with the jaws. **2.** n. Act, sound, of scrunching.

scruple (I.), n. [1. skrṓōpl; 2. skrúpl]. Fr., fr. Lat. *scrūpulus*, 'small, sharp stone; weight, one-twenty-fourth of the ounce; sharp stone in one's shoe; troublesome thing; doubt, scruple', dimin. of *scrūpus*, 'broken, sharp piece of stone'. Etymol. uncertain. **1.** **a** A weight, 20 grains, ⅓ of a drachm, a unit of apothecaries' weight; **b** (archaic or obs.) a very small amount, a trifle. **2.** Doubt, hesitation as to course of action, opinion &c., arising from difficulty of determining what is right or expedient; objection arising from conscientious motives; compunction, qualm of conscience: *to have scruples about doing something*; *ready to break the most solemn promises without scruple*; *determined to make no scruple of stamping out the rebellion ruthlessly*; *(a man) of no scruples*, unscrupulous.

scruple (II.), vb. intrans. & trans., fr. prec. **1.** intrans. To have scruples; to hesitate, doubt, about one's actions, decisions, opinions, owing to scruples &c.; to be reluctant to do, feel compunction in doing, something: *to scruple to charge more than a thing is worth*; *he would not scruple to make the most unfounded accusations*; *don't scruple to ask for anything you want.* **2.** trans. (obs.) To have, make, scruples about, to hesitate at; to question, doubt: *to scruple doing something*; *he scrupled the honesty of their motives.*

scrupulosity, n. [1. skrōōpūlósiti; 2. skrùpjulɔ́siti], fr. Lat. *scrūpulōsitāt-(em)*. See **scrupulous** & **-ity**. Quality of being scrupulous; esp. exaggerated, meticulous and conscientious exactness in thought, conduct, method &c.

scrupulous, adj. [1. skrōōpūlus; 2. skrúpjuləs], fr. O. Fr. *scrupuleux*, fr. Lat. *scrūpulōsus*, 'full of sharp, pointed stones; rough, jagged; precise, exact, careful'. See **scruple** (I.) & **-ous**. **1.** **a** (of persons) Paying great attention to scruples or points of conscience; affected by, inclined to, scruples in matters of conscience; strictly, conscientiously, punctiliously, upright and honest: *he was most scrupulous in all business relations*; *a person not likely to be scrupulous if his interests were at stake*; **b** (of actions &c.) marked by conscientious scruples; strictly, punctiliously careful and correct: *scrupulous honesty*; *a scrupulous adherence to the truth*; *not over-scrupulous*, very unscrupulous. **2.** **a** (of persons) Precise, exact, careful of details; punctiliously accurate and correct; thorough: *a scrupulous editor, proof-reader*; *most scrupulous in one's dress*; **b** (of actions &c.) characterized by, performed with, precision, care, exactness: *scrupulous neatness, cleanliness*; *to pay scrupulous attention to orders.*

scrupulously, adv. Prec. & **-ly**. In a scrupulous manner; with scrupulous attention or care.

scrupulousness, n. See prec. & **-ness**. Quality of being scrupulous; minute, meticulous, exactness in thought, conduct, performance of duty &c.; scrupulosity.

scrutator, n. [1. skrōōtátur; 2. skrūtéitə]. Lat., 'searcher, scrutinizer, investigator', fr. *scrūtāt-(um)*, P.P. type of *scrūtāri*, 'to search carefully, investigate, examine', & **-or**; fr. *scrūta*, 'broken fragments, trash, rubbish'; cogn. w. O.E. *scrūd*, 'dress, clothing', see **shroud**, & w. O.E. *scrēad*, 'shred, paring', see **shred**. One who scrutinizes or who examines carefully; careful investigator.

scrutineer, n. [1. skrōōtinḗr; 2. skrūtiníə]. **scrutiny** & **-eer**. A scrutinizer, examiner, esp. one who makes a scrutiny of ballot papers at an election.

scrutinize, vb. trans. [1. skrōōtinīz; 2. skrútinaiz]. **scrutiny** & **-ize**. **a** To look closely and carefully at; **b** to examine, look into, with minuteness.

scrutinizingly, adv. [1. skrōōtinīzingli; 2. skrútinàiziŋli] Pres. Part. of prec. & **-ly**. In a scrutinizing manner; by careful examination or scrutiny.

scrutiny, n. [1. skrōōtini; 2. skrútini], fr. Lat. *scrūtinium*, 'close examination, scrutiny'; fr. base seen in *scrūtāri*, 'to search carefully, investigate' &c., see **scrutator**. **1.** **a** A careful, minute, examination of anything, made with the eyes: *a scrutiny of the morning papers, of racing results, of a person's face*; **b** specif., careful, detailed, examination of the voting-papers, to ascertain which candidate has been elected; demanded by defeated candidate after a re-count, and where there is a suspicion of any irregularity. **2.** A penetrating, searching, look or gaze directed at something for the purpose of examining thoroughly and forming a judgement concerning it.

scry, vb. intrans. [1. skrī; 2. skrai]. Shortened form of **descry**. To practise crystal-gazing; to gaze fixedly into a crystal, pool of ink &c., and see or claim to see significant scenes of past or future.

scryer, n. [1. skríer; 2. skráiə]. Prec. & **-er.** One who practises crystal-gazing.

scrying, n. [1. skríing; 2. skráiiŋ]. See prec. & **-ing.** Crystal-gazing.

scud (I.), vb. intrans. [1. skud; 2. skad]. Scand.; cp. Norw. *skudda*, 'to shove, push', cp. Dan. *skyde*, 'to shoot, glide', cogn. w. **scoot** & **shoot**, cp. **scuttle** (IV.). To move along, be driven along, rapidly; to glide, dart, with swift, smooth, easy motion: *a ship scuds before the breeze*; *clouds scud across the moon*; *a stone is sent scudding over the ice*; *rabbits scud across the short turf* &c.

scud (II.), n., fr. prec. **1.** Act of scudding; swift, smooth movement as of ship running before a gale. **2. a** Light, vapoury cloud or mist driving before the wind; **b** a short, sharp shower of rain or snow.

scudo, n. [1. skōōdō; 2. skūdou]. Ital., lit. 'shield'. See **scutum.** An old Italian silver coin and money of account worth about 4s.

scuff, vb. intrans. [1. skuf; 2. skaf]. Scand.; cp. Swed. *skuffa*, 'to shove, push', see **shove.** To walk without lifting the feet; to shuffle.

scuffle (I.), vb. intrans. & trans. [1. skúfl; 2. skáfl]. Freq. of prec. & **-le. 1.** intrans. To struggle, push roughly; to engage in a rough, irregular, confused fight. **2.** trans. To hoe up, roughen surface of (gravel), so as to destroy weeds, and freshen its appearance, before rolling down afresh.

scuffle (II.), n., fr. prec. A confused fight, a rough-and-tumble.

scull, n. & vb. trans. & intrans. [1. skul; 2. skal]. Etymol. doubtful; possibly same as **skull**, & so named fr. shape of the blade. **1.** n. A light oar pulled with one hand, so that one person pulls a pair; distinguished from an *oar* by being shorter, lighter, and having a more concave blade than this. **2.** vb. **a** trans. To propel (a boat) with sculls or a scull; **b** intrans., to propel a boat with sculls or a scull.

sculler, n. [1. skúler; 2. skálə]. Prec. & **-er. a** One who sculls; **b** light boat built to be rowed by sculls.

scullery, n. [1. skúleri; 2. skáləri], fr. O. Fr. *escuellerie*, the office of an *escuelier*, 'keeper of the plates and dishes of a household': fr. Med. Lat. *scutellārius*, fr. *scutella*, 'salver, tray'. See **scuttle** (I.) & **-(e)ry.** A room behind or off the kitchen, where kettles, pots, and pans are cleaned and kept, dishes and plates washed up, and the rough work of the kitchen and household is done.

scullery-maid, n. A maid who washes up dishes &c., and works in the scullery.

scullion, n. [1. skúliun; 2. skáliən], fr. O. Fr. *escovillion*, *escouillon*, 'a swab, dishclout', dimin. of O. Fr. *escove*, 'a broom', fr. Lat. *scōpa*, 'a thin twig', pl. *scōpae*, 'a bundle of twigs, broom', cogn. w. Lat. *scāpus*, 'stem, stalk, shaft', cogn. w. **shaft** (I.) & **sceptre.** (archaic) A boy who cleans pots and pans &c., and does the menial, rough work in the kitchen.

sculp, vb. intrans. & trans. [1. skulp; 2. skalp]. Back-formation fr. **sculpture** (I.). (colloq.) **a** intrans. To sculpture, to carve in stone, wood &c.; to be a sculptor, **b** trans., to carve, model; *to sculp busts.*

sculpin, n. [1. skúlpin; 2. skálpin]. Etymol. doubtful; possibly corrupt. of Fr. *scorpène*, or Ital. *scorpina*, fr. Lat. *scorpaena*, 'the sea-scorpion', also a spiny fish, & perh. influenced by **skull.** A spiny sea-fish of the N. American Atlantic coast with large head and gaping mouth.

sculpsit, vb. [1. skúlpsit; 2. skálpsit]. Lat., 'he carved', 3rd pers. sing. perf. indic. of *sculpere*, 'to carve'; connected w. Lat. *scalpere*, 'to scratch, tear', see **scalpel**; further cogn. w. O.E. *scalu*, 'shell, husk', lit. 'something which is torn off', see **scale.** Placed on engravings, followed by artist's name; (he, So-and-so) engraved this.

sculptor, n. [1. skúlptur; 2. skálptə]. Lat., fr. *sculpt-(um)*, P.P. type of *sculpere*, 'to carve'. See prec. & **-or.** Artist who models in clay, and carves stone, metal, wood &c.; a maker of sculpture.

sculptress, n. [1. skúlptres; 2. skálptris]. Prec. & **-ess.** A woman sculptor.

sculptural, adj. [1. skúlpchural; 2. skálptʃərəl]. **sculpture** & **-al.** Of, pertaining to, sculpture; resembling sculpture, plastic.

sculpturally, adv. Prec. & **-ly.** In a sculptural manner.

sculpture (I.), n. [1. skúlpchur; 2. skálptʃə]. Fr., fr. Lat. *sculptūra*, formed fr. stem *sculpt-*, as in **sculptor**, & **-ure.** See **sculpsit. 1. a** The art of carving, or cutting with a chisel, in stone or wood, any kind of figures, designs, and representations of natural objects whether in the round or in relief; the term is also extended to the art of modelling in clay, and casting in bronze; plastic art; **b** example of this art; **a** carved or modelled figure &c. **2. a** (bot. and zool.) Markings, in relief or impressed, on the surface of a plant or on a shell &c.; **b** (physical geog.) markings left on rocks, shape of ground formed by weathering, erosion &c.

sculpture (II.), vb. trans. & intrans., fr. prec. **A.** trans. **1. a** To cut, carve, (stone &c.) into designs and figures; **b** to portray by means of sculpture: *to sculpture a head*; (also fig. of the action of weather on rocks &c.) to erode. **2.** To decorate, adorn with sculptured figures or work: *a sculptured pillar.* **B.** intrans. To practise the art of sculpture.

sculpturesque, adj. [1. skùlpchurésk; 2. skàlptʃərésk]. **sculpture** (I.) & **-esque.** Having the character of, resembling, sculpture; shapely, well modelled, statuesque.

scum (I.), n. [1. skum; 2. skam]. Scand., fr. Dan. *skum*, 'froth, foam, scum', cp. O.H.G. *scūm*, Mod. Germ. *schaum*, 'foam'; according to Kluge fr. base meaning 'to cover, protect', whence also Lat. *scūtum*, 'shield', see **scutum**, & second element in **obscure. 1.** Froth, foam rising to the surface of a liquid during boiling or in the process of fermentation, esp. the impurities and refuse which rise to the surface and remain floating there as a film. **2. a** Offscourings, refuse; the worthless part of anything; dregs; **b** (fig.) riff-raff, dregs of the population; Phr. *the scum of the earth*, the lowest, most degraded people; also as term of abuse, *you filthy scum* (to a single person).

scum (II.), vb. trans. & intrans., fr. prec. **1.** trans. To remove the scum from, to skim. **2.** intrans. To form into, develop, scum.

scumble, vb. trans. & n. [1. skúmbl; 2. skámbl]. Prec. & **-le. 1.** vb. To soften the outlines of a painting by adding a thin opaque or semi-opaque coat of almost dry colour. **2.** n. **a** Coat of colour added for this purpose; **b** softening of outline by scumbling.

scummy, adj. [1. skúmi; 2. skámi]. **scum** (I.) & **-y.** Covered with scum; like, consisting of, scum.

scuncheon, n. [1. skúnshun; 2. skánʃən]. Also spelt *sconcheon*, fr. Fr. *esconçon*, dimin. of **sconce.** One of the stones or arches resting upon the angles of a square tower, and supporting the sides of an octagonal spire.

scupper (I.), n. [1. skúper; 2. skápə]. Orig. *scupper-hole*, fr. O. Fr. *escope*, 'a baling scoop', of Gmc. origin; cp. Swed. *scopa*, see **scoop.** An opening cut through a ship's side to allow water to run off from the deck into the sea.

scupper (II.), vb. trans., fr. prec., prob. in sense of throwing a ship on to her scuppers. (slang) To disable, throw into disorder.

scurf, n. [1. skĕrf; 2. skāf], fr. O.N. *skurfur*, pl., cogn. w. O.E. *scurf*, *sceorf*, 'scurf', & *sceorfan*, 'to scrape, scarify', & cp. **scurvy. 1.** Thin, dry scales or flakes of dead skin, esp. such coming from the scalp; dandruff. **2.** Anything loose and scaly or flaky, e.g. the dry pubescence on a leaf &c.

scurfiness, n. [1. skĕrfines; 2. skāfinis]. **scurfy** & **-ness.** Scurfy condition.

scurfy, adj. [1. skĕrfi; 2. skāfi]. **scurf** & **-y.** Affected, covered, with scurf, or with any flaky matter resembling it.

scurrile, adj. [1. skúril; 2. skáril], fr. Lat. *scurrilis*, 'like a buffoon, scurrilous', fr. *scurra*, 'buffoon, jester'; cogn. w. Gk. *skairein*, 'to leap, dance'; cp. further M.H.G. *scherz*, 'jest, sport', & see **scherzo.** (archaic) Scurrilous.

scurrility, n. [1. skuríliti; 2. skaríliti], fr. Lat. *scurrilitāt-(em)*, 'buffoonery'. Prec. & **-ity. 1.** Quality of being scurrilous. **2.** A scurrilous remark; scurrilous language, abuse.

scurrilous, adj. [1. skúrilus; 2. skáriləs]. **scurrile** & **-ous. 1.** (of persons) Using low, vulgar, abusive, indecent language; coarsely abusive. **2.** (of language &c.) Containing, consisting of, low, vulgar abuse.

scurrilously, adv. Prec. & **-ly.** In a scurrilous manner.

scurry (I.), vb. intrans. [1. skúri; 2. skári]. Prob. formed fr. **scour** (I.) & **-y.** To run, hurry with quick, short steps, to scamper, scuttle.

scurry (II.), n., fr. prec. **1. a** Hasty, rapid, movement; **b** haste, flurry. **2.** Sudden, violent, shower of rain or snow.

scurvily, adv. [1. skĕrvili; 2. skāvili]. **scurvy** & **-ly.** In a scurvy manner; (chiefly fig.) meanly, contemptibly, shabbily.

scurviness, n. [1. skĕrvines; 2. skāvinis]. See next word & **-ness.** Condition, quality, of being scurvy (lit. and fig.).

scurvy (I.), adj. [1. skĕrvi; 2. skāvi]. **scurf** & **-y. 1.** (obs.) Scurfy. **2.** (of persons and actions) Mean, low, shabby, contemptible: *a scurvy fellow*; *scurvy tricks, treatment.*

scurvy (II.), n., fr. prec., in sense of 'pitiful, low state of health'. Cp. **scorbutic.** A disease of malnutrition, due to lack of fresh vegetables, fruits &c. in diet, occurring formerly among sailors on long voyages; the symptoms being spongy, swollen gums, bleeding from mucous membranes, great debility and dry, livid skin.

scurvy grass, n. Prec. & substitution for **cress.** A perennial herb, *Cochlearis officinalis*, growing near the sea, with fleshy root-stock and stems, spoon-shaped leaves, and clustered white flowers, used as a salad; reputed to be a cure for scurvy.

scut, n. [1. skut; 2. skat]. Prob. fr. O.N. *skott*, 'fox's brush'. Cp. **scruff.** The short, stumpy tail of an animal, esp. of a hare or rabbit.

scutage, n. [1. skūtij; 2. skjūtidž], fr. Med. Lat. *scūtāgium*, see **scutum**, & **-age.** (feudal law) Sum of money paid to the Crown by holder of a knight's fee, in lieu of military service.

scutal, adj. [1. skūtl; 2. skjūtl]. **scutum** & **-al.** (bot. and zool.) Pertaining to a scutum or shield.

scutate, adj. [1. skūtāt; 2. skjūteit], fr. Lat. *scūtātus*, 'armed with a *scūtum* or shield', see **scutum**, & **-ate. a** (bot., of leaves) Shaped like a shield; **b** (zool.) covered with shield-like plates or scales.

scutch (I.), vb. trans. [1. skuch; 2. skatʃ], fr. O. Fr. *escouche*, 'a scutcher or swingle'; etymol. doubtful, perh. fr. O. Fr. *escousser*, 'to shake out', fr. Lat. *excussāre*, *ex* & *quatere*, *quass-(um)*, 'to shake', see **quash**; perh. influenced by *couch grass* & *quitch.* To free the fibres of flax, cotton &c., of woody and other particles, dust &c., by beating.

scutch (II.), n., fr. prec. Implement or machine used for beating and dressing fibres; scutcher, swingle.

scutcheon, n. [1. skúchun; 2. skátʃən]. Abbr. form of **escutcheon. 1.** Escutcheon. Specif. **2. a** a metal name-plate; **b** the movable shield or cover for a keyhole.

scutcher, n. [1. skúcher; 2. skátʃə]. **scutch** (I.) & **-er.** A scutch, swingle.

scute, n. [1. skūt; 2. skjūt], fr. **scutum.** (zool.) A scutum.

scutellate, adj. [1. skūtélāt; 2. skjūtéleit]. **scutellum** & **-ate.** (bot. and zool.) Covered with scutella or small scales or plates.

scutellum, n., pl. **scutella** [1. skūtélum, -a; 2. skjūtéləm, -ə]. Neo-Lat., 'little shield', dimin. of **scutum**. (bot. and zool.) A small horny scale or plate, as on lichens, birds' claws, the thorax of insects &c.

scutiform, adj. [1. skū́tifòrm; 2. skjū́tifɔ̄m]. See **scutum** & **-form**. (bot. and zool.) Shaped like a shield or scutum.

scuttle (I.), n. [1. skútl; 2. skátl]. O.E. *scutel*, 'dish, bowl', fr. Lat. *scutula*, also *scutella*, 'square tray or salver', dimin. of *scutra*, 'flat dish, platter'; prob. orig. 'leather dish or vessel', connected w. **scutum**. A metal or other receptacle for carrying and holding small supply of coal for a fire in a room.

scuttle (II.), n., fr. O. Fr. *escoutilles*, pl., 'hatches of a ship', fr. Span. *escotilla*, 'hatchway', fr. *escotar*, 'to cut out a hole', esp. in a garment at the neck so as to fit, fr. *escote*, 'opening at the neck, tucker in a garment'; of Gmc. origin, cp. Du. *schoot*, 'bosom, lap', cogn. w. O.E. *scēat*. **a** An opening in a wall or roof of a house with a cover to it; trap-door; specif. **b** (naut.) a square opening or hatchway in a deck, large enough to admit a man's body.

scuttle (III.), vb. trans. To cut holes in the bottom or sides of a ship in order to sink it; to sink (a ship) by making holes in it.

scuttle (IV.), vb. intrans. & n. Earlier *scuddle*, freq. of **scud**. **1.** vb. To run away, to hurry, scurry off; esp. to run away from danger, difficulty &c. **2.** n. A hasty flight, hurried departure, a bolt.

scutum, n., pl. **scuta** [1. skū́tum, skū́ta; 2. skjū́təm, skjū́tə]. Lat., 'shield'; prob. cogn. w. Lat. *cutis*, 'hide, skin', see **cuticle**, & meaning orig. 'shield of hide or leather', or else fr. primary meaning of the base, 'that which covers or protects'; cp. **obscure**. **1.** (Rom. antiq.) The oblong shield of wood covered with leather and strengthened with iron borne by the heavy armed infantry of the legions. **2.** (anat.) The knee-cap, patella. **3.** (zool.) A horny, shield-like plate or scale as found in certain reptiles, on the thorax of insects &c.; a scute.

Scylla, n. [1. síla; 2. sílə]. Gk. name of a she-monster with six heads dwelling on a rock on Italian side of the Straits of Messina, opposite to the whirlpool Charybdis, q.v.; hence Phr. *between Scylla and Charybdis*, to be caught between two fires, between the devil and the deep sea, in allusion to the difficulty of steering through the passage without being caught by one or other, as in Homer's Odyssey.

scyphi-, scypho-, pref., fr. Gk. *skúphos*, 'cup', see **scyphus**, used in compounds: *scyphiform*, cap-shaped; *scyphomedusae, scyphozoa*, of various forms of jelly-fish &c.

scyphus, n. [1. sífus; 2. sáifəs]. Gk. *skúphos*, 'drinking-cup'; perh. related to Gk. *skáptein*, 'to hollow out', but the *u* is difficult to explain. **1.** (Gk. antiq.) A form of cup without a base or foot and with two handles with flat tops projecting from the sides. **2.** (bot.) A corona of a flower; cup-like formation in lichens.

scythe (I.), n. [1. sīdh; 2. saið]. O.E. *siğþe*, *sīþe*, 'scythe', fr. **segiþe*, M.E. *sithe*; O.S. *segisna*; O.N. *sigðr*; O.H.G. *segansa*, Mod. Germ. *sense*, 'sickle or scythe'; Gmc. base **seχ-*, 'to cut', cogn. w. Lat. *secāre*, cp. **section**, & Engl. **saw** (III.) & **sickle**. Tool for mowing, consisting of a long, slightly curved, tapering blade, the inner edge of which is sharpened, the back being relatively thick, set at right angles to a long wooden stock, which has two short handles projecting from it.

scythe (II.), vb. trans. & intrans., fr. prec. **a** trans. To cut (grass) with a scythe; **b** intrans., to use a scythe for cutting grass &c.

Scythian, adj. & n. [1. síthian; 2. síþiən], fr. Lat. *Scythia*, Gk. *Skuthía*, *Skúthēs*, 'a Scythian', & **-an**. **1.** adj. Of, pertaining to, ancient Scythia, which lay north and east of the Black Sea. **2.** n. Inhabitant, language, of ancient Scythia.

'sdeath, interj. [1. zdeth; 2. zdɛþ]. Euphemistic abbr. of 'God's death'. Oath now obsolete, expressing anger, impatience &c.

se-, pref. Lat *sē-*, occurring in a certain number of Lat. words, for *sēd-*, wh. remains before vowels; the particle denotes separation or division: *secure, separate, sedition*. It is identical w. the conj. *sēd* (w. shortening of the vowel), 'but, yet' &c.; the basal meaning is 'for itself alone', & it is ultimately fr. the reflex. pronominal stem **suē-*, 'self', see **sui**; the *-d* is prob. the old abl. suff.

sea, n. [1. sē; 2. sī]. O.E. *sǣ*, 'sea, lake', M.E. *see*; O.S. & O.H.G. *seo*; O. Fris. *sē*, O.N. *sǣr*; Goth. *saiws*; O.H.G. (*gi*)*sig*, 'lake, marsh', a gradational variant, points to an orig. Gmc. **saigwi-*, wh. apparently rules out the attractive proposal to connect the word w. Lat. *saevus*, 'fierce, raging, wild'. **1.** The ocean, the body of salt water which covers the larger part of the surface of the globe; **a** contrasted with freshwater rivers and lakes &c.: *animals, plants, which live in the sea*; *chemical constituents of the sea*; *salmon return from the sea to fresh water to breed*; **b** contrasted with dry land: *by land and sea*; *beyond, across, the sea(s)*, away from one's own country, separated from one's home by the sea; *by the sea*, on the coast, by the seaside, close to any body of salt water; *to be buried at sea*; *to put out to sea*, to sail from land. Phrs. *the high seas*, the ocean, as the highway of commerce by sea, esp. of the ocean outside territorial waters or outside the three-mile limit and jurisdiction; *the narrow seas*, the seas between Great Britain and Ireland, or between England and France, or the Netherlands; *the freedom of the seas*, the right of states to trade by sea without interruption, even in time of war, as neutrals; *at sea*, (i.) (lit.) out of sight of land; (ii.) (fig.) *all at sea*, not knowing where one is or what one is doing; perplexed, confused, about anything; *to go to sea, follow the sea*, to adopt profession of a sailor; *to go* (*down*) *to the sea*, go to the coast, the seaside. **2. a** Any of various tracts of the sea, considered as less than an *ocean* or as more or less defined or enclosed by the land or as part of an ocean: the *Mediterranean, Baltic Sea*; *the Caribbean Sea, Japan, China Seas* &c.; Phrs. *the four seas*, those surrounding Great Britain; *the seven seas*, the Arctic and Antarctic, N. and S. Atlantic, N. and S. Pacific, and the Indian Oceans; **b** one of the large, entirely enclosed, salt-water or brackish lakes: *the Caspian, Dead, Sea*; more rarely of a freshwater lake: *Sea of Galilee*. **3. a** (also *seas*) State, condition, of the sea, in relation to wind or weather: *a calm, stormy sea*; *heavy, choppy seas*; **b** a wave, billow: *a high, short, long, sea*; *to ship a sea*, (of vessel) to be flooded by a wave. **4.** A large expanse of anything; a sheet, flood; **a** (of material things) *sea of flame, blood, of faces* &c.; **b** (of non-material things) *a sea of troubles*. **5.** (Bib.) The great metal laver or basin for the use of the priests in Solomon's Temple: *the brazen, molten, sea*.

sea-acorn, n. Acorn shell, a species of acorn-shaped barnacle.

sea-air, n. Air at the seaside, or at sea, as distinct from that inland.

sea-anchor, n. A floating, expanding anchor, usually of canvas, used to prevent a ship drifting and to keep her head to the wind; a drag- or drift-anchor.

sea-anemone, n. Any of various marine polyps, with expanding and often brightly coloured, flower-like tentacles, belonging to the order *Actinaria*, of the class Anthozoa.

sea-angel, n. The angel-fish, a species of Atlantic shark, *Squatina*, with wing-like, pectoral fins.

sea-ape, n. **1.** The sea-otter. **2.** The thresher shark.

sea-bank, n. **1.** The shore of the sea. **2.** A bank, mole, or wall to keep off the sea and prevent encroachment on the land.

sea-beach, n. A beach of shingle or sand by the sea.

sea-bear, n. A fur-bearing seal, *Otaria ursina*, of the Pacific.

sea-beet, n. Wild beet, *Beta maritima*.

sea-bells, n. Popular name of *Convolvulus soldanella*, with pink flowers, growing by the seashore, the sea bindweed.

sea-belt, n. A large seaweed, with long belt-like fronds, growing in masses on rocky shores, *Laminaria saccharina*.

sea-bird, n. Any bird whose usual habitat is the sea-coast and rocky islands in the sea.

seaboard, n. [1. sḗbord; 2. síbɔ̄d]. The coast bordering the sea; sea-coast; line of coast.

sea-born, adj. Born of or from the sea: *the sea-born goddess*, Aphrodite; *the sea-born town*, Venice.

sea-borne, adj. Borne, brought, by sea: *sea-borne commerce*; *sea-borne coal*, sea-coal.

sea-breeze, n. A breeze blowing landwards from the sea; a breeze at sea.

sea-calf, n. The common seal.

sea-canary, n. Sailor's name for the white whale, from the whistling noise it makes.

sea-captain, n. **a** The captain of a sea-going vessel; a naval as distinguished from an army captain; **b** a great naval commander.

sea-cat, n. **1.** The common seal. **2.** The sea-wolf.

sea-chestnut, n. The sea-urchin.

sea-coal, n. Sea-borne coal; old name in south of England, in areas remote from coal-mines, for mineral coal as distinguished from *charcoal*.

sea-coast, n. Land adjacent to the sea, line of coast at the sea.

sea-cock, n. A valve or cock in a ship's side which opens and shuts, a pipe leading from the sea to the condenser.

sea-coconut, n. The double or bilobed coconut of the Seychelles.

sea-colander, n. A greenish seaweed, the fronds of which are perforated with small holes.

sea-cook, n. A ship's cook; used as a term of abuse or contempt by sailors, esp. of landsmen.

sea-cow, n. **1.** The manatee or the dugong. **2.** The walrus.

sea-crow, n. Popular name for various sea-birds, as the black-headed gull, the cormorant &c.

sea-cucumber, n. Sea-slug, one of the holothurians, esp. the *bêche-de-mer* or trepang.

sea-devil, n. **1.** The devil fish, a large kind of ray. **2.** The angler fish, fishing frog or monk.

sea-dog, n. **1.** The dogfish. **2.** The common seal. **3.** An old, experienced sailor, generally *old sea-dog*.

sea-dragon, n. Name applied to various fish, esp. to the Australian pipe fish.

sea-duck, n. One of a kind which frequents salt water.

sea-eagle, n. **1.** A large fishing eagle, *Haliaetus*, including the Old World *H. albicilla*, the white-tailed eagle, and *H. leucocephalus*, the bald or white-headed eagle of N. America. **2.** The osprey.

sea-elephant, n. The largest of the seals, of the S. Atlantic, *Macrorhinus proboscideus*; the males have a short dilatable proboscis.

sea-fan, n. A coral, genus *Gorgonia*, with fan-like branches.

seafarer, n. [1. sḗfàrer; 2. sífɛ̀ərə]. **sea** & **fare** (III.) & **-er**. (poet.) One who travels by sea; a sailor, mariner.

seafaring (I.), adj., fr. Pres. Part. [1. sḗfàring; 2. sífɛ̀əriŋ]. Chiefly in Phr. *seafaring man*, a sailor; *seafaring life*, that of a sailor.

seafaring (II.), vbl. n. Act of travelling by, of going to, sea; specif., the profession of a sailor, a sailor's life.

sea-fennel, n. Samphire.

sea-fight, n. A naval battle.

sea-fire, n. Phosphorescence in the sea.

sea-foam, n. **a** Foam of the sea; **b** meerschaum.

sea-fog, n. Fog coming inland from the sea.

sea forces, n. pl. A nation's navy, as distinguished from the army or land forces.

sea-fowl, n. Any bird that lives near or on the sea and gets its food from it.
sea-fox, n. The thresher shark, sea-cat.
sea-front, n. That part of a seaside town which faces and skirts the sea; esp. a marine parade.
sea-gauge, n. **1.** An automatic gauge used in deep-sea soundings. **2.** The draught of a ship.
sea-gherkin, n. The sea-cucumber.
sea-gilliflower, n. The sea-pink, thrift.
sea-girt, adj. (poet.) Girdled, surrounded, by the sea: *this sea-girt isle.*
sea-god, -goddess, n. A deity of the sea.
sea-going, adj. **a** *Sea-going vessel, craft,* sailing, and built to sail, on the open sea for long voyages, and not merely for coastal trips; **b** *sea-going fisherman* &c., going out to sea, not working only in estuaries &c.
sea-grape, n. **1.** Gulf-weed, sargasso. **2.** Name of a shrubby tree with clustered berries growing on sand-dunes. **3.** (pl.) The egg-clusters of the cuttle-fish.
sea-grass, n. Collective name for various grass-like plants growing by the sea, as thrift, and esp. eel-grass, *Zostera marina.*
sea-green, adj. & n. **1.** adj. Of a pale bluish green colour, as of the sea in shallow waters with sandy bottom. **2.** n. This colour.
sea-gull, n. Any one of the sea-birds constituting the family *Laridae*, a gull.
sea-hawk, n. **1.** The skua. **2.** The osprey.
sea-hedgehog, n. The sea-urchin.
sea-hog, n. The porpoise.
sea-holly, sea-holm, n. A variety of holly growing by the sea, *Eryngium maritimum.*
sea-horse, n. **1.** (zool.) A small fish, *Hippocampus,* found in warm seas; allied to the pipe-fishes, with head and upper part of the body resembling those of a horse, prehensile tail, and plated body. **2.** (mythol.) A fabulous monster, half horse, half fish, depicted as harnessed to a sea-god's chariot.
sea-island cotton, n. A fine, long-haired variety of cotton, producing a long staple, originally cultivated in the islands and coast regions of Georgia and S. Carolina.
sea-kale, n. A colewort, with white roots used as a vegetable.
sea-king, n. Ancient Scandinavian chieftain, esp. one who was a leader in piratical, free-booting expeditions.
seal (I.), n. [1. sēl; 2. sīəl], fr. O.E. *sēole-*, inflected type of *seolh,* M.E. *sēle,* O.H.G. *selah,* O.N. *selr,* cp. Swed. *sjöl,* Dan. *sæl.* **1.** The general name for a group of marine, amphibious, fish-eating mammals with long tapering bodies and stunted limbs ending in flippers or paddle-like webbed feet; the true seals, *Phocidae,* have no external ear, and are hunted for their hides and oil; the fur-bearing or eared seals, *Otariidae,* of N. and S. Pacific, include the sea-bear and sea-lion. **2.** Seal-skin: *a coat made of seal.*
seal (II.), vb. intrans., fr. prec. To hunt seals: (chiefly in Pres. Part.) *to go sealing*; *a sealing expedition.*
seal (III.), n. M.E. *seel, sele,* fr. O. Fr. *seel,* fr. Lat. *sigillum,* 'little sign, mark, figure, a seal', dimin. of *signum.* See **sigillate & sign. 1. a** Heraldic or other device stamped upon wax, lead, or other plastic material by means of an engraved die, affixed to a document &c. as a mark or proof of its authenticity; Phr. *under my hand and seal,* i.e. with signature and seal; **b** small wafer, circular ring made by a pen, impression directly stamped on paper, used as the legal equivalent of an impressed wax seal on documents requiring such. **2.** A piece of metal, pebble &c. upon which an initial, crest, coat of arms, or other device is engraved, used as a die for stamping on wax &c.: *the Great Seal,* of Great Britain, in charge of the Lord Chancellor, formerly Lord Keeper, used for treaties, parliamentary writs, and other important State documents; *the Seal of the Fisherman,* that of the Papacy, bearing a figure of St. Peter as a fisherman. **3.** A device for closing a pipe to prevent the passing of air or gas, esp. a quantity of water in a trap or bend. **4.** (fig.) **a** That which authenticates, confirms, or identifies; a token, guarantee; prophetic mark: *a kiss as the seal of his love*; *to bear upon his face the seal of fate*; **b** that which closes or secures, that which ensures secrecy or silence: *a seal upon his lips*; *under the seal of confession, secrecy* &c.
seal (IV.), vb. trans., fr. prec. **1. a** To affix a seal to, as authentication; to mark with official stamp as of standard pattern &c.: *to seal a document*; *the treaty has been signed and sealed* (cp. *sealed book* &c. below); **b** to close, fasten, secure, by means of a seal or seals; also *seal up*: *to seal (up) a letter*; *officials have sealed (up) all drawers, doors* &c. **2.** To close completely, so as to prevent access or passage of air, gas &c.: *to seal a pipe*; *windows hermetically sealed.* **3.** (in fig. or transf. senses) **a** To mark as settled, set apart, decide finally; to determine: *his fate is sealed*; **b** to confirm, ratify; bear witness: *he sealed the bargain with a kiss*; **c** to close tightly, shut up: *eyes sealed in death, sleep*; *his lips were sealed,* he was unable to speak; he was bound by a promise of secrecy.
sea-law, n. Maritime law, (esp. pl.) any of various ancient codes of maritime law.
sea-lawyer, n. **1.** Argumentative person with some slight, inaccurate smattering of legal knowledge; one fond of pedantic refinements and quibbles which he believes to be in accordance with the principles of law. **2.** A shark.
sealed book, n. [1. sēld bóok; 2. sīəld búk]. **1.** (hist.) A standard copy of the Book of Common Prayer, issued in 1662 under the Great Seal and ordered to be kept in all cathedrals and collegiate churches. **2. a** A book the contents of which are secret; hence, **b** something difficult to know or understand: *metaphysical arguments are a sealed book to most people.*
sealed orders, n., pl. Instructions issued to a commander of a ship, esp. in time of war, in a sealed envelope, only to be opened at a stated time or place: *to sail under sealed orders,* of ship sailing with such instructions.
sealed pattern, n. A regulation pattern, of uniforms &c., adopted by the Admiralty or War Office and kept as a standard.
sea-legs, n. Only in such Phr. as *to find, get, one's sea-legs,* to become accustomed to the motion of a ship; in allusion to the habitual rolling gait of sailors, adopted in order to preserve balance when ship is tossing; to get accustomed to life at sea, and be free from sickness.
sea-leopard, n. A spotted or blotched seal of the South Pacific seas, *Ogmorhinus leptonyx*; also used of Weddell's seal (*Leptonyx weddellii*).
sealer, n. [1. sēler; 2. sīlə]. **seal (II.) & -er. a** Person engaged in seal-hunting; **b** vessel used by seal-hunters.
sealery, n. [1. sēleri; 2. sīləri]. **seal (I.) & -ery.** Breeding-place of seals.
sea-letter, n. A document or passport issued from the custom-house to a neutral ship in time of war, giving full description of the vessel, cargo, destination &c.
sea-level, n. Level taken midway between high- and low-water mark; also called *mean sea-level,* and used as standard for measurements of heights and depths.
seal-fishery, n. **a** The business of hunting and killing seals for their fur and oil; **b** seals' habitat, where they are killed by sealers.
sea-line, n. The horizon at sea.
sealing, n. [1. sēling; 2. sīliŋ]. Trade of hunting seals; seal-fishery.
sealing-wax, n. Substance made of a mixture of shellac and resin, variously coloured, which becomes plastic when heated and hardens as it cools, thus easily receiving and preserving the impression of a seal; used for sealing and closing letters, documents &c.
sea-lion, n. Large, maned, and eared kind of fur-bearing seal of the Pacific Ocean, of which there are several species, belonging to the family *Otariidae.*
Sea Lord, n. One of the four naval members of the Board of Admiralty, as distinguished from the two Civil Lords or non-professional members.
seal-ring, n. Finger-ring having an armorial or other device engraved upon its stone, or on part of the metal, and used as a seal.
seal-rookery, n. A breeding-place of seals.
sealskin, n. [1. sēlskin; 2. sīəlskin]. **a** The coat of one of various species of the eared seal dressed and prepared as a fur; **b** a garment made of this; a sealskin coat.
Sealyham, n. [1. sēliam; 2. sīliəm], fr. name of place in Pembrokeshire, Wales. A breed of wire-haired terriers with very short legs and a long body.
seam (I.), n. [1. sēm; 2. sīm]. O.E. *sēam,* M.E. *seme*; O.H.G. *soum,* O.N. *saumr*; fr. base *seu- &c. See **sew & suture. 1.** Line at junction of two pieces of cloth or leather where they are sewn together. **2.** The juncture of two boards or planks, esp. of a ship's planking, filled in, or caulked, with oakum: *leaking seams.* **3.** A suture; **a** (anat.) an articulation in the bones of the skull; **b** (surg.) the line where the two edges of a wound are stitched together; a scar, cicatrix: *seam of an old wound.* **4.** Line resembling a seam, specif., a line or wrinkle in the face. **5.** (geol. and min.) A thin layer or stratum between two thicker strata; a vein of ore, coal &c. between two thicker veins.
seam (II.), vb. trans., fr. prec. **1.** To join together to form a seam. **2.** To mark with scars or lines resembling seams, to furrow with wrinkles: *a face seamed with scars, with care, old age* &c.
seam (III.), n. O.E. *sēam,* 'burden, load', fr. L. Lat. *sauma,* fr. Lat. *sagma,* 'horse's load', fr. Gk. *ságma,* 'a pack-saddle'. See **sumpter & breastsummer.** (obs. or provinc.) An old measure of weight for wheat, manure, sand, timber, of varying amount, usually as much as a horse would carry or draw.
seaman, n. [1. sēman; 2. sīmən]. O.E. *sǣman.* **sea & man. 1.** A sailor, mariner; specif. **a** (merchant service) anyone employed on board a ship on the sea other than the master, pilot, or apprentices; **b** (nav.) one below the rank of officer; *able-bodied seaman* (A.B.), a fully qualified sailor, with higher rating and pay than an *ordinary seaman.* **2.** A person regarded from the point of view of his skill in the management of a ship at sea: *a good, poor, seaman.*
seamanlike, adj. [1. sēmanlīk; 2. sīmənlaik]. Prec. & **-like.** Like a seaman; having, showing, the skill of a good seaman.
seamanly, adj. [1. sēmanli; 2. sīmənli]. See prec. & **-ly.** Seamanlike.
seamanship, n. [1. sēmanship; 2. sīmənʃip]. **seaman & -ship.** Skill in handling or navigating a ship; the sailor's craft.
sea-mark, n. A mark consisting of a conspicuous object on shore, a beacon or the like, serving as a guide for a ship's course when approaching land, a harbour &c.
sea-mat, n. A kind of flat, matted coral.
sea-mew, n. A sea-gull.
sea-mile, n. A nautical or geographical mile, one minute of the great circle of the earth, 6080 ft.
seaming, n. [1. sēming; 2. sīmiŋ]. **seam (II.) & -ing. 1.** A kind of gimp lace, also called *seam lace* or *seaming lace,* used for ornamenting the seams in upholstery. **2.** A rope or cord at the edge of a fishing-net.
seamless, adj. [1. sēmles; 2. sīmlis]. **seam (I.) & -less.** Without seams, woven in a single piece.
sea-monster, n. Any large, strange, monstrous, usually fabulous, animal of the sea.
sea-mouse, n. Popular name of a marine, annelid worm, covered with minute iridescent bristles or setae, belonging to the genus *Aphrodite.*

seamstress, sempstress, n. [1. sém(p)stres; 2. sém(p)stris]. O.E. *sēamestre*, fr. *sēam*, see **seam (I.)**, & *-estre*, fem. agent-suff., cp. **spinster**, additional fem. suff. **-ess**. A woman who seams or sews, needlewoman.

seamy, adj. [1. sémi; 2. sími]. **seam (I.)** & **-y**. (of cloth &c.) Showing the rough, unpressed underside part of a seam. Phr. *the seamy side*, the underside, the least attractive or pleasant side or aspect of life and experience.

Seanad Eireann, n. [1. shánadh āran; 2. ʃǽnəð éərən]. Ir., 'Senate of Ireland'. The Senate or Upper House of the Irish Free State Parliament.

séance, n. [1. sáahns; 2. séiɑ̃s]. Fr., 'a sitting', fr. Lat. *sedens*, Pres. Part. of *sedēre*, 'to sit'; cp. **sedentary**. **1.** A session, meeting, of a public body, society &c. **2.** Specif., meeting of spiritualists, attended by a medium, for the investigation of psychical phenomena.

sea-nettle, n. A stinging jelly-fish or medusa.

sea-onion, n. Popular name of the squill, *Urginea Scilla*, the bulbs of which are used medicinally.

sea-otter, n. A carnivorous, amphibious mammal of the N. Pacific, *Latax lutra*, allied to the true otters, with flipper-like hind limbs and valuable dark-brown fur.

sea-pen, n. A kind of polyp with feathery shape, like the shaft of a quill-pen.

sea-pie, n. The oyster-catcher.

sea-piece, n. A picture of a scene at sea; a seascape.

sea-pig, n. The porpoise.

sea-pink, n. A plant, *Statice armeria*, also called thrift, with pink and white flowers, which grows by the seashore.

seaplane, n. [1. séplān; 2. síplèin]. An aeroplane fitted with floats to enable it to alight on and rise from the sea; a hydroplane.

seaport, n. [1. séport; 2. sípōt]. A town with a harbour, having access to the sea for ocean-going vessels.

sea-power, n. **1.** [1. sé póur; 2. sí páuə] A nation with a powerful navy and a large mercantile marine. **2.** [1. sé pour; 2. sí pauə] **a** The possession of a powerful navy and mercantile marine; **b** the actual naval strength, and resources in trading ships collectively, of a nation at a given time.

sea-purse, n. The egg-case of the skate.

seaquake, n. [1. sékwāk; 2. síkweik]. A seismic disturbance in a part of the earth's crust forming the bed of the sea.

sear (I.), sere, adj. [1. sēr; 2. siə]. O.E. *sēar*, 'withered, barren', M.E. *sēre*; cp. O.D. *sore*, Du. *zoor*, L.G. *soor*; cogn. w. Gk. *aûos*, 'dry', for **sausos*; Lith. *sausas*; cp. **austere**. (poet.) Dry, shrivelled, faded, withered, esp. of plants, flowers, leaves. Phr. '*the sere and yellow leaf*', the autumn of life, advanced age (from Shakespeare, 'Macbeth', v. 3).

sear (II.), vb. trans. O.E. *sēarian*, 'to wither, pine away'. See prec. **1.** To wither, dry up: *cold wind sears the leaves*. **2. a** To scorch, parch, so as to render dry and hard; to cauterize: *to sear a wound with a hot iron*; **b** (fig.) to take away freshness from, to give faded appearance to: *a countenance seared by grief and weeping*. **3.** To render callous or hard: *conscience seared by crimes*.

sear (III.), sere, n., fr. O. Fr. *serre*, 'a grasp', fr. Lat. *sera*, 'bar of a door', fr. *serere*, 'to join, fasten', see **serried** & **seraglio**. Catch in the lock of a gun which holds the hammer at half or full cock.

search (I.), vb. trans. & intrans. [1. sērch; 2. sǝ̄tʃ]. M.E. *serchen*, fr. O. Fr. *cerchier*, fr. Lat. *circāre*, 'to go round, about', formed fr. *circum*, 'around'. See **circum-** & **circus**. **A.** trans. **1.** To go through and examine carefully, by eye and touch, in order to find, or on the chance of finding, something, or to ascertain what is there; to rummage, ferret about in, overhaul, ransack: *to search premises, a house, a cupboard, a drawer, one's pockets*; specif., *to search a person*, go through his clothes, run the hand over his person, in order to find out what he carries; *to search a wound*, to explore it with a probe. **2. a** To scrutinize carefully, scan, peer at, reconnoitre: *to search the horizon with a glass*; *to search a person's face*, look fixedly, piercingly, at, as though trying to read his thoughts; *to search a book*, read it carefully through in order to find a passage; **b** to apply moral scrutiny to, to examine carefully, test, try: *to search one's heart, conscience &c.*; *to search one's memory*, try hard to recall something to mind. **3.** To penetrate thoroughly, to rake, sweep through, along, across: *the wind searched every cranny of the hovel*; *the hail of bullets searched the trench.* **B.** intrans. To seek, look for, try to find, something: *you are sure to find your purse if you search properly*. **C.** Followed by prepositions. *Search after*, trans., to seek, try to find or obtain, pursue in hope of finding what is lacking or lost: *to search after health and happiness. Search for*, trans., to seek, look for. *Search out*, trans., **a** to seek, inquire whereabouts of, and find; to look up, ferret out: *to search out an old friend, some books that have been put away*: **b** (archaic and Bib.) to try, examine thoroughly: '*Lord, thou has searched me out and known me*'.

search (II.), n., fr. prec. Cp. O. Fr. *cerche*. **1.** Act of searching; effort, endeavour, to find, or regain (what is lost): *the search for the missing aviators has been discontinued*; *to make a careful search for a lost ring*; *in search of health*, trying to regain health. **2.** Attempt to gain; quest, pursuit: *the search for truth, for wealth*; *in search of a wife*. **3.** *Right of search*, (internat. law) right of a belligerent to stop neutral vessels at sea and examine or search them for contraband.

searchable, adj. [1. sérchabl; 2. sǝ́tʃəbl]. **search (I.)** & **-able**. (rare) Capable of being searched for; to be found.

searcher, n. [1. sércher; 2. sǝ́tʃə]. **search (I.)** & **-er**. One who searches, examines, or investigates: *a searcher in the public records*; specif. **a** a person, male or female, employed by the Custom House to search passengers for smuggled articles, or by the police to search prisoners on arrest; **b** an implement (i.) for probing or examining a wound, an internal organ &c., a probe, sound; (ii.) for examining the bore of a gun for defects.

searching, adj. [1. sérching; 2. sǝ́tʃiŋ], fr. Pres. Part. of **search (I.)**. Penetrating, keen, piercing: *a searching glance*; *a searching scrutiny, examination*, thorough, careful, rigorous; *a searching wind, gunfire &c.*

searchlight, n. [1. sérchlīt; 2. sǝ́tʃlait]. Large, powerful, movable ray of light, directed from electrical apparatus, used in war for discovering hostile aircraft, for observing enemy movements on land, passing ships &c.

search-party, n. A party, body of persons sent out to search or look for someone or something lost or hidden.

search-warrant, n. A warrant issued by a magistrate, giving authority to police to enter and search a house or premises for stolen goods, articles not lawfully kept &c., such as firearms &c., suspected persons &c.

sea-risk, n. Risk of loss or injury at sea.

sea-robin, n. The common red gurnard of the N. Atlantic.

sea-room, n. Room, free space at sea in which a ship can be sailed and steered without danger of collision or running aground.

sea-rover, n. A pirate or pirate ship.

sea-salt, n. Salt obtained from sea-water by evaporation.

seascape, sea-scape, n. [1. séskāp; 2. sískeip]. Formed on anal. of **landscape**. A picture of a scene at sea.

sea-serpent, n. **1.** A sea-monster, resembling in appearance and movement a gigantic serpent, often reported to have been seen at sea, but never authenticated to the satisfaction of zoologists. **2.** A sea-snake.

seashore, n. [1. séshór; 2. síʃɔ́]. **1.** Land close to the sea; sea-coast, beach. **2.** (law) Land between high- and low-water mark; foreshore.

sea-sick, adj. Suffering from sea-sickness.

sea-sickness, n. Nausea, vomiting, accompanied by giddiness, and in severe cases by prostration, brought on by the rolling and pitching of a vessel at sea.

seaside, n. [1. sésīd; 2. sísáid]. Land by the side of the sea, on or close to the seashore; a watering-place or town at the sea: *to go to the seaside for the holidays*.

sea-sleeve, n. Cuttle-fish.

sea-snail, n. **1.** Any of various snail-like marine gastropod molluscs. **2.** A small slimy fish, genus *Liparis*, with a ventral sucker.

sea-snake, n. A poisonous tropical marine snake, family *Hydrophinae*, of the Indian and Pacific Oceans.

sea-snipe, n. **a** The dunlin; **b** the snipe-fish, an eel-like fish with long snipe-like snout.

season (I.), n. [1. séz(u)n; 2. síz(ə)n]. M.E. *sesoun*, fr. O. Fr. *seson, seison*, Fr. *saison*, fr. Lat. *satiōn-(em), satio*, 'a sowing', in L. Lat. 'sowing time, the spring, season', fr. *sat-(um)*, P.P. type of *serere*, 'to sow', fr. base **sē-* &c. See further under **semen, seed, sow (II.)**. **1.** One of the divisions of the year, spring, summer &c., distinguished respectively by differences of temperature and weather, in the relative length of day and night, determined by the position of the earth's axis in relation to the sun; *the seasons*, these periods collectively. **2. a** A part of the year in which specific processes of nature occur, or in which certain human activities related to, and conditioned by, these take place: *the season of harvest*; *the blossoming season*; *nesting, breeding, season*; *the season for pruning &c.*; **b** part of the year during which, by custom and convenience, specific occupational or social activities take place: *the publishing, the theatrical, season*; *the holiday season*; specif. *the (London) season*, the early summer, when the Royal Court is in London and social gaiety in the fashionable world is at its height; any period of social activity at a specified place: *the Bath, Brighton, Cheltenham, season*; **c** the period of the year devoted to particular sports and amusements: *the hunting, football, cricket, season*. **3.** A period of the year **a** when specific crops are most plentiful or at their prime: *the asparagus, strawberry, season*; **b** when certain animals are fit for eating or are allowed to be caught, hunted, or shot, as opposed to *close time*; Phr., *in, out of, season*: *oysters are supposed to be out of season when there is no R in the month*; *grouse are in season after the 12th of August*. **4.** Suitable, appropriate, convenient, time for anything: *there is a season for work and for play*; *a word (of advice) in season*, at time when most useful or likely to be effective. Phr. *in season and out of season*, at any time, at all times, without discrimination. **5.** (archaic) An indefinite space of time; a relatively short period, a while: '*The devil departed from Him for a season*' (Luke iv. 13); *to enjoy the pleasures of sin for a season*. **6.** (colloq.) A season-ticket.

season (II.), vb. trans. & intrans., fr. prec. **A.** trans. **1. a** To bring into a fit, proper, condition for use, to render mature by special processes, exposure to air &c.: *to season timber*; *wine seasoned in the wood*; **b** to bring into good, sound, hard condition, by training, exposure to climate &c.; to habituate, acclimatize, accustom; *to season oneself to cold, hunger, fatigue*; *cattle seasoned to diseases*; *a seasoned soldier*; *a seasoned old toper*. **2. a** To make (food) agreeable to the taste, render palatable; to flavour, to add salt, sauce, condiments to, to give a relish to; **b** (fig.) to give intellectual zest, flavour, point, to: *to season conversation with wit*; *he has not failed to season the narrative with some humorous sallies*. **3.** (archaic) To make less harsh or severe; to qualify, moderate, temper: '*When mercy seasons justice*' (Shakespeare, 'Merchant of Venice'). **B.** intrans. To mature, to become seasoned: *timber seasons best when exposed to the weather.*

seasonable, adj. [1. sḗzunabl; 2. sízənəbl]. **season (I.)** & **-able**. **1.** Of the kind expected at, or usual and suitable for, a particular season of the year: *seasonable weather*; *a seasonable frost at Christmas.* **2.** Appropriate to, suitable for, the occasion; occurring, done, at the proper time; opportune: *a seasonable gift; the money, help, came at a most seasonable time; the advice was good, but hardly seasonable.*

seasonableness, n. Prec. & **-ness**. State, quality, of being seasonable.

seasonably, adv. See prec. & **-ly**. In a seasonable manner; at the appropriate season; opportunely.

seasonal, adj. [1. sḗzunal; 2. sízənəl]. **season (I.)** & **-al**. Connected with, pertaining to, the seasons, or a season; occurring at special seasons of the year: *the seasonal migration of birds; seasonal changes of climate.*

seasonally, adv. Prec. & **-ly**. According to the seasons, at a special season, or at seasons.

seasoning, n. [1. sḗzuning; 2. sízəniŋ]. **season (II.)** & **-ing**. **1.** Act, process, by which anything is seasoned, made fit or palatable: *timber, food, needs seasoning.* **2.** (lit. and fig.) That which seasons or renders palatable; condiment, spice: *add a little more seasoning; wit is the seasoning of good talk.*

seasonless, adj. [1. sḗzunles; 2. sízənlis]. Having no season or seasons; having a climate without distinct seasonal changes.

season-ticket, n. **a** A ticket issued by a railway company, &c., at a reduced rate for a stated period, entitling the holder to take as many journeys between two specified stations as he chooses during that period; **b** ticket giving right of entry to a series of entertainments &c., costing less than a series of tickets for individual performances.

sea-spider, n. **a** A spider crab; **b** a marine, spider-like arthropod of the order *Pycnogonida.*

sea-squirt, n. An ascidian.

sea-sunflower, n. A sea-anemone.

sea-swallow, n. **a** The common tern; **b** the stormy petrel.

seat (I.), n. [1. sēt; 2. sīt]. O.E. *sǣt* means 'ambush'; M.E. *sēte*, 'seat', owes its meaning to the cogn. O.N. *sǣti*, fr. wh. indeed the word may be borrowed. Both the O.E. & O.N. words represent the same gradational form fr. the base wh. gives us **sit**. **1.** That on which one sits, specif. **a** anything made to sit upon, such as a chair, bench, stool &c., or suitable for sitting on, as a pile of cushions &c.; accommodation for sitting; occupation of a seat: *all the seats in the room are occupied; you must take a seat on the floor; an old-fashioned carved seat; to take a seat*, to sit down; *to rise from one's seat; the king then took his seat upon the throne*; **b** in symbolical Phr.: *the seat of judgement, of mercy* &c.; *the seats of the mighty.* **2. a** That part of a stool, chair &c. on which a person's body rests when sitting: *the seat of a chair, stool* &c.; **b** the part of the person upon which one rests when sitting; the buttocks; **c** that part of the clothing covering this: *the seat of one's trousers*; **d** (mach.) a part of a machine on which another part rests or moves: *seat of an engine, valve* &c. **3. a** Sitting accommodation; right to sit in a certain place: *a seat at a theatre, in a church; to buy, reserve, seats for a play, cricket match* &c.; **b** rank, position, membership of a specific body implied by occupation of particular seat, or one in particular place: *a seat on the bench*, position of a judge; *a seat on a board of directors, in the House of Lords* &c.; Phr. *to take one's seat in the House of Commons* or *Lords*, to go through the formalities necessary after election, succession, or elevation; *to lose one's seat*, fail to be re-elected; *a safe seat*, constituency to which a particular person, or a member of a particular party, is certain to be elected. **4.** Manner, way, of sitting, esp. when riding: *he has a good, poor, seat on a horse; a firm seat in the saddle.* **5.** Place occupied by anything; site, location, habitat; principal, central, place where anything takes place or is carried on: *the seat of Government is at Westminster; news from the seat of war; the seat of the Muses; the lungs are the seat of the disease.* **6.** A large house, esp. one in the country, forming the principal residence on a private estate, regarded as the home of an individual, or of a family: *an old family seat in Somerset; many of the finest country seats are empty.*

seat (II.), vb. trans., fr. prec. **1. a** To place in, or on, a seat: *to seat a person in an arm-chair*; Phr. *to be seated*, to sit down; **b** (reflex.) *to seat oneself*, to sit down. **2. a** To accommodate (person, oneself) with a seat or seats: *the vergers seated the large congregation; the public had to seat themselves where they could*; **b** to furnish (building &c.) with seats: *the theatre is seated for about 800*; **c** (of building) to provide seats for (so many): *the theatre will seat 800.* **3.** To repair, put a new seat to; to reseat: *to seat a cane-bottomed chair; to seat a pair of old breeches.* **4.** To settle, plant with inhabitants, (usually reflex. or in pass.) to dwell, live in: *the Phoenicians began to seat themselves along the Mediterranean coasts; a family long seated in Somerset.*

-seated, adj. [1. sḗted; 2. sítid]. In compounds; **a** having specified kind of seat: *cane-seated*; **b** in *deep-seated*, (of disease) well established; involving large area of the body.

-seater, n. [1. sḗter; 2. sítə]. In compounds. Having so many seats (of motor-car &c.): *a two-, four-seater (car).*

seating, vbl. n. [1. sḗting; 2. sítiŋ]. **1.** Act of providing with seats or a seat, or settling into seats: *the seating of the audience took a long time.* **2.** Provision, arrangement, of seats for a building: *the seating of a theatre, church* &c.

seatless, adj. [1. sḗtles; 2. sítlis]. Without, not provided with, a seat.

sea-trout, n. Salmon trout; a true trout, *Salmo trutta*, which ascends rivers from the sea to breed.

sea-unicorn, n. The narwhal.

sea-urchin, n. See **urchin**. A marine animal belonging to the class of echinoderms with organs enclosed in a globular, brittle, spiny shell, living on the sea-bottom.

sea-valve, n. A sea-cock.

sea-wall, n. A wall or embankment built to protect land from encroachment by the sea, or from being eroded by storms.

seaward, adj. & n. [1. sḗward; 2. sīwəd]. **sea** & **-ward**. **1.** adj. Directed, situated, toward the sea: *a seaward aspect.* **2.** n. Position toward the sea: *look to the seaward.*

seaward(s), adv. [1. sḗward(z); 2. síwəd(z)]. Toward the sea: *looking, travelling, seaward(s).*

sea-water, n. The salt water of the sea.

sea-way, n. **1.** The progress made by a ship through the water; headway: *to make sea-way.* **2.** Place, position, in which a ship lies with the sea rolling: *in a heavy sea-way.*

seaweed, n. [1. sḗwēd; 2. síwīd]. Any marine alga; any plant growing in the sea or on rocks covered by the sea according to the tide.

sea-wife, n. Popular name for the wrasse.

sea-wind, n. A sea breeze, wind blowing from the sea.

sea-wolf, n. **1.** A large sea-fish belonging to the blenny family of the N.E. Atlantic; also called sea-cat or wolf-fish. **2.** A viking, pirate, sea-robber.

seaworthiness, n. [1. sḗwërdhines; 2. síwʌ̄ðinis]. See next word & **-ness**. State, quality, of being seaworthy.

seaworthy, adj. [1. sḗwërdhi; 2. síwʌ̄ði]. **sea** & **-worthy**. (of ships) Fit to go to sea; well built, rigged &c.

sea-wrack, n. Floating seaweed; specif., this when thrown up by the sea in large quantities.

sebaceous, adj. [1. sebā́shus; 2. sibéiʃəs]. Neo-Lat. *sēbāceus*, cp. Lat. *sēbāceus*, 'a tallow candle', fr. *sēbum*, fr. **sēvum*, 'fat, tallow', prob. connected w. **soap** & **-aceous**. (physiol.) Fatty; resembling, secreting, fat: *sebaceous secretions; sebaceous glands*, small glands in the skin, usually associated with the hair follicles and sweat glands.

sebestan, -en, n. [1. sebéstan; 2. səbéstən]. Arab., fr. Pers. *sipistan*, fr. *sapista*, 'smelling badly'. The plum-like fruit of an Assyrian and Indian tree, *Cordia*, used in the East for pickles and in medicine.

sebundy, n. [1. sebúndi; 2. sibʌ́ndi]. Hind. & Pers. *sebandī*. Class of irregular soldiers in the Indian Army.

sec (I.), adj. [1. sek; 2. sɛk]. Fr., fr. Lat. *siccus*, 'dry'. See **siccative**. (of wine) Dry, unsweetened.

sec (II.), n., abbr. of **secant**.

secant, adj. & n. [1. sékant; 2. sékənt]. fr. Lat. *secant-(em)*, Pres. Part. of *secāre*, 'to cut', see **section**. (geom.) **1.** adj. Cutting; *secant line*, one cutting a line or curve. **2.** n. **a** A secant line; **b** abbr. *sec*, ratio of the secant line to the radius, reciprocal of *cosine.*

sécateurs, n. [1. sékatërz; 2. sékətʌ̄z]. Fr., wrongly formed fr. Lat. *sect-(um)*, P.P. type of *secarē*, 'to cut', see **section (I.)**. Pair of strong pruning scissors.

secco, n. [1. sékō; 2. sékou]. Ital., 'dry'. See **sec (I.)**. Tempera painting, on dry plaster; contrasted with *fresco.*

secede, vb. intrans. [1. sesḗd; 2. sisíd], fr. Lat. *sēcēdere*, 'to go away, withdraw, separate from, revolt, secede'. See **se-** & **cede**. To withdraw, cut oneself off, by a voluntary act, from a body of which one is a member; specif., to withdraw from membership of a religious body or, as a state, from a federation.

seceder, n. [1. sesḗder; 2. sisídə]. Prec. & **-er**. One who secedes, specif. (cap. and pl.), *the Seceders*, Presbyterians who seceded from the established Church of Scotland in 1733.

secernent, adj. & n. [1. sesërnent; 2. sisʌ́nənt]. Lat. *secernent-(em)*, Pres. Part. of *secernere*, 'to sift apart, to separate; to distinguish', see **secrete** & **discern**. (physiol.) **1.** adj. Secreting: *secernent organs.* **2.** n. **a** A secernent or secreting organ; **b** drug acting as a stimulant of secretion.

secession, n. [1. seséshun; 2. siséʃən], fr. Lat. *sēcessiōn-(em)*, 'withdrawal, separation, secession', fr. *sēcess-(um)*, P.P. type of *sēcēdere.* See **secede** & **-ion**. Act of seceding (from a political or religious body &c.).

secessionism, n. [1. seséshunizm; 2. siséʃənizəm]. Prec. & **-ism**. Doctrines, principles, policy, of a secessionist.

secessionist, n. [1. seséshunist; 2. siséʃənist]. See prec. & **-ist**. One who advocates secession from some specific religious or political body.

seck, adj. [1. sek; 2. sɛk]. See **sec (I.)**. (law) Dry, barren, unprofitable; only in *rent seck*, one without power of distress.

seclude, vb. trans. [1. seklṓōd; 2. siklúd], fr. Lat. *sēclūdere*, 'to shut up, shut off, seclude'; fr. **se-** (I.) & *claudere*, 'to shut, close', see **close (I.)**. **1.** To shut up, apart from others; to keep away from others, to keep in seclusion: *Moslems seclude their wives in the harem; the prisoners were carefully secluded from intercourse with each other.* **2.** (reflex.) *Seclude oneself*, to withdraw, retire from society, or from intercourse with others; to live a retired and solitary life.

secluded, adj. [1. seklṓōded; 2. siklúdid]. Prec. & **-ed**. Solitary, retired, remote, withdrawn from the world; esp. of place: *a secluded spot.*

secludedly, adv. Prec. & **-ly**. In a secluded, retired manner; in retirement.

seclusion, n. [1. seklṓōzhun; 2. siklúžən], fr. L.Med. Lat. *sēclūsiōn-(em)*, fr. Lat. *sēclūs-(um)*, P.P. of *sēclūdere.* See **seclude** & **-ion**. **1.** Act of secluding: *Moslems still practise seclusion of their wives.* **2.** State of being secluded; retirement, privacy: *in the seclusion of one's own house*; aloofness from society: *to live in seclusion.*

second (I.), adj. [1. sékund, sékunt; 2. sékənd, sékənt]. Fr., fr. Lat. *secundus*, 'following, second', fr. base **sekʷ-*, 'to follow', w. gerundive suff.; see **sequela.** **1.** Ordinal number of two; immediately following the first in a series or of two things: *the second day of the month; the second finger of the right hand; second chapter of a book; here endeth the second lesson.* **2.** Next to, following, the first in order of time: *the second person to swim the Channel; to go by the second train; the second child of his parents; second teeth,* those which grow after the first or milk teeth are shed; *the second king of the name.* Phr. *in the second place,* secondly. **3.** Next to, following, the first in space, position, or place: *take the second turning to the right; the second floor or storey,* one above the first. **4. a** Occurring again; repeated, done over again: *do it, say it, a second time; the second time of asking,* of banns of marriage; Phr. *second thoughts,* opinions formed after reconsideration; **b** supplementary, additional to the first; another: *ask for a second helping; you need a second pair of boots.* **5.** Next to the first in order of rank, dignity &c.: *the second lady in the land,* next to the Queen; *a second secretary of legation; a second lieutenant,* lowest rank of commissioned officer in the army. **6.** Inferior only to the first, lower than the first in number, size, importance, quality &c.: *the second city of the empire; goods of second grade or quality.* Phr. *second to none,* without a superior, equal to the best or first. **7.** Exactly, closely resembling another; serving as a counterpart: *he thinks himself a second Napoleon.*

second (II.), adv., fr. prec. In the second place, second in order, in importance &c.: *will you play second?,* after first player. Phr. *to come second* (*in one's estimation, affections* &c.), to occupy a subordinate place.

second (III.), n., fr. **second** (I.). **1.** (in various elliptical uses of adj.) **a** (of things) *The second of July,* the second day of July; *get into a second,* second class of a train; *to get a second in Greats,* a second class in the examination so called at Oxford; Phr. *second of exchange,* the second copy of a bill of exchange; **b** (of persons) *to be the second* (*man*) *in a race; the horse was a poor, good, second,* some distance from, close to, the winner at the finish: *James II., the Second,* the second king of that name. **2.** Person next or inferior to the first in rank, position &c.: *content to be a second to his rival; the second in command,* an officer next in rank to the commanding officer. **3.** One who attends on and acts as supporter or assistant to another: *to act as a most useful second,* to support, back up another in any matter; specif., *one's seconds in a duel,* those who represent one in making the preliminary arrangements, delivering challenges, and giving support and attendance on the field &c. **4.** (mus.) **a** Interval between two tones of the diatonic scale; next tone above or below; **b** a lower part for voice or instrument arranged in harmony with that of the first voice or instrument which sings or plays the melody.

second (IV.), n. usually [1. sékunt; 2. sékənt], but [1. sékund; 2. sékənd] in careful, studied speech; fr. Fr. *seconde,* fr. Med. Lat. *minuta secunda,* the secondary division of the minute. **1.** (as unit of time) **a** The sixtieth part of a minute, the second subdivision of the hour; **b** a very short period of time; moment: *done in a few seconds; wait a second for me; we mustn't lose a second.* **2.** (as unit of angular measure) The sixtieth part of a minute, second subdivision of the degree, *symbol* ″.

second (V.), vb. trans., fr. **second** (III.). **1. a** To support, back, up: *to second a person's efforts;* specif. **b** to act as second to, in a duel. **2.** (in Parliament, public meeting &c.) To support a motion, proposal, vote of thanks &c. immediately after the mover of the motion &c., either by a speech, or merely by rising and formally stating intention of supporting it. **3.** [1. sekónd; 2. sikónd]. To place (an officer) on temporary list for special service, military or civil, outside his ordinary regimental or army service, for which he draws pay assigned to the special service, but not his regimental pay, through retaining regimental rank and seniority: (chiefly in P.P.) *seconded for service on the staff* &c.

Second Advent, n. The second coming or return of Christ to the world, as judge and king, to establish His personal reign; the millennium.

Second Adventist, n. Prec. & **-ist.** One of a sect believing in the near approach of the Second Advent of Christ, or the millennium.

secondarily, adv. [1. sékundarili; 2. sékənd-ərili]. **secondary** & **-ly.** In a secondary manner; not primarily; not originally.

secondariness, n. [1. sékundarines; 2. sékənd-ərinis]. **secondary** & **-ness.** State, quality, of being secondary.

secondary (I.), adj. [1. sékundari; 2. sékənd-(ə)ri], fr. Lat. *secundārius,* 'belonging to the second class, inferior'. See **second** & **-ary.** **1.** Second in order of rank or importance; inferior, subordinate, contrasted with *primary*: *of secondary weight, importance* &c.; *a secondary post; secondary evidence,* (law) indirect evidence. **2.** Coming after the first in time, in the second stage: *secondary symptoms of a disease; Secondary School,* one coming after Primary or Elementary School, and leading to the University. **3.** In various specific uses: **a** (astron.) revolving round a primary planet: *a secondary planet,* satellite; **b** (biol.) of differences between the sexes, not directly connected with the reproductive processes: *secondary sexual characteristics,* such as voice, colouration &c.; **c** (chem.) having some quality in the second degree, of second valency: *secondary salts.*

secondary (II.), n., fr. prec. **a** Person who is secondary, subordinate, to another; one acting as deputy of another; **b** secondary thing; specif. feather on second joint of wing.

second-best, adj. & n. **second,** adv., & **best.** **1.** adj. Next to the best; of quality inferior to the best: *one's second-best clothes.* Phr. *to come off second-best,* to get the worst of it. **2.** n. That which is second-best: *we ought not to be content with the second-best.*

second cabin, n. A second-class cabin or accommodation on board ship.

second cause, n. A cause which is the effect of, or caused by, something else.

Second Chamber, n. The upper house in a legislature which consists of two chambers or houses.

second childhood, n. Feebleness, childishness, of mind and body which comes in extreme old age; dotage, senility.

second class (I.), n. **1.** The class in an honours examination next to the first: *to take, get, a second class in law.* **2.** Second-class compartment, ticket &c. on a train or steamship: *can only afford a second class.*

second-class (II.), adj. & adv. **1.** adj. **a** inferior in quality, not of highest order; second-rate: *a second-class hotel, mind* &c.; **b** belonging to the class below the first; specif. (i.) belonging to a kind of accommodation in railway, or steamship, lower in price, and less luxurious than the first class; (ii.) *Second-Class Honours* (in University Degree Examination) awarded for attainments and performance not of the first order. **2.** adv. Chiefly in Phr., *to travel, go, second-class,* by railway, steamer &c.

Second Coming, n. See **Second Advent.**

second cousin, n. The child of a parent's first cousin.

second distance, n. (paint.) The portion of a picture between the foreground and background; middle distance.

seconde, n. [1. sekónd; 2. sekónd]. Fr. The second, parrying position in fencing.

seconder, n. [1. sékunder; 2. sékəndə]. **second** (IV.) & **-er.** Person who seconds, or supports; specif., person who seconds a motion.

second-hand (I.), adj. & adv. [1. sékund hánd; 2. sékənd hǽnd]. **1.** Bought, or for sale, after use by previous owner; not new: *second-hand clothes, books* &c. **2.** (of knowledge, ideas &c.) Derived from others, not discovered or invented for oneself; unoriginal. Phr. *at second-hand,* by hearsay, not from personal knowledge or information. **3.** (as adv.) *To buy second-hand,* buy at reduced price, after use by another; *to know, have, something second-hand,* get by hearsay.

second hand (II.), n. [1. sékund hànd; 2. sékənd hǽnd]. Rapidly moving, small hand on a watch or clock which marks the seconds, revolving in a small circle in the dial, and separate from the other hands.

secondly, adv. [1. sékundli; 2. sékəndli]. **second** (I.) & **-ly.** In the second place.

second nature, n. A habit, custom, tendency so long established that it has become instinctive and natural and unconsciously exercised: *avarice has become second nature in him.*

secondo, n. [1. sekóndō; 2. sekóndou]. Ital., 'second'. (mus.) The second or lower part, second performer, singer, or instrumentalist, in a concerted piece, esp. in a duet, for the pianoforte.

second-rate, adj. & n. **1.** adj. **a** Not of the first or superior rate or class: *a second-rate ship,* one rated in the second class; **b** inferior in quality, position &c.: *a second-rate mind; a second-rate hotel* &c. **2.** n. Something which is second-rate: *the second-rate,* inferiority, the mediocre.

second rater, n. **1.** A second-rate ship. **2.** (colloq.) A second-rate person; a person of inferior quality or standing.

second sight, n. The faculty, claimed by, or attributed to, certain persons, of seeing, as in a vision, events, such as deaths, fatal accidents &c., before they occur, or objects such as corpse lights, shrouds &c. giving warning of a coming death.

secrecy, n. [1. sékresi; 2. síkrəsi]. See **secret** & **-cy.** **1.** Secret conditions, state of concealment; state in which something happens, or is done, without common knowledge; freedom from observation; seclusion, privacy: *the Expeditionary Force was despatched with absolute secrecy;* (fig.) *in the secrecy of one's own heart.* **2.** Secretiveness; fidelity in keeping a secret: *I must rely on your secrecy in so confidential a matter.*

secret (I.), adj. [1. sékret; 2. síkrit]. O. Fr., fr. Lat. *sēcrētus,* 'separated, set apart; secluded, secret', P.P. of *sēcernere,* 'to set apart, sever, separate'. See **secrete.** **1.** Deliberately hidden from the eye, and from common knowledge; designed to escape observation: *a secret door, staircase, drawer.* **2. a** Done, made, carried out, or on, in secret, and without the fact being generally known: *a secret treaty; secret diplomacy* &c.; **b** (in bad sense) clandestine, surreptitious: *a secret traffic in drugs;* **c** (of persons) furtive: *secret in his habits.* **3.** Remote, retired, secluded, hidden: *a secret pool, valley; the secret depths of the sea;* '*in secret shades Of woody Ida's inmost grove*' (Milton, 'Il Penseroso', 28-9). **4.** Mysterious, not revealed, difficult to discover or understand; inscrutable: *the secret ways of God; the secret workings of nature, of the human heart* &c. **5.** Containing, based on, working by means of, a secret process: *a secret code; a secret padlock.*

secret (II.), n., fr. prec. **1.** A fact known to, knowledge possessed by, a single person, or a small body of persons, which is not, and must not be divulged or disclosed, or be made common property; confidential information: *let us have no secrets between us.* Phrs. *to keep a secret,* not to divulge it; *an open secret,* piece of information, supposed to be confidential, but which is widely known; *in the secret,* sharing, possessed of, a secret. **2.** The true method by which something may be attained: *the secret of health is moderation in all things.* **3.** The true explanation of something which is obscure; key to understanding; hidden meaning: *shall we ever know the secret of Shakespeare's sonnets?* **4.** Something obscure and difficult to find out, something not commonly revealed and understood; a mystery: *the secrets of nature, of human motive.*

secretaire, n. [1. sèkretā́r; 2. sèkritéə]. Fr. form of **secretary.** A writing-desk, escritoire, bureau.

secretarial, adj. [1. sèkretā́rial; 2. sèkritéəriəl]. **secretary** & **-al.** Connected with, pertaining to, a secretary: *secretarial duties; the office needs secretarial assistance; secretarial staff,* members of an organization who perform the functions of secretaries.

secretariate, n. [1. sèkretā́riat; 2. sèkritéəriət]. Fr. *secrétariat.* See next word & **-ate. a** The office of secretary; **b** body, staff, of secretaries; a secretarial staff.

secretary, n. [1. sékretari; 2. sékritəri], fr. Fr. *secrétaire,* fr. L. Med. Lat. *sēcrētārius,* 'confidential, official'. See **secret (II.)** & **-ary. 1.** A person employed by another to help him in his correspondence, literary, or other work, and to act generally for him in a confidential capacity; also *private secretary.* **2.** Official of a company, or other corporation, in charge of correspondence, records, minutes &c., and acting generally as official representative; *honorary secretary,* one performing such duties without remuneration. **3.** One of the principal assistants to an ambassador or minister, often acting as his deputy: *secretary of embassy, legation.* **4. a** A Cabinet Minister, head of one of the great departments of State; the full official title being *Secretary of State* (see below): *Home Secretary, Foreign Secretary* &c.; **b** the second responsible minister of a department, usually sitting in that House in which his principal does not sit: *Financial Secretary to the Treasury, Parliamentary or Under-Secretary;* **c** the permanent official in charge of a department: *permanent (under-) secretary,* or one of his principal assistants: *assistant secretary.* **5.** An escritoire, a secretaire. **6.** (typog.) A form of type resembling hand-writing.

secretary-bird, n. A long-legged, large African bird, *Serpentarius secretarius,* bluish-grey and black in colour, with pen-like tufts behind the ears, whence its name.

Secretary of State, n. The full, official title of the responsible minister at the head of certain great departments of state; **a** (in Great Britain) now seven in number: *Secretary of State for Home Affairs, Foreign Affairs, the Dominions and Colonies, for War, for India,* and (recently added) *for Air,* and *for Scotland;* usually styled *Foreign Secretary, Colonial Secretary* &c.; **b** (U.S.A.) the member of the President's Council or Cabinet at the head of the department of foreign affairs; **c** (papacy) the Cardinal at the head of the administration and foreign department of the Vatican, acting as the Pope's chief minister.

secrete, vb. trans. [1. sekrḗt; 2. sikrī́t], fr. Lat. *sēcrēt-(um),* P.P. type of *sēcernere,* 'to set apart, separate'; fr. *sē,* 'apart', see **se-,** & base **(s)kʷrēi-* &c., q.v. under **critic, crisis, certain,** & cp. **riddle,** 'sieve'. **1.** To put in a secret place; to hide away, conceal: *to secrete stolen goods, the corpse of a murdered person; to secrete oneself,* to hide. **2.** (physiol. and biol., of glands and organs) To gather from the system by chemical process and give out as a secretion.

secretion, n. [1. sekrḗshun; 2. sikrī́ʃən]. Lat. *sēcrētiōn-(em).* See prec. & **-ion. 1.** Act of secreting, concealing, or hiding; concealment: *the secretion of stolen goods.* **2.** (physiol.) **a** Process carried out by the glands in secreting; **b** that which is secreted and given out by the glands.

secretive (I.), adj. [1. sekrḗtiv, sḗkretiv; 2. sikrī́tiv, sī́kritiv]. **secret (I.)** & **-ive.** (of persons, character &c.) Inclined to conceal from others one's thoughts, feelings, intentions, plans &c.; unduly reserved or reticent, uncommunicative; furtive.

secretive (II.), adj. [1. sekrḗtiv; 2. sikrī́tiv]. **secrete** & **-ive.** Promoting, causing, secretion; secretory.

secretively, adv. **secretive (I.)** & **-ly.** In a secretive manner; reticently; furtively.

secretiveness, n. See prec. & **-ness.** Secretive habit of mind; practice of being secretive.

secretly, adv. [1. sḗkretli; 2. sī́kritli]. **secret (I.)** & **-ly.** In secret, not openly; privately, covertly.

secretory, adj. [1. sekrḗturi; 2. sikrī́təri]. **secrete** & **-ory.** Secreting; connected with, producing, the physiological process of secretion: *secretory glands, organs.*

secret service, n. **1.** Secret work or duties on behalf of the state, in obtaining information of political, military, naval, character, and concerning foreign states, of discovering political crimes &c.; espionage. **2.** Official department undertaking such service; those engaged in such service.

sect, n. [1. sekt; 2. sɛkt], fr. O. Fr. *secte,* fr. Lat. *secta,* 'a path; a method; a school of thought, a following', &c.; fr. base *seq-,* 'follow', see **sequela,** but early associated w. *sect-,* the P.P. type of *secāre,* 'to cut', see **section (I.)**, & words there referred to. Body of persons who hold certain philosophical or religious doctrines in common, esp. a body whose beliefs are at variance with those commonly held, or which are in contrast to those of other schools of thought; the word is now usually applied specifically to a group of persons holding peculiar opinions on religion, and in particular to a schismatic body which has seceded from the Church of England, or of Scotland; (gen. used disparagingly) *a mere sect* &c.

sectarian, adj. & n. [1. sektā́rian; 2. sɛktéəriən]. **sectary** & **-an. 1.** adj. Pertaining to, characteristic of, a sect or sects; tending towards the formation of a sect; supporting, devoted to, the interests and principles of a sect (usually in disparaging sense): *sectarian animosities; sectarian education; parties in the Church may easily become sectarian.* **2.** n. An adherent of a sect; a sectary.

sectarianism, n. [1. sektā́rianizm; 2. sɛktéəriənizəm]. Prec. & **-ism. 1.** Habit of mind, mode of thought, line of conduct, conducive to the formation of sects, or of a sect. **2.** Condition in which sects develop; fact of sectarian tendencies being in existence; reverse of uniformity or catholicity.

sectarianize, vb. trans. [1. sektā́rianīz; 2. sɛktéəriəndiz]. See prec. & **-ize.** To make sectarian; to imbue with sectarian tendencies and principles.

sectary, n. [1. sḗktari; 2. sḗktəri]. See **sect** & **-ary.** A sectarian; member of a religious sect or faction; applied specifically by the Cavaliers to a member of the body called Independents at the time of the Great Rebellion.

sectile, adj. [1. sḗktīl; 2. sḗktail], fr. Lat. *sectilis,* 'cut, cleft, divided', fr. *sect-(um),* P.P. type of *secāre,* 'to cut', see **section (I.)**, & **-ile.** Capable of being cut; esp. (of mineral such as mica) capable of being cut smoothly with a knife.

section (I.), n. [1. sḗkshun; 2. sḗkʃən], fr. Lat. *sectiōn-(em),* 'a cutting, a cutting off, or up', formed fr. *sect-(um),* P.P. type of *secāre,* 'to cut'. See further derivatives fr. same base under **segment, saw (III.), sax, scythe, sickle** &c. **1.** Act, process, of cutting: *the section of bones and muscles.* **2.** That which is cut off from anything; a severed portion of anything: *a triangular section of cloth, cheese* &c.; *wood cut into sections;* specif., a thin slice of an object prepared for microscopic examination: *section of rock, diseased bone* &c. **3.** Any one of a set of separable parts of a whole; one of the separate parts of something, made to be joined or fitted together to form a whole: *the jointed sections of a cane, plant-stem; a section of a lead pipe, of a fishing-rod; a wooden hut, boat, machine &c., built in sections.* **4.** Any distinct, separate part of anything, as of surface, area, distance, time &c.: *a section of a road, railway, journey, day* &c. **5.** A subdivision of a written treatise, of a speech; of a subject &c.; a heading; specif., a subdivision of a chapter, statute, legal document, or other writing; usually marked by the symbol §. **6.** A definite, distinct part, division, class, of a community; group of individuals having some characteristic in common: *a section of the population; the various sections of Christendom.* **7. a** (mil.) One of the four subdivisions of a platoon of infantry, troop of cavalry, or battery of artillery; **b** (zool.) a natural subdivision of a genus, group, family &c., not used as a strict term of classification. **8.** (geom.) The cutting, intersection, of a solid by a plane; figure so produced; specif., *conic section,* one of the three curves, ellipse, parabola, and hyperbola, formed by the cutting of the surface of a cone by a plane; (in pl.) *conic sections,* the branch of geometry treating of such curves. **9.** Plan, representation, view of an object, such as a geological formation, earthwork, building, machine &c., regarded as having been cut through by an intersecting plane and thus showing its interior or internal structure, styled *horizontal, longitudinal, vertical, section,* according to the direction of the intersecting plane.

section (II.), vb. trans., fr. prec. **1.** To cut, divide, into sections. **2.** To arrange in sections. **3.** To show, exhibit, represent, by a section.

sectional, adj. [1. sḗkshunal; 2. sḗkʃənəl]. **section (I.)** & **-al. 1.** Pertaining to, having reference to, a section or sections, to part or parts of a whole; individual, local: *sectional arrangement of a subject; sectional differences, quarrels, interests* &c. **2.** Divided, cut up, into sections; composed of, arranged in, sections or by a section: *a sectional boat, boiler* &c.; *a sectional plan of a building.*

sectionalism, n. [1. sḗkshunalizm; 2. sḗkʃənəlizəm]. Prec. & **-ism.** Tendency to lay stress on a section or part of whole, or tendency to regard disproportionately the interests of a section or class of the community.

sectionally, adv. [1. sḗkshunali; 2. sḗkʃənəli]. See prec. & **-ly.** By, in sections, in a sectional manner.

section mark, n. The symbol § used to mark a section in a book &c.

sector, n. [1. sḗkter; 2. sḗktə]. Lat., 'a cutter', *sect-* as in **section (I.)**, & **-or. 1. a** An astronomical instrument for measuring differences of declination; **b** a mathematical measuring instrument or jointed rule, marked with various scales. **2.** (geom.) Portion of a circle enclosed between the arc and two radii drawn from the centre to the arc. **3.** (mil.) A section or division of a fortified line.

sectorial, adj. & n. [1. sektṓrial; 2. sɛktɔ́riəl]. **sector** & **-ial. 1.** adj. Referring to the teeth of carnivorous animals; adapted for cutting, like scissors, with corresponding tooth in the other jaw. **2.** n. A sectorial tooth.

secular (I.), adj. [1. sḗkūlar; 2. sḗkjulə], fr. O. Fr. *seculer,* fr. Lat. *saeculāris,* 'of, belonging to, a *saeculum* or age'; hence, 'worldly, temporal, secular', fr. *saeculum, sēculum, saeclum,* 'age, period of a man's life; generation; period of a hundred years; an indefinitely long period'; the older form was **səi-tlom,* & the first syll. is fr. base **sēi-,* 'seed, sowing' &c., q.v. under **semen, season;** for the development of meaning cp. the cogn. Goth. *sēþs,* 'seed', see **seed** & **sow (II.)**, wh. occurs in compound *mana-sēþs,* lit. 'seed of man', hence 'humanity; the world'. Cp. also etymol. of **world. 1.** (Rom. antiq.) Of, belonging to, occurring once in, a generation or age, occurring once in a very long time, esp. *secular games (ludi saeculares),* celebrated at long intervals of from 100 to 120 years; *secular hymn, ode,* poem written for and recited at the celebration of the secular games. **2.** Continued through the ages, extending over, lasting a very long or indefinite period of time; occurring in, accomplished during, a very long period of time; contrasted with *recurrent* or *periodical*; **a** (of astron. and physical phenomena or processes) *secular cooling of the earth, changes in temperature*; *secular acceleration of the moon's motions* &c.; **b** (poet.) extremely old; aged: *the secular oaks*; **c** (of states of mind &c.) permanent, persistent, age-long: *the secular enmity of Slav and Teuton.* **3. a** Pertaining to this world, concerned with worldly things; worldly, temporal; contrasted with *spiritual*. or *religious*: *concerned only with secular affairs*; *secular music*; *secular education*, education which excludes all definite religious teaching; specif. **b** not ecclesiastical; apart from, not owned by, an ecclesiastical organization, authority &c.; civil, lay: *the secular power*; *secular property*; *secular courts*; *handed over to the secular arm for punishment.* **4.** (R.C. Ch.) Not monastic, not bound by a monastic vow or rule; contrasted with *regular*: *the secular orders, priesthood, clergy*, parish priests &c. **5.** Connected with, pertaining to, secularism and its principles.

secular (**II.**), n., fr. prec. (R.C. Ch.) A secular or parish priest.

secularism, n. [1. sékūlarizm; 2. sékjuləriz̆əm]. **secular** (**I.**) & **-ism. a** Theory, doctrine, that the definite separation of the State from ecclesiastical and religious matters is desirable; contrasted with *clericalism*; **b** specif. (cap.) a system of political philosophy or social ethics, founded on natural, practical morality, wholly divorced from religious faith or teaching; so called by its chief exponent, G. J. Holyoake.

secularist, n. & adj. [1. sékūlarist; 2. sékjulərist]. See prec. & **-ist. 1.** n. A believer in, supporter of, secularism. **2.** adj. Based on, pertaining to, advocating, secularism.

secularity, n. [1. sèkūláriti; 2. sèkjulǽriti]. **secular** (**I.**) & **-ity.** State, quality, of being secular; secularism.

secularization, n. [1. sèkūlarīzā́shun; 2. sèkjuləraizéiʃən]. **secularize** & **-ation.** Act of secularizing; state of being secularized; conversion from ecclesiastical or religious to civil or lay ownership, use &c.

secularize, vb. trans. [1. sékūlarīz; 2. sékjuləraiz]. **secular** (**I.**) & **-ize.** To render, make, secular. Specif. **1.** to transfer from ecclesiastical or spiritual ownership, use, authority &c., to secular, temporal, civil, or lay ownership &c.: *to secularize church property, courts* &c. **2.** To make worldly or unspiritual; to exclude religion, or religious teaching or worship from: *to secularize education*; *a secularized Sunday.* **3.** (R.C. Ch.) To absolve from monastic or regular vows: *to secularize a monk, a regular priest.*

secularly, adv. [1. sékūlarli; 2. sékjuləli]. **secular** (**I.**) & **-ly.** In a secular manner.

secund, adj. [1. sē̆kund; 2. síkand]. Lat. *secundus*, 'following'. See **second** (**I.**). (bot., of flowers, leaves &c.) Growing, arranged, on one side of the stem only.

secundine, n. [1. sékundīn; 2. sékəndain]. Formed fr. Lat. *secundus*, see **second** (**I.**), & **-ine. 1.** (bot.) The second membrane or integument covering an ovule or nucleus. **2.** (med.) Placenta, afterbirth.

secundum, prep. [1. sekúndum; 2. sikándəm]. Lat. See **second.** According to; in Phrs. *secundum artem*, according to art, science, skill; skilfully, scientifically; *secundum legem*, according to law, legally; *secundum naturam*, according to nature, naturally; *secundum quid*, according to something; in some, one, respect; with a certain limitation.

securable, adj. [1. sekū́rabl; 2. sikjɔ́rəbl]. **secure** & **-able.** Capable of being secured.

secure (**I.**), adj. [1. sekū́r; 2. sikjɔ́]. Lat. *sēcūrus*, 'free from care, free from danger, safe, secure'. See **se-** & **cure. 1.** Free from care, anxiety, or apprehension; easy in mind, not fearing for the future; undisturbed, untroubled, as to the future: *to have one's mind secure*; *to feel secure about, as to, the future*; *a peaceful and secure old age.* **2. a** (of persons) *Secure of*, confident, certain, assured, having no doubt about: *secure of success, victory*; **b** (of hopes, beliefs &c.) certain, well-founded, firmly fixed: *we live in the secure hope of immortality.* **3.** Free from, not exposed to, danger; made safe; capable of resisting an attack: *the danger is past and the town is now secure*; also *secure from, against*: *secure from, against, attack, all enemies.* **4.** Firm, stable, not likely to fall, collapse, or give way: *the foundations of the house do not seem very secure*; *make the fastening more secure.* **5.** In safe keeping; firmly held or fastened; secured: *to hold a secure position*; *keep the prisoners secure.*

secure (**II.**), vb. trans., fr. prec. **1.** To make safe or secure; to put into a condition of safety, to guard, protect, against danger: *to secure a town against assault, starvation*; *to secure oneself against the cold.* **2.** To make safe against loss or damage, to insure; to guarantee: *a fully secured debt or loan*; *to secure oneself against accidents, risks* &c. Phr. (mil.) *to secure arms*, hold a rifle in a position, as under the armpit, with muzzle down, to protect the breech mechanism or lock from wet. **3. a** To confirm, make certain, the possession and enjoyment of (rights, privileges &c.): *Magna Charta secured for ever the liberties of Englishmen*; **b** to devise, make succession of certain by will: *to secure one's property to one's son.* **4. a** To make fast or secure; to fasten firmly: *to secure a door, window*; **b** to confine, keep in safe custody: *the prisoner was at once secured.* **5.** To get hold of, obtain possession of: *I have at last secured a house, a good bargain*; *I managed to secure an excellent horse, a good dinner* &c.

securely, adv. [1. sekū́rli; 2. sikjɔ́li]. **secure** (**I.**) & **-ly.** In a secure manner; safely.

secureness, n. [1. sekū́rnes; 2. sikjɔ́nis]. See prec. & **-ness. a** State of being secure; **b** sense of security, freedom from anxiety or danger.

securiform, adj. [1. sekū́riform; 2. sikjɔ́rifɔ̄m], fr. Lat. *secūris*, 'axe'; fr. base **sekʷ-*, 'to cut', see **section**, & **-form.** (bot. and zool.) Shaped like an axe; hatchet-shaped.

security, n. [1. sekū́riti; 2. sikjɔ́riti]. Fr. *sécurité*, fr. Lat. *sēcūritāt-(em)*, 'freedom from care; unconcern; safety'. See **secure** & **-ity. 1.** State of being secure; safety, freedom from danger, injury, harm of any sort: *during the war some spies managed to live in England in security for a long time*; *Magna Charta gives us security against infringement of our liberties.* **2.** Sense of being secure; belief, conviction, that one is safe: *one feels great security in the presence of a strong and brave personality.* **3.** That which gives security; protection, defence, safeguard; **a** (in physical sense) *strong bolts and a good watchdog are my securities against burglars*; **b** (in moral sense) *the law and the man's own cowardice are sufficient security against any further molestation from him.* **4.** (commerc.) **a** Something of value deposited as pledge of repayment, and as protection against financial loss; guarantee: *security for a loan* &c.; **b** person who guarantees repayment, undertakes to indemnify in case of another's default; a surety. **5.** (usually pl.) *Securities*, bonds, share certificates, title-deeds of land or houses, or other evidence of ownership of property: *my securities are all lodged in the bank.*

sedan-chair, n. [1. sedán chā́r; 2. sidǽn tʃéə], fr. Sedan, in France, where first used. A portable covered chair for one person, borne by two chairmen by means of poles; used in the 17th and 18th cents.

sedate, adj. [1. sedā́t; 2. sidéit], fr. Lat. *sēdātus*, 'composed, calm, sedate', fr. P.P. type of *sēdāre*, 'to calm, allay, still'; fr. base *sēd-*, gradational variant of *sed-*, 'sit', q.v. under **sedentary.** (of persons, manner, mode of expression) Calm, unruffled, composed, tranquil; staid, decorous; reverse of *boisterous, excitable* &c.

sedately, adv. Prec. & **-ly.** In a sedate manner.

sedateness, n. See prec. & **-ness.** State, quality, of being sedate.

sedative, adj. & n. [1. sédativ; 2. sédətiv]. Fr. *sédatif.* See **sedate** & **-ive. 1.** adj. Having the property of calming, soothing, composing, bodily or mental pain or excitement. **2.** n. Something which produces a sedative effect; (med.) a sedative drug.

se defendendo, adv. [1. sē dĕfendéndō; 2. sī dīfɛndéndou]. Lat., 'in defending himself, in self-defence'. (law) Plea in cases of homicide.

sedentarily, adv. [1. sédentarili; 2. sédəntərili]. **sedentary** & **-ly.** In a sedentary manner.

sedentariness, n. [1. sédentarines; 2. sédəntərinis]. See prec. & **-ness.** State of being sedentary; sedentary habits.

sedentary (**I.**), adj. [1. sédentari; 2. sédəntəri], fr. Lat. *sedentārius*, fr. *sedent-(em)*, Pres. Part. of *sedēre*, 'to sit', & **-ary**; the base **sed-*, **sēd-* &c., 'to sit', is found in various forms in most Aryan languages; Scrt. *sádas*, 'seat' &c.; Gk. *hézomai*, 'to sit', for **sed-jo-*, *hédos*, 'seat', also *hédra*, see **cathedral**; cp. further **sedate, sit, seat, set** (**I.**). **1.** Sitting, keeping still; contrasted with active, mobile, bustling; specif. **a** involving prolonged periods of sitting and enforced bodily inactivity: *sedentary occupation*; *clerks lead a sedentary life*; **b** (of persons) compelled, or choosing, to lead a life of bodily inactivity; not taking much exercise; **c** *sedentary habits*, those of sitting still, not moving about, of taking little or no exercise. **2.** (of birds and animals) **a** Remaining in one country, not migratory; **b** remaining fixed to one spot, not moving, or able to move, about.

sedentary (**II.**), n. Person or animal of sedentary habits.

sederunt, n. [1. sedḗrunt; 2. sedíərənt]. Lat., 'they sat, there sat', 3rd pers. pl., past tense of *sedēre*, 'to sit'. See **sedentary. a** A formal meeting of a deliberative or legislative body; a session, a sitting; **b** (gen.) a formal, or informal, meeting of any body of persons, for discussion or ordinary conversation.

sedge, n. [1. sej; 2. sedž]. O.E. *secg*, M.E. *segge*; prob. fr. base **seg-*, **seχ-*, 'to cut', variant of **sekʷ-*, see **section**; cogn. w. **sax, saw** (**III.**), **scythe**; the meaning is 'cutting grass'; cp. the name *sword grass*, a species of sedge. Any of various species of coarse perennial, grass-like plants, growing in tufts in marshy or swampy places, of the genus *Carex*, with long, narrow, sharp-edged or serrated leaves and flowering spikelets; often used loosely of marsh or swamp grasses generally.

sedge-warbler, n. A small brown and white European bird, one of the warblers, building in sedges and reeds.

sedgy, adj. [1. séji; 2. sédži]. **sedge** & **-y.** Overgrown, fringed, with sedge; resembling sedge.

sedilia, n. pl. [1. sedília; 2. sedáiliə]. Lat., pl. of *sedīle*, 'seat, stool, bench', fr. base *sed-*, 'sit'. See **sedentary.** A set of seats, usually of stone, and three in number, set or recessed in the wall on the south side of the chancel of a church; intended originally for the priest, deacon, and subdeacon, and often surmounted by a stone canopy and otherwise decorated.

sediment, n. [1. sédiment; 2. sédimənt]. Fr., fr. Lat. *sedimentum*, 'subsidence, settling down', fr. base *sed-*, 'sit'. See **sedentary.** That which settles to the bottom of a liquid; matter deposited by a liquid or by action of water; dregs, lees of wine &c.

sedimentary, adj. [1. sèdiméntari; 2. sèdiméntəri]. Prec. & **-ary.** Pertaining to, of the nature of, containing, sediment; (geol.) *sedimentary rocks*, formed by sedimentation, as sandstones, limestones &c.

sedimentation, n. [1. sèdimentā́shun; 2. sèdimentéiʃən]. **sediment** & **-ation.** Process of depositing sediment; precipitation of solid matter from solution.

sedition, n. [1. sedíshun; 2. sidíʃən]. O. Fr., fr. Lat. *sēditiōn-(em)*, 'a going apart or aside; civil dissension or discord, sedition', see **se-**; the second element is *itiōn-(em)*, 'a going, travelling', fr. base *it-*, extension of base **i-*, 'to go', see **itinerate** & cp. **exit**. **1.** An offence against the crown and government, not amounting to treason, and therefore not capital; any act, writing, speech &c. directed unlawfully against state authority, the government or constitution, or one calculated to bring it into contempt or to incite others to hostility, ill-will, or disaffection. **2.** Tumult, public commotion, riot, not amounting to insurrection or rebellion.

seditious, adj. [1. sedíshus; 2. sidíʃəs], fr. Lat. *sēditiōsus*, fr. *sēdit-*, as in prec., & **-ous**. **1.** Pertaining to, of the nature of, likely to cause or arouse, sedition: *a seditious assembly, society; seditious acts, speech; seditious libel.* **2.** (of persons) Guilty of, imbued with, sedition.

seditiously, adv. Prec. & **-ly**. In a seditious manner.

seditiousness, n. See prec. & **-ness**. Quality of being seditious.

seduce, vb. trans. [1. sedūs; 2. sidjūs], fr. Lat. *sēdūcere*, 'to lead, draw away or apart, to separate'; in eccles. Lat., 'to lead astray, seduce', fr. **se-** & *dūcere*, 'to lead, draw', see **duct**. **1. a** To corrupt, debauch, lead astray, persuade, entice (away from virtue and good conduct): *to seduce a person from loyalty, into idleness* &c.; specif. **b** to persuade (a woman) to surrender chastity. **2.** (in innocent sense) To attract greatly, charm, entice: *I was seduced by the beauty of the evening into staying out of doors till past midnight.*

seducement, n. [1. sedūsment; 2. sidjūsmənt]. Prec. & **-ment**. (not much used) **1.** Act of seducing, seduction. **2.** That which seduces, attracts, charms.

seducer, n. [1. sedūser; 2. sidjūsə]. See prec. & **-er**. One who seduces; specif., one who seduces a woman.

seducing, adj. [1. sedūsing; 2. sidjūsiŋ], fr. Pres. Part. of **seduce**. Having power to seduce; seductive.

seducingly, adv. Prec. & **-ly**. In a seducing manner.

seduction, n. [1. sedúkshun; 2. sidákʃən]. Fr., fr. Lat. *sēductiōn-(em)*, fr. *sēduct-(um)*, P.P. type of *sēdūcere*, see **seduce**, & **-ion**. **1. a** Act of seducing; specif. **b** act, crime, of seducing a woman. **2.** That which seduces; means taken to seduce; **a** (in bad sense) wiles, blandishments; temptations, arts employed to seduce, corrupt, lead astray: *in spite of the seductions which ingenuity could devise, or which promised wealth could provide, he remained loyal to his allegiance*; **b** (in innocent sense) powerful attraction, charm, allurement: *the seductions of country life, of one's favourite study* &c.

seductive, adj. [1. sedúktiv; 2. sidáktiv]. See prec. & **-ive**. **a** Providing, exhibiting, full of, seductions; alluring, charming, winning; (chiefly in innocent sense): *a seductive smile; the cool shade of the forest was most seductive after the heat of the sun*; **b** persuasive: *seductive eloquence.*

seductively, adv. Prec. & **-ly**. In a seductive manner.

seductiveness, n. See prec. & **-ness**. Quality of being seductive.

sedulity, n. [1. sedūliti; 2. sidjūliti], fr. Lat. *sēdulitāt-(em)*, 'assiduity, application, zeal'. See **sedulous** & **-ity**. Quality of being sedulous.

sedulous, adj. [1. sédūlus; 2. sédjuləs], fr. Lat. *sēdulus*, 'diligent, industrious, assiduous', lit. 'without deceit, craft, or fraud', hence, 'honest, showing application and devotion (to duty &c.)'; fr. *sēd-*, 'without', see **se-**, & *dolus*, 'device, artifice, deceit' &c.; cogn. w. Gk. *dólos*, 'craft, cunning'; O.H.G. *zāl*, 'snare, trap'; further connexions are doubtful. (of persons and actions) Diligent, persistent, assiduous; careful, painstaking in pursuit and accomplishment of an object.

sedulously, adv. Prec. & **-ly**. In a sedulous manner.

sedulousness, n. See prec. & **-ness**. Quality of being sedulous; sedulous action.

sedum, n. [1. sēdum; 2. sídəm]. Lat. *sedum*, 'house-leek', prob. fr. **sed-*, root of *sedēre*, 'to sit'. See **sedentary**. (bot.) A very large genus of perennial herbs, including the stonecrops, with fleshy stems and leaves and white, yellow, or pink flowers, growing chiefly on rocks or walls.

see (I.), vb. trans. & intrans. [1. sē; 2. sī]. O.E. *sēon*, fr. **sehwan* (cp. Goth. *saihwan*, 'to see'); M.E. *seen* &c.; O.S., O.H.G. *sehan*. The view that this Gmc. word was derived fr. the base **sekʷ-*, 'to follow', cp. **sequela**, & that the orig. sense was 'to follow with the eyes', is now abandoned. Etymologists prefer to relate the word to **say (I.)**; the basal meaning is 'to see', & 'say' is a derivative sense; see further under **sign**. **A.** trans. **1.** To perceive with the eyes, obtain a visual impression of: *animals appear to see things invisible to human sight; we see many things whose use we do not know.* Phrs. *first saw the light*, was born; *I don't see it in that light*, don't regard it in that way; *to see the last of* (person or thing), get rid of, have done with; *to see one's way to doing something*, feel disposed to do it; manage to do it; *to come, go, and see*, or *to see* (a person), to pay a visit to, call upon; *see p. 50* &c., look at, refer to, mode of reference to passage in a book &c.; *to see a person home, to the door, as far as the station* &c., accompany him; *to see a person further, damned, first*, i.e. before consenting to his suggestion &c.; expressing absolute refusal; *to see something through*, attend to it until it is completed and done; to wait on to the end; *to see a person through his troubles* &c., give him full support. **2.** To perceive with the intelligence, grasp intellectually; understand, appreciate bearing of: *to see the meaning of; to see an argument, a point in discussion; I see what you mean; now you see why I did that; I see how it is; I see that I'm not wanted.* Phrs. *to see a joke*, perceive humour of; *he can't see a joke*, has no sense of humour; *as I see it*, as it appears to me; *not to see the use, the good, the fun, of* (something), to doubt whether it be of any use &c. **3.** To have experience of, live through, to witness, come across; to have brought to one's knowledge, or under one's observation: *he has seen a good deal in his long life; to see war at close quarters; I have seen the time when the poor could not afford meat; I never saw such rudeness.* Phrs. *to see life*, gain experience of the world; *to see service*, to serve, esp. as a soldier or sailor, or in some other official capacity; *he, it, has seen better days*, (i.) (of person) he has been prosperous, but is now poor; (ii.) (of object) it is old and shabby, or worn out. **4.** To have the illusion, hallucination, that one sees; to have a vision of: *to see things in dreams.* Phrs. *to see stars*, have impression of flashes of light before the eyes, through excessive stimulus of optic nerve caused by blow on the head &c.; *to see snakes*, suffer from delusions through delirium tremens. **5.** To perceive by imagination; to visualize, form, call up, mental conception of; to imagine: *poets see many things in man and in nature to which the ordinary man is blind; I can't quite see myself at a ball; 'I see thee old and formal, fitted to thy petty part'* (Tennyson, 'Locksley Hall'). **6. a** To look at, be a spectator of: *to see a play, the latest actress* &c.; **b** to become acquainted with, to study, understand, learn appearance and character of, by seeing, inspecting, and examining: *to see the sights; to see Rome; Americans manage to see Oxford in a few hours; to see a house before taking it*; **c** specif., to examine for purpose of discovering what is wrong: *he seems very ill, the doctor ought to see him at once; have in a man to see the drains.* **7. a** To meet, come across, come into social contact with (persons): *I haven't seen you for ages; I hope to see him for a few minutes tomorrow; I am very pleased to see you*; **b** to come upon, have under one's notice, observe, take cognizance of (things): *I have just seen the book, but haven't yet read it; have you seen today's paper?; I saw an interesting story the other day.* **8. a** To interview, grant an interview or audience to: *the Rector will see those wishing to consult him in the vestry; I'm too busy to see you now*; **b** to have an interview with, to consult: *to see one's lawyer about something; I should like to see a doctor.* **9.** To take care that, take steps to secure that, make sure that: *kindly see that everything is properly done; I'll see that he comes to no harm*; also *see to it that.* **B.** intrans. **1. a** To have the faculty of sight: *very young animals do not see; 'eyes have they, but they see not'* (Ps. cxv. 5). **b** to make use of the eyes for a given purpose, or at a given moment: *I can't see to read; I can't see as far as that*; Phr. *to see no further than one's nose*, (fig.) to be mentally obtuse, lack penetration. **2.** To have an intellectual perception, to understand; to grasp a meaning, perceive significance of a fact, statement &c.: *the whole thing was a mistake, don't you see?; oh, I see now, he was only joking all the time.* **3.** To look in order to find out something; to reconnoitre, make survey; to make inquiry: *I think the post has come, I will go and see.* Phr. *to see for oneself*, make inquiries at first-hand. **4.** To consider, reflect, think things over, deliberate: *will you come to dinner tomorrow? well, I'll see; let me see, what was I saying?* **C.** Followed by preposition or adverb. *See about*, to attend to, pay attention to, look, inquire into, to take steps to do: *we must see about the matter at once; do see about packing; I will see about it at some time or other. See after*, trans., to take care of, pay heed to: *to see after one's own interests. See into*, intrans., to examine, make inquiries about, investigate: *to see into the state of a business. See off*, trans., to accompany, attend a person till he goes away: *to see one off at the station; to see a man off the premises. See out*, trans., to wait till the end of; to see a thing finished: *to see out a long play; whatever happens I will see the struggle out. See over*, intrans., to examine, inspect thoroughly: *to see over a house, the premises* &c. *See through*, intrans., to understand thoroughly: *to see through a person, his motives, game* &c., to perceive the duplicity of; Phr. *to see through a brick wall*, to have uncommon power of mental penetration. *See to*, to attend to: *I will leave you to see to the business.*

see (II.), n., fr. O. Fr. *se, sie, sied*, fr. Lat. *sēdes*, 'seat', fr. base *sed-*, 'to sit', see **sedentary**. The ecclesiastical unit over which a bishop or archbishop rules; geographical area covered by this; diocese: *the See of Oxford, Lincoln, Rome* &c.; *bishops reside in their sees for the greater part of the year.*

seed (I.), n. [1. sēd; 2. sīd]. O.E. *sǣd*, M.E. *sēde*; O.S. *sād*; O.H.G. *sāt*; fr. base **sē-*, **se-*, cp. Lat. *sēmen*, see **semen**, *serere*, 'to sow'. Cogn. w. Lith. *sėju*, 'to sow', *sėkla*, 'seed'; O. Slav. *sěją*, 'to sow'. See further under **sow (II.)**. **1.** (bot.) **a** Fertilized germ produced by a plant, and capable of developing into, and reproducing another plant of the same kind: *'of fifty seeds She often brings but one to bear'* (Tennyson, 'In Memoriam', LV.); **b** a number of seeds collectively: *to sow seed in the ground*; used also of potato tubers whence new plants are produced: *potato seed*; Phr. *to run to seed*, (of plants) to produce seed in abundance, and cease sending up shoots, and producing flowers for the season; (also fig., of persons) to become intellectually sterile, or physically feeble; *to sow the good seed*, to disseminate good influence, sound doctrines and principles, specif., those of the Gospel. **2.** The fertilizing, reproductive element, in male animals; sperm, milt; hence (fig.) descendants, offspring, posterity: *the seed of Abraham.*

3. (fig.) Germ, source, origin of anything; first principle; fructuating idea &c.: *the seeds of decay, disease, enmity* &c.; *implant in him the seeds of virtue.*

seed (**II.**), vb. intrans. & trans., fr. prec. **A.** intrans. **1.** To grow to maturity and produce seed; to go, run, to seed. **2.** To shed, let fall, the seed. **B.** trans. **1.** (gen.) *Seed down*, to lay (a field) down in seed, to sow it. **2.** To remove the seed from (a plant, fruit &c.). **3.** Specif. (in games, such as lawn-tennis) to arrange, select the names of competitors in the draw for a tournament, so that certain of them, whether as belonging to a particular nation or to a specially high class in skill, should not meet in the early rounds: *to seed the draw*; *competitors seeded in the draw.*

seed-cake, n. One containing caraway seeds as a flavouring.

seed-case, n. Seed vessel.

seed-coat, n. The integument covering a seed.

seed-coral, n. Small, irregular pieces of coral, used for ornaments.

seed-corn, n. Corn kept for sowing.

seed-drill, n. Drill made for dropping seeds into prepared furrows when sowing.

seed-eater, n. Name of various small finches of S. America and Africa.

seeder, n. [1. sḗder; 2. sídə]. **seed** (**II.**) & **-er.** **1.** Seed-drill. **2.** Machine for seeding raisins &c.

seed-fish, n. Fish ready to spawn.

seedily, adv. [1. sḗdili; 2. sídili]. **seedy** & **-ly.** In a seedy manner; poorly, shabbily.

seediness, n. [1. sḗdines; 2. sídinis]. See prec. & **-ness.** State of being seedy; **a** state of having, containing, an abundance of seeds (e.g. a fruit, jam); **b** shabbiness of appearance; **c** indisposition, ill health.

seed-leaf, n. (bot.) The first small leaf put out by a seed when germinating; a cotyledon.

seedless, adj. [1. sḗdles; 2. sídlis]. **seed** (**I.**) & **-less.** Containing, producing, no seeds.

seedling, n. [1. sḗdling; 2. sídliŋ]. **seed** (**I.**) & **-ling.** A young plant grown from a seed and not from a cutting.

seed-oysters, n. pl. Oyster spat; young, immature oysters ready for transplanting.

seed-pearl, n. A very small, seed-like pearl.

seed-plot, n. **a** Piece of ground in a garden set apart for raising plants from seed; **b** (fig.) a nursery, nest, hotbed, as of vice, sedition &c.

seed-potatoes, n. pl. Small, mature potatoes kept for planting.

seedsman, n. [1. sḗdzman; 2. sídzmən]. A dealer in flower and vegetable seeds, and in garden requisites.

seed-time, n. The time at which seeds are sown; late spring, early summer.

seed-vessel, n. Pod or capsule holding the ripe seeds; seed-case; also called *pericarp.*

seed wool, n. Raw cotton before being cleaned of its seeds.

seedy, adj. [1. sḗdi; 2. sídi]. **seed** (**I.**) & **-y.** **1.** Full of seeds; run to seed. **2.** (colloq.) **a** Shabby, worn out; of shabby appearance: *in seedy clothes*; *a seedy individual*; **b** out of sorts; indisposed: *to feel, look, seedy.* **3.** (specif., of brandy) Having a peculiar flavour, attributed to the seeds of the weeds growing among the vines.

seeing (**I.**), vbl. n. [1. sḗing; 2. síiŋ]. **see** (**I.**) & **-ing.** **a** Faculty, sense, of sight; **b** act of perceiving with the eyes; Phr. *seeing is believing*, the best proof of anything is one's own sight or direct knowledge of it; don't believe anything until you know it yourself as a fact.

seeing (**II.**), conj. & prep., fr. Pres. Part. of **see** (**I.**). **a** conj. Considering, in view of the fact that, since, inasmuch as: *seeing (that) these men are murderers they deserve to be hanged*; **b** prep., in view of, on account of: *he was unfitted for the post seeing his youth and inexperience.*

seek, vb. trans. & intrans. [1. sēk; 2. sik]. O.E. *sēċan*, fr. **sōkjan*, 'to try to find; try to get; try to find out, investigate, inquire; to visit, go to; to attack'; M.E. *sēchen*, & *sēken*; the latter, the ancestor of present form, is due to the anal. of O.E. *sēcst*, *sēcþ* (with [k]), 2nd & 3rd pers. sing., whereas *sēchen*, & present-day *beseech*, are due to the infin. & 1st pers. sing.; cp. O.S. *sōkian*; Goth. *sōkjan*; O.H.G. *suohhan*, Gmc. **sōk-* is fr. Aryan **săg-*, as in Lat. *săgire*, 'to perceive keenly', *săga*, 'female diviner, fortune-teller', & *sagax* (different grade), 'keen-witted', see **sagacious**; perh. also Gk. *hēgéomai*, fr. **săg-*, 'lead; believe', basal meaning perh., 'to be keen-witted', see **hegemony.** **A.** trans. **1.** (archaic or poet.) To try to find; search, look, for: '*Why seek ye the living among the dead?*' Phr. *to seek a quarrel*, try to start one; *to seek safety*, to take shelter; *(the reason is) not far to seek*, (pass.) does not need to be sought after, is easy to find, obvious; *to be sadly to seek*, be lacking. **2.** (chiefly poet.) To set out for, go to, visit, resort to: *to seek another and a happier clime*; *to seek a home beyond the sea.* **3.** **a** To look out for, go in search of, try to obtain: *to seek a place as clerk*; *to seek one's fortune*; **b** to pursue, aim at, make efforts to attain to: *to seek wealth, power*; '*seek ye first the kingdom of God, and His righteousness*'; '*seeking the bubble reputation*'. **4.** To ask for, demand: *to seek advice, an explanation of a person's conduct* &c. **5.** To inquire into; to investigate, try to discover by research: *to seek the causes of disease*; *to seek the solution, explanation, of a problem, a mystery* &c. **6.** Followed by infin., to endeavour, make an attempt: *he sought to draw his sword, to grasp the drowning man* &c. **B.** intrans. To make a search, perform the act of seeking: '*seek and ye shall find*'. **C.** Followed by preposition or adverb. *Seek after*, to hunt for; pursue; try to attain to. *Seek for*, to seek, to search for. *Seek out*, to seek with particular care; to look up, hunt out. *Seek through*, to search (place &c.) thoroughly, from end to end.

seeker, n. [1. sḗker; 2. síkə]. Prec. & **-er.** One who seeks; searcher; inquirer: *an earnest seeker after truth.*

seel, vb. trans. [1. sēl; 2. sīəl], fr. O. Fr. *siller*, *ciller*, fr. *cil*, 'eyelid', fr. Lat. *cilium*, see **cilia.** (archaic or obs.) **1.** To close the eyes (of a young hawk) with threads drawn through upper lids. Hence **2**, to blind, blindfold; to hoodwink.

seem, vb. intrans. [1. sēm; 2. sīm]. M.E. *sēmen*, in Mod. sense; also 'to beseem, befit'; the first sense is prob. Scand.; cp. O.N. *sǿma*, 'to conform to'; the cogn. O.E. *sēman* means 'to bring (persons) to agreement; to settle (dispute)'; the word is cogn. w. **same.** **1.** **a** To appear to be, have the appearance of being; to look like; to be in appearance if not in reality; to give the impression of being: *he seemed an honest man*; *the tale seems incredible*; *this wine seems rather good*; *things are not always what they seem*; Phr. *it seems good to (me &c.) to do* &c., I choose, I intend, to do so and so; **b** (in 1st pers. followed by infin.) *I seem to hear someone calling*, I have the impression that I hear; *I always seem to get on better with the husband than with the wife*, I appear to myself to, it seems to me that I &c. **2.** (impers.) *It seems*, **a** it appears, it gives one the impression: *it seems that the weather is improving*; *I have been out in the rain*; *so it seems*, i.e. that is certainly the impression I get from your wet clothes; **b** it appears from reports, it is stated, the fact is, that: *it seems (that) the bank was robbed last night*; Phr. *meseems, meseemed*, archaic impers. construction, it seems, seemed, to me; I have, had, the impression, or illusion that; I fancy, fancied, that: *meseemed that I was walking in a wood.*

seeming (**I.**), adj. [1. sḗming; 2. símiŋ], fr. Pres. Part. of **seem.** Apparent, having an appearance or semblance, whether true or not; ostensible: *his seeming loyalty, friendship.*

seeming (**II.**), n. **seem** & **-ing.** (archaic) Outward appearance, what is external and ostensible: '*My love is strengthened though more weak in seeming; I love not less, though less the show appear*' (Shakespeare, Sonnet cii.).

seemingly, adv. **seeming** (**I.**) & **-ly.** In appearance, apparently; ostensibly.

seemliness, n. [1. sḗmlines; 2. símlinis]. **seemly** & **-ness.** Quality of being seemly; decency, propriety.

seemly, adj. [1. sḗmli; 2. símli]. M.E. *sēmlich*, fr. O.N. *sǿmiligr*, 'fit, becoming'. See **seem.** Suitable, fit, proper; appropriate; decent, comely, becoming.

seen, adj. [1. sēn; 2. sin], fr. P.P. of **see** (**I.**). (archaic) *Well, ill, seen in*, equipped, provided with; instructed in: *the house was very well seen in conveniences of every sort*; *a man well seen in classical learning.*

seep, vb. intrans. [1. sēp; 2. sīp]. Cp. O.E. *sīpian*, 'to soak, take in moisture'. (provinc. and U.S.A., of liquids) To ooze, percolate, leak.

seer (**I.**), n. [1. sēr; 2. sīə]. **see** (**I.**) & **-er.** **a** One who sees; specif., one who sees visions, person gifted with imagination &c.: *a dreamer of dreams and a seer of visions*; hence **b** one who sees into the future, a prophet: '*some bold seer in a trance*' (Tennyson, 'Lady of Shalott').

seer (**II.**), n. Hind. *sēr.* An Indian measure of weight, varying in different districts and at different times; roughly about 2 lb.

seerband, n. [1. sḗrband; 2. síəbænd]. Hind. *sirband*, 'turban'. A kind of Indian muslin used for turbans.

seersucker, n. [1. sḗrsuker; 2. síəsakə], fr. Hind., Pers. *shir shakar*, *shir*, 'milk', & *shakar*, 'sugar'. A thin cotton or linen blue and white striped Indian cloth.

seesaw (**I.**), n. [1. sḗsaw; 2. sísɔ̄]. Prob. reduplication of **saw** (**III.**), fr. the motion. Wooden plank fastened by the middle to an upright support, in such a way that each end can alternately rise and fall; used by children, one of whom sits at either end, and as his end falls thrusts it upwards again with his feet.

seesaw (**II.**), vb., adj., & adv., fr. prec. **1.** vb. **a** To go, ride, on a seesaw; **b** to move up and down like a seesaw; **c** (fig.) to fluctuate, to rise and fall alternately (of prices, temperature &c.). **2.** adj. Resembling the movement of a seesaw; alternately rising and falling. **3.** adv. In a fluctuating manner; up and down.

seethe, vb. trans. & intrans. [1. sēdh; 2. sīð]. O.E. *sēoðan*, 'to boil, cook; to afflict', M.E. *sēthen*, O.H.G. *siodan*, O.N. *sjōða*, cogn. w. Goth. *saups*, 'burnt offering, sacrifice'. **1.** trans. **a** (archaic) To boil (meat) in water, to cook by boiling; **b** to steep, soak (leather) in water in order to soften it. **2.** intrans. **a** (of water &c.) To boil, to bubble up, be in a state of violent commotion: *seething waters, whirlpool* &c.; **b** (fig.) to bubble over with, be deeply stirred by, be violently agitated by, thrown into state of great excitement by: *the whole country is seething with discontent and rebellious tendencies*; *his mind, bosom, was seething with conflicting emotions.*

segar, n. Obs. form of **cigar.**

segment (**I.**), n. [1. ségment; 2. ségmənt], fr. Lat. *segmentum*, fr. base **seg-*, 'to cut', cogn. w. *secāre*, 'to cut', see **section** & **saw** (**III.**). **1.** One of the parts into which a body is, or can be, divided; a separable, or separated part; part cut off, section: *the jointed, ringed segments of a worm, crustacean* &c.; *the cranial segments*, the three sections into which the bones of the skull are divided by the sutures; *a segment of an orange.* **2.** (biol.) A cell formed by cleavage or segmentation. **3.** (geom.) A part cut off from any figure by a line or plane: *segment of a circle* &c.

segment (**II.**), vb. trans. & intrans., fr. prec. **1.** trans. To divide, cut, into segments. **2.** intrans. To split up, become divided, into segments; to undergo segmentation.

segmental, adj. [1. segméntal; 2. segméntəl]. **segment** & **-al.** **a** Of, pertaining to, resembling, a segment; **b** composed of segments; segmentary.

segmentally, adv. Prec. & **-ly**. In segments.
segmentary, adj. [1. ségmentari ; 2. ségmentəri]. **segment (I.)** & **-ary**. Segmental.
segmentation, n. [1. sègmentáshun ; 2. sègmentéiʃən]. **segment (II.)** & **-ation**. **1.** Act, process, of dividing or splitting up into segments. **2.** Specif. (biol.) formation of cells by cleavage.
segmented, adj. [1. segménted ; 2. segméntid]. **segment (II.)** & **-ed**. Divided, separated, marked off in segments ; jointed, articulated.
segment gear, n. Gear, wheel, with cogs on a segment only of the circle.
segment saw, n. **a** One made in form of segment of a circle ; **b** one made in segments ; **c** one for cutting material into segments.
segregate (I.), vb. trans. & intrans. [1. ségregāt ; 2. ségrigeit]; pedantically [1. sḗgregāt ; 2. sígrigeit] on account of Lat. *sē-* ; fr. Lat. *sēgregāt-(um)*, P.P. type of *sēgregāre*, 'to set apart, separate from others', fr. **se-** & *greg-*, stem of *grex*, 'a flock'. See **gregarious**. **1.** trans. To cut off, separate from others or the main body or mass ; to set apart ; isolate. **2.** intrans. To become separated from a main body or mass, specif. (of crystals &c.) to separate and collect round a nucleus or line of fracture.
segregate (II.), adj., fr. prec. Segregated, set apart, solitary.
segregation, n. [1. sègregáshun ; 2. sègrigéiʃən], fr. Lat. *sēgregātiōn-(em)*. See prec. & **-ion**. **a** Act, process, of segregating ; **b** state of being segregated ; **c** segregated group of persons or objects &c.
segregative, adj. [1. ségregātiv ; 2. ségrigeitiv]. **segregate (I.)** & **-ive**. **a** Tending to segregate ; **b** characterized by segregation.
seiche, n. [1. sāsh ; 2. seiʃ]. Swiss Fr., etymol. doubtful ; either a dialectal variant of Fr. *sèche*, 'dry', see **sec**, or fr. Germ. *seiche*, 'sinking'. Slight variation in level, oscillation of the surface of a lake, or land-locked sea, due to changes in atmospheric pressure.
Seidlitz powder, n. [1. sédlits póuder ; 2. sédlits páudə], fr. name of village and mineral spring in Czechoslovakia. A saline aperient medicine ; an artificial powdered preparation from the mineral water of Seidlitz, mixed with powdered tartaric acid as an effervescent.
seignior, seigneur, n. [1. sányōr, sányēr ; 2. séinjɔ̄, sèinjə́]. O. Fr., fr. Lat. See **senior, sir, sire**. Feudal lord, lord of the manor ; *grand seigneur*, a great nobleman ; person of distinguished appearance, manners &c.
seigniorage, n. [1. sányurij ; 2. séinjəridž]. O. Fr. Prec. & **-age**. **a** Right, due, of a feudal overlord ; **b** percentage, royalty ; specif. **c** right to a percentage on all bullion brought to the royal mint for coining ; profit made on coins issued at a rate above their intrinsic value.
seignioralty, n. [1. sányuralti ; 2. séinjərəlti]. Prec. & **-ty**. Seigniory.
seigniorial, adj. [1. sānyṓrial ; 2. seinjɔ́riəl]. **seignior** & **-ial**. Of, pertaining to, a seignior, to a feudal lord, or to a lord of a manor ; manorial.
seigniory, n. [1. sányori ; 2. séinjəri]. O. Fr. *seignieurie*. See **seignior** & **-y**. **a** Jurisdiction, authority, of a seignior or feudal lord ; **b** territory, domain, over which this extends ; **c** (hist.) the municipal council of a mediaeval Italian city republic.
seine, n. & vb. trans. & intrans. [1. sān ; 2. sein]. M.E. *seyne*, fr. O. Fr. *seigne*, Mod. Fr. *seine*, fr. Lat. *sagēna*, fr. Gk. *sagḗnē*, 'a fishing-net' ; origin obscure. **1.** n. Large fishing-net, the upper edge of which is kept near surface of water by floats, while the net is kept in vertical position by sinkers attached to lower edge ; the net is drawn in together with the fish inside. **2.** vb. **a** trans. To catch (fish) with a seine ; **b** intrans., to fish with a seine.
seise, vb. See **seize**.
seisin, n. See **seizin**.
seismal, adj. [1. sízmal ; 2. sáizməl]. **seismo-** & **-al**. Seismic.
seismic, adj. [1. sízmik ; 2. sáizmik]. **seismo-** & **-ic**. Pertaining to, caused by, an earthquake or earthquakes.
seismo-, pref., fr. Gk. *seismós*, 'earthquake', fr. *seíein*, 'to shake', for **tweis-* ; cp. Scrt. *tvēšāmi*, 'to be violently shaken, be upset' ; used in scientific compound words expressing ideas connected with earthquakes.
seismogram, n. [1. sízmogram ; 2. sáizməgræm]. **seismo-** & **-gram**. Record of an earthquake or tremor made by a seismograph.
seismograph, n. [1. sízmograhf ; 2. sáizməgrāf]. **seismo-** & **-graph**. Instrument which records in diagrammatic form the motions or oscillation of an earthquake.
seismographer, n. [1. sīzmógrafer ; 2. saizmɔ́grəfə]. Prec. & **-er**. One who uses a seismograph ; recorder, observer, of earthquakes.
seismographic(al), adj. [1. sìzmográfik(l) ; 2. sàizməgrǽfik(l)]. See prec. & **-ic** & **-al**. **a** Pertaining to, shown by, a seismograph ; **b** pertaining to seismography.
seismography, n. [1. sīzmógrafi ; 2. saizmɔ́grəfi]. **seismo-** & **-graphy**. Art of observing and recording earthquakes by means of a seismograph.
seismological, adj. [1. sìzmolójikl ; 2. sàizməlɔ́dzikl]. **seismo-** & **-logical**. Pertaining to seismology.
seismologist, n. [1. sīzmólojist ; 2. saizmɔ́lədžist]. **seismo-** & **-logist**. One who studies, specializes in, seismology.
seismology, n. [1. sīzmóloji ; 2. saizmɔ́lədži]. **seismo-** & **-logy**. The science of earthquakes.
seismometer, n. [1. sīzmómeter ; 2. saizmɔ́mitə]. **seismo-** & **-meter**. Instrument for measuring the direction and intensity of earthquakes.
seismometric, adj. [1. sìzmométrik ; 2. sàizməmétrik]. Prec. & **-ic**. Of, pertaining to, a seismometer or seismometry.
seismometry, n. [1. sīzmómetri ; 2. saizmɔ́mitri]. **seismo-** & **-metry**. Measurement of the intensity &c. of earthquake shocks.
seismoscope, n. [1. sízmoskōp ; 2. sáizməskoup]. **seismo-** & **-scope**. Apparatus used for detecting occurrence of earthquakes and earth tremors.
seizable, adj. [1. sézabl ; 2. sízəbl]. **seize** & **-able**. Capable of being seized.
seize, vb. trans. & intrans. [1. sēz ; 2. sīz]. M.E. *seisen* &c., 'to put in, take possession ; to give seizin of land &c.', fr. O. Fr. *seisir* &c., fr. L. Lat. *sacīre*, 'to take possession of' ; etymol. doubtful. **A.** trans. **1.** (law) **a** (the orig. sense) To put into possession of, put into seizin of : (with *of* and usually in P.P.) *to stand, be, seized of the manor &c. of A* &c. ; **b** to take possession of by warrant or other legal process ; to impound, attach, confiscate. **2.** To take possession of suddenly or by force ; also *seize on* : *to seize the throne, reins of power*. Phrs. *to seize an idea*, appropriate it (from someone else), adopt it ; *to seize on, upon, a suggestion*. **3.** To grasp with the hand, take hold of forcibly ; to clutch, grab : *to seize a rope, a stick* ; *to seize a person by the arm, throat* &c. ; also *seize hold of*. Phr. *to seize an opportunity, the occasion*, to make use of, avail oneself of it, with alacrity. **4.** Only in construction *to be seized with*, to be suddenly affected, struck, attacked, by (disease) : *to be seized with gout, a fit of coughing, a mortal illness* &c. ; also *to be seized with remorse, terror, pity* &c. **5.** To understand, see, grasp firmly and rapidly with the mind, to get into one's head : *I can't quite seize your meaning* ; *to seize the importance of a statement* &c. **6.** (naut.) To lash, fasten together (ropes), with small pieces of cord &c. : *to seize up*, to tie (a man) up with cords, esp. to tie up to rigging or mast to flog him. **B.** intrans. (of mach. or part of it) To stick, adhere, jam, bind, esp. from great heat, undue friction &c. ; also *seize up*.
seizin, seisin, n. [1. sézin ; 2. sízin]. O. Fr. *saisine, seisine*. See **seize**. (law) **a** Freehold possession of land ; **b** act of taking legal possession of freehold estates.
seizings, n. pl. [1. sézingz ; 2. síziŋz]. **seize** & **-ing**. Ropes lashed or seized together with small cords and tarred.
seizor, n. [1. sézōr ; 2. sízɔ̄]. **seize** & **-or**. (law) Person who seizes, takes possession of, freehold estates.
seizure, n. [1. sézhur ; 2. sížə]. **seize** & **-ure** ; cp. *pleasure*. **1.** Act of seizure ; forcible appropriation : *the seizure of another's property*. **2.** Something seized or forcibly appropriated. **3.** Sudden attack of illness ; specif., a paralytic stroke, apoplectic fit.
sejant, adj. [1. séjant ; 2. sídžənt]. A.-Fr., Pres. Part. of *seier*, 'to sit' ; fr. Lat. *sedēre*, 'to sit', see **sedentary**. (her., of lion or other beast) Sitting.
sekos, n. [1. sékos ; 2. síkɔs]. Gk. *sēkós*, 'shrine, enclosure, pen' ; etymol. doubtful. (Gk. archit.) The adytum or sacred enclosure of a temple.
selachian, n. & adj. [1. selákian ; 2. seléikiən], fr. Gk. *sélakhos*, 'any cartilaginous fish, a shark', cogn. w. Gk. *sélas*, 'flash, bright light', cp. **selenium**, & **-ian**. (zool.) **a** n. Any fish of the sub-class *Selachii*, including the sharks, dog-fishes, and rays ; **b** adj., of, pertaining to, like, this class of fishes.
selah, n. [1. sélah ; 2. sílā]. A Hebrew word found at end of a verse in the Psalms, of unknown meaning, but usually taken as a musical direction, indicating a pause or break.
selamlik, n. [1. seláhmlik ; 2. selámlik]. Turk. The men's quarters in a Turkish house.
seldom, adv. [1. séldum ; 2. séldəm]. O.E. *seldum, seldan*, dat. pl. used adverbially fr. **seld*, 'rare, strange', cogn. w. O.H.G. *seltan* ; Goth. *silda-(leiks)*, 'seldom' ; the base is apparently unknown outside Gmc. Rarely, not often, infrequently : *very seldom* ; *seldom or never*, hardly ever, on the rarest occasions.
select (I.), adj. [1. selékt ; 2. silékt]. Lat. *sēlect-(um)*, P.P. of *sēligere*, 'pick out, choose'. See **se-** & **lecture**. **1.** Chosen, picked out, selected, from among a number ; specif., chosen on account of excellence, merits, suitability for particular purpose : *dinner consisting of a few select dishes* ; *a library of select books* ; *a few select friends*. Phr. *select committee* (of the House), one appointed by Parliament from all parties to inquire into desirability of proposed legislation &c. **2.** Specif., careful in selecting friends and associates ; fastidious, exclusive : *Mrs. Jones is very select in the people she invites* ; *we are very select in the garden city* ; *a select club, select circles*, exclusive, consisting of select persons.
select (II.), vb. trans. See prec. To pick out, choose, for some particular purpose, on account of excellence, suitability for particular purpose &c. : *to select the books one wants, a hat to wear in the sun, a candidate for a post* &c.
selected, adj. [1. selékted ; 2. siléktid], fr. P.P. of prec. Carefully chosen ; choice.
selection, n. [1. selékshun ; 2. silékʃən], fr. Lat. *sēlectiōn-(em)*. **select (II.)** & **-ion**. **1.** **a** Act or process of selecting, choice : *to make one's own selection* ; specif. **b** (biol.) (i.) natural process by which certain individuals of a species are eliminated, and therefore do not propagate, owing to their inability to adapt themselves to their environment ; also called *natural selection* ; (ii.) artificial process whereby breeders match together pairs of animals who possess the characteristics which it is desired to perpetuate in the species. **2.** **a** That which, he who, has been selected, picked out, chosen, for any given purpose : *the selections for a match*, those chosen as members of a team ; *these shrubs are my selections for the border* ; **b** something, a limited number, picked out, or specially chosen from among many of the same kind : *the catalogue contains only a selection of our stock* ; **c** specif., collection of selected, representative examples : *selections*

from the writings of De Quincey; *selections from the poets*, i.e. from their works.

selective, adj. [1. seléktiv; 2. siléktiv]. **select (II.) & -ive.** Having the power of selection; tending to select; specif. (wireless) *selective system* (of transmitting and receiving messages), one so devised that two messages can be sent and received at once without confusion.

selectively, adv. Prec. & **-ly.** In a selective manner; by selection.

selectivity, n. [1. sèlektíviti; 2. sèlektíviti]. See prec. & **-ity.** (specif., wireless) Reception of any particular wave-length to the exclusion of others.

selectman, n. [1. seléktman; 2. siléktmæn]. **select (I.) & man.** (U.S.A.) One of a board of officers chosen in various New England states to manage municipal affairs.

selectness, n. [1. seléktnes; 2. siléktnis]. **select (I.) & -ness.** Quality of being select.

selector, n. [1. selékter; 2. siléktə]. **select (II.) & -or.** **a** One who selects; **b** specif. (in Australia) a small farmer or squatter; **c** (wireless) device for eliminating certain wave-lengths.

selenate, n. [1. sélenāt; 2. sélənеit]. See next word & **-ate.** (chem.) A salt of selenic acid.

selenic, adj. [1. selḗnik; 2. silínik]. See **selenium & -ic.** (chem.) Pertaining to, containing, the element selenium; specif., *selenic acid*, an acid formed by the oxidation of selenium, of higher valency than *selenious acid*.

selenide, n. [1. sélinīd; 2. sélinaid]. **selenium & -ide.** (chem.) A compound of selenium and another element.

seleniferous, adj. [1. sèliníferus; 2. sèlinífərəs]. **selenium & -ferous.** (chem.) Yielding, containing, selenium.

selenious, adj. [1. selḗnius; 2. silíniəs]. **selenium & -ous.** (chem.) Containing the element selenium; specif., *selenious acid*, acid formed by oxidation of selenium, of lower valency than *selenic acid*.

selenite, n. [1. sélenīt; 2. sélənait]. Sense **1.** fr. **selenium & -ite.** **1.** A salt of selenious acid. **2.** (mineral.) A variety of gypsum, crystallizing in thin, transparent plates.

selenitic, adj. [1. sèlinítik; 2. sèlinítik]. Prec. & **-ic.** Of, pertaining to, selenite.

selenium, n. [1. selḗnium; 2. silíniəm], fr. Gk. *selḗnē*, 'the moon', & Lat. suff. on anal. of names of other elements; the Gk. word for 'moon' contains base **swel-*, 'to glow, be bright'; cp. also Gk. *sélas*, 'light, brightness, flash' &c.; cogn. w. O.E. *swelan*, 'to burn, be hot', q.v. under **swelter & sultry.** Non-metallic element resembling sulphur and tellurium, discovered in 1817; its electric conductivity is increased by light, and is thus used in the transmission of photographic telegraphy.

seleno-, pref., fr. Gk. *selḗnē*, 'the moon'. See prec.; used to form scientific words referring to the moon, its shape &c.

selenocentric, adj. [1. selḗnosént rik; 2. səlínə-séntrik]. Prec. & **-centric.** (astron.) Relating to the centre of the moon; viewed as if from the centre of the moon; referring to the moon as a centre.

selenodont, adj. & n. [1. selḗnodònt; 2. səlínədònt]. **seleno- & -odont.** (zool.) **a** adj. Having molar teeth with crescent-shaped, ridged crowns; **b** n., mammal with such teeth.

selenograph, n. [1. selḗnograhf; 2. səlínəgrāf]. **seleno- & -graph.** A chart or other representation of the moon's surface.

selenographic, adj. [1. selḕnográfik; 2. səlìnəgrǽfik]. **seleno- & -graphic.** Of, pertaining to, selenography: *selenographic chart, map.*

selenography, n. [1. sèlinógrafi; 2. sèlinógrəfi]. **seleno- & -graphy.** Science which deals with the physical geography of the moon, with the mapping of the moon's surface &c.

selenology, n. [1. sèlinóloji; 2. sèlinólədži]. **seleno- & -logy.** The branch of astronomy dealing with the moon.

selenotropic, adj. [1. sèlinotrópik; 2. sèlinətrópik]. **seleno- & -tropic.** (bot., of plants) Turning towards the moon.

selenotropism, -tropy, n. [1. sèlinótropi(zm); 2. sèlinótrəpi(zəm)]. See prec. & **-ism.** (bot.) Tendency to curve upwards under moonlight.

Seleucid, n. [1. selū́sid; 2. seljū́sid], fr. Seleucus & **-id.** (hist.) A member of the dynasty which ruled over a greater part of Asia Minor, Syria, and Persia from 312 to c. 65 B.C., founded by Seleucus Nicator, general of Alexander the Great.

self, n. [1. self; 2. self]. O.E. *self* &c., M.E. *self*; O.S., O. Fris. *self*, Goth. *silba*; etymol. unknown. **1.** One's own individual personality, and identity, as distinct from those of others; the ego: *to be conscious of self*; *one's own self*. **2.** One's own individual interests, advantage; things connected with and affecting oneself thought of to the exclusion of everything else: *thoughts centred on self*; *to have no thought of self*; *to put self first*. **3.** The essential quality, character, genius, quintessence, inmost nature, of anything: *some believe that we get a glimpse of Shakespeare's very self in the Sonnets*; *Keats's Odes seem to be the expression of beauty's self*. **4.** Various commercial or vulgar uses: **a** for *me, myself*: *a room for self and wife*; **b** (on cheques) *pay to self*, to the person who signs the cheque; **c** Phr. (commerc., in letters) *your good selves*, you, that is, the heads of the firm, to whom the letter is addressed.

self-, pref. expressing (1) reflexive action, direct or indirect: *self-defence, self-sacrificing* &c.; (2) relation with the self: *self-conscious*; (3) action independent of external agency, automatic: *self-fertilize*; *self-sown*; (4) natural, uniform, unmixed, pure condition: *self-coloured*. The number of possible formations with this prefix is almost infinite.

-self, suff. Used to form a reflexive personal pronouns: *to hurt oneself* &c.; **b** emphatic pronouns: *if you want something done you had better do it yourself*; *I myself have known sorrow* &c.

self-abandoned, adj. [1. sélf abándund; 2. sélf əbǽndənd]. Abandoned, given up to oneself, and one's own desires, impulses &c.

self-abasement, n. [1. sélf abā́sment; 2. sélf əbéismənt]. **a** Abasement, shame, humiliation, as result of consciousness of guilt &c.; **b** act of humiliating oneself.

self-abhorrence, n. [1. sélf abhórens; 2. sélf əbhórəns]. Abhorrence, detestation, of oneself.

self-absorbed, adj. [1. sélf absórbd; 2. sélf əbsṓbd]. Absorbed in, taken up with, one's own thoughts, interests, and affairs.

self-adjustment, n. [1. sélf ajústment; 2. sélf ədžástmənt]. Automatic adjustment (of parts of machinery &c.).

self-adornment, n. [1. sélf adórnment; 2. sélf ədṓnmənt]. Adornment of oneself.

self-applause, n. [1. sélf apláwz; 2. sélf əplṓz]. Applause of oneself, self-praise.

self-appointed, adj. [1. sélf apóinted; 2. sélf əpóintid]. Appointed by oneself.

self-assertion, n. [1. sélf asérshun; 2. sélf əsə́ʃən]. The asserting, putting forward, of oneself, one's opinions, claims, or rights.

self-assertive, adj. [1. sélf asértiv; 2. sélf əsə́tiv]. Given to self-assertion; pushing, bumptious.

self-binder, n. [1. sélf bínder; 2. sélf báində]. **a** An agricultural machine, with automatic attachment for binding sheaves as they are reaped; **b** portfolio fitted with an easily manipulated device for holding together loose sheets &c.

self-blinded, adj. [1. sélf blínded; 2. sélf bláindid]. Deluded by one's own stupidity.

self-centred, adj. [1. sélf sénterd; 2. sélf séntəd]. Centred in, preoccupied with, oneself, one's own interests and affairs.

self-closing, adj. [1. sélf klṓzing; 2. sélf klóuziŋ]. (of door &c.). Closing automatically.

self-collected, adj. [1. sélf kulékted; 2. sélf kəléktid]. Self-possessed; calm, cool, having presence of mind.

self-coloured, adj. [1. sélf kùlurd; 2. sélf kàləd]. **1.** (of textile materials &c.) Of one colour throughout. **2.** (of flowers) **a** Of one colour; **b** of its natural, wild colour before cultivation.

self-command, n. [1. sélf kumáhnd; 2. sélf kəmā́nd]. Control, command, of oneself; self-possession; power of controlling one's feelings.

self-communion, n. [1. sélf kumū́niun; 2. sélf kəmjū́njən]. Communion with oneself; meditation upon one's own spiritual condition; introspection.

self-complacence, -cy, n. [1. sélf kumplā́sens(i); 2. sélf kəmpléisəns(i)]. State, quality, of being self-complacent; self-satisfaction.

self-complacent, adj. [1. sélf kumplā́sent; 2. sélf kəmpléisənt]. Unduly satisfied with oneself, one's abilities, appearance &c.

self-conceit, n. [1. sélf kunsḗt; 2. sélf kənsít]. Conceit; exaggerated opinion of one's own powers, appearance, merits &c.

self-confidence, n. [1. sèlf kónfidens; 2. sèlf kónfidəns]. Confidence in oneself, one's own power, strength &c.; self-reliance.

self-confident, adj. [1. sèlf kónfident; 2. sèlf kónfidənt]. Confident of oneself, one's powers &c.; self-reliant.

self-confidently, adv. In a self-confident manner.

self-conscious, adj. [1. sèlf kónshus; 2. sèlf kónʃəs]. **1.** Over-conscious of oneself, of one's movements, behaviour &c., in the presence of others; easily embarrassed, awkward, shy. **2.** (philos.) [1. sélf-; 2. sélf-] Conscious of the self or ego, as both subject and object of experience.

self-consciously, adv. **1.** In a self-conscious manner. **2.** (philos.) By, through, the self-conscious mind or self-consciousness.

self-consciousness, n. **1.** State of being self-conscious. **2.** (philos.) The faculty of apprehending subjective experiences or phenomena.

self-contained, adj. [1. sèlf kuntā́nd; 2. sèlf kəntéind]. **1.** (of persons) Reserved, uncommunicative; self-controlled. **2.** (of things) Contained in itself, compact; specif. **a** (of houses, flats &c.) having all necessary rooms, domestic offices &c. together and separate from another house or flat; esp. having a separate entrance and staircase; **b** (of machines) having all the working parts in one framework or case.

self-contradiction, n. [1. sélf kòntradíkshun; 2. sélf kòntrədíkʃən]. **a** Act or state of contradicting oneself or itself; specif. **b** a proposition containing two terms, one of which contradicts the other.

self-contradictory, adj. [1. sélf kòntradíkturi; 2. sélf kòntrədíktəri]. Containing, expressing, a self-contradiction.

self-control, n. [1. sèlf kontrṓl; 2. sèlf kəntróul]. Control of oneself, one's emotions, temper &c.; self-command, self-restraint.

self-deceit, n. [1. sèlf desḗt; 2. sèlf disít]. The deceiving of oneself; state of being deceived or misled by oneself; self-deception, self-delusion.

self-deception, n. [1. sèlf desépshun; 2. sèlf disépʃən]. Self-deceit.

self-defence, n. [1. sèlf deféns; 2. sèlf diféns]. Defence of oneself, one's property, rights, person &c. Phrs. *the art of self-defence*, boxing; *in self-defence*, in order to defend oneself, not as an aggressive action.

self-delusion, n. [1. sèlf delū́zhun; 2. sèlf diljū́žən]. Self-deception, self-deceit.

self-denial, n. [1. sèlf denīal; 2. sèlf dináiəl]. Act, practice, of refusing to gratify one's desires; abstention from pleasure.

self-denying, adj. [1. sèlf denīing; 2. sèlf dinái-iŋ]. Practising self-denial; of the nature of self-denial; *self-denying ordinance*, (hist.) a resolution of the Long Parliament, 1645, declaring that no members should hold any civil or military office or command.

self-destruction, n. [1. sèlf destrúkshun; 2. sèlf distrákʃən]. Suicide.

self-determination, n. [1. sélf detèrmináshun; 2. sélf dɪtʌ̄minéiʃən]. **1.** Determination by one's own mind as to one's actions, without subjection to or interference by external influence; free will as opposed to determinism or fatalism. **2.** Specif., right, power, of a race or nation to determine its own form of government without interference by, or reference to, any foreign power.

self-devotion, n. [1. sèlf devṓshun; 2. sèlf dɪvóuʃən]. Devotion of oneself and one's interests to the good of others; self-sacrifice.

self-display, n. [1. sèlf displā́; 2. sèlf dɪspléi]. Display, showing off of oneself, one's wealth &c.

self-distrust, n. [1. sèlf distrúst; 2. sèlf dɪstrʌ́st]. Distrust, want of confidence, in oneself; reverse of *self-confidence*.

self-educated, adj. [1. sèlf édūkàted; 2. sèlf édjukèitɪd]. Educated by oneself, without teachers or without pecuniary help; self-taught.

self-elective, adj. [1. sèlf eléktiv; 2. sèlf ɪléktɪv]. **a** (of an assembly or body of persons) Having the right of electing its own members by co-optation; **b** (of a person) having the right to nominate or elect himself to a position, membership of a body &c.

self-esteem, n. [1. sèlf estḗm; 2. sèlf ɪstím]. Esteem, good opinion, of oneself; self-respect; self-conceit.

self-evident, adj. [1. sèlf évident; 2. sèlf évɪdənt]. Evidently true without proof or argument; producing conviction upon mere statement.

self-evidently, adv. Without proof or reasoning.

self-examination, n. [1. sélf egzàmináshun; 2. sélf ɪgzæ̀mɪnéiʃən]. Examination of one's own mind, conscience, motives &c.

self-existent, adj. [1. sèlf egzístent; 2. sèlf ɪgzístənt]. (of God) Existing of or by the self; existing independently of a cause external to self.

self-explanatory, adj. [1. sèlf eksplánaturi; 2. sèlf ɪksplǽnətəri]. Explaining itself; carrying its own explanation with it without further demonstration.

self-feeding, adj. [1. sèlf fḗding; 2. sèlf fídɪŋ]. (of machine, boiler &c.) Supplying itself with fuel &c. automatically.

self-fertilization, n. [1. sélf fèrtilīzáshun; 2. sélf fʌ̀tɪlaizéiʃən]. The fertilization of flowers with pollen from the same or other flowers on same plant.

self-governing, adj. [1. sèlf gúverning; 2. sèlf gʌ́vənɪŋ]. **1.** Governing oneself, exercising self-control. **2.** Specif., having, exercising, independent political government; autonomous: *the self-governing Dominions and the Crown Colonies.*

self-government, n. [1. sèlf gúvernment; 2. sèlf gʌ́vənmənt]. **1.** Self-control. **2.** Independent, democratic, political government; autonomy.

self-heal, n. [1. sèlf hḗl; 2. sèlf híəl]. (bot.) A perennial herb with purple flowers, *Prunella vulgaris*, allied to sage, marjoram, thyme &c., formerly supposed to heal wounds &c.

self-help, n. [1. sèlf hélp; 2. sèlf hélp]. Use of one's own powers, unaided by other agency, to secure one's improvement and success in life.

self-importance, n. [1. sèlf impórtans; 2. sèlf ɪmpɔ́təns]. **a** Exaggerated sense of one's own importance or worth; self-conceit; **b** pomposity of manner.

self-important, adj. [1. sèlf impórtant; 2. sèlf ɪmpɔ́tənt]. Having, exhibiting, self-importance.

self-induction, n. [1. sèlf indúkshun; 2. sèlf ɪndʌ́kʃən]. (elect.) The production of counter-electro-motive force by the variation of direction in an alternating current.

self-inductive, adj. [1. sèlf indúktiv; 2. sèlf ɪndʌ́ktɪv]. (elect.) Capable of producing, tending to produce, self-induction.

self-indulgence, n. [1. sèlf indúljens; 2. sèlf ɪndʌ́ldʒəns]. Indulgence, gratification, of one's own appetites and passions, without due self-restraint.

self-indulgent, adj. [1. sèlf indúljent; 2. sèlf ɪndʌ́ldʒənt]. Giving way to self-indulgence.

self-inflicted, adj. [1. sélf inflikted; 2. sélf ɪnflɪ́ktɪd]. Inflicted on or by oneself.

self-interest, n. [1. sèlf ínterest; 2. sèlf íntərɪst]. Consideration of one's own interests; selfishness.

self-interested, adj. [1. sèlf ínterested; 2. sèlf íntərɪstɪd]. Animated by self-interest.

selfish, adj. [1. sélfish; 2. sélfɪʃ]. **self** & **-ish**. **1. a** Considering primarily oneself and one's desires and pleasures; consulting and indulging one's own desires and interests without regard to how such conduct may affect others; **b** (of conduct and action) based upon, arising from, regard taken primarily of one's own desires and interests. **2.** (of ethical system and theory) Regarding, adducing, self-interest and the gratification of self as the mainspring of human conduct.

selfishly, adv. Prec. & **-ly**. In a selfish manner; having regard only to oneself.

selfishness, n. See prec. & **-ness**. State, quality, of being selfish.

self-knowledge, n. [1. sèlf nólej; 2. sèlf nɔ́lɪdʒ]. Knowledge of self; knowledge of one's own powers, character, motives, limitations &c.

selfless, adj. [1. sélfles; 2. sélflɪs]. Forgetful of, having no regard for, self; unselfish.

selflessness, n. Quality of being selfless.

self-limited, adj. [1. sèlf límited; 2. sèlf límɪtɪd]. Limited, defined, by one's own or its own character, esp. (med.) of certain diseases running their natural course within a specified period.

self-love, n. [1. sèlf lúv; 2. sèlf lʌ́v]. **1.** Love of oneself; instinctive impulse to protect one's own life and happiness. **2.** Self-indulgence, selfishness.

self-made, adj. [1. sèlf mā́d; 2. sèlf méid]. Made by oneself, esp. having risen from a humble position to one of wealth, influence &c., by one's own efforts, without money or help from others: *a self-made man; self-made career.*

self-mastery, n. [1. sèlf máhsteri; 2. sèlf mā́stəri]. Mastery of self; self-command, self-control.

self-murder, n. [1. sèlf mèrder; 2. sèlf mʌ́də]. Suicide.

self-neglect, n. [1. sèlf neglékt; 2. sèlf nɪglékt]. **1.** Neglect of one's own interests; unselfishness. **2.** Neglect of one's own person; uncleanliness.

self-opinionated, adj. [1. sèlf ōpínyunāted; 2. sèlf oupínjəneitɪd]. Sticking obstinately to one's own opinions; self-willed.

self-opinioned, adj. [1. sèlf ōpínyund; 2. sèlf oupínjənd]. Self-opinionated.

self-possessed, adj. [1. sèlf puzést; 2. sèlf pəzést]. Having self-possession; cool, collected.

self-possession, n. [1. sèlf puzéshun; 2. sèlf pəzéʃən]. Possession of, control over, one's emotions, behaviour &c.; self-command, self-control; coolness, composure, in emergencies.

self-preservation, n. [1. sélf prèzerváshun; 2. sélf prèzəvéiʃən]. Preservation of oneself from injury or death; instinctive impulse to save one's own life and escape injury.

self-raising, adj. [1. sèlf rā́zing; 2. sèlf réizɪŋ]. (of flour) Containing a certain proportion of baking-powder.

self-realization, n. [1. sélf rèalīzáshun; 2. sélf rɪəlaizéiʃən]. Accomplishment of, freedom to develop to the utmost, all that of which one is capable in view of one's character, natural faculties, powers, passions &c.; esp. regarded as the end of ethical action.

self-recording, adj. [1. sèlf rekórding; 2. sèlf rɪkɔ́dɪŋ]. Self-registering.

self-regard, n. [1. sèlf regárd; 2. sèlf rɪgā́d]. Regard for oneself and one's interests.

self-registering, adj. [1. sèlf réjistring; 2. sèlf rédʒɪstrɪŋ]. (of instruments) Registering, recording, variations of phenomena automatically.

self-regulating, adj. [1. sèlf régūlāting; 2. sèlf régjuleitɪŋ]. (of mach.) Regulating, correcting, its movements automatically.

self-reliance, n. [1. sèlf relíans; 2. sèlf rɪláiəns]. Reliance on oneself, on one's own powers and faculties.

self-reliant, adj. [1. sèlf relíant; 2. sèlf rɪláiənt]. Relying on one's own powers, faculties, judgement &c.

self-renunciation, n. [1. sélf renùnsiáshun; 2. sélf rɪnànsiéiʃən]. Renunciation of one's own desires and interests for the sake of others, or for a cause or ideal.

self-reproach, n. [1. sèlf reprṓch; 2. sèlf rɪpróutʃ]. Reproach, censure, of oneself; remorse, prickings of conscience.

self-respect, n. [1. sèlf respékt; 2. sèlf rɪspékt]. Due regard for one's own dignity, conduct, position, character, reputation &c.; regard for decency of behaviour and for a certain fitting or worthy standard of conduct.

self-respecting, adj. [1. sèlf respékting; 2. sèlf rɪspéktɪŋ]. Having, exhibiting, self-respect.

self-restraint, n. [1. sèlf restrā́nt; 2. sèlf rɪstréint]. Restraint, control, of oneself; self-control.

self-righteous, adj. [1. sèlf ríchus; 2. sèlf ráitʃəs]. Righteous, virtuous, upright, in one's own opinion; pharisaical.

self-righteousness, n. Quality, state, of being self-righteous; pharisaism.

self-sacrifice, n. [1. sèlf sákrifīs; 2. sèlf sǽkrɪfais]. Sacrifice of oneself for the good of others; surrender of one's interest, advantage &c., to those of others; self-denial.

self-sacrificing, adj. [1. sèlf sákrifīsing; 2. sèlf sǽkrɪfaisɪŋ]. Sacrificing, surrendering, oneself for the good of others; exhibiting self-sacrifice.

self-same, adj. [1. sélf sām; 2. sélf seim]. The very same, precisely the same, identical, an emphatic form of **same**.

self-satisfaction, n. [1. sèlf satisfákshun; 2. sèlf sætɪsfǽkʃən]. **1.** State of feeling satisfied with oneself; self-complacency. **2.** Satisfaction of one's desires, appetites &c.

self-satisfied, adj. [1. sèlf sátisfīd; 2. sèlf sǽtɪsfaid]. Satisfied with oneself; smugly conceited.

self-satisfying, adj. [1. sèlf sátisfīing; 2. sèlf sǽtɪsfaiɪŋ]. Giving satisfaction to oneself.

self-seeker, n. [1. sèlf sḗker; 2. sèlf síkə]. One who is perpetually thinking of how to further his own interests, and whose chief motive is self-advancement; a pushing person with an axe to grind.

self-seeking, adj. & n. [1. sèlf sḗking; 2. sèlf síkɪŋ]. **1.** adj. Seeking primarily one's own advantage; striving to advance one's own interests. **2.** n. Act, conduct, of a self-seeker.

self-sown, adj. [1. sèlf sṓn; 2. sèlf sóun]. (of plants) Sprung from seed scattered by natural processes direct from parent plant.

self-starter, n. [1. sèlf stárter; 2. sèlf stā́tə]. **1.** Any one of various electric or other devices for automatically starting the internal combustion engine of a motor-car &c. without the use of a crank-handle. **2.** A motor-car &c. fitted with such device.

self-sterile, adj. [1. sèlf stérīl; 2. sèlf stérail]. (bot.) Not capable of self-fertilization, needing pollen from other plants in order to become fertilized.

self-styled, adj. [1. sèlf stī́ld; 2. sèlf stáild]. Called, denominated, by oneself, but without any right; soi-disant: *a self-styled 'professor' of conjuring.*

self-sufficiency, n. [1. sèlf sufíshensi; 2. sèlf səfíʃənsi]. Quality, state, of being self-sufficient or self-sufficing; **a** capability of getting, doing, what one wants without external aid; **b** self-importance, presumptuousness.

self-sufficient, adj. [1. sèlf sufíshent; 2. sèlf səfíʃənt]. Sufficient, sufficing, for oneself; **a** capable of getting what one wants without others; **b** self-important, presumptuous.

self-sufficing, adj. [1. sèlf sufísing; 2. sèlf səfáisɪŋ]. Sufficing to oneself; independent of others for help, advice, society &c.

self-suggestion, n. [1. sèlf sujéschun ; 2. sèlf sədžéstʃən]. Auto-suggestion, suggestion arising from oneself, as when hypnotized.
self-supporting, adj. [1. sèlf supórting ; 2. sèlf səpɔ̃tiŋ]. Supporting, maintaining, oneself or itself.
self-surrender, n. [1. sèlf surénder ; 2. sèlf səréndə]. Surrender of oneself, of one's will, to another.
self-sustained, adj. [1. sèlf sustánd ; 2. sèlf səstéind]. Sustained, supported, by oneself or itself.
self-taught, adj. [1. sèlf táwt ; 2. sèlf tɔ̃t]. Taught by oneself, self-educated.
self-torture, n. [1. sèlf tórchur ; 2. sèlf tɔ̃tʃə]. Torture deliberately inflicted on oneself.
self-will, n. [1. sèlf wíl ; 2. sèlf wíl]. Obstinacy, pig-headedness.
self-willed, adj. [1. sèlf wíld ; 2. sèlf wíld]. Obstinate, pig-headed.
self-winding, adj. [1. sèlf wínding ; 2. sèlf wáindiŋ]. (of clock) Winding itself automatically at certain intervals by an electric device &c.
Seljuk, n. [1. seljóōk; 2. seldžúk]. Turk. *Seljuq*. A member of a Turkish Moslem dynasty, founded by Seljuk, A.D. 1000, which ruled in Central and Western Asia from the 11th to the 13th cents.
sell (I.), vb. trans. & intrans. [1. sel ; 2. sɛl]. O.E. *sellan*, 'to give; give up, surrender; to sell', M.E. *sellen* ; O.S. *sellian*, O.H.G. *saljan*, O.N. *selja*, Goth. *saljan*, 'to offer'; prob. cogn. w. Gk. *heleîn*, 'to take with the hand, grasp; to take', fr. *sel- &c.; the Gmc. vb., it is suggested, was orig. a causative, meaning 'to cause to take, hand over to, offer, give'; the sense 'give in exchange for something, sell', is much later. Cp. also **consult**. **A.** trans. **1.** To transfer the ownership of (goods, property &c.) to another in return for a valuable consideration, usually for money; to dispose of by sale, to hand over in return for a price; the correlative of *buy*: *to sell one's pigs at the market*; *to sell a horse for £100*. Phrs. *to sell one's life dearly*, to make an enemy pay dearly by killing as many as possible before being killed oneself; (colloq.) *to sell a person a pup*, cheat him, take him in, let him in for a bad bargain; *to sell the pass*, be unfaithful to one's trust; give opponents an advantage, give away some important point in a dispute. **2.** To deal in, be engaged in the sale of; to stock, keep (goods) for sale: *grocers often sell wine and spirits*; *do you sell postage-stamps?*; *we sell only articles of the first quality*. **3.** To help in the sale of, cause to be sold: *good advertising will sell goods*. **4.** To part with, give up, surrender, sacrifice (something non-material) in exchange for a bribe or material inducement: *to sell one's honour, self-respect, peace of mind* &c. **5.** To betray, be a traitor to, break one's faith with, be disloyal to: *to sell one's country, one's party*. **6.** (colloq.) To play a trick upon; to cheat, deceive, disappoint; (usually in pass.) *to be sold over a bargain*; *sold again*, as exclamation of disappointment &c. if of oneself, of triumph if referring to another. **B.** intrans. **1.** (of persons) To be ready to sell; to deal in: *if you will sell, I will buy*. **2.** (of goods) To become object of sale, to find buyers, to be sold: *wheat is selling well*; *goods of that quality will never sell*. **C.** Followed by preposition or adverb. *Sell off*, to dispose of (the remainder of a stock of goods) at bargain prices. *Sell out*, intrans., **a** to sell one's stock of goods, shares in a company &c.; **b** (obs.) to retire from the army by selling one's commission, in the days of purchase. *Sell up* (person or goods), trans., to sell the goods of a debtor, under a distraint or legal process: *to be sold up*, have one's goods sold to satisfy creditors.
sell (II.), n., fr. prec. (colloq. slang) **a** A disillusionment, a disappointment: *we were too late for the luncheon, which was rather a sell*; *it was an awful sell going twenty miles only to find our friends had left*; **b** a hoax, trick, catch: *the much-vaunted weed-killer was just a sell*.
sellanders, n. See **sallenders**.
seller, n. [1. séler ; 2. sélə]. **sell (I.)** & **-er**. **1. a** Person who sells, who deals in, goods: *a bookseller*; **b** one who offers (something) for sale or is ready to sell: *are you a seller?* **2.** Something which sells or is sold: *a good, a poor, seller*. Phr. *a best-seller*, book that is largely bought.
seltzer water, n. [1. séltser wàwter ; 2. séltsə wɔ̀tə], fr. Pl. N. Selters, near Wiesbaden, Germany. Aerated mineral water consumed alone or mixed with spirits.
selvage, also **selvedge**, n. [1. sélvij ; 2. sélvidž], fr. M. Du. *selfegge*. **self** & **edge**. **1.** An edge or border of cloth, so woven as to prevent ravelling. **2.** The edge plate of a lock into which the bolt is shot. **3.** Selvagee.
selvagee, n. [1. sèlvajḗ; 2. sèlvidží], fr. **selvage**. A coil of rope-yarn wound tightly together by lashings; used for slings, collars &c.
semantics, n. pl. [1. semántiks ; 2. simǽntiks], fr. Fr. *sémantique*, fr. Gk. *sēmantikós*, 'significant, meaning', fr. *sēmainein*, 'to signify', fr. *sêma*, 'a sign'; cogn. w. Scrt. *dhyāma*, 'thought', *dhyāti*, 'to reflect upon'. Branch of linguistic study which deals with the development of meaning.
semaphore (I.), n. [1. sémafōr ; 2. séməfɔ̄], fr. Fr. *sémaphore*, word coined fr. Gk. *sêma*, 'sign', see **semantics**, & *phorá*, 'a carrying, bearing', see **-phore**. **1.** An apparatus used for signalling, consisting of a post with two movable arms at the top which can be swung into various positions, each representing a letter of the alphabet; **a** (hist.) device of this kind used to send messages from station to station over long distances, until superseded by the telegraph; **b** (nav.) similar device still used at sea for sending short messages from ship to ship. **2.** Similar device, with red and green lights for night, used for signalling on railways.
semaphore (II.), vb. trans. & intrans., fr. prec. To signal, send (messages), by semaphore.
semasiology, n. [1. sèmāzióloji ; 2. simeiziɔ́lədží], fr. Gk. *sēmasía*, 'significance, meaning', fr. *sêma*, 'sign', & **-logy**. Semantics.
sematic, adj. [1. semátik ; 2. simǽtik], fr. Gk. *sēmat-(os)*, *sêma*, 'sign', see **semantics**, & **-ic**. (biol.) Serving as a sign, of warning or attraction: *sematic colouration*.
semblable, adj. [1. sémblabl ; 2. sémbləbl]. Fr. See next word & **-able**. (archaic) Having semblance; resembling, like, similar.
semblance, n. [1. sémblans ; 2. sémbləns]. Fr., fr. Lat. *simulant-*, Pres. Part. stem of *simulāre*, 'to make like, copy, represent', see **simulate**, & **-ce**. **1.** Likeness, image, similitude: *Satan appeared to Eve in the semblance of a serpent*. **2.** Outward show or appearance: *to have at least the semblance of virtue, honesty* &c.
semble, vb. intrans. [1. sémbl ; 2. sémbl]. Fr. *il semble*, 'it seems'; 3rd pers. pres. indic. See prec. (law) It seems, it would appear; contracted as *semb.*, *sem.*; used in a judgement to express an obiter dictum.
semé, adj. [1. sémā ; 2. sémei]. Fr., 'sown', P.P. of *semer*, 'to sow', see **semen**. (her., of the field) Sown, powdered, strewn: *semé of fleur-de-lis* &c.
semeio-, pref. Form in compounds of Gk. *sēmeîon*, 'sign', fr. *sêma*, see **semantics**.
semeiological, adj. [1. sèmīōlójikl ; 2. simaiolɔ́džikl]. Prec. & **-logical**. Pertaining to semeiology.
semeiologist, n. [1. sèmīólojist ; 2. simaiɔ́lədžist]. See prec. & **-ist**. Student of, expert in, semeiology.
semeiology, semiology, n. [1. sèmīóloji ; 2. simaiɔ́lədži]. See prec. & **-logy**. **1.** Art of using symbols to express ideas. **2.** (med.) The study of the symptoms of disease.
semeiotics, n. pl. [1. sèmīótiks ; 2. simaiɔ́tiks], fr. Gk. *sēmeiotikós*, fr. *sēmeîon*, 'sign'. See prec. words & **-ic**. Semeiology.
semen, n. [1. sḗmen ; 2. símɛn]. Lat., 'seed'; fr. base *sē-, *se-, cp. Lat. *serere*, 'to sow', & the words given under **seed** & **sow (II.)**. Spermatic fluid of male animal.
semester, n. [1. seméster ; 2. siméstə]. Germ., fr. Fr. *semestre*, fr. Lat. *semestris*, 'every six months'; for *sex-*, fr. *sex*, 'six', see **sex-**, & *mensis*, 'month', see **menses**. A half-year, period of six months; esp. as applied to the two terms into which the educational year is divided in German and other continental universities and schools.
semi-, pref. [1. sémi; 2. sémi]. Lat. *sēmi-*, 'half'; cogn. w. Gk. *hēmi-*, see **hemi-**; Scrt. *sāmi-*; O.H.G. *sāmi-*, O.E. *sōm-* (as in O.E. *sōmcwicu*, 'half-alive', O.H.G. *sāmiquek*). Living pref. capable of being used before any n. & adj. in Engl.; having the sense **a** half: *semicircle, semicircular*; **b** partly, to some extent, more or less: *semi-opaque, semi-idiotic*.
semi-annual, adj. Half-yearly; occurring, published, once every six months or twice a year.
semi-automatic, adj. Acting, operated, partly automatically, partly by hand.
semi-barbarian, adj. & n. **1.** adj. Half-civilized, only partly civilized. **2.** n. Person in a state of semi-barbarism.
semi-barbarism, n. State, quality, of being half or only partly civilized.
semi-barbarous, adj. Semi-barbarian.
semibreve, n. [1. sémibrēv ; 2. sémibrīv]. (mus.) A note of half the duration of a breve, equivalent to two minims or four crotchets, a whole note.
semi-bull, n. A bull issued by a Pope between his election and enthronement.
semi-centennial, n. & adj. **1.** n. Celebration of a fiftieth anniversary. **2.** adj. Occurring once every fifty years; pertaining to the end of a half-century.
semi-chorus, n. (mus.) **a** A passage to be sung by half or part of a choir or chorus; **b** music composed for a semi-chorus.
semicircle, n. [1. sémisẽrkl ; 2. sémisʌ̄kl]. **1. a** A half circle; **b** group of persons or objects arranged so as to form a semicircle. **2.** A surveying instrument for measuring angles.
semicircular, adj. [1. sèmisẽ́rkūlar ; 2. sèmisʌ̄́kjulə]. **a** Having the shape of, **b** arranged in, a semicircle.
semi-civilized, adj. Half, partly, civilized; not fully civilized.
semicolon, n. [1. sèmikólun, sémikōlun ; 2. sèmikóulən, sémikoulən]. A mark of punctuation (;), indicating a more marked separation than the comma, and less than the full stop or colon.
semi-conscious, adj. Half, partially, conscious.
semi-demisemiquaver, n. (mus.) A note of half the duration of a demisemiquaver.
semi-detached, adj. (of a house) Having another built so as to be joined to it on one side.
semi-diurnal, adj. Lasting half a day; lasting half the time between the rising and setting of a heavenly body.
semi-double, adj. (of flowers) Having an extra number of floral leaves of which, however, only the outer ones are converted into full petals.
semi-final, adj. & n. **a** adj. (of a round in a match) Played immediately before the final round; **b** n., the round before the final.
semi-fluid, adj. & n. **1.** adj. Partially fluid, viscous. **2.** n. Semi-fluid substance.
semi-fluidity, n. State, quality, of being semi-fluid.
semilunar, adj. [1. sémilúnar ; 2. sémiljúnə]. Shaped like a half-moon or crescent; crescent-shaped; specif. (anat.) *semilunar bone, cartilage, valves* &c.
semi-monthly, adj. & n. **1.** adj. Occurring, made, done, twice in a month. **2.** n. Something occurring, appearing, twice a month; specif., journal or magazine published twice a month.

semi-mute, adj. Having only partial power of speech; nearly, practically dumb, usually owing to congenital deafness.

seminal, adj. [1. sḗminal; 2. símịnəl]. Lat. *sēminālis*. See **semen** & **-al**. **1.** Of, pertaining to, containing, producing, the seed of plants or the semen of male animals: *seminal leaf*, a cotyledon; *seminal fluid*, semen; *seminal ducts, glands* &c. **2.** Of, relating to, reproduction; germinal, reproductive; **a** (in physical sense) *seminal power, weakness* &c.; **b** (of non-physical things) productive, pregnant, potential: *seminal thoughts, principle* &c. **3.** Contained in the seed; rudimentary, primary: *in the seminal stage of life*; also fig.

seminally, adv. Prec. & **-ly**. In a seminal manner; originally, primarily.

seminar, n. [1. sèminár; 2. sèmịnā́]. Borrowed fr. Mod. Germ. See **seminary**. A class or group of students, at a university, engaged in learning the methods of research under the direction of a professor.

seminarist, n. [1. séminarist; 2. sémịnərist]. See next word & **-ist**. One trained in a Roman Catholic seminary; a seminary priest.

seminary, n. [1. séminari; 2. sémịnəri], fr. O. Fr. *seminaire*, fr. Lat. *sēminārium*, 'seed-plot, nursery garden, seminary', neut. sing. as n. of *sēminārius*, 'relating to seed'. See **semen** & **-ary**. **1. a** A place of education, formerly a high-sounding name for a school; an academy: *a seminary for young ladies*; **b** (fig.) a nursery, training-ground, school: *a seminary of revolution, vice* &c. **2.** Specif., a training college for the Roman Catholic priesthood.

semination, n. [1. sḕ-, sèminā́shun; 2. sì-, sèminéiʃən], fr. Lat. *sēminātiōn-(em)*, fr. *sēmināt-(um)*, P.P. type of *sēmināre*, 'to beget, procreate', see **semen**, & **-ion**. **1.** Act of sowing or spreading; dissemination. **2.** (bot.) Process, mode, of seeding.

seminiferous, adj. [1. sèminíferus; 2. sìmínífərəs]. See **semen** & **-ferous**. **a** (of plants) Seed-bearing; **b** (animal physiol.) Conveying semen: *seminiferous tubes*.

semi-official, adj. Not fully official, having some official authority only; not directly or officially authorized: *a semi-official report in the press*.

semio-, pref. See **semeio-**.

semi-opal, n. A variety of opal without the opalescent quality of the true opal.

semi-oviparous, adj. Not completely viviparous, producing the young not completely out of the egg-stage, as marsupials.

semi-Pelagianism, n. A theological doctrine of the 9th cent., which combined the free-will principles of Pelagius with the predestination of Augustine.

semi-plume, n. (ornith.) A feather with the shaft of a true feather, but with a downy web.

semi-precious, adj. (of gems) Referring to those of inferior value to precious stones; e.g. the garnet, aquamarine, carbuncle &c.

semiquaver, n. [1. sémikwā̀ver; 2. sémikwèivə]. (mus.) A note having half the duration of the quaver, one-sixteenth of a semibreve.

Semite, n. [1. sḗmīt; 2. símait], fr. Gk. *Sēm*, translating Heb. *Shem*, & **-ite**. Member of any one of several Asiatic races, including Jews, Arabs, and in ancient times, the Assyrians, Babylonians, Phoenicians &c.

Semitic, adj. & n. [1. semítik; 2. simítik]. Prec. & **-ic**. **1.** adj. Pertaining to, connected with, the Semites or their languages. **2.** n. A Semitic language.

Semitism, n. [1. sḗmitizm; 2. símitizəm]. **Semite** & **-ism**. **1.** Semitic characteristics, racial or linguistic. **2.** A Semitic idiom.

Semitize, vb. trans. [1. sḗmitīz; 2. símitaiz]. **Semite** & **-ize**. To give a Semitic character to: *many parts of London are largely Semitized*.

semitone, n. [1. sémitōn; 2. sémitoun]. (mus.) A half-tone, one of the lesser intervals of the diatonic scale.

semi-tropical, adj. (of climate, vegetation &c.) Nearly tropical; bordering on the tropics.

semi-uncial, adj. Designating a handwriting between the uncial and the cursive.

semi-vowel, n. Misleading term best avoided, applied by some philologists **a** to certain original sounds [w, j], which either remain as consonants (before vowels), or become the vowels [i, u] (before consonants, and finally); **b** to [w, j], when uttered with very weak consonantal friction.

semolina, n. [1. sèmolḗna; 2. sèməlínə], fr. Ital. *semolina*, dimin. of *semola*, 'bran', fr. Lat. *simila*, 'the finest wheat flour after being sifted', fr. Gk. *semídalis*, wh. is prob. also a loan-word. A meal which is a coarsely ground product of wheat, used for making macaroni, and otherwise in cookery.

Sempervivum, n. [1. sèmpervívum; 2. sémpəváivəm]. Neo-Lat., fr. *semper*, 'always', & *vivum*, 'living'. See next word & **vivacious**. (bot.) A genus of plants with very fleshy leaves, including the houseleek.

sempiternal, adj. [1. sémpitḗrnal; 2. sémpitə́nəl], fr. Fr. *sempiternel*, Lat. *sempiternus*, 'everlasting, perpetual'; fr. *semper*, 'always,' derived fr. *sem-*, 'one', as in Lat. *semel*, 'once, a single time', see words in **simul-**, & *per*, 'through'; cp. also **sengreen**; for second element see **eternal**. (archaic, rhet., or poet). Everlasting, never-ending, eternal.

semplice, adj. [1. sémplichā; 2. sémplitʃɛ]. Ital., 'simple': cp. **simple**. (mus.) A direction that the music is to be rendered simply, without embellishments.

sempre, adv. [1. sémprā; 2. sémprɛ]. Ital., 'continually', fr. Lat. *semper*, 'always'. See under **sempiternal**. (mus.) A direction that the music is to be played throughout as directed; as *sempre forte*, loudly throughout &c.

sempstress, n. See **seamstress**.

sen, n. [1. sen; 2. sɛn]. Jap., fr. Chinese *chi'en*, 'coin'. A Japanese copper coin, one hundredth part of the yen.

senarius, n. [1. senā́rius; 2. sɛnɛ́əriəs]. Lat., 'consisting of six each'; a verse consisting of six feet', sc. *versus*; fr. *sēnī*, distrib. for **sex-ni*. See **sex-** & **-ary**. A Latin verse of six iambic feet.

senary, adj. [1. sḗnari; 2. sínəri]. Engl. form of prec. Containing, pertaining to, six.

senate, n. [1. sénat; 2. sénit], fr. Fr. *sénat*, fr. Lat. *senātus*, lit. 'council of elders', fr. base *sen-*, as in *senex*, 'old'. See **senile**. **1.** A council, assembly of elders, specif. **a** (anct. Rome) the chief council of the republic and of the Empire, consisting originally of the heads of the patrician families, but at an early date admitting representatives of the plebeians, having administrative, legislative, and judicial functions; **b** name given to deliberative, legislative bodies in many countries, esp. the Upper House of such bodies. **2.** The legislature considered as a whole with reference to its legislative functions, hence politics: *distinguished both at the bar and in the senate*. **3.** Chief academic deliberative body in some universities; applied to such bodies, although they are variously constituted and have differing functions, in Cambridge and the newer English Universities; *Senate house*, the building in which the senate meets, as at Cambridge University.

senator, n. [1. sénater; 2. sénətə], fr. Lat. *senātōr*. See prec. & **-or**. A member of a senate.

senatorial, adj. [1. sènatórial; 2. sènətɔ́riəl]. Prec. & **-ial**, cp. Fr. *sénatorial*. Pertaining, relating, to a senate or to a senator: *senatorial rank, powers* &c.

senatorship, n. [1. sénatership; 2. sénətəʃip]. **senator** & **-ship**. **1.** Office, rank, position of a senator. **2.** Period of such office.

senatus, n. [1. senā́tus; 2. sɛnéitəs]. Lat., 'senate', fr. base *sen-*, as in *senex*, 'old', see **senile**. **1.** The Roman Senate, q.v.; esp. in Phr. *Senatus populusque Romanus*, abbr. S.P.Q.R., the full title of the ancient Roman state, the senate and people of Rome. *Senatus consultum* (pl. *consulta*), a decree of the senate. **2.** Name given to chief academic deliberative body in Scottish universities, corresponding to what is elsewhere called a *senate*.

send (I.), vb. trans. & intrans. [1. send; 2. sɛnd]. O.E. *sendan*, fr. **sandjan*, M.E. *senden*; O.S. *sendian*, O.H.G. *senten*; O.N. *senda*; Goth. *sandjan*; the orig. sense is 'to cause to go'; cp. the O.E. *sīþ*, 'journey; time', fr. **sinþ-*, Goth. *sinþs*, 'time'; O.E. *gesīþ*, 'travelling companion', Goth. *gasinþja*; O.E. *sīþian*, 'to travel, depart, go'; a cogn. of Gmc. **sinþ-*, fr. earlier **sent-*, is believed to exist also in Lat. *sentīre*, 'to feel, perceive'. See **scent, sentiment, sense**. **A.** trans. **1.** To cause to go, or be carried, to dispatch, cause to be conveyed; to arrange for transit of: *to send a letter, a parcel, by post*; *to send goods by train*; *I will send you home in my car*; *to send troops by sea*; *to send one's boots to be mended*; *to send aid, relief, help, to*; *to send a message, an answer*. Phr. *to send word*, to have a message conveyed by any method: *send me word of your arrival*. **2.** To cause (person) to go from one place to another, by requesting or commanding: *if you are noisy, I shall send you to bed*; *send the children into the garden*; *send him to me at once*; *to send a missionary to the Jews*; *to send a messenger*; *to send an ambassador abroad* &c. Phr. *to send a person about his business, packing, to the right about*, dismiss him abruptly, get rid of him. **3. a** To cause (object) to move in a certain direction or manner, to a certain spot, by throwing, striking, propelling in any way: *send the ball over here, will you*; *to send a ball (at cricket) to the boundary*; *we sent several shots into the enemy*; *to send a stone rolling down the hill*; **b** to pass, hand &c. (an object): *send the wine round again*; *send your plates (up) for a second helping*. **4.** To bestow, give, grant, cause to come as a benefit, or the reverse: *God sent plagues upon the Egyptians*; *He sends the former and the latter rain*; (archaic) *God send you better health*; also in construction, *God send his life may be spared* &c., God grant that . . . Phr. *God send you a good deliverance*, formerly used by a judge in pronouncing sentence of death. **5.** To cause to be or become; to drive, only in such Phr. as **a** *to send a person mad, off his head, out of his mind*; **b** '*Send him victorious . . . Long to reign over us*', grant him long to reign (National Anthem). **B.** intrans. To send a messenger, message, or missive: *if you want me, please send*; *I sent and let him know his father was dead*. **C.** Followed by preposition or adverb. *Send away*, **1.** trans., **a** to dismiss (one's cook &c.); **b** to dispatch to a distance: *to send away one's garden produce*; **2.** intrans., to send a message, or order for to another place: *I have to send away for my groceries*. *Send down*, trans., **1.** to expel for a period from a college or the university; **2.** to lower, cause to fall; **a** *to send down temperature*; **b** (fig.) *to send down prices*. *Send for*, intrans., **a** to summon (person), ask, order, tell to come: *to send for the doctor*; **b** to order (things) to be brought to one: *to send for some more coal, a taxi* &c.; *to send to the butcher for some chops*; **c** to make request for dispatch of: *to send for help*. *Send forth*, trans., **a** to send out: *to send forth the labourers into the harvest*; **b** to give out, emit: *the sun sends forth light and heat*. *Send in*, trans., to forward, dispatch, hand in (to particular person or place): *to send in one's name as a candidate*; *to send in one's bill*; Phrs. *to send in one's papers*, to resign one's commission in army or navy; *to send in one's resignation*, to resign formally. *Send off*, trans., **a** to send away, dispatch (things): *to send off one's luggage*; **b** to dismiss, expel, drive away (persons). *Send out*, trans., **1.** (of human action) **a** to dispatch, commission (person): *to send out young men as missionaries*; **b** to enable to go away, arrange for journey of (persons): *to send boys* *out to the colonies*; **c** to disseminate, give out, cause to be received: *to send out invitations, notices* &c; **2.** (of natural processes) **a** to give off or out, emit: *a stove sends out heat*; *lamp sends out light*; **b** to put forth: *a plant sends out a new shoot* &c. *Send up*, trans., **a** to cause (a given person) to go to or reach: *to send up a report* (to headquarters &c.); **b** to throw, propel &c., to a given person or place: *to send the ball up to the bowler*; *send the red (ball) up to balk.*

send (II.), vb. intrans. & n. Origin doubtful; prob. same as prec. (naut.) **1.** vb. (of ship) **a** To plunge, be borne forward from one wave to another; **b** to lift up, heave upward in a heavy sea, contrasted with *pitch*. **2.** n. The driving, impelling movement of a wave: *the send of the sea.*

sendable, adj. [1. séndabl; 2. séndəbl]. **send** (I.) & **-able**. Capable of being sent.

sendal, n. [1. séndl; 2. séndl]. O. Fr., also *cendal*, fr. Low Lat. *cendalum*, cp. Gk. *sindṓn*, 'fine cloth from India'; Scrt. *sindhu-*, 'of, from, the Indus, or Sind.' A fine silk textile of the Middle Ages used for flags, rich costumes &c.

sender, n. [1. sénder; 2. séndə]. **send** (I.) & **-er**. **a** One who sends: *the sender of a letter, message* &c.; **b** that which sends or transmits, a telegraphic or telephonic transmitter.

send-off, n. Behaviour, esp. of a kindly, affectionate sort, on the departure of travellers by those who stay behind; expression of good wishes at starting: *to give a good send-off to.*

senega, seneka, n. [1. sénega, -ka; 2. sénegə, -kə], fr. *Seneca*, name of a N. Am. Indian tribe. (med.) The dried root of the Seneca snake-root, *Polygala senega*, used as an expectorant, and as a diuretic.

senescence, n. [1. senésens; 2. senésəns]. See next word & **-ce**. State of growing old; the beginning of old age.

senescent, adj. [1. senésent; 2. senésənt], fr. Lat. *senescent-(em)*, Pres. Part. of *senescere*, 'to grow old', formed fr. base of *senex*, 'old', q.v. under **senile**. In process of growing old.

seneschal, n. [1. séneshl; 2. sénəʃəl]. O. Fr., cp. Ital. *siniscalco*, Span. *senescal*; of Gmc. origin; first element is seen in Goth. *sineigs*, 'old', cogn. w. Lat. *senex*, see **senile**, & **senior**; the second element means 'servant', cp. O.H.G. *scalc*, O.E. *scealc*, Goth. *skalks*, for wh. see second element of **marshal**. A steward, majordomo, bailiff of a royal palace, noble's castle &c., in the Middle Ages; one of the great officers of state under the early French monarchy.

sengreen, n. [1. séngrēn; 2. séngrīn]. O.E. *singrēne*, 'green vegetables; the houseleek', *sin- is a widespread element in Gmc. occurring chiefly in compounds w. force of 'lasting, great', or simply as intens.; cp. O.E. *sincieldu*, 'great, enduring, cold'; Goth. *sinteins*, 'everlasting; occurring every day'; O.H.G. *sin-vluot*, 'the great flood', wh. in Mod. Germ. has by popular etymol. become *sündflut*, as though it meant 'the flood caused by man's sin', fr. *sünde*, 'sin'; the element is cogn. w. Lat. *semper*, 'ever'; cp. **sempiternal**. (archaic) The houseleek.

senhor, senhora, senhorita, n. [1. senyór, -yóra, -yoréta; 2. senjór, -jóra, -joríta]. Port., equiv. of Span. *señor*, Ital. *signor*, see **senior**. Title of courtesy used in addressing, or speaking of, a Portuguese gentleman or lady; Sir, Madam; Mr., Mrs., Miss.

senile, adj. [1. sénīl; 2. sínail], fr. Lat. *senīlis*, 'belonging to old people, senile', fr. base of *sen-ex*, 'old', & **-ile**; the base **sen-*, 'full of years, old', is found also in Gk. *hénos*, 'old,' fr. **sénos*; in Scrt. *sánaš*, 'old'; Lith. *senas*, 'old'; in Goth. *sineigs*; cp. **senate, seneschal**. Characteristic of, arising from, old age; marked by the signs of age; specif., showing the mental and bodily weakness and decay associated with old age; infirm, doting: *he has become perfectly senile*; *senile decay*, that of mind and body in old age; *senile dementia*, decay of mental faculties from old age.

senilely, adv. Prec. & **-ly**. In a senile manner.

senility, n. [1. seníliti; 2. siníliti, -áiliti]. **senile** & **-ity**. **a** Condition of being senile; extreme old age accompanied by decay of mental and physical powers; dotage, second childhood; **b** senile behaviour.

senior (I.), adj. [1. sénier; 2. síniə]. Lat., 'older', compar. of *senex*, *sen-is*, 'old', also as n., 'old man, an elder', see **senile**. **1.** Older, opposite of *junior*; abbr. *sen.*, *senr.*, *sr.*, attached to a name to distinguish the elder of two of a family having the same Christian and surnames, as father and son: *Mr. Thomas Jones, senr.*, also at schools to distinguish the elder of two brothers: *Jones, senior*. **2. a** Older in age; more advanced in years: *he is several years senior to me*; *the senior members of the family*; **b** belonging to the main stock, descended from elder son of the original founder: *the senior branch of a family*, as distinguished from *cadet branches*. **3. a** Older in standing, whether actually so in age or not; having belonged to an institution &c. for a longer time: *the senior members of a club*; *a senior man*, at a university, contrasted with *freshman*; **b** more advanced in education: *senior pupils, classes*, of a school; *a senior examination*, for seniors. **4.** Of higher degree, rank, position; superior in standing: *a senior captain, lieutenant*; *senior counsel*, leading barrister, opposite of *junior counsel*; *senior partner*, the head of a firm, partnership &c. Phr. *the senior service*, the Navy. **5.** (Cambridge Univ.) *Senior Classic*, head of the Classical Tripos; *Senior Wrangler*, holder of first place in Mathematical Tripos; the terms are no longer used.

senior (II.), n. See prec. **1.** A person who is older than another: *to have respect for our seniors*; *the seniors of the family, town* &c. **2.** One of older standing, of higher rank, position, degree &c.: *the seniors of a profession, school* &c.; *he was my senior at Oxford by two years*; *promotion went to the seniors in rank.*

seniores priores [1. sèniórēz prīórēz; 2. sìnióriz praióriz]. Lat., 'seniors, elders, first'. See **senior** & **prior** (I.). Phr. indicating the respect due from the young to their elders.

seniority, n. [1. sènióriti; 2. sìnióriti]. **senior** (I.) & **-ity**. **1.** State of being old, or older than another: *abashed by the seniority of his fellows*. **2.** Priority, precedence, superiority in length of membership, service, rank, position &c.: *promotion goes by seniority, not by merit.*

senna, n. [1. séna; 2. sénə]. M.E. *senee*, fr. O. Fr. *senné*; later *sena*, fr. Ital.; fr. Arab. *sanā*, *senā*. (pharm.) An aperient drug obtained from the dried leaflets of Arabian and African species of cassia; *senna tea*, infusion of dried senna leaflets, or seed-pods, used as a mild aperient.

sennet, n. [1. sénet; 2. sénit], fr. O. Fr. *senet*, *sinet*, *segnet*, dimin. of *seing*, *signe*, 'sign'. See **signet & signal**. (archaic) A trumpet-call, as a signal, used to indicate the entrance and exits of players on the stage: '*Sennet. Enter Lear*' &c. (Shakespeare, 'Lear', I. i. 33).

sennight, se'nnight, n. [1. sénīt; 2. sénait], for *seven-*. Cp. **fortnight**. (archaic) Week: *next, last, Monday sennight.*

sennit, sinnet, n. [1. sénit, sínit; 2. sénit, sínit]. Etymol. uncertain; prob. for *seven-knit*. (naut.) Rounded or square braided small cordage of rope yarn.

señor, señora, señorita, n. [1. senyór, -yóra, -yoréta; 2. senjór, -jóra, -joríta]. Span. Cp. **senhor, signor**, & see **senior & sir**. Title of courtesy used in addressing or speaking of a Spanish gentleman or lady; Sir, Madam; Mr., Mrs., Miss.

Senoussi, Senussi, n. [1. senóosi; 2. senúsi], fr. name of Sidi Mohammed es Senussi, the founder. A religious and political Moslem fraternity or sect of N.E. Africa, founded in 1835.

sensation, n. [1. sensáshun; 2. senséiʃən]. Fr., fr. Lat. *sensāt-(us)*, 'gifted with sense, intelligent', formed fr. *sensus*, 'perception, sense'. See **sense** & **-ate** & **-ion**. **1. a** Impression conveyed to the nervous system and thence to consciousness by an external stimulus derived through any of the organs of sense: *a pleasant, disagreeable, sensation*; *a sensation of heat, cold* &c.; **b** power of experiencing sensation; feeling: *to lose all sensation of feeling in one's feet* &c. **2.** General, indefinite, bodily or mental feeling: *a sensation of weariness*; *a sensation of awe, fear*. **3. a** State of excited emotion, aroused interest, or strong feeling generally, esp. such a condition existing in the public mind: *the news of the assassination caused a profound sensation in the city*; **b** event, action &c. which causes such a state of mind: *the press recognized in the assassination a sensation of the first magnitude.*

sensational, adj. [1. sensáshunal; 2. senséiʃənəl]. Prec. & **-al**. **1.** (rare) Connected with, causing, transmitting, physical sensations; sensory: *sensational phenomena, nervous reaction* &c. **2.** Connected with, based on, sensationalism: *the sensational theory of knowledge*. **3. a** Of such a nature as to cause a sensation; arousing excitement and emotion in the mind: *a sensational crime*; *sensational news, rumours* &c.; **b** dealing with exciting, stirring, events &c., tending and intended to provoke powerful interest and emotion: *sensational literature, fiction* &c.; **c** (journalistic style) surprising, striking, remarkable: *a sensational victory*; *sensational play at Lords.*

sensationalism, n. [1. sensáshunalizm; 2. senséiʃənəlizəm]. Prec. & **-ism**. **1.** Philosophical doctrine that physical sensation is the sole ultimate basis of knowledge. **2. a** The search for, treatment of, what is sensational in literary or other artistic expression; **b** sacrifice of truth and good sense to emotional appeal in writing, speaking, political action &c.

sensationalist, n. [1. sensáshunalist; 2. senséiʃənəlist]. See prec. & **-ist**. **1.** An adherent of the philosophical doctrine of sensationalism. **2.** One who practises literary, artistic, or political sensationalism.

sensationally, adv. [1. sensáshunali; 2. senséiʃənəli]. **sensational** & **-ly**. In a sensational manner; so as to create a sensation.

sense (I.), n. [1. sens; 2. sens], fr. Fr. *sens*, fr. Lat. *sensus*, 'feeling, sense; meaning', fr. *sens-(um)*, P.P. type of *sentīre*, 'to feel, perceive, think'; the full form of this base was **senew-*, whence fr. grade **snow-* some wd. derive Gk. *noûs*, 'mind, intelligence', fr. **nowos*, earlier **snowos*, see **nous**; on the other hand, it is fairly certain that the O.H.G. *sinn*, 'sense', is cogn., & philologists prefer now to connect this w. Goth. *sinþs*, 'a going, journey'; see words mentioned under **send** (I.), the meanings of wh. rule out connexion w. the Gk. word. **1. a** The general faculty of bodily sensation; power to feel, perceive, or be conscious of the objective, external world: *impressions, perceptions, of sense*; *this world of sense*; *the physiological basis of sense*; '*devoid of sense and motion*' (Milton, 'P. L.' II. 151); specif. **b** any one of the bodily faculties of perception, sight, hearing, touch, smell, taste, associated with specialized organs and nerves; Phr. *sixth sense*, (i.) sense, perception of specific muscular tension or effort; (ii.) term applied jocularly to an intuitive, non-logical mode of reasoning; *the seven senses*, (archaic, except in such expressions as *scared out of one's seven senses*) the seven properties together forming the inward body of man, formerly supposed to be under the influence of the seven planets; *the senses*, the bodily, sensual appetites, the body as opposed to the spiritual nature of man; *in, out of, one's senses*, in, not in, a normal, ordinary state of mind; *in one's right senses*; *to bring (person) to his senses*, (i.) to make him see reason, recognize facts; (ii.) make him behave properly; *to lose one's* *senses*, become foolish; behave foolishly; irresponsibly. 3. Perception, feeling, discernment, recognition of, a by the senses: *a sense of pleasure, pain*; *to have a sense of warmth, of bodily comfort* &c.; b through the mind: *a sense of injury, of wrong*; *a sense of one's own importance*; *sense of failure*. 4. Faculty of appreciating, recognizing, distinguishing things external to oneself; intuitive, natural instinct, perception, discrimination; a physical: *a sense of locality, height, time, distance*; b intellectual, moral and spiritual: *a sense of beauty, style, rhythm* &c.; *a sense of humour*; *the political sense*; *a sense of honour, duty, responsibility*; *no sense of right or wrong, of decency*; *a sense of spiritual values*; specif. use: *the moral sense*, the natural, a priori instinct of man to approve what is good and dislike what is evil. 5. Emotional feeling or impression: *a sense of awe, dread* &c. 6. Good, sound, practical judgement; normal mental power or understanding; brains: *common, sound, sense*; *a man of sense*; *to talk sense*; *no sense in what you say*; *what is the sense of doing that?*; *he hadn't sufficient sense to get out of danger*; *you should have had more sense than to talk such rubbish*. 7. a Meaning, signification, import, interpretation: *the sense of a word, passage* &c.; *in a narrow sense*; *if I may use the term in that sense*; Phrs. (*true* &c.) *in a* or *one sense*, with qualifications or limitations, in one specified or particular sense only; *to make sense of*, find intelligible meaning in; *in the best sense of the term*, giving the word its widest or most favourable interpretation; b intended, implied, significance; tendency, purport of what is said, done &c.: *I hardly know in what sense to reply*; *you mistake the sense in which I spoke*. 8. General, prevailing feeling, mental attitude, opinion, view, sentiment, towards or about anything; consensus of opinion: *to take the sense of a (public) meeting*.

sense (II.), vb. trans., fr. prec. 1. (rare) To perceive by the organs of sense. 2. (U.S.A.) To perceive, be aware of, intuitively; to realize, understand, the meaning of; to feel something concerning: *he sensed the approaching disaster*; *she fully sensed the danger of her position*.

senseless, adj. [1. sénsles; 2. sénslis]. **sense** (I.) & **-less**. 1. Deprived, incapable, of sensation and power of feeling; insensible, unconscious: *he fell senseless on the floor*. Phr. *to knock senseless*, to stun. 2. a Lacking, deficient, in good sense and judgement; foolish: *a senseless person*; b not inspired by good sense; arising from, due to, folly and stupidity: *a senseless action, proposal* &c.

senselessly, adv. Prec. & **-ly**. In a senseless manner.

senselessness, n. See prec. & **-ness**. State, quality, of being senseless; folly.

sensibility, n. [1. sènsibíliti; 2. sènsibíliti], fr. Fr. *sensibilité*, fr. L. Lat. *sensibilitāt-(em)*. See **sensible** & **-ity**. State, quality, of being sensitive. 1. a (in living organisms) Capacity of sensation; power of responding to external stimuli; sensitiveness: *the sensibility of the eye and ear, of the nerves*; b (fig., of inanimate objects) property of being easily affected by modifying agencies: *sensibility of a thermometer, a balance* &c. 2. a Capacity to respond to, be affected by, an appeal to the aesthetic taste; delicacy of emotional or intellectual perception: *the sensibility of the artist*; b (i.) sensitiveness to, keen appreciation of, moral facts, conditions, conceptions; delicacy, refinement of moral sense: *moral and religious sensibility*; (ii.) delicate spiritual sense of, and respect for, what is seemly, decent, in accordance with good taste: *his sensibilities were deeply wounded by irreverence*.

sensible, adj. [1. sénsibl; 2. sénsibl]. Fr., fr. Lat. *sensibilis* (late and rare), 'perceptible by the senses; capable of perceiving or feeling'. See **sense** & **-ible**. 1. a Capable of being perceived by the senses or of arousing or exciting sensations: *the sensible world around us*; '*Art thou not, fatal vision, sensible to feeling as to sight?*' (Shakespeare, 'Macbeth'); b capable of being distinguished, perceived, computed; appreciable, marked, distinct: *a sensible difference in the temperature*; *a sensible change for the better, worse*. 2. (rare) Capable of sensation or feeling or of receiving impressions; sensitive: *sensible to pain*. 3. Having possession of one's senses; conscious, not insensible: *the injured man was still sensible when picked up*. 4. *Sensible of*, a aware of, alive to, conscious of; able to perceive with the senses: *sensible of one's surroundings*; *sensible of a voice calling one from afar*; b able to realize, understand, appreciate, with the intellect or emotions: *fully sensible of one's own shortcomings*; *sensible of the affection and loyalty of one's friends*; *sensible of the risk one is running*. 5. a (of persons) Possessing good sense and judgement; shrewd, reasonable, sagacious, canny, judicious: *not brilliant, but a very sensible fellow*; b (of actions, ideas, utterances &c.) based on, evincing, inspired by, good sense; wise, prudent, practical: *a very sensible thing to do*; *a sensible remark, suggestion* &c.

sensibleness, n. Prec. & **-ness**. Quality of being sensible, wise, prudent &c.; reasonableness, sagacity, prudence.

sensibly, adv. See prec. & **-ly**. 1. To a sensible degree; appreciably, perceptibly: *he looked sensibly older than last time I saw him*; *the patient has grown sensibly weaker*. 2. With good sense; reasonably, wisely: *he spoke and behaved very sensibly*.

sensitive (I.), adj. [1. sénsitiv; 2. sénsitiv]. Fr. *sensitif*, fem. *-ive*; formed irregularly fr. the Lat. group of words related to *sensus* (see **sense** (I.)), w. suff. **-ive**. 1. a Keenly sensible of bodily sensations; feeling readily and acutely; acutely perceptive of stimuli communicated through the senses: *eyes sensitive to light*; *a skin that is sensitive to heat*; *his sensitive ear caught the slightest sound*; specif. b over-sensitive, hence tender, easily hurt: *a sensitive skin*; *a partly-healed wound is very sensitive*. 2. a (of intellectual sense) Highly refined, acute, delicate, responding readily to ideas; keenly perceptive, discriminating, nice: *a sensitive taste, appreciation, of art, literature, nice points of scholarship* &c.; b (in emotional and moral sense) easily wounded, readily shocked; susceptible, delicate, tender: *a sensitive heart, conscience*; *a sensitive child*, one that is highly strung, liable to feel harsh treatment; Phr. *a sensitive ear*, specif. highly trained, discriminating; sense of different shades of musical or speech sounds; c easily offended, touchy: *sensitive about one's poverty, personal appearance* &c. 3. (of non-sentient things) a Reacting readily to external conditions, to the effects of natural or mechanical processes; delicately adjusted: *a sensitive thermometer, spring, balance* &c.; specif. b *a sensitive film, plate*, photographic film &c., specially sensitized, i.e. covered with a chemical substance which reacts to light rays; c (commerc., of markets &c.) liable to fluctuate in relation to political or other conditions.

sensitive (II.), n., fr. prec. A sensitive person; specif., one liable, susceptible, to so-called psychic influence.

sensitively, adv. **sensitive** (I.) & **-ly**. In a sensitive manner.

sensitiveness, n. See prec. & **-ness**. State, quality, of being sensitive.

sensitive plant, n. (bot.) Any plant whose leaves &c. react to, and move at, a touch, specif., a species of mimosa, *Mimosa pudica, sensitiva*, whose leaves curl up and whose leaf-stalks droop when touched.

sensitivity, n. [1. sènsitíviti; 2. sènsitíviti]. **sensitive** (I.) & **-ity**. Sensitiveness, esp. in physical or material sense, susceptibility to physiological, chemical, action: *the sensitivity of a nerve, photographic plate, film* &c.

sensitization, n. [1. sènsitīzā́shun; 2. sènsitaizéiʃən]. **sensitize** & **-ation**. (chem., photog.) Act, process, of sensitizing; result of this.

sensitize, vb. trans. [1. sénsitīz; 2. sénsitaiz]. Irregular formation, fr. stem *sensit-*, as in **sensitive**, & **-ize**. To render (paper, film &c.) sensitive to actinic light.

sensitizer, n. [1. sénsitīzer; 2. sénsitaizə]. Prec. & **-er**. A sensitizing chemical agent.

sensitometer, n. [1. sènsitómeter; 2. sènsitómitə]. See **sensitive** & **-meter**. Instrument for testing the sensitivity of photographic plates, films &c.

sensori-, pref., fr. **sensorium** or **sensory**, used to form compound physiological or psychological terms, as *sensori-motor*, of nerves, area of brain &c.

sensorial, adj. [1. sensórial; 2. sensóriəl]. See next word & **-al**. Sensory.

sensorium, n. [1. sensórium; 2. sensóriəm]. Formed fr. Lat. *sensus*, see **sense**, for suff. see **-ory**. The grey matter of the brain, regarded as the seat of physical sensations; the nervous system as a whole, including the organs of sense.

sensory, adj. [1. sénsuri; 2. sénsəri]. **sense** (I.) & **-ory**. Connected with, pertaining to, the sensorium, to sensation, or to the senses.

sensual, adj. [1. sénsūal; 2. sénsjuəl], fr. L. Lat. *sensuālis*, fr. *sensu-*, stem of *sensus*. See **sense** (I.) & **-al**. (archaic, poet.) 1. Pertaining to, affecting, perceived by, the bodily senses; sensuous: '*Sound, sound the clarion, fill the fife! To all the sensual world proclaim...*' (quoted by Scott in 'Old Mortality'); '*Therefore, ye soft pipes, play on, Not to the sensual ear...*' (Keats, 'Ode on a Grecian Urn'). Chiefly now in unfavourable sense: 2. Pertaining to the body, carnal, earthy; contrasted with *spiritual*: *sensual appetites, affections* &c. 3. Connected with the gratification of the bodily senses, gross; specif. a connected with gratification of, appealing to, sexual appetite: *a sensual attraction, charm* &c.; b inclined to gratify sexual appetite; lustful, licentious, voluptuous: *a sensual person*. 4. (philos.) Pertaining to the doctrine of sensationalism: *a purely sensual origin of knowledge*.

sensualism, n. [1. sénsūalizm; 2. sénsjuəlizəm]. Prec. & **-ism**. 1. Sensual indulgence, gratification of the senses. 2. (philos.) Sensationalism.

sensualist, n. [1. sénsūalist; 2. sénsjuəlist]. **sensual** & **-ist**. 1. Person fond of, given to, sensual indulgence; a voluptuary. 2. (rare) A sensationalist.

sensuality, n. [1. sènsūáliti; 2. sènsjuǽliti]. **sensual** & **-ity**. Cp. Fr. *sensualité*. a Love of, proneness to, sensual indulgence; b state, quality, of being sensual.

sensualization, n. [1. sènsūalīzā́shun; 2. sènsjuəlaizéiʃən]. See next word & **-ation**. Act, process, of sensualizing; state of being sensualized.

sensualize, vb. trans. [1. sénsūalīz; 2. sénsjuəlaiz]. **sensual** & **-ize**. To make sensual; to degrade by sensual indulgence; to despiritualize.

sensually, adv. [1. sénsūali; 2. sénsjuəli]. **sensual** & **-ly**. In a sensual manner.

sensuous, adj. [1. sénsūus; 2. sénsjuəs]. See **sensual** & **-ous**. Pertaining to, arising from, based on, affecting, appealing to, the bodily senses; connected with experience derived from the senses; distinguished from *sensual* in that it conveys no sense of grossness or lewdness: *sensuous impressions*; *Milton said that poetry should be 'simple, sensuous, passionate'*.

sensuously, adv. Prec. & **-ly**. In a sensuous manner; by, through, the senses.

sensuousness, n. See prec. & **-ness**. Quality of being sensuous.

sent, vb. [1. sent; 2. sent]. O.E. *sende(ġe)send(ed)*, M.E. *sende, sente*, Pret. & P.P. of **send** (I.).

sentence (I.), n. [1. séntens; 2. séntəns]. Fr., fr. Lat. *sententia*, 'way of thinking, opinion;

judgement, decision; meaning; sentence', for *sententia, fr. *sentient-(em)*, Pres. Part. type of *sentīre*, 'to feel, be of opinion', see **sense** & words there referred to. **1.** (archaic) **a** Meaning, interpretation: '*The sentence of this Latin is, Woman is mannes joy, and al his bliss*' (Chaucer, 'Nonne Preestes Tale', 345–6): **b** decision, opinion: '*My sentence is for open war*' (Milton, 'P. L.', ii. 51); **c a** maxim, proverb, short saying giving some moral teaching; **d** (theol.) the opinion, briefly expressed, of the Fathers or Doctors of the Church on specific subjects; *Master of the Sentences*, Peter Lombard. **2.** (law) **a** The judgement, decision of a court, generally a criminal court, declaring the punishment or penalty to be inflicted on a prisoner found guilty of a crime or offence: *to pass sentence of death*; *to be under sentence of*; *the sentence of the court is that . . .*; **b** punishment so declared: *to receive a heavy sentence*; *to undergo a sentence of penal servitude.* Phr. *to pass sentence upon*, (i.) to declare the decision of the court as to the punishment of a convicted prisoner; (ii.) to express an opinion or judgement, esp. an unfavourable one. **3.** (gram.) The unit of rational speech, series of words, or, occasionally, only one word, which makes a statement, asks a question, expresses a wish or command, or is merely exclamatory.

sentence (II.), vb. trans., fr. prec. To pronounce, pass formal, judicial, sentence upon; to impose punishment upon; to condemn: *to sentence a man to death*; *the accused was sentenced for theft ten years ago.*

sentential, adj. [1. senténshal; 2. senténʃəl], fr. Lat. *sententiālis*. See **sentence & -ial.** (rare) **1.** Pertaining to, of the nature of, a judicial sentence, a decision, decided opinion: *sentential powers.* **2.** (gram.) Pertaining to sentences or a sentence, in the form of a sentence: *a sentential clause*, subordinate clause.

sententious, adj. [1. senténshus; 2. senténʃəs], fr. Fr. *sententieux*, fr. Lat. *sententiōsus*, 'full of meaning, pithy'. See **sentence & -ous.** (of persons and their mode of expression) Abounding in maxims and moral utterances; (chiefly in derogatory sense) turgid and trite; high-flown, ponderous, pompous.

sententiously, adv. Prec. & **-ly.** In a sententious manner.

sententiousness, n. See prec. & **-ness.** Quality of being sententious.

sentience, n. [1. sénshens; 2. sénʃəns]. **sentient & -ce.** Capacity, power, of feeling or perception by sense; consciousness.

sentient, adj. [1. sénshent; 2. sénʃənt], fr. Lat. *sentient-(em)*, Pres. Part. of *sentīre*, 'to feel'. See **sense** (I.). Having the capacity, faculty, of perceiving by the senses; experiencing sensation.

sentiently, adv. Prec. & **-ly.** In a sentient manner; by sense-perception.

sentiment, n. [1. séntiment; 2. séntimənt], fr. L. Lat. *sentimentum*, fr. Lat. *sentīre*, 'to feel', see **sense** (I.), & **-ment.** **1.** Whole body of feelings constantly entertained by a person towards some particular ideal, institution &c.; emotionalized thought or firmly held principle concerning; persistent disposition and attitude of mind: *religious, patriotic, family, sentiment*; *to have friendly, hostile, sentiments towards*; *animated by lofty sentiments.* **2. a** A refined, emotional feeling, sensibility to emotional appeal; tendency to be influenced by emotion rather than by reason or by fact: *a man of sentiment*; *sentiment must be eliminated in business discussions*; *to appeal to sentiment*; *sentiment is stronger than logic*; **b** (in derogatory sense) maudlin, ill-directed emotion; sentimentality: *a new film remarkably free from sentiment.* **3.** Opinion, judgement, view, arrived at as a result of deliberation: *to ascertain a person's sentiments with regard to a proposal* &c. Phr. (jocular) *them's my sentiments*, that is what I think. **4.** (archaic) A short, aphoristic sentence expressing (usually) a trite thought or wish: *Mr. Jones was called on for a sentiment.*

sentimental, adj. [1. sèntiméntl; 2. sèntiméntəl]. Prec. & **-al.** **1.** Of the nature of, characterized by, animated by, arising from, sentiment or feeling, rather than from cold logic, or purely utilitarian motives: *I have sentimental reasons for my action, for wishing to buy the place* &c.; *who does not become sentimental when he remembers his childhood and his parents?*; *to strike a sentimental note* (in a speech &c.). **2.** (in derogatory sense) Foolishly emotional; giving way to, expressing, weak, ill-restrained, ill-directed, sickly, emotion; mawkishly sensitive and tender, maudlin: *a sentimental young ass*; *a rubbishy, sentimental novel.*

sentimentalism, n. [1. sèntiméntalizm; 2. sèntiméntəlizəm]. **sentimental & -ism.** (usually in derogatory sense) **a** Weakly sentimental habit of mind; **b** expression of this in behaviour and action.

sentimentalist, n. [1. sèntiméntalist; 2. sèntiméntəlist]. **sentimental & -ist.** **a** One inclined to sentimentalism; **b** one swayed primarily by sentiment rather than by logic.

sentimentality, n. [1. sèntimentáliti; 2. sèntimentǽliti]. **sentimental & -ity.** Quality of being sentimental (in bad sense); sentimentalism.

sentimentalize, vb. intrans. & trans. [1. sèntiméntalīz; 2. sèntiméntəlaiz]. **sentimental & -ize.** **1.** intrans. To become sentimental; to act, think, in a sentimental way: *to sentimentalize over, about, the past, the woes of humanity* &c. **2.** trans. **a** To regard, explain, in a sentimental way; read sentiment into: *to sentimentalize history, nature* &c.; **b** to cause to become sentimental, impart a sentimental character to: *the actor sentimentalized his part*; *to sentimentalize a story.*

sentimentally, adv. [1. sèntiméntali; 2. sèntiméntəli]. **sentimental & -ly.** In a sentimental manner.

sentinel, n. [1. séntinel; 2. séntinəl], fr. O. Fr. *sentinelle*; prob. a dimin. form of O. Fr. *sentine*, itself dimin. of O. Fr. *sente*, 'path', orig. sense 'sentinel's beat', the ground on wh. he walks up & down when on duty; *sente* is fr. Lat. *sēmita*, 'path', fr. *sē-*, pref., 'apart, aside', see **se-**, & **mita*, fr. *meāre*, 'to go', see **meatus.** **1.** A military guard, or sentry; a rhetorical or poetical term; also of animals, such as seals and birds, which post guards to give warning of danger. **2.** A watch, guard: *to stand sentinel over*, to guard.

sentry, n. [1. séntri; 2. séntri]. Prob. fr. O. Fr. *senteret*, a form of *sentier*, 'path', fr. L. Lat. *sēmitārius*, 'pertaining to paths or byways', fr. *sēmita*, 'path'. See **sentinel.** Armed military guard who paces up and down between fixed points to give warning in case of danger.

sentry-box, n. A small narrow wooden hut just high enough for a man to stand up in, used to protect sentries from the weather.

sentry-go, n. **1.** A sentry's beat. **2.** Duty as a sentry; guard duty.

Senussi, n. See **Senoussi.**

senza, prep. [1. séntsa; 2. séntsa]. Ital., 'without', fr. Lat. See **sine die.** Musical direction indicating that something can be dispensed with or disregarded: *senza stromenti*, without instruments; *senza tempo*, not in strict time.

sepal, n. [1. sépal; 2. sépəl], fr. Fr. *sépale*, Neo-Lat. *sepalum*; coined word, said by inventor to have been formed fr. Gk. *sképē*, 'covering' (possibly cogn. w. Lith. *kepùrė*, 'hat'), but now felt to be connected w. **petal.** (bot.) One of the group of leaves forming the calyx of a flower.

-sepalous, suff. [1. sépalus; 2. sépələs]. Prec. & **-ous.** Having (specified number of) sepals: *polysepalous*, having many sepals; *gamosepalous*, with sepals joined &c.

separability, n. [1. sèparabíliti; 2. sèpərəbíliti]. **separable & -ity.** Quality of being separable; separableness; divisibility.

separable, adj. [1. séparabl; 2. sépərəbl], fr. Lat. *sēparābilis*. See **separate & -able.** Capable of being separated or divided.

separableness, n. Prec. & **-ness.** Quality of being separable; separability.

separably, adv. See prec. & **-ly.** So as to be separable.

separate (I.), adj. [1. séparit; 2. sépərit]. Lat. *sēparāt-(um)*, P.P. of *sēparāre*, 'to put apart, divide, separate', fr. *sē-*, 'apart', see **se-**, & *parāre*, 'to prepare; arrange, contrive' &c., see **pare.** **1.** Divided, disjoined, distinct, physically; **a** (of parts of a whole or things formerly joined) no longer joined; disunited, disconnected, cut, divided one from the other: *cut the cake into three separate parts*; **b** (of individual, different, objects) distinct, placed apart one from the other: *three separate trees*; *a book in two separate volumes*; *to sleep in separate beds.* **2.** Thought of, looked at, as distinct, having distinctive form and function, though occurring in proximity, and forming a unity: *the separate organs of the body*; *separate parts of a machine.* **3.** Isolated, secluded, shut off, from others: *to live separate from others*; *prisoners are kept separate one from the other.* **4.** Not in relation with others; individual, particular, independent: *each member of the family has a separate fortune.* **5.** Kept apart, distinguished one from the other in the mind: *to keep two sets of ideas separate*; *these are two entirely separate questions.*

separate (II.), vb. trans. & intrans. [1. séparāt; 2. sépəreit]. See prec. **A.** trans. **1. a** To make separate, sever, disunite, by cutting &c.: *to separate a bough from the trunk, a head from a body* &c.; **b** to remove by sifting or other eliminating process: *to separate chaff from grain, dross from ore*; specif., *to separate milk*, to remove cream from it in a separator. **2.** To divide (persons) from each other, cause separation between; **a** to remove (person) from society or propinquity of another (person, place &c.): *to separate a mother from her child*; *to separate a man from his home*; **b** to cause disagreement, be source of difference, between; to estrange, divide in feelings, opinions &c.: *two old friends separated for a time by spiteful gossip*; *there are but a few minor points which separate us.* **3. a** To divide, cut up, by physical barriers, place dividing lines, boundaries &c., between: *to separate a tract of land (up) into small plots* &c.; **b** to serve as a barrier, intervene, between: *the channel, a few miles of sea, separate(s) England from France*; *each field is separated from the next by a stone wall.* **4.** To distinguish between intellectually, discriminate, perceive, difference between: *to separate sense from nonsense*; *I am unable to separate the two arguments*; *it is difficult to separate the different degrees of guilt one from another.* **B.** intrans. **1.** To be, become, separate; to come apart, break: *the rope separated under the strain.* **2. a** To go apart; go in different directions, abandon company of another or others and pursue different road: *we walked a mile together and then separated*; *we did not separate till midnight*; **b** to cease living together or in association (specif. of husband and wife). **3.** To secede from, dissolve partnership, membership of same body, political unity &c.: *various sects have separated from the Church of England at different times*; *America separated from the old country late in the 18th century.*

separate (III.), n., fr. **separate** (I.). **1.** (obs.) A person living a separate, esp. a religious, monastic life. **2.** (bibliog.) Reprint, off-print, separate copy of an article published in a journal or volume of Transactions &c.

separately, adv. [1. séparitli; 2. sépəritli]. **separate** (I.) & **-ly.** In a separate manner; distinctively, singly.

separateness, n. [1. séparitnes; 2. sépəritnis]. See prec. & **-ness.** Quality of being separate or independent.

separation, n. [1. sèparáshun; 2. sèpəréiʃən], fr. Lat. *sēparātiōn-(em)*, 'a parting, severing; division, separation'. See **separate** (II.)

& -ion. **1.** Act, process, of separating; state of being separated or separate (in various senses of vb.). **2.** (specif., law) Formal arrangement, not amounting to a dissolution of marriage, whereby married persons cease to live together, whether by mutual agreement or by an order of the court. *Separation allowance*, allowance made to a wife living separate from her husband, esp. one paid by the State when the husband is serving as a soldier or sailor in war.

separationist, n. [1. sèparáshunist; 2. sèpəréiʃənist]. Prec. & **-ist**. One who is in favour of political separation, between two states or parts of an empire, or between a group of members of a religious body and the main body; separatism.

separatism, n. [1. séparitizm; 2. sépəritizəm]. **separate (I.)** & **-ism**. Principles and aims of political or religious separatists.

separatist, n. [1. séparatist; 2. sépəritist]. **separate (I.)** & **-ist**. One who advocates political or religious separatism; separationist.

separative, adj. [1. séparativ; 2. sépərltiv], fr. Lat. *sēparātīvus*. **separate (I.)** & **-ive**. Tending to cause separation.

separator, n. [1. séparàter; 2. sépərèitə]. **separate (II.)** & **-or**. **1.** One who separates. **2.** Mechanical device for separating cream from milk.

separatory, adj. [1. séparaturi; 2. sépərətəri]. **separate (I.)** & **-ory**. (rare) Separative.

Sephardic, adj. [1. sefárdik; 2. səfádik]. Next word & **-ic**. Pertaining to the Sephardim.

Sephardim, n. pl. [1. sefárdim; 2. səfádim]. Heb. Descendants of Jews anciently settled in Spain and Portugal.

sepia, n. [1. sépia; 2. sípiə]. Lat., fr. Gk. *sēpía*, 'cuttle-fish'; connected w. base **sēp-*, 'decay', see **sepsis**; cp. Gk. *sḗps*, 'a venomous snake'. **a** The black inky fluid secreted by the cuttle-fish; **b** a dark brown pigment made from this, used in water-colour drawing &c.; *sepia-drawing*, a drawing in sepia.

sepoy, n. [1. sépoi; 2. sípɔi], fr. Hind., Pers. *sipāhi*, 'soldier', fr. Pers. *sipah*, 'army'; cp. Fr. *spahi*. A native Indian soldier, esp. one trained in and for a European army; a soldier of a native regiment in British India: *the Sepoy Mutiny*, the Indian Mutiny of 1857–58.

seps, n. [1. seps; 2. sɛps]. Lat., fr. Gk. *sḗps*, 'a venomous snake, a lizard', fr. *sḗpein*, 'to make putrid, to rot'. See next word. Mediterranean snake-like lizard, genus *Chalcides*.

sepsis, n. [1. sépsis; 2. sépsis]. Gk. *sêpsis*, 'putrefaction, decay', fr. *sḗpein*, 'to rot'; cogn. w. Gk. *saprós*, 'rotten, destroyed' (with different grade), see **sapro-** & **septic**; other relationships doubtful. Putrefaction; specif. (pathol.) a general term including various forms of infection of the blood by micro-organisms or their products; blood-poisoning, septic infection.

sept, n. [1. sept; 2. sɛpt], fr. O. Fr. *septe*, variant of *secte*, **sect**, possibly influenced by Lat. *saeptum*, 'enclosure, fence', see **septum**. One of the old Irish clans or tribes.

sept-, septem-, septen-, septi-, prefs. Forms meaning 'seven', fr. Lat. *septem*, 'seven', cogn. w. Scrt. *saptá*; Gk. *heptá*; all fr. Aryan **septm̥*; cp. Goth. *sibun*, & see **seven**.

septa, n., pl. of **septum**.

septal (I.), adj. [1. séptal; 2. sépt(ə)l]. **septum** & **-al**. (zool.) Pertaining to a septum or to septa.

septal (II.), adj. **sept** & **-al**. Pertaining to an Irish sept.

septan, adj. [1. séptan; 2. séptən]. **sept-** & **-an**; formed on anal. of **quartan**. (of fever) Recurring every seventh day.

septangle, n. [1. séptànggl; 2. séptæŋgl]. **sept-** & **angle**. (geom.) A figure having seven sides and seven angles; heptagon.

septangular, adj. [1. sèptánggūlar; 2. sèptǽŋgjulə]. **sept-** & **angular**. Having seven angles; septagonal.

septate, adj. [1. séptāt; 2. sépteit], fr. Lat. *saeptāt-(us)*. **septum** & **-ate**. (anat.) Having, divided by, a septum or septa.

September, n. [1. septémber; 2. sɛptémbə]. Lat., 'the seventh month', according to the old pre-Julian calendar. See **sept-** &c. & **December**. The ninth month of the year.

Septembrist, n. [1. septémbrist; 2. sɛptémbrist], fr. Fr. *Septembriste*. (hist.) One of those who took an active part in the *September Massacres* of Royalists in Paris, 1792.

septempartite, adj. [1. sèptempártīt; 2. sèptɛmpátait]. **sept-** &c. & **partite**. Divided into seven parts.

septenarius, n. [1. sèptenárius; 2. sèptɛnέəriəs]. Lat., fr. *septēni*, 'seven each, by sevens'. See **sept-** &c. (prosody) A verse of seven feet.

septenary, adj. & n. [1. septénari; 2. sɛptínəri]. **sept-** &c. & **-ary**. **1.** adj. Consisting of, related to, seven. **2.** n. The number seven; group of seven things.

septennate, n. [1. septénāt; 2. sɛpténeit], fr. Fr. *septennat*. **sept-** &c., & **septennial** for second element, & **-ate**. **a** A period of seven years; **b** period of office held for seven years.

septennial, adj. [1. septénial; 2. sɛpténiəl], fr. Lat. *septennium*, 'period of seven years', & **-al**, fr. *septennis*, 'of seven years', see **septennium**, & **-al**. **a** Lasting seven years: *septennial parliaments*; *Septennial Act*, statute of 1716 extending the life of a Parliament from three to seven years; **b** happening, recurring, every seven years: *a septennial valuation of property*; *septennial elections*.

septennially, adv. Prec. & **-ly**. Once every seven years.

septennium, n. [1. septénium; 2. sɛpténiəm]. Lat., 'period of seven years'. See **sept-** &c.; second element fr. *annus*, 'year', see **annual**. Period of seven years.

septentrional, adj. [1. septéntrional; 2. sɛpténtriənəl]. Lat., 'northern, of the North', fr. *septentriōnes*, 'the seven bright stars of Ursa Major or the Plough, the northern regions as a quarter of the heavens', fr. *septem*, 'seven', see **sept-** &c., & *triōnes*, 'plough-oxen', perh. fr. base **tri-*, 'rub, grind', see **trite**. Northern; coming from, situated in, the north.

septet, septette, n. [1. septét; 2. sɛptét]. **sept-** & **et(te)**, on anal. of **duet**. (mus.) A composition for seven players or singers.

septic, adj. & n. [1. séptik; 2. séptik], fr. Gk. *sēptikós*, 'causing putrefaction', fr. *sēptós*, 'putrid, rotten'. See **sepsis** & **-ic**. **1.** adj. Connected with, promoting, of the nature of, sepsis; poisoned, infected with putrefactive organisms. **2.** n. Substance or organism tending to cause sepsis.

septicaemia, n. [1. sèptisémia; 2. sèptisímiə]. Formed fr. Gk. *sēptikós*, 'decayed, putrid', see **septic**, & *haîma*, 'blood', see **haemal**, & **-ia**. A septic condition of the blood stream caused by bacteria; blood-poisoning.

septically, adv. [1. séptikali; 2. séptikəli]. **septic** & **-al** & **-ly**. In a septic manner; by septic infection.

septicity, n. [1. septísiti; 2. sɛptísiti]. **septic** & **-ity**. **a** Quality of being septic; **b** tendency to become septic or cause septic infection.

septilateral, adj. [1. sèptiláteral; 2. sèptilǽtərəl]. See **sept-** & **lateral**. Seven-sided.

septillion, n. [1. septíliun; 2. sɛptíliən]. Fr. *septillion*, fr. **sept-** & *-illion*, on anal. of **million**. **a** A million raised to the seventh power, 1 followed by 42 ciphers; **b** (in Fr. and Am. usage) a thousand raised to eighth power, 1 followed by 24 ciphers.

septimal, adj. [1. séptimal; 2. séptiməl], fr. Lat. *septimus*, 'seventh', see **septimus**, & **-al**. Relating, pertaining, to the number seven.

septime, n. [1. séptēm; 2. séptīm]. Fr. See next word. The seventh position in fencing.

septimus, adj. [1. séptimus; 2. séptiməs]. Lat., 'seventh'. See **sept-** &c. Seventh, esp. in schools, of the seventh of a series of boys having the same name, cp. *primus*; sometimes used as Christian name of a seventh son.

septuagenarian, n. & adj. [1. séptūajenárian; 2. séptjuədžinέəriən]. See next word & **-an**. **1.** n. **a** A person seventy years old; **b** person between the ages of 70 and 80. **2.** adj. Septuagenary.

septuagenary, adj. [1. sèptūajénari; 2. sèptjuədžínəri], fr. Lat. *septuāgēnārius*, fr. *septuāgēni*, 'seventy each', *septuāginta*, 'seventy', & **-ary**. **a** Consisting of seventy; **b** seventy years old; pertaining to a person seventy years old.

Septuagesima, n. [1. sèptūajésima; 2. sèptjuədžésimə]. Lat. *septuāgēsima (dies)*, 'seventieth (day)', form of *septuāgēsimus*, see prec.; loosely, as nearly seventy days before Easter, cp. **Quadragesima**; see **sept-** &c., & the suff. *gēs-(imo-)*, fr. **gens-* for **-gent-s*, cp. **-gint-* under next word. *Septuagesima (Sunday)*, the Sunday before Sexagesima; third Sunday before Lent.

Septuagint, n. [1. séptūajint; 2. séptjuədžint], fr. Lat. *septuāginta*, 'seventy'; **sept-** &c. & *-gint-* (cp. Lat. *viginti*, '20'), wh. is for Aryan **k̑m̥t-*, 'decade, group of ten', as in Lat. *decem* &c., see **deci-**. (abbr. LXX) The Hellenistic Greek version of the Old Testament and the Apocrypha, made according to the legend by seventy (two) writers in the 3rd cent. B.C.

septum, n., pl. **septa** [1. séptum, -ta; 2. séptəm, -tə]. Lat., also *saeptum*, 'hedge, enclosure', P.P. type of *sēpīre*, *saepīre*, 'to enclose, fence', fr. *saepes*, 'hedge'; cogn. w. Gk. *haimós* for **saimós*, 'thicket', fr. **saipm-*. A dividing partition, a membrane or wall; specif. **a** such a partition dividing two cavities or masses of tissue in the body; **b** (bot.) one dividing the chambers of a seed-vessel &c.

septuple, adj., n. & vb. trans. [1. septúpl; 2. sɛptjúpl]. Fr., fr. Lat. *septuplus*, see **sept-**, & suff. *-ple*, as in **quadruple** &c., & cp. **double**. **1.** adj. Multiplied by seven; sevenfold. **2.** n. A sevenfold amount. **3.** vb. To multiply by seven.

sepulchral, adj. [1. sepúlkral; 2. sipálkrəl]. O. Fr., fr. Lat. *sepulchrālis*. See **sepulchre** & **-al**. **1.** Connected with, pertaining to, a sepulchre, to the grave, to a burial or to the dead: *sepulchral monuments, rites* &c.; *sepulchral remains, pottery* &c. **2.** Suggestive of the grave; melancholy, dismal, funereal: *sepulchral visage, look* &c.; *sepulchral voice*, one that is deep in tone and suggestive of mental gloom.

sepulchrally, adv. Prec. & **-ly**. In a sepulchral manner.

sepulchre (I.), n. [1. sépulker; 2. sépəlkə], fr. O. Fr. *sepulcre*, fr. Lat. *sepulcrum*, fr. *sepul-(tum)*, P.P. type of *sepelīre*, 'to bury, inter'; the origin of this vb. is doubtful. **1.** A burial-place, grave, tomb, esp. a grave cut in rock or built of stone &c.; a vault. Phr. *a whited sepulchre*, hypocrite, see Matt. xxiii. 27. *Easter Sepulchre*, a small vaulted or arched niche on the north side of the sacrarium in a church in which the consecrated elements of the Eucharist were kept from Thursday in Easter week till Easter Sunday; *Holy Sepulchre*, the rock tomb in which Christ was laid, the place for which the Crusades were fought and to which pilgrims resort. **2.** (fig., rare) Place where something is lost or buried: *the sepulchre of one's hopes, ambitions* &c.; *grave* is the more usual word here.

sepulchre (II.), vb. trans., fr. prec. To lay in a sepulchre or tomb; to bury, inter: *to sepulchre the dead*; (also fig.) *there all his ambitions lay sepulchred*.

sepulture, n. [1. sépulchur; 2. sépəltʃə]. O. Fr., fr. Lat. *sepultūra*. See *sepult-*, as in **sepulchre (I.)**, & **-ure**. Act, mode, of burying the dead; burial, interment.

sequacious, adj. [1. sekwáshus; 2. sikwéiʃəs]. Lat. base *sequ-*, 'to follow', see **sequela**, & **-ious**. (rare) **1.** Following, attendant, not independent; pliable, ductile. **2.** Logically consistent, following as effect on cause.

sequaciously, adv. Prec. & **-ly**. In a sequacious, logically consistent manner.

sequaciousness, n. See prec. & **-ness**. Quality of being sequacious.

sequel, n. [1. sékwel; 2. síkwəl], fr. O. Fr. *sequele*, fr. Lat. *sequēla*, 'a follower, that which follows, consequence, result, sequel'. See next word & cp. **sociable**. That which follows. **1.** A continuation, resumption, after a break or pause: *the sequel of a novel*; '*Paradise Regained*' *is not a mere sequel to* '*Paradise Lost*'. **2.** A following, subsequent event, whether causally connected with the preceding one or not: *is the sequel to (of) the war to be preparation for another?*; *the sequel to this unhappy marriage is well known.* Phr. *in the sequel*, as events have proved, as things turned out, as it has happened. **3.** A consequence, result; effect: *the sequel of such a speech can be foreseen*; *the inevitable sequel of his folly.*

sequela, n. [1. sekwéla; 2. sikwílə]. Lat., 'follower; that which follows, consequence, result', fr. base *sequ-*, as in *sequi*, 'to follow'; cogn. w. Gk. *hépomai*, 'I follow'; Sert. *saččati*, 'accompanies, follows'; cp. the related Lat. *socius*, 'fellow, companion', see **sociable**. (med., usually pl. *sequelae*) Condition, state, esp. abnormal, morbid state, left as the consequence of a disease or injury: *scarlet fever often has deafness as one of its sequelae.*

sequence, n. [1. sékwens; 2. síkwəns]. **sequent** & **-ce**. **1. a** Order in which events succeed each other; **b** series of events or phenomena occurring in succession. **2. a** (implying natural or causal connexion) *The sequence of the seasons*; *the inevitable sequence of a crime and punishment*; **b** (implying logical connexion) *one could wish a little more sequence in the arguments.* **3.** Specific uses: **a** (cards) series of cards of same suit in order of value; **b** (gram.) principles according to which the tenses of a subordinate are adjusted to those of a principal clause; **c** (mus.) a succession of tones of graduated pitch, up or down the scale.

sequent, adj. [1. sékwent; 2. síkwənt], fr. Lat. *sequent-(em)*, 'following', Pres. Part. of *sequi*, 'to follow', see **sequela**. **a** Following, succeeding, subsequent: '*a sequent king*' (Milton, 'P. L.', xii. 165); **b** resulting, consequent.

sequentes, n. [1. sekwéntēz; 2. sikwéntīz]. Lat. nom. masc. pl. **sequentia** [1. sekwénshia; 2. sikwénʃiə]. Neut. pl. See prec. (abbr. *seq.*, *seqq.*) The following pages, verses, lines &c., used in giving references.

sequential, adj. [1. sekwénshal; 2. sikwénʃəl]. **sequent** & **-ial**. Sequent, succeeding; following in order of time or place; occurring as a consequence or result.

sequentiality, n. [1. sekwènshiáliti; 2. sikwènʃiǽliti]. Prec. & **-ity**. Quality, state, of being sequential.

sequentially, adv. [1. sekwénshali; 2. sikwénʃəli]. **sequential** & **-ly**. In a sequential manner; subsequently, consequently.

sequester, vb. trans. & intrans. [1. sekwéster; 2. sikwéstə], fr. O. Fr. *sequestrer*, fr. L. Lat. *sequestrāre*, 'to hand over to another for safe custody, to surrender; to take away, separate from', fr. *sequester*, 'a depository, custodian, trustee', *sequestrum*, 'deposit of property which is a subject of dispute, with a third party as trustee, till the dispute is settled'; etymol. uncertain; prob. fr. base *sequi*, 'to follow', see **sequela** &c. **A.** trans. **1.** (now usually *sequestrate*) **a** (law) To take possession of (the property of another) for a certain time and purpose; **b** to cause (one's property) to be sequestered: *he has sequestered his estates*; **c** (gen.) to seize, confiscate. **2.** (reflex.) *To sequester oneself*, to withdraw, set apart, seclude: *he sequestered himself from society*; (or P.P. as adj.) *to live a sequestered life*; '*Along the cool sequestered vale of life*' (Gray's 'Elegy'). **B.** intrans. (law, of widow) To sequestrate.

sequestrable, adj. [1. sekwéstrabl; 2. sikwéstrəbl]. **sequester** & **-able**. Capable of being sequestrated; subject to sequestration.

sequestral, adj. [1. sekwéstral; 2. sikwéstrəl]. **sequestrum** & **-al**. (med.) Pertaining to, of the nature of, a sequestrum.

sequestrate, vb. trans. & intrans. [1. sékwestrāt, sekwéstrāt; 2. síkwəstreit, sikwéstreit], fr. L. Lat. *sequestrāt-(um)*, P.P. of *sequestrāre*, see **sequester**. **A.** trans. **1.** (law) **a** To remove (property) from the possession of its owner, by process of law, and hold it, taking profits for the purpose of paying a debt, satisfying a claim &c.; specif. (used of bishop) to hold (an ecclesiastical benefice) till claims against the incumbent are satisfied; **b** to cause (one's property) to be sequestrated, to hand over to a sequestrator; **c** (internat. law, of a belligerent State) to appropriate the debts due from its own nationals to the enemy State; **d** (Scots law) to take possession of a bankrupt's property for the purpose of realization for the benefit of the creditors. **2.** (obs.) To sequester (**A. 2**). **B.** intrans. (law, of widow) To renounce all claims upon the estate of her deceased husband.

sequestration, n. [1. sèkwestráshun; 2. sìkwəstréiʃən], fr. L. Lat. *sequestrātiōn-(em)*. See **sequestrate** & **-ion**. **1.** Act, process, of sequestrating or taking possession of the property of another and holding it for the benefit of creditors or of the State. **2.** (rare) State of being sequestered or withdrawn, seclusion.

sequestrator, n. [1. sékwestràter; 2. síkwəstrèitə]. Lat. See **sequestrate** & **-or**. One who sequestrates; specif. (law) person appointed to hold sequestrated property till claims against it are satisfied &c.; applied specifically to a bishop who sequestrates a benefice.

sequestrum, n. [1. sēkwéstrum; 2. sīkwéstrəm]. Med. Lat., lit. 'a sequestered thing'. See **sequester**. (med.) A piece of dead or diseased bone which becomes separated by necrosis from the healthy bone, and has to be removed by an operation.

sequin, n. [1. sékwin; 2. síkwin]. Fr., fr. Ital. *zecchino*, 'coin', fr. *zecca*, 'a mint', fr. Arab. *sikkah*, 'a die for stamping coins'. **1.** A Venetian gold coin, value about 9s. 3d., struck first in the 13th cent., later struck elsewhere in Italy and circulating in Turkey and the Levant &c. **2.** A disk or spangle made of bright metal, tinfoil &c., used as an ornamental trimming for women's dresses.

Sequoia, n. [1. sekwóia; 2. sikwóiə], fr. *Sequoyah*, name of a Cherokee Indian. (bot.) Genus of Californian evergreen coniferous trees of great height, including *Sequoia sempervirens*, the redwood, and *Sequoia gigantea*, the Californian 'big tree'; the latter, grown as an ornamental tree, is called in England Wellingtonia.

ser, also **seer**, n. [1. sēr; 2. siə]. Hind. *sēr*. An Indian measure of weight, one-fortieth of a *maund*, slightly over 2 lb.

sérac, n. [1. sérak; 2. séræk]. Fr., properly (in the Alps) the name of a cheese. A pointed mass or pinnacle of ice formed by crevasses crossing a glacier at steep slopes.

seraglio, n. [1. seráhliō; 2. serάliou], fr. Ital. *serraglio*, orig. 'enclosure, place enclosed by palisades', later, 'a Turkish palace', formed w. suff. *-aglio* (Lat. *-āculum*), fr. *serrare*, 'to lock, close, shut', fr. L. Lat. *serāre*, 'to bolt, bar', fr. *sera*, 'bolt, bar to a door', fr. *serere*, 'to join'. See **series** & **serried** & cp. **sear (III.)**; the ordinary meaning is due to a confusion w. Pers. *serāi*, 'a sultan's palace', see **serai**. **1. a** (hist., cap.) The name of the old palace of the Sultan of Turkey in Constantinople, including his residence and harem, official and government buildings &c.: *the Old Seraglio*; **b** (not cap.) any palace of a sultan of Turkey or Moslem ruler; esp. with reference to the harem. **2. a** Harem, the place where a Moslem keeps his wives &c. in seclusion; **b** (fig.) the wives and esp. concubines of an Oriental or other monarch: *Charles II. and his seraglio.* **3.** The system of the harem or seclusion of wives &c.; concubinage.

serai, n. [1. serí; 2. serái]. Pers., 'palace'. A place where travellers may be accommodated in India and the East; a caravanserai.

serang, n. [1. seráng; 2. səræŋ], fr. Pers. *sarhang*, 'commander'. The name given in the East Indies to the native, usually Malay, boatswain of a ship.

serape, n. [1. seráhpā; 2. sərάpei], fr. Mexican Span. *sarape*. A blanket worn as a kind of riding cloak or used as a saddle-cloth in Mexico and Spanish S. America.

seraph, n. [1. séraf; 2. sérəf], pl. *seraphs*, Heb. *seraphim* [1. sérafim; 2. sérəfim], fr. Heb. *serāphīm* (only in pl.), 'the exalted ones', cogn. w. Arab. *sharaf*, 'high, noble'. Cp. **Shereef.** **1.** (Bib.) A celestial being, having human form and three pairs of wings (Isaiah vi. 2, 6). **2. a** An angel of the highest of the nine angelic orders; **b** a representation in art of such an angel, usually a head surrounded by three pairs of wings.

seraphic, adj. [1. seráfik; 2. səræfik]. Prec. & **-ic**. **1.** Pertaining to a seraph or to the order of seraphs: '*the great seraphic lords*' (Milton, 'P. L.'). **2.** Sublime, angelic, serene: *a seraphic smile. The Seraphic Doctor*, Saint Bonaventura, General of the Franciscans, 1221–74, renowned for his ardent preaching.

seraphically, adv. [1. seráfikali; 2. səræfikəli]. Prec. & **-al** & **-ly**. In a seraphic manner.

seraphim, n. pl. [1. sérafim; 2. sérəfim]. Heb.; used as pl. of **seraph**. Seraphs. *Order of the Seraphim*, the principal Swedish order of knighthood.

seraphine, n. [1. sérafēn; 2. sérəfīn]. **seraph** & **-ine**. (mus.) An early form of reed instrument played by a keyboard and bellows, succeeded by the melodeon and harmonium.

seraskier, n. [1. sèraskḗr; 2. sèrəskíə]. Turk. *serasker*, fr. Pers. *sīr*, 'chief, head', & Arab. '*asker*, 'army'. A Turkish general; the commander-in-chief, or minister of war, in the Turkish Empire.

Serb, n. [1. sërb; 2. sāb]. Serb. *Srb*, *Srp*. **a** A native of Serbia (or Servia); **b** language of this people.

Serbian, adj. & n. [1. sërbian; 2. sābiən], fr. prec. & **-ian**. **1.** adj. Of or pertaining to Serbia or the Serbian language. **2.** n. **a** A Serb; **b** the Serbian language.

Serbonian bog, n. [1. sërbónian bòg; 2. sābóuniən bɔ̀g], fr. Lake Serbonis, a boggy lake in the delta of the Nile, in which whole armies were said to be swallowed up; cp. Milton, 'P. L.', ii. 592. (lit. and fig.) A difficult, confused position from which escape is almost impossible.

sere (I.), adj. [1. sēr; 2. siə]. See **sear (I.)**. Dry, withered.

sere (II.), n. See **sear (III.)**. A catch of a gun-lock.

serecloth, n. See **cerecloth.**

serein, n. [1. serán; 2. seréin]. **Fr.** See **serene (I.)**. A fine, misty rain falling from a clear sky.

serenade (I.), n. [1. sèrenád; 2. sèrinéid], fr. Fr. *sérénade*, fr. Ital. *serenata*, fr. Lat. *serēnāt-(um)*, P.P. of *serēnāre*, 'to make calm, clear, or serene', fr. *serēnus*, see **serene (I.)**; the meaning is due to the confusion of Lat. *serēnus* w. *sērus*, 'late' (cp. Ital. *sera*, 'evening'), & the application of former to the evening or night. **1. a** Music sung or played at night by a lover beneath a lady's window; **b** music composed for such a song. **2.** (mus.) **a** A cantata; **b** an early form of the instrumental symphony, a development of the suite.

serenade (II.), vb. trans. & intrans., fr. prec. **1.** trans. To play, sing, a serenade to: *to serenade one's lady-love.* **2.** intrans. To perform, sing, play, serenades: *the young Spaniards go serenading every night.*

serenata, n. [1. sèrenáhta; 2. sèrenάtə]. **Ital.** See prec. Serenade.

serendipity, n. [1. sèrendípiti; 2. sèrəndípiti]. Coined by Horace Walpole, Letters to Mann, Jan. 1754; fr. *Serendib, -dip*, Arab. name of Ceylon, in tale of three princes of Ceylon. The faculty of finding interesting or valuable things by chance or where one least expects them.

serene (I.), adj. [1. serḗn; 2. sərín], fr. Lat. *serēnus*, 'clear, fair, cloudless, bright; joyous, glad'; fr. **kseresnos*; prob. cogn. w. Gk. *xērós, xerós*, 'dry'; Scrt. *kṣáyati*, 'it burns'; cp. Lat. *serescere*, 'to grow dry'. **1. a** (of sky, air, weather; of celestial bodies &c.) Clear, unclouded: *the sky is serene and bright*; *in the clear sky the moon shines serene*; **b** (of sea, weather) calm, unruffled, placid: *into the serene waters of the Pacific*; *a bright, serene October*. **2.** (of condition of mind and body) **a** Calm, placid, tranquil; undisturbed, unruffled: *a serene old age*; *the serene dignity of his face*; *serene courage*; *he kept his temper serene in the most trying circumstances*; **b** slang Phr. *all serene!*, everything is quiet, there is no danger; all right! **3.** (as title) *Serene Highness*, abbr. H.S.H., *His, Her, Serene Highness*, used of members of certain princely European families; the Lat. *serēnissimus*, 'most serene', was used as a title of honour in the Byzantine Empire and also by the Doges of Venice.

serene (II.), n. & vb. trans., fr. prec. (poet. and archaic) **1.** n. A serene expanse of sky or sea: *into the vast serene*; '*But never did I breathe its pure serene, Till I heard Chapman speak out loud and bold*' (Keats). **2.** vb. To make serene, to make clear or calm.

serenely, adv. [1. serḗnli; 2. serínli]. **serene** (I.) & **-ly.** In a serene manner; clearly; calmly, without perturbation or agitation of mind.

sereneness, n. [1. serḗnnes; 2. serínnis]. See prec. & **-ness.** Serenity.

serenity, n. [1. seréniti; 2. seréniti], fr. Lat. *serēnitāt-(em)*. See **serene** (I.) & **-ity. 1.** State, quality, of being serene; **a** (of sky, sea &c.) clearness, brightness: *the serenity of the weather*; **b** (of mind &c.) tranquillity, composure: *the serenity of old age*. **2.** As title, referring to a Serene Highness: *Their Serenities the Prince and Princess of X.*

serf, n. [1. sërf; 2. sə̄f]. Fr., fr. Lat. *servus*, 'slave'. See **serve** (I.). **1.** (hist.) **a** In the earlier pre-Conquest Middle Ages a slave belonging personally to a thegn, and working his land; **b** one who, as formerly in Russia, while personally free, is bound to the soil, which he cannot leave without his master's consent; a serf can be sold only with the land to which he is attached. **2.** (fig.) Term applied to one who is conceived of as being in a humiliating and degrading state of dependence upon another and living under conditions supposed to resemble those of a serf; e.g. a wage-earner who works for a master is compared by some to a serf.

serfage, n. [1. sërfij; 2. sə̄fidž]. Prec. & **-age.** Serfdom.

serfdom, n. [1. sërfdum; 2. sə̄fdəm]. **serf** & **-dom. a** State, condition, of a serf; servitude; **b** system of tilling the land by serfs; villeinage.

serge, n. [1. sërj; 2. sə̄dž]. Fr., fr. Lat. *sērica*, 'silk material, silken garments', fem. of *sēricus*, 'silken'. See **sericeous.** Formerly a silken fabric, now a hard-wearing, twilled, woollen material, used for men's and women's outer garments.

sergeant, serjeant, n. [1. sárjent; 2. sádžənt], fr. O. Fr. *sergant*, fr. L. or Med. Lat. *servient-(em)*, n. 'servant', Pres. Part. of *servīre*, 'to serve', see **servant** & **serve** (I.). The spelling w. *g* is usual in military & police senses; that w. *j* in the legal sense; the rule in other cases varies. **1.** (Med. hist., in various uses) **a** Of various royal or court officials, surviving in *sergeant-at-arms*; **b** a fully armed mounted man-at-arms, ranking below a squire; **c** a legal official of the king; **d** a tenant holding by *sergeanty*. **2.** (mil.) **a** Non-commissioned officer in British Army, ranking above a corporal and below a *sergeant-major*, responsible for drill and discipline; **b** a police-officer ranking below an inspector and above a constable. **3.** (legal, in full *Serjeant-at-law*) A member of an order of barristers, now abolished, ranking in precedence before King's Counsel, enjoying exclusive rights of pleading in certain courts, and wearing originally a coif or white lawn cap, later a small black silk patch on the top of the wig; the privileges were abolished finally in 1873, and the order is extinct except in Ireland; *Common Serjeant*, a judicial officer of the City of London, who also sits as a judge in the Central Criminal Court. **4.** Sergeant-fish.

sergeant-, serjeant-at-arms, n. Usually w. *j*. **1.** The name of various ceremonial officials of the Royal Household. **2.** Specif., name of two officials in charge of the mace, **a** of the Lord Chancellor in the House of Lords; **b** of the Speaker of the House of Commons, responsible for carrying out disciplinary orders, conveying messages from the Crown, and other ceremonial duties.

sergeant-fish, n. A deep-sea fish of the Atlantic and Pacific Oceans, resembling the mackerel, bearing stripes like those of a sergeant's chevron.

sergeant-major, n. (mil.) A warrant officer of which there is one to each company in infantry battalions, ranking above a sergeant; in the cavalry and artillery, the senior non-commissioned officer of a troop, squadron, or battery; *regimental sergeant-major*, the senior warrant officer of a battalion.

sergeanty, serjeanty, n. [1. sárjenti; 2. sádžənti]. Usually w. *j*; fr. O. Fr. *sergantie*. See **sergeant** & **-y.** (feudal law) A tenure of land by the rendering of various services, to the Crown, or superior lord, other than military or knight service; *grand serjeanty*, performance of personal service or attendance on the lord; still surviving in ceremonial duties at coronations: *petty serjeanty*, annual tribute of some article of war; surviving in some tenures, by presentation of a flag &c.

serial (I.), adj. [1. sḗrial; 2. síəriəl]. See **series** & **-al. 1.** Pertaining to, arranged in, forming, a series: *currency notes bearing serial numbers*; *in serial order*. **2. a** Appearing, issued, published, at specific intervals or periods; issued in a series of parts or instalments: *a serial story, film* &c.; **b** referring to a publication so issued: *serial rights*; *serial publication*.

serial (II.), n., fr. prec. **a** A serial publication of any kind; **b** specif., a story, novel &c. published in serial form.

serially, adv. [1. sḗriali; 2. síəriəli]. **serial** (I.) & **-ly. a** In a series, in successive order: *the numbers follow serially*; **b** in succeeding numbers or parts: *the novel will appear serially*.

seriate, adj. [1. sḗriāt; 2. síərieit], fr. Med. Lat. *seriāt-(um)*, P.P. of *seriāre*, 'to arrange in a series'. See **series** & **-ate. a** Arranged in a series or in order of successive numbers; **b** pertaining to a series.

seriatim, adv. [1. sēriátim; 2. siəriéitim]. Med. Lat.; prec. & *-im*, old form of acc. suff., used to form adv., cp. Lat. *statim*, 'immediately'. In regular order, serially; specif., point by point, taking things one by one in their order: *to deal with arguments seriatim*; *to take the numbers seriatim*.

seriation, n. [1. sēriáshun; 2. siəriéiʃən]. **seriate** & **-ion.** Arrangement in series; formation of a series; position in a series.

sericate, adj. [1. sérikāt; 2. sérikeit]. See next word & **-ate.** Sericeous.

sericeous, adj. [1. seríshus; 2. seríʃəs], fr. L. Lat. *sericeus* & **-ous**; Lat. *sēricus*, 'silken'; cp. *sēricum*, 'silk', fr. Gk. *sērikón*, fr. *sērikós*, pertaining to the *Seres*, an E. Asiatic people mentioned by Gk. & Lat. writers as making silk; now gen. identified w. the Chinese. Resembling silk, having a silky appearance or feel; specif. (bot.) covered with soft, silky hairs.

sericite, n. [1. sérisīt; 2. sérisait], fr. Lat. *sēricus*, 'silken', & **-ite.** (mineral.) A species of muscovite with a silky, lustrous surface, resembling talc.

sericultural, adj. [1. sèrikúlchural; 2. sèrikáltʃərəl]. Next word & **-al.** Pertaining to sericulture.

sericulture, n. [1. sérikùlchur; 2. sérikàltʃə]. Lat. *sēricum*, 'silk'. See **sericeous** & **culture.** The breeding and management of silkworms for the production of raw silk.

sericulturist, n. [1. sérikulchurist; 2. sérikaltʃərist]. Prec. & **-ist.** One engaged in the production of raw silk.

seriema, n. [1. sèriḗma; 2. sèriímə]. Native S. Am. name. A large, long-legged, crested Brazilian bird, of yellowish-grey colour, with red legs and bill, related to the bustards.

series, n. [1. sḗrēz; 2. síərīz]. Lat., 'row, succession, order, sequence, series'; fr. *serere*, 'to join, fasten together, to arrange in order', cogn. w. Gk. *heirein* for **ser-j-*, 'to fasten together in rows, to string together, to bind'; O.E. *searu*, 'device, contrivance; armour'; cp. **seraglio** & **serried.** A number, set of things, or events, similar to each other or having some common characteristic or relationship, arranged, or standing, in order of succession, following in time, or next in space; a sequence, row, set, succession; **a** (of material things or persons) *a series of columns, arches* &c.; *series of coins*; *a series of able statesmen*; **b** (of non-material things) *a series of defeats, victories*; Phr. *in series*, arranged in order of. **2.** Specific or technical uses: **a** (bibliog.) a number of works having similar size and scope, published successively from same firm, dealing with related subjects, different aspects of a subject &c., edited according to some common plan; **b** (biol.) a group as a form of classification, less wide than order; **c** (elect.) arrangement, set, of batteries connected end to end and not parallel; **d** (chem.) a group of compounds having a common radical, as the hydrocarbons; **e** (geol.) a formation, group, of allied strata forming a subdivision of a system; **f** (math.) a succession of terms arranged according to a common law; a progression.

serif, n. See **ceriph.**

serin, n. [1. sérin; 2. sérin]. Fr.; etymol. unknown. A yellow or greenish-yellow finch, *Serinus hortulanus*, of Central and South Europe, akin to the canary.

serinette, n. [1. serinét; 2. sèrinét]. Fr., prec. & dimin. **-ette.** A musical instrument used in training serins and other song-birds.

seringa, n. [1. seríngga; 2. səríŋgə]. Port. See **syringa.** A Brazilian rubber tree of various species.

serio-comic, adj. [1. sḗriō kómik; 2. síəriou kómik]. See **serious** & **comic.** Half serious, half comic; combining the serious and comic; mock serious.

serious, adj. [1. sḗrius; 2. síəriəs]. O. Fr. *serieux*, fr. L. Lat. *sērius*, 'grave, earnest, not jocular, serious', & **-ous**; orig. sense, 'heavy', whence 'weighty, in importance and in behaviour'; cogn. w. O.H.G. *swār*, 'heavy, severe', Mod. Germ. *schwer*; O.E. *swǣr*, 'excessive, heavy, grievous'; Goth. *swērs*, 'honoured', fr. earlier sense 'weighty; making an imposing impression'; further Lith. *svarùs*, 'heavy', *svoras*, 'weight'. **1. a** Of a solemn, sober, thoughtful turn of mind; not given to levity; grave, sedate, staid: *he is strangely serious for so young a man*; also, *a serious mind, a serious thought* &c.; **b** in a solemn, serious mood; not for the moment inclined to jest; filled with grave thoughts: *the news of the disaster rendered him serious in a moment*; *you look very serious this morning*; also expressing, revealing, a serious mood: *his face became suddenly serious*; *we must have a serious talk.* **2. a** Meaning what one says, wishing to be taken literally; not ironical: *you cannot be serious when you say you are thirty-five*;

b (of things said or done) meant in earnest, intended, whole-hearted: *is this a serious offer?*; *make a serious attempt to swim the Channel.* 3. Genuine, thorough, to be reckoned with in specified capacity; reverse of superficial, perfunctory, amateurish: *a serious student, scholar, painter*; *a serious opponent, rival.* 4. Important, grave, not to be disregarded; bringing important results; demanding consideration and care; demanding considered action; **a** as involving difficulty, effort: *a serious matter*; *a serious step to take*; *a serious offence, mistake, oversight* &c.; **b** attended with risk and danger; giving rise to anxiety; critical: *the situation is serious*; *a serious menace*; *a serious illness, wound*; *the patient is in a serious condition.* 5. Concerned, dealing, with grave intellectual or spiritual questions: *many people cannot read serious books*; *a mind accustomed to dwell on serious subjects*; *the play was too serious for me.*

seriously, adv. Prec. & **-ly**. 1. In a serious manner, **a** gravely, solemnly, impressively: *he warned them seriously*; *we must treat, take, the matter seriously*; **b** not lightly; in earnest: *do you seriously mean what you say?*; *seriously speaking*; *now, seriously* (as introducing a statement &c.), joking apart. 2. To a serious degree, so as to cause anxiety or danger; dangerously; severely: *seriously wounded, seriously ill*; *seriously affected by the coal strike*; to a considerable extent, gravely: *seriously offended.*

seriousness, n. See prec. & **-ness**. 1. Quality, state, of being serious, grave, earnest; not frivolous or jocular: *his life was marked by an unrelaxing seriousness*; *the seriousness of his mind*; *we must regard the matter in all seriousness.* 2. State or quality of being attended with danger, causing anxiety: *seriousness of our position, of the news*; *seriousness of an illness* &c.

serjeant, serjeanty. See **sergeant** &c.

sermon, n. [1. sêrmun; 2. sə́mən]. M.E., fr. Fr., fr. Lat. *sermōn-(em)*, 'speech, discourse, conversation, discussion'; prob. cogn. w. Goth. *swaran*, 'to answer; to swear, affirm', q.v. under **swear**, & second element of **answer**. **a** Discourse on moral and religious subjects delivered from the pulpit of a church; *the Sermon on the Mount*, the teaching of Christ embodied in the discourse related in Matt. v., vi., and vii. and Luke vi.; **b** (iron.) tedious harangue, pronouncement of a moralizing and admonitory character uttered by one having no special mission to preach.

sermonize, vb. trans. & intrans. [1. sêrmunīz; 2. sə́mənaiz]. **sermon** & **-ize**. **a** trans. To preach at; to lecture; **b** intrans., to preach; to deliver harangues.

sero-, pref. See **serum**; used in compounds: *sero-therapy*, treatment by serum.

serosity, n. [1. sērósiti; 2. siərɔ́siti]. **serous** & **-ity**. 1. State of being serous. 2. A serous fluid.

serotine, n. [1. sérotin; 2. sérətin]. Fr., fr. Lat. *sērōtinus*, 'happening, coming late or in the evening', fr. *sērus*, 'late'; cogn. w. Scrt. *sāyám*, 'evening'; O. Ir. *sīr*, 'enduring, everlasting'; Goth. *seiþus*, 'late'; O.E. *siððan*, 'since, later', see **since**. The base is *sēi- &c., 'to come late, come slowly'. A small European and N. African bat, *Vespertilio serotinus*, chestnut brown in colour with yellowish underparts.

serotinous, adj. [1. serótinus; 2. sərɔ́tinəs]. Prec. & **-ous**. (bot. and zool.) Appearing later in the season than is usual.

serous, adj. [1. sḗrus; 2. síərəs]. **serum** & **-ous**. Having the character of serum; secreting serum.

serpent, n. [1. sêrpent; 2. sə́pənt]. Fr., fr. Lat. *serpent-(em)*, 'serpent, snake', lit. 'a creeping thing', fr. Pres. Part. of *serpere*, 'to wind; crawl', cogn. w. Scrt. *sarpati*, 'he creeps', & *sarpaś*, 'serpent', Gk. *hérpein*, 'to creep'. 1. A snake. Phr. *the Serpent*, the devil in the form of the tempter. 2. A malevolent, venomous person. 3. Specif. **a** (astron., cap.) one of the northern constellations; **b** (mus.) an obsolete bass wood wind instrument, with long tube curved or bent like a snake.

serpent-bearer, n. A constellation to the south of Hercules, represented pictorially by a man strangling a serpent, also called *Ophiuchus.*

serpent-charmer, n. A snake-charmer.

serpent-eater, n. **a** The secretary-bird; **b** the markhor or Himalayan wild goat.

serpent-fish, n. A ribbon fish.

serpent-grass, n. The Alpine bistort, a polygonaceous perennial herb with twisted root.

serpentiform, adj. [1. sërpéntiform; 2. səpéntifɔ̄m], fr. Lat. *serpent-(is)*, 'serpent', & **-form**. Serpent-like in form.

serpentine (I.), adj. & n. [1. sêrpentīn; 2. sə́pəntain], fr. Fr. *serpentin(e)*, fr. Lat. *serpentīnus*. See **serpent** & **-ine**. 1. adj. Resembling a serpent; specif. **a** twisting, winding, sinuous: *the serpentine turnings of the road*; **b** (fig., of character &c.) crooked, tortuous, treacherous, unreliable. 2. n. (cap.) *The Serpentine*, sheet of water in Hyde Park; so called from its former shape.

serpentine (II.), n., fr. prec. 1. (geol.) A rock or mineral consisting of hydrous magnesium silicate, found in a fibrous state as *asbestos* or in masses of soft rock, of deep green or red colour, taking a high polish and used as a form of marble for ornamental work; named from its mottled appearance. 2. An old form of cannon.

serpent-like, adj. **serpent** & **-like**. Resembling a serpent (lit. and fig.).

serpent-lizard, n. The seps.

serpent's tongue, n. (bot.) A fern, also known as *adder's tongue.*

serpiginous, adj. [1. sërpíjinus; 2. səpídžinəs], fr. Lat. *serpīgin-(em)*. Stem of next word & **-ous**. Of the nature of serpigo; resembling this.

serpigo, n. [1. sërpígō; 2. səpáigou]. Lat., 'a creeping skin disease', fr. base *serp-*, 'to creep', see **serpent**. **a** Ringworm; **b** herpes or shingles.

serpula, n. [1. sêrpūla; 2. sə́pjulə]. Lat., 'little snake'. See **serpent**. A brightly coloured marine worm living in a tubular shell.

serra, n. [1. séra; 2. sérə]. Lat., 'saw'; etymol. doubtful; perh. imitative of sound of sawing; Isidore says of the word '*nomen de sono factum est*'. A saw-like organ; a serrated edge of an organ or part of the body, as of the saw-fish or saw-fly.

serradella, serradilla, n. [1. sèradéla, -díla; 2. sèrədélə, -dílə]. Port. & Span., fr. *serrado*, 'serrated'. See prec. word. A kind of clover, also called 'bird's foot clover', used for fodder.

serrate, adj. [1. sérāt; 2. séreit], fr. Lat. *serrātus*. See **serra** & **-ate**. Having notches on the edge like the teeth of a saw; serrated; esp. of leaves.

serrated, adj. [1. serā́ted; 2. seréitid]. Prec. & **-ed**. Serrate; more usual in common parlance.

serration, n. [1. serā́shun; 2. seréišən]. Prec. & **-ion**. Formation resembling the edge of a saw.

serricorn, n. [1. sérikorn; 2. sérikɔ̄n]. **serra** & Lat. *cornu*, 'horn'. See **corn** (III.). A beetle with serrated antennae.

serried, adj. [1. sérid; 2. sérid], fr. Fr. *serré*, P.P. of *serrer*, 'to press close together', & **-ed**; *serrer* is fr. Lat. *serāre*, 'to bolt, shut', formed fr. Lat. *sera*, 'bolt, bar', wh. is in gradational relation to Lat. *sūrus*, 'branch of a tree, bar (for a door)'; cogn. w. Scrt. *sváruš*, 'long piece of wood; a post'; O.E. *swēor*, 'pillar, column', & *swēora*, 'neck'; cp. **series** & **seraglio**. Packed, pressed, closely together, in compact order; closely knit; esp. in Phr. *in serried ranks* (of soldiers &c.); *serried rows of spectators.*

serriferous, adj. [1. seríferus; 2. seríferəs]. See **serra** & **-ferous**. (bot. and zool.) Having serrated edges; bearing a serrated organ or appendage.

serriform, adj. [1. sériform; 2. sérifɔ̄m]. **serra** & **-form**. Shaped like, resembling, a saw; having a serrated edge.

serrirostrate, adj. [1. sēriróstrāt; 2. sèrirɔ́streit]. **serra** & **rostrate**. (of birds) Saw-billed.

serrulate, adj. [1. sérūlāt; 2. sérjuleit], fr. Lat. *serrula*, 'a little saw', dimin. of **serra**, & **-ate**. Finely toothed or serrated.

serum, n. [1. sḗrum; 2. síərəm]. Lat. *serum*, 'whey, watery fluid', cogn. w. Gk. *orós*, 'whey', fr. **sorós*; Scrt. *saraš*, 'flowing'; the base **ser-*, **sor-*, is a simpler form of **srew-*, 'to flow', q.v. under **rheo-** & **stream**. **a** Watery fluid remaining from the fluids of the body, esp. from blood, after coagulation; **b** specif. (pathol.) such a fluid prepared by culture for immunization by inoculation; cp. *vaccine.*

servable, adj. [1. sêrvabl; 2. sə́vəbl]. **serve** (I.) & **-able**. Capable of being served.

serval, n. [1. sêrvl; 2. sə́vl], fr. native name. An African wild cat, *Felis serval*, of brownish-yellow colour with black spots, long limbs, and ringed tail.

servant, n. [1. sêrvant; 2. sə́vənt]. O. Fr., fr. Lat. *servant-(em)*, Pres. Part. of *servāre*, 'to protect, keep watch over' &c.; the Fr. infin. *servir*, corresponds to Lat. *servīre*, 'to be a servant'. See **serve** (I.). One who serves, is in service of, another. 1. A person in the service of the Crown or State: *the Ministers are His Majesty's servants*; *a public servant*; *civil servant*, member of the Civil Service. 2. A person employed by another, his master, under a contract, written or implied, to perform certain duties and to be under his control and obedient to his orders, esp. **a** one, male or female, in personal service to such master, and attached to his house or estate: *a domestic servant*; *outdoor, indoor, general, servant*; *man-, maid-servant* &c.; **b** of a member of the official staff of a company, or of an employee of a company performing public services: *the servants of a railway company*, including all the employees; in general the term is contrasted with *employee, workman, labourer*, which are applied to persons employed in trades, businesses &c. 3. **a** As form of ending an official letter whether to a superior or not: *your obedient servant*, (formerly in full) *your humble and obedient servant*; **b** (obs. or semi-jocular) as form of greeting, or acknowledgement: *madam, your obedient, humble servant!*; *your servant, sir!* 4. **a** (as transl. of Lat. *servus*, in religious or eccles. usage) A devoted adherent or follower of another, one ready and eager to do service, fulfil the will of another: *a humble servant of Christ*; '*Servant of God, well done*' (Milton, 'P. L.' vi. 29); *servant of the servants of God*, (Lat. *servus servorum Dei*), title adopted for the Popes by Gregory the Great; **b** (by transf.) one devoted to the service or interests of others or of some special duty or interest: *a servant of art, literature* &c.; *he professed to conduct his business solely as a servant of the public.* 5. Something which aids, helps, or serves, if put to proper use and kept under control, esp in Phr. *a good servant, but a bad master*, of money, fire &c.

servant-maid, -girl, n. A maidservant; girl, maid, in domestic service.

servants' hall, n. Special room in a private house used as sitting-room for the domestic servants, for their meals &c.

serve (I.), vb. trans. & intrans. [1. sërv; 2. sə̄v]. M.E. *serven*, fr. O. Fr. *servir*; there are two vbs. in Lat. the meanings of wh. are to some extent combined in the Fr. vb., *servīre*, 'to serve, be in service, be a servant', & *servāre*, 'to save, deliver, preserve, protect', cp. **observe, preserve, conserve**; both Lat. vbs. are formed fr. *servus*, 'slave, servant' &c., the primitive sense of wh. is 'guardian, watcher', specif., 'guardian of cattle' &c.;

hence, 'attendant, slave' &c.; cp. cogn. Gk. *oûros*, 'watcher, guardian', for **sorwos*; cp. also Lith. *sergiu*, 'I watch'; on the other hand, Gk. *eireros*, 'servitude', orig. perh. 'place where something is guarded'; the idea of servitude, slave &c., may be arrived at either direct fr. that of 'one employed as a guardian', or fr. the sense 'person under guard, one who is kept from escaping'. Another form of the same base, in the sense of 'to watch', hence, 'to be troubled' &c., is prob. found in **sorrow**. **A.** trans. **1. a** To act as servant to, to be employed by, to work for: *to serve a master*; **b** to render spiritual service and obedience to, to worship and obey: *to serve God*; Phr. *to serve two masters*, to owe divided allegiance. **2. a** To perform service, duties, for; give one's service to: *to serve the king, one's country* &c.; **b** to be of service to; to help, assist, forward interests of: *I am only too glad if I can serve you in any way*; **c** to be of use, to avail: *there are occasions when we feel that no human power can serve us.* **3. a** To supply with goods &c., to attend, wait, upon: *to serve customers*; *what can we serve you with?*; *is there anyone to serve me?*; **b** to supply, satisfy, the wants of: *our branch (railway) line serves a large district.* **4. a** To prepare and present (food) at table: *dinner is served*; *to serve goose with plenty of stuffing*; **b** to distribute, hand round: *to serve coffee in Sèvres cups*; *serve it to his lordship first.* **5.** To be adequate to, fulfil; (chiefly) *to serve its purpose*, do what is required; *that will serve my purpose*, perform the duties or functions which I need; (also) *serve its, my &c., turn.* **6. a** To perform, fulfil, the duties necessary for or required in: *one doctor serves a large district*; **b** (i.) to assist at (a service); (ii.) give assistance to in a subordinate position: *an acolyte to serve Mass, to serve the priest at Mass.* **7.** To go through, pass time in, undergo punishment &c.: *to serve an apprenticeship*; *to serve one's full term in office, prison* &c.; *he served seven years.* Phr. *to serve time.* **8.** To treat, to behave to; chiefly in Phr. *it serves you right*, you have got what you deserve; (otherwise rather vulg.) *he served his father very badly*; *you have no business to serve me like that.* **9.** To handle, work, operate: *to serve a, the, gun(s).* **10.** (of stallion) To cover: *to serve a mare.* **11.** (law) **a** (of legal processes) To make legal service of, to bring to the notice of person affected, to deliver, execute, put into effect: *to serve a summons, writ, notice (upon)*, to deliver it personally or by substitution; *to serve a warrant*, to read it to and arrest person named in it; *to serve an attachment, execution*, to levy by attachment of person or seizure of goods; **b** to make legal service of processes on: *to serve a person with a writ, summons* &c. **12.** (naut.) To wind, wrap, pieces of cord, wire, canvas &c. round (rope) to protect it from wear, fraying, or against the weather &c. **13.** (tennis and similar games) To deliver (ball to opponent) by striking with racquet into his court &c. **B.** intrans. **1. a** To be, act as, a servant, to be employed by another, to be in domestic service: *to serve in the house, garden, kitchen* &c.; *he served as a footman before the war*; **b** to be in subjection or servitude, to obey, have to be obedient to another: '*Better to reign in Hell than serve in Heaven*' (Milton, 'P. L.', i. 263). **2.** Specif. **a** to be a soldier or sailor, perform military or naval duties: *to serve in India, in the ranks, in a flag-ship* &c.; **b** to be in any public service, act as official or public servant: *to serve as a judge in India.* **3.** To perform services, duties &c.; to be of service: '*They also serve who only stand and wait*' (Milton, 'On his Blindness'). **4.** To be all that is needed; to suffice, to avail, for particular purpose; **a** *a single horse will serve*; *the car is old, but it will serve for my purpose*; *this will serve for the moment*; (also) *it will serve to do what I want* &c.; *a single example will serve to illustrate the point*; *his rags hardly served to cover him*; **b** to be convenient, favourable, to suit: *the tide serves (for setting sail &c.)*; *as, where occasion, the time, serves*, at the earliest and most favourable opportunity. **5.** *Serve as*, to supply the place of, perform functions of, act as substitute for: *a crutch served John Silver as a deadly weapon*; *an old blanket served as a curtain.* **6.** (tennis &c.) To deliver the ball to opponent before each point is scored: *it is your turn to serve.*

serve (II.), n., fr. prec. Act of serving; style of serving; turn to serve, at tennis &c.

server, n. [1. sĕ́rver; 2. sʌ́və]. **serve (I.)** & **-er.** One who serves; specif. **a** (eccles.) one who serves the officiating priest at the Mass; acolyte; **b** (tennis &c.) the player who serves.

-server, suff. Prec. in compounds: *time-server* &c.

Servian, adj. & n. See **Serbian**, wh. is better.

service, n. [1. sĕ́rvis; 2. sʌ́vis]. M.E. *servise*, fr. O. Fr. *servise, service*, fr. Lat. *servitium*, 'state of a slave, servitude', fr. *servus.* See **serve (I.)**. **1. a** Act of serving or being a servant; occupation, employment, position, of a servant, esp. of a domestic servant to a master or mistress: *domestic service*; *to be in, go into, out to, service*, to be, become, a domestic servant; **b** employ: *he was in his master's service for many years*; *the cook left our service last week.* Phr. *at your service*, at your disposal, for your use. **2.** Devotion to, worship of, God. **3.** Any one of the various duties which a feudal tenant owed to his lord as a condition of tenure of land: *a knight's service.* Phr. *to do yeoman('s) service*, good, useful service or work; valuable help or assistance when in need. **4. a** Public work, official duty, esp. of a Government or State department or of the Crown; department performing such duties, staff employed: *the Civil, Consular, Diplomatic, Service*; *On His Majesty's Service*, O.H.M.S., form for franking official letters; *the services*, also *the fighting services*, the Army and Navy; **b** performance of the duties of any of such services, esp. in Army or Navy: *(to be) on active service*; *to see service.* **5.** Act performed for the benefit or advantage of a person, institution, or cause; action, effort, carried out as an assistance to a person, institution, or in furtherance of a cause &c.; benefit arising from such action: *to render services to one's fellow-townsmen, one's country*; *his services to the cause of learning deserve recognition*; *I shall be happy to render you any service in my power*; *you have done me a great service.* Phr. *to be of service to*, be useful, advantageous, to. **6.** Any activity of public utility, regularly carried on to supply public need: *train service*; *tramway, telephone, service*; *a service of trains*, all trains collectively running regularly between certain places. **7.** (eccles.) An office, order, a part of the liturgy set down for religious worship: *the Church services*; *divine service*; *the Communion, Eucharistic, Service*; *marriage, burial, service* &c.; **a** performance of this: *to hold a daily service*; *to attend morning service*; **b** musical setting for those parts of the liturgy which are to be sung: *Tallis's Service in the Dorian Mode.* **8. a** The serving of a meal, attendance, waiting, as at a restaurant, hotel &c.: *the food is good, but is spoiled by bad service*; **b** a set of all the dishes, plates, cups, and saucers &c. necessary for the serving of a particular meal: *a dinner, tea, breakfast, service*; **c** a set of spoons, forks &c., in silver or gold plate: *a service of plate.* **9.** (law) The serving of a writ or other legal process or notice in a suit so that it shall come to the knowledge of the person concerned, by personal delivery of a copy of the document, *personal service*, or by publication in a newspaper or other such means or by delivery to an authorized person, *substituted service.* **10.** (naut.) Material, such as yarn, small cord &c. used in serving a rope. **11.** (tennis &c.) **a** Act of serving the ball; **b** ball so served; manner, style in which it is served; **c** turn for serving.

serviceable, adj. [1. sĕ́rvisabl; 2. sʌ́visəbl]. **service** & **-able.** **a** (of persons) Fit, able, willing, to render service; **b** (of things) useful; fit for use; lasting.

serviceableness, n. Prec. & **-ness.** Quality of being serviceable.

serviceably, adv. See prec. & **-ly.** In a serviceable manner.

service-book, n. A book containing a church service or liturgy; a prayer-book, missal.

service court, n. That court on a tennis-lawn, part of tennis court, into which the ball must be served.

service dress, n. Uniform worn on active service, or when on ordinary routine duties; contrasted with full dress or parade order.

service flat, n. A flat, set of rooms in a building of residential flats &c., in which meals and attendance are supplied from a common kitchen and by a central staff of servants.

service line, n. Line marking limit of service court in lawn-tennis.

service pipe, n. Pipe conveying water or gas from the main into a building.

service tree, n. M.E. *serves*, pl., 'service berries', O.E. *syrf(e)*, 'the service tree', fr. Lat. *sorbus*, 'the tree', *sorbum*, pl. *sorba*, 'its fruit'; etymol. doubtful. A rosaceous tree, found in Europe and Asia Minor, *Pyrus sorbus*, allied to, and resembling, the mountain ash, with greenish-brown berries.

servient, adj. [1. sĕ́rvient; 2. sʌ́viənt], fr. Lat. *servient-(em)*, Pres. Part. of *servīre*, see **serve.** Serving, subordinate to; specif. (law) of estate or property which carries a servitude or easement due to a dominant estate or property.

serviette, n. [1. sĕrviét; 2. sʌviét]. Fr., fr. *servir*, 'to serve (at table)'. (vulg.) A table napkin; better called simply a napkin.

servile, adj. [1. sĕ́rvīl; 2. sʌ́vail]. O. Fr., fr. Lat. *servīlis.* See **serf, serve (I.)** & **-ile.** **1.** Connected with, pertaining to, a slave, slaves, or slavery. **2. a** (of persons) Having the character of, behaving like, a slave; hence cringing, fawning, abjectly submissive or obsequious; **b** expressing servility: *servile manners, behaviour, action* &c. **3.** Specif. uses: **a** (R.C. Ch.) pertaining to bodily, rather than mental labour: *servile works*, such as are performed by servants or hired workmen, forbidden on Sundays &c. except as permitted by custom; **b** (feudal law, of tenure) not free.

servilely, adv. Prec. & **-ly.** In a servile manner; with servility.

servility, n. [1. sĕrvíliti; 2. sʌvíliti]. See prec. & **-ity.** State, quality, of being servile; **a** servitude, serfdom, slavery; **b** obsequious behaviour, subserviency, sycophancy.

serving man, n. [1. sĕ́rving măn; 2. sʌ́viŋ mæn]. (archaic) Manservant.

servitor, n. [1. sĕ́rviter; 2. sʌ́vitə], fr. O. Fr. *servitour*, fr. Lat. *servītor*, 'servant'. See **serve (I.)** & **-or.** (archaic and poet.) **1. a** A male attendant or servant; **b** an adherent, partisan, henchman. **2.** (Oxford University) Formerly a poor undergraduate, supported by a college in return for certain menial services rendered to the fellows and gentlemen commoners.

servitorship, n. [1. sĕ́rvitership; 2. sʌ́vitəʃip]. Prec. & **-ship.** Position of a servitor.

servitude, n. [1. sĕ́rvitūd; 2. sʌ́vitjūd]. O. Fr., fr. Lat. *servitūdo*, 'slavery'; fr. *servus*, 'slave', see **serve (I.)** & **-tude**; in the legal sense the Lat. word is *servitūs.* **1.** Condition, state, of a slave; slavery, serfdom, bondage; *penal servitude*, imprisonment for a term of three years or longer; (also fig.) compulsory subjection to the will of another or any compelling influence: *a life of toil and servitude*; *in servitude to one's evil passions* &c. **2.** (Rom., civil and Scots law) A burden affecting land or other heritable property, equivalent of the English *easement.*

sesame, n. [1. sésami; 2. sésəmi]. In M.E., fr. O. Fr. *sisame, sesame*, fr. Lat. *sēsama*, also *sisamum*, fr. Gk. *sēsámē*, prob. of Eastern origin. **a** An annual East Indian herb,

Sisamum Indicum, with white flowers, spotted with red or yellow, and small, ovoid two-celled seeds yielding an oil, used as a substitute for olive or almond oil and also in medicine; **b** the seeds of this plant; the oil extracted therefrom; Phr. *Open Sesame* (fr. tale of 'Ali Baba' in 'Arabian Nights'), magic formula, a method of gaining entrance or access, where these are normally difficult or impossible.

sesamoid, adj. & n. [1. sésamoid; 2. sésəmɔid]. Prec. & **-oid.** (anat.) **a** adj. Shaped like a sesame seed, used of small bone of kneecap &c.; **b** n., a sesamoid bone.

sesqui-, pref. Lat. *sesqui*, adv., chiefly as pref., 'one half more, (one) and a half'; fr. *sēmis*, 'half a unit, a half', see **semi-**, and *que*, 'and'.

sesquialter(al), adj. [1. sèskwiálter(al); 2. sèskwiǽltə(rəl)]. Lat. *sesquialter*, prec. & *alter*, 'another, second'. See **alter.** In the ratio of 1½ to 1, 3 to 2 &c.

sesquicentennial, adj. & n. [1. sèskwisenténial; 2. sèskwisenténiəl]. **sesqui-** & **centennial. a** adj. Pertaining to, of, a century and a half, of 150 years; **b** n., a one-hundred-and-fiftieth anniversary.

sesquipedalian, adj. [1. sèskwipedálian; 2. sèskwipedéiliən], fr. Lat. *sesquipedālis*. See **sesqui-** & **pedal** & **-ian.** Measuring, containing, a foot and a half; a foot and half long or broad; esp. used humorously of words containing many syllables; very long.

sess, n. See **cess.**

sessile, adj. [1. sésil; 2. sésail], fr. Lat. *sessilis*, 'of sitting, fit for sitting on; low, dwarfish, growing low', fr. *sess-(um)*, P.P. type of *sedēre*, 'to sit'. See **sedentary** & **-ile.** (bot. and zool.) Attached directly to the main stem or base, without stalk or peduncle.

session, n. [1. séshun; 2. séʃən]. Lat. *sessiōn-(em)*, 'a sitting; a sitting for discussion'; fr. *sess-(um)*, P.P. type of *sedēre*, 'to sit'. See **sedentary** & **sederunt** & **-ion. 1. a** A formal assembly or meeting, of a legislative or deliberative body for the transaction of business; specif., a meeting of Parliament; Phr. *in session*, assembled, sitting; **b** period during which a legislative body meets, or sits, regularly, without a break, for the transaction of business; specif., period during which Parliament sits. **2.** (in Scotland, and the newer universities of England) That part of each year, usually about seven months broken by short vacations, during which the university is officially in residence; academic year. **3.** (legal) *Sessions*, name given to certain meetings of courts of justice, presided over by judges, or magistrates, to try cases, grant licences &c., as *Brewster, Petty, Quarter, Sessions.* **4.** *Court of Session*, the supreme court of justice in Scotland. **5.** *Kirk Session*, lowest body in the Church of Scotland, consisting of the minister and elders of a particular church, which deals with matters concerning that church and parish.

sessional, adj. [1. séshunal; 2. séʃənəl]. Prec. & **-al.** Pertaining to a session or sessions; specif., *sessional orders, rules*, orders or rules applicable only to a specific session of Parliament.

sesterce, n., pl. *sesterces* [1. séstĕrs; 2. séstʌs], fr. Lat. *sestertius*, pl. *sestertii*, properly an adj., sc. *nummus*, 'coin', fr. *sēmis-tertius*, 'two and a half', see **semi-** & **tertius.** Ancient Roman coin and money of account, originally of silver, later of bronze or copper, ¼ of a denarius, 2½, later 4, asses, value about 2d.

sestertium, n., pl. **sestertia** [1. sestĕrshium, -ia; 2. səstʌ́ʃiəm, -iə]. Lat., properly genit. pl. of *sestertius*, sc. *(mille) nummōrum.* See prec. Ancient Roman money of account, 1000 sesterces, value about £8 : 17s.

sestet, n. [1. sèstét; 2. sèstét], fr. Ital. *sestetto*, fr. *sesto*, 'sixth', fr. Lat. *sextus*, 'sixth'. See **sextet. a** (mus.) A sextet; **b** the last six lines of a sonnet.

sestina, n. [1. sèstēna; 2. sèstínə]. Ital. See prec. & **-ine.** A complicated verse form, invented by the French troubadours of the 12th cent., consisting of six stanzas of six lines each with a triplet or envoy; it may be unrhymed; the words ending each stanza begin the next, but with the order changed, the triplet containing all these words.

set (I.), vb. trans. & intrans. [1. set; 2. set]. O.E. *settan*, fr. **sættjan*, 'to put, place; set down (what one is carrying); plant; lay foundations of, build &c.; to decree, appoint'; M.E. *sette(n)*; O.S. *settian*, O.H.G. *sezzen*, O.N. *setja*, Goth. *satjan*; formed in Gmc. fr. **sat-*, grade of *sittan*, 'to sit', see **sit.** The basal sense is to put, place, lay; hence, to bring into a specified position or condition. In the vast majority of sentences where *set* is used in a general sense, *put* could be used with exactly the same force, the former being, however, perhaps less colloquial, and belonging to a more refined and studied type of diction. On the other hand, there is a large number of idiomatic phrases in which *set* is fixed. In the examples of such phrases given below, only those are included in which *set* is habitually used in the particular idiom; those in which it might be and occasionally is used, although *put* &c. is more usual, are omitted. **A.** trans. **1.** To put, lay, (an object in a specified place or position) by a bodily effort or movement; **a** *to set a cup on a table*; *to set a stake in the ground*; *to set wine before a person*; **b** to move a limb, or part of the body into, or on to, a specified place: *to set one's foot in the stirrup, on a step*; *to set one's hand on a person's shoulder*; Phr. *to set eyes on*, to see, catch sight of; meet, come across; *to set one's foot on (a spark, a worm &c.)* to tread, stamp, on; *not to set foot (in a person's house, a certain place &c.)*, not to go there; *to set one's hand to the plough*, undertake to do something, and begin to do it; *to set one's hand, name, to a document*, sign it. **2.** To move something into contact with something else, apply, bring in contact or juxtaposition with: *to set a glass to one's lips, one's lips to a glass* &c.; *to set a match, a light, to a fire.* Phr. *to set fire, light, to*, burn; *to set pen to paper*, to write. **3.** To move (something), cause it to incline, turn (it) in a certain direction: *to set one's face towards the sun*; *to set one's horse's head homewards.* Phr. (fig.) *to set one's face against* (proposal &c.), to oppose strongly; *to set one's cap at*, endeavour to attract, make overtures to; esp. try to gain love of. **4.** To adjust, (machine, mechanism, implement &c.), put, fix, it into the right position, or condition, for functioning; various specif. uses: **a** *to set a clock*, put its hands at proper time; *to set the hands of a clock*; *to set a trap*; *to set the sails of a ship*; **b** *to set a razor*, put a keen edge on it; *to set a saw*, to sharpen the teeth with a file; **c** *to set a palette*, to squeeze out colours on to it, ready for painting. **5.** Specif. (of jeweller's craft) **a** *to set stones, diamonds* &c. to mount, embed, them firmly in some article of jewellery &c. so that they are seen to advantage; (fig.) *an island set in a sea of silver*; **b** *to set gold &c. with jewels*, to encrust it. **6.** To cause to become hard, solid, fixed, rigid &c.; **a** *the wind will soon dry up the mortar and set it*; *to set the white of an egg by boiling it*; *rennet sets milk*; **b** *to set one's teeth*, to clench the jaws tightly; (fig.) to come to a firm determination, to adopt an unbending, obstinate attitude of mind; **c** specif. (med.) *to set a broken bone*, fix the two edges in such a position that they will unite; **d** (i.) (of the body, its movements &c., chiefly in P.P.) to make mature, no longer liable to growth and change: *her figure is hardly set yet*; *the bowler is set*, has become fixed and invariable in his action; (ii.) (in moral sense) fixed, inflexible, rigid, lacking pliability, or adaptability: *his mind and character are completely set.* **7.** Specif., *to set a (broody) hen*, put her on eggs; *to set eggs under a hen.* **8. a** To lay out, arrange in desired way; plan out, place in position, for particular purpose: *the scene is set for the drama, tragedy* &c.; *all the properties and details are set for the picture*; *to set a table for dinner*; specif. **b** *to set a butterfly, moth* &c., pin it down, and fasten its wings in desired position, until they become stiff and retain this. **9.** (print.) *To set type*, to arrange it in proper order for printing. **10. a** To bring into specified physical condition, position, order, movement; to dispose in particular way; in various senses, determined by following adverb or adverbial phrase: *to set a room in order*; *set your hat straight*; *to set in motion*; *to set a top spinning*; *to set one's heart beating*; *to set free, at liberty*; Phr. *to set (the whole room, the table) in a roar*, make everybody present roar with laughter; **b** also in non-material sense: *to set one's affairs in order*; *to set things going*, to start a series of events, initiate course of action; *to set things right, straight* &c.; *to set (a question, affair) at rest*, settle it, bring it to an end. **11.** (mus.) **a** To compose air for: *to set words, a song, to music*; **b** to arrange, adapt: *to set a piece of music for the violin* &c. **12.** To bring (persons) into a specified state of mind, feeling, emotion, to influence them intellectually or emotionally in a particular way; to influence the mind or feelings in a particular way: *to set a person right*, correct his errors or mistakes; *to set a person at ease*; *to set people by the ears, at variance*; *to set one's mind at rest*; *to set a person thinking*, start him on a train of thought; *that sets me thinking*, gives me food for thought, suggests certain ideas, causes me to reconsider my position &c.; *to set people wondering.* **13. a** To order (person) to do something, introduce him to, start him on, some task: *to set a man to saw wood, to catch rats, to dig a field* &c.; **b** to propose, submit, prescribe, as a task, duty, as something to be dealt with: *you have set me a difficult job, an easy task* &c.; *to set a person a sum, a problem*, ask him to calculate, solve it &c.; specif., *to set an examination paper, questions in an examination* &c., to offer for written answer, as test of knowledge. **14.** To direct the thoughts or emotions into a particular channel; concentrate, fix, them on particular object: *to set one's mind, brain, (on) to a subject*; *to set one's thoughts on lofty themes*; *all my hopes are set on winning.* Phr. *to set one's heart on*, to desire earnestly, be intent on; *to set one's affections on*, to conceive strong liking for (thing), a desire to obtain. **15.** To estimate, rate, rank, attach a value to: *I set the value of the horse at £100.* Phr. *to set great, very little, store by*, to value highly, low; *to set at naught*, to disregard, defy. **16. a** To assign a place for, order to be stationed: *to set a guard at the door*; **b** to impose, place: *to set a limit, boundary* &c.; Phr. (fig.) *set a limit to*, curtail (extravagance &c.). **17.** To provide, introduce, exhibit for imitation: *to set a standard, model, a fashion*; *to set an example.* Phr. *to set the fashion* (of), to fix, make current; *to set the pace*, to determine the rate of speed by imposing one's own pace; also (fig.) to set a standard of conduct, expenditure &c. **18.** To appoint, fix, determine: *to set a time, date* &c. **B.** intrans. **1.** (of celestial bodies) To sink below the horizon, to decline: *the sun has set, moon is setting*; (also fig.) *his star has set.* **2.** (of fruit or fruit-blossom) To develop from the blossom into fruit as result of fertilization: *the apples*, or *the apple-blossom, won't set this year.* **3.** To become firm, solid: *the cream, jelly, mortar &c. has set.* **4.** To have a certain direction, to flow, move: *the tides set strongly off the shore*; *the wind sets from the north-east.* **5.** (of sporting dogs, orig. of *setter*) To indicate position of game by lying or crouching down and pointing. **C.** Followed by preposition or adverb. *Set about*, **1.** intrans., **a** to make a start with, begin (to do), put in hand: *to set about one's work for the day, getting dinner ready*; *to set about one's packing*; **b** (slang) to start fighting with, to hit, knock about: *they then set about each other in fine style*; **2.** trans., to start going, to spread abroad : *to set a rumour about that* ; *to set about gossip, scandal* &c. *Set aside,* trans., **a** to put on one side, to lay by, to reserve : *to set money aside for one's children's education* ; **b** to disregard for the moment : *setting aside your errors,* or *setting &c. aside* ; **c** to reject : *he set all their offers aside* ; **d** to quash, annul : *to set aside a verdict. Set apart,* trans., **a** to set aside, reserve : *to set some food apart for further use* ; **b** to separate, part : *to set the dogs apart (from each other). Set back,* trans., to put back, reverse ; to stop advance, progress, of : *to set back the clock* ; *all their efforts have been set back. Set by,* trans., **a** to set aside ; **b** (archaic) to value, regard, esteem : *his name was much set by in former days. Set down,* trans., **a** to put out of one's hand, lay, put, down (what one is carrying) : *he set down his spade and seized a rifle* ; **b** to stop, and deposit at a specified place : *this bus will set you down at your destination* ; **c** *set down as,* to reckon, esteem, put in a particular category : *to set a person down as a knave or a fool* ; **d** to put down on paper, enter in writing : *it is all set down in the book* ; *set me down as a subscriber* ; **e** to put down, attribute, to : *to set down a person's bad manners to his ignorance* ; **f** to set forth, fix, prescribe : *rules have been set down and must be obeyed* ; **g** (colloq.) to snub, rebuke, humiliate : *bumptious, pushing people need to be set down. Set forth,* **1.** trans., **a** to state, expound, make known : *to set forth one's opinions at length* ; **b** to lay out, expose to view or for exhibition &c. : *the wedding presents were tastefully set forth for all to see* ; **2.** intrans., to set out, to start, on a journey : *to set forth on one's travels. Set forward,* **1.** trans., **a** to help forward, assist the progress of, promote : *to set forward the cause of the oppressed* ; **b** to put forward, declare, make known, set forth : *to set forward proposals* ; **2.** intrans., to start, go, forward, set out : *if we don't set forward soon, darkness will overtake us. Set in,* intrans., **1.** to begin, start : *winter has set in very early this year* ; **2.** to become fixed, settled, in a particular state : *it, the weather, has set in rainy* ; *it set in to freeze very early* ; **3.** to move, flow, towards : *the current, tide, sets in to the shore. Set off,* **1.** trans., **a** to discharge, to explode : *to set off a rocket* ; *to set off a gun, charge of dynamite, mine* ; **b** to start, set going : *to set people off on a journey* ; *to set one off laughing* ; **c** to heighten the qualities of by contrast, to intensify ; **d** to match against, counterbalance by : *you can set off this loan against what you owe me* ; **2.** intrans., to set out, to start off, on a journey : *they set off* ; *the runners set off at a great pace. Set on,* **1.** trans., **a** to urge on, incite ; to instigate : *to set a dog on a person* ; *to set a person on to attack another* ; **b** to put on the trail or track of : *to set detectives on a person or on his track* ; **2.** intrans., **a** (archaic) to go, move, forward to the attack : *the order came to set on* ; **b** to attack, to set upon : *the dog set on me savagely. Set out,* **1.** trans., **a** to state, set forth, give an exposition of : *to set out one's reasons for* ; *the details are clearly set out in an appendix* ; **b** to adorn, embellish, set off : *the beauty set out by the contrast of the simple surroundings* ; **2.** intrans., **a** to start, begin, a journey ; to set forth : *let us set out before it gets dark* ; **b** to have the intention to do, plan to do : *he set out to write a history of civilization. Set over,* trans., to place in authority over : *they asked for a king to be set over them. Set to,* trans., **1.** to apply oneself vigorously ; to begin, start, in earnest : *it is getting late, it is time to set to* ; **2.** to start doing something ; specif. **a** to start fighting ; **b** to start eating : *if you are so hungry, you'd better set to at once. Set up,* **1.** trans., **a** to erect, raise, place in position or in view : *to set up a post, a fence, a monument* ; (fig.) *to set up the standard of revolt,* to start, raise, a revolution ; **b** to place in power, exalt : *he was set up above his rivals* ; *he set himself up over his people* ; **c** to found, establish, start going : *to set up a government, school, business* &c. ; **d** to establish in, start in, enable to go on in : *he set up his son in business* ; *a timely legacy set him up in his profession* ; **e** to put forward, propose, propound : *to set up a defence* ; *the latest theory to be set up* ; **f** to raise, utter loudly : *to set up a hullabaloo, a howl, clamour* &c. ; **g** to equip, provide, furnish with : *to be well set up with clothes for an expedition* ; **h** to train, develop, the body or figure, as by drill, physical exercise &c. : *a month in the ranks sets up a recruit wonderfully* ; (also in P.P.) *a well-set-up figure* ; **i** to stimulate, rouse, act as a tonic to : *a holiday will soon set you up again* ; **j** to put into type, to compose : *to set up a book, a page* &c. ; **2.** intrans., **a** to start in business, to begin business &c., as : *to set up in trade, set up as a lawyer, grocer* &c. ; Phr. *to set up for oneself,* start in business, or profession, on one's own account, not as an employee or assistant ; **b** *set up for,* to profess, have pretensions to be : *he sets up for a profound scientist, a religious reformer. Set upon,* trans., to set on, attack : *the dog set upon and bit me* ; *they were set upon by a lot of roughs in the dark.*

set (II.), n., fr. prec. **1.** (poet.) Act of setting or sinking below the horizon : *at set of sun,* i.e. sunset. **2.** Way in which anything is set or placed ; **a** pose, position, carriage : *the set of one's head, shoulders* ; **b** way in which anything sits or fits : *the set of a coat, cloak, hat* ; **c** direction, course, in which anything flows or moves : *the set of a current, tide, wind* ; **d** inclination, bias : *the spire has a distinct set away from the perpendicular* ; hence (fig.) **e** general trend, tendency, or drift : *the set of one's mind, of public opinion.* **3.** A cutting, young plant ready to be set or planted out : *a set of blackthorn, privet* &c., cp. *quickset.* **4.** In certain specific uses of above : **a** act of setting, pointing, at game by a setter or other sporting dog ; also in Phr. *to make a dead set at,* (i.) to attack vigorously, with determination or concerted action ; (ii.) to endeavour strenuously to obtain influence over (a person) ; make vigorous efforts to capture support, friendship, confidence of ; **b** the setting or hardening of a liquid or semi-liquid substance, as of plaster, glue &c. ; **c** the lateral deflection or spread to right and left alternately of the teeth of a saw ; **d** (print.) amount of margin or width in type determining space between letters. **5.** A number of objects or persons, of a similar kind, or considered together as a group : *a set of men, cattle, houses* &c. ; specif. **a** (of things) a collection or series of objects similar or related to each other, used for the same purpose and together forming a whole of which each member or unit serves the common purpose or is complementary to the other : *a set of tools, surgical instruments, golf clubs* &c. ; *a set of chessmen, of teeth* &c. ; *a set of Shakespeare's plays, Hardy's novels* &c. ; *a tea, dinner, toilet, set,* service of cups, plates, basin, jug &c. for a specific meal, special use &c. ; **b** (of persons) a group of persons regarded as united, associated, or classed together by some common characteristic, by similar opinions, pursuits, tastes &c. ; (often in disparaging sense) gang, clique : *an artistic, literary, fashionable, smart, golfing, racing, set,* in a community, town &c. ; *he's not of my set* ; *he belonged to the best, worst, set in the college* ; *luckily there are no sets in the club* ; *a mischievous set of hooligans* ; *the old, corrupt set of officials has been dismissed.* **6.** Specific uses : **a** the series of figures or movements which form a square dance ; music composed for this ; number of persons necessary for such dance : *a set of lancers, quadrilles* ; *a set of partners, dancers* ; **b** number of eggs laid by or placed under a bird for hatching out ; a clutch : *hatched ten out of the set of twelve* ; **c** (tennis or lawn-tennis) number, series, or group of games forming one of the three or five units of a match. **7.** In various technical uses (also spelt *sett*) : **a** a name given to various implements or mechanical devices, as a kind of punch or wrench, a riveting implement, an angled iron used in forging &c. ; **b** a squared, flat stone used in paving streets ; **c** the last coat of plaster on a wall before the paper &c. is laid on ; **d** the timber framing of the shaft of a coal mine ; **e** stage scenery built up and fitted together, a carpenter's scene.

set (III.), adj., P.P. of **set** (I.). (in vbl. senses) Specif. **1.** Fixed in position, rigid, immovable : *a set stare* ; *set, glassy eyes* ; *a stern, set, countenance.* **2.** Fixed, unchanging in opinion, obstinate, determined : *of set opinions.* **3.** Determined, arranged beforehand : *at the set time* ; *he did the deed of set purpose.* **4.** Prescribed, ordered, established by authority or usage : *a set form of service, prayer* ; regular, formal : *a set speech* ; *in set terms.*

seta, n., pl. **setae** [1. sḗta, -tē ; 2. sītə, -tī]. Lat., better *saeta,* 'a stiff hair, bristle' ; cogn. w. Scrt. *si-nati,* 'he binds' ; O.H.G. *seito,* O.E. *sāda,* 'noose, snare'. (bot. and zool.) A small stiff hair or bristle, as on certain mosses, hairy caterpillars &c.

setaceous, adj. [1. sētáshus ; 2. sītéiʃəs]. Prec. & **-aceous.** Bristly ; **a** set with, consisting of, setae or bristles ; **b** bristle-like, having the form or feel of bristles.

set-back, n. **1.** A check, reverse, upset. **2.** (archit.) An off-set.

setiferous, adj. [1. sētíferus ; 2. sitífərəs]. See **seta** & **-ferous.** Bearing, producing, bristles ; bristly.

setiform, adj. [1. sḗtiform ; 2. sítifɔ̄m]. **seta** & **-form.** Having the shape or form of a bristle.

setigerous, adj. [1. sētíjerus ; 2. sitídžərəs]. Lat. *sētiger,* 'bristle-bearing' &c. **seta** & **-gerous.** Bristly, having bristles.

set-off, n. **1.** That which sets off, enhances appearance of something else ; an ornament. **2.** (law) Settlement of a debt by a claim on behalf of debtor.

seton, n. [1. sḗtn ; 2. sítn]. Fr. *séton,* cp. Ital. *setone.* See **seta** & **-on.** (surg.) A twist of horse-hairs, silk or linen thread, drawn through the skin by a large needle and left to form an issue and act as counter-irritant &c.

setose, setous, adj. [1. sḗtōs, sḗtus ; 2. sítous, sítəs]. See **seta** & **-ose, -ous.** Bristly, setaceous.

set square, n. A flat piece of wood, vulcanite &c., shaped as a right-angled triangle, showing various angles, for use by draughtsmen &c.

sett, n. [1. set ; 2. sɛt]. Spelling variant of **set** (II.). Rare, except in technical senses, esp. of a small block of stone for paving roads or streets : *granite setts.*

settee (I.), n. [1. setḗ ; 2. sɛtí], fr. **set** (I.) & dimin. ending **-ee.** An upholstered seat with arms and back ; a combination of the sofa and the chair, usually of medium size for two or three people.

settee (II.), n., fr. Fr. *scétie, setie,* fr. Ital. *saetta,* fr. Lat. *sagitta,* 'arrow', see **sagittal.** A long sharp-prowed Mediterranean vessel with two or more masts carrying lateen sails.

setter, n. [1. séter ; 2. sétə]. **set** (I.) & **-er.** One who sets. **1.** (in vbl. senses) **a** usually with adverbs, as *setter-on,* one who incites or instigates, instigator ; *setter-up,* one who sets up or establishes &c. ; **b** as second element of compounds : *bone-setter, type-setter.* **2.** One of several varieties of sporting dogs, with long silky coat like a spaniel, trained to point at game ; the *English setter* is white with liver and black markings, the *Gordon setter* black with tan markings, and the *Irish setter* of dark red or chestnut colour.

setterwort, n. [1. séterwërt ; 2. sétəwāt]. First element prob. fr. **seton,** the roots of the plant being used as setons for cattle. (bot.) Bear's-foot or stinking hellebore, *Helleborus foetidus.*

setting, n. [1. séting ; 2. sétiŋ]. **set** (I.) & **-ing.** **1.** Act or process of setting (in various senses of the vb.) ; specif. **a** *the setting of the sun* &c. ; **b** process of hardening, solidification &c. : *the setting of plaster, mortar* &c. ; **c** act of mounting gems &c. : *stones are some-*

times injured in the setting; **d** act of sharpening, putting fine edge on, razors &c.; **e** act of putting songs to music, of composing airs for them: *the setting of a great lyric to music is a matter of considerable delicacy.* **2.** That in which anything is set; in various specific senses: **a** the general surroundings, background, environment, decoration, accessories &c.; (i.) (lit.) *modern theatre managers give a magnificent setting to plays*; (ii.) (fig.) actual physical surroundings, accompanying events: *the tragedy of the murders of the Russian Imperial family had a lurid and terrible setting*; **b** that in which gems are set; mounting. **3.** The bed upon which machinery, a heavy gun &c. rests; emplacement.

setting-block, -board, n. Board with grooved layer of cork, upon which butterflies &c. are set.

settle (I.), n. [1. sétl; 2. sétl]. O.E. *setl,* M.E. *setel, setil,* 'seat', cogn. w. O.H.G. *sezzal*; Goth. *sitls,* 'throne'; fr. **set-,* the base in **sit.** A long wooden bench or seat with high back and arms.

settle (II.), vb. trans. & intrans. So far as the form goes, & the meanings connected w. reconcilement, the word may be derived fr. a very late O.E. *sehtlian,* 'to bring, come, to an agreement', formed fr. O.E. *seht,* 'agreement, settlement (of disputes &c.); peace, friendship'. On the other hand, the meanings 'to establish firmly, place securely, alight upon', & so on, & derived senses, are more akin to O.E. *setl,* 'a seat', see **settle (I.).** M.E. has *settlen* in the latter meanings. The two strands of meaning, 'to sink down, alight upon, place firmly' &c., whence, in fig. sense, 'to be at, bring to, peace' &c., & 'to reconcile, allay disputes' &c., have become intertwined, & the latter might have developed fr. the former without the existence of *sehtlian* at all. The O.E. n. *seht* is connected w. *sacu,* 'dispute, lawsuit' &c., see **sake,** the basal meaning being 'a quarrel smoothed over and disposed of by discussion, or disputation, or by means of a lawsuit', hence 'a reconciliation'. **A.** trans. **1.** To place, plant, firmly and securely, on or in: *to settle one's hat on one's head*; *to settle one's feet in the stirrups*; (also reflex.) *to settle oneself in a chair, in the saddle* &c. **2. a** To plant, place, give place of abode to (persons), as inhabitants in a country; to people: *King James settled Ulster with families from Scotland*; *a family long settled in the country*; **b** to resort to and take up abode in: *the Jutes settled Kent, part of Hampshire, and the Isle of Wight.* **3. a** To establish (persons) in an occupation, a post, office, position: *to settle one's son in business*; *the government is quite settled in power*; **b** to install, help (person) to establish himself: *she went to settle her son in his new quarters.* **4.** To restore calm to, to soothe down, pacify; to compose: *to settle a disordered brain, a heated imagination*; *a draught to settle one's stomach.* **5.** To bring to an issue or decision; **a** to determine, resolve, decide, what is uncertain, and under discussion or in dispute: *to settle points of difficulty and doubt*; *to settle difficulties, problems, questions* &c.; **b** to dispose, fix, arrange, order: *to settle affairs of state, the future, fate, of the country* &c. **6.** To make up one's mind concerning, fix, decide on, determine: *to settle one's route, which way to go, what to take, what to say, the date of one's return* &c. Phr. *that settles it* (referring to something which has happened, been done or said), that decides the matter, determines what should be done, proves what is the fact &c. **7.** To come to an agreement or understanding concerning, to compose, make up: *to settle one's quarrels, differences* &c. **8. a** To deal with so as to dispose of finally, to put out of the way, bring to a conclusion once for all; finish: *his arguments soon settled his opponent*; *the affair is settled and done with*; *to settle one's affairs before one dies*; specif. **b** *to settle a claim, bill, account,* to pay it; Phrs. *to have an account to settle with,* an affair of an unpleasant character to discuss; *to settle a person's hash,* prevent him once for all from being troublesome. **9.** To clarify by causing dregs, sediment &c. to sink to the bottom: *a drop of cold water will settle boiling coffee.* **10.** To bestow with legal formality, endow with (property &c.), to take legal steps to secure to: *the throne was settled upon the heirs of Henry VII.*; *to settle one's estate upon one's son.* **B.** intrans. **1.** To fix one's abode, go to reside, establish oneself as inhabitant; to make one's home: *to settle in one's native country, in London, at Brighton* &c.; *to settle in a Crown Colony*; *I can't make up my mind where to settle.* **2.** To assume, pass into, a permanent, lasting, stable condition, position, direction &c.: *the weather has settled at last*; *the wind seems to have settled in the south-west.* **3.** To apply oneself or one's mind to, concentrate upon, fix one's attention on, occupy oneself continuously with: *at last he has settled to his work in earnest*; *I fear he will never settle to anything for long.* **4.** To decide, determine, resolve: *we had settled to start yesterday but were prevented*; *I can't settle finally till I know more details.* **5.** To descend, alight, rest: *a butterfly settled on my hand*; *a bird settled on the topmost bough*; *the last rays of the sun settled for a moment on the mountain peak.* **6.** To subside, sink down to a lower level; to give way: *the foundations have settled, and the walls are beginning to crack*; *the ship was settling by the stern.* **7. a** (of sediment) To fall to the bottom (of vessel containing liquid); **b** (of liquid) to become clear through the settlement of sediment. **C.** Followed by preposition or adverb. *Settle down,* intrans., **1. a** to fix one's home somewhere permanently, to cease moving about the world and adopt a fixed place of residence; **b** to become tranquil in mind and accustomed to one's surroundings, to cease to be restless and unhappy: *to settle down at a new school, in one's job* &c.; **c** to adopt a regular, ordered mode of life and conduct: *to marry and settle down*; **2. a** to sink, subside (of earth, foundations &c.); **b** (of ship) to settle, sink, become immersed; **c** (of sediment) to fall to the bottom of liquid, or of vessel containing it. *Settle in,* **1.** intrans., to move in (to new premises &c.) and put everything in order preparatory to taking up one's abode: *I have taken the house but shan't settle in till the autumn*; **2.** trans., to cause, help, to settle in: *my wife is staying with her son, to settle him in to his new house.* *Settle up,* **1.** trans., **a** to complete, carry through (business): *to settle up one's affairs*; **b** to pay: *to settle up one's debts, tradesmen's bills* &c.; **2.** intrans., **a** to complete, conclude, business &c.; **b** to pay debts, bills &c. *Settle upon,* trans., **a** to decide, resolve to do &c.: *to settle upon a plan*; **b** make up one's mind to have: *to settle upon one's future home* &c. *Settle with,* trans., **a** to come to an understanding with; **b** to pay; **c** to discuss, conclude, business with.

settled, adj. [1. sétld; 2. sétld], fr. P.P. of **settle (II.).** Fixed, established, permanent: *a settled melancholy brooded on her face.*

settlement, n. [1. sétlment; 2. sétlmənt]. **settle (II.)** & **-ment.** **1.** Act of settling (in various senses); **a** *the settlement of a new country* &c.; **b** *settlement of a dispute*; **c** formal conveyance of property &c.: *to make a settlement of one's estates*; *Act of Settlement,* that which settled the Crown on the Electress Sophia and her heirs; **d** payment of debts, creditors &c. **2.** Something which is settled (in various senses); **a** a group of settlers, colonists &c.; the place, tract of country, where they settle; their dwellings &c. collectively; **b** an understanding, agreement, concerning disputed questions; a reconcilement of disputing parties: *to reach a settlement of one's differences*; *terms of settlement*; **c** property conveyed, secured, to, settled on, some person.

settler, n. [1. sétler; 2. sétlə]. **settle (II.)** & **-er.** **1.** One who settles, specif. one who settles as a colonist in a newly discovered or newly opened country; a planter, colonist: *the early settlers in Virginia.* **2.** (colloq., slang) That which settles or finishes anything; a deciding blow, argument &c.

settling-day, n. [1. sétling dā; 2. sétliŋ dei]. (Stock Exchange) Day appointed for periodical settling of accounts.

settlor, n. [1. sétler; 2. sétlə]. **settle (II.)** & **-or.** (law) One who makes a settlement of property, esp. a marriage settlement.

set-to, n. **set (I.)** & **to.** (colloq.) A vigorous fight with fists; a hotly contested argument.

setwall, n. [1. sétwawl; 2. sétwɔ̄l]. M.E. *setewale, cetewale,* fr. O. Fr. *citoual,* also *citouar,* fr. Med. Lat. *zedoāria,* fr. Pers. *zedwar,* cp. **zedoary.** Old, popular name for valerian, formerly used in medicine.

seven, adj. & n. [1. sévn; 2. sévn]. O.E. *seofon,* Goth. *sibun,* O.H.G. *sibun,* Du. *zeven*; Scrt. *saptá,* Gk. *heptá,* see **hepta-**; Lat. *septem,* see **sept-.** **1.** adj. One more than six and less than eight; often used with omission of noun, as *it is just on seven,* nearly seven o'clock; *only seven (persons) turned up*; *seven and six,* seven shillings and sixpence &c. Phrs. (of various groups, historical or legendary, of seven persons or things): *Seven Bishops,* tried in 1688 for protesting against James II.'s Declaration of Indulgence; *Seven Champions of Christendom,* the patron saints of England, Scotland, Ireland, and Wales, and of France, Italy, and Spain; *Seven Churches,* of Asia (see Rev. i. 11); *Seven Deadly Sins,* Pride, Covetousness, Lust, Gluttony, Anger, Envy, Sloth; *City of the Seven Hills,* Rome; *Seven League Boots,* in the fairy tale, boots in which the wearer could cover seven leagues at each step; *Seven Liberal Arts,* the subjects of the mediaeval *Quadrivium* and *Trivium*; *Seven Principal Virtues,* Faith, Hope, Charity, Prudence, Justice, Fortitude, Temperance; *Seven Seas,* the Arctic and Antarctic, N. and S. Atlantic, N. and S. Pacific, and Indian Oceans; *Seven Sisters,* the Pleiades; *Seven Sleepers,* in early Christian legend, seven young men of high rank who during a time of persecution, A.D. 250, took refuge in a cave and slept for 200 years, to awake and find the Roman Empire Christian and then die; *Seven Weeks' War,* between Prussia and Austria, 1866; *Seven Wonders of the World,* various great buildings &c., such as the Colossus of Rhodes, the Pyramids &c., of the ancient world; *Seven Years' War,* war of chief European powers, 1756–63, in which Frederick the Great established the power of Prussia in Europe, and England gained from France her colonial possessions in America and India. **2.** n. **a** The figure or symbol representing the number seven, 7, vii.; **b** a playing card with seven pips: *the seven of hearts*; **c** a person, object, holding the seventh place in a series, usually, *number seven*; **d** set of persons or things numbering seven: *in sevens,* in groups of seven; Phr. *at sixes and sevens,* confused, in confusion, upside-down.

sevenfold, adj. & adv. [1. sévnfōld; 2. sévnfould]. **seven** & **-fold.** Seven times repeated; seven times as many.

seventeen, adj. & n. [1. sèvntḗn; 2. sèvntī́n]. O.E. *seofon-týne.* **seven** & **ten.** Seven plus ten; one less than eighteen or more than sixteen; the sum of ten and seven. Phr. *sweet seventeen,* of girl nearly grown up, in the flower of her youth and beauty.

seventeenth, adj. & n. [1. sèvntḗnth; 2. sèvntī́nþ]. Prec. & **-th.** **a** adj. Following sixteen others in a series; **b** n., the last of seventeen persons or things; one of seventeen equal parts.

seventh, adj. & n. [1. sévnth; 2. sévənþ]. **seven** & **-th.** **1.** adj. Following six others in a series, next after the sixth, often used with omission of the noun: *the seventh of October,* of day of the month. Phrs. *the Seventh Day,* the Sabbath of the Jews and of such sects as keep Saturday instead of Sunday as day of rest &c.; the Quaker name for Saturday; *Seventh Day Baptists*, a Baptist sect which observes Saturday as the Sabbath; *the seventh heaven*, the highest of the seven heavens; regarded by the Jews as the dwelling-place of God. Phr. *in the seventh heaven*, in a state of extreme happiness, satisfaction &c. **2.** n. **a** The last of a series of seven persons or things; **b** one of seven equal parts, a seventh part; **c** (mus.) a musical interval a tone or semitone lower than an octave.

seventhly, adv. Prec. & **-ly**. In the seventh place.

seventieth, adj. & n. [1. séventieth; 2. sévəntiiþ]. **seventy** & **-th**. **1.** adj. Following sixty-nine in a series; forming one of seventy equal parts. **2.** n. One next in order after the sixty-ninth; a seventieth part.

seventy, adj. & n. [1. sévnti; 2. sévnti. O.E. *seofontig*. **seven** & **-ty**. **1.** adj. Seven times ten; one more than sixty-nine. Phr. *seventy times seven*, a very large number of times, from Matt. xviii. 22; *seventy-four*, an old line-of-battle ship with seventy-four guns; *a seventy-five*, translation of French *soixante-quinze*, the ·75 cm. gun of the French artillery. **2.** n. Number equal to ten times seven; symbol of this. Phr. *the seventies*, the years seventy to seventy-nine of a particular century, esp. of the 19th cent.

sever, vb. trans. & intrans. [1. séver; 2. sévə]. M.E. *severen*, fr. O. Fr. *sevrer*, fr. Lat. *sēparāre*; see **separate**. **A.** trans. **1.** To separate, cut off, disunite, break or cut in two, divide; **a** (in physical sense) *to sever a limb from the body, a bough from the trunk* &c.; *the sudden jerk severed the rope*; **b** (in spiritual or moral sense) to cause estrangement between, part: *slight misunderstandings may sever lifelong friends*; to break up, shatter: *to sever an ancient friendship, alliance, partnership*; *to sever one's connexion with*, cease to have social or business relations with; (also reflex.) *to sever oneself from* (a party &c.), to separate oneself from. **2.** To divide, come, lie, between: *the Channel severs England from France*. **3.** Specif. (law) to divide; treat as separate and independent: *to sever an estate, liabilities* &c. **B.** intrans. **1.** To perform the action, carry out the process, of severing. **2.** To become severed: *this rope will stand a tremendous strain without severing*.

severable, adj. [1. séverabl; 2. sévərəbl]. Prec. & **-able**. Capable of being severed or divided.

several (I.), adj. [1. séveral; 2. sévərəl]. O. Fr., fr. L. Lat. *sēparāle*, 'a separate thing'. See **sever** & **-al**. **1.** Separate, individual, and distinct; respective, various: *the several items in an account*; *examine the several reasons urged by different persons*; *we are all busy at our several tasks*, i.e. each at his own individual task. **2.** (law) Able to be separated or treated as separate, not shared with others: *a joint and several liability*; *the bond, promissory note &c. is joint and several*; *a several estate*. **3.** More than two in number, but not very many; more than a few: *several people left the room*; *I have said the same thing several times*; *he missed several chances of scoring*.

several (II.), n., fr. prec. A few; several, a moderate number of, persons or things: *in the struggle several received injuries*; *fish began to rise and we caught several in a few minutes*.

severally, adv. [1. séverali; 2. sévərəli]. **several** (I.) & **-ly**. Separately, distinctly, apart from others; not together or jointly: *the guests were received, the prisoners tried, severally*; *the bond was signed jointly and severally*.

severalty, n. [1. séveralti; 2. sévərəlti]. **several** (I.) & **-ty**. State, character, of being several, separate or distinct; specif., *in severalty*, of estate held by owner in his own right and not jointly or in common with others.

severance, n. [1. séverans; 2. sévərəns]. A.-Fr., fr. O. Fr. *sevrance*. See **sever** & **-ance**. Act of severing; state of being severed (in all senses).

severe, adj. [1. sevḗr; 2. sivíə]. O. Fr., fr. Lat. *sevērus*, 'serious, grave; strict, austere'. Etymol. very doubtful. **1.** (of persons, disposition &c.) **a** Harsh, stern, rigorous, strict: *a severe judge*; **b** grave, serious; not inclined to levity: '*From grave to gay, from lively to severe*' (Pope, 'Essay on Man,' Epistle iv. 379). **2.** (of human actions &c.) **a** Exhibiting sternness and rigour; reverse of lenient: *severe punishment, sentence* &c.; **b** searching, rigorous, exacting: *a severe cross-examination, criticism* &c. **3.** (of natural processes and phenomena) Violent, intense, exerting powerful effect; not slight: *a severe frost, thunderstorm* &c.; *a severe illness, attack of gout* &c. **4.** (of artistic expression) Plain, austere; reverse of florid: *a severe literary style*; *the beauty of severe lines*.

severely, adv. Prec. & **-ly**. **a** In a severe manner, with severity: *he has been punished too severely*; *discipline was severely enforced*; **b** intensely, to a considerable degree: *to suffer severely from the cold*; *to be severely ill*; Phr. *to leave* (person or thing) *severely alone*, to avoid, have no association or connexion with, have nothing to do with.

severeness, n. See prec. & **-ness**. Quality of being severe; severity.

severity, n. [1. severíti; 2. sivériti], fr. Fr. *sévérité*, fr. Lat. *sevēritāt-(em)*. See **severe** & **-ity**. **1.** Quality of being severe; severe treatment; harshness, rigour; austerity. **2.** State of being severe; intensity, gravity (of weather &c.; of an illness &c.).

Seville orange, n. [1. sévil órinj; 2. sévil ɔ́rindž], fr. name of Spanish town. The bitter orange.

Sèvres, n. [1. sā́vr; 2. séivr]. Name of town near Paris, France, seat of porcelain manufacture since 1756. Porcelain made at Sèvres.

sew, vb. trans. & intrans. [1. sō; 2. sou]. O.E. *sēowian*, M.E. *sowen, sewen*; O.H.G. *siuwan*; Goth. *siujan*; cogn. w. Lat. *suere*, 'to stitch, sew', see **suture**. **1.** trans. To fasten, put together, by needle and thread, to unite by stitches; put stitches into: *to sew on a button*, or, *a button on*; *sew up*, fasten up, close, with stitches. **2.** intrans. To practise sewing; to work with the needle and thread or with a sewing-machine: *to be taught to sew*.

sewage, n. [1. sū́ij; 2. sjúidž]. For *sewerage*. See **sewer** (II.) & **-age**. Waste matter, water &c. carried off by sewers; *sewage farm*, farm in which the sewage of a town is disposed of by being utilized as manure.

sewen, n. See **sewin**.

sewer (I.), n. [1. sōer; 2. sóuə]. **sew** & **-er**. One who sews; a needlewoman, seamstress.

sewer (II.), n. & vb. trans. [1. sūer; 2. sjúə], fr. O. Fr. *seuwiere*, 'sluice for draining a pond', L. Lat. *exaquatorium*, 'contrivance for letting water out', see **ex-, aquatic, & -ory**. **1.** n. Large underground conduit, main drain of a town or district, into which smaller drains empty themselves, for carrying off waste water, excreta &c. **2.** vb. To furnish with sewers and drains; to install a system of sewers in: *to sewer a town, district*.

sewer (III.), n. [1. sūer; 2. sjúə], fr. O. Fr. *asseour*, 'one who sets a table', fr. *asseoir*, 'to seat, set', fr. Lat. *assidēre*, 'to sit beside, to wait upon', fr. **ad-**, 'near, by', & *sedēre*, 'to sit', cp. **assiduous**. A servant, household official in the Middle Ages, who set the dishes on the table and generally attended to the service of guests at meals.

sewerage, n. [1. sūerij; 2. sjúəridž]. **sewer** (II.) & **-age**. **1.** System of sewers and drains in a town, district &c.; public drainage. **2.** Construction of sewers and drains. **3.** Disposal of waste matter by sewers.

sewer-gas, n. Gas generated in sewers, drains, and cesspools.

sewer-rat, n. Rat infesting sewers; common brown or Norway rat.

sewin, sewen, n. [1. sūin; 2. sjúin]. W. *sewyn*. A variety of the sea or salmon trout, sometimes regarded as a distinct species, *Salmo cambricus*.

sewing, n. [1. sōing; 2. sóuiŋ]. **sew** & **-ing**. Act, art, occupation, of one who sews; product of this; needlework.

sewing-machine, n. Mechanical contrivance for sewing fabric.

sex, n. [1. seks; 2. seks], fr. Fr. *sexe*, fr. Lat. *sexus*, 'sex', prob. orig. meaning 'division', fr. *secāre*, 'to cut', see **section**. **1.** The sum of physiological differences in form and function which distinguish the male from the female in animals and plants. **2.** One of the two groups of individuals, male or female, distinguished by sex. Phr. *the sex*, women. **3.** Everything arising out of, or determined by, sexual differences in human beings; passion, social relations &c.: *many modern novelists are obsessed by what they call problems of sex*.

sex-, sexi-, pref. Lat., 'six'; Gk. *hex*, see **hexa-**. See further under **six**.

sexagenarian, adj. & n. [1. sèksajenā́rian; 2. sèksədžinéəriən]. **sexagenary** & **-an**. **1.** adj. Sixty years old, between the age of sixty and seventy. **2.** n. Person of this age.

sexagenary, adj. & n. [1. sèksajḗnari; 2. sèksədžínəri], fr. Lat. *sexāgēnārius*, fr. *sexāgēni*, 'sixty each', distributive of *sexāginta*, 'sixty', fr. *sex*, 'six', see **sex-**. **1.** adj. Pertaining to the number sixty; containing sixty; arranged in sixties, based on the number sixty. **2.** n. **a** That which is composed of sixty parts; **b** a sexagenarian.

Sexagesima, n. [1. sèksajésima; 2. sèksədžésimə]. Lat., fem. of *sexāgēsimus* (for *gens-), 'sixtieth', fr. *sexāginta*, 'sixty'. See prec. *Sexagesima Sunday*, the second Sunday before Lent, as preceding *Quinquagesima Sunday*, roughly, the 60th day before Easter.

sexagesimal, adj. & n. [1. sèksajésimal; 2. sèksədžésiməl]. Prec. & **-al**. **1.** adj. Pertaining to, based on, the number sixty: *a sexagesimal fraction*, one whose denominator is sixty or a multiple of sixty, as $\frac{7}{60}$. **2.** n. A sexagesimal fraction.

sexangle, n. [1. séksàngl; 2. séksæŋgl]. **sex** & **angle**. A hexagon.

sexangular, adj. [1. sèksánggūlar; 2. sèksǽŋgjulə]. Prec. & **-ar**. Hexagonal.

sexcentenary, adj. & n. [1. sèksentḗnari; 2. sèksentínəri]. **sex-** & **centenary**. **1.** adj. Of, pertaining to, six hundred years. **2.** n. A six-hundredth anniversary.

sexdigitate, adj. [1. sèksdíjitāt; 2. sèksdídžiteit]. **sex-** & **digitate**. (zool.) Having six fingers or toes.

sexed, adj. [1. sekst; 2. sekst]. **sex** & **-ed**. Having sex: (usually in combination) *fully sexed, over-sexed* &c.

sexennial, adj. [1. seksénial; 2. sekséniəl], fr. Lat. *sexennium*, 'a period of six years', & **-al**. See **sex-** & **annual**. Lasting six years; occurring once every six years.

sexillion, n. See **sextillion**.

sexisyllabic, adj. [1. sèksisilábik; 2. sèksisilǽbik]. **sex-** & **syllabic**. Having six syllables.

sexisyllable, n. [1. séksisìlabl; 2. séksisiləbl]. **sex-** & **syllable**. A word of six syllables.

sexless, adj. [1. séksles; 2. sékslis]. **sex** & **-less**. **1.** Without sex; neither male nor female; neuter. **2.** Not having the natural feelings and passions of sex; cold, frigid.

sexlessness, n. [1. sékslesnes; 2. sékslisnis]. Prec. & **-ness**. State of being sexless.

sexpartite, adj. [1. sèkspártīt; 2. sèkspátait]. **sex-** & **partite**. Divided into, made up of, six parts.

sext, n. [1. sekst; 2. sekst]. Fr. *sexte*, fr. Med. Eccles. Lat. *sexta* (*hora*), 'sixth hour', fem. of *sextus*, 'sixth'; see **sex-**. One of the canonical hours or offices recited at noon, the 6th hour, or rather earlier.

sextain, n. [1. sékstān; 2. sékstein]. Formed on anal. of **quatrain**, fr. Lat. *sextus*, 'sixth', cp. Ital. *sestina*. A stanza of six lines.

sextan, adj. [1. sékstan; 2. sékstən], fr. Lat. *sext-(us)*, 'sixth', & -an. Recurring every sixth day, as an intermittent fever.

sextant, n. [1. sékstant; 2. sékstənt]. Lat. *sextant-(em)*, 'sixth part of a unit'. **1.** (math.) The sixth part of a circle. **2.** Instrument used by navigators and others for determining the latitude and longitude.

sextet(te), n. [1. sekstét; 2. sekstét], fr. Lat. *sext-(us)*, 'sixth', & **-et(te)**, cp. **quartet.** (mus.) **1.** A composition for six voices or six instruments. **2.** A set of six singers or instrumentalists for the performance of such composition. **3.** Performance by such singers &c.

sextillion, sexillion, n. [1. sekstíliun, seksíliun; 2. sekstíliən, seksíliən]. Lat. *sextus*, see prec. w. ending on anal. of **billion** &c. **a** (Engl. usage) Sixth power of a million, 1 followed by 36 ciphers; **b** (Fr. and U.S.A.) seventh power of a thousand, 1 followed by 21 ciphers.

sexto, n. [1. sékstō; 2. sékstou]. Lat., abl. sing. of *sextus*, 'sixth'; see **sex-**. Cp. **quarto.** A size of book made up of sheets folded in six.

sextodecimo, n. [1. sèkstōdésimō; 2. sèkstoudésimou]. Abl. sing. of Lat. *sextōdecimus*, 'sixteenth', fr. *sextus*, 'sixth', & *decimus*, 'tenth'. See **sex-** & **decimal.** Cp. prec. (abbr. 16mo, 16°) **a** Sheet of paper folded into 16 leaves; **b** size of book of sheets so folded.

sexton, n. [1. sékstun; 2. sékstən]. M.E. *sekesteyn, sexteyn*, an early modification of **sacristan.** Man employed in a parish to open, warm, and light the church, ring the bells, and dig graves.

sextuple, adj. & vb. trans. [1. sekstúpl; 2. sekstjúpl], fr. Lat. *sextus*, 'sixth', see **sex-**, on anal. of **quadruple. 1.** adj. Sixfold, six times as much. **2.** vb. To multiply by six.

sexual, adj. [1. sékshooal; 2. sékʃuəl], fr. Lat. *sexuālis*, fr. *sexus*, see **sex**, & **-al. 1.** Pertaining to, arising from, sex, and the distinction of sex. **2.** (bot.) *Sexual system of classification*, that of Linnaeus, which classified plants according to the number of stamens.

sexualist, n. [1. sékshooalist; 2. sékʃuəlist]. Prec. & **-ist. 1.** Person obsessed by sex. **2.** Follower of Linnaeus in classifying plants.

sexuality, n. [1. sèkshooáliti; 2. sèkʃuǽliti]. **sexual** & **-ity.** Quality of being distinguished by sex.

sexualize, vb. trans. [1. sékshooalīz; 2. sékʃuəlaiz]. **sexual** & **-ize.** To assign sex to; to distinguish by sex.

sexually, adv. [1. sékshooali; 2. sékʃuəli]. **sexual** & **-ly.** From the point of view of, by means of, sex.

Seym, n. [1. sām; 2. seim]. Pol., 'diet, assembly'. The legislature or parliament of the republic of Poland.

sforzando, adv. [1. sfortsándō; 2. sfɔ̄tsǽndou]. Ital., 'to be emphasized'. A musical direction indicating that a note is to be played with sudden force or emphasis.

sfumato, adj. [1. sfōōmáhtō; 2. sfūmā́tou]. Ital., P.P., 'smoked'. (of paint.) Having indistinct, blurred, outlines.

shabbily, adv. [1. shábili; 2. ʃǽbili]. **shabby** & **-ly.** In a shabby manner; **a** poorly, raggedly &c.; **b** meanly.

shabbiness, n. [1. shábines; 2. ʃǽbinis]. **shabby** & **-ness. a** Shabby appearance &c.; **b** shabby behaviour, treatment.

shabby, adj. [1. shábi; 2. ʃǽbi]. O.E. *sceabb*, 'scab', & **-y.** Cp. **scab. 1.** (of external appearance) **a** (of persons) Wearing old, dilapidated, worn-out, threadbare, clothes; **b** (of things) showing signs of hard wear, well worn, ragged, disreputable, deteriorated; reverse of *smart, new* &c.; **c** mean, poverty-stricken, squalid, neglected: *a shabby neighbourhood, street* &c. **2.** (in moral sense) **a** Mean, trifling, parsimonious, stingy; **b** ungenerous, ignoble, despicable.

shabby-genteel, adj. Poor and shabby, but making brave efforts to retain something of the dignity and decency of earlier, more prosperous days.

shabrach, shabrack, n. [1. shábrak; 2. ʃǽbræk], fr. Germ. *schabracke*, fr. Turk. *chābrāq.* A saddle-cloth or housing, usually covered with a leopard skin, used in parade uniform by a cavalry officer.

shack, n. [1. shak; 2. ʃæk]. Etymol. uncertain. (Canadian, Am.) A hut, shanty.

shackle (I.), n. [1. shákl; 2. ʃǽkl]. O.E. *sceacol*, 'a loose link in a chain, a bond', fr. *sceacan*, 'to shake', M.E. *shakkyl*; cp. M. Du. *schakel*, 'link', O.N. *skökull*, 'a loose pole or shaft for a cart'. See **shake (I.). 1.** A link joining the metal rings fastened round the wrists or ankles of a prisoner or slave, sufficiently long to allow a certain amount of movement. **2.** (pl.) **a** Fetters, chains: *a prisoner's, slave's, shackles*; **b** (fig.) that which hampers, fetters, or binds; that which constrains or restrains: *shackles of debt, vice*; *to break through the shackles of habit, convention* &c. **3.** Applied to various objects or devices for fastening and coupling.

shackle (II.), vb. trans., fr. prec. **a** To put shackles upon, fasten with shackles; **b** (fig.) to hamper, impede &c.

shad, n. [1. shad; 2. ʃæd]. O.E. *sceadd*, 'a kind of fish', similar forms in various languages. Etymol. unknown. Edible marine fish of herring family, chiefly used in America.

shaddock, n. [1. sháduk; 2. ʃǽdək]. Named after Captain Shaddock, who brought the fruit fr. the East to the West Indies at end of 17th cent. **a** Tropical fruit usually globular in shape, much resembling a lemon in taste and smell, and having a pale yellow rind; also called *grape-fruit*; **b** tree bearing this.

shade (I.), n. [1. shād; 2. ʃeid]. O.E. *sceadu*, 'shadow, shade, darkness'; M.E. *schāde*; O.S. *skado*; O.H.G. *skato*; Goth. *skadus*; cogn. w. Gk. *skótos*, 'darkness'. **1. a** Partial darkness caused by intervention of something between the light and a given spot; Phr. *to put* (person or thing) *into the shade*, cause to appear insignificant, unimportant, undesirable, by contrast; **b** diminution of light, partial darkness caused by waning of the day: *the shades of evening* &c. **2.** (poet.) An obscure, remote, retired place: '*In vain to deserts thy retreat is made, The muse attends thee to that silent shade*' (Pope, Epistle to Robt. Earl of Oxford, 28-9). **3.** Reproduction of shade or shadow in painting or drawing, by more sombre, less vivid colour, or by darkening, blackening &c. Phr. *light and shade*, (fig.) strong contrast in artistic expression, in emotional feelings &c. **4. a** Something which affords shelter, protection, from excessive light: *the shade of trees*; *no shade from the burning sun*; specif. **b** a piece of silk &c. stiffened with cardboard, attached to the forehead, so as to project outwards above the eyes; **c** any one of various devices attached to lamps of all kinds to intercept or direct the light. **5. a** The spirit, ghost, of a dead person; hence **b** (pl.) *the shades* (i.) (poet.), the abode of spirits; death, the grave, (ii.) wine vaults, hotel bar. **6.** Slight difference of colour, variety of intensity, depth &c., or of luminosity, paleness &c. **7. a** A slight amount or degree, a suspicion, tinge: *a certain shade of disapproval*; *not a shade of doubt, hesitation*; **b** a slight difference, minute variation: *many English words have innumerable shades of meaning.*

shade (II.), vb. trans. & intrans. See prec. **A.** trans. **1.** To cast shade upon: *the tree shades the house too much.* **2. a** To shelter, protect, from light or heat: *to shade one's head, eyes, from the sun, with a broad-brimmed hat*; to cover: *to shade one's face with one's hand*; **b** to cut, keep off (light) from: *to shade the light from one's eyes.* **3.** To indicate, express, light and shade in (a drawing) by darkening some parts and leaving others light. **B.** intrans. *Shade away, off, into*, to exhibit gradually varying shades of colour, meaning &c.; to grade off; fade away by gradually lessening intensity; to pass into by imperceptible degrees of difference.

shadeless, adj. [1. shādles; 2. ʃéidlis]. **shade (I.)** & **-less.** Without shade; destitute of, deprived of, shade; unshaded.

shadily, adv. [1. shādili; 2. ʃéidili]. **shady** & **-ly.** In a shady manner.

shadiness, n. [1. shādines; 2. ʃéidinis]. **shady** & **-ness.** Quality, state, of being shady.

shading, n. [1. shāding; 2. ʃéidiŋ]. **shade (II.)** & **-ing. 1.** Act or process of giving shade. **2. a** Act of giving light and shade to a picture; **b** contrast of light and shade depicted in a picture.

shadoof, n. [1. shadōōf; 2. ʃædū́f]. Arab. *shādūf.* Device for raising water from rivers &c., consisting of a pivoted pole with bucket at one end and counterbalancing weight at the other, used in Egypt and the East.

shadow (I.), n. [1. shádō; 2. ʃǽdou], fr. O.E. *sceadwe* &c., M.E. *schadewe*, fr. type in oblique cases of O.E. *sceadu.* See **shade (I.). 1. a** Patch of shade; obscure area of limited extent and definite shape produced upon a more or less illuminated surface by the intervention of a solid body between this and the light: *her face was in deep shadow*; **b** specif., such a patch of shade, of definite shape, produced by the intervention of some particular object between an illuminated surface and the light: *the shadow of a dog, a house* &c.; Phrs. *afraid, frightened, of one's own shadow*, very timid, easily startled, alarmed by trifles; *to grasp at the shadow and lose the substance*, to sacrifice a solid advantage for a visionary unattainable ideal; *coming events cast their shadows before*, give an indication or warning of their approach. **2.** Person who attends or follows another closely, like his shadow. **3. a** A number of shadows, partial darkness, gloom, as of gathering twilight: *the shadows of evening are falling*, night is coming on; (fig.) **b** mental or moral gloom, depression, of spirits; obscuring of the intellect: *the shadows of old age*; *Cowper's later years were passed amid the shadows of a disordered mind*; *the shadow of death.* **4.** The pictorial representation of shade or shadow; the darker parts of a picture. **5. a** An apparition, a phantom, a shade; **b** something unreal, fleeting, and transitory: '*. . . what shadows we are, and what shadows we pursue.*' (Burke). **6.** An imperfect image, reproduction, of something; something which but faintly and vaguely represents another person or thing; an unreal, unsubstantial, feeble, reflexion of something: *kings have now but the shadow of their former power*; *the Protector's son was only the shadow of his father.* Phrs. *worn to a shadow*, exceedingly tired and exhausted; *the mere shadow of one's former self*, very much altered (by sickness, sorrow &c.). **7.** A very slight amount or degree: *not a shadow of difference between them*; *I have not the slightest shadow of doubt.* **8.** (archaic and Bib.) Shelter, protection: '*Hide me under the shadow of Thy wings*'.

shadow (II.), vb. trans., fr. prec. **1.** To cast a shadow upon, throw into shade: *a grove of trees shadowed the house to the west.* **2.** (rare) To shade (drawings &c.). **3.** Usually *shadow forth*, **a** to indicate in outline, adumbrate; **b** to be a type of, typify, symbolize. **4.** To follow closely, to dog footsteps of.

shadowiness, n. [1. shádōines; 2. ʃǽdouinis]. **shadowy** & **-ness.** State, quality, of being shadowy.

shadowless, adj. [1. shádōles; 2. ʃǽdoulis]. **shadow (I.)** & **-less.** (rare) **a** Not covered by shadow, having no shade; **b** not casting a shadow.

shadowy, adj. [1. shádōi; 2. ʃǽdoui]. **shadow** & **-y. 1.** Surrounded by, placed, standing, amid, shadows; producing shadows; umbrageous: *shadowy woods.* **2.** Resembling a shadow; unsubstantial; dim, indistinct: *a shadowy form, outline.* **3.** (in non-material sense) **a** Vague, but faintly remembered, far off: *the shadowy past*; **b** unreal, unlikely to be realized; visionary: *a shadowy hope.*

shady, adj. [1. shādi; 2. ʃéidi]. **shade (I.)** & **-y. 1. a** Affording shade: *a shady tree*; **b** standing in shade, sheltered from full light or heat of the sun: *a shady spot*; *the shady side of a street.* Phr. *on the shady side* *of forty* &c., older than forty, the other side of forty &c. 2. (in moral sense) Not able to stand the light of inquiry; hence, dubious, equivocal, disreputable, of doubtful character: *a shady person, character*; *a shady transaction*; *shady conduct*.

shaft (I.), n. [1. shahft; 2. ʃâft]. O.E. *sceaft*, 'shaft (of an arrow or spear); a spear; a pole'; M.E. *s(c)haft*; O.H.G. *scaft*; cogn. w. Gk. *skâpton*, 'staff, sceptre'; cp. also Gk. *skâpos*, 'stick, staff'; Lat. *scāpus*, 'shaft, stem, stalk' &c., cp. **scape**; Gk. *sképtein*, 'to prop, support (with a stick or pole)', is a cogn., cp. **sceptre**, but there is no reason to assume that 'prop, support', was a primitive sense of the base. Connexion w. **shave** & its cognates is improbable, & the suggestion that a *shaft* was orig. 'a shaved, sharpened rod' appears fantastic. Basal meaning: a rod, pole, stake. Specific uses: **1.** Stem, stock, handle, of certain weapons; a *shaft of a spear, of an arrow*; hence **b** (poet.) an arrow, a spear; **c** (fig.) *shafts of wit*, sallies, thought of as aimed at, and piercing someone. **2.** Handle, haft, of tools and implements: *shaft of an axe, a hammer, a golf-club* &c. **3.** (pl.) *The shafts*, the two poles attached to the front of a horse vehicle, between which the horse is placed in order to pull the vehicle. **4.** Applied to several objects which are long or tall in proportion to their thickness; e.g. **a** an iron, steel, or wooden bar used to support moving parts in machinery, or to transmit motion; **b** the main part of a column, between the capital and the base; **c** the main part of a tall column-shaped chimney; **d** the upright trunk or stalk of a plant; **e** the central rib of a feather. **5.** A beam or ray of light; cp. the use of *beam* and *ray* in similar sense.

shaft (II.), n. Ultimately the same as prec., but in application to mines, borrowed fr. L.G. **1.** Vertical opening or excavation, narrow in proportion to its length, made in the ground, leading to the main workings of a mine. **2.** Channel, conduit, conveying air, used in ventilation.

shaft-horse, n. A draft-horse harnessed between the shafts of a vehicle.

shafting, n. [1. sháhfting; 2. ʃáftiŋ]. **shaft** & **-ing.** (mechan.) System of shafts, belts &c., used in the transmission of power or motion.

shag (I.), n. [1. shag; 2. ʃæg]. O.E. *sceacga*, 'rough hair'; cogn. w. O.N. *skegg*, 'the beard', fr. *skaga*, 'to jut out, project', cp. *skegi*, 'cape, headland'. **1.** (archaic or rare) **a** A rough mass or mop of hair; **b** coarse, long-napped cloth. **2.** A fine cut, coarse, strong kind of tobacco.

shag (II.), n. Prob. same as prec. A small crested cormorant, *Phalacrocorax graculus*.

shaggily, adv. [1. shágili; 2. shǽgili]. **shaggy** & **-ly.** In a shaggy manner.

shagginess, n. [1. shágines; 2. ʃǽginis]. See prec. & **-ness.** State, quality, of being shaggy; roughness.

shaggy, adj. [1. shági; 2. ʃǽgi]. **shag** (I.) & **-y.** (of hair, animal's coat, growing bush &c.) Rough, unkempt; having long hair, fur &c. sticking out untidily; growing long and straggly: reverse of *smooth, sleek, well kept*.

shagreen, n. [1. shagrḗn; 2. ʃægrín, ʃəgrín], fr. Fr. *chagrin*, fr. Pers. & Turk. *saghri*, 'the back, rump, of a horse or ass, leather obtained from this, esp. of the wild ass', cp. **chagrin**. **1.** A kind of untanned leather made from the hide of a horse, ass, or camel, with a roughened, granulated surface produced artificially by embedding small seeds in the skin while soft; often dyed green and used for making small ornamental cases, covering handles of daggers &c. **2.** Shark-skin used for similar purposes, the granulated surface being natural.

shah, n. [1. shah; 2. ʃā]. Pers., 'king, ruler', in full *padshah*, 'lord king'. See **padishah** & **pasha**; fr. O. Pers. *khsayathiya*, 'power', fr. *khsi*, 'to rule', cp. Scrt. *kshatram*, 'rule'. See **satrap** & cp. **checkmate**. The title of the sovereign rulers of Persia; *shah-in shah*, 'king of kings'.

shahzada, n. [1. shàhzáhda; 2. ʃâzádə]. Pers., 'son of a king'. The title of the heir-apparent of the Ameer of Afghanistan.

shakable, adj. [1. shā́kabl; 2. ʃéikəbl]. **shake** & **-able.** Capable of being shaken.

shake (I.), vb. trans. & intrans. [1. shāk; 2. ʃeik]. O.E. *scacan*, 'to shake, brandish; to depart; flee away', M.E. *shāken*; O.S. *skakan*, 'to move off, depart'. Prob. cogn. w. O. Slav. *skakati*, 'to leap, spring'. Used to express movements of various degrees of violence, and rapidity, also movement of very various kinds, but generally implying movement to and fro, backwards and forwards, up and down; trembling, vibrating motion; swaying, waving, brandishing. **A.** trans. **1.** (of movement imparted to external objects) **a** *to shake a closed door* (or other fixed object), to seize it by the handle &c., and attempt to move it towards, or away from one, alternately pulling and pushing with some violence; *to shake a person, shake him* (*gently* or *roughly*) *by the shoulder*; *to shake a tree and bring the fruit down*; **b** to take in the hand and agitate first in one direction then in another: *to shake a bottle of medicine, gently* or *violently*; **c** to cause to sway: *the wind shakes the trees*; **d** to cause to vibrate rapidly, impart a tremulous, vibratory motion to: *a reed shaken by the wind*; *the blast shook the windows*, caused them to rattle; **e** to flap, wave, agitate with jerky up-and-down movements: *to shake a carpet, a coat* &c. **2. a** (of effect of falling weight, heavy blow, explosion &c. upon a heavy fixed object) To cause to tremble; to jar: *his step shook the room*; **b** to upset, weaken stability of, cause to rock: *the explosion shook the house to its foundations*; **c** (fig.) to unsettle, cause to become precarious, to lessen stability of: *many thrones were sorely shaken in the Great War, and some fell*. **3.** (of movement imparted to one's person, or part of it, to limbs &c.) Specific usages: *to shake oneself*, agitate one's whole body more or less violently; *to shake one's finger* (*at*), to wag the first finger rapidly (towards a person), expressing menace, warning, mild reproof &c.; *to shake one's head*, move it repeatedly from side to side, esp. as expressing refusal, disapproval &c.; (fig.) *to shake one's head at*, or *over*, to express doubt, hesitation, disapproval; *to shake one's fist* (*at*), hold it up and move it rapidly, alternately towards, and away from oneself, esp. as expressing denunciation of, threat to, a person; Phr. *to shake hands* (*with*), grasp the hand of another, in greeting, bidding farewell, or in token of reconciliation: *let us shake hands and be friends*; *to shake one's sides* (with laughing), to laugh heartily; *to be badly shaken* (by a fall &c.), to receive a nervous shock, be jarred; *to shake oneself free*, to free oneself by an abrupt movement; (fig.) to get rid of by decisive action. **4.** (in moral sense) To upset, disturb, weaken, render less firm or intense: *to shake one's faith, confidence, courage, resolution*; *to shake the credit of* (a bank &c.). **B.** intrans. **1.** To be moved, rapidly or violently to and fro; to vibrate, rock, sway: *the earth shook violently*; *the room shakes as he walks*; *the trees shake in the wind*. **2. a** To tremble, quiver: *to shake with cold, fever, fright* &c.; *his hand was shaking*; Phr. *to shiver and shake*; *to shake in one's shoes*, to be very frightened; **b** (of the voice) to become tremulous, be produced with a quavering sound. **3.** To execute shakes with the voice, in singing, or on a musical instrument; to trill, warble. **C.** Followed by preposition or adverb. *Shake down*, **1.** trans., **a** to cause to fall down by shaking or violent and rapid movement: *to shake down apples from a tree*; **b** to cause to settle down into a close, compact form: *to shake down grain in a sack*; **c** to throw, spread on the floor: *to shake down blankets, straw* &c., to make a bed; **2.** intrans., **a** to become firm and compact, to settle into a compact mass; **b** to settle down, in or with: *we will shake down on the floor with a blanket or two*; **c** to become settled in mind; become calm and peaceful: *the boy will soon shake down at his new school*; *things are shaking down very quickly*. *Shake off*, trans., **1.** to remove by shaking: *to shake off rain from one's hair* &c., *a person's hand from one's arm*; Phr. *to shake off the dust of* (place, person's house &c.) *from one's feet*, to leave for good, resolve never to visit again; **2.** to get rid of, become emancipated from (an illness, bad habit &c.); **3.** to out-distance, get away from, elude (pursuers, pursuit); **4.** to get rid of, cease to be troubled by, drive away, by resolute action: *to shake off a disreputable acquaintance* &c. *Shake out*, trans., **a** to spread out, open, to unfurl: *to shake out a sail, flag*; **b** to spread out and shake, for airing, getting rid of dust, wet &c.: *to shake out a carpet, one's coat* &c.; **c** to cause to fall out by shaking: *shake the dust and grit out of one's shoes*; *shake the pepper out of the pot*. *Shake up*, trans., **1.** to mix, cause to mix thoroughly, by shaking: *to shake up the ingredients in a bottle*; **2.** to restore to shape by shaking: *to shake up a pillow, cushion* &c.; **3.** to rouse, stir up; stimulate, enliven: *an idle wretch like that needs to be well shaken up*.

shake (II.), n., fr. prec. **1.** Act of movement made in shaking (in various senses): *a shake of the head*, negative gesture; *a shake of the hand*, a handshake; *to give a person a good shake*, submit him to a rapid rocking to and fro, by shaking him roughly. **2.** A tremulous, uncertain, quivering movement, or effect: *a shake in the walk, hand, head, voice*; *a shake in one's writing*. **3.** A trill, rapid alternation on two notes, executed by the voice, or on an instrument. **4.** (colloq.) The time occupied in shaking something; a very brief space of time, a moment. Phr. *in two shakes, half a shake*, in a moment, instantly.

shakedown, n. [1. shā́kdoun; 2. ʃéikdaun]. A rough, temporary, make-shift bed of blankets spread on the floor.

shaken, vb. [1. shā́ken; 2. ʃéikən]. P.P. of **shake**; O.E. (*ge*)*scacen*; M.E. *shāken*.

shaker, n. [1. shā́ker; 2. ʃéikə]. **shake** (I.) & **-er.** **1. a** One who or that which shakes; **b** that in which something is shaken: *a cocktail shaker*. **2.** (cap.) Member of a religious sect founded c. 1770, calling themselves the *Millennial Church*, who exhibited their religious emotions by violent bodily movements, and by dances.

Shakeress, n. [1. shā́keres; 2. ʃéikəres]. Prec. & **-ess.** A female Shaker.

Shakerism, n. [1. shā́kerizm; 2. ʃéikərizəm]. **shaker** & **-ism.** Religious system and beliefs of the Shakers.

shakily, adv. [1. shā́kili; 2. ʃéikili]. **shaky** & **-ly.** In a shaky manner; totteringly, tremulously.

shakiness, n. [1. shā́kines; 2. ʃéikinis]. **shaky** & **-ness.** State of being shaky.

shaking (I.), n. [1. shā́king; 2. ʃéikiŋ]. **shake** (I.) & **-ing.** Act of one who or that which shakes; process of being shaken: *the shaking of the trees, of head or hand*; *give the carpet a good shaking*; *the boy deserves a good shaking*.

shaking (II.), adj., fr. Pres. Part. of **shake** (I.). Trembling; specif. *shaking palsy*, a form of paralysis accompanied by nervous twitchings and uncontrollable movements of the limbs.

shako, n. [1. shákō; 2. ʃǽkou]. Fr., fr. Hung. *czako*. A flat-topped, cylindrical, peaked soldier's cap, with a plume.

shaky, adj. [1. shā́ki; 2. ʃéiki]. **shake** (I.) & **-y.** **1. a** (of fixed objects) Liable to be upset, not firm or stable; flimsy; wobbly, cranky: *a shaky wall, tree*; also **b** (non-material) *his position in the Cabinet, his credit, was shaky*; **c** (of mental conditions, knowledge &c.) uncertain, doubtful, vague, unreliable: *his Latin has got rather shaky*; *a bit shaky in his grammar*. **2. a** (of movements, physical actions, or persons in movement) Tottery, wavering, uncertain, feeble; tremulous: *a shaky walk, gait, steps; his hand is getting shaky; shaky on one's legs; a shaky handwriting; a shaky voice*, quavering, trembling; **b** (in moral sense) shifty, unreliable, wavering: *shaky in one's principles, veracity* &c.

shale, n. [1. shāl; 2. ʃeil], fr. Germ. *schale*, 'shell, scale, shale', O.H.G. *scala*, cogn. w. **scale (III.)** A clay rock formation of many varieties, which splits readily into plates or laminae.

shale oil, n. Oil derived from bituminous shale.

shall, vb. auxil. [1. shal; 2. ʃæl] when stressed; when unstressed [1. shl; 2. ʃl]; neg. form *shan't* [1. shahnt; 2. ʃānt]. O.E. *sċeal*, Pret. type used as pres. sing. (1st & 3rd pers.) of *sċeolan*; a so-called Pret.-Pres. vb.; the pres. pl. in O.E. is *sculon, sċeolon*; M.E. *schal* &c., *schullen*; the distinction is preserved sporadically till near the end of the 15th cent. Corresponding forms are found in the other old Gmc. languages—O.S. & O.H.G. *skolan, skal*; Goth. *skulan* (infin.), *skal*. The orig. sense is 'to owe, be under an obligation'; a sense still preserved in O.E. & the other old Gmc. languages. See further under **should**, orig. the Pret. of *shall*. The base is seen in O.E. *sċyld*, 'guilt, fault', fr. **skuldi-*, cogn. w. O.S. & O.H.G. *sculd*, 'guilt, sin' &c.; further cogn. w. Lith. *skelëti*, 'to be guilty'. Connexion w. Lat. *scelus*, 'crime', formerly widely accepted, is now considered improbable by Walde & by Kluge. *Shall* is followed by the vb. directly without intervening *to*. **1.** Expressing the future tense pure and simple; only with the 1st. pers. sing. and pl.; for other persons see **will**: *I shall arrive by the first train tomorrow; we shall be away next winter; shall I be in your way if I stay?* **2.** Expressing intention to do something in the future: *I shall come home every week; we shall not call on our new neighbours; I shall whip you if you don't behave better; I was told not to smoke at all but I certainly shall; shall you be here tomorrow?* **3. a** Expressing obligation or compulsion; must; (with stress on *shall*): *you shall do what you are told; he said he didn't want to come with us, but I say that he shall*; **b** (in neg., expressing a prohibition) *thou shalt not kill; you shan't have your own way in everything.* **4.** Expressing a promise of something in the future: *if you are a good boy you shall have a pony to ride.* **5.** (in interrog. sentences and polite formulae) Asking permission, ascertaining another's wishes &c.: *shall I get you some more tea?; shall we go for a walk; shall we have another game?; have another cigar; shall I?* = had I better have one?

shalloon, n. [1. shalōōn; 2. ʃəlún], fr. Fr. *chalon*, fr. Châlons, town in France where the material was made. A light, loosely woven worsted fabric.

shallop, n. [1. shálup; 2. ʃǽləp], fr. Fr. *chaloupe*, fr. Du. *sloep*. See **sloop**. A light, undecked boat; (poet.) any small boat.

shallot, n. [1. shalót; 2. ʃəlɔ́t], fr. O. Fr. *eschalote*, a variant or corrupt. of *escalogne*, fr. Lat. *ascalōnia*, sc. *caepa*, 'onion', fr. Ascalon, in Palestine. A plant of the onion family, *Allium ascalonicum*, with mild-flavoured, clustered bulbs; used for pickling, and in cooking for flavouring.

shallow (I.), adj. [1. shálō; 2. ʃǽlou]. Not in O.E.; M.E. *schalowe*; etymol. doubtful, prob. cogn. w. O.N. *skjalgr*, 'sloping, oblique', see **shoal (III.)**. **1.** Not deep, having little or not much depth: *a shallow stream; in shallow seas; a shallow vessel.* **2. a** (of thought, knowledge, feeling, character) Lacking depth, intensity, thoroughness; superficial, slight, trivial; **b** (of persons) possessing a shallow character, knowledge &c.

shallow (II.), n., fr. prec. A shallow place in a body of water; a shoal; (often pl.) *the shallows*, a tract of shallow water.

shallow (III.), vb. intrans. & trans., fr. **shallow (I.)**. **1.** intrans. To become shallow, to grow gradually less in depth: *the river shallows at this point.* **2.** trans. To cause to become shallow: *the sand-banks here shallow the channel.*

shallow-brained, -minded, adj. Having a shallow, superficial brain or mind.

shallowness, n. [1. shálōnes; 2. ʃǽlounis]. **shallow (I.) & -ness.** State, quality, of being shallow.

sham (I.), vb. trans. & intrans. [1. sham; 2. ʃæm]. A Nthn. variant of **shame**; in early usage, now obs., 'to trick, delude, deceive'. **1.** trans. To assume the character of, to imitate, simulate, feign; to pretend to be in a state of: *to sham illness, stupidity; to sham madness, courage* &c. **2.** intrans. **a** To practise simulation; to make pretences, to pretend: *take no notice, he is only shamming*; **b** (followed directly by adj.) to pretend to be: *to sham dead, sick.*

sham (II.), n., fr. prec. **1.** A thing made to appear something it is not; a counterfeit, an imitation, a pretence, a fake: *these pearls are all shams; his illness was only a sham.* **2.** Disingenuous, hypocritical conduct; an assumed virtue; an act of hypocrisy: *his religion, philanthropy, is all a sham.* **3. a** A person who pretends to be what he is not; a fraud, a charlatan; **b** a person who shams (illness &c.).

sham (III.), adj., fr. prec. Not genuine; bogus, counterfeit, feigned, spurious: *a sham diamond*; (also of qualities &c.) *sham piety*; (of persons) *a sham doctor*, a quack; *a sham gentleman*, a pretender to gentility.

shaman, n. [1. sháman; 2. ʃǽmæn]. Etymol. doubtful; prob. Pers. *shaman*, 'idolater'. A priest-magician or medicine man among the primitive Ural-Altaic tribes of N. Asia; also applied to witch-doctors &c. of other primitive tribes &c.

Shamanism, n. [1. shámanizm; 2. ʃǽmænizəm]. Prec. & **-ism.** The religion, religious practices &c. of various primitive tribes in N.E. Asia, based on the belief in good and evil spirits which can only be controlled by the spells and rites of the shamans; also applied to other primitive religions of this type.

shamble, vb. intrans. & n. [1. shámbl; 2. ʃǽmbl], fr. O. Du. *schampelen*, 'to slip, stumble', *schampen*, 'to slip away, decamp', fr. O. Fr. *escamper*, Ital. *scampare*, 'to decamp, escape', fr. Lat. *ex-*, 'out of, away', & *campus*, 'field'; cp. **scamper**. **1.** vb. To walk with a stumbling or shuffling gait; to walk as if the knees were weak and the feet could hardly be lifted. **2.** n. A shambling, shuffling gait; an ungainly, clumsy walk.

shambles, n. pl., used as sing. [1. shámblz; 2. ʃǽmblz]. O.E. *sċamel*, 'stool', M.E. *schamel*, 'bench', fr. Lat. *scamellum*, 'bench, stool'; dimin. of *scamnum*, 'step, throne', for **scapnom*, fr. base seen in Lat. *scāpus*, 'stem &c.', q.v. under **scape, shaft**. **1. a** A butcher's stall or bench in which meat is exposed for sale; **b** a slaughter-house. **2.** (fig.) A place of slaughter, carnage, or bloodshed; place covered in blood: *the deck of a ship in action is a veritable shambles.*

shame (I.), n. [1. shām; 2. ʃeim]. O.E. *sċamu*, M.E. *schāme*; O.S. & O.H.G. *scama*; O.N. *skömm*; Goth. has the vb. *skaman*, 'to be ashamed'; Goth *skanda*, O.H.G. *scanta*, in same sense, are fr. same base. Further connexions in Gmc. & outside are doubtful. **1.** Powerful and painful emotion of regret and contrition, arising from a consciousness of guilt, or from something which shocks the sense of modesty, propriety &c.; sense that one has offended against decency and seemliness of behaviour &c.: *to feel shame at the recollection of one's conduct; the sight brought a blush of shame to her cheek.* **2. a** Disgrace, dishonour, reproach; ignominy suffered; contemptuous, dishonouring treatment: *to bring shame on one's family; to suffer the shame of being inferior to one's fellows*; Phr. *to put to shame*, cause to feel ashamed; *bring to shame*, to disgrace, cause to suffer ignominy; **b** (colloq.) hard luck, unfair treatment: *what a shame to treat you like that! it is a horrid shame not to give children enough to eat.* **3.** Cause, source, of shame, reproach, disgrace: '*Erasmus ... The glory of the priesthood, and its shame*' (Pope, 'Ess. on Crit.', 693-4).

shame (II.), vb. trans., fr. prec., O.E. *sċamian, sċeamian*. **1.** To make to feel shame, to make ashamed: *his industry and success shamed all his detractors.* **2.** To bring shame or disgrace upon, to disgrace, put to shame: *openly detected as a thief, and shamed before the whole school.* **3.** To urge, drive, cause to do by shame or reproach: *he was shamed into working, out of his bad habits.*

shamefaced, adj. [1. shāmfāst; 2. ʃéimfèist]. Popular etymol. for *shamefast*, O.E. *sċamfæst*, 'ashamed, modest'. **shame (I.) & fast (I.)**, as in *steadfast*. **a** (in good sense) Bashful, shy, easily put out of countenance, diffident, modest; **b** (more usually in unfavourable sense) ashamed of oneself, sheepish, exhibiting consciousness of some shortcoming.

shamefacedly, adv. [1. shāmfāsedli; 2. ʃéimfèisidli]. Prec. & **-ly.** In a shamefaced manner.

shamefacedness, n. [1. shāmfāstnes, shāmfāsednes; 2. ʃéimfeistnis, ʃeimféisidnis]. See prec. & **-ness.** State of being shamefaced.

shameful, adj. [1. shāmfool; 2. ʃéimful]. **shame (I.) & -ful.** **1.** Causing, bringing, shame or disgrace; disgraceful: *a shameful defeat; shameful conduct.* **2.** Arousing feelings of shame; outrageous, disgusting, indecent: *a shameful book, sight* &c.

shamefully, adv. Prec. & **-ly.** In a shameful manner; disgracefully.

shamefulness, n. See prec. & **-ness.** State of being shameful.

shameless, adj. [1. shāmles; 2. ʃéimlis]. **shame (I.) & -less.** **1.** Feeling no shame; destitute of modesty, insensible to shame, reproach, or disgrace; impudent, brazen: *a shameless liar, rogue.* **2.** Exhibiting no sense of shame, no regard for propriety or decency; outraging all natural feelings of shame; immodest: *a shameless play, picture; shameless conduct.*

shamelessly, adv. Prec. & **-ly.** In a shameless manner.

shamelessness, n. See prec. & **-ness.** Quality of being shameless.

shammer, n. [1. shámer; 2. ʃǽmə]. **sham (I.) & -er.** One who shams; impostor, humbug.

shammy (leather), n. [1. shámi; 2. ʃǽmi]. Variant spelling of **chamois**.

shampoo (I.), vb. trans. [1. shàmpōō; 2. ʃæmpú], fr. Hind. *chāmpo*, imperat. of *chāmpnā*, 'to knead, squeeze, press; to shampoo'. **1.** To massage the limbs, by kneading, pressing &c.; one of the principal stages in the Oriental or Turkish bath. **2.** To wash (the head or hair) by soaping and rubbing under a spray of water, or with a soapy, alcoholic preparation, known as a *dry shampoo*.

shampoo (II.), n., fr. prec. **1.** Act or process of shampooing. **2.** Special soap-powder &c. used in shampooing the head.

shamrock, n. [1. shámrok; 2. ʃǽmrɔk], fr. Ir. *seamrog*, 'trefoil'. **a** The white clover, *Trifolium repens*, with three heart-shaped leaflets to each leaf; **b** this or similar trefoil as the badge or emblem of Ireland, worn on St. Patrick's Day in memory of his adoption of a trefoil, probably the wood-sorrel, as a symbol of the Trinity.

shandrydan, n. [1. shándridàn; 2. ʃǽndridæn]. Etymol. unknown. **1.** Specif. (obs.) a light, two-wheeled Irish cart. **2.** A shabby, old-fashioned chaise or carriage.

shandygaff, n. [1. shándigaf; 2. ʃǽndigæf]. Etymol. unknown. A drink of beer mixed with ginger-beer.

shanghai, vb. trans. [1. shàng-hí; 2. ʃæŋhái], fr. the town and port in China. (sailors' slang) To make a man insensible by drink, drugs, or other methods, and ship him on board an outgoing ship as a sailor.

shank (I.), n. [1. shangk; 2. ʃæŋk]. O.E. *sċ(e)anca*, 'the leg', M.E. *schanke*; cp. Mod. Germ. *schenkel*, 'the leg, thigh', fr. **skank-il*, dimin. fr. same base; also O.H.G. *scinko*, Mod. Germ. *schinken*, 'ham'. **1.** The leg, esp. the shin, of man or such animals as horses and cows; chiefly used in derogatory sense: *long, thin, lean, shanks* &c. Phr. *to go on Shanks's mare*, to use one's own legs, instead of riding, driving &c. **2.** Part between the top &c. and the working end of tools and implements; handle, shaft, stem: *shank of a spoon, scissor-blade, key* &c.

shank (II.), vb. intrans., fr. prec. (usually *shank off*, of flower) To drop off, decay and fall off, from the shank or footstalk.

shanny, n. [1. sháni; 2. ʃǽni]. Etymol. unknown. Green sea-fish, *smooth blenny*.

shan't, vb. [1. shahnt; 2. ʃānt]. Contraction of *shall not*, see **shall**.

shantung, n. [1. shántúng; 2. ʃǽntáŋ]. Name of Chinese province. A coarse silk obtained from undomesticated silk-worms; tussore silk, usually left in its natural colour when woven.

shanty (I.), n. Sailor's song. See **chantey**.

shanty (II.), n. [1. shánti; 2. ʃǽnti]. Etymol. doubtful; perh. Fr. *chantier*, 'shed; timber-yard'. A small shed or hut; a poor, mean, tumble-down dwelling.

shapable, adj. [1. shā́pabl; 2. ʃéipəbl]. **shape** (I.) & **-able**. Capable of being shaped.

shape (I.), n. [1. shāp; 2. ʃeip]. O.E. *(ge)sċeap*, 'creation; created thing, creature; form, shape; destiny, decree (of fate)'; M.E. *s(c)hāpe*; fr. base **skăb-*, 'to scrape, cut' &c., cp. Lat. *scabere*, 'to scratch, scrape', *scaber*, 'rough', see **scabrous**; Lith. *skabus*, 'sharp'; related also to a group of words fr. a variant **skap-*, cp. Gk. *skáptein*, 'to dig'; Lith. *skùpti*, 'to hollow out' &c. See also **-ship** & **shave** (I.). **1.** Outward form, outline, contour: *the shape of one's head, face; shape of a cloud, tree* &c. Phrs. *in the shape of*, in the form, in the guise, of: *a fiend in human shape; a reward in the shape of £100; not in any shape or form*, in no way whatever, not at all. **2.** Something having an outward, visible form, esp. something vague, mysterious, and uncanny; an apparition: *strange shapes appeared from the shadows.* **3.** Clear, definite conception, orderly arrangement in the mind: *to put one's ideas into shape; the plan is taking shape in my head.* **4.** a Practical expression of an idea, plan &c. in action: *Foch's long-prepared schemes at last took shape in a concerted attack along an immense front*; b embodiment in artistic form: *the poet's dreams find a shape in his poetry.* **5.** a Pattern to be copied in making anything; mould for shaping anything; model: *a hat shape; iron-moulder's shape*; b that which is formed or turned out of a mould: *cornflour shape.*

shape (II.), vb. trans. & intrans. A new formation fr. prec.; not derived fr. O.E. *sċieppan*, non-W.S. *sċeppan*, 'to create, form, appoint, decree', either in form or meaning; the O.E. vb. is formed fr. Gmc. base **skap-*, for wh. see prec. **1.** trans. To give a specific shape to, to form, mould (in material and non-material senses): *to shape a piece of wood; to shape a stone into an axe; to shape a garment; to shape one's ideas; shape one's rough material into a book.* Phr. *to shape one's course*, direct it. **2.** intrans. To take on, assume, a shape, appearance; to become ordered, disposed, adapted; to turn out, develop: *the box I am making is shaping quite well; I don't like the way events are shaping at all; the boy is shaping very satisfactorily.*

shaped, adj. [1. shāpt; 2. ʃeipt]. Prec. & **-ed**. Having a given or specified shape: *shaped like a pear.*

-shaped, suff. Same as prec., in compounds: *pear-shaped, boat-shaped* &c.

shapeless, adj. [1. shā́ples; 2. ʃéiplis]. **shape** (I.) & **-less**. Without shape or form; lacking order and arrangement; amorphous.

shapelessly, adv. Prec. & **-ly**. In a shapeless form.

shapelessness, n. See prec. & **-ness**. Quality of being shapeless.

shapeliness, n. [1. shā́plines; 2. ʃéiplinis]. Next word & **-ness**. Quality of being shapely.

shapely, adj. [1. shā́pli; 2. ʃéipli]. **shape** (I.) & **-ly**. Having a good, pleasing, shape; well-proportioned, symmetrical.

-shapen, suff. [1. shā́pen; 2. ʃéipən]. Old strong P.P. of **shape**. O.E. *(ġe)sċapen.* Having a specified shape: *ill-shapen, mis-shapen.*

shaper, n. [1. shā́per; 2. ʃéipə]. **shape** (II.) & **-er**. One who, that which, shapes; specif., a hand- or machine-tool for cutting moulds, patterns &c.

shapka, n. [1. shápka; 2. ʃǽpkə], fr. Pol. *czapka*. A cylindrical, conical cap with a flat top, the typical head-dress of lancer regiments.

shard, n., also **sherd** [1. shard, shĕrd; 2. ʃād, ʃǝ̄d]. O.E. *sċeard*, 'notched, broken'; fr. base seen in *sċieran*, 'to cut', see **shear** (I.). **1.** (archaic) A fragment of pottery, or of a broken pot; a potsherd; (gardener's term) piece of crock placed over hole at bottom of a flower-pot. **2.** The hard wing-case of a beetle.

share (I.), n. [1. shār; 2. ʃɛə]. O.E. *sċ(e)aru*, 'a cutting'; in compounds, 'that which is cut off, apportioned' &c.; gradational variant of **shear** (I.). **1.** a Portion, part, amount of a thing or quality in possession of which several participate: *to have a share in the spoils; he has some share of his father's genius; a share of luck*; b part, division, of specific and limited size, and amount allotted, awarded, assigned, to a person in distribution, or to be contributed by him as part of a joint payment: *his share of his father's fortune was smaller than that of his brothers; your share of the expenses is five shillings*; Phr. *lion's share*, largest portion. **2.** Part, rôle, played, contribution made, by a person in an action: *what share had he in the victory?; he took no share in the plot.* **3.** a Ownership of part of property, business, undertaking &c. together with others: *to have a share in a mining speculation; a share in some house property, in a shipping business* &c.; specif. b any one of the equal parts into which the invested capital of a joint-stock company is divided, entitling the owner to a proportion of the profits as interest, and of the assets if and when the company is wound up; c (loosely) document which gives evidence of ownership of such a share; in full, *share certificate.*

share (II.), vb. trans. & intrans., fr. prec. **A.** trans. **1.** *Share out*, to distribute, apportion, hand out in shares: *to share out food and clothing to the poor.* **2.** *Share with*, to give a share of to (another person) and retain a portion for oneself: *to share one's dinner with a beggar, one's purse with a friend.* **3.** a To participate in use or possession of, enjoy in common with others; to have a share or portion of, together with others: *we had better share the food, profit, glory; let us share what is left between us*; Phr. *to share the bed of*, sleep with; b to participate in, experience, incur, together with others: *to share the toils and hardships of a campaign; to share losses, expenses; to share the blame, responsibility* &c. **B.** intrans. To have a share; to take, play, a part in; to participate in: *to share alike in the hopes and anxieties of parenthood*; Phr. *share and share alike*, (of several persons) to participate equally in use or enjoyment of something distributed.

share (III.), n. O.E. *sċear*, 'ploughshare', fr. same base as prec., & cp. **shear** (II.). That part of a plough or similar implement which cuts the furrow; ploughshare.

share-beam, n. **share** (III.) & **beam**. The part of a plough in which the share is fixed.

shareholder, n. [1. shā́rhōlder; 2. ʃɛ́əhòuldə]. One who holds, or owns, shares in a joint-stock company.

sharer, n. [1. shā́rer; 2. ʃɛ́ərə]. **share** (II.) & **-er**. One who shares, takes part, participates.

shark (I.), n. [1. shark; 2. ʃāk]. Etymol. uncertain; possibly an adaptation of Lat. *carcharus*, 'the dog-fish', fr. Gk. *karkharias*, 'a sea-fish with sharp teeth, shark', fr. *kárkharos*, 'jagged, sharp'; the Gk. word shows reduplication, cp. Scrt. *kharaš*, 'hard, rough, sharp'. **1.** The general name for any one of a very large group of extremely voracious sea-fishes, allied to the rays and including the dog-fishes; chiefly characterized by a long, rounded and tapering body, and a powerful tail; having gills placed laterally, the mouth on the underside, a tough skin, usually of a slaty grey colour, and being covered with hard tubercles instead of scales; some varieties, such as the man-eating shark, *Carcharodon carcharias*, of tropical waters, the basking shark, hammer-head, thresher, the porbeagle, are dangerous to man. **2.** (fig.) A rapacious, greedy person; one who preys on others; a swindling rogue, a sharper.

shark (II.), vb. intrans. & trans. See prec. **1.** intrans. To prowl about in search of plunder; to play the shark, swindler or plunderer. **2.** trans. a To devour voraciously, like a shark; b to plunder, swindle, cheat.

sharker, n. [1. shárker; 2. ʃā́kə]. **shark** (II.) & **-er**. One who sharks or plunders; swindler, sharper.

sharking, adj. [1. shárking; 2. ʃā́kiŋ], fr. Pres. Part. of **shark** (II.). Inclined to shark; rapaciously dishonest: *a sharking rogue, money-lender* &c.

shark oil, n. Oil obtained from the liver of certain sharks or dog-fishes, used as a substitute for cod-liver oil.

shark-ray, n. The angel-fish.

shark-skin, n. Shagreen.

shark's mouth, n. An opening in an awning on a ship's deck through which the mast &c. passes.

sharp (I.), adj. [1. sharp; 2. ʃāp]. O.E. *sċearp*; M.E. *scherpe, scharpe*; O.S. *skarp*; O.N. *skarpr*; cogn. w. O.E. *sċeorpan*, 'to scrape', & *sċrepan* in same sense; further Lat. *scrobis*, 'a ditch, a trench'. **1.** a (of edges, or edged tools &c.) Keen, cutting; b (of points, or pointed tools &c.) fine, piercing; reverse of *blunt*; c (of sand &c.) composed of spiky, pointed grains. **2.** (referring to form and shape) a Acute, pointed, not obtuse or rounded: *a sharp peak, ridge; a sharp nose, features*; b (of curves) turning abruptly and suddenly: *a sharp corner of a road; a sharp turn*; c (of gradients) steep, abrupt: *a sharp ascent, descent, fall.* **3.** (of visual images) Clearly seen, distinctly defined or outlined; standing out clearly, clean-cut, not blurred: *a sharp outline* &c. **4.** Producing a physical sensation resembling or suggestive of cutting, biting, piercing &c.; intense: *a sharp frost; a sharp pain, twinge* &c. **5.** (of sound) Shrill, piercing. **6.** (of taste and smell) Acrid, intensely bitter, sour. **7.** (of the senses) Acute, keen, sensitive, alert, quick to perceive and distinguish: *sharp eyes, sight, ears, hearing; a sharp nose, sense of smell* &c.; *to have a sharp eye, ear, nose, for anything; to keep a sharp lookout.* **8.** (of sensations, appetites &c.) Eager, keen to be satisfied: *a sharp hunger, thirst.* **9.** (of actions and movements) Brisk, rapid, swift; sudden; performed quickly and briskly, vigorously: *a sharp walk; a sharp game, set* &c. Phr. *short and sharp*, brief but intense. **10.** (referring to mental qualities) a Quick, keen, penetrating, alert, clever, smart: *sharp wits, intelligence; a sharp lad; he was very sharp at figures*; Phr. *sharp as a needle*, very keen, alert &c.; also b (in bad sense) keen and unscrupulous: *a very sharp customer; he was much too sharp for me.* **11.** (of actions, expression, affecting the feelings) Piercing, biting, cutting; wounding; severe: *a sharp rebuke, criticism, cross-examination; a sharp* *sentence*; Phr. *to have a sharp tongue*, one ready to make cutting, biting, remarks. **12.** (mus., opposed to *flat*) **a** (of note) Raised a semitone in pitch (expressed by ♯): *C sharp*; **b** (of voice, tone) above the true pitch, out of tune by being too high; **c** (of key) with the signature in sharps: *sonata in F sharp*.

sharp (II.), adv., fr. prec. **1.** Punctually, to the moment: *at ten o'clock sharp*; *train left sharp to time*. **2.** Quickly, briskly; Phr. *look sharp!*, be quick, hurry.

sharp (III.), n., fr. **sharp** (I.). **1.** (mus.) Symbol ♯; contrasted with *flat*; **a** a sharp tone, note; **b** symbol for this in musical notation; **c** one of the black keys on an organ or piano. **2.** (colloq. or slang) A swindler, cheat, sharper. **3.** (pl.) See **sharps.**

sharp (IV.), vb. trans. & intrans., fr. prec. **A.** trans. **1.** (obs. or provinc.) To sharpen, to whet. **2.** (mus.) To raise above the proper pitch, to make sharp: *to sharp a tone*. **3.** (colloq., slang) To swindle, cheat: *he sharped me out of my winnings*. **B.** intrans. **1.** (mus.) To sing or play sharp. **2.** (colloq., slang) To play the sharp or swindler: *he sharps at cards*.

sharp-cut, adj. Sharply, clearly, cut or defined; having a clear, defined outline.

sharpen, vb. trans. & intrans. [1. shárpen; 2. ʃápən]. **sharp** (I.) & **-en**. **A.** trans. To make sharp. **1.** To whet, to put a sharp edge or point on to: *to sharpen a knife, razor, pencil*. **2.** (fig.) **a** To make keen, quick, and ready: *to sharpen one's wits*; **b** to intensify (the appetite &c.); **c** to make more biting or malicious: *to sharpen one's tongue*. **B.** intrans. To become, grow, sharp.

sharpener, n. [1. shárpener; 2. ʃápənə]. Prec. & **-er**. That which sharpens; which puts a keen edge or point to something: *a knife-, pencil-sharpener*.

sharper, n. [1. shárper; 2. ʃápə]. **sharp** (II.) & **-er**. (colloq.) One who sharps or swindles, esp. at cards; a swindler, cheat.

sharp-eyed, adj. Having sharp, keen eyes; sharp-sighted.

sharply, adv. [1. shárpli; 2. ʃápli]. **sharp** (I.) & **-ly**. In a sharp manner.

sharpness, n. [1. shárpnes; 2. ʃápnis]. **sharp** (I.) & **-ness**. State, quality, of being sharp; (in non-material sense) severity, bitterness, intense suffering &c.: *the sharpness of death*.

sharps, n. pl. [1. sharps; 2. ʃáps]. **1.** Sewing-needles with very fine slender points. **2.** Grain middlings.

sharp-set, adj. Very hungry, having a keen appetite.

sharpshooter, n. [1. shárpshōōter; 2. ʃápʃùtə]. A skilled, specially trained marksman.

sharp-sighted, adj. Having sharp, keen sight; sharp-eyed.

sharp-witted, adj. Having sharp, keen wits; very quick and intelligent.

Shastra, n. See **Sastra.**

shatter, vb. trans. & intrans. [1. sháter; 2. ʃǽtə], fr. L.G. source, cp. O.D. *schetteren*, 'to scatter; to burst'; **scatter** is apparently a variant of *shatter*. **A.** trans. **1. a** To break into fragments, to smash, cause to fly in pieces; esp. applied to the breaking of brittle objects and substances such as porcelain, glass, earthenware &c.; **b** (fig.) to destroy, crush, dispel, cause to crumble: *to shatter one's hopes, illusions, ideals*; *to shatter a country's power, influence, discipline* &c. **2.** To deprive of power; to weaken, to disable, cripple: *shattered nerves, health*. **B.** intrans. To break in pieces, to become broken, to fall apart into fragments.

shave (I.), vb. trans. & intrans. [1. shāv; 2. ʃeiv]. O.E. *sc(e)afan*, 'to scrape; to shave', M.E. *s(c)hāven*; cogn. w. O.H.G. *scaban*, 'to scratch, scrape'; Goth. *skaban*, 'to shave'; fr. a base meaning 'to cut' &c., allied to that discussed under **shape** (I.). **A.** trans. **1. a** To remove hair from with a razor: *to shave one's face, chin*; *to shave one-self*, remove hair from one's face with a razor; *to shave a customer*, remove his beard &c. with a razor; **b** *to shave one's beard*, also *shave off*, to cut it off with a razor. This, which is probably now felt to be the essential meaning of the word, is a secondary and specialized development from the original sense 'to scrape'. **2.** To cut thin slices off surface of; to pare, whittle. **3.** To pass close to but without touching; to miss narrowly; to graze: *the wheel of the car shaved the kerb*. **B.** intrans. **1.** To shave oneself: *he looks as though he hadn't shaved for a week*. **2.** (of razor or knife) To perform the action of shaving: *it is very hard to get hold of a razor that will shave properly*.

shave (II.), n., fr. prec. In sense **4**, fr. O.E. *scafa*, 'a shaving tool, plane'. **1.** Act, operation, process, of shaving (the beard &c.): *he needs a shave badly*; *a clean shave*. **2.** A thin slice or paring, a shaving: *take a shave off the surface of the wood*. **3.** A close, near, approach to anything without actually touching it; a narrow miss or escape: *a narrow, near, shave of being killed*; *that was a close shave!* **4.** A cutting tool for shaving or paring wood, cutting thin slices &c., esp. a knife-blade fixed in two handles, a spoke-shave.

shave-hook, n. A plumber's or metal-worker's implement for scraping metal before soldering.

shaveling, n. [1. shāvling; 2. ʃéivliŋ]. **shave** (II.) & **-ling**. (archaic) **a** A shaven person, as term of contempt for a monk or priest; **b** (attrib.) *a shaveling priest*.

shaven, adj. [1. shāven; 2. ʃéivən]. Old strong P.P. of **shave** (I.). (archaic, except as adj.) **a** Having been shaved: *a shaven cheek*; **b** (as P.P., chiefly preceded by adv.) *well, closely, shaven*; also in Phr. *all shaven and shorn*.

shaver, n. [1. shāver; 2. ʃéivə]. **shave** (I.) & **-er**. **1. a** One who shaves (himself or others); **b** that which shaves. **2.** (colloq.) Boy, lad: *a lively young shaver*.

Shavian, adj. [1. shāvian; 2. ʃéiviən]. After, in the manner of, G. Bernard Shaw.

shaving, n. [1. shāving; 2. ʃéiviŋ]. **shave** (I.) & **-ing**. **1.** Act of one who shaves: *shaving is a nuisance*. **2.** Something shaved off; a thin slice or paring of wood cut off by a plane &c.

shaving-brush, n. Brush in form of a tuft of badger's hair &c. fixed in a short handle, used for applying soap to the face before shaving.

shaw, n. [1. shaw; 2. ʃɔ̄]. O.E. *scaga*, 'a wood, copse', M.E. *schawe*, *shawe*, cp. O.N. *skōgr*, prob. cogn. w. base seen in **sky** & **obscure.** (archaic or poet., except in Place-Names) A thicket, small wood, or copse.

shawl, n. [1. shawl; 2. ʃɔ̄l], fr. Pers. *shāl*. Piece of silk or woollen material, folded, and worn over the shoulders, chiefly by women; a plaid; piece of material in which very young children are rolled.

shawm, n. [1. shawm; 2. ʃɔ̄m]. M.E. *shalmye*, fr. O. Fr. *chalamie*, also *chalameau*, 'a small reed-pipe,' fr. *chaume* for **chalme*, 'straw', fr. Lat. *calamus*, 'reed-pipe', fr. Gk. *kálamos*, 'reed'. See **calumary** & **haulm.** An obsolete double-reed musical instrument, the predecessor of the modern oboe.

shay, n. [1. shā; 2. ʃei]. Back-formation fr. **chaise**; cp. **pea**, fr. *pease*. (obs. or jocular) A chaise or low four-wheeled carriage: *a one-horse shay*.

she, nom. sing. of fem. pron. of 3rd pers., when stressed [1. shē; 2. ʃī]; otherwise [1. shi; 2. ʃi]. Origin doubtful; first appears as *scæ* in 'Peterborough Chronicle' (c. 1154); various forms in M.E., *scō*, *scheo*, *s(c)hē* &c. Prob. a special development of O.E. *hēo*, 'she'. See **he.** **1.** The pronoun denoting **a** a woman or female animal; **b** something personified as feminine, as the moon, a ship &c. **2.** (as n.) A woman, female: '*the cruellest she alive*' ('Twelfth Night'); *is the baby a she or a he?* **3.** As prefix before nouns denoting the female sex: *she-devil, she-goat, she-ass* &c.

shea, n. [1. shē; 2. ʃī]. West African native name, *shi* or *si*. A West African tree, the butter-tree, from the seeds of which a yellow fat is obtained, called *shea-butter*.

sheading, n. [1. shēding; 2. ʃídiŋ], fr. base of O.E. *scēadan*, 'to divide, part'. See **shed** (I.), & **-ing**. One of the six administrative divisions of the Isle of Man.

sheaf (I.), n. [1. shēf; 2. ʃīf]. O.E. *scēaf*, M.E. *s(c)heef* &c.; cp. O.H.G. *scoub*, Mod. Germ. *schaube*, 'bundle of hay or straw'; prob. fr. same base as O.E. *scūfan*, 'to thrust, push', q.v. under **shove.** **1.** Large pile or bundle of reaped grain, together with the stalks, tied together and set on end to dry before carrying. **2.** A bundle of things laid or tied together: *a sheaf of papers* &c.; specif., *sheaf of arrows*, number of arrows sufficient to fill a quiver, usually taken as 24.

sheaf (II.), vb. trans., fr. prec. To put (corn) into a sheaf.

shealing, n., also **sheeling, shieling** [1. shēling; 2. ʃíliŋ]. Origin doubtful; perh. connected w. **shell**, but cp. O.N. *skāli*, 'hut', *skjōl*, 'shelter'. (provinc. or poet.) A small hut or shelter, used by shepherds, fishermen &c. during the summer.

shear (I.), vb. trans. & intrans. [1. shēr; 2. ʃiə]. O.E. (non-W.S.) *scēran*, M.E. *s(c)hēren*, cp. Du. & Germ. *scheren*, O.N. *skera*; cogn. w. Gk. *keírein*, 'to cut, shear', for **skʷer-*; also Lat. *caro*, 'flesh, piece of flesh', see **carnal.** **A.** trans. **1.** To cut; specif. **a** cut with shears: *to shear a sheep*, remove its fleece; *to shear cloth*, remove nap; **b** (poet.) to cut with sword or axe. **2.** (archaic P.P.) *Shorn* (used of human hair): *you have been too closely shorn*. **3.** *Shear off*, to cut off **a** with shears, or **b** by striking with sword or axe. **B.** intrans. **1.** To remove fleece from sheep with shears. **2.** (mechan.) To come apart under the action or strain of a shear (see **shear** (II.) 2).

shear (II.), n. Cp. O.E. *scēar*, 'ploughshare', & *scēareru*, 'scissors, shears'. See prec. **1.** (pl.) *Shears, pair of shears*, one of several varieties of large cutting implement with two blades crossing like scissors, usually fastened together in the middle and worked with handles held in either hand, used for trimming hedges &c., or worked with one hand for shearing sheep. **2. a** A strain or alteration of shape in elastic bodies under pressure; **b** stress, pressure, which causes the successive layers of a body to shift and slide over one another.

shear-bill, n. A name given to **a** the skimmer, **b** the shearwater.

shearer, n. [1. shērer; 2. ʃíərə]. **shear** (I.) & **-er.** One who shears, esp. sheep: *the sheep-shearers*.

shear-grass, n. Any of various grasses with sharp, cutting edges.

shearhog, n. [1. shērhog; 2. ʃíəhɔg]. A shear-ling.

shear-hulk, n. See **sheer-hulk.**

shearing, n. [1. shēring; 2. ʃíəriŋ]. **shear** (I.) & **-ing**. **1.** Act, process, of cutting off the wool of sheep with shears: *sheep ready for the shearing*. **2.** Proceeds of shearing, wool clipped off; wool clip: *a heavy shearing*.

shear-legs, sheer-legs, shears, n. [1. shēr legz; 2. ʃíə legz]. Kind of crane for hoisting heavy weights in or out of ships, consisting of a movable set of two or more long spars, lashed together at the top and spread out at the bottom like an open pair of shears.

shearling, n. [1. shērling; 2. ʃíəliŋ]. **shear** (I.) & **-ling**. A sheep after its first shearing, a shearhog.

shears, n. See **shear** (II.) & **shear-legs.**

shear-steel, n. A form of blister-steel, cut or sheared into lengths, brought to a great heat and hammered or rolled; used for cutting tools.

shear-tail, n. A species of humming-bird with long, forked tail, resembling in shape a pair of open shears.

shearwater, n. [1. shḗrwàwter; 2. ʃíəwɔ̄tə]. So called from its shearing or cutting the water as it swims. **1.** A sea-bird, genus *Puffinus*, of many varieties, allied to the petrels and albatross; the Manx shearwater is the only species that breeds in the British Isles. **2.** The skimmer or shear-bill.

sheat-fish, n. [1. shḗt fish; 2. ʃít fiʃ]. First element perh. fr. O.E. *scēota*, 'a trout', fr. *scēot*, 'rapid', see **shoot.** A very large, freshwater, edible fish of the catfish family, found in the Danube and other Central European rivers.

sheath, n. [1. shēth; 2. ʃīþ]. O.E. *scǣð*, fr. **skaiþi-*, 'sheath', M.E. *schēthe*; O.S. *skēðia*, O.H.G. *sceida*; orig. sense 'separation', whence 'means of separation; separating covering' &c.; fr. base in O.E. *sc(e)ād-an*, 'divide, separate' &c., q.v. under **shed (I.)**. **1.** A case or covering, esp. one made to fit blade of a knife, dagger, or other sharp tool or weapon; the scabbard of a sword. **2.** Any close-fitting, enveloping membrane, or sheath-like structure, in plants or animals.

sheathe, vb. trans. [1. shēdh; 2. ʃīð], fr. prec. **1.** To put, replace, in a sheath or scabbard. Phr. *to sheathe the sword*, (fig.) to make peace. **2.** To cover with a protective sheath or casing: *to sheathe a ship's bottom with copper.*

sheathing, n. [1. shḗdhing; 2. ʃíðiŋ]. **sheathe & -ing. 1.** Act of placing or replacing in a sheath or scabbard: *the sheathing of the sword*, (fig.) cessation of hostilities. **2.** That which sheathes, covers, or encases: *the copper sheathing*, of a ship's bottom.

sheath-knife, n. A knife with a fixed blade, fitting into a sheath, as contrasted with *clasp-knife.*

sheave (I.), n. [1. shēv; 2. ʃīv], fr. unrecorded O.E. **scǣf*, fr. **skaiƀi-*, gradational variant of M.E. *shive*, 'slice'; cp. O.H.G. *scība*, Mod. Germ. *scheibe*, 'slice' &c., & Du. *schijf*. The grooved wheel of a pulley over which the rope runs.

sheave (II.), vb. trans., fr. **sheaf.** To collect, put, (grain) into sheaves.

sheaved (I.), adj. [1. shēvd; 2. ʃīvd], fr. **sheave (I.) & -ed.** (of pulleys) Having sheaves.

sheaved (II.), adj. **sheave (II.) & -ed.** Shaped like a sheaf of corn, having top flared, and rather wider than base.

shebang, n. [1. shibáng; 2. ʃibǽŋ]. Variant of **shebeen.** (slang) House, dwelling, shop.

shebeen, n. & vb. intrans. [1. shēbḗn; 2. ʃibín]. Ir.; dimin. of *siopa*, 'shop'. **1.** n. A low public-house; an unlicensed drinking shop. **2.** vb. To carry on illicit traffic in drink.

shebeener, n. [1. shēbḗner; 2. ʃibínə]. Prec. & **-er.** One who carries on traffic in drink without a licence.

shed (I.), vb. trans. [1. shed; 2. ʃed]. O.E. *sc(e)ādan*, 'to divide, separate; to distinguish; to scatter'. M.E. *schōden, scheden*; cogn. w. O.S. *skēðan*, O. Fris. *skētha*, O.H.G. *sceidan*; cogn. w. Gk. *skhízein*, 'to cleave, split'. See **schism, rescind,** & cp. **water-shed. 1.** To let fall, allow to flow: *to shed tears*; (poet.) *leaves shed their dewdrops*; *clouds shed rain.* **2. a** To cast, slough, off, become divested of, lose, by natural process of moulting &c.: *animals shed their coats in summer*; *snakes shed their skins*; *stags shed their antlers*; *flowers shed their petals*; **b** to take off, leave off, divest oneself of: *to shed one's winter clothes*; also (fig.) to get rid of, abandon, free oneself from (habits, mannerisms, titles, acquaintances). **3.** To cause to flow; hence in Phrs. *to shed blood*, to kill, to deprive (man or other animal) of life; *to shed one's blood*, sacrifice one's life. **4.** To pour forth, to scatter; to radiate; to diffuse: *to shed light, radiance, warmth*; *roses shed their fragrance*; (also of non-material things) *to shed a benediction*; *to shed peace and happiness around*; *to shed a good influence* &c.

shed (II.), n. Apparently an unlengthened form of O.E. *scead*, 'shade, protection'. See **shade (I.).** A low, one-storeyed structure, large or small, temporary or permanent, whether of stone or wood, roofed with stone, tiles, or thatch; usually near a dwelling-house; an outhouse: *a shed for cattle, for bicycles, for tools*; *a potting-shed* &c.

shedder, n. [1. shéder; 2. ʃédə]. **shed (I.) & -er. 1.** One who sheds: *shedder of blood*, a murderer. **2.** Specif., an animal, in the initial stages of shedding or moulting.

shedding (I.), n. [1. shéding; 2. ʃédiŋ]. **shed (I.) & -ing. 1.** Act of one who or that which sheds or pours forth: *the shedding of blood, tears* &c. **2.** Something shed, cast off: *the sheddings of a lobster.* **3.** A parting, division: *shedding of waters* (cp. *watershed.*)

shedding (II.), n. **shed (II.) & -ing.** A collection of sheds or huts.

sheeling, n. See **shealing.**

sheen, n. [1. shēn; 2. ʃīn], fr. O.E. adj. (non-W.S.) *scēne*, 'beautiful', M.E. *schēne*, O.S., O.H.G. *scōni*; Goth. *skauns*, 'beautiful'; further relations outside Gmc. doubtful; mistakenly associated w. *shine*, wh. has influenced the meaning. **a** (rare and poet.) Brightness, flash: *the sheen of spears*; **b** gloss, glossiness, lustre: *sheen on satin* &c.

sheeny (I.), adj. [1. shḗni; 2. ʃíni]. Prec. & **-y.** Glossy, bright; possessing a sheen.

sheeny (II.), n., also **sheeny man.** Origin doubtful. (colloq. and disparaging) A Jew.

sheep, n. [1. shēp; 2. ʃīp]. O.E. *scēap, scēp*, M.E. *scheep*; only in W. Gmc.; O.S. *skāp*, O.H.G. *scāf*; no cognates traced. **1. a** Any of various species of ungulate, ruminant mammals, genus *Ovis*, with woolly coat or fleece, and often having curved, hollow horns; specif., domesticated species bred for flesh and wool; **b** the form is also pl.: *five sheep* &c., and collective: *to keep sheep*; Phr. *the black sheep of the family*, one who is different, in a bad sense, from the rest of his family or associates; a bad lot, a rogue; *a wolf in sheep's clothing*, from the fable, an avaricious, grasping, rapacious person concealing his real nature under a mask of simplicity and innocence; *to cast sheep's eyes at*, to look at with shy, sidelong, amorous glances; *to follow like sheep*, to follow a leader blindly or without thinking; *to separate the sheep and the goats*, to distinguish between the good and the bad; *a lost, wandering, sheep*, one who has strayed from the flock, esp. in a religious sense, a sinner who, it is hoped, may one day be reformed and restored to the fold; *sheep without a shepherd*, helpless people, without a leader; *one may as well be hanged for a sheep as a lamb*, if you are going to commit a crime or sin, you may as well risk punishment for a solid, satisfying one as for a petty one, so 'go the whole hog'. **2.** The skin of sheep, dressed as leather or parchment; sheepskin. **3. a** A spiritless, timid, feeble person; **b** the member(s) of a church or other religious community, regarded as the 'flock' of a minister or pastor.

sheep-dip, n. A chemical preparation in which sheep are dipped to free them from parasites and other vermin and to preserve the fleece; sheep-wash.

sheep-dog, n. A dog trained and used by a shepherd to help him in herding his sheep; usually either a collie, or the so-called *Old English sheep-dog*, with long, woolly rough coat, and a bobbed tail.

sheepfold, n. [1. shḗpfōld; 2. ʃípfould]. An enclosure in which sheep are penned.

sheep-hook, n. A shepherd's crook.

sheepish, adj. [1. shḗpish; 2. ʃípiʃ]. **sheep & -ish. a** Bashful, shy, awkward, self-conscious, in manner; **b** silly, dull-witted.

sheepishly, adv. Prec. & **-ly.** In a sheepish manner.

sheepishness, n. See prec. & **-ness.** State, quality, of being sheepish.

sheep-master, n. A breeder of sheep, a sheep-farmer.

sheep-pen, n. A pen or fold for enclosing sheep; sheepfold.

sheep-run, n. A large expanse of land on which sheep are pastured; a large sheep-walk, esp. in Australia.

sheep's fescue, n. A kind of fescue grass, *Festuca ovina*, valuable as a pasture and lawn grass.

sheep's head, n. **1. a** The head of a sheep, esp. as a dish for the table; **b** a dull, stupid person. **2.** A large food fish of the Atlantic coast of N. America, *Sargus ovis.*

sheep-shearer, n. One who shears sheep.

sheep-shearing, n. **1.** Act of shearing or clipping sheep. **2.** Time when sheep are sheared; a feast held at this time.

sheepskin, n. [1. shḗpskin; 2. ʃípskin]. **1.** A coat or rug made of the skin of a sheep with the fleece left on. **2. a** Parchment made from the skin of sheep; **b** (by transf.), a deed, document, engrossed on such parchment. **3.** Leather made of sheepskin, used in bookbinding &c.

sheep-tick, n. Tick which infests sheep; called also sheep-louse.

sheep-walk, n. A tract of land on which sheep are pastured; a small sheep-run.

sheep-wash, n. Sheep-dip.

sheer (I.), adj. [1. shēr; 2. ʃiə]. M.E. *scheere*, 'bright, clear'; of Scand. origin, cp. O.N. *skærr*, 'bright'; cogn. w. O.E. *scīr*, 'bright, shining', Goth. *skeirs*; prob. same base as **shine. 1.** (obs.) Bright, clear, shining: '*The sheer . . . silver fountain*' (Shakespeare, 'Richard II.'). **2.** Clear, unmixed, undiluted; plain, mere, absolute; downright: *sheer waste of time*; *sheer nonsense, roguery* &c.; *a sheer impossibility*; *this means sheer ruin for me.* **3.** Uninterrupted, clear, perpendicular, precipitous: *a sheer rock, cliff*; *a sheer descent, fall.* **4.** (of textiles) Transparent; thin, diaphanous: *sheer muslin* &c.

sheer (II.), adv., fr. prec. **1.** Completely, absolutely, outright. **2.** Straight down, perpendicularly: *he fell sheer down 300 feet*; *the cliff descends sheer to the sea.*

sheer (III.), vb. intrans., fr. Du. *scheren*, 'to shear, cut; to move away or aside, to warp'; cogn. w. **shear (I.). 1.** (of ship) To deviate from proper course, to swerve aside. **2.** *Sheer off*, to move, turn aside; to depart, go away.

sheer (IV.), n., fr. prec. **1.** Deviation from proper or normal course of a ship. **2.** The upward curve of the lines or deck of a ship from amidships to stem or stern, as viewed from the side.

sheer-hulk, n. Spelling due to association w. **sheer (I.)**, in sense of 'mere'. An old, dismasted ship or hulk, provided with shear-legs for hoisting heavy weights in and out of other vessels in a harbour &c.

sheer-legs, n. See **shear-legs.**

sheet (I.), n. [1. shēt; 2. ʃīt]. O.E. *scēat*, 'piece of cloth, cloak; lap, bosom; surface (of ground), region'; O.H.G. *scōz*, cp. Mod. Germ. *schoss*, 'bosom'; O.N. *skaut*, 'corner, lappet'; Goth. *skauts*, 'hem, edge, of a garment'; perh. fr. same base as **shoot**, but the path of development of meaning is uncertain; perh. orig. that part of a **garment** wh. hangs down, or projects. **1.** A rectangular piece of linen or cotton cloth used **a** in pairs, as the inner part of the bed-clothes, coming between the body and the blankets; Phr. *to get between the sheets*, go to bed; **b** as a shroud for wrapping a dead body, usually *winding sheet*; **c** as a white garment or robe for penitents; Phr. *to put on, stand in, a white sheet*, to recant, repent, publicly for an offence. **2.** A piece of paper. Phr. *a blank sheet*, applied (fig.) to a character or mind, as of a young person, ready to receive impressions by education, environment &c.; *clean sheet*, the record of a person under discipline, which contains no entry of breaches of rules, offences, or misconduct; hence, a good character; **a** (gen.) any such piece, whether blank or written or printed upon: *a sheet of notepaper*; *several sheets of MS.* &c.; **b** (techn.) a piece of paper as it comes from the manufacturer, of various sizes, demy, foolscap &c., before folding; when folded it becomes *a sheet in folio, quarto* &c., of so many leaves and pages; *in sheets*, of book before binding; **c** (by transf.) printed matter, a pamphlet, newspaper: *a news sheet*; *fly sheet*; *to sell sheets hot from the press*; *a contemptible, libellous sheet.* **3.** Any broad, flat, and thin piece of metal or other material; specif., one of less thickness than a *plate*: *a sheet of tin, iron, glass* &c.; also *sheet-iron, sheet-lead* &c., iron, lead &c. in sheets. **4.** (by transf.) A broad, continuous, flat expanse or surface: *a sheet of water, ice, snow* &c.; *a sheet of flame, fire*; *rain fell in sheets.*

sheet (**II.**), vb. trans., fr. prec. **1.** To furnish with sheets: *to sheet a bed.* **2.** To wrap, cover, in a sheet: *to sheet a corpse*; '*the sheeted dead*'.

sheet (**III.**), n. Same word as **sheet** (**I.**). **1.** A rope or chain fastened to the lower corner of a sail used for shortening or extending it to the wind: *let out, haul in, the sheet*; *with flowing sheets*, with sails fully expanded, not close-hauled. Phr. *three sheets in the wind* (slang), drunk; from a ship with all three sheets left free or uncontrolled, and so staggering and veering about like a drunken man. **2.** (pl.) The inside, angular parts at the bow or stern of an open boat, not occupied by thwarts: *fore-sheets, stern-sheets.*

sheet (**IV.**), vb. trans., fr. prec. To haul, pull upon a sail by the sheet: *to sheet home*, to haul hard on the sheets of a square sail so as to get it to expand to the full.

sheet anchor, n. For earlier *shoot anchor.* **1.** A large, heavy anchor carried outside the waist or middle part of a ship, ready to be 'shot' or cast in case of great danger or emergency. **2.** (fig.) A person, thing, circumstance &c., upon which one can thoroughly depend in time of trouble or emergency; a sure, last support, hope, or security.

sheet glass, n. A kind of crown glass, made in cylinders, then cut and flattened out while hot into sheets; in distinction to *plate glass.*

sheeting, n. [1. shḗting; 2. ʃítiŋ]. **sheet** (**I.**) & **-ing.** **1.** Linen or cotton fabric, used for making sheets; material such as lead &c., made into sheets. **2.** Timber lining for an embankment, river or canal banks &c.

sheet lightning, n. A diffused flash of lightning; lightning appearing in sheet-like form, mainly visible as reflected from the clouds; contrasted with *forked lightning.*

Sheffield plate, n. [1. shéfēld plā̆t; 2. ʃéfīəld pléit], fr. Sheffield, Yorkshire, where it was first made c. 1758. Plate first made in 18th cent., of a thin sheet of copper enclosed between two sheets of silver which were brought together and welded at the edges.

sheik, sheikh, n. [1. shāk, shēk; 2. ʃeik, ʃīk]. Arab., *sheikh, shaykh*, lit. 'an old man, an elder, chief'. A title of respect used by Arabs and Moslems generally of the Nearer East, hence the head or chief of a family, tribe, or clan; the head of a village, responsible for law and order &c.; also applied to heads of religious communities &c.; *Sheikh-ul-Islam*, the grand mufti, the chief authority on religious law in Turkey and the countries formerly under the Caliphate.

shekaree, n. See **shikari.**

shekel, n. [1. shékl; 2. ʃékl]. Heb. *sheqel*, fr. *shāqal*, 'to weigh'. **1.** **a** An old Jewish unit of weight of about half an ounce; **b** a coin of silver, worth about two shillings and ninepence. **2.** (colloq. or slang, pl.) Money, cash, coins: *to rake in the shekels.*

Shekinah, Shechinah, n. [1. shekína; 2. ʃikáinə], fr. Heb. *shekhinah*, 'the dwelling place', fr. *shākhan*, 'to dwell, inhabit'; in the Targums, not in O.T. The visible presence and glory of God.

sheldrake, n. [1. shéldrāk; 2. ʃéldreik]. In M.E., fr. *shēld*, 'shield', see **shield**, & **drake** (**I.**); old dialects have *sheld*, 'dappled, spotted, piebald'; the meaning is due to the resemblance of the markings on the bird to the gay blazonings on a shield or coat of arms; cp. O.N. *skjöldungr*, 'sheldrake', fr. *skjöldr*, 'shield, spot, patch'; cp. Germ. *schildern*, 'to paint, depict', as on a shield. A genus of wild ducks, *Tadorna*, with red beak, dark green head, and bands of white, brown, and green on the neck; the bird comes between the true ducks and the wild geese; it is found on sandy shores by the sea, feeding on shell-fish and marine worms.

shelf, n. [1. shelf; 2. ʃelf]. O.E. *scylfe, scelfe*, 'plank, shelf', origin & formation doubtful; the dictionaries assert a connexion w. **scale** (**III.**) & **shell**, wh. does not throw much light on the meaning. **1.** **a** A narrow, projecting, flat piece of wood or other material fastened to, or hung from a wall at right angles to this, and parallel to the floor or ground, used for holding various articles of ornament or use, books &c.; **b** one of a set of such boards fitted into a framework, a cupboard, cabinet, bookcase &c.; *shelves*, a set of such boards; Phr. *to be (put, laid) on the shelf*, to be set, laid aside as not in use or not worth using, of persons past useful service &c. **2.** **a** A flat, projecting, horizontal ledge or layer of rock on the face of a cliff &c.; **b** a flat submerged reef or sandbank in the sea or a river; **c** *continental shelf*, elevated submarine zone fringing continent; this may possibly be a distinct word. See **shelve** (**II.**).

shelfful, n. [1. shélffòol; 2. ʃélfful]. Prec. & **-ful.** Amount, quantity, number of things, such as books &c., sufficient to fill a shelf.

shell (**I.**), n. [1. shel; 2. ʃel]. O.E. (non-W. Sax.) *scell*, M.E. *schell*; cogn. w. **scale** (**III.**) & **shale.** **1.** The hard, outer covering of many vegetable or animal objects, retaining its hollow shape when removed from what it contains; **a** the husk of a nut, pod of peas, beans &c.; **b** the hard, calcareous outer covering of a bird's egg; **c** the wing case of a beetle &c.; **d** specif., the test or carapace of invertebrates, such as molluscs; or of vertebrates, such as tortoises &c., forming a protection to their soft bodies; Phr. *to come out of, retire into, one's shell*, to cease to be, to become, shy, reserved, or uncommunicative. **2.** Any kind of shell used for commercial purposes: *(pearl) shell, (tortoise) shell* &c. **3.** Anything resembling a shell, or husk, as being hollow, emptied of its contents and fittings; **a** the outer walls of a house or building, which has been gutted by fire or ruined by time: *only the shell of the castle remains*; **b** the hull of a ship or boat; (in U.S.) a light racing skiff; **c** a light coffin, placed inside the outer or more solid coffin proper. **4.** (by transf. or fig.) Empty show, outward semblance, anything without substance or reality: *some regard ritual as the mere shell of religion.* **5.** **a** A metal or paper cartridge case for rifles, sporting-guns &c., to be filled with charge of powder, bullet or shot; (in U.S.) a filled, complete cartridge; **b** similar case used for fireworks. **6.** (artillery) A cylindrical projectile of hardened steel with conical head, fired from a gun; filled with a bursting charge which explodes by action of time-fuse, in flight, or impact, or after penetrating the object aimed at; shells produce their destructive effect by the shrapnel, bullets, or poison-gas which they contain, by the fragments of the casing itself, or by the concussive shock of the high-explosive bursting charge. **7.** In various special uses: **a** (poet.) the lyre, as originally made from the shell of a tortoise: '*When Jubal struck the chorded shell*' (Dryden, 'S. Cecilia's Day'); **b** the semicircular hand plate or guard of a sword; **c** an intermediate form at certain schools, coming usually between the fourth and fifth forms; **d** a shell-jacket.

shell (**II.**), vb. trans. & intrans., fr. prec. **A.** trans. **1.** **a** To remove, take off the shell from; to take out from the shell or pod: *to shell peas or beans*; *to shell an egg*; *shelled oysters*; Phr. *as easy as shelling peas*, (colloq.) of some absurdly easy task; **b** to remove, strip grain, as wheat, maize, from the ear or cob. **2.** To cover with shells, to fix shells in or upon, for decoration &c. **3.** Specif., to bombard, fire at with shells or artillery: *to shell a town, line of trenches, road* &c.; *the troops were shelled unceasingly.* **B.** intrans. To cast, throw off the shell, to become free from the shell. **C.** *Shell out*, trans. & intrans. (slang) to pay out or over; to hand over money: *shell out your money*; *he hopes that his uncle will shell out handsomely.*

shellac, n. & vb. trans. [1. shélak, shelák; 2. ʃélæk, ʃelǽk]. **shell** (**I.**) & **lac** (**II.**). **1.** n. Lac melted and strained and spread into thin shells or flakes used in making varnishes, sealing-wax &c. **2.** vb. To coat with shellac.

shell-back, n. (slang) An old sailor; old salt.

shell-bark, n. A variety of hickory with peeling bark.

shell-bit, n. A kind of auger or gouge attached to a brace for boring.

-shelled, adj. [1. sheld; 2. ʃeld]. **shell** (**I.**) & **-ed.** Having a specified kind, or quality, of shell: *hard-shelled, soft-shelled.*

shellfish, n. [1. shélfish; 2. ʃélfiʃ]. Any marine mollusc or crustacean having a hard outer shell, as the oyster, lobster, crab &c., esp. of such as are used for food.

shell-heap, n. A kitchen midden.

shell-jacket, n. A tight-fitting, short-backed military jacket, as worn in undress uniform by the household cavalry and horse artillery, or as a mess-jacket by officers.

shell-less, adj. [1. shélles; 2. ʃéllis]. **shell** (**I.**) & **-less.** Having no shells; lacking, deprived of, a shell.

shell-out, n. (billiards) A variety of the game of pyramids.

shell-proof, adj. Proof against the effect of explosive shells or bombs.

shell-work, n. Ornamentation formed of shells, or with pattern resembling shells.

shelly, adj. [1. shéli; 2. ʃéli]. **shell** (**I.**) & **-y.** **1.** Abounding in, covered with, shells: *a shelly beach* &c. **2.** Resembling, having the form or composition of, shells.

shelta, n. [1. shélta; 2. ʃélta], i.e. Celtic. Kind of traditional, secret back slang, mostly of great antiquity, based on Old Irish, still spoken by Irish, Welsh, and Gaelic travelling cairds or tinkers, also known to some gipsies.

shelter (**I.**), n. [1. shélter; 2. ʃéltə]. O.E. *scēld-truma*, lit. 'shield troop', that is, a body of men armed w. shields; a phalanx; later, the compound got to mean 'shielding, protecting, troop or force', hence 'a guard; a protection'; the M.E. form was normally *schĕltrum*, w. shortening of *ē* in first element before the combination of consonants; this became *schel(d)troun, scheltren*, whence the present form. For first element see **shield**; the second, a regular word in O.E. for a body of troops, is formed fr. *trum*, 'strong, firm, steadfast'. See this under **trim** (**I.**). **1.** Protection, cover, screen; state of safety, from physical or moral attack, annoyance, injury &c.: *to take, provide, shelter from rain, cold, wind* &c.; *to find shelter from insult, bad influence, the worries of life* &c.; *to lend the shelter of one's name and position to.* **2.** **a** Place where shelter is obtained; place of refuge and safety; something which affords shelter; specif. **b** a cabin, hut, shed, constructed for the purpose: *cabmen's shelter.*

shelter (**II.**), vb. trans. & intrans., fr. prec. **A.** trans. **1.** To give, afford, shelter to; **a** to give a place of shelter, safety, rest &c., to: *to shelter a person for the night*; **b** to give moral support and protection to; to save: *I cannot shelter you from the results of your folly, from hostile criticism* &c. **2.** To afford cover to, to screen, come between (person or thing and physical injury &c.): *the wood shelters the house to the north.* **3.** (reflex.) *Shelter oneself* (chiefly in moral sense), to seek safety, excuse, justification; to shift responsibility from oneself: *to shelter oneself behind one's superior in office.* **B.** intrans. To seek, take, shelter: *let us shelter till the storm is over*; *to shelter behind a hedge* &c.

sheltie, shelty, n. [1. shélti; 2. ʃélti]. Modification of **Shetland** & **-y**. A Shetland pony.

shelve (I.), vb. trans. [1. shelv; 2. ʃɛlv], fr. **shelf**. 1. To place, arrange, on a shelf: *to shelve books* &c. 2. (fig., commonest sense) To put aside, as if on a shelf and not wanted for use; **a** to get rid of (persons), cease to employ, to supersede, dismiss, force to retire from service &c.: *to shelve an official*; **b** to put (questions, action) on one side, postpone, defer, put off, indefinitely: *officials like to shelve awkward questions*. 3. To furnish, fit, with shelves: *to shelve a recess in a wall, cupboard* &c.

shelve (II.), vb. intrans. Origin doubtful; prob. fr. **shelf** in sense 'to form a ledge or shelf'. To slope, dip, incline, gently: *the shore shelves gradually into deep water*; *a shelving beach*.

she-oak, n. **she** & **oak**. An Australian hardwood tree, of genus *Casuarina*.

Sheol, n. [1. shḗōl; 2. ʃíoul]. Heb. *sheōl*, fr. *shā'al*, 'to dig'. The Hebrew place of departed spirits; the grave, Hades; translated *hell* in A.V. of O.T., cp. Psalm xvi. 10.

shepherd (I.), n. [1. shéperd; 2. ʃépəd]. O.E. *scēap-, scēpherde*, M.E. *schepherde*. See **sheep** & **herd** (II.). 1. **a** Man who looks after sheep; **b** (fig.) a spiritual pastor. Phr. *the Good Shepherd*, Jesus Christ.

shepherd (II.), vb. trans., fr. prec. **a** To look after, protect, as a shepherd does his sheep; **b** to guide, direct along, induce to take, a particular road: *the police shepherded the crowd safely out of the park*.

shepherdess, n. [1. shéperdes; 2. ʃépədɛs, -is]. **shepherd** (I.) & **-ess**. A woman who tends sheep; a figure rather of pastoral poetry than of real life.

shepherd's clock, n. The common pimpernel.

shepherd's club, n. Mullein, *Verbascum*.

shepherd's crook, n. **a** A shepherd's staff with hook at one end; a sheep-hook; **b** a pastoral staff.

shepherd's knot, n. Potentilla.

shepherd's pie, n. A dish of minced meat, chopped onions &c. with a thick covering of mashed potatoes, baked in a pie-dish.

shepherd's plaid, n. **a** A woollen cloth woven with a black and white check pattern; **b** fabric with a pattern of black and white checks.

shepherd's purse, n. An annual, cruciferous, wild plant, *Capsella Bursa-pastoris*, with minute white flowers and heart-shaped, double-valved seed-case.

shepherd's rod, n. A small teasel.

Sheraton, adj. & n. [1. shératun; 2. ʃérətən], fr. Thomas Sheraton, cabinet-maker & designer, d. 1806. **a** adj. Designating a style of domestic furniture made by, or after the designs of, the above: *Sheraton furniture, style* &c.; **b** n., *a genuine piece of Sheraton*.

sherbet, n. [1. shẽrbet; 2. ʃʌ́bət], fr. Pers. *sharbat*, fr. Arab. *sharbah*, 'a drink', *shariba*, 'to drink'. Cp. **syrup** & **shrub** (II.). 1. An Eastern drink of fruit juice, sugar, and water, cooled with snow. 2. Popular name for an effervescent drink made by adding water to a powder of sugar, tartaric acid, and bicarbonate of soda, variously flavoured.

sherd, n. Variant of **shard**.

Shereef, Sherif, n. [1. sherḗf; 2. ʃeríf], fr. Arab. *sharīf*, 'noble, exalted', also as n., 'prince, chief'. 1. A descendant of Mahomet, through his daughter Fatima and her husband Ali; used as a title. 2. The title of the governor of Mecca, the guardian of the Holy Places, usually *Grand Shereef*.

Shereefian, Sherifian, adj. [1. sherḗfian; 2. ʃerífiən]. Prec. & **-ian**. Pertaining to a Shereef: *His Shereefian Majesty*, the Sultan of Morocco; *Shereefian family*.

sheriff, n. [1. shérif; 2. ʃérif]. O.E. *scīr-ȝerēfa*, a king's officer presiding over a shire; M.E. *shereve*. See **shire** & **reeve** (II.). 1. (hist.) An official representative of the Crown in the various counties or shires of England and Wales, Scotland, and Ireland, with various important, chiefly judicial and police, functions. 2. **a** (usually in full) *High Sheriff*, an honorary official of a county or shire in England, Wales, and Ireland, also in certain old cities of England, appointed yearly by the Crown or the cities, having various administrative and judicial functions, such as those of returning officer at elections, attendance on the judges of assize &c., and the issue and execution of writs, custody of prisoners &c., such being performed by his *under-sheriff* and *sheriff's officers* or bailiffs; **b** (Scotland) sheriff-depute, q.v.; **c** (U.S.A.) an elective officer of a county with certain judicial functions, esp. those of keeping the peace, and having the power to call out his *posse comitatus*.

sheriff court, n. (Scotland) The court held by the sheriff-depute or sheriff-substitute.

sheriff-depute, n. [1. shérif depū́t; 2. ʃérif dɛpjū́t]. (Scotland) A judicial officer of a county or stewartry having jurisdiction in minor criminal and civil cases, and administrative functions corresponding to those of the English high sheriff.

sheriffdom, n. [1. shérifdum; 2. ʃérifdəm]. **sheriff** & **-dom**. (Scotland) The office and jurisdiction of a sheriff-depute or sheriff-substitute.

sheriff-substitute, n. (Scotland) The deputy of the sheriff-depute.

sherris, n. [1. shéris; 2. ʃéris]. See **sherry**. (archaic) Sherry, esp. in *sherris-sack*.

sherry, n. [1. shéri; 2. ʃéri]. Earlier *sherris*, regarded as a pl. fr. *Xeres* (=[ʃɛríz]), now called *Jerez de la Frontera* (=[χɛrɛð]), town, near Cadiz, Spain, the centre of the district where the wine is made; fr. Lat. *Caesaris*, genit. sing. of *Caesar*. A still, dry wine of Spain, yellowish brown or dark brown in colour, made in the district of Xeres or in Southern Spain generally.

sherry-cobbler, n. Drink made of sherry, sugar, and lemon with broken ice; usually drunk through a straw.

Shetland, adj. [1. shétland; 2. ʃétlənd]. Name of a group of islands, lying with Orkney, N.N.E. of Scotland. Specif. **a** *Shetland pony*, a breed of small, sturdy pony, with long coat, mane, and tail, originally bred in the islands; **b** *Shetland wool*, a soft fleecy wool spun in the islands.

shew, vb. See **show** (I.).

shewbread, n. [1. shṓbred; 2. ʃóubrɛd]. See **show** (I.) & **bread**. (Jewish relig.) Twelve loaves of unleavened bread, 'shown' or presented to the Lord in the sanctuary of the tabernacle by the high priest each Sabbath.

shewn, vb. See **shown**.

Shiah, Shiite, n. [1. shḗa, shḗīt; 2. ʃíə, ʃíait]. Arab. *shia(h)*, 'sect'. A member of one of the two great divisions of the Moslem faith, which rejects the first three Caliphs and regards Ali, the husband of Fatima, daughter of the Prophet, as his lawful successor; opposed to *Sunnah*.

shibboleth, n. [1. shíboleth; 2. ʃíbəlɛþ]. Heb., 'a river', also 'ear of corn', fr. *shibal*, 'to flow, to grow'. 1. (Jewish hist.) A test word used to distinguish the Gileadites from the Ephraimites, who could not pronounce *sh* (see Judges xii. 6). 2. **a** A cant catchword or formula used as a kind of test of genuineness and loyalty by the adherents of a sect or party, as supposed to embody some principle or ideal; **b** any arbitrary test of social status, conformity to which is exacted from those who desire to come up to the standard.

shield (I.), n. [1. shēld; 2. ʃīld]. O.E. (non-W.S.) *scēld*, M.E. *schēld*; O.S. *scild*, O.H.G. *scilt*, Goth. *skildus*, O.N. *skjolde*; etymol. uncertain; according to some authorities, orig. 'a board', & cogn. w. O.N. *skilja*, 'to split'; also Lith. *skelti*, 'to split' &c., ultimately connected w. **scale** (III.). 1. **a** A piece of portable, protective armour of various shapes and sizes; term applied specifically to the long, kite-shaped or triangular type carried on the left arm, as distinguished from the round *buckler* or *target* held by the left hand; **b** (her.) the field on which a coat of arms is blazoned, representing the surface of a shield. 2. (fig.) That which serves as a protection or defence; **a** (of persons) a defender, protector: '*Our soul waiteth for the Lord: he is our help and our shield*' (Ps. xxxiii. 20); **b** (of things) a defence, protection: '*Above all, taking the shield of faith*' (Ephes. vi. 16). 3. Any object which serves to protect or guard; **a** a guard protecting workers from the moving parts of a machine; **b** a pad for protecting a limb against injury, as the arm after vaccination &c. 4. In various specific uses: **a** (engin.) a steel cylinder with cutting edge used in tunnelling; **b** (ordnance) a screen of armour-plate protecting the men serving a gun; **c** (zool.) a plated or horny covering of certain animals, as of a tortoise; a carapace.

shield (II.), vb. trans., fr. prec. 1. To protect, guard, defend, as with a shield; **a** (of physical things) *the hedge shields the cattle from the wind*; *we can trust the fleet to shield us from invasion*; **b** (of non-physical things) *her youth and innocence shielded her from danger*. 2. To screen, cover, save, from punishment or rebuke: *who is shielding this notorious swindler from prosecution?*

shield-bearer, n. A young squire or page who carried his knight's shield.

shield-fern, n. A fern, *Dryopteris*, with a shield-shaped cover or *indusium* to the clusters of sporangia or fruit-cases.

shield-hand, n. The left hand.

shieldless, adj. [1. shḗldles; 2. ʃíldlis]. **shield** (I.) & **-less**. **a** Without, deprived of, a shield; **b** undefended, unprotected.

shieling, n. See **shealing**.

shier (I.), adj. [1. shíer; 2. ʃaiə]. Compar. of **shy** (I.), less usual than *shyer*.

shier (II.), n. **shy** (II.) & **-er**. A horse inclined to shy.

shift (I.), vb. trans. & intrans. [1. shift; 2. ʃift]. O.E. *sciftan*, 'to divide, separate', M.E. *s(c)hiften*, 'to divide, change, remove', cp. O.N. *skipta*, 'to divide, change, shift', Du. *schiften*, 'to divide, turn', cogn. w. **sheave** & **shiver** (II.). A. trans. 1. To remove, get rid of; **a** (of material objects) *shift this rubbish out of the way*; **b** (of non-material things) to lay aside, to transfer from oneself to another and get rid of: *to shift a burden, blame, responsibility on to someone else*; *to shift off a load of anxiety*. 2. **a** To move (something) from one position to another; to change the position of: *to shift the helm*, to put the helm hard over from port to starboard, or *vice versa*; *to shift furniture from one room to another*; *to shift a rifle from the right to the left shoulder* &c.; *to shift the scenes (on the stage)*; *to shift one's lodgings*, move into another house &c. Phrs. *to shift one's ground*, stand in another place, change one's position; (also fig.) to adopt another point of view, change one's mind; *to shift one's clothes* (archaic or provinc.), change them &c.; *shift oneself* (provinc.), to change one's clothes. B. intrans. 1. **a** (of persons) To move, change, one's position: *to shift from side to side, from one foot to another*; **b** (colloq.) to go away. 2. **a** (of things) To move out of original position, to slip, slide, away from a given place: *sandbanks are constantly shifting*; *cargo shifts in a ship's hold*; **b** (of wind) to veer from one quarter to another. 3. (new formation from n.) *To shift for oneself*, manage without assistance from others, be cast on one's own resources.

shift (II.), n., fr. prec. 1. A change, in position, direction, in conditions &c., change, fluctuation, of mood. 2. **a** (archaic or provinc.) A change of clothes, esp. of underclothing; **b** (archaic) a woman's undergarment, a chemise. 3. A change from one resource to another; an expedient, contrivance, dodge: *to try every shift available*. Phr. *to make (a) shift*, to manage, contrive, with any resource available: to get along as best one can. 4. **a** Set of workmen working at one time at a specific job; **b** time worked by these: *day-shift, night-shift*; *the working day is divided into three shifts.* **5.** (various techn. uses) **a** Rotation of crops; **b** method of laying bricks &c. so that the joints of the rows do not coincide; **c** (min.) a fault, dislocation, or slip in a vein or lode; **d** (mus.) a change of position of the hand on the finger-board of a violin.

shifter, n. [1. shífter; 2. ʃíftə]. **shift (I.) & -er.** **1.** In *scene-shifter*, one who shifts. **2.** A shifty person.

shiftily, adv. [1. shíftili; 2. ʃíftili]. **shifty & -ly.** In a shifty manner.

shiftiness, n. [1. shíftines; 2. ʃíftinis]. **shifty & -ness.** Quality of being shifty.

shiftless, adj. [1. shíftles; 2. ʃíftlis]. **shift (II.) & -less.** **1.** (of persons) Without resource or expedients; lacking foresight and power of management; feckless, inefficient, incapable. **2.** (of something done or made) Exhibiting lack of resource in the doer or maker.

shiftlessly, adv. Prec. & **-ly.** In a shiftless way.

shiftlessness, n. See prec. & **-ness.** Quality of being shiftless.

shifty, adj. [1. shífti; 2. ʃífti]. **shift (II.) & -y.** **a** Not abiding by one's decisions or promises; tricky; **b** evasive, unreliable, dishonest: *a shifty fellow*; *too shifty to be trusted*; furtive, wavering, not steady; hence, conveying impression of dishonesty: *shifty eyes, a shifty glance.*

Shiite, n. See **Shiah.**

shikar, n. [1. shikár; 2. ʃikā́]. Hind. Hunting, sport.

shikari, shikaree, n. [1. shikáhri; 2. ʃikā́ri]. Hind. Hunter; specif., a native hunter acting as guide &c. for a hunting or shooting party in India.

shillelagh, shillelah, n. [1. shilála; 2. ʃiléilə]. Irish; name of a barony in Co. Wicklow, famed for its oak trees. A stout cudgel, esp. one of oak or blackthorn.

shillibeer, n. [1. shílibēr; 2. ʃílibiə]. After G. Shillibeer (1797-1866), coachbuilder. (obs.) An omnibus; a funeral coach.

shilling, n. [1. shíling; 2. ʃíliŋ]. O.E. *sćilling*, 'a coin worth about fivepence'; O.S. & O.H.G. *scilling*, Goth. *skilliggs*, O.N. *skillingr*; etymol. doubtful; perh. connected w. Gmc. base **skel-*, 'to ring, resound', cp. O.H.G. *scellan*, O.N. *skjalla*, in wh. case *shilling* wd. be orig. 'the ringing coin'. A silver coin and money of account, $\frac{1}{20}$ of the pound sterling, equal to 12 pence, abbr. *s.* Phrs. *to cut (a person) off with a shilling*, to disinherit; to leave an expectant heir merely a derisory sum in a will, as a sign of displeasure &c.; *to take the Queen's (King's) shilling*, to enlist in the army, from the former custom of giving a recruit a shilling on enlistment; *shilling shocker*, a cheap sensational novel.

shilly-shally, n. & vb. intrans. [1. shíli shàli; 2. ʃíli ʃæ̀li]. For *shall I?, shall I?* repeated as in hesitation. **1.** n. Indecision, inability to make up one's mind, hesitation, needless delay. **2.** vb. To hesitate, vacillate, to refuse to decide or make up one's mind.

shily, adv. See **shyly.**

shim, n. & vb. trans. [1. shim; 2. ʃim]. Etymol. unknown. **1.** n. A thin slip of wood, metal &c. used as a wedge to make two parts of a machine fit, to fill in a joint &c. **2.** vb. To fit, fill, with a shim.

shimmer, vb. intrans. & n. [1. shímer; 2. ʃímə]. O.E. *sćimrian*, 'to glitter', freq. of *sćīmian, sćīman*, 'to shine', fr. *sćīma*, 'brightness, light', O.H.G. *scīmo*, Goth. *skeima*, 'a light, a torch'; cp. also Mod. Germ. *schimmern*, Du. *schemeren*, 'to glitter, shimmer, shine'; ultimately fr. same base as **shine.** **1.** vb. To shine with a tremulous, fitful light; to glint, glisten. **2.** n. A faint, tremulous light, a glimmer.

shimmery, adj. [1. shímeri; 2. ʃíməi Prec. & **-y.** Emitting a tremulous light.

shimmy, n. [1. shími; 2. ʃími], fr. **chemise.** Childish word for shirt or chemise.

shin (I.), n. [1. shin; 2. ʃin]. O.E. *sćinu*, 'shin', O.H.G. *scina*, cp. Mod. Germ. *schien(bein)*, 'shin-bone'; etymol. uncertain; possibly connected w. **shank.** **a** The front part of the leg from the knee to the ankle, the sharp edge of the front of the shin-bone; **b** the lower part of the foreleg of an ox, as a butcher's term; distinct from *shank.*

shin (II.), vb. intrans. & trans., fr. prec. **1.** intrans. *Shin up*, to climb, swarm (pole &c.), esp. by using legs and arms to grasp with: *to shin up a tree, wall* &c. **2.** trans. **a** To strike, hit, the shin: *to shin oneself against a rock* &c.; **b** to kick the shin of, hack.

shin-bone, n. The tibia.

shindy, n. [1. shíndi; 2. ʃíndi]. Etymol. doubtful; possibly variant of **shinty.** (colloq.) A row, noise; a noisy disturbance: *to kick up a shindy*, to make a disturbance, cause a row.

shine (I.), vb. intrans. & trans. [1. shīn; 2. ʃain]. O.E. *sćīnan*, M.E. *schīnen*, O.S. & O.H.G. *scīnan*, O.N. *skīna*, Goth. *skeinan*; relations outside Gmc. doubtful; but cp. **scintilla.** **A.** intrans. **1.** To emit, reflect, light: *the sun, the stars, a lamp, shine(s)*; *jewels, armour, shine(s) in the sun.* **2.** **a** To be luminous, be visibly bright, to glow, to illuminate: *a light shines in the window* &c.; **b** (fig.) *goodness and contentment shone in his face.* **3.** **a** (of eyes) To sparkle, be lustrous; **b** to convey the impression of moral brightness, cheerfulness, intelligence &c.: *his face shone with happiness.* **4.** To be conspicuous, form a striking contrast to: *her beauty shines out amid sordid surroundings.* Phr. *a shining example*, conspicuous and notable example. **5.** **a** To be intellectually brilliant: *he is a sound sort of fellow, but does not exactly shine*; **b** to excel in, be conspicuous for, some particular attainment: *to shine as a teacher, as a half-back, as an administrator*; **c** to excel under particular circumstances: *to shine in society.* **B.** trans. (colloq.) To polish, make bright: *to shine boots, the plate.*

shine (II.), n., fr. prec. **1.** Sunshine, bright, fine weather: *in rain or shine.* **2.** (poet.) Brightness, lustre. **3.** (colloq.) Polish, gloss: *get a shine put on one's shoes* &c.; *his top-hat had lost its shine.* Phr. *to take the shine out of*, (i.) to spoil the brightness or newness of; (ii.) to impair effect of, cause to appear inferior by contrast. **4.** (slang, prob. different word) A row, disturbance, shindy: *to kick up a shine*, to make a row.

shiner, n. [1. shíner; 2. ʃáinə]. **shine (I.) & -er.** **1.** One who shines. **2.** (slang) A bright, shining coin, esp. a sovereign. **3.** (zool.) Popular name of various small freshwater fishes of N. America, of the carp family, with gold or silver scales.

shingle (I.), n. [1. shíngl; 2. ʃíŋgl]. Etymol. doubtful; perh. of Scand. origin, cp. Norw. *singl, singling*, 'small round pebbles, coarse gravel', fr. *singla*, 'to make a ringing, rattling sound', as made by waves on a beach, cp. **sing.** Coarse, rounded stones or pebbles as found on sea-beaches.

shingle (II.), n. & vb. trans. In M.E.; for *shindle*, f Lat. *scindula*, 'roofing shingle', fr. *scindere*, to split, cleave' &c.; cogn. w. **schedule, schism, & w. shed (I.).** **1.** n. **a** A small rectangular piece of split wood, thicker at one end than the other, forming a wooden tile for roofing, covering outside walls &c., the thicker ends of one row overlapping the thin ends of the row below; **b** a method of dressing women's hair, cut short behind, close to the neck, and waved so as to form curving lines like those of a roof or wall covered with wooden tiles. **2.** vb. **a** To cover with shingles; **b** to cut, dress, (hair) so as to form a shingle.

shingles, n. pl. [1. shínglz; 2. ʃíŋglz]. Earlier *sengle*, fr. O. Fr. *cengle*, 'girth, belt', fr. Lat. *cingulum*, 'girdle', fr. *cingere*, 'to gird', see **cincture.** An eruptive, inflammatory disease of the skin (*herpes zoster*) which, among other symptoms, is characterized by a ring of vesicles, following the course of a nerve, round the body.

shingly, adj. [1. shíngli; 2. ʃíŋgli]. **shingle (I.) & -ly.** Covered with shingle, pebbly; resembling shingle: *a shingly beach, path.*

shin-guard, -pad, n. A guard or pad worn at football or hockey to protect the front lower part of the leg.

shininess, n. [1. shínines; 2. ʃáininis]. **shiny & -ness.** State, quality, of being shiny.

shinny, n. See **shinty.**

Shinto, n. [1. shìntṓ; 2. ʃìntóu]. Jap., 'the divine way', fr. Chin. *shĕn*, pl. *shin*, 'god', & *tao*, 'way, teaching'. The very ancient national religion of Japan, consisting primarily in the worship of tribal ancestors and heroes.

Shintoism, n. [1. shìntṓizm; 2. ʃìntóuizəm]. Prec. & **-ism.** Religious principles of Shinto.

Shintoist, n. [1. shìntṓist; 2. ʃìntóuist]. See prec. & **-ist.** One who practises Shintoism.

shinty, shinny, n. [1. shínti, shíni; 2. ʃínti, ʃíni]. Etymol. uncertain; perh. fr. **shin.** A rough, rudimentary form of hockey, played in Scotland and the north of England with curved sticks and a leather-covered ball with a cork core.

shiny, adj. [1. shíni; 2. ʃáini]. **shine (II.) & -y.** **1.** Bright, clear, full of sunshine: *a hot, shiny day.* **2.** **a** Glossy, polished, lustrous: *a shiny hat, shoes*; *face shiny with soap and water*; **b** polished by wear, having the nap worn down: *a shiny pair of trousers.*

ship (I.), n. [1. ship; 2. ʃip]. O.E. *sćip*, M.E. *s(c)hip*; O.S. *scip*, O.H.G. *scif*, O.N. & Goth. *skip*; origin & further connexions entirely doubtful. **1.** Any large vessel used for navigating the sea, propelled by sails, steam, or other mechanical means. Phrs. *on board ship*, in, or on, a ship; *to take ship*, to go on board a ship; *ship of the line*, a ship of 74 guns or over, of the old wooden sailing navy, that could take its place in the line of battle, the equivalent of the modern *battleship*; Phr. *ship of the desert*, the camel. **2.** Specif., a sailing-vessel with bowsprit, three masts, square-rigged, each divided into lower, top-mast, and topgallant masts.

ship (II.), vb. trans. & intrans., fr. prec. **A.** trans. **1.** **a** Specif., to send (goods &c.) by ship; **b** to cause (goods &c.) to be transported by any means; *ship off*, to send away, whether by ship or otherwise: *to ship a young man off to the colonies* &c. **2.** To engage for service on board a vessel: *to ship a new crew at the next port.* **3.** **a** To place in its proper position for use at sea: *to ship a mast, tiller* &c.; **b** to remove from the rowlocks and place inboard ready for use: *to ship oars.* **4.** (of vessel) To take on board: *to ship a sea.* **B.** intrans. **1.** (of sailors) To agree to serve on board a vessel: *to ship as bo'sun* &c. **2.** (of passengers &c.) To go on board, embark, sail: *we ship from Marseilles tomorrow.*

-ship, suff. O.E. *-sćipe*, M.E. *-schipe*; cogn. w. O.H.G. *-scaf*; fr. base meaning 'to form, make', cp. **shape & -scape.** Suff. forming abstract ns. **1.** From ns., indicating **a** office, dignity, status, tenure of the same: *premiership, judgeship*, also of individual holding such office &c.: *his lordship*; **b** condition, state, quality: *friendship, companionship*; **c** skill, capacity: *seamanship, marksmanship*; many words w. this suff. combine these meanings: *scholarship, fellowship* &c. **2.** From adjs., as *worship* for *worth-ship, hardship.*

ship-biscuit, n. A kind of hard biscuit, used on long voyages when bread cannot be made regularly; hard tack.

shipboard, n. [1. shípbord; 2. ʃípbɔ̄d]. Only in advbl. Phr. *on shipboard*, on board ship.

ship-breaker, n. A person who buys up old, worn-out ships and breaks them up in order to sell the material of which they are made.

ship-broker, n. **1.** The agent of a shipping company, transacting business for their vessels when in port, securing cargoes &c. **2.** One engaged in the buying and selling or chartering of vessels &c. **3.** An agent for marine insurance business.

shipbuilder, n. [1. shípbilder; 2. ʃípbìldə]. One whose business it is to build ships; a naval architect.

shipbuilding, n. [1. shípbìlding; 2. ʃípbìldiŋ]. **1.** The art or business of building ships; naval architecture. **2.** Attributively, as *shipbuilding yard*, a shipyard.

ship-canal, n. A canal large enough for sea-going vessels to pass through.

ship-chandler, n. One who deals in cordage, canvas, or other things which go to furnishing a ship.

ship-fever, n. An old name for typhus.

ship-letter, n. A letter conveyed by a vessel other than a mail-steamer.

shipload, n. [1. shíplōd; 2. ʃíploud]. A full cargo or load for a ship; such quantity of cargo as a ship can carry.

shipman, n. [1. shípman; 2. ʃípmən]. (archaic) A sailor, seaman, mariner.

shipmaster, n. [1. shípmàhster; 2. ʃípmàstə]. The master, captain, skipper, of a merchant vessel.

shipmate, n. [1. shípmāt; 2. ʃípmeit]. One who serves with another on board the same ship; fellow-sailor, messmate.

shipment, n. [1. shípment; 2. ʃípmənt]. **ship (II.)** & **-ment**. **1.** Act, process, of shipping or placing goods on board ship for transportation by sea: *goods awaiting shipment*. **2.** A quantity of goods transported by sea; consignment.

ship-money, n. (hist.) An old tax on seaports and towns to provide money for national defence; specif., tax revived without consent of Parliament by Charles I. and levied on inland counties in time of peace in 1634, 1635, and 1636; one of the causes of the Great Rebellion.

shipowner, n. [1. shípòner; 2. ʃípòunə]. An owner of a ship or ships, or of shares in a ship or ships.

shippen, n. [1. shípen; 2. ʃípən]. O.E. *scypen*, fr. **scuppin-*, cp. O.E. *sćoppa*, 'shed, booth'. See **shop**. A cowhouse, stable.

shipper, n. [1. shíper; 2. ʃípə]. **ship (II.)** & **-er**. **1.** One who imports or exports goods by sea. **2.** A shipowner.

shipping, n. [1. shíping; 2. ʃípiŋ]. **ship (II.)** & **-ing**. **1.** Act, business, of importing and transporting goods &c. by ship. **2.** All the ships collectively, belonging to, using, a port, or belonging to a country.

shipping agent, n. Person representing a shipowner at a seaport.

shipping-articles, n. pl. Articles of agreement between the captain of a vessel and the crew, as to wages, time of the voyage &c.

shipping-bill, -note, n. Document sent by the shipper to the master of the vessel containing all necessary details as to goods to be shipped.

ship-rigged, adj. Rigged as a ship, with three square-rigged masts.

ship's company, n. The crew of a naval or mercantile ship, not including the officers.

ship's corporal, n. A petty officer on a war-vessel who assists the master-at-arms in police and disciplinary duties.

shipshape, adj. & adv. [1. shípshāp; 2. ʃípʃeip]. **a** adj. After the manner of a ship; in good order, arranged as a good seaman would approve of; hence trim, tidy, orderly; **b** adv., in a shipshape manner.

ship's husband, n. The agent of a shipowner at a seaport who looks after the repairs, equipment, stores, and general seaworthiness of the vessel, settles contracts, enters into charter-parties, and keeps regular books of the business &c.

ship's papers, n. pl. The documents which every merchant vessel must carry, as required by the country of registry and by the law of nations, such as certificate of registry, bills of lading, shipping-articles, bills of health, passport &c.

ship-way, n. The inclined way or track on which a ship is built and down which she passes to the water on launching.

ship-worm, n. Any of various worm-like marine molluscs, esp. *Teredo navalis*, which bores into, and destroys, submerged ship's timbers, wooden piles &c.

shipwreck (I.), n. [1. shíprek; 2. ʃíprɛk]. **1.** The loss or destruction of a vessel at sea by storm, collision, sinking, running on shore or against rocks &c. **2.** Vessel so lost or destroyed. **3.** (fig.) Ruin, destruction; complete failure or loss: *the shipwreck of one's ambitions, plans, hopes* &c. Phr. *to make shipwreck of*, to ruin, destroy.

shipwreck (II.), vb. trans. & intrans., fr. prec. **A.** trans. **1.** a To destroy, cause destruction, loss, of (vessel) by shipwreck; **b** to cause (persons) to undergo shipwreck. Rare, except in P.P. pass., *to be shipwrecked* &c. **2.** (fig.) To bring to ruin, to destroy utterly: *shipwrecked hopes, plans* &c. **B.** intrans. **a** To suffer shipwreck; **b** (fig.) to come, be brought, to ruin and destruction.

ship-wright, n. **ship (I.)** & **wright**. One who builds or repairs ships; shipbuilder; ship's carpenter.

shipyard, n. [1. shípyard; 2. ʃípjād]. **ship (I.)** & **yard**. A place, yard, establishment, where ships are built or repaired.

shir(r), n. & vb. trans. [1. shër; 2. ʃʌ̄]. Etymol. unknown. (U.S.A.) **1.** n. Gathered material, esp. on elastic. **2.** vb. To gather, make gathers in (fabric).

shire, n. [1. shīr, 2. ʃáiə]. O.E. *sćir*, 'business, office, administration; district, shire'; O.H.G. *sćira*, 'business, charge'; etymol. unknown; it is impossible to connect w. O.E. *sćeran*, 'to cut, divide' &c., as O.E. *ě* can have no historical relation to *ī*. **1.** A county, now chiefly as termination of names, **a** of certain counties in Great Britain, as *Lancashire, Ayrshire, Flintshire* &c.; **b** of certain districts in Yorkshire, as *Hallamshire*; Phr. *the shires*, (i.) a general name of those counties in England which terminate in *-shire*; (ii.) specif., of certain midland counties famous for their grassland and fox-hunting, as Leicestershire, Northamptonshire, and Rutlandshire, also sometimes including Warwickshire. **2.** A shire horse.

shire horse, n. One of an English breed of heavy draught horses, with long hair on fetlocks.

shire-mote, -moot, n. O.E. *sćirgemōt*. **shire** & **moot**. (hist.) **a** An ancient deliberative assembly of a shire or county in Anglo-Saxon times; **b** a county court held before the *ealdorman* twice a year.

shirereeve, n. See **sheriff**.

shirk (I.), vb. trans. & intrans. [1. shërk; 2. ʃʌ̄k]. Earlier *sherk*; possibly a variant of **shark (II.)**, 'to cheat, swindle'. **1.** trans. To evade, try to get out of, to refuse to face (duty, responsibility, danger, difficulties, and the like). **2.** intrans. To practise, or attempt, evasion of duty, difficulty, danger &c.

shirk (II.), n., fr. prec. A shirker.

shirker, n. [1. shërker; 2. ʃʌ̄kə]. **shirk (I.)** & **-er**. One who shirks or avoids danger, responsibility, hard work &c.

shirra, n. [1. shíra; 2. ʃírə]. Pronunciation of **sheriff** in certain parts of Scotland.

shirt, n. [1. shërt; 2. ʃʌ̄t]. O.E. *scyrte*, 'skirt, tunic'; M.E. *schirte, sherte*; cp. Mod. Germ. *schürze*, 'apron'; fr. **scurti*, 'the short garment', see **short**, & cp. **skirt**. **1.** A loose-fitting, sleeved under-garment of linen, cotton, flannel &c., worn by men beneath the waistcoat and coat, extending from the neck to the middle of the thigh, to the neck-band of which a collar is attached, while the sleeves terminate in wristbands or cuffs. Phrs. *stripped to the shirt*, (lit. and fig.) reduced to the barest necessaries; *to have one's shirt out*, (slang) to lose one's temper; *to put one's shirt on (a horse* &c.), (racing slang) to bet heavily, all one can possibly raise, on a particular horse. **2.** A woman's plain, tailored blouse.

shirt-front, n. The front (archaic, the 'bosom') of a shirt, esp. a stiff starched or pleated front worn with evening dress under a low-cut waistcoat.

shirting, n. [1. shërting; 2. ʃʌ̄tiŋ]. **shirt** & **-ing**. (shop term) Textile material, of cotton, linen &c., suitable for making shirts.

shirtless, adj. [1. shërtles; 2. ʃʌ̄tlis]. **shirt** & **-less**. **a** Without a shirt; deprived of, not wearing, not possessing, a shirt; **b** (fig.) reduced to direst poverty.

shirt-waist, n. (Am.) A woman's blouse.

shirty, adj. [1. shërti; 2. ʃʌ̄ti]. **shirt** & **-y** (slang) Out of temper, irritable, peppery fr. Phr. *to have one's shirt out*.

shittah, n. [1. shítah; 2. ʃítā]. Heb., pl. *shittim*. A tree, probably a species of acacia, of which the Ark of the Covenant and various parts of the Tabernacle were made.

Shivaism, n. See **Sivaism**.

shiver (I.), vb. intrans. [1. shíver; 2. ʃívə]. Etymol. doubtful. **1.** intrans. To be agitated by involuntary vibratory muscular movement; to tremble, shake, quiver, as with cold, fear &c. **2.** trans. (naut.) To cause (sails) to shake in the wind by close steering.

shiver (II.), n., fr. prec. Tremulous involuntary muscular movement, a tremor, as from cold or violent emotion. Phr. (colloq.) *the shivers*, the creeps.

shiver (III.), n. Dimin. of obs. *shive*, 'thin slice of wood', cogn. w. **sheave** & **shift**. (usually in pl.) A splinter, fragment, small piece into which an object is broken by a blow, fall &c.: *the glass fell and broke into shivers*; *smashed to shivers*.

shiver (IV.), vb. trans., fr. prec., but cp. M.E. *scirren*, vb. To break, smash, into fragments; to shatter, dash, to pieces. Phr. *shiver my timbers*, an old nautical exclamation.

shivery, adj. [1. shíveri; 2. ʃívəri]. **shiver (II.)** & **-y**. Inclined to shiver, having a sensation of cold and shuddering, as with fever &c.

shoal (I.), n. [1. shōl; 2. ʃoul]. O.E. *sćolu*, 'crowd, throng', O.S. *skola*, 'troop', Du. *school*, 'shoal of fish', cp. **school (III.)**; fr. Gmc. base **skel-*, 'to divide', cp. O.N. *skilja*, 'to divide, separate', see **skill**. A crowd, large number, or quantity; **a** specif., a large mass of fish, such as herrings, swimming together; **a** school; also **b** (colloq., pl.) a large number or quantity: *I saw shoals of people I knew*; *we have shoals of butter left*; **c** plenty of, more than enough; esp. *shoals of time*.

shoal (II.), vb. intrans., fr. prec. (of fish) To form, and swim together in, shoals.

shoal (III.), adj. & n. A variant of **shallow**, fr. O.N. *skjālgr*. **1.** adj. Shallow, not deep: *shoal water*. **2.** n. **a** A place in a river or sea where the water gets shallow; a shallow: *the deeps and shoals*; **b** a submerged sand-bank, bar, or piece of rising ground which causes the water to become shoal or shallow: *to strike on a shoal*. **3.** (fig.) A concealed danger, a pitfall: *the shoals of public life*.

shoal (IV.), vb. intrans., fr. prec. (of water, river-bed &c.) To become more shallow, to decrease in depth.

shoaliness, n. [1. shṓlines; 2. ʃóulinis]. **shoaly** & **-ness**. State, quality, of being shoaly.

shoaly, adj. [1. shṓli; 2. ʃóuli]. **shoal (III.)** & **-y**. Full of shoals or shallows.

shock (I.), n. [1. shok; 2. ʃɔk]. Either fr. L.G., cp. Du. *schok*, 'jolt', cogn. w. O.H.G. *scoc*, 'jolt, swing', prob. cogn. w. **shake**, or fr. Fr. *choc*, the origin of wh. is uncertain, & wh. may be a Gmc. loan-word. The Engl. n. was perh. derived fr. the vb. See next word. **1.** **a** A sharp, violent concussion, causing oscillation or shaking; a violent jolt or jar, as of an explosion, earthquake &c.; **b** a violent collision or impact of meeting bodies: *the shock of a blow, fall*; *the shock of arms, battle*. *shock action, tactics*, the employment of masses of troops, for attack in close formation, relying on physical weight and impact for success rather than on fire; *shock troops*,

troops specially selected and trained to lead an attack on a defensive position, push it home at all costs and bear the brunt and shock of such tactics. **2.** (elect.) Sensation as of a concussion or blow accompanied by contraction of the muscles and stimulation of the nerves, caused by the discharge of electricity through an animal body. **3.** A sudden disturbance, or total upset, of the vital functions and nervous system of the body, accompanied by collapse, caused by severe injuries, such as an operation, accident, explosion &c., or by violent emotion: *to die of shock.* **4. a** Moral or emotional agitation, bewilderment, surprise, offence, disgust, suddenly and violently caused by some unexpected, overwhelming event or experience; **b** event or experience which produces such moral effects. **5. a** Sudden violent disturbance in human affairs and circumstances; **b** that which causes such disturbance.

shock (II.), vb. trans. & intrans. See prec. **A.** trans. **1. a** To cause physical shock to; to shake, jar, cause to tremble or oscillate by severe impact, collision; **b** to give an electric shock to. **2. a** To produce mental or moral shock in; to produce a sudden sense of stupefaction, bewilderment, grief &c. in; specif. **b** to wound moral susceptibilities of, excite strong disapproval in; outrage person's sense of propriety &c.: *I was shocked by his callousness and cynicism*; *I hope you won't be shocked at* (or *by*) *his coarse stories.* **B.** intrans. To come into violent contact, to collide with a shock: *the two bodies of cavalry shocked, and reeled for a moment*; also *shock together*: *spears and bucklers shocked together in the fight.*

shock (III.), n. & vb. trans. M.E. *schokke*, cp. M. Du. *schocke*; Swed. *skock*, 'heap, pile, of corn sheaves'; etymol. doubtful. **1.** n. A pile, group, stook, usually of twelve sheaves, of corn placed upright in a field to dry and mature before carting. **2.** vb. To arrange, pile, (sheaves of corn) in shocks.

shock (IV.), n. Etymol. doubtful; possibly variant of **shag** (I.). **1.** A rough, unkempt, shaggy mass or mop of hair. **2.** (attrib.) *A shock head*, a head with a shock of shaggy hair.

shocker, n. [1. shóker; 2. ʃɔ́kə]. **shock** (II.) & **-er.** One who, that which, shocks; something very startling or sensational; specif., a sensational novel; often *shilling shocker.*

shock-headed, adj. Having a shock of shaggy, unkempt hair.

shocking, adj. [1. shóking; 2. ʃɔ́kiŋ], fr. Pres. Part. of **shock** (II.). In various senses developed from, but no longer clearly associated with, the idea of giving a moral shock, except Nos. 1 & 2. **1.** Improper, scandalous: *shocking conduct*; *shocking indecency.* **2.** Horrifying, disgusting, revolting: *shocking cruelty*; *a shocking story of crime and folly*; **3.** Of poor quality, inferior; bad: *a shocking dinner, sermon, voice.* **4.** As intensive: **a** *a shocking coward*; *a shocking cold in the head*; **b** as intensive adverb: very, extremely; in Phrs. *shocking bad*; *shocking poor* (*play*) &c.

shockingly, adv. Prec. & **-ly.** In a shocking manner; so as to shock.

shod (I.), adj. [1. shod; 2. ʃɔd], fr. P.P. of **shoe** (II.). See next word. Furnished with shoes: *a shod horse*; also as second element of a compound preceded by qualifying word: *dry-shod*; also, *a stick, pole, shod with iron.*

shod (II.), vb. Pret. of **shoe**, vb.; M.E. *schood, schodd*, Pret. & P.P. of *schōen*, O.E. *sc(e)ōian*, 'to shoe', see **shoe** (II.).

shoddy (I.), n. [1. shódi; 2. ʃɔ́di]. Etymol. unknown. **1.** Fibrous material made from old, worn woollen cloth, or from waste woollen material, shredded or ground up and respun and woven to form a cheap woollen cloth. **2.** Cloth made of shoddy or similar cheap material. **3.** (by extension) Anything of inferior quality; esp. inferior thing, work &c., made to counterfeit excellence.

shoddy (II.), adj., fr. prec. **1.** Made of shoddy: *shoddy cloth, clothes* &c. **2.** Sham, counterfeit; making great pretensions, but actually inferior; cheap and nasty: *shoddy buildings*; *his much vaunted learning proves to be very shoddy stuff*; *a shoddy character.*

shoe (I.), n. [1. shōō; 2. ʃū]. O.E. *sċeōh*, M.E. *s(c)hō*, O.S. *skōh*; O.H.G. *scuoh*; O.N. *skōr*, Goth. *skōhs*; cogn. w. Goth. *skēwjan*, 'to wander about'; cp. also O. Slav. *skokŭ*, 'a leaf', *skočiti*, 'to leap, run'. **1.** An outer covering for the foot, usually of leather, reaching to but not covering the ankle, thus distinguished from *boot*. Phrs. *another pair of shoes*, something quite different; quite another matter; *to stand in another man's shoes*, to occupy another man's place or position; to enjoy another's honours; to be in the same condition or plight as another; *to wait for dead men's shoes*, to wait for a man's death in expectation of inheriting his wealth; *to die in one's shoes*, (rare) to die while still active, working to the last, without lingering illness; *to know where the shoe pinches*, to know by personal experience what causes trouble or grief, and what this means; *to put the shoe on the right foot*, to accuse the right person; to place blame, responsibility &c. where it is due; *to shake in one's shoes*, to tremble, be nervous, esp. in anticipation of evil to befall. **2.** A flat metal band shaped to a horse's hoof and fastened to it with nails. **3.** One of various objects resembling a shoe in shape or function as: **a** a wooden or iron block placed under the wheel of a vehicle to act as a brake when going down a hill; **b** that part of the brake of a bicycle or motor which presses on the rim of the wheels; **c** the metal or wooden rim on the under side of the runner of a sleigh; **d** the metal socket or ferrule of a pile or staff; **e** a small piece of lead or iron at the end of a gutter or pipe to throw off water in a particular direction.

shoe (II.), vb. trans. O.E. *sċ(e)ōian*, 'to shoe', fr. *sċōh*. See prec. **a** To fasten shoes on to (a horse); **b** in P.P., protect end of a stick or staff with iron; see **shod** (I.).

shoebill, n. [1. shōōbil; 2. ʃúbil]. An enormous kind of heron, genus *Balaeniceps*, of the White Nile, with large, flat, hooked bill, shaped rather like a shoe.

shoeblack, n. [1. shōōblak; 2. ʃúblæk]. Person who, for a small charge, cleans boots and shoes for passers-by in the street.

shoe-block, n. (naut.) A block with double sheaves at right angles to each other.

shoe-buckle, n. A silver or metal buckle on a shoe, now worn chiefly as an ornament on dress shoes.

shoehorn, n. [1. shōōhòrn; 2. ʃúhɔ̀n]. Implement of horn, ivory, metal &c. with a hollowed blade for easing the heel into the back of a shoe.

shoe-lace, n. A lace for fastening shoes.

shoe-latchet, n. (obs.) Strap used for fastening a shoe or sandal.

shoe-leather, n. **1.** Leather suitable for making shoes. **2.** Shoes or boots.

shoeless, adj. [1. shōōles; 2. ʃúlis]. **shoe** (I.) & **-less.** Wearing no shoes, barefoot; possessing no shoes.

shoemaker, n. [1. shōōmàker; 2. ʃúmèikə]. Maker of shoes and boots; bootmaker.

shoemaking, n. [1. shōōmàking; 2. ʃúmèikiŋ]. Trade, business, of a shoe or bootmaker.

shoe-string, n. (archaic) Shoe-lace.

shofar, n. [1. shófar; 2. ʃóufā]. Heb. *shōphar.* A ram's horn trumpet, blown on the day of atonement in the synagogue.

shogun, n. [1. shógōōn; 2. ʃóugùn]. Jap. *sho-gūn*, 'generalissimo', fr. Chin. *chiang-chūn*, 'leader of an army'. (Jap. hist.) The title of the real, military, rulers of Japan, who, from the 12th cent. till their abolition in 1868, usurped all the powers of the Emperor; the office was hereditary in certain families.

shogunate, n. [1. shógoonāt; 2. ʃóuguneit]. Prec. & **-ate. a** Office, government, rank, of a shogun; **b** period of such office; **c** period of the rule of the shoguns in Japan.

shone, vb. [1. shon; 2. ʃɔn]. Pret. & P.P. of **shine.** O.E. Pret. sing. *scān*, M.E. *schoon*; cp. O.E. P.P. (*ġe*)*sċinen*; M.E. *schine(n)*.

shoo, interj. & vb. trans. & intrans. [1. shōō; 2. ʃū]. Imitative. **1.** interj. Sound used for driving away or frightening animals or birds. **2.** vb. **a** trans. To drive away by uttering 'shoo'; to drive, frighten, away with an energetic sound or gesture; **b** intrans., to utter the sound 'shoo'.

shook (I.), n. & vb. trans. [1. shook; 2. ʃuk]. Etymol. unknown. **1.** n. **a** A set of staves to make a barrel or cask; **b** a shock or set of sheaves of corn. **2.** vb. To arrange, pack (staves), in a shook.

shook (II.), vb. O.E. *scōc*; M.E. *s(c)hook.* Pret. of **shake.**

shoon, n. Archaic pl. of **shoe.**

shoot (I.), vb. trans. & intrans. [1. shōōt; 2. ʃūt]. O.E. *sċēotan*, trans., 'to shoot (missile); hit with missile; to push, throw'; intrans., 'to rush, flow, shoot out' &c.; M.E. *schēten* (cp. **sheet anchor**) & *schōten*, the former derived fr. O.E. type w. stress on first element of diphthong *sċéotan*, in wh. case *ēo* normally becomes *ē* in M.E. except in the Western areas; the latter fr. O.E. *sċ(e)ṓtan*, wh. becomes M.E. *schōt-*, Mod. Engl. [ʃūt]. The word is found in O.H.G. as *sciozzan*, O.S. *skeotan*, O.N. *skjōta.* The base is widely used in Gmc. in forming words, but outside connexions are very doubtful. **A.** trans. **1.** To cast, hurl, propel, forward with a sudden, forcible, jerky, movement: *to be shot out of a car, over a horse's head*; *to shoot rubbish, gravel &c. on to a heap.* **2.** *Shoot out*, thrust forward, protrude suddenly and with some force (some limb or member of the body): *to shoot out one's tongue*; *he suddenly shot out a leg, his fist* &c. **3.** To emit, flash out, dart (ray of light &c.): *the sun shoots its beams through the mist*; *the search-light shot a long ray across the harbour.* Phr. (fig.) *to shoot a look, glance*, to cast the eyes, look, at, suddenly and swiftly. **4.** Specif. (referring to use of missiles, firearms &c.) **a** to send forth (a missile) from a weapon of propulsion: *to shoot an arrow from a bow, a bullet from a rifle, a shell from a cannon* &c.; **b** to use, discharge, fire (a weapon of propulsion): *to shoot a rifle, gun*; also *shoot off*; **c** (i.) to hit with a missile, or by firing a missile: *to shoot game, a bird on the wing*; *to shoot a man through the head* &c.; (ii.) to execute by shooting: *condemned to be shot for cowardice*; *it is less disgraceful to be shot than to be hanged*; Phr. (slang) *to shoot up* (a person), shoot at, fire at, try to kill by shooting; *to shoot the moon*, remove one's furniture &c. from a house, and leave without paying one's rent. **5.** To kill game in (a particular area) by shooting: *to shoot a covert.* **6.** To be carried rapidly through, or over: *to shoot a rapid in a canoe.* **B.** intrans. **1.** To flash, dart, suddenly: *a meteor suddenly shot across the sky.* **2.** To throb, produce sharp, sudden, darting, stabbing pain: *the pain of sciatica shoots up the back of the leg*; *shooting pains in the limbs.* **3. a** To bud, germinate, break: *the rose will shoot again if you cut it back hard*; **b** *shoot up*, (i.) grow strongly and rapidly: *the child has shot up wonderfully*; (ii.) to rise, tower up, abruptly: *the cliff shoots up to a height of several hundred feet.* **4.** To let fly a missile from a bow &c.; to discharge a fire-arm, to fire: *the king bade the archers to shoot low*; *hands up! or I'll shoot.* **5.** To practise shooting as a sport: *he hunts and shoots, but doesn't fish.* Phr. *to shoot over a dog*, use him to retrieve game when shooting. **6.** (of a fire-arm) To discharge a bullet &c.: *my old revolver doesn't shoot very straight.* **7. a** (of player at football) To kick the ball at the goal; **b** (of cricket ball &c.) to gain suddenly increased speed after striking the ground.

shoot (II.), n., fr. prec. **1. a** Act of shooting with a gun &c.; **b** party assembled to shoot game; a shooting party; **c** area, tract of land over which game is shot; land rented for the shooting of game. **2.** A new growth on a plant, from the root, or from a bud; a newly sprouted branch. **3.** Same as **chute**, with which it is confused. **4.** A spurt, jet, sudden gush of water.

shootable, adj. [1. shōōtabl; 2. ʃútəbl]. **shoot** (I.) & **-able**. Capable of being shot or shot over.

shooter, n. [1. shōōter; 2. ʃútə]. **shoot** (I.) & **-er**. One who, that which, shoots; specif. **a** (in compounds) revolver &c. holding and firing so many cartridges: *a six-shooter*; also *pea-shooter*, small metal tube from which peas are shot by the breath; **b** (of cricket ball &c.) one that keeps low and close to the ground and does not bounce.

shooting, vbl. n. [1. shōōting; 2. ʃútiŋ]. **1. a** Act of one who shoots; specif. of one who shoots for sport: *to be fond of shooting*; **b** opportunity for, practice of, shooting: *good shooting is obtainable quite near London.* **2.** Tract of land over which game is preserved; such land rented for the shooting of game; a shoot: *to take a shooting in Scotland.*

shooting-boots, n. pl. Strong, thick boots worn for shooting.

shooting-box, n. Lodge, smallish house, near a shooting, used during the season.

shooting-gallery, n. Place where shooting at targets with miniature rifles is practised.

shop (I.), n. [1. shop; 2 ʃɔp]. O.E. *sceoppa*, 'stall, booth at a market' &c., M.E. *shoppe*, in mod. sense; O.H.G. *scopf*, 'shed', L.G. *schup*, Germ. *schupfen*, 'shed, barn'; etymol. uncertain; prob. fr. same base as **shape**. **1.** a Place, set of rooms, where goods are displayed, and sold by retail; retail tradesman's place of business; whole building in which retail trade is carried on; Phr. *to talk shop*, to talk about one's own special profession, business, subject of study and interest; *to shut up shop*, retire from business, cease to carry on a given form of activity; *to keep a shop*, be engaged in retail trade; **b** (fig.) retail trade generally. **2.** A workshop of a joiner; engineering works or yard &c. Phr. *the Shop*, Royal Military Academy, Woolwich. **3.** (loosely, slang) A place, building, generally, a dwelling, place of employment &c. Phr. (*things*) *all over the shop*, in disorder, out of place, scattered in confusion.

shop (II.), vb. intrans. & trans., fr. prec. **1.** intrans. To visit shops to make purchases; to make purchases at a shop: *to go shopping*; *we shop at the Stores.* **2.** trans. (slang) To get (person) put in prison.

shop assistant, n. An employee in a retail shop.

shop-girl, n. A girl or young woman employed as an assistant in a shop.

shop hours, n. pl. Hours during which a shop may be open for sales and the employees kept at work, under various Acts of Parliament known as *Shop Hours Acts.*

shopkeeper, n. [1. shópkēper; 2. ʃɔ́pkīpə]. **a** One who owns or keeps a shop for the sale of goods by retail; **b** a small retail trader, as contrasted with *merchant*; Phr. *a nation of shopkeepers*, quoted by Napoleon I. of the English, from Adam Smith's 'Wealth of Nations', iv. 7.

shop-keeping, n. **a** Business of keeping a shop for retail trade; **b** retail trade.

shoplifter, n. [1. shópliftér; 2. ʃɔ́pliftə]. See special sense of **lift**. Thief who specializes in stealing articles from shops under the guise of a customer.

shoplifting, n. [1. shóplifting; 2. ʃɔ́pliftiŋ]. Stealing from shops, under pretence of being a customer.

shopman, n. [1. shópman; 2. ʃɔ́pmən]. **a** A shopkeeper; **b** man who serves in a shop.

shopper, n. [1. shóper; 2. ʃɔ́pə]. **shop** (II.) & **-er**. One who shops.

shopping, n. [1. shóping; 2. ʃɔ́piŋ]. **shop** (II.) & **-ing**. Act of purchasing goods at a shop.

shoppy, adj. [1. shópi; 2. ʃɔ́pi]. **shop** (I.) & **-y**. **1. a** Pertaining to, characteristic of, the shop, or of retail trade: *shoppy manners*; **b** full of shops: *a shoppy neighbourhood.* **2.** (colloq., of persons, conversation &c.) Pertaining to one's own special business, profession, interests, or to some technical branch of knowledge.

shop-soiled, adj. [1. shóp sòild; 2. ʃɔ́p sɔ̀ild]. (of goods) Grown dingy, shabby, soiled, from being exposed for sale.

shop-steward, n. An official of a trade union, in a workshop or factory, elected by his fellow-workers, to see that their union rules are carried out &c., and to represent them in disputes and negotiations with the employers as to wages, hours &c.

shopwalker, n. [1. shópwàwker; 2. ʃɔ́pwɔ̀kə]. A man employed in a large shop as a person of some authority; to supervise junior assistants, direct customers to the department they require &c.

shop window, n. Large front window of a shop where samples of goods for sale within are displayed: *to dress a shop window*, to arrange goods in a shop window for purposes of display. Phr. *to put all one's goods in the shop window*, to make an obtrusive display of all one's knowledge, talents &c., and have nothing behind the superficial show.

shop-worn, adj. Shop-soiled.

shore (I.), n. [1. shōr; 2. ʃɔ]. M.E. *schōre*, perh. fr. a grade of O.E. *sceran*, see **shear** (I.), cp. P.P. *scoren*, 'shorn', w. sense of 'something cut off'. Edge of the land abutting on the sea, an estuary, or on a large lake. Phr. *on shore*, on the land, as contrasted with *on the water*; *to come on shore*, to land from a vessel at sea; used also of coming to land from a boat on a river; *in shore* (naut.), near to the shore, in shallow water.

shore (II.), n. & vb. trans. Either fr. Du. *schoor*, 'prop', or fr. O.N. *skorða*, 'a stay, prop' &c., w. initial cons. influenced by the Engl. cogn. *shorn* &c. See prec., **shear** (I.), & **shorn**. **1.** n. Large, thick beam, or balk of timber used to prop a shaky building &c., or one of a series of smaller timbers used to prop a ship of any sort, in dry dock, or drawn up on shore, while in process of construction or repair &c. **2.** vb. Usually *shore up*, to support, prop, with a shore or series of shores.

shore (III.), vb. Archaic pret. of **shear** (I.).

shoreless, adj. [1. shórles; 2. ʃɔ́lis]. **shore** (I.) & **-less**. (poet.) Without a shore or coast; limitless, not bounded, of indefinite extent: *launched on a shoreless sea.*

shoreward, adj. & adv. [1. shórward; 2. ʃɔ́wəd]. **shore** (I.) & **-ward**. Moving, going, towards the shore; **a** adj., *a shoreward set of the tide*; **b** adv., *to row shoreward.*

shoring, n. [1. shōring; 2. ʃɔ́riŋ]. **shore** (II.) & **-ing**. **1.** The supporting, propping of a ship, building &c. with shores. **2.** System of shores for support of a building &c.; shores collectively.

shorn, adj. [1. shorn; 2. ʃɔn]. O.E. *scoren*, P.P. of *sc(i)eran*. See **shear** (I.). (archaic) Closely cut, or shaved; of the hair, grass, sheep; chiefly in Phrs. such as *shaven and shorn*, *closely shorn* &c.; also *God tempers the wind to the shorn lamb.*

short (I.) adj. [1. short; 2. ʃɔt]. O.E. *sc(e)ort*, 'short in length; brief in time'; cp. O.H.G. *scurz*, 'short garment'; O.E. *scyrte*, 'skirt, tunic', see **shirt** & **skirt**. The Gmc. words are early loan-forms fr. Lat. *excurtus*, q.v. under **ex-** & **curt**. **1.** (of spatial extension) Not having great length, extending but a small way, not reaching far, occupying but a limited space between starting-point and end; reverse of *long*: *a short street, road, piece of rope, stick*; *short skirts, hair*; *a short journey*, involving but little distance and lasting only a little time; *a short cut*, near, direct way of reaching one's objective; (special sense) *short sight*, vision which does not carry far, inability to see at a distance; myopia; *short story*, a piece of fiction, not of the length of a novel, usually concerned with a single episode, development of a single phase of a character &c. **2. a** Of less than normal height, below the average height; reverse of *tall*: *a short man*; **b** of less than normal or proportionate length: *his legs ar very short*; *short legs are ugly*; **c** of less tha the desired, requisite, length; not long enoug for a particular purpose: *why do fat wome so often wear skirts that are short for them?*; *I can't tie a proper knot, the string is short.* **3. a** (of periods of time) Brief, of limited duration, lasting only a little time; not protracted or spun out: *a short life, reign, visit*; *a short winter*, one in which the cold begins late and ends early; *the nights are getting shorter*, period of darkness is becoming less; *the pain will be sharp but short*; Phr. *a short life and a merry one*; **b** (of actions and events in relation to time) not taking long to happen, or be performed; soon completed and over: *a short war*; *a short sermon, address, prayer* &c.; specif. *a short memory*, one that retains only for a short time; *a short temper*, one that is quickly aroused. **4.** Concise, brief, not lengthy: *in speaking one should be short and to the point.* Phr. *to cut a long story short*, to put in as few words as possible. **5.** (of persons, their speech or manner) Abrupt, curt. **6.** Not reaching a required amount or standard: **a** *short weight*; *to be short in one's accounts, in payments*; *short time*, reduced hours of work in an industry, adopted for economic reasons; **b** (*short of*) not reaching to, or as far as: *we were some miles short of our destination*; *all the shells fell short of the mark*; Phrs. *to fall, come, short of*, to fail to reach, as a required or expected standard; *nothing short of*, nothing less than; **c** (of ball in cricket &c.) not pitched, not falling, near enough to wicket. **7.** (of persons) Inadequately supplied, deficient, lacking sufficient quantity: *if I give you all this money it will leave me rather short*; also *short of money, food* &c. Phrs. *to run short (of)*: (i.) (of persons) not to have enough (of); (ii.) (of things, supplies &c.) to fail or run out, become exhausted; *short commons*, insufficient or less than normal amount of food &c. **8. a** (phonetics, of vowels, syllables, and consonants) Of relatively brief duration, compared with others in the same language; **b** (prosody, of vowels or syllables) (i.) (in languages having quantitative metres) reverse of *long* in phonetic sense; (ii.) (in many languages, including English) unstressed, weak. **9.** (commercial) **a** (of negotiable instruments) Maturing early: *a short bill, note*, to be paid or met very soon; *at short date*, dated to mature early; **b** (of dealers) not having sufficient stocks or shares or goods in hand for delivery when such have been sold forward; **c** (of stocks &c.) not available on the market at the price at which they have been sold forward: *copper is very short today.* **10.** (of clay, metal, pastry &c.) Not tough or tenacious; brittle, friable, crumbling. **11.** (of drink, esp. spirits) Undiluted, strong.

short (II.), adv., fr. prec. In a short manner; abruptly, suddenly: *to stop short*; *to cut a man short*, interrupt him; *to pull a horse up short*; (colloq.) *to be taken short*, to be seized with a sudden need of evacuating the bowels; *short of*, except, apart from: *short of what is dishonourable, I will do anything to help you.*

short (III.), n., fr. **short** (I.). **1.** That which is short or not long: only in Phrs. *for short*, for brevity's sake, as abbreviation: *called Sam for short*; *in short*, in a few words, summarily, to sum up; *the long and the short of it is*, to put the matter briefly or in a few words. **2.** (phon. and prosody) A short vowel or syllable. **3.** (pl.) Loose knickerbockers cut short above the knee: *football, rowing, running shorts.* **4.** (pl.) Middlings, milled grain less coarse than offal or bran.

shortage, n. [1. shórtij; 2. ʃɔ́tidž]. **short** (I.) & **-age**. Condition of being short or deficient;

deficiency, insufficient amount: *shortage of food, rain, fighting men* &c.

short-armed, adj. **a** Having short arms; **b** delivered with a short, bent, or unextended arm: *a short-armed blow* or *punch.*

shortbread, shortcake, n. [1. shórtbred, -kāk; 2. ʃɔ́tbred, -keik]. A friable, crisp, brittle kind of biscuit or cake, made of wheat flour with butter and sugar.

short-circuit (I.), n. (elect.) A new path made by a current where it encounters a smaller resistance than in the normal circuit, thus allowing a much larger current to flow through and causing dangerous overheating, fusing &c.

short-circuit (II.), vb. trans. To cause a short circuit in.

short-coat, vb. trans. To put a child into short clothes or a short coat from the long clothes of a young baby.

shortcoming, n. [1. shórtkuming; 2. ʃɔ́tkamiŋ]. **1.** Failure to reach a required standard; **a** defect of character, failure in performance of a duty: *the shortcomings of Charles I. as a king*; **b** defect, inadequacy, in the way some piece of work is carried out; unsatisfactory feature, drawback; imperfection: *a comfortable house in spite of some shortcomings.* **2.** A falling below expected yield in a crop &c.

short-dated, adj. [1. shórt dāted; 2. ʃɔ́t déitid]. (of negotiable instruments) Having an early date for maturity; coming to maturity shortly after being drawn.

short-eared, adj. Having short or small ears; *short-eared owl*, a brown owl, *Asio accipitrinus*, with short ear-tufts.

shorten, vb. trans. & intrans. [1. shórtn; 2. ʃɔ́tn]. **short** (I.) & **-en**. **A.** trans. **1.** To reduce length or extent of (material objects; period of time &c.): *to shorten a rope*; *to shorten sail*, lessen spread of; *his life was shortened by trouble.* Phr. *to shorten one's arm, sword*, or anything held extended in the hand, hold it nearer one's body. **2.** To abbreviate, cut down (a chapter, lecture, speech &c.) **B.** intrans. To become, grow, shorter; to shrink, contract: *the days are rapidly shortening.*

shorthand, n. [1. shórt-hand; 2. ʃɔ́thænd]. **short** (I.) & **hand**, in sense of 'writing'. Stenography, system of graphic notation designed to make possible the recording of speech with much greater speed than with ordinary writing, economy of labour being secured partly by the character of the symbols used, partly by contractions, partly by eliminating all superfluous letters.

short-handed, adj. Short of, lacking, the usual or necessary number of hands, workmen, servants, or assistants.

shorthand writer, n. Person employed to make verbatim report of speeches, debates &c. in shorthand; stenographer.

short-headed, adj. (ethnol.) Having a head which is short, or broad in proportion to its length; brachycephalic; contrasted with *long-headed* or *dolichocephalic.*

shorthorn, n. [1. shórt-horn; 2. ʃɔ́thɔ̄n]. An English breed of large, heavy cattle with short, curved horns, valuable for rapid fattening qualities and as good milk producers.

shortish, adj. [1. shórtish; 2. ʃɔ́tiʃ]. **short** (I.) & **-ish**. Rather short.

short list, n. Brief enumeration of names &c., compiled, selected, from longer list.

short-lived, adj. **short** (I.) & **-lived**. **a** Having a short life; not living long: *a short-lived family, race*; **b** not lasting long, of brief duration, transitory: *short-lived happiness, triumph*; *his jubilation was short-lived.*

shortly, adv. [1. shórtli; 2. ʃɔ́tli]. **short** (I.) & **-ly**. **1.** In a short time, soon, before long: *the guests will arrive shortly*; *events will shortly happen which will prove that I am right.* **2.** Briefly, succinctly: *to put it shortly*, in a few words. **3.** Abruptly, sharply, curtly: *he took the questioner up shortly*; *answered me very shortly.*

shortness, n. [1. shórtnes; 2. ʃɔ́tnis]. **short** (I.) & **-ness**. State, quality, of being short (in all its senses); specif., *shortness of breath*, liability, tendency, to get out of breath.

short rib, n. One of the false ribs.

short sea, n. A broken, choppy sea.

short-sighted, adj. **1.** Having short sight; not able to see objects at a distance; near-sighted, myopic. **2.** (fig.) **a** Lacking imagination and vision; deficient in foresight; incapable of preparing for future developments; **b** exhibiting, based on, lack of vision and foresight: *a short-sighted policy.*

short-sightedly, adv. Prec. & **-ly**. In a short-sighted way.

short-sightedness, n. See prec. & **-ness**. State, quality, of being short-sighted.

short-spoken, adj. Speaking in a short, abrupt, curt manner.

short temper, n. A temper easily and soon roused, provoked, excited.

short-tempered, adj. Having a short or quick temper; losing control of one's temper easily or quickly.

short-waisted, adj. **a** (of persons) Having comparatively short space between the ribs and the hips; **b** (of garments) made so as to produce the impression of a short waist in the wearer.

short-winded, adj. [1. shórt winded; 2. ʃɔ́t windid]. Becoming breathless after comparatively slight exertion.

short-windedness, n. Prec. & **-ness**. Condition of being short-winded.

shot (I.), adj. [1. shot; 2. ʃɔt], fr. P.P. of **shoot** (I.); O.E. (*ge*)*scoten*; M.E. *shote*(*n*). Variegated, streaked, with another colour or colours; (of fabrics) woven with the warp and the weft of different colours, so that an iridescent effect is produced, and the material appears to change colour when seen from different angles.

shot (II.), vb., Pret. & P.P. of **shoot**, fr. M.E. P.P. type *shoten.* See prec. Cp. O.E. Pret. *scēat*, M.E. *sheet.*

shot (III.), n. O.E. *gesc*(*e*)*ot*, in gradational relation to *scēotan.* See **shoot** (I.). **1. a** One of the small lead pellets with which the cartridge of a sporting or 'shot gun' is filled; **b** (coll. pl.) a number of such pellets: *a cartridge filled with shot*; *a few shot*; **c** a solid ball, formerly of stone, later of metal, used as the missile of a cannon: contrasted with *shell*: *shot and shell*; *to fire a shot*; Phrs. *a shot in the locker*, (naut. slang) money in one's pocket; any personal resource in an emergency: *there's hope while there's a shot in the locker*; **d** iron ball in form of a shot used as a trial of skill and strength, held in the hand, and propelled by extending the arm from the shoulder: *to put the shot.* **2.** Act of firing a fire-arm; the discharge of a fire-arm; sound of this: *was that a shot I heard?* Phrs. (*to do it*) *like a shot*, at once; willingly: *off like a shot*, instantly, at great speed. **3.** Range, distance, to which a shot will carry, or over which it is fired: *a long shot.* **4.** Aim, attempt, to hit with a shot from a fire-arm: *to take, have, a shot at*; *that was a good shot*; *a flying shot*, one at a moving object; *pot shot*, one at any easy mark which one can hardly miss. **5. a** A stroke, hit, throw &c., attempt to hit with any kind of missile: *a lucky shot off the red* (at billiards); *a neat shot through the slips* (at cricket); *a beautiful shot at goal* (at football &c.); *a random shot with a stone broke the window*; **b** (colloq.) attempt to do anything: *to have a shot for* (or *at*) *the prize*; *I'll have a shot for the train*, try to catch it; **c** a chancy, random guess: *as a shot, I should say she's about forty*; *don't make shots at the questions.* **6.** One who shoots, considered in relation to his proficiency: *a good shot with a sporting gun is often a poor one with a rifle*; *he is not much of a shot.* **7.** Specific uses: **a** cast of a net in sea-fishing; **b** (min. &c.) a charge of blasting explosive; discharge of this.

shot (IV.), n. Variant of **scot** (I.). Share, contribution, reckoning; chiefly in Phr. *to pay one's shot*, pay one's share of expenses &c.

shot-gun, n. A smooth-bore gun, often double-barrelled, used for killing birds and other small game, firing cartridges filled with varying sizes of small shot.

shotted, adj. [1. shóted; 2. ʃɔ́tid]. **shot** (III.) & **-ed**. Loaded, weighted, with shot.

shotten, adj. [1. shótn; 2. ʃɔ́tn]. O.E. *scoten*, P.P. of *scēotan.* See **shoot** (I.). (of fish) Having shot or ejected its spawn, and therefore of inferior food value: *a shotten herring.*

shot-tower, n. A lofty, cylindrical tower used for making shot by pouring molten lead from the top through a sieve, so that the streams of metal form round drops in the fall.

should, auxil. vb. [1. shood; 2. ʃud]; unstressed [ʃəd]. O.E. *sceolde*, Pret. of *sceal*, fr. base *scul-*, in gradational relation to *sceal*, see **shall**, & *-de*, suff. of Pret. **1.** (forming conditional mood) *I should be glad to play if I could.* **2.** (expressing future intention) *I said I should be at home next week.* **3.** (expressing obligation) *You are not behaving as you should*, as you ought to (behave); *children should be taught to speak the truth.* **4.** (expressing expectation or probability) *They should arrive by one o'clock, I think.*

shoulder (I.), n. [1. shṓlder; 2. ʃóuldə]. O.E. *sculdor*; O.H.G. *scultarra*; Swed. *skuldra*, Dan. *skulder*, ultimate orig. doubtful. **1. a** That part of the body of a man or lower animal where the arm or foreleg is attached to the trunk, articulating with the collar-bone and shoulder-blade; either one of the two projecting parts of the body below, and on either side of, the neck: *to put one's shoulder out*, to dislocate it; Phrs. *to give the cold shoulder to*, to give a cold reception to; to shun, avoid; to show distaste for the company of (possibly derived from a cold shoulder of mutton, as an unappetizing dish); *head and shoulders*, in comparison of height; (in physical or moral sense) *he stands head and shoulders above his colleagues*; *to put one's shoulder to the wheel*, to put all one's energies into a task &c.; to make a strenuous, earnest effort; *shoulder to shoulder*, (i.) close together, side by side; (ii.) (fig.) in close, united, co-operative effort; **b** the upper part of the foreleg of a slaughtered animal; as butcher's term: *a shoulder of lamb.* **2.** (pl.) *Shoulders*, the upper part of the back just below the neck: *a man with broad shoulders.* Phrs. *to shift the blame, responsibility, on to other shoulders*, to let others take the blame &c.; *his shoulders are broad enough to bear the responsibility, blame* &c., he is sufficiently strong, courageous &c. **3.** One of various things supposed to resemble a shoulder in shape: *the shoulder of a mountain*, detached part sloping into the plain; *shoulders of a bottle.*

shoulder (II.), vb. trans. & intrans., fr. prec. **1. a** To place (burden, bundle) upon the shoulder in order to carry; **b** (mil.) in Phr. *shoulder arms*, to hold rifle vertically in front of shoulder, the butt resting in palm of hand, the arm being fully extended downwards; **c** (fig.) *to shoulder a task, responsibilities* &c., to undertake, assume, deal with. **2. a** To push, thrust, aside: *to shoulder a person out of the way*; also **b** to make a path for oneself by pushing &c.: *to shoulder* (*one's way*) *through a crowd.*

shoulder-belt, n. A belt worn with military uniform, passing over one shoulder and under the other arm, to support weight of sword &c.

shoulder-blade, n. Either of the two broad flat bones of the upper part of the back; the scapula.

-shouldered, adj. [1. shṓlderd; 2. ʃóuldəd]. Having shoulders of specified shape &c.: *broad-shouldered* &c.

shoulder-knot, n. A knot of lace, ribbon &c., worn on the point of the shoulder by servants in livery.

shoulder-strap, n. A small, narrow strap worn extending from base of collar to point of shoulder in military uniforms, through which is passed the shoulder belt; it bears badge of rank in case of commissioned officers, in that of non-commissioned ranks a regimental mark &c.

shout (I.), vb. intrans. & trans. [1. shout; 2. ʃaut]. M.E. *shouten*; origin unknown. **A.** intrans. **1.** To utter a loud cry, call out; to bawl: *to shout with pain, laughter*; *to shout for, with, joy.* **2.** To call something out loudly, utter words with a shout: *to shout for the waiter, shout to a man to come* &c.; also *shout out.* **3.** To speak loudly, to raise the voice when speaking: *I'm not deaf, you needn't shout*; *please don't shout at me.* **B.** trans. **1.** To say, utter, with a shout, in a very loud voice: *to shout one's orders, an insult, a person's name* &c.; also *shout out.* **2.** *To shout (a person) down*, to speak so loudly as to drown what another says; to silence by loud speech.

shout (II.), n., fr. prec. A loud outcry, sudden call of a single person or a crowd; a loud, vehement expression of various emotions; a burst of vocal sound: *greeted with shouts of laughter, applause*; *to give a shout of warning.*

shouter, n. [1. shóuter; 2. ʃáutə]. **shout** (I.) & **-er.** One who shouts; a loud, noisy speaker.

shouting, n. [1. shóuting; 2. ʃáutiŋ]. **shout** (I.) & **-ing.** Act of calling out loudly; outcry, clamour, shouts: '*The tumult and the shouting dies*' (Kipling, 'Recessional'). Phr. *it's all over bar the shouting*, the race, contest, struggle &c. is concluded, and nothing is left to do but to cheer.

shove (I.), vb. trans. & intrans. [1. shuv; 2. ʃav]. O.E. *scūfan*, trans., 'to thrust', intrans., 'to fall', M.E. *shouven*; O.H.G. *sciupan*; O.N. *skūfa, skȳfa*, Goth. *skiuban*, 'to thrust'; cogn. w. Lith. *skùbti*, 'to hasten', *skubùs*, 'hasty, quick'. Cp. also **sheaf. A.** trans. Implies rough, hasty action. Not now, as in O.E., a dignified word; used in place of *push* and *put.* **1.** To push, thrust, roughly: *to shove a person off the pavement, over a cliff, into the water* &c.; *to shove a boat into the water*; *who are you shoving?* **2.** (colloq. and coarse) Instead of *to put*: *to shove one's clothes on, a plate on the table, a book back in the shelves*; *to shove something down on paper*, to write. **B.** intrans. **1.** To push, exert pressure against, person or thing; to thrust roughly: *don't shove, wait your turn*; *if you pull, I'll shove.* **2.** In various Phrs., followed by adverb or preposition: *shove along, up* (a bench), to move to a different place upon it; *shove off, out*, to leave the shore in a boat, by thrusting it out into the water; *shove past* (a person), pass by pushing roughly against or aside.

shove (II.), n., fr. prec. **1.** Act of shoving; a vigorous push, thrust.

shovel (I.), n. [1. shúvl; 2. ʃávl]. O.E. *scofl*, M.E. *schŏvel*, fr. **skuf-al*, in gradational relation to O.E. *scūfan*, see **shove** (I.), cp. P.P. *scofen* & **-el. a** A tool somewhat resembling a spade in general shape but not used for digging, having a broad, slightly hollowed blade with a blunt edge, used for shifting loose earth, gravel, small coal, grain &c.; also **b** one of several much smaller implements; a scoop, for sugar; a scoop for lifting coals from a scuttle.

shovel (II.), vb. trans., fr. prec. **a** To take up, collect, shift, with a shovel; also *shovel up*; **b** (colloq.) *to shovel up, down, food*, to put it into the mouth hastily and voraciously. Phr. *to shovel up, in, money*, make it rapidly and in large quantities.

shovelboard, n. [1. shúvlbòrd; 2. ʃávlbɔ̀d]. **1. a** A game played on a marked board with coins or disks, formerly called *shove halfpenny*; **b** board on which the game is played. **2.** Game played on the deck of a ship with wooden disks shoved by a sort of cue or mace into divisions marked by chalk &c.

shovelful, n. [1. shúvlfool; 2. ʃávlful]. **shovel** (I.) & **-ful.** Enough to fill a shovel; amount which a shovel will hold at one time.

shovel hat, n. A broad-brimmed hat looped up at the side, as worn by Church dignitaries.

shoveller, n. [1. shúvler; 2. ʃávlə]. **shovel** (II.) & **-er.** A bright-coloured, freshwater duck, with broad, flat bill; also called the *spoon-bill duck.*

shovel-nosed, adj. Having a broad, flat nose or bill: *shovel-nosed duck*, the shoveller; *shovel-nosed shark, sturgeon.*

show (I.), archaic spelling **shew**, vb. trans. & intrans. [1. shō; 2. ʃou]. O.E. *scēawian*, 'to look at, scrutinize; to watch, spy' (Mod. sense, 'to display', is first found in E.M.E.); O.S. *skauwōn*, O.H.G. *scouwōn*; all in sense of looking; cp. Goth. *us-skaus*, 'on the look-out, wary'; cogn. w. Lat. *cavēre*, 'to beware', see **cave** (III.) & cp. **caution**; Gk. *koéein*, 'to observe'; O. Slav. *čuti*, 'to feel, perceive'. **A.** trans. **1. a** To bring before, present to, the sight; to exhibit: *to show the contents of one's pockets*; *show your tongue to the doctor*; *to show one's passport at the frontier*; Phrs. *(not) to show one's face (head)*, (not) to appear or be seen; *to show one's teeth*, to give signs of anger, hostile intentions &c.; *to show one's hand*, to disclose one's plans and intentions; *to show fight*, exhibit hostile intentions or disposition; **b** to allow to be seen, permit a sight of: *a dress showing the petticoat below*; *to show oneself*, to appear; **c** to point out, indicate: *show me the best way to the village.* **2.** Specif., to display for inspection and examination at an exhibition: *to show dogs, fat cattle, roses.* **3.** To bring before, present to, the mind; **a** to evince, give proof of possessing: *to show a noble spirit*; **b** to prove, make manifest, by argument and logical proof: *Bopp was the first to show the existence of an Aryan family of languages.* **4. a** To guide, conduct, to: *to show a visitor into the drawing-room*; *to show a person to the door*, attend, accompany, him; Phr. *to show a person the door*, turn him out of the house; **b** to explain, make clear to the mind; to reveal, make known: *show me the best way to learn languages*; *show me the truth and I will follow it.* **5.** To bestow, confer: *to show kindness to the oppressed.* **B.** intrans. To be visible, noticeable, permit itself to be seen: *the scar on his cheek hardly shows now.* **C.** Followed by preposition or adverb. *Show off*, **1.** trans., to display, exhibit; **2.** intrans., to make a display of one's abilities, talents, attainments; to behave in a way that one hopes will excite admiration. *Show out*, trans., **a** to conduct (a person) to the door of room or house; **b** to accompany (person) to the door, and turn him out. *Show up*, **1.** trans., to expose, show true character of: *to show up a swindler, a fraud*; **2.** intrans., **a** to appear, be clearly seen, esp. by contrast: *the house shows up against the western sky*; **b** (colloq.) to come, be present at, some specific place &c.: *he never shows up at balls.*

show (II.), n., fr. prec. **1.** (rare) Act of showing; chiefly in Phr. *(to vote by) show of hands*, holding up of one's hand to signify the side on which one votes. **2. a** Something shown, exhibited, to be looked at, admired, as a spectacle &c.: *a picture, flower, cattle, dog, show*; *wild beast show, travelling show*, a menagerie; a pageant, procession &c.: *Lord Mayor's show*; **b** (slang) any institution, organized undertaking, concern, establishment, business &c.: *the present government is rather a poor show*; *the party was rather a dull show*; Phrs. *to give the (whole) show away*, reveal defects, weakness, shortcomings, of anything; (i.) to do this of deliberate intent; to betray; (ii.) to do it unconsciously and inadvertently; *a one-horse show*, a poor, inefficient concern; **c** a contemptible, pitiable, spectacle; person or thing whose appearance, behaviour, condition, evokes contempt and derision: '*And swift expires a driveller and a show*' (Johnson, 'Vanity of Human Wishes', 317). **3. a** Something which shows, which presents itself to view; a natural collocation of objects which arrest attention; a display: *a fine show of blossom on the trees this year*; *not much of a show of apples in this orchard*; **b** trace, vestige, indication, promise: *I don't see the slightest show of bud as yet*; *considerable show of new growth.* **4.** Vain pomp, hollow, gaudy, display; ostentation: *fond of show*; *all done for show.* **5. a** Appearance, semblance: *there is some show of justice in his claim, of sense in his remarks*; **b** pretence, fallacious appearance: *not even the show of affection between them.*

showbread, n. See **shewbread.**

show-card, n. A small placard or card for advertising goods in a shop &c.

show-case, n. A case with glass sides or top for exhibiting goods for sale in a shop or small objects in a museum &c.

shower (I.), n. [1. shour; 2. ʃáuə]. O.E. *scūr*, M.E. *schour, shour*; O.H.G. *scūr*, O.N. *skūr*; Goth. *skūra windis*, 'gale, storm of wind'; perh. related to Lat. *caurus*, 'north-west wind'; Lith. *sziaurỹs*, 'north wind', *sziaure*, 'north'. See further under **obscure** & **sky. 1. a** A brief fall, or storm, of rain, sleet, hail; **b** a single, light fall or scattering of water or moisture, coming otherwise than from the sky; a sprinkle: *a shower of spray*; *a shower of snow sliding off a roof.* **2.** A copious, uninterrupted discharge, flight, cloud, rain (of arrows, bullets, dust &c.). **3.** (fig.) An abundant, copious, rush of things arriving all at once, or in rapid succession: *a shower of presents, blessings*; *a shower of invitations.*

shower (II.), vb. trans. & intrans., fr. prec. **A.** trans. **1. a** To send down, discharge, let fall, pour, in a shower or in showers: *to shower rain upon the field*; *the wave showered spray over us*; *to shower stones* &c.; **b** to drench, wet, with or as with a shower: *to shower plants, the fields, with rain* &c. **2.** To bestow copiously, plenteously, give lavishly: *to shower gifts, benefits, kindness, affection, blessings &c. upon.* **B.** intrans. (of rain, sleet &c.) To fall in showers.

shower-bath, n. **a** A device whereby water falls in a shower from above upon the person, through a perforated plate; **b** (fig.) a thorough drenching.

showeriness, n. [1. shóuerines; 2. ʃáuərinis]. **showery** & **-ness.** Showery state of weather.

showery, adj. [1. shóueri; 2. ʃáuəri]. **shower** (I.) & **-y.** (of weather) Characterized by constant showers.

showily, adv. [1. shṓili; 2. ʃóuili]. **showy** & **-ly.** In a showy manner; in a manner to attract attention; ostentatiously; gaudily.

showman, n. [1. shṓman; 2. ʃóumən]. Owner, organizer, producer, of a travelling show, menagerie, circus; person who takes part in exhibiting attractions at a show.

shown, vb. [1. shōn; 2. ʃoun]. P.P. of **show** (I.); formerly always weak. The new strong P.P. is on the anal. of **blown** &c.

show-place, n. A large, famous or beautiful house, park &c. open to the public to view.

showroom, n. [1. shṓroom; 2. ʃóurum]. A room in a shop or warehouse where goods or samples are exhibited for sale.

show-window, n. Window in a shop &c. where goods are displayed.

showy, adj. [1. shṓi; 2. ʃóui]. **show** (II.) & **-y. a** Making a great show or display; noticeable and attractive; **b** possessing superficial qualities which attract attention; gaudy, ostentatious.

shrank, vb. [1. shrangk; 2. ʃræŋk]. O.E. *scranc*; M.E. *shrank*; Pret. of **shrink.**

shrapnel, n. [1. shrápnel; 2. ʃrǽpnəl], fr. General H. Shrapnel, 1761–1842, the inventor A shell which bursts in the air and scatters bullets or pieces of metal: *piece of shrapnel*, missile from such a shell.

shred (I.), n. [1. shred; 2. ʃrɛd]. O.E. *scrēad(e)*, 'shred, paring', M.E. *shrēde*; O.H.G. *scrōt*, 'piece cut off'; prob. cogn. w. O.E. *scrūd*, 'a cloth; a garment', see **shroud. 1.** A small piece torn, cut, or pared off; a strip, paring, tattered fragment, scrap: *a shred of cloth, of orange peel*; *in shreds and tatters*; *torn to shreds.* **2.** (fig.) A fragment, particle, iota: *left without a shred of reputation*; *not a shred of evidence for the charge.*

shred (II.), vb. trans. & intrans. O.E. *scrēadian*, 'to cut'; O.H.G. *scrōtan*. See prec. **a** trans. To pare, cut up, into shreds; **b** intrans., to peel, flake, off, into shreds or strips.

shrew, n. [1. shrōō; 2. ʃrū]. O.E. *scrēawa*, 'shrew-mouse'; M.E. *schrēwe*, 'a bad, malicious person, a scoundrel'; etymol. unknown. Cp. **beshrew**. **1.** A nagging, scolding woman; virago, termagant. **2.** (zool.) Also *shrew-mouse*, a small, mouse-like, insectivorous mammal, genus *Sorex*, with long pointed snout, shortish tail, and brownish silky fur; its bite was long supposed to be poisonous to animals.

shrewd, adj. [1. shrōōd; 2. ʃrūd]. M.E. *shrēwed*, P.P. of *shrēwen*, 'to curse', fr. *schrēwe*, 'malicious person', see prec. **1.** (archaic) **a** (of persons) Malicious, wicked, mischievous, shrewish: '*as curst and shrewd As Socrates' Xanthippe*' (Shakespeare, 'Taming of the Shrew'); **b** (of things) biting, keen, sharp, penetrating: *a shrewd wind, pain; a shrewd thrust*. **2.** Penetrating in mind; astute, sharp-witted, sagacious; having sound practical common sense.

shrewdly, adv. Prec. & **-ly**. **a** In a shrewd manner, sagaciously; **b** (archaic) bitingly, penetratingly: '*The air bites shrewdly*' (Shakespeare).

shrewdness, n. See prec. & **-ness**. Quality of being shrewd.

shrewish, adj. [1. shrōōish; 2. ʃrūiʃ]. **shrew & -ish**. Ill-tempered, malicious; given to biting, ill-natured speech.

shrewishly, adv. Prec. & **-ly**. In a shrewish manner.

shrewishness, n. See prec. & **-ness**. Condition, quality, of being shrewish.

shrew-mouse, n. See **shrew**.

shriek (I.), vb. intrans. & trans. [1. shrēk; 2. ʃrīk]. M.E. *schriken, shriken, scriken*, fr. O.N. *skrækja*, see **screech**. **A.** intrans. To utter a loud, piercing, shrill cry; to scream, screech: *to shriek with pain, terror*; *to shriek with laughter*, to laugh loudly, shrilly, or hysterically. **B.** trans. To utter with a shriek: *to shriek curses at one*.

shriek (II.), n., fr. prec. A loud, shrill, piercing cry; a scream, screech.

shrievalty, n. [1. shrēvalti; 2. ʃrīvəlti], fr. *shrieve*, obs. form of **sheriff**, & **-alty**. Office, rank, of a sheriff; tenure, period, of the same.

shrift, n. [1. shrift; 2. ʃrift]. O.E. *scrift*, 'legal penalty; penance', fr. *scrīfan*, see **shrive**. Confession and absolution; obs. except in Phr. *short shrift*, **a** (obs.) the very short time allowed to a condemned criminal to make his confession to a priest and be shrived before execution; **b** *to give, get, short shrift*, to treat, be treated, summarily; to make short work of, be soon disposed of.

shrike, n. [1. shrīk; 2. ʃraik], fr. O.N. *skrīkja*, 'shrieker, shrike'; cogn. w. O.E. *scrīc*, 'the missel thrush', & w. **shriek**. The general name given to the genus *Lanius* or butcher-birds, as the great grey shrike, *Lanius excubitor*, or the red-backed shrike, *L. collurio*.

shrill (I.), adj. [1. shril; 2. ʃril]. Not in O.E.; M.E. *s(c)hril(l)*, prob. fr. L.G. source; cogn. w. O.E. *scrallettan*, intrans., 'to sound loudly'; of imitative origin. **1.** (of sound, voice) High-pitched and thin, penetrating, piercing. **2.** (fig.) Petulant, plaintive, complaining; insistent.

shrill (II.), vb. intrans. & trans. M.E. *schrillen*. See prec. **a** intrans. To make a shrill noise; **b** trans., (rare) to utter on a shrill note, with a shrill voice.

shrilly, adv. [1. shrílli; 2. ʃrílli]. **shrill** (I.) & **-y**. On a shrill note; with a shrill voice.

shrimp (I.), n. [1. shrimp; 2. ʃrimp]. In M.E.; cogn. w. O.E. *scrimman*, 'to dry up, wither, to shrink', cp. M.H.G. *schrimpfen*, Germ. *schrumpfen*, 'to shrink'. See **scrimp & shrink**. **1.** A small, decapod, long-tailed crustacean belonging to the division *Macrura*, esp. one belonging to the edible genus *Crangon*, frequenting shallow, sandy shores; of pale greyish transparent colour, with brown spots, turning a pinkish brown when boiled. **2.** A small, poorly developed man; esp. one who appears to lack virility. **3.** A pale-pinkish colour, resembling that of a boiled shrimp.

shrimp (II.), vb. intrans., fr. prec. To fish for, to catch, shrimps.

shrimper, n. [1. shrímper; 2. ʃrímpə]. Prec. & **-er**. One who catches or fishes for shrimps.

shrimp net, n. Net used for catching shrimps.

shrine (I.), n. [1. shrīn; 2. ʃrain]. O.E. *scrīn*, used of the ark of the Covenant, fr. Lat. *scrīnium*, 'case, box for papers, books, letters' &c., see **scrinium**. **1. a** A casket or box, often richly ornamented and sometimes elaborated into a large architectural feature of a church &c., in which are kept the relics of a saint, a reliquary: *the shrine of St. Thomas at Canterbury*; **b** the sculptured tomb of a saint or hero. **2. a** An altar, chapel, church, temple, or other sacred holy place; **b** (fig.) a place made sacred by reason of the events or ideas associated with it; something held sacred in the memory: *the shrine of liberty, beauty, art* &c.

shrine (II.), vb. trans., fr. prec.; more usually **enshrine**. (poet.) To place in a shrine or sacred place; to enshrine.

shrink, vb. intrans. & trans. [1. shringk; 2. ʃriŋk]. O.E. *scrincan*, M.E. *s(c)hrinken*; similar words occur in Du. & Swed. Origin unknown. **A.** intrans. **1.** (of materials, fabric &c.) To contract, become smaller in superficial area by becoming denser and closer in texture: *unseasoned wood is apt to shrink; flannel shrinks in the wash*. **2.** To become less, diminish, in amount or extent: *the streams have shrunk from the drought; our resources are gradually shrinking; his property had shrunk almost to nothing through his extravagance*. **3.** *Shrink back, away, from*, **a** to recoil, start, suddenly back, or away, from: *to shrink back from the heat of the fire*; *to shrink away from* (a person), as though in fear or disgust; also *to shrink away* (from a crowd &c.), to retreat, retire, withdraw, seek solitude; **b** (in moral sense) to feel reluctant to encounter; to dread, flinch from, avoid: *to shrink from danger, responsibility, publicity*; *I rather shrink from meeting him*, feel unwilling to meet. **B.** trans. To cause to shrink, contract, diminish: *the washerwoman has kindly shrunk all my underclothes; summer has shrunk the streams*.

shrinkage, n. [1. shríngkij; 2. ʃríŋkidž]. **shrink & -age**. Process of shrinking; contraction in area; diminution, reduction, in bulk, quantity &c.: *there has been much shrinkage of clothes in the wash; the long drought has caused a shrinkage in the water supply; a shrinkage in values*.

shrinking, adj. [1. shríngking; 2. ʃríŋkiŋ], fr. Pres. Part. of **shrink**. (in moral sense) Reluctant, retiring; timid, sensitive.

shrinkingly, adv. Prec. & **-ly**. Timidly, diffidently.

shrive, vb. trans. [1. shrīv; 2. ʃraiv]. O.E. *scrīfan*, M.E. *s(c)hrīven*, 'to shrive, impose penance, to judge', loan-word fr. Lat. *scrībere*, 'to write', see **scribe**; cp. **shrift & Shrovetide**. (archaic) **1.** To receive the confession of a penitent, impose penance, and grant absolution to. **2.** (reflex., very rare) To obtain absolution by confession and penance.

shrivel, vb. intrans. & trans. [1. shrívl; 2. ʃrívl]. Not in O.E. or M.E.; etymol. uncertain; cp. Swed. *skryvla*, 'to wrinkle, shrivel up'. **1.** intrans. To curl, roll, up, become wrinkled, to shrink, by the action of heat, frost, dryness, decay &c.; of thin, flat objects and substances, such as leaves, the skin &c.; also *shrivel up*, to shrivel considerably. **2.** trans. To cause to shrivel.

shroff, n. [1. shrof; 2. ʃrɔf], fr. Arab. *çarrāf*. A money-changer in India and the Far East, esp. one who is expert in currency and the testing of good and bad coins.

shroud (I.), n. [1. shroud; 2. ʃraud]. O.E. *scrūd*, 'a dress, a garment', M.E. *s(c)hroud*; in gradational relation to O.E. *scrēad*, q.v. under **shred**; orig. meaning 'a piece, a fragment' (of cloth); etymol. doubtful; perh. the base ultimately means 'tear, cut', then it is used of 'torn, stripped-off skin'; cp. O.N. *skrydda*, 'shrivelled skin', & Lith. *scraudùs*, 'brittle'. **1.** Sheet or cloth in which dead bodies are wrapped for burial; a winding-sheet. **2. a** Something which enfolds, covers, conceals; a covering, cloak, veil, mask: *a shroud of snow, mist, darkness* &c.; also **b** something which conceals from the understanding: *a shroud of mystery*. **3.** (naut.) *Shrouds*, the set of ropes, usually in pairs, leading from the mast-heads of a vessel to the sides, acting as lateral supports (cp. O.N. *skrūð* in same sense; the word is applied in O.E. poetry to a ship's sails and rigging).

shroud (II.), vb. trans. A new formation fr. prec.; O.E. *scrȳdan*, fr. **scrūd-jan*, wd. give **shride* in Mod. Engl. **1.** To wrap (a dead body) in a shroud. **2.** To hide, cover, enwrap, enfold: **a** *mountains shrouded in mist*; **b** *a crime shrouded in mystery*.

shroudless, adj. [1. shróudles; 2. ʃráudlis]. **shroud** (I.) & **-less**. Without a shroud or winding-sheet.

shroud plate, n. **a** One of the chain plates at the side of a ship to which the shrouds are fastened; **b** one of the side plates of the buckets of a water-wheel.

Shrovetide, n. [1. shrṓvtīd; 2. ʃróuvtaid]. *Shrove*, representing an O.E. **scrāf*, is not used in this connexion, the gradational type occurs as the Pret. sing. of *scrīfan*, see **shrive**; see also **tide** (I.). The season for being shriven, extending from the Saturday to the Tuesday before Ash Wednesday, the commencement of Lent.

Shrove Tuesday, n. The Tuesday before Ash Wednesday.

shrub (I.), n. [1. shrub; 2. ʃrab]. O.E. *scrybb*, 'underwood, low-growing bushes', M.E. *sc(h)rub*; origin unknown; **scrub** (I.) is fr. the O.N. variant. Low-growing woody plant, smaller than what is specifically called a tree, having a number of separate stems growing from near the ground.

shrub (II.), n., fr. Arab. *sharab*, 'drink, beverage'. See **sherbet & syrup**. A drink made of the juice of lemons or other fruit, sugar, and spirit, usually rum.

shrubbery, n. [1. shrúberi; 2. ʃrábəri]. **shrub** (I.) & **-ery**. **a** Collection, mass, of shrubs; **b** a walk planted with shrubs on either side.

shrubbiness, n. [1. shrúbines; 2. ʃrábinis]. **shrubby & -ness**. Quality, habit, in plants, of growing thickly like a shrub.

shrubby, adj. [1. shrúbi; 2. ʃrábi]. **shrub** (I.) & **-y**. Having the habit of growth of a shrub; growing thickly, bushy.

shrug (I.), vb. trans. & intrans. [1. shrug; 2. ʃrag]. Cp. Dan. *skrugge*, 'to stoop, sit huddled up'; origin unknown. **1.** trans. To lift and draw (the shoulders) up, slightly, as sign of doubt, hesitation, disapprobation, nonchalance, helplessness &c.: *to shrug one's shoulders*. **2.** intrans. To shrug the shoulders.

shrug (II.), n., fr. prec. Act of, gesture made in, shrugging.

shrunk, vb. [1. shrungk; 2. ʃraŋk]. P.P. of **shrink**. O.E. *(ge)scruncen*; M.E. *shrunke(n)*.

shrunken, adj. [1. shrúngken; 2. ʃráŋkən], fr. old P.P. of **shrink**. See prec. Giving an impression of having grown smaller and thinner; shrivelled, withered, pinched: *shrunken limbs; a shrunken face*.

shuck, n. & vb. trans. [1. shuk; 2. ʃak]. Etymol. unknown. (rare or provinc.) **1.** n. Husk, pod, shell of maize, nuts, peas &c. **2.** vb. To remove the shucks of.

shudder (I.), vb. intrans. [1. shúder; 2. ʃádə]. M.E. *shoderen, s(c)huderen*; prob. fr. a L.G. source; cp. M. Du. *shudden*; fr. similar source, Mod. Germ. *schaudern*, 'to shudder'; cogn. w. O.S. *skuddian*, 'to shake, rattle'. **1.** To be powerfully agitated or shaken, as by a qualm involving the whole being; to quake violently, as with great horror or disgust. **2.** *Shudder at*, to feel violent aversion to, be filled with disgust at: *to shudder at the thought of*; *shudder to think of*.

shudder (II.), n., fr. prec. An agitation, shaking, of the body, resembling, but more powerful and deep-seated than, shivering or trembling, caused by strong feeling of horror or disgust.

shudderingly, adv. [1. shúderingli; 2. ʃádəriŋli], fr. Pres. Part. of **shudder** (I.) & **-ly**. With a shudder.

shuffle (I.), vb. trans. & intrans. [1. shúfl; 2. ʃáfl]. A variant of **scuffle**, & perh. formed fr. **shove**. Cp. **shovel**. **1.** trans. **a** To move rapidly and aimlessly backwards and forwards: *to shuffle one's feet*; specif. **b** *to shuffle cards*, mix them so that the order is changed, before dealing; **c** *shuffle off*, get rid of. **2.** intrans. **a** (also *shuffle along*) To drag the feet in walking, to walk with a stumbling gait, without lifting the feet properly; **b** to shuffle cards; **c** (fig.) to equivocate, prevaricate, answer in such a way as to mislead.

shuffle (II.), n., fr. prec. Act of shuffling; shuffling movement. **1. a** A sliding, scraping, dragging movement of the feet in walking; **b** a dancing step, usually *double shuffle*, consisting of a rapid backward and forward scrape, made twice, first with one foot and then with the other. **2.** Act of shuffling cards. **3.** An evasion, equivocation; trick, swindle.

shuffle-board, n. See **shovelboard**.

shuffler, n. [1. shúfler; 2. ʃáflə]. **shuffle** (I.) & **-er**. One who shuffles (in any sense).

shuffling, adj., fr. Pres. Part. of **shuffle** (I.). Shifty, evasive.

shun (I.), vb. trans. [1. shun; 2. ʃan]. O.E. *scunian*, 'to avoid, fear'; etymol. not clear. To avoid, keep clear of; to eschew: *to shun danger, evil company, vice, temptation*; *a person to be shunned*.

'shun, abbr. of **attention**, as drill word of command.

shunt (I.), vb. trans. & intrans. [1. shunt; 2. ʃant]. Suggested connexion w. O.E. *scyndan*, 'to hasten, cause to hasten, to urge, incite', seems improbable; cp. M.E. *shunten*, the origin of which is obscure. **A.** trans. **1.** To turn off, to shift to one side; specif. **a** to turn, switch a train, waggons &c. from one line on to another; **b** (elect.) to provide a current with an alternative circuit by means of a 'shunt'. **2.** (gen., colloq.) To put, push, on one side; to remove, get rid of, dismiss, to put off, to shelve. **B.** intrans. To be shunted.

shunt (II.), n., fr. prec. Act of shunting, process of being shunted (in various senses); specif. (elect.) alternative circuit for a current, a conductor, switch, or other contrivance for turning a current in to another circuit.

shunter, n. [1. shúnter; 2. ʃántə]. **shunt** (I.) & **-er**. One who shunts, specif., a railway employee who shunts trains.

shut, vb. trans. & intrans. [1. shut; 2. ʃat]. O.E. *scyttan*, 'to shoot the bolt of a door'; M.E. *schutten, shutten*, 'to shut'; cp. Du. *schutten*, 'to shut', M.H.G. *schützen*, 'to dam up (water); to protect, guard'; formed fr. **skutt-jan*, a gradational variant of the base of O.E. *scēotan*, q.v. under **shoot**. **A.** trans. **1.** To close; used of various physical actions and movements resulting in the closing, covering, of an opening, of an entrance or exit of any kind; in the exclusion of light, air, sound &c.; or in the fastening of a receptacle and the safe enclosure of something; **a** (of action exerted on external objects) *to shut a door, gate*, by pulling or pushing it to, so that the catch or lock falls into position; *shut a window*, pull to, as in a casement, slide up or down, as in a sash-window; *shut the lid of a box*, close it down, so that it covers the opening; *shut a drawer*, push it back into position; **b** (of action on bodily organs) *to shut one's eyes*, close, draw the lids; *shut one's mouth*, close the lips; **c** to prevent entrance to or exit from by closing door or window; to cover with lid &c.: *to shut (up) a house, stable, shop* &c.; *to shut a box*; specif., *the shops are shut*, no longer open to customers; Phrs. *to shut the door on, to (a person)*, to exclude, refuse him admission; also *to shut the door on proposals, measures* &c., refuse finally to consider, make it impossible to carry them out; *to shut one's eyes*, to be wilfully blind, to refuse to see what is plain and obvious; *to shut one's eyes to*, to be wilfully blind to, refuse to notice; *to shut one's mouth*, to hold one's tongue, be silent; to refuse to divulge a secret &c.; *shut your mouth, face*, rude way of saying, 'stop talking'; *to shut a person's mouth*, to persuade or compel him to be silent about something; *to shut one's ears to*, refuse to listen to or hear; **d** (in non-material sense) *to shut one's mind to*, refuse to admit or to try to understand (ideas &c.); *to shut one's heart to (pity &c.)*, refuse to be moved by. **2.** To fold, fasten, bring together, close what is open, expanded, or unfolded: *to shut a book, knife, fan, umbrella* &c. **B.** intrans. To be shut, close itself: *the door won't shut*; *shuts of itself* &c. **C.** Followed by preposition or adverb. *Shut down*, **a** trans., to pull, push down: *shut down a window, lid of a box*; to cease activity, stop work: *to shut down a business, factory*; **b** intrans., to cease working, come to a stop: *some mines will have to shut down*. *Shut in*, trans., to enclose, keep out view, light &c.; to prevent from access to &c.: *the house is much shut in by trees, hills* &c.; *a harbour shut in by sandbanks*. *Shut off*, to cut, turn off, to stop, check flow of: *to shut off water, gas, electricity, steam* &c. *Shut out*, to exclude by making access difficult: *to shut out a view, air, light* &c. *Shut to*, trans. & intrans., to close, fasten; to become fastened or shut: *shut the box to*; *the door shut to behind me*. *Shut up*, **1.** trans., **a** to close firmly or securely: *shut up the box, window* &c.: **b** to close the windows, doors of: *to shut up a room, house*, close it, and cease to use or live in it; Phr. *to shut up shop*, to close down a business, cease doing business; **c** to shut in, enclose: *to shut a person up in prison*; *shut up the silver in the safe*; **d** (colloq.) to make a person stop talking; to disconcert and reduce to silence, by ready retort, invective, or physical force &c.: *the interrupters were quickly shut up*; **2.** intrans., (colloq.) to cease, stop talking or doing anything: *I wish that old bore would shut up*; *oh! shut up! it is time to shut up*.

shutter (I.), n. [1. shúter; 2. ʃátə]. **shut** & **-er**. That which shuts; specif. **a** wooden or steel panel on a hinge, made to close over a window for the purpose of excluding light and heat, or to give greater security against burglars &c.; **b** small movable flap in a photographic camera for admitting and shutting off light to and from the sensitized plate or film; **c** device for regulating volume of sound in the swell-box of an organ.

shutter (II.), vb. trans., fr. prec. **1.** To fit, furnish (a window), with shutters. **2.** To close (a window) with a shutter.

shutterless, adj. [1. shúterles; 2. ʃátəlis]. Prec. & **-less**. Without shutters.

shuttle (I.), n. [1. shútl; 2. ʃátl]. O.E. *scytel(s)*, 'bolt, bar', as 'shot' into a lock &c.; M.E. *s(c)hutel* &c., 'bolt, weaver's shuttle'; formed fr. O.E. base *scut-*, gradational variant of *scēot-*, see **shoot**, & **-el**. **1.** The weft carrier in a loom, a boat- or cigar-shaped wooden implement, metal pointed and capped, with hollowed centre to hold the weft thread, formerly thrown or 'shot' from hand to hand by the weaver, now moving by mechanical power, backwards and forwards across and through the warp. **2.** The sliding plate carrying the under thread in a lock-stitch sewing machine.

shuttle (II.), vb. intrans., fr. prec. (rare) To move backwards and forwards like a weaver's shuttle.

shuttle-cock, n. O.E. *scytel*, 'a missile'. Formed as **shuttle** (I.) & **cock** (I.), as being fitted w. feathers & kept flying in the air. **1.** Object made from a piece of weighted cork, with feathers projecting in a ring from one side and struck backwards and forwards across a net, by a battledore in the old game of *battledore and shuttlecock*, and by a racket in *badminton*. **2.** (fig.) An object of controversy, bandied to and fro by contending parties; a person who wavers between different opinions, tossed about by conflicting interests and desires &c., a mere plaything or sport of circumstances or passion.

shuttle-train, n. A train which moves backwards and forwards on a set of rails.

shy (I.), adj. [1. shī; 2. ʃai]. O.E. *scēoh*, 'timid'; M.E. *schey, shȳ* &c., 'shy', of a horse; cp. O.H.G. *sciuhen*, 'to avoid, fight shy of'; O.H.G. adj. **scioh*, 'shy' &c., whence M.H.G. *schiech*, Germ. *scheu*, is not recorded. **1.** (of animals) Timid, easily scared; keeping away or at a distance; evading observation: *partridges are shy this year*; *the shy small beasts of the woodlands*. **2.** (of persons) **a** Bashful, retiring, diffident, farouche; extremely self-conscious, and uncomfortable in society; **b** (of manner, character &c.) expressing, animated by, shyness: *a shy glance, smile*; *of shy disposition*. **3.** *Shy of*, reluctant, hesitating, chary: *shy of committing oneself*. Phr. *to fight shy of*, to keep aloof from (a person); to avoid (doing something).

shy (II.), vb. intrans., fr. prec. **1.** (of a horse) To start and swerve aside nervously: *this horse has never been known to shy*; *some horses shy at running water*. **2.** (of human beings) Generally *shy at*, to recoil from as in alarm or disgust, to refuse to do, or to entertain; to have scruples about: *many who are not over nice will shy at sheer treachery*.

shy (III.), n., fr. prec. A sudden start or swerve aside of a horse.

shy (IV.), vb. trans. & intrans. Etymol. unknown. **A.** trans. (usually colloq.) To fling, throw: *to shy a stone, cricket ball* &c. **B.** intrans. To perform the act of shying: *he must learn to shy straight*.

shy (V.), n., fr. prec. **1. a** A throw, fling of a stone, ball &c.: *three shies a penny*; *a good, long shy*; **b** object thrown at; usually in combination, *cockshy*. **2.** (colloq.) Aim, chance, try, shot: *to have a shy at doing something*.

shyer (I.), more usual than **shier** [1. shīer; 2. ʃáiə]. Comparative of **shy** (I.)

shyer (II.), n. **shy** (II.) & **-er**. A horse addicted to shying.

Shylock, n. [1. shīlok; 2. ʃáilɔk], fr. character in 'Merchant of Venice'. A grasping, rapacious, merciless money-lender; one who drives the hardest possible bargain.

shyly, adv. [1. shīli; 2. ʃáili]. **shy** (I.) & **-ly**. In a shy, diffident manner.

shyness, n. [1. shīnes; 2. ʃáinis]. See prec. & **-ness**. Condition, quality, of being shy.

shyster, n. [1. shīster; 2. ʃáistə]. Etymol. unknown. (Am. slang) A disreputable, unscrupulous lawyer, one who undertakes business of doubtful honesty and respectability.

si, n. [1. sē; 2. si]. Prob. fr. the initials of *Sancte Ioannes*, in old verses for the **gamut**. (mus.) The seventh note of the diatonic scale in the sol-fa system.

siamang, n. [1. sīamàng; 2. sáiəmæ̀ŋ]. Malay. A large, long-armed black ape or gibbon, *Hylobates syndactyla*, of Sumatra and the Malay Archipelago.

Siamese, n. & adj. [1. sīaméz; 2. saiəmíz]. Siam & **-ese**. **1.** n. A native, the language, of Siam. **2.** adj. Belonging to, coming from, Siam.

Siamese cat, n. A distinct breed of domesticated cat, of a cream colour with chocolate or seal-brown head, tail, and feet, usually with a shortish, kinked tail.

Siamese twins, n. pl. Pair of human beings joined together from birth by a fleshy ligature; so called from a notorious pair born in Siam (1811–74).

sib, adj. [1. sib; 2. sib]. O.E. *sib, sibb*, 'relationship; friendliness; peace; happiness', also ġesibb, 'related'; O.S. *sibbia*; O.H.G. *sippa*; Goth. *sibja*, 'blood-relationship', cp. Mod. Germ. *sippe*, 'race, family, stem'; cogn. w. Scrt. *sabhā*, 'race; relationship'. Cp. second element of **gossip**, n. (archaic and rare) Related, of the same kin.

Siberian, n. & adj. [1. sībérian; 2. saibíəriən]. Siberia & **-an**. **1.** n. Inhabitant, native, of Siberia. **2.** adj. Belonging to, coming from, Siberia.

Siberian dog, n. A breed of dogs, resembling the Eskimo dog, used for drawing sledges &c.

Siberian sable, n. **a** The true Russian sable, as distinguished from the American marten; **b** the fur or skin of this.

sibilance, -cy, n. [1. síbilans(i); 2. síbiləns(i)]. **sibilant** & **-ce, -cy**. Quality, state, of being sibilant; sibilation.

sibilant, adj. & n. [1. síbilant; 2. síbilənt], fr. Lat. *sibilant-(em)*, Pres. Part. of *sībilāre*, 'to make a hissing sound, to hiss', fr. *sībilus*, 'hissing', imitative in origin. **1.** adj. Having, making, a hissing sound; sounding like, producing, a hiss (of the consonants [s, z, ʃ, ž]). **2.** n. (popular phon.) One of the above consonants.

sibilate, vb. trans. & intrans. [1. síbilāt; 2. síbileit], fr. Lat. *sībilāt-(um)*, P.P. type of *sībilāre*, 'to hiss'. See prec. & **-ate**. **a** trans. To utter with a hissing sound; **b** intrans., to hiss.

sibilation, n. [1. sìbiláshun; 2. sìbiléiʃən]. Prec. & **-ion**. Utterance with a hissing sound; sibilance; a hissing sound, a hiss.

sibyl, n. [1. síbil; 2. síbil], fr. Lat. *Sibylla*, Gk. *Sibulla*; etymol. uncertain; the class. explanation is that the word is fr. Dor. Gk. *Siobólla*, for Attic, *theoû boulḗ*, 'will of God'. **1.** (class. mythol.) One of several women of the ancient world, having the power of delivering prophecies or oracles under the inspiration of some god, established in various countries or places, from which they were named, as the *Babylonian, Egyptian, Delphian sibyls*; the most famous was the *Cumaean sibyl*, who kept the *Sibylline books*. **2. a** A wise woman, fortune-teller, soothsayer; **b** a witch, sorceress; an ugly old hag, a crone.

Sibylline, adj. [1. síbilin; 2. síbilain], fr. Lat. *Sibyllīnus*. Prec. & **-ine**. Pertaining to, uttered, written, by a sibyl or the sibyls; oracular: *Sibylline books*, collection of Greek oracles brought to Rome from Cumae, by the influence of which Roman religion was largely transformed.

sic, adv. [1. sik; 2. sik]. Lat. *sīc*, 'so, thus'; for *sī*, 'if', & *-ce*, 'there'; *sī* is fr. **sei*, orig. 'then', perh. ultimately identical w. demonst. pron.; for *-ce*, see under **he**. Thus; generally italicized and in brackets, used to call attention to a word, phrase, or expression, which looks wrong or doubtful but is quoted verbatim and literatim; also, loosely, to express a writer's surprise at some statement &c. which he is quoting.

siccative, adj. & n. [1. síkativ; 2. síkətiv], fr. Lat. *siccātīvus*, 'tending to dry, drying', fr. *siccāt-(um)*, P.P. type of *siccāre*, 'to dry', fr. *siccus*, 'dry', & **-ive**; the etymol. of *siccus* is disputed. The earlier proposal to derive it fr. **sitkʷos*, & connect it w. Lat. *sitis*, 'thirst', is now rather discredited, & Walde prefers to derive it, strange as this may seem, fr. a base meaning orig., 'wet, fluid', the development of meaning being 'flowing, drained away, dried out'; cp. Lith. *sèkti*, 'to drip', *(nu)sèkti*, 'to flow away, to become dry'. **1.** adj. Having property of drying (things) up. **2.** n. A substance which promotes drying.

sice (I.), n., also **sise, size** [1. sīz; 2. saiz], fr. O. Fr. *sis*, **six**. The six on dice.

sice (II.), n., also **syce** [1. sīs; 2. sais], fr. Hind. & Arab. *sāyis*. Term for groom used esp. in Bengal.

Sicel, also **Sikel, Siculian**, n. & adj. [1. síkl, sikū́lian; 2. síkl, sikjū́liən], fr. Gk. *Sikeloi*, Lat. *Siculi*. **1.** n. One of an early immigrant race into Sicily, coming probably from Italy before Greek colonization began. **2.** adj. Of, pertaining to, the Sicels.

Siceliot, also **Sikeliot**, n. & adj. [1. sikéliot; 2. sikéliət], fr. Gk. *Sikeliṓtēs*, fr. *Sikelia*, 'Sicily.' **1.** n. One of the early Greek colonizers or settlers in ancient Sicily. **2.** adj. Of, pertaining to, the Siceliots.

Sicilian, n. & adj. [1. sisílian; 2. sisíliən], fr. Lat. *Sicilia*. Sicily & **-an**. **1.** n. A native of Sicily. **2.** adj. Of, pertaining to, Sicily or its inhabitants; *Sicilian Vespers*, the massacre, at vespers on Easter Monday, 1282, of the French by the Sicilians, leading to the expulsion of the Angevin kings and the beginning of Spanish rule.

sick, adj. [1. sik; 2. sik]. O.E. *sēoc*, 'sick, ill', M.E. *sēke, sik*, 'ill'; O.S. *siok*, O.H.G. *sioh*, Mod. Germ. *siech*; O.N. *sjūkr*; Goth. *siuks* 'ill', cp. *siukan*, 'to be ill'. **1. a** (pred.; archaic and Bib.) In sense ill, not well, suffering; only used in certain Biblical or archaic Phrs. *he is sick unto death*; *sick of a fever*; *sick at heart*, very sad, filled with misgiving; and in a few colloquial Phrs. *sick and sorry*; *to fall sick*, become ill; *go, report, sick*, (mil.) report oneself as unfit for duty. (*N.B.*, the word is superseded by *ill*, and the Phrs. *to be sick, feel sick, look sick* are hardly used now in England in sense of *unwell, ill*, though normal in America); **b** (attrib., in ordinary Engl. usage) *a sick man, dog, cow*, rather than *ill*; Phr. *the sick man of Europe*, of the now extinct Turkish Empire, also the Sultan; *on the sick-list*, ill, and unable to perform one's duties (from mil. usage); *the sick*, sick persons. **2.** (pred.) Vomiting, ready, inclined, to vomit, suffering from nausea: *I'm going to be sick*, am about to vomit; *to feel, turn, sick*, to feel that one is going to vomit; *to make (a person) sick*, cause him to vomit. **3.** Filled with longing (only pred., *sick for*): '*when sick for home, She stood in tears amid the alien corn*' (Keats, Nightingale). **4.** (pred.) *Sick of*, tired of, sated with: '*I am half sick of shadows, said The Lady of Shalott*' (Tennyson); *sick of doing nothing*. Phrs. *sick to death (of)*; *sick and tired (of)*. **5.** (colloq., chiefly pred.) Disgusted, annoyed, exasperated; disappointed, disconcerted: *it makes me sick to think of that fellow living in my old house*; *I was awfully sick at missing you*; *he was sick with me for being so late*; *he was rather sick at missing the train*. **6.** In various special senses: **a** (of wine) undergoing a chemical process while maturing which gives it an unpleasant taste; **b** (of cast iron or other wrought metal) in a peculiar physical condition which renders it brittle.

sick-bed, n. That upon which a sick person lies.

sicken, vb. intrans. & trans. [1. síken; 2. síkən]. **sick** & **-en**. **A.** intrans. **1. a** (i.) To become sick or ill: *he sickened and died*; (ii.) (of plants) to wither, fade, cease to flourish; **b** to begin to be ill; to show signs of an on-coming attack of illness: *he is sickening for mumps*. **2.** To be disgusted, feel sick, be nauseated by; to be filled with physical or moral loathing: *to sicken at the sight of blood*; *to sicken at the mere idea of cruelty*. **3.** To weary, grow tired of, become satiated by: *he soon sickened of his wife*; *he is amused with his new possessions for the moment, but he will soon sicken (of them)*. **B.** trans. **1.** To cause to feel sick or inclined to vomit; to make, turn, sick; to nauseate: *rich food sickens me*; *a sickening draught of medicine*. **2.** To cause to feel (physical or moral) disgust, abhorrence, loathing; to nauseate: *to be sickened by the sight of blood*; *a sickening sight*; *his cowardice and cruelty are enough to sicken decent people*.

sickener, n. [1. síkener; 2. síkənə]. Prec. & **-er**. **1.** (schoolboy slang) A sickening, annoying, disagreeable, person. **2.** (colloq.) Feeling of disgust; fact of being disgusted, wearied, bored: *six months of prison ought to have given him a sickener of the life*.

sickeningly, adv. [1. síkeningli; 2. síkəniŋli]. Pres. Part. of **sicken** & **-ly**. In a sickening manner, to a sickening extent.

sick-headache, n. Headache accompanied by nausea; migraine.

sickish, adj. [1. síkish; 2. síkiʃ]. **sick** & **-ish**. **1.** Somewhat sick or nauseated: *to feel sickish*. **2.** Somewhat sickening or nauseating: *a sickish smell, taste* &c.

sickle, n. [1. síkl; 2. síkl]. O.E. *sicol*, M.E. *sikil*, fr. Lat. *secula*, 'sickle', fr. *secāre*, 'to cut', see **secant** & **section**; native Engl. words fr. same Aryan root are **saw (I.)** & **scythe**; Gmc. words, as Du. *sikkel*, Germ. *sichel* &c., are also fr. Lat. Hook used for reaping corn by hand; reaping-hook.

sickle-bill, n. Popular name of various birds such as some humming-birds, birds of paradise, with bill shaped like a sickle.

sickle-feather, n. One of the long curved feathers in the tail of a cock.

sickle-wort, n. Popular name of a plant, *Prunella vulgaris*, also called *heal-all*.

sickliness, n. [1. síklines; 2. síklinis]. **sickly** & **-ness**. **1. a** Bad, feeble, health; **b** nausea. **2.** Washed-out appearance, lack of intensity, in a colour.

sickly, adj. [1. síkli; 2. síkli]. **sick** & **-ly**. **1. a** Inclined, disposed, to be sick or ill; chronically ailing; unhealthy, poorly, invalidish: *a sickly child, family*; **b** having the appearance of ill-health or sickness; pale, wan: *a sickly complexion*; hence **c** (of light and colour) lacking intensity, faint, pale, feeble, washy; also **d** *a sickly smile*. **2. a** Connected with sickness; unhealthy, marked by prevalence of sickness: *a sickly season*; **b** producing, tending to produce, sickness or disease: *a sickly climate, region* &c. **3. a** Causing, tending to produce, a feeling of nausea from faintness and insipidity; sickening: *a sickly taste, smell*; **b** (fig.) nauseating, mawkish: *sickly sentimentality*.

sickness, n. [1. síknes; 2. síknis]. **sick** & **-ness**. **1. a** State, quality, of being ill; ill-health, disease; **b** a specific disease: *sleeping sickness*. **2.** A sick feeling, inclination to vomit; vomiting itself.

sick-room, n. Room in which a sick person lies.

side (I.), n. [1. sīd; 2. said]. O.E. & M.E. *sīde*; O.H.G. *sīta*; O.N. *sīða*; connected w. O.E. *sīd*, 'spacious, broad'; relationships outside Gmc. unknown. **1. a** (i.) Any one of the external surfaces of anything: *a box has usually four sides*; *the north side of the house*; also (ii.) one of the corresponding internal surfaces (of a box &c.); **b** boundary line of a geometrical figure: *a triangle has three sides*. **2. a** One of the two halves or divisions of an object or portion of space, right and left of a central line: *on one side of the head, body* &c.; *the other side of the room, road, playground* &c.; **b** either of two opposite surfaces of a flat, thin object: *two sides of a coin, wall* &c.; *the right and wrong sides of a piece of cloth* &c.; Phr. *born on the wrong side of the blanket*, of illegitimate birth. **3.** Specif., that part of the body extending from immediately below the ribs to the hips, between the backbone and the abdomen: *a pain in the side*. Phrs. *to shake, split, one's sides with laughing*, to laugh very heartily; *to stand by a person's side*, (i.) not in front of or behind him; (ii.) (fig.) to support him morally; *side by side*, close together; also (fig.) in mutual agreement; *by the side of*, (i.) near; (ii.) compared with. **4. a** One of the two lateral boundaries of anything rectangular, specif. contrasted with top or bottom, front or back: *a drawer with oak sides, a deal bottom, and a mahogany front*; **b** the wall, the bounding, enclosing portion of a curved receptacle, in distinction to the bottom, the rim, or the mouth: *the sides of a flower-pot, cup, jug* &c. **5.** That part of a space, or object of definite shape and limit, which is near one of the bounding lines; edge, margin: *by the side of the road, pavement*; *the river side* &c.; distinguished from the middle or centre. Phr. *on all sides, from every side*, everywhere, from all directions; *to put a question on one side*, disregard it. **6.** Area situated on either extremity of something which divides one area from another: *on this side of the Channel*; *the house is on the* *other side of the river, street.* **7.** Slope, declivity, sloping shoulder of mountain or hill. **8.** Aspect, view, regarded as partial only, and as differing from, or contrasted with, another aspect: *to look at the bright, gloomy, side of life*; *to study a question from every side*; *a side of his character not generally known.* **9. a** One of two groups of persons holding respectively contrasting views, ideals, doctrines; one of two opposing or contending parties or groups of persons; a party, faction: *on the side of the moderates against the extremists*; '*Who is on my side? who?*' (2 Kings ix. 32); *neither side has strong leaders*; Phr. *to take sides* (in a dispute &c.), be, declare oneself, a supporter of one side or the other; **b** a team of players in a match. **10.** A line of descent traced through one or other parent: *on the father's, mother's, paternal, maternal, side.* **11.** (billiards) Tendency to spin or twist aside from the straight course on coming in contact with another ball, imparted to a ball by the manner of striking it with the cue. **12.** (colloq.) Pretentiousness, arrogance of manner; swagger: *much too much side about the man*; *to put on side,* to swagger; cp. use of *face, cheek,* in somewhat similar sense. **13.** (football) *On side, off side,* right or wrong position of player when receiving or playing the ball in reference to position of other players; *no side,* call of time at Rugby football.

side (II.), vb. intrans., fr. prec. **1.** *Side with,* to support, be on the side of (a person, party &c.). **2.** (colloq., slang, rare) To put on side, to swagger.

side-arms, n., pl. Such weapons, as bayonet or sword, as are worn at the (left) side by soldiers or sailors.

side-bar, n. A supporting bar or plate on the side of various objects; e.g. either of the two plates which join the pommel to the cantle of a saddle; a side piece of a waggon or cart &c.

sideboard, n. [1. sídbord; 2. sáidbōd]. Piece of furniture of various design, but essentially a long table, placed against a wall at one side of a dining-room; used for displaying plate &c., and also for holding glasses, dessert &c. required during the service of a meal.

side-bone, n. **1.** The hip-bone. **2.** One of the two small forked bones beneath the wing of a fowl. **3.** A bony cartilage, causing lameness, on the hinder side of a horse's hoof.

side-car, n. **1.** An Irish jaunting car. **2.** A small car for a passenger attached to the side of a motor-bicycle.

side-chain, n. (chem., bacter.) A chain of atoms branching off from the main or central chain of a molecule; *side-chain theory,* a theory of Ehrlich accounting for the immunity produced by anti-toxins.

-sided, adj. [1. síded; 2. sáidid]. **side (I.) & -ed.** Having specified number of sides: *a three-sided figure*; *one-sided argument*; *a many-sided character* &c.

side-dish, n. Extra dish or course at a dinner.

-sidedly, adv. [1. sídedli; 2. sáididli]. **-sided & -ly.** In *one-sidedly* &c.

-sidedness, n. [1. sídednes; 2. sáididnis]. **-sided & -ness.** *One-, many-sidedness.*

side-glance, n. A glance or look to or from one side; a sidelong glance.

side-issue, n. Result, point in question, which is to the side of or away from the main result or point.

sidelight, n. [1. sídlīt; 2. sáidlait]. **1.** A lamp, lantern &c. placed on or at the side, as on a ship, carriage, motor-car &c. **2. a** Light coming or shining from one side, as from windows other than the main window or a top or skylight; **b** something, apart from the main stream of fact or knowledge, which throws light on a subject incidentally.

side-line, n. **1.** A rope attached to the side of anything. **2.** Specif., a class or line of goods sold as subsidiary to the main line of goods stocked; any business, course of action &c., subsidiary to the main one.

sidelong, adv. & adj. [1. sídlong; 2. sáidlɔŋ]. **side (I.) & -long.** **1.** adv. Sideways, in the direction of, towards, on the side; obliquely, laterally: *to move, look, sidelong.* **2.** adj. Coming, directed, from or to the side; lateral, oblique: *a sidelong movement, glance.*

sideral, adj. [1. sídera1; 2. sáidərəl], fr. Lat. *sīderālis.* See **sidereal.** (rare and poet.) Pertaining to the stars, sidereal; (esp. astrol.) exerting a baleful influence, as do the stars.

sidereal, adj. [1. sīdḗreal; 2. saidíəriəl]. Variant of the earlier **sideral**; fr. Lat. *sīdereus,* 'of, belonging to, the stars, starry, heavenly', & **-al**; fr. *sīder-,* stem of *sīdus,* 'star, esp. group of stars, constellation'; prob. cogn. w. Lith. *svidùs,* 'shining'. **1.** Of, relating to, the constellations or the fixed stars; starry, astral: *sidereal light.* **2.** Measured by, measuring, the apparent motion of the fixed stars: *sidereal clock,* an astronomical clock, regulated by marking sidereal time; *sidereal day,* a day, less than the solar day of 24 hours, by about 4 minutes, measured by the interval between two transits of Aries across the meridian; *sidereal time,* time measured by the axial rotation of the earth in reference to a fixed star, as one in Aries; *sidereal year,* the time occupied by a complete revolution of the earth round the sun, and measured by the recurrence of a fixed star, 365 days, 6 hours, and about 9-10 minutes, 20 minutes more than the *tropical year.*

siderography, n. [1. sìderógrafi; 2. sàidərógrəfi], fr. Gk. *sídēros,* 'iron', the origin of which is unknown, & **-graphy.** A kind of engraving on steel.

siderolite, n. [1. síderolīt; 2. sáidərəlait], fr. Gk. *sídēros,* 'iron', see prec., & **-lite.** A meteorite, mainly composed of meteoric iron or siderite, but with some stony matter.

side-saddle, n. A saddle for women, so made that both legs of rider are on the same side of the horse.

side-show, n. **a** A small, subsidiary show at a larger exhibition carried on at the same time as the main show; **b** (fig.) a subsidiary event or activity, one of secondary importance to some more extensive form of action &c.

side-slip, n. & vb. intrans. **1.** n. A slip, skid, to one side; esp. of a motor-car or aeroplane. **2.** vb. To make such a slip.

sidesman, n. [1. sídzman; 2. sáidzmən]. Person whose business it is to look after, and find seats for, a certain section of a church congregation, usually that in a particular aisle.

side-step (I.), n. A step to one side, step taken sideways, so as to avoid a blow or get out of the way.

side-step (II.), vb. intrans. & trans. **1.** intrans. To take a side-step, to step to one side. **2.** trans. To avoid (blow &c.) by making a side-step.

side-stroke, n. The stroke made when swimming on the side; contrasted with *breast-stroke.*

side-table, n. A small table placed against the wall or at one side of a main or principal table; used for carving &c. during a meal.

side-track (I.), n. A railway siding.

side-track (II.), vb. trans. **1.** To shunt, turn into a siding or off the main line. **2.** (colloq.) **a** To divert (person) from his purpose, or from some important line of action, or from pursuing a career of importance; **b** to postpone, shelve (a proposal &c.).

side-view, n. View of anything taken from the side; profile.

side-walk, n. Path for foot passengers by the side of a street or road; pavement.

sideward(s), adv. & adj. [1. sídward(z); 2. sáidwəd(z)]. **side (I.) & -ward(s).** Sideways.

sideways, adv. & adj. [1. sídwāz; 2. sáidweiz]. **1.** adv. **a** Towards the side: *to look sideways*; from the side, obliquely: *to look sideways at*; **b** side first, edgewise: *to walk, move, come in, sideways.* **2.** adj. **a** From the side: *a sideways glance*; **b** edgewise: *a sideways walk.*

side-wind, n. **1.** A wind blowing from one side or obliquely. **2.** (fig.) An indirect influence, agency, or means: *I only learnt the news by a side-wind.*

siding, n. [1. síding; 2. sáidiŋ]. **side (I.) & -ing.** A set of rails, or short track, by the side of a main line, to which a train, goods-waggons &c. can be shunted by points in order to clear the main line for another train, or for purpose of unloading &c.

sidle, vb. intrans. [1. sídl; 2. sáidl]. Formed fr. obs. adv. *sidling,* 'sidelong'. **a** To move, walk, sideways or with one side forward; **b** to advance or retreat in a furtive, fawning, cringing, or apologetic, nervous manner: *to sidle up to a person*; *to sidle away.*

siècle, n. [1. siákl; 2. siékl]. Fr., fr. Lat. *saeculum,* 'age, century'. See **secular.** Century; age; in Phr. *fin de siècle,* q.v., end of the century.

siege (I.), n. [1. sēj; 2. sīdž]. M.E. *sēge,* 'seat; siege', fr. O. Fr. *sege, siege,* Mod. Fr. *siège,* cp. Ital. *seggio,* 'seat', fr. assumed Low Lat. **sedicum,* **sedicāre,* fr. *sēdes,* 'seat', *sedēre,* 'to sit', see **sedentary.** **1. a** (obs.) A seat, throne: '*from lofty siege*' (Spenser, 'F. Q.' II. ii. 39); *the siege perilous,* seat of danger at King Arthur's round table; (also fig.) rank, station: '*of royal siege*' (Shakespeare, 'Othello'); **b** (in techn. senses) a workman's bench; floor of a glass-blower's furnace. **2. a** The investment of a fortified place, town &c. by a military force for the purpose of taking it either by direct attack or compelling its surrender by cutting off supplies of ammunition, food &c.; **b** period of such investment; **c** act of besieging, state of being besieged. Phrs. *to lay siege to,* to besiege; (also fig.) *to lay siege to a lady's heart* &c., attempt to win by persistent attentions; *to press a siege,* to force it on more vigorously; *to raise a siege,* (of besieging army) to give up, abandon, the investment of a fortified place; (of relieving army) to force the investing army to abandon a siege; *to stand, undergo, a siege,* to be besieged.

siege (II.), vb. trans., fr. prec. (archaic) To besiege.

siege-artillery, n. Heavy artillery used in a siege of a fortified place.

siege-money, n. Money minted in a town undergoing a siege, usually of special shape and device to distinguish it from the current coinage not available.

siege-piece, n. A coin struck during a siege.

siege-train, n. Artillery &c. used by a besieging army.

siege-works, n., pl. Trenches, gun-emplacements &c. constructed for a siege.

Sienese, Siennese, n. & adj. [1. sēenḗz; 2. sienīz]. Sien(a), town in Italy, & **-ese.** **1.** n. An inhabitant, native, of Siena. **2.** adj. Pertaining to Siena; *Sienese school,* of painting, 13th-16th cents.

sienna, n. [1. siéna; 2. siénə], fr. Ital. *terra di Siena,* 'earth of Siena'. An earthy ochreous pigment, containing oxides of iron and manganese, yellowish-brown, *raw sienna*; reddish-brown, *burnt sienna.*

sierra, n. [1. siéra; 2. siérə]. Span., fr. Lat. *serra,* 'saw'. See under **serrate.** A range of hills, mountain chain, with saw-like or jagged ridges.

siesta, n. [1. siésta; 2. siéstə]. Span., fr. Lat. *sixta (hora),* 'sixth hour, noon'. See **sext.** A short nap, esp. one taken at mid-day or after the mid-day meal in hot countries.

sieve (I.), n. [1. siv; 2. siv]. O.E. *sife,* M.E. *sive,* cogn. w. Du. *zeef,* O.H.G. *sib,* Mod. Germ. *sieb*; prob. connected w. O.E. *sēon,* fr. **sihan,* 'to strain, filter', & *sīgan,* 'to fall', though the final consonants present difficulties. **1.** Utensil consisting of a framework across which is stretched a fine network of wire, or horsehair, or a thin perforated sheet of metal; used for separating the finer from the coarser particles of a granulated substance, the former passing through, the latter remaining behind, when the sieve is shaken. Phr. *like putting water into a sieve,* said of a fruitless, unprofitable task; *a head, memory, like a sieve*, incapable of retaining anything. **2.** A coarse basket containing about a bushel, used as a measure. **3.** (fig.) A person who cannot keep information to himself, and who lets out a secret.

sieve (II.), vb. trans., fr. prec. To pass through a sieve; to sift.

sift, vb. trans. & intrans. [1. sift; 2. sift]. O.E. *siftan*, fr. *sife*. See **sieve**. **A.** trans. **1. a** To pass through a sieve or riddle: *to sift cinders*; **b** *sift out*, to separate, eliminate, by sifting: *to sift out gravel from gold dust.* **2.** To sprinkle (sugar, pepper &c.) through a sifter. **3.** To examine carefully and critically so as to separate the true from the false, the useful from the worthless &c.: *to sift evidence*; *to sift a question to the bottom.* **B.** intrans. (of dust, sand, snow &c.) To pass, filter, percolate, through or as through a sieve: *sand sifts through one's clothes, into one's shoes*; *snow sifts through a chink in the windows.*

sifter, n. [1. sífter; 2. síftə]. Prec. & **-er.** (often preceded by defining word) Object used for sifting or sprinkling: *a sugar-sifter* &c.

sigh (I.), vb. intrans. & trans. [1. sī; 2. sai]. O.E. *sīcan*; M.E. *siken, sīghen*, 'to sigh', the latter a new formation in infin. & pres., fr. Pret. type *sīhte*; prob. imitative; cp. **sough. A.** intrans. **1. a** To draw into the lungs, and expel slowly and audibly, a deep, long breath; often thus expressing weariness, sadness, or of relief after an effort &c.: *to sigh with fatigue, for grief, with satisfaction, relief, repletion* &c.; **b** to make a sound resembling sighing: *the wind sighs through the trees.* **2.** *Sigh for*, **a** to pine after, long for: *it is no good sighing for the unattainable*; *to sigh for the country amid the heat and noise of London*; **b** to lament, grieve for: *to sigh for a misspent youth.* **B.** trans. (rare) To utter with a sigh; also *sigh out.*

sigh (II.), n., fr. prec. **a** Act of sighing; **b** sound made in sighing: *sighs and sobs*; *a sigh of satisfaction*; *to heave a sigh of relief.*

sighing, n. [1. síing; 2. sái-iŋ]. **sigh** (I.) & **-ing. 1.** Sighs; act, sound, of sighs, of human beings, or of the wind &c. **2.** (fig.) Grief: '*sorrow and sighing shall flee away*' (Isa. xxxv. 10).

sighingly, adv., fr. Pres. Part. of **sigh** (I.) & **-ly.** With sighs.

sight (I.), n. [1. sīt; 2. sait]. O.E. (*ġe-*)*sihþ, -siht*, 'power of seeing; act of seeing; what is seen, a vision, apparition', fr. W. Gmc. **siχ-iþu*, formed fr. base **seχ-*, 'to see', see **see**, & abstract suff., q.v. under **-th**; M.E. *siht, sight*; O.H.G. *gisiht* in sense of O.E. *ġesiht*, Mod. Germ. *gesicht*, 'countenance'. **1. a** Faculty of seeing, vision, ability to see; *long sight*, ability to see clearly at a distance; *near, short, sight*, inability to see things clearly except when close to the eyes. Phr. *to know (a person) by sight*, to be familiar with the appearance of, although not having his personal acquaintance. **2. a** Act of seeing, perception by the eye of physical objects: *the sight of a total eclipse of the sun is one which one will always remember*; Phrs. *to have, catch, gain, get, sight of*, to manage, begin, to see; *to have sight of*, to see; *to lose sight of*, (i.) cease to see; (also fig.) (ii.) to omit to see or take heed or regard of; forget: *such points must not be lost sight of*; (iii.) lose track of, allow to pass out of one's ken, cease to meet or hear from: *I've lost sight of him for several years*; *at, on, sight*, when or as soon as seen, inspected, or examined: *a draft payable on sight*; (also attrib.) *sight draft*, one payable on presentation; *to shoot a person at sight*, directly he is seen; *to read (a passage in a foreign language) at sight*, without previous preparation; *to play, read, music at sight*, to play without previous practice; *at first sight*, on first seeing a thing, without further examination, *prima facie*; **b** (of mental vision) point of view, judgement, estimation: *in the sight of God all men are equal*; *to gain, lose, favour in a person's sight*; *to do what is right in one's own sight.* **3.** Range of vision, visibility; space, region, distance over or to which the vision reaches, or penetrates: *in, within, sight*, visible, able to be seen, or to see: *the land came in sight*; *to come in sight of land*; (also fig.) *within sight of victory*, victory is near at hand; *peace is now in sight*, approaching; *out of sight*, invisible, not to be seen, out of range; *get out of my sight!*, begone!; *to put* (something) *out of sight*, to hide it. Phr. *out of sight, out of mind*, forgotten when absent. **4. a** That which is seen or visible; a spectacle, a view: *a pleasant, beautiful, memorable, horrid, awful, sight*; Phrs. *quite a sight*, something worth looking at; *a sight for sore eyes*, something that is pleasant to see, that one is glad to see; *the sights*, noteworthy, interesting, curious, objects, esp. such as are to be seen in a particular place: *the sights of London* &c.; **b** (colloq.) something conspicuous, odd or which attracts attention and (usually unfavourable) notice: *these clothes make you look a perfect sight.* **5.** (colloq. and illit.) A multitude, large number, quantity; a great deal: *it must have cost a sight of money*; *not by a long sight*, not nearly. **6.** Any of various devices for helping the vision; **a** a small piece of metal placed on the central line at one or both ends of the barrel of a rifle to assist the eye in taking aim at an object: *a fore-, back-sight*; **b** optical apparatus attached to artillery for the same purpose: *a gun sight*; **c** an aperture attached to an optical instrument, as a prismatic compass, through which the object observed can be aligned to a bearing.

sight (II.), vb. trans. & intrans., fr. prec. **A.** trans. **1.** To get sight of; to come in sight of; to see by approaching near to: *to sight land, a fox breaking covert*; *to sight a town from the air.* **2.** To look at, observe through an optical sight: *to sight a star*; *to sight an objective point, landmark* &c., so as to get a bearing upon it. **3. a** To aim at over or through the sights of a rifle: *to sight a target, objective*; **b** to adjust the sights of, so as to get the right elevation and aim: *to sight a rifle*; **c** to equip, furnish, with sights. **B.** intrans. To take aim by a sight: *a sighting shot*, one taken with a rifle to get the range and elevation &c.

sighted, adj. [1. sīted; 2. sáitid]. **sight** (II.) & **-ed.** (of rifles or guns) **a** Having sights fitted to it; **b** aligned on a mark, by adjustment of sights.

-sighted, adj. **sight** (I.) & **-ed.** Having sight of a specified kind: *short-, keen-, quick-sighted.*

sightless, adj. [1. sítles; 2. sáitlis]. **sight** (I.) & **-less. 1.** Lacking sight, blind. **2.** (rare or poet.) Not appearing to sight, invisible.

sightlessly, adv. Prec. & **-ly.** In a sightless manner; blindly.

sightlessness, n. See prec. & **-ness.** State of being sightless; blindness.

sightliness, n. [1. sítlines; 2. sáitlinis]. **sightly** & **-ness.** Quality of being sightly; comeliness.

sightly, adj. [1. sítli; 2. sáitli]. **sight** (I.) & **-ly.** Pleasing to the eye, comely, of pleasing appearance.

sight-reader, n. One who reads and plays or sings music at sight.

sight-reading, n. The reading and playing or singing of music at sight.

sightseeing, n. [1. sítsēing; 2. sáitsīiŋ]. Act of going to see places or objects of special interest, beauty, rarity &c.

sightseer, n. [1. sítsēr; 2. sáitsīə]. Person who visits places and objects of interest &c. as a spectator.

sightworthy, adj. [1. sítwẽrdhi; 2. sáitwə̄ði]. Worth seeing.

sigillate, adj. [1. síjilāt; 2. sídžileit], fr. Lat. *sigillāt-(um)*, P.P. type fr. *sigillāre*, 'to mark with a seal or sign', fr. *sigillum*, 'seal', earlier **signolom*, dimin. of *sīgnum*, 'a mark, token, sign'. See **sign** (I.). **1.** (bot.) Having marks resembling seals or stamps. **2.** (of pottery) Decorated with impressed marks.

sigma, n. [1. sígma; 2. sígmə]. Gk. The 18th letter of the Greek alphabet (Σ, earlier C, σ or ς), expressing the sound [s].

sigmate, adj. & vb. trans. [1. sígmāt; 2. sígmeit]. Prec. & **-ate. 1.** adj. Shaped like a Greek sigma or *s*. **2.** vb. To add sigma or *s* to.

sigmatic, adj. [1. sigmátik; 2. sigmǽtik], fr. stem of **sigma** & **-ic.** (of tenses, esp. aorist) Formed by addition of a sigma.

sigmoid, adj. & n. [1. sígmoid; 2. sígmɔid]. **sigma** & **-oid. 1.** adj. Shaped like the letter S, with two reversed curves; specif. (anat.) *sigmoid flexure*, of the intestine between the colon and the rectum; *sigmoid cavity*, of the elbow &c. **2.** n. A double, reversed curve.

sigmoidal, adj. [1. sigmóidl; 2. sigmɔ́idl]. Prec. & **-al.** Sigmoid.

sign (I.), n. [1. sīn; 2. sain], fr. O. Fr. *signe*, fr. Lat. *signum*, 'mark, token, sign'; cp. **sigillate**; prob. fr. base of *secāre*, 'to cut'. See **secant, sect, & section. 1.** (in widest and most general senses) Anything whether a material, visible object, mark, occurrence, natural phenomenon, or an action, state, or condition &c. which conveys a meaning to the mind, by the sight or otherwise; indication, token, symbol, evidence, symptom: *a flag as the sign of one's nation*; *animals leave signs and traces behind them*; *there are signs of ill-health in his face*; *the weather shows signs of change*; *the gift was a sign of his forgiveness.* **2.** A visible mark, written or inscribed on anything, having some definite, accepted meaning, conveying a message, or expressing some idea, thought &c.: *pictorial signs representing things*; *conventional signs to represent sounds*; *bore the sign of his caste painted on his forehead*; *he could read the signs the tramp had marked on the wall*; *the broad arrow is the sign on government property*; specif., an arbitrary, conventional character or symbol; **a** (math.) one of the symbols representing a mathematical process: *the positive or plus sign*, + &c.; **b** (mus.) any of the characters indicating a sharp, flat, key &c. **3.** Any agreed word, gesture, object &c., understood only by certain people: *the freemason's sign*; *a sign and countersign*, pass-word. **4.** A bodily gesture, used to express an idea, conception, emotion, instead of words or writing: *to talk in signs*; *a sign of assent*; *he made a sign to me to leave the room.* Phr. *to make the sign of the cross*, to make gesture tracing the shape of a cross with the hand, either in the air, over an object, or by touching successively one's forehead, one's breast, one's left and right shoulders, in token of consecrating, blessing, or as an act of reverence, in memory of the Cross of Christ. **5.** Any device, such as a painted or lettered board, a carved or painted object &c., used to indicate that a particular trade or business is carried on, as an advertisement &c.: *an inn sign*; *a pawnbroker's sign*, three gold balls &c. **6.** (astron.) *Sign of the zodiac*, one of its twelve divisions, represented by a conventional symbol representing a constellation, which occupied it formerly but has changed its position owing to precession of the equinoxes. **7. a** Something done, act performed, something which occurs, of such a nature as to give evidence of the possession of supernatural power, or of supernatural forces at work; miracle, portent, omen: *they asked him for a sign*; *signs and wonders*; **b** (theol.) an external rite &c., having a spiritual force, or meaning: *a sacrament is an outward and visible sign of an inward and spiritual grace* (Church Catechism).

sign (II.), vb. trans. & intrans. Cp. Fr. *signer*, fr. Lat. *signāre*, 'to sign'. See prec. **A.** trans. **1.** To mark with a sign or symbol, esp. to mark with the sign of the cross in baptism: *we do sign (this child) with the sign of the cross in token* &c. (Baptismal Service). **2. a** To write (one's name) as signature: *to sign one's name to a cheque, petition* &c.; **b** to ratify, indicate one's consent to, acknowledge as one's own &c., by affixing one's name or signature to, or allowing such to be published: *to sign a cheque, receipt, letter*; *to sign a petition*; *a picture, article, signed by the artist, author* &c.; *the treaty was signed today*; **c** (fig.) to confirm, assure, fix: *by this act he has signed his doom.* **3.** To express, indicate, communicate, make known, by signs, as a gesture &c.; to signify: *to sign one's assent, dissent* &c. **4.** *Sign away*, to assign, convey, transfer, by affixing one's signature to document &c.: *to sign away one's property, interests, rights* &c.; *to sign away one's liberty, freedom* &c., (fig.) to act in such a way as to produce this effect. **5.** *Sign on*, to engage, hire, obtain, the service of, by securing the signature of to a contract of service: *to sign on a hundred more workmen, fresh crew* &c. **B.** intrans. **1.** To affix one's signature to a document: *to refuse to sign*; *all are requested to sign.* **2.** To signify, communicate, by signs or signals: *she signed to the other ladies to leave the room.* **3.** *Sign on*, to undertake, engage oneself for service by affixing one's signature to an agreement or contract: *to sign on for a new job*; *to sign on for a voyage.*

signable, adj. [1. sínabl; 2. sáinəbl]. **sign (II.)** & **-able.** Capable of being signed; ready for, requiring, signature: *a document signable by special persons.*

signal (I.), n. [1. sígnal; 2. sígnəl]. Fr., fr. L. Lat. *signāle*, 'a signal', neut. sing. of *signālis*, 'of, belonging to, of the nature of, a sign'. See **sign (I.)** & **-al. 1. a** Message conveyed to a distance by means of visible or audible signs such as waving of flags, flashing lights, or firing guns &c.: *a signal of distress*; **b** apparatus, object, whereby a signal is conveyed: *the signals are against our train*; *the signals are up, down* &c.; **c** specif., *Royal Corps of Signals*, the army organization in charge of all means of communication in time of war. **2.** Act, behaviour, occurrence, phenomenon, which is an indication, warning, premonition, of something else: *his rising was a signal that the meeting was over*; *fainting is a signal of ill-health.* **3.** Any action or event which serves to provoke, cause, or incite some other action: *a shot fired by an unknown hand was the signal for indiscriminate fighting.*

signal (II.), vb. trans. & intrans., fr. prec. **1.** trans. To send, notify, communicate, announce by means of signals: *to signal an order, a message*; *the ship signalled its distress, position.* **2.** intrans. To make a signal or signals: *to signal by means of rockets.*

signal (III.), adj. Fr., fr. Med. Lat., fr. **sign (I.)** & **-al.** Distinguished, marked out, standing out, from others; noticeable, conspicuous, remarkable: *a signal success, failure*; *a man of signal virtues*; *he must receive signal punishment*; *a signal instance of courage.*

signal-book, n. A book containing the code of signals used esp. in the army and navy.

signal-box, n. A building on a railway line containing the levers and other apparatus used in the control of the signals, points &c.

signal gun, n. **a** A gun carried on board a ship to be fired as a signal in case of distress &c.; **b** the report of such a gun.

signalize, vb. trans. [1. sígnalīz; 2. sígnəlaiz]. **signal (III.)** & **-ize.** To make signal, noteworthy, remarkable or conspicuous; to mark out as noteworthy; to give distinction to: *to signalize a victory by public rejoicing*; *signalized by great courage.*

signaller, n. [1. sígnaler; 2. sígnələ]. **signal (II.)** & **-er.** One who signals, esp. a soldier &c. of the corps of signals in an army.

signally, adv. [1. sígnali; 2. sígnəli]. **signal (III.)** & **-ly.** In a signal or noteworthy manner; conspicuously, remarkably: *to fail signally.*

signalman, n. [1. sígnalman; 2. sígnəlmən]. Railway official in charge of the signals and points.

signary, n. [1. sígnari; 2. sígnəri]. **sign (I.)** & **-ary.** (archaeol.) A systematic arrangement of signs, used in the writing of a language, as of ideographs, hieroglyphics &c.

signatary, n. Spelling variant of **signatory.**

signatory, adj. & n. [1. sígnaturi; 2. sígnət(ə)ri], fr. Lat. *signātōrius*, 'of, belonging to, seals or sealing', fr. *signāt-(um)*, P.P. type of *signāre*, 'to sign, seal'. See **sign (I.)** & **-ory. 1.** adj. **a** (rare) Pertaining to a seal or signature, used in sealing or signing; **b** signing or sealing, taking part in the signing or sealing of a document, esp. of a treaty or other interstate document: *the signatory powers to the Treaty of Versailles.* **2.** n. Person, representative of a party or state, who signs a document, agreement, treaty &c.

signature, n. [1. sígnachur; 2. sígnətʃə]. Fr., fr. L. Lat. *signātūra.* See prec. word & **-ure. 1.** Person's name written by himself; autograph. **2.** (archaic) Characteristic mark, feature, appearance; esp. in ancient medicine, some external feature of a disease found also in the herb &c. which was used in its treatment, e.g. yellow flowers of a herb supposed to cure jaundice; red colour of the bloodstone, which was supposed to stop bleeding. **3.** (mus.) The symbol or mark placed at the beginning of the stave to indicate the key, *key signature*, or rhythm, *time signature.* **4.** (print.) **a** The mark, letter, numeral, or both, placed by the printer at the foot of each sheet before folding as guide to the binder; **b** the folded sheet, thus marked.

signboard, n. [1. sínbord; 2. sáinbɔ̄d]. A board bearing a sign or notice; esp. a painted board bearing a device suggestive of the name of an inn.

signet, n. [1. sígnet; 2. sígnit]. Fr., dimin. of *signe*, 'seal, stamp'. See **sign (I.)** & **-et.** A private seal, used for sealing documents &c. with or without signature; *the privy signet*, the private seal of the sovereign, used by him for personal letters and documents, and for certain bills, writs &c. under the sign manual, esp. for the authentication of writs issued in Scotland, whence, *Writer to the Signet*, a Scottish law officer, equivalent to the English solicitor.

signet-ring, n. A finger-ring bearing crest, coat of arms &c., used as a seal.

significance, n. [1. signífikans; 2. signífikəns]. Next word & **-ce. 1.** Quality of being significant; expressiveness: *a look, voice, words, of great significance.* **2.** That which is signified; meaning, import: *the real significance of his words was not grasped at the time.* **3.** Importance, weight, consequence: *a person, matter, of little or no significance.*

significant, adj. [1. signífikant; 2. signífikənt], fr. Lat. *significant-(em)*, Pres. Part. of *significāre.* See **signify, -fic** & **-ant. 1.** Having a meaning or significance; expressing, conveying something: *the -t- in Fr. 'a-t-on' is not a significant element of speech.* **2. a** Conveying, suggesting, a covert meaning: *a significant glance*; **b** full of import, not negligible; momentous, likely to have an effect: *your success today may be significant for your whole future.*

significantly, adv. Prec. & **-ly.** In a significant manner (with various shades of meaning).

signification, n. [1. sìgnifikáshun; 2. sìgnifikéiʃən]. Fr., fr. Lat. *significātiōn-(em).* See **signify,** & **-fication. 1.** Act of signifying, indicating, making known. **2.** That which is signified; meaning, significance: *the signification of a word, sentence* &c.; *of an action, look.*

significative, adj. [1. signífikativ; 2. signífikətiv], fr. Fr. *significatif, (-ive)*, fr. Lat. *significātīvus*; fr. *significāt-(um)*, P.P. type of *significāre.* See **signify** & **-ive.** Significant; having significance or signification.

signify, vb. trans. & intrans. [1. sígnifī; 2. sígnifai], fr. Fr. *signifier*, fr. Lat. *significāre*, 'to show by signs, to notify, signify'. See **sign (I.)** & **-fy. A.** trans. **1.** To indicate, announce, make known: *to signify one's satisfaction, approval, one's intentions* &c. **2.** To be a sign or indication of; to imply, portend: *a red sunset signifies fine weather*; *few people realized what the event signified.* **3.** To have, express, as a meaning; to mean: *this notice signifies that we mustn't talk here*; *what does K.G. signify?* Phr. *what does it signify?*, what does it matter? **B.** intrans. To have significance or importance; to matter: *he doesn't signify*, is of no importance; *never mind, it doesn't signify.*

signior, n. [1. sínyōr; 2. sínjɔ̄]. Anglicized form of Ital. **signor** or Span. **señor.** (archaic) Sir, as form of address of Italian or Spanish gentlemen: *the Grand Signior*, the Grand Turk, archaic title of the Sultan of Turkey.

sign manual, n. A signature written by one's own hand, an autograph signature, esp. that of a sovereign or official head of a state, affixed, to give validity, to certain State documents before passing the Great or Privy Seal.

signor, n. [1. sényōr; 2. sínjɔ̄], when = Mr.; [1. sènyṓr; 2. sìnjɔ́] when = Sir. Ital. See **senior.** Title and form of address of an Italian gentleman, equivalent to *Sir* and *Mr.*

signora, n. [1. sēnyṓra; 2. sìnjɔ́ra]. Ital. Title &c. of an Italian married lady, equivalent to *Madam* and *Mrs.*

signorina, n. [1. sènyōrḗna; 2. sìnjɔ̄ríːna]. Title &c. of an Italian unmarried lady, equivalent to *Miss.*

sign-painter, n. One who paints inn-signs, signboards, inscriptions on shop fronts &c.

signpost, n. [1. sínpōst; 2. sáinpoust]. A post bearing a sign, esp. one placed at cross-roads, bearing the names and distances of towns &c. on arms pointing in their direction.

Sikh, n. [1. sēk; 2. sīk]. Hind., 'disciple'. Member of a religious community in the Punjab and N.-W. Provinces of India, founded in the 16th cent., rejecting the polytheism and caste system of Hinduism, with a sacred book, *the Granth*, and ruled by *gurus* or teachers; the Sikhs became a military power in the Punjab in the 17th cent.

Sikhism, n. [1. sḗkizm; 2. síkizəm]. Prec. & **-ism.** The religious and other tenets of the Sikhs.

silage, n. & vb. trans. [1. sílij; 2. sáilidž]. **silo** & **-age. 1.** n. Fodder packed green in a silo or pit, ensilage. **2.** vb. To pack fodder in a silo.

silence (I.), n. [1. sílens; 2. sáiləns]. Fr., fr. Lat. *silentium.* See **silent** & **-ce.** State of being or keeping silent: **1.** Forbearance from speaking or from making a sound or noise; absence of speech or sound; taciturnity: *silence is golden*; *they listened in dead silence.* **2.** Absence of sound or noise; stillness, quiet; **a** *the silence of the desert*; *in the silence of the night*; *not one moment of silence all day or night*; **b** (fig.) *the silence of death, of the grave.* **3. a** Failure to make known, mention, or communicate: *the silence of history as to Shakespeare's life*; *we cannot understand your long silence*; **b** secrecy, withholding of information: *to buy a person's silence*; **c** oblivion, absence of mention or knowledge: *the rest is silence.*

silence (II.), vb. trans., fr. prec. **1.** To cause to be silent, to reduce to silence; to cause (person) to cease speaking or making a noise; to put an end to (sounds or noise): *to silence a speaker, a crying child*; *to silence the roar of machinery*; Phr. *to silence the enemy's guns*, cause them to cease firing by putting out of action. **2.** (fig.) To put down, crush; put to shame: *to silence captious criticism, popular complaints, malicious traducers* &c.

silencer, n. [1. sílenser; 2. sáilənsə]. Prec. & **-er.** That which silences, specif., device for reducing or muffling noise of machinery or firearms.

silent, adj. [1. sílent; 2. sáilənt]. Lat. *silent-(em)*, Pres. Part. of *silēre*, 'to be still, to keep silence; not to speak of'; cogn. w. Goth. *(ana)-silan*, 'to be silent'; & w. the (rare) O.E. *sālnes*, 'silence'. Cp. w. different formative element, Lat. *sinere*, 'to leave, leave off', see **desinence. 1. a** Not actually speaking; preserving silence, holding one's tongue, mum: *children must be absolutely silent during the sermon*; *he was silent the whole* *evening*; **b** given habitually to speaking little; disinclined to speak; taciturn, uncommunicative: *a strong silent man*; **c** no longer vocal, having ceased to speak: '*The trumpet's silver sound is still, The warder silent on the hill*' (Scott, Introd. to Canto I. of 'Marmion'); *that eloquent voice is silent now*; Phr. *silent as the grave*, quite silent; *silent prayer*, not uttered aloud; *silent thought*, carried on in silence. **2.** *Silent about, concerning, respecting, on*: *he is silent about his past*, says nothing about, does not mention; *biographers are silent concerning the less creditable episodes in his career*; *on these things history is silent*. **3.** Quiet, still, not uttering sound, not making, causing, a noise; not heard; **a** (of living things) *the birds are silent on the trees*; **b** (of inanimate things) *the engine is very silent and runs quite smoothly*; **c** (popular phon.) not uttered: *final t is usually silent in French*. (An absurdity, because if a sound is not uttered it has no existence; if the reference is to the 'letter', it is more absurd, since 'letters' can have no sound.) **4.** Pervaded by silence: *the silent hills*; *the streets of cities are never silent*.

silently, adv. Prec. & **-ly**. In a silent manner; without speaking, noiselessly.

silent partner, n. A sleeping partner.

Silenus, n. [1. sīlḗnus; 2. sailínəs]. Lat., fr. Gk. *Seilēnós*, one of the companions of Dionysus (Bacchus), one of the older Satyrs, depicted as a drunken old man with goat's legs. A jovial, rather debauched old fellow, whose appearance suggests that he is fond of good living.

silesia, n. [1. sīlḗsha; 2. sailíʃə]. Name of Prussian province, where it was made. A thin, twilled cotton or linen cloth, used for linings &c.

silhouette (I.), n. [1. silooét; 2. siluét]. Fr., so named in mockery of E. de Silhouette, a Fr. 18th-cent. finance minister, notorious for his petty economies. **1.** A portrait in outline or profile, either cut out of black paper and mounted on white ground or drawn in outline and filled in with black paint &c. **2.** Profile or outline of a person or object, esp. as seen against a light or a light background; *in silhouette*, in outline, as portrait or figure.

silhouette (II.), vb. trans., fr. prec. **1.** To depict in silhouette. **2.** (usually in P.P.) To project, show up in outline against a background: *a figure silhouetted against the sky*.

silica, n. [1. sílika; 2. síləkə]. Neo-Lat., fr. Lat. *silic-(em), silex*, 'flint or other hard stone', perh. dissimilated fr. **gsilek-*, & cogn. w. O.H.G. *kisil, chisil*, Mod. Germ. *kiesel*, 'gravel'; O.E. *ċisil, ċeosol*, 'gravel', wh. survives in Place-Names, *Chislehurst, Chesil Beach* &c. Hard, white mineral, varieties of which are flint and quartz, forming principal constituent of sandstone, feldspar, and other rocks.

silicate, n. [1. sílikat; 2. sílikit]. Prec. & **-ate**. (chem.) A salt of silicic acid or compound of silica and a metallic base.

silicated, adj. [1. sílikàted; 2. sílikèitid]. Prec. & **-ed**. Impregnated, combined with silica.

siliceous, silicious, adj. [1. silíshus; 2. silíʃəs]. **silica** & **-ous**. (chem.) Of, pertaining to, containing, silica.

silicic, adj. [1. silísik; 2. silísik]. **silica** & **-ic**. Derived from, pertaining to, silica; esp. of compounds of silica or silicon: *silicic acid*.

siliciferous, adj. [1. silisíferus; 2. silisífərəs]. **silica** & **-ferous**. Containing, producing, combined with, silica.

silicify, vb. trans. & intrans. [1. silísifī; 2. silísifai]. **silica** & **-fy**. **1.** trans. To convert into, impregnate with, silica. **2.** intrans. To be converted into, impregnated with, silica; to become silicified.

silico-, pref., fr. **silica**, used to form compounds indicating the presence of silica or silicon.

silicon, n. [1. sílikon; 2. sílikən, -ən]. **silica** & **-on**. (chem.) A non-metallic element, symbol *Si*, not found in uncombined state, but in silica or various silicates, and forming one of the principal constituents of the earth's surface.

siliqua, n. [1. sílikwa; 2. sílikwə]. Lat., 'pod, husk of various leguminous plants'; for **skeliqua*, fr. base **skel-*, 'to split, cleave', whence also O. Slav. *skolĭka*, 'oyster'; see also **scale** (III.) & **shale**; more remotely connected is Lat. *calx*, 'small stone, limestone'. See **calcareous** &c. (bot.) The long, narrow seed pod of plants belonging to the mustard or cress family.

silique, n. [1. silḗk; 2. silík]. Fr. form of prec. Siliqua.

silk (I.), n. [1. silk; 2. silk]. O.E. *seolc*, for **siluc*, w. change fr. *r* to *l*, cp. also O.N. *silki*, fr. Lat. *sēricum*, 'silk', the fabric associated w. the *Sēres*, Gk. *Sêres*, 'the Chinese' see **sericate, serge**; prob. ultimately fr. a Chinese word, variously transliterated *se, sai, sze* &c., for the substance & fabric. **1. a** The fine, lustrous, strong filament produced, to form their cocoons, by the caterpillars or so-called 'silk-worms' of a moth, *Bombyx mori*, also by other caterpillars, and wound off and spun into fibrous threads; **b** similar filament produced by spiders for webs &c.; **c** similar lustrous filament or fibre obtained, by chemical processes, from cellulose, *artificial silk* or *rayon*. **2. a** Thread spun from natural or artificial silk; **b** lustrous fabric, cloth, woven from natural or artificial silk thread. **3.** A dress, robe, gown made of silk: *dressed in silks and satins*; specif. **a** the silk gown worn in Court by King's Counsel, K.C., to distinguish them from Junior Counsel. Phr. *to take silk*, to be called within the bar and become a K.C.; **b** a K.C.: *to sit among the silks*. **4.** A lustre resembling that of silk, seen in defective gem-stones, esp. in rubies and sapphires.

silk (II.), adj., fr. prec. Made of silk, silken: *silk cloth, dress, stockings* &c.

silken, adj. [1. sílken; 2. sílkən]. **silk** (I.) & **-en**. **1.** (archaic or poet.) Made of silk: *arrayed in silken robes*. **2.** Resembling silk; silky, soft, lustrous, gleaming: *her silken locks*. **3.** (by transf.) Soft, smooth, silky: *a silken voice, manner*.

silk gland, n. One of the two glands in a silkworm which secrete the viscous fluid that hardens in the air and becomes silk.

silk gown, n. Specif., the gown or robe of silk, worn by a King's Counsel, as contrasted with the stuff-gown of a junior barrister.

silk hat, n. A tall or top hat, with a covering of silk plush stretched over a stiff calico framework.

silkiness, n. [1. sílkines; 2. sílkinis]. **silky** & **-ness**. Quality, state, of being silky.

silkworm, n. [1. sílkwērm; 2. sílkwʌm]. The silk-producing larva or caterpillar of various Eastern moths, genus *Bombyx*, esp. of *Bombyx mori*. domesticated since ancient times in China and now in Europe and elsewhere; the caterpillar feeds on mulberry leaves.

silky, adj. [1. sílki; 2. sílki]. **silk** (I.) & **-y**. Like silk, resembling silk in texture and appearance; glossy, lustrous, fine, soft, smooth to the touch; **a** (of hair, fur &c.) *a horse's silky coat*; **b** (of taste) smooth, soft to the palate: *a silky wine*; **c** (of voice or manner) suave, smooth, and soft, caressing, (usually in depreciatory sense) oily.

sill, n. [1. sil; 2. sil]. O.E. *syll*, 'foundation beam or plank; base, support', fr. **sullj-*; M.E. *sille*, O.N. *syll, svill*; cp. Goth. *(ga)suljan*, 'to lay a foundation for'; cp. w. different grade O.H.G. *sūl*, Mod. Germ. *säule*, 'pillar, column'; cp. Goth. *sauls*, 'pillar'; perh. cogn. w. O.H.G. *swelli*, 'threshold', related to Lat. *solum*, 'ground, earth; base', for **svolom*, see **soil** (I.); further connected w. Gk. *xúlon*, 'piece of wood, timber', see **xyl(o)-**, & *hū́lē*, 'a wood', also 'piece of wood'. **1.** The horizontal block, shelf, or slab of stone or wood at the foot of a window or door. **2.** In various technical uses: **a** the floor of a seam of coal; **b** the timber across the bottom of the entrance to a lock on a canal or river against which the gates close; **c** a sheet of igneous rock intruded between the strata of older rocks.

sillabub, syllabub, n. [1. sílabùb; 2. síləbàb]. Etymol. doubtful; earlier form *sillibouk*, where second element is obs. or dial. *bouk*, O.E. *būc*, 'belly', cp. **bulk**; the first element being **silly**, in sense of 'happy, merry'; Skeat cites a Derbyshire variant *merribouk* for the dish. A mixture of cream, or of milk fresh from the cow, with wine and sugar.

siller, n. [1. síler; 2. sílə]. Scots variant of **silver**. Silver; money.

Sillery, n. [1. síleri; 2. síləri]. Name of village near Rheims, France. A sparkling or still brand of champagne.

sillily, adv. [1. síli li; 2. síli li]. **silly** & **-ly**. In a silly manner.

silliness, n. [1. sílines; 2. sílinis]. See next word & **-ness**. Quality of being silly; a silly act, word &c.

silly (I.), adj. [1. síli; 2. síli]. O.E. *sǣliġ*, 'fortunate, happy', M.E. *sēly*; fr. O.E. *sǣl*, 'time, occasion, good fortune, happiness'; O.S. *sālig*, 'happy, good, blessed'; O.H.G. *sālik*, Mod. Germ. *selig*, 'blessed'; O.N. *sǣll*; Goth. *sēls*, 'good, kind'; ultimate origin obscure. **1.** (archaic or obs. senses) Blessed, innocent, simple; weak. **2. a** Lacking wisdom and experience, foolish, frivolous, trivial, stupid: *a silly girl, child*; **b** arising from, expressing, folly and frivolity: *a silly book, joke*; *a silly laugh*. Phr. *silly season*, (obs.) holiday, summer, season, when newspapers are short of news and publish correspondence &c. on trivial matters. **3.** Imprudent, injudicious: *it was silly (a silly thing to do) to offend your best friend*; *you were very silly to trust him*. **4.** Weak-minded, imbecile, senile: *he is getting quite silly in his old age*. **5.** Specif. (cricket, of fieldsman) placed close to the wicket so as to entrap an unwary batsman: *silly point* &c.

silly (II.), n., fr. prec. (colloq.) A silly, foolish, credulous, imprudent person: *you are a silly*.

silo (I.), n. [1. sílō; 2. sáilou]. Span., fr. Lat. *sīrus*, fr. Gk. *sirós, seirós*, 'pit for storing grain'; etymol. unknown. A pit, trench, or building from which air is excluded, used for storing and preserving fodder in a green compressed state.

silo (II.), vb. trans., fr. prec. To store, preserve (fodder) in a silo.

silt (I.), n. [1. silt; 2. silt]. M.E. *silte*, etymol. doubtful; prob. of Scand. origin, cp. M. Swed. *sylta*, 'mud, marsh', Dan. *sylt*, 'salt marsh', Norw. *sylta*, 'coast-land washed by the sea', cogn. w. L.G. *sulte*, 'brine-pit', Germ. *sülze*, 'brine-pit, brine'; in this case the word is cogn. w. **salt**. On the other hand, an orig. connexion might be suggested between the Gmc. **sultja-* & Gk. *hū́lē*, 'mud, sediment'; cp. also Gk. *hūlízein*, 'to filter, clarify', & *hūlṓdēs*, 'muddy, full of sediment', fr. a base **sūl-*. Mud, fine earth or sand deposited as sediment by water, as at the mouth or in the bed of a river, at entrance to an estuary, harbour &c.

silt (II.), vb. trans. & intrans., fr. prec. **1.** trans. (usually *silt up*) To choke, fill up, block, with silt. **2.** intrans. **a** *Silt up*, to become choked or blocked with silt; **b** *silt through*, to percolate, ooze through.

Silurian, adj. [1. silū́rian; 2. sailjṓriən], fr. Lat. *Silures* & **-ian**. **1.** The name of an ancient British people or tribe living in Glamorgan, Monmouth, and Brecon. **2.** (geol.) A Palaeozoic rock series and geological period above or following the Ordovician, and below or preceding the Devonian.

silvan, sylvan, adj. [1. sílvan; 2. sílvən], fr. Lat. *silvānus*, fr. *silva*, less correctly *sylva*, 'wood, forest'; etymol. obscure. (poet.) Connected with, pertaining to, woods, forests; rural: *silvan glades, scenes* &c.

silver (I.), n. [1. sílver; 2. sílvə]. O.E. *seolfor*; O.S. *silubar*; O.H.G. *silabar, silbar*; O.N. *silfr*; Goth. *silubr*; cp. Russ. *serebro*; origin doubtful. **1.** An element and one of the precious metals, symbol Ag (fr. Lat. *argentum*), white and taking a high, lustrous polish, malleable and ductile, and giving a clear ringing sound when struck. **2.** Articles made of silver (or of plate), esp. those in domestic use, as spoons, forks, cups, dishes &c.: *to clean the silver*; *a sale of 17th-century silver.* **3.** Coins of silver; silver money: *change this note into silver.* Phr. *loose silver*, a number of silver coins. **4.** (chem.) Any salt, as the bromide, chloride, nitrate &c. of silver, esp. as used in photography for its sensitizing effect. **5.** The sheen, lustre, of or as of silver; the white or grey colour of silver: *the silver of the moon's reflection in water*; *the flashing silver of a salmon*; '*His golden locks time hath to silver turn'd*' (Peele, A Sonnet).

silver (II.), vb. trans. & intrans., fr. prec. **A.** trans. **1.** To cover, coat, with a plating of silver, as by electro-plating &c.: *to silver copper articles* &c. **2. a** To coat the back (of glass) with a metallic mixture, as of tin and mercury, in order to form a mirror; **b** (photog.) to coat and sensitize a plate or film with a salt of silver. **3. a** To give the appearance, brightness, or sheen of silver to: *the water of the lake silvered by the moonbeams*; **b** to cause (hair) to grow, turn, grey or white: *age has silvered his hair.* **B.** intrans. To become, turn, grey or white in colour: *her locks have silvered with age.*

silver (III.), adj. Attrib. use of n. **1. a** Made of silver: *silver plate*; *a silver cup*; *silver coins, currency* &c.; **b** (chem.) combining with silver to form a salt: *silver nitrate*, nitrate of silver &c. **2.** Resembling silver, silvery; **a** (in appearance) shining, lustrous, bright, gleaming: (also fig.) *the silver rays of the moon*; Phr. *every cloud has a silver lining*, there is a bright side to the darkest situation; **b** of the colour of silver, silvered, white, grey, as from old age: *silver hair*; **c** (of sound) ringing clear and soft, as silver when it is struck: '*The trumpet's silver sound is still*' (Scott, 'Marmion'); *the silver tone of a voice.* Phr. *a silver tongue*, power of speaking with a clear, well-modulated voice; eloquence. **3.** *Silver Age* (in art and liter.), as contrasted with *Golden Age*, following, subsequent to, inferior to this.

silver-bath, n. A shallow tray or bath containing salts of silver for sensitizing in photography; solution of salts of silver for such purpose.

silver birch, n. The common white birch, *Betula alba*, from colour of the bark.

silver fir, n. A tall, true fir, *Abies pectinata*, with silvery bark and white under-side to the leaves.

silver-fish, n. **1.** A white or silvery variety of the gold-fish. **2.** A small, flattish, wingless insect, *Lepisma*, with silvery scales, found in dark corners of houses &c.

silver-fox, n. A variety of N. American fox, with black fur tipped with silvery white.

silver-gilt, adj. Silver or silver plate washed over or coated with gold; gilded silver.

silver-grey, adj. & n. **a** adj. Having a grey colour with a silvery or lustrous sheen; **b** n., a silver-grey colour.

silver-haired, adj. Having silver or white or grey hair.

silveriness, n. [1. sílverines; 2. sílvərinis]. **silvery & -ness.** State, quality, of being silvery in colour, or sound.

silver-leaf (I.), n. & adj. **1.** n. Any of various plants having silvery leaves. **2.** adj. Silver-leaved: *silver-leaf maple* &c.

silver-leaf (II.), n. Disease in plum trees, characterized by a silvery sheen on the leaves.

silver-leaved, adj. Having silvery leaves: *silver-leaved poplar* &c.

silvern, adj. [1. sílvern; 2. sílvən]. O.E. *sielfren*, 'made of silver', M.E. *silfren*. **silver (I.) & -en.** (archaic or poet.) Made of silver; silvery in colour.

silver-paper, n. **a** A fine white tissue-paper; **b** tin-foil.

silver-plate, n. **a** Articles of domestic use made of silver; **b** articles coated with silver, electro-plate.

silver-point, n. **a** A stylus or pencil tipped with silver, used for drawing on specially prepared paper; **b** process of drawing with this; **c** drawing made by this process.

silver-print, n. A photographic print on paper sensitized by a salt of silver.

silver sand, n. A white, silvery, pure quartz sand, used in glass-making for polishing &c., also mixed with soil for assisting the growth of certain plants.

silver-side, n. The top side of a round of beef, used for salting; a salted round of beef.

silversmith, n. [1. sílversmith; 2. sílvəsmiþ]. A worker in silver; one who manufactures and sells articles of silver.

silver standard, n. Silver taken as the standard of monetary value.

silver-stick, n. Title of the field-officer-in-waiting of the Household Cavalry at Court ceremonies, who carries a silver-plated rod of office.

silver-tail, n. The insect known as the silver-fish.

silver thaw, n. Phenomenon occurring when a warm, damp wind comes very suddenly upon a prolonged hard frost and is succeeded by a light frost.

silver-tongued, adj. Eloquent, mellifluous.

silver-top, n. A disease, caused by various insects, affecting the tops and seed-cases of grasses.

silver-tree, n. A small, S. African tree with long, silvery, hairy leaves, used for making everlasting wreaths &c.

silver ware, n. Articles made of silver; silver-plate.

silver-weed, n. A common perennial weed or herb, genus *Potentilla*, with silvery leaves.

silvery, adj. [1. sílveri; 2. sílvəri]. **silver** (I.) **& -y.** **1.** Resembling, like, silver in colour and appearance: *silvery leaves*; *a silvery light*; *silvery hair.* **2.** (of sounds) Resembling the note given out by a thin piece of silver when struck; clear, ringing, sweet-toned, mellow: *a silvery tone, note, voice* &c.

silviculture, n. [1. sílvikùlchur; 2. sílvikàltʃə], fr. Lat. *silva*, 'wood, forest', see **silvan, & culture.** Forestry, arboriculture; study and cultivation of trees for timber.

simian, adj. & n. [1. símian; 2. símiən], fr. Lat. *sīmia*, 'ape', cogn. w. *sīmus*, fr. Gk. *sīmós*, 'flat-nosed, snub-nosed', wh. is said to be cogn. w. O.H.G. *sīman*, 'to tumble down, crumble, collapse', & **-an.** **1.** adj. **a** (zool.) Of, pertaining to, a family of anthropoid apes, including the chimpanzees, orang-utangs &c.: *our simian ancestors*; **b** resembling an ape in appearance, character &c.; ape-like: *a simian cast of countenance.* **2.** n. An anthropoid ape.

similar, adj. & n. [1. símilar; 2. símilə], fr. Fr. *similaire*, fr. Lat. *similis*, 'like', cogn. w. Lat. *simul*, 'together', see **simultaneous**; Gk. *homós*, 'the same', *hómoios*, 'like', see **homo-**, O.E. *same*, 'similarly', see further under **same, & -an.** **1.** adj. **a** Like, resembling; having certain qualities in common; nearly corresponding; somewhat the same as, of nearly the same kind as; **b** (geom.) having the same shape, but differing in size or position. **2.** n. **a** That which is similar to something else; something resembling another thing, in appearance, quality &c.; **b** (pl., *similars*) similar things.

similarity, n. [1. similáriti; 2. similǽriti]. Prec. & **-ity.** State, quality, of being similar; resemblance, likeness.

similarly, adv. [1. símilarli; 2. símiləli]. **similar & -ly.** In a similar manner; in the same way; likewise.

simile, n. [1. símili; 2. símili]. Lat., neut. sing. as n. of *similis*, 'like', see **similar.** Rhetorical figure and a poetic ornament whereby one thing is directly compared to another; an imaginative comparison; e.g. the likening by Heber (Palestine) of the building of the temple to the growth of a tree: '*Like some tall palm the noiseless fabric sprung*'; or Milton's comparison of the devils' palace in hell: '*Anon out of the earth a fabric huge Rose like an exhalation*' ('P. L.' i. 710-11). Contrasted with *metaphor.*

similitude, n. [1. simílitūd; 2. simílitjūd], fr. Lat. *similitūdō*, 'likeness, resemblance', fr. *similis*, 'like', see **similar, & -tude.** **1.** Quality, state, of being similar; likeness, similarity; similar appearance; resemblance: *I see no similitude between the portrait and the original.* **2.** (rare) Something which is like something else; a representation, a counterpart. **3.** (rare) A simile.

similize, vb. intrans. & trans. [1. símilīz; 2. símilaiz]. **simile & -ize.** (rare) **1.** intrans. To use similes. **2.** trans. To illustrate by similes.

simmer (I.), vb. intrans. & trans. [1. símer; 2. símə]. Of imitative origin. **A.** intrans. **1. a** To be on, or just below, the point of boiling; to boil gently with a bubbling, humming sound: *a kettle simmering on the hob*; **b** *simmer down*, to come off the boil, to cool down gradually. **2.** (fig., of feelings &c.) **a** To be on the point of bursting out or boiling over; in a condition of suppressed rage: *to simmer with anger*; *his indignation began to simmer over*; **b** *simmer down*, to cool down, to become moderated, to abate. **B.** trans. To boil gently, to keep (water, food &c.) gently boiling.

simmer (II.), n., fr. prec. State of simmering or gently boiling: *bring* (*water*) *to, keep at, a simmer.*

simnel, n. [1. símnel; 2. símnəl], fr. O. Fr. *simenel*, 'fine wheaten bread or cake', fr. L. Lat. *siminellus* for **similellus*, fr. Lat. *simila*, 'fine wheat flour', fr. Gk. *semidālis*; perh. fr. some foreign tongue; but if orig. Aryan, prob. related to O.H.G. *semōn*, 'to eat', also O.S. *sumbel*, O.E. *symbel*, 'feast'; the latter words are prob. fr. Aryan base **bhs-em*, fr. **bhsa-* &c., 'to grind, triturate'. see **sand,** & cp. Gk. *psōmós*, 'a morsel, scrap' (of meat or bread). Usually *simnel-cake*, a fine, rich plum cake, highly spiced, first boiled and then baked, and covered with almond paste; made esp. for Mid-Lent Sunday, Easter, or Christmas.

simoniac, n. [1. simóniak; 2. saimóuniæk], fr. O. Fr. *simoniaque.* See **simony & -ac.** Person guilty of simony.

simoniacal, adj. [1. simoníakl; 2. saimənáiəkl]. Prec. & **-al.** **a** Of the nature of simony; **b** guilty of simony.

simoniacally, adv. Prec. & **-ly.** In a simoniacal manner; with, by, simony.

Simon Pure, n. [1. símun pūr; 2. sáimən pjóə]. Name of character in Mrs. Centlivre's play, 'A Bold Stroke for a Wife' (1718). In Phr. *the real Simon Pure*, the genuine, real, authentic person or article.

simony, n. [1. símuni; 2. sáiməni], fr. Fr. *simonie*, fr. L., eccles., Lat. *simōnia*, fr. *Simon* (*Magus*), who offered Peter money for the gift of the Holy Spirit (Acts viii. 18-24). **a** Traffic in, making a profit out of, spiritual things; specif. **b** (law) the ecclesiastical offence of corruptly presenting any person to an ecclesiastical benefice for money, gift, or reward.

simoom, n. [1. simóōm; 2. saimúm], fr. Arab *samūm*, fr. *samma*, 'to poison'. A hot, dry suffocating desert wind, of Arabia, N. Africa &c., usually accompanied by clouds of dust and sand; a desert sand-storm.

simper (I.), vb. intrans. [1. símper; 2. símpə]. Perh. of Scand. origin; cp. Swed. & Norw. *semper*, 'fine, smart, affected, coy'. To smile affectedly or vacuously; to smile with an expression of coyness and demureness; to smirk.

simper (II.), n., fr. prec. An affected, coy, silly smile or smirk.

simperer, n. [1. símperer; 2. símpərə]. **simper** (I.) **& -er.** One who simpers.

simperingly, adv. [1. símperingli; 2. símpəriŋli], fr. Pres. Part. of **simper** (I.) **& -ly.** In a simpering manner; with a simper.

simple (I.), adj. [1. símpl; 2. símpl]. Fr., fr. Lat. *simplus*, 'simple', fr. *simplex*; cp. relation of Lat. *duplus* & *duplex*, 'double'; the first element of *simplex* is *sem-*, 'one', as in Lat. *semel*, 'once'; cp. Gk. *hén*, neut., 'one', for **sem*; Goth. *simlē*, 'once'; see also under **similar**; the second element is *plic-*, 'fold' &c., see **plicate & ply (I.)**. **1.** Not compounded, combined, or differentiated; consisting of a single substance, part, element; not complex. **2. a** Not intricate, complicated, or difficult to understand; clear, intelligible, easy to follow: *a simple statement, argument*; *a simple arrangement*; **b** easy to perform or to do: *a simple task*. **3.** Not elaborate, highly wrought, or ornamented; plain, unadorned; **a** (of material things) *simple mode of dress, of arranging the hair*; **b** (of liter. and artistic expression) not flowery, rhetorical, highly coloured, or bombastic; straightforward: *a simple style* (*of writing*). **4.** Not luxurious, expensive, rich, or lavish; plain, austere: *a simple mode of life*; *simple food*; *simple furniture*. **5.** (of character, disposition &c.) Sincere, natural, unaffected, artless, unsophisticated; undesigning, not artful, not given to duplicity; ingenuous: *an honest, simple soul, nature &c.*; *as simple as a child*. **6.** Foolish, credulous, easily deceived and imposed upon: *you must be very simple to be taken in by such a story*; *I'm not quite so simple as to believe that*. **7.** Of plebeian, humble, undistinguished birth; contrasted with *gentle* in special sense. **8.** Sheer, mere, nothing else than, neither more nor less than: *such an act is simple madness*. Phr. (*fraud, murder, ruin &c.*) *pure and simple*, out and out.

simple (II.), n., fr. prec. A simple, uncompounded medicine or remedy; specif., a medicinal herb; medicine made from such.

simple-hearted, adj. Having a simple heart; ingenuous, frank, open, natural, artless.

simple-minded, adj. Having a simple mind; **a** straightforward, free from duplicity, ingenuous; **b** easily taken in; unsophisticated, credulous.

simple-mindedness, n. Prec. & **-ness.** State, quality, of being simple-minded.

simpleness, n. [1. símplnes; 2. símplnis]. **simple (I.) & -ness.** (rare) Quality, condition, of being simple.

simpleton, n. [1. símpltun; 2. símpltən], fr. Fr. *simplet*, dimin. of *simple*, & *-on*. A simple, foolish, silly, weak-minded person; one who is credulous and easily gulled.

simpliciter, adv. [1. simplísiter; 2. simplísitə]. Lat., 'simply, plainly, directly; openly, honestly'; adv. formed fr. *simplic-*, stem of *simplex*, 'simple', see **simple (I.)**. Absolutely, wholly; not relatively.

simplicity, n. [1. simplísiti; 2. simplísiti], fr. Fr. *simplicité*, fr. Lat. *simplicitāt-(em)*, formed fr. *simplic-*, see **simple (I.), & -ity.** Quality, state, of being simple; **a** state of being uncompounded or not made up of different parts or elements: *theories based on the supposed simplicity of the atom*; **b** freedom from complexity or elaboration; easiness of working: *simplicity in a machine*; **c** (i.) freedom from difficulty in understanding; intelligibility, clearness: *the simplicity of a problem, argument*; (ii.) freedom from difficulty in performance: *simplicity of a task*; **d** freedom from ornament, unnecessary luxuries &c.; plainness: *simplicity in dress, style, way of living &c.*; **e** freedom from cunning or duplicity; naturalness, artlessness, innocence, ingenuousness: *the sweet simplicity of a child*.

simplification, n. [1. simplifikáshun; 2. simplifikéiʃən]. See **simplify & -fication.** Act, process, of simplifying; that which is simplified.

simplifier, n. [1. símplifier; 2. símplifaiə]. **simplify & -er.** One who, that which, simplifies.

simplify, vb. trans. [1. símplifi; 2. símplifai]. See **simple (I.) & -fy**; cp. Fr. *simplifier*. To make simple or simpler; to make less complicated; to make easier to understand, use, or to do.

simplism, n. [1. símplizm; 2. símplizəm]. **simple (I.) & -ism.** Effort after simplicity; sham simplicity.

simplistic, adj. [1. simplístik; 2. simplístik]. **simple (I.) & -ist & -ic.** Tending to an exaggerated simplification; tending to adopt a single and too simple an explanation for a complex problem.

simply, adv. [1. símpli; 2. símpli]. **simple (I.) & -y.** In a simple manner (in all senses); **a** without complexity: *a machine simply constructed*; **b** without difficulty, easily: *a question answered quite simply*; **c** without subtlety, plainly, clearly: *arguments very simply stated*; **d** without adornment; without expense, luxury &c., unostentatiously: *dressed simply*; *in spite of his wealth he lived quite simply*; **e** merely, just, so much and no more than: *all it amounts to is simply this*; **f** (as intens.) *the cold was simply awful*.

simulacrum, n. [1. simūlákrum; 2. simjuléikrəm]. Lat., 'likeness, image, representation, portrait; a phantom, an apparition; a shadow, semblance'; formed fr. *simulāre*, 'to make like' &c., see **simulate.** **1.** Image, likeness; something made in the form of another person or object. **2.** A deceptive, shadowy likeness; a sham, pretence.

simulant, adj. [1. símūlant; 2. símjulənt], fr. Lat. *simulant-(em)*, Pres. Part. of *simulāre*, see **simulate.** Simulating, imitating, like; having an appearance of something else (esp. in biol.): *colouration simulant of surroundings &c.*

simulate, vb. trans. [1. símūlāt; 2. símjuleit], fr. Lat. *simulāt-(um)*, P.P. of *simulāre*, 'to make like, to imitate; to pretend', fr. *simul*, 'at the same time, together'; cogn. w. *similis*, 'like', cp. **similar & same.** To imitate, assume appearance of without reality; to feign; **a** to pretend to be, to mimic: *to simulate a person or character on the stage*; *pride may simulate humility*; **b** to pretend to have or to feel: *to simulate affection, madness, illness &c.*

simulation, n. [1. simūláshun; 2. simjuléiʃən], fr. Lat. *simulātiōn-(em)*, 'false show, feigning, pretence'. **simulate & -ion.** Act of simulating; pretence, feigning.

simultaneity, n. [1. simultanḗiti; 2. siməlteinîiti]. See **simultaneous & -ity.** Quality of being simultaneous; simultaneousness.

simultaneous, adj. [1. simultáneus; 2. siməltéiniəs], fr. L. Lat. *simultāneus*, formed fr. L. Lat. *simultim*, 'at the same time', fr. Lat. *simul*, 'together, at the same time', see **simulate, & -aneous.** Occurring, done, at the same time: *simultaneous events, actions.*

simultaneously, adv. Prec. & **-ly.** In a simultaneous manner; at one and the same time.

simultaneousness, n. See prec. & **-ness.** Quality, fact, of being simultaneous.

simurg, n. [1. sémërg; 2. símə̄g], fr. Pers. *sīmurgh*. A gigantic bird of Oriental mythology, probably to be identified with the roc of the 'Arabian Nights'.

sin (I.), n. [1. sin; 2. sin]. O.E. *synn*, 'wrongdoing, injury; hostility', M.E. *sunne, sinne*; O.H.G. *suntea*, Mod. Germ. *sünde*; cogn. w. Lat. *sont-(em)*, stem of *sons*, 'guilty, criminal'; perh. also w. Gk. *átē* (if for **aswn̥tā*), 'folly, delusion; ruin, mischief'; the etymol. is much disputed. Many etymologists connect the word w. **sooth**, 'true', in wh. case it is ultimately derived fr. a participial form of the base **es-*, 'to be', see **esse**, & the orig. sense wd. be, according to Kluge, 'that which is really true, and which is revealed in confession'; fr. the point of view of semantics this seems rather far-fetched. **1. a** Transgression of the divine law, in thought, word, or deed; disobedience to God's will; spiritual wickedness, iniquity; transgression of a moral code, neglect of a moral duty; moral depravity: *the consciousness of sin*; *original sin*, that which man inherits from Adam through the Fall; inherited disposition to evil: *we are all born in sin*; **b** a specific example, instance, act, of such transgression: *to commit a sin*; *sins of omission and commission*; *the deadly, mortal, sins*, such as are deliberate and wilful, involving loss of salvation and death of the soul: *the sin against the Holy Ghost*, the unpardonable sin (see Matt. xii. 32); *besetting sin*, that by which one is most often tempted. Phr. *like sin*, (colloq.) vigorously, vehemently, in earnest: *to hate a person like sin*. **2. a** Any offence in general; a breach of good manners: *the social sins*; **a** *sin against good manners*; **b** something which is not sensible or reasonable: *it is a sin to be indoors on such a fine day.*

sin (II.), vb. intrans. & trans. O.E. *syngian*, M.E. *sinȝen, sinnen*, fr. prec. **1.** intrans. (often with *against*) To commit sin or a sin; to be sinful; to transgress the Divine law; to violate a moral code &c.: *man's nature is to sin*; '*I have sinned against heaven and before thee*' (Luke xv. 18); '*More sinned against than sinning*' (Shakespeare, 'King Lear'). **2.** trans. (rare) To commit as a sin: *repent of the sins ye have sinned.*

Sinaitic, adj. [1. sināítik; 2. sainei-ítik], fr. Mod. Lat. *Sinaiticus*. Of, pertaining to, Mount Sinai: *the Sinaitic peninsula.*

Sinanthropus, n. [1. sinanthrṓpus; 2. sinænþróupəs]. See **sinology & anthropo-.** Member of a hypothetical semi-human species, known from fossilized remains found near Pe-king, China.

sinapism, n. [1. sínapizm; 2. sínəpizəm]. Fr., fr. Lat. *sināpismus*, fr. Gk. *sināpismós*, fr. Lat. *sināpi*, 'mustard', borrowed fr. Gk.; there is a variant Gk. form *nâpu*, wh. is said to be an Egyptian loan-word. This word is found also in Lat. *nāpus*, 'turnip', wh. was borrowed by O.E. in form of *nǣp*; see *-nip*, in **parsnip & turnip.** A mustard plaster or poultice.

since, adv., prep., & conj. [1. sins; 2. sins]. Contracted form of M.E. *sithen(e)s*, w. adv. ending *-(e)s*, cp. *besides*; O.E. *siððan*, 'after that, since', is a compound word, in wh. the second element, *ðon*, is the instrumental case of the demonstr. pron. **that**; the first element, *sīð*, as adj. 'late', as adv. 'after', is cogn. w. O.S. *sīð*, O.H.G. *sīt*, Germ. *seit*, cp. *seitdem*, exactly parallel to O.E. *siððan*; Goth. *seiþus*, adj., 'late', *seiþu*, adv., 'since'; cp. W. *hīr*, 'long', Lat. *sēro*, 'late in the day, late', Scrt. *sāyam*, 'in the evening'; cp. **desinence.** **1.** adv. **a** After, subsequent to, at some time after a specified or implied date, time, or event, and before now or the present: *the building fell down in 1920 and has since been rebuilt*; *he disappeared last week and has not been seen since*; **b** from a specified time in the past until now; throughout a specified period up to the present: *he had a bad accident and has not been well since*; *the family settled in Norfolk in 1770 and has been there ever since*; **c** before the present time, before now, ago: *a word that has long since been out of use*; *he died many years since*. **2.** prep. After, subsequently to, during the time following, succeeding (a specified date): *since my last letter I have decided &c.*; *nothing like it has happened since the war*; *since my coming to London I have not been well*; *I have not seen him since last year*. **3.** conj. **a** From the time that, after the time when: *how long is it since I saw you last?*; **b** seeing that, because, inasmuch as: '*Since there's no help, come let us kiss and part*' (Drayton, Sonnet); *since force is no remedy, let us try conciliation*; also ellipt., as being: *a useless, since impossible, proposal.*

sincere, adj. [1. sinsḗr; 2. sinsíə]. O. Fr., fr. Lat. *sincērus*, 'clean, pure, uninjured, whole; genuine; sound, uncorrupted'; first element *sine*, 'without', see under **sine die**; the second is cogn. w. Lat. *cariēs*, 'rottenness, decay', see **caries**; thus the word orig. means 'without decay'; cp. Gk. *akḗratos*, 'unmixed, pure; incorrupt, upright', fr. *a-*, 'not, un-', & the base seen in Gk. *kḗr*, 'destruction, death', & in *keraízein*, 'to lay waste, destroy'. Being what one appears to be, being in reality the same as in appearance or profession; a (of persons, character &c.) honest, true, genuine, frank, straightforward; loyal, really meaning what one says or does: *a sincere friend*; *he was quite sincere in his professions of loyalty*; b (of actions &c.) free from deceit or pretence, real, genuine, not assumed: *a sincere devotion*; *is his grief sincere?*

sincerely, adv. Prec. & **-ly**. In a sincere manner; genuinely, earnestly, with sincerity, truthfully: *I am sincerely grateful*; *I sincerely hope you are right*. Phr. *yours sincerely*, formula in terminating a letter, less formal than *yours truly* or *faithfully* &c.

sincereness, n. See prec. & **-ness**. State, condition, of being sincere; sincerity.

sincerity, n. [1. sinsériti; 2. sinsériti], fr. Fr. *sincérité*, fr. Lat. *sincēritāt-(em)*. See **sincere** & **-ity**. Quality of being sincere; honesty, genuineness of character, purpose, motive &c.; freedom from pretence, deceit, or dissimulation: *to doubt a person's sincerity*; *the sincerity of one's grief, professions* &c.

sinciput, n. [1. sínsiput; 2. sínsipat]. Lat., 'half the head, one of the smoked cheeks of a pig'; the first element is either *sēmi-*, 'half', see **semi-**, or, as Walde suggests, possibly for *s(u)īno-*, 'pig', see **swine**; the second element is *caput*, 'head', see **capital** & cp. **occiput**. (anat.) The forehead, the upper half of the skull.

sine, n. [1. sīn; 2. sain], fr. Lat. *sinus*, 'fold of garment, bosom; curve, bay, gulf', see **sinus**; in L. Lat. used to translate Arab. *jība*, 'chord of an arc, sine', also written *jaib* & confused w. word meaning 'fold of garment'. (math., abbr. *sin*) a Perpendicular or its length drawn from one extremity of an arc to diameter drawn through the other extremity; b ratio of this perpendicular to the radius of the circle.

sin-eater, n. One who professed, according to an old custom, to take upon himself the sins of a dead person by eating bread laid on the bier, for a money payment.

sinecure, n. [1. sínekūr, sínekūr; 2. sáinikjǝ, sínikjǝ], fr. Lat. *sine cūrā*, 'without a cure (of souls)', Lat. *sine*, 'without', see **sine die**, & *cūra*, 'care', see **cure (I.)**. 1. An ecclesiastical benefice without a cure of souls. 2. Any office or position with emoluments or rank, but with few or no duties attached to it. Phr. *hardly a, not a, no, sinecure*, a very busy job.

sinecurism, n. [1. sínekūrizm; 2. sáinikjǝrizǝm]. Prec. & **-ism**. Conditions under which sinecures are prevalent; principle of taking emoluments without work or performance of any duty.

sinecurist, n. [1. sínekūrist; 2. sáinikjǝrist]. See prec. & **-ist**. One who holds a sinecure.

sine die, adv. [1. síni, síni, díē; 2. sáini, síni, dáii]. Lat., 'without a day', *sine*, 'without', & abl. of *dies*, 'day', see **dies non**; *sine* is cogn. w. Scrt. *sanitur*, 'without'; Gk. *áter*, without'; O.E. *sundor*, 'in two', see **asunder** & **sunder**. Without a day or date fixed: *to adjourn business sine die*, to postpone it indefinitely.

sine prole, adv. [1. síni prōlē; 2. sáini próulī], Lat., abl. sing. of *prōles*, 'offspring, descendant'. See under **proletariat(e)**. Without issue, leaving no children.

sine qua non, n. [1. síni kwā nón; 2. sáini kwèi nɔ́n]. Lat., lit. 'without which not'. An indispensable condition; a necessity.

sinew, n. [1. sínū; 2. sínjū]. O.E. *seonu, sinu*, M.E. *senewe, sinewe*; Du. *zenuw*, O.N. *sinar*, pl.; O.H.G. *senawa*, Mod. Germ. *sehne*; possibly cogn. w. Scrt. *snāva(s)*, 'tendon'. 1. A tendon, fibrous tissue, connecting muscle and bone. 2. (pl.) Muscles, muscular power, strength, brawn: *a man of mighty sinews*. Phr. *the sinews of war*, money and material resources.

sinewed, adj. [1. sínūd; 2. sínjūd]. (poet.) Having sinews of specified kind: *iron-sinewed*.

sinewiness, n. [1. sínūines; 2. sínjuinis]. **sinewy** & **-ness**. State, quality, of being sinewy.

sinewless, adj. [1. sínūles; 2. sínjulis]. **sinew** & **-less**. Without, deprived, devoid of, sinew or sinews; without strength, flabby, weak.

sinewy, adj. [1. sínūi; 2. sínjui]. **sinew** & **-y**. 1. Containing sinew or sinews; having many sinews; stringy: *a sinewy piece of beef*. 2. a Muscular, physically strong and vigorous: *sinewy arms*; *a strong, sinewy frame*; b (fig. of style) well-knit, terse, not diffuse.

sinfonia, n. [1. sìnfṓnia; 2. sìnfóuniǝ]. Ital. A symphony.

sinful, adj. [1. sínfool; 2. sínful]. O.E. *synfull*. **sin (I.)** & **-ful**. 1. (of persons) Full, guilty, of sin; wicked: *poor, sinful mortals*. 2. (of actions &c.) Tainted with, characterized by, of the nature of, sin: *a sinful act, thought* &c.

sinfully, adv. Prec. & **-ly**. In a sinful manner.

sinfulness, n. See prec. & **-ness**. State, quality, of being sinful.

sing, vb. intrans. & trans. [1. sing; 2. siŋ]. O.E. *singan*; O.S. & O.H.G. *singan*, 'to sing; to crow'; O.N. *syngja*; Goth. *siggwan*, 'to sing, to read out' = *singwan*; cogn. w. Gk. *omphḗ*, 'voice, oracle, report', fr. **soŋghwā*; orig. meaning of vb. is 'to use the voice'. See **singe** & **song**. A. intrans. 1. To use the voice so as to produce musical sounds and modulations, so as to render an air or tune; also simply, to utter musical notes: *to learn, be taught, to sing*; *to sing in tune*; *to sing at a concert*. Phrs. *to sing for one's supper*, to contribute something to one's entertainment; to pay in some way for what one gets; *to sing in the choir*, form one of the choir at a particular church; *to sing small*, to behave modestly and humbly, refrain from arrogance as though conscious of error and fearing a rebuff. 2. (of birds &c.) To utter their natural cries, to pipe, twitter &c. 3. (fig.) To rejoice, show signs of exultation: '*When the morning stars sang together*' (Job); *her heart sang for joy*. 4. To be capable of, be adapted for, being sung: *these words don't sing very well*. 5. To make a humming, buzzing noise or shrill sound: *the wind sings through the trees*; *a kettle singing on the fire*; *the mosquitoes sing round one's head*; *to make one's head sing*, produce sensation of humming &c. by a blow. 6. (poet.) a To write, compose, poetry, to be a poet: '*I do but sing because I must*' (Tennyson, 'In Mem.' xxi.); b *sing of*, to celebrate, tell of, something in verse: *poets shall sing of their glory*. 7. *Sing out* (chiefly colloq.), to shout, call out loudly: *sing out if you want anything*. B. trans. 1. a (of persons) To utter (words) with musical inflections and modulations of the voice: *sing us one of the old songs*; *let us now sing* '*God save the King*'; *sing the part of Tristan*; Phr. *to sing another tune, song*, to change one's tone, take another line, esp. to be less exultant or arrogant; b (of birds &c.) to utter with their natural cries: *the birds sang their merry notes*. 2. To intone, chant: *the psalms may be said or sung*; *to sing Mass*. 3. (poet.) To tell of, celebrate, in verse: '*Arms and the man I sing*' (Dryden, transl. of Virgil's 'Aeneid'); '*I celebrate myself, I sing myself*' (Whitman). Phr. *to sing a person's praises*, to praise enthusiastically or continually. 4. (reflex.) To go naturally into a song; to be perfectly adapted for singing: *Moore's lyrics sing themselves*. 5. To attend, accompany, with songs and singing: *to sing the harvest home*; *sing a bride to her new house*; *sing the Old Year out, New Year in*. 6. To bring to a certain state by singing: *to sing a child to sleep*. Phr. *the song has been sung to death*, sung so often that one is tired and sick of it.

singable, adj. [1. singabl; 2. síŋǝbl]. Prec. & **-able**. Adapted, suitable, for singing; easy to sing.

singe (I.), vb. trans. & intrans. [1. sinj; 2. sindž]. O.E. *sengan*, 'to singe, scorch', M.E. *sengen*; fr. **sang-jan*, a gradational form of **sing-*, see **sing**; orig. sense 'to cause to sing, hiss' &c., in reference to the sound made in the process of scorching &c.; for change of *-eng* to *-ing*, cp. **wing**, & the pronunciation of *England* &c. A. trans. 1. a To burn, scorch lightly and superficially: *the hot iron has slightly singed the cloth*; *a moth gets singed in a candle*; Phr. *to singe one's wings*, (i.) to injure one's reputation; (ii.) to suffer loss, by some action or enterprise; b to remove feathers, fluff, bristles &c. from, by singeing or scorching: *to singe a fowl, pig* &c. 2. Specif., *to singe hair*, to burn the ends slightly after cutting. B. intrans. To become singed or scorched: *I can smell something singeing*.

singe (II.), n., fr. prec. A superficial burn or scorch; mark of this.

singer, n. [1. sínger; 2. síŋǝ]. **sing** & **-er**. 1. a One who sings, esp. one who sings in public as a profession; b a person who can sing: *I fear I'm not a singer*. 2. A poet.

Singh, n. [1. sing; 2. siŋ]. Hind., fr. Scrt. *simha*, 'lion'. Patronymic or title borne by Sikhs after initiation into the community.

Singhalese, adj. & n. [1. sìnggalḗz; 2. sìŋgǝlíz], also spelt **Sinhalese**. Scrt. *simhala*, 'Ceylon'. 1. adj. a Pertaining to, coming from, Ceylon; b pertaining to, uttered, written in, the language of Ceylon. 2. n. a A native of Ceylon; b the language of Ceylon.

singing, n. [1. singing; 2. síŋiŋ]. **sing** & **-ing** a Act of, sound made by, one who sings; b art of the singer.

singing-bird, n. A song bird.

singingly, adv. [1. síngingli; 2. síŋiŋli], fr. Pres. Part. of **sing** & **-ly**. In a singing manner; with a sound as if singing or sung.

singing-man, n. A man employed in a choir to sing the services; choir-man.

singing-master, n. A teacher of singing.

singing-voice, n. Voice as used in, or trained for, singing.

single (I.), adj. [1. singgl; 2. síŋgl]. M.E. & O. Fr. *sengle*; fr. L. Lat. *singulus* (Class. Lat. only in pl. *singuli*), 'one to each, one apiece; single, separate, individual'; fr. **sem-*, 'one', as in Lat. *semel*, 'once', *simplex*, 'onefold', see **simple**, & *-go-* & *-lo-*, elements found also in Goth. *ain-ak-l-s*, 'single'. 1. a One only: '*And beauty draws us with a single hair*' (Pope, 'Rape of Lock', ii. 28); b as emphatic, preceded by negative: *not a single thing of value*, not even one; also *hardly a single man to be seen*, hardly any at all, hardly one even. 2. Not double or compound; not more than one; consisting of one thing or part only: *a single valve, single ply, a single burner* &c. 3. (various specialized uses) a Designed for use for one person only; suitable for one person: *a single bed*; *single room*; b performed by one person on either side: *challenged to single combat*; *a single game at tennis*; *single court*, court for such game; c done, performed, once only: *to keep accounts, books, by single entry*, i.e. entered under one account only; d levied on one species of property: *single tax*, on land value only; e to be used for one journey only: *a single ticket*, on railway, contrasted with *return*; also *a single*, as noun. 4. Alone, solitary; specif., unmarried: *are you married or single?*; *a single man, woman*; *a single life*; *to live and die single*. Phrs. *single blessedness*, the unmarried state; *to remain single*, not to marry. 5. United, shared in common with others; devoted to one thing only: *the party worked with a single purpose, for a single object*; *the nation spoke with a single voice*. 6. Not animated by unworthy motives, untinged by self-interest; simple, ingenuous, sincere: *a single eye, heart, mind*.

single (II.), n., fr. prec. (in various games) a (cricket) A hit for which one run is scored; b (lawn tennis) a game between only two players.

single (III.), vb. trans., fr. prec. *Single out,* **a** to choose, pick out, select, from among several, for some purpose, or as possessing some quality: *to single out the biggest apples for dumplings; he was singled out to succeed his uncle;* **b** to indicate as most suitable for a particular purpose; cause to appear superior to others: *his abilities soon singled him out for promotion.*

single-breasted, adj. [1. singgl brésted; 2. síŋgl bréstid]. (of coat, waistcoat) Made to button on one side only, having only a single row of buttons and buttonholes.

single entry, n. Simple method of book-keeping in which transactions are entered under one account only in the ledger; contrasted with *double entry.*

single-eyed, adj. **1.** Having only one eye, one-eyed. **2.** Devoted exclusively to a single purpose; honest, sincere.

single-handed, adj. & adv. **1.** adj. **a** Having only one hand; **b** unassisted; with no help from others; **c** done, performed, with one pair of hands, by one person, without assistance from others. **2.** adv. Without assistance, unaidedly, alone: *did the job single-handed.*

single-hearted, adj. Having an honest, simple character; faithfully devoted to one purpose or cause; sincere; single-minded.

single-minded, adj. Single-hearted.

singleness, n. [1. síngglnes; 2. síŋglnis]. **single** (I.) & **-ness.** State, quality, of being single, esp. of being single in heart or mind: *singleness of purpose.*

single phase, adj. (elect.) Having an alternating current of one phase.

singlestick, n. [1. sínggistik; 2. síŋglstik]. Prob. fr. the cudgel wielded by one hand, as contrasted w. the *quarter-staff,* with two. **1.** A stick about the length of a sword, provided with basket hilt, used in a rough kind of fencing. **2.** The use of the singlestick.

singlet, n. [1. síngglet; 2. síŋglit]. **single** (I.) & **-et,** as contrasted w. *doublet.* (shop term) Garment worn under a shirt; a vest.

singleton, n. [1. sínggltun; 2. síŋgltən]. **single** (I.) & **-ton,** cp. **simpleton.** A single card of any suit occurring in a hand at whist.

singly, adv. [1. síinggli; 2. síŋgli]. **single** (I.) & **-ly. 1.** Individually, separately, one at a time, one by one: *deal with the questions singly.* **2.** Alone, without associate, wife &c.: *to live singly.* **3.** By oneself, alone, unassisted, single-handed: *he attacked the enemy singly.*

sing-song, n., adj., & vb. [1. síng song; 2. síŋ sɔŋ], fr. **sing** & **song. 1.** n. **a** A droning, monotonous, expressionless utterance, or delivery; a speech, reading, utterance, rising and falling in tone with monotonous regularity, undiversified by expressive modulation: *many churches are emptied by the dreary sing-song of the clergy;* **b** an informal impromptu concert, in which members of the audience are the performers. **2.** adj. Uttered, delivered, in a sing-song; hence, also, lacking freshness of ideas, dull, commonplace. **3.** vb. To speak in a sing-song.

singular (I.), adj. [1. sínggūlar; 2. síŋgjulə]. Lat. *singulāris,* 'alone, one at a time; solitary; of the singular number; unique, unparalleled'. See **single** (I.) & **-ar. 1.** Of, relating to, a single person or thing; **a** (gram.) contrasted with *plural* or *dual*: *in the singular number; first person singular;* **b** (law) each, separate, individual, not taken together: *all and singular interests, parcels* &c.; **c** (log.) considered by itself, individual, referring to a single thing, not general: *a singular term, proposition* &c. **2.** (rare) Alone of its kind, unexampled, unique: *a specimen singular of its kind.* **3. a** Rare, unusual, uncommon, strange, remarkable, extraordinary: *a most singular phenomenon; a singular coincidence; they all agreed with singular unanimity;* **b** above the usual or common standard; of high degree; eminent: *a man of singular ability;* **c** not in accord with general customs, eccentric, unconventional, peculiar, odd: *he has rather singular habits; dressed in singular fashion.*

singular (II.), n., fr. prec. The singular number; word not in the plural: *in the singular; give the singular of mice.*

singularity, n. [1. sìnggūláriti; 2. sìŋgjulǽriti], fr. Fr. *singularité,* fr. Lat. *singulāritāt-(em).* **singular** (I.) & **-ity.** Quality, state, of being singular, esp. of being rare, peculiar; unusualness, strangeness, or eccentricity: *the singularity of such an occurrence; singularity in dress, manner* &c.

singularization, n. [1. sìnggūlarīzáshun; 2. sìŋgjuləraizéiʃən]. **singularize** & **-ation.** Act, process, of singularizing.

singularize, vb. trans. [1. sínggūlarīz; 2. síŋgjuləraiz]. **singular** (I.) & **-ize.** To make singular; to turn into a supposed singular form: *the word pea has been singularized from pease.*

Sinhalese. See **Singhalese.**

sinister, adj. [1. sínister; 2. sínistə]. Lat., 'on the left hand or side; awkward, wrong, perverse, improper; lucky, favourable' (because the Romans faced south when taking auspices, so that the left side was to the East, or fortunate quarter); also, according to Gk. custom, 'unlucky, inauspicious'; the first element is perh. cogn. w. Scrt. *sáṇīyān,* 'more profitable, more advantageous'; cp. also Scrt. *sanóti,* 'he gains, acquires'; further, Gk. *(h)anúein,* 'to accomplish, complete'; the second element is comparable to that in Lat. *dexter,* 'right', see **dexter,** & in O.E. *winstre,* 'left hand', O.H.G. *winistar* &c., & is ultimately a compar. suff. **1. a** (archaic) On the left-(hand) side; **b** (her.) on the right side of the shield as seen from the front, that is as depicted, but on the left of the supposed bearer who stands behind; for *bend (bar) sinister* see under **bend** (II.). **2. a** Evil, inauspicious, portending or suggesting coming disaster: *a sinister beginning to an enterprise; sinister symptoms;* **b** forbidding, malignant, malevolent, conveying an impression of evil: *a sinister countenance, expression, glance;* **c** mysteriously, covertly, evil; conveying a sense of lurking wickedness, treachery, or danger: *a sinister design, plot; a sinister character, reputation* &c.

sinisterly, adv. Prec. & **-ly.** In a sinister manner.

sinistral, adj. [1. sínistral; 2. sínistrəl]. **sinister** & **-al.** (zool., of shells) Having the whorls turning leftwards.

sinistrally, adv. Prec. & **-ly.** Towards the left hand.

sinistro-, pref. Form of **sinister** used in compounds; pertaining to, towards, the left hand.

sinistrorse, adj. [1. sìnistrórs; 2. sìnistrɔ́s]. Lat. *sinistrorsus,* fr. **sinistroversus,* 'turned towards the left'. See prec. & **versus.** (bot.) Twisting spirally from right to left, of climbing plants as the hop; contrasted with *dextrorse.*

sinistrous, adj. [1. sínistrus; 2. sínistrəs]. **sinister** & **-ous.** Sinistral.

sink (I.), vb. intrans. & trans. [1. singk; 2. siŋk]. O.E. *sincan,* only intrans., the old trans. **senċan* is lost; M.E. *sinken,* O.S. *sincan;* O.H.G. *sinchan;* Goth. *sigqwan* for **sin(g)-kwan;* cogn. w. Lith. *sekti, senktu,* 'to drain away'. See also **siccative. A.** intrans. **1.** To fall gradually or slowly downwards, descend, as by weight or gravity: *heavy clouds began to sink lower and lower;* **a** to appear to the sight as descending or disappearing: *the sun sinks in the west, below a cloud, beneath the horizon; the land sank slowly as the ship sailed away;* **b** to be or become submerged in a liquid or semi-liquid; to disappear beneath the surface of water: *the ship sank with all her crew; swimmer sank like a stone; to sink up to one's knees in mud, in a quicksand;* Phr. *sink or swim,* of a desperate chance, in which there is no choice but to succeed or fail absolutely. **2.** (of liquids) To subside, fall gradually to a lower level; to diminish, shrink in quantity: *the floods are sinking rapidly; the lake has sunk much below its level.* **3.** (of ground, buildings &c.) **a** To slope, fall away gradually to a lower level: *the land sinks at this point towards sea-level;* **b** to subside, fall in, give way: *the road suddenly sank in; ground sank under my feet, the building has sunk slightly at one corner.* **4.** To diminish in degree, intensity &c.; **a** (of voice, sound &c.) to fall to a lower pitch, to become less in volume, to become less loud: *his voice sank to a whisper;* **b** (of value, prices) to become lower, to diminish, lose former price: *the shares have sunk to nothing;* **c** (of numbers &c.) to grow less, diminish: *have figures of unemployment sunk since last year?;* **d** to become less in force, violence; to abate, die down: *the storm, wind, is beginning to sink.* **5. a** To fall, slide, allow oneself to fall down gradually from an upright position: *to sink into a chair; they sank into each other's arms; to sink exhausted on the ground; to sink back on to the pillows;* Phr. *to sink into the grave,* to die; **b** (of part of the body) to droop forward or down; to drop: *his head sank on his breast; he let his arms sink from weariness;* Phr. *my heart sank,* I lost all hope, spirits, buoyancy; I was in despair; **c** (of eye, look &c.) to droop, be cast down, to turn downwards: *his eyes sank before that stern glance.* **6.** To become, or appear, hollow, shrunken, or deeply withdrawn: *his eyes seemed to sink into his head.* **7.** To pass into a mental or bodily condition of reduced vitality, robustness, vigour, activity: *to sink into a consumption, into a faint, a deep sleep;* specif. in Phr. *he is sinking (fast)* &c., is dying. **8.** To decline from a higher, better position, condition, mode of life &c. into a lower and worse one: *to sink into poverty, degradation, vicious habits* &c.; *to sink to the lowest depths of humiliation, baseness* &c.; *to sink in another's estimation,* be less esteemed by. **9.** To percolate, penetrate, enter gradually into, to be absorbed by; to become impressed on; **a** (in physical sense) *dye sinks into the fabric; water will sink through sand but not clay;* also, **b** (of intellectual process) *let the lesson sink into your mind; his early privations have sunk deeply into his memory.* **B.** trans. **1.** To cause, allow to sink; to submerge, send below the surface of water: *the battleship was sunk by gunfire; the submarine sank two vessels on her first voyage; the captain sank his ship by opening the cocks.* **2.** To lower below the surface of the ground; to fix firmly and deeply into: *to sink a post ten feet into the ground.* **3.** To let fall into a lower position: *to sink one's head on one's arms; to sink one's eyes,* to cast them down. **4.** To excavate from above downwards; to make, construct, by digging or boring: *to sink a well, shaft, mine.* **5.** To cause to subside, reduce volume of, drain away: *a week of fine weather will soon sink the floods; a leakage has sunk the water in the well.* **6.** To lower the pitch; reduce volume of: *to sink one's voice.* **7. a** To reduce, extinguish, by annual payments or by a sinking fund, q.v.: *to sink a (national) debt;* **b** to invest (money) in some business, undertaking &c. from which it may prove difficult to withdraw it; to lose, waste (money) in a speculative investment: *he sank all his capital in house-building.* **8.** To conceal from sight or notice; to keep withdrawn or concealed; to suppress, ignore: *to sink one's identity; he generously chose to sink his personal interests; let us sink our differences, enmities* &c. **9.** In technical senses: **a** (minting &c.) to engrave: *to sink a die;* **b** (naut.) to cause to disappear from view by moving away: *to sink the land;* **c** (print.) to set lower than the top of a page or line.

sink (II.), n., fr. prec. **1.** A shallow, rectangular trough or basin of stone, porcelain, lead &c. with a drainage outlet, placed beneath a water tap or taps in a scullery, pantry &c., for washing up dishes &c., getting rid of dirty water &c. **2.** A place in which filth, drainage &c. is collected; a cesspool; (usually only fig.) *a sink of iniquity; the slum* *is a sink for all the dregs of humanity.* **3.** Any place, such as a marsh, hole in rock &c., through which water drains or percolates away and disappears. **4.** A trap or opening in the stage of a theatre, through which scenery is raised or lowered.

sinkable, adj. [1. síngkabl; 2. síŋkəbl]. **sink (I.)** & **-able.** Capable of being sunk, liable to sink.

sinker, n. [1. síngker; 2. síŋkə]. **sink (I.)** & **-er.** **1.** One who sinks, esp. one who sinks or engraves dies: *a die-sinker.* **2.** That which sinks something, esp. a leaden weight on a fishing net or line, or sounding line.

sinking, n. [1. síngking; 2. síŋkiŋ]. **sink (I.)** & **-ing.** Specif., an internal sensation of collapse, as from weakness, hunger, fear &c.: *a sinking in the stomach, at the heart.*

sinking fund, n. A fund formed by setting apart yearly certain sums of money out of revenue for the sinking or paying off of a national debt, a municipal loan or a company's debentures &c.

sinless, adj. [1. sínles; 2. sínlis]. **sin (I.)** & **-less.** Free from sin; innocent.

sinlessly, adv. Prec. & **-ly.** In a sinless manner; without sin.

sinlessness, n. See prec. & **-ness.** Quality, condition, of being sinless.

sinner, n. [1. síner; 2. sínə]. **sin (II.)** & **-er.** **1.** One who sins; one who has transgressed the law of God or refuses to obey His will. **2.** One guilty of a breach of social conventions, of regulations, or unwritten laws of any kind; an offender against these: *occupants of the stalls are the worst sinners in disturbing a performance by their late arrival.*

Sinn Fein, n. [1. shín fán; 2. ʃin féin]. Ir., lit. 'we ourselves'. An Irish political social and economic movement, aiming at complete independence from Great Britain.

sin offering, n. **sin (I.)** & **offering.** An offering, sacrifice, in expiation of sin.

sinologist, n. [1. sinólojist; 2. sinɔ́lədžist]. See **sinology** & **-ist.** Student of, specialist in, sinology.

sinologue, n. [1. sínològ, -òg; 2. sínəlòug, -ɔ̀g]. Fr. See next word. Sinologist.

sinology, n. [1. sinóloji; 2. sinɔ́lədži], fr. Lat. *Sinae,* fr. Gk. *Sinai,* 'the Chinese people', & **-logy.** Study of Chinese language, history, literature, art &c.

sinter, n. [1. sínter; 2. síntə], fr. Mod. Germ., 'dross', fr. Lat. See under **cinder.** A siliceous or calcareous deposit from mineral springs.

sinuate, adj. [1. sínūāt; 2. sínjuèit], fr. Lat. *sinuāt-(um),* P.P. type of *sinuāre,* 'to wind, bend', see **sinus.** Winding in and out; sinuous; specif. (bot.) having a wavy edge, of leaves with regular and strongly marked indentations.

sinuosity, n. [1. sìnūósiti; 2. sìnjuɔ́siti]. **sinuous** & **-ity.** **a** State of being sinuous; **b** a bend, or winding, as in a river, road &c.

sinuous, adj. [1. sínūus; 2. sínjuəs]. fr. Lat. *sinuōsus,* see **sinus.** Bending, winding; snaky, serpentine, undulating.

sinuously, adv. Prec. & **-ly.** In a sinuous manner.

sinus, n. [1. sínus; 2. sáinəs], Lat. *sinus,* 'a curve, hollow; fold, esp. of a garment across the breast, hence bosom; a gulf, bay'. Prob. cogn. w. Lat. *sīnum,* 'round drinking-vessel with swelling sides', & *situla,* 'a bucket'; fr. base **sweit-, *swit-,* further etymol. uncertain. **1.** (zool. and anat.) A cavity, esp. in substance of a bone, or soft tissue. **2.** (pathol.) A cavity in which pus forms, a fistula. **3.** (bot.) Depression, curve, between the lobes of a leaf.

Siouan, adj. [1. sóoan; 2. sūən]. **Sioux** & **-an.** Pertaining to the language spoken by tribes of N. American Indians of the same stock as the Sioux.

Sioux, n. & adj. [1. sóō; 2. sū]. Fr., form of native name. **1.** n. **a** One of the chief tribes or families of N. American Indians; **b** a member of this tribe or family; **c** its language. **2.** adj. Of, pertaining to, the Sioux or their language.

sip (I.), vb. trans. & intrans. [1. sip; 2. sip]. O.E. *sȳpian,* 'to absorb moisture'; cp. also O.E. *sūpan,* 'to absorb, to drink'; O.H.G. *sūfan,* Mod. Germ. *saufen,* 'to drink deep'; cp. **sup (I.).** **1.** trans. To drink in repeated and very small quantities; to drink drop by drop, or a very little at a time; specif., to drink wine in this way, so as to taste each mouthful thoroughly: *he sat sipping his wine for hours.* **2.** intrans. To drink a small quantity of liquid at a time; to take a sip.

sip (II.), n., fr. prec. **a** A very small mouthful of any liquid; **b** act of sipping.

sipahee, n. Obs. form of **sepoy.**

siphon (I.), n. [1. sífun; 2. sáifən]. Fr., fr. Lat. *sīphōn-(em),* fr. Gk. *síphōn,* 'a small pipe or tube'; perh. fr. **twībh-,* & cogn. w. Lat. *tībia,* 'shin-bone, pipe'. See **tibia.** **1.** A tube with one short end bent downwards, by means of which, if the bent end is placed in a vessel of liquid, and the longer end allowed to hang downwards outside the vessel, the liquid is made to drain away down the outside piece of pipe by atmospheric pressure, provided that the lower extremity be lower than the bottom of the vessel. **2.** Glass bottle containing aerated water, fitted with an internal glass tube, and an external lever which opens a valve and allows the water to flow out from the pressure of the gas within. **3.** (zool.) Any of various kinds of tubular organs, as in molluscs, insects &c., used for drawing in and ejecting water or air, sucking &c.

siphon (II.), vb. trans. & intrans., fr. prec. **a** trans. *Siphon out,* to draw off (water &c.) by means of a siphon; **b** intrans., to be drawn from higher to lower level through the action of a siphon.

siphonet, n. [1. sífunet; 2. sáifənet]. **siphon** & **-et.** One of the suction tubes of the green-fly or of similar insects.

siphuncle, n. [1. sífungkl; 2. sáifaŋkl], fr. Lat. *sīphunculus,* dimin. See **siphon.** **1.** The tube connecting the inner chamber of the shell of some cephalopods. **2.** Sucking tube of insects; siphonet.

sippet, n. [1. sípet; 2. sípit]. **sip** & **-et,** cp. **sop.** **a** A small piece of bread, toast, biscuit &c., dipped in soup, milk, or other liquid and eaten; a sop; **b** small triangular piece of toast, or fried bread, used for garnishing a dish of mince &c.

sir (I.), n. [1. sěr; 2. sʌ̄]. In M.E., form of **sire,** occurring orig. in unstressed position in the sentence. **1.** As form of address: **a** (obs.) as polite form in addressing a friend or equal; **b** polite form of address for a stranger; **c** expressing respect to a superior, servant to master, pupil to teacher, officer to his colonel, and to any superior officer when on parade &c.; **d** official form used in addressing the Speaker, in House of Commons, either directly or in course of debate; **e** in writing formally on business or to a stranger, as *Dear Sir,* or *Sir*; *gentlemen* is now used for the plural rather than *sirs.* **2.** As title of knights and baronets, in written communications, prefixed to the Christian name, followed by surname: *Sir John Jones*; in speaking, to Christian name alone: *Sir John*; and in writing, *Dear Sir John*; or more formally, *Dear Sir John Jones*; in addressing letters to baronets: *Sir X. Y., Bart.*; to knights or baronets, *Sir* follows another title, e.g. *The Hon. Sir X. Y.*; *The Rev. Sir X. Y., Bart.*; *General, Colonel &c., Sir X. Y.* **3.** (obs. and hist.) Translating Latin *dominus,* as titular prefix to the name of a priest, equivalent to modern *Reverend,* as *Sir Hugh Evans,* in Shakespeare, 'Merry Wives'. (*Sir* is always unstressed when it precedes a name. and the latter is strongly stressed, as [sə džɔ́n]; when a second name follows, this has chief stress, first name having secondary stress. [sə džɔ̀n džóunz].)

sir (II.), vb. trans., fr. prec. To address as *sir*: *don't sir me quite so much.*

sircar, sirkar, n. [1. sěrkar; 2. sʌ́kā], fr. Hind. & Pers. *sarkār,* 'chief', fr. Pers. *sar,* 'head', & *kār,* 'work'. **a** (as title) Master, lord; **b** the supreme government of India.

sirdar, n. [1. sěrdar; 2. sʌ́dā]. Hind. & Pers. *sardār,* 'commander', fr. Pers. *sar,* 'head', & *dār,* 'possessing, holding'. A military commander; specif., the British Commander-in-chief of the Egyptian army.

sire (I.), n. [1. sīr; 2. sáiə]. Fr., variant of *sieur,* earliest O. Fr. form *senre,* fr. Lat. *senior,* 'older'. See **senior** & cp. **sir (I.).** **1.** As form of address, to a monarch, equivalent of 'Your Majesty'. **2.** (poet. or rhet.) Father or other male ancestor: *buried with his sires.* **3.** **a** Male parent of horse or bullock, also of a dog; specif. **b** a stallion.

sire (II.), vb. trans., fr. prec. (of stallions &c.) To beget, be the sire of.

siren, n. [1. síren; 2. sáiərən]. Lat. *sīrēn,* fr. Gk. pl. *seirên-(es)*; etymol. doubtful. **1.** (class. mythol.) One of two or three sea-nymphs, half-woman, half-bird, who with their song lured mariners to destruction on the rocks where they dwelt. **2.** (fig.) **a** An alluring, dangerous woman; a fascinating temptress; female seducer; **b** a woman with a charming voice; **c** mermaid. **3.** A hooter or whistle, operated by steam or air driven through a revolving perforated disk, giving various sounds. **4.** (zool.) **a** An eel-like batrachian, with small forelegs and no hindlegs, having gills and lungs; found in swamps in U.S.A. **5.** (attrib.) Of, pertaining to, the siren; fascinating, alluring: *siren song, voice.*

sirenian, adj. & n. [1. sīrénian; 2. sairíniən]. Mod. Lat. *sirēnia* & *-an,* see **siren**; so called fr. their resemblance to a mermaid. (zool.) **1.** adj. Of, belonging to, the order *Sirenia,* of marine mammals; the sea-cows, the manatee and dugong. **2.** n. A sirenian mammal.

sirgang, n. [1. sěrgang; 2. sʌ́gæŋ]. Native name. A bright green or blue East Indian or Asiatic bird, allied to the jackdaw, with long tail and red bill and feet.

siriasis, n. [1. sirīasis; 2. siráiəsis], fr. Gk. *seiriāsis,* fr. *seirios,* 'hot, scorching'; cp. Scrt. *tvēsāmi,* 'to be strongly agitated; to sparkle, burn'; & Lith. *tviskéti,* 'to waver (of a flame), to shine'. **a** Sunstroke; **b** a sun-bath.

Sirius, n. [1. sírius; 2. síriəs]. Lat., fr. Gk. *Seírios.* See prec. The dog-star.

sirloin, n. [1. sěrloin; 2. sʌ́lɔin]. Variant spelling of *surloin,* fr. O. Fr. *surlonge,* 'upper part of the loin'. See **sur-** & **loin.** Upper part of a loin of beef, with meat above and below the bone.

sirocco, n. [1. sirókō; 2. sirɔ́kou]. Ital. *s(c)irocco,* fr. Arab. *shoruq,* fr. *sharq,* 'the East, rising of the sun', fr. *sharaqa,* 'to rise'. A hot wind blowing from the Libyan deserts, experienced on the northern coasts of Mediterranean, dry or moist according to the season.

sirrah, n. [1. síra; 2. sírə], fr. Provençal *sira,* fr. Fr. *sire,* see **sire** & **sir.** (obs.) Sir, fellow, used contemptuously in speaking to an inferior.

sirup, n. See **syrup.**

sirvente, n. [1. sěrváhnt; 2. siəvā́t]. Fr., fr. Provenç., Pres. Part. of Lat. *servīre,* see **serve.** A mediaeval Provençal form of lay often satirical.

sisal grass, hemp, n. [1. sísl gràhs, hèmp; 2. sísl grās, hèmp], fr. Sisal, seaport in Yucatan. A strong fibre, used for making rope and cords, obtained from the American agave, henequen.

siskin, n. [1. sískin; 2. sískin], fr. M. Du. *cijsken, sijsken,* fr. L.G. *zieske,* fr. Pol. *czyżik,* dimin. of *czyż,* name of the bird. A species of finch, of Asia and Europe, of olive green plumage with black and yellow markings, often kept as a caged song-bird.

sissoo, n. [1. sísōō; 2. sísū]. Hind. *sīsō.* East Indian tree yielding strong, dark-coloured timber.

sister (I.), n. [1. síster; 2. sístə]. M.E. *sister* &c.; prob. fr. O.N. *systir*; the native O.E. forms were *sweostor*, *swuster* &c., M.E. *suster* &c.; O.S. & O.H.G. *swestar*, Mod. Germ. *schwester*; Goth. *swistar*; Gmc. type **swestr-*, fr. Aryan **swesr-*; cp. Lat. *soror*, fr. **swozōr*, & **swesōr*; Gk. (Hesychius) *héōr*, fr. **swesōr*, 'first cousin'; Scrt. *svasa*; O. Slav. *sestra*; ultimately prob. fr. reflex. **swe-*, 'self, own', as in Lat. *suus*, see **sui.** **1. a** A woman born of the same parents as oneself: *my sister*; a female having same parents as one or more persons of either sex: *the two are sisters*; *brother and sister*; (also used of animals); *to be like sisters*, very intimate, having great affection for each other; **b** a half-sister; also applied to stepsister; *the weird sisters*, the witches, in 'Macbeth'; *the three sisters*, the Fates. **2. a** Woman who bears an affection resembling that of a sister to another person; **b** a fellow human being of the female sex: *our sisters of other lands and races.* **3.** A member of a religious or charitable community; specif., a professed nun: *Sisters of Mercy*, charitable religious order so called; *Little Sisters of the Poor*; *the Clewer Sisters* &c. **4.** A senior hospital nurse; usually in charge of a ward. **5.** One of exactly the same kind or type, (usually attrib.) *sister ship.* **6.** A language or family of languages, sprung from a common ancestral type; used esp. attrib.: *sister languages.*

sister (II.), vb. trans., fr. prec. (rare) To act like a sister to.

sisterhood, n. [1. sísterhood; 2. sístəhud]. **sister (I.)** & **-hood.** **1.** State of being a sister; mutual relation of sisters: *they lived in loving sisterhood.* **2.** A community or order of women living under religious vows and performing works of religion, charity &c.

sister-hooks, n. Pair of hooks, each having a looped shank, hung from a ring with the openings facing, and made so that they close over each other.

sister-in-law, n. [1. síster in law; 2. sístər in lɔ̄]. **a** Husband's or wife's sister; **b** brother's wife; **c** brother-in-law's wife.

sisterless, adj. [1. sísterles; 2. sístəlis]. **sister (I.)** & **-less.** Having no sister; having lost a sister.

sisterliness, n. [1. sísterlines; 2. sístəlinis]. **sisterly** & **-ness.** Quality of being sisterly; sisterly character, action &c.

sisterly, adj. [1. sísterli; 2. sístəli]. **sister (I.)** & **-ly.** **a** Like a sister; affectionate as a sister; **b** resembling the conduct of, becoming, suitable for, a sister.

Sistine, adj. [1. sístīn; 2. sístain], fr. Ital. *Sistino*, fr. *Sisto*, 'Sixtus', name of popes & saints, fr. Lat. *sextus*, 'sixth', see **sext-**, & **-ine.** **1.** Of, pertaining to, built by &c., one of the Popes, named *Sixtus*; **a** *Sistine Chapel*, private chapel of the Popes in the Vatican, built by Sixtus IV., d. 1484, decorated by Michelangelo and others; **b** *Sistine Vulgate*, edition revised under the Papacy of Sixtus V., d. 1590. **2.** *Sistine Madonna*, painting by Raphael, now in Dresden, formerly in the church of *San Sisto*, Piacenza.

sistrum, n., pl. **sistra** [1. sístrum, -tra; 2. sístrə(m)]. Lat., fr. Gk. *seîstron*, fr. *seíein*, 'to shake'. See **seismo-.** An ancient form of rattle, used by the Egyptians in the religious rites of Isis, consisting of a metal oval frame with rods passing through holes, which jingled when shaken.

Sisyphean, adj. [1. sìsiféan; 2. sìsifíən], fr. Gk. *Sisúpheios*, fr. *Sísuphos*, Lat. *Sisyphus*, prob. fr. a redupl. form of *sophós*, 'wise, crafty', q.v. under **sophist.** Of, pertaining to, Sisyphus, a crafty king of ancient Corinth, condemned in the underworld to roll for ever up a hill a huge rock which at once rolled down again; hence *Sisyphean task, labour* &c., one that is tedious, useless, and can never be completed.

sit, vb. intrans. & trans. [1. sit; 2. sit]. O.E. *sittan*; M.E. *sitten*; O.S. *sittian*; O.H.G. *sizzan*; Mod. Germ. *sitzen*; O.N. *sitja*; Goth. *sitan*; all fr. Gmc. **set-jan-*; fr. base **sed-jō*; cp. Gk. *hédzomai*; Lat. *sedēre.* See further under **sedentary**; cp. **seat, set (I.), settle.** **A.** intrans. **1. a** (of men) To assume, be in, a position in which the thighs are more or less at right angles to the trunk, while the body itself is upright, with its weight resting upon, and supported by, some object serving as a seat; contrasted with both *to stand* and *to lie*; Phrs. *to sit on the throne*, reign, be king; *to sit on the fence*, hesitate to commit oneself by taking a definite side, adopting an opinion, embarking on a line of action; *to sit tight*, (colloq.) (i.) to seat oneself firmly in the saddle; (ii.) to adhere firmly to one's opinions, purpose &c., and refuse to be shaken; **b** (of quadrupeds) to rest the weight of the body on the haunches and hocks, with the hind legs stretched out in front and the front legs kept upright; **c** (of birds, loosely used) to rest, perch, on anything, the weight of the body being sometimes partly supported by the object on which the bird sits: *to sit on a bough*; *a jackdaw sitting on a roof*; contrasted with *to fly.* **2.** Specif. (of birds) to remain covering eggs uninterruptedly, so as to hatch them: *the hens won't sit this year*; *don't disturb hens when they are sitting.* **3. a** To occupy a seat, as indicating official functions: *to sit on the bench*, be a judge or magistrate; *the judge will not sit on Saturday*, will not hold a court on that day; Phr. *to sit in judgement on*, to take upon oneself the function of a judge, esp. in matters of morals; to judge, censure; **b** to be a member of (a body): *to sit on a jury, committee* &c.; *to sit in parliament*, be an M.P. or peer of the realm; *to sit for a constituency*, represent it in House of Commons; **c** (of law court, deliberative or legislative body) to be in session; to meet, be convened, for transaction of business: *Law Courts do not sit from August till October*; *Parliament will sit in the autumn*; *the House was still sitting at 8 o'clock this morning.* **4.** To do something in which a sitting position is usually involved; specif. **a** *to sit for an examination* &c., to submit oneself, enter, for an examination &c.; **b** *to sit to an artist, a photographer* &c.; *to sit for one's portrait*, have one's portrait painted. **5.** To press, bear, weigh, upon; to be felt as a weight or burden; **a** (in physical sense) *food at night is likely to sit heavy on one's stomach*; **b** (in non-material sense) *his losses, his responsibilities, sit but lightly upon him*; '*care Sat on his faded cheek*' (Milton, 'P. L.' i. 601). **6. a** To fit, hang, well: *the coat does not sit properly across the shoulders*; **b** (fig.) to be suitable to, to become; to befit: *his new dignities sit rather awkwardly upon him.* **7.** (archaic or poet., esp. of the wind) To have a certain position or direction, to set: *in what quarter sits the wind?* **B.** trans. **1.** (reflex.) *Sit oneself*, to sit, take a seat, be seated, place oneself: *we sat ourselves (down) on a mossy bank*; *he came and sat himself beside me.* **2. a** (riding) To keep one's seat on; to ride, bestride: *to sit a horse like a gentleman*; **b** (rowing) to sit in, so that the boat does not roll; to keep (boat) trimmed by even swing and good watermanship: *to sit a light eight.* **C.** Followed by adverbs and prepositions. *Sit down*, intrans., **a** to encamp before and besiege: *to sit down before a town, fortress* &c.; **b** *sit down to (one's work)*, settle down to, concentrate on; **c** (of speaker in public) to conclude a speech, make an end of speaking; **d** *sit down under (an insult* &c.), to submit to, suffer without protest or reply. *Sit on, upon*, intrans., **a** to be a member of (a committee, deliberative body &c.); **b** to inquire into, investigate, as member of a jury, commission &c.: *to sit on a case*; *to sit upon a body found drowned*; **c** (colloq., slang) to rebuke, repress, snub: *to sit upon a bumptious person.* *Sit out*, **1.** trans., **a** to stay to the end of, sit through: *to sit out a play, concert* &c.; **b** to stay longer than (others): *which of the visitors will sit out the other?*; **c** to refrain from taking part in; to remain seated during: *to sit out a dance*; **2.** intrans., specif., not to dance, but to sit and talk to one's partner while a dance is in progress: *if you are tired, let us sit out.* *Sit through*, intrans., to stay to the end of, sit out: *it is an ordeal to sit through a long sermon.* *Sit under*, intrans., to be a member of the congregation of a particular minister, esp. as a listener to his preaching: *he was proud to have sat under the great Mr. Spurgeon.* *Sit up*, intrans., **a** (of a dog &c.) to sit upright upon hind quarters with forelegs held up in the air: *she taught Fido to sit up and beg*; **b** to raise oneself from a lying position: *to sit up in bed*; **c** to keep the backbone erect when sitting; not to lounge or sit with a bent back: *in the days of our great-grandmothers decent people sat up straight, and didn't lean back in arm-chairs*; **d** (colloq.) (i.) to be startled, suddenly shocked, surprised, frightened &c.: *the sudden pain made me sit up, I can tell you*; (ii.) to become suddenly alert and expectant; to be startled into activity: *some of the country clergy need the bishop to drop in on them suddenly now and then, and make them sit up a bit*; **e** to stay up beyond, not go to bed at, the usual time: *to sit up all night playing cards*; *children are allowed to sit up later than usual for a treat on Christmas day.* *Sit upon*, to sit on.

site, n. [1. sīt; 2. sait]. Fr., fr. Lat. *situs*, 'situation, local position'; formerly supposed to be formed fr. P.P. type of *sinere*, 'to set down; leave; to let', though Walde rejects this, & connects the word w. Scrt. *kšēti*, *kšiyáti*, 'he dwells, abides', cp. also Scrt. *kšitiš*, 'dwelling, settlement', & *kšētram*, 'landed property, dwelling-place'; cogn. also w. Gk. *ktízein*, 'to found, build' &c. Ground, specific space of ground, on which anything is, or is to be, built; local position: *the site of a church*; *a good site for a house*; *to buy a site for building.*

sited, adj. [1. sīted; 2. sáitid]. Prec. & **-ed.** (rare) Situated, placed, usually with qualification: *a well-, badly-sited house.*

sith, conj. [1. sith; 2. siþ]. O.E. *siþþan*, 'since, afterwards', M.E. *sith.* See **since.** (obs.) Since, seeing that.

sitology, n. [1. sītóloji; 2. saitɔ́lədži], fr. Gk. *sîtos*, 'wheat, corn, meal; food'; cp. also *siteîn*, 'to feed'; the etymol. is disputed; an ingenious & attractive suggestion is that the word is borrowed fr. the so-called *šatam* branch of Aryan speech, & represents a form **swītos*, fr. Aryan *k̑weit-* &c., wh. survives in Gmc. in *hwaiteis*, 'wheat', for wh., however, Aryan **k̑woid-* must be postulated. See under **wheat** & **white**; for suff. see **-logy.** Study of food, its values &c.; dietetics.

sitophobia, n. [1. sītōfóbia; 2. sàitoufóubiə]. Gk. *sito-*, 'food', see prec., & **-phobia.** Morbid aversion to food; refusal to take proper nourishment.

sitter, n. [1. síter; 2. sítə]. **sit** & **-er.** One that sits; specif. **a** person who is sitting for a portrait &c.; **b** a broody hen incubating her eggs: *a good, bad, sitter*; **c** a sitting game-bird or other animal, hence (colloq.) an easy shot; also of anything easy to do, as an easy catch at cricket.

sitting, n. [1. síting; 2. sítiŋ]. **sit** & **-ing.** **1.** Act of one who sits (in various senses); **a** general: *sitting becomes more fatiguing than standing if too much prolonged*; **b** a session of a deliberative body: *a sitting of Parliament*; **c** act of posing for a portrait: *to give a sitting to a painter, photographer.* **2.** Time occupied by a sitting; occasion on which a sitting in any sense takes place. **3.** Time during which some piece of sedentary work is uninterruptedly carried out; a spell, bout, of work: *to finish a job at a, one, sitting.* **4.** Seat reserved in a church for a particular person in return for rent; right thus acquired in such a seat.

5. Collection of eggs covered by a bird when sitting (in specif. sense); a clutch.

sitting-room, n. [1. síting room; 2. sítiŋ rum]; 1 A room in a house used for sitting in; contrasted with *bedroom, offices, bathroom* &c. 2. Space reserved for sitting; space sufficient to sit in: *there is very little sitting-room in a small aeroplane; sitting-room for two only.*

situate, adj. [1. síchooāt; 2. sítʃueit], fr. L. Lat. *situāt-(um)*, P.P. of *situāre*, 'to place', fr. *situs*, see **site**. (house agent's word) Situated.

situated, adj. [1. síchooāted; 2. sítʃueitid]. Prec. & **-ed**. Placed; having a particular site or position; **a** (in physical sense) *a pleasantly, badly, situated house, town* &c.; **b** (in non-physical sense) placed in certain conditions, circumstanced: *I am rather awkwardly situated having no house to go to.*

situation, n. [1. sichooáshun; 2. sitʃuéiʃən]. Fr. **situate** & **-ion**. 1. Place, locality, site, position, of anything in relation to other things, surroundings &c.: *a delightful situation for a house.* 2. **a** State, condition, position, of affairs; circumstances: *the political situation seems quiet; the situation at the front is critical; he found himself in a very delicate situation;* **b** specif., momentous combination of circumstances, clash of passions or personalities at a critical moment in a drama, or in life: *a thrilling, a tense, situation.* 3. Employment, job, place, position, in which specific duties are to be performed; chiefly used now of the humbler kinds of employment: *a situation as head porter, gardener, cook, butler* &c.

sitz-bath, n. [1. síts bàhth; 2. síts bàþ], fr. Mod. Germ. *sitz-bad*, fr. *sitzen*, 'to sit', q.v. A hip-bath.

Sivaism, Shivaism, n. [1. séva-, shévaizəm; 2. sívə-, ʃívəizəm], fr. Hind. *Shiva*, fr. Scrt. *śivāś*, 'propitious, gracious'; cogn. w. Lat. *cīvis*, q.v. under **civic**. The worship, by the Hindus, of Shiva as the supreme god of the Brahman triad, with Brahma and Vishnu.

Sivaist, Shivaist, n. [1. séva-, shévaist; 2. sívə-, ʃívəist]. See prec. & **-ist**. Worshipper of Siva.

Sivaistic, Shivaistic, adj. [1. sèva-, shèvaístik; 2. sivə-, ʃivəístik]. Prec. & **-ic**. Of, pertaining to, Sivaism.

six, adj. & n. [1. siks; 2. siks]. O.E. *six, seox, siex*, M.E. *six*; O.S. & O.H.G. *sehs*, O.N. *sex*; Goth. *saihs*; Lat. *sex*, see **sex-**, Gk. *héx* for **séx*, see **hexa-**, Scrt. *šaš*; O. Slav. *šesti*; W. *chwech*. 1. adj. **a** One more than five or less than seven: *six feet high, yards long; six years old* &c.; **b** elliptically, with noun understood: *six o'clock; half-past six*, 6.30; *six and six*, 6/6; *bet six to one against; the child is only six; a party of six.* Phr. *six of one and half a dozen of the other*, nothing to choose between two alternatives. 2. n. **a** The cardinal number six; the symbol for this number, 6, vi.; Phr. *at sixes and sevens*, upside-down, in confusion &c.; **b** a card, domino, dice, with six pips: *the six of hearts; play the double six or six blank; to throw a six;* **c** a hit for six runs at cricket; **d** a size of gloves, shoes; **e** (pl. *sixes*) candles running six to the pound.

sixain, n. [1. síkzān; 2. síkzein]. Fr., fr. *six*, Lat. *sex*, & **-ain**. A stanza of six lines; sextain.

sixer, n. [1. síkser; 2. síksə]. **six** & **-er**. (colloq.) A hit for six runs at cricket.

sixfold, adj. & adv. [1. síksfōld; 2. síksfould]. O.E. *sixfald*. **six** & **-fold**. Six times as much; six times over.

six-foot, adj. [1. síks foot; 2. síks fut]. Six feet in height, length &c.: *a six-foot plank* &c.

six-footer, n. [1. siks fóoter; 2. siks fútə]. (colloq.) Person six feet in height.

sixpence, n. [1. síkspens; 2. síkspəns]. **six** & *pence*, see **penny**. **a** A silver coin of the value of six pennies; half a shilling: *put a sixpence in the plate;* **b** value of this: *it cost me sixpence.* Phrs. *I don't care (a) sixpence about it*, care nothing at all; *it doesn't matter sixpence*, is of no consequence.

sixpenny, adj. [1. síkspeni; 2. síkspəni]. **a** Of the value of six pennies: *a sixpenny piece, bit*, a sixpence; **b** costing, worth, sixpence: *a sixpenny toy.*

six-score, adj. & n. Six times twenty, 120.

six-shooter, n. A revolver with six chambers.

sixte, n. [1. sikst; 2. sikst]. Fr., fr. Lat. *sextus*, 'sixth'. One of the parries in fencing.

sixteen, adj. & n. [1. síkstḗn; 2. sikstín]. O.E. *sixtȳne, sixtēne*. **six** & **-teen**. 1. adj. Six more than ten. 2. n. Sum of ten and six; symbol of this, 16, xvi.

sixteenth, adj. & n. [1. síkstḗnth; 2. síkstínþ]. New formation fr. **sixteen** & **-th**; O.E. form *sixtēoða*. 1. adj. Ordinal of sixteen; **a** next after fifteenth; **b** consisting of a sixteenth: *sixteenth part.* 2. n. One of sixteen equal parts.

sixth, adj. & n. [1. siksth; 2. siksþ]. New formation fr. **six** & **-th**, on anal. of *fourth*; O.E. *sixta*, M.E. *sixte, sexte*; *sixt* was used in 16th cent. 1. adj. **a** Ordinal of six; next in order after fifth: *the sixth day of the week* &c.; *in the sixth form;* **b** being one of six equal parts or divisions: *took a sixth share;* **c** as noun with ellipse of word: *the sixth of August; was in the sixth (form) at school; the sixth in the class.* 2. n. Specif. (mus.) interval between a tone and the sixth tone above or below, reckoned inclusively, on the diatonic scale.

sixthly, adv. Prec. & **-ly**. In the sixth place (only in enumeration).

sixtieth, adj. & n. [1. síkstieth; 2. síkstiiþ]. **sixty** & **-eth**. 1. adj. **a** Next in order after fifty-ninth; **b** forming one of sixty equal parts. 2. n. **a** The ordinal number following the fifty-ninth; **b** one of sixty equal parts.

sixty, adj. & n. [1. síksti; 2. síksti]. O.E. *sixtiġ*. **six** & **-ty**. 1. adj. Six times ten, also elliptically as noun: *not more than sixty were present (persons* understood); *I'll take sixty for the horse (pounds* understood). 2. n. **a** The sum of six times ten; **b** symbol representing this, 60, lx.

sizable, adj. [1. sízəbl; 2. sáizəbl]. **size** & **-able**. Of considerable size; of a suitable or reasonable size.

sizar, n. [1. sízər; 2. sáizə]. Earlier spelt *sizer*; fr. **size** (I.), in sense of a 'ration of bread and drink', & **-er**. In use at Cambridge and Trinity College, Dublin; an undergraduate student, corresponding to the Oxford servitor, who, after examination, was exempted from certain fees and other payments, and performed certain duties, now abolished, as the distribution of the 'size' or ration to the students of a higher grade, receiving his own 'size' free of charge.

sizarship, n. [1. sízərship; 2. sáizəʃip]. Prec. & **-ship**. Position, emoluments, of a sizar.

size (I.), n. [1. sīz; 2. saiz]. Shortened form of **assize**, in the old sense of 'that which is fixed or assessed'. Cp. **assess**. 1. (hist.) A fixed quantity, allowance, ration, of anything; specif., at Cambridge University, a ration of food or drink served from the buttery of a college. 2. (hist.) A standard measure of length, weight, or quantity, fixed by an assize; now, one of the conventional relative dimensions into which certain articles, as gloves, shoes, hats, ready-made clothes &c., are divided. 3. **a** Relative dimensions, magnitude, mass or bulk of an object: *a building of the largest size; the size of the book makes it awkward to hold; type of such small size is difficult to read; of what size is our future army to be?* Phr. *that's about the size of it*, (colloq.) that's the real fact, the true explanation; **b** also of intellectual and spiritual bulk or magnitude: *we want a man of a considerable size for the position of ruler.* 4. Specif., instrument used by dealers to grade and measure the size of pearls.

size (II.), vb. trans. & intrans., fr. prec. 1. trans. **a** To classify, arrange, grade according to size, esp. of soldiers, to arrange them in rank according to height, so that the tallest men are at each flank and the smaller in the centre: *to size a platoon, company* &c.: **b** *size up*, (colloq.) to estimate the value, character, ability &c. of; to form a general judgement about: *to size up a man, a situation.* 2. intrans. (obs.) To draw a 'size' or ration, as at Cambridge University.

size (III.), n. & vb. trans., fr. Ital. *sisa*, abbr. form of *assisa*, 'painter's glue, size', fr. P.P. fem. of *assidere*, 'to make to lie or sit down', fr. Lat. *assidēre*. See **assize** & **assess**. 1. n. A thin kind of glue or gelatinous solution used to glaze and stiffen paper, textiles &c. 2. vb. To apply size to; to glaze with size.

-sized, adj. [1. sīzd; 2. saizd]. **size** (II.) & **-ed**. (in compounds) Having a certain size or magnitude: *medium-sized* &c.

sizy, adj. [1. sízi; 2. sáizi]. **size** (III.) & **-y**. Of the nature of, covered with, size; gelatinous, viscous, gluey.

sizzle, vb. intrans. & n. [1. sízl; 2. sízl]. Of imitative origin. 1. vb. To make a hissing, spluttering sound, as of things frying or very hot; to fizzle. 2. n. A sizzling sound.

sjambok, n. & vb. trans. [1. shámbok; 2. ʃǽmbək]. S.A., fr. Du., fr. Malay *chamboq*, fr. Pers. *chābuq*, 'whip', also adj. 'quick, alert'. 1. n. A heavy whip with lash of rhinoceros hide. 2. vb. To flog with a sjambok.

skald, scald, n. [1. skawld; 2. skōld]. O.N. *skāld*; etymol. doubtful. One of the old Scandinavian bards; a composer and singer of poems in honour of the heroes and their deeds.

skat, n. [1. skaht; 2. skāt]. Mod. Germ.; according to Kluge, a 19th cent. loan-word, orig. *sca(r)t*, fr. Ital. *scartare*, 'to reject a card', *skat-karte* being the rejected or discarded card. Cp. **ecarté** & **card** (II.). A three-handed card game, played with a thirty-two card pack; one of the predecessors of bridge.

skate (I.), n. [1. skāt; 2. skeit], fr. O.N. *skata*, wh. is perh. fr. Lat. *squātus*, 'a flat fish'; cogn. w. Gk. *psêtta*, 'sole or turbot'. An edible flat fish, genus *Raia*, of the ray family.

skate (II.), n. Back-formation fr. *skates*; fr. Du. *schaatz(en)*, M.D. *schaetz(en)*, fr. O. Fr. *eschace*, 'stilt', Fr. *échasse*, fr. L.G. *shake*, 'leg', see **shank**; the word meant something wh. raised the leg off the ground & lengthened the stride. 1. One of a pair of sharp-edged steel blades fitted into a metal or wooden frame, and fastened by clamps, screwed plates, or straps to the boot, used for moving rapidly over a sheet of ice. 2. One of a pair of objects furnished with four small solid wheels, or rollers, attached to the feet, and used for moving rapidly over a smooth, flat surface, esp. in a rink; called also *roller-skate.*

skate (III.), vb. intrans., fr. prec. To move on skates over ice &c. Phr. *to skate over thin ice*, to treat a difficult or dangerous subject or situation with skill and tact.

skater, n. [1. skā́ter; 2. skéitə]. Prec. & **-er**. One who skates, esp. one who skates well.

skating, n. [1. skā́ting; 2. skéitiŋ]. **skate** (II.) & **-ing**. Act of moving on ice, or on a rink, with skates.

skating-rink, n. **a** Specially prepared surface on which roller skating is practised; **b** (rare) generally *ice-rink*, specially made sheet of ice used for skating.

skean, skene, n. [1. skēn; 2. skīn], fr. Gael. *sgian*, 'knife'. A short dagger or dirk, generally with an ornamented silver handle, as worn by Scottish Highlanders with native dress.

skean-dhu, n. [1. skḗn dū; 2. skín djū]. Prec. & Gael. *dubh*, 'black'. A small dirk or knife, worn in the stocking by Highlanders in native costume.

skedaddle, vb. intrans. & n. [1. skedádl; 2. skidǽdl]. Etymol. unknown. 1. vb. (colloq. and slang) To run away, to bolt; to depart in haste, to clear out. 2. n. (rare) A hasty flight or departure; a bolt.

skein, n. [1. skān; 2. skein]. M.E. *skeyn*, fr. O. Fr. *escaigne*; prob. of Celt. origin, cp. Gael. *sgeinnidh*, 'hemp or flax thread', Ir. *sgainne*, 'skein of thread'; possibly cogn. w. Gk. *skhoinos*, 'rope, cord'. **1.** A quantity of yarn, of wool, cotton, silk &c., coiled and knotted. **2.** A flock of wild geese or swans in flight.

skeletal, adj. [1. skéletal; 2. skélitəl]. See **skeleton** & **-al.** (anat.) Pertaining to the skeleton; of the nature of a skeleton: *skeletal muscles*, those attached to the bones; *a skeletal structure* &c.

skeleto-, pref. Form of **skeleton** used in compounds, indicating some relation to the skeleton or bony structures.

skeletology, n. [1. skèletóloji; 2. skèlɛtólədži]. Prec. & **-logy.** Study of the skeleton; osteology.

skeleton, n. [1. skéletun; 2. skélit(ə)n]. Gk., neut. sing. of *skeletós*, 'dried up, parched', as n., 'mummy'; cp. *skéllein*, 'to dry up, parch', cogn. w. *sklērós*, 'dry, hard', see **scler(o)-. 1.** The bony framework of the human or animal body; specif., the bones of the body as a whole, from which all the soft tissues have decayed or been removed: *of the body nothing was left but the skeleton*; *skeletons of men and animals are exhibited in museums.* Phr. *skeleton at the feast*, a person whose presence casts a gloom on an occasion of rejoicing; *a, the, skeleton in the cupboard, family skeleton*, some distressing, shameful, or discreditable fact, affecting an individual or family, the secret of which is carefully guarded by him or them; *reduced to a skeleton*, very thin and emaciated by illness; *worn to a skeleton*, thin and worn from toil, want, anxiety &c.; *a mere skeleton*, a thin, emaciated person. **2.** The fine lace-like fibrous framework of a leaf from which all the tissue has disappeared. **3. a** The framework of a building: *many modern buildings are constructed upon steel skeletons*; **b** the remaining framework or other remnants of a building &c. wh. survive after some destructive agent, such as fire or natural decay, has brought it to ruin; a shell. **4.** An outline, preliminary, general plan, of a piece of literary or scientific work, of a speech, lecture &c., the details of which have still to be filled in.

skeleton army, n. An army with a few men representing each unit of a large force and marking their presence by flags or other signals extended over a wide area.

skeleton crew, n. A crew reduced in numbers to the minimum required for keeping a ship seaworthy, and ready to be enlarged to full complement when required.

skeleton drill, n. Practice drill, for officers, with only flank men of a line present.

skeletonize, vb. trans. [1. skéletunīz; 2. skélitəndīz]. **skeleton** & **-ize. 1.** To reduce (an animal body) to a skeleton by removing the tissues, muscles &c.; to prepare (a body) for exhibition as a skeleton. **2.** To put down in outline; to reduce to a brief sketch or abstract.

skeleton key, n. A key with parts of the bit filed away, and capable of opening a large variety of locks; a form of master-key.

skene, n. See **skean.**

skep, n. [1. skep; 2. skɛp], fr. O.N. *skeppa*, 'basket, bushel'. **1. a** A light kind of basket, of wicker-work or wood, used for carrying or measuring light farm or garden produce; **b** a measure of capacity for such, varying in different districts. **2.** A beehive of straw.

skeptic &c. See **sceptic.**

skerry, n. [1. skéri; 2. skéri]. Scand., fr. O.N. *sker*; cp. **scar (II.), scaur.** A small, isolated rock or reef in the sea.

sketch (I.), n. [1. skech; 2. skɛtʃ]. Du. *schets*, fr. Ital. *schizzo*, through Lat. *schedium*, 'extempore poem', fr. Gk. *skhédios*, 'extempore'; see further under **scheme. 1. a** A rapidly executed drawing of an object, scene, landscape &c., made in outline or simple washes, in pencil, chalk, water-colour &c., serving as a study for a finished picture or as a note for further use in aiding the memory; also **b** a drawing or painting in a slight or broad manner, not intended to be worked on further. **2.** A rough preliminary draft, synopsis, outline, epitome, of a plan, literary work &c. **3. a** A short musical or dramatic play; **b** a short, descriptive article.

sketch (II.), vb. trans. & intrans., fr. prec. **1.** trans. **a** To make a sketch of: *to sketch a scene, person's head* &c.; **b** (also with *out*) to draw up a sketch or outlined plan of, to make a rough draft of; to plan, indicate, by giving only essential details: *to sketch (out) a scheme, plan*; *he sketched the situation in a few vivid words.* **2.** intrans. To practise the art of making sketches; to paint landscapes &c. in water-colours.

sketch-book, n. **a** A book containing paper suitable for making sketches on; **b** book containing an artist's sketches.

sketcher, n. [1. skécher; 2. skétʃə]. **sketch (II.)** & **-er.** One who sketches.

sketchily, adv. [1. skéchili; 2. skétʃili]. **sketchy** & **-ly.** In a sketchy manner.

sketchiness, n. [1. skéchines; 2. skétʃinis]. **sketchy** & **-ness.** State, quality, of being sketchy.

sketching, n. [1. skéching; 2. skétʃiŋ]. **sketch (II.)** & **-ing.** Art, practice, of making sketches.

sketchy, adj. [1. skéchi; 2. skétʃi]. **sketch (I.)** & **-y.** Depicted in outline or roughly; having only an outline and few or no details; hence, unfinished, incomplete, inadequate: *only a sketchy knowledge of philology*; *a rather sketchy meal*; *the lecture was too sketchy to be much good.*

skew, adj. & n. [1. skū; 2. skjū], fr. obs. vb. *skew, skue*, M.E. *skewen*, 'to turn, move, to one side; to shy', fr. M. Du. *schouwen*, 'to avoid, shun,', cogn. w. O.H.G. *sciuhen*, 'to avoid, escape', cp. Germ. *scheu*, 'shy', see **shy (I.). 1.** adj. **a** Oblique, sloping; turned, twisted, to one side, crooked, chiefly in compounds, in technical terms; see below and cp. **askew; b** (math.) unsymmetrical, distorted. **2.** n. (archit.) A sloping stone cut to hold the coping of a gable &c.; the upper, sloping top of a buttress.

skewback, n. [1. skúbak; 2. skjúbæk]. The sloped face of part of an abutment used to carry the thrust of an arch which projects beyond the vertical line of the opening.

skewbald, adj. [1. skúbawld; 2. skjúbɔld]. **skew**, in sense of 'irregular', & **bald**, cp. **piebald.** (of horse &c.) Marked with irregular patches of different colours; used by some to imply black and white, by others to mean a patchiness in which black does not occur; sometimes distinguished from *piebald.*

skew-bridge, n. A bridge with an arch or arches set obliquely to the abutments.

skew-chisel, n. **a** A chisel with oblique edge; **b** chisel with bent shank to allow the edge to work in a sunk groove &c.

skew-curve, n. (math.) A curve in three dimensions.

skewer, n. & vb. trans. [1. skúer; 2. skjúə]. Scand., cp. Swed. *skifer*, 'a slate'; provinc. Engl. *skiver*, 'skewer'; variant of **shiver (III.)**, 'splinter'. **1.** n. **a** A thin pointed rod or pin of wood or metal used for fastening a piece of meat together and keeping it in shape for cooking; **b** humorous term for a sword, dagger. **2.** vb. To fasten (meat &c.) with a skewer.

skew-eyed, adj. **skew** & **eyed.** Squinting.

ski, n. & vb. intrans. [1. shē, skē; 2. ʃī, skī]. Norw. & Dan., fr. O.N. *skīð*, 'billet of wood, snow-shoe'; cogn. w. **skid (I.). 1.** n. One of a pair of long, narrow strips of hard wood, strapped to the feet and used as runners for moving over frozen snow, and for racing and jumping &c. as a form of sport. **2.** vb. To use skis for travelling &c. over snow.

skiagram, n. See **sciagram.**

skiagraph, n. See **sciagraph.**

skid (I.), n. [1. skid; 2. skid], fr. O.N. *skīð*, 'wooden billet'; the Engl. cogn. is seen in M.E. *shide*, 'billet, thin piece of board', obs. except in dial. & some techn. uses; cogn. w. **sheath** & **shed (I.). 1.** A drag, shoe, clog of any kind placed under a wheel of a heavy cart to reduce speed downhill. **2.** A side-slip or slide of wheel of bicycle or motor-car on a slippery road.

skid (II.), vb. intrans. & trans., fr. prec. **1.** intrans. To slip sideways (of wheels). **2.** trans. (rare) To retard speed of by means of a skid or drag.

skier, n. [1. shéer; 2. ʃíə]. **ski** & **-er.** One who skis; user of skis to travel or run over snow.

skiff, n. [1. skif; 2. skif], fr. Fr. *esquif*, fr. Ital. *schifo*, 'little boat', fr. O.H.G. *skif*, cogn. w. **ship. a** A light rowing or sculling boat, usually for a single rower or sculler; **b** (poet. or obs.) any small boat.

ski-ing, n. [1. shéing; 2. ʃíiŋ]. **ski** & **-ing.** Act of moving along on skis; this considered as a sport.

skilful, adj. [1. skílfool; 2. skílful]. **skill (I.)** & **-ful. a** Possessing skill: *a skilful surgeon*; **b** performed with skill: *a skilful cross-examination* &c.

skilfully, adv. Prec. & **-ly.** In a skilful manner; with skill.

skilfulness, n. Prec. & **-ness.** Quality of being skilful; skill.

skill (I.), n. [1. skil; 2. skil]. In M.E., fr. O.N. *skil*, 'discernment', cp. *skilja*, 'to separate, distinguish, discriminate'; orig. sense of base 'to split'. See also under **shell. 1.** Manual dexterity and deftness, proficiency, resulting from training, practice, experience: *skill in fencing, boxing*; *skill in watch-making, carpentry*; *the skill of a surgeon.* **2.** Intellectual adroitness, resourcefulness, cleverness, ingenuity: *skill in diplomacy, lecturing, teaching*; *skill in debate* &c.

skill (II.), vb. intrans., fr. O.N. *skilja.* See prec. word. (archaic; impers.) *It skills not*, it makes no difference, it matters not; *what skills it that we die?*

skilled, adj. [1. skild; 2. skild]. **skill (I.)** & **-ed. a** Possessing manual or intellectual skill, esp. of some specified kind: *a skilled watch-maker*; *a skilled debater* &c.; **b** specif. (of workmen) trained and practised in some particular trade or handicraft, and having gone through an apprenticeship in it; also *skilled work*, such as requires special training to perform; contrasted with *unskilled*, in specific sense.

skilless, adj. [1. skílles; 2. skíllis]. **skill (I.)** & **-less.** (rare or archaic) Lacking skill.

skillet, n. [1. skílet; 2. skílit], fr. O. Fr. *escuellete*, dimin. of *escuelle*, 'dish, pan', fr. Lat. *scutella*, dimin. of *scūta*, 'dish'. Cp. also **scuttle (I.).** A small metal cooking-pot with long handle and three or four legs.

skilly, n. [1. skíli; 2. skíli]. Shortened form of earlier *skilligalee*; etymol. unknown. Thin oatmeal gruel or thin broth mixed with some meat, as formerly served in workhouses or prisons.

skim, vb. trans. & intrans. [1. skim; 2. skim]. The word looks like a form produced by *i*-mutation fr. O.N. *skūm*, w. shortening as in the loan-word **scum. A.** trans. **1.** To remove the scum, cream, fat, or other substance floating on the surface of a liquid: *to skim the cream off milk*; also *to skim milk*, remove cream from surface. **2.** To glide over the surface of; to pass lightly or swiftly over; to touch or nearly touch the surface of, in passing over it: *a gull skims the water*; *a skater skims the ice*; *a swift runner seems to skim the ground.* **3.** To read, run through (a book &c.) rapidly and perfunctorily. **B.** intrans. **1.** *Skim over*, to become coated with a film, scum &c., on the surface. **2.** To move, glide, along, lightly and rapidly: *the boat, a bird, skims before the breeze*; also *skim along, over, through*; *a skater, a stone, skims along the ice.* **3.** To read a book rapidly and perfunctorily, to skip: *read carefully, don't skim*; also *to skim through a book.*

skimmer, n. [1. skímer; 2. skímə]. **skim** & **-er**. **1. a** One who skims; specif. **b** a long-winged sea-bird, genus *Rhynchops*, with the lower mandible longer than the upper, with which it skims up fish near the surface of the water as it flies. **2.** Utensil used for skimming liquids, such as milk.

skim-milk, n. Milk from which the cream has been skimmed.

skimp, vb. trans. & intrans. [1. skimp; 2. skimp]. Etymol. doubtful; prob. allied to O.N. *skemma*, 'to make short, shorten', & to **scant** & **scamp** (II.). **1.** trans. **a** To stint, grudge, act meanly towards (a person); **b** to supply (things) in too small an amount; give, allow, insufficient quantity of. **2.** intrans. To be parsimonious, practise petty economies. Phr. *to skimp and screw.*

skimpily, adv. [1. skímpili; 2. skímpili]. **skimpy** & **-ly**. In a skimpy manner; stingily, meagrely.

skimpy, adj. [1. skímpi; 2. skímpi]. **skimp** & **-y**. Scant, skimped, inadequate, meagre, in quantity, amount, amplitude: *a skirt which is skimpy round the hips.*

skin (I.), n. [1. skin; 2. skin]. Found as *scinn* in Late O.E., borrowed fr. O.N. *skinn*; O.H.G. has *scintan*, 'to take the skin off, to flay', though the n. does not occur. Etymol. unknown. **1.** The outer, flexible covering or integument of the animal body; consisting of the epidermis or cuticle and the corium or true skin, with its sebaceous glands, hair follicles &c. Phrs. *to save one's skin*, to escape with one's life; escape uninjured in body, reputation &c.; *with a whole skin*, uninjured; *with, by, the skin of one's teeth*, by the narrowest margin of safety; *to have a thick, thin, skin*, to be insensitive, or the reverse, to criticism, insults &c.; *to be mere skin and bone*, to be emaciated, excessively thin or skinny. **2.** The stripped, dressed, and preserved outer covering of an animal or bird, including the actual cuticle, and the hair, fur, or feathers growing from this; hide, pelt. **3.** (slang) **a** A horse or other beast; **b** specif., a poor, worn-out, emaciated horse; hence, **c** (jocose) a person: *the headmaster isn't a bad old skin.* **4.** A receptacle for wine, water &c., made from an animal's skin. **5.** The rind of a fruit. **6.** A thin film which has formed on a liquid, and acquired a certain toughness and consistency. **7.** The outermost layer, covering, surface, of various objects; **a** the outer layer of planks or plates on the hull of a ship; **b** the outer layer of nacre on a pearl.

skin (II.), vb. trans. & intrans., fr. prec. **A.** trans. **1. a** To remove, strip off, the skin from; to flay: *to skin a tiger* &c.; **b** to remove the peel or rind from; to peel: *skin a walnut*; Phrs. *to skin a flint*, to be exceedingly miserly and penurious; *to keep one's eyes skinned* (colloq.), to be very watchful and alert; **c** to abrade, graze, scrape off, skin from: *fell and skinned his knee.* **2.** (slang) To fleece, swindle, do out of money or other possessions: *the gamblers skinned him of every shilling.* **B.** intrans. *Skin over*, to become covered with skin; to cicatrize: *the wound has skinned over too quickly.*

skin-bound, adj. With skin stretched too tightly over, or adhering too closely to, the flesh.

skin-deep, adj. Not penetrating deeper than the skin, not affecting the tissues; superficial; esp. of wounds.

skinflint, n. [1. skínflint; 2. skínflint]. One who extracts the utmost profit or advantage from a transaction; a mean, avaricious, niggardly, stingy person.

skin friction, n. Friction exerted upon the surface of a body moving through a liquid, e.g. that upon the sides of a ship moving through water.

skinful, n. [1. skínfool; 2. skínful]. **skin** (I.) & **-ful**. Chiefly used in Phr. *skinful of drink*, as much drink as one can hold.

skink, n. [1. skingk; 2. skiŋk], fr. Lat. *scincus*. fr. Gk. *skígkos*. A kind of lizard, with thickish body and short tail and limbs, found in N. Africa in dry sandy places.

-skinned, adj. [1. skind; 2. skind]. **skin** (II.) & **-ed**. Having a skin of specified kind: *thin-skinned*; *clear-skinned* &c.

skinner, n. [1. skíner; 2. skínə]. **skin** (I.) & **-er**. A dealer in pelts and hides.

skinny, adj. [1. skíni; 2. skíni]. **skin** (I.) & **-y**. Very thin or emaciated; reduced to skin and bone; scraggy.

skip (I.), vb. intrans. & trans. [1. skip; 2. skip]. In M.E.; origin uncertain; prob. Scand. **A.** intrans. **1.** To leap, or bound lightly about, like a child or young animal; to frisk, frolic, gambol; commonly, *skip about.* **2.** Specif., to bound or hop lightly, at the same time swinging a rope with both hands so that the middle of it passes with a circular motion alternately over the head and under the feet. **3.** (colloq.) **a** To depart, disappear, hastily and suddenly; to bolt; **b** to travel rapidly, undertake a brief journey: *to skip over, across, to France for a week.* **4.** To read a book through hastily and perfunctorily, omitting large portions of it. **B.** trans. **1.** To jump, bound, lightly over or across; more often *skip over, across*; *to skip (over) a brook.* **2. a** To read perfunctorily or omit altogether; pass rapidly over in reading: *to skip the dull parts of a book*; **b** to leave out, omit to mention, in narration: *I shall skip the events of the next few days.* **3.** Colloquial Phr. *skip it*, to go away, skedaddle, hook it.

skip (II.), n., fr. prec. A light jump or bound; specif., a quick leap from one foot to the other: *a hop, skip, and a jump.*

skip (III.), n., prob. for **skipper** (II.). The captain of a team or side at bowls and curling.

skip (IV.), n., variant of **skep**. An iron bucket used for hoisting coal in a mine; also small iron truck or tub running on rails in a coal-mine.

skip (V.), n.; etymol. doubtful, prob. fr. **skip** (I.). A college servant at Trinity College, Dublin; equivalent to the Oxford *scout* and Cambridge *gyp.*

skipjack, n. [1. skípjak; 2. skípdžæk]. **skip** (I.) & **Jack** (I.). **1.** Small doll formed from the wish-bone of a fowl, made to leap into the air by means of a piece of elastic. **2.** Popular name for any of several small animals which have a quick, jumping movement.

skipper (I.), n. [1. skíper; 2. skípə]. **skip** (I.) & **-er**. **a** One who, that which, skips; **b** a skipjack.

skipper (II.), n. [1. skíper; 2. skípə], fr. Du. *schipper*, fr. *schip*, cogn. w. **ship**. Captain, master, of a small merchant ship; hence (colloq.) the captain of any ship.

skippet, n. [1. skípet; 2. skípit]. Dimin. of **skep**. A case or box used to enclose and protect the large pendent seal attached to an official document.

skipping-rope, n. [1. skíping rōp; 2. skípiŋ ròup]. A rope with a wooden handle at each end, used for skipping.

skirl, vb. intrans. & n. [1. skërl; 2. skāl]. Scots variant of **shrill**. **1.** vb. To make a shrill, piercing sound, like that of the bagpipes. **2.** n. The shrill, piercing flourish of the bagpipes.

skirmish, vb. intrans. & n. [1. skërmish; 2. skāmiʃ]. M.E. *skirmishen*, fr. O. Fr. *eskermiss-*, stem of *eskermir*, 'to fence, fight'; fr. O.H.G. *scirman*, 'to fight under cover', Germ. *schirmen*, 'to defend', fr. *scirm*, 'shield, defence, cover'. Cp. also **scaramouch** & **scrimmage**. **1.** vb. To engage in a skirmish. **2.** n. **a** A fight between small, detached bodies of troops or as incidental to a battle; any slight, unimportant, or unexpected engagement between detachments of opposing armies; **b** any slight, brief contest, argument.

skirmisher, n. [1. skërmisher; 2. skāmiʃə]. **skirmish** & **-er**. One who skirmishes; specif., one of a body of detached troops sent forward or to a flank, in extended order, to cover a movement of the main body.

skirret, n. [1. skíret; 2. skírit]. Earlier spelt *skirwhit*, as though fr. O.N. *skírr*, 'bright, clear', see under **sheer** (I.) & **white**; more prob. a modification of O. Fr. *eschervis*, Fr. *chervis*, fr. Span. *chirivia*, fr. Arab. *karawia*. See **caraway**. A plant, allied to the celery and parsnip, with edible tuberous root; the water-parsnip.

skirt (I.), n. [1. skërt; 2. skāt], fr. O.N. *skyrt*, 'kirtle, skirt', cogn. w. **shirt**. **1. a** Lower part of any garment, as coat, shirt &c., which hangs below the waist: '*Laid hold upon the skirt of his mantle*' (1 Sam. xv. 27); **b** specif., outer garment worn by women covering the legs. **2.** (vulg. slang) A woman. **3.** (often pl.) The outer edge, margin, border, of anything: *on the skirts of the wood, town*; *the skirts of a cloud.* **4.** In various technical senses: **a** the leather flaps of a saddle covering the iron loops to which the stirrups are attached; **b** butcher's term for the midriff of beef &c.; **c** skirting-board.

skirt (II.), vb. trans. & intrans., fr. prec. **1.** trans. **a** To form the border, edge, or margin of; to be situated on the margin of: *the road skirts the wood*; **b** to move, pass along, or close to, the border of: *ship skirted the coast.* **2.** intrans. (w. preps.) To move, go close, to border &c.: *to skirt along the edge of a cliff.*

skirt-dancing, n. Dancing with long, full skirts, which are waved rhythmically.

-skirted, adj. [1. skërted; 2. skātid]. **skirt** (I.) & **-ed**. Having a skirt of specified kind: *short-, full-skirted* &c.

skirting-board, n. [1. skërting bòrd; 2. skātiŋ bɔ̀d]. A board running round the bottom of the walls of a room.

skit, n. [1. skit; 2. skit], fr. an old word meaning 'to shoot, to taunt, jibe at'; of Scand. origin, cp. O.N. *skjōta*, 'to shoot, to dart'; cogn. w. **shoot**. A light, humorous, satirical, literary or dramatic sketch or burlesque; a parody, *upon, on*, any subject &c.

skitter, vb. intrans. [1. skíter; 2. skítə]. Freq., fr. prec. & **-er**. **a** (of sea-bird, wild duck &c.) To skim rapidly over the surface of water with splashing touches, of wings or legs, as in rising; **b** (in fishing) to draw the hook and bait along near the surface of the water.

skittish, adj. [1. skítish; 2. skítiʃ]. See **skit** & **-ish**. **1.** (of a horse) Playful, lively, frisky, fresh; inclined to jump about in harness or with rider. **2.** (of persons) Lively and playful; frolicsome; said esp. of a woman past her first youth who affects the airs and graces and sprightliness of girlhood.

skittishly, adv. Prec. & **-ly**. In a skittish manner.

skittishness, n. See prec. & **-ness**. Quality of being skittish; skittish behaviour.

skittle, vb. trans. [1. skítl; 2. skítl]. See next word. **1.** (colloq.) *Skittle away* (one's money, resources, chances in life &c.), to waste, squander, lose by foolish conduct. **2.** *Skittle out*, (cricket) to bowl (batsmen) out easily or quickly.

skittles, n. pl. (1. skítlz; 2. skítlz), not used in sing. except attributively, fr. Dan. *skyttel*, 'a child's earthen ball', Scand. form of **shuttle**. **a** Set of ninepins used in the game of skittles; **b** game resembling ninepins, in which a heavy wooden disk, 'cheese', is bowled along a wooden course at the skittles. Phrs. *not all beer and skittles*, not all fun and amusement; (slang) *skittles!*, exclamation of contempt.

skive, vb. trans. & n. [1. skīv; 2. skaiv]. Scand.; cp. O.N. *skīfa*, 'slice', cogn. w. **sheave**. (rare) **1.** vb. **a** To pare, split, cut (hide, leather &c.), into thin slices; **b** to grind (gem-stones) on a skive. **2.** n. A diamond wheel for grinding gem-stones.

skiver, n. [1. skíver; 2. skáivə]. Prec. & **-er**. **a** Cheap leather made from split sheepskin; used for bindings, linings &c.; **b** knife used in skiving leather

skua, n. [1. skúa; 2. skjúə], fr. O.N. *skūfr*, also *skūmr*, prob. so called fr. its dark colour, cp. O.N. *skūmi*, 'shade, dusk'. One of several large, dark-brown gulls of the N. Atlantic and Arctic and Antarctic seas.

skulk, vb. intrans. & n. [1. skulk; 2. skalk]. Scand., cp. Dan. *skulke*, 'to skulk', cogn. w. O.N. *skolla*, see **scowl**, & cp. Swed. *skolka*, 'to shirk', L.G. *schulen*, 'to skulk'. **1. a** To seclude oneself, hide; to lurk in concealment; **b** to slink furtively away or about. **2.** Specif., to shirk duties and dangers; keep oneself out of the way so as to avoid danger &c. **3.** n. (rare) One who skulks.

skulker, n. [1. skúlker; 2. skálkə]. Prec. & **-er**. One who skulks; a shirker.

skulking, adj. [1. skúlking; 2. skálkiŋ], fr. Pres. Part. of **skulk**. Inclined to evade and avoid danger or dangerous duties; cowardly, evasive, shirking: *a skulking coward, rogue.*

skull, n. [1. skul; 2. skal]. M.E. *sculle, skulle*; of Scand. origin; cp. Swed. dial. *skulle*, variant of Norw. *skult*; fr. Gmc. base a different grade of wh. appears in **scale (I.)** & **shell**; cp. also **scull**. **1. a** The bony case containing the brain of animals; Phr. *to have a thick skull*, to be stupid and impervious to ideas; **b** the bones of the head as a whole when stripped of flesh. **2.** A pictorial, or other representation of a skull, as a symbol of death; *skull and cross-bones*, a skull with two thigh bones crossed below it, on a black ground, the typical pirate's flag.

skull-cap, n. **1.** The upper part of the cranium; brain-pan. **2.** A close-fitting brimless cap, worn in the house to protect bald heads from cold or draughts.

-skulled, adj. [1. skuld; 2. skald]. **skull** & **-ed**. Having a skull of a specified kind: *thick-skulled; broad-, long-skulled.*

skunk, n. [1. skungk; 2. skaŋk]. Shortened form of native N. Am. Indian name, *seganku*. **1.** A small carnivorous N. American mammal, *Mephitis*, allied to the weasel and polecat, with bushy tail and black fur, striped on back with white, which when attacked emits from anal glands a secretion with a very offensive odour. **2.** (colloq.) An offensive, mean, contemptible person.

Skupshtina, n. [1. skóopshtina; 2. skúpʃtina]. Serb. fr. *skupiti*, 'to meet'. The parliament of Yugo-Slavia.

sky (I.), n. [1. skī; 2. skai]. M.E. (Chaucer & Gower) *skie*, 'cloud', fr. O.N. *ský*; cogn. w. O.E. *scēo*, 'cloud'. See further under **obscure**, **shower**, & **cutis**. **1.** The vault of heaven, the upper atmosphere. Phrs. *under the open sky*, the open air, with no roof or shelter above one; *to praise to the skies*, praise excessively. **2.** (often pl.) Place of clouds, storms, and other meteorological phenomena; climate, weather: *under brighter skies than ours.* **3.** (in the language of devotion) Heaven, the dwelling-place of God.

sky (II.), vb. trans., fr. prec. **1.** To place in a lofty position; specif., to hang (a picture) at an exhibition somewhere near the ceiling, where it can hardly be seen, thus implying that it is an inferior work. **2.** To hit (a ball) high into the air.

sky-blue, adj. & n. **1.** adj. Having the bright blue colour of the clear, cloudless sky. **2.** n. This colour.

Skye terrier, n. [1. skī térier; 2. skái tériə], fr. the Isle of Skye, Hebrides. A variety of Scotch terrier, with long body, short legs, and long, silky, grey- or fawn-coloured hair.

sky-high, adj. & adv. (colloq.) As high as the sky, very high.

skylark (I.), n. [1. skīlark; 2. skáilāk]. The common lark of the open fields and downs, *Alauda arvensis*, nesting on the ground, and famous for its song as it rises almost perpendicularly into the air.

skylark (II.), vb. intrans. & n., fr. prec. **1.** vb. **a** (orig. naut.) To cut capers in the rigging of a ship, high above the deck; **b** to romp, engage in boisterous play. **2.** n. Boisterous merriment or play; usually *skylarking.*

skyless, adj. [1. skīles; 2. skáilis]. **sky (I.)** & **-less**. With no sky visible; cloudy.

skylight, n. [1. skīlīt; 2. skáilait]. A glazed opening in a roof, or in a ceiling, which admits light to a hall, passage, or room.

sky-line, n. **a** The line which, to the eye, separates earth and sky; visible horizon; **b** outline, silhouette, of an object seen against the sky.

sky-pilot, n. (slang) A clergyman; esp. a ship's chaplain.

skysail, n. [1. skīsàl; 2. skáisèil]. A small sail set above the royals in square-rigged sailing-vessels.

skyscape, sky-scape, n. [1. skīskāp; 2. skáiskeip]. On anal. of *landscape*. A picture, study, of sky and clouds.

sky-scraper, n. **sky (I.)** & **scraper**. **1.** A skysail. **2.** A very lofty building, containing a large number of storeys; used esp. of such as are built in America.

skyward(s), adv. & adj. [1. skīward(z); 2. skáiwəd(z)]. **sky (I.)** & **-ward(s)**. Toward(s) the sky, upwards.

slab (I.), n. & vb. trans. [1. slab; 2. slæb], fr. O. Fr. *esclape*, 'thin fragment of wood', of doubtful etymol.; cogn. w. Provenç. *esclapa*, Ital. *schiappare*, 'to split, cleave'; possibly fr. *es-* (*ex-*), as intens. pref., & L.G. *klappen*, 'to clap, go off with explosive sound, as of split wood'. **1.** n. **a** A flat, relatively thin slice of any solid material; esp. of wood, stone, meat, bread, cake; specif. **b** the outside piece sawn off a timber log in squaring it for cutting it into planks. **2.** vb. To saw the slab off (log &c.).

slab (II.), n. & adj., fr. O.N. *slabb*, 'mud'. **1.** n. (archaic or dial.) Slime, mud, a puddle. **2.** adj. Thick and sticky, viscous, slimy; chiefly familiar from '*Make the gruel thick and slab*' ('Macbeth').

slabber (I.), n. [1. sláber; 2. slǽbə]. **slab (I.)** & **-er**. A saw for cutting the slabs off logs; slabbing saw.

slabber (II.), vb. See **slobber**.

slab-stone, n. **slab (I.)** & **stone**. Stone, such as sandstone, which splits easily into slabs.

slack (I.), adj. [1. slak; 2. slæk]. O.E. *sleac, slæc*, 'slow, slack', cogn. w. O.N. *slakr*, O.S. *slak*, O.H.G. *slah*; allied to **lax (I.)** & **slake**. **1.** Slow, sluggish, not moving rapidly: *at a slack pace, speed*; specif., *slack water*, **a** (of tide) dead, not moving on the surface, as at period between end of ebb and beginning of flood tide; **b** (of stream) with no visible current, as at head of dam &c., or under shelter of curving bank; Phr. (naut.) *slack in stays*, (of sailing-vessel) slow in going about. **2. a** Relaxed, left or let loose; not taut or tight: *a slack rope; leave your muscles slack; ride, drive, with a slack rein; keep only a slack hand on the rein*; **b** specif. (phon.) *slack vowels*, those uttered with the tongue in a slack condition; contrasted with *tense*; also called, rather misleadingly, *open vowels*, and by other phoneticians *wide vowels*. **3.** Not energetic or active; lazy, listless; negligent, remiss: *to feel slack; to be slack in one's duties, work.* **4.** Not brisk or active or busy; having no life or movement; dull: *trade, business, is slack; a slack season.* **5. a** Not sufficiently baked or dried: *slack bread, hops*; **b** slaked: *slack lime.*

slack (II.), n., fr. prec. **1.** Part of anything left slack or loose: *slack of a rope, sail* &c.; *to pull in, up, the slack*, tighten it. **2.** (pl. *slacks*) Loose trousers or overalls worn by soldiers on fatigue duty &c. **3.** Slack water; period of this: *at the slack of the tide.* **4.** (colloq.) Bout, spell, of slackness, inactivity, or rest: *to have a good slack.*

slack (III.), vb. trans. & intrans., fr. **slack (I.)**. **A.** trans. **a** To slacken; **b** *slack off* (*rope* &c.), to loosen, remove strain from by lengthening or loosening. **B.** intrans. **1.** To become loose or slack; to sag: *rope, sail, slacks.* **2. a** To work slackly; to be idle, lazy, remiss, or negligent: *to slack at one's job*; *to slack for the whole afternoon*; **b** *slack off*, to diminish one's efforts, slow down, preparatory to ceasing work &c.; **c** *slack up*, to reduce speed, to go more slowly.

slack (IV.), n. L.G. *slacke*. See also **slag**. Small coal; coal-dust.

slack-, adv. Only in *slack-baked, slack-dried* &c. See **slack (I.)**, **5.**

slacken, vb. trans. & intrans. [1. sláken; 2. slǽkən]. **slack (I.)** & **-en**. **A.** trans. **1.** To cause to be slack and unbraced; to loosen, relax: *to slacken a rope, one's muscles.* **2.** To diminish, abate; to make less intense; to lessen the energy or force of: *to slacken one's efforts; to slacken speed.* **B.** intrans. **1.** To become slack or loose: *rope slackens.* **2.** To become less energetic or active: *to slacken in one's efforts, work* &c. **3.** To diminish gradually in violence, to abate &c.: *the wind, fire, has slackened.*

slacker, n. [1. sláker; 2. slǽkə]. **slack (III.)** & **-er**. (colloq.) One who slacks or takes things easy; one who is slack, lazy, negligent, or remiss at work, games &c.; an idle fellow, lacking energy and vigour; a shirker.

slackly, adv. [1. slákli; 2. slǽkli]. **slack (I.)** & **-ly**. In a slack manner; **a** loosely, floppily; **b** lazily, negligently.

slackness, n. [1. sláknes; 2. slǽknis]. **slack (I.)** & **-ness**. **1.** Slack condition; looseness, lack of tenseness, state of being unbraced. **2.** Quality of being slack in action or mind; lack of energy; laziness; negligence.

slag, n. & vb. trans. & intrans. [1. slag; 2. slæg], fr. Swed. *slagg*, 'dross', cogn. w. Norw. *slagga*, 'to flow over', L.G. *slakke*, Germ. *schlacke*, 'scoria'; linguistic variant of **slack (IV.)**. **1.** n. **a** The dross, cinder, refuse, left after smelting metallic ore; **b** volcanic scoria. **2.** vb. To form, be formed into, slag; to convert, be converted into or combine as slag.

slaggy, adj. [1. slági; 2. slǽgi]. Prec. & **-y**. Of the nature of slag.

slain, vb. [1. slān; 2. slein]. O.E. (*ġe*)*sleġen*, *-slæġen*; M.E. *sleȝen*, 'slain'; P.P. of **slay**.

slake, vb. trans. [1. slāk; 2. sleik]. O.E. *sleacian*, 'to grow slack, slacken', M.E. *slāken*, 'to make, slack'. See **slack (I.)**, of wh. it is a variant. **1.** To render less intense; to assuage, satisfy, quench, allay: **a** (in physical sense) *to slake one's thirst*; **b** (fig.) *to slake one's longing for vengeance*; *to slake one's lust of blood* &c. **2.** To mix with water, so as to form a chemical compound: *to slake lime.*

slakeless, adj. [1. slākles; 2. sléiklis]. Prec. & **-less**. (poet.) Unquenchable, quenchless, not to be assuaged or satisfied: *slakeless desire, vengeance* &c.

slam (I.), vb. trans. & intrans. [1. slam; 2. slæm]. Cp. Swed. *slemma*, 'to bang'; of imitative origin. **1.** trans. **a** To shut, close, violently, with a bang; also *slam to*: *to slam* (*to*) *a door, window* &c.; **b** to put, throw, down hastily and violently, or noisily: *to slam down the lid of a trunk*; *to slam one's hand on the table, hat on one's head* &c.; **c** to beat, hit: *he got badly slammed about the head*; *cricketer slams the bowling.* **2.** intrans. To be shut, to close with a bang: *to hear a door slam.*

slam (II.), n., fr. prec. **1.** A loud bang or noise, as of a door slamming. **2.** (cards) The taking, winning, of all tricks in one deal, as at bridge &c.

slander (I.), n. [1. sláhnder; 2. slā́ndə]. M.E. *sclaundre*, fr. O. Fr. *esclandre*, for earlier *escand(e)le, escandre*, fr. Lat. *scandalum*, see **scandal**. **1.** (law) Malicious defamation, by words, of a person, in his reputation, character, profession, or trade; utterance of false statements about a person with intent to injure or defame, cp. **libel**; *slander of title*, false, malicious statement casting doubt on a person's title to property; (loosely) any false statement likely to damage the value of property. **2.** A false tale, report &c.; disparaging, untrue statement about a person.

slander (II.), vb. trans., fr. prec. To utter slander concerning; to defame, injure, by malicious tales &c.

slanderer, n. [1. sláhnderer; 2. sláːndərə]. Prec. & **-er**. One who slanders; an utterer of slander.

slanderous, adj. [1. sláhnderus; 2. sláːndərəs]. **slander** (I.) & **-ous**. **1.** Uttering, given to uttering, slanders: *slanderous accusers*; *a slanderous tongue*. **2.** Containing, imputing, slander or slanders: *slanderous rumours, statements* &c.

slanderously, adv. Prec. & **-ly**. In a slanderous manner.

slang (I.), n. [1. slang; 2. slæŋ]. Etymol. doubtful; used in 18th cent.; prob. fr. or cogn. w. **sling** (I.); cp. Norw. *slengja kjeften*, 'to sling the jaw, to abuse'; *slengja-ord*, 'a new slang word'; *slengja-namn*, 'nickname'. **1.** (orig. use) Words, phrases &c. used only among a particular community, class, section of society; jargon, argot, cant &c.: *schoolboy slang*; *thieves' slang* &c.; also technical terms peculiar to a particular profession, or to a special branch of study: *doctors' slang*; *biological slang* &c. **2. a** A new word, phrase, or idiom introduced into, and used in, colloquial speech, but not yet recognized as sufficiently dignified for literary usage, esp. on solemn occasions or in elevated style, whether in speaking or writing; **b** peculiar idiomatic use of a word in a new way to impart variety, picturesqueness, point, to familiar colloquial style, but felt to be trivial or flippant on serious occasions. While slang is essentially part of familiar and colloquial speech, it is not necessarily either 'incorrect' or vulgar in its proper place. On the other hand, slang may be vulgar, either from its own character, or because it is associated with the usage of vulgar people. **3.** (attrib.) Belonging to, of the nature of, slang: *a slang word, expression* &c.

slang (II.), vb. trans., fr. prec. To scold, vituperate; to censure loudly in abusive terms.

slangily, adv. [1. slángili; 2. slǽŋili]. Next word & **-ly**. In a slangy manner.

slangy, adj. [1. slángi; 2. slǽŋi]. **slang** (I.) & **-y**. **a** Given to using slang when speaking; **b** of the nature of slang: *a slangy phrase*.

slank, vb. [1. slangk; 2. slæŋk]. O.E. *slanc*; M.E. *slank*; Pret. of **slink**; now usually **slunk**.

slant (I.), vb. intrans. & trans. [1. slahnt; 2. slānt]. M.E. *slenten*, 'to slope, glide'; Scand., cp. Norw. *slenta*, 'to fall slanting or obliquely, to fall on one side'. **1.** intrans. To slope; to incline away from the perpendicular. **2.** trans. To cause to slant; to put, place, obliquely.

slant (II.), n., fr. prec. Oblique position; a slope.

slanting, adj. [1. sláhnting; 2. sláːntiŋ], fr. Pres. Part. of **slant** (I.). Sloping, oblique, aslant.

slantingly, adv. Prec. & **-ly**. In a slanting direction or position.

slap (I.), vb. trans. [1. slap; 2. slæp]. Imitative; cp. L.G. *slappe*, Germ. *schlappe*, & cp. **slam** (I.). **1.** To smack, strike, smartly with the open hand: *to slap a naughty child*; *to slap a person's face*; *slap him in the face* &c.; *to slap person on the back*, by way of hearty greeting. **2.** *Slap down*, to throw down with force: *to slap down a piece of steak on to the counter*; *slap on*, to put on violently: *to slap a hat on* (*to*) *one's head*.

slap (II.), n., fr. prec. A smack, a smart blow, given with the open hand. Phr. *a slap in the face, eye*, an unexpected snub, a rebuff; a disappointment, a check, repulse.

slap (III.), adv., fr. **slap** (I.) (colloq.) Straight, directly, full: *hit him slap in the eye*; *car ran slap into the wall*.

slap-bang, adv. (colloq.) Violently, noisily.

slap-dash, adv. & adj. (colloq.) **1.** adv. Impetuously, headlong, carelessly. **2.** adj. **a** (of persons &c.) Impetuous, headlong, careless, happy-go-lucky; **b** (of actions, work &c.) performed hastily or carelessly.

slapstick, n. [1. slápstik; 2. slǽpstik]. A wooden stick with flapping ends used in rough, knockabout farce &c.; also attrib.: *slapstick comedy*.

slap-up, adj. [1. sláp up; 2. slǽp ap]. (slang) First-rate, first-class; of the finest quality, of the best of its kind: *a slap-up establishment, dinner* &c.

slash (I.), vb. trans. & intrans. [1. slash; 2. slæʃ]. M.E. *slaschen*, fr. O. Fr. *esclachier*, 'to break, split up'; etymol. doubtful, possibly fr. *es-* (*ex-*), as intens., & M.H.G. *klecken*, 'to break with a sharp, clicking noise'; prob. influenced by O. Fr. *esclichier*, 'to slice', see **slice**. **A.** trans. **1. a** To cut gashes in with a cutting instrument, to slit with a downward blow of a sword, knife &c.; specif. **b** to make cuts or slits in a garment, by way of ornament, so as to show another garment underneath. **2.** To lash, strike violently at, with a whip. **B.** intrans. (often *slash at*) To strike fiercely at with a sword, knife, whip &c.

slash (II.), n., fr. prec. **1.** A violent, cutting blow. **2.** A slit, gash.

slashing, adj. [1. sláshing; 2. slǽʃiŋ]. **slash** (I.) & **-ing**. Specif., cutting, severe, destructive: *a slashing review, attack, criticism* &c.

slat (I.), n. [1. slat; 2. slæt]. Variant of **slate** (I.). A thin, flat, narrow piece of wood or metal, a lath; esp. **a** one of the set of such pieces forming a Venetian blind; **b** one of the cross-pieces of a bedstead on which a mattress rests; (slang) the ribs.

slat (II.), vb. intrans. & trans. Prob. imitative, cp. **slap**. **a** intrans. To flap, strike object, with noisy sound, esp. of sails, ropes &c.; **b** trans., to strike against with such sound.

slate (I.), n. [1. slāt; 2. sleit]. M.E. *sclat, slat*, fr. O. Fr. *esclat*, 'a split piece of wood, lath; wooden tile or shingle', fr. *esclater*, 'to split, burst, into splinters', apparently fr. a presumed L. Lat. **exclapitāre*, fr. *es-* (*ex-*), intens. pref., & L.G. *klappen*, see **clap** (I.), & cp. **éclat**. **1.** (geol.) A hard, grey or greenish-grey shaly rock which splits easily into thin flat layers. **2.** Piece of this rock split into a flat plate and used as a roofing tile. **3.** A sheet of slate, usually with a narrow wooden frame, used for writing on, esp. in schools. Phr. *a clean slate*, a good, clean record. **4.** Grey colour resembling that of slate.

slate (II.), vb. trans., fr. prec. To cover (a roof) with slates.

slate (III.), vb. trans., fr. **slate** (I.), fr. idea of throwing slates at, pelting. Connexion w. O.E. *slǣtan*, 'to rend', is improbable. **a** To submit to severe censure: *to slate a book*, review it harshly; **b** to blame severely, to rate, to pitch into: *to slate a person*.

slate club, n. A voluntary, unofficial benefit or thrift society, to which small sums are paid in weekly.

slate-coloured, adj. Of the colour of slate; dark grey.

slate-grey, adj. Slate-coloured.

slate-pencil, n. A thin pencil of soft slate, used for writing on slates.

slater, n. [1. slāter; 2. sléitə]. **slate** (II.) & **-er**. Tradesman who lays slates on roofs.

slat(e)y, adj. [1. slāti; 2. sléiti]. **slate** (I.) & **-y**. **a** Resembling a slate in colour; **b** of the nature and consistency of slate; **c** full of slate.

slating (I.), n. [1. slāting; 2. sléitiŋ]. **slate** (II.) & **-ing**. **a** Act of covering a roof with slates; **b** slates collectively as used for roofing.

slating (II.), n. **slate** (III.) & **-ing**. Rebuke, scolding; severe criticism: *to give, get, a severe slating*.

slattern, n. [1. slátern; 2. slǽtən]. Etymol. doubtful. An untidy, dirty, sluttish woman.

slatternliness, n. [1. sláternlines; 2. slǽtənlinis]. **slatternly** & **-ness**. Quality, state, of being slatternly.

slatternly, adj. [1. sláternli; 2. slǽtənli]. **slattern** & **-ly**. Untidy, dirty, sluttish.

slaty, adj. See **slat(e)y**.

slaughter (I.), n. [1. sláwter; 2. slɔ́tə]. M.E. *slauhter* &c., fr. O.N. *slātr*, 'slain flesh', influenced by the cogn. *slaht*, fr. O.E. *sleaht*, 'a killing, slaughter'; formed fr. O.E. base *slag-, slah-*, q.v., under **slay**. The act or fact of slaying or killing; specif. **a** the butchering of animals for food; **b** the killing of human beings, esp. on a large scale, in battle, or by putting to death in a massacre: *the battle was attended by a terrible slaughter on both sides*; *Herod ordered the slaughter of the Innocents*.

slaughter (II.), vb. trans., fr. prec. **1.** Specif. **a** to kill cattle, sheep, or pigs for market; **b** to kill wild animals ruthlessly and wantonly. **2.** To kill, massacre (human beings), in large numbers, either in battle, or as an act of cruelty inflicted on a civilian population.

slaughterer, n. [1. sláwterer; 2. slɔ́tərə]. Prec. & **-er**. One who slaughters, specif. one who slaughters cattle.

slaughter-house, n. **a** Place where cattle are butchered for market; an abattoir, shambles; **b** (fig.) place of carnage or massacre.

slaughterous, adj. [1. sláwterus; 2. slɔ́tərəs]. **slaughter** (I.) & **-ous**. (rhet.) Murderous; wantonly, ruthlessly destructive of life.

Slav, n. & adj. [1. slahv, slav; 2. slāv, slæv], fr. Germ. *Sklave*, fr. L. Byzantine Gk. *Sklábos, Esklabînos*, name given to various Slavonic races in S. Russia & the Balkans; origin unknown. **1.** n. A member of various races, widespread over E. and S.E. Europe, speaking different forms of the Slavonic language, including Russians, Poles, Serbians, Croats, Czechs, Bulgarians &c. **2.** adj. Of, belonging to, the Slavs; Slavonic.

slave (I.), n. [1. slāv; 2. sleiv], fr. Fr. *esclave*, fr. L. Lat. *Sclavus*, fr. Gk. *Sklábos*, see **Slav**, term first applied to captives of various S.E. European Slavonic races. **1.** One held in bondage to another; a human chattel; one whose person, family, life, labour, or skill is in the absolute ownership of another, by capture, purchase &c., and whose status as such is recognized by law and custom; a bondman, serf, thrall. Phr. *to work like a slave*, to toil hard. **2. a** Any one who is subject to the will of another person; a member of a subject race or nation: '*Britons never shall be slaves*'; **b** one who works like a slave; a drudge; also a workman, regarded as economically entirely under the control of employers or the employing class: *the worker in the early days of the industrial revolution was a slave*. **3. a** *Slave to*, or *of*, one who is dominated by desires, habits, passions, to the point of being no longer master of himself: *a slave to one's passions, to vice, drink* &c.; *a slave to his own ambitions, to convention, fashion* &c.; **b** (in favourable sense) person completely devoted to, and dominated by, a cause or a principle: *a slave to duty* &c.; **c** a person entirely devoted to another: *he professed to be her devoted slave*; *a willing slave*, one who submits cheerfully to another's domination.

slave (II.), vb. intrans., fr. prec. To work, labour, like a slave; to toil very hard: *to slave for one's family*.

slave-driver, n. **a** Superintendent or overseer of slaves at work; **b** a hard, merciless taskmaster, one who forces people to work to the last ounce of their strength and ability.

slave-driving, n. Action, behaviour, methods, of a slave-driver.

slaver (I.), n. [1. slāver; 2. sléivə]. **slave** (I.) & **-er**. **1.** Person who trades in slaves. **2.** A ship engaged in the slave trade.

slaver (II.), vb. intrans. & trans. [1. slāver; 2. sléivə], fr. O.N. *slafra*; cogn. w. L.G. *slabbern*, cp. variants **slobber** & **slubber**. **1.** intrans. To dribble with saliva, to let saliva dribble from the mouth; to foam at the mouth. **2.** trans. **a** To cover with saliva; let saliva drop on to; **b** (fig.) to be effusively servile and fulsome to.

slaver (**III.**), n., fr. prec. **1.** Saliva dropping or dribbling from mouth. **2.** (fig.) Servile, fulsome flattery &c.

slavery (**I.**), adj. [1. sláveri; 2. slǽvəri]. Prec. & **-y.** Covered with, dripping with, slaver.

slavery (**II.**), n. [1. sláveri; 2. sléivəri]. **slave** (**I.**) & **-ery.** **1. a** Status, condition, of a slave; bondage, serfdom; **b** (also fig.) domination by one's desires &c. **2.** The institution, custom, of owning slaves. **3.** Hard, toilsome work or labour; drudgery.

slave-ship, n. Ship engaged in the slave-trade; a slaver.

slave-states, n. pl. Those Southern States of N. America in which slave-owning predominated before the Civil War of 1861.

slave-trade, n. Traffic in slaves; esp. that formerly prevalent, involving the purchase or capture of West African negroes and the transporting of them to the West Indies and America for sale to planters.

slave-trader, n. One engaged in the slave-trade; a slaver.

slavey, n. [slávi; 2. sléivi]. **slave** (**I.**) & **-y.** (familiar, slang) A young servant-girl.

Slavic, adj. & n. [1. slávik; 2. slǽvik]. **Slav** & **-ic.** **a** adj. Connected with, pertaining to, the Slavs, or to their language; **b** n., the language of the Slavs; Slavonic.

slavish, adj. [1. slávish; 2. sléiviʃ]. **slave** (**I.**) & **-ish.** Characteristic of, befitting, a slave; servile; abject: *a slavish follower, flatterer.* Phr. *slavish imitation*, one that is blind and uncritical, reproducing the object copied exactly, without discrimination or originality.

slavishly, adv. Prec. & **-ly.** In a slavish, servile, manner.

Slavism, n. [1. sláhvizm; 2. slávizəm]. **Slav** & **-ism.** **1.** Devotion to the political ideal of a national unity for the Slavic races; insistence on this as a principle of statesmanship. **2.** A Slavonic idiom.

Slavonian, adj. & n. [1. slavónian; 2. sləvóuniən], fr. Med. Lat. *S(c)lavonia*, the country inhabited by the Slavs, & **-an.** **1.** adj. Slavonic. **2.** n. **a** Member of, language of, the Slavonic races; **b** inhabitant of the district of the old Austrian Empire, Slavonia.

Slavonic, adj. & n. [1. slavónik; 2. sləvɔ́nik]. See prec. & **-ic.** **a** adj. Belonging to, connected with, the Slav races, or their language; **b** n., the language of the Slavs.

Slavophil, n. & adj. [1. slávofil; 2. slǽvəfil]. **Slav** & **-phil.** **a** n. Lover, admirer, of the Slavs; **b** adj., loving, admiring, the Slavs.

Slavophobe, n. & adj. [1. slávōfōb; 2. slǽvoufòub]. **Slav** & **-phobe.** **a** n. One who fears or hates the Slavs; **b** adj., fearing, hating, the Slavs.

slay, vb. trans. [1. slā; 2. slei]. M.E. *sleien*, a new formation on the anal. of O.E. *sleġþ*, (M.E. *slei(e)þ* &c.) 3rd pers. sing. pres. indic. of *slēan*, 'to strike; to kill', wh. also survives directly in M.E. as *slē(n)*. O.E. *slēan* is fr. W. Gmc. **slahan*; cp. O.S., O.H.G., & Goth. *slahan*, 'to strike'. From the base **slah-* comes also **slaughter**, & fr. the variant **slag-* comes **sledge-hammer.** To deprive of life, to kill. The word is now chiefly confined to poetry, elevated prose style, and to technical legal usage; in ordinary use it has been replaced by *kill.*

slayer, n. [1. sláer; 2. sléiə]. Prec. & **-er.** One who slays; a killer, murderer; also in combination, as *man-slayer* &c.

sled, n. & vb. intrans. & trans. [1. sled; 2. sled]. M.E. *slede*, fr. M. Du. *sledde*, cogn. w. **slide**; for variants see **sledge** & **sleigh.** **1.** n. Small, low wooden framework with runners, for travelling on ice, or on snow-covered roads; a small sledge. **2.** vb. To travel, convey, by sled.

Sledge, n. & vb. intrans. & trans. [1. slej; 2. sledž]. Prob. earlier *sleds*, pl. of **sled.** **1.** n. A vehicle of different shapes and sizes, furnished with runners, for travelling over snowy roads, varying from an elaborately built carriage with a hood and padded seats, drawn by horses, to a simple wooden framework upon which persons or goods slide down a mountain road, or down a specially made track of ice. **2.** vb. To travel, convey, by sledge.

sledge-hammer, n. O.E. *sleċġ*, 'a heavy hammer', fr. earlier **slagjō-*, fr. the base seen in O.E. *slæġen, slegin* &c., P.P. of *slēan*, 'to strike', see **slay.** A heavy hammer, with a long handle; wielded with both hands, used by blacksmiths. Phr. *a sledge-hammer blow*, a very violent, powerful blow; (also fig.) a powerful, destructive attack.

sleek, adj. & vb. trans. [1. slēk; 2. slīk]. M.E. *slēke*, w. lengthening fr. *slike*, fr. O.N. *slikr*, 'smooth'; variant of **slick**, w. differentiation of meaning, cp. **slight** (**I.**). **1.** adj. **a** (of animal's coat, person's hair) Smooth, glossy; (also of general appearance) very neat and trim; **b** (of manner) smooth, oily, unctuous, smug. **2.** vb. To make sleek; to smooth, press down.

sleekly, adv. Prec. & **-ly.** In a sleek manner.

sleekness, n. See prec. & **-ness.** Quality, condition, of being sleek; smoothness, glossiness; smugness.

sleeky, adj. [1. sléki; 2. slíki]. **sleek** & **-y.** Sleek.

sleep (**I.**), n. [1. slēp; 2. slīp]. O.E. *slǣp*, M.E. *slēpe*; O.S. *slāp*; O.H.G. *slāf*; Goth. *slēps*; orig. sense, 'drowsiness, lethargy' is preserved in Mod. Germ. *schlaff*, 'loose, slack, weak, feeble'; cogn. w. O. Slav. *slabŭ*, 'weak', Lith. *slopstù*, 'become weak'. **1. a** The natural and healthy temporary suspension of consciousness and activity necessary to complete repose in man and the lower animals, recurring normally at least once every twenty-four hours, and lasting for several hours; slumber; Phr. *to go to sleep*, fall into the state of sleep; *to put to sleep*, place (a person) under conditions which induce and finally produce sleep; *one's last sleep*, death; **b** closing up of leaves or petals of plants at night; **c** prolonged state of quiescence, and cessation or partial cessation of bodily functions in certain animals; hibernation. **2.** Period during which one is asleep. Phr. *beauty sleep*, the first and most refreshing period of sleep. **3.** (fig.) A condition of mental inactivity, insensibility, indifference.

sleep (**II.**), vb. intrans. & trans. O.E. *slǣpan*, M.E. *slēpen.* See prec. **A.** intrans. **1. a** To pass into a state of sleep; to take rest by sleeping; to slumber: *to sleep well, badly*; *I hardly slept all night*; Phrs. *to sleep the clock round*, sleep for twelve hours on end; *sleeping dogs*, unpleasant awkward facts, memories of these, dormant and half-forgotten; *to sleep like a top*, sleep very soundly; *sleep on, upon* (a question, problem, proposal), to take a night to consider and decide; **b** to behave as though one were asleep, to be indifferent, torpid. **2.** To pass the night: *I shall sleep in London tonight*; *to sleep out of doors.* **3.** To be dormant, not to show signs of activity, to be quiescent: *for the moment feuds and animosities are sleeping.* **4.** (fig.) To be dead: *to sleep in the grave, with one's fathers.* **5.** (of a top) To spin so rapidly and steadily that it stands perfectly upright, the motion being imperceptible **B.** trans. **1.** In such constructions as *to sleep the sleep of the just, to sleep one's last sleep* &c.; '*such a sleep They sleep the men I loved*' (Tennyson); or *to sleep one's life away*, to spend in sleeping. **2.** (colloq.) To provide sleeping accommodation for: *a hotel that can sleep 300 people*; *we can dine you and sleep you.* **3.** *Sleep off*, to get rid of by sleeping: *to sleep off the effects of a debauch.*

sleeper, n. [1. sléper; 2. slípə]. **sleep** (**II.**) & **-er.** **1. a** One who is asleep; **b** (preceded by adj.) one who sleeps in a specified way: *a good sleeper*; *a heavy, light, sleeper.* **2.** A stout, squared wooden timber used as a support for the rails of a railway line. **3.** A sleeping-car on a railway.

sleepily, adv. [1. slépili; 2. slípili]. **sleepy** & **-ly.** In a sleepy manner; drowsily, lazily, indolently.

sleepiness, n. [1. slépines; 2. slípinis]. **sleepy** & **-ness.** Quality, condition, of being sleepy; drowsiness, somnolence.

sleeping-car, n. [1. sléping kar; 2. slípiŋ kā]. Railway carriage fitted with beds or berths.

sleeping-draught, n. An opiate or other narcotic medicine for inducing or promoting sleep.

sleeping partner, n. A partner with financial interest in a business who takes no active part in the control and management.

sleeping sickness, n. A tropical African disease, trypanosomiasis, caused by a parasite introduced by the bite of a species of tsetse-fly, accompanied by extreme drowsiness and headache, often lasting several years, and usually terminating fatally.

sleepless, adj. [1. sléples; 2. slíplis]. **sleep** (**I.**) & **-less.** **1. a** Not attended by sleep; wakeful: *a sleepless night*; **b** not enjoying sleep, unable to sleep, suffering from insomnia. **2. a** Unremitting, untiring, ever alert: *sleepless care*; **b** ever in motion, never at rest: *the sleepless ocean.*

sleeplessly, adv. Prec. & **-ly.** In a sleepless manner.

sleeplessness, n. See prec. & **-ness.** Quality, condition, of being sleepless; lack of sleep; insomnia.

sleepwalker, n. [1. slépwàwker; 2. slípwɔ̀kə]. One who walks in his sleep; a somnambulist.

sleep-walking, n. [1. slép wàwking; 2. slíp wɔ̀kiŋ]. Somnambulism.

sleepy, adj. [1. slépi; 2. slípi]. **sleep** (**I.**) & **-y.** **1.** (of persons) **a** Inclined to sleep; overcome by sleep, drowsy, somnolent; **b** mentally sluggish; not alert in mind. **2.** (of places) Characterized by an absence of business and bustle; lifeless, very quiet; reverse of stirring. **3.** (of fruit, esp. of pears) Grown soft and squashy, yet juiceless, without ripening properly.

sleepyhead, n. [1. slépihed; 2. slípihed]. A sleepy person, esp. a child who has stayed up beyond its usual hour, and is overcome by sleep.

sleepy sickness, n. Popular name of a disease, *encephalitis lethargica*, a form of inflammation of the brain, usually accompanied by intense drowsiness, and sometimes leaving mental and nervous degeneration.

sleet, n. & vb. intrans. [1. slēt; 2. slīt]. In M.E.; origin uncertain. **1.** n. A fine, grain-like form of ice, or frozen rain, smaller and softer than hail. **2.** vb. *It is sleeting*, sleet is falling.

sleety, adj. [1. sléti; 2. slíti]. Prec. & **-y.** Consisting of, resembling, sleet.

sleeve, n. [1. slēv; 2. slīv]. O.E. (non-W.S.) *slēf*, W.S. *slīef*, sleeve'; cp. *slīefan, slēfan*, 'to put on a dress'; prob. fr. a variant form of base in O.E. *slīepan, slēpan*, 'to slip (a thing) off, or on'; see **slip** (**I.**). **1.** That part of a garment which covers the arm; (in several phrases) *to have something up one's sleeve*, to have some plan, or decisive fact, in one's possession ready to be used when needed; originally of cards, concealed in sleeves by sharpers; *to wear one's heart upon one's sleeve*, to show one's private feelings to the world; *to laugh in, up, one's sleeve*, to chuckle inwardly, exult secretly; from the old-fashioned wide loose sleeves with which one could hide one's face. **2.** Any of various mechanical devices, in which a tube is used to fit or slip over a smaller tube or rod.

sleeved, adj. [1. slēvd; 2. slīvd]. Prec. & **-ed.** Provided with sleeves.

-sleeved, adj., fr. prec. Having sleeves of specified kind: *loose-, full-sleeved* &c.

sleeve-fish, n. A squid or cuttle-fish.

sleeveless, adj. [1. slévles; 2. slívlis]. **sleeve** & **-less.** Having no sleeves.

sleigh, n. & vb. intrans. & trans. [1. slā; 2. slei]. Variant of **sled**; perh. fr. Du. *slee.* **1.** n. A sledge. **2.** vb. To travel, convey, by sleigh.

sleigh-bell, n. Small, jingling bell attached to the harness of an animal drawing a sleigh.

sleight, n. [1. slīt; 2. slait]. M.E. *sleiȝtə, sleȝþe*, fr. O.N. *slægð*, 'cunning, slyness', fr. *slægr*, 'sly, cunning', see **sly**, & **-th**. Dexterity, craft, cunning; a dexterous trick or device; now, chiefly in *sleight-of-hand*, deftness, dexterity, of the hand, esp. in performing conjuring tricks; legerdemain.

slender, adj. [1. slénder; 2. sléndə]. M.E. *slendre*, fr. O. Du. *slinder*, 'thin, slender'; origin doubtful. **1.** Thin, slim, tenuous, narrow; small in circumference or width, as compared with height; reverse of *stout, thickset, cobby*: *a slender figure*; *slender fingers, waist* &c.; *a slender girl*; *a slender stem, tree* &c. **2. a** Slight, feeble: *slender hopes of success*; **b** scanty, meagre, inconsiderable: *a person of slender means*; *a slender income*; *my knowledge of the subject is of the slenderest*; *a slender meal.*

slenderly, adv. Prec. & **-ly**. In a slender manner; to a slender degree; sparely, meagrely, slightly.

slenderness, n. See prec. & **-ness**. Quality, condition, of being slender.

slept, vb. [1. slept; 2. slept]. Pret. & P.P. of **sleep**. O.E. *slǣpte*; M.E. *slepte*. O.E. has also a strong Pret. *slēp*.

sleuth (I.), n. [1. slōōth; 2. slūþ]. Perh. fr. O.N. *slōð*. See **slot** (I.). **1.** (archaic) The slot or track of an animal or man. **2. a** Also *sleuth-hound*, a bloodhound or other hound that tracks by scent; **b** (colloq.) a detective.

sleuth (II.), vb. trans. & intrans., fr. prec. **a** To track by scent (of hounds); **b** to follow, track down, as a detective.

slew (I.), vb. [1. slōō; 2. slū]. Pret. of **slay**; M.E. *slēw*, a new formation on the anal. of *grew, knew* &c.; M.E. has *slōg, slouh*, fr. O.E. *slōg, slōh*.

slew (II.), **slue**, vb. trans. & intrans. Etymol. unknown. Often *slew round*; **a** trans., to cause to swing round; **b** intrans., to swing round.

slice (I.), n. [1. slīs; 2. slais]. M.E. *sclice*, fr. O. Fr. *esclice*, 'splinter', fr. *esclicier*, 'to split, shiver, slit', fr. O.H.G. *slizzen, slīzan*, 'to slit'; cogn. w. O.E. *slītan*. See **slit** (I.). **1.** A flat piece, thin in proportion to its breadth, cut off from anything: *a slice of cake, meat, bread* &c.; *a slice of rock for microscopic examination.* **2.** A part, piece, share, of or in anything: *all demanded a slice of the booty, profits* &c.; *a slice of luck*, a piece of good fortune. **3.** Any thin, broad, flat implement for cutting slices. **4.** A cutting, slicing, stroke, esp. in ball-games.

slice (II.), vb. trans. & intrans., fr. prec. **A.** trans. **1. a** To cut into slices; also *slice up*; **b** *slice off*, to cut off as a slice: *to slice off a man's head, arm.* **2.** To strike with a drawing, cutting, blow: *to slice the water with an oar*; *to slice a ball at golf.* **B.** intrans. To make a slicing drive at golf, or slicing stroke in rowing.

slick, adj. & adv. [1. slik; 2. slik]. M.E. *slike*, 'smooth', fr. O.N. See also **sleek** & **slight** (I.). (colloq.) **1.** adj. (rare) **a** Rapid; smooth-running, moving easily; **b** clever, adroit. **2.** adv. Directly, straight, full tilt: *his car ran slick into mine.*

slid, vb. [1. slid; 2. slid]. Pret. & P.P. of **slide** (I.); fr. M.E., P.P. *slide(n)*; O.E. *(ȝe)sliden*; cp. O.E. Pret. *slād*; M.E. *slōd*.

slide (I.), vb. intrans. & trans. [1. slīd; 2. slaid]. O.E. *slīdan*, 'to slide, glide; to make a false step, to err'; cogn. w. O.E. *slider*, 'slippery'; cp. O.H.G. *slita*, 'sledge'; cogn. w. Lith. *slidùs*, 'smooth, slippery'. **A.** intrans. **1.** To move along with a gliding movement while preserving contact with a surface; to slip, glide, easily and smoothly; **a** to slip down or off: *to slide down a slope*; *the book slid off my knee*; **b** to move, slip, easily into a given place or position: *the window-catch slides backwards and forwards*; *a sword slides into its scabbard.* **2.** Specif., to glide along over the smooth slippery surface of ice or hard snow without moving the feet. **3.** (fig.) To pass lightly over without dwelling upon: *to slide over delicate questions.* **4.** To pass gradually, and without being conscious of the process, into a specified condition, to come gradually to adopt a specified line of conduct: *to slide into a state of lethargy*; *to slide into bad habits.* **B.** trans. **1.** To cause to slide; to propel (something) along a surface or push it into a receptacle: *to slide a decanter along a table*; *to slide a drawer back into its place.* **2.** To thrust slowly, with a sliding movement: *he slid his hands, purse, back into his pocket.*

slide (II.), n., fr. prec. **1.** Act of sliding: *a slide on the ice.* **2.** Strip of smooth ice, or hard snow, rendered extra slippery by persons sliding upon it. **3.** An inclined plane down which heavy objects are made to slide as a means of moving them; a shoot. **4.** Something which slides; specif., a round shallow vessel of silver with smooth cloth on the under surface, in which a wine decanter is placed for sliding along a polished table. **5. a** A slip of glass, which is slid into place, used as a mount for specimens for examination under a microscope; **b** a glass plate bearing a picture, to be projected on to a screen by a magic-lantern. **6.** Kind of flat brooch used in a woman's hair. **7.** A fall of rock, earth, ice, or snow down a mountain-side: *a landslide.*

slider, n. [1. slīder; 2. sláidə]. **slide** (I.) & **-er**. **a** One who slides; **b** the sliding part of a machine &c.

slide-rule, n. [1. slīd rōōl; 2. slaid rūl]. Ruler with graduated sliding part attached, for making mathematical calculations.

slide-valve, n. A valve which opens and shuts an aperture by sliding over, or away from it, as in a steam-engine &c.

slide-way, n. An inclined plane or chute.

sliding-rule, n. See **slide-rule.**

sliding-scale, n. A scale or schedule for raising or lowering taxes, wages, prices &c. automatically in accordance with fluctuations in economic conditions.

sliding-seat, n. A seat, moving on runners, used in racing boats, to increase the length of the stroke.

slight (I.), adj. [1. slīt; 2. slait]. M.E. *sliht* &c.; fr. O.L.G. *sligt*, 'even, smooth; simple; poor, bad'; cp. O.H.G. *sleht*, 'smooth', Germ. *schlecht*, 'bad'; Goth. *slaihts*, 'smooth'; prob. cogn. w. Gk. *lissós*, 'smooth', fr. **slikʷjos*; cp. also O.N. *slikr*, 'smooth'. See **slick** & **sleek**. **1. a** Slim, slender; not thick or stout: *a slight figure*; **b** fragile, frail; not strong: *the platform is too slight for the weight it carries.* **2.** Mild, not severe or intense: *a slight attack of the gout*; *a slight cold.* **3.** Inconsiderable in amount or extent: *a slight meal*; *a slight difference of opinion*; *not the slightest doubt.* **4.** Intellectually inadequate; not weighty; trivial, insignificant: *his book is so slight as to be negligible.*

slight (II.), vb. trans., fr. prec. To treat, speak of (persons), with less than the deserved degree of respect; to neglect, disregard, claims to attention and respect; to belittle: *to ignore his greeting was to slight him publicly.*

slight (III.), n., fr. prec. Action with regard to another which constitutes a breach of due respect; a neglect of deference due to a person; act or utterance expressing disrespect; a humiliation inflicted upon another.

slighting, adj. [1. slīting; 2. sláitiŋ]. **slight** (II.) & **-ing**. Of the nature of a slight; expressing, conveying, a slight.

slightingly, adv. Prec. & **-ly**. In a slighting manner.

slightish, adj. [1. slītish; 2. sláitiʃ]. **slight** (I.) & **-ish**. Somewhat slight.

slightly, adv. [1. slītli; 2. sláitli]. **slight** (I.) & **-ly**. In a slight manner; to a slight degree.

slightness, n. [1. slītnes; 2. sláitnis]. **slight** (I.) & **-ness**. Quality, condition, of being slight (in various senses).

slily, adv. See **slyly.**

slim, adj. [1. slim; 2. slim], fr. Du.; cp. also M.H.G. *slimp*, 'crooked, oblique'; same word as Mod. Germ. *schlimm*, 'bad'. Origin uncertain. **1.** Slender, slight, in girth and build; reverse of *stout, thick*: *a slim figure, leg, tree trunk* &c. **2.** Slight in degree or amount: *very slim chances of success.* **3.** (introduced from Cape Dutch during last Boer War) Crafty, wily, cunning.

slime, n. & vb. trans. [1. slīm; 2. slaim]. O.E. *slīm*; M.H.G. & O.N. *slīm*; cogn. w. Lat. *līmus*, 'mud'; Gk. *leîos*, 'smooth'. See also **lime** (I.). **1.** n. **a** Any soft, moist, sticky, slippery, substance, such as thin, oozy mud, moisture secreted by snails &c.; **b** (fig.) moral degradation. **2.** vb. To cover, bedaub, with slime.

slimily, adv. [1. slīmili; 2. sláimili]. **slimy** & **-ly**. In a slimy manner.

sliminess, n. [1. slīmines; 2. sláiminis]. **slimy** & **-ness**. Condition, quality, of being slimy.

slimly, adv. [1. slímli; 2. slímli]. **slim** & **-ly**. **1.** Slenderly, slightly: *slimly built.* **2.** With cunning, craftily.

slimness, n. [1. slímnes; 2. slímnis]. See prec. & **-ness**. **1.** Slenderness. **2.** Wiliness, cunning.

slimy, adj. [1. slīmi; 2. sláimi]. **slime** & **-y**. **1.** Of the nature of, like, slime: *a slimy liquid* &c. **2.** Covered, smeared, with slime: *a slimy road.* **3.** (colloq.) Obsequiously servile, unctuous, fawning: *slimy manners* &c.

sling (I.), vb. trans. [1. sling; 2. sliŋ]. O.E. *slingan*, 'to creep'; M.E. in mod. sense; cp. O.H.G. *slingan*, 'to creep'; O.N. *slyngva*, 'to throw, sling'; cogn. w. Lith. *slenkù*, 'to creep'. See also **slink**. The M.E. & Mod. Engl. sense perh. due to the influence of **fling**. **1.** To throw with a free, swinging movement of the arm. Phrs. *to sling ink*, to write copiously and frequently; *sling out*, to hurl (esp. a person) out of a room &c.; to eject; *to sling a man out of the room*, to thrust out with a violent action. **2.** Specif., to cast by means of a sling; probably from noun. **3. a** To suspend by means of a sling: *to sling a sword from a belt*; **b** to lift and leave hanging; to lift and move by means of a sling: *to sling a sick cow from the roof of a shed*; *to sling a crate on board a ship*; **c** specif., to suspend (wounded limb), place in a sling; **d** *sling oneself up* (a tree), climb, hoist, oneself up by rapid easy movements.

sling (II.), n., fr. prec. **1.** Primitive device for throwing stones or other small missiles, used as weapon of offence, consisting of a short strip of leather or other material, held so as to form a loop in which the stone &c. is placed; as it is brought sharply forward by a rapid movement of the arm as in throwing, one end of the band is released. **2.** A throw, cast, stroke, from, or as from, a sling; (also fig.) a blow, stroke, attack: '*The slings and arrows of outrageous fortune*' (Shakespeare). **3.** A band of material passed round an object in order to lift or suspend it; **a** such a band used for holding heavy weights which have to be hoisted by tackle; **b** a scarf or strip of cloth passed round the neck and hanging down in a loop in front for supporting an injured arm.

sling (III.), n. Etymol. doubtful; but cp. Mod. Germ. *schlingen*, 'to swallow'; an Am. term. A drink made of spirits, usually gin and water, sweetened and iced.

sling dogs, n. A pair of grappling irons or cramps, slung by ropes, used for hoisting blocks of stone &c.

slinger, n. [1. slínger; 2. slíŋə]. **sling** (I.) & **-er**. **1.** Man armed with or using a sling, as a weapon. **2.** Man in charge of slings used as hoisting tackle &c.

slink (I.), vb. intrans. [1. slingk; 2. sliŋk]. O.E. *slincan*, 'to creep'; prob. a variant of **sling** (I.). To move, proceed, in a furtive, secretive, sneaking manner; (commonly) *slink away, about, off.*

slink (II.), vb. intrans. & trans. & n.; variant of **sling** (I.). **1.** vb. (of animals, esp. cows) **a** intrans. To miscarry, abort; **b** trans., to cast, slip, give birth to (offspring) prematurely. **2.** n. A prematurely born calf or other animal.

slip (I.), vb. intrans. & trans. [1. slip; 2. slip]. M.E. *slippen*, 'to slip, glide; to escape'; either fr. O.L.G. or formed in Engl. fr. the base in O.E. *slipor*, 'slippery', & *slipig*, 'slimy'. A cogn. exists in O. & M.H.G. *slīfan*, 'to glide; to make smooth, polish', Mod. Germ. *schleifen*, 'to sharpen'. **A.** intrans. **1.** To slide, move, be moved, slowly from one place or position to another by weight or pressure, or owing to absence of friction on a smooth surface: *a table-napkin slips off one's knee*; *a stone slips down the face of a cliff, over the edge of a grassy slope*; *the bolt slips quite easily into its catch.* **2.** To miss one's footing through treading on something slippery or slimy; to stumble, trip, lose one's balance in walking or running: *to slip on the stairs, on the ice*; *my foot slipped*; also *slip up*, to trip, stumble. **3.** a To slide out of, away from, a normal or desired position: *a window-catch slips out of its place*; *a paper has slipped down behind the bookcase*; *a tie is apt to slip up over the collar if not properly held in place*; b to slide suddenly, and with a jerk, in an unexpected direction: *the knife slipped and cut my hand.* **4.** a To run, slide, fall, away from a grasp or fastening: *the sword slipped from his nerveless hand*; *the rope slipped through my fingers*; b to become relaxed or untied: *the knot is so firm that it can't slip*; c to pass from one's mental grasp: *all these points had entirely slipped from my mind.* **5.** To go, steal, away, escape swiftly and quietly, without attracting attention: *I slipped out just before the sermon*; *you had better slip away while the hymn is being sung*; *the dog slipped off after a hare*; (also fig.) *to let opportunities slip.* **6.** a To move, progress, glide, along, swiftly, smoothly, and easily: *the boat slips through the water*; *the car is slipping along splendidly*; Phr. *to slip into another suit, dress, one's evening clothes* &c., to put on a suit &c. rapidly; b (of periods of time) to pass, esp. to pass rapidly and imperceptibly: *life is slipping away and we get very little done*; *the years slip by and the seasons soon come round again.* **B.** trans. **1.** To cause to slip or glide on, off &c.; to pull on or off quickly: *to slip a ring on to a finger*; *slip one's shoes off*; *to slip one's clothes on, off.* **2.** a To put in, insert, take out, remove, quietly &c. with smooth, gliding movement: *to slip a cartridge into (breech of) a gun*; *to slip one's hand into, out of, a pocket*; b implying stealthy, furtive movement: *to slip money into a person's hand*; *to slip a pair of handcuffs on a man's wrists.* **3.** To let go, release; a (of dogs) to let free from the leash: *to slip greyhounds on the hare*; b (naut.) to let go overboard by releasing tackle: *to slip an anchor, cable* &c.; c to detach (railway carriage) from coupling and leave behind when moving. **4.** a To escape from: *a prisoner slips his captors*; b to get rid of by slipping out of: *a dog slips his collar, a horse his bridle, a prisoner his handcuffs*; c (of mental process) *to slip the memory*, pass out of, be forgotten. **5.** (of animals) To give birth to prematurely; to slink: *the cow has slipped her calf.*

slip (II.), n., fr. prec. **1.** Act of slipping; an involuntary sliding action of the foot caused by treading upon something slippery; a stumble caused by a slip of the foot. **2.** a A slipping, sliding movement of anything, out of straight line of progress, away from normal position &c.: *the slip of a wheel on a slippery road*; *a sudden slip of a portion of a cliff.* Phrs. *a slip of the pen*, a graphic error; error of expression in writing; *slip of the tongue*, slight error in utterance; *many a slip 'twixt the cup and the lip*, many things may possibly occur between the beginning of an action, and its completion, to prevent the latter; *to give (a person) the slip*, to escape from, evade him; b an error in judgement, defect of knowledge; an error in conduct, a moral lapse. **3.** One of various kinds of loose garment easily slipped on. **4.** A loose outer linen cover or case, for a pillow or bolster. **5.** a A cutting, live shoot, taken from a plant for grafting, or planting; scion; hence b (i.) (archaic, poet.) a descendant, a youthful member of a family &c.; (ii.) a young, undeveloped person; chiefly in Phr. *a (mere) slip of a boy, girl.* **6.** (usually *slips*, pl.) The leash or coupling by which a dog or couple of dogs, as greyhounds, is held. **7.** a A thin, narrow strip or piece of anything: *a slip of paper, wood* &c.; b specif., a galley proof, printed in single column on a long slip of paper, for revision before being set up in page form. **8.** A small, young sole or plaice. **9.** An inclined plane on which a vessel is built or hauled up for repair; a slipway. **10.** (cricket) One of the fielders, two or more in number, placed behind the wicket on the offside, in position to stop balls which slip or glance off the bat: *short, long slip*, placed close to or at a distance from the wicket; *in the slips*, in this position on the field. **11.** Clay in a semi-liquid state, used to cover earthenware or for decorations &c.

slip-carriage, n. A carriage, coach, on an express train which is detached or 'slipped' at a station where the rest of the train does not stop.

slip-knot, n. a A running knot, one that slips up and down and tightens or loosens a loop; b form of knot which can be untied by a pull.

slipper (I.), n. [1. slíper; 2. slípə]. **slip** (I.) & **-er.** A new formation; cp., however, O.E. *slīepes-sceōh*, lit. 'slip shoe', where the first element is unconnected w. *slip.* A light, loose, easy shoe, worn indoors, esp. while dressing and undressing; a light, lady's shoe, worn in the evening, for dancing &c.

slipper (II.), n. **slip** (I.) & **-er.** **1.** Man who slips greyhounds in coursing. **2.** A shoe or drag, placed or slipped under the wheel of a cart or waggon to take the weight off the horse when going downhill.

slipper (III.), vb. trans., fr. **slipper** (I.). (colloq.) To chastise with a slipper.

slipper-bath, n. Obsolete kind of bath shaped like a shoe, having a cover over lower part of the body and the legs.

slippered, adj. [1. slíperd; 2. slípəd]. **slipper** (I.) & **-ed.** Wearing slippers.

slipperily, adv. [1. slíperili; 2. slípərili]. **slippery** & **-ly.** In a slippery manner.

slipperiness, n. [1. slíperines; 2. slípərinis]. See prec. & **-ness.** Condition, quality, of being slippery.

slipper-wort, n. The calceolaria; also called *lady's slipper.*

slippery, adj. [1. slíperi; 2. slípəri]. O.E. *slipor*, 'slippery' & **-y.** **1.** (of a surface) Affording no purchase, producing only very slight friction in contact with other bodies, by reason of extreme smoothness, sliminess, iciness &c., hence, liable to cause slipping and skidding if trodden or walked upon: *a slippery slope, deck, path, road, plank* &c. **2.** Affording no purchase when grasped, liable to slip through the fingers; difficult to hold: *a slippery rope.* Phr. *as slippery as an eel*, very slippery; (also in fig. sense, see **3**). **3.** (in moral sense) Unreliable, undependable; evasive; hard to pin down to a bargain; unscrupulous. Phr. *a slippery customer*, unreliable, unscrupulous person.

slippy, adj. [1. slípi; 2. slípi]. **slip** & **-y.** (colloq.) Quick, nimble, active; esp. in Phr. *look slippy, be slippy about it*, be smart, quick in going somewhere, or doing something.

slip-rope, n. A rope, or hawser, so fastened that it can be easily slipped and freed.

slipshod, adj. [1. slípshod; 2. slípʃɔd]. **slip** (I.) & **shod** (I.). **1.** (archaic) Wearing shoes or slippers trodden or worn down at heel. **2.** Slovenly, careless in dress, manners, style of writing, speaking, or in action generally.

slipslop, n. & adj. [1. slípslòp; 2. slípslɔ̀p]. Imitative. **1.** n. a Weak, sloppy liquor or other beverage; b sentimental, sloppy writing, talk &c.; trashy, futile gossip &c. **2.** adj. Feeble, weak, sentimental, trashy.

slipway, n. [1. slípwā; 2. slípwei]. An inclined plane or slip in a dock or shipbuilder's yard.

slit (I.), vb. trans. & intrans. [1. slit; 2. slit]. M.E. *slitten*, new weak formation, fr. *slīten*, O.E. *slītan*, (strong), 'to tear, cut', cp. O.H.G. *slīzan*, O.N. *slīta*, cp. **slice.** **1.** trans. To cut open, make an incision in, with a sharp, cutting instrument: *to slit a person's throat*; *to slit open an envelope*; *to slit one's coat up the back.* **2.** intrans. To be slit: *the coat has slit in two places.*

slit (II.), n., fr. prec. **1.** A narrow, clean-cut incision: *a slit in one's coat* &c. **2.** A narrow opening: *the window was a mere slit in the wall*; *he appears to have two slits for eyes.*

slither, vb. intrans. [1. slídher; 2. slíðə]. O.E. *slidrian*, 'to slip', M.E. *slideren*, cp. O.E. *slidor*, 'slippery'; fr. gradational variant of base in **slide.** **1.** To slip and slide continually as in walking upon a hard, slippery road, or through liquid, slimy mud. **2.** To slide slowly along, or down, a surface, preserving continuous contact with it: *to slither along a bench*; *the car began to slither down the hill.*

slithery, adj. [1. slídheri; 2. slíðəri]. Prec. & **-y.** Slippery; causing one to slither; slimy.

sliver, n. & vb. trans. & intrans. [1. slíver, slíver; 2. sláivə, slívə]. M.E. *slīver*, 'part, portion', cp. M.E. *sliven*, fr. O.E. *slīfan*, 'to cut, slice'. **1.** n. Small, narrow piece, cut, torn, or split off anything. **2.** vb. a trans. To cut, tear, off a sliver from; to cut into slivers; b intrans., to split into slivers.

slobber (I.), vb. intrans. & trans. [1. slóber; 2. slɔ́bə]. M.E. *sloberen*, apparently of Du. origin; perh. cogn. w. **slaver** (II.). **1.** intrans. To allow saliva to run out of the mouth; to dribble; Phr. *to slobber over a person*, cover him with fulsome caresses; speak to or of him with sentimental enthusiasm. **2.** trans. To cover, wet, with saliva.

slobber (II.), n., fr. prec. a Dribbling saliva, slaver; b maudlin, drivelling, sentimental talk &c.

slobberiness, n. [1. slóberines; 2. slɔ́bərinis]. **slobbery** & **-ness.** State, quality, of being slobbery.

slobbery, adj. [1. slóberi; 2. slɔ́bəri]. **slobber** & **-y.** **1.** a Inclined to slobber; b wet with saliva. **2.** Maudlin, drivelling, sentimentally emotional.

sloe, n. [1. slō; 2. slou]. O.E. *slā*, M.E. *slō*; cognates occur in other Gmc. languages; origin doubtful; possibly cogn. w. Lith. *slywa*, Russ. *sliva*, 'wild plum', & w. Lat. *līvidus*, 'blue', see **livid.** The acrid, bluish-black fruit of the blackthorn or wild plum, *Prunus spinosa.*

sloe-gin, n. A liqueur made from sloes steeped in gin.

sloe-worm, n. See **slow-worm.**

slog, vb. intrans. & trans. & n. [1. slog; 2. slɔg]. Etymol. doubtful. **1.** vb. a intrans. To hit hard; esp. at cricket, to hit a ball, or at a ball, hard and wildly; *slog at*, to work hard, exert effort to accomplish: *to slog at one's work*; *to slog away*; b trans., to strike with violence: *to slog a ball at cricket*; *to slog a man over the head.* **2.** n. A hard, rather random stroke; a violent blow.

slogan, n. [1. slṓgan; 2. slóugən], fr. Gael. *sluagh-gairm*, fr. *sluagh*, 'host, army', & *gairm*, 'cry, shout'. **1.** The gathering call or war-cry of a Highland clan; a battle-cry. **2.** a Word or phrase embodying, or standing as a symbol of, some principle or cause advocated by a political or other party; b similar phrase &c., used in advertising: *our slogan is 'high quality and low prices'.*

slogger, n. [1. slóger; 2. slɔ́gə]. **slog** & **-er.** **1.** One who slogs; a hard, wild hitter, esp. at cricket; a hard, steady worker.

sloid, sloyd, n. [1. sloid; 2. slɔid], fr. Swed. *slöjd*, 'skill, dexterity', cp. **sleight.** Sys em of elementary manual training based upon the making of small wooden articles with the aid of simple tools.

sloop, n. [1. slōop; 2. slūp], fr. Du. *sloep*, L.G. *sluup*, fr. *slupen*, 'to glide, slip along', cogn. w. O.E. *slūpan*, 'to glide'; the base is seen outside Gmc. in Lat., see **lubricate**. A single-masted fore-and-aft rigged vessel, with jib, mainsail, staysail, and gaff-topsail.

sloop of war, n. A small war vessel furnished with sails as well as steam.

sloop-rigged, adj. Rigged as a sloop.

slop (I.), n. [1. slop; 2. slɔp]. M.E. *sloppe*, 'puddle'; O.E. *-sloppe*, in combin. *cū-sloppe*, 'cow's droppings', fr. *slūpan*, 'to slip'. See **sloop**. **1.** A pool of spilt liquid, as produced by upsetting a cup or other vessel of any kind. **2.** (pl. *slops*) Water which has been used for washing, and liquid from other utensils, removed from bedrooms. Phr. *to empty the slops*, remove water from hand-basins &c. **3.** *Slops*, liquid food, milk, broth, milky puddings &c., as given to invalids: *to live on slops*.

slop (II.), vb. intrans. & trans., fr. prec. **1.** intrans. To be spilt, to overflow: *some water has slopped on the floor*; also *slop over*. **2.** trans. To spill, cause to overflow.

slop (III.), n., fr. O.N. *sloppr*, 'loose robe', cogn. w. **slip**. (only in pl. *slops*) **1.** (archaic) Loose, wide trousers or breeches. **2.** Ready-made clothing; esp. clothes, bedding &c. issued to sailors.

slop (IV.), n. For *ecilop*, back slang for police. (thieves' slang) A policeman.

slop-basin, n. Small china basin, forming part of a breakfast- or tea-service, into which the dregs from teacups &c. are poured.

slop clothes, n. **slop** (III.) & **clothes**. Sailor's slops; ready-made clothes.

slope (I.), n. [1. slōp; 2. sloup]. In M.E.; first in *aslope*, 'ready to slip, on an incline'; formal development obscure; perh. connected w. O.E. *slūpan*, 'to glide'. Cp. **sloop**. **1. a** Inclined, oblique direction or position; line away from the horizontal or perpendicular: *the slope of a roof*; *to give a slope to anything*; **b** degree of inclination from the perpendicular or horizontal or from ground level: *the road rises at a slope of 1 in 20*. Phr. *on the slope*, obliquely, aslope, aslant. **2.** Sloping ground; ground rising or falling; an incline, a declivity: *the grassy slopes of the downs*. **3.** Position of rifle when sloped: *at the slope*.

slope (II.), vb. intrans. & trans., fr. prec. **1.** intrans. **a** To lie in an oblique direction, to incline; to slant: *the ground slopes sharply at this point*; *a sloping roof, forehead &c.*; **b** (slang) (i.) to go away; also *slope off*; (ii.) *slope about*, to loaf, lounge, saunter, idly and aimlessly about. **2.** trans. To give a slope to; to place at a slope or obliquely; to cause to slope or slant: *to slope the ground so that the water can run away*; *to slope a roof*; *to slope a ladder at a safe angle*; Phr. (mil.) *to slope arms*, to hold rifle at the slope upon the shoulder.

sloping, adj. [1. slōping; 2. slóupiŋ], fr. Pres. Part. of **slope** (II.). Inclined, inclining, slanting, oblique.

slopingly, adv. Prec. & **-ly**. In a sloping direction, or position, at a slope, obliquely.

slop pail, n. A pail or bucket for holding the slops of a bedroom &c.

sloppily, adv. [1. slópili; 2. slɔ́pili]. **sloppy** & **-ly**. In a sloppy manner.

sloppiness, n. [1. slópines; 2. slɔ́pinis]. **sloppy** & **-ness**. Condition, quality, of being sloppy (in various senses).

sloppy, adj. [1. slópi; 2. slɔ́pi]. **slop** (I.) & **-y**. **1. a** Of a thin, liquid, watery consistency; impregnated with liquid; reverse of *firm*: *a sloppy pudding, sloppy food, sloppy ground*; **b** covered with liquid, or semi-liquid; liable to splash: *sloppy roads*. **2.** (fig.) **a** Carelessly, loosely, put together, or performed: *sloppy work*; lacking sound, well-knit, terse construction: *sloppy style*; **b** lacking restraint, sincerity, depth: *sloppy sentiment*.

slop-room, n. **slop** (III.) & **room**. Room on board ship from which slops &c. are issued.

slop-shop, n. **slop** (III.) & **shop**. Shop where ready-made clothes or slops are sold.

slosh, n. [1. slosh; 2. slɔʃ]. Variant of **slush**.

slot (I.), n. [1. slot; 2. slɔt]. A.-Fr. *esclot*, borrowed fr. M.E. *slooth*, 'track', see **sleuth**. Track, trail of an animal, esp. of a deer, as shown by marks of feet in mud, snow &c.

slot (II.), n. & vb. trans. Etymol. doubtful. **1.** n. **a** A groove, slit, incision in any object into which something fits or along which something may slide; **b** a narrow aperture or slit, esp. in an automatic machine, into which a coin is inserted to start the lever working the machine which delivers a small article, such as a packet of cigarettes &c. **2.** vb. To make a slot in, provide with slots.

sloth (I.), n. [1. slōth; 2. slouþ]. O.E. *slǣwþ*, M.E. *slēwþ*, also *slōwþ*. The latter is a new formation fr. adj. *slōw*, whence present form, see **slow** & **-th**. Disinclination to, absence of, bodily or mental activity; indolence, laziness.

sloth (II.), n., fr. prec. One of several species of nocturnal, long-haired, slow-moving arboreal mammals found in the forests of S. America.

sloth-bear, n. Bear with long black coat, and long claws, feeding on honey and insects, found in India and Ceylon.

slothful, adj. [1. slōthfool; 2. slóuþful]. **sloth** (I.) & **-ful**. Indolent, lazy, inactive.

slothfully, adv. Prec. & **-ly**. In a slothful manner.

slothfulness, n. See prec. & **-ness**. Quality of being slothful; sloth.

slot-machine, n. An automatic machine which delivers small packages of cigarettes, sweets &c. through an opening upon the working of a lever set in motion by a coin placed in a slot.

slouch (I.), n. [1. slouch; 2. slautʃ]. The development of the form is obscure, though there is apparently some connexion, as the dictionaries suggest, w. O.N. *slōkr*, 'slouching, lazy fellow', fr. *slōka*, 'to hang down, to droop, fall slack or loose', wh. is prob. in gradational relation to **slack**. **1.** A crouching, bent, stooping, attitude of head, shoulders, and back, in walking or sitting; a careless, clumsy, slovenly gait. **2.** (rare) Downward droop of a broad soft hat-brim.

slouch (II.), vb. intrans., fr. prec. **a** To hold oneself with a slouch in sitting, standing, or walking; to move with a slovenly, clumsy gait; also *slouch along*; **b** *slouch about*, to hang idly about, to loaf, to loll in a lazy, aimless manner.

slouch-hat, n. Hat of soft material, with a broad, turned-down brim.

slough (I.), n. [1. slou; 2. slau]. O.E. *slōh*, fr. **slaŋχ-*, cogn. w. *schlingel* & *geschlinge*, 'a small valley, gorge', found in Germ. Pl.-Ns.; connexion w. Mod. Germ. *schlingen*, 'to swallow up, devour', is problematical, since in O.H.G. the form was *slinden*; w. this cp. O.H.G. *slunt*, 'throat, swallow', Mod. Germ. *schlund*, 'gullet; abyss'. A swamp, quagmire, a marshy, muddy place, a bog. Phr. *Slough of Despond*, the bog of sin in which Christian flounders at beginning of Bunyan's 'Pilgrim's Progress'; hence any state of hopeless despondency &c.

slough (II.), n. [1. sluf; 2. slaf]. M.E. *slūghe*, *slouh*; origin obscure; cp. the cogn. O.H.G. *slūch*, Mod. Germ. *schlauch*, 'skin; bag, wallet'. **1.** The skin of a snake cast off at certain periods; any part periodically shed or cast by an animal &c. **2.** Dead, injured tissue which comes away from a wound as this heals.

slough (III.), vb. trans. & intrans., fr. prec. **1.** trans. **a** To shed, cast, throw off as a slough: *a snake sloughs its skin*; *wound sloughs dead tissue*; **b** (fig.) to cast away, discard as worthless or dead: *to slough off old prejudices, habits &c.* **2.** intrans. To form a slough; *slough off*, to come away, be shed, in form of a slough.

sloughy (I.), adj. [1. slóui; 2. sláui]. **slough** (I.) & **-y**. (rare) Resembling a slough; boggy, marshy.

sloughy (II.), adj. [1. slúfi; 2. sláfi]. **slough** (II.) & **-y**. (rare) Of the nature of, resembling, the slough of a snake, or the dead tissue cast off from a wound &c.

Slovak, n. [1. slōvak; 2. slóuvæk]. Czech *Slowak*, 'Slavic'. See **Slav**. **1.** Member of a western Slav race inhabiting the region south-east of Moravia, now included in Czechoslovakia. **2.** Slavic language spoken by this race.

Slovakian, adj. [1. slōvákian; 2. slouvéikiən]. Prec. & **-ian**. Connected with, pertaining to, the Slovaks and their language.

sloven, n. [1. slúvn; 2. slávn]. M.E. *sloveyn*, fr. M. Du. *slof*, *sloef*, 'a sloven, careless person', cogn. w. L.G. *sluf*, 'slovenly' & *-ein*, Fr. *-ain*, Lat. *-ānus*, see **-an**. **a** An untidy, dirty, lazy person, a male slattern; **b** one who is slipshod, unmethodical, or careless in work &c.

Slovene, n. [1. slōvēn, slōvén; 2. slóuvīn, slouvín], fr. *Slowene*, the people's own name; cp. Gk. *Sklabēnos*, & see **Slav**. A member of a South Slavonic race, inhabiting Carinthia and Styria, formerly included in the Austrian Empire, now one of the peoples forming, with the Serbs and Croats, Yugo-Slavia.

Slovenian, adj. & n. [1. slōvénian; 2. slouvíniən]. Prec. & **-ian**. **1.** adj. Of, pertaining to, the Slovenes, their language &c. **2.** n. Language of the Slovenes, a Southern Slavonic language.

slovenliness, n. [1. slúvnlines; 2. slávnlinis]. **slovenly** & **-ness**. Condition, quality, of being slovenly.

slovenly, adj. [1. slúvnli; 2. slávnli]. **sloven** & **-ly**. **1.** Having the habits, character, of a sloven; **a** untidy, neglected, in appearance, clothes &c.; **b** careless, negligent, slipshod, in performance of duties, work &c. **2.** (of work &c.) Performed in a careless, slipshod way.

slow (I.), adj. [1. slō; 2. slou]. O.E. *slāw*; M.E. *slōwe*; O.S. *slēu*; O.H.G. *slēo*, 'dull, blunt'; O.N. *sljōr*, *slǣr*; further relations obscure; connexion w. Lat. *laevus*, 'left-hand', is doubtful. Reverse of *fast, quick, rapid*. In physical, material senses: **1. a** Moving at a low rate of speed; traversing only a small space or short distance in a relatively long time: *a slow runner, walker*; *a slow ball* (at cricket); *a slow horse*; *one of the slower vessels of the line*; Phr. *a slow train*, one that stops at intermediate stations between terminal points, contrasted with *express* or *fast train*; **b** taking, occupying, a considerable time to complete: *a slow journey, crossing &c.* **2.** Taking a considerable time, or longer than the average or usual time, to perform some action: *a slow worker, speaker, reader &c.*; *a slow bowler*, one who delivers a slow ball at cricket. **3.** Taking some time to develop, to accomplish a process, to take effect: *a slow growth of timber*; *a slow poison*. **4.** In such a state as to cause an object travelling over it to move at a low rate of speed: *a slow cricket-pitch, tennis-court, billiard-table, golf-green &c.* **5.** Taken at, performed at, a rate or rhythm below that of the average or common rate: *in slow time*; *at a slow pace*; *a slow step*. Phr. *slow march*, of soldiers, as at a funeral or as a parade exercise. **6.** (of time) **a** (of clock or watch) Behind the correct time: *the clock is slow, ten minutes slow*; **b** late, not punctual: *the guests are slow in arriving*; *to be slow in keeping an appointment*. In non-material senses: **7. a** (of mental capacity) Not quick or alert; not able readily and rapidly to take in an idea or to understand; dull, sluggish, stupid: *slow of wits*; *slow of speech*; *very slow in grasping one's meaning, in learning lessons &c.*;

b (of temperament) not quickly or easily moved or excited; not hasty or rash; deliberate: *slow to wrath or anger*; *slow to take offence*; Phr. *slow and sure*; c inactive, inert, dilatory, reluctant: *the nation was not slow to take up arms*. 8. Not causing the time to pass quickly; not stimulating to the mind; monotonous, uninteresting, tedious, dull, boring; not lively or entertaining: *to find life slow in the country*; *this book is rather slow*; *to pass a very slow evening*. 9. Not brisk; inactive: *a slow season*; *markets are rather slow*.

slow (II.), vb. intrans. & trans. O.E. *slāwian*, 'become slow'. See prec. 1. intrans. *Slow down, slow up*, to reduce speed; to go slower: *you had better slow down, slow up, going through the village*. 2. trans. To reduce the speed of; cause to go slower: *to slow down an engine, motor-car* &c.

slow (III.), adv., fr. **slow** (I.). Slowly: *how slow the time passes*; *speak slow over the telephone*. Phr. *to go slow*, (fig.) to show caution, avoid rashness.

slow (IV.), n., fr. **slow** (I.). A slow ball, as at cricket.

slowcoach, n. [1. slṓkōch; 2. slóukoutʃ]. Person who moves, thinks, does things slowly; an old-fashioned dull person; one averse to changes, rapid action &c.

slowly, adv. [1. slṓli; 2. slóuli]. **slow** (I.) & **-ly**. In a slow manner; at a slow or low rate of speed; not quickly.

slow-match, n. Match or fuse made to burn slowly, for igniting an explosive, blasting charge &c.

slowness, n. [1. slṓnes; 2. slóunis]. **slow** (I.) & **-ness**. State, quality, of being slow.

slow-worm, n. O.E. *slā-wyrm*; first element prob. cogn. w. *slēan*, 'to strike', see **slay**; the animal was for long considered venomous. The blind-worm, *Anguis fragilis*, a limbless lizard, resembling a snake, with shiny scales and somewhat brittle body, feeding on worms, insects &c. and perfectly harmless.

sloyd, n. See **sloid**.

slub, n. & vb. trans. [1. slub; 2. slab]. Etymol. unknown. 1. n. Roll of wool, cotton, or other fibre, slightly twisted as prepared for spinning. 2. vb. To twist wool into slub, in preparation for spinning.

slubber (I.), n. [1. slúber; 2. slábə]. Prec. & **-er**. That which slubs or twists wool &c.; a slubbing machine.

slubber (II.), vb. Variant of **slobber**.

slubbing machine, n. [1. slúbing mashèn; 2. slábiŋ məʃín]. **slub** & **-ing**. Machine used for slubbing or twisting wool &c.

sludge, n. [1. sluj; 2. sladž]. M.E. *sluche*, also *slich*, cogn. w. *sleck*, & cp. **slush** & provinc. Engl. *slud*, 'mud'. 1. Thick, greasy mud; slush, mass of melting snow. 2. Any thick, slimy, muddy deposit, as in ore-dressing, paraffin distillation &c. 3. Small floating pieces of ice.

sludgy, adj. [1. slúji; 2. sládži]. Prec. & **-y**. Consisting of sludge; muddy, slushy.

slue, vb. See **slew** (II.).

slug (I.), n. [1. slug; 2. slag]. M.E. *slugge*. See **sluggard**. 1. (obs. or archaic) Sluggard. 2. Any of various kinds of gastropod molluscs without external shell, a kind of shell-less snail, exuding a slimy mucus, and feeding voraciously on garden plants &c.; (also loosely) soft, smooth, creeping larva of various flies or moths. 3. (possibly a different word) a A small, roughly shaped bullet of lead or other metal, used in old shot-guns, boys' catapults, air-guns &c.; b (print.) line of type produced by linotype or similar type-composing machine.

slug (II.), vb. intrans., fr. M.E. *sluggen*, 'to be slothful'. See **sluggard**. 1. (colloq.) To be slothful, to lie in bed, be lazy: *to slug in bed, indoors* &c. 2. To gather, destroy, slugs, as in a garden &c.

slug-a-bed, n. [1. slúg a bed; 2. slág ə bed]. One who slugs or lies late in bed; sluggard.

sluggard, n. [1. slúgard; 2. slágəd], fr. M.E. *sluggen*, 'to go slowly, be lazy', & **-ard**; of Scand. origin, cp. Dan. *slug*, in compounds *slugöret*, 'with drooping ears', Swed. *slogga*, 'be sluggish', Norw. *slōka*, 'to hang down, slouch', cogn. w. **slouch**. A lazy, sluggish person; a confirmed idler.

sluggish, adj. [1. slúgish; 2. slágiʃ]. **slug** (I.) & **-ish**. 1. Slow to move, having slow movement: *a sluggish stream*. 2. Inert, inactive, not functioning properly: *a sluggish liver*; also (in commerc. circles) *a sluggish market*, not brisk, not showing activity in sales or purchases. 3. Lazy, disinclined to move or be active: *a sluggish idler*; *to have a sluggish temperament*.

sluggishly, adv. Prec. & **-ly**. In a sluggish way.

sluggishness, n. See prec. & **-ness**. Quality, condition, of being sluggish.

slug-horn, n., fr. Lowland Scots *slogorne*, see **slogan**. A war horn or trumpet; word due to Chatterton ('Battle of Hastings'), who took *slogorne* to mean a kind of horn blown in battle; also followed by Browning ('Childe Roland').

sluice (I.), n. [1. slōōs; 2. slūs], fr. O. Fr. *escluse*, 'flood-gate', fr. L. Lat. *exclūsa*, sc. *aqua*, lit. 'water shut out', fr. Lat. *exclūsus*, P.P. *exclūdere*, 'to shut out', see **exclude**. 1. a An artificial passage for regulating the flow and level of water, as in a mill-stream, canal, river &c., by means of a sliding valve or moving gate &c.; a flood-gate; b body of water passing through such passage or blocked above it; any fast-flowing stream; Phr. *to open, let loose, free, the sluices* (lit. and fig.). 2. An inclined trough used for washing out gold and other metals from ore. 3. (colloq.) A bathe, thorough wash down with water.

sluice (II.), vb. trans. & intrans., fr. prec. 1. trans. a To provide with sluices; b to drench, flood, with water by opening the sluices; c (colloq.) to wash down with, pour, splash, water over. 2. intrans. (of water, liquid) To flow out freely, as through a sluice.

sluice-gate, n. A movable gate controlling the flow of water in a sluice.

sluice-valve, n. A sliding valve serving as a sluice-gate.

sluice-way, n. Artificial channel for passage of water, controlled by a sluice-gate or valve.

slum, n. & vb. intrans. [1. slum; 2. slam]. Etymol. doubtful, possibly form of **slump**, in provinc. sense of 'swamp, bog, muddy place'. 1. n. A street or area which is in an insanitary, dirty, dilapidated, and neglected condition, inhabited by the poorest and most thriftless of the population, and usually greatly overcrowded; a low, dirty court, back alley &c; *the slums*, area in a town or city covered with squalid houses of the poorest kind. 2. vb. To visit the slums of a town for charitable or social purposes; it is doubtful if such a verb actually exists except in present participle or verbal noun in such Phrs. as *to go slumming*; *to be fond of slumming*.

slumber (I.), vb. intrans. & trans. [1. slúmber; 2. slámbə]. M.E. *slumeren*, freq. form of *slumen*, 'to doze, slumber', formed fr. *slūme*, 'doze', O.E. *slūma*; Late M.H.G. *slummeren*; fr. base *slau-, *slu-, 'to be silent', cp. Goth. *slawan*, 'to be silent'; no connexions apparently outside Gmc. 1. intrans. a (poet., or with slight suggestion of deliberate affectation) To sleep; the shade of meaning given in some dictionaries, to sleep lightly, can hardly be supported, since we can perfectly well say: *he slumbered long and deeply*; b (fig.) to be quiescent, lie dormant: *one's conscience may slumber on occasions*. 2. trans. *Slumber away*, to pass, spend, in slumber or inactivity: *to slumber one's life away*.

slumber (II.), n., fr. prec. (often poet., but common in ordinary speech) Sleep: *a profound slumber*; *a broken, troubled, fitful, slumber*.

slumberer, n. [1. slúmberer; 2. slámbərə]. **slumber** (I.) & **-er**. One who slumbers.

slumb(e)rous, adj. [1. slúmb(e)rus; 2. slámb(ə)rəs]. **slumber** (II.) & **-ous**. a Inclined to slumber, sleepy, drowsy; b tending to cause slumber, inviting to slumber: *a slumberous atmosphere, heat* &c.

slumb(e)rously, adv. Prec. & **-ly**. In a slumberous manner.

slump, n. & vb. intrans. [1. slump; 2. slamp]. In provinc. Engl., 'bog, muddy place'; imitative; cp. Norw. *slump*, 'plump', noise made by falling into water. 1. n. a (obs. or dial.) A bog, swamp; also fall into water, through ice or snow &c.; b (i.) (commerc.) sudden fall in the value of shares, in prices of goods, in demand for such; contrasted with *boom*; (ii.) decline in esteem in which a person or thing is held: *the slump in Tennyson is passing away*. 2. vb. a (i.) (obs. or dial.) To step suddenly into a bog; break, fall, through ice into water; (ii.) to sit down heavily; remain sitting as though thoroughly exhausted and in state of collapse; b (of prices &c.) to fall suddenly and heavily.

slung, vb. [1. slung; 2. slaŋ]. Pret. & P.P. of **sling**; fr. M.E., P.P. *slunge(n)*; O.E. *(ġe)slungen*; cp. O.E. Pret. *slang*.

slung-shot, n. P.P. of **sling**, & **shot** (III.). A ball or lump of metal attached to a leather strap or thong and used by criminals as a weapon.

slunk, vb. [1. slungk; 2. slaŋk]. Pret. & P.P. of **slink**, fr. M.E. P.P. *slunke(n)*; O.E. *(ġe)sluncen*. Cp. O.E. Pret. *slanc*, see **slank**.

slur (I.), vb. trans. & intrans. [1. slėr; 2. slʌ], fr. M. Du. *sleuren*, *slooren*, 'to draggle, trail', cp. E. Fris. *slūron*, 'to go about carelessly'. A. trans. 1. a To pronounce indistinctly, by running syllables together, or by speaking so rapidly that the sounds cannot be clearly distinguished; b to run two or more letters or words together in writing so as to cause illegibility. 2. (mus.) a To sing, or play legato: *passage to be slurred*; b to sing (syllable) on more than one note; c to mark (passage) with a 'slur'. 3. a (archaic or obs.) To put a slur upon a person; to disparage by innuendo or insinuation; to speak slightingly of; b *slur (over)*, to pass lightly over, to minimize, to refrain from alluding to: *to slur (over) a person's faults, crimes*; *the more dangerous accusations were cleverly slurred by the speaker*. B. intrans. 1. To pronounce, speak, inarticulately. 2. To sing, play, a passage &c. *legato*.

slur (II.), n., fr prec. 1. a Act of slurring in pronunciation, singing, writing &c.; b (mus.) mark, ⌒, ‿, indicating that a passage is to be slurred or read *legato*. 2. A stain, stigma, imputation of blame, suggestion of disgrace: *a slur upon a person's reputation, good name* &c.; *to put a slur upon a person*.

slush, n. [1. slush; 2. slaʃ]. Variant of **sludge**, cp. Swed. *slask*, 'filth, mud'. 1. Liquid mud; melted, thawing, snow. 2. (colloq.) a Sickly, mawkish sentiment; b trash, drivel.

slushy, adj. [1. slúshi; 2. sláʃi]. Prec. & **-y**. a Abounding in slush; covered with, of the nature of, slush; b rubbishy, trashy.

slut, n. [1. slut; 2. slat]. M.E. *slutte*; cp. Swed. dial. *slåta*, 'slatternly, idle woman', cp. *slåter*, 'idle fellow', fr. *slota*, 'to be lazy'; cogn. w. O.N. *slota*, 'to droop, flag'; cp. **slattern**. 1. A slattern; an idle, slovenly, disreputable woman. 2. (colloq. and semi-humorous) A young girl, a puss: *a saucy slut*.

sluttish, adj. [1. slútish; 2. slátiʃ]. Prec. & **-ish**. Slovenly, slatternly; idle and dirty.

sluttishly, adv. Prec. & **-ly**. In a sluttish manner.

sluttishness, n. See prec. & **-ness**. State, quality, of being sluttish.

sly, adj. [1. slī; 2. slai]. M.E. *sleigh*, *sleh*, *slī*, fr. O.N. *slægr*, *slogr*, 'cunning, crafty'; Mod. Germ. *schlau*, & Du. *sluw*, 'crafty', wh. do not appear in the old languages, must be ultimately cogn. w. the O.N. word. Connexion w. **slay** in old sense 'strike' is suggested, though the vowel sounds present some difficulty. 1. a Cunning, underhand, wily, stealthily artful; b not frank or open; Phr. *on the sly*, secretly, surreptitiously. 2. Arch, playfully roguish, bantering: *sly jokes.*

slyboots, n. [1. slíbōōts; 2. sláibūts]. a A playful name given to a roguish child or pet animal &c.; also b (as mildly reproachful term) a secretive person, one who is not perfectly frank.

slyly, slily, adv. [1. slíli; 2. sláili]. **sly** & **-ly.** In a sly manner.

slyness, n. [1. slínes; 2. sláinis]. **sly** & **-ness.** Quality of being sly.

slype, n. [1. slīp; 2. slaip]. May be fr. M.E. *slīp, fr. O.E. type *slȳp-, mutated form of the base in O.E. *slūpan*, 'to move, glide, smoothly'; perh. connected w. **slop (I.)**, but not w. **slip.** The orig. meaning was apparently simply 'a passage'. A narrow covered passage-way leading between two walls, specif., one from the transept of a cathedral or monastic church to the deanery or chapter-house.

smack (I.), n. [1. smak; 2. smæk]. O.E. *smæc*, M.E. *smak*, 'taste, flavour'; cp. M. Du. *smaeck*; O.H.G. *smac*, Mod. Germ. (*ge*)*schmack*. Origin obscure. 1. The quality which gives a distinctive flavour or taste to anything; small quantity, trace, of any substance which gives a taste: *a smack of garlic in a salad, of resin in rough Italian wines; add a smack of pepper, spice &c. to a dish.* 2. (in non-material sense) Significant trace, tinge, suggestion, of some quality: *a smack of the pedant about him; a smack of insincerity in his character; a smack of the sea in the man's garb and walk.*

smack (II.), vb. intrans.; new formation fr. prec.; the O.E. vb. *smæccan*, 'to taste', wd. give *smatch in Mod. Engl. 1. To have a smack of; to taste slightly of; to indicate the presence of a substance by the taste or flavour: *southern cookery always smacks of oil; medicinal waters smacking of sulphur.* 2. (in non-material sense) To suggest the presence of (some quality); to have the air of, be tinged with, suggest: *his manner smacks of self-conceit; a style which smacks of pedantry.*

smack (III.), n. Of imitative origin; cp. Dan. *smæk*, 'smack, rap', Swed. *smäk*, 'slap', & cp. vb. below. 1. A smart explosive sound, a (of lips) in kissing or tasting anything: *a smack of the lips*; b *a smack of the whip*, crack; c (of palm or flat of open hand) *brought his hand down with a smack on the table.* 2. a A loud, hearty kiss: *gave the girl a good smack on the lips*; b smart blow from a whip, slap with open hand: *caught the horse a smack; he got a smack in the face for his trouble.* Phr. *a smack in the eye*, a disconcerting fact, rebuff &c.

smack (IV.) vb. trans. & intrans. Cp. M. Du. *smacken*, Du. *smakken*, 'to fling, throw, down', Dan. *smække*, 'slam, bang'. 1. trans. a To part (lips) with slight explosive noise, esp. as a sign of enjoyment over food, wine &c., or in anticipation; Phr. *to smack one's lips over (something)*; (also fig.) to dwell on with satisfaction, to gloat over; b to crack, make a loud noise with: *to smack a whip*; c to strike, slap, smartly, but not severely, with the flat of the hand: *to smack the table; smack a naughty child.* 2. intrans. a To make a sharp noise, as with lips; b to crack, as a whip.

smack (V.), adv. See **smack (III.)**. (colloq. or slang) As if with a smack or slap; suddenly, directly; bang, slap: *to run smack into something; fell smack on to his back; caught him smack on the point of the chin.*

smack (VI.), n., fr. M. Du. *smacke*, Du. *smak*, L.G. *smakke*, 'a boat, hoy, smack'; origin obscure. A small fishing-boat, usually sloop-rigged.

smacker, n. [1. smáker; 2. smǽkə]. **smack (IV.)** & **-er.** (colloq. or vulg.) a A loud-sounding kiss or slap; b anything very fine, large, or splendid; a stunner.

smacking, vbl. n. [1. smáking; 2. smǽkiŋ]. **smack (IV.)** & **-ing.** Act of smacking or slapping; punishment inflicted by a smack or slap: *the child wants a good smacking.*

small (I.), adj. [1. smawl; 2. smōl]. O.E. *smæl*, 'narrow, slender; fine, small', M.E. *smal*; O.S., O.H.G. *smal*, 'narrow, slight'; Mod. Germ. *schmal*, 'narrow, slender'; Goth. *smals*; cp. O.N. *smali*, 'small cattle', i.e. sheep or goats; cogn. w. O. Slav. *malŭ*, 'small'; Gk. *mêlon*, 'a small beast, sheep'. 1. a Little; not large; of inconsiderable bulk, height, extent: *a small dog, house, field, estate, piece of paper* &c.; b of less than average, usual, normal, size; not so large as other things of the same kind; of a size less than is desired; too small, undersized: *a small man is often very self-important; the cuckoo, though a large bird, lays small eggs; I find my house rather small, all the rooms are small; a small size in hats; a breed of small sheep; her nose was small but finely shaped;* Phrs. *on the small side*, rather too small, not large enough; *a small whisky*, half the usual portion; *a small soda, small bottle of soda (water)*, a small size, half usual size; c specif., young, undeveloped, not fully grown, esp. in *small birds*; *a small boy*, quite a child, a little boy. 2. a Inconsiderable in number, amount, quantity; reverse of *numerous, large*: *a small audience, dinner-party; small profits; a small present; a small sum of money; a small helping of pudding*; b of inferior strength, quality, value, volume, or the like: *small beer*, q.v.; Phrs. *small change*, coins of low face value; *a small voice*, weak, not powerful. 3. Not lasting long; of short duration: *a small time, while.* 4. a Insignificant, trivial, unimportant, petty: *small cares and worries; thankful for small mercies; matters too small to be worth notice; small errors;* Phrs. *to feel small*, feel rebuffed or snubbed; *to look small*, appear foolish; b involving but slight or inconsiderable interests; conducted on a petty scale: *a small business; to keep a small shop; a small tradesman*, one having a small business; Phrs. *in a small way of business*, doing only a small business; *to live in a small way*, poorly, unostentatiously. 5. Narrow-minded, petty; reverse of *magnanimous*; mean, ungenerous: *small jealousies; a person of small mind; to enjoy a small triumph.* 6. Not much, but little: *to have small cause for gratitude; to pay small heed to what is said.* Phr. *small blame to him*, he was quite justified.

small (II.), n., fr. prec. 1. The small, slender part of anything, esp. of the part of the back above the waist: *small of the back.* 2. (pl. *smalls*) Small-clothes. 3. *Smalls*, (Oxford Univ.) popular name for the examination *Responsions*, q.v.

small (III.), adv., fr. **small (I.)**. Only in Phr. *to sing small*, (fig.) to express oneself with modesty and diffidence, to assume a humble attitude of mind, esp. to cease boasting and asserting oneself as result of a rebuff, failure, humiliation &c.

smallage, n. [1. smáwlij; 2. smōlidž]. M.E. *smalache*, *smalege*, fr. **small (I.)** & Fr. *ache*, 'parsley', fr. Lat. *apium*, etymol. doubtful. Old popular name for wild celery.

small-arms, n. A collective term, applied in widest sense to all military weapons that are wielded and carried by a single man, but more usually confined to all fire-arms other than field or other artillery or machine-guns.

small beer, n. (obs.) a A thin, weak beer; b (by transf.) anything trivial or unimportant; trifling gossip: '*To suckle fools and chronicle small beer*' (Shakespeare, 'Othello'); c an unimportant person: *he is very small beer*; Phr. *to think no small beer of oneself*, have a high opinion of one's own abilities and importance.

small capital, n. (typog.) Capital letter of smaller size than the ordinary capital letter used.

small-clothes, n. (archaic) Knee-breeches.

small coal, n. Broken coal; coal in small lumps.

small debts, n. (law) Debts of such amount as can be sued for in a county court.

small fry, n. a Diminutive, young fish; b persons, things, of no importance.

small-hand, n. Ordinary handwriting, as distinguished from *text-hand.*

small-holder, n. A tenant of a small-holding.

small-holding, n. A small plot of land let at special rents and under special terms to agricultural workers for their own cultivation.

small hours, n. pl. The hours from 1 o'clock to 3 or 4, after midnight.

smallish, adj. [1. smáwlish; 2. smōliʃ]. **small (I.)** & **-ish.** Rather, somewhat, small.

small-minded, adj. Having a small, narrow mind; narrow-minded; mean, not magnanimous.

small-mindedness, n. Prec. & **-ness.** State, quality, of being small-minded.

smallness, n. [1. smáwlnes; 2. smōlnis]. **small (I.)** & **-ness.** 1. State, quality, of being small. 2. a Pettiness of mind, meanness; b petty, mean, action or motive: *his conduct revealed many unsuspected smallnesses.*

small pica, n. Size of type between long primer and pica.

smallpox, n. [1. smáwlpoks; 2. smōlpɔks]. **small (I.)** & **pox**, as distinct fr. the 'great pox', syphilis. See **pox.** An acute infectious and contagious disease, *variola*, often epidemic in occurrence, accompanied by high fever and an eruption of pustules or pocks, which in severe cases leave permanent scars.

small-sword, n. A light sword for thrusting only; a rapier.

small-talk, n. Easy, urbane, trivial conversation on general subjects of trifling importance.

small-wares, n. pl. Small articles of commerce, esp. such as are sold by drapers, e.g. tapes, reels of cotton, ribbons, thimbles &c.

smalt, n. [1. smawlt; 2. smōlt], fr. Ital. *smalto*, 'enamel'; of Gmc. origin; fr. O.H.G. *smalz*, 'butter, grease'; connected w. O.H.G. *smelzan*, 'to smelt'. See under **smelt (I.)** & cp. **enamel.** a A deep blue pigment obtained by fusing oxide of cobalt with silica and potash and reducing the glass thus formed into powder; b deep blue glass formed thus.

smart (I.), vb. intrans. [1. smart; 2. smāt]. O.E. *smeortan*, M.E. *smerten*, 'to give pain'; O.H.G. *smerzan*, Mod. Germ. *schmerzen*, 'to pain'; cp. O.H.G. *smerzo*, 'a pain, smart'; prob. Lat. *mordēre* for *smordēre, 'to bite, sting', see **mordant**; & Gk. *smerdnós*, *smerdaléos*, 'terrible'. 1. a To feel, be affected by, a sharp, tingling, but comparatively slight and superficial pain; to feel sore and painful: *eyes smart with tears, smoke* &c.; *his back smarted after five strokes of the cane; finger smarts from a sting, throat from scalding drink* &c.; *a smarting wound*; b (rare) to be the cause of a sharp pain: *a strong, carbolic dressing smarts when applied to a wound.* 2. To experience mental pain; a (rare) to suffer the sting of conscience, feel self-reproach: *I only hope your conscience is smarting*; b to feel hurt or resentful: *he was still smarting from the insult*; c *smart under*, to suffer from; to resent: *to smart under an injustice; to smart under the jibes of one's fellows, under the lash of reviewers* &c. 3. *Smart for*, to receive punishment for, be punished on account of: *he must be made to smart for his impudence; you shall smart for this.*

smart (II.), n., fr. prec. 1. a Sensation of smarting; a slight tingling, pricking pain, as from a superficial injury: *the smart of a broken blister*; b (poet.) pain generally, whether slight and superficial, or severe and deep-seated: *the smart of his wounds.* 2. Mental distress; wounded feeling caused by insult; resentment; grief felt at calamity: *the smart of ancient wrongs, of former sorrow.*

smart (III.), adj., fr. prec. 1. a Sharp, forcible, severe; delivered with energy and vigour: *a smart punishment; a smart blow*; b occurring suddenly and with intensity; sharp: *a smart pain in the side.* 2. Characterized by, involving, rapid, vigorous action or movement; brisk, quick: *a smart walk, gallop; you'd better be pretty smart about the job.* **3. a** Alert, rapid, and dexterous in performance of an action; quick and clever: *a smart cricketer, bowler, hockey player; a smart carpenter; smart at his work, job* &c.; **b** performed with celerity and skill: *a smart piece of work; to make a smart job of it,* do something neatly and well. **4.** (of persons) Mentally quick and alert; **a** ready, clever, acute, sharp-witted, on the spot, quick to see a point or grasp a situation: *it was rather smart of him to seize the occasion and profit by it; he is as smart as his brother is slow and stupid;* **b** witty, and ready of speech, but superficial; given to clever, pointed sayings uttered for effect; superficially clever, pert: *you are merely trying to be smart; I hate your smart man who thinks a problem is settled by an epigram;* **c** shrewd, keenly alive to one's own interests and quick to further them; clever and unscrupulous: *he was inclined to be smart in his dealings, and few trusted him; more smart than honest.* **5. a** (of sayings) Witty, pungent, pointed, but superficial; said for effect without regard to sincerity and truth: *he is very young, and too fond of saying smart things;* **b** (of actions) displaying unscrupulous shrewdness and cleverness; tricky: *his methods were altogether too smart for an honest man.* **6.** Neat and spruce; fresh, clean; bright, gay, in appearance; reverse of *shabby* or *dingy*; **a** (of persons) well dressed, carefully groomed, brushed-up: *go and make yourself smart; he looked quite smart with white spats and a flower in his button-hole;* specif. (mil.) having uniform and kit, accoutrements &c., clean and in good order, also with an implication of alertness and competence in performance of duties (see No. **3** above): *the regiment was not as smart as one could wish; the general expressed pleasure at their smart appearance;* **b** (of dress) well made, well fitting; in good order, fresh, clean; hence striking, gay, showy: *his clothes were not new, but still looked smart; a smart tie and a dirty collar don't go well together;* **c** (of other objects) tidy, in good order; clean, bright, fresh: *the lawn was mown and the paths swept, and the garden made smart for the party; a car painted sealing-wax red looks very smart.* **7.** In accordance with the latest conventions of the moment among what is accepted as, or what claims to be, the most highly civilized and fashionable society; expressing, embodying, agreeing with, conventional standards of behaviour and action; belonging to the latest ton, modish, fashionable, good form: *it is no longer smart to wear long hair and a beard; smart men do not wear frock-coats now; at one time it is smart to pronounce 'r' like 'w', at another to pronounce '-in' for '-ing', and to make certain slips in grammar; the smart set.* **8.** (colloq.) Considerable; fairly large, extensive, intense &c.: *a smart number of people present; a smart frost.* Phr. *a smart few,* a good, fairly large, number.

smarten, vb. trans. & intrans. [1. smártn; 2. smátn]. **smart (III.)** & **-en. 1.** trans. To make smart; to give smart, spruce appearance; also *smarten up (one's house, one's clothes, oneself).* **2.** intrans. Chiefly *smarten up;* **a** to become smart, be smartened up; **b** to brisk up, become alert.

smartish, adj. & adv. [1. smártish; 2. smátiʃ]. **smart (III.)** & **-ish. 1.** adj. Rather smart, fairly smart. Phr. *a smartish few,* a good number. **2.** adv. (colloq.) To some considerable extent: *it hurt smartish; it froze smartish last night.*

smartly, adv. [1. smártli; 2. smátli]. **smart (III.)** & **-ly.** In a smart manner (in various senses); **a** sharply, severely: *he ought to be smartly censured, punished;* **b** rapidly, briskly: *bring the hands smartly to the sides;* **c** readily, intelligently, alertly; wittily: *to answer smartly;* **d** (i.) sprucely, neatly; gaily, showily: *smartly, but not fashionably dressed;* (ii.) (more rarely) fashionably: *to dress, speak, and behave smartly,* i.e. in accordance with the conventions of the smart set.

smart-money, n. (mainly obs. or hist.) **1. a** Money paid as damages or compensation for injuries, esp. when excessive or vindictive; **b** money exacted from or paid by a person to escape from an unpleasant situation or severe penalty. **2.** (mil. and nav.) **a** Money allowed to a soldier or sailor for wounds received on active service; **b** money paid by a recruit before being sworn in, to escape formal enlistment.

smartness, n. [1. smártnes; 2. smátnis]. **smart (III.)** & **-ness.** Quality, condition, of being smart (in all senses of the adj.).

smartweed, n. [1. smártwēd; 2. smátwīd]. The water-pepper, *Polygonum,* which has sharp, acrid juice.

smash (I.), vb. trans. & intrans. [1. smash; 2. smæʃ]. Prob. of imitative origin, cp. *clash, dash* &c.; Norw. has *smaska,* 'to break to bits'. **A.** trans. **1. a** To break, dash, to pieces, shatter: *to smash a window; she dropped a plate and smashed it to atoms;* **b** *smash in,* to break, burst, through with violence, cause to fall or open inwards: *to smash in a door;* **c** *smash up,* to break up: *to smash up the furniture.* **2.** (colloq.) To deal a heavy blow to; to hit hard: *to smash a man on the nose, in the ribs, over the head.* **3.** (lawn-tennis &c.) To hit (ball &c.) downwards with hard, overhead stroke so that it is impossible to return. **4.** To defeat utterly, annihilate, destroy, crush, bring to nothing: **a** *to smash an attack;* **b** *to smash an argument, an opponent in argument;* **c** specif., to ruin financially; to break, bankrupt. **B.** intrans. **1.** To break up into pieces; to be shattered; to fall to pieces: *the cup fell and smashed to pieces.* **2.** To collide with, rush into, or on to, something: *the car smashed into a wall; ship smashed on to the rocks* &c. **3.** To come to grief, disintegrate, be destroyed, go to pieces; also *smash up,* (i.) to lose one's health utterly; specif. (ii.) to be financially ruined. **4.** (slang) To make counterfeit coin.

smash (II.), n., fr. prec. **1. a** Process of smashing; a violent shattering, a breaking to pieces; **b** sound caused by a violent fall, or by the process of something being smashed; a clatter; Phr. *to go, come, to smash,* to be ruined, destroyed; specif., to be financially ruined. **2.** Also *smash-up;* **a** a violent collision, fall &c.: *broke his ribs as a result of a smash in, with, his car; he's bound to have a smash-up if he drives so recklessly;* **b** failure, bankruptcy, ruin: *the smash-up of a great business;* **c** a catastrophe of any kind: *there will be a smash-up in that household before long.* **3.** (colloq.) An iced drink of brandy or other spirit and water, sweetened and flavoured with mint &c.

smash (III.), adv., fr. prec. (colloq., after vbs. of movement) With a smash; equivalent to bang, slap, crash: *the cars ran smash into each other.*

smasher, n. [1. smásher; 2. smǽʃə]. **smash (I.)** & **-er.** One who, that which, smashes; Specif. (slang) **1. a** a crushing, smashing, blow; **b** a convincing, decisive, argument &c. **2.** One who utters counterfeit coin; counterfeiter.

smashing, adj. [1. smáshing; 2. smǽʃiŋ], fr. Pres. Part. of **smash (I.)**. Tending to smash; destructive, disastrous; crushing, overwhelming, shattering: *a smashing blow; a smashing argument, defeat; a smashing victory,* one in which the enemy is smashed.

smatter, vb. intrans. [1. smáter; 2. smǽtə]. M.E. *smatteren,* 'to make a noise; to talk, prate, ignorantly'; Scand., cp. Swed. *smattra,* 'to clatter'; imitative in origin. (obs. or archaic) **1.** To talk, chatter, about something of which one is ignorant. **2.** To have only a slight or superficial knowledge of anything; to dabble in: *to smatter in Latin.*

smatterer, n. [1. smáterer; 2. smǽtərə]. Prec. & **-er.** One who has only a superficial, slight knowledge of a subject; a dabbler.

smattering, n. [1. smátering; 2. smǽtəriŋ]. **smatter** & **-ing.** A slight, superficial knowledge of a subject.

smear (I.), n. [1. smēr; 2. smiə]. O.E. *smeoru, smeru,* 'fat, grease', M.E. *smēre;* O.H.G. *smero;* O.N. *smjǫr,* 'grease, fat'; Goth. *smairþr,* 'fatness'; cogn. w. Lith. *smarsas,* 'fat'; Gk. *múron,* 'ointment, unguent'; O. Ir. *smir,* 'marrow'. A spot, stain, blotch, mark, made by a rub or touch from a greasy, sticky, staining, or dirty substance: *a smear of greasy fingers on the glass; a smear on one's face.*

smear (II.), vb. trans. & intrans. O.E. *smierwan, smeorwan,* M.E. *smēren.* See prec. **A.** trans. **1. a** To put a smear upon; to soil by contact with greasy, dirty substance: *to smear one's face;* **b** to rub, daub, with grease, dirt &c.: *to smear one's face with grease-paint; to smear a plate with butter;* **c** (rare) to sully, stain, morally. **2.** To rub (grease or sticky substance, dirt &c.) on to: *to smear butter on to a plate.* **3.** To blur, render indistinct by a rubbing, brushing movement: *to smear the address on a letter.* **B.** intrans. **a** (of greasy, sticky substance) To cause a smear; **b** to be liable, tend, to blur, or to be smeared: *anything written with a soft pencil smears easily.*

smeariness, n. [1. smērines; 2. smíərinis]. **smeary** & **-ness.** State, quality, of being smeary.

smeary, adj. [1. smēri; 2. smíəri]. **smear (I.)** & **-y. 1.** Covered, stained, blurred, with smears; having the appearance of having been rubbed with something greasy or sticky: *a smeary window-pane; a woman's face smeary with paint and powder.* **2.** Likely, tending, to become smeared; sticky, greasy: *the paint is still wet and smeary.*

smee, n. See **smew**.

smegma, n. [1. smégma; 2. smégmə], fr. Gk. *smēgma,* 'soap', fr. *smḗkhein,* 'to wipe off', fr. *smáein,* 'to wipe'; cognates doubtful. A soapy, sebaceous secretion from the glands, in folds of the skin.

smell (I.), n. [1. smel; 2. smel]. Not recorded in O.E.; in M.E. occurs in the dialectal variant forms *smel, smil, smul,* the first of wh. is the ancestor of the present form, & must be of the Essex or S.E. dial. type, fr. **smuli-*; perh. cogn. w. **smoulder (I.)**. **1.** That one of the five senses which perceives odours through stimulation of the olfactory nerve conveyed through the nose: *taste and smell are closely connected.* **2.** That which is perceived by the olfactory organs; an odour whether pleasant or unpleasant, a scent, **a** perfume: **a** *the pleasing smell of newly broken earth;* **b** a stink, a stench: *sulphur fumes have a disgusting smell.* **3.** Act of smelling, a sniff: *to take a smell at a nosegay* (prob. formed fr. the vb.).

smell (II.), vb. trans. & intrans. M.E. *smellen, smillen, smullen.* See prec. **A.** trans. **1. a** To perceive (odours) by means of the olfactory organs, to be conscious of the odour of: *do you smell something burning?; I don't smell anything;* Phrs. *to smell a rat,* have suspicions, suspect, that something is wrong; *to smell powder,* to have experience of warfare; **b** to be vaguely conscious of, to suspect, to scent: *to smell treason.* **2.** To direct one's sense of smell upon; to sniff, inhale, the odour of: *just smell this rose.* **3.** *Smell out,* **a** to track, discover, by means of the sense of smell: *hounds soon smelt out the fox;* **b** (fig.) to track, discover, unravel: *to smell out a mystery.* **B.** intrans. **1. a** To have the sense of smell, to have the capacity of perceiving odours: *one cannot smell with a cold in the nose;* Phr. *to smell round, come smelling round,* to poke and pry, to try to pick up odds and ends of information; **b** *smell at,* to sniff the odour of: *to smell at a flower.* **2. a** To emit an odour (good or bad): *the old-fashioned roses often smell deliciously, many of the new* *ones don't smell at all*; **b** specif., to emit an unpleasant odour, to stink: *in hot weather meat soon begins to smell*; *the room is so stuffy, it positively smells*; **c** (often followed by adj. or adv.) *to smell good*, have a pleasant smell; *smell bad, nasty*; *to smell vilely, delightfully* &c. **3.** *Smell of*, **a** to have a smell characteristic of, be redolent of, fragrant with: *the house smells of paint*; *your clothes smell of tobacco smoke, of camphor* &c.; *to smell of drink* &c.; Phr. *to smell of the lamp*, to show signs of having cost much labour; (cp. Phr. *to burn the midnight oil*); **b** to suggest, to smack of: *the whole affair smells of plotting and intrigue.*

smellable, adj. [1. smélabl; 2. sméləbl]. **smell (II.)** & **-able.** Capable of being smelt.

smeller, n. [1. sméler; 2. smélə]. **smell (II.)** & **-er.** (vulg. slang) **1.** The nose. **2. a** A heavy fall; **b** a severe blow.

smelling-bottle, n. [1. sméling bòtl; 2. smélıŋ bɔ̀tl]. Bottle filled with smelling-salts.

smelling-salts, n. An aromatic compound of carbonate of ammonia crystals, mixed with some strong pungent essence; used for faintness, headache, &c.

smell-less, adj. [1. smél les; 2. smél lıs]. **smell (I.)** & **-less. 1.** Deprived of, lacking the sense of, smell. **2.** Having no smell; scentless, odourless.

smelly, adj. [1. sméli; 2. sméli]. **smell (I.)** & **-y.** (colloq.) Having a disagreeable smell; whiffy.

smelt (I.), vb. trans. [1. smelt; 2. smelt]. Scand., cp. Swed. *smälta*, 'to smelt iron ore'; cogn. w. O.H.G. *smelzan*, 'to melt, become fluid', & *smelzan*, 'to cause to melt'; a primitive variant of **melt. a** To subject (ore) to intense heat and reduce it to fluid state in order to extract the metal from it; **b** to extract (metal) from ore by smelting: *to smelt copper.*

smelt (II.), n. In O.E.; perh. fr. same base as O.E. *smolt*, 'calm, smooth'. A small edible fish with silvery sides, belonging to the genus *Osmerus*, found in tidal waters.

smelter, n. [1. smélter; 2. sméltə]. **smelt (I.)** & **-er.** One who smelts ore; a worker in a smeltery or at a smelting-furnace.

smeltery, n. [1. smélteri; 2. sméltəri]. Prec. & **-y.** Establishment where ore is smelted.

smelting-furnace, n. [1. smélting fêrnis; 2. sméltıŋ fʌ̂nis]. Furnace in which ore is smelted.

smew, n. [1. smū; 2. smjū], also **smee.** Origin very doubtful. A small diving sea-duck with black and white plumage, allied to the merganser.

smilax, n. [1. smílaks; 2. smáilæks]. Gk. *smilax*, 'bindweed, convolvulus'; etymol. doubtful. (bot.) **a** (cap). A genus of climbing plants, with small greenish flowers, some tropical species of which yield sarsaparilla; **b** a climbing or twining S. African vine, grown in green-houses for its beautiful foliage.

smile (I.), vb. intrans. & trans. [1. smīl; 2. smail]. M.E. *smīlen*; prob. Scand., cp. Swed. *smīla*; perh. ultimately fr. base **smi-* &c. seen in Scrt. *smēraš*, 'smiling'; Lat. *mīrāri*, 'to wonder'. See **mirror. A.** intrans. **1.** To allow the features to assume an expression indicative of mild amusement, joy, pleasure, benevolence &c., by drawing up the corners of the mouth and generally relaxing the facial muscles, esp. those round the eyes; reverse of *to frown*: *he smiled to see the children's frolics*; *to smile through one's tears*; *what are you smiling at?*; *what is making you smile?* **2.** *Smile at*, (fig.) to regard with indifference or mild contempt; to disregard: *I can afford to smile at your threats.* **3.** *Smile on, upon*, (fig.) to regard with favour, to be propitious to: *he rejoiced when the lady of his choice smiled upon him*; *fortune has smiled upon him from his birth.* **4.** To convey an impression of joy, cheerfulness, prosperity, well-being &c.: *all nature smiled*; *a smiling landscape.* **B.** trans. **1.** To express by a smile: *to smile farewell, forgiveness.* **2.** (w. cogn. object) *To smile a bitter smile.* **3.** Such constructions as, *to smile away his grief*, to dispel by a smile &c., are possible but rare.

smile (II.), n. See prec. **1.** Act of smiling; facial expression somewhat resembling that in a laugh, but unaccompanied by any vocal sound, while the lips are closed and curve upwards at the corners: *greet one with a smile*; *to raise a smile on the face of the audience*; '*The tear which enjoyment may gild with a smile*' (Moore); *a face wreathed in smiles*; the word denotes an expression indicating mild, placid, amusement, joy, benevolence &c., unless some qualifying word or phrase shows the contrary; e.g. *a bitter, cruel, smile, a smile of contempt, derision* &c; also in *I can afford to regard your threats with a smile* &c. **2.** (usually pl.) Favour, support, favourable attitude: *the smiles of fortune*; *he long enjoyed the smiles of his sovereign.* **3.** External appearance of nature which suggests and promotes feelings of cheerfulness, gaiety &c.: *the smile of spring.*

smileless, adj. [1. smílles; 2. smáillıs]. Prec. & **-less.** Without a smile.

smiling, adj. [1. smíling; 2. smáiliŋ], fr. Pres. Part. of **smile (I.). 1.** Wearing a smile: *a pleasant, smiling face*; *I wish the portrait was more smiling, and less stern.* **2.** (of landscape) Conveying an impression of placid cheerfulness and prosperity; radiant, peaceful, serene: '*To scatter plenty o'er a smiling land*' (Gray).

smilingly, adv. [1. smílingli; 2. smáiliŋli], fr. Pres. Part. of **smile (I.)** & **-ly.** In a smiling manner; with a smile.

smirch, vb. trans. & n. [1. smĕrch; 2. smʌ̄tʃ]. Apparently formed fr. **smear**, but the nature of the ending is obscure. **1.** vb. To smear, stain, tarnish, soil, sully (esp. in fig. sense): *to smirch a person's fair name, fame, reputation* &c. **2.** n. Stain, blot (esp. fig.): *it has left a smirch on his reputation.*

smirk, vb. intrans. & n. [1. smĕrk; 2. smʌ̄k]. In O.E. *smearcian*, 'to smile'; M.E. *smirken* is connected w. this, but not derived fr. it. Origin entirely uncertain. **1.** vb. To contort the lips into a disagreeable expression of low satisfaction, or self-conceit; to simper in a self-satisfied manner. **2.** n. A disagreeable gesture, or contortion, of the lips, partly resembling a smile, but expressing or suggesting fatuous self-complacency, would-be archness, and so on.

smite, vb. trans. & intrans. [1. smīt; 2. smait]. O.E. *smītan*, M.E. *smīten*; O.H.G. *smīzan*, 'to stroke, to strike', Goth. (*bi*)*smeitan*, 'to anoint'; the orig. meaning was perh. 'to throw', thence 'throw down'; Walde derives the Gmc. words fr. an Aryan base **smeid-*, 'throw', fr. a variant of wh. **(s)meit-* &c., comes Lat. *mittere*, 'to send', q.v. under **miss (II.).** (archaic or poet.) **A.** trans. **1.** To strike, hit, hard; to deal a heavy blow upon or to: *to smite a person on the cheek, head*; *Moses smote the rock with his rod*; *to smite the drum*; *smite one's hands together*; *to smite a person's head off*, decapitate him. **2. a** To defeat, rout with slaughter; to slay: '*go and smite Amalek and spare not*'; **b** to afflict with: '*I will smite the Egyptians with pestilence*'; *smitten with palsy.* **3.** To affect, fall upon, strike, the senses, powerfully: *a blinding glare smote our eyes*; *our ears were smitten by a deafening roar*; *a horrible stench smote our nostrils.* **4. a** To affect strongly, distress the mind, cause a moral twinge or pang to: *my conscience smites me*; *smitten with remorse*; **b** (only in P.P. pass.) *to be smitten by*, to have the affections and emotions deeply stirred, be struck by: *he was much smitten by the charms of Miss X*; *to be smitten by Miss X*, to be in love with; *I am suddenly smitten with a desire for a pipe*, am strongly desirous of. **B.** intrans. **1.** To strike, deal, a heavy blow; to slay: *smite and spare not*; '*That two-handed engine at the door Stands ready to smite once, and smite no more*' (Milton, 'Lycidas'). **2.** *Smite on, upon*, to strike, beat, hammer, upon: *he smote on the door*; *sound smites on one's ears*; *sunlight smiting on one's eyes* &c.; *smite together*, to knock one against the other: *his knees smote together in his terror.*

smiter, n. [1. smíter; 2. smáitə]. Prec. & **-er.** One who smites: *to turn one's cheek to the smiter.*

smith, n. [1. smith; 2. smiþ]. O.E. *smiþ*, M.E. *smith*; Goth. (*aiza-*)*smiþa*, '(copper-) smith'; O.N. *smiðr*, 'a worker in wood or metal'; the orig. sense seems to have been 'worker, wright, craftsman'; perh. fr. a base **smĕi-*, **smī-* &c., 'to hew, cut'; cp. Gk. *smílē*, 'knife', & perh. Goth. *mailan* (fr. (*s*)*mai-*), 'to hack, hew'; O.H.G. *meizan*, 'cut', & *meizel*, 'hacking tool'. The Gmc. specialization of *smith* as 'metal-worker' is a later process. A worker in metal, usually one who works in and forges iron, in full, *blacksmith*; also in compounds, as *tinsmith, goldsmith, silversmith* &c.

smithereens, n. pl. [1. smìdherḗnz; 2. smìðərínz]. Origin unknown; the suff. appears to be the Ir. dimin. as in *colleen*, 'a girl' &c. (colloq., slang) Small pieces, fragments, atoms: *to blow, smash, to smithereens.*

smithy, n. [1. smídhi; 2. smíði]. New formation fr. **smith** & **-y**, perh. on anal. of **stithy.** The O.E. form for a forge, smith's workshop, was *smiþþe*, cp. O.N. *smiðja*, wh. wd. become simply **smith* in Mod. Engl. A blacksmith's shop, a forge.

smitten, vb. [1. smítn; 2. smítn]. P.P. of **smite**, q.v. for special uses. O.E. (*ġe*)*smiten*; M.E. *smiten.*

smock (I.), n. [1. smok; 2. smɔk]. O.E. *smoc(c)*, 'smock-frock; woman's shift', M.E. *smok*, cogn. w. O.N. *smokkr*, O.H.G. *smoccho*, connected w. O.E. *smūgan*, 'to creep into', cp. O.N. *smjūga*, 'to creep into', esp. to get into a garment by putting it over one's head. Cogn. w. Lith. *smùkti*, 'to slip down'; O. Slav. *mučati*, 'to creep'; for probable further cognates see **mucus.** Cp. **smuggle. 1.** (archaic) A woman's shift or chemise. **2. a** A loose, sleeved, linen garment worn outside other clothes, formerly much worn by workers on the land; also called a *smock-frock*; **b** an overall similarly shaped, worn by small children and young girls.

smock (II.), vb. trans. Back-formation fr. **smocking.** To decorate (garment) with smocking.

smock-frock, n. A long outer garment of linen, with pleated gathers at neck and shoulders, and ornamented at front and back of the neck with 'smocking', formerly worn by farm-labourers, milkmen &c.

smocking, n. [1. smóking; 2. smɔ́kiŋ]. **smock (I.)**, 2, & **-ing.** Needlework in which the material is stitched into very small pleats or gathers, forming a kind of honeycomb ornamentation.

smock-mill, n. A form of windmill, in which the cap alone moves round to the wind with the sails; contrasted with *post-mill*, where the whole body of the mill revolves.

smokable, adj. [1. smṓkabl; 2. smóukəbl]. **smoke (II.)** & **-able.** Capable of being, fit to be, smoked.

smoke (I.), n. [1. smōk; 2. smouk]. O.E. *smoca*, M.E. *smōke*; in gradational relation to M.H.G. *smouch*, Mod. Germ. *schmauch*, 'thick smoke; whiff of smoke'; cp. Lith. *smaugti*, 'to choke'; cp. further O.E. *smēocan*, 'to smoke; to fumigate'; cogn. w. Gk. *smúkhein*, 'to burn with a smouldering flame'. **1.** The volatile gaseous product of the combustion of any organic substances, rendered visible by unconsumed particles of carbon, suspended in it and deposited as soot. Phrs. *no smoke without a fire*, no rumour or scandal without some foundation for it; *to end in smoke*, come to, end in, nothing; *like smoke*, (slang) at once, quickly; readily. **2.** Anything which resembles the smoke of burning substances, as heavy cloud of steam, vapour, spray &c.: *the smoke of a volcano, of a water-*

fall &c. **3.** (fr. vb.) **a** Act of smoking tobacco: *to long for a smoke*; **b** (colloq., vulg.) something to be smoked, a cigar, cigarette: *a box of good smokes.*

smoke (**II.**), vb. intrans. & trans. New formation fr. prec. The O.E. vb. *smēocan* wd. become **smeek* in Mod. Engl. **A.** intrans. **1.** To emit, discharge, smoke: *on every hill a bonfire smoked.* **2.** Specif. **a** to discharge smoke in a wrong direction: *the study chimney, fire, fireplace, smokes,* i.e. discharges its smoke downwards into the room, instead of upwards into the air; **b** to give off smoke, through imperfect combustion, where there should be none: *oil lamps smoke if they are not properly trimmed.* **3.** To give off, exhale, steam or vapour; to reek: *the horses were smoking after the gallop*; *their swords smoked with blood.* **4.** To suck tobacco smoke into the mouth from a pipe, cigar, cigarette, and blow it out again: *everyone smokes nowadays*; *you must not smoke in this carriage.* **5.** (schoolboy slang) To blush. **B.** trans. **1. a** To impregnate (meat &c.) with wood smoke in order to cure and preserve it: *to smoke a ham, salmon, herrings*; **b** to impart the taste and smell of smoke to; to spoil taste of (food) by allowing smoke to reach it when cooking: *the milk has been smoked.* **2.** To darken by depositing carbon upon, by exposing to, or impregnating with, smoke: *smoked glasses.* **3.** Gen. *smoke out*; **a** to fumigate, purify, by impregnating thoroughly with chemical fumes: *to smoke out a sick-room*; **b** to drive away, expel, by a discharge of smoke or poisonous vapour upon: *to smoke rats out of a barn.* **4. a** To breathe in and out the smoke of, by means of a pipe, or in form of cigarette &c.: *to smoke tobacco, opium* &c.; **b** to draw at, for purpose of sucking smoke into the mouth: *to smoke a pipe, cigarette* &c. **5.** (reflex.) To bring into a specified condition by smoking tobacco: *to smoke oneself sick, silly* &c. **6.** (archaic or obs.) To have an inkling of, suspect existence or character of, be suspicious of, to detect (as one suspects fire from getting a whiff of smoke): *to smoke a plot*; *I smoked his intentions at once*; *I smoked him as a traitor.* **7.** (obs. or liter.) **a** To tease, chaff, quiz (as it were to pester by discharging smoke at): *they smoked the young man rarely on the subject of his intrigue*; **b** to bamboozle, take in, hoax, deceive (as by blinding with smoke): *they smoked him that the lady was a fortune.*

smoke-ball, n. **a** A smoke-bomb; **b** small ball used in trap-shooting which emits a puff of smoke when hit.

smoke-bomb, n. Bomb or other missile filled with chemical which on ignition by explosion throws out dense clouds of smoke, which serve as a screen in warfare.

smoke-box, n. A hollow space or chamber between the end of the boiler of a steam engine and the funnel or smoke-stack.

smoke-consumer, n. Apparatus or device for consuming the solid particles in the smoke from a furnace &c. before it is allowed to be discharged into the air.

smoke-dried, adj. [1. smṓk drīd; 2. smóuk draid]. Dried and cured in wood smoke.

smoke-jack, n. A jack or spit for roasting meat in which the motive power is obtained from a small fly-wheel placed in the chimney of the kitchen range and turned by the ascending heated air.

smokeless, adj. [1. smṓkles; 2. smóuklis]. **smoke (I.) & -less.** Not producing smoke; making little or no smoke; not attended by smoke; esp. *smokeless powder*, an explosive, such as cordite, which explodes with little or no smoke; *smokeless fuel.*

smokelessly, adv. Prec. & **-ly.** In a smokeless manner, without producing smoke.

smokelessness, n. See prec. & **-ness.** State, quality, of being smokeless.

smoker, n. [1. smṓker; 2. smóukə]. **smoke (II.) & -er.** **1.** One who smokes, esp. one who habitually smokes tobacco: *smoker's heart, throat,* affections of the heart or throat, due to excessive smoking of tobacco. **2.** (colloq.) **a** A carriage or compartment on a railway train reserved for smokers; **b** a smoking concert.

smoke-screen, n. A cloud of thick smoke spread by smoke-bombs or other devices, used in land or sea warfare to conceal movements from the enemy.

smoke-stack, n. The funnel of a steamship; factory chimney.

smokily, adv. [1. smṓkili; 2. smóukili]. **smoky & -ly.** In a smoky manner.

smokiness, n. [1. smṓkines; 2. smóukinis]. **smoky & -ness.** State, quality, of being smoky.

smoking-carriage, n. [1. smṓking kàrij; 2. smóukiŋ kǽridž]. Carriage or compartment on a railway train reserved for smokers.

smoking-concert, n. Concert at which smoking is allowed.

smoking-jacket, n. A jacket, usually braided &c., worn formerly by smokers to prevent the smell of tobacco smoke affecting their clothes.

smoking-room, n. Room in house, hotel &c. in which smoking is allowed.

smoky, adj. [1. smṓki; 2. smóuki]. **smoke (I.) & -y.** **1.** Emitting, giving off, smoke, esp. in excessive quantities or of black, dense quality: *smoky chimneys*; *a smoky chimney* is also one which discharges smoke into the room. **2.** Filled, dense, with, covered by, smoke: *a smoky town, room* &c.; *a smoky atmosphere.* **3.** Stained with, of the colour of, smoke.

smolt, n. [1. smōlt; 2. smoult]. O.E., 'calm, serene', in dial. use, 'shining', orig. 'liquid, smooth'; perh. a gradational variant of **smelt (II.).** A young salmon in its second year, when its silvery scales are developed.

smooth (**I.**), adj. [1. smo͞odh; 2. smūð]. O.E. *smōþ*, fr. wh. our present form comes, is only noted once, & then in the sense of 'serene' applied to the human countenance; the regular form is *smēþe*, a mutated form, fr. **smōþi-.* The old meanings were 'smooth, polished; soothing; flattering, suave; harmonious; pleasant, comfortable'. The Gmc. form was **smanþ-*, whence O.E. *smōþ-* by a well-known & regular change (cp. *tooth*, O.E. *tōþ*, fr. **tanþ-*); cogn. w. M.H.G. *smant*, 'cream', wh., however, is apparently orig. a Slav. loan-word, cp. Czech *smant*, & Russ. *smetana*, 'cream' (fr. **sment-*); Scrt. *manth-*, 'butter'. The ultimate meaning was apparently 'buttery'; O.E. is the only Gmc. language wh. preserves the word, & then only in derived senses. In M.E. the mutated form *smēthe* was gradually ousted by the unmutated *smōthe*; it survives, however, in such names as *Smeeth* & *Smedley.* In general sense, the reverse of *rough.* **1.** (of surfaces in general) Free from roughness or irregular projections perceptible to touch or sight; glossy, polished, glabrous, silky: *a smooth paper, bark of tree, plank of wood, floor* &c.; *smooth sheet of ice*; *smooth as marble.* **2.** (of edge) Not jagged or indented; even: *the smooth edge of a table, razor* &c. **3.** (of ground &c.) Level, even, not broken by undulations or sudden depressions and elevations: *a smooth lawn*; *smooth slope of a hill*; *a smooth road,* one easy to travel on. Phr. *to make things smooth for a person,* to make them easy, get rid of difficulties, obstacles, &c.; *the way is now smooth* (*for further progress* &c.), obstacles have been removed. **4.** (of water) Not agitated and broken by waves or ripples; calm, unruffled: *a smooth sea, stream, lake*; *a smooth passage, crossing,* one across a smooth, calm sea; *to get to, reach, smooth water,* to come safely through difficulties &c. **5. a** (of skin) (i.) Not hairy or bristly, whether made so by nature, or by shaving: *a smooth face, chin*; (ii.) unwrinkled, as by age: *the smooth cheeks of youth*; **b** (of animal's coat &c.) not long or rough or shaggy; sleek; **c** (of hair) sleek, glossy; well brushed; not ruffled up; **d** (bot.) having no pubescence or down, not prickly. **6.** (of consistency) Well, evenly, mixed; of the same fine texture throughout; not coarse or lumpy: *a smooth paste.* **7.** (of taste) Soft, soothing, bland, not harsh or acrid or astringent: *good wine should be silky and smooth.* **8.** (of melody, style) Flowing easily, rhythmical; not disjointed, harsh, or discordant: *smooth verses*; *a smooth phrase,* in music &c. **9.** (of motion) Not interrupted; not subject to friction, jars, jolts; moving easily and freely, like well-oiled machinery: *the smooth running of an engine.* **10. a** Suave, soothing, bland; calm, unruffled: *a smooth temper, disposition* &c.; *smooth, polished courtiers*; **b** flattering, conciliatory, often with suggestion of insincerity: *to speak smooth words,* such as are pleasant and flattering to another's susceptibilities; or words which gloze over real difficulties; *a smooth tongue,* one ready with smooth, flattering words.

smooth (**II.**), n., fr. prec. **1.** That which is smooth; something smooth; esp., smooth ground: '*O'er rough and smooth she trips along*' (Wordsworth, 'Lucy Gray'). Phr. *to take the rough with the smooth,* to take things as they come, the unpleasant with the pleasant, to accept the ups and downs of life. **2.** (from vb.) Act of making smooth: *give one's hair a smooth*; (also fig.) *his temper is ruffled and needs a smooth down.*

smooth (**III.**), also **smoothe,** vb. trans. & intrans., fr. **smooth (I.).** **A.** trans. **1.** To make smooth or level; to remove roughnesses, projections &c. from the surface of: *to smooth rough ground* &c.; *to smooth wood with a plane.* **2. a** To arrange neatly and evenly by brushing, patting, or pressing down: *smooth one's hair, ruffled clothing, a rumpled sheet* &c.; also **b** *smooth out, away, down,* to remove so as to make smooth: *to smooth out wrinkles from a coat*; *death has smoothed away the lines from his face.* **3.** To make easy by removing obstructions &c.: *to smooth a path, road*; (also fig.) *to smooth difficulties away.* **4.** *Smooth down,* to soothe, render calm: *to smooth down a person, his temper*; *to smooth down quarrels, differences.* **5.** *Smooth over,* to gloze, minimize: *to smooth over faults.* **B.** intrans. *Smooth down,* **a** to become smooth or calm: *the sea gradually smoothed down*; **b** (fig.) become easier, less disturbed: *affairs have smoothed down since the cause of trouble was removed.*

smooth (**IV.**), adv., fr. **smooth (I.).** Smoothly: *the engine is running very smooth today*; *things have gone smooth with me.*

smooth bore, n. Gun with barrel not rifled.

smooth breathing, n. (Gk. gram.) **a** Sound of initial vowel when not aspirated; **b** symbol, ', of this before such vowel.

smooth-faced, adj. [1. smo͞odh fāst; 2. smūð feist]. **a** Having a smooth or hairless face; clean-shaven; **b** (fig.) having a suave, bland manner, usually with sense of insincerity.

smoothing-iron, n. [1. smo͞odhing īern; 2. smūðiŋ aiən]. A tailor's flat-iron for smoothing and pressing clothes.

smoothing-plane, n. [1. smo͞odhing plān; 2. smūðiŋ plein]. A small carpenter's plane with closely set blade for finishing work.

smoothly, adv. [1. smo͞odhli; 2. smūðli]. **smooth (I.) & -ly.** In a smooth manner (in various senses of adj.).

smoothness, n. [1. smo͞odhnes; 2. smūðnis]. See prec. & **-ness.** State, quality, of being smooth (in various senses of adj.).

smote, vb. [1. smōt; 2. smout]. O.E. *smāt*; M.E. *smoot*; Pret. of **smite.**

smother (**I.**), vb. trans. & intrans. [1. smúdher; 2. smáðə]. M.E. *smortheren*; the O.E. form is *smorian*, 'to choke, suffocate'; the formation of the M.E. word is obscure, as is the origin of the O.E. form. Alleged connexion w. **smoulder** is very doubtful as the words agree neither in sense nor form. **A.** trans. **1. a** To suffocate, choke, stifle, prevent access of air to the lungs of, cause difficulty of breathing to: *to be smothered by thick smoke*; *the fog was smothering me*; **b** to kill by suffocation, as by pressure of something over mouth and nose: *the princes were smothered in the Tower*; also fig., *smothered by unwelcome attentions.* 2. a To put out, damp down (fire), by heaping ashes &c. on it so as to prevent free passage of air; b to cover up (light) so as to prevent visibility; c (fig.) to conceal, suppress, stifle: *to smother a yawn*; *smother one's boredom*; also *to smother (up) a crime, scandal.* 3. a To cover, wrap up, entirely and thickly: *town smothered in smoke, fog*; *smother the patient in blankets*; b to spread, heap, thickly upon: *to smother a salad with oil*; *coffin smothered in flowers*; c (fig.) to heap on, cover, overwhelm: *she smothered the child with kisses.* B. intrans. To feel choked, suffocated, be unable to breathe, to stifle: *I shall smother if I stay in this hot room.*

smother (II.), n. See prec. 1. (archaic) A smouldering fire, ashes. 2. a A choking, stifling, cloud of smoke, fog, or dust; b a heavy cloud of steam, spray.

smothery, adj. [1. smúdheri; 2. smáðəri]. **smother (I.)** & **-y.** Stifling, suffocating.

smoulder (I.), vb. intrans. [1. smṓlder; 2. smóuldə]. M.E. *smolderen*, cp. L.G. *smölen*, Du. *smeulen*; perh. cogn. w. **smell** (I.). 1. (of fire) To burn slowly, with smoke but little or no flame. 2. (of emotions &c.) To be felt inwardly, without outward sign; to be in a latent or suppressed condition: *hatred smouldered in his heart*; *the rebellion smouldered for some time and then broke out afresh.*

smoulder (II.), n., fr. prec. A smouldering fire; smother.

smudge (I.), vb. trans. & intrans. [1. smuj; 2. smadž]. M.E. *smogen*, variant of **smutch.** 1. trans. a To make a dirty mark or smear on; to smear with dirt: *to smudge the wall-paper with one's finger*; *with face smudged with soot*; b to smear, blot, blur (writing, a drawing &c.). 2. intrans. To be liable to be, to become, smudged or blurred: *this spongy paper smudges badly.*

smudge (II.), n., fr. prec. A smear, dirty mark; a blur, blot.

smudge (III.), n. Origin doubtful. A fire of weeds &c. kept smouldering to drive away insects, as in a garden &c.

smudgily, adv. [1. smújili; 2. smádžili]. **smudgy** & **-ly.** In a smudgy, blurred, manner.

smudginess, n. [1. smújines; 2. smádžinis]. See prec. & **-ness.** State, quality, of being smudgy.

smudgy, adj. [1. smúji; 2. smádži]. **smudge (II.)** & **-y.** Covered with smudges; smudged, smeared, blurred, blotted with dirty marks or smudges.

smug (I.), adj. [1. smug; 2. smag], fr. L.G. & Du. *smuk*, 'neat, spruce'; cp. Germ. *schmuck*, 'ornament', & *schmücken*, 'to dress, adorn', cogn. w. M.H.G. *smiegen*, 'to creep into, put on (clothes) over the head'; see **smock** & **smuggle.** 1. (archaic) Neat, trim, spruce. 2. a Pedantically, affectedly, precise in appearance, manner, or conduct; b scrupulous in keeping up the appearance of respectability; absurdly self-satisfied and complacent; prim, narrow-minded: *smug smile*; *content to live in smug respectability*; *such forms of social interference will always find smug supporters.*

smug (II.), n., fr. prec. 1. A smug person. 2. (school or univ. slang) One who does not mix freely in the ordinary life of the place, esp. one who takes an unwilling part in games and devotes himself to work.

smuggle, vb. trans. & intrans. [1. smúgl; 2. smágl], fr. L.G. *smuggeln*, in Engl. sense cogn. w. Dan. *smugla* in same sense; Swed. *smuga*, 'hole to creep into', cogn. w. O.E. *smūgan*, 'to creep', q.v. under **smock.** A. trans. 1. Specif., to import or export (goods) into or out of a country in a way that contravenes the laws of the country, as forbidding all trading in such commodities or as levying a customs duty on them, which is thereby evaded: *to smuggle silk, tobacco, cocaine* &c. 2. (by transf.) To introduce, convey, pass, secretly or clandestinely; to conceal, hide away: *to smuggle a letter into, out of, a prison*; *to smuggle a person into a meeting.* B. intrans. To smuggle goods; to practise smuggling.

smuggler, n. [1. smúgler; 2. smáglə]. Prec. & **-er.** a One who practises smuggling; b vessel employed in smuggling.

smuggling, n. [1. smúgling; 2. smágliŋ]. **smuggle** & **-ing.** a Act of one who smuggles; b practice of bringing into or out of a country goods which are prohibited or without paying the lawful customs duty.

smut (I.), n. [1. smut; 2. smat]. Scand., cp. Swed. *smuts*, 'dirt'; cogn. w. M.E. *(bi)-smoteren*, 'to make dirty'; cp. M.H.G. *smuz*, Mod. Germ. *schmutz*, 'dirt, filth'. 1. a A small piece or flake of soot, coal-dust, or other dirty, black substance; b stain, spot, mark left by such substance. 2. A disease of wheat and other cereal plants, caused by a parasitic fungus breaking out into masses of brownish-black spores resembling soot. 3. Obscene conversation or writing.

smut (II.), vb. trans. & intrans., fr. prec. 1. trans. a To mark, stain, with smuts; b to infect (wheat &c.) with the smut disease. 2. intrans. To become infected with smut.

smutch, vb. & n. [1. smuch; 2. smatʃ]. Perh. connected w. prec.; now rarely used, but the usual form **smudge** is a later variant.

smuttily, adv. [1. smútili; 2. smátili]. **smutty** & **-ly.** In a smutty manner.

smuttiness, n. [1. smútines; 2. smátinis]. **smutty** & **-ness.** State, quality, of being smutty.

smutty, adj. [1. smúti; 2. smáti]. **smut (I.)** & **-y.** 1. Marked, stained, with smuts; sooty, dirty. 2. Obscene.

snack, n. [1. snak; 2. snæk]. Cp. M. Du. *snakken*, & see **snatch.** 1. (obs.) A share, portion; something snatched. Phr. *to go snacks*, to go shares (used by Pope). 2. A hasty, light meal.

snaffle, n. & vb. trans. [1. snáfl; 2. snǽfl], fr. Du. *snavel*, 'horse's muzzle', dimin. of O.D. *snabbe*, 'bill, beak of bird'; cp. O.H.G. *snabul*, Mod. Germ. *schnabel*, 'beak, snout'. See **snub.** 1. n. A bit for a horse consisting of two slightly curved, rounded bars, each tapering towards the point where it is joined to the other by a loop in the metal which allows considerable play between the parts; externally, the snaffle is attached to the reins either by large rings alone, or by straight bars with movable rings, into which the reins are buckled; this bit sometimes has the reins permanently attached. 2. vb. a To put snaffle on (horse); b (slang) to steal, pinch.

snag, n. & vb. trans. [1. snag; 2. snæg]. Scand., cp. Norw., 'projecting point, spike'; O.N. *snagi*, 'clothes-peg'. 1. n. a A rough, jagged projection, such as of a broken branch, stump of a tree, tooth &c.; esp. the trunk or branch of a tree embedded in a river with jagged end sticking upwards; b (fig., colloq.) an unforeseen obstacle or difficulty; an unexpected drawback: *it seems an ideal plan, but there is sure to be a snag somewhere.* 2. vb. a To run (boat) on to a snag; b to clear (river) of snags.

snaggy, adj. [1. snági; 2. snǽgi]. Prec. & **-y.** a Of the nature of a snag; b abounding in snags.

snail, n. [1. snāl; 2. sneil]. O.E. *snæġl*, *sneġel*, dimin. of *snaca*, **snake**; cp. O.N. *snegil*, 'snail'; O.H.G. *snecko* is the same word without the *-il* suff. 1. Any of various kinds of air-breathing gastropod molluscs, bearing a spiral shell into which the body can be retracted for protection and sealed up by a membrane during hibernation &c.; very slow of movement, leaving a slimy track, and with retractile eye-stalks; usually applied to the land-snails, family *Helicidae*, as distinguished from pond or freshwater snails or sea-snails, and from the shell-less 'slugs'. Phr. *at a snail's pace*, exceedingly slowly. 2. A slow, sluggish person. 3. A spiral cam or wheel with notches, controlling the striking movement in a clock; a snail-wheel.

snail-clover, n. A kind of lucerne with pods shaped like a snail's shell.

snailery, n. [1. snā́leri; 2. snéiləri]. Place where edible snails are bred and fattened.

snail-fish, n. The sea-snail.

snail-like, adj. Like a snail, either in appearance &c., or in slowness of movement.

snail-paced, adj. Slow-moving, like a snail, moving at a snail's pace.

snail-wheel, n. Notched spiral cam or wheel, controlling the striking movement of a clock.

snake, n. [1. snāk; 2. sneik]. O.E. *snaca*, M.E. *snāke*; M.H.G. *snāke*, Mod. Germ. *schnake*, 'ringed snake'; O.N. *snākr*, 'serpent'; connected w. O.H.G. *snahhan*, 'to creep, crawl'; apparently related to Scrt. *nāgaš*, 'serpent'. Origin obscure. See also **snail.** 1. The general name for any member of the zoological order *Ophidia*, or scaly, limbless reptiles or serpents; also loosely applied to certain snake-like lizards with rudimentary limbs, as the *glass snake* &c. Phrs. *a snake in the grass*, a lurking, concealed enemy or danger; *to see snakes*, (colloq.) to have delirium tremens. 2. (fig.) A treacherous, cold-blooded, malevolent person.

snake-berry, n. The bryony and its fruit.

snake-bird, n. A fish-eating bird with long snakelike neck, belonging to the genus *Plotus*, of America, allied to the cormorant and shag.

snake bite, n. The bite of a poisonous snake; the pathological results of this.

snake-charmer, n. One who claims to charm and tame poisonous snakes, esp. by music of a pipe &c.

snake-charming, n. The art of charming poisonous snakes, as practised in the East.

snake-eater, n. Another name of the secretary-bird.

snake-fly, n. Popular name of a neuropterous insect, *Raphidia*, with large head and elongated prothorax.

snakelike, adj. [1. snā́klīk; 2. snéiklaik]. Resembling a snake, esp. in form and movement.

snake-lizard, n. Any lizard with rudimentary limbs, resembling a snake.

snake-root, n. Popular name for various American plants whose root is supposed to be an antidote for snake bite.

snake's head, n. The fritillary, so called from the markings on the petals, which resemble those on the head of a snake.

snake-stone, n. a An ammonite; b any stone supposed to act as a charm or antidote for snake bite.

snake-weed, n. A herb allied to buckwheat, with tall spike of flowers and curiously twisted root-stock; called also bistort.

snake-wood, n. The hard, ornamental wood of a tall Brazilian tree, with markings like those of a snake's skin.

snakily, adv. [1. snā́kili; 2. snéikili]. **snaky** & **-ly.** In a snaky manner.

snakiness, n. [1. snā́kines; 2. snéikinis]. **snaky** & **-ness.** State, quality, of being snaky.

snaky, adj. [1. snā́ki; 2. snéiki]. **snake** & **-y.** 1. Pertaining to a snake or snakes; resembling a snake: *a snaky tail*; *snaky locks.* 2. Winding, serpentine: *a snaky stream.* 3. Wily, treacherous, cold-blooded, cruel.

snap (I.), vb. trans. & intrans. [1. snap; 2. snæp]. Either Scand., cp. Swed. *snappa*, or fr. Du. *snappen*; Mod. Germ. *schnappen* is of L.G. origin. Prob. related to O.H.G. *snabul*, 'beak, muzzle', &, more remotely, w. O.E. *nebb*, 'nose, beak, front', see **neb.** A. trans. 1. (also *snap off*) To bite, snatch, with the teeth or beak: *shark snapped the man's leg off*; *dog snapped a piece out of my trousers*; *parrot snapped my finger.* Phr. *to snap a person's head, nose, off*, to take up, cut short, interrupt him curtly or rudely; to speak sharply, angrily, to. **2.** *Snap up*, **a** to snatch, grasp, seize, pick up, hastily, greedily, or eagerly: *dog snaps up a piece of meat; to snap up odds and ends*; Phr. *to snap a person up*, to interrupt curtly or rudely; to cut short in an argument &c.; **b** to seize, take possession of, acquire, early and eagerly: *all the best houses have been snapped up by this time.* **3. a** To break quickly or sharply, to break with a sharp, wrenching movement: *to snap a sword across his knee; snap a stick, piece of thread, in two*; (also fig.) *the ties of affection were snapped*; **b** *snap off*, to break off, detach by a snapping movement: *to snap off a piece of stick.* **4.** To cause to make a sharp report or crack, to make a sharp noise with; to crack: *to snap a whip; to snap a pistol, gun*, release the trigger with click of falling hammer but without exploding the charge. Phr. *to snap one's fingers at*, (lit. or fig.) to show complete contempt for, or indifference to. **5. a** To close, bring together, with a short, sharp noise: *to snap the teeth, beak* &c.; **b** to shut, close, fasten, also to open, with a click: *to snap down the lid of a box; snap open a watch; snap to the clasp of a necklet* &c.; *snapped the handcuffs on person's wrists.* **6.** To take an instantaneous photograph or snapshot of: *he was snapped falling off his horse.* **7.** To catch (batsman) out smartly from a glance or snick: *snapped at the wicket.* **B.** intrans. **1.** Often *snap at*, **a** to make a hasty, sudden bite at; to try to bite or seize with the jaws; to make a sudden rapid movement with the jaws towards something, as though about to seize or bite: *a fish snaps at the bait; I hate a dog that snaps*; **b** to grasp at, accept, eagerly; to try and seize or get hold of: *to snap at a bargain, offer, invitation* &c. **2.** To speak curtly, crossly, irritably: *to snap and snarl; always snapping at one.* **3.** To break in two, part, suddenly, with a sharp noise: *stick snapped under the weight; branch snapped off the tree in a wind; knife snapped as he struck; a chain, rope, snaps at its weakest point.* **4.** To make a sharp noise or crack: *whip, pistol, snaps.* **5.** To close to, shut, become fastened, with a sharp click: *the bolt snapped into its place; door, lid, window-catch, snaps to.*

snap (II.), n. See prec. **1.** Act of snapping with teeth &c.; sound made in snapping: *felt a snap at my legs; heard snaps and snarls.* **2.** Process of something breaking, or being broken suddenly; sound made thus: *the snap of twigs under one's feet.* **3.** Sharp clicking sound as of a bolt being shot home; movement producing this. **4.** A catch, clasp: *the snap of a bracelet, necklace* &c. **5.** Liveliness, spirit, point, bite: *a style without much snap.* **6.** A short, sudden spell (of weather &c.): *a cold snap.* **7.** A crisp cake of gingerbread: *ginger snaps.* **8.** An instantaneous photograph, snapshot. **9.** A child's simple game of cards.

snap (III.), adj. Done quickly, taken, done, without notice, by surprise; (esp. parl.) *a snap division; to take a snap vote.*

snapdragon, n. [1. snápdràgun; 2. snǽpdrægən]. **1.** A herbaceous perennial or biennial plant, *Antirrhinum*, with showy red, yellow, or white flowers, of tubular, lipped shape, opening like a mouth. **2.** An old-fashioned Christmas game of picking out raisins from a dish of burning brandy.

snaphance, n. [1. snáp-hàns; 2. snǽphæ̀ns], fr. Du. *snaphaan*, lit. 'snapping hen', of the cock of the weapon. An old form of pistol or musket with a flint-lock and spring.

snap-lock, n. A lock fastening with a snap or catch.

snapper, n. [1. snáper; 2. snǽpə]. **snap** (I.) & **-er.** **1. a** A dog or other animal given to snapping; **b** person given to snapping, i.e. making sharp, irritable, caustic remarks. **2.** Popular name for various kinds of sea-fish; also called *Schnapper.*

snappily, adv. [1. snápili; 2. snǽpili]. **snappy** & **-ly.** In a snappy manner.

snapping-turtle, n. [1. snáping tě̀rtl; 2. snǽpiŋ tə̀tl]. A large voracious freshwater turtle of North America, with powerful jaws with which it snaps its prey.

snappish, adj. [1. snápish; 2. snǽpiʃ]. **snap** & **-ish.** **1.** (of dog) Inclined to snap. **2.** (of person) Irritable, given to making sharp, ill-natured remarks or replies.

snappishly, adv. Prec. & **-ly.** In a snappish manner.

snappishness, n. See prec. & **-ness.** State, quality, of being snappish.

snappy, adj. [1. snápi; 2. snǽpi]. **snap** (II.) & **-y.** **1.** Snappish. **2.** Full of snap, vigour, or life; brisk, lively: *a short, snappy article, paragraph* &c.

snapshooter, n. [1. snápshòoter; 2. snǽpʃùtə]. **snap** & **shooter.** One who takes a snap shot or one with little or no aim at an object with a gun or rifle.

snapshot, n. & vb. trans. [1. snápshot; 2. snǽpʃɔt]. **1.** n. **a** (usually *snap shot*) [1. snap shót; 2. snǽp ʃɔ́t] A quick shot fired with little or no aim; **b** an instantaneous photograph taken with a hand camera and usually without posing &c. **2.** vb. To take an instantaneous photograph of.

snare (I.), n. [1. snār; 2. snɛə]. M.E. *snāre*, prob. fr. O.N. *snara*, 'snare, noose, halter'; cogn. w. O.E. *snearh*, 'cord, string'; cp. O.H.G. *snarahha*, 'noose'; in gradational relation to Goth. *snōrjō*, 'woven basket, basket-work; O.H.G. *snuor*, 'a string, rope, band'; Mod. Germ. *schnur*; orig. base **snēu-* &c., 'to twist'; prob. cogn. w. O.E. *sinu*, see **sinew**, & O.E. *snōd*, see **snood.** A variant base, **snē(i)-*, w. loss of *s-*, is seen in Lat. *nēre*, 'to sew'. See **Nemesis** & **needle.** **1.** A device for catching birds, rabbits &c., consisting usually of a noose of wire or cord; a trap, gin. **2.** (in moral sense) Anything which seduces, beguiles, entraps, entangles one, or brings one into difficulties, trouble, or disgrace; allurement, enticement, temptation: *the snares of the devil, of the wicked; beauty and charm too often prove a snare.* **3.** A string of gut stretched across the under head of a side-drum to increase the rattling sound and give resonance.

snare (II.), vb. trans., fr. prec. **1.** To catch in a snare: *to snare a bird, rabbit.* **2.** (in moral sense) To seduce from duty, good conduct &c.; to entangle, inveigle, to entrap: *to be snared by the wiles of a designing female.*

snare drum, n. A side-drum with snares stretched across the under end to increase resonance and rattling sound.

snarer, n. [1. snárer; 2. snɛ́ərə]. Prec. & **-er.** One who, that which, snares; usually in combination: *bird-, rabbit-snarer.*

snark, n. [1. snark; 2. snāk]. Invented by Lewis Carroll in 'The Hunting of the Snark', 1876. Imaginary mysterious creature whose appearance and character are only hinted at.

snarl (I.), vb. intrans. & trans. [1. snarl; 2. snāl]. Freq. form of earlier *snarre, snar*; fr. or cogn. w. M. Du. *snarren*; Germ. *schnarren*, 'to growl; to roll the *r* in speaking'. Cp. **sneer** & **snort.** **A.** intrans. **1.** (of animals) To growl with a sharp, high tone and showing the teeth, as a dog when angry. **2.** (of human beings) To speak in a harsh, grating voice and with angry, savage tone. **B.** trans. (rare) To utter with a snarl; also *snarl out.*

snarl (II.), n., fr. prec. Facial expression adopted, and sound made, in snarling.

snarl (III.), n. & vb. trans. & intrans. In M.E., fr. O. Swed. *snarel*, 'noose, halter'; dimin. of *snara*, q.v. under **snare** (I.). **1.** n. (archaic or obs.) A tangle, entanglement; (also fig.) complication, intricacy. **2.** vb. trans. **a** To entangle: *snarled hair, skein (of wool)* &c.; also **b** (fig.) to ornament (metal ware) by beating out a design in relief from the inside with a snarling-iron. **3.** vb. intrans. To become entangled.

snarler, n. [1. snárler; 2. snálə]. **snarl** (I.) & **-er.** Animal or person that snarls.

snarling-iron, n. [1. snárling ìern; 2. snáliŋ àiən]. **snarl** (III.) Tool used in making ornaments in relief on metal ware.

snarlingly, adv. [1. snárlingli; 2. snáliŋli], fr. Pres. Part. of **snarl** (I.) & **-ly.** In a snarling tone or manner; with a snarl.

snatch (I.), vb. trans. & intrans. [1. snach; 2. snætʃ]. M.E. *snacchen*; prob. fr. a L.G. word such as M. Du. *snakken*, 'to seize', w. final cons. influenced by M.E. *lacchen*, 'to seize', see **latch**, or by *cacchen*, see **catch.** Connected w. **snack, sneck.** **A.** trans. **1. a** To seize with a sudden, rapid, more or less violent movement of the hand; to grab, snap: *to snatch a thing from a person's hand*; **b** to grab, seize suddenly, with the jaws, beak &c.: *a fish may snatch a worm from the hook; one bird will snatch food out of the beak of another*; Phr. *to snatch a kiss*, take, give, one, without permission. **2.** *Snatch up*, to pick up, seize hurriedly. **3. a** To take, obtain, take to oneself, with haste: *to snatch a hurried meal*; **b** (fig.) to secure, grasp, obtain, carry off, with difficulty, or as by chance; to seize the opportunity of enjoying: *to snatch a few hours of sleep; 'They hear a voice in every wind, And snatch a fearful joy'* (Gray, 'Eton Coll.' 4); *'And snatch a grace beyond the reach of art'* (Pope, 'Ess. on Crit.' 155); also *to snatch a victory from a seeming defeat.* **4.** *Snatch away*, carry off, remove, by the exercise of sudden force; **a** (in physical sense) *to snatch food away from a starving person; to snatch a knife away from a would-be assassin*; **b** (in non-material sense) *'O, snatched away in beauty's bloom!'* (Byron); *all hope of happiness has been snatched away.* **B.** intrans. **1.** To seize, or attempt to seize, by a sudden movement of the hand; to grab: *children are not allowed to snatch.* **2.** *Snatch at*, to make a sudden, eager, movement towards, in an attempt to seize: *the thief snatched at the purse in the lady's hand*; (also fig.) *to snatch at the chance of*, to avail oneself eagerly of it.

snatch (II.), n., fr. prec. **1.** Act of snatching; a grab; sudden more or less violent movement in an attempt to seize something: *he made a snatch at my watch.* **2.** (often pl.) **a** Short period or spell of activity: *to work in, by, snatches*; **b** disconnected fragment, or portion: *short snatches of song; a snatch of melody.*

snatchily, adv. [1. snáchili; 2. snǽtʃili]. **snatchy** & **-ly.** In a snatchy manner; by snatches.

snatchy, adj. [1. snáchi; 2. snǽtʃi]. **snatch** (II.) & **-y.** Performed, done, in snatches; not continuous; disconnected, interrupted; broken.

snathe, n. [1. snādh; 2. sneið], fr. O.N. *sneið*, 'a portion, a slice'; cogn. w. O.E. *snǣd*, see next word. (obs. or provinc.) The wood stock or shaft, to which a scythe-blade is fastened.

snead, n. [1. snēd; 2. snīd]. O.E. *snǣd*, 'a morsel, slice', lit. 'something cut off', M.E. *snēde*; fr. **snādi-*, fr. base of O.E. *snīþan*, 'to cut', Pret. *snāþ*; cogn. w. O.N. *sneið*. See prec. Cp. O.S. *snīthan*; O.H.G. *snīdan*; Goth. *sneiþan*, 'to cut'. (obs. or provinc.) Snathe.

sneak (I.), vb. intrans. & trans. [1. snēk; 2. snīk], presupposes a M.E. **snēke*, wh. is not found. The word cannot possibly be derived, formally, fr. O.E. *snīcan*, M.E. *snīke*, 'to creep, crawl'. It is apparently connected in some way w. these, but how, is entirely obscure. It is still more difficult to connect O.E. *snīcan* w. **snail** or **snake.** **A.** intrans. (usually w. various advs.) **1. a** To creep, move silently or furtively; to move so as not to be observed or as if in fear of detection or observation; to slink, lurk, steal: *to sneak into, out of, a room; he sneaked off round the corner; he was found sneaking about the place*; **b** *sneak out of* (fig.), to contrive to avoid, withdraw oneself from, escape from, *danger, responsibility, difficulty* &c., by stealth, craft &c. **2.** (schoolboy slang) To tell (a master) of something which other boys desire to hide; esp. to inform against another boy, and reveal his offences to a master; to peach, blow the gaff. **B.** trans. (slang) To steal, pinch: *my watch was sneaked in the crowd.*

sneak (II.), n., fr. prec. **1.** A mean, underhand, furtive, cowardly person. **2.** (schoolboy slang) An informer, a tell-tale. **3.** (cricket) A ball bowled so as to travel along the ground.

sneaking, adj. [1. snéking; 2. sníkiŋ], fr. Pres. Part. of **sneak** (I.). **1.** Furtive, underhand; mean. **2.** Unavowed, secret: *a sneaking sympathy for certain kinds of criminals.*

sneakingly, adv. [1. snékingli; 2.eníkiŋli]. Prec. & **-ly.** In a sneaking, furtive manner.

sneak-thief, n. One who steals small articles which he finds lying about, or which he can pick up through open doors and windows, without breaking in.

sneck, n. & vb. trans. [1. snek; 2. snɛk]. Connected w. **snatch.** (provinc.) **1.** n. Latch, catch of a window or door. **2.** vb. To make fast with a sneck.

sneer (I.), vb. intrans. & trans. [1. snēr; 2. sniə]. M.E. *snēren,* 'to scorn, deride'; cp. Dan. *snærre,* 'to grin like a dog', connected w. **snarl. A.** intrans. **1.** To smile mockingly, ironically, or scornfully; to show contempt by a contraction or contortion of the facial muscles. **2.** To utter remarks intended to belittle and disparage; to express contempt in words, esp. by innuendo: '*Damn with faint praise, assent with civil leer, And without sneering, teach the rest to sneer*' (Pope). **3.** *Sneer at,* to feel and express contempt for, esp. in words. **B.** trans. (rare) **1.** To express with a sneer or in sneering words: *to sneer one's contempt for.* **2.** To affect by a sneer: *to sneer person down, out of countenance* &c.

sneer (II.), n., fr. prec. **1.** A sardonic, ironical, scornful smile or change of facial expression. **2.** Verbal expression of covert contempt; a bitter suggestion of disparagement; a gibe, flout.

sneerer, n. [1. snérer; 2. sníərə]. **sneer** (I.) & **-er.** One who sneers.

sneeringly, adv. [1. snéringli; 2. sníəriŋli]. Pres. Part. of **sneer** (I.) & **-ly.** In a sneering manner; with sneers.

sneeze (I.), vb. intrans. [1. snēz; 2. sniz]. M.E. *snēsen.* The O.E. form is *fnēosan,* perh. cogn. w. O.H.G. *niesen* (fr. *fnies-* ?), but in any case w. Gk. *pnéein,* 'to breathe', fr. **pnew-,* & *pneûma,* 'breath, spirit'; see **pneuma.** *Fnēsen* is still found in M.E.; the change in initial consonant is due to the influence of such words as **sniff, snort.** To undergo a sudden involuntary convulsion of throat and soft palate, accompanied by the noisy expulsion of air through the vocal chords and nose, as a result of irritation in the mucous membrane of the nose, from catarrh, effect of pepper, dust &c. Phr. *not to be sneezed at,* not to be despised, worth consideration or acceptance.

sneeze (II.), n., fr. prec. **a** Act of sneezing; **b** sound thus produced.

sneezewort, n. [1. snézwěrt; 2. snízwʌt]. **sneeze** & **wort** (I.). Popular name of a strongly scented perennial herb, *Achillea ptarmica,* or wild pellitory, with large white flowers, allied to the yarrow; the leaves were once powdered and used as snuff.

snell, n. [1. snel; 2. snɛl]. Origin unknown. A short piece of gut or horsehair used to attach the hook to a fishing-line.

snick (I.), vb. trans. [1. snik; 2. snik]. Scand.? Cp. O.N. *snikka,* 'to cut'. Origin obscure. **1.** To cut a small notch or nick in. **2.** (cricket) To hit (ball) with a glancing stroke; to touch (ball) slightly with bat.

snick (II.), n., fr. prec. **1.** A small notch or nick in a piece of wood &c. **2.** A glancing stroke, slight touch of a cricket ball with the bat.

snicker, vb. [1. sníker; 2. sníkə]. Variant of **snigger.**

snickersnee, n. [1. sníkersné; 2. sníkəsní]. Prob. fr. obs. *snick and snee,* 'a fight with knives'; lit. 'stab and cut'; it is suggested that the first element is fr. Du. *steken,* 'to stab, stick', *st-* being assimilated to the *sn-* of the second element, wh. is fr. Du. *snijen* or *snijden,* 'to cut', cogn. w. O.E. *snīþan,* 'to cut', see **snead.** Humorous term for a cutting weapon, knife, dagger, or sword.

Snider, n. [1. snider; 2. snáidə]. Inventor's name. An obsolete type of breech-loading rifle.

sniff (I.), vb. intrans. & trans. [1. snif; 2. snif]. Apparently of late Scand. origin, cp. Dan. *snive,* in same sense. The M.E. vb. is *snēvien,* the precise origin of wh. is obscure. The word is imitative. Cp. also **snivel** & **snuffle.** On the other hand, the word may have been formed direct fr. **snivel** by omission of the suffix. **A.** intrans. **1. a** To draw in air sharply and audibly through the nose, as a person with a cold &c.; **b** to draw in air thus, sharply and nervously, as though to express contempt, disapproval &c.; to affect an air of superiority, with or without actually sniffing; also, *sniff at,* to express contempt for or disapproval of. **2.** *Sniff at,* to smell at perfunctorily, or hesitatingly and delicately; to test the scent of with quick, slight drawing in of air through the nose: *to sniff at a flower; sniff at this egg and see if it is fresh.* **B.** trans. **1.** To breathe in through the nose, to inhale: *to sniff the sea air.* **2.** *Sniff up,* to draw up into the nose by inhalation: *to sniff up cocaine.* **3. a** To perceive (odour of) by sniffing: *I can sniff something burning; to sniff the drains;* **b** (fig.) to have an inkling or suspicion of; to suspect presence of: *to sniff treason, danger.*

sniff (II.), n., fr. prec. **1.** Act, sound, of sniffing. **2.** That which is sniffed or inhaled.

sniffy, adj. [1. snífi; 2. snífi]. Prec. & **-y.** (colloq.) **1.** Inclined to sniff at or be contemptuous of; disdainfully superior or critical; disapproving. **2.** Smelly; malodorous, whiffy.

snifting-valve, n. [1. snifting vàlv; 2. sníftiŋ vælv], fr. obs. *snift,* 'to snivel, whimper', variant of **sniff.** A valve in a steam-engine which allows steam or air to escape from the condenser or cylinder, so called from the noise made.

snigger, vb. intrans. & n. [1. sníger; 2. snígə]. Variant of earlier *snicker;* possibly form of **nicker,** or an independent imitative word. **1.** vb. To utter a silly, half-suppressed laugh, to giggle; to laugh furtively and slyly, as at something improper, or suggestive of impropriety. **2.** n. A half-suppressed laugh; a giggle.

sniggle, vb. intrans. [1. snígl; 2. snígl]. Dimin. of provinc. *snig,* 'eel', found in 15th cent.; perh. connected w. **snake.** To fish for eels by dropping or pushing a baited hook into their holes.

snip (I.), vb. trans. & intrans. [1. snip; 2. snip]. L.G., cp. Du. *snippen,* & L.G. *snippeln,* 'to cut in small pieces', Germ. *schnippen,* 'to snap'; connected w. **snap. 1.** trans. To cut, clip, with scissors, shears; to pinch, nip, with the nails: *snip a piece out of, a hole in, cloth; snip a bud off a stem; snip off the ends of hair* &c. **2.** intrans. To make a cut or snip at.

snip (II.), n., fr. prec. **1.** A short, quick cut or clip with shears or scissors. **2.** Small piece cut off or out by snipping. **3.** (colloq.) A tailor.

snipe (I.), n. [1. snīp; 2. snaip]. In M.E., fr. O.N. *snīpa;* cp. Dan. *sneppe,* Du. *snip,* Mod. Germ. *schnepfe;* the meaning is 'the snapping bird', cogn. w. **snap.** The O.E. word is *snite,* still preserved in some dialects. Any bird of the genus *Gallinago,* allied to the plover, curlew, sandpiper, woodcock &c., haunting marshes in which it probes for its food with a long and sensitive bill; its curious zigzag flight makes it a favourite bird for shooting; the plumage is mottled black and brown, with buff or grey under parts; the three best-known species are the common, *G. caelestis,* the solitary, *G. major,* and the small jack-snipe, *G. gallinula.*

snipe (II.), vb. intrans. & trans., fr. prec. **1.** intrans. **a** To shoot snipe, go snipe-shooting; **b** specif. (mil.) to shoot at, and pick off, single men of the enemy forces from a concealed position, usually at long range, with specially sighted rifle. **2.** trans. To hit, kill (man) in this way.

snipe-eel, n. A long, slender marine eel with long, curved beak.

snipe-fish, n. **a** Garfish; **b** snipe-eel.

sniper, n. [1. sníper; 2. snáipə]. **snipe** (II.) & **-er.** One who snipes; specif., a trained marksman who picks off single men of an enemy's forces, from a concealed position and at long range; *sniper's post,* concealed, camouflaged position for a sniper.

snippet, n. [1. snípet; 2. snípit]. **snip** & **-et. a** A small piece snipped or cut off anything; a snipping, clipping; **b** any small fragment or scrap of anything: *snippets of news, information* &c.; a short extract or passage selected from a literary work &c.: *so many anthologies consist of mere snippets.*

snippety, adj. [1. snípeti; 2. snípiti]. Prec. & **-y.** Consisting of snippets; fragmentary.

snipping, n. [1. sníping; 2. snípiŋ]. **snip** & **-ing.** Piece snipped off; a snippet, clipping.

snip-snap, adv. Descriptive of the action and the sound made by scissors &c.: *snip-snap went the scissors and her golden locks fell.*

snivel (I.), vb. intrans. [1. snívl; 2. snívl]. The O.E. words connected w. this are *snyflung,* fr. **snufil-ung,* 'mucus from the nose', & *snofl* for **snufol-,* w. same sense. From the base or stem **snufil-,* a vb. *snuvelen, snivelen, snefelen,* according to dial., was formed in M.E. The mod. form is derived fr. the *sniv-* type. See also **sniff** & **snuffle. 1.** (rare) To run, have a running at the nose; to sniff continually. **2.** (chief present uses) **a** To whine, whimper, fret, like a peevish or frightened child; **b** to complain in a fretful, whimpering manner; **c** to exhibit feeble, maundering, canting, often hypocritical and insincere regret, contrition &c.

snivel (II.), n., fr. prec. **1.** (rare) Running at the nose. **2.** Fretful, whimpering complaint; canting expression of sorrow &c.

sniveller, n. [1. snívler; 2. snívlə]. **snivel** (I.) & **-er.** One who snivels.

snob, n. [1. snob; 2. snɔb]. Also in Scots dial. *snab;* orig. sense 'cobbler's mate or boy'; also *snap,* 'boy, lad'; Scand., cp. O.N. *snāpr,* 'dolt, impostor', Swed. dial. *snöpp,* 'boy', Dan. *snopp,* 'silly, foolish'; cogn. w. **snub. 1.** (archaic or obs.) **a** Person belonging to the so-called vulgar or lower classes; person of no breeding or social position; in Phr. *a snob or a nob;* **b** (obs. university slang) townsman. **2. a** A person who pretends, from vulgar ostentation, to be better than he is; one who pretends to belong to or be familiar with people of high social standing or of great wealth or reputation; one who puts an exaggerated and vulgar estimate on rank, wealth, fashionable society or distinction and endeavours to conceal his own supposed inferior position or connexions; **b** also applied to persons who adopt a similar attitude in intellectual or artistic spheres. **3.** A cobbler.

snobbery, n. [1. snóberi; 2. snɔ́bəri]. Prec. & **-ery.** Quality of being a snob; snobbishness.

snobbish, adj. [1. snóbish; 2. snɔ́biʃ]. **snob** & **-ish.** Characteristic of a snob; pertaining to a snob.

snobbishly, adv. Prec. & **-ly.** In a snobbish manner.

snobbishness, n. See prec. & **-ness.** State, quality, of being snobbish; snobbery.

snood, n. [1. snōōd; 2. snūd]. O.E. *snōd,* 'fillet, head-dress'; fr. same base as **snare** though w. different gradation & formative element. **1.** (Scots or poet.) A fillet or ribbon for the hair, worn formerly by unmarried girls. **2.** A short piece of gut or silk fastening the hook to a fishing line; a snell.

snook (**I.**), n. [1. snook; 2. snuk], fr. Du. *snoek*; prob. gradationally related to O.E. *snaca*, see **snake**. Popular name of various sea-fishes with long beak-like snouts, as the garfish, sea-pike, barracouta &c.

snook (**II.**), n. Etymol. unknown. (slang) Impudent, boyish gesture of derision, made by placing thumb on tip of the nose and stretching out the fingers. In Phr. *to cock a snook at.*

snooker pool, n. [1. snóoker pōōl; 2. snúkə pūl]. Origin unknown; also called *Snooker's pool*, as if fr. a personal name. A game played on a billiard table, combining pyramids and ordinary pool.

snoop, vb. intrans. [1. snōōp; 2. snūp]. Imit. (U.S.A. slang) To pry inquisitively, meddle.

snooze (**I.**), vb. intrans. & trans. [1. snōōz; 2. snūz]. Etymol. doubtful; Swed. dial. has *snusa*, 'to take snuff, to sniff, breathe loud in sleep'. **1.** intrans. To take a light, short sleep or nap; to doze. **2.** trans. *Snooze away*, to spend, occupy (time) in dozing; to laze; to be lazy or indolent over.

snooze (**II.**), n., fr. prec. A light, short sleep; a nap, doze.

snore (**I.**), vb. intrans. & trans. [1. snōr; 2. snɔ]. M.E. *snōren*, fr. L.G., of imitative origin. **1.** intrans. To breathe heavily, stertorously, with vibrating or snorting noise, when asleep, a practice usually due to sleeping with mouth open on account of obstructed nasal passages. **2.** trans. (rare) **a** *Snore away*, to spend, pass (time &c.) in snoring; **b** (reflex.) to bring (oneself) into specific state by snoring: *to snore oneself awake.*

snore (**II.**), n., fr. prec. Act, sound, of snoring.

snort (**I.**), vb. intrans. & trans. [1. snort; 2. snɔ̄t]. M.E., fr. L.G. *snorten*; cogn. w. Dan. *snorke*, Swed. *snorka*, 'to snort, fume with anger', Germ. *schnarchen*, 'to snore, snort'. Of imitative origin & connected w. **snarl** & **snore**. **A.** intrans. **1. a** (of living creatures) To make a sound by drawing in the air violently and noisily through the nose; nervous action due to sudden fear, rage, surprise &c., esp. of horses; **b** (of steam engines &c.) to make a loud noise in emitting steam, gas &c. **2.** (of human beings) To show signs of contempt, surprise, impatience, disapproval &c., and to express such feelings by snorting, or merely in words. **B.** trans. (rare) *Snort out*, to express by or with a snort: *to snort out words of contempt* &c.

snort (**II.**), n., fr. prec. Act, sound, of snorting.

snorter, n. [1. snórter; 2. snɔ̄tə]. **snort** (**I.**) & **-er**. **1.** Person or animal that snorts. **2.** (slang) **a** (i.) Something or someone big, violent, vulgar, noisy &c.; (ii.) a harsh, severe, outspoken rebuke: *his letter was a regular snorter*; **b** person who, thing which, is specially good, surprising, admirable &c., in a particular class.

snorty, adj. [1. snórti; 2. snɔ̄ti], fr. **snort** (**I.**). **1.** Given to snorting; uttering snorts. **2.** (fig., of persons) Contemptuous, angry, disapproving.

snot, n. [1. snot; 2. snɔt]. O.E. (*ġe*)*snot*, cp. L.G. *snotte*, cogn. w. **snout**. (vulg.) Mucus from the nose.

snotty, adj. & n. [1. snóti; 2. snɔ́ti]. Prec. & **-y**. **1.** adj. (vulg.) Befouled with nasal mucus. **2.** n. (nav. slang) A midshipman.

snout, n. [1. snout; 2. snaut]. O.E. **snūt*, unrecorded; M.E. *snūte, snoute*; cp., however, O.E. *snȳtan*, 'to wipe the nose'; cp. L.G. *snūte*, Du. *snuit*, Mod. Germ. *schnauze*, 'muzzle', & *schneuzen*, 'to blow the nose'; fr. **snūt-jan*; belongs to the group of imitative words wh. includes **sniff, snuff, snort, snore** &c. **1. a** The projecting nose and muzzle of an animal, such as the pig; **b** (colloq. and vulg.) the human nose; the face. **2.** Projecting nozzle of a pipe; a projecting cliff, end of glacier &c.

snouted, adj. [1. snóuted; 2. snáutid]. Prec. & **-ed**. Furnished with, having, a snout; esp. in combination, *long-snouted* &c.

snow (**I.**), n. [1. snō; 2. snou]. O.E. *snāw*; M.E. *snōw* &c.; found in all Gmc. languages & in most of the other Aryan families. Gmc. type **snaiȝʷ-*, fr. Aryan **snoigʷ-*, **sneigʷ-*; the Gmc. cognates are O.S. & O.H.G. *snēo*; Goth. *snaiws*; O.N. *snǣr*, fr. **snaiwi-z*; in other Aryan languages, Scrt. *snihyati*, 'it becomes damp or sticky'; *snēhaś*, 'stickiness, slipperiness; grease'; Gk. *nipha*, 'snow', *niphás*, 'snowflake', fr. **snigʷh-*, Lat. *nix*, 'snow', for **snigʷh-s*, genit. *nivis*, O. Slav. *snĕgŭ*; Lith. *snẽgas*, 'snow'. **1. a** Vapour frozen in the atmosphere into crystals and falling upon the earth in white flakes; **b** a fall of snow: *heavy snow is reported in the North*; *snow is expected soon. Red snow*, snow-plant, q.v. **2.** (poet.) Bright, pure whiteness: *the snows of venerable age*, white hairs; *the snow of a maiden's breast* &c. **3.** Anything white and powdery, esp. (slang) powdered cocaine.

snow (**II.**), vb. intrans. & trans. New formation fr. n.; O.E. *snīwan*, 'to snow', represents a different gradational type fr. that in the n. See prec. **1.** intrans. **a** (impers.) To discharge snow from the sky: *it is snowing*, snow is falling; *it will snow tonight*; *it was snowing in the North yesterday*; **b** (by transf.) to fall, come, down in heavy showers or in large numbers: *complaints, congratulations &c., came snowing in.* **2.** trans. **a** To scatter, shower, cause to fall as or like snow: *it snowed petitions* &c.; **b** (usually in P.P.) *snow in, up, under*, (lit. or fig.) *to be snowed in, up*, to be prevented from going out by heavy fall of snow; *to be snowed under by complaints, letters* &c., overwhelmed by.

snowball (**I.**), n. [1. snṓbawl; 2. snóubɔ̄l]. **snow** (**I.**) & **ball** (**I.**). **1.** A round mass of snow moulded by the hands and used as a missile; a mass of snow rolled on ground in the snow and growing larger as it rolls and collects more snow round it. **2.** A form of collecting money &c. by an ever-widening group of subscribers, each of whom enlists the support of others. **3.** The flower of the guelder rose. **4.** Humorous name for a white-haired negro.

snowball (**II.**), vb. intrans. & trans., fr. prec. **1.** intrans. To throw snowballs. **2.** trans. To pelt, hit, with snowballs; to throw snowballs at.

snowball-tree, n. The guelder rose.

snow-berry, n. A garden ornamental shrub, *Symphoricarpus racemosus*, with small pink flowers and round white berries.

snow-bird, n. The snow-bunting or snowflake.

snow-blind, adj. Having become temporarily blind or partly blind from the effects of prolonged exposure of the eyes to the dazzling glare of snow on the ground.

snow-blindness, n. Total or partial temporary blindness, caused by the glare of a large expanse of snow-covered country.

snow-blink, n. Reflection on the horizon of sunlight from a field of ice or snow.

snow-boot, n. A boot of rubber and felted cloth worn over the ordinary boot in heavy snow.

snow-bound, adj. Snowed up, shut in, prevented from travelling &c., by a heavy fall of snow.

snow-bunting, n. A bird of the finch family, *Plectrophanes nivalis*, breeding in polar regions and visiting N. Europe and America in winter, with white and brown plumage, also called 'snowflake'.

snow-cap, n. **1.** Cap, crown, of snow on the top of a mountain. **2.** Name of a very small humming-bird, with white crown, inhabiting Central America.

snow-capped, adj. [1. snṓ kapt; 2. snóu kæpt]. (of mountains) Capped, crowned, with snow.

snow-drift, n. A heap, bank, of snow, drifted or blown together by the wind.

snowdrop, n. [1. snṓdrop; 2. snóudrɔp]. A bulbous plant, *Galanthus nivalis*, with drooping white bell-like flowers, appearing in late winter or early spring.

snowfall, n. [1. snṓfawl; 2. snóufɔ̄l]. **a** A fall of snow; **b** amount of snow falling at a certain place or during a certain period.

snow-field, n. A large expanse of permanent snow, on Alpine heights, in Arctic regions &c.

snowflake, n. [1. snṓflāk; 2. snóufleik]. **1.** A flake of snow, the form in which snow falls to the ground, being a group of frozen crystals massed together. **2.** The snow-bunting. **3.** A plant, *Leucojum*, like a large snowdrop.

snow-goggles, n. Spectacles with darkened glass worn amid snow-fields to prevent snow-blindness.

snow-goose, n. An arctic wild goose, with white plumage and black-tipped wing feathers.

snow-grouse, n. The ptarmigan.

snow-ice, n. White, opaque ice formed by the freezing of half-melted snow or ice.

snowily, adv. [1. snṓili; 2. snóuili]. **snowy** & **-ly**. In a snowy manner.

snowiness, n. [1. snṓines; 2. snóuinis]. **snowy** & **-ness**. Quality, state, of being snowy.

snow-leopard, n. The ounce, *Felis uncia*, of the mountains of Central Asia.

snowless, adj. [1. snṓles; 2. snóulis]. **snow** (**I.**) & **-less**. Without snow.

snow-like, adj. **snow** (**I.**) & **-like**. Like, as white as, snow.

snow-line, n. The imaginary line of altitude above which snow never melts; the line of perpetual snow.

snow-on-the-mountain, n. Popular name for various plants with closely set white flowers, as arabis, the N. American spurge &c.

snow-owl, n. See **snowy owl**.

snow-plant, n. A minute alga, *Protococcus nivalis*, with reddish spores, found in the snow-fields of arctic and subarctic regions.

snow-plough, n. A device of various kinds for clearing a road, railway track &c., of snow.

snow-shoe, n. & vb. intrans. **1.** n. Long, narrow, flat framework in form of a racquet, with cross-pieces of strips of leather &c., attached to the foot, enabling wearer to walk over soft snow without sinking. **2.** vb. To travel over snow in snow-shoes.

snowstorm, n. [1. snṓstorm; 2. snóustɔ̄m]. Heavy fall of snow, esp. one accompanied by a strong wind.

snow-white, adj. White as snow.

snow-wreath, n. A circular drift of snow.

snowy, adj. [1. snṓi; 2. snóui]. **snow** (**I.**) & **-y**. **1.** Covered with snow: *snowy mountains.* **2.** Characterized by, abounding in, snow: *a snowy day, snowy weather.* **3.** White as snow, snow-white: *snowy breast*; *a long snowy beard.*

snowy owl, n. A large species of Arctic owl, *Nyctea scandiaca*, with white plumage, mottled with black, visiting N. Europe and America in winter.

snub (**I.**), vb. trans. [1. snub; 2. snab]. M.E. *snubben*, also *snibben*; of Scand. origin, cp. Dan. *snubbe*, Swed. *snubba*, 'to nip off, to check, rebuke, snub', O.N. *snubba*, 'to check, chide'; cogn. w. **snuff** (**III.**). **1.** To check, slight, put down, rebuff, by a sharp, sarcastic, or contemptuous remark, or by a show of coolness or indifference. **2.** (naut.) To stop, check, the way of a ship suddenly by means of a rope tautened round a bollard or 'snubbing post'.

snub (**II.**), n., fr. prec. Act of snubbing; rebuke, rebuff.

snub (**III.**), adj. & n., fr. prec. words. **1.** adj. (applied only to the nose) Short, thick, blunt, and somewhat flat and turned up at the end. **2.** n. A snub nose.

snubbing, n. [1. snúbing; 2. snábiŋ]. **snub** (**I.**) & **-ing**. A snub, sharp rebuff or reproof.

snubbingly, adv. Prec. & **-ly**. In a snubbing manner; by means of a snub.

snubbing post, n. A bollard or post on a wharf or quayside round which a rope may be thrown and tautened to 'snub' or check the way of a vessel.

snub-nosed, adj. Having a snub nose.

snuff (**I.**), vb. trans. & intrans. [1. snuf; 2. snaf], fr. M. Du. *snuffen*, 'to blow, clear, the nose', cp. Du. *snuiven*, 'to snort', Swed. *snuffla*, 'to snuffle', Mod. Germ. *schnupfen*, 'a cold in the head'; connected w. **sniff**; orig. imitative. **1.** trans. To sniff, inhale, breathe in through the nose: *to snuff (up) the scent of* &c.; *to snuff sea-breezes, to snuff tobacco.* **2.** intrans. To sniff.

snuff (II.), n., fr. prec., & vb. intrans., a new formation fr. n. in sense **b**. **1.** n. **a** A sniff; **b** (i.) powdered, grated tobacco, for sniffing up the nose; a pinch of tobacco thus inhaled; Phr. *up to snuff* (colloq., slang), wide-awake, knowing, sharp; not to be taken in; (ii.) any powdered drug used for inhaling medicinally. **2.** vb. To take snuff.

snuff (III.), vb. trans. & intrans. M.E. *snuffen*, 'to snuff a candle'; origin doubtful. **A.** trans. **1.** To nip off that part of the wick of the antiquated type of tallow candle which had ceased to be incandescent, and which curled over and prevented flame burning brightly: *to snuff a candle.* **2.** *Snuff out*, **a** to extinguish, put out (candle), by squeezing wick with snuffers &c.; **b** (fig., colloq.) to destroy, do away with, put down, suppress: *to snuff out a rebellion.* **B.** intrans. *Snuff out*, (colloq.) to die, be extinguished.

snuff (IV.), n., fr. prec. The charred wick of a tallow candle, which prevents it burning clearly or brightly.

snuff-and-butter, adj. & n. **snuff** (II.) & **butter**. **1.** adj. **a** Brownish yellow in colour; specif. **b** (colloq.) of mixed European and E. Indian blood. **2.** n. **a** The colour itself; **b** mixed European and E. Indian descent.

snuff-box, n. A small box of horn or metal &c., often highly decorated and used for carrying snuff in the pocket.

snuff-coloured, adj. **snuff** (II.) & **coloured**. Of the colour of snuff; brownish yellow.

snuffers, n. pl. [1. snúferz; 2. snáfəz]. **snuff** (III.) & **-er**. Instrument of silver or other metal, shaped like a pair of scissors, having broad short blades, one of which had a raised rim on the outer edge, formerly used for removing that part of the wick of a now obsolete type of candle, which had ceased to be incandescent.

snuffiness, n. [1. snúfines; 2. snáfinis]. **snuffy** & **-ness**. Condition, quality, of being snuffy.

snuffle (I.), vb. intrans. & trans. [1. snúfl; 2. snáfl]. Freq. of **snuff** (I.), cp. **snivel** & **sniff**. **1.** intrans. **a** To sniff constantly and continually; to keep on sniffing, make a sniffing noise; to breathe rapidly in and out, audibly through the nose, esp. when the nasal passages are partially blocked; **b** to speak through the nose; (in transf. sense) to speak with a nasal, whining, sing-song and canting, hypocritical tone of voice. **2.** trans. (rare) To utter with a snuffle.

snuffle (II.), n., fr. prec. **1.** Act of snuffling; sound made by snuffling. **2.** *The snuffles*, kind of persistent nasal catarrh, affecting babies and young children.

snuff-mill, n. **snuff** (II.) & **mill** (I.). A small hand-mill for grinding tobacco into snuff.

snuffy, adj. [1. snúfi; 2. snáfi]. **snuff** (II.) & **-y**. **1.** Resembling snuff in colour &c. **2.** Covered, stained, with snuff; untidy, grimy, dingy, in personal appearance. **3.** (colloq.) Offended, cross.

snug (I.), adj. [1. snug; 2. snag]. Early & provinc. use, 'trim, neat, compact', of Scand. origin; cp. O.N. *snoggr*, 'smooth-haired, tidy'; Swed. *snygg*, 'neat, trim'. **1.** Warm, sheltered, comfortable; protected from draughts or cold; cosy: *a snug seat by the fire; to lie snug in bed.* **2.** **a** Of comfortable, adequate, size: *a snug income*; **b** convenient, compact, trim: *a snug little cottage, farm* &c. **3.** Protected from view or notice, hidden, concealed: *he lay snug for some time before his retreat was found out.* **4.** Neatly and closely arranged, coiled down; furled; fitting closely: *make ropes, sails &c., snug.*

snug (II.), n., fr. prec. A snug place, snuggery.

snug (III.), vb. intrans. & trans. **1.** intrans. To make oneself snug, to snuggle. **2.** trans. To make snug, esp. of ropes, sails &c.

snuggery, n. [1. snúgeri; 2. snágəri]. **snug** (I.) & **-ery**. A snug, cosy place or room; place in which one can be snug and undisturbed; one's own private study or 'den'.

snuggle, vb. intrans. & trans. [1. snúgl; 2. snágl], fr. **snug** (III.) & **-le**. **1.** intrans. To nestle, get, lie, close and snug to, or comfortable in: *to snuggle up to a person; snuggle down in bed.* **2.** trans. To bring close to one, to cuddle: *snuggled the baby in her arms.*

snugly, adv. [1. snúgli; 2. snágli]. **snug** (I.) & **-ly**. In a snug manner; cosily, comfortably.

snugness, n. [1. snúgnes; 2. snágnis]. **snug** (I.) & **-ness**. State, quality, of being snug.

so, adv., pron., & conj. [1. sō; 2. sou]. O.E. *swā*, M.E. *sō*; O.H.G. *sō*; Gk. *hṓs*, 'so, thus'; the word belongs ultimately to the reflex. base **swo-* &c., seen in Lat. *suus*. See **sui**. **1.** **a** (archaic) To the extent, in the way, stated, indicated, or about to be stated; thus: *so spake he*; **b** in this or that way: *you must not behave so; so, and in no other way*; **c** in accordance with what has been stated or expected; in that case: *is he really ill? if so, send for the doctor; he states that you struck him—kindly tell me if that is so; do do you say so?*, expressing surprise; *just so, quite so*, expressing agreement with what has been said. **2.** **a** To such an extent or degree; to that extent or degree: *I was so hot (that) I took my coat off; he is so stupid that he can't understand a plain statement*; **b** followed by correlative *as* (chiefly in neg. sentences): *he is not so stupid as he looks; not so hot as yesterday.* **3.** To such a great degree or extent; how much: (chiefly colloq.) *it was so kind of you to write; I am so tired.* **4.** (partly pronominal in function) In that way, thus (=that which has been stated or referred to): *I don't think so; I hope so; he promised to clean the car but has not yet done so; I never said so; I told you so.* **5.** In the same proportion, in like manner, to the same extent; in the same way; in correlation with preceding clause introduced by *as*: *just as we have been unprepared for war in the past, so we are now; as the father was a degenerate, so the son is a criminal; 'as thy days, so shall thy strength be'; as you treat me, so will I treat you.* **6.** For the reason specified, on that account, therefore: *the manager was out, so I left a message with his secretary; the train leaves in half an hour, so you had better hurry.* **7.** (exclamatory) Well!, *so you came after all!; so the great dictionary is finished at last!* **8.** In the same way, to the same extent; also, as well: *my father was a Tory, and so am I; we were wrong, so were you.* **9.** *Or so*, more or less, thereabouts, approximately: *he must be forty or so; it will cost you five pounds or so.* **10.** (as impers. pron.) *So-and-so*, **a** referring to some specific person, whose name is not mentioned: *we all know what So-and-so will say*; **b** referring to some person unknown, considered as a type; people, somebody or other, anybody: *don't be afraid to do your duty because So-and-so will laugh at you.* **11.** *So much*, **a** a definite but unspecified sum, amount &c.: *you can board at so much a day; so much brandy, so much wine, and so much of several other things*; **b** in Phr. *so much nonsense, rubbish* &c., all nonsense &c.; **c** *so much for*, that is the end of, that concludes, there is nothing more to be said or done about: *so much for Mr. Jones, he won't trouble us again; every one of his statements was refuted—so much for his case.* **12.** *So long as*, provided that, on the understanding that: *I will pay you five pounds so long as you admit that you have no legal claim; you may have leave this time so long as it does not form a precedent.* **13.** *So on, so forth*, as abbreviation of an enumeration &c.; more (things) of the same kind, etcetera: *he told me his age, where he lived, how many children he had, and so on*; also emphatic: *and so on and so on; and so on and so forth.* **14.** *So as*; **a** in such a way as: *he struck the snake so as to break its back*; **b** in order: *come early so as to have plenty of time.* **15.** *So that*, in order that: *I stayed on so that he might not feel lonely.*

soak (I.), vb. trans. & intrans. [1. sōk; 2. souk]. O.E. *socian*, fr. **sukōjan*, M.E. *soken*; in gradational relation to O.E. *sūcan*, q.v. under **suck**. **A.** trans. **1.** To steep, allow to lie in liquid, to impregnate thoroughly with liquid: *to soak bread in milk.* Phr. *to soak oneself in a subject* (of study), *an author* &c., to immerse oneself in, saturate oneself with, study with such intensity as to become thoroughly familiar with. **2.** To wet thoroughly, to drench, saturate: *the shower soaked us to the skin.* **3.** *Soak up*, **a** (i.) to absorb (liquid), become saturated with, suck up: *sponges readily soak up water; parched ground soaks up rain*; (ii.) also in non-material sense, *to soak up information* &c., to imbibe it, acquire it readily; **b** to remove (liquid) from a given position by absorption: *soak up that pool of ink with some blotting-paper.* **B.** intrans. **1.** To remain in liquid so as to become saturated; to steep: *put the clothes in water and allow them to soak for several hours.* **2.** (colloq.) To drink (alcoholic liquor) steadily and persistently in large quantities; to drink to excess. **3.** (of liquids) **a** *Soak through*, to penetrate, percolate through: *blood from the wound has soaked through the bandages*; **b** *soak into*, to pass into from elsewhere, by soaking, oozing &c.: *water has soaked into the cellar from the soil.*

soak (II.), n., fr. prec. **1.** Act of soaking; state of being soaked: *give the clothes a thorough soak.* **2.** (colloq.) A downpour of rain, drenching rain; a spell of wet weather: *'If ash is out before the oak, In summer we shall have a soak'.* **3.** (colloq.) A steady spell of hard drinking; a booze.

soakage, n. [1. sókij; 2. sóukidž]. **soak** (I.) & **-age**. **1.** Act of soaking or percolating through or into anything. **2.** Amount of liquid percolating through or into anything.

soaker, n. [1. sóker; 2. sóukə]. **soak** (I.) & **-er**. One who, that which, soaks; specif. (colloq.) **a** a downpour of rain; drenching rain; **b** a hard drinker, boozer.

soap (I.), n. [1. sōp; 2. soup]. O.E. *sāpe*, M.E. *sōpe*; O.H.G. *seifa*, Du. *zeep*; O.N. *sāpa* is fr. O.E.; Lat. *sāpo, sāpōnem*, see **saponaceous**, is borrowed fr. Gmc. Cp. further the related O.E. *sīpian*, 'to macerate, be soaked'; the true Lat. cogn. is *sēbum*, 'tallow, suet', see **sebaceous**. **1.** The substance used for washing and cleansing, composed of a combination of caustic soda or potash, and animal or vegetable oils and fats, often scented and moulded into bars or cakes. Phrs. *to wash one's hands in invisible soap*, to rub one hand over the other, as though washing them, esp. as a nervous or ill-bred person wishing to be ingratiating, or when merely embarrassed; *soft soap*, (i.) a semi-liquid form of potash soap; (ii.) (fig.) flattery. **2.** Specif. (chem.) any compound of an alkali with a fatty acid.

soap (II.), vb. trans. & intrans., fr. prec. **1.** trans. **a** To use soap upon, apply soap to for washing, to rub with soap and water; **b** (fig.) to flatter: *to soap a person down.* **2.** intrans. To use soap for washing.

soap-bark, n. Name of various American tropical trees, the bark of which is soapy and used for washing and medicinally.

soap-berry, n. A tropical tree of America genus *Sapindus*, the berries of which, soaked in water, produce a lather, used for washing.

soap-boiler, n. A manufacturer of soap.

soap-boiling, n. The process or industry of manufacturing soap.

soap-bubble, n. A hollow, iridescent ball or bubble of air enclosed in a film of soap.

soapily, adv. [1. sópili; 2. sóupili]. **soapy** & **-ly**. In a soapy manner; specif. (fig.) with obsequious politeness.

soapiness, n. [1. sṓpines; 2. sóupinis]. See prec. & **-ness**. State, quality, of being soapy (in both senses).

soap-plant, n. Any plant which yields substances capable of being used as soap.

soap-root, n. Name of various bulbous plants used as soap.

soapstone, n. [1. sṓpstōn; 2. sóupstoun]. A soft stone which is soapy to the touch, esp. steatite.

soap-suds, n. **soap** & **suds**. Frothy scum of soap floating on water; soapy water.

soap-wort, n. **soap** & **wort** (I.). Popular name of a plant, *Saponaria officinalis*, the leaves of which when bruised and steeped in water yield a soapy lather.

soapy, adj. [1. sṓpi; 2. sóupi]. **soap (I.)** & **-y**. **1.** Covered with, impregnated with, full of, soap: *a soapy face; soapy water*. **2.** Resembling soap in consistency and texture; slimy, greasy to the touch. **3.** (fig., of bearing and manners) Obsequious, flattering; designed to propitiate; oily, unctuous.

soar, vb. intrans. [1. sōr; 2. sɔ̄]. M.E. *sōren*, fr. O. Fr. *essorer*, 'to expose (wings) to the air, to soar', orig. a hawking term; fr. L. Lat. **exaurāre*, fr. **ex-**, 'out', & *aura*, 'air', see **aura**. **1.** (of birds) To rise from the ground &c. and mount high into the air. **2.** (fig.) To aspire in mind; to rise to heights of feeling, imagination &c.; to attain great elevation of thought, feeling, expression.

soave, adv. [1. sōáhvā; 2. soáve]. Ital., fr. Lat. *suāvis*, 'sweet'. See **suave**. (musical direction) Sweetly, gently, softly.

sob (I.), vb. intrans. & trans. [1. sob; 2. sɔb]. M.E. *sobben*, fr. an unrecorded O.E. **sobbian*; prob. related to O.E. *seofian*, 'to sigh, lament', & apparently to O.H.G. *siufzen*, 'to sigh, groan', though the phonology is by no means clear. Prob. of imitative origin. **A.** intrans. **1.** To weep convulsively and noisily. **2.** To labour for breath, to breathe in short, rapid, convulsive breaths, as after prolonged, violent exertion. **3.** To produce either **a** a series of rapid convulsive sounds, such as the palpitations of an engine, or **b** a mournful, intermittent sound such as the breaking of waves on rocks, a fitful gust of wind &c. **B.** trans. Usually *sob out*, to express, utter, in sobs or by sobbing: *to sob out one's grief* &c. Phr. *to sob one's heart out*, to weep convulsively and noisily as from heart-rending grief.

sob (II.), n., fr. prec. Act of, sound of, sobbing.

sobbing, n. [1. sóbing; 2. sɔ́biŋ]. **sob (I.)** & **-ing**. Act, sound, of one who, that which, sobs.

sobbingly, adv., fr. Pres. Part. of **sob (I.)** & **-ly**. In a sobbing manner, with sobs.

sober (I.), adj. [1. sṓber; 2. sóubə], fr. Fr. *sobre*, fr. Lat. *sōbrius*, wh. is believed to come fr. **sō(d)*, 'without', a variant of *sēd*, see **sed-**, & *ēbrius*, 'drunk', see **ebriety**. **1. a** Not drunk; not under the influence of strong drink; unaffected in mind or power of movement by alcohol: *not completely sober at the time of the accident; drunk or sober, he is a dismal man*; **b** not given to habitual excess in the use of strong drink; temperate, abstemious: *the man was sober, honest, and thrifty; the sober army and navy of today*. Phr. *as sober as a judge*, completely sober. **2.** Moderate in character or temperament; of sound, cool judgement; not given to extremes in opinions and prejudices; habitually avoiding vehemence of feeling and expression, or violence in action; not easily carried away by emotion or passion: *the more sober of his supporters were not so confident of success; a sober critic*. **3.** Characterized by moderation and not excited or exaggerated; not fanciful or visionary: *of sober mind, judgement; no man in his sober senses would act thus; gave a sober statement of the facts*. **4.** Quiet, subdued in colour; not bright or garish: *clad in sober raiment*.

sober (II.), vb. trans. & intrans., fr. prec. **1.** trans. To make sober; **a** to bring out of condition of drunkenness or other excess; **b** to cool the judgement of; to reduce to a reasonable state of mind, to reduce to moderation from a state of mental exaltation, from extremes of passion, prejudice &c. **2.** intrans. *Sober down*, to become sober in mind, opinions, conduct.

soberly, adv. [1. sṓberli; 2. sóubəli]. **sober (I.)** & **-ly**. In a sober manner.

sober-minded, adj. Having a sober, calm, self-controlled mind and character; not rash or impetuous.

sober-mindedly, adv. Prec. & **-ly**. In a sober-minded manner.

sober-mindedness, n. See prec. & **-ness**. State, quality, of being sober-minded.

sobersides, n. [1. sṓbersīdz; 2. sóubəsaidz]. (colloq.) A solemn, sedate, serious person; one not given to frolics, light jests, jollification &c.

Sobranje, n. [1. sōbráhnyā; 2. soubrǽnjɛ]. Bulg., 'assembly', fr. *so*, 'together', & base **ber-*, 'to bring, bear', see **bear (I.)**. The national legislative assembly of Bulgaria.

sobriety, n. [1. sōbríeti; 2. soubráiəti], fr. Fr. *sobriété*, fr. Lat. *sōbrietāt-(em)*. See **sober** & **-ty**. State, quality, of being sober, in all its senses.

sobriquet, soubriquet, n. [1. sṓbrikā; 2. sóubrikei]. Fr.; etymol. obscure; O. Fr. had *soubzbriquet*, 'chuck under the chin'; fr. *soubz, sous*, 'under', cp. **sub**, & Norm. Fr. *briquet*, fr. *brechet*, 'brisket, chest'. A nickname; an assumed name.

sob-stuff, n. (Am. slang) Mawkish sentimentality, exaggerated pathos, esp. in journalism, acting on the stage, and in films.

soc, n. [1. sok; 2. sɔk]. O.E. or early M.E. *sōc*, a legal term, apparently a variant of *sōcn*, 'inquiry, right of inquiry, jurisdiction; place, area, over which jurisdiction extends'; borrowed fr. O.N. & cogn. w. O.E. *sēcan*, 'to seek', see **seek**. (feudal law) **1.** Right and power of judicial inquiry and decision; jurisdiction; esp. in Phr. *sac and soc*, power of hearing and deciding legal causes and disputes. **2.** Area in which such power is exercised, surviving as *soke*, q.v. **3.** Freedom from certain personal, esp. military, services or burdens, as basis of tenure of land.

socage, soccage, n. [1. sókij; 2. sɔ́kidž]. L., Med. Lat. *soc(c)āgium*. See prec. & **-age**. (legal hist.) A form of tenure of agricultural land in which the tenant performed certain fixed, definite services other than military, or paid in kind in lieu of such, developing into freehold and copyhold tenures.

soccer, also spelt **socker**, n. [1. sóker; 2. sɔ́kə]. Popular abbr. of **association football**.

sociability, n. [1. sōshabíliti; 2. souʃəbíliti]. **sociable** & **-ity**. Quality of being sociable.

sociable (I.), adj. [1. sṓshabl; 2. sóuʃəbl]. Fr., fr. Lat. *sociābilis*, 'easily joined; sociable', fr. base of *sociāre*, 'to accompany, be a companion to', fr. *socius*, 'companion, fellow', fr. base **sokʷ-*, 'to follow', in gradational relation to Lat. *sequi*, 'to follow', see **sequela**; Lat. *socius* is exactly cogn. w. O.E. *secġ*, 'man. warrior', fr. Gmc. **saȝʷja-*, Aryan **sokʷjó-*; cp. also Scrt. *saci*, 'together'. **1.** (of persons &c.) Fond of company and society; companionable; agreeable to meet; inclined to be friendly and genial; ready to talk and mix with others, affable: *the English are not a very sociable people*. **2.** Characterized, marked, by friendliness and affability; not stiff or formal: *sociable manners, disposition* &c. **3.** Affording opportunity for friendly talk and companionship: *a sociable evening, meeting, party*.

sociable (II.), n., fr. prec. **1.** (colloq.) A friendly, social, informal, meeting, party &c. **2.** A vehicle, sofa, tricycle, with seats for two persons side by side.

sociably, adv. [1. sṓshabli; 2. sóuʃəbli]. **sociable (I.)** & **-ly**. In a sociable manner; *sociably inclined*, fond of society; convivial.

social (I.), adj. [1. sṓshl; 2. sóuʃl], fr. Lat. *sociālis*, fr. *socius*, 'companion, partner, ally', q.v. under **sociable**. **1.** Pertaining to, concerned with, the mutual relations of mankind as living in an organized, interdependent body or society: *social laws, relations; social progress, reform* &c.; *the social good*. Phr. *the Social Contract*, translating Rousseau's 'Contrat Social,' theoretical contract by which men obtained true freedom by mutual agreement to substitute a state of law for a state of individualism and nature; *the social evil*, prostitution; *social science*, sociology. **2. a** (of human beings) Living in mutual relations, sharing work, duties &c. with, or in dependence on, others: *when did man become social?*; **b** (zool., esp. of insects) living in communities, gregarious, contrasted with *solitary*: *social wasps, ants, bees* &c. **3. a** Pertaining to organized human society: *the social customs of the Hindus*; specif. **b** pertaining to the ranks, grades, of society: *one's social equals; to long for social advancement*. **4.** Composed of persons meeting on terms of social equality, tastes &c.: *a social club*. **5.** Enjoyed, spent, in company with others: *a social evening*. **6.** Friendly, sociable: *he has a nice, social character*. **7.** (Gk. and Rom. hist.) Taking place between allies: *the Social Wars*.

social (II.), n. (colloq. or vulg.) A social evening.

socialism, n. [1. sṓshalizm; 2. sóuʃəlizəm]. **social (I.)** & **-ism**. **1.** A political and economic theory and movement for the reform of society by the substitution of collective for individual ownership of capital and property; contrasted with, and opposed to, *capitalism* or *individualism*; state or municipal ownership of the means of production, distribution, and exchange.

socialist, n. [1. sṓshalist; 2. sóuʃəlist]. See prec. & **-ist**. **1. a** One who believes in socialism as a political and economic theory; **b** a member of a political party which advocates and endeavours to introduce socialism as a form of government. **2.** (attrib.) Pertaining to socialism or socialists: *socialist organization, members of Parliament* &c.

socialistic, adj. [1. sōshalístik; 2. souʃəlístik]. Prec. & **-ic**. Pertaining, relating, to socialists or socialism.

socialistically, adv. [1. sōshalístikali; 2. souʃəlístik(ə)li]. Prec. & **-al** & **-ly**. In a socialistic manner, by way of socialism.

sociality, n. [1. sōshiáliti; 2. souʃiǽliti]. **social (I.)** & **-ity**. **a** State, quality, of being social or sociable; sociability; **b** instinct, tendency, to become social.

socialization, n. [1. sōshalīzáshun; 2. souʃəlaizéiʃən]. See next word & **-ation**. **a** Act, process, of socializing; **b** state of being socialized.

socialize, vb. trans. [1. sṓshalīz; 2. sóuʃəlaiz]. **social (I.)** & **-ize**. **1.** To make, render, social; to subordinate to the interests of a society; to incorporate in a society. **2.** To make socialistic; to make to conform to the principles of socialism; to change from individual or private ownership to state or municipal ownership.

socially, adv. [1. sṓshali; 2. sóuʃəli]. **social (I.)** & **-ly**. **1.** After the manner of, according to the principles and customs of, organized society: *man has lived socially from the moment at which he became man*. **2.** In social or sociable manner; affably, companionably. **3.** According to the ranks, grades, divisions, of society: *ranks socially inferior, superior*.

society, n. [1. sosíeti; 2. səsáiəti]. Fr. *société*, fr. Lat. *societāt-(em)*, 'fellowship, association, community; a political league, alliance', fr. base in *socius*, 'companion' &c., see under **sociable**, & abstract suff., q.v. under **-ty**. **1.** System whereby men live in organized communities, regulated by custom and law, for purposes of mutual protection, help, government &c., with division of labour to ensure that the various necessities of life are provided and its essential activities carried on: *the dawn of human society; primitive society*. **2.** Any organized group of human beings forming a community, more or less closely united by common customs or laws, and living under some form of common government: *the society of the Ancient Egyptians was based upon kingship closely related with religion.* **3.** Human life, customs, behaviour, in general, considered as existing in organized communities, and subject to the conditions governing organized social life: *the habits and morality of society have changed greatly since the Great War.* **4.** Some particular grade or stratum of society; **a** some group of persons associated together, and marked out from the community as a whole, by the possession of particular interests and capacities or by following some special occupation: *literary, scientific, academic, society*; **b** specif. (i.) those sections of the community distinguished by birth, high rank, considerable wealth, and sometimes by education and refinement of manners; those circles which are fashionable and (more or less) exclusive: *society with a capital S*; *anxious to get into society*; (ii.) (attrib.) belonging to, frequenting, fashionable society: *a society woman, hostess.* **5.** Companionship, company, of, social association with, another or others: *to enjoy the society of one's friends*; *I was glad to be quit of his unwelcome society.* **6.** A group, party, company, posse, of persons, standing or walking, at a given moment, in sufficiently close proximity to each other to form a band or unit: '*There entertain him all the saints above, In solemn troops and sweet societies*' (Milton, 'Lycidas', 178-9). **7.** (cap.) A group or association of persons united under a set of regulations, conditions of membership &c., for the furtherance of a particular cause, set of interests &c.: *the Royal Society*; *Archaeological Society*; *Society for the Propagation of the Gospel* &c.

Socinian, adj. & n. [1. sōsínian; 2. sousíniən]. Formed fr. *Socinus*, the Latinized form of the name of the Italian Fausto Sozzini (1539–1604) & his uncle Lelio S. (1525–62) who taught anti-Trinitarian doctrines, & denied the Atonement. Socinus's views are virtually those held by modern Unitarians. **a** adj. Pertaining to, based on, embodying, the doctrines of Socinus; **b** n., an adherent of these doctrines.

Socinianism, n. [1. sōsínianizm; 2. sousíniənizəm]. Prec. & **-ism.** The doctrines and theological system taught by Socinus.

sociological, adj. [1. sōsiōlójikl; 2. sousiəlódžikl]. See **sociology** & **-ic** & **-al.** Pertaining to sociology.

sociologically, adv. Prec. & **-ly.** From the point of view of sociology.

sociologist, n. [1. sōsiólojist; 2. sousiólədžist]. **sociology** & **-ist.** Student of sociology.

sociology, n. [1. sōsióloji; 2. sousiólədži], fr. Lat. *socius.* See **social** (I.) & **-logy.** Scientific and systematized study of mankind considered as social beings, living in organized communities; the study of human society; social science.

sock (I.), n. [1. sok; 2. sɔk]. O.E. *socc*, fr. Lat. *soccus*, 'a light shoe or slipper', worn by comic actors; fr. Gk., cp. *sukkhis*, 'kind of shoe'; prob. of Oriental origin. **1.** (archaic and poet.) The comic actor's shoe; hence, comedy, the comic muse: '*If Jonson's learned sock be on*' (Milton, 'L'Allegro', 132). **2.** A short stocking reaching to the middle of the calf of the leg, as worn by men and young children. **3.** An inner sole, usually with a woolly upper surface, inserted in a boot or shoe for the sake of warmth or to effect a better fit.

sock (II.), vb. trans. Etymol. obscure, possibly abbr. fr. **sockdologer.** (slang) To hit, strike, with missile, fist, or weapon.

sock (III.), n. Etymol. unknown. (schoolboy slang) Food, such as pastry, sweets &c., obtained in school tuck-shop &c.; grub, tuck.

sockdologer, n. [1. sokdólojer; 2. sɔkdólədžə]. Corrupt. of **doxology.** (Am. slang) Something which finally settles or ends anything, such as a blow, decisive argument &c.

socker, soccer, n. [1. sóker; 2. sɔ́kə]. Popular abbr. of **association football.**

socket, n. & vb. [1. sóket; 2. sɔ́kit]. M.E., fr. O. (Norm.) Fr. *soket*; dimin. of *souche*, 'stock, stump, of a tree'; of Gmc. origin, cp. M. Du. *schocke*, 'cock, heap, shock, of corn', &c., see **shock** (III.); Ital. has *ciocco*, 'stump', fr. same source. **1.** n. A hollow chamber, cavity, recess, formed by nature or art, adapted for the reception of another object or a portion of this, whether so as to hold it immovable, or to allow a certain play or movement: *a bolt often fits into a socket cut in the wood of the door frame*; *the head of a joint works in a socket*; *the eye-sockets.* **2.** vb. To furnish with, fix into, a socket.

socketed, adj. [1. sóketed; 2. sɔ́kitid]. P.P. of prec. Fixed into, provided with, a socket.

socle, n. [1. sókl; 2. sɔ́kl]. Fr., fr. Ital. *zoccolo*, fr. L. Lat. *socculus*, dimin. of *soccus.* See **sock** (I.). (archit.) **a** A plain, rectangular base or plinth, forming the pedestal of a statue, column &c.; **b** a low, plain, projecting plinth at the base of a wall.

socman, n. [1. sókman; 2. sɔ́kmən]. **soc** & **man.** (legal hist.) Person holding agricultural land by tenure of socage.

Socratic, adj. & n. [1. sōkrátik; 2. soukrǽtik], fr. Gk. *Sōkratikós.* **1.** adj. Connected with, pertaining to, Socrates, the Greek philosopher and teacher (469–399 B.C.); *Socratic dialectic* or *method*, method of argument and proof by means of question and answer; *Socratic irony*, assumption of ignorance on the part of questioner, thus leading the questioned into contradictions and display of his own ignorance. **2.** n. (usually pl.) Follower of the teaching and philosophy of Socrates.

Socratically, adv. [1. sōkrátikali; 2. soukrǽtik(ə)li]. Prec. & **-al** & **-ly.** In the manner of Socrates or the Socratics.

sod (I.), n. [1. sod; 2. sɔd]. The word is prob. of L.G. origin in the present sense, cp. L.G. *sode*, 'turf'. It is, however, connected w. **seethe** & **sodden**, the orig. sense of the base being 'to boil, bubble'. Cp. also the O.E. cogn. *sēaþ*, 'a pond, well', L.G. *sood*, 'a well'. Thus the chain of meaning wd. be 'a spring; ground through which water springs; moist ground; grass growing on such ground'. **1.** Grassy surface of earth; turf, sward. Phr. *under the sod*, in the grave, buried. **2.** A piece of cut turf.

sod (II.), vb. trans., fr. prec. To cover with sods.

sod (III.), vb. Pret. of **seethe.** Obs. or very archaic.

sod (IV.), n. Contraction of **Sodomite.** An obscene and vulgar term of abuse.

soda, n. [1. sóda; 2. sóudə]. Ital., orig. applied to the ash used in making glass; fem. sing. of *sodo*, 'firm, hard', fr. Lat. *solidus*, see **solid.** **1.** Any of the various compounds of sodium, esp. **a** *sodium carbonate*, common soda, used in various industries, as glass-making, soap-boiling &c., and for washing purposes; **b** *sodium bicarbonate*, used for baking powders and medicinally; **c** *sodium hydroxide*, caustic soda. **2.** Soda-water: *a whisky and soda.*

soda-fountain, n. Apparatus for holding and supplying soda-water or other effervescing mineral waters and beverages.

sodalite, n. [1. sódalit; 2. sóudəlait]. Fr. See **soda** & **-lite.** Name of a group of rock-forming minerals, of which the type is a silicate of sodium and aluminium.

sodality, n. [1. sōdáliti; 2. soudǽliti], fr. Lat. *sodālitāt-(em)*, fr. *sodālis*, 'comrade, companion', fr. **swedhālis*; cp. Scrt. *svadhá*, 'peculiar manner, custom', & Gk. *êthos*, 'custom, habit'. See **ethos.** A fraternity or fellowship, brotherhood, esp. one of laymen in the Roman Catholic Church, existing for charitable or devotional purposes.

soda-water, n. **a** Water highly charged with carbonic acid gas, forming an effervescing drink, often used mixed with brandy, whisky, wine, milk &c.; **b** formerly, a weak effervescing solution of bicarbonate of soda.

sodden (I.), adj. [1. sódn; 2. sɔ́dn], fr. O.E. *soden*, P.P. of *sēoþan*, 'to boil, cook'. See **seethe.** **1.** (archaic) Boiled in water, seethed. **2. a** Soaked, saturated, with water; **b** specif. (of food) badly cooked, so as to be damp, soft, and squashy. **3.** (fig.) **a** Soaked in, having partaken to excess of, alcoholic drink; **b** heavy, dull in mind, stupid, from habitual intemperance.

sodden (II.), vb. trans. & intrans. Prec., or new formation fr. form *sod* & suff. **-en**, as in *deepen* &c. **1.** trans. (usually in P.P.) *Soddened*, to make sodden, to saturate, soak. **2.** intrans. To become sodden.

soddenness, n. [1. sódennes; 2. sɔ́dənnis]. Condition, quality, of being sodden.

sodium, n. [1. sódium; 2. sóudiəm]. Mod. coinage fr. **soda.** A metallic, alkaline element, having symbol *Na* (for *natrium*), of a silvery white colour, and waxy soft consistency, only found in combination, as *sodium chloride*, common salt; *sodium nitrate*, Chile saltpetre &c.

Sodomite, n. [1. sódumīt; 2. sɔ́dəmait]. Fr., fr. Lat. *Sodomīta*, fr. Gk. *Sodomítēs*, 'inhabitant of Sodom'. **1.** (cap.) Inhabitant of Sodom. **2.** (without cap.) One guilty of the crime of sodomy.

sodomitic(al), adj. [1. sodumítik(l); 2. sɔdəmítik(l)]. Prec. & **-ic** & **-al.** Pertaining to sodomites or to sodomy.

sodomy, n. [1. sódumi; 2. sɔ́dəmi]. Sodom & **-y.** See Gen. xix. Unnatural sexual crime between males.

soever [1. sōéver; 2. souévə]. **so** & **ever.** Adverbial suffix, appended to, but separable from, relative pronouns and pronominal adjectives and adverbs, giving them a wider or more indefinite meaning, or adding emphasis: *who-*, *what-*, *when-*, *howsoever*; *how wide soever the difference may be* &c.

sofa, n. [1. sófa; 2. sóufə], fr. Arab. *suffa(h)*, 'bench, couch'. Piece of furniture in form of a long seat or couch on which to recline; sofas are made in various shapes, but all have in common that they are upholstered, have a layer of thick soft material placed over springs, on which the user lies, and are intended primarily for repose during the day-time.

soffit, n. [1. sófit; 2. sɔ́fit], fr. Fr. *soffite*, fr. Ital. *soffitta*, 'ceiling', fem. sing. of *soffitto*, 'fixed underneath'; fr. Lat. *suffixum*, P.P. of *suffigere*, 'to fasten underneath'. See **suffix.** The *-t-* is due to confusion w. Lat. *fictum*, P.P. of *fingere*, 'to shape, fashion'; but the Ital. P.P.s are normally formed as fr. Lat. *-to-* type. (archit.) The under surface of an arch, vault, cornice &c.

soft (I.), adj. [1. sawft, soft; 2. sɔ̄ft, sɔft]. O.E. *sōfte*, 'quiet; luxurious, comfortable; not stern, gentle'; also as adv. fr. **samfto-*; the more usual form of the adj. in O.E. is, however, *sēfte*, w. *i*-mutation fr. **samfti-*; O.S. *sāfti*, adj., *sāfto*, adv.; O.H.G. *semfti*, adj., *samfto*, adv.; Germ. *sanft*; the word may be fr. base **sam-*, seen in Goth. *samjan*, 'to please'; cp. further Gk. *hḗmeros*, 'mild, calm', fr. *sēm-*, Scrt. *sāman*, 'mildness', cp. O. Ir. *saim*, 'mildness'. Referring to material qualities. **1.** Offering little or no resistance to pressure; easily compressed or squeezed; readily worked or cut; the opposite of *hard* or *tough*: *soft as clay, butter*; *a soft bed, pillow*, one comfortable and yielding to lie upon, as being packed with light substances &c.; *soft ground, pitch*, not rolled or trampled hard; also damp, sodden, or slow; (specific uses) *soft coal*, bituminous coal, as opposed to anthracite; *soft goods*, textiles, as opposed to hardware; *soft metal*, one that is malleable, such as lead &c.; *soft money*, paper money; *soft palate*, the velum, the back membranous part of the roof of the mouth, between the pharynx and the mouth cavity; *soft sawder*, soft solder, also (fig.) flattery, soft soap; *soft soap*, semi-liquid potash soap, also (fig.) flattery, soft sawder; *soft solder*, solder used for soldering soft, easily fused metals; *soft tack*, (sailor's slang) white bread, as contrasted with *biscuit* or *hard tack*; *soft woods*, timber of coniferous trees, which is light and not closely grained, and thus easily sawn. **2.** Not rough or harsh in texture; smooth; **a** smooth to the touch: *skin soft as silk*; *a soft hand, cheek.* Phrs. *as soft as silk*; (*clad in*) *soft raiment*, luxurious, as made of silk &c.; **b** smooth to the palate or taste, not astringent or sour: *a soft wine*; *soft as milk.* **3.** (of bodily condition) Not firm, hard or well-braced &c.; flabby, weak: *muscles grow soft through want of exercise.* **4.** (of physical action) **a** Gentle, light; not violent: *a soft tap on the head*; **b** (colloq.) easy, not demanding great exertion or expenditure of energy to perform: *a soft job.* Phr. *a soft thing*, a transaction in which money can be easily earned. **5.** (of weather &c.) **a** Mild, balmy, gentle; not cold or boisterous, not excessively hot: *he had to live in a softer climate*; *a soft breeze from the west*; *a soft rain*, one which falls gently; **b** moist, damp, and warm: *a soft day.* **6.** (referring to chemical quality, constituents &c.) **a** *Soft water*, one free from such mineral salts as prevent the easy lathering of soap; **b** (colloq.) not alcoholic: *soft drinks.* **7. a** (of colour) Not too bright, vivid, glaring, or garish; subdued, low in tone: *soft shades of green and blue*; **b** (of outline &c.) not sharply defined; indistinct; merging into other lines, or into the background: *soft contours of the distant hills*; *soft lines of a statue.* **8.** (of sound) Low, modulated, not loud or harsh: *a soft voice*; *to speak in soft tones*; *the soft murmur of a stream*; *soft rustle of the leaves.* **9.** (as popular and misleading phon. term; very vaguely and inaccurately used) **a** Voiced: *the soft th*=[ð]; **b** not a stop: *the soft sound of c*=[s]; *b is often soft in Spanish*, i.e. is pronounced not as a lip stop, but as a lip open consonant. (Such terminology should be avoided.) Referring to non-material qualities. **10.** (of disposition &c.) **a** Gentle, merciful, tender, averse to giving pain or distress, reverse of *harsh* or *obdurate*: *a soft heart*; *appeal to the softer side of his character*; **b** expressing such a disposition: *a soft glance, smile.* Phr. '*A soft answer turneth away wrath*' (Proverbs); *soft words*, ingratiating, mollifying expressions. **11. a** (of mental capacity, colloq.) Weak, feeble: *a bit soft in the head*; **b** (of character) not virile; not energetic; enfeebled, effeminate, easy-going, luxurious: *the softer races of the East*; *Northerners look on Southerners as soft*; **c** lacking severity and sternness; humane; lenient: *it is a mistake to be soft with inveterate rogues and criminals*; *a soft sentence.*

soft (II.), adv. & interj., fr. prec. **1.** adv. Softly, gently: *soft falls the snow*; *speak softer.* **2.** interj. (archaic) Be quiet, be still, stop, go slowly or quietly: *soft! someone comes.*

soft (III.), n., fr. **soft** (I.). (colloq.) A weak-minded, soft-headed person.

softa, n. [1. sófta; 2. sɔ́ftə]. Turk. A Moslem student of theology and law.

soften, vb. trans. & intrans. [1. sáwfn; 2. sɔ́fn]. **soft** (I.) & **-en. 1.** trans. To make, cause to become, soft, pliable &c. (in various senses): *to soften leather*; *to soften water*; *to soften one's voice*; *to soften a person's heart.* **2.** intrans. To become soft or softer.

softener, n. [1. sáwfner; 2. sɔ́fnə]. Prec. & **-er.** One who, that which, softens; specif., some chemical substance or device by which hard water is softened: *water-softener.*

softening, n. [1. sáwfning; 2. sɔ́fniŋ]. **soften** & **-ing.** Act, process, of making or of becoming soft; **a** (in material sense) specif., *softening of the brain*, a chronic disease of the brain marked by a morbid, gradual degeneration of certain parts of the brain tissue; **b** process of becoming milder, of relenting, of becoming less harsh, stern &c.: *the cruel tyrant showed no signs of softening.*

soft-hearted, adj. **soft** (I.) & **hearted.** Having a soft, tender heart; gentle, pitiful, merciful.

soft-heartedness, n. Prec. & **-ness.** Quality of being soft-hearted.

softish, adj. [1. sáwftish; 2. sɔ́ftiʃ]. **soft** (I.) & **-ish.** Rather, inclined to be, soft.

softly, adv. [1. sáwftli; 2. sɔ́ftli]. **soft** (I.) & **-ly.** In a soft manner.

softness, n. [1. sáwftnes; 2. sɔ́ftnis]. **soft** (I.) & **-ness.** Quality, condition, of being soft (in various senses).

soft-spoken, adj. **soft** (I.) & **-spoken.** Speaking softly, having a soft, gentle voice; usually fig., saying pleasant things, mild in expression.

sogginess, n. [1. sóginés; 2. sɔ́ginis]. **soggy** & **-ness.** Condition of being soggy.

soggy, adj. [1. sógi; 2. sɔ́gi]. Cp. O.N. *soggr*, 'damp'; prob. cogn. w. **soak.** (of soil) Saturated with water, sodden.

soho, interj. [1. sòhó; 2. sòuhóu]. Earlier *sa ho*, fr. Fr. *ça*, 'here', & *ho!* as call. Sportsman's call, indicating position of game; a halloa.

soi-disant, adj. [1. swáh dézon; 2. swá dízã]. Fr. Self-styled, self-named; hence, would-be, pretended: *a soi-disant poet.*

soil (I.), n. [1. soil; 2. sɔil]. M.E. *soile*, *soyle*, fr. A.-Fr. *soil*, fr. O. Fr. *soel*, *suel*, 'threshold, sill of a door', fr. Lat. *solea*, 'sole of the foot, sandal', wh. in L. Lat. is used also in sense of 'ground, soil', thus taking the place of Lat. *solum*, 'ground', w. wh. it is cogn. The words go back to a base **swol-* &c., whence also O.H.G. *swelli*, 'threshold'. O.E. *syll*, 'foundation', see **sill**, & also Goth. (*ga-*)*suljan*, 'to base, found', are prob. early loan-words fr. Lat. *solea*. **1.** The surface earth or top layer of ground in which plants grow, consisting of loose, broken-down rock and decayed organic, chiefly vegetable, matter; mould. **2.** Rare, except in *night-soil*, sewage cleared from cess-pits at night. **3.** Ground, land, country: *one's native soil*; *on foreign soil*; *a friendly soil*; '*Is this the region, this the soil, the clime, . . . this the seat . . . That we must change for Heaven?*' (Milton, 'P. L.', I. 241).

soil (II.), vb. trans. & intrans. M.E. *soilen*, fr. A.-Fr. *soyler*, O. Fr. *soillier*, Mod. Fr. *souiller*, fr. *soil*, *souil*, 'place where a pig has wallowed'; fr. Lat. *suillus*, adj., 'of, pertaining to, swine', fr. *sus*, 'pig'; cogn. w. O.E. *sū*, see **sow** (I.); cp. also **sully. A.** trans. **1.** (in material sense) **a** To make dirty, to stain or smear with dirt; to put dirty marks upon: *to soil one's hands, one's linen, clothes* &c.; Phr. *to soil one's hands with*, to degrade oneself by; **b** (rare, influenced by **soil** (I.)) to cover with manure, to put soil on: *to soil a field* &c. **2.** (in non-material sense) To defile, tarnish, besmirch, sully: *his character was soiled by serious crimes.* **B.** intrans. To become soiled, stained, or dirty: *such delicate fabrics soil only too quickly.*

soil (III.), n., fr. prec. **1.** (archaic) Lair, wallowing place of a boar or wild pig. **2.** That which soils; dirt, a stain; also fig.

soil (IV.) vb. trans., fr. O. Fr. *saoler*, *saouler*, *soeler*, fr. Lat. *satullus*, 'filled with food', dimin. of *satur*, 'full, satiated', see **saturate.** To feed, fatten (cattle or horses) in stall with green food or fresh grass.

soil-pipe, n. **soil** (I.) & **pipe** (I.). Large pipe which conveys sewage from a house &c. into the drain or sewer.

soirée, n. [1. swáhrā; 2. swárei]. Fr., 'evening party', fr. *soir*, 'evening', fr. Lat. *sērus*, 'late', see **serotine.** A social gathering in the evening.

sojourn, vb. intrans. & n. [1. sújern; 2. sádžən], fr. O. Fr. *sojorner*, *sojourner*, Mod. Fr. *séjourner*, fr. assumed Low Lat. **subdiurnāre*, fr. Lat. *sub*, 'under', see **sub-**, & *diurnāre*, 'to stay, dwell', fr. *diurnus*, 'daily', see **diurnal**, & cp. **journey.** (archaic or liter.) **1.** vb. To stay, live, dwell, have one's abode in for a season, reside temporarily in, at, among: *to sojourn in Ireland*; *sojourn among strange peoples.* **2.** n. A temporary residence in, or visit to, a place or country.

sojourner, n. [1. sújerner; 2. sádžənə]. Prec. & **-er.** One who sojourns; a temporary resident or visitor.

soke, n. [1. sōk; 2. souk]. O.E. *soca.* See **soc** & cp. **socage. 1.** (legal hist.) Right to hold a court and exercise jurisdiction. **2.** An administrative district over which soke is exercised; still surviving in the *Soke of Peterborough.*

sokol, n. [1. sókol; 2. sɔ́kɔl]. Czech, 'falcon'. An athletic and gymnastic association, organized for national and patriotic purposes in pre-war Bohemia &c., now Czechoslovakia.

Sol (I.), n. [1. sol; 2. sɔl]. Lat., 'sun'; fr. **sāwel*, cp. Gk. cogn. *hḗlios*, *hēélios*, 'sun', for **sāwelios*, see **heliacal**; Goth. *sauil*; O.E. *sōl* may be a cogn. or a direct borrowing fr. Lat. O.E. *swelan*, 'to burn, to glow' &c., cp. **sultry**, may be connected. The sun; only in vulgar journalese, or as frankly facetious—*old Sol.*

sol (II.), n. The first syll. in Lat. *solve.* See **sol-fa.** (mus.) **a** The fifth tone in diatonic scale in the *sol-fa* system; **b** the fifth note, G, in scale of C major.

sola, n. [1. sóla; 2. sóulə]. Bengali, fr. Hind. *shola.* **a** An East Indian plant with pithy stem; **b** pith of this plant used for making sun helmets.

solace, n. & vb. trans. & intrans. [1. sólas; 2. sɔ́lis, -əs]. M.E. *solas*, 'satisfaction, pleasure', fr. O. Fr. *solaz*, fr. Lat. *sōlātium*, 'a soothing, assuaging; comfort, solace', formed fr. *sōlāt-*(*um*), P.P. type of *sōlāri*, 'to comfort, console', cogn. w. Lat. *sollus*, 'whole'; cogn. w. Gk. *hólos*, 'entire, whole, intact'; Scrt. *sarvaś*, 'intact, entire'; closer in meaning to Lat. *sōlātium* are O.E. *sǣl*, '(favourable) occasion; happiness'; *sǣliġ*, 'happy, prosperous', see **silly**; Goth. *sēls*, 'good'. Cp. further **salvation, solid,** & second element of **console** (I.). **1.** n. That which provides comfort, consolation &c.; a relief, consolation; a pleasure, a recreation: *to find solace from grief in religion*; *my chief solace in old age is the affection of my friends*; *his sole solace in his loneliness and ill-health was the company of books.* **2.** vb. **a** trans. To provide solace for, bring solace to; esp. *solace oneself* (*with*); **b** intrans., to provide, be a source of, solace: *the older we grow, the more we find that great literature solaces and supports.*

solan goose, n. [1. sólan gōōs; 2. sóulən gūs]. Scots *soland*, fr. O.N. *sūla.* The gannet, a large fish-eating sea-bird of the North Atlantic, found in a few spots in Northern Britain, such as Ailsa Craig and the Bass Rock.

Solanum, n. [1. solánum; 2. səléinəm]. Lat., 'deadly nightshade'; formed fr. Lat. *sōl*, 'sun'. See **Sol** (I.). (bot.) The typical genus of the family *Solanaceae*, which includes the nightshade, potato, tomato, henbane, capsicum, tobacco &c.

solar (I.), adj. [1. sólar; 2. sóulə], fr. Lat. *sōlāris*, 'belonging to the sun'. See **Sol** (I.) & **-ar. 1.** Pertaining to, concerned with, the sun: *the solar system*, the system of planets, including the earth, satellites, comets &c., of which the sun is the centre; *solar eclipse*, eclipse of the sun; *solar myth*, myth or tale explained as originating from various natural phenomena in which the sun is the cause &c. **2.** Caused by, produced by, emanating from, the sun: *solar heat, rays* &c. **3.** Measured by the revolution of the earth in relation to the sun: *solar year* &c.

solar (II.), n., fr. Lat. *sōlārium*, 'flat house-top, balcony exposed to the sun'; also 'a sun-dial'. See prec. Living-room on the upper storey of a mediaeval house.

solarization, n. [1. sòlarīzáshun; 2. sòuləraizéiʃən]. Next word & **-ation. a** Act, process, of solarizing; **b** state of being solarized.

solarize, vb. trans. [1. sólarīz; 2. sóuləraiz]. **solar** (I.) & **-ize.** To expose or over-expose to the heat of the sun's rays.

solar plexus, n. [1. sólar pléksus; 2. sóulə plɛ́ksəs]. A network or mass of nerves situated in the abdomen behind the stomach; so-called as being the centre of the nervous system of the abdominal viscera.

solatium, n., pl. **solatia** [1. sōláshium, -ia; 2. souléiʃiəm, -iə]. Lat. See **solace.** Something, money, or other gift, presented to a person as compensation or reward for trouble incurred or injury suffered.

sola topi, n. [1. sṓla tṓpi; 2. sóulə tóupi]. See **sola** & **topi**; also, by a natural popular association of meaning, often spelt *solar topi.* A hat or helmet, made from the pith of the *sola* plant, worn by Europeans in India, Mesopotamia, Africa &c., as a protection against the sun.

sold, vb. [1. sōld; 2. sould]. Pret. & P.P. of **sell**; O.E. Pret. *sālde* (cp. W.S. *sealde*); P.P. (*ġe*)*sāld*; M.E. *sōld*(*e*).

solder, n. & vb. trans. [1. sáwder, sóder, sṓlder; 2. sɔ́də, sódə, sóldə]. M.E. *sowdere*, fr. O. Fr. *soudure*, 'solder', fr. *souder*, 'to fasten together, to solder', fr. Lat. *solidāre*, 'to make firm', fr. *solidus*, 'firm', see **solid**, & **-ure**; the Mod. Engl. vb. is fr. the n.; M.E. has *souden*, fr. O. Fr. *souder*. See also **sawder.** **1.** n. Fusible metal alloy used for uniting two metal surfaces or edges, and for filling holes in metal objects; metallic cement. **2.** vb. To unite, fasten together, the surfaces or edges of (metal, metal vessel &c.) by means of solder.

soldering, n. [1. sáwdering; 2. sɔ́dəriŋ]. Prec. & **-ing.** Act, process, of using solder for uniting two metallic surfaces &c.; *soldering-iron*, tool used in this process.

soldier (I.), n. [1. sṓljer; 2. sóuldžə]. M.E. *soudiour*, *souldier*, fr. O. Fr. *soldoier*, *soldier*, fr. L. Lat. *soldārius*, fr. L. Lat. *soldum*, 'pay', fr. L. Lat. *solidus*, 'a coin', see **solidus** & **sou**; L. Lat. *soldāt-*(*um*), P.P. of *soldāre*, 'to pay', gives Mod. Fr. form *soldat*, 'soldier'. **1.** a One who is enrolled or enlisted in the military forces of a country, member of an army, as contrasted with *sailor*, of the navy; Phrs. *soldier of fortune*, a person of adventurous character and restless nature, willing to go, and to serve, anywhere where his services are well paid; *soldier of Christ*, an earnest Christian; b specif., a private or non-commissioned officer, one of the rank and file: *officers and soldiers*; Phrs. *go for a soldier*, (colloq. and popular) to enlist; *an old soldier*, empty bottle of wine or other liquor. **2.** Person having specific military qualities, abilities, or fame; esp. as a commander or general: *the great soldiers of history*; *no one thought he would make a soldier*; *he turned out a very fine soldier.* **3.** One of a class or caste of white ants or termites, also of red or black ants, with large jaws and head, a specialized form of worker ant adapted for fighting, raiding other ants &c. **4.** (colloq.) A red herring.

soldier (II.), vb. intrans., fr. prec. To serve as a soldier: *he has soldiered all over the world*; *to go soldiering.*

soldier-ant, n. A fighting ant or termite.

soldier-crab, n. A hermit-crab.

soldierlike, adj. [1. sṓljerlīk; 2. sóuldžəlaik]. **soldier** (I.) & **-like.** Having the appearance, bearing, qualities, of a soldier; soldierly.

soldierly, adj. [1. sṓljerli; 2. sóuldžəli]. **soldier** (I.) & **-ly.** **1.** (of persons) a Having a military appearance and bearing; well set up; b having the qualities of mind and character usually associated with a soldier; courageous, determined, restrained, and well-disciplined. **2.** (of qualities, appearance &c.) Characteristic of a soldier; esp. a upright, neat, smart: *soldierly appearance*; b evincing coolness, courage, endurance, loyalty &c.: *soldierly mind, character* &c.

soldiery, n. [1. sṓljeri; 2. sóuldžəri]. **soldier** (I.) & **-y.** a Soldiers collectively, the military troops of a state; b any body of troops or soldiers: *at the mercy of an undisciplined soldiery.*

soldo, n., pl. **soldi** [1. sóldō, -ē; 2. sɔ́ldou, -ī]. Ital., fr. Lat. See **solidus** & **sou.** A small Italian coin, $\frac{1}{20}$ of a lira, 5 centesimi, equivalent to French *sou*, halfpenny.

sole (I.), n. [1. sōl; 2. soul]. In O.E. & M.E.; fr. Lat. *solea*, 'sole of sandal, of the foot; a flat fish; sill', fr. or cogn. w. *solum*, 'bottom of anything, ground, floor'. See further under **soil** (I.) **1.** a The under surface of the foot of men and plantigrade animals; b strip of leather or other material forming the under part, upon which one walks, of a boot, shoe, or sandal. **2.** The bottom or lower part of various objects; that part on which they rest: *the sole of a plough, wooden golf-club, carpenter's plane* &c.

sole (II.), vb. trans., fr. prec. To provide (boot &c.) with (new) sole.

sole (III.), n., fr. Fr., fr. L. Lat. *sola*, fr. Lat. *solea*, 'a flat fish, the sole', see **sole** (I.), fr. its shape. A marine flat fish, *Solea vulgaris*, one of the most valuable of food-fishes; often styled *Dover sole* to distinguish it from the *lemon sole*, or limande, which is a variety of plaice.

sole (IV.), adj. M.E. *sool*, fr. O. Fr. *sol*, Mod. Fr. *seul*, fr. Lat. *sōlus*, 'alone', wh. is prob. fr. **swōlos*, formed fr. base of reflex. pron. Lat. *suus*, 'belonging to him, her, itself; one's own', see **sui.** The primary sense of *sōlus* wd. therefore be '(existing) for, and by, itself, without connexion with others'. **1.** (archaic or poet.) Alone, solitary, without companions: '*Sole sitting by the shores of old Romance*' (Wordsworth). **2.** One and only, single; acting, being, without another: a (of persons) *the sole heir to an estate*; b (of actions &c.) *it was done on your sole authority*; *the sole argument he brought forward.* **3.** (law) a Single, unmarried; only in Phr. *feme sole*, as contrasted with *feme co*(*u*)*vert*; b having one individual member only: *corporation sole.*

solecism, n. [1. sólesizm; 2. sɔ́lisizəm], fr. Fr. *solécisme*, fr. Lat. *soloecismus*, fr. Gk. *soloikismós*, fr. *soloikízein*, 'to speak (Greek) ungrammatically or badly', fr. *sóloikos*, 'speaking badly' like the people of *Soloi*, town in Cilicia, colonized by Greeks who soon began to speak a corrupt form of Attic Greek. **1.** A grammatical or idiomatic error or blunder in speaking or writing; esp. the use of a phrase, word, pronunciation &c. which is regarded as vulgar or provincial. **2.** A social mistake or impropriety in manners &c.; an offence against the conventions of polite society; a piece of ill-breeding.

solecist, n. [1. sólesist; 2. sɔ́lisist]. See prec. & **-ist.** One who commits a solecism.

solecistic, adj. [1. sòlesístik; 2. sɔ̀lisístik]. Prec. & **-ic.** Of the nature of, containing, a solecism.

solecistically, adv. [1. sòlesístikali; 2. sɔ̀lisístik(ə)li]. Prec. & **-al** & **-ly.** In a solecistic manner.

solely, adv. [1. sṓlli; 2. sóulli]. **sole** (IV.) & **-ly.** **1.** Alone; apart from, to the exclusion of, others: *he is solely responsible.* **2.** *Solely because, on account of*, for this reason alone: *he left the Army solely because he couldn't afford it*; *solely on account of ill-health.*

solemn, adj. [1. sólem; 2. sɔ́ləm]. M.E. & O. Fr. *solempne*, fr. Lat. *sollemnis*, *sōlemnis*, later *sollennis*, *sōlennis*, 'taking place every year, annual; religious, solemn', an old compound, the first element of wh. is *sollus*, 'whole, entire', see under **solace**, & the second element *annus*, 'year', q.v. under **annual.** **1.** Kept and observed at stated intervals, whether annually or not; regular, according to established, esp. religious, usage: *solemn festivals of the Church* &c. **2.** Observed, performed, with due formalities; formal: *a solemn oath, act* &c.; *to prove a will in solemn form*; Phr. *this is the solemn truth*, as if sworn on oath; *the Solemn League and Covenant*, of 1643, establishing Presbyterianism in Scotland and England. **3.** Serious, grave, important, weighty: *on such solemn occasions as these*; *to give a solemn warning.* **4.** (of persons, manner, action &c.) a Grave, serious, not smiling or cheerful; impressively calm and deliberate: *a solemn judge*; *you look very solemn, what's the matter?*; *a solemn voice*; '*with solemn tread and slow*'; b affectedly, exaggeratedly grave and serious; pompous: *the usual letter in the papers from some solemn ass.* **5.** (of things, places &c.) Causing, arousing a feeling of awe, seriousness, or gravity: *a solemn sight*; *a solemn place, building* &c.

solemnity, n. [1. solémniti; 2. səlémniti]. M.E. & O. Fr. *solempnite*, fr. Lat. *sol*(*l*)*emnitāt-*(*em*). See **solemn** & **-ity.** **1.** State, quality, of being solemn; solemn appearance, character, emotion, behaviour &c.: *the solemnity of the occasion, place, awed him*; *you do not treat the matter with the solemnity it deserves*; *a ribald laugh somewhat detracted from the speaker's pompous solemnity.* **2.** Ceremonial observance; due, formal rite: *performed with all the historic solemnities.*

solemnization, n. [1. sòlemnīzáshun; 2. sɔ̀ləmnaizéiʃən]. **solemnize** & **-ation.** Act of solemnizing or celebrating; due, formal, performance: *the solemnization of a marriage* &c.

solemnize, vb. trans. [1. sólemnīz; 2. sɔ́ləmnaiz]. **solemn** & **-ize.** **1.** To celebrate, keep with due rites and ceremonies: *to solemnize Easter by going to Communion, Christmas with old-fashioned feasting* &c. **2.** To perform with proper, legal formalities: *to solemnize a marriage.* **3.** To make solemn; to impart a grave, serious, or awful character to: *sacred memories solemnize the place.*

solemnly, adv. [1. sólemli; 2. sɔ́ləmli]. **solemn** & **-ly.** In a solemn manner; with due solemnity; formally, ceremoniously; gravely.

solemnness, n. [1. sólemnes; 2. sɔ́ləmnis]. See prec. & **-ness.** Quality, condition, of being solemn.

Solen, n. [1. sṓlen; 2. sóulən]. Gk. *sōlḗn*, 'pipe, channel, gutter; also a shell-fish'; prob. for **twōl-*, w. gradational variants **twel-* &c.; cogn. w. O.H.G. *dola*, 'pipe, drain', fr. Gmc. **þ*(*w*)*ula*, wh. was prob. borrowed in O. Fr. in the form *tuel.* See **tewel.** (zool.) A genus of shell-fish, the razor-clam.

solenoid, n. [1. sṓlenoid; 2. sóulənɔid]. See prec. & **-oid.** (elect.) A coil of insulated wire through which an electric current is passed, magnetizing iron within the coil, used in constructing magnetic brakes, electro-magnets &c.

sol-fa, n. & vb. [1. sòl fáh; 2. sɔ̀l fá], fr. *sol*(*ve*) & *fa*(*muli*), words in Lat. mnemonic. See **gamut.** **1.** n. System of using certain syllables, *do* (*ut*), *re*, *mi*, *fa*, *sol*, *la*, *si*, for, and associating them in sound with, the notes of the scale, solmization; cp. also *tonic sol-fa.* **2.** vb. To pronounce, sing these syllables, use this system in singing.

solfatara, n. [1. sòlfatáhra; 2. sɔ̀lfatára]. Ital., fr. *solfo*, 'sulphur'. A vent or fissure in the ground, in or near a dormant volcano, from which sulphureous fumes issue.

solfeggio, n. [1. solféjiō; 2. sɔlfédžiou]. Ital. See **sol-fa.** Exercise for the singing voice based upon the syllables (and corresponding notes) *do*, *re*, *mi*, *fa*, &c.

solicit, vb. trans. & intrans. [1. solísit; 2. səlísit]. M.E. *soliciten*, M. Fr. *soliciter*, fr. Lat. *sollicitāre*, 'to arouse, excite, urge; to solicit', fr. *sollicitus*, 'violently, lit. wholly, moved, agitated; anxious, solicitous', formed fr. *sollus*, 'whole', see **solace**, & *citus*, P.P. of *ciēre*, 'to arouse', see **cite.** **A.** trans. **1.** a To beg, ask earnestly of; to petition (person) for something: *to solicit a person for help, money, his custom, his support* &c.; b (in bad sense) to beg persistently of, to importune; specif. (of woman) to accost (man) in the street or a public place &c. for immoral purposes. **2.** To beg, ask earnestly for: *to solicit favours, custom &c. of or from a person.* **B.** intrans. a To practise solicitation; specif. b to accost persons in public places for immoral purposes.

solicitation, n. [1. sōlisitáshun; 2. soulisitéiʃən]. Prec. & **-ation.** Act of soliciting; persistent, earnest, invitation or request; specif., offence of soliciting or accosting men in streets for an immoral purpose.

solicitor, n. [1. solísiter; 2. səlísitə]. Formed fr. **solicit** & **-or**; cp., however, O. Fr. *soliciteur*. **1.** (rare) One who solicits or asks earnestly for: *a solicitor for one's favour, custom* &c. **2.** An officer of the Supreme Court of Judicature, admitted to practise law on behalf of clients, by advice, and in the briefing of barristers, but allowed to plead only in the lower courts; the term was at one time distinguished from *attorney*, but is so no longer, and it is now the general term for all legal practitioners other than barristers.

Solicitor-General, n. One of the principal law officers of the Crown, ranking next to the Attorney-General, a member of the Ministry of the day, but not of the Cabinet.

solicitous, adj. [1. solísitus; 2. səlísitəs], fr. Lat. *sollicit-(us)*, 'disturbed, agitated, anxious'. See **solicit** & **-ous**. **1.** Eager, desirous to do, obtain, or avoid something: *solicitous to please*; *solicitous to gain esteem* &c. **2.** Anxious, concerned: *solicitous about, concerning, one's health, safety* &c.

solicitously, adv. Prec. & **-ly**. In a solicitous manner.

solicitude, n. [1. solísitūd; 2. səlísitjūd]. Fr., fr. Lat. *sollicitūdo*. See **solicitous** & **-ude**. State of being solicitous or anxious; anxiety, concern.

solid (I.), adj. [1. sólid; 2. sɔ́lid], fr. Fr. *solide*, fr. Lat. *solid-(us)*, 'firm, solid', cogn. w. *sollus*, 'whole, complete'. See under **solace**. **1.** Not liquid, fluid, or gaseous; maintaining its shape, size, volume under pressure, or immediately regaining it when pressure is removed; firm; capable of resisting penetration by other substances: *solid bodies*; *lava becomes solid on cooling*; *a solid block of ice*. Phr. *solid food*, meat, bread &c.; contrasted with liquid nourishment. **2.** Compact, of firm consistency, hard; able to support weight; stable: *solid ground*. Phrs. *a solid meal*, a substantial one; *rather a solid pudding*, stiff, heavy, substantial. **3. a** Opposite of *hollow*; not having empty spaces or cavities within it: *a solid ball, globe*; *a solid wall*; *a solid tire*, contrasted with pneumatic; **b** of the same material throughout; not merely having a casing or coating of some material: *a dinner service of solid gold*. **4.** Firmly, strongly built, substantial, massive: *a man of solid frame, build*; *some of these new houses don't look very solid*. **5.** (math.) **a** Of three dimensions, cubic: *a solid figure*; *a solid or cubic foot, yard* &c.; **b** concerned with solid figures: *solid geometry*. **6.** (of persons) **a** Of sound, sterling character, reliable, trustworthy, not superficial or flashy: *English voters like a good solid man as their member*; *he's a very plausible speaker but hardly a solid politician*. **7.** Of sound financial position; substantial: *a solid merchant of the City of London*; *a solid business, firm* &c., one well-established and safe. **8.** Logically sound, well-established; based upon, characterized by, good reasoning; reasonable, well grounded: *solid arguments*; *he had no solid ground for his actions*. **9.** United in opinions, feelings, beliefs; unanimous: *the meeting was solid in his favour*; *England is said to be solid for Protestantism*.

solid (II.), adv., fr. prec. Chiefly *vote solid*, unanimously.

solid (III.), n., fr. **solid** (I.). **1.** (phys.) A solid body; contrasted with *a liquid* or *a gas*. **2.** (geom.) A figure which has three dimensions, such as a cube or sphere.

solidarity, n. [1. sòlidáriti; 2. sɔ̀lidǽriti], fr. Fr. *solidarité*, 'mutual interdependence between persons', formed fr. *solidaire*, 'having common interests' &c., fr. Lat. *solidus*, see **solid**. Complete union of interests and responsibilities; solid community in feeling and action; fellowship: *the solidarity of the nations, classes* &c.

solid colour, n. **a** Colour covering an object completely; **b** a uniform colour.

solid drawn, adj. Of tubes &c., formed out of a solid bar or rod of iron or steel.

solid hoofed, adj. Having a solid, not cleft hoof, as the horse &c.; solidungulate.

solid horned, adj. Having solid horns, like deer &c.; not hollow horns like oxen.

solidifiable, adj. [1. solídifīabl; 2. səlídifaiəbl]. See **solidify** & **-able**. Capable of being solidified.

solidification, n. [1. solìdifikáshun; 2. səlìdifikéiʃən]. See next word & **-fication**. **a** Act, process, of solidifying; **b** state of being solidified.

solidify, vb. trans. & intrans. [1. solídifī; 2. səlídifai], fr. Fr. *solidifier*, fr. **solid** (I.) & **-fy**. **1.** trans. To make, cause to become, solid, compact, or firm. **2.** intrans. To become solid.

solidity, n. [1. solíditi; 2. səlíditi], fr. Fr. *solidité*, fr. Lat. *soliditāt-(em)*. See **solid** (I.) & **-ity**. Quality, condition, of being solid (in various material and non-material senses).

solidly, adv. [1. sólidli; 2. sɔ́lidli]. **solid** (I.) & **-ly**. In solid form; in a solid manner.

solid matter, n. Specif. (print.) type set without leads between the lines.

solidness, n. [1. sólidnes; 2. sɔ́lidnis]. **solid** (I.) & **-ness**. Quality of being solid; solidity.

solidungulate, adj. [1. sòlidúnggūlāt; 2. sɔ̀lidáŋgjuleit]. See **solid** & **ungulate**. Solid hoofed.

solidus, n., pl. **solidi** [1. sólidus, -ī; 2. sɔ́lidəs, -ai]. L. Lat., fr. Lat. *solidus*, adj. See **solid**. **1.** A gold coin of the Late Empire, replacing the *aureus*, called the *Byzantine solidus* or *bezant*, q.v. **2.** A silver coin of the Franks, worth twelve *denarii*, twenty going to the *libra*, or pound, whence s. for shilling in £ s. d., or /- (the old long *ſ*) in 6/8; cp. Ital. *soldo*, $\frac{1}{20}$ of lira, and Fr. *sol*, modern *sou*, $\frac{1}{20}$ of the livre or franc.

solifidian, n. [1. sòlifídian; 2. sòulifídiən]. Formed fr. Lat. *sōlus*, 'alone' see **sole** (IV.), & *fidi-*, stem of *fides*, 'faith'. See **fidelity**, & **-ian**. (theol.) One who holds that man can be justified by faith alone without works.

soliloquist, n. [1. solílokwist; 2. səlíləkwist]. **soliloquy** & **-ist**. (rare) Soliloquizer.

soliloquize, vb. intrans. [1. solílokwīz; 2. səlíləkwaiz]. **soliloquy** & **-ize**. **a** To utter a soliloquy, as on the stage &c.; **b** to speak to oneself.

soliloquizer, n. [1. solílokwīzer; 2. səlíləkwaizə]. Prec. & **-er**. One who utters a soliloquy or speaks to himself.

soliloquy, n. [1. solílokwi; 2. səlíləkwi], fr. Lat. *sōliloquium*, fr. *sōlus*, 'alone', see **sole** (IV.), & *loqui*, 'to speak', see **loquacious**. **1.** The utterance of one's thoughts aloud; talking to oneself. **2.** Declamation in which he utters his thoughts, by a character in a play when alone on the stage; speech uttered by an actor as for himself, in the presence of other characters who are supposed not to hear; actual passage uttered in soliloquy. **3.** Talk, a monologue, by one person only who monopolizes the conversation in a company.

solipsism, n. [1. sólipsizm; 2. sóulipsizəm]. Formed fr. Lat. *sōlus*, 'alone', see **sole** (IV.), & *ipse*, 'he himself, self', & **-ism**. A term in metaphysics for the doctrine that nothing exists outside the cognition of the self, and that the self can know nothing outside its own experience.

solitaire, n. [1. sòlitár; 2. sɔ̀litéə]. Fr. See **solitary**. **1. a** A single stone, such as a diamond &c., set as a stud, ring, earring &c.; **b** (obs.) a loose lace cravat worn by men in the 18th cent. **2. a** A game played by a single person with a board with small cups or hollows in which marbles are placed, one being left vacant, the object being to clear the board by 'taking' the marbles one by one as in draughts; **b** (U.S.A.) the game of patience. **3.** (zool.) **a** An extinct flightless bird, resembling the dodo, whose remains are found in the island of Rodriguez; **b** any of various shy, singing thrushes of the W. Indies and Southern United States.

solitarily, adv. [1. sólitarili; 2. sɔ́litərili]. **solitary** & **-ly**. In a solitary manner.

solitariness, n. [1. sólitarines; 2. sɔ́litərinis]. See prec. & **-ness**. Quality, condition, of being solitary.

solitary, adj. [1. sólitari; 2. sɔ́litəri]. M.E. & A.-Fr. *solitarie*, Mod. Fr. *solitaire*, fr. Lat. *sōlitārius* for **sōlitātārius*, formed w. suff. *-ārius*, see **-ary**, fr. *sōlitāt-(em)*, *sōlitas*, 'solitariness, loneliness', fr. *sōlus*, 'alone', see **sole** (IV.). **1. a** Living, being, alone, not accompanied by others; alone, lonely: *a solitary monk*; *a solitary horseman on the lonely road*; *now all the guests have gone we feel quite solitary*; **b** (of animals, esp. insects) not living in communities, opposed to *social* or *gregarious*: *the solitary wasp* &c. **2.** Passed, spent, performed, alone; not shared with others: *to lead a solitary life, take a solitary walk, a solitary task*; *solitary confinement*, form of imprisonment in which the prisoner is isolated, works in his cell and takes exercise alone. **3.** Not much frequented; lonely, remote, secluded: *a solitary village, house*; *a gloomy, solitary moor*. **4.** Single, sole, not having anything similar: *not a solitary instance of such a thing in history*.

solitude, n. [1. sólitūd; 2. sɔ́litjūd]. Fr., fr. Lat. *sōlitūde*, fr. *sōlus*, 'alone', see **sole** (IV.) & **-tude**. **1.** State of being solitary; state of being, or living alone, of being isolated from others: *to live in solitude*; '*O solitude, where are the charms, That sages have seen in thy face?*' (Cowper). **2.** A lonely, deserted place; a wilderness: '*He makes a solitude and calls it peace*' (Byron, 'Bride of Abydos,' II. 20).

solive, n. [1. solḗv; 2. səlív]. O. Fr., etymol. uncertain; perh. formed fr. Fr. *soulever*, 'to raise up', fr. Lat. *sublevāre*, 'to lift up', fr. **sub-** & *levāre*, 'to lift', formed fr. Lat. *levis*, 'light, not heavy', see **lever** & **levitate** &c. A secondary timber, or joist, resting on beams, and supporting a floor.

solleret, n. [1. sóleret; 2. sɔ́lərət]. O. Fr. *sol(l)eret*, dimin. of *sol(l)er*, Mod. Fr. *soulier*, 'shoe, slipper', fr. Lat. *solea*, see **sole** (I.). A steel shoe, made with jointed, flexible plates, worn with armour in the Middle Ages.

solmization, n. [1. sólmizáshun; 2. sɔ̀lmizéiʃən], fr. *sol*, *mi*, see **sol-fa**, **-ize**, & **-ation**. Sol-fa system of musical notation and singing.

solo (I.), n. [1. sṓlō; 2. sóulou]. Ital., 'alone'; fr. Lat. *sōlus*. See **sole** (IV.). (mus.) Piece, passage, sung or played by a single performer, whether accompanied or not; (also attrib.).

solo (II.), n., see prec. (also *solo whist*) **a** A card game for four players, resembling whist; **b** a declaration by a player that he will take five tricks.

soloist, n. [1. sṓlōist; 2. sóulouist]. **solo** (I.) & **-ist**. Player, singer, of a solo.

Solomon, n. [1. sólomun; 2. sɔ́ləmən]. Gk. *Solomōn*, Heb. *Shelōmōh*; name of David's son, King of Israel, famed for his wisdom. A wise man, a sage: *the Solomon of his age*; *looked up to as a regular Solomon*.

Solomon's seal, n. **1.** A magic symbol formed of two interlaced triangles, making a six-pointed star. **2.** (bot.) A perennial liliaceous herb, *Polygonatum*, with arching stems from which depend greenish white bell-shaped flowers.

Solon, n. [1. sṓlon; 2. sóulɔn]. Gk. *Solōn*. **a** Name of Athenian statesman and lawgiver, of 7th and 6th cents., B.C., one of the seven sages of the ancient world; hence, **b** any very wise man, a wise lawgiver.

so-long, interj. [1. sṑ lóng; 2. sòu lɔ́ŋ]. Said to be a corrupt. of *salaam*, but associated w. the Engl. words, & felt as meaning 'until we meet again'. (colloq.) Good-bye, au revoir.

solstice, n. [1. sólstis; 2. sɔ́lstis]. Fr., fr. Lat. *solstitium*, lit. 'standing still of the sun', fr. *sol*, 'sun', see **Sol** (I.), & *stit-*, stem of *sistere*, 'to make to stand', fr. *stāre*, 'to stand', see **stand**. Point in the ecliptic at which the sun reaches the limit of extreme N. or S. declination and appears to stand still, as on June 21, *summer*, and Dec. 21, *winter, solstice*, corresponding with the longest and shortest days of the year.

solstitial, adj. [1. sòlstíshal; 2. sɔlstíʃəl]. See prec. & **-al**. Pertaining to, occurring at time of, a solstice.

solubility, n. [1. sòlūbíliti; 2. sɔljubíliti]. See next word and **-ity**. Quality, condition, of being soluble.

soluble, adj. [1. sólūbl; 2. sɔ́ljubl]. Fr., fr. Lat. *solūbilis*, formed w. suff. *-bilis*, see **-able**, **-ible**, fr. *solu-*, stem of *solvere*, 'to loosen, break up' &c. See **solve**. **1**. Capable of being dissolved, capable of solution. **2.** (rare) Capable of being solved; solvable.

solution, n. [1. solúshun; 2. səljúʃən]. Fr., fr. Lat. *solūtiōn-(em)*, 'a loosening, dissolution; an explanation', fr. *solūt-(um)*, P.P. type of *solvere*, see **solve**, & **-ion**. **1**. Act or process of loosening, separating, or dividing up a body or substance into its component parts. **2. a** That condition of an originally solid substance in which it is broken up, or dissolved, into its component parts or elements, so that it may be absorbed by a different substance, esp. a liquid: *many chemical substances are held in solution in water*; **b** a substance broken up and held in solution. **3. a** The act or process of resolving, explaining, making clear, finding the answer to, a problem, mystery, riddle &c., act of overcoming, finding a way out of, a difficulty; **b** an explanation, clearing up, making plain, of a problem, mystery, riddle &c.; method discovered for overcoming a difficulty &c.

Solutrian, adj. [1. solútrian; 2. səljútriən], fr. Solutré, Saône-et-Loire, France, where characteristic fossil remains of palaeolithic culture & extinct animals were discovered, & **-ian**. **a** (of palaeolithic culture, implements &c.) Belonging to, found in, the rock-shelter at Solutré; **b** belonging to the same type and period as the fossil remains at Solutré, succeeding the Mousterian.

solvability, n. [1. sòlvabíliti; 2. sɔlvəbíliti]. See next word & **-ity**. State, quality, of being solvable.

solvable, adj. [1. sólvabl; 2. sɔ́lvəbl]. Next word & **-able**. Capable of being solved or explained.

solve, vb. trans. [1. solv; 2. sɔlv], fr. Lat. *solvere*, 'to loosen, untie; to break up; to pay; to explain; to free, release', for **selvere*, fr. *sē(d)*, prep. expressing separation, see **sed-**, & *luere*, 'to loose, release'; orig. 'to wash, wash away, purge' &c.; cp. Lat. *lues*, 'a spreading, contagious disease', see **lues** & words there referred to. **1**. (rare or obs. in physical sense) To untie, unravel. **2**. To discover an answer to, explanation of (a problem, riddle, mystery &c.); to contrive to overcome, find a way out of (a difficulty).

solvency, n. [1. sólvensi; 2. sɔ́lvənsi]. **solvent (I.)** & **-cy**. State, quality, of being solvent; ability to pay one's debts.

solvent (I.), adj. [1. sólvent; 2. sɔ́lvənt], fr. Lat. *solvent-(em)*, Pres. Part. of *solvere*, see **solve**. **1. a** Having the property of dissolving another substance or of forming a chemical solution: *solvent liquids* &c.; **b** (fig.) having power of loosening, disintegrating, or of modifying, mitigating, an emotion, state of mind &c.: *the solvent power of laughter, flattery* &c. **2**. Having sufficient funds to pay all debts, claims &c.: *was the defendant solvent when the debt was incurred?*; *a solvent firm* &c.

solvent (II.), n., fr. prec. **1**. Substance having the property of dissolving other substances. **2**. Action, fact, circumstance, which modifies, relieves, explains, other acts, circumstances &c.

somatic, adj. [1. sōmátik; 2. soumǽtik], fr. Gk. *sōmatikós*, fr. *sōmat-*, stem of *sôma*, 'body', & **-ic**; *sôma* stands for **twōmn̥t-*, fr. a base **tewa-* &c., 'to swell', variants of wh. are seen also in Lat. *tumēre*, 'to swell', see **tumour**, *tōtus*, 'whole', see **total**. **a** Pertaining to the body; bodily, corporeal, physical, contrasted with *mental* or *psychical*; specif. **b** (biol.) *somatic cells*, those which form the body of the individual organism, as distinct from the *reproductive cells*.

somato-, pref. Form used in compounds, fr. Gk. *sōmat-*, see prec.

somatology, n. [1. sòmatóloji; 2. sòumətɔ́lədži]. Gk. *sōmat-*, see **somatic** & **-logy**. Study of the bodily structure of individuals, races &c.

sombre, adj. [1. sómber; 2. sɔ́mbə]. Fr., etymol. uncertain; Span. *sombra*, 'shade'; *sombrio*, 'shady, gloomy, sombre', point to a L. Lat. **exumbrāre*, 'to cast shade upon, to darken', fr. **ex-** & *umbra*, 'shadow, shade'. See **umbra**. **1**. Dark, dismal, in appearance; **a** reverse of *bright* or *sunny*; not cheerful; gloomy, overcast: *a sombre sky, cloud* &c.; *a sombre landscape*; **b** dark in colour, subdued: *sombre raiment* &c.; *a sombre shade of colour* &c. **2. a** Expressing, exhibiting, suggesting, a depressed, gloomy state of mind: *a sombre countenance, expression* &c.; **b** melancholy, sinister: *a sombre character*; **c** depressing, sad, dismal: *my life just now is rather sombre*; *the future outlook is sombre indeed*.

sombrely, adv. Prec. & **-ly**. In a sombre manner.

sombreness, n. See prec. & **-ness**. Condition, quality, of being sombre.

sombrero, n. [1. sombrárō; 2. sɔmbréərou]. Span., fr. *sombra*, 'shade', see **sombre**. A broad-brimmed felt hat, esp. as worn in Spain, S. America &c.

sombrous, adj. [1. sómbrus; 2. sɔ́mbrəs]. **sombre** & **-ous**. (poet., rare) Sombre.

some (I.), adj., (when stressed) [1. sum; 2. sam], (when unstressed) [səm]. O.E. *sum*, 'a certain one; some'; M.E. *sōme*; O.S. & O.H.G. *sum*; O.N. *sumr*; Goth. *sums*; cogn. w. **same**. **1. a** A certain, particular (person, thing, event &c.) not specifically named or known: *some mischievous boy has broken the window*; *some unscrupulous person has borrowed my umbrella*; *some car or other broke down our fence*; **b** emphatic: *some people don't know when they are well off*, there are those who &c.; *some houses are very damp in winter*. **2.** *Some day, some time*, on a certain future day, at a certain future time, not precisely determined: *some day we will visit the Zoo*; *I'll come some time when I'm less busy*. **3**. (unstressed) A certain, indefinite number or quantity of (persons, things &c.): *I must get some new clothes*; *have some more tea*; *I would like some strawberries*; *I saw some people walking on the lawn as I passed*. **4**. Nearly so many or so much; so much as, more or less, about: *there were some 20 persons present*; *some 40 tons in weight*; *some 15 more miles to go*. **5. a** (stressed or unstressed) Of a considerable or appreciable amount, number, degree, or quantity: *some miles still to walk*; *you'll need some courage to face this*; **b** (stressed) (colloq., slang) *some battle*, a great one; *some scholar*, a good one.

some (II.), pron. See prec. Certain number, quantity, not specified, of persons, &c.: *some say it is true, some not*; *I want some of those strawberries*; *this is good—will you have some?*

-some (I.), [1. sum; 2. səm], suff., fr. O.E. *-sum*, cogn. w. O.H.G. *-sam*, Du. *-zaam*, O.N. *-samr*, Goth. *-sams*, see **same**, forming **a** adjectives from nouns, verbs, and adjectives, indicating a likeness with, or aptness or tendency for, or to, as *handsome, quarrelsome, irksome, tiresome* &c.; also **b** with numerals to form nouns, now chiefly in *foursome*, q.v.

-some (II.), [1. sōm; 2. soum] suff., fr. Gk. *sôma*, 'body', see **somatic**, chiefly in biol. terminology, as **chromosome**.

somebody, n. [1. súmbòdi, súmbudi; 2. sámbɔdi, sámbədi]. **some** & **body**. **1**. Some person not identified, or unknown; someone: *somebody has disclosed the secret*. **2**. A person of importance: *he thinks he is (a) somebody*; *nobodies posing as somebodies*.

somehow, adv. [1. súmhou; 2. sámhau]. **some** & **how**. In some way, by some means, not otherwise specified or not yet known, in one way or another: *he had to get money somehow*; *we must get home somehow even if we have to walk*; *somehow or other he always managed to get the best of his opponent*; *somehow I don't trust him*, for some reason or other.

someone, n. [1. súmwun; 2. sámwan]. Somebody.

somersault, n. & vb. intrans. [1. súmersàwlt; 2. sáməsɔ̀lt], fr. O. Fr. *sombre sault*, Fr. *soubre saut*; Lat. *suprā*, 'above', see **supra-**, & *saltus*, 'a leap', see **saltation** & **salient**. **1. n.** A leap, or fall, in which the performer turns completely head over heels while in the air. **2.** vb. To turn, fall, head over heels in the air.

something (I.), n. [1. súmthing; 2. sámþiŋ]. **1**. Some thing or event &c., thing &c., of some kind, anything indefinite, uncertain, undetermined, or vague: *I must get something to eat, read* &c.; *take something hot the last thing at night*; *he has something on his mind*; *something dreadful has happened*; *there is something about it in the papers*; *something in the city*; **a** (followed by *of*) an indefinite quantity or degree: *he is something of a liar*; *there is something of uncertainty in his self-confidence*; **b** preceded by *or*, expressing vagueness, lack of precise information: *he's a stockbroker or something*; *she can't play today, she's got a cold or something*; *he turned dizzy or something and fell out*. **2**. That which is of importance; thing or (rarely) person that matters: *it is something at any rate to be out of the rain*; *it is something at least that the income-tax has not gone up*; *he thinks he is something and puts on airs*.

something (II.), adv., fr. prec. **a** (archaic) to some extent, rather: *he is getting something stout round the waist*; **b** (colloq.) *something like*; (i.) bearing some, though not a strong, resemblance to: *he is something like what his father was at that age*; (ii.) nearly, more or less, round about, approximately: *it must be something like six o'clock*; *he left something like a million*; (iii.) in such Phrs. as, *Kean was something like an actor!*, a superlatively good one; *to become a millionaire and a peer at forty-five is something like success!*, a very considerable success; *Scott was something like an author!*, a very great one. (In such Phrs. *like* is always strongly stressed.)

sometime, adv. [1. súmtīm; 2. sámtaim]. **1**. At some date or at a time hereafter, not specified: *I will do it sometime or other*. **2**. Formerly, at one time: *he was sometime professor of chemistry at the university*; also as adjective: *X, the sometime professor at* &c.

sometimes, adv. [1. súmtīmz; 2. sámtaimz]. Prec. w. advbl. suff. *-s*. At some times; at times, occasionally, now and then: *sometimes he seemed very depressed*; *sometimes rich, sometimes poor*.

somewhat, adv. & pron. [1. súmwot; 2. sámwɔt]. **1**. adv. In some degree, to some extent, rather: *you are somewhat rash in making such promises*; *he was somewhat hard to follow*. **2**. pron. A certain amount or degree of: *he was somewhat of a connoisseur*.

somewhere, adv. [1. súmwār; 2. sámwɛə]. In, to, at some place not specified, or unknown: *I have left my umbrella somewhere*; *you should go somewhere for a holiday*; *you will find the quotation somewhere in Pope*.

somite, n. [1. sṓmīt; 2. sóumait], fr. Gk. *sôma*, 'body'. See **somatic** & **-ite**. (anat. and biol.) One of the series of similar segments of which the bodies of many articulated animals are composed; a metamere.

somitic, adj. [1. sōmítik; 2. soumítik]. Prec. & **-ic**. Pertaining to a somite.

somnambulant, adj. [1. somnámbūlant; 2. sɔmnǽmbjulənt], fr. Lat. *somnus*, 'sleep', see **somnolent**, & *ambulant-(em)*, Pres. Part. of *ambulāre*, 'to walk', see **ambulance**. (rare) Walking, having a tendency to walk, in one's sleep.

somnambulate, vb. intrans. [1. somnámbūlāt; 2. sɔmnǽmbjuleit]. See prec. & **-ate**. (rare) To walk in one's sleep.

somnambulism, n. [1. somnámbūlizm; 2. səmnǽmbjulizəm]. See **somnambulant** & **-ism.** Sleep-walking; a kind of trance in which a person may move about, speak, and perform various actions of which he has no recollection in his normal waking state.

somnambulist, n. [1. somnámbūlist; 2. səmnǽmbjulist]. See prec. & **-ist.** One who walks in his sleep; person liable to somnambulism.

somnambulistic, adj. [1. somnàmbūlístik; 2. səmnæ̀mbjulístik]. Prec. & **-ic.** Pertaining to somnambulism or walking in one's sleep.

somni-, pref. Form of Lat. *somnus*, 'sleep', used in compounds. See **somnolent.**

somniferous, adj. [1. somníferus; 2. səmníferəs]. See prec. & **-ferous**, cp. Lat. *somnifer.* Sleep-producing; inducing sleep, soporific.

somniloquence, n. [1. somnílokwens; 2. səmníləkwəns]. **somni-** & Lat. *loquent-*, 'speaking', Pres. Part. stem of *loqui*, 'to speak', see **loquacious.** (rare) Speech uttered in one's sleep.

somniloquy, n. [1. somnílokwi; 2. səmníləkwi]. See prec., cp. ending of **soliloquy.** (rare) A talk in one's sleep.

somnolence, -cy, n. [1. sómnolens(i); 2. sómnələns(i)]. Fr., fr. Lat. *somnolentia.* Next word & **-ce, -cy.** Tendency, inclination, to fall asleep; sleepiness, drowsiness.

somnolent, adj. [1. sómnolent; 2. sómnələnt], fr. base of Lat. *somnolentus*, formed w. adj. suff. *-lentus*, fr. *somnus*, 'sleep', for **sopnus*, fr. **swepnos*, cp. Scrt. *svapna-*, 'sleep', Gk. *húpnos*, see **hypno-**, & O.E. *swefn*, 'a dream, a vision'; cp. also **soporific. 1.** Inclined to fall asleep; sleepy, drowsy. **2.** Tending to induce sleepiness: *a somnolent tone of voice, sermon* &c.

somnolently, adv. Prec. & **-ly.** In a somnolent manner.

son, n. [1. sun; 2. san]. O.E. *sunu*; M.E. *sune, sone*; O.H.G. *sunu*; Mod. Germ. *sohn*; Du. *zoon*; O.N. *sunr, sonr*; Goth. *sunus*; cogn. w. Lith. *sūnus*; O. Slav. *synŭ*; Scrt. *sūnu-*, 'a son'; fr. **sū-*, 'to beget, bear'; cp. Gk. *huiós*, fr. **suiós*; O. Ir. *suth*, 'birth'. **1. a** A male offspring of a specified parent; Phr. *the Son*, the second Person of the Trinity; **b** one closely resembling his father in body, mind, or character: *he is a true son of his father, his father's own son*; **c** one who feels for another, older, person the kind of affection and respect that he might bear to his own father; **d** descendant, male offspring: *the sons of Adam*, mankind; *the sons of Abraham*, the Jews. **2. a** A member of a particular nation, one born and bred in a specified country: *a faithful son of England*; **b** a member of a specified institution, movement, society, regarded chiefly as having been trained and formed by it: *the great public schools may be proud of their sons*; *the young Wordsworth was a son of the French Revolution*; **c** person regarded as engaged in a particular mode of life, addicted to certain pursuits, having certain interests &c.: *a son of toil*; *a son of the Muses*, a poet. **3.** As form of address; **a** from a priest to a male member of his flock; or from an ecclesiastical superior to an inferior; chiefly *my son*; **b** (colloq.) affectionate or playful, to a friend: *my son*; *old son.*

-son, suff., of Fr. origin, as in *poison, reason*, representing Lat. *-s-ion, -t-ion*, used to form ns. fr. vb. stems.

sonance, -cy, n. [1. sónans(i); 2. sóunəns(i)]. See next word & **-ce.** Quality of being sonant.

sonant, adj. & n. [1. sṓnant; 2. sóunənt], fr. Lat. *sonant-(em)*, Pres. Part. type of *sonāre*, 'to sound', fr. *sonus*, 'sound'; fr. **swonos*, fr. **swenos*; cogn. w. Scrt. *svánati*, 'it sounds'; also w. O.E. *swan*, name of the bird, see **swan.** & cp. **sound (I.). 1.** adj. **a** Sounding, giving forth a sound; **b** (specif. phon.) voiced. **2.** n. A voiced speech-sound.

sonata, n. [1. sonáhta; 2. sənátə]. Ital., lit. 'a sounding, thing sounded', i.e. played on musical instrument, as contrasted w. *cantata*, 'something sung'; fem. sing. of P.P. of *sonare*, 'to sound'; fr. Lat. See prec. A special type of musical composition, for one or two instruments, consisting of three or four movements, varying in rhythm, but so related as to form a unity.

sonatina, n. [1. sònatḗna; 2. sɔ̀nətínə]. Ital., dimin. of prec. A short or simplified form of the sonata proper.

song, n. [1. song; 2. sɔŋ]. O.E. *sāng*, M.E. *sǫng*; O.H.G. *sanc*; Goth. *saggws*; in gradational relation to **sing**; perh. cogn. w. Gk. *omphḗ*, 'voice', fr. **songʷhē*. **1.** Musical, rhythmic, variously modulated utterance produced by the human voice, or by that of birds; more rarely used of sounds made by insects: *to break into song.* **2. a** A musical composition forming a setting for words intended to be sung by the human voice; **b** a rendering by the voice of such a composition; Phrs. *not worth an old song*, valueless; (slang) *nothing to make a song about*, of something not worth troubling about or of little or no importance; **c** such a composition reduced to a graphic notation, whether printed or in manuscript: *be sure to bring some songs with you.* **3. a** A lyrical poem intended to be set to music and sung; **b** (poet.) a poem of any kind; poetry in general.

song-bird, n. A singing bird, such as a thrush, nightingale &c.

song-book, n. Book consisting of a collection of songs, esp. one containing both words and music.

songful, adj. [1. sóngfool; 2. sɔ́ŋf(u)l]. **song** & **-ful. a** Melodious; **b** inclined to sing; in the habit of singing frequently.

songless, adj. [1. sóngles; 2. sɔ́ŋlis]. **song** & **-less. a** Lacking song; **b** not able to sing; not in the habit of singing.

song-sparrow, n. The hedge sparrow.

songster, n. [1. sóngster; 2. sɔ́ŋstə]. O.E. *sangestere.* See **song** & **-ster.** One who sings; esp. a singing bird, but applied also to a human singer.

songstress, n. [1. sóngstres; 2. sɔ́ŋstris]. Prec. & **-ess.** A female singer.

song-thrush, n. The throstle or mavis, *Turdus musicus.*

soniferous, adj. [1. soníferus; 2. sənífərəs], fr. Lat. *sonus*, see **sonant**, & **-ferous.** Producing, conveying, sound.

son-in-law, n. [1. sún in law; 2. sán in lɔ̄]. A daughter's husband.

sonless, adj. [1. súnles; 2. sánlis]. **son** & **-less.** Without a son.

sonnet, n. [1. sónet; 2. sɔ́nit]. Fr., fr. provinc. *sonet*, Ital. *sonetto*, 'sonnet', dimin. of *sono*, 'sound', fr. Lat. *sonus*, see **sonant**, & **-et.** Short poem of fourteen iambic lines, the regular or Petrarchan form being divided into an octave of eight lines, rhyming *a b b a a b b a*, and a sestet of six lines with two or three rhymes variously arranged; the Shakespearean or irregular sonnet has three quatrains followed by a rhymed couplet.

sonneteer, n. [1. sònetḗr; 2. sɔ̀nitíə], fr. Ital. *sonettiere.* See prec. & **-eer.** A writer of sonnets; sometimes in derogatory sense.

sonnet sequence, n. A series of sonnets bound together by a common theme running through them, and sometimes by the last line of one being repeated as the first of the following sonnet.

sonny, n. [1. súni; 2. sáni]. **son** & **-y.** Term of familiar or affectionate address to a boy or to an inferior.

sonometer, n. [1. sonómeter; 2. sənɔ́mitə], fr. Lat. *sonus*, see **sonant**, & **-meter. 1.** Instrument for measuring sounds, their audibility and intensity and mathematical relations. **2.** Instrument for testing the power of hearing.

sonorescence, n. [1. sònorésens; 2. sɔ̀nərésəns]. See next word & **-ce.** Quality of being sonorescent.

sonorescent, adj. [1. sònorésent; 2. sɔ̀nərésənt], fr. Lat. *sonor*, 'a noise, a sound', fr. base seen in **sonant**, & **-escent.** (phys., of certain substances) Capable of emitting sound under the stimulus of radiations of heat or light.

sonority, n. [1. sonóriti; 2. sənɔ́riti], fr. Lat. *sonōritāt-(em)*, Lat. *sonor*, 'sound' &c., see prec., & **-ity.** Quality of being sonorous; fullness of sound; resonance, sonorousness.

sonorous, adj. [1. sonṓrus; 2. sənɔ́rəs], fr. Lat. *sonōrus*, 'resounding', fr. *sonor*, 'sound', see **sonant**, & **-ous. 1. a** (of the voice) Full, loud, resonant in quality; **b** (of instruments or other objects) emitting a powerful, resonant note or sound when played on, struck &c. **2. a** (of verse or prose) High-sounding, melodious; **b** (of style in general) rhetorical, orotund, imposing.

sonorously, adv. Prec. & **-ly.** In a sonorous manner; with full, resonant sound.

sonorousness, n. See prec. & **-ness.** Sonority.

sonship, n. [1. súnship; 2. sánʃip]. **son** & **-ship.** Filial relationship; relation of a son to his father; used in both a literal and a spiritual sense.

sonsy, adj. [1. sónzi; 2. sɔ́nzi]. Scots, fr. Gaelic. Buxom, comely, good-natured.

soon, adv. [1. sōōn; 2. sūn]. O.E. *sōna*, 'immediately', M.E. *sǫne*; cp. O.S. *sāna*, O.H.G. *sān*, Goth. *suns*, 'at once'. **1.** In a short time from now, before very long, shortly after the present time; shortly after some specified time in the past or future: *come as soon as you can*; *summer will soon be here*; *it will soon be time to go*; *I shall soon have to get a new hat*; *the train arrives soon after six o'clock*; *he soon repented his hasty marriage*; *I shall come soon after you arrive.* Phr. *sooner or later*, some day, but inevitably in the long run. **2.** Before the expected or usual right time, early: *winter has come rather soon this year*; *if we arrive too soon, we shall have to wait.* **3.** In no long time; without trouble, effort, or delay; readily, quickly: *he soon took his adversary's measure*; *you will soon get the better of that fellow.* Phr. *least said, soonest mended*, talking may only make things worse, cause irritation. **4.** *As soon as, so soon as*, at the very same moment, without delay, immediately: *be ready to start as soon as I give the signal*; *as soon as I spoke I felt I had committed a blunder*; *so soon as I saw him I knew he was a rogue*; *no sooner. . . . than*, immediately after: *he had no sooner arrived than he fell ill.* Phr. *no sooner said than done*, of an action accomplished immediately after it is suggested. **5.** In various constructions; **a** expressing preference: *I would sooner stay where I am than go to such a place*; *I would as soon leave at once if I'm not wanted*; in such Phr. as *he would as soon cut his throat as disoblige a lady* = he would never disoblige a lady; **b** expressing capacity, *he could as soon write an epic as drive a car* = he could never drive a car.

soot, n. & vb. trans. [1. soot; 2. sut]. O.E. & M.E. *sōt*, also in O.N.; cp. Lith. *sōdis*, 'soot', *sodzotas*, 'sooty'; fr. Aryan **sōd-*, gradational variant of base **sed-*, 'to sit, settle', See **sedentary, sederunt, sit. 1.** n. Black, flaky or powdery substance, consisting chiefly of carbon, produced through imperfect combustion of coal, wood, oil &c., and deposited in chimneys or on buildings, trees, and the ground; used as a garden manure. **2.** vb. To cover with soot.

sooth, n. [1. sōōth; 2. sūþ]. O.E. *sōð*, adj., 'true'; n., 'truth'; M.E. *sōth*, adj. & n.; the O.E. word is fr. Gmc. **sanþ-*, cp. the O.N. cogn. *sannr*, 'true', for **sanþ-r.* The literal sense is 'that which is', & the word is fr. a participial base **essont-* of **es-*, 'to be'. See **esse, essence**; also second element of **presence**; cp. **am, is.** (archaic) That which is true or a fact; truth; chiefly in Phrs. *in sooth, sooth to say*, truly, really, in fact; cp. *forsooth.*

soothe, vb. trans. [1. sōōdh; 2. sūð]. O.E. *ġesōðian*, 'to prove, show the truth of'; fr. *sōþ*, 'true', see prec., M.E. *sōðien*, 'to assent to, confirm, verify', lit. 'to say "yes" to, agree with'. **1.** To exert a pacifying influence on the mind, to restore calm to; **a** to appease; placate by kind or flattering words: *to soothe a person's injured dignity, vanity* &c.; **b** to calm down, put to rest; to quiet, comfort: *to soothe a crying baby, a restless patient, person's nerves* &c. **2.** To allay, mitigate, assuage (physical suffering): *to soothe the pain of a toothache* &c.

soothfast, adj. & adv. [1. sōōthfahst; 2. súþfāst]. O.E. *sōþfæst*, 'truthful, just, righteous'. See **sooth & fast (I.)**. (archaic) Truthful, honest, trustworthy, loyal.

soothingly, adv. [1. sōōdhingli; 2. súðiŋli], fr. Pres. Part. of **soothe & -ly**. In a soothing manner; so as to soothe.

soothsay, vb. intrans. [1. sōōthsā; 2. súþsei]. Back-formation fr. next word. (rare) To tell the truth; to foretell, predict, what is coming.

soothsayer, n. [1. sōōthsàer; 2. súþsèiə]. Cp. M.E. *sōþsiggere*, 'a speaker of truth'. See **sooth & say (I.) & -er.** One who predicts the future; a diviner, a prophet.

soothsaying, n. [1. sōōthsāing; 2. súþsei-iŋ]. Cp. M.E. *sōþsaȝe*, 'a true saying'. **sooth & saying.** The foretelling of the future; prediction, prognostication.

sootily, adv. [1. sóotili; 2. sútili]. **sooty & -ly.** In a sooty state or manner.

sootiness, n. [1. sóotines; 2. sútinis]. **sooty & -ness.** A sooty state or condition.

sooty, adj. [1. sóoti; 2. súti]. **soot & -y.** **1. a** Pertaining to soot, of the nature of soot; **b** impregnated, covered, soiled, stained, with soot: *sooty smoke, fog; a sooty face; sooty London buildings.* **2.** Dark, black, like soot; dusky; sometimes used as descriptive of sea-birds &c.: *sooty albatross* &c.

sop (I.), n. [1. sop; 2. sɔp]. O.E. *sopp*, M.E. *soppe, sop*, cp. O.N. *soppa*, M. Du. *soppe*, cogn. w. **sup (I.)**, O.E. *sūpan*, & cp. **soup.** **1.** Piece of bread or similar substance, dipped and soaked in broth, milk &c., and eaten. **2.** (fig.) From mythological tale, *a sop to Cerberus* (the watch-dog of hell), something given to pacify, or meet demands of another; a bribe, concession. **3.** Anything sopped or soaked, wet with rain or other water: *the ground is a mere sop.* **4.** (colloq. slang) A soppy person, a milksop.

sop (II.), vb. trans., fr. prec. **1. a** To dip and soak (bread &c.) in broth, milk &c.; **b** *sop up*, to mop, soak up, absorb (water) &c., as with a sponge or other absorbent substance &c. **2.** To drench, saturate, with water, rain &c.: *sopped to the skin.*

soph, n. [1. sof; 2. sɔf]. Abbr. form of *sophister* or *sophomore*, qq.v.

sophism, n. [1. sófizm; 2. sɔ́fizəm], fr. Fr. *sophisme*, fr. Lat., fr. Gk. *sóphisma*, formed fr. Gk. *sophós*, 'clever, skilled, in any art or craft; prudent, shrewd, cunning; learned, wise'; perh. for **twogʷhós*, 'clear-sighted, intelligent', & possibly cogn. w. Lat. *tueor*, 'to look at, examine; to look after; to watch, guard, defend', see **tutor**; for the suff. see **-ism.** **1.** Form of reasoning or dialectic, as practised by the Greek sophists. **2.** Sophistical reasoning; fallacious, captious, argument; plausible, deceptive reasoning; ingenious quibble.

sophist, n. [1. sófist; 2. sɔ́fist], fr. Fr. *sophiste*, fr. L. Lat. *sophista*, fr. Gk. *sophistḗs*, 'a clever, skilful man; a wise, prudent person; statesman'; specif. later, in sense **1.** below; fr. Gk. *sophós*, discussed under prec., & **-ist.** **1.** (hist.) One of a class of professional paid teachers of grammar, rhetoric, dialectic, philosophy, politics &c., in ancient Greece, who were often accused, as by Socrates, of being skilled in 'making the worse appear the better cause'. Hence, **2.** A fallacious, plausible, captious reasoner; a quibbler; one skilled in persuasion by unsound though plausible arguments.

sophister, n. [1. sófister; 2. sɔ́fistə], fr. O. Fr. *sophistre*, an irregular variant of *sophiste.* See **sophist.** (obs.) Student in his second or third year at Cambridge University and Trinity College, Dublin.

sophistic(al), adj. [1. sofístik(l); 2. sɔfístik(l)], fr. Gk. *sophistikós.* See **sophist & -ic & -al.** **1.** Pertaining to a sophist or the class of Sophists in ancient Greece: *the sophistic school, teaching* &c. **2.** Usually *sophistical*, **a** (of arguments &c.) fallacious, though plausible, subtly deceptive; based on, involving, sophistry; **b** (of persons) using sophistry, arguing in a fallacious way.

sophistically, adv. Prec. & **-ly.** In a sophistical or sophistic manner.

sophisticate, vb. trans. & intrans. [1. sofístikāt; 2. səfístikeit], fr. L. or Med. Lat. *sophisticāt-(um)*, P.P. type of *sophisticāre*, fr. *sophisticus.* See **sophistic & -ate.** Rare, except as P.P. used as adj.; see **sophisticated. A.** trans. **1.** To render, make, sophistical; to treat sophistically, use sophistical arguments about; to use sophistry concerning: *a subtle controversialist able to sophisticate the simplest question of morals.* **2. a** To spoil the purity of, to adulterate (a substance, esp. an article of commerce); specif. **b** to change, tamper with (the text of an author). **B.** intrans. To use sophistry, be sophistical.

sophisticated, adj. [1. sofístikāted; 2. səfístikeitid], fr. P.P. of prec. (of persons) Artificial, not genuine or natural; lacking in natural simplicity; disingenuous; worldly-wise.

sophistication, n. [1. sofistikáshun; 2. səfistikéiʃən]. **sophisticate & -ion. a** Act of rendering sophisticated; **b** state of being sophisticated.

sophistry, n. [1. sófistri; 2. sɔ́fistri]. M.E. *sophistrie*, fr. O. Fr. *sophisterie.* See **sophist & -ry. a** Art, skill, practice, of a sophist; **b** plausible but specious reasoning.

sophomore, n. [1. sófomōr; 2. sɔ́fəmɔ̄]. Invented word, supposed to be fr. Gk. *sophós*, 'wise', & *mōrós*, 'dull, stupid, foolish', cp. **sophister.** A second-year man at an American university.

soporiferous, adj. [1. sòp-, sòporíferus; 2. sɔ̀p-, sòupəríf ərəs]. See next word & **-ferous,** & cp. Lat. *sopōrifer.* Causing, tending to cause, sleep; soporific.

soporific, adj. & n. [1. sòp-, sòporífik; 2. sɔ̀p-, sòupəríf ik], fr. Lat. *sopōri-*, stem of *sopor*, 'sleep'; derived, w. different formative elements, fr. same base as Lat. *somnus*, 'sleep', see **somnolent. 1.** adj. Causing, tending to cause, sleep. **2.** n. A drug or other agent which causes sleep; a narcotic.

sopping, adj. & adv. [1. sóping; 2. sɔ́piŋ], fr. Pres. Part. of **sop (II.). 1.** adj. Thoroughly drenched with moisture, soaking, wet through: *if you were out in that shower you must be simply sopping.* **2.** adv. Gen. *sopping wet*, very wet, soaked through, drenched.

soppy, adj. [1. sópi; 2. sɔ́pi]. **sop (I.) & -y. 1.** Like a sop; saturated with moisture; soft, sloppy, squashy. **2.** (fig., colloq.) Lacking spirit and vigour; weakly sentimental.

soprano, n. [1. sopráhnō; 2. səprā́nou]. Ital. pl. *soprani* [1. sopráhnē; 2. səprā́nī]. Ital., 'supreme, sovereign'; also in musical sense, fr. L. Lat. *superānus.* See **sovereign.** (mus.) **1. a** The female voice of the highest range and clear, bird-like quality; **b** a boy's treble voice of similar quality. **2. a** Woman singer with such voice; **b** one of the singers in a choir taking the treble parts. **3.** The treble part in a musical composition for several voices, which indicates the air and is sung by the sopranos.

sora, n. [1. sóra; 2. sɔ́rə]. Native Indian name. A small, short-billed bird, like a rail, which frequents the marshes of the Southern Atlantic States in its autumn migrations.

sorb, n. [1. sorb; 2. sɔ̄b], fr. O. Fr. *sorbe*, fr. Lat. *sorbus* for **sordhos*, cp. Lith. *saŕ-tàs*, 'foxy in colour'. The service tree or its fruit.

sorbefacient, adj. & n. [1. sòrbefáshient; 2. sɔ̀biféiʃiənt], fr. Lat. *sorbēre*, 'to suck in, swallow', cogn. w. Gk. *hropéō*, 'I swallow', & **-facient.** See also **absorb.** (med.) **1.** adj. Causing, promoting, absorption; sucking up moisture. **2.** n. Drug or other substance which absorbs or promotes absorption.

sorbet, n. [1. sórbet; 2. sɔ́bɛt]. A French variant of **sherbet.** A water-ice.

sorcerer, n. [1. sórserer; 2. sɔ́sərə], fr. O. Fr. *sorcier*, fr. L. Lat. *sortiārius*, 'teller of fortunes by casting of lots, sorcerer', fr. *sortiāre*, 'to cast lots', fr. *sort-(em), sors*, 'lot', see **sort (I.).** Magician, wizard, practitioner of the black arts.

sorceress, n. [1. sórseres; 2. sɔ́sərɛs]. See prec. & **-ess.** Female sorcerer, a witch.

sorcery, n. [1. sórseri; 2. sɔ́səri]. O. Fr. *sorcerie.* See **sorcerer & -ry.** Magic, witchcraft; enchantment.

sordamente, adv. [1. sòrdaméntā; 2. sɔ̀daménte]. Ital., fr. *sordo*, 'deaf', fr. Lat. *surdus*, see **surd, & -ment.** Musical direction to play in a muted or muffled manner or with use of a sordine.

sordes, n. [1. sórdēz; 2. sɔ́dīz]. Lat., 'filth'; cogn. w. O.E. *sweart*, 'black, dark', O.H.G. *swarz*, see next word. (med.) The foul, yellowish crust which forms on the lips, teeth, and gums of patients suffering from typhoid and other acute fevers.

sordid, adj. [1. sórdid; 2. sɔ́did], fr. Fr. *sordide*, fr. Lat. *sordidus*, 'dirty, squalid, mean', fr. base **sord-*, as *sordēre*, 'to be dirty, mean; to seem base'; *sordēs*, 'filth' &c., see prec.; cogn. w. O.E. *sweart*, 'black, dark', O.H.G. *swarz.* See **swart. 1.** Filthy, squalid, mean, low: *a sordid district; in sordid surroundings.* **2.** Base-minded, mean; arising from, animated by, ignoble, unworthy ideals, motives; characterized by low, mean aims and methods: *sordid desires; a sordid quarrel; sordid practices* &c.

sordidly, adv. Prec. & **-ly.** In a sordid manner.

sordidness, n. See prec. & **-ness.** State, quality, of being sordid; material or spiritual squalor.

sordine, n. [1. sordḗn; 2. sɔdín]. Fr., fr. Ital. *sordino* for *sordo*, 'deaf, dull-sounding', fr. Lat. *surdus*, 'deaf, noiseless', see **surd.** Any of various devices used to reduce resonance and produce a muffled tone in musical instruments.

sore (I.), adj. [1. sōr; 2. sɔ̄]. O.E. *sār*, 'painful', M.E. *sōr*; O.H.G. *sēr*, 'painful'; Du. *zeer*, 'sore', O.N. *sārr*, 'sore, painful'. See **sorry. 1.** Painful to the touch, tender, esp. of inflamed or wounded surfaces of the body; *a sore finger, foot* &c.; *sore throat*, inflamed condition due to a cold; *a sore head*, one that is cut or bruised as from fighting. Phr. *like a bear with a sore head*, surly, grumpy. **2.** Grieved, sad, filled with sorrow; woeful: *there were many sore hearts at home after the great victory.* **3.** Grieved, wounded in spirit; having a feeling of resentment as from a slight or affront: *to feel sore about*, to resent, feel hurt at. Phr. *a sore subject*, topic which causes awkwardness, irritation, resentment when broached. **4.** Extreme, intense, severe: *in sore need, distress.*

sore (II.), adv. O.E. *sāre.* See prec. (archaic and poet.) Sorely, severely, grievously: *sore troubled, oppressed* &c.

sore (III.), n. O.E. *sār*, 'pain of body or mind'; fr. the adj., see **sore (I.). 1.** A place on the body where the skin has been broken or has perished, esp. a painful, inflamed, suppurating open place on which a crust forms, caused by injury or disease. Phr. *an open sore*, a standing evil, an abuse, a cause of scandal. **2.** A feeling of mental irritation; rancour, a grudge; a painful memory: *time does not always heal old sores.*

sorel. See **sorrel (I.).**

sorely, adv. [1. sórli; 2. sɔ̄́li]. **sore (I.) & -ly. a** Grievously, severely: *he is very sorely tried by his wife's temper;* **b** exceedingly, very much: *I felt sorely inclined to hit him on the head.*

soreness, n. [1. sórnes; 2. sɔ̄nis]. **sore (I.)** & **-ness**. State, quality, of being sore. **1.** Painfulness, sensitiveness, to the touch: *abrasions of the skin cause considerable soreness.* **2. a** Resentment, grudge, sense of injury: *I no longer feel any soreness at his ingratitude*; **b** strained relations between persons; unfriendliness, ill-feeling: *there was some soreness between father and son over the former's second marriage.*

sorghum, n. [1. sórgum; 2. sɔ̄gəm]. Latinized form, also *sorgum*, prob. fr. an East Indian word; Ital. has *sorgo*. The name of a tall cereal grass, of which the chief and most valuable species, *S. vulgare*, is Indian millet; *S. saccharatum* is Chinese sugar-cane.

soricine, adj. [1. sórisīn; 2. sɔ́risain], fr. Lat. *soricīnus*, fr. *sōric-*, stem of *sōrex*, 'shrew-mouse', cogn. w. Gk. *húrax*, see **hyrax** & **-ine**. Pertaining, related to, belonging to, the genus of shrew-mice.

sorites, n. [1. sōrītēz; 2. sourάitīz]. Lat., fr. Gk. *sōreítēs*, 'heaped up', also (sc. *sullogismós*) 'a heap, pile of syllogisms, a sorites', fr. *sōrós*, 'a heap', wh. is for **twōros*, fr. a base **tewā-* &c., 'to swell', found also in Lat. *tumēre*, 'to swell', see **tumid, tumour**. (log.) A series of condensed syllogisms, the predicate of each proposition becoming the subject of the next, and so on; the conclusion having the subject of the first and the predicate of the last proposition; e.g. *English is a Germanic language*; *Germanic speech is a branch of Aryan*; *all Aryan languages are inflexional*; *therefore English is an inflexional language.*

Soroptimist, n. [1. sōróptimist; 2. sōrɔ́ptimist]. Concocted term, fr. Lat. *soror*, q.v. under **sister, & optimist**. A member of a woman's Rotary Club.

sorosis, n. [1. sorósis; 2. sɔróusis], fr. Gk. *sōrós*, 'heap'. See prec. (bot.) A clustered, compound pulpy fruit, such as the pineapple, bread-fruit, mulberry &c.

sorrel (I.), adj. & n. [1. sórel; 2. sɔ́rəl], fr. O. Fr. *sorel*, 'sorrel horse', dimin. of *sor*, 'sorrel horse', also the colour itself, also as adj., Mod. Fr. *saur*, 'reddish brown', of Gmc. origin; cp. L.G. *soor*, Du. *zoor*, 'dried, withered', cp. **sear (I.)**; the sense is derived fr. the colour of autumn leaves. **1.** adj. Reddish brown in colour, esp. of horses. **2.** n. **a** A sorrel horse; **b** (obs.) also *sorel*, a third-year buck.

sorrel (II.), n., fr. O. Fr. *sorel*, Mod. Fr. *surelle*, dimin. form fr. M.H.G. *sūr*, 'sour', see **sour**. **1.** A plant, *Rumex Acetosa*, allied to the dock, with arrow-shaped leaves, which have an acid taste, and reddish-brown flowers; it is a common weed in meadows and pastures. **2.** A plant of the genus *Oxalis*, usually called *wood-sorrel*, with acid trefoil leaves and small, white, delicately veined, cup-like flowers.

sorrily, adv. [1. sórili; 2. sɔ́rili]. **sorry** & **-ly**. In a sorry manner.

sorriness, n. [1. sórines; 2. sɔ́rinis]. See prec. & **-ness**. Condition or quality of being sorry; inferior, poor, quality.

sorrow (I.), n. [1. sórō; 2. sɔ́rou]. O.E. *sorg*, *sorh*, M.E. *sorwe*, cogn. w. O.N. *sorg*, Du. *zorg*, Germ. *sorge*, 'care, anxiety'; Goth. *saurga*, 'sorrow, grief'; Gmc. type **sorgā*, 'care'; cp. Lith. *sirgti*, 'to be ill, in pain', O. Ir. *serg*, 'sickness'; perh. related also to **serve (I.)**, w. a different formative element. The word has no historical connexion w. **sore** or **sorry**, but the latter has been to some extent influenced by it in sense owing to resemblance in sound. **1.** Grief, pain of mind, sadness, unhappiness, felt for or aroused by one's own or another's misfortune, disappointments, loss &c.: *to feel sorrow for*; *the people's sorrow at her death was deep.* **2. a** Regret for what has been done; penitence, contrition: *sorrow for one's sins of omission or commission*; *he expressed his sorrow for his mistake*; **b** regret for what one has lost or is losing: *we left the place without much sorrow.* **3.** Experience of that which causes sorrow; occasion of such; misfortune, affliction: '*a man of sorrows and acquainted with grief*' (Isaiah liii. 3); *these repeated sorrows broke his heart.* **4.** Expression, display, of sorrow; mourning, lamentation: *his exaggerated sorrow for his rival's misfortunes was somewhat ridiculous.*

sorrow (II.), vb. intrans. O.E. *sorgian*, M.E. *sorwhen*, *sorowen*, cp. Goth. *saurgan*, 'to grieve'. See prec. To feel, show, sorrow; to grieve, regret, mourn.

sorrower, n. [1. sórōer; 2. sɔ́rouə]. **sorrow (II.)** & **-er**. One who sorrows; a mourner.

sorrowful, adj. [1. sórofool; 2. sɔ́rəfl, -ful]. **sorrow (I.)** & **-ful**. **a** Full of, experiencing, sorrow; melancholy, unhappy: *and left us all very sorrowful*; **b** expressing sorrow and sadness, mournful: *such sorrowful tales, hymns &c.*; **c** exciting or causing sorrow, grievous: *a sorrowful sight.*

sorrowfully, adv. Prec. & **-ly**. In a sorrowful manner, with sorrow.

sorrowfulness, n. See prec. & **-ness**. Condition of being sorrowful.

sorry, adj. [1. sóri; 2. sɔ́ri]. O.E. *sārig*, 'feeling, expressing, grief; sad', fr. *sār*; M.E. *sǭry*; not related historically to **sorrow**, but partially influenced in meaning through association w. this word. See also **sore (I.)**. **1. a** Grieved, distressed in mind: *we were sorry to hear of your sad bereavement*; **b** feeling deep regret, repentant, contrite: '*we are heartily sorry for these our misdoings*'; *say you are sorry and I'll forgive you*; (colloq.) *sorry!*, expressing mild apology; **c** mildly regretful: *I'm so sorry I can't accept your kind invitation*; *(I am) sorry you can't stay longer.* **2.** (archaic) **a** Of poor, inferior, quality: *a sorry performance, exhibition*; **b** contemptible, mean: *a sorry rogue*; *a sorry jade*; **c** miserable, unfortunate, wretched: *in a sorry plight.*

sort (I.), n. [1. sort; 2. sɔ̄t], fr. O. Fr. *sorte*, 'kind, sort; manner', cp. also Fr. *sort*, 'lot, fate', fr. Lat. *sort-(em)* &c., stem of *sors*, 'fate, lot, condition, state'; prob. cogn. w. *sert-(um)*, P.P. type of *serere*, 'to join, connect', see **series**. **1. a** Number or group of persons or things possessing certain common qualities of character, appearance; a class, category, kind, species: *we have every sort of boots in stock*; '*all sorts and conditions of men*'; *the latest sort of music*; *he is not the sort of man to do a mean thing*; *he's not my sort*, not the kind of man I like; **b** kind, quality, something in the nature of (that): *that's the sort of thing I want*; *we discussed art and that sort of thing*; *I don't believe anything of the sort*; *nothing of the sort*, as a strong negative; *he is a politician of a sort*, something like one, but of a doubtful kind; *a sort of a peace*, not a very satisfactory one. Phrs. *a good sort*, (colloq.) a good, kind, genial, decent person; *sort of* (with advbl. force, colloq.): *he sort of hinted he'd like a tip*, in a kind of way. **2.** Manner, quality, fashion, condition: *after a sort*, to a certain degree. Phr. *out of sorts*, not very well, seedy; not in good fettle. **3.** (print., in pl.) Letters, stops, and other marks of a particular fount of type.

sort (II.), vb. trans. & intrans., fr. O. Fr. *sortir*, 'to get by lot, to obtain, choose'; fr. Lat. *sortīri*, 'to assign by lot, to divide'. See prec. **A.** trans. To separate things of one sort or kind from others, and group them together; to classify, select, pick out, arrange in groups: *to sort the sheep from the goats*; *to sort letters*; *sort out your cards*, arrange them in suits. **B.** intrans. **1.** (archaic) To associate with others of same kind or character, to consort. **2.** To suit, agree with, fit, be in accord with: *such conduct sorts ill with his position.*

sortable, adj. [1. sórtabl; 2. sɔ̄təbl]. **sort (II.)** & **-able**. Capable of being sorted.

sorter, n. [1. sórter; 2. sɔ̄tə]. **sort (II.)** & **-er**. One who sorts; specif., an employee of Post Office who sorts letters.

sortes, n. pl. [1. sórtēz; 2. sɔ̄tīz]. Lat., pl. of *sors*, 'lot' &c., see **sort (I.)**. The lots, cp. *sortilege*, hence determination of line of action by choosing, haphazard, passages from a book, as *Sortes Virgilianae*, fr. Virgil; *Sortes Biblicae*, fr. the Bible &c.

sortie, n. [1. sórtē; 2. sɔ̄ti]. Fr., fem. sing. of P.P. of *sortir*, 'to go forth, to sally'; cp. Ital. *sortita*, Span. *surtida*, in same sense; etymol. doubtful, but prob. to be referred to a Low Lat. **surrectīre*, 'to rise up', fr. Lat. *surrect-(um)*, P.P. of *surgere*, 'to rise', see **surge** & cp. **source**. A sally made by troops besieged in a town or fortress upon the besieging army.

sortilege, n. [1. sórtilij; 2. sɔ̄tilidž]. Fr., fr. Med. Lat. *sortilegium*, fr. *sort-(em)*, *sors*, 'lot', see **sort (I.)**, & *legere*, 'to pick out, select; read', see **legend**. Divination by drawing lots.

sorus, n., pl. **sori** [1. sórus, -ī; 2. sɔ̄rəs, *-ai*]. Neo-Lat., fr. Gk. *sōrós*, 'heap', see **sorites**. (bot.) Group, cluster, of spore-cases at the back of ferns.

so-so, adj. [1. só sō; 2. sóu sou]. Reduplication of **so**. (colloq.) Not very good; not very well: *his play was only so-so*; *how do you feel? Just so-so.*

sostenuto, adv. [1. sòstenóotō; 2. sɔ̀stenúːtou]. Ital., P.P. See **sustain**. (mus.) Sustained, prolonged, so as to give each note its full value.

sot, n. [1. sot; 2. sɔt]. In M.E. in sense of 'foolish', fr. L. Lat. *sottus*, 'stupid', prob. of Gmc. origin; cp. M. Du. *zoot*, M.H.G. *sote*. Person stupefied by drinking; persistent, habitual drunkard.

Sothic, adj. [1. sóthik; 2. sóuþik], fr. Gk. *Sôthis*, the Egyptian name of Sirius, the dog-star, & **-ic**. Named after, pertaining to, Sothis; esp. *Sothic year*, the Egyptian year, of 365 days 6 hours, reckoned by the heliacal rising of the dog-star; *Sothic period* or *cycle*, of 1460 Sothic years = 1461 years.

sottish, adj. [1. sótish; 2. sɔ́tiʃ]. **sot** & **-ish**. Like a sot; given to excessive drinking; bemused by this; foolish.

sottishly, adv. Prec. & **-ly**. In a sottish manner.

sottishness, n. See prec. & **-ness**. Condition of being sottish.

sotto voce, adv., Anglicized to [1. sótō vóchā; 2. sɔ́tou vóutʃei]. Ital., lit. 'under the voice'. In an undertone, so as not to be overheard, aside.

sou, n. [1. sōō; 2. sū]. Fr., in O. Fr. *sol*, fr. **solidus**. Five centimes, $\frac{1}{20}$ of the franc, nickel or copper coin of this value; halfpenny; in Phr. *he hasn't a sou*, is penniless.

soubrette, n. [1. sōōbrét; 2. sūbrét]. Fr., fem. fr. O. Fr. *soubret*, 'sober, cunning, sharp'. Type of female character in light comedy &c., usually depicted as an arch, pert, and pretty chambermaid.

soubriquet, n. See **sobriquet**.

soucar, n. [1. sóukar; 2. sáukā]. Hind. *sāukār*, 'honest.' Hindu banker.

souchong, n. [1. sōōchóng; 2. sūtʃɔ́ŋ]. Fr., fr. Chin. *hsiao chung*, 'small, fine kind'. A kind of black Chinese tea, of small leaf and fine quality.

Soudanese. See **Sudanese**.

souffle, n., Anglicized to [1. sōōfl; 2. sūfl], Fr. [sufl]. Fr., fr. *souffler*, 'to blow', fr. Lat. *sufflāre*, fr. **sub-** & *flāre*, see **flatus, blow (I.)** & words there referred to. (med.) Soft, low murmur or sound, as of blowing, heard through the stethoscope in the examination of the heart, lungs, or other organs.

soufflé, n. [1. sōōflā; 2. súflei]. Fr., P.P. of *souffler*. See prec. A dish, either sweet or savoury, made of the white of eggs, milk or cream, beaten to a froth and baked.

sough, n. & vb. intrans. [1. suf, sou; 2. saf, *sau*]. M.E. *swogh*, *swowgh*; cp. O.E. *swōgan*, 'to sound, make, a noise', also O.E. *swēg*, 'sound, melody', fr. **swōgi-*; prob. imitative. **a** n. A low, murmuring, moaning, or sighing sound, as of wind in trees &c.; **b** vb. (of wind) to make such a sound.

sought, vb. [1. sawt; 2. sɔ̄t]. O.E. *sōhte*, M.E. *souht*; Pret. & P.P. of **seek**.

soul, n. [1. sōl; 2. soul]. O.E. *sāwol*, M.E. *sāule*, *sōule*; O.S. *sēola*, O.H.G. *sēula*, Mod. Germ. *seele*; Goth. *saiwala*; relation has been suggested w. Gk. *aiólos*, 'quick-moving, rapid', wh. wd. be plausible if this were for

saiwolos*, but this is rendered improbable by Scrt. *āyúš*, 'quick-moving'. **1. The non-material part in man which thinks and wills; the personal entity of an individual regarded as separate and separable from the body and distinguishing him from others; psychologically the inner activity of which one is directly conscious; theologically the immortal substance of man which distinguishes him from the beasts: *the transmigration of souls*; *the immortality of the soul*; *a corporation has not a body to be kicked nor a soul to be saved.* **2.** The vital, mental principle without which consciousness either totally or partially ceases: *an idiot can hardly be said to have a soul*; *to keep body and soul together.* **3.** The ethical or emotional nature of man, as contrasted with his bodily, or intellectual, powers and desires: *do it with all your heart and soul*; *a soul which no appeals could touch*; *he has a soul above mere money-grubbing.* **4.** That which expresses the essential part of anything; quality, property, which gives life and energy to anything: *in translation the soul of the book has been lost*; *dull copies of ancient art without any soul.* **5. a** A person regarded as giving vitality, enthusiasm, animation to anything; inspirer, the moving, active spirit: *he was the life and soul of the party, place, company* &c.; **b** person regarded as the embodiment of some quality: *the soul of generosity, kindness* &c. **6.** A departed, disembodied spirit: *the souls of the blessed in heaven*; *pray for the souls of the departed.* **7.** A human being, a person: *ship was lost with 500 souls on board*; *not a soul was saved*; *I have not spoken to a soul all day*; also with qualifying epithet: *a kind, good soul*; *a jolly old soul*; *poor soul, she has had a lot of trouble.*

-souled, adj. [1. sōld; 2. sould]. Prec. & **-ed.** Having a soul of a specified kind, as *great-*, *high-souled* &c.

soulful, adj. [1. sṓlfool; 2. sóulful]. **soul** & **-ful.** Full of soul; emotional; sentimental.

soulfully, adv. Prec. & **-ly.** In a soulful manner.

soulfulness, n. See prec. & **-ness.** Condition of being soulful.

soulless, adj. [1. sṓles; 2. sóullis]. **soul** & **-less.** Having no soul; without emotion, sentiment, or feeling.

soullessly, adv. Prec. & **-ly.** In a soulless manner.

soullessness, n. See prec. & **-ness.** Condition of being soulless.

sound (I.), n. [1. sound; 2. saund]. M.E., fr. O. Fr. *soun*, fr. Lat. *sonus*, see **sonant.** The final *-d* in the present form is due to a tendency to develop this finally, after *-n*, wh. is traceable fr. the 15th cent. onwards; cp. the now vulg. *gownd.* **1.** That which is or can be heard; the sensation resulting from stimulation of the auditory nerves through the ear: *the sound of running water, of a drum, of the human voice*; *not a sound was heard*; *what was, what made, that sound?* Phr. *within sound of*, at a distance within which sound can be heard, within earshot. **2.** The external causes of auditive sensation, namely, the vibrations set up in a vibrating body, and transmitted through the air, water, or other elastic medium: *the physics of sound*; *sound is impossible in a vacuum*; *regularity of vibration distinguishes sound from noise.* **3. a** An auditive impression which, by reason of its characteristic quality, conveys a definite impression as to its cause or source or character: *'There was a sound of revelry by night'* (Byron); *a cheerful, melancholy, sound*; **b** meaningless noise: *'full of sound and fury, signifying nothing'.* **4.** Specif., a sound produced by the vocal organs: *the sounds of speech.* **5.** Meaning, mental impression, conveyed by the voice, or (fig.) as read or understood: *the rumours have a sinister sound.*

sound (II.), vb. intrans. & trans. M.E. *sounen*, fr. O. Fr. *soner*, Fr. *sonner*, fr. Lat. *sonāre.* See prec. **A.** intrans. **1.** To make a sound or noise; to produce an audible effect: *the organ sounds*; *I cannot make this bell sound.* **2.** To have a specific acoustic quality, to convey a particular auditive impression: *how sweet the music sounds*; *the poem sounds better when read than sung.* **3. a** To produce an auditive impression which suggests that some specific thing is taking place, or that that which makes a sound is in some specified condition: *it sounded as if someone was running away*; *his voice sounds as if he had a cold*; **b** to suggest to the mind, to seem, to appear: *the statement sounds improbable*; *how does this proposal sound to you?* **4.** (law) To have or tend to have the effect of, in Phr. *to sound in damages*, when the action is brought for unascertained damages. **B.** trans. **1.** To cause to sound, to produce sound from: *sound a trumpet, a bell.* **2. a** To utter, express by the voice: *to sound a note of fear*; **b** to express, utter, by any means: *the first note of danger was sounded by the press.* **3.** To give a signal for by means of a sound: *the tocsin sounded an alarm*; *to sound the retreat, the réveillé* &c. **4.** To spread abroad, publish, celebrate in speech, or otherwise: *to sound a man's praises* &c.

sound (III.), adj. O.E. *sund*, 'uninjured, in good condition'; O.H.G. *gisunt*, 'strong, healthy', Mod. Germ. *gesund*; these words are prob. connected w. O.E. *swīþ*, 'strong', cp. Goth. *swinþs*; the base is prob. unrelated to Lat. *sānus*, 'healthy', see **sane. 1. a** Physically healthy, in good bodily condition, not diseased: *of sound body and mind*; *his heart is not sound*; *horse hasn't a sound leg to stand on*; **b** not decayed, over-ripe, or rotten: *sound fruit, timber*; **c** not defective; undamaged, in good, workable condition, not worn out: *a sound building*; *the bridge is no longer sound.* **2.** (of the mind and mental faculties and activities) **a** In healthy, normal condition; unimpaired; **b** well-founded, reliable, sagacious: *a sound opinion, judgement*; **c** based on reason, in accordance with logic; valid, logical: *sound argument.* **3.** (of actions) **a** In accordance with good judgement; judicious, safe: *a sound policy to adopt*; **b** (of specific acts, movements, activities) skilfully and efficiently carried out; likely to effect its purpose: *a sound stroke at cricket* &c.; *a sound way of operating*; **c** (of conduct) morally unexceptionable; correct, right: *sound behaviour.* **4.** Financially stable; solvent, commercially solid, firmly established, safe: *a sound investment*; *his financial position is perfectly sound.* **5.** (of persons) Exhibiting soundness in thought, action, conduct &c.; reliable, competent, efficient in a specified way: *a sound reasoner, cricketer, member of society*; *a sound strategist* &c. **6. a** Complete, thorough: *a sound thrashing, beating*; **b** *a sound sleep*, one that is profound, unbroken, undisturbed. **7.** Legally valid; without a flaw, unassailable: *sound title to land.*

sound (IV.), adv., fr. prec. **5.** In a sound, unbroken manner; soundly: *to sleep sound*; *the more noise there was the sounder he slept.*

sound (V.), n. O.E. *sund*, 'capacity of swimming; act of swimming; that in which swimming takes place, the sea'; specif., 'narrow strait of sea'; the latter is perh. primarily an O.N. sense, prob. orig. a piece of water that one can swim across; fr. **swum-d*; cogn. of **swim. 1.** A narrow channel or strait, as between an inland sea or lake and the high sea or between an island and mainland; *the Sound*, one of the entrances to the Baltic. **2.** The swim or air-bladder of a fish.

sound (VI.), vb. trans. & intrans. M.E. *sounden, sonden*, 'to use a sounding-lead', formed fr. prec. or fr. Fr. *sonder*, in same sense; the Fr. word is almost certainly derived fr. Gmc. The word *sund*, see prec., is used w. sense of testing depth in the O.E. compound *sund-ġierd*, 'a sounding pole'. **A.** trans. **1.** To find out the depth of (water); to explore nature of bottom of (water) by means of a line and plummet, the sailor's lead, or other mechanical device: *to sound the entrance to a harbour*; *sound the depths of the ocean* &c. **2.** (med.) To probe, examine, by a sound &c. *to sound the bladder, urethra*; also *to sound a person's chest, heart* &c., to test with a stethoscope; perhaps influenced by **sound** (II.). **3.** To ascertain, or try to ascertain, the opinions, feelings, wishes of (a person) by cautious, tactful questions, the purpose of which is rather hinted at than fully expressed: *will you sound X as to whether he would accept the post if offered?* **4.** (fig.) To know by experience; to explore: *to sound the depths of human misery.* **B.** intrans. **1.** To use the lead or other sounding apparatus to ascertain depth of water &c.: *ship moved slowly forward sounding as she went.* **2.** (of whale &c.) To plunge, dive suddenly from surface of the sea.

sound (VII.), n., fr. prec. Surgeon's probe used for examination of bladder or other cavity of the body.

sound-board, n. See **sounding board.**

sound boarding, n. Extra boarding under a floor to deaden sound.

sounder (I.), n., fr. **sound** (II.) & **-er.** That which sounds; specif., a device in a telegraphic instrument which transmits the message by means of clicks.

sounder (II.), n., fr. **sound** (VI.) & **-er.** Device for taking soundings without stopping a ship.

sounder (III.), n. [1. sóunder; 2. sáundə]. O.E. *sūnor*, 'herd of swine'; fr. base in **sow** (I.) & **swine.** (archaic) Herd of wild swine: erroneously applied to a single young wild boar.

sound-film, n. Cinematograph film accompanied by mechanically reproduced effects of sound, dialogue &c., vulgarly styled *talkies.*

sounding (I.), adj. [1. sóunding; 2. sáundiŋ]. Pres. Part. of **sound** (II.). **a** Full of sound, making a sound, resonant, resounding; esp. **b** having much sound but without much meaning, magnificent in sound only: *sounding oratory.*

sounding (II.), n., fr. **sound** (VI.) & **-ing. 1.** Act, process, of ascertaining or measuring the depth of water in a channel &c., by the lead or other methods. **2.** (pl.) **a** Measurements of depth of water at specific places; **b** places where such measurements have been, or can be, taken.

sounding board, n. **sounding** (I.) & **board. a** A contrivance placed above a pulpit or rostrum &c. which prevents the sound of a speaker's voice from being dissipated, and throws it forward and down towards the audience; **b** a thin plate of wood or metal which increases the resonance of a musical instrument.

soundless, adj. [1. sóundles; 2. sáundlis]. **sound** (I.) & **-less.** Without sound; noiseless.

soundlessly, adv. Prec. & **-ly.** In a soundless manner; noiselessly.

soundlessness, n. See prec. & **-ness.** State, quality, of being soundless.

soundly, adv. [1. sóundli; 2. sáundli]. **sound** (III.) & **-ly.** In a sound manner.

soundness, n. [1. sóundnes; 2. sáundnis]. See prec. & **-ness.** State, quality, of being sound.

sound-wave, n. **sound** (I.) & **wave** (II.). One of the longitudinal vibratory disturbances of air which produce upon the auditive nerves the sensation of sound.

soup, n. [1. sōōp; 2. sūp], fr. Fr. *soupe*; of Gmc. origin. See **sup** (I.) & **supper** & cp. **sop. 1.** A clear or thick liquid food, made by boiling down bones, meat, or vegetables in water, variously seasoned and served hot or, more rarely, cold; usually distinguished by the name of its principal ingredient, as *pea soup, turtle soup* &c. Phr. (slang) *in the soup*, in trouble, in a fix. **2.** (legal slang) Certain briefs at the Central Criminal Court, the Old Bailey, distributed in rotation among the junior barristers.

soupçon, n. [1. sóopson; 2. súpsɔ̃]. Fr., 'suspicion; slight trace', see **suspicion**. A suspicion, suggestion, mere trace, or taste, of anything, material or non-material: *a soupçon of garlic is the making of a salad*; *a soupçon of humour will enliven the driest of lectures*.

soup-kitchen, n. Public charitable institution where soup and other food is supplied free among the poor in times of distress.

soup-plate, n. Plate with deep centre for serving soup.

soup-ticket, n. Ticket entitling a person to obtain soup &c. from a soup-kitchen.

sour (I.), adj. [1. sour; 2. sauə]. O.E. *sūr*, M.E. *soure*; O.H.G. *sūr*, Mod. Germ. *sauer*; Du. *zuur*; O.N. *sūrr* &c.; cogn. w. Lith. *súrus*, 'salt to the taste', O. Slav. *syrŭ*, 'rough, raw'; possibly cogn. w. Lat. *rūta*, 'a bitter herb', & *rumex*, 'sorrel', if fr. **srū-*, & Gk. *rhuté*, 'a bitter herb'; cp. also **sorrel (II.)**. **1.** (of taste or smell) **a** Acid, acrid, sharp, tart to the taste, as vinegar, lemon juice, unripe fruit &c.; **b** (of milk) rancid, turned. **2.** (of the temper &c.) Morose, cross, crabbed, disagreeable, bitter, acrimonious: *sour looks*; *a sour temper* &c.; also of persons, *a sour old maid*. **3.** (of soil) Poor, cold, and damp; impoverished, unproductive.

sour (II.), n., fr. prec. That which is sour; esp. fig. that which is unpleasant or bitter, in Phr. *to take the sweet with the sour*, accept all the changes and chances of life as they come.

sour (III.), vb. trans. & intrans. See **sour (I.)**. **1.** trans. **a** To turn, make sour, acid, or rancid: *thunder will sour beer, milk* &c.; **b** (fig.) to make morose and gloomy; to render unhappy: *a temper soured by disappointments*. **2.** intrans. To become sour or rancid: *milk sours quickly in heat* (also fig.).

source, n. [1. sors; 2. sɔ̄s]. M.E. *sours*, fr. O. Fr. *sorse, surse* (later & Mod. Fr. *source*), fem. of *sors*, P.P. of *sordre*, 'to rise', fr. Lat. *surgere*, see **surge**. **1. a** The point at which a river or stream rises; the fount; a spring at its rising point; **b** (poet.) a stream, a rill, generally. **2.** The starting-point, place of origin of anything, esp. when regarded as the cause: *literature is a source of endless pleasure to many thousands*; *the sources of political unrest are often obscure*. **3. a** Documents or other means of knowledge from which information, esp. historical, is directly derived: *sources of knowledge*; *historical sources*; **b** literary works which have supplied later poets with inspiration, models, plots &c.: *many of Chaucer's sources are to be sought in France and Italy*.

source-book, n. Collection of historical documents of primary authority as sources of our knowledge of certain events, transactions &c.

sourdine, n. See **sordine**.

sourish, adj. [1. sóurish; 2. sáuəriʃ]. **sour (I.)** & **-ish**. Somewhat, tending to become, sour.

sourly, adv. [1. sóurli; 2. sáuəli]. See prec. & **-ly**. In a sour manner; chiefly (fig.) with ill-temper, morosely: *he looked sourly on the merriment of others*.

sourness, n. [1. sóurnes; 2. sáuənis]. See prec. & **-ness**. Condition, quality, of being sour.

souse (I.), n. [1. sous; 2. saus]. In M.E. fr. O. Fr. *sause*. See **sauce**. **1. a** Salt pickle; **b** something steeped in such pickle, as herrings, pigs' trotters &c. **2. a** A soaking, drenching with water or other liquid: *to get a thorough souse in a thunderstorm*; **b** a plunge, dip into water &c.; a ducking: *pitch him into the pond and give him a souse*.

souse (II.), vb. trans., fr. prec. **1.** To pickle, steep in souse: *soused herring* &c. **2. a** To soak, drench with water &c.: *we were soused to the skin*; **b** to plunge, duck in water: *souse him thoroughly in the pond*.

souse (III.), vb. intrans., fr. O. Fr. *sorse*, 'swoop, spring', fr. *sordre*, 'to rise'. See **source**. (obs. or archaic) Of bird &c., to swoop, spring upwards or downwards.

souse (IV.), adv., fr. prec. but confused w. **souse (I.)**. Down with a plunge, with a splash: *to fall souse into the water*.

soused, adj. [1. soust; 2. saust], fr. P.P. of **souse (II.)**. (slang) Drunk, half-seas over, pickled.

soutane, n. [1. sóotáhn; 2. sūtán]. Fr., in O. Fr. *sotane*, fr. Med. L. Lat. *subtāneus*, also L. Lat. *subtāna*, 'under garment', fr. *sub*, 'beneath', see **sub-**. Long black outer garment resembling a cassock, worn as walking dress by Roman Catholic priests in France and other foreign countries.

souteneur, n. [1. sóotenër; 2. sūtənʌ̄]. Fr., 'supporter, protector'; also specif. in sense below. Man who lives on the immoral earnings of a woman; a bully.

south (I.), n. [1. south; 2. sauþ]. O.E. *sūð*, adj. for **sunð*, *sūða*, n., *sūðan*, adv.; M.E. *sūþ*, *south*; O.N. *sunnr*, *sūðr*; O.H.G. *sund*, adj., *sundan*, n. & adv; Germ. *süd*; Du. *zuid*; prob. fr. same base as **sun**. **1.** One of the four cardinal points of the compass; the point facing one, N. of the equator, when turned towards the sun at midday; the point opposite to the north. **2.** The southern hemisphere; the Antarctic regions; southern parts of the earth generally; also people living in southern regions of the globe: *the tropical south*; '*bright and fierce and fickle is the south*' (Tennyson). **3.** That part of a country, town, district &c. which lies south of a specified line or towards the south: *the south of England, of France* &c.; *the Solid South*, the Southern States of U.S.A., which seceded in 1862 at Civil War, usually voting for Democratic party.

south (II.), adj., fr. prec. **1. a** Situated at, lying in or towards, the south; southern: *the south country*, southern part of England &c.; so *south countryman*; *south latitudes*; *the South Pole*; **b** directed towards the south, facing south: *a south aspect, window* &c.; *south side*, of church, that side which is on the right hand of one looking towards the altar; the Epistle side; **c** coming from the south: *a south wind*. **2.** In combination (cap.), as part of the name of the southern part of a sea, country, district &c., or of peoples living in the South: *South Atlantic*; *South America*; *South Africans*; *to live in South London*; *the South Seas*, Pacific Ocean; *the South Downs*, the chalk hills of Sussex; also applied to the Hampshire downs.

south (III.), adv., see **south (I.)**. Towards the south, in a southerly direction: *to sail, go south*.

south (IV.), vb. intrans., fr. prec. **1.** To move, go, towards the south or in a southerly direction, esp. of ships. **2.** (of the moon) To cross the meridian.

Southdown, adj. & n. [1. sóuthdoun; sáuþdaun]. See **south (II.)**, **2**. **1.** adj. Pertaining to a breed of sheep of the South Downs of Sussex and Hampshire: *Southdown mutton*. **2.** n. A Southdown sheep: *flock of Southdowns*.

south-east, southeast, also **sou'east**, n., adj., & adv. [1. sóu(th) ést; 2. sáu(þ) íst]. **1.** n. Point of the compass half-way between due south and east; region, district &c. towards this point: *the south-east of London*; *south-east by east* or *by south*, one point east or south of due south-east. **2.** adj. **a** Situated in or towards the south-east, facing, directed towards the south-east: *south-east London, aspect* &c.; **b** coming from the south-east: *a south-east wind*. **3.** adv. Towards the south-east: *to sail south-east*.

south-easter, n. [1. sòuth éster; 2. sàuþ ístə]. Prec. & **-er**. A strong wind blowing from the south-east.

south-easterly, adj. & adv. Prec. & **-ly**. **1.** adj. **a** Situated in or towards, pertaining to the south-east; **b** coming from the south-east: *south-easterly wind*. **2.** adv. In a south-easterly direction, towards the south-east.

south-eastern, adj. **south** & **eastern**. Situated in, pertaining to, the south-east.

south-eastward, adj., adv., & n. **south** & **eastward**. **a** adj. Situated in or towards the south-east; **b** adv., in a south-east direction; **c** n., the south-east.

south-eastwardly, adv. South-eastward.

southerly, adj. & adv. [1. súdherli; 2. sáðəli]. See next word & **-ly**. **1.** adj. **a** Toward the south: *a southerly course*; **b** coming from the south: *a southerly breeze*. **2.** adv. **a** Towards the south: *sail southerly*; **b** from the south: *wind blows southerly*.

southern, adj. [1. súdhern; 2. sáðən]. O.E. *sūðerne*, see **south (I.)**, & **-ern**. Pertaining to, situated in, characteristic of, the south: *Southern railway*; *Southern States of U.S.A.*; *Southern Cross*, bright constellation of the *Southern hemisphere*; *southern habits, customs*.

southerner, n. [1. súdherner; 2. sáðənə]. Prec. & **-er**. Person belonging to the south; specif., inhabitant of the Southern States of U.S.A.

southernmost, adj. [1. súdhernmōst; 2. sáðənmoust]. **southern** & **-most**. Most southern; farthest south.

southernwood, n. [1. súdhernwood; 2. sáðənwud]. O.E. *sūðerne wudu*; it first came from S. Europe. A shrubby plant, *Artemisia*, with scented leaves, allied to wormwood.

southing, n. [1. sóudhing; 2. sáuðiŋ]. **south (I.)** & **-ing**. (of ships) Difference in latitude south from last point of reckoning.

south-polar, adj. **south** & **polar**. Antarctic: *south-polar regions, exploration* &c.

southron, n. [1. súdhrun; 2. sáðrən]. Variant of **southern**. (archaic) Inhabitant of a southern part of a country, one who lives south of one, a southerner, esp. applied by the Scots to the English.

south-south-east, n., adj., & adv. [1. sóu(th) sou(th) ést; 2. sáu(þ) sau(þ) íst]. (In or towards) direction, point, midway between south and south-east.

south-south-west, n., adj., & adv. [1. sóu(th) sou(th) wést; 2. sáu(þ) sau(þ) wést]. (In or towards) direction, point, midway between south and south-west.

southward, southwards, adv., adj., & n. [1. sóuthward(z); 2. sáuþwəd(z)]. O.E. *sūðweard*; **south (I.)** & **-ward**; *-s* is advbl. Toward the south; southerly: *sailing southward(s)*; *take a southward direction*; *to the southward*.

southwardly, adv. [1. súdherdli; 2. sáðədli]. Prec. & **-ly**. Southward, southerly.

southwards, adv. Variant of **southward**.

south-west, southwest, also **sou'west**, n., adj., & adv. [1. sòu(th) wést; 2. sàu(þ) wést]. **1.** n. Point of the compass half-way between due south and west; region, district, towards this point: *in the south-west of London*; *south-west by west* or *by south*, one point west or south of due south-west. **2.** adj. Situated in or towards the south-west, facing or coming from the south-west: *the south-west district*; *a south-west aspect, wind* &c. **3.** adv. Towards the south-west.

southwester, sou'wester, n. [1. sóu(th)wéster; 2. sáu(þ)wéstə]. Prec. & **-er**. **1.** A strong south-west wind. **2.** (always *sou'wester*) A waterproof hat with broad flap behind to protect the neck, worn by sailors &c. in stormy and wet weather.

south-westerly, sou'westerly, adv. & adj. Prec. & **-ly**. Towards or from the south-west.

south-western, adj. [1. sòu(th) wéstern; 2. sàu(þ) wéstən]. **south** & **western**. Situated in, pertaining to, the south-west.

south-westward(s), adv., adj., & n. [1. sóu(th) wéstward(z); 2. sáu(þ) wéstwəd(z)]. **a** adv. In a south-west direction; **b** adj., situated in or toward the south-west; **c** n., the south-west.

souvenir, n. [1. sóovenër; 2. sūvəníə]. Fr., fr. vb. *souvenir*, 'to remember', fr. Lat. *subvenīre*, 'to come up in, recur to, the mind'; see **sub-** & **venue**. An object preserved, or serving, as a reminder or memento of a place, event &c., keepsake.

sovereign (I.), adj. [1. sóvrin; 2. sɔ́vrin], fr. O. Fr. & M.E. *soverain*; later spelling influenced by **reign**; fr. L. Lat. *superānus*, 'chief, principal', fr. Lat. *super*, 'above', see **super-**. **1.** Supreme, superior to others, paramount, chief: *sovereign authority, power, rights.* **2.** Possessing, wielding, supreme power and dominion; royal, reigning: *a sovereign prince; a sovereign state,* one exercising supreme, independent, unlimited power and jurisdiction within its own territories. **3.** Excellent; efficacious, effectual to a high degree: *a sovereign remedy.*

sovereign (II.), n., fr. prec. **1. a** One who exercises supreme rule; a monarch, king, emperor; **b** (in political science or jurisprudence) a sovereign State; the body or person in whom sovereign power is vested and by whom it is exercised. **2.** A gold coin of Great Britain, value 20 shillings, £1 sterling; *half-sovereign,* smaller gold coin, value 10s.; both so called from the sovereign's head on the obverse.

sovereignty, n. [1. sóvrinti; 2. sɔ́vrinti], fr. O. Fr. *souveraineté.* See prec. & **-ty. 1.** State, position, of holding and exercising sovereign power; state of being a sovereign. **2. a** Supreme, sovereign power in a State; **b** power exercised over other States.

soviet, n., Engl. pronunc. [1. sóviet; 2. sɔ́viet], Russ. [1. suvyét; 2. savjét], 'council'. A council of workers and soldiers, the political unit of the Communist, proletarian (Bolshevik) federated republic of Russia, the official title of which is *the Union of Soviet Socialist Republics,* U.S.S.R.

sovietism, n. [1. sóvietizm; 2. sɔ́vietizəm]. Prec. & **-ism.** Principles, system, of government by Soviets or workers' councils; Bolshevism.

sovietist, n. [1. sóvietist; 2. sɔ́vietist]. See prec. & **-ist.** Supporter, adherent, of Sovietism.

sovietize, vb. trans. [1. sóvietīz; 2. sɔ́vietaiz]. **soviet** & **-ize.** To give the form of a soviet to a government.

sovran, adj. [1. sóvran; 2. sɔ́vrən]. Archaic form and spelling of **sovereign (I.).** Sovereign, esp. in sense of effectual, efficacious: *sovran remedies.*

sow (I.), n. [1. sou; 2. sau]. O.E. *sugu, sū*, M.E. *sūwe, sowe*; O.H.G. *sū*; O.N. *sýr*; cogn. w. Lat. *sūs*; Gk. *hûs* or *sûs*; Ir. *suig*; fr. Aryan base **su-*, 'to bring forth, produce'. See also **son** & **swine. 1.** A fully grown female pig. Proverb. Phrs. *to take, get, the wrong sow by the ear,* (i.) to attribute an action, mistake &c. to the wrong person; (ii.) to settle on the wrong thing as the cause; *you cannot make a silk purse out of a sow's ear,* it is impossible to make a good thing, or get a good result, from bad or poor materials; esp., impossible to make a rough, ill-bred person into a polished gentleman. **2. a** One of the large or main channels or moulds into which molten metal, as iron, is run, the smaller branches being styled 'pigs'; **b** large bar of iron cast in such channel or mould; any bar of cast iron larger than a 'pig'. **3.** A movable covering for besiegers in attacking a wall in ancient warfare.

sow (II.), vb. trans. & intrans. [1. sō; 2. sou]. O.E. *sāwan*, M.E. *sōwen*; O.H.G. *sāwen*, O.N. *sā*; Goth. *saian*; cogn. w. Lat. *sēmen*, 'seed', see **semen**; cp. also **seed** & cognates there referred to. **A.** trans. **1. a** To scatter, cast (seed or specific kind of seed) on the ground so that it shall grow and produce: *to sow seed in autumn and spring; sow wheat, oats* &c. Phrs. *to sow one's wild oats,* indulge in youthful follies before settling down in life; *to sow the wind and reap the whirlwind,* to find that one's actions produce a greater and more violent result than one anticipated or desired; **b** (fig.) *to sow the seeds of (hatred, revolution* &c.), to spread abroad, disseminate, inculcate &c. **2.** To scatter, cast, seed upon; to plant with seed: *to sow a field with wheat; sow a garden with annuals.* **3.** Only in P.P.: *sown with pearls,* thickly studded or embroidered with; *a sky sown with stars,* densely bespangled. **B.** intrans. To perform the act of sowing seed: *not yet time to sow.* Phr. *as a man sows, so he shall reap,* our own actions determine the future course of our lives for good or ill.

sowar, n. [1. sowár; 2. səwā́]. Pers. & Hind. *sāwar*, 'rider'. A trooper of native Indian cavalry; a mounted orderly; member of a mounted escort.

sow-bread, n. **sow (I.)** & **bread.** Popular name of the wild cyclamen.

sower, n. [1. sóer; 2. sóuə]. **sow (II.)** & **-er. a** One who sows seed: '*a sower went forth to sow his seed*'; **b** (fig.) one who spreads, disseminates: *a sower of discord.*

sowing, n. [1. sóing; 2. sóuiŋ]. **sow (II.)** & **-ing. a** Act, process, of scattering seed in the ground; **b** that which is sown; seed.

sown, vb. [1. sōn; 2. soun]. O.E. *(ġe)sāwen*; M.E. *sōwe(n)*; P.P. of **sow (II.).**

sow-thistle, n. **sow (I.)** & **thistle.** Popular name for various species of a perennial or annual wild herb or plant, genus *Sonchus*, with spiked leaves, yellow flowers, and milky juice.

soy, n. [1. soi; 2. sɔi]. Jap. *shōyū*, 'sauce from soya-bean', fr. Chin. *shi*, 'beans', & *yin*, 'oil'. A Chinese and Japanese sauce for fish made from fermented soya-beans pickled in brine.

soya-, soy-bean, n. [1. sóia, sói, bēn; 2. sóiə, sói, bīn], fr. prec. An Asiatic leguminous plant, the beans of which yield a rich oil, which is used in making margarine, and also an oil-cake for feeding cattle.

spa, n. [1. spah, spaw; 2. spā, spɔ̄], fr. Spa, town in Belgium. **1.** Health resort having a mineral spring. **2.** Mineral spring.

space (I.), n. [1. spās; 2. speis], fr. O. Fr. *espace*, fr. Lat. *spatium*, 'space, room, extent, distance'; cp. Scrt. *sphāyati*, 'increases'; O. Slav. *spěją*, 'to be successful'; *spěšiti*, 'to hasten'; Lett. *spēt*, 'to be able'; *spēks*, 'power'; O.H.G. *spuot*; O.S. *spōd*; O.E. *spēd*, 'success', see **speed**; cp. also Gk. *spáein*, 'to draw, draw out', see **spasm**; *spádion*, 'racecourse'; fr. Aryan base **spē(i)-*, **spə(i)-*, **sphē-* &c., 'to stretch out, extend in time or space'. See **spadix, span, spathe. 1.** One of the conditions of material existence, characterized by dimension; limitless extension considered with or without reference to what it contains: *our existence is governed by conditions of time and space.* **2.** A portion of extension; interval between two or more objects; distance: *a space of 100 yards; not enough space between the houses; an open space; an enclosed space.* **3.** Specif. (print.) **a** blank interval between words; **b** the type which effects this. **4.** (mus.) Interval between the lines on a score. **5.** Portion, interval, duration, of time: *to live in London for a space; the space of a month* &c.

space (II.), vb. trans. & intrans., fr. prec. **1.** trans. To set, place, arrange, with space(s) between: *to space men in a line, lines of type, words in line of type* &c. **2.** intrans. *Space out,* (print.) to arrange with specially large spaces between: *to space out words, head-lines* &c.

space-bar, n. Flat bar in typewriter &c. pressed down to make a space between words &c.

space-key, n. Key taking place of space-bar in typewriter &c.

spaceless, adj. [1. spā́sles; 2. spéislis]. **space (I.)** & **-less.** Having no space, deficient in space.

spacer, n. [1. spā́ser; 2. spéisə]. **space (II.)** & **-er.** One who, that which, spaces; specif. **a** space-bar; **b** instrument for reversing telegraphic current.

space-time, n. (phys.) An amalgamation of space and time into one system or continuum of four dimensions.

space-writer, n. Journalist &c. paid for articles according to the space they occupy in print.

space-writing, n. Journalistic articles paid for in proportion to the space they occupy.

spacial, adj. [1. spā́shal; 2. spéiʃəl]. Variant of **spatial.**

spacing, n. [1. spā́sing; 2. spéisiŋ]. **space (II.)** & **-ing. 1.** Act, method, of placing or arranging with fixed or suitable spaces between, arrangement at intervals. **2.** Space between words, lines &c. in printing &c.

spacious, adj. [1. spā́shus; 2. spéiʃəs], fr. Fr., fr. Lat. *spatiōs-(us)*, 'roomy, ample, extensive', fr. *spati-(um)*, 'space', see **space (I.),** & **-ous. 1.** Of large or considerable extent, affording ample space; extensive, roomy: *a spacious plain, hall, realm* &c. **2.** (fig.) Of great capacity, breadth; ample; not narrow, limited, or restricted: *of spacious intellect.*

spaciously, adv. Prec. & **-ly.** In a spacious manner.

spaciousness, n. See prec. & **-ness.** State or quality of being spacious; ample room.

spadassin, n. [1. spádasin; 2. spǽdəsin], fr. Fr., fr. Ital. *spadacchino*, fr. Lat. *spatha*, 'spade', see **spathe.** Man expert in swordsmanship, esp. one making use of his skill in acts of violence; bravo.

spade (I.), n. [1. spād; 2. speid]. O.E. *spadu*; M.E. *spāde*; cp. O.S. *spado*; cogn. w. Gk. *spáthē*, 'flat wooden instrument', see **spathe.** Cp. also Gk. *spidés*, 'long, extensive'; fr. Aryan base **spēi-*, **spəi-*, **spī-*, 'to press or stretch out, extend'; see **space (I.). 1.** Tool, used for digging, with broad, nearly flat blade of metal with sharpish edge, attached to long handle; similarly shaped implement of wood, esp. one of small size used by children at the seaside. Phr. *to call a spade a spade,* speak plainly and unambiguously; to call things by their right names. **2.** Flat-bladed tool resembling a spade; specif. **a** spade-like tool for breaking ice; **b** tool used in cutting cameos; **c** instrument for cutting whale's blubber.

spade (II.), vb. trans., fr. prec. To dig or cut with a spade.

spade (III.), n., fr. Span. *espada*, 'sword', fr. Lat. *spatha*, 'spade; broad two-edged sword', see **spathe.** (cards) **1. a** Conventional representation of a spade, consisting of a black heart-shaped figure with projection below, as distinctive mark on playing-card; **b** card bearing one or more of these marks: *to lead a spade.* **2.** (usually pl.) Suit of cards marked with spade(s): *spades are trumps.*

spade (IV.), n., fr. **spado.** Castrated animal, gelding.

spade-bayonet, n. Broad-bladed bayonet used as tool and weapon.

spade-bone, n. Shoulder-blade, scapula.

spade-foot, n. Kind of toad with spade-like projection on hind feet used for burrowing.

spadeful, n. [1. spā́dfool; 2. spéidful]. **spade (I.)** & **-ful.** Amount taken up by, and contained in, a spade.

spade-guinea, n. Guinea issued 1787–99, having on the reverse a shield shaped like spade on a playing-card.

spade-husbandry, n. Method of cultivation in which deep digging is substituted for subsoil ploughing.

spade-work, n. (fig.) Laborious, detailed work, drudgery, necessary as the basis of higher, constructive work.

spadger, n. [1. spájer; 2. spǽdžə], fr. **sparrow.** (slang) Sparrow.

spadiceous, adj. [1. spādíshus; 2. speidíʃəs], fr. Lat. *spādic-*, stem of *spādix*, 'broken branch'. See **spadix** & **-eous.** (bot.) Of, having, of the nature of, a spadix.

spadicose, adj. [1. spā́dikōs; 2. spéidikous], fr. Lat. *spādic-*, stem of **spadix, & -ose.** Spadiceous.

spadille, n. [1. spadíl; 2. spədíl], fr. Fr., fr. Span. *espadilla*, dimin. of *espada*, 'spade', see **spade (III.).** Ace of spades in ombre or quadrille.

spadix, n. [1. spā́diks; 2. spéidiks]. Lat. *spādix*, 'broken palm-branch with its fruit', fr. Gk. *spā́dix*; cp. Gk. *spáein*, 'to tear away, rend'; *spásma*, 'spasm, convulsion', see **spasm**; *spadṓn*, 'eunuch'; *spádion*, 'race-course'; fr. Aryan base **spē(i)*-, **spə(i)*- &c., 'to spread or stretch out', see **space, spade (I.), speed, span.** Spike of flowers round a fleshy axis, usually wholly or partially surrounded by a spathe.

spado, n. [1. spā́dō; 2. spéidou], fr. Lat. *spado*, fr. Gk. *spadṓn*, 'eunuch', fr. *spá-(ein)*, 'to tear, destroy'. See **spadix.** Person incapable of procreation.

spaghetti, n. [1. spagéti; 2. spagéti]. Ital., pl. of *spaghetto*, dimin. of *spago*, 'cord', fr. its appearance. Kind of thin macaroni.

spahi, spahee, n. [1. spáhhē; 2. spáhi], fr. Fr. *spahi*, fr. Turk., fr. Pers. *sipahi*, 'soldier', see **sepoy. 1.** Member of Turkish irregular cavalry corps founded in 14th cent. and disbanded in 1835. **2.** Member of native Algerian cavalry corps in French army.

spake, vb. [1. spāk; 2. speik]. Archaic or obs. Pret. of **speak.** M.E. *spāk(e)*, fr. earlier *spak*, O.E. *sp(r)æc*, w. vowel lengthened through the influence of the infin., Pret. pl., & P.P., all of wh. had long vowels in M.E.

spalder, n. [1. spáwlder; 2. spɔ́ldə]. M.E. *spald-(en)*, 'to split', see **spall (II.)** & **-er.** Man employed in spalling stone or ore.

spall (I.), n. [1. spawl; 2. spɔl], fr. next word. Flake, chip, splinter, esp. of stone.

spall (II.), vb. trans. & intrans. M.E. *spalden*, 'to chip, split'; cp. Germ. *spalten*, 'to split'; M. Du. *spalden*; O.N. *spjald*, 'plank'; Goth. *spilda*, 'writing-tablet'; Scrt. *sphatáti*, 'tears'; Gk. *sphélas*, 'block of wood'; prob. cogn. w. Lat. *pellis*, 'skin', orig. 'flayed skin'. See **pellicle. A.** trans. **1.** To break up roughly in preparation for sorting: *to spall ore.* **2.** To give preliminary dressing to: *to spall stone.* **B.** intrans. **1.** To spall ore. **2.** (of stone) To splinter, chip.

spalpeen, n. [1. spáwlpēn; 2. spɔ́lpín]. Ir. *spailpīn*, 'rascal', fr. *spailp*, 'dandy; pride, conceit'; cp. *spailp*, 'to strut'. Rascal, ne'er-do-well.

spalt, n. [1. spawlt; 2. spɔlt], fr. Germ., fr. *spalten*, 'to split', q.v. under **spall (II.)** Scaly mineral used in fusing metals.

span (I.), vb. trans. & intrans. [1. span; 2. spæn]. O.E. *spannan*, 'to clasp, enfold, fasten, stretch'; M.E. *spannen*; cp. O.H.G. *spannan*; O.H.G. *spanna*; O.E. *spann*, 'span, measure'; O.N. *spǫnn*; Du. *spannen*, 'to span; fasten'; fr. same base as **space. A.** trans. **1.** To stretch thumb and finger(s) around or across for measurement &c.; to encircle: *to span one's wrist.* **2.** To measure, determine, breadth of: *his eye spanned the intervening space.* **3. a** To cross, extend over, stretch across: *the bridge spans the river*; hence, **b** (fig.) to extend over, cover: *imagination will span the gap in our knowledge.* **4.** (naut.) To fasten with ropes; esp. *to span a boom.* **B.** intrans. (of span-worm &c.) To advance by a series of contractions and extensions.

span (II.), n. O.E. *spann*, 'span'. See prec. **1. a** Distance between tip of thumb and tip of little finger when hand is fully extended; **b** average span as measure, 9 inches; **c** (fig.) short period or distance: *how brief is the span of human life.* **2. a** Extreme measurement, full extent, length from end to end: *the span of one's arms, of a bridge, girder* &c.; **b** specif., extreme lateral measurement of an aeroplane from tip to tip; **c** (fig.) the whole extent of a period of time: *his life had well-nigh completed its span.* **3.** Space between bases or supports of arch, abutments of bridge &c. **4.** (naut.) Rope fastened at both ends, leaving loop in centre free to take a purchase on. **5.** (U.S.A., S. Afr.) Pair or team of horses, mules, oxen &c.

spancel, vb. trans. [1. spánsl; 2. spǽnsl], fr. M. Du. *spansel*, fr. *spannen*, 'to stretch', see **span (I.).** To tether, hobble, hindlegs of, to prevent kicking while milking: *to spancel a cow.*

span-dogs, n. Pair of hooked bars used in hauling timber.

spandrel, n. [1. spándrel; 2. spǽndrəl], fr. O. Fr. *espandre*, q.v. under **expand,** & **-el. 1.** Triangular space between shoulder of arch and right angle of frame surrounding it. **2.** Triangular space between the curves of adjoining arches and a straight cornice &c. above them.

spandrel-wall, n. Wall built above arches and filling in spandrels between them.

spangle (I.), n. [1. spánggl; 2. spǽŋgl]. M.E. *spangel*, fr. O.E. *spang*, 'clasp, buckle'; cp. Germ. *spange*; perh. cogn. w. Gk. *sphíggein*, 'to bind'; *sphigktḗr*, 'band, bond', see **sphincter**; Lett. *spaiglis*, 'fork for catching crabs'; O.N. *spīkr*, 'nail'. See further **spica, spike, spile, spire. 1.** Very small, thin disc of brilliant metal, usually with hole in centre, attached to dress &c. for ornament. **2.** Hence, any small, esp. round, glistening object. **3.** (bot.) Small, spongy excrescence on oak-leaf.

spangle (II.), vb. trans., fr. prec. To adorn with, as with, spangles; to cover, sprinkle, with a number of shining objects: *a spangled scarf*; *grass spangled with dewdrops*; *the heavens spangled with stars.*

spangly, adj. [1. spánggli; 2. spǽŋgli]. **spangle (I.)** & **-y.** Of, like, adorned with, spangles.

Spaniard, n. [1. spányerd; 2. spǽnjəd], fr. M.E. *Spa(y)gn-(el)*, 'Spanish', w. change of suff.; cp. O. Fr. *espaignard.* See next word & **-ard.** Native of Spain.

spaniel, n. [1. spányel; 2. spǽnjəl]. M.E. *spa(i)gnel*, 'Spanish; spaniel', fr. O. Fr. *espagneul*; fr. Span. *español*, 'Spanish', fr. *España*, 'Spain', fr. Lat. *Hispānia.* Any of many closely related breeds of dogs, with long, silky hair and large, drooping ears. Phr. *a tame spaniel*, person who is at another's beck and call; a fawning flatterer.

Spanish, adj. & n. [1. spánish; 2. spǽniʃ]. M.E. *Spainisch*; fr. *Spain*, fr. Lat. *Hispānia*, & **-ish. 1.** adj. Of, pertaining to, coming from, Spain; *Spanish Armada*, see **Armada**; *Spanish bayonet*, kind of yucca; *Spanish broom*, Mediterranean shrub with showy yellow flowers; *Spanish black*, pigment obtained from charred cork; *Spanish brown*, dark reddish-brown earth used as pigment; *Spanish chalk*, kind of talc; *Spanish chestnut*, see **chestnut**; *Spanish fly*, kind of beetle from which cantharides, used for blistering, is obtained; *Spanish fowl*, breed of greenish-black domestic fowl; *Spanish grass*, esparto grass; *Spanish main*, see **main (I.). 2.** n. Language of Spain.

Spanish American, adj. & n. **1.** adj. Of, pertaining to, a part of America in which Spanish or a form of Spanish is spoken. **2.** n. Person of Spanish descent inhabiting Spanish America.

spank (I.), vb. trans. & intrans. [1. spangk; 2. spæŋk]. Cp. Dan. *spanke*, 'to strut'. **A.** trans. **1.** To strike, slap, smack, with open hand or other flat object, as punishment. **2.** To urge on, drive forward, esp. by slapping, striking, with flat object. **B.** intrans. *Spank along*, to move along swiftly; (of horses) to move with a brisk, spirited action.

spank (II.), n., fr. prec. Single slap with flat of hand &c.

spanker, n. [1. spángker; 2. spǽŋkə]. **spank (I.)** & **-er. 1.** One who, that which, spanks; specif. **a** a horse that moves with a fast, spirited, showy action; **b** (slang) a brilliant, spirited, striking person. **2.** (naut.) Fore-and-aft sail extended by spars from after side of mizzen-mast.

spanking (I.), n. [1. spángking; 2. spǽŋkiŋ]. **spank (I.)** & **-ing.** Series of slaps administered as punishment.

spanking (II.), adj., fr. Pres. Part. of **spank (I.). 1.** Brisk, rapid: *a spanking trot.* **2.** (slang) Fine, strong, striking; esp. *a spanking breeze.*

spanless, adj. [1. spánles; 2. spǽnlis]. **span (II.)** & **-less.** (poet.) Not capable of being spanned; measureless.

spanner, n. [1. spáner; 2. spǽnə]. **span (I.)** & **-er.** One of various tools for tightening or loosening nuts and bolts; a wrench.

span-roof, n. Roof with two slopes inclining towards a common ridge.

span-worm, n. Larva of geometer moth.

spar (I.), n. & vb. trans. [1. spar; 2. spā]. M.E. *sparre*, 'spar, beam, rafter'; cp. O.E. *spearrian*, 'to shut, bar'; O.N. *sparri*; O.H.G. *sparro*; M. Du. *sparre.* **1.** n. (naut.) Pole for supporting or extending sail(s); mast, yard, gaff &c. **2.** vb. **a** To furnish with, support on, a spar; **b** to take (a ship) over bar, through shallows &c., by means of spars and tackle.

spar (II.), n. O.E. *spær(stān)*, 'gypsum'; cp. O.E. *spæren*, 'chalky'; M.H.G. *spār*, 'gypsum'. One of various kinds of crystalline mineral; esp. *fluor-spar*, calcium fluoride; *Greenland spar*, cryolite; *Iceland spar*, transparent calcite used in making optical instruments.

spar (III.), vb. intrans., fr. O. Fr. *esparer* (of cock), 'to strike with spurs', prob. of Gmc. origin. See **spur. 1.** To fight with the fists; to box; *spar at*, to make motions with the fists towards (a person) as though about to strike. **2.** (fig.) To engage in dispute; to wrangle. **3.** (of cocks) To fight, esp. with protected spurs.

spar (IV.), n., fr. prec. **a** Act of sparring; boxing-match; **b** wordy dispute, quarrel, wrangling; **c** a cock-fight.

sparable, n. [1. spárabl; 2. spǽrəbl], fr. earlier *sparrow-bill*, fr. shape of nail. Small, headless nail used in shoemaking.

spar-buoy, n. Buoy consisting of, or supporting, vertical spar to indicate channel &c.

spar-deck, n. Upper deck of ship, including quarter-deck and forecastle.

spare (I.), adj. [1. spār; 2. spɛə]. O.E. *spær*, 'sparing, frugal'; M.E. *spāre*; cp. O.N. *sparr*; O.H.G. *spar*, 'frugal' &c.; O.E. *sparian*, 'to abstain from; to show **mercy** to'; formed fr. base **spa*-, **spō*-, **meaning** 'to prosper, succeed, promote advance' **&c.** See further under **speed. 1.** Not plentiful; scanty, meagre: *spare diet.* **2.** Lean, thin, having little flesh: *a spare form, frame.* **3.** In excess of absolute necessity, additional to what is in ordinary use; available at will, after usual requirements are fulfilled; *spare time*, leisure time, left over after discharge of duties or completion of other work; *spare cash*, that left after supplying one's needs, paying one's legal debts &c.; *spare wheel* (on motor-car), an extra, additional, wheel carried to take the place of one of those in use, in case of emergency; *spare parts*, extra parts of machine, esp. of a motor-car, kept in stock or reserve for replacement; *spare room, spare bed-room*, specif., room in a house unoccupied under ordinary circumstances and reserved for visitors; a guest-room.

spare (II.), vb. trans. & intrans. O.E. *sparian*, 'to show mercy to; abstain from; preserve'. See prec. **A.** trans. **1.** To refrain from using, to withhold use or expenditure of; to grudge: *to spare neither trouble nor expense.* Phr. *spare the rod and spoil the child*, discipline and punishment are necessary in the training of the young. **2.** To dispense with, do without; to lose use or services of; to afford: *could you spare a poor man a copper, sir?*; *a public servant of a kind that can ill be spared*; *I have no time to spare today.* Phr. *enough and to spare*, sufficient for all needs and something over. **3. a** To show mercy, leniency, consideration, to; to refrain from killing, injuring, destroying &c.: *the victorious enemy spared neither young nor old*; *he doesn't spare his dearest friends when he is roused*; Phrs. *spare my life*, don't kill me; *if we are spared* (i.e. by Providence), if we are still alive; **b** (i.) *to spare oneself*, to economize one's strength, reserve oneself for a later effort; to take things easily, not to exert oneself; (ii.) *not to spare oneself*, to be severe or exacting with oneself; to put forth all one's efforts, show great zeal in performance of a task; **c** to secure, preserve (a person) against, or from, some specified misfortune; to save from, protect from undergoing: *I want to spare you all the suffering I can*; *I will spare you the humiliation of a public exposure*; *pray spare me the tedium of hearing your story all over again.* **B.** intrans. **1.** To be frugal, practise economy. **2.** To exercise mercy, refrain from inflicting injury &c.

sparely, adv. [1. spárli; 2. spéəli]. **spare (I.)** & **-ly**. In a spare manner; scantily, meagrely.

spareness, n. [1. spárnes; 2. spéənis]. See prec. & **-ness**. State, quality, of being spare; leanness; scantiness.

sparerib, n. [1. spárrib, spárib; 2. spéərib, spǽrib]. Part of ribs of pork so trimmed that very little meat is left on the bones.

sparger, n. [1. spárjer; 2. spádžə], fr. rare or obs. *sparge*, 'to sprinkle', fr. Lat. *sparg-(ere)*, 'to scatter, sprinkle'; cogn. w. O.E. *spearca*, 'spark', see **spark (I.)**; O. Ir. *arg*, 'drop'; Scrt. *parjányaš*, 'rain'; Lith. *sproga*, 'spark'; Gk. *spargáein*, 'to swell'. See **asperges**, **asparagus**. Apparatus for sprinkling; specif. (brewing) machine for sprinkling hot water in mash-tub.

spar-hawk, n. [1. spár hawk; 2. spá hōk], fr. **sparrow-hawk**. Sparrow-hawk.

sparing, adj. [1. spáring; 2. spéəriŋ], fr. Pres. Part. of **spare (II.)**. Moderate, frugal, restricted; not copious or excessive: *a sparing use of alcohol*; *be sparing of your epithets in writing.*

sparingly, adv. Prec. & **-ly**. In a sparing manner, with restraint and moderation.

spark (I.), n. [1. spark; 2. spāk]. O.E. *spearca*; M.E. *sparke*; cp. M. Du., M.L.G. *sparke*; cp. also M. Du. *spranken*, 'to sparkle'; Lith. *sproga*, 'spark'; Lat. *spargere*, 'to scatter, sprinkle', see **sparger**; further cogn. w. O.E. *spræc*, 'shoot, twig'; O.E. *spræc*, O.N. *sprakr*, 'lively'; cp. Gk. *aspháragos*, see **asparagus**; perh. also O.E. *sprecan*, 'to speak, give forth utterance', see **speak**. **1.** Small glowing particle thrown off by a body in combustion or in a state of incandescence: *sparks fly out of the fire*; *to strike a spark from flint.* Phrs. *as the sparks fly upward*, in accordance with an irresistible tendency; *the vital spark*, life. **2.** (in various fig. senses) **a** Animating, kindling principle, germ: *the spark of life, of learning, religious zeal* &c.; **b** slight vestige, trace: *he showed not a spark of interest, intelligence* &c. **3.** **a** Light, brief flash accompanying an electric discharge; **b** (pl., naut. slang) wireless operator on a ship.

spark (II.), vb. intrans. O.E. *spearcian*, fr. *spearc-(a)*, 'spark'. See prec. **a** To give out sparks; **b** specif., to produce electric sparks and secure ignition.

spark (III.), n. & vb. intrans., fr. O.N. *sparkr*, 'lively'; cogn. w. **spark (I.)**. **1.** n. Gay, dashing fellow; **a** gallant, a beau: *a gay young spark.* **2.** vb. To play the spark.

spark-arrester, n. [1. spárk arésterr; 2. spák əréstə]. Device to prevent sparking in part of electric circuit when this is not desired.

sparking-plug, n. [1. spárking plùg; 2. spákiŋ plàg]. Device for securing electric ignition in an internal-combustion engine.

sparkish, adj. [1. spárkish; 2. spákiʃ]. **spark (III.)** & **-ish**. Like, having the character of, a spark; lively, gay; apt to make love.

sparkle (I.), vb. intrans. [1. spárkl; 2. spákl]. M.E. *sp(e)arclen*, freq. fr. **spark (I.)** & **-le**. **1.** To give forth shifting sparks of light; to flash, scintillate, coruscate: *a thousand gems, bright eyes, sparkled*; (of intellectual brilliance) *his wit, he, sparkles in society.* **2.** To give out bubbles of gas; to effervesce (of champagne &c.).

sparkle (II.), n. M.E. *sparcle*, fr. prec. Physical or intellectual scintillation, coruscation, shifting flash, glitter.

sparkler, n. [1. spárkler; 2. spáklə]. **sparkle (I.)** & **-er**. That which sparkles; **a** (thieves' slang) a diamond; **b** a brilliant, beautiful, showy person.

sparkless, adj. [1. spárkles; 2. spáklis]. **spark** & **-less**. Emitting no sparks.

sparklet, n. [1. spárklet; 2. spáklit]. **spark (I.)** & **-let**. **a** Small spark; **b** trade or proprietary name for small metal capsule filled with carbonic acid gas, used in conjunction with a special type of syphon for aerating water.

sparkling, adj. [1. spárkling; 2. spákliŋ]. **sparkle (I.)** & **-ing**. **1.** **a** Giving off sparks, flashing, glittering, scintillating; **b** intellectually brilliant. **2.** (of wines &c.) Giving out continuously small bubbles of gas; effervescing; contrasted with *still.*

sparklingly, adv. Prec. & **-ly**. In a sparkling manner.

sparring-match, n. [1. spáhring màch; 2. spáriŋ mæ̀tʃ]. Pres. Part. of **spar (III.)** & **match (I.)**. Boxing-match, esp. for exhibition or exercise.

sparring-partner, n. See prec. & **partner**. Boxer with whom professional boxer spars as part of training.

sparrow, n. [1. spárō; 2. spǽrou]. O.E. *spearwa*; M.E. *sparewe*; cp. Goth. *sparwa*; O.H.G. *sparo*; O.N. *spörr*, 'sparrow'; O.S. *sprā*, 'starling'; Lat. *parra*, 'a bird of ill omen'; Gk. *sporgílos*, 'sparrow'; *sparásion*, 'sparrow'; O. Prussian *spurglis*, 'sparrow'; cp. **spavin**. One of various small passerine birds, allied to the finches, with dull-coloured, plain, streaked, or speckled plumage; esp. *house-sparrow* (*Passer domesticus*), small brown kind found frequently in neighbourhood of human habitations; the *hedge-sparrow, Accentor modularis*, is not of the same family, but is allied to the thrushes.

sparrow-bill, n. Sparable.

sparrow-grass, n. By popular etymol. fr. **asparagus**. (vulg.) Asparagus.

sparrow-hawk, n. O.E. *spear-hafoc*. **sparrow** & **hawk**. Small species of hawk, *Accipiter nisus*, which hunts sparrows and other small birds as prey; it has shortish wings and a light grey barred breast.

sparry, adj. [1. spáhri; 2. spári]. **spar (II.)** & **-y**. Of, like, containing, abounding in, spar.

sparse, adj. [1. spars; 2. spās], fr. Lat. *spars-(um)*, P.P. type of *spargere*, 'to scatter', q.v. under **sparger**; prob. cogn. w. many words beginning w. *sp(r)-*. See also **asperges**, **spark**. Occurring here and there, singly, or in scattered groups; planted, growing, thinly; reverse of *dense, close*: *a sparse population*; *a sparse vegetation*; *a sparse beard.*

sparsely, adv. Prec. & **-ly**. In a sparse manner.

sparseness, n. See prec. & **-ness**. State of being sparse.

sparsity, n. [1. spársiti; 2. spásiti]. See prec. & **-ity**. Sparseness; scarcity, lack.

Spartacist (I.), n. [1. spártasist; 2. spátəsist], fr. *Spartac-(us)*, leader of army of slaves who rebelled against Rome in 73–71 B.C., & **-ist**. Adherent of Liebknecht, who adopted the pen-name of Spartacus, and was leader of the extreme revolutionary Socialist party organized in Germany in 1918.

Spartacist (II.), adj., fr. prec. Connected with, pertaining to, the Spartacists.

Spartan (I.), adj. [1. spártan; 2. spátən], fr. Lat. *Spartān-(us)*, 'of Sparta', fr. Lat. *Sparta*, fr. Gk. *Spártē*, capital of Laconia, the people of wh. were noted for their hardihood, endurance, & the simplicity of their lives. **1.** Of, pertaining to, Sparta or Laconia. **2.** Characteristic of, resembling, the Spartans: *Spartan courage, simplicity*; hence, austere, hardy; the reverse of luxurious: *a Spartan diet.*

Spartan (II.), n., fr. prec. **1.** Native, inhabitant, of Sparta, characterized by courage, severe discipline &c. **2.** (fig.) A hardy, robust, courageous person; one who lives a rigorous, austere, simple life.

spartein, sparteine, n. [1. spártiin, -ēn; 2. spátiin, -īn], fr. Mod. Lat. *sparta*, 'broom', fr. Gk. *spártos*, 'esparto grass'; cp. Gk. *speîra*, 'net, cordage'; cogn. w. Lith. *spartas*, 'thong'. See **spire (III.)**. Colourless, oily liquid obtained from the broom and used as a narcotic.

sparterie, n. [1. spárteri; 2. spátəri], fr. Fr., fr. Span. *espartería*. **esparto** & **-ery**. **a** Fabric woven from esparto grass; **b** mats, ropes &c. made from this fabric.

spasm, n. [1. spázm; 2. spǽzəm], fr. Fr. *spasme*, fr. Lat. *spasmus*, fr. Gk. *spasmós*, 'spasm, convulsion'; fr. *spá-(ein)*, 'to draw, drag, tear; to contract violently; to tear out', fr. base **spē(i)-*, **spə(i)-* &c., 'to stretch or press out, extend, prolong'. See also **space**, **span**, **speed** &c. **1.** Sudden, violent, involuntary contraction of the muscles. **2.** Sudden, violent, convulsive mental or physical reaction to shock, powerful emotion &c.: *a spasm of fear, pain* &c.

spasmodic, adj. [1. spazmódik; 2. spæzmódik], fr. Gk. *spasmōd-(ēs)*, 'of the nature of a spasm', fr. *spasm-(ós)*, 'spasm', see prec., **-oid**, & **-ic**. **1.** Characteristic of, characterized by, of the nature of, a spasm; convulsive: *spasmodic twitching of the limbs*; *spasmodic sobs* &c. **2.** Taking place, carried out, from time to time, at no fixed period, and by fits and starts; intermittent: *spasmodic attempts.*

spasmodical, adj. [1. spazmódikl; 2. spæzmódikl]. Prec. & **-al**. (rare) Spasmodic.

spasmodically, adv. Prec. & **-ly**. In a spasmodic manner.

spasmology, n. [1. spazmóloji; 2. spæzmólədži]. **spasm** & *-o-* & **-logy**. Branch of pathology dealing with spasms.

spastic, adj. [1. spástik; 2. spǽstik], fr. Gk. *spastik-(ós)*, 'afflicted with a spasm', fr. *spá-(ein)*, 'to tear, draw; to contract, convulse', see **spasm**. (med.) Spasmodic.

spasticity, n. [1. spastísiti; 2. spæstísiti]. Prec. & **-ity**. Tendency to spasms or to spasmodic action.

spat (I.), n., vb. intrans. & trans. [1. spat; 2. spæt]. Prob. cogn. w. **spit (III.)**. **1.** n. **a** Spawn of shellfish, esp. of oyster; **b** young oyster before it becomes fixed in position. **2.** vb. **a** intrans. (of oyster &c.) To spawn; **b** trans., to deposit (spawn).

spat (II.), n., abbr. of **spatterdashes**. Short gaiter of cloth &c. covering upper part of boot or shoe, buttoned a short way up the ankle, and strapped under the instep.

spat (III.), vb. O.E. *spǣtte*, fr. *spǣtan*, 'to spit', Pret. of **spit (III.)**.

spatchcock, n. & vb. trans. [1. spáchkok; 2. spǽtʃkɔk]. Either *dispatch-cock* or variant of **spitchcock**. **1.** n. (rare) Bird killed and cooked immediately in an emergency &c. **2.** vb. (colloq.) To interpolate, put in, as an afterthought, between or amongst other things &c.: *to spatchcock a sentence into a letter.*

spate, n. [1. spāt; 2. speit], fr. O. Fr. *espoit*, fr. Du. *spuiten*, 'to flow, flood, spout', cogn. w. **spout**. Flood, esp. sudden flood of river after rain, when it is said to be *in spate.*

spathaceous, adj. [1. spathā́shus; 2. spæþéiʃəs]. Next word & **-aceous**. **a** Having a spathe; **b** of the nature of, resembling, a spathe.

spathe, n. [1. spādh; 2. speið], fr. Lat. *spatha*, fr. Gk. *spáthē*, 'broad, flat wooden instrument for stirring &c.; broad, flat sword; spathe of palm tree'; cogn. w. O.E. *spadu*, see **spade**, & cognates given under **space**. Large leaf-like, single or double sheath surrounding flower-cluster, bract enfolding spadix.

spathic, adj. [1. spáthik; 2. spǽþik], fr. Mod. Germ. *spat(h)*, 'spar', M.H.G. *spāt*, possibly cogn. w. **spar (II.)**, & **-ic**. Of, resembling, of the nature of, spar.

spathiform, adj. [1. spáthifòrm; 2. spǽþifɔ̀m], fr. Germ. *spat(h)*, 'spar', see prec., & *-i-* & **-form**. Having the character or appearance of spar.

spathose (I.), adj. [1. spā́thōs; 2. spéiþous]. **spathe** & **-ose**. Of, pertaining to, of the nature of, a spathe.

spathose (II.), adj. [1. spáthōs; 2. spǽþous], fr. Mod. Germ. *spat(h)*, 'spar', see **spathic**, & **-ose**. Spathic.

spathous, adj. [1. spā́thus; 2. spéiþəs]. **spathe** & **-ous**. Spathose (I.).

spatial, adj. [1. spā́shal; 2. spéiʃəl], fr. Lat. *spati-(um)*, 'space', see **space**, & **-al**. Pertaining to, connected with, involving, space, or relations in space.

spatiality, n. [1. spāshiáliti; 2. spèiʃiǽliti]. Prec. & **-ity**. State of being spatial.

spatially, adv. [1. spā́shali; 2. spéiʃəli]. See prec. & **-ly**. In relation to space.

spatter (I.), vb. trans. & intrans. [1. spáter; 2. spǽtə]. Perh. fr. Du. *spatten*, 'to sprinkle'. **A.** trans. **1.** To sprinkle, splash, drops of liquid upon: *spattered with mud* &c. **2.** To splash, scatter, in drops: *to spatter water on a surface.* **3.** (fig.) To smirch, defame, reputation of. **B.** intrans. To fall, splash, in form of intermittent drops.

spatter (II.), n., fr. prec. Light splash, sprinkling; slight shower.

spatterdashes, n. pl. [1. spáterdàshez; 2. spǽtədæʃiz]. Prec. & **dash**. (obs.) Leggings worn as protection from rain, mud &c. (cp. **spat** (II.)).

spatula, n. [1. spátūla; 2. spǽtjulə]. Lat. *spat(h)ula*, dimin. of *spatha*, 'broad, flat instrument or weapon', see **spathe**, & **-ule**. Knife-like instrument with broad, usually flat, blade and often rounded end, used for mixing or spreading plaster, enamel, artist's pigments &c.

spatular, adj. [1. spátūlar; 2. spǽtjulə]. Prec. & **-ar**. Connected with, resembling, a spatula.

spatulate, adj. [1. spátūlàt; 2. spǽtjulèit]. Next word & **-ate**. Having the form of a spatula; specif. (bot., of leaf) having a narrow base and broad, rounded end.

spatule, n. [1. spátūl; 2. spǽtjūl], fr. Fr., fr. Lat. *spatula*. See **spatula**. (zool.) Spatulate formation.

spatuliform, adj. [1. spátūlifòrm; 2. spǽtjulifɔ̄m]. See **spatula** & *-i-* & **-form**. Having the shape of a spatula.

spavin, n. [1. spávin; 2. spǽvin]. M.E. *spaveine*, fr. O. Fr. *esparvin*, fr. Med. Lat. **sparvānus*, fr. O.H.G. *sparw-*, nom. *sparo*, 'sparrow', see **sparrow**, fr. jerky movement of spavined horse. Disease of hock-joint of horse; **a** *blood-, bog-spavin*, distension of joint with lymph &c.; **b** *bone-spavin*, stiffening of the joint through a morbid bony deposit.

spavined, adj. [1. spávind; 2. spǽvind]. Prec. & **-ed**. Affected with spavin.

spawn (I.), vb. trans. & intrans. [1. spawn; 2. spɔ̄n]. M.E. *spaunen*, fr. A.-Fr. *espaundre*, O. Fr. *espandre*, 'to expand', see **expand**. **A.** trans. **1.** (of fish, crustaceans, amphibians &c.) To produce, lay, deposit (eggs &c.). **2.** (contemptuously) To generate, bring forth as offspring: *the lowest types of humanity spawned in some reeking slum.* **B.** intrans. **1.** To produce spawn. **2.** (of young fish &c.) To be produced in the form of spawn.

spawn (II.), n., fr. prec. **1.** Eggs of fish, amphibians, crustaceans &c. **2.** (contemptuously) Offspring: *the spawn of the ghetto.* **3.** Thread-like substance from which mushrooms or other fungi are developed.

spawner, n. [1. spáwner; 2. spɔ̄nə]. **spawn** (I.) & **-er.** Female fish at spawning time.

spay, vb. trans. [1. spā; 2. spei], fr. Romance, fr. L. Lat. *spadāre*, 'to castrate', fr. *spado*, 'castrated person or animal', see **spado**. To remove ovaries of (female animal).

speak, vb. intrans. & trans. [1. spēk; 2. spīk]. O.E. *sp(r)ecan*; M.E. *spēken*; cp. O.H.G. *sprechan*; Du. *spreken*, 'to speak'. Gmc. is the only branch of Aryan speech wh. uses this word in the specialized sense of uttering language; the orig. & more general sense of the base was 'to start, spring, burst forth'; many cognates occur w. varying meanings; cp. further O.E. *spræc*, 'shoot of a plant'. See the words cited under **spark.** **A.** intrans. **1.** To make use of vocal language; to utter intelligible words and sentences without musical modulation of the voice; contrasted with *sing*: *the baby hasn't yet learnt to speak; to speak clearly; to speak in a whisper; he refused to speak; to teach a parrot to speak.* Phrs. *so to speak*, as one might say; *strictly, properly, speaking*, in the exact, true, sense of the words; *roughly speaking*, without strict accuracy as to detail; *to speak (a person) fair*, speak politely, or flatteringly, and reassuringly, to; *to speak for oneself*, (i.) to express one's own sentiments &c. in one's own way; (ii.) to express one's personal views which are different from those of others; (iii.) to speak only of what affects oneself; *I will now let Mr X speak for himself*, I won't anticipate what he is going to say; *speak for yourself*, don't include others in, or associate them with, what you have said; don't attribute such sentiments as you have uttered to them; *that speaks for itself*, is so clear, or so excellent, that it carries its own explanation, or justification &c. **2.** To address an audience, pronounce a discourse, harangue: *to speak in public; the president will now speak.* **3.** To express, convey, an idea, emotion, &c., be expressive, significant: *actions speak louder than words.* **4.** (of musical instrument) To produce sounds: *the trumpets spoke.* **B.** trans. **1.** To utter with the vocal organs: *to speak words of wisdom.* Phr. *to speak volumes (for)*, be very significant (of). **2.** To convey, express, make known, in words: *to speak the truth.* Phr. *to speak one's mind*, say exactly what one thinks. **3.** To express oneself in, use as medium of oral expression: *to speak French, Standard English; to speak several languages.* **4.** (archaic) To bespeak, show, indicate, proclaim, be significant, afford evidence of the fact: *his action speaks him a rogue.* **5.** (naut.) To hail for the purpose of communicating with: *to speak a ship.* **C.** Followed by adverb or preposition. *Speak for*, to speak, give evidence on behalf of: *to speak well for*, witness favourably to. *Speak of*, to mention in speaking, talk about; Phr. *nothing to speak of*, nothing worth mentioning. *Speak out*, **a** to speak, produce the voice, clearly and distinctly; **b** to speak freely, without fear of consequences &c. *Speak to*, **a** to address or converse with; **b** to witness, testify to, to attest. *Speak up*, to speak loudly and distinctly.

speak-easy, n. [1. spḗk ḕzi; 2. spík ìzi]. (U.S.A. slang) Illicit drinking-place.

speaker, n. [1. spḗker; 2. spíkə]. **speak** & **-er.** One who speaks; **a** person actually engaged in speaking: *the voices of (the) speakers in the next room could be faintly heard*; **b** (i.) one who speaks in public; a maker of speeches: *a poor, a timid, speaker* &c.; (ii.) a good speaker, an orator: *he is a good administrator but no speaker*; specif. **c** (cap.) *the Speaker*, presiding officer in British House of Commons; addressed in the House as *Mr. Speaker*; similar officer in U.S. House of Representatives and other legislative assemblies.

speakership, n. [1. spḗkership; 2. spíkəʃip]. Prec. & **-ship.** Office, tenure of office, of Speaker.

speaking, adj. [1. spḗking; 2. spíkiŋ], fr. Pres. Part. of **speak.** **1.** Used in, adapted for, ordinary speech, as distinct from singing: *a good speaking voice.* **2.** Various special uses: **a** *speaking acquaintance*, formal acquaintance, sufficient to admit of conversation; **b** *not on speaking terms*, (i.) not having a speaking acquaintance with; (ii.) having quarrelled with, renounced acquaintance of; **c** *a speaking knowledge of a language*, one enabling one to speak it. **3.** Very expressive: *a speaking look; a speaking likeness*, lifelike portrait.

speaking-trumpet, n. Instrument for collecting and intensifying the tones of the voice: **a** for enabling a deaf person to hear; **b** for enabling the voice to carry to a distance.

speaking-tube, n. Tube through which the voice can be heard, carried along or through walls and floors, from one part of a building to another; short tube passing from the inside to the outside of a closed carriage or motor-car, enabling the occupants to speak with the driver.

spear (I.), n. [1. spēr; 2. spiə]. O.E. *spere*; M.E. *spēre*; cp. M. Du. *spere*; O.H.G. *sper*; cogn. w. Lat. *sparus*, 'short hunting-spear'; perh. orig. 'something thrown or tossed forward'; cp. Lat. *spernere*, 'to push away, reject'; O.E. *spurnan*, 'to strike with the foot, kick away', see **spurn.** **1.** Weapon with sharply pointed, usually metal, head and wooden shaft, used in hunting or fighting, for throwing or stabbing. Phr. (archaic) *spear side*, male branch of family, contrasted with *distaff* or *spindle side.* **2.** Man armed with spear.

spear (II.), vb. trans. & intrans., fr. prec. **1.** trans. **a** To pierce, stab, with spear; **b** to catch with spear: *to spear fish.* **2.** intrans. (of plant) To develop a long tapering shoot.

speargrass, n. [1. spḗrgrahs; 2. spíəgrās]. One of various kinds of meadow grass.

spearhead, n. [1. spḗrhed; 2. spíəhed]. Pointed metal or flint head for spear.

spearman, n. [1. spḗrman; 2. spíəmən]. Man armed with spear.

spearmint, n. [1. spḗrmint; 2. spíəmint]. Aromatic herb of Europe &c., common garden mint.

spear-thistle, n. Purple-flowered thistle.

spear-thrower, n. Instrument used by primitive races for hurling a spear; throwing-stick.

spearwort, n. [1. spḗrwẽrt; 2. spíəwʌt]. One of several varieties of crow's-foot with long tapering leaves.

spec, n. [1. spek; 2. spek]. Abbr. fr. **speculation.** Phr. *on spec*, as a speculation, on the chance of a successful result.

special (I.), adj. [1. spéshl; 2. spéʃl], fr. O. Fr. *(e)special*, fr. Lat. *speciāl-(is)*, 'individual, particular', fr. *speci-(ēs)*, 'sight, view; shape, appearance; kind, sort', see **species.** **1.** **a** Of particular, individual character or importance; having distinctive character; particular, exceptional: *a day of special thanksgiving; as a special favour; for a special purpose; to receive special care*; **b** devoted to a particular purpose; specialized; particular, minute, detailed, intensive; contrasted with *general*: *special study, work; one's special subject*, that to which one has devoted special study and attention; *a special subject* (in an examination), one selected for special, intensive, study. Phr. *special jury*, one drawn from particular social class. **2.** Peculiar, individual, private, not for public or general use or attention: *my special chair; one's special work, duty* &c. **3.** Designed for, applied to, special use or purpose; appointed, prepared, for specific purpose, duty &c.; limited in scope, duty, application &c.: *special agent, correspondent, train* &c.; *special anatomy*, of specific part of body; *special case*, (legal) agreed written statement presented jointly by contesting parties to a court for decision; *special constable*, civilian enrolled in police force in time of civil emergency; *special edition*, of newspaper, published later than ordinary edition, usually to include special news; *special hospital*, treating particular class of cases; *special licence*, sanctioning marriage of specified persons at any place or time, and without publication of banns; *special logic*, rules of thinking to be applied to particular subject; *special pleader*, counsel employed to give an opinion on special points submitted to him, and to prepare papers dealing with proceedings out of the usual course; *special pleading*, (i.) new evidence brought up in law court to oppose evidence offered by other side; (ii.) (colloq.) specious, unfair, biassed, argument; *special verdict*, one stating facts proved in evidence, but leaving the court to draw conclusions from them. **4.** Definite, specific: *do you want to come on any special day?*

special (II.), n., fr. prec. Person or thing appointed or prepared for a special purpose; specif. **a** special constable; **b** special edition of newspaper; **c** special train.

specialism, n. [1. spéshalizm; 2. spéʃəlizəm]. **special & -ism.** Devotion of effort to a special line of study, research &c., or to some special branch of a profession.

specialist, n. [1. spéshalist; 2. spéʃəlist]. **special & -ist.** Person engaging in special line of study, research &c., or in special branch of a profession; one who has special knowledge in some field of learning or science: *a specialist in geology, diseases of the heart* &c.

specialistic, adj. [1. speshalístik; 2. spɛʃəlístik]. Prec. & **-ic.** Characteristic of, pertaining to, a specialist, or specialism.

speciality, n. [1. spèshiáliti; 2. spɛ̀ʃiǽliti], fr. O. Fr. *specialite*, fr. Lat. *speciālitāt-(em)*, 'peculiarity', fr. *speciāl-(is)*, 'peculiar, individual'. See **special** (I.) & **-ity. 1.** Distinctive feature, characteristic, peculiarity. **2.** Object, occupation, branch of study, to which special attention is given. **3.** Article of commerce in selection or manufacture of which the vendor takes special care and pride.

specialization, n. [1. spèshalizáshun; 2. spɛ̀ʃəlaizéiʃən]. Next word & **-ation.** Act of specializing, state of being specialized.

specialize, vb. trans. & intrans. [1. spéshalīz; 2. spéʃəlaiz]. **special** (I.) & **-ize. A.** trans. **1. a** To give a special definition to, make special or specific, to qualify, limit: *to specialize a statement, application* &c.; **b** to direct, and limit, to a particular object: *to specialize a course of study* &c. **2.** (biol.) To develop, evolve (an organ or part), in particular direction, or adapt to specific function. **3.** To limit to a particular purpose or function; reverse of *generalize*: *the word 'shroud' has a specialized meaning in Modern English.* **B.** intrans. **1.** To particularize. **2.** To engage in special study, occupation &c. **3.** (biol.) To assume, develop, a special character or function.

specially, adv. [1. spéshali; 2. spéʃəli]. **special** (I.) & **-ly. 1.** In a special manner; particularly, individually: *he was specially mentioned.* **2.** For specific purpose: *specially selected, appointed* &c.

specialty, n. [1. spéshalti; 2. spéʃəlti], fr. O. Fr. *specialte*. See **speciality. 1.** Speciality. **2.** (law) A contract embodied in a document bearing a seal.

specie, n. [1. spésh(i)ē; 2. spíʃ(i)ī], fr. Lat. *specie*, abl. of **species.** Money in metal form, coin, as distinct from paper money.

species, n. [1. spésh(i)ēz; 2. spíʃ(i)īz]. Lat. *speciēs*, 'sight, look; appearance, shape, form; kind, class; ornament, beauty'; cp. Lat. *specere*, 'to see, look at'; Gk. *sképtomai*, 'to look closely at', for *spek-*, see **sceptic**; *skopós* for *spok-*, 'one who sees', see **scope**; Scrt. *spáçati*, 'sees'; O.H.G. *spehōn*, 'to watch', cp. **spy. 1.** (theol.) The appearance as presented to the senses of either of the consecrated elements in the Eucharist. **2.** (log.) A group of individuals possessing common attributes, and designated by a common name. **3.** (biol.) A term of classification used to denote a group of animals or plants, larger than a *variety* and smaller than a *genus*, possessing certain distinctive characters in common, capable of interbreeding and of transmitting their distinctive characters to their offspring. **4.** Sort, kind: *a species of fierce egotism which one hopes is rare.*

specifiable, adj. [1. spésifīabl; 2. spésifaiəbl]. **specify & -able.** Capable of being specified.

specific (I.), adj. [1. spesífik; 2. spisífik]. Med. Lat. *specificus*; Lat. *speci-(ēs)*, see **species, & -fic. 1.** Characteristic of a species; possessing the distinguishing features of a species: *specific forms, variations, characters, in animals or plants*; *specific difference*, one constituting a species. **2.** Characteristic of a particular, distinct, class, sort, kind: *there is no specific distinction between a language and a dialect*; *specific gravity*, see **gravity. 3. a** (of drugs) Acting upon some particular organ or part of the body; **b** (of disease) produced by a particular micro-organism. **4. a** Clearly defined or formulated; precise, explicit, definite: *a specific statement*; *to have a specific aim and object in view*; *specific performance*, carrying out of strict terms of contract, esp. at the order of court of equity; **b** definitely limited in force and application: *the word 'whisper' is used by phoneticians with a perfectly specific meaning.*

specific (II.), n., fr. prec. A specific drug or medicine.

specifically, adv. [1. spesífikali; 2. spisífikəli]. **specific** (I.) & **-al & -ly.** In a specific manner; precisely, definitely.

specification, n. [1. spèsifikáshun; 2. spɛ̀sifikéiʃən]. See **specify & -fication. 1.** Act of specifying. **2.** A detailed descriptive statement; esp. **a** one made in reference to the design and particulars of a building, piece of machinery, or other constructive work; **b** a statement embodying a definition of specific charges brought against a person; a specific enumeration of the terms of a contract &c. **3.** (law) Working up of material into a different form, character, product, adjudged not to be the property of the owner of the material.

specificity, n. [1. spèsifísiti; 2. spɛ̀sifísiti]. **specific** (I.) & **-ity.** Specificness.

specificness, n. [1. spesífiknes; 2. spisífiknis]. **specific** (I.) & **-ness.** State or quality of being specific.

specify, vb. trans. [1. spésifī; 2. spésifai], fr. O. Fr. *specifier*, fr. Med. Lat. *specificāre*, 'to specify'. See **species & -fy. 1.** To make specific; to make definite and particular mention of, state, indicate, precisely, enumerate: *to specify the grounds of complaint*; *to specify those to whom invitations are to be sent.* **2.** To include, insert, in a specification.

specimen, n. [1. spésimen; 2. spésimin]. Lat. *specimen*, 'indication, distinctive mark, sign', fr. *spec-(ere)*, 'to look at', see **species, & -i- & -men. 1. a** One of a class, taken and regarded as possessing the characteristic features, qualities &c. of the whole class, and serving as a representative example: *a fine specimen of English manhood*; *a specimen of the first issue of English postage stamps*; **b** specif., an example of any kind of natural object preserved, classified, and exhibited as a sample of its kind: *a museum specimen*; *his house was full of stuffed specimens, and specimens in spirits.* **2. a** A part of anything, taken as an example or pattern of the whole: *a specimen of fourteenth-century handwriting*; **b** isolated characteristic instance: *a specimen of a person's manners, of English weather*; *specimen page*, of book or other publication, one showing style, size of type &c., esp. one printed in publisher's prospectus. **3.** (colloq.) An eccentric, unusual person; one exhibiting some marked characteristic; a remarkable type: (usually in unfavourable sense) *a queer, a rum, specimen.*

speciological, adj. [1. spèshiolójikl; 2. spiʃiəlódžikl]. Next word & **-ic & -al.** Of, pertaining to, speciology.

speciology, n. [1. spèshióloji; 2. spiʃiólədži]. **species & -o- & -logy.** The science of the origin and development of species.

speciosity, n. [1. spèshiósiti; 2. spiʃiósiti], fr. Lat. *speciōsitāt-(em)*, 'beauty', fr. *speciōs-(us)*, 'beautiful', see next word, & **-ity.** State or quality of being specious; speciousness.

specious, adj. [1. spéshus; 2. spíʃəs], fr. Lat. *speciōs-(us)*, 'beautiful, showy; plausible', fr. *speci-(ēs)*, 'appearance', see **species, & -ose.** Having superficial beauty or excellence; seeming good on the surface, but deceptive and lacking genuineness; plausible, meretricious: *a specious appearance of prosperity*; *a specious excuse, plea* &c.; *a specious refinement.*

speciously, adv. Prec. & **-ly.** In a specious manner.

speciousness, n. See prec. & **-ness.** Speciosity.

speck (I.), n. [1. spek; 2. spɛk]. O.E. *specca*, 'speck, spot', M.E. *specke*. **1. a** Small spot, stain, dot, mark; **b** specif., a small spot in fruit caused by disease &c. **2. a** Minute object; a small grain, a particle: *a speck of dust*; **b** something which appears like a speck from being remote; *the ship became a mere speck in the distance.*

speck (II.), vb. trans., fr. prec. To mark with small spots or specks.

speck (III.), n. O.E. *spic*, 'bacon'; cp. O.N. *spik*; O.H.G. *spec*; Du. *spek*. Blubber of whales or seals; also (U.S.A. and S. Afr.) fat meat, esp. bacon.

speckle, n. & vb. trans. [1. spékl; 2. spékl]. **speck** (I.) & **-le. 1.** n. Small spot or mark distinct in colour from surrounding surface. **2.** vb. (chiefly in P.P.) To mark, cover, with speckles; to dot, variegate with spots.

speckless, adj. [1. spékles; 2. spéklis]. **speck** (I.) & **-less.** Without a speck; spotless; also fig.

specktioneer, specksioneer, n. [1. spekshunḗr; 2. spɛkʃəníə], fr. Du. *speksnijer*, fr. *spek*, 'blubber', see **speck** (III.), & *snij-(den)*, 'to cut', & **-er.** The Gmc. stem **snīþ-*, 'cut', appears in O.E. *snīðan*, Mod. Germ. *schneiden*, 'to cut' &c., but apparently has no cognates outside Gmc. Chief harpooner in whaler.

specky, adj. [1. spéki; 2. spéki]. **speck** (I.) & **-y.** Marked with specks, esp. of fruit with spots of rottenness.

specs, n. [1. speks; 2. spɛks]. Abbr. fr. *spectacles*, see next word. (colloq.) Pair of spectacles.

spectacle, n. [1. spéktakl; 2. spéktəkl], fr. Fr., fr. Lat. *spectāculum*, 'show, sight; public spectacle', fr. *spect-(āre)*, 'to see, watch', fr. *spect-(um)*, P.P. type of *specere*, 'to look', see **species. 1.** Something looked at; specif., something exhibited to public view; a show, a remarkable display. **2.** Something unusual, esp. that which arouses pity, contempt, reprobation &c. when seen: *he is a sad spectacle in his infirm old age.* **3.** (pl.) (*Pair of*) *spectacles*, pair of optical lenses for correcting the sight, fitted into a frame, supported by the nose, and held in place by thin bars of metal or tortoiseshell passing behind the ears; (colloq., cricket slang) a failure to score in both innings; a duck in both innings.

spectacled, adj. [1. spéktakld; 2. spéktəkld]. Prec. & **-ed. a** Wearing spectacles; **b** having markings resembling a pair of spectacles: *spectacled bear, cobra* &c.

spectacular, adj. [1. spektákūlar; 2. spɛktǽkjulə], fr. Lat. *spectācul-(um)*, 'show', see **spectacle, & -ar.** Of, pertaining to, of the nature of, characteristic of, a spectacle: *a spectacular display.*

spectacularism, n. [1. spektákūlarizm; 2. spɛktǽkjulərizəm]. Prec. & **-ism.** State or quality of being spectacular.

spectacularly, adv. [1 spektákūlarli; 2. spɛktǽkjuləli]. See prec. & **-ly.** In a spectacular manner.

spectator, n. [1. spektátur; 2. spɛktéitə], fr. Lat. *spectātor*, 'observer, spectator', fr. *spectāt-(um)*, P.P. type of *spectāre*, 'to see, watch', see **spectacle, & -or. 1.** Person who watches, sees, looks on at, a performance, an action, an event; an observer, an onlooker: *a crowd of spectators at a football match*; *he remained a mere spectator of the great occurrences of his time.* **2.** (cap.) Title of periodical.

spectatorial, adj. [1. spektatórial; 2. spɛktətóriəl]. Prec. & **-ial.** Of, pertaining to, a spectator.

spectatorship, n. [1. spektátурship; 2. spɛktéitəʃip]. See prec. & **-ship.** State of being a spectator.

spectatress, n. [1. spektátres; 2. spɛktéitris]. See prec. & **-ess.** Female spectator.

spectra, pl. of **spectrum.**

spectral, adj. [1. spéktral; 2. spéktrəl]. See **spectre, spectrum, & -al. 1.** Pertaining to, resembling, of the nature of, a spectre; ghostly. **2.** Pertaining to the spectrum: *spectral analysis, colours.*

spectrally, adv. Prec. & **-ly.** Like, after the manner of, a spectre.

spectre, n. [1. spékter; 2. spéktə], fr. O. Fr. *spectre*, fr. Lat. *spectrum*, 'appearance, form; apparition'. See **spectrum. 1.** Disembodied spirit in visible form; apparition, ghost.

2. *Spectre of the Brocken*, huge, ghost-like image of spectator projected on mist at the summit of mountain, as on the Brocken in the Harz Mountains.

spectre-bat, n. S. American leaf-nosed bat.

spectre-crab, n. The transparent larva of certain crustaceans.

spectre-insect, n. Walking-stick insect.

spectre-lemur, n. The tarsier.

spectre-shrimp, n. Shrimp with long, slender body.

spectro-, pref. Form of **spectrum**, used in compounds.

spectrogram, n. [1. spéktrogràm; 2. spéktrəgræm]. Prec. & **-gram**. Reproduction of a spectrum by means of a spectrograph.

spectrograph, n. [1. spéktrogràhf; 2. spéktrəgràf]. See prec. & **-graph**. Instrument for representing or reproducing a spectrum photographically &c.

spectrographic, adj. [1. spèktrográfik; 2. spèktrəgræfik]. Prec. & **-ic**. Of, pertaining to, by means of, a spectrograph.

spectrography, n. [1. spèktrógrafi; 2. spèktrógrəfi]. See prec. & **-y**. Art of reproducing spectra by means of a spectrograph.

spectrological, adj. [1. spèktrolójikl; 2. spèktrəlódžikl]. See **spectrology & -ic & -al**. Pertaining to spectrology.

spectrologically, adv. Prec. & **-ly**. By means of spectrology.

spectrology, n. [1. spèktróloji; 2. spèktrólədži]. **spectro- & -logy**. Science of spectral analysis.

spectrometer, n. [1. spèktrómeter; 2. spèktrómitə]. See prec. & **-meter**. Instrument for measuring angular deviation of ray of light passing through prism.

spectrophone, n. [1. spéktrofòn; 2. spéktrəfòun]. See prec. & **-phone**. Form of spectroscope in which the different light-rays are made to produce distinctive sounds.

spectroscope, n. [1. spéktroskōp; 2. spéktrəskoup]. See prec. & **-scope**. Instrument for analysing the spectra of rays emitted by luminous bodies.

spectroscopic(al), adj. [1. spèktroskópik(l); 2. spèktrəskópik(l)]. Prec. & **-ic & -al**. Of, pertaining to, formed by, a spectroscope.

spectroscopically, adv. Prec. & **-ly**. By means of a spectroscope.

spectroscopist, n. [1. spektróskopist; 2. spektróskəpist]. **spectroscope & -ist**. Student of, one learned in, spectroscopy.

spectroscopy, n. [1. spektróskopi; 2. spektróskəpi]. See prec. & **-y**. **1**. Use of the spectroscope. **2**. Science of spectral phenomena and analysis.

spectrum, n., pl. **spectra** [1. spéktrum, -a; 2. spéktrə(m)]. Lat. *spectrum*, 'form, image'; formed fr. *spect-(um)*, P.P. type of *specere*, 'to look', see **species**. **1**. Image presented by a ray of light which has passed through, and been broken up by, a prism, consisting of a series of bands of the different colours forming the constituents of the ray; *spectrum analysis*, chemical analysis carried out by examination of the spectrum of a compound; also *spectral analysis*. **2**. Image retained by the retina of the eye, after the object which caused the stimulus to the optic nerve is removed; after-image.

specular, adj. [1. spékūlar; 2. spékjulə], fr. Lat. *speculār-(is)*, 'of, of the nature of, a mirror'. See **speculum & -ar**. Of, pertaining to, having the property of, a speculum; *specular iron*, lustrous variety of haematite.

speculate, vb. intrans. [1. spékūlāt, 2. spékjulèit], fr. Lat. *speculāt-(um)*, P.P. type of *speculāri*, 'to observe, examine', fr. *specula*, 'watch-tower', fr. base **spec-*, 'to look at', see **species**. **1**. To consider, form theory about, ruminate, ponder, meditate: *to speculate concerning the future life*. **2**. To invest money in uncertain security, under circumstances involving risk of loss or possibility of gain: *to speculate in mining shares*.

speculation, n. [1. spèkūlāshun; 2. spèkjuléiʃən], fr. Lat. *speculātiōn-(em)*, 'observation, contemplation'. **speculate & -ion**. **1**. Act or process of speculating mentally. **2**. **a** Theory, opinion, arrived at by speculation; **b** conjecture, unconfirmed hypothesis. **3**. Investment of money in hope of gain but with risk of loss: *to engage in speculation*; *to buy land* &c., as a speculation. **4**. Kind of card game.

speculative, adj. [1. spékūlativ; 2. spékjulətiv]. **speculate & -ive**. **1**. Pertaining to, derived from, given to, mental speculation. **2**. Of the nature of, given to, financial speculation; hence, risky, uncertain.

speculatively, adv. Prec. & **-ly**. In a speculative manner.

speculativeness, n. See prec. & **-ness**. State or quality of being speculative.

speculator, n. [1. spékūlātur; 2. spékjulèitə]. **speculate & -or**. Person engaging in speculation, esp. in finance.

speculum, n. [1. spékūlum; 2. spékjuləm]. Lat. *speculum*, 'mirror', fr. *spec-(ere)*, 'to look at', see **species, & -ule**. **1**. (med.) Instrument for dilating a cavity &c., of the body, to facilitate the inspection of the interior. **2**. Mirror, usually of polished metal, used as reflector in telescope &c. **3**. (ornith.) Patch of distinct colour on bird's wing.

speculum-metal, n. Hard alloy of copper and tin, capable of taking a brilliant polish, used for making the speculum of a telescope.

sped, vb. [1. sped; 2. sped]. O.E. *spēdde*, M.E. *spedde*. Pret. & P.P. of **speed (II.)**.

speech, n. [1. spēch; 2. spītʃ]. O.E. *sp(r)ǣc*, M.E. *spēche*; cp. O.H.G. *sprāhha*; O.S. *sprāka*; O. Fris. *sprēke*; in gradational relation to O.E. *sprecan*, 'to speak'; wh. has also the type *sprǣc-* in Pret. pl. See **speak**. **1**. **a** The expression of ideas and thoughts by means of articulate sounds produced by the vocal organs; language; Phr. *figure of speech*, see **figure**; **b** the faculty of thus expressing ideas and thoughts. **2**. **a** Particular form of language used by the people of a given country; a tongue, a language: *English speech*; *the native speech of Ireland*; **b** manner of speaking, dialect, jargon, in vogue among a limited section of the community: *the speech of the proletariat*; **c** mode of utterance, articulation, enunciation: *his speech was very indistinct.* **3**. Act of speaking: *speech is silver, silence is golden*. Phr. *to have speech of (a person)*, to converse with. **4**. A formal public utterance, an address, harangue. **5**. Sound produced by musical instrument, esp. organ or organ-pipe.

speech basis, n. (philol.) The group of mental and physical habits, esp. habits of using the vocal organs, peculiar to an individual speaker, or to the speakers of a given language or dialect.

speech-day, n. Annual school celebration at which prizes are presented &c.

speechification, n. [1. spèchifikāshun; 2. spìtʃifikéiʃən]. See **speechify & -fication**. Act of speechifying.

speechifier, n. [1. spéchifīer; 2. spítʃifaiə]. Next word & **-er**. Person given to speechifying.

speechify, vb. intrans. [1. spéchifī; 2. spítʃifai]. **speech & -i- & -fy**. (contemptuous or facet.). To make (public) speeches; esp. to make long, or frequent, speeches.

speechifying, n. [1. spéchifīing; 2. spítʃifaiiŋ]. Prec. & **-ing**. Act of making speeches; the making of long or frequent speeches: *do not let us have too much speechifying after dinner*.

speechless, adj. [1. spéchles; 2. spítʃlis]. **speech & -less**. **1**. Lacking the faculty of speech, dumb. **2**. Not actually speaking at a given moment; temporarily unable to speak: *he remained speechless the whole evening*; *speechless with indignation*; (slang) dead drunk. **3**. Not expressed, not expressible in speech: *speechless fear, grief* &c.

speechlessly, adv. Prec. & **-ly**. In a speechless manner; without speaking.

speechlessness, n. See prec. & **-ness**. State of being speechless.

speech-maker, n. Person who makes a speech; one given to making speeches.

speech-reading, n. Interpretation of speaker's words by observation of movements of mouth &c., as practised by the deaf &c.; lip-reading.

speech-sound, n. Single articulate sound produced by the vocal organs and forming an element of language.

speed (I.), n. [1. spēd; 2. spīd]. O.E. *spēd*, fr. **spōdi-*, 'success, prosperity'; M.E. *spēd*, 'speed'; cp. O.S. *spōd*; O.H.G. *spuot*, 'success'; cogn. w. O.E. *spōwan*; O.H.G. *spuon*, 'to prosper, succeed'; cp. further O. Slav. *spěja*, 'to be successful'; *spěšiti*, 'to hasten'; Lith. *spēt*, 'to be able'; Scrt. *sphāyati*, 'increases'; *sphārás*, 'spread out, broad'; Lat. *spatium*, 'extent'. See **space**. **1**. (obs., except in archaic Phr.) *To wish good speed (to)*; *God send you, give you, good speed*, prosperity, luck, success. **2**. Quick motion, swiftness, rapidity: *to move with incredible speed*; *at full speed*. **3**. Rate of motion; velocity: *with gradually increasing speed*; *at a reasonable speed*.

speed (II.), vb. trans. & intrans., fr. O.E. *spēdan*, 'to succeed, make successful', fr. *spēd*, 'success'. See prec. **A**. trans. **1**. **a** To wish good luck, or success to: *to speed the parting guest*; **b** to help forward, be propitious to, give, grant, success to: *God speed you*; '*What recks it them? What need they? They are sped*' = they have succeeded, have got what they want (Milton, 'Lycidas', 122). **2**. To accelerate, increase speed of; also *speed up*. **B**. intrans. **1**. To go with speed, to move swiftly forward, to hasten, hurry: *a boat speeds across the waves*; *the arrow sped forth on its flight*. **2**. To make progress, fare, get on; to prosper: *how have you sped?*

speeder, n. [1. spéder; 2. spídə]. **speed & -er**. Attachment to machine for regulating or increasing its speed.

speedily, adv. [1. spédili; 2. spídili]. **speedy & -ly**. In a speedy manner; rapidly, promptly.

speediness, n. [1. spédines; 2. spídinis]. See prec. & **-ness**. Haste, rapidity; promptitude.

speed-limit, n. Legal limit of speed at which a vehicle, esp. a motor, may travel.

speedometer, n. [1. spēdómeter; 2. spīdómitə]. **speed & -o- & -meter**. Instrument which registers the speed at which a vehicle, esp. a motor, is travelling.

speedway, n. [1. spédwā; 2. spídwei]. Public track for motor-cycle racing; dirt-track.

speedwell, n. [1. spédwel; 2. spídwel]. Genus, *Veronica*, of low-growing herbs, with small, blue, pink, or white flowers.

speedy, adj. [1. spédi; 2. spídi]. O.E. *spēdiġ*, 'prosperous'; M.E. *spēdi*. **speed & -y**. **1**. Characterized by swiftness of motion; rapid, quick: *a speedy flight*. **2**. Undelayed, prompt; made or occurring soon: *a speedy recovery, return, retribution* &c.

speiss, n. [1. spīs; 2. spais], fr. Germ. *speise*, 'food, meal'; amalgam of metal', fr. Med. Lat. *spēsa*, 'food, provisions', fr. Lat. *expensa*, 'disbursement'. See **expense**. Arsenical compound of copper, iron, nickel, &c. produced in smelting certain ores.

spelaean, adj. [1. spēlḗan; 2. spilíən], fr. Lat. *spēlae-(um)*, fr. Gk. *spélaion*, 'cave'; cp. Gk. *spēlugx*, *spéos*, 'cave'; etymol. doubtful. Of, pertaining to, inhabiting, a cave.

spelaeology, n. [1. spèlēóloji; 2. spìliólədži]. See prec. & **-logy**. The science or study of caves.

spelican, n. [1. spélikan; 2. spélikən]. See **spillikin**.

spell (I.), n. [1. spel; 2. spel]. O.E. *spell*, 'saying, narrative, discourse'; cp. O.H.G. *spel*; O.N. *spjall*; Goth. *spill*, 'tale, saying'; Goth. *spillōn*; O.H.G. *spellōn*, 'to tell'; possibly cogn. w. Lat. *appellāre*, 'to speak to', see **appeal**; Gk. *apeilḗ*, 'threat'; cp. second element of **gospel**. **1**. Magical formula, incantation, charm. **2**. Irresistible fascination, sway, overpowering attraction: *under the spell of beauty, eloquence* &c.

spell (II.), vb. trans. & intrans., fr. O. Fr. *espeler*, fr. L.G. *spellen*, 'to say'; cogn. w. O.E. *spellian*, 'to tell, narrate'; *spell*, 'tale'. See prec. **A.** trans. **1.** To name, or write, in succession, the letters used to express (a word) in writing: *to spell a word; how do you spell your name?; is 'harass' spelt with one r or two?; spell out*, (i.) to decipher slowly and with difficulty; (ii.) (as direction to printer) spell in full, not in contracted form. **2.** (of letters) To form a word when arranged in specific order: O-N-E, *spells 'one'*. **3.** To involve, result in, have as consequence; signify: *such an error spells the ruin of our hopes.* **B.** intrans. To put down, or mention the right letters of a word in the right order; to express words in writing, in the correct, recognized, conventional manner: *learn to spell; we do not pronounce as we spell.*

spell (III.), n., fr. next word. **1.** Single period, bout, turn, of activity, esp. as coming in rotation: *to take a spell at the oars; a spell of work.* **2.** Short period, interval, brief space; a season: *to sleep for a spell; a spell of fine weather.*

spell (IV.), vb. trans. O.E. *spelian*, 'to act, deputize, for another'; prob. related to *spilian*, 'to play'; cogn. w. O.H.G. *spilōn*; O.N. *spila*, 'to play'; O. Fris. *spil, spel*, 'sport, game'. (rare) To take turns with in working, give temporary relief from duty to.

spell-binder, n. (U.S. slang) Speaker able to hold an audience spell-bound.

spell-bound, adj. **a** Overcome by, or as by, a spell; fascinated, entranced; hence **b** amazed, dumbfounded.

speller, n. [1. spéler; 2. spélə]. **spell** (II.) & **-er**. **1.** One who spells; (usually qualified): *a good, careless, speller* &c. **2.** Spelling-book.

spelling, n. [1. spéling; 2. spéliŋ]. **spell** (II.) & **-ing**. **1.** Act of naming or writing down in order the letters which express a word graphically. **2.** Way in which a word is spelt: *an incorrect spelling; variant spellings.*

spelling-bee, n. Competitive exercise in spelling.

spelling-book, n. Book of exercises for teaching children to spell.

spelt, n. [1. spelt; 2. spelt]. O.E. *spelt*; cp. O.H.G. *spelza*; Lat. *spelta* is prob. a loan-word fr. Gmc. Kind of wheat, resembling both wheat and barley, grown in the mountains of Switzerland, Germany, and Spain; German wheat.

spelter, n. [1. spélter; 2. spéltə], fr. L.G. *spialter*, 'pewter'; cp. Du. *spiauter*; perh. cogn. w. **pewter**. Zinc.

spence, spense, n. [1. spens; 2. spens]. M.E. *spens, spence*, fr. O. Fr. *spense*, abbr. fr. *despense*. See **dispense**. (archaic) Larder, pantry.

spencer (I.), n. [1. spénser; 2. spénsə]. Named after Earl Spencer, d. 1845. **1.** Short overcoat, esp. of early 19th cent. **2.** Short woollen jacket.

spencer (II.), n. Etymol. unknown. (naut.) Trysail.

Spencerian, adj. & n. [1. spensérian; 2. spensíəriən], fr. Herbert Spencer (1820–1903), & **-ian.** **a** adj. Pertaining to, connected with, Herbert Spencer or his synthetic philosophy; **b** n., a follower of Herbert Spencer.

Spencerianism, n. [1. spensérianizm; 2. spensíəriənizəm]. Prec. & **-ism.** Philosophic doctrines and system of Herbert Spencer.

Spencerism, n. [1. spénserizm; 2. spénsərizəm]. See prec. & **-ism.** Spencerianism.

spend, vb. trans. & intrans. [1. spend; 2. spend]. O.E. *spendan*, fr. Lat. *dispend-(ere)*, 'to weigh out', fr. **dis-** & *pendere*, 'to weigh, pay out; to ponder'. See **pendant.** **A.** trans. **1.** To give out in payment, pay out, for thing(s) bought: *to spend a penny on sweets; how much have you spent?* **2.** To use up gradually, consume, expend: *to spend one's efforts, strength, to no purpose*; **b** to pass: *to spend one's life, the time; to spend a sleepless night.* **3.** To wear out, exhaust, consume, work itself out: *to spend one's strength; the storm has spent itself*; also (archaic) *the night is far spent*, far advanced. **4.** (naut.) To lose: *to spend a mast.* **B.** intrans. **1.** To pay out, disburse, money: '*Getting, and spending, we lay waste our powers*' (Wordsworth). **2.** (of fish &c.) To emit spawn.

spendable, adj. [1. spéndabl; 2. spéndəbl]. Prec. & **-able.** Capable of being spent; available for spending.

spender, n. [1. spénder; 2. spéndə]. **spend** & **-er.** One who spends money: *a lavish spender.*

spendthrift, n. & adj. [1. spén(d)thrift; 2. spén(d)þrift]. **1.** n. One who spends lavishly, and extravagantly; a wastrel, a prodigal, a squanderer. **2.** adj. Characteristic of a spendthrift; extravagant, prodigal, thriftless: *spendthrift lavishness.*

spense, n. See **spence.**

Spenserian, adj. [1. spensérian; 2. spensíəriən], fr. Edmund Spenser (1552–99) & **-ian.** Pertaining to, characteristic of, Edmund Spenser; esp. *Spenserian stanza*, that used in the *Faerie Queene*, consisting of nine lines, the first eight having ten syllables, the last being an alexandrine.

spent, adj. [1. spent; 2. spent], fr. P.P. of **spend.** **1.** Worn out by effort, exhausted; *spent bullet* &c., with speed reduced after traversing distance. **2.** (of fish &c.) Having deposited spawn.

sperm (I.), n. [1. spěrm; 2. spəm], fr. Fr. *sperme*, fr. Lat. *sperma*, fr. Gk. *spérma*, 'seed; germ; sperm'; cogn. w. Gk. *speírein*, 'to sow'; *sporá*, 'sowing'; *sporás*, 'scattered, sparse'. See also **spray** & words there referred to. Male generative substance.

sperm (II.), n. Abbr. of **spermaceti.** **1.** Also *sperm-whale*, whale yielding spermaceti. **2.** Spermaceti.

spermaceti, n. [1. spěrmaséti; 2. spəməséti], fr. Lat. *sperma*, 'sperm', see **sperm** (I.), & *cēti*, gen. of *cētus*, 'whale', see **cetacean.** White, waxy substance obtained from the oil in the head of the sperm-whale, used as basis for ointments, and in making candles &c.

spermary, n. [1. spěrmari; 2. spə́məri]. **sperm** & **-ary.** Male generative gland.

spermatic, adj. [1. spěrmátik; 2. spəmǽtik], fr. Gk. *spérmat-*, stem of *spérma*, 'sperm'. See **sperm** (I.) & **-ic.** **1.** Pertaining to, containing, sperm. **2.** Pertaining to the spermary.

spermatism, n. [1. spěrmatizm; 2. spə́mətizəm]. See **spermatic** & **-ism.** **1.** Discharge of seminal fluid. **2.** Spermism.

spermatist, n. [1. spěrmatist; 2. spə́mətist]. See prec. & **-ist.** Spermist.

spermatize, vb. intrans. [1. spěrmatīz; 2. spə́mətaiz]. See **spermatic** & **-ize.** To emit seminal fluid.

spermato-, pref. representing Gk. *spérmat-*, stem of *spérma*, 'seed, sperm'. See **sperm** (I.).

spermatoblast, n. [1. spěrmatōblàhst; 2. spə́mətoublàst]. Prec. & Gk. *blastós*, 'bud, sprout', see **blastoderm.** Cell from which spermatozoon develops.

spermatogenesis, n. [1. spěrmatōjénesis; 2. spə́mətoudžénisis]. See prec. & **genesis.** Development of spermatozoa.

spermatogenous, adj. [1. spěrmatójenus; 2. spə̀mətódžinəs], fr. **spermato-** & base **gen-*, 'produce', see **genesis,** & **-ous.** Producing sperm.

spermatogeny, n. [1. spěrmatójeni; 2. spə̀mətódžini]. See prec. & **-y.** Formation of sperm.

spermatological, adj. [1. spěrmatōlójikl; 2. spə̀mətoulódžikl]. See next word & **-ic** & **-al.** Pertaining to spermatology.

spermatologist, n. [1. spěrmatólojist; 2. spə̀mətólədžist]. Next word & **-ist.** Student of spermatology.

spermatology, n. [1. spěrmatóloji; 2. spə̀mətólədži]. **spermato-** & **-logy.** Branch of biology treating of the properties and character of the male generative principle.

spermatophore, n. [1. spěrmatōfōr; 2. spə́mətoufɔ̄]. **spermato-** & **-phore.** Case containing spermatozoa in some invertebrates.

spermatorrhoea, n. [1. spěrmatōréa; 2. spə́mətouríə]. **spermato-** & **rheo-.** Involuntary emission or flow of sperm.

spermatozoal, adj. [1. spěrmatōzṓal; 2. spə́mətouzóuəl]. See **spermatozoon** & **-al.** Of, pertaining to, a spermatozoon.

spermatozoan, adj. [1. spěrmatōzṓan; 2. spə́mətouzóuən]. See next word & **-an.** Spermatozoal.

spermatozoon, n., pl. **spermatozoa** [1. spěrmatōzṓon, -a; 2. spə́mətouzóuən, -ə]. **spermato-** & Gk. *zôon*, 'animal.' See **zoo-.** One of the germ-cells forming the fertilizing elements in the semen of male animals.

spermism, n. [1. spěrmizm; 2. spə́mizəm]. **sperm** (I.) & **-ism.** Theory that the spermatozoon contains the complete germ of the future animal.

spermist, n. [1. spěrmist; 2. spə́mist]. **sperm** (I.) & **-ist.** Adherent of the theory of spermism.

spermo-, pref. representing Gk. *spérm-(a)*, 'seed'. See **sperm** (I.). Seed; sperm.

spermoblast, n. [1. spěrmoblàhst; 2. spə́məblàst]. Prec. & Gk. *blastós*, 'bud'. See **blastoderm.** Spermatoblast.

spermological, adj. [1. spěrmolójikl; 2. spə̀məlódžikl]. **spermology** & **-ic** & **-al.** Pertaining to spermology.

spermologist, n. [1. spěrmólojist; 2. spəmólədžist]. Next word & **-ist.** Student of spermology.

spermology, n. [1. spěrmóloji; 2. spəmólədži]. **spermo-** & **-logy.** **1.** Spermatology. **2.** Branch of botany treating of seeds.

sperm-whale, n. Large whale or cachalot, the head of which contains spermaceti.

spew, spue, vb. intrans. & trans. [1. spū; 2. spjū]. O.E. *spēowan*; M.E. *spēwen*, 'to vomit, to spit'; cp. Germ. *speien*; O.N. *spȳja*; Gk. *ptúein*; Lat. *spuere*; Lith. *spiáuju*, 'to spit'. Prob. imitative. **A.** intrans. **1.** To vomit. **2.** (of gun) To sink at the muzzle after too quick firing. **B.** trans. To vomit up, eject.

sphacelate, vb. trans. & adj. [1. sfáselāt; 2. sfǽsileit], fr. Gk. *sphákel-(os)*, 'gangrene; convulsive movement, spasm'; prob. fr. Aryan base **sphē-*, **sphə-*, 'to stretch, draw out'; cp. parallel base **spē(i)-* &c. See **space.** **1.** vb. (of flesh or bone) To be affected with necrosis; to mortify, become gangrenous. **2.** adj. Mortified, gangrenous.

sphacelation, n. [1. sfàseláshun; 2. sfæ̀siléiʃən]. Prec. & **-ion.** Mortification, necrosis.

sphaer(o)-, pref. representing Gk. *sphaîr-(a)*, 'ball; sphere'; cp. Gk. *sphurón*, 'ankle'; *spairein*, 'to move convulsively, gasp'; Lith. *spiriù*, 'I kick'; Scrt. *sphuráti*, 'to kick, trample'; Lat. *spernere*, 'to reject, spurn'; O.E. *spurnan*, 'to spurn', see **spurn;** fr. base **sp(h)er-*, **sp(h)erē-*, 'muscular contraction, tension, spasmodic movement', fr. **sp(h)ē-* &c., 'to stretch or spread out'. See **space, spasm.** Spherical shape; esp. in botanical terms, e.g. *sphaerella*, a genus of fungi.

sphagnum, n. [1. sfágnum; 2. sfǽgnəm], fr. Gk. *sphágn-(os), sphákos*, 'kind of fragrant moss'; also, 'sage'; prob. named fr. the astringent properties of the latter; cp. Gk. *sphákelos*, 'convulsive movement; gangrene'. See **sphacelate.** Gen. *sphagnum moss*, genus of mosses; peat-moss.

sphen(o)-, pref. representing Gk. *sphḗn*, 'wedge'; cogn. w. Scrt. *sphyáś*, 'splinter of wood'; O.N. *spānn*; O.H.G. *spān*, 'splinter', O.E. *spōn*, 'chip, shaving'; M.H.G. *spāt*, 'splinter'; cogn. w. **spathe.** **1.** Wedge-shaped. **2.** Of the sphenoid bone.

sphenoccipital, adj. [1. sfénoksípitl; 2. sfìnəksípitl]. Prec. & **occipital.** Of the sphenoid and occipital bones.

sphenocephalous, adj. [1. sfēnōséfalus; 2. sfìnouséfələs]. **sphen(o)-** & **-cephalous.** Having a wedge-shaped head.

sphenogram, n. [1. sfénōgràm; 2. sfínougræ̀m]. **sphen(o)-** & **-gram**. Cuneiform character.

sphenographic, adj. [1. sfènōgráfik; 2. sfìnougrǽfik]. See prec. & **-graphic**. Of, pertaining to, written in, cuneiform characters.

sphenography, n. [1. sfēnógrafi; 2. sfīnɔ́grəfi]. See prec. & **-graphy**. Cuneiform writing.

sphenoid, adj. & n. [1. sfénoid; 2. sfínɔid], fr. Gk. *sphḗn*, 'wedge', see **sphen(o)-**, & **-oid**. **1.** adj. **a** Wedge-shaped, esp. *sphenoid bone*, large bone at base of skull; **b** of the sphenoid bone. **2.** n. (anat.) Sphenoid bone.

sphenoidal, adj. [1. sfēnóidl; 2. sfīnɔ́idl]. Prec. & **-al**. Of, pertaining to, the sphenoid bone.

sphenoido-, pref. representing **sphenoid** & *-o-*. Of the sphenoid bone, e.g. *sphenoido-parietal*, of the sphenoidal and parietal diameters of the skull.

sphere (I.), n. [1. sfēr; 2. sfiə], fr. Lat. *sphaera*, fr. Gk. *sphaîra*, 'ball, globe, sphere'. See **sphaero-**. **1.** Solid figure of such a form that every point on its surface is equidistant from a fixed point (the centre) within; *doctrine of the sphere*, spherical geometry and trigonometry. **2.** Any completely or approximately spherical solid; ball, globe; specif. **a** one of the heavenly bodies; **b** globe representing the earth or the apparent surface of the heavens; **c** one of the spherical, hollow bodies, revolving round the earth, in which ancient astronomers believed the heavenly bodies to be enclosed; esp. *music of the spheres*, produced by movements of the spheres. **3. a** *Celestial sphere*, spherical surface on which the heavenly bodies appear to be set; **b** (poet.) sky, heavens. **4. a** Scope, range, compass, province; field of action, knowledge, or influence; **b** normal circumstances, condition of life, social circle: *to remain in one's proper sphere*.

sphere (II.), vb. trans., fr. prec. To enclose in, form into, a sphere.

spheric, adj. & n. [1. sférik; 2. sférik], fr. Gk. *sphairik-(ós)*, 'spherical'. **sphere** (I.) & **-ic**. **1.** adj. **a** (poet.) Connected with, pertaining to, the heavenly bodies; celestial; **b** spherical. **2.** n. (pl.) Spherical geometry and trigonometry.

spherical, adj. [1. sférikl; 2. sférikl]. Prec. & **-al**. **1.** Shaped like a sphere; round, globular. **2.** Pertaining to spheres: *spherical geometry*; *spherical triangle, polygon* &c., on the surface of a sphere and bounded by arcs of great circles.

spherically, adv. Prec. & **-ly**. In spherical form.

sphericity, n. [1. sferísiti; 2. sfɛrísiti]. **spheric** & **-ity**. State of being a sphere.

spheriform, adj. [1. sférifòrm; 2. sférifɔ̀m]. **sphere** (I.) & *-i-* & **-form**. Shaped like a sphere.

spherograph, n. [1. sfērograhf; 2. sfiərəgrāf]. **sphere** (I.) & *-o-* & **-graph**. Device for finding spherical triangles.

spheroid, n. [1. sféroid; 2. sfíərɔid], fr. Gk. *sphairoeidés*, 'spherical'. **sphere** (I.) & **-oid**. Solid generated by revolution of an ellipse about either of its axes; body which is nearly but not quite spherical; *prolate, oblate, spheroid*, slightly lengthened, slightly flattened, sphere.

spheroidal, adj. [1. sfērōidl; 2. sfiərɔ́idl]. Prec. & **-al**. Of, pertaining to, shaped like, a spheroid.

spheroidally, adv. See prec. & **-ly**. In a spheroidal manner.

spheroidic(al), adj. [1. sfēróidik(l); 2. sfiərɔ́idik(l)]. **spheroid** & **-ic** (& **-al**). Spheroidal.

spheroidicity, n. [1. sfèroidísiti; 2. sfìərɔidísiti]. Prec. & **-ity**. State of being a spheroid.

spherometer, n. [1. sfērómeter; 2. sfiərɔ́mitə]. **sphere** (I.) & *-o-* & **-meter**. Instrument for measuring curvature or radius of spherical surface or body.

spherular, adj. [1. sféroolar; 2. sférulə]. **spherule** & **-ar**. Of, pertaining to, shaped like, a sphere.

spherulate, adj. [1. sféroolat; 2. sférulət]. Next word & **-ate**. Of, pertaining to, bearing spherules.

spherule, n. [1. sféro͞ol; 2. sférūl], fr. Lat. *sphaerula*, 'small ball'. **sphere** (I.) & **-ule**. Minute sphere.

spherulite, n. [1. sféroolīt; 2. sférulait]. Prec. & **-ite**. Spherical group of minute crystals found in siliceous rock.

spherulitic, adj. [1. sfèroolítik; 2. sfèrulítik]. Prec. & **-ic**. Of, pertaining to, containing, spherulites.

spherulitize, vb. trans. [1. sféroolitīz; 2. sférulitaiz]. **spherulite** & **-ize**. To form into spherulites.

sphery, adj. [1. sfēri; 2. sfíəri]. **sphere** (I.) & **-y**. **1.** Pertaining to, resembling, a sphere. **2.** (poet.) Belonging to the heavens; celestial.

sphincter, n. [1. sfíngkter; 2. sfíŋktə]. Lat. *sphincter*, fr. Gk. *sphigktḗr*, 'band'; cp. Gk. *sphiggein*, 'to bind tightly'; *sphígma*, 'knot'; *sphígx*, 'sphinx'; prob. a nasalized form of base **sp(h)eig-* &c., expanded fr. **sp(h)ē(i)-* &c., 'to stretch'. See **spasm, space, speed**. Muscular ring surrounding an orifice of the body and serving to close it.

sphincteral, adj. [1. sfíngkteral; 2. sfíŋktərəl]. Prec. & **-al**. Of, pertaining to, a sphincter.

sphincterial, adj. [1. sfingktérial; 2. sfìŋktíəriəl]. **sphincter** & **-ial**. Sphincteral.

sphincteric, adj. [1. sfingktérik; 2. sfìŋktérik]. **sphincter** & **-ic**. Sphincteral.

sphinx, n. [1. sfingks; 2. sfíŋks]. Lat. *sphinx*, fr. Gk. *sphígx*, 'sphinx', q.v. under **sphincter**. **1.** (cap., Gk. mythol.) Monster, usually represented with a woman's head and the body of a winged lion, who sat on a rock near Thebes and strangled all passers-by who could not solve the riddle which she put to them. **2.** (cap.) Egyptian sculptured figure of wingless lion with head of man, ram, or hawk; esp. *the Sphinx*, colossal, human-headed sphinx of Gizeh. **3.** (fig.) Person of mysterious or enigmatic character; inscrutable person. **4.** (zool.) **a** Hawk-moth; **b** Guinea baboon.

sphinx-like, adj. Resembling a sphinx.

sphinx-moth, n. Hawk-moth.

sphragistics, n. [1. sfrajístiks; 2. sfrədʒístiks], fr. Gk. *sphrāgistik-(ós)*, 'of seals', fr. *sphrāgízō*, 'I seal', fr. *sphrāgís*, 'seal, signet-ring, engraved stone'. Etymol. unknown. Study of engraved seals.

sphygmic, adj. [1. sfígmik; 2. sfígmik]. See **sphygmo-** & **-ic**. Pertaining to, resembling, the action of the pulse.

sphygmo-, pref. representing **sphygmus** & *-o-*. Pulse.

sphygmogram, n. [1. sfígmogràm; 2. sfígməgræ̀m]. Prec. & **-gram**. Graphic record of pulse-beats made by a sphygmograph.

sphygmograph, n. [1. sfígmogràhf; 2. sfígməgrāf]. **sphygmo-** & **-graph**. Instrument recording the force and rate of the pulse and its variations.

sphygmographic, adj. [1. sfìgmográfik; 2. sfìgməgrǽfik]. **sphygmo-** & **-graphic**. Pertaining to, recorded by, sphygmography.

sphygmography, n. [1. sfigmógrafi; 2. sfigmɔ́grəfi]. **sphygmo-** & **-graphy**. **a** Use, art of using, the sphygmograph; **b** study of sphygmograms.

sphygmology, n. [1. sfigmóloji; 2. sfigmɔ́lədži]. **sphygmo-** & **-logy**. The study of the pulse.

sphygmometer, n. [1. sfigmómeter; 2. sfigmɔ́mitə]. **sphygmo-** & **-meter**. Instrument for measuring blood-pressure in the arteries.

sphygmophone, n. [1. sfígmofòn; 2. sfígməfòun]. **sphygmo-** & **-phone**. Instrument for making the pulse-beat audible.

sphygmoscope, n. [1. sfígmoskòp; 2. sfígməskòup]. **sphygmo-** & **-scope**. Instrument representing the pulse-beat in visible form.

sphygmus, n. [1. sfígmus; 2. sfígməs]. Mod. Latinized form of Gk. *sphugmós*, 'pulsation'; cp. Gk. *sphúzein*, 'to beat, pulsate'; *ásphuktos*, 'pulseless, lifeless'; prob. fr. a variant **sphuk-*, of the base **sphək-* &c. seen in Gk. *sphákelos*, 'convulsive movement'. See **sphacelate**. **Pulse**.

spica, n. [1. spíka; 2. spáikə]. Lat. *spīca*, 'ear of corn'; cp. Lat. *spīna*, 'thorn'; cogn. w. Lett. *spīle*, 'wooden fork'; M. Du. *spīcher*, 'nail'; O.N. *spīkr*, 'spike, nail', see **spike**; O.H.G. *spënala*, 'needle'; O.E. *spinl*, 'spindle', see **spindle**. Cp. further O.E. *spitu*, 'spit', see **spit** (I.); Lith. *spitnà*, 'tongue of buckle'; Lat. *pinna*, 'pinnacle', see **pinna**; fr. base **(s)pi-*, **spei-*, 'point'. **1.** (bot.) Spike, flower-spike. **2.** (surg.) Spiral bandage with turns arranged in herring-bone pattern.

spicate(d), adj. [1. spíkāt, spīkāted; 2. spáikeit, spaikéitid]. Prec. & **-ate** & **-ed**. (bot.) Arranged in form of, forming, consisting of, a spike.

spice (I.), n. [1. spīs; 2. spais], fr. O. Fr. *espice*, *espece*, fr. Lat. *speciēs*, 'kind, sort'. See **species**. **1. a** Pungent, aromatic preparation, usually dried, of vegetable root, seed, &c., used for flavouring; **b** spices collectively. **2.** (fig.) Quality, feature, giving a characteristic touch or flavour: *a spice of malice in one's words*; *a spice of the devil in one's character*.

spice (II.), vb. trans., fr. prec. **1.** To flavour with spice. **2.** (fig.) To give a characteristic tinge or piquancy to.

spice-box, n. Box in which spices are kept; esp. ornamental box of china &c.

spicebush, n. [1. spísboosh; 2. spáisbuʃ]. Aromatic American shrub, *Lindera Benzoin*, of the laurel family.

spicery, n. [1. spíseri; 2. spáisəri]. **spice** & **-ery**. Spices generally.

spicewood, n. [1. spíswood; 2. spáiswud]. Spicebush.

spicily, adv. [1. spísili; 2. spáisili]. **spicy** & **-ly**. In a spicy manner.

spiciness, n. [1. spísines; 2. spáisinis]. **spicy** & **-ness**. State or quality of being spicy; pungency.

spick and span, adj. [1. spík an(d) spán; 2. spík ən(d) spæ̀n]. Formerly *spick-and-span-new*; perh. variant of **spike** & **spoon**= new and fresh as a chip or spike just made. Very smart, fresh, and spruce; bright, clean, and tidy: *he looked very spick and span*; *the whole place is thoroughly spick and span*.

spicular, adj. [1. spíkūlar; 2. spíkjulə]. **spicule** & **-ar**. Having the shape of, covered with, spicules.

spiculate, adj. [1. spíkūlāt; 2. spíkjuleit]. Next word & **-ate**. Having, covered with, divided into, spicules.

spicule, n. [1. spíkūl; 2. spáikjūl], fr. Lat. *spīcul-(um)*, 'small, sharp point; dart, arrow'; dimin. of *spīca*, 'ear of corn', see **spica**, & **-ule**. Any small, sharply pointed object; specif. **a** (bot.) small, secondary spike; **b** (zool.) small, hard, often needle-shaped, granule found in invertebrates, esp. as forming skeleton of sponge.

spicy, adj. [1. spísi; 2. spáisi]. **spice** (I.) & **-y**. **1.** Flavoured or perfumed with spice; pungent, aromatic. **2.** (fig.) Piquant, racy: *spicy conversation*; *spicy bits of scandal*.

spider, n. [1. spíder; 2. spáidə]. M.E. *spīþre*; prob. fr. earlier **spinþer*, fr. base of *spinnan*, 'to spin', & agent suff.; cp. Dan. *spinder* & see **spin**. **1.** A member of the order *Araneida*, with eight legs in four pairs and body of two segments, furnished with silk glands and spinnerets with which they spin webs for catching insects, thus distinguished from other arachnids, to which class they belong. **2.** Utensil, framework &c. resembling a spider in having long slender legs; specif. **a** trivet; **b** long-handled frying pan with feet to support it above a fire.

spider-catcher, n. [1. spíder kàcher; 2. spáidə kæ̀tʃə]. Kind of East Indian bird.

spider-crab, n. Sea-crab with long, slender legs.

spider-like, adj. Resembling a spider, esp. in having long, thin legs.

spider-line, n. Thread of spider's web used in delicate weighing instruments or to form reticle of telescope.

spider-monkey, n. Thin, long-legged, long-tailed monkey of S. and Central America.

spider-wasp, n. Wasp that provides in its nest a store of spiders &c. for its young.

spider-web, n. Web spun by spider to catch flies &c.; also *spider's web.*

spiderwort, n. [1. spíderwêrt; 2. spáidəwɅt]. Plant of the genus *Tradescantia*, esp. American perennial, deep-blue variety.

spidery, adj. [1. spíderi; 2. spáidəri]. **spider & -y.** 1. Connected with, pertaining to, a spider; resembling a spider in shape; *spidery handwriting*, with thin, sprawling strokes. 2. Infested with spiders.

spied, vb. [1. spīd; 2. spaid]. Pret. & P.P. of **spy.**

spiegeleisen, n. [1. spḗgl-īzen; 2. spígl-áizn], fr. Germ. *spiegel*, 'mirror', fr. O.H.G. *spiagal*, fr. Lat. *speculum*, 'mirror', see **speculum**, & *eisen*, 'iron', cogn. w. **iron.** Hard, brittle, white cast iron, containing manganese, used in making steel by Bessemer process.

spif(f)licate, vb. trans. [1. spíflikāt; 2. spíflikeit]. Etymol. unknown. (slang) a To squash, scotch; b to confound, disconcert.

spif(f)lication, n. [1. spìflikā́shun; 2. spìflikéiʃən]. Prec. & **-ion.** Act of spifflicating; state of being spifflicated.

spigot, n. [1. spígut; 2. spígət]. In M.E.; perh. fr. Provenç. *espigot*, 'ear of corn', fr. Lat. *spīca*, 'ear', see **spica**, & dimin. suff. Small plug for stopping air-hole in a cask; vent-peg.

spike (I.), n. [1. spīk; 2. spaik]. Partly fr. Lat. *spīca*, 'ear of corn,' see **spica**; chiefly fr. O.N. *spīk*, 'nail'; cp. O.H.G. *speihha*; O.E. *spāca*, 'spoke', see **spoke** (I.); Lett. *spikis*, 'bayonet'; M. Du. *spīcher*, 'nail'. See also **spire, spindle.** 1. Any tapering, sharp-pointed rod, bar, projection; specif. a a sharp-pointed metal projection on top of wall, railing &c.; b on soles of shoes &c. to prevent slipping. 2. Strong, stout metal nail, esp. as used in fixing railway lines. 3. Steel pin or stopper used for plugging vent of cannon. 4. Ear of corn. 5. (bot.) Inflorescence consisting of small sessile flowers arranged about an axis. 6. (slang) A High-Churchman, a ritualist.

spike (II.), vb. trans., fr. prec. 1. To provide, furnish, set, with spike(s): *spiked shoes*; *a spiked pole.* 2. To stop up vent of (cannon) with spike. Phr. (fig.) *to spike a person's guns*, to upset, frustrate, his plans, bring his devices to naught. 3. To pierce, fix, impale, with spike.

spike-lavender, n. French lavender, from which spike-oil is obtained.

spikelet, n. [1. spíklet; 2. spáiklit]. **spike** (I.) & **-let.** Small spike; esp. (bot.) secondary spike of inflorescence.

spike-nail, n. Large nail used for fastening thick planks together.

spikenard, n. [1. spíknàrd; 2. spáiknȧd]. M.E. *spikenard*, fr. O. Fr. *spiquenard*, fr. Lat. *spica nardi*, 'spike of nard'. See **spica, nard.** 1. Perennial aromatic herb resembling valerian. 2. Fragrant, costly ointment anciently prepared from this herb. 3. Kind of aromatic, vegetable oil.

spike-oil, n. Oil obtained from a species of lavender.

spike-plank, n. Platform before mizzen-mast of ship in polar regions.

spikewise, adv. [1. spíkwīz; 2. spáikwaiz]. **spike** (I.) & **-wise.** In the form of a spike.

spiky, adj. [1. spíki; 2. spáiki]. **spike** (I.) & **-y.** 1. a Set, bristling, with spikes; b (fig., of persons) difficult to deal with, cantankerous, touchy. 2. Resembling a spike in form.

spile (I.), n. [1. spīl; 2. spail]. Cp. Du. *spijl*, 'bar'; Germ. *speiler*, 'skewer'; cp. M.H.G. *spille*, 'peg'; O.N. *spila*, 'narrow piece of wood'. Cp. further Lat. *spīna*, 'thorn', see **spine**; *spīca*, 'ear of corn', see **spica.** See also **spoke** (I.), **spire, spindle** (II.). 1. Timber driven into ground as foundation for building or other erection; pile. 2. Wooden spigot, a vent-peg.

spile (II.), vb. trans., fr. prec. To pierce hole in (a cask) for spile; to vent: *to spile a cask.*

spiling, n. [1. spíling; 2. spáiliŋ]. Prec. & **-ing.** 1. Set of piles for building; spiles collectively. 2. (naut.) Curve of plank in ship's hull.

spill (I.), vb. trans. & intrans. [1. spil; 2. spil]. L.O.E. *spillan*, 'to destroy', fr. O.N. *spilla*; cp. O.E. *spildan*, 'to kill'; M. Du. *spillen, spilden*; O.H.G. *spaltan*, 'to split'; O.N. *spjald*, 'plank'; M.H.G. *spélte*, 'splinter'; M.E. *spalden*, 'to split, chip'. See **spall** (II.). A. trans. 1. To allow (liquid &c.) to splash or run out of vessel, esp. unintentionally, permit to escape or be wasted: *to spill gravy, salt, a glass of milk, on the tablecloth*; Phr. (slang) *to spill the beans*, divulge a secret, blow the gaff. 2. (colloq.) To throw out or off, upset: *to be spilt from vehicle, horse &c.* 3. (naut.) To empty of wind before reefing &c.: *to spill a sail.* B. intrans. (of liquid &c.) To flow, splash, be upset, out of a vessel.

spill (II.), n., fr. prec. (colloq.) A fall, esp. from a horse or vehicle; a toss, a tumble.

spill (III.), n. Cp. O.E. *speld*, 'a splinter of wood; a torch'; Goth. *spilda*, 'writing-tablet'; O.N. *spjald*, 'plank', q.v. under **spall** (II.). A thin, narrow shaving or strip of wood, or paper, used for lighting pipes &c.

spiller, n. [1. spíler; 2. spílə]. Etymol. doubtful. Small mackerel-seine let down into larger one to remove the fish.

spillikin, n. [1. spílikin; 2. spílikin], fr. M.E. *spelleken*, fr. M. Du., dimin. of *spelle*, 'pin, peg', prob. cogn. w. O.E. *speld*, 'splinter of wood', q.v. under **spall** (II.). a Slender strip of wood, ivory &c. used in the game of spillikins; b (pl.) the game itself.

spilling-line, n. [1. spíling līn; 2. spíliŋ lain]. (naut.) Rope used for spilling a square-sail.

spillway, n. [1. spílwā; 2. spílwei]. **spill** (I.) & **-way.** Passage in a dam to carry off overflow of water.

spilth, n. [1. spilth; 2. spilþ]. **spill** (I.) & **-th.** (archaic) Surplus, overflow, excess.

spin (I.), vb. trans. & intrans. [1. spin; 2. spin]. O.E. *spinnan*; M.E. *spinnen*; cp. O.H.G. *spinnan*; O.N. *spinna*; Goth. *spinnan*, 'to spin'; cogn. w. Lith. *pinù*, 'to stretch, draw, tie'; O. Slav. *pęto*, 'fetter'; cp. further O.E. *spannan*, 'to clasp, enfold', see **span** (I.) &, further, **space**, & cp. **spindle.** A. trans. 1. To draw out and twist (yarn, wool, fibre) into threads. 2. a To make (thread) by spinning; Phrs. *to spin a yarn*, tell a story; *to spin out*, protract unduly; b (of silkworm &c.) *to spin a cocoon*, to form by exuding silk. 3. a To cause to revolve rapidly, to twirl, twist, rotate: *to spin a ball, a top*; specif., *to spin a coin*, to toss up; b (slang) to reject, plough (examination candidate). B. intrans. 1. To practise the art, engage in occupation of, spinning thread: '*the lilies of the field . . . toil not, neither do they spin*'. 2. To revolve rapidly, rotate, turn, on axis. Phr. *to send (person or thing) spinning*, to strike forcibly and cause to fall, roll, stagger.

spin (II.), n., fr. prec. 1. Act of spinning, rapid rotation, whirl; twist given to a ball. 2. Short spell of rapid, brisk exercise or movement: *to go for a spin in a car, on a horse &c.*

spinaceous, adj. [1. spinā́shus; 2. spinéiʃəs]. **spinach & -aceous.** Pertaining to, resembling, spinach.

spinach, spinage, n. [1. spínij; 2. spínidž], fr. O. Fr. *espinache*; fr. Span., fr. Arab. *aspanakh*, fr. Pers. Annual garden herb, *Spinacia oleracea*, with hollow stems, and edible, bitter, fleshy leaves, used as a vegetable.

spinach beet, n. Vegetable resembling and cooked to look like spinach, but having a different flavour.

spinal, adj. [1. spínl; 2. spáinl], fr. L. Lat. *spīnāl-(is)*, 'spinal'. **spine & -al.** Pertaining to, connected with, the spine: *spinal injury, curvature &c.*; *spinal column*, spine, backbone; *spinal cord*, structure of nerve-fibres and cells passing down the spinal column and forming an important part of the nervous system.

spindle (I.), n. [1. spíndl; 2. spíndl]. O.E. *spinl*; M.E. *spindle*; cp. O.H.G. *spinala*, 'spindle'; *spēnala*, 'needle'; fr. base seen in **spine, spike**; possibly having orig. connexion w. **spin** (I.), but in any case associated w. it. 1. Slender rod on which the thread from the distaff is wound in hand-spinning; Phr. *spindle side*, maternal side, female line. 2. Rod holding the bobbin of a spinning-machine. 3. Rod, pin, shaft, axis, on which anything rotates; e.g. *the spindle of a lathe.*

spindle (II.), vb. intrans., fr. prec. To grow into, assume, a long slender shape.

spindle-legged, adj. Having long, slender legs.

spindle-shanked, adj. [1. spíndl shàngkt; 2. spíndl ʃæ̀ŋkt]. Spindle-legged.

spindle-shanks, n. [1. spíndl shàngks; 2. spíndl ʃæ̀ŋks]. Spindle-shanked person.

spindle-shaped, adj. Shaped like a spindle; in the form of a slender cylinder tapering at both ends.

spindle-tree, n. Shrub, *Euonymus*, with close-grained wood used for spindles, skewers &c.

spindle-whorl, n. Perforated disk of stone, pottery &c. used to weight a spindle.

spindly, adj. [1. spíndli; 2. spíndli]. **spindle** (I.) & **-ly.** Spindle-shaped; long and thin.

spindrift, n. [1. spíndrift; 2. spíndrift]. Variant of *spoon-drift*, earlier *spoom-drift*, fr. Lat. *spūma*, 'foam', see **spume, & drift.** Spray blown over water from crests of waves; (attrib.) *spindrift clouds*, light, feathery clouds.

spine, n. [1. spīn; 2. spain], fr. O. Fr. *espine*, fr. Lat. *spīna*, 'thorn; spine, prickle; backbone', fr. base *(s)pī-, *(s)pei-, 'point', as in **spica, spike** &c. 1. Bony column composed of series of small bones or vertebrae, jointed together, running from the back of the head to the hips in vertebrates, and in animals other than man, being continued to form the tail. 2. Any stiff, pointed, spiky structure on the surface of an animal's body: *the spines of a porcupine.* 3. (bot.) Sharply pointed, slender projection resulting from modification of a leaf or other organ; thorn: *the spines of a fir tree.*

spineback, n. [1. spínbak; 2. spáinbæk]. Fish with spines on ridge of back.

spined, adj. [1. spīnd; 2. spaind]. **spine & -ed.** Having a spine or spines.

spinel (I.), n. [1. spinél; 2. spinél], fr. O. Fr. *espinelle*, dimin. of *espine*, 'spine', see **spine.** Kind of vitreous, crystalline mineral, red, blue, green, or brown; *spinel ruby*, red variety.

spinel (II.), n. [1. spínel; 2. spínəl]. Origin unknown. Linen yarn used for making tape.

spineless, adj. [1. spínles; 2. spáinlis]. **spine & -less.** 1. Having no backbone; invertebrate. 2. (fig.) Lacking moral backbone; irresolute, lacking in force of character. 3. (bot.) Without spines: *spineless cactus.*

spinet, n. [1. spínet, spinét; 2. spínet, spinét], fr. M. Fr. *espinette*, fr. Ital. *spinetta*, dimin. of *spina*, 'thorn, spine', see **spine**, named fr. the quills w. wh. the strings were plucked; or fr. the name of the alleged inventor, G. Spinetti, of Venice (c. 1500). Small keyboard instrument of 16th, 17th, and 18th cents., ancestor of the harpsichord and piano.

spini-, pref. representing Lat. *spīna*, 'thorn; spine; backbone', see **spine.** 1. Backbone. 2. Thorn, spine.

spinicerebrate, adj. [1. spínisérebrāt; 2. spàinisérəbreit]. Prec. & **cerebro- & -ate.** Having a brain and spinal cord.

spiniferous, adj. [1. spiníferus; 2. spainífərəs]. **spini- & -ferous.** Producing spines, thorns.

spinifex, n. [1. spínifeks; 2. spínifeks]. Kind of Australian grass with stiff, sharply pointed leaves.

spiniform, adj. [1. spínifòrm; 2. spáinifɔ̀m]. **spini- & -form.** Having the shape of a spine, or thorn.

spininess, n. [1. spínines; 2. spáininis]. **spiny & -ness.** State or quality of being spiny.

spinitis, n. [1. spīnítis; 2. spaináitis]. **spini-** & **-itis**. Inflammation of the spinal cord.

spinnaker, n. [1. spínaker; 2. spínəkə]. Possibly connected w. **spin**. Large triangular sail carried on the side opposite the mainsail by racing-cutters &c. when running before the wind.

spinner, n. [1. spíner; 2. spínə]. **spin (I.)** & **-er**. **1.** One who, that which, spins; specif. **a** one who shapes cups &c. on a revolving lathe; **b** spinning-machine. **2.** Spinneret.

spinneret, n. [1. spíneret; 2. spínərɛt]. Prec. & **-et**. Silk or thread-spinning organ of silk-worm, spider &c.

spinney, n. [1. spíni; 2. spíni], fr. O. Fr. *espinoye*, fr. Lat. *spīnētum*, 'thorn-hedge, thicket', fr. *spīna*, 'thorn', see **spine**, & cp. suff. in **arboretum**. Copse, thicket.

spinning-house, n. [1. spíning hous; 2. spíniŋ haus]. (hist.) Women's house of correction, the inmates of which were made to spin.

spinning-jenny, n. Machine for spinning several threads at the same time.

spinning-wheel, n. Instrument used for household spinning, with spindle rotated by fly-wheel usually worked by a treadle.

spinose, adj. [1. spínōs; 2. spáinous], fr. Lat. *spīnōsus*, 'thorny, prickly'. **spine** & **-ose**. Full of, covered with, spines; spiny, prickly.

spinosity, n. [1. spīnósiti; 2. spainósiti], fr. L. Lat. *spīnōsitātem*, 'thorniness'. Prec. & **-ity**. State of being spinose.

spinous, adj. [1. spínus; 2. spáinəs]. **spine** & **-ous**. **1.** Having, producing, spines; spinose. **2.** Having the shape of a spine; spiniform; *spinous process*, part of vertebra projecting backwards.

Spinozism, n. [1. spī-, spinózizm; 2. spai-, spinóuzizəm], fr. Benedict de Spinoza, d. 1677, & **-ism**. Philosophical system of Spinoza.

Spinozist, n. [1. spin-, spinózist; 2. sp(a)inóuzist]. See prec. & **-ist**. Adherent of Spinoza.

Spinozistic, adj. [1. spìn-, spìnōzístik; 2. sp(à)inouzístik]. Prec. & **-ic**. Pertaining to, resembling, Spinozism.

spinster, n. [1. spínster; 2. spínstə]. M.E. *spinnester*, 'woman who spins'. **spin (I.)** & **-ster**. Unmarried woman; (popularly) esp. elderly unmarried woman.

spinsterhood, n. [1. spínsterhood; 2. spínstəhud]. Prec. & **-hood**. State of being a spinster.

spinthariscope, n. [1. spinthárisköp; 2. spinþǽriskoup], fr. Gk. *spintharís*, 'spark'; cp. Gk. *spinthḗr*, 'spark'; Lith *spìstu*, 'to shine, sparkle'; Lett. *spīdu*, 'to shine'; *spudrs*, 'brilliant'; & **-scope**. Instrument for exhibiting the scintillations caused by the impact of products of radium disintegration against a screen.

spinule, n. [1. spínūl; 2. spáinjūl], fr. Lat. *spīnula*, 'little thorn'. **spine** & **-ule**. Small spine, prickle.

spinuliferous, adj. [1. spìnūlíferus; 2. spàinjulíferəs]. Prec. & **-i-** & **-ferous**. Bearing spinules.

spinulose, adj. [1. spínulōs; 2. spáinjulous]. **spinule** & **-ose**. Having, covered with, spinules.

spinulous, adj. [1. spínūlus; 2. spáinjuləs]. **spinule** & **-ous**. Of, like, covered with, small spines.

spiny, adj. [1. spíni; 2. spáini]. **spine** & **-y**. **1.** Having, covered with, full of, spines; *spiny ant-eater*, echidna; *spiny rat*, genus of rats of Central and South America, with spines among the hair. **2.** (fig.) Difficult, perplexing, harassing: *a spiny subject to discuss*.

spiracle, n. [1. spírakl; 2. spáiərəkl], fr. Lat. *spīrāculum*, 'breathing-hole', fr. *spīrāre*, 'to breathe', see **spirant**, & **-cule**. External orifice used in respiration; breathing-hole, air-hole; specif. **a** external opening of trachea of insect; **b** blow-hole of cetacean.

spiracular, adj. [1. spīrákūlar; 2. spairǽkjulə], fr. Lat. *spīrāculum*, see prec., & **-ar**. Pertaining to, of the nature of, a spiracle.

spiraculate, adj. [1. spīrákūlāt; 2. spairǽkjuleit], fr. Lat. *spīrāculum*, see **spiracle**, & **-ate**. Having a spiracle or spiracles.

spiraea, n. [1. spīréa; 2. spairíə]. Lat. *spīraea*, fr. Gk. *speiraiā*, 'meadow-sweet'; cp. Gk. *speîra*, 'spiral; net; tissue', see **spire (III.)**. Genus of small rosaceous shrubs or herbs with feathery clusters of small white or pink flowers.

spiral (I.), adj. [1. spíral; 2. spáiərəl], fr. Lat. *spīrālis*, 'spiral', fr. *spīra*, 'coil', see **spire (III.)**, & **-al**. **1.** Forming a curve that winds continually about a centre from which it constantly recedes. **2.** Winding constantly about a centre while undergoing continual change of plane, as on surface of cylinder or cone: *spiral staircase, spring, thread of screw* &c.; *spiral balance*, instrument measuring weight by the torsion of a spiral spring.

spiral (II.), n., fr. prec. **1. a** Spiral curve remaining in one plane; **b** spiral curve that changes its plane continuously, forming a cone or cylinder. **2.** Object or series of objects arranged to form a spiral; specif. **a** spiral spring; **b** spiral or whorled shell.

spiral (III.), vb. trans. & intrans., fr. prec. **1.** trans. To form into, arrange as, a spiral; to make spiral. **2.** intrans. To move in, form, a spiral.

spirality, n. [1. spīráliti; 2. spaiərǽliti]. **spiral (I.)** & **-ity**. State of being spiral.

spirally, adv. [1. spírali; 2. spáiərəli]. See prec. & **-ly**. In a spiral manner, so as to form a spiral.

spirant, n. & adj. [1. spírant; 2. spáiərənt], fr. Lat. *spīrantem*, Pres. Part. of *spīrāre*, 'to breathe, blow'; cp. Lat. *spīritus*, 'breath; spirit'; prob. fr. base *(s)peis-, 'to blow', as in O. Slav. *piskŭ*, 'to pipe'; see **spirit (I.)** & cp. **despair**. **1.** n. (phon.) A consonantal sound formed by a constriction, but not a total closure, of the air-passage, so that the air-stream passes continuously, and the sound can be prolonged indefinitely; called also *open consonant*; contrasted with *stop*. **2.** adj. Of the nature of a spirant.

spirated, adj. [1. spírāted; 2. spáiəreitid]. **spire (III.)** & **-ate** & **-ed**. Twisted into spiral form.

spire (I.), n. [1. spīr; 2. spaiə]. O.E., M.E. *spīr*, 'sprout; spire'; cp. M.L.G. *spīr*; O.N. *spīra*, 'point, ear of corn'; fr. base *spī-, *spei-, 'point'. Seen also in **spike**, **spine** &c. **1.** Tall, slender prolongation of a tower, which tapers to a point. **2.** Any of various objects tapering to a point, e.g. flower-cluster of this shape; an ear of corn; the upper part of a tapering tree such as a poplar.

spire (II.), vb. intrans. & trans., fr. prec. (rare) **1.** intrans. To taper upwards, shoot up, in a spire. **2.** trans. To furnish with, build with, a spire.

spire (III.), n., fr. Fr., fr. Lat. *spīra*, fr. Gk. *speîra*, 'coil, twist; braid; net'; cp. Gk. *speirāma*, 'fold of a serpent'; *speíron*, 'web, tissue'; *speiraiā*, 'spiraea'; cp. further Gk. *spártos*, 'esparto grass'; *spurís*, 'woven basket'; Lith. *spartas*, 'bond'. **a** Spiral coil, esp. rising spiral; **b** single coil or twist of a spiral; whorl.

Spirillum, n., pl. **Spirilla** [1. spīríllum, -a; 2. spairílə(m)]. Mod. Lat., dimin. of Lat. *spīra*, 'coil, twist', see **spire (III.)**. A genus of bacteria, of spiral or twisted thread-like shape; one species is the cause of cholera.

spirit (I.), n. [1. spírit; 2. spírit]. M.E. *spirit*, *sprit*, fr. O. Fr. *espirit*, fr. Lat. *spīritus*, 'breath; breeze; breath of life; life; soul, mind, spirit; energy, courage; pride, arrogance', fr. *spīrāre*, 'to breathe', see **spirant**. **1.** The life-giving principle; breath of life, conceived of as animating the body. **2. a** The immortal, non-material part of, or element in, man, which wills, thinks, and feels; thought of as a gift of God; contrasted with *body*; intelligence, soul; (translating Gk. *pneûma*, or Lat. *spiritus*, and *anima*): *the spirit shall return to God who gave it*; *to lead the life of the spirit*; **b** this element or principle thought of as separated from the body; disembodied intelligence: *the spirits and souls of the righteous*; *the abode of spirits*. **3.** Life, will, and consciousness thought of as existing apart from matter, and as never being associated with a body, and yet as pervading all things; contrasted with *matter*: *God is pure spirit*; (specif.) *the Holy Spirit*, the third Person of the Trinity; Holy Ghost. **4.** A materialized, sometimes visible, disembodied spirit; an apparition, spectre, ghost: *are the phenomena of the séance room really the work of spirits?* **5.** Individual human being, a person, thought of as exhibiting certain qualities of mind, character, disposition: *Dr. Johnson is recognized as one of the greatest spirits of his day*. **6.** Temper, mood, disposition; mental attitude, frame of mind: '*His spirits do not seem to have been high, but they were singularly equable*' (Macaulay, on Milton); *a noble spirit animates all Burke's speeches*; *to show a mean, a proper, the right, spirit*; *high spirits*, cheerfulness, elation; *low spirits*, dejection, depression, of mind. **7.** Vigour, energy of mind and character; liveliness, vivacity, fire; noble pride and courage; contempt for what is mean and base: *a young man of spirit*; *a cowardly wretch who shows no spirit*; *the king faced his accusers with spirit*. **8.** Real meaning, true intention, underlying principle; contrasted with *letter*: *he obeyed the true spirit of the law*; *you must understand this in the spirit in which it was written*. **9. a** A volatile distilled essence, alcohol: *to burn spirit in a lamp*; **b** *spirits*, (i.) powerful alcoholic drink; (ii.) any powerful distilled alcoholic liquor: *anatomical specimens are often preserved in spirits*. **10.** (obs.) An aspirate, a rough breathing; translating Lat. *spiritus asper*.

spirit (II.), vb. trans., fr. prec. **1.** Usually *spirit away, off*, to carry off, remove, secretly, swiftly, and mysteriously. **2.** To give spirit to, animate, cheer.

spirit-blue, n. Kind of aniline dye soluble in alcohol.

spirit-duck, n. Kind of wild duck with unusually rapid dive.

spirited, adj. [1. spírited; 2. spíritid]. **spirit** & **-ed**. **1.** Vigorous, animated, full of life, spirit, or courage: *spirited dialogue*; *a spirited attack, defence*; *a spirited horse*. **2.** (in compounds) **a** Having specified character or disposition: *poor-, high-spirited*; *public-spirited*; **b** showing specified mood: *low-spirited*.

spiritedly, adv. Prec. & **-ly**. **1.** In a spirited manner. **2.** (in compounds) In a manner showing specified kind of spirit(s): *high-spiritedly*.

spiritedness, n. See prec. & **-ness**. **1.** State or quality of being spirited. **2.** (in compounds) State of having specified spirit(s).

spirit-gum, n. Gum dissolved in alcohol, used by actors &c. to affix false beard &c.

spiritism, n. [1. spíritizm; 2. spíritizəm]. **spirit** & **-ism**. **1.** Spiritualism. **2.** Animism.

spiritist, n. [1. spíritist; 2. spíritist]. **spirit** & **-ist**. Believer in spiritism, spiritualist.

spirit-lamp, n. One in which alcohol is burnt.

spiritless, adj. [1. spíritles; 2. spíritlis]. **spirit** & **-less**. Lacking spirit, animation, energy, vigour, or courage; listless, apathetic.

spiritlessly, adv. Prec. & **-ly**. In a spiritless manner.

spiritlessness, n. Prec. & **-ness**. State or quality of being spiritless; listlessness.

spirit-level, n. Glass tube almost completely filled with spirit, and used in surveying &c. to show any deviation from the level.

spiritoso, adv. [1. spìritósō; 2. spìritóusou]. Ital.; **spirit** & **-ose**. (mus.) With spirit, with animation.

spirit-rapping, n. [1. spírit ràping; 2. spírit rǽpiŋ]. **a** Raps on table &c., made at spiritualist séances, as it is alleged, by disembodied spirits; **b** (loosely) the physical phenomena generally, said to be produced by spirits.

spirit-room, n. Paymaster's storeroom.

spirit(s) of wine, n. [1. spírit(s) uv wīn; 2. spírit(s) əv wáin]. Pure alcohol.

spirit-stove, n. Stove for cooking &c., heated by burning spirit.

spiritual (I.), adj. [1. spírichooal; 2. spíritʃuəl], fr. O. Fr., fr. Lat. *spīrituālis*, 'of breathing; of the spirit', fr. *spīritus*, 'breath, spirit'. See **spirit** (I.), & **-al**; see also **spirant**. **1.** Pertaining to, of the nature of, spirit; contrasted with *material*; incorporeal: *spiritual beings.* **2. a** Pertaining to the soul or spirit; connected with the inner life and being; contrasted with *physical, carnal*, or *bodily*: *the spiritual life*; *spiritual concerns, ideals*; *spiritual growth*; **b** preoccupied with the things of the spirit; expressing, animated by, thoughts and interests connected with the spirit; not centred in material, or worldly things: *a spiritual mind*; *a spiritual face, expression* &c. **3.** Proceeding from, inspired by, the Holy Spirit: *spiritual gifts*; *psalms and hymns and spiritual songs.* **4.** Of, pertaining to, the Church or to religion; ecclesiastical as opposed to secular or temporal: *a spiritual court*; *Lords Spiritual*, peers of Parliament who are bishops.

spiritual (II.), n., fr. prec. Also *negro spiritual*, a sacred song or hymn as sung by the negroes in the U.S.A.

spiritualism, n. [1. spírichooalizm; 2. spíritʃuəlizəm]. **spiritual** (I.) & **-ism**. **1.** Philosophical theory that spirit is the ultimate reality; idealism. **2. a** Belief that the spirits of the dead can and do communicate with the living by means of material manifestations; **b** the system of belief, beliefs collectively, of spiritualists; practices based on these beliefs.

spiritualist, n. [1. spírichooalist; 2. spíritʃuəlist]. **spiritual** (I.) & **-ist**. Believer in spiritualism; **a** in sense **1**; **b** in sense **2**.

spiritualistic, adj. [1. spìrichooalístik; 2. spìritʃuəlístik]. Prec. & **-ic**. Of, pertaining to, a spiritualist or to spiritualism.

spirituality, n. [1. spìrichooáliti; 2. spìritʃuǽliti], fr. O. Fr., fr. L. Lat. *spīrituālitātem*, 'spirituality'. **spiritual** (I.) & **-ity**. **1.** Quality of being spiritual; spiritual character or nature; contrasted with *materiality, sensuality* &c. **2. a** The spiritual jurisdiction belonging to the Church or to an ecclesiastical office; **b** fees and revenues due to the holder, as such, of an ecclesiastical benefice.

spiritualization, n. [1. spìrichooalīzáshun; 2. spìritʃuəlaizéiʃən]. Next word & **-ation**. Act of spiritualizing; state of being spiritualized.

spiritualize, vb. trans. [1. spírichooalīz; 2. spíritʃuəlaiz]. **spiritual** (I.) & **-ize**. **1.** To render spiritual; to purify; to give a spiritual, elevated, non-material character to (a person, belief &c.). **2.** To give a spiritual meaning to; contrasted with *literalize*.

spiritually, adv. [1. spírichooali; 2. spíritʃuəli]. **spiritual** (I.) & **-ly**. In a spiritual manner.

spiritualness, n. [1. spírichualnes; 2. spíritʃuəlnis]. See prec. & **-ness**. State or quality of being spiritual.

spirituelle, adj. [1. spìritūél; 2. spìritjuél]. Fr. *spirituelle*, fem. form of *spirituel*, fr. Lat. *spīrituālis*, 'of a spirit', see **spiritual**. **1.** Delicate, graceful, ethereal. **2.** Delicately and gracefully witty.

spirituous, adj. [1. spíritūus; 2. spíritjuəs], fr. O. Fr. *spiritueux*, fr. Lat. *spiritus*, 'breath; spirit', see **spirit** (I.) & **-ous**. Containing a large percentage of alcohol; esp. of distilled liquor as distinct from fermented.

spirituousness, n. Prec. & **-ness**. State or quality of being spirituous.

spiritus, n. [1. spíritus; 2. spáiəritəs]. Lat. *spiritus*, 'breath; (gram.) breathing, aspiration', see **spirit**. (Gk. gram.) *Spiritus asper*, rough breathing, aspiration; *spiritus lenis*, smooth breathing.

spirivalve, adj. [1. spírivàlv; 2. spáiərivæ̀lv], fr. Lat. *spīra*, 'coil, spiral', see **spire** (III.), & *-i-* & **valve**. **1.** Having a spiral shell. **2.** (of shell) Spiral, whorled.

spirket, n. [1. spérket; 2. spə́kit]. Etymol. unknown. Space between floor-timbers of a ship, forward and aft.

spirketing, n. [1. spérketing; 2. spə́kitiŋ]. Prec. & **-ing**. Part of inside planking of a ship.

spiro- (I.), pref. representing Lat. *spīra*, 'coil', see **spire** (III.). Spiral, whorled; e.g. *Spirochaete*, a thread-like bacterium of the genus *Spirochaeta*, of the *Spirillum* type, one species, *S. pallida*, is the cause of syphilis; *Spirodela*, genus of aquatic plants including the great duckweed.

spiro- (II.), pref. representing Lat. *spīr-(āre)*, 'to breathe'. See **spirant**. Breath, breathing.

spirograph, n. [1. spírōgràhf; 2. spáiərougràf]. **spiro-** (II.) & **-graph**. Instrument recording movements made in breathing.

spirometer, n. [1. spīrómeter; 2. spairɔ́mitə]. **spiro-** (II.) & **-meter**. Instrument for measuring the capacity of the lungs.

spirometric, adj. [1. spìrōmétrik; 2. spáiəroumétrik]. Prec. & **-ic**. Pertaining to, recorded by, a spirometer.

spirometry, n. [1. spìrómetri; 2. spàirɔ́mitri]. **spiro-** (II.) & **-metry**. The measurement of the breathing capacity of the lungs.

spirophore, n. [1. spírōfòr; 2. spáiəroufɔ̀]. **spiro-** (II.) & **-phore**. Instrument for inducing artificial respiration.

spirt (I.), **spurt**, vb. intrans. & trans. [1. spërt; 2. spə̄t]. Metathesized form of O.E. *spryttan*, 'to shoot forth, sprout'; cp. O.E. *sprūtan*, 'to sprout', see **sprout**. **1.** intrans. (of liquid) To shoot out, gush out, in a small, sudden jet or stream. **2.** trans. To squirt out, pour out in a sudden jet.

spirt (II.), **spurt**, n., fr. prec. See also **spurt** (I.) w. special sense. Sudden, small, but strong jet or stream of liquid.

spiry (I.), adj. [1. spīri; 2. spáiəri]. **spire** (I.) & **-y**. **a** Of, pertaining to, having the form of, having, a spire; **b** abounding in spires.

spiry (II.), adj. **spire** (III.) & **-y**. Spiral, coiled.

spit (I.), n. [1. spit; 2. spit]. O.E. *spitu*; M.E. *spite*; cp. O.H.G. *spiz*; M. Du. *spit, spet*; cp. also O.H.G. *spizzi*; Mod. Germ. *spitz*, 'point'; cogn. w. Lith. *spitnà*, 'tongue of a buckle'; Lat. *pinna*, 'pinnacle'; *bipinnis*, 'two-edged'; fr. base **(s)pi(d)-, *(s)pi(t)-*, 'point', expanded fr. **(s)pei-, *spī-*, 'point', see **spine, spike**. **1.** Long, thin pointed bar of iron thrust through and supporting meat to be roasted before a fire. **2.** Long, narrow point of land or sandbank extending into the sea, separating lagoon from sea &c.

spit (II.), vb. trans., fr. prec. To pierce, penetrate, transfix, with, or as with, a spit.

spit (III.), vb. intrans. & trans. O.E. *spittan*; M.E. *spitten*; fr. *spit-*, gradational variant of base in O.E. *spǣtan*, 'to spit', wh. is for **spāt-jan*, earlier **spait-*; ultimately related to **spew** & **sputum**. **A.** intrans. **1. a** To eject saliva from the mouth; Phr. *spit upon* (fig.), to treat, regard, with contempt; **b** (of an angry cat) to make a noise like that of spitting, or hissing. **2.** (of boiling liquid, fat &c.) To sputter, hiss, spirt out in minute drops. **3.** To rain intermittently and lightly. **B.** trans. **1. a** Often *spit out*, to eject from the mouth; *to spit blood*, cough it up from the lungs or throat; **b** (vulg.) to utter, say, tell; esp. in Phr. *spit it out*, out with it. **2.** To utter violently, as in anger, contempt, malice: *he spat his words at his hearers.*

spit (IV.), n., fr. prec. **1.** Act of spitting. **2.** Saliva, spittle; Phr. *the dead spit of* (a person), another who resembles him exactly, living image. **3.** Frothy secretion of certain insects. **4.** A sprinkle of rain.

spit (V.), n. Prob. fr. Du. *spit*, 'a spit'; cp. O.E. *spittan*, 'to dig'. Depth of earth equal to blade of spade.

spitchcock, n. & vb. trans. [1. spíchkok; 2. spítʃkɔk]. Etymol. doubtful. **1.** n. Eel split and broiled. **2.** vb. To split and broil (eel, bird &c.).

spite (I.), n. [1. spīt; 2. spait]. Abbr. of despite. **1.** Malice, malevolence, mean or petty hatred: *the victim of another's spite*; *to do something out of spite*; Phr. *spite of, in spite of*, notwithstanding, in defiance of. **2.** Cause of dislike or desire to injure; grudge: *to have a spite against one.*

spite (II.), vb. trans., fr. prec. To injure, annoy, through malevolence; to act maliciously towards: *it is only done to spite me.*

spiteful, adj. [1. spítfool; 2. spáitful]. **spite** (I.) & **-ful**. Full of, caused by, spite; malicious, malevolent, meanly hostile.

spitefully, adv. Prec. & **-ly**. In a spiteful manner.

spitefulness, n. See prec. & **-ness**. Quality of being spiteful.

spitfire, n. [1. spítfīr; 2. spítfaiə]. **spit** (III.) & **fire** (I.). Sharp-tongued person; one given to hasty, biting speech.

spittle, n. [1. spítl; 2. spítl]. O.E. *spātl*; M.E. *spōtel*; remodelled on **spit** (III.). Secretions of the glands of the mouth, saliva, esp. when ejected.

spittoon, n. [1. spitóon; 2. spitúːn]. **spit** (III.) & **-oon**. Receptacle for saliva ejected by smokers.

spitz, n. [1. spits; 2. spits], fr. Germ. *spitzhund*, fr. *spitz*, 'point', q.v. under **spit** (I.). Also *spitz-dog*, breed of small dog, with narrow, tapering muzzle and long, silky hair; Pomeranian.

splanchnic, adj. [1. splángknik; 2. splǽŋknik], fr. Gk. *splágkhna*, 'viscera'. See next word & **-ic**. Of, pertaining to, the abdominal viscera, esp. the intestines.

splanchno-, pref. representing Gk. *splágkhnon*, 'viscera'; prob. cogn. w. *splḗn*, 'spleen', see **spleen**, cogn. w. Scrt. *plīhán-*; Lat. *liēn*; O. Slav. *slezena*, 'spleen'. The abdominal viscera.

splanchnology, n. [1. splàngknóloji; 2. splæ̀ŋknɔ́lədʒi]. Prec. & **-logy**. The science or study of the viscera.

splanchnoskeleton, n. [1. splángknōskéletun; 2. splǽŋknouskélitən]. **splanchno-** & **skeleton**. Part of the skeleton surrounding the viscera.

splanchnotomy, n. [1. splàngknótumi; 2. splæ̀ŋknɔ́təmi]. **splanchno-** & **-tomy**. Dissection of the viscera.

splash (I.), vb. trans. & intrans. [1. splash; 2. splæʃ]. Of imitative origin. **A.** trans. **1.** (of liquid) To scatter, fly about, and fall in drops upon: *the mud has splashed my dress.* **2.** To cause (liquid) to fly or scatter in drops or small streams: *to splash ink on to one's fingers.* **3.** To cause liquid to scatter or fall in drops upon: *to splash a page with ink.* **4.** To achieve, effect, by splashing: *to splash one's way through the mud.* **5.** To adorn with scattered ornament irregularly placed. **B.** intrans. **1.** (of liquid) To fly about, scatter, in drops or small streams, esp. as result of sudden pressure of falling body: *the mud splashed up at every step.* **2.** To strike liquid so as to cause it to fly or scatter in drops. **3.** To pass, go, so as to cause splashing: *to splash through the stream.*

splash (II.), n., fr. prec. **1.** Act of splashing: *to fall into water with a splash.* Phr. *to make a splash*, to create a sensation by display &c. **2.** Sound produced by splashing. **3. a** Spot, streak, or patch of liquid splashed on to a surface: *a splash of ink on the carpet*; **b** patch or streak of colour on a surface. **4.** Kind of white face-powder.

splash-board, n. Screen or guard protecting passengers in a vehicle from splashes caused by wheels &c.

splasher, n. [1. splásher; 2. splǽʃə]. **splash** (I.) & **-er**. **1.** One who, that which, splashes. **2.** Screen &c. giving protection from splashes; specif. **a** splash-board; **b** mudguard over wheel of locomotive; **c** curtain &c. protecting wall behind wash-stand.

splashy, adj. [1. spláshi; 2. splǽʃi]. **splash** & **-y**. Liable to splash; wet, muddy.

splatter, vb. intrans. & trans. [1. spláter; 2. splǽtə]. Variant of **spatter**. **A.** intrans.

1. To make a sound as of lightly falling liquid; to splash. 2. To strike liquid lightly so as to cause it to splash. 3. To speak, chatter, unintelligibly; to jabber. B. trans. To utter, speak, unintelligibly.

splay, vb. trans., n., & adj. [1. splā; 2. splei]. M.E. *splayen*, 'to turn outwards, spread out', abbr. fr. **display**. 1. vb. a (archit.) To slope, slant, bevel, form with oblique surface: *to splay the sides of a window outwards*; b (veter. surg.) to dislocate: *a splayed shoulder-bone*. 2. n. Sloping or bevelled edge, angle, or surface; esp. sloping side of splayed window, embrasure. 3. adj. Sloping, oblique, forming an angle, spreading out.

splay-foot(ed), adj. Having flat feet turned outwards to an abnormal degree.

splay-mouth, n. Wide, or widely opened, mouth.

spleen, n. [1. splēn; 2. splīn]. Lat. *splēn*, fr. Gk. *splḗn*, earlier **splegkh*; prob. cogn. w. *splágkhnon*, 'entrails', see **splanchno-**, cogn. w. Lat. *liēn*; Scrt. *plīhán-*; O. Slav. *slezena*, 'spleen'. 1. Small, soft, vascular ductless gland situated near the stomach, which modifies the character of the blood; formerly supposed to be the seat of certain emotions. 2. a Ill-humour, spite; b dejection, melancholy.

spleenful, adj. [1. splḗnfool; 2. splínful]. **spleen** & **-ful**. Characterized by, showing, ill-temper; peevish, fretful, irascible.

spleenfully, adv. Prec. & **-ly**. In a spleenful manner.

spleenish, adj. [1. splḗnish; 2. splíniʃ]. **spleen** & **-ish**. Peevish, ill-tempered.

spleenishly, adv. Prec. & **-ly**. In a spleenish manner.

spleenless, adj. [1. splḗnles; 2. splínlis]. **spleen** & **-less**. Having no spleen; (chiefly fig.) lacking malice, good-tempered.

spleenwort, n. [1. splḗnwërt; 2. splínwɑ̄t]. Genus, *Asplenium*, of ferns with pinnate leaves, formerly used medicinally.

spleeny, adj. [1. splḗni; 2. splíni]. **spleen** & **-y**. Spleenful.

splen-, pref. representing Lat. *splēn*, 'spleen', see **spleen**. Spleen.

splenalgia, n. [1. splenáljia; 2. splinǽldʒə]. Prec. & Gk. *álgos*, 'pain', & **-ia**; cp. Gk. *alégein*, 'to suffer', q.v. under **neglect**. Pain in the spleen.

splenalgic, adj. [1. splenáljik; 2. splinǽldʒik]. Prec. & **-ic**. Pertaining to, of the nature of, splenalgia.

splendent, adj. [1. spléndent; 2. spléndənt], fr. Lat. *splendent-(em)*, Pres. Part. of *splendēre*, 'to shine, gleam, glisten', cogn. w. Lith. *spléndžiu*, 'I shine'; M. Ir. *lainn*, 'bright'; more remotely connected w. Scrt. *sphuliṅgaś*, 'spark'; Germ. *flinken*, 'to glitter', fr. **(s)pleŋk-*. Lustrous, glossy; brilliant, gleaming.

splendid, adj. [1. spléndid; 2. spléndid], fr. Fr., fr. Lat. *splendidus*, 'bright, brilliant; gorgeous, magnificent; eminent, illustrious', fr. *splend-(ēre)*, 'to shine', see **splendent**, & **-id**. 1. Magnificent, gorgeous, making a striking impression on the senses: *a splendid scene*. 2. Worthy of honour or fame; eminent, illustrious, admirable: *splendid heroism*. 3. (colloq.) Very satisfactory, excellent: *a splendid idea*; *fir-cones make splendid fuel*.

splendidly, adv. Prec. & **-ly**. 1. In a splendid manner. 2. (colloq.) Excellently, very well.

splendiferous, adj. [1. splèndíferus; 2. splèndífərəs]. As though fr. **splendour** & **-ferous**. (slang or facet.) Gorgeous, magnificent.

splendour, n. [1. spléndur; 2. spléndə], fr. O. Fr., fr. Lat. *splendōr-(em)*, 'brilliance; magnificence; grandeur', fr. *splendēre*, 'to shine', see **splendent**, & **-our**. 1. Brilliance, radiance, dazzling lustre, brightness. 2. Magnificence, gorgeousness, sumptuousness. 3. Intellectual or moral magnificence; impressiveness, pre-eminence, greatness: *the splendour of his achievements, exploits*.

splenectomy, n. [1. splenéktumi; 2. splinéktəmi]. **splen-** & Gk. *ek*, 'out of', q.v. under **ecto-**, & **-tomy**. Removal of the spleen.

splenetic (I.), adj. [1. splenétik; 2. splinétik], fr. O. Fr. *splenetique*, fr. L. Lat. *splēnēticus*, 'affected with spleen', w. Gk. suff., fr. *splḗn*, 'spleen', see **spleen**, & **-ic**. 1. Of, pertaining to, the spleen; splenic. 2. Ill-tempered, fretful or sulky.

splenetic (II.), n., fr. prec. 1. Person affected with spleen; one who is peevish, ill-humoured. 2. Person suffering from a splenic disorder. 3. Medicine for disorder of the spleen.

splenetically, adv. [1. splenétikali; 2. splinétikəli]. Prec. & **-al** & **-ly**. In a splenetic manner, ill-humouredly.

splenial, adj. [1. splḗnial; 2. splíniəl]. **splenius** & **-al**. 1. Of, pertaining to, the splenius. 2. Of, shaped like, serving as, a splint.

splenic, adj. [1. splḗnik; 2. splínik], fr. O. Fr. *splenique*, fr. Lat. *splēnicus*, fr. Gk. *splēnikós*, 'splenetic', fr. *splḗn*, 'spleen', see **spleen**, & **-ic**. Pertaining to, situated near, the spleen.

splenitic, adj. [1. splenítik; 2. splinítik]. See next word & **-ic**. Pertaining to, of the nature of, splenitis.

splenitis, n. [1. splenítis; 2. splináitis]. **splen-** & **-itis**. Inflammation of the spleen.

splenius, n. [1. splḗnius; 2. splíniəs]. Mod. Lat., fr. Gk. *splḗnion*, 'bandage', dimin. of *splḗn*, 'spleen; absorbent bandage', see **spleen**. Large, strong muscle on either side of back of the neck.

splenization, n. [1. splēnīzā́shun; 2. splinaizéiʃən], fr. Lat. *splēn*, 'spleen', see **spleen**, & **-ize** & **-ation**. (pathol.) Morbid development of organ into tissue resembling that of the spleen, esp. of the lung in certain pulmonary diseases.

splenoid, adj. [1. splḗnoid; 2. splínɔid], fr. Lat. *splēn*, 'spleen', see **spleen**, & **-oid**. Resembling spleen in character and appearance.

splenological, adj. [1. splḗnolójikl; 2. splīnəlɔ́dʒikl]. Next word & **-ic** & **-al**. Pertaining to splenology.

splenology, n. [1. splēnóloji; 2. splīnɔ́lədʒi]. **splen-** & *-o-* & **-logy**. The study of the spleen.

splenotomy, n. [1. splēnótumi; 2. splīnɔ́təmi]. **splen-** & *-o-* & **-tomy**. a Removal of the spleen; b dissection of the spleen.

splice (I.), vb. trans. [1. splīs; 2. splais], fr. M. Du. *splissen*, 'to splice'; fr. *splijten*, 'to split; to unravel'; cogn. w. **split** (I.). 1. To join (two ropes or ends of rope) end to end, by unlaying and then interweaving the strands; Phr. *to splice the main-brace*; a to drink; b to serve out an allowance of spirits. 2. To join up, connect, timbers &c., by overlapping the ends, or fitting one end into the other, and binding. 3. (slang) To perform marriage ceremony for, join in marriage.

splice (II.), n., fr. prec. 1. Join made in two ropes or two parts of rope by interweaving the strands. 2. Joining of timbers &c. by overlapping, or fitting the ends, and binding.

spline, n. [1. splīn; 2. splain]. Etymol. unknown. 1. Square end of a wheel shaft which fits into a similarly shaped opening in hub of a wheel, and ensures that the shaft revolves with the wheel. 2. Long, flexible strip of wood or solid rubber used by mechanical draughtsmen for drawing large curves, esp. in shipbuilding &c.

splint (I.), n. [1. splint; 2. splint], fr. Sw. *splint*, 'spike, pointed rod'; cp. Swed. *splinta*, 'to split'; Dan. *splint*, 'splinter'; Mod. Germ. *splint*, 'steel strip'; nasalized form of stem **split*, 'to tear asunder', see **split** (I.). 1. Padded strip of wood or other appliance for keeping the two ends of a fractured bone in position. 2. Flexible strip of split wood used for basket-making or other wickerwork. 3. Also *splint-bone*, a (anat.) fibula; b (of horse) one of two bones lying near cannon-bone. 4. (veter. surg.) Bony tumour on horse's splint-bone caused by disease.

splint (II.), vb. trans., fr. prec. To furnish with, hold in place by means of, splint(s).

splint-coal, n. Bituminous coal found in slaty masses.

splinter (I.), vb. trans. & intrans. [1. splínter; 2. splíntə], fr. Swed. *splinta*, 'to split', see **splint** (I.), & **-er**. 1. trans. To break into long, thin pieces, split, shiver, divide into slivers, as by a violent blow &c. 2. intrans. To break, split up, into splinters.

splinter (II.), n., fr. prec. Thin, sharp, irregularly shaped fragment of wood or other harder substance, torn or split from a larger mass.

splinter-bar, n. 1. Crossbar supporting springs of vehicle. 2. Rigid bar of gun-carriage &c., to which traces are attached.

splinter-bone, n. Splint-bone (see **splint** (I.)).

splinter-proof, adj. Proof against flying shell-splinters.

splintery, adj. [1. splínteri; 2. splíntəri]. **splinter** (II.) & **-y**. 1. Of the nature of, like, splinters. 2. Liable to splinter.

split (I.), vb. intrans. & trans. [1. split; 2. split], fr. M. Du. *splitten*; cp. Dan. *splitta*; Mod. Germ. *spleissen*; Du. *splijten*, 'to split'; fr. base **splīt-*, 'to tear asunder', not known outside Gmc. A. intrans. 1. a (of hard substances) To be ruptured, cloven, shivered; to divide, into two or more parts with long narrow crack or cracks between, as a result of pressure, a sudden impact or blow, the insertion of a wedge, changes of temperature &c.; Phr. *the rock on which we split*, (i.) the subject of disagreement between us; (ii.) the cause of our misfortunes; b (of soft, thin substance) to burst, gape, open suddenly, as result of excessive lateral strain: *gloves often split the first time they are worn*. 2. a To become disunited, to undergo division, become alienated, in sympathies, opinions &c.: *the old Liberal party split over the question of Irish Home Rule*; b to undergo differentiation, divide up into two or more different entities: *a primitive language splits into several dialects*; *the crowd is splitting into small groups*. B. trans. 1. To cause to split; to shiver, rupture, crack suddenly; to cleave, burst, apart: *to split wood, to split one's skull open*. Phrs. *to split hairs*, to make subtle distinctions; *to split one's sides*, to laugh uncontrollably; *a splitting headache*, one that is very severe. 2. To divide into parts; to share: *to split a bottle of wine with a person*; *to split the profits*. Phr. *to split the difference*, to take the mean between two amounts &c. in dispute. 3. To cause dissension, disunion, disagreement, between; to provoke differences of opinion among or between: *the Church is split by parties and factions*. C. Followed by adverb or preposition with special meanings. *Split off*, a trans., to break off by splitting; b intrans., to become separated, to divide off by fission; (in material and non-material senses). *Split on*, intrans. (slang) to inform against a person. *Split up*, (in material and non-material senses) 1. trans., to divide, break up, into parts, to disunite; 2. intrans., to be broken up, forcibly divided.

split (II.), n., fr. prec. 1. a Process of splitting; b result of splitting; a narrow fissure, a crack, a cleft, a tear (in fabric). 2. Moral or physical separation, disunion. 3. a Flexible strip of wood for basket-making &c.; b wooden strip forming part of reed of loom. 4. Single thickness of hide split horizontally. 5. (slang) a A half-glass or portion of brandy, whisky &c.; b a small bottle of soda water. 6. (colloq.) *The splits*, acrobatic feat in which the legs are opened until both lie almost flat, upon the ground, the trunk being kept upright. 7. (Corn.) Small soft roll or scone, split and spread with cream and jam.

split cloth, n. Surgical bandage with four, six, or more tails, used for head or face.

split infinitive, n. Construction in which an adverb is inserted between the particle *to* and the infinitive; e.g. *I wish to highly recommend him for the post.*

split-moss, n. Family of mosses whose seed-capsules split open when ripe.

split peas(e), n. Peas shelled, dried, and split in halves for cooking.

split shot, stroke, n. (croquet) Stroke by which two balls are driven in different directions.

splitter, n. [1. splíter; 2. splítə]. **split (I.)** & **-er.** One who, that which, splits; sometimes in compounds, e.g. *side-splitter*.

splodge, n. [1. sploj; 2. splɔdž]. Variant of next word. Irregular patch, smear, blotch, splash.

splotch, n. [1. sploch; 2. splɔtʃ]. Cp. O.E., M.E. *splot*, 'spot'; but perh. a blend of **spot** & **splash.** Splodge.

splotchy, adj. [1. splóchi; 2. splɔ́tʃi]. Prec. & **-y.** Marked with splotches.

splurge, n. & vb. intrans. [1. splërj; 2. splʌ̄dž]. Prob. imitative. (colloq., slang) **1.** n. Ostentation, obtrusive display. **2.** vb. To show off, make a splurge.

splutter (I.), vb. intrans. & trans. [1. splúter; 2. splátə]. Variant of **sputter. 1.** intrans. **a** To eject, throw off, liquid, saliva &c. with succession of spitting sounds; to sputter; **b** to speak hastily and indistinctly, as from anger or other form of excitement. **2.** trans. To utter in a sputtering manner.

splutter (II.), n., fr. prec. Spluttering noise.

splutterer, n. [1. splúterer; 2. splátərə]. See prec. & **-er.** One who splutters.

Spode, n. [1. spōd; 2. spoud]. Name of maker, Josiah Spode (1754–1827), of Stoke-on-Trent, Staffordshire. Also *Spode ware*, a highly decorated form of chinaware.

spoil (I.), n. [1. spoil; 2. spɔil]. M.E. *spoile*, fr. O. Fr. *espoille*, fr. Lat. *spolium*, 'skin or hide stripped from animal; arms taken from defeated enemy; prey, booty'; cogn. w. Gk. *spolás*, 'flayed skin; leather jerkin'; Scrt. *phálaš*, 'ploughshare'; O. Slav. *plěvą*, 'to weed out'. **1.** Property, goods, taken by violence; loot, plunder, booty: *the thieves escaped with their spoil*; (also in pl.) *the spoils of war*. **2.** (fig.) Profit, benefit, arising from contest with, or effort against, another; (specif. U.S.A.) public offices and their emoluments given by political party as rewards to their adherents; *spoils system*, political service given in hope of reward.

spoil (II.), vb. trans. & intrans., fr. M.E. *spoilen*, fr. O. Fr. *espoillier*, fr. Lat. *spoliāre*, 'to strip, rob, plunder', fr. *spolium*, 'spoil', see prec. **A.** trans. **1.** (archaic) To take spoils from; plunder, rob with violence: *to spoil the Egyptians*. **2. a** (of physical effect) To injure, impair, do harm to; to injure the appearance of; to detract from the beauty, value, or usefulness of: *the fresh paint has been spoilt by the rain*; *the picture is spoilt by too much detail*; *the damp has spoilt my watch*; *don't spoil your new clothes by wearing them too much*; Phrs. *to spoil one's appetite*, reduce desire for a meal by eating beforehand; *to spoil one's dinner*, lessen appetite for, enjoyment of, by eating beforehand; **b** (in non-material sense) to detract from extent or merit of, lessen enjoyment of: *to spoil one's pleasure*; *he spoilt the effect of his genuine kindness of heart by his rudeness and moroseness*; **c** to cause to deteriorate, to make bad: *his temper had been spoilt by petty worries*. **3.** Specif., to injure character of; to cause character of to develop badly, to encourage growth of selfishness and unruliness in, by wrong modes of training, by lack of discipline, over-indulgence &c.; esp. *to spoil a child*; *she had been thoroughly spoilt by adulation and flattery*. **B.** intrans. To deteriorate, to become impaired, lose quality, value, usefulness: *delicate fabric soon spoils if exposed to the sun*. Phr. *to be spoiling for (a fight &c.)*, be eager for.

spoilage, n. [1. spóilij; 2. spɔ́ilidž]. **spoil** & **-age.** Paper spoilt or wasted in printing.

spoiler, n. [1. spóiler; 2. spɔ́ilə]. **spoil** & **-er.** Person who takes spoils; plunderer.

spoil-five, n. Card game for three or more persons, to each of whom five cards are dealt.

spoilsman, n. [1. spóilzman; 2. spɔ́ilzmən]. Person engaging in political career in the hope of financial gain.

spoil-sport, n. A dismal, disagreeable person who objects to, and tries to prevent, other people enjoying themselves; the skeleton at the feast.

spoke (I.), n. [1. spōk; 2. spouk]. O.E. *spāca*; M.E. *spōke*, 'spoke'; cp. M.L.G. *spēke*; O.H.G. *speicha*; cogn. w. **spike. 1.** Any one of the bars radiating from the hub of a wheel and joining this to the outer rim or felly. **2.** Rung of ladder. **3.** Bar of wood used to prevent the wheels of a cart &c. from turning, acting as a drag downhill. Phr. *to put a spoke in a person's wheel*, to upset or delay his plans. **4.** (naut.) One of the handles projecting from the rim of the steering-wheel.

spoke (II.), vb. trans., fr. prec. **1.** To supply, fit, with spokes. **2.** To hinder movement of (wheel &c.) with spoke.

spoke (III.), vb. Pret. of **speak**, fr. P.P. **spoken.**

spoke-bone, n. Bone extending from elbow to wrist; radius.

spoken, vb. [1. spóken; 2. spóukən]. P.P. of **speak**; M.E. *spōken*, formed on the anal. of **broken**; cp. O.E. *sp(r)ecen*, P.P.

-spoken, adj., fr. prec. (in compounds) Characterized by specific manner of speech: *ill-*, *fair-*, *soft-spoken* &c.

spoke-shave, n. Small blade set in the middle of a piece of wood which, grasped by a hand at either end, is used for planing and smoothing curved wood articles.

spokesman, n. [1. spóksman; 2. spóuksmən], fr. *spoke*, Pret. of **speak**, & *-es* & **-man.** Person who speaks as representative of others.

spokewise, adv. [1. spókwīz; 2. spóukwaiz]. **spoke (I.)** & **-wise.** Arranged as spokes; in the position of a spoke; radiating.

spolia opima, n. pl. [1. spólia opíma; 2. spóuliə ɔpáimə]. Lat., fr. pl. of *spolium*, 'booty', see **spoil (I.)**, & *opīmus*, 'rich; fat'; prob. cogn. w. Gk. *pīmelḗ*, 'fat', Lat. *pinguis*, 'rich, fat', see **pinguid.** Arms taken by Roman general from enemy's commander in single combat; hence, rewards, honours, received as result of contest.

spoliation, n. [1. spòliáshun; 2. spòuliéiʃən], fr. Lat. *spoliātiōnem*, fr. *spoliātum*, P.P. type of *spoliāre*, 'to pillage', see **spoil (II.)**, & **-ion. 1.** Robbery with violence, plunder, esp. plunder of neutral trading-vessel by nation at war. **2.** (eccles.) Illegal appropriation of tithes &c. **3.** (legal) Wilful destruction, mutilation &c., of document liable to be put in evidence.

spoliator, n. [1. spóliātur; 2. spóulieitə], fr. Lat. *spoliātum*, P.P. type of *spoliāre*, 'to pillage', see **spoil (I.)**, & **-or.** Plunderer, spoiler.

spoliatory, adj. [1. spóliaturi; 2. spóuliətəri], fr. Lat. *spoliātum*, see prec., & **-ory.** Of the nature of, causing, spoliation.

spondaic, adj. [1. spondáik; 2. spɔndéiik], fr. O. Fr. *spondaique*, fr. L. Lat. *spondaicus*, *spondīacus*, fr. Gk. *spondeiakós*, 'spondaic', fr. *spondeios*, 'spondee', see next word. Pertaining to, composed in, spondees; *spondaic hexameter*, one that has a spondee in fifth foot.

spondee, n. [1. spóndē; 2. spɔ́ndī], fr. Lat. *spondēus*, fr. Gk. *spondeîos (poús)*, 'metrical foot used at a libation, esp. in making a treaty'; cp. *spéndein*, 'to pour forth as a libation'; *spondḗ*, 'libation; treaty, alliance'; Lat. *spondēre*, 'to promise', see **sponsion.** Metrical foot consisting of two long syllables.

spondulics, n. pl. [1. spondúliks; 2. spɔndjúliks]. Origin doubtful; Weekley suggests that first element may be fr. Du. *spaan*, 'a chip', see **spoon (I.)**, used also in sense of 'money'. (Am. slang) Money; equivalent to *dibs*.

spondyl(e), n. [1. spóndil; 2. spɔ́ndil], fr. Fr., fr. Lat. *spondylus*, fr. Gk. *spónd-*, *sphóndulos*, 'vertebra'; cp. Gk. *sphendónē*, 'sling'; prob. related to Gk. *sphadázein*, 'to move convulsively'; Scrt. *spandatē*, 'to start up'. One of the bones of the spinal column; vertebra.

spondyl(o)-, pref. representing prec. & *-o-*. Vertebra; e.g. *spondylitis*, inflammation of the vertebrae.

sponge (I.), n. [1. spunj; 2. spandž], fr. O. Fr. *esponge*, fr. Lat. *spongia*, fr. Gk. *spoggiá*, 'sponge'; etymol. doubtful. **1.** Marine animal, belonging to the phylum *Porifera*, with tough, fibrous skeleton and without tentacles, usually found fixed to a rock. **2.** Elastic, absorbent, fibrous network left after removal of living matter from a sponge, used for applying water to the body or other surface for cleansing &c. Phr. *to throw up the sponge*, (of boxer and fig.) to admit defeat; to give up a struggle of any kind. **3.** Object or substance resembling a sponge in structure, appearance, or use; specif. **a** light, porous mass of fermented dough before kneading; **b** sweet cake of light, soft, elastic consistency; **c** soft pad &c. used for cleaning bore of cannon. **4.** Person living at another's expense; hanger-on, parasite, a cadger.

sponge (II.), vb. intrans. & trans., fr. O. Fr. *espongier*, fr. L. Lat. *spongiāre*, 'to sponge', fr. *spongia*, 'sponge'; see prec. **A.** intrans. **1.** To collect, gather, sponges. **2.** To play the part of a social sponge; to live at the expense of others. **B.** trans. To apply water to, wash, wipe, cleanse, by means of a sponge. **C.** Followed by adverb or preposition, with special meanings. *Sponge down*, trans., to wash, pour water over, with a sponge. *Sponge on*, intrans., to live in dependence on, as parasite of. *Sponge out*, trans. (lit. and fig.), to erase, efface, wipe out, with or as with a sponge. *Sponge up*, trans., To absorb, take up, with a sponge.

sponge (III.), n., fr. prec. Act of sponging; process of being sponged: *to have a sponge (down)*.

sponge-cake, n. Soft, light, sweet cake made of eggs, sugar, and flour.

sponge-cucumber, n. Tropical plant producing a large gourd, the fibrous network of which is dried and used as a rubber in Turkish baths.

sponge-gourd, n. Sponge-cucumber.

spongelet, n. [1. spúnjlet; 2. spándžlit]. **sponge (I.)** & **-let.** Spongiole, q.v.

sponger, n. [1. spúnjer; 2. spándžə]. **sponge (II.)** & **-er. 1.** One who sponges; apparatus for sponging. **2.** Parasite, hanger-on.

sponge tree, n. Tropical tree with round clusters of sweet-scented yellow flowers.

spongiform, adj. [1. spúnjiform; 2. spándžifɔ̄m]. **sponge (I.)** & *-i-* & **-form.** Resembling a sponge in form, structure, or texture.

sponginess, n. [1. spúnjines; 2. spándžinis]. **spongy** & **-ness.** State of being spongy.

sponging-house, n. [1. spúnjing hòus; 2. spándžiŋ hàus]. Bailiff's house where debtors were formerly detained in custody before being committed to prison.

spongiole, n. [1. spúnjiōl; 2. spándžioul]. **sponge (I.)** & *-i-* & dimin. *-ole*, as in **aureole, foliole.** Protective tissue covering the tip of the root of a plant.

spongiopiline, n. [1. spùnjiopílīn; 2. spàndžiəpáil(a)in], fr. Lat. *spongia*, 'sponge', see **sponge**, & *-o-* & Gk. *pīlos*, 'felt'; cp. Lat. *pilleus*, 'felt cap', & see **pile (VII.).** Material made of small pieces of sponge and vegetable fibre, waterproofed on one side; used wet as a poultice.

spongo-, pref. representing Gk. *spóggos*, *spoggiá*, 'sponge', see **sponge (I.).** Sponge.

spongoid, adj. [1. spónggoid; 2. spɔ́ŋgɔid]. See prec. & **-oid.** Like, of the nature of, a sponge.

spongologist, n. [1. spònggólojist; 2. spɔ̀ŋgɔ́lədžist]. Next word & **-ist.** Student of, one versed in, spongology.

spongology, n. [1. spònggóloji; 2. spɔ̀ŋgɔ́lədži]. **spongo-** & **-logy.** Study of sponges.

spongy, adj. [1. spúnji; 2. spándži]. **sponge (I.)** & **-y. 1.** Like a sponge in structure; elastic and porous. **2.** (of land) Wet, marshy, absorbent. **3.** (of metal) Of open texture, loosely coherent.

sponsion, n. [1. spónshun; 2. spɔ́nʃən], fr. Lat. *spōnsiōnem*, 'engagement, covenant', fr. *spōnsum*, P.P. type of *spondēre*, 'to warrant, give, assurance, promise'; cp. Lat. *respondēre*, 'to promise in return; to reply', see **respond**; cogn. w. Gk. *spéndein*, 'to pour out a libation; to promise'; *spondḗ*, 'libation; treaty'. **1.** Act of becoming surety for another, of entering into an engagement on another's behalf. **2.** (legal) International agreement made on behalf of a state by an official not fully empowered to enter into it.

sponson, n. [1. spónsun; 2. spɔ́nsən]. Possibly a popular modification of **expansion.** Curved projection from side of vessel; specif. **a** outward curve of planking before and behind each wheel of paddle-steamer; **b** projection on side of warship to enable gun to be swung round to a different angle.

sponsor, n. [1. spónsur; 2. spɔ́nsə], fr. Lat. *spōnsor*, 'surety', fr. *spōnsum*, P.P. type of *spondēre*, 'to bind oneself', see **sponsion**, & **-or.** **a** Person who enters into an agreement on another's behalf; one who makes himself responsible for another's obligations, or who vouches for his character; specif. **b** godfather or godmother.

sponsorial, adj. [1. sponsórial; 2. spɔnsɔ́riəl]. Prec. & **-ial.** Pertaining to a sponsor.

sponsorship, n. [1. spónsurship; 2. spɔ́nsəʃip]. **sponsor** & **-ship.** State of being a sponsor.

spontaneity, n. [1. spòntanéiti; 2. spɔ̀ntəníiti]. See next word & **-ity.** State or quality of being spontaneous; spontaneous action.

spontaneous, adj. [1. spontáneus; 2. spɔntéiniəs], fr. Lat. *spontāneus*, 'of one's free will, voluntary', fr. *sponte*, 'of one's own accord', fr. **spons*, 'free will, desire'; cp. O.H.G. *spanst*, 'charm, allurement'; *spanan*, 'to entice'; O.E. *spanan*, 'to entice'. **1.** Arising from one's own internal tendency, disposition, inclination, without external influence, constraint, compulsion; voluntary: *a spontaneous expression of admiration*; *spontaneous generosity.* **2.** Self-acting; produced by internal, natural impulse or energy; not due to external agency or stimulus: *spontaneous movement, action, growth.*

spontaneous combustion, n. See **combustion.**

spontaneous generation, n. Process, the existence of which is no longer believed in, whereby life, as it was held, originated spontaneously, in non-living matter, under certain conditions, without the presence of pre-existing living organisms.

spontaneously, adv. [1. spontáneusli; 2. spɔntéiniəsli]. **spontaneous** & **-ly.** In a spontaneous manner.

spontaneousness, n. [1. spontáneusnes; 2. spɔntéiniəsnis]. See prec. & **-ness.** State or quality of being spontaneous.

spontoon, n. [1. spontōōn; 2. spɔntū́n], fr. Fr. *sponton*, fr. Ital. *spontone*, fr. *spontāre*, fr. Lat. **expunctāre*, 'to blunt the point', fr. **ex-** & *punctum*, 'point', see **point.** (hist.) Kind of halberd, usually with hook, sometimes carried by infantry officers.

spoof, vb. trans. & n. [1. spōōf; 2. spūf]. Invented by Arthur Roberts, the comedian, b. 1852. (slang) **1.** vb. To deceive, hoax, swindle. **2.** n. Hoax, swindle.

spook, n. [1. spōōk; 2. spūk], fr. Du. *spook*; cp. Germ. (dial.) *spuk*; Dan. *spøg.* Ghost, apparition, wraith.

spookish, adj. [1. spōōkish; 2. spúkiʃ]. Prec. & **-ish.** Of, like, a ghost.

spooky, adj. [1. spōōki; 2. spúki]. **spook** & **-y.** Pertaining to, resembling, a ghost; suggesting the presence of ghosts; haunted.

spool (I.), n. [1. spōōl; 2. spūl], fr. M. Du. *spoele*; cp. Germ. *spule*; etymol. doubtful. Bar, cylinder &c., on which thread &c. is wound; a reel for cotton &c.; specif., bar of reel on fishing-rod, on which line is wound.

spool (II.), vb. trans., fr. prec. To wind on a spool.

spoon (I.), n. [1. spōōn; 2. spūn]. O.E. *spōn*, 'a shaving, chip of wood'; cp. Du. *spaan*; O.H.G. *spān*; O. Fris. *spōn*; O.N. *spánn*, *spōnn*, 'chip, splinter'; cogn. w. Gk. *sphḗn*, 'wedge'; Scrt. *sphyáś*, 'splinter of wood'; fr. base **sp(h)ei-*, **sp(h)i-* &c., 'to spread out, stretch', seen in **spathe, spade** (I.) &c. **1.** Implement made of wood, iron, nickel &c., or (esp. for table use) of silver, with long handle ending in a shallow oval or round bowl, used for measuring or stirring liquid &c., in cooking &c., and for conveying food to the mouth; often in compounds, named according to use &c.: *egg-, tea-, dessert-, table-, mustard-spoon* &c.; Phr. *wooden spoon*, specif. **a** that formerly given to candidate placed lowest in Cambridge mathematical tripos; **b** man attaining this distinction. **2.** Instrument somewhat resembling a spoon in form; specif. **a** kind of oar with curved blade; **b** (golf) kind of wooden-headed club; **c** spoon-bait.

spoon (II.), vb. trans. & intrans., fr. prec. **A.** trans. **1.** To use a spoon for; to lift, convey, with a spoon: *to spoon up liquid*; *to spoon liquid out of a vessel.* **2.** To lift, move, as with a spoon; (specif. croquet) to push or scoop with mallet. **B.** intrans. To fish with spoon-bait.

spoon (III.), n. Prob. same as **spoon** (I.), cp. use of **stick** or **pump** as terms for a stupid, empty-headed person. **1.** Foolish fellow, simpleton. **2.** One who makes love in a foolish and demonstrative manner.

spoon (IV.), vb. intrans. & trans., fr. prec. (vulg. slang) **1.** intrans. To make love. **2.** trans. To make love to, to court.

spoon-bait, n. Bright piece of metal, shaped like bowl of spoon with hook at one end, attached by swivel to fishing-line and drawn through the water.

spoonbill, n. [1. spōōnbil; 2. spū́nbil]. Family of wading birds resembling ibises, having a broad, flat bill expanded at the end in the shape of a spoon.

spoondrift, n. [1. spōōndrift; 2. spū́ndrift]. Spindrift, q.v.

Spoonerism, n. [1. spōōnerizm; 2. spū́nərizəm], fr. name of the Rev. W. A. Spooner, D.D., formerly Warden of New College, Oxford. Involuntary transposition of sounds in successive words; e.g. *bilging buns*, for *bulging bins*; *queer dean*, for *dear queen* &c.

spoon-fed, adj. **a** Fed (as infant, invalid &c.) with a spoon; **b** (fig., of industries &c.) encouraged, aided, by artificial financial support; **c** (of pupils) taught by the repeated administration of small doses of information, cut and dried, and carefully adapted to the comprehension of the recipients.

spoon-food, n. Food taken with a spoon, esp. by infants or invalids.

spoonful, n. [1. spōōnfool; 2. spū́nful]. **spoon** (I.) & **-ful.** Amount contained in a spoon.

spoonily, adv. [1. spōōnili; 2. spū́nili]. **spoony** & **-ly.** In a spoony manner.

spooniness, n. [1. spōōnines; 2. spū́ninis]. See prec. & **-ness.** State of being spoony.

spoon-meat, n. Soft or liquid food, esp. infant's food.

spoon-net, n. Fisherman's landing-net.

spoony, adj. [1. spōōni; 2. spū́ni]. **spoon** (III.) & **-y.** Amorous; inclined for love-making.

spoor (I.), n. [1. spōr, spoor; 2. spɔ̄, spuə]. Du. *spoor*; cp. Germ. *spur*, 'track'; O.N. *spor*; O.E. *spor*; perh. cogn. w. O.E. *spora*, 'spur'; see **spur** (I.). **1.** Trail, track, succession of footprints, of wild animals. **2.** Animal's scent.

spoor (II.), vb. trans. & intrans., fr. prec. **1.** trans. To follow the track or scent of. **2.** intrans. To follow a spoor.

sporadic(al), adj. [1. sporádik(l); 2. spərǽdik(l)], fr. Gk. *sporadikós*, fr. *sporád-*, stem of *sporás*, 'scattered'; cp. Gk. *spóros*, 'sowing'; *speírein*, 'to sow, scatter'; *spérma*, 'seed, germ', see **sperm.** Occurring at irregular intervals; scattered; (esp. of disease) not epidemic or widely prevalent, occurring in single cases.

sporadically, adv. [1. sporádikali; 2. spərǽdikəli]. Prec. & **-ly.** In a sporadic way.

sporadicalness, n. [1. sporádiklnes; 2. spərǽdikəlnis]. See prec. & **-ness.** State of being sporadic.

sporange, n. [1. spóranj; 2. spɔ́rændž], fr. next word. Sporangium.

sporangium, n. [1. sporánjium; 2. spərǽndžiəm], fr. **spore** & Gk. *aggeíon*, dimin. of *ággos*, 'vessel, receptacle'. Sac within which spores are developed.

sporation, n. [1. spōráshun; 2. spɔ̄réiʃən]. Next word & **-ation.** Production of spores.

spore, n. [1. spōr; 2. spɔ̄], fr. Gk. *sporá*, 'sowing, seed'; cp. Gk. *spóros*, 'sowing', & see **sporadic, sperm** (I.). (biol.) **a** Minute reproductive organism of flowerless plant, capable of developing into a new individual; **b** minute animal organism as in bacteria &c. developing into a new individual.

sporo-, pref. representing **spore** & *-o-*. Spore.

sporogenesis, n. [1. spōrojénesis; 2. spɔ̄rədžénisis]. Prec. & **genesis.** Reproduction by means of spores.

sporogenous, adj. [1. spōrójenus; 2. spɔ̄rɔ́džinəs]. **sporo-** & **-genous.** Reproducing by means of spores.

sporran, n. [1. spóran; 2. spɔ́rən], fr. Gael. *sporan.* Leather pouch, usually having the fur left on, worn by Scottish Highlanders with the kilt, slung round the waist by a leather thong and hanging down in front.

sport (I.), n. [1. sport; 2. spɔ̄t]. Abbr. of **disport.** **1.** Any of various forms of activity, engaged in as recreation; **a** hunting, shooting, fishing; sailing a boat; **b** outdoor games; **c** athletics, swimming, boxing, fencing, wrestling &c.; **d** (vulg.) a sporting person. **2.** *Sports*, meeting for athletic contests: *school sports*; *sports day* &c. **3.** **a** Jest, raillery, fun: *to say a thing in sport*; **b** plaything; object, victim, of caprice: *to become the sport of fortune*; (fig.) *the sport of the waves.* **4.** A diverting action, occurrence, or experience: *children think it great sport to dress up, and pretend to be grown up.* **5.** (biol.) Plant or animal varying spontaneously from the normal type; a freak.

sport (II.), vb. intrans. & trans., fr. prec. **1.** intrans. To frolic, disport oneself; to dally: '*To sport with Amaryllis in the shade*' (Milton, 'Lycidas', 68). **2.** trans. To wear or carry, esp. ostentatiously, for display: *to sport a rose in one's buttonhole*; (Phr., university) *to sport one's oak*, shut the outer (oaken) door of college rooms, as indication that one must not be disturbed.

sporting, adj. [1. spórting; 2. spɔ̄́tiŋ]. Pres. Part. of **sport** (II.). **1.** Of, pertaining to, engaging in, addicted to, sport. **2.** Characteristic of a sportsman; sportsmanlike; enterprising, willing to take risks; Phr. *a sporting chance*, one involving risk, but offering possibility of success.

sportingly, adv. Prec. & **-ly.** In a sporting manner.

sportive, adj. [1. spórtiv; 2. spɔ̄́tiv]. **sport** & **-ive.** Inclined to sport, playful, frolicsome.

sportively, adv. Prec. & **-ly.** In a sportive manner.

sportiveness, n. See prec. & **-ness.** State or quality of being sportive.

sportless, adj. [1. spórtles; 2. spɔ̄́tlis]. **sport** (I.) & **-less.** (of country, region &c.) Giving no opportunity for sport.

sportsman, n. [1. spórtsman; 2. spɔ̄́tsmən]. **1.** Person engaged in, or addicted to, sport. **2.** (fig.) Person possessing the qualities attributed to a sportsman; a chivalrous, fair-minded person; one willing to incur risks, and prepared to suffer defeat in fair competition without complaining.

sportsmanlike, adj. [1. spórtsmanlīk; 2. spɔ̄́tsmənlaik]. Prec. & **-like.** Of the nature of, characteristic of, suitable for, a sportsman.

sportsmanship, n. [1. spórtsmanship; 2. spɔ̄́tsmənʃip]. **sportsman** & **-ship.** Skill in, devotion to, sport; sportsmanlike quality or character.

sporular, adj. [1. spórūlar; 2. spɔ́rjulə]. Next word & **-ar**. Of, pertaining to, a sporule.

sporule, n. [1. spórūl; 2. spɔ́rjūl]. **spore** & **-ule**. Small spore.

spot (I.), n. [1. spot; 2. spɔt]. M.E.; also in O. Du. Origin unknown. **1. a** A patch, speck, fleck on a surface, differing in colour from the rest: *a black dog with white spots*; **b** a stain, discolouration: *a spot of ink, blood* &c.; **c** (specif.) a pimple, pustule on the skin: *his face was covered with spots.* **2.** A moral stain, flaw, blemish; defect of character, matter of reproach: *a character without spot or stain.* **3.** A definite part of space; a specific place, locality, region: *a lovely spot on which to build a house.* Phr. *on the spot*, at a given place: *the doctor was on the spot a few minutes after the accident*; *the people on the spot*, those who live in a given place, and who know the facts &c. connected with it; *a tender spot*, (fig.) subject on which one's feelings are easily aroused. **4.** (specif., billiards) **a** One of the black spots on the table upon which balls are placed on opening and on other occasions during the game; *spot barred*, game in which players are not allowed to place the red ball on the spot and continue to hole it indefinitely; Phr. *to be on the spot*, (fig.) alert, wide-awake, equal to the situation; *to act on the spot*, there and then without delay; **b** small black spot on one of the white balls to distinguish it from the other; *the spot ball*, that bearing the spot; *spot* (contrasted with *plain*) the spot ball. **5.** (colloq.) **a** Small quantity of liquor; **a** splash: *won't you have a spot of whisky?* **b** small quantity of food: *how about a spot of lunch?* **6.** (commerc.) *Spot cash*, paid on delivery; *spot price*, price for spot cash; *spot goods, wheat, cotton* &c., sold for immediate delivery; *spots*, spot goods.

spot (II.), vb. trans. & intrans., fr. prec. **A.** trans. **1.** To mark, stain, with spots: *to spot one's fingers with ink.* **2.** To mar, impart moral blemish to. **3.** (colloq.) **a** To identify, pick out, recognize, at sight: *it is difficult to spot people in a crowd*; **b** to detect, find out, perceive true character of: *I spotted his roguery as soon as I met him.* **B.** intrans. To become discoloured or injured by spots: *a delicate fabric which spots very easily.*

spotless, adj. [1. spótles; 2. spɔ́tlis]. **spot** (I.) & **-less**. **1.** Without spot or stain; hence, scrupulously clean: *the room was absolutely spotless*; *a spotless white shirt-front.* **2.** Free from moral stain; immaculate, irreproachable.

spotlessly, adv. Prec. & **-ly**. To the degree of being spotless: *spotlessly clean.*

spotlessness, n. See prec. & **-ness**. State or quality of being spotless.

spotlight, n. [1. spótlīt; 2. spɔ́tlait]. **1.** Strong beam of light thrown on to a performer on the stage &c. **2.** Electric searchlight used in theatre &c. to project such a beam.

spotted, adj. [1. spóted; 2. spɔ́tid]. **spot** (II.) & **-ed**. Marked with, characterized by, spots, esp. in names of birds, fishes, and other animals, plants &c.: *spotted bass, flycatcher* &c.; *spotted dog*, (slang) plain, boiled suet pudding with currants &c.

spotted fever, n. Cerebro-spinal meningitis.

spottedness, n. [1. spótednes; 2. spɔ́tidnis]. **spotted** & **-ness**. State of being spotted.

spottiness, n. [1. spótines; 2. spɔ́tinis]. Next word & **-ness**. State of being spotty.

spotty, adj. [1. spóti; 2. spɔ́ti]. **spot** (I.) & **-y**. Marked, covered, with spots (in various senses); **a** patchy, diversified by patches of different colours: *seen from a distance the different uniforms produced a spotty effect*; **b** pimply: *a spotty complexion.*

spousal, n. [1. spóuzl; 2. spáuzl]. Variant of **espousal**. (archaic) Marriage, nuptials; also *spousals.*

spouse, n. [1. spouz; 2. spauz], fr. O. Fr. *espous(e)*, 'spouse', fr. Lat. *spōns(um), spōns(a)*, 'bride(groom)', fr. P.P. type of *spondēre*, 'to engage oneself, promise', see **sponsion**; cp. Lat. *sponsāre*, 'to marry', *sponsālia*, 'marriage'. Either of two persons joined by marriage; a husband or a wife.

spouseless, adj. [1. spóuzles; 2. spáuzlis]. Prec. & **-less**. Without a spouse.

spout (I.), vb. intrans. & trans. [1. spout; 2. spaut]. M.E. *spouten*; cp. M. Du. *spuiten*; O.N. *spȳta*; O.H.G. *spiutzen*, 'to spout'; perh. remotely connected w. **spit** (III.). **A.** intrans. **1.** To burst, gush, spurt, pour forth, be discharged, in a copious stream: *blood spouted from the wound.* **2.** To discharge liquid forcibly: *the whale spouts.* **3.** To make speeches, harangue, copiously and often: *a good fellow but too fond of spouting.* **B.** trans. **1.** To pour out in a stream, discharge forcibly, cause to gush forth in a jet: *the volcano spouts lava*; *the whale spouts water*; *the chimney spouted smoke and flame.* **2.** (colloq.) To utter, recite, esp. in a fluent and declamatory manner: *to spout one's own verses.* **3.** (slang) To pawn, pledge.

spout (II.), n., fr. prec. **1. a** Narrow, specially shaped, projecting part, orifice, mouth of a receptacle, through which the liquid contents are poured out; piece of projecting pipe discharging water: *the spout of a tea-pot, jug*; *spout of a pump*; **b** (archit.) carved or moulded projection of stone or lead for conveying water from a roof. **2.** Shoot, or small lift, in pawnbroker's shop, by means of which pledged articles are conveyed to place of storage; (hence vulgar) *up the spout*, in pawn. **3.** Blow-hole of whale &c. **4.** Stream, jet, gush, of water or other liquid, esp. one discharged or escaping with considerable force and volume; (specif.) **a** column of water shot into the air by whale &c., in breathing; **b** water-spout. **5.** A copious, sudden discharge, burst, gust, of vapour, steam, smoke, dust.

spout-hole, n. Blow-hole of cetacean; spiracle.

spoutless, adj. [1. spóutles; 2. spáutlis]. **spout** (I.) & **-less**. Without a spout.

sprag, n. [1. sprag; 2. spræg]. Dan. *sprag*, 'twig, sprig'; cogn. w. **spray** (I.). Billet or block of wood, bar of steel &c., used to check movement of wheel &c., as prop in mining &c.

sprain, vb. trans. & n. [1. sprān; 2. sprein], fr. O. Fr. *esprein-*, stem of *espreindre*, 'to press out', fr. Lat. *exprimere*, 'press out; to squeeze, wring', fr. **ex-** & *premere*, 'to press', see **press**. **1.** vb. To strain excessively, but without dislocation, by a sudden twist or wrench, the tendons and muscles connected with a joint; esp. those of the ankle or wrist. **2.** n. **a** Violent wrench or twist given to the muscles, ligaments, or tendons of a joint, without dislocation; **b** inflammation and swelling resulting from such a wrench.

spraints, n. [1. sprānts; 2. spreints], fr. O. Fr. *espraintes*, fr. P.P. of *espreindre*, 'to press out', see **sprain**. Otter's dung.

sprang, vb. [1. sprang; 2. spræŋ]. O.E., M.E. *sprang*, Pret. of **spring** (I.).

sprat, n. [1. sprat; 2. spræt]. O.E., M.E. *sprott*; cp. L.G. *sprotte*, 'sprat'; prob. a gradational form of base in **sprout**. The present-day form shows unrounding of M.E. *ŏ*, as in **gad** (I.) & **strap**. Small, edible fish of the herring family, found off W. Europe.

sprat-day, n. November 9th, on which sprat season begins.

spratter, n. [1. spráter; 2. sprǽtə]. **sprat** & **-er**. Man or vessel engaged in fishing for sprats.

sprawl (I.), vb. intrans. & trans. [1. sprawl; 2. sprɔl]. Connected w. O.E. *sprēawlian*, 'to move convulsively', M.E. *spraulen*; cp. Norw. *sprala*; origin unknown. **A.** intrans. **1. a** (of person) To lie or sit with limbs relaxed and spread out in careless ungainly manner; to loll; **b** (of limbs) to be stretched out in an ungainly manner. **2.** To be spread out irregularly, so as to cover considerable space; to straggle: *handwriting in which a single word sprawls half across a page*; *sprawling shoots of roses.* **B.** trans. To cause to sprawl.

sprawl (II.), n., fr. prec. Sprawling position or movement.

spray (I.), n. [1. sprā; 2. sprei]. M.E. *sprai*; cp. Dan. *sprag*; O.E. *spræc*, 'twig, shoot'; O.N. *sprek*; cogn. w. Gk. *spargáein*, 'to be swollen, be ripe', Lith. *sprógti*, 'to bud'; *spùrgas*, 'sprout'; Scrt. *sphūrjati*, 'breaks forth'; cp. also Lat. *spargere*, 'to scatter', & see **sparse** & **spark**. See also next word. **1.** Small branch or stem of tree or plant, sprig, twig, with flowers or smaller branches spreading from it. **2. a** Design, pattern, ornament, representing spray of flowers &c.; **b** similar design representing other objects.

spray (II.), n., fr. L.G. *sprei*, 'spray, drizzle'; cp. O.H.G. *spriu*, 'spray'; M.H.G. *spraewen*; M. Du. *spraeien*, 'to spray, scatter'; cogn. w. O.E. *sprūtan*, 'to sprout', see **sprout** (I.); fr. base **sper-*, **sprē-* &c., 'to scatter, sow; to grow up, sprout'; see **sparger, spring, spark**. **1.** Fine particles of water, larger than those of vapour, carried in a cloud from a breaking wave, or from a waterfall. **2. a** Liquid disinfectant, chemical disease-killer, or perfume &c., driven in fine particles resembling spray by an atomizer; **b** mechanical device for producing such a spray.

spray (III.), vb. intrans. & trans., fr. prec. **1.** intrans. To form spray. **2.** trans. To treat with liquid in the form of spray: *to spray one's throat, an apple tree* &c.

spray-board, n. Board on gunwale of boat to throw off spray.

spray-drain, n. Trench filled with branches and covered in with earth, to serve as drain.

sprayer, n. [1. sprāer; 2. spréiə]. **spray** (III.) & **-er**. One who, that which, sprays; device for spraying.

sprayey (I.), adj. [1. sprāi; 2. spréii]. **spray** (I.) & **-y**. In the form of, consisting of, sprays.

sprayey (II.), adj. **spray** (II.) & **-y**. Resembling, in the form of, full of, spray.

spread (I.), vb. trans. & intrans. [1. spred; 2. spred]. O.E. *sprǣdan*, M.E. *sprēden*; evidently fr. **spraidjan*, cp. O.H.G. *spreiten*, 'to extend' &c. Origin of base unknown. **A.** trans. **1.** To cause (a substance) to cover a larger surface, **a** by pressing and smearing: *to spread butter on bread*; **b** by laying or scattering on, and scraping it out thin: *to spread mortar on a stone, manure over a field*; **c** to cover a surface by unfolding, and stretching: *to spread a carpet on a floor, a cloth on a table.* **2.** To cover (surface) with a substance or material: *to spread bread with honey, butter* &c.; *to spread a table with a cloth, with a meal.* **3.** To extend, stretch out, reach out: *to spread one's hands to the fire*; *a bird spreads its wings*; *a tree spreads its branches to the light.* **4.** To diffuse, disseminate, hand on, extend, cause to be widely circulated; **a** (of material things) *to spread disease*; **b** (of non-material things) *to spread news, learning, knowledge, a love of virtue*; *to spread one's interests over too many subjects*; also *to spread oneself*, engage in variety of activities; (slang) **a** to talk, write, at length, or self-assertively; **b** be profuse in hospitality. **B.** intrans. **1.** To extend, cover larger surface: *the floods have spread over the valley.* **2.** To extend in time, be prolonged during: *the course of study spreads over three years.* **3.** To open out, be extended or displayed: *a broad plain spread before us.* **4.** (of material and non-material things) To be diffused, disseminated, circulated, handed on: *measles has spread to the school*; *the bad news, rumour, spread like wildfire.* **C.** Followed by adverb with special meanings. *Spread out*, **1.** trans., **a** to unfold: *to spread out a carpet*; **b** to stretch out, extend: *to spread out one's hands, arms, legs*; **c** to scatter, sprinkle, here and there over a surface: *to spread out manure over a field* &c.; **2.** intrans., to be extended, unfolded, displayed: *the branches spread out like a fan.*

spread (II.), n., fr. prec. **1.** Process of extending over wider area; extension, expansion, increase: *the alarming spread of the floods.* **2.** Process of circulation, diffusion, dissemination; increased prevalence: **a** (material) *the spread of disease*; **b** (non-material) *the spread of religion, scientific knowledge.* **3.** Extent, amount, of expansion: *the spread of a bird's wings.* **4.** (colloq.) A copious repast; a feast, banquet: *he gave us a regular spread.*

spread eagle (I.), n. **1.** (her.) Figure of an eagle with wings raised and legs spread out; an eagle displayed. **2.** Bird split open lengthwise and broiled.

spread-eagle (II.), vb. trans. To tie up (person) with arms and legs spread out; specif., to tie up thus for punishment by flogging.

spread-eagle (III.), adj. (Am., not Engl.) Extravagant, bombastic.

spreader, n. [1. spréder; 2. sprédə]. **spread** (I.) & **-er.** One who, that which, spreads; specif., one of various mechanical devices for spreading flame of lamp, scattering water from hose-pipe for spraying lawn &c.

spread over, n. In industry, esp. mining, an arrangement by which the workers can spread the allotted number of working hours per week over a longer period, e.g. instead of working 45 hours in each of two successive weeks, they can work 60 hours in one and 30 in the other.

spree, n. & vb. intrans. [1. sprē; 2. sprī]. Cp. Ir. *spre*, Gael. *spraig*, 'spark; spirit'; perh. fr. O.N. *sprakr*; cp. **spark. 1.** n. **a** A bout of dissipation, a drunken frolic; Phrs. *on the spree*, engaged in a drinking bout; *to go on the spree*, give oneself up temporarily to drinking and dissipation; **b** a spell of innocent amusement; an amusing experience; a lark: *it would be rather a spree to run up to town for a few theatres.* **2.** vb. To indulge in a spree.

sprent, adj. [1. sprent; 2. sprent], also **besprent.** M.E. *spre(i)nt*, P.P., fr. O.E. *sprengan*, 'to sprinkle'; cp. O.H.G. *sprengan*; O.N. *sprengja*; fr. **sprang-*, Pret. stem of **spring-*, 'to spring, jump', see **spring** (I.). (archaic) Sprinkled, scattered, over: *sprent with dew.*

sprig, n. [1. sprig; 2. sprig]. M.E. *sprigge*; precise origin not clear; prob. related to **spray** (I.). **1.** Small branching twig, spray, cluster. **2.** Small spray-like design, branching pattern, e.g. on a fabric, wall-paper &c. **3.** Small headless nail, brad. **4. a** Scion, offshoot of a family: *a sprig of nobility*; **b** a young man, young spark: *a lively young sprig.*

sprigged, adj. [1. sprigd; 2. sprigd]. Prec. & **-ed.** Covered, beset, with sprigs.

spriggy, adj. [1. sprígi; 2. sprígi]. **sprig** & **-y.** Full of, covered with, consisting of, sprigs.

sprightliness, n. [1. sprítlines; 2. spráitlinis]. Next word & **-ness.** State or quality of being sprightly; liveliness, animation.

sprightly, adj. [1. sprítli; 2. spráitli]. **sprite** & **-ly.** Gay, vivacious, lively, lightly animated.

sprigtail, n. [1. sprígtāl; 2. sprígteil]. Kind of sharp-tailed duck or grouse.

spring (I.), vb. intrans. & trans. [1. spring; 2. spriŋ]. O.E. *springan*; M.E. *springen*; cp. O.H.G. *springan*, 'to spring, rise'; O.N. *springa*, 'to burst'; fr. base **sprē-*, **sper-* &c., 'to scatter, sow; to shoot forth, grow up'; see **sparger, spark, spray,** & words there referred to. **A.** intrans. **1. a** To jump, leap, bound; move upwards or forwards &c. by sudden contraction of the muscles: *to spring up into the air, over a gate, out of bed &c.*; *to spring to one's feet*, rise rapidly and suddenly from sitting posture; *to spring at, upon, a person*, attack suddenly; **b** hence, to move swiftly, rush, dart: *his hand sprang to his sword-hilt.* **2.** To come, pass, suddenly and rapidly into a different condition, set of circumstances &c.: *to spring into fame, notoriety &c.* **3.** To move suddenly and rapidly by, as if by, the action of a spring, as result of reaction, recoil: *the doors spring open.* **4.** a (of water, stream &c.) To rise from, or as from, a source, to bubble up, gush, flow forth; to well; (also of tears) to gather suddenly; **b** (also *spring up*; of plants) to grow from root or seed; to show above ground, sprout up: *daisies spring on every side*; *weeds spring up as fast as one exterminates them*; **c** (fig.; also *spring up*) to come into existence, arise, emerge suddenly, become apparent: *new factions sprang up in the state*; *dangers and difficulties spring up on every side*; **d** (sometimes *spring up*) to grow, rise, in the mind: *strange thoughts spring from lonely contemplation*; '*Hope springs eternal in the human breast*' (Pope, 'Ess. on Man', i. 95). **5.** To arise from, have as cause, motive &c.: *all our errors have sprung from carelessness*; *his actions spring from malice and fear.* **6.** (of arch) To start from the impost. **7.** (of timber) To become warped or bent. **B.** trans. **1.** To cause to act, move, close, open &c. by reaction, recoil of spring &c.: *to spring a trap.* **2. a** To discharge, explode: *to spring a mine* (often fig.); **b** (fig.) to reveal, disclose, bring to notice, unexpectedly and suddenly: *to spring a surprise, a new proposal, on one.* **3.** To overstrain, cause to split or warp. Naut. Phrs. *to spring a butt*, loosen end of timber through heavy seas; *to spring a leak*, begin leaking.

spring (II.), n., fr. prec. **1.** Act of springing; a leap, jump, bound. **2.** Elastic body or appliance, often a curve or spiral of metal, tending to return to its original shape or position on release from pressure; used **a** to supply motive power: *spring of a watch*; **b** to reduce effects of concussion: *spring of a carriage*; **c** to ascertain weight of object, by the amount of resistance offered to pressure or pulling. **3.** Elastic movement, recoil, rebound. **4. a** Elastic quality, resilience: *the spring of a bow*; *a spring in one's step*; **b** mental resilience; spirit; initiative: *his mind had lost its spring.* **5. a** Source, well, fount, in the ground, from which water rises naturally; **b** small stream, flow of water from its source. **6.** (fig.) Motive, cause of action; impelling power: *springs of action.* **7.** (fig.) Source, origin: *the springs of affection.* **8.** Time of year between winter and summer, when the new growth of vegetation begins. **9.** (naut. &c.) **a** Warp, split, crack, in timber; **b** leak caused by warping or cracking. **10.** (archit.) Lower part, starting-point, of curve of arch, vault &c.

springal(d), n. [1. springal(d); 2. spríŋəl(d)]. M.E. *springal(d)*; connected w. **spring** (I.). (archaic or obs.) Young man, youth, stripling.

spring-balance, n. Balance measuring weight by action on spring.

spring-beam, n. Beam spanning considerable space without intermediate support.

spring-bed, n. Spring-mattress.

spring-board, n. Elastic board having one end off the ground and the other firmly fastened; used to give impetus for leap, dive &c.

springbok, n. [1. springbŏk; 2. spríŋbɔk]. S. Afr. Du. See **spring** (I.) & **buck.** Small S. African gazelle, named from its habit of springing vertically into the air when alarmed.

spring-carriage, n. Carriage with body mounted on springs.

spring-cart, n. Cart with body mounted on springs.

springe, n. [1. sprinj; 2. sprindž]. Variant of **spring** (II.). Snare, noose, attached to branch &c. for catching small game.

springer, n. [1. springer; 2. spríŋə]. **spring** (I.) & **-er. 1.** One who, that which, springs. **2.** Small variety of spaniel used in pheasant-shooting &c. **3.** Springbok. **4.** Grampus. **5.** (archit.) **a** Lowest part of curve of arch; **b** rib in vaulted roof &c.; **c** lowest stone in coping of gable.

spring-gun, n. Gun set to go off when struck accidentally by trespasser, animal &c.

spring-halt, n. Involuntary jerk of horse's hind leg in walking.

springiness, n. [1. springines; 2. spríŋinis]. **springy** & **-ness.** State or quality of being springy.

springless, adj. [1. springles; 2. spríŋlis]. **spring** (II.) & **-less. 1.** Without springs. **2.** Having no natural fountains of water.

springlet, n. [1. springlet; 2. spríŋlit]. **spring** (II.) & **-let.** Small spring of water.

springlike, adj. [1. springlīk; 2. spríŋlaik]. **spring** (II.) & **-like.** Resembling, characteristic of, the season of spring.

spring-mattress, n. Mattress made of a series of spiral springs set in a rigid frame.

spring-tail, n. Small wingless insect with two stiff, elastic bristles on the tail, which by bending and extending impart a springing movement.

springtide, n. [1. springtīd; 2. spríŋtaid]. Springtime.

spring-tide, n. [1. spring tīd; 2. spríŋ táid]. The tide occurring at new and full moon, when the distance between high- and low-water marks is greatest, cp. *neap.*

springtime, n. [1. springtīm; 2. spríŋtaim]. Season of spring.

spring-water, n. Water obtained from spring.

springy, adj. [1. springi; 2. spríŋi]. **spring** (II.) & **-y.** Having spring; elastic, resilient.

sprinkle (I.), vb. trans. & intrans. [1. springkl; 2. spríŋkl]. M.E. *sprenkelen*, fr. *sprengan*, 'to scatter'; freq. of *springan*, see **spring** (I.), & **-le. A.** trans. **1.** To cause to fall in small drops or particles; to scatter, strew: *to sprinkle salt, water &c. on an object.* **2.** To cause small drops or particles to fall upon, besprinkle: *to sprinkle a dish with flour.* **B.** intrans. To fall in small, scattered particles or drops.

sprinkle (II.), n., fr. prec. Light, scattered shower of liquid or particles of dry matter: *a sprinkle of snow.*

sprinkler, n. [1. springkler; 2. spríŋklə]. **sprinkle** (I.) & **-er.** One who, that which, sprinkles; object, vessel, device, for sprinkling liquid &c.

sprinkling, n. [1. springkling; 2. spríŋkliŋ]. **sprinkle** (I.) & **-ing. 1.** Small quantity of liquid or dry substance falling in scattered drops or particles; a sprinkle: *a sprinkling of snow.* **2.** Small number of persons, or objects, scattered here and there: *a sprinkling of visitors among the usual inhabitants.*

sprint (I.), vb. intrans. & trans. [1. sprint; 2. sprint]. Cp. O.N. *spretta.* **1.** intrans. To run at full speed for short distance. **2.** trans. To run (distance) at top of one's speed.

sprint (II.), n., fr. prec. Short run performed at full speed throughout.

sprinter, n. [1. sprínter; 2. spríntə]. **sprint** (I.) & **-er.** One who sprints; specif., athlete specializing in sprinting.

sprint-race, n. Foot-race run at top speed, usually up to or under 440 yards.

sprit, n. [1. sprit; 2. sprit]. O.E. *sprēot*; M.E. *sprēte*; cp. M.L.G. *sprēt*; M. Du. *spriet*, 'sprit, pole'; cogn. w. **sprout** (I.). Spar extending diagonally upwards from mast.

sprite, n. [1. sprīt; 2. sprait]. M.E. *sprīte*, variant of **spirit.** Small supernatural being; fairy, elf.

spritsail, n. [1. sprítsl; 2. sprítsl]. Triangular sail extended by sprit.

sprocket, n. [1. spróket; 2. sprɔ́kit]. Etymol. unknown. Projecting tooth on rim of wheel, engaging with links of chain &c.; *sprocket-wheel*, one fitted with sprockets.

sprout (I.), vb. intrans. & trans. [1. sprout; 2. spraut]. O.E. *sprūtan*; M.E. *sprūten*, 'to sprout'; cp. O. Fris. *sprūta*; M. Du. *spruiten*; M.H.G. *spriuzen*; cp. also O.E. *sprytlan*; M.H.G. *sprützen*, 'to sprout'; fr. base **spreu-*, **spru-* &c., 'to sprout', expanded fr. **sper-*, **sprē-* &c., 'to scatter, sow; to sprout, germinate', see **spark, sparger, sperm** (I.), & words there referred to. **1.** intrans. (of plant, bud, seed &c.) To put forth shoots, develop, begin to grow. **2.** trans. To put forth, develop, as, or in the manner of, a sprout.

sprout (II.), n., fr. prec. **1.** Young shoot, new growth from bud, seed &c. **2.** *Sprouts*, for *Brussels sprouts* see **Brussels.**

spruce (I.), adj. [1. sprōōs; 2. sprūs]. Prob. as **spruce** (III.), w. special reference to Prussian leather, fashionable in 16th cent. Neat, smart, trim, dapper.

spruce (II.), vb. trans., fr. prec. Usually *spruce up*, to make spruce, tidy, smarten.

spruce (III.), n. Abbr. fr. *spruce-fir*, for Prussian fir, fr. M.E. (*s*)*pruce*, O. Fr. *Pruce*, 'Prussia'; see **Prussian. 1.** (also *spruce-fir*) Coniferous tree of the pine family, genus *Picea*, indigenous to northern hemisphere, of many kinds, as the *black* and *white spruce*, *Norway spruce*, *Douglas fir* &c. **2.** Timber of this tree.

spruce-beer, n. Beer made from leaves and twigs of spruce-fir.

sprue (I.), n. [1. sprōō; 2. sprū]. Etymol. unknown. **a** Aperture through which molten metal is poured into a mould; **b** piece of metal remaining in this.

sprue (II.), n., fr. Du. *spruw*, 'thrush' (the disease). Tropical disease characterized by inflammation and ulceration of the mouth and throat, and by enteritis.

sprung, adj. [1. sprung; 2. spraŋ]. P.P. of **spring** (I.); O.E. (*ġe*)*sprungen*. **1.** (of bat, racquet) Split, cracked. **2.** (slang) Slightly intoxicated, tipsy.

spry, adj. [1. sprī; 2. sprai]. Cp. Swed. *sprygg*; O.N. *sprakr*; O.E. *spræc*, 'lively', q.v. under **spark.** Active, nimble, and alert in movement, agile; also alert in mind; smart. Phr. *look spry*, hurry up, look sharp.

spud (I.), n. [1. spud; 2. spad]. M.E. *spudde*; cp. Dan. *spyd*; O.N. *spjot*, 'spear'. **1.** Small spade or chisel-shaped tool for digging up weeds &c. **2.** (colloq.) Potato.

spud (II.), vb. trans., fr. prec. To remove, dig up, with a spud.

spuddle, vb. intrans. [1. spúdl; 2. spádl]. Prob. freq. of prec. (dial.) To use a spud; esp. to dig carelessly or desultorily, potter about with a spade.

spuddy, adj. [1. spúdi; 2. spádi]. **spud** (I.) & **-y.** Short, plump, thickset.

spue, vb. See **spew.**

spume, n. [1. spūm; 2. spjūm], fr. Lat. *spūma*, 'foam, froth'; perh. cogn. w. Lat. *pūmex*, 'pumice-stone', see **pumice**; cogn. w. Scrt. *phḗnaś*, 'foam'; O.H.G. *feim*; O.E. *fām*, 'foam', see **foam**; cp. Lith. *spáine*, 'foam'. Foam, froth, scum.

spumescence, n. [1. spūmésens; 2. spjūmésəns]. See next word & **-ence.** State or quality of being frothy, foaming.

spumescent, adj. [1. spūmésent; 2. spjūmésənt], fr. Lat. *spūmescent-(em)*, Pres. Part. of *spūmescere*, 'to grow frothy', fr. *spūma*, 'foam', see **spume.** Producing or resembling foam; frothy.

spuminess, n. [1. spúmines; 2. spjúminis]. **spumy** & **-ness.** State or quality of being spumy.

spumous, adj. [1. spúmus; 2. spjúməs], fr. Lat. *spūmōsus*, 'full of foam'; **spume** & **-ous.** Of, pertaining to, resembling, covered with, foam.

spumy, adj. [1. spúmi; 2. spjúmi]. **spume** & **-y.** Spumous.

spun, adj. [1. spun; 2. span]. P.P. of **spin** (I.); O.E. (*ġe*)*spunnen*. *Spun glass*, stretched into threads while hot; *spun gold*, thread of gold-covered fibre for weaving &c.; *spun silk*, material woven of thread spun from short fibres of silk; *spun yarn*, (naut.) rope made of two or four loosely twisted strands.

spunge. Archaic spelling variant of **sponge.**

spunk, n. [1. spungk; 2. spaŋk], fr. Ir. *sponc*, 'tinder', fr. Lat. *spongia*, 'sponge', see **sponge. 1.** Touchwood, tinder made from dried fungus impregnated with inflammable substance. **2.** (Scots) **a** Courage, spirit; **b** hot temper, irascibility.

spunky, adj. [1. spúngki; 2. spáŋki]. Prec. & **-y. 1.** Resembling, of the nature of, spunk or tinder. **2. a** Courageous, mettlesome; **b** angry, ill-tempered.

spur (I.), n. [1. spër; 2. spā]. O.E. *spura*, *spora*; M.E. *spur*, *spore*; cp. O.H.G. *sporo*; O.N. *spori*; Du. *spoor*; Germ. *sporn*, 'spur'; cogn. w. Gk. *sphurón*, 'ankle'; cp. also O.H.G. *spornōn*, 'to strike with the heels'; O.E. *spurnan*, 'to drive away, reject', see **spurn. 1. a** Instrument fitted to rider's heel, with sharp point, or series of points on revolving wheel or rowel, for pricking horse's flanks; **b** (hist.) specif., spur, esp. of gold, as emblem of knighthood. Phr. *to win one's spurs*, (i.) attain the rank of knight; (ii.) (fig.) achieve honour and reputation. **2.** Sharply pointed, spur-like object; specif. **a** stiff, pointed projection on wing of bird or leg of bird or insect, esp. horny projection on leg of cock; **b** projection from, or elongated part of, flower; **c** projecting cliff, ridge, or part of mountain range &c.; **d** wall connecting part of rampart with interior work. **3.** (fig.) Keen impulse, instigation, stimulus, incitement: *ambition is an excellent spur for the young.* Phr. *on the spur of the moment*, without previous intention or preparation.

spur (II.), vb. trans. & intrans., fr. prec. **A.** trans. **1.** To strike, prick, urge on, with spurs. **2.** To provide, equip, with spurs: *booted and spurred.* **3.** (fig.) To stimulate, incite, urge on: *to spur a person into action.* **B.** intrans. **a** To use spurs to urge on a horse; hence, **b** to ride fast and urgently.

spurge, n. [1. spërj; 2. spādž], fr. O. Fr. *espurge*, fr. *espurger*, 'to purge', fr. Lat. *expurgāre*, 'to cleanse, purge'; see **expurgate.** Genus of plants, *Euphorbia*, usually having fleshy stems containing a highly acrid, milky juice.

spurge-laurel, n. Evergreen shrub, *Daphne laureola*, with yellow flowers and poisonous berries.

spurious, adj. [1. spúrius; 2. spjɔ́riəs], fr. Lat. *spurius*, 'of illegitimate birth; false, spurious'; prob. fr. Gk. *sporá*, 'sowing; seed; generation; birth'; see **sperm** (I.). **1.** Of origin different from that claimed, not genuine; false, counterfeit, sham: *spurious bank-notes*; *spurious sentiment.* **2.** (biol.) Having superficial resemblance to some organ, limb &c., but differing in function or origin.

spuriously, adv. Prec. & **-ly.** In a spurious manner.

spuriousness, n. See prec. & **-ness.** State or quality of being spurious.

spurless, adj. [1. spërles; 2. spális]. **spur** (I.) & **-less.** Without spurs.

spurling-line, n. [1. spërling līn; 2. spáliŋ làin]. Etymol. unknown. (naut.) Cord attached to helm and serving to show position of the latter on an indicator.

spurn, vb. trans. & intrans. [1. spërn; 2. spān]. O.E. *spurnan*, *spornan*, 'to kick, thrust at with foot; to drive away, reject'; cp. O.N. *spyrna*, 'to drive away'; O.H.G. *spornōn*, 'to kick'; cogn. w. **spur** (I.), & further w. Scrt. *sphurati*, 'to push with the foot', Lat. *spernere*, 'to repulse'; Gk. *spairein*, 'to palpitate'; see also **sphaero-. A.** trans. **1.** (archaic) To thrust at with the foot; chiefly now in Phr. *to spurn the ground*, to leap. **2.** To drive away roughly or rudely, repel: *to spurn a poor relation from one's door.* **3.** To reject scornfully, refuse with disdain, show contempt for: *to spurn one's offers, affection* &c. **B.** intrans. *Spurn at*, (rare) to reject with scorn.

spurrier, n. [1. spërier, spúrier; 2. spária, spáriə]. **spur** (I.) & **-ier.** Maker of spurs.

spur-royal, n. Gold coin of James I., worth about 15s., having on the reverse side a star resembling a rowel.

spurry, spurrey, n. [1. spúri; 2. spári], fr. O. Fr. *spurrie*; cp. Med. Lat. *spergula*. Genus, *Spergula*, of small, slender, annual, herbaceous plants with small white or pink flowers.

spurt (I.), vb. intrans. & n. [1. spërt; 2. spāt]. See also **spirt. 1.** vb. To make a sudden violent effort, put forward all one's strength for a short spell, in racing &c. **2.** n. Sudden, short spell of violent exertion, esp. at the end of a race &c.

spurt (II.), vb. intrans. & trans. & n. O.E. *spryttan*; M.E. *sprutten*, *spritten*, 'to shoot forth', see **spirt** (I.). Same as **spirt** (I.) and (II.).

spur-wheel, n. Gear-wheel with toothed rim.

spurwort, n. [1. spërwërt; 2. spáwāt]. Madder, from the whorls of leaves encircling the stem.

sputter (I.), vb. intrans. & trans. [1. spúter; 2. spátə], fr. M.E. *spouten*, 'to spout', see **spout** & **-er. A.** intrans. **1.** To make a series of spitting sounds or light explosive noises; to splutter. **2.** To speak rapidly, jerkily, and indistinctly. **B.** trans. To utter rapidly and indistinctly, jabber.

sputter (II.), n., fr. prec. Sputtering noise or speech.

sputteringly, adv. [1. spúteringli; 2. spátəriŋli], fr. Pres. Part. of **sputter** (I.) & **-ly.** In a sputtering manner, with a sputter.

sputum, n. [1. spūtum; 2. spjūtəm]. Lat. *spūtum*, 'spittle', fr. neut. P.P. of *spuere*, 'to spit'; cogn. w. Gk. *ptúō*; Goth. *speiwan*; O.N. *spȳja*; Lith. *spiáuju*, 'to spit', see **spew. 1.** Saliva. **2.** (often pl., *sputa*) Matter that has been expectorated, esp. when considered as characteristic of specific disease.

spy (I.), vb. trans. & intrans. [1. spī; 2. spai]. M.E. *spien*, fr. O. Fr. *espier*, fr. O.H.G. *spehōn*, 'to see, spy'; cp. O.H.G., O.S. *spāhi*, 'wise, discriminating, prudent'; Scrt. *spáçati*, 'sees'; Lat. *specere*, 'to see'; *speciēs*, 'appearance'; see **species. 1.** trans. To see, discern, perceive, make out, espy. Phr. *I spy strangers*, used in British House of Commons by a Member who wishes to have the galleries cleared. **2.** intrans. To act as a spy: *he spies for the enemy.* **3.** Followed by adverbs and prepositions in special senses. *Spy into*, to examine, investigate, carefully and secretly: *to spy into one's actions. Spy out*, to make clandestine investigations in, explore secretly: *to spy out the land. Spy upon*, to keep a secret watch upon, examine closely and secretly: *to spy upon a person.*

spy (II.), n. M.E. *spie*, fr. O. Fr. *espie*, fr. *espier*, 'to spy', see prec. **a** Person keeping secret watch on another's speech, conduct, actions; specif. **b** person employed to obtain secret information about another country, its social conditions, military preparations, political intentions &c.

spy-glass, n. Small hand telescope.

spy-hole, n. Hole through which one can see without being seen; peep-hole.

squab, adj. & n. [1. skwob; 2. skwɔb]. Cp. Swed. *sqvabb*, 'loose flesh'. **1.** adj. Short, plump and thick; stumpy. **2.** n. Short, fat, round object; specif. **a** young, unfledged pigeon or rook; **b** short, stout person; **c** small, stuffed cushion.

squabble (I.), n. [1. skwóbl; 2. skwɔ́bl]. Cp. Swed. *skvabbel*, 'a dispute'. Undignified quarrel, a petty wrangle; a bicker.

squabble (II.), vb. intrans. & trans., fr. prec. **1.** intrans. To engage in squabbles; to quarrel, to bicker. **2.** trans. (print.) To disarrange, upset, disturb position of (composed type).

squabby, adj. [1. skwóbi; 2. skwɔ́bi]. **squab** & **-y.** Short, plump, and stumpy.

squab-chick, n. Young bird, fledgeling.

squab-pie, n. **1.** Pigeon-pie; rook-pie. **2.** Pasty made of mutton, apples, and onions.

squacco, n. [1. skwákō; 2. skwǽkou]. Imitative. Small crested heron of Southern Europe, Africa, and Asia.

squad, n. [1. skwod; 2. skwɔd], fr. M. Fr. *esquadre*, fr. Ital. *squadra*, 'square', fr. L. Lat. **exquadrāre*, 'to form into a square'; see **square** (I.). **1.** Small detachment of troops &c. for drill. Phr. *awkward squad*, body of new, and still raw, recruits; (chiefly fig.) of inefficient group of people &c. **2.** Small group of persons acting together.

squadron (I.), n. [1. skwódrun; 2. skwɔ́drən], fr. M. Fr. *esquadron*, fr. Ital. *squadrone*, fr. *squadra*, 'square', see **squad,** & **-oon. 1.** Body of cavalry, consisting of 120 to 200 men; two troops. **2. a** Group or detachment of ships of war detached for special service; **b** group of twelve military aeroplanes. **3.** Organized group of persons; squad.

squadron (**II.**), vb. trans., fr. prec. To form into squadrons, organize as squadron.

squadron-leader, n. Officer in Royal Air Force commanding a squadron of twelve aeroplanes, ranking with a major in the army.

squail, n. [1. skwāl; 2. skweil]. Etymol. unknown; cp. dial. *squail*, 'to strike, pelt'; see **squailer**. **1.** Small wooden counter used in the game of squails. **2.** (pl.) Table game played by snapping small discs from the edge to centre of a board.

squail-board, n. Round board used in the game of squails.

squailer, n. [1. skwáler; 2. skwéilə], fr. dial. *squail*, 'to strike, pelt', of doubtful origin. Stick with weighted knob used as missile in hunting animal &c.

squalid, adj. [1. skwólid; 2. skwɔ́lid], fr. Lat. *squālidus*, 'rough; neglected; filthy', fr. *squālēre*, 'to be stiff with dirt or dryness'; cogn. w. Gk. *pēlós*, 'clay', fr. **skʷēlos*; O. Slav. *kalŭ*, 'mud, loam, clay'. **a** Filthy and degraded; foul, unclean, dingy: *a squalid slum*; *squalid surroundings*; **b** (in moral sense) base, sordid, mean: *a squalid quarrel*.

squalidity, n. [1. skwolíditi; 2. skwɔlíditi]. Prec. & **-ity**. State or quality of being squalid.

squalidly, adv. [1. skwólidli; 2. skwɔ́lidli]. See prec. & **-ly**. In a squalid manner.

squalidness, n. [1. skwólidnes; 2. skwɔ́lidnis]. See prec. & **-ness**. Squalor.

squall (**I.**), vb. intrans. & trans. [1. skwawl; 2. skwōl], fr. O.N. *skvala*, 'to squeal'; cp. Swed. *sqvala*, 'to gush out'; prob. imitative in origin. **1.** intrans. **a** To cry out loudly and shrilly; to bawl; **b** to sing loudly, unmelodiously. **2.** trans. To utter with a squall.

squall (**II.**), n., fr. prec. **1.** Loud, discordant cry; harsh, shrill shriek; a squawk. **2.** Sudden, violent brief storm of wind, whether accompanied or not with rain or snow. Phr. *look out for squalls*, be on your guard against trouble, esp. that due to another's temper.

squally, adj. [1. skwáwli; 2. skwɔ́li]. Prec. & **-y**. Liable to, abounding in, characterized by, squalls.

squaloid, adj. [1. skwáloid; 2. skwéilɔid], fr. Mod. Lat. *squalus*, 'shark', fr. Lat. *squalus*, 'kind of large fish'; cp. O.N. *hvalr*; O.E. *hwæl*, 'whale', see **whale**; perh. cogn. w. Gk. *skúlion*, 'kind of shark'; & **-oid**. Of, pertaining to, resembling, a shark.

squalor, n. [1. skwóler; 2. skwɔ́lə]. Lat. *squālor*, 'stiffness, roughness, filth', fr. *squālēre*, 'to be stiff with dirt', see **squalid**, & **-or**. State or quality of being squalid; physical or moral uncleanness, filth, sordidness.

squama, n. [1. skwáma; 2. skwéimə]. Lat. *squāma*, 'scale'; etymol. doubtful. Scale, or scale-like structure or object.

squami-, squamo-, prefs. representing Lat. *squāma*, 'scale'; see prec. Scale.

squamiferous, adj. [1. skwāmíferus; 2. skweimífərəs]. Prec. & **-ferous**. Bearing scales.

squamiform, adj. [1. skwámiform; 2. skwéimifōm]. **squami-** & **-form**. In the form of a scale.

squamoid, adj. [1. skwámoid; 2. skwéimɔid]. **squama** & **-oid**. Like, having the form of, a squama.

squamose, adj. [1. skwámōs; 2. skwéimous], fr. Lat. *squāmōsus*, 'scaly'; **squama** & **-ose**. Of the nature of, resembling, covered with, scales.

squamo-temporal, adj. [1. skwámō témpural; 2. skwéimou témpərəl]. Of the squamous part of the temporal bone.

squamous, adj. [1. skwámus; 2. skwéiməs]. **squama** & **-ous**. Squamose.

squamule, n. [1. skwámūl; 2. skwéimjūl]. Lat. *squāmula*, 'little scale'; **squama** & **-ule**. Small scale.

squander, vb. trans. [1. skwónder; 2. skwɔ́ndə]. Etymol. dubious. To spend wastefully and extravagantly; to dissipate; to disperse, expend foolishly and to no purpose: *to squander money, time, talents* &c.

squanderer, n. [1. skwónderer; 2. skwɔ́ndərə]. Prec. & **-er**. Person given to squandering.

squanderingly, adv. [1. skwónderingli; 2. skwɔ́ndəriŋli]. Pres. Part. of **squander** & **-ly**. Extravagantly.

squandermania, n. [1. skwóndermánia; 2. skwɔ́ndəméiniə]. A journalistic invention. Mania for spending money, esp. applied to any government expenditure on objects of which the user of the word disapproves.

square (**I.**), n. [1. skwār; 2. skwɛə], fr. O. Fr. *esquarre*, fr. Low Lat. **exquadrāre*, 'to form into a square', fr. **ex-** & *quadra*, 'square'; cp. Lat. *quadru-*, *quadri-*, 'four' (in compounds), & see **quadri-**. **1. a** Plane rectangular figure enclosed by four equal sides; **b** four equal lines, at right angles to each other, enclosing such a figure. **2. a** Object having the shape of a square: *a square of glass, linen* &c.; **b** specif., division of chessboard &c. **3. a** Square or oblong open space in town usually laid out as a garden, fenced in and bounded by a street of houses on at least two sides; **b** large open space, or place in a town, bounded by streets, and usually with several important buildings looking into it, used for fairs, markets &c. **4.** Body of troops &c. drawn up to form a square. **5.** Measure for flooring &c. = 100 square feet. **6.** Instrument for measuring or determining right angles, consisting of two wooden or metal bars at right angles to each other, in form of **L** or **T**. Phr. *on the square*, honest, sincere, genuine. **7.** (arith.) Product of quantity multiplied by itself.

square (**II.**), adj., fr. prec. **1.** Having, bounded by, four equal sides and four right angles; rectangular. **2.** Forming, having, a right angle; placed at right angles: *square corners*. Phr. *a square meal*, a solid, substantial one. **3.** (of shape) **a** Having a firm outline suggestive of a square: *square shoulders*; *a square chin* &c.; **b** broad in proportion to height, square-built. **4.** (lit. and fig.) On equal terms, with debit and credit balanced; even: *to get one's accounts square*. Phrs. *to get square with*, get even with, retaliate upon; *all square*, (golf) with neither side leading; even. **5.** Honest, genuine, straightforward, just: *square dealing*; *he is absolutely square*. **6.** Unequivocal, unambiguous, clear: *a square refusal*. **7.** (arith.) **a** Of, pertaining to, quantity multiplied by itself; having two equal factors: *square number*; *square inch, foot* &c., surface area equal to square each of whose sides measures one inch, foot &c.; **b** *square measure*, giving table of measurement of superficial area; **c** *square root*, see **root**.

square (**III.**), vb. trans. & intrans., fr. **square** (**I.**). **A.** trans. **1.** To make square, give square shape to. Phr. *to square the circle*, (i.) to construct a square equal in area to a given circle; (ii.) to express or determine the exact area of a circle in terms of its radius; (iii.) (fig.) to perform an impossibility. **2. a** To make square, form into a right angle: *to square the edge of a board*; **b** to raise, place, so as to form a horizontal line: *to square one's shoulders, elbows*, esp. in preparation for fighting. **3.** To settle, make even, balance: *to square accounts with*. **4. a** To induce, persuade, by illicit means, to act in a certain way, or to abstain from hostile action; to bribe: *it was said that the police had been squared*; **b** to persuade by legitimate means; to satisfy, convince; to settle with: *to square one's creditors by paying them*. **5.** To adapt, reconcile, bring into line: *to square one's theories with ascertained facts*. **6.** (arith.) To multiply (quantity) by itself. **7.** (naut.) **a** To get (dead-eyes &c.) in line with each other; **b** to lay (yards &c.) parallel to deck and at right angles to ship's length. **B.** intrans. **1.** To be at right angles, form a right angle. **2.** To assume an attitude with squared elbows &c., assume boxer's preliminary position: *to square up to a person*. **3.** To harmonize, be in agreement with: *statement does not square with the facts*.

square (**IV.**), adv., fr. **square** (**II.**). **1.** At right angles, so as to form a right angle; squarely: *to stand square*. **2.** Honestly, fairly: *fair and square*.

square-built, adj. Broad in proportion to height, and with straight outlines.

square-head, n. (U.S. slang) Scandinavian immigrant in America.

square-leg, n. (cricket) Fielder standing at right angles to wicket on the on-side.

squarely, adv. [1. skwárli; 2. skwɛ́əli]. **square** (**II.**) & **-ly**. **1.** So as to form a right angle. **2.** Directly opposite: *to face a person squarely*. **3.** Unambiguously, without equivocation. **4.** Honestly, equitably, on the square.

squareness, n. [1. skwárnes; 2. skwɛ́ənis]. See prec. & **-ness**. **1.** State of being square. **2.** Honesty, sincerity, square dealing.

square-rigged, adj. (of ship) Having the yards horizontal and at right angles to keel; opposed to *fore-and-aft*.

square-rigger, n. [1. skwár ríger; 2. skwɛ́ə rìgə]. Square-rigged vessel.

squaresail, n. [1. skwársl; 2. skwɛ́əsl]. Four-cornered sail extended by yard lying across mast, esp. on fore-and-aft rigged ship.

square-shouldered, adj. Having shoulders which give the impression of being approximately at right angles to the neck; contrasted with sloping.

square-toed, adj. **1.** (of shoes &c.) Having square toes. **2.** (fig.) Puritanical, over-rigid, and scrupulous.

square-toes, n. [1. skwár tōz; 2. skwɛ́ə touz]. Exact, punctilious, conventional, puritanical person.

squarish, adj. [1. skwárish; 2. skwɛ́əriʃ]. **square** (**II.**) & **-ish**. Nearly square.

squarrose, adj. [1. skwárōs; 2. skwǽrous], fr. L. Lat. *squarrōsus*, 'scaly, scurfy', prob. w. assimilation to **squama**, fr. Gk. *eskhára*, 'scab'. With rough, scale-like projections.

squarrous, adj. [1. skwárus; 2. skwǽrəs]. See prec. & **-ous**. Squarrose.

squarson, n. [1. skwársun; 2. skwɑ́sən]. Coinage fr. a blend of **squire** & **parson**. Clergyman who is also a landowner, esp. one who is both the squire and the incumbent of his parish.

squash (**I.**), vb. trans. & intrans. [1. skwosh; 2. skwɔʃ]. M.E. *squacchen*, fr. O. Fr. *esquacher*, fr. **ex-** & Low Lat. **coacticāre*, 'to press together', fr. Lat. *coactus*, P.P. of *cōgere*, 'to drive together; to compel'. See **cogent**. **A.** trans. **1. a** To crush, press, to a shapeless mass or pulp; **b** to compress, crush, jam, press or squeeze flat. **2.** (fig., colloq.) To disconcert, crush, abash, by sarcastic speech &c. **B.** intrans. **1.** To become crushed, squeezed, compressed to a soft or pulpy mass: *the fruit will squash if it is badly packed*. **2.** To squeeze, force one's way by pressure.

squash (**II.**), n., fr. prec. **1.** Condition of being closely packed and crushed; a jam. **2.** Mass of soft, moist substance which has been crushed and bruised: *the strawberries have all gone to squash*. **3. a** Closely packed crowd of persons &c.; **b** process, or sensation, of being squeezed in a crowd. **4.** Drink made of the juice of crushed fruit; chiefly in the compounds, *lemon-squash, orange-squash*. **5.** Squash racquets.

squash (**III.**), n., fr. Am. Indian *askutasquash*. Thick fleshy fruit of various kinds of trailing plant, eaten as vegetable &c.

squash-hat, n. Soft felt hat with broadish brim.

squashiness, n. [1. skwóshines; 2. skwɔ́ʃinis]. **squashy** & **-ness**. State or quality of being squashy.

squash-rackets, n. Game resembling rackets, but played in a smaller court, by two persons, with a soft india-rubber ball.

squashy, adj. [1. skwóshi; 2. skwɔ́ʃi]. **squash** (II.) & **-y.** Tending, liable, to become squashed; soft and pulpy; reduced to a soft moist mass.

squat (I.), vb. intrans. [1. skwot; 2. skwɔt]. M.E. *squatten*, fr. O. Fr. *esquatir*, fr. **ex-** & *quatir*, 'to flatten', fr. Lat. *coactus*, P.P. of *cōgere*, 'to drive together; to compel'. See **cogent.** **1.** (of person) To sit back, resting on the heels, or, generally, to crouch on the ground with the feet drawn up to the body. **2.** (of animal) To crouch with legs close to body. **3. a** To settle down on land without permission of owner, or on common land without authorization; **b** to occupy land as a settler in a wild, thinly populated country; esp. a settler on Government land in Australia.

squat (II.), adj., fr. prec. Short and thick, stumpy and square.

squatter, n. [1. skwóter; 2. skwɔ́tə]. **squat** (I.) & **-er.** **1.** Person or animal that squats. **2.** Person who settles on common land, on outlying portion of an estate, without right or permission. **3.** (in Australia) Person who settles on Government land with a view to eventual ownership.

squaw, n. [1. skwaw; 2. skwɔ̄], fr. N. Am. Ind. *squa*, 'woman'. North American Indian woman.

squawk, vb. intrans. & n. [1. skwawk; 2. skwɔ̄k]. Imitative. **1.** vb. To utter a short, shrill, harsh cry. **2.** n. Short, harsh cry.

squaw-man, n. White man married to American Indian woman.

squeak (I.), vb. intrans. & trans. [1. skwēk; 2. skwīk]. In Shakespeare; of Scand. origin; cp. M. Swed. *sqvǣka* in same sense. **A.** intrans. **1.** To utter a squeak. **2.** (slang) To betray secrets, inform on a person &c. **B.** trans. To utter, pronounce, in a squeak.

squeak (II.), n., fr. prec. Weak, thin, high-pitched cry of fright or excitement, as made by small animals such as rats, mice, bats, or by young children; high piercing, grating sound, such as that made by a pencil on a slate, an unoiled hinge or wheel &c. Phr. *a narrow squeak*, narrow margin of success, performance, escape from danger &c.

squeaker, n. [1. skwḗker; 2. skwíkə]. **squeak** (I.) & **-er.** **1.** One who, that which, squeaks; specif., young pigeon. **2.** (slang) An informer, esp. a criminal who betrays his companions to the police.

squeakily, adv. [1. skwḗkili; 2. skwíkili]. Next word & **-ly.** With a squeaky sound.

squeaky, adj. [1. skwḗki; 2. skwíki]. **squeak** (II.) & **-y.** Producing, of the nature of, a squeak; liable to squeak.

squeal (I.), vb. intrans. & trans. [1. skwēl; 2. skwīəl]. M.E. *squēlen*; of Scand. origin, cp. M. Swed. *sqvǣla*; prob. connected w. **squeak** & **squall.** **1.** intrans. **a** To utter a high, shrill, but ringing, prolonged cry; **b** to complain. **2.** (slang) To act as informer, betray confederates &c. **3.** trans. To utter with a squeal.

squeal (II.), n., fr. prec. High, shrill, prolonged cry, louder and stronger than a squeak.

squealer, n. [1. skwḗler; 2. skwílə]. **squeal** & **-er.** One who, that which, squeals; specif. **a** young bird, esp. pigeon; **b** a person who is always complaining.

squeamish, adj. [1. skwḗmish; 2. skwímiʃ]. M.E. *squeimous*, fr. A.-Fr. *escoimous*, 'squeamish, disdainful', etymol. doubtful, & **-ish.** **1.** Easily affected by nausea; slightly nauseated. **2.** Highly fastidious or scrupulous; easily offended or disgusted; very sensitive.

squeamishly, adv. Prec. & **-ly.** In a squeamish manner.

squeamishness, n. See prec. & **-ness.** State or quality of being squeamish.

squeegee (I.), n. [1. skwḗjḗ; 2. skwídʒí], fr. popular form of **squeeze** & **-ee.** **1.** Long-handled wooden instrument with rubber blade for clearing water, mud &c., from smooth surface of a road, deck &c. **2.** Small implement in form of a rubber roller for drying photographic prints &c.

squeegee (II.), vb. trans., fr. prec. To treat, dry, sweep, with a squeegee.

squeezability, n. [1. skwēzabíliti; 2. skwīzəbíliti]. See next word & **-bility.** State or quality of being squeezable.

squeezable, adj. [1. skwḗzabl; 2. skwízəbl]. Next word & **-able.** **a** Capable of being squeezed; yielding to pressure; **b** capable of being persuaded or coerced.

squeeze (I.), vb. trans. & intrans. [1. skwēz; 2. skwīz]. Prob. fr. O.E. (non-W.S.) *cwēsan*, 'to bruise, dash against; to squeeze', w. O. Fr. pref. *es-*, fr. Lat. **ex-**, as intens.; further connexions of *cwēsan* are doubtful. **A.** trans. **1.** To compress (esp. a soft substance) between two or more surfaces or between the fingers; to press firmly; to mould, knead: *to squeeze moist clay; to squeeze a person's hand.* **2. a** To exert pressure upon for the purpose of extracting moisture: *to squeeze a sponge; to squeeze a lemon dry*; **b** to extract (moisture) by squeezing: *to squeeze juice from a lemon.* **3.** (fig.) **a** To bring moral pressure of persuasion or fear to bear upon, constrain; to practise extortion upon: *a usurer squeezes his victims*; **b** to extort, extract, by moral pressure, threats &c.: *to squeeze money, a confession, from a person.* **4.** To pack tightly, cram, compress; jam in, by pressing: *to squeeze things into a box; to squeeze oneself into a room* &c. **5.** To gain, force, by pushing and pressing: *to squeeze one's way through a crowd.* **6.** To take an impression of (moulded, engraved, inscribed object &c.) on a plastic surface. **B.** intrans. To go, move, pass, force one's way by squeezing and compressing: *to squeeze through a narrow opening.*

squeeze (II.), n., fr. prec. **1.** Act of squeezing: *to give one's hand a squeeze.* **2.** Crowding, compression, state of being packed closely together: *it was a tight squeeze to get everything in.* **3.** Impression of inscription, coin &c., taken by pressure on soft surface, such as on damp paper.

squeezer, n. [1. skwḗzer; 2. skwízə]. **squeeze** (I.) & **-er.** **1.** One who, that which, squeezes; specif. **a** device for extracting juice from fruit &c.; **b** machine for removing air-bubbles from puddled iron. **2.** *Squeezers*, playing-cards with value indicated in top right-hand corner.

squelch (I.), vb. intrans. [1. skwelch; 2. skwel(t)ʃ]. Imitative. **1.** To produce a splashing, gurgling sound, or a sound of suction, as by walking in wet boots through adhesive mud &c. **2. a** To crush, annihilate, as by treading upon; **b** (fig.) to disconcert, reduce to silence by rebuke or irony.

squelch (II.), n. See prec. **1.** Sound of suction made in walking through wet, thick mud &c. **2.** Act of squelching; **a** a crushing extermination; **b** rebuke or retort which silences opposition, disconcerts, and abashes &c.

squib (I.), n. [1. skwib; 2. skwib], fr. next word. **1.** Small firework which, when lighted, gives off a series of sparks, ending with a loud but harmless explosion. **2.** Tube of gunpowder used to fire a charge. **3.** Short satirical composition, a lampoon.

squib (II.), vb. trans. Perh. a dialectal variant fr. M.E. *swippen*, 'to move quickly, vibrate', fr. O.N. *svipa*, 'quick movement; sharp blow; flash'; cp. O.H.G. *sweifan*, 'to swing, give turning movement to'; O.E. *swāpan*, 'to move, sweep'; see **sweep.** To attack with squibs.

squid (I.), n. [1. skwid; 2. skwid]. Origin uncertain; perh. related to O.N. *skvetta*, 'squirt'. **1.** Kind of cuttle-fish with a slender body and long arms and tentacles; esp. the common squid, used as bait. **2.** Kind of artificial bait, sometimes made of metal in imitation of a squid.

squid (II.), vb. intrans., fr. prec. To fish with squid as bait.

squiffer, n. [1. skwífer; 2. skwífə]. Etymol. unknown. (slang) Concertina.

squiffy, adj. [1. skwífi; 2. skwífi]. Etymol. unknown. Slightly intoxicated, tipsy.

squilgee, n. & vb. trans. [1. skwíljē; 2. skwíldʒī]. See **squeegee**; origin of variant unknown.

squill, n. [1. skwil; 2. skwil]. M.E., fr. M. Fr. *squille*, fr. Lat. *squilla*, fr. Gk. *skilla*, 'squill, sea-onion'. **1.** Genus, *Scilla*, of plants of the lily family with blue or purplish, bell-shaped flowers; the bulb of some species is used medicinally. **2.** Dried and sliced bulb of the squill, used as purgative and emetic drug. **3.** Genus of crustaceans, esp. kind of shrimp.

squinancy, n. [1. skwínansi; 2. skwínənsi]. The quinsy-wort; see **quinsy.**

squinch, n. [1. skwinch; 2. skwintʃ]. Variant of **sconce.** Arch or series of arches across interior right angle, esp. of square tower, to support octagonal spire &c.

squint (I.), n. [1. skwint; 2. skwint]. Occurs in Early M.E. in adv. *asquint*; cp. O. Fris. *schün*, 'oblique', & *schünte*, 'obliquity'; also Dan. *paa skōns*, 'aslant'. Prob. connected w. **askance.** **1.** Condition in which both eyes cannot look, at the same time, straight at an object; condition in which the eyes tend to converge or to diverge, caused by an affection of the eye-muscles or nerves; strabismus: *to have a bad squint.* **2.** (colloq.) Look, peep, glance: *let me have a squint at it.* **3.** Small tunnel open at either end, made through the thickness of the wall of church to enable the high altar to be seen from transepts, side-chapels &c.

squint (II.), vb. intrans. & trans., fr. prec. **A.** intrans. **1.** To be affected with strabismus or squint; to look in different directions with the two eyes. **2.** *Squint at*, **a** to look hastily and sideways at; **b** (colloq.) to glance, look, at. **B.** trans. (rare) To cause (eyes) to squint: *to squint the eyes.*

squint (III.), adj., fr. **squint** (I.). (rare) Affected with strabismus, squinting.

squint-eyed, adj. **1.** Affected with squint. **2.** Having an evil, malicious look; malevolent, evil, spiteful.

squinting, adj. [1. skwínting; 2. skwíntiŋ], fr. Pres. Part. of **squint** (II.). **a** Affected with squint, with distorted vision; **b** awry, out of the straight.

squintingly, adv. [1. skwíntingli; 2. skwíntiŋli]. Prec. & **-ly.** In a squinting manner.

squire (I.), n. [1. skwīr; 2. skwaiə], fr. **esquire.** **1.** (hist.) Man of gentle or noble birth in attendance on knight. **2.** Member of landed gentry, owner of country estate, esp. *the squire*, chief landowner of particular village &c. **3.** Man escorting or attentive to woman: *squire of dames*, man often in attendance on women.

squire (II.), vb. trans., fr. prec. To act as squire, escort, be attentive to: *to squire a lady.*

squirearch, n. [1. skwírark; 2. skwáiərāk], fr. **squire** & Gk. *arkhós*, 'leader, chief', see **arch-.** Member of squirearchy.

squirearchal, -archical, adj. [1. skwíràrk(ik)l; 2. skwáiərāk(ik)l]. **squirearchy** & **-ic** & **-al.** Pertaining to, of the nature of, a squirearchy.

squirearchy, n. [1. skwíràrki; 2. skwáiərāki]. **squire** & **-archy.** **1.** Landed gentry, country landowners, collectively. **2.** Government by landed classes.

squireen, n. [1. skwīrḗn; 2. skwaiərín]. **squire** & Ir. dimin. suff. *-een, -īn.* Small landowner in Ireland; esp. a rough country gentleman with little education or experience of the world.

squirehood, n. [1. skwírhood; 2. skwáiəhud]. **squire** & **-hood.** Rank of squire.

squirelet, n. [1. skwírlet; 2. skwáiəlit]. **squire** & **-let.** Petty squire.

squireling, n. [1. skwírling; 2. skwáiəliŋ]. **squire** & **-ling.** Squirelet.

squirely, adj. [1. skwírli; 2. skwáiəli]. **squire** (I.) & **-ly.** Pertaining to a squire.

squireship, n. [1. skwírship; 2. skwáiəʃip]. **squire** (I.) & **-ship.** State of being a squire, rank of squire.

squirm (I.), vb. intrans. [1. skwērm; 2. skwʌ̄m]. Etymol. doubtful; perh. imitative. **1.** To twist the body, wriggle, writhe. 2. (fig.) To exhibit a sense of humiliation, embarrassment, discomfiture; to feel and betray impatience and silent dislike of what is said or of something which occurs.

squirm (II.), n., fr. prec. 1. Squirming, writhing motion; wriggle. 2. (naut.) Kink in rope.

squirrel, n. [1. skwírel; 2. skwírəl]. M.E. *squirel*, fr. O. Fr. *escurel*, fr. L. Lat. *scurellus*, fr. *sciūrus*, 'squirrel', fr. Gk. *skíouros*, fr. *skiá*, 'shadow', see **sciagraphy**, & *ourá*, 'tail'; cp. Gk. *ourakhós*, 'point'; cogn. w. Lat. *urruncum*, 'lowest part of ear of corn'; see also **uro-**. Small, arboreal, bushy-tailed, hibernating rodent, genus *Sciurus*, with reddish, dark-brown, or grey fur; *barking squirrel*, prairie-dog; *flying squirrel*, species with extensible, lateral membranes serving as parachutes.

squirrel-fish, n. Reddish fish of West Indies.

squirrel-grass, n. Wild barley.

squirrel monkey, n. a Small, long-tailed monkey of S. America; b marmoset.

squirrel-tail, n. Kind of grass resembling barley.

squirt (I.), vb. trans. & intrans. [1. skwërt; 2. skwʌt]. Cp. L.G. *swirtjen*. 1. trans. To eject (liquid) in a thin but fairly powerful stream, or jet. 2. intrans. To spurt out, be forced out, in a jet.

squirt (II.), n., fr. prec. 1. Jet, stream, of liquid &c. 2. Instrument for ejecting liquid in a jet; syringe. 3. (colloq. and vulg.) Conceited, bumptious, insignificant upstart; pert, self-satisfied person.

squish, n. [1. skwish; 2. skwiʃ]. Prob. variant of **squash** (II.). (colloq.) Marmalade.

stab (I.), vb. trans. & intrans. [1. stab; 2. stæb]. Etymol. doubtful; perh. fr. Swed. *stabbe*, 'a stub, stump'. A. trans. 1. To pierce, wound, penetrate flesh or substance of, with stick, or pointed weapon (esp. with a knife or dagger): *to stab one in the arm*. Phr. *to stab in the back*, to disparage, injure, in underhand way, to backbite. 2. To cause to pierce; to stick, jab: *to stab a weapon into*. 3. (fig.) To attack, assail, injure maliciously: *to stab one's reputation*. 4. To roughen surface of (wall &c.) by blows from a pick, to enable it to hold a coat of plaster. B. intrans. 1. To aim a blow, to make a thrust, with pointed weapon: *to stab at a person*. 2. (of wound, pain) To produce sensation of stabbing, to shoot, throb suddenly and painfully.

stab (II.), n., fr. prec. a Sharp, sudden, violent blow, thrust, with pointed weapon: *a stab in the breast*; Phr. (fig.) *a stab in the back*, a malicious, treacherous attempt to injure; b a sudden sharp shoot, or throb, of pain.

Stabat Mater, n. [1. stáhbat máhter; 2. stǽbət mátə]. Lat. *stābat māter (dolorōsa)*, 'the mother stood', first words of hymn. 1. Mediaeval Latin sequence on the Crucifixion. 2. Musical setting of this.

stabber, n. [1. stáber; 2. stǽbə]. **stab** (I.) & **-er**. 1. One who stabs; an assassin, one who kills by stabbing. 2. That which stabs, esp. instrument for stabbing or piercing.

stability, n. [1. stabíliti; 2. stəbíliti]. Lat. *stabilitāt-(em)*, 'firmness', fr. *stabilis*, 'firm, stable', see **stable** (I.), & **-ity**. State or quality of being stable; steadiness, firmness.

stabilization, n. [1. stàbilizáshun; 2. stæbilaizéiʃən]. Next word & **-ation**. Act of stabilizing; state of being stabilized; esp. of a country's currency, by fixing a definite gold value for it.

stabilize, vb. trans. [1. stáb-, stábilīz; 2. stǽb-, stéibilaiz], fr. Lat. *stabilis*, 'firm', see **stable** (I.), & **-ize**. To make stable, bring into a state of stability or equilibrium, specif., *to stabilize a currency*.

stabilizer, n. [1. stábilīzer; 2. stǽbilaizə]. Prec. & **-er**. One who, that which, stabilizes; specif., an additional plane or fin attached to aeroplane &c. to maintain stability in flight.

stable (I.), adj. [1. stábl; 2. stéibl], fr. Lat. *stabilis*, 'firm, steady, constant', fr. *sta-, fr. base *stā-, *stə-, 'to stand', see **stand, state**, & **-ble**. 1. (of material and non-material things) Fixed, firmly established, steady; not easily moved or upset: *stable foundations*; *a stable government*; *stable currency*; reverse of *shifting, uncertain, fluctuating*. 2. Resolute, unwavering, steadfast, tenacious of purpose. 3. (mechan.) *Stable equilibrium*, tendency of body to return to position of rest when moved or disturbed.

stable (II.), n., fr. O. Fr. *estable*, fr. Lat. *stabulum*, 'stable, stall, lair, hive; hut, hovel', fr. *stə-dhlo-, expanded fr. *stā-, *stə-, 'to stand'; cogn. w. **stall** (I.). See also **stand, state**, & prec. 1. Building fitted and used as shelter for cattle or, more usually, for horses. 2. Group of horses kept in any particular stable, and belonging to a given owner.

stable (III.), vb. trans. & intrans., fr. prec. 1. trans. To put into a stable. 2. intrans. To be kept in, occupy, a stable.

stable-boy, n. Boy employed in stable.

stable-call, n. Signal in cavalry regiment for watering and grooming horses.

stableman, n. [1. stáblman; 2. stéiblmən]. Man employed in or about a stable.

stableness, n. [1. stáblnes; 2. stéiblnis]. **stable** (I.) & **-ness**. Quality of being stable; stability.

stabling, n. [1. stábling; 2. stéibliŋ]. **stable** (II.) & **-ing**. Set of stables, accommodation for horses &c.

stablish, vb. trans. [1. stáblish; 2. stǽbliʃ]. Abbr. fr. **establish**. (archaic) To make firm, set stably; to found, establish.

stably, adv. [1. stábli; 2. stéibli]. **stable** (I.) & **-ly**. In a stable manner, firmly.

staccato, adv. & adj. [1. stakáhtō; 2. stəkátou]. Ital., P.P. of *staccare*, fr. *distaccare*, 'to detach'; cp. **detach** & see **tack** (I.). (mus.) 1. adv. With each note played in a sharply detached, abrupt manner. 2. adj. (of passage, note &c.) To be played staccato: *staccato mark*, dot above or below musical note to show that it is to be played staccato.

stack (I.), n. [1. stak; 2. stæk]. M.E. *stac*, fr. O.N. *stakkr*, 'stack'; cogn. w. Lith. *stókas*, 'pillar'; O. Prussian *staklan*, 'support'; fr. base *stə-k- &c., expanded fr. *stə-, *stā- &c., 'to stand'; see **stand**, & words there referred to. 1. Large, symmetrical pile of hay, straw, or unthrashed corn, usually round or rectangular, with top sloping to a peak or ridge; rick. 2. Any orderly heap, pile, or group: *a stack of wood* &c.; specif. a pyramidal pile of rifles &c., with muzzles upwards; b cluster of chimneys projecting above a roof. 3. Also, *smoke-stack*, chief chimney or funnel of locomotive engine, furnace &c. 4. (esp. Scots) Tall, detached shaft of rock. 5. (as measure of firewood &c.) One hundred and eight cubic feet. 6. (colloq.) Any large pile, heap: *a stack of papers, books*.

stack (II.), vb. trans., fr. prec. To place, arrange, pile up, in a stack. Phr. *stack arms!*, (mil.) command to pile rifles &c. in a stack.

stack-funnel, n. Vertical, cylindrical opening down centre of haystack &c., to prevent overheating.

stack-stand, n. Rough platform on short stone or wooden posts, faggots &c., to raise stack above ground to prevent injury from damp, rats &c.

stack-yard, n. Enclosure in farm &c., within which stacks are erected.

stacte, n. [1. stáktē; 2. stǽkti]. Lat. *stactē*, 'oil of myrrh', fr. Gk. *staktḗ*, fr. *stázein*, 'to drop, drip'; cp. Gk. *stagṓn*, 'flowing drop'; cogn. w. Lat. *stagnum*, 'pond', see **stagnant**. Spice used by ancient Jews in making incense (cp. Exodus xxx. 34).

stactometer, n. [1. staktómeter; 2. stæktómitə], fr. Gk. *staktós*, 'flowing in drops', fr. *stázein*, 'to flow', see prec., & **-meter**. Tubular instrument pierced with minute hole for measuring liquid in drops.

stadium, n. [1. stádium; 2. stéidiəm]. Lat. *stadium*, fr. Gk. *stádion*, 'racecourse, stadium', apparently, through the influence of *stádion*, 'firm', fr. base *stə-, 'to stand', q.v. under **stand** (I.), for earlier *spádion*, 'racecourse', fr. *spáein*, 'to draw out, stretch', q.v. under **spathe, spasm, span, speed**. 1. (Gk. antiq.) Foot racecourse at Olympia &c., where games were held. 2. Course specially prepared for foot-races, consisting of a large open space enclosed by walls and tiers of seats for spectators. 3. Length of Olympic stadium from end to end, as ancient Greek measure of length, equal to nearly 203 yards. 4. (med.) Specific phase or stage of disease.

stad(t)holder, n. [1. stáhd-, stád-, stáht-hōlder; 2. stád-, stǽd-, státhouldə], fr. Du. *stadhouder*, but influenced by **holder**, & partly by Germ. *stadt*, 'town', q.v. under **stead**. (Du. hist.) 1. Governor or lieutenant of town or province. 2. Chief magistrate of the seven United Provinces.

stad(t)holderate, n. [1. stáhd-hōlderit; 2. stád-houldərit]. Prec. & **-ate**. Office of stadtholder.

stad(t)holdership, n. [1. stáhd-hōldership; 2. stádhouldəʃip]. See prec. & **-ship**. Stadholderate.

staff (I.), n. [1. stahf; 2. stāf]. O.E. *stæf*; M.E. *staf*, 'stick, staff; letter, verse', cp. O. Fris. *stef*; O.N. *stafr*; O.H.G. *stab*; cogn. w. Scrt. *stabhnā́ti*, 'supports'; *stambhaś*, 'post'; Lith. *stė̃bas*, 'staff, pole', & further w. **stem** (I.). 1. a (archaic) Strong, relatively slender stick, rod, pole, esp. for aid in walking &c., or as weapon; b staff or wand in various forms as a badge of office, or authority &c.: *pastoral staff* (of a bishop). 2. Tall pole serving as a support: *flagstaff*. 3. Instrument used a in surveying; b (naut.) for taking altitudes. 4. (surg.) Curved steel instrument for guiding knife into bladder. 5. (fig.) Support, prop, stay: *bread is the staff of life*; *a son should be the staff of his father's old age*. 6. Organized group of persons working under central direction; esp. in a factory, an educational or other institution &c.: *the nursing, medical, staff of a hospital*; *the staff of a college*; *teaching staff* &c. 7. (mil.) Group of officers of various ranks, not themselves in command, serving at the headquarters of a military unit larger than a regiment, under the commander of the unit, and engaged in administrative or executive duties connected with the various branches of military operations and organization; *General Staff*, that for the army as a whole. 8. (mus.) Group of five parallel horizontal lines and intermediate spaces used for indicating pitch of notes.

staff (II.), n. Etymol. unknown. Plastic compound of plaster-of-Paris, glycerine, cement &c., used as material for building, architectural ornament &c.; esp. for temporary structures.

staff captain, n. Junior staff officer of a military unit higher than a regiment.

staff college, n. Establishment for instruction and training of officers for the General Staff.

staffed, adj. [1. stahft; 2. stāft]. **staff** (I.) & **-ed**. Having, provided with, a staff: *a well-staffed institution*.

staff notation, n. Musical notation in which the pitch of the notes is indicated by position on the staff.

staff officer, n. Officer serving on the General Staff.

staff sergeant, n. Non-commissioned officer serving on regimental staff.

staff tree, n. Genus, *Celastrus*, of small trees and climbing shrubs with brightly coloured fruit.

staff work, n. a Work of organization and direction carried out by military staff; hence b organization and management of any undertaking.

stag, n. [1. stag; 2. stæg]. Scand., cp. O.N. *steggr*, 'male bird; male cat'. 1. Male of red deer, esp. in and after fifth year. 2. Male of other varieties of large deer. 3. Bull castrated when full-grown. 4. (Stock Exchange)

Person applying for an allotment of shares in a new company in order to sell immediately on allotment at a profit.

stag-beetle, n. Genus of beetles with large, strong, branched mandibles.

stage (I.), n. [1. stāj; 2. steidž], fr. O. Fr. *estage*, fr. Low Lat. **staticum*, fr. *statum*, P.P. type of *stāre*, 'to stand', see **state** (I.). **1.** Platform for raising, supporting or displaying any object, person &c.; specif. **a** platform supported by scaffolding, slung by ropes, &c., for workmen at work; **b** small adjustable shelf of microscope, supporting object to be examined; **c** usually *landing-stage*, part of dock or wharf, on which passengers disembark from vessel. **2. a** Raised platform in theatre on which dramatic performance &c. takes place; Phr. *to go on the stage*, take up acting as profession; **b** any space, surface, enclosure &c. for dramatic performance. **3.** Dramatic literature; the drama: *the mediaeval stage*. **4.** Acting as a profession; occupation of an actor: *to give up the law for the stage* &c. **5.** (fig.) Scene of action, place where plans are carried out, events happen &c. **6.** Period of development; specific point of progress &c.: *at an early stage in his career; different stages of education; negotiations had reached their final stage*. **7. a** One of a series of stopping-places in a journey, of a public vehicle on a regular course &c.: *to travel to the last stage*; **b** distance between two successive stopping-places: *to travel by short stages*. **8.** Stage-coach.

stage (II.), vb. trans., fr. prec. **1.** To arrange, prepare (play &c.) for public performance on the stage, put on the stage. **2.** To arrange the sequence of events in a pageant or other public show so as to produce the greatest dramatic effect.

stage-coach, n. Large, public conveyance plying regularly by stages, as means of communication between two places.

stage-coachman, n. Driver of stage-coach.

stage-craft, n. Skill in writing plays for performance on the stage; skill and experience in everything connected with the production of plays in public.

stage-direction, n. Instruction to the actors of a play regarding their entrances, exits, their relative positions on the stage, and the like, written or printed on the copies of a play.

stage-door, n. Door leading to back of theatre for the use of actors, workmen &c.

stage-effect, n. Effect produced on, characteristic of, or suitable for, the stage.

stage-fever, n. Infatuation for everything connected with the theatre; esp. a strong desire to embark on an actor's career.

stage-fright, n. Nervousness experienced by actor or speaker on facing an audience.

stage-manager, n. Person superintending the acting of a play.

stager, n. [1. stājer; 2. stéidžə]. **stage** (I.) & **-er**. In Phr. *old stager*, person of long experience.

stage-right, n. Right of producing a play.

stage-struck, adj. Infatuated with the theatre; desirous of embracing a theatrical career.

stag-evil, n. Lock-jaw in horses.

stage whisper, n. Loud whisper as of actor on stage, intended to be heard by audience.

staggard, n. [1. stágard; 2. stǽgəd]. **stag** & **-ard**. Stag of the fourth year.

stagger (I.), vb. intrans. & trans. [1. stáger; 2. stǽgə]. M.E. *stakkeren*, fr. O.N. *stakra*, 'to cause to reel'; cp. O.N. *staka*, 'to push'; M. Du. *staggeren*. **A.** intrans. **1.** To move with an unsteady, uneven, uncertain gait, as from weakness, shock, intoxication &c.; to reel, walk stumblingly. **2.** (fig.) To become irresolute, vacillating, hesitant. **B.** trans. **1.** (fig.) To disconcert, overwhelm, as by amazement, horror &c., by the shock of something unexpected &c.: *I was positively staggered by the news; the size of the bill staggered him*. **2.** (mechan.) To set (wheel spokes) inclined alternately to right and left.

stagger (II.), n., fr. prec. **1.** Staggering, tottering, unsteady, jerky movement. **2.** *The staggers*, **a** feeling of giddiness; vertigo; **b** often *blind staggers*, nervous disease of cattle and horses, characterized by staggering movements in walking.

staggerer, n. [1. stágerer; 2. stǽgərə]. **stagger** (I.) & **-er**. **a** One who, that which, staggers or disconcerts; specif. **b** disconcerting or difficult question &c.; poser.

staggering, adj. [1. stágering; 2. stǽgəriŋ], fr. Pres. Part. of **stagger** (I.). **1.** Tottering, reeling, unsteady: *staggering gait*. **2.** Causing one to stagger: *a staggering blow*. **3.** Of a kind, size, amount, to produce a shock of amazement; overwhelming, gravely disconcerting: *a staggering piece of news, sum, misfortune*.

staggeringly, adv. Prec. & **-ly**. To an extent which staggers one.

stag-horn, n. **1.** Kind of branching moss or fern. **2.** Kind of large coral.

staghound, n. [1. stág-hound; 2. stǽghaund]. One of a large, swift breed of dogs used for stag-hunting.

stag-hunting, n. The chase of the stag on horseback, with pack of hounds.

staginess, n. [1. stājines; 2. stéidžinis]. **stagy** & **-ness**. State or quality of being stagy; theatricality.

staging, n. [1. stājing; 2. stéidžiŋ]. **stage** (I.) & **-ing**. **1.** Temporary platform or scaffolding for use of men at work on the face of a building. **2.** Method or process of presenting a play on the stage.

Stagirite, n. [1. stájirīt; 2. stǽdžirait], fr. Lat. *Stagīrītes*, fr. Gk. *Stageirítēs*, fr. *Stágeira*, town in Macedonia, & **-ite**. Native of Stageira; esp. *the Stagirite*, Aristotle.

stagnancy, n. [1. stágnansi; 2. stǽgnənsi]. **stagnant** & **-cy**. Condition of being stagnant.

stagnant, adj. [1. stágnant; 2. stǽgnənt], fr. Lat. *stagnantem*, Pres. Part. of *stagnāre*, 'to become a pool', fr. *stagnum*, 'pool'; cogn. w. Gk. *stagṓn*, 'drop'; *stázein*, 'to drip'; cp. **stacte**. **1.** (of water) **a** Not moving or flowing; having no current, remaining stationary as in a pond, ditch &c.; **b** esp. stale, foul, unhealthy, through lack of motion. **2.** Inactive, remaining in a dull, inefficient state; torpid, sluggish; reverse of *brisk, lively*: *trade is stagnant; a stagnant brain*.

stagnantly, adv. Prec. & **-ly**. In a stagnant manner.

stagnate, vb. intrans. [1. stágnāt; 2. stǽgneit], fr. Lat. *stāgnāt-(um)*, P.P. type of *stagnāre*, 'to become a pool', fr. *stagnum*, 'pool', see **stagnant**. **1.** (of water) To remain stationary, without current or flowing motion; esp. to become foul through remaining in a pond, ditch, barrel &c. without inlet or outlet. **2.** (fig.) To be and remain inactive; to become dull and lifeless through lack of use; to lack variety and movement.

stagnation, n. [1. stagnāshun; 2. stægnéiʃən]. Prec. & **-ion**. (lit. and fig.) Act or process of stagnating; condition of being stagnant.

stagnicolous, adj. [1. stagníkulus; 2. stægníkələs], fr. Lat. *stagnum*, 'pond, swamp', see **stagnant**, & *-i-*, & *colere*, 'to inhabit', see **colony**, & **-ous**. Living in or near stagnant water, marsh &c.

stag's-horn fern, n. Genus, *Platycerium*, of evergreen ferns, with broad, antler-like fronds.

stagy, adj. [1. stāji; 2. stéidži]. **stage** (I.) & **-y**. Characteristic of the stage; (usually in unfavourable sense) over-emphatic in manner or mode of speech; producing an effect of unreality and insincerity; artificial, theatrical.

staid, adj. [1. stād; 2. steid]. Variant of *stayed*, P.P. of **stay** (I.). Steady, sober, sedate; reverse of frivolous or flighty.

staidly, adv. Prec. & **-ly**. In a staid manner.

staidness, n. See prec. & **-ness**. Quality of being staid.

stain (I.), vb. trans. & intrans. [1. stān; 2. stein]. M.E. *steinen*, abbr. fr. *disteinen*, fr. O. Fr. *disteindre*, 'to colour', fr. **dis-** & Lat. *tingere*, 'to dye, stain', see **tinct**. **A.** trans. **1.** To make a stain on surface of; to discolour: *to stain one's fingers with ink, one's coat with blackberry juice*. **2.** To impart colour, esp. by a deliberate process, to the surface of (substance): *to stain wood, glass* &c. **3.** To colour (part of tissue &c.) for greater distinctness in examination under a microscope, by staining with a substance whose chemical reaction affects some cells &c. but not others. **4.** To mar, impart moral blemish to: *his character was stained by cruelty and rapacity*. **B.** intrans. **1.** To be affected by, susceptible of, discolouration; to be liable to staining: *the cloth will not stain*. **2.** To be liable to cause a stain, or produce discolouration: *ink stains worse than almost anything*.

stain (II.), n., fr. prec. **1.** Discolouration; dirty mark; patch, streak, spot, of distinct colour, or foreign substance, esp. upon the surface of some other substance or material: *a stain on the cloth; petrol will remove stains of grease; ink-stains; blood-stains* &c. **2.** Colour given to wood, glass, wall-paper &c. by staining or dyeing. **3.** Pigment, colouring-matter, used for staining. **4.** Moral defect, blemish, spot: *without a stain on one's character*.

stainable, adj. [1. stānabl; 2. stéinəbl]. **stain** (I.) & **-able**. Capable of being stained.

stainer, n. [1. stāner; 2. stéinə]. **stain** (II.) & **-er**. One who, that which, stains; specif., colouring-matter used in staining.

stainless, adj. [1. stānles; 2. stéinlis]. **stain** (I.) & **-less**. **1.** Without a stain; (esp. in moral sense) spotless, immaculate, unstained. **2.** Not liable to become stained: *stainless steel*.

stainlessly, adv. Prec. & **-ly**. In a stainless manner, without causing stains or becoming stained.

stainlessness, n. See prec. & **-ness**. State or quality of being stainless.

stair, n. [1. stār; 2. steə]. O.E. *stǣger*, 'stair, ladder'; M.E. *steire*; fr. **stāg-ir-*, earlier **staig-*, cp. M. Du. *stēger*; cp. same base in Goth. *staiga*; O.H.G. *steiga*, 'path'; in gradational relation w. O.E. *stīgan*; O.H.G. *stīgan*, 'to climb, go up', cp. **stile** (I.); cogn. w. Scrt. *stighnōti*, 'to ascend'; Lett. *staigát*, 'to go, walk'; *stiga*, 'path'; O. Slav. *stĭgna*, 'street'; Gk. *steikhein*, 'to go'; *stikhos*, 'rank, line'; see **stichic**. **1.** One of a series of steps leading from one floor to another in a building: *a short passage and then three stairs*. **2. a** (in sing.) A flight, series, of steps forming part of the structure of house or other building, leading from one floor to another: *a winding stair; a short stair leads to the first floor; the stair is very steep*; more commonly, **b** (pl.) *stairs*: *the stairs are steep; a flight of stairs*; Phr. *below stairs*, in the lower floor of a house; specif., the kitchen and servants' quarters in a house with a basement.

stair-carpet, n. Carpet woven in narrow strip for laying on stairs.

staircase, n. [1. stārkās; 2. stéəkeis]. **1.** The part of a building in which the stairs are constructed. **2.** The stairs themselves, including the banisters; flight of stairs in any one part of a house, forming a continuous series: *a narrow staircase; the principal staircase; large houses often have several staircases; corkscrew staircase*, flight of stairs winding spirally round central pillar; also *spiral staircase*.

stair-rod, n. Metal or wooden bar for holding stair-carpet in position at bottom of each riser.

stairway, n. [1. stārwā; 2. stéəwei]. Staircase, flight of steps.

staith, n. [1. stāth; 2. steiþ]. O.E. *stæþ*; M.E. *stāþe*, *staþ*, 'bank, shore'; cp. O.N. *stōth*, 'landing-stage'; cogn. w. O.E. *stede*, 'place'; see **stead** & **stand**. Wharf with apparatus for loading coal &c.

staithe, n. [1. stādh; 2. steið]. Variant of prec.

stake (I.), n. [1. stāk; 2. steik]. O.E. *staca*; M.E. *stāke*, 'stake'; cp. O. Fris. *stake*; O.N. *stjaki*; O.H.G. *stehho*, 'pillar, stake'; cogn. w. Lett. *stēga*, 'stake'; prob. also w. Lat. *tignum*, 'beam'; gradational variant of **stick** (II.). **1.** Bar of wood, strong but slender relatively to its length, pointed for driving into the ground: *to tether an animal to a stake*; *to tie a plant to a stake*; *to fix a row of stakes*. **2. a** Stout post to which person was tied when being burnt alive: *burnt at the stake*; hence, **b** *the stake*, death by burning: *some died by the axe, some perished at the stake*. **3.** Small anvil used by tinsmith &c. **4.** Money &c. risked on a bet &c.; amount or object wagered; esp. (pl.), money &c. deposited with third person until wager is decided. Phr. *at stake*, risked, depending, on the outcome of an event &c. **5.** (pl.) **a** Money offered as prize for horse-race &c.; **b** race run for such a prize. **6.** Interest, share in chances of profit or loss; concern: *a stake in an undertaking, in the country*.

stake (II.), vb. trans., fr. prec. **1. a** To fasten, support, secure, with stake(s): *dahlias and Michaelmas daisies should be staked long before they attain their full growth*; **b** to pierce, impale, with a stake: *my horse got staked in trying to jump a very big fence*. **2.** Usually *stake off, out*, to mark (boundary &c.) by driving in stakes: *to stake out a boundary* &c. Phr. *to stake out a claim*, (i.) (lit.) mark out the piece of land which one claims as one's own (in a new settlement, minefield &c.); (ii.) (fig.) to set up, make, a claim, generally. **3.** To put on as a stake, to wager, hazard, risk, as a bet: *to stake a fortune on a single race*; (also fig.) *to stake one's future on a single chance*; *I stake my reputation on his honesty*, will forfeit my reputation if he be not honest.

stake-boat, n. Boat anchored or moored to post at starting point or as winning post in boat race.

stakeholder, n. [1. stákhōlder; 2. stéikhōuldə]. Person appointed to hold the stakes for a wager &c.

stake-net, n. Fishing-net stretched on stakes in shallow water near shore of river or estuary.

stalactic, adj. [1. staláktik; 2. stæléktik], fr. Gk. *stalaktós*, fr. *stalássein*, 'to drop, drip'; cp. Gk. *télma*, 'stagnant water, marsh'; cogn. w. M.L.G. *stal*, 'urine of horses', see **stale** (II.). Of, pertaining to, in the form of, containing, stalactites.

stalactiform, adj. [1. staláktiform; 2. stæléktifōm]. See prec. & *-i-* & **-form**. Having the structure or appearance of a stalactite.

stalactite, n. [1. stálaktīt, staláktīt; 2. stǽləktait, stæléktait], fr. Gk. *stalaktós*, 'dripping', see **stalactic**, & **-ite**. Long, tapering or cylindrical, calcareous formation, resembling an icicle in form, hanging from roof of cavern, produced by continuous deposits of limy matter dissolved in the water which percolates through; distinguished from *stalagmite*.

stalactitic, adj. [1. stàlaktítik; 2. stæ̀ləktítik]. Prec. & **-ic**. Same as **stalactic**; *stalactitic column*, formed by the uniting of a stalactite with a stalagmite.

stalagmite, n. [1. stalágmīt, stálagmīt; 2. stælǽgmait, stǽləgmait], fr. Gk. *stalagmós*, 'dripping', fr. *stalássein*, 'to drip', see **stalactic**, & **-ite**. Formation analogous to stalactite, but formed from below, by limy matter deposited on the floor of a cavern by water dropping from roof; a stalagmite often becomes united into a continuous column with the stalactite forming from above.

stalagmitic, adj. [1. stàlagmítik; 2. stæ̀ləgmítik]. Prec. & **-ic**. Of, pertaining to, of the nature of, a stalagmite.

stalagmitically, adv. [1. stàlagmítikali; 2. stæ̀ləgmítikəli]. Prec. & **-al** & **-ly**. In the manner of a stalagmite, as a stalagmite.

stale (I.), adj. [1. stāl; 2. steil]. M.E. *stāle*, 'stale'; prob. fr. next word. **1.** Not fresh, having lost some original, vital quality; specif. **a** (of air) heavy, close, stagnant, vitiated; **b** (of food &c.) beginning to decay, or grow sour &c.; *stale bread*, dry, not freshly baked; **c** (of wine) flat, insipid. **2.** Having lost bodily or mental freshness, vigour, spring; grown out of condition; fatigued by prolonged strain or monotony: *one's mind gets stale with too much teaching*; *an athlete becomes stale through overtraining*. **3.** (fig.) Lacking in interest or originality; no longer new and fresh; grown tedious from frequent repetition or long familiarity: *a stale joke*; *stale news*.

stale (II.), n. Cp. M.L.G. *stal*, 'urine of horses'; L.G. *stallen*; Lith. *telžu*, 'to make water'; cogn. w. Gk. *télma*, 'stagnant water'; *stalássein*, 'to drip'; cp. **stalactic**. Urine of cattle and horses.

stale (III.), vb. trans., fr. **stale** (I.). (rare) To make stale; (chiefly in spiritual sense).

stale (IV.), vb. intrans. Cp. **stale** (II.). (of horses and cattle) To discharge urine.

stale (V.), n. O.E. *stalu*; M.E. *stāle*, 'theft'; cp. O.H.G. *stala*, 'theft'; gradational variant of **steal**. (rare or archaic) Victim of deception; dupe, gull; laughing-stock, butt.

stalely, adv. [1. stālli; 2. stéilli]. **stale** (I.) & **-ly**. In a stale manner.

stalemate, n. & vb. trans. [1. stálmāt; 2. stéilmeit]. **stale** (I.) & **mate** (I.), in chess. **1.** n. **a** (chess) Position in which one player can make no move without bringing his king into check; **b** (fig.) a deadlock, an impasse in negotiations. **2.** vb. To put (opponent) into this position.

staleness, n. [1. stálnes; 2. stéilnis]. **stale** (I.) & **-ness**. State or quality of being stale.

stalk (I.), n. [1. stawk; 2. stōk]. M.E. *stalke*, 'stalk, reed'; formed w. dimin. suff. *-oc*, *-uc*, cp. **bullock**, fr. O.E. *stela*, *stæla*, 'stalk, support'; cp. O.H.G. *stil*, Mod. Germ. *stiel*, 'stem, stalk'; poss. cogn. w. Lat. *stilus*, 'a stake' (but see alternative explanation of this under **style** (I.)); perh. also Gk. *steleós*, 'handle of an axe', & *stélekhos*, 'trunk, log'; cp. further the gradational variant Lat. *stolō*, 'shoot from a root, sucker'. The last is connected by Walde w. Lat. *lātus*, 'broad, expansive', fr. **stlātos*, q.v. under **latitude**. **1.** (bot.) **a** Central support, stem, axis, of a plant, esp. of herbaceous plant; **b** any secondary stem, petiole &c. supporting a leaf, flower, fruit, or other part of a plant. **2.** (zool.) Slender part supporting an organ; stem; peduncle. **3.** Object or part of object resembling a stalk in appearance or function; specif. **a** stem of a glass, goblet &c.; **b** shaft of feather; **c** tall, slender chimney. **4.** (archit.) Moulding, fluting &c., resembling a stalk.

stalk (II.), vb. intrans. & trans. O.E. *stealcan*, M.E. *stalken*, 'to walk carefully'; perh. orig. 'to walk lifting the feet high at each step'; the word has been connected w. O.E. *stealc*, 'steep, lofty'. **A.** intrans. **1. a** To walk with a lofty, stately, dignified stride; to move with a certain pride and arrogance; **b** (fig. of disease, death, misfortune) to sweep silently but irresistibly along: *pestilence and famine stalked unchecked through the land*. **2.** To practise the stalking of game. **B.** trans. **1.** To pursue, approach, get close to (game &c.) cautiously and noiselessly, without being seen, heard, or winded. **2.** To stride through, across, along: *to stalk the land, the streets*.

stalk (III.), n., fr. prec. **1.** Stiff, imposing gait. **2.** Act of stalking game; stealthy pursuit.

stalked, adj. [1. stawkt; 2. stōkt]. **stalk** (I.) & **-ed**. Having, supported by, a stalk.

stalker, n. [1. stáwker; 2. stṓkə]. **stalk** (II.) & **-er**. One who stalks; esp. one who pursues game by stalking; esp. *deer-stalker* &c.

stalk-eyed, adj. (of crustacean &c.) Having the eyes supported on stalk-like structures.

stalking-horse, n. [1. stáwking hòrs; 2. stṓkiŋ hòs]. **1.** Horse used as cover by hunter in stalking game. **2.** (fig.) Alleged motive, pretext concealing real intention.

stalkless, adj. [1. stáwkles; 2. stṓklis]. **stalk** (I.) & **-less**. Without, unsupported by, a stalk.

stalklet, n. [1. stáwklet; 2. stṓklit]. **stalk** (I.) & **-let**. Small stalk.

stalky, adj. [1. stáwki; 2. stṓki]. **stalk** (I.) & **-y**. **1.** Like a stalk. **2.** (of plant) Having a long stalk with few or no leaves; leggy.

stall (I.), n. [1. stawl; 2. stōl]. O.E. *steall*, *stall*, 'stable', M.E. *stall*; O.H.G. *stall*; O.N. *stallr*; all fr. Gmc. **staðla-*; cp. also O.E. *staðol*, O.H.G. *stadal*, 'foundation, base'; fr. Aryan type **stədhlo-*, whence also Lat. *stabulum*, see **stable** (II.). The word is extended fr. the base **stā-*, **stə-* &c., q.v. under **stand** (I.); **state** (I.) &c. **1.** Division, compartment, in stable, cow-house &c., in which horse or beast is kept, fed &c. **2. a** Small recess with seat, in choir of cathedral, church, chapel &c., sometimes assigned by right of office to specific church dignitary: *canons' stalls* &c.; hence, **b** ecclesiastical office, dignity, entitling holder to a stall in a cathedral &c.: *to hold a prebendal stall*. **3. a** Small shelter or enclosed space, compartment, booth, in market, fair, or other public place, for sale of goods: *a stall at a bazaar*; also in compounds; *book-stall* &c.; **b** table, counter &c. in a booth on which goods for sale are displayed. **4.** Theatre seat forming one of a series, usually with arms, on ground floor of auditorium and nearest the stage; *orchestra stalls*, those in front; *pit stalls*, those in rear. **5.** Covering, sheath, for injured finger &c.; usually compounded: *finger-*, *thumb-stall* &c. **6.** Recess for single workman in coal-mine &c.

stall (II.), vb. trans. & intrans., fr. prec. **A.** trans. **1. a** To place, keep, in a stall; specif. **b** to fatten (cattle) in a stall. **2.** To furnish (stable &c.) with, divide into, stalls. **B.** intrans. **a** (of horse, vehicle, train &c.) To be brought to a standstill, stuck, obstructed, by snow, mud &c.; **b** (of engine, esp. of motor) to stop working; **c** (of aeroplane) to lose speed to such an extent that the machine becomes out of control.

stall (III.), n. Variant of **stale** (V.). Thief's accomplice, who distracts victim's attention during perpetration of theft &c.

stallage, n. [1. stáwlij; 2. stṓlidž]. **stall** (I.) & **-age**. **1. a** Space for stall in market &c.; **b** rent paid for such space. **2.** Right of erecting stalls in market-place &c.

stall-fed, adj. (of cattle) Fed, fattened, in a stall instead of in the open fields.

stall-feed, vb. trans. To keep and feed (cattle) in a stall, esp. for fattening.

stallion, n. [1. stáliun; 2. stǽliən]. M.E. *stalun*, fr. O. Fr. *estalon*, lit. 'horse kept in a stall', fr. O.H.G. *stal*, 'stall', see **stall** (I.), & **-oon**. Uncastrated male horse; an entire horse, esp. a sire for breeding.

stalwart (I.), adj. [1. stáwlwart; 2. stṓlwət]. O.E. *stælwierðe*, 'able to stand one in good stead; serviceable', M.E. *stālewurþe*, *stalwurþe* &c., also once *staðelwurþe*, 'firm'; the O.E. form may be for **staðolwierþe*, 'firm on its base', or may simply be fr. a Gmc. **stǣl-*, cp. O.E. *stǣl*, 'place, relation; assistance', wh. is a gradational variant of **stall-* as in Mod. Germ. *stellen* (fr. **stalljan*), 'to place'; cp. also Gk. *stéllein*, 'to arrange, set in order' &c. (with orig. *e*). The base is an extension of **stə-* &c., 'stand'; see **stall** (I.) & **stand** (I.); see second element under **worth**. **1.** Tall and muscular; robust, strong. **2.** Staunch, reliable, unflinchingly loyal to a person or cause: *stalwart defenders*.

stalwart (II.) n., fr. prec. A staunch, reliable person, who is unshakable in defence and support of a cause, of a party in politics &c.

stalwartly, adv. Prec. & **-ly**. In a stalwart manner.

stalwartness, n. See prec. & **-ness**. State or quality of being stalwart.

stamen, n. [1. stámen; 2. stéimen]. Lat. *stāmen*, 'warp in upright loom'; cp. Gk. *stḗmōn*, 'warp'; fr. base **stā-*, 'to stand', see **stand** (I.). Cp. further Scrt. *sthā́man-*, 'station'; Goth. *stōma*, 'material'; Lith. *stomũ*, 'stature'. (bot.) Pollen-bearing organ of flower.

stamened, adj. [1. stámend; 2. stéimənd]. Prec. & **-ed**. Having stamens.

stamina, n. [1. stámina; 2. stǽminə]. Lat. *stāmina*, pl. of *stāmen*, 'warp of upright loom', see **stamen**. Vigour of constitution, vitality, staying power.

staminal, adj. [1. stá-, stáminal; 2. stéi-, stǽminəl], fr. Lat. *stāmin-*, stem of **stamen**, & **-al**. **1.** (bot.) Of, pertaining to, stamens. **2.** Of, pertaining to, giving, stamina.

staminate, adj. [1. stáminăt; 2. stéimineit], fr. Lat. *stāmin-*, stem of **stamen**, & **-ate**. (bot.) Having stamens; esp. having stamens but no pistils.

stamineal, adj. [1. stâminéal; 2. stèiminíəl]. See next word & **-al**. Staminal.

stamineous, adj. [1. stāmíneus; 2. steimíniəs], fr. Lat. *stāmin-*, stem of **stamen**, & **-eous**. Of, pertaining to, stamens.

staminiferous, adj. [1. stâminíferus; 2. stèiminífərəs], fr. Lat. *stāmin-*, stem of **stamen**, & **-i-** & **-ferous**. Producing stamens.

stammer (I.), vb. intrans. & trans. [1. stámer; 2. stǽmə]. M.E. *stameren*; cp. M. Du. *stameren*; O.H.G. *stammalōn*; in gradational relation w. O.S., & O.H.G. *stum*, 'dumb'. **1.** intrans. **a** Specif., to speak with a nervous impediment or hesitation, esp., to utter certain sounds repeatedly, pause on certain sounds, through inability to complete the articulation; to stutter; **b** to speak incoherently, jerkily, and brokenly through nervousness; to hesitate, hum and haw in speaking. **2.** trans. To utter, pronounce, with a stammer: *to stammer, stammer out, a few words.*

stammer (II.), n., fr. prec. Nervous defect in articulation arising from a kind of partial paralysis in, and lack of control of, the tongue and lips, resulting in the speaker dwelling unduly on the beginning or end of a sound through inability, sometimes to begin, sometimes to complete it, and pass on to the next sound of a series; a stutter.

stammerer, n. [1. stámerer; 2. stǽmərə]. **stammer (I.)** & **-er**. Person afflicted with a stammer.

stammering, adj. [1. stámering; 2. stǽməriŋ], fr. Pres. Part. of **stammer (I.)**. **1.** Specif., afflicted with, speaking with, a stammer. **2.** a (of speaker) Halting, hesitating; **b** uttered with hesitation: *a stammering speech.*

stammeringly, adv. Prec. & **-ly**. In a stammering manner.

stamp (I.), vb. trans. & intrans. [1. stamp; 2. stæmp]. M.E. *stampen*; cp. O.E. *stempan*; M.L.G., M. Du. *stampen*; O.H.G. *stamfōn*, 'to pound'; O.N. *stappa*, 'to stamp'; cogn. w. Gk. *stémbein*, 'to crush with the feet'; nasalized variant of base in **step (II.)**. **A.** trans. **1. a** To imprint (inscription, pattern, mark &c. on) by means of a die &c.: *to stamp a document with the address and date*; *metal stamped with a design*; *goods stamped with the maker's name*; **b** to imprint on a surface by means of a die &c.: *to stamp one's name on a title-page.* **2.** To affix a postage-stamp to (letter, document &c.). **3.** To crush, pulverize (ore &c.), by pressure, esp. in a stamp-mill. **4.** Usually *stamp out*, to cut out, give shape to (piece of metal, dough &c.), by means of die, cutter &c. **5.** To imprint, impress, upon the mind: *the scene is stamped on my memory.* **6.** (fig.) To distinguish, characterize, mark, give specific character to; reveal true nature of: *his manners stamp him as a cad.* **7.** To bring down (one's foot) heavily to the ground, strike ground violently with (foot), esp. as indication of anger, impatience &c. **8.** *Stamp down, flat* &c., to crush, flatten &c. by stamping heavily upon with the foot: *to stamp the grass flat.* Phr. *to stamp out*, (i.) to destroy, extinguish, by crushing with foot: *to stamp a fire out*; (ii.) (fig.) to suppress, extirpate, by drastic measures: *to stamp out disease, a rebellion* &c. **B.** intrans. To strike the ground violently with the foot: *to stamp with rage*; '*the wild ass Stamps o'er his head, but cannot break his sleep*' (Fitzgerald, 'Omar Khayyam', xviii.

stamp (II.), n., fr. prec. **1.** Act of stamping, heavy blow of foot on ground &c. **2. a** Design, mark, signature &c. impressed or printed upon the surface of something by means of a die &c.; **b** specific mark &c. stamped on goods &c. by maker, owner &c. as sign of genuineness, ownership &c.: *every article bears the stamp of the maker.* **3.** Object used for stamping, having a design incised or in relief upon it. **4. a** Official device imprinted on certain documents, goods &c. to indicate that the necessary duty, fee &c. has been paid; **b** paper label, often adhesive, bearing such a device to be affixed to documents &c. in proof of payment of fee &c.; specif., stamped piece of paper bearing value engraved on it attached to letters for the post; also *postage-stamp.* **5.** Machine, part of machine, implement, for stamping, crushing &c. **6.** Characteristic indication, sign or mark, evidence, of specific quality, kind, nature: *to bear the stamp of breeding, learning* &c. **7.** Kind, class, character: *men of the same stamp.*

stamp act, n. Act of Parliament &c., imposing stamp-duty; specif. (cap.) act of 1765, imposing stamp-duty on colonists in N. America.

stamp-album, n. Book in which stamp-collector preserves his specimens.

stamp-collector, n. Person who collects postage-stamps &c. as hobby; philatelist.

stamp-duty, n. Tax levied upon certain legal instruments, payment of which is indicated by an official stamp impressed upon, or affixed to, the document.

stampede (I.), n. [1. stampéd; 2. stæmpíd], fr. Span. *estampido*, fr. *estampar*, 'to stamp', of Gmc. origin; see **stamp (I.)**. **1.** Sudden, combined, headlong rush of horses, cattle &c. caused by fright. **2. a** Panic-stricken rush or scattering of crowd of people, soldiers &c.; **b** any confused, unreasoning rush on the part of a crowd of people &c.

stampede (II.), vb. intrans. & trans., fr. prec. **1.** intrans. To take part in a stampede. **2.** trans. To cause to stampede.

stamper, n. [1. stámper; 2. stǽmpə]. **stamp (I.)** & **-er**. One who, that which, stamps; esp. machine for pulverizing stone, ore &c.

stamp-machine, n. Machine for stamping or crushing material; esp. machine for reducing rags to pulp in the manufacture of paper.

stamp-mill, n. Machine for crushing ore &c.

stamp-office, n. Office where government stamps are issued and the revenue from stamp-duties received.

stance, n. [1. stans; 2. stæns], fr. O. Fr. *estance*, fr. L. Lat. *stantia*, 'place, abode', fr. *stāre*, 'to stand'; variant of **stanza**. Position, attitude, assumed by player when making a stroke, at such games as golf, cricket &c.

stanch (I.), **staunch**, vb. trans. [1. stahnch, stawnch; 2. stān(t)ʃ, stōn(t)ʃ]. M.E. *sta(u)nchen*, fr. O. Fr. *estanchier*, fr. Low Lat. **stagnicāre*, 'to stop the flow', fr. *stagnāre*, 'to be or cause to become stagnant', see **stagnant**. **a** To stop or retard flow of (blood) from wound &c., esp. by use of absorbents, pads &c.; **b** to plug, bandage, or otherwise treat (a wound), so as to arrest bleeding.

stanch (II.), adj. See **staunch (I.)**.

stanchion (I.), n. [1. stánshun, stáhnshun; 2. stǽnʃən, stánʃən], fr. Norm. Fr. *estanchon*, fr. O. Fr. *estance*, 'place, situation', see **stance** & **stanza**. Upright post or bar acting as support &c.; specif. a iron rod fixed in masonry &c. for support; **b** bar or pair of bars, usually removable, for fastening cattle &c. in a stall; **c** (naut.) post supporting deck-beam &c.

stanchion (II.), vb. trans., fr. prec. **1.** To furnish, support, with stanchions. **2.** To fasten (cattle) in a stall with stanchions.

stand (I.), vb. intrans. & trans. [1. stand; 2. stænd]. O.E. *standan*; M.E. *standen*; cp. O.L.G., Goth. *standan*; O.N. *standa*; O.H.G. *stantan*, 'to stand'; cogn. w. Lat. *stāre*; Gk. *histēmi*, 'I stand'; Lith. *stójūs*; O. Slav. *stają*, 'I place myself'; fr. base **stā-*, **stə-*, 'to stand', wh. appears in many words in all the Aryan languages; see **stable (I.)**, **state**, **station**, **stead**, **stolid**, **locus**, **stool** &c. **A.** intrans. **1. a** (of men and quadrupeds) To place the body and limbs in such a position that the weight of the body rests, and is balanced, upon the feet, the legs being more or less straightened and braced; contrasted with *sit, kneel, lie*: *very young children cannot stand without support*; *so giddy that one cannot stand*; *no one may sit down as long as the king is standing*; *the cow is so weak that she can't stand*; **b** specif. (of human beings) to support weight of body on the feet, the back being relatively straight and the head erect; contrasted with *crouch, squat* &c.: *stand straight, don't stoop.* **2.** To assume a standing position, to rise to the feet from a sitting or recumbent posture: *everyone stood as the king entered*; *the congregation shall now stand.* **3.** To remain standing, without moving from one place to another; contrasted with *go, walk, run, trot* &c.: *it is more tiring to stand for long periods than to walk a long distance*; *a horse that won't stand is a great nuisance.* **4.** (of inanimate objects) To be upright, remain vertical: *the glass stands on a stem*; *the table will not stand without support*; *one's hair stands on end.* **5.** (archaic) To halt, cease motion, stop: *stand and deliver!* **6.** To move into particular position: *to stand aside, back, clear, down, out* &c. **7.** To be in a specific place, position, situation; to be placed or situated: *the stuffed parrot stands on the table*; *the house stands by the river*; *the chairs stand by the wall*; *a Roman camp once stood on the hill-top*; *the stones stand in a circle.* **8.** To remain in, maintain, be left in, original position, be undisturbed: *the walls of the keep still stand*; *not a stone was left standing*; *to stand fast*; Phr. *to stand pat*, in poker, to play the hand dealt without drawing cards; also Am. polit. slang, to stick firmly to one's party's politics and platform, esp. on tariff matters. Phr. *it stands to reason*, is a logical deduction, can be proved logically. **9. a** To be in specified state or condition: *to stand in awe of*; *to stand ready for anything*; *to stand accused of murder, convicted of treason*; Phrs. *to stand alone*, (i.) to be unequalled, pre-eminent; (ii.) to be without supporters &c.; *to stand corrected*, accept correction; *to stand well with*, be on good terms with, esteemed by; *to stand one in good stead*, be of use, come in handy; **b** to be at, reach, particular price, measure, degree &c.: *the thermometer stands at 90°*; *he stands six feet.* **10.** To remain valid, hold good, be in force: *the order will still stand*; *his resolution still stands*; *that translation may stand.* **11.** (of dog) To point. **12.** (naut.) To steer, lay, a course: *to stand in, off* &c. **B.** trans. **1.** To put into a more or less upright position, cause to remain vertical, or nearly so: *to stand a ladder against a wall.* **2.** To remain firmly at, or on, resist attempts to remove from; esp. in Phr. *to stand one's ground.* **3.** (of physical action or process) **a** To tolerate, endure, be able to bear: *I cannot stand great heat*; *she will not stand another winter in England*; **b** to remain uninjured by, to resist, be proof against: *your coat won't stand much rain*; *these boots have stood a good deal of wear.* **4.** (of moral attitude) To tolerate, bear, with patience, to suffer willingly: *I can stand a good deal, but I won't have insolence*; *I will not stand any nonsense.* Phr. *I can't stand (such and such a person or thing)*, I detest, dislike extremely. **5.** To undergo, be subjected to: *to stand one's trial.* **6.** To treat (person) to, pay for on behalf of: *to stand one's friend a dinner.* **C.** Followed by adverbs and prepositions with special meanings. *Stand by*, **a** to remain as an onlooker, refrain from interfering; **b** to support, aid, be loyal to: *to stand by one's friends*; **c** to adhere to, refrain from breaking or abandoning: *to stand by one's promise, faith* &c.; **d** (naut.) to remain near in order to help: *to* *stand by a sinking ship* (of another ship), also absol. *Stand for*, **a** to support, be adherent of, strive for: *I stand for liberty*; **b** to symbolize, be typical of: *the olive branch stands for peace*; **c** to represent, be significant of: *what do the initials stand for?*; **d** to be a candidate for, aim at election to: *to stand for Parliament*; **e** to tolerate, put up with: *I won't stand for that. Stand in*, (colloq.) **a** to cost, cause expense of: *it stood me in a lot of money*; **b** to participate in, take a share, give help: *if you are starting a movement for brighter streets, I'll stand in. Stand in with*, **a** to be in agreement with, to support, ally oneself to: *to stand in with the progressive party*; **b** to take a share in along with: *I'll stand in with you in this expense. Stand off*, (lit. and fig.) to be aloof, withdraw, keep one's distance. *Stand off and on*, (naut.) to tack along a coast. *Stand on*, (naut.) to follow a specific course. *Stand out*, **a** to be in clear relief, be distinctly outlined: *to stand out against a background*; **b** to remain firm, be obstinate in objecting, refuse to yield. *Stand to*, to adhere to, abide by: *to stand to one's word*; Phr. (fig.) *to stand to one's guns*, to stick to one's principles, decision &c. *Stand up*, **a** to be on one's feet, be standing; **b** to assume an erect position, rise to one's feet; **c** to hold oneself erect, refrain from stooping. *Stand up for*, to defend, maintain: *to stand up for oneself, for the truth. Stand up to*, to face boldly, meet courageously. *Stand upon*, to take one's stand on, rely upon, insist upon: *to stand upon one's rights.*

stand (II.), n., fr. prec. **1.** Halt, stoppage, arrest, cessation of progress: *to come to, be at, a stand.* Phr. *to make a stand (against)*, offer determined resistance. **2. a** Position, situation: *to take one's stand on the platform*; **b** moral position, that on which one relies for support: *my stand is on the strict interpretation of the law.* **3.** Place appointed for vehicles to stand; parking-place; also in compounds: *cab-stand* &c. **4. a** Any structure, framework &c. on which objects are kept, supported, displayed &c.; also in many compounds: *hat-stand, music-stand, wash-stand* &c.; specif. **b** stall, table &c. for display of goods for sale: *a stand for fruit in a market-place.* **5.** Raised platform or enclosure on which persons may sit or stand: *bandstand*; *grand stand.* **6.** Growing crop in specific area, year's growth &c.: *a stand of clover.*

standard (I.), n. [1. stándard; 2. stǽndəd], fr. O. Fr. *estandard*, 'banner', of Gmc. origin, cp. **stand** (I.); or connected w. **extend**; also in some senses fr. Engl. *stand.* **1.** A flag, banner; *royal standard*, that bearing the royal, national arms, flown only by the Sovereign; specif., flag of cavalry regiment, contrasted with *colours* of infantry. Phrs. *raise the standard of revolt* &c., initiate revolt; *to march under the standard of*, to be a follower, adherent, of. **2.** That which is constituted by authority as a fixed basis of comparison by which weights, measures, values (of gold and silver) are tested and tried; fixed rule, official gauge, criterion. Hence, **3.** Style, mode, type, accepted and recognized by convention, within a community, at a given time, as the criterion of what is best in speech, behaviour, conduct, action, taste, morality &c.; test, criterion, pattern, approved model: *to sin against, fall short of, accepted standards*; *up to, below, standard*; *society punishes those who will not conform to its standards.* **4.** Any of various upright shafts, poles, columns serving as supports &c.; e.g. upright stand supporting a lamp; perpendicular pole used in scaffolding &c. **5.** (hort.) A shrub or other plant growing with an upright, tree-like stem or growing from a bud grafted upon an upright stem; contrasted with a *bush, tree, climber* &c.

standard (II.), adj., fr. prec. **1.** In accordance with, serving as, a recognized standard: *standard weights, measures*; *standard English.* **2.** Having permanent, undisputed value: *a standard writer*; *the standard books on history* &c. **3. a** Supported by a standard, standing on but raised above the ground: *a standard lamp*; **b** (hort.) growing, grown, in form of a standard: *a standard tree, rose, apple* &c.

standard-bearer, n. **1. a** Member of regiment, army &c., who carries the standard; hence, **b** leader of party, movement, cause &c. **2.** (cap.) Hereditary officer who bears the king's standard on great ceremonial occasions, esp. at a coronation.

standard bread, n. Bread containing at least four-fifths of whole meal.

standardization, n. [1. stàndardīzā́shun; 2. stæ̀ndədaizéiʃən]. Next word & **-ation.** Act of standardizing; state of being standardized.

standardize, vb. trans. [1. stándardīz; 2. stǽndədaiz]. **standard** (II.) & **-ize.** **a** To reduce to an unvarying standard: *to standardize English speech*; **b** to regard as standard, recognize as the standard type, measure, value &c.: *one type of English has been standardized as the proper form for literature.*

stand-by, n. [1. stánd bī; 2. stǽnd bai]. Person, object, line of action &c., to which one has recourse in an emergency &c.; trustworthy, reliable, person or thing.

standing (I.), adj. [1. stánding; 2. stǽndiŋ], fr. Pres. Part. of **stand** (I.). **1.** Remaining in an erect position: *standing corn.* Phr. *standing jump*, one made without preliminary run. **2.** Permanent, lasting, perennial, remaining always in being; contrasted with *temporary*: *a standing joke, menace*; *standing orders*; *a standing army.* **3.** (print.) Remaining set up, not distributed: *standing type.*

standing (II.), n. **stand** (I.) & **-ing.** **1.** Position, rank, reputation: *a person of high standing.* **2.** Duration, period, of existence: *a custom of long standing.*

standing gear, rigging, n. (naut.) The shrouds and stays which are more or less permanent, and support the masts, bowsprit &c.

standing part, n. (naut.) That part of a rope &c. which is made fast; fixed end.

standing room, n. Room, space, for person(s) to stand.

standing stone, n. Vertical monolith of unhewn stone.

standish, n. [1. stándish; 2. stǽndiʃ]. **stand** (II.) & **dish.** (archaic) Inkstand.

stand-offish, adj. [1. stánd áwfish; 2. stǽnd ɔ́fiʃ]. Aloof, distant, reserved, repellent, in manner, character &c.; haughty.

stand-offishly, adv. Prec. & **-ly.** In a stand-offish manner.

stand-offishness, n. See prec. & **-ness.** Quality of being stand-offish.

standpatter, n. [1. stándpàter; 2. stǽndpæ̀tə]. (Am. polit. slang) One who stands pat, i.e. sticks firmly to his party platform, esp. in tariff matters.

stand-pipe, n. Vertical pipe for water, steam, gas &c.

standpoint, n. [1. stándpoint; 2. stǽndpɔint]. **a** Position from which a thing is seen, point of view; **b** mental attitude; point of view.

stand-rest, n. Sloping seat supporting person in half-standing position.

standstill, n. [1. stándstil; 2. stǽndstil]. Complete cessation of progress; halt: *to come to a standstill*; *work was at a standstill.*

stand-up, adj. [1. stánd up; 2. stǽnd ap]. **1.** Erect, upright: *a stand-up collar.* **2.** Done, taken, while standing: *a stand-up meal.* Phr. *stand-up fight*, serious fight or scuffle in which blows are exchanged.

stanhope, n. [1. stánup; 2. stǽnəp], fr. name of inventor. Light, open, two- or four-wheeled carriage, usually with single seat.

Stanhope-lens, n. Lens with differently curved, convex faces, invented by the Earl of Stanhope (1753–1816).

Stanhope-press, n. Iron printing press invented by Lord Stanhope, as prec.

staniel, n. [1. stányel; 2. stǽnjəl]. O.E. *stāngella*, fr. *stān*, 'stone', see **stone**, & *ġella*, 'screamer', fr. *ġellan*, 'to yell', see **yell.** Kind of small falcon; kestrel.

stank, vb. [1. stangk; 2. stæŋk]. Pret. of **stink**; O.E. *stanc.*

stannary, n. & adj. [1. stánari; 2. stǽnəri], fr. Med. Lat. *stannārius*, fr. Lat. *stagnum, stannum*, 'an alloy of silver and lead; tin'; possibly cogn. w. Gk. *staphúlē*, 'plummet'; but perh. of Celt. origin, cp. W. *ystaen*, 'tin'. **1.** n. **a** Tin-mine; **b** district in which tin-mines are situated. **2.** adj. Of, pertaining to, tin-mines; *stannary courts*, tin-miners' courts held in Cornwall.

stannate, n. [1. stánat; 2. stǽnət], fr. Lat. *stannum*, 'tin', see prec., & **-ate.** (chem.) Salt of stannic acid.

stannic, adj. [1. stánik; 2. stǽnik], fr. Lat. *stannum*, 'tin', see **stannary**, & **-ic.** Of, derived from, tin.

stanniferous, adj. [1. staníferus; 2. stænífərəs], fr. Lat. *stannum*, 'tin', see **stannary**, & **-i-** & **-ferous.** Containing, producing, tin.

stannite, n. [1. stánīt; 2. stǽnait], fr. Lat. *stannum*, 'tin', see **stannary**, & **-ite** (I.). Grey or black mineral compound of tin, copper, iron, and sulphur.

stannous, adj. [1. stánus; 2. stǽnəs], fr. Lat. *stannum*, 'tin', see **stannary**, & **-ous.** Of, pertaining to, containing, tin.

stanza, n. [1. stánza; 2. stǽnzə], fr. Ital. *stanza*, fr. L. Lat. *stantia*, 'place, situation', see **stance.** Group of four or more rhymed verse-lines arranged according to a specific metrical scheme; esp. one of series of such groups; a strophe: *Spenserian stanza.*

stanzaed, adj. [1. stánzad; 2. stǽnzəd]. Prec. & **-ed.** Arranged in, consisting of, stanzas; (in compounds) consisting of stanzas of a specific type.

stanzaic, adj. [1. stanzáik; 2. stænzéiik]. **stanza** & **-ic.** Of, pertaining to, consisting of, arranged in, stanzas.

stapes, n. [1. stápēz; 2. stéipiz]. Med. Lat. *stapes*, 'stirrup'. Du Cange has *stapes, stapedium, stapeda, straphes* (once each); possibly fr. a form of Lat. *stāre*, 'to stand', see **state**, & Lat. *ped-(em)*, 'foot', see **pedal.** Stirrup-shaped bone of the middle ear; stirrup-bone.

staple (I.), n. [1. stápl; 2. stéipl]. O.E. *stapul*; M.E. *stapel*, 'pillar, prop; step'; cp. O. Fris. *stapul*; M. Du. *stapel*; O.H.G. *stafol*, 'rung'; cogn. w. O.E. *stōpol*, 'footprint', & O.H.G. *stuofa*, 'threshold'; cp. Mod. Germ. *stufe*, 'degree, stage in development'; fr. same base as **step** (II.). One of various objects used for fastening; specif. **a** metal bar, wire &c., pointed at both ends and bent into U-shape, used as fastening for holding end of bolt &c.; **b** metal tube holding ends of reeds in oboe and similar musical instruments; **c** bent wire used in bookbinding for stitching with wire.

staple (II.), vb. trans., fr. prec. To fasten, hold, with a staple.

staple (III.), n., fr. O. Fr. *estapel*, 'market, staple', fr. L.G. *stapel*, 'step; pile; market', cogn. w. **staple** (I.). **1.** (hist.) Centre of trade, principal market of district &c. **2.** Leading article of commerce, principal commodity, of country, district, town &c. **3.** Leading factor, element, chief material: *the staple of diet, conversation* &c. **4.** Raw material; stuff, matter, ready for manufacture. **5.** Thread, fibre, of wool or cotton: *wool of fine staple.*

staple (IV.), adj., fr. prec. Of the nature of a staple; forming an important factor or part; leading, principal: *staple products of a country*; *the staple topic of conversation.*

staple (V.), vb. trans., fr. **staple** (III.). To sort, classify, grade (wool &c.) according to quality of fibre.

stapler, n. [1. stápler; 2. stéiplə]. Prec. & **-er.** Person who grades wool &c., esp. *wool-stapler.*

stapling-machine, n. [1. stápling mashēn; 2. stéipliŋ məʃīn]. (bookbinding) Machine for wire-stitching.

star (I.), n. [1. star; 2. stā]. O.E. *steorra*; M.E. *sterre*; cp. O.H.G. *sterro*, *sterno*; O.N. *stjarna*; Goth. *stairnō*; cogn. w. Lat. *stēlla*, 'star', see **stellar**; Gk. *astḗr*, *ástron*, 'star', see **astral**; Scrt. *star-*, 'star'. **1. a** One of the distant, luminous, heavenly bodies, appearing to be of small size as compared with sun and moon; Phr. *to see stars*, to have the sensation of seeing luminous flashes, as after a severe blow on the eye, back of the head &c.; **b** specif., a fixed heavenly body, contrasted with a planet. **2.** Any of various objects or figures resembling a star in shape or appearance; specif. **a** five- or six-pointed device formed by producing sides of pentagon or hexagon, used as ornament, emblem &c.; Phr. *stars and stripes*, flag of U.S.A., bearing a pattern of stars and stripes; **b** jewel or personal ornament in the shape of a star; object of this shape in precious metal, and highly decorated, forming the regalia, or part of it, of an order of knighthood; also the order itself: *the Star of India* &c.; **c** an asterisk used in printing; **d** white mark on a horse's forehead. **3.** Heavenly body considered as influencing person's character, fortunes &c.: *to be born under a lucky star*; *one's star is in the ascendant*; *to thank one's stars*, to be thankful, consider oneself lucky. **4.** Person who excels, is eminent, in particular field, profession &c.: *a literary, operatic, film, star* &c.; specif., leading actor or actress in theatrical production.

star (II.), vb. trans. & intrans., fr. prec. **A.** trans. **1.** To mark, adorn, set, with design of stars. **2.** To mark, distinguish, with an asterisk. **3.** To present as a star or theatrical celebrity in a play. Phr. *to star it*, to play the part of theatrical star. **B.** intrans. To appear as leading actor on the stage or in a film play: *to star in the provinces*.

star-apple, n. **1.** Evergreen tree of tropical America producing an apple-like fruit whose carpels exhibit a star-shaped figure when the fruit is cut open. **2.** The fruit of this tree.

starblind, adj. [1. stárblīnd; 2. stáblaind]. O.E. *stær-*, *stareblind*, 'quite blind'; cp. O. Fris. *stareblind*; O.H.G. *starablind*; cp. O.E. *stær*, 'stiff'; *starian*, 'to gaze fixedly', see **stare** (I.). Half blind; having dim sight.

starboard, n., adj., & vb. trans. [1. stárbord; 2. stábəd]. O.E. *stēorbord*; M.E. *sterbord*; fr. O.E. *stēor*, 'rudder', q.v. under **steer** (I.), & **board**. **1.** n. Right-hand side of ship, from point of view of observer standing on ship and looking towards bow. **2.** adj. Situated on, pertaining to, the starboard. **3.** vb. To turn (helm) to starboard.

starch (I.), n. [1. starch; 2. stātʃ]. M.E. *starche*, O.E. **sterče*, 'stiff'; cp. *sterčed-*, 'resolute'; fr. *stearc*, 'strong, stiff'; see **stark**. **1. a** White, tasteless substance found in all vegetables except fungi, esp. in grain, beans, potatoes &c., and forming a valuable constituent of food; **b** starch in granular or powdered form as extracted from vegetable matter. **2.** Sticky, thick, jelly-like preparation of starch with boiling or cold water, used for stiffening clothes in washing &c. **3.** (fig.) Stiffness, formality, rigidity, of manner, mind, or character.

starch (II.), adj. See prec. (archaic, lit. and fig.) Stiff, rigid.

starch (III.), vb. trans., fr. prec. To make (linen &c.) stiff with starch.

Star-chamber, n. So called fr. decoration of ceiling. (cap.) Civil and criminal court abolished in 1641, characterized by arbitrary methods of procedure.

starched, adj. [1. starcht; 2. stātʃt], fr. P.P. of **starch** (III.). (fig.) Stiff, formal, rigid, precise, in manner.

starchedly, adv. [1. stárchedli; 2. státʃidli]. Prec. & **-ly**. In a starched manner.

starchedness, n. [1. stárchednes; 2. státʃidnis]. See prec. & **-ness**. Quality of being starched.

starchily, adv. [1. stárchili; 2. státʃili]. **starchy** & **-ly**. In a starchy manner.

starchiness, n. [1. stárchines; 2. státʃinis]. Next word & **-ness**. State or quality of being starchy.

starchy, adj. [1. stárchi; 2. státʃi]. **starch** (I.) & **-y** (IV.). **1.** Containing, composed of, starch: *starchy food*. **2.** Stiffened with starch. **3.** (fig.) Prim, precise, formal, stiff, in manner &c.

star-drift, n. United motion in the same direction by a group of fixed stars in a particular region of the heavens.

stare (I.), vb. intrans. & trans. [1. stār; 2. stɛə]. O.E. *starian*, 'to look, gaze, upon'; M.E. *stāren*, 'to look fixedly; to gleam, shine'; cp. O.H.G. *storrēn*, 'to stand out, project'; M.H.G. *starren*, 'to be stiff'; Mod. Germ. *starr*, 'stiff'; Goth. *andstaúrran*, 'to be opposed to, murmur at'; O.N. *stōrr*, 'proud'; cogn. w. Gk. *stereós*, 'stiff, firm'; *strēnés*, 'hard, rough'; Lat. *strēnuus*, 'vigorous', see **strenuous**; Scrt. *sthirás*, 'hard, firm'; Lith. *stóras*, 'thick'; *styru*, 'to be stiff'; O. Slav. *starŭ*, 'old'. See also **stern** (I.), **sterile**, **stark**. **1. a** (i.) To look or gaze intently, fixedly, as though with curiosity: *it is very rude to stare*; (ii.) to gaze abstractedly: *to stare straight in front of one*; **b** *stare at*, to contemplate, gaze at intently, as with surprise or curiosity. Phr. (*the fact, thing &c.*) *stares you, is staring you, in the face*, it is perfectly plain and obvious; *to make people stare*, surprise, shock, them; '*And paid a tradesman once to make him stare*' (Pope, Moral Essays, Epist. ii. 56); *to stare a person out of countenance*, stare at him until he becomes confused. **2.** (of colour &c., rare except as adj. in Pres. Part.) See **staring**.

stare (II.), n., fr. prec. **1.** A prolonged, fixed, intent, look, or gaze, expressive of curiosity, surprise, contempt &c. **2.** Peculiar fixed expression of the eyes when the lids are widely opened and the eyes immovable; a glare: *the eyes of the dead man were fixed in a terrifying stare*.

starfinch, n. [1. stárfinch; 2. stáfin(t)ʃ]. Bird of the warbler family, redstart.

starfish, n. [1. stárfish; 2. stáfiʃ]. Kind of echinoderm, esp. one with a central body from which five or more rays or arms project in the form of a star.

star-gazer, n. [1. stár gàzer; 2. stá gèizə]. (facet.) **a** Astronomer; **b** an absent-minded, dreamy person.

star-gazing, n. [1. stár gàzing; 2. stá gèiziŋ]. **a** Practice of observing the stars; **b** absent-mindedness, abstraction.

staring, adj. & adv. [1. stáring; 2. stéəriŋ], fr. Pres. Part. of **stare** (I.). **1.** (of the eyes) Fixed as in a stare; wide open and glaring. Phr. *stark, staring mad*, completely mad. **2.** (of colours) Presenting too violent a contrast to surroundings; brilliant to excess. **3.** (of animal's coat) Bristling, rough, esp. in illness.

staringly, adv. Prec. & **-ly**. In a staring manner, with a fixed gaze.

stark (I.), adj. [1. stark; 2. stāk]. O.E. *stearc*; M.E. *stark*, 'strong'; cp. O. Fris. *sterk*; O.H.G. *starch*; O.N. *starkr*, 'strong'; Goth. *gastaúrknan*, 'to stiffen'; cogn. w. Lith. *stregti*, 'to stiffen, freeze'. Cp. further O.E. *stær*; Mod. Germ. *starr*, 'stiff'; & see **stare** (I.), **stern** (I.), **sterile**. **1.** Stiff, rigid, esp. in, or as in, death: *stark and cold*. **2.** (archaic and poet.) **a** Strong, powerful, firm; **b** resolute, unyielding. **3.** Absolute, utter, downright: *stark madness*.

stark (II.), adv., fr. prec. Absolutely, thoroughly: *stark mad*.

stark (III.), adj., for *stark-naked*.

stark-naked, adj. M.E. *stert-nāked*, fr. O.E. *steort*, 'tail'; cp. O. Fris. *stert*; O.H.G. *sterz*, 'tail; plough handle'; M.H.G. *sterzen*, 'to stick out stiffly'; fr. base **ster-* &c., 'stiff'; see **stare** (I.), **stern** (I.), & cp. **redstart**. Completely naked.

starless, adj. [1. stárles; 2. stális]. **star** (I.) & **-less**. Without stars.

starlet, n. [1. stárlet; 2. stálit]. **star** (I.) & **-let**. Small star.

starlight, n. & adj. [1. stárlīt; 2. stálait]. **1.** n. Light given by stars. **2.** adj. Lighted by stars: *a starlight night*.

star-like, adj. Resembling a star in shape, appearance, brilliance &c.

starling (I.), n. [1. stárling; 2. stáliŋ]. O.E. *stær(ling)*; M.E. *stare(ling)*; cp. O.H.G. *stāra*, O.N. *stari*; cogn. w. Lat. *sturnus*, 'starling'. Genus, *Sturnus*, of birds with glossy iridescent black plumage, of gregarious habits and often nesting near human dwellings.

starling (II.), n. Cp. Swed. *stōr*, 'stake'; but perh. fr. earlier *staddling*, fr. O.E. *staðolung*, 'foundation', fr. *staðol*, 'support, foundation', q.v. under **stall** (I.). Ring of piles surrounding and protecting the pier of a bridge &c.

starlit, adj. [1. stárlit; 2. stálit]. **star** (I.) & **lit**. Lit up, illuminated, by stars: *a starlit landscape*.

star of Bethlehem, n. [1. stár uv béthlēem; 2. stár əv béþliəm]. Herbaceous plant, *Ornithogalum umbellatum*, of lily family, with long narrow leaves and six-petalled white flowers having green stripes on the back.

starred, adj. [1. stard; 2. stād], fr. P.P. of **star** (II.). **1.** Marked, set, adorned, with a star or stars; specif., to mark with an asterisk. **2.** Affected by influence of stars; esp. in compounds: *ill-starred*, unlucky, unfortunate.

starriness, n. [1. stáhrines; 2. stárinis]. Next word & **-ness**. State of being starry.

starry, adj. [1. stáhri; 2. stári]. **star** (I.) & **-y** (IV.). **1.** Pertaining to, covered with, stars: *the starry sky*. **2.** Bright, shining like stars: *starry eyes*.

star-shell, n. (mil.) Metal cylinder filled with illuminating explosives, fired so as to burst in the air and light up enemy's lines.

star-spangled, adj. Studded, adorned, with stars; esp. *star-spangled banner*, U.S.A. flag, the Stars and Stripes.

star-stone, n. Variety of corundum, esp. kind of sapphire, showing starlike markings when cut.

start (I.), vb. intrans. & trans. [1. start; 2. stāt]. M.E. *sterten*, 'to start, leap'; fr. O.N. *sterta*; cp. Du. *storten*; O.H.G. *sturzen*, 'to overthrow'; perh. fr. same base as O.E. *steort*, 'tail', see under **stark-naked**; for meaning cp. Fr. *culbuter*, 'to upset'. **A.** intrans. **1.** To make a sudden, involuntary movement as from fear, shock, surprise &c.: *to start at the sound of a rifle-shot*. **2.** To move, jump, suddenly, in specified direction: *to start back, forward* &c. **3. a** To begin a journey &c., set out: *we must start early, as we have a long way to go*; *to start for the continent*; **b** to begin to move forward: *the train has just started*; to begin to work: *I can't get the engine* (of motor-car) *to start*; **c** specif., to begin to run, be among those who come up to scratch, in a race. **4.** To begin, embark on, a course of action, begin to do something: *to start on a course of study*; *he started to whistle a tune*. **5.** To come into existence, begin to exist, to have origin: *the fire started in the cellar*. **6.** To get out of position, be displaced, or warped: *the timbers have started*. **B.** trans. **1.** To begin (an action), set out on (a journey): *to start work, a meal*; *to start crying*; *start one's travels*. **2.** To cause to start, put in motion, set going: *to start an engine, car* &c. **3.** To give signal for starting to: *to start runners in a race*. **4.** To give a start to, enable to start: *to start a person in life*. **5.** To arouse, put up: *to start a hare*; (also fig.) *to start another hare*, to raise a fresh, irrelevant, subject for discussion. **6. a** To be the cause of, cause to begin, bring into existence: *to start a fire*; **b** to originate, initiate: *to start an idea, a discussion* &c. **7.** To displace, cause to move suddenly from position: *the damp has started the timbers*. **8.** To tap, cause contents to flow from. **C.** Followed by adverbs and prepositions with special meanings. *Start in*, intrans. (colloq.), to begin, set to work: *just start in and clean out the stables*. *Start out*, intrans. (colloq.), to have the intention, propose to oneself (to do something): *he* *started out to reform the society.* *Start up,* **1.** intrans., **a** to spring suddenly to one's feet, jump up; **b** to come suddenly into existence, appear abruptly: *a new leader, idea &c. has started up*; **2.** trans., to cause to begin working, put into motion: *to start up an engine.*

start (**II.**), n., fr. prec. **1.** Slight shock, caused by some sudden, unexpected occurrence, a fright &c.; involuntary jerky muscular movement resulting from this: *your sudden, silent appearance gave me quite a start*; Phr. *by fits and starts,* irregularly, intermittently. **2. a** Act of setting out on journey &c.: *to make an early start; to prepare for the start*; Phrs. *a start in life,* beginning of one's career; *to give one a start in life,* help one, afford one an opportunity for making a good beginning; **b** beginning of race &c.: *to line up for the start.* **3.** Commencement of action, work &c.: *the workmen looked on for several hours before making a start on the job.* **4.** Place at which a start is made, esp. starting-point of race &c. Phr. *from start to finish,* from beginning to end. **5.** Advantageous position, distance in advance, allowed or obtained at beginning of race, pursuit &c.: *to have a few yards' start*; *you must give me a start if I'm to race you.*

starter, n. [1. stárter; 2. stā́tə]. **start** (**I.**) & **-er.** **1.** Person who gives signal for a race to start. **2.** Person, or horse, who starts in a race as a competitor. **3. a** Device for causing an engine to start working; esp. *self-starter*; **b** motor-car provided with such a device.

starting-gate, n. [1. stárting gāt; 2. stā́tiŋ gèit]. Movable barrier at starting-post in horse-race, for ensuring a fair start.

starting-point, n. Place or point at which a start or beginning is made; **a** of a journey or a race; **b** of a course of action, line of thought, argument &c.

starting-post, n. Post or mark from which a race is begun.

starting price, n. Odds offered immediately before start of race.

startle, vb. trans. [1. stártl; 2. stā́tl]. O.E. *steartlian,* 'to stumble', M.E. *stertlen,* 'to rush along'; mod. vb. prob. a new formation fr. **start** (**I.**) & freq. **-le.** **1. a** (i.) To cause to start; to scare, frighten, alarm suddenly: *to startle a herd of deer*; (ii.) to cause slight shock to, by a sudden, and unexpected appearance, noise, movement, action &c.: *you startled me by bursting in so suddenly*; **b** to cause shock of surprise to (usually in bad sense) as by an unexpected occurrence, piece of news &c.: *I was startled by the news of his death, by the magnitude of the demands made* &c. **2.** To rouse, stimulate, goad (into action) by startling: *to startle a person out of his apathy, into doing some hard work.*

startling, adj. [1. stártling; 2. stā́tliŋ], fr. Pres. Part. of prec. Causing alarm or astonishment: *startling events, developments* &c.

startlingly, adv. Prec. & **-ly.** In a startling manner; to a startling degree.

starvation, n. [1. starvā́shun; 2. stāvéiʃən]. Next word & **-ation**; a hybrid word dating fr. late 18th cent. Act or process of starving; state of being starved.

starve, vb. intrans. & trans. [1. starv; 2. stāv]. O.E. *steorfan,* 'to die', M.E. *sterven*; cp. O. Fris. *sterva*; O.H.G. *sterban*; 'to die'; cp. O.N. *starf,* 'toil; effort', *stjarfe,* 'tetanus', *stirfenn,* 'stubborn'; cogn. w. Gk. *stérphos,* 'thick, hard skin; leather'; fr. an expansion of base **ster-,* 'stiff', see **stare, stark**; possibly also remotely cogn. w. O. Slav. *tirpstŭ,* 'to stiffen'; Lat. *torpēre,* 'to be numb, torpid, sluggish'; see **torpid.** **A.** intrans. **1.** Original, general sense of to die preserved only in Phr. *starving with cold.* **2.** To die from insufficient food: *he bolted to America and left his family to starve.* **3.** To suffer from lack of food; to be reduced to extreme weakness and emaciation by hunger: *many live in luxury while others are starving*; Phr., (colloq.) *I'm simply starving, you must be starving* = to be very hungry. **4.** To abstain from food temporarily: *when one is ill it is very good to starve for a bit.* **5.** *To starve for,* long for, hunger after; to feel the lack of: *to be starving for companionship*; *a mind starving for knowledge.* **B.** trans. **1.** To cause to suffer greatly; to kill; only in Phr. *starved with cold.* **2.** To kill by depriving of food. **3.** To supply with insufficient food, to nourish inadequately; Phr. *to starve into submission, surrender,* induce, compel, to submit, surrender, by starvation.

starveling, n. & adj. [1. stárvling; 2. stā́vliŋ]. **starve** & **-ling** (**I.**). **1.** n. Thin, weak, underfed person or animal. **2.** adj. Hungry, emaciated, ill-fed.

stasis, n. [1. stā́sis; 2. stéisis], fr. Gk. *stásis,* 'a standing still', see **state** (**I.**). Stoppage of the circulation of any of the fluids of the body.

statable, adj. [1. stā́tabl; 2. stéitəbl]. **state** (**III.**) & **-able.** Capable of being stated.

state (**I.**), n. [1. stāt; 2. steit], fr. O. Fr. *estat,* see **estate,** fr. Lat. *status,* 'posture, attitude; place, position; condition, circumstances; public affairs; constitution; form of government', fr. P.P. type of *stāre,* 'to stand'; cp. Lat. *stō,* 'I stand', earlier **stājō*; cogn. w. O. Slav. *stają,* 'I stand'; Lith. *stóju̇s,* 'I put myself'; Lith. *statau͂,* 'to place'; Scrt. *sthitáš,* 'standing'; Gk. *statós,* 'placed'; Scrt. *sthítiš,* 'act of standing'; Gk. *stásis,* 'standing'; O.E. *stede,* 'place', see **stead.** All fr. base **stə-,* **stā-* &c., 'to stand', seen also in **stall** (**I.**), **still** (**I.**), **stamen, status, stool, stand, locus** &c. **1. a** Temporary or permanent set of circumstances: *a building in an unfinished state*; *affairs in a state of confusion*; physical or mental condition: *a wonderful state of preservation*; *in a state of coma*; *a poor state of health*; *an unhappy state of mind*; (colloq.) **b** bad condition of body or mind: *to get oneself into such a state that one is unfit to be seen*; **c** agitation, anxiety: *in a terrible state.* **2. a** Rank, position, social circumstances: *persons in every state of life*; **b** specif., high station, dignity: *to live in a style befitting one's state.* **3.** Elaborate style of living, pomp, ceremony: *to keep up considerable state*; *the state with which he is surrounded.* Phr. *in state,* with great pomp and circumstance, ceremony. **4.** (often cap.) Body of persons inhabiting an area, or country, with defined limits or frontiers, organized as political unity under one supreme ruler or government: *to fight for the State*; *the State declared war*; *to be a menace to the State.* Phr. *States of the Church, Papal States,* parts of Italy formerly under the temporal authority of the Pope. **5.** Partially autonomous division of federal republic; specif., one of the states forming the United States of America; *free states,* part of U.S.A. in which slavery did not exist, as opposed to *slave states.* **6. a** Government, political authority, of state: *schools provided by the State*; **b** specif., civil, as distinct from ecclesiastical, government: *Church and State.* **7.** (pl.) **a** Legislative body in islands of Jersey and Guernsey; **b** *States General,* legislative body of the Netherlands, and of France before 1879. **8.** (biol.) Organized community of insects, organisms &c. **9.** (archaic) **a** Dais or throne; **b** canopy above throne. **10.** (engraving) Any one of the stages through which a plate passes in the process of engraving.

state (**II.**), adj., fr. prec. **1.** Pertaining to the State: *state papers, state prisoner,* person arrested for or convicted of felony, esp. for political crime; *state trial,* that of person prosecuted by the State, esp. on political charge. **2. a** Performed upon, used for, intended for, occasions of special ceremony: *state coach*; **b** intended, reserved for persons of exalted rank: *state apartments.*

state (**III.**), vb. trans., fr. **state** (**I.**). **1.** To express in words, affirm, relate, say: *the witness stated that he was struck on the head*; *it is sometimes stated that English weather is uncertain*; *travellers state that the wild boar is more ferocious than the tiger.* **2.** To put down clearly in words, to expound, give a reasoned exposition of: *to state one's case*; *he stated Verner's Law with great lucidity.* **3.** (math.) To express (problem &c.) in algebraic symbols.

state bank, n. Bank under the control of the state.

statecraft, n. [1. stā́tkrahft; 2. stéitkrāft]. **state** (**I.**) & **craft.** The art of government; statesmanship.

stated, adj. [1. stā́ted; 2. stéitid], fr. P.P. of **state** (**III.**). Appointed, established, definitely fixed: *at a stated time*; *at stated intervals*; *a stated meeting.*

statedly, adv. Prec. & **-ly.** In a stated manner.

stateliness, n. [1. stā́tlines; 2. stéitlinis]. Next word & **-ness.** Quality of being stately.

stately, adj. [1. stā́tli; 2. stéitli]. **state** (**I.**) & **-ly.** Grand, impressive and dignified; imposing; nobly proportioned; well balanced: *a stately manner, walk*; *stately dances*; *stately buildings*; *stately rhythm, phraseology* &c.

statement, n. [1. stā́tment; 2. stéitmənt]. **state** (**III.**) & **-ment.** **1.** Act of stating; utterance; verbal expression: *belief and statement are two different things.* **2.** That which is stated; **a** expression of a judgement, belief, opinion, in words; assertion, affirmation: *to make a statement*; *an astonishing statement*; **b** a reasoned exposition, a setting forth; mode of stating: *a new statement of old truths is often necessary*; *an admirable statement of the case.* **3.** Official report or summary of financial position issued by commercial firm &c.

stater, n. [1. stā́ter; 2. stéitə]. Lat. *statēr,* fr. Gk. *statḗr,* 'stater'; orig. 'a weight'; cp. Scrt. *sthā́tṛ,* 'upright object'; fr. base **stā-,* **stə-,* 'to stand', see **state** (**I.**). Ancient Greek coin of different values, esp. **a** Persian gold coin worth about 22s.; **b** later silver coin worth four drachmas.

stateroom, n. [1. stā́troom; 2. stéitrum]. Private cabin on ship.

statesman, n. [1. stā́tsman; 2. stéitsmən]. **state** (**I.**), & genit. *-es* & **-man.** **1.** Person taking part in state government; specif., who has constructive ability and foresight in the management of public affairs; often contrasted with *politician,* which is used in sense of one interested merely in party politics. **2.** Small landowner, farming his own land, in the North of England.

statesmanlike, adj. [1. stā́tsmanlīk; 2. stéitsmənlaik]. Prec. & **-like.** Characteristic of, befitting, a statesman.

statesmanly, adj. [1. stā́tsmanli; 2. stéitsmənli]. See prec. & **-ly.** Statesmanlike.

statesmanship, n. [1. stā́tsmanship; 2. stéitsmənʃip]. **statesman** & **-ship.** Art of a statesman; statecraft.

state trial, n. Trial in which the state is the prosecuting party, esp. for a political offence.

static(al), adj. [1. stā́tik(l); 2. stǽtik(l)], fr. Gk. *statikós,* 'causing to stand', fr. stem **stat-,* in Gk. *statós,* 'placed; standing', fr. base **stə-,* 'to stand', see **state** (**I.**) & **-ic** & **-al.** **1.** At rest, not in motion; stationary. **2.** Pertaining to, connected with, bodies in a state of rest; contrasted with *dynamic,* or *kinetic*; *static pressure,* that caused solely by weight without motion. **3.** (elect.) Shortened form of electro-static.

statically, adv. Prec. & **-ly.** In a static manner; by means of pressure.

statice, n. [1. stā́tisē; 2. stǽtisī], fr. Gk. *statikós,* 'stanching blood', see **static.** (bot.) Genus of plants, including the sea-lavender, a shore plant with lilac flowers.

statics, n. [1. stā́tiks; 2. stǽtiks], fr. **static.** **a** Branch of mechanics dealing with bodies remaining at rest, and the equilibrium of forces; contrasted with *dynamics*; **b** (wireless) name given to naturally produced ether waves, causing irregular disturbances in reception, cp. *atmospherics.*

station (**I.**), n. [1. stā́shun; 2. stéiʃən], fr. Lat. *statiōn-(em),* 'act of standing; place, position; abode, office', fr. *stat-(um)*, P.P. type of *stāre*, 'to stand', see **state** (I.), & **-ion**. **1.** Place, position, situation, esp. spot chosen by or assigned to person for particular purpose: *to take up one's station*; *one's appointed station*. **2.** Place, enclosure, building, &c., forming local headquarters of some official organization; often in compounds *police-*, *coastguard-*, *lifeboat-*, *dressing-station* &c. **3.** Regular stopping-place of public vehicle in a road or street. **4.** Also *railway-station*, the whole group of buildings, offices, sheds, platforms &c., used in the working and administration of a railway for the taking up and setting down of passengers and goods at a regular halting-place on a railway line, bearing the name of the place, or district in which it is situated. **5.** (Australia) Farm, estate, run, for sheep &c.; stock farm. **6. a** (India) Place at which English troops and officials reside; military post; official headquarters; **b** administrative centre or base assigned to a fleet or naval unit: *naval stations*. **7.** (eccles.) **a** (pl.) Also *stations of the Cross*, series of fourteen pictures &c., placed at intervals around walls of church, esp. Roman Catholic church, and representing scenes of the Passion; **b** (R.C. Ch.) church to which a procession makes its way for devotions &c.; **c** fast appointed for Friday (R.C. Ch.) or Wednesday and Friday (Gk. Ch.). **8. a** Position of an individual in relation to society; condition, rank, status, walk in life: *to have ideas above one's station*; *a lowly, an exalted, station in life*; **b** specif., high social or official position: *several men of station*. **9.** (surv.) **a** Point from which measurements are taken; **b** distance adopted as unit for surveying. **10.** (zool. and bot.) Area of specific character regarded as the habitat of particular animal or plant.

station (II.), vb. trans., fr. prec. **a** To place in a specific spot, assign a station to: *to station a guard at the gate*; *to station oneself at a window*; **b** specif. (mil.) *a regiment stationed at Quetta*.

stational, adj. [1. stā́shunal; 2. stéiʃənəl]. **station** (I.) & **-al**. Relating to a station.

stationariness, n. [1. stā́shunarines; 2. stéiʃənərinis]. Next word & **-ness**. State of being stationary.

stationary (I.), adj. [1. stā́shunari; 2. stéiʃənəri], fr. Lat. *statiōnārius*, 'pertaining to a post or station'; **station** (I.) & **-ary**. **1.** At rest, remaining in one place or position, not in motion, not moving from one place to another: *to remain stationary*; *a row of stationary vehicles*; *stationary air*, that remaining in lungs during normal respiration; *stationary diseases*, local ailments appearing and disappearing in accordance with specific atmospheric conditions. **2.** Remaining at the same degree, amount, value, size &c.; neither increasing nor diminishing: *the population has remained stationary since the last census*; *the glass is stationary for the moment*. **3.** Acting, or intended to act, in one fixed position; not capable of being, or liable to be, moved: *a stationary crane*; *stationary troops*.

stationary (II.), n., fr. prec. Stationary object or person, esp. member of stationary force.

station-bill, n. (naut.) Document showing post allotted to each member of the crew in specific operations.

stationer, n. [1. stā́shuner; 2. stéiʃənə]. M.E. *stacyonere*, 'a bookseller', fr. Med. Lat. *statiōnārius*, 'bookseller'; so called fr. his **station** or stall. **1.** Old meaning survives only in *Stationers' Hall*, the headquarters of the guild of stationers or booksellers, at which, until 1911, every book published in England had to be 'entered' or registered for purposes of copyright. **2.** (present use) A dealer in all kinds of writing materials.

stationery, n. [1. stā́shuneri; 2. stéiʃənəri]. Prec. & **-ery**. All those classes of goods, collectively or separately, in which a stationer deals; specif., writing paper; in Phr. *stationery and envelopes*.

station-house, n. Building used as station, esp. police-station.

station-master, n. Official of railway staff in charge of railway station.

station-pointer, n. Three-armed protractor used in determining point on chart from given data.

statist, n. [1. stā́tist; 2. stéitist]. **state** (I.) & **-ist**. **1.** (obs.) Politician. **2.** Statistician.

statistic(al), adj. [1. statístik(l); 2. stətístik(l)]. Prec. & **-ic** & **-al**. Pertaining to, consisting of, based on, statistics.

statistically, adv. Prec. & **-ly**. According to, by means of, statistics.

statistician, n. [1. stàtistíshan; 2. stæ̀tistíʃən]. **statistic** & **-ian**. Person skilled in collecting, dealing with, interpreting, statistics.

statistics, n. [1. statístiks; 2. stətístiks]. **statist** & **-ics**. **1.** Systematic collection and arrangement of numerical facts: *statistics of crime, disease, births and deaths* &c. **2.** Science of collecting and tabulating numerical facts, esp. such as bear upon social conditions.

statistology, n. [1. stàtistóloji; 2. stæ̀tistóləd͡ʒi]. See prec. & **-logy**. Science of collecting and classifying statistics.

statoscope, n. [1. státoskōp; 2. stǽtəskoup], fr. Gk. *statós*, 'placed, fixed', q.v. under **state** (I.), & **-scope**. Instrument showing minute variations in atmospheric pressure.

statuary (I.), adj. [1. státūari; 2. stǽtjuəri], fr. Lat. *statuārius*, 'of statues'; **statue** & **-ary**. Connected with, pertaining to, suitable for, statues: *statuary marble*.

statuary (II.), n., fr. Lat. *statuārius*, 'maker of statues'; *statuāria*, 'art of making statues'; **statue** & **-ary**. **1.** Art of making or carving statues. **2.** Statues collectively; sculpture; group of sculptured figures. **3.** Maker of statues; a sculptor.

statue, n. [1. státū; 2. stǽtjū, stǽtʃū]. M.E., fr. O. Fr. *statue*, fr. Lat. *statua*, 'image, statue', fr. *statum*, P.P. type of *stāre*, 'to stand', see **state** (I.). Human or animal figure, approaching or exceeding life-size, carved or modelled, in the round.

statued, adj. [1. státūd; 2. stǽtjūd]. Prec. & **-ed**. Having, adorned with, statues.

statuesque, adj. [1. stàtūésk; 2. stæ̀tjuésk]. **statue** & **-esque**. Resembling, having the dignity, noble proportions or serenity, of a statue: *a lady of statuesque beauty*.

statuesquely, adv. Prec. & **-ly**. In a statuesque manner.

statuesqueness, n. See prec. & **-ness**. State or quality of being statuesque.

statuette, n. [1. stàtūét; 2. stæ̀tjuét]. **statue** & **-ette**. A small statue.

statu quo. See **status quo**.

stature, n. [1. stáchur; 2. stǽtʃə], fr. Fr., fr. Lat. *statūra*, 'statue', fr. *stat-(um)*, P.P. type of *stāre*, 'to stand', see **state** (I.) & **-ure**. **a** Bodily proportion, height, size: *of imposing stature*; *to grow in stature*; **b** intellectual proportions, mental or moral calibre.

statured, adj. [1. stáchurd; 2. stǽtʃəd]. Prec. & **-ed**. Having specified stature, chiefly in compounds, *small-statured* &c.

status, n. [1. stā́tus; 2. stéitəs]. Lat. *status*, 'mode of standing, posture; position, circumstances; civil standing; rank', fr. P.P. type of *stāre*, 'to stand', see **state** (I.). **1. a** Standing, rank, social position; **b** relative position in regard to others in attainments, professional reputation and the like: *a man's status as a scholar*. **2.** (law) Legal position of a person; **a** in relation to the state; **b** in relation to other persons.

status lymphaticus, n. [1. stā́tus limfátikus; 2. stéitəs limfǽtikəs]. Lat.; see prec. & **lymphatic**. A pathological condition of the lymphatic vessels, associated with an enlargement of the thymus gland.

status quo, in quo, n. [1. stā́tus (in) kwō; 2. stéitəs (in) kwou]. Lat.; see **status**. (lit.) Position, condition in which; state, condition in which things were before certain date or event; unaltered condition; esp. in such Phrs. as *to preserve the status quo*; *in statu quo*; also in full *in statu quo ante (bellum)*, in state as before the war.

statutable, adj. [1. státūtabl; 2. stǽtjutəbl]. **statute** & **-able**. Statutory.

statutably, adv. Prec. & **-ly**. According to, by means of, statutes.

statute, n. [1. státūt; 2. stǽtjūt], fr. O. Fr. *statūt*, fr. L. Lat. *statūtum*, 'law, decree', fr. P.P. type of *statuere*, 'to cause to stand, set up, erect; to establish, constitute; to determine', fr. *statum*, P.P. type of *stāre*, 'to stand', see **state** (I.). **1.** Enactment of a legislative body, expressly stated and fully authorized; act of parliament: *declaratory statute*, giving authoritative explanation of previous statute; *private statute*, applying to individuals only; *statutes at large*, statutes of legislative body, in full as originally enacted, and not abridged. **2.** Decree, ordinance, rule, of corporation, founder of institution &c., made as permanent rule.

statute-book, n. Register of statutes.

statute-law, n. Law expressed in statutes; contrasted with *common law*.

statutory, adj. [1. státūturi; 2. stǽtjutəri]. **statute** & **-ory**. Pertaining to, in the form of, depending on, enacted by, a statute.

staunch (I.), **stanch**, adj. [1. stawnch, stahnch; 2. stōn(t)ʃ, stān(t)ʃ], fr. O. Fr. *estanche*, 'seaworthy, watertight; staunch, reliable'; cp. O. Fr. *estanchier*, 'to stop the flow', & see **stanch** (I.). Reliable, dependable, trustworthy, loyal.

staunch (II.), vb., variant of **stanch** (I.).

staunchly, adv. **staunch** (I.) & **-ly**. In a staunch manner; loyally.

staunchness, n. See prec. & **-ness**. Quality of being staunch.

stauroscope, n. [1. stṓroskōp; 2. stṓrəskoup], fr. Gk. *staurós*, 'stake, pile; cross'; cogn. w. Lat. *staurāre*, 'to stand', see **restore**; cp. O.N. *staurr*, 'post', see **steer** (I.), fr. base **stāu-*, **stū-*, 'to be upright', parallel to **stā-*, **stə-*, 'to stand', see **stand**, **state**, & **-scope**. Instrument for determining the direction of polarized light in crystals.

stauroscopic, adj. [1. stṓroskópik; 2. stṓrəskópik]. Prec. & **-ic**. Pertaining to, carried out by, a stauroscope.

stave (I.), n. [1. stāv; 2. steiv]. M.E. *stāve*, fr. inflected form of O.E. *stæf*, 'bar, staff', see **staff** (I.). **1.** Curved and shaped strip of wood forming part of wall of cask, pail &c. **2.** Rung of ladder. **3.** Stanza, verse, section, of poem or song. **4.** (mus.) Group of lines and intermediate spaces used for showing relative pitch of notes; staff.

stave (II.), vb. trans., fr. prec. **1.** To furnish with staves. **2.** *Stave in*, to break, strike a hole in, break through: *to stave in a cask, side of boat* &c. **3.** *Stave off*, to keep off, defer, delay progress or performance of: *to stave off bankruptcy, arrest, starvation* &c.

stave-rhyme, n. After Germ. *stabreim*. Alliteration, esp. as prominent feature of verse.

stavesacre, n. [1. stā́vzāker; 2. stéivzeikə], fr. O. Fr. *stavesaigre*, fr. Med. Lat. *staphisagria*, fr. Gk. *(a)staphís*, 'raisins'; cp. Gk. *staphulḗ*, 'bunch of grapes'; prob. cogn. w. Scrt. *stambhaš*, 'pillar'; *stabhnāti*, 'to lean'; Lith. *stébas*, 'rod'; O.E. *stæf*, 'rod, staff', see **staff** (I.). The second element is Gk. *agría*, 'wild', cogn. w. *agrós*, 'field', q.v. under **agronomy**. Kind of Southern European larkspur, the seeds of which have emetic properties.

stay (I.), vb. trans. & intrans. [1. stā; 2. stei], fr. O. Fr. *estayer*, fr. M. Du. *stade*, 'support, prop'; cogn. w. O.H.G. *stat*; Goth. *staþs*; O.E. *stede*, 'place'; see **stead**. **A.** trans. **1. a** To check, restrain, hold back, stop or hinder progress of: *to stay the spread of a disease*; Phr. *to stay one's hand*, refrain from action; **b** specif. (law) to delay, defer, suspend, postpone: *to stay judgement, proceedings*. **2.** To retain one's energy, continue, last out, during: *to stay the course*. **B.** intrans. **1.** To remain, stop, refrain, from departure; be continuously in specified place or condition: *to* *have no time to stay; to stay where one is; to stay in bed; to stay still; the fine weather has come to stay.* **2.** To have a temporary abode, reside for a time, be a guest, visitor: *to stay at the seaside; to stay with friends, at a hotel* &c.; (colloq.) *I don't live here, I'm only staying.* **3.** (in imperat., archaic) To stop, halt, cease motion, speech &c.: *stay! not so fast!* **4.** To be capable of prolonged effort, endure, last out: *to be unable to stay to the end of a race; staying power.*

stay (II.), n., fr. prec. **1.** Act of staying, period of continuance in one place &c.: *to make a long stay.* **2.** Restraint, controlling influence: *to put a stay on one's thoughts.* **3.** (legal) Postponement, suspension, of proceedings &c.: *stay of execution,* of writ &c. **4.** (fig.) Endurance, persistence, power of sustained effort.

stay (III.), n. In specif. naut. sense, fr. O.E. *stæg,* 'rope for supporting mast'; but cp. also O. Fr. *estai,* 'prop', borrowed fr. Gmc. word, e.g. O. Du. *stag,* cogn. w. the O.E. Largely confused w. **stay** (I.). **1.** (naut.) Rope supporting mast or spar. Phr. *in stays,* going about. **2. a** A prop, support, strut; **b** a moral support; a stand-by: *religion is the stay of thousands in times of trouble.* **3.** (pl.) *Stays,* tightly fitting garment, stiffened with whalebone, worn by women on the upper portion of the body to give support to the figure; corset.

stay (IV.), vb. trans., fr. prec., influenced by **stay** (I.). **1.** To support, prop, by means of a stay or stays. **2.** To support, sustain; to satisfy: *to stay one's stomach; to stay one's appetite.* **3.** *Stay up,* to support by means of a stay or prop.

stay-at-home, adj. & n. [1. stá at hōm; 2. stéi ət houm]. **1.** adj. Addicted to staying at home. **2.** n. Stay-at-home person.

stay-bar, n. Bar used as support in building, machinery &c.

stayer, n. [1. stáer; 2. stéiə]. **stay** (I.) & **-er.** One who stays; specif. (colloq.) person, horse &c. capable of prolonged effort.

stay-lace, n. Cord for lacing stays.

stayless, adj. [1. stáles; 2. stéilis]. **stay** (II.) & **-less.** **1.** Without support. **2.** Not wearing stays.

stay-maker, n. Manufacturer of stays or corsets.

stay-rod, n. Stay-bar.

staysail, n. [1. stásl; 2. stéisl]. Sail extended on a stay.

stead, n. [1. sted; 2. sted]. O.E., M.E. *stede,* 'place'; O.H.G. *stat;* cp. Goth. *staþs;* O.N. *staðr,* 'place'; cogn. w. Lat. *status,* 'position', see **status** &c. **1.** Place, in Phr. *I am come in his stead, in the stead of,* as substitute for; cp. **instead.** **2.** Service, advantage; in Phr. *it will stand, has stood, me in good stead.*

-stead, fr. prec.; in compounds *farmstead, homestead* &c.

steadfast, adj. [1. stédfəst; 2. stédfəst]. O.E. *stedefæst;* **stead** & **fast** (I.). **1. a** (archaic) Firmly fixed, unshakable: *'the stedfast ground'* (Spenser, 'F. Q.'); **b** intent, steady, unwavering: *a steadfast gaze.* **2.** (in moral sense) Firm, constant, steady; enduring, unwavering: *a steadfast faith* &c.

steadfastly, adv. Prec. & **-ly.** In a steadfast manner.

steadfastness, n. See prec. & **-ness.** Quality of being steadfast.

steadily, adv. [1. stédili; 2. stédili]. **steady** (I.) & **-ly.** In a steady manner.

steadiness, n. [1. stédines; 2. stédinis]. See prec. & **-ness.** State or quality of being steady.

steading, n. [1. stéding; 2. stédiŋ]. **stead** & **-ing.** Farmstead.

steady (I.), adj. [1. stédi; 2. stédi]. M.E. *stēdi,* 'stable, steady'; **stead** & **-y** (IV.). **1.** Firmly supported, not liable to fall, shake, or totter: *hold the ladder steady; a steady hand,* (i.) one which does not tremble; (ii.) (fig.) resolute leadership, guidance, command. **2.** Uniform, regular, constant, not fluctuating; uninterrupted: *a steady light, improvement, flow of talk* &c. **3.** Firm, unwavering, constant: *a steady look, faith* &c. **4.** Sober and regular in conduct &c.; not erratic or dissipated: *a very steady young man.* **5.** (naut.) In Phr. *keep her steady,* order to keep ship on her course. **6.** *Steady!,* command to slacken speed, to be cautious, prepare for careful action &c.

steady (II.), vb. trans. & intrans., fr. prec. **1.** trans. (lit. and fig.) To make, cause to become, steady (in various senses of adj.). **2.** intrans. To become steady.

steady (III.), n., fr. **steady** (I.). Rest for supporting hand, tool &c., when at work.

steak, n. [1. stāk; 2. steik]. M.E. *stēke,* fr. O.N. *steik,* lit. 'something stuck on a spit; a steak'; cp. O.N. *steikja,* 'to roast on a spit'; cogn. w. O.E. *stician,* 'to stab, pierce'; see **stick** (I.). **a** Thick slice of meat or fish for grilling or frying; often preceded by specifying word: *beef-steak, cod-steak, rump-steak* &c.; **b** specif., beef-steak.

steal, vb. trans. & intrans. [1. stēl; 2. stil]. O.E. *stelan;* M.E. *stēlen,* 'to steal; hide; move stealthily'; cp. Goth. *stilan;* O.H.G. *stelan;* O.N. *stela,* 'to steal, hide'; origin uncertain. **A.** trans. **1.** To seize (the property of another) unlawfully, and appropriate it to one's own use or purpose. Phr. *to steal a march on,* gain an advantage over another by anticipating a move of his. **2. a** To gain by stealth or art, obtain without permission: *to steal a kiss, a glance at* &c.; **b** to win subtly by art or cunning: *to steal a person's heart.* **B.** intrans. **1.** To practise stealing; to thieve: *'Too proud to beg but not ashamed to steal'.* **2. a** To pass, glide, move, furtively, silently: *he stole cautiously round to the back-door; clouds stole across the face of the moon;* **b** to invade, overwhelm gradually: *a sense of peace and happiness stole over him.* **3.** *Steal away,* to slip, go, away, furtively and silently; *steal out,* slip out silently &c.

stealth, n. [1. stelth; 2. stelþ]. Prec. & **-th** (I.). Secret, concealed, furtive action or movement: *'Do good by stealth and blush to find it fame'* (Pope, Epilogue to Satires).

stealthily, adv. [1. stélthili; 2. stélþili]. **stealthy** & **-ly.** In a stealthy manner; secretly, furtively.

stealthiness, n. [1. stélthines; 2. stélþinis]. Next word & **-ness.** State or quality of being stealthy.

stealthy, adj. [1. stélthi; 2. stélþi]. **stealth** & **-y** (IV.). Characterized by, performed with, stealth; furtive, secret; cautious: *a stealthy tread, glance, whisper* &c.

steam (I.), n. [1. stēm; 2. stim]. O.E. *stēam,* 'exhalation, vapour, steam'; M.E. *stēm,* 'steam, flame'; cp. M. Du. *stoom,* further connexions unknown. **1.** Water in the form of vapour; transparent elastic gas produced from water by boiling; used for heating, cooking, and under pressure as motive power &c.; *dry, wet, steam,* steam without or with a mixture of suspended particles of water; *saturated steam,* in contact with water at the same temperature; *superheated steam,* not in contact with water but with addition of heat, thus increasing volume and temperature. Phr. *to get up steam,* (colloq., fig.) to prepare oneself for special effort. **2.** Cloudy mass or film, mist, formed by partially condensed vapour: *windows covered with steam.*

steam (II.), vb. intrans. & trans. O.E. *stēman,* 'to give out an odour'; see prec. **A.** intrans. **1. a** To give out steam: *the kettle was steaming on the hob;* **b** to give out vapour: *the fields are steaming in the frosty air; a horse steams after a hard gallop; he wiped his steaming forehead; steam away,* (of water) to become exhausted, dissipated, in the form of steam or vapour. **2.** To move along by means of steam: *the train steamed into the station.* **B.** trans. To subject to the influence of, bring into contact with, steam; specif., to cook (food) by this means.

steamboat, n. [1. stḗmbōt; 2. stímbout]. Vessel driven by steam.

steam-boiler, n. Boiler in which steam is generated for engine &c.

steam-box, n. Chamber through which steam passes from boiler to cylinder of engine.

steam-brake, n. Brake worked by steam.

steam-chest, n. Steam-box.

steam-colour, n. Colour printed on material &c. by action of steam.

steam-engine, n. Engine worked by action of steam.

steamer, n. [1. stḗmer; 2. stímə]. **steam** & **-er.** One who, that which, steams; specif. **a** steamship; **b** domestic utensil for cooking food by steam.

steam-gas, n. Gas produced by superheating steam.

steam-gauge, n. Device for indicating the pressure of steam.

steam-hammer, n. Powerful machine hammer worked by steam.

steam-heat, n. **1.** Heat required to convert water at freezing-point into steam. **2.** Heat given off by steam.

steaminess, n. [1. stḗmines; 2. stíminis]. **steamy** & **-ness.** State or quality of being steamy.

steam-jacket, n. Chamber filled with steam, enclosing a cylinder in machinery.

steam-navvy, n. Excavating machine worked by steam.

steam-port, n. Opening for the passage of steam, esp. between steam-chest and cylinder.

steam-power, n. Steam employed as motive power &c.

steam-roller, n. Heavy roller, propelled by steam, for levelling roads.

steamship, n. [1. stḗmship; 2. stímʃip]. Large vessel driven by steam.

steam-tight, adj. Capable of resisting passage or pressure of steam.

steam-whistle, n. Powerful whistle worked by a jet of steam.

steamy, adj. [1. stḗmi; 2. stími]. **steam** (I.) & **-y.** **a** Of the nature of, resembling, steam; vaporous; **b** covered with, enveloped in, steam; teeming with, giving off, vapour; misty, hazy.

stearate, n. [1. stḗarāt; 2. stíəreit]. See **stearin** & **-ate.** A salt of stearic acid.

stearic, adj. [1. stēárik; 2. stiǽrik]. See next word & **-ic.** Of, derived from, stearin; *stearic acid,* fatty acid obtained from stearin and used for making candles &c.

stearin, n. [1. stḗarin; 2. stíərin], fr. Gk. *stéar,* 'fat'; see under **steat(o)-,** & **-in.** **1.** White, fatty, crystalline compound contained in many animal and vegetable fats. **2.** Stearic acid.

stearinery, n. [1. stḗarineri; 2. stíərinəri]. Prec. & **-ery.** Manufacture of stearin.

steatite, n. [1. stḗatīt; 2. stíətait]. **steat(o)-** & **-ite.** Massive variety of talc, usually white or yellow; soapstone.

steatitic, adj. [1. stēatítik; 2. stiətítik]. Prec. & **-ic.** Of, pertaining to, resembling, containing, composed of, steatite.

steat(o)-, pref. representing Gk. *stéāt-,* stem of *stéar,* 'fat'; cp. Gk. *staîs,* 'dough'; *stîā,* 'pebble'; *stiphrós,* 'hard, firm'; cogn. w. Lat. *stīpāre,* 'to press together, cram', see **stipate;** Scrt. *styā́yatē,* 'to congeal, coagulate, harden'; fr. base **stī-, *st(e)jā-,* 'to condense, congeal', seen also in Goth. *stains;* see under **stone;** cp. also **stiff;** perh. ultimately allied to the base **stā-* &c., 'to stand'; see **stand** (I.). Fat, fatty.

steatopygia, n. [1. stēatōpíjia; 2. stíətoupáidžiə]. Prec. & Gk. *pūgḗ,* 'buttocks'; prob. w. orig. sense 'swelling', & cogn. w. Scrt. *pūgaś,* 'heap, crowd'. Abnormal accumulation of fat on the buttocks, esp. as in some primitive African races.

steatopygous, adj. [1. stēatōpígus; 2. stíətoupáigəs]. Prec. & **-ous.** Affected by, exhibiting, steatopygia.

steatosis, n. [1. stēatṓsis; 2. stiətóusis]. **steato-** & **-osis.** Fatty degeneration of an organ.

steed, n. [1. stēd ; 2. stīd]. O.E. *stēda*, 'horse, stallion' ; M.E. *stēde* ; cp. O.E. *stōd*, 'stud', see **stud** ; cp. O.N. *stōð*, 'stud' ; O.E. *stōd*, Pret. sing. of *standan*, 'to stand', see **stand** (I.). (poet. or facet.) Horse.

steedless, adj. [1. stḗdles ; 2. stídlis]. Prec. & **-less**. Without a steed.

steel (I.), n. [1. stēl ; 2. stīl]. O.E. *stēle*, (W.S. *stīele*) ; O.H.G. *stahal* ; M. Du. *stael* ; O.N. *stāl*, 'steel' ; O. Prussian *stakla*, 'steel' ; Kluge connects w. Zend *stuχra*, 'firm, strong'. **1.** Form of iron, containing a certain proportion of carbon alloy, hardened and toughened by heating to a very high temperature and cooling suddenly. **2.** Any of several objects made of steel ; specif. **a** sword, cutting weapon ; Phrs. *cold steel*, weapons of steel &c., as distinct from fire-arms ; *a foeman worthy of one's steel*, (chiefly fig.) a redoubtable opponent ; **b** bar of steel with roughened or fluted surface for sharpening knives ; **c** thin, flexible strip of steel for stiffening dress, corsets &c. ; **d** piece of steel for striking fire from flint.

steel (II.), adj., fr. prec. Made of, resembling, containing, steel.

steel (III.), vb. trans., fr. prec. **1.** To cover, strengthen, edge, with steel. **2.** (fig.) To harden, make obdurate, firm, unyielding ; esp. *to steel one's heart*.

steel-clad, adj. Covered with steel ; clad in armour.

steel-engraving, n. Engraving by means of a steel plate.

steelify, vb. trans. [1. stḗlifī ; 2. stílifai]. **steel** (I.) & *-i-* & **-fy**. To convert into steel.

steeliness, n. [1. stḗlines ; 2. stílinis]. **steely** & **-ness**. State or quality of being steely.

steel-plated, adj. [1. stēl plāted ; 2. stīl pleitid]. Covered with steel plates, armoured : *a steel-plated ship* &c.

steel-points, n. Small steel studs or nails fixed in soles of shoes to prevent slipping.

steelwork, n. [1. stḗlwërk ; 2. stílwāk]. Tools and other goods made of steel.

steely, adj. [1. stḗli ; 2. stíli]. **steel** (I.) & **-y** (IV.). **a** Of, pertaining to, like, made of, steel ; **b** (fig.) obdurate, relentless, unyielding.

steelyard, n. [1. stḗlyard ; 2. stíljād], fr. the Steelyard, London meeting-place of German traders ; fr. Germ. *stahlhof*, 'sample yard', misunderstood as 'steel yard'. Instrument with a short arm for supporting object to be weighed, and a weight moving on long, graduated arm.

steen, vb. trans. [1. stēn ; 2. stīn]. Cp. O.E. *stǣnan*, 'to pelt with stones ; to set with stones ; to bejewel' ; fr. **stān-jan*, fr. O.E. *stān*, see **stone** (I.). To line a (well) with stone or brick.

steenbok, n. [1. stḗnbok ; 2. stínbɔk]. Du. *steenbok*, fr. *steen*, 'stone', q.v. under **stone** (I.), & *bok*, 'buck', see **buck**. Small S. African rock-dwelling antelope.

steening, n. [1. stḗning ; 2. stíniŋ]. **steen** & **-ing**. Material used for lining a well.

steenkirk, n. [1. stḗnkërk ; 2. stínkāk]. Named after battle of Steenkerke, in Belgium, 1692. (hist.) Kind of lace cravat, wig, buckle &c. of late 17th cent.

steep (I.), adj. [1. stēp ; 2. stīp]. O.E. *stēap*, 'lofty, tall ; prominent' ; M.E. *stēp(e)*, 'steep, difficult' ; cp. O. Fris. *stāp*, & see **stoop** (I.). **1.** Having a pronounced slope, making a considerable angle with the level, ascending or descending sharply : *a steep hill, roof* &c. ; *steep stairs*. **2.** (colloq.) Exorbitant, excessive, considerably above what is normal or expected : *steep prices, demands* &c. ; hence, preposterous, intolerable : *I thought his conduct a bit steep*.

steep (II.), n., fr. prec. (chiefly poet.) Precipitous slope, hill ; steep ascent or descent : *the rugged steeps of the mountains*.

steep (III.), vb. trans. M.E. *stēpen*, 'to steep', fr. O.N. *steypa*, 'to pour ; to rush down ; to overthrow' ; cogn. w. **stoop** (I.). **1.** To soak in liquid. **2.** To bathe, wet thoroughly, saturate, with liquid. **3.** (fig.) To soak, immerse, imbue, impregnate : *steeped in crime, blood, sorrow* &c. ; *to steep oneself in a subject, a language* &c.

steep (IV.), n., fr. prec. **1.** Act of steeping ; state of being steeped. **2.** Liquid in which anything is steeped.

steepen, vb. trans. & intrans. [1. stḗpen ; 2. stípən]. **steep** (I.) & **-en** (V.). **1.** trans. To make steep. **2.** intrans. To become, grow, steep or steeper.

steeper, n. [1. stḗper ; 2. stípə]. **steep** (III.) & **-er**. Vessel containing articles in steep.

steeple, n. [1. stḗpl ; 2. stípl]. O.E., M.E. *stēpel*, 'steeple', fr. **stēapil*, cp. O.E. *stēap*, 'lofty', see **steep** (I.). Tall, tapering structure, usually surmounted by a spire, rising above roof of a building, esp. a church, and often containing a belfry.

steeplechase, n. [1. stḗplchās ; 2. stípltʃèis]. Horse-race across country, over hedges, walls, &c., or on a fixed track with built-up obstacles ; so called because the first race of the kind was across country in a bee-line for a distant steeple.

steeplechaser, n. [1. stḗplchāser ; 2. stípltʃèisə]. Horse running, man riding, in steeplechase.

steeplechasing, n. [1. stḗplchāsing ; 2. stípltʃèisiŋ]. Steeplechases as a form of sport.

steeple-crowned, adj. [1. stḗpl kròund ; 2. stípl kràund]. (of hat) Having a tall, tapering crown.

steepled, adj. [1. stḗpld ; 2. stípld]. **steeple** & **-ed**. Having, surmounted by, a steeple.

steeplejack, n. [1. stèpljāk ; 2. stípldžǽk]. Man employed to scale steeples, chimneys, and other tall structures for purposes of repair &c.

steeple-top, n. Bowhead whale.

steeplewise, adv. [1. stḗplwīz ; 2. stíplwàiz]. Like a steeple.

steeply, adv. [1. stḗpli ; 2. stípli]. **steep** (I.) & **-ly**. In a steep manner ; with a steep slope.

steepness, n. [1. stḗpnes ; 2. stípnis]. See prec. & **-ness**. State or quality of being steep.

steepy, adj. [1. stḗpi ; 2. stípi]. **steep** (I.) & **-y** (IV.). (poet.) Steep, sheer.

steer (I.), vb. trans. & intrans. [1. stēr ; 2. stiə]. O.E. *stēoran*, 'to steer, guide' ; M.E. *stēren* ; cp. O.H.G. *stiuran* ; O. Fris. *stiura* ; O.N. *stýra*, 'to steer' ; Goth. *stiurjan*, 'to confirm, maintain' ; cp. O.E. *stēor*, 'rudder' ; O.N. *staurr*, 'post' ; O.H.G. *stiura*, 'pillar' ; Gk. *staurós*, 'pole' ; see **stauroscope** ; fr. base **st(h)ēu-r-*, **st(h)əu-r-*, &c., 'firm', parallel to base **stā-* &c., 'to stand', see **stand** (I.), **state** (I.) ; see further **stow, style** (III.). **A.** trans. **1.** To direct movements and direction of (vessel) by means of rudder or instrument used as rudder. **2. a** To guide movements of (oneself, motor-car &c.), keep on a definite course ; **b** (fig.) to direct, bring, guide, to specified position or condition : *to steer one's country to peace and prosperity*. **3.** To pursue, pick out, find, by steering : *to steer one's way* ; *to steer a steady course* (lit. and fig.). **B.** intrans. To direct course of vessel &c. by means of a rudder or other instrument ; Phr. *to steer clear of*, (chiefly in fig. sense) to avoid ; (colloq.) *where are you steering for?*, where are you going, heading?

steer (II.), n. O.E. *stēor* ; M.E. *steer* ; cp. Goth. *stiur* ; O.H.G. *stior* ; cp. further O.H.G. *stūri*, 'strong, heavy' ; L.G. *stūr*, 'large' ; cogn. w. Scrt. *sthūrás*, 'thick, dense, heavy' ; Gk. *stúrax*, 'butt of lance' ; *staurós*, 'pole, pillar' ; see **stauroscope, steer** (I.). The connexion with Lat. *taurus*, 'bull', see **Taurus**, is improbable. Young ox, bullock.

steerable, adj. [1. stḗrabl ; 2. stíərəbl]. **steer** (I.) & **-able**. Capable of being steered.

steerage, n. [1. stḗrij ; 2. stíəridž]. **steer** (I.) & **-age**. **1. a** Act or process of steering ; **b** the manner in which a vessel answers to the helm. **2. a** The end of a vessel from which she is steered ; the stern ; hence, **b** that part of a vessel in which are the quarters of passengers paying the lowest rates ; **c** part of berth-deck of warship used as quarters for junior officers &c.

steerage-way, n. Movement of vessel sufficient to enable it to answer to the helm.

steerer, n. [1. stḗrer ; 2. stíərə]. **steer** (I.) & **-er**. One who steers.

steering-gear, n. [1. stḗring gḗr ; 2. stíəriŋ gìə]. Mechanism controlling the steering of a vessel, the rudder &c.

steering-wheel, n. Wheel controlling the rudder of ship, motor-car &c.

steersman, n. [1. stḗrzman ; 2. stíəzmən]. Person steering a vessel.

steersmanship, n. [1. stḗrzmanship ; 2. stíəzmənʃip]. Skill in steering.

steeve (I.), vb. intrans. & trans. [1. stēv ; 2. stīv]. Scots variant of **stiff**. (naut.) **1.** intrans. (of bowsprit) To form an angle with the plane of the horizon. **2.** trans. To cause (bowsprit) to steeve.

steeve (II.), n., fr. prec. (naut.) Angle made by bowsprit with plane of horizon.

steeve (III.), vb. trans., fr. O. Fr. *estiver*, 'to cram', fr. Lat. *stīpāre*, 'to press closely ; to cram', see **stipate** ; cp. also **stevedore**. To pack, stow (cargo), with a steeve.

steeve (IV.), n., fr. prec. Spar with block at one end used in stowing cargo.

steganography, n. [1. stèganógrafi ; 2. stègənɔ́grəfi], fr. Gk. *steganós*, 'covered', fr. *stégein*, 'to cover closely ; to conceal' ; cp. Gk. *stégos*, 'roof, house' ; cogn. w. Lat. *tegere*, 'to cover', see **tegument** ; O.E. *þæc*, 'roof', see **thatch** ; for the second element, see **-graphy**. Art, science or practice of writing in cipher.

Steinberger, n. [1. stínbërger ; 2. stáinbāgə], fr. Steinberg, near Wiesbaden. Kind of white, Rhenish wine produced on the estate of Steinberg.

steinbock, n. [1. stínbok ; 2. stáinbɔk]. Germ., fr. *stein*, 'stone, rock', q.v. under **stone** (I.), & *bock*, 'buck', see **buck**. Steenbok.

stelar, adj. [1. stḗlar ; 2. stílə]. Next word & **-ar**. Pertaining to, executed on, a stele.

stele, n. [1. stḗlē ; 2. stílī]. Gk. *stḗlē*, 'block of stone, as gravestone, buttress, for inscription &c.' ; cp. Gk. *stéllein*, 'to arrange, set in order' ; *stolḗ*, 'adjustment, equipment ; clothing', cp. **stole** (I.) ; *steleón*, 'handle' ; cogn. w. O.E. *stela*, 'handle', *still*, 'quiet', see **still** (I.) ; Scrt. *sthálati*, 'stands' ; Lat. *stolidus*, 'stupid', see **stolid**. Ancient Greek inscribed or sculptured upright stone slab, as monument, gravestone &c.

stelene, adj. [1. stḗlēn ; 2. stílīn]. Prec. & **-ene**. Stelar.

stellar, adj. [1. stélar ; 2. stélə], fr. L. Lat. *stēllāris*, 'of a star', fr. Lat. *stēlla*, 'star', fr. **stēr-lā* ; cogn. w. Gk. *astḗr*, 'star', see **astral**, & w. O.E. *steorra*, 'star', see **star**. Connected with, pertaining to, the stars : *stellar light* &c.

stellate(d), adj. [1. stélāt(ed) ; 2. stéleit(id)], fr. Lat. *stēllāt-(um)*, P.P. type of *stēllāre*, 'to set with stars', fr. *stēlla*, 'star', see **stellar**, & **-ed**. Star-shaped, radiating from a centre.

stellately, adv. [1. stélātli ; 2. stéleitli]. Prec. & **-ly**. In a stellate manner.

stelliferous, adj. [1. stelíferus ; 2. stelífərəs], fr. Lat. *stēlla*, 'star', see **stellar**, & *-i-* & **-ferous**. Set with many stars.

stelliform, adj. [1. stéliform ; 2. stélifōm], fr. Lat. *stēlla*, 'star', see prec., & *-i-* & **-form**. Star-shaped.

stellular, adj. [1. stélūlar ; 2. stéljulə], fr. Lat. *stēllula*, 'little star', fr. *stēlla*, 'star', see **stellar**, & **-ule** & **-ar**. **a** Shaped like a small star ; **b** set with small stars.

stellulate, adj. [1. stélūlāt ; 2. stéljuleit], fr. Lat. *stēllula*, 'little star', see prec., & **-ate**. Stellular.

stem (I.), n. [1. stem ; 2. stɛm]. O.E. *stæfn, stefn, stemn*, 'stem of tree ; prow of ship ; family' ; M.E. *stam, stem* ; cp. O.N. *stafn* ; O.L.G. *stamn* ; O.H.G. *stam*, 'stem, prow' ; Du. *stam*, 'trunk' ; cogn. w. O.E. *stæf*, see **staff** (I.). **1.** Main part, body, support ; trunk or stalk of tree, plant &c., as distinct from branches &c., usually ascending and aerial, but sometimes prostrate and subterranean.

2. Slender branch from main stem of plant, supporting flower, fruit, or leaf; secondary stalk. 3. Slender, stem-like part or growth; anything resembling a stem in form or function; specif. a slender part between foot and bowl of wineglass, egg-cup &c.; b short perpendicular line projecting above or below certain notes in written or printed music; c rod projecting from top of watch, by means of which the watch is wound; d (zool.) slender stalk supporting organ &c.; e (print.) vertical stroke forming part of letter. 4. (archaic) Family, stock, ancestry, lineage: *the stem of Jesse.* 5. Part of word to which inflexional endings are added. 6. (naut.) Upright, usually curved, timber or metal bar, to which timbers of both sides of ship are joined at the bow; *false stem*, sharp-edged timber in front of stem, serving as cutwater. Phr. *from stem to stern*, throughout whole length of ship.

stem (II.), vb. trans., fr. prec. To remove stem(s) of.

stem (III.), vb. trans. M.E. *stemmen*, 'to stop'; cp. M.H.G. *stemmen*; O.N. *stemma*, 'to stop'; prob. cogn. w. **stammer** (I.). 1. To check, hold back, dam up: *to stem a torrent, flood, the flow of water, of blood* &c.; (also fig.) *to stem the flood of a person's eloquence.* 2. To make progress, headway, against; chiefly in Phr. *to stem the tide*; often indistinguishable from No. 1 in fig. uses: *to stem the tide of opposition* &c.

stemless, adj. [1. stémles; 2. stémlis]. **stem** (I.) & **-less**. Without a stem.

stemlet, n. [1. stémlet; 2. stémlit]. **stem** (I.) & **-let**. Small stem or stalk.

stemma, n. [1. stéma; 2. stémə]. Lat. *stemma*, 'garland; pedigree; nobility', fr. Gk. *stémma*, 'wreath', fr. *stéphein*, 'to surround, wreathe, crown'; cp. Gk. *stéphanos*, 'crown'; cognates in other languages doubtful. 1. a Pedigree, genealogical tree; b hence family, descent, lineage. 2. (zool.) Simple eye or single facet of compound eye.

stemmed, adj. [1. stemd; 2. stɛmd]. **stem** (I.) & **-ed**. Having a stem; usually of specified character: *short-, rough-stemmed* &c.

stemmer, n. [1. stémer; 2. stémə]. **stem** (II.) & **-er**. Person employed in removing stems from tobacco-plants in making tobacco.

stemple, n. [1. stémpl; 2. stémpl]. Mod. Germ. *stempel*, 'a prop'; connected w. **stamp** (I.). 1. One of a series of cross-timbers forming steps in a shaft. 2. Timber supporting platform &c.

stem-winder, n. Keyless watch.

stench, n. [1. stench; 2. stɛn(t)ʃ]. O.E. *stenc*, 'smell, odour'; M.E. *stench*; fr. **stanki-*, gradational variant of O.E. *stincan*, 'to smell', see **stink** (I.). Strong, offensive smell. (Politer word than *stink*, n.)

stench-trap, n. Trap in sewer to prevent noxious smells from rising.

stencil (I.), n. [1. sténsil; 2. sténsil, sténsl]. Prob. fr. O. Fr. *estenceler*, 'to spangle', fr. *estencele*, 'spark', fr. Lat. *scintilla*, 'spark', see **scintillate**. 1. Thin metal plate perforated with series of holes forming a design through which colouring-matter is applied to a surface. 2. Pattern, design, produced by stencilling.

stencil (II.), vb. trans., fr. prec. 1. To apply, produce (design &c.), by means of a stencil. 2. To apply design to, produce pattern on, by means of a stencil.

stencil-plate, n. Stencil.

steno-, pref. representing Gk. *stenós*, 'narrow'; cp. Gk. *steinos*, 'confined space'; no certain cognates. Narrow; e.g. *stenosis*, constriction of the pores or other orifice.

stenochrome, n. [1. sténokrōm; 2. sténəkroum]. **steno-** & **chrome**. Print produced by stenochromy.

stenochromy, n. [1. stenókrumi; 2. stenɔ́krəmi]. Prec. & **-y** (I.). Art of printing in several colours at one impression by means of a group of pigment-blocks.

stenograph, n. [1. sténograhf; 2. sténəgrāf]. **steno-** & **-graph**. 1. Character used in shorthand. 2. Script in shorthand. 3. Machine for writing in a form of shorthand.

stenographer, n. [1. stenógrafer; 2. stenɔ́grəfə]. Prec. & **-er**. Shorthand writer.

stenographic, adj. [1. stènográfik; 2. stènəgrǽfik]. **stenograph** & **-ic**. Connected with, written in, shorthand.

stenographically, adv. [1. stènográfikali; 2. stènəgrǽfikəli]. Prec. & **-al** & **-ly**. By means of shorthand.

stenographist, n. [1. stenógrafist; 2. stenɔ́grəfist]. Next word & **-ist**. Stenographer.

stenography, n. [1. stenógrafi; 2. stenɔ́grəfi]. **steno-** & **-graphy**. Shorthand; art of writing shorthand.

stenolalism, n. [1. stenólalizm; 2. stenɔ́ləlizəm], fr. **steno-** & Gk. *lálein*, 'to speak, chatter', see **alalia**, & **-ism**. Formation of a name or term from the initial letters or syllables of full title; e.g. *Anzac* (Australian and New Zealand Army Corps), *Cheka* (Chrezvychainaya Komisiya).

stenotype, n. [1. sténotīp; 2. sténətaip]. **steno-** & **type**. Letter, group of letters, representing in shorthand a word or phrase.

Stentor, n. [1. sténtōr; 2. sténtɔ̄]. Lat. *Stentor*, fr. Gk. *Sténtōr*. Person with unusually powerful voice; so called from the Greek herald of this name in Trojan war.

stentorian, adj. [1. stentṓrian; 2. stentɔ́riən]. Prec. & **-ian**. Very loud or powerful: *a stentorian voice; stentorian tones.*

step (I.), n. [1. step; 2. stɛp]. O.E. *stæpe*, 'a step; a tread in stairs; degree'. See next word. 1. Movement in walking, involving lifting the foot and putting it down further forward. Phrs. *step by step*, gradually; *to turn one's steps (towards* &c.*)*, to go; *to retrace one's steps*, go back, return; *to watch one's steps*, act cautiously and prudently. 2. a Space covered by a step; a pace; b a short distance: *it is only a step to the inn.* Phr. *unable to walk a step*, not able to walk at all. 3. Sound of a footfall: *steps were heard approaching.* 4. Mark made by a foot on the ground; footprint; (chiefly fig.) *to tread in the steps of*, follow example of, adopt same career &c. as. 5. Mode of walking, tread: *a light, heavy, ponderous &c. step.* 6. One of a series of characteristic movements executed by the feet in a dance. 7. Regular, rhythmical pace made in marching or walking; esp. one made simultaneously by each of two or of more persons walking or marching together, so timed that each person advances the left or right leg at the same moment as all the others: *in step, out of step; to keep step (with).* 8. An act performed with a view to securing some object; means, mode of procedure, measures. Phrs. *to take steps*, adopt means, measures &c.; *to take steps to avoid the repetition of an offence, to abolish a nuisance* &c.; *a false step*, wrong, foolish, measure. 9. (fig.) A degree, stage, in progress, advance, or retrogression: *we have made a great step forward in our negotiations; a few steps nearer the grave.* 10. An object designed as, or serving for, a support for the feet in moving from one level to another; one of rising or falling series of shelves, ledges, spars &c., upon which the foot is placed in ascending or descending; specif. a one of the treads in a set of stairs: *a flight of steps*, a staircase; b ledges cut on face of a rock, bank &c. for placing the feet upon; c small projecting metal or wooden ledge, some few inches from the ground, to facilitate entering or leaving a vehicle; d (i.) one of the rungs of a ladder; (ii.) *steps, pair of steps*, light short ladder, with hinged prop which keeps it upright when opened; step-ladder; e object in nature resembling a step, e.g. a plateau, esp. one of a series of plateaux, on the side of a hill &c. 11. Higher or lower grade in rank: *a step in the peerage, in army rank* &c. Phr. *to get one's step*, be promoted to superior rank; *to rise a step in one's opinion, estimation* &c., be more highly thought of. 12. (mus.) Degree, interval, between notes of a scale. 13. (naut.) Socket in which lower end of mast rests. 14. (mechan.) Socket or support for shaft &c.

step (II.), vb. intrans. & trans. O.E. *stæppan, steppan*; M.E. *steppen*; cp. O.H.G. *steffan*; O. Fris. *steppa*; cp. O.E. *stæpe*, 'a step'; & further w. nasal, O.H.G. *stampfōn*, O.E *stempan*, 'to stamp with the feet', see **stamp** (I.). A. intrans. 1. To take a step or series of steps: *to step forward, back, over an obstacle, into a carriage, on a person's toe* &c. Phrs. *to step high*, raise foot high in taking a step; *to step out*, take long step, increase length of step; *to step short*, take too short a step. 2. To move forward, walk, esp. a short distance, or in specified manner: *to step lightly; to step out briskly.* In various colloq. Phrs.: *will you step inside*, come in (to the house or room); *step outside*, go out; *step upstairs*; (also fig.) *to step aside*, withdraw in favour of another; *step in*, intervene. B. trans. 1. To perform, execute, steps of (dance). Phr. *to step it*, to go on foot, to walk. 2. Also *step out*, to measure by stepping: *to step (out) the length of a room* &c. 3. To insert (mast) in socket &c., fix in position.

step-, pref. representing O.E. *stēop-*; M.E. *stēp-*; cp. O.N. *stiūp-*; O.H.G. *stiuf-, stiof-*; O. Fris. *stiap-, stiep-*, 'step'; cp. further O.H.G. *stiufan*, 'to bereave of parents, orphan'. Related by remarriage of one parent, e.g. *stepson, stepbrother, stepfather* &c.

stepbrother, n. [1. stépbrùdher; 2. stépbràðə]. Son of one's stepfather or stepmother.

stepchild, n. [1. stépchīld; 2. stéptʃaild]. Child of a husband or wife by a previous marriage.

stepdame, n. [1. stépdām; 2. stépdeim]. (archaic) Stepmother.

step-dance, n. Dance in which characteristic steps are executed.

stepdaughter, n. [1. stépdàwter; 2. stépdɔ̀tə]. Daughter of a husband or wife by a previous marriage.

stepfather, n. [1. stépfàhdher; 2. stépfàðə]. Second or subsequent husband of one's mother.

stephanotis, n. [1. stèfanótis; 2. stèfənóutis], fr. Gk. *stéphanos*, 'wreath, crown', q.v. under **stemma**, & *ōt-*, stem of *oûs*, 'ear', see **otalgia**. Genus of tropical, twining shrubs with very fragrant, waxy flowers.

step-ladder, n. Ladder with flat steps which is not leant up against a wall &c., but has a folding support opening at an angle.

stepmother, n. [1. stépmùdher; 2. stépmàðə]. One's father's second or subsequent wife; sometimes with implication of being unfeeling or negligent; also fig.: '*Oxford Street, stony-hearted stepmother*' (De Quincey).

stepmotherly, adj. [1. stépmùdherli; 2. stépmàðəli]. Prec. & **-ly**. Pertaining to, befitting, like, a stepmother, often in bad sense, unfeeling, neglectful.

stepney, n. [1. stépni; 2. stépni], fr. name of inventor. Also *stepney-wheel*, spare wheel carried on motor-car.

step-parent, n. Stepfather or stepmother.

steppe, n. [1. step; 2. stɛp]. Fr. or Germ., fr. Russ. *step.* Broad, open, treeless, uncultivated plain, esp. of Russia and Siberia.

stepped, adj. [1. stept; 2. stɛpt]. **step** (I.) & **-ed**. Having, furnished with, forming, a series of steps: *stepped gables.*

stepper, n. [1. stéper; 2. stépə]. **step** (II.) & **-er**. One who, that which, steps, esp. in specified manner: *a high stepper.*

stepping-stone, n. [1. stéping stòn; 2. stépiŋ stòun]. 1. One of a series of stones placed in stream so as to rise above water and form means of crossing. 2. (fig.) Means or instrument to an end; position which leads to further advancement: *a stepping-stone to promotion, fame* &c.

stepsister, n. [1. stépsìster; 2. stépsìstə]. Daughter of one's stepfather or stepmother.

stepson, n. [1. stépsun; 2. stépsan]. Son of a person's husband or wife by a previous marriage.

stepwise, adv. [1. stépwīz; 2. stépwaiz]. **step** (I.) & **-wise.** In steps, so as to form steps.

-ster, suff. representing O.E. *-estre*, agent suff.; in O.E. restricted to fem. ns. (cp. **spinster**), but in M.E. & Mod. Engl. used to form ns. of either gender; denoting a trade, occupations, e.g. *brewster*, but esp. **a** in surnames, *Webster*, *Baxter* &c., derived from these, & **b** (in depreciatory sense) *punster*, *rhymester*, *youngster* &c.

stercoraceous, adj. [1. stērkurā́shus; 2. stākəréiʃəs], fr. Lat. *stercor-*, stem of *stercus*, 'dung', perh. cogn. w. Lith. *trisziu*, 'to manure the ground'; Gk. *tárganon*, 'sour wine'; O.N. *þrekkr*, 'excrement'; for the second element see **-aceous.** Connected with, pertaining to, dung or excrement.

stercoral, adj. [1. stērkural; 2. stā́kərəl], fr. Lat. *stercor-*, stem of *stercus*, 'dung', see prec., & **-al.** Stercoraceous.

stereo, n. [1. stéreō, stḗrēō; 2. stériou, stíəriou]. Abbr. fr. **stereotype** (I.). Stereotype.

stereo-, pref. representing Gk. *stereós*, 'firm, stiff, solid'; cogn. w. O.H.G. *storrēn*, 'to rise stiffly'; cp. Goth. *(and)staurran*, 'to complain'; O.E. *stierne*, 'stiff, stern', see **stern** (I.). See also **stare**, & words there referred to. Solid.

stereobate, n. [1. stéreobàt; 2. stériəbèit]. **stereo-** & Gk. *bátēs*, 'that which treads, steps', cogn. w. **base** (I.). Solid or continuous substructure of building.

stereochemistry, n. [1. stéreōkémistri; 2. stérioukémistri]. **stereo-** & **chemistry.** Branch of chemistry dealing with the arrangement of atoms in the molecule.

stereochromy, n. [1. stéreōkrṑmi; 2. stérioukròumi]. **stereo-** & **chrome** & **-y** (I.). Process of painting with colours fixed by waterglass.

stereogram, n. [1. stéreogram; 2. stériəgræm]. **stereo-** & **-gram.** Drawing made by stereographic means.

stereographic(al), adj. [1. stèreográfik(l); 2. stèriəgrǽfik(l)]. **stereo-** & **-graphic** & **-al.** Relating to, executed by means of, stereography.

stereographically, adv. Prec. & **-ly.** By stereographic means.

stereography, n. [1. stèreógrafi; 2. stèriɔ́grəfi]. **stereo-** & **-graphy.** The art of representing solids on a plane surface.

stereome, n. [1. stéreōm; 2. stérioum], fr. Gk. *steréōma*, 'a solid body'; see **stereo-.** Strengthening or supporting tissue of the cells of plants.

stereometer, n. [1. stèreómeter; 2. stèriɔ́mitə]. **stereo-** & **-meter.** **1.** Instrument measuring volume of a body, capacity of a vessel &c. **2.** Instrument for determining specific gravity of liquids &c.

stereometric(al), adj. [1. stèreométrik(l); 2. stèriəmétrik(l)]. **stereo-** & **-metric** & **-al.** Relating to, done by means of, stereometry.

stereometry, n. [1. stèreómetri; 2. stèriɔ́mitri]. **stereo-** & **-metry.** The art of determining the dimensions of solid bodies.

stereopticon, n. [1. stèreóptikun; 2. stèriɔ́ptikən]. See **stereo-** & **optic.** Double magic-lantern for exhibiting dissolving views.

stereoscope, n. [1. stéreoskṑp; 2. stériəskòup]. **stereo-** & **-scope.** Optical instrument for representing to the eye as single object in relief two views of the object taken from slightly different angles.

stereoscopic, adj. [1. stèreoskópik; 2. stèriəskɔ́pik]. Prec. & **-ic.** Pertaining to, suitable for, of the nature of, a stereoscope.

stereoscopically, adv. [1. stèreoskópikali; 2. stèriəskɔ́pikəli]. Prec. & **-al** & **-ly.** By stereoscopic means.

stereoscopy, n. [1. stèreóskopi; 2. stèriɔ́skəpi]. **stereoscope** & **-y.** Art of making or using a stereoscope.

stereotype (I.) n. [1. stéreotīp; 2. stériətàip]. **stereo-** & **-type.** (print.) Metal plate cast in mould taken from page &c., set up in ordinary type.

stereotype (II.), vb. trans., fr. prec. **1. a** To cast (printing-plate) from a mould; **b** to print (book &c.) from stereotypes. **2.** (fig.) To fix once for all; reproduce always according to one and the same fixed pattern; to repeat unalterably as though always from the same mould: *stereotyped features, ideas, phrases, lectures* &c.

stereotyper, n. [1. stéreotīper; 2. stériətàipə]. Prec. & **-er.** Person engaged in printing from or making stereotypes.

stereotypist, n. [1. stéreotīpist; 2. stériətàipist]. **stereotype** & **-ist.** Stereotyper.

stereotypography, n. [1. stéreōtīpógrafi; 2. stérioutaipɔ́grəfi]. **stereotype** & *-o-* & **-graphy.** Art or practice of printing from stereotypes.

stereotypy, n. [1. stéreōtīpi; 2. stérioutàipi]. **stereotype** & **-y** (I.). Art of making stereotypes.

sterile, adj. [1. stéril; 2. stérail], fr. Lat. *sterilis*, 'unfruitful'; cogn. w. Scrt. *stariś*, 'barren cow'; Gk. *steîra*; Goth. *stairō*, 'sterile'; perh. fr. base **ster-*, 'to be stiff, rigid', q.v. under **stare, stereo-, stern** &c. **1.** (of animal, plant &c.) Incapable of reproducing itself in offspring; barren. **2.** (of soil, country &c.) Unproductive, infertile, unfruitful. **3.** (of food, liquid &c.) Containing no living bacteria, microbes &c. **4.** (of action, work &c.) Producing no result; ineffective. **5.** (of literary style &c.) Without life or interest; not stimulating; barren of suggestive ideas.

sterility, n. [1. sterı́liti; 2. sterı́liti], fr. Lat. *sterilitāt-(em)*, 'sterility'; **sterile** & **-ity.** State or quality of being sterile.

sterilization, n. [1. stèrilīzā́shun; 2. stèrilaizéiʃən]. Next word & **-ation.** Act of sterilizing; state of being sterilized.

sterilize, vb. trans. [1. stérilīz; 2. stérilaiz]. **sterile** & **-ize.** To make sterile; specif. **a** to deprive (animal) of reproductive power; **b** to render free of living organisms, esp. of bacteria: *to sterilize milk, surgical instruments* &c.

sterilizer, n. [1. sterilīzer; 2. stérilàizə]. Prec. & **-er.** One who, that which, sterilizes; esp. instrument, device, for sterilizing.

sterlet, n. [1. stḗrlet; 2. stā́lit], fr. Fr., fr. Russ. *sterlyadi*, apparently borrowed fr. a Fr. or Germ. form; cp. **sturgeon.** Kind of small sturgeon, yielding a superior variety of caviare.

sterling, adj. [1. stḗrling; 2. stā́liŋ]. In M.E., formerly supposed to be fr. *Easterling*, name given to traders of the Hanseatic League; in M.H.G. *sterlinc* was the name of a coin. Origin uncertain. **1.** (of British money, coinage, and of gold or silver) Of standard value, of quality fixed by Government: *sterling silver*; *five pounds sterling*. **2.** (fig.) Genuine, true, dependable, not sham or counterfeit: *sterling worth, qualities, sense* &c.

stern (I.), adj. [1. stērn; 2. stān]. O.E. *steorne*, W.S. *styrne*; M.E. *sterne*, 'stern, severe'; cp. O.H.G. *storrēn*, 'to rise stiffly'; M.H.G. *starren*, 'to stiffen'; Goth. *andstaurran*, 'to complain of'; cogn. w. Gk. *stereós*, 'firm, stiff'; see **stereo-, stare, stark.** Austere, rigid, unyielding, relentless, severe: *stern parents, discipline, necessity, resolve* &c.; *a stern look, command* &c.

stern (II.), n. [1. stērn, starn; 2. stān, stān]. M.E. *stern*, fr. O.N. *stjorn*; cp. O. Fris. *stiorne*, 'rudder'; cogn. w. O.E. *stēoran*, 'to steer', see **steer** (I.); O.N. *stýra*; O.H.G. *stiurjan*, 'to steer, guide'. **1.** Back part of ship, part farthest from bow or stem. Phrs. *a stern chase*, in which pursuing ship follows in wake of pursued; *stern foremost*, backwards; *stern on*, with stern turned to observer &c. **2. a** Rump of animal; **b** tail of animal, esp. of foxhounds.

sternal, adj. [1. stḗrnl; 2. stā́nəl]. **stern(o)-** & **-al.** Of, pertaining to, situated near, the sternum.

sternalgia, n. [1. stērnā́ljia; 2. stānǽldžiə], fr. **stern(o)-** & **-algia**; cp. Gk. *alégein*, 'to suffer', q.v. under **neglect.** Pain near the breast-bone.

stern-chase(r), n. Gun mounted in stern of vessel for defence against pursuing ship.

sterned, adj. [1. stērnd; 2. stānd]. **stern** (II.) & **-ed.** (chiefly in compounds) Having a stern of specified kind.

stern-fast, n. Rope, chain &c. for mooring vessel by the stern.

sternly, adv. [1. stḗrnli; 2. stā́nli]. **stern** (I.) & **-ly.** In a stern manner.

sternmost, adj. [1. stḗrnmōst; 2. stā́nmoust]. **stern** (II.) & **-most.** Nearest to the stern.

sternness, n. [1. stḗrnnes; 2. stā́nnis]. **stern** (I.) & **-ness.** State or quality of being stern.

stern(o)-, pref. representing **sternum.** Sternum; near the sternum.

sternoclavicular, adj. [1. stērnōklavíkūlar; 2. stānouklәvíkjulə]. **stern(o)-** & **clavicular.** Of the sternum and clavicle.

sternocostal, adj. [1. stērnōkóstal; 2. stānou kɔ́stəl]. **stern(o)-** & **costal.** Of the sternum and ribs.

sternoscapular, adj. [1. stērnōskápūlar; 2. stānouskǽpjulə]. **stern(o)-** & **scapular.** Of the sternum and scapula.

sternothyroid, adj. [1. stērnōthīroid; 2. stānouþáiərɔid]. **stern(o)-** & **thyroid.** Of the sternum and thyroid cartilage.

stern-post, n. Upright timber at vessel's stern, attached to keel, and usually supporting rudder.

stern-sheets, n. Part of boat between stern and rowers' thwarts.

sternum, n. [1. stḗrnum; 2. stā́nəm]. Lat. *sternum*, fr. Gk. *stérnon*, 'chest'; cp. Scrt. *stīrnáś*, 'spread out'; O.H.G. *stirna*, 'forehead'; O.E. *steornede*, 'having a forehead'; Gaul. *sarn*, 'paved way'; O. Slav. *strand*, 'side, place'; fr. base **st(e)rē-*, **stor-*, **stṛ-* &c., 'to spread out, extend', seen also in **stratum, strath, strand** (I.), **strew** &c. Breast-bone, vertical bone in front of thorax, to which the upper ribs are joined.

sternutation, n. [1. stērnūtā́shun; 2. stānjutéiʃən], fr. Lat. *sternūtātiōn-(em)*, 'act of sneezing', fr. *sternūtāt-(um)*, P.P. type of *sternūtāre*, 'to sneeze', fr. *sternuere*, 'to sneeze'; cogn. w. Gk. *ptárnūmi*; W. *ystrewi*, 'to sneeze'; O. Ir. *sren(n)im*, 'to snore'. Act of sneezing.

sternutative, adj. [1. stērnū́tativ; 2. stānjū́tətiv], fr. Lat. *sternūtāt-(um)*, P.P. type of *sternūtāre*, 'to sneeze', see prec., & **-ive.** Causing, tending to cause, sneezing.

sternutatory, adj. & n. [1. stērnū́taturi; 2. stānjū́tətəri], fr. Lat. *sternūtāt-(um)*, see prec. & **-ory.** **1.** adj. Sternutative. **2.** n. Substance causing, or intended to cause, sneezing.

sternward, adj. & adv. [1. stḗrnward; 2. stā́nwəd]. **stern** (II.) & **-ward.** **1.** adj. Situated near or towards the stern. **2.** adv. Towards the stern.

sternwards, adv. [1. stḗrnwardz; 2. stā́nwədz]. **stern** (II.) & **-wards.** Towards the stern.

stern-way, n. Backward motion of ship.

stern-wheeler, n. (U.S.A.) Steamboat with single paddle-wheel at stern.

stertorous, adj. [1. stḗrtorus; 2. stā́tərəs], fr. Lat. *stertere*, 'to snore', & **-or** & **-ous**; etymol. doubtful; possibly fr. the same base as Lat. *sternuere*, 'to sneeze'; cp. O. Ir. *sren(n)im*, 'to snore', & see **sternutation.** (of breathing or person breathing) Characterized, accompanied by, producing sound like, snoring.

stertorously, adv. Prec. & **-ly.** In a stertorous manner.

stertorousness, n. See prec. & **-ness.** Quality of being stertorous.

stet, imperat. (intrans.) & vb. trans. [1. stet; 2. stet]. Lat. *stet*, 'let it stand', 3rd sing. pres. subj. of *stāre*, 'to stand', see **state.** **1.** imperat. Direction to printer &c., written in margin of a proof to cancel correction made in text, the letters thus replaced being dotted under. **2.** vb. trans. To cancel (correction in text) by placing dot(s) beneath and writing '**stet**' in margin.

stethoscope, n. & vb. trans. [1. stéthoskôp; 2. stéþəskòup], fr. Gk. *stêthos*, 'breast'; cogn. w. Scrt. *stánaś*, 'breast'; for the second element see **-scope**. **1.** n. Slender tube with one flat and one bell-shaped end for auscultation of heart, lungs &c.; also more elaborate apparatus for same purpose. **2.** vb. To examine with a stethoscope.

stethoscopic, adj. [1. stèthoskópik; 2. stèþəskópik]. Prec. & **-ic**. Of, pertaining to, a stethoscope or stethoscopy.

stethoscopically, adv. [1. stèthoskópikali; 2. stèþəskópikəli]. Prec. & **-al** & **-ly**. In a stethoscopic manner; by means of the stethoscope.

stethoscopist, n. [1. stèthóskopist; 2. stèþóskəpist]. **stethoscope** & **-ist**. Person using or skilled in use of a stethoscope.

stethoscopy, n. [1. stèthóskopi; 2. stèþóskəpi]. **stethoscope** & **-y (I.)**. Art or practice of using a stethoscope.

stevedore, n. [1. stḗvedôr; 2. stívidɔ̄], fr. Span. *estivador*, fr. *estivar*, 'to pack, stow', fr. Lat. *stīpāre*, 'to pack tightly', see **steeve (III.)** & **stipate**; the Span. suff. *-dor*, corresponds to Lat. **-tor**, expressing the agent. Person employed at docks to stow and unload cargoes.

stew (I.), n. [1. stū; 2. stjū]. M.E. *stuve*, *stue*, fr. O. Fr. *estuve*, 'hot bath, bath-room; stew', of Gmc. origin; cp. Germ. *stube*, 'room'; M. Du. *stove*; O.E. *stofa*, 'heated room; bath-room'; see **stove (I.)**. Public baths were formerly, in many countries, the resort of persons of ill-fame. (archaic, usually pl. *stews*). A brothel.

stew (II.), vb. trans. & intrans. M.E. *stu(w)en*, 'to stew', fr. *stue*, 'hot bath', see prec. **1.** trans. To cook slowly by simmering in a small proportion of liquid, esp. in covered vessel: *to stew beef*; *stewed fruit*. **2.** intrans. (of food) To be cooked, be in process of cooking, by this method. Phr. *to let a person stew in his own juice*, abandon him to his fate, withhold help.

stew (III.), n., fr. prec. **1.** Dish of meat, fish, vegetables &c. cooked by stewing, usually with considerable number of ingredients; *Irish stew*, thick stew of mutton, onions, and potatoes. **2.** (slang) State of restless anxiety and excitement: *in a regular stew*.

stew (IV.), n. M.E. *stēwe*; cp. M.L.G. *stouwe*, 'fish-pond'; *stauen*, 'to dam'; O.H.G. *stowan*, *stūan*, 'to accuse, blame, take into custody'; Goth. *stōjan*, 'to judge', & see **stow**. Fish-pond serving as store for fish for the table.

steward, n. [1. stūard; 2. stjūəd]. O.E. *stigweard*; M.E. *stiward*, 'steward'; fr. O.E. *stiġ*, 'sty, hall', see **sty**, & **ward**. **1. a** (hist.) An officer on the estate of a feudal lord having charge and management of the cattle; **b** generally, manager and administrator of a large estate and of all the business connected with it, agricultural, legal, and financial. **2.** Salaried manager of a large household and estate belonging to another. **3.** Person whose business it is to arrange for the supply of provisions in a college, club, or similar institution. **4.** Servant on a ship who waits on and attends to the passengers. **5.** One of a body of officials employed on various public occasions, e.g. at race meetings, at public balls. **6.** One of various high officers of State: *Lord High Steward of England*; *Lord Steward of the Household*.

stewardess, n. [1. stūardes; 2. stjūədis]. Prec. & **-ess**. Female steward, esp. on passenger-ship.

stewardship, n. [1. stūardship; 2. stjūədʃip]. **steward** & **-ship**. **a** Rank, office, functions of a steward; Phr. *to give an account of one's stewardship*, make a statement relative to the way in which one has discharged one's duties and responsibilities; **b** tenure of office of steward.

stew-pan, n. Covered vessel for stewing food.

stew-pot, n. Stew-pan.

sthenic, adj. [1. sthénik; 2. sþénik], fr. Gk. *sthénos*, 'strength'; etymol. doubtful. (pathol.) Abnormally active; applied to a state of morbid activity of some vital process.

stibial, adj. [1. stíbial; 2. stíbiəl], fr. Lat. *stibi*, *stibium*, fr. Gk. *stíbi*, 'a sulphuret of antimony', fr. Egyptian, & **-al**. Of, containing, consisting of, like, antimony.

stibialism, n. [1. stíbializm; 2. stíbiəlizəm]. Prec. & **-ism**. Poisoning by antimony.

stibium, n. [1. stíbium; 2. stíbiəm]. Lat., see **stibial**. (chem.) Antimony.

stichic, adj. [1. stíkik; 2. stíkik]. Gk. *stikhikós*, fr. *stíkhos*, 'file of soldiers; line of verse'; cp. Gk. *stoîkhos*, 'row, rank'; *steíkhein*, 'to advance'; cogn. w. Scrt. *stighnōti*, 'ascend'; Goth. *steigan*; O.N. *stīga*; O.E. *stīgan*, 'to ascend'; O.E. *stǣger*, 'stair', see **stair**. Connected with, consisting of, lines as metrical units.

stichomyth, n. [1. stíkomith; 2. stíkəmiþ], also **stichomythia** [1. stìkomíthia; 2. stìkəmíþiə]. Gk. *stikhomūthia*, 'conversation in alternate lines', fr. *stíkhos*, 'line of verse', see **stichic**, & *mūthos*, 'word, speech', see **myth**. Verse dialogue as in Greek plays.

stick (I.), vb. trans. & intrans. [1. stik; 2. stik], fr. two M.E. vbs., w. forms & meanings confused; (1) M.E. *steken* (str. vb.), 'to prick, fix, fasten'; cp. O.S. *stecan*; O.H.G. *stechan*, 'to prick'; (2) M.E. *stikien* (wk. vb.), 'to be infixed, to prick'; fr. O.E. *stician*, 'to prick, goad, stab'; to remain fixed, be infixed'; both cogn. w. Goth *stiks*; O.H.G. *stih*, 'prick, point'; cp. O.E. *sticca*, 'stick, peg, point'; see **stick (II.)**, L.G. *stikke*, 'to stick on', cp. **etiquette**; further, Gk. *stízein*, 'to prick, puncture'; *stiktós*, 'embroidered; variegated'; *stígma*, 'mark made by pointed instrument; scar; brand', see **stigma**; Lat. *instīgāre*, 'to goad', see **instigate**; Scrt. *tijatē*, 'is sharp'; *tigmáś*, 'pointed'; O. Pers. *tigra-*, 'sharp', see **tiger**. Cp. also **stake (I.)**. **A.** trans. **1. a** To pierce, thrust pointed object or instrument into or through: *to stick a pincushion full of pins*; **b** specif., *to stick a pig*, to kill it by sticking knife into its throat. Phr. *to stick pigs* (as sport), to hunt wild pigs on horseback with spear. **2.** To cause to penetrate, thrust into: *to stick a fork into a potato, a needle into one's finger* &c. **3.** (colloq.) To place, put, set, thrust: *stick it on the shelf*; *to stick one's hands into one's pockets*; *to stick one's tongue out*; *to stick a rose in one's buttonhole*; *to stick one's head round the door*. **4. a** To cause to adhere, cause to cling or cleave, fix in position, attach: *to stick a stamp on a letter*; *to stick bills, a notice, on a wall* &c.; **b** to mend, fasten together; *stick a thing, broken pieces &c., together with glue*. **5.** (slang) To tolerate, endure, stand: *I simply can't stick a whole summer in a town*. Phr. *to stick it*, to bear patiently (circumstances &c.), go through with, see it through. **B.** intrans. **1.** To remain fixed in, be held in position by point penetrating an object: *pins sticking in a pincushion*; *a dagger sticking in the corpse*. **2. a** To remain attached to, adhere, cleave, cling closely: *stamps stick together, to one's fingers* &c.; *burrs stick to one's clothes*; *to stick fast, like a limpet* &c.; (colloq.) *to stick on a horse*, be firmly seated on, not to fall off; **b** (fig.) to cling, cleave, remain in close association, avoid estrangement: *friends stick together*; **c** to remain, stop: *to stick at home, in the house* &c.; **d** to remain attached, become permanent, always used: *the nickname stuck*. **3. a** To become embedded, held fast, fixed; to be caught, entangled, attached: *to stick in the mud*; *the key has stuck in the lock*; *the door sticks*; *a fish-bone stuck in my throat*; Phr. *to stick in one's throat*, (fig.) be difficult to accept, acknowledge, utter &c.; **b** (fig.) to come to, be forced to, a standstill, be unable to proceed: *he tried to repeat Gray's 'Elegy', but stuck after the first few verses*. **C.** Followed by adverbs or prepositions with special meanings. *Stick at*, intrans., **1.** to remain at, persist in: *to stick at a piece of work*; **2.** to be checked, daunted by; to hesitate about, have scruples concerning: *he will stick at nothing to gain his ends*; *to stick at trifles*. *Stick out*, **1.** intrans., to project, stand out: *his ears stick out*; *buried in the sand with only his head sticking out*; **2.** trans., to cause to project, thrust out, force into prominence: *to stick out one's chest*. *Stick out for*, intrans., to persist in demanding, insist on having: *to stick out for higher wages*. *Stick to*, intrans., **a** to persevere in, continue at, refrain from abandoning: *to stick to one's work, post* &c.; Phr. *to stick to one's guns*, (fig.) adhere to one's opinions, refuse to be deflected from one's purpose, in spite of opposition; **b** (fig.) to be loyal, faithful, constant, to: *to stick to one's friends, one's word* &c. *Stick up*, **1.** intrans., to project upwards, stand upright: *hair sticking up on end*; *a head sticking up out of the water*; **2.** trans., **a** to cause to project upwards, put into upright position: *to stick up a post*; **b** (slang) to hold up, stop, or threaten for the purpose of robbing; **c** (slang) to puzzle, perplex. *Stick up for*, intrans., to defend, uphold; speak, or act in defence of: *to stick up for a friend, oneself, one's rights* &c.

stick (II.), n. O.E. *sticca*, 'stick, peg'; M.E. *sticke*; see prec. **1.** Slender, stiff shoot or twig of tree or shrub, light enough to be lifted or carried in the hand: *to collect dry sticks for the fire*; *to put a stick in the ground to mark a point*. Phrs. *to cut one's stick*, (colloq.) take one's departure; *in a cleft stick*, (fig.) dilemma, position from which one cannot extricate oneself; *to give one the stick*, cane him; *to get hold of the wrong end of the stick*, to misunderstand a situation, form a wrong idea concerning a matter; specif. **a** a stick seasoned, shaped &c. for support or defence, as symbol of office &c.; rod, staff: *to walk with, lean on, a stick*; **b** (usually in compounds) stick prepared or adapted for specific purpose: *fiddlestick, singlestick, broomstick, drumstick, hockey-stick* &c. **2.** Slender, usually cylindrical, bar or piece of some plastic substance: *a stick of sealing-wax, barley-sugar* &c. **3.** (print.) Composing-stick. **4.** (mus.) Conductor's baton. **5.** Stick-insect. **6.** (fig., colloq.) Dull, stiff, starched, unresponsive person: *he's a regular stick*; *a dry old stick*.

stick (III.), vb. trans., fr. prec. **1.** To support with a stick; to fasten to, supply with, sticks as support: *to stick peas*. **2.** (print.) To set up (type) in composing-stick.

sticker, n. [1. stíker; 2. stíkə]. **stick (I.)** & **-er**. **1.** One who, that which, sticks (in various senses); specif. **a** butcher &c. who sticks pigs; **b** one who fastens objects with adhesive compound: *bill-sticker* &c.; **c** (cricket) batsman who stays in for a long period but makes few runs. **2.** Person who sticks to, persists in, a piece of work, line of conduct &c.; a persistent, assiduous, persevering person. **3.** Wooden rod connecting two reciprocating levers in an organ &c.

stickful, n. [1. stíkfool; 2. stíkful]. **stick (II.)** & **-ful**. (print.) Amount of type that fills a composing-stick.

stickily, adv. [1. stíkili; 2. stíkili]. **sticky** & **-ly**. In a sticky manner.

stickiness, n. [1. stíkines; 2. stíkinis]. See prec. & **-ness**. State or quality of being sticky.

sticking-place, -point, n. [1. stíking plās, pòint; 2. stíkiŋ plèis, pòint]. (chiefly fig.) Point at which something sticks, holds fast, remains fixed; esp. in Phr. *to screw one's courage to the sticking-point*.

sticking-plaster, n. Adhesive plaster for covering cuts &c. on the face &c.

stick-insect, n. Any of several kinds of insect resembling a twig or small stick.

stick-in-the-mud, adj. & n. [1. stík in dhe mùd; 2. stík in ðə màd]. **1.** adj. Unprogressive, dull, without imagination, initiative &c. **2.** n. Stick-in-the-mud person, place &c.

stickjaw, n. [1. stíkjaw; 2. stíkdžɔ̄]. (slang) Sweetmeat, pudding, which is sticky and difficult to masticate.

stickleback, n. [1. stíklbàk; 2. stíklbæ̀k], fr. O.E. *sticel*, 'sting', fr. *stician*, 'to prick', see **stick (I.)**, & **-le** & **back**. Small, fresh- and salt-water fish with a ridge of sharp dorsal spines.

stickler, n. [1. stíkler; 2. stíklə]. Obs. sense, 'umpire'; fr. M.E. *stihtlen*, 'to rule, dispose, set in order', fr. *stihten*, O.E. *stihtan*, 'to arrange, dispose', fr. **stik-tan*; cp. M. Du. *stichten*; O.H.G. *stiftan*, 'to arrange'. Only in Phr. *stickler for*, person who insists on, is punctilious about: *a stickler for ceremony, etiquette* &c.

sticky, adj. [1. stíki; 2. stíki]. **stick (I.)** & **-y (IV.)**. **a** Adhesive, glutinous, tending to cling to surfaces; **b** (in moral sense) difficult to move or influence; given to making objections, having scruples and hesitations: *rather sticky about giving his consent* &c.

stiff (I.), adj. [1. stif; 2. stif]. O.E. *stīf*; M.E. *stif*, 'stiff, strong'; cp. M.L.G. *stīf*; Du. *stijf*; O.N. *stīfr*, 'stiff'; cogn. w. Lat. *stīpāre*, 'to pack closely, cram', see **stipate**; *stīpes*, 'pillar'; Lith. *stiprùs*, 'strong'; cp. further Gk. *stiphrós*, 'thick, firm'; *steíbein*, 'to thicken'; fr. base **sti-*, **stei-* &c., 'to press close together'; see also **steato-**, **stone (I.)**. **1.** Rigid, firm, not easily bent; not flexible or pliant: *a stiff bar of iron*; *standing straight and stiff*; *stiff and cold in death*; *a stiff piece of cardboard*; *a stiff collar*. **2.** Dense in texture, only slightly plastic; thick: *stiff dough, paste, clay* &c. **3. a** Not moving freely, working with difficulty, owing to excessive friction &c.: *stiff joints, hinges* &c.; *a stiff neck*, rheumatism of muscles of neck; Phr. *to keep a stiff face, lip*, remain grave; (fig.) remain unmoved; *to keep a stiff upper lip*, remain firm in trouble or difficulty; **b** (of part of body) painful when moved through over-exertion; **c** (of person) suffering from stiffness of limb, muscle &c. through over-exertion: *feeling rather stiff*. **4. a** Formal, constrained, distant; reverse of natural, cordial, or easy in manner or character: *a stiff bow, greeting* &c.; *a stiff manner, style* &c.; **b** morally unyielding, not easily persuaded or influenced; severe. **5.** Requiring physical or mental effort; difficult: *a stiff climb, examination*. **6.** Of considerable strength, volume, amount &c.; specif. **a** *a stiff gale, breeze* &c., strong and steady; **b** *a stiff drink* &c., containing large proportion of spirit, drug &c.; **c** excessive: *a stiff demand, price* &c.; **d** (colloq.) startling, difficult to acquiesce in; preposterous; thick, steep (in colloq. senses).

stiff (II.), n., fr. prec. (slang) **1.** Paper money &c. **2.** A corpse.

stiff-bit, n. Horse's bit consisting of a single, rigid bar.

stiffen, vb. trans. & intrans. [1. stífen; 2. stífən]. **stiff (I.)** & **-en (V.)**. **A.** trans. **1.** To make stiff; specif. **a** to make rigid, difficult to bend: *to stiffen linen with starch*; **b** to increase density of, make less plastic: *to stiffen paste* &c. **2.** To render more resolute and unyielding; to inspire with power or will to resist: *the king tried to stiffen his wavering generals*. **B.** intrans. **1.** To become stiff; specif. **a** to grow rigid, lose flexibility; **b** to become less plastic; hard. **2.** To become colder in manner, more formal, distant, constrained. **3. a** To increase in intensity, force, volume: *the breeze stiffened*; **b** (fig.) to become firmer, more determined and unyielding: *one's resolution stiffens*.

stiffener, n. [1. stífener; 2. stífənə]. Prec. & **-er**. Something which causes stiffening; **a** (in material sense) specif. (slang) **a** stimulant, a tonic; **b** (in moral sense) circumstance which stiffens the courage, resolution &c.

stiffening, n. [1. stífening; 2. stífəniŋ]. See prec. & **-ing**. Material used to stiffen substance or object.

stiffish, adj. [1. stífish; 2. stífiʃ]. **stiff (I.)** & **-ish (I.)**. Fairly stiff.

stiffly, adv. [1. stífli; 2. stífli]. **stiff (I.)** & **-ly**. In a stiff manner.

stiff-necked, adj. [1. stíf nekt; 2. stíf nékt]. (fig.) Stubborn, unyielding, obstinate.

stiffness, n. [1. stífnes; 2. stífnis]. **stiff (I.)** & **-ness**. State or quality of being stiff.

stifle (I.), vb. trans. & intrans. [1. stífl; 2. stáifl], fr. O.N. *stīfla*, 'to choke', fr. *stīva*, 'to stiffen'; cogn. w. M.L.G. *stīven*; M. Du. *stijven*, 'to stiffen'; cp. O.N. *stīfr*; O.E. *stīf*, 'stiff'; see **stiff (I.)**. **A.** trans. **1. a** To choke, suffocate; kill, destroy, by stopping air supply; **b** to render breathing difficult, deprive of adequate supply of fresh air. **2. a** To suppress, damp down, cause to die down, to extinguish, to quench: *to stifle fire, flames*; **b** (fig.) to quell, put down: *to stifle complaints, rebellion* &c. **3. a** To repress (feelings &c.), to crush down, keep in check, control, refrain from giving vent to or expressing: *to stifle one's hopes, fears, affection* &c.; **b** *to stifle a noise, laughter, sobs* &c. **B.** intrans. To experience sensation of stifling.

stifle (II.), n. Prob. fr. O.N. *stīva*, 'stiffen', see prec. **1.** Joint in hind leg of horse or dog, above the hock; also *stifle-joint*. **2.** Disease of stifle-joint or stifle-bone.

stifle-bone, n. Horse's knee-pan.

stifled, adj. [1. stífld; 2. stáifld]. **stifle (II.)** & **-ed**. Affected with stifle.

stifle-joint, n. See **stifle (II.)**.

stifle-shoe, n. Horseshoe designed to correct a stifled joint.

stifling, adj. [1. stífling; 2. stáifliŋ]. **stifle (I.)** & **-ing**. Tending to stifle; suffocating; stuffy, airless; also in moral sense.

stiflingly, adv. Prec. & **-ly**. So as to stifle.

stigma, n. [1. stígma; 2. stígmə], pl. *stigmas*; (eccles., anat.) *stigmata* [1. stígmata; 2. stígmətə]. Lat., fr. Gk. *stígma*, 'puncture; brand', fr. stem of *stízein*, 'to prick, brand, tattoo'; cogn. w. Lat. *instīgāre*, 'to goad', see **instigate**; also w. O.E. *stician*, 'to prick', see **stick (I.)**. **1.** (archaic) Mark made with branding-iron on slave or criminal; brand. **2.** Moral reproach, brand of disgrace or infamy: *the stigma of illegitimacy*. **3.** (eccles., commonly in pl., *stigmata*) Marks, or periodically bleeding wounds, corresponding to the five wounds of the Saviour, appearing miraculously on the bodies of some saints and other persons. **4.** (anat.) Any small mark or scar on the body; specif., small spot that bleeds periodically or under certain mental or physical stimuli. **5.** (bot.) That part of a pistil which receives the pollen.

stigmatic, adj. [1. stigmátik; 2. stigmǽtik], fr. Lat., fr. Gk. *stigmat-*, stem of *stígma*, 'brand', see **stigma**, & **-ic**. Of the nature of a stigma.

stigmatiferous, adj. [1. stìgmatíferus; 2. stìgmətífərəs], fr. Gk. *stigmat-*, as in prec., & **-i-** & **-ferous**. Bearing stigmas.

stigmatism, n. [1. stígmatizm; 2. stígmətìzəm], fr. Gk. *stigmat-*, as in prec., & **-ism**. **1.** Condition of bearing stigmata. **2.** Property of an optical lens, or of that of the eye, of focussing rays of light upon a single point.

stigmatist, n. [1. stígmatist; 2. stígmətist], fr. Gk. *stigmat-*, see prec., & **-ist**. (eccles.) Person supposed to bear the marks of the stigmata.

stigmatization, n. [1. stìgmatizáshun; 2. stìgmətaizéiʃən]. Next word & **-ion**. Act of stigmatizing; state of being stigmatized.

stigmatize, vb. trans. [1. stígmatīz; 2. stígmətaiz], fr. Gk. *stigmat-*, see **stigmatic**, & **-ize**. **1.** (fig.) To designate, brand, as (something discreditable); to describe by an opprobrious name: *to stigmatize a person as a rogue*. **2.** (eccles.) To impress, mark, stigmata upon; to mark with stigmata.

stigmatose, adj. [1. stígmatōs; 2. stígmətous], fr. Gk. *stigmat-*, see prec., & **-ose**. Bearing, marked with, having, a stigma.

stilbite, n. [1. stílbīt; 2. stílbait]. Formed fr. Gk. *stilbein*, 'to glitter'; cp. Gk. *stilpnós*, 'shining'; perh. cogn. w. O. Ir. *sell*, 'eye'. A white, crystalline mineral.

stile (I.), n. [1. stīl; 2. stail]. O.E. *stigel*, 'place for climbing over fence; stile'; M.E. *stile*; cp. M.H.G. *stigele*; M.L.G. *stegel*, 'stile'; cp. further O.E. *stīgan*, 'to climb'; P.P. *(ge)stigen*; & see **stair** & **sty (I.)**. Device for facilitating the climbing of a wall or fence, usually consisting of a bar or rail, and more or less rough steps of wood or stone placed permanently on either side.

stile (II.), n. Origin unknown. Upright piece in frame of door &c.

stiletto, n. & vb. trans. [1. stilétō; 2. stilétou], fr. Ital. *stiletto*, dimin. of *stilo*, fr. Lat. *stilus*, 'pointed instrument', see **style (I.)**. **1.** n. **a** Small, slender, continuously tapering dagger; **b** small pointed instrument of metal, ivory &c. for making eyelet-holes in textile fabric &c. **2.** vb. (rare) To pierce, make holes in, stab, with a stiletto.

still (I.), adj. [1. stil; 2. stil]. O.E. *stille*, 'at rest; silent; secret'; cp. M. Du. *stille*; O.H.G. *stilli*, 'still'; cogn. w. Gk. *stéllein*, 'to set in order'; *stḗlē*, 'pillar', see **stele**; *stélekhos*, 'stem'; Scrt. *sthálam*, 'place, position'; Lat. *locus*, O. Lat. *stlocus*, 'place', see **locus**; fr. base **stĕl-*, **stŏl-*, **stl-* &c., 'to place'; expansion of **stā-*, **stə-*, 'to stand'; see **stand**, **state**. **1. a** Devoid of motion: *still water*; *the air is perfectly still*; *a still evening*; **b** no longer moving, having come to rest: *keep your feet still*; *never still for a moment*. **2.** (of wine) Not sparkling or effervescent. **3.** Devoid of sound, no longer heard; silent: '*The trumpet's silver sound is still*' (Scott, Introd. to Canto I. of 'Marmion').

still (II.), n., fr. prec. Cp. O.H.G. *stillī*, 'stillness'. (rare and poet.) Stillness, quiet, calm.

still (III.), vb. trans. & intrans., fr. **still (I.)**. **1.** trans. To make still; **a** to cause to be quiet or silent; to calm, hush: *to still the clamours of envy*; **b** to soothe, assuage: *to still the pain of a wound*. **2.** intrans. (rare) To become still.

still (IV.), adv. O.E. *stille*, 'quietly', see **still (I.)**. **1.** (archaic or obs.) Continuously, constantly. **2.** Right up to specified time, even now or even then: *he is still asleep*; *will you still be here when I return?* **3.** Nevertheless, even, granting that, notwithstanding: *he is an awful bore—still we are bound to ask him*. **4.** (after or before a compar. adj.) Even, yet, more, to an increasing degree: *he is tall enough, but his brother is still taller*, or *taller still*.

still (V.), vb. trans. & intrans. Abbr. fr. **distil**; but cp. also Lat. *stillāre*, 'to fall in drops; to cause to fall in drops', fr. *stīlla*, 'a small drop', dimin. of *stīria*, 'small drop, icicle'; cogn. w. *stīpāre*, 'to press together', q.v. under **stiff**, & cp. **stipate**. **1.** trans. To distil; produce (spirit) from a still. **2.** intrans. (poet.) To fall drop by drop, trickle.

still (VI.), n. M.E. *stillatorie*, fr. *stillāt-(um)*, P.P. type of *stillāre*, see prec., & **-ory**. Apparatus for distilling; apparatus in which the more volatile parts of a liquid are separated from it by heat and subsequently condensed.

stillage, n. [1. stílij; 2. stílidž]. Formed fr. base of **stilling**, **stillion**, & **-age**. Framework, bench, stool &c. for raising things off the floor, e.g. yarn &c. while draining, goods ready for packing &c.

still-birth, n. Birth of a dead child.

still-born, adj. Dead when born.

still-fish, vb. intrans. To fish from an anchored boat.

stilling, n. [1. stíling; 2. stíliŋ], fr. L.G. *stelling*, fr. *stellen*, 'to place', cogn. w. **stall (I.)**, & **-ing (I.)**. Stand, framework, supporting cask &c.

stillion, n. [1. stílyun; 2. stíljən]. Variant of prec. Stilling.

still life, n. Pictorial representation of inanimate objects.

stillness, n. [1. stílnes; 2. stílnis]. **still (I.)** & **-ness**. State or quality of being still.

still-room, n. **1.** Room in which distilling is carried on. **2.** Housekeeper's store-room; one where home-made preserves &c. are kept.

stilly (I.), adv. [1. stílli; 2. stílli]. **still (I.)** & **-ly**. In a still manner, quietly.

stilly (II.), adj. [1. stíli; 2. stíli]. **still (I.)** & **-y (IV.)**. (poet.) Still, quiet, silent.

stilt, n. [1. stilt; 2. stɪlt], fr. Swed. *stylta*; cp. Germ. *stelze*, 'stilt'. **1.** (usually pl.) *Stilts*, device used for raising a walker above the ground, consisting of a pair of long, light poles, with supports for the feet eighteen inches or so from the ground, the upper part of each resting in crook of elbow and grasped lower down by the hand. **2.** Also *stilt-bird*, *stilt-plover*, genus of three-toed wading birds, with long, slender legs.

stilt-bird, n. See **stilt, 2.**

stilted, adj. [1. stílted; 2. stíltɪd]. **stilt** & **-ed.** **1.** Stiff, pretentious, bombastic (of style and manner); literally resembling gait of person on stilts. **2.** (archit.) *Stilted arch*, one springing from a series of horizontal courses of masonry above the impost, and not from the impost itself.

stiltedly, adv. Prec. & **-ly.** In a stilted manner.

stiltedness, n. See prec. & **-ness.** State or quality of being stilted.

Stilton, n. [1. stíltun; 2. stíltən], fr. Stilton, Hunts. Kind of rich cheese.

stilt-petrel, n. Long-legged petrel.

stilt-plover, n. See **stilt, 2.**

stilt-sandpiper, n. Kind of North American sandpiper.

stimulant (**I.**), adj. [1. stímūlant; 2. stímjulənt], fr. Lat. *stimulāre*, 'to prick with a goad; to stimulate', fr. *stimulus*, 'goad', see **stimulus**, & **-ant.** Serving to stimulate; acting as a stimulant.

stimulant (**II.**), n., fr. prec. Something which stimulates; specif. **a** a drug or other agent which increases the activity of some bodily organ or function, or which excites emotions; in Phr. *to take stimulants*, refers specifically to alcohol; **b** some motive or influence which incites (persons) to action: *ambition is often a stimulant of industry.*

stimulate, vb. trans. [1. stímūlāt; 2. stímjuleit], fr. Lat. *stimulāt-(um)*, P.P. type of *stimulāre*, 'to prick with a goad; to rouse up, stimulate', fr. *stimulus*, 'goad', see **stimulus. 1.** To cause activity in, rouse up, excite, act as stimulus to; specif. **a** to excite a nerve: *light stimulates the optic nerve*; **b** to increase, arouse, provoke, an emotion: *to stimulate one's curiosity*; **c** to increase action of a bodily organ: *to stimulate (the action of) the heart.* **2.** To provide a motive or incentive to human action; to urge, incite: *I couldn't stimulate him into a display of spirit or courage.*

stimulating, adj. [1. stímūlāting; 2. stímjulèitiŋ]. Prec. & **-ing.** Acting as stimulus, exciting, provoking, increasing, bodily or mental activity; bracing.

stimulation, n. [1. stìmūlāshun; 2. stìmjuléiʃən]. **stimulate** & **-ion.** Act of stimulating; state of being stimulated.

stimulative, adj. [1. stímūlativ; 2. stímjulətiv]. **stimulate** & **-ive.** Tending to stimulate.

stimulator, n. [1. stímūlàter; 2. stímjulèitə]. **stimulate** & **-or.** One who, that which, stimulates, esp. object or substance used for stimulating.

stimulose, adj. [1. stímūlōs; 2. stímjulous], fr. Lat. *stimulōsus*, 'stimulative'; see **stimulus** & **-ose.** (bot.) Having a sting.

stimulus, n. [1. stímūlus; 2. stímjuləs]. Lat. *stimulus*, 'goad, sting; pang; spur, incentive'; cp. Lat. *stilus*, 'pointed instrument'; fr. base **sti-*, **stei-*, **stoi-* &c., 'sharp'; cp. Avest. *staēra*, 'peak'. From the same base w. addition of formative element *-g-*, cp. Lat. *(in)stīgāre*, 'to goad', see **instigate**; Gk. *stígma*, 'prick', see **stigma**; O.E. *sticca*, 'stick, peg', see **stick** (**I.**). **1.** Anything which excites action or reaction in tissue, muscle, nerve &c. **2.** (bot.) Plant's sting. **3.** (eccles.) Point at end of ecclesiastical staff. **4. a** Substance, drug &c. which increases and provokes activity of bodily function; a stimulant; **b** something which incites to mental or moral action; an incentive, a motive, an inducement: *interest and curiosity provide a sufficient stimulus to industry; without the stimulus of poverty and ambition he would never have reached success.*

stimy. See **stymie.**

sting (**I.**), vb. trans. & intrans. [1. sting; 2. stiŋ]. O.E. *stingan*; M.E. *stingen*; cp. O.N. *stinga*; Goth. *-stiggan*, 'to sting'; prob. a nasalized form of base in **stick** (**I.**). **A.** trans. **1.** (of insect, plant &c.) To pierce, wound, with a sting: *to be stung by a bee.* **2.** To cause a sharp, smarting, tingling sensation or pain to: *a stinging blow; the hail stings one's face.* **3.** (fig.) **a** To give keen mental pain to, cause to suffer acutely: *to be stung by remorse, an insult* &c.; **b** to stimulate, provoke: *the insult stung him into a reply.* **B.** intrans. **1.** (zool., bot.) **a** To have a sting; **b** to inflict a sting. **2.** To feel a sharp, smarting sensation, to tingle: *the blow made his hand sting.* **3.** (fig.) To give acute mental pain: *reproach stings.*

sting (**II.**), n. O.E. *sting*, see prec. **1.** (zool.) Sharply pointed organ of offence or defence of an animal, as insect, reptile &c. **2.** (bot.) Sharp, stiff hair, containing tube leading from poison-gland; as in a nettle. **3. a** Act of stinging; **b** wound or puncture caused by sting. **4.** Sharp pain caused by, or as by, a sting: *to feel a sharp sting; the sting of the wind; the stings of hunger.* **5.** Property of, capacity for, inflicting keen mental or moral suffering: '*O Death, where is thy sting?*' **6.** Stimulating force, keenness, power to rouse, excite; bite, tang: *the breeze has a sting in it.*

stingaree, n. [1. stínggarē; 2. stíŋgərī], fr. **sting-ray.** Sting-ray.

sting-bull, n. Kind of sharp-spined fish; weever.

stinger, n. [1. stínger; 2. stíŋə]. **sting** (**I.**) & **-er.** One who, that which, stings; esp. stinging blow.

sting-fish, n. Sting-bull.

stingily, adv. [1. stínjili; 2. stíndžili]. **stingy** & **-ly.** In a stingy manner.

stinginess, n. [1. stínjines; 2. stíndžinis]. See prec. & **-ness.** State or quality of being stingy.

stinging, adj. [1. stínging; 2. stíŋiŋ], fr. Pres. Part. of **sting** (**I.**). **1.** (of plant, insect &c.) Having a sting; able to sting. **2.** Producing a sharp, smarting, painful sensation: *a stinging blow.* **3.** (fig.) Causing acute exasperation, irritating like a sting: *stinging words.*

stingingly, adv. Prec. & **-ly.** So as to sting: *to retort briefly but stingingly.*

stinging-nettle, n. Species of nettle with stings on leaf.

stingless, adj. [1. stíngles; 2. stíŋlis]. **sting** (**II.**) & **-less.** Without a sting.

stingo, n. [1. stínggō; 2. stíŋgou], fr. **sting.** (archaic) Strong beer.

sting-ray, n. Kind of ray with a sharp spine near the base of the long whip-like tail.

sting-winkle, n. Kind of shellfish that perforates the shells of other shellfish.

stingy, adj. [1. stínji; 2. stíndži], fr. O.E. **stingiġ*, 'stinging'. See **sting** (**II.**) & **-y** (**IV.**). Disinclined to spend money; not in the habit of giving; penurious, mean, niggardly; reverse of *open-handed, generous, liberal.*

stink (**I.**), vb. intrans. & trans. [1. stingk; 2. stiŋk]. O.E. *stincan*, 'to emit vapour; to give forth odour (good or bad)'; M.E. *stinken*; cp. O.H.G. *stinchan*; M.L.G. *stinken*, 'to smell'; prob. cogn. w. Gk. *taggós*, 'rancid'; fr. a nasalized form of base seen in O.N. *stǫ̈kr*, 'stinking'. See also **stench. 1.** intrans. To give out a strong, unpleasant smell, have an offensive odour. Phrs. (fig.) *to stink of money*, be conspicuously rich; *to stink in one's nostrils*, be highly offensive to one. **2.** trans. Only in *stink out*, to drive out by stinking.

stink (**II.**), n., fr. prec. **1.** (not a refined word) Strong, offensive, disgusting smell; a stench. **2.** (slang) *Stinks*, chemistry; natural science.

stink-alive, n. Kind of fish, whiting pout.

stinkard, n. [1. stíngkard; 2. stíŋkəd]. **stink** (**I.**) & **-ard.** Stinking person, animal; esp. the stinking badger, teledu.

stink-ball, n. Ball or vessel filled with explosives or combustibles, designed to produce noxious fumes, formerly used to fling on to hostile ships in naval warfare.

stinker, n. [1. stíngker; 2. stíŋkə]. **stink** (**I.**) & **-er.** **1.** One who, that which, stinks; stinkard. **2.** Kind of petrel, esp. giant fulmar.

stink-horn, n. Kind of fungus growing on decayed vegetable matter.

stinking, adj. [1. stíngking; 2. stíŋkiŋ], fr. Pres. Part. of **stink** (**I.**). Emitting an offensive odour; e.g. *stinking badger*, E. Indian badger secreting a malodorous fluid, the teledu; *stinking cedar*; *stinking crane's-bill*, *night-shade* &c.; *stinking elder*, common elder; *stinking-weed*, kind of W. Indian cassia.

stinkingly, adv. Prec. & **-ly.** In a stinking manner.

stink-pot, n. **1.** Stink-ball. **2.** Term of abuse.

stink-stone, n. Kind of rock, esp. limestone, which emits a fetid odour when struck or split.

stink-trap, n. Contrivance to prevent escape of effluvia from drains.

stink-wood, n. Valuable, durable, but ill-smelling timber obtained from a South African tree.

stint (**I.**), vb. trans. [1. stint; 2. stint]. O.E. *styntan*, 'to stupefy'; M.E. *stinten*, 'to stop, stint'; fr. O.E. *stunt*, 'dull'; cp. O.N. *stuttr*, 'short'; cogn. w. Lat. *tundere*, 'to beat'. Cp. Scrt. *tundatē*, 'pricks, pushes', &, without the nasal, Lat. *tudēs*, 'hammer'; cp. the same base w. a different formative element in **type**; & cp. **toil** (**II.**). See also **stunt** (**I.**) & cp. **contuse.** **1.** To be chary of bestowing, to limit, be too sparing in bestowal of: *he does not stint his praise.* **2.** To grudge, be niggardly with, dole out inadequate quantities of (thing), to (person): *to stint one's children of food*; also *to stint oneself (of).*

stint (**II.**), n., fr. prec. **1.** Restriction, limitation; chiefly in Phr. *without stint*, unrestrictedly, ungrudgingly, lavishly. **2.** (archaic) Limited, appointed, assigned proportion or task. **3.** Small sandpiper, esp. the dunlin.

stinting, adj. [1. stínting; 2. stíntiŋ], fr. Pres. Part. of **stint** (**I.**). Grudging, niggardly.

stintingly, adv. Prec. & **-ly.** Grudgingly, sparingly.

stintless, adj. [1. stíntles; 2. stíntlis]. **stint** (**II.**) & **-less.** Without stint, unlimited.

stipate, adj. [1. stípāt; 2. stáipeit], fr. Lat. *stīpāt-(um)*, P.P. type of *stīpāre*, 'to press together, compress'; cp. Lat. *stīpes*, 'pillar; stem'; cogn. w. **stiff** (**I.**). (bot.) Compressed, crowded.

stipe, n. [1. stīp; 2. staip]. Fr., fr. Lat. *stīpes*, 'stem', see prec. Stalk, stem, support; specif. (bot.) **a** stalk of fern-frond; **b** stem-like part of mushroom or similar fungus.

stipel, n. [1. stípel; 2. stáipel]. Prec. & **-el.** Small, secondary stipule, esp. at base of leaflet in compound leaf.

stipellate, adj. [1. stípelāt; 2. stáipeleit]. Prec. & **-ate.** (bot.) Having a stipel.

stipend, n. [1. stípend; 2. stáipənd], fr. Lat. *stīpendium*, 'tax, impost; pay, stipend; income', earlier **stipipendium*, fr. *stips*, 'payment, donation'; the orig. sense may possibly have been 'stem, rod; specif., bar of copper used as form of currency'; cp. Lat. *stipula*, 'stalk, straw', see **stipule** & **stipate.** Regular periodical payment made for services rendered in some permanent post or employment; salary.

stipendiary, adj. & n. [1. stīpéndiari; 2. staipéndiəri], fr. Lat. *stīpendiārius*, 'of tribute; receiving pay', fr. *stīpendium*, 'tax; payment'. See prec. & **-ary.** **1.** adj. Receiving periodical payment, serving for pay. **2.** n. In full, *stipendiary magistrate*, one appointed by Home Secretary and paid by Government, presiding in certain metropolitan or other borough police courts.

stipes, n. [1. stípēz; 2. stáipīz]. Lat., '**stalk,** stem'. See under **stipate**. Stipe.

stipiform, adj. [1. stípiform; 2. stáipifōm]. **stipe** & *-i-* & **-form**. Having the form of a stipe.

stipitate, adj. [1. stípitāt; 2. stáipitèit], fr. Lat. *stīpit-*, stem of *stīpes*, 'stem', see **stipe** & **-ate**. Having, supported by, a stipe.

stipitiform, adj. [1. stipítiform; 2. stáipitifōm], fr. Lat. *stīpit-*, stem of *stīpes*, 'stalk', see **stipes** & *-i-* & **-form**. Stipiform.

stipple (I.), vb. trans. & intrans. [1. stípl; 2. stípl], fr. Du. *stippelen*, fr. *stippel*, dimin. of *stip*, 'point, dot'; cp. M. Du. *stippen*, 'to prick'; fr. base **sti-*, **stoi-* &c., 'sharp, pointed', seen in **stimulus, stigma, stick** &c. **1.** trans. To execute, draw, engrave &c. in stipple. **2.** intrans. To work in stipple.

stipple (II.), n., fr. prec. Method of painting or engraving in which dots are used in place of lines.

stipple-graver, n. Instrument for making dots in stippling.

stippler, n. [1. stípler; 2. stíplə]. **stipple** (I.) & **-er**. **1.** Painter, engraver, using stipple. **2.** Paint-brush used in stippling.

stippling, n. [1. stípling; 2. stípliŋ]. **stipple** (I.) & **-ing**. Etching or engraving in which effect is produced by dots and points; work done in stipple.

stipulaceous, adj. [1. stìpulā́shus; 2. stìpjuléiʃəs]. **stipule** & **-aceous**. Stipular.

stipular, adj. [1. stípūlar; 2. stípjulə]. **stipule** & **-ar**. Pertaining to, of the nature of, a stipule.

stipulary, adj. [1. stípūlari; 2. stípjuləri]. **stipule** & **-ary**. Stipular.

stipulate (I.), vb. intrans. & trans. [1. stípūlāt; 2. stípjuleit], fr. Lat. *stipulāt-(um)*, P.P. type of *stipulāri*, 'to demand a formal promise; to bargain, stipulate', fr. O. Lat. *stipulus*, 'firm'; cp. Lat. *stīpes*, 'trunk, stem'; *stīpāre*, 'to press together, make compact'. See **stipate**. **1.** intrans. To make stipulations, esp. in Phr. *to stipulate for*, make a necessary condition of an agreement &c., insist expressly on: *the contract stipulates for the use of seasoned timber; the witness, before telling his story, stipulated that his name should be kept secret.* **2.** trans. To demand as essential part of agreement or contract: *an increase in the working hours was not stipulated; to use the stipulated material.*

stipulate (II.), adj. **stipule** & **-ate**. (bot.) Having a stipule.

stipulation (I.), n. [1. stìpūlā́shun; 2. stìpjuléiʃən]. **stipulate** (I.) & **-ion**. **1.** Act of stipulating. **2.** That which is stipulated; point, condition, undertaking, insisted on in a contract, agreement, bargain &c.

stipulation (II.), n. **stipule** & **-ation**. (bot.) Character, formation, arrangement, of stipules.

stipulator, n. [1. stípūlāter; 2. stípjuleitə]. **stipulate** & **-or**. Person who makes a stipulation.

stipule, n. [1. stípūl; 2. stípjūl], fr. Lat. *stipula*, 'stalk, stem, blade, straw', dimin. of *stīpes*, 'stem, trunk'. See **stipes** & **-ule**. Appendage at the base of a leaf-stalk, usually in the form of a small leaf, or of a scale, or tendril.

stipuliform, adj. [1. stípūlifòrm; 2. stípjulifōm]. Prec. & *-i-* & **-form**. Having the shape of a stipule.

stir (I.), vb. trans. & intrans. [1. stĕr; 2. stʌ̄]. O.E. *styrian*, 'to set in action; to agitate'; M.E. *stiren*; cp. O.H.G. *-stōren*, 'to disturb'; Germ. *stören*, 'to disturb'; *sturz*, 'plunge, overthrow'; cp. also **storm**; cogn. w. Lat. *trua*, 'scoop, ladle, spoon for stirring', see **trowel**. **A.** trans. **1.** To set in motion, cause to move, alter position of: *the wind stirs the leaves.* Phrs. *to stir one's stumps* (lit. and fig.), move or act briskly, energetically; *to stir the fire*, poke it, move pieces of burning fuel &c.; *not to stir an eyelid*, remain perfectly motionless; *not to stir a finger*, make no effort. **2.** To give circular motion to (fluid, semi-fluid, or dry particles) in a vessel with a spoon, cause to move round and round, to mix thoroughly, make or keep smooth: *to stir one's tea, soup, porridge, mincemeat.* **3.** To affect the emotions (of); to move, rouse: *he was deeply stirred by the news; to stir the imagination, enthusiasm* &c. Phr. *to stir the blood*, rouse to excitement, enthusiasm &c. **B.** intrans. **1.** To move, be in motion: *not a wind was stirring; something stirred in the wood.* **2.** To shift from one position to another: *don't stir for a moment; the cat lay the whole day on the chair without stirring.* **C.** Followed by adverbs or prepositions, with special meanings. *Stir up*, trans., **1.** to mix, stir thoroughly, cause particles of to intermingle; **2.** to disturb, cause to rise, by stirring: *don't stir up the dregs;* **3.** to rouse, excite, bring into existence or action: *to stir up interest in a subject; to stir up strife.*

stir (II.), n., fr. prec. **1.** Act of stirring; stirring movement or action: *to give the fire, porridge &c. a stir.* **2.** Mental excitement, disturbance, commotion; esp. public excitement, sensation: *the news created a tremendous stir in the country.*

stirabout, n. & adj. [1. stĕrabòut; 2. stʌ́rəbàut]. **1.** n. Kind of porridge. **2.** adj. Active, busy, bustling.

stirless, adj. [1. stĕrles; 2. stʌ́lis]. **stir** (II.) & **-less**. (rare) Without a stir, motionless.

stirpiculture, n. [1. stĕrpikùlchur; 2. stʌ́pikàltʃə], fr. Lat. *stirp-*, stem of *stirps*, 'stock', see next word, & *-i-* & **culture**. Breeding of animals &c. from special strains or with special characteristics.

stirps, n. [1. stĕrps; 2. stʌ̄ps]. Lat. *stirps*, 'roots and stem of tree, stock; stem; branch of family, race; foundation'; etymol. unknown. (law) Person from whom a family descends; common ancestor of a group of persons.

stirrer, n. [1. stĕrer; 2. stʌ́rə]. **stir** (I.) & **-er**. One who, that which, stirs; (specif.) instrument for stirring food &c.

stirring, adj. [1. stĕring; 2. stʌ́riŋ], fr. Pres. Part. of **stir** (I.). **1.** Having the property of affecting, rousing the emotions; exciting, moving: *a stirring incident, speech, song* &c. **2. a** Active, brisk, busy: *a stirring person, a stirring body;* **b** characterized by, filled with, incident, activity, business &c.: *stirring times.*

stirringly, adv. Prec. & **-ly**. In a stirring manner.

stirrup, n. [1. stírup; 2. stírəp]. O.E. *stigrāp*, 'stirrup'; M.E. *stirop, stirep*; cp. O.N. *stigreip*; O.H.G. *stegereif*, 'stirrup'; cp. O.E. *stīgan*, 'to climb'; *stigel*, 'stile', see **stair, stile** (I.). For the second element see **rope**. **1. a** One of two metal hoops or rings, with flat base, hung by straps, one either side, from a saddle to support foot of rider; also *stirrup iron*: *to have one's feet in the stirrups;* **b** strap from which stirrup-iron is suspended: *to shorten, lengthen, one's stirrups;* called also *stirrup-leather.* **2.** (naut.) Rope which supports the foot-rope below a ship's yard.

stirrup-bar, n. Short, horizontal iron bar, let into rider's saddle, to which stirrup-leather is attached.

stirrup-bone, n. Stirrup-shaped bone of the middle ear; stapes.

stirrup-cup, n. Parting cup of wine &c. drunk by rider mounted for departure.

stirrup-iron, n. The metal ring in which the foot of a rider is placed; stirrup; contrasted with *stirrup-leather.*

stirrup-leather, n. Strap attaching stirrup to saddle.

stirrupless, adj. [1. stíruples; 2. stírəplis]. **stirrup** & **-less**. Without stirrups.

stirrup-piece, n. (mechan., carpentry &c.) Hanging, metal loop supporting bar, beam &c.

stirrup-strap, n. Stirrup-leather.

stitch (I.), n. [1. stich; 2. stitʃ]. O.E. *stiće*, 'stab, prick, puncture'; M.E. *stiche*; cp. O.E. *stician*, 'to prick'; fr. **stiki-*, see **stick** (I.). **1.** Single, complete in-and-out action of needle in sewing; act of passing needle through material from above and bringing point out to upper surface again by a forward movement. **2. a** Piece of thread &c. drawn through material by needle, and left to cover part of material, used for ornamentation, for joining two pieces or parts of material together &c.: *to make small, long, neat, stitches; to put a stitch in a garment* &c., make slight repair in; Phr. *without a stitch of clothing, not a stitch on*, completely naked; **b** specif., stitch made by surgeon to close wound &c.: *to put in several stitches; to take out the stitches* &c. **3.** Single, complete loop or knot made by needle or hook in knitting, crochet &c. Phr. *to drop a stitch*, allow it to slip off needle. **4. a** Method of forming, character, structure, of stitch in sewing, knitting, crochet &c.: *to learn a new stitch*; esp. in compounds, *buttonhole-, feather-, slip-, satin-stitch* &c.; **b** style of work produced by characteristic stitch, chiefly in compounds, *cross-, stocking-stitch* &c. **5.** (bookbinding) Loop of thread, wire &c., securing sheets of book &c. **6.** Sudden, sharp, stabbing pain in the side.

stitch (II.), vb. trans. & intrans., fr. prec. **1.** trans. **a** To secure, fasten together, with stitch(es), sew; **b** to ornament with stitches, embroider. **2.** intrans. To make stitches, sew.

stitching-horse, n. [1. stíching hòrs; 2. stítʃiŋ hōs]. Saddler's clamp for holding harness steady during stitching.

stitch-wheel, n. Saddler's toothed wheel for marking position for series of holes in leather &c.

stitchwort, n. [1. stíchwĕrt; 2. stítʃwʌ̄t]. O.E. *stićwyrt*; **stitch** (I.) & **wort** (I.), so called from its supposed efficacy for a stitch in the side. Genus of herbaceous plants, *Stellaria*, esp. *greater stitchwort*, with white star-like flowers and grass-like leaves.

stithy, n. [1. stídhi; 2. stíði], fr. M.E. *stithe, stethe*, 'anvil', fr. O.N. *steði*, 'anvil'; cogn. w. **stead**. (archaic) Smith's workshop, smithy, forge.

stiver, n. [1. stíver; 2. stáivə], fr. Du. *stuiver*, small coin formerly current in the Netherlands. A trifling amount; worthless object: *not worth a stiver; to lose every stiver one possesses.*

stoa, n. [1. stṓa; 2. stóuə]. Gk. *sto(i)á*, 'colonnade, cloister, portico', prob. fr. the base **sthū-*, **sthau-* &c., 'to be upright', seen in Gk. *stûlos*, 'column', see **style** (III.); cogn. w. Scrt. *sthū́nā*, 'pillar'; O.E. *stōw*, 'place'; see **stow** & words there referred to. Cp. also **stoic**. (Gk. archit.) Cloister; colonnade walled at the back, with the front opening upon a public place.

stoat, n. [1. stōt; 2. stout]. M.E. *stōte*, inflected form of *stot*, 'stoat; bullock; male animal'; cp. Swed. *stut*; Dan. *stud*, 'bullock'; cogn. w. Goth. *stautan*; O.H.G. *stōzan*, 'to push'; Lat. *tundere*, 'to beat'; cp. further O.E. *stunt*, 'dull'; *styntan*, 'to stupefy', see **stint**. **1.** Small animal, *Mustela erminea*, resembling weasel, esp. in russet summer coat; also called ermine in white winter coat. **2.** Any animal of weasel family.

stock (I.), n. [1. stok; 2. stɔk]. O.E. *stocc*, 'trunk, log, stock'; M.E. *stoc(k)*; cp. O. Fris. *stok*; O.N. *stokkr*; O.H.G. *stoc*, 'trunk, stock', orig. 'hewn stump; log chopped off'; cp. Norw. *stauka*, 'to strike, push'; O.N. *stūka*, 'to push'; cogn. w. Scrt. *tuñjati*, 'strikes, pushes'; Lith. *tūzgénti*, 'to knock at'. Cp. further, w. different formative element, Gk. *stúpos*, 'stock'; *túptein*, 'to strike'; *túpos*, 'stamp, impression', see **type**; O.N. *stufr*, 'stump'; O. Slav. *tŭpati*, 'to beat, palpitate'. See also **stint, stub, stump, stupid**. **1. a** Main stem of tree or plant; esp. lower part of trunk; bole, stem; Phr. *stocks and stones*, inanimate, insensible, objects; **b** (fig.) only in *laughing-stock*, butt, target, object, of attack, ridicule &c. **2.** Main body, base, solid part, serving as support, handle &c., of an object, piece of mechanism &c.: *stock of a rifle, plough, plane* &c.; specif. **a** *stock of an anvil*, support, heavy block, on which it stands; **b** *stock of an anchor*, wooden cross-piece into which the shank is fastened. **3.** (pl.) Framework of solid timbers supporting ship in course of construction. Phr. *on the stocks*, in process of making, undergoing construction. **4.** (pl., hist.) Heavy wooden framework to which offenders were fastened by having their feet passed through holes in the timbers. **5. a** Stem into which a graft is inserted; **b** plant from which cuttings are taken. **6. a** Descent, ancestry, lineage: *to come of good, noble, talented, stock* &c.; **b** (biol.) colony, related group, of organisms. **7.** (of material and non-material things) **a** Supply on which one may draw, material ready for use; equipment, store, effects: *to lay in a stock of flour*; *a contribution to the common stock*; *the general stock of human knowledge*; Phrs. *live stock*, domestic animals kept on farm &c.; *dead stock*, agricultural implements &c. as part of equipment of farm; *to take stock*, (lit. and fig.) to make an inventory of, review, one's stock, assets; *to take stock of*, (fig.) estimate character &c. of, by observation; specif. **b** supply of articles of commerce kept in reserve at a given moment, by a shopkeeper, from which to supply his customers. Phr. *to have, keep, in stock*, have in store, on hand, and available for sale. **8.** Raw or partially prepared material for manufacture &c.; specif. **a** also *paper-stock*, rags, pulp &c., for making paper; **b** also *soup-stock*, broth, liquor, in which bones, vegetables &c. have been boiled, used in cooking for making soup, gravy &c. **9. a** Broad band of leather or stiffened silk &c., formerly worn by men round neck; now largely superseded by a collar and tie, though still worn in modified forms; **b** woman's upright collar. **10.** Genus, *Matthiola*, of half-shrubby garden plants, usually having brightly coloured, scented flowers. **11.** (finance) **a** Originally a wooden tally representing a sum of money lent to the king; hence, **b** money lent at specified rate of interest to a government, usually divided into shares or units of £100; *the stocks*, the total of the money lent to a State upon which interest is paid: *to have money in the stocks*; **c** capital of a company or corporation divided into units, often of £100, entitling holders to a proportion of the profits.

stock (II.), vb. trans. & intrans., fr. prec. **A.** trans. **1.** To supply with stock, equip, store: *to stock a shop with goods*; *to stock a farm*; *a mind well stocked with information.* **2.** To keep in stock, have as part of regular stock: *the shop only stocks cheap goods.* **3.** To fit, supply (gun &c.), with stock. **4.** To put in the stocks as punishment. **5.** To sow, plant (land). **B.** intrans. (of plant) To produce suckers.

stock (III.), adj., fr. **stock (I.)**. **a** Constantly kept in stock: *stock sizes in boots*; hence, **b** (fig.) habitually produced, stereotyped, commonplace, hackneyed: *stock examples, jokes, arguments.*

stockade, n. & vb. trans. [1. stokā́d; 2. stɔkéid]. Fr. *estacade, estocade*, cp. O. Fr. *estaque*, 'a stake', of Gmc. origin, see **stake**; cp. Ital. *steccata*, 'palisade'; Fr. form w. *o*, & present Engl. form influenced by **stock (I.)** or its continental cognates. **1.** n. Barrier, enclosure, wooden fence, for defence, consisting of a series of stakes or posts planted upright in the ground; a palisade. **2.** vb. To defend, supply, with a stockade, set up a stockade around.

stock-book, n. Commercial register of goods bought and sold.

stock-breeder, n. Person engaged in breeding live stock.

stock-broker, n. Member of Stock Exchange who buys and sells stocks and shares for clients.

stock-broking, n. Business, occupation, of a stock-broker.

stock-car, n. Railway truck for transporting cattle &c.

stockdove, n. [1. stókduv; 2. stɔ́kdav]. Small, dark, European wild pigeon, without the white markings of the ring-dove; so called as nesting in stocks of trees or as supposed to be of the original stock from which domestic pigeons were bred.

Stock Exchange, n. **a** Organized body or association of stock-brokers, the membership of which is limited and regulated by various conditions imposed by the governing body; **b** the building in which stock-brokers meet to discuss and transact their business.

stock-farm, n. Farm used for the raising of live-stock.

stock-farmer, n. Farmer engaged in the rearing of cattle, sheep &c.

stockfish, n. [1. stókfish; 2. stɔ́kfiʃ]. Cod, hake &c., prepared for keeping by being split and dried without salt.

stock-gang, n. Set of saws in saw-mill cutting log into series of planks by single simultaneous action.

stock-gillyflower, n. Genus of half-shrubby garden plants with scented flowers, now usually *stock*; see **stock (I.), 10.**

stock-holder, n. (finance) Owner of stock.

stockily, adv. [1. stókili; 2. stɔ́kili]. **stocky & -ly.** In a stocky manner.

stockiness, n. [1. stókines; 2. stɔ́kinis]. See prec. & **-ness.** Quality of being stocky.

stockinet, n. [1. stókinèt; 2. stɔ́kinèt]. Next word & **-et.** Elastic knitted or woven material for dresses, underclothing &c.

stocking, n. [1. stóking; 2. stɔ́kiŋ]. **stock (I.) & -ing (III.)**; cp. earlier (*nether*)-*stocks*, from knee downwards, regarded as cut off from original long hose, from waist downwards. **1.** Knitted or woven, elastic, close-fitting covering for leg and foot, made of wool, silk, cotton thread &c.; often *pair of stockings.* Phrs. *to stand six feet in one's stockings*, i.e. without additional height given by heel of shoe; *elastic stocking* &c., surgical device, shaped like a stocking or part of stocking, woven with rubber &c., for compressing part of leg. **2.** Lower part of leg of horse &c., when of distinct colour from upper part: *a horse with one white stocking.*

stockinged, adj. [1. stókingd; 2. stɔ́kiŋd]. Prec. & **-ed.** Wearing, covered with, stocking(s); chiefly in compounds, *silk-stockinged* &c.

stocking-feet, n. pl. *In (his) stocking-feet*, without boots or shoes.

stocking-frame, n. Machine for knitting stockings.

stockingless, adj. [1. stókingles; 2. stɔ́kiŋlis]. **stocking & -less.** Without stocking(s).

stocking-loom, n. Machine for knitting stockings.

stock-in-trade, n. **a** Stock goods, appliances, equipment, tools &c. required for the carrying on of particular trade, business, occupation: *books are a scholar's stock-in-trade*; **b** (fig.) any habitual, stereotyped trick, mannerism, trite utterance, set phrase &c., characteristic of a particular profession or individual: *grimaces and posturings are part of an actor's stock-in-trade*; *catchwords, and promises never to be fulfilled, are the stock-in-trade of the professional politician.*

stock-jobber, n. Member of the Stock Exchange from whom the broker buys and to whom he sells stocks and shares on behalf of his clients.

stockless, adj. [1. stókles; 2. stɔ́klis]. **stock (I.) & -less.** Without a stock, esp. of gun &c.

stock-list, n. Periodical list of current prices of stocks and shares.

stock-man, n. (chiefly Australian) Man in charge of stock on farm &c.

stock-market, n. **a** Stock Exchange; **b** business transacted on Stock Exchange.

stock-owl, n. Eagle-owl.

stock-pot, n. Vessel in which bones &c. are boiled to make stock.

stock-raising, n. [1. stók rā̀zing; 2. stɔ́k rèiziŋ]. The raising of live-stock on a farm &c.

stock-rider, n. (chiefly Australian) A mounted herdsman.

stock-still, adv. As still as a stock; absolutely motionless: *to stand stock-still.*

stock-taking, n. Periodical taking of inventory of stock in a shop &c.

stock-whip, n. Herdsman's short-handled, long-lashed whip.

stocky, adj. [1. stóki; 2. stɔ́ki]. **stock (I.) & -y (IV.).** Short and thickset, sturdy.

stock-yard, n. Enclosure fitted with pens &c., where cattle &c. are kept for market &c.

stodge, n. & vb. intrans. [1. stoj; 2. stɔdž]. Possibly imitative. **1.** n. **a** Heavy, solid food; **b** substantial, heavy meal; **c** (fig.) dull, heavy intellectual pabulum. **2.** vb. To eat heartily and greedily; to stuff and cram.

stodginess, n. [1. stójines; 2. stɔ́džinis]. Next word & **-ness.** State or quality of being stodgy.

stodgy, adj. [1. stóji; 2. stɔ́dži]. **stodge & -y (IV.).** **1.** (of food &c.) Heavy, solid, substantial. **2.** (of literary style &c.) Dull, heavy, uninteresting, difficult to read; verbose; lacking lightness of touch.

stoep, n. [1. stōōp; 2. stūp]. S. Afr. Du., in European Du. = 'a threshold'; cogn. w. O.H.G. *stuopa*, 'threshold'; Mod. Germ. *stufe*, 'stage, degree'; cp. **step (I.)**. Verandah in front of African Dutch house.

stoic (I.), n. [1. stóik; 2. stóuik], fr. Gk. *stōikós*, 'Stoic', fr. *stoá*, 'cloister, colonnade', specif., the *Stoá Poikílē*, 'Painted Porch', the colonnade at Athens where Zeno and his followers taught; see **stoa & -ic.** **1.** (cap.) Follower of the philosopher Zeno of Citium (c. 340–260 B.C.), who taught that virtue or conformation to the divine will was the highest good and insisted on complete submission to the divine will with indifference to external pleasure and pain. **2.** Person who does not feel, or controls, personal emotions; person of rigid calm, fortitude, or impassivity.

stoic (II.), adj., fr. prec. (often cap.) Of, pertaining to, characteristic of, a Stoic: *Stoic doctrines*; *stoic calm* &c.

stoical, adj. [1. stóikl; 2. stóuikl]. **stoic (I.) & -al.** Pertaining to, characteristic of, resembling, a Stoic; hence, impassive, indifferent to external conditions and circumstances.

stoically, adv. Prec. & **-ly.** In a stoical manner; like a Stoic.

stoichiometry, n. [1. stòikiómetri; 2. stɔ̀ikiɔ́mitri], fr. Gk. *stoikheîon*, 'base, element', fr. same as *stoikhos*, 'row', see **stichic & -metry.** That branch of chemistry which deals with determination of atomic and molecular weights of elements &c.

stoicism, n. [1. stóisìzm; 2. stóuisìzəm]. **stoic (I.) & -ism.** **1.** (cap.) Doctrine, philosophy, of the Stoics. **2.** Stoical impassivity, calm fortitude, rigid indifference.

stoke, vb. trans. & intrans. [1. stōk; 2. stouk], fr. **stoker. 1.** trans. **a** To feed (furnace, fire &c.) with fuel; **b** to feed furnace of (engine &c.). **2.** intrans. **a** To tend a furnace, act as stoker; **b** (slang, also *stoke up*) to eat, take, a meal.

stokehold, n. [1. stókhōld; 2. stóukhould]. Space, compartment, from which ship's boilers are fed.

stoke-hole, n. Small room or enclosure near a furnace in which a stoker works.

stoker, n. [1. stóker; 2. stóukə], fr. Du., fr. *stoken*, 'to light a fire', fr. *stok*, 'stick', cogn. w. **stock (I.)**. **1.** Person employed in feeding a furnace, esp. of boiler on ship, steam-engine &c.; a fireman. **2.** Mechanical device for supplying a furnace with fuel.

Stokes mortar, n. [1. stóks mórtar; 2. stóuks mɔ́tə], fr. inventor, Sir Wilfrid Stokes (1860–1927). Light, easily transported, trench mortar; also *Stokes gun.*

stole (I.), n. [1. stōl; 2. stoul], fr. Lat. *stola*, fr. Gk. *stolḗ*, 'equipment; apparel; garment'; cp. Gk. *stéllein*, 'to put in position; to arrange, equip, prepare; to array, dress'; *stḗlē*, 'column'; see **stele**, & words there referred to. **1.** (also in Lat. form, *stola*) Long outer garment of Roman matron. **2.** Long strip of coloured cloth or silk, usually embroidered and having fringed ends, part of the Eucharistic vestments, worn over the neck so that the ends hang down in front on either side, and reach to just above the knee. **3.** Woman's long, narrow wrap of fur &c. worn round the neck with the ends hanging down.

stole (II.), n., fr. **stolon.** Stolon.

stole (III.), vb. Pret. of **steal**; fr. P.P.

stoled, adj. [1. stōld; 2. stould]. **stole** (I.) & **-ed.** Wearing a stole.

stolen, vb. [1. stōlen; 2. stóulən]. P.P. of **steal**; O.E. (*ġe*)*stolen*; M.E. *stōlen.*

stolid, adj. [1. stólid; 2. stɔ́lid], fr. Lat. *stolidus*, 'slow, dull, obtuse'; cp. Lat. *stultus*, 'foolish', see **stultify**; cogn. w. O.E. *still*, 'motionless', see **still** (I.); cp. further Lat. *locus*, O. Lat. *stlocus*, 'place', see **locus**; Gk. *stéllein*, 'to place', see **stele.** Dull and impassive, not betraying emotion; lifeless, lacking animation or agitation.

stolidity, n. [1. stolíditi; 2. stɔlíditi], fr. Lat. *stoliditātem*, 'obtuseness'; prec. & **-ity.** State or quality of being stolid.

stolidly, adv. [1. stólidli; 2. stɔ́lidli]. **stolid** & **-ly.** In a stolid manner.

stolidness, n. [1. stólidnes; 2. stɔ́lidnis]. See prec. & **-ness.** Quality of being stolid; stolidity.

stolon, n. [1. stṓlon; 2. stóulən]. Lat. *stolōn-*, nom. *stolō*, 'shoot; sucker'; possibly, according to Walde, fr. base *(*s*)*telā-*, **stolā-* &c., 'broad, extended', whence Lat. *lātus*, earlier **stlātus*, 'broad', see **latitude.** Prostrate shoot, or sucker from a plant, which roots; a runner, an offset.

stolonate, adj. [1. stṓlunāt; 2. stóulənèit]. Prec. & **-ate.** Having, producing, a stolon.

stoloniferous, adj. [1. stōloníferus; 2. stòulənífərəs]. **stolon** & *-i-* & **-ferous.** Producing a stolon.

stoma, n. [1. stṓma; 2. stóumə]. Gk. *stóma*, 'mouth'; see **stomach** (I.). Minute mouth-like orifice in one of the lower animals, or in a plant cell.

stomach (I.), n. [1. stúmak; 2. stámək]. M.E. *stomak*, fr. O. Fr. *estomac*, fr. Lat. *stomachus*, 'gullet; stomach; taste' (lit. and fig.), fr. Gk. *stómakhos*, 'gullet', fr. *stóma*, 'mouth'; cogn. w. Goth. *stibna*; O. Fris. *stifne*; O.E. *stefn*, 'voice'. **1.** Internal sac in the animal body within which the chief part of the process of digestion is carried on, formed by an enlargement of the alimentary canal, connected with the mouth by the gullet, and passing on the digested food into the intestine. **2.** The lower external front part of the body below the diaphragm; the belly, abdomen: *to get a kick in the stomach*; *a pain in the stomach.* **3. a** Desire for food; appetite; **b** desire, inclination, generally: *no stomach for fighting.* **4.** (archaic) Disposition, character; bearing and deportment as expressive of these: *a man of a proud and haughty stomach.*

stomach (II.), vb. trans., fr. prec. **1.** To deal with in the stomach, to digest; hence to relish, manage to eat (food). **2.** (fig.) To tolerate, put up with, accept without protest: *to stomach an insult*; *insolence from an insignificant scoundrel is more than I will stomach.*

stomach-ache, n. Pain in stomach or bowels.

stomachal, adj. [1. stúmakl; 2. stáməkl]. **stomach** (I.) & **-al.** Of, pertaining to, the stomach.

stomach-cough, n. Cough caused by irritation in digestive organs.

stomacher, n. [1. stúmaker; 2. stáməkə]. **stomach** (I.) & **-er.** Part of woman's dress in 15th-17th cents., consisting of a piece of material, triangular in shape, often embroidered or otherwise ornamented, covering breast and upper part of abdomen.

stomachful (I.), n. [1. stúmakfool; 2. stáməkful]. **stomach** (I.) & **-ful.** Amount sufficient to fill the stomach.

stomachful (II.), adj. (archaic or obs.) Proud, haughty.

stomachic, adj. & n. [1. stomákik; 2. stəmǽkik]. **stomach** (I.) & **-ic.** **1.** adj. **a** Pertaining to, connected with, arising from, the stomach; **b** promoting action of the stomach; digestive. **2.** n. Medicinal substance with stomachic properties.

stomachless, adj. [1. stúmakles; 2. stáməklis]. **stomach** (I.) & **-less.** **a** Without a stomach; **b** without appetite.

stomach-pump, n. Apparatus with india-rubber tube attached used for washing out the stomach.

stomach-staggers, n. Apoplexy in horses, caused by paralysis of the stomach.

stomach-tooth, n. Infant's lower canine tooth.

stomach-tube, n. One of the tubes of a stomach-pump.

stomatitis, n. [1. stṓmatítis; 2. stòumətáitis]. See next word & **-itis.** Inflammation of the mucous membrane of mouth, as in thrush &c.

stomato-, pref. representing Gk. *stómat-*, stem of *stóma*, 'mouth', q.v. under **stomach** (I.). Mouth; e.g. *stomatogastric*, of mouth and stomach.

stomatology, n. [1. stṓmatóloji; 2. stóumətɔ́lədži]. **stomato-** & **-logy.** The study of the diseases of the mouth.

stomatoscope, n. [1. stṓmatoskōp; 2. stóumətəskòup]. **stomato-** & **-scope.** Instrument for inspecting the mouth.

stone (I.), n. [1. stōn; 2. stoun]. O.E. *stān*; M.E. *stōn*; cp. O.H.G. *stein*; O. Fris. *stēn*; Du. *steen*; O.N. *steinn*; Goth. *stains*, 'stone'; cp. further O. Slav. *stěna*, 'wall'; fr. base **stei*(*ā*)-, **sti-*, &c., 'to stiffen, become thick, compressed'; seen also in Lat. *stīpāre*, 'to pack closely', see **stipate**; Gk. *stía*, 'pebble'; Lith. *stings*, 'stiff'; Lat. *stīpes*, 'stem, pillar'; see **stipes**; O.E. *stif*, see **stiff** (I.). **1.** Single lump or piece of rock of comparatively small size: *to throw stones*; *to trip over a stone*; *the horse has a stone in its hoof*; *a heap of stones.* Phrs. *rolling stone*, person of restless temperament and habits; esp. one who is constantly changing his occupation, situation, and place of abode; *to leave no stone unturned*, use every effort; *to throw a stone at*, (fig.) make an imputation against, to censure; *to mark (a day) with a white stone*, record as exceptionally happy or fortunate; *stone of Sisyphus*, task involving constant, but unsuccessful effort; *a stone's throw*, short distance; *as cold, as hard, as a stone*, very cold, or hard; *precious stone*, a gem of high value, such as a diamond, ruby, sapphire &c. **2.** Solid mineral matter, rock, esp. as material for building &c.: *a wall of stone*; *a floor paved with stone*; *blocks of stone*; also in compounds: *sandstone, limestone* &c. Phr. *a heart of stone*, an unfeeling, callous nature. **3.** Block or slab of stone cut or shaped for some specific purpose; usually in compounds, e.g. *paving-, stepping-stone, millstone, oilstone, keystone* &c.; specif. **a** for sharpening tools &c.: *whetstone, grindstone* &c.; **b** as memorial, often inscribed: *tombstone, gravestone, headstone* &c.; **c** curling-stone; **d** stone used for lithographing. **4.** Specif., a precious stone of any kind, a gem: *a ring set with five stones.* **5.** A hail-stone. **6.** (bot.) **a** Hard shell enclosing the kernel of certain fruits; e.g. *peach-, plum-, cherry-stone* &c.; **b** hard, grain-like seed of the grape. **7.** (med.) **a** Hard concretion formed in an organ of the body, calculus, esp. *gall-stone*; **b** disease characterized by such a concretion: *an operation for stone.* **8.** (archaic) A testicle. **9.** (with invariable pl., 10 stone &c.) Measure of weight differing in different substances: avoirdupois weight, 14 lb.; in weighing meat, 8 lb.; cheese, 16 lb.; hay, 22 lb.; wool, 24 lb.

stone (II.), vb. trans., fr. prec. **1.** To throw stones at, pelt with stones: *to stone a man to death.* **2.** To supply with stone paving, lining, facing &c.: *to stone a wall, well* &c. **3.** To remove stone from (cherries, raisins &c.).

stone (III.), adj., fr. **stone** (I.). Connected with, pertaining to, made of, stone(s): *a stone wall*; *stone implements.*

Stone Age, n. Prehistoric period in which stone was used for weapons, cutting-tools &c.

stone-axe, n. Heavy axe with short handle at right angles, having one blunt edge for breaking and one sharper edge for shaping stone.

stone-blind, adj. Quite blind.

stone-blue, n. Mixture of indigo and whiting.

stone-boiling, n. Primitive method of heating water for cooking by placing hot stones in it.

stone-borer, n. Kind of bivalve.

stone brash, n. Limy subsoil containing detached pieces of stone of varying size.

stone-break, n. Saxifrage.

stone-breaker, n. **a** One who breaks stones, esp. for road-making &c.; **b** machine for crushing stones.

stone-buck, n. Steenbok.

stone-butter, n. Variety of alum.

stone-cast, n. As far as one can fling a stone, short distance, stone's cast.

stonechat, n. Small European bird, *Pratincola rubicola*, black above, with reddish breast and white collar, allied to the wheatear.

stone-circle, n. Prehistoric ring of upright megaliths.

stone-coal, n. **a** Mineral coal, as opposed to *charcoal*; **b** hard coal, anthracite.

stone-cold, adj. Very cold, quite cold.

stonecrop, n. [1. stṓnkrop; 2. stóunkrɔp]. Sedum; esp. *common stonecrop*, small creeping plant with fleshy leaves and yellow flowers.

stone-curlew, n. Large species of plover, the thick-kneed curlew or plover, *Oedicnemus.*

stone-cutter, n. Person employed in shaping stone for architectural purposes &c.

stoned, adj. [1. stōnd; 2. stound]. **stone** (I.) & **-ed.** (of fruit) With stone(s) removed: *stoned raisins.*

stone-dead, adj. Quite dead.

stone-deaf, adj. Completely deaf.

stone-dresser, n. Person employed in dressing stone for building &c.

stone-eater, n. Stone-borer.

stone fence, n. (U.S. slang) Mixed alcoholic drink, esp. whisky and cider.

stone-fern, n. Kind of fern growing on stone walls.

stone-fly, n. Kind of insect used as fishing-fly.

stone-fruit, n. Fruit containing a stone; drupe, e.g. plum, damson &c., as opposed to *soft fruit.*

stone-gall, n. Clayey mass sometimes found in sandstone.

stone-horse, n. (archaic) Stallion.

stoneless, adj. [1. stṓnles; 2. stóunlis]. **stone** (I.) & **-less.** (esp. of fruit) Without a stone.

stone-lily, n. Fossil crinoid.

stone-man, n. Cairn.

stone-mason, n. Man employed in hewing, dressing, and laying building-stone.

stone-parsley, n. Tall herb of parsley family, with clusters of creamy flowers.

stone-pine, n. Umbrella-shaped pine of Mediterranean coast, with edible seeds.

stone-pit, n. Pit from which stone is quarried.

stone-pitch, n. Hard pitch.

stone-plover, n. Stone-curlew.

stone-rag, n. Kind of lichen.

stone-rue, n. Kind of fern.

stone-saw, n. Instrument for cutting stone.

stone-snipe, n. North American bird, yellow legs.

stone-still, adj. As still as a stone, very still.

stone-walling, n. [1. stṓn wáwling; 2. stóun wɔ́liŋ]. **1.** (cricket) Batting with little effort to make runs. **2.** (politics) Opposition by obstruction.

stone-ware, n. Kind of coarse, glazed pottery, made of siliceous clay.

stone-weed, n. Kind of plant with stony seeds, lithospermum, gromwell.
stone-work, n. Masonry.
stonewort, n. [1. stṓnwërt; 2. stóunwə̄t]. Kind of wild parsley.
stonily, adv. [1. stṓnili; 2. stóunili]. **stony** & **-ly**. In a stony manner.
stoniness, n. [1. stṓnines; 2. stóuninis]. Next word & **-ness**. State or quality of being stony.
stony, adj. [1. stṓni; 2. stóuni]. **stone (I.)** & **-y (IV.)**. **1.** Of, containing, full of, stones: *stony ground*; *a stony path*. Phr. (slang) *stony broke*, financially ruined. **2.** (fig.) **a** Like stone, hard, unfeeling: *a stony heart*; **b** fixed, unmoving: *a stony stare*.
stony-hearted, adj. Unfeeling, pitiless.
stood, vb. [1. stood; 2. stud]. O.E. *stōd*, M.E. *stood*, Pret. & P.P. of **stand (I.)**.
stook, n. & vb. trans. [1. stook; 2. stuk]. M.E. *stouke*, 'pile of sheaves'; cp. L.G. *stūke*, 'bundle'. **1.** n. Group of sheaves of corn set up in field; shock. **2.** vb. To set up, arrange (sheaves, corn &c.), in stooks.
stool (I.), n. [1. stōōl; 2. stūl]. O.E., M.E. *stōl*; cp. Goth. *stōls*; O.N. *stōll*; O.H.G. *stuol*, 'stool, seat'; cogn. w. O. Slav. *stolŭ*, 'throne, seat'; Lith. *pastólas*, 'stand'; fr. base **stā-*, **stə-* &c., 'to stand', as in **stand**; **state (I.)** &c. **1.** Seat for one person, consisting of a flat top supported by one, three, or four legs, and without a back. Phr. *to fall between two stools*, lose an opportunity by hesitating between two courses. **2.** Low stool or bench for resting feet or kneeling on; also *footstool*. **3. a** Seat used for evacuation of the bowels; Phr. *to go to stool*, evacuate the bowels; **b** act of evacuating bowels; **c** faeces discharged. **4.** Portable framework to which a wooden pigeon is attached to serve as decoy. **5.** Root from which a sprout or sucker springs.
stool (II.), vb. intrans., fr. prec. **1.** (of plant) To produce shoots or suckers. **2.** (archaic or obs.) To evacuate the bowels.
stool-ball, n. Game resembling cricket, popular in 17th cent., and now played in Sussex and elsewhere, chiefly by women.
stool-pigeon, n. Wooden pigeon used as decoy; also fig., chiefly U.S.A., of persons.
stoop (I.), vb. intrans. & trans. [1. stōōp; 2. stūp]. O.E. *stūpian*; M.E. *stūpen*; cp. O.N. *stūpa*; M. Du. *stuipen*; cogn. w. **steep (I.)**. **A.** intrans. **1.** To curve, bend, the upper part of the body forwards and downwards towards the ground: *to stoop to pick a flower*; *the doorway is so low that you must stoop*. **2.** (fig.) To demean oneself by unworthy conduct; lower oneself by an action below one's dignity and character; to condescend: *to stoop to meanness and duplicity*; rarely absol., but cp. title of Goldsmith's play, '*She Stoops to Conquer*'. **3.** To hold, carry, oneself with the back and shoulders curved and bent forward: *sit up straight and don't stoop*; *to stoop over one's books*. **4. a** (of hawk &c.) To swoop; **b** hence (fig.) to pounce, make swooping attack. **B.** trans. To bend (head and neck) forward and downwards.
stoop (II.), n., fr. prec. Act, position, of stooping; curved, hunched attitude of the back and shoulders: *he has a shocking stoop*.
stoop (III.), n. See **stoup**.
stoop (IV.), n. Variant spelling of **stoep**. (U.S.A.) Uncovered verandah, porch, platform &c. at door of house.
stooping, adj. [1. stōōping; 2. stūpiŋ], fr. Pres. Part. of **stoop (I.)**. Bent forward and downward; bowed, humped: *stooping shoulders*.
stoopingly, adv. Prec. & **-ly**. In a stooping manner.
stop (I.), vb. trans. & intrans. [1. stop; 2. stɔp]. O.E. (*for*)*stoppian*, 'to stop up, close'; M.E. *stoppen*; cp. O.N. *stoppa*; M. Du. *stoppen*; M.H.G. *stopfen*; fr. L. Lat. *stuppāre*, 'to stuff, stop up', fr. Lat. *stuppa*, 'tow', fr. Gk. *stúppē*, 'tow'; possibly cogn. w. Scrt. *stupáś*, 'tuft of hair'. **A.** trans. **1. a** To stuff up, close, place obstruction in, so as to check egress or ingress: *to stop a hole, leak, crack* &c.; Phrs. *to stop one's ears*, (i.) place hands &c. over them to prevent hearing; (ii.) (fig.) refuse to listen; *to stop a gap*, (fig.) act as substitute in emergency &c.; take someone's place; *to stop a person's mouth*, (colloq.) prevent his speaking; *to stop the way*, (lit. and fig.) hinder progress or passage; **b** specif., to stanch, check: *to stop the flow of blood*; **c** to fill up, pack tightly with cement &c.: *to stop a tooth*. **2. a** To cause (moving object) to cease motion; to arrest motion of, cause to come to rest, bring to a standstill: *to stop the traffic, a runaway horse*; *stop the train!*; *he was running too fast to stop himself*; *the fielder stopped the ball*; **b** to cause to cease operation, put out of action: *to stop an engine, watch* &c. **3.** To arrest progress or course of, cause cessation of, hold up (action or process): *to stop a fight*; *the rain stopped further play*; *frost has stopped the growth of plants*. Phr. *to stop a cheque*, order bank not to pay it. **4.** To prevent, hinder (person &c.) from action: *nothing will stop his, him from, interfering*; *what is to stop me from coming?* **5.** (of agent) To discontinue, leave off, cease from (an action which one is in course of performing): *to stop work*; *to stop talking*; *stop that chatter!* **6.** To discontinue supply of, cut off, deprive of: *to stop one's allowance, wages* &c. Phr. *to stop payment*, (i.) to stop a cheque &c., (ii.) (of bank), be unable to continue financial operations. **7.** (mus.) To alter pitch of musical note by pressing down string, closing hole &c., to change rate of vibration: *to stop a string* &c. **8.** (naut.) To make fast, lash firmly. **B.** intrans. **1. a** To cease movement or advance, come to rest, halt: *the train stops at all stations*; *to stop short, stop dead*; *it's time we stopped to rest*; **b** (of mechanism, organ &c.) to cease operation, cease to function: *the clock has stopped*; *his heart had stopped*. **2. a** To break off, discontinue, make an end of action; to pause: *he began to speak, but suddenly stopped*; *we will work for an hour and then stop*; **b** to be discontinued, come to an end: *the music, rain, rush of visitors &c., has stopped*. **3.** (colloq.) To stay, remain for a time: *to stop at home, in bed* &c.; *don't stop out too long*; *to stop with friends, at a hotel* &c., be a guest, visitor. **C.** Followed by adverbs or prepositions, with special meanings. *Stop down*, trans., (photog.) to reduce exposed part of (lens) by partially covering with a diaphragm. *Stop off*, intrans., (founding) to fill up part of mould with sand. *Stop out*, trans., (etching) to cover part of (plate &c.), with some substance which prevents action of acid upon that part. *Stop up*, trans., to obstruct, choke, close, fill up: *to stop up a hole*; *the drain is stopped up*.
stop (II.), n., fr. prec. **1.** Act of stopping; state of being stopped; cessation of movement or action: *to come to a sudden stop*; *the train goes through without a stop*; *Oxford is the first stop*, i.e. place of first stop. Phr. *to put a stop to*, cause to cease, bring to an end. **2.** (mus.) **a** Key or other device for depressing string, closing hole, &c. to alter pitch of note; **b** lever, movable knob &c., for opening or closing particular set of organ pipes, and producing specific quality or volume of tone; **c** (fig.) quality, character, of speech; style, tone &c. designed to produce specific effect: *to pull out the sympathetic stop*. **3.** Punctuation mark; *full stop*, dot indicating end of sentence, an abbreviation &c.; a period. Phr. *to come to a full stop*, (fig.) be obstructed or checked in action, be unable to continue. **4.** (joinery) Peg, block &c., checking movement of drawer, window-sash, door &c., at specific point. **5.** (phon.) Also *stop consonant*, consonant formed by complete stoppage of air-stream at some point, followed by its sudden release. **6.** (photog.) Diaphragm reducing aperture of lens. **7.** (naut.) Line used for lashing.
stop (III.), vb. trans., fr. prec. To put in the stops (in a piece of writing); to punctuate.
stop-cock, n. Tap for opening or closing pipe, cask &c.
stop-collar, n. Ring limiting motion of shaft &c.
stop-cylinder, n. Kind of mechanical printing press.
stop-drill, n. Drill with collar stopping its operation at specific depth.
stope, n. [1. stōp; 2. stoup]. Perh. connected w. **step**. (min.) Space cut through seam, usually roughly in the form of steps, between two galleries in a mine.
stopgap, n. [1. stópgap; 2. stɔ́pgæp]. Person or object supplying the place of another in an emergency.
stop-knob, n. Knob controlling organ-stop.
stopless, adj. [1. stóples; 2. stɔ́plis]. **stop (II.)** & **-less**. Without stops.
stop-motion, n. Mechanical device for arresting motion of machine automatically at certain point(s).
stop-order, n. Order fixing the prices above or below which stock is to be bought or sold, in order to limit losses.
stoppage, n. [1. stópij; 2. stɔ́pidž]. **stop (I.)** & **-age**. Act of stopping, state of being stopped; cessation of action, movement, or progress.
stopper (I.), n. [1. stóper; 2. stɔ́pə]. **stop (I.)** & **-er**. **1.** One who, that which, stops; specif. **a** object designed to fit into and close an opening, esp. the mouth of bottle &c.; **b** *tobacco-stopper*, instrument for packing tobacco into pipe. **2.** (naut.) Line for lashing, checking motion of, or shortening a cable &c.
stopper (II.), vb. trans., fr. prec. To fit, close, with a stopper: *to stopper a bottle*.
stopping (I.), adj. [1. stóping; 2. stɔ́piŋ], fr. Pres. Part. of **stop (I.)**. Specif. (of train &c.) calling at intermediate stations; contrasted with *non-stop, fast, express, train*.
stopping (II.), n. **stop (I.)** & **-ing**. **1.** Act of one who, that which, stops; specif. (mus.) act of pressing a string or closing hole &c.; *double-stopping*, simultaneous stopping of two strings. **2.** Material used for stopping; specif., cement, gold &c. used to stop a tooth.
stop-plate, n. Plate fixed to the end of an axle to prevent too great lateral play of the wheel.
stopple, n. & vb. trans. [1. stópl; 2. stɔ́pl]. **stop (I.)** & **-le**. **1.** n. Object for closing mouth of bottle &c.; stopper. **2.** vb. To close with a stopple.
stop-press, n. Late news inserted in special column of a newspaper after printing has begun.
stop-valve, n. Valve for controlling volume of water or steam passing through a pipe.
stop-watch, n. Watch, the hands of which can be instantaneously stopped or started by pressing a knob in the rim, in order to measure the exact duration of an action or event.
storable, adj. [1. stṓrabl; 2. stɔ́rəbl]. **store (II.)** & **-able**. Capable of being stored, suitable for storing.
storage, n. [1. stṓrij; 2. stɔ́ridž]. **store (II.)** & **-age**. **1.** Act of storing, state of being stored: *in cold storage*, in refrigerator. **2.** Space devoted to, available for, storing goods. **3.** Charge made for storing of goods.
storage battery, n. (elect.) Accumulator.
storax, n. [1. stṓraks; 2. stɔ́ræks]. Lat. *storax*, fr. Gk. *stúrax*, 'kind of resin'; Semitic loanword. **1.** Resin with scent like vanilla, formerly used in medicine; *liquid storax*, kind of balsam. **2.** Tree from which this resin is obtained.
store (I.), n. [1. stōr; 2. stɔ̄]. M.E. *stōr*, fr. O. Fr. *estōr*, fr. L. Lat. (*in*)*staurum*, fr. Lat. *instaurāre*, 'to renew, restore, repair', q.v. under **restore, steer (I.), stauroscope**. **1. a** Reserve supply, stock, accumulation of goods, material, provisions, kept for use when needed: *a store of food, fuel* &c.; *to lay in stores for the winter*; Phrs. *to set store by*, consider valuable; *to set no (great) store by*, regard as unimportant; **b** (pl.) supply of goods of specific kind, or needed for specific purpose: *naval, military, ship's stores* &c.; *marine stores*, old ship materials, cables &c., offered for sale; **c** accumulation of knowledge in the mind: *a store of learning, information* &c.

2. Place in which goods are stored; a depôt, warehouse, magazine &c. Phr. *in store*, (i.) reserved for future use; (ii.) (fig.) reserved by fate; destined to come or happen in the future: *to have a disappointment in store for one*; *who knows what the future may hold in store?* 3. Place in which goods are sold; specif. a *stores*, large general shop containing a number of departments for sale of goods of various kinds; b (Am.) *a store*, a shop; *to buy candy and crackers at the store*, to buy sweets and biscuits at the shop. 4. (usually pl.) Store-cattle.

store (II.), vb. trans. M.E. *stōren*, fr. O. Fr. *estorer*, fr. *estor*, 'store', see prec. 1. To fill, furnish, stock, with supplies, reserves; a (in material sense) *to store one's cupboards with food*; b *to store the mind with knowledge, with pleasant memories* &c. 2. a Often *store up* (in material and non-material sense), to put away, lay up, set aside carefully, reserve, for future use, consideration &c.: *to store up fuel for the winter*; *to store up a fact in one's mind*; specif., b to place, deposit (furniture &c.), temporarily in warehouse &c., for safe-keeping; c (of elect.) to accumulate. 3. To hold, provide storage room for: *the shed will store 20 ton of coal.*

store-cattle, n. Cattle kept for future fattening for killing.

storehouse, n. [1. stórhous; 2. stɔ́haus]. a Building in which goods &c. are stored; warehouse, repository; also b (fig., of person, mind &c.), *he is a storehouse of information.*

store-keeper, n. 1. Official in charge of stores, esp. naval and military stores. 2. (Am.) Shopkeeper.

store-room, n. Room in which supplies are kept, esp. for household use.

store-ship, n. Vessel carrying supplies for fleet &c.

storey, story, n. [1. stóri; 2. stɔ́ri]. Earlier, 'building', fr. O. Fr. *estorée*, P.P. of *estorer*, 'to build, construct; to repair, renew', fr. Lat. *(in)staurāre*, 'to renew', see **store (II.)**; or perh. fr. Med. Anglo-Lat. *(h)istoria* (as **history**) in the sense of storey marked by paintings, painted windows, carving &c. Single horizontal section of house or other building, the whole set of rooms, passages &c. on the same level. Phr. *the upper storey*, (slang) the brain, mind.

storeyed, storied, adj. [1. stórid; 2. stɔ́rid]. Prec. & **-ed.** (of building) Having specified number of storeys: *three-storeyed* &c.

storey-post, n. Upright post supporting floor-beam &c.

storiated, adj. [1. stōriāted; 2. stɔ̄rieitid], fr. **historiated.** (of letter, page, of book or manuscript) Decorated with elaborate design.

storied (I.), adj. [1. stórid; 2. stɔ́rid]. **story** (I.) & **-ed.** 1. Celebrated, made famous, in story. 2. Ornamented with, bearing, significant design or inscription, adorned with scene(s) from history &c.: '*Storied windows richly dight*' (Milton, 'Il Penseroso', 158); '*Can storied urn, or animated bust, Back to its mansion call the fleeting breath?*' (Gray's 'Elegy').

storied (II.), adj. See **storeyed.**

storiette, n. [1. stōriét; 2. stɔ̄riét]. **story** (I.) & **-ette.** Story in miniature, very short tale.

storiology, n. [1. stōriólоji; 2. stɔ̄riɔ́lədži]. **story** (I.) & *-o-* & **-logy.** The study of folk-tales.

stork, n. [1. stork; 2. stɔk]. O.E., M.E. *storc*; cp. O.N. *storkr*; M.L.G. *stōrk*; O.H.G. *storch*, 'stork'; cogn. w. Gk. *tórgos*, 'vulture'; prob. fr. base **ster-g-*, 'strong', expanded fr. **ster-* &c., 'stiff, firm, strong', q.v. under **stare** (I.), **stark** (I.). Large, long-legged, long-necked, long-billed, wading bird resembling heron, ibis &c.; esp. *common* or *white stork*, *Ciconia alba*, migratory European stork, often frequenting human habitations, nesting on housetops &c.

stork's bill, n. Plant of genus *Erodium* or *Pelargonium*.

storm (I.), n. [1. storm; 2. stɔm]. O.E., M.E. *storm*; cp. M.L.G., M. Du. *storm*; O.H.G. *sturm*; O.N. *stormr*, 'storm, tumult'; fr. base seen in O.E. *styrian*, 'to stir up, put in motion, whirl round', see **stir** &c. 1. Violent atmospheric disturbance involving strong wind, with or without rain, sleet &c., and sometimes accompanied by thunder and lightning; sometimes in compounds, indicating specific character of storm, e.g. *thunder-storm*; *sand-*, *dust-storm*, clouds of sand, dust, carried and whirled round, by the wind; *cyclonic storm*, cyclone; *magnetic storm*, disturbance of magnetic field, indicated by oscillation of magnetic needle. Phr. *a storm in a tea-cup*, a fuss about trifles. 2. Violent atmospheric precipitation, with or without wind: *a storm of rain, hail*; also in compounds, *hail-*, *rain-*, *snow-storm* &c. 3. (naut. and meteorol.) Wind of specific velocity, usually 70-80 miles per hour, between gale and hurricane. 4. Dense shower or volley of objects flying through the air: *a storm of arrows, missiles* &c. 5. Loud, repeated, tumultuous expression of emotion by persons, voices &c., in unison: *a storm of cheers, applause, hisses* &c. 6. a Violent mental or emotional agitation, disturbance, commotion, gust of passion; esp. one affecting a large number of people: *a storm of indignation swept over the country*; cp. *brain-storm*; Phr. *storm and stress*, period of restlessness, agitation, or revolutionary change, in intellectual development &c.; b violent upheaval in social or political conditions: *the storm of revolution.* 7. (mil.) Sudden violent assault on fortified post &c. Phr. *to take by storm*, (i.) capture by sudden attack; hence (ii.) (fig.) captivate instantaneously and completely: *he took her, her affections, by storm.*

storm (II.), vb. trans. & intrans., fr. prec. A. trans. (mil.) To take by storm, capture by sudden assault. B. intrans. 1. (of wind &c.) To be boisterous, violent, tempestuous. 2. (fig.) To give violent expression to anger, agitation &c., to rage; also, *storm at*, to upbraid loudly and violently; to scold, vituperate.

storm-beaten, adj. Injured by storms.

storm-belt, n. Area in which storms are specially frequent.

storm-bird, n. Bird supposed to presage approach of storm, esp. stormy petrel.

storm-bound, adj. Delayed by storms.

storm-card, n. Chart indicating position of ship in relation to storm-centre.

storm-centre, n. a Point of lowest atmospheric pressure in a storm area; b (fig.) person or group of persons who form a centre and starting-point of unrest and disturbance.

storm-cloud, n. a Cloud portending or accompanying storm; hence, b (fig.) signs of approaching danger or disturbance.

storm-cock, n. Kind of bird, esp. fieldfare or missel-thrush.

storm-cone, n. Large canvas cone hoisted as storm-signal.

storm-door, n. Supplementary outer door to protect entrance to building &c. in a storm.

storm-drum, n. Canvas-covered cylinder used, in conjunction with storm-cone, as storm-signal.

stormer, n. [1. stórmer; 2. stɔ́mə]. **storm** (II.) & **-er.** One who, that which, storms, esp. member of storming-party.

storm-finch, n. Stormy petrel.

stormful, adj. [1. stórmfool; 2. stɔ́mful]. **storm** (I.) & **-ful.** (rare) Abounding in storms.

storm-glass, n. Glass-tube containing a chemical solution, the precipitate of which changes in appearance in varying atmospheric conditions.

stormily, adv. [1. stórmili; 2. stɔ́mili]. **stormy** & **-ly.** In a stormy manner.

storminess, n. [1. stórmines; 2. stɔ́minis]. See prec. & **-ness.** State or quality of being stormy.

storming-party, n. [1. stórming pàrti; 2. stɔ́miŋ pàti]. Member of military party detailed to storm fortified post &c.

stormless, adj. [1. stórmles; 2. stɔ́mlis]. **storm** (I.) & **-less.** Without, free from, storms.

storm-petrel, n. Stormy petrel.

storm-proof, adj. Not liable to be injured, affected, or penetrated by storm.

storm-sail, n. Heavy canvas sail used in rough weather.

storm-signal, n. Signal displayed on coast &c. to give warning of storm.

storm-tossed, adj. [1. stórm tost; 2. stɔ́m tɔst]. (lit. and fig.) Suffering from effects of storm.

storm-wind, n. Violent wind, constituting or accompanying a storm.

storm-window, n. Extra, external window for protection in a storm.

stormy, adj. [1. stórmi; 2. stɔ́mi]. **storm** (I.) & **-y** (IV.). 1. Of, pertaining to, characteristic of, agitated by, storms: *stormy weather, winds, sea.* 2. Indicating presence or approach of storm: *a stormy sunset, sky* &c.; *stormy petrel*, kind of petrel thought to portend a storm, called by sailors 'Mother Carey's chicken'. 3. Characterized by violent emotion; passionate, agitated by strong contending feeling, opinions &c.: *a stormy discussion*; *the meeting was rather stormy.*

storm-zone, n. Storm-belt.

stort(h)ing, n. [1. stórting; 2. stɔ́tiŋ]. Norw., lit. 'the great meeting or place of discussion'; fr. O.N. *stōrr*, 'great; proud', see under **stare** (I.), & O.N. *þing*, 'meeting', see under **thing**. Norwegian parliament.

story (I.), n. [1. stṓri; 2. stɔ́ri]. M.E., fr. A.-Fr. *storie*; O. Fr. *estoire*, fr. Lat. *historia*, see **history.** 1. a History; account and description of a series of past events and actions: *the story of the rise of England's sea-power*; '*In this harsh world draw thy breath in pain, To tell my story*' ('Hamlet'); b what is told in the form of traditional, often legendary, recital, concerning the lives and adventures of heroes and other great personages of the past: *a name famous in story*; *the story goes that.* 2. a Piece of imaginative writing, whether in prose or verse, shorter than a novel, describing adventures and episodes in the lives of a group of personages; esp. an account of a complete action or adventure with a rounded-off conclusion; also *short story*; b a recital by word of mouth of such an action or adventure; a tale: *please tell us a story*; *children like to listen to a story.* Phr. *a very different story*, something quite different. 3. An interesting series of events, adventures, actions, associated with a person or object: *there is often a story connected with a famous jewel.* 4. A brief, pointed, narrative, relating a single saying, adventure, or action of a specific person; an anecdote: *he told some good stories of Oxford dons.* 5. The plot, intrigue, dénouement of a work of fiction or of a drama: *a novel with very little story.* 6. Childish word for lie; untrue statement, fib.

story (II.), n. See **storey.**

story-book, n. Collection of short stories; book containing a single story; a novel, a romance.

story-teller, n. 1. One who relates a story; writer or reciter of stories. 2. (childish) Liar, fibber.

story-writer, n. Writer of stories.

stoup, n. [1. stōōp; 2. stūp]. Cp. O.N. *staup*; Du. *stoop*; O.E. *stēap*, 'flagon'. 1. Drinking-vessel, flagon, goblet. 2. Vessel or basin for holy water.

stout (I.), adj. [1. stout; 2. staut]. M.E. *stout*, fr. O. Fr. *estout*, fr. M. Du. *stolt*, 'stout, strong, bold'; cp. O.N. *stoltr*; O.H.G. *stolz*, 'proud'; the Gmc. words are possibly for Lat. *stultus*, 'foolish'; see **stultify** 1. Strong, tough, durable, able to stand strain or pressure: *stout cords*; *a stout staff*; *a stout ship.* 2. Brave, resolute; capable of, characterized by, endurance: *a stout fellow*; *a stout fighter*; *a stout heart*; *stout resistance.* 3. Full-bodied; fat, plump, corpulent, obese.

stout (II.), n., fr. prec. A dark, strong, superior kind of porter.
stout-hearted, adj. Having a stout heart; courageous, resolute.
stout-heartedly, adv. Prec. & **-ly**. In a stout-hearted manner.
stout-heartedness, n. See prec. & **-ness**. State or quality of being stout-hearted.
stoutish, adj. [1. stóutish; 2. stáutiʃ]. **stout** (I.) & **-ish** (I.). Fairly stout.
stoutly, adv. [1. stóutli; 2. stáutli]. **stout** (I.) & **-ly**. In a stout manner; resolutely.
stoutness, n. [1. stóutnes; 2. stáutnis]. See prec. & **-ness**. State or quality of being stout; **a** obesity; **b** toughness; **c** resoluteness.
stove (I.), n. [1. stōv; 2. stouv]. O.E. *stofa*; M.E. *stōve*, 'bathroom, heated room'; O.H.G. *stuba*, 'heated chamber; bath', Mod. Germ. *stube*, 'room'; cp. further Ital. *stufa*, Fr. *étuve*, 'heated chamber; stove'; fr. Low Lat. **stūba*, prob. fr. *extufāre*, whence Fr. *étouffer*, 'suffocate', & Ital. *tufo*, 'vapour'. Ultimately fr. Gk. *tûphos*, 'mist, vapour, cloud'. This is fr. base **dhŭ-*, q.v. also under **dust** & **fume**. Apparatus, burning different kinds of fuel, as coke, gas, oil, electricity, of various shapes and sizes, for heating and cooking.
stove (II.), vb. trans., fr. prec. To raise (plants) in a stove.
stove (III.), vb. Pret. & P.P. of **stave** (II.).
stove-pipe, n. Metal pipe carrying off smoke &c. from stove; *stove-pipe hat*, (U.S.A.) top-hat.
stow, vb. trans. [1. stō; 2. stou]. O.E. *stōwian*; M.E. *stōwen*, 'to place, stow away'; fr. O.E. *stōw*, 'place'; cp. O.N. *stō*, 'place'; Goth. *stōjan*, 'to direct'; cogn. w. Lith. *stovà*, 'position'; Lett. *stāwēt*, 'to stand'; Scrt. *sthinā*, 'pillar'; Gk. *stoá*, 'colonnade', see **stoa**; fr. base **st(h)ĕu-*, **st(h)ŏu-* &c., 'to stand firm', seen also in **steer** (I.), **restore**. **a** To pack carefully, closely, and compactly in a receptacle: *to stow clothes into a box* &c.; Phr. (vulg. slang) *stow it!*, shut up!; **b** to fill (receptacle) with goods: *to stow the hold with cargo.*
stowage, n. [1. stṓij; 2. stóuidž]. **stow** & **-age**. **a** Method of stowing; **b** space for stowing; **c** charge for stowing.
stowaway, n. [1. stṓawā; 2. stóuəwei]. Person who conceals himself in outward-bound ship in order to obtain a free passage.
stow-wood, n. Wooden blocks for wedging and steadying casks in ship's hold &c.
strabismal, adj. [1. strabízmal; 2. strəbízməl]. See **strabismus** & **-al**. Of, pertaining to, affected with, strabismus; cross-eyed.
strabismic, adj. [1. strabízmik; 2. strəbízmik]. See next word & **-ic**. Strabismal.
strabismus, n. [1. strabízmus; 2. strəbízməs]. Mod. Lat. fr. Gk., fr. *strabós*, 'crooked, squinting'; cp. Gk. *stróbilos*, 'spinning, whirling', see **strobile**; *stróbos*, 'whirlpool'; *streblós*, 'twisted; squinting'. Cp. further Gk. *stréphein*, 'to turn, twist'; *strophḗ*, 'action of turning'. See **strophe**. Affection of eye-muscles which makes it impossible for both eyes to look straight at an object at the same time; squint, cast, in the eye.
strabotomy, n. [1. strabótumi; 2. strəbɔ́təmi], fr. Gk. *strabós*, 'squinting', see prec., & **-tomy**. Surgical operation of cutting contracted muscle of eyeball to cure squint.
Strad, n. [1. strad; 2. stræd]. Abbr. fr. **Stradivarius**.
straddle (I.), vb. intrans. & trans. [1. strádl; 2. strǽdl]. Perh. a freq. fr. **stride**; vowel unexplained. **A.** intrans. **1.** To sit, stand, or walk with feet far apart, to stretch the legs out widely. **2.** (fig.) To assume a doubtful or hesitating position; to hedge, vacillate. **3.** (naut.) To drop shots of known range beyond and short of an object in order to determine the range of the latter. **B.** trans. **1.** To sit or stand with a leg on either side of: *to straddle a fence.* **2.** To double (the opening stakes), at poker, before examining one's cards.
straddle (II.), n., fr. prec. **1.** Act of straddling; straddling position. **2. a** (poker) A doubling of opening stakes before looking at one's cards; **b** (Stock Exchange) a form of contract which gives right of calling for or delivering stock at an agreed price.
straddle-legged, adj. Having the legs wide apart.
Stradivarius, n. [1. stràdivárius, -váhrius; 2. strædivéəriəs, -vāriəs], fr. name of Antonio Stradivari, violin-maker of Cremona, d. 1737. Violin, viola, or violoncello made by this maker.
strafe, vb. trans. & n. [1. strahf; 2. strāf], fr. Germ. Phr. *Gott strafe England*, 'God punish England', used in Great War. (slang) **1.** vb. **a** To shell, bombard, heavily; hence, **b** (i.) to damage, punish; (ii.) to scold severely. **2.** n. **a** Heavy gunfire, bombardment; hence, **b** punishment, injury.
straggle, vb. intrans. [1. strágl; 2. strǽgl]. Origin uncertain. **1. a** To loiter, stray, wander in the rear of a group; to loiter along in isolated, irregular groups: *children straggling home from school*; **b** to stray irregularly from the rest of a mass, bunch, bundle, plait &c.: *a wisp of hair straggled across her ear.* **2.** To extend, in isolated, scattered, groups: *the town straggles out into the country*; *a few houses straggling along the road.*
straggler, n. [1. strágler; 2. strǽglə]. Prec. & **-er**. One who, that which, straggles.
straggling, adj. [1. strágling; 2. strǽgliŋ]. Pres. Part. of **straggle**. **1.** Detached from the main body, forming an irregular, outlying portion; scattered: *a straggling line of soldiers, of houses, of bushes.* **2.** Drooping, projecting, untidily from its place: *a straggling wisp of hair*; *a shrub with straggling shoots.*
stragglingly, adv. Prec. & **-ly**. In a straggling manner.
straggly, adj. [1. strágli; 2. strǽgli]. **straggle** & **-y** (IV.). Straggling.
straight (I.), adj. [1. strāt; 2. streit]. M.E. *streiht*, fr. O.E. *streht*, P.P. of *streććan*, 'to extend'. See **stretch** (I.). **1.** Extending constantly, throughout its length, in one direction; lying evenly between its extreme points; contrasted with *crooked, bent*, or *curved*: *a straight line, road, stick, hedge* &c.; *straight arch*, having sides without curve; *straight hair*, without curl or wave. **2.** Upright; not bent, stooping, or inclined; vertical: *a straight back, tree-trunk* &c. **3.** Level, not crooked, esp. parallel to a given line or surface: *to put a picture, mat, one's hat, straight.* **4.** In order, properly arranged, worked out, balanced &c.: *to put a room straight*; *to get one's affairs straight.* **5.** Direct, frank, not ambiguous or equivocal, without concealment: *a straight question, answer, look* &c. **6.** Morally upright; honest, sincere; equitable: *a thoroughly straight fellow*; *a person who is not quite straight*; *straight dealing*; *to keep straight.* **7.** (slang) Authoritative, reliable: *a straight tip for a race.*
straight (II.), n., fr. prec. **1.** State, quality, of being straight; esp. *out of the straight*, crooked. **2.** Straight stretch of road, river &c.; specif., final straight part of racecourse. **3.** A sequence, in card games, esp. poker.
straight (III.), adv., fr. **straight** (I.). **1.** In a straight line; directly; without forming or following a curve or angle: *the smoke rises straight upwards*; *to fly straight as an arrow*; *to look straight ahead*; *he can't walk straight.* Phrs. *to hit, shoot, straight*, take accurate aim; *to ride straight*, ride across country after hounds, taking all fences &c. and not stopping to go through gates; *to run straight*, (fig.) behave as an honest man. **2.** Upright, not crouching or stooping: *to stand straight.* **3. a** Directly, by direct route, without making a detour; without intermediate stages, without breaking the journey: *I shall go straight to Paris without stopping at Dover*; **b** directly in thought or speech, without circumlocution, digression, or ambiguity: *to come straight to the point*; *tell me straight what you think*; also *to say, tell, something straight out.* **4. a** (archaic) At once, immediately, straightway; **b** (*I will do it*) *straight off*, straight away, immediately, without delay, hesitation, or reflection; at once.
straight-cut, adj. (of tobacco) Made from leaf cut lengthwise.
straight-edge, n. Wooden or metal bar or strip with one straight edge for testing straightness of line, level surface &c.
straighten, vb. trans. & intrans. [1. strātn; 2. stréitn]. **straight** (I.) & **-en** (V.). **1.** trans. To make, put, straight. **2.** intrans. To become straight.
straightforward, adj. [1. strātfórward; 2. streitfɔ́wəd]. **1.** Acting, speaking, openly, without concealment or ambiguity; made, done, in this way; frank, candid, honest: *a straightforward person, answer*; *straightforward behaviour.* **2.** Not elaborate or complicated; simple: *a straightforward piece of work.*
straightforwardly, adv. Prec. & **-ly**. In a straightforward manner.
straightforwardness, n. See prec. & **-ness**. State or quality of being straightforward.
straightness, n. [1. strātnes; 2. stréitnis]. **straight** (I.) & **-ness**. State or quality of being straight (in material and moral sense).
straightway, adv. [1. strātwā; 2. stréitwei]. (archaic) Immediately, at once.
strain (I.), vb. trans. & intrans. [1. strān; 2. strein]. M.E. *streinen*, 'to strain, stretch; to constrain', fr. O. Fr. *estreign-*, Pres. stem of *estreindre*, 'to strain', fr. Lat. *stringere*, 'to draw tightly'. See **stringent**. **A.** trans. **1.** To stretch tightly, make taut: *to strain a wire in a fence.* **2.** To exert (bodily faculty) to the utmost, use, tax, to the utmost capacity: *to strain one's ears to catch a sound.* Phr. *to strain every nerve*, use every effort, employ every means. **3.** To over-exert, over-tax, put too great a strain or tax upon (bodily faculty); to fatigue by excessive use: *to strain one's eyes by reading small print.* **4. a** To wrench, tear, sprain, cause injury to, by sudden or too violent effort or movement: *to strain a tendon*; **b** to twist, pull awry, cause to warp (part of a structure): *to strain the timbers of a ship.* **5.** To presume too much upon; to exact too much from, try too far: *to strain a person's patience, good temper, politeness* &c. **6.** To wrest, pervert (meaning) of; to put an interpretation upon, read a meaning into (words), different from, or wider than, what appears to be the natural implication; Phr. *to strain a point* (esp. *in a person's favour*), to interpret a statement, rule, as liberally as possible. **7.** To embrace tightly, clasp, press closely: *to strain a person to one's heart.* **8. a** To filter by passing through perforated object or porous substance: *to strain wine, soup* &c.; **b** to remove by straining, also *strain out.* **B.** intrans. **1.** To make a violent effort, exert all one's forces, strive with difficulty: *a swimmer straining to reach the shore*; *eyes straining through the mist.* **2.** To become strained or clarified; to percolate slowly through filtering object or substance. **C.** Followed by adverbs or prepositions in special senses. *Strain after*, intrans., to strive laboriously for, make utmost efforts to obtain or produce: *a writer who strains after effect.* *Strain at*, intrans., **a** to apply exertion to, push or pull at: *to strain at a rope*; *the horse strains at his collar*; **b** (with reference to Matt. xxiii. 24) to make a fuss about tolerating or accepting: *one shouldn't strain at a few tactless words.* *Strain off*, trans., to remove (impurities &c.) from liquid by passing through strainer &c.
strain (II.), n., fr. prec. **1. a** Condition of tension; tautness, tightness: *to keep a strain on a rope*; **b** amount of force exerted on an object by tension: *the rope broke under the strain.* **2.** Severe bodily or mental effort: *it was a hard strain to reach the top of the mountain*; *the constant strain of anxiety.* **3.** Effect on body or mind of an excessive strain; **a** bodily injury, lesion, sprain;

b nervous fatigue resulting from prolonged and severe tension. **4.** (mechan.) Effect exerted upon, alteration caused in shape of, material, by pressure, stress, thrust.

strain (III.), n. Neither spelling nor pronunciation can be derived fr. O.E. *strēon*, 'treasure; propagation, offspring, progeny', as many dictionaries appear to suggest, & as there is no connexion in sense w. **strain** (I.) there is no ground for assuming that this word could have influenced the form, wh. remains a puzzle. The old word in its normal modern form is used by Spenser: '*yborne of heauenly strene*', race, lineage ('F. Q.' v. 9. 32). **1.** a Breed, stock, ancestry: *he comes of a noble strain*; b inherited characteristics, line of descent from a particular stock: *Alsatian dogs seem to have a wolf strain in their ancestry.* **2.** a Cast of mind, disposition, tendency; characteristic quality; tinge, streak: *a strain of melancholy, cruelty &c. in a man's character*; b characteristic mode of expression; style, manner, tenor: *he spoke in a dismal strain*; *he said he had been grossly betrayed, and much more in the same strain.* **3.** a (often pl.) A song, melody, musical air, note: *the strains of the human voice, of a harp*; *the melancholy strains of the bagpipe*; *strains of mirth* &c.; b (poet.) poetry, minstrelsy, song: '*Soul-animating strains, alas, too few!*' (Wordsworth, of Milton's Sonnets).

strainable, adj. [1. strânabl; 2. stréinəbl]. **strain** (I.) & **-able.** Capable of being strained.

strained, adj. [1. strānd; 2. streind], fr. P.P. of **strain** (I.). **1.** (in moral sense) Warped, distorted, awry; awkward, constrained: *relations between us have become strained.* **2.** Produced with effort; forced, unnatural: *strained merriment*; *his jokes were rather strained.*

strainer, n. [1. strâner; 2. stréinə]. **strain** (I.) & **-er.** One who, that which, strains; specif., device with a mesh for removing solids or impurities from liquid.

strait (I.), adj. [1. strāt; 2. streit]. M.E. *streit*, fr. A.-Fr. *estreit*, 'narrow', fr. Lat. *strictum*, P.P. type of *stringere*, 'to draw together'; see **strict, stringent.** **1.** (archaic) Narrow, restricted; in Phr. *the strait gate* (Matt. vii. 13). **2.** (archaic) Strict, scrupulous, rigorous.

strait (II.), n., fr. prec. **1.** Narrow channel of water connecting two larger bodies of water: *Menai Strait*; (also pl.) *the Straits of Dover.* **2.** Position, circumstances, of difficulty and perplexity; an awkward fix, situation of stringency; (often pl.) *to be in a strait*; *in great straits.*

straiten, vb. trans. [1. strâtn; 2. stréitn]. **strait** (I.) & **-en** (I.). **1.** (archaic) To make narrow, confine, limit. **2.** (chiefly in P.P. as adj.) To restrict, make difficult, put into difficulties, embarrass: *in straitened circumstances.*

strait jacket, n. Strait waistcoat.

strait-laced, adj. (fig.) Rigid, severe, strict, austere in morals or opinions.

straitly, adv. [1. strâtli; 2. stréitli]. **strait** (I.) & **-ly.** (archaic) Strictly, narrowly.

straitness, n. [1. strâtnes; 2. stréitnis]. See prec. & **-ness.** (archaic) Strictness.

strait waistcoat, n. Kind of coat made to confine arms and used to restrict movements of dangerous lunatic or criminal.

strake, n. [1. strāk; 2. streik]. Variant of **streak.** Single breadth of plank or plating running continuously from stem to stern of ship, and forming a section of her side.

stramineous, adj. [1. stramíneus; 2. strəmíniəs], fr. Lat. *strāmineus*, 'like, made of, straw', fr. *strāmin-*, stem of *strāmen*, 'straw, litter'; cp. Gk. *strōma*, 'straw, litter; cover', see **stroma**; Scrt. *stárīman*, 'spreading out'; cp. further Lat. *strātum*, 'something spread out, layer'; see **stratum,** & words there referred to. (archaic) Of, like, straw; esp. of the colour of straw.

stramonium, n. [1. stramṓnium; 2. strəmóuniəm]. Etymol. doubtful. Poisonous narcotic drug obtained from the *Datura* or thorn-apple, used medicinally for asthma &c.

strand (I.), n. [1. strand; 2. strænd]. O.E., M.E. *strand*; cp. M.H.G. *strant*; prob. cogn. w. Lat. *sternere*, P.P. *strātum*, 'to spread, scatter', see **stratum**; O. Slav. *strana*, 'region'; Scrt. *stṛnāti*, 'strews'; see also **straw, strew.** (chiefly poet.) Shore, beach, of sea, lake, or river.

strand (II.), vb. trans. & intrans., fr. prec. **1.** trans. To run (ship) aground, cause to run aground. **2.** intrans. (of ship &c.) To run aground.

strand (III.), n., fr. O. Fr. *estran*, fr. O.H.G. *streno*, 'skein'; cp. Du. *streen*, 'skein'; prob. cogn. w. Lat. *stria*, 'furrow, channel, fluting'; see **stria**; cp. also O.H.G. *strīmo*, 'stripe, streak'. Single thread, fibre, or part twisted with another or others to form yarn, rope &c.

strand (IV.), vb. trans., fr. prec. **1.** To break a strand of (rope &c.). **2.** To make (rope, yarn &c.) by twisting strands together.

stranded, adj. [1. stránded; 2. strǽndid], fr. P.P. of **strand** (II.), fr. idea of ship & crew left on a rock, barren shore &c. Left destitute or helpless, without means of escape or extrication from difficulty; left without resources.

strange, adj. [1. strānj; 2. streindž]. M.E. *strānge*, fr. O. Fr. *estrange*, fr. Lat. *extrāneus*, 'strange, foreign', see **extraneous.** **1.** Not known, unfamiliar, not recognizable, not previously seen, heard, experienced &c.: *a strange man, face, voice, handwriting* &c.; *to wake in a strange place*; *the language is quite strange to me.* **2.** Foreign, alien, exotic, not one's own: *to visit strange lands*; *to follow strange gods.* **3.** Remarkable from its newness or unexpectedness; unusual, uncommon, singular; difficult to explain: *what a strange thing!*; *to see strange sights*; *it's very strange that you haven't heard from him*; *a strange expression on one's face*; *a strange thing to say*; *to speak with a strange reluctance.* Phr. *strange to say*, it is surprising that. **4.** (of persons) Inexperienced, raw; unfamiliar, unaccustomed, out of one's element: *he is still strange to the job, place* &c.; *to feel strange.*

strangely, adv. Prec. & **-ly.** In a strange manner; esp. remarkably, unusually; to a remarkable degree: *strangely silent about it.*

strangeness, n. See prec. & **-ness.** State or quality of being strange; esp. a unfamiliarity; b remarkableness, queerness.

stranger, n. [1. strânjer; 2. stréindžə]. M.E. *stranger*, fr. O. Fr. *estrangier*; **strange** & **-er.** **1.** Person unknown to one; one who is unfamiliar, not an acquaintance: *a stranger came to the door*; *he is a stranger to me*; *to be shy in the presence of strangers.* Phrs. *to see, spy, strangers*, said in House of Commons in order to have House cleared of all but members; *you are quite a stranger*, you have not been here, or to see us, for a long time. **2.** Person coming from another place or country; foreigner, alien: *I'm a stranger in these parts*; *a stranger in a strange land.* **3.** Person unfamiliar with, not experienced in, unaccustomed to, some particular condition, circumstances, occupation: *no stranger to sorrow*; *a stranger to your way of thinking.*

strangle, vb. trans. [1. stránggl; 2. strǽŋgl], fr. O. Fr. *estrangler*, fr. Lat. *strangulāre*, 'to strangle, choke; to check, constrain', see **strangulate.** **1.** a To kill by suffocation caused by constriction of windpipe; hence, b of anything placed or worn round neck, to be uncomfortably tight for, choke. **2.** (fig.) To suppress, keep back, stifle: *to strangle a sob, oath, sigh* &c.

strangle-hold, n. Hold in wrestling involving the temporary choking of one's opponent (also fig.).

strangles, n. [1. strángglz; 2. strǽŋglz], fr. **strangle.** Infectious catarrhal disease in horses.

strangulate, vb. trans. [1. stránggūlāt; 2. strǽŋgjulèit], fr. Lat. *strangulātum*, P.P. type of *strangulāre*, 'to strangle; to stifle, suppress', fr. Gk. *straggaloûn*, 'to twist, strangle'; cp. Gk. *straggálē*, 'cord, lace'; *strágx*, 'drop squeezed out'; cogn. w. Lett. *stringt*, 'to dry up, stiffen'; Ir. *sreang*, 'cord'; cp. further O.E. *streng*, 'cord', see **string**; O.N. *strangr*, 'rough, strong', see **strong.** See also **stringent.** To strangle; hence, (specif. med. and surg.) to compress, constrict (vein, duct, intestine &c.), so as to obstruct passage.

strangulation, n. [1. strànggūlâshun; 2. stræŋgjuléiʃən]. Prec. & **-ion.** (med.) Compression, constriction, of some channel or tube in the body, which prevents passage of air, liquid &c.

strangurious, adj. [1. strànggū́rius; 2. stræŋgjǝ́riəs]. Next word & **-ous.** Of, pertaining to, characteristic of, strangury.

strangury, n. [1. stránggūri; 2. strǽŋgjuri], fr. Lat. *strangūria*, fr. Gk. *straggouría*, 'strangury', fr. Gk. *stragg-*, stem of *strágx*, 'drop', q.v. under **strangle,** & *oûron*, 'urine', q.v. under **urine,** & **-ia.** Difficult and painful urination.

strap (I.), n. [1. strap; 2. stræp]. O.E. *stropp*, 'thong'; M.E. *strop*; fr. Lat. *struppus*, 'thong, strap', fr. Gk. *stróphos*, 'cord, band'; see **strophe.** **1.** Strip of flexible material, usually of leather; esp. such a strip furnished with a buckle, used for fastening and securing; (fig.) *the strap*, corporal punishment, from use of strap in castigation. **2.** Flat piece of metal for holding timbers, or parts of a machine, together. **3.** Blade of grass-leaf.

strap (II.), vb. trans., fr. prec. **1.** To fasten, secure, bind, with a strap. **2.** To fasten with strips of adhesive plaster; esp. to fasten (edges of wound) together in this way; also, *strap up (a wound).* **3.** To chastise with a strap. **4.** To sharpen on a strap; to strop.

strap-hanger, n. Passenger in train, bus, or tram who cannot obtain a seat and has to hold on to a strap.

strap-laid, adj. *Strap-laid rope*, flat band made of several ropes laid side by side and fastened in position.

strappado, n. & vb. trans. [1. strapâdō; 2. stræpéidou], fr. Ital. *strappata*, fr. *strappare*, 'to pull'. **1.** n. Punishment or torture in which the victim is raised above the ground by a rope fastened to his wrists, and then allowed to fall to the length of the rope. **2.** vb. To torture by this method.

strapped, adj. [1. strapt; 2. stræpt], fr. P.P. of **strap** (II.). Fastened, secured, with a strap; *strapped trousers*, fastened down by straps passing under insteps; ornamented by straps or flat bands of material.

strapper, n. [1. stráper; 2. strǽpə]. **strap** (I.) & **-er.** **1.** a One who fastens or fixes straps; specif. b one who harnesses horses; stableman. **2.** (colloq.) Large, robust, strapping person.

strapping (I.), adj. [1. stráping; 2. strǽpiŋ]. **strap** (II.) & **-ing** (II.). (colloq.) Tall, robust, largely made and well-proportioned; bouncing: *a fine strapping wench, girl.*

strapping (II.), n. **strap** (II.) & **-ing** (I.). a Material used for straps; b specif. (surg.) strips of adhesive plaster used to bring edges of a wound together, to hold bandages in place &c.

strap-work, n. (archit.) Ornamentation representing a series of narrow, interlacing bands.

strapwort, n. [1. strápwërt; 2. strǽpwə̄t]. Maritime plant with white flowers, *Corrigiola littoralis.*

strata, pl. of **stratum.**

stratagem, n. [1. strátajem; 2. strǽtədžəm], fr. O. Fr. *stratageme*, fr. Lat. *stratēgēma*, fr. Gk. *stratḗgēma*, 'piece of generalship; device, stratagem', fr. *stratēgein*, 'to lead as general', fr. *stratēgós*, 'general'; see **strategus.** Cunning device intended to deceive; artifice, clever trick.

stratal, adj. [1. strâtl; 2. stréitl]. See **stratum** & **-al.** Pertaining to, arranged in, characteristic of, strata.

strategic(al), adj. [1. stratḗjik(l); 2. strətídž-ik(l)], fr. Gk. *stratēgikós*, 'of a general', fr. *stratēgós*, 'general', see **strategus**, & **-ic** (& **-al**). Of, pertaining to, carried out by, characterized by, strategy: *a strategic retreat.*

strategically, adv. Prec. & **-ly**. In a strategic manner.

strategics, n. [1. stratḗjiks; 2. strətídžiks], fr. Gk. *stratēgós*, 'general', see **strategus**, & **ics**. Science of strategy.

strategist, n. [1. strátejist; 2. strǽtidžist]. **strategy** & **-ist**. Person skilled in strategy.

strategus, n. [1. stratḗgus; 2. strətígəs]. Lat. *stratēgus*, fr. Gk. *stratēgós*, 'strategus', fr. *stratós*, 'army; crowd; division of people'; cp. Scrt. *str̥taš*, 'spread out'; cogn. w. Lat. *strātum*, 'layer'; see **stratum**, & *ágein* 'to lead': see **act** (I.). General commanding ancient Greek army; esp. one of the ten Athenian officers elected yearly to commands in army and navy.

strategy, n. [1. stráteji; 2. strǽtidži], fr. Gk. *stratēgía*, 'office of general; skill of general', fr. *stratēgós*, 'general', see prec., & **-ia**. The art of conducting a military campaign; specif., the art of preparing, moving, and using armed forces in a war so as to secure the initiative and ultimately to win the war; distinguished from *tactics*; also fig.

strath, n. [1. strath; 2. stræþ]. Gael. *srath*, 'valley'; cp. M. Ir. *srath*, 'shore; valley'; W. *(y)strad*, 'plain'; cogn. w. Lat. *strātum*, 'layer', see **stratum**; Gk. *strôma*, 'layer, carpet', see **stroma**; O.E. *strēawian*, 'to spread', see **strew**. (Scots) A broad, open valley through which a river runs.

strathspey, n. [1. strathspā́; 2. stræþspéi], fr. name of district in Eastern Scotland. **a** Kind of Scottish dance, rather slower than **reel**; **b** music for this dance.

strati-, pref. representing **stratum**. Stratum or strata.

straticulate, adj. [1. stratíkūlāt; 2. strætík-juleit]. Prec. & **-cule** & **-ate**. (geol.) Having, arranged in, deposited as, a series of thin layers.

stratification, n. [1. stràtifikā́shun; 2. strǽtifi-kéiʃən]. See **stratify** & **-fication**. Process of stratifying; state of being stratified; specif., deposition of sediment in distinct layers by the action of water, wind, or other agency; relative position or arrangement of such layers in specific type of rock.

stratiform, adj. [1. strátiform; 2. strǽtifɔ̄m]. **strati-** & **-form**. Having the character of, forming, a stratum.

stratify, vb. trans. [1. strátifī; 2. strǽtifai]. **strati-** & **-fy**. To arrange, deposit, in layers; specif., *stratified rock*, deposited in the form of layers of sediment by the action of water &c.

stratigraphic, adj. [1. stràtigráfik; 2. strǽti-grǽfik]. **strati-** & **-graphic**. Of, pertaining to, stratigraphy.

stratigraphically, adv. [1. stràtigráfikali; 2. strǽtigrǽfikəli]. Prec. & **-al** & **-ly**. According to the methods of stratigraphy.

stratigraphy, n. [1. stratígrafi; 2. strætígrəfi]. **strati-** & **-graphy**. Science or description of relative position of strata of rock.

strato-, pref. representing **stratus** & *-o-*. Stratus; e.g. *strato-cirrus, -cumulus*, cloud formations resembling cirrus or cumulus and stratus.

stratocracy, n. [1. stratókrasi; 2. strətɔ́krəsi], fr. Gk. *stratós*, 'army; division of people', q.v. under **strategus**, & **-cracy**. Government by the army; military domination in a state.

stratum, n., pl. **strata** [1. strā́tum, -a; 2. stréitəm, -ə]. Lat. *strātum*, 'covering; blanket; bed'; orig. 'thing spread out', fr. P.P. type of *sternere*, 'to spread out, stretch out; to scatter, strew; to cover'; fr. base **ster-*, **stor-*, **str̥-* &c., 'to spread out, extend'; cp. Lat. *strāmen*, 'straw', see **stramineous**; Gk. *stórnūmi*, 'to spread out'; *strôma*, 'layer, carpet', see **stroma**; Scrt. *str̥ṇā́ti*, 'scatters'; Goth. *straujan*; O.E. *strēawian*, 'to scatter', see **strew**; Gk. *stérnon*, 'surface; breast', see **sternum**; O. Slav. *stĭrą*, 'to spread out'; *strana*, 'region'; see also **street**. Layer, bed, horizontal division of distinct character; specif. **a** (geol.) layer of deposited rock distinguished from layers above and below; **b** (fig.) anything thought of as resembling a stratum or layer: *a stratum of society*, social division, class; *the various strata of Latin loan-words in English*, groups of words of Latin origin, each containing a number of words borrowed from the same source at the same period.

stratus, n., pl. **strati** [1. strā́tus, -ī; 2. stréi-təs, -ai]. Lat. *strātus*, masc. sing. of P.P. of *sternere*, see prec. Low, horizontal, uniform layer of cloud.

straw (I.), n. [1. straw; 2. strɔ̄]. O.E. *strēaw*; M.E. *strau*, 'straw'; cp. O.N. *strā*; O. Fris. *strē*; O.L.G. *strō*; O.H.G. *strō, strou*; cp. further O.E. *strēawian*, 'to scatter', see **strew**; cogn. w. Lat. *strāmen*, 'straw', see **stramineous**; see also **stratum**, & words there referred to. **1.** Hollow stem, stalk, or portion of stalk, of grain, esp. that of wheat, oats, barley, rye &c.; Phrs. *to catch at a straw*, resort desperately to any expedient available; *the last straw*, (fig.) final addition to a burden, hardship &c., which renders it unendurable; *not worth a straw*, worth nothing; *not to care a straw*, to be indifferent; *straws which show the way the wind blows*, slight indications of the trend of events, of public opinion &c. **2.** Stalks of grain collectively, esp. after drying and threshing, used for thatching, bedding, for making textile fabric for mats, hats &c.: *stuffed, thatched &c., with straw*. Phr. *man of straw*, effigy made of or stuffed with straw; hence (i.) imaginary person regarded as opponent in controversy &c.; (ii.) an unreliable person, with no solidity or strength of character; (iii.) person of no financial substance. **3.** Straw hat.

straw (II.), vb. trans. M.E. *strāwen*, 'to scatter', variant of *strēwen*, see **strew**. (archaic) To scatter, strew.

strawberry, n. [1. stráwberi; 2. strɔ́bəri]. O.E. *strēawberige*; perh. so called because the runners were supposed to resemble straw, or because straw was used to keep the fruit off the ground; this name may, however, be due to an anct. popular etymol., & it has been suggested that the first syll. is fr. Aryan **sraghʷo-*, whence Gmc. **straʒʷ-*; cp. Lat. *frāgum* for **srāghom*, 'strawberry'; Gk. *hrāgós*, fr. **srāgos*, 'a grape'; Scrt. *sraj-*, 'wreath, crown'. **a** Fruit of any plant of genus *Fragaria*, consisting of a pulpy, sweet, juicy, red or yellowish body bearing seeds on the surface; *crushed strawberry*, dull crimson colour; **b** plant bearing these berries.

strawberry-leaf, n. **a** Triple leaf of strawberry; **b** representation of this forming part of ornamentation of the coronet of a duke, marquess, or earl; hence specif., *strawberry leaves*, ducal rank.

strawberry-mark, n. Dull reddish birth-mark.

strawberry-pear, n. Red pear-shaped fruit of a tropical American cactus.

strawberry-roan, adj. & n. Reddish roan.

strawberry-tree, n. Small S. European, evergreen tree, *Arbutus unedo*, with edible fruit which resembles a strawberry in appearance.

straw-board, n. Kind of coarse cardboard made of straw pulp.

straw-colour, n. Clear, pale yellow; the colour of straw.

straw-coloured, adj. Of the colour of straw.

straw-stem, n. Wineglass stem made in one piece with the bowl, by drawing out part of the material of the latter.

straw-worm, n. Caddis.

strawy, adj. [1. stráw-i; 2. strɔ́i]. **straw** (I.) & **-y** (IV.). Connected with, resembling, full of, covered with, straw.

stray (I.), vb. intrans. [1. strā; 2. strei]. M.E. *straien*, 'to stray, wander', fr. O. Fr. *estraier*, prob. fr. Lat. *strāta*, 'way, road', see **street**. **1. a** To go or wander beyond appointed limits, leave enclosure or recognized path: *don't stray too far from the path*; *the sheep have strayed (from a field &c.)*; *a child that has strayed from home*; **b** (poet.) to wander, roam, rove: *to stray aimlessly through the woods*. **2.** To wander from the path of virtue and rectitude; to fall into sin. **3.** (of thoughts, affections &c.) To wander; not to be concentrated on a single object, or the subject of study or discussion.

stray (II.), n., fr. prec. **1.** Domestic animal that has strayed. **2.** Person or child who is lost, has wandered from its home, or is without a proper home, esp. in Phr. *waifs and strays*. **3.** (law, in pl. *strays*) Property passing to Crown in default of heirs to deceased owner. **4.** (wireless, in pl. *strays*) Atmospherics.

stray (III.), adj., fr. prec. **1.** Having strayed; wandering, lost: *stray cattle*; *a stray dog*. **2.** Occurring here and there, at irregular and infrequent intervals; scattered, sporadic.

strayed, adj. [1. strād; 2. streid], fr. P.P. of **stray** (I.). Having strayed, wandering, astray: *a strayed horse*.

streak (I.), n. [1. strēk; 2. strīk]. Cannot be derived fr. O.E. *strica*, 'mark, stroke of the pen', though it may come fr. a cogn. of this, & of **strike** (I.) & **stroke** (I.); we may assume an O.E. **strǣċ-*, fr. **strāki*, wh. wd. normally give M.E. *strēch*; the final *-k* may be due to anal. w. *strike, stroke* &c. **1.** Long, narrow, usually irregular, mark, line, stripe on a surface, distinct in colour: *an apple with a red streak*; *streaks of light in the east*; *streak of lightning*, a flash. Phr. *off like a streak (of lightning)*, very swiftly. **2.** (fig.) Tendency, strain: *he hasn't a streak of humour in him*.

streak (II.), vb. trans., fr. prec. To mark with streaks.

streakily, adv. [1. strḗkili; 2. stríkili]. See next word & **-ly**. In a streaky manner.

streakiness, n. [1. strḗkines; 2. stríkinis]. Next word & **-ness**. State or quality of being streaky.

streaky, adj. [1. strḗki; 2. stríki]. **streak** & **-y** (IV.). Arranged in, marked with, showing, streaks: *streaky bacon*, with alternate layers of fat and lean.

stream (I.), n. [1. strēm; 2. strīm]. O.E. *strēam*, 'current; river'; M.E. *strēme*; cp. O.H.G. *stroum*; O. Fris. *strām*; O.N. *straumr*; fr. Gmc. **straum-*; cogn. w. Scrt. *srávati*, 'flows'; *srṓtaš*, 'stream'; Gk. *rhóos*, 'stream'; *rhéein*, 'to flow', fr. Aryan **srow-, srew-*, see **rheo-**. **1.** Body of running water, flowing naturally from its source, in a bed or channel; rivulet, brook; river: *the Thames is a noble stream*. Phr. *the stream of time*. **2. a** A flow of water or other liquid; a jet, gush: *water flowing from the burst main in a great stream*; *a stream of blood*; **b** flow of molten matter: *a stream of lava*. **3. a** Direction in which a stream or river moves; current: *with, against, the stream*; **b** (fig.) trend, drift, of events, of popular feeling or opinion &c.; direction in which events, feelings &c. tend, are moving: *the stream of popular prejudice is against what is new*. **4.** Continuous series of moving objects: *a stream of people, motor-cars*; *the stream of traffic*.

stream (II.), vb. intrans. & trans., fr. prec. **A.** intrans. **1.** (of fluid) To flow in, or as in, a stream, to flow freely, form a continuous line of moving matter, pour forth: *tears streamed down her cheeks*; *people streamed out of the building*; *light streamed through the window*. **2.** To pour forth liquid in a stream, be suffused with, run with, liquid: *eyes that streamed with tears*; *a streaming cold*, one accompanied by copious discharge from eyes and nose. **3.** To fly out, be extended; float (on the air); to trail: *hair streaming in the wind*; *the comet's tail streams behind it*. **B.** trans. To pour out, cause to issue, emit, in a stream: *wounds streaming blood &c.*

stream-anchor, n. Anchor of medium size.

streamer, n. [1. strēmer; 2. strímə]. **stream (II.)** & **-er.** **1.** Strip of material designed to hang down, be extended, float, in the air &c., esp. flag, ribbon &c., attached at one end. **2.** Ray of light seen shooting up or across the sky in the aurora borealis.

streamless, adj. [1. strḗmles; 2. strímlis]. **stream (I.)** & **-less.** Without, lacking in, streams.

streamlet, n. [1. strḗmlet; 2. strímlit]. **stream (I.)** & **-let.** Small stream, brook.

stream-line, n., adj., & vb. trans. **1.** n. Natural flow of current in air or water without eddying. **2.** adj. (of shape of fish, aircraft, motor-car &c.) Such as to offer the least resistance to currents in air or water. **3.** vb. To give a stream-line form to (submarine, body of car &c.).

streamy, adj. [1. strḗmi; 2. strími]. **stream (I.)** & **-y (IV.).** Of, like, flowing in, a stream; abounding in streams.

street, n. [1. strēt; 2. strīt]. O.E. *strǣt*; M.E. *strēte*, 'paved road'; cp. O.L.G. *strāta*; O.H.G. *strāza*; Du. *straat*; borrowed in continental period, fr. Lat. *strāta (via)*, 'paved way', fr. P.P. of *sternere*, 'to spread, scatter; to cover, pave', see **stratum.** **1.** Formerly applied to the old Roman roads in England; cp. *Watling Street, Akeman Street.* **2.** Properly constructed, metalled road in a town or large village, with buildings on one or both sides: *the chief street of the town*; *to live in a quiet street*; *the village street*; *to run out into the street*; *High Street.* Phrs. *street arab*, homeless waif; *street cries*, of hawkers calling their wares; *on the streets*, earning a living as a prostitute; *not in the same street with*, not to be compared with, not nearly as good as.

street-door, n. That door of a house which opens on to a street.

street-orderly, n. Street scavenger.

street-sweeper, n. **a** Person occupied in sweeping streets; **b** machine with revolving brushes for sweeping streets.

street-walker, n. Prostitute.

streetward, adj. & adv. [1. strḗtward; 2. strítwəd]. **street** & **-ward.** **1.** adj. Situated in or near the street. **2.** adv. Towards the street.

strength, n. [1. strength; 2. strɛŋþ]. O.E. *strengþ(o)*, 'strength; severity; efficacy'; M.E. *strengþ*; fr. **strang-iþu*; **strong** & **-th (I.).** **1. a** Quality, condition, of being strong; bodily or intellectual vigour, power; capacity for exertion or endurance: *a man of enormous strength*; *the strength of his mind was such that he overcame all obstacles*; **b** special quality, aptitude, talent, that in which one excels; forte: *his strength lay in lucid exposition rather than in original discovery.* **2.** Quality in materials which enables them to resist strains, bear weights &c.; toughness, durability; opposite of *fragility*: *the strength of a beam, bridge* &c. **3.** Power of resisting attack; impregnability: *the strength of a fortified place.* **4.** Large numbers; power, efficiency, completeness considered as depending on numbers: *the enemy were in great strength.* Phrs. *up to, below, strength*, of a regiment, or other body of fixed size, having full complement, or less than full complement, of men; (mil.) *on the strength*, on the muster-roll. **5.** Source of power, efficiency &c.; that which makes one strong in some specified way: *high courage and cheerfulness are a great strength to a general*; *he was a strength and support to his father in old age.* **6.** Intensity, potency; degree of capacity for producing characteristic effects: *the strength of a poison*; *the strength of colour*; *the strength of one's affections.* **7.** Power to effect an intellectual or moral result; compelling power, cogency: *the strength of an argument.* Phr. *on the strength of (what was said, of a promise* &c.), having regard to, relying on, influenced, persuaded, by.

strengthen, vb. trans. & intrans. [1. stréngthen; 2. strέŋþən]. Prec. & **-en (I.).** **1.** trans. To make strong, increase strength of, reinforce. **2.** intrans. To grow strong, increase in strength.

strengthening, adj. [1. stréngthening; 2. strέŋþəniŋ]. Prec. & **-ing.** Tending, serving, to strengthen; invigorating: *strengthening food.*

strengthless, adj. [1. stréngthles; 2. strέŋþlis]. **strength** & **-less.** (rare) Devoid of strength; weak.

strenuous, adj. [1. strénūus; 2. strénjuəs], fr. Lat. *strēnuus*, 'brisk, active, vigorous'; cp. Gk. *strēnés*, 'keen, strong'; *strēnos*, 'haughtiness'; cp. O.E. *styrne*, 'hard, keen, severe', see **stern (I.)**; O. Slav. *strada*, 'labour'; the base **st(e)rē-* &c., 'vigorous, powerful', is prob. expanded fr. **ster-*, **str̥-* &c., 'stiff, strong', see **stare, stark, sterile.** Characterized by, putting forth, continuous, intense, unremitting effort; unrelaxing and vigorous: *strenuous supporters of a cause*; *a strenuous worker*; *strenuous efforts*; *the strenuous life.*

strenuously, adv. Prec. & **-ly.** In a strenuous manner.

strenuousness, n. See prec. & **-ness.** Quality of being strenuous.

Strephon, n. [1. stréfun; 2. stréfən]. Shepherd lover in Sidney's *Arcadia.* Lover; counterpart of Chloe.

strepitoso, adv. [1. strèpitṓsō; 2. strèpitóusou]. Ital., fr. Lat. *strepit-(us)*, 'confused noise', fr. P.P. type of *strepere*, 'to make a noise; to clatter, rattle, roar'; perh. related to *strīdēre*, 'to hiss, creak, buzz' &c., see **strident**, fr. base **stre(i)-*, 'to make a harsh noise'. (mus.) Boisterously, loudly, vigorously.

strepto-coccus, n. [1. stréptō kókus; 2. stréptou kɔ́kəs]. Coined fr. Gk. *streptós*, 'easy to bend, pliant', fr. base **strebh-* in Gk. *stréphein*, 'to twist, turn'; cp. gradational form *strophḗ*, 'a turn, twist', see **strophe**; *coccus* is Neo-Lat. fr. Gk. *kókkos*, 'a kernel, a berry'; see **coccus & cochineal.** One of a genus of bacteria of virulent character found in the blood in several diseases, such as pneumonia, septicaemia &c.

stress (I.), n. [1. stres; 2. strɛs]. M.E. *stresse*, 'force', fr. O. Fr. *estrecier*, fr. Low Lat. **strictiāre*, 'to constrain', fr. Lat. *strict-(um)*, P.P. type of *stringere*, 'to draw tight', see **stringent.** **1.** Strain, tension, intense effort: *in times of stress.* **2.** Impelling force, pressure, power or influence exercising constraint or compulsion: *under stress of weather, circumstances* &c. **3.** Importance, weight, emphasis; esp. in Phr. *to lay stress on*, indicate importance of, bring into prominence. **4. a** Relative force with which a word or syllable is uttered; accent: *strong, secondary, weak, stress*; esp. **b** highest degree of force used in uttering a group of syllables or words; strong stress: *the stress is on the first syllable*; *to put special stress on a word*; *there are two stresses in each half-line.* **5.** (mechan.) Force(s) exerted on a solid body and tending to alter its shape.

stress (II.), vb. trans., fr. prec. **1.** To lay stress on, emphasize, indicate importance or prominence of: *St. Paul specially stresses charity as the greatest of the virtues.* **2.** To utter (word or syllable) with stress, esp. with strong stress; to accentuate: *stressed syllables.* **3.** (mechan.) To subject to stress.

stressless, adj. [1. strésles; 2. strέslis]. **stress** & **-less.** Without stress.

stretch (I.), vb. trans. & intrans. [1. strech; 2. strɛtʃ]. O.E. *streććean*, M.E. *stre(t)chen*; O.H.G. *strecchan*; perh. fr. base **srak-*, a parallel form of **rak-* in **reach**; or connected w. **stark**, &, more remotely, w. **strong**; cp. also O.E. *strec*, 'strong, vehement, violent'. **A.** trans. **1. a** To cause to increase in length or breadth by forcibly pulling longitudinally or laterally: *to stretch a pair of gloves to make them fit*; also **b** (fig.) *to stretch the law, a rule*, to strain it, so as to make it more inclusive. Phr. *to stretch a point (in a person's favour)*, to go beyond what is strictly and literally legal or legitimate. **2. a** To pull or spread (object or material) tightly to its fullest extent, without attempting to increase this: *to stretch a rope between two posts*; *to stretch a carpet upon the floor*; *to stretch one's neck in order to see over the heads of a crowd*, to crane it, extend it fully; *to stretch (out) one's arm, hand*, reach it out, extend it; *to stretch oneself*, extend one's muscles fully by stretching out one's limbs. Phr. *to stretch one's legs*, exercise them; to go for a walk after a period of inactivity; **b** (reflex.) *stretch oneself*, to extend the limbs forcibly as far as muscles and tendons will allow, as on waking from sleep. **3.** To knock down, cause to lie at full length on the ground: *a blow behind the ear stretched him unconscious on the floor.* **4.** (slang) **a** To hang by the neck; **b** to lay out for burial. **B.** intrans. **1.** To be capable of extension, to have elastic properties; to become larger by being stretched: *my gloves are too tight, but no doubt they'll stretch*; *iron may stretch slightly, but not stone.* **2. a** To extend, reach, lie spread out: *the plain stretches for miles*; *the range of mountain stretches across the frontier*; also, **b** (of time) to last; to extend: *the Middle English Period stretches (down) roughly to the early years of the 15th century*; *a dreary life stretches before prisoners.* **3.** To stretch oneself, extend one's limbs to the utmost, as after sleep or prolonged inactivity, to stretch oneself: *he sat up in bed, yawned, and stretched.*

stretch (II.), n., fr. prec. **1. a** Act of stretching: *to give, make, a stretch of the arm*; *a stretch of the imagination*; **b** state of being stretched, strained, tightened; specif., bodily or mental tension or strain: *nerves on the stretch.* **2. a** Unbroken period or spell of time: *to work for six hours at a stretch*; **b** (slang) period, term of imprisonment, esp. of penal servitude. **3. a** Uninterrupted tract of space; a reach, extent, expanse: *a fine stretch of country, of water*; **b** (sailing) distance traversed on a single tack.

stretcher, n. [1. strécher; 2. strétʃə]. **stretch (I.)** & **-er.** **1.** One who, that which, stretches; esp. **a** apparatus for stretching something, also in compounds, *glove-stretcher, boot-stretcher*; **b** wooden frame for stretching and tautening artist's canvas. **2.** Apparatus, consisting of a light wooden framework covered with canvas &c., for carrying injured or wounded person, hence *stretcher-bearer.* **3.** Crosspiece in boat, against which the rower braces his feet. **4.** (masonry) Brick or stone laid longitudinally along line of wall. **5.** (slang) Exaggerated or untrue statement.

stretcher-bond, n. (masonry) Method of building in which bricks or stones are laid lengthwise in successive courses.

stretchiness, n. [1. stréchines; 2. strétʃinis]. Next word & **-ness.** State or quality of being stretchy.

stretchy, adj. [1. stréchi; 2. strétʃi]. **stretch** & **-y (IV.).** Capable of being stretched, liable to stretch; pliant, elastic.

strew, vb. trans. [1. stroo; 2. strū]. O.E. *strēawian*; M.E. *strēwen*, 'to scatter'; cp. Goth. *straujan*, 'to scatter'; see **straw, stratum.** **1.** To scatter, drop, or fling hither and thither in small quantities; to sprinkle, spread irregularly: *to strew rushes on the floor.* **2.** To cover lightly and irregularly, scatter, bestrew: *to strew a grave with flowers*; *the road was strewn with stones.*

stria, n., pl. **striae** [1. stría, strīē; 2. stráiə, stráiī]. Lat. *stria*, 'furrow, channel, fluting'; cogn. w. O.H.G. *strīmo*, 'stripe'; *streno*, 'skein', see **strand (III.)**; cp. also Lat. *striga*, 'stroke, stripe, swath', see **strigil**; see also **stringent.** (zool., bot., geol. &c.) Narrow, lengthwise mark, stripe, channel, groove &c.; thread-like or flute-like marking.

striate (I.), adj. [1. stríat; 2. stráiət], fr. Lat. *striāt-(um)*, P.P. type of *striāre*, 'to groove, flute', fr. *stria*, 'furrow', see prec. **1.** Marked with striae; striped, fluted, variegated. **2.** Of, resembling, forming, striae.

striate (II.), vb. trans. [1. stríāt; 2. stráieit], fr. Lat. *striātum*, see prec. To mark with striae.

striated, adj. [1. strīā́ted; 2. straiéitid], fr. P.P. of **striate (II.).** Striate.

striately, adv. [1. stríatli; 2. stráiətli]. **striate (I.)** & **-ly.** In striae.

striation, n. [1. strīáshun; 2. straiéiʃən]. **striate (II.)** & **-ion**. **1.** Act of striating; state of being striated; variegation; arrangement of striae. **2.** Stria.

striature, n. [1. stríachur; 2. stráiətʃə]. **striate (I.)** & **-ure**. Arrangement of striae; striation.

stricken, adj. [1. striken; 2. strikən]. Archaic P.P. of **strike**. **1.** (archaic) Wounded, injured by missile &c.; struck down: *a stricken deer.* **2.** Smitten, affected by grief, illness &c.; *stricken with disease* &c.; sometimes in compounds, *terror-stricken; stricken field,* pitched battle, or the place where it was fought. **3.** *Stricken in years,* of advanced age, old.

strickle, n. [1. strikl; 2. strikl]. O.E. *stricel,* 'rod', cogn. w. **strike**. Rod used for levelling grain in a heaped vessel to ensure accurate measure; see **strike-measure**.

strict, adj. [1. strikt; 2. strikt]. Lat. *strictus,* 'drawn together, tight; close-knit, narrow'; fr. P.P. of *stringere,* 'to draw tight', see **stringent**, & cp. **strait (I.)**. **1. a** Precise, accurate, exact; reverse of lax, loose, equivocal: *the strict truth; take the words in their strict sense; a strict interpretation; in strict accuracy, law* &c.; **b** punctilious, nice, rigidly conscientious; admitting no deviation from what is correct: *a strict observer of rules, of the truth; a strict Protestant.* **2. a** Admitting no infringement; inflexible, exacting: *a strict system of government; the game laws are very strict; a school must have strict rules;* **b** rigorous in preserving law and order, insistent on discipline; stern, severe, austere: *schoolmasters should be strict but just; it doesn't do to be too strict with very young children.*

strictly, adv. Prec. & **-ly**. **1. a** Precisely, exactly, with rigid accuracy: *strictly (speaking) you ought not to leave;* **b** punctiliously: *he stuck strictly to his own business.* **2.** Severely, sternly, rigidly: *he preserved discipline strictly, but with fairness.*

strictness, n. See prec. & **-ness**. Quality of being strict in all senses.

stricture, n. [1. stríkchur; 2. stríktʃə], fr. Lat. *strictūra,* 'contraction, compression; suffering', fr. *stric-(tum),* P.P. type of *stringere,* 'to draw together, bind tightly', see **stringent**, & **-ure**. **1.** (med.) Constriction, contraction, of a duct or vessel of the body, esp. of the urethra. **2.** (fig., often pl.) Severe criticism, reflection, censure: *strictures were passed on his conduct.*

strictured, adj. [1. stríkchurd; 2. stríktʃəd]. Prec. & **-ed**. Affected by stricture.

stridden, vb. [1. strídn; 2. strídn]. P.P. of **stride (I.)**. O.E. *(ge)striden.*

stride (I.), vb. intrans. & trans. [1. strīd; 2. straid]. O.E. *strīdan;* M.E. *strīden,* 'to stride, step'; cp. M. Du. *strīden;* cogn. w. O.H.G. *strītan,* 'to fight'; O.S. *strīd,* 'eagerness'; O.N. *strīðr,* 'strong, firm, obstinate'; fr. base **ster-, *str-,* 'to stiffen, become strong'; see **stare, stark**, & words there referred to. **A.** intrans. **1.** To walk with long, swinging, or measured steps. **2.** To take a single long step in crossing a space, obstacle &c.: *to stride over an obstacle, across a brook* &c. **B.** trans. **1.** To cross, pass over, with a single long step. **2.** To bestride, stand or sit with a leg on either side of.

stride (II.), n., fr. prec. **1.** Long step in walking: *to walk with rapid strides;* Phr. *to make great, rapid, strides* (in learning &c.), to progress rapidly; *to take something in one's stride,* to do something easily, without special effort, without going out of one's way. **2. a** Distance between feet when standing astride; **b** greatest length of pace.

strident, adj. [1. strident; 2. stráidənt], fr. Lat. *strīdent-(em),* Pres. Part. of *strīdēre,* 'to make a shrill, harsh, or creaking sound'; cogn. w. Gk. *trizein,* 'to utter a shrill sound'; cp. also Gk. *strix,* 'owl'; Lat. *strix,* 'screech owl'. (of sound, voice &c.) Loud, harsh, jarring.

stridently, adv. Prec. & **-ly**. In a strident manner.

stridulant, adj. [1. strídūlant; 2. strídjulənt]. Lat. *strīdulus,* 'creaking', see next word & **-ant**. (of insect) Producing stridulations.

stridulate, vb. intrans. [1. strídūlāt; 2. strídjuleit]. fr. Lat. *strīdulus,* 'creaking, grating', fr. *strīdēre,* 'to make a shrill, harsh sound', see **strident**, & **-ule**, & **-ate**. (Of crickets, locusts, grasshoppers &c.) To produce a shrill chirping or creaking noise by rubbing parts of the hard integument together.

stridulation, n. [1. stridūláshun; 2. stridjuléiʃən]. Prec. & **-ion**. **1.** Act of stridulating. **2.** Noise produced by stridulating.

stridulator, n. [1. strídūlātur; 2. strídjuleitə]. **stridulate** & **-or**. Insect that stridulates.

stridulous, adj. [1. strídūlus; 2. strídjuləs]. See **stridulant** & **-ous**. Resembling, characterized by, stridulation.

strife, n. [1. strīf; 2. straif]. M.E. *strīf,* fr. O. Fr. *estrīf,* fr. O.N. *strīþ,* 'oppression, pain'; cp. O.N. *strīðr,* 'strong, obstinate'; see **stride (I.)**. Conflict, struggle, combat, controversy; reciprocal hostile action; quarrelling, war.

striga, n. [1. strīga; 2. stráigə]. Lat. *striga,* 'furrow, stroke, stripe'; see **strigil**. (bot.) Short bristle or hair-like scale.

strigil, n. [1. stríjil; 2. strídžil], fr. Lat. *strigilis,* 'scraper'; cp. Lat. *striga,* 'swath, furrow, stroke, stripe'; cogn. w. O. Slav. *strigą,* 'to shear'; O.E. *strīcan,* 'to rub'; see **strike (I.)**, **stringent**. (Rom. antiq.) Instrument of metal, bone, or horn used for scraping the skin after the bath.

strigose, adj. [1. strīgōs; 2. stráigous], fr. Lat. *striga,* 'swath, furrow', q.v. under **strigil**, & **-ose**. (bot.) Covered with short, stiff bristles or hair-like scales.

strigous, adj. [1. strīgus; 2. stráigəs], fr. Lat. *striga,* 'swath', see prec., & **-ous**. (bot.) Strigose.

strike (I.), vb. trans. & intrans. [1. strīk; 2. straik]. O.E. *strīcan,* 'to rub; to move, go'; M.E. *strīken,* 'to strike, stroke, rub'; cp. M.L.G. *strīken,* M. Du. *strȳken;* O.H.G. *strīhhan;* O.N. *strȳkna,* 'to rub, stroke'; cp. further Goth. *striks;* O.E. *strica,* 'stroke of pen'; cogn. w. O. Slav. *strigą,* 'stripe, stroke, swath'; Lat. *strigilis,* 'scraper', see **strigil**; cp. w. infixed nasal Lat. *stringere,* 'to touch, graze; to draw out; to draw together', see **stringent**; Gk. *strígx,* 'line, ray, channel'. Cp. further Lat. *stria,* 'channel, furrow', see **stria**; O.H.G. *strīmo,* 'stripe'; *streno,* 'skein', see **strand (III.)**; see also **stroke (I.)**. The word expresses generally violent, or sudden, & rapid action or movement. **A.** trans. **1.** To hit, smite, give a blow to; bring (an object) violently into contact with (another): *to strike the table with one's fist; to strike a person a violent blow; to strike a ball with a racket; the wall sounds hollow when struck;* Phr. *to strike hands,* (archaic) make a bargain or agreement. **2.** To cause to hit or impinge upon, bring (object) violently into contact with another: *to strike one's head against the lintel.* **3.** To pierce, penetrate, by a blow: *to strike a person to the heart with a dagger.* **4.** To give, deal, aim, deliver: *to strike a blow; to strike the first blow;* Phr. *to strike a blow for,* make an effort in support of. **5.** To come suddenly in contact with, impinge upon: *the ship struck a rock; a falling rock struck his head; the ball struck him in the eye.* **6. a** To come upon, to reach, to find: *we shall strike the main road beyond the wood;* **b** to come across, happen upon, to discover as by chance: *I struck a good place for a holiday; to strike a bad hotel, an amusing book;* Phr. *to strike oil,* (i.) to discover a gusher; (ii.) (fig.) to make a lucky hit, make one's fortune. **7.** To produce by striking: *to strike a light; to strike sparks from flint.* **8.** To produce by striking musical instrument; cause to sound: *to strike a chord, note;* Phr. *to strike a note,* to convey a specific impression, emotion &c. **9.** To make by stamping, to coin: *to strike a medal.* **10.** To pull down, take down, lower: *to strike a sail, tent* &c.; *to strike camp,* remove, break up, encampment; *to strike one's flag,* esp. in token of surrender &c. **11.** To bring suddenly into a specific condition, affect suddenly and violently: *to be struck dumb, blind, with disease* &c.; Phr. *to strike dumb,* (fig.) make speechless with amazement, terror &c.; *to strike one all of a heap,* (colloq.) to astound. **12.** To inspire, instil, with (some violent emotion): *to strike terror and dismay into every heart.* **13. a** To affect the judgement, produce an impression on the mind of; to impress: *how does his playing strike you?; the idea strikes me as a good one; the humorous side of it struck me very forcibly;* specif. **b** to make a favourable, deep, lasting, impression upon: *to be struck by a person's beauty, ability* &c.; **c** (of ideas &c.) to come into the mind of, occur to: *an idea has just struck me; it strikes me that . . .* **14.** To assume, put oneself into (esp. by a sudden, rapid movement): *to strike an attitude.* **15.** (of clock) To sound, announce by striking: *the clock strikes the hours and quarters; it has just struck four.* **16.** To make (measure) level, by smoothing of piled-up grain &c. from the top by means of a rod &c. **17.** To come to, make, arrive at, by reckoning, agreement &c.: *to strike a balance, a bargain, an average* &c. **18.** (fishing) To fix hook in mouth of (fish), by quick, upward stroke of the rod: *to strike a fish.* **19. a** To cause to take root; set, plant: *to strike cuttings;* **b** (of plant) *to strike root,* to form roots. **20.** To tap, broach (cask). **21.** *To strike work,* **a** to cease work; specif. **b** to go on strike. **B.** intrans. **1.** To hit, smite, deliver blow(s): '*Willing to wound, and yet afraid to strike*' (Pope, Epistle to Dr. Arbuthnot, 203). Phr. *to strike while the iron's hot,* act promptly, and at appropriate moment. **2.** To come sharply into contact with an object or surface: *the ship struck (on a rock &c.); his foot struck against a stone.* **3.** To be kindled by striking: *the match wouldn't strike.* **4.** To direct one's course, turn; to penetrate, pass: *to strike to the left; the disease struck inwards; the light strikes through the darkness, the clouds* &c.; *the damp strikes through the walls.* **5. a** (of plant) To take root; **b** (of oyster &c.) to become fixed, adhere to rock &c. **6.** To strike one's flag as sign of surrender or respect. **7. a** (of clock) To announce hour &c. by specific number of strokes: *I didn't hear the clock strike;* **b** (of hour) be recorded by striking of clock: *the hour has struck;* Phr. *his hour has struck,* he is about to die. **C.** Followed by adverbs or prepositions, with special meanings. *Strike at,* intrans., to aim at, aim blow or attack at, direct blow towards; Phr. *to strike at the root of,* try to destroy or exterminate utterly. *Strike down,* trans., **a** to fell with a blow; **b** to attack, prostrate by illness &c. *Strike in,* intrans., **1.** (of disease) to affect internal organs instead of surface of body or extremities; **2.** to interrupt, interpose: *here someone struck in with a question. Strike into,* **1.** intrans., **a** to turn off abruptly into: *to strike into the fields;* **b** to break into, start off suddenly into: *to strike into a gallop;* **2.** trans., to cause to penetrate, drive: *to strike spurs into a horse. Strike off,* trans., **1.** to remove by striking: *to strike off a person's head;* **2.** to cancel, remove by drawing stroke through &c.: *to strike a name off a list;* **3.** to print: *to strike off a hundred copies. Strike out,* **1.** intrans., to aim a blow, hit out; **2. a** (of swimmer, skater) to make a stroke, esp. in specific direction: *to strike out for the shore;* **b** (fig.) to begin action, make a start: *to strike out in a line of one's own;* **3.** trans., **a** to cancel, erase, cross out (word &c.); **b** to produce, originate: *to strike out a new idea, a line of one's own. Strike through,* trans., to cross out, cancel, by stroke of pen &c. *Strike up,* trans., **1.** to begin to play or sing: *to strike up a song;* **2.** to begin, bring into being *to strike up a friendship;* **3.** intrans., to begin to play or sing: *now then, strike up; the band struck up as the King entered.*

strike (II.), n. & vb. intrans. Noun fr. prec., in specialized sense, as in Phr. *to strike work*; vb., a new formation fr. n. **1.** n. Legalized method for workers of dealing, and bargaining for terms, with employers, by an organized general stoppage of work among all workers in a given trade or industry, or in a branch of a trade &c., until agreement is reached regarding wages, hours of work, or other matters in dispute. **2.** vb. To engage, take part, in a strike.

strike-a-light, n. [1. strík a līt; 2. stráik ə lait]. Apparatus for producing spark from flint and steel &c.

strike-breaker, n. Worker brought in from outside to replace striker.

strike-measure, n. Method of measuring grain &c., in which the surplus is levelled off from a heaped vessel with a rod.

strike-pay, n. Allowance made by trade union to workmen during a strike.

striker (I.), n. [1. stríker; 2. stráikə]. **strike** (I.) & **-er.** **1.** One who strikes; specif. (tennis &c.), player to whom ball is served. **2.** Instrument, device, mechanism, for striking.

striker (II.), n., fr. **strike** (II.) & **-er.** Workman, employee, who takes part in a strike.

striking, adj. [1. stríking; 2. stráikiŋ], fr. Pres. Part. of **strike** (I.). Producing an effect on, impressing, appealing to, the mind, or imagination; hence, arresting, remarkable; provoking wonder, admiration &c.: *a striking face, portrait, likeness* &c.; *a striking example of folly* &c.

strikingly, adv. Prec. & **-ly.** In such a manner as to impress; remarkably.

strikingness, n. See prec. & **-ness.** Quality of being striking.

striking-plate, n. Metal plate securing latch when door is closed.

string (I.), n. [1. string; 2. striŋ]. O.E. *streng*, 'string of bow, of harp; rope, cable; sinew'; M.E. *streng, string*; cp. O.N. *strengr*; M.L.G. *streng*; fr. **strangi-*, see **strong** (I.). **1. a** Slender, tough line of twisted fibre &c. used for tying; cord, twine: *a piece, ball, of string*; *to tie a parcel up with string*; *to pull a toy along by a string*; Phrs. *to pull strings*, use one's influence to bring about some result; specif. **b** cord of bow, bow-string. Phr. *to have two strings to one's bow*, have more than one expedient or means for attaining one's end; *first, second, string*, person or thing that main, alternative, reliance is placed upon. **2.** Slender cord of stretched gut or wire, in certain musical instruments, tightened until it gives forth a specific musical note when made to vibrate: *the strings of a harp, violin* &c. Phrs. *to touch the strings*, to play (harp &c.); *to be for ever harping on the same string*, dwelling on the same subject, idea &c. **3.** Narrow strip of ribbon or other textile fabric used for tying parts of wearing apparel &c. together &c.: *the strings of a bonnet, apron* &c. **4.** Strong, slender, string-like object or substance; specif. **a** tendon: *the string of the tongue, eyes* &c.; **b** fibre connecting the two halves of a pod. **5.** Series of objects threaded on a string; a chain: *a string of beads, pearls* &c. **6.** Long succession of persons, objects &c.: *a string of people, horses*; also *a string of oaths*, series uttered in rapid succession. **7.** (mus., in pl.) *The strings*, group of stringed instruments in an orchestra &c.

string (II.), vb. trans. & intrans., fr. prec. **A.** trans. **1. a** To supply, furnish, with a string or strings: *to string a bow*; **b** (fig.) usually *string up*, to tune; key up, brace: *to string oneself up to a high pitch of expectancy* &c.; *nerves strung up to the highest pitch.* **2.** To join, link, by a string; to thread, suspend, on a string &c.: *to string beads*; *beads strung on wire.* Phr. *to string up*, to hang. **3.** To remove string or fibre from (beans &c.). **B.** intrans. (of glue) To become stringy. **C.** Followed by adverb with special meaning. *String out*, to extend in a long line, form into a series: *to string out scouts along the road.*

string-alphabet, n. Alphabet in which each letter is represented by a specific knot or group of knots tied in a cord.

string-band, n. Orchestra of stringed instruments.

string-bark, n. Kind of eucalyptus tree with fibrous bark.

string-board, n. Board running up side of staircase, at right angles to and receiving ends of steps.

string-course, n. Projecting moulding running horizontally along the wall of a building.

stringed, adj. [1. stringd; 2. striŋd]. **string** (I.) & **-ed.** Having a string or strings: *stringed instruments*; also *four-stringed* &c.

stringency, n. [1. strínjensi; 2. stríndžənsi]. See **stringent** & **-ency.** State or quality of being stringent; specif. **a** severity; **b** scarcity of money.

stringendo, adv. [1. strinjéndō; 2. strindžéndou]. Ital., fr. Lat. *stringent-(em)*, see next word. (musical direction) Increasing the tempo, accelerating.

stringent, adj. [1. strínjent; 2. stríndžənt], fr. Lat. *stringent-(em)*, Pres. Part. of *stringere*, 'to draw or bind tightly; to touch lightly, graze; to pull or cut off; to draw from the sheath; to check, restrain'; according to Walde, fr. two orig. distinct vbs.: (1) earlier **strengere*, 'to draw tightly'; cogn. w. Gk. *straggaloûn*, 'to twist, strangle', see **strangle**; O.N. *strangr*, 'violent', see **strong** (I.) & **string** (I.); (2) fr. base **strei-g-*, **stri-g-* &c., 'to rub, scrape', seen also in Lat. *strigilis*, 'scraper', see **strigil**; O. Slav. *strigą*, 'to shear'; O.E. *strīcan*, 'to rub', see **strike**; cp. base **streu-*, 'to rub', seen in **strip** (I.), **stripe** (I.). **1.** Requiring exact obedience or fulfilment, binding, not to be evaded; rigid, rigorous, severe: *stringent regulations.* **2.** (finance) Marked by shortage or scarcity of money; tight: *a stringent money-market.*

stringently, adv. Prec. & **-ly.** In a stringent manner.

stringer, n. [1. strínger; 2. stríŋə]. **string** (II.) & **-er.** **1.** One who, that which, strings. **2.** Timber forming part of framework and supporting other parts of the same structure.

string-halt, n. Disease of muscles in horse's hind leg causing a jerky action; spring-halt.

stringiness, n. [1. stríngines; 2. stríŋinis]. **stringy** & **-ness.** State or quality of being stringy.

stringless, adj. [1. stríngles; 2. stríŋlis]. **string** (I.) & **-less.** Without a string or strings.

string-orchestra, n. Orchestra composed of stringed instruments.

string-piece, n. String-board.

string quartet, n. **1.** Quartet of players on stringed instruments, usually two violins, a viola, and a violoncello. **2.** Piece of music composed for such a combination of players.

stringy, adj. [1. stríngi; 2. stríŋi]. **string** (I.) & **-y** (IV.). **1.** Resembling string; consisting of, containing, tough fibres: *stringy meat*; *a stringy throat*, one in which the tendons are very apparent. **2.** (of glue &c.) Forming thick, viscous strings; ropy.

stringy-bark, n. String-bark.

strip (I.), vb. trans. & intrans. [1. strip; 2. strip]. O.E. *strȳpan*; M.E. *strīpan*, 'to strip'; cp. O.H.G. *stroufen*, 'to flay'; M. Du. *stroopen*; etymol. obscure; perh. ultimately connected w. base seen in **strike.** **A.** trans. **1. a** To tear off (skin, outer covering &c.): *to strip the bark from a tree, paper off a wall, the hide from a carcass* &c.; **b** to deprive (object) of outer covering, skin, or some external appendage: *to strip a tree of its bark, leaves* &c.; *the birds have completely stripped the currant bushes.* **2.** *Strip* (*person or thing*) *of*, to deprive of, remove, take away from, bereave, despoil; *to strip a man of his honours, wealth, possessions, pretensions* &c.; *to strip a house of its furniture.* **3.** Phr. *to strip a cow*, milk her dry, remove all the milk from her. **B.** intrans. **1.** To take one's clothes off; to undress. **2.** Specif. (of a screw) to have the thread torn off.

strip (II.), n., fr. prec., perh. partially influenced in meaning by **stripe** (I.). **1.** Long, narrow, flat piece of thin material; **a** an irregular piece torn, or partially torn, from something; a tatter, a shred: *paper hanging in strips from the wall*; **b** narrow piece of anything, cut or shaped into more or less regular breadth: *a strip of wood nailed over a crack*; *a strip of paper as a book-mark*; *a dress trimmed with strips of velvet.* **2.** Long narrow piece of land or vegetation &c. distinct from surroundings: *a strip of garden, woodland, turf, gravel* &c.

stripe (I.), n. [1. strīp; 2. straip]. M.E. *strīpe*, fr. M. Du. *strijpe*; cp. O.H.G. *strīf*; Germ. *streifen*, 'to touch lightly, graze; to strip off; to mark with stripes'; Du. *strippen*, 'to strip off leaves'; prob. related to **strip.** **1. a** Long, narrow mark, line, band, division visibly distinct in colour or character from the surface on which it appears; a streak, stria, variegation: *the stripes of a tiger, zebra*; *the material is blue with yellow stripes*; specif. **b** stripe or chevron worn on sleeve of uniform as symbol of military rank: *a sergeant's stripes.* Phr. *to get, lose, one's stripes*, be promoted from, degraded to, the ranks. **2.** Blow, stroke, delivered by a rod, lash.

stripe (II.), vb. trans., fr. prec. To impose stripes upon, to mark with a stripe.

striped, adj. [1. strīpt; 2. straipt]. **stripe** (I.) & **-ed.** Having, marked with, stripes: *striped cloth* &c.; also specif. of animals, e.g. *striped squirrel.*

stripiness, n. [1. strípines; 2. stráipinis]. **stripy** & **-ness.** State or quality of being stripy.

strip-leaf, n. Tobacco with stalks removed.

stripling, n. [1. strípling; 2. strípliŋ]. **strip** (II.) & **-ling** (I.). Young man, youth, lad.

stripper, n. [1. stríper; 2. strípə]. **strip** (I.) & **-er.** One who, that which, strips; esp. a mechanical device for stripping off bark &c.

stripy, adj. [1. strípi; 2. stráipi]. **stripe** (I.) & **-y** (IV.). Having, marked with, stripes.

strive, vb. intrans. [1. strīv; 2. straiv]. M.E. *strīven*, fr. O. Fr. *estriver*, fr. O. Fr. *estrif*, 'strife, effort'; see **strife.** **1.** To make great efforts, try earnestly, exert oneself: *the swimmer strives to reach the shore*; *to strive to understand*; *to strive for victory.* **2.** To fight, struggle, engage in combat: *to strive with, against, an enemy, temptation* &c.

strobile, n. [1. stróbil, stróbīl, -il; 2. stróbil, stróub(a)il], fr. L. Lat. *strobilus*, 'pine-cone', fr. Gk. *stróbīlos*, 'anything twisted or whirling; whirlwind; pirouette; pine-cone'; cp. *stróbos*, 'a twisting round'; *streblós*, 'twisted'; *strabós*, 'crooked', see **strabismus.** (bot.) Pine-cone, fir-cone.

strode, vb. [1. strōd; 2. stroud]. O.E. *strād*, M.E. *strōd.* Pret. of **stride** (I.).

stroke (I.), n. [1. strōk; 2. strouk]. O.E. *strāc*; M.E. *strōk*, 'stroke'; cp. M.H.G. *streich*; cp. also O.E. *strīcan*, 'to rub, stroke', Pret. sing. *strāc*; & see **strike** (I.). **1.** Action of one who strikes; a blow: *with one stroke of the axe*; '*How bowed the woods beneath their sturdy stroke*' (Gray's 'Elegy'). Phrs. *a stroke of genius*, action inspired by genius; *a stroke of luck*, fortunate event or experience; piece of good fortune. **2. a** Single movement of the hand(s), or of an instrument guided by hand, in performing some operation, esp. in games: *a stroke in cricket, tennis, golf, billiards* &c.; *a backhand stroke*; *to do a hole in three strokes*; **b** single movement forming part of rhythmical series: *the stroke of a bird's wing, of person swimming, of an oar in rowing* &c. **3. a** Movement of the striking mechanism or hammer in a clock in sounding the hour, blow &c.; **b** sound made by such a blow. Phr. *on the stroke of* (*five* &c.), as the hour is being struck or is about to strike. **4.** Line produced by single movement of pen, pencil, brush &c.: *straight thick,* *fine, strokes* &c. **5.** Sudden attack or access of illness; esp. *paralytic, apoplectic, stroke*; also without qualifying word: *to have a stroke.* **6.** Oarsman nearest stern of boat, and setting time of stroke: *to row stroke.*

stroke (II.), vb. trans., fr. prec., **6.** *To stroke a boat,* row stroke in it.

stroke (III.), vb. trans. O.E. *strācian*; M.E. *strōken,* 'to stroke'; fr. O.E. *strāc,* 'stroke', see **stroke** (I.). **1.** To draw one's hand with gentle pressure over surface of, to caress: *to stroke one's hair, a cat.* Phrs. *to stroke one (up) the wrong way,* irritate him; *to stroke one down,* soothe him, allay irritation. **2.** To smooth, set in order (gathers in needlework &c.), by drawing point of needle &c. down each.

stroke (IV.), n., fr. prec. Act of stroking.

strokingly, adv. [1. strṓkingli; 2. stróukiŋli], fr. Pres. Part. of **stroke** (III.) & **-ly.** In the manner of one who strokes; caressingly.

stroll (I.), vb. intrans. [1. strōl; 2. stroul]. Origin unknown. To take a short, leisurely walk; to saunter, walk quietly and without hurry.

stroll (II.), n., fr. prec. A quiet, leisurely walk; a saunter.

stroller, n. [1. strṓler; 2. stróulə]. **stroll** (I.) & **-er.** One who strolls; specif. (rare) strolling player.

strolling, adj. [1. strṓling; 2. stróuliŋ], fr. Pres. Part. of **stroll** (I.). Going from place to place, itinerant: *a strolling player, minstrel* &c.

stroma, n. [1. strṓma; 2. stróumə]. Gk. *strôma,* 'covering'; cp. Gk. *strōtós,* 'spread out'; *stórnūmi,* 'I extend, spread out; spread a covering over'; Lat. *strātus,* 'layer, covering'; see **stratum,** & words there referred to. (biol.) Fine network of connective tissue forming the framework of an organ or cell.

stromatic, adj. [1. strōmátik; 2. stroumǽtik], fr. Gk. *strômat-,* stem of *strôma,* 'covering', see prec., & **-ic.** Of, pertaining to, forming, of the nature of, a stroma.

strong (I.), adj. [1. strong; 2. strɔŋ]. O.E., M.E. *strang, strong*; cp. O.N. *strangr*; O.H.G. *strang, streng,* 'strong, severe, powerful'; prob. cogn. w. M. Ir. *srengim,* 'I draw, drag'; Gk. *straggaloûn,* 'twist, strangle', see **strangle**; Lett. *stringt,* 'to stiffen'; see also **string** (I.). **1. a** Physically powerful, capable of exerting great force; muscular: *strong arms*; *he is enormously strong*; Phr. *with a strong hand,* forcibly; **b** morally powerful, possessing great force of character, tenacity of purpose: *the strong man of the government*; *a strong, silent man*; **c** intellectually powerful, capable of vigorous, clear thinking: *a strong brain, intelligence, imagination.* **2. a** Tough, firm, stout, durable; not easily broken; resisting strains: *a strong chain, branch*; *strong cord, wall* &c.; **b** difficult to capture, capable of resistance, well protected, easy to defend: *a strong fortress, position* &c. Phr. *one's strong point,* something in which one excels; a good quality &c. **3.** Producing considerable effect, rigorous, drastic, acting powerfully: *strong remedies*; *to take strong measures.* **4.** Robust, vigorous, hale; in good health and physical condition; sound: *he is far from strong, quite strong again*; *a strong constitution.* **5.** Not weak or diluted; containing a large proportion of essential quality: *strong tea, coffee, whisky* &c.; *strong drink,* alcoholic liquor. **6.** Affecting the senses powerfully and keenly: *a strong smell, taste* &c.; specif. **b** rank, ill-smelling. **7. a** Deeply felt, vigorously held; pronounced, decided, intense; *strong opinions, suspicions*; *a strong sense of disappointment*; *strong feeling*; **b** appealing powerfully to the mind; cogent, conclusive: *strong reasons, arguments.* **8.** Expressing ideas and emotions vigorously and unambiguously: *a strong expression.* Phr. *strong language,* swearing, blasphemy. **9.** Possessing a stated strength; amounting to, reckoned at, a specified number or figure: *an army 10,000 strong.* **10.** (of wind) Moving rapidly, of considerable velocity. **11.** (gram.) **a** *Strong verb,* in Germanic languages, one which exhibits gradational changes in conjugation; **b** *strong noun,* in Germanic and Aryan, one which had originally a vowel stem. **12.** (commerc.) *Markets, prices, are strong,* tending to rise.

strong (II.), adv., fr. prec. (slang) Strongly, vigorously; esp. in Phr. *(he is) going strong,* continues to be vigorous, healthy &c.; still in action; *that is coming it rather strong,* making an extravagant claim, proposal &c.; *going it rather strong,* behaving in an extravagant manner.

strong-box, n. Strong chest of iron for storing deeds and other important documents.

stronghold, n. [1. stróng-hōld; 2. strɔ́ŋhould]. Place of defence or refuge, fortified or defensible position: *a robber's stronghold in the mountains*; (also fig.) *a stronghold of superstition* &c., place where it flourishes.

strongish, adj. [1. stróngish; 2. strɔ́ŋiʃ]. **strong** (I.) & **-ish** (I.). Fairly strong.

strongly, adv. [1. stróngli; 2. strɔ́ŋli]. **strong** (I.) & **-ly.** In a strong manner, vigorously.

strong-minded, adj. **a** Having capable, vigorous, resolute mind; **b** specif., *strong-minded woman,* one who is free, or supposed to be free, from ordinary feminine weaknesses.

strong-room, n. Fire-proof or burglar-proof room, usually built in thickness of a wall, and provided with heavy iron door, for storing valuables.

strontia, n. [1. strónsha; 2. strɔ́nʃə]. See **strontium** & **-ia.** Oxide of strontium.

strontian, n. & adj. [1. strónshan; 2. strɔ́nʃən]. See **strontium** & **-an.** **1.** n. Oxide of strontium. **2.** adj. Pertaining to, consisting of, strontia or strontium.

strontium, n. [1. strónshum; 2. strɔ́nʃəm], fr. Strontian, in Argyllshire, where the metal was first found, & **-ium.** Yellowish, ductile, metallic element, whose salts burn with a red flame.

strop, n. & vb. trans. [1. strop; 2. strɔp]. O.E., M.E. *stropp*; see **strap** (I.). **1.** n. a Leather strap, or a piece of wood covered with leather &c., for putting an edge on razors; **b** (naut.) band of leather, rope, or iron round pulley. **2.** vb. To put an edge on to (a razor) by applying it to a strop.

strophanthus, n. [1. strofánthus; 2. strɔfǽnþəs], fr. Gk. *strophḗ,* see **strophe,** & *ánthos,* 'flower', see **anther.** **a** A genus of tropical African plants; **b** a poisonous drug made from the seeds of this, used in heart disease, also called *strophanthin.*

strophe, n. [1. strṓfi; 2. stróufi], more rarely [1. strófi; 2. strɔ́fi]. Gk. *strophḗ,* 'a turning, twisting'; cp. Gk. *stróphos,* 'cord'; *stréphein,* 'to turn'; fr. base *strebh-; cp. the parallel form *streb-, 'to turn, twist', in Gk. *streblós,* 'twisted'; *stróbos,* 'whirlpool'; *strabós,* 'squinting'; see **strobile, strabismus,** & **strepto-coccus.** **1.** (Gk. theatre) **a** Specif., the dancing of chorus in Greek play towards one side of scene; **b** song sung during this evolution. **2.** A regular arrangement or group of metrical lines in a poem; **a** loosely, a verse, a stanza; **b** strictly, former of two corresponding stanzas, in an ode, of which the second is the antistrophe.

strophic, adj. [1. strṓfik, strófik; 2. stróufik, strɔ́fik]. Prec. & **-ic.** Pertaining to, characteristic of, written in, strophes.

strove, vb. [1. strōv; 2. strouv]. Pret. of **strive,** formed on the anal. of the Engl. strong vb. *drive, drove* &c.

strow, vb. trans. [1. strō; 2. strou]. O.E. *strāwian, strēawian*; M.E. *strōwian,* variant of **strew.** (archaic) To strew, scatter.

struck, vb. [1. struk; 2. strak]. Pret. & P.P. of **strike.** The form *struck* occurs fr. the early 17th cent., perh. on the anal. of **stuck.** Cp. O.E. *strāk,* M.E. *strook.*

structural, adj. [1. strúkchural; 2. stráktʃərəl]. **structure** & **-al.** Pertaining to, connected, associated, with, structure: *the structural beauties of a building, a play* &c.

structurally, adv. Prec. & **-ly.** From the point of view of structure, as regards structure.

structure, n. [1. strúkchur; 2. stráktʃə]. Lat. *structūra,* 'mode of building, construction; edifice, erection; arrangement, order', fr. *struct-(um),* P.P. type of *struere,* 'to put together, construct, erect, build'; cp. Lat. *struēs,* 'heap, pile; series of layers'; Lat. *strātum,* 'layer'; cogn. w. O.E. *strēawian,* 'to scatter', see **strew, straw** (I.). **1.** Way in which a body is built up; arrangement and mode of connexion of the parts of an organic whole; formation, construction, organization of component parts: *the structure of a building, cell, organ* &c.; *the structure of rocks*; *the structure of a sentence, of a language.* **2.** Something that is constructed; specif., a building: *a tall, top-heavy structure*; *the earthquake shook the structure to its foundations.*

structured, adj. [1. strúkchurd; 2. stráktʃəd]. Prec. & **-ed.** Having a structure of specific kind; having carefully designed mode of arrangement.

structureless, adj. [1. strúkchurles; 2. stráktʃəlis]. **structure** & **-less.** Without structure; lacking any specific arrangement of parts.

struggle (I.), vb. intrans. [1. strúgl; 2. strágl]. M.E. *strogelen,* 'to struggle'; origin uncertain; perh. connected w. **strike** (I.) & **stroke** (I.). **1. a** To fight, offer resistance; to attempt to free oneself from physical constraint by violent bodily movements: *the prisoner struggled fiercely with the police before being arrested*; *the rabbit struggled to escape from the snare*; **b** to grapple with, attempt to solve or overcome, intellectual difficulty: *to struggle with mathematical problems* &c. **2.** To move the limbs and body violently and convulsively: *he struggled for a moment and then died*; *to struggle to one's feet.* **3.** To make a strenuous effort, attempt vigorously, to accomplish something: *to struggle to get a position in society*; *to struggle to make oneself heard.*

struggle (II.), n., fr. prec. **1.** Act of struggling; **a** violent movement, effort to free oneself from constraint, or against odds, or to reach a position in spite of opposition; a fight, **a** rough-and-tumble: *a violent struggle to escape*; *a sharp struggle with the police*; **b** convulsive movement of limbs: *the wounded animal made a short struggle, and then lay still.* **2.** Effort of any kind, strenuous attempt to overcome difficulties: *a desperate struggle to make both ends meet*; *the struggle for existence*; *a hard struggle to get one's work done in time.*

struggling, adj. [1. strúgling; 2. strágliŋ], fr. Pres. Part. of **struggle** (I.). Engaged in a struggle; esp. striving with difficulty to overcome poverty or obscurity &c.: *a struggling painter, genius* &c.

strugglingly, adv. Prec. & **-ly.** With, by means of, a struggle.

struldbrug, n. [1. strúldbrug; 2. stráldbrag]. Arbitrary coinage. One of a class of human beings in Luggnagg, described in Swift's *Gulliver's Travels* (Vge. to Laputa, ch. x.), who were unable to die, but who, after the age of eighty, exhibited all the signs of senility, gradually lost both physical and mental vigour, and were unable to remember the words of their own language, or to understand that spoken by the younger generation.

strum (I.), vb. intrans. & trans. [1. strum; 2. stram]. Prob. fr. **thrum** (II.). **1.** intrans. To play musical instrument by thumping heavily, or plucking the strings violently; to play noisily and carelessly: *to strum on a piano, on a banjo*; *he strums from morning to night.* **2.** trans. To strum on: *to sit for hours strumming the piano.*

strum (II.), n., fr. prec. Act of strumming; noisy, careless playing on a piano or plucking instrument.

struma, n. [1. strōōma; 2. strúmə]. Lat. *strūma,* 'scrofulous tumour; swollen neck'; prob. cogn. w. Gk. *strūphnós,* 'hard, firm'; O.N. *str(j)ūpi,* 'throat'; O.H.G. *strūbēn,* 'to stand stiffly'. **1.** Scrofula. **2.** Morbid enlargement of the thyroid gland; goitre. **3.** (bot.) Small, soft swelling at the base of an organ.

strumose, adj. [1. stróōmōs; 2. strúmous], fr. Lat. *strūmōsus*, 'scrofulous'; prec. & **-ose.** Strumous.

strumous, adj. [1. stróōmus; 2. strúməs]. **struma** & **-ous.** a Resembling, of the nature of, struma; b afflicted with struma.

strumpet, n. [1. strúmpet; 2. strámpit]. M.E. *strumpet*, possibly fr. O. Fr. *strupe, stupre*, fr. Lat. *stuprum*, 'dishonour, violation'; orig. 'punishment, banishment', cogn. w. Gk. *túptein*, 'to strike'; *túpos*, 'blow, imprint', see **type** (I.); O. Fris. *stūpa*, 'chastisement'. A prostitute.

strung, vb. [1. strung; 2. straŋ]. Pret. & P.P. of **string**, vb.

strut (I.), vb. intrans. & n. [1. strut; 2. strat]. O.E. *strūtian*, 'to stand stiffly'; M.E. *strouten*, 'to swell out, strut'; cp. M.H.G. *strūz*, 'swelling, contention'; cogn. w. Lat. *trūdere*, 'to push, press', see **intrude**; O. Slav. *truditi*, 'to trouble'; cp. also without initial *s-*, O.E. *þrēatian*, 'to threaten', see **threat** & **thrust** (I.); O.H.G. *drīozan*, 'to oppress'. **1.** vb. To walk with stiff, pompous, affected, self-conscious gait. **2.** n. Act of strutting; self-satisfied, swaggering, pompous gait.

strut (II.), n. & vb. trans. Cp. L.G. *strutt*, 'stiff, rigid'; cogn. w. prec. **1.** n. A prop, stay, or support, esp. for a wooden structure, consisting of a piece of timber placed at an angle and pressing in the contrary direction from the strain or thrust. **2.** vb. To support, keep in position by a strut.

struthious, adj. [1. stróōthius; 2. strúþiəs], fr. Lat. *strūthio*, fr. Gk. *strouthós*, 'sparrow; ostrich'; prob. earlier **strousthos*, & cogn. w. O.H.G. *drōsca*; O.E. *þrysće*, 'thrush', see **throstle**; Lat. *turdus*, 'thrush', see **turdine**; O. Prussian *tresde*, 'thrush'. Pertaining to, connected with, the ostrich.

strutting, adj. [1. strúting; 2. strátiŋ], fr. Pres. Part. of **strut** (I.). Performed with, characterized by, a strut: *a strutting walk.*

struttingly, adv. Prec. & **-ly.** In a strutting manner.

strychnia, n. [1. stríknia; 2. stríkniə], fr. Lat. *strychnos*, fr. Gk. *strúkhnos*, 'kind of nightshade', etymol. unknown, & **-ia.** (archaic) Strychnine.

strychnic, adj. [1. stríknik; 2. stríknik], fr. Lat. *strychnos*, 'nightshade', see prec., & **-ic.** Pertaining to, caused by, strychnine.

strychnin(e), n. [1. stríknin, -ēn; 2. stríknin, -in], fr. Lat. *strychnos*, 'nightshade', see **strychnia**, & **-ine.** White, crystalline, highly poisonous alkaloid, obtained from tropical plants of the genus *Strychnos*, especially *S. Nux vomica*; used medicinally in minute quantities as a stimulant for the nerves.

strychn(in)ism, n. [1. strikn(in)izm, -ēnizm; 2. stríkn(in)izəm, -īnizəm]. Prec. & **-ism.** Strychnine poisoning, characterized by spasm and violent contraction of the muscles.

stub (I.), n. [1. stub; 2. stab]. O.E. *stybb*; M.E. *stubbe*, 'stock of tree'; cp. M.L.G. *stubbe*; O.N. *stubbi*; cogn. w. O.N. *stūfr*, 'stump'; Gk. *stúpos*, 'stump, stick'; Lett. *stups*, 'stump'; cp. further Gk. *túptein*, 'to strike'; *túpos*, 'blow; imprint'; & see **type** (I.), **stump** (I.). **1.** Lower part of trunk or stalk of a tree left when upper part is cut off; a stump. **2.** Short, thick, portion, or stump, of such an object as a pencil, cigar, &c., the main part of which has been worn down, used, or consumed.

stub (II.), vb. trans., fr. prec. **1.** To clear (land) of stumps, roots &c. **2.** (usually, *stub up*) To remove (stumps &c.) from ground. **3.** a To strike (foot) accidentally against a hard object; esp. *to stub one's toe*; b to thrust, poke, with, or as with, a stub.

stubble, n. [1. stúbl; 2. stábl]. M.E. *stuble, stobul*; fr. O. Fr. *estouble*, fr. Lat. *stipula*, 'stalk, stem; straw; stubble', see **stipule.** **1.** Short, stiff stalks of grain left standing in the field after reaping. **2.** Anything resembling stubble, esp. short, stiff, bristling growth of hair on the chin.

stubbly, adj. [1. stúbli; 2. stábli]. Prec. & **-y** (IV.). **1.** Of, covered with, full of, stubble. **2.** Like stubble, short and bristling.

stubborn, adj. [1. stúbern; 2. stábən]. M.E. *stoburn, stiborn*, prob. fr. O.E. *stybb*, 'stump of tree', see **stub** (I.). **1.** Resolute, determined, inflexible; not easily overcome, staunch: *stubborn courage*; *a stubborn resistance.* **2.** (of persons) Not accessible to reason; obstinate, intractable, pig-headed.

stubbornly, adv. Prec. & **-ly.** In a stubborn manner.

stubbornness, n. See prec. & **-ness.** Quality of being stubborn.

stubby, adj. [1. stúbi; 2. stábi]. **stub** (I.) & **-y** (IV.). Like a stub; short, thick, stumpy, squat: *a stubby bit of pencil*; *a short stubby figure.*

stub-iron, n. Iron refashioned from old horseshoe nails and used for gun-barrels.

stucco, n. & vb. trans. [1. stúkō; 2. stákou]. Ital., fr. O.H.G. *stucchi*, 'crust; piece, fragment'; cp. O.E. *stock*, 'stump, piece', see **stock** (I.). **1.** n. Fine white plaster used as external coating for walls, for architectural ornaments in relief &c. **2.** vb. To cover (wall, house &c.) with stucco.

stuck, vb. [1. stuk; 2. stak]. Pret. & P.P. of **stick**, perh. on the anal. of **stung**, Pret. of **sting.**

stuck-up, adj. [1. stúk up; 2. sták ap], fr. P.P. of **stick.** (colloq.) Vain, conceited, haughty.

stud (I.), n. [1. stud; 2. stad]. O.E., M.E. *stōd*, 'stud, herd of horses'; cp. O.N. *stōð*, O.H.G. *stuot*, 'stud', Mod. Germ. *stute*, 'mare'; cp. also O.E. *stēda*, 'a stallion', see **steed**; the word is fr. base **stā-* &c., 'to stand', & the orig. sense was prob. 'standing-place (for horses)'; cp. similar transference of sense in **stable** (II.) a Number of horses and mares kept for breeding; b collection of horses for hunting, racing &c.

stud (II.), n. O.E. *studu*, 'post, buttress'; M.E. *stude*, 'stud, button'; cp. O.H.G. *(unter)stuzzen*, 'to prop, support'; O.N. *styðia*, 'to establish, support'; fr. base **stŭ-* as Gk. *stūlos*, 'pillar', see **style** (III.). **1.** One of a series of supporting posts in a framework &c. **2.** Large-headed, projecting nail or peg used to strengthen or ornament a surface. **3.** Kind of button consisting of a short neck, with a flattened base and a smaller round or flat head, used to fasten collar, shirt-front &c.; similar object used for buttoning two edges of leather &c. together. **4.** Cross-bar strengthening a link in a chain cable.

stud (III.), vb. trans., fr. prec. (chiefly in P.P.) **1.** To cover, ornament with short, projecting studs: *an iron-studded door.* **2.** a To set thickly, encrust: *a box studded with gems*; b to sprinkle, bespangle: *sky studded with stars*; *a plain studded with trees.*

stud-book, n. Register of pedigrees of thoroughbred horses.

studding-sail, n. [1. stúnsl; 2. stánsl]. Etymol. unknown. Narrow, auxiliary sail set beyond outer edge of square sail in light wind.

student, n. [1. stūdnt; 2. stjūdnt], fr. Lat. *student-(em)*, Pres. Part. of *studēre*, 'to apply oneself to, engage in, occupy oneself with'; either cogn. w. Goth. *stiwiti*, 'patience, endurance', fr. **stewedjo-*, cp. Lat. *studium*, 'zeal, eagerness', see **study**, or, w. orig. sense, 'to strive after, aim at something', connected w. Lat. *tundere*, 'to strike', & *tudes*, 'hammer', see **stint** (I.). **1.** Specif., person engaged in the acquisition of knowledge, esp. one not yet a graduate, at a university, college &c.; person engaged in a course of study at a learned institution: *a medical student*; *a hostel for students.* **2.** One who studies; a a person who is devoted to learning, who pursues study or investigation in any special branch of knowledge or human experience: *a profound student of theology, archaeology* &c.; *a student of life, human nature* &c.; b a person of studious habits: *he is a man of action rather than a student.* **3.** (cap.) At Christ Church, Oxford, senior member of the foundation, and of the governing body of the college; equivalent to a Fellow at other colleges.

studentship, n. [1. stūdntship; 2. stjūdntʃip]. Prec. & **-ship.** **1.** Endowment for scholarship at certain colleges. **2.** Position of a student at Christ Church, Oxford.

stud-farm, n. Farm where horses are bred.

stud-groom, n. Groom employed in looking after a stud; esp. head-groom.

stud-horse, n. Horse kept for breeding, a stallion.

studied, adj. [1. stúdid; 2. stádid], fr. P.P. of **study** (II.). Carefully planned, deliberate, intentional, premeditated: *studied indifference*; *a studied insult*; *a style which is too studied*, mannered, over-careful, lacking spontaneity.

studiedly, adv. Prec. & **-ly.** In a studied manner; deliberately.

studio, n. [1. stūdiō; 2. stjūdiou]. Ital., fr. Lat. *studium*, 'zeal, eagerness, exertion, study'; see **study** (I.), **student.** Work-room of painter, sculptor, photographer &c.

studious, adj. [1. stūdius; 2. stjūdiəs], fr. Lat. *studiōsus*, 'zealous, assiduous; devoted to study', fr. *studium*, 'zeal, application, study', see **study** (I.), & **-ous.** **1.** Devoted to, occupied with, engaged in, study. **2.** Deliberate, careful, studied: *studious politeness.* **3.** Eager, careful, zealous: *studious to obey.*

studiously, adv. Prec. & **-ly.** In a studious manner.

studiousness, n. Prec. & **-ness.** State or quality of being studious.

study (I.), n. [1. stúdi; 2. stádi]. M.E. *studie*, 'thought, study'; fr. O. Fr. *estudie*, fr. Lat. *studium*, 'zeal, eagerness; assiduity, application; application to learning, study'. Cp. **student.** **1.** Object of solicitude; earnest endeavour, deliberate intention: *his constant study is to please.* **2.** Act of applying the mind to the acquisition of erudition and knowledge; systematic cultivation and pursuit of science and learning: *fonder of sport than of study.* **3.** a Systematic attention to, and pursuit of, knowledge in some specific branch of learning or science: *the study of history, ancient languages, electricity, politics* &c.; *to begin, interrupt, one's studies*; b careful examination, scrutiny, critical consideration, concentration of the attention: *the study of a document*; *the study of human nature*; Phr. *in a brown study*, in an abstracted state of mind, distrait. **4.** Subject studied; branch of learning, department of knowledge: *philology and archaeology are comparatively modern studies*; *humane studies.* **5.** Something deserving or attracting attention, interest, or observation: *his face was a perfect study.* **6.** An excursus, dissertation, essay, embodying the results of a special investigation: *Froude's 'Short Studies in Great Subjects'.* **7.** A drawing, painting, sketch, a exhibiting an experimental treatment of an object, as part of a training; or b an experimental, tentative, essay to portray some particular aspect or part of a subject. **8.** Musical composition designed as an exercise in technique. **9.** Actor considered from the point of view of his faculty for memorizing a part in a play: *a quick study* &c. **10.** Room in which studies are carried on; specif., a room in a private house devoted to one person, generally containing a library, in which reading, writing, and the transaction of private business is carried out.

study (II.), vb. trans. & intrans. M.E. *studien*, fr. O. Fr. *estudier*, fr. *estudie*, 'study', see prec. **A.** trans. **1.** a To pay great attention to, be concerned with or for, act in regard to: *to study one's own interests, another's comfort* &c.; b to show deference, solicitude, regard, respect, consideration, for: *he studies his parents in every possible way.* **2.** To seek to acquire knowledge of, apply oneself to learning: *to study history, medicine* &c. **3.** a To examine, investigate, make a study of: *to study social conditions at first hand*; **b** specif., to scrutinize, gaze carefully at, examine in detail: *to study a map, a person's face* &c. **4.** To learn by heart, memorize (part in play &c.). **B.** intrans. **1.** To endeavour, direct one's efforts, apply one's mind to: '*May he ever study to preserve thy people committed to his charge*'; *study to be wise.* **2.** To engage in study; be a student; **a** to carry out the process of acquiring knowledge, to receive one's intellectual training and education: *to study at a university*; **b** to work at, endeavour to increase one's knowledge by study: *he never studied after he left the university.* **3.** (archaic) To reflect, contemplate, meditate. **C.** Followed by adverbs or prepositions with special meanings. *Study for,* to undertake special course of instruction or training for: *to study for the Bar, the Church* &c. *Study out,* to elucidate by study; to puzzle out: *to study out a plan, a problem* &c.

stuff (I.), n. [1. stuf; 2. staf]. M.E. *stuffe, stoffe,* fr. O. Fr. *estoffe,* fr. Lat. *stuppa,* 'coarse part of flax, tow', q.v. under **stop** (I.). **1. a** Substance, matter of all sorts: *dynamite is queer stuff to play with*; *rhubarb is nasty stuff to take*; (also of non-material things) *his poems are poor stuff.* Phrs. (colloq.) *the sort of stuff, the stuff, to give them,* the proper treatment, the right way to deal with, the right thing to say; *green stuff,* vegetables; *doctor's stuff,* medicine; **b** (disparaging or contempt.) (i.) rubbish, worthless, heterogeneous material or objects: *what shall I do with all this stuff from the cupboard?*; (ii.) silly, fantastic nonsense: *all stuff! I don't believe a word of it*; *stuff and nonsense!* **2. a** That from which anything, material or non-material, is constructed or made: *tallow is the stuff of which candles are made*; *to collect the stuff for a book*; (fig.) *he is made of sterner stuff than his father,* has a more resolute character; *not the stuff of which poets are made,* not possessing the mental qualities, temperament &c.; **b** essential quality, character, content, constituent elements: *a man with plenty of good stuff in him.* **3.** Textile fabric: *I don't like the stuff that your dress is made of*; specif., woollen fabric: *a dress made of stuff.*

stuff (II.), adj., fr. prec. Made of woollen fabric: *stuff gown,* specif., gown worn by barrister before becoming a king's counsel and adopting a silk gown.

stuff (III.), vb. trans. & intrans., fr. **stuff** (I.). **A.** trans. **1. a** (i.) To fill tightly, pack, cram, with: *to stuff a box with old clothes, a sack with leaves* &c.; (ii.) (fig.) *to stuff one's mind, head, with facts* &c., fill full, overload; (colloq.) *to stuff a person,* tell him what is untrue, hoax him, play on his credulity; specif. **b** to fill (a pillow, mattress, seat of a chair &c.) as an upholsterer does: *this cushion ought to be freshly stuffed*; *a mattress stuffed with horsehair*; **c** to fill with food: *to stuff oneself,* overeat. **2.** To preserve (a dead animal, bird &c.) by packing the skin with tow &c., treating with preservatives, placing limbs in a lifelike attitude, and mounting. **3.** To put spices, condiments &c. into: *to stuff a duck with sage and onions* &c. **4.** To thrust, crowd, cram, ram, press (objects), with force into a receptacle or into a narrow space: *to stuff one's clothes into a trunk*; *just stuff a cushion behind my head, please.* **B.** intrans. To eat to excess; to eat voraciously, overeat; to cram, guzzle, eat like a pig.

stuffiness, n. [1. stúfines; 2. stáfinis]. **stuffy** & **-ness**. State of being stuffy.

stuffing, n. [1. stúfing; 2. stáfiŋ]. **stuff** (III.) & **-ing**. Material with which something is stuffed or packed: **a** *the stuffing of a cushion, doll* &c.; Phr. (colloq.) *to knock the stuffing out of,* (i.) take self-confidence or conceit out of, disconcert, discompose (a person); (ii.) to unnerve, render weak & shaky, as by a shock, illness &c.; (iii.) show (argument &c.) to be worthless; render ineffective; **b** compressed mass of pungent, savoury spices, herbs, chopped meat &c., inserted and cooked in a bird or joint of meat to impart flavour.

stuffing-box, n. Chamber filled with packing to reduce leakage of steam, water &c. from the hole in which a piston-rod moves.

stuffy, adj. [1. stúfi; 2. stáfi]. **stuff** (I.) & **-y** (IV.). **1. a** (of room) Ill-ventilated, imperfectly supplied with fresh air; close, airless, fusty, frowsty; **b** (of air) exhausted, reverse of fresh, used-up, musty; **c** (of weather) close, steamy, reverse of bracing. **2.** (of persons, mind) Not easily accessible to new ideas; dull, stodgy; sticky.

stuggy, adj. [1. stúgi; 2. stági]. Prob. a variant of **stocky**. Stocky.

stultification, n. [1. stùltifikáshun; 2. stàltifikéiʃən]. See next word & **-fication**. Act of stultifying; state of being stultified.

stultify, vb. trans. [1. stúltifi; 2. stáltifai], fr. L. Lat. *stultificāre,* 'to make foolish', fr. *stultus,* 'foolish', & **-fy**; cp. Lat. *stolō,* 'useless sucker'; *stolidus,* 'dull, stupid', see **stolid**; cogn. w. Scrt. *sthūlāś,* 'thick, coarse, stupid'; O.E. *stille,* 'motionless, silent', see **still** (I.). To make of no effect, cause to appear in a foolish light; make inconsistent, destroy value or weight of, spoil effect of: *to go back on one's word now would be to stultify oneself hopelessly*; *this clause is stultified by what follows.*

stum, n. & vb. trans. [1. stum; 2. stam], fr. Du. *stom,* 'stum', fr. adj. *stom,* 'silent, still'; cp. Mod. Germ. *stumm,* 'dumb'; cp. **stammer** & **stem** (III.). **1.** n. Wholly or partially unfermented grape-juice. **2.** vb. To prevent or hinder fermentation of (grape-juice) by adding sodium sulphite &c.

stumble (I.), vb. intrans. & trans. [1. stúmbl; 2. stámbl]. M.E. *stom(b)len*; cp. M. Du. *stomelen*; cp. M.E., M. Du. *stameren*; O.H.G. *stammalōn,* 'to stammer', see **stammer** & prec. **A.** intrans. **1. a** To trip up, miss one's footing, lose balance, in walking, running &c., esp. by catching foot in, or striking foot against, an object, or from weakness &c.: *to stumble and fall*; *to stumble over a stone*; **b** (fig.) to err, make a mistake, to be guilty of a moral or intellectual lapse. **2.** To speak, read, recite &c. haltingly, with frequent mistakes, hesitations &c.; to falter, blunder: *to stumble over one's words*; *to stumble through a speech, lesson* &c. **B.** trans. (archaic) To disconcert, perplex, trouble. **C.** Followed by adverbs or prepositions with special meanings. *Stumble across,* intrans., to come upon, discover, by chance. *Stumble along,* intrans., to walk or run with a stumbling gait. *Stumble at,* intrans., to hesitate over, be disconcerted, perplexed, embarrassed by. *Stumble* (*up*)*on,* stumble across.

stumble (II.), n., fr. prec. Act of stumbling; sudden loss of foothold, halt in progress due to catching one's foot &c.

stumbling, adj. [1. stúmbling; 2. stámbliŋ], fr. Pres. Part. of **stumble** (I.). Hesitating, unsteady, faltering: *a stumbling gait*; *a stumbling speech.*

stumbling-block, n. (fig.) Something that hinders progress; impediment, obstacle: *a stumbling-block to faith.*

stumblingly, adv. [1. stúmblingli; 2. stámbliŋli]. **stumbling** & **-ly**. In a stumbling manner.

stumer, n. [1. stûmer; 2. stjûmə]. Etymol. unknown. (slang) Worthless, forged, counterfeit, coin, note, or cheque.

stump (I.), n. [1. stump; 2. stamp]. M.E. *stumpe, stompe,* fr. O.N. *stumpr*; cp. M. Du. *stomp*; M.L.G. *stump*; M.H.G. *stumpf*; cogn. w. Scrt. *tu(m)páti,* 'strikes, pushes'; cp. further, without *m,* O.N. *stūfr,* 'stump'; Gk. *stúpos,* 'stick'; *túptein,* 'to strike'; *túpos,* 'blow', see **type** (I.); cp. Lett. *stupe,* 'broomstick'. **1. a** Lower part of trunk of tree left in ground when upper part has fallen or been felled; stock, stub; specif. **b** tree-stump or similar object from which speaker addresses crowd &c. Phr. *stump oratory, speeches* &c., bombastic, ranting speeches, esp. on political affairs, such as are made from a stump; Phr. *to go, be, on the stump,* engage in a campaign of stump oratory. **2.** Any short, thick, more or less cylindrical body left when the remainder has been removed, worn off &c.: *the stump of a tooth, amputated limb, mast, pencil, candle* &c. Phr. *to stir one's stumps,* move the legs, walk, hurry. **3.** (cricket) One of three upright sticks forming the wicket. **4.** Pointed, rubber stick, or stiff cylinder of paper, used to apply or soften charcoal &c. in drawing.

stump (II.), vb. trans. & intrans., fr. prec. **A.** trans. **1. a** (cricket) To put batsman out by striking the bails from the wicket while he is outside his ground; **b** (fig., colloq.) to puzzle, disconcert, defeat, esp. by asking questions which cannot be answered, or presenting difficulties which cannot be resolved: *to be stumped by an examination question*; *I was completely stumped when the car began to slide backwards down the hill.* **2.** (drawing &c.) To apply (pigment), tone down, soften, with a stump. **3.** (See prec. **1. b.**) In Phr. *to stump the country, a constituency,* to travel about addressing meetings in support of a political or other cause: *to stump the country on Tariff Reform* &c. **B.** intrans. To walk with stiff, heavy steps; esp. *stump along.* **C.** Followed by adverb. *Stump up,* trans., (slang) to pay out.

stumper, n. [1. stúmper; 2. stámpə]. **stump** (II.) & **-er**. One who, that which, stumps; specif. (colloq.) puzzling problem, question &c.; a poser.

stumpily, adv. [1. stúmpili; 2. stámpili]. **stumpy** & **-ly**. In a stumpy manner.

stumpiness, n. [1. stúmpines; 2. stámpinis]. Next word & **-ness**. Quality of being stumpy.

stumpy, adj. [1. stúmpi; 2. stámpi]. **stump** (I.) & **-y** (IV.). Short and thickset, stubby, stocky, cobby.

stun, vb. trans. [1. stun; 2. stan]. M.E. *stonien* &c., 'to stun, astonish', fr. O. Fr. *estoner,* 'to stun, resound', fr. L. Lat. *extonāre,* 'to resound'; cp. also O.E. *stunian,* 'to resound, dash against'; O.N. *stynia,* 'to groan'; cogn. w. Gk. *sténein,* 'to groan'; Scrt. *stánati,* 'thunders'; *tányati,* 'rustles, roars'; Lat. *tonāre,* 'to thunder'; O.E. *þunor,* 'thunder', see **thunder**. **1.** To inflict a severe physical shock to, as by a heavy blow or impact, which temporarily destroys consciousness and power of movement. **2.** To cause a shock to the nerves; to amaze, astound, by unexpected news &c., to the point of producing momentary confusion of mind: *completely stunned by the (news of the) disaster.*

Stundism, n. [1. stóondizm; 2. stúndizəm], fr. Germ. *stunde,* 'hour; lesson'; cp. O.E., O.N. *stund*; O. Fris. *stunde,* 'moment, time, hour'. Doctrine of the Stundists.

Stundist, n. [1. stóondist; 2. stúndist]. See prec. & **-ist**. Member of a body of dissenters from the Russian Orthodox Church, rejecting all forms and ceremonies, and basing their doctrines entirely on the Modern Russian translation of the Bible (1861).

stung, vb. [1. stung; 2. staŋ]. Pret. & P.P. of **sting**; O.E. (*ġe*)*stungen,* P.P.

stunk, vb. [1. stungk; 2. staŋk]. Pret. & P.P. of **stink**; O.E. (*ġe*)*stuncen,* P.P.

stunner, n. [1. stúner; 2. stánə]. **stun** & **-er**. (slang) Person or object that surprises and delights by his or its qualities of beauty or excellence.

stunning, adj. [1. stúning; 2. stániŋ]. Pres. Part. of **stun**. **1.** Producing physical or mental shock; causing loss or partial loss of consciousness: *a stunning blow on the head*; (also fig.) *stunning blow,* terrible, paralysing shock. **2.** (slang) Producing a pleasant surprise; hence highly delightful, splendid; topping.

stunningly, adv. Prec. & **-ly**. In a stunning manner.

stunsail, n. [1. stúnsl; 2. stánsl]. Contracted fr. **studding-sail.** Studding-sail.

stunt (I.), vb. trans. [1. stunt; 2. stant], fr. M.E., O.E. *stunt*, 'dull, foolish'; cp. O.N. *stuttr*; M.H.G. *stunz*, 'short'; see **stint (I.)**. To check growth, development, of; to dwarf: *stunted trees, intelligence* &c.

stunt (II.), n. Introduced fr. America; orig. athletic slang; fr. Germ. *stunde*, 'lesson'; see **Stundism.** (slang) A showy, striking performance; feat, display, of skill.

stuntedness, n. [1. stúntednes; 2. stántidnis], fr. P.P. of **stunt (I.)** & **-ness.** Condition, state, of being stunted or dwarfed.

stupa, n. [1. stōōpa; 2. stúpə]. Scrt. *stūpa*, 'mound'; cp. Hind. *top*. A round, domed tumulus in India, containing a Buddhist shrine; a tope.

stupe, n. & vb. trans. [1. stūp; 2. stjūp], fr. Lat. *stūpa*, variant of *stuppa*, 'tow', see **stop (I.)**. **1.** n. Compress, cloth wrung out in hot water &c., as fomentation for wound &c. **2.** vb. To apply a stupe to; to poultice, foment.

stupefacient, adj. & n. [1. stūpefáshent; 2. stjūpiféiʃənt]. See **stupefy** & **-facient.** **1.** adj. Tending to stupefy. **2.** n. (med.) Stupefacient substance; a narcotic.

stupefaction, n. [1. stūpefákshun; 2. stjūpifǽkʃən]. See **stupefy** & **-faction.** **a** Act of stupefying; state of being stupefied; **b** specif., amazement; cause of amazement.

stupefactive, adj. [1. stūpefáktiv; 2. stjūpifǽktiv]. See prec. & **-ive.** Having the power of stupefying; stupefacient.

stupefy, vb. trans. [1. stūpefī; 2. stjūpifai], fr. Lat. *stupefacere*, 'to make senseless, benumb, deaden', fr. *stupēre*, 'to be stunned, stupefied; to be amazed', q.v. under **stupid.** **a** To deaden the faculties or senses of, make stupid, dull, deprive of perceptive power; **b** to stun with astonishment, to amaze.

stupendous, adj. [1. stūpéndus; 2. stjūpéndəs], fr. Lat. *stupendus*, 'amazing', gerundive of *stupēre*, 'to be benumbed, amazed', see **stupid,** & **-ous.** Possessing some quality in an extraordinary degree; astonishing by virtue of size, volume, force &c.: *stupendous height; a stupendous mistake.*

stupendously, adv. Prec. & **-ly.** In a stupendous manner.

stupendousness, n. See prec. & **-ness.** Quality of being stupendous.

stupeous, adj. [1. stūpeus; 2. stjūpiəs], fr. Lat. *stūpeus*, 'of tow', fr. *stūpa*, 'tow', see **stupe,** & **-eous.** Having, bearing, long, loose, thread-like hairs or scales.

stupid (I.), adj. [1. stūpid; 2. stjūpid, stjúpid], fr. Lat. *stupidus*, 'struck senseless, amazed; dull, stupid', fr. *stupēre*, 'to be stunned, senseless; to be amazed'; cogn. w. Scrt. *tu(m)páti*, 'strikes, pushes'; Gk. *túpos*, 'blow; imprint', see **type (I.)**; see **stub (I.) stump (I.)**, & words there referred to. **1.** With senses or faculties deadened, dull, benumbed; stupefied; in a state of stupor: *to be stupid with sleep.* **2.** Characterized by, evincing, lack of intelligence, wisdom, prudence &c.; dull, foolish, slow-witted: *a stupid person, action, book; a stupid thing to do.*

stupid (II.), n., fr. prec. (colloq.) Stupid person.

stupidity, n. [1. stūpíditi; 2. stjupíditi], fr. Lat. *stupiditātem*, 'dullness, stupidity', fr. *stupidus*, 'dull', see prec., & **-ity.** Quality of being stupid; mental dullness, lack of intelligence, slowness of wit.

stupidly, adv. [1. stūpidli; 2. stjūpidli]. Prec. & **-ly.** In a stupid manner.

stupor, n. [1. stūper; 2. stjūpə], fr. Lat. *stupor*, 'numbness, insensibility; dullness', fr. *stupēre*, 'to be senseless; to be amazed', see **stupid,** & **-or.** **1.** Partial insensibility, torpor, deadened condition of faculties and senses; state of coma. **2.** Mental dullness or helplessness caused by intense astonishment, shock &c.

stuporous, adj. [1. stūporus; 2. stjūpərəs]. Prec. & **-ous.** Of, characteristic of, affected with, stupor.

stupose, adj. [1. stūpōs; 2. stjūpous], fr. Lat. *stūpa*, 'tow', see **stupe,** & **-ose.** Having tufts of tow-like filaments.

sturdied, adj. [1. stérdid; 2. stə́did]. **sturdy (II.)** & **-ed.** Affected with sturdy.

sturdily, adv. [1. stérdili; 2. stə́dili]. **sturdy (I.)** & **-ly.** In a sturdy manner.

sturdiness, n. [1. stérdines; 2. stə́dinis]. See prec. & **-ness.** State or quality of being sturdy.

sturdy (I.), adj. [1. stérdi; 2. stə́di]. M.E. *stourdi*, 'sturdy, stubborn', fr. O. Fr. *estourdi*, 'astounded'; etymol. uncertain. **1.** Strong, vigorous, robust, well developed, stout: *a sturdy youngster; a sturdy oak; sturdy beggar*, specif., one able, but unwilling, to work. **2.** Characterized by, evincing, strength, vigour, robustness: *a sturdy common sense, resistance, faith.*

sturdy (II.), n., fr. O. Fr. *estourdie*, 'giddiness', fr. *estourdi*, 'amazed', see prec. Disease of sheep characterized by giddiness and stupor.

sturgeon, n. [1. stérjun; 2. stə́dʒən]. M.E. *sturgiun*, fr. O. Fr. *esturgeon*, fr. Med. Lat. *sturiōnem*, fr. O.H.G. *sturjo*, 'sturgeon'; cp. O.E. *styria*, 'sturgeon'; origin obscure. Large fish, genus *Acipenser*, of N. Atlantic coasts and N. American and N. European rivers, from which caviare and isinglass are obtained.

sturnoid, adj. [1. stérnoid; 2. stə́nɔid], fr. Lat. *sturnus*, 'starling', see **starling (I.)**, & **-oid.** Pertaining to, like, the starlings.

stutter (I.), vb. intrans. & trans. [1. stúter; 2. státə], fr. M.E. *stutten*, 'to hesitate, stammer'; cp. O.N. *stauta*; Du. *stotteren*, 'to stutter'; Goth. *stautan*; O.H.G. *stōzzan*, 'to strike'; cp. further O.E. *styntan*, 'to stupefy', see **stint (I.)**; O.N. *stuttr*, 'short'. **1.** intrans. To speak with involuntary, spasmodic hesitations and repetitions; to stammer. **2.** trans. To pronounce, utter, with hesitation: *to stutter (out) an apology.*

stutter (II.), n., fr. prec. Speech-defect characterized by spasmodic repetition of initial sounds; a stammer.

stuttering, adj. [1. stútering; 2. státəriŋ], fr. Pres. Part. of **stutter (I.)**. Characterized by a stutter.

stutteringly, adv. Prec. & **-ly.** In a stuttering manner.

sty (I.), n. [1. stī; 2. stai]. O.E. *stiġ*, M.E. *stī*, 'sty'; fr. the base in O.E. *stīgan*, 'to rise, mount'; also in O.S. & O.H.G.; Goth. *steigan*; cogn. w. Gk. *steíkhein*, 'to walk, go'; Scrt. *stighnati*, 'he climbs'. See also **stair, steward, & stile (I.)**. Enclosure, pen, for pig.

sty (II.), vb. trans., fr. prec. (rare) To enclose, keep, in a sty.

sty (III.), **stye**, n. [1. stī; 2. stai]. M.E. *stī(en)*, 'sty'; O.E. *stīgend*, 'sty in the eye'; prob. fr. O.E. *stīgan*, 'to rise', q.v. under **sty (I.)**. Small, inflamed swelling on the eyelid.

Stygian, adj. [1. stíjian; 2. stídʒiən], fr. Lat. *Stygius*, fr. Gk. *Stúgios*, 'Stygian', fr. *stug-*, stem of *Stúx*, 'Styx, river of the nether regions'; cp. Gk. *stugein*, 'to hate'; *stugnós*, 'hateful'. Of, pertaining to, characteristic of, the Styx or the infernal regions, esp. in Phr. *Stygian gloom, darkness* &c.

style (I.), n. [1. stīl; 2. stail]. M.E. *stīle*, 'style, pen'; fr. O. Fr. *stile, style*, fr. Lat. *stilus*, 'pointed instrument, spike, pale; instrument for writing on waxed tablets; writing; composition; mode of expression, style'; cogn. w. Lat. *stimulus*, 'point, goad'; fr. base **sti-, *stoi-*, 'sharp, pointed', whence also Lat. *instīgāre*, 'to goad, prick', see **instigate**; O.E. *sticca*, 'stick, peg', see **stick (I.)** &c. **1. a** Small, slender, pointed instrument anciently used for inscribing letters on waxed tablets; hence, **b** (archaic) pen, pencil. **2.** Object or formation resembling a style in shape; specif. **a** engraving tool; **b** etching needle; **c** (zool.) small, pointed projection or process. **3. a** Mode of verbal expression, way of putting ideas into words in speech or writing; manner: *a concise, rhetorical, turgid, style; a style of one's own*; **b** distinguished, good, clear, graceful, style &c.: *a writer without style*; **c** specific mode of expression characteristic of an individual, a period, a school &c.: *in the Elizabethan, eighteenth-century, style; in the style of Pope.* **4.** Mode, method, of execution, expression, in any of the fine arts; esp. method characteristic of specific person, country, period &c.: *the Byzantine, Romanesque, style; in the style of Rubens; classical styles of architecture; furnished in Mid-Victorian style.* **5.** Way of moving in carrying out some skilled action or series of actions, e.g. in games &c.: *the style of a cricketer, fencer, lawn-tennis player* &c. **6.** Fashion in dress, mode: *all the latest styles from Paris.* **7. a** Way of carrying and behaving oneself; general bearing, manner, deportment, in relation to the usages of good society: *ladies tell me that the new Mayoress is shocking bad style*; **b** specif., good style; distinction of bearing and manner; good breeding: *a woman who naturally has style can afford to be plain.* **8.** Sort, kind, particular variety: *just the style of dinner I detest; he called me a fool, and more in the same style.* Phrs. *style of thing*, way of behaving, speaking; the way things happen, particular kind of event &c.: *I've had quite enough of that style of thing.* **9.** Mode of address, proper title, designation: *what is the proper style of a bishop?* **10.** Mode of reckoning date; *Old Style*, with reference to date reckoned according to Julian calendar; *New Style*, according to Gregorian calendar.

style (II.), vb. trans., fr. prec. To call, name, designate, address, speak of, by title of: *the heads of several Oxford Colleges are styled Warden; an impostor styling himself a baronet.*

style (III.), n., fr. Gk. *stûlos*, 'pillar'; cp. Gk. *stūō*, 'I set upright'; *staurós*, 'stake', see **stauroscope**; O.N. *staurr*, 'post'; O.E. *stōw*, 'place'; see **stow, steer (I.)**, & words there referred to. **1.** Gnomon, pointer, of sun-dial. **2.** (bot.) Slender part of pistil, between ovary and stigma.

style (IV.). See **stile.**

stylet, n. [1. stílet; 2. stáilɛt], fr. O. Fr. *stilet*, fr. Ital. **stiletto.** **1.** Small, slender, pointed instrument or weapon. **2.** (med.) Wire extending and stiffening catheter.

styliform, adj. [1. stíliform; 2. stáilifɔ̄m]. **style (I.)** & *-i-* & **-form.** Having the shape of a style.

stylish, adj. [1. stílish; 2. stáiliʃ]. **style (I.)** & **-ish (I.)**. (often vulg.) **a** Having social style: *a stylish woman*; **b** fashionable, smart: *a stylish hat; a coat of stylish cut.*

stylishly, adv. Prec. & **-ly.** In a stylish manner.

stylishness, n. See prec. & **-ness.** Quality of being stylish.

stylist, n. [1. stílist; 2. stáilist]. **style (I.)** & **-ist.** Writer or other artist who has a good, or a characteristic, style; one who pays great attention to style.

stylistic, adj. [1. stīlístik; 2. stailístik]. Prec. & **-ic.** Of, pertaining to, literary style.

stylistically, adv. [1. stīlístikali; 2. stailístikəli]. Prec. & **-al** & **-ly.** From a stylistic point of view.

stylite, n. [1. stílīt; 2. stáilait], fr. L. Gk. *stūlītēs*, 'stylite', fr. *stûlos*, 'pillar', see **style (III.)**, & **-ite (I.)**. One of a class of religious ascetics of the early Middle Ages, who lived without shelter on the tops of pillars.

stylize, vb. trans. [1. stílīz; 2. stáilaiz]. **style (I.)** & **-ize.** To conventionalize.

stylo, n. [1. stílō; 2. stáilou]. Abbr. form of **stylograph.**

stylo-, pref. representing **style (I.)** & *-o-*. Styloid process; e.g. *stylohyoid*, (muscle &c.) of the styloid process and the hyoid bone.

stylobate, n. [1. stílobāt; 2. stáiləbeit], fr. L. Lat. *stylobates*, fr. Gk. *stūlobátēs*, 'pedestal of a row of columns', fr. **style (III.)** & *-o-* & *-batēs*, fr. *bainein*, 'to go', see **basis.** Continuous foundation, base, for two or more columns.

stylograph, n. [1. stílograhf; 2. stáilə-, stáiləgrâf]. **style (I.)** & *-o-* & **-graph.** Kind of fountain-pen with needle-like point.

stylographic, adj. [1. stìlográfik; 2. stàiləgræ̀fik]. Prec. & **-ic.** Of, pertaining to, of the nature of, a stylograph: *stylographic pen.*

stylographically, adv. [1. stìlográfikali; 2. stàiləgræ̀fikəli]. Prec. & **-al** & **-ly.** By means of a stylograph.

styloid, adj. & n. [1. stíloid; 2. stáiloid]. **style (I.)** & **-oid. 1.** adj. (anat.) *Styloid process*, spiny projection at the base of the temporal bone. **2.** n. Styloid process.

stymie, stimy, n. & vb. trans. [1. stími; 2. stáimi]. Etymol. unknown. (golf) **1.** n. Position in which the opponent's ball lies between that of player and the hole. **2.** vb. trans. **a** (of opponent's ball) To lie between (ball of player) and the hole; **b** (of player) to leave ball between that of (opponent) and the hole.

styptic, adj. & n. [1. stíptik; 2. stíptik], fr. Fr., fr. Lat. *stypticus*, fr. Gk. *stūptikós*, 'astringent, styptic'; cp. Gk. *stúphein*, 'to contract'; to be astringent'; *stûpsis*, 'contraction'; fr. base *stău-, *stŭ- &c., 'to condense', parallel w. *st(h)ā- &c., 'to stand', see under **stand (I.)**, **state (I.)**. **1.** adj. Tending to check bleeding, esp. by contraction of blood-vessels. **2.** n. Styptic substance.

styrax, n. [1. stíraks; 2. stáiræks], fr. Lat. *styrax*, fr. Gk. *stúrax*, 'styrax'; Semitic loan-word. **1.** Genus of trees and shrubs yielding a fragrant resin. **2.** Gum obtained from this plant.

Styx, n. [1. stiks; 2. stiks]. Lat. *Styx*, fr. Gk. *Stúx*, 'Styx', see **Stygian.** (Gk. mythol.) River of the infernal regions, across which the shades of the departed had to pass. Phr. *to cross the Styx*, to die.

Suabian. See **Swabian.**

suability, n. [1. sùabíliti; 2. sjûəbíliti]. See next word & **-bility.** State of being suable.

suable, adj. [1. sûabl; 2. sjûəbl]. **sue** & **-able.** Capable of being, liable to be, sued.

suasion, n. [1. swâzhun; 2. swéižən]. Lat. *suāsiōnem*, 'advice, persuasion', fr. *suāsum*, P.P. type of *suādēre*, 'to advise, recommend, persuade', q.v. under **suave.** Act of persuading; persuasion; now chiefly in Phr. *moral suasion*, as opposed to force.

suasive, adj. [1. swâsiv; 2. swéisiv]. See prec. & **-ive.** Persuasive, tending to persuade.

suave, adj. [1. swāv; 2. sweiv], fr. Fr., fr. Lat. *suāvis*, 'sweet, pleasant, agreeable', earlier **swādwis*; cp. Lat. *suādēre*, 'to recommend, persuade'; Scrt. *svādúš*, 'pleasant to the taste'; Gk. *hēdús*, see **hedonic**; O.E. *swēte*, 'sweet', see **sweet (I.)**. **1.** Possessing, exhibiting, a smooth, ingratiating courtesy; bland, urbane, gracious, affable: *suave manners, smile* &c. **2.** (of wine &c.) Smooth, reverse of acid or astringent.

suavely, adv. Prec. & **-ly.** In a suave manner.

suavity, n. [1. swáviti; 2. swæ̀viti], fr. Lat. *suāvitātem*, 'sweetness'; **suave** & **-ity.** Quality of being suave; urbanity.

sub (I.), n. [1. sub; 2. sab]. Abbr. fr. **subaltern.** (colloq.) Subaltern. Not in military usage.

sub (II.), prep. Lat. *sub, subs*, 'under'; cp. Lat. *super*, 'above', prob orig., 'from below, upwards', see **super.** According to Walde, fr. base **upo-* &c., 'to, towards, up to' &c., see **up**, w. pref. **ks-*; see **sub-.** In Latin Phrs., e.g. *sub judice*, under consideration, awaiting decision; *sub rosa*, in secret; in confidence, privately; *sub voce*, under the word specified.

sub-, pref. Lat. *sub*, (*subs*), (1) expressing spatial relations: below, under, beneath; near, at the foot of; (2) expressing relations of time: towards, about; just after. **A.** In compounds derived fr. Lat., *sub-* has the following senses: **1. a** Under, as in *submergere*, 'to dip under'; hence, **b** inferiority, as in *subcenturion*; **c** diminution, *subrīdēre*, 'to laugh slightly, smile'; **d** secrecy, as in *subornare*, 'to instigate secretly, suborn'; **e** substitution, *succēdere*, 'to come into another's place'. **2. a** From below, up, *suscipere*, 'to take up'; **b** assistance, *succurrere*, 'to run up (in order to help), to succour'. **3.** Propinquity, immediate succession, *subsequi*, 'to follow closely'. *Sub-* remains unaltered in form before vowels, & *b, d, j, l, n, s, t, v*; before *c, f, g, p, r*, the *b* is usually assimilated, thus *sub-* appears as *suc-, suf-, sug-* &c.; before *m* it appears sometimes as *sum-*, sometimes as *sub-*. It is assumed by Brugmann that the orig. form was *sup*, & the meaning, in Aryan, was 'from below, upwards, towards', hence he connects Lat. *super*, 'above', see **super-**; cp. also Gk. *hupó*, 'under', & *hupér*, 'over', see **hypo-** & **hyper-.** The Lat. **sup* is assumed to be formed fr. *(*e*)*ks-*, 'from', see **ex- (I.)**, & **upo*, for wh. cp. Scrt. *úpa*, 'towards; on'; & the group of Gmc. words wh. includes Goth. *iup*, 'upwards', & O.E. *upp*, see **up. B.** *Sub-*, as living pref. in Engl., same as prec. in origin, having the following senses: **1.** Below, lower in degree or intensity: *subconscious, subnormal, subhuman*, less than human &c. **2.** Situated below, underneath: *subsoil, substratum.* **3.** Inferior in size, importance, rank &c.: *subdivision, subarea, subcommittee.* **4.** Approaching, bordering on; partly, to some extent, slightly (on anal. of genuine Lat. *subacidus*): *subtropical*; *subfebrile* &c.

subabdominal, adj. [1. sùbabdóminal; 2. sàbæbdóminəl]. Situated beneath the abdomen.

subacid, adj. [1. sùbásid; 2. sàbæ̀sid]. Lat. *subacidus*, 'sourish'; **sub-** & **acid (I.)**. **1.** Moderately acid, tending to sourness. **2.** (fig.) Somewhat acid or biting.

subacidity, n. [1. súbasíditi; 2. sábəsíditi]. Prec. & **-ity.** Quality of being subacid.

subacute, adj. [1. sùbakût; 2. sàbəkjût]. Moderately acute, less acute than normal.

subadar, soubadar, n. [1. sōōbadar; 2. súbədā]. Hind., fr. Pers. *sūbadār*, 'one holding a province', fr. *subah*, 'province', & *dār*, 'master'. Native officer commanding a company in a native regiment in India.

subaerial, adj. [1. sùbârial; 2. sàbéəriəl]. Existing, formed, on the surface of the earth, contrasted with *subterranean, aerial.*

subaerialist, n. [1. subârialist; 2. sabéəriəlist]. Prec. & **-ist.** One who attributes geological formations to changes produced subaerially.

subaerially, adv. [1. subâriali; 2. sabéəriəli]. See prec. & **-ly.** On the surface of the ground.

subagency, n. [1. sùbâjensi; 2. sàbéidžənsi]. Office or position of a subagent.

subagent, n. [1. sùbâjent; 2. sàbéidžənt]. Person acting as representative of or employed by an agent.

subalpine, adj. [1. sùbálpīn; 2. sàbæ̀lpain]. (bot., zool.) Of, pertaining to, part of mountainous district between Alpine region and timber-line.

subaltern, n. & adj. [1. súbaltern; 2. sábəltən], fr. Fr. *subalterne*, fr. Med. Lat. *subalternus*, **sub-** & *alternus*, 'one after the other', see **alternate (I.)**. **1.** n. Any commissioned officer in the army, below rank of captain. **2.** adj. Of less importance, subordinate, of lesser rank, inferior; (esp. log.) specific, individual, particular, opposed to *universal, general.*

subandean, adj. [1. sùbandéan; 2. sàbændíən]. Pertaining to, characteristic of, the lower slopes of the Andes mountains.

subapennine, adj. [1. sùbápenīn; 2. sàbæ̀pinain]. Pertaining to, characteristic of, the lower slopes of the Apennines.

subapostolic, adj. [1. súbàpostólik; 2. sábæ̀pəstólik]. Of, pertaining to, the period immediately following that of the Apostles.

subaquatic, adj. [1. sùbakwátik; 2. sàbəkwǽtik]. Partially aquatic.

subaqueous, adj. [1. sùbákweus; 2. sàbéikwiəs]. Existing, formed, intended for use, under water.

subarctic, adj. [1. sùbárktik; 2. sàbáktik]. Of, pertaining to, a region bordering on the Arctic.

subastral, adj. [1. sùbástral; 2. sàbæ̀strəl]. Situated, existing, below the stars; terrestrial.

subaudition, n. [1. sùbawdíshun; 2. sàbōdíʃən], fr. L. Lat. *subaudīt-(um)*, P.P. type of *subaudīre*, 'to understand, supply, a word omitted'; **sub-** & **audition.** Mental process of supplying, understanding, something implied, but not expressed in words.

subaural, adj. [1. sùbóral; 2. sàbɔ́rəl]. Situated below the ear.

subaxillary, adj. [1. sùbaksílari; 2. sàbæksíləri]. **a** Situated below the armpit; **b** (bot.) growing beneath the axil.

sub-base, n. [1. súb bās; 2. sáb bèis]. (archit.) Lowest division of a base divided horizontally.

subcaudal, adj. [1. sùbkáwdl; 2. sàbkɔ́dl]. Situated beneath or near the tail.

subcentral, adj. [1. sùbséntral; 2. sàbséntrəl]. Situated near or beneath the centre.

subcerebral, adj. [1. sùbsérebral; 2. sàbséribrəl]. Of, pertaining to, originating in, part of the body or nervous system below the brain.

subclass, n. [1. súbklahs; 2. sábklās]. (biol.) Subdivision of a class.

subclavian, adj. [1. sùbklâvian; 2. sàbkléiviən]. Situated beneath the clavicle.

subclavicular, adj. [1. sùbklavíkūlar; 2. sàbkləvíkjulə]. Subclavian.

subcommittee, n. [1. súbkumìti; 2. sábkəmìti]. Committee formed as adjunct to general committee for specific purpose.

subconcave, adj. [1. sùbkónkāv; 2. sàbkónkeiv]. Slightly concave.

subconical, adj. [1. subkónikl; 2. sabkónikl]. Nearly conical; tapering slightly.

subconscious, adj. [1. sùbkónshus; 2. sàbkónʃəs]. Present in the consciousness, and capable of being the subject of, or involving, mental activity, but not fully perceived and recognized by the mind, or completely and clearly present to the attention: *subconscious ideas, reasoning.*

subconsciously, adv. Prec. & **-ly.** In a subconscious manner.

subconsciousness, n. See prec. & **-ness.** That region of the mind, the margin of consciousness, which lies outside attention and introspection.

subcontiguous, adj. [1. súbkontígūus; 2. sábkəntígjuəs]. Nearly, but not quite, touching.

subcontinent, n. [1. sùbkóntinent; 2. sàbkóntinənt]. Mass of land, large enough to be regarded as a separate continent, but not usually so called.

subcontract, n. [1. sùbkóntrakt; 2. sàbkóntrækt]. Contract subordinate to or forming part of a larger contract.

subcontrariety, n. [1. súbkòntraríeti; 2. sábkòntrəráiiti]. (log.) Relation of subcontraries.

subcontrary, adj. & n. [1. sùbkóntrari; 2. sàbkóntrəri]. **1.** adj. Contrary in some, though not all, respects (esp. in log. and geom.). **2.** n. (log.) A subcontrary proposition; e.g. *some Englishmen are fair—some Englishmen are dark*, are subcontraries; but *all Englishmen are dark—no Englishmen are dark*, are contraries.

subconvex, adj. [1. sùbkónveks; 2. sàbkónveks]. Slightly convex.

subcorneous, adj. [1. sùbkórneus; 2. sàbkɔ́niəs]. **1.** Somewhat horny. **2.** Situated beneath horn or horny growth, nail &c.

subcostal, adj. [1. sùbkóstl; 2. sàbkóstl]. Situated behind or between the ribs.

subcranial, adj. [1. sùbkrânial; 2. sàbkréiniəl]. Situated beneath the cranium.

subcrystalline, adj. [1. sùbkrístalīn; 2. sàbkrístəlain]. Only partially crystallized.

subcutaneous, adj. [1. sùbkūtâneus; 2. sàbkjūtéiniəs]. Existing, applied, beneath the skin.

subcutaneously, adv. Prec. & **-ly.** Beneath the skin.

subcuticular, adj. [1. sùbkūtíkūlar; 2. sàbkjūtíkjulə]. Situated beneath the cuticle.

subcylindrical, adj. [1. sùbsilíndrikl; 2. sàbsilíndrikl]. Nearly cylindrical.
subdeacon, n. [1. súbdēkun; 2. sábdíkən]. Minister next below deacon in rank, in Roman Catholic and Eastern Churches.
subdean, n. [1. súbdēn; 2. sábdīn]. Assistant or deputy of a dean.
subdecuple, adj. [1. sùbdékūpl; 2. sàbdékjupl]. In the ratio of 1 to 10.
subdelirium, n. [1. súbdelírium; 2. sábdilíriəm]. Condition bordering on delirium; intermittent delirium.
subdermal, adj. [1. sùbdérmal; 2. sàbdʌ́məl]. Beneath the skin.
subdiaconate, n. [1. sùbdiákunat; 2. sàbdaiǽkənit]. Rank or office, tenure of the office, of subdeacon.
subdititious, adj. [1. sùbditíshus; 2. sàbditíʃəs], fr. Lat. *subditīcius*, 'substituted, spurious', fr. P.P. type of *subdere*, 'to place under; to substitute', fr. **sub-** & *dāre*, 'to give', q.v. under **date (I.)**. Secretly substituted, insinuated, foisted on in place of something else.
subdivide, vb. trans. & intrans. [1. sùbdivíd; 2. sàbdiváid], fr. L. Lat. *subdīvidere*, 'to subdivide'. **sub-** & **divide (I.)**. **1.** trans. To divide still further a part resulting from a previous division. **2.** intrans. To become subdivided, separated into lesser or subordinate parts.
subdivisible, adj. [1. sùbdivízibl; 2. sàbdivízibl]. Capable of being subdivided.
subdivision, n. [1. súbdivìzhun; 2. sábdivìžən]. **1.** Act of subdividing; state of being subdivided. **2.** Part, section, area, produced by subdividing.
subdominant, n. [1. súbdóminant; 2. sábdóminənt]. (mus.) Fourth note of the scale.
subdorsal, adj. [1. sùbdórsl; 2. sàbdɔ́sl]. Situated nearly on or near the back.
subdouble, adj. [1. sùbdúbl; 2. sàbdábl]. In the ratio of 1 to 2.
subduable, adj. [1. subdúabl; 2. səbdjúəbl]. **subdue** & **-able**. Capable of being subdued.
subdual, n. [1. subdúal; 2. səbdjúəl]. **subdue** & **-al**. Act of subduing; state of being subdued.
subduce, vb. trans. [1. subdús; 2. səbdjús], fr. Lat. *subdūcere*, 'to draw away; to withdraw', fr. **sub-** & *dūcere*, 'to lead', see **duke**. To take away, remove, withdraw, draw off.
subduct, vb. trans. [1. subdúkt; 2. səbdákt], fr. Lat. *subductum*, P.P. type of *subdūcere*, 'to draw away', see prec. To subduce.
subdue, vb. trans. [1. subdú; 2. səbdjú]. M.E. *sodewe*, 'to subdue', later *subdewe*, through influence of **sub-**; fr. O. Fr. *soduire*, 'to seduce', fr. Lat. *subdūcere*, 'to draw up, draw away', see **subduce**; the Engl. word has the sense of Lat. *subdere*, 'to place under', see **subdititious**. **1.** To conquer, repress, bring into subjection, gain authority over by force or effort: *to subdue one's enemies, one's passions* &c. **2.** To reduce, lessen, force, intensity, vigour of, diminish effect of, limit power of: *subdued light, voices, spirits.*
subduedness, n. [1. subdúdnes; 2. səbdjúdnis], fr. P.P. of prec. & **-ness**. State or quality of being subdued.
subduple, adj. [1. subdúpl; 2. sabdjúpl]. In the ratio of 1 to 2; subdouble.
subduplicate, adj. [1. sùbdúplikat; 2. sàbdjúplikit]. (math., of ratio) Expressed by the square root.
sub-edit, vb. trans. [1. sùb édit; 2. sàb édit]. To act as sub-editor of, prepare (copy &c.), for the press as assistant of editor.
sub-editor, n. [1. sùb éditor; 2. sàb éditə]. Assistant editor.
subepidermal, adj. [1. sùbepidérml; 2. sàbepidʌ́məl]. Situated beneath the epidermis.
subequal, adj. [1. sùbḗkwal; 2. sàbíkwəl]. **1.** Nearly equal, approximating in value &c. **2.** (of numbers in a group) Of such value that no one number equals the sum of the rest.
subequilateral, adj. [1. sùbēkwiláteral; 2. sàbīkwilǽtərəl]. Nearly equilateral.
suberect, adj. [1. sùberékt; 2. sàbirékt]. Nearly upright; tending to become erect.
subereous, adj. [1. sūbḗreus; 2. s(j)ūbíəriəs], fr. Lat. *sūbereus*, 'of cork, of the cork tree', fr. *sūber*, 'cork, cork tree', etymol. doubtful, & **-ous**. Of, pertaining to, like, cork.
suberic, adj. [1. sūbérik; 2. s(j)ūbérik], fr. Lat. *sūber*, 'cork', see prec. & **-ic**. Of, pertaining to, obtained from, cork.
suberin, n. [1. sūberin; 2. s(j)ūbərin], see prec. & **-in**. Waxy substance contained in cork tissue.
suberose, adj. [1. sūberōs; 2. s(j)ūbərous], fr. Lat. *sūber*, 'cork', see **subereous**, & **-ose**. Subereous.
subfamily, n. [1. súbfámili; 2. sábfǽmili]. (bot., zool. &c.) Division of a family, consisting of a genus or group of genera.
subfebrile, adj. [1. sùbfébril; 2. sàbfíbrail]. Slightly or intermittently febrile.
subflavour, n. [1. súbflávur; 2. sábflèivə]. Secondary or underlying flavour.
subfusc, adj. [1. sùbfúsk; 2. sàbfásk], fr. next word. Subfuscous.
subfuscous, adj. [1. sùbfúskus; 2. sàbfáskəs], fr. Lat. *sub-*, *suffuscus*, 'brownish, dusky', fr. **sub-** & *fuscus*, 'dusky, tawny', see **fuscous**. Dull or dark in colour.
subgelatinous, adj. [1. sùbjelátinus; 2. sàbdžilǽtinəs]. Somewhat gelatinous in character.
subgeneric, adj. [1. sùbjenérik; 2. sàbdžinérik]. Pertaining to a subgenus.
subgenus, n. [1. súbjēnus; 2. sábdžīnəs]. (bot., zool. &c.) Division of a genus, consisting of one or more species.
subglacial, adj. [1. sùbglásial; 2. sàbgléisiəl]. **1.** Existing, formed, under a glacier. **2.** (of climate &c.) Partially glacial, verging on glacial conditions.
subglobular, adj. [1. sùbglóbūlar; 2. sàbglɔ́bjulə]. Nearly globular.
subheading, n. [1. súbhèding; 2. sábhèdiŋ]. Heading of minor division of newspaper article &c.
subhepatic, adj. [1. sùbhepátik; 2. sàbhipǽtik]. Situated under the liver.
subhuman, adj. [1. sùbhúman; 2. sàbhjúmən]. Less than, inferior to, human.
sub-imago, n. [1. sùb imágō; 2. sàb iméigou]. (zool.) Stage between pupa and imago in the development of some insects.
subinfeudation, n. [1. sùbinfūdáshun; 2. sàbinfjūdéiʃən]. Grant of land by a vassal to a dependent.
subintestinal, adj. [1. sùbintestínal; 2. sàbintəstáinəl]. Situated beneath or near the intestines.
subjacent, adj. [1. sùbjásent; 2. sàbdžéisənt], fr. Lat. *subjacent-(em)*, Pres. Part. of *subjacēre*, 'to lie under or near', fr. **sub-** & *jacēre*, 'to lie', see **adjacent**. **1.** Situated, lying, directly below; underlying. **2.** Situated below, at the foot.
subject (I.), adj. [1. súbjekt; 2. sábdžikt], fr. Lat. *subjectum*, P.P. type of *sub(j)icere*, 'to place or throw under; to submit, subject; to include, comprise; to subjoin, append', fr. **sub-** & *jacere*, 'to throw', see **jactitation** & **jet**. **1.** Under authority, not a free agent, owing or giving obedience: *subject nations, States; a State subject to another; subject to the law.* **2.** Having a tendency to; exposed, liable, to: *subject to sudden changes of temperature, fits of depression* &c. **3.** *Subject to*, conditional upon some other action or event: *a proposal subject to the approval of a higher authority.*
subject (II.), adv., fr. prec. *Subject to*, conditionally upon: *this can only be done subject to the consent of the king.*
subject (III.), n., fr. Lat. *subjectus*, 'an inferior, dependent', *subjectum*, 'grammatical subject', fr. P.P. type of *sub(j)icere*, 'to place under; to submit, subject', see **subject** (I.). **1.** Person owing, or giving, allegiance to a sovereign, or a sovereign State: *we in England are all the subjects of His Majesty King George.* **2. a** That which is treated or dealt with in specific way; person or object submitted to treatment, or process: *a hypnotic subject; to make a person the subject of an experiment;* specif. **b** dead body for anatomical dissection &c.; **c** person liable to specific disease, condition &c.: *a hysterical, gouty, subject.* **3. a** That which is dealt with in writing, painting &c.; matter written or spoken of; theme; leading figure, idea &c., in literary or artistic composition: *the subject of a story, play; to choose the subject of a dissertation; a painter with a leaning to mythological subjects; a subject for discussion;* **b** (mus.) short musical phrase, sentence, theme upon which a composition is founded. **4.** Cause, occasion, originating circumstance: *a subject for rejoicing* &c. **5.** (gram.) The nominative of a sentence; word or group of words in a sentence representing the person or thing about which something is predicated. **6.** (log.) That part of a proposition corresponding to the subject of a grammatical sentence, the person or thing concerning which a statement is made, or judgement expressed. **7.** (philos.) **a** The substance of anything, the thing in itself; substantive reality, as opposed to its qualities and attributes; that of which an attribute is affirmed, or in which it inheres; **b** the Ego, the self, the mind which thinks.
subject (IV.), vb. trans. [1. subjékt; 2. səbdžékt], fr. **subject** (I.). **1.** To bring under authority, make subject, subordinate, subdue: *to subject a nation to one's rule.* **2. a** To cause to undergo, submit; to cause to be affected by some action, treatment, process: *to subject a person to cross-examination; to subject an object to extreme pressure; to subject a statement to criticism;* **b** to render liable: *to subject oneself to ridicule, insult* &c. **3.** To present, submit, place before: *to subject one's plans to another's consideration.*
subject-heading, n. Reference heading to a subject in a catalogue, index &c.
subjection, n. [1. subjékshun; 2. səbdžékʃən]. **subject** (IV.) & **-ion**. Act of subjecting; state of being subjected; dependence, subordination: *she was in a state of complete subjection to her husband's authority.*
subjective (I.), adj. [1. subjéktiv; 2. səbdžéktiv], fr. Lat. *subjectīvus*, 'pertaining to the subject of a proposition'; **subject** (I.) & **-ive**. **1.** (philos.) Arising from, originating in, the mind itself; not produced by something external to one's own mind; opposed to *objective*: *subjective impressions; many believe the phenomena of spiritualism to be purely subjective.* **2.** (gram.) Pertaining to the grammatical subject; *subjective case*, the nominative.
subjective (II.), n., fr. prec. Subjective case, nominative.
subjectively, adv. **subjective** (I.) & **-ly**. (philos.) In a subjective manner, from a subjective point of view.
subjectiveness, n. See prec. & **-ness**. State, quality, of being subjective.
subjectivism, n. [1. subjéktivizm; 2. səbdžéktivizəm]. **subjective** (I.) & **-ism**. Doctrine that all knowledge is the result of subjective experience, and that there is no objective test of truth.
subjectivist, n. [1. sùbjéktivist; 2. sabdžéktivist]. **subjective** (I.) & **-ist**. Adherent of subjectivism.
subjectivity, n. [1. sùbjektíviti; 2. sàbdžiktíviti]. **subjective** (I.) & **-ity**. **1.** Subjective quality or state. **2.** Doctrine that religious belief should be based upon subjective experience rather than upon external revelation.
subjectless, adj. [1. súbjektles; 2. sábdžiktlis]. **subject** (III.) & **-less**. Without a subject.
subject-matter, n. Theme, that which is discussed or treated of.
subjoin, vb. trans. [1. sùbjóin; 2. sàbdžɔ́in], fr. O. Fr. *subjoindre*, fr. Lat. *subjungere*, 'to append, affix', fr. **sub-** & *jungere*, 'to join', see **join**. To add (statement) to what has already been stated.

subjoint, n. [1. súbjoint; 2. sábdžɔint]. Secondary joint, division of limb of animal &c.

subjugable, adj. [1. súbjoogabl; 2. sábdžugəbl], fr. Lat. *subjugāre*, 'to subjugate', see next word, & **-able**. Capable of being subjugated.

subjugate, vb. trans. [1. súbjoogāt; 2. sábdžugeit], fr. Lat. *subjugātum*, P.P. type of *subjugāre*, 'to subjugate', fr. **sub-** & *jugum*, 'yoke', see **jugate**. To bring under a yoke; force under control, subdue, bring into subjection.

subjugation, n. [1. sùbjoogáshun; 2. sàbdžugéiʃən]. Prec. & **-ion**. Act of subjugating; state of being subjugated.

subjugator, n. [1. súbjoogātur; 2. sábdžugeitə]. See prec. & **-or**. One who subjugates; conqueror.

subjunctive, adj. & n. [1. subjúngktiv; 2. səbdžáŋktiv], fr. Lat. *subjunctīvus*, 'connecting; subjunctive', fr. *subjunct-(um)*, P.P. type of *subjungere*, 'to append, subjoin, subordinate', see **subjoin**, & **-ive**. **1.** adj. (gram.) *Subjunctive mood*, that mood of a verb expressing an action or state of existence as hypothetical, contingent on something else, conditional; virtually obs. in English. **2.** n. Subjunctive mood.

subjunctively, adv. Prec. & **-ly**. By means of, as, a subjunctive.

subkingdom, n. [1. sùbkíngdom; 2. sàbkíŋdəm]. (biol.) Subdivision of a kingdom.

sublanceolate, adj. [1. sùbláhnseolāt; 2. sàblánsiəleit]. (bot.) Somewhat lanceolate.

sublapsarian, adj. & n. [1. sùblapsárian; 2. sàblæpséəriən], fr. **sub-** & Lat. *lapsus*, 'act of falling', see **lapse (I.)**, & **-arian**. **1.** adj. Pertaining to the Calvinist doctrine that the Fall of man was permitted, but not foredetermined, by God. **2.** n. Person believing in this doctrine.

sublapsarianism, n. [1. sùblapsárianizm; 2. sàblæpséəriənizəm]. Prec. & **-ism**. The doctrine of the sublapsarians.

sublate, vb. trans. [1. sublát; 2. sabléit], fr. **sub-** & Lat. *lāt-(um)*, P.P. type of *tollere*, 'to carry'; see **ablation** & **tolerate**. (log.) To deny, refuse to regard as fact, opposed to *posit*.

sublation, n. [1. sùbláshun; 2. sàbléiʃən]. Prec. & **-ion**. (log.) Act of sublating.

sublease (I.), n. [1. súblēs; 2. sáblīs]. Lease granted by tenant or lessee to another person.

sublease (II.), vb. trans. [1. sublḗs; 2. sablís]. To grant a sublease of.

sublessee, n. [1. sùblesḗ; 2. sàblesí]. Person holding a sublease.

sublessor, n. [1. sùblésor; 2. sàblésə]. Person granting a sublease.

sublet, vb. trans. & intrans. [1. súblét; 2. sáblét]. To let to another, a house, land &c., of which one is oneself a tenant.

sublibrarian, n. [1. sùblībrárian; 2. sàblaibréəriən]. Person acting as assistant to a librarian.

sublieutenant, n. [1. sùbleftḗnant; 2. sàbleftḗnənt]. Junior officer in the Navy holding rank next below that of a lieutenant.

sublimate (I.), vb. trans. [1. súblimāt; 2. sáblimeit], fr. Lat. *sublīmātum*, P.P. of *sublīmāre*, 'to lift up', fr. *sublīmis*, 'high, lofty, elevated', see **sublime (I.)**, **limen**. **1.** (fig.) To refine, etherealize, elevate. **2.** (chem.) To purify by heating from solid to vaporous state and subsequently restoring solidity.

sublimate (II.), adj. & n. [1. súblimat; 2. sáblimət], fr. Lat. *sublīmātum*, see prec. **1.** adj. (chem.) Refined by sublimation. **2.** n. Sublimated substance.

sublimation, n. [1. sùblimáshun; 2. sàbliméiʃən]. **sublimate (I.)** & **-ion**. Act of sublimating, state of being sublimated.

sublime (I.), adj. [1. sublím; 2. səbláim], fr. Lat. *sublīmis*, 'high, lofty, elevated, exalted', prob. fr. **sub-** & *līmen*, 'threshold, lintel', see **limen**. **1.** Characterized by extreme nobility and grandeur; majestic, grandiose, impressive, exalted, awe-inspiring: *sublime beauty, strength, valour, self-sacrifice.* **2.** a Lofty, haughty, Olympian, supercilious; as though raised above ordinary human qualities: *sublime insolence, contempt*; b hence, showing, evincing, an indifference arising from a sense of superiority: *sublime ignorance, self-conceit.* **3.** (anat.) Situated near the surface: *sublime nerves.*

sublime (II.), n., fr. prec. *The sublime*, a sublime thing or quality; that which inspires a sense of awe and reverence and impresses by virtue of its vastness, nobility, majesty.

sublime (III.), vb. trans. & intrans., fr. Med. Lat. *sublīmāre*, 'to sublimate', fr. Lat. *sublīmāre*, 'to exalt', see **sublimate (I.)**. **1.** trans. (lit. and fig.) To sublimate. **2.** intrans. (lit. and fig.) To refine, purify, by, or as by, sublimation.

sublimely, adv. [1. sublímli; 2. səbláimli]. **sublime (I.)** & **-ly**. In a sublime manner; to a sublime degree.

Sublime Porte, n. [1. sublím pórt; 2. səbláim pɔ́t]. Fr., translating Turkish name of the Government central office. See **Porte**.

subliminal, adj. [1. sublíminal; 2. sablíminəl], fr. **sub-** & **liminal**, fr. Lat. *līmin-*, stem of *līmen*, 'threshold', see **limen**, & **-al**. (psychol.) Present in the consciousness, but not consciously apprehended; *subliminal self*, the subconscious mind, regarded as a domain of the individual's personality distinct from, and unrecognized by, the ordinary waking consciousness.

sublimity, n. [1. sublímiti; 2. səblímiti], fr. Lat. *sublīmitātem*, 'loftiness, elevation'; **sublime (I.)** & **-ity**. State or quality of being sublime; sublime character.

sublingual, adj. [1. sùblínggwal; 2. sàblíŋgwəl]. Situated, existing, below the tongue.

sublittoral, adj. [1. sùblíteral; 2. sàblítərəl]. (zool.) Existing near the shore-line.

sublunar(y), adj. [1. subloōnar(i); 2. sablúnə(ri)]. (poet.) Beneath the moon; belonging to this world; terrestrial, mundane.

submammary, adj. [1. sùbmámari; 2. sàbmǽməri]. Situated below the mammae.

submarine, adj. & n. [1. súbmarēn; 2. sábmərīn]. **1.** adj. Existing, living, designed for use, below the surface of the sea: *submarine plants*; *submarine vessel* &c., one capable of being sunk and moved about below the surface of the sea, used esp. in war, for firing torpedoes &c. **2.** n. Submarine vessel.

submaster, n. [1. súbmàhster; 2. sábmàstə]. Second master in certain schools.

submaxillary, adj. [1. sùbmaksílari; 2. sàbmæksíləri]. Situated under the lower jaw.

submembranous, adj. [1. sùbmémbranus; 2. sàbmémbrənəs]. Somewhat membranous in character.

submental, adj. [1. sùbméntl; 2. sàbméntl]. Situated below the chin.

submerge, vb. trans. & intrans. [1. submérj; 2. səbmə́dž], fr. Lat. *sub-*, *summergere*, 'to plunge under, sink, overwhelm', fr. **sub-** & *mergere*, to dip, plunge', see **merge**. **1.** trans. To cause to plunge, dip, below surface of water; to cover with water or other liquid: *rocks submerged at high tide.* Phr. *the submerged tenth*, completely destitute, hopelessly poor class. **2.** intrans. To go, sink, beneath the surface of water; esp. of submarines.

submergence, n. [1. submérjens; 2. səbmə́džəns]. Prec. & **-ence**. Act or process of submerging; state of being submerged.

submergible, adj. [1. submérjibl; 2. səbmə́džibl]. (rare) Capable of being submerged.

submerse (I.), vb. trans. [1. submérs; 2. sabmə́s], fr. Lat. *submersum*, P.P. type of *submergere*, 'to plunge under, sink', see **submerge**. To cause to sink under water; rare except in P.P., (bot.) see next word.

submerse (II.), adj., fr. Lat. *submersum*, see prec. Also *submersed*, (bot.) growing under water.

submersible, adj. [1. submérsibl; 2. sabmə́sibl]. Prec. & **-ible**. Capable of being submersed or submerged.

submersion, n. [1. submérshun; 2. sabmə́ʃən]. **submerse (I.)** & **-ion**. Act or process of submerging; state of being submerged.

submetallic, adj. [1. sùbmetálik; 2. sàbmitǽlik]. Somewhat metallic in character.

submission, n. [1. submíshun; 2. səbmíʃən], fr. Lat. *submiss-(um)*, P.P. type of *submittere*, 'to put or place below; to furnish, provide; to transfer, resign', see **submit**. **1.** Act or process of submitting; state of being submitted. **2.** Spirit of readiness to submit; resignation, surrender, acquiescence. Phr. *with all due submission*, with respect and humility.

submissive, adj. [1. submísiv; 2. səbmísiv], fr. Lat. *submissum*, see prec., & **-ive**. Ready to submit, expressing submission, acquiescing, resigned, docile.

submissively, adv. Prec. & **-ly**. In a submissive manner.

submissiveness, n. See prec. & **-ness**. State or quality of being submissive.

submit, vb. trans. & intrans. [1. submít; 2. səbmít], fr. Lat. *sub-*, *summittere*, 'to place, set, below; to furnish, provide; to transfer, resign; to reduce, moderate', fr. **sub-** & *mittere*, 'to send, place', see **missile**. **A.** trans. **1.** (reflex.) To yield, surrender, resign: *to submit oneself to another's authority.* **2.** To present, place before person, tribunal &c. for consideration, judgement &c.: *to submit a scheme, case* &c. **3.** To suggest, put forward, urge: *I submit, with all respect, that what you propose is contrary to the statutes.* **B.** intrans. To give in to authority, superior force &c.; to yield, surrender, resign oneself, be submissive: *to refuse to submit tamely*; *to submit to control*; specif., *to submit to the Pope, the Church*, to acknowledge the absolute supremacy of.

submontane, adj. [1. sùbmóntān; 2. sàbmɔ́ntein]. Situated, formed, at the foot of a mountain or mountain-range.

submucous, adj. [1. sùbmū́kus; 2. sàbmjū́kəs]. Somewhat mucous in character.

submultiple, n. [1. sùbmúltipl; 2. sàbmáltipl]. Number contained in another an exact number of times; factor.

subnarcotic, adj. [1. sùbnarkótik; 2. sàbnākɔ́tik]. Slightly narcotic.

subnasal, adj. [1. sùbnázl; 2. sàbnéizl]. Situated beneath the nose.

subnatural, adj. [1. sùbnáchural; 2. sàbnǽtʃərəl]. Less than natural, opposed to *supernatural.*

subnormal, adj. [1. sùbnórml; 2. sàbnɔ́məl]. Below normal.

suboccipital, adj. [1. sùboksípitl; 2. sàbɔksípitl]. Situated below the occiput.

suboceanic, adj. [1. sùbōshiánik; 2. sàbouʃiǽnik]. Situated, formed, beneath the surface of the ocean.

subocellate, adj. [1. sùbosélāt; 2. sàbɔséleit]. Somewhat ocellate in appearance.

suboctuple, adj. [1. sùbóktūpl; 2. sàbɔ́ktjupl]. In the ratio of 1 to 8.

subocular, adj. [1. sùbókūlar; 2. sàbɔ́kjulə]. Situated beneath the eye.

suborbital, adj. [1. sùbórbitl; 2. sàbɔ́bitl]. Situated beneath the orbit of the eye.

suborder, n. [1. súbórder; 2. sábɔ́də]. (biol.) Subdivision of an order.

subordinal, adj. [1. sùbórdinal; 2. sàbɔ́dinəl]. Pertaining to, ranking as, a suborder.

subordinate (I.), adj. [1. subórdinat; 2. səbɔ́dinit], fr. **sub-** & Lat. *ordinātum*, P.P. type of *ordināre*, 'to ordain, appoint', see **ordain**. **1.** Placed below, inferior in rank and importance, subject to the authority of another: *subordinate rank, position* &c. **2.** Inferior in importance, dependent upon, subject to: *pleasure should be subordinate to duty.* **3.** (gram.) *Subordinate clause*, part of a sentence introduced by a subordinative conjunction; dependent clause.

subordinate (II.), n., fr. prec. Person in a subordinate position; an inferior.

subordinate (III.), vb. trans. [1. subórdināt; 2. səbɔ́dineit], fr. prec. **a** To bring under control of, make subservient to: *to subordinate one's own interest to the public good*; **b** to place in inferior, less important, position; regard as inferior: *it is sometimes necessary to subordinate an elderly official to one who is his junior in service.*

subordinately, adv. [1. subórdinatli; 2. səbɔ́dinitli]. **subordinate (I.)** & **-ly**. In a subordinate manner.

subordination, n. [1. subòrdináshun; 2. səbɔ̀dinéiʃən]. **subordinate (III.)** & **-ion**. Act of subordinating; state of being subordinated.

subordinationism, n. [1. subòrdináshunizm; 2. səbɔ̀dinéiʃənizəm]. Prec. & **-ism**. Doctrine of the superiority of the first Person of the Trinity over the second and third.

subordinative, adj. [1. subórdinativ; 2. səbɔ́dinitiv]. **subordinate (I.)** & **-ive**. Tending to, expressing, subordination: *a subordinative conjunction*, one introducing a subordinate clause.

suborn, vb. trans. [1. subórn; 2. səbɔ́n], fr. Fr. *suborner*, fr. Lat. *subornāre*, 'to provide, furnish; to instigate, incite secretly', fr. **sub-**, & *ornāre*, 'to equip', see **ornate**. To procure (a person) by bribery or other illicit means, to commit a crime, esp. that of perjury.

subornation, n. [1. sùbornáshun; 2. sàbɔ̄néiʃən], fr. Lat. *subornātum*, P.P. type of *subornāre*, 'to incite secretly', see prec., & **-ion**. Act of suborning; state of being suborned.

suboval, adj. [1. sùbóvl; 2. sàbóuvəl]. Nearly oval, somewhat egg-shaped.

subovate, adj. [1. sùbóvat; 2. sàbóuvət]. Suboval.

subparietal, adj. [1. sùbparíetl; 2. sàbpəráiitl]. Situated beneath the parietal bones.

subphrenic, adj. [1. sùbfrénik; 2. sàbfrénik]. Situated beneath the diaphragm.

subpilose, adj. [1. sùbpílōs; 2. sàbpáilous]. Somewhat hairy.

subpleural, adj. [1. sùbplóoral; 2. sàbplúərəl]. Situated beneath the pleura.

subpoena, n. & vb. trans. [1. sùbpḗna; 2. sàbpínə], fr. first words of the document; Lat. *sub poena*, 'under the penalty'; see **sub-**, **penal**. **1.** n. Writ summoning person to attend in court of justice. **2.** vb. To summon by subpoena.

subpolar, adj. [1. sùbpólar; 2. sàbpóulə]. **1.** Near the North or the South Pole. **2.** (astron.) Situated directly beneath the celestial pole.

subprefect, n. [1. sùbprḗfekt; 2. sàbprífekt]. Official acting as assistant to prefect.

subprior, n. [1. sùbpríor; 2. sàbpráiə]. Official in religious house ranking next to prior.

subpyramidal, adj. [1. sùbpirámidl; 2. sàbpirǽmidl]. Nearly pyramidal in shape.

subquadrate, adj. [1. sùbkwódrat; 2. sàbkwɔ́drət]. Nearly square.

subquadruple, adj. [1. sùbkwódroopl; 2. sàbkwɔ́drupl]. In the ratio of 1 to 4.

subquintuple, adj. [1. sùbkwíntūpl; 2. sàbkwíntjupl]. In the ratio of 1 to 5.

subramose, adj. [1. sùbrámōs; 2. sàbréimous]. Slightly branching.

subrational, adj. [1. sùbráshunal; 2. sàbrǽʃən(ə)l]. Nearly rational.

subrectangular, adj. [1. sùbrektánggūlar; 2. sàbrektǽŋgjulə]. Almost rectangular.

subrector, n. [1. sùbréktor; 2. sàbréktə]. Rector's assistant or deputy.

subregion, n. [1. súbrējun; 2. sábrīdžən]. Subdivision of a region, esp. with reference to distribution of fauna or flora.

subreption, n. [1. subrépshun; 2. sabrépʃən], fr. Lat. *sub-*, *surreptiōn-(em)*, 'theft', fr. *subreptum*, P.P. type of *subripere*, 'to steal or snatch away', & **-ion**; fr. **sub-** & *rapere*, 'to seize, snatch', see **rape (I.)**. Obtaining of favour, property &c. by fraudulent concealment, misrepresentation of fact.

subretinal, adj. [1. sùbrétinal; 2. sàbrétin(ə)l]. Situated beneath the retina.

subrhomboidal, adj. [1. sùbrombóidl; 2. sàbrɔmbɔ́idl]. Nearly rhomboidal in shape.

subrogation, n. [1. sùbrogáshun; 2. sàbrəgéiʃən]. (law) Substitution of one creditor for another.

subsacral, adj. [1. sùbsákral; 2. sàbséikrəl]. Situated beneath the sacrum.

subscapular, adj. [1. sùbskápūlar; 2. sàbskǽpjulə]. Situated beneath the scapula.

subscribe, vb. trans. & intrans. [1. subskríb; 2. səbskráib], fr. Lat. *subscrībere*, 'to write below; to sign; to agree to, approve of', fr. **sub-** & *scrībere*, 'to write', see **scribe (I.)**. **A.** trans. **1.** To write (one's name &c.) at end of document, as attestation &c. **2.** To sign one's name at end of (document &c.), esp. to indicate consent, attestation &c. **3.** To pay, guarantee to pay, contribute (sum of money) to fund &c.: *to subscribe money to charities.* **B.** intrans. **1.** To signify one's agreement, approval, assent: *to subscribe to a proposal, opinion* &c. **2.** To contribute, pay or engage to pay sum of money, as one of a group of contributors, to fund, for publication of book &c., for regular receipt of periodical &c.: *to subscribe to a fund, journal* &c.; *to subscribe for a book.*

subscriber, n. [1. subskríber; 2. səbskráibə]. Prec. & **-er**. One who subscribes; specif. **a** person who contributes, or undertakes to contribute, periodically, a specific sum for a specified purpose; **b** a person who undertakes to receive and pay for a publication appearing at stated intervals.

subscript, adj. [1. súbskript; 2. sábskript], fr. Lat. *subscript-(um)*, P.P. type of *subscrībere*, 'to write below', see **subscribe**. *Iota subscript*, (in Gk.) a small iota written below *ā*, *ē*, *ō*, expressing originally the second element of a diphthong.

subscription, n. [1. subskrípshun; 2. səbskrípʃən], fr. Lat. *subscriptiōn-(em)*, 'something written below; signature' &c.; see prec. & **-ion**. **1.** Act of subscribing; state of being subscribed. **2.** Signature to a document. **3. a** Sum paid or subscribed at regular intervals for a particular cause or purpose; a contribution; **b** sum charged or paid for a periodical publication.

subsection, n. [1. súbsèkshun; 2. sábsèkʃən]. Division of a section.

subsellium, n. [1. subsélium; 2. sabséliəm]. Lat. *subsellium*, 'bench, seat', fr. **sub-** & *sella*, 'seat', fr. earlier **sedlā*, cp. *sedēre*, 'to sit', & see **sedate**; cp. further O.E. *setl*, 'seat', see **settle (I.)**. Low bench; ledge below a hinged seat; a misericord.

subsensible, adj. [1. sùbsénsibl; 2. sàbsénsibl]. Beyond the range of, not capable of being perceived by, the senses.

subseptuple, adj. [1. sùbséptūpl; 2. sàbséptjupl]. In the ratio of 1 to 7.

subsequence, n. [1. súbsekwens; 2. sábsikwəns]. See next word & **-ence**. Condition of being subsequent.

subsequent, adj. [1. súbsekwent; 2. sábsikwənt], fr. Lat. *subsequentem*, Pres. Part. of *subsequor*, 'I follow, succeed', fr. **sub-** & *sequor*, 'I follow', see **sequela**. **1.** Following; occurring, appearing, at a later time, coming after: *subsequent events showed that I was right*; *subsequent to his death.* **2.** *Subsequent upon*, following as a result, consequent upon. **3.** (geol., of stream) Forming a primary tributary to main stream of river-system, and flowing in hollow formed by denudation.

subsequently, adv. Prec. & **-ly**. At a subsequent time; later on, later.

subserous, adj. [1. sùbsḗrus; 2. sàbsíərəs]. Somewhat serous in character.

subserve, vb. trans. [1. subsérv; 2. səbsʌ́v], fr. Lat. *subservīre*, 'to be subject to, serve'; **sub-** & **serve**. To promote, help on, be a useful adjunct to; to fulfil: *to subserve a useful purpose.*

subservience, **-cy**, n. [1. subsérviens(i); 2. səbsʌ́viəns(i)]. See **subservient** & **-ence** & **-cy**. State of being subservient.

subservient, adj. [1. subsérvient; 2. səbsʌ́viənt], fr. Lat. *subservient-(em)*, Pres. Part. of *subservīre*, 'to be subject to', see **subserve**. **1.** Obsequious, servile. **2.** Adapted to promote or forward, serving as means to an end; acting in subordination to, as ancillary to.

subserviently, adv. Prec. & **-ly**. In a subservient manner.

subsessile, adj. [1. sùbsésīl; 2. sàbsésail]. Nearly sessile.

subsextuple, adj. [1. sùbsékstūpl; 2. sàbsékstjupl]. In the ratio of 1 to 6.

subside, vb. intrans. [1. subsíd; 2. səbsáid], fr. Lat. *subsīdere*, 'to sit, sink, or settle down', fr. **sub-** & *sīdere*, 'to sit down'; cp. Scrt. *sīdati*, 'sits'; fr. base **si-zd-*, redupl. fr. **sed-* &c., 'to sit'; see **sit, sedate**. **1. a** To fall, pass, sink, to a lower level; to settle or sink down: *the floods have subsided*; **b** (of ground) to collapse, cave in, sink, esp. as result of undermining &c. **2.** To allow oneself to sink gradually: *to subside into a chair.* **3.** To decrease in volume, intensity, vigour &c., abate, slacken, diminish: *the gale, one's fury, fever &c. subsides.*

subsidence, n. [1. súbsidens; 2. sábsidəns]. Prec. & **-ence**. Process of subsiding.

subsidiarily, adv. [1. subsídiarili; 2. səbsídiərili]. Next word & **-ly**. In a subsidiary manner.

subsidiary (I.), adj. [1. subsídiari; 2. səbsídiəri], fr. Lat. *subsidiārius*, 'forming a reserve', fr. *subsidium*, 'line of reserve, auxiliary troops; help, succour', see **subsidy**, & **-ary**. **1.** Serving as support or supplement, additional, auxiliary, esp. in an inferior or subordinate position; secondary. **2.** Pertaining to, of the nature of, a subsidy.

subsidiary (II.), n., fr. prec. (often pl.) Persons or things serving as or giving supplementary aid or support; auxiliaries.

subsidize, vb. trans. [1. súbsidīz; 2. sábsidaiz]. See **subsidy** & **-ize**. To give subsidy to, support by subsidy.

subsidy, n. [1. súbsidi; 2. sábsidi], fr. Lat. *subsidium*, 'reserve troops; support, help', fr. *subsidēre*, 'to be in reserve', fr. **sub-** & *sedēre*, 'to sit', see **sedate, sit**. **1.** Grant of public money to support or assist private industry or enterprise. **2.** (hist.) Grant of money by Parliament to Sovereign for State needs.

subsist, vb. intrans. & trans. [1. subsíst; 2. səbsíst], fr. Lat. *subsistere*, 'to stand still; to stop, halt; to remain', fr. **sub-** & *sistere*, 'to stand', redupl. form of base **stā-* &c., 'to stand', see **state** & **stand (I.)**. **1.** intrans. **a** To remain in existence, be extant, continue in being: *a country where superstition still subsists*; **b** to remain alive, sustain life: *we are unable to subsist without air and water.* **2.** trans. (rare) To provide food for, give sustenance to.

subsistence, n. [1. subsístens; 2. səbsístəns]. Prec. & **-ence**. **1.** Act of subsisting; state of being subsisted. **2.** Means of supporting life, that on which one subsists.

subsoil, n. [1. súbsoil; 2. sábsɔil]. Layer, stratum, of earth immediately below the top layer of the ground.

subspecies, n. [1. súbspèshēz; 2. sábspìʃiz]. A division of a species.

subspecific, adj. [1. sùbspesífik; 2. sàbspisífik]. Characteristic of a subspecies.

subspherical, adj. [1. sùbsférikl; 2. sàbsférikl]. Nearly spherical.

subspinous, adj. [1. sùbspínus; 2. sàbspáinəs]. Somewhat spinous.

substage, n. [1. súbstāj; 2. sábsteidž]. Attachment below the stage of a microscope to hold diaphragm, mirror, condenser &c.

substance, n. [1. súbstans; 2. sábstəns]. Lat. *substantia*, 'that of which a thing consists, material; property, fortune'; fr. *substant-(em)*, Pres. Part. of *substāre*, 'to stand firm' &c., see **sub-**, **state (I.)**, & **-ce**. **1.** (philos.) The underlying permanent reality and cause of all outward phenomena; the subject, essence, reality of anything in which properties, accidents, attributes inhere. **2.** The essential, most important elements or components of anything; the true meaning, purport: *give me briefly the substance of his speech*; *though differently expressed, the two* *statements agree in substance.* **3.** **a** The material of which a thing consists; a portion of solid matter; stuff: *soils consist of various chemical substances*; **b** (i.) solid character, firm consistency, body: *this fabric lacks substance*; also (ii.) (in non-material sense) intellectual or moral worth and value or content: *a piece of writing which lacks substance.* **4.** Material possessions, means, resources, property: *a man of substance*; *to waste one's substance.*

substantial, adj. [1. substánshal; 2. səbstǽnʃəl], fr. Lat. *substantiālis*, 'of the essence or substance', fr. *substantia*, 'substance', see prec., & **-al.** **1.** **a** Pertaining to, of the nature of, possessing, substance; material: *no mere apparition, but a substantial being*; **b** solid, firm, stout: *a substantial building*; *a substantial meal*, one that is solid, ample, satisfying. **2.** Considerable, weighty, important, valuable: *a substantial improvement, contribution*; *substantial additions.* **3.** Pertaining to, expressing, containing, agreeable to, the pith, essential meaning, true import: *in substantial agreement*; *substantial compliance with the law.* **4.** Possessing property, commanding resources; wealthy, well-to-do: *a substantial farmer.*

substantialism, n. [1. substánshalizm; 2. səbstǽnʃəlizəm]. Prec. & **-ism.** Doctrine that a permanent substratum of reality, or substance, underlies all phenomena.

substantialist, n. [1. substánshalist; 2. səbstǽnʃəlist]. **substantial & -ist.** Adherent of substantialism.

substantiality, n. [1. substànshiáliti; 2. səbstænʃiǽliti]. **substantial & -ity.** State or quality of being substantial.

substantialize, vb. trans. [1. substánshalīz; 2. səbstǽnʃəlaiz]. **substantial & -ize.** To make substantial, give substance or reality to.

substantially, adv. [1. substánshali; 2. səbstǽnʃəli]. **substantial & -ly.** In a substantial manner; to a substantial degree.

substantiate, vb. trans. [1. substánshiāt; 2. səbstǽnʃieit], fr. Lat. *substantia*, 'substance', see **substance, & -ate.** To give substance or reality to; to prove, confirm, establish; to show to be true or genuine, give evidence of the truth of: *to substantiate a statement, claim* &c.

substantiation, n. [1. substànshiáshun; 2. səbstænʃiéiʃən]. Prec. & **-ion.** Act of substantiating; state of being substantiated.

substantival, adj. [1. sùbstantívl; 2. sàbstəntáivəl]. **substantive (II.) & -al.** (gram.) Pertaining to, of the nature of, a substantive.

substantivally, adv. Prec. & **-ly.** As a substantive.

substantive (I.), adj. [1. súbstantiv; 2. sábstəntiv], fr. Lat. *substantīvus*, 'self-existent', fr. *substantia*, 'substance', see **substance, & -ive.** **1.** Existing independently, of individual importance, having distinct or real existence: *a substantive being*; (mil.) *substantive rank*, one which entitles the holder to full pay, or pension of that rank; contrasted with honorary or brevet rank: *a substantive major* &c. **2.** (gram.) **a** Expressing existence: *the verb 'to be' is the substantive verb*; **b** *noun substantive*, one which is the name of a specific object, idea &c.

substantive (II.), n., fr. prec. Noun substantive.

substantively, adv. **substantive (I.) & -ly.** Substantivally.

substation, n. [1. súbstāshun; 2. sábsteiʃən]. Subsidiary or subordinate station.

substernal, adj. [1. sùbstérnal; 2. sàbstə́n(ə)l]. Situated below the sternum.

substitute (I.), n. [1. súbstitūt; 2. sábstitjūt], fr. Lat. *substitūt-(um)*, P.P. type of *substituere*, 'to put instead of', fr. **sub-** & *statuere*, 'to place, put', see **statute.** **a** Something put in the place of, used instead of, something else; **b** person taking the place of, acting instead of, acting as deputy for, another.

substitute (II.), vb. trans., fr. Lat., see prec. To put, use, in place of another person or thing: *to erase a word and substitute another.*

substitution, n. [1. sùbstitúshun; 2. sàbstitjúʃən], fr. Lat. *substitūtiōnem*, 'a putting in the place of another'; prec. & **-ion.** Act of substituting; state of being substituted.

substitutional, adj. [1. sùbstitúshunal; 2. sàbstitjúʃənəl]. Prec. & **-al.** Of, pertaining to, substitution; serving as substitute.

substitutionally, adv. Prec. & **-ly.** As a substitute, by means of substitution.

substitutionary, adj. [1. sùbstitúshunari; 2. sàbstitjúʃənəri]. **substitution & -ary.** Substitutional.

substitutive, adj. [1. súbstitūtiv; 2. sábstitjūtiv]. **substitute (II.) & -ive.** Capable of being substituted; liable to substitution.

substratum, n. [1. súbstrātum; 2. sábstréitəm]. **a** Lower stratum, underlying layer: *a substratum of rock*; **b** (also in non-material sense) underlying basis, foundation: *a substratum of fact, truth.*

substructural, adj. [1. sùbstrúkchural; 2. sàbstrák tʃərəl]. Next word & **-al.** Pertaining to a substructure.

substructure, n. [1. súbstrùkchur; 2. sábstràktʃə]. Lower or basic structure, foundation; lowest part of structure.

subsume, vb. trans. [1. sùbsúm; 2. sàbsjúm], fr. **sub-** & Lat. *sūmere*, 'to take, lay hold of', see **assume & sumption.** To classify, include, under, regard as belonging to, a specific category; to include in a specific class.

subsumption, n. [1. sùbsúmpshun; 2. sàbsámpʃən]. **sub- & sumption.** **1.** Act of subsuming; state of being subsumed. **2.** That which is subsumed, special instance &c. classified under a general category.

subsumptive, adj. [1. sùbsúmptiv; 2. sàbsámptiv]. See prec. & **-ive.** Pertaining to, of the nature of, a subsumption.

subtemperate, adj. [1. sùbtémperat; 2. sàbtémpərit]. (of region, climate &c.) Of, approaching, bordering on, the temperate zone; slightly colder than the temperate zone.

subtenancy, n. [1. súbtènansi; 2. sábtènənsi]. Next word & **-cy.** **1.** **a** Act of holding property as a subtenant; **b** period, duration, of such holding.

subtenant, n. [1. súbtènant; 2. sábtènənt]. Person who holds a lease from one who is himself a tenant.

subtend, vb. trans. [1. sùbténd; 2. sàbténd], fr. Lat. *subtendere*, 'to stretch underneath', fr. **sub-** & *tendere*, 'to stretch', see **tense (II.).** (geom., of side of triangle) To extend under, be opposite to.

subtense, n. [1. sùbténs; 2. sàbténs]. **sub- & tense (II.).** (geom.) Line subtending an arc or angle.

subter-, pref. representing Lat. *subter*, 'below, beneath', fr. **sub-** & compar. suff. *-ter*, cp. **inter-.** Lower, beneath, less than; e.g. *subterhuman* &c., contrasted with *superhuman* &c.

subterfuge, n. [1. súbterfūj; 2. sábtəfjūdž], fr. L. Lat. *subterfugium*, 'subterfuge', fr. *subterfugere*, 'to depart secretly; to evade, avoid', fr. **subter-** & *fugere*, 'to flee', see **fugitive.** An artifice, means of evasion, disingenuous pretext; prevarication, sophistry, equivocation.

subterminal, adj. [1. subtérminal; 2. sabtə́minəl]. Approaching, near, the end.

subterposition, n. [1. sùbterpozíshun; 2. sàbtəpəzíʃən]. State of being below, underneath, some substance or thing.

subterranean, subterraneous, adj. [1. sùbteránean, -eus; 2. sàbtiréiniən, -iəs], fr. Lat. *subterrāneus*, 'underground', fr. **sub- & terra & -aneous & -an.** Situated, existing, underground: *a subterranean dwelling*; *subterranean fire.*

subterraneously, adv. [1. sùbteráneusli; 2. sàbtiréiniəsli]. See prec. & **-ly.** Beneath the surface of the earth, underground.

subterrestrial, adj. [1. sùbteréstrial; 2. sàbtiréstriəl]. Subterranean, underground.

subthoracic, adj. [1. sùbthorásik; 2. sàbþərǽsik]. Situated under the thorax.

subtil(e), adj. [1. sútl; 2. sátl]. Archaic spelling of **subtle.**

subtilization, n. [1. sùtilīzáshun; 2. sàtilaizéiʃən]. Next word & **-ation.** Act of subtilizing; state of being subtilized.

subtilize, vb. trans. & intrans. [1. sútilīz; 2. sátilaiz]. **subtil(e) & -ize.** **1.** trans. **a** To make subtle, refined, ethereal; **b** to make subtle distinctions in (thought &c.). **2.** intrans. To make subtle distinctions.

subtilty, n. [1. sútlti; 2. sátlti], fr. Lat. *subtīlitātem*, 'fineness, acuteness, simplicity'; **subtil(e) & -ity.** Archaic for **subtlety.**

subtitle, n. [1. súbtītl; 2. sábtaitl]. Secondary, additional, title of book &c.

subtle, also (archaic) **subtil(e)**, adj. [1. sútl; 2. sátl], fr. Lat. *subtīlis*, 'fine, thin; delicate, subtle; clear, simple', earlier **subtexlis*, 'finely woven', fr. **sub-** & **tex-*, stem of *texere*, 'to weave', see **textile**; cp. Lat. *tēla*, 'web', fr.* *texlā*; see **tela.** **1.** Rarefied, highly refined, delicate; elusive, indefinable: *a subtle delight.* **2.** **a** (of the mind and its operations) Keen, penetrating, nicely critical and discriminating; **b** (in bad sense) crafty, designing, underhand. **3.** Possessing, exhibiting, delicacy of touch and exquisite skill in craftsmanship; deft, highly accomplished: *a subtle artist*; *a subtle bit of work.*

subtlety, n. [1. sútlti; 2. sátlti]. Prec. & **-ty (I.).** **1.** State or quality of being subtle (in various senses of the adj.). **2.** Something that is subtle; esp. nice distinction, over-refined point or argument; a quibble, a splitting of hairs.

subtly, adv. [1. sútli; 2. sátli]. **subtle & -ly.** In a subtle manner.

subtonic, n. [1. súbtónik; 2. sábtónik]. (mus.) Seventh note of the scale.

subtract, vb. trans. [1. subtrákt; 2. səbtrǽkt], fr. Lat. *subtractum*, P.P. type of *subtrahere*, 'to draw off, carry away, withdraw', fr. **sub-** & *trahere*, 'to carry, draw', see **tract (I.).** To take away (a part, amount, quantity) from another amount or number; to lessen an amount or number by: *to subtract 2 from 4.*

subtraction, n. [1. subtrákshun; 2. səbtrǽkʃən]. Prec. & **-ion.** Act of subtracting; specif., (math.) process of taking away a number from another number.

subtractive, adj. [1. subtráktiv; 2. səbtrǽktiv]. **subtract & -ive.** Tending, having the power, to subtract.

subtrahend, n. [1. súbtrahend; 2. sábtrəhend], fr. Lat. *subtrahendum*, gerundive of *subtrahere*, 'to remove', see **subtract.** (arith. &c.) Amount, number, to be subtracted.

subtransparent, adj. [1. sùbtrahnspárent; 2. sàbtrānspέərənt]. Almost transparent.

subtriangular, adj. [1. súbtriánggūlar; 2. sábtraiǽŋgjulə]. Nearly triangular in shape.

subtribe, n. [1. súbtrīb; 2. sábtraib]. A subdivision of a tribe.

subtriple, adj. [1. súbtrìpl; 2. sábtrìpl]. In the ratio of 1 to 3.

subtriplicate, adj. [1. sùbtríplikat; 2. sàbtríplikit]. (of ratio) Expressed by cube roots.

subtropical, adj. [1. sùbtrópikl; 2. sàbtrópikl]. Verging on the tropical, slightly colder than tropical region &c.; intermediate between temperate and tropical.

subulate, adj. [1. súbūlat; 2. sjúbjulət], fr. Lat. *sūbula*, 'awl'; cp. O. Slav. *šilo*, 'awl'; O.H.G. *siula*, 'awl, needle'; cp. further Lat. *suere*, 'to sew', & see **suture (I.).** (zool., bot.) Slender and pointed, awl-shaped.

subuliform, adj. [1. súbūliform; 2. sjúbjulifɔ̄m], fr. Lat. *sūbula*, 'awl', see prec., & *-i-* & **-form.** Awl-shaped.

subungulate, adj. [1. sùbúnggūlat; 2. sàbáŋgjulət]. (zool.) With hoof divided into digits.

suburb, n. [1. súbĕrb; 2. sábāb], fr. Lat. *suburbium*, 'suburb', fr. **sub-** & *urb-*, stem of *urbs*, 'city', see **urban.** Part of town lying on its outskirts; residential area outside boundaries of a town; (often pl.) *to live in the suburbs* &c.

suburban, adj. [1. subérban; 2. səbábən], fr. Lat. *suburbānus*, 'near the city'; prec. &

-an. Pertaining to, situated in, living in, a suburb; characteristic of a suburb or of the inhabitants of a suburb; often (in derogatory sense), prejudiced, limited in intellectual outlook; having the good qualities neither of the town, nor of the country.

subursine, adj. [1. sùbĕrsīn; 2. sàbʌ́s(a)in]. Somewhat ursine in character or appearance.

subvention, n. [1. subvénshun; 2. səbvénʃən], fr. Lat. *subventiōn-(em)*, 'assistance', fr. *subvent-(um)*, P.P. type of *subvenīre*, 'to come to the aid of', fr. **sub-** & *venīre*, 'to come', see **venue**, & **-ion.** Grant of money, esp. one made by a government, or public body, in support of industry, institution, enterprise &c.; a subsidy.

subversion, n. [1. subvĕrshun; 2. sabvʌ́ʃən], fr. Lat. *subversiōn-(em)*, 'overthrow', fr. *subversum*, P.P. type of *subvertere*, 'to overthrow', see **subvert**, & **-ion.** Act of subverting; state of being subverted.

subversive, adj. [1. subvĕrsiv; 2. səbvʌ́siv], fr. Lat. *subvers-(um)*, see prec. & **-ive.** Tending to subvert; destructive.

subvert, vb. trans. [1. subvĕrt; 2. səbvʌ́t], fr. Lat. *subvertere*, 'to overthrow, destroy, ruin', fr. **sub-** & *vertere*, 'to turn', see **version.** To destroy, overthrow, bring to ruin.

subvertebral, adj. [1. sùbvĕrtebral; 2. sàbvʌ́tibrəl]. Situated under the vertebrae.

subvertical, adj. [1. sùbvĕrtikl; 2. sàbvʌ́tikl]. Nearly vertical.

subvitreous, adj. [1. sùbvítreus; 2. sàbvítriəs]. Somewhat glassy.

subway, n. [1. súbwā; 2. sábwei]. A road, path, passage, under another road, or under railway lines &c.

suc-, pref. Form of **sub-** used in compounds before *-c-*.

succades, n. pl. [1. sukādz; 2. sakéidz], fr. Lat. *succus*, *sūcus*, 'juice, sap'; cp. Lat. *sūgere*, O.E. *sūcan*, 'to suck'; see **suck (I.)**, & **-ade.** (commerc.) Candied fruits.

succedaneous, adj. [1. sùksedāneus; 2. sàksidéiniəs], fr. Lat. *succēdāneus*, 'following, supplying place of, substituted for, something', fr. *succēdere*, 'to follow', see **succeed**, & **-aneous.** Of, pertaining to, serving as, a succedaneum.

succedaneum, n. [1. sùksedāneum; 2. sàksidéiniəm]. Lat. *succēdāneum*, neut. form of *succēdāneus*, see prec. Something used, serving, acting, in place of another; substitute.

succeed, vb. trans. & intrans. [1. suksḗd; 2. səksíd], fr. Lat. *succēdere*, 'to go under or from under; to follow in space or time; to be successful, prosper', fr. **suc-** & *cēdere*, 'to go', see **cede** & **cease (I.)**. **A.** trans. **1.** To follow, come, occur, appear after; contrasted with *precede*: *night succeeds day*; *the storm was succeeded by calm*; *one exciting event succeeded another*; *as fast as one man was shot down he was succeeded by another.* **2. a** To follow (a person) in an office, rank, employment &c.: *Asquith succeeded Campbell-Bannerman as Premier*; **b** specif., to follow as heir, obtain property, honours, rank, office of, as lawful hereditary successor to: *the late peer left none to succeed him*; *King George V. succeeded his father King Edward.* **3.** (rare, poet.) to grant success to, cause to succeed or prosper: '*Pallas from the skies Accords their vow, succeeds their enterprise*' (Pope, 'Iliad'). **B.** intrans. **1.** To follow, come immediately after, another (person, thing, event &c.): *the storm died down, and a great calm succeeded*; often *succeed to*: *a long period of peace succeeded to the stormy days of the Napoleonic wars.* **2. a** To take up another's office, duties &c., after him: *to succeed to the Archiepiscopal throne, to the office of Lord Chancellor* &c.; **b** specif., to acquire property, office, rank, as hereditary successor or heir: *when a peer dies his eldest son succeeds*; *to succeed to one's father's estate*; *no woman could succeed to the throne of Hanover.* **3. a** To attain one's object, be successful, have success; to accomplish, complete, one's purpose: *if you try often enough you'll succeed at last*; *succeed in* (*doing* &c.), contrive to do; **b** (of action, attempt &c.) to be satisfactorily accomplished, attain object for which it was undertaken, be crowned with success: *the attack succeeded beyond all expectations*; *half-hearted attempts rarely succeed.* **4.** To become prosperous, be fortunate in one's career; to acquire wealth: *to succeed in life, as a doctor, politician* &c.

succentor, n. [1. sukséntor; 2. səkséntə], fr. L. Lat. *succentor*, 'one who accompanies in singing', **suc-** & Lat. *cantor*, 'singer', see **cantoris** & **cant (I.)**. **1.** Leading bass, bass soloist, in a choir. **2.** Sub-precentor, precentor's deputy.

succès d'estime, n. [1. sóoksā destḗm; 2. syksɛ dɛstīm]. Fr. Applause accorded to a work, performance &c., on account of the respect in which the performer is held, rather than on account of the merits of the work itself.

success, n. [1. suksés; 2. səksés], fr. O. Fr. *succes*, fr. Lat. *successus*, 'advance, approach; good result', fr. *success-(um)*, P.P. type of *succēdere*, 'to go under, from under; to march up to; to follow; to prosper'; see **succeed.** **1.** Fortunate accomplishment of an aim, or attempt; attainment of desired object, or result: *my efforts were crowned with success.* **2.** Prosperity, good fortune: *he has had great success in life.* **3. a** Person who, that which, attains success: *he was not a success as a speaker*; *my holiday in Switzerland was a great success*; **b** action in which one has been successful; a triumph, lucky hit: *I count that speech, book, among my successes*; *Marlborough's battles were a series of successes.*

successful, adj. [1. suksésfool; 2. səksésful, -fəl]. Prec. & **-ful.** **1. a** Having attained one's object, having succeeded in an attempt: *I tried to persuade him but was not successful*; **b** (of action, effort &c.) producing, resulting in, a desired effect. **2.** Fortunate, happy in one's career, prosperous: *he had all the appearance of a successful man.*

successfully, adv. Prec. & **-ly.** In a successful manner.

successfulness, n. See prec. & **-ness.** Quality of being successful.

succession, n. [1. sukséshun; 2. səkséʃən]. Lat. *successiōn-(em)*, 'a coming into the place of; a succession in office &c.', fr. *success-(um)*, P.P. type of *succēdere*, see **succeed**, & **-ion.** **1.** Act or process of succeeding, or following; **a** in office, employment &c.: *a man's succession to another as editor* &c.; *Apostolic Succession*, continuous transmission of the spiritual authority of the Apostles through bishops; **b** act, or right of succeeding as heir, lawful descendant, hereditary successor: *the succession of King Charles II. to the throne of his ancestors*; *War of the Spanish Succession*; *law of succession*, that which defines and regulates conditions for the inheritance of property; *succession duties*, those payable by an heir on succeeding to property. **2.** Number of persons, objects, events, actions which follow one another in time or space; a series, sequence: *a succession of remarkable victories*; *famous personages rode past in rapid succession.*

successional, adj. [1. sukséshunal; 2. səkséʃənəl]. Prec. & **-al.** Pertaining to a succession; coming, occurring, in regular sequence.

successionist, n. [1. sukséshunist; 2. səkséʃənist]. See prec. & **-ist.** One who attaches great importance to lawful and regular succession; specif. one who holds Apostolic Succession to be essential to the validity of the Christian Ministry.

successive, adj. [1. suksésiv; 2. səksésiv]. See **success** & **-ive.** Coming in immediate succession; consecutive: *on three successive occasions*; *in successive reigns.*

successively, adv. Prec. & **-ly.** In a successive manner; in succession.

successiveness, n. See prec. & **-ness.** State of being successive.

successor, n. [1. suksésur; 2. səksésə]. See **success** & **-or.** **1. a** Person who follows another in an office, employment &c.: *when a great public servant dies or retires, it is not always easy to find a worthy successor*; **b** one who succeeds another as lawful heir, by descent, according to fixed rule &c.: *King George is the regular successor of William the Conqueror.* **2.** Object, event, which comes after another as part of a sequence, which takes the place of another as representing a stage in regular progress &c.: *the tank and the aeroplane are to a great extent the successors of cavalry in warfare*; *the summer before last was dryer than its successor.*

succinct, adj. [1. suksíngkt; 2. səksíŋkt], fr. L. Lat. *succinct-us*, 'prepared, ready; concise', fr. P.P. type of *succingere*, 'to gird; to prepare, equip', fr. **suc-** & *cingere*, 'to gird'; see **cincture (I.)**. **1.** Concisely expressed, terse. **2.** (archaic and poet.) Girded, tucked up: '*with garbs succinct*', with clothes tucked up (Pope, translating Homer).

succinctly, adv. Prec. & **-ly.** In a succinct manner.

succinctness, n. See prec. & **-ness.** Quality of being succinct.

succory, n. [1. súkuri; 2. sákəri]. Variant of **chicory.** Chicory plant.

succose, adj. [1. súkōs; 2. sákous], fr. Lat. *succus*, 'juice, sap', see **succades**, & **-ose.** Full of juice, sappy.

succotash, n. [1. súkotash; 2. sákətæʃ], fr. Amer. Ind. *msiquatash.* (U.S.A.) Dish of green corn and beans boiled together, usually with pieces of salt pork.

succour (I.), vb. trans. [1. súkur; 2. sákə]. M.E. *socouren*, fr. O. Fr. *succurre*, fr. Lat. *succurrere*, 'to run under; to run to the aid of; to help, assist', fr. **suc-** & *currere*, 'to run'. See **courier.** To help, aid, assist, relieve.

succour (II.), n. M.E. *socour*, fr. O. Fr. *socors*, fr. Lat. *succursus*, 'help', fr. P.P. type of *succurrere*, 'to help'. See prec. **1.** Help, relief, support, given to one in difficulty or danger. **2.** (pl., archaic) Auxiliary troops, reinforcements.

succourless, adj. [1. súkurles; 2. sákəlis]. Prec. & **-less.** Without succour, helpless.

succuba, **succubus**, n. [1. súkūba, -us; 2. sákjubə, -əs]. Lat *succuba*, *succubus*, 'succuba', fr. *succu(m)bere*, 'to lie down, lie under'. See **succumb.** A lascivious spirit supposed to have the power of acquiring a material body, and of having sexual intercourse with human beings; *succuba*, a female spirit of this kind; *succubus*, used either of male or female. See **incubus.**

succulence, n. [1. súkūlens; 2. sákjuləns]. Next word & **-ce.** State or quality of being succulent.

succulent, adj. [1. súkūlent; 2. sákjulənt], fr. Lat. *succulentus*, 'juicy', fr. *succus*, 'juice, sap', see **succades.** Juicy, full of juice or sap.

succulently, adv. Prec. & **-ly.** In a succulent manner, with succulent material, food &c.: *to feed succulently.*

succumb, vb. intrans. [1. sukúm; 2. səkám], fr. Lat. *succumbere*, 'to lie down, sink down; to submit, surrender', fr. **suc-** & *-cumbere*, 'to lie down', q.v. under **cubicle.** **a** To yield, submit, be overcome (by), give way (to), cease to resist: *to succumb to superior force*; *to be forced to succumb*; *to succumb to temptation*; **b** specif., to die.

succursal, adj. [1. sukĕrsl; 2. sakʌ́səl], fr. Fr. *succursale*, fr. L. Lat. *succursus*, 'help', see **succour (I.)** & **course (I.)** & **-al.** (of church, chapel of ease &c.). Subsidiary, ancillary.

such (I.), adj. [1. such; 2. satʃ]. O.E. *swylć*, *swilć*; *swelće*; M.E. *such*, *swu(l)ch*, 'such'; earlier **swilīc*, **swalīc*; cp. O.H.G. *solich*; Goth. *swāleiks*; **so** & **-like.** **1. a** Of that or similar kind; of the same nature, quality, degree &c.; of kind, like that, specified, or implied: *I never saw such a sight before*; *I know of no such place*; *there are few such towns* *as this*; *children such as these*; *such was the force of the explosion that all the windows were broken*; *how can he say such things?*; *another such disaster and he will be ruined*; **b** of that kind, of the kind just stated: '*Such were the words thy once-loved poet sung*' (Pope). **2.** Emphatic; **a** possessing a specified quality to so great a degree: *such a good man!*; *we had such a kind reception*; **b** not followed by another adjective= so great, good &c., or so bad &c. according to the context: *she possessed beauty, and such beauty!*; *did you ever see such weather?*

such (II.), pron., fr. prec. **1.** Such person(s) or things(s): '*All such as have erred and are deceived*'; '*Peace to all such, but were there one whose fires*' &c. (Pope). **2.** (commerc. or vulg.) It, them, those: *we note your remarks, and in reply to such* . . .

such-and-such, adj. [1. súch an(d) sùch; 2. sátʃ ən(d) sàtʃ]. Certain, particular but not expressly stated: *the payment of such-and-such sums to such-and-such persons.*

suchlike, adj. [1. súchlīk; 2. sátʃlaik]. Similar, of the same kind: *avoid pork and suchlike indigestible food.*

suck (I.), vb. trans. & intrans. [1. suk; 2. sak]. O.E. *sūcan*; M.E. *souken*; cp. O.E. *sūgan*; O.N. *sūga*; O.H.G. *sūgan*, 'to suck'; cogn. w. Lat. *sūgere*, 'to suck'; *sūcus, succus*, 'juice, sap'; Lett. *sūkt*, 'to suck'; cp. further, w. different formative element, Scrt. *sūpaś*, 'broth'; O.E. *sūpan*, 'to sup', see **sup (I.)**. **A.** trans. **1. a** To draw (liquid) into the mouth by an inward rush of air following a partial vacuum formed by action of lips: *to suck lemonade through a straw*; *to suck the juice from an orange*; *vampires that suck one's blood*; **b** to absorb, take up (liquid &c.) by action resembling sucking: *bees suck honey.* **2.** To draw liquid into the mouth from, by means of action of lips &c.: *to suck oranges*; *to suck the breast.* **3.** To dissolve in the mouth or hold in the mouth and lick repeatedly with tongue: *to suck a lozenge*; *to suck one's thumb.* **4.** (fig.) **a** To take into the mind, absorb, imbibe: *to suck knowledge into one's mind*; **b** to draw, absorb (profit, advantage &c.). **B.** intrans. **1. a** To perform the action of sucking liquid &c. into the mouth; specif. **b** (of child, young animal) to draw milk into the mouth from breast, udder &c. **2.** To make sound as of person, &c. sucking, draw in air with this sound: *a pump that sucks.* **C.** Followed by adverbs or prepositions with special meanings. *Suck at*, intrans., to apply lips to, and carry out action of sucking: *to suck at a pipe* &c. *Suck in*, trans., **a** to draw (liquid, air &c.) into mouth; **b** to draw in and down, to engulf, by suction: *to be sucked in by a quicksand*; **c** (of porous substance) to absorb. *Suck out*, trans., to draw out by suction. *Suck up*, trans., **a** to draw up by, or as by suction: *the sun sucks up the mist*; **b** (of porous substance) to absorb, draw into itself: *blotting-paper sucks up ink*; (Phr., colloq.) intrans., *suck up to (person)*, try to propitiate by flattery, cajolery &c.

suck (II.), n., fr. prec. **1.** Act of sucking; state of being sucked; sucking action: *the suck of the whirlpool.* Phr. *to give suck (to)*, suckle. **2.** (slang) **a** Small drink, mouthful of liquid; **b** a sell, hoax.

sucker (I.), n. [1. súker; 2. sákə]. **suck (I.)** & **-er.** **1.** One who, that which, sucks; specif. **a** sucking-pig; **b** newly born whale; **c** (Am. slang) a person easily duped or swindled; a greenhorn. **2. a** Genus of freshwater, edible fish with thick, protractile lips; **b** one of several other varieties of fish. **3. a** Flexible, usually concave disk, which is made to adhere to a surface by atmospheric pressure; specif., **b** organ by which shellfish &c. adhere to a surface; acetabulum; sucking-disk. **4.** Piston of suction-pump. **5.** (bot.) **a** Shoot from subterranean stem; **b** abnormal shoot from axis of branch &c.

sucker (II.), vb. trans. & intrans., fr. prec. (bot.) **1.** trans. To remove suckers from. **2.** intrans. To produce suckers.

sucking, adj. [1. súking; 2. sákiŋ], fr. Pres. Part. of **suck (I.)**. **a** (of child, young animal) Being suckled, not yet weaned; **b** (fig.) incipient, inexperienced.

sucking-disk, n. Same as **sucker (I.) 3.**

sucking-pig, n. Young pig, sucker.

suckle, vb. trans. [1. súkl; 2. sákl]. M.E. *sokelen*; **suck (I.)** & **-le.** To give suck to; to feed with milk from the breast.

suckling, n. [1. súkling; 2. sákliŋ]. M.E. *sokelinge*; **suck (I.)** & **-ling (I.)**. **a** Unweaned child or other young mammal; hence (fig.) **b** inexperienced, unsophisticated person; esp. in Phr. *babes and sucklings.*

sucrose, n. [1. sūkrōs; 2. sjūkrous], fr. Fr. *sucre*, q.v. under **sugar (I.)**, & **-ose.** (chem.) White, sweet, crystalline compound obtained from various plants but identical in composition; sugar.

suction, n. [1. súkshun; 2. sákʃən], fr. Lat. *suctum*, P.P. type of *sūgere*, 'to suck', q.v. under **suck (I.)**, & **-ion.** **a** Act or process of sucking; **b** specif., act or process of causing fluid to pass in a given direction by exhausting the air behind it over a small surface, so that it is driven by atmospheric pressure.

suction-fan, n. Rotating fan which separates chaff from grain by a process of suction.

suction-pipe, n. Pipe through which fluid is drawn by suction.

suction-plate, n. Plate holding artificial teeth in place by suction.

suction-pump, n. Pump raising water by suction.

suctorial, adj. [1. suktórial; 2. saktɔ́riəl], fr. Lat. *suct-(um)*, P.P. type of *sūgere*, 'to suck', q.v. under **suck (I.)**, & **-ory** & **-al.** **1.** Of, pertaining to, adapted for, sucking. **2.** (zool.) Having, adhering by means of, a sucker.

Sudanese, adj. & n. [1. sōōdanéz; 2. sūdəníz]. **1.** adj. Of, belonging to, the Sudan, Africa. **2.** n. Native of the Sudan.

sudarium, n. [1. sūdárium; 2. sjūdéəriəm]. Lat. *sūdārium*, 'a cloth for wiping off perspiration, a handkerchief', fr. *sūd-(or)*, 'sweat', see next word, & **-ary.** **1. a** St. Veronica's handkerchief which received a miraculous impression of the face of Christ on His way to Calvary; hence, **b** portrait of Christ produced by miraculous means. **2.** Napkin wrapped about the head of Christ in the sepulchre.

sudation, n. [1. sūdáshun; 2. sjūdéiʃən], fr. Lat. *sūdātiōn-(em)*, 'sweating', fr. *sūdāt-(um)*, P.P. type of *sūdāre*, 'to sweat'; cp. Lat. *sūdor*, 'sweat'; fr. base **swoid-*, **sweid-*, **swīd-*, 'sweat', whence also Scrt. *svidyati*, 'sweats'; Lett. *swēdri*; Gk. *hīdrṓs*, 'sweat', fr. **swīd-*; O.S. *swēt*; O.E. *swāt*, 'sweat', see **sweat (I.)**. **a** Process of sweating; **b** sweat, perspiration.

sudatorium, n. [1. sūdatórium; 2. sjūdətɔ́riəm]. Lat. *sūdātōrium*, 'sweating-bath', fr. *sūdātum*, see prec., & **-ory.** Hot room for inducing perspiration in Roman bath.

sudatory, adj. & n. [1. sūdaturi; 2. sjūdətəri], fr. Lat. *sūdātōrius*, 'sudatory', see prec. **1.** adj. Connected with, promoting, perspiration. **2.** n. (med.) Sudatory substance, sudorific.

sudd, n. [1. sud; 2. sad]. Arab. *sudd*, 'barrier'. Floating mass of water-weeds, reeds &c., forming obstruction on White Nile.

sudden, adj. & n. [1. súdn; 2. sádn]. M.E. *sodein*, fr. O. Fr. *soudain*, fr. Lat. *subitāneus*, 'sudden', fr. *subitus*, 'sudden, happening unexpectedly', fr. P.P. type of *subīre*, 'to go under, up to; to advance secretly; to occur', fr. **sub-** & *īre*, 'to go', see **itinerant.** **1.** adj. **a** Happening, occurring, done unexpectedly, without previous indication or warning: *a sudden shout, shock, idea*; *sudden death*; **b** acting unexpectedly, abrupt: *to be sudden in one's actions.* **2.** n. State of being sudden; sudden happening; only in Phr. *(all) of, on, a sudden*, suddenly.

suddenly, adv. Prec. & **-ly.** In a sudden manner, with suddenness.

suddenness, n. See prec. & **-ness.** State or quality of being sudden.

sudoriferous, adj. [1. sūduríferus; 2. sjūdərífərəs], fr. Lat. *sūdōri-*, stem of *sūdor*, 'sweat', see **sudation**, & **-ferous.** (of gland) Secreting sweat.

sudorific, adj. & n. [1. sūdurífik; 2. sjūdərífik], fr. Lat. *sūdōri-*, 'sweat', see prec. & **sudation**, & **-fic.** **1.** adj. Promoting perspiration. **2.** n. Sudorific medicine, drug &c.

Sudra, n. [1. sōōdra; 2. sūdrə]. Hind., fr. Scrt. *śūdra-*. Member of lowest Hindu caste, originally non-Aryan.

suds, n. pl. [1. sudz; 2. sadz]. Cp. O.E. *sēoðan*, 'to boil', P.P. *soden*; see **seethe, sodden (I.)**. Frothy substance from dissolved soap, which floats on surface of water.

sue, vb. trans. & intrans. [1. sū; 2. sjū], fr. O. Fr. *suir*, 'to follow', fr. L. Lat. *sequere*, variant of *sequi*, 'to follow', see **sequela,** & cp. second element in **ensue, pursue.** **A.** trans. **1.** To bring a legal action against, prosecute: *to sue a person for libel.* **2.** To beseech, entreat. **B.** intrans. **1.** To take legal action, prosecute claim &c. by legal proceedings. **2.** To make entreaties, beg, plead: *to sue for peace.*

suède, n. [1. swād; 2. sweid]. Fr. *Suède*, 'Sweden'. Soft, undressed leather made of kid-skin, used for gloves &c.

suet, n. [1. sūet; 2. sjūit], fr. O. Fr. *seu*, fr. Lat. *sēbum, sēvum*, 'tallow, suet', see **sebaceous,** & **-et.** Cogn. w. O.H.G. *seifa*; O.E. *sāpe*, 'soap', see **soap (I.)**. Solid fatty tissue formed around kidneys &c. of oxen, sheep &c.

suety, adj. [1. sūeti; 2. sjūiti]. Prec. & **-y (IV.)**. Like, abounding in, greasy with, suet.

suf-, pref. Form of **sub-**, w. assimilation of *b* when compounded w. words beginning w. *f-*.

suffer, vb. trans. & intrans. [1. súfer; 2. sáfə]. M.E. *suffren*, fr. O. Fr. *sufrir*, fr. Lat. *sufferre*, 'to submit to; to undergo, endure'; fr. **suf-** & *ferre*, 'to carry, bear, endure', see **-ferous.** **A.** trans. **1.** To experience (something painful or unpleasant), undergo, be subjected to: *to suffer pain, torture, hardship, wrong, death, punishment, loss.* **2.** To allow, permit, tolerate: *if I suffer you to be present, you must remain silent*; chiefly with negative: *I will not suffer such conduct*; *one cannot easily suffer ingratitude and treachery in a friend.* Phr. *not to suffer fools gladly*, to be impatient and intolerant of folly and stupidity in others. **B.** intrans. **1. a** To experience mental or physical pain: *men are born to suffer*; *learn to suffer without complaining*; **b** *suffer from*, to be liable to, be afflicted by: *to suffer from gout*; *he is now suffering from measles*; *I do not suffer from shyness.* **2.** To be the worse, be injured, harmed, impaired: *neither car nor passengers suffered much in the accident*; *his reputation suffered greatly by his failure at a critical moment.* **3. a** To be punished: *we must all suffer sooner or later for our sins and follies*; **b** to be executed, esp. to undergo martyrdom: *King Charles I. suffered on Jan. 30th, 1649.*

sufferable, adj. [1. súferabl; 2. sáfərəbl]. Prec. & **-able.** Capable of being tolerated.

sufferance, n. [1. súferans; 2. sáfərəns], fr. Lat. *sufferentia*, 'suffering, toleration'; **suffer** & **-ence.** **1.** (archaic) Submission, endurance, passive resignation. **2.** Tacit consent, acceptance, permission, implied by failure to forbid or object; esp. in Phr. *on sufferance*, without explicit consent, merely tolerated or acquiesced in.

sufferer, n. [1. súferer; 2. sáfərə]. **suffer** & **-er.** One who suffers; **a** one suffering from disease, pain &c.: *sufferers in hospitals*; *a great sufferer from rheumatism*; **b** one who has been injured, one who has suffered loss or other injury in some way specified or implied: *the poor are the greatest sufferers in times of famine*; *he tried to injure others, but was himself the sufferer.*

suffering, n. [1. súfering; 2. sáfəriŋ]. **suffer** & **-ing.** Experience of, process of undergoing, physical or mental pain; anguish, agony, of body or mind; tribulation: *the sufferings of Napoleon's army in Russia were indescribable*; *it is hard to be patient under severe suffering*.

suffete, n. [1. súfēt; 2. sáfīt], fr. Lat. *sūfet-*, stem of *sūfes*, 'suffete', fr. Carthaginian. (antiq.) Chief Carthaginian magistrate.

suffice, vb. intrans. & trans. [1. sufís; 2. səfáis]. M.E. *suffisen*, fr. stem of O. Fr. *suffire*, 'to suffice', fr. Lat. *sufficere*, 'to put, supply, as a substitute; to give, supply; to satisfy, be enough'; fr. **suf-** & *-facere*, 'to make', see **fact. 1.** intrans. To be sufficient, be enough, be adequate; to satisfy demand or requirements: *a small amount of food suffices for old people*; *a brief statement will suffice*. **2.** trans. To be enough for, satisfy, be adequate for needs or purpose of: *nothing would suffice him but the whole story*.

sufficiency, n. [1. sufíshensi; 2. səfíʃənsi], fr. L. Lat. *sufficientia*; see **sufficient (I.)** & **-cy. 1. a** That which suffices; sufficient quantity, adequate amount, ample supply; specif. **b** adequate pecuniary resources, competency. **2.** (archaic) Efficiency, capability.

sufficient (I.), adj. [1. sufíshent; 2. səfíʃənt], fr.Lat. *sufficient-(em)*, Pres. Part. of *sufficere*, 'to suffice', see **suffice. 1.** Adequate in size or quantity, enough; capable of meeting demands; as much as is requisite for particular purpose: *to lack sufficient food*; *the rain was not sufficient to do any harm*; *I have not sufficient room for my family*. **2.** (archaic) Capable, efficient, well qualified, for specific task.

sufficient (II.), n., fr. prec. (colloq.) A sufficient quantity: *thank you, I have quite sufficient*.

sufficiently, adv. **sufficient (I.)** & **-ly.** To a sufficient degree, in sufficient amount: *sufficiently provided with means* &c.

sufficingly, adv. [1. sufísingli; 2. səfáisiŋli], fr. Pres. Part. of **suffice** & **-ly.** Sufficiently, so as to suffice.

suffix (I.), n. [1. súfiks; 2. sáfiks], fr. Lat. *suffixum*, P.P. of *suffigere*, 'to attach, affix', fr. **suf-** & *fīgere*, 'to fasten, fix', see **fix (I.)**. Syllable or group of syllables appended as formative element to end of word or stem.

suffix (II.), vb. trans. [1. sufíks; 2. safíks], fr. prec. To add as a suffix, add to end of word or stem.

suffocate, vb. trans. & intrans. [1. súfokāt; 2. sáfəkèit], fr. Lat. *suffōcātum*, P.P. type of *suffōcāre*, 'to choke, stifle, strangle', fr. **suf-** & dial. form of *fauc-*, stem of *faux*, 'throat', see **faucal. A.** trans. **1.** To deprive of fresh air, cause difficulty in breathing to: *to be suffocated by close atmosphere*. **2.** To kill by depriving of air; to choke: *to be suffocated by poisonous fumes, by a pillow pressed over one's mouth and nose*. **B.** intrans. To have difficulty in breathing, choke, stifle.

suffocating, adj. [1. súfokāting; 2. sáfəkèitiŋ], fr. Pres. Part. of **suffocate.** Liable to cause, causing, suffocation; stifling, very close: *a suffocating atmosphere*; *suffocating heat*.

suffocatingly, adv. Prec. & **-ly.** So as to suffocate; to the point of suffocation.

suffocation, n. [1. sufokāshun; 2. sàfəkéiʃən]. **suffocate** & **-ion. a** Act or process of suffocating; **b** state of being suffocated.

suffragan, adj. & n. [1. súfragan; 2. sáfrəgən], fr. Med. Lat. *suffrāgāneus*, 'assistant', fr. Lat. *suffrāgor*, 'I vote for, support', fr. *suffrāgium*, 'vote', see **suffrage**, & **-an. 1.** adj. **a** *Suffragan bishop*, or *bishop suffragan*, one appointed as assistant to a diocesan, esp. for work in specific part of diocese; **b** of any bishop considered in relation to his archbishop; **c** (of see) under suffragan bishop. **2.** n. Suffragan bishop.

suffraganship, n. [1. súfraganship; 2. sáfrəgənʃip]. Prec. & **-ship.** Rank, office of, period of work as, suffragan.

suffrage, n. [1. súfrij; 2. sáfridž], fr. Fr., fr. Lat. *suffrāgium*, 'voting-tablet; vote; right of voting; assent, support', prob. orig. 'concerted cheer or shout of agreement or approval', fr. **suf-** & stem **frāg-*, seen in *frāgor*, 'noise, din, crash', *frangere*, 'to break' &c.; see **fragment, fragile. 1. a** Vote given on a question of controversy; **b** approval, assent, support, signified by vote or otherwise: *I hope to secure your suffrages in my candidature*. **2.** The right to express an opinion by voting on political questions; esp. the right to vote at parliamentary elections: *manhood suffrage*.

suffragette, n. [1. sufrajét; 2. sàfrədžét]. Prec. & **-ette.** (derisive) Woman who insisted on the right of women to have a parliamentary vote, and to be elected to Parliament, in the days before this right was secured by law; esp. a woman who emphasized her claims by violent words and acts.

suffragist, n. [1. súfrajist; 2. sáfrədžist]. **suffrage** & **-ist.** Person advocating some extension of the right of voting.

suffuse, vb. trans. [1. sufúz; 2. səfjúz], fr. Lat. *suffūsum*, P.P. type of *suffundere*, 'to pour into, overspread; to mingle, blur', fr. **suf-** & *fundere*, 'to pour', see **fuse (I.)**. (of fluid, light, colour) To spread over surface of, flood, cover: *sky suffused with light*; *eyes suffused with tears*; *blushes suffused her face*.

suffusion, n. [1. sufúzhun; 2. səfjúžən], fr. Lat. *suffūsiōnem*, 'a pouring or spreading over', prec. & **-ion.** Act of suffusing; state of being suffused.

sufi, sofi, n. [1. sōōfi, sófi; 2. súfi, sóufi], fr. Arab. Member of a class of Mohammedan mystics, philosophic and pantheistic.

sufic, sofic, adj. [1. sōō-, sófik; 2. sú-, sóufik]. Prec. & **-ic.** Of, pertaining to, a sufi.

sufism, sofism, n. [1. sōō-, sófizm; 2. sú-, sóufizəm]. **sufi** & **-ism.** Doctrines, practices, of a sufi.

sug-, pref. Form of **sub-** w. assimilation of *b* when compounded w. words beginning w. *g-*.

sugar (I.), n. [1. shóogar; 2. ʃúgə]. M.E. *sugre, suger*, fr. O. Fr. *sucre*, fr. Arab. *sukkar*; cp. Scrt. *čarkarā*; Pers. *shakar*. Cp. **sacchar-** & **crocodile. 1.** A sweet, white, or pale brown, crystalline substance extracted from the juice of various plants, esp. from the sugar-cane or from beetroot; often with qualifying noun or adjective, indicating **a** source, e.g. *cane-, beet-, maple-sugar*; **b** place of origin, e.g. *Demerara sugar*; **c** appearance, character &c., e.g. *white, lump, granulated, castor sugar* &c.; **d** use or purpose, e.g. *icing, preserving, sugar*. **2.** (chem.) One of many varieties of sweet, soluble carbohydrates found esp. in plants, including glucose, lactose, saccharose &c. **3.** Substance resembling sugar in appearance or taste; esp. *sugar of lead, of milk*. **4.** (fig.) Flattery, smooth-speaking, words designed to please.

sugar (II.), vb. trans., fr. prec. **1. a** To sweeten with sugar; **b** to cover, coat, sprinkle, with sugar. **2.** (fig.) **a** To flatter, speak honeyed words to; **b** to disguise nature of, make alluring, by flattery &c.

sugar-basin, n. Small basin of metal or china for holding sugar at table.

sugar-bean, n. Kind of kidney-bean.

sugar-beet, n. Kind of beetroot from the juice of which sugar is obtained.

sugar-bird, n. Bird that sucks honey from flowers.

sugar-candy, n. Sugar crystallized in large, hard lumps.

sugar-cane, n. Tall, perennial grass, with strong, jointed stalk, from 6 to 20 ft. in height, from the juice of which sugar is extracted.

sugar-gum, n. Large Australian eucalyptus with sweet leaves.

sugar-house, n. Factory for manufacture of sugar.

sugariness, n. [1. shóogarines; 2. ʃúgərinis]. **sugary** & **-ness.** State or quality of being sugary.

sugarless, adj. [1. shóogarles; 2. ʃúgəlis]. **sugar (I.)** & **-less.** Without, containing no, sugar.

sugar-loaf, n. **1.** Hard, conical mass of sugar. **2.** Anything resembling sugar-loaf in shape, e.g. conical hill; sometimes in compounds, *sugar-loaf hat* &c.

sugar-maple, n. Kind of maple from which sugar is obtained.

sugar-mill, n. Establishment in which juice is extracted from sugar-cane &c.

sugar-mite, n. Mite sometimes infesting unrefined sugar.

sugar-orchard, n. Plantation of sugar-maples.

sugar-planter, n. Owner of a plantation of sugar-cane.

sugar-plum, n. A small hard ball or cylinder of sugar, sometimes enclosing a caraway seed.

sugar-refiner, n. Person engaged in refining sugar.

sugar-refinery, n. Establishment in which raw sugar is refined.

sugar-tongs, n. pl. Small metal tongs for lifting lump sugar from sugar-basin.

sugary, adj. [1. shóogari; 2. ʃúgəri]. **sugar (I.)** & **-y (IV.). 1.** Containing, abounding in, covered with, tasting of, sugar. **2.** (fig.) Flattering, honeyed, excessively sweet: *a sugary voice, compliments* &c.

suggest, vb. trans. [1. sujést; 2. sədžést], fr. Lat. *suggestum*, P.P. type of *suggerere*, 'to lay beneath; to furnish, supply; to suggest, prompt', fr. **sug-** & *gerere*, 'to carry, bring', see **gest, gesture (I.). 1. a** To bring into the mind, call up idea of; to imply: *his skill suggests long training*; *his appearance suggests an open-air life*; specif. **b** to arouse in the mind by association &c.: *does the name suggest anything to you?*; **c** (reflex.) to come into the mind, present itself: *an idea suggests itself to me*. **2.** To put forward, lay before a person, as hypothesis, possible course of action &c.; to introduce, present for consideration: *to suggest a plan*; *to suggest a walk*; *what do you suggest we should do?*; *have you nothing further to suggest?* **3.** To imply, intimate, state, as completed action, motive, fact, &c.: *I suggest that you are not speaking the truth*.

suggestibility, n. [1. sujèstibíliti; 2. sədžèstibíliti]. See next word & **-ity.** State or quality of being suggestible.

suggestible, adj. [1. sujéstibl; 2. sədžéstibl]. **suggest** & **-ible. 1.** Capable of being suggested. **2.** Capable of being acted upon by suggestion.

suggestio falsi, n. [1. sujéstiō fálsī; 2. sədžéstiou fǽlsai]. Lat., see next word & **false (I.).** Suggestion of falsehood; statement which, without actually being false, nevertheless conveys a false impression, and allows the hearer to believe what is untrue.

suggestion, n. [1. sujéschun; 2. sədžéstʃən], fr. Lat. *suggestiōnem*, 'suggestion'; **suggest** & **-ion. 1. a** Act of suggesting; specif. **b** act or process of conveying an idea or impulse to the mind by hypnotic influence. **2. a** Something suggested, implied, hinted, intimated, called up in the mind by association &c.: *a suggestion of a nautical roll in his gait*; *there is no suggestion of provincial accent in his speech*; *a building calling up suggestions of the past*; *to make a suggestion*; *his suggestion was approved*; **b** specif., something, idea, impulse of action, conveyed to the mind by hypnotic influence. **3.** A suggesting of, or tendency to suggest, what is indecent or improper.

suggestionization, n. [1. sujèschunīzáshun; 2. sədžèstʃənaizéiʃən]. Prec. & **-ation. a** Act or process of suggestionizing; **b** state of being suggestionized.

suggestionize, vb. trans. [1. sujéschunīz; 2. sədžéstʃənaiz]. Prec. & **-ize.** To subject to, influence by, suggestion; esp. to incite to action by hypnotic suggestion.

suggestive, adj. [1. sujéstiv; 2. sədžéstiv]. **suggest** & **-ive. 1.** Tending to suggest, arousing mental associations: *a melody suggestive of the rolling of waves*. **2.** Full of suggestion; **a** stimulating to the mind, provoking thought and ideas: *a suggestive article on educational method*; **b** specif., tending to suggest what is evil; smacking of impropriety.

suggestively, adv. Prec. & **-ly.** In a suggestive manner.

suggestiveness, n. See prec. & **-ness.** Quality of being suggestive (in good and bad senses).

sui, pron. [1. sŭī; 2. sjúai]. Lat. *suī*, genit. of *suus*, 'his', fr. Aryan pronominal form **s(e)wo-*, **swe-*, **se-* &c.; cp. Gk. *heós*, 'his'; Scrt. *svayám*, 'self'; O.H.G. *swās*; O.E. *swǣs*, 'own, familiar'; O.E. *sīn*, 'his'; O. Prussian *se*, 'self' &c. Cp. **custom**. In Latin Phrs. *sui generis*, of his, its &c. own special kind; unique, highly characteristic; *sui juris*, in his &c. own law or right; legally independent, of age to act for oneself.

suicidal, adj. [1. sŭisīdl; 2. sjúisaidl]. **suicide & -al**. **1.** Of, pertaining to, inclining to, suicide. **2.** (fig.) Tending to one's own ruin, destruction, downfall: *his life of debauchery and extravagance was utterly suicidal.*

suicidally, adv. Prec. & **-ly**. In a suicidal manner, by means of suicide.

suicide, n. [1. sŭisīd; 2. sjúisaid], fr. Lat. *suī*, genit. of *suus*, 'his; himself', see **sui**, & **-cide**, on anal. of **matricide** &c. **1.** Person who deliberately takes his own life. **2.** Crime of self-murder: *to commit suicide.* **3.** (fig.) Act tending to one's own downfall and ruin, moral, political, or social.

suilline, adj. [1. sŭilīn; 2. s(j)úilain], fr. Lat. *suillus*, 'of swine', fr. stem seen in *sūs*, 'swine'; cp. Scrt. *sūkaras*, 'boar'; Gk. *hûs*; O.E. *sū*, *sugu*, 'sow', see **sow (I.)**; cp. further Lat. *suīnus*, 'of a pig'; O. Slav. *svinŭ*, 'of swine'; O.H.G., O.E. *swīn*, 'swine', see **swine**. Of, pertaining to, like, the pig family; pig-like.

suint, n. [1. sŭint, swint; 2. sjúint, swint], fr. Fr., fr. O. Fr. *suint*, fr. *suer*, 'to sweat', fr. Lat. *sūdāre*, 'to sweat', see **sudation**. The natural grease of sheep's wool, containing potassium salts and used as a source of potash.

suit (I.), n. [1. sūt; 2. sjūt], fr. O. Fr. *suite*, 'following', fr. Lat. *secūta*, fem. P.P. of *sequi*, 'to follow', see **sequela**. **1. a** Act of suing; request, prayer, solicitation: *to grant one's suit*; **b** specif., act of seeking woman's hand in marriage: *to press one's suit*; *to fail, prosper, in one's suit.* **2.** (law) Judicial action to enforce claim or redress grievance, often *law-suit.* **3. a** Set of clothes to be worn together, esp. man's outer garments, including coat, waistcoat, and trousers or breeches &c., made of same material: *a suit of clothes, a new suit*; **b** complete set of harness for a horse: *a suit of harness*; **c** complete set of armour. **4.** (naut.) Set of sails to be used simultaneously. **5.** (cards) **a** One of the four distinctive sets of cards, hearts, diamonds, clubs, and spades, composing a pack; Phr. *to follow suit*, (i.) to play a card of same suit as that led; hence, (ii.) to follow another's example, do as he does; **b** number of cards of one suit held by one player; *long suit*, consisting of four or more cards; *short suit*, less than four cards.

suit (II.), vb. trans. & intrans., fr. prec. **A.** trans. **1.** To be satisfactory, or convenient to; to meet requirements or wishes of: *the plan, date, arrangement &c. suits me well*; *when will it suit you to start?*; *to try to suit everybody, all tastes* &c.; *to suit oneself*, act in accordance with one's own wishes or convenience. **2.** To be appropriate to, befit, be in accordance with character of: *buffoonery does not suit an old man.* **3.** To be adapted to temperament or abilities &c. of: *the rôle does not suit him.* **4.** To be becoming to, be in harmony with, improve, appearance of: *this hat, colour &c. suits me.* **5.** To conduce to health of, agree with: *climate, food, that suits one.* **6.** To cause to conform to, make appropriate, adapt: *to suit one's matter to one's hearers*; *suiting the action to the word.* **B.** intrans. To be convenient, satisfactory: *will that time suit?*

suitability, n. [1. sūtabĭliti; 2. sjūtəbíliti]. See **suitable** & **-ity**. State, quality, of being suitable.

suitable, adj. [1. sūtabl; 2. sjūtəbl]. **suit (II.)** & **-able**. Appropriate to character, position, or circumstances; fitting, proper; adapted for specific purpose: *to say a few suitable words*; *clothes suitable for the country.*

suitableness, n. Prec. & **-ness**. Suitability.

suitably, adv. See prec. & **-ly**. In a suitable manner.

suit-case, n. Portable, flat, shallow, oblong case of leather, fibre &c., for carrying clothes &c. for travelling.

suite, n. [1. swēt; 2. swīt], fr. O. Fr. *suite*, 'following'; see **suit (I.)**. **1.** Band of retainers; group of attendants and servants in the train of a person of rank &c.; train. **2.** Group or set of things standing in proximity to each other, or of similar design, and forming a unity of some kind; specif. **a** set of rooms connecting, or intended for the use of one person or party: *a suite of apartments*; **b** set of furniture made to match. **3.** (mus., orig.) Musical composition consisting of a series of dances in one key; (now often) series of movements of which some at least are in dance rhythm, and the first and last are in the same key.

suited, adj. [1. sūted; 2. sjūtid], fr. P.P. of **suit (II.)**. *Suited to, for*, adapted to, having qualifications for, fitted for: *not suited to the teaching profession*; *hardly suited for such a post.*

suiting, n. [1. sūting; 2. sjūtiŋ]. **suit (I.)** & **-ing**. (tailor's word) Material for making suits of clothes.

suitor, n. [1. sūter; 2. sjūtə]. **suit (I.)** & **-or**. **1.** Person instituting a lawsuit. **2. a** One who presents a petition, asks a favour, proffers a request; specif. **b** person seeking woman's hand in marriage.

suivez, vb. [1. swḗvā; 2. swívei]. Fr. *suivez*, 'follow', imperat. of *suivre*, 'to follow', fr. L. Lat. *sequere*, 'to follow', see **sue**. (mus.) Direction to accompanist to follow soloist in tempo &c.

sulcate, adj. [1. súlkāt; 2. sálkeit], fr. Lat. *sulcus*, 'furrow, trench'; cp. Gk. *holkós*, 'furrow'; *hélkein*, 'to draw'; O.E. *sulh*, 'plough'. (anat. and bot.) Marked with long, narrow grooves; fluted.

sulk, vb. intrans. & n. [1. sulk; 2. salk]. Back-formation, fr. **sulky (I.)**. **1.** vb. To be sulky. **2.** n. (usually pl.) Sulky mood: *in the sulks*; *a fit of the sulks.*

sulkily, adv. [1. súlkili; 2. sálkili]. **sulky (I.)** & **-ly**. In a sulky manner.

sulkiness, n. [1. súlkines; 2. sálkinis]. Next word & **-ness**. State of being sulky; sulky behaviour.

sulky (I.), adj. [1. súlki; 2. sálki], fr. a base seen in O.E. *āseolcan*, 'to be slothful or remiss', P.P. *asolcen*; cp. N. Fris. *sulke*, 'to sulk'. Sullen; showing ill-temper and resentment by silent, gloomy, moroseness, and by shunning conversation and society.

sulky (II.), n., fr. prec. Light, two-wheeled vehicle for one horse and one person.

sullen, adj. & n. [1. súlen; 2. sálin]. M.E. *solein*, fr. O. Fr. *solain*, 'lonely', fr. Lat. *sōlus*, 'alone', see **sole (IV.)** & **-an**. **1.** adj. **a** Obstinately gloomy and ill-tempered, morose, surly; persistently sulky; **b** making, conveying, a gloomy, depressing, sombre impression; lowering; *a sullen landscape*; **c** expressing sullenness: *a sullen face, expression* &c. **2.** n. (pl.) *The sullens*, sulks, gloomy ill-temper.

sullenly, adv. Prec. & **-ly**. In a sullen manner.

sullenness, n. See prec. & **-ness**. State or quality of being sullen.

sully, vb. trans. [1. súli; 2. sáli]. O.E. *sylian*; M.E. *sulien*, 'to soil'; cp. O.L.G. *sulian*, 'to defile'; cp. O.E. *sol*, 'dirty'; O.E. *sol*, 'muddy pool'; Lith. *sulà*, 'flowing sap'. To impair, mar, tarnish, the purity or freshness of; to stain, soil, defile: (chiefly in non-material or fig. sense) *to sully one's hands by an infamous action*; *a reputation sullied by many crimes.*

sulph(o)-, pref. representing **sulphur (I.)**. Sulphur; e.g. *sulphacid*, acid of sulphur; *sulphocyanic*, derived from sulphur and cyanogen.

sulphate, n. [1. súlfāt, -it; 2. sálfeit, -it]. Prec. & **-ate**. Salt of sulphuric acid; *calcium sulphate*, gypsum; *magnesium sulphate*, Epsom salts; *sodium sulphate*, Glauber's salts; *sulphate of copper, iron, zinc*, varieties of vitriol.

sulphide, n. [1. súlfīd; 2. sálfaid]. **sulph(o)-** & **-ide**. Compound of sulphur with another element; *sulphide of iron*, pyrites; *sulphide of mercury*, cinnabar.

sulphite, n. [1. súlfīt; 2. sálfait]. **sulph(o)-** & **-ite (I.)**. Salt of sulphurous acid.

sulphonal, n. [1. súlfonal; 2. sálfənəl], fr. **sulph(o)-**. Crystalline compound used as anaesthetic and hypnotic.

sulphur (I.), n. [1. súlfur; 2. sálfə]. Lat. *sulphur*, *sulfur*, *sulpur*, 'sulphur'; prob. fr. earlier **sulkʷ-*; cp. Goth. *swibls*; O.H.G. *swebal*; O.E. *swefel*, 'sulphur'. **1.** Non-metallic, light-yellow, inflammable, fusible crystalline or amorphous element, burning with a blue flame, and used for making sulphuric acid, for matches, gunpowder, vulcanized rubber, and medicinally; *flowers of sulphur*, sulphur in the form of fine powder, condensed from sulphur vapour; *roll, stick, sulphur*, purified sulphur moulded in the form of rolls or sticks; *sulphur dioxide*, suffocating gas produced by burning sulphur. **2.** Kind of yellow butterfly.

sulphur (II.), adj., fr. prec. Of the colour of sulphur, pale lemon yellow.

sulphur (III.), vb. trans., fr. prec. To fumigate with burning sulphur.

sulphurate, vb. trans. [1. súlfūrāt; 2. sálfjureit]. **sulphur (I.)** & **-ate**. **1.** To combine, mix, impregnate, with sulphur. **2.** To bleach by means of sulphurous acid, or by fumes of burning sulphur.

sulphuration, n. [1. sùlfūráshun; 2. sàlfjuréiʃən]. Prec. & **-ion**. Process of sulphurating; state of being sulphurated.

sulphurator, n. [1. súlfūrātur; 2. sálfjureitə]. **sulphurate** & **-or**. Apparatus for bleaching by sulphur fumes.

sulphureous, adj. [1. sùlfúreus; 2. sàlfjɔ́riəs], fr. Lat. *sulphureus*; **sulphur (I.)** & **-eous**. **1.** Of, pertaining to, like, sulphur; having the colour or smell of burning sulphur. **2.** (bot.) Pale yellow, sulphur-coloured.

sulphuretted, adj. [1. súlfūrĕted; 2. sálfjurètid], fr. obs. *sulphuret*, 'sulphide'; **sulphur (I.)** & **-et** & **-ed**. Combined with sulphur: *sulphuretted hydrogen*, hydrogen sulphide.

sulphuric, adj. [1. sulfúrik; 2. salfjɔ́rik]. **sulphur (I.)** & **-ic**. Of, pertaining to, containing, derived from, sulphur; *sulphuric acid*, colourless, corrosive, oily, liquid compound, used extensively as basis of chemical operations and manufactures; oil of vitriol: *sulphuric ether*, liquid derived from alcohol by the action of sulphuric or other acid, used as anaesthetic.

sulphurization, n. [1. sùlfūrīzáshun; 2. sàlfjuraizéiʃən]. Next word & **-ation**. Act of sulphurizing; state of being sulphurized.

sulphurize, vb. trans. [1. súlfūrīz, súlfurīz; 2. sálfjuraiz, sálfəraiz]. **sulphur (I.)** & **-ize**. To sulphurate.

sulphur-ore, n. Sulphide of iron, pyrites.

sulphurous, adj. [1. súlfūrus, súlfurus; 2. sálfjurəs, sálfərəs]. **sulphur (I.)** & **-ous**. **1.** Of, derived from, impregnated with, sulphur. **2.** (fig.) Heated, imflammable, pervaded by intense passion: *the atmosphere of the meeting became rather sulphurous towards the close.*

sulphur-spring, n. Natural spring impregnated with sulphur.

sulphur-wort, n. Herb with sulphur-coloured flowers.

sulphury, adj. [1. súlfuri; 2. sálfəri]. **sulphur (I.)** & **-y (IV.)**. Resembling, pertaining to, sulphur.

sultan, n. [1. súltan; 2. sáltən], fr. Fr., fr. Arab. *sulṭān*, 'victorious; ruler'. **1.** Mohammedan prince or king; specif., *the Sultan*, former sovereign of the Turkish Empire. **2.** Kind of purple gallinule. **3.** Breed of small domestic hen, originally from Turkey. **4.** Kind of garden annual, *Centaurea*, with yellow (*yellow sultan*) or purple (*sweet sultan*) flowers.

sultana, n. [1. sultáhna ; 2. saltánə]. Ital., fr. Arab.; see prec. **1.** Sultan's wife, daughter, or sister. **2.** Mistress of king or prince. **3.** Kind of small, seedless raisin from Smyrna.

sultanate, n. [1. súltanāt ; 2. sáltəneit]. **sultan** & **-ate**. **1.** Rank, authority, of a sultan. **2.** Jurisdiction, dominion, of a sultan.

sultaness, n. [1. súltanes ; 2. sáltənis]. **sultan** & **-ess**. Sultana.

sultriness, n. [1. súltrines ; 2. sáltrinis]. Next word & **-ness**. State of being sultry.

sultry, adj. [1. súltri ; 2. sáltri], fr. obs. *sweltry* ; **swelter** (**I.**) & **-y** (**IV.**). **a** (of weather, climate, atmosphere &c.) Hot and damp, moist and stuffy, close, oppressive; also **b** (fig.) of temper, language &c.; violent, hectic, lurid.

sum (**I.**), n. [1. sum ; 2. sam], fr. Fr. *somme*, fr. Lat. *summa*, 'top, summit; chief place, highest rank, chief point, essence; amount, quantity; total', fr. fem. form of *summus*, 'highest', assimilated fr. **sup-mo-*; cp. Lat. *super*, 'above'; *sub*, 'below', see **sub-**; Scrt. *upamáś*, 'the highest'; Gk. *húpatos*, 'the first'; O.E. *ufema*, 'highest'. **1.** Amount produced by adding two or more numbers, magnitudes, quantities, together; the total, also *sum total*. **2.** Group of related ideas, facts, points, considered together, total result, compendium of such points &c.; the essence: *the sum of the whole matter*. **3.** A quantity, or amount, of money: *to spend large sums*. **4. a** A problem in arithmetic; **b** (pl.) *sums*, arithmetical calculation: *to do sums*; *good at sums*.

sum (**II.**), vb. trans. & intrans., fr. Fr. *sommer*, fr. *somme*, 'sum', see prec. **A.** trans. **1.** Often *sum up*, to add up, give total of, give result of addition of, reckon up: *to sum up one's takings*. **2.** Also *sum up*, to present in the form of a brief review, summarize, recapitulate shortly: *to sum up facts, statements, evidence, arguments* &c. **B.** intrans. *Sum up*, specif. (of a judge) to review and comment upon facts proved in evidence, &c.

sumac(h), n. [1. shóomak ; 2. ʃúmæk], fr. Fr., fr. Span. *zumaque*, fr. Arab. *summāq*. **1.** Shrub or small tree of the genus *Rhus*, with pinnate or trifoliate leaves and clusters of small flowers. **2.** Dried leaves of some species of sumac, used in dyeing and tanning.

Sumerian, adj. & n. [1. sūmérian ; 2. sjūmíəriən], fr. *Sumer*, ancient district of Babylonia, & **-ian**. **1.** adj. Pertaining to, characteristic of, the civilization of Sumer. **2.** n. **a** The language of the Sumerian inscriptions &c.; **b** an inhabitant of Sumer.

summarily, adv. [1. súmarili ; 2. sáməril*i*]. **summary** (**I.**) & **-ly**. In a summary manner.

summarist, n. [1. súmarist ; 2. sáməríst]. **summary** (**I.**) & **-ist**. Person who prepares a summary.

summarize, vb. trans. [1. súmariz ; 2. sáməraiz]. **summary** (**I.**) & **-ize**. To make, present, a summary of, present in a brief review; to epitomize.

summary (**I.**), adj. [1. súmari ; 2. sáməri], fr. Lat. *summārium*, 'summary, abstract'; **sum** (**I.**) & **-ary**. **1.** Condensed, brief, giving the substance or gist: *summary reports*. **2.** Carried out without many formalities, effected without delay or debate: *summary justice, punishment*; specif. *summary jurisdiction*, that of petty sessions, exercised by justices of the peace, in cases of trivial, more or less light, offences &c.

summary (**II.**), n., fr. prec. Brief statement of leading points of argument, book &c.; epitome, digest, concise review.

summation, n. [1. sumáshun ; 2. saméiʃən], fr. Fr. *sommation*; **sum** (**II.**) & **-ation**. Act of summing, of reckoning a total; summing up, computation.

summer (**I.**), n. [1. súmer ; 2. sámə]. O.E. *sumor*; M.E. *somer*; cp. O.H.G. *sumar*; O. Fris. *sumur*; O.N. *sumarr*, 'summer'; cogn. w. Scrt. *sámā*, 'year, season'; O. Ir. *sam*, 'summer'. **1.** Season in which the sun has the greatest power, usually (in Northern Hemisphere) considered to include June, July, and August; astronomically, June 21 to Sept. 22; Phr. *Indian summer*, short spell of warm, dry weather in the autumn, with hazy atmosphere; *St. Luke's, St. Martin's, summer*, short periods of mild, dry weather sometimes occurring about October 18th (St. Luke's Day) and November 11th (St. Martin's Day). **2.** (fig.) Prime, best part, most flourishing period of life. **3.** (pl.) Years of age: *a young woman of some twenty summers*.

summer (**II.**), vb. intrans. & trans., fr. prec. **1.** intrans. To spend the summer: *to summer in Scotland*. **2.** trans. To feed, graze (cattle) during the summer.

summer (**III.**), adj., fr. **summer** (**I.**). Of, pertaining to, suitable for, occurring in, the summer: *summer holidays*.

summer (**IV.**), n., fr. Fr. *sommier*, 'beam'; see **breastsummer**. **a** Large, horizontal beam or girder supporting a superstructure; **b** stone resting on a column, and supporting an arch &c.

summer-house, n. Small, ornamental building used in a garden as a place to sit in.

summerless, adj. [1. súmerles ; 2. sáməlis]. **summer** (**I.**) & **-less**. Without a summer, having no summer.

summer lightning, n. Sheet lightning without audible thunder.

summerlike, adj. [1. súmerlik ; 2. sáməlaik]. **summer** (**I.**) & **-like**. Like summer.

summerly, adj. [1. súmerli ; 2. sáməli]. **summer** (**I.**) & **-ly**. Like, characteristic of, summer.

summersault, -set, n. See **somersault**.

summer school, n. Organized course of lectures &c. at a university during long vacation.

summer-time, n. **1.** Season of summer. **2.** Time as reckoned during spring and summer, one hour in advance of Greenwich mean time, adopted for daylight-saving (q.v.) purposes.

summery, adj. [1. súmeri ; 2. sáməri]. **summer** (**I.**) & **-y** (**IV.**). Of, like, characteristic of, suitable for, summer.

summing-up, n. [1. súming úp ; 2. sámiŋ áp]. Review, recapitulation, of, comments upon, the chief points of evidence, made by a judge at the conclusion of a trial, before the jury retire to consider their verdict.

summit, n. [1. súmit ; 2. sámit], fr. Fr. *sommet*, 'summit', fr. *som*, 'top', fr. Lat. *summum*, 'top', neut. form of *summus*, 'highest', see **sum** (**I.**), & **-et**. **1.** Highest part of hill or mountain &c., top, peak: *to climb to the summit*. **2.** (in non-material sense) Highest point, acme, maximum: *to reach the summit of fame*.

summitless, adj. [1. súmitles ; 2. sámitlis]. Prec. & **-less**. Without a summit.

summit-level, n. Highest point (of railway, road &c.).

summon, vb. trans. [1. súmun ; 2. sámən], fr. O. Fr. *somoner*, fr. Lat. *sub-*, *summonēre*, 'to remind, hint', fr. **sub-** & *monēre*, 'to warn', see **monition** & **mental** (**I.**). **1. a** To call authoritatively for, demand presence of, send for: *to summon a servant*; **b** specif. to require attendance of, in court of law as witness, defendant, or juror. **2.** To call upon with insistence and authority, require, to carry out some action: *to summon a garrison to surrender*. **3.** To bring into play; to collect, gather together: *to summon all one's energy*; also, *to summon up* (*one's courage* &c.).

summons, n. & vb. trans. [1. súmunz ; 2. sámənz], fr. A.-Fr. *somonse*, fr. O. Fr. *semonse*, fr. P.P. of *somoner*, see prec. **1.** n. **a** Call to appear or attend, demand for presence at specific time or place: *to receive a summons*; *to answer one's summons*; specif. **b** notice, citation, to appear before a judge or magistrate. **2.** vb. To issue a summons to, cite.

summum bonum, n. [1. súmum bŏnum ; 2. sáməm bóunəm], fr. Lat. *summum bonum*, 'highest good'; see **sum** (**I.**) & **bonus**. Supreme good, chief end of being.

sump, n. [1. sump ; 2. samp]. Cp. Dan. *somp*, 'swamp'; Germ. *sumpf*, 'bog', & see **swamp**. **1.** Lowest part of mine, pool at the bottom of a mine from which water is pumped. **2.** Reservoir for superfluous lubricating oil in a motor-car.

sumpitan, n. [1. súmpitan ; 2. sámpitən]. Malay. Blow-pipe used by natives of Borneo for shooting arrows.

sumpter, n. [1. súmpter ; 2. sámptə], fr. O. Fr. *sommetier*, fr. Low Lat. **sagmatarius*, fr. Lat. *sagmārius*, fr. *sagma*, 'pack-saddle', fr. Gk. *ságma*, 'equipment; pack-saddle'; cp. Gk. *sáttein*, 'to pack, press, equip'; *saktós*, 'crammed'; cp. **summer** (**IV.**) & **breastsummer**. (archaic) Beast of burden, pack-horse; usually *sumpter-horse, -mule* &c.

sumption, n. [1. súmpshun ; 2. sámpʃən], fr. Lat. *sumptiōn-(em)*, 'major premise', fr. *sumpt-(um)*, P.P. type of *sūmere*, 'to take hold of; to select; to assume', earlier **subs-emere*, fr. **sub-** & *emere*, 'to take, buy', see second element of **exempt** (**I.**). (log.) Major premise.

sumptuary, adj. [1. súmptūari ; 2. sámptjuəri], fr. Lat. *sūmptuārius*, 'of expense', fr. *sūmpt-(um)*, P.P. type of *sūmere*, 'to take hold of; to select; to acquire; to spend', see prec., & **-ary**. Of, pertaining to, regulating, expense; esp. *sumptuary laws* &c., regulating expenditure and intended to check extravagance.

sumptuous, adj. [1. súmptūus, súmpchoous ; 2. sámptjuəs, sámptʃuəs], fr. Lat. *sūmptuōsus*, 'costly', fr. *sūmptus*, 'expense', fr. P.P. type of *sūmere*, 'to take; to spend', see **sumption**, & **-ous**. Luxurious, rich, costly; involving or indicating expenditure on a lavish scale: *sumptuous clothes, food* &c.

sumptuously, adv. Prec. & **-ly**. In a sumptuous manner.

sumptuousness, n. See prec. & **-ness**. Quality of being sumptuous.

sun (**I.**), n. [1. sun ; 2. san]. O.E. *sunne*, M.E. *sonne*; cp. O.L.G., O.H.G., O.N. *sunna*; Goth. *sunnō*, 'sun'; fr. stem **su-n-*, **swe-n-*; fr. same base, but having formative *-l-*, are Goth. *sauil*; O.E. *sōl*; Lat. *sōl*, 'sun', see **sol** (**I.**); O.E. *swegle*, 'shining'; O.E. *swelan*, 'to glow'; cp. also Gk. *selḗnē*, 'moon', see **selenium**. **1.** Heavenly body forming the centre of, and chief source of light and heat in, the solar system. Phrs. *midnight sun*, as seen from polar regions; *mock-sun*, sun-dog, parhelion; *sun's backstays, eyelashes, sun drawing water*, (naut.) appearance in sky of parallel lines of dust particles lit up by sun shining through rifts in clouds; *the sun rises*, is brought into view above the horizon by the earth's rotation; *the sun sets*, disappears from view below horizon through earth's motion; *one's sun is set*, one's day is over; one's reputation has declined; *the Sun of Righteousness*, Christ; *against the sun*, counter-clockwise; *with the sun*, in direction of sun's apparent course; *to hold a candle to the sun*, perform useless or superfluous action; *a place in the sun*, prominent position; *to rise with the sun*, get up at daybreak; *to see the sun*, be born; *to take, shoot, the sun*, (naut.) to determine sun's altitude by means of a sextant; to determine latitude from sun's altitude; (*everything* &c.) *under the sun*, in the world, on earth. **2.** Direct rays of sun; sunlight: *to sit in the sun*; *to have the sun in one's eyes*; *no sun ever gets into this room*. **3.** (poet.) Period of earth's revolution about the sun; year: '*A thousand suns will stream on thee, A thousand moons will quiver*' (Tennyson, 'A Farewell'). **4.** Any star forming the centre of a system, with planets revolving about it. **5.** (her.) Disk, or representation of human face, with rays radiating from it. **6.** Circular group of gas-jets &c., arranged to reflect downwards.

sun (**II.**), vb. trans. & intrans., fr. prec. **1.** trans. **a** To expose to rays of sun, place in the sun; **b** (reflex.) *sun oneself*, go into, remain in the sunlight. **2.** intrans. To be exposed to sun's rays, bask in the sun.

sun-and-planet, n. [1. sún an(d) plánet ; 2. sán ən(d) plǽnit]. Combination of two toothed wheels, so adjusted that one on a central axis (sun-wheel) imparts its motion to the other or planet wheel.

sun-bath, n. Exposure of body to direct rays of the sun.

sun-bathing, n. Act, habit, or cult of the sun-bath.

sunbeam, n. [1. súnbēm; 2. sánbīm]. Single distinct ray of sunlight becoming visible through its shining on dust-particles through aperture.

sun-bird, n. Brightly coloured bird of Asia, Africa, and Australia, with long, slender beak and protractile tongue.

sun-bittern, n. Bird of Central and South America, resembling the crane and heron, and elaborately striped or mottled with brown, black, and white.

sun-blind, n. Movable, outside shade or awning, protecting window &c. from direct rays of sun.

sun-bonnet, n. Linen bonnet, with a projecting brim to shade the face and eyes, and flap to protect back of neck.

sun-bow, n. Rainbow produced by sun shining on spray of waterfall &c.

sunburn, n. [1. súnbĕrn; 2. sánbʌ̄n]. Darkening of skin through exposure to sun.

sunburned, sunburnt, adjs. [1. súnbĕrnd, -bĕrnt; 2. sánbʌ̄nd, -bʌ̄nt], fr. prec. Affected, tanned, by exposure to sun.

sun-burner, n. Circular group of gas jets or electric lights.

sun-burst, n. Sudden flood of light caused by sun coming out suddenly from behind clouds.

sundae, n. [1. súndi, -ē; 2. sándi, -ī]. Etymol. unknown. An ice-cream with crushed fruit, fruit-juice &c.

sun-dance, n. N. American Indian religious dance.

Sunday, n. [1. súndi; 2. sándi]. O.E. *sunnan dæġ,* 'sun's day'; M.E. *sonnedai;* **sun** (I.) & **day.** 1. First day of the week, kept as day of special worship and of rest from business &c.; *Low Sunday,* Sunday after Easter; *Mid-Lent, Refreshment, Mothering, Sunday,* fourth Sunday of Lent; *Palm Sunday,* Sunday before Easter; *Show Sunday,* (Oxford University) Sunday before Commemoration; *a month of Sundays,* long time. Phr. (colloq.) *to look two ways to find Sunday,* to squint. 2. (attrib.) Of, pertaining to, suitable for, characteristic of, Sunday: *Sunday clothes, dinner* &c. Phr. *one's Sunday best,* (colloq. or facet.) best clothes worn on Sunday.

Sunday school, n. School for religious instruction held for children on Sundays, under direction of authorities of church, chapel &c.

sunder, vb. trans. & intrans. [1. súnder; 2. sándə]. O.E. *syndrian,* 'to separate', M.E. *sundren,* fr. *sunder,* 'apart'; cp. O.H.G. *suntar;* O.S. *sundor;* O.N. *sundr,* 'apart', either **a** fr. base **sem-, *sm̥-,* 'alone', see **simple** (I.), **single** (I.); or **b** cogn. w. Lat. *sine,* 'without'; Scrt. *san-utár,* 'away'. 1. trans. To put apart, separate, prevent union of, sever. 2. intrans. To separate, keep apart.

sunderance, n. [1. súnderans; 2. sándərəns]. Prec. & **-ance.** Act of sundering, state of being sundered.

sundew, n. [1. súndū; 2. sándjū]. Low-growing herb, genus *Drosera,* found in bogs &c., with clusters of small flowers, and hairy leaves exuding a viscous liquid which serves to catch insects on which the plant feeds.

sundial, n. [1. súndīal; 2. sánddaiəl]. Instrument for indicating the hour by means of the shadow of a pointer or gnomon, cast by the sun on to a numbered plate.

sun-dog, n. Mock-sun, parhelion.

sundown, n. [1. súndoun; 2. sándaun]. Sunset, evening.

sundowner, n. [1. súndòuner; 2. sánddunə]. Prec. & **-er.** (Australia) A tramp arriving at a station after sundown, to secure food and lodging for the night.

sun-dried, adj. [1. sún drīd; 2. sán draid]. (of fruit &c.) Dried by natural, as distinct from artificial heat.

sundry, adj. & n. [1. súndri; 2. sándri]. O.E. *syndriġ,* 'separate, several', fr. *sundor,* 'apart', see **sunder,** & **-y** (IV.). 1. adj. Several, various, of indefinite number: *to talk of sundry matters.* 2. n. **a** (pl.) Unspecified items, odds and ends: *hotels charge considerable sums for what they call sundries;* **b** Phr. *all and sundry,* everyone, collectively and individually: *to extend a welcome to all and sundry.*

sunfish, n. [1. súnfish; 2. sánfiʃ]. Large, N. Atlantic fish with nearly spherical body flattened at the back.

sunflower, n. [1. súnflòur; 2. sánflduə]. Plant of the genus *Helianthus,* with large flowers having bright yellow petals radiating from a centre.

sung, vb. [1. sung; 2. saŋ]. O.E., M.E. *sungen,* P.P. of **sing.**

sun-glow, n. Corona of sun.

sun-god, n. Personification of the sun worshipped as a god.

sun-hat, n. Large, shady, broad-brimmed hat.

sun-helmet, n. Helmet of pith, with brim to give protection to the head and neck from sun.

sunk, adj. [1. sungk; 2. saŋk]. P.P. of **sink;** O.E. *(ġe)suncen;* M.E. *sunke(n).* Placed, existing, below normal level of surface: *sunk fence,* placed along bottom of ditch.

sunken, adj. [1. súngken; 2. sáŋkən]. P.P. of **sink,** see prec. (of cheeks, eyes &c.) Abnormally depressed, fallen in, hollow.

sunless, adj. [1. súnles; 2. sánlis]. **sun** (I.) & **-less.** Receiving little or no light and heat from the sun.

sunlessness, n. Prec. & **-ness.** State of being sunless.

sunlight, n. [1. súnlīt; 2. sánlait]. Light radiated by the sun.

sunlike, adj. [1. súnlīk; 2. sánlaik]. **sun** (I.) & **-like.** Like the sun; bright, glowing.

sunlit, adj. [1. súnlit; 2. sánlit]. Illuminated by the sun.

sun-myth, n. Solar myth.

sunn, n. [1. sun; 2. san], fr. Hind. *san.* Also *sunn hemp,* fibre obtained from inner bark of a leguminous Indian plant.

Sunna(h), n. [1. súna; 2. sánə]. Arab. *sunna,* 'tradition'. Part of Mohammedan law based on tradition of Mohammed's actions and teaching, accepted by orthodox as equal in authority to the Koran and rejected by the Shiites. See **Shiah.**

Sunni, n. [1. súnē; 2. sánī]. See prec. Orthodox Mohammedan, accepting the authority of the Sunnah.

sunnily, adv. [1. súnili; 2. sánili]. **sunny** & **-ly.** In a sunny manner.

sunniness, n. [1. súnines; 2. sáninis]. **sunny** & **-ness.** State or quality of being sunny.

Sunnite, n. [1. súnīt; 2. sánait]. **Sunna(h)** & **-ite** (I.). Sunni.

sunny, adj. [1. súni; 2. sáni]. **sun** (I.) & **-y** (IV.). 1. Illuminated, made bright, by the light of the sun; pervaded by, bathed in, sunlight: *sunny days, weather; a sunny room, hill-side* &c. Phr. *to look on the sunny side of things,* take a cheerful view of life &c. 2. (fig.) Cheerful, genial, bright: *a sunny disposition, smile* &c.

sun-picture, n. Photograph.

sun-power, n. Power obtained by concentrating the heat of the sun.

sunproof, adj. [1. súnproof; 2. sánprūf]. Impervious to, unaffected by, rays of sun.

sun-recorder, n. Instrument for recording duration and intensity of sunlight.

sunrise, n. [1. súnrīz; 2. sánraiz]. **a** Appearance of sun above the horizon at daybreak; **b** time at which this takes place.

sun-rose, n. Kind of rock-rose, *Helianthemum.*

sunset, n. [1. súnset; 2. sánsεt]. **a** Disappearance of sun below horizon in the evening; **b** time at which this takes place; **c** appearance, colour(s), of sky at sunset; **d** (fig.) decline, end, final period: *the sunset of life.*

sunshade, n. [1. súnshād; 2. sánʃeid]. Light umbrella carried as protection against sun; parasol.

sunshine, n. [1. súnshīn; 2. sánʃain]. 1. **a** Rays of sun, bright light of sun; **b** fine, bright weather. 2. Cheerfulness, brightness; enlivening or animating influence: *the sunshine of her smile, presence.*

sunshiny, adj. [1. súnshīni; 2. sánʃaini]. Prec. & **-y** (IV.). Of, pertaining to, like, sunshine.

sun-snake, n. Ornament typical of early N. European art, snake curved in form of letter S with small circle at the centre.

sun-spot, n. 1. Dark, irregular, fluctuating spot, the origin of which is uncertain, sometimes visible on surface of sun. 2. Freckle.

sun-star, n. Kind of starfish.

sun-stone, n. Kind of feldspar.

sunstroke, n. [1. súnstrōk; 2. sánstrouk]. Illness characterized by severe fever, headache, and nervous prostration, caused by prolonged exposure to the fierce heat of the sun.

sun-up, n. [1. sún up; 2. sán ap]. (U.S.A.) Sunrise.

sunward, adj. & adv. [1. súnward; 2. sánwəd]. **sun** (I.) & **-ward.** 1. adj. Facing, toward, the sun. 2. adv. Sunwards.

sunwards, adv. [1. súnwardz; 2. sánwədz]. **sun** (I.) & **-wards.** Towards, in the direction of, the sun.

sunwise, adv. [1. súnwīz; 2. sánwaiz]. **sun** & **-wise.** In the direction of the sun's apparent course through the sky.

sun-worship, n. Adoration of the sun as a deity, or as the symbol of a god.

sun-worshipper, n. One practising sun-worship.

sup (I.), vb. trans. & intrans. [1. sup; 2. sap]. O.E. *sūpan,* M.E. *sūpen,* 'to sup, drink'; cp. O.N. *sūpa;* O.H.G. *sūfan,* 'to sup'; cogn. w. Scrt. *sūpaś,* 'broth'; cp. w. different formative element Lat. *sūcus,* 'sap'; Lat. *sūgere,* O.E. *sūcan,* 'to suck'; see **suck** (I.). 1. trans. To eat or drink in small mouthfuls; to sip. 2. intrans. To take drink or liquid food in small mouthfuls.

sup (II.), n., fr. prec. Small amount, mouthful, taste, of liquid or semi-liquid food: *a sup of broth; neither bite nor sup.*

sup (III.), vb. intrans. & trans., fr. Fr. *souper,* O. Fr. *soper,* 'to sup'; see **supper.** 1. intrans. To take supper. 2. trans. To furnish, supply, supper for.

sup-, pref. Form of **sub-** in compounds where the second element begins w. *p-.*

super, n. [1. sūper; 2. sjūpə]. Abbr. fr. **supernumerary.** (slang) Supernumerary actor.

super-, pref. representing Lat. *super,* 'above', prob. w. earlier sense 'from below upwards'; cogn. w. **sub-;** cp. **hyper-.** In words derived fr. Lat. or formed on analogy of Lat. words, in following senses: **a** implying action of placing above or outside: *superimpose, superscribe, supersede;* **b** position above, something placed above: *superaltar, supercolumniation, superstructure;* **c** situated above or at top of specified part or level: *superaqueous, supercilious, supercretaceous, superficial;* **d** being, moving, acting, at higher level: *superincumbent, supernatant;* **e** from above: *superintend, supervise;* **f** at top as distinct from bottom, affecting surface only: *superembattled, superdentate, supercarbonize;* **g** transcending, superior to, more than: *superhuman, supernatural, supersubstantial, superman, super-Dreadnought;* **h** exceeding the normal in quality or degree: *superfine, superacute, supersensible;* **i** excessive, beyond normal limit: *superabundance, supererogation, superheat, supernumerary, supersaturate;* **j** addition: *superadd, superinduce;* **k** in secondary degree: *superfeudation, superparasite, superreflexion;* **l** including subordinate classes &c.: *superclass, superfamily;* **m** higher in pitch: *supertonic, superdominant:* **n** (math.) indicating some ratio, e.g. *superbipartient,* in the ratio 5 : 3; *superbiquintal,* 7 : 5.

superable, adj. [1. sūperabl; 2. sjūpərəbl], fr. Lat. *superābilis,* 'superable', fr. *superāre,* 'to surmount', fr. *super*, 'over', see **super-**, & **-able.** (rare) Capable of being overcome, not insurmountable.

superably, adv. Prec. & **-ly**. To a superable degree; so as to be superable.

superabound, vb. intrans. [1. sûperabóund; 2. sjûpərəbáund]. To have an abundance, abound greatly.

superabundance, n. [1. sûperabúndans; 2. sjûpərəbándəns]. Next word & **-ce**. State of being superabundant; excessive amount, excess, superfluity.

superabundant, adj. [1. sûperabúndant; 2. sjûpərəbándənt], fr. L. Lat. *superabundant-(em)*, 'superabundant'; **super-** & **abundant**. In excess of requirements or of normal amount; abounding, copious.

superabundantly, adv. Prec. & **-ly**. In a superabundant manner.

superadd, vb. trans. [1. sûperád; 2. sjûpərǽd], fr. Lat. *superaddere*, 'to add besides'; **super-** & **add**. To add to something already added, make a further addition.

superaddition, n. [1. sûperadíshun; 2. sjûpərədíʃən]. Prec. & **-ition**. Act of superadding; state of being superadded.

superaltar, n. [1. sûperàwltar; 2. sjûpərɔ̀ltə]. Consecrated stone slab used as portable altar, and placed upon unconsecrated altar.

superangelic, adj. [1. sûperanjélik; 2. sjûpərændʒélik]. More than, transcending, above, the angels.

superannuate, vb. trans. [1. sûperánūāt; 2. sjûpərǽnjueit], fr. **super-** & Lat. *annus*, 'year', see **annual** (I.), & **-ate**. **a** To put on retired list, pension off, require retirement of, on account of age; **b** to request, or insist on, the withdrawal of (a boy) from school because he has not reached the required standard of his age.

superannuated, adj. [1. sûperánūāted; 2. sjûpərǽnjueitid], fr. P.P. of prec. **a** Incapacitated by age, past work; **b** out-of-date, no longer current.

superannuation, n. [1. sûperànūáshun; 2. sjûpərænjuéiʃən]. Prec. & **-ion**. **1.** Act of superannuating; state of being superannuated. **2.** Pension given to official &c. retiring on account of age.

superaqueous, adj. [1. sûperákweus; 2. sjûpəréikwiəs]. Situated, existing, above water.

superb, adj. [1. sūpérb; 2. sjūpə́b], fr. Lat. *superbus*, 'haughty, proud'; prob. fr. **super-**, & stem **bhwe-*, **bhū-* &c., 'to be'; cp. Gk. *huperphués*, 'overgrown', & see **be**, **future** (I.). Of the finest quality, magnificent; of highest excellence, value, beauty.

superbipartient, adj. [1. sûperbīpárshent; 2. sjûpəbaipáʃənt]. (of number or quantity) Standing to another in the ratio of 5 to 3.

superbiquintal, adj. [1. sûperbīkwíntl; 2. sjûpəbaikwíntl]. In the ratio of 7 to 5.

superbitertial, adj. [1. sûperbītérshal; 2. sjûpəbaitə́ʃəl]. In the ratio of 5 to 3.

superbly, adv. **superb** & **-ly**. In a superb manner.

superbness, n. See prec. & **-ness**. Quality of being superb.

supercalendered, adj. [1. sûperkálenderd; 2. sjûpəkǽləndəd]. (of paper) Finished with a high polish by means of repeated rollings.

supercanopy, n. [1. sûperkánupi; 2. sjûpəkǽnəpi]. Arch or gable placed above another.

supercapital, n. [1. sûperkápitl; 2. sjûpəkǽpitl]. Capital placed above another to support a superstructure &c.

supercargo, n. [1. sûperkárgō; 2. sjûpəkágou], fr. Span. *sobrecarga*; **super-** & **cargo**. Agent in merchant ship travelling in charge of cargo and superintending its sale &c.

supercelestial, adj. [1. sûperseléstial; 2. sjûpəsiléstiəl]. **1.** Existing, situated, above the sky or firmament. **2.** Above, transcending, the angels.

supercharger, n. [1. sûperchàrjer; 2. sjûpətʃàdʒə]. Blowing apparatus, in motor-car &c., for forcing extra amount of petrol vapour into the cylinders.

superciliary, adj. [1. sûpersíliari; 2. sjûpəsíliəri], fr. Lat. *supercilium*, 'eyebrow', fr. **super-** & *cilium*, 'eyelid, eyelash', see **cilia**, & **-ary**. Situated above the eyebrow; *superciliary ridge*, projecting curve of frontal bone above the eye.

supercilious, adj. [1. sûpersílius; 2. sjûpəsíliəs], fr. Lat. *superciliōsus*, see prec. & **-ous**. Showing haughtiness and contempt for others, their capacity, belongings &c., as though looking down on them from the height of one's own superiority; loftily arrogant and superior.

superciliously, adv. Prec. & **-ly**. In a supercilious manner.

superciliousness, n. See prec. & **-ness**. Quality of being supercilious.

supercivilized, adj. [1. sûpersívilīzd; 2. sjûpəsívilaizd]. Over-civilized.

superclass, n. [1. sûperklàhs; 2. sjûpəklàs]. Group or class comprising more than one class.

supercolumnar, adj. [1. sûperkolúmnar; 2. sjûpəkəlámnə]. Characterized by, built with, supercolumniation.

supercolumniation, n. [1. sûperkolùmniáshun; 2. sjûpəkəlàmniéiʃən]. Arrangement of one architectural order above another.

supercooled, adj. [1. sûperkōōld; 2. sjûpəkûld]. (chem.) Having temperature brought to a point below freezing-point without freezing.

supercretaceous, adj. [1. sûperkretáshus; 2. sjûpəkritéiʃəs]. **super-** & **cretaceous**. (geol.) Lying above the chalk.

superdentate, adj. [1. sûperdéntāt; 2. sjûpədénteit]. Having teeth in upper jaw only.

superdominant, n. [1. sûperdóminant; 2. sjûpədɔ́minənt]. (mus.) Note immediately above dominant.

super-Dreadnought, n. [1. sûper drédnawt; 2. sjûpə drédnɔ̄t]. Large and powerful type of battleship, superior to the Dreadnought class.

supereminence, n. [1. sûperéminens; 2. sjûpəréminəns]. Supreme eminence.

supereminent, adj. [1. sûperéminent; 2. sjûpəréminənt]. Supremely, conspicuously, eminent.

supereminently, adv. Prec. & **-ly**. Eminently to a supreme degree.

supererogation, n. [1. sûperèrogáshun; 2. sjûpərèrəgéiʃən], fr. Lat. *superērogāt-(um)*, P.P. type of Lat. *superērogāre*, 'to spend in addition', fr. **super-** & *ērogāre*, 'to pay out', fr. **e-** & *rogāre*, 'to ask, demand, beg, borrow', see **rogation**. (theol.) *Work(s) of supererogation*, pious works performed by good men over and above what is necessary for their own salvation; these are held to constitute a fund in the general treasury of the Church, which is available for the benefit of others who have need of it.

supererogatory, adj. [1. sûpererógaturi; 2. sjûpərirɔ́gətəri], fr. Lat. *superērogāt-(um)*, see prec., & **-ory**. Of, pertaining to, of the nature of, supererogation.

super-ethical, adj. [1. sûper éthikl; 2. sjûpər éþikl]. Transcending, above the scope of, ethics.

superexcellence, n. [1. sûperékselens; 2. sjûpəréksələns]. Next word & **-ce**. Extreme, unusual, excellence.

superexcellent, adj. [1. sûperékselent; 2. sjûpəréksələnt]. Of more than normal excellence.

superexcitation, n. [1. sûperèksitáshun; 2. sjûpərèksitéiʃən]. Excitation to an abnormally high degree.

superfamily, n. [1. sûperfàmili; 2. sjûpəfæ̀mili]. (zool. and bot.) Category of classification larger than a family; a suborder.

superfatted, adj. [1. sûperfáted; 2. sjûpəfǽtid]. (of soap) Containing a large proportion of fat.

superfecundation, n. [1. sûperfèkundáshun; 2. sjûpəfèkəndéiʃən]. Superfetation.

superfetation, n. [1. sûperfētáshun; 2. sjûpəfitéiʃən]. Second conception by female already pregnant.

superficial, adj. [1. sûperfíshl; 2. sjûpəfíʃl], fr. Lat. *superficiālis*, 'of the surface', fr. *superficiēs*, 'surface', see **superficies**, & **-al**. **1.** Of, pertaining to, affecting, existing on, the surface: *superficial colour, wounds, appearance* &c. **2.** (of non-material things) Slight, shallow, not deep or thorough: *superficial knowledge, character*; *a superficial writer*.

superficiality, n. [1. sûperfishiáliti; 2. sjûpəfiʃiǽliti]. Prec. & **-ity**. State or quality of being superficial.

superficially, adv. [1. sûperfíshali; 2. sjûpəfíʃəli]. See prec. & **-ly**. In a superficial manner.

superficies, n. [1. sûperfíshiēz; 2. sjûpəfíʃiīz]. Lat. *superficiēs*, 'surface', fr. **super-** & *faciēs*, 'face', see **face** (I.). Surface, outer or upper face.

superfine, adj. [1. sûperfīn; 2. sjûpəfáin]. **1.** Over-subtle, refined to excess. **2.** (commerc.) Of the finest quality, extra fine.

superfineness, n. Prec. & **-ness**. State or quality of being superfine.

superfluity, n. [1. sûperflōōiti; 2. sjûpəflûiti]. See next word & **-ity**. **1.** State or quality of being superfluous. **2. a** Something which is superfluous: *to keep a carriage as well as a motor-car is a superfluity*; specif. **b** pecuniary surplus, wealth beyond one's needs: *to give of one's superfluity*.

superfluous, adj. [1. sûpérfloous; 2. sjûpə́fluəs], fr. Lat. *superfluus*, 'unnecessary', fr. **super-** & *fluere*, 'to flow', see **fluent** (I.), & **-ous**. Beyond requirements, forming a surplus or unnecessary adjunct; more than is necessary; redundant.

superfluously, adv. Prec. & **-ly**. In a superfluous manner.

superfluousness, n. See prec. & **-ness**. State of being superfluous; superfluity.

superheat, vb. trans. [1. sûperhḗt; 2. sjûpəhít]. To raise (vapour) to a temperature above that of boiling-point of water.

superheater, n. [1. sûperhḗter; 2. sjûpəhítə]. Prec. & **-er**. Apparatus in a steam-engine for raising temperature of steam after leaving the boiler or when no longer in contact with the water.

superhive, n. [1. sûperhīv; 2. sjûpəhaiv]. Hive placed above or fitting on to top of another.

superhuman, adj. [1. sûperhûman; 2. sjûpəhjûmən]. Exceeding normal human power, wisdom, size &c.; possessing more than human capacity.

superhumanly, adv. Prec. & **-ly**. In a superhuman manner.

superhumeral, n. [1. sûperhûmeral; 2. s(j)ûpəhjûmərəl], fr. **super-** & Lat. *humerus*, 'shoulder', see **humerus**, & **-al**. Vestment worn on the shoulders; specif. **a** priest's amice; **b** bishop's pallium; **c** Jewish ephod.

superimpose, vb. trans. [1. sûperimpṓz; 2. sjûpərimpóuz]. To lay, place, establish, on top of something else: *to superimpose a building on the remains of another*; *a superimposed mass*.

superimpregnation, n. [1. sûperìmpregnáshun; 2. sjûpərimpregnéiʃən]. Superfetation.

superincumbent, adj. [1. sûperinkúmbent; 2. sjûpərinkámbənt]. Lying, resting, on top of something else: *a superincumbent weight*.

superinduce, vb. trans. [1. sûperindûs; 2. sjûpərindjûs]. To induce, develop, give rise to, as an addition to something else.

superinduction, n. [1. sûperindúkshun; 2. sjûpərindákʃən]. Act of superinducing; state of being superinduced.

superinstitution, n. [1. sûperìnstitûshun; 2. sjûpərinstitjûʃən]. The institution of a priest in a benefice already in the possession of an incumbent.

superintend, vb. trans. & intrans. [1. sûperinténd; 2. sjûpərinténd], fr. **super-** & Lat. *intendere*, 'to stretch out; to pay attention to', see **intend**. To direct, guide, control, working of; to supervise functioning or organization of, regulate progress of.

superintendence, n. [1. sûperinténdens; 2. sjûpərinténdəns]. Next word & **-ce**. Act or quality of superintending; state of being superintended.

superintendent, n. [1. sûperinténdent; 2. sjûpərinténdənt]. **super-** & Pres. Part. of Lat. *intendere*, see **intend**. **a** Person who superintends, esp. some specific official organization, institution, department &c.; manager, overseer, director; specif. **b** police officer above the rank of inspector.

superior (I.), adj. [1. sûpérier; 2. sjûpíəriə], fr. Lat. *superior*, compar. of *superus*, 'higher', see **super-**. **1.** Higher in physical position, above, more elevated; specif. **a** (bot., anat., zool. &c.) situated nearer the head or upper side; growing above another organ &c.: *superior wings, calyx* &c.; **b** (print., of letter or figure) printed above the line. **2.** Of higher rank or grade; of more authoritative position: *superior officer, court* &c.; *superior genus*, including more categories; *superior planets*, those revolving beyond the earth's orbit. **3. a** Of better quality, of greater skill, power, capability, excellence &c., surpassing in quantity or degree: *superior strength, skill, knowledge* &c.; **b** of great excellence, eminently satisfactory, reliable &c.; of excellent quality or attainments; above the average: *made of superior cloth*; *a very superior man*. **4.** Larger in number or amount: *the enemy attacked with superior forces*; *a superior volume of fire*. **5.** *Superior to*, rising above influence of, not affected, swayed or biassed by: *superior to temptation*; *to rise superior to hardship, obstacles* &c.; *to be superior to prejudice*.

superior (II.), n., fr. prec. **1. a** Person placed over another; person of greater rank, position, authority &c.: *to look up to one's superiors*; **b** person surpassing another in merit, in intellectual or spiritual qualities, skill &c.: *he was his brother's superior in every way*. **2.** (cap.) Person presiding over religious house; director of monastery, convent &c.: *Father, Mother, Superior*.

superioress, n. [1. sûpèrieres; 2. sjûpíəriəris]. Prec. & **-ess**. Mother Superior.

superiority, n. [1. sûpèrióriti; 2. sjûpìərióriti]. **superior** (I.) & **-ity**. State or quality of being superior.

superiorly, adv. [1. sûpérierli; 2. sjûpíəriəli]. **superior** (I.) & **-ly**. (bot. &c.) In a superior position.

superjacent, adj. [1. sûperjásent; 2. sjûpədžéisnt], fr. **super-** & Lat. *jacent-(em)*, Pres. Part. of *jacēre*, 'to lie', see **adjacent**. Lying above, resting upon, something else.

superlative (I.), adj. [1. sûpérlativ; 2. sjûpə́lətiv], fr. Lat. *superlātīvus*, 'exaggerated'; in the superlative degree', fr. **super-** & *lātum*, P.P. type of Lat. *ferre*, 'to carry', fr. **tlāt-*, fr. base **tel-*, **tol-* &c.; see **tolerate** & **-ive**. **1.** Of the highest degree of excellence; of supreme quality or merit: *superlative beauty, goodness, virtue* &c. **2.** (gram.) *Superlative degree*, highest degree of comparison of adjective or adverb, expressing the existence of a quality in the highest degree.

superlative (II.), n., fr. prec. **a** (gram.) Superlative degree, form indicating this degree; **b** word in the superlative: *to speak in superlatives*, implying exaggeration, over-enthusiasm &c.

superlatively, adv. Prec. & **-ly**. To a superlative degree.

superlativeness, n. See prec. & **-ness**. State or quality of being superlative.

superlunar(y), adj. [1. sûperlúnər(i); 2. sjûpəljúnər(i)]. **super-** & **lunar**. **a** Beyond the moon, celestial; specif. **b** not earthly, transcending things of this world.

superman, n. [1. sûpermàn; 2. sjûpəmæ̀n]. Hypothetical being possessing supreme physical and mental powers; the overman, q.v.

supermedial, adj. [1. sûpermédial; 2. sjûpəmídiəl]. Situated above the middle.

supermolecule, n. [1. sûpermólekūl; 2. sjûpəmólikjūl]. Group of molecules regarded as a unit.

supermundane, adj. [1. sûpermúndān; 2. sjûpəmándein]. Above, superior to, transcending, mundane things.

supernacular, adj. [1. sûpernákūlar; 2. sjûpənǽkjulə]. See next word & **-ar**. (of wine) Worthy to be drunk supernaculum; first-rate.

supernaculum, adv. & n. [1. sûpernákūlum; 2. sjûpənǽkjuləm], fr. **super-** & Latinized form of Germ. *nagel*, 'nail', q.v. under **nail** (I.), w. reference to custom of reversing emptied wine-glass &c. & pouring last drop on finger-nail. **1.** adv. To the last drop, so as to finish completely. **2.** n. Wine of fine quality, worthy of being drunk supernaculum.

supernal, adj. [1. sūpérnal; 2. sjûpə́nəl], fr. Lat. *supernus*, 'celestial', fr. *super*, 'above', see **super-**, & **-al**. (poet.) Heavenly, celestial.

supernatant, adj. [1. sûpernátant; 2. sjûpənéitənt], fr. **super-** & *natant-(em)*, Pres. Part. of Lat. *natāre*, 'to swim, float', see **natation**. Floating on the surface.

supernatural, adj. [1. sûpernáchural; 2. sjûpənǽtʃərəl]. Existing outside of, transcending, effected by, a force above the normal laws of nature; miraculous.

supernaturalism, n. [1. sûpernáchuralizm; 2. sjûpənǽtʃərəlizəm]. Prec. & **-ism**. Belief in the supernatural.

supernaturalist, n. [1. sûpernáchuralist; 2. sjûpənǽtʃərəlist]. **supernatural** & **-ist**. Believer in the supernatural.

supernaturalistic, adj. [1. sûpernàchuralístik; 2. sjûpənæ̀tʃərəlístik]. Prec. & **-ic**. Characteristic of a supernaturalist.

supernaturalize, vb. trans. [1. sûpernáchuralīz; 2. sjûpənǽtʃərəlaiz]. **supernatural** & **-ize**. To make, regard as, supernatural, bring into the domain of the supernatural.

supernaturally, adv. [1. sûpernáchurali; 2. sjûpənǽtʃərəli]. See prec. & **-ly**. In a supernatural manner.

supernaturalness, n. [1. sûpernáchuralnes; 2. sjûpənǽtʃərəlnis]. See prec. & **-ness**. State or quality of being supernatural.

supernormal, adj. [1. sûpernórmal; 2. sjûpənɔ́məl]. Above the normal.

supernumerary, adj. & n. [1. sûpernúmerari; 2. sjûpənjúmərəri], fr. L. Lat. *supernumerārius*, 'supernumerary', fr. **super-** & *numerus*, 'number', see **number** (I.), & **-ary**. **1.** adj. Exceeding, beyond, the normal or necessary number; extra. **2.** n. Person or thing in excess of the normal, necessary, or appointed number.

supernutrition, n. [1. sûpernūtríshun; 2. sjûpənjūtríʃən]. Extra or excessive feeding.

superoctave, n. [1. sûperóktāv; 2. sjûpərɔ́kteiv]. Organ-stop coupling any note with its octave.

superorder, n. [1. sûperòrder; 2. sjûpərɔ̀də]. Group comprising more than one order.

superordinal, adj. [1. sûperórdinal; 2. sjûpərɔ́dinəl]. Of, pertaining to, a superorder.

superordinary, adj. [1. sûperórdinari; 2. sjûpərɔ́dinəri]. Above the ordinary.

superorganic, adj. [1. sûperorgánik; 2. sjûpərɔgǽnik]. Above, superior to, not dependent upon, a physical organism; psychical.

superparasite, n. [1. sûperpárasīt; 2. sjûpəpǽrəsait]. The parasite of a parasite.

superparasitic, adj. [1. sûperpàrasítik; 2. sjûpəpæ̀rəsítik]. Prec. & **-ic**. Characteristic of, pertaining to, a superparasite.

superphosphate, n. [1. sûperfósfāt; 2. sjûpəfɔ́sfeit]. (chem.) **a** An acid phosphate; **b** a fertiliser consisting of soluble phosphates.

superphysical, adj. [1. sûperfízikl; 2. sjûpəfízikl]. Not to be explained by known physical laws.

superpose, vb. trans. [1. sûperpóz; 2. sjûpəpóuz]. To lay, deposit, place (one thing) above another.

superposition, n. [1. sûperpozíshun; 2. sjûpəpəzíʃən]. Act of superposing; state of being superposed; (geol.) *law of superposition*, principle that in stratified rock underlying beds are older than those which are above them.

superquadripartient, adj. [1. sûperkwòdripárshent; 2. sjûpəkwɔ̀dripáʃənt]. In the ratio of 9 to 5.

superquadriquintal, adj. [1. sûperkwòdrikwíntl; 2. sjûpəkwɔ̀drikwíntl]. In the ratio of 9 to 5.

superroyal, adj. [1. sûperóial; 2. sjûpərɔ́iəl]. (of paper) Of a size larger than *royal*.

supersacral, adj. [1. sûpersákral; 2. sjûpəséikrəl]. Situated above the sacrum.

supersaturate, vb. trans. [1. sûpersáchurāt; 2. sjûpərsǽtʃəreit]. (chem.) To saturate beyond the normal degree.

supersaturation, n. [1. sûpersàchuráshun; 2. sjûpəsæ̀tʃəréiʃən]. Prec. & **-ion**. State of being supersaturated.

superscribe, vb. trans. [1. sûperskríb; 2. sjûpəskráib], fr. Lat. *superscrībere*, 'to write above'; see **super-** & **scribe** (I.). To write, engrave &c. (name, inscription &c.), on the outer or upper side of anything.

superscript, adj. [1. sûperskrìpt; 2. sjûpəskrìpt], fr. Lat. *superscriptum*, see **super-** & **script**. (of letter, figure &c.) Written above, over the top.

superscription, n. [1. sûperskrípshun; 2. sjûpəskrípʃən]. Prec. & **-ion**. **1.** Act of superscribing. **2.** Something superscribed.

supersede, vb. trans. [1. sûperséd; 2. sjûpəsíd], fr. Fr. *superséder*, 'to desist', fr. Lat. *supersedēre*, 'to forbear, refrain, desist', fr. **super-** & *sedēre*, 'to sit, remain', see **sedentary** (I.). **1.** To put or use in the place of; replace by some other person, thing, method &c.: *to supersede a general*. **2.** To take the place of, supplant, be adopted instead of: *the use of machinery has largely superseded manual labour*.

supersedeas, n. [1. sûperséedeas; 2. sjûpəsídiæs], fr. Lat. *supersedeas*, 2nd sing. subj. Pres. of *supersedēre*, 'to desist, refrain', see **supersede**. (legal) Writ issued to stay proceedings or stop execution of another writ.

supersedence, n. [1. sûperséedens; 2. sjûpəsídəns]. **supersede** & **-ence**. (rare) Act of superseding; state of being superseded.

supersensible, adj. [1. sûpersénsibl; 2. sjûpəsénsibl]. Above, beyond the range of, the senses.

supersensitive, adj. [1. sûpersénsitiv; 2. sjûpəsénsitiv]. Highly, abnormally, sensitive.

supersensual, adj. [1. sûpersénsūal, -sénshooal; 2. sjûpəsénsjuəl, -sénʃuəl]. Supersensible.

supersensuous, adj. [1. sûpersénsūus; 2. sjûpəsénsjuəs]. Supersensual.

supersesquialteral, adj. [1. sûpersèskwiálteral; 2. sjûpəsèskwiǽltərəl]. In the ratio of 5 to 2.

supersesquitertial, adj. [1. sûpersèskwitérshal; 2. sjûpəsèskwitə́ʃəl]. In the ratio of 7 to 3.

supersession, n. [1. sûperséshun; 2. sjûpəséʃən], fr. Lat. *supersess-(um)*, P.P. type of *supersedēre*, 'to refrain', see **supersede**, & **-ion**. Act of superseding; state of being superseded.

supersolar, adj. [1. sûpersólar; 2. sjûpəsóulə]. Situated above the sun.

supersolid, n. [1. sûpersòlid; 2. sjûpəsɔ̀lid]. A solid body of more than three dimensions.

superspiritual, adj. [1. sûperspírichooal; 2. sjûpəspíritʃuəl]. More than normally spiritual.

superspirituality, n. [1. sûperspìrichooáliti; 2. sjûpəspìritʃuǽliti]. Prec. & **-ity**. Quality of being superspiritual.

superstition, n. [1. sûperstíshun; 2. sjûpəstíʃən], fr. Lat. *superstitiōn-(em)*, 'superstition', orig. 'prophesy, soothsaying'; fr. *superstāre*, 'to stand over', see **super-**, & **station** (I.). **1.** Irrational dread of the supernatural; excessive credulity with regard to what is mysterious and unexplained; belief in magic and in the influence of inanimate objects on human life and destiny. **2.** Opinion, act, practice, based on superstition: *heathen superstitions*.

superstitious, adj. [1. sûperstíshus; 2. sjûpəstíʃəs], fr. Lat. *superstitiōsus*, 'full of superstition; prophetical', fr. *superstitio*, see prec., & **-ous**. Pertaining to, influenced by, involving, based on, superstition: *superstitious people, beliefs, customs* &c.

superstitiously, adv. Prec. & **-ly**. In a superstitious manner.

superstitiousness, n. See prec. & **-ness**. Quality of being superstitious.

superstratum, n. [1. sûperstrấtum; 2. sjûpəstréitəm]. Stratum imposed upon, overlying, another.

superstructural, adj. [1. sûperstrúkchural; 2. sjûpəstráktʃərəl]. Of, pertaining to, a superstructure.

superstructure, n. [1. sûperstrùkchur; 2. sjûpəstràktʃə]. Any structure built upon another.

supersubstantial, adj. [1. sûpersubstánshal; 2. sjûpəsəbstǽnʃəl]. Above, transcending, outside the sphere of, mere substance or matter.

supersubtle, adj. [1. sûpersútl; 2. sjûpəsátl]. Over-subtle.

supersubtlety, n. [1. sûpersútlti; 2. sjûpəsátlti]. Prec. & **-ty (I.)**. Quality of being supersubtle.

supertax, n. [1. sûpertàks; 2. sjûpətæ̀ks]. A tax paid on incomes in excess of a certain figure, paid in addition to, but separate from, the ordinary income-tax.

supertelluric, adj. [1. sûpertèlúrik; 2. sjûpətèljʊ̃rik], fr. **super-** & Lat. *tellūr-*, stem of *tellūs*, 'earth', see **tellurium**. Above, beyond, the earth's atmosphere.

supertemporal, adj. [1. sûpertémporal; 2. sjûpətémpərəl]. **1.** Beyond the limits of time. **2.** Situated above the temporal bone.

superterrene, adj. [1. sûpertérēn; 2. sjûpətérīn]. Above the earth, celestial; supermundane.

superterrestrial, adj. [1. sûperteréstrial; 2. sjûpəteréstriəl]. Superterrene.

supertonic, n. [1. sûpertònik; 2. sjûpətɔ̀nik]. (mus.) Note immediately above the tonic of the scale.

supertripartient, adj. [1. sûpertrìpárshent; 2. sjûpətràipáʃənt]. In the ratio of 7 to 4.

supertriquartal, adj. [1. sûpertrìkwórtl; 2. sjûpətràikwɔ̃tl]. Supertripartient.

supertuberation, n. [1. sûpertûberáshun; 2. sjûpətjûbəréiʃən]. Development of young tubers from one still growing.

supervacaneous, adj. [1. sûpervakáneus; 2. sjûpəvəkéiniəs], fr. Lat. *supervacāneus*, 'superfluous', fr. **super-** & *vacāre*, 'to be empty', see **vacant**, & **-aneous**. Superfluous, redundant.

supervene, vb. intrans. [1. sûpervḗn; 2. sjûpəvīn], fr. Lat. *supervenīre*, 'to follow, come after, follow upon', fr. **super-** & *venīre*, 'to come', see **venue**. To come directly after, to come into existence, occur, as an addition to, or in consequence of, some other condition, event &c.; to be introduced as something additional or extraneous.

supervention, n. [1. sûpervénshun; 2. sjûpəvénʃən], fr. Lat. *superventum*, P.P. type of *supervenīre*, 'to follow', see prec., & **-ion**. Act or process of supervening.

supervise, vb. trans. [1. sûpervíz; 2. sjûpəváiz], fr. **super-** & Lat. *vīsum*, P.P. type of *vidēre*, 'to see', see **vision (I.)**. To superintend, give oversight to, direct, the work or progress of.

supervision, n. [1. sûpervízhun; 2. sjûpəvížən]. Prec. & **-ion**. Act of supervising; state of being supervised.

supervisor, n. [1. sûpervìzer; 2. sjûpəvàizə]. **supervise** & **-or**. Person who supervises.

supervisory, adj. [1. sûpervízeri; 2. sjûpəváizəri]. Prec. & **-y**. Pertaining to, characteristic of, a supervisor, or of supervision: *supervisory duties*.

supinate, vb. trans. [1. sûpināt; 2. sjûpineit], fr. Lat. *supīnātum*, P.P. type of *supīnāre*, 'to bend back, turn over', fr. *supīnus*, 'on the back', see **supine (I.)**. To place (hand) with palm upwards; reverse of *pronate*.

supination, n. [1. sûpinấshun; 2. sjûpinéiʃən]. Prec. & **-ion**. Act of supinating; state of being supinated; rotation of the hand at the wrist so that the palm is turned upwards; reverse of *pronation*.

supinator, n. [1. sûpinàter; 2. sjûpinèitə]. **supinate** & **-or**. Muscle of the fore-arm by means of which supination is produced.

supine (I.), adj. [1. sûpīn, sūpín; 2. sjûpain, sjūpáin], fr. Lat. *supīnus*, 'thrown backwards; on the back, backwards, indolent, negligent', fr. stem **sup-*, 'beneath', seen in **sub-**, **super-**. **1.** Lying on the back, with face upwards, opposed to *prone*. **2.** Averse to, not taking, action; inactive.

supine (II.), n., fr. Lat. (*verbum*) *supīnum*. See prec. Latin verbal noun formed from P.P. stem.

supinely, adv. **supine (I.)** & **-ly**. In a supine manner or position.

supineness, n. See prec. & **-ness**. State or quality of being supine.

supper, n. [1. súper; 2. sápə], fr. O. Fr. *soper*, fr. vb. *soper*, 'to sup', fr. L.G. *sūpen*, 'to sup', cogn. w. **sup (I.)**. Last meal of the day, substituted for, or following, dinner. Phrs. *the Last Supper*, the last meal of Christ with His disciples before the Crucifixion; *the Lord's Supper*, the Holy Eucharist.

supperless, adj. [1. súperles; 2. sápəlis]. Prec. & **-less**. Without supper.

supplant, vb. trans. [1. supláhnt; 2. səplánt], fr. O. Fr. *supplanter*, fr. Lat. *supplantāre*, 'to trip up', fr. **sup-** & *planta*, 'sole of the foot', see **plantar**. To take the place of, oust, usurp position or function of, esp. by art or fraud.

supple (I.), adj. [1. súpl; 2. sápl], fr. O. Fr. *souple*, fr. Lat. *supplex*, 'submissive, supplicating', fr. **sup-** & *plic-*, stem of *plicāre*, 'to bend, fold', see **plicate**; & cp. ending of *double*, *triple*. **1.** Pliant, flexible, easily bent: *supple leather*; *a supple cane, bow* &c.; *supple limbs*. **2. a** Docile, amenable, easily led or influenced; **b** cunningly compliant; sly, adroit.

supple (II.), vb. trans. & intrans., fr. prec. **1.** trans. **a** To make supple: '*Their joints they supple with dissolving oil*' (Pope, 'Homer'); **b** to train (horse) to be docile, quickly obedient. **2.** intrans. To grow supple.

supple-jack, n. **a** One of several varieties of climbing plant with tough, woody, pliant stems; **b** walking-stick cut from the wood of this plant.

supplement (I.), n. [1. súplement; 2. sáplimənt], fr. Fr., fr. Lat. *supplēmentum*, 'that which supplies, fills up', fr. *supplēre*, 'to fill out, make good', fr. **sup-** & *plēre*, 'to fill', q.v. under **plenum**, & **-ment**. **1. a** Something added to supply a deficiency; that which is added to fulfil requirements, ensure adequacy &c.; specif. **b** (i.) additional matter included at the end of a book giving fuller or later details on subjects dealt with in the body of the work; (ii.) special additional number or part of a periodical devoted to a particular range of subjects. **2.** (math.) Angle that must be added to another to make two right angles.

supplement (II.), vb. trans. [1. sùplemént; 2. sàplimént], fr. prec. To add something to in order to make up deficiencies in, to provide something additional for.

supplemental, adj. [1. sùpleméntl; 2. sàpliméntl]. **supplement (I.)** & **-al**. Supplementary.

supplementary, adj. [1. sùpleméntari; 2. sàpliméntəri]. **supplement (I.)** & **-ary**. Of the nature of a supplement; supplying deficiencies, adding something that was lacking.

supplementation, n. [1. sùplementấshun; 2. sàplimentéiʃən]. **supplement (II.)** & **-ation**. Act of supplementing; state of being supplemented.

suppleness, n. [1. súplnes; 2. sáplnis]. **supple (I.)** & **-ness**. State or quality of being supple.

suppliance, n. [1. súplians; 2. sápliəns]. See next word & **-ce**. (rare) Act of supplicating; state of being suppliant.

suppliant, adj. & n. [1. súpliant; 2. sápliənt], fr. Fr., fr. *supplier*, 'to beg', fr. Lat. *supplicāre*, 'to kneel down, beg, beseech', see **supplicate**. **1.** adj. Entreating, beseeching; making, uttering, supplication. **2.** n. One who supplicates; person making humble entreaty.

suppliantly, adv. Prec. & **-ly**. In a suppliant manner; as a suppliant.

supplicate, vb. trans. & intrans. [1. súplikàt; 2. sáplikèit], fr. Lat. *supplicāt-(um)*, P.P. type of *supplicāre*, 'to kneel down, humble oneself, beg, beseech', fr. *supplic-*, stem of *supplex*, 'kneeling, entreating, suppliant', see **supple (I.)**. **1.** trans. **a** To ask humbly and earnestly for; to pray, beg, entreat for: *to supplicate pardon*; **b** to address entreaty to, pray, petition: *to supplicate a person*. **2.** intrans. To make supplication, proffer humble entreaties, beg earnestly: *to supplicate for mercy*.

supplicating, adj. [1. súplikàting; 2. sáplikèitiŋ]. Prec. & **-ing**. Of, consisting of, expressing, supplication.

supplicatingly, adv. Prec. & **-ly**. In a supplicating manner; with supplication.

supplication, n. [1. sùplikấshun; 2. sàplikéiʃən]. **supplicate** & **-ion**. Act of supplicating; humble request, prayer, petition.

supplicatory, adj. [1. súplikaturi; 2. sáplikətəri]. **supplicate** & **-ory**. Of the nature of, expressing, supplication.

supply (I.), vb. trans. [1. suplí; 2. səplái], fr. O. Fr. *supploier*, 'to fill up', fr. Lat. *supplēre*, 'to fill out, make good', see **supplement (I.)**. **1.** To equip with, provide, furnish, satisfy needs and requirements of: *cows supply us with milk*; *the butcher supplies us with meat*. **2.** To provide, produce, yield, afford for use: *the cow supplies milk*; *trees supply shade in summer*. **3.** To make good, make up for, compensate for: *to supply a need, deficiency* &c.; Phr. *to supply the place of*, to replace, act as substitute for.

supply (II.), n., fr. prec. **1.** Something which is supplied; amount, store, stock: *a supply of food, water* &c. **2.** (pl.) *Supplies*, specif., the whole of the necessities of life supplied to a large body of men, esp. an army, the inhabitants of a country. **3.** (econ.) Total quantity of an article or commodity, available at a given price; contrasted with *demand*. **4.** Person who takes the place of another, a (temporary) substitute; esp. a teacher temporarily in charge of a school, or of a class in a school, in an emergency.

supply (III.), adv. [1. súpli; 2. sápli]. **supple (I.)** & **-ly**. In a supple manner.

support (I.), vb. trans. [1. supórt; 2. səpɔ̃t], fr. Fr. *supporter*, 'to bear, endure', fr. Lat. *supportāre*, 'to convey', fr. **sup-** & *portāre*, 'to carry', see **port (IV.)**. **1.** To bear weight of, prevent from falling or sinking, hold up from below: *a roof supported by pillars*; *to support one's chin on one's hand*; *to support oneself with a stick*. **2. a** To sustain, maintain, keep vigorous: *air is necessary to support life*; **b** to maintain mental or spiritual vigour of, uphold: *to be supported by courage, vigour* &c. **3. a** To have dependent on one, provide subsistence for, maintain: *to support a family*; **b** to subscribe to, give financial help to: *to support hospitals by voluntary subscriptions*. **4.** To bear, endure, submit to, put up with: *to support fatigue* &c. **5. a** To give help, sanction, approval to, assist, further, promote progress of: *to support a cause, leader, motion* &c.; **b** to show approval of, aid, by one's presence: *the speaker was supported on the platform by the mayor*. **6.** To confirm, corroborate, show proof of, vindicate: *to support an argument, claim* &c. **7.** To assume and carry out (part, rôle &c.); to represent successfully.

support (II.), n., fr. prec. **1.** Act of supporting, state of being supported: *to walk, stand, without support*; Phr. *in support of*, in order to uphold, promote, advocate &c. **2. a** One who, that which, supports: *the neck forms a support for the head*; *to provide a structure with supports*; **b** means of maintenance or sustenance: *the sole support of an aged mother*. **3. a** Spiritual or moral help, prop, stay; sustaining power: *the support of a good conscience*;

b moral influence, backing : *I shall hope for your support in my candidature.*

supportable, adj. [1. supórtabl ; 2. səpɔ́təbl]. **support (I.)** & **-able.** Capable of being endured ; tolerable, endurable.

supportably, adv. Prec. & **-ly.** In a supportable manner.

supporter, n. [1. supórter ; 2. səpɔ́tə]. **support (I.)** & **-er. 1.** Person who supports another person, or a cause ; an adherent, a partisan. **2.** (her.) One of two human or animal figures represented on either side of a shield.

supportless, adj. [1. supórtles ; 2. səpɔ́tlis]. **support (II.)** & **-less.** Without support.

supposable, adj. [1. supózabl ; 2. səpóuzəbl]. **suppose** & **-able.** Capable of being supposed ; conceivable.

supposably, adv. Prec. & **-ly.** As is to be supposed ; presumably.

suppose, vb. trans. [1. supóz ; 2. səpóuz], fr. Fr. *supposer*, fr. **sup-** & *poser*, 'to place', see **pose (I.)** ; corresponding to Lat. *supponere* in meaning. **1.** To assume tentatively, as a hypothesis, for the sake of argument : *let us suppose for a moment that what you say is true.* **2.** To imagine, conjecture, fancy, believe, to be : *I should suppose him to be about fifty* ; *I never supposed him (to be) a hero* ; *I suppose you like London* ; *I don't suppose I shall be very long.* **3.** To require as a natural or logical result or concomitant, to presuppose, to involve as a necessary presumption : *success in any walk of life supposes both ability and careful training.* **4. a** In imperat., introducing a proposal or suggestion : *suppose we take a holiday next week* ; **b** in Pres. Part., having force of *if* : *supposing you miss your tiger, he is not likely to miss you* ; Phr. *always supposing*, provided that.

supposed, adj. [1. supózd ; 2. səpóuzd]. Prec. & **-ed.** Accepted as, believed to be, genuine ; assumed : *the supposed prince turned out to be a draper's assistant.*

supposedly, adv. [1. supózedli ; 2. səpóuzidli]. Prec. & **-ly.** According to what is, or may be, supposed ; as may be assumed : *he was supposedly grateful for your kindness.*

supposition, n. [1. sùpozíshun ; 2. sàpəzíʃən]. **suppose** & **-ition. 1.** Act of supposing. **2.** That which is supposed, hypothetical conjecture ; assumption : *the whole story is based on mere supposition* ; *on the supposition*, on the assumption, assuming, in the expectation.

suppositional, adj. [1. sùpozíshunal ; 2. sàpəzíʃənəl]. Prec. & **-al.** Based on, of the nature of, supposition.

suppositionally, adv. Prec. & **-ly.** As a supposition, by way of supposition.

supposititious, adj. [1. supòzitíshus ; 2. səpɔ̀zitíʃəs], fr. Lat. *suppositīcius*, 'substituted', fr. *supposit-(um)*, P.P. type of *suppōnere*, 'to put in place of another', fr. **sup-** & *pōnere*, 'to place' ; see **pose (I.)** & **-ious. 1.** Substituted for genuine object or person with intent to defraud ; spurious : *supposititious writings.* **2.** (rare) Suppositional.

supposititiously, adv. Prec. & **-ly.** In a supposititious manner.

supposititiousness, n. See prec. & **-ness.** Quality of being supposititious.

suppositive, adj. [1. supózitiv ; 2. səpɔ́zitiv], fr. Lat. *supposit-(um)*, see **supposititious** & **-ive.** Of the nature of, implying, based on, supposition.

suppository, n. [1. supózituri ; 2. səpɔ́zitəri], fr. L. Lat. *suppositōrius*, 'something placed underneath', fr. *supposit-(um)*, P.P. type of *suppōnere*, 'to place under or instead of another', see **supposition**, & **-ory.** Stick or lump of solid medicinal, or nutritive substance, inserted and allowed to dissolve and be absorbed, in a canal or organ of the body.

suppress, vb. trans. [1. suprés ; 2. səprés], fr. Lat. *suppress-(um)*, P.P. type of *supprimere*, 'to keep back, restrain ; to check, repress', fr. **sup-** & *premere*, 'to press', see **press (I.)**. **1. a** To restrain, check, keep back, prevent, the development or occurrence of : *to suppress a smile, a yawn, an involuntary movement* ; **b** to keep back, repress, stifle, smother, silence, the expression or manifestation of (an emotion &c.) : *to suppress an inclination to laugh, a sob, a sigh, an exclamation of astonishment* &c. **2.** To put down by force, to quell, subdue, crush : *to suppress a heresy, a popular rising, a rebellion, mutiny* &c. **3. a** To disallow the publication of : *to suppress a newspaper, a book* ; **b** to cut out, eliminate : *to suppress a phrase, a passage, in a book, article* &c. **4.** To conceal, refuse to reveal or divulge, to keep back, prevent statement of : *to suppress important facts, the truth.*

suppressed, adj. [1. suprést ; 2. səprést], fr. P.P. of prec. **1.** (of disease) Arrested in development, checked in its normal development, not manifesting usual external symptoms : *suppressed scarlet fever* &c. **2.** Checked in process of utterance ; muffled : *sounds of suppressed laughter.*

suppressible, adj. [1. suprésibl ; 2. səprésibl]. Prec. & **-ible.** Capable of being suppressed.

suppression, n. [1. supréshun ; 2. səpréʃən], fr. Lat. *suppressiōn-(em)*, 'restraint' ; **suppress** & **-ion.** Act of suppressing ; state of being suppressed.

suppressio veri, n. [1. suprésiō vḗrī ; 2. səpréṣiou viərai]. Lat. *suppressio vērī*, 'suppression of the truth' ; see prec., & **veracious.** Concealment of the truth ; esp. the withholding of facts, a knowledge of which is essential to the formation of a correct judgement.

suppressive, adj. [1. suprésiv ; 2. səprésiv]. **suppress** & **-ive.** Tending to suppress.

suppurate, vb. intrans. [1. súpūrāt ; 2. sápjurèit], fr. Lat. *suppūrātum*, P.P. type of *suppūrāre*, 'to form pus', fr. **sup-** & *pūr-*, stem of *pūs*, 'pus, matter', see **pus.** (of wounds, sores &c.) To produce pus.

suppuration, n. [1. sùpūráshun ; 2. sàpjuréiʃən]. Prec. & **-ion.** Process of suppurating.

suppurative, adj. [1. súpūrativ ; 2. sápjurətiv]. **suppurate** & **-ive.** Tending to suppurate ; causing, characterized by, suppuration.

supra-, pref. representing Lat. *suprā*, 'on the top, above' ; cp. Lat. *super*, 'above', apparently orig. 'from below upwards' ; Lat. *sub*, 'below', see **sub-.** In its modern use, the pref. is usually interchangeable w., but rarer than, **super-. 1.** Forming scientific terms denoting position above part, structure, or organ specified ; e.g. *supraciliary*, above the eyebrow ; *supraclavicular*, situated above the clavicle ; *supracretaceous*, (geol.) lying above the chalk ; *supradorsal*, situated on the back ; *supra-orbital*, above the orbit of the eye ; *suprarenal*, situated above the kidneys. **2.** Before, at a prior time ; e.g. *supralapsarian*, member of a group of Calvinists who regard predestination as preceding the Creation and the Fall. **3.** Above, transcending, superior ; e.g. *supramortal*, beyond the power or attributes of mortals ; *supramundane*, above the world or worldly things ; *suprasensible*, beyond the range of the senses.

supremacy, n. [1. sūprémasi ; 2. s(j)upréməsi], fr. O. Fr. *supremalie*, fr. Lat. *suprēmus*, 'supreme', see next word, & **-acy.** State or quality of being supreme ; supreme power or authority, domination. Phr. *Act of Supremacy*, Parliamentary Act of 1534, declaring the Sovereign of England to be supreme head on earth of the Church of England.

supreme, adj. [1. sūprḗm ; 2. s(j)uprím], fr. Lat. *suprēmus*, 'highest', superl. form of *superus*, 'above', see **superior (I.)** ; *-mo-* is an old superl. suff., seen also in **-most. 1.** Above, superior to, all others, in rank, power, jurisdiction &c. : *supreme head, ruler, tribunal* &c. Phr. *the Supreme Being*, God ; *the Supreme Court of Judicature*, High Court of Justice ; *supreme good*, highest possible good. **2.** Exceeding all others in degree, quality, intensity &c. ; utmost : *supreme sacrifice, devotion, goodness* &c.

supremely, adv. Prec. & **-ly.** In a supreme manner ; to a supreme degree or extent.

sur- (I.), form of **sub-**, w. assimilation of *-b* in compounds where the second element begins w. *r-*.

sur- (II.), pref. representing O. Fr. *sur-*, 'above, over, beyond', fr. Lat. **super-** ; **a** in loan-words fr. O. Fr., e.g. *surcoat, surface, surprise* &c. ; **b** in some scientific or technical terms &c., in place of **supra-, super-**, e.g. *surangular, surbase* &c.

sura(h), n. [1. sŏŏra ; 2. súrə], fr. Arab. *sūra*, 'step'. Chapter, section, of the Koran.

surah, n. [1. sūra ; 2. sjúərə]. Prob. fr. Surat, in Western India, see **surat.** Also *surah silk*, soft twilled silk fabric.

sural, adj. [1. sūral ; 2. sjúərəl], fr. Lat. *sūra*, 'calf of the leg' ; cp. Gk. (Ionic) *(h)órē*, 'calf of the leg'. Pertaining to, connected with, the calf of the leg.

surat, n. [1. soorát ; 2. surǽt], fr. Surat, town in Western India, north of Bombay. **1.** Kind of cotton grown in Bombay Presidency **2.** Coarse cotton fabric made in Surat district.

surbase, n. [1. sérbās ; 2. sə́bèis]. **sur- (II.)** & **base (I.).** (archit.) Moulding, cornice, above base of pedestal &c.

surcease, n. & vb. intrans. [1. sërsḗs ; 2. səsís], w. assimilation to **cease** (I.), fr. A.-Fr. *sursise*, P.P. of *surseer*, 'to delay, restrain', fr. O. Fr. *surseoir*, fr. Lat. *supersedēre*, 'to refrain from, forbear', see **supersede.** (archaic) **1.** n. Complete cessation, end. **2.** vb. To stop, cease finally.

surcharge (I.), n. [1. surchárj ; 2. sətʃádž], fr. O. Fr., **sur- (II.)** & **charge (I.). 1.** Excessive, additional, extra, load, burden, charge ; specif. **a** sum added to price &c. ; extra charge ; **b** extra charge of electricity &c. beyond requirements. **2. a** Additional charge made on property by assessors of taxes, as penalty for inaccurate return ; **b** extra charge on letter or parcel for understamping ; **c** special charge made on the individual members of a local authority by the auditor on account of expenditure wrongly incurred. **3.** Additional imprint, superimposed upon original design &c., showing change of value &c. on postage-stamp &c.

surcharge (II.), vb. trans., fr. prec. **1.** To overcharge, charge to excess or beyond requirements. **2.** To demand additional payment or surcharge from. **3.** To print a surcharge upon.

surcingle (I.), n. [1. sérsinggl ; 2. sə́siŋgl], fr. O. Fr. *surcengle*, fr. **sur- (II.)** & *cengle*, 'girth', fr. Lat. *cingula, -um*, 'girdle, girth', see **cinch, cingulum. 1.** Belt or strap round body of horse &c. to hold saddle, blanket &c. in position. **2.** A priest's girdle.

surcingle (II.), vb. trans., fr. prec. **a** To gird, surround ; **b** to fasten with a surcingle.

surcoat, n. [1. sérkōt ; 2. sə́kout]. M.E., O. Fr. *surcote* ; **sur- (II.)** & **coat. 1.** Loose gown worn over armour in Middle Ages. **2.** Short coat worn by women in 14th-15th centuries.

surculose, adj. [1. sérkūlōs ; 2. sə́kjulous], fr. Lat. *surculus*, 'shoot, sprout', dimin. of *surus*, 'twig, branch', & **-ose** ; cogn. w. Scrt. *svárus*, 'pole' ; O.E. *swēr*, M.H.G. *swir*, 'pillar'. (bot.) Producing suckers.

surculous, adj. [1. sérkūlus ; 2. sə́kjuləs], fr. Lat. *surculus*, 'shoot, sprout', see prec., & **-ous.** Surculose.

surd (I.), adj. [1. sërd ; 2. səd], fr. Lat. *surdus*, 'deaf, dull-sounding', earlier 'dull, dark, in colour' ; cp. Lat. *sordēre*, 'to be soiled, become dull, dirty', see **sordid. 1.** (math., of number, quantity) Irrational. **2.** In antiquated phonetic terminology, (of consonants) voiceless ; uttered without accompanying vibration of vocal chords.

surd (II.), n., fr. prec. **1.** (math.) Irrational number. **2.** Voiceless consonant.

sure (I.), adj. [1. shōr, shŏŏr ; 2. ʃɔ, ʃuə]. M.E. *sur*, fr. O. Fr. *seur*, fr. Lat. *sēcūrus*, 'free from care, untroubled ; heedless, careless ; free from danger, safe', see **secure (I.)**.

1. a Certain to produce a particular result; unfailing in action, effectiveness &c.: *a sure way to injure oneself*; *a sure method*; *a sure shot*; *slow and sure*; '*our defence is sure*'; **b** reliable, dependable: *to send a letter by a sure hand*; *sure grounds for belief*; **c** safe, secure, trustworthy: *a sure footing*. **2.** Certain to do some specific thing, action, or to undergo specific experience, be in specific condition: *he is sure to come*; *it's sure to be wet*. Phrs. *be sure to*, take care to, be certain to: *be sure to tell me*. **3.** Positively true, well authenticated as a fact, undoubted: *a sure and certain hope*. Phrs. *to make sure*, (i.) to feel sure, be convinced, persuaded: *I made sure it would rain today*: (ii.) to ascertain beyond doubt, satisfy oneself: *I believe the line is from* '*Lycidas*', *but you had better make sure*; *to make sure of*, (i.) to secure evidence of reliability of: *to make sure of one's facts*; (ii.) to secure possession of, make certain of obtaining: *I must make sure of a house for the winter*; (iii.) to ascertain that one can count on support &c. of: *I fancy X will vote for us, but we must make sure of him*; *to be sure*, **a** (implying concession) indeed; it is granted, admitted; **b** (as exclamation) denoting surprise, *well, to be sure!*, just fancy that! **4.** Having reasonable grounds for belief, basing one's opinion on positive or apparent fact; confident, free from doubt or uncertainty: *to be sure of one's facts*; *I am sure he is honest*; *I am not sure if I can do it*; Phrs. *to feel sure (that)*, be convinced, be confident that; *I'm not so sure*, I don't feel absolute confidence; *sure of*, having good reasons for expecting or depending on: *to be sure of a living, a welcome* &c.; *sure of oneself*, having self-confidence.

sure (II.), adv., fr. prec. Surely, certainly; archaic, except in colloq. Phr. *as sure as*, as certainly, truly, as; *sure enough*, certainly, in fact.

sure-footed, adj. Not liable to stumble or slip: *mountain ponies are very sure-footed*.

surely, adv. [1. shórli, shŏŏrli; 2. ʃɔ́li, ʃúəli]. **sure** (I.) & **-ly**. **1.** Without danger, safely, securely. **2.** Without doubt, inevitably: *he must surely fail*. **3.** Expressing strong hope or belief in the probability, though not absolute certainty, that something is so, that it will happen or be done: *you surely don't mean to be cruel*; *surely something can be done to help him*; *surely this drought can't last much longer*.

sureness, n. [1. shórnes, shŏŏrnes; 2. ʃɔ́nis, ʃúənis]. See prec. & **-ness**. State or quality of being sure.

surety, n. [1. shórti, shŏŏrti; 2. ʃɔ́ti, ʃúəti]. Doublet of **security**; M.E. *seurtee*, fr. O. Fr. *seurte*, fr. Lat. *sēcūritāt-(em)*, 'safety, security'; see **sure** (I.) & **-ty**. **1.** State of being sure; certainty, sureness. Phr. (archaic) *of a surety*, certainly. **2.** Person who makes himself responsible for the good conduct of another, for his appearance in court, payment of a debt &c.

suretyship, n. [1. shórti-, shŏŏrtiship; 2. ʃɔ́ti-, ʃúətiʃip]. Prec. & **-ship**. Position, obligation, of person acting as surety.

surf, n. [1. sërf; 2. sʌ̄f]. Earlier *suffe*, perh. a variant of **sough**. Foamy spray produced by waves breaking on the shore or on a reef of rocks.

surface (I.), n. [1. sërfis; 2. sʌ́fis], fr. O. Fr. *surface*; **sur-** (II.) & **face**; cp. **superficies**. **1.** Outer part of anything having length and breadth; any two-dimensional limit of a solid object; outside, exterior: *the surface of the earth, ocean*; *wood with a polished surface*; *beneath the surface*. **2.** (geom.) Part of space existing in two dimensions, having length and breadth but not depth; *plane surface*, plane. **3.** (in material and non-material sense) Outward appearance, outward part, exterior, that part or aspect of anything which meets the eye, which is obvious, or apparent on a cursory inspection, or to the inner perception from a brief experience or contemplation: *his cleverness is only on the surface*; *to look below the surface of things*; Phr. *on the surface*, so far as appearances go.

surface (II.), adj., fr. prec. Existing only on, affecting only, pertaining only to, the surface; superficial: *surface appearance, politeness* &c.

surface (III.), vb. trans., fr. **surface** (I.). To produce a specific kind of surface on; to finish off, dress, surface of.

surface-current, n. Current of little depth at surface of water.

surfaced, adj. [1. sërfist; 2. sʌ́fist], fr. P.P. of **surface** (III.). Having, provided with, finished with, a specific kind of surface.

surface-flow, n. (geol.) Flow of lava &c. over a land-surface.

surfaceman, n. [1. sërfisman; 2. sʌ́fismən]. Workman employed on railway to keep permanent way in repair.

surface-printing, n. Printing on textile fabric from a plate with design in relief.

surface-tension, n. Property of liquids, due to molecular action, which causes the outer, exposed surface to contract to a minimum area, thus forming a very thin film of appreciable toughness.

surface-water, n. Water lying on or drained from surface of ground.

surf-bird, n. Bird resembling plover, found on west coast of America.

surf-board, n. Oblong board used for surf-riding.

surf-boat, n. Boat specially constructed for use in surf.

surf-duck, n. Kind of sea-duck of northern regions.

surfeit (I.), n. [1. sërfit; 2. sʌ́fit]. M.E. *surfēt*, fr. O. Fr. *sorfait*, fr. P.P. of *sorfaire*, 'to increase, cause to exceed', fr. **sur-** (II.) & Lat. *facere*, 'to do', see **fact**. **1.** Excess, esp. in feeding; overeating or overdrinking. **2.** Result of over-indulgence in food or drink; satiety, repletion. **3.** Excess of intellectual or spiritual experience: *a surfeit of concerts, of detective novels*.

surfeit (II.), vb. trans. & intrans., fr. prec. **1.** trans. To over-indulge, overfeed; to satiate, cloy, with excessive indulgence. **2.** intrans. To indulge (oneself) to excess; to become satiated, experience satiety.

surf-man, n. Man engaged or skilled in management of surf-boat.

surf-riding, n. A form of sport in which one endeavours to balance oneself on an oblong board while being swept along by heavy surf.

surfy, adj. [1. sërfi; 2. sʌ́fi]. **surf** & **-y**. Abounding in, resembling, of the nature of, surf.

surge (I.), vb. intrans. [1. sërj; 2. sʌ̄dž], fr. O. Fr. *surgir*, fr. Lat. *surgere*, 'to raise; to rise', fr. **sur-** (I.) & *-rigere*, fr. *regere*, 'to guide, direct', see **regent, rex**. **1.** (of water, waves &c.) To swell, rise, with violent, tumultuous motion. **2. a** To move to and fro, billow, like waves: *surging crowds*; **b** (fig., of emotion &c.) to rise tumultuously.

surge (II.), n., fr. prec. **1.** Act, process, of surging. **2. a** Mass of heaving, billowing water, tumultuous waves; **b** (poet.) the sea.

surgeon, n. [1. sërjun; 2. sʌ́džən]. M.E. *surgien*, contracted fr. *cirurgien*, fr. O. Fr. *cirurgien*, see **chirurgeon**. **1.** Medical practitioner in that branch of the profession which treats diseases and injuries by operation and manipulation; contrasted with *physician*. **2.** General term for a doctor in the army and navy; also a doctor on a merchant-ship.

surgeon-dentist, n. Dentist holding diploma of Royal College of Surgeons.

surgeon-fish, n. Brightly coloured fish of West Indies &c., with sharp spines at either side of the tail.

Surgeon-General, n. (cap.) Military surgeon holding the rank of a general in the army.

surgery, n. [1. sërjeri; 2. sʌ́džəri]. M.E. *surgerie*, fr. O. Fr. *cirurgie*, fr. L. Lat. *chirurgia*, 'surgery', see **surgeon**. **1.** The art and science of treating diseases and injuries by operation and manipulative means. **2.** Doctor's office or consulting-room and dispensary.

surgical, adj. [1. sërjikl; 2. sʌ́džikl]. See **surgeon** & **-ic** & **-al**. Connected with, pertaining to, characteristic of, surgery or surgeons: *surgical treatment, training, knowledge* &c.; *surgical instruments*, those used in surgical operations.

surgically, adv. Prec. & **-ly**. By means of, according to the methods of, surgery.

suricate, n. [1. sūrikāt; 2. sjúərikeit], fr. native name. South African four-toed burrowing mammal allied to the mongoose; the meerkat.

Surinam toad, n. [1. sūrinam tōd; 2. sjúərinæm tòud], fr. Surinam, Dutch Guiana. Large aquatic toad of Brazil and Guiana, the eggs of which develop in the back of the female.

surlily, adv. [1. sërlili; 2. sʌ́lili]. **surly** & **-ly**. In a surly manner.

surliness, n. [1. sërlines; 2. sʌ́linis]. See prec. & **-ness**. State or quality of being surly.

surloin. Variant of **sirloin**.

surly, adj. [1. sërli; 2. sʌ́li]. Not found before 16th cent.; used by Spenser & Shakespeare. Origin doubtful; derivations fr. *sir-like*, in sense of haughty, & *sour* & *-ly* have been suggested. Sullen, morose, gloomy, gruff and churlish.

surmaster, n. [1. sërmahster; 2. sʌ́māstə]. **sur-** (II.) & **master** (I.). (rare) The second master in some schools.

surmisable, adj. [1. sërmízabl; 2. sʌmáizəbl]. **surmise** (II.) & **-able**. Capable of being surmised; conjecturable.

surmise (I.), n. [1. sërmíz; 2. sʌmáiz], fr. O. Fr. *surmise*, fr. P.P. of *surmettre*, 'to lay to one's charge, accuse', fr. **sur-** (II.), & *mettre*, 'to put', fr. Lat. *mittere*, 'to send', see **mission**. Conclusion, inference, formed from data which do not amount to absolute proof; a conjecture, a guess.

surmise (II.), vb. intrans. & trans., fr. prec. **1.** intrans. To form a surmise, to conjecture. **2.** trans. To guess, reach by a surmise: *to surmise the truth*.

surmount, vb. trans. [1. sërmóunt; 2. sʌmáunt], fr. O. Fr. *surmonter*; **sur-** (II.) & **mount** (II.). **1.** To overcome, get the better of, rise superior to (difficulties, obstacles &c.). **2.** To rise, stand, be placed over the top of, be above: *elaborate carving surmounts the entrance*; (chiefly used in P.P.) *his head was surmounted by a tuft of feathers*.

surmountable, adj. [1. sërmóuntabl; 2. sʌmáuntəbl]. Prec. & **-able**. Capable of being surmounted, overcome.

surmullet, n. [1. sërmúlet; 2. sʌmálit], fr. O. Fr. *surmulet*, fr. *sor*, 'reddish-brown', see **sorrel** (II.), & **mullet** (I.). European edible fish with two barbels below the mouth; red mullet.

surname, n. & vb. trans. [1. sërnām; 2. sʌ́neim]. **sur-** (II.) & **name** (I.), on anal. of Fr. *surnom*, fr. **sur-** (II.) & Lat. *nōmen*, 'name', see **nominal**. **1.** n. **a** (formerly) A distinctive personal appellation, often a nickname, bestowed upon an individual in addition to his baptismal name; **b** permanent, hereditary name borne by all the members of a family, and usually transmitted through direct male ancestors from father to son. **2.** vb. To give a surname (in sense **a**) to, call (person) by surname: *they surnamed King Edward VII.* '*the Peacemaker*'; *King John was surnamed Lackland*.

surpass, vb. trans. [1. sërpáhs; 2. sʌpás, səpás], fr. O. Fr. *surpasser*, 'to excel'; **sur-** (II.) & **pass** (I.). To rise above, go beyond, excel, in degree, quality, intensity &c.: *the reality surpassed all their expectations*; *he surpassed all his brothers in strength and comeliness*.

surpassing, adj. [1. serpáhsing; 2. səpásiŋ], fr. Pres. Part. of prec. Exceeding or excelling others, pre-eminent, matchless: *surpassing beauty*.

surpassingly, adv. Prec. & **-ly**. To a surpassing degree.

surplice, n. [1. sérplis; 2. sɅ́plis, -əs]. M.E. *surplis*, fr. O. Fr. *surplis, surpliz*, fr. Med. Lat. *superpelliceum*, fr. **super-** & Lat. *pelliceum*, 'tunic of skins'; see **pelisse** & **pellicle.** Loose, white vestment of varying length, with wide sleeves, worn by clergy, and usually by a choir, at divine service.

surpliced, adj. [1. sérplist; 2. sɅ́plist]. **surplice** & **-ed.** Wearing a surplice.

surplice-fee, n. Clergyman's fee for marriage, baptism &c.

surplus, n. & adj. [1. sérplus; 2. sɅ́pləs], fr. O. Fr. *surplus*, fr. Med. Lat. *superplus*, 'excess'; **super-** & **plus. 1.** n. Amount over and above what is required; quantity or sum left over; excess, residue. **2.** adj. Remaining as residue; forming a redundant amount or supply: *surplus food* &c.

surplusage, n. [1. sérplusij; 2. sɅ́pləsidž]. Prec. & **-age.** Surplus, overplus.

surprisal, n. [1. surprízl; 2. səpráizl]. **surprise (II.)** & **-al.** (rare) Act of surprising.

surprise (I.), n. [1. surpríz; 2. səpráiz], fr. O. Fr. *surprise*, fr. P.P. of *surprendre*, 'to surprise'; see **sur- (II.)** & **prize (III.). 1.** Emotion aroused by sudden, unexpected action, circumstance, or event; wonder, astonishment. **2.** That which arouses surprise; unexpected action, circumstance, or event: *his arrival was a great surprise.* **3.** Act of seizing, overcoming, taking (person &c.) unawares; unexpected attack: *to capture a force by surprise.* Phr. *to take one by surprise*, take unawares, surprise.

surprise (II.), vb. trans., fr. prec. **1.** To come upon, attack, capture, or overcome unexpectedly; to take, overcome by surprise: *to surprise the enemy's camp.* **2. a** To cause surprise to, excite surprise in; to astonish: *it takes a good deal to surprise an experienced man of the world*; *nothing he can do would surprise me*; **b** to shock, startle: *I am surprised at you*, am shocked by your conduct &c. Phr. *I shouldn't be surprised if*, I rather expect that . . . **3.** *Surprise into*, to cause (person) to do something, by startling him, taking him unawares, by making a sudden unexpected challenge &c.: *to surprise a person into a confession.*

surprise (III.), adj., fr. **surprise (I.).** Occurring as a surprise, unexpected; done without previous warning: *a surprise visit* &c.

surprisedly, adv. [1. surprízedli; 2. səpráizidli], fr. P.P. of **surprise (II.)** & **-ly.** In a manner expressing surprise.

surprising, adj. [1. surprízing; 2. səpráiziŋ], fr. Pres. Part. of **surprise (II.).** Causing, exciting, surprise; astonishing.

surprisingly, adv. Prec. & **-ly.** In a surprising manner; to a surprising degree.

surra, n. [1. sōōra; 2. súrə], fr. Marathi *sūra.* A disease of horses, cattle, and camels in India and Burma; a form of pernicious anaemia, caused by a parasitic trypanosome.

surrebut, vb. intrans. [1. sùrebút; 2. sàribát]. **sur- (II.)** & **rebut.** To make a surrebutter.

surrebutter, n. [1. sùrebúter; 2. sàribátə]. **sur- (II.)** & **rebutter.** (law) Plaintiff's reply to defendant's rebutter.

surrejoin, vb. intrans. [1. sùrejóin; 2. sàridžóin]. **sur- (II.)** & **rejoin.** To make a surrejoinder.

surrejoinder, n. [1. sùrejóinder; 2. sàridžóində]. **sur- (II.)** & **rejoinder.** (law) Plaintiff's reply to defendant's rejoinder.

surrender (I.), vb. trans. & intrans. [1. surénder; 2. səréndə], fr. O. Fr. *surrendre*, fr. **sur- (II.)** & *rendre*, 'to give', see **render. A.** trans. **1. a** To give up, yield possession of, relinquish, under pressure or compulsion: *to surrender a fort to the enemy*; *to surrender one's sword*; **b** to give up voluntarily, relinquish, resign, cease claim to: *to surrender one's freedom, rights, position, a lease* &c.; specif., to give up a claim under an insurance policy, on repayment of proportion of premiums paid, i.e. the *surrender value.* **2.** (reflex.) To give oneself over, abandon oneself, to a specified mood, state of mind: *to surrender oneself to despair.* **B.** intrans. To yield oneself, or something in one's possession or keeping, to superior force &c.; to submit, cease to resist: *the fort, ship &c. surrendered*; *to surrender to the enemy.*

surrender (II.), n., fr. prec. Act of surrendering: *there must be no surrender.*

surreptitious, adj. [1. sùreptíshus; 2. sàreptíʃəs], fr. Lat. *surrepticius*, 'secret, surreptitious', fr. *surreptum*, P.P. type of *surripere*, 'to creep, steal, along', fr. **sur- (I.)** & *rapere*, 'to seize, snatch', see **rapid (I.).** Done, formed, in a secret, underhand manner, with intent to avoid observation; clandestine, stealthy, furtive.

surreptitiously, adv. Prec. & **-ly.** In a surreptitious manner.

surrogate, n. [1. súrogit, -gāt; 2. sárəgit, -geit], fr. Lat. *surrogāt-(um)*, P.P. type of *surrogāre*, 'to elect in another's place, substitute', fr. **sur- (I.)** & *rogāre*, 'to ask, demand', see **rogation.** Substitute, deputy; specif., an ecclesiastical officer acting as deputy for the bishop, or his chancellor, in granting marriage licences.

surrogateship, n. [1. súrogātship; 2. sárəgeitʃip]. Prec. & **-ship.** Office, rank, period of tenure of office, of surrogate.

surround (I.), vb. trans. [1. suróund; 2. səráund], fr. obs. *surround*, 'to overflow', fr. O. Fr. *surrunder*, fr. **sur- (II.)** & Lat. *undāre*, 'to rise in waves, surge, swell', fr. *unda*, 'wave'; see **undulate (I.)**; cp. **abound**; the present meaning is influenced by **round (I.). 1. a** To extend round about on all or nearly all sides; to circumscribe, enclose, encircle, encompass: *a wall surrounds the garden*; *hills surround the plain*; *a crowd surrounded him*; **b** specif. (mil.) to invest, beset (fortress, body of troops &c.); **c** to stand round, be present in numbers at: *all his family surrounded his death-bed.* **2.** To cause to be surrounded; to fence round, place a boundary round: *to surround a park with a wall.* **3.** (fig.) **a** To bring into contact with, subject to influence of, encompass; to lap in: *to surround a person with every comfort, with luxury, affection* &c.; **b** (i.) to beset, press in upon, be ready to assail: *many dangers surround us*; (ii.) to be close at hand, be readily available: *surrounded with, by, hosts of friends* &c.

surround (II.) n., fr. prec. Floor-covering between carpet and walls.

surrounding, adj. [1. suróunding; 2. səráundiŋ], fr. Pres. Part. of prec. Lying adjacent to, extending in proximity on all sides: *surrounding country* &c.

surroundings, n. pl. [1. suróundingz; 2. səráundiŋz]. **surround** & **-ing. 1.** Things, objects, persons, area, lying, existing, in immediate proximity or relation; surrounding country &c.: *a fine house in ugly surroundings*; *pleasant social surroundings.* **2. a** External circumstances and conditions of existence; material environment: *unhealthy surroundings*; *surroundings favourable to work*; **b** moral and intellectual environment, surrounding influences: *the stimulating surroundings of college life*; *to live amid religious surroundings.*

surtax, n. & vb. trans. [1. sértàks; 2. sɅ́tæ̀ks]. **sur- (II.)** & **tax (I.). 1.** n. A term used, since 1929–30, for the tax previously called 'supertax'; unlike the latter, it is assessed not separately, but for the same year and on the same return as the ordinary income-tax. **2.** vb. To impose an extra tax on.

surtout, n. [1. sërtōō; 2. sɅtú], fr. Fr. *surtout*, 'long coat', lit. 'an overall', fr. **sur- (II.)** & *tout*, 'all', fr. Lat. *tōtus*, 'all', see **total.** (archaic or obs.) Man's overcoat; an old-fashioned style of frock-coat.

surveillance, n. [1. sërvályens; 2. sɅvéiljəns], fr. Fr. *surveillance*, fr. *surveiller*, 'to watch over', fr. **sur- (II.)** & *veillant*, Pres. Part. of *veiller*, 'to watch', fr. Lat. *vigilāre*, 'to be watchful', see **vigilant**, & **-ce.** Constant supervision, watch, observation, kept over person's movements: *under surveillance.*

survey (I.), vb. trans. [1. servá; 2. səvéi], fr. A.-Fr. *surveier*, fr. O. Fr. *surveeir*, 'to look over', fr. **sur- (II.)** & *veeir*, 'to see', fr. Lat. *vidēre*, 'to see', see **vision (I.)**, & words there referred to. **1.** To look over, view full extent of, take comprehensive view of: *to survey the scene, a landscape* &c. **2.** To take a general view of, consider at large, review (circumstances, facts &c.): *to survey the situation.* **3.** specif. **a** To inspect carefully, measure by geometrical and trigonometrical methods (a tract of country, coast, a piece of land &c.), and record the exact extent, shape, contours, natural features &c.; **b** to inspect (house, piece of property) in order to ascertain its condition and to estimate its value.

survey (II.), n. [1. sérvā; 2. sɅ́vei], fr. prec. **1.** General view, comprehensive examination, of a scene, group of objects &c.: *to make a rapid survey of a house and grounds.* **2.** General review, consideration, of facts, circumstances, situation &c.: *a survey of our present position.* **3.** Specif. **a** (i.) act, process, of surveying a country, tract of land &c. from the point of view of its size and physical features; (ii.) department of government &c. carrying out a series of surveying operations; (iii.) record of result of such survey; **b** (i.) inspection, examination, of condition, extent &c. of buildings, esp. for purposes of valuation; (ii.) record of result of such examination.

surveying, n. [1. serváing; 2. sɅ-, səvéiiŋ]. **survey (I.)** & **-ing.** Science or practice of determining extent, physical features &c. of a part of the earth's surface by means of measurements and mathematical calculations.

surveyor, n. [1. serváer; 2. sɅ-, səvéiə]. **survey (I.)** & **-or. a** Person employed in land-surveying; specif. **b** official inspector or superintendent.

surveyorship, n. [1. serváership; 2. sɅ-, səvéiəʃip]. Prec. & **-ship.** Position, office, of a surveyor.

survival, n. [1. servívl; 2. sɅ-, səváivl]. **survive** & **-al. 1.** Act of surviving; state of being alive after specific event or after period of existence of another person, animal &c. Phr. *survival of the fittest*, (biol.) theory that as a result of natural selection only those organisms which can adapt themselves to their environment can survive, the others being eliminated. **2.** That which survives, something continuing in existence after specific event or period: *survivals of mediaeval customs.*

survive, vb. trans. & intrans. [1. servív; 2. sɅ-, səváiv], fr. Fr. *survivre*, fr. Lat. *supervīvere*, 'to outlive', fr. **super-** & *vīvere*, 'to live', see **vital. A.** trans. **1.** To live longer than, outlive; live, exist, beyond term of existence of: *he survived his wife for many years*; *his mental faculties survived his physical powers.* **2.** To continue to live or exist after, and in spite of, a specified event or experience: *to survive a shipwreck* &c. **B.** intrans. To continue to exist, be still in existence or operation: *not one of the family survives*; *the custom still survives.*

survivor, n. [1. servíver; 2. sɅ-, səváivə]. **survive** & **-or.** One who survives; **a** one who outlives another or others; **b** one who survives an event: *the survivors of the earthquake.*

survivorship, n. [1. servíversh ip; 2. sɅ-, səváivəʃip]. Prec. & **-ship. 1.** State of being a survivor. **2.** (law) Right of surviving tenant of jointly held property to claim entire estate.

sus-, pref. Form of **sub-**, perh. fr. the earlier form *subs*, w. loss of *-b-*, used in Lat. compounds where the second element begins w. *c-, p-, t-.*

susceptibility, n. [1. susèptibíliti; 2. səsèptibíliti]. See **susceptible** & **-ity. 1.** State or quality of being susceptible. **2.** (pl.) *Susceptibilities*, responsiveness to, capacity for reacting to, emotional stimulus; sensibility.

susceptible, adj. [1. suséptibl; 2. səséptibl], fr. Lat. *suscept-(um)*, P.P. type of *suscipere*, 'to take up, receive, hold up', fr. **sus-** & *capere,* 'to take', see **captive,** & **-ible. 1. a** Easily accessible, keenly responsive to, emotional appeal; readily influenced by feelings and emotions; highly sensitive: *he is a susceptible fellow where the ladies are concerned; a too susceptible heart is often troublesome;* **b** *susceptible to,* capable of feeling, readily influenced by, accessible to: *susceptible to flattery, to kind treatment.* **2.** (pred. only, followed by *of*) Patient of, admitting, allowing: *to be susceptible of proof, of several interpretations.*

susceptibly, adv. Prec. & **-ly.** In a susceptible manner.

susceptive, adj. [1. suséptiv; 2. saséptiv], fr. Lat. *susceptum,* P.P. type of *suscipere,* 'to receive', see **susceptible,** & **-ive.** Connected with, pertaining to, the reception of emotional impressions or influences.

susceptiveness, n. Prec. & **-ness.** Quality of being susceptive.

susceptivity, n. [1. sùseptíviti; 2. sàseptíviti]. See prec. & **-ity.** Quality of being susceptive.

susi, n. [1. sōōsi; 2. súsi]. Hind. E. Indian striped fabric of cotton and silk.

suslik, n. [1. sōōslik; 2. súslik]. Russ. Greyish-brown ground squirrel of Northern Europe and Asia.

suspect (I.), adj. & n. [1. súspekt; 2. sáspekt], fr. Fr., fr. Lat. *suspectum,* P.P. type of *suspicere,* 'to look upwards, to look secretly at; to mistrust, suspect', fr. **sub-** & *specere,* 'to look', see **species. 1.** adj. Open to suspicion; liable to be mistrusted, of doubtful character. **2.** n. Suspected person.

suspect (II.), vb. trans. & intrans. [1. suspékt; 2. səspékt]. Lat. *suspectāre,* 'to look at secretly; to mistrust', freq. of *suspicere,* see prec. **A.** trans. **1.** To have a vague idea or inkling of the existence of; to feel persuaded of existence of, or of the future occurrence of: *I suspected the presence of fire from the odour; from the symptoms one might suspect measles; I strongly suspect an underhand plot.* **2.** To have misgivings regarding, to doubt, mistrust, be inclined to disbelieve in: *I strongly suspect the truth of the story, the genuineness of his professions, the authenticity of the document.* **3.** To believe guilty, to attribute guilt to; to consider the guilt of (a person) probable: *to suspect a person of murder, of lying; to suspect an innocent man; suspect* in such connexion may involve various degrees of moral certainty short of absolute conviction based upon proof. **4.** To suppose, presume, expect; to think it probable, to feel persuaded (that): *I suspect that we shall have rain before night; I suspect he was only too glad not to be asked to sing;* also absol. *you are pretty tired after your journey, I suspect.* **B.** intrans. To entertain suspicions, to be suspicious.

suspectable, adj. [1. suspéktabl; 2. səspéktəbl]. Prec. & **-able.** Capable of being suspected; liable to suspicion.

suspend, vb. trans. [1. suspénd; 2. səspénd], fr. Lat. *suspendere,* 'to hang up; to check, interrupt, suspend', fr. **sus-** & *pendere,* 'to hang', see **pendant. 1.** To hang up, cause to hang from above: *to suspend a bird-cage from the ceiling.* **2.** To postpone, defer, arrest, delay (a physical or mental action): *to suspend judgement, proceedings, business* &c. Phrs. *to suspend payment* (of a bank &c.), fail to meet financial obligations; *to suspend one's judgement,* delay coming to a decision pending further information and consideration. **3.** (i.) To debar, prohibit, temporarily, from exercise of privileges or functions; (ii.) remove from position: *to suspend a clergyman for misconduct; to suspend a clergyman from preaching.*

suspended, adj. [1. suspénded; 2. səspéndid], fr. P.P. of prec. **1.** Held in fixed position within the atmosphere, or in a fluid, without either rising or sinking: *dust suspended in the air; salt suspended in water.* **2.** Temporarily inactive, in state of abeyance: *suspended animation,* unconsciousness.

suspender, n. [1. suspénder; 2. səspéndə]. Prec. & **-er.** That which suspends; specif. **a** device for holding a sock or stocking in position on the leg; **b** (Am. usage, pl.) braces.

suspense, n. [1. suspéns; 2. səspéns], fr. Fr., fr. P.P. of *suspendre,* 'to hang', fr. Lat. *suspendere,* 'to hang', see **suspend. 1.** State of mental uncertainty and anxiety as to the result of some action or event; anxious expectation: *to keep a person in suspense; to be unable to endure the suspense.* **2.** (law) Temporary cessation of a right. **3.** (book-keeping) *suspense account,* account in which items are entered temporarily until their proper place is settled.

suspensibility, n. [1. suspènsibíliti; 2. səspènsibíliti]. See next word & **-ity.** State or quality of being suspensible.

suspensible, adj. [1. suspénsibl; 2. səspénsibl], fr. Lat. *suspens-(um),* P.P. type of *suspendere,* 'to hang', see **suspense,** & **-ible.** Capable of being suspended.

suspension, n. [1. suspénshun; 2. səspénʃən]. **suspense** & **-ion.** Act of suspending; state of being suspended (in various senses of vb.).

suspension-bridge, n. Bridge suspended from chains or cables which are supported by towers at either end, or by a series of piers.

suspensio per collum, n. [1. suspénsiō për kólum; 2. səspénsiou pā kóləm]. Lat., 'hanging by the neck'. (law) Hanging as capital punishment; usually abbr. *sus. per coll.*

suspensive, adj. [1. suspénsiv; 2. səspénsiv], fr. Lat. *suspensum,* P.P. type of *suspendere,* 'to hang', see **suspend,** & **-ive. a** Tending, having the power, to suspend temporarily; **b** pertaining to, resulting from, characterized by, mental suspense.

suspensively, adv. Prec. & **-ly.** In a suspensive manner.

suspensory, adj. [1. suspénsuri; 2. səspénsəri], fr. Lat. *suspensum,* P.P. type of *suspendere,* 'to hang', see **suspend,** & **-ory. 1.** Of, pertaining to, forming a means of, suspension: *suspensory bandage.* **2.** Tending to delay, suspend, arrest, operation.

suspicion, n. [1. suspíshun; 2. səspíʃən], fr. O. Fr., fr. Lat. *suspīciōn-(em),* 'mistrust, suspicion', earlier **suspēcio-,* fr. **sub-** & stem **spĕc-,* seen in Lat. *specere,* 'to see', see **species;** cp. **suspect** (I.). **1.** Feeling of vague belief in, inkling, glimmering, of, the existence or occurrence of something: *I had a suspicion of the truth though I was not certain; the disguise was so good that I had no suspicions of his real identity.* **2.** Act of suspecting; **a** feeling of doubt, mistrust; impression that something is probably not true, not genuine &c.: *I have grave suspicions of the man's integrity;* **b** belief in a person's guilt, tendency to suspect a person. **3.** State of being suspected: *to be under suspicion, above suspicion.* **4.** Slight trace, touch, hint, flavour, small portion: *just a suspicion of brandy in the pudding; a suspicion of arrogance in his manner.*

suspicionless, adj. [1. suspíshunles; 2. səspíʃənlis]. Prec. & **-less.** Without suspicion; unsuspecting.

suspicious, adj. [1. suspíshus; 2. səspíʃəs], fr. Lat. *suspīciōsus,* 'feeling or exciting suspicion', fr. *suspicio,* 'mistrust', see **suspicion,** & **-ous. 1.** Inclined to, feeling, expressing, suspicion: *a suspicious nature* &c. **2.** Arousing, tending to excite, suspicion: *a suspicious character; suspicious actions; under suspicious circumstances.*

suspiciously, adv. Prec. & **-ly.** In a suspicious manner; **a** so as to express suspicion: *to glance suspiciously at a person;* **b** so as to excite suspicion: *to behave suspiciously.*

suspiciousness, n. See prec. & **-ness.** State or quality of being suspicious.

suspiration, n. [1. sùspiráshun; 2. sàspiréiʃən], fr. Lat. *suspīrātiōn-(em),* 'a sighing'; next word & **-ation.** Act or process of suspiring; a sigh.

suspire, vb. intrans. [1. suspír; 2. səspáiə], fr. O. Fr. *souspirer,* fr. Lat. *suspīrāre,* 'to draw a deep breath, to sigh', fr. **sub-** & *spīrāre,* 'to breathe', see **spirant.** (poet.) To draw a deep breath; to sigh.

sustain, vb. trans. [1. sustán; 2. səstéin]. M.E. *susteinen,* fr. O. Fr. *sustein-,* Pres. stem. of *sustener,* 'to hold up', fr. Lat. *sustinēre,* 'to hold up; to check, restrain; to uphold, maintain; to undergo, endure', fr. **sus-** & *tenēre,* 'to hold', see **tenable. 1.** To support, carry weight of, hold up: *pillars sustain the arch.* **2. a** To undergo, endure, suffer (physical or mental experience): *to sustain injuries, a shock* &c.; specif. **b** to be able to endure without giving way or collapsing; to bear: *to be unable to sustain a shock.* **3.** To enable to endure, give physical, moral, or mental strength or support to: *food sufficient to sustain life; hope alone sustained him.* **4.** To uphold, support, approve as right or just: *the court sustained his claim.* **5.** To support, confirm, corroborate, help to prove: *the recently discovered facts sustain the contention.* **6. a** To keep up, maintain: *to sustain one's rôle; sustained efforts;* **b** to prolong, keep going: *to sustain a note.*

sustainable, adj. [1. sustánabl; 2. səstéinəbl]. Prec. & **-able.** Capable of being sustained.

sustainment, n. [1. sustánment; 2. səstéinmənt]. **sustain** & **-ment.** Act of sustaining; state of being sustained.

sustenance, n. [1. sústenans; 2. sástinəns], fr. O. Fr., fr. L. Lat. *sustinentia,* 'endurance', fr. *sustinent-(em),* Pres. Part. of *sustinēre,* 'to hold up; to uphold, maintain; to endure', see **sustain,** & **-ce,** w. spelling altered on anal. of words in **-ance,** e.g. *governance* &c. **1.** (rare) Act of sustaining by nourishment, maintenance of strength. **2.** That which sustains or supports life or strength; nourishment.

sustentation, n. [1. sùstentáshun; 2. sàstintéiʃən], fr. O. Fr., fr. Lat. *sustentātiōnem,* 'maintenance', fr. *sustent-(um),* P.P. of *sustinēre,* 'to uphold, support', see **sustain,** & **-ation.** Act or process of sustaining life; subsistence; *sustentation fund,* fund for supplying sustenance, or more generally for supporting, maintaining, an institution and the group of persons connected with it.

susurrant, adj. [1. sūsúrant; 2. sjusárənt], fr. Lat. *susurrant-(em),* Pres. Part. of *susurrāre,* 'to buzz', see next word. Whispering, murmurous.

susurration, n. [1. sūsuráshun; 2. sjūsəréiʃən], fr. Lat. *susurrāt-(um),* P.P. type of *susurrāre,* 'to buzz, murmur, whisper', fr. *susurrus,* 'hum, whisper'; a reduplicated base cogn. w. Scrt. *svárati,* 'sounds, resounds'; O. Slav. *svirati,* 'to pipe'; Mod. Germ. *schwirren,* 'to buzz'; see also **swarm** (I.). Soft murmur, whisper, or rustle.

susurrous, adj. [1. sūsúrus; 2. sjusárəs], fr. Lat. *susurrus,* 'whispering', fr. *susurrus,* 'a whisper', see prec., & **-ous.** Producing a soft murmuring or rustling sound.

sutler, n. [1. sútler; 2. sátlə], fr. Du. *zoetelaar,* 'sutler; camp cook; scullion'; cp. Mod. Germ. *sudeln,* 'to daub, sully'; according to Kluge, orig. 'to cook badly', cogn. w. **seethe, suds.** Camp-follower who sells goods, esp. food, to troops.

Sutra, n. [1. sōōtra; 2. sūtrə], fr. Scrt.; cp. Scrt. *sūtram,* 'thread'; cogn. w. Lat. *suere,* 'to sew'; *sūtor,* 'cobbler'; *sūtūra,* 'seam', see **suture** (I.). Series of aphoristic formulae, collection of precepts, in Sanscrit.

suttee, sati, n. [1. sutḗ, sútē; 2. satí, sáti], fr. Scrt. *satī,* 'faithful wife'. **1.** Custom of self-immolation formerly practised by high-caste Hindu widows on their husbands' funeral pyre. **2.** Hindu widow who sacrifices herself in this way.

sutteeism, n. [1. sutḗizm; 2. satíizəm]. Prec. & **-ism.** Practice of suttee.

sutural, adj. [1. sūchural; 2. sjūtʃərəl]. **suture** (I.) & **-al.** Of, pertaining to, situated near, a suture.

suturally, adv. Prec. & **-ly**. In the manner of a suture.

suturation, n. [1. sùchuráshun; 2. sjûtʃəréiʃən]. **suture (I.)** & **-ation**. Joining by means of, formation of, a suture.

suture (I.), n. [1. sûchur; 2. sjûtʃə], fr. Lat. *sūtūra*, 'a sewing together, seam', fr. *sūt-(um)*, P.P. type of *suere*, 'to sew', cogn. w. Scrt. *syūtáś*, 'stitched'; Gk. (*kas*)*súein*, 'to patch'; Goth. *siujan*; O.E. *sēowan*, 'to sew', see **sew**; O.N. *saumr*, O.E. *sēam*, 'seam', see **seam (I.)**; & **-ure**. **1.** (anat.) Interlocking joint of two bones along their edges; esp. articulation of bones of skull. **2.** (bot., zool.) Line of junction between two adjacent parts. **3. a** Act or process of joining edges of incised wound &c. by stitching; **b** stitch of thread, wire &c., used in surgical suture.

suture (II.), vb. trans., fr. prec. To join with a suture.

sutured, adj. [1. sûchurd; 2. sjûtʃəd]. **suture (I.)** & **-ed**. Having, united by, a suture.

suzerain, n. [1. sûzerān; 2. s(j)ûzərein], fr. O. Fr. *suzerain*, formed on the anal. of *suverain*, see **sovereign (I.)**, fr. *sus-*, 'over', fr. Lat. *su(r)sum*, 'from below, upwards, over, above', fr. *subs-*, see **sub-**, & **-vorsum*, 'turned'; cp. Lat. *vertere*, 'to turn', see **version, vertex, vortex**. **1.** One who has supreme power, dominant authority, esp. in feudal system. **2.** State exercising general, nominal, or limited control over another.

suzerainty, n. [1. sûzerānti; 2. s(j)ûzəreinti]. Prec. & **-ty**. Rank, authority, of, or exercised by, a suzerain.

svelte, adj. [1. svelt; 2. svelt]. Fr. *svelte*, 'slim, slender', fr. **ex-** & L. Lat. *vellit-(um)*, used as P.P. of *vellere*, 'to pull, pluck, stretch', see **vellicate**. (of a woman's figure) Slender and graceful, lissom, willowy.

swab (I.), vb. trans. [1. swob; 2. swɔb], fr. **swabber**. **1.** To clean, wash out, with a swab: *to swab (down) the decks*. **2.** *To swab up*, to mop up, take up (liquid) with a swab.

swab (II.), n., fr. prec. **1.** Mop or pad of absorbent substance for cleaning. **2.** (naut.) Naval officer's epaulet. **3.** (naut. slang) Awkward, clumsy, unskilful fellow.

swabber, n. [1. swóber; 2. swɔ́bə], fr. Du. *zwabber*, 'one who does dirty work'. **1.** One who uses a swab. **2.** Awkward, clumsy fellow.

Swabian, Suabian, adj. & n. [1. swábian; 2. swéibiən], fr. Swabia, Germ. *Schwaben*, cp. Lat. *Suevi*, & **-an**. **1.** adj. Of, pertaining to, Swabia. **2.** n. **a** Inhabitant of Swabia; **b** Swabian dialect.

swaddle, vb. trans. [1. swódl; 2. swɔ́dl]. M.E. *swathlen*, 'to swaddle, bind', fr. O.E. *swæðel*, 'bandage', fr. *swaðu*, 'band, track'. Cp. **swath**. To wrap up in long bandages or garments, bind, swathe, bundle up.

swaddling-bands, -clothes, n. [1. swódling bàndz, klòdhz; 2. swɔ́dliŋ bæ̀ndz, klòuðz]. Long strip of material formerly used for wrapping round very young infants. Phr. (fig.) *still in, hardly, just, out of swaddling clothes*, very young and inexperienced; still under, just escaping from, strict parental supervision and control.

swadeshi, n. [1. swadáshi; 2. swadéiʃi]. Bengali, 'native country'. Indian nationalists' boycott of foreign, esp. British, goods, for the purpose of furthering their political aims.

swag (I.), n. [1. swag; 2. swæg], fr. obs. or provinc. *swag*, 'to sway'; prob. of Scand. origin; cp. Norw. *svaga*, 'to sway'; cogn. w. **sway (I.)**. (slang) Plunder, booty, anything acquired by robbery or fraud.

swag (II.), n. See prec. A hanging wreath or festoon as an architectural or other ornament.

swage, n. & vb. trans. [1. swāj; 2. sweidž]. Origin uncertain. **1.** n. Kind of die or tool for shaping wrought-iron &c. **2.** vb. To shape (metal) with a swage.

swage-block, n. Kind of anvil with hollows or perforations for shaping wrought-iron &c.

swagger (I.), vb. intrans. & trans. [1. swáger; 2. swǽgə], fr. obs. *swag*, 'to sway', see **swag (I.)**, & **-er**. **A.** intrans. **1.** To walk, bear oneself, with a jaunty, self-satisfied air, strut about with an air of insolent superiority. **2. a** To show off, give oneself airs; to affect superiority in bearing and speech; **b** *swagger about (one's) exploits, possessions* &c., to boast of. **B.** trans. (rare) To influence, affect, bluff, by boastful talk or bluster.

swagger (II.), n., fr. prec. **1.** Swaggering gait. **2.** Boastful, self-important manner, talk &c.

swagger (III.), adj., fr. prec. Smart, swell, ultra-fashionable or splendid: *swagger clothes*.

swagger-cane, n. Cane carried by soldier in uniform when not on parade.

swaggering, adj. [1. swágering; 2. swǽgəriŋ], fr. Pres. Part. of **swagger (I.)**. Inclined to swagger, boastful.

swaggeringly, adv. Prec. & **-ly**. With (a) swagger.

Swahili, n. [1. swahhéli; 2. swahíli]. Arab., 'of the coast'. **a** Bantu inhabitants of Zanzibar and the neighbouring coasts; **b** dialect of these tribes.

swain, n. [1. swān; 2. swein]. M.E. *swein*, fr. O.N. *sveinn*, 'young man', cp. O.E. *swān*, 'herdsman', also as second element in **boatswain & coxswain**, etymol. doubtful. **a** (chiefly poet.) Country lad, young yokel; **b** rustic lover; hence, **c** lover, admirer: *a lady surrounded by adoring swains*.

swallet, n. [1. swólet; 2. swɔ́lit]. Prob. fr. next word. (provinc.) Underground rock-fissure through which a stream flows.

swallow (I.), vb. trans. & intrans. [1. swólō; 2. swɔ́lou]. M.E. *swolwen, swolgen, swelwen*, fr. O.E. *swelgan*, 'to swallow, engulf'; cp. O.H.G. *swelgan*; O.N. *svelga*, 'to swallow'; apparently has no cognates outside Gmc. **A.** trans. **1.** To receive (food, drink &c.) into the mouth, and pass into the stomach, through the gullet, by the action of the muscles of the throat. Phrs. *to swallow one's words*, withdraw what one has said, recant; *to swallow the bait*, (fig.) to fall into the trap, to allow oneself to be deceived by a specious hope of advantage. **2.** *Swallow up*, of the sea, mist, the earth (in an earthquake), to cover over, overwhelm, engulf; to conceal from sight, envelop, enshroud. **3.** *Swallow up*, to use up, exhaust, absorb: *the expenses swallowed up most of the profits*. **4.** To tolerate, put up with, receive patiently: *to swallow an insult*. **5.** To believe, receive with credulity, accept as true: *he is so credulous that he swallows everything that is told him*; *such stories are rather hard to swallow*. **B.** intrans. To carry out the muscular action of swallowing.

swallow (II.), n., fr. prec. **1.** Act of swallowing. **2.** Amount swallowed at one time; mouthful: *to take a swallow of water*. **3. a** Food passage in throat; gullet; **b** capacity of this in respect of size to allow a mouthful to pass: *to have a small swallow*. **4.** Swallow-hole.

swallow (III.), n. O.E. *swalwe*; M.E. *swaluwe, swolwe*; cp. O.H.G. *swalawa*; M. Du. *swaluwe*; O.N. *svala*, 'swallow'; perh. fr. **swalgwō-*, in wh. case cogn. w. Gk. *alkuṓn*, 'kingfisher', for **swalkwōn*, see **halcyon**. Insectivorous, migratory bird, genus *Hirundo*, with long, pointed wings, forked tail, and short, broad beak.

swallowable, adj. [1. swólōabl; 2. swɔ́louəbl]. **swallow (I.)** & **-able**. Capable of being swallowed.

swallow-fish, n. Kind of gurnard, with much elongated pectoral fins.

swallow-hawk, n. Swallow-tailed hawk.

swallow-hole, n. Funnel-shaped, water-worn hole in limestone rock; rock-fissure through which stream flows underground.

swallow-plover, n. Pratincole.

swallow-shrike, n. Swallow-tailed bird of Australia and E. Indies.

swallow-tail, n. **1.** Object, projection &c., with deep fork as in swallow's tail; specif. **a** *swallow-tails*, swallow-tailed coat; **b** small pennant with forked end. **2.** Kind of humming bird. **3.** Kind of butterfly with long projection from each lower wing.

swallow-tailed, adj. Prec. & **-ed**. Having a forked, pointed tail like that of a swallow; *swallow-tailed coat*, evening dress coat.

swallow-wort, n. **1.** Herb of milkweed family. **2.** Celandine.

swam, vb. [1. swam; 2. swæm]. O.E. *swam*, Pret. of **swim**.

Swami, n. [1. swáhmē; 2. swámī]. Hind. Title given to, form of address to, Brahmin.

swamp (I.), n. [1. swomp; 2. swɔmp], cp. Du. *zwamp*; Mod. Engl. *sump*; Mod. Germ. *sumpf*, 'pond'; O.N. *svoppr*, 'sponge'; cp. also Goth. *swamm*; O.H.G. *swamp*, 'sponge'; Gk. *somphós*, 'spongy, porous'. Level tract of land saturated with moisture; marsh, bog.

swamp (II.), vb. trans., fr. prec. **1.** To fill, overwhelm, cover, with water: *a wave swamped the boat*. **2.** (chiefly in P.P.) To overwhelm, inundate; bestow upon to excess: *to be swamped with invitations*.

swampy, adj. [1. swómpi; 2. swɔ́mpi]. **swamp (I.)** & **-y**. Resembling, of the nature of, a swamp; boggy, marshy.

swan, n. [1. swon; 2. swɔn]. O.E., M.E. *swan*, cp. Mod. Germ. *schwan*; O.S. *swan*; Du. *zwaan*; cogn. w. Scrt. *svánati*, 'it sounds'; *svanáś*, 'tone'; Lat. *sonāre*, 'to sound'; *sonus*, 'sound'; see **sonant**; cp. also O.E. *swinsian*, 'to sing'. **1.** Large, web-footed, long-necked bird, genus *Cygnus*, usually white in Northern Hemisphere; *black swan*, Australian black genus; according to an ancient tradition the swan is supposed to sing very melodiously just before its death. Phr. *the swan of Avon*, Shakespeare. **2.** The constellation Cygnus.

swan-flower, n. Variety of tropical American orchid.

swan-goose, n. Chinese goose.

swan-herd, n. Official in charge of swan-marks of royal swans.

swank, vb. intrans. & n. [1. swangk; 2. swæŋk]. Etymol. unknown. (slang) **1.** vb. To swagger, to show off; to behave or speak in a manner adopted to show one's superiority and importance. **2.** n. Behaviour, mode of speech, of one who swanks; swagger, side.

swan-like, adj. **swan** & **-like**. Resembling a swan, specif., in whiteness, grace of form, neck &c.

swan-maiden, n. (in folk-tales) Maiden capable of becoming a swan by assuming a magic robe of feathers.

swan-mark, n. Mark of ownership, usually on swan's upper mandible.

swan-neck, n. Curved end of pipe &c. resembling in outline the curve of a swan's neck.

swannery, n. [1. swóneri; 2. swɔ́nəri]. **swan** & **-ery**. Place where swans are kept or bred.

swan's-down, n. **1.** Down of swan, esp. as trimming for dress &c. **2.** Fine, thick, woollen cloth.

swan-shot, n. Large size of shot.

swan-skin, n. Soft, fine flannel.

swan-song, n. **1.** Fabled song of dying swan. **2.** Last work, pronouncement, or utterances, esp. of a poet or orator, before his death or retirement from productiveness or activity.

swan-upping, n. [1. swón ùping; 2. swɔ́n àpiŋ]. Annual marking of swans in royal herd by a notch cut in the skin of the upper mandible.

swap. See **swop**.

Swaraj, n. [1. swaráhj; 2. swarádž], fr. Scrt. *svaraj*, 'self-ruling', fr. *svá-*, 'own', cogn. w. Lat. *suus*, 'one's own', see **sui**, & **raj**. Self-government for India, as aim of Indian Nationalists.

sward, n. [1. sword; 2. swɔd]. O.E. *sweard*, 'skin, rind'; M.E. *sward*; cp. O. Fris. *swarde*; M.H.G. *swarte*; O.N. *svörðr*, 'skin, scalp'; Du. *zwoord*, 'rind of bacon'. Grass-covered surface of ground, expanse of turf.

swarded, adj. [1. swórded; 2. swɔ́did]. Prec. & **-ed**. Covered with sward.

sware, vb. [1. swār; 2. swɛə]. (archaic) Pret. of **swear.**

swarm (I.), n. [1. sworm; 2. swɔ̄m]. O.E. *swearm*; M.E. *swarm*; cp. M.H.G. *swarm*; O.N. *svarmr*, 'swarm, tumult'; Mod. Germ. *schwarm*, 'swarm of bees'; prob. cogn. w. Scrt. *svárati*, 'sounds, rings'; Lat. *susurrus*, 'hum, buzz', see **susurration**; O. Slav. *svirati*, 'to whistle'. **1. a** Large number or mass of insects, esp. with continuous, irregular movement within the group; specif. **b** cluster of bees, including a queen, leaving the parent hive to seek a new home. **2. a** Large body, throng, of moving persons, animals &c.; large irregular cluster: *a swarm of sightseers*; *a swarm of children*; **b** large group, multitude, of inanimate objects: *a swarm of letters.*

swarm (II.), vb. intrans., fr. prec. **1. a** To come, cluster, throng, together in great numbers, as in a swarm; to crowd in an irregular mass: *a crowd of people swarmed to the spot, all over the ground*; *children came swarming round*; **b** (specif. of bees) to cluster together round queen in preparation for leaving parent hive. **2. a** To be present, frequent a place, exist, in swarms, or large numbers; to abound: *brigands simply swarm in the mountains*; **b** *swarm with*, to abound in, be much frequented by, thronged: *the place is swarming with strangers*; *a garden swarming with pests.*

swarm (III.), vb. trans. & intrans. Etymol. unknown. **a** trans. To climb by clasping with hands and legs: *to swarm a rope, a pole*; also *swarm up*; **b** intrans., to perform the act of swarming.

swarm-cell, n. Spore having power of independent motion; zoospore.

swarm-spore, n. Zoospore.

swart, adj. [1. swort; 2. swɔ̄t]. O.E. *sweart*; M.E. *swart*, 'dark'; cp. O.H.G. *swarz*; Goth. *swarts*; O.N. *svartr*; Du. *zwart*, 'dark'; cp. also O.N. *sorta*, 'dark colour'; prob. cogn. w. Lat. *sordēre*, 'to be soiled', see **sordid**; *surdus*, 'dark; dull; deaf', see **surd** (I.). Dark in colour, swarthy.

swarthily, adv. [1. swórdhili; 2. swɔ̄́ðili]. **swarthy** & **-ly.** In a swarthy manner.

swarthiness, n. [1. swórdhines; 2. swɔ̄́ðinis]. Next word & **-ness.** State or quality of being swarthy.

swarthy, adj. [1. swórdhi; 2. swɔ̄́ði], fr. obs. *swarth*, variant of **swart**, & **-y.** Dark-skinned, of brown, black, or sunburnt complexion.

swash (I.), vb. trans. & intrans. [1. swosh; 2. swɔʃ]. Imitative. (of liquid) **a** trans. To dash, splash, against; **b** intrans., to make a splash in, or as in, striking solid object, dash, wash.

swash (II.), n., fr. prec. Noise of dashing or splashing water.

swashbuckler, n. [1. swóshbùkler; 2. swɔ́ʃbàklə]. See next word. A bold, dashing, adventurous, rather unscrupulous fighting man.

swashing, adj. [1. swóshing; 2. swɔ́ʃiŋ], fr. **swash** (I.), in obs. or archaic sense, 'to strike violently'. (of blow) Violent, crushing.

swash-plate, n. Revolving disk set at an oblique angle to its shaft, used for communicating an up and down motion to a rod parallel to its shaft.

swastika, n. [1. swástika; 2. swǽstikə]. Scrt., lit. 'fortunate', fr. *svastiš*, 'welfare', fr. *su-*, 'well', & *asti*, 'being', cogn. w. Gk. *esti*, Lat. *est*, 'is' &c.; see **esse.** Very primitive and widespread symbol consisting of cross with arms of equal length, each arm having a prolongation at right angles; said to have been primitively a sun-symbol, but it is also used in Christian decoration; also called a fylfot.

swat, vb. trans. [1. swot; 2. swɔt]. Imitative. (colloq.) To crush, squash (a wasp, fly &c.).

swath, n. [1. swawth, swath; 2. swɔ̄þ, swæþ]. O.E. *swaðu*, 'track, band'; M.E. *swāðe*; cp. M. Du. *swade*; cogn. w. **swaddle. 1. a** The amount of grass cut with a single sweep of a scythe, and removed to one side by the blade; **b** the mark left by the scythe at each stroke. **2.** The space cleared by a mower in the whole course in a given direction.

swathe, vb. trans. & n. [1. swādh; 2. sweið]. M.E. *swāðen*, 'to bind', fr. O.E. *swaðu*, 'band, track', see prec. **1.** vb. To wrap, bind up, wind round, with long bandages or drapery. **2.** n. Bandage, wrapping.

sway (I.), vb. intrans. & trans. [1. swā; 2. swei]. M.E. *sweien*; cp. O.N. *sveigja*, 'to bend, swing'. Cp. **swag** (I.). **A.** intrans. To swing unsteadily, lean to either side alternately with irregular motion, oscillate: *branches sway in the wind*; *the bridge swayed as the train passed over it.* **B.** trans. **1.** To cause to sway, give irregular swinging motion to: *the wind sways the branches.* **2. a** To move, incline, influence, by moral power: *to sway the minds of men*; *he is not to be swayed by argument or entreaty*; **b** (poet.) to have dominion over; to rule, govern, by authority: *to sway the realm*; *to sway the sceptre.*

sway (II.), n., fr. prec. **1.** Swaying movement, oscillation. **2.** Influence, power to move or direct; rule, dominion, jurisdiction; royal or other authority: *King Alfred held sway over all England*; *to own love's sway.*

sway-backed, adj. Of horses and cattle, having the back abnormally hollowed.

swayed, adj. [1. swād; 2. sweid], fr. P.P. of **sway** (I.). Sway-backed.

swear (I.), vb. trans. & intrans. [1. swār; 2. swɛə]. O.E. *swerian*; M.E. *swēren*; cp. O.H.G. *swer(i)en*; O.N. *sverja*; Goth. *swaran*, 'to swear'; earlier sense, 'to speak'; cp. O.E. & O.S. *andswearian*, 'to address, answer', see **answer** (I.); O.N. *svara*, 'to answer (for); to stand surety'; cogn. w. Lat. *sermo*, 'conversation', see **sermon**; O. Slav. *svara*, 'dispute'. **A.** trans. **1. a** To assert, vow, promise solemnly, on one's oath: *I believe it to be true, but I can't swear it*; *to swear allegiance, eternal friendship*; **b** specif., *swear an oath*, (i.) to make a solemn vow, take one's oath, (ii.) to utter a profane oath, curse, imprecation; Phr. *to swear a charge, accusation, against*, accuse on oath. **2. a** To make a solemn promise, pledge, bind, oneself by an oath (that something is, or to do something): *to swear to speak the truth, that what one says is true*; *to swear to be faithful*; **b** (colloq.) to assert emphatically, express a strong conviction that: *I swear I'll never go near the place again*; *I'd swear that picture was never painted by Turner.* **3. a** To obtain a solemn promise from under oath, cause to take an oath: *to swear a person to secrecy*; specif. **b** to administer a legal oath to: *to swear a jury, a witness* &c.; also *swear in.* **B.** intrans. To utter profane or blasphemous oaths or imprecations; to curse; to vent one's rage by uttering blasphemies: *he began to curse and swear*; *it is enough to make one swear.* **C.** Followed by adverbs and prepositions with special meanings. *Swear at*, intrans., to address oaths or imprecations to; to curse at, vituperate. *Swear by*, intrans., **a** to invoke as witness of oath: *to swear by all that's holy*; **b** to have entire confidence in, recommend highly: *he swears by quinine for preventing colds*; Phr. *not enough to swear by*, a very small amount. *Swear in*, trans., to administer oath of office to: *the members of the jury were sworn in. Swear off*, intrans., to promise or swear to renounce: *to swear off smoking* &c. *Swear to*, intrans., to affirm on oath: *I believe that is true, but I could not swear to it.*

swear (II.), n., fr. prec. (colloq., rare) An oath, blasphemy, imprecation.

swear-word, n. (colloq.) A profane oath.

sweat (I.), n. [1. swet; 2. swɛt]. O.E. **swǣt*, fr. **swāti*, variant of *swāt*, 'sweat'; M.E. *swēt*; cp. O.H.G. *sweiz*; O.S. *swēt*, 'sweat'; cogn. w. Lat. *sūdor*, 'sweat', see **sudation**; Gk. *idos*; Scrt. *svéda-*, 'sweat'; *svídyati*, 'he sweats'; Lett. *swēdri*, 'sweat'. The word in a physiological sense is often avoided in polite conversation, *perspiration* being commonly used instead in sense **1. 1. a** Moisture exuded by pores of skin; perspiration; Phr. *by the sweat of one's brow*, by hard work; **b** moisture resembling sweat exuded from any substance, and condensing on the surface. **2. a** Process of sweating: *a good sweat often cures a cold*; **b** state characterized by pronounced sweating: *to be in a sweat*; *a cold sweat*, accompanied by chilly feeling, induced by fear &c. **3.** (colloq.) Something that promotes sweat; work, toil, heavy labour; troublesome, tedious work; a grind: *compiling a dictionary is an awful sweat.*

sweat (II.), vb. intrans. & trans. O.E. *swǣtan*, 'to sweat', fr. *swāt*, 'sweat', see prec. The word is often avoided, esp. in physiological sense, *perspire* being substituted. **A.** intrans. **1. a** (of animals) To exude sweat, to perspire; Phr. *to sweat with fear, emotion* &c., to be strongly moved or affected; **b** (of other objects and substances) to give out moisture from a surface in drops like sweat: *apples sweat after they are gathered*; *a new house is apt to be damp till the stone has sweated thoroughly.* **2.** To work hard, toil: *to sweat (away) at one's job.* **B.** trans. **1.** To give out, exude, in form of, or as, sweat: *to sweat blood.* Phr. *to sweat out (a cold* &c.), get rid of it by sweating. **2.** To cause to sweat, cause to perspire freely, by drugs or physical exercise: *doctors sweat their patients*; *to sweat a horse.* **3.** To remove, scrape, sweat from (horse &c.). **4.** To force hard work from (workmen &c.) at insufficient wages. **5.** To wear down edges or surface of (coins &c.) by friction.

sweat-band, n. Strip of leather &c. forming lining for hat.

sweat-cloth, n. Cloth placed under horse's collar or saddle.

sweat-duct, n. Duct carrying sweat from sweat-gland to surface of skin.

sweated, adj. [1. swéted; 2. swétid], fr. P.P. of **sweat** (II.). **a** (of persons) Forced to work at inadequate wage; **b** (of labour) inadequately paid; **c** (of commodities) made, produced, by workers who are inadequately paid.

sweater, n. [1. swéter; 2. swétə]. **sweat** (II.) & **-er. 1.** One who sweats excessively. **2.** Employer who sweats his workpeople. **3.** Heavy jersey worn by athletes after severe exercise &c.

sweat-gland, n. Small subcutaneous gland which secretes sweat.

sweatily, adv. [1. swétili; 2. swétili]. **sweaty** & **-ly.** In a sweaty manner.

sweatiness, n. [1. swétines; 2. swétinis]. See prec. & **-ness.** Sweaty condition.

sweating-bath, n. [1. swéting bàhth; 2. swétiŋ bàþ]. Bath intended to increase perspiration.

sweating-iron, n. Metal scraper for removing sweat from horse.

sweating room, n. Hot room in Turkish bath.

sweating-sickness, n. Fatal, inflammatory fever, epidemic in Europe in 15th and 16th cents.

sweatless, adj. [1. swétles; 2. swétlis]. **sweat** (I.) & **-less.** Without, producing no, sweat.

sweaty, adj. [1. swéti; 2. swéti]. **sweat** (I.) & **-y. a** Covered with sweat; inclined to sweat; **b** resembling sweat.

Swede, n. [1. swēd; 2. swīd]. **1.** Native of Sweden. **2.** (without cap.) The Swedish turnip, with yellow, edible root.

Swedenborgian, adj. & n. [1. swēdenbórjian; 2. swīdənbɔ̄́dʒiən], fr. Swedish philosopher Swedenborg, d. 1772. **1.** adj. Pertaining to the system of philosophy and religious mysticism established by Swedenborg, or to the church founded by him. **2.** n. Adherent of Swedenborg or the Swedenborgian church.

Swedenborgianism, n. [1. swēdenbórjianizm; 2. swīdənbɔ̄́dʒiənizəm]. Prec. & **-ism.** Doctrine, philosophy, of Swedenborg.

Swedish, adj. & n. [1. swḗdish; 2. swídiʃ]. **Swede** & **-ish. 1.** adj. Pertaining to Sweden or the Swedes. **2.** n. Language of Sweden.

sweeny, n. [1. swḗni; 2. swíni]. Origin doubtful. Muscular atrophy in horses.

sweep (I.), vb. intrans. & trans. [1. swēp; 2. swīp]. M.E. *swēpan*, 'to sweep, move rapidly', wh. presupposes an O.E. **swǣpan*, (unrecorded) fr. base **swāp-* w. *i*-mutation, cp. O.E. *swāpan*, 'to sweep with a broom; to brandish (sword); to rush, dash (of wind)'; cp. also O.E. *swipu*, 'a whip'; O.H.G. *sweifan*; see further under **swift (I.)**, **swipe (I.)**, & **swoop (I.)**. **A.** intrans. **1. a** (i.) To move along, pass, with a swift, impetuous rush; to rush, dash, drive: *a pestilence swept over the land*; '*Your manly hearts shall glow, As ye sweep through the deep, While the stormy winds do blow*' (Campbell); *the cavalry swept down the valley*; (ii.) to be driven with irresistible force: *snow, rain, wind, sweeps across the country*; **b** (of non-material process) *a wave of indignation swept through the country*; *a deadly fear swept over him.* **2.** To walk with vigorous motion, and a stately, proud, important bearing, to sail along, sail in: *the archbishop swept up the aisle in his flowing robes.* **3.** To extend, be shaped, in a wide, bold, curve: *the coast-line sweeps away to the east in a deep bay.* **4.** Specif., to perform the action of sweeping, brushing, with a broom: *I can't sweep without a broom.* Phr. *a new broom sweeps clean*, new men, new measures. **B.** trans. **1.** To descend upon, traverse, pass along, through, over, impetuously, with violence, irresistibly: *the waves swept the deck*; *the storm swept the whole countryside.* **2. a** To execute a rapid, abrupt gesture with; to brush: *to sweep one's hand over one's face, across the strings of a harp* &c.; **b** to touch, brush, with a rapid gesture: *to sweep the notes of a piano, the strings of a harp* &c. **3.** To pass searchingly over or through; to traverse in all directions: *our ships swept the sea for weeks but could not find the enemy*; *to sweep the horizon with a telescope*; *to sweep the faces of an audience with a hasty glance.* **4.** Specif. **a** to clean, remove dirt, dust, rubbish &c. from with a broom: *to sweep (out) a room, the pavements, a chimney* &c.; Phr. *to sweep the board*, win all stakes on gaming-table; hence, (fig.) to win all the prizes, be victorious in all contests &c.; **b** to collect together and remove by sweeping with a broom: *to sweep away, up, dust, snow, rubbish* &c. **5.** (gen.) **a** To remove, drive, brush, away, eliminate, cause to disappear, by violent or drastic action: *death sweeps away great and small*; *the waves swept away the breakwater*; *our troops swept the enemy before them*; *to be swept along in the crowd*; *the wind swept his hat off his head*; *to be swept off one's feet (by a wave* &c.); (also fig.) to be carried away, overcome, by emotion &c.; **b** to obliterate, wipe out, destroy, abolish: *to sweep away slum areas, trees which obstruct the view* &c.

sweep (II.), n. See prec. **1.** Act of sweeping with a broom: *to give a room a good sweep.* Phr. *to make a clean sweep of*, to get rid of, do away with utterly. **2. a** Person who sweeps a chimney; Phr. *as black as a sweep*, very black, grubby; **b** a dirty, grubby person, esp. *a regular little sweep*, a grubby child; **c** (slang) a mean, ill-mannered, ill-conditioned, disagreeable person. **3. a** A steady, irresistible movement, flux, flow: *the sweep of the tide*; **b** a steady, spacious, movement, esp. of progress, in affairs, events, intellectual development &c.: *the onward sweep of civilization.* **4. a** A wide sweeping movement, swing, stroke, made or delivered by a weapon, implement &c.: *the sweep of a sword, scythe*; **b** large, vigorous bodily gesture: *a sweep of the arm*; **c** a wide searching inspection with a telescope &c. of the heavens. **5. a** The extent of a sweeping movement; range, reach: *a two-handed sword had a wide sweep*; **b** intellectual range, scope, grasp, comprehensiveness: *a mind of wonderful sweep.* **6.** A long, heavy oar, moved with a sweeping action, used for propelling or steering heavy barges, sailing-boats &c. **7.** A long, flowing curve: *the graceful sweep of draperies.* **8.** (colloq.) Abbr. of *sweepstake.*

sweeper, n. [1. swēper; 2. swīpə]. **sweep (I.)** & **-er.** **a** Mechanical device for sweeping (floors, streets); **b** person employed in sweeping; esp. in compound *crossing-sweeper.*

sweeping, adj. [1. swēping; 2. swīpiŋ], fr. Pres. Part. of **sweep (I.)**. **a** Comprehensive, of wide range; unqualified; of too great inclusiveness: *a sweeping statement*; **b** complete, thorough-going, radical: *sweeping changes.*

sweepingly, adv. Prec. & **-ly.** In a sweeping manner.

sweepingness, n. See prec. & **-ness.** Quality of being sweeping.

sweepings, n. pl. [1. swēpingz; 2. swīpiŋz]. **sweep (I.)** & **-ing.** **a** Matter such as rubbish or refuse swept up from floor, ground &c.; **b** (fig.) *the sweepings of the gutter*, the lowest dregs of the population.

sweep-net, n. **1.** Large fishing-net paid out in an arc of a circle and drawn ashore. **2.** Net with handle, swept to and fro above bushes &c., for catching insects.

sweep-seine, n. Sweep-net, **1.**

sweepstake(s), n. [1. swēpstāk(s); 2. swīpsteik(s)]. Form of gambling on horse-race &c. in which those taking part pay money into a common fund which is afterwards divided between those who have drawn numbered tickets representing winning or placed horses.

sweet (I.), adj. [1. swēt; 2. swīt]. O.E., M.E. *swēte*, fr. **swōti-*, 'sweet, pleasant'; cp. O.S. *swōti*; O.H.G. *suozi*; O.N. *sǿtr*; Goth. *sūts*; cogn. w. Lat. *suāvis*, fr. **swādwi-*, 'sweet, pleasant', see **suave**; Gk. *hēdús*, fr. **swādu-*, 'sweet', see **hedonic**; Scrt. *svādúś*, 'pleasant in taste'. **1.** Having the taste of sugar; reverse of *bitter* or *sour*: *sweet cakes, apples*; *to be fond of sweet things*; *the pudding is too sweet*; *sweet wine*, reverse of *dry*. Phr. *to have a sweet tooth*, like sweet things. **2.** Pleasing to sense of smell or taste; fresh, pure; reverse of *tainted, stale, stinking, rancid*: *the milk, water, meat, air &c. is quite sweet.* **3.** Pleasing to sense of smell; fragrant, agreeably scented: *sweet flowers*; *a sweet smell*; *the rose smells sweet*; *sweet herbs*, culinary herbs. **4. a** Pleasing to sense of hearing, gentle, soothing, melodious: *a sweet voice*; *sweet melodies*; **b** having a sweet, pleasant voice: *a sweet singer.* **5.** Agreeable, pleasant, gratifying, to body or mind; delightful or restful: *sweet sleep*; *sweet words*; *praise was sweet to him.* **6. a** Kind, tender, gentle: *a sweet temper, disposition* &c.; Phr. *sweet on* (a person), in love with; **b** having or revealing a sweet disposition: *a sweet woman*; *a sweet face.* **7.** (colloq.) Pretty, charming, delightful: *a sweet frock*; *a sweet little dog*; *he was perfectly sweet to her.*

sweet (II.), n., fr. prec. **1.** Anything with sweet taste, esp. **a** small sweetmeat; **b** sweet dish as course at dinner &c. **2.** Something sweet, delightful &c.: *the sweet of the year*, i.e. sweet season. **3.** (usually pl.) Enjoyment, delight, pleasure, joy: *the sweets of life, victory, success.* **4.** Sweet, beloved, person, darling: **a** '*She is coming, my own, my sweet*' (Tennyson, 'Maud'); **b** (as form of address) '*Sweet, be not proud of those two eyes Which starlike sparkle in their skies*' (Herrick).

sweetbread, n. [1. swētbred; 2. swītbrɛd]. Pancreas or thymus, esp. of calf, used as food.

sweet-brier, -briar, n. Species of brier-rose with aromatic leaves.

sweeten, vb. trans. & intrans. [1. swētn; 2. swītn]. **sweet (I.)** & **-en.** **A.** trans. **1.** To make sweet, impart sweetness (in any sense) to: *to sweeten sauce* &c.; *a temper sweetened by sympathy.* **2.** To render pleasant, make more endurable: *to sweeten toil.* **B.** intrans. To become sweet.

sweetening, n. [1. swētn-ing; 2. swītn-iŋ]. Prec. & **-ing.** That which sweetens; sweet substance added to food &c.

sweet-flag, n. A plant of the Arum family, with sword-shaped leaves and aromatic root, growing in marshy ground.

sweet-gale, n. A plant of the myrtle family, with aromatic leaves, growing in marshy ground; bog-myrtle.

sweetheart, n. & vb. intrans. [1. swēt-hart; 2. swīthāt]. The suff. orig. **-ard**, cp. **drunkard**, but associated w. **heart (I.)**. **1.** n. **a** Lover; **b** (as form of affectionate address) beloved, darling. **2.** vb. Esp. in Phr. *to go sweethearting*, to go courting, love-making.

sweeting, n. [1. swēting; 2. swītiŋ]. **sweet (I.)** & **-ing.** **1.** A sweet apple. **2.** (archaic) Sweetheart, darling.

sweetish, adj. [1. swētish; 2. swītiʃ]. **sweet (I.)** & **-ish.** Fairly sweet.

sweet-john, n. Narrow-leaved variety of sweet-william.

sweetly, adv. [1. swētli; 2. swītli]. **sweet (I.)** & **-ly.** **1. a** In a sweet manner: *to speak, sing, sweetly*; **b** to the extent of being sweet; in Phr. *sweetly pretty.* **2.** (of machines) Smoothly, easily: *the engine runs sweetly.*

sweetmeat, n. [1. swētmēt; 2. swītmīt]. Small piece of sweet confection made of or containing sugar, chocolate &c.

sweetness, n. [1. swētnes; 2. swītnis]. **sweet (I.)** & **-ness.** Quality of being sweet.

sweet-oil, n. Olive oil.

sweet-pea, n. Cultivated annual of pea family with white or brightly coloured, very fragrant flowers.

sweet-potato, n. Creeping plant, *Ipomaea*, of warm climates, with sweetish, farinaceous, edible root.

sweet-root, n. Liquorice.

sweet-rush, n. Sweet-flag.

sweet-scented, adj. Having sweet odour, fragrant.

sweet-sop, n. Sweet, pulpy, egg-shaped fruit of tropical American tree.

sweet-sultan, n. Garden annual, variety of the plant sultan, with purple flowers.

sweet-tempered, adj. Amiable, gracious, gentle in disposition.

sweet-water, n. Kind of white grape.

sweet-william, n. [1. swēt wílyum; 2. swīt wíljəm]. A perennial pink, *Dianthus*, with clusters of small, white, red, pink, or particoloured flowers.

sweet-willow, n. Sweet-gale.

sweetwood, n. [1. swētwood; 2. swītwud]. The bay, the wood of which is fragrant when crushed.

sweety, n. [1. swēti; 2. swīti]. **sweet (I.)** & **-y.** Sweetmeat.

swell (I.), vb. intrans. & trans. [1. swel; 2. swɛl]. O.E. *swellan*, M.E. *swellen*; O.H.G. *swellan*; cp. O.E. *swyle*, fr. **swuli-*, 'tumour'; cogn. w. Lat. *(in)solens*, 'immoderate, haughty', see **insolent**. **A.** intrans. **1. a** To expand, dilate, become larger by pressure exerted from within, as by inflation; to be blown out, puffed out: *a tire swells as it is filled with air*; **b** specif., to become tumefied and puffy from inflammation, accumulation of purulent matter &c.: *his legs swelled with dropsy.* Phr. *to have, suffer from, swelled head*, to have an exaggerated idea of one's own importance. **2.** To be increased in size, volume, number, by external addition: *the book has now swelled to an inordinate size*; *all the streams have swelled since the thaw*; *population in many places has swelled beyond the limits of actual housing accommodation.* **3. a** (of surface of the ground or of water) To rise into a curved protuberance above surrounding level; to billow; **b** (of sails &c.) to be filled with wind; to belly; **c** (of a contour) to bulge out, become larger at a given point: *the vase swells into a beautiful curve in the middle*; (often in Pres. Part. as adj.) *the swelling sides of a ship.* **4.** (of sound) To increase in volume and intensity: *the first occasional twitter of birds at dawn soon swells into a full-voiced chorus.* **5.** To have a sense of elation, of mental or moral excitement under the stress of powerful emotion: *to swell with pride, with indignation.* **B.** trans. **1.** To cause to swell (in various senses); **a** to add to amount of: *to swell the national debt*; **b** to augment numbers of: *to swell the popu-*

lation; c to increase volume of: *the melting snow swells the rivers*; d to increase size or bulk of: *new notes and additions of all kinds have swelled the book out to monstrous size*; e to render arrogant, puff up morally; (chiefly in P.P.) *swollen with pride* &c. 2. (mus.) To increase the loudness, volume, intensity of (a note &c.): '*The pealing anthem swells the note of praise*' (Gray's 'Elegy'). Phr. *to swell the chorus* (*of admiration* &c.), join one's voice, add one's opinion, to that of others (perhaps also under 1. b above).

swell (II.), n., fr. prec. 1. (rare) Process of swelling, increase in magnitude or volume. 2. Slow, steady, continuous, undulation of the sea unbroken by waves after a storm. 3. a (mus.) Gradual increase in volume of sound; b gradual increase and diminution of volume and loudness of a note. 4. Mechanical device in an organ producing alternate increase and diminution of loudness at the will of the player. 5. (colloq. slang) a A person who is smartly, richly, fashionably, dressed; a dandy, a buck, a blood; b a person of eminence, position, and distinction: *the Bishop and the other swells sat on the platform*; c person who excels in some particular bodily or mental accomplishment: *a swell at tennis, at polo*; *a swell at Latin prose.*

swell (III.), adj., fr. prec. (colloq.) a Specif., smart, dandified, extremely fashionable: *swell clothes*; *a swell walking-stick*; b (gen.) of excellent quality; first-rate; admirable, meritorious: *a swell tennis-player*; *a swell speech, book.*

swell-blind, n. One of the shutters of a swell-box.

swell-box, n. Chamber enclosing organ-box and fitted with movable slats or shutters to release or muffle the sound.

swelldom, n. [1. swéldum; 2. swéldəm]. **swell** (II.) & **-dom**. (colloq.) Fashionable society.

swell-fish, n. Fish capable of inflating itself.

swelling (I.), n. [1. swéling; 2. swéliŋ]. **swell** (I.) & **-ing**. 1. Something which is swollen; specif., swelled part of the body; a tumour. 2. That which swells; specif. a an undulation of the ground, a hillock; b an increase in size of one part of an object, part that is more prominent than the rest: *the swelling of a cask.*

swelling (II.), adj., fr. Pres. Part. of **swell** (I.). 1. Rising in an undulation, sloping, curving, into a mound: *the swelling turf.* 2. Formed so as to curve outwards, having a bulge: *the swelling sides of a ship.*

swellish, adj. [1. swélish; 2. swéliʃ]. **swell** (II.) & **-ish**. (colloq.) Of, pertaining to, a swell; ultra-fashionable.

swell-mob, n. (coll.) Well-dressed criminals.

swell-organ, n. Organ fitted with swell-box.

swell-pedal, n. Pedal controlling shutter of swell-box.

swell-rule, n. (print.) Diamond-shaped rule with elongated ends.

swelter (I.), vb. intrans. [1. swélter; 2. swéltə]. O.E. *sweltan*; M.E. *swelten*, 'to grow faint, die', & **-er**; cp. O.N. *svelta*; Goth. *swiltan*, 'to die'; see also **sultry**. To be, feel, extremely hot.

swelter (II.), n., fr. prec. Sweltering state or condition.

swept, vb. [1. swept; 2. swɛpt]. Pret. & P.P. of **sweep** (I.).

swerve (I.), vb. intrans. & trans. [1. swërv; 2. swʌ̄v]. O.E. *sweorfan*, 'to scrub, file'; M.E. *swerven*, 'to swerve'; cp. O.N. *sverfa*, 'to scour'; Goth. (*af*)*svairban*, 'to wipe out'; O.H.G. *swerban*, 'to wipe, rub, dry'; M. Du. *swerven*, 'to wander'. A. intrans. 1. To deviate from a straight line of progress; to start aside from one's course: *the runner swerved suddenly*; *some bowlers can make the ball swerve in the air.* 2. To depart, deviate, from a straight line of conduct: *to swerve from the path of duty.* B. trans. (rare) To cause (esp. a ball) to swerve.

swerve (II.), n., fr. prec. Act of swerving; turning aside, divergence from straight course; specif., turn or twist of cricket-ball in the air.

swerveless, adj. [1. swérvles; 2. swʌ́vlis]. **swerve** (II.) & **-less**. Not liable to swerve.

swift (I.), adj. [1. swift; 2. swift]. O.E., M.E. *swift*, 'swift', fr. Gmc. **swip-ta-*; cp. O.E. *swipa*, O.N. *svipa*, 'whip'; O.H.G. *sweif*, 'rotation'; O.N. *svīfa*, 'to sweep'; O.E. *swīfan*, 'to move, sweep'; *swāpan*, 'to sweep, rush', see **sweep** (I.). 1. a Moving or capable of moving quickly; rapid, fleet: *a swift runner, horse*; *as swift as thought*; *swift feet*; b (of time) *swift years.* 2. (of motion) Rapid, quick: *a swift movement, glance* &c.; *birds of swiftest flight.* 3. Acting or happening promptly; not delayed, speedy: *swift revenge*; *a swift response.* 4. Acting readily and promptly: *swift to take offence.*

swift (II.), adv. O.E. *swifte*, fr. prec. Swiftly; chiefly in compounds: *swift-passing* &c.

swift (III.), n., fr. **swift** (I.). Swift-moving bird, insect, object &c.; specif. a genus, *Cypselus*, of swallow-like birds with long, pointed wings, capable of rapid and prolonged flight; b breed of pigeons; c common European newt; d ghost-moth or other species of the *Hepialidae*; e reel for winding yarn.

swift-footed, adj. Moving on rapid feet, walking or running quickly; also fig. of time &c.

swift-handed, adj. a Quick and deft in action; b (fig., of justice, vengeance &c.) coming promptly, not delayed.

swiftlet, n. [1. swíftlet; 2. swíftlit]. **swift** (III.) & **-let**. Small kind of swift (*Cypselus*).

swiftly, adv. [1. swíftli; 2. swíftli]. **swift** (I.) & **-ly**. Rapidly, quickly.

swiftness, n. [1. swíftnes; 2. swíftnis]. See prec. & **-ness**. Quality of being swift; speed, rapidity, quickness.

swift-winged, adj. Flying on swift wings.

swig, vb. trans. & intrans. & n. [1. swig; 2. swig]. Etymol. unknown. (now, vulg. slang) 1. vb. a trans. (i.) To drink, esp. in large quantities; (ii.) cp. Dryden's usage: '*but the bleating lambs Securely swig the dug, beneath the Dams*' ('Æneid', ix. 72-3); b intrans., to imbibe drink. 2. n. Draught of liquor; a pull: *to take a swig at.*

swill (I.), vb. trans. & intrans. [1. swil; 2. swil]. O.E. *swilian*; M.E. *swilen*, 'to swill, wash'. A. trans. 1. To rinse, wash out, drench, with water; also *swill out.* 2. (vulg.) To drink large quantities of: *to swill beer.* B. intrans. To absorb liquor in large quantities, greedily.

swill (II.), n., fr. prec. 1. Act of swilling; rinse, wash. 2. Liquid mixture of kitchen refuse &c., as food for pigs &c.; wash. 3. Draught of liquor, esp. of poor quality.

swim (I.), vb. intrans. & trans. [1. swim; 2. swim]. O.E. *swimman*, 'to swim, float'; cp. O.H.G. *swimman*; O.N. *svimma*, 'to swim'; O.N. *svamla*, 'to swim'; cp. further Goth. *swumfsl*, 'pool'; *swamms*, 'sponge'; O.E. *sund*, 'swimming; sea'; see **sound** (V.). A. intrans. 1. (of living creatures) To proceed through water by movements of the limbs, tail, fins, or other parts of the body: *to swim across the river*; *to swim about in the sea*; *to swim on one's back*; *to swim under water.* Phrs. *to swim like a stone*, sink; *to swim with the tide, stream*, follow popular custom or convention; *sink or swim*, fail, be ruined, or succeed, prosper. 2. a To be supported upon surface of water, float: *the leaf swims down the river*; b to be supported, held in suspension: *specks of dust that swim in sunbeams.* 3. To move with or as with smooth, gliding, buoyant motion: '*like some watcher of the skies When a new planet swims into his ken*' (Keats, 'Chapman's Homer'). 4. To be deluged in, saturated with: *food swimming in butter.* 5. To overflow, be flooded, with: *eyes that swam with tears*; see **swim** (III.). B. trans. 1. To cause, compel, to swim: *to swim a horse across a river.* 2. To traverse by swimming: *to swim the Channel.* 3. To swim for (specified distance): *to swim a mile.* 4. a To engage in (swimming-race); b to oppose (person) in swimming-race.

swim (II.), n., fr. prec. 1. a Act of swimming: *to enjoy a swim*; b spell of swimming: *to go for a long swim.* Phr. *in the swim*, familiar with current events, tendencies, activities. 2. Deep pool in river, abounding in fish.

swim (III.), vb. intrans. Now felt as belonging to **swim** (I.), but partly influenced in meaning by obs. O.E. *swīma*, M.E. *swīme*, 'giddiness'; cp. **swindler**. 1. To feel giddy; to reel, spin: *his head swam.* 2. To produce a visual impression of revolving, rocking, oscillating; to be seen hazily, as through a mist by one who is giddy: *everything swam before his eyes.*

swimmer, n. [1. swímer; 2. swímə]. **swim** (I.) & **-er**. One who swims: *a poor, strong, swimmer.*

swimmeret, n. [1. swímeret; 2. swímərɛt]. Prec. & **-et**. Abdominal appendage used by crustacean for swimming.

swimming-bath, n. [1. swíming bàhth; 2. swímiŋ bāþ]. Large tank filled with water, usually under cover, used for swimming.

swimming-bell, n. Bell-like swimming organ of jelly-fish &c.

swimming-belt, n. Pneumatic belt for supporting a person in the water.

swimming-bladder, n. Fish's air-bladder; sound.

swimming-foot, n. Swimmeret.

swimmingly, adv. [1. swímingli; 2. swímiŋli], fr. Pres. Part. of **swim** (I.) & **-ly**. With easy, unhindered, progress; successfully, prosperously: *everything went swimmingly*; *to get on swimmingly.*

swimming-stone, n. Light, porous variety of quartz.

swindle (I.), vb. trans. & intrans. [1. swíndl; 2. swíndl]. Back-formation fr. **swindler**. 1. trans. a To cheat, defraud: *you've been swindled*; b to obtain (money, &c.) by swindling: *to swindle money out of a person.* 2. intrans. To practise swindling, to cheat.

swindle (II.), n., fr. prec. 1. Act of swindling; a fraudulent transaction: *he carried out a series of gigantic swindles.* 2. Something which is different from, and inferior to, what it is represented to be; something of which the nature and qualities have been deliberately misrepresented with intent to defraud; a take-in: *a cheap watch advertised as made of gold is usually a swindle.*

swindler, n. [1. swíndler; 2. swíndlə], fr. Germ. *schwindler*, 'one who plans extravagant schemes; swindler, cheat', fr. *schwindeln*, 'to be giddy', O.H.G. *swintilōn*, 'to be giddy'; cp. O.H.G. *swintan*, 'to be faint; to vanish'; cogn. w. O.E. *swīma*, 'dizziness', see **swim** (III.); O.N. *svīmi*, 'giddiness'. Person who swindles; a cheat, a sharper.

swindlingly, adv. [1. swíndlingli; 2. swíndliŋli], fr. Pres. Part. of **swindle** (I.) & **-ly**. By means of a swindle, fraudulently.

swine, n. [1. swīn; 2. swain]. O.E., M.E. *swīn*; cp. Germ. *schwein*; Goth. *swein*; cogn. w. Lat. *suīnus*, 'of swine', see **suilline**; O. Slav. *svinija*, 'swine'; Gk. *huénós*, 'of swine'. 1. (archaic in sing.) a Hoofed, omnivorous mammal, wild or domesticated, of subfamily *Suinae*, esp. of genus *Sus scrofa*; a pig; b (as pl.) pigs collectively: *a herd of swine*; *some sheep and several swine.* 2. Term of violent abuse; a detestable, disgusting person; one guilty of low, mean, or dishonourable conduct.

swine-bread, n. Truffle.

swine-fever, n. Contagious disease which attacks the lungs and intestines of domestic swine.

swineherd, n. [1. swínhërd; 2. swáinhʌ̄d]. Man in charge of swine.

swine-plague, n. Swine-fever.

swine-pox, n. Form of chicken-pox.

swinery, n. [1. swíneri; 2. swáinəri]. **swine** & **-ery**. Place in which swine are kept.

swine's-snout, n. Dandelion.

swing (**I.**), vb. intrans. & trans. [1. swing; 2. swiŋ]. O.E. *swingan*; M.E. *swingen*, 'to swing'; cp. O.S., O.H.G. *swingen*; Du. *zwenken*, 'to swing'; Goth. (*af*)*swaggwjan*, 'to cause to waver'. **A.** intrans. **1. a** To carry out the movement characteristic of a hanging object; to move backwards and forwards; to sway to and fro, oscillate: *to let one's legs swing*; *to swing by one hand from a branch*; *a lamp swung from a hook*; Phr. (slang) *to swing for* (a person), be hanged for murdering him; **b** specif. (as form of recreation) to move rhythmically backwards and forwards on a seat suspended by ropes &c. **2. a** To turn, move, on or as on a pivot or hinge: *the door swung open, back* &c.; *to swing to*, close; *he swung round on his heel*; *the ship swung slowly round*; **b** to move freely, as with the movements of water, about a fixed point: *the boat swings at her moorings*. **3.** To walk, run &c. with smooth, steady, easy, swaying motion: *the troops went swinging past.* **B.** trans. **1. a** To cause, allow, to swing; to impart swinging motion to; to wave to and fro: *to swing a cane, one's arms*; **b** to hold suspended and allow to dangle: *to swing a parcel from one's finger*; *to swing a lamp from the ceiling*; Phr. *no room, not large enough, to swing a cat* (*in*), (of room, enclosed space) very small and confined; *to swing the lead*, soldiers' and sailors' slang, to pretend to work hard, to malinger; **c** to cause to swing to and fro, in regular curves &c., as a form of exercise: *to swing Indian clubs*; **d** to give a rhythmic motion to (person &c.) on a swing, in a hammock &c., by pushing or pulling. **2.** To sling, hoist, up, with a rapid swinging motion: *to swing a child on to one's shoulder.* **3.** To cause to wheel from a fixed point, to cause to move on or as on a pivot: *to swing a battalion into line*; *the tide swung the boat round on its moorings.*

swing (**II.**), n., fr. prec. **1.** Act, process, of swinging; swinging movement, motion to and fro; **a** *the swing of a pendulum*; Phr. *the swing of the pendulum*, inevitable ebb and flow, action and reaction, in human affairs, opinions &c.; *in full swing*, at the height of activity or operation; **b** mode of swinging, e.g. in playing golf, tennis &c. **2.** Free, easy, swaying gait: *to walk with a swing.* **3.** Rhythm, rhythmic movement: *the swing of music, verse, a dance*; Phr. *to go with a swing*, (i.) (of a tune, verse &c.) run with easy, rapid movement; (ii.) (fig., of an event, organized action, entertainment &c.) to pass off satisfactorily, cheerfully, with zest &c. **4.** Freedom to swing without obstruction or hindrance. **5.** Specif. **a** apparatus consisting of a seat &c. suspended by ropes &c., on which one may sit and swing backwards and forwards as recreation; **b** act of swinging in such an apparatus; **c** spell of such swinging. **6.** Distance swung, compass of swing; sweep.

swing-boat, n. Boat-shaped swing with seats for two or more persons.

swing-bridge, n. Bridge moving on a pivot to allow passage of boats &c.

swinge, vb. trans. [1. swinj; 2. swíndž]. O.E. *swengan*, fr. **swang-jan*, 'to strike, fling aside'; cp. Goth. (*af*)*swaggwjan*, 'to cause to waver'; see **swing** (**I.**). (archaic) To strike, give heavy blow to.

swingeing, adj. [1. swínjing; 2. swíndžiŋ], fr. Pres. Part. of prec. **1.** (of blow &c.) Heavy, forcible. **2.** (colloq.) Large, huge, very considerable.

swinging, adj. [1. swínging; 2. swíŋiŋ], fr. Pres. Part. of **swing** (**I.**). Having, performed with, a swing; **a** rapid, vigorous; active, buoyant: *a swinging stride*; **b** lilting, leaping, swiftly moving: *a swinging rhythm.*

swingingly, adv. Prec. & **-ly.** With a swing.

swingle, n. & vb. trans. [1. swínggl; 2. swíŋgl]. swing (I.) & **-le. 1.** n. Wooden instrument used for beating flax to separate woody part from fibre. **2.** vb. To dress flax by beating with a swingle.

swingle-tree, n. Horizontal bar to which traces, chains &c. of cart, plough &c. are attached; whipple-tree.

swingling-tow, n. [1. swíngglìng tō; 2. swíŋgliŋ tòu]. Coarse, woody part of flax.

swing-plough, n. Plough without wheels.

swinish, adj. [1. swínish; 2. swáiniʃ]. **swine** & **-ish.** Resembling, befitting, swine.

swinishly, adv. Prec. & **-ly.** In a swinish manner.

swinishness, n. See prec. & **-ness.** State or quality of being swinish; disgusting, mean, or dishonourable conduct.

swink, vb. intrans. & n. [1. swingk; 2. swiŋk]. O.E. *swincan*, 'to work'; M.E. *swinken.* (obs. or deliberately archaic) **1.** vb. To toil, labour. **2.** n. Toil, drudgery.

swipe (**I.**), vb. intrans. & trans. [1. swīp; 2. swaip]. O.E. *swīpian*, 'to beat, vibrate'; cp. O.E. *swipe*, 'whip; stroke'; O.N. *svipa*, 'whip'; see **swift** (**I.**); **sweep** (**I.**). **1.** intrans. **a** To hit hard, deliver a powerful blow, esp. at cricket; **b** *swipe at*, to aim a powerful blow at, hit out wildly at. **2.** trans. To strike (ball) hard with a bat.

swipe (**II.**), n., fr. prec. Strong, violent blow, given with full swing of arm.

swipes, n. [1. swīps; 2. swaips]. Prob. fr. prec. in obs. sense, 'drink off'. Weak, muddy, inferior beer.

swirl (**I.**), vb. intrans. & trans. [1. swërl; 2. swʌ̄l], fr. O.N. *svirla*, 'to whirl', fr. *sverra*, 'to whirl; to hum'; cp. Germ. *schwirren*, 'to buzz', cogn. w. **swarm** (**I.**). **1.** intrans. (of spray, water, dust, snow) To be whirled, or whisked, into an eddy; to eddy; to revolve rapidly and in spirals. **2.** (rare) trans. To cause to swirl; to whirl.

swirl (**II.**), n., fr. prec. **1.** Eddying motion of water, snow &c. **2.** Swift, darting movement of fish through water.

swish (**I.**), vb. trans. & intrans. [1. swish; 2. swiʃ]. Imitative. **A.** trans. **1.** To whirl, flirt, flick, quickly through the air with an audible, whistling sound: *the cow swished her tail.* **2. a** To thrash, strike, flog; **b** *swish off*, to strike, cut, off, with a swishing blow. **B.** intrans. To pass, cut, through the air with sweeping movement and whistling, hissing, sound: *the sword-blade swished past my ear.*

swish (**II.**), n., fr. prec. **1.** Sharp, whistling, hissing sound produced by slender, flexible body moving quickly through the air. **2.** Quick movement producing swishing sound: *a swish of a cow's tail.*

Swiss (**I.**), adj. [1. swis; 2. swis], fr. Fr. *suisse*, fr. M.H.G. *swiz.* Pertaining to Switzerland, its inhabitants or dialects.

Swiss (**II.**), n., fr. prec. **1. a** Native of Switzerland; **b** one of the German, French, or Italian dialects spoken in Switzerland. **2.** Specif. **a** a Swiss porter, or guard, formerly employed by the French kings, now only by the Pope; **b** a porter or guard generally.

swiss-roll, n. Thin layer of light, spongy cake spread with jam and rolled up while hot.

switch (**I.**), n. [1. swich; 2. switʃ]. Perh. partly imitative of sound; cp. also M. Du. *swick*, 'whip'. **1. a** Small, slender, flexible shoot, twig, rod; **b** specif., such a rod used as a riding-whip. **2.** Tress of false hair, fastened at one end. **3.** Device for making or breaking electric circuit or transferring current. **4.** Device for moving short section of railway-line, to allow train &c. to pass from one track to another.

switch (**II.**), vb. trans. & intrans., fr. prec. **A.** trans. **1.** To strike, lash with switch or other slender, flexible object. **2.** To move, swing, with a quick jerk or flick; to whisk: *the horse switched its tail.* **3. a** To transfer, shift, (train) to another track; **b** to make or break electric or other similar circuit: *to switch electric light on, off*; *to switch* (*person*) *on, off*, make, break, telephone connexion for. **B.** intrans. **a** To transfer, be transferred to another track; **b** to turn (electric current) by means of a switch; (also fig.) *to switch off to another line of thought.* Phr. *to switch off*, cut off telephone connexion.

switchback, n. [1. swíchbak; 2. swítʃbæk]. **1.** Railway laid in zigzags to facilitate ascension by trains of very steep slope. **2.** Steeply undulating track up and down which a car moves on runners or rollers, at great speed, by its own impetus; form of amusement at fairs &c.

switchboard, n. [1. swíchbord; 2. swítʃbɔ̄d]. Set of switches, at a telephone exchange, for connecting a series of electric circuits.

switch-lever, n. Lever for operating a switch.

switch-man, n. Man working railway switches.

switch-signal, n. Device, usually automatic, for indicating position of railway switch.

Switzer, n. [1. swítser; 2. swítsə], fr. Swiss-Germ. form corresponding to Germ. *Schweizer*, fr. *Schweiz*, 'Switzerland', & **-er.** (archaic) Swiss native.

swivel (**I.**), n. [1. swívl; 2. swívl], fr. next word. Part of an attachment made to turn round, such as the shank of a hook which turns in a ring, being secured by a nut or bolt from slipping through.

swivel (**II.**), vb. intrans. & trans., fr. O.E. *swīfan*, 'to move, turn', see **swift** (**I.**), **sweep** (**I.**), & **-le.** To turn on or as on a swivel.

swivel-eye, n. (colloq.) An eye which looks in a different direction when the other is directed on an object; an eye with a strong cast.

swivel-gun, n. Gun mounted on a pivot.

swob, n. [1. swob; 2. swɔb]. Variant of **swab.**

swollen, vb. [1. swṓlen; 2. swóulən]. O.E. (*ġe*)*swollen*; M.E. *swollen*; P.P. of **swell.**

swoon (**I.**), vb. intrans. [1. swōōn; 2. swūn]. M.E. *swōghnen*, *swownen*, 'to swoon', fr. O.E. *swōgan*, 'to sigh, sough', see **sough.** **1.** To faint, be overcome by syncope. **2.** (poet., of sound) To fade gradually, die away.

swoon (**II.**), n., fr. prec. Fainting-fit.

swooningly, adv. [1. swṓōningli; 2. swū́niŋli]. Pres. Part. of **swoon** (**I.**) & **-ly.** As though swooning; in a die-away manner.

swoop (**I.**), vb. intrans. & trans. [1. swōōp; 2. swūp]. O.E. *swāpan*, q.v. under **sweep** (**I.**), M.E. *swōpen*, w. alteration of *ō* due to the influence of *w-.* **1.** intrans. To sweep, pounce down suddenly and impetuously, descend in sudden attack (esp. of bird of prey): *the eagle was about to swoop, swooped,* (*down*) *upon its prey*; *the robbers swooped down on the unsuspecting travellers.* **2.** trans. (colloq.) Usually *swoop up*, to snatch up, seize with sweeping motion.

swoop (**II.**), n., fr. prec. Act of swooping; sudden, swift, sweeping descent of, or as of, bird of prey.

swop, swap (**I.**), vb. trans. & intrans. [1. swop; 2. swɔp]. Prob. fr. M.E. *swappen*, 'to strike', fr. *swap*, O.E. *swāp*, 'blow'; cp. O.N. *svipa*, 'whip'; see **sweep** (**I.**), **swift** (**I.**). **1.** trans. To give as reciprocal equivalents; to exchange: *to swop hats*; *to swop yarns*; *to swop a penknife for a guinea-pig.* Now colloquial, but formerly in literary use in this sense, cp. Dryden, 'Cleomenes': '*I would have swopped Youth for old age*'. **2.** intrans. To carry out an exchange.

swop, swap (**II.**), n., fr. prec. Act of swopping; exchange.

sword, n. [1. sord; 2. sɔ̄d]. O.E. *sweord*, *sword*; M.E. *swerd*; cp. O. Fris. *swerd*; O.H.G. *swert*; O.N. *sverðr*; Du. *zwaard.* **1.** Cutting and thrusting weapon of attack and defence, with a long blade, sharpened on one or both edges, fixed in a hilt; *cavalry sword*, sabre; *duelling-*, *small-sword*, light, straight, triangular-bladed sword; *sword of state*, sword carried before sovereign on state occasions. Phrs. *sword of Damocles*, a danger which is constantly threatening; *fire and sword*, general destruction by invading army; *at the point of the sword*, under compulsion, under threat of death; *to cross, measure, swords with*, to oppose; *to draw, sheathe, the sword*, to begin, end, hostilities; *to put to the sword*, kill, massacre. **2.** *The sword*, military methods or power; warfare.

sword-arm, n. That used in wielding a sword, the right arm.
sword-bayonet, n. Bayonet with a handle and a sword-like blade, capable of being used as sword.
sword-bearer, n. Official carrying a sword before the sovereign at ceremonies.
sword-belt, n. Belt to which sword-sheath is attached.
sword-bill, n. South American humming-bird with long, slender beak.
sword-cane, n. Sword-stick.
sword-cut, n. **a** Cut delivered by sword-blade; **b** scar left by this.
sword-dance, n. Dance in which swords are used, esp. one with elaborate steps performed in and out between the blades of two crossed swords laid on the ground.
sword-dollar, n. Scottish silver coin of James VI., with a sword on the reverse.
sworded, adj. [1. sórded; 2. sɔ̃did]. **sword & -ed.** Having, equipped with, a sword.
sword-fish, n. Large ocean fish, *Xiphias*, allied to the mackerel, with upper jaw elongated to form a long sword-like projection.
sword-flag, n. Water-flag, yellow iris.
sword-flighted, adj. [1. sórd flīted; 2. sɔ̃d flàitid]. (of bird) Having wing-feathers of distinct colour, producing effect of a sword at the side when folded.
sword-grass, n. Kind of sedge.
sword-guard, n. Part of a sword-hilt which protects the hand.
sword-hand, n. Hand used in wielding sword; the right hand.
sword-knot, n. Loop of leather attached to the hilt of a sword, through which the hand is passed when grasping the sword for use, so that if the grasp be relaxed the sword is not dropped, but can be seized again; a sword-knot may also be purely ornamental and made of gold wire.
sword-law, n. Military rule.
swordless, adj. [1. sórdles; 2. sɔ̃dlis]. **sword & -less.** Without, not relying upon, a sword.
sword-like, adj. **sword & -like.** Resembling a sword in shape, keenness &c.
sword-lily, n. Gladiolus.
sword-play, n. Fencing.
sword-proof, adj. Not liable to be pierced by sword.
swordsman, n. [1. sórdzman; 2. sɔ̃dzmən]. Man skilled in use of sword; skilful fencer.
swordsmanship, n. [1. sórdzmanship; 2. sɔ̃dzmənʃip]. Prec. & **-ship.** Skill in the use of the sword.
sword-stick, n. Hollow walking-stick containing a thin sword-blade.
swore, vb. [1. swōr; 2. swɔ̃]. O.E. *swōr*, M.E. *swōr*, Pret. of **swear.**
sworn, adj. [1. sworn; 2. swɔ̃n], fr. P.P. of **swear**; O.E., M.E. *sworen*. Under a vow, pledged: *sworn brothers, friends; sworn enemies*, bitter, irreconcilable.
swot, vb. intrans. & n. [1. swot; 2. swɔt]. Prob. a variant of **sweat.** (slang) **1.** vb. To work hard, toil. **2.** n. Hard mental work, drudgery.
swum, vb. [1. swum; 2. swam]. P.P. of **swim**; O.E. (*ģe*)*swummen*; M.E. *swumme*(*n*).
swung, vb. [1. swung; 2. swaŋ]. Pret. & P.P. of **swing**; O.E. (*ģe*)*swungen*, P.P.; M.E. *swunge*(*n*).
sy-, pref. representing Gk. **syn-** before *s* & consonant, or *z*; e.g. *system, systole, syzygy.*
sybarite, n. & adj. [1. síbarīt; 2. síbərait], fr. Lat. *Sybarīta*, fr. Gk. *Subarítēs*, inhabitant of Sybaris, in Italy, near the Gulf of Tarentum, noted for the luxury of the inhabitants. **1.** n. Person given up to luxury and effeminacy. **2.** adj. Luxurious and effeminate.
sybaritic, adj. [1. sìbarítik; 2. sìbərítik]. Prec. & **-ic.** Pertaining to, characteristic of, a sybarite.
sybaritically, adv. [1. sìbarítikali; 2. sìbərítikəli]. Prec. & **-al** & **-ly.** In a sybaritic manner.
sybaritism, n. [1. síbarītizm; 2. síbəraitizəm]. **sybarite & -ism.** Sybaritic life or habits.
sybil, n. See **sibyl.**
sycamine, n. [1. síkamin, -mīn; 2. síkəmin, -main], fr. Lat. *sȳcamīnus*, fr. Gk. *sūkámīnos*, Semitic loan-word, influenced by Gk. *sūkon*, 'fig', see **syconium**; cp. Heb. *šiqmā*, 'mulberry'. Black mulberry.
sycamore, n. [1. síkamōr; 2. síkəmɔ̃], fr. Lat. *sȳcomorus*, fr. Gk. *sūkómoros*, 'mulberry tree', prob. of Semitic origin, see prec., influenced by Gk. *sûkon*, 'fig', see **syconium,** *móron*, 'mulberry', see under **mulberry. 1.** Also *sycamore fig*, Egyptian and Syrian tree of fig family. **2.** Also *sycamore maple*, broad-leaved maple of Northern Europe.
syce, sice, n. [1. sīs; 2. sais]. Hind., fr. Arab. An Indian groom.
sycee, n. [1. sīsḗ; 2. saisí], fr. Chinese *si szĕ*, 'fine silk'. Ingots of silver, varying in size, used in China as medium of exchange; also *sycee silver.*
sychnocarpous, adj. [1. sìknōkárpus; 2. sìknoukā́pəs], fr. Gk. *sukhnós*, 'many; frequent; dense, compact', earlier **tuk-sno-*, fr. stem **twekʷ-, *tukʷ-*, seen in Gk. *sáttein*, 'to pack, press; to equip'; & Gk. *karpós*, 'fruit', see **carpel.** (bot.) Producing fruit for several seasons; perennial.
syconium, n. [1. sī-, sikónium; 2. sai-, sikóuniəm]. Mod. Lat., fr. Gk. *sûkon*, 'fig', prob. borrowed fr. a Mediterranean language. Fleshy fruit with seeds borne in a hollow receptacle, as in the fig.
sycophancy, n. [1. síkofansi; 2. síkəfənsi]. Next word & **-cy.** Character, method, practice, of a sycophant.
sycophant, n. [1. síkofant; 2. síkəfənt], fr. Lat. *sȳcophanta*, fr. Gk. *sūkophántēs*, 'informer', perh. orig. 'one who informed against persons exporting figs', fr. *sûkon*, 'fig', see **syconium,** & *-phant-*, fr. stem of *phaínein*, 'to show', see **phantasm.** Servile flatterer, toady.
sycophantic, adj. [1. sìkofántik; 2. sìkəfǽntik]. Prec. & **-ic.** Of, pertaining to, characteristic of, a sycophant.
sycosis, n. [1. sī-, sikṓsis; 2. sai-, sikóusis], fr. Lat., fr. Gk. *sukōsis*, 'fig-shaped ulcer', fr. *sûkon*, 'fig', see **syconium,** & **-osis.** Eruption on scalp or bearded part of face; barber's itch.
syenite, n. [1. síenīt; 2. sáiinait], fr. Lat. *Syēnītes* (*lapis*), a kind of red granite, fr. *Syēnē*, in Upper Egypt. Crystalline, igneous, alkaline rock containing little or no quartz.
syenitic, adj. [1. sìenítik; 2. sàiinítik]. Prec. & **-ic.** Pertaining to, resembling, syenite.
syl-, pref. representing Gk. **syn-** before *-l*; e.g. *syllable, syllogism.*
syllabary, n. [1. sílabari; 2. síləbəri], fr. Lat. *syllaba*, 'syllable', see **syllable** (**I.**), & **-ary.** List of syllabic characters used in some languages in place of an alphabet.
syllabic, adj. [1. silábik; 2. silǽbik], fr. Lat. *syllaba*, 'syllable', see **syllable** (**I.**), & **-ic. 1.** Connected with, pertaining to, a syllable. **2.** Representing a syllable: *syllabic character, symbol.* **3.** Forming, constituting, a separate syllable: *the sound l is syllabic in 'bottle'.*
syllabically, adv. [1. silábikali; 2. silǽbikəli]. Prec. & **-al** & **-ly.** In a syllabic manner; according to syllables; syllable by syllable.
syllabicate, vb. trans. [1. silábikāt; 2. silǽbikeit]. **syllabic & -ate. 1.** To divide into syllables. **2.** To articulate syllable by syllable.
syllabication, n. [1. silàbikā́shun; 2. silæ̀bikéiʃən]. Prec. & **-ion.** Act of syllabicating; state of being syllabicated.
syllabification, n. [1. silàbifikā́shun; 2. silæ̀bifikéiʃən]. See next word & **-fication.** Syllabication.
syllabify, vb. trans. [1. silábifi; 2. silǽbifai], fr. Lat. *syllaba*, 'syllable', see **syllable** (**I.**) & *-i-* & **-fy.** To treat, pronounce, as a syllable.
syllabize, vb. trans. [1. sílabīz; 2. síləbaiz], fr. Lat. *syllaba*, 'syllable', see **syllable** (**I.**), & **-ize.** To syllabify.
syllable (**I.**), n. [1. sílabl; 2. síləbl]. M.E., fr. O. Fr. *sillabe*, fr. Lat. *syllaba*, fr. Gk. *sullabḗ*, 'that which holds together; syllable', fr. **syl-** & *lab-*, stem of *lambánein*, 'to take, seize', cogn. w. Scrt. *lábhatē, rábhatē*, 'seizes'; *rábhaš*, 'vehemence'; Lat. *rabiēs*, 'rage, madness'; see **rabid, catalepsy,** & **-le. 1. a** Any sound or combination of sounds, the utterance of which produces upon the ear the impression of an unbroken unity, the principal condition of which is that the sonority shall be either gradually reduced or gradually increased during the utterance, but not reduced and then increased again; such a new increase would constitute a fresh syllable; **b** graphic representation of a syllable. **2.** Verbal utterance; in such Phr. as: *he never uttered a syllable*, did not speak at all; *I don't understand a syllable of what you say*, I understand nothing.
syllable (**II.**), vb. trans., fr. prec. **1.** To pronounce syllable by syllable. **2.** To utter, pronounce: '*Airy tongues that syllable men's names*' (Milton, 'Comus', 208).
syllabled, adj. [1. sílabld; 2. síləbld]. **syllable** (**I.**) & **-ed.** Having specified number of syllables: *a three-syllabled word.*
syllabub, n. See **sillabub.**
syllabus, n. [1. sílabus; 2. síləbəs], fr. L. Lat. *syllabus*, fr. Gk. *súllabos*, 'list, syllabus', fr. *sullambánein*, 'to gather together', fr. **syl-** & *lambánein*, 'to take', see **syllable** (**I.**). **1. a** An outline, summary, containing the principal subjects to be dealt with in a course of lectures or other form of instruction; programme of studies; **b** such course of instruction &c. itself. **2.** (R.C. Ch.) Summary of decrees of Roman Curia; specif. (cap.) list of eighty heretical doctrines &c. given in the encyclical letter of Pius IX., 1864.
syllepsis, n. [1. silépsis, silḗpsis; 2. silépsis, silípsis]. Lat. *syllepsis*, fr. Gk. *súllēpsis*, 'a taking together, comprehension', fr. **syl-** & **lēp-*, a form of the base of *lambánein*, 'to take, seize', see **syllable** (**I.**). Figure of rhetoric in which a word is used in two different senses at the same time, esp. in both a literal and a metaphorical sense; e.g. *his temper was as short as his coat-tails.*
sylleptic, adj. [1. siléptik; 2. siléptik], fr. Gk. *sullēpt-*, see prec., & **-ic.** Pertaining to, forming, of the nature of, a syllepsis.
sylleptically, adv. [1. siléptikali; 2. siléptikəli]. Prec. & **-al** & **-ly.** By means of syllepsis.
syllogism, n. [1. sílojìzm; 2. sílədžìzəm], fr. Lat. *syllogismus*, fr. Gk. *sullogismós*, 'conclusion, inference from premises', fr. *sullogízomai*, 'to collect, bring before the mind, sum up, draw conclusions', fr. **syl-** & *logízomai*, 'to reckon, compute; to conclude, infer', fr. *lógos*, 'word, speech, thought', see **logos.** (log.) Formal statement of an argument, consisting of three propositions, called respectively the major and minor premises and the conclusion; e.g. *water is wet; rain is water; therefore rain is wet.*
syllogistic, adj. [1. silojístik; 2. silədžístik], fr. adj. stem of Gk. *sullogizomai*, 'to infer', see prec., & **-ic.** Pertaining to, of the nature of, in form of, a syllogism.
syllogistically, adv. [1. silojístikali; 2. silədžístikəli]. Prec. & **-al** & **-ly.** In a syllogistic manner or form.
syllogize, vb. intrans. & trans. [1. sílojīz; 2. sílədžaiz], fr. Gk. *sullogízomai*, 'to infer', see **syllogism. 1.** intrans. To reason by syllogisms. **2.** trans. To put into syllogistic form.
sylph, n. [1. silf; 2. silf], fr Fr. *sylphe*, perh. fr. Gk. *sílphē*, 'insect, beetle, bookworm'; etymol. doubtful. **1.** Air-spirit, elemental spirit existing in the air. **2.** Slender, graceful woman. **3.** Humming-bird with long, brightly coloured tail.
sylph-like, adj. Prec. & **-like.** Resembling a sylph; slender and graceful.
sylvan, adj. See **silvan.**
sym-, pref. representing Gk. *sum-*; form of **syn-**, before *b-, p-, m-*; e.g. *symbol; symmetry.*

symbion(t), n. [1. símbion(t); 2. símbiən(t)], fr. Gk. *sumbiōn*, stem *sumbiōnt-*, Pres. Part. of *sumbióein*, 'to live together', fr. **sym-** & *bíos*, 'life', see **bio-**. Organism living in symbiosis.

symbiosis, n. [1. sìmbiōsis; 2. sìmbaióusis], fr. Gk. *sumbiōn*, see prec., & **-osis**. (biol.) A living together, in intimate relation, for purposes of nutrition, of two dissimilar organisms; a form of parasitism.

symbiotic, adj. [1. sìmbiótik; 2. sìmbiɔ́tik]. See prec. & **-otic**. Pertaining to, characterized by, symbiosis.

symbiotically, adv. [1. sìmbiótikali; 2. sìmbiɔ́tikəli]. Prec. & **-al** & **-ly**. By means of symbiosis.

symbol, n. [1. símbl; 2. símbl], fr. Fr. *symbole*, fr. Lat. *symbola*, fr. Gk. *súmbolon*, 'token; pledge; covenant', fr. *sumbállein*, 'to throw together, unite; to compare; to correspond', fr. **sym-** & *bállein*, 'to throw', see **ballistic**. **1.** Something which represents or typifies another thing, quality &c.; outward sign, emblem of a person, cause, quality, principle, ideal &c.: *the owl was the symbol of Minerva*; *a circle is the symbol of eternity*; *a cross is the symbol of Christianity*. **2.** Specif., a graphic character, letter, figure, sign, used to express a sound, a mathematical quantity &c.

symbolic(al), adj. [1. sìmbólik(l); 2. sìmbɔ́lik(l)]. Prec. & **-ic** & **-al**. Of, pertaining to, serving as, a symbol.

symbolically, adv. Prec. & **-ly**. In a symbolic manner; by means of a symbol.

symbolics, n. [1. sìmbóliks; 2. sìmbɔ́liks]. **symbol** & **-ics**. Study of symbols.

symbolism, n. [1. símbolizm; 2. símbəlizəm]. **symbol** & **-ism**. **1.** Representation by symbols. **2.** System or group of symbols representing specific group of ideas &c.: *religious symbolism* &c. **3.** Doctrines of a certain 19th cent. school of French poets and painters, denoting revulsion from the realistic or naturalistic school.

symbolist, n. [1. símbolist; 2. símbəlist]. **symbol** & **-ist**. **a** Person who is versed in the use of symbols; **b** person who makes use of symbols; **c** member of the French school of symbolism in art and literature.

symbolization, n. [1. sìmbolīzáshun; 2. sìmbəlaizéiʃən]. Next word & **-ation**. Act of symbolizing; state of being symbolized.

symbolize, vb. trans. [1. símboliz; 2. símbəlaiz]. **symbol** & **-ize**. **1.** To be a symbol of, typify, represent symbolically: *the peacock symbolizes pride*. **2.** To represent by a symbol: *how shall we symbolize cunning?*

symbology, n. [1. simbóloji; 2. simbɔ́lədži]. **symbol** & **-logy**. Study of symbols; art of symbolic representation.

symbololatry, n. [1. símbolólatri; 2. símbəlɔ́lətri]. **symbol** & *-o-* & **-latry**. Worship of symbols; excessive reverence given to symbols.

symbolology, n. [1. símbolóloji; 2. símbəlɔ́lədži]. **symbol** & *-o-* & **-logy**. Symbology.

symmetrian, n. [1. simétrian; 2. simétriən]. **symmetry** & **-an**. Symmetrist.

symmetric(al), adj. [1. simétrik(l); 2. simétrik(l)]. **symmetry** & **-ic** & **-al**. Having, exhibiting, the quality of symmetry; duly proportioned, harmonious; conforming exactly in opposite parts.

symmetrically, adv. Prec. & **-ly**. In a symmetrical manner.

symmetrician, n. [1. sìmetríshan; 2. sìmitríʃən]. **symmetry** & **-ician**. Symmetrist.

symmetrist, n. [1. símetrist; 2. símitrist]. **symmetry** & **-ist**. Person who is careful of, insistent on, symmetry.

symmetrization, n. [1. sìmetrīzáshun; 2. sìmitraizéiʃən]. Next word & **-ation**. Act of symmetrizing; symmetrical construction or arrangement.

symmetrize, vb. trans. [1. símetrīz; 2. símitraiz]. **symmetry** & **-ize**. To make symmetrical; construct, arrange, symmetrically.

symmetrophobia, n. [1. simétrofóbia; 2. simétrəfóubiə]. **symmetry** & *-o-* & **-phobia**. Fear, dislike, or avoidance of symmetry, esp. in architecture.

symmetry, n. [1. símetri; 2. símitri], fr. O. Fr. *symmetrie*, fr. Lat. *symmetria*, fr. Gk. *summetría*, 'symmetry, due proportion', fr. *súmmetros*, 'commensurate; in due proportion; symmetrical', fr. **sym-** & *métron*, 'measure', see **metre**. **1.** Such due proportion of the parts of a body or structure in relation to each other as conveys an impression of fitness and beauty, and produces a sense of pleasure. **2.** Correspondence, similarity in or between the opposing sides of an object, considered as halves on either side of a central line, in form and dimensions: *the symmetry of a face is marred by a bulge in one cheek*.

sympalmograph, n. [1. simpálmograhf; 2. simpǽlməgrāf], fr. **sym-** & Gk. *palm-(ós)*, 'vibration', fr. *pállein*, 'to shake, throw', cogn. w. Gk. *pelemízein*, 'to shake, move violently', *pólemos*, 'fight, struggle' (see **polemic**); & *-o-* & **-graph**. Instrument recording sound-vibrations.

sympathetic (I.), adj. [1. sìmpathétik; 2. sìmpəþétik], fr. Gk. *sumpathētikós*, 'sympathetic'; **sym-** & **pathetic**. **1.** Pertaining to sympathy; feeling, expressing, sympathy; arising from sympathy: *a sympathetic person, look, nature, understanding* &c.; *sympathetic words*. **2.** In accordance with one's sympathies; consonant with one's tastes, feelings, opinions &c.; hence, congenial: *to live in sympathetic surroundings*. **3.** *Sympathetic vibrations*, such as are set up indirectly by those occurring in another vibrating body, and transmitted by the air or other medium. **4.** *Sympathetic sensation*, one due to an indirect stimulus applied at a different point from that at which it is felt; *sympathetic nerve*, one of the smaller nervous ganglia which connect the main nerves of the cerebro-spinal system. **5.** *Sympathetic ink*, one which is invisible until exposed to heat, or treated with a chemical reagent.

sympathetic (II.), n., fr. prec. **1.** Sympathetic nerve. **2.** Person yielding easily to hypnotic influence.

sympathetically, adv. [1. sìmpathétikali; 2. sìmpəþétikəli]. Prec. & **-al** & **-ly**. In a sympathetic manner.

sympathize, vb. intrans. [1. símpathīz; 2. símpəþaiz]. **sympathy** & **-ize**. **1.** To feel sympathy; to be affected by similar or corresponding ideas or emotions: *to sympathize with a person in his grief or in his joy*; *I can quite sympathize with your delight at your success*; *my father never sympathized with my desire to see the world*. **2.** To express sympathy; to speak sympathetically; to condole, commiserate.

sympathizer, n. [1. símpathīzer; 2. símpəþaizə]. Prec. & **-er**. **1.** One who sympathizes; **a** person who shares another's opinions &c.; an adherent, supporter; **b** one who supports a cause, movement &c. **2.** Person who shares the afflictions &c. of another, who expresses sympathy, who gives consolation.

sympathy, n. [1. símpathi; 2. símpəþi], fr. Lat. *sympathīa*, fr. Gk. *sumpátheia*, 'fellow-feeling, sympathy', fr. *sympathés*, 'sympathizing with', fr. **sym-** & *páthos*, 'suffering', see **pathos**. **1.** Community, identity, of feeling; fellow-feeling; **a** agreement with another in tastes, opinions, aspirations, or with the tastes and opinions, aspirations, of another: *I have every sympathy with you in your love of country life*, or *with your love* &c.; *he had small sympathy with the idle and frivolous*, or *with idleness and frivolity*; Phr. *in, out of, sympathy with*, in, out of, agreement with; **b** conformity of temperament, spiritual harmony, and understanding: *perfect sympathy should exist between husband and wife*. **2.** Specif. **a** the sharing of another's grief, sorrow, misery, misfortune &c.; feeling of compassion and pity, tenderness, aroused by the sufferings of others: *his infirmities and poverty could but excite sympathy in those who knew him*; *one should feel sympathy for* (or *with*) *misfortune even when it arises from misconduct*; *a man of ready sympathies*; **b** expression of sympathy; condolence, commiseration, consolation: *letters and messages of sympathy*. **3.** (physiol.) Increase or diminution of activity in an organ as a result of a similar condition in another organ. **4.** (phys.) **a** Correlation existing between vibrating bodies whereby the vibrations of one are transmitted indirectly to the other through a medium; **b** tendency of certain substances to act one upon the other, or to unite, e.g. the attraction of a magnet for steel.

sympelmous, adj. [1. simpélmus; 2. simpélməs], fr. **sym-** & Gk. *pélma*, 'sole of foot', see under **film** (I.), & **-ous**. (of bird) Having the flexor tendons united.

sympetalous, adj. [1. simpétalus; 2. simpétələs]. **sym-** & **petal** & **-ous**. (bot.) With petals united.

symphonic, adj. [1. simfónik; 2. simfɔ́nik]. **symphony** & **-ic**. Pertaining to, resembling, in the form of, a symphony.

symphonious, adj. [1. simfónius; 2. simfóuniəs]. Next word & **-ous**. Characterized by harmony of sound; harmonious.

symphony, n. [1. símfuni; 2. símfəni], fr. O. Fr. *symphonie*, fr. Lat. *symphōnia*, fr. Gk. *sumphōnía*, 'concord of sound; harmony', fr. *súmphōnos*, 'agreeing in sound', fr. **sym-** & *phōnḗ*, 'sound', see **phone** (I.). **1.** (archaic) Harmony of sounds, harmonious blending of sound. **2.** (mus.) Sonata for an orchestra; orchestral composition in two or more contrasted movements.

symphoricarpous, adj. [1. sìmforikárpus; 2. sìmfɔrikápəs], fr. **sym-** & Gk. *phorós*, 'bearing', see **-phore**, & Gk. *karpós*, 'fruit', see **carpel**, & **-ous**. Bearing fruit in clusters.

symphyllous, adj. [1. simfílus; 2. simfíləs], fr. **sym-** & Gk. *phúll-(on)*, 'leaf', see **phyllo-**, & **-ous**. Having leaves united.

symphyseal, adj. [1. simfízeal; 2. simfíziəl]. See next word & **-al**. Pertaining to a symphysis.

symphysis, n. [1. símfisis; 2. símfisis]. Gk. *súmphusis*, 'a growing together', fr. **sym-** & Gk. *phúsis*, 'nature, form, development', fr. *phúein*, 'to grow', see **physic** (I.). Union, line of junction, between two parts of the skeleton, directly or by means of connecting cartilage &c.

sympiesometer, n. [1. sìmpiezómeter; 2. sìmpiizɔ́mitə], fr. Gk. *sympíes-(is)*, 'compression', fr. *sympiézein*, 'to compress', fr. **sym-** & *piézein*, 'to compress', see **piezometer**; & *-o-* & **-meter**. **a** Instrument measuring velocity or force of current of water; **b** barometer indicating atmospheric pressure by compression of gas in a tube.

sympodium, n. [1. simpódium; 2. simpóudiəm]. Mod. Lat., fr. **sym-** & Gk. *pódion*, dimin. of *poûs*, stem *pod-*, 'a foot', see **pedal** (I.). (bot.) Apparent main stem composed of a succession of branches.

symposiac, adj. [1. sìmpóziak; 2. sìmpóuziæk]. See **symposium** & **-ac**. Symposial.

symposial, adj. [1. simpózial; 2. simpóuziəl]. See **symposium** & **-al**. Of, pertaining to, a symposium.

symposiarch, n. [1. simpóziárk, simpóziàrk; 2. simpóuziàk, simpóziàk], fr. Gk. *symposiarkh-(os)*, 'symposiarch', fr. *sumpósion*, see next word, & *arkhós*, 'leader', see **arch-**. Director of a symposium; toast-master.

symposium, n. [1. simpózium, simpózium; 2. simpóuziəm, simpóziəm]. Lat., fr. Gk. *sumpósion*, 'drinking-party', fr. **sym-** & *pósis*, 'drinking', cogn. w. Lat. *pōtio*, see under **potion**. **1. a** Drinking-feast, often with music &c., following dinner in ancient Greece; **b** drinking-party. **2.** Meeting for philosophical discussion. **3.** Collection of essays or comments by different writers upon a given subject.

symptom, n. [1. símptum; 2. símptəm], fr. O. Fr. *symptome*, fr. Gk. *súmptōma*, 'chance, casualty', fr. *sumpíptein*, 'to fall in with; to happen', fr. **sym-** & *píptein*, 'to fall'; see **ptosis** & **ptero-**. **1.** Perceptible change in an organ, or organic function, due to, and indicating, presence or development of disease: *the symptoms point to poisoning; to develop alarming symptoms; he has all the symptoms of malaria.* **2.** Outward, recognizable, sign, indication, of the presence or existence of something else: *to show symptoms of fear, joy; hesitation is not infrequently a symptom of cowardice.*

symptomatic, adj. [1. simptomátik; 2. simptəmǽtik], fr. Gk. *sumptōmat-*, stem of *súmptōma*, 'chance', see prec., & **-ic.** Pertaining to, of the nature of, a symptom; forming, to be regarded as, a symptom; indicative.

symptomatically, adv. [1. simptomátikali; 2. simptəmǽtikəli]. Prec. & **-al** & **-ly.** According to symptoms.

symptomatology, n. [1. símptomatóloji; 2. símptəmætɔ́lədži], fr. Gk. *sumptōmat-*, stem of *súmptōma*, 'chance', see **symptom**, & *-o-* & **-logy.** Study of symptoms; investigation and classification of symptoms and their relation to disease.

syn-, pref. representing Gk. *sún*, 'with'; etymol. unknown. Found in compounds, usually representing or derived fr. Gk. words w. the sense of 'with, together'.

syn(a)eresis, n. [1. sinéresis; 2. siníərisis]. Gk. *sunaíresis*, 'a taking, drawing, together', see **syn-** & **heresy.** Coalescence, contraction, of two vowels or syllables.

synagogic(al), adj. [1. sinagógik(l), -gójik(l); 2. sinəgɔ́gik(l), -gɔ́džik(l)]. **synagogue** & **-ic** & **-al.** Pertaining to a synagogue.

synagog(u)al, adj. [1. sínagògal; 2. sínəgòugəl]. Next word & **-al.** Synagogical.

synagogue, n. [1. sínagòg; 2. sínəgɔ̀g], fr. Fr., Lat. *synagōga*, 'congregation of Jews', fr. Gk. *sunagōgḗ*, 'a bringing together; place of assembly, synagogue', fr. *sunágein*, 'to bring together', fr. **syn-** & *ágein*, 'to bring', see **agonistic.** **a** Congregation or assembly of Jews organized for religious observances and instruction; **b** meeting-place, place of worship, of Jewish congregation.

synallagmatic, adj. [1. sinalagmátik; 2. sinælәgmǽtik], fr. **syn-** & Gk. *allagmat-*, stem of *állagma*, 'thing taken in exchange', fr. stem of *allássein*, 'to exchange, barter', fr. *állos*, 'other', see under **alias.** Expressing, setting out, mutual obligations.

synal(o)epha, n. [1. sinoléfa; 2. sinəlífə]. Lat. *synaloepha*, fr. Gk. *sunaloiphḗ*, 'contraction of two syllables', fr. **syn-** & *aleíphein*, 'to anoint, smear over'; cp. Gk. *lípos*, 'fat', & see **adipose.** Elision of final vowel before following initial vowel.

synantherous, adj. [1. sinántherus; 2. sinǽnþərəs], fr. **syn-** & **anther** & **-ous.** (bot.) Having the anthers united.

synanthous, adj. [1. sinánthus; 2. sinǽnþəs], fr. **syn-** & Gk. *ánth-(os)*, 'flower', see under **anther**, & **-ous.** (bot.) Producing flowers and leaves at the same time.

synaphe(i)a, n. [1. sinaféa; 2. sinəfíə], fr. **syn-** & Gk. *haphḗ*, 'touch', fr. *háptein*, 'to touch, fasten'; no cognates outside Gk. Metrical continuity between lines or half-lines of verse.

synarthrosis, n. [1. sinarthrósis; 2. sināþróusis]. Gk. *sunárthrosis*, fr. **syn-** & *árthr-(on)*, 'a joint', see **arthritis**, & **-osis.** Joint permitting of no movement between articulating bones.

syncarp, n. [1. sínkarp; 2. sínkāp], fr. **syn-** & Gk. *karp-(ós)*, 'fruit', see **carpel.** Multiple or aggregate fruit, e.g. blackberry, mulberry.

syncarpous, adj. [1. sinkárpus; 2. sinkāpəs]. Prec. & **-ous.** Pertaining to, characterized by, syncarps.

synchondrosis, n. [1. sinkondrósis; 2. sinkəndróusis]. Gk. *sugkhóndrōsis*, 'a growing together into one cartilage', fr. **syn-** & *khóndr-(os)*, 'cartilage', see **chondri-**, & **-osis.** Articulation of bones by means of a layer of cartilage, forming an almost immovable joint.

synchronism, n. [1. sínkronizm; 2. sínkrənizəm]. See **synchronize** & **-ism.** State of being synchronous; simultaneous occurrence or existence.

synchronistic, adj. [1. sinkronístik; 2. sinkrənístik]. See prec. & **-ist** & **-ic.** Synchronous.

synchronistically, adv. [1. sinkronístikali; 2. sinkrənístikəli]. Prec. & **-al** & **-ly.** So as to synchronize; synchronously.

synchronization, n. [1. sinkronīzáshun; 2. sinkrənaizéiʃən]. Next word & **-ation.** Act of synchronizing; state, condition, of being synchronized.

synchronize, vb. intrans. & trans. [1. sínkronīz; 2. sínkrənaiz], fr. Gk. *súgkhronos*, 'contemporary', fr. **syn-** & *khrónos*, 'time', see **chronic**, & **-ize.** **A.** intrans. **1.** To agree in date or time, occur or exist at same period or point of time, be coincident. **2.** (of clocks &c.) To keep the same time. **B.** trans. **1.** To show (events &c.) to coincide in date, prove simultaneous existence or occurrence of. **2.** To regulate (a number of clocks), esp. by electric or other mechanical device, so that they all keep the same time.

synchronous, adj. [1. sínkrunus; 2. sínkrənəs], fr. Lat. *synchronus*, fr. Gk. *súgkhronos*, 'contemporary', see **synchronize**, & **-ous.** Occurring, existing, at the same time; simultaneous, coincident, contemporary.

synchronously, adv. Prec. & **-ly.** At the same point of time.

synchrony, n. [1. sínkruni; 2. sínkrəni]. See **synchronous** & **-y.** (rare) Agreement in point of time; synchronism.

synclastic, adj. [1. sinklástik; 2. sinklǽstik], fr. **syn-** & Gk. *klastós*, 'broken', fr. *kláein*, 'to break'; see **cataclasm.** Curving similarly in all directions, convex or concave on all sides.

synclinal, adj. [1. sinklínal; 2. sinkláinəl]. Next word & **-al.** (geol.) Forming a syncline.

syncline, n. [1. sínklin; 2. sínklain], fr. **syn-** & Gk. *klínein*, 'to slope; to lie'; see **clinical.** Geological formation with beds dipping down to the axis of a fold.

syncopate, vb. trans. [1. síngkopāt; 2. síŋkəpèit], fr. Lat. *syncopāre*, 'to faint away', fr. *syncopē*, 'a swoon', see **syncope**, & **-ate.** **1.** (gram.) To shorten (a word) by omitting medial sound or syllable. **2.** (mus.) **a** To alter musical rhythm by beginning (a note) on a normally unaccented beat and holding it into next accented beat; **b** to disturb rhythm of (musical composition) by syncopation.

syncopation, n. [1. singkopáshun; 2. siŋkəpéiʃən]. Prec. & **-ation.** Act of syncopating; state of being syncopated.

syncope, n. [1. síngkopi; 2. síŋkəpi]. Lat. *syncopē*, 'swoon; syncope', fr. Gk. *sugkopḗ*, 'a cutting short; syncope', fr. **syn-** & *kopḗ*, 'act of cutting'; cp. Gk. *kóptein*, 'to strike, cut'; *kópos*, 'blow'; *kómma*, 'piece cut off', see **comma.** **1.** Fainting-fit, sudden loss of consciousness. **2.** (gram.) Contraction of a word by loss of medial sound or syllable. **3.** (mus.) **a** Syncopation; **b** correspondence of two or more notes in one voice-part &c. to one note in another part.

syncopic, adj. [1. sinkópik; 2. sinkɔ́pik]. Prec. & **-ic.** Of, pertaining to, of the nature of, affected by, syncope.

syncoptic, adj. [1. sinkóptik; 2. sinkɔ́ptik], fr. Gk. *sugkóptein*, 'to cut up', fr. **syn-** & *kóptein*, 'to strike, cut', see **syncope**, & **-ic.** Syncopic.

syncotyledonous, adj. [1. sinkotilédunus; 2. sinkɔtilídənəs]. **syn-** & **cotyledon** & **-ous.** (bot.) Having the cotyledons united.

syncretic, adj. [1. sinkrétik; 2. sinkrítik]. See next word & **-ic.** Syncretistic.

syncretism, n. [1. sínkretizm; 2. sínkritizəm]. Gk. *sugkrētismós*, fr. *sugkrētízein*, 'to combine against a common enemy', fr. **syn-**, & the base seen in Gk. *keránnūmi*, 'to mix, blend', *krâsis*, 'mixture', q.v. under **crasis.** Attempt to reconcile or unite varying religious or philosophic systems (often in disparaging sense).

syncretistic, adj. [1. sinkretístik; 2. sinkritístik]. See prec. & **-ist** & **-ic.** Pertaining to syncretism.

syncretize, vb. trans. & intrans. [1. sínkretīz; 2. sínkritaiz], fr. Gk. *sugkrētízein*, see **syncretism.** **1.** trans. To carry out syncretism of; to attempt to harmonize. **2.** intrans. (of conflicting religious or philosophic systems &c.) To come into harmony, be reconciled.

syncytium, n. [1. sinsíshium, -sítium; 2. sinsíʃiəm, -sítiəm], fr. **syn-** & Gk. *kút-(os)*, 'hollow; urn, vessel', see under **cutis.** (biol.) Mass of tissue containing many nuclei but not divided into separate cells.

syndactyl, adj. [1. sindáktil; 2. sindǽktil], fr. **syn-** & Gk. *dáktulos*, 'finger', see **dactyl.** Having two or more digits united.

syndactylism, n. [1. sindáktilizm; 2. sindǽktilizəm]. Prec. & **-ism.** State of being syndactyl.

syndactylous, adj. [1. sindáktilus; 2. sindǽktiləs]. See prec. & **-ous.** Syndactyl.

syndesmosis, n. [1. sindezmósis; 2. sindezmóusis], fr. **syn-** & Gk. *desmós*, 'band', fr. *déein*, 'to bind', see **diadem**, & **-osis.** Union of two parts of the skeleton by means of ligaments.

syndetic, adj. [1. sindétik; 2. sindétik], fr. **syn-** & Gk. *detós*, 'bound', fr. *déein*, 'to bind', see prec., & **-ic.** (gram.) Connecting, being connected, by means of conjunctions.

syndic, n. [1. síndik; 2. síndik], fr. Fr., fr. Lat. *syndicus*, 'representative of a corporation', fr. Gk. *súndikos*, 'public advocate', fr. **syn-** & *díkē*, 'judgement, justice', see **dicast.** **1.** An officer having magisterial functions in some European countries. **2.** (Cambridge University) Member of a special committee of the senate; corresponding to a *delegate* in Oxford.

syndicalism, n. [1. síndikalizm; 2. síndikəlizəm]. Prec. & **-al** & **-ism.** **1.** Government, management of business, by a syndicate. **2.** Specif., system advocated by some trade-unionists whereby the ownership and management of an industry would be in the hands of the trade unions, the capitalist owner being abolished; the term is derived from French *syndicat*, 'trade union'.

syndicate (I.), n. [1. síndikat; 2. síndikət], fr. Med. Lat. *syndicātus*; **syndic** & **-ate.** **1.** Body of syndics, council. **2.** Group of financiers, merchants &c. combining to carry out a commercial enterprise, esp. in the preliminary stages of forming a limited liability company prior to the issue of shares to the public; group of persons &c. that buy up news &c. for simultaneous publication in different periodicals.

syndicate (II.), vb. trans. [1. síndikāt; 2. síndikeit], fr. prec. **a** To combine into a syndicate; **b** to publish (news &c.) in several papers at the same time.

syndication, n. [1. sindikáshun; 2. sindikéiʃən]. Prec. & **-ion.** Act of syndicating; state of being syndicated.

syne, n. [1. sīn; 2. sain]. Scots for **since.** *Auld lang syne*, the days of long ago.

synecdoche, n. [1. sinékdoki; 2. sinékdəki], fr. Lat. *synecdochē*, fr. Gk. *sunekdokhḗ*, 'synecdoche', fr. **syn-** & Gk. *ek*, 'out of', see under **ex-**, & Gk. *dokhḗ*, 'reception' fr. *dék(h)omai*, 'I receive', fr. base **dek-*, see **dogma.** Figure of speech in which a part is used to imply a whole; e.g. *blade* for *sword*; *sail, keel, bottom*, for *ship*; *hand* for *workman.*

synedrium, n. [1. sinédrium; 2. sinédriəm]. Lat., fr. Gk. *sunédrion*, 'assembly, council', fr. **syn-** & *hédra*, 'a seat; a sitting', see under **cathedral** & **seat (I.).** Council, assembly; specif., the Jewish sanhedrim.

synesis, n. [1. sínesis; 2. sínisis], fr. Gk. *súnesis*, 'coming together, union; comprehension, undertaking', fr. *suniēmi*, 'I bring together', fr. **syn-** & *hiēmi*, 'I move forward, throw, send'; cogn. w. Lat. *jacere*, 'to throw', see **jactitation**. Construction in which there is a departure from strict syntax owing to the attraction exercised by some conception expressed in the sentence, e.g. *these sort of things, these* being affected by the plural *things*.

syngenesis, n. [1. sìnjénesis; 2. sìndžénisis]. **syn-** & **genesis**. Development of embryo from union of male and female elements.

syngnathous, adj. [1. singnā́thus, síngnathus; 2. siŋnéiþəs, síŋnəþəs], fr. **syn-** & Gk. *gnáth-(os)*, 'jaw', see **gnathic**, & **-ous**. (of fish) With mouth forming a tube.

synizesis, n. [1. sìnizḗsis; 2. sinizísis]. Gk. *synízēsis*, fr. **syn-** & *hízein*, 'to seat', cogn. w. Gk. *hézomai*, 'to sit', see under **sedentary (I.)**. Contraction of two vowels, each originally forming a separate syllable, into one syllable.

synod, n. [1. sínod; 2. sínəd], fr. Fr., fr. Lat. *synodus*, 'ecclesiastical assembly', fr. Gk. *súnodos*, 'meeting, junction, assembly', fr. **syn-** & *hodós*, 'way', see **hodometer**. **1.** Ecclesiastical council, whether local or general. **2.** Council in Presbyterian Church, intermediate between General Assembly and presbyteries. **3.** Deliberative assembly, council. **4.** (astron., archaic) Conjunction.

synodal, adj. [1. sínodl; 2. sínədl]. Prec. & **-al**. Pertaining to a synod.

synodic(al), adj. [1. sinódik(l); 2. sinɔ́dik(l)]. **synod** & **-ic** & **-al**. Synodal.

synodically, adv. Prec. & **-ly**. After the manner of, by means of, a synod.

synoecious, adj. [1. sinḗsius; 2. sinísiəs], fr. **syn-** & Gk. *oîkos*, 'house', see **economy**. (bot.) Having male and female elements in the same flower-head, or within the same receptacle.

synonym, n. [1. sínonim; 2. sínənim], fr. Lat. *synōnyma*, fr. Gk. *sunṓnumos*, 'synonymous', fr. **syn-** & *ónoma*, 'name', see **onomatopeia**, & **name (I.)**. **1.** Word identical in meaning with another, or only slightly differentiated in sense or usage. **2.** Word identical in meaning with another in one or more of its senses, but not all.

synonymatic, adj. [1. sinònimátik; 2. sinɔ̀nimǽtik], fr. **syn-** & Gk. *onomat-*, stem of *ónoma*, 'name', see prec., & **-ic**. Of, pertaining to, making use of, constituting, a synonym.

synonymic, adj. [1. sìnonímik; 2. sìnənímik]. **synonym** & **-ic**. Synonymatic.

synonymity, n. [1. sìnonímiti; 2. sìnənímiti]. **synonym** & **-ity**. State of being synonymous; similarity or identity in meaning.

synonymous, adj. [1. sinónimus; 2. sinɔ́niməs]. **synonym** & **-ous**. Of the nature of, constituting, a synonym; expressing the same or almost the same meaning, conveying the same or a similar idea: *the two terms are synonymous*; *high is synonymous with lofty*; *his name is synonymous with cowardice*.

synonymously, adv. Prec. & **-ly**. By means of, in the manner of, synonyms.

synonymy, n. [1. sinónimi; 2. sinɔ́nimi], fr. Gk. *sunōnumía*, fr. *sunṓnumos*, 'synonymous'; **synonym** & **-y**. Synonymity.

synopsis, n. [1. sinópsis; 2. sinɔ́psis], fr. Gk. *súnopsis*, 'general view', fr. **syn-** & *ópsis*, 'sight, view', see under **optic**. Comprehensive summary, general view, outline.

synoptic, adj. & n. [1. sinóptik; 2. sinɔ́ptik], fr. Gk. *sunoptikós*, 'taking a general view'; **syn-** & **optic**. **1.** adj. **a** Pertaining to, of the nature of, giving, a synopsis; *the Synoptic Gospels*, those of St. Matthew, St. Mark, and St. Luke, which present similarity of treatment, as opposed to that of St. John; hence, **b** of, pertaining to, the Synoptic Gospels. **2.** n. Writer of one of the Synoptic Gospels.

synoptical, adj. [1. sinóptikl; 2. sinɔ́ptikl]. Prec. & **-al**. Synoptic.

synoptically, adv. Prec. & **-ly**. In a synoptic manner, in outline, as a summary.

synoptist, n. [1. sinóptist; 2. sinɔ́ptist]. See **synoptic** & **-ist**. Writer of one of the Synoptic Gospels.

synosteology, n. [1. sìnosteóloji; 2. sìnɔstiɔ́lədži]. **syn-** & **osteology**. Study of the joints of the body.

synost(e)osis, n. [1. sìnost(e)ósis; 2. sìnɔst(i)óusis], fr. **syn-** & Gk. *osté-(on)*, 'bone', see **osteo-** & **os**, & **-osis**. Anchylosis.

synostotic, adj. [1. sìnostótik; 2. sìnɔstɔ́tik]. See prec. & **-otic**. Pertaining to anchylosis.

synovia, n. [1. sinṓvia; 2. sinóuviə], fr. **syn-** & perh. Lat. *ōv-(um)*, 'egg', see **ovum**, & **-ia**. Albuminous fluid secreted by glands between joints and acting as lubricator.

synovial, adj. [1. sinṓvial; 2. sinóuviəl]. Prec. & **-al**. Of, pertaining to, secreting, synovia: *synovial membrane, fluid*.

synovitis, n. [1. sìnovī́tis; 2. sìnəváitis]. See **synovia** & **-itis**. Inflammation of the synovial membrane.

syntactic(al), adj. [1. sintáktik(l); 2. sintǽktik(l)], fr. Gk. *suntaktikós*, fr. **syn-** & *tássein*, 'to arrange, put together'; see **tactics**. Pertaining to syntax.

syntactically, adv. Prec. & **-ly**. From the point of view of, as regards, syntax.

syntactics, n. [1. sintáktiks; 2. sintǽktiks]. See **syntactic** & **-ics**. Branch of mathematics treating of the number of ways of putting things together, e.g. permutations and combinations.

syntax, n. [1. síntaks; 2. síntæks], fr. Fr. *syntaxe*, fr. Lat. *syntaxis*, fr. Gk. *súntaxis*, 'arrangement; grammatical construction', fr. **syn-** & *táxis*, 'arranging', see **taxis**. Arrangement and grammatical relation of words as members of a sentence; sentence construction.

synthesis, n. [1. sínthesis; 2. sínþisis], fr. Lat. *synthesis*, 'compound, mixture', fr. Gk. *súnthesis*, 'a putting together'; **syn-** & **thesis (I.)**. **1. a** The act or process of putting together, of combining; **b** the result of such a process; combination; the reverse of *analysis*. **2.** (chem.) The process of building up a substance by combining the elements of which it is formed, or of forming compounds by bringing together a number of simpler compounds. **3.** (philos.) The mental process of uniting the separate elements of thought or sensation into a complex conception. **4.** (philol.) The process of combining into an inflected word various elements supposed to have been originally distinct, e.g. a base, secondary formative elements including the stem, and the suffix or inflexion.

synthesist, n. [1. sínthesist; 2. sínþisist]. Prec. & **-ist**. One who makes a synthesis.

synthesize, vb. trans. [1. sínthesīz; 2. sínþisaiz]. See **synthesis** & **-ize**. To synthetize.

synthetic(al), adj. [1. sinthétik(l); 2. sinþétik(l)], fr. Gk. *sunthetikós*, 'constructive', fr. *súnthetos*, 'compound', fr. **syn-** & *thetós*, 'placed', see **thesis**. **1.** Pertaining to, of the nature of, a synthesis. **2. a** Produced by, resulting from, a synthesis; specif. **b** (chem.) produced by artificial process of synthesis in a laboratory, and not by the ordinary process of nature: *synthetic wine, silk, rubber* &c.

synthetically, adv. Prec. & **-ly**. In a synthetic manner; by means of synthesis.

synthetist, n. [1. sínthetist; 2. sínþitist], fr. Gk. *súnthetos*, 'compound', see **synthetic**, & **-ist**. One who makes a synthesis.

synthetize, vb. trans. & intrans. [1. sínthetīz; 2. sínþitaiz], fr. Gk. *súnthetos*, 'compound', see **synthetic**, & **-ize**. **a** trans. To combine (things or ideas) by a process of synthesis; **b** intrans., to make a synthesis.

syntonic, adj. [1. sintónik; 2. sintɔ́nik]. **syntony** & **-ic**. (of wireless transmitter and receiver) Tuned to the same wave-length.

syntonization, n. [1. sìntonīzā́shun; 2. sìntənaizéiʃən]. Next word & **-ation**. Process of syntonizing, tuning of wireless receiver and transmitter to a certain wave-length.

syntonize, vb. trans. [1. síntōnīz; 2. síntənaiz]. **syntony** & **-ize**. (wireless) To adjust (transmitter and receiver) to the same wave-length.

syntonizer, n. [1. síntonīzer; 2. síntənaizə]. Prec. & **-er**. Device for syntonizing wireless apparatus.

syntony, n. [1. síntoni; 2. síntəni], fr. Gk. *suntonía*, 'agreement'; see **syn-** & **tone (I.)**. State of being syntonized; specif., in wireless, the adjustment or tuning of one circuit to another so that their time-periods or frequencies are similar, see **resonance**.

sypher, vb. trans. [1. sífer; 2. sáifə]. Etymol. unknown. To join (planks) by overlapping the edges so as to produce a smooth surface.

sypher-joint, n. Joint made by syphering.

syphilis, n. [1. sífilis; 2. sífilis], fr. Fr., fr. *Syphilus*, name of a character in the 16th cent. Lat. poem of Frascatorius. Highly infectious venereal disease which starts with local symptoms and gradually, unless promptly treated, affects the whole system; caused by the micro-organism *Spirochaeta pallida*.

syphilitic, adj. [1. sìfilítik; 2. sìfilítik]. See prec. & **-itic**. Connected with, pertaining to, of the nature of, affected with, due to, syphilis.

syphilize, vb. trans. [1. sífilīz; 2. sífilaiz]. See **syphilis** & **-ize**. To inoculate with the virus of syphilis.

syphiloid, adj. [1. sífiloid; 2. sífilɔid]. See **syphilis** & **-oid**. Resembling syphilis.

syphilology, n. [1. sìfilóloji; 2. sìfilɔ́lədži]. See **syphilis** & **-o-** & **-logy**. Study of syphilis and its treatment.

syphilous, adj. [1. sífilus; 2. sífiləs]. See **syphilis** & **-ous**. Syphilitic.

syphon, n. See **siphon**.

syren, n. See **siren**.

Syriac, n. & adj. [1. síriàk; 2. síriæ̀k], fr. Lat. *Syriacus*, fr. Gk. *Suriakós*, fr. *Suria*, 'Syria'. **1.** n. Ancient Syrian dialect, western Aramaic. **2.** adj. Of, pertaining to, written in, Syriac.

Syriacism, n. [1. síriasìzm; 2. síriəsìzəm]. Prec. & **-ism**. Syriac idiom or characteristic in Hebrew.

Syrian, adj. & n. [1. sírian; 2. síriən]. Syria & **-an**. **1.** adj. Of, pertaining to, Syria. **2.** n. Native of Syria.

syringa, n. [1. siríngga; 2. siríŋgə]. Mod. Lat., fr. *sȳring-*, stem of Lat. *sȳrinx*, 'pipe', see **syrinx**. Ornamental shrub, *Philadelphus*, with clusters of sweet-scented white flowers; mock orange.

syringe, n. & vb. trans. [1. sírinj; 2. síríndž], fr. Lat. *sȳring-*, stem of *sȳrinx*, 'pipe', fr. Gk. *sūrigx*, 'pipe', see **syrinx**. **1.** n. Tube into which liquid is drawn by suction, and ejected in a jet by pressure; *hypodermic syringe*, small, needle-pointed syringe used by surgeons &c. for subcutaneous injections. **2.** vb. To apply a jet or spray of liquid to, by means of a syringe.

syringeal, adj. [1. sirínjeal; 2. siríndžiəl], fr. Lat. *sȳring-*, stem of *sȳrinx*, 'pipe', see **syrinx** & **-al**. Of, pertaining to, the syrinx.

syringeful, n. [1. sírinjfòol; 2. síríndžfùl]. **syringe** & **-ful**. Amount of liquid contained in a syringe.

syringitis, n. [1. sìrinjítis; 2. sìrindžáitis], fr. Lat. *sȳring-*, stem of *sȳrinx*, 'pipe', see **syrinx** & **-itis**. Inflammation of Eustachian tube.

syringotomy, n. [1. sìringótomi; 2. sìriŋgɔ́təmi], fr. Lat. *sȳring-*, stem of *sȳrinx*, 'pipe', see **syrinx**, & **-o-** & **-tomy**. Operation on fistula.

syrinx, n. [1. síringks; 2. síriŋks]. Lat. *sȳrinx*, fr. Gk. *sūrigx*, 'shepherd's pipe'; cp. Gk. *sōlēn*, 'channel, pipe', see **Solen**. **1.** Ancient wind-instrument consisting of a set of hollow tubes of varying lengths; Pan-pipes. **2.** Song-organ of birds, at the base of the windpipe. **3.** Eustachian tube. **4.** (surg.) Fistula. **5.** (archaeol.) Narrow, horizontal, rock-hewn gallery in ancient Egyptian tomb.

Syro-, pref. representing Gk. *Súros*, 'Syrian', fr. *Suria*, 'Syria'. Syrian; Syriac; e.g. *Syro-arabian*, including Syriac and Arabic.

syrtis, n. [1. sértis; 2. sǽtis]. Lat. *Syrtis*, fr. Gk. *Súrtis*, sand-bank on Libyan coast; cp. Gk. *súrtēs*, 'drag-rope'; *sūrein*, 'to draw'. Quicksand.

syrup, sirup, n. [1. sírup; 2. sírəp], fr. O. Fr. *syrop*, fr. Arab. *sharāb*, 'drink', see **sherbet** & **shrub (II.)**. **1. a** Water saturated with sugar; **b** solution of sugar and water flavoured or mixed with fruit juice, medicinal substance &c. **2. a** Condensed juice of sugar-cane &c. before separation of crystallizable sugar; **b** uncrystallizable part of juice of sugar-cane &c., separated from crystals by the process of refining; treacle; *golden syrup*, pale yellow syrup obtained from sugar-cane; *maple-syrup*, obtained from sap of sugar-maple.

syrupy, adj. [1. sírupi; 2. sírəpi]. Prec. & **-y**. Resembling syrup in consistency, stickiness, sweetness &c.

sys-, pref. representing Gk. **syn-** before *s*-followed by vowel.

syssarcosis, n. [1. sìsarkṓsis; 2. sìsākóusis], fr. Gk. *sussárkōsis*, fr. **sys-** & *sarkóein*, 'to make like flesh', fr. *sark-*, stem of *sárx*, 'flesh', see **sarco-**, & **-osis**. Union of two adjoining parts of the skeleton by means of intervening muscle.

syssitia, n. [1. sisítia, sisítia; 2. sisítiə, sisáitiə], fr. Gk. *sussītía*, 'public mess', fr. **sys-** & *sītia*, pl. of *sītion*, 'food'; cp. Gk. *sîtos*, 'grain; food', & see **sitology**. Communal meals in ancient Sparta, intended to promote discipline, economy, patriotism &c.

systaltic, adj. [1. sistáltik; 2. sistǽltik], fr. L. Lat. *systalticus*, fr. Gk. *sustaltikós*, 'drawing together', fr. *sustéllein*, 'to draw in', fr. **sy-** & *stéllein*, 'to place', see under **stole (I.)**. Alternately contracting and dilating.

system, n. [1. sístem; 2. sístim], fr. Lat. *systēma*, fr. Gk. *sústēma*, 'whole compounded of parts; organized government', fr. **sy-** & *histēmi*, 'I place, stand', see **static**, & **-m**. **1.** Group, association, aggregation, of things or objects, between which there exists connexion, relation, interaction, and which together form a unity: *solar system, nervous system, tramway system*. **2.** A collection of related facts, principles, ideas, exhibited and arranged so as to show the relations and bearings of each in respect of others and of the whole: *a system of philosophy, of grammar* &c. **3.** A plan, scheme, for arranging and classifying objects, facts, ideas, according to general principles determined by the mutual relations of the objects &c. so arranged: *a system of botanical, zoological, classification*. **4.** Method, orderly mode of procedure, regularity of action: *system is necessary to success in business and affairs of every kind*; *studies conducted without a proper system are apt to lead to confusion of mind*. **5.** Specif., the body as a whole considered in relation to efficient performance of all its functions: *too much tea is bad for the system*; *burgundy is highly recommended for the system*; *his system was much impaired by excesses*.

systematic, adj. [1. sistemátik; 2. sìstimǽtik], fr. Gk. *sustēmat-*, stem of *sústēma*, 'compound, organized whole', see **system**, & **-ic**. Made, carried on, performed in accordance with system, or a system; based on a system.

systematically, adv. [1. sìstemátikali; 2. sistimǽtikəli]. Prec. & **-al** & **-ly**. In a systematic manner.

systematism, n. [1. sístematìzm; 2. sístimətìzəm], fr. Gk. *sustēmat-*, see **systematic** & **-ism**. **a** Systematic arrangement or method; **b** exaggerated, blind, adherence to a system.

systematist, n. [1. sístematist; 2. sístimətist]. See prec. & **-ist**. **a** Person working according to system; **b** person who pursues a system too blindly and rigidly.

systematization, n. [1. sístematīzáshun; 2. sìstimətàizéiʃən]. Next word & **-ation**. Act of systematizing; state of systematizing.

systematize, vb. trans. [1. sístematīz; 2. sístimətàiz], fr. Gk. *sustēmat-*, see **systematic**, & **-ize**. To arrange in accordance with a system, reduce to a system.

systemic, adj. [1. sistémik; 2. sistémik]. **system** & **-ic**. Pertaining to the human system, or body as a whole.

systemically, adv. [1. sistémikali; 2. sistémikəli]. Prec. & **-al** & **-ly**. In respect of the human system.

systemless, adj. [1. sístemles; 2. sístimlis]. **system** & **-less**. Without system.

systole, n. [1. sístoli; 2. sístəli], fr. Gk. *sustolé*, 'contraction', fr. *sustéllein*, 'to draw together', see **systaltic**. Periodic contraction of heart and arteries, alternating with diastole, q.v.

systolic, adj. [1. sistólik; 2. sistólik]. Prec. & **-ic**. Of, pertaining to, the contraction of the heart &c.

systyle, adj. [1. sístīl; 2. sístail], fr. Lat. *systylos*, fr. Gk. *sústūlos*, 'systyle', fr. **sy-** & *stūlos*, 'pillar', see **style (III.)**. (archit., of columns) Placed two diameters apart.

systylous, adj. [1. sístilus; 2. sístiləs]. Prec. & **-ous**. (bot.) Having the styles united.

syzygy, n. [1. síziji; 2. sízidži], fr. Lat. *sȳzigia*, fr. Gk. *sūzugía*, 'yoke, pair', fr. *sūzugos*, 'yoked', fr. **sy-** & *zugón*, 'yoke', see **zygo-**. (astron.) Point in an orbit at which a heavenly body is in conjunction with or opposition to, the sun, or, in the case of the moon, to the earth.

T

T, t [1. tē; 2. tī]. The twentieth letter of the English alphabet; for use in abbreviations &c. see list at end of Dictionary. In Phrs. (*it suits me*) *to a T*, as well as possible, exactly; *to cross one's t's*, pay careful attention to very minute points.

T-. Used before names of various objects shaped like the letter T; *T-bandage, -bar, bolt* &c.

ta, vb. [1. tah; 2. tā]. Imitative of *thank* (*you*). (baby language) Thank you; (also in anticipation) please; a vulgarism when used by adults to each other.

taal, n. [1. tahl; 2. tāl]. Du. *taal*, 'language', see under **tale**. Dutch dialect spoken in S. Africa, esp. at the Cape; Cape Dutch.

tab, n. [1. tab; 2. tæb]. Etymol. unknown. Small flap, strip of cloth &c. attached to surface or edge of larger piece, to part of a garment &c.

tabard, n. [1. tábard; 2. tǽbəd], fr. O. Fr. *tabard*; etymol. doubtful. **a** (hist.) Cloak worn by lower classes in 15th cent. &c.; **b** short sleeveless garment worn by knights in Middle Ages over their armour, often emblazoned with arms of wearer; **c** similar garment worn by heralds, emblazoned with royal arms.

tabarder, n. See **taberdar**.

tabaret, n. [1. tábaret; 2. tǽbərɛt]. Possibly connected w. **tabby**. Fabric of satin and watered silk in alternate stripes, used in upholstery.

tabasheer, tabashir, n. [1. tàbashḗr; 2. tæbəʃíə]. Hind. & Pers. *tabāshīr*, 'sugar of bamboo'. Siliceous substance found in joints of the bamboo, formerly used in medicine.

tabby, n. [1. tábi; 2. tǽbi], fr. Fr. *tabis*, fr. Span. *tabi*, fr. Arab. **1.** Kind of coarse, watered silk. **2.** Also *tabby cat*, **a** brownish or brindled cat; cat with dark stripes on brown or grey; **b** hence, cat, esp. female cat. **3.** Gossiping and spiteful old woman. **4.** Kind of concrete made of lime, gravel &c.

tabby-moth, n. Kind of moth with streaked or mottled wings.

tabefaction, n. [1. tàbefákshun; 2. tæbifǽkʃən], fr. Lat. *tābefact-(um)*, P.P. type of *tābefacere*, 'to melt, dissolve'; fr. *tābē-(s)*, 'a wasting away'. See **tabes** & **-faction**. Emaciation caused by disease.

tabellion, n. [1. tabéliun; 2. təbéliən], fr. Fr., fr. Lat. *tabelliōn-(em)*, 'notary, scrivener', fr. *tabell-(a)*, 'tablet; deed, document', dimin. of *tabula*, 'tablet', see **table**. Official scrivener in ancient Rome; also, until 18th cent. in France.

taberdar, -er, n. [1. táberdar; 2. tǽbədə]. **tabard** & **-er**, fr. tabard formerly worn by taberdar. Name given to certain foundation scholars of Queen's College, Oxford.

tabernacle (I.), n. [1. tábernàkl; 2. tǽbənækl], fr. Fr., fr. Lat. *tabernāculum*, 'tent', fr. *taberna*, 'hut, booth, dwelling, shop', see **tavern**, & **-cule**. **1. a** Temporary shelter, habitation; specif., light, portable temple used by the Israelites during their wanderings; *feast of tabernacles*, Jewish annual feast held in commemoration of the wanderings through the wilderness; **b** dissenting chapel or place of worship; **c** (fig.) human body thought of as temporary dwelling-place of the soul. **2. a** (eccles.) Receptacle in which the Host is reserved in churches; **b** (archit.) canopied niche for the image of a saint &c. **3.** (naut.) Socket in deck of vessel for a mast.

tabernacle (II.), vb. trans. & intrans., fr. prec. **1.** trans. To furnish, provide with, a temporary dwelling or shelter. **2.** intrans. To take up a temporary abode.

tabernacle-work, n. (archit.) Series of carved and ornamented canopies over stalls &c.

tabernacular, adj. [1. tàbernákūlar; 2. tæbənǽkjulə], fr. Lat. *tabernācul-(um)*, 'tent', see **tabernacle**, & **-ar**. Of, pertaining to, of the nature of, characteristic of, a tabernacle.

tabes, n. [1. tábēz; 2. téibīz], fr. Lat. *tābēs*, 'a wasting away, dwindling; moisture of decaying matter'; cp. Lat. *tābēre*, 'to waste, be consumed'; supposed to be an extension w. *-bh* of base **tāw-*, 'to melt away'; cp. O. Slav. *tajati*, 'to melt'; also O.E. *þwīnan*, 'to dwindle', & cp. **thaw**. (med.) Wasting, emaciation; specif. *tabes dorsalis*, locomotor ataxia.

tabescence, n. [1. tabésens; 2. təbésəns]. See next word & **-ce**. State of emaciation.

tabescent, adj. [1. tabésent; 2. təbésənt], fr. Lat. *tābescent-(em)*, Pres. Part. of *tābescere*, 'to waste away', inchoative of *tābēre*, see **tabes**. Wasting away, tending to become emaciated.

tabetic, adj. & n. [1. tabétik; 2. təbétik], fr. **tabes**, on anal. of adjs. in **-etic**. **1.** adj. Pertaining to, of the nature of, suffering from, tabes. **2.** n. Person suffering from tabes.

tabic, adj. [1. tábik; 2. téibik], fr. **tabes** & **-ic**. Tabetic.

tabid, adj. [1. tábid; 2. téibid], fr. Lat. *tābid-(us)*, 'wasting'; see **tabes** & **-id**. Tabetic.

tabidly, adv. Prec. & **-ly**. In a tabid manner.

tabinet, n. [1. tábinet; 2. tǽbinɛt], fr. Fr.; etymol. doubtful. Watered fabric of silk and wool, used in upholstery.

tabitude, n. [1. tábitūd; 2. tǽbitjūd], fr. Lat. *tābitūd-(o)*, 'wasting away, consumption', see **tabes**, & *-i-* & **-tude**. State of being tabescent; emaciation.

tablature, n. [1. táblachur; 2. tǽblətʃə], fr. Fr., fr. Lat. *tabula*, 'plank; writing-tablet; painted panel', see **table**, & **-ate** & **-ure**. Ancient name for instrumental musical notation.

table (I.), n. [1. tábl; 2. téibl]. Fr., fr. Lat. *tabula*, 'board, plank; writing tablet';

etymol. uncertain; the suggested relations seem purely speculative. **1.** **a** Piece of household furniture consisting of a flat surface of wood supported on legs, used for eating and working at when sitting; **b** (in compounds) such piece of furniture used for a specified purpose, e.g. *billiard-, card-, dressing-table* &c. **2.** **a** A table considered primarily as a piece of furniture at which people sit at meals; Phrs. *at table,* (i.) in the act of partaking of a meal; (ii.) at, or for, meals; *the Lord's Table,* (chiefly Evangelical) (i.) the altar; (ii.) the Eucharist; **b** hence, the food itself consumed at table: *a liberal, good, table,* plentiful, good, food; **c** the persons seated at a table at a given time for a meal: *to set the table in a roar.* **3.** Inscribed flat slab of stone, wood, metal &c.; hence, **a** the inscription on such a slab: *the tables of the law,* the Ten Commandments, originally delivered to Moses on tables of stone; **b** a systematic list of figures, facts &c. arranged according to some definite plan: *a table of births and deaths; table of contents* (of a book &c.); *tables of weights and measures; mathematical tables,* of logarithms &c.; *multiplication table,* list of results of multiplying numbers, usually 1 to 12, by a given number: *twice two are four* &c. Phr. *to learn one's tables,* learn multiplication table, tables of weights and measures, by heart. **4.** A flat surface; in various specific and technical senses; e.g. **a** a flat elevated tract of land, a plateau; **b** the cut, flat surface of a gem; **c** either of two flat bony surfaces in the skull &c.

table (II.), vb. trans., fr. prec. **1.** To place upon a table; specif. **a** *to table a motion,* submit it for future discussion; **b** to inscribe upon a writing tablet; enter as a note &c.

tableau, n. [1. táblō; 2. tǽblou], fr. Fr. *tableau,* 'picture', dimin. of O. Fr. *table,* 'plank, table, panel, picture' &c., see **table (I.)**. **a** Representation of some well-known picture, a striking historical scene &c., by living persons suitably dressed and posed in fixed attitudes; called also *tableau vivant*: **b** (fig.) dramatic situation.

table-clamp, n. Clamp for fastening object to table.

table-cloth, n. Piece of material for covering table; esp. one of white linen for use at meals.

table-cut, adj. (of diamond &c.) Cut with flat top and usually bevelled border.

table-d'hôte, n. [1. táhbl dṓt; 2. tā́bl dóut]. Fr., lit. 'table of the host'. **1.** Public table for guests at hotel &c. **2.** Also *table-d'hôte breakfast, dinner* &c., meal in a hotel for which a fixed price is charged, consisting of a series of courses chosen and ordered by the management.

table-flap, n. Leaf of a table, on a hinge, which can be raised or lowered.

tableful, n. [1. tā́blfool; 2. téiblful]. **table (I.)** & **-ful.** **a** Amount, number of objects, required to cover a table; **b** number of persons that may be seated round a table.

table-knife, n. Knife for use at meals.

table-land, n. Elevated plain, plateau.

table-leg, n. One of the vertical supports of a table.

table-linen, n. Table-cloths, napkins &c., used at table.

table-money, n. Allowance made to general officers in the Army, and flag-officers in the Navy for expenses of official hospitality.

table-spoon, n. Large spoon used for eating soup, and for helping vegetables &c.

tablespoonful, n. [1. tā́blspōōnfool; 2. téiblspūnful]. As much as can be contained in a table-spoon.

tablet, n. [1. táblet; 2. tǽblit], fr. O. Fr. *tablette,* fr. Med. Lat. *tabulēta*; **table (I.)** & **-et.** **1.** Small flat slab of stone or metal inscribed with a design, inscription &c. **2.** Thin sheet of wood, ivory, metal &c., covered with wax or otherwise prepared, formerly used for writing upon; esp. one of a set of two or more sheets hinged or tied together at top or side. **3.** Small flat, compressed cake, usually round, containing medicinal drug.

table-talk, n. **a** Informal conversation at meals; **b** book containing record of such conversation.

table-tomb, n. Flat-topped burial-chest found in catacombs at Rome.

tablette, n. [1. táblet; 2. tǽblɛt], fr. Fr. *tablette,* see **tablet.** (archit.) Flat coping-stone of wall &c., projecting at either side.

table-turning, n. Act or process of causing a table to move by the unconscious action of a number of persons who place their hands lightly upon it.

tablier, n. [1. tábliā; 2. tǽbliei], fr. Fr. *tablier,* 'apron', fr. Lat. *tabulāri-(us),* fr. *tabula,* see **table (I.)** & **-ary.** Small apron used as part of the trimming of a woman's dress.

tabling, n. [1. tā́bling; 2. téibliŋ]. **table (II.)** & **-ing.** **1.** (carpentry) Projection on piece of timber, designed to fit into corresponding groove or mortice in another piece. **2.** (naut.) Broad hem on sail.

tabloid, n. [1. tábloid; 2. tǽblɔid]. **table** & **-oid.** Copyright trade-name. Small, round, flat, compressed cake, containing a drug &c.; tablet. Phr. *in tabloid form,* (fig.) in concentrated, compressed form.

taboo (I.), n. [1. tabṓō; 2. təbū́], fr. Polynesian *tapu.* **1.** (in Polynesian tribes) Custom of setting apart certain persons or objects as either sacred or accursed; this usually implies that such persons or things may not be touched, and that their names may not be uttered. **2.** Religious or social system characterized by taboo. **3.** Prohibition, ban, restraint.

taboo (II.), adj., fr. prec. (only predic.) **1.** **a** Set apart as sacred or accursed under taboo; **b** forbidden to be touched or spoken of. **2.** Prohibited, ruled out by convention, proscribed: *such things are taboo in decent society.*

taboo (III.), vb. trans., fr. **taboo (I.).** To prohibit, interdict; to avoid (a word, practice &c.) as taboo.

tabor, n. [1. tā́bor; 2. téibə, -ō], fr. O. Fr. *tabour,* fr. Arab., see **tambour.** Small drum resembling a tambourine or timbrel; used to accompany pipe.

tabouret, n. [1. táboret, táboorā; 2. tǽbərɛt, tǽburei], fr. O. Fr., 'stool', dimin. of O. Fr. *tabour,* 'drum', see **tabor.** **1.** Small stool. **2.** Embroidery frame. **3.** Needle-case. **4.** Small tabor; tabret.

tabret, n. [1. tábret; 2. tǽbrɛt]. Variant of prec. Small tabor; tabouret.

tabula, n. [1. tábūla; 2. tǽbjulə]. Lat. *tabula,* 'board, plank, writing-table; panel', see **table (I.).** (zool.) Flat plate of bone &c.; esp. horizontal plate in some corals.

tabula rasa, n. [1. tábūla ráhza; 2. tǽbjulə rā́zə]. Lat., 'erased tablet'. **a** Used of the mind before any impressions or ideas have been received; **b** complete obliteration, a blank; **a** clean sweep of what already exists.

tabular, adj. [1. tábūlar; 2. tǽbjulə], fr. Lat. *tabulār-(is),* 'of boards or plates', fr. *tabula,* 'board, tablet', see **table (I.),** & **-ar.** **1.** **a** Having a flat table-like surface; **b** consisting of thin plates, laminated. **2.** **a** Arranged, set out, in tables: *in tabular form;* **b** stated, exhibited, by means of tables: *tabular results.*

tabularly, adv. Prec. & **-ly.** (rare) In tabular form; by means of a table.

tabulate (I.), vb. trans. [1. tábūlāt; 2. tǽbjuleit]. **tabula** & **-ate.** **1.** To arrange, display, in tabular form; to set out in systematic grouping: *to tabulate data, results* &c. **2.** To give a flat surface to.

tabulate (II.), adj. **tabula** & **-ate.** **1.** Having a broad flat surface. **2.** Arranged in series of thin plates; laminated.

tabulation, n. [1. tàbūlā́shun; 2. tæ̀bjuléiʃən]. **tabulate (I.)** & **-ion.** Act of tabulating; state of being put into tabular form.

tabulator, n. [1. tábūlātur; 2. tǽbjuleitə]. **tabulate (I.)** & **-or.** **a** Person who tabulates; **b** typewriter attachment for tabulating figures.

tacamahac, n. [1. tákama-hak; 2. tǽkəməhæk]. S. American Indian. **1.** Yellowish, bitter, aromatic gum-resin yielded by certain tropical trees; used in incense, ointment &c. **2.** Balsam poplar of N. America.

tac-au-tac, n. [1. ták ō ták; 2. tǽk ou tǽk], fr. Fr., imitative. (fencing) **a** Parry followed immediately by riposte; **b** series of swift attacks and parries.

tace, vb. intrans., imperat. [1. tā́si; 2. téisi]. Lat. *tacē,* imperat. of *tacēre,* 'to be silent'; cogn. w. Goth. *þahan*; O.N. *þegja*; O.S. *thagian*; O.H.G. *dagēn,* 'to be silent'. Be silent.

tacet, vb. intrans. [1. tā́set, táset; 2. téisɛt, tǽsɛt]. Lat. *tacet,* 3rd sing. pres. of *tacēre,* 'to be silent', see prec. (in musical score) Direction for instrument to remain silent.

tache, n. [1. tahsh, tash; 2. tāʃ, tæʃ], fr. O. Fr. *tache,* 'spot', of Gmc. origin, see **tack (I.).** Coloured spot or blemish on the skin; **a** freckle.

tachometer, n. [1. takómeter; 2. tækɔ́mitə], fr. Gk. *tákho-(s),* 'speed', etymol. doubtful, & **-meter.** Instrument for measuring speed.

tachometry, n. [1. takómetri; 2. tækɔ́mitri], fr. Gk. *tákho-(s),* 'speed', see prec., & **-metry.** Art or practice of measuring speed.

tachycardia, n. [1. tàkikárdia; 2. tæ̀kikā́diə], fr. Gk. *takhú-(s),* 'swift', see **tachometer,** & *kardía,* 'heart', see **cardiac.** (med.) Abnormally rapid action of the heart.

tachygraphic(al), adj. [1. tàkigráfik(l); 2. tæ̀kigrǽfik(l)]. **tachygraphy** & **-ic** & **-al.** Of, pertaining to, written in, tachygraphy.

tachygraphy, n. [1. takígrafi; 2. tækígrəfi], fr. Gk. *takhú-(s),* 'swift', q.v. under **tachometer,** & **-graphy.** System or use of shorthand; specif., one of the systems of notation used by ancient Greeks and Romans.

tachylyte, n. [1. tákilīt; 2. tǽkilait], fr. Gk. *takhú-(s),* 'swift', see **tachometer,** & *lut-(ós),* fr. *lúein,* 'to loosen, dissolve', q.v. under second element of **analysis**; so called because easily decomposed by acids. Kind of black, opaque, basaltic glass.

tachylytic, adj. [1. tàkilítik; 2. tæ̀kilítik]. Prec. & **-ic.** Of, of the nature of, consisting of, tachylyte.

tachymeter, n. [1. takímeter; 2. tækímitə], fr. Gk. *takhú-(s),* 'swift', see **tachometer,** & **-meter.** Instrument used in surveying for the speedy measuring of distances, fixing of points &c.

tachymetry, n. [1. takímetri; 2. tækímitri]. See prec. & **-metry.** The use of a tachymeter.

tacit, adj. [1. tásit; 2. tǽsit], fr. Lat. *tacit-(um),* P.P. type of *tacēre,* 'to be silent', see **tace.** Unspoken; understood without being expressed, implied by silence: *tacit approval; a tacit understanding.*

tacitly, adv. Prec. & **-ly.** In a tacit manner.

taciturn, adj. [1. tásitĕrn; 2. tǽsitə̄n], fr. Lat. *taciturn-(us),* 'quiet, taciturn', fr. *tacit-(um),* see **tacit.** Habitually silent, speaking little, of few words, reserved in speech.

taciturnity, n. [1. tàsitĕrniti; 2. tæ̀sitə́niti], fr. Lat. *taciturnitāt-(em),* 'taciturnity'; prec. & **-ity.** Quality of being taciturn.

taciturnly, adv. [1. tásitĕrnli; 2. tǽsitə̄nli]. **taciturn** & **-ly.** In a taciturn manner.

tack (I.), n. [1. tak; 2. tæk], fr. A.-Fr. *taque,* 'nail'; cp. O. Fr. *tache,* 'point, spot'; of Gmc. origin; cp. Germ. *zacken,* 'tooth, prong'; Du. *tak,* 'twig'; cp. **attach.** **1.** Short, sharp, broad-headed, weakish nail; *tin-tack,* one made of iron coated with tin; Phr. (vulg.) *(come down to) brass tacks,* facts. **2.** (needlework) Long stitch used in making temporary seam or fastening. **3.** (naut.) **a** Rope for fastening corner of sail; **b** corner of sail to which this is attached; **c** ship's course in relation to position of sails; Phr. *on the port, starboard, tack,* with wind on port, starboard, side; **d** change of course produced by shifting sails to take advantage of wind. Phr. *tack and tack,* by a succession of tacks. **4.** (fig.) Course of action; policy: *on the wrong, right, tack.* **5.** (of varnish, printing-ink &c.) Viscous condition, stickiness.

tack (II.), vb. trans. & intrans., fr. prec. **A.** trans. **1.** To fasten with tack(s): *to tack the carpet down*; *to tack a notice to the wall.* **2.** To make a temporary seam or fastening in a garment or fabric, stitch together with long stitches: *to tack two pieces of silk together.* **3.** (fig.) To attach, link on, as a supplementary part; to append: *to tack a moral on to the end of a story.* **B.** intrans. **1.** To change ship's direction by bringing a different side to the wind. **2.** (fig.) To change one's line of action, one's opinions &c.; to adopt a new policy.

tack (III.), n. Etymol. unknown. Food, fare, provisions; esp. *hard tack*, ship's biscuits; *soft tack*, bread, as distinct from biscuit &c.; good food.

tackiness, n. [1. tákines; 2. tǽkinis]. **tacky** & **-ness**. State of being tacky; stickiness.

tackle (I.), n. [1. tákl; 2. tǽkl]. M.E. *takel*, fr. L.G. *takel*, fr. O.N. *taka*, 'to seize, grasp', & **-le**; see **take** (I.). **1.** Mechanical contrivance for moving, esp. for raising, heavy weights; specif., system of ropes, pulleys &c.; **a** for raising weights; **b** for handling ship's sails, spars &c. **2.** Gear, equipment, used in specific occupation; often in compounds, *fishing-tackle* &c. **3.** (fr. vb.) Act of tackling opposing player in football.

tackle (II.), vb. trans. & intrans., fr. prec. **A.** trans. **1.** To fasten, hoist, with tackle. **2.** (lit. and fig.) **a** To seize, grapple, come to grips with, attack; specif. (football) to seize and try to stop (opponent); **b** (fig.) to approach, deal with, confront, engage in argument with: *I tackled him on the question of free trade.* **3.** To turn one's attention to (a piece of work, a problem) with a view to completion, or solution; to undertake, start dealing with. **B.** intrans. To carry out the operation of tackling.

tackle-block, n. Pulley forming part of tackle.

tackle-fall, n. Rope connecting blocks.

tackling, n. [1. tákling; 2. tǽkliŋ]. **tackle** & **-ing**. Apparatus for hoisting &c.; tackle.

tacky, adj. [1. táki; 2. tǽki]. **tack** (I.) & **-y**. (of varnish &c.) Thick, sticky, viscous.

tact, n. [1. takt; 2. tækt], fr. Lat. *tact-(us)*, 'touch; sense of touch; effect, influence', fr. P.P. type of *tangere*, 'to touch', see **tangent**. **1.** Keen, natural perception of what is right and fitting; quick apprehension of the right thing to say or do; instinctive skill, adroitness, discretion, in dealing with persons or difficult situations. **2.** (mus.) Most emphatic beat in a bar.

tactful, adj. [1. táktfool; 2. tǽktful]. Prec. & **-ful**. Possessing, exhibiting, tact.

tactfully, adv. Prec. & **-ly**. In a tactful manner.

tactical, adj. [1. táktikl; 2. tǽktikl]. See **tactics** & **-al**. Concerned with, pertaining to, tactics.

tactically, adv. Prec. & **-ly**. By means of, from the point of view of, according to the methods of, tactics.

tactician, n. [1. taktíshan; 2. tæktíʃən]. See **tactics** & **-ian**. Student of, one skilled in, tactics.

tactics, n. [1. táktiks; 2. tǽktiks], fr. Gk. *taktik-(á)*, 'tactics', cp. *tássein*, fr. **tak-jo-*, 'to arrange'; cp. also *tagḗ*, 'order of battle'; *táxis*, 'arrangement; ordinance; post, rank; levy'; see **taxis** & **-ic**. **1.** Art of handling troops in the field, in presence of enemy; also art of handling ships in a naval action: contrasted with *strategy*. **2.** Art of handling a political situation; adroit method of dealing with persons and circumstances so that a desired end may be gained as easily and smoothly as possible.

tactile, adj. [1. táktīl, -il; 2. tǽktail, -il], fr. Lat. *tactil-(is)*, 'tangible', fr. *tact-(um)*, P.P. type of *tangere*, 'to touch', see **tangent**, & **-ile**. **1.** Concerned with, pertaining to, affected by, the organs, or the sense, of touch. **2.** Capable of being touched; tangible.

tactility, n. [1. taktíliti; 2. tæktíliti]. Prec. & **-ity**. **1.** State or quality of being tactile. **2.** Tangibility.

tactless, adj. [1. táktles; 2. tǽktlis]. **tact** & **-less**. Lacking in tact.

tactlessly, adv. Prec. & **-ly**. In a tactless manner.

tactlessness, n. See prec. & **-ness**. Lack of tact.

tactual, adj. [1. táktūal; 2. tǽktjuəl], fr. Lat. *tactu-(s)*, 'touching', see **tact**, & **-al**. Pertaining to, derived from, the sense of touch.

tactually, adv. Prec. & **-ly**. By means of touch.

tadpole, n. [1. tádpōl; 2. tǽdpoul]. M.E. *tadpolle*, fr. O.E. *tād*, 'toad', see **toad**, & **poll** (I.). Larva of frog, toad &c., having a tail and external gills, later absorbed into the body.

tadpole-fish, n. Fish with broad, flat head.

taedium vitae, n. [1. tḗdium vītē; 2. tídiəm váitī]. Lat. *taedium vītae*, 'weariness of life'; see **tedium**, **vital**. (med.) Suicidal tendency caused by depression or weariness.

tael, n. [1. tāl; 2. teil]. Port., fr. Malay *tahil*, 'weight'. **a** Chinese ounce, 1½ oz. avoirdupois; **b** this weight in pure silver, as monetary unit.

ta'en, vb. [1. tān; 2. tein]. Contracted fr. **taken**. (poet.)

taenia, n. [1. tḗnia; 2. tíniə]. Lat. *taenia*, 'ribbon, band, fillet; ribbon-fish; tapeworm'; fr. Gk. *tainía*, 'band, fillet, bandage', fr. a form **tain-(ós)*, 'narrow', earlier **tan-jo-*; cp. Gk. *teínein*, *tanúein*, 'to stretch'; *tónos*, 'cord'; see **tone** & **thin**. **1.** (Gk. and Rom. archaeol.) Hair-band, fillet. **2.** (archit.) Fillet above architrave on Doric column. **3.** (anat.) Ribbon-like organ, arrangement of muscle &c. **4.** Tape-worm.

taenioid, adj. [1. tḗnioid; 2. tíniɔid]. Prec. & **-oid**. **1.** Ribbon-shaped. **2.** Connected with a tapeworm.

tafferel, n., usually **taffrail** [1. táfril; 2. tǽfril], fr. Du. *tafereel*, dimin. of *tafel*, 'table', fr. Lat. *tabula*, 'tablet, slab', see **tabula**, **table** (I.). Upper part of ship's stern.

taffeta, n. [1. táfeta; 2. tǽfitə], fr. Fr. *taffetas*, fr. Ital. *taffetà*, fr. Pers. *taftah*. Fabric of silk, or silk and linen.

taffrail, n. [1. táfril; 2. tǽfril], fr. Du. *tafereel*, 'tafferel', see **tafferel**, assimilated to *rail*. Rail round ship's stern.

Taffy (I.), n. [1. táfi; 2. tǽfi]. Welsh form of Davy, fr. David. (colloq.) Welshman.

taffy (II.), n. See **toffee**. American for toffee.

tafia, n. [1. táfia; 2. tǽfiə]. W. Indian. Kind of rum distilled from refuse of sugar manufacture &c.

tag (I.), n. [1. tag; 2. tæg]. Prob. Scand.; cp. Swed. *tagg*, 'spike, prickle, tooth'; Norw. *tagge*, 'tooth'. **1.** Appendage, something forming an end, point, or projecting flap, point &c.; specif. **a** metal point of lace; **b** tip of animal's tail; **c** loop or flap at back of boot to give purchase in drawing it on; **d** label tied by string &c.; **e** loose, hanging end, flap or torn edge; **f** ragged or matted lock of wool on sheep. **2.** Refrain of song or poem. **3.** Epilogue of play. **4.** Hackneyed phrase or quotation.

tag (II.), vb. trans., fr. prec. **1.** To furnish with a tag, add a tag to: *a tagged lace.* **2.** To join on, add, as an appendage, tack on; esp. to add something on to a literary composition. **3.** To cut tags from wool of: *to tag sheep.* **4.** (colloq.) To pursue closely, dog.

tag (III.), n. & vb. trans. Prob. fr. prec. **1.** n. Children's game in which one pursues and tries to touch others. **2.** vb. To overtake and touch another player in this game.

Tagetes, n. [1. tajḗtēz; 2. tædžítiz]. Mod. Lat., origin doubtful; the name of an Etruscan deity *Tages* is suggested as possible source. Genus of plants of the aster family, with bright yellow or orange flowers; e.g. French marigold.

tagger, n. [1. táger; 2. tǽgə]. **tag** & **-er**. (pl.) Thin sheet-iron, esp. one without coating of tin.

Taic, adj. & n. [1. táh-ik; 2. tấik], fr. *Tai*, a race of the Indo-Chinese peninsula, including Siamese &c., & **-ic**. **1.** adj. Of, pertaining to, the Tai. **2.** n. Language of the Tai.

taiga, n. [1. tíga; 2. táigə]. Siberian. Belt of coniferous forest lying to the south of the tundra in N. Europe and Asia.

tail (I.), n. [1. tāl; 2. teil]. O.E. *tæg(e)l*; M.E. *teil*; cp. O.N., Goth. *tagl*; O.H.G. *zagel*, 'tail'. **1.** Prolongation of the spine in vertebrates, which extends beyond the body and constitutes a separate and distinctive part. Phrs. *to turn tail*, to show cowardice, run away from danger, a fight &c.; *with his tail between his legs*, (of dog, or fig. of person) cowed; dispirited, discouraged, as having suffered a rebuff; *to be unable to make head or tail of*, find unintelligible; *to twist the tail of*, to subject to annoyance, to torment; *close on a person's tail*, close behind him, as in pursuit. **2.** Any of several objects supposed to resemble a tail; **a** *a tail of hair*, a plait, a wisp; **b** *tail of kite*, length of string with series of twisted strips of paper knotted to it, attached to lowest point of kite; **c** *tail of comet*, luminous train extending behind the nucleus; **d** *tail of a letter*, line or loop extending below the line; **e** *tail of a note*, stroke extending above or below the line as part of a symbol of a musical note; **f** *tail of a wing*, slender point of a butterfly's lower wing. **3.** Lowest, hindmost, or subordinate part of object or group; specif. **a** *tail of a coat*, part below waist, skirt; half of skirt when divided; **b** *tail of a procession*, rear portion; **c** *tail of a cart*, back of cart; **d** *tail of one's eye*, outer corner; **e** *tail of a storm, gale*, comparative calm when gale has slackened; **f** *tail of a stream*, comparatively calm water after current or rough water; **g** exposed end of roofing-tile, slate &c.; **h** concealed end of brick &c. in wall; **i** (of coin) reverse side. **4.** Retinue, train, band of followers. **5.** (mil.) *Tail of the trenches*, part first dug by advance party. **6.** Horse-tail, formerly an emblem of rank in Turkey: *a Pasha with three tails.*

tail (II.), vb. trans. & intrans., fr. prec. **A.** trans. **1.** To provide with a tail. **2.** To follow (a person) closely, to track, esp. for the purpose of watching, and preventing escape of. **3.** To cut or pull stalk or lower end off: *to tail fruit.* **B.** intrans. (naut.) *To tail to the tide, tail up and down stream* (of anchored ship), to take up position according to direction of tide or current. **C.** Followed by adverbs and prepositions with special meanings. *Tail after*, intrans., to follow closely, esp. in line or procession. *Tail away*, intrans., to diminish gradually, fade away, grow sparser and sparser; straggle. *Tail in*, trans., to fix (timbers &c.) into wall or other structure by one end. *Tail off*, same as *tail away*. *Tail on*, trans., to join on as appendage or supplement.

tail (III.), n. & adj., fr. O. Fr. *taille*, 'notch, cutting', see **tailor** & **entail**. **1.** n. Limitation of inheritance of an estate to descendants in particular line, of a particular person: *an estate in tail*; *in tail male.* **2.** adj. Limited, in respect of inheritance, in a particular way.

tail-bay, n. Part of lock between tail-gate and lower pond.

tail-board, n. Movable board forming back of cart.

tail-coat, n. Coat with tails, with division between them, and a button at the top of each, just below the waist.

-tailed, adj. [1. tāld; 2. teild]. **tail** (I.) & **-ed**. Having a particular kind of tail: *long-tailed*; *bob-tailed* &c.

tail-end, n. Last part, fag-end: *tail-end of a procession, of a speech* &c.

tail-feather, n. Longest or most conspicuous feather in a bird's tail.

tail-gate, n. Lower gate of canal lock.

tailing, n. [1. tāling; 2. téiliŋ]. **tail** (II.) & **-ing**. In various senses; **a** concealed end of brick &c. in wall; **b** fault in calico-printing; **c** refuse separated from grain in threshing &c.; **d** inferior, useless part of ore.

tailless, adj. [1. tâlles ; 2. téilis]. **tail** (I.) & **-less.** Without a tail.

tail-margin, n. Margin at foot of page of book &c.

tailor (I.), n. [1. tâler ; 2. téilə], fr. M.E. *tailleur* &c., fr. O. Fr. *tailleor*, lit. ' cutter ', fr. Low Lat. *tăliāre*, fr. Lat. *tălea*, ' rod ; cutting for planting ' ; orig. ' sprout, fresh growth ' ; cogn. w. Gk. *têlis*, ' fenugreek ' ; Lith. *(at)tólas*, ' aftermath '. **a** Person who cuts out and makes clothes, esp. outer garments made from cloth ; **b** tradesman who sells coats, and suits, esp. for men, which he employs others to make.

tailor (II.), vb. trans. & intrans. **1.** trans. **a** To work upon (clothes) as a tailor ; to sew, press, and otherwise get ready, cloth garments; **b** to make clothes for. **2.** intrans. To ply the trade of tailor.

tailor-bird, n. Oriental bird that stitches leaves together to form a receptacle for its nest.

tailoress, n. [1. tâlores ; 2. téilərəs]. **tailor** & **-ess.** Female tailor.

tailoring, n. [1. tâloring ; 2. téiləriŋ]. **tailor** & **-ing. a** Occupation, business, of a tailor ; **b** the work of a tailor as exhibited in a particular garment.

tailor-made, adj. **a** (of woman's dress) Made by tailor ; hence, cut like a man's suit, plain, well-fitting, and without trimmings, flounces &c. ; **b** (of a woman) dressed in tailor-made clothes.

tail-piece, n. **1.** Longish, narrow piece of ebony on instruments of the violin class, to which the lower ends of the strings are fastened after passing over the bridge. **2.** Ornamental design on the lower half of the page of a book, at the end of a chapter or of the book itself.

tail-pipe, n. Suction-pipe in a pump.

tail-race, n. Part of mill-stream below water-wheel.

tain, n. [1. tān ; 2. tein]. Origin doubtful ; M.E. *tein*, fr. O.N. *teinn*, ' twig ', relationship w. O.E. *tān*, Goth. *tains*, 'rod, twig ', the origin of wh. is also unknown, is suggested by some dictionaries, but connexion in sense appears to be lacking ; Lat. *taenia*, ' ribbon ', see **taenia**, is hardly more convincing. Thin sheet of tin-foil used for the backing of mirrors.

taint (I.), n. [1. tānt ; 2. teint], fr. Fr. *teinte*, fem. P.P. of *teindre*, ' to tinge, dye ', fr. Lat. *tingere*, ' to stain, colour ', see **tinge** & **tint.** Trace of physical corruption or decay ; moral degeneration, imperfection ; contamination, pollution.

taint (II.), vb. trans. & intrans., fr. prec. **1.** trans. To impart a taint to ; to infect with physical or moral deterioration and corruption ; to render unwholesome or noxious : *air tainted by smoke* ; *character tainted by self-seeking* ; *tainted meat*, incipiently putrescent. **2.** intrans. To become infected, corrupted, by something noxious, by decay &c.

taintless, adj. [1. tántles ; 2. téintlis]. Prec. & **-less.** Without taint ; uncorrupted, pure.

taintlessly, adv. Prec. & **-ly.** In a taintless manner.

Tai-ping, Tae-ping, n. [1. tí píng ; 2. tái píŋ], fr. Chinese *t'ai p'ing*, ' great peace '. One taking part in Chinese Rebellion of 1850, finally crushed by Gordon in 1864.

taj, n. [1. tahj ; 2. tādž]. Pers. *tāj*, ' crown '. Tall, conical cap worn by Mohammedan dervishes.

take (I.), vb. trans. & intrans. [1. tāk ; 2. teik]. M.E. *tāken* ; L.O.E. *tacan*, fr. O.N. *taka*, ' to touch, seize ' ; prob. cogn. w. Goth. *tēkan*, ' to touch ', w. different grade ; perh. remotely connected w. same base as Lat. *digitus*, ' finger ', see **digit. A.** trans. **1.** (of bodily action) **a** To seize, lay hold of, grasp, esp. with the hand : *to take a person's head between one's hands* ; *to take a person by the hand, by the nose* ; Phrs. *to take one's arm*, lay hand on person's arm for guidance, support &c. ; *to take arms*, arm oneself, prepare to fight ; *to take in hand*, undertake ; **b** to grasp, catch hold of, grip, otherwise than with the hand : *to take something between one's knees* ; *to take (a person) to one's arms, to one's heart, breast*, (i.) to embrace him ; (ii.) to admit, receive, him into one's affections. **2.** To receive, accept, have given, handed, transferred to one, receive into one's grasp or possession : *to take presents, what is offered* ; *I can't take money from you* ; Phrs. *to take things as they come* ; *to take people as they are* ; *to take the rough with the smooth* ; *to take one's chance.* **3. a** To remove ; pick up, and convey away : *some one has taken my pen* ; *take the knife from the baby* ; **b** (math.) to deduct, subtract : *to take 4 from 10.* **4.** To convey with one, **a** to convey in one's grasp or keeping, to carry : *to take a letter to the post* ; *to take one's umbrella in case of rain* ; **b** to conduct, cause to accompany one : *take me with you* ; *to take the dog for a walk.* **5. a** To gain, obtain, possession of, power over, (i.) by one's efforts or skill in a transaction ; to win, earn : *he took £100 at Ascot* ; *large sums were taken at the gate* ; (ii.) to obtain by force, to capture : *to take a fort, ship, a prisoner* ; **b** to catch in trap, snare, with bait &c. : *to take fish* ; **c** to gain, win, as result of contest : *to take a prize* ; **d** (games, cards, chess, cricket &c.) to win : *to take a trick, a pawn, a wicket* &c. ; **e** to affect, strike, make impression upon, (i.) bodily, to affect, hit : *the blow took him on the nose* ; *the cold takes me in the chest* ; (ii.) mentally : *to take one by surprise* ; **f** to attract, charm : *to take one's fancy* ; *to be much taken by something.* **6.** To draw, absorb, receive, into the system **a** to inhale : *to take a deep breath* ; *to take breath* ; *to take the air* ; *to take a pinch of snuff* ; **b** to eat, drink, swallow, consume : *to take one's medicine* ; *I never take wine* ; *he can take no food* ; *do you take sugar ?* **7. a** To make use of, employ, procure, or select for use : *take a larger spoon* ; *take a dozen eggs and a pound of flour* ; **b** to select and associate oneself with : *take your partners* ; **c** to select and acquire by marriage : *to take a wife.* **8.** To enter and avail oneself of for conveyance : *to take a train, car* &c. ; *to take ship*, embark. **9. a** To make use of, occupy, spend, avail oneself of (time and amount) : *he took an hour over his dinner* ; *take as long as you like* ; Phr. *to take one's time (over)*, to act, work, slowly and deliberately, be slow and unhurried ; **b** (impers.) to require, demand, call for : *it takes too long* ; *it only takes five minutes to walk there* ; *it takes patience and industry to learn a language* ; *it takes many men to build a house* ; Phr. *it takes two to make a quarrel*, both parties are usually responsible. **10. a** To acquire, gain possession of, by payment ; to purchase : *I will take as many eggs as you can supply* ; **b** to reserve, engage, gain right to, by payment &c. ; to hire : *to take seats at a theatre, tickets* ; *to take a house, rooms* &c. ; **c** to subscribe to, receive regularly : *to take a newspaper.* **11.** To be infected by, catch, have communicated to one : *to take cold* ; *to take fire.* **12. a** To select, adopt, accept, for one's own use : *to take a seat*, sit down ; *please take my seat* ; Phrs. *to take the chair*, preside at meeting &c. ; *to take a back seat*, occupy inferior or obscure position, play a less important part ; **b** to assume, place oneself in, undertake, occupy oneself with : *to take one's proper position* ; *to take command, charge, the lead, precedence* ; *to take sides* ; *to take part* ; *the army takes the field* ; **c** to adopt, transfer to oneself : *to take an assumed name.* **13.** To assume, gain attribute of, come into possession of as part of one's mental condition : *to take courage, heart, fright, offence, comfort, a dislike to, exception to* &c. ; *to take care*, be careful ; *take care of*, attend carefully to. **14.** To enjoy, use : *to take a rest, a holiday.* **15.** To perform a given action, act in specified way : *to take a leap, a look round, a step, flight* ; *to take steps, measures, precautions* ; *to take vengeance* ; *to take one's leave, one's choice* ; *to take account of, no notice of* ; *a disease takes its course* ; *the river takes its rise.* **16.** To adopt specified attitude towards : *to take it easy, calmly* ; *to take something ill, amiss.* **17. a** To receive into the mind, have communicated to one ; to grasp mentally and act upon : *to take a thing to heart* ; *to take a hint, advice* ; **b** to understand, comprehend : *to take one's meaning* ; *do you take me ?* **18.** To accept mentally, assume, presume : *I take him to be an honest man* ; *I take it that you are fully acquainted with the facts of the case* ; Phr. *you may take it from me*, you may assume it to be a fact. **19.** To observe as an example, point of argument &c. ; to consider, turn one's attention to : *take the case of your brother, for instance* ; *let us take the facts in order.* **20.** To ascertain, find out, determine : *to take measurements* ; Phr. *to take a person's measure*, make an estimate of his character &c. **21.** To set down, record on, transfer to, paper or other surface : *to take notes, photographs* &c. **22.** To jump over, pass across : *the horse took the hedge* ; *to take a stream in one's stride.* **23.** (gram.) **a** To have as inflexion : *most nouns take -s in the plural* ; **b** to be followed by : *in O.E. verbs expressing deprivation take a genitive of the thing, and a dative of the person.* **B.** intrans. **1.** To have required effect, work effectively : *the vaccine did not take.* **2.** To become popular, capture general fancy : *the play did not take.* **3.** To make photographic impression of specified kind, give specific result when photographed : *to take well* &c. **C.** Followed by adverbs and prepositions, with special meanings. *Take aback*, trans., to disconcert, throw into confusion, surprise, startle. *Take after*, intrans., to resemble in features, character &c., have hereditary resemblance to : *to take after one's father. Take away*, trans., **a** to remove, cause to depart, convey away ; **b** to deduct, subtract. *Take back*, trans., to retract, withdraw : *to take back one's words. Take down*, trans., **a** to lower, remove by lifting down : *to take down a picture from the wall* ; **b** to take apart, pull down : *to take down a building* ; *take down one's hair*, to undo fastenings of, and allow to flow down the back ; **c** to swallow, gulp down ; **d** to humble, reduce conceit of ; esp. *to take a person down a peg* ; **e** to record in writing, set down on paper &c. : *to take down a speech in shorthand. Take for*, trans., **a** to believe, consider to be : *what do you take me for ?* ; *do you take me for a fool ?* ; **b** to consider erroneously, mistake : *to be taken for one's sister. Take from*, intrans., to reduce, diminish, lessen amount or quality of : *the size of her hat takes from her height* ; *his fortunate circumstances take from the merit of his achievements. Take in*, trans., **1.** to admit, receive, give entrance or welcome to : *to take in a homeless traveller, lodgers* ; **2.** to receive, undertake, to do at home : *to take in washing* ; **3.** to receive into the mind, grasp, comprehend : *he listens to the lectures without taking them in* ; **4.** to reduce to smaller size, compass, extent : *to take in a dress* ; *to take in a sail*, furl it ; **5.** to deceive, impose upon, swindle : *he took me in over the purchase of a horse* ; **6.** to subscribe to, receive regularly : *to take in a journal. Take into*, trans., *to take it into one's head, mind*, be seized with a sudden idea, notion, intention. *Take off*, **A.** trans. **1. a** to remove, lead, conduct, convey away : *to take oneself off* ; *he took me off to the garden* ; **b** to remove, lift or draw off, esp. from the body : *to take off one's hat*, esp. as salute ; *to take off one's shoes* ; **c** to lift, and move to another position : *please take your hand off me* ; *take your foot off my toe* ; to deduct, reduce by specified amount : *to take a penny off the price* ; **2.** to swallow, take down ; **3.** to mimic, burlesque. **B.** intrans., to leave ground in jumping, begin a leap. *Take on*, **1.** trans., **a** to engage in, undertake : *to take on a piece of work* ; **b** to accept as opponent in a contest : *to take a man on at golf* ; **2.** intrans., (colloq.)

to give way to emotion, be greatly agitated: *keep calm, don't take on so.* *Take out,* trans., **1.** to remove from within, extract, take away: *to take a stain out*; *hot water will take out the stiffness*; Phr. *to take the nonsense out of a person*; *to take it out of one,* weary, exhaust; **2.** to obtain, procure, have issued for one: *to take out a licence, insurance policy* &c. *Take over,* **1.** trans., to have transferred to one, assume control of: *to take over the business, duties, responsibilities*; **2.** intrans., to assume, have transferred to one, duties and responsibilities: *the new general will take over immediately from the retiring one.* *Take to,* intrans., **1.** to feel attracted by, form a liking for: *to take to a person*; **2.** to engage in, form a habit: *to take to drink, gardening.* *Take up,* trans., **1.** to raise, lift up, pick up: *to take up a book*; Phr. *to take up arms, the gauntlet, the cudgels* &c. (see **arm, cudgel** &c.); **2.** to catch end of and make secure: *to take up an artery, a dropped stitch*; **3.** to receive, admit, into a vehicle: *to take up a passenger*; **4. a** to absorb: *the blotting-paper takes up ink*; **b** to fill, occupy: *it takes up a lot of room, time*; **5.** to take into custody, arrest; **6. a** to engage in, adopt as occupation &c.: *to take up gardening*; **b** to turn one's attention to, pursue, deal with: *to take up a matter*; **c** to resume, return to: *to take up one's story.* *Take up with,* intrans., to adopt as companion &c., associate with. *Take upon,* trans., *to take (it) upon oneself to,* to assume responsibility of, presume to.

take (II.), n., fr. prec. **1.** Amount of fish, game &c. taken at one time or in specific period. **2.** Amount of money received at theatrical performance &c. **3.** (print.) Portion of copy allotted to a compositor to set up.

take-in, n. [1. ták ín; 2. téik ín]. A deception, fraud, imposition, swindle.

taken, vb. [1. táken; 2. téikən]. P.P. of **take** (I.); L.O.E. (*ġe*)*tacen,* M.E. *tāke*(*n*).

take-off, n. [1. ták awf; 2. téik ōf]. **1.** Caricature, mimicry, burlesque imitation. **2.** Place at which the feet leave the ground in jumping, often *a good, bad, take-off,* suitable, unsuitable, place for beginning a jump.

taker, n. [1. táker; 2. téikə]. **take** (I.) & **-er.** One who, that which, takes, specif., person who accepts a bet.

take-up, n. [1. ták up; 2. téik ap]. One of various mechanical devices for tightening thread in machine, taking in slack of rope &c.

takin, n. [1. táhkin; 2. tákin]. Assam. Large, heavy, reddish-brown, horned ruminant of Tibet, allied to the antelope.

taking (I.), n. [1. táking; 2. téikiŋ]. **take** (I.) & **-ing.** **1.** (pl. *takings*) That which is taken, something received as payment; earnings, receipts, gains. **2.** (colloq.) State of mental agitation, fuss, perplexity: *in a terrible taking.*

taking (II.), adj., fr. Pres. Part. of **take** (I.). **1.** Attractive, charming, captivating: *a taking manner.* **2.** (of disease) Infectious, catching.

takingly, adv. Prec. & **-ly.** In a taking manner; attractively.

takingness, n. See prec. & **-ness.** State of being taking; attractiveness.

talapoin, n. [1. tálapoin; 2. tǽləpɔin], fr. E. Indian. **1.** Buddhist priest or monk in Siam, Burma &c. **2.** Small W. African monkey.

talaria, n. pl. [1. talária; 2. təléəriə]. Lat. *tālāria,* 'ankles; winged shoes', neut. pl. form of adj. *tālārius,* 'of the ankle', fr. *tāl-*(*us*), 'ankle', see **talus,** & **-ary.** Winged sandals represented in classical art as attributes of Hermes, and also of Iris, Perseus, Eros &c.

talbot, n. [1. táwlbot; 2. tɔ́lbət]. Origin unknown; perh. fr. name of family in whose arms talbots figure. Extinct breed of hound, with pendulous ears, somewhat resembling a bloodhound.

Talbot House, n. Society with branches all over the world for mutual help and service on Christian lines in memory of the Great War, founded in memory of Gilbert Talbot, killed 1915; usually styled Toc H., the signaller's pronunciation of T. H.

talc, n. [1. talk; 2. tælk], fr. Fr., fr. Arab. *talq.* Mineral, magnesium silicate, capable of being split into thin, transparent sheets, which are elastic and do not fracture, and are used for protecting the light in lanterns, for windscreens of motors &c.

talcky, adj. [1. tálki; 2. tǽlki]. **talc** & **-y.** Talcous.

talcoid, adj. [1. tálkoid; 2. tǽlkɔid]. **talc** & **-oid.** Of, pertaining to, having the appearance of, talc.

talcose, adj. [1. tálkōs; 2. tǽlkous]. **talc** & **-ose.** Talcoid.

talcous, adj. [1. tálkus; 2. tǽlkəs]. **talc** & **-ous.** Of, composed of, containing, talc.

tale, n. [1. tāl; 2. teil]. O.E. *talu,* 'story, tale', *tæl,* 'number'; cp. O.N. *tal,* 'talk', *tala,* 'number'; Germ. *zahl,* 'number'; Du. *taal,* 'speech', cp. **taal**; O. Fris. *tale,* see **tell.** **1.** (chiefly archaic) Number, total, amount: *the tale of dead and wounded*; *the tale is complete.* **2.** Connected oral or written narrative of any length; account, record, of true or fictitious events &c.: *to tell the tale of one's adventures*; *a stirring tale*; *a fairy-tale.* Phrs. *old wives' tale,* incredible legend &c.; *tells its own tale,* is self-explanatory, is obvious record of events &c. **3.** Rumour, report (esp. of malicious reports). Phr. *to tell tales (out of school),* (i.) reveal, esp. with malicious intent, something which should be kept secret or private; (ii.) to inform concerning another's faults and peccadilloes.

talebearer, n. [1. tálbārer; 2. téilbɛ̀ərə]. Person who tells tales of others with malicious or mischievous intent; informer.

talebearing, n. [1. tálbāring; téilbɛ̀əriŋ]. Prec. & **-ing.** Act of telling tales; the spreading of malicious reports.

talent, n. [1. tálent; 2. tǽlənt], fr. Fr., fr. Latin *talent-*(*um*), fr. Gk. *tálanton,* 'pair of scales, balance; a weight; sum of money representing a talent of silver', cp. Gk. *tálanta,* 'scales of balance', fr. *tálant-,* neut. stem of *tálās,* 'suffering, enduring, unhappy', fr. stem seen in archaic form *talássai,* 'to take upon oneself, support, undergo'; cogn. w. Scrt. *tulā́,* 'balance'; Lat. *tollere,* 'to lift up'; *tolerāre,* 'to support, endure'; see **tolerate**; O.E. *þolian,* 'to endure'; see **thole.** See also **atlas, tantalus.** **1.** Ancient weight and sum of money, varying in different places and periods, e.g. *the Attic, Roman, Egyptian, talent.* **2. a** Special gift or faculty, marked aptitude in a specific direction: *a talent for languages, for drawing*; *to develop one's talents*; Phr. *to hide one's talents in a napkin,* allow one's gifts and abilities to lie idle (cp. Matt. xxv. 15); **b** persons possessing talent: *the best talent in the country*; *to encourage local talent.*

talented, adj. [1. tálented; 2. tǽləntid]. Prec. & **-ed.** Possessing talent, naturally gifted.

talentless, adj. [1. tálentles; 2. tǽləntlis]. **talent** & **-less.** Without talent, having no special gifts or aptitude.

tales, n. [1. tálēz; 2. téiliz], fr. Lat. *tālēs,* 'such', first word of writ, pl. form of *tālis,* 'such', fr. pronominal stem **to-,* whence also **the, that** &c. (law) **1.** Writ summoning additional jurors to make up deficiency. **2.** List of persons who may thus be called upon to serve on a jury.

talesman, n. [1. tál(ē)zman; 2. téil(ī)zmən]. Prec. & **man.** Person summoned by a tales to serve on a jury.

taleteller, n. [1. tálteler; 2. téiltelə]. **1.** One who relates true or fictitious stories; narrator. **2.** One who makes malicious reports; talebearer.

taliacotian, adj. [1. tàliakóshan; 2. tæ̀liəkóuʃən], fr. the Italian surgeon Tagliacozzi (d. 1599) & **-an.** *Taliacotian operation,* formation of a new nose by grafting skin from the arm or forehead, the grafted skin being severed only when it has begun to grow in its new position.

talion, n. [1. tálion; 2. tǽliən], fr. Fr., fr. Lat. *tāliōn-*(*em*), 'retaliation in kind', fr. *tāl-*(*is*), 'such', see **tales** & cp. **retaliate.** Also called *lex taliōnis*; law of punishment by inflicting the same kind of injury as that suffered, on the principle of Levitical law, an eye for an eye, a tooth for a tooth &c.

talionic, adj. [1. tàliónik; 2. tæ̀liɔ́nik]. Prec. & **-ic.** Of, pertaining to, the law of talion.

taliped, adj. & n. [1. táliped; 2. tǽliped]. Mod. Lat., fr. *tālus,* 'ankle', see **talus,** & *-i-* & Lat. *ped-,* stem of *pēs,* 'foot', see **pedal.** **1.** adj. **a** Suffering from talipes; club-footed; **b** (zool.) having the feet placed at peculiar angle &c., as the sloth. **2.** n. **a** Taliped person; **b** taliped animal; the sloth.

talipes, n. [1. tálipēz; 2. tǽlipiz]. See prec. **1. a** Club-foot; **b** state of having a club-foot. **2.** Peculiar position, formation, or distortion of foot.

talipot, n. [1. tálipot; 2. tǽlipɔt], fr. Hind. *talpat,* fr. Scrt. *tala,* 'palm', & *patra,* 'leaf'. East-Indian palm with large fan-shaped leaves.

talisman, n. [1. tálizman; 2. tǽlizmən], fr. Span., fr. Arab. *ṭilsaman* (pl.), fr. Gk. *télesma,* 'payment'; Late Gk. 'consecration, sacred rite, mystery', fr. *teléein,* 'to pay; to fulfil, perform; to initiate into mysteries', fr. *tél-os,* 'fulfilment, completion, end', see **tele-.** Object regarded as possessing supernatural power of influencing, protecting &c., the wearer; charm, amulet.

talismanic, adj. [1. tàlizmánik; 2. tæ̀lizmǽnik]. Prec. & **-ic.** Pertaining to, of the nature of, having the power of, a talisman.

talk (I.), vb. intrans. & trans. [1. tawk; 2. tōk]. M.E. *talken,* cp. E. Fris. *talken*; connected w. O.E. *talian,* 'to reckon'; see **tale** & **tell.** **A.** intrans. **a** To express ideas &c. by means of language; to speak: *to learn to talk*; *to talk to a friend*; *stop talking*; *to talk too much*; Phrs. *to talk big,* boast; *to talk at,* refer pointedly to, direct remarks at (person), without addressing him directly; **b** specif. to gossip, comment on other people's affairs in a malicious spirit: *people are beginning to talk.* **B.** trans. **1.** To give expression to in words, utter in speech: *to talk scandal, treason, nonsense, business.* **2.** To use (a language) as means of expression; to speak: *to talk French* &c. **3.** To bring into specified condition by talking: *to talk oneself hoarse.* Phr. *to talk a donkey's hind leg off,* talk incessantly, with great volubility. **C.** Followed by adverbs and prepositions with special meanings. *Talk about,* intrans., to talk upon the subject of, discuss, debate. *Talk down,* trans., to silence by louder or more effective talking. *Talk of,* intrans., **a** to discuss, talk about; Phr. *talking of,* à propos of, with reference to; **b** to put forward as a suggestion or intention: *they are talking of going abroad.* *Talk over,* trans. **a** to discuss, debate, hold council upon; **b** to persuade, win over, by talking. *Talk round,* **a** intrans., to discuss (subject) at some length without coming to the real point; **b** trans., to bring (person) over to one's own view by talking. *Talk to,* intrans., **a** to address in speech, converse with; **b** specif., to address reproaches to, reprove. *Talk up,* intrans., to speak loudly or clearly.

talk (II.), n., fr. prec. **1. a** Act of talking, mutual communication of ideas in speech; conversation: *fond of good talk*; **b** a conversation, a chat: *to have a long, friendly talk*; **c** an informal lecture or address. **2.** Specif., frivolous, idle, futile talk or discussion which leads to nothing: *he is all talk*; *we've had enough talk, it is time to act.* **3.** Subject of conversation; gossip: *the talk of the town.*

talkative, adj. [1. táwkativ; 2. tɔ́kətiv]. **talk** & **-ative.** Given to, fond of, talking; loquacious; reverse of *taciturn.*

talkatively, adv. Prec. & **-ly**. In a talkative manner.

talkativeness, n. See prec. & **-ness**. Loquacity.

talkee-talkee, n. [1. táwki táwki; 2. tɔ̄ki tɔ̄ki]. **talk**, & *-ee*, to suggest broken English. **1.** Broken English, esp. of negroes &c. **2.** Incessant, futile, idle chatter; useless, empty loquacity.

talker, n. [1. táwker; 2. tɔ̄kə]. **talk (I.)** & **-er.** **1.** One who talks, esp. of specified kind: *a good talker.* **2.** One who talks too much; one who talks but does not act.

talkies, n. pl. [1. táwkiz; 2. tɔ̄kiz], fr. **talk (I.)** on the anal. of **movies.** (vulg. slang) Sound-films.

talking, adj. [1. táwking; 2. tɔ̄kiŋ], fr. Pres. Part. of **talk (I.)**. **1.** Having, using, the power of speech or of imitating speech: *a talking parrot* &c.; *talking doll*, one emitting squeaks when pressed &c. **2.** Speaking, expressive.

talking-film, n. Sound-film.

talking-to, n. [1. táwking tōō; 2. tɔ̄kiŋ tū]. A reprimand, a reproof, a scolding: *I'll give him a good talking-to.*

tall (I.), adj. [1. tawl; 2. tɔ̄l]. Origin uncertain; no cognates in other languages. **1.** Above the average in stature; high in relation to the average, or to surroundings: *a tall man; a tall house, tower, tree, chimney, ship* &c. **2.** Of a specified height: *six feet tall.* **3.** (slang) Excessive, extravagant, inordinate, difficult to believe: *a tall story*; Phr. *a tall order*, task, undertaking, difficult of fulfilment.

tall (II.), adv., fr. prec. (slang) Extravagantly, boastfully: *to talk tall.*

tallage, talliage, n. [1. tálij, táliij; 2. tǽlidž, tǽliidž]. M.E. *tall(i)age*, fr. O. Fr. *taillage*, fr. *tailler*, 'to cut', see **tail (III.)**, & **-age.** Form of taxation, including customs and subsidies, established by Parliament in 1340.

tallboy, n. [1. táwlboi; 2. tɔ̄lbɔi]. **tall** & **boy.** Chest of drawers about double the usual height.

tallith, n. [1. tálith; 2. tǽliþ]. Heb., 'covering'. Scarf, originally fringed mantle, worn by Jews round the neck, or on the head, while at prayer.

tallness, n. [1. táwlnes; 2. tɔ̄lnis]. **tall (I.)** & **-ness.** Quality of being tall; height.

tallow (I.), n. [1. tálō; 2. tǽlou]. M.E. *tal(u)gh*; cp. Du. *talgh*; M.L.G., Germ., Swed. *talg*; O.N. *tólgr.* The coarser and harder animal fats melted down for making common kind of candles, for lubricating machinery &c.; *vegetable tallow*, similar substance made from vegetable fats.

tallow (II.), vb. trans., fr. prec. **1.** To grease with tallow. **2.** To fatten: *to tallow sheep.*

tallow-chandler, n. One who makes and sells tallow candles.

tallow-drop, n. Method of cutting precious stones so that one, or both sides are dome-shaped.

tallow-faced, adj. [1. tálō fāst; 2. tǽlou feist]. Having a pale, unhealthy complexion.

tallowish, adj. [1. tálōish; 2. tǽlouiʃ]. **tallow (I.)** & **-ish.** Somewhat tallowy.

tallow-tree, n. One of various trees yielding vegetable tallow.

tallowy, adj. [1. tálōi; 2. tǽloui]. **tallow (I.)** & **-y.** Pertaining to, like, containing, smeared with, tallow.

tally (I.), n. [1. táli; 2. tǽli]. M.E. *tail*, fr. O. Fr. *taille*, 'notch, cut', see **tail (III.).** **1. a** Piece of wood with notches cut to indicate numbers, amount owing &c.; hence, **b** one of two accounts kept in duplicate. **2.** A label, tag of identification.

tally (II.), vb. trans. & intrans., fr. prec. **A.** trans. **1.** To reckon, register, keep account of, by tally. **2.** (naut.) To put aft: *to tally a sheet* &c. **B.** intrans. To correspond, conform exactly, agree: *his statement does not tally with the facts.*

tally-ho, n. & vb. intrans. [1. tàli hṓ; 2. tæ̀li hóu], fr. Fr. *taïaut.* **1.** n. Huntsman's cry to hounds. **2.** vb. To utter this cry.

tallyman, n. [1. táliman; 2. tǽlimən]. **tally** & **man.** One who keeps a tally-shop.

tally-sheet, n. Paper on which tally is kept.

tally-shop, n. Shop where accounts are kept by tally and goods are paid by instalment.

talma, n. [1. tálma; 2. tǽlmə], fr. François Talma, French actor, d. 1826. Long, sometimes hooded, man's or woman's cloak, worn in early part of 19th cent.

talmi-gold, n. [1. tálmi gōld; 2. tǽlmi gòuld]. Origin unknown. Kind of thinly gilt brass.

Talmud, n. [1. tálmud; 2. tǽlməd]. Heb. *talmūd*, 'instruction'. Whole body of Jewish civil and canonical law and commentary thereupon, apart from that in the Pentateuch.

Talmudic(al), adj. [1. talmū́dik(l), talmúdik(l); 2. tælmjū́dik(l), tælmádik(l)]. Prec. & **-ic** & **-al.** Of, pertaining to, contained in, the Talmud.

Talmudist, n. [1. tálmudist; 2. tǽlmədist]. **Talmud** & **-ist.** **a** One of the compilers of the Talmud; **b** student of, one versed in, the Talmud.

Talmudistic, adj. [1. tàlmudístik; 2. tæ̀lmədístik]. Prec. & **-ic.** Of, pertaining to, the Talmud or a Talmudist.

talon, n. [1. tálun; 2. tǽlən], fr. Fr., fr. Lat. *tālōn-(em)*, 'ankle; heel'; see **talus.** **1. a** Claw of bird of prey; **b** human finger nails when long and supposed to resemble a bird's claws. **2.** Heel of sword-blade. **3.** (archit.) Ogee moulding. **4.** (cards) Part of pack left after dealing. **5.** Certificate attached to a bond exchangeable for a further sheet of coupons.

taloned, adj. [1. tálund; 2. tǽlənd]. Prec. & **-ed.** Having, furnished with, talon(s).

taluk, talook, n. [1. talōōk; 2. təlū́k]. Hind. *taluk*, fr. Arab. **1.** Government district in southern and western India, paying fixed revenue in lieu of taxes. **2.** Proprietary landed estate on special tenure, esp. in Oudh.

talukdar, n. [1. talōōkdar; 2. təlū́kdā]. Hind. Administrator of, owner of, a taluk.

talus, n. [1. tálus; 2. téiləs]. Lat. *tālus*, 'ankle, ankle-bone, heel'; etymol. doubtful. **1. a** Ankle-bone, bone of tarsus which articulates with leg-bones; **b** ankle. **2.** Slope of wall or fortification. **3.** (geol.) Sloping mass of fallen fragments at foot of cliff.

tamability, n. [1. tàmabíliti; 2. tèiməbíliti]. Next word & **-ity.** State of being tamable.

tamable, adj. [1. tā́mabl; 2. téiməbl]. **tame** & **-able.** Capable of being tamed.

tamableness, n. Prec. & **-ness.** Tamability.

tamale, n. [1. tamáhlā; 2. təmā́le]. Span., fr. Mexican. Dish made of crushed Indian corn, meat, red peppers &c.

tamandua, n. [1. tamándūa; 2. təmǽndjuə]. Brazilian. Small, arboreal ant-eater with prehensile tail.

tamanoir, n. [1. támanwar; 2. tǽmənwā], fr. Fr., fr. prec. Great ant-eater of S. America, with long hair and snout.

tamanu, n. [1. támanōō; 2. tǽmənū]. East Indian. Gamboge tree of East Indies and Pacific islands, yielding tacamahac.

tamarack, n. [1. támarak; 2. tǽməræk]. Am. Indian. **1.** N. American black larch. **2.** Kind of N. American pine.

tamarin, n. [1. támarin; 2. tǽmərin]. S. Am. Indian. S. American marmoset.

tamarind, n. [1. támarind; 2. tǽmərind], fr. Span. *tamarindo*, fr. Arab. *tamr Hindi*, fr. *tamr*, 'date', & *Hind*, 'India'. **1.** Tropical tree with pinnate leaves and yellow flowers. **2.** Pod of this tree, containing a brownish pulp used in cookery, medicine, for making cooling drinks &c.

tamarisk, n. [1. támarisk; 2. tǽmərisk], fr. Lat. *tamarisc-(us)*, *tamarix*, 'tamarisk'. Genus of shrubs, esp. evergreen variety with minute leaves and pink and white flowers arranged in spikes.

tamasha, n. [1. tamáhsha; 2. təmā́ʃə]. Arab. (Anglo-Indian) Elaborate function, entertainment.

tambour (I.), n. [1. támboor; 2. tǽmbuə], fr. Fr., fr. Arab. *ṭambūr*, 'drum, lute'. **1.** Drum, esp. bass-drum. **2.** One of various objects resembling drum in shape; specif. **a** wooden frame for stretching material for embroidery; **b** (archit.) cylindrical stone forming part of column; drum; **c** kind of fish. **3.** (archit.) Vestibule in church porch designed to prevent draughts. **4.** Palisade defending gate &c. **5.** Material embroidered in tambour.

tambour (II.), vb. trans., fr. prec. To embroider in a tambour.

tambourin, n. [1. támborin; 2. tǽmbərin], fr. Fr., dimin. of prec. **1.** Kind of Provençal drum. **2. a** Dance accompanied by tambourin; **b** music for this dance.

tambourine, n. [1. tàmborḗn; 2. tæ̀mbərī́n], fr. Fr., prob. fr. prec. **1.** Light instrument played by shaking and rapping, consisting of a round shallow frame with skin stretched over one side, and having jingling metal disks attached. **2. a** Provençal dance; **b** music for this dance. **3.** S. African wild pigeon, white, with black-tipped wings and tail.

tambour-work, n. Embroidery done in frame.

tame (I.), adj. [1. tām; 2. teim]. O.E. *tam*, M.E. *tāme*; cp. Du. *tam*; Germ. *zahm*, 'tame'; cogn. w. Lat. *domāre*; Gk. *damáein*, 'to tame, subdue'; cp. Lat. *domus*, 'house'; see **dome** & words there referred to. **1.** (of animal, bird) Brought under human authority, made friendly and tractable; reverse of *fierce, wild.* **2. a** Subdued, spiritless, passive; **b** dull, flat, uninspiring: *a tame affair, retort, surrender* &c.

tame (II.), vb. trans. New formation fr. prec.; cp. O.E. *temian*, 'to tame'; this stem has been lost. **1.** To make tame; reduce to domesticated state; bring under human influence; make docile and tractable: *to tame a wild animal, bird* &c. **2.** To bring into subjection, gain authority over; curb, subdue: *to tame one's spirit, tongue, ardour* &c.

tameless, adj. [1. tā́mles; 2. téimlis]. **tame (II.)** & **-less.** (poet.) Incapable of being tamed.

tamely, adv. [1. tā́mli; 2. téimli]. **tame (I.)** & **-ly.** In a tame manner; without offering resistance: *to submit tamely to discipline* &c.

tameness, n. [1. tā́mnes; 2. téimnis]. See prec. & **-ness.** State or quality of being tame.

tamer, n. [1. tā́mer; 2. téimə]. **tame (II.)** & **-er.** One who tames: *a tamer of wild animals*; (often in compounds) *lion-tamer* &c.

Tamil, n. [1. támil; 2. tǽmil]. Native. **1.** One of the Dravidian dialects of Ceylon and S. India. **2.** Inhabitant of S. India or Ceylon.

Tamilian, n. [1. tamílian; 2. tæmíliən]. Prec. & **-ian.** Of, pertaining to, the Tamils or their language.

tamis, n. [1. támi(s); 2. tǽmi(s)]. Fr. *tamis*, 'sieve'; etymol. doubtful. Bag, cloth, for straining liquids, fruit-pulp &c.

Tammany, n. [1. támani; 2. tǽməni], fr. Tammany Hall, in New York, headquarters of Tammany Society; name is supposed to be that of an Indian chief. Also *Tammany Society*, organized Democratic party in New York City.

Tammanyism, n. [1. támaniizm; 2. tǽməniizəm]. Prec. & **-ism.** Tammany policy and principles.

tam-o'-shanter, n. [1. tám o shánter; 2. tǽm ə ʃǽntə], fr. hero of Burns's poem of this name. Round woollen cap fitting closely round the head and having a flat, baggy top.

tamp, vb. trans. [1. tamp; 2. tæmp]. Perh. fr. **tampon.** To pound, stamp, ram down; specif., to ram down clay &c. on top of charge so as to plug the hole in blasting.

tampan, n. [1. támpan; 2. tǽmpən]. Native. Poisonous S. African tick, biting flesh between fingers and toes.

tamper, vb. intrans. [1. támper; 2. tǽmpə]. Variant of **temper.** Usually *tamper with*, to interfere, meddle, with; specif. **a** to make changes in (a document) with fraudulent intent; **b** to attempt to corrupt, to suborn (a witness).

tamping, n. [1. támping; 2. tǽmpiŋ]. **tamp & -ing.** Material used to ram down a charge of explosive, to fill blast-hole &c.

tampion, n. [1. támpiun; 2. tǽmpiən]. Variant of **tampon**. Disk or plug; **a** one for stopping the mouth of a gun; **b** a stopper for the end of an organ-pipe &c.

tampon, n. & vb. trans. [1. támpun; 2. tǽmpən], fr. O. Fr., variant of *tapon*, 'bung, plug', fr. Du. *tap*, & **-oon. 1. n.** Plug of lint &c. to stop haemorrhage. **2. vb.** To plug with a tampon.

tamponade, n. [1. tamponád; 2. tæmpənéid]. Prec. & **-ade.** Use of a tampon to arrest haemorrhage.

tamponage, n. [1. támponij; 2. tǽmpənidž]. **tampon & -age.** Use of, method of applying, tampons.

tamponment, n. [1. támponment; 2. tǽmpənmənt]. **tampon & -ment.** Tamponade.

tamtam. See **tomtom.**

tan (I.), n. [1. tan; 2. tæn], fr. Fr., either fr. Germ. *tanne*, 'fir-tree', or fr. Celt., cp. Bret. *tann*, 'oak'. **1.** Bark of oak &c. bruised to extract tannic acid for use in tanning. **2.** Bark from which tannic acid has been extracted; also called *spent tan*. **3.** The colour of tan, i.e. yellowish brown.

tan (II.), vb. trans. & intrans., fr. prec. **A.** trans. **1.** To make (hides) into leather by steeping in a solution of tannic acid. **2.** To make brown: *complexion tanned by the sun.* **3.** To toughen with tannic acid: *to tan fish-nets* &c. **4.** (slang) To beat, flog. **B.** intrans. (of complexion &c.) To become brown through exposure to sun.

tan (III.), adj., fr. **tan** (I.). Having the colour of tan; yellowish brown.

tan (IV.). Abbr. of **tangent** (II.), 2.

tana, tanna, n. [1. táhna; 2. tánə], fr. Hind. *thāna.* (in India) **a** Military post; **b** police station.

tanager, n. [1. tánajer; 2. tǽnədžə], fr. Brazilian *tangara.* Group of American birds of finch family, usually brilliantly coloured.

Tanagra, adj. [1. tánagra; 2. tǽnəgrə], fr. Tanagra in Boeotia, Greece, where many statuettes of this type have been found. Made at, coming from, Tanagra, esp. applied to a type of small coloured terra-cotta figurines or statuettes, usually of maidens &c., found in ancient graves and temples at Tanagra and elsewhere in Greece and Italy.

tanagrine, adj. [1. tánagrin; 2. tǽnəgrin]. Prec. & **-ine.** Of, pertaining to, the tanagers.

tanagroid, adj. [1. tánagroid; 2. tǽnəgroid]. **tanager & -oid.** Of, pertaining to, resembling, a tanager.

tan-ball, n. Compressed lump of spent tan used as fuel.

tandem, adv. & n. [1. tándem; 2. tǽndəm]. Orig. as pun, fr. Lat. *tandem*, 'at length', earlier **tamdem*, fr. *tam*, 'so', fr. pronominal stem **to-* &c., see under **the**, & pronominal stem **dĕ*, see **de-. 1.** adv. (of two horses) Harnessed one behind another: *to drive tandem*, with horses so harnessed. **2.** n. **a** Pair of horses harnessed tandem; **b** carriage drawn by horses placed tandem; **c** bicycle with seats for two persons, one behind another. **3.** (attrib., of bicycle) Having seats for two persons, one behind another.

tändstickor, n. [1. tándstiker; 2. tǽndstikə], fr. Swed. *tändstickor*, 'matches', fr. *tända*, 'to kindle', cp. **tinder**, & *sticka*, 'slip of wood'; cp. **stick** (II.). Wooden match.

tang (I.), n. [1. tang; 2. tæŋ]. M.E. *tange*, fr. O.N. *tange*, 'dagger'; cp. O.E. *tange*, 'pair of tongs', see **tongs. 1.** Spike, pointed shank, projecting from upper end of blade of tool, knife, dagger &c., to fit into handle. **2.** Strong, penetrating, pungent taste or smell; (also in non-material sense).

tang (II.), vb. trans., fr. prec. To furnish with a tang or spike.

tang (III.), n., fr. Dan. *tang*, 'seaweed'; cp. O.N. *þang*, 'seaweed'. Kind of seaweed.

tang (IV.), vb. intrans. & trans. Imitative. **1.** intrans. To make a harsh, ringing sound, clang. **2.** trans. **a** To clash (metal) together; **b** *to tang bees*, cause them to settle when swarming by clanging metal, beating cans &c.

tang (V.), n., fr. prec. Harsh, ringing sound.

tangency, n. [1. tánjensi; 2. tǽndžənsi]. **tangent** (I.) & **-cy.** State of being tangent.

tangent (I.), adj. [1. tánjent; 2. tǽndžənt], fr. Lat. *tangent-(em)*, Pres. Part. of *tangere*, 'to touch'; cp. Lat. *integer*, 'whole, untouched'; *tagax*, 'thievish'; cogn. w. Gk. *tetagṓn*, 'grasping'; cogn. w. Goth. *tēkan*, 'to touch', see also **tact.** Meeting at a point without intersecting: *a line tangent to a curve, sphere* &c.

tangent (II.), n., fr. prec. **1.** Straight line touching a curve at one point only. Phr. *to go off, fly off, at a tangent*, to pass suddenly to an entirely different line of thought. **2.** (trig.) Tangent line subtending angle, expressed as ratio to radius of circle.

tangent-balance, n. Balance in which the weight is indicated by a pointer on a graduated arc.

tangential, adj. [1. tanjénshal; 2. tændžénʃəl]. **tangent** (II.) & **-ial.** Of, pertaining to, forming, a tangent.

tangentially, adv. Prec. & **-ly.** In a tangential manner; as, in the direction of, a tangent.

Tangerine (I.), adj. [1. tànjerén; 2. tæ̀ndžəríːn], fr. Fr., fr. *Tanger*, 'Tangiers', & **-ine.** Of, pertaining to, coming from, Tangiers.

Tangerine (II.), n., fr. prec. **1.** Native, inhabitant, of Tangiers. **2.** (without cap.) A Tangerine orange; small thin-skinned, flattish orange from Tangiers; cp. *mandarine.*

tanghin, n. [1. tánggin; 2. tǽŋgin], fr. Fr., fr. native *tangena.* Evergreen tree of Madagascar, bearing poisonous fruit.

tangibility, n. [1. tànjibíliti; 2. tæ̀ndžibíliti]. **tangible & -ity.** State or quality of being tangible.

tangible, adj. [1. tánjibl; 2. tǽndžibl], fr. L. Lat. *tangibilis*, 'that may be touched', fr. *tang-(ere)*, 'to touch', see **tangent** (I.), & **-ible. 1. a** Capable of being touched, perceptible by sense of touch; having material substance; specif. **b** (law, of property &c.) material, corporeal. **2.** (fig.) Clearly defined in the mind; definite, practical; not vague, illusory, or visionary: *a tangible reason, ground of complaint.*

tangibleness, n. Prec. & **-ness.** Tangibility.

tangibly, adv. See prec. & **-ly.** In a tangible manner.

tangle (I.), n. [1. tánggl; 2. tǽŋgl]. Perh. fr. Dan. *tang*, 'seaweed', see **tang** (III.), & **-le**; but cp. M.E. *tagle*, Swed. dial. *taggla*, 'to entangle'. **1.** Confused knot or mass of interwoven threads; intricate, disorderly, irregular interweaving of flexible materials: *a tangle of wool, briars* &c.; *to get one's hair in a tangle.* **2.** (in non-material sense) State of confusion, disorder, perplexity: *his affairs, thoughts, were in a tangle.* **3.** Device, consisting of iron frame with lines, hooks &c. attached, for drawing up seaweeds &c. from sea-bottom. **4.** Kind of seaweed.

tangle (II.), vb. trans. & intrans., fr. prec. **A.** trans. **1.** To form into an intricate, confused mass, to intertwine confusedly: *tangled threads.* **2.** (fig.) To complicate, confuse, make perplexing. **3.** To ensnare, catch, entangle. **B.** intrans. To become tangled, be inextricably twisted together.

tanglesome, adj. [1. tángglsum; 2. tǽŋglsəm]. **tangle** (I.) & **-some.** Intricately interwoven.

tangly, adj. [1. tánggli; 2. tǽŋgli]. **tangle** (I.) & **-y.** Tangled, full of tangles.

tango, n. [1. tánggō; 2. tǽŋgou]. Span.-American. **a** S. American dance of Spanish origin; **b** dance for two persons, derived from this, and introduced into Europe at the beginning of the 20th cent.

tangram, n. [1. tángram; 2. tǽngræm]. Etymol. unknown. Chinese puzzle consisting of a square cut into seven specific shapes to be put together to form different figures.

tangy, adj. [1. tángi; 2. tǽŋi]. **tang** (I.) & **-y.** Having a tang; producing a sharp, distinct flavour or odour.

tanist, n. [1. tánist; 2. tǽnist], fr. Ir. *tanaiste*, 'prince's heir', fr. *tan*, 'territory'. Heir elect to Celtic chief.

tanistry, n. [1. tánistri; 2. tǽnistri]. Prec. & **-ry.** System under the Brehon laws of ancient Ireland whereby the chieftaincy of a clan, although hereditary in a particular family, was fixed by the election of an individual from the members of the family.

tank, n. [1. tangk; 2. tæŋk], fr. Port. *tanque* for *estanque*, 'pond'; cp. Fr. *étang*, fr. earlier *estang*, fr. Lat. *stagnum*, 'pool, pond'; see **stagnant. 1. a** Vessel, receptacle, cistern, for holding or storing water, oil, or gas; **b** specif., part of tender holding water-supply for locomotive engine; **c** artificial reservoir for water in India &c. **2.** (mil.) Heavy, armoured car carrying guns and moving on caterpillar wheels.

tankage, n. [1. tángkij; 2. tǽŋkidž]. **tank & -age. 1.** Storage of water, oil, gas &c. in tanks. **2.** Price charged for this. **3.** Cubic capacity of tank. **4.** Substance, used as fertilizer, obtained by rendering down refuse fat &c.

tankard, n. [1. tángkard; 2. tǽŋkəd]. Cp. Du. *tanckaert*; O. Fr. *tancquard*; origin uncertain; perh. connected w. **tank. 1.** Large drinking-vessel of metal, porcelain, or wood, sometimes with cover attached. **2.** Amount contained in tankard.

tank engine, n. Locomotive engine carrying its own supplies of water and coal instead of drawing a tender.

tanker, n. [1. tángker; 2. tǽŋkə]. **tank & -er.** Vessel used for carrying and distributing oil as fuel to ships driven by oil, thus serving as a reservoir.

tan-liquor, n. Infusion of bark used for steeping hides in tanning.

tannable, adj. [1. tánabl; 2. tǽnəbl]. **tan** (II.) & **-able.** Capable of being tanned.

tan(n)adar, n. [1. tánadar; 2. tǽnədā]. Hind. Officer in charge of a tana.

tannage, n. [1. tánij; 2. tǽnidž]. **tan** (II.) & **-age.** Action, process, of tanning.

tannate, n. [1. tánāt; 2. tǽneit]. **tan** (I.) & **-ate.** (chem.) A salt of tannic acid.

tanner (I.), n. [1. táner; 2. tǽnə]. **tan** (II.) & **-er.** Person engaged in the business of tanning.

tanner (II.), n. Etymol. unknown. (slang) A sixpence.

tannery, n. [1. táneri; 2. tǽnəri]. **tan** (II.) & **-ery.** Establishment for tanning.

tannic, adj. [1. tánik; 2. tǽnik]. **tan** (I.) & **-ic.** Of, pertaining to, obtained from, tan; esp. *tannic acid*, astringent substance obtained from oak-bark, gall-nuts &c., and used in preparation of leather, in medicine, and in making ink.

tanniferous, adj. [1. taníferus; 2. tænífərəs]. **tan** (I.) & *-i-* & **-ferous.** Yielding tannic acid.

tannin, n. [1. tánin; 2. tǽnin]. **tan** (I.) & **-in.** Tannic acid.

tanning, n. [1. táning; 2. tǽniŋ]. **tan** (II.) & **-ing.** Art or process of preparing leather from hides.

tan-ooze, n. Tan-liquor.

tan-pickle, n. Tan-liquor.

tanrec, tenrec, n. [1. tánrek; 2. tǽnrɛk], fr. Fr., fr. Malagasy *tandraka.* Small insectivorous mammal of Madagascar, with a tailless body covered with spines.

tansy, n. [1. tánzi; 2. tǽnzi], fr. O. Fr. *tanasie*, fr. L. Lat., fr. Gk. *athanasia*, 'immortality', fr. neg. pref. **a-** & *thána-(tos)*, 'death', see **thanato-.** Bitter, aromatic, perennial herb, *Tanacetum*, with fine, deeply indented leaves and large heads of small, closely set yellow flowers.

tantalization, n. [1. tàntalizáshun; 2. tæ̀ntəlaizéiʃən]. Next word & **-ation.** Act of tantalizing; state of being tantalized.

tantalize, vb. trans. [1. tántalīz; 2. tǽntəlaiz]. See **tantalus** & **-ize.** To torment by constant, alternate renewal of hope and disappointment; to tease, harass, by repeated disappointments in attainment of some object.

tantalizing, adj. [1. tántalīzing; 2. tǽntəlaiziŋ], fr. Pres. Part. of prec. Having the power to tantalize; inspiring hope which is repeatedly renewed and disappointed.

tantalizingly, adv. Prec. & **-ly**. In a tantalizing manner.

tantalum, n. [1. tántalum; 2. tǽntələm], fr. **tantalus**. Rare, silvery, hard, ductile metallic element used in making filaments for electric lamps.

tantalus, n. [1. tántalus; 2. tǽntələs]. Lat. *Tantalus*, fr. Gk. *Tántalos*, son of Zeus, condemned to stand up to his chin in water with fruit suspended above his head, both food and drink receding when he tried to reach them; formed by reduplication fr. stem **tal-*, fr. **tl-*, **tel-*, 'to endure', seen in Gk. *tálās*, 'suffering', *tálanta*, 'scales of a balance', see **talent**. **1.** Stand containing spirit decanters, open at the sides, with a bar which prevents removal of the bottles unless it is unlocked. **2.** Wood-ibis.

tantamount, adj. [1. tántamount; 2. tǽntəmaunt], fr. A.-Fr. *tant amunter*, 'to amount to so much', fr. O. Fr. *tant*, fr. Lat. *tant-(us)*, 'so much', fr. pronominal stem **to-*, seen in Lat. *tam*, 'so', see **tandem**, & **amount**. Of equal value or effect; equivalent: *an invitation which is tantamount to a command.*

tantara, n. [1. tantáhra; 2. tæntárə]. Imitative; cp. **tarantara**. Blast or series of notes on trumpet, horn &c.

tantivy, n., vb. intrans., adj., adv. [1. tantívi; 2. tæntívi]. Prob. imitative of hunting-horn. (all archaic or obs.) **1.** n. **a** Hunting cry; **b** swift gallop or rush. **2.** vb. To gallop at full speed. **3.** adj. Swift, rushing. **4.** adv. Swiftly, headlong.

tantra, n. [1. tántra; 2. tǽntrə]. Scrt. *tantra(m)*, 'thread; rule'; cp. *tantrá*, 'relaxation'; cogn. w. Lat. *tendere*, 'to strain, stretch', see **tend (II.)**. See further **tone**, **thin**, & words there referred to. One of the later Sanskrit religious text-books, chiefly on magic.

tantrism, n. [1. tántrizm; 2. tǽntrizəm]. Prec. & **-ism**. Doctrines enunciated in the tantras.

tantrist, n. [1. tántrist; 2. tǽntrist]. **tantra** & **-ist**. Student, adherent, of tantrism.

tantrum, n. [1. tántrum; 2. tǽntrəm]. Etymol. unknown. (colloq.) Fit, outburst, of violent temper; exhibition of petulance: *to fly, go, into a tantrum.*

tan-yard, n. Establishment for conversion of hides into leather.

Taoism, n. [1. táh-ōizm, tóuizm; 2. táouizəm, táuizəm], fr. Chinese *tao*, 'way', & **-ism**. Chinese religious system founded upon the teaching of Lao-tsze (c. 500 B.C.).

tap (I.), n. [1. tap; 2. tæp]. O.E. *tæppa*, M.E. *tappe*, cp. O.N. *tappi*. **1.** Device with turning valve or screw for controlling flow of liquid from pipe, cask &c.; cock. Phr. *on tap*, (of liquor) kept in a cask fitted with tap and ready to be drawn off. **2.** Liquor obtained from particular cask; special brew of liquor. **3.** Tap-room. **4.** Instrument for cutting internal screw-threads, in a nut &c.

tap (II.), vb. trans. O.E. *tæppan*, M.E. *tappen*, fr. O.E. *tæppa*, 'tap', see prec. **1. a** To supply with a tap; to fit a tap into (a cask &c.) and draw liquor from it; **b** to pierce and draw liquid from a swelling in the body: *to tap a person for dropsy*; **c** (slang) to extract, borrow, money from: *he tried to tap me for a fiver yesterday.* **2.** (by extension, in various senses) To obtain access to, to make available: *to tap new sources of information*; *to tap a telephone wire*, to fix receiver to and listen to messages passing over it.

tap (III.), vb. trans. & intrans. M.E. *tappen*, fr. O. Fr. *taper*, prob. of Gmc. origin. **A.** trans. **1. a** To strike lightly, with slight, rapid blow: *to tap the floor with one's toe*; *to tap a person on the shoulder*; **b** to make use of (an object) in tapping: *to tap one's crutch on the floor.* **2.** To fix a piece of leather on to, in repairing: *to tap the heel of a shoe.* **B.** intrans. To knock lightly with a quick blow or series of blows; to rap: *to tap on the door.*

tap (IV.), n., fr. prec. **1. a** Light, quick blow; **b** sound made by such a blow. **2.** (pl. *taps*, mil.) Signal for extinguishing of lights in soldiers' quarters. **3.** Small piece of leather used to repair sole or heel of boot &c.

tapa, n. [1. táhpa; 2. tápa]. Polynesian. Paper-like fabric made by Pacific Islanders from the bark of a kind of mulberry and used for mats, hangings &c.

tape (I.), n. [1. tāp; 2. teip]. O.E. *tæppe*; M.E. *tappe, tape*, 'tape, fillet'; cp. O.E. *tæppet*, 'cloth', fr. Lat. *tapēte*, 'cloth, carpet, hangings', fr. Gk. *tápēt-*, 'hangings, carpet'; prob. fr. Pers. or Armenian; cp. Med. Pers. *tāftan*, 'to spin'; ultimately fr. base **ten-*, 'to stretch', cp. **tend (II.)** & **thin**. **1.** Linen or cotton thread woven into a strong narrow strip, used for tying things into bundles, binding edges of material, fastening garments &c.: *red tape*, that formerly used for tying up legal documents, hence, (fig.) pedantic formality and insistence on routine in legal and other business. **2.** Length of tape &c. stretched between winning-posts on race-track. Phr. *to breast the tape*, reach winning post in foot-race. **3.** Narrow strip of paper on which message is printed in self-recording telegraph instrument.

tape (II.), vb. trans., fr. prec. **a** To join, fasten, bind, supply, with tape; **b** specif. (bookbinding) to fasten together with bands of tape: *to tape the sections of a book.*

tape-line, n. Tape-measure.

tape-machine, n. (colloq.) Self-recording telegraph instrument.

tape-measure, n. Length of tape or strip of flexible metal, marked in inches, feet, yards &c., and used for measuring.

taper (I.), n. [1. tāper; 2. téipə]. O.E. *tapur*; perh. Celt.; cp. Ir. *tapar*. **a** Wick thinly coated with wax or tallow, used for lighting lamps &c.; **b** a thin candle.

taper (II.), adj., fr. prec. (chiefly poet.) Tapering.

taper (III.), vb. intrans. & trans., fr. **taper (I.)**. **1.** intrans. To narrow, contract, diminish, gradually to a point in one direction; also *taper off.* **2.** trans. To cause to taper, give tapering shape to; also *taper off.*

tapering, adj. [1. tāpering; 2. téipəriŋ]. Prec. & **-ing**. Growing gradually thinner, narrower, more contracted, towards one end, in one direction; narrowing to a point.

taperingly, adv. Prec. & **-ly**. In a tapering manner.

taperness, n. [1. tāpernes; 2. téipənis]. **taper (II.)** & **-ness**. (rare) State of being tapering.

taperwise, adv. [1. tāperwīz; 2. téipəwaiz]. **taper (I.)** & **-wise**. In a tapering manner, so as to taper.

tapestried, adj. [1. tápestrid; 2. tǽpistrid]. Next word & **-ed**. Adorned, hung, covered, with tapestry.

tapestry, n. [1. tápestri; 2. tǽpistri]. M.E. *tapicerie*, fr. O. Fr. *tapisserie*, fr. *tapiss-(er)*, 'to hang with tapestry', fr. *tapis*, 'tapestry, carpet', see **tapis**, & **tape (I.)**. **a** Fabric of linen or some such material, upon which designs are wrought in wool by hand; **b** fabric with designs woven upon it in imitation of tapestry.

tapeworm, n. [1. tāpwĕrm; 2. téipwə̄m]. Kind of ribbon-shaped worm, genus *Taenia*, infesting alimentary canal of vertebrates.

tapioca, n. [1. tàpióka; 2. tæ̀pióukə], fr. Port., fr. Brazil. *tipioca*, 'cassava juice'. Starchy substance, in the form of rough, white grains obtained by drying manioc, boiled and used as food.

tapir, n. [1. tāper, tāpēr; 2. téipə, téipiə], fr. Brazil. *tapira*. Herbivorous, pig-like mammal with short flexible proboscis, found in S. and C. America and E. Indies.

tapiroid, adj. [1. tāpiroid; 2. téipiroid]. Prec. & **-oid**. Like, related to, the tapirs.

tapis, n. [1. táhpē; 2. tápi], fr. Fr. *tapis*, 'carpet, tapestry', fr. Lat. *tapēte*, 'carpet' &c., see **tape (I.)**. Only in Phr. *on the tapis*, under consideration and discussion.

tapotement, n. [1. tapṓtment; 2. təpóutmənt], fr. Fr., fr. *tapoter*, 'to tap', freq. fr. *taper*, 'to tap', see **tap (III.)**, & **-ment**. (med.) Light manual percussion as form of massage.

tappet, n. [1. tápet; 2. tǽpit]. Prob. **tap (III.)** & **-et**. (mechan.) Projecting arm &c. transmitting intermittent motion from moving part of machine to another part.

tappet-loom, n. Loom in which hammers are worked by tappets.

tap-room, n. **tap (I.)** & **room**. Place in public-house &c. where liquor is sold and drunk.

tap-root, n. Principal descending root of a plant.

tapster, n. [1. tápster; 2. tǽpstə]. O.E. *tæppestre*; **tap (I.)** & **-ster**. Man employed in tap-room to serve beer from cask &c.

tapu. Variant of **taboo**.

tar (I.), n. [1. tar; 2. tā]. O.E. *te(o)ru*; M. *terre*; cp. O.N. *tjara*; Dan. *tjære*, 'tar'; perh. ultimately cogn. w. **tree**. Thick, black, strong-smelling, viscous liquid obtained by distillation from wood and bituminous minerals such as coal &c.; used as preservative and antiseptic, and in manufacture of aniline dyes. Phr. *a touch of the tar brush*, a dash of negro blood in one's veins.

tar (II.), vb. trans., fr. prec. To coat, smear, treat, with tar. Phrs. *tarred with the same brush*, having the same defects of character as someone else; *to tar and feather*, smear (person) with tar, and then roll in feathers, as an unofficial punishment.

tar (III.), n. Abbr. fr. **tarpaulin**. (colloq.) A sailor; chiefly in Phrs. *a jolly tar, an old tar*; also *Jack tar.*

tara, n. [1. táhra; 2. tárə]. Native. See **tara-fern**.

taradiddle. See **ta(r)radiddle**.

tara-fern, n. [1. táhra fĕrn; 2. tárə fə̄n]. Native. Kind of New Zealand bracken with edible rhizome.

tarantara, n. [1. tárentáhra; 2. tǽrəntárə]. Lat.; imitative in origin; cp. **tantara**. Blast on horn or trumpet.

tarantass, n. [1. tárantas; 2. tǽrəntæs], fr. Russ. *tarantas*. Large four-wheeled vehicle hung on bars instead of springs.

tarantella, **tarantelle**, n. [1. tàrentél(a); 2. tæ̀rəntél(ə)], fr. Ital. *tarantella*, fr. Taranto in S. Italy. **1.** Lively Italian dance for two persons, formerly considered a cure for tarantism. **2.** Music for this dance, usually in 6-8 time.

tarantism, n. [1. tárantizm; 2. tǽrəntizəm], fr. Taranto, town in S. Italy, & **-ism**. Nervous disease ending in dancing mania, formerly supposed to be caused by the bite of the tarantula, common in Italy in 15th to 17th centuries.

tarantula, n. [1. tarántūla; 2. tərǽntjulə], fr. Ital. *tarantola*, fr. *Taranto*. See prec. Large, black, hairy, venomous spider found in Southern Europe; also a similar spider found in America.

tarantular, adj. [1. tarántūlar; 2. tərǽntjulə]. Prec. & **-ar**. Of, resembling, produced by, the tarantula.

taratantara, n. [1. táratantáhra; 2. tǽrətæntárə]. Lat.; imitative. Trumpet or bugle call.

taraxacum, n. [1. taráksakum; 2. tərǽksəkəm]. Prob. fr. Pers. **a** Genus of plants, including dandelion, with toothed leaves, and yellow composite flowers supported on hollow scapes; **b** laxative drug obtained from this.

tar-board, n. Strong millboard made from tarred rope &c.

tarboosh, n. [1. tárbōōsh; 2. tábúʃ]. Arab. *ṭarbūsh*. Brimless, tasselled, felt cap worn by Turks and Egyptians; fez.

tardamente, adv. [1. tardaménte; 2. tādəméntɛ]. Ital., fr. Lat. *tard-(us)*, 'slow'. See **tardo**. (mus.) Slowly.

Tardenoisean, adj. [1. tardenóizean; 2. tādənóiziən]. (archaeol.) Pertaining to the late palaeolithic culture represented by the finds at Tardenois, Aisne, France.

tardigrade, adj. & n. [1. tárdigrād; 2. tádigreid], fr. Lat. *tardigrad-(us)*, 'slow-paced', fr. *tard-(us)*, 'slow', see **tardo**, & *grad-(i)*, 'to walk', see **gradus**. (zool.) **1.** adj. Moving slowly, sluggish. **2.** n. Tardigrade animal; including the sloths.

tardily, adv. [1. tárdili; 2. tádili]. **tardy** & **-ly**. In a tardy manner, so as to be behind-hand; dilatorily.

tardiness, n. [1. tárdines; 2. tádinis]. **tardy** & **-ness**. Quality of being tardy; lateness; dilatoriness.

tardo, adj. & adv. [1. tárdō; 2. tádou]. Ital., fr. Lat. *tard-(us)*, 'slow; late; dull'; prob. cogn. w. Lat. *terere*, 'to rub', see **teredo** & **trite**. (mus.) **1.** adj. Slow. **2.** adv. Slowly, slackening speed.

tardy, adj. [1. tárdi; 2. tádi], fr. O. Fr. *tardif*, fr. Lat. *tard-(us)*, 'slow; dull; late', see prec., & **-ive**. **1. a** Slow in action, sluggish; **b** reluctant to act, dilatory. **2.** Coming, arriving, performed, late; late in the day, behind the time, belated: *a tardy repentance*; *to make a tardy appearance*.

tare (I.), n. [1. tār; 2. tɛə]. M.E. *tāre*; etymol. unknown. **1.** Kind of vetch, esp. common vetch. **2.** (in Matt. xiii. 25 &c.) Unidentified weed, possibly the darnel.

tare (II.), n., fr. Fr., fr. Span. *tara*, fr. Arab. *ṭarḥah*, 'what is rejected'. **1.** Allowance made for weight of box, crate, sacks &c., in which goods are packed, in reckoning customs duties &c.; *tare and tret*, rules for calculating tare. **2.** Weight of a vehicle, after deducting that of the load, fuel &c. **3.** (chem.) Weight of vessel in which substance is weighed.

tare (III.), vb. trans., fr. prec. To reckon or determine weight for tare.

targe, n. [1. tarj; 2. tādž], fr. O. Fr. *targe*, *targue*, fr. O.N. *targe*, 'shield'; cp. O.E. *targe*, 'shield'; Germ. *zarge*, 'frame, rim'; O. Slav. *(po)dragŭ*, 'border'; cogn. w. Gk. *drássomai*, 'I take in the hand', orig. 'I enclose'; *drágma*, 'sheaf'; *drakhmḗ*, 'drachma', orig. 'handful', see **drachma**. Small round shield, buckler, target.

target, n. [1. tárget; 2. tágit], fr. O. Fr. *targuete*, dimin. of *targue*, see prec. **1.** Shield, buckler, targe. **2. a** Object to be aimed at in shooting-practice; esp. a flat circular board, or sheet of iron, painted with circles, the central and smallest one of which is known as the bull's eye; **b** any object at which one aims in shooting. **3.** (fig.) Person who, theory, action &c. which, is the object of attack: *to be a target for criticism*. **4.** Small, usually circular, railway-signal placed near switches &c. **5.** Neck and breast of lamb, cut in one piece as a joint for cooking.

target-card, n. Card marked like shooting target for recording score.

targeted, adj. [1. tárgeted; 2. tágitid]. **target** & **-ed**. Armed with a buckler.

targeteer, n. [1. tàrgetḗr; 2. tàgitíə]. **target** & **-eer**. Soldier armed with a shield.

target-ship, n. Ship used as target for naval gunnery practice.

Targum, n. [1. tárgum; 2. tágəm]. Chaldean *targum*, 'interpretation'; cp. **dragoman**. Any of several ancient Aramaic translations or paraphrases of Hebrew Old Testament.

Targumic, adj. [1. targúmik; 2. tāgjúmik]. Prec. & **-ic**. Of, pertaining to, the Targums.

Targumist, n. [1. tárgumist; 2. tágəmist]. See prec. & **-ist**. **1.** Composer, writer, of a Targum. **2.** Student of the Targums.

Targumistic, adj. [1. tàrgūmístik; 2. tàgjumístik]. Prec. & **-ic**. Of, pertaining to, the Targums or Targumists.

tariff (I.), n. [1. tárif; 2. tǽrif], fr. O. Fr. *tariffe*, 'arithmetic', fr. Span., fr. Arab. *ta'rīf*, fr. *'irf*, 'knowledge'. **1. a** List of articles upon which duties are charged by government when exported or imported; **b** the rate of duty charged according to tariff. **2.** List of prices and charges made for food, accommodation &c., together with the articles, rooms &c. for which the charges are made, esp. by a hotel; statement of terms, price-list.

tariff (II.), vb. trans., fr. prec. **1.** To include in a tariff, make list of duties payable on: *to tariff goods*. **2.** To put a price on; to value.

tarlatan, n. [1. tárlatan; 2. tálətən], fr. Fr. *tarlatane*, etymol. doubtful. Kind of open, transparent muslin.

tar-macadam, n. **tar (I.)** & **macadam**. (usually abbr. *tar-mac.*) Layer of broken stone mixed with tar &c. as road-surface.

tarn (I.), n. [1. tarn; 2. tān], fr. O.N. *tjörn*, 'small lake'; cp. Swed. dial. *tjärn*. Small lake high among mountains or on a moor.

tarn (II.). See **tern**.

tarnish (I.), vb. trans. & intrans. [1. tárnish; 2. tániʃ], fr. Fr. *tern-(ir)*, 'to tarnish', fr. M.H.G. *ternen*, 'to darken', fr. O.H.G. *tarni*, 'dark'; cp. O.E. *derne*, 'hidden, secret'; O.N. *dāra*, 'to deceive'; O.H.G. *terren*, 'to harm'; see **darn (I.)**. **A.** trans. **1.** To spoil, dull, the brightness or lustre of by exposure to air, damp &c. **2.** (fig.) To diminish lustre of, to sully (reputation &c.): *to tarnish one's name, honour, fair fame* &c. **B.** intrans. To become tarnished; to be liable to become tarnished.

tarnish (II.), n., fr. prec. **1.** (lit. and fig.) Loss of brightness; blemish. **2.** Characteristic film of colour forming on face of mineral when exposed to the air.

tarnishable, adj. [1. tárnishabl; 2. tániʃəbl]. Prec. & **-able**. Liable to tarnish.

taro, n. [1. táhrō; 2. tárou]. Polynesian. **a** Tropical plant of arum family, with edible root and leaves; **b** root of this plant boiled and used as food in Pacific Islands.

taroc, n. [1. tárok; 2. tǽrək], fr. Ital. *tarocchi*; etymol. unknown. Tarot.

tarot, n. [1. tárō; 2. tǽrou], fr. Fr. *tarots*, fr. Ital. *tarocchi*, see prec. **1.** Each card of a pack of 78 painted playing-cards, used in Italy from 14th century onwards. **2.** Game played with such a pack.

tarpan, n. [1. tárpan; 2. tápæn]. Tartar. Small wild horse of Russian steppes.

tarpaulin, n. [1. tarpáwlin; 2. tāpɔ́lin]. **tar (I.)** & *palling*, 'covering', fr. obs. *pall*, 'to cover', fr. **pall (I.)**. **1.** Waterproofed cloth or canvas, esp. canvas coated with tar. **2.** Sheet of this material as protection against rain &c. **3.** Sailor's oilskin or tarpaulin hat, coat &c. **4.** (obs.) Sailor, tar.

Tarpeian, adj. [1. tarpḗan; 2. tāpíən], fr. Lat. *Tarpēi-(us) (mons)*, '(rock) of Tarpeia', who was said to have been buried at its foot, & **-an**. *Tarpeian Rock*, cliff on Capitoline Hill at Rome from which state criminals were thrown.

tarpon, n. [1. tárpon; 2. tápən]. Prob. Am. Indian. Large game fish, *Tarpon*, or *Megalops atlanticus*, belonging to the herring family, with broad, silvery scales, of West Indies and Southern U.S.A.

tar(r)adiddle, n. [1. tàradídl; 2. tæ̀rədídl]. A modern invention. Prevarication, lie.

tarragon, n. [1. táragon; 2. tǽrəgən], fr. Span. *taragona*, fr. Arab. *tarkhūn*, fr. Gk. *drákōn*, 'dragon, large serpent', see **dragon**. **a** Perennial herb with aromatic leaves used in flavouring salads &c., and in making tarragon oil and vinegar; **b** vinegar made from this.

tarragona, n. [1. taragṓna; 2. tærəgóunə]. Province of N.E. Spain. Spanish wine resembling port.

tarras. See **trass**.

tarrock, n. [1. tárok; 2. tǽrək]. Supposed to be of Greenlandish origin. One of several kinds of sea-bird; **a** young kittiwake; **b** guillemot; **c** tern.

tarry (I.), adj. [1. táhri; 2. tári]. **tar (I.)** & **-y**. Resembling, covered with, of the nature of, tar.

tarry (II.), vb. intrans. & trans. [1. tári; 2. tǽri]. M.E. *tarien*, 'to vex, irritate; to hinder, delay', fr. O.E. *tergan*, 'to vex', confused in meaning with M.E. *targen*, 'to delay', fr. O. Fr. *targer*, fr. L. Lat. *tardicāre*, fr. Lat. *tardāre*, 'to delay', see **tardo**. (chiefly archaic) **A.** intrans. **1.** To linger, be slow in coming, delay: '*Why tarry the wheels of his chariots?*' (Judg. v. 28). **2.** To remain, stay, stop, in a place: *to tarry at home*. **3.** (rare) To wait, expect, be in expectation. **B.** trans. (rare) To await, wait for: *I will tarry his arrival*.

tarsal, adj. [1. társal; 2. tásəl]. **tarsus** & **-al**. Of, pertaining to, near, the tarsus.

tarsi-, pref. representing **tarsus**. Tarsus; e.g. *tarsitis*, inflammation of tarsus of eyelid.

tarsia, n. [1. társia; 2. tásiə]. Ital. See **tarsus**. Mosaic of coloured wood.

tarsier, n. [1. társier; 2. tásiə], fr. Fr., fr. **tarsus**, fr. peculiar structure of foot. Small, arboreal lemur of the East Indies, with large eyes and long tail, and with one of the tarsal bones much elongated.

tarso-, pref. representing **tarsus** in various anatomical terms.

tarsus, n. [1. társus; 2. tásəs]. Mod. Lat., fr. Gk. *tars-(ós)*, 'wicker-work; reed-mat; any flat surface'; cp. Gk. *trasiá*, 'crate for drying figs'; O.H.G. *darra*, 'drying oven', fr. stem **ters-*, 'to dry', seen in Gk. *térsomai*, 'to dry'; O.E. *þyrst*, 'thirst', see **torrid** & **thirst**. **1.** That part of the skeleton which lies between the leg and the metatarsus; the ankle. **2.** (ornith.) Shank of bird's leg. **3.** (zool.) Final segment of leg of insect or crustacean. **4.** Sheet of connective tissue in eyelid.

tart (I.), adj. [1. tart; 2. tāt]. O.E. *teart*, 'acid', perh. related to O.E. *teran*, see **tear (I.)**. **1.** Acid, sour. **2.** (fig., of the temper, manner, mode of expression) Caustic, biting; sour, crabbed: *a tart reply*.

tart (II.), n., fr. O. Fr. *tarte*, but Mod. Fr. *tourte*; perh. variant of *torte*, fr. Lat. *tort-(um)*, P.P. type of *torquere*, 'to twist'; see **torque**. **a** Fruit cooked in a dish with top covering of pastry: *apple tart, damson tart* &c.; **b** fruit or jam cooked in flattish dish, with pastry below it but not covering it; called *an open tart*.

tartan (I.), n. [1. tártn; 2. tátən]. Etymol. unknown. **1.** Woollen fabric of various colours, with stripes of different widths and colours intersecting at right angles; esp. used for making kilts and plaids worn in Highland dress. **2.** Tartan of distinctive pattern peculiar to specific Highland clan. **3.** (attrib.) Made of tartan: *a tartan plaid* &c.

tartan (II.), n., fr. Fr. *tartane*, prob. fr. Arab. *tarīdah*, 'small ship'. Single-masted Mediterranean vessel carrying lateen sail.

tartar (I.), n. [1. tártar; 2. tátə], fr. Fr. *tartre*, fr. L. Lat. *tartarum*, fr. Arab. *durd*, 'dregs'. **1.** Compound of potash and lime deposited in the form of a crust by fermented wine; *cream of tartar*, purified form of this used medicinally and in cooking. **2.** *Tartar emetic*, compound of tartrate of potassium and antimony, used as emetic, in dyeing &c. **3.** Incrustation forming on the teeth, composed chiefly of calcium phosphate.

Tartar (II.), **Tatar**, adj. & n. [1. tártar; 2. tátə], fr. Pers. *Tatar*; the common spelling *Tartar* is influenced by **Tartarus**. **1.** adj. Of, pertaining to, the Tartars or Tatars. **2.** n. **a** Member of a branch of the Ural-Altaic family, including Turks, Cossacks &c., originally from Eastern Asia; **b** a savage, violent, intractable person; an awkward customer; Phr. *to catch a Tartar*, to have to do with an intractable, unmanageable person.

Tartarean, adj. [1. tartárean; 2. tātéəriən], fr. Lat. *Tartare-(us)*, 'of the infernal regions', see **Tartarus**, & **-an**. Of, pertaining to, characteristic of, Tartarus.

Tartarian, adj. [1. tartárian; 2. tātéəriən]. **Tartar (II.)** & **-ian**. Of, pertaining to, characteristic of, the Tartars.

tartaric, adj. [1. tartárik; 2. tātǽrik]. **tartar (I.)** & **-ic**. Of, pertaining to, derived from, containing, tartar.

tartarization, n. [1. tàrtarīzáshun; 2. tàtəraizéiʃən]. Next word & **-ation**. **1.** Act of tartarizing, state of being tartarized. **2.** Formation of tartar.

tartarize, vb. trans. [1. tártarīz; 2. tátəraiz]. **tartar (I.)** & **-ize**. To treat with tartar.

tartarous, adj. [1. tártarus; 2. tátərəs]. **tartar (I.)** & **-ous**. Of, pertaining to, containing, tartar.

Tartarus, n. [1. tártarus; 2. tátərəs]. Lat. *Tartarus*, fr. Gk. *Tártaros*. (Gk. mythol.) **1.** Dark abyss below Hades to which the Titans were consigned as a punishment. **2.** Place of punishment for the wicked; hell.

tartlet, n. [1. tártlet; 2. tátlit]. **tart (II.)** & **-let.** Small open tart.

tartly, adv. [1. tártli; 2. tátli]. **tart (I.)** & **-ly.** In a tart manner; rudely, abruptly, crabbedly.

tartness, n. [1. tártnes; 2. tátnis]. See prec. & **-ness. 1.** Sourness, acidity. **2.** Tart manner; abruptness, crabbedness, of speech or manner.

tartrate, n. [1. tártrāt; 2. tátreit]. **tartar (I.)** & **-ate.** Salt of tartaric acid.

Tartuf(f)e, n. [1. tartóof; 2. tātýf]. Fr. [tartyf], fr. name of character in Molière's comedy of same name. One who conceals a base nature under the guise of meekness and sanctity; a hypocrite.

Tartuf(f)ism, n. [1. tartóofizm; 2. tātýfizəm]. Prec. & **-ism.** Character of a Tartuffe; hypocrisy.

tar-water, n. Infusion of tar used as antiseptic.

taseometer, n. [1. tàseómeter; 2. tæsiómitə], fr. Gk. *tase-*, stem of *tásis*, 'stretching, tension'. See next word & *-o-* & **-meter.** Device for determining strains in buildings.

tasimeter, n. [1. tasímeter; 2. tæsímitə], fr. Gk. *tási-(s)*, 'stretching, tension', fr. stem of *teinein*, 'to stretch'; see **tend (II.), tone,** & **-meter.** Electrical apparatus for measuring changes in pressure caused by changes in moisture or temperature.

tasimetric, adj. [1. tàsimétrik; 2. tæsimétrik]. Prec. & **-ic**; see **metric.** Of, pertaining to, tasimetry.

tasimetry, n. [1. tasímetri; 2. tæsímitri]. **tasimeter** & **-y.** Measurement of pressure.

task (I.), n. [1. tahsk; 2. tāsk], fr. O. Nthn. Fr. *tasque*, Fr. *tasche*, fr. L. Lat. *tasca*, fr. Lat. *taxāre*, 'to censure; to touch'; see **tax (I.). 1.** Specific piece or amount of work of any kind imposed by authority; specif., a piece of work, or 'lesson', prescribed for pupils by teachers at school. Phr. *to take a person to task*, find fault with him. **2.** Any piece of work, whether imposed or undertaken voluntarily, which has to be accomplished.

task (II.), vb. trans., fr. prec. **1.** To assign a piece of work to, set to a task. **2.** (rare) To try, put a strain on, tax, mental or physical powers; to overtax: *to task one's memory, powers of endurance* &c.

taskmaster, n. [1. táhskmàhster; 2. táskmàstə]. An exacting master, teacher, or other person having authority to prescribe the work of others; esp. *a severe taskmaster*.

taskmistress, n. [1. táhskmìstres; 2. táskmìstris]. Feminine of prec.

taskwork, n. [1. táhskwěrk; 2. táskwʌ̄k]. Piecework.

Tasmanian, adj. & n. [1. tazmánian; 2. tæzméiniən], fr. Tasmania, named after the Dutch navigator Tasman, d. 1659. **1.** adj. Pertaining to Tasmania; specif., *Tasmanian devil*, a fierce, nocturnal, carnivorous marsupial, *Dasyurus ursinus*. **2.** n. Inhabitant of Tasmania.

tass, n. [1. tas; 2. tæs], fr. O. Fr. *tasse*, 'cup', perh. fr. Arab. *tass*. Small draught, dram, esp. of spirits.

tassel (I.), n. [1. tásl; 2. tǽsl]. M.E. & O. Fr. *tassel*, prob. fr. Lat. *taxillus*, 'small die', dimin. of *tālus*, 'ankle, knuckle-bone, heel'; see **talus.** The dimin. is prob. formed on the anal. of **axilla**, fr. *āla*, see **alar, aileron. 1.** Bunch of silk or other threads knotted or bound together at one end, used as ornament for dress, cap, banner &c. **2.** Any of various objects resembling a tassel, e.g. the arrangement of inflorescence in some plants, such as Indian corn. **3.** Narrow ribbon fastened to top of book to serve as marker. **4.** Thin gold plate on back of bishop's glove.

tassel (II.), vb. trans., fr. prec. **1.** To provide, adorn, with tassel(s). **2.** To cut off tassels from (Indian corn) to strengthen the plant.

tastable, adj. [1. tástabl; 2. téistəbl]. **taste** & **-able.** Capable of being tasted.

taste (I.), vb. trans. & intrans. [1. tāst; 2. teist]. M.E. *tasten*, fr. O. Fr. *taster*, 'to handle, feel, taste', prob. fr. Low Lat. **taxitāre*, fr. Lat. *taxāre*, 'to appraise, value; to handle, touch', see **tax (I.). A.** trans. **1. a** To test, judge, appraise, flavour of by taking some into the mouth: *taste this coffee to see if you like it*; **b** specif., to act as professional taster of. **2.** To perceive, distinguish, detect, the specific flavour of with the organs of taste: *I can taste pepper in this pudding*. **3.** To partake of, eat or drink a small quantity of: *he hadn't tasted food for many hours*. **4.** To experience, try: *to taste the joys of freedom*. **B.** intrans. **1.** To experience the sensation of taste, be able to distinguish flavours: *I am quite unable to taste on account of my cold*. **2.** (archaic) To eat or drink a small portion, partake: *to taste of strange dishes*. **3.** (archaic) To experience, undergo: *to taste of danger, of death*. **4.** To have particular flavour, convey specific sensation of taste to, have specific effect upon, the organs of taste: *the milk tastes sour*; *this sauce tastes of nothing at all*.

taste (II.), n. M.E. *tāst*, fr. O. Fr. *tast*, fr. *taster*, 'to taste'; see prec. **1.** One of the five senses; the faculty of experiencing, perceiving, and discriminating different flavours on the tongue and palate: *a fine taste in wines*. **2.** The characteristic sensation, other than that of texture, or of differences of temperature, produced upon the tongue by something coming into contact with it; flavour, gust, sapidity: *an unpleasant taste*. Phr. (fig.) *to leave a bad taste in the mouth*, to produce a bad impression, a feeling of disgust and repulsion. **3.** Something which is tasted; specif. **a** a small portion of food or drink: *I'll have just a (small) taste of ham*; hence, **b** a slight suggestion; a touch, a tinge, a trace, a faint smack: *just a taste of sadness in his remarks*. **4.** Intellectual, aesthetic, moral, discrimination; discernment, sensibility, trained judgement, critical appreciation: *a man of taste*; *a house furnished in the best taste*; *a cultivated taste in poetry, painting* &c. **5.** Manner and expression as evincing sensibility and refinement; tact, delicacy of feeling; sense of what is fitting: *his speech was in excellent taste*; *his conduct was in the worst taste*. **6.** Tendency, bias, towards; preference, predilection for; fondness, liking: *a taste for low company, for dissipation*; *a taste for the theatre, for horse-racing* &c. Phrs. *not at all to my taste*, not what I like; *very much to my taste*, just what I like. **7.** An experience of anything; a sample, evidence: *he gave me a taste of his skill, of his bad manners* &c.

tasteful, adj. [1. tástfool; 2. téistful]. **taste (II.)** & **-ful.** Having, showing, good taste.

tastefully, adv. Prec. & **-ly.** In a tasteful manner.

tastefulness, n. See prec. & **-ness.** Quality of being tasteful.

tasteless, adj. [1. tástles; 2. téistlis]. **taste (II.)** & **-less. 1.** Without distinctive flavour; insipid, flat. **2.** (rare) Lacking, having lost, the sense of taste. **3.** Having bad taste; possessing, evincing, exhibiting, no discernment or discrimination; tactless.

tastelessly, adv. Prec. & **-ly.** In a tasteless manner.

tastelessness, n. See prec. & **-ness.** Quality of being tasteless.

taster, n. [1. táster; 2. téistə]. **taste (I.)** & **-er. 1.** One who tastes; specif. **a** (hist.) servant employed to taste his master's food and drink before it was served; **b** person employed professionally to test quality of articles of food and drink by tasting; esp. *tea-*, *wine-taster*. **2.** (fig., colloq.) Publisher's reader. **3.** Vessel or other device used in tasting or sampling; specif. **a** small metal cup for wine; **b** long-handled scoop for extracting sample from cheese &c.

tastily, adv. [1. tástili; 2. téistili]. Next word & **-ly.** (vulg. or colloq.) In a tasty manner.

tasty, adj. [1. tásti; 2. téisti]. **taste (II.)** & **-y. 1.** Having a distinctive, usually agreeable, flavour; savoury, pungent. **2.** (vulg.) Tasteful, smart, attractive.

tat (I.), vb. intrans. & trans. [1. tat; 2. tæt]. Prob. back-formation fr. **tatting. 1.** intrans. To do tatting. **2.** trans. To make by tatting.

tat (II.), n. Hind. Coarse Indian canvas.

tata, interj. [1. tatáh; 2. tætá, tātá]. (child's word) Good-bye.

Tatar. See **Tartar (II.).**

tatter, n. [1. táter; 2. tǽtə]. Cp. O.N. *tǫturr*; L.G. *tater*, 'rag'. Rag, shred, torn fragment (usually in pl.): *his coat was in tatters, hanging in tatters*. Phr. *to tear (an argument, statement* &c.) *to tatters*, demolish, disprove, refute it.

tatterdemalion, n. [1. tàterdemálliun; 2. tætədiméiliən]. Etymol. doubtful. A ragged, disreputable person.

tattered, adj. [1. táterd; 2. tǽtəd]. **tatter** & **-ed. 1.** Ragged, hanging in tatters. **2.** Clothed in ragged garments.

Tattersall's, n. [1. tátersalz; 2. tǽtəsəlz], fr. name of founder, Richard Tattersall, d. 1795. **1.** London market for sale of hunters, racehorses &c. **2.** This market regarded as the headquarters of racing and betting.

tattery, adj. [1. táteri; 2. tǽtəri]. **tatter** & **-y.** Tattered, ragged.

tatting, n. [1. táting; 2. tǽtiŋ]. Etymol. doubtful. Lace-like trimming of knotted and looped threads.

tattle (I.), vb. intrans. & trans. [1. tátl; 2. tǽtl]. Imitative; cp. L.G. *tateln*, 'to gabble'. **1.** intrans. To chatter idly, to gossip. **2.** trans. To utter in idle chatter, gossip about.

tattle (II.), n., fr. prec. Idle or indiscreet talk, chatter, gossip; more often *tittle-tattle*.

tattler, n. [1. tátler; 2. tǽtlə]. Earlier *tatler*; **tattle** & **-er. 1.** One who gossips or tattles. **2.** Kind of sand-piper.

tattling, adj. [1. tátling; 2. tǽtliŋ]. **tattle** & **-ing.** Given to idle chatter, gossiping.

tattoo (I.), n. [1. tatóo; 2. tætū́], fr. Du. *taptoe*, 'tattoo'; orig., of public-house, 'the tap is closed', fr. *tap*, 'tap-room'; see **tap (I.), to. 1. a** Drum-beat or bugle-call summoning soldiers &c. to quarters at nightfall; Phr. *to beat the devil's tattoo*, drum with fingers on table &c.; **b** the hour at which tattoo is sounded. **2.** Loud and prolonged knocking: *a loud tattoo on the door*. **3.** Military display or pageant, performed, usually at night, to musical accompaniment.

tattoo (II.), vb. intrans., fr. prec. To sound a tattoo.

tattoo (III.), vb. trans. [1. tatóo; 2. tætū́], fr. Tahitian *tatau*. **1.** To mark (the skin) indelibly with pigments introduced into punctures arranged in a desired pattern. **2.** To produce (designs) on the skin by tattooing: *to tattoo a butterfly on one's arm*.

tattoo (IV.), n., fr. prec. Design on skin produced by tattooing.

tatty, n. [1. táti; 2. tǽti], fr. Hind. *ṭaṭṭi*, 'wicker frame'. Matting of cuscus-grass hung in doorway, window &c. and kept wet to cool the air.

tau, n. [1. taw; 2. tɔ̄]. Gk. *taû*, loan-word fr. Semitic; cp. Heb. *tāw*. **1.** Greek letter corresponding to T; *tau cross*, T-shaped cross. **2.** Fish with T-shaped markings; esp. toad-fish.

taube, n. [1. tóube; 2. táubə]. Germ., 'dove'; cogn. w. **dove.** German military monoplane.

taught, vb. [1. tawt; 2. tɔ̄t]. O.E. *tǣht(e)*, *getǣht*, M.E. *taught(e)*; Pret. & P.P. of **teach.**

taunt (I.), vb. trans. & n. [1. tawnt; 2. tɔ̄nt], fr. O. Fr. *tanter*, variant of *tenter*, 'to provoke, tempt', see **tempt. 1.** vb. To reproach contemptuously; to twit, gibe at; *taunt with*, reproach with. **2.** n. **a** A spiteful, sarcastic, sneering remark levelled at another; a jeer, a gibe; **b** object of taunts.

taunt (II.), adj. & adv., fr. adv. *ataunt*, (naut.) 'fully rigged', fr. Fr. *autant*, 'so much', fr. Lat. *tant-(us)*, 'so much'; see **tantamount.** (naut.) **a** adj. (of mast) Tall; **b** adv., fully rigged.

taunting, adj. [1. táwnting; 2. tɔ́ntiŋ]. Pres. Part. of **taunt** (I.). Provoking by spiteful criticism and insult; mocking, gibing.

tauntingly, adv. Prec. & **-ly.** In a taunting manner.

tauriform, adj. [1. tṓriform; 2. tɔ́rifɔ̄m]. See **Taurus** & **-form.** Having the form or appearance of a bull.

taurine, adj. [1. tṓrin, tṓrīn; 2. tɔ́rin, tɔ́rain], fr. Lat. *taurīn-(us)*, 'taurine', fr. *taur-(us)*, 'bull', see **Taurus**, & **-ine. 1.** Pertaining to, resembling, a bull; bovine. **2.** Of, pertaining to, Taurus as a sign of the zodiac.

tauromachy, n. [1. tōrómaki; 2. tɔrɔ́məki], fr. Gk. *taũros*, 'bull'; cp. Lat. *taurus*, see **Taurus**, & **-machy. a** Bull-fighting; **b** a bull fight.

Taurus, n. [1. tṓrus; 2. tɔ́rəs]. Lat. *taurus*, 'bull'; cp. Gk. *taũros*, 'bull'; Lith. *tauras*, 'aurochs'; O.N. *þiorr*, 'bull'; prob. fr. base **tou-*, **tu-*, 'to swell'; see **tumid** & words there referred to. (cap.) **1.** A constellation, containing the Pleiades. **2.** One of the signs of the zodiac.

taut, adj. [1. tawt; 2. tɔ̄t]. M.E. *togt, toht*, 'firm, tight', fr. P.P. of *tōgen, tōwen*, O.E. *togian*, 'to draw, pull', see **tow** (I.), & *-t*, suff. of a weak P.P. **1.** (of rope, sail &c.) Stretched tightly, tense. **2.** In good condition, trim.

tauten, vb. trans. & intrans. [1. táwtn; 2. tɔ́tn]. Prec. & **-en. 1.** trans. To stretch tightly, make taut. **2.** intrans. To become taut.

tautly, adv. [1. táwtli; 2. tɔ́tli]. **taut** & **-ly.** In a taut manner; **a** tightly, tensely; **b** trimly.

tautness, n. [1. táwtnes; 2. tɔ́tnis]. See prec. & **-ness.** State of being taut.

tauto-, pref. representing Gk. *tautó*, contracted fr. *tò autó*, 'the same'; see under **the** & **auto-.** The same.

tautochrone, n. [1. táwtokrōn; 2. tɔ́təkroun]. Prec. & Gk. *khrónos*, 'time', see **chronic.** Curve on which a body, moving from any point thereon by the force of gravity, will always reach the lowest point in the same space of time.

tautochronism, n. [1. tawtókronizm; 2. tɔtɔ́krənizəm]. Prec. & **-ism.** Property of being tautochronous.

tautochronous, adj. [1. tawtókronus; 2. tɔtɔ́krənəs]. See prec. & **-ous.** Having the nature of, pertaining to, a tautochrone.

tautog, n. [1. tawtóg; 2. tɔtɔ́g]. N. Am. Indian *tautaúog*. Edible fish of Atlantic coast of N. America.

tautologic(al), adj. [1. tàwtolójik(l); 2. tɔ̀təlɔ́džik(l)]. **tautology** & **-ic** & **-al.** Connected with, of the nature of, tautology.

tautologically, adv. Prec. & **-ly.** In a tautological manner.

tautologist, n. [1. tawtólojist; 2. tɔtɔ́lədžist]. **tautology** & **-ist.** Person given to tautology.

tautologize, vb. intrans. [1. tawtólojīz; 2. tɔtɔ́lədžaiz]. **tautology** & **-ize.** To express oneself tautologically.

tautology, n. [1. tawtóloji; 2. tɔtɔ́lədži], fr. Gk. *tautología*; **tauto-** & **-logy.** Pleonastic repetition of the same idea in a sentence; e.g. *to speak all at once together.*

tautophony, n. [1. tawtófuni; 2. tɔtɔ́fəni]. **tauto-** & **-phone** & **-y.** Constant repetition of the same sound.

tavern, n. [1. távern; 2. tǽvən], fr. Fr. *taverne*, fr. Lat. *taberna*, 'hut; shop, booth; tavern'; prob. fr. earlier **traberna*, fr. stem of *trabs*, 'beam, timber'; cogn. w. O.W. *treb*, 'dwelling'; cp. *Tre-* in Corn. Pl.-Ns.; see also **tabernacle** & **trabeated.** Public house for retail of food and drink; an inn, hostelry.

taw (I.), vb. trans. [1. taw; 2. tɔ̄]. O.E. *tāwian, tēawian*; M.E. *tāwen, tēwen*, 'to prepare, dress' (leather, hemp &c.); cp. O.H.G. *zawan, zouwan*; Goth. *(ga)tēwjan*, 'appoint, arrange', & *tēwa*, 'order'; cp. **tool.** To prepare, dress (skins), make them into leather.

taw (II.), n. Etymol. unknown. **1.** Line from which players shoot in game of marbles. **2.** Game of marbles. **3.** A marble.

tawdrily, adv. [1. táwdrili; 2. tɔ́drili]. See **tawdry** & **-ly.** In a tawdry, flashy, manner.

tawdriness, n. [1. táwdrines; 2. tɔ́drinis]. Next word & **-ness.** State or quality of being tawdry.

tawdry, adj. [1. táwdri; 2. tɔ́dri], fr. St. Audry (pronounced [sən tɔ́dri]), O.E. *Aeðelðrȳð*, on whose day, Oct. 17th, a fair was held, where gay finery was sold. Showy but of inferior quality; flashy, gaudy: *tawdry garments, decorations* &c.

tawer, n. [1. táw-er; 2. tɔ́ə]. **taw** (I.) & **-er.** One who taws skins.

tawery, n. [1. táw-eri; 2. tɔ́əri]. **taw** (I.) & **-ery.** Place where skins are tawed.

tawniness, n. [1. táwnines; 2. tɔ́ninis]. Next word & **-ness.** State of being tawny; tawny colour.

tawny, adj. [1. táwni; 2. tɔ́ni]. M.E. *tauni, tanni*, fr. O. Fr. *tanné*, P.P. of *tanner*, 'to tan', see **tan** (I.). Light brownish yellow, tan, or sand-coloured; *tawny port*, one that has been matured in the cask and has become pale.

taws(e), n. [1. tawz; 2. tɔ̄z]. Perh. cogn. w. **taw** (I.). (Scots) Strap for chastising children.

tax (I.), vb. trans. [1. taks; 2. tæks], fr. Fr. *taxer*, fr. Lat. *taxāre*, 'to estimate, compute; to censure, reproach; to touch'; prob. fr. Gk. *tássein*, 'to arrange, put in order; to appoint; to impose; to fix as payment'; cp. **taxis. 1. a** To impose tax upon (persons), compel to pay a tax; **b** to put a tax upon (articles of commerce). **2.** To subject to a strain, make heavy demands upon: *to tax one's resources, memory, energies* &c. **3.** *Tax with*, to accuse of, charge with, impute to: *to tax a person with rudeness, trickery.*

tax (II.), n., fr. prec. **1.** Compulsory duty or impost levied by the State upon property, income, certain business transactions, articles of commerce, the right to use certain things &c. **2.** Strain, serious burden, heavy demand: *a tax on one's endurance, strength, resources* &c.

taxability, n. [1. taksabíliti; 2. tæksəbíliti]. See next word & **-bility.** State of being taxable.

taxable, adj. [1. táksabl; 2. tǽksəbl]. **tax** (I.) & **-able.** Capable of being taxed; subject to taxation.

taxableness, n. Prec. & **-ness.** Taxability.

taxation, n. [1. taksáshun; 2. tækséiʃən]. **tax** (I.) & **-ation.** Act of taxing; system of raising revenue by means of taxes; whole body of taxes payable at a given time.

tax-cart, n. Light, tradesman's or farm cart exempt from taxation.

tax-collector, n. Official whose business it is to collect taxes.

tax-farmer, n. Person who buys from the government the right to collect taxes in a specific district.

tax-free, adj. **a** Exempt from taxation; **b** (of dividends or interest) having the income-tax paid by the company and not deducted when dividend or interest is paid to the shareholders; as some British war loans.

tax-gatherer, n. [1. táks gàdherer; 2. tǽks gæ̀ðərə]. (archaic) Tax-collector.

taxi (I.), n. [1. táksi; 2. tǽksi]. Abbr. of **taximeter** (cab). Also *taxi-cab*, motor-cab for public hire, fitted with taximeter; by extension, any motor-car plying for hire.

taxi (II.), vb. intrans., fr. prec. **1.** To travel in a taxi. **2.** (of aeroplane) To move on surface of land or water under its own power.

taxidermal, adj. [1. tàksidérmal; 2. tæ̀ksidə́məl]. **taxidermy** & **-al.** Of, pertaining to, taxidermy.

taxidermic, adj. [1. tàksidérmik; 2. tæ̀ksidə́mik]. **taxidermy** & **-ic.** Taxidermal.

taxidermist, n. [1. táksidèrmist; 2. tǽksidə̀mist]. **taxidermy** & **-ist.** Person who cures, stuffs, and mounts the skins of animals and birds so as to represent them as in life.

taxidermy, n. [1. táksidèrmi; 2. tǽksidə̀mi], fr. Gk. *táxi-(s)*, 'arrangement', see **taxis**, & **-derm** & **-y.** Art of preparing, stuffing, and mounting skins of dead animals, birds &c. so as to represent them as they appeared when alive.

taximeter, n. [1. táksimèter; 2. tǽksimìtə]. Fr. *taximètre*, fr. *taxe*, 'charge, tariff, tax', see **tax** (II.), & **-meter.** Instrument fixed to a motor-car plying for hire, having a dial indicating automatically the distance travelled and the corresponding fare.

taxin, n. [1. táksin; 2. tǽksin], fr. Lat. *tax-(us)*, 'yew', & **-in.** Etymol. uncertain. See under **toxic.** Poisonous, resinous compound obtained from leaves and berries of yew.

taxis, n. [1. táksis; 2. tǽksis]. Gk. *táxis*, 'arrangement; battle array; order, relative position'; cp. Gk. *tássein*, 'to arrange'; no further cognates known certainly. **1.** (Gk. antiq.) Division of Greek army, varying in size in different states. **2.** (zool.) System of classification. **3.** (surg.) Application of manual pressure to restore displaced organs &c. to their positions. **4.** (gram.) Order, arrangement.

taxless, adj. [1. táksles; 2. tǽkslis]. **tax** (II.) & **-less.** Without taxes, not liable to taxation.

taxology, n. [1. taksóloji; 2. tæksɔ́lədži], fr. Gk. *táx-(is)*, 'arrangement', see **taxis**, & *-o-* & **-logy.** Science of classification.

taxonomic(al), adj. [1. taksonómik(l); 2. tæksənɔ́mik(l)]. **taxonomy** & **-ic** & **-al.** Of, pertaining to, taxonomy.

taxonomist, n. [1. taksónomist; 2. tæksɔ́nəmist]. Next word & **-ist.** Student of, one skilled in, taxonomy.

taxonomy, n. [1. taksónomi; 2. tæksɔ́nəmi], fr. Fr., fr. Gk. *táx-(is)*, 'arrangement', see **taxis**, & *nóm-(os)*, 'law, ordinance &c.', see **Nemesis.** Science of classification.

taxpayer, n. [1. tákspàer; 2. tǽkspèiə]. Person liable for payment of tax.

tazza, n. [1. tátsa, táhtsa; 2. tǽtsə, tā́tsə]. Ital., 'cup'; cp. Fr. *tasse*, see **tass.** Ornamental, decorated, flattish, shallow bowl mounted on a pedestal which forms a part of the vessel.

tea, n. [1. tē; 2. tī], fr. Fr. *thé*, fr. Chinese *chai*. **1. a** Also *tea-plant*, evergreen shrub or small tree grown in China, Ceylon, Assam &c.; **b** leaves of tea-plant dried and used in infusion as a beverage. **2.** The drink made by steeping the leaves of the tea-plant in boiling water. **3.** Light meal, taken esp. in afternoon or evening, at which tea is drunk. **4. a** Strong broth made by stewing down meat in a closed vessel: *chicken-, beef-tea*; **b** *black-currant tea*, drink made by soaking black-currant jam in boiling water.

tea-caddy, n. Air-tight box in which small supply of tea is kept for daily use.

tea-cake, n. Flat, slightly sweetened cake, toasted, buttered, and eaten at tea.

teach, vb. trans. [1. tēch; 2. titʃ]. O.E. *tǣcan*, fr. **tāhjan*; M.E. *tēchen*; cp. O.E. *tāc(e)n*, 'sign', see **token**; cogn. w. Gk. *deĩgma*, 'proof, example', fr. base **deig-*, **doig-*, 'to show', parallel to **deik-* &c., 'to show', seen in Goth. *gateihan*, 'to announce', &c.; cp. Lat. *dīcere*, 'to show, tell', see **diction. 1. a** (i.) To give instruction to, guide studies of, impart knowledge, experience, skill, to: *to teach children, apprentices* &c.; (ii.) (with two objects) to give instruction to (person &c.) in (a subject &c.): *to teach a child to read; to teach a class singing; to teach one French*; **b** to accustom, train, habituate: *to teach a child to obey, to tell the truth; to teach the ear to distinguish sounds*; **c** to train: *to teach a dog to beg.* **2.** To give instruction in, to bring one to a knowledge of or skill in (a subject): *to teach music, riding* &c.

teachability, n. [1. tèchabíliti; 2. tìtʃəbíliti]. See next word & **-ity.** State of being teachable.

teachable, adj. [1. téchabl; 2. títʃəbl]. **teach & -able.** Capable of being taught, susceptible to training.

teachableness, n. Prec. & **-ness.** State of being teachable.

teacher, n. [1. tēcher; 2. títʃə]. **teach & -er.** a One who teaches; trainer of the mind, instructor: *a child's first teacher is usually his mother*; specif. b one who does this as a profession: *a teacher of drawing*; *a school-teacher.*

teachership, n. [1. téchership; 2. títʃəʃip]. Prec. & **-ship.** Office of a teacher.

tea-chest, n. Light wooden, metal-lined box in which tea is imported from the country in which it is grown.

teaching, n. [1. téching; 2. títʃiŋ]. **teach & -ing.** 1. Act, occupation, of a teacher: *to take up teaching.* 2. That which is taught, specific doctrine: *the teaching of the apostles.*

tea-cloth, n. 1. Small cloth for tea-table. 2. Cloth for drying tea-things &c. when washed.

tea-cup, n. 1. Small cup used, as used, at tea. 2. Tea-cupful.

tea-cupful, n. Amount contained in a tea-cup.

tea-fight, n. (slang) Tea-party.

tea-garden, n. Garden containing an open-air restaurant where tea and other light refreshments are obtainable.

tea-gown, n. Woman's loose gown worn for tea &c.

Teague, n. [1. tēg; 2. tīg]. Ir. name. (contemptuously) Irishman.

tea-house, n. Restaurant in China or Japan where tea &c. is consumed.

teak, n. [1. tēk; 2. tīk], fr. Port. *teca*, fr. Malayalam *tekka.* 1. Large East Indian tree, *Tectona grandis.* 2. The wood of this tree, a valuable kind of timber, used in shipbuilding &c.

tea-kettle, n. Smallish kettle as used to boil water for tea.

teal, n. [1. tēl; 2. tīəl]. M.E. *tēle*; etymol. doubtful. Kind of small wild-duck, genus *Nettion*, frequenting rivers and lakes.

tea-leaf, n. 1. Leaf of tea-plant; specif., the same dried and prepared for infusing and making into the beverage. 2. (pl.) *Tea-leaves*, a collection of leaves of the tea-plant left after infusion.

team (I.), n. [1. tēm; 2. tīm]. O.E. *tēam*, 'progeny, family; team of oxen'; M.E. *tēme*; prob. connected (in Mod. sense) w. **tow** (I.), **tug**, & w. Lat. *dūcere*, 'to draw', see **duct, duke**; cp. also **teem** (I.). 1. Two or more beasts of burden or draught harnessed together: *a team of horses*; *a sledge drawn by a dog-team.* 2. Group of persons acting together in specific work, game &c.; players forming one side.

team (II.), vb. trans., fr. prec. 1. To harness together to form a team. 2. (colloq.) To let out (work, job &c.) to contractor employing team of horses, men &c.

teaming, n. [1. téming; 2. tímiŋ]. Prec. & **-ing.** (colloq.) System, method, of hiring out work to contractors employing gangs of workmen.

teamster, n. [1. témster; 2. tímstə]. **team** (I.) & **-ster.** a Driver of team of animals; b an animal in a team.

teamwise, n. [1. témwīz; 2. tímwaiz]. **team** (I.) & **-wise.** In the form or manner of a team.

team-work, n. Organized joint effort, co-operation.

tea-party, n. Social gathering at afternoon tea.

tea-pot, n. Earthenware or metal vessel, with a lid, handle, and spout, in which tea is infused before being poured into cups.

teapoy, n. [1. tépoi; 2. típɔi], fr. Hind. *tīpāi*, fr. Pers. *sipai*; associated popularly w. **tea.** Small three- or four-legged table, esp. one used as tea-table.

tear (I.), vb. trans. & intrans. [1. tăr; 2. tɛə]. O.E. *teran*; M.E. *tēren*; cp. Goth. *gatairan*, 'to break'; O.N. *tæra*; Germ. *zehren*, 'to consume'; Goth. *-taúrnan*, 'to tear'; cogn. w. Scrt. *dṛṇáti*, 'splits'; Lith. *dirù*; Gk. *dérein*, 'to flay'; Gk. *dérma*, 'skin'; see **derm(a).** A. trans. 1. a To pull apart, cause to divide along a gradually lengthening, straight or irregular line; to rend, rip; contrasted with *cut*: *to tear one's coat*; *to tear a thing to pieces*; Phrs. *to tear up*, destroy by tearing to pieces; *to tear one's hair*, pull it violently; (fig.) to show signs of despair, rage, or distress &c.; *to tear a hole*, make one by tearing; b to wound by tearing; lacerate: *to tear one's hands on barbed wire.* 2. To pull violently away, remove by violent effort, drag off or up: *to tear (plants) up by the roots*; *to tear open an envelope*; *to tear one's clothes off.* Phr. *to tear oneself away*, depart reluctantly. 3. (fig.) a To make divisions or discord in, set at variance, destroy peace of: *a country torn by civil war, rival parties* &c.; b to agitate, disturb: *a heart torn by anxiety.* 4. *Torn between*, divided in mind between, attracted equally by, two alternative choices, lines of action &c. B. intrans. 1. To be torn, undergo tearing: *paper tears easily.* 2. To pull violently, attempt to rend: *he tore at the covering of the parcel.* 3. To run quickly and impetuously; to rush: *to tear about in excitement*; *to tear down, along, the road.*

tear (II.), n., fr. prec. Rent, division, caused by tearing: *a tear in fabric, a garment* &c.

tear (III.), n. [1. tēr; 2. tiə]. O.E. *tēar*, M.E. *tēre*; O.H.G. *zahar*; Goth. *tagr*; cogn. w. Gk. *dákru*; Lat. *lacrima*, 'tear', fr. *dacruma*; see **lachrymal.** 1. Single drop of the saline secretion of the lachrymal gland, which normally serves to moisten the eye-ball, but whose flow is increased by emotion or by violent contraction of the eye-muscles in coughing &c.: *to shed tears*; *to wipe away one's tears*; *eyes filled with tears.* Phr. *in tears*, weeping; *crocodile tears*, sham, hypocritical grief. 2. Drop or drop-like particle of liquid or transparent solid, e.g. drop of dew, resin, amber &c.; *tears of strong wine*, drops forming on side of glass partly filled with port &c.

tear-drop, n. Single tear falling from the eye.

tear-duct, n. Duct passing from lachrymal gland to nose-passage.

tearful, adj. [1. tērfool; 2. tíəful]. **tear** (III.) & **-ful.** 1. Shedding tears; given to weeping, lachrymose. 2. Causing tears; sad, lamentable.

tearfully, adv. Prec. & **-ly.** In a tearful manner, with tears.

tearfulness, n. See prec. & **-ness.** State of being tearful.

tear-gas, n. Poison gas, contained in shells or otherwise discharged, causing violent watering of the eyes and temporary blindness.

tearing, adj. [1. tăring; 2. tɛəriŋ]. **tear** (I.) & **-ing.** (colloq.) Violent, raging, furious: *a tearing rage*; *a tearing hurry*; *a tearing gale.*

tearless, adj. [1. tērles; 2. tíəlis]. **tear** (III.) & **-less.** Not weeping; not causing the shedding of tears.

tea-room, n. Restaurant in which tea, coffee, and light refreshments are obtainable; room in hotel &c., set apart for tea.

tea-rose, n. Variety of China rose with scent supposed to resemble that of tea.

tear-shell, n. Explosive shell containing tear-gas that causes the eyes to water painfully.

tear-stained, adj. [1. tēr stānd; 2. tíə steind]. Showing signs of recent tears.

tease (I.), vb. trans. [1. tēz; 2. tīz]. O.E. *tǣsan*, 'to pluck, pull apart'; M.E. *tēsen*; cp. Dan. *tæse*; M. Du. *teesen.* 1. To tear apart fibres of, separate into parts: *to tease flax* &c. 2. To raise a nap on (cloth), by scratching with teasels. 3. a To worry, annoy, harass, bait, twit, make a mockery of; b to subject to good-natured chaff; to poke fun at, banter. 4. To pester, importune, with persistent demands to do something: *he was always teasing her to marry him.*

tease (II.), n., fr. prec. Person given to teasing; one indulging in arch banter.

teasel, teazel, teazle (I.), n. [1. tēzl; 2. tīzl]. O.E. *tǣsel*, 'teasel', fr. base of *tǣsan*, 'to tease, pluck', see **tease** (I.) & **-el.** 1. a Plant, genus *Dipsacus*, with large burrs, or heads covered with hooked prickles; b one of these heads used in raising nap on cloth &c. 2. Machine, brush &c., used in place of teasel.

teasel (II.), vb. trans., fr. prec. To dress, raise nap on (cloth), with teasel.

teaseler, teazler, n. [1. téz(e)ler; 2. tíz(ə)lə]. Prec. & **-er.** Person employed in, machine used in, teaseling.

teaser, n. [1. téser; 2. tízə]. **tease** (I.) & **-er.** 1. Person given to teasing. 2. (colloq.) Puzzling problem or task.

tea-service, n. Tea-set.

tea-set, n. Set of cups, plates &c., for use at tea.

teasing, adj. [1. tézing; 2. tíziŋ], fr. Pres. Part. of **tease** (I.). Harassing, tormenting, causing petty annoyance.

teasingly, adv. Prec. & **-ly.** So as to tease.

teaspoon, n. [1. téspōōn; 2. tíspūn]. Small spoon, of size used for stirring tea &c.

teaspoonful, n. [1. téspōōnfool; 2. tíspūnful]. Amount contained in a teaspoon, one-fourth of tablespoon.

teat, n. [1. tēt; 2. tīt]. M.E. & O. Fr. *tete*, fr. L.G. *titte*; cp. O.E. *titt*; Germ. *zitze*; cogn. w. Gk. *títthē*, 'nurse'; fr. base **dhē-*, 'suck', & ultimately cogn. w. *thēlḗ*, 'teat'; *thêsthai*, 'to milk'; Scrt. *dhātri*, 'nurse'; Lat. *fēlāre*, 'to suck'; *fēmina*, 'woman'; see **feminine & filial.** Pointed projection on the breast of a mammal through which milk passes; nipple.

tea-table, n. Small table used for tea.

tea-things, n. Utensils prepared for use at tea.

teatlike, adj. [1. tḗtlīk; 2. títlaik]. **teat & -like.** Resembling a teat.

tea-tray, n. Small tray on which tea-things are set out, and carried.

tea-urn, n. Urn in which water is boiled for making tea.

teazel. See **teasel.**

tec, n. [1. tek; 2. tɛk]. Abbr. of **detective.** (slang) Detective.

techily, adv. See **tetchily.**

techiness, n. See **tetchiness.**

technic, adj. & n. [1. téknik; 2. téknik], fr. Gk. *tekhnik-(ós)*, 'made by art', fr. *tékhn-(ē)*, 'art, skill', & **-ic**; cp. Gk. *téktōn*, 'carpenter, workman'; Scrt. *tákṣan*, 'carpenter'; O.H.G. *dehsala*, 'axe'; O. Slav. *tesla*; Perh. cogn. w. Lat. *texere*, 'to weave, construct'; see **text.** 1. adj. Technical. 2. n. a Technique; b (pl. *technics*) the arts in general, branches of knowledge dealing with the mechanical arts; c (pl.) vocabulary or rules of the arts.

technical, adj. [1. téknikl; 2. téknikl]. Prec. & **-al.** 1. Connected with, pertaining to, based on, the industrial or mechanical arts: *technical education.* 2. Pertaining to, occurring, specially used in, some specific art, industry, branch of knowledge &c.: *technical knowledge, difficulty, terms*; *the technical use of a word.*

technicality, n. [1. tèknikáliti; 2. tèknikǽliti]. Prec. & **-ity.** 1. State of being technical. 2. Something, a term, method, procedure &c., connected with, and peculiar to, some specific art, science, branch of knowledge, occupation &c.

technically, adv. [1. téknikali; 2. téknikəli]. See prec. & **-ly.** In a technical manner; in a technical sense; from a technical point of view.

technician, n. [1. tekníshan; 2. tɛkníʃən]. **technic & -ian.** Technicist.

technicist, n. [1. téknisist; 2. téknisist]. **technic & -ist.** Student of, one skilled in, technics.

technicon, n. [1. téknikon; 2. téknikɔn], fr. Gk. *tekhnikón*, neut. form of *tekhnikós*, see **technic.** Device or apparatus for exercising fingers of pianist.

techniphone, n. [1. téknifōn; 2. téknifoun], fr. Gk. *tékhn-(ē)*, 'art, skill', see **technic,** & *-i-* & Gk. *phōnḗ*, 'sound'; see **-phone.** Instrument with keyboard producing no sound, for exercising pianist's fingers; dumb piano.

technique, n. [1. teknḗk; 2. tɛkník]. Fr., fr. Gk. *tekhnik-(ós)*, 'of art', see **technic. 1.** Systematic and special method employed in carrying out some particular operation. **2.** Skill in, practical acquaintance with, the methods of some particular art, specialized procedure, operation, and the like.

technologic(al), adj. [1. tèknolójik(l); 2. tèknəlɔ́džik(l)]. **technology** & **-ic** & **-al.** Of, pertaining to, technology.

technologist, n. [1. teknólojist; 2. tɛknɔ́lədžist]. **technology** & **-ist.** Student of, one versed in, technology.

technology, n. [1. teknóloji; 2. tɛknɔ́lədži], fr. Gk. *tékhn-(ē)*, 'art', see **technic**, & **-logy.** Science and history of the mechanical and industrial arts, contrasted with the fine arts.

techy. See **tetchy.**

tecnology, n. [1. teknóloji; 2. tɛknɔ́lədži], fr. Gk. *tékno-(n)*, 'child', see under **teknonymy**, & **-logy.** The study of the development of the child.

tectological, adj. [1. tektolójikl; 2. tɛktəlɔ́džikl]. Next word & **-ic** & **-al.** Of, pertaining to, tectology.

tectology, n. [1. tektóloji; 2. tɛktɔ́lədži], fr. Gk. *téktōn*, 'carpenter, builder', see **technic** & *-o-* & **-logy.** (biol.) Structural morphology.

tectonic, adj. & n. [1. tektónik; 2. tɛktɔ́nik], fr. Lat., fr. Gk. *tektonik-(ós)*, 'skilled in building', fr. *téktōn*, 'carpenter', see **technic** & **-ic. 1.** adj. **a** Of, pertaining to, the art of building; **b** (geol.) of, relating to, depending on, the structure of the earth. **2.** n. (pl. *tectonics*) The art of designing and constructing implements, vessels, furniture, weapons &c., that combine usefulness with artistic merit.

tectorial, adj. [1. tektṓrial; 2. tɛktɔ́riəl], fr. Lat. *tectōri-(us)*, 'of, forming, a cover', fr. *tect-(um)*, P.P. type of *tegere*, 'to cover', see **tegument**, & **-ory** & **-al.** Of, forming, a covering; esp. *tectorial membrane*, covering part of inner ear.

tectrices, n. [1. téktrisēz; 2. téktrisiz]. Mod. Lat., pl. of *tectrix*, 'that which covers'; fr. *tect-*, P.P. type of *tegere*, 'to cover'; see **tegument.** (ornith.) Feathers covering base of tail-feathers; tail coverts.

ted, vb. trans. [1. ted; 2. tɛd], fr. O.N. *teðja*, 'to spread manure'; fr. *tað*, 'manure'; cogn. w. Gk. *datéomai*, 'to distribute, scatter', fr. base **dā-*, **də-*, 'to share', seen in Gk. *daiomai*, 'to share', & in **demon.** To toss, spread out and turn over (hay), in order to dry it.

tedder, n. [1. téder; 2. tédə]. Prec. & **-er.** Machine for tedding hay &c.

teddy bear, n. [1. tédi bār; 2. tédi béə]. Named after Theodore Roosevelt, President of U.S.A., and big-game hunter (1858–1919). Child's furry toy bear.

Te Deum, n. [1. tē dḗum; 2. tí díəm]. Lat. *Tē Deum (laudāmus)*, '(we praise) Thee, O God', opening words of hymn. **a** Hymn ascribed to St. Ambrose, sung at Matins, or as a special thanksgiving hymn; **b** musical setting for this.

tedious, adj. [1. tḗdius; 2. tídiəs], fr. O. Fr. *tedieux*, fr. Lat. *taediōs-(us)*, 'tedious', fr. *taedium*, 'weariness', see **tedium**, & **-ous.** Wearying by length or monotony; dull, tiresome, boring: *a tedious discourse, journey.*

tediously, adv. Prec. & **-ly.** In a tedious manner.

tediousness, n. See prec. & **-ness.** Quality of being tedious.

tedium, n. [1. tḗdium; 2. tídiəm]. Lat. *taedium*, 'weariness, tediousness', fr. *taed-(et)*, 'it wearies, irks'; cp. Lith. *tingùs*; O. Slav. *tęžą*, 'dull, slow', *tęžiti*, 'to be unhappy'. Weariness, irksomeness, monotony.

tee (I.), n. [1. tē; 2. tī], from letter T. **1.** Letter T. **2.** Anything in the shape of a T.

tee (II.), n., fr. Burmese *h'ti*, 'umbrella'. Umbrella-shaped finial on top of pagoda, usually gilded and hung with bells.

tee (III.), n. Prob. fr. mark T used to mark the place. **1.** Mark aimed at in playing quoits, curling &c. **2.** (golf) Small cone of sand, or of rubber &c., on which ball is placed for driving off at start and after each hole.

tee (IV.), vb. trans. & intrans., fr. prec. **1.** trans. To place on a tee. **2.** intrans. *Tee off*, to play ball from tee.

teem (I.), vb. trans. & intrans. [1. tēm; 2. tīm]. O.E. *tēman*, 'to breed'; M.E. *tēmen*; fr. O.E. *tēam*, 'family, progeny', see **team. A.** trans. (archaic) To bear, bring forth, produce. **B.** intrans. **1.** To bring forth young: '*A teeming mistress, but a barren bride*' (Pope, 'To a Lady', 72). **2.** To be highly productive of, full to overflowing with, to abound in: *rivers teeming with fish.* **3.** To be abundant, prolific: *wild life teems in the forest; the teeming population of the slums.*

teem (II.), vb. trans. M.E. *tēmen*, fr. O.N. *tœma*, 'to pour out', fr. *tōmr*, 'empty'; cp. O.E. *tōm*; L.G. *tōm*, 'free from'. (in steel-making) To pour from the crucible: *to teem molten steel.*

teen, n. [1. tēn; 2. tīn]. O.E. *tēona*, 'accusation, injustice, injury, grief'; M.E. *tēne*; cp. O.L.G. *tīona*, 'injury'; O.E. *tēon*, O.H.G. *zīhan*, 'to accuse'; Goth. *gateihan*, 'to announce'; cogn. w. Gk. *deiknūmi*, 'I show'; Lat. *dīcere*, 'to say', see **diction.** (archaic) Misfortune, sorrow, grief.

-teen, suff. representing O.E. *tēne*, 'ten', see **ten**, forming cardinal numbers fr. 13 to 19 inclusive, indicating 10+3, 4 &c.

teens, n. [1. tēnz; 2. tīnz], fr. prec. (pl.) Those years of human life counted in numbers ending in *-teen*; age between 12 and 20: *to be in, just out of, one's teens.*

teeny, adj. [1. tḗni; 2. tíni]. Variant of **tiny.** Often used as intensive form of *tiny*, very tiny, minute; also (colloq.) *teeny weeny.*

teepee, n. See **tepee.**

teeth, n. [1. tēth; 2. tīþ]. Pl. of **tooth**; O.E. *tēþ*, fr. **tōþ-i.*

teethe, vb. intrans. [1. tēdh; 2. tīð]. As though fr. O.E. **tēðan*, fr. **tōþjan*, formed fr. *tōþ*, see **tooth.** To develop or cut teeth.

teething, n. [1. tḗdhing; 2. tíðiŋ]. Prec. & **-ing.** Process or period of cutting of teeth; dentition.

teetotal, adj. [1. tētṓtal; 2. tītóutl]. Popular, reduplicated form of **total. 1.** Of, pertaining to, advocating, devoted to the cause of, total abstinence from intoxicants. **2.** (colloq.) complete, absolute.

teetotalism, n. [1. tētṓtalizm; 2. tītóutəlizəm]. Prec. & **-ism.** Adherence to, support of, doctrine of, total abstinence.

teetotaller, n. [1. tētṓtaler; 2. tītóutələ]. **teetotal** & **-er.** Advocate of, one who practises, total abstinence from intoxicants.

teetotally, adv. [1. tētṓtali; 2. tītóutəli]. See prec. & **-ly. a** After the manner of a teetotaller; **b** (colloq.) totally, completely.

teetotum, n. [1. tètṓtum; 2. tītóutəm], fr. letter T (for Lat. *tōtum*) marked on one side of toy, & *tōtum*, neut. form of Lat. *tōtus*, 'all': see **total.** Small, four-sided toy top, lettered on each side to indicate player's score.

teg(g), n. [1. teg; 2. tɛg]. Etymol. unknown. Sheep in its second year.

tegular, adj. [1. tégūlar; 2. tégjulə], fr. Lat. *tēgul-(a)*, 'tile', see **tegument** & **tile**, & **-ar.** Of, shaped like, used as, placed like, a tile.

tegularly, adv. Prec. & **-ly.** In a tegular manner, as a tile.

tegulated, adj. [1. tégūlāted; 2. tégjulèitid], fr. Lat. *tēgul-(a)*, 'tile'. See **tegular** & **-ate** & **-ed.** (zool.) Having scales or plates overlapping like tiles.

tegument, n. [1. tégūment; 2. tégjumənt], fr. Lat. *tegument-(um)*, 'covering', fr. *teg-(ere)*, 'to cover', & **-ment.** Cp. Lat. *tegulum*, 'roof'; *tēgula*, 'tile'; *toga*, 'robe', see **toga.** Cogn. w. Gk. *stégein*, 'to cover'; Scrt. *sthágati*, 'conceals'; O.H.G. *dah*; O.N. *þak*; O.E. *þæc*, 'roof', see **thatch.** Envelope of membrane enclosing animal body or organ; integument.

tegumental, adj. [1. tègūméntl; 2. tègjuméntl]. Prec. & **-al.** Of, forming, a tegument.

tegumentary, adj. [1. tègūméntari; 2. tègjuméntəri]. **tegument** & **-ary.** Of, pertaining to, of the nature of, a tegument.

tehee, n. & vb. intrans. [1. tēhḗ; 2. tīhī]; in Chaucer as interj.: '*Tehee, quod she, and clapt the window to*' ('Miller's Tale', 554). Imitative. **1.** n. A shrill, foolish, cackling laugh. **2.** vb. To utter a high, shrill laugh.

Teian, Tean, adj. [1. tḗan; 2. tí(i)ən], fr. Lat. *Tēi-(us)*, fr. Gk. *Té-(ōs)*, in Ionia, & **-an. a** Of Teos; **b** of Anacreon, born at Teos, c. 550 B.C.

teil, n. [1. tēl; 2. tīl], fr. O. Fr., fr. Lat. *tilia*, 'lime-tree'; cogn. w. M. Ir. *teile*, 'lime-tree'. Lime-tree.

teind, n. [1. tēnd; 2. tīnd], fr. O.N. *tīund*, cogn. w. **tithe.** (Scots) Tithe.

teknonymous, adj. [1. teknónimus; 2. tɛknɔ́niməs]. Next word & **-ous.** Of, pertaining to, teknonymy.

teknonymy, n. [1. teknónimi; 2. tɛknɔ́nimi], fr. Gk. *téknon*, 'child', cogn. w. Scrt. *tákma*, 'descendant'; O.E. *þegen*; O.N. *þegn*; O.H.G. *degan*, 'warrior', see **thane**; & Gk. *ónuma*, 'name', see **onomatopoeia.** Custom of certain savage races of naming the parent from the child.

tela, n. [1. tḗla; 2. tílə]. Lat., 'web, tissue', earlier **texlā*, cogn. w. *texere*, 'to weave'. See **text.** (anat.) Web-like membrane.

telaesthesia, n. [1. tèlesthḗzia; 2. tèlīsþíziə], fr. **tele-**, & Gk. *aisthēsis*, 'perception', fr. *aisthánomai*, 'perceive', see **aesthete**, & **-ia.** (psychol.) Perception of objects, events &c., at a distance, not perceptible to the physical senses.

telaesthetic, adj. [1. tèlesthétik; 2. tèlīsþétik]. See prec. & **-etic.** Of the nature of, pertaining to, telaesthesia.

telamon, n. [1. télamon; 2. téləmən]. Lat. *telamon*, fr. Gk. *telamṓn*, 'strap, leather band; male figure supporting entablature'; fr. Aryan base **telā-*, **telə-* &c., 'to carry, support', seen in archaic Gk. *talássai*, 'to undertake'; *tálanta*, 'balance'; see **talent**; *tlḗmōn*, 'one who endures'; see base under **tolerate**; cogn. w. **thole (I.).** (archit.) Male figure supporting entablature; cp. *caryatid.*

telary, adj. [1. tḗlari; 2. tíləri]. Lat. *tēlāris*, fr. *tēla*, 'web', see **tela**, & **-ary. 1.** Pertaining to, of the nature of, a web. **2.** Spinning webs; e.g. of spiders.

telautogram, n. [1. teláwtogram; 2. tɛlɔ́təgræm]. **tele-** & **auto-** & **-gram.** Writing, message, transmitted by telautography.

telautograph, n. [1. teláwtograhf; 2. tɛlɔ́təgrāf]. See prec. & **-graph.** Electric instrument reproducing writing &c. at a distance.

telautographic, adj. [1. tèlawtográfik; 2. tèlɔ̄təgræfik]. See prec. & **-graphic.** Pertaining to, effected by means of, telautography.

telautography, n. [1. tèlawtógrafi; 2. tèlɔ̄tɔ́grəfi]. See prec. & **-graphy.** The use of a telautograph.

tele-, pref. representing Gk. *tēle*, 'far off, at a distance'; cp. Gk. *télos*, 'end, result', prob. orig. in the sense of 'place where one stops and turns back', fr. base **kʷel-*, **kʷol-*, 'to turn', whence also **cycle, pole (III.), wheel.** At a distance, from far off.

telebarograph, n. [1. tèlebárograhf; 2. tèlibærəgrāf]. **tele-** & **barograph.** Self-recording telebarometer.

telebarometer, n. [1. tèlebarómeter; 2. tèlibərɔ́mitə]. **tele-** & **barometer.** Barometer that transmits its readings to a distant point by means of electricity.

teledu, n. [1. téledōō; 2. télidū]. E. Indian. Small, burrowing animal of Java and Sumatra; the stinking badger.

telegonic, adj. [1. tèlegónik; 2. tèligɔ́nik]. Next word & **-ic.** Pertaining to, characterized by, telegony.

telegony, n. [1. telégoni; 2. tɛlégəni], fr. **tele-** & Gk. *gónos*, 'procreation', cogn. w. *génos*, 'birth', q.v. under **genus.** Theory of the supposed transmission of characteristics from a previous male to offspring of the same mother by a later sire.

telegram, n. [1. télegram; 2. téligræm]. **tele-** & **-gram**. Message sent by telegraph.

telegraph (I.), n. [1. télegrahf; 2. téligrāf]. **tele-** & **-graph**. **1**. Electrical apparatus for transmitting messages to a distance either with or without a wire. **2**. Any of various devices for signalling or announcing something so as to be seen from a distance.

telegraph (II.), vb. intrans. & trans., fr. prec. **A**. intrans. **1**. To send a message by electric telegraph. **2**. (fig.) To make signals, communicate by signs with person without speaking. **B**. trans. **1**. To send (message &c.) by means of electric telegraph: *to telegraph the news* &c. **2**. To convey (one's wishes &c.) to a person by signs, without speaking.

telegrapher, n. [1. telégrafer; 2. telégrəfə]. Prec. & **-er**. Person skilled in telegraphy; person employed in transmitting telegrams.

telegraphese, n. [1. tèlegrahféz; 2. tèligrāfíz]. **telegraph** & **-ese**. Compressed style commonly used in telegrams.

telegraphic, adj. [1. tèlegráfik; 2. tèligrǽfik]. **telegraph** & **-ic**. Of, pertaining to, sent as, suitable for, telegram: *telegraphic message, code*; *telegraphic brevity*; *telegraphic address*, registered short form of address used in sending telegrams to a firm &c.

telegraphically, adv. [1. tèlegráfikali; 2. tèligrǽfikəli]. Prec. & **-al** & **-ly**. **1**. **a** By means of the telegraph; **b** by means of signs. **2**. In a manner suitable to, usual in, telegraphic messages; briefly, concisely.

telegraphist, n. [1. telégrafist; 2. telégrəfist]. **telegraph** & **-ist**. Telegrapher.

telegraph-line, n. Telegraphic connexion.

telegraphone, n. [1. telégrafōn; 2. telégrəfoun]. See **telegraph** & **-phone**. Instrument which records telephone messages and afterwards reproduces these phonographically.

telegraph-plant, n. East Indian plant of the bean family, the leaves of which jerk spontaneously.

telegraph-pole, n. Pole supporting telegraph wires.

telegraph-post, n. Telegraph-pole.

telegraph-wire, n. Wire along which telegraphic messages are transmitted.

telegraphy, n. [1. telégrafi; 2. telégrəfi]. **tele-** & **-graphy**. Art, process, of communicating by telegraph; art of constructing telegraphic apparatus.

telekinesis, n. [1. tèlekīnésis; 2. tèlikainísis]. **tele-** & Gk. *kīnēsis*, 'movement', fr. *kineîn*, 'to move', see **kinesis**. Motion produced in, movement of, an object without apparent physical connexion with any possible physical agent, esp. as a spiritualistic phenomenon.

telemark, n. [1. télemark; 2. télimāk]. Norw. Place-Name. A swinging turn in ski-ing.

telemechanics, n. [1. tèlemekániks; 2. tèlimikǽniks]. **tele-** & **mechanic** & **-s**. Mechanical control from a distance by rays.

telemeter, n. [1. telémeter; 2. telémitə]. **tele-** & **-meter**. Apparatus for determining distances; range-finder.

telemetric, adj. [1. telemétrik; 2. tèlimétrik]. See prec. & **-metric**. Pertaining to, determined by means of, telemetry.

telemetry, n. [1. telémetri; 2. telémitri]. See prec. & **-metry**. Art of using a telemeter.

teleologic(al), adj. [1. tèleolójik(l); 2. tèliəlɔ́džik(l)]. **teleology** & **-ic** (& **-al**). Of, pertaining to, teleology.

teleologically, adv. Prec. & **-ly**. From a teleological point of view.

teleologism, n. [1. tèleólojizm; 2. tèliɔ́lədžizəm]. **teleology** & **-ism**. Belief in final causes.

teleologist, n. [1. tèleólojist; 2. tèliɔ́lədžist]. See prec. & **-ist**. Student of, believer in, final causes.

teleology, n. [1. tèleóloji; 2. tèliɔ́lədži], fr. Gk. *télos*, genit. *téleos*, 'end; result', see **tele-** & **-logy**. **a** Doctrine that all things in nature were created to fulfil a specific purpose; **b** systematic study of the evidences of this.

teleosaurus, n. [1. tèleosórus; 2. tèliəsɔ́rəs], fr. Gk. *téle-(os)*, 'complete', fr. *tél-(os)*, 'end', see **tele-**, *-o-* & *saûros*, 'lizard', see **sauro-**. Genus of fossil mesozoic crocodiles.

teleostean, n. [1. tèleóstean; 2. tèliɔ́stiən], fr. Gk. *téleos*, 'complete', see **tele-**, & Gk. *osté-(on)*, 'bone', see **osteo-** & **os** & **-an**. Pertaining to the order of fishes which have true bony skeletons.

telepathic, adj. [1. tèlepáthik; 2. tèlipǽþik]. **telepathy** & **-ic**. Of, pertaining to, acting by, telepathy.

telepathically, adv. [1. tèlepáthikali; 2. tèlipǽþikəli]. Prec. & **-al** & **-ly**. By means of telepathy.

telepathist, n. [1. telépathist; 2. telépəþist]. **telepathy** & **-ist**. Student of, one who believes in, or who practises, telepathy.

telepathize, vb. trans. & intrans. [1. telépathīz; 2. telépəþaiz]. Next word & **-ize**. **1**. trans. To influence by telepathy. **2**. intrans. To communicate by telepathy.

telepathy, n. [1. telépathi; 2. telépəþi]. **tele-** & **-pathy**. Communication between mind and mind, influence of one mind upon another, without the physical medium of the senses; thought transference.

telephone (I.), n. [1. télefōn; 2. télifoun]. **tele-** & **-phone**. Instrument by means of which the vibrations caused by sound are converted into an electric current which passes along a wire and is re-converted into sound-vibrations at the other end.

telephone (II.), vb. intrans. & trans., fr. prec. **1**. intrans. To communicate by, make use of, a telephone. **2**. trans. **a** To send, convey (a message), by telephone: *to telephone a message*; **b** to communicate with by telephone: *telephone me tomorrow*.

telephonic, adj. [1. tèlefónik; 2. tèlifɔ́nik]. **telephone** (I.) & **-ic**. Of, pertaining to, conveyed by, telephone.

telephonically, adv. [1. tèlefónikali; 2. tèlifɔ́nikəli]. Prec. & **-al** & **-ly**. By telephone, by means of a telephone.

telephonist, n. [1. teléfunist; 2. teléfənist]. **telephone** (I.) & **-ist**. Person operating telephone.

telephony, n. [1. teléfuni; 2. teléfəni]. **telephone** (I.) & **-y**. Process, method, of transmitting sounds, and communicating, by telephone.

telephote, n. [1. télefōt; 2. télifout], fr. **tele-** & Gk. *phōt-*, stem of *phôs*, 'light', see **phosphorus**. Apparatus for electrical reproduction of photographs at a distance.

telephoto, adj. [1. tèlefótō; 2. tèlifóutou]. Telephotographic.

telephotograph, n. [1. tèlefótograhf; 2. tèlifóutəgrāf]. **tele-** & **photograph**. Photograph **a** made with a telephoto lens; **b** reproduced by means of a telephote.

telephotographic, adj. [1. télefòtográfik; 2. télifòutəgrǽfik]. Prec. & **-ic**. Pertaining to, effected by, telephotography.

telephotography, n. [1. tèlefotógrafi; 2. tèlifətɔ́grəfi]. **tele-** & **photography**. **a** Method of photographing distant objects with a telephoto or telescopic lens; **b** the use of a telephote.

telergy, n. [1. télerji; 2. télədži]. Invented fr. **tele-** & **energy**. Force effecting telepathy.

telescope (I.), n. [1. téleskōp; 2. téliskoup]. **tele-** & **-scope**. Instrument consisting in its simplest, typical form of an arrangement of lenses in a tube, for enabling the observer to see objects or details at a distance.

telescope (II.), vb. trans. & intrans., fr. the form of construction of smaller, portable, telescopes. **1**. trans. To press, drive, together, so that various sections slide one into the other, as into a series of sockets. **2**. intrans. To close, slide together, like the sections of a portable telescope; to be forced one into the other: *the trains telescoped*.

telescopic, adj. [1. tèleskópik; 2. tèliskɔ́pik]. **telescope** & **-ic**. **1**. Of, pertaining to, obtained by means of, a telescope: *telescopic investigation, knowledge*. **2**. Visible only with a telescope. **3**. Having, consisting of, sections sliding one into the other.

telescopically, adv. [1. tèleskópikali; 2. tèliskɔ́pikəli]. Prec. & **-al** & **-ly**. By means of a telescope; in a manner resembling that made possible by a telescope.

telescopiform, adj. [1. tèleskópiform; 2. tèliskɔ́pifōm]. **telescope** & *-i-* & **-form**. Having the form or construction of a telescope.

telescopist, n. [1. teléskopist; 2. teléskəpist]. **telescope** & **-ist**. Person skilled in the use of a telescope.

telescopy, n. [1. teléskopi, téleskopi; 2. teléskəpi, téliskɔpi]. **telescope** & **-y**. Science of the use or construction of telescopes.

telescriptor, n. [1. téleskrìpter; 2. téliskrìptə]. **tele-** & **script** & **-or**. Telegraphic instrument worked by a lettered keyboard.

teleseme, n. [1. télesēm; 2. télisīm], fr. **tele-** & Gk. *sêma*, 'sign', see first element in **semantics**. System of transmitting signals by electricity, used in hotels &c.

telespectroscope, n. [1. tèlespéktroskōp; 2. tèlispéktrəskoup]. **tele-** & **spectroscope**. Combined telescope and spectroscope.

telethermometer, n. [1. tèlethërmómeter; 2. tèliþāmɔ́mitə]. **tele-** & **thermometer**. Thermometer which transmits its readings to a distance by electricity.

television, n. [1. tèlevízhun; 2. tèlivížən]. **tele-** & **vision**. The act or process of seeing objects or events at a distance by means of electricity transmitted over a wire or by wireless waves.

tell, vb. trans. & intrans. [1. tel; 2. tel]. O.E. *tellan*, 'to reckon, calculate; consider (a thing to be so and so); to impute; to enumerate; later, to narrate, say'; M.E. *tellen*; fr. **tælljan*, cp. *tæl*, 'number', & *talu*, 'series; statement; discussion; claim; excuse; action at law'; see **tale**. **A**. trans. **1**. (archaic) To count, reckon, compute: '*He telleth the number of the stars*' (Ps. cxlvii. 4). Phrs. *to tell one's beads*, say one's prayers (with rosary); see **bead**; *all told*, in all, altogether. **2**. **a** To narrate, recount: *to tell a tale, story*; **b** to utter, express, in form of words: *to tell a lie, the truth*. Phr. *to tell fortunes*. **3**. **a** To divulge, proclaim, reveal, express; impart information concerning: *tell me all you know*; *I can't tell you how sorry I am*; '*she never told her love*'; *to tell a secret*; *a man's face may tell a great deal about his character*; Phrs. *this tells its own tale*, explains itself, makes things clear; *to tell tales*, act as informer; **b** to point out, indicate, instruct as to: *tell me the best thing to do*; *to tell one the shortest way*; *clocks tell the time*; **c** to state positively, to affirm: *I tell you I'm sick of the whole thing*; *people are very angry let me tell you*. **4**. **a** To make out, reckon out, find explanation of, account for, elucidate: *to tell the cause, the reason, of*; *difficult to tell how it is done*; *I can't tell what's the matter with him*; **b** to distinguish, discriminate: *to tell the true from the false*; *I can't tell one from the other*. **5**. To order, give command to: *tell him to do as he's bid*; *I told you to be home by ten*. **B**. intrans. **1**. *Tell of*, to make a report concerning, give an account: '*I will tell of all thy wondrous works*'. **2**. To act as tale-bearer, to publish, divulge (secrets, news &c.): *I promise not to tell*; also (childish, colloq.) *tell on*, inform against. **3**. **a** To produce an appreciable effect, to have a definite result: *blood tells in the long run*; *his unselfish work is at last beginning to tell*; **b** (of visual and auditive impressions) to have a value in contrast with other sounds, colours &c.; to show up, stand out, be distinctive compared with others: *a painter knows how to make every mass of colour tell*; *the tenor part in a part-song tells remarkably*. **4**. *Tell on, upon*, to affect for the worse, to exhaust, wear out: *a youth of poverty and hardship told upon him in middle age*; *his age is beginning to tell upon him*.

tellable, adj. [1. télabl; 2. téləbl]. Prec. & **-able**. Capable of being told.

teller, n. [1. téler; 2. télə]. **tell** & **-er**. One who tells; specif. **a** any one of four officials counting votes in House of Commons; **b** bank official whose duty it is to pay out money.

tellership, n. [1. télership; 2. téləʃip]. Prec. & **-ship**. Office of teller.

telling, adj. [1. téling; 2. téliŋ], fr. Pres. Part. of **tell**. Producing a marked effect; impressive, striking.

tellingly, adv. Prec. & **-ly**. In a telling manner.

telltale (I.), n. [1. téltāl; 2. télteil]. **1. a** Person inclined to divulge the private affairs of others; a gossip; **b** one who tells things to another's discredit; a sneak, an informer. **2.** (fig.) Thing conveying information; a token, sign, evidence.

telltale (II.), adj., fr. prec. Acting as telltale; tending to betray or reveal a secret, hidden feelings &c.: *a telltale blush.*

tellural, adj. [1. telūral; 2. teljṓrəl], fr. Lat. *tellūr-*, stem of *tellus*, 'earth', see **tellurium**, & **-al**. Of, pertaining to, the earth or its inhabitants.

tellurate, n. [1. télūrāt; 2. téljureit]. See **tellurium** & **-ate**. A salt of telluric acid.

telluret, n. [1. télūret; 2. téljurit]. See **tellurium** & **-et**. Compound of tellurium.

telluretted, adj. [1. télūrèted; 2. téljurètid]. Prec. & **-ed**. Containing tellurium.

tellurian, adj. & n. [1. telūrian; 2. teljṓriən], fr. Lat. *tellūr-*, stem of *tellūs*, 'earth', see **tellurium**, & **-ian**. **1.** adj. Of, pertaining to, the earth. **2.** n. Inhabitant of the earth.

telluric, adj. [1. telūrik; 2. teljṓrik]. See **tellurium** & **-ic**. Of, derived from, tellurium.

telluride, n. [1. télūrīd; 2. téljuraid]. See **tellurium** & **-ide**. Telluret.

tellurion, n. [1. telūrion; 2. teljṓriən], fr. Lat. *tellūr-*, stem of *tellūs*, 'earth', see **tellurium**. Apparatus illustrating motions of earth.

tellurium, n. [1. telūrium; 2. teljṓriəm], fr. Lat. *tellūr-*, stem of *tellūs*, 'earth', & **-ium**; cp. Scrt. *talam*, 'surface'; O. Slav. *tĭlo*, 'ground'. (chem.) Rare, brittle, lustrous, crystalline element resembling sulphur and selenium.

tellurous, adj. [1. télūrus; 2. téljurəs]. See **tellurium** & **-ous**. Containing tellurium.

telotype, n. [1. télotīp; 2. télətaip]. See **tele-** & **type**. **1.** Electric telegraphic instrument which prints automatically. **2.** Telegram printed by this instrument.

telpher, adj. & n. [1. télfer; 2. télfə]. Contracted fr. **tele-** & **-phore**. **1.** adj. Conveying, transporting, by electricity: *telpher line, road* &c. **2.** n. An electrically driven truck or carrier for conveying goods &c.

telpherage, n. [1. télferij; 2. télfəridž]. Prec. & **-age**. Transportation by electricity.

telson, n. [1. télsun; 2. télsən]. Gk. *télson*, 'limit'; prob. like *télos*, 'end', see **tele-**, fr. base *k^wel-, 'to turn'; see **cycle** & **wheel**. Last abdominal section of some crustaceans.

Telugu, n. [1. téloogōō; 2. télugū]. Native. A Dravidian language of Southern India.

temenos, n. [1. témenos; 2. téminɔs]. Gk. *témenos*, 'sacred enclosure'; cp. *témnein*, 'to cut'; *tómos*, 'part, portion; volume'; see **tome** & cp. also **temple** (I.). (Gk. archaeol.) Sacred enclosure round temple &c.

temerarious, adj. [1. tèmerārius; 2. tèmərέəriəs]. Lat. *temerārius*, 'rash', see **temerity** & **-ary** & **-ous**. Foolishly venturesome, rash, reckless.

temerariously, adv. Prec. & **-ly**. In a temerarious manner.

temerariousness, n. See prec. & **-ness**. Quality of being temerarious; rashness, foolhardiness.

temerity, n. [1. teméritі; 2. timériti], fr. Lat. *temeritāt-(em)*, 'rashness', fr. *temere*, 'rashly, headlong', fr. **temes-*, 'dark'; cp. Lat. *tenebrae*, 'darkness'; Scrt. *támisrā*, 'darkness'; O.H.G. *dinstar*, 'dark'; Lith. *tamsà*, 'darkness'; cp. **tenebrae**. **a** Rashness, daring; **b** audacity, presumptuousness.

temp., adv. [1. temp; 2. temp], abbr. of Lat. *tempore*, abl. of *tempus*, 'time', see **temporal** (I.). In the time of: *temp. Edw. I.*

Tempean, adj. [1. tempēan; 2. tempíən], fr. Gk. *Témpē*, valley in Thessaly, & **-an**. Of, pertaining to, as beautiful as, the valley of Tempe.

temper (I.), vb. trans. & intrans. [1. témper; 2. témpə]. O.E. *temprian*, 'to mingle, moderate, regulate', M.E. *temperen*; fr. Lat. *temperāre*, 'to combine in due proportion; to rule, regulate; to be moderate', fr. *tempor-*, stem of *tempus*, 'portion of time; due season; time'; see **tempus**. **A.** trans. **1. a** (archaic) To blend, compound; **b** to moderate, regulate; to diminish, mitigate, potency of, by mingling with another ingredient: *to temper strong drink with water*; (also in non-material sense) *to temper justice with mercy*. Phr. *to temper the wind to the shorn lamb*, to make allowances, show consideration, for weakness, poverty, misfortune. **2.** To reduce (clay) to desired consistency, by moistening and kneading. **3.** To toughen and harden (metal or glass) by heating, sudden cooling, and reheating. (*N.B.*—Meanings **2** and **3** are probably influenced by Fr. *tremper*, 'to soak, temper steel' &c.). **B.** intrans. To have, attain, a desired quality or state; esp. to become soft and pliable.

temper (II.), n., fr. prec. **1.** Consistency of clay, mortar &c. obtained by tempering. **2.** Condition and degree of hardness and toughness in metal produced by tempering. **3.** Disposition, cast, attitude, of mind; character, nature: *a stubborn, fiery, equable, uncertain, temper*. Phr. *to lose one's temper*, become suddenly angry; *recover, regain, one's temper*, become calm and equable again. **4.** Particular mood, transient humour: *to be in a good, bad, temper*. **5.** State of irritation of mind; anger, passion: *to get into a temper*; *to show signs of temper*. **6.** Calmness, equable state of mind: '*To fall with dignity, with temper rise*' (Pope, 'Essay on Man', 378).

tempera, n. [1. témpera; 2. témpərə]. Ital. Distemper, esp. as used in fresco painting.

temperable, adj. [1. témperabl; 2. témpərəbl]. **temper** & **-able**. Capable of being tempered.

temperament, n. [1. témperament; 2. témpərəmənt], fr. Lat. *temperāment-(um)*, 'mixing in due proportion; disposition, constitution', fr. *temperā-(re)*, 'to mix, mingle, temper', see **temper** (I.), & **-ment**. **1. a** Characteristic combination of bodily, mental, and moral qualities, which together constitute the character and disposition of an individual, and predispose him to act and behave in a particular manner: *excitable, placid, easy-going &c., by temperament*; *the artistic temperament*; **b** specif., an intense, passionate nature and character: *a woman lacking temperament.* **2.** Adjustment of the tones of the scale in instruments of fixed tone (e.g. piano &c.), so as to adapt the scale for use in all keys.

temperamental, adj. [1. tèmperaméntl; 2. tèmpərəméntəl]. Prec. & **-al**. Pertaining to, depending on, arising from, the temperament, esp. in sense **1, b.**

temperamentally, adv. Prec. & **-ly**. By reason of temperament: *temperamentally disinclined for work.*

temperance, n. [1. témperans; 2. témpərəns], fr. O. Fr., fr. Lat. *temperantia*, 'temperance'; **temper** (I.) & **-ance**. **1.** State or quality of being temperate; moderation, self-restraint, self-control, in action, conduct, speech, and, esp., in eating and drinking. **2.** Specif. **a** Moderation in use of alcoholic liquor; **b** total abstinence from intoxicants; *temperance movement, society* &c., aiming at restriction or prohibition of intoxicating drinks; *temperance hotel*, one in which alcoholic liquors are not sold.

temperate, adj. [1. témperat; 2. témpərit]. **temper** & **-ate**. **1.** (of persons) **a** Exercising self-restraint in pleasures; abstemious, not self-indulgent; **b** moderate in opinions; restrained in action, and expression &c. **2.** (of ideas, opinions &c.) Not violent or excessive, not extreme. **3.** (of climate) Not exhibiting extremes either of heat or cold; moderate, fairly equable.

temperately, adv. Prec. & **-ly**. In a temperate manner.

temperateness, n. See prec. & **-ness**. State of being temperate.

temperative, adj. [1. témperativ; 2. témpərətiv]. **temper** (I.) & **-ative**. Having the power of tempering.

temperature, n. [1. témperachur; 2. témp(ə)rətʃə], fr. L. Lat. *temperātūra*, 'temperature', see **temper** & **-ure**. **1.** Degree of heat or cold: *the temperature of the room was intolerably hot.* **2.** Degree of heat possessed by a living body. Phrs. *to take one's temperature*, measure and ascertain this by means of a clinical thermometer; *to have a temperature*, (colloq.) have a temperature above normal; to be feverish.

-tempered, adj. [1. témperd; 2. témpəd]. **temper** (II.) & **-ed**. Having a temper of specified kind: *good-, bad-, hot-tempered* &c.

-temperedly, adv. Prec. & **-ly**. In a manner characteristic of specific temper: *ill-temperedly* &c.

temperer, n. [1. témperer; 2. témpərə]. **temper** (I.) & **-er**. One who, that which, tempers; specif., machine for blending potter's clay.

tempest (I.), n. [1. témpest; 2. témpist]. M.E. fr. O. Fr. *tempeste*, fr. Low Lat. **tempesta*, Lat. *tempestas*, 'portion, space, of time, season, period; a storm'; see **tempus**, **temporal** (I.). **1.** Violent agitation of the elements; rough, tumultuous state of the weather; violent storm of wind, rain &c. **2.** (fig.) Something resembling a tempest in violence; violent disturbance of the emotions; uncontrolled, tumultuous, expression of such disturbance: *a tempest of sobs, weeping* &c.

tempest (II.), vb. intrans. & trans., fr. prec. **a** intrans. To move violently and tumultuously, like a tempest: *to tempest through the house*; **b** trans., to cause a tempest in; raise to the fury of a tempest: '*Tempest the ocean*' (Milton).

tempestuous, adj. [1. tempéstūus; 2. tempéstjuəs]. O. Fr. *tempestueux*, w. substitution of **-ous**; see **tempest** (I.). **a** Resembling a tempest in violence; of the nature of a tempest; stormy: *a tempestuous wind*; **b** (fig., of the emotions, or behaviour) violent, turbulent, powerfully excited, agitated: *a tempestuous sitting of Parliament* &c.

tempestuously, adv. Prec. & **-ly**. After the manner of a tempest; violently, agitatedly.

tempestuousness, n. See prec. & **-ness**. State, quality, of being tempestuous.

Templar, n. [1. témplar; 2. témplə]. M.E. *templere*, L. Lat. *templarius*; see **temple** (I.) & **-ar**. **1.** Member of the military religious Order, founded 1119 for the protection of the Holy Sepulchre; so called from headquarters of the Order, known as Solomon's Temple in Jerusalem; also called *Knight Templar.* **2.** Law student; esp. one having chambers in the Temple in London, which formerly belonged to the Knights Templars: '*And wits and templars every sentence raise*' (Pope, 'To Arbuthnot', 211). **3. a** Member of an order in modern Freemasonry styled *Knights Templars*; **b** member of a temperance society known as *Good Templars.*

template. See **templet**.

temple (I.), n. [1. templ; 2. templ]. Fr., fr. Lat. *templum*, 'place or space of observation, marked off by the Augur with his staff; any open space (poet.); place set apart for public functions; consecrated, sacred, place; place of refuge; place devoted to a particular deity; a fane'. Walde sees as the kernel of meaning, 'stretched, expectant', & connects the word w. Lat. *tendere*, 'to stretch', see **tend** (II.) & **tense** (II.); other authorities regard the central meaning as 'place set apart, cut off, from surroundings', & connect w. Gk. *témenos*, 'sacred enclosure', see **temenos**, fr. Gk. *témnein*, 'to cut', connected w. *tomé*, 'slice', see **tome**. **1.** A building set apart for worship; **a** a heathen fane; **b** place of Christian worship; a church; esp. a Protestant church (in France); **c** a Mormon place of worship. **2.** Specif., *the Temple*, the chief place of worship of Jehovah, built in Jerusalem by the ancient Jews. **3.** *The Temple*, **a** the Inns of Court, Inner and Middle Temple, in London, the site of which formerly belonged to the Knights Templars; **b** the Temple Church in London; **c** former headquarters of Templars in Paris. **4.** Place or object sanctified by the Divine Presence; the body thought of as *the temple of the Holy Ghost*.

temple (II.), n. O. Fr. *temple*, fr. Lat. *tempora*, pl., 'the fatal spot', fr. *tempus*, 'period of time; the fitting time'; in pl. 'the fatal spot; the temples of the head'; see **tempus**. One of the sides of the head on either side of the forehead in front of the ear.

temple (III.), n. See **templet**. Device for keeping cloth taut on a loom.

templed, adj. [1. témpld; 2. témpld]. **temple** (I.) & **-ed**. Supplied with, abounding in, temples.

templet, n. [1. témplet; 2. témpl*i*t]. Fr. dimin. of *temple*; prob. fr. Lat. *templum*, in sense of 'small rafter, purlin', see **temple** (I.). **1.** Thin plate of wood or metal used as a pattern or guide in cutting wood or stone. **2.** Timber used under end of a girder or beam, to distribute weight. **3.** Wedge under block on keel of a ship in process of construction.

tempo, n. [1. témpō; 2. témpou]. Ital., 'time', see **tempus**. (mus.) Degree of speed at which a passage is to be played.

temporal (I.), adj. [1. témporal; 2. témpərəl]. Lat. *temporālis*, 'belonging to time; lasting only for a time, temporary'; fr. *tempor-*, stem of **tempus**, & **-al**. **1.** Belonging to, existing under, the limitation of time; contrasted with *spatial*. **2.** Pertaining to, limited by, time; lasting only during the lifetime of humanity upon the earth; earthly, transient; contrasted with *eternal*. **3.** Pertaining to civil affairs as distinguished from ecclesiastical: *the temporal power of the Pope*. **4.** (gram.) Pertaining to tense.

temporal (II.), adj. & n. Cp. **temple** (II.). **1.** adj. (anat.) Connected with, lying near, forming part of, the temples. **2.** n. A temporal bone.

temporality, n. [1. tèmporáliti; 2. tèmpərǽl*i*ti]. **temporal** (I.) & **-ity**. Material rights and possessions; esp. those pertaining to an ecclesiastical authority; generally pl., *temporalities of the Church*.

temporalty, n. [1. témporalti; 2. témpərəlt*i*]. See prec. (rare) Temporality.

temporarily, adv. [1. témporarili; 2. témpərər*i*li]. **temporary** & **-ly**. For a time only.

temporariness, n. [1. témporarines; 2. témpərər*i*nis]. See prec. & **-ness**. State of being temporary.

temporary, adj. [1. témporari; 2. témpərər*i*]. Lat. *temporārius*, 'belonging to time; lasting only for a time'; *tempor-*, stem of *tempus*, see **tempus**. **a** Lasting only for a time; transient, fleeting: *temporary pleasures, good fortune* &c.; contrasted with *lasting*; **b** held, occupied, during a limited time only; not permanent: *a temporary job, employment, post, appointment*; *temporary possession*.

temporization, n. [1. tèmporīzáshun; 2. tèmpəraizéiʃən]. Next word & **-ation**. Act of temporizing.

temporize, vb. intrans. [1. témporīz; 2. témpəraiz], fr. *tempor-*, stem of Lat. *tempus*, see **tempus**, & **-ize**. **1.** To pursue a non-committal line of conduct or action, give evasive, indecisive reply, so as to gain time before coming to irrevocable decision. **2.** To play the part of time-server; comply, or appear to comply, with the requirements of the time and occasion.

temporizer, n. [1. témporīzer; 2. témpəraizə]. Prec. & **-er**. Person given to temporizing.

temporizing, n. [1. témporīzing; 2. témpər*aiziŋ*]. **temporize** & **-ing**. Act of temporizing; temporization.

temporizingly, adv. Pres. Part. of **temporize** & **-ly**. In a temporizing manner.

temporo-, pref. Lat. *tempora*, see **temple** (II.). Connected with the head or facial areas, e.g. *temporo-maxillary*, pertaining to the temple and upper jaw.

tempt, vb. trans. [1. tempt; 2. tɛmpt]. M.E. *tempten, tenten*, fr. O. Fr. *tempter, tenter*, 'to try, attempt; to tempt'; Lat. *tentāre*, 'to handle, touch, feel; to prove, put to the test, try; to essay, attempt; to urge, incite'; the base is said by Walde to be an intens. of *tendere*, 'to stretch, stretch out; to aim, strive, direct one's course towards'; see **tend** (II.). **1.** **a** (archaic, Bib.) To test, try, prove; **b** (poet.) to attempt. **2.** (of human action) **a** To persuade, or endeavour to persuade, to do something, esp. something wrong, by holding out certain inducements; to seduce, incite, urge on, to evil: '*the woman tempted me*'; *to tempt a man to steal*; **b** (in innocent sense) to persuade, induce: *can't I tempt you to have another helping*; *I am almost tempted to accept*. Phr. *nothing would tempt me to (leave England)*, I am determined not to. **3.** (of effect of inanimate things, of circumstances &c.) To attract, allure, entice, excite desire in: *your offer doesn't tempt me at all*; *everything to tempt the appetite*.

temptation, n. [1. temptáshun; 2. tɛmptéiʃən]. Prec. & **-ation**. **1.** **a** Act of tempting; **b** state of being tempted. **2.** That which tempts; an attraction, allurement, inducement; **a** (in bad sense) *one should not put temptation in the way of others*; *many temptations beset the young*; **b** (in innocent sense) *I am so comfortable here, that there is no temptation to leave*.

tempter, n. [1. témpter; 2. témptə]. **tempt** & **-er**. Person who tempts; specif., *the Tempter*, the Devil, Satan.

tempting, adj. [1. témpting; 2. témpt*i*ŋ], fr. Pres. Part. of **tempt**. Attractive, alluring, seductive: *a tempting offer*; *this peach looks very tempting*.

temptress, n. [1. témptres; 2. témptr*i*s]. **tempter** & **-ess**. Woman who tempts (chiefly in bad sense).

tempus, n. [1. témpus; 2. témpəs]. Lat., 'time; a period of time', stem *tempor-*, see **temporal** (I.) &c.; the etymol., like the orig. conception, whence the meaning springs, is doubtful. Some regard this as being 'a particular region of the sky', & connect w. **temple** (I.); others believe the basal idea to be 'that which lasts', & connect w. *tendere*, 'to stretch out, extend', & Scrt. *tanōti*, 'it lasts', & w. Goth. *þeihs*, fr. *þeŋχ-, 'time, season'; others again believe the orig. sense to have been 'particular, specific, period or point of time', still connecting w. *tendere*, & *þeihs*, & also w. O.N. *þing*, 'meeting held at fixed times', see **thing**. Time as thought of in connexion with music and prosody.

tempus fugit, phr. [1. témpus fūjit; 2. témpəs fjūdžit]. Lat. Time flies.

ten, numeral adj. & n. [1. ten; 2. tɛn]. O.E. *tīen, tēn*, O.H.G. *zehan*, Mod. Germ. *zehn*; O.S. *tehan*; Goth. *taihun*; all fr. Aryan **dek̑m̥*, whence also Gk. *déka*; Scrt. *dáśa*; Lat. *decem*, cp. **decimal**. **1.** adj. One more than nine; twice five. Phrs. *ten times the man you are*, a much better man; *ten times as big*, a great deal bigger; *I'd ten times rather*, much rather. **2.** n. **a** The number one more than nine; **b** the figure 10, or X, expressing this; **c** a collection of ten objects: *to arrange things in tens*. Phr. *the upper ten*, for *ten thousand*, the aristocracy.

tenable, adj. [1. ténabl, ténabl; 2. tínəbl, tɛ́nəbl]. Fr., fr. Lat. stem *ten-*, 'to hold', & **-able**. Lat. *tenēre*, 'to hold, grasp; have in one's power, have, keep, possession of; to hinder, restrain; to hold in the mind, to know; to take in, understand', is ultimately fr. same base as *tendere*, 'to stretch', q.v. under **tend** (II.) & cp. **tendon** & **tense** (II.). **1.** (of a fortress, position &c.) Capable of being defended, maintained, held in possession. **2.** (of opinions, ideas &c.) Capable of being reasonably held by the mind; in accordance with facts or with common sense; logical.

tenace, n. [1. tenás; 2. tɛnéis]. Fr., see next word. (whist) Combination of first and third best, or second and fourth best cards of the suit which has been led, held by the same hand.

tenacious, adj. [1. tenáshus; 2. tɛnéiʃəs]. Lat. *tenāci-*, stem of *tenax*, 'holding fast; sticky; stubborn', see base under **tenable**, & **-ous**. **1.** Holding, grasping, firmly: *a tenacious grip*. **2.** Holding together firmly; **a** tough, cohesive; **b** adhesive, sticky. **3.** (of the mind and mental condition) **a** Grasping and keeping firmly; retentive: *a tenacious memory*; **b** adhering firmly to a purpose; unyielding, stubborn: *a tenacious foe*; *to be tenacious of one's rights*.

tenaciously, adv. Prec. & **-ly**. In a tenacious manner.

tenaciousness, n. See prec. & **-ness**. Quality, fact, of being tenacious (in physical and moral sense).

tenacity, n. [1. tenásiti; 2. tɛnǽs*i*ti]. Lat. *tenācitāt-(em)*, 'a holding fast', fr. *tenāc-*, see **tenacious**, & **-ity**. **a** Resolution, fixity of purpose, stubbornness; **b** power of retaining; retentiveness.

tenaculum, n. [1. tenákūlum; 2. tɛnǽkjuləm]. Lat., 'a holder', formed fr. *tenāc-*, see **tenacious**. Sharp, slender hook used by surgeons.

tenail(le), n. [1. tenál; 2. tɛnéil]. Fr., fr. prec. (fort.) Outwork in main ditch between two bastions.

tenancy, n. [1. ténansi; 2. tɛ́nəns*i*]. Next word & **-cy**. **1.** **a** Act of holding property as a tenant; **b** period, duration, of such holding. **2.** Property, land, or house, held by a tenant.

tenant (I.), n. [1. ténant; 2. tɛ́nənt]. Fr., fr. Pres. Part. of *tenir*, 'to hold', fr. Lat. *tenēre*, see **tenable**. **1.** (law) Person possessing real estate by any kind of right, whether for life, or for a term of years, or at the will of another. **2.** Person who holds house or land belonging to another on payment of rent; contrasted with *landlord*. **3.** Inhabitant, dweller, denizen: *tenants of the woods, trees* &c., birds.

tenant (II.), vb. trans., fr. prec. To occupy, hold, possess, as a tenant; chiefly used in P.P.

tenantable, adj. [1. ténantabl; 2. tɛ́nəntəbl]. **tenant** (II.) & **-able**. Capable of being, fit to be, occupied by a tenant.

tenantless, adj. [1. ténantles; 2. tɛ́nəntlis]. **tenant** (I.) & **-less**. Empty, unoccupied, devoid of tenants or inhabitants.

tenantry, n. [1. ténantri; 2. tɛ́nəntr*i*]. **tenant** (I.) & **-ry**. Body of tenants collectively.

tench, n. [1. tensh; 2. tɛnʃ]. O. Fr. *tenche*, L. Lat. *tinca*. A freshwater, cyprinid fish, *Tinca vulgaris*.

tend (I.), vb. trans. [1. tend; 2. tɛnd]. Form of **attend**. **1.** To watch over, guard, look after, provide for the wants of: *to tend the sick and wounded*; *to tend sheep*. **2.** (naut.) To stand by, in readiness to attend to (a rope &c.).

tend (II.), vb. intrans. Fr. *tendre*, fr. Lat. *tendere*, 'to stretch, extend; to direct oneself, or one's course'; cogn. w. *teinein*, fr. **tenjō-*, 'stretch'; Scrt. *tanṓti*, 'he stretches' &c.; also w. Gk. *tónos*, see **tone**; Lat. *tenuis*, 'thin'; Scrt. *tamiś*, 'thin, tender'; cp. also **tantra, tender** (IV.), **thin** &c. **1.** To move, be directed, in a certain direction. **2.** To have an inclination, tendency, bias, in a certain direction; **a** (of human action) *he tends to become tedious and long-winded*; *I naturally tend towards conservatism*; **b** (of other processes) *it tends to become very cold at night now*; *the lowest rabble tend to get the upper hand in revolutions*. **3.** To have the effect of, have a tendency to: *too much smoking tends to injure the voice*.

tendance, n. [1. téndans; 2. tɛ́ndəns]. Form of **attendance**; see **tend** (I.). **a** Act of tending, caring for; **b** care, attention.

tendencious, tendentious, adj. [1. tendénshus; 2. tɛndɛ́nʃəs], fr. Germ. *tendenziös*, see next word & **-ous.** (of writings, utterances) Having a distinct aim or purpose, or tendency; biassed, not impartial.

tendency, n. [1. téndensi; 2. téndənsi]. Fr. *tendance*; **tend (II.)** & **-ance** & **-cy.** Process of tending towards; inclination, bent; drift, trend: *a tendency to corpulence, to insomnia, to drink too much*; *the tendency of events is towards war.*

tender (I.), n. [1. ténder; 2. téndə]. **tend (I.)** & **-er.** **1.** Person who tends (in various senses); specif., person who looks after the sick or young children. **2.** Small ship in attendance upon a larger vessel for supplying stores, conveying messages &c. **3.** Truck carrying fuel attached to locomotive.

tender (II.), vb. trans. & intrans. [1. ténder; 2. téndə], formed fr. next word. **A.** trans. **1.** To offer in payment of amount due: *to tender a sum in satisfaction of a claim.* **2.** To offer, present for acceptance: *to tender one's apologies, thanks* &c. **B.** intrans. To make a tender; to offer to carry out work at a specified price.

tender (III.), n., fr. Fr. infin. *tendre*, 'to reach out; offer', used as n., fr. Lat. *tendere*, 'to stretch', see **tend (II.).** **1.** Offer made by a contractor, to carry out work according to specification at a fixed price. **2.** Money tendered or offered in payment of a debt, satisfaction of a claim &c. Phr. *legal tender*, any form of currency recognized by law in a given country as acceptable in payment of debt: *Russian roubles are not legal tender in England.*

tender (IV.), adj. M.E., fr. Fr. *tendre*, fr. Lat. *tener*, 'soft, delicate; susceptible; weak'; either fr. base **ten-* &c., 'to stretch', see **tend (II.)**; or for **teren-*, influenced by *tenuis*, 'thin', cogn. w. Gk. *térēn*, 'delicate, tender'; Scrt. *tárunaś*, 'young, tender'; connected w. Lat. *terere*, 'to rub, wear down', see **trite** & cp. **teredo.** **1. a** (of food, esp. meat) Soft, easily broken up by chewing; reverse of *tough*; **b** easily injured, broken, or torn, by rough handling; flimsy; not firm, strong, or resistent: *a tender structure, fabric* &c.; *a tender skin*; **c** (of colour) soft, delicate. **2. a** Constitutionally delicate; not able to resist severe cold; feeble, liable to injury; reverse of *strong* or *hardy*: *a tender shoot, plant, blossom* &c.; also **b** immature, young: *of tender age*; *tender buds* &c. **3.** Susceptible to pain, sensitive to pressure &c., as after an injury &c.: *a tender place on one's head*; *my bruise is still tender.* **4. a** Morally susceptible, full of compunction; scrupulous: *a tender conscience*; **b** sensitive to, easily moved by, the suffering of others; pitiful, compassionate: *a tender heart.* **5. a** Kind, loving, solicitous; feeling, expressing, affection: *a tender glance, touch* &c.; *tender care*; **b** careful not to wound; considerate: *be tender of his conscientious scruples*; *tender of hurting his feelings* &c.

tenderfoot, n. [1. ténderfoot; 2. téndəfut]. (Colonial slang) A new-comer, esp. in a newly formed, rough, settlement, camp &c.; an inexperienced novice, a greenhorn.

tender-hearted, adj. Having a tender heart; susceptible to, easily moved by, pity; kindly, compassionate.

tenderloin, n. [1. ténderloin; 2. téndəlɔin]. **tender (IV.)** & **loin.** (U.S.A.) **1.** Undercut of sirloin. **2.** District of New York or other city regarded as the centre of amusement.

tenderly, adv. [1. ténderli; 2. téndəli]. **tender (IV.)** & **-ly.** In a tender manner; with tenderness.

tenderness, n. [1. téndernes; 2. téndənis]. See prec. & **-ness.** State, quality, of being tender (in various senses). **1.** Delicacy, softness, of texture. **2.** Sensitiveness to pain. **3. a** Sensitiveness to suffering of others; compassionateness: *tenderness of heart*; **b** moral scruple: *tenderness of conscience.* **4. a** Affection, love, solicitude; **b** expression of these in action and behaviour; kindness, gentleness.

tendinous, adj. [1. téndinus; 2. téndinəs], fr. Mod. Lat. *tendin-*, stem of *tendo*, see next word, & **-ous.** Pertaining to, connected with, resembling, a tendon.

tendon, n. [1. téndun; 2. téndən]. Lat. *tendo*, fr. base in *tendere*, 'stretch, extend'; see **tend (II.).** (anat.) Tough, fibrous connective tissue which joins a muscle to some other part; a sinew. *Achilles tendon*, or *tendo Achillis*, that which connects the heel with the calf (so called because the heel was the one vulnerable spot of Achilles).

tendril, n. [1. téndril; 2. téndril, téndrəl], cp. Fr. *tendrille*, fr. **tender (IV.).** A slender organ in climbing plants, which coils in a spiral round neighbouring objects, parts of other plants &c., and serves to anchor and support the plant whence it grows.

tendrillar, adj. [1. téndrilar; 2. téndrilə]. Prec. & **-ar.** Pertaining to, playing part of, a tendril.

tenebrae, n. pl. [1. ténebrē; 2. ténibrī]. Lat., 'darkness'; for **temefrā*, fr. **temesrā*; cogn. w. Scrt. *támisrā*, 'darkness'; cp. O.H.G. *dinstar*, 'dark'; O.S. *thima*, 'dark'; cp. **temerity**, see also **dust.** Matins and lauds for the last three days of Holy Week, commemorating the passion and death of Christ, at which the candles are extinguished.

tenebrous, adj. [1. ténebrus; 2. ténibrəs]. Prec. & **-ous.** Dark, gloomy, dusky, shady.

tenement, n. [1. ténement; 2. ténimənt]. L. Lat. *tenementum*, fr. *tenēre*, 'to hold', see **tenant (I.).** **1.** (law) That which is held by tenure, the possessor of which is a tenant; hence land, houses, and forms of incorporeal property held of another, whether for life or for a term of years; houses, rents, an office, a peerage &c. **2. a** A dwelling-house; **b** one of a set of apartments in a building, each occupied by a separate family; also *tenement house*, one so occupied. **3.** (fig., poet.) A dwelling-place: *the soul's tenement*, the body.

tenemental, adj. [1. tèneméntl; 2. tènimɛ́ntl]. Prec. & **-al.** Pertaining to a **tenement**; held by tenants.

tenementary, adj. [1. tèneméntari; 2. tènimɛ́ntəri]. See prec. & **-ary.** Tenemental; to be leased to tenants.

tenet, n. [1. tḗnet, ténet; 2. tīnit, ténit]. Lat. 3rd pers. sing. indic. pres. of *tenēre*, 'to hold' &c.; see **tenable** & **tenant.** A principle, opinion, dogma, held and taught as true.

tenfold, adj. & adv. [1. ténfōld; 2. ténfould]. **ten** & **-fold.** Ten times repeated; ten times as many.

tenner, n. [1. téner; 2. ténə]. (colloq.) A ten-pound note; ten pounds.

tennis, n. [1. ténis; 2. ténis]. M.E. *teneis*; in one 15th cent. MS. *tenetz*; origin obscure; possibly fr. A.-Fr. *tenetz*, imper., 'hold, receive', i.e. 'play'. **1.** Ancient ball game for two or four players, played in a specially made covered court, divided by a net, the ball being originally struck by the hand, later with racquets. **2.** Somewhat similar game played on an open court: *lawn tennis.*

tennis ball, n. Ball used in playing tennis or lawn tennis.

tennis court, n. Court in or on which tennis or lawn tennis is played.

tennis elbow, n. Inflammatory condition of the elbow joint, caused by strain in playing tennis.

tenon, n. & vb. trans. [1. ténun; 2. ténən]. M.E., fr. O. Fr. *tenoun*, fr. *tenir*, 'to hold', fr. Lat. *tenēre*; see **tenable, -oon.** **1.** n. Projection formed at the end of a piece of timber by cutting away wood around it, made to fit into a mortice cut in another timber. **2.** vb. To shape (end of a timber) for insertion in a mortice.

tenor (I.), n. [1. téner; 2. ténə]. Lat., 'a holding on; uninterrupted course or career'; fr. base *ten-*, 'to hold'; see **tenable, tenant.** **1.** Course, general direction followed, career: '*the noiseless tenor of their way*' (Gray). **2.** General bearing, meaning, drift, of a statement, speech, document.

tenor (II.), n. Fr., fr. Ital. *tenore*, fr. Lat. *tenor*, see prec.; so called because this voice sang and kept the principal part. **1.** The higher of the two adult types of male singing voice. **2.** The part in a song sung in harmony, taken by this voice. **3. a** The person who sings the tenor part; **b** an instrument which plays this part; the viola.

tenor (III.), adj., fr. prec. Pertaining to the tenor part, or to the quality of voice possessed by tenors.

tenorino, n. [1. tènorḗnō; 2. tènərínou]. Ital. dimin. of *tenore*, see **tenor (II.).** Falsetto; sham soprano produced by a male voice.

tenotomy, n. [1. tenótumi; 2. tenɔ́təmi]. Gk. *ténōn*, 'tendon', & **-tomy**, 'a cutting'. Operation of cutting a tendon.

tense (I.), n. [1. tens; 2. tɛns]. O. Fr. *tens*, 'time', fr. Lat. *tempus*, see **tempus.** (gram.) That form in verbs which expresses the time—past, present, future—in which the action takes place.

tense (II.), adj., fr. Lat. *tensum*, P.P. of *tendere*, 'to stretch'; see **tend (II.).** **1.** (of material object or substance) Tightly stretched, strained; braced up. **2.** Specif. (phon.) *tense vowel*, one uttered with the tongue braced up, in a tense condition; contrasted with *slack.* **3. a** (of the mind and emotions) Strained, keyed up; on the qui vive, alert; **b** (of the manner) expressing such a state of mind; strained, stiff, unnatural.

tense (III.), vb. trans., fr. prec. To brace, make tense (esp. the muscles); specif., to make a vowel sound tense by bracing up the tongue.

tensely, adv. [1. ténsli; 2. tɛ́nsli]. **tense (II.)** & **-ly.** In a tense manner.

tenseness, n. [1. ténsnes; 2. tɛ́nsnis]. See prec. & **-ness.** Condition of being tense.

tensibility, n. [1. tènsibíliti; 2. tɛ̀nsibíliti]. Next word & **-ity.** Quality of being tensible; capacity for extension.

tensible, adj. [1. ténsibl; 2. tɛ́nsibl]. **tense (II.)** & **-ible.** Capable of being stretched out or extended.

tensile, adj. [1. ténsīl; 2. tɛ́nsail]. **tense (II.)** & **-ile.** **1. a** Pertaining to tension; **b** (of musical instrument) producing notes from tightened strings. **2.** Capable of being stretched; tensible.

tension, n. [1. ténshun; 2. tɛ́nʃən]. Lat. *tensiōn-(em)*, fr. *tens-*, P.P. type of *tendere*, 'to stretch', see **tense (II.)**, & **-ion.** **1. a** Act or process of straining, stretching, tightening; **b** state of being tightly stretched: *the tension of a fiddle-string.* **2. a** Mental or emotional stress and strain; suppressed excitement; **b** social atmosphere of uneasiness, stiffness, in which those present exhibit emotional strain; **c** (elect.) only in compounds, *high-*, *low-tension.*

tensional, adj. [1. ténshunal; 2. tɛ́nʃənəl]. Prec. & **-al.** Pertaining to, of the nature of, tension.

tensive, adj. [1. ténsiv; 2. tɛ́nsiv]. See **tense (II.)** & **-ive.** Producing a feeling of tension or stiffness.

tenson, tenzon, n. [1. ténsn, -zn; 2. tɛ́nsn, -zn]. Ital. *tensione*; see **tension.** Contest of verse-making between troubadours.

tensor, n. [1. ténser; 2. tɛ́nsə]. See **tense (II.)** & **-or.** Muscle which stretches a part or renders it tense.

tent (I.), n. & vb. trans. & intrans. [1. tent; 2. tɛnt]. Fr. *tente*; Med. Lat. *tenta*, prob. orig. 'something stretched'; see **tend (II.).** **1.** n. Protection, shelter, covering, formed of canvas stretched over poles and kept tight by ropes pegged to the ground. **2.** vb. (rare) **a** trans. To cover with or as with a tent; (in P.P.) *tented field*, having tents pitched in it; **b** intrans., to lodge in a tent, to encamp.

tent (II.), vb. trans. & n., fr. O. Fr. *tenter*, 'to try, probe', see **tempt.** **1.** vb. To dilate (orifice of a wound or natural opening) by inserting a plug of lint, sponge &c. **2.** n. Plug of lint, linen &c. used for keeping open a wound or dilating natural orifice.

tent (III.), n. Span. *tinto*, fr. Lat. *tinctum*, P.P. of *tingere*, 'to dye', see **tinge** & **tincture**. A sweet, dark-red Spanish wine, chiefly used for ecclesiastical purposes.

tentacle, n. [1. téntakl; 2. téntəkl]. Lat. *tentāculum*, fr. *tentāre*, 'to feel, handle'; see **tempt**. Any long, slender, flexible organ, or feeler, often prehensile, and used also for aiding movement, borne by many lower forms of animals.

tentacled, adj. [1. téntakld; 2. téntəkld]. Prec. & **-ed**. Possessing, bearing, tentacles.

tentacular, adj. [1. tentákūlar; 2. tentǽkjulə]. See **tentacle** & **-ar**. Resembling, of the nature of, a tentacle.

tentaculate(d), adj. [1. tentákūlāt(ed); 2. tentǽkjuleit(id)]. See **tentacle** & **-ate** (& **-ed**). Furnished with tentacles.

tentative, adj. & n. [1. téntativ; 2. téntətiv], fr. *tentāt-*, P.P. type of *tentāre*, 'to try' &c., see **tempt**, & **-ive**. **1.** adj. Of the nature of a trial; experimental; done, made, as an experiment. **2.** n. Something done, opinion, theory, put forward as a test or experiment.

tentatively, adv. Prec. & **-ly**. In a tentative manner; experimentally, by way of a test or trial.

tent-bed, n. Bed with a canopy.

tenter (I.), n. [1. ténter; 2. téntə], fr. Scots *tent*, form of **tend** (I.). Person in charge of machinery.

tenter (II.), n. M.E. *tenture*, *tentoure*, fr. Fr. *tenture*, 'hangings, tapestry'; fr. Lat. *tentum*, P.P. of *tendere*, 'to stretch', see **tend** (II.). Frame for stretching cloth so that it may dry square.

tenter-hook, n. One of the hooks that hold cloth on a tenter; Phr. *on tenter-hooks*, in a state of excitement, expectation, anxiety &c.

tenth, adj. & n. [1. tenth; 2. tenþ]. New formation fr. **ten** & **-th**, the O.E. being *tēoða*; see **tithe**. **1.** adj. **a** Next after the ninth; **b** referring to one of ten equal parts of a whole: *tenth part*. **2.** n. **a** A tenth part; **b** the object in a series next in order to, and immediately following, the ninth.

tent-pegging, n. [1. tént pèging; 2. tént pègiŋ]. Act, practised as part of cavalry exercise, of approaching at a gallop, lifting, and carrying off on the point of a lance a peg firmly fixed in the ground.

tenuis, n., pl., **tenues** [1. ténūis, -ēz; 2. ténjuis, -īz]. Lat., 'thin, fine'; used by grammarians to translate Gk. *psilós*, 'bare; unaspirated'; the word is cogn. w. Gk. *tanu-*, 'slender, thin'; Scrt. *tanúš*, 'long, stretched out'; O.E. *þynn*, see **thin**; the orig. base is **ten-*, as seen in extended form in *tendere*, 'to stretch', see **tend** (II.). Antiquated grammatical or phonetic term applied to any one of the sounds expressed respectively by *p*, *t*, *k*; now usually called *voiceless stops*.

tenuity, n. [1. tenūiti; 2. tenjūiti]. Fr. *tenuité*, Lat. *tenuitāt-(em)*, 'thinness, slenderness, fineness'; see prec. & **-ity**. Quality, state, of being tenuous; **a** rarity, thinness (of air, gas, liquid); **b** fineness, slenderness (of hair &c.); **c** thinness, lack of substance (in something flat); **d** simplicity, thinness, lack of grandeur (of style).

tenuous, adj. [1. ténūus; 2. ténjuəs]. Stem of **tenuis** & **-ous**. **a** (of material things) Fine, slender, thin; **b** (of distinctions) too subtle, over-refined.

tenure, n. [1. ténūr; 2. ténjə]. O. Fr. *teneure*, fr. *tenir*, 'to hold'; see **tenable** & **tenant**. **1.** **a** Act of holding, right to hold, property; esp. holding of real estate, formerly from a superior or over-lord; **b** act, fact, of holding an office, dignity &c. **2.** Manner in which, condition on which, property, a right, an office, is held.

tenurial, adj. [1. tenúrial; 2. tenjúəriəl]. Prec. & **-al**. Connected with, dependent on, tenure.

tenuto, adj. [1. tenōōtō; 2. tenúto]. Ital., 'held', P.P. of *tenēre*. (mus. direction) Sustained, given its full duration; contrasted with *staccato*.

teocalli, n. [1. tēōkáli; 2. tioukǽli]. Aztec (Mexican), lit. 'house (*calli*) of the God (*teotl*)'. An ancient Aztec temple.

tepee, n. [1. tḗpē; 2. tīpī], fr. N. Am. Indian *tipi*. A tent, hut, or wigwam of the N. American Indians.

tepefy, vb. trans. & intrans. [1. tépifī; 2. tépifai]. Lat. *tepēre*, 'to be lukewarm', see **tepid**, & **-fy**. **a** trans. To make tepid; **b** intrans., to become tepid.

tephrite, n. [1. téfrīt; 2. téfrait]. Gk. *téphrā*, 'ashes', & **-ite**; *téphrā* stands for **théphrā*, fr. earlier **dhegʷhrā*, cp. Scrt. *dáhati*, 'it burns'; fr. same base come Lat. *fovēre*, 'to warm; to foster', see **foment**, Lat. *febris*, 'fever', see **febrile**; see also **day**. Ash-coloured volcanic rock.

tepid, adj. [1. tépid; 2. tépid]. Lat. *tepidus*, 'warm'; cogn. w. Scrt. *tápati*, 'it warms, burns'; O. Slav. *topiti*, 'to warm', *teplŭ*, 'warm'. Slightly warm, lukewarm: *tepid water*; also of the feelings.

tepidarium, n. [1. tèpidárium; 2. tèpidéəriəm]. Lat., see prec. & **-ary**. Intermediate room of moderate temperature in a Roman bath.

tepidity, n. [1. tepíditi; 2. tepíditi]. **tepid** & **-ity**. Quality, state, of being tepid.

ter, adv. [1. tër; 2. tā]. Lat., 'thrice'; see **tri-** & **three**. (mus.) Three times; indicating that a passage is to be played three times successively.

teraphim, n. pl., as coll. sing. [1. térafim; 2. térəfim]. Heb. Small idol or idols used in divination as a kind of household oracle among the ancient Jews.

terato-, pref. Gk., stem of *téras*, 'a monster'; fr. *(*s*)*kʷer-*; cp. O.N. *skars*, 'monster', *skyrse*, 'bad omen; phantom, dreadful apparition'; cp. **scare**.

teratoid, adj. [1. tératoid; 2. térətoid]. Prec. & **-oid**. Of the nature of a monster; of abnormal, pathological, growth.

teratologist, n. [1. tèratólojist; 2. tèrətóləǆist]. Next word & **-ist**. Student of teratology.

teratology, n. [1. tèratóloji; 2. tèrətóləǆi]. **terato-** & **-logy**. The scientific study of animal and vegetable freaks and monstrosities and malformations.

terbium, n. [1. térbium; 2. tábiəm]. Mod. Lat., fr. Ytterby, Sweden. A metallic element, one of the rare earths.

terce. See **tierce**.

tercel, n. [1. tërsl; 2. tásl]. Fr., fr. Lat. *tertiolus*, dimin. of *tertius*, 'third'; see **tertian**; fr. belief that the third egg of a hawk produced a small male bird. Male falcon.

tercentenary, adj. & n. [1. tërsentēnari; 2. tāsentīnəri]. **ter** & **centenary**. **1.** adj. Pertaining to a period of three hundred years. **2.** n. **a** Three hundredth anniversary of an event; **b** celebration of, commemorative festivity in connexion with, such an anniversary.

tercet, n., also **tiercet** [1. tërset, tërset; 2. táset, tíəset]. Fr., fr. Ital. *terzetto*, dimin. of *terzo*, fr. Lat. *tertium*, 'third'. (mus. or pros.) A triplet.

terebene, n. [1. térebēn; 2. térebīn]. See next word & **-ene**. Disinfecting substance made from turpentine treated with sulphuric acid.

terebinth, n. [1. térebinth; 2. térebinþ]. Gk. *terébinthos*. European balsamic tree which yields Chian turpentine.

terebra, n. [1. térebra; 2. térebrə]. Lat., 'instrument for boring, a gimlet'; fr. *terere*, 'to rub, wear, away; to bore'; see **toreutic** & cp. **trite** & **triturate**. (zool.) A boring, egg-depositing organ of certain insects.

teredo, n. [1. terḗdō; 2. terídou]. Gk. *terēdṓn*, 'wood-worm', fr. base **ter-*, 'to bore'; cogn. w. Lat. *terere*, see prec. Worm-like mollusc which bores into the timbers of ships; the ship-worm.

tergal, adj. [1. tërgal; 2. tágəl], fr. Lat. *tergum*, 'back; covering of the back; skin, hide, leather'; cp. Gk. *térphos*, 'skin, hide, esp. that on hind quarters of beasts'. Belonging to the back; dorsal.

tergiversate, vb. intrans. [1. tërjivërsāt; 2. tāǆivāseit]. Lat. *tergiversāri*, *tergiversāt-(um)*, P.P. type of 'to turn the back; to practise evasion', fr. *tergum*, 'back', see prec., & *versāri*, 'to turn oneself about', freq. of *vertere*, 'to turn', see **version**. To shuffle, behave in an evasive manner; to vacillate in one's opinions and intentions.

tergiversation, n. [1. tërjivërsāshun; 2. tāǆivāséiʃən]. Prec. & **-ion**. Act of tergiversating; vacillation; shifty conduct.

term (I.), n. [1. tërm; 2. tām]. M.E., fr. O. Fr. *terme*, fr. Lat. *termen*, also *terminus* 'boundary, limit, end'; cogn. w. Gk. *térma* *térmōn*, 'boundary, end'; fr. base **ter-*, 'to pass beyond, reach a point on the other side'; cp. Scrt. *tárati*, 'wins through'; ultimately connected w. **through**. **1.** A limit, esp. of time: *to set a term to the existence of*. **2.** (geom.) A limiting point, line, or surface. **3.** **a** A fixed, limited period of time: *during one's term of office*; specif. **b** continuous period, officially fixed, during which instruction is given at a university or at a school; **c** continuous, specified period during which cases are heard in the courts of law. **4.** (law) **a** Continuous, limited period of time during which, by agreement, certain rights are to be enjoyed: *to let a house for a term of years*; **b** day fixed for payment of rents &c.; quarter-day. **5.** (med.) Menses. **6.** (log.) One of the three parts of a syllogism: *major term*, predicate of the conclusion; *minor term*, subject of conclusion; *middle term*, the part common to both premises. **7.** **a** Word expressing a definite object or conception; one in use in a particular branch of study, in a specific profession &c.: *hero is hardly the term to apply to him*; *terms of law*; *botanical terms* &c.; **b** (pl.) mode of expression, style of language: *he spoke in terms of approval*, *in flattering terms*. Phrs. *in set terms*, definitely; *contradiction in terms*, self-contradictory statement. **8.** **a** Conditions of a contract: *the terms of an agreement*; Phrs. *terms cash*, conditions of business are payment on delivery; *to come to terms with*, reach an agreement, an understanding, with; **b** financial payment demanded for services &c. rendered: *the terms asked for lodgings are too high*; *terms for private lessons are so much an hour*. **9.** **a** Personal relations: *on good or bad terms with*; *not on speaking terms*; **b** good, friendly, relations: *we are not on terms*; *to come to terms with*; see also **8, a.** **10.** (Rom. antiq.) A boundary post, usually taking the form of a tapering, square, or rectangular pillar supporting the head and shoulders of the god *Terminus*; cp. the corresponding Greek *herm*.

term (II.), vb. trans., fr. prec. To apply a term to; to designate, call: *his life might be termed happy*.

termagant, n. [1. tërmagant; 2. táməgənt]. M.E. *termagant*, *tervagant*, fr. O. Fr. *tervagant*; cp. Ital. *trivigante*; fr. Lat. **ter** or **tri-**, 'thrice', & Pres. Part. of *vagāri*, 'to roam about, wander'; see **vagrant**. *Termagant* was a fictitious personage, supposed by Christians to be a Mohammedan deity, and was represented as a boisterous, turbulent character. A noisy, quarrelsome, scolding woman.

termer, -or, n. [1. tërmer; 2. támə]. **1.** (law) *Termor*, person holding an estate for a term of years or for life. **2.** *Termer*, person serving a term of imprisonment: *second, third, termer*.

terminability, n. [1. tërminabíliti; 2. tāminəbíliti]. See next word & **-ity**. Quality of being terminable.

terminable, adj. [1. tërminabl; 2. táminəbl]. See **terminate** & **-able**. Capable of being, liable to be, terminated; capable of being terminated after a specified time.

terminableness, n. [1. tërminablnes; 2. táminəblnis]. See prec. & **-ness**. State of being terminable.

terminal (I.), adj. [1. tẽrminal; 2. tʌ́minəl]. Lat. *termināl̄is*, see **term** (I.) & **-al**. **1.** Connected with, pertaining to, situated at or near, a term, limit, end: *a terminal ornament, leaf* &c.; *terminal figure*, a term, see **term** (I.), **10**. **2.** Connected with a term or fixed period of time: *a terminal rent*; specif., connected with, occurring in or at end of, a university or school term: *terminal fees, examinations* &c.

terminal (II.), n., fr. prec. **1.** Something forming the end or extremity of anything; specif. **a** (archit. &c.) an ornamental termination of a feature; a terminal figure; **b** the end of a wire conducting an electric current; **c** the end or terminus of a railway line. **2.** Examination occurring in or at end of a term at a school or university.

terminally, adv. [1. tẽrminali; 2. tʌ́minəli]. **terminal** (I.) & **-ly**. **1.** At the end or extremity; finally. **2.** At fixed intervals; every school or university term.

terminate, vb. trans. & intrans. [1. tẽrminàt; 2. tʌ́mineit], fr. Lat. *termināt-(um)*, P.P. of *termināre*, 'to set bounds to; to bring to an end'; fr. *termen*, see **term** (I.) **1.** trans. **a** To put a bound or limit to; **b** to bring to an end, finish, conclude. **2.** intrans. To come to an end, reach a close; *terminate in*, **a** to have as a final phase or feature; to have as a terminal; **b** (gram.) to have as a final sound, syllable &c.

termination, n. [1. tẽrmináshun; 2. tʌminéiʃən]. Prec. & **-ion**. **1.** Act or process of terminating; of bringing or coming to a close: *the termination of an agreement, of an enterprise, of a lease* &c. **2.** That which forms the end or close; conclusion, completion; **a** in space: *the termination of a journey*; **b** in time: *the termination of one's life*; **c** of a series of events or actions: *the termination of an adventure, a quarrel, of a game* &c. **3.** (of material objects) The end, extremity, final portion: *the termination of a line, a pillar*. **4.** (gram.) Ending of a word; final sound or syllable; inflexion, final suffix.

terminational, adj. [1. tẽrmináshunal; 2. tʌminéiʃənəl]. Prec. & **-al**. Connected with, relating to, of the nature of, a termination, esp. in grammatical sense.

terminative, adj. [1. tẽrminativ; 2. tʌ́minətiv]. **terminate** & **-ive**. **a** Serving to terminate; **b** (gram., of verbal forms) distinguishing between beginning or end of action.

terminator, n. [1. tẽrminàter; 2. tʌ́mineitə]. See prec. & **-or**. Person who, or thing which, terminates; specif. (astron.) line dividing illuminated and unilluminated portion of disk of a heavenly body.

terminatory, adj. [1. tẽrminaturi; 2. tʌ́minətəri]. **terminate** & **-ory**. Terminative.

terminer, n. [1. tẽrminer; 2. tʌ́minə]. Fr. infin., 'to end', fr. Lat. *termināre*, see **terminate**. (law) A determining; for the writ of *oyer and terminer* see under **oyer**.

terminism, n. [1. tẽrminizm; 2. tʌ́minizəm]. Lat. *termin-*, stem of *termen*, 'limit' &c., q.v. under **term** (I.), & **-ism**. Doctrine that the period during which a human being has the opportunity and offer of divine grace is limited.

terminist, n. [1. tẽrminist; 2. tʌ́minist]. Stem of prec. & **-ist**. Adherent of the doctrine of terminism.

terminological, adj. [1. tẽrminolójikl; 2. tʌminəlɔ́dʒikl]. **terminology** & **-ic** & **-al**. Connected with terminology, or the use of terms.

terminologically, adv. Prec. & **-ly**. From the point of view of terminology.

terminology, n. [1. tẽrminóloji; 2. tʌminɔ́lədʒi]. Lat. *termino-*, stem of *terminus*, 'limit; term', see **terminus**, & **-logy**. System of special or technical terms used in some particular branch of learning, art, science, or in a specialized occupation, in a form of sport &c.

terminus, n. [1. tẽrminus; 2. tʌ́minəs]. Lat., 'boundary-line, boundary, limit'; see **term** (I.). **1.** (rare) Goal, final point reached or aimed at. **2.** Station at the end of a line of railway: *Paddington is the London terminus of the G.W.R.* Lat. Phrs. *terminus ad quem*, goal of a line of action or argument; *terminus a quo*, starting-point of these. **3. a** (cap.) The Roman God of boundaries; **b** a terminal figure or term.

termitary, n. [1. tẽrmitari; 2. tʌ́mitəri]. See next word & **-ary**. A nest, mound, of termites.

termite, n. [1. tẽrmīt; 2. tʌ́mait]. Lat. *termes*, 'wood worm', see base under **teredo**, & **-ite**. One of a family of insects, popularly and wrongly called 'white ants', living in communities and often, in tropical countries, building large mounds for nests; they are extremely destructive to wood, textiles, paper &c.

termless, adj. [1. tẽrmles; 2. tʌ́mlis]. **term** (I.) & **-less**. Having no term or boundary; limitless; unending.

tern (I.), n. [1. tẽrn; 2. tʌ̄n]. O.N. *þerna*. One of various sea-birds of the gull family, often living in colonies; the common tern, *Sterna hirundo*, or sea-swallow, has forked tail and black head.

tern (II.), n. & adj., fr. Lat. *terni*, 'three each'; see **ter** & **tri-**. **1.** n. Group of three; specif., group of three numbers in a lottery which win special prize if drawn together. **2.** adj. Ternate.

ternal, **ternary**, adj. [1. tẽrnal, tẽrnari; 2. tʌ́nəl, tʌ́nəri]. Prec. & **-al**, or **-ary**. **1.** adj. Threefold; (of numbers) consisting of, proceeding by, threes. **2.** n., *Ternary*, the number three; a triad.

ternate, adj. [1. tẽrnāt; 2. tʌ́neit]. See **tern** (II.) & **-ate**. (bot., of leaves) Arranged in groups of three.

terne, n. [1. tẽrn; 2. tʌ̄n], fr. Fr. *terne*, 'dull, lustreless', see **tarnish**. Alloy of tin and lead; *terne-plate*, sheet of iron coated with terne.

ternery, n. [1. tẽrneri; 2. tʌ́nəri]. **tern** (I.) & **-ery**. Breeding-place of terns.

terpene, n. [1. tẽrpēn; 2. tʌ́pīn]. A combination of **terebinth** & **turpentine**. (chem.) One of a group of hydrocarbons, found in the volatile oils obtained by distillation from coniferous and other plants.

Terpsichorean, adj. [1. tẽrpsikoréan; 2. tʌpsikəríən]. Lat., fr. Gk. *Terpsikhórē*, the muse of dancing, & **-an**. Pertaining to dancing: *the Terpsichorean art*.

terra, n. [1. téra; 2. térə]. Lat. (or Ital.) *terra*, 'land, ground, soil; the earth'; fr. **tersa-*, 'dry'; cogn. w. Lat. *terrēre*, 'to burn, parch', fr. **tors-*, see **torrid** & **toast**; see also **thirst**. In various Latin words and phrases: *Terrae filius* [1. térē filius; 2. térī fáiliəs], lit. 'son of the soil'; person of humble origin. *Terra firma* [1. téra fẽrma; 2. térə fʌ́mə], lit. 'firm earth'; dry land, contrasted with water. *Terra incognita* [1. téra inkógnita; 2. térə inkɔ́gnitə], lit. 'unknown country'; unexplored country; (also fig.) an unfamiliar, uninvestigated, region of thought or knowledge.

terrace (I.), n. [1. téras; 2. térəs]. O.Fr. *terrace*, fr. Ital. *terrazza*; see **terra**, 'earth'. **1.** A long, raised, flat platform of earth, either built up and levelled, or cut in sloping ground; often forming a feature in gardens and pleasure-grounds. **2.** (geol.) A flat, raised surface with steep side, bordering a river or lake, marking the ancient water-level. **3.** A row of houses, properly one built on high level ground which slopes away immediately from the houses; often applied to any row of high houses standing back from a thoroughfare.

terrace (II.), vb. trans., fr. prec. To build up, or cut, into the form of a terrace: *a terraced walk*.

terra-cotta, n. [1. téra kóta; 2. térə kɔ́tə]. Ital., 'baked earth'; see **terra**, & *cotta* fr. Lat. *cocta*, P.P. fem. of *coquere*, 'to boil' &c., see **cook**. Reddish or pale brown hard but porous pottery.

terrain, n. [1. térān; 2. terein]. Fr., fr. Lat. *terrēnus*, 'made of earth'; see **terrene**. A tract of land; specif. (mil.) a tract of ground considered in relation to its uses for a battle, or for fortifications.

terramara, n. [1. téramára; 2. térəméərə]. Ital., fr. Lat. *terra amara*, 'bitter land'. **a** Earthy deposit, especially from prehistoric mounds, suitable for use as a fertilizer; **b** (cap.) an early type of bronze age culture, found in lake dwellings &c. in Northern Italy.

terraneous, adj. [1. teráneus; 2. teréiniəs]. **terra** & **-aneous**. Growing on, belonging to, the earth.

terrapin, n. [1. térapin; 2. térəpin], fr. Am. Indian word for 'turtle'. Edible turtle, found in fresh or tidal water of the North Atlantic American coast.

terraqueous, adj. [1. teràkweus; 2. teréikwiəs]. See **terra** & **aqueous**. (of the earth) Consisting of, comprising, both land and water.

terrene, adj. [1. terēn; 2. terīn]. Lat. *terrēnus*, fr. *terra*, 'earth'; see **terra**. Connected with the earth; earthly, mundane.

terrestrial (I.), adj. [1. teréstrial; 2. teréstriəl]. O. Fr. *terrestriel*, fr. Lat. *terrestri-*, see **terra**, & **-al**. **1.** Belonging to the earth; earthly, earthy; contrasted with *celestial*: *a terrestrial body*; *terrestrial preoccupations*. **2. a** Consisting of this earth: *this terrestrial ball*; **b** made to represent the earth: *a terrestrial globe*. **3.** Inhabiting, living upon, the dry land; contrasted with *aquatic, arboreal* &c.

terrestrial (II.), n., fr. prec. An inhabitant of the earth.

terret, n. [1. téret; 2. térit]. M.E. *teret*, also *toret*; etymol. doubtful; prob. fr. O. Fr. *toret, touret*, 'ring for falcon's leash', cf. **tour** (I.). One of the rings on a (driven) horse's harness-pad, or saddle, through which the reins pass.

terrible, adj. [1. téribl; 2. térəbl, téribl]. Fr., fr. Lat. *terribilis*, 'frightful, dreadful', fr. base of *terrēre*, 'to frighten'; for **ters-*, **teres-*; cogn. w. Gk. *tréein*, 'to tremble'; Scrt. *trásati*, 'trembles'; Goth. *þrasa(balþei)*, 'audacity'; the base is an extension of **ter-*, 'to tremble', as in Lat. *tremere*, 'to tremble', see **tremble**, & *trepidus*, 'agitated, alarmed', see **trepidation**. **1.** Inspiring, calculated to inspire, terror, dread, awe; fearful, frightful: *the terrible sufferings caused by war*; *terrible in anger*. **2.** (colloq.) Excessive, tremendous: *a terrible heat, frost*; *a terrible man to drink*.

terribleness, n. Prec. & **-ness**. Quality, state, of being terrible.

terribly, adv. See prec. & **-ly**. In a terrible manner; horribly; to a terrible extent: *terribly injured, shocked*; (colloq.) excessively: *terribly afraid of dogs*; *terribly hungry*.

terrier (I.), n. [1. térier; 2. tériə]. Fr. *(chien) terrier*, 'a burrowing dog', fr. L. Lat. *terrārium*, 'a burrow, hillock'; see **terra** & **-ier**. One of several breeds of small or medium-sized dogs kept as pets, very lively, courageous, and affectionate, and good at killing rabbits and rats.

terrier (II.), n. Fr. *(papier) terrier*, Lat. *(liber) terrārius*, 'book relating to land', fr. **terra**. Document or book setting forth extent, boundaries, rents, and rights in land.

terrific, adj. [1. terífik; 2. terífik]. Lat. *terrificus*, 'causing terror, frightful'; see **terrify**. Striking terror, of a nature to terrify; appalling, dreadful, awe-inspiring, esp. by reason of size or violence.

terrifically, adv. [1. terífikali; 2. terífikəli]. Prec. & **-al** & **-ly**. To a terrific extent.

terrify, vb. trans. [1. térifī; 2. térifai]. Fr. *terrifier*, fr. Lat. *terrificāre*, 'to frighten'; see **terror** & **-fy**. To strike terror in, to fill with fright, cause great alarm to.

terrigenous, adj. [1. teríjenus; 2. terídʒinəs]. Lat. *terrigena*, 'born of the earth'; see **terra** & **-genous**. Earth-born; produced by the earth; native of the soil.

terrine, n. [1. térēn; 2. térīn]. Fr., fr. L. Lat. *terrineus*, 'made of earth', see **terra.** Vessel, dish, jar, of earthenware, esp. one used for containing and preserving some delicacy such as foie-gras, and sold with this.

territorial (I.), adj. [1. tèritṓrial; 2. tèritṓriəl]. **territory** & **-al.** **1.** Connected with, consisting of, territory: *territorial owner, property* &c. **2.** Pertaining, limited, to some particular region or country under control of a state: *territorial rights, waters, boundaries* &c. **3.** (mil., cap.) Relating to a force of soldiers raised, by voluntary enlistment, in a particular area or county and serving as a second line to the Regular Army: *Territorial Army.*

territorial (II.), n., fr. prec. Member of the Territorial Army.

territorialism, n. [1. tèritṓrializm; 2. tèritṓriəlizəm]. Prec. & **-ism.** System of Church government, under which the ruler of a territory has religious jurisdiction over his subjects.

territorialize, vb. trans. [1. tèritṓrialīz; 2. tèritṓriəlaiz]. **territorial** (I.) & **-ize.** **1.** To extend (domains) by addition of fresh territory. **2.** To reduce to condition of a territory.

territorially, adv. [1. tèritṓriali; 2. tèritṓriəli]. See prec. & **-ly.** From the point of view of, according to, territory.

territory, n. [1. térituri; 2. téritəri]. Lat. *territōrium*, 'land round a town; domain'; see **terra.** **1.** Large tract of land; region, district. **2.** Amount of land, country, under jurisdiction of a single ruler or government. **3.** Part of a state ruled as a dependency and not having yet attained full rights as an independent state.

terror, n. [1. téror; 2. térə]. Lat., 'great fear, dread, alarm'; see under **terrible.** **1.** Extreme, overwhelming, fear. **2.** Person or thing which inspires terror: *Cromwell was a terror to his country's foes.* Phrs. *the king of terrors*, death; *the Reign of Terror, the Terror*, the period from May 1793 to July 1794 of the French Revolution, characterized by countless executions &c. **3.** (colloq.) A troublesome, unmanageable person; a pest, a nuisance: *a perfect terror, a holy terror.*

terrorism, n. [1. térorizm; 2. térərizəm]. Prec. & **-ism.** Method of government by inspiring terror by acts of brutality and savagery.

terrorist, n. [1. térorist; 2. térərist]. **terror** & **-ist.** One who practises, or believes in, terrorism.

terrorization, n. [1. tèrorīzā́shun; 2. tèrəraizéiʃən]. See next word & **-ation.** Act of terrorizing; state of being terrorized.

terrorize, vb. trans. [1. térorīz; 2. térəraiz]. **terror** & **-ize.** To reduce to state of terror by threats or acts of cruelty; to intimidate.

terry, n. [1. téri; 2. téri]. Connected w. Fr. *tirer*, 'to pull'? Loop left uncut from nap of velvet or other fabric.

terse, adj. [1. tẽrs; 2. tʌ̄s]. Lat. *tersum*, P.P. of *tergēre*, 'to rub, wipe, off'; prob. connected w. *terere*, 'to rub'; see **trite.** **a** (of mode of expression) Concise, succinct, and polished; free from redundancy; **b** (of a speaker or writer) employing terse style.

tersely, adv. Prec. & **-ly.** In a terse, succinct manner.

terseness, n. See prec. & **-ness.** Quality of being terse.

tertial, adj. [1. tẽrshial; 2. tʌ̄ʃiəl]. Lat. *tertius*, see next word, & **-al.** (zool.) Referring to flight feathers of third row in a bird's wing.

tertian, adj. & n. [1. tẽrshan; 2. tʌ̄ʃən]. Fr., fr. Lat. *tertiānus*, fr. *tertius*, 'third', cogn. w. Goth. *þridja*, see **third**, & cp. **tri-** & **three.** **1.** adj. (med.) Recurring every other day: *tertian fever.* **2.** n. An intermittent disease; a tertian fever.

tertiary (I.), adj. [1. tẽrshari; 2. tʌ̄ʃəri]. Lat. *tertius*, 'third', see prec. & **-ary.** **1.** Third in order, rank, occurrence, importance. **2.** (geol., cap.) Pertaining to the era immediately following the Mesozoic, which was formerly called *Secondary.*

tertiary (II.), n., fr. prec. Member of third order in a monastic system.

tertium quid, n. [1. tẽrshium kwíd; 2. tʌ̄ʃiəm kwíd]. Lat., 'a third something'. Something intermediate between two other alternative, incompatible things, positions, possibilities.

tertius, adj. [1. tẽrshus; 2. tʌ̄ʃəs]. Lat. 'third'. See **tertian** & words there referred to. Used in some schools, after surname, to distinguish the youngest of three boys of the same name or family: *Smith tertius.*

terza rima, n. [1. tā́rtsa rḗma; 2. téətsə rīmə]. Ital., 'third, triple, rhyme'; fr. Lat. *tertia*, 'third', see **tertian**, & **rhyme.** System of verse in which the rhymes are arranged thus: *aba; bcb; cdc.*

terzetto, n. [1. tārtsétō; 2. teətsétou]. Ital. dimin. of *terzo*, 'third'. Part-song for three voices.

tessellar, adj. [1. téselar; 2. tésilə]. Lat. *tessella*, 'little cube', see **tessellate**, & **-ar.** Composed of tesserae.

tessellate, vb. trans. [1. téselāt; 2. tésileit]. Lat. *tessellātus*, 'composed of small stones or *tesserae*'; fr. *tessella*, 'small piece of stone, little cube', dimin. of **tessera**, & **-ate.** To pave by inlaying small blocks of stone in mosaic work.

tessellated, adj. [1. téselāted; 2. tésileitid], fr. P.P. of prec. Paved with small blocks of stone in form of a mosaic.

tessellation, n. [1. tèselā́shun; 2. tèsiléiʃən]. **tessellate** & **-ion.** Work, esp. pavement, composed of tesserae; mosaic work.

tessera, n., pl. **tesserae** [1. tésera, -rē; 2. tésərə, -rī]. Lat., 'a square piece of stone, a die', fr. Gk. *téssares*, 'four', wh. is for **kʷetwar-*, cp. Scrt. *čatur*; Lat. *quātuor*, see **quater-**, & **four.** Small, approximately square piece of marble, glass &c. used in mosaic work.

tessitura, tessiture, n. [1. tèsitóōra, tésitūr; 2. tèsitúra, tésitjuə]. Ital.; Fr., see **texture.** (mus.) Compass, range, within which the characteristics of a voice lie; compass of a voice part.

test (I.), n. [1. test; 2. test]. O. Fr., fr. Lat. *testum*, 'pot', cp. *testa*, 'piece of burnt clay, potsherd, shell, covering'; cogn. w. Scrt. *tašta*, 'shell, cup'. The starting-point of the Mod. meanings is a cup for refining metal. **1. a** Movable bottom of furnace, also called *cupel*, in which precious metals are refined; **b** portion of refined metal isolated for weighing. **2.** Process designed to try, or prove; a critical, searching examination; Phr. *put to the test*, prove quality of. **3. a** (chem.) Process adopted to discover and distinguish the various substances of which anything is composed; an analysis; **b** (hist.) the oath taken under the *Test Act*, q.v.; **c** (colloq.) a test match, q.v. **4.** Any method adopted to try and prove the extent of knowledge: *written examinations are the main test applied to candidates for degrees.* **5.** Circumstances, experiences, trials, which when undergone by an individual, serve to show his real character, degree of moral worth, intelligence &c.; touchstone: *poverty is often a severe test of a man's integrity.*

test (II.), vb. trans., fr. prec. **1.** (chem.) To analyse by application of reagents. **2.** To put to the test; **a** to ascertain by searching scrutiny the truth, validity, soundness (of a statement, argument, theory &c.); **b** to prove the quality, extent (of knowledge &c.), or the moral worth, reliability &c. (of a person); **c** to ascertain the value, genuineness, quality (of a thing); *to test*, implies in all cases the application of a fixed principle to the person or thing tested, and the consideration of how far he, or it, conforms to a chosen standard.

test (III.), n. Lat. *testa*, 'shell', see **test** (I.). The hard shell or covering of molluscs, crustaceans, and many other invertebrates.

testable (I.), adj. [1. téstabl; 2. téstəbl]. **test** (II.) & **-able.** Capable of being tested.

testable (II.), adj. See **testament** & **-able.** (law) Capable of being disposed of by will.

testaceous, adj. [1. testā́shus; 2. testéiʃəs]. Lat. *testaceus*, see **test** (III.), & **-aceous.** **1.** Connected with, of the nature of, a shell; formerly applied to molluscs and brachiopods; in distinction to *crustaceous.* **2.** (zool. and bot.) Brick red, brownish yellow; from original meaning of Latin *testa*, 'piece of burnt clay'.

Test Act, n. A statute of 1672, repealed 1828, requiring persons, before holding an office, to take the oaths of allegiance and supremacy, receive Communion according to the rites of the Church of England, and abjure transubstantiation.

testacy, n. [1. téstasi; 2. téstəsi]. See **testate** & **-cy.** State of being testate.

testament, n. [1. téstament; 2. téstəmənt]. Lat. *testāmentum*, 'declaration of one's will'; formed fr. Lat. *testāri*, 'to witness, testify', fr. *testis*, 'a witness'; according to Walde formed fr. **tristo-*, 'the third', cp. Lat. *trēs*, 'three', see **-tri.** The orig. sense was 'third party present at a transaction', as distinct fr. those actually engaged in it. **1.** Translating Gk. *diathḗkē*, 'last will; covenant'; cp. Fr. use in this case, & **testamentary**; (obs. except Bib.) **a** either of the two covenants of God known respectively as the *Old* and *New Testament*; **b** (colloq.) the New Testament. **2.** (law) Only in Phr. *last will and testament*, document in which a person sets forth his wishes for the disposal of his property after his death.

testamental, adj. [1. tèstaméntal; 2. tèstəméntəl]. Prec. & **-al.** Pertaining to a testament; testamentary.

testamentary, adj. [1. tèstaméntari; 2. tèstəméntəri]. **testament** & **-ary.** Pertaining to, bequeathed in, appointed by, a will or testament.

testamur, n. [1. testā́mur; 2. testéimə]. Lat., 'we attest, testify', fr. *testāri*, see **testament.** University certificate stating officially that a person has passed a specified examination.

testate, adj. & n. [1. téstāt; 2. tésteit]. Lat. *testātus*, P.P. of *testāri*, see **testament.** (law) **a** adj. Having died leaving a valid will; **b** n., person in this position.

testator, n. [1. testā́ter; 2. testéitə]. Lat., 'one who makes a will', fr. *testāt-(um)*, P.P. type of *testāri*, see **testament**, & **-or.** Male person who makes a will; the maker of a particular will: *the testator.*

testatrix, n. [1. testā́triks; 2. testéitriks]. Lat., fem. of prec. Female who makes a will.

tester (I.), n. [1. téster; 2. téstə]. **test** (II.) & **-er.** **a** Person who tests (in various specific senses); **b** one of various mechanical devices for testing quality &c. of substances.

tester (II.), n. M.E. *testere*, 'headpiece, helmet', fr. O. Fr. *testiere* &c., fr. Lat. *testa*, 'potsherd; shell, skull'; whence O. Fr. *teste*, 'head'; see **test** (I.). Canopy for a bed, supported on posts.

tester (III.), n.; also *teston*, fr. O. Fr., fr. *teste*, Mod. Fr. *tête*, 'head', see prec. The name of the shilling of Henry VIII., which was later reduced to sixpence.

testicle, n. [1. téstikl; 2. téstikl]. Lat. *testiculus*, dimin. of *testis*, 'testicle'; etymol. uncertain. Male gland secreting spermatozoa.

testiculate, adj. [1. testíkūlāt; 2. testíkjuleit]. Lat. *testiculus*, see prec., & **-ate.** **a** Having testicles, or (of plants) organs corresponding to these; **b** shaped like a testicle.

testification, n. [1. tèstifikā́shun; 2. tèstifikéiʃən]. See **testify** & **-fication.** **a** Act of testifying; **b** testified statement, evidence.

testify, vb. intrans. & trans. [1. téstifī; 2. téstifai]. Fr. *testifier*, fr. Lat. *testificāri*, 'to bear witness', fr. *testis*, 'witness', see **testament**, & **-fy.** **1.** To make a solemn declaration, to bear witness that something has happened, to give evidence: *to testify that one has seen so-and-so*; also *to testify to the fact that* &c.; *testify against*, give, provide, evidence against. 2. (law) To state in accordance with legal procedure, give evidence of, affirm, on oath. 3. To indicate, tend to show, make manifest, be evidence of: *his manner testified his eagerness to be off.*

testily, adv. [1. téstili; 2. téstili]. **testy & -ly.** In a testy manner.

testimonial, n. [1. tèstimónial; 2. tèstimóuniəl]. Lat. (*literae*) *testimōniālēs*, '(letters, document) containing testimony'; see **testimony & -al.** 1. Uttered or written statement setting forth a person's merits and qualities of character, his capacities and abilities, esp. a document stating a person's qualifications for an appointment. 2. A tribute in the form of a written expression, of respect and admiration, or of appreciation and gratitude for services rendered, often accompanied by a public presentation of a gift and a list of names of subscribers.

testimonialize, vb. trans. [1. tèstimónialīz; 2. tèstimóuniəlaiz]. Prec. & **-ize.** To write a testimonial for; to present a testimonial to.

testimony, n. [1. téstimuni; 2. téstiməni]. Lat. *testimōnium*, 'evidence, attestation', fr. *testis*, 'a witness', see **testament. 1.** Solemn statement made to establish a fact; evidence given by a witness under oath in a court of law; *to bear testimony (to)*, to affirm (truth of), state as a fact. 2. a Series of statements; general bearing, tenor, drift of such a series of statements: *the testimony of the Fathers of the Church*; b the conclusion to which a series of actions, events, facts, points; evidence, indication, afforded by such a series of events &c.: *the testimony of the rocks is sometimes held to refute the Mosaic account of the Creation*; *to bear testimony*, to indicate, point to truth of, help to establish, certain facts. 3. Tables of the law; divine revelation; the Scriptures: *the testimonies of the Lord.*

testiness, n. [1. téstines; 2. téstinis]. **testy & -ness.** Condition of being testy.

testis, n., usually pl. **testes** [1. téstis, -ēz; 2. téstis, -īz]. Lat., see **testicle.** Testicle.

test match, n. A cricket match played between representative elevens of two countries.

test-tube, n. Slender tube of thinnish glass, usually closed at one end, used in chemical experiments.

testudinarious, adj. [1. tèstūdinárius; 2. tèstjūdinéəriəs]. Lat. *testūdin-*, stem of *testūdo*, 'tortoise', see **testudo, & -arious.** Mottled with the colours seen in tortoise-shell.

testudinate, adj. [1. testúdināt; 2. testjúdineit]. Lat. *testūdin-*, see prec., & **-ate.** Vaulted, arched, like the shell of a tortoise.

testudineous, adj. [1. tèstūdíneus; 2. tèstjūdíniəs]. Lat. *testūdin-*, see prec., & **-eous.** Resembling the shell of a tortoise.

testudo, n. [1. testúdō; 2. testjúdou]. Lat., 'tortoise', formed fr. Lat. *testa*, 'shell', see under **test (I.) & (III.). 1.** (Rom. antiq.) Shed, covering, of wood used to protect besieging troops. 2. (Rom. archit.) An arched, vaulted, roof. 3. Land tortoise.

testy, adj. [1. tésti; 2. tésti]. M.E. *testif*, fr. O. Fr. *testu*, 'headstrong', fr. *teste*, 'head', fr. Lat. *testa*, 'shell; skull, head', see **test (I.) & (III.).** Easily angered; irascible, irritable.

tetanic, adj. & n. [1. tetánik; 2. tətǽnik]. See **tetanus & -ic.** a adj. Connected with, arising from, of the nature of, tetanus; b n., a substance, such as strychnine, which produces muscular spasms similar to those of tetanus.

tetanization, n. [1. tètanīzáshun; 2. tètənaizéiʃən]. See **tetanus, & -ize, & -ation.** a Process of causing tetanic contractions in a muscle; b state of being affected by, or as by, tetanus.

tetanus, n. [1. tétanus; 2. tétənəs]. Gk. *tétanos*, 'a stretching, straining', redupl. form fr. base **ten-*, 'to stretch' &c., see **tend (II.).** a Disease caused by a specific bacillus, in which the muscles are violently contracted and affected with spasmodic movements; when tetanus affects the muscles of the jaw, it is popularly called *lockjaw*; b violent muscular contraction caused by drugs such as strychnine.

tetchily, adv. [1. téchili; 2. tétʃili]. **tetchy & -ly.** In a tetchy manner.

tetchiness, n. [1. téchines; 2. tétʃinis]. See next word & **-ness.** Condition of being tetchy.

tetchy, techy, adj. [1. téchi; 2. tétʃi]. O. Fr. *tache*, 'speck, blemish', & **-y.** Touchy, thin-skinned; irritable, testy, petulant.

tête-à-tête, adv., adj., n., Anglice [1. tát ah tát; 2. téit ā téit]. Fr., lit. 'head to head', cp. *cheek by jowl.* 1. adv. Privately, with one other person: *to see a person tête-à-tête.* 2. adj. Private, alone with one other person; confidential. 3. n. A private meeting or conversation with one other person; a confidential talk, private confab.

tether, n. & vb. trans. [1. tédher; 2. téðə]. M.E. *tedir*, fr. O.N. *tjōðr.* 1. n. A long rope or chain by which a grazing animal is made fast to a peg fixed in the ground, to prevent it from straying; Phr. *at the end of one's tether*, a at the end of one's physical and mental resources, on the verge of a break-down; b at the end of one's financial resources; c having done the utmost of what can be tolerated; having reached the limits of another's indulgence. 2. vb. To fasten with a tether.

tetra-, pref. Gk., form used in compounds, fr. *téttares*, variant *téssares*, 'four'; see this numeral under **tessera, four, quater-.**

tetrachord, n. [1. tétrakord; 2. tétrəkɔ̄d]. See prec. & **chord**, cp. Gk. *tetrákhordos*, 'four-stringed'. Series of four tones with interval of a fourth between first and last.

tetrad, n. [1. tétrad; 2. tétræd]. Lat. *tetrad-(em)*, fr. Gk. *tetrad-*, see **tetra-.** a The number four; b group, set, of four things.

tetragon, n. [1. tétragon; 2. tétrəgən]. **tetra- & -gon.** (geom.) Plane figure with four angles.

tetragonal, adj. [1. tetrágonal; 2. tətrǽgənəl]. Prec. & **-al.** Pertaining to a tetragon; having four angles.

tetragram, n. [1. tétragram; 2. tétrəgræm]. **tetra- & -gram.** Word of four letters.

tetragrammaton, n. [1. tètragrámaton; 2. tètrəgrǽmətən]. Gk., see prec. The four consonants forming the Hebrew name for God, the original pronunciation of which was lost as the word was only pronounced with vowels taken from other names for the Deity, no vowel symbols being written; the word was variously reconstructed as *Jahaveh, Jahveh* &c.

tetragynous, adj. [1. tetrájinus; 2. tətrǽdžinəs]. **tetra- & -gynous.** (bot.) Having four pistils.

tetrahedral, adj. [1. tètra-hédral; 2. tètrəhídrəl]. See next word & **-al.** Connected with, belonging to, of the form of, a *tetrahedron.*

tetrahedron, n. [1. tètra-hédron; 2. tètrəhídrən]. Gk., fr. **tetra-**, 'four', & *hédra*, 'seat, base', wh. is cogn. w. Lat. *sedēre*, 'to sit', see **sedentary, & w. seat & sit.** Solid, four-sided figure; a triangular pyramid.

tetralogy, n. [1. tetráloji; 2. tətrǽlədži]. Gk. *tetralogía*, 'series of four dramas'; see **tetra- & -logy.** Series of four connected dramas, as found in Greek theatre, or in Wagner's 'Ring'.

tetrameter, n. [1. tetrámeter; 2. tətrǽmitə]. See **tetra- & -meter.** Verse, line, of four measures or feet.

tetrandrous, adj. [1. tetrándrus; 2. tətrǽndrəs]. **tetra- & -androus.** (bot.) Having four stamens.

tetrarch, n. [1. tétrark, tétrark; 2. tītrāk, tétrāk]. Gk. *tetrárkhes, -arkhos*, see **tetra- & -arch.** (Rom. antiq.) The governor of a part, orig. the fourth part, of a province.

tetrarchy, n. [1. tétrarki; 2. tétrəki]. Gk. *tetrarkhía*, see prec. a The district ruled by a tetrarch; b office of a tetrarch.

tetrastich, n. [1. tétrastik; 2. tétrəstik]. Gk. *tetrástikhon*; cp. **distich.** Poem of four lines.

tetter, n. [1. téter; 2. tétə]. O.E. & M.E. *teter*, 'ringworm, skin disease'; cogn. w. Scrt. *dadru*, 'skin disease'. A disease of the skin such as ringworm, eczema &c.

Teucrian, adj. [1. túkrian; 2. tjúkriən], fr. *Teucer*, Gk. *Teûkros*, the first King of Troy. a Pertaining to Teucer; b pertaining to the ancient Trojans.

Teuton, n. [1. tútun; 2. tjútən]. Lat. *Teutones*, the name of an anct. Gmc. people; fr. Gmc. *þeuda-*, 'people, race', cp. Goth. *þiuda*, O.E. *þēod*; O.S. *thioda*; O.H.G. *diota*; fr. this word comes *deutsch* (= *þiudisk-*, 'belonging to the people'), & **Dutch.** a Member of the Germanic race; b specif. (colloq.) a German.

Teutonic, adj. & n. [1. tūtónik; 2. tjūtónik]. Prec. & **-ic.** 1. adj. a Pertaining to the Germanic race; b to the primitive Germanic language; c to a or any Germanic language. 2. n. Germanic speech, esp. primitive Germanic.

tew, vb. See **taw (I.).**

tewel, n. [1. túel; 2. tjúəl]. M.E. *tuel*, 'funnel, chimney', fr. O. Fr. *tuiel, tuel*, 'pipe', Mod. Fr. *tuyau*; prob. fr. Gmc. source; cp. Mod. Germ. *tüte, düte*, & see **Solen.** The pipe or chimney which carries away the smoke; tuyère.

text, n. [1. tekst; 2. tekst]. M.E., fr. O. Fr. *texte*, fr. Lat. *textus*, 'texture, structure; grammatical construction; context'; formed fr. *text-(um)*, P.P. of *texere*, 'to weave, to plait, to fit together, contrive'; cogn. w. Scrt. *takšati*, 'he fashions, constructs'; *taštar*, 'carpenter'; Gk. *tékhnē*, 'handicraft, art', cp. **technic.** The Lat. shows a specialization of meaning fr. an elementary sense 'construct, fashion'. 1. The original words of an author; contrasted with *paraphrase, commentary* &c.: *innumerable scholars have laboured to restore the text of Beowulf.* 2. a A verse or short passage of Scripture: '*And many a holy text around she strews*' (Gray's 'Elegy'); specif. b a verse of Scripture taken as the heading and general theme of a sermon; hence, c the theme, subject, topic, of any discourse, argument, dissertation. 3. The principal part of a literary composition, as distinct from preface, notes &c. 4. Large type of handwriting; also *text-hand*, in which the main part of a book was formerly written, the notes being in smaller writing.

text-book, n. A manual for instruction; a compendious general treatise on a branch of learning; applied both to elementary, introductory treatises, and to advanced, standard works.

text-hand, n. Large style of handwriting formerly used for the body or main part of a book.

textile, adj. & n. [1. tékstīl; 2. tékstail]. Lat. *textilis*, 'woven, wrought', also as n., 'a fabric'; see **text & -ile.** 1. adj. Connected with weaving, or with woven material: *textile industries.* 2. n. A woven fabric.

textual, adj. [1. tékstūal; 2. tékstjuəl]. M.E., fr. Fr. *textuel*, see **text.** a Pertaining to, concerned with, based on, derived from, the text of an author: *textual criticism, emendation* &c.; hence b literal, word for word: *a textual quotation.*

textualism, n. [1. tékstūalizm; 2. tékstjuəlizəm]. Prec. & **-ism.** Insistence upon a strict adherence to an author's text.

textualist, n. [1. tékstūalist; 2. tékstjuəlist]. See prec. & **-ist.** 1. A student of an author's text; a textual critic. 2. One who insists on rigid adherence to an author's text.

textural, adj. [1. tékschural; 2. tékstʃərəl]. Next word & **-al.** Connected with texture.

texture, n. [1. tékschur; 2. tékstʃə]. Lat. *textūra*, 'a web, texture; fabric; structure'; see **text & -ure.** 1. That which is woven; a woven fabric. 2. a (i.) Way in which the threads of a fabric or constituent elements of a substance are arranged and put together: *a coarse, fine, harsh, texture* (of cloth &c., also of wood, rock &c.); (ii.) sensation produced by this upon the sense of touch; b (of the mind) general disposition, quality, capacity, esp. with respect to degree of fineness of perception and discrimination displayed.

-th (I.), Engl. suff. of Gmc. origin, forming abstract ns.; **a** fr. adj., as *health*, O.E. *hǣlu* (*-th* being a M.E. addition), fr. **hāli*, fr. *hāl*, see **whole**; *breadth*, fr. O.E. *brǣdu*, fr. *brād*, 'broad'; *youth*, O.E. *ġeoguþ*, fr. **juŋgunþ-*, cp. O.E. *ġeong*, 'young'; cp. Lat. suff. *-tūt-* in *juven-tūt-(em)*, 'youth'; **b** fr. vbs., expressing result of action, as *tilth*, *growth* &c. The suff. appears as *-t-* in *height*, earlier *heighth*, *highth*, O.E. *hēhþu*.

-th (II.), suff. O.E. *-þa*, forming ordinal numbers, as *fourth*, O.E. *feorþa*; the later ordinals in *-th* are new formations; cp. Gk. *-tos*, Lat. *-tus*.

thalamus, n. [1. thálamus; 2. þǽləməs]. Lat., 'chamber', fr. Gk. *thálamos*, 'inner chamber, women's apartment; bride-chamber'; cogn. w. Gk. *thólos*, 'vault, vaulted building, a round chamber'; also cogn. w. O.E. *dæl*, 'valley', see **dale**. (anat.) Generally *optic thalamus*, that part of the brain from which the optic nerve springs.

thaler, n. [1. táhler; 2. tálə]. Du. *daler*, whence **dollar**. Obsolete German coin formerly worth about three shillings.

Thalia, n. [1. thalía; 2. þəláiə]. Gk. *Tháleia*, one of the Muses, Muse of comedy and bucolic poetry; the word means 'the blooming, luxuriant one'; cp. Gk. *thalein*, 'to bloom, to flourish'; *thalía*, 'abundance, wealth; good cheer'; *thallós*, 'a young shoot'; perh. cogn. w. O.E. *deall*, 'proud, resplendent'.

thallic, adj. [1. thálik; 2. þǽlik]. See next word & **-ic**. Pertaining to thallium, esp. of compounds containing the element with less proportion of oxygen than thallous compounds.

thallium, n. [1. thálium; 2. þǽliəm], fr. Gk. *thallós*, 'young shoot', see **Thalia**; so called fr. the bright green line in its spectrum. Rare element connected with aluminium, resembling lead in its properties.

thallophyte, n. [1. thálofit; 2. þǽləfait]. See **thallus** & **-phyte**. (bot.) A plant belonging to the class *Thallophyta*, which includes the algae, lichens, fungi &c.

thallous, adj. [1. thálus; 2. þǽləs]. See prec. & **-ous**. Pertaining to thallium, of compounds; contrasted with *thallic*.

thallus, n. [1. thálus; 2. þǽləs]. Gk. *thallós*, 'young shoot', q.v. under **Thalia**. (bot.) Mass of undifferentiated vegetable tissue; the plant body found in algae, lichens, fungi.

than, conj. [1. dhan; 2. ðæn], when stressed; more usual in unstressed form [ðən]; O.E. *þonne*, *þon*, *þænne*; M.E. *thonne*, *thon*, *thenne*, *then*; prob. connected w. **the, then, there.** Particle used in the comparison of inequality, after the comparative adjective before the noun or pronoun representing the second of two things compared: *this is bigger than that*; *children are smaller than grown-up people* &c.; *you have more money than I have.*

thanage, n. [1. thānij; 2. þéinidž]. **thane** & **-age**. **1.** Rank, status, of a thane. **2.** Land held by a thane from the king.

thanato-, pref. Form used in compounds, fr. Gk. *thánatos*, 'death'; cogn. w. Scrt. *ádhvanīt*, 'becomes, is, extinguished', *dhvāntaš*, shrouded, dark'; prob. also W. *dyn*, 'man', i.e. 'mortal': *thanatophobia*, morbid fear of death.

thanatoid, adj. [1. thánatoid; 2. þǽnətɔid]. Prec. & **-oid**. **a** Death-like; **b** deadly.

thane, n. [1. thān; 2. þein]. O.E. *þeġn*, *þeġen*; M.E. *thein*; O.S. *thegan*, 'follower'; O.H.G. *degan*; O.N. *þegn*; cogn. w. Gk. *téknon*, 'child'; connected w. Gk. *tiktein*, aorist *étek-on*, 'to beget, produce, offspring'; cp. also Gk. *tókos*, 'birth; child, offspring'. Member of a class of nobles among the Anglo-Saxons and ancient Scandinavians who were members of the king's household and in attendance upon his person, esp. in war; in O.E. poetry the word is used to designate the faithful follower and companion-in-arms of a prince or superior lord.

thank (I.), n. [1. thangk; 2. þæŋk]. O.E. *þanc*, 'thought; favour, grace; pleasure, satisfaction; delight, thanks'; in gradational relation to O.E. *þynċan*, 'to seem', see under **think**. Now only in pl. *thanks*: **1.** Gratitude, grateful feeling: *thanks be to God*; *to express one's thanks.* Phr. *thanks to*, owing to, on account of, through the agency of: *thanks to his obstinacy he was landed in disaster*; *thanks to your help I was able to do it*; Phr. *we succeeded, small thanks to him*, it was not through his help that we succeeded; *no, thanks*, polite formula for declining an offer. **2.** Expression of gratitude, grateful acknowledgement of obligation: *please accept my best thanks*; (also in colloq. construction) *thanks very much.*

thank (II.), vb. trans. O.E. *þancian*, M.E. *thankie(n)*, *thanke(n)*, see prec. To express one's thanks or gratitude to, acknowledge gratefully the services, help, kindness &c. of: *to thank a person for what he has done*; *thank you*, common form of *I thank you*; *no, thank you*, form of declining an offer; *thank you for nothing*, ironical formula acknowledging refusal to help &c.; *I will thank you to be a little more polite*, urbane but peremptory request, almost amounting to a command; *you have only yourself to thank* (*for the mess you are in* &c.), it is no one's fault but your own.

thankful, adj. [1. thángkfool; 2. þǽŋkful]. **thank** (I.) & **-ful**. Grateful, having a due sense of kindness received, and being eager to express it: *a thankful heart.* Phr. *I'm thankful (that it is no worse, that I saw him before he died* &c.), expressing satisfaction, relief &c.

thankfully, adv. Prec. & **-ly**. Gratefully; with gratitude.

thankfulness, n. See prec. & **-ness**. Gratitude; feeling of satisfaction, relief.

thankless, adj. [1. thángkles; 2. þǽŋklis]. **thank** (I.) & **-less**. **1.** (of persons) Devoid of gratitude; not feeling or expressing gratitude. **2.** (of actions) Not arousing gratitude; not appreciated by others: *it is a thankless job, task, to tell people of their faults.*

thanklessly, adv. Prec. & **-ly**. In a thankless manner.

thanklessness, n. See prec. & **-ness**. Quality, state, of being thankless.

thank-offering, n. Offering made as an expression of gratitude.

thanksgiver, n. [1. thángksgiver; 2. þǽŋksgivə]. Person who gives thanks.

thanksgiving, n. [1. thángksgiving; 2. þǽŋksgiviŋ]. **1.** Act of expressing gratitude. **2.** Formula expressing gratitude, esp. for divine goodness. **3.** (cap.) Thanksgiving Day.

Thanksgiving Day, n. Day appointed for public thanksgiving for mercies vouchsafed by Providence; esp. annual thanksgiving in U.S.A., usually the last Thursday in November.

that (I.), demonstr. pron. [1. dhat; 2. ðæt]. O.E. *þæt*, neut. sing. nom. & acc. of the def. art. *se, sēo, þæt*, wh. already in O.E. has a certain demonstr. force; see **the. 1.** The object, or idea, just referred to, or evidently to be understood from the context or circumstances: *that is what I want to know*, what you, we, have just mentioned; *that's no way to behave*; *his manner was that of a gentleman*, i.e. the manner of; *I can't agree to that*, to what you have just proposed. In colloq. speech also used contemptuously and disparagingly of persons: *do you call that an officer and a gentleman?* (prob. for *that thing*). **2.** The thing, object, over there, or more remote; contrasted with *this*, the one here: *which will you have, this or that?* Phrs. *to talk of this, that, and the other*, various things, all sorts of matters; *none of that, now*, don't talk or behave in such a manner.

that (II.), demonstr. adj.; same as prec. **1.** The one over there, the one we formerly saw, referred to &c.; contrasted with *this one here*: *I don't like that room you showed me first, I prefer this one.* **2.** Indicating something familiar and generally recognized: *that stately bearing, that benevolent expression, that sonorous voice which we knew so well.*

that (III.), rel. pron.; chiefly unstressed & pronounced [ðət]. **1.** The person or persons who, the thing or things which: *the man that I want to see*; *the woman that he loved*; *we have done those things that we ought not to have done.* **2.** (adverbially) On which, in which: *the last time that I saw you*; *the year that King Edward died.*

that (IV.), conj.; chiefly unstressed [ðət]; derived fr. rel., **that** (III.). **1.** Introducing a subordinate clause: *I fear that I cannot come*; *I am sorry that you should attribute such motives to me*; *it seems that you have forgotten me*; *he said that he disliked exercise*; *he knew that it was impossible*; *there is no doubt that we were wrong from the start.* **2.** Expressing purpose: '*So run that ye may attain*'; *he only rested that he might engage in more arduous labours*; *he only fled that he might fight another day*; also *so that*; *to the end that*; *in order that.* **3.** Expressing cause; because: *if I find fault it is that I want you to improve.* **4.** Expressing result, effect: *I am so tired that I can hardly stand*; *he had lived so long abroad that he had got out of English ways.* **5.** Introducing a sentence expressing surprise, indignation, a strong wish: *to think that I never knew you were here all this time!*; *O that, would that, I had never been born!*; *O that I might see him once more!*

that (V.), adv. (colloq. and illit. or facet.) To such an extent, so much: *I can't walk that far*; *he was that drunk he could scarcely stand*; *I'm that sleepy I can't keep my eyes open.*

thatch (I.), n. [1. thach; 2. þætʃ]. O.E. *þæċ*, 'roof, thatch'; O.N. *þak*; O.H.G. *dah*, 'cover, roof'; cogn. w. Lat. *tegere*, 'to cover', see **tegument**; *tēgula*, 'tile', see **tile, toga**; cp. further under **deck** (I.). **a** Roofing for a house, protective covering for a rick, composed of straw, reeds &c., arranged in rows of bundles and pegged and tied down; **b** (colloq.) thick covering of hair on the head.

thatch (II.), vb. trans. A new formation fr. prec. The O.E. vb. is *þeċċan*, 'to cover', fr. **þæċċ-jan*. To cover with thatch, fix thatch on to (roof of a house or top of a rick).

thatching, n. [1. tháching; 2. þǽtʃiŋ]. Straw, reeds &c. used as thatch for a roof &c.

thauma(to)-, pref. Gk. *thaûmat-*, fr. *thaûma*, 'a wonder, marvel, wondrous thing; a juggler's trick'; see further **theatre**.

thaumatrope, n. [1. tháwmatrōp; 2. þɔ́mətroup]. Prec. & *trópos*, 'a turning', see **trope**. Optical instrument, consisting either of a disk with two different pictures one on either side, which when the disk is rapidly spun round, appear to merge into a single picture, e.g. if a fish is on one side of the disk, and a bowl on the other, the fish appears to be inside the bowl; or a series of pictures on a flat disk, of the same object in slightly different positions, which when the disk is revolved appear to be moving.

thaumaturge, n. [1. tháwmatērj; 2. þɔ́mətɑ̀dž]. Fr., fr. Gk. *thaumatourgós*, 'wonder-working', fr. **thauma(to)-** & *érgon*, 'work', see **erg**. A worker of miracles; a magician.

thaumaturgic(al), adj. [1. thàwmatḗrjik(l); 2. þɔ̀mətɑ́džik(l)]. Prec. & **-ic** (& **-al**). Pertaining to, of the nature of, magic.

thaumaturgist, n. [1. tháwmatērjist; 2. þɔ́mətɑ̀džist]. Next word & **-ist**. One who practises thaumaturgy; a magician.

thaumaturgy, n. [1. tháwmatērji; 2. þɔ́mətɑ̀dži]. Gk. *thaumatourgía*, 'magic'; **thaumaturge** & **-y**. Magic, conjuring, wonder-working.

thaw (I.), vb. intrans. & trans. [1. thaw; 2. þɔ̄]. O.E. *þāwian*, cp. O.N. *þeyja*, 'to melt'; connected w. Germ. *(ver)dauen*, 'to digest'; possibly also w. Lat. *tābēre*, 'to melt', see **tabes**; no connexion w. **dew** or Germ. *tau*, 'dew'. A. intrans. 1. a (of the weather) *It is thawing*, passing to a degree of temperature sufficiently high for frost to disperse and ice to turn to water; b (of frozen matter, objects) to turn to water; to become liquid, to melt: *the ice is thawing*; *the snow on Scottish mountains thaws in summer*; c (colloq., of persons) to become warm, pass from state of extreme chill to normal temperature: *I was half frozen after my drive, but I'm gradually thawing.* 2. (fig., of persons, manner, mental attitude &c.) To become genial, cordial, frank; to pass from frigidity, embarrassment, and stiffness to ease and naturalness. B. trans. To cause to thaw, to increase temperature of (frozen object) till liquefaction is produced.

thaw (II.), n., fr. prec. Process of becoming warmer, of passing from freezing-point to open, mild weather; change from frozen condition to liquefaction: *a thaw has set in and the snow is melting.*

the (I.), def. art. [1. dhē; 2. ðī] when stressed; normally, when unstressed [1. dhi; 2. ð*i*], before words beginning w. a vowel; [1. dhe; 2. ðə] before words beginning w. a cons. Already in early M.E. *ðē* is used as indeclinable art. This is a new formation fr. the O.E. nom. masc. *se*, w. þ (*th-*) introduced fr. the other O.E. cases, all of wh., in all numbers & genders, begin w. þ- (*th-*), except nom. sing. masc. (*sē*), & nom. sing. fem. (*sēo*). Orig. a demonstr. pron. Cp. Lat. *is-te*, *is-tum* &c., 'that'; Gk. *tó*, neut. sing. of def. art., also other cases *tón*, *tén* &c.; Scrt. *ta*, *tam*, *tad* &c. See also **that** (I.), **their**, **them**. 1. Indicating some particular person or thing; contrasted with the indef. art. *a*: *the man I loved*; *the King of England*; *the author of 'Hamlet'*; *the man for my money*; *the day that first we met* &c. 2. Before a noun expressing some well-known object, thing, or personage: *the Thames*; *now they bring in the Boar's Head*; *the Wrekin*; *the Devil*; *the Pope*; *the King*, indicating either the Sovereign of one's own country, or of some other country about which one is speaking, or in which one is. 3. a Used before titles: *the Lord Bishop of Oxford*; *the Venerable the Archdeacon of London*; *the Mayor of Yarmouth*; *the Duke of Wellington*; *the Earl of Oxford*; b used before the family name of the head of certain ancient families or clans, esp. in Scotland and Ireland: *the Mackintosh*; *the Chisholm*; *the Macgillicuddy.* 4. Before a noun used to designate a whole class or genus: *the wild boar*; *the laughing jackass*; *the horse and the dog are faithful servants of mankind.* 5. a Before adjectives referring to a person or to persons possessing the qualities which it denotes: '*The young, the beautiful, the brave*' (Byron, 'Bride of Abydos', ii. 1); *the living and the dead*; *a book much prized by the learned*; b before adjectives expressing an abstract idea: '*We needs must love the highest when we see it*' (Tennyson, 'Guinevere'); *the sublime and the beautiful*; *the public loves the sensational*; *the picturesque* &c. 6. With stress [ðī] before a noun, denoting some unique object or person: *thé specialist on liver complaints*; *thé poet of the day*; *cider is thé drink for hot weather.*

the (II.), adv. [1. dhe; 2. ðə]. O.E. *þȳ*. Instrumental of def. art. By so much, by that amount: *the more the merrier*; *the more I practise, the worse I sing.*

theandric, adj. [1. thēándrik; 2. þīǽndrik]. Gk. *theós*, 'God', see **theo-**, & *andr-*, stem of *anḗr*, 'man', see first element of **androgynous**, & **-ic**. Pertaining to, based on, the combination of divine and human nature, as in Jesus Christ.

theanthropic(al), adj. [1. thēanthrópik(l); 2. þīænþrɔ́pik(l)]. Gk. *theós*, 'God', see **theo-**, & *ánthrōpos*, 'man', see **anthropo-**, & **-ic** (& **-al**). Divine and human; embodying God in human form.

theanthropism, n. [1. thēánthropizm; 2. þīǽnþrəpizəm]. a Anthropomorphism; b belief in the embodiment of God in human form.

theanthropist, n. [1. thēánthropist; 2. þīǽnþrəpist]. Believer in theanthropism.

thearchic, adj. [1. thēárkik; 2. þīákik]. Next word & **-ic**. Pertaining to, based on, of the nature of, thearchy.

thearchy, n. [1. thḗarki; 2. þīāki]. See **theo-** & **-archy**. a Divine rulership; b government claiming direct divine authority and guidance, claiming to act as God's vicegerent; theocracy.

theatre, n. [1. thḗater; 2. þíətə]. Fr., fr. Lat. *theātrum*, fr. Gk. *théatron*, fr. *theā́*, 'sight, a spectacle'; cp. also *theáomai*, 'I gaze at, behold', & *theātós*, 'to be seen'; prob. related to Gk. *thaûma*, 'object of wonder' &c., see **thauma(to)-**. 1. A building containing a large chamber, with a stage for the performance of dramatic pieces, and seats for spectators. 2. A hall arranged like a theatre, with a dais, and rows of seats rising towards the back, for lectures, scientific demonstrations, surgical operations &c., or for public ceremonies: *operating*, *lecture*, *theatre*; *the Sheldonian Theatre* (at Oxford). 3. The scene of important events or actions, region where these take place: *the theatre of war*; *the theatre of his early triumphs.* 4. Dramatic literature collectively; esp. the dramatic writings of a particular author or period: *Goethe's theatre*; *the Elizabethan theatre.*

theatric, adj. [1. theátrik; 2. þiǽtrik]. Prec. & **-ic**. (rare, chiefly poet.) Showy; see next word.

theatrical, adj. [1. theátrikl; 2. þiǽtrikl]. Prec. & **-al**. 1. Pertaining to, connected with, the theatre, or with dramatic representation. 2. a (of manner) Affected, studied, not natural; adopted for the purpose of impressing; not restrained; b (of appearance) showy, unreal, artificial, meretricious.

theatricality, n. [1. theàtrikáliti; 2. þiæ̀trikǽliti]. Prec. & **-ity**. Quality of being theatrical; affectation of manner &c.

theatrically, adv. [1. theátrikali; 2. þiǽtrikəli]. See prec. & **-ly**. In a theatrical manner; as though performing on the stage; affectedly, unnaturally.

theatricals, n. pl. [1. theátriklz; 2. þiǽtriklz]. Dramatic performances, esp. those executed by amateurs.

Thebaid, n. [1. thḗbaid; 2. þíbei-id]. Gk. *Thēbai*, 'Thebes'. a District round or near Thebes in Egypt; b poem (esp. that by Statius) upon the siege of Thebes in Boeotia.

theca, n., pl. **thecae** [1. thḗka, -kē; 2. þíkə, -kī]. Lat., fr. Gk. *thḗkē*, 'case in which to put anything'; fr. *títhēmi*, 'I place', see **theme**. (bot. and zool.) Sheath, case, capsule, as of mosses &c.; the case of the pupa of an insect &c.

thee, pron. Objective case of **thou**.

theft, n. [1. theft; 2. þεft]. O.E. *þīefþe*, *þēofþe*, see **thief** & **-th** (I.). a Act of stealing; b object stolen.

thegn, n. [1. thān; 2. þein]. O.E. See **thane**.

theine, n. [1. thḗin; 2. þíin], fr. *thea*, Latinized form of Gk. *theā́*, 'goddess', invented by Linnaeus, as scientific name for **tea**, & **-ine**. Caffeine as it occurs in tea.

their, pron. [1. dhār; 2. ðεə]. O.N. *þeirra*, possess. pl. of 3rd pers. pron. See **they**.

theirs, pron., fr. prec., *-s* added on anal. of *his*. Form of *their* used absolutely: *this is yours and that is theirs*; also when preceded by *of*: *a favourite habit of theirs.*

theism (I.), n. [1. thḗizm; 2. þíizəm]. *Thea*, see **theine**, & **-ism**. Pathological condition due to excessive use of tea.

theism (II.), n. [1. thḗizm; 2. þízəm]. Gk. *theós*, 'God', see **theo-** & **-ism**. Belief in a personal God capable of making Himself known by supernatural revelation.

theist, n. [1. thḗist; 2. þíist]. See **theo-** & **-ist**. Adherent of theism.

theistic, adj., rarer **theistical** [1. thēístik(l); 2. þiístik(l)]. Prec. & **-ic** (& **-al**). Connected with theism or theists.

them, pron. [1. dhem; 2. ðεm, ðəm]. M.E. *þeim*, *þem*, fr. O.N. *þeim*, cogn. w. O.E. *þǣm*, dat. pl. of def. art. See **the**, **they**. Form of pron. of 3rd pers. used both as dat. & acc. pl.

thematic, adj. [1. thematik; 2. þimǽtik], fr. Gk. *themat-*, see **theme**, & **-ic**. 1. (gram.) Pertaining to the stem or theme of a word. 2. (mus.) Pertaining to the theme or melodic subject; *thematic catalogue*, one which gives, in addition to the title and full reference, also the opening measures of musical compositions. 3. (rare) Relating to a theme or topic.

theme, n. [1. thēm; 2. þīm]. M.E., fr. O. Fr. *teme*, Mod. Fr. *thème*, fr. Lat. *thema*, fr. Gk. *théma*, fr. *títhēmi*, 'I place', fr. base **dhē-* &c., whence also **deed**, **do** (I.), & Lat. *facere*, see **fact**; cp. also **thesis**. 1. Subject of thought, writing, discourse. 2. (gram.) That part of a word to which the inflexions are suffixed; a stem. 3. (mus.) A brief melody occurring and recurring in a composition, subsequently elaborated in variations.

Themis, n. [1. thémis; 2. þḗmis]. Gk., name of the goddess of law and order, 'Justice'; fr. the same word meaning 'that which is fixed, settled, agreed upon'; hence 'law, right' &c., fr. base **dhē-* &c., 'to place, set', see prec. Personification of law and justice.

themselves, pron. [1. dhemsélvz; 2. ðəmsélvz]. 1. Emphatic form of pron. of 3rd pers. pl.: *they had often done the same thing themselves*, or *they themselves had* &c. 2. Reflex. pron. pl.: *they were ashamed of themselves*; *they felt themselves to be in the wrong.*

then (I.), adv. & conjunc. [1. dhen; 2. ðεn]. Same in origin as **than**; O.E. *þonne*. A. adv. 1. a At that (specified) time in the future: '*now I know in part; but then shall I know even as also I am known*' (1 Cor. xiii. 12); *when I know what the price is, then I shall be able to decide*; *I shall see you on Monday, and will then tell you the facts*; b at some former time, in the past; in the old days; contrasted with *now*, *at present*: *ah, we were still young then*; Phrs. *there and then*, at that very moment; *now and then*, from time to time, occasionally. 2. Next in order of time; immediately afterwards: *Queen Anne died in 1702, and then the first Hanoverian sovereign succeeded to the throne of England*; *he made a few convulsive movements and then died*; *take a hot drink and then go to bed.* 3. At another, subsequent, time; later on: *he used to behave like a lunatic when he was in a rage, then, when the fit had passed, he would be full of contrition.* 4. In that case, that being so: *if you are tired, then you had better stay at home*; *well then, please yourself about it*; *if you didn't understand, then you should have told me*; expressing rather unwilling acquiescence: *oh, all right then, do what you like.* 5. Expressing condition; under the circumstances, from what you say: *you don't want to go after all, then*; *then you didn't expect me today.* 6. *Now then*, expressing protest, warning &c.: *now then, what are you doing?*; *now then, don't hit me in the eye!*; *now then, a little less noise there.* B. conj. Moreover, in addition, also, further: *then there's the General still to be invited*; *then what about French, can you speak that language?*

then (II.), adj., fr. prec. Existing, acting, at a specified time: *the then governor was a man of probity and honour.*

then (III.), n. See prec. That (specified) time: *by then*, *till then*, *up to then*, *from then onwards.*

thenar, n. [1. thḗnar; 2. þínə]. Gk. *thénar*, 'palm of the hand', cogn. w. O.H.G. *tenar*, 'palm'. The palm of the hand; the protuberance in the palm at the base of the thumb.

thence, adv. [1. dhens; 2. ðεns]. O.E. *þanon*, O.H.G. *danān* &c.; M.E. *þennes*, w. suff. of genit. used adverbially. 1. From that place: *we went to Geneva, and thence to the Rhone Valley.* 2. (rare) From that time, thenceforth: *a year thence*; contrasted with *a year hence.* 3. On that account, for that reason; from what has been said; therefore: *thence it follows that we were wrong*; *he was very old, and thence very feeble.*

thenceforth, adv. [1. dhènsfórth; 2. ðènsfɔ̄̀þ]. From that time or place, onwards; often *from thenceforth.*

thenceforward, adv. [1. dhènsfórward; 2. ðènsfɔ̄̀wəd]. Thenceforth.

theo-, pref. Form used in compounds, fr. Gk. *theós*, 'god', later of the God of the Jews or of the Christians. The etymol. is disputed; some authorities derive the word fr. the base **dhwes-*, 'to breathe; breath, spirit, life', & connect w. Lat. *bēstia*, see **beast**, & w. **deer**; also w. Lat. *fūmus*, 'smoke', see **fume** & **dust**; others derive fr. **dhēs-* &c., 'religious act', & connect w. Lat. *fēriae*, 'religious festivals', see **ferial** & **fair** (I.), & w. Lat. *festus*, 'connected with holidays; solemn, festal' &c., & *festum*, 'festival, feast', see **feast**, **festive** &c.; also Lat. *fānum*, 'place consecrated to a deity', see **fane**.

theocentric, adj. [1. thèōséntrik; 2. þìouséntrik]. Prec. & **centric**. Considering God as the centre of the universe.

theocracy, n. [1. theókrasi; 2. þiɔ́krəsi]. **theo-** & **-cracy**. a System of state government by direct guidance of God; b government by priests as purporting to represent God, and interpret His will.

theocrasy, n. [1. theókrasi, theokrā́si; 2. þiɔ́krəsi, þiɔkréisi], fr. **theo-** & *krāsis*, 'a mixing', see **crasis**. Union of the soul with God in mystical contemplation.

theocrat, n. [1. thḗōkrat; 2. þíoukræt]. **theo-** & **-crat**. A ruler under a system of theocracy.

theocratic, adj. [1. thèōkrátik; 2. þìoukrǽtik]. Prec. & **-ic**. Pertaining to, based on, theocracy.

theodicy, n. [1. theódisi; 2. þiɔ́disi]. **theo-** & Gk. *díkē*, 'justice', see **dicast**. Vindication of divine justice in permitting existence of evil.

theodolite, n. [1. theódolīt; 2. þiɔ́dəlait]. Origin unknown. Instrument used by surveyors for measuring angles.

theogony, n. [1. theóguni; 2. þiɔ́gəni]. Gk. *theogonía*, 'genealogy of the gods'; fr. **theo-** & *gónos*, 'race, offspring; begetting'; see under **genus**. Branch of ancient heathen theology, dealing with the origin and descent of the various gods.

theologian, n. [1. thèolṓjian; 2. þìəlóudž(i)ən]. Gk. word is *theológos*; our word fr. Fr. *théologien*; fr. *théologie*, see **theology** & **-an**. Student of, authority on, theology.

theological, adj. [1. thèolójikl; 2. þìəlɔ́džikl]. **theology** & **-ic** & **-al**. Connected with, based upon, of the nature of, theology.

theologically, adv. Prec. & **-ly**. From the point of view of theology, or of theologians.

theologico-, pref. Form of **theological** used in compounds: *theologico-philosophical.*

theologue, n. [1. thèōlṓg; 2. þìoulóug]. Fr., Lat. *theologus*, fr. Gk., see **theologian**. (archaic or obs.) Theologian.

theology, n. [1. theóloji; 2. þiɔ́lədži]. Gk. *theologia*, see **theo-** & **-logy**. Systematic study and inquiry into the nature and attributes of God; also the systematic study of religion and the foundations of belief.

theomachy, n. [1. theómaki; 2. þiɔ́məki], fr. Gk. *theomakhía*, see **theo-** & **-machy**. A battle with or among the gods.

theomorphic, adj. [1. thèōmórfik; 2. þìoumɔ̄́fik], fr. Gk. *theómorph-(os)* & **-ic**, see **theo-** & first element in **morphology**. Having the form or appearance of a god; in the form of a god.

theophany, n. [1. theófani; 2. þiɔ́fəni], fr. Gk. *theopháneia*, fr. **theo-** & base discussed under **phantasm**. An appearance, manifestation of God in human or divine form to men.

theorbo, n. [1. theórbō; 2. þiɔ́bou]. Fr. *théorbe*, fr. Ital. *tiorba*. Origin unknown. Obsolete kind of lute, of large size, and having two necks, and sets of pegs and strings.

theorem, n. [1. thḗorem; 2. þíərɛm]. Gk. *theṓrēma*, 'a sight, speculation', see **theory**. 1. Something established as a law or general principle; a speculative truth. 2. (math.) A general statement: a proposition to be established by reasoning.

theorematic(al), adj. [1. thèoremátik(l); 2. þìərɛmǽtik(l)], fr. *theoremat-*, stem of prec., & **-ic** (& **-al**). Pertaining to theorems.

theoretic(al), adj. [1. thèorétik(l); 2. þìərétik(l)]. Gk. *theōrētikós*; see **theory**. a Pertaining to, based upon, theory; b speculative, not based on actual experience; contrasted with *practical.*

theoretically, adv. Prec. & **-y**. In theory, as a theory; from the point of view of theory.

theorist, n. [1. thḗorist; 2. þíərist]. **theory** & **-ist**. One given to forming theories; an unpractical person.

theorize, vb. intrans. [1. thḗorīz; 2. þíəraiz]. **theory** & **-ize**. To form, put forward, theories.

theory, n. [1. thḗori; 2. þíəri]. Fr. *théorie*, Lat. *theōria*, fr. Gk. *theōría*, 'a spectacle, contemplation, speculation'; cp. *theōrós*, 'spectator', & *theā́sthai*, 'to see'; see also **theatre**. 1. A general principle, a supposition, advanced to explain a group of phenomena; esp. one which has been tested, and is regarded as supplying an acceptable explanation; distinct from *hypothesis*, which is an assumption not yet verified. 2. General principles underlying a body of facts; contrasted with *practice*: *a theory of education, government; the theory of music.* 3. Contemplation, speculation, as distinct from actual experience: *foreign travel is all very well in theory.* 4. (popular usage) Opinion, fanciful belief; fad, whimsy: *I have a theory that a hot bath at night makes one sleepless.*

theosophic(al), adj. [1. thèosófik(l); 2. þìəsɔ́fik(l)]. **theosophy** & **-ic** (& **-al**). Connected with, relating to, theosophy.

theosophist, n. [1. theósofist; 2. þiɔ́səfist]. **theosophy** & **-ist**. Believer in theosophy.

theosophy, n. [1. theósofi; 2. þiɔ́səfi]. Gk. *theosophía*, 'knowledge of divine things'; *theós*, 'God', see **theo-** & *sophía*, 'skill, wisdom', fr. *sophós*, 'skilled, clever, wise', see **sophist**. Mystic form of religious thought which aims at establishing a direct relation between the individual soul and the divine principle by contemplation and ecstasy, and thereby gaining superior spiritual insight and knowledge.

-ther, compar. suff., fr. base **ter-*, **tr-*, seen in Gk. *-teros*, Lat. *-ter(us)*, see **inter-**; found in prons. & advbs. implying comparison, alternative possibility, distinction &c., e.g. *either, other, whether, hither, nether.*

therapeutic(al), adj. [1. thèrapū́tik(l); 2. þèrəpjū́tik(l)]. Gk. *therapeutikós*, 'attentive, obedient; able to cure', *therapeutikḗ*, 'the healing art'; cp. *therapeúein*, 'to serve, attend upon'; fr. *therápōn*, 'an attendant, servant'; the orig. sense is perh. 'prop, support', cp. Gk. *thrā̃nos*, 'a bench, form', & Lat. *firmus*, 'strong, firm', see **firm** (I.), & *frē-tus*, 'trusting to, relying on'. Connected with the art of healing, with the cure of disease.

therapeutics, n. pl. [1. thèrapū́tiks; 2. þèrəpjū́tiks]. That side of medicine which is concerned with the treatment and cure of disease.

-therapy, suff. [1. thérapi; 2. þérəpi]. Gk. *therapeia*, 'service, attendance; medical attendance'; see **therapeutic**. Curative treatment, e.g. *radio-therapy*, cure by radium.

there, adv. & interj. [1. dhār; 2. ðɛə]. O.E. *ðǣr*; belongs to the group of demonstrative words including **the**, **that**, **then**. 1. a In that place, referring to one other than that in which the speaker actually is; contrasted with *here*: *when we reached London my brother remained there, while I came on here;* b to, towards, that place: *I've never been to Rome, but I'm going there at Easter.* Phrs. *look there*, look at that, in that direction &c.; *there it is!* = what you are looking for &c. 2. a At that point, stage (in action, discourse, argument &c.): *don't stop there, go on and tell us all about it;* b towards a certain point (in action &c.): *I have not yet reached your intellectual position, but I may get there in time.* Phrs. (slang) *to get there*, attain one's object, do what one is trying to do; *there it is*, that is the situation. 3. Pronominally and impersonally, as subject of a verb, introducing a sentence: *there was once a great king*, at beginning of a narrative; *there was a sudden drop in the temperature; there was no excuse for his rudeness; what is there to do here?; there are plenty of foxes to be killed;* also archaic or poet., *a king there was* &c. 4. (as interj.) *There, there!*, in soothing a child &c.; *there now, I told you it would land you in a mess!; there now, it has turned out all right after all!*

thereabouts, adv. [1. dhàrabóuts; 2. ðɛ̀ərəbáuts]. 1. Near that (specified) place: *he lives in Wantage or thereabouts.* 2. Near to that amount, extent, degree, position &c.: *a thousand a year, or thereabouts; top of his school or thereabouts.*

thereafter, adv. [1. dhāráhfter; 2. ðɛərā́ftə]. O.E. *þǣræfter*. 1. After that time. 2. (rare) According to, in accordance with, that: *listen to his advice, and behave yourself thereafter.*

thereat, adv. [1. dhārát; 2. ðɛərǽt]. (archaic) At, on account of, by means of, that.

thereby, adv. [1. dhārbī́; 2. ðɛəbái]. 1. Near to that place. 2. By that means: *I have learnt my lesson, and hope to profit thereby.*

therefor, adv. [1. dhārfṓr; 2. ðɛəfɔ́]. (archaic) For it, for that, or this; in exchange for that.

therefore, adv. [1. dhā́rfōr; 2. ðɛ́əfɔ̄]. On this, or that, account; for this, or that, reason.

therefrom, adv. [1. dhārfróm; 2. ðɛəfrɔ́m]. From, away from, that; by means of that.

therein, adv. [1. dhārín; 2. ðɛərín]. a In that thing, or place; b in this, that, particular.

thereinafter, adv. [1. dhāriną́hfter; 2. ðɛ̀ərinā́ftə]. In that part which follows (in a speech, or document).

thereof, adv. [1. dhāróv, -óf; 2. ðɛəróv, -ɔ́f]. (archaic) Of it, of that: *thou shalt not eat thereof.*

thereon, adv. [1. dhārón; 2. ðɛərɔ́n]. (archaic) On this, on that.

thereto, adv. [1. dhārtōō; 2. ðɛətū́]. (archaic) 1. To it, to that, to that place. 2. Moreover, in addition to that.

theretofore, adv. [1. dhàrtoofṓr; 2. ðɛ̀ətufɔ́]. (archaic) Until then, up to that time.

thereunder, adv. [1. dhārúnder; 2. ðɛəránd ə]. (archaic) Under that.

thereunto, adv. [1. dhàruntōō; 2. ðɛ̀ərantū́]. (archaic, or obs.) To that, to it.

thereupon, adv. [1. dhàrupón; 2. ðɛ̀ərəpɔ́n]. 1. Upon that. 2. In consequence, as result, of that. 3. At that point (of time); immediately after that.

therewith, adv. [1. dhārwídh, -wíth; 2. ðɛəwíð, -wíþ]. (archaic) 1. With that. 2. Forthwith, at that moment, thereupon.

therewithal, adv. [1. dhàrwidhawl; 2. ðɛ̀əwiðɔ́l]. Besides, moreover; therewith.

theriac, n. [1. thḗriak; 2. þíəriæk]. Lat. *Theriaca (Andromachi)*, fr. Gk. *thēriakḗ*, 'antidote'; formed fr. *thḗrion*, 'wild beast', dimin. of *thḗr*, 'wild beast'; fr. **ghwēr-*, & cogn. w. Lat. *ferus*, 'wild', see **feral**, & **ferocious**; cp. **treacle**. Ancient antidote for poison, composed of certain drugs mixed with honey.

therianthropic, adj. [1. thèrianthrópik; 2. þìəriænþrɔ́pik]. Gk. *thḗr*, 'animal, beast', see **therio-** & *ánthrōpos*, 'man', see **anthropo-**. Combining human and animal form, as the centaur.

therio-, pref., fr. Gk. *thḗrion*, 'beast, animal', fr. *thḗr*, 'wild beast', see **theriac**.

theriomorphic, theriomorphous, adj. [1. thèriōmórfik, -mórfus; 2. þìərioumɔ̄́fik, -mɔ̄́fəs]. Prec. & Gk. *morphḗ*, 'form', see first element in **morphology**. Having the form of an animal.

-therium, suff. Mod. Lat., fr. Gk. *thḗrion*, 'animal', see **theriac**: *megatherium* &c.

therm, n. [1. thërm; 2. þām]. Gk. *thérmē*, 'heat', cp. *thermós*, 'hot, warm'; fr. base *ghwerm-, *ghworm-, & cogn. w. Lat. *formus*, 'warm', also w. **warm**. Term for British thermal unit, or unit of heat, being the amount of heat required to raise a pound of water at maximum density, 1° Fahrenheit; abbreviated B.T.U.

thermae, n. pl. [1. thërmē; 2. þámī]. Lat., 'hot springs', fr. Gk. *thérmai*, pl. of *thérmē*, 'heat', see prec. Hot springs, or baths; specif., the springs connected with ancient Roman public baths, also the baths themselves.

thermaesthesia, n. [1. thërmesthḗzia; 2. þàmespízia], fr. **thermo-** & Gk. *aisthēsis*, 'sensation', see **aesthete**, & **-ia**. (physiol.) Sensitiveness to heat.

thermal, adj. [1. thërmal; 2. þám(ə)l]. See **therm** & **-al**. **a** Pertaining to thermae; **b** pertaining to heat; hot: *thermal waters, springs* &c.

thermantidote, n. [1. thërmántidōt; 2. þàmǽntidout]. See **therm** & **antidote**. Apparatus used in hot countries for cooling the air.

thermic, adj. [1. thërmik; 2. þámik]. See **therm** & **-ic**. Connected with, caused by, heat.

Thermidor, n. [1. thërmidōr; 2. þámidō]. Fr., fr. Gk. *thérmē*, 'heat', see **therm**, & *dôron*, 'gift', base of wh. see under **donate**. Name given in French Revolution to the eleventh month of their calendar, from July 19th to August 17th.

Thermidorian, n. [1. thërmidṓrian; 2. þàmidṓriən]. Prec. & **-an**. One of those who took part in, or favoured, the overthrow of Robespierre on 9th Thermidor (July 27th), 1794.

thermionic, adj. [1. thërmiónik; 2. þàmiɔ́nik], fr. **therm** & **-ion** & **-ic**. Term applied to a vacuum tube, *thermionic valve*, used in wireless, in which electrons given off by a heated filament carry current in one direction, thus converting the alternating current of the radio waves into wire-directional current which can be made to work a telephone and produce sound.

thermit(e), n. [1. thërmit, -īt; 2. þámit, -ait]. **thermo-** & **-ite**. A mixture of finely granulated aluminium with an iron oxide, used in welding.

thermo-, pref. Form used in compounds, fr. Gk. *thermós*, 'hot', or *thérmē*, 'heat', see **therm**.

thermobarometer, n. [1. thërmobarómeter; 2. þàmoubərɔ́mitə]. Apparatus for measuring a height by determining the boiling-point of water at that altitude.

thermochemistry, n. [1. thërmōkémistri; 2. þàmoukémistri]. Branch of chemistry treating of relation between heat and chemical action.

thermo-couple, n. [1. thërmō kùpl; 2. þámou kàpl]. Thermopile.

thermodynamics, n. [1. thërmōdīnámiks; 2. þàmoudainǽmiks]. Branch of science dealing with the relation between thermal and mechanical energy.

thermoelectric(al), adj. [1. thërmōeléktrik(l); 2. þàmouiléktrik(l)]. Pertaining to thermoelectricity.

thermoelectricity, n. [1. thërmōelektrísiti; 2. þàmoueliktrísiti]. Electricity produced by the action of heat, by differences in temperature &c.

thermoelectrometer, n. [1. thërmōèlektrómeter; 2. þàmouèliktrɔ́mitə]. Instrument for determining the power of an electric current by measuring the heat which it produces.

thermogenesis, n. [1. thërmōjénesis; 2. þàmoudžénisis]. The production of heat in the human body &c.

thermogenetic, adj. [1. thërmōjenétik; 2. þàmoudžinétik]. **thermo-** & **-genetic**. Pertaining to thermogenesis.

thermogenic, adj. [1. thërmōjénik; 2. þàmoudžénik]. **thermo-** & **-gene** & **-ic**. Relating to the production of heat.

thermogenous, adj. [1. thërmójenus; 2. þàmɔ́džinəs]. See prec. & **-ous**. Producing heat.

thermogram, n. [1. thërmōgràm; 2. þámougrǽm]. **thermo-** & **-gram**. Record produced by a thermograph.

thermograph, n. [1. thërmōgràhf; 2. þámougrâf]. **thermo-** & **-graph**. Self-registering thermometer.

thermology, n. [1. thërmóloji; 2. þàmɔ́lədži]. **thermo-** & **-logy**. The science of heat.

thermometer, n. [1. thermómeter; 2. þəmɔ́mitə]. **thermo-** & **-meter**. Instrument for measuring degrees of temperature.

thermometric(al), adj. [1. thërmōmétrik(l); 2. þàmoumétrik(l)]. Prec. & **-ic** & (**-al**). Pertaining to, measured by, a thermometer.

thermometrically, adv. [1. thërmōmétrikali; 2. þàmoumétrikəli]. Prec. & **-ly**. By means of a thermometer.

thermometry, n. [1. thërmómetri; 2. þàmɔ́mitri]. **thermo-** & **-metry**. The measurement of heat.

thermomotive, adj. [1. thërmōmṓtiv; 2. þàmoumóutiv]. Pertaining to motion produced by heat.

thermomotor, n. [1. thërmōmṓtor; 2. þàmoumóutə]. An engine worked by heat, usually by hot air.

thermophilic, adj. [1. thërmófilik; 2. þàmɔ́filik]. **thermo-** & **-phil** & **-ic**. (of bacteria) Heat-loving; developing best at a comparatively high temperature.

thermophore, n. [1. thërmōfōr; 2. þámoufɔ̄]. **thermo-** & **-phore**. Apparatus for conveying warmth; heating appliance.

thermopile, n. [1. thërmōpīl; 2. þámoupail]. **thermo-** & **pile (III.)**. Thermoelectric battery, used as delicate form of thermometer, consisting of junctions of dissimilar metals which produce an electric current on the application of heat.

thermoplegia, n. [1. thërmōplḗjia; 2. þàmouplídžiə]. **thermo-** & Gk. *plēgē*, 'blow, stroke', see under **plectrum** & **-ia**. A heat-stroke.

thermoscope, n. [1. thërmōskōp; 2. þámouskoup]. **thermo-** & **-scope**. Instrument for indicating differences of temperature without exact measurement.

thermoscopic(al), adj. [1. thërmōskópik(l); 2. þàmouskɔ́pik(l)]. Prec. & **-ic** & (**-al**). Pertaining to, shown by, a thermoscope.

thermos flask, n. [1. thërmos flàhsk; 2. þáməs flâsk]. Proprietary trade name, fr. Gk. *thermós*, 'hot', see **therm**. A kind of vacuum flask or bottle used for keeping liquids contained in it hot or cold; also *thermos*.

thermostat, n. [1. thërmōstàt; 2. þámoustǽt]. See **thermo-** & **static**. Device for regulating temperature automatically.

thermostatic, adj. [1. thërmōstátik; 2. þàmoustǽtik]. Prec. & **-ic**. Pertaining to, carried out by, a thermostat.

thermostatics, n. [1. thërmōstátiks; 2. þàmoustǽtiks]. See prec. & **-ics**. Branch of the science of heat dealing with the equilibrium of heat.

thermotaxic, adj. [1. thërmōtáksik; 2. þàmoutǽksik]. **thermo-** & **taxis** & **-ic**. Pertaining to the regulation of bodily heat.

thermotensile, adj. [1. thërmōténsil; 2. þàmouténsil]. Pertaining to variation in tensile force when affected by temperature.

thermotherapy, n. [1. thërmōthérapi; 2. þàmoupérəpi]. The treatment of disease by heat.

thermotype, n. [1. thërmōtīp; 2. þámoutaip]. Impression of an object, e.g. a section of wood &c., produced by damping the object with dilute acid, taking a print from it, and developing this print by the application of heat.

theroid, adj. [1. thḗroid; 2. þíərɔid]. Gk. *thḗr*, 'wild beast', see **theriac**, & **-oid**. Resembling a beast; like an animal in appearance and habits: *theroid idiot*.

therology, n. [1. thēróloji; 2. þiərɔ́lədži]. Gk. *thḗr*, '(wild) beast', as in prec., & **-logy**. Study of mammals.

thesaurus, n. [1. thēsṓrus; 2. þisɔ́rəs]. Lat., fr. Gk. *thēsaurós*, 'treasure; treasure house'; origin unexplained; prob. a primitive compound. A treasury; esp. a treasury or collection of words, phrases, literary extracts or the like; a lexicon.

these, demonstr. pron. [1. dhēz; 2. ðīz]. Pl. of **this**.

thesis (I.), n. [1. thésis; 2. þésis]. Gk. *thésis*, 'a setting, placing, arranging', fr. base in *tithēmi*, 'I set, place'; cogn. w. Engl. **do (I.)** & Lat. *facere*, 'do, make', see **fact**, & cp. **theme**. (pros.) The accented part of a metrical foot; contrasted with *arsis*, the unaccented part.

thesis (II.), n. [1. thḗsis; 2. þísis]; more rarely [1. thésis; 2. þésis]. Same as prec. **1.** Something advanced, maintained, laid down; a proposition. **2.** Specif., formerly, a proposition advanced and publicly disputed, defended, or maintained by a candidate for a university degree; hence, a dissertation, essay, treatise, written for purposes of a degree examination, embodying the candidate's research.

Thespian, adj. & n. [1. théspian; 2. þéspiən], fr. Gk. *Théspis*, supposed founder of Gk. drama, & **-an**. **1.** adj. Connected with the drama, or with acting. **2.** n. An actor.

theurgic(al), adj. [1. theẽrjik(l); 2. þiádžik(l)]. **theurgy** & **-ic** (& **-al**). Magical.

theurgist, n. [1. thḗẽrjist; 2. þíàdžist]. **theurgy** & **-ist**. A magician.

theurgy, n. [1. thḗẽrji; 2. þíàdži]. Gk. *theourgía*, 'miracle', see **theo-**, 'God', & *érgon*, 'work', see **erg**. **a** Divine work, miracle; **b** sorcery, magic.

thewed, adj. [1. thūd; 2. þjūd]. See **thews**. Having thews of specified kind.

thewless, adj. [1. thūles; 2. þjúlis]. **thew(s)** & **-less**. Lacking physical strength; lacking mental or moral fibre.

thews, n. pl. [1. thūz; 2. þjūz]. O.E. *þēaw*, 'custom, habit'; later, 'strength'; still used by Spenser in sense of 'manners, behaviour': *three daughters, well upbrought In goodly thewes, and godly exercise* ('F. Q.' I. x. 4); cogn. w. O.S. *thau*, 'habit, custom'; O.H.G. *thau*, 'discipline'; etymol. doubtful. **1.** Sinews, muscles; esp. *thews and sinews*. **2.** Moral or mental fibre, robustness, vigour.

thewy, adj. [1. thūi; 2. þjúi]. See prec. & **-y**. Muscular, sinewy.

they, pers. pron. of 3rd pers. pl. nom. [1. dhā; 2. ðei]. M.E. *þei*, *thei* &c., fr. O.N. *þeirr*, wh. gradually takes the place of M.E. *hii* &c., fr. O.E. *hīe*; cogn. w. **the**.

thiasus, n. [1. thíasus; 2. þáiəsəs]. Lat., fr. Gk. *thíasos*, etymol. doubtful. (Gk. antiq.) **a** Religious brotherhood formed in honour of a god; **b** the sacrifice, festival, of such a brotherhood.

thick (I.), adj. [1. thik; 2. þik]. M.E. *thikke* &c., prob. fr. O.N. *þykkr*; the O.E. cogn. *þiċċe* wd. result in **thitch*; O.S. *thikki*; O.H.G. *dicchi*; relations outside Gmc. doubtful. **1. a** (i.) Of great circumference relatively to length: *a thick bough, trunk; thick neck, legs, fingers*; (ii.) of great, or relatively great, depth laterally, from one surface to that opposite; reverse of *thin*: *a thick slice of meat, sheet of paper; thick cloth*; Phrs. (colloq.) *a bit thick*, of conduct, demands &c., hardly tolerable, too much of a good thing; of circumstances, fortune &c., hard to bear, exigent; **b** having, of, a specified thickness: *five-foot thick* &c. **2. a** (of fluids, vapours &c.) Having considerable density; of semi-solid consistency; inspissated; having component particles closely packed together; **b** (of a group of objects) placed close together, having small space between; dense: *a thick wood; corn standing thick*. **3.** (of water &c.) Muddy, turbid; reverse of *clear, limpid*: *the river looks thick after the rain*. **4. a** Frequent, occurring rapidly one after another, repeated; crowded, numerous: *with honours thick upon him; a thick shower of blows*; **b** full of, abounding in: *the air thick with rain, snow* &c. **5.** (of the voice, of sound) Dull; not distinct, resonant or ringing; reverse of *clear*. **6.** Dull of intellect, slow-witted, obtuse, dense. **7.** Intimate, much together, closely associated: *he and I are very thick*; Phr. *as thick as thieves*.

thick (**II.**), n., fr. prec. **1.** *The thick*, thickest, densest, part; place where most is taking place: *to plunge into the thick of the fight, of politics* &c. Phrs. *in the thick of it*, in the midst of, taking active part in, events, or affairs &c.; *to go through thick and thin*, face and overcome great difficulties, hardships &c. **2.** A person of thick wits, a blockhead.

thick (**III.**), adv., fr. **thick** (**I.**). Thickly: *the snow fell thick.*

thicken, vb. trans. & intrans. [1. thíken; 2. þíkən]. **thick** (**I.**) & **-en.** **a** trans. To make thick (in various senses); **b** intrans., to become thick.

thickening, n. [1. thíkening; 2. þík(ə)niŋ]. Prec. & **-ing. 1.** Process of becoming thick, or thicker: *a thickening of the tissues.* **2.** Some thing or part which has become thick. **3.** Something which serves to thicken a liquid &c.

thicket, n. [1. thíket; 2. þíkit]. O.E. *þiččet*; Mod. form recast on type of **thick** (**I.**). Thickly wooded area, esp. one with dense undergrowth of low-growing shrubs and trees.

thicketed, adj. [1. thíketed; 2. þíkitid]. Prec. & **-ed.** Rich in thickets; covered with thicket.

thickhead, n. [1. thíkhed; 2. þíkhɛd]. A stupid person; a blockhead.

thickish, adj. [1. thíkish; 2. þíkiʃ]. **thick** (**I.**) & **-ish.** Rather thick.

thick-knee, n. Popular name of the stone-curlew.

thickly, adv. [1. thíkli; 2. þíkli]. **thick** (**I.**) & **-ly.** In a thick manner; **a** densely, closely; in such a way as to be, lie, thick: *thickly covered with snow*; **b** indistinctly: *to speak thickly*; **c** frequently, in rapid succession.

thickness, n. [1. thíknes; 2. þíknis]. See prec. & **-ness. 1.** Quality of being thick (in various senses): *the thickness of his arms showed great muscular development*; *thickness of speech*; *thickness of intellect.* **2.** Amount by which, extent to which, a thing is thick; measurement other than in length and breadth: *a thickness of ten feet*; *three inches in thickness.* **3.** Thickest part of anything: *wounded in the thickness of the back.* **4.** Layer, fold, ply: *three thicknesses of felt.*

thickset, adj. **1.** [1. thíkset; 2. þíksɛt] Closely, densely, planted: *a thickset hedge.* **2.** [1. thík-sét; 2. þíksét] Stumpy, stocky, short, and broadly, solidly, built; reverse of *slim, tall*: *a man who is sturdy and thickset.*

thick-skinned, adj. (chiefly fig.) Insensitive, having obtuse, blunted, sensibilities; slow to perceive or recognize subtle shades of feeling; not sensitive to the opinion of others.

thick-skulled, adj. Dense, stupid, mentally obtuse.

thief, n. [1. thēf; 2. þīf]. O.E. *þēof*, M.E. *þēf, thēf* &c.; O.S. *thiof*; O.H.G. *diob*; Goth. *þiufs*; etymol. unknown. **1.** Person who steals. **2.** (colloq.) Flaw in wick of a candle which causes this to gutter, thus wasting the wax.

thieve, vb. intrans. & trans. [1. thēv; 2. þīv]. O.E. *þēofian.* See prec. **a** intrans. To play the thief, be guilty of theft; **b** trans., to steal (a thing).

thievery, n. [1. thḗveri; 2. þívəri]. **thief** & **-ry.** The act of stealing; theft.

thievish, adj. [1. thḗvish; 2. þíviʃ]. **thief** & **-ish. 1.** Addicted to thieving. **2.** Of the nature of theft: *thievish habits.*

thievishly, adv. Prec. & **-ly.** In a thievish manner; like a thief, dishonestly.

thievishness, n. See prec. & **-ness.** **a** Habit of stealing; **b** fact of being a thief.

thigh, n. [1. thī; 2. þai]. O.E. *þēoh*; M.E. *þēh, þīh*; O. Fris. *thiah*; O.H.G. *dioh*; cp. Lith. *táukas*, 'animal fat'; fr. base **teu-*, 'to swell', as in Lat. *tumēre*, 'to swell', see **tumid, tumour. a** The thick part of the leg in man, apes, and birds, and of the hind leg in quadrupeds, between the hip and the knee; **b** the bone of the thigh, the femur: *to break one's thigh.*

thigh-bone, n. Bone of the thigh; the femur.

thighed, adj. [1. thīd; 2. þaid]. Having specified kind of thigh: '*ostrich-thighed*' (Browning); *large thighed.*

thill, thiller, n. [1. thil(er); 2. þil(ə)]. O.E. *þille*, 'structure of planks, flooring' (fr. **þeli*); M.E. *thille*; cogn. w. O.E. *þel*, 'plank'; O.H.G. *dili*; O.N. *þilja*, 'plank'; cp. Mod. Germ. *diele*, & **deal** (**IV.**) (plank). Shaft of a cart.

thimble, n. [1. thímbl; 2. þímbl]. O.E. *þȳmel*, 'thumbstall', fr. *þūma*, see **thumb**, w. dimin. suff., see **-le. 1.** Small cap of metal, bone &c. used to protect the finger when sewing. **2.** (naut.) Metal ring having the outer edge or surface grooved, fitted into a rope or sail, to prevent chafing.

thimbleful, n. [1. thímblfool; 2. þímblful]. Prec. & **-ful.** As much (liquid) as could be contained in a thimble; hence, a very small quantity of liquid.

thimblerig, n. & vb. intrans. [1. thímblrig; 2. þímblrig]. See prec. & **rig** (**III.**). **1.** n. Usually *thimblerigging*, swindling game at fairs &c., in which a player bets that he will detect under which of three small thimble-shaped cups a small pea or ball of pith is concealed, after the operator has rapidly and dexterously shifted it from one to the other many times; the swindle consists in the fact that there is often no ball under any of the cups. **2.** vb. To play this game; to swindle.

thimblerigger, n. [1. thímblrìger; 2. þímbl-rìgə]. Practitioner of thimblerigging.

thimblerigging, n. [1. thímblrìging; 2. þímbl-rìgiŋ]. **a** The game described under **thimble-rig**; **b** (fig.) dishonest, unscrupulous practice.

thin (**I.**), adj. [1. thin; 2. þin]. O.E. *þynne*, M.E. *thinne*; O.H.G. *dunni*; O.N. *þunnr*; cogn. w. Lat. *tenuis*, 'thin, slender', see **tenuis**; Gk. *tanúein*, 'to stretch', & *tanu-* as in *tanú-glōssos*, 'long-tongued'; fr. base **ten-*, 'stretch', see **tend** (**II.**), **tense** (**II.**), & cp. **tone. 1.** (of flat objects) Having small depth in relation to extent of surface; reverse of *thick*: *thin paper*; *a thin layer of butter*; *a thin blanket*; *a thin slice*; *thin clothes.* **2.** (of long objects) Having small circumference in relation to length; slender slim, tenuous: *a thin rope, chain*; *thin branch*; *thin fingers.* **3.** (of the animal body) Not thickly covered with fat or soft tissue; lean, gaunt, emaciated; reverse of *plump, stout, fat*: *arms too thin for beauty*; *thin in face*; *to look thin after an illness.* **4.** Widely spaced; not placed close together; sparse, scattered; reverse of *thick*, or *dense*: *hair rather thin on the top*; *thin growth of herbage*; also, *a thin audience, congregation* &c. **5. a** (of liquids, and gases) Rarefied, having small specific density; **b** (fig.) easily penetrated, refuted, or unmasked; transparent, flimsy: *a thin excuse, disguise, deception* &c. **6. a** Lacking in body, substance, richness: *thin ale, soup, porridge*; **b** (in non-material sense) lacking weightiness, solidity, intellectual substance and force: *the style of the book is elegant, but the matter is rather thin.*

thin (**II.**), vb. trans. & intrans., fr. prec. **1.** trans. To make thin (in various senses); **a** to reduce thickness of, make fine; **b** to weaken, make less dense; **c** to make sparser, by removing some: *to thin the branches of a tree*; *to thin out the shoots on a tree* &c. **2.** intrans. To become thinner (in various senses); also *thin down*, (of the body) to become thinner; *thin out*, (of an audience) to become sparser.

thine, possess. pron. of 2nd pers. sing. [1. dhīn; 2. ðain]. O.E. *þīn*, orig. genit. of **thou**; also declined as an adj. In M.E. *-n* is lost before words beginning with a consonant. See **thy.** (archaic, Bib., and liturgical) **1.** Possessive pronoun before vowel. **2.** Used absolutely: '*all that is in the heaven and in the earth is thine*' (1 Chron. xxix. 11).

thing, n. [1. thing; 2. þiŋ]. O.E., M.E. *þing*, also O.S. & O.N.; O.H.G. *ding*; the old meanings included those of 'object; action; event; condition; meeting'; cogn. w. O.E. *þingian*, 'to determine; settle, arrange; perh. connected w. Goth. *þeihs*, 'time, season', & *þeihan*, 'to advance, thrive', fr. Gmc. base **þiŋχ-*, Aryan **tenkkʷ-*, & further to be related to Lat. *tempus*, 'time', see **temporary** & **tempus.** At this rate the orig. meaning of *thing* wd. be 'something occurring at a given or fixed time, or under certain conditions', hence, 'event, circumstance, condition' &c., cp. Germ. *bedingen*, 'to make conditions, determine'. This is one of the words most highly generalized in meaning. **1. a** Any object that exists or is thought of as existing; whatever is conceived of as a separate object of thought; fact, idea; in the most general sense: *things of the intellect*; *the good things of life*; **b** a subject, topic, matter: *there's another thing I should like to speak to you about*; *he spoke of many things.* **2.** An inanimate object or what appears to be such: *to lose one's mind is to become a mere thing, devoid of life*; *what are those black things in the field?*; *not a thing to be seen anywhere.* **3.** (in pl.) **a** Personal property, belongings, baggage &c.: *I must collect my things at the station*; *take your things and go*; **b** specif., wearing apparel, clothes: *put on your things and come out for a walk.* **4.** (usually in pl.) **a** Circumstances, events, conditions of life &c.: *things are looking rather black for me*; *I want to think things over*; *I fear things are going wrong*; *I have many things to worry me*; Phrs. *that's a nice thing!*, ironic, expressing indignation; *it's a strange thing* (*that he doesn't write*); **b** (in sing.) action, aim: *the best thing* (*to do*); *the thing is* (*to say nothing for the moment*). **5. a** What is fitting or seemly: *it is not at all the thing to stare at people*; **b** what one wants, what is adapted to one's purpose: *a nice trout stream is the very thing for a holiday*; *a good thrashing would be the thing for him*; *just the thing*, exactly what is wanted. Phr. *not to look, feel, quite the thing*, to look, feel, unwell, out of sorts. **6.** (applied to persons) Expressing: **a** mild contempt, or indignation: *he's rather a stupid old thing*; *you're a horrid, mean, thing*; **b** affection, admiration (of women or children): *a dear little thing*; *a pretty little thing*; *a dear old thing*; **c** pity: *oh, poor thing!*; *the poor thing lost her husband in the War.*

thingamy, thingummy, n. [1. thíngumi; 2. þíŋəmi], also **thingumajig** [1. thíngumijig; 2. þíŋəmidžig], **thingumbob** [1. thíngumbòb; 2. þíŋəmbòb]. Used for name of person or thing, when these escape the memory momentarily; equivalent to *what's-his-name, what-d'you-call-it.*

think, vb. intrans. & trans. [1. thingk; 2. þiŋk]. The form is derived fr. O.E. *þynčan*, 'to seem', see **methinks**, but the meanings come fr. the O.E. cogn. *þenčan*, 'to think' &c.; O.S. *thunkian, thenkian*; O.H.G. *denkan*; Goth. *þugkjan, þagkjan*, w. sense of corresponding O.E. vbs.; **thank** is also cogn. Outside Gmc. cp. Lat. *tongēre*, 'to know' (rare), wh. must be cogn., but other suggested connexions are purely speculative. **A.** intrans. **1.** To exercise the mental faculties, esp. to judge, draw inferences; to reason, ponder, reflect: *take time to think*; *learn to think clearly*; *unfortunately, he never thinks.* **2.** *Think about* (a person or thing): **a** to allow the mind to dwell upon: *to think about one's home and friends*; **b** to turn over in the mind, reflect upon: *I must think about it and let you know my decision.* **3.** To hold an opinion, to surmise, believe, expect; often contrasted with *know*: *I'm not sure, but I rather think so*; *I don't think, I know.* **4.** *Think of*, **a** to reflect upon: *think of what I told you*; **b** to allow to enter the mind, have in mind, contemplate: *it is so dreadful that I don't want to think of it*; Phr. *I shouldn't think of* (*doing such a thing*), emphatic for *I would not do*; **c** to dwell upon, have vividly before one: *to think of old times*; **d** to hit upon, invent, discover: *to think of a way out of a difficulty*; *what genius first thought of cooking?*; **e** to have an opinion concerning: (followed by qualifying adv.) *to think highly of a man*; *I don't think much of him.* Phrs. *to* *think better of,* reverse one's opinions, alter one's intentions; *to think nothing of,* to disregard, attach no importance to. **5.** *Think on, upon,* (archaic) same as *think of.* **B.** trans. **1.** To conceive, imagine, have in mind: *to think evil; to think no harm.* **2.** To hold, esteem, consider, regard as: *I thought him a charming person; to think oneself all-important.* Phr. (archaic) *to think scorn of,* to despise. **3.** To surmise, believe, expect, that: *I don't think it will be very hot today; are you coming with us? I don't think I will.* **4.** To reduce to specified condition by thinking: *to think oneself into a fever.*

thinkable, adj. [1. thíngkabl; 2. þíŋkəbl]. Prec. & **-able.** That can be thought of; conceivable.

thinker, n. [1. thíngker; 2. þíŋkə]. See prec. & **-er.** One who thinks; a rational being; a philosopher.

thinking, vbl. n. & adj. [1. thíngking; 2. þíŋkiŋ]. **1.** n. The act of one who thinks; thought, reflection: *you had better do a little hard thinking* **2.** adj. Capable of thought, rational: *man is a thinking animal.*

thinly, adv. [1. thínli; 2. þínli]. **thin (I.)** & **-ly.** In a thin manner; sparingly; flimsily.

thinness, n. [1. thínnes; 2. þínnis]. See prec. & **-ness.** Quality, condition, of being thin.

thin-skinned, adj. (chiefly fig.) Sensitive; easily offended, touchy.

thio-, pref. Form used in compounds, representing Gk. *theîon,* 'fumes of sulphur', earlier **thweseion,* fr. base **dhwes-, *dhwos-,* &c., 'spirit, breath', see **theo-.** Containing sulphur; e.g. *thio-acid,* an acid produced by substituting sulphur for oxygen in an oxygen acid; *thionin,* the dark blue solution of a sulphur compound, used as a stain in microscopy.

third (I.), adj. [1. therd; 2. þɜ̄d]. O.E. *þridda,* M.E. *þridde;* cp. Du. *derde;* Goth. *þridja;* Lat. *tertius;* Gk. *trítos;* see **three. 1.** Coming after the second; specif. in *third person,* that expressed by pronouns *he, she, it, they.* **2.** Forming one of three equal parts or divisions: *the third part of a ton.*

third (II.), n., fr. prec. **1.** The person or thing coming next after the second in a series. **2.** Third part; one of three equal parts into which a thing or amount may be divided. **3.** (mus.) Interval of four semitones.

third degree, n. (chiefly U.S.A.) Severe examination or treatment of prisoner by police to extort an admission.

thirdly, adv. [1. thérdli; 2. þɜ̄dli]. **third (I.)** & **-ly.** In the third place.

third man, n. (cricket) Fielder placed rather deep on the offside between point and slip.

third party, n. (law) A party in a case other than the two principals; *third party risks,* (insurance) of damage to persons not mentioned in policy.

third-rate, adj. Third in order of merit or quality; hence, inferior, mediocre.

thirst (I.), n. [1. thërst; 2. þɜ̄st]. O.E. *þyrst,* M.E. *thurst, thirst;* O.S. *thurst;* O.H.G *darst,* Goth. *þaurstei;* cp. also Goth. *þaursus,* 'parched, dry'; cogn. w. Lat. *torrēre* for **tors-,* 'to parch, dry up', see **torrid;** Gk. *térsomai,* 'I become dry'. **1. a** (in living animals) Sensation caused by prolonged abstinence from drinking; natural craving for liquid; **b** (fig., of ground, plant life &c.) condition of extreme dryness caused by prolonged lack of moisture, condition in which the earth &c. rapidly absorbs moisture. **2. a** Craving for spiritual or intellectual nourishment: *a thirst for knowledge, for ghostly comfort* &c.; hence, **b** powerful desire, yearning, craving in general: *a thirst for pleasure, excitement* &c.

thirst (II.), vb. intrans., fr. prec. **1.** (absol., archaic) To experience thirst, to have a need of liquid in the system, to crave for something to drink: *I thirst,* now replaced by *I am thirsty.* **2.** *Thirst for:* **a** to experience a powerful craving for liquid refreshment: *to be thirsting for a drink;* **b** to crave, desire strongly and eagerly: *to thirst for information, for new sensations, for amusement* &c.; also (rarer, except in fig. sense) *thirst after; to thirst after new experiences.*

thirsty, adj. [1. thérsti; 2. þɜ̄sti]. O.E. *þyrstig;* see **thirst (I.)** & **-y. 1. a** Experiencing thirst, desiring to drink; **b** causing thirst: *haymaking is thirsty work.* **2.** Lacking moisture; parched, dried up: *thirsty soil.*

thirteen, adj. & n. [1. thertén; 2. þɜ̄tín]. O.E. *þrēotēne;* see **three** & **ten. 1.** adj. Cardinal numeral, one more than twelve. **2.** n. **a** The number greater by one than twelve, or by three than ten; **b** symbol representing this number.

thirteenth, adj. & n. [1. therténth; 2. þɜ̄tínþ]. New formation fr. prec. & **-th;** O.E. *þrēotēoþa.* **1.** adj. **a** Next in order after the twelfth; **b** being one of 13 equal parts. **2.** n. One of thirteen equal parts.

thirtieth, adj. & n. [1. thértieth; 2. þɜ̄tiiþ]. See next word & **-th. 1.** adj. **a** Next in order to twenty-ninth; **b** being, making, one of thirty equal parts. **2.** n. One of thirty equal parts.

thirty, adj. & n. [1. thérti; 2. þɜ̄ti]. O.E. *þrittig,* M.E. *þritty, thritty, therty* &c.; see **three** & **-ty. 1.** adj. Being the amount of three times ten. **2.** n. **a** A cardinal number, the sum of three tens; **b** symbol expressing this; **c** *the thirties,* (i.) that part of a century covering the time from the years thirty to thirty-nine of the century; (ii.) period of a person's life from the ages of thirty to thirty-nine: *just out of one's thirties.*

this, demons. adj. & pron. [1. dhis; 2. ðis]. O.E. *þis,* neut. sing.; cp. **the** & **that. 1.** adj. **a** Referring to, indicating, person or thing actually present, or near to, the speaker; often to something pointed to or touched when referred to in uttered speech; contrasted with *that;* **b** (i.) referring to present time or a current period: *this very moment; this week, year* &c.; (ii.) referring to a specified time, or if several periods or points of time are mentioned, to the last of these: *by this time* (that which I have just referred to) *the king was past all earthly help.* **2.** pron. **a** In senses corresponding to above; for *this one,* the thing here, near me, which I now point out to you: *the last house you had was charming, but this is not nearly so nice;* **b** often referring to facts, actions, circumstances, situations &c., just mentioned, and assumed to be uppermost in the minds of hearers, and immediate to them: *what's all this?* = this confusion &c.; *this will never do; you mustn't behave like this* (as you are behaving); *I don't like this at all,* what has just happened, is happening, or of which you have just told me.

thisness, n. [1. dhísnes; 2. ðísnis]. Prec. & **-ness.** (philosophical term) Quality of being this; feeling of present reality.

thistle, n. [1. thísl; 2. þísl]. O.E. *þistel;* cp. O.H.G. *distila;* O.N. *þistell.* One of various plants with purple flowers and prickly leaves and stalks. Phrs. *to grasp the thistle firmly,* to face, and deal with, difficulties, awkward situations &c. resolutely; *Order of the Thistle,* the Scottish order of knighthood.

thistle-down, n. Light substance from ripe seed-vessel of the thistle which floats in the air and carries the seeds far and wide.

thistly, adj. [1. thísli; 2. þísli]. **thistle** & **-ly. a** Resembling a thistle; prickly; **b** abounding in thistles.

thither, adv. & adj. [1. dhídher; 2. ðíðə]. O.E. *þider;* fr. demonstr. base as in **that, the, this,** & adv. suff. *-þra, -ō,* cp. Goth. *þaþrō,* 'thence', & see **hither. 1.** adv. **a** To that specified place; **b** to, towards, that direction, place, point, stage, result: *he has not yet joined the Church of Rome, but is tending thither.* **2.** adj. (rare) **a** Lying beyond, on the other side (from the speaker): *the thither side of the stream;* **b** being beyond, farther from a specified point of time: *on the thither side of 40.*

thlipsis, n. [1. thlípsis; 2. þlípsis]. Gk. *thlîpsis,* 'pressure; oppression, affliction'; cp. *thlíbein,* 'to press, crush', also *phlíbein,* the *th-* being prob. due to the influence of *thláō,* 'crush' &c.; the orig. form of *phlīb-* is **bhlīgʷ-,* whence also Lat. *flīgere,* 'strike', see **afflict, inflict;** Goth *bliggwan,* 'to strike, kill', is prob. not connected. (med.) External compression of blood-vessels.

tho'. See **though.**

thole (I.), vb. trans. [1. thōl; 2. þoul]. O.E. *þolian,* 'to endure, suffer', M.E. *tholien, thōlen;* O.S. *tholōn,* O.H.G. *dulēn;* Goth. *þulan;* fr. base **tel-, *tol-* &c., 'to bear'; see further under **tolerate.** (archaic or provinc.) **1.** To endure, bear, sustain, undergo. **2.** To tolerate, suffer, permit, to stand.

thole (II.), thole-pin, n. O.E. *þol,* 'rowlock'; cp. Dan. *tol,* 'a stopple, thole, pin'; Swed. *tull,* 'thole'; *tall,* 'pine tree'; O.N. *þollr,* 'fir tree'; prob. fr. the base **tu-,* 'to swell'; see **tumid.** Peg in the gunwale of a rowing-boat, serving as fulcrum for the oar; generally *thole-pin.*

Thomism, n. [1. tōmizm; 2. tóumizəm]. After St. Thomas Aquinas (1225–74). Doctrines of Thomas Aquinas and his followers in philosophy and theology.

Thomist, adj. & n. [1. tōmist; 2. tóumist]. See prec. & **-ist. 1.** adj. Also *Thomistic(al);* pertaining to the doctrines or followers of Thomism. **2.** n. Adherent of Thomism.

thong, n. [1. thong; 2. þoŋ]. O.E. *þwāng,* M.E. *þwōng;* cp. O.N. *þvengr,* 'thong, latchet'; perh. cogn. w. **twinge.** Narrow strip of leather, a strap, as used for a rein, or for fastening harness &c. together, as a lash to a whip &c.

thoracic, adj. [1. thōrásik; 2. þɔrǽsik]. *thorac-,* stem of **thorax,** & **-ic.** Connected with, situated on or in, the thorax.

thoraco-, pref. Form of **thorax** used in compounds, e.g. *thoracotomy,* (surg.) opening of the chest cavity.

thorax, n. [1. thōraks; 2. þɔ́ræks]. Gk. *thṓrax,* 'breastplate; the chest'; Boisacq connects w. Scrt. *dhāráyati,* 'he holds, supports'. **a** That part of the body of vertebrates between the neck and the abdomen, consisting of the ribs and breast-bone and the cavity enclosed by these; **b** the second or middle segment of the body of an insect.

thorite, n. [1. thórīt; 2. þɔ́rait], fr. name of *Thor,* anct. Scand. god, see **Thursday,** & **-ite.** Mineral of blackish-brown colour found in Norway, a silicate of thorium.

thorium, n. [1. thórium; 2. þɔ́riəm]. Mod. Lat., formed fr. prec. A rare metallic element, occurring in combination in thorite &c.; it is highly radio-active, and the oxide is used in making incandescent gas-mantles.

thorn, n. [1. thorn; 2. þɔ̄n]. O.E. *þorn,* 'a thorn, prickle; thorn tree', also *þyrne,* 'thorn tree'; O.S. *thorn;* Goth. *þaurnus;* cogn. w. O. Slav. *trŭnŭ;* Scrt. *tṛna-,* 'grass blade'. **1.** A spiky excrescence, spine, prickle, growing from the stems and boughs of certain trees; specif., one growing on a *thorn tree,* a rose, a bramble &c. Phrs. *no rose without a thorn,* all beautiful and pleasant things are liable to possess other, less desirable, qualities; pleasure is often attended with pain; *a thorn in one's side,* person or thing which is a constant source of annoyance; *thorn in the, one's, flesh,* a secret but disabling infirmity. **2.** The typical thorn-bearing tree, the hawthorn, or may tree. **3.** The Old English name for the letter þ.

thornbill, n. [1. thórnbil; 2. þɔ́nbil]. S. American humming-bird with long, pointed bill.

thornless, adj. [1. thórnles; 2. þɔ́nlis]. **thorn** & **-less.** Having no thorns.

thorny, adj. [1. thórni; 2. þɔ́ni]. See prec. & **-y. 1.** Plentifully furnished with thorns. **2.** (fig.) Difficult, arduous, painful: *a thorny subject,* one giving rise to differences of opinion and controversy. Phr. (*to tread*) *a thorny path,* pursue a difficult, arduous course of action.

thorough, adj. [1. thúro; 2. þárə]. O.E. *þuruh*, variant of *þurh*, see **through**. Complete, absolute, out-and-out, to the core, through and through: *a thorough blackguard*; *a thorough rest, holiday* &c.

thorough-bass, n. **1**. System of musical notation in which chords are expressed by figures placed beneath the bass part. **2**. Theory of harmony.

thorough-bred, adj. & n. **1**. adj. **a** (of animals) Pure-bred; specif., sprung entirely from ancestors who are in the official pedigrees of the particular species, e.g. in the Stud Book in case of horses; **b** (of human beings) having the characteristics of aristocratic lineage; hence high-spirited, of lofty and dauntless character and distinguished bearing. **2**. n. A thoroughbred animal or person.

thoroughfare, n. [1. thúrofār; 2. þárəfɛə]. A street or road through which traffic, on foot or wheels, may pass uninterruptedly, as contrasted with a cul-de-sac or a private road.

thorough-going, adj. Carried out completely, uncompromising, out-and-out: *thorough-going reforms*; *a thorough-going disciplinarian*.

thoroughly, adv. [1. thúroli; 2. þárəli]. **thorough** & **-ly**. In a thorough manner; completely: *a thoroughly bad man*; *to do a thing thoroughly*.

thoroughness, n. [1. thúrones; 2. þárənis]. See prec. & **-ness**. Quality of being thorough; completeness.

thorough-paced, adj. Originally of a horse, thoroughly trained in all its paces; hence thorough, out-and-out: *a thorough-paced rascal*.

thorp(e), n. [1. thorp; 2. þōp]. O.E. *þorp*, 'village'; O.S. *thorp*; O.N. *þorp*; cogn. w. Germ. *dorf*, 'village'; Goth. *þaurp*; cogn. w. Lith. *trobà*, 'house, building'; W. *tref*, 'hamlet'; some authorities regard this group of words as cogn. w. Lat. *trabs*, 'beam', see **trabeated**; others deny this, & connect *thorp* w. Lat. *turba*, 'crowd, mob', see **turbulent**. Obs. except in Place-Names, orig. in sense of 'village'; occurring also in forms *-thrup*, *-trup*; *-threp*, *-trip*; cp. O.E. variants *þrop*, *-þrep*.

those, demons. pron. [1. dhōz; 2. ðouz]. O.E. *þās*, nom. & acc. pl. of *þes* &c., 'this'. Pl. of **that**.

thou, pron. of 2nd pers. sing. [1. dhou; 2. ðau]. O.E. *þū*, M.E. *thū*, *thou*; O.S. *thu*; Goth. *þu*; cogn. w. Lat. *tū*; Gk. (Doric) *tu*, (Attic) *su*; O. Slav. *toi*. Now entirely replaced by *you*, & obs. except in dial., poet., Bib., & Liturgical Engl., or in prayers to God; formerly used by the Quakers, who, however, now use *thee* as nom. in addressing a single person.

though, tho', conj. & adv. [1. dhō; 2. ðou]. M.E. *þogh*, *though* &c., fr. O.N. *þō*; cp. O.S. *thōh*; Goth. *þauh*; O.H.G. *doh*; the O.E. cogn. *þēah*, *þēh* &c. wd. produce **they* or **thy* in Mod. Engl., & survives as *thei* &c. in M.E. **1**. Although, notwithstanding that: *he seems perfectly healthy, though his heart is said to be weak*; *he made a number of debts though he had a large income*. **2**. *As though*, as if: *I felt as though I should die of hunger*; *it looks as though he wasn't coming after all*. **3**. (archaic) Even if, notwithstanding that: *though I were starving, I would not ask a favour of him*. **4**. (introducing a statement) All the same, nevertheless, in spite of this: *I will come, though I don't expect to enjoy myself*; (also absol.) *I'll come and see you tomorrow—I can only stay a few minutes, though*.

thought (I.), n. [1. thawt; 2. þōt]. O.E. n. is *(ge)þeaht*; M.E. *þought* is due to association w. P.P. type of **think**. **1**. **a** Act or process of thinking; reflection, cogitation: *to spend whole hours in thought*; *absorbed in thought*; **b** chain of reasoning, series of consecutive reasonings and reflections: *a pity he does not put more thought into his books*; **c** body of ideas and opinions based on consecutive reasoning which are current at a given time, esp. about a given subject: *modern thought rejects many of the old theological dogmas*; *scientific thought in the 19th century*. **2**. Solicitude, care, as resulting from reflection: *to take thought for*, be anxious about; *I am grateful for your kind thought of me in sending back my umbrella*. **3**. **a** The result of thinking and reflection; an idea, conception: *a great and noble thought*; *a striking and original thought*; *my mind is full of dismal thoughts*; **b** an opinion, belief: *I have very few thoughts on the subject*. Phrs. *on second thoughts*, after thinking it over; *second thoughts are best*. **4**. A slight, trifling, amount: *he looked a thought more serious than when I saw him last*.

thought (II.), vb. O.E. *þōht(e)*, M.E. *þōught(e)*; Pret. & P.P. of **think**.

thoughtful, adj. [1. tháwtfool; 2. þōtful]. **thought** (I.) & **-ful**. **1**. (of persons and the mind) **a** Given to thought; reflective, contemplative; **b** serious, sad, pensive. **2**. **a** Expressing thought; full of thoughts: *a thoughtful lecture, book*; **b** characterized by thought: *a thoughtful ramble*. **3**. Solicitous, anxious, considerate (for others): *it was kind and thoughtful of you to call*.

thoughtfully, adv. Prec. & **-ly**. In a thoughtful manner.

thoughtfulness, n. See prec. & **-ness**. Quality, fact, of being thoughtful; solicitude.

thoughtless, adj. [1. tháwtles; 2. þōtlis]. **thought** (I.) & **-less**. **1**. Not given to thought; heedless, careless. **2**. Lacking consideration for others; inconsiderate.

thoughtlessly, adv. Prec. & **-ly**. In a thoughtless manner.

thoughtlessness, n. See prec. & **-ness**. Quality of being thoughtless.

thought-reader, n. One who reads a person's thoughts; esp. one who practises thought-reading.

thought-reading, n. The power or practice of reading people's thoughts by telepathy or thought-transference.

thought-transference, n. Telepathy.

thought-wave, n. Supposed telepathic vibration.

thousand, n. & adj. [1. thóuzand; 2. þáuzənd]. O.E. *þūsend*, M.E. *thūsend*; O.S. *thusind*; O.H.G. *tūsunt*; Goth. *þūsundi*; origin unexplained. **1**. n. **a** The number of 100 multiplied by 10: *many thousands of times*; Phr. *one in a thousand*, unique, extremely good, person or thing; **b** symbol for this number. **2**. adj. **a** Consisting of ten times one hundred; **b** used to express an indefinite number: *I have told you a thousand times not to do that*.

thousand-fold, adj. & adv. [1. thóuzan(d) fōld; 2. þáuzən(d) fould]. **1**. adj. A thousand times as much or as many. **2**. adv. A thousand times; to a thousand-fold degree.

thousandth, adj. & n. [1. thóuzanth; 2. þáuzənþ]. **1**. adj. **a** Next in order to the nine hundred and ninety-ninth in a series; **b** occurring after a large number: *I told him for the thousandth time*; **c** consisting of, being, one of a thousand equal parts. **2**. n. One of a thousand equal parts.

thraldom, n. [1. thráwldum; 2. þrōldəm]. Next word & **-dom**. State of being a thrall; servitude, bondage.

thrall, n. [1. thrawl; 2. þrōl]. L.O.E. *þrǣl*, fr. O.N. *þrǣll*, 'bondsman'; M.E. *þrall*; fr. **þrahil*, cp. O.E. *þrǣgan*; & Goth. *þragjan*, 'to run'; cogn. w. Gk. *trékhein*, 'to run', & perh., remotely, w. Lat. *trahere*, 'to draw'. **1**. **a** A slave, bondman; **b** (fig.) intellectual, moral, emotional, slave. **2**. Servitude, thraldom.

thrapple. See **thropple**.

thrash, see also **thresh**, vb. trans. & intrans. [1. thrash; 2. þræʃ]. O.E. *þerscan*, 'to beat, batter; thrash corn', M.E. *threschen*, O.H.G. *dreskan*; O.N. *þreskja*; Goth. *þriskan*. **A**. trans. **1**. **a** To beat, flog; **b** (colloq.) to surpass, outdo, win victory over in a contest. **2**. To beat the grain out of (wheat and other cereals), either with a flail or mechanically; also *thresh*. **3**. (fig.) *Thrash out*, to discuss thoroughly and elucidate; to clear up (a problem, difficulty &c.) by discussion. **B**. intrans. **1**. To thrash wheat &c. **2**. To move, toss, about violently.

thrasher, n. [1. thrásher; 2. þrǽʃə]. Prec. & **-er**. **1**. Person who, thing &c. which, thrashes; specif. **a** person who thrashes wheat &c.; **b** one who flogs (boys &c.); **c** agricultural implement for thrashing grain. **2**. A kind of large shark with long, whip-like tail; also called *fox-shark*.

thrasonical, adj. [1. thrāsónikl; 2. þreisɔ́nikl], fr. Gk. *Thrásōn*, name of a braggart, fr. *thrasús*, 'over-bold', & **-ic** & **-al**; *thrasús* is cogn. w. Gk. *thársos*, *thrásos*, 'courage, rashness'; cp. Scrt. *dhárṣati*, 'to dare'; & Goth. *(ga-)dars*, 'dared', Pret. of *daursan*, q.v. under **dare**. Boastful.

thread (I.), n. [1. thred; 2. þred]. O.E. *þrǣd*, M.E. *thrēd(e)*; O.H.G. *drāt*; fr. same base as O.E. *þrāwan*, 'to twist'; see **throw** (I.). **1**. A very fine cord of twisted fibres of flax, cotton, silk &c., used for sewing. **2**. A very fine line or filament of any substance; a fibre: *gold thread*; *a thread of light*. Phrs. *the thread of life*; *to hang by a thread*, to be in a precarious, dangerous, state or position. **3**. Spiral groove with sharp edges; cut in a screw. **4**. Consecutive, connected, series of thoughts, train of reasoning; sequence of ideas, statements: *the thread of a narrative, discourse* &c.

thread (II.), vb. trans., fr. prec. **1**. To put (a thread) through the eye of: *to thread a needle*. **2**. To put upon a thread; to string: *to thread beads*. **3**. **a** To make one's way along, cautiously, deliberately, or through difficulties and intricacies: *to thread the paths of a wood*; **b** to pick out, select, and traverse with care: *to thread one's way*.

threadbare, adj. [1. thrédbār; 2. þrédbɛə]. **1**. **a** (of fabric, clothes &c.) Worn down, rubbed by wear, so that the nap or upper surface is worn off and the thread of woof becomes visible; **b** (of persons) wearing threadbare garments; shabby. **2**. (fig.) Well worn, lacking novelty; hackneyed: *threadbare arguments, jokes* &c.

threader, n. [1. thréder; 2. prédə]. **thread** (II.) & **-er**. Specif., machine for putting thread on screws.

threadlike, adj. [1. thrédlīk; 2. þrédlaik]. **thread** (I.) & **-like**. Filamentous; resembling a fine thread.

threadworm, n. [1. thrédwërm; 2. þrédwɜ̄m]. Minute, threadlike, intestinal worm.

thready, adj. [1. thrédi; 2. þrédi]. **thread** (I.) & **-y**. **a** Composed of, covered with, thread; **b** resembling a thread in fineness.

threat, n. [1. thret; 2. þret]. O.E. *þrēat*, 'crowd, troop; violence, punishment; threat'; cp. also O.E. *þrēatian*, 'to afflict, threaten, compel by threats'; O.H.G. *(ir)driozan*; Goth. *(us)þriutan*, 'to vex'; cogn. w. Lat. *trūdere*, 'to thrust'; O. Slav. *truditi*, 'to afflict', & *trudŭ*, 'oppression'; see also words ending in *-trude*, as **intrude, extrude** &c., & see **thrust**. **1**. Statement of intention to injure, punish, cause pain to &c.; menace: *to utter threats of violence, revenge* &c. **2**. Situation, circumstance, set of conditions, which seems to make probable the occurrence of something undesired; menace: *a threat of rain, drought* &c.

threaten, vb. trans. & intrans. [1. thrétn; 2. þrétn]. O.E. *þrēatnian*, 'to urge, compel'; see prec. **A**. trans. **1**. To utter a threat to (a person), state intention of injuring, punishing &c.; also *threaten with*, to express intention of hurting, punishing &c. in a specified way: *he was threatened with imprisonment if he should ever transgress in the same way again*. **2**. To state intention to inflict: *to threaten immediate retribution upon evil-doers*. **3**. To present appearance, manifest a probability, of immanent occurrence, approach &c.; to menace: *the look of the sky threatens rain*; *danger and disaster threaten us on every side*. **B**. intrans. **1**. To utter threats: *Sir, do you mean to threaten?* **2**. To appear likely to occur, approach &c.: *if danger threatens, it* *is all the more important to keep an unmoved mind.*

threatening, adj. [1. thrétning; 2. þrétniŋ]. **a** Menacing, expressing threats; **b** portending, indicating, disaster or some unwished-for occurrence: *a threatening sky.*

three, adj. & n. [1. thrē; 2. þrī]. O.E. *þrēo*, fem., *þrī*, masc., O.S. *thria, threa*; O.H.G. *drī*; Goth. *þreis*; Lat. *trēs, tria*; Gk. *treîs, tria*; Scrt. *tri.* **1.** adj. One more than two. Phr. *the three R's*, reading, writing, and arithmetic. **2.** n. **a** The number greater by one than two; **b** symbol representing this number. Phr. *rule of three*, in arithmetic, a sum in simple proportion.

three-colour process, n. Method or process of printing in colours, by use of three blocks, yellow, red, and blue, produced by photography.

three-cornered, adj. Having three corners or angles; triangular.

three-decker, n. **1.** Old-fashioned ship with three decks one above another. **2.** Obsolete form of pulpit having three floors.

threefold, adj. & adv. [1. thréfōld; 2. þrífould]. **a** adj. Thrice repeated; triple; **b** adv., triply.

three-halfpence, n. [1. thrē hā́pens; 2. þrī héipəns]. **a** The sum of a penny halfpenny; **b** obsolete coin worth this amount.

three-legged race, n. [1. thrē légd, léged, rās; 2. þrī légd, légid, reis]. Race in which those taking part are linked together in pairs, in such a way that the right leg of one person is tied to the left leg of another, so that they must move at one and the same time.

three-master, n. Sailing-ship with three masts.

threepence, n. [1. thrépens, thrípens; 2. þrépəns, þrípəns]. The sum of three pennies considered as a monetary unit.

threepenny-bit, n. [1. thrépeni, thrípeni, bít; 2. þrépəni, þrípəni, bít]. The smallest English silver coin, of the value of three pence.

three-per-cents, n. British Government bonds yielding 3% interest.

three-ply, adj. Having, woven with, three strands (of thread, yarn &c.); also *three-ply wood*, of three thin plates or layers of wood glued together with grain arranged transversely.

three-quarter, n. One of the four backs in Rugby football, playing between the half-backs and the full-back.

threescore, n. [1. thréskōr; 2. þrískɔ́]. Three times twenty; sixty; *threescore years*, 60 years.

threesome, n. [1. thrésum; 2. þrísəm]. Game of golf played by three persons.

thremmatology, n. [1. thrèmatóloji; 2. þrèmətɔ́lədži], fr. Gk. *thremmat-*, stem of *thrémma*, 'nurseling', & **-logy**; *thrémma* is connected w. vb. *tréphein*, 'to fatten, nourish', for **dhrebh-*, see **trophic** & cp. **thrombosis.** The science and art of breeding domestic animals.

threnetic(al), adj. [1. thrēnétik(l); 2. þrīnétik(l)]. Gk. *thrēnētikós*, fr. *thrēnos*, 'a dirge', fr. a variant of base **dhrew-* as in *thréomai*, 'I shout'; cp. Goth. *drunjus*, 'droning sound'; connected w. O.E. *drān*, see **drone (I.)**; cp. also O.E. *drēam*, 'revelry, joy', q.v. under **dream (I.)**. Mournful; of the nature of a dirge or lamentation.

threnode, also **threnody**, n. [1. thrḗnōd, thrḗnōdi; 2. þrínoud, þrínoudi]. Gk. *thrēnōidía*, fr. *thrēnos*, 'dirge', see prec. & **ode.** Funeral song, dirge, chant of lamentation.

threnodial, adj. [1. thrēnṓdial; 2. þrīnóudiəl]. Prec. & **-al.** Threnodic.

threnodic, adj. [1. thrēnṓdik; 2. þrīnóudik]. **threnode** & **-ic.** Pertaining to a threnody.

threnodist, n. [1. thrḗnōdist; 2. þrínoudist]. **threnode** & **-ist.** One who sings or composes a threnody.

threnody, n. [1. thrḗnōdi; 2. þrínoudi]. Threnode.

threpsology, n. [1. threpsóloji; 2. þrepsɔ́lədži]. Gk. *thrépsis*, 'nourishment', see **thremmatology** & **trophic**, & **-logy**. (med.) Theory of diet; treatise on this.

thresh, vb. trans. & intrans. [1. thresh; 2. þreʃ]. See **thrash.** Same as **thrash**; more commonly used of beating grain; (also fig.) *thresh out*, see *thrash out.*

thresher, n. [1. thrésher; 2. þréʃə]. Prec. & **-er.** Thrasher.

threshold, n. [1. thréshōld; 2. þréʃould]. O.E. *þerscold, -wold*, M.E. *threshwold*; cp. O.N. *þreskjöldr*; fr. base *þersc-*, see **thrash.** **1.** Stone or plank immediately below a door; hence, entrance, to a building, house, room. **2.** (fig.) The entrance to, starting-point of something: *on the threshold of life*; *the threshold of new experiences, of a new order.* **3.** (psychol.) Usually *threshold of consciousness*, translating German *schwelle*, the lowest stage at which sensation becomes noticeable, the limen; cp. *subliminal.*

threw, vb. [1. thrōō; 2. þrū]. O.E. *þrēow*; M.E. *þrēw*; Pret. of **throw.**

thrice, adv. [1. thrīs; 2. þrais]. M.E. *thrīes*, fr. O.E. *þriga, þriwa*, 'three times', & genit. suff., used adverbially. See **three.** **1.** Three times. **2.** To a threefold degree; hence, merely as intensive, very much, thoroughly, fully: *thrice blessed, thrice happy.*

thrift, n. [1. thrift; 2. þrift], fr. O.N. *þrift*, 'prosperity'; connected w. **thrive.** **1.** Frugality; good, economical management; reverse of *extravagance, waste.* **2.** Genus of plant, *Statice*, esp. the sea-pink.

thriftily, adv. [1. thríftili; 2. þríftili]. **thrifty** & **-ly.** In a thrifty, careful manner; economically.

thriftiness, n. [1. thríftines; 2. þríftinis]. See prec. & **-ness.** Quality of being thrifty.

thriftless, adj. [1. thríftles; 2. þríftlis]. Wasteful, extravagant.

thrifty, adj. [1. thrífti; 2. þrífti]. **thrift** & **-y.** **a** Practising thrift; **b** exhibiting, betokening, thrift.

thrill (I.), vb. trans. & intrans. [1. thril; 2. þril]. O.E. *þȳr(e)lian*, 'to pierce, perforate', M.E. *thirlen, thrillen*; still used in sense of 'pierce' by Spenser; cp. *þȳrel*, 'hole', fr. *þurh*, 'through'; see **through (I.)**. **1.** trans. To cause profound emotional excitement in; to touch, cause glow of excitement in, stir, excite, penetrate deeply: *great actors thrill an audience to the point of pain*; *our hearts were thrilled by tales of heroism.* **2.** intrans. **a** To feel great emotional excitement; to be deeply stirred; to glow with enthusiasm, joy, indignation or the like; **b** to vibrate, tremble, tingle: *his voice thrilled through the hall.*

thrill (II.), n., fr. prec. Sensation of being thrilled; intense emotional stirring; a throb, glow: *a thrill of anticipation, of disgust, of terror* &c.

thriller, n. [1. thríler; 2. þrílə]. **thrill (I.)** & **-er.** One who, that which, thrills; specif., a highly sensational and exciting novel or play.

thrilling, adj. [1. thríling; 2. þríliŋ], fr. Pres. Part of **thrill (I.)**. **a** Causing a thrill; stirring, exciting: *thrilling news*; **b** vibrant, penetrating: *a thrilling voice.*

thrips, n. [1. thrips; 2. þrips]. Gk., 'woodworm'; perh. having as fundamental meaning 'the borer', & fr. same base as O.E. *drīfan*, q.v. under **drive (I.)**. Name of various small insects which injure plants by sucking the vital juices.

thrive, vb. intrans. [1. thrīv; 2. þraiv]. M.E. *thrīven*, fr. O.N. *þrífa*, 'to grasp', prob. fr. reflex. *þrifask*, 'to grasp oneself', hence 'to have oneself well in hand'. See also **thrift.** **1.** (of persons and businesses) To prosper, flourish, do well, be successful; specif., as a result of industry and thrift; (also in gen. sense) to flourish, grow strong: *wickedness of all kinds thrives in big cities.* **2.** (of living organisms) To prosper in health, grow fat and strong; to develop healthily and luxuriantly: *children thrive in good air*; *roses thrive in a heavy soil.*

thriven, vb. [1. thríven; 2. þrív(ə)n]. M.E. *þriven*; P.P. of **thrive.**

thriving, adj. [1. thrīving; 2. þráiviŋ], fr. Pres. Part. of **thrive.** Prosperous, flourishing, successful.

throat (I.), n. [1. thrōt; 2. þrout]. O.E. *þrote*, M.E. *thrōte*; cp. O.H.G. *drozza*, 'throat', Mod. Germ. *drossel*; prob. cogn. w. Du. *strot(e)*, 'throat'. **1. a** The passage from the back of the mouth to the stomach and the lungs; gullet, windpipe: *sore throat*, inflamed condition of the lining of the throat; Phrs. *to stick in one's throat*, of words &c., (i.) to be difficult of utterance; (ii.) to be uttered with reluctance; (iii.) (of circumstances, actions &c.) to be repugnant to; *to ram, thrust, down another's throat*, force to accept against his will; **b** the external, front part of the neck, which covers the jugular vein: *to cut one's throat*, to commit suicide by severing the jugular vein, (also fig.) to adopt a dangerous or destructive course of action; *to take, seize, by the throat*, to strangle, throttle. **2.** A constricted passage, neck, as the narrowed part of a river, valley, pass &c.; the orifice of a vase &c.; specif. (archit.) a groove, channel, in or under the surface of a projection.

throat (II.), vb. trans., fr. prec. (archit., rare) To provide with a throat or groove.

-throated, adj. [1. thrṓted; 2. þróutid]. Having a throat of specified kind: *red-throated*; *brazen-throated* &c.

throatiness, n. [1. thrṓtines; 2. þróutinis]. See next word & **-ness.** Quality of being throaty.

throaty, adj. [1. thrṓti; 2. þróuti]. **throat (I.)** & **-y.** **1.** (of the voice) Sounding as though produced in the back of the throat; muffled, not clear. **2.** (of persons) Having a sore, or sensitive throat; having a throaty voice.

throb, vb. intrans. & n. [1. throb; 2. þrɔb]. M.E. *throbben*; origin doubtful; possibly cogn. w. Lat. *trepidus*, 'agitated, anxious', & *trepidāre*, 'to bustle anxiously about; to move noisily and irregularly'; see **trepidation.** **1.** vb. **a** To beat, pulsate (as the heart, or a pulse): *his heart had ceased to throb*, i.e. he was dead; **b** to beat, palpitate, with abnormal rapidity or violence, as the heart &c., under stress of strong exertion or emotion: *his temples throbbed.* **2.** n. **a** A beat, pulsation, palpitation (of the heart &c.); **b** (fig.) a thrill, qualm.

throe, n. [1. thrō; 2. þrou]. O.E. *þrawu*, 'pain, punishment, affliction'; M.E. *throwe*, perh. influenced by the gradational variants O.E., M.E. *þrowung*, 'affliction', *þrōwian*, 'to suffer'; cp. O.N. *þrā*, 'pain, throe'. Great pain, anguish, access of pain, pang: *the throes of toothache, childbirth.* Phrs. *in the throes of*, in very general sense, struggling with, having come to grips with &c.: *in the throes of a spring-cleaning, a move* &c.

thrombosis, n. [1. thrombṓsis; 2. þrɔmbóusis]. Gk. *thrómbōsis*, 'clot, coagulation'; cp. Gk. *tróphis*, 'fat, well-nourished'; see **trophic** & cp. **thremmatology.** Stoppage of a blood-vessel by a clot.

throne (I.), n. [1. thrōn; 2. þroun]. Lat. *thronus*, fr. Gk. *thrónos*, 'seat, chair; chair of state, throne; teacher's chair'; cp. also *thrânos*, 'a bench', *thrênus*, 'footstool'; cogn. w. Scrt. *dhāráyati*, 'to support'; *dhárman-*, 'prop'; Lat. *firmus*, 'fast, firm', see **firm (I.)**. **1.** Chair, seat of state; specif. **a** official seat with canopy, occupied on ceremonial occasions by a king or other sovereign ruler; **b** official seat of archbishop or bishop, in a cathedral. **2. a** Royal power and authority: *loyalty to the king's throne and person*; **b** the king, or other sovereign ruler of a State: *it is rare in England that the throne is publicly attacked.* **3.** Superior order in the hierarchy of angels: '*Thrones, dominations, princedoms, virtues, powers*' (Milton, 'P. L.' v. 601).

throne (II.), vb. trans. & intrans., fr. prec. **1.** trans. **a** To place upon a throne, to enthrone; **b** (fig.) to accord a position of honour and dignity to; to esteem, venerate. **2.** intrans. (rare, lit. and fig.) To occupy a throne or position of honour.

throneless, adj. [1. thrónles; 2. þróunlis]. **throne** (I.) & **-less**. Without a throne; used of a deposed monarch.

throng, n. & vb. intrans. & trans. [1. throng; 2. þroŋ]. O.E. (ġe)*þrang*, 'crowd, tumult'; cp. *þringan*, 'to press on, crowd; to afflict; to throng'; O.S. *thringan*; Goth. *þreihan*, fr. **þriŋχan*, 'to crowd round, press upon'. Etymol. doubtful; prob. not connected w. Lat. *truncus*, 'mutilated', see **truncate**. **1.** n. A crowd, a press of people; a multitude, host. **2.** vb. **a** intrans. To form, gather, into a throng; to crowd: *multitudes thronged to hear the new preacher*; **b** trans., to press, crowd into; to fill with a throng: *to throng the churches* &c.; (rarely) to crowd upon, press.

thropple, thrapple, n. [1. thrópl, thrápl; 2. þrópl, prǽpl], fr. O.E. *protbolla*, 'gullet, windpipe'; see **throat** & **boll**. (provinc. or rare) The throat.

throstle, n. [1. thrósl; 2. þrósl]. O.E. *þrostle*, M.E. *þrostel*; cp. Germ. *drossel* & O.N. *þrōstr*; cogn. w. Lat. *turdus*, *turda*, 'thrush', for *(*s*)*tṛzdos*; cp. Lith. *strãzdas*, 'thrush'; Gk. *strouthós*, 'sparrow'; **-le** is dimin.; see also **thrush** (I.). **1.** The common song-thrush, mavis, *Turdus musicus*. **2.** Machine for spinning wool, cotton &c.; so called from the noise it makes.

throttle (I.), n. [1. thrótl; 2. þrótl]. Dimin. of **throat** (I.). **1.** (colloq.) The throat. **2.** Valve in a machine which regulates flow of steam, gas &c.

throttle (II.), vb. trans., fr. prec. **1.** To impede breathing of, choke, by compressing the wind-pipe; to strangle. **2.** (fig.) To suppress, check: *to throttle discussion*; *to throttle trade* &c. **3.** (mechan.) To reduce flow of steam &c. in an engine or other machine; to lessen the speed in this way.

through (I.), prep. [1. thrōō; 2. þrū]. O.E. *þurh*, M.E. *thurgh, thurugh* &c.; O.S. *thurh*; O.H.G. *durh*; Goth. *þairh*; see **thorough**, & **thrill** (I.), also *-tril* in **nostril**. **1.** From one end to the other; traversing entire length, breadth, or depth; entering at one side or surface and coming out at opposite side &c.; penetrating the outer surface: *to get a bullet through the head*; *a wound passing through the cheek*; *to hammer a nail through the lid of a box*. **2.** Across; passing over the whole surface or extent of: *to travel through a country, continent* &c. **3. a** Along, surrounded by, moving in the midst of: *flying through the air*; *sailing through the water*; *walking through a wood*; **b** (also in non-material sense) *to pass, come, through dangers, tribulations, anxieties* &c. **4.** By way of; expressing penetration, traversing, of an intervening medium, opening, channel &c.: *to look through a window, through the keyhole* &c.; *hear sounds through a thin wall*; *to look through a telescope, listen through an ear-trumpet*. Phrs. *one can't see through a brick wall*, can't do what is impossible; (also fig.) *to see through a man, his character, a plot, scheme* &c., to detect faults and flaws in; not to be deceived by. **5.** Indicating channel, medium: '*But looks through Nature up to Nature's God*' (Pope, 'Ess. on Man', iv. 332). **6.** Expressing duration of time; during the whole of a specified period: *he won't last through the night*; *to stay through the autumn*; *to sit through a long sermon*. **7.** By agency of, by means of; by reason of; on account of: *I succeeded chiefly through your help*; *all his sorrows arose through the conduct of his son*.

through (II.), adv. See prec. **1.** From end to end, from side to side, so as to traverse entire extent from one end to the other: *to shoot, pierce, something through*. **2. a** From beginning to end: *to sing a song through*; *to read a book through*; **b** (of time) for the whole extent or duration of: *to sleep the whole night through*. **3.** Expressing completion; to the very end: *to carry one's plans through*; *to see a thing through*; *through and through*, in the whole substance, in all its parts, completely: *good sound material through and through*; *an honest man through and through*. Phr. *to be through with*, to have done with; to have completed, be quit of.

through (III.), adj. See prec. **1.** Going, passing, extending, through: *a through passage, way, channel*. **2.** Travelling direct from one place, station, or port, to another: *a through train, carriage, coach, boat*.

throughly, adv. [1. thrōōli; 2. þrūli]. Prec. & **-ly**. (obs. and liturg. and Bib.) Completely, thoroughly: '*Wash me throughly from my wickedness*' (Psalm li. 2).

throughout, prep. & adv. [1. thrōōóut; 2. þrū-áut]. **1.** prep. **a** Through every part of: *throughout the house*; **b** for whole duration of: *throughout one's life, the night, the war* &c. **2.** adv. **a** In, through, every part of; right through; in every particular: *this peach is ripe throughout*; *an honest man throughout*; **b** during the whole time: *it was a tedious discourse, but he sat perfectly still throughout*.

throve, vb. [1. thrōv; 2. þrouv]. Pret. of **thrive**, fr. O.N. *þrīfa*; M.E. *þrōf*, on the anal. of **drove** (I.) &c. Cp. the O.N. Pret. *þreif*, wh. is etymologically equiv. to the unrecorded O.E. **þrāf*, wh. wd. have become M.E. *þrōf*.

throw (I.), vb. trans. & intrans. [1. thrō; 2. þrou]. O.E. *þrāwan*, trans., 'to twist'; intrans., 'to revolve'; M.E. *þrōwen*; cogn. w. Lat. *terere*, 'to rub, wear away', see **termite** & **trite**; Gk. *terein*, 'to bore, turn', & *teirein*, 'to rub, wear, away', see **teredo**. **A.** trans. **1. a** To cause to fly through the air by a forcible movement, or jerk of the arm; to hurl, cast, fling, chuck: *to throw stones*; *to throw a ball*; *to throw a bone to a dog*; Phrs. (fig.) *to throw stones at*, to asperse, make imputations against; *to throw dust in the eyes of*, to hoodwink, deceive; *to throw a fly* (in fishing), make a cast; *to throw dice*, to fling them out upon the table; *to throw cold water on* (*a plan* &c.), to discourage (a person) in, make little of; **b** of other rapid movements, to cast &c.: *to throw a cloak round one*; **c** to upset (an opponent) in wrestling. **2.** To cast, propel, by mechanical means: *a big gun throws a heavy shell*; *a pump throws water*. **3. a** To direct, concentrate; to cause to appear: *to throw an angry, hasty, glance at*; *to throw a light on the scene*; *to throw a gloom on the proceedings*; **b** to cast: *to throw a veil of mystery over*; *the trees throw long shadows in the moonlight*. **4.** (of a horse) To dislodge from the saddle: *a horse that throws its rider*. **5.** To cast off, cast, slough: *a snake throws its old skin*. **6.** (of animals) To bring forth, give birth to: *a cow throws its calf, a mare its foal*. **7.** To bring into a specified condition, esp. suddenly, and by violent means: *to throw into confusion, into a state of agitation, into a fever* &c. **8.** To wind, twist (silk). **B.** intrans. To execute, carry out the act or process of throwing: *a long field must be able to throw*; *the fast bowler was thought by some to throw* (not bowl fairly). **C.** Followed by prepositions or adverbs. *Throw about*, trans., to fling in various directions, to scatter; also in special uses: *to throw one's arms about*, wave them; *to throw money about*, squander it. *Throw away*, trans., to waste, part with unwisely, sacrifice, lose through one's own act: *to throw money away*; *to throw away one's advantages*. *Throw back*, intrans., to reproduce, revert to the type of, a remote ancestor. *Throw down*, trans., **a** to overthrow, upset, overturn, cast down on the ground; pull down; Phr. *to throw down the gauntlet, glove*, to utter a challenge, to defy; **b** *throw oneself down*, to lie down with a sudden, forcible movement. *Throw in*, trans., to give over and above, in addition to what is bargained for, in return for an agreed price. *Throw off*, **1.** trans., **a** to fling aside, cast off, remove hastily: *to throw off one's clothes*; *to throw off one's disguise*; **b** to discard, repudiate, get rid of: *to throw off an acquaintance*; **c** to shake off, get rid of, recover from: *to throw off a cold, an illness* &c.; **d** to compose, utter, easily, without effort: *to throw off brilliant sayings, an epigram* &c.; **2.** intrans., to make a start with hounds at a hunt. *Throw* (*oneself*) *on, upon*, to trust to, commit oneself to; in Phr. *to throw oneself* (*up*)*on the mercy of*. *Throw open*, trans., **a** to open widely and suddenly: *to throw open a door*; Phr. *to throw open the door to* (*abuses* &c.), run the risk of, render possible; **b** to make widely accessible, permit entrance to: *to throw open the public parks on Sundays*; *to throw open one's house to all and sundry*. *Throw out*, trans., **a** to fling, cast out; specif., to eject, turn out: *to throw a rowdy out of a meeting*; **b** to reject, refuse to pass: *to throw out a bill in Parliament*; **c** to utter lightly and casually in passing: *to throw out a suggestion, a hint* &c.; **d** to build on; extend (a building) into: *to throw out a new wing, a bay window* &c. *Throw over*, trans., to abandon, give up: *to throw over a friend, a plan*; also *throw overboard*. *Throw up*, trans., **a** to toss into the air; Phrs. *to throw up the sponge*, acknowledge defeat, abandon the struggle; *to throw up a window*, lift the lower sash vigorously; **b** to pitch (a ball) in to a particular point, e.g. in cricket: *to throw the ball up to the wicket-keeper*; **c** to vomit, eject from the stomach.

throw (II.), n., fr. prec. Act or process of throwing something (in various special senses); **a** *a good, a straight, throw* (at cricket); *a throw of the hammer*; Phr. *a stone's throw*, a very short distance; **b** act of casting a fishing line; **c** act of casting dice: *it's your throw*; **d** act, manner, of throwing an opponent in wrestling.

throw-back, n. An individual of any species which reverts physically or mentally to an ancestral type.

thrower, n. [1. thrṓer; 2. þróuə]. **throw** (I.) & **-er**. One that throws; specific uses: **a** one who twists silk; a throwster; **b** person who shapes vessels on a potter's wheel.

thrown, vb. [1. thrōn; 2. þroun]. P.P. of **throw** (I.); O.E. (*ġe*)*þrāwen*; M.E. *þrōwen*.

throw-off, n. The start of a hunt.

throwster, n. [1. thrṓster; 2. þróustə]. **throw** (I.) & **-ster**. One who twists silk.

thrum (I.), n. & vb. trans. [1. thrum; 2. þram]. M.E., fr. O.N. *þrōmr*, 'edge, brim'; cogn. w. Lat. **terminus**. **1.** n. **a** The end of threads of warp on a loom after the web is cut; **b** any loose thread or yarn. **2.** vb. To cover with, provide with, thrums or fringe.

thrum (II.), vb. intrans. & trans. O.N. *þrumma*, 'to rattle'; prob. imitative in origin. **1.** intrans. To play carelessly, idly, noisily, or incorrectly (on a musical instrument); to strum; also *thrum on*. **2.** trans. To play (an instrument) badly, carelessly, incorrectly.

thrum-eyed, adj. (bot.) Having the anthers exserted, and visible at the throat of the corolla; contrasted with *pin-eyed*.

thrumming, n. [1. thrúming; 2. þrámiŋ]. **thrum** (I.) & **-ing**. **a** Act of, noise made by, one who thrums; **b** recurring beat, and accompanying sound, made by an engine when run.

thrush (I.), n. [1. thrush; 2. þraʃ]. O.E. *þrysċe*; see **throstle**. One of several varieties of medium-sized singing birds, genus *Turdus*, with darkish plumage save on throat and belly, which are pale with dark spots; esp. the song thrush, *T. musicus*, and the missel-thrush, *T. viscivorus*.

thrush (II.), n. Cp. Dan. *trōske*; cogn. w. O.E. *þyrre*, 'dry', & *þyrst*; see **thirst** (I.) & **torrid**. (med.) Inflammatory affection of mouth and throat, occurring most frequently in young children.

thrust (I.), vb. trans. & intrans. [1. thrust; 2. þrast]. M.E. *thrusten*, fr. O.N. *þrȳsta*; cogn. w. Lat. *trūdere*, 'to push, thrust'; see *-trude* in **extrude**, **intrude** &c., & cp. **threat**. **A.** trans. **1.** To push, shove, with a sudden, violent action: *to thrust a sword, a bayonet, a knife* &c., *into, or through, a body*; *to thrust one's fist in a person's face*; *he thrust his face into, close to, mine*; *to thrust a chair forward*; *to thrust one's hands into one's pockets, one's feet into a pair of slippers*; *thrust on*, put on with sudden, impulsive movement. Phrs. *to thrust one's way* (*through a crowd* &c.), to advance by pushing, and thrusting obstacles aside; *thrust one's nose into* (*other people's affairs* &c.), interfere in, or with, uninvited. **2.** (reflex.) *Thrust oneself*, in various Phrs.: *to thrust oneself into* (*a good place* &c.), force one's way there; *thrust oneself forward*, (fig.) deliberately make oneself conspicuous, obtrude oneself; *thrust oneself into the society of*, obtrude oneself, force oneself into, intrude. **B.** intrans. **1.** To make a thrust *at* (person &c.). **2.** To force oneself *through, past* &c.

thrust (**II.**), n., fr. prec. **1.** Act of thrusting; **a** sudden, violent push: *a thrust with the elbow*; **b** onset with a pointed weapon; a lunge: *a thrust with a sword*; blow delivered in this way: *a sword thrust.* **2.** (archit.) Outward pressure (e.g. against a wall) exerted by a weight from above. **3.** (min.) Breakdown of the roof of a gallery under weight from above.

thruster, n. [1. thrúster; 2. þrástə]. **thrust** (**I.**) & **-er.** Person who rides too close to, or over, hounds when hunting.

thud, n. & vb. intrans. [1. thud; 2. þad]. Cp. O.E. *þyddan*, 'to strike, thrust'. **1.** n. Dull sound, as of a heavy, solid, but not very hard, body falling from a height upon the ground. **2.** vb. **a** To make the sound of a thud; **b** to fall with a thud; also *thud down.*

thug, n. [1. thug; 2. þag]. Hind. *ṭhag*, 'a deceiver, a robber'; Scrt. *sthaga*, 'a swindler'. **1.** Member of a fraternity of assassins and robbers in Northern India, suppressed in the late thirties of the 19th cent., whose method was to strangle their victims with a bowstring or a strip of linen, to plunder, and then bury, the body. **2.** An assassin, a ruffian.

thuggee, n. [1. thúgē; 2. þágī]. Hind. *ṭhagī*, 'the act of a thug'. System of murder by strangling as carried out by thugs.

thuggery, thuggism, n. [1. thúgeri, thúgizm; 2. þágəri, þágizəm]. **thug** & **-ery**, or **-ism.** Thuggee; ruffianism.

thuja, n. [1. thūya; 2. þjūjə]. Gk. *thuía*, Afr. tree with scented wood. The arbor vitae.

Thule, n. [1. thūlē; 2. þjūlī]. Name given by ancient geographers to the most northern of known lands, now only in Phr. *ultima Thule*, q.v. under **ultima.**

thumb, n. & vb. trans. [1. thum; 2. þam]. O.E. *þūma*, M.E. *þūme, thoumbe* &c.; O.H.G. *dūmo*, Mod. Germ. *daumen*; O.N. *þūmall*; fr. base ***tūm-**, 'to swell'; see **tumid**; cp. also **thimble. 1.** n. **a** The short, thick digit of the hand, opposable to the fingers; Phrs. *his fingers are all thumbs*, said of a clumsy person lacking manual dexterity; *rule of thumb*, any rough-and-ready, practical way of doing anything, a method not based on principles; *under the thumb of*, in power of; ruled, influenced, by; **b** the corresponding digit of animals; **c** the division of a glove which covers the thumb. **2.** vb. To wear, make dirty (the pages of a book &c.), by constant handling; to make thumb-marks upon.

thumb-mark, n. Dirty mark made by a person's thumb.

thumb-nut, n. One with a flattened top so that it can be turned by the thumb.

thumb-screw, n. Ancient instrument of torture, the functions of which are indicated by its name.

thumb-stall, n. Covering of leather &c. for protecting the thumb.

thummim. See under **urim and thummim.**

thump, n. & vb. trans. & intrans. [1. thump; 2. þamp]. Of imitative origin. **1.** n. Heavy blow inflicted with the fist or with a cudgel &c. **2.** vb. To inflict a thump or thumps upon, to pound with the fist.

thumping, adj. [1. thúmping; 2. þámpiŋ]. (colloq.) Very large, possessing to a marked degree some characteristic quality: *a thumping lie*; as adv., *a thumping* (*good, great*) *dinner.*

thunder (**I.**), n. [1. thúnder; 2. þándə]. O.E. *þunor*, M.E. *þuner, thunder* &c.; O.H.G. *donar*; cogn. w. Lat. *tonitrus*, 'thunder', *tonāre*, 'to thunder', & cp. **Thursday.** See also **astound. 1.** Loud, crashing, or rumbling sound caused by electrical disturbance in the air. **2.** Loud sound bearing some resemblance to thunder: *thunders of applause*; *the thunder of the cataract.*

thunder (**II.**), vb. intrans. & trans. O.E. *þunrian*, see prec. **1.** intrans. **a** To emit thunder: *it is thundering*; *it thunders*; **b** to give forth a sound like that of thunder: *the waves thunder upon the shore*; *to thunder at the door*, knock loudly; **c** to speak in a loud voice, with powerful resonance; to roar: *preachers thunder weekly from a thousand pulpits.* **2.** trans. To utter with a loud, powerful voice: *to thunder words of warning in a person's ears.*

thunderbolt, n. [1. thúnderbōlt; 2. þándəboult]. **1.** Discharge of lightning and accompanying clap of thunder; so called from belief that the noise was caused by a bolt hurled by a god. Phrs. *it came upon me like a thunderbolt, was a regular thunderbolt*, a matter of overwhelming surprise, something entirely unexpected. **2.** Any of certain kinds of stone or fossils, supposed to have fallen from the clouds as a result of discharges of lightning. **3.** (her.) Representation of supposed thunderbolt, consisting of a bar with blazing ends, and four darts issuing from the centre.

thunder-clap, n. Clap of thunder.

thunderer, n. [1. thúnderer; 2. þándərə]. One who thunders; specif., *the thunderer*, one of the names of Jove.

thundering, adj. [1. thúndering; 2. þándəriŋ]. **1.** Making a sound like, as loud as, thunder. **2.** (colloq.) Very large, excessive; same as *thumping*, q.v.: *a thundering mistake*; *a thundering ass* &c.

thunderous, adj. [1. thúnderus; 2. þándərəs]. **thunder** (**I.**) & **-ous. 1.** Thundery. **2.** As loud as, loud like, thunder.

thunder-storm, n. Storm of thunder and lightning.

thunder-struck, adj. Struck by lightning; (usually fig.) amazed, astonished, astounded.

thundery, adj. [1. thúnderi; 2. þándəri]. **thunder** (**I.**) & **-y.** (of weather) Tending to thunder, oppressive with thunder.

thurible, n. [1. thūribl; 2. þjúəribl]. Lat. *thūribulum*, formed fr. *thūri-*, stem of *thūs*, 'frankincense', fr. Gk. *thúos*, 'sacrifice'; cp. *thúein*, 'to sacrifice'; orig. 'to cause to smoke', fr. base ***dhu-**, as in Gk. *thūmós*, 'passion, courage'; Lat. *fūmus*, 'smoke'; see **fume** (**I.**) & cp. **thyme.** A censer.

thurifer, n. [1. thūrifer; 2. þjúərifə], fr. *thuri-*, as in prec., & **-fer.** Person who carries a censer; an acolyte.

Thursday, n. [1. thérzdi; 2. þə́zdi]. O.E. *Þūres dæġ*, fr. O.N. *Þōrr*, 'the god of thunder'; contracted fr. earlier ***þonraz**, see **thunder** (**I.**). Day of the week following Wednesday and preceding Friday.

thus, adv. [1. dhus; 2. ðas]. O.E. *þus*, cp. **this, the,** & **that. 1.** In this (specified) way: *he spoke thus.* **2.** To this extent: *thus far shalt thou go.*

thwack, vb. trans. & n. [1. thwak; 2. þwæk]. Prob. a dialectal variant of **whack** (**I.**). **1.** vb. To thrash, flog, beat, belabour. **2.** n. A blow, a slap or thump.

thwaite, n. [1. thwāt; 2. þweit]. O.N. *þveit*, 'piece of enclosed land, i.e. land set apart or cut off from surrounding area'; cogn. w. O.E. *þwītan*, 'to cut', q.v. under **whittle** (**I.**). (northern provinces and in northern Place-Names and surnames) Piece of wild or forest land cleared and cultivated.

thwart (**I.**), adv., prep., & adj. [1. thwort; 2. þwōt]. M.E. as adv., fr. O.N. *þvert*, neut. of *þverr*, 'across'; cogn. w. O.E. *þweorh*, 'across, crosswise; perverse, angry'; Goth. *þwairhs*, 'angry'; prob. connected w. Lat. *torquēre*, 'to twist' &c.; see **torque.** (obs. or archaic) Passing, lying, across. See **athwart.**

thwart (**II.**), n. See prec. Seat for oarsman in a boat.

thwart (**III.**), vb. trans. See **thwart** (**I.**). **a** To oppose will of; **b** to hinder, obstruct, prevent, fulfilment of (wishes, designs, intentions).

thy, possess. pron. of 2nd pers. sing. [1. dhī; 2. ðai]. See **thine** & **thou.** Of thee, belonging to thee.

thylacine, n. [1. thílasin; 2. þáiləsin], fr. Gk. *thúlax*, 'sack, pouch', & *kun-*, stem of *kúōn*, 'dog'. Tasmanian marsupial, resembling a dog in appearance; greyish brown with darker stripes across back and hind quarters.

thyme, n. [1. tīm; 2. taim]. M.E. *tyme*, fr. O. Fr., fr. Lat. *thymus*, fr. Gk. *thúmos*; connected w. *thúein*, 'to sacrifice'; see **thurible.** Pungent, aromatic plant, *Thymus*, common in English gardens, with palish purple flowers; the leaves are used for flavouring in cookery; also the wild thyme growing on chalk downs &c.

thymol, n. [1. tímol; 2. táimɔl]. Prec. & **-ol.** An aromatic substance obtained from the essential oil of thyme and other plants, also made synthetically, used medicinally as an antiseptic &c.

thymus, n. [1. thímus; 2. þáiməs], fr. Gk. *thúmos*, 'thyme', q.v., fr. resemblance to shape of a bud of thyme. A small ductless gland, in upper part of the chest; it is one of the so-called sweetbreads of calves or lambs; its functions are obscure, but its enlargement is associated with 'status lymphaticus', q.v.

thymy, adj. [1. tími; 2. táimi]. **thyme** & **-y.** Scented with, covered with, thyme.

thyroid, adj. & n. [1. thíroid; 2. þáiərɔid]. Gk. *thureoeidḗs*, 'shield-shaped'; fr. *thureós*, 'a large, oblong shield'; cogn. w. Gk. *thúrā*, 'a door'; see under **door** & **forum**; for ending see **-oid. 1.** adj. Indicating **a** the ductless gland in the neck of vertebrates, which has an important effect on growth and metabolism: *thyroid gland*; *thyroid extract*, of sheep, used for metabolic diseases, such as goitre &c.; **b** the Adam's apple: *thyroid cartilage.* **2.** n. The thyroid gland or cartilage.

thyrsus, n. [1. thérsus; 2. þə́səs]. Gk. *thúrsos*, 'a light wand'; etymol. unknown. A wand or staff; specif., a rod surmounted by a pine cone, and twined round with ivy or vine leaves and berries; the attribute of Bacchus.

thyself, pers. pron. [1. dhīsélf; 2. ðaisélf]. Reflex. & emphatic of **thou.**

tiara, n. [1. tiáhra, tiáhra; 2. taiárə, tiárə]. Lat., fr. Gk. *tiárā*; of Pers. origin. **1.** Ancient Persian head-dress. **2.** **a** Official head-dress of the Pope, consisting of a high conical cap, surmounted by three crowns, emblematical of the threefold sovereignty claimed by the Papacy, temporal, spiritual, purgatorial; **b** (fig.) the dignity and power of the Papacy. **3.** Jewelled head ornament or kind of coronet worn by women.

tibia, n. [1. tíbia; 2. tíbiə]. Lat. *tībia*, 'shinbone; a flute'; Walde derives it fr. ***twībh-**, whence also Gk. *síphōn*, see **siphon** (**I.**). (anat.) The larger of the two bones between the knee and the foot.

tibial, adj. [1. tíbial; 2. tíbiəl]. Prec. & **-al.** Pertaining to, connected with, the tibia.

tibio-, pref. Form of *tibia* used in compound words, e.g. *tibiofemoral*, pertaining to the tibia and femur.

tic, n. [1. tik; 2. tik]. Fr., origin doubtful. Often *tic douloureux* [dūlūrā], a convulsive twitching of the facial muscles, associated with neuralgic pains.

tick (**I.**), n. [1. tik; 2. tik]. For **ticket** (**I.**). (slang) Credit: *to buy on tick*; *to get tick.*

tick (**II.**), n. Low Lat. *tēca*, Lat. *thēca*, fr. Gk. *thḗkē*, 'a case, cover'; fr. base of *títhēmi*, 'I put', cogn. w. **do** (**I.**) & Lat. *facere*, 'to do, make', see **fact. a** Outside cover of mattresses, bolsters, pillows; **b** coarse striped material of which this is made.

tick (**III.**), n. M.E. *tike, tēke*; cp. L.G. *teke*; Germ. *zecke*, origin unknown. Any of various parasitic arachnids, order *Acari*, which attach themselves to the skin of men or other animals and suck the blood of their hosts. Phr. *as full as a tick.*

tick (**IV.**), vb. intrans. & trans. & n. Imitative of sound. **1.** vb. **a** intrans. To make a slight, sharp, reiterated clicking, or tapping noise; specif. of a clock or watch, also of tape machine, to make the sound characteristic of the movements of the works; **b** trans., (i.) to mark with a small stroke of the pen or pencil placed against a word, name, letter &c.; Phr. (slang) *to tick off*, to reprimand; (ii.) also *tick out*, of tape machine, to give out the news on the roll of tape. **2.** n. **a** Sound made by clock or watch in ticking; **b** small mark or scratch of a pen &c.

ticker, n. [1. tíker; 2. tíkə]. Prec. & **-er.** (slang) **a** A watch; **b** a tape-machine.

ticket (**I.**), n. [1. tíket; 2. tíkit], fr. O. Fr. *estiquet*, see **etiquette**. **1.** Small piece of cardboard bearing necessary printed inscription, showing **a** that owner has paid the price charged for entrance to, and seat at, a concert, theatre, or other entertainment, or that he is for any reason entitled to go in; **b** that possessor has paid his fare for a railway or tram journey &c. Phrs. *to take tickets for the opera*; *to take one's ticket to Edinburgh* &c. **2.** Any of various short notices, announcements, printed on small cards or sheets of paper; e.g. a label indicating price of goods exhibited for sale: *price ticket*; brief document issued by pawnbroker when advancing money on an article left as a pledge: *pawn ticket*; or issued as certificate of share in a lottery &c.: *take a ticket in a sweepstake.* **3. a** List of political candidates for election, belonging to a particular party; **b** (fig.) the principles of a political party: *the Tory ticket.* Phrs. *the proper ticket*, orthodox ideas, behaviour &c.; *not quite the ticket*, not quite the right thing.

ticket (**II.**), vb. trans., fr. prec. To mark with a ticket, to affix a ticket to.

ticket-of-leave, n. [1. tíket uv lēv; 2. tíkit əv lív]. Permission granted to a convict to be at liberty, with certain restrictions, before expiry of his sentence. Phrs. *out* (*of prison*) *on ticket-of-leave*; *ticket-of-leave man*, prisoner released with such a ticket.

tickle (**I.**), vb. trans. & intrans. [1. tíkl; 2. tíkl]. Possibly freq. of **tick** (**IV.**). **A.** trans. **1.** To excite, irritate, the superficial nerves and cause peculiar sensation, involuntary laughter, or slight spasm, by touching lightly and repeatedly some part of the skin; to titillate. **2. a** To please, gratify: *to tickle one's palate*; **b** to amuse, cause laughter, excite risibility in: *I was immensely tickled by his good stories.* **B.** intrans. **a** To experience a sensation of tickling, or irritation, on some part of the surface of the body; to itch, tingle: *my throat, nose &c. tickles*; **b** to cause, provoke, sensation of tickling: *nothing tickles so intolerably as a hair in the throat.*

tickle (**II.**), n., fr. prec. Sensation of tickling; tingling, irritation of superficial nerves: *a tickle in the throat.*

tickler, n. [1. tíkler; 2. tíklə]. **tickle** (**I.**) & **-er.** A puzzle, a difficult problem.

tickling, n. [1. tíkling; 2. tíkliŋ]. See prec. & **-ing.** A tickle.

ticklish, adj. [1. tíklish; 2. tíkliʃ]. **tickle** (**I.**) & **-ish. 1.** Sensitive to tickling, easily excited to laughter or irritation by tickling. **2. a** (of persons) Touchy, difficult to deal with; **b** (of affairs) delicate, hazardous, requiring skilful handling.

tick-tack, -tock, n. [1. tík tak, -tok; 2. tík tæk, -tɔk]. Reduplication of **tick** (**IV.**). **1.** Childish name for a watch or clock. **2.** (slang, usually *tick-tack man*) A bookmaker's assistant who signals the change of odds and other news of a race from different parts of the course.

tidal, adj. [1. tídl; 2. táidl]. **tide** (**I.**) & **-al.** Connected with the tide or tides; specif. **a** experiencing alterations of tide: *a tidal river*; **b** caused by the tide: *tidal waves*; **c** sailing at times determined by the tide: *tidal steamer.*

tiddly-winks, n. [1. tídli wìngks; 2. tídli wìŋks]. Child's game played on a table, in which counters are flipped from the edge into a receptacle in the centre.

tide (**I.**), n. [1. tīd; 2. taid]. O.E. *tīd*, 'time'; also O.S. & O. Fris.; O.H.G. *zīt*; see base under **time** (**I.**). **1.** Period, season; obsolete except in *eventide, Christmastide, Whitsuntide, yule-tide*, and in proverb '*Time and tide wait for no man*'. **2.** Alternate rise and fall, ebb and flow, of the surface of the sea: *high, low, half, tide*; cp. also **neap-** (**I.**) and **spring-tide** (**II.**). **3.** Trend, flow, tendency, **a** (in feeling and emotion) *the full tide of pleasure, passion* &c.; **b** (of circumstances and affairs) *the high tide of fortune.* Phr. *the turn of the tide*, reversal of fortune.

tide (**II.**), vb. intrans., fr. prec. **1.** (rare) To drift with the tide. **2.** Chiefly *tide over* (a difficulty &c.), to surmount, manage to overcome.

tideless, adj. [1. tídles; 2. táidlis]. **tide** (**I.**) & **-less.** Having no tide: *the Mediterranean is a tideless sea.*

tide-waiter, n. Custom-house official who boards vessels and watches landing of cargoes, to secure payment of duties.

tidewater, n. [1. tídwawter; 2. táidwɔ̄tə]. **tide** (**I.**) & **water.** (U.S.A.) **1. a** Water on sea-coast or in estuary &c., affected by tides; hence, **b** sea-coast. **2.** (attrib.) On, belonging to, the sea-coast.

tide-way, n. **a** Channel through which tide ebbs and flows; **b** ebb and flow of tide through such channel.

tidily, adv. [1. tídili; 2. táidili], fr. **tidy** (**I.**) & **-ly.** In a tidy manner.

tidiness, n. [1. tídines; 2. táidinis]. See prec. & **-ness.** State, quality, of being tidy.

tidings, n. pl. [1. tídingz; 2. táidiŋz]. Takes vb. either in pl. or sing. M.E. *tidinge, tīthinge, tīthinde*; prob. fr. O.N. *tíðindi*, cp., however, O.E. *tīdung*, fr. O.E. *tīdan*, 'to happen'; see **betide.** Piece of news, intelligence: *the good tidings*; *evil tidings.*

tidy (**I**), adj. & n. [1. tídi; 2. táidi], fr. **tide** (**I.**) & **-y**, in sense of 'timely'; cp. Mod. Germ. *zeitig.* **1.** adj. **a** Orderly, neat, well-arranged; **b** (colloq.) considerable, of some size, amount &c.: *a tidy income*; *to leave a tidy sum to one's heirs.* **2.** n. **a** A small antimacassar or chair cover; **b** small receptacle in which odds and ends of the dressing-table may be placed.

tidy (**II.**), vb. trans., fr. prec. To make tidy, to put in order: *to tidy a room, a garden*; *to tidy oneself*; also *tidy up* (*a room, myself* &c.); intrans., *I must just tidy up a bit*, put things in order.

tie (**I.**), n. [1. tī; 2. tai]. O.E. *tēah, tēh*, 'bond, chain; enclosure', M.E. *tēh, tē3(e), tīe*; cogn. w. O.N. *taug*, 'a string, a tie'; fr. Gmc. base **teuh-, *tauh-* &c., 'to pull, draw'; cp. O.E. *tēon* (fr. **tēoh-*), 'to draw, pull', Goth. *tiuhan*, see **tow** (**I.**), cogn. w. Lat. *dūcere*, 'to pull; to lead', see **duke**, & **duct. 1.** A knot, ligature, bond; rope, chain, string &c. used to fasten something. **2.** Specif., a strip of white lawn, or black silk, tied in a bow (evening tie), or folded piece of silk or other ornamental coloured material worn knotted round the neck; necktie. **3.** A bond, connecting piece, of wood, iron &c., used to hold together and make firm, or give support to, different parts of a structure; e.g. a wooden rod or spar fastened between two legs of a table or chair; a piece of timber, or an iron rod, used to hold together larger timbers in a building &c. **4.** A spiritual bond, connecting link of feeling between persons; a moral obligation: *the ties of parenthood, patriotism, friendship* &c. **5.** Object or circumstance the existence of which imposes certain duties and obligations that restrict one's actions, curb one's freedom &c.; a burden: *I find my large establishment rather a tie*; *a dog is a considerable tie if one has sole charge of it.* **6.** Equality of scores between two competitors in a sporting contest, or of votes between candidates in an election &c. **7.** Match or game played between pairs of opponents or teams, the loser or losing side being eliminated from the contest, the winner subsequently being matched against another winner, until all are eliminated but the winner in the final bout. **8.** (mus.) A curved line joining two notes of same pitch, indicating that the note is sustained for a period equivalent to the duration of both.

tie (**II.**), vb. trans. & intrans. O.E. *tēgan*, M.E. *tē3en, tī3en*; see prec. **A.** trans. **1.** To fasten, bind, attach, by means of a string, cord, rope: *to tie a branch of a rose to a trellis*; *to tie a horse to a tree* &c. Phrs. (fig.) *to tie the hands of*, to hamper, curtail freedom of; *to be tied hand and foot*, be completely hampered and hindered in freedom of action. **2. a** To form (a cord, string, strip of material &c.) into some kind of knot: *to tie one's tie*; *to tie a piece of ribbon into a knot or bow* &c.; **b** to form knot, twist &c.: *to tie a knot, a bow, a loop* &c. **3.** To make firm by connecting with a tie: *to tie the legs of a table.* **4. a** To bind, impose an obligation upon, force to act in a certain way: *I won't tie you too rigidly, but I expect you to do what I wish*; **b** to keep occupied, to engage; to hinder complete liberty of action: *my professional duties tie me for the greater part of each day.* **5.** To unite, bind: *to be tied to a wife.* **B.** intrans. **1.** To be capable of being tied or formed into a knot: *this rope won't tie.* **2.** (of two competitors in a contest) To make an equal score, obtain same number of votes &c. **C.** Followed by preposition or adverb. *Tie down*, trans., **1.** to fasten by tying so as to prevent from rising; **2.** to bind, restrain (a person), by conditions, obligations, to exact an undertaking from. *Tie up*, trans., **1.** to fasten securely together: *to tie up a truss of hay, a parcel* &c.; **2.** to bind up, swathe round, wrap up: *to tie up a person's head*; **3.** to take such measures as will restrict (a person's) freedom of action, to impose conditions, obligations, restrictions upon; **4.** to secure (property) by will &c. in such a way that it cannot be alienated or squandered, or so that it must pass to a certain line of heirs, or can only be enjoyed under certain conditions.

tied house, n. [1. tíd hóus; 2. táid háus]. Public-house the liquor for which must, by contract, be purchased from a single, specified, firm of brewers.

tier, n. [1. tēr; 2. tiə]. O. Fr. *tiere*, 'row, rank, series'; origin uncertain. **a** Originally, a row of guns (in a ship); **b** a row, series, of objects, forming one of several rows, also one of several shelves &c., placed one above another.

tierce, n. [1. tērs; 2. tiəs]. Fr. *tiers*, 'third', fr. Lat., see **tertius. 1.** Wine cask containing 42 gallons; one-third of a pipe. **2.** The third of the canonical hours; service said at that hour (9 A.M.). **3.** Position in fencing, both in attacking and parrying, in which the point of the weapon is on a level with the eye; the third position.

tiercel, tiercet. See **tercel, tercet.**

tiers état, n. [1. tyárz ātáh; 2. tjéər(z) eitá]. Fr., 'third estate'. The common people; the class coming after, and inferior to, the nobility and the clergy.

tiff, n. & vb. intrans. [1. tif; 2. tif]. Supposed to be fr. O.N. *þēfr*, 'a smell', with vb. *þēfa*, 'to sniff'; Mod. Norw. *teft*, 'a scent'. **1.** n. **a** A slight, passing, quarrel, trifling dispute; **b** (obs. or provinc.) a small draught or taste of liquor. **2.** vb. (rare or obs.) To be peevish, pettish.

tiffany, n. [1. tífani; 2. tífəni]. O. Fr. *tiffanie*, fr. L. Lat. *theophania*, 'manifesting of God'; fr. Gk., see **theophany** & cp. **epiphany.** Thin silk gauze; originally a dress for wearing on Twelfth Night.

tiffin, n. [1. tífin; 2. tífin]. Said to be for *tiffing*, fr. **tiff, 1, b.** Luncheon; word current among the English in India and the Far East.

tige, n. [1. tēzh; 2. tīž]. Fr., 'a stalk', fr. Lat.; see **tibia. 1.** (archit.) The shaft of a column. **2.** (bot.) Stalk, stem, of a plant.

tiger, n. [1. tíger; 2. táigə]. M.E., fr. O. Fr. *tigre*, fr. Lat. *tigris*, Gk. *tígris*; said to be fr.

an old Pers. word *tigra*, meaning 'an arrow'. **1.** Large, fierce, Asiatic carnivorous animal of the cat tribe, *Felis tigris*, measuring from 9 to 10 ft. to tip of tail, having a white throat and belly, and tawny yellow back and sides, with narrow black stripes; *American tiger*, the jaguar. **2.** (fig.) A violent, cruel, ruthless man. **3.** A small groom or page-boy in livery; probably so called because formerly these boys wore yellow waistcoats with black stripes. **4.** A yell, or supplementary cheer, at the end of a round of cheering: *three cheers and a tiger*.

tiger-beetle, n. One of several kinds of carnivorous beetles with stripes on the back.

tiger-cat, n. Large kind of wild cat, partly striped, such as the ocelot or the margay.

tiger-flower, n. Plant of iris family, *Tigridia*, the flowers of which are streaked with darker colour.

tig(e)rish, adj. [1. tíg(e)rish; 2. táig(ə)riʃ]. **tiger** & **-ish.** Like a tiger in character; fierce, rapacious, cruel, bloodthirsty.

tig(e)rishly, adv. Prec. & **-ly.** In a tigerish manner.

tiger-lily, n. Lily of Chinese origin, *Lilium tigrinum*, cultivated in English gardens, with orange-coloured flowers spotted with black.

tiger-moth, n. One of several varieties of large moths, found in England, with variegated wings, mottled with dark reddish-brown, yellow, and buff spots.

tiger('s)-eye, n. A chatoyant stone, yellowish brown in colour; polished and used as an ornament.

tiger-wood, n. Tree from British Guiana used in cabinet-making.

tight (I.), adj. [1. tīt; 2. tait]. M.E. *ti(g)ht* & *thiht*; prob. of Scand. origin, cp. O.N. *þéttr*, '(water-)tight'; cp. Mod. Germ. *dicht*, 'thick'; related to **thick** (I.); orig. sense 'thickly set, dense, firm' &c. **1.** Drawn close, firm, compact: *a tight knot*. **2.** So compactly and closely put together as not to allow the passage of liquid; not leaky; esp. *a tight ship, cask*; cp. *water-tight*. **3.** Having all loose parts arranged to lie close and compact; hence trim, snug, neat: *a tight little vessel*; '*A right little, tight little island*'. **4.** (of a cord, line, chain &c.) Firmly held, pulled, and strained from either end; kept fully stretched; taut; reverse of *slack, loose*: *a tight rein*, one drawn so as to put a strain on the bit. Phr. (fig.) *to keep a tight rein, hand, on (a person)*, treat with severity. **5. a** Entirely filled with the contents, so as to be stretched from within; specif., clinging so close as to compress what is within or underneath; scanty, too small; reverse of *loose, easy*: *a tight boot, hat, coat*; *my coat is tight across the chest*; *a tight squeeze*; **b** (fig., of external conditions) cramped, making action difficult, hard to deal with; dangerous, oppressive; specif., *a tight corner*, difficult, dangerous, situation. **6. a** (of money) Scarce, difficult to obtain; **b** (of persons) close-fisted, stingy, niggardly. **7.** (slang) Drunk, intoxicated, tipsy. **8.** (of artistic method, treatment &c.) Lacking largeness and breadth; petty, finicky.

tight (II.), adv., fr. prec. Tightly, firmly: *a coat made to fit tight round the waist*; *to keep one's mouth tight shut*; *to sit tight (on a horse) over a fence*. Phr. *to sit tight*, to stick tenaciously to one's rights, position, opinions &c.

tighten, vb. trans. & intrans. [1. títn; 2. táitn]. **1.** trans. To draw, make, tight or tighter: *to tighten one's grip, the reins, a strap* &c. **2.** intrans. To become tight or tighter: *a tent-rope tightens when it gets wet*; *the grip of the enemy upon the small force of defenders tightened daily*.

tightly, adv. [1. títli; 2. táitli]. **tight** (I.) & **-ly.** In a tight manner; so as to constrict; compactly; firmly.

tightness, n. [1. tītnes; 2. táitnis]. See **tight** (I.) & **-ness.** Quality, state, fact, of being tight; constriction.

tight-rope, n. Rope or wire tightly stretched some distance above the ground, upon which acrobats walk; *tight-rope dancer*, performer upon such a rope.

tights, n. pl. [1. tīts; 2. taits]. Garments made to fit tight to the skin; specif., garments fitting tight to the trunk and legs, worn by professional dancers, gymnasts &c.

tigress, n. [1. tígres; 2. táigris]. **tiger** & **-ess.** **1.** Female tiger. **2.** A fierce, cruel, violent woman.

tike, tyke, n. [1. tīk; 2. taik]. M.E. *tīke*, 'dog; rustic', fr. O.N. **1.** A rough dog of no particular breed; a cur. **2.** A rough, uncultivated, ill-bred, mannerless, boorish fellow. Phr. *Yorkshire tike*, a rough, loutish Yorkshireman.

tilbury, n. [1. tílburi; 2. tílbəri], fr. name of inventor. A kind of high two-wheeled carriage with a hood.

tilde, n. [1. tíldā; 2. tíldɛ]. Span., fr. Lat. *titulo*, see **title. a** Mediaeval mark (~) placed over a letter to indicate that *n* follows; **b** mark (~) placed over *n* in Spanish writing indicating that this expresses a front nasal consonant, i.e. the sound written *gn(e)* in French and Italian.

tile, n. & vb. trans. [1. tīl; 2. tail]. O.E. *tigele*, fr. Lat. *tēgula*, formed fr. base *teg-, 'to cover', as in *tegere*, 'to cover'; see **tegument** & cp. **thatch** (I.). **1.** n. **a** A flat, generally rectangular, cake of baked clay or earthenware, used for roofing; or one made of finer clay or porcelain, and glazed, used for covering inside walls &c.; **b** (colloq.) a top hat. **2.** vb. **a** To cover with tiles; **b** to guard the entrance door of a masonic lodge.

tiler, n. [1. tíler; 2. táilə]. Prec. & **-er.** **1.** Man who makes tiles; one who lays tiles on roofs &c. **2.** External guard of the door of a masonic lodge while in session.

tilery, n. [1. tíleri; 2. táiləri]. Prec., sense **1**, & **-y.** Place where tiles are made and baked in a kiln.

tilestone, n. [1. tílstōn; 2. táilstoun]. A flat stone used for roofing.

tiliaceous, adj. [1. tiliáshus; 2. tiliéiʃəs], fr. Lat. *tilia*, 'linden tree', & **-aceous.** (bot.) Belonging to the family *Tiliaceae*, which includes the linden tree, bass-wood &c.

till (I.), prep & conj. [1. til; 2. til]. O.E. (Nthn. dial.) & M.E. 'to, up to'; perh. fr. O.N. *til* in same sense; cogn. w. O.H.G. *zil*, 'limit, end, aim'; cp. Goth. *(ga)tilon*, 'to obtain, reach', & *(ga)tils*, 'convenient, fit'; O.E. *til*, 'good', is the same word. **a** prep. To, up to, down to, up to the time when: *till tomorrow*; *till next week*; *till then*; *till now*; *true till death*; **b** conj., in same sense as the prep.: *wait till I come*; *till the day breaks*; '*till death us do part*'.

till (II.), vb. trans. O.E. *tilian*, 'to strive after; to provide for; to treat medically; to cultivate (land)'; fr. same base as prec. To cultivate (the land); to prepare (land) for sowing by ploughing &c.

till (III.), n. Connected w. M.E. *tillen*, 'to pull'; cp. O.E. *(for-)tyllan*, 'to draw, lead astray'; see also **tiller** (II.). Small drawer in a shop counter where money is kept.

tillable, adj. [1. tílabl; 2. tíləbl]. **till** (II.) & **-able.** Capable of being tilled.

tillage, n. [1. tílij; 2. tílidž]. **till** (II.) & **-age. a** Act, process, of tilling or cultivating the ground; **b** tilled land.

tiller (I.), n. [1. tíler; 2. tílə], fr. **till** (II.) & **-er.** One who tills (the soil).

tiller (II.), n. Connected w. **till** (III.). Bar, lever, fixed to head of rudder, worked by hand in a small vessel; or by tiller-chains or ropes fixed to steering wheel in larger vessels.

tiller (III.), n. & vb. intrans. O.E. *telgor*, 'shoot, twig'; cp. *telga*, 'branch'. **1.** n. A shoot, sucker, from a plant. **2.** vb. To shoot, put forth young shoots from root.

tilt (I.), vb. trans. & intrans., & n. [1. tilt; 2. tilt]. Cp. O.E. *tealtian*, 'to be unsteady'; O.E. *tealt*, 'unsteady, heaving', M.E. *tilten*, 'to totter, fall'. **1.** vb. **a** trans. To cause to slope, to tip; also *tilt up*; **b** intrans., to assume a sloping position, stand or lie at an angle, to slope; to heel over. **2.** n. A sloping position: *to give a tilt to a barrel*.

tilt (II.), vb. intrans. & n. Apparently same word as prec. **1.** vb. To take part in a tournament; specif., to make a charge on horseback with a lance; also *tilt at*, (chiefly fig.) to attack, protest, inveigh, against: *to tilt at abuses*. **2.** n. **a** Exercise of tilting; **b** thrust, charge, in tilting. Phr. *to run full tilt into, at, anything*, at full speed.

tilt (III.), n. M.E. *telt*, 'tent', loan-word fr. some other Gmc. tongue, the O.E. word being *teld*; O.H.G. *zelt*; the etymol. is obscure; perh. connected w. **tent** (I.). A light canopy or covering, esp. one of canvas on a wooden frame, placed over a cart, a boat, or a street stall.

tilth, n. [1. tilth; 2. tilþ]. In O.E., see **till** (II.) & **-th. a** Act of tilling; **b** tilled land; tillage.

tilt-hammer, n. fr. **tilt** (I.). A large heavy hammer used in iron-forging, raised or tilted and let fall by a wheel.

tilt-yard, n., fr. **tilt** (II.). Place, courtyard, in which tilting was practised.

timbal, n. [1. tímbl; 2. tímbl]. See next word. A kettle-drum.

timbale, n. [1. tambáhl; 2. tǣbāl]. Fr., fr. Span. *timbal*, 'kettle-drum', fr. Arab. *atabal*; perh. influenced by Fr. *timbre*, see **timbre.** A highly flavoured dish of chicken, fish, lobster &c., cooked in a mould of rounded shape.

timber (I.), n. [1. tímber; 2. tímbə]. O.E. *timber*, 'timber; a building'; cp. also O.E. *timbrian*, 'to build'; O.H.G. *zimbar*, 'wooden building'; Mod. Germ. *zimmer*, 'room, chamber', cogn. w. Lat. *domus*, 'house' &c., see **dome** (I.); also **tame** (I.). **1. a** Wood cut up and prepared for building; **b** growing trees thought of as wood with commercial value for building. **2.** A shaped, fitted piece of wood designed to form, or actually forming, a structural element in a building, specif. in a house &c., or a ship.

timber (II.), vb. trans. O.E. *timbrian*, 'to build', see prec. To build up with timber; to furnish with timbers; to prop, support, pin, with timber.

timbered, adj. [1. tímberd; 2. tímbəd]. **a** Built of or with timber; **b** supplied with growing timber: *well-timbered land*.

timbering, n. [1. tímbering; 2. tímbəriŋ]. Timbers of a building collectively; timber work.

timber-toes, n. [1. tímber tōz; 2. tímbə touz]. (colloq. and facet.) Person with a wooden leg.

timbre, n. [1. támbr; 2. tǣmbr]. Fr., 'bell sounded by being struck with a hammer; quality of sound, voice &c.'; see **tympanum** & next word. (mus.) The characteristic quality of the sound of an instrument, or of a human voice.

timbrel, n. [1. tímbrel; 2. tímbrəl]. See prec. & **tympanum.** Kind of small drum played by being struck by the hand; a tambourine.

time (I.), n. [1. tīm; 2. taim]. O.E. *tīma*, 'time, date; proper time; period of time; lifetime; season of the year'; M.E. *tīme*; O.N. *tīmi*; fr. Gmc. base *tī-, & cogn. w. **tide** (I.), q.v., w. different suff. The fundamental sense of the orig. base *dā(i)-, *dī- &c., is 'to divide; division'; cp. Lat. *daps*, 'religious feast'; Gk. *dêmos*, 'district; people', see **demos**; Scrt. *dāpayati*, 'he divides'; see also **damn** (I.). **1.** A fundamental conception, involving recognition of the ideas of before and after, past, present, and future, in the sequence of events: *space and time are sometimes called 'categories of sense'*. Phr. *time and tide wait for no man*. **2.** Time regarded theoretically, as having a beginning and an end, as something limited by the duration of the external universe, or of man and human existence; contrasted with *eternity*: '*A rose-red city half as old as time*' (Burgon). **Phrs.**

from time immemorial, time out of mind, from the remotest period; (of legal memory) '*from time whereof the memory of man runneth not to the contrary*'. **3.** Duration of time; a length, portion, of time; a period: *I've only been here a short time*; *that will take a long time.* Phrs. *in no time,* very soon, in a brief space; *take your time,* don't hurry; *in one's own time,* in one's leisure moments, during time for which one is not paid; *there is no time to lose,* **a** the matter is urgent; **b** there is need of hurry; *to have no time to spare, to be pressed for time,* to have no leisure, to be very busy, to be compelled to hurry to get something done; *have I time* (*to catch the train* &c.)*?*, i.e. enough time; *to do time,* (colloq.) undergo period of imprisonment; *to serve one's time,* the agreed period of apprenticeship; *what time,* (archaic and poet.) at the moment when; while: '*What time the laboured ox In his loose traces from the furrow came*' (Milton, 'Comus', 291-2). **4.** (often pl.) Period distinguished by the occurrence of specific, memorable, historical events, by the activities of historical characters &c.; age, epoch: '*The spacious times of great Elizabeth*' (Tennyson, 'Dr. of Fair W.', v. 2); *life and times of Queen Victoria.* Phr. *the good old times,* the past. **5.** A portion of time characterized by specified conditions, or considered in relation to the kind of events that occur: *hard times*; *to pass through a terrible time*; *what wonderful times we live in.* Phrs. *to have a good time,* to enjoy oneself; *to have the time of one's life,* a period of extreme and exceptional happiness and enjoyment; *time was when . . .*, it used formerly to be that . . . **6. a** Lifetime, duration of one's life: *the house will last my time*; *such things never happened in the old squire's time*; **b** period in which one was associated with particular persons, places &c., or was engaged in some particular activities &c.: *he was no longer head of the college in my time,* that is, not while I was there; *all these things happened in my time.* **7.** Particular point or moment of time; esp. the customary, normal moment for something to happen; a time fixed for something to be done or to happen; season; the proper time: *I was ill at the time*; *he arrived in due time*; *the time has come when . . .*; *will you kindly fix a time to call?* Phrs. *there are times when . . .*, sometimes, at certain moments; *your, my, time has come,* you are, I am, going to die; *time of life,* age; (of a woman) *near her time,* shortly to be delivered; (*glad to see you*) *at all times,* always; *to do something in one's own good time,* when one chooses; *to be in (good) time (for),* early enough, punctual; *all in good time,* soon enough, there's no hurry!; *time!*, (at contests &c. where a given time is allowed for performance) time is up!; stop! **8. a** Mode of computing, of reckoning, lapse of time: *Greenwich time*; *Summer time*; **b** specif., some particular hour in the day, or fraction of it, as reckoned in a given latitude: *what's the time?*; *the right time*; *the time of day.* Phrs. *to pass* (*him*) *the time of day,* to greet, salute, exchange formal greetings with; *at this time of day,* (fig.) so late, after all that has happened; (of a timepiece) *to keep good time,* show the hour correctly. **9. a** Portion of time in which an action is repeated, or an event recurs; occasion: *each time I see him I dislike him more and more*; *many a time, many times,* often, on many occasions; *time after time,* again and again, repeatedly; **b** (in pl.) as a sign of multiplication: *three times four is twelve.* Phr. *many times as large,* much larger. **10. a** (mus.) Measurement based on the periodicity of accents, and classified according to the subdivision of the beats; Phr. *to beat time,* indicate proper time by motions made with a baton; **b** (prosody) duration of utterance, including pause, as an element of metre.

time (**II.**), vb. trans., fr. prec. **1.** To calculate time that an action will take to perform, and adjust one's movements accordingly; to do something at, or within, the right, or a suitable, time: *to time one's arrival opportunely*; *to time one's start so as just to catch a train*; *to time one's blows skilfully.* **2.** To observe and note length of time taken in performing an action; esp. time taken in a race to run a given distance.

time-ball, n. Ball which falls at a given hour, usually at noon, as an indication of the time.

time-bargain, n. Contract to sell stocks, shares &c. at an agreed price at a fixed future time.

time-expired, adj. [1. tīm ekspīrd; 2. táim ikspáiəd]. Having completed the term of service (of soldiers and sailors).

time-honoured, adj. [1. tīm ònurd; 2. táim ɔ̀nəd]. Long respected or observed; respected on account of its antiquity: *a time-honoured custom.*

time-keeper, n. **a** Person who keeps, observes, notes, measures, time, esp. that spent by men at their work; **b** a timepiece.

timeless, adj. [1. tīmles; 2. táimlis]. **time** (**I.**) & **-less.** **1.** (poet.) **a** Not to be measured by time; unending, interminable; **b** (archaic) unseasonable. **2.** Pertaining to no fixed time.

timelessly, adv. Prec. & **-ly.** Unendingly.

timelessness, n. See prec. & **-ness.** State, quality, of being timeless.

timely, adj. & adv. [1. tīmli; 2. táimli]. **time** (**I.**) & **-ly.** **1.** adj. Occurring at a suitable time; opportune: *timely help.* **2.** adv. (rare) In good, at a suitable, time; opportunely.

timenoguy, n. [1. tīménogī; 2. taiménəgai]. Origin unknown; cp. **guy rope** &c. (naut.) Taut rope over which running rigging slides, used to prevent fouling.

timeous, timous, adj. [1. tīmus; 2. táiməs]. **time** (**I.**) & **-ous.** (rare, or Scots, esp. Scots law) In good time; opportune; seasonable.

timeously, adv. Prec. & **-ly.** Seasonably, opportunely.

timepiece, n. [1. tīmpēs; 2. táimpīs]. A watch or clock.

time-saving, adj. Serving to save time.

time-server, n. Person who in his behaviour and actions subordinates duty and principle to self-interest and expediency; an obsequious unprincipled toady who readily adapts his opinions and conduct to those which are popular at the time at which he lives, and among the more powerful people with whom he is brought in contact.

time-serving, adj. Practising the behaviour of a time-server; obsequious, pliant.

time-sheet, n. Record of time spent on a job of work or at work by a workman.

time-table, n. **1. a** List, in tabular form, showing the days and hours at which particular duties and work of any kind have to be done, or for which engagements, appointments &c. have been fixed; **b** the whole series of duties, engagements &c. assigned to particular days and hours. **2.** Specif. **a** table, book containing a list, showing hours of the arrival and departure of trains, boats, trams &c.; **b** the total number of departures and arrivals, at fixed hours, of trains, boats &c. running under direction of a particular company.

time-work, n. Work, esp. manual labour, which is paid at certain rates by the hour or day; contrasted with *piece-work.*

timid, adj. [1. timid; 2. tímid]. Fr. *timide,* fr. Lat. *timidus,* 'faint-hearted, cowardly'; cp. also *timēre,* 'to be afraid'; the origin is uncertain; connexion w. Lat. *tenebrae,* 'darkness', see **tenebrae**, has been suggested. Easily frightened, lacking in courage, nerve, or spirit; lacking self-confidence and enterprise; diffident, shy. Phr. *as timid as a hare.*

timidity, n. [1. timíditi; 2. timíditi]. Lat. *timiditāt-(em).* Prec. & **-ity.** Lack of courage and self-confidence; nervousness; shyness, diffidence.

timidly, adv. See prec. & **-ly.** In a timid manner; shyly, hesitatingly.

timidness, n. See prec. & **-ness.** Condition of being timid; shyness, timidity.

timist, n. [1. tīmist; 2. táimist]. **time** (**I.**) & **-ist.** **1.** Musical performer considered according to the manner in which he observes the time of the piece which he is playing: *a good, poor, timist.* **2.** (prosody) One who emphasizes the importance of time as an element in metre.

timocracy, n. [1. tīmókrasi; 2. taimɔ́krəsi]. Gk. *tīmokratia,* fr. *tīmḗ,* 'price, worth; moral worth, honour in which one is held; esteem, respect', & base **krat-*, 'strength; government, rule', see **-cracy**; *tīmḗ* contains the same base **tī-* as in Gk. *tíein,* 'to place a value on; to honour, esteem' &c., wh. is fr. **kʷei-*, **kwi-* &c., 'to respect', whence also Scrt. *cā́yati,* 'he worships, has high respect for'; it is possible that the first syllable of Lat. *caerimōnia,* 'religious awe, reverence; religious usage', is fr. the same source; see **ceremony.** **1.** A state in which the love of honour and glory is the ruling principle. **2.** A state in which political power is in proportion to the amount of property possessed.

timocratic, adj. [1. tìmokrátik; 2. tàiməkrǽtik]. See prec., w. substitution of suff. **-crat** & **-ic.** Pertaining to, based on, timocracy.

timorous, adj. [1. tímorus; 2. tímərəs], fr. Lat. *timor,* 'fear', see **timid**, & **-ous.** Exceedingly timid, easily startled, prone to take fright; apprehensive, faint-hearted.

timorously, adv. Prec. & **-ly.** In a timorous manner.

timorousness, n. See prec. & **-ness.** State, quality, of being timorous.

timothy (**grass**), n. [1. tímuthi (grahs); 2. tíməþi (grās)]. fr. name of introducer, Timothy Hanson. A grass with long spikes grown for hay in America and Europe.

timous, adj. See **timeous.**

timpano, n. [1. tímpanō; 2. tímpənou]. Ital., see **tympanum.** A kettle-drum.

tin (**I.**), n. [1. tin; 2. tin]. O.E. *tin*; in most Gmc. languages, e.g. O.N. *tin*; O.H.G. *zin* &c.; origin unknown; not related to Lat. *stagnum, stannum,* 'tin'. **1.** A white, malleable metal, taking a high polish, and almost unaffected by atmosphere. **2. a** Thin iron plate or sheet coated with tin, used for making vessels, cases &c. of various kinds: *a box made of tin,* made of tin plates: (also attrib.) *a tin box, saucepan* &c. Phr. *a little tin god,* an insignificant person who on the strength of his position or other accidental circumstances is regarded by others, or by himself, as being very important; *tin hat,* (slang) a soldier's steel helmet; **b** a receptacle made of such plates: *a tin for biscuits*; **c** the contents of a tin box or other receptacle; so much as such a box &c. will hold: *to eat a whole tin of sardines, of biscuits* &c. **3.** (slang) Money; wealth.

tin (**II.**), vb. trans., fr. prec. **1.** To coat with tin. **2.** To pack, preserve, in a box or case, made of tin-covered plates: *to tin fruit, fish* &c.

tinamou, n. [1. tínamōō; 2. tínəmū]. S. Am. word. S. American bird, member of the family *Tinamidae,* resembling a quail.

tincal, tinkal, n. [1. tíngkl; 2. tíŋkl]. Malay. word. Crude borax.

tin-clad, n. (facet.) An ironclad vessel; an ironclad.

tinct, adj. & n. [1. tingkt; 2. tiŋkt], fr. Lat. *tinctus,* P.P. of *tingere,* 'to wet, moisten; to soak, steep; to soak in colour, to dye'; earlier **tengere,* cp. Gk. *téngein,* 'to moisten'; cogn. w. O.H.G. *dunkōn,* 'to steep, immerse'. (poet. and archaic) **1.** adj. Coloured, tinged. **2.** n. A colour, hue, shade of colour.

tinction, n. [1. tíngkshun; 2. tíŋkʃən]. Prec. & **-ion.** Act or process of staining or dyeing.

tinctorial, adj. [1. tingktórial; 2. tiŋktɔ́riəl]. Lat. *tinctōrius,* fr. *tinctor,* 'dyer', see **tinct**, & **-al.** **a** Connected with, pertaining to, dyeing; **b** pertaining to colour or colours; **c** tending to impart a colour.

tincture (**I.**), n. [1. tíngkchur; 2. tíŋktʃə]. Lat. *tinctūra,* 'dyeing', see **tinct** & **-ure.** **1.** A tinge, shade of colour, a tint. **2.** (her.)

The word used for colour on shields and bearings, but including, beside the heraldic colours, also *metals* and *furs*. **3.** (med.) A solution of some substance, esp. of vegetable character, used as a drug. **4.** (fig.) **a** (material sense) A slight trace, faint taste, or colour; smack: *a faint tincture of tobacco, vanilla, of red &c.*; **b** (in moral sense) a superadded quality or characteristic; a veneer: *some tincture of education, civilization, of good breeding.*

tincture (II.), vb. trans., fr. prec. **1.** To impart a tincture to; to communicate a slight taste, shade of colour, to. **2.** (in moral sense) To affect slightly, imbue faintly; to impart a quality to in a small degree: *his character is but slightly tinctured with humanity.*

tindal, n. [1. tíndal; 2. tíndəl], fr. Malay. *tandal*. A petty officer of a lascar crew, subordinate to the serang.

tinder, n. [1. tínder; 2. tíndə]. O.E. *tynder, tyndre*, M.E. *tinder* &c.; O.H.G. *zuntara*; O.N. *tundr*; cp. O.E. (*on-*)*tendan*, fr. **tand-jan*, 'to kindle; to inflame'; O.H.G. *zunten*, 'to burn, glow'; Goth. *tandjan*, 'to kindle'; cp. Swed. *tända*, see **tändstickor**, & Goth. *tunnan*, 'to become kindled, enflamed'. Inflammable material, esp. such as was formerly used for obtaining a light from a spark, consisting of scorched linen &c., impregnated with saltpetre. Phr. *to burn like tinder*, to blaze up and burn furiously.

tinder-box, n. Case used before the invention of modern matches, for obtaining a light, containing tinder, flint, and steel.

tindery, adj. [1. tínderi; 2. tíndəri]. **tinder** & **-y**. Like tinder; very dry and inflammable.

tine, n. [1. tīn; 2. tain]. O.E. *tind*, 'prong, spike'; O.N. *tindr*; cogn. w. O.E. *tōþ*, 'tooth', fr. **tanþ-*, of wh. base it is a gradational variant, w. *-d* instead of *-þ*, on account of the conditions of accent formulated under Verner's Law; see **tooth**. **a** One of the prongs of a fork; **b** one of the projecting spikes of a harrow; **c** a prong of a stag's antler.

tinea, n. [1. tínea; 2. tíniə]. Lat., 'worm, moth'. Prob. fr. **twinea*, & cogn. w. Gk. *sínomai*, 'to injure, damage'; & w. O.E. *þwīnan*, 'to dwindle', also w. O.E. *þwǣnan*, 'to moisten, soften'. The base, according to Walde, meant 'moisture, injury caused by damp' &c., & *tinea* meant 'a worm produced from damp mould'. See also **tabes**. **1.** (entom.) The genus of clothes-moths. **2.** (med.) One of various skin diseases, esp. ringworm.

tin-foil, n. & vb. trans. **1.** n. Very thin sheet of tin, used for wrapping and packing. **2.** vb. To wrap up in, coat with, tin-foil.

ting, n. & vb. intrans. & trans. [1. ting; 2. tiŋ]. Imitative word. **1.** n. A tinkle, sound, made by a bell. **2.** vb. **a** intrans. To tinkle, sound as a bell; **b** trans., to ring, tinkle (a bell).

tinge (I.), vb. trans. & intrans. [1. tinj; 2. tin(d)ž], fr. Lat. *tingere*, 'to dye' &c., see **tinct**. **A.** trans. **1.** To colour slightly, to tint, imbue: *the setting sun tinges the sky with a rosy flush.* **2.** (fig., chiefly in P.P.) To affect faintly but perceptibly, to cast a shadow, shed a brightness upon, to colour: *memories of past events tinged with melancholy; present sorrow tinged with brighter hopes for the future.* **B.** intrans. (rare) To become tinged.

tinge (II.), n., fr. prec. **1.** Some degree of colour, usually a faint amount; a tincture. **2.** Admixture, addition, of some extraneous feeling, passion &c., to a prevailing state of mind; a spice, a touch: *his piety had no tinge of hypocrisy; his banter contained a tinge of malice.*

tingle (I.), vb. intrans. [1. tínggl; 2. tiŋgl]. Prob. freq. of **ting**. **1.** To experience a sensation as of slight pricking, smarting, tickling, or stinging: *ears tingling with the cold; the blow made my cheek tingle.* **2.** To thrill, be excited, stirred, roused; to throb, flutter: *we were all tingling with eagerness and excitement.* **3.** To produce a sensation comparable to pricking or tingling; **a** to tremble, shimmer: *the tingling heat and sunlight of an August noon*; **b** to vibrate, throb: *the air still tingled with the sound of distant bells.*

tingle (II.), n., fr. prec. **a** The physical sensation of tingling; **b** the emotional condition of tingling.

tinker (I.), n. [1. tíngker; 2. tíŋkə]. In M.E.; lit. 'one who tinks', i.e. who makes a tinkling sound, as by striking a metal vessel with another piece of metal, as itinerant menders of pots and pans used formerly to do, to announce their coming. *Tink* was an imitative word; see **tinkle**. **1.** A mender of metal articles such as kettles, pots, and pans, esp. an itinerant mender of these. **2.** A clumsy botcher, an unskilful workman. **3.** (re-formed from **tinker** (II.)) Act of tinkering; clumsy, unskilful attempt to mend or fix: *to have a tinker at the electric light.*

tinker (II.), vb. trans. & intrans., fr. prec. **1.** trans. **a** To apply the craft of a tinker to; **b** to mend roughly, unskilfully; to botch: *I've merely tinkered the pipe anyhow for the time being.* **2.** intrans. To ply the trade of a tinker: (fig.) *to tinker with (anything)*, try to improve by hesitating, unskilful means; also *tinker away (at)*, to make prolonged, clumsy, ineffectual efforts at repairing; to fiddle with; *tinker up*, to get, or try to get, into working order, at least temporarily, by hasty, insufficient means: *to tinker up a broken-down car; his doctor tinkered him up so that he could make his promised speech.*

tinkle, vb. intrans. & trans. & n. [1. tíngkl; 2. tiŋkl]; freq. of imitative *tink*. **1.** vb. **a** intrans. To give out a series of clear, light, metallic sounds as of a bell, or of a succession of light pieces of metal falling one upon another; to fall with a tinkling sound; **b** trans., to cause to tinkle: *to tinkle a bell.* **2.** n. The sound of a small bell; sound of pieces of metal &c. falling with ringing noise; a jingle.

tinkling, vbl. n. [1. tíngkling; 2. tíŋkliŋ], fr. prec. Sound of that which tinkles; succession of tinkles: '*Drowsy tinklings lull the distant folds*' (Gray's 'Elegy').

tinman, n. [1. tínman; 2. tínmən]. Craftsman who works in tin-plate; one who repairs articles made of this; manufacturer of tin-plate goods.

tinned, adj. [1. tind; 2. tind], fr. P.P. of **tin** (II.). **1.** Preserved in tins: *tinned salmon.* **2.** Coated with tin.

tinning, n. [1. tíning; 2. tíniŋ]. **1.** Act, trade, **a** of covering (iron plates &c.) with tin; **b** of enclosing and preserving (food) in tins. **2.** Lining of tin.

tinnitus, n. [1. tinítus; 2. tináitəs]. Lat., formed fr. *tinnītum*, P.P. of *tinnīre*, 'to ring, jingle, tinkle'; imitative. (med.) Affection of the organs of audition, which causes a sensation of a continuous ringing in the ears.

tin-plate, n. Thin sheet of iron coated with tin.

tinsel (I.), n. [1. tínsl; 2. tínsl], fr. O. Fr. *estencele*, 'spark', fr. Lat. **scintilla**. **1. a** Glittering material composed of thin strips or shreds of metal, used for trimming, esp. of theatrical costumes &c.; **b** a thin textile material interwoven with metal threads. **2.** (fig.) Anything gaudy, outwardly and superficially showy, but really cheap and meretricious; sham splendour; hollow pretence.

tinsel (II.), adj., fr. prec. **1.** Made of tinsel. **2.** (fig.) Resembling tinsel; gaudy, cheaply showy; flashy.

tinsel (III.), vb. trans., fr. **tinsel** (I.). To cover, trick out, with tinsel.

tinsmith, n. [1. tínsmith; 2. tínsmiþ]. Worker in tin or tin-plate.

tint (I.), n. [1. tint; 2. tint], fr. earlier **tinct**; see also **taint** (I.). **1. a** A colour, a dye; **b** a particular shade, variety of a colour. **2.** A faint shade of colour, a slight tinge.

tint (II.), vb. trans., fr. prec. To impart (a slight) colour to; to stain, dye; to tinge.

tinter, n. [1. tínter; 2. tíntə]. Prec. & **-er**. **a** Person who, thing which, tints; specif. **b** coloured slide used with another in a magic lantern, to impart a particular tint.

tintinnabular(y), adj. [1. tìntinábūlar(i); 2. tìntinǽbjulə(ri)]; see **tintinnabulum** & **-ary**. **a** Connected with bells, with the sound of bells; **b** producing a sound of ringing.

tintinnabulation, n. [1. tìntinabūláshun; 2. tìntinæbjuléiʃən]. Lat. *tintinnāt-*, P.P. type of *tintinnāre*, 'to ring, jingle' &c., fr. *tinnīre*, q.v. under **tinnitus**, & **-ion**. Ringing sound of bells.

tintinnabulum, n. [1. tìntinábūlum; 2. tìntinǽbjuləm]. Lat., 'a door bell, a cattle bell'; formed fr. *tintinnāre*, 'to ring' &c. See prec. The ringing, clanging sound, of bells.

tintometer, n. [1. tintómeter; 2. tintɔ́mitə]. See **tint** (I.) & **-meter**. Instrument for testing and determining tints.

tiny, adj. [1. tíni; 2. táini]. Origin unknown. See also **teeny**. Minute, very small, diminutive; often *tiny little* (*piece* &c.).

-tion, suff. [1. shn; 2. ʃən]. Lat. suff. expressing action or state; used to form ns. fr. vbl. stems; *-t-* is the termination of the stem of the P.P. See also **-ion** & **-ation**.

tip (I.), n. [1. tip; 2. tip]. In M.E.; cp. M.H.G. *zippel*, 'point, peak'; origin doubtful. **1.** Pointed or tapering upper part of anything: *the tips of the ears; a mountain tip.* **2.** The pointed lower or outer end, extremity of anything: *the tips of one's fingers, toes, tongue; the tip of an animal's tail, of wing &c.; the tip of a spear; the tip of one's stick* &c. Phrs. *to touch with the tips of one's fingers*, touch very lightly; barely touch; *to have something at the tips of one's fingers* (or *finger-tips*), handy, ready for use; *to the tips of one's fingers* (or *finger-tips*), through and through, completely; *at, on, the tip of one's tongue*, just about to be uttered. **3.** Various technical uses: e.g. a ferule for a stick or umbrella; upper section of a fishing-rod &c.

tip (II.), vb. trans., fr. prec. **1. a** To put a special tip or end to: *to have one's rod &c. tipped*; **b** (poet.) to affect, touch, adorn, the tip of: '*And tipped with silver every mountain-head*' (Pope, 'Il.', viii.). **2.** To cut off the tip(s) of: *to tip a bush* (in pruning); *to have one's hair tipped.* **3.** To touch very lightly, tap, as though with the tip of something. [Possibly should go under **tip** (IV.).]

tip (III.), n., fr. prec. in sense **3.** A slight, light touch, tap, or pat; *tip and run*, a form of primitive cricket, in which the batsman must run if the bat touches the ball.

tip (IV.), vb. trans. & intrans. M.E. *tipen*, 'to overthrow'; origin doubtful, perh. ultimately fr. **tip** (I.) & w. sense of 'to bend, press, the tip over', hence 'to upset'. **A.** trans. **1.** To cause to lean away from the vertical, to make to slant; to tilt, cant: *to tip a barrel; to tip a cart.* Phr. *to tip the scale*, to cause one scale to be lower than the other, to be heavier than something else; (fig.) to outweigh, preponderate over, have the advantage of. **2.** To cause to shoot out of a receptacle by tipping; to upset, empty out (a load) in this way: *to tip rubbish.* **B.** intrans. To lean out of the straight, to tilt, slant. **C.** Followed by prepositions or adverbs. *Tip off*, trans., to pour out (liquor) by tilting the vessel. *Tip out*, **a** trans., to cause to fall out by tilting; to upset: *to be tipped out of a cart*; **b** intrans., to fall out through being tilted; to be tipped out. *Tip over*, **a** trans., to upset, overturn; **b** intrans., to be upset, to capsize. *Tip up*, **1.** trans., **a** to cause to fall over, to upset; **b** to tilt backwards so that the lighter end rises: *to tip up a cart*; hence, *tip-up seat*, that allows free passage; **2.** intrans., to lose one's balance when leaning backwards; to fall over through being top-heavy; to topple over.

tip (V.), n. Place where rubbish &c. is tipped.

tip (VI.), n. & vb. trans. & intrans. Origin doubtful. **1.** n. **a** A present, voluntary gift of money, a gratuity; esp. a payment not legally enforceable, made to an inferior for some slight extra service; **b** a useful hint, piece of advice, supposed to be based upon private information, recommending a certain line of action; esp. regarding the probable winner of a horse race or concerning a financial speculation: *to get a good tip for the Derby; to get the tip to buy copper.* Phrs. *take my tip,* do what I advise; *to give a man the tip* (*to do something*), recommend him (to); *the straight tip,* a definite, unambiguous hint; sound advice. **2.** vb. **a** trans. (i.) To give a tip or present to: *to tip a waiter, a schoolboy;* (ii.) (colloq.) to give, bestow, communicate; (in restricted usage) *to tip the company a song.* Phrs. *to tip the wink,* give a hint, make a sign to; *to tip a winner,* indicate beforehand the horse which will win a race; **b** intrans., to give tips: *travelling is made easy if one tips freely.*

tip-cart, n. One made to tip backwards from the shafts.

tip-cat, n. Boys' game in which a small piece of wood is struck with a bat or stick, so as to cause it to fly into the air, and is then struck again so that it flies several yards.

tippet, n. [1. típet; 2. típit]. O.E. *tæppet,* fr. Lat. *tapēte,* 'tapestry, coverlet'; see **tapestry. a** Short cape covering shoulders and chest worn by women; **b** specif., cape or scarf worn officially by judges and by the clergy.

tipple (**I.**), vb. intrans. & trans. [1. típl; 2. típl]. Freq., fr. **tip** (**IV.**). **1.** intrans. To drink frequently; specif., to drink alcoholic liquor to excess. **2.** trans. To drink; implying excess in strong liquor: *to tipple brandy all day long.*

tipple (**II.**), n., fr. prec. **a** Strong drink; **b** (facet.) any kind of drink.

tippler, n. [1. típler; 2. típlə]. **tipple** (**I.**) & **-er.** One who tipples; person who partakes, frequently, and to excess, of strong drink; a drunkard, a bibber.

tipsily, adv. [1. típsili; 2. típsili]. **tipsy** & **-ly.** In a tipsy, drunken manner; as though tipsy.

tipsiness, n. [1. típsines; 2. típsinis]. **tipsy** & **-ness.** State of being tipsy; tipsy habits.

tipstaff, n. [1. típstahf; 2. típstāf]. **a** Rod tipped with metal, used as the badge of a sheriff's officer; **b** official who carries such a rod.

tipster, n. [1. típster; 2. típstə]. **tip** (**VI.**) & **-ster.** One who lives by selling tips on likely winners (of horse-races).

tipsy, adj. [1. típsi; 2. típsi]. **tip** (**IV.**) & **-sy.** (refined and slightly old-fashioned; lady's word) Drunk, intoxicated; the politest and mildest term, often implying only an early stage of intoxication.

tipsy-cake, n. Sponge cake soaked in wine, covered with jam, over which whipped cream is spread, the whole garnished with small macaroons or almonds.

tiptoe, adv. & vb. intrans. [1. típtō; 2. típtou]. Used by Chaucer. **1.** adv. Usually *on tiptoe:* **a** on the points, tips, of the toes; *to stand on tiptoe,* as though trying to see over something; **b** (fig.) nervously wrought up, stirred, eagerly expectant, agog: (*to be*) *on tiptoe with curiosity, excitement.* **2.** vb. To walk on tiptoe: *to tiptoe into the room, tiptoe about,* to walk gingerly as though to avoid making a noise or arousing attention.

tiptop, n. & adj. [1. típtóp; 2. típtɔ́p]. **1.** n. **a** The highest point; esp. **b** (fig.) the highest point of excellence: *at the tiptop of his profession.* **2.** adj. (colloq.) First-rate, most excellent: *a tiptop lecture, dinner, rider* &c.

tirade, n. [1. tirād; 2. tiréid]. Fr., fr. Ital. *tirata,* 'a pulling; a lengthening; a long speech'; fr. *tirāre,* 'to draw'; see second element in **retire,** & cp. **tier.** Long, impassioned, or intemperate speech, esp. one in denunciation of a person or policy &c.

tirailleur, n. Compromise for Fr. pronunciation [1. tìrī(l)yĕr; 2. tìrai(l)jʌ́]. Fr., 'skirmisher, sharp-shooter', fr. *tirailler,* 'to skirmish', fr. *tirer,* 'to draw (trigger), to shoot'. In French army, sharpshooter, an infantry skirmisher, esp. of the native, or colonial infantry.

tire (**I.**), vb. trans. & intrans. [1. tīr; 2. táiə]. Origin doubtful; the vowel in M.E. *tiren,* & in the present form, is difficult to explain if we derive them fr. O.E. *teorian,* 'to fail; not to be up to the mark; to be tired; to make tired'. Even if we suppose that the word was partly influenced by O.E. *tergan,* 'to irritate, annoy, afflict', it does not help us much for the present form. See **tarry** (**II.**). **A.** trans. **1.** To render weary, to fatigue, exhaust: *walking tires me; tire out,* render very weary, to exhaust completely. **2.** To render weary, sick of; to bore: *he tired me with his long speeches.* **B.** intrans. **1.** To become weary, grow fatigued; to become exhausted: *he tires very soon if he exerts himself.* **2.** *Tire of,* to become sick of, bored by, to lose patience over, and interest in: *I soon tire of listening to classical music.*

tire (**II.**), n. In sense **3** often **tyre.** Form of **attire** (**II.**). **1.** (archaic) Raiment, apparel. **2.** (archaic) Apparatus, equipment, furnishing, trapping. **3. a** Circular iron band surrounding the outside of the wheel of a vehicle, and forming the tread; **b** thick solid band of rubber on outside of carriage wheels; relatively thick, cushion-like inflated tube fixed to the outside of wheels of bicycles and motor vehicles.

tire (**III.**), vb. trans., fr. prec. **1.** (archaic) To attire, adorn, dress: '*she painted her face, and tired her head*' (II. Kings, 9. 30). **2.** To put a tire on (a wheel).

tire (**IV.**), n. See **tiara.** (archaic and poet.) A tiara.

tired, adj. [1. tīrd; 2. táiəd], fr. P.P. of **tire** (**I.**). **1.** Fatigued, exhausted, weary, in mind or body, as from exertion. **2.** *Tired of,* uninterested in, out of patience with, sick of, bored with: *tired of life, of doing, hearing, the same thing so often; to get very tired of constant complaints* &c.; (also absol.) *you can shout till you are tired,* i.e. tired of shouting &c. Also frequently, *sick and tired of,* thoroughly disgusted with and bored by.

tiredness, n. [1. tīrdnes; 2. táiədnis]. Prec. & **-ness.** Fatigue, weariness.

tireless, adj. [1. tīrles; 2. táiəlis]. **tire** (**I.**) & **-less. 1.** (of persons) Unwearied, not easily fatigued; hence, very energetic, active, industrious. **2.** (of actions and activities) Showing no weariness on the part of performer; unwearying, ceaseless, unabated: *tireless energy, zeal, solicitude, industry* &c.

tirelessly, adv. Prec. & **-ly.** In a tireless manner.

tirelessness, n. See prec. & **-ness.** Quality of being tireless.

tiresome, adj. [1. tīrsum; 2. táiəsəm]. **tire** (**I.**) & **-some. 1.** Annoying, worrying, provoking, irritating, plaguy: *a tiresome child, illness, piece of work.* **2.** Tedious, devoid of interest, dull: *a tiresome lecture, sermon.*

tiresomely, adv. Prec. & **-ly.** In a tiresome way.

tiresomeness, n. See prec. & **-ness.** Quality of being tiresome.

tire-woman, n., fr. **tire** (**III.**). (archaic) Female attendant, lady's maid; esp. a dresser in a theatre.

tiring, adj. [1. tīring; 2. táiəriŋ], fr. Pres. Part. of **tire** (**I.**). **1.** Tending to produce fatigue, exhausting: *a very tiring job.* **2.** (more rarely) Tedious, boring.

tiring-room, n., fr. **tire** (**III.**). (archaic) Dressing-room in a theatre.

tiro, tyro, n. [1. tīrō; 2. táiərou], fr. Lat. *tīro,* 'young, newly enlisted soldier; recruit; hence, beginner', etymol. doubtful. A beginner, a new, unskilled hand, one who is inexperienced in some particular occupation, craft, exercise &c.

tirocinium, n. [1. tìrōsínium; 2. tàirousíniəm]. Lat., 'the first military service or campaign of a young soldier; military inexperience'; fr. *tīro,* see prec. Apprenticeship; first steps in, elements of, an art or accomplishment.

tirra-lirra, n. [1. tíra líra; 2. tírə lírə]. Imitative of a bird's note. Used to designate a gay, light-hearted carolling; equivalent to *tralala* and such combinations, substituted for words in a song: '*Tirra-lirra by the river Sang Sir Lancelot*' (Tennyson, 'Lady of Shalott', iii. 4).

tir-wit, n. [1. tĕ́r wit; 2. tíə wit]. Imitative. Peewit, lapwing.

tisane, n. [1. tizán; 2. tizǽn]. See **ptisan.** A medicinal tea, herbal decoction.

tissue (**I.**), n. [1. tíshū, tísū, tíshōō; 2. tíʃju, tísju, tíʃū]. Fr. *tissu,* 'woven fabric', formed fr. *tisser,* 'to weave', fr. Lat. *texere,* 'to weave', q.v. under **text. 1. a** A woven fabric; generally used only of finely woven material; specif. **b** light, gauzy silken material, esp. one interwoven with gold or silver threads. **2.** (biol.) The structural material of the body of plants or animals, consisting of groups of cells and the intercellular substance. **3.** Complicated, interwoven, series; web: esp. *a tissue of lies, falsehoods, absurdities.* **4.** Tissue-paper.

tissue (**II.**), vb. trans., fr. prec. (rare) To form into a tissue.

tissued, adj. [1. tísūd, tíshūd; 2. tísjūd, tíʃjūd], fr. P.P. of prec. **a** Clothed, covered, with tissue; **b** variegated like tissue.

tissue-paper, n. Kind of very thin, soft paper, used to wrap or protect delicate, fragile articles.

tit (**I.**), n. [1. tit; 2. tit]. Variant of **teat.**

tit (**II.**), n., in M.E. cp. O.N. *tittr,* 'a bird; a small thing'. **1.** Any of various kinds of small, bright-coloured birds. **2.** (archaic, rare) **a** A poor, small horse; **b** a child, girl.

tit (**III.**). Origin unknown. Cp. Fr. *tant pour tant.* Only in Phr. (to give, pay) *tit-for-tat,* blow for blow; an equivalent for something received; retaliation.

Titan, n. [1. tī́tan; 2. táitən]. Gk. mythol. *Tītán,* name of one of the primitive deities, the gigantic children of Uranus & Gaea; fr. two of these, Cronos & Rhea, Zeus & the Olympians descended. The name is cogn. w. Lat. *titio,* 'a burning brand'; see **entice.** A person of heroic size and strength, or of surpassing genius and intellect; (also attrib.) gigantic, enormous: *Titan strength* &c.; specif., *Titan crane,* a large crane for hoisting and moving very heavy weights, travelling on rails under its own motive power.

Titanesque, adj. [1. tītanésk; 2. tàitənésk]. Prec. & **-esque.** Resembling, characteristic of, a Titan, or the Titans.

Titaness, n. [1. tī́tanes; 2. táitənes]. **Titan** & **-ess.** Female Titan.

titanic, adj. [1. tītánik; 2. taitǽnik]. **Titan** & **-ic. 1.** Huge, gigantic, colossal. **2.** (chem.) Connected with, derived from, titanium: *titanic acid.*

titanite, n. [1. tī́tanīt; 2. táitənait]. See prec. & **-ite.** A mineral containing titanic acid, found in igneous rocks.

titanium, n. [1. tītā́nium; 2. taitéiniəm]. See prec. & **-ium.** A grey-coloured metallic element, somewhat resembling silicon, found only in combination.

titbit, n. [1. títbìt; 2. títbit]. See **tit** (**II.**) = 'small', & **bit** (**I.**). A choice morsel, extra delicate or tender piece of food; (fig.) a spicy item of news &c.

tithable, adj. [1. tī́dhabl; 2. táiðəbl]. **tithe** & **-able.** (of land) Subject to tithes.

tithe (**I.**), n. [1. tīdh; 2. taið]. O.E. *teogoþa, tēoþa,* 'tenth part', M.E. *tīthe, tīthe;* fr. primitive **tigunþa,* cp. Goth. *taihunda;* O.N. *tīund,* formed fr. numeral **tegun,* '10', see **ten** & **-th; tenth** is a later formation. **1.** A tenth part; specif., a portion of the supposed yearly profit derived from a given piece of land, from stock &c., anciently set apart for the support of the Church. **2.** (popular usage) A small portion or proportion of anything, a fraction; in Phr. *not a tithe of,* only a very small part.

tithe (II.), vb. trans., fr. prec. To impose a tithe upon.

tithe-barn, n. One in which the grain representing the tithe payable by a parish was anciently stored.

tithe-pig, n. Pig set apart as tithe.

tithing, n. [1. tídhing; 2. táiðiŋ]. O.E. *tēoþung*, 'a group of ten (men)'; see **tithe** (I.) & **-ing**. Ancient administrative unit, consisting formerly of ten households living near together.

titillate, vb. trans. [1. títilāt; 2. títileit]. Lat. *titillāt-(um)*, P.P. of *titillāre*, 'to tickle'; prob. imitative of rapid movement. To tickle; usually in non-physical sense, to stimulate the mind, excite pleasurably; to exhilarate.

titillation, n. [1. titiláshun; 2. titiléiʃən]. Prec. & **-ion**. **1.** Act, process, of titillating. **2.** **a** Sensation of tickling; **b** sense of being stimulated, exhilarated.

titillative, adj. [1. títilativ; 2. títilətiv]. **titillate** & **-ive**. Serving to titillate, producing titillation.

titivate, **tittivate**, vb. trans. & intrans. [1. títivāt; 2. títiveit]. Origin unknown. **1.** trans. To smarten up, to make clean and tidy, and adorn. **2.** intrans. To smarten oneself up, put finishing touches to one's toilet.

titivation, n. [1. titiváshun; 2. titivéiʃən]. Prec. & **-ion**. **a** Act of titivating; **b** results of this process; smartness, extra adornment.

titlark, n. [1. títlark; 2. títlāk]. See **tit** (II.). Name of a bird; the meadow pipit.

title, n. [1. títl; 2. táitl]. M.E., fr. O. Fr. *title*, fr. Lat. *titulus*, 'inscription, superscription, label, title; honourable appellation'; the etymol. is entirely uncertain, & none of the various suggestions appears even at all plausible. **1.** Distinguishing, descriptive designation, or inscription, placed on the front page &c. of a book, pamphlet, or other literary work, at the head of a chapter of a book &c.; also, such a distinctive appellation given to a musical composition, to a picture, sculpture &c.; appellation, name by which any of these things is known and identified. **2.** Appellation of honour and distinction, whether inherited, or conferred upon an individual, borne by him, and used in addressing, and referring to him, in addition to, or instead of, his name; in specific sense, *a title* means either an hereditary dignity, e.g. that of *duke, earl, baron* &c., that of *baronet*, or one specifically conferred by the sovereign or his representative, e.g. that of *knight*; more generally, the term is used in reference to appellations indicating rank, status, such as *General, Admiral* &c., to those indicating some particular office such as *Professor, Judge* &c., and to others designating a degree conferred by a university, such as *Doctor*. **3.** (law) The heading forming the name of an act or statute. **4.** **a** An admitted, recognized claim or right; the ground, reason, of such a claim: *the Odes of Keats would alone be a sufficient title to a place among the greatest poets*; specif. **b** (law) the elements as a whole which constitute right of ownership of property, esp. in land; also the document whereby such rights are established; title-deed. **5.** (eccles.) Usually defined as sphere of work and source of maintenance, evidence of which is required by a bishop before he admits a candidate to Holy Orders, that is, evidence that such a candidate has been nominated to a curacy, College Fellowship, chaplaincy &c. **6.** (bookbinding) Panel on back of book which bears the name.

titled, adj. [1. títld; 2. táitld]. Prec. & **-ed**. Possessing a title; specif., possessing a title of nobility, a baronetcy, or a knighthood.

title-deed, n. Document which establishes ownership, esp. of land.

title page, n. Front page of a book, which bears the title.

title-rôle, n. That part or character in a play from which it takes its name; e.g. the part of Hamlet in the play of that name.

titling, n. [1. títling; 2. táitliŋ]. **title** & **-ing**. Act, process, of stamping the title on the back of a book.

titmouse, n. [1. títmous; 2. títmaus]. M.E. *titemōse*, fr. **tit** (II.) & O.E. *māse*, 'titmouse'; cp. O.H.G. *meisa*; the modern form has been influenced by *mouse*. Any one of the small birds belonging to the family *Paridae*, allied to the nuthatch.

titrate, vb. trans. [1. títrāt; 2. táitreit]. Fr. *titre*, see **title**, & **-ate**. To subject to titration.

titration, n. [1. titráshun; 2. taitréiʃən]. Prec. & **-ion**. Process of ascertaining the strength of a chemical solution by noting the amount of a standardized solution which requires to be added to it in order to produce a definite chemical reaction.

titter, vb. intrans. & n. [1. títer; 2. títə]. Imitative of sound made. **1.** vb. To utter a partially smothered laugh, to giggle. **2.** n. A shrill, smothered laugh.

tittle, n. [1. títl; 2. títl]. M.E. *titel*, 'superscription' &c., see **title**. **1.** (obs.) Diacritical mark over a letter or word to indicate contraction &c. **2.** A minute amount, particle: *not a tittle of evidence against him*.

tittle-tattle, n. & vb. intrans. Redupl. of **tattle** (I.). **1.** n. Gossip, idle talk; chatter, rumour. **2.** vb. To gossip, to put rumours about.

tittup, vb. intrans. & n. [1. títup; 2. títəp]. Perh. popular form of **titubate**. **1.** vb. To behave in a gay, frolicsome manner; to prance gaily about. **2.** n. Light-hearted frolic; lively, frisky movement.

tittuppy, adj. [1. títupi; 2. títəpi]. Prec. & **-y**. **1.** Gay, frolicsome, cheerful, and lively. **2.** Shaky, tottery, rocky, groggy.

titubate, vb. intrans. [1. títūbāt; 2. títjubeit]. Lat. *titubāt-(um)*, P.P. of *titubāre*, 'to stagger, totter; to stammer'; according to Walde, fr. base **steub-* &c.; cogn. w. **stumble**. (obs. or rare) **a** To reel in one's walk; to totter; **b** to stammer.

titubation, n. [1. titūbáshun; 2. titjubéiʃən]. Prec. & **-ion**. **a** Act of reeling, staggering &c.; specif. **b** (med.) unsteadiness in the gait due to some nervous disorder.

titular, adj. & n. [1. títūlar; 2. títjulə]. Lat. *titulus*, see **title**, & **-ar**. **1.** adj. **a** Connected with, of the nature of, a title: *a titular distinction*; **b** existing in name only, nominal; holding a title without in fact enjoying the dignity it connotes, or performing the functions of the office: *Charles Stuart, the Young Pretender, was titular Prince of Wales*; *titular bishop*, bishop who holds the title of an extinct see, esp. one the seat of which is now in Mohammedan possession. **2.** n. The nominal holder of a title of an office, who does not perform the functions of the office: *titular prince, professor, bishop*.

titulary, adj. & n. [1. títūlari; 2. títjuləri]. Prec. & **-y**. Titular.

tityre-tu, n. [1. títirā tū; 2. táitirei tjú], fr. the opening words of Virgil's 1st Eclogue, 'O Tityrus, thou &c.'. Name of a class or gang of young, noisy, and ruffianly men of fashion, infesting the streets of London during the late 17th cent., esp. during reign of Charles II.

tizzy, n. [1. tízi; 2. tízi]. Familiar form of **tester** (III.). (obsolesc. slang) A sixpence.

tmesis, n. [1. tmēsis; 2. tmísis]. Gk. *tmēsis*, 'a cutting'; *tm-* is the 'vanishing' grade of Gk. base *tem-, tom-*, cp. *témnein*, 'to cut', & *tomḗ*, 'a cutting'; see under **tome**. (gram.) The interpolation of one or more words between the parts of a compound, thus dividing the word; e.g. *what name soever*; or (vulg.) *abso-blooming-lutely*.

to (I.), prep. [1. too; 2. tū] when stressed; the unstressed forms are [tə] before cons., & [tu] before vowels. O.E., O.S., & O. Fris. *tō*; O.H.G. *za, zuo* &c.; Germ. *zu*; outside Gmc. cp. Lat. *dḗ*, 'from; concerning' &c., see **de-**; O. Slav. *do*, 'up to, to, till'. **1.** Expressing movement towards, in the direction of; **a** (not implying arrival): *turn, keep, to the right*; *go to the south*; *on the way to London*; **b** (implying arrival) as far as: *I am going to London tomorrow, and leaving next day*; *you can't possibly get to Oxford tonight*; *to fall to the ground*; *to go to sea*; Phr. *to and fro*, backwards and forwards, there and back; see **fro**. **2.** Expressing a progress, change, trend, in direction of particular state, set of conditions or circumstances: *from bad to worse*; *brought to poverty*; *to sink to the worst depths of misery*; *to put to death*; **b** movement into and retention of certain position; starting and continuance of an action: *stand to attention*; *to horse!*; *to arms!* **3.** Expressing **a** some precise stage, phase, point, reached; just as far as: *done to a turn*; *expressed to a nicety, shade*; *frozen to the marrow*; *wet to the skin*; **b** extent, intensity, of some quality or action: *an Englishman to the core*; *sick to death*; *cut to the heart*. **4.** Expressing a final point of duration in time; until: *from Saturday to Monday*; *stay to the end of June*; *conscious to the last*; *to the end of his life he refused to see his brother*. **5.** Indicating the dative case relation; denoting the indirect object of an action, that to which the action is directed; person or thing affected by the action expressed by the verb; indicating the recipient, possessor, one to whom something is imparted &c.: *to do harm to a person*; *listen to me*; *I look to you for help*; *attend to what is said*; *hand round the wine to the company*; *to give money to the poor*; *it belongs to me*; *I wouldn't tell this to everybody*; *I put it to you*. **6.** Expressing comparison; compared with: *nothing to what it might have been*; *all former wars were mere child's play to the Great War*; *he's quite rich to what he once was*. **7.** In numerous phrases and constructions expressing various relations and conditions; **a** effect, consequence: *to my great distress*; *to my delight, horror*; *to his cost*; *to his credit be it said* &c.; **b** opposition: *hand to hand*; *face to face*; **c** amount, extent; *it comes to ten pounds*; *the park extends to several thousand acres*; **d** agreement: *quite to my taste*; *to the best of my belief*; *to my way of thinking*; **e** adaptation, suitability: *boots made to any foot*; *drawn to scale*; **f** addition, advantage: *put this to what you already have*; *to have a handle to one's name*; *five pounds to one's credit*; *all to the good*; **g** intention, purpose: *to that end*; *to the end that*. **8.** Followed by unaltered form of verb to form infinitive; **a** expressing purpose: *I said that to test you*; *everything was done to please her*; *he fights to win*; *have come to see you*; *I bought this house to live in*; *this was made to be used*; (archaic or provinc.) *for to do*, see &c.; **b** used before the second of two verbs: *I want to see*; *to refuse to stay*; *begin to talk* &c.; also elliptically at end of sentence, with verb omitted when it has been previously mentioned: *he asked me to go to dinner, but I don't want to, haven't time to* &c. (*go to dinner* understood); **c** forming with following verb the equivalent of a noun: '*To err is human, to forgive divine*' (Pope, 'Ess. on Crit.', ii. 526), = error, forgiveness; *to defy the law is a crime*, = defiance of; *it is foolish to speak of what one does not understand* &c.

to (II.), adv. Same as prec. **1.** Towards, into, the normal, desired, position, condition &c., esp. condition of repose: *push the door to*; *shut the window to*; *I can't get the lid of my trunk quite to*. **2.** After certain verbs: *bring to, come to, go to, fall to, heave to* &c.; see these verbs.

toad, n. [1. tōd; 2. toud]. O.E. *tādde*; usually *tādige*; etymol. unknown. Cp. **tadpole**. **1.** Amphibian, genus *Bufo*, shaped like a frog, but terrestrial in habits except at breeding season, more squat in shape, and having a rough skin, and less apt to leap. **2.** **a** A disgusting, loathsome person; **b** (archaic) applied playfully and affectionately to a person, esp. a child, without intention of disparagement: *the poor toad was delighted to see his mother again*.

toad-eater, n. **1.** Originally, a mountebank's assistant who pretended to swallow toads in order to show his master's skill at curing him of the poisonous effects. **2.** A flatterer, an obsequious sycophant.

toad-eating, n. Sycophancy, servility, obsequiousness.

toad-flax, n. Common European plant, *Linaria*, one species of which has flowers of two shades of yellow; called also *butter-and-eggs*.

toad-in-the-hole, n. [1. tōd in dhe hōl; 2. tòud in ðə hóul]. Beef-steak cooked in batter.

toadstone, n. [1. tṓdstōn; 2. tóudstoun]. Stone formerly supposed to be formed in body of a toad, and to possess powers as a charm.

toadstool, n. [1. tṓdstōōl; 2. tóudstūl]. Any of various fungi other than mushrooms, esp. those of supposedly poisonous species.

toady, n. & vb. trans. [1. tṓdi; 2. tóudi]. Prob. fr. **toad-eater**. **1.** n. A servile flatterer, a truckling sycophant of the rich and powerful. **2.** vb. To truckle to, and flatter grossly, with ulterior motives of self-interest.

toast (**I.**), vb. trans. & intrans. [1. tōst; 2. toust]. O. Fr. *toster*, fr. Lat. *tostum*, P.P. of *torrere*, 'to parch, roast'; see **torrid**. **A.** trans. **1.** To render brown and dry by direct exposure to fire. **2.** To warm thoroughly: *to toast oneself, one's feet, before the fire*. **B.** intrans. **1.** To become toasted, become brown by exposure to the fire. **2.** To toast oneself.

toast (**II.**), n. O. Fr. *tostée*, 'toasted bread', P.P. See prec. **1. a** Slices of bread made brown and crisp on the outside by exposure to fire; **b** specif., such a slice soaked in hot wine; the wine together with the toast. **2. a** A person's health, a patriotic or other sentiment proposed, and honoured by the company raising their glasses and drinking in agreement: *to propose the toast of the King*; **b** person whose health is drunk; specif., a woman whose beauty and charm are frequently celebrated in toasts: *Mary Lepel was a favourite toast in the mid 18th century*; **c** act of proposing or honouring a toast.

toast (**III.**), vb. trans. & intrans., fr. prec. **1.** trans. To propose and drink the health of. **2.** intrans. To drink toasts.

toaster, n. [1. tṓster; 2. tóustə]. Any of various devices for toasting bread &c.

toasting-fork, n. [1. tṓsting fork; 2. tóustiŋ fɔ̄k]. Fork with a long handle with which bread is held before the fire to be toasted.

toast-master, n. Official who announces the toasts about to be proposed at a public dinner &c.

toast-rack, n. Small rack for holding slices of toast in vertical position on the table.

toast-water, n. Drink made by steeping well-browned toast in boiling water.

tobacco, n. [1. tobákō; 2. təbǽkou]. Span. *tabaco*; fr. a Carib. (Haiti) native word. **1.** A solanaceous plant, genus *Nicotiana*, grown for its leaves, which are smoked in a pipe; grown also in gardens for its flowers. **2.** The leaves of this plant, dried and variously treated, used for chewing, for smoking in pipes and cigarettes, rolled into cigars, and reduced to a fine powder and used as snuff.

tobacco heart, n. Affection of the heart due to excessive tobacco smoking.

tobacconist, n. [1. tobákunist; 2. təbǽkənist]. An irregular formation. **1.** Person who sells tobacco in all forms retail. **2.** (obs.) In 17th and 18th cents., one who smoked tobacco.

tobacco-pipe, n. Small tube of wood, meerschaum, clay &c., with mouth-piece at one end, and a receptacle or bowl at the other, in which tobacco is smoked.

tobacco-pouch, n. Bag or case of india-rubber, leather, or other air-tight material, in which tobacco is carried in the pocket.

toboggan, n. & vb. intrans. [1. tobógan; 2. təbɔ́gən], fr. Am. Indian name. **1.** n. Kind of sledge with flat bottom, without runners, having the forward end curved upward, much used in Switzerland for coasting down snow-covered slopes. **2.** vb. To use, travel, coast on, a toboggan.

toby jug, n. [1. tṓbi jug; 2. tóubi džag]. Jug or tankard of porcelain, used for ale, in form of a fat squat man gaily dressed in 18th century style, wearing a three-cornered hat which forms the brim of the vessel.

toccata, n. [1. tokáhta; 2. təkā́tə]. Ital., P.P. fem. of *toccāre*, see **touch** (**I.**). Old musical composition for organ or piano, formerly intended as an exercise for the touch.

toccatella, n. [1. tòkatéla; 2. tɔ̀kətélə]. Ital. dimin. of prec. Short or simple toccata.

tocology. See **tokology**.

tocsin, n. [1. tóksin; 2. tɔ́ksin]. Fr., 'alarm-bell'; earlier *toquesing*, cp. Fr. *touquer*, 'to strike', see **touch** (**I.**), & **sign** (**I.**). **a** Bell sounded to give an alarm; **b** the sound of, alarm sounded by, such a bell.

tod, n. [1. tod; 2. tɔd]. O.N. *toddi*, 'mass, tuft'. **1.** (archaic) Bush, thick foliage. **2.** (provinc., from its bushy tail) A fox. **3.** (archaic) Weight of wool; usually 28 lbs.

Toda, n. [1. tṓda; 2. tóudə]. Member of a tribe in the Nilgiri Hills of Hindustan, speaking a Dravidian language, and characterized by a fair complexion and regular features.

today, adv. & n. [1. tudā́; 2. tədéi]. O.E. *tō dæge*, also uninflected *tōdæġ*; see **to** (**I.**) & **day**. **1.** adv. **a** On this day; **b** at this present time, in the age in which we live: *our ideas today differ much from those prevalent in the 18th century*. **2.** n. This present time: *the writers of today*.

toddle (**I.**), vb. intrans. [1. tódl; 2. tɔ́dl]. Freq. of **totter**. **1.** To walk with short, hesitating, uncertain steps, as a child does; to walk like a very young child. **2.** (colloq.) **a** To walk, stroll, in a quiet unhurried manner: *do you feel inclined to toddle down to the club?*; **b** to take one's departure: *it's getting late, we must be toddling*.

toddle (**II.**), n., fr. prec. **a** Act of toddling; **b** a quiet, leisurely walk, stroll.

toddler, n. [1. tódler; 2. tɔ́dlə]. **toddle** (**I.**) & **-er**. Person who toddles; specif., a young child just learning, or having just learnt, to walk.

toddy, n. [1. tódi; 2. tɔ́di]. Hind. *tārī*, 'juice of palmyra tree'. A drink composed of spirits, sugar, lemon, and hot water; punch.

to-do, n. [1. tu dōō; 2. tə dū́]. See **to** (**I.**) & **do** (**I.**). An ado, a fuss, commotion: *to make a terrible to-do about losing one's luggage*.

tody, n. [1. tṓdi; 2. tóudi], fr. Fr. *todier*, fr. Lat. *todus*, 'kind of small bird'. A small bright-coloured W. Indian bird allied to the king-fishers, living on insects and nesting in the banks of streams and rivers.

toe (**I.**), n. [1. tō; 2. tou]. O.E. *tā*, *tāhe*, M.E. *tō*; O.H.G. *zēha*; orig., 'the pointer'; cogn. w. Lat. *digitus* (fr. **dicitus*), 'finger, toe', see **digit**; fr. base **doikʷ-*, **dikʷ-* &c.; see also **diction, teach, token**. **1. a** (in man and monkey) One of the digits of the feet, corresponding to the fingers of the hand; Phrs. *to tread on a person's toes*, wound his susceptibilities; *to turn up one's toes*, to die; *from top to toe*, from head to foot; *big, great, toe*, largest of the toes on a human foot, corresponding to the thumb of the hand; *little toe*, smallest, outside, toe of human foot; **b** (in other animals) one of the digits on fore or hind feet. **2. a** That part of a boot, shoe, stocking &c. which covers the toes; **b** projecting point on under side of a horse-shoe, designed to prevent slipping. **3.** The fore part of the foot, contrasted with *heel*. **4.** (colloq.) The foot of man as a whole: *to toast one's toes*, warm one's feet. **5.** The outer end of the head of a golf-club.

toe (**II.**), vb. trans., fr. prec. **1.** To put a toe (cap) on to: *boots to be toed and heeled*. **2.** To bring the toes level with: *to toe the line*, originally of line marked at starting-point of a race; (fig.) to submit to discipline, conform to orders, custom &c. **3.** (slang) To kick with the toes: *to toe a person out of the room* &c. **4.** (golf) To strike (a ball) with part of club too near the toe.

toe-cap, n. That part of a boot or shoe which covers the toes, usually made separate from the rest of the boot.

-toed, suff. [1. tōd; 2. toud]. **toe** (**I.**) & **-ed**. As second element of compounds, having a particular kind of toe or certain number of toes: *square-toed*; *three-toed* &c.

toe-drop, n. Paralysis of foot muscles which causes inability to raise the toes.

toe-nail, n. Nail growing upon a toe.

toff, n. [1. tof, tawf; 2. tɔf, tɔ̄f]. Origin unknown. (lower class slang) **a** A swell, a dandy; **b** a person of the better classes; **a** gentleman.

toffee, toffy, n. [1. tófi; 2. tɔ́fi]. Also Scots & U.S.A. *taffy*; origin doubtful. Compound of sugar and butter, boiled till it becomes thick, then poured into a dish and allowed to cool and harden.

toft, n. [1. toft; 2. tɔft]. In O.E., 'piece of ground; hillock', fr. O.N. *topt*, 'a green knoll; site marked out for a house'. (only provinc., and in place-names) **a** A knoll, hillock; **b** a homestead.

tog, vb. trans. [1. tog; 2. tɔg], fr. **togs**. (slang) Chiefly *tog out*, to dress, esp. carefully and elaborately: *togged out in full uniform*.

toga, n. [1. tṓga; 2. tóugə]. Lat. *toga*, 'garment'; esp. the outer garment of a Roman citizen in peace, assumed at age of 14 as sign of manhood'; connected w. *tegere*, 'to cover'; see this base under **tegument**; cp. **thatch** (**I.**).

togaed, adj. [1. tṓgad; 2. tóugəd]. Clad in, wearing, a toga.

together, adv. [1. togédher; 2. təgéðə]. O.E. *tōgædere*; see **to** (**I.**) & **gather** (**I.**). **1.** In company, associated one with another: *to go about together*; *to live together*, specif. of persons of opposite sex, to live as man and wife. **2.** Against each other, in mutually hostile conjunction: *I can't have you two boys always fighting together*. **3.** Towards each other, into conjunction, so as to form a contact: *the opposing forces rushed together*; *to bring the blades of a pair of scissors together*. **4.** (of time) **a** (of divisions of time) In continuous succession, uninterruptedly, on end: *to ponder for hours together*; **b** (of events happening in time) at one and the same time or moment; synchronously: *all my troubles seem to come upon me together*. **5.** *Together with*, in combination with; also, as well as, in addition to: *I am sending you a dozen new-laid eggs, together with some fresh butter*.

togger, n. [1. tóger; 2. tɔ́gə]. Oxford University slang for **torpid** (**II.**), college boat in the Lent Term races. Pl. *toggers*, inter-collegiate boat-races in Lent Term.

toggery, n. [1. tógeri; 2. tɔ́gəri]. See **togs** & **-ery**. (colloq.) Clothes collectively; esp. some special kind of dress, uniform &c.: *an actor's, a bishop's, general's, toggery*.

toggle, n. & vb. trans. [1. tógl; 2. tɔ́gl]. Etymol. uncertain; perh. connected w. **tug** (**I.**). **1.** n. A metal pin fixed at right angles in the strands of a rope and projecting at either side, to serve as a means for holding another rope hitched over it. **2.** vb. To fasten by means of a toggle.

toggle-joint, n. Device for applying pressure sideways, consisting of two bars crossing each other near the ends, and pivoted or jointed together, so that force directed to straighten the joint is transmitted to the other end of each bar.

togs, n. pl. [1. togz; 2. tɔgz], fr. **toga**? (slang, esp. naut.) Clothes, dress: *fine new togs*.

toil (**I.**), n. [1. toil; 2. tɔil]. Fr. *toile*, 'cloth', fr. Lat. *tēla*, 'woven stuff, web'; fr. **texla*, cp. Lat. *texere*, 'to weave'; see **text**. Only used in pl. *toils*; net, meshes, snare; *in the toils*, lit. netted, caught; (fig.) deeply fascinated, charmed, under a spell &c.

toil (**II.**), vb. intrans. M.E. *toilen*, fr. O. Fr. *toillier*, 'to pull, drag about; cause to roll' &c., Lat. *tudiculāre*, 'to stir', fr. *tuditāre*, 'to thrust, push'; fr. *tudit-* stem of *tudēs*, 'hammer', connected w. the nasalized *tundere*, 'to strike', Both nasalized & unnasalized forms of this base occur in other languages, cp. Scrt. *tundatē*, & *tudáti*, 'he pushes, strikes, pricks'.

See also **contuse**. **1.** To exert strength, to work hard, labour; also *toil at*, to work at laboriously. **2.** To go along, walk, painfully and with effort: *to toil up hill*; *to toil along the road* &c.

toil (III.), n., fr. prec. Severe, tedious labour, exacting, fatiguing work, drudgery.

toiler, n. [1. tóiler; 2. tɔ́ilə]. **toil (I.)** & **-er.** One who toils; a hard worker.

toilet, n. [1. tóilet; 2. tɔ́ilit], fr. *toilette*, dimin. of *toile*, 'cloth', see **toil** (I.). **1.** (formerly, now obs.) A cloth for covering something; **a** one put over the shoulders while the hair was being dressed; **b** bag for night clothes. **2. a** Process of dressing: *to spend time on one's toilet*; **b** mode of dressing; a female costume: *colour was given by the brilliant toilets of the ladies.*

toilet-cover, n. Cloth or sheet placed over dressing-table.

toilet-paper, n. Thin sheets used in the privy.

toilet-powder, n. Soothing powder applied to the skin after shaving &c.

toilet-set, n. Set of articles and utensils used in the toilet.

toilet-table, n. Dressing-table.

toilful, adj. [1. tóilfool; 2. tɔ́ilful]. **toil (III.)** & **-ful.** Involving toil; toilsome.

toilfully, adv. Prec. & **-ly.** With toil; laboriously.

toilsome, adj. [1. tóilsum; 2. tɔ́ilsəm]. **toil (III.)** & **-some.** Laborious, wearying; involving toil.

toilsomely, adv. Prec. & **-ly.** Laboriously.

toilsomeness, n. See prec. & **-ness.** Quality of being toilsome; laboriousness.

toison d'or, n. [1. twahzon dŏr; 2. twazɔ̃ dɔ́r]. Fr. The Golden Fleece.

Tokay, n. [1. tōká; 2. toukéi], fr. place in Hungary. **1.** A rich, scarce, Hungarian wine coming from Tokay. **2.** A kind of grape used in the making of this wine.

token, n. [1. tōken; 2. tóukən]. O.E. *tācn*, 'sign, token, emblem' &c.; M.E. *tōken*; O.S. *tēkan*; O.H.G. *zeihhan*; Goth. *taikns*; all fr. Gmc. **taikn-*, see also **teach**, fr. base **deik-*, **dīk-* &c., 'to show, tell, point out' &c.; cp. Gk. *deiknūmi*, 'I show' &c.; Lat. *dīcere*, 'to show, say, tell'; see **diction**. **1.** A symbol, evidence: *a token of respect, regard, affection* &c.; *in token of*, as a sign, as evidence of. Phr. *by the same token*, to introduce additional or amplifying statement. **2.** Object used, or given, as a symbol and sign of some quality, feeling, value &c.; specif., a piece of metal formerly used by tradesmen and others instead of, but representing, money; (also attrib.) *token-money*, see preceding sense; *token vote*, money vote taken in Parliament for specific purpose, with nominal sum stated, the full amount being afterwards voted under a supplementary estimate.

tokenless, adj. [1. tōkenles; 2. tóukənlis]. Prec. & **-less.** Without, lacking, a token.

tokology, tocology, n. [1. tokóloji; 2. təkɔ́lədži], fr. Gk. *tókos*, 'birth, offspring, child', fr. base **tek-*, cp. *tiktein*, 'to produce, beget offspring', *téknon*, 'child'; cp. **thane** & see **-logy.** The science of obstetrics; midwifery.

tola, n. [1. tóla; 2. tóulə]. Hind., fr. Scrt. *tulā*, 'weight'. An Indian weight, 180 grains troy.

tolbooth, n. See **tol(l)booth.**

told, vb. [1. tōld; 2. tould]. O.E. *talde*, (*ge*)*tald* (cp. W.S. *tealde*); M.E. *tōld*(*e*); Pret. & P.P. of **tell.**

Toledo, Toledo blade, n. [1. tōlḗdō (blād); 2. toulídou (bleid)]. Sword-blade of finely tempered steel made at Toledo in Spain.

tolerability, n. [1. tòlerabíliti; 2. tɔ̀lərəbíliti]. See next word & **-ity.** Quality, state, of being tolerable.

tolerable, adj. [1. tólerabl; 2. tɔ́lərəbl]. Lat. *tolerābilis*, see **tolerate** & **-able.** **1.** Endurable, capable of being borne: *the pain was severe but tolerable.* **2. a** Fairly good, neither of the highest excellence nor such as to merit severe condemnation: *the food was good and the company tolerable*; **b** (colloq.) in fairly good health, pretty well.

tolerably, adv. Prec. & **-ly.** Moderately, fairly; to a moderate degree or extent; (usually in favourable sense) *tolerably well*; *tolerably satisfied.*

tolerance, n. [1. tólerans; 2. tɔ́lərəns]. Lat. *tolerantia*, see **tolerant** & **-ce.** Disposition of mind which is inclined to tolerate, and show forbearance to, opinions, beliefs, which one does not share, or a line of action which one does not approve of; toleration; reverse of *bigotry.*

tolerant, adj. [1. tólerant; 2. tɔ́lərənt], fr. Lat. *tolerant-*(*em*), Pres. Part. of *tolerāre*, 'to bear, endure', see **tolerate.** **1.** Disposed to tolerate; forbearing, indulgent; esp. to opinions and lines of conduct which are not one's own. **2.** (med.) Capable of bearing the action of a drug; inured by habit to considerable doses of poisonous drugs without suffering injury.

tolerate, vb. trans. [1. tólerāt; 2. tɔ́ləreit], fr. Lat. *tolerāt-*(*um*), P.P. of *tolerāre*, 'to bear, sustain, endure' &c.; fr. same base as *tollere*, 'to lift up; to accept'; cogn. w. Gk. *tálanton*, 'weight', see **talent**; also w. Lat. *lātus* for **tlātus*, 'borne', & Gk. *tlḗmōn*, 'enduring'; O.E. *þolian*, 'to endure', see **thole** (I.). **1. a** To endure, show forbearance to, bear with, put up with: *to tolerate a person's presence*; **b** to show toleration of the opinions, beliefs &c. of others. **2.** To be able to resist or endure: *his delicate constitution could not tolerate the severities of a northern climate.* **3.** To permit, suffer to be done without attempting to prevent: *I will not tolerate interference in my affairs*; *no responsible government can tolerate disregard of the law.*

toleration, n. [1. tòleráshun; 2. tɔ̀ləréiʃən]. Prec. & **-ion.** Act of tolerating; mental disposition to allow freedom of opinion and belief &c. to others; tolerance; practice of allowing such freedom, esp. in religious beliefs.

tolerationist, n. [1. tòleráshunist; 2. tɔ̀ləréiʃənist]. Prec. & **-ist.** One who advocates toleration, esp. in religion.

toll (I.), vb. trans. & intrans. [1. tōl; 2. toul]. In M.E.; etymol. uncertain; partly imitative. **1.** trans. To cause to sound or ring in a series of strokes repeated at regular intervals: *to toll a bell*; *to toll a funeral knell.* **2.** intrans. To sound, ring, clang, with a series of regularly repeated strokes (of a bell).

toll (II.), n., fr. prec. The sound made by the tolling of a bell.

toll (III.), n. O.E. *toll*, 'a tax; money due for rent' &c.; O.S. *tol*, O.H.G. *zol*; all fr. L. Lat. *tolōnium*, Lat. *telōneum*, 'toll-house', fr. Gk. *telṓnion*, cp. *telṓnēs*, 'tax-collector', & *télos*, 'tax'. **1. a** Tax, duty, paid for some privilege; specif., one paid for the right to pass along a road, or over a bridge, for use of a market &c.; **b** the right to exact a toll. **2.** Portion of grain kept by miller in payment for grinding; hence Phr. *to take toll of*, to exact something from.

tollable, adj. [1. tōlabl; 2. tóuləbl]. Prec. & **-able.** Subject to toll.

tollage, n. [1. tōlij; 2. tóulidž]. See prec. & **-age.** Payment, exaction, of toll.

toll-bar, n. Toll-gate.

tol(l)booth, n. [1. tòlbōōth; 2. tɔ̀lbúþ]. Scots. **1.** Formerly, temporary shed erected at a market &c. for payment of tolls. **2.** (Scots) Town prison.

toll-gate, n. Gate placed across high road, kept closed to prevent persons and vehicles from passing until the toll is paid.

toll-house, n. House at a toll-gate, where the keeper of this lives.

Toltec, n. [1. tóltek; 2. tɔ́ltɛk]. Race possessing considerable civilization, who preceded the Aztecs in Mexico.

tolu, n. [1. tōlōō; 2. toulú], fr. Santiago de Tolu. Also *tolu balsam*, an aromatic resin obtained from a S. American tree, used medicinally and in perfumery.

toluene, toluol, n. [1. tólooēn, tólūol; 2. tɔ́luīn, tɔ́ljuəl], fr. prec. & second element of **benzene, benzol.** An aromatic hydrocarbon obtained by distillation of tolu balsam, and from coal tar; used in dyeing and manufacture of explosives.

tom, n. [1. tom; 2. tɔm]. Abbr. of *Thomas.* **1.** (cap.) *Tom, Dick, and Harry*, all sorts and conditions, people in general without selection, anybody and everybody. **2.** Denotes the male of certain animals, esp. of the cat.

tomahawk, n. & vb. trans. [1. tóma-hawk; 2. tɔ́məhɔ̄k]. Am. Indian. **1.** n. A light axe or hatchet used by American Indians, often made with a hollow handle, the passage in which communicates with a bowl on reverse side of handle to the blade, so that the weapon can also be used as a tobacco pipe. **2.** vb. To strike, kill, with a tomahawk.

tomalley, n. [1. tomáli; 2. təmǽli], fr. **tourmalin**, on account of colour. Liver of a lobster, which turns green when boiled.

toman, n. [1. tomáhn; 2. təmán]. Pers., 'heap; ten thousand'. Persian gold coin worth about 7s.

tomato, n., pl. *tomatoes* [1. tomáhtō; 2. təmátou]. Span. *tomate*, fr. Mex. *tomatl.* **a** A trailing plant, *Lycopersicum esculentum*, native of S. America, bearing juicy, acid fruit, red or yellow when ripe; **b** fruit of this, much used for salads.

tomb (I.), n. [1. tōōm; 2. tūm]. M.E., fr. O. Fr. *tombe*, fr. Lat. *tumba*, fr. Gk. *túmbos*, cogn. w. **tumulus.** **1. a** A grave in which the dead are buried; **b** a cavity in the earth, vault, in which the dead are deposited; **c** a monument erected over a grave or vault. **2.** (fig.) *The tomb*, death; cp. *the grave.*

tomb (II.), vb. trans. (rare) To place in a tomb; to entomb.

tombac, n. [1. tómbak; 2. tɔ́mbæk]. Port. *tambaca*, fr. Malay. *tambāga*, 'copper'. Alloy of copper and zinc, used in making cheap jewellery.

tombola, n. [1. tómbōla; 2. tɔ́mboulə]. Ital., fr. *tombolare*, see **tumble** (I.). Kind of lottery.

tomboy, n. [1. tómboi; 2. tɔ́mbɔi]. A noisy, romping girl; (not in derogatory sense).

tombstone, n. [1. tōōmstōn; 2. túmstoun]. Stone placed over a grave recording the name, dates of birth and death &c. of the deceased.

tomcat, n. [1. tómkát; 2. tɔ́mkǽt]. Male cat.

tome, n. [1. tōm; 2. toum]. Fr., fr. Lat. *tomus*, fr. Gk. *tómos*, 'piece cut off, section'; cogn. w. Gk. *témnein*, 'to cut'; cp. **tmesis**; O. Russ. *timeti*, 'he strikes'; cp. also **-tomy.** **1.** A volume, a book, esp. a large, ponderous volume. **2.** A part, a volume, of a large work, usually bound separately.

-tome, suff. See prec. Form used in compounds, in sense of **a** section, part; **b** instrument for cutting.

tomentose, adj. [1. tōmentos; 2. tóumentous]. See next word & **-ose.** Covered with long or matted hairs.

tomentum, n. [1. tōméntum; 2. touméntəm]. Lat., 'stuffing for cushions' (of wool, hair &c.); for **tovementum*, fr. same base as in *tōtus*, 'all', see **total** (I.), & *tumēre*, 'to swell', see **tumid.** (bot.) Covering of dense, matted, woolly hairs.

tomfool, n. [1. tómfōōl; 2. tɔ́mfúl]. A great fool, perfect fool; a silly buffoon.

tomfoolery, n. [1. tómfōōleri; 2. tɔ́mfúləri]. Prec. & **-ery.** Buffoonery; stupid, senseless behaviour, nonsense.

tommy, n. [1. tómi; 2. tɔ́mi]. Familiar form of *Thomas.* **1.** (cap.) A private soldier; also *Tommy Atkins.* **2.** Provisions given to workmen in lieu of wages; *tommy shop*, one where practice of providing tommy prevails. **3.** (slang) *tommy rot*, rank foolishness, absurd nonsense.

tomorrow, n. & adv. [1. tumórō; 2. təmɔ́rou]. **to** (I.) & **morrow.** **1.** n. The day which follows today: *let us hope tomorrow will be fine.* **2.** adv. On the day following today: *we shall meet tomorrow.*

tompion, n. [1. tómpiun; 2. tɔ́mpiən]. Variant of **tampion.** Pad for inking, used in lithography.

tomtit, n. [1. tómtít; 2. tɔ́mtít]. Name of a bird; also called blue *titmouse*.

tomtom, n. [1. tómtom; 2. tɔ́mtɔm]. Hind. *tamtam*; imitative. Primitive kind of drum used in India.

-tomy, suff. fr. Gk. *-tomía*, fr. *tomé*, 'a cutting, section'; see **tome**. Indicates 'cutting', e.g. *anatomy, ovariotomy* &c.

ton (I.), n. [1. tun; 2. tan]. Variant spelling of **tun**. **1. a** A weight consisting of 20 hundredweights; *the long* or *gross ton*, of 2240 lb. avoirdupois; the *short, American, ton*, of 2000 lb.; *metric ton*, 1000 kilograms, 2204·6 lb.; **b** (colloq. and loosely) (i.) a very heavy weight: *this box of yours weighs a ton*, i.e. is very heavy; (ii.) a large quantity: *tons of money*; *you have tons of time*, plenty of time; *with tons of love* &c. **2.** A measure of amount, volume, or capacity, varying with the article, as of timber, gravel, coke, wheat &c. **3.** (naut.) **a** *Displacement ton*, 35 cubic feet of water; **b** *freight ton*, 40 cubic feet; **c** *register ton*, 100 cubic feet.

ton (II.), n. [1. ton; 2. tɔ̃]. Fr., see **tone** (I.). Style; fashion, vogue.

tonal, adj. [1. tṓnal; 2. tóun(ə)l]. **tone** (I.) & **-al**. Connected with, pertaining to, tone or tonality.

tonality, n. [1. tōnáliti; 2. tounǽliti]. **tonal** & **-ity**. **1.** (mus.) Quality of a composition derived from its key or from its system of tones. **2.** (paint.) Quality, scheme, of colour.

tondo, n. [1. tóndō; 2. tɔ́ndou]. Ital., 'round plate', fr. Lat. *rotundus*, see **rotund**. **a** A circular painted panel or canvas; **b** a sculptured relief in circular form.

tone (I.), n. [1. tōn; 2. toun]. Fr. *ton*, fr. Lat. *tonus*, 'sound, tone, of an instrument', fr. Gk. *tónos*, 'that which tightens, or which can itself be strained or tightened; a cord, rope; a tightening, strain; a pitching of the voice; hence, a musical note'; cp. Gk. *teinein*, 'to stretch, strain, extend', fr. **ten-jo-*; base **ten-*, **ton-*, whence also **thin**; also Lat. *tenuis*, 'slight', see **tenuis**, & **tenuity**; & cp. **tend** (II.) &c. **1.** Sound, esp. conceived of as possessing a certain quality, resonance, pitch &c.; a musical sound: *the tones of the voice, of a harp* &c.; *sweet, silvery, harsh, gentle, tones*. **2.** Pitch of the voice; modulation of this in speaking, as expressing varying emotion: *angry, loving, tones*; *a tone of entreaty, apology* &c. **3.** (mus.) The larger interval between the notes of the diatonic scale, as distinguished from *semitone*. **4.** (phon.) One kind of accent; an intonation, degree of pitch in the voice in speaking; the note on which a given word or syllable is uttered; contrasted with *stress*. **5.** (med.) State of body or mind in which the organs and functions are vigorous. **6.** Prevailing spirit, mental attitude, moral atmosphere: *a school with a good, healthy, tone*; *the tone of a letter*; *the general tone of the speech was gloomy, frivolous, solemn* &c. **7.** Shade, degree of intensity of colour, hue.

tone (II.), vb. trans. & intrans., fr. prec. **A.** trans. **1.** To impart tone to: **a** of sound; **b** of colour. **2.** Specif. (photog.) to modify colour of by treating chemically. **B.** Followed by adverb or preposition. *Tone down*, **1.** trans., **a** to reduce intensity of colouring of; **b** (fig.) to mitigate, diminish violence, intensity, of (passions, opinions &c., or their expression); to subdue, render less marked and noticeable; **2.** intrans., to become softened, less intense, less marked; *tone in with*, **a** trans., to cause to blend; **b** intrans., to blend, become mingled, harmonize with; *tone up*, **1.** trans., to intensify, emphasize **a** colour of; **b** form of expression; **2.** intrans., to become intensified.

toned, adj. [1. tōnd; 2. tound], fr. P.P. of prec. Slightly tinted.

-toned, adj. Having a particular kind of tone: *loud-toned*; *sweet-toned* &c.

toneless, adj. [1. tṓnles; 2. tóunlis]. **tone** (I.) & **-less**. **1.** Giving forth no tone or sound; silent; lacking resonance. **2.** Lacking colour, character; spiritless.

tonelessly, adv. Prec. & **-ly**. In a toneless manner.

tonelessness, n. See prec. & **-ness**. Quality of being toneless.

tong, n. [1. tong; 2. tɔŋ]. Chinese *t'ang*, 'hall'. A Chinese secret society or club.

tonga, n. [1. tóngga; 2. tɔ́ŋgə]. Hind. *tānga*. Light two-wheeled carriage.

tongs, n. pl. [1. tongz; 2. tɔŋz]. O.E. *tange*, 'tongs, forceps'; O.H.G. *zanga*; O.N. *tǫng*; cogn. w. Gk. *dáknein*, 'to bite'. See **tang** (I.). One of various kinds of objects, mostly consisting of two legs of metal joined by a pivot or by a spring, used for gripping, lifting, twisting &c.: *tongs for lifting pieces of coal*; *sugar tongs* &c. Phr. *I wouldn't touch him, it, with a pair of tongs*, he, it, is too disgusting to handle; (also fig.) it is the kind of business to avoid as much as possible.

tongue, n. [1. tung; 2. taŋ]. O.E. *tunge*, M.E. *tunge, tonge* &c.; O.S. *tunga*; O.H.G. *zunga*; Goth. *tungō*; cogn. w. Lat. *lingua*, 'tongue', fr. *dingua*, see **lingual**. **1.** Long, narrow, muscular, highly sensitive, and mobile organ in the mouth by means of which the act of licking is performed, and which plays a part in swallowing; the chief organ of taste, and, in man, of speech. Phrs. *to give tongue*, (i.) to shout, speak loud or vehemently; (ii.) to bark, as hounds on the scent; *to have a ready tongue*, be an easy, fluent speaker. **2.** (fig.) **a** Mode of speech, way of speaking: *a gentle tongue*; **b** mode of verbal expression: *the silver tongue of the orator*. **3.** A human language: *the ancient tongues*. **4.** The tongue of an animal, thought of as, and prepared for, food. **5.** Any of various things shaped, approximately, like a tongue; **a** thin leather flap fixed by lower end, under the laces of a boot or shoe, lying between them and the foot; **b** hinged or otherwise movable pin in a buckle, which passes through a hole in the strap; **c** thin, movable strip of metal occurring in various wind instruments; **d** clapper of a bell; **e** a narrow strip of land, esp. one that juts out into the water; **f** a thin, long, narrow flame; **g** thin projecting portion of a piece of wood, fitting into a corresponding groove or hollow in another piece.

tongue (II.), vb. trans. & intrans., fr. prec. **1.** trans. **a** To use the tongue in playing (a flute); **b** to execute (piece of music) by using the tongue. **2.** intrans. To produce staccato notes with the tongue (on a flute).

-tongued, adj. [1. tungd; 2. taŋd]. **tongue** (I.) & **-ed**. Having a particular kind of tongue, voice, sound &c.: *silver-tongued*; *dry-tongued*.

tongueless, adj. [1. túngles; 2. táŋlis]. **tongue** (I.) & **-less**. **1.** Lacking a tongue. **2.** Not using the tongue to speak; silent.

tongue-tied, adj. [1. túng tīd; 2. táŋ taid]. **a** Having an impediment in one's speech; **b** unable to speak, esp. through embarrassment; **c** not inclined to speak, taciturn, silent.

tonguing, n. [1. túnging; 2. táŋiŋ]. Staccato effect produced by tip of the tongue in playing a wind instrument.

tonic (I.), adj. [1. tónik; 2. tɔ́nik]. Fr. *tonique*, fr. Gk. *tonikós*; **tone** (I.) & **-ic**. **1.** (phon.) Pertaining to tones; *tonic accent*, one depending on alterations of pitch; contrasted with *stress accent*. **2.** (med.) **a** Distinguished by muscular contraction: *tonic spasms, convulsions*; **b** having an invigorating, stimulating effect upon the system: *a tonic drug* &c.; also, stimulating to the mind. **3.** Pertaining to colour tone, to light and shade, in a picture or landscape.

tonic (II.), n., fr. prec. **1.** The syllable in a word distinguished by the chief tonic accent. **2.** (mus.) The keynote. **3. a** An invigorating medicine; **b** something which stimulates the mind or character.

tonically, adv. [1. tónikali; 2. tɔ́nikəli]. **tonic** (I.) & **-al** & **-ly**. **1.** In respect of tone or pitch. **2.** As a tonic, so as to stimulate or invigorate.

tonicity, n. [1. tonísiti; 2. tɔnísiti]. **tonic** (I.) & **-ity**. Property of possessing tone; a condition of normal healthy muscular tension and elasticity; vigour; **b** musical tone.

tonic sol-fa, n. [1. tónik sòl fáh; 2. tɔ́nik sɔ̀l fá]. System of musical notation based on tonality, consisting of a series of syllables, *do, re, mi* &c.

tonight, adv. & n. [1. tunī́t; 2. tənáit]. **to** (I.) & **night**. **1.** adv. On this night; on the night of today. **2.** n. This night; the night coming after this day.

tonite, n. [1. tṓnīt; 2. tóunait], fr. base of Lat. *tonāre*, 'to thunder', see **thunder** (I.), & **-ite**. Explosive used for blasting.

tonka bean, n. [1. tóngka bēn; 2. tɔ́ŋkə bīn]. Native word. Aromatic seed of a plant growing in Guiana, used in perfumery.

tonnage, n. [1. túnij; 2. tánidž]. **ton** (I.) & **-age**. **a** Freight-carrying capacity of a ship, in tons; **b** total amount of a country's shipping calculated in tons; **c** duty payable on ships according to their tonnage.

tonneau, n. [1. tónō; 2. tɔ́nou]. Fr., 'cask', see **tun**. Rear part, containing back seats, of a motor-car.

-tonner, n. [1. túner; 2. tánə]. Having capacity of so many tons: *300-tonner* (of ships); weighing so many tons.

tonometer, n. [1. tōnómeter; 2. tounɔ́mitə]. See **tone** (I.) & **-meter**. Device for measuring tone or pitch.

tonsil, n. [1. tónsl, -il; 2. tɔ́nsl, -il]. Fr. *tonsille*, fr. Lat. *tonsillae* (pl.); connected w. Lat. *tōlēs*, 'goitre'; perh. ultimately fr. base **twen-*, 'to swell', see **tumid**. One of a pair of masses of lymphoid tissue on either side of the back of the throat.

tonsillar, adj. [1. tónsilar; 2. tɔ́nsilə]. Prec. & **-ar**. Connected with, pertaining to, the tonsils.

tonsillitic, adj. [1. tònsilítik; 2. tɔ̀nsilítik]. See next word & **-ic**. Pertaining to, of the nature of, tonsillitis.

tonsillitis, n. [1. tònsilī́tis; 2. tɔ̀nsiláitis]. See **tonsil** & **-itis**. Inflammation of the tonsils; quinsy.

tonsorial, adj. [1. tonsórial; 2. tɔnsɔ́riəl]. Lat. *tonsōrius*, 'pertaining to shearing', fr. *tonsor*, 'shearer, shaver, barber', & **-al**; fr. *tons-(um)*, P.P. type of *tondēre*, 'to shear, clip; to act as barber'; connected w. Gk. *téndein*, 'to gnaw, nibble'; the base **tend-*, **tond-*, is an extension of **tem-* &c., 'to cut', q.v. under **tmesis** & **tome**. Pertaining to a barber or his craft; (facet.) *tonsorial artist*, a barber, hairdresser.

tonsure, n. & vb. trans. [1. tónshur; 2. tɔ́nʃə]. Lat. *tonsūra*, 'a shearing, clipping'; fr. *tons-*, see prec., & **-ure**. **1.** n. **a** Act of shaving the crown of the head or part of it; a rite administered in Roman Church, to a person on admission to priest's orders, and to a monastic order; **b** that part of the head from which the hair has been removed. **2.** vb. To shave part of the head of; to administer the tonsure to; to make a tonsure on.

tonsured, adj. [1. tónshurd; 2. tɔ́nʃəd]. Prec. & **-ed**. **a** Having a tonsure; **b** shaven and shorn.

tontine, n. [1. tóntēn; 2. tɔ́ntīn]. Ital. *tontina*, fr. Tonti, the inventor (17th cent.). Arrangement whereby a number of persons share an annuity or other financial benefit, the share of each increasing as the number is diminished by death, until the last survivor obtains the whole sum.

too, adv. [1. tōō; 2. tū]. Stressed form of **to** (I.). **1. a** Denoting superfluity; excessively; more than enough, in excess of what is required: *a hat far too big for him*; *too good to last*; *too good for him*; *too fat for beauty*; *too much*; *too little*, not enough; **b** (as intens.) equivalent to very: *you are really too kind*; *I shall be only too pleased to help you*. **2.** In addition, as well, moreover: *I had some food, and some wine too*; *to play, and sing too*; *won't you come too?* Phr. *very nice too*, strongly affirmative.

took, vb. [1. took; 2. tuk]. L.O.E. *tōc*; M.E. *tōk*; Pret. of **take**.

tool (I.), n. [1. to͞ol; 2. tūl]. O.E. *tōl*, not found in other Gmc. languages; prob. formed fr. the base seen in O.E. *tāwian*, 'to prepare land for sowing'; *ġetāwe*, 'apparatus', see **taw (I.)**; cp. Goth. *taujan*, 'to make, do, effect'; *tēwa*, 'order, arrangement'; *tawi*, 'work'. **1. a** Any of a large variety of implements, instruments, utensils, used in making things, in shaping, working, preparing material &c.; esp. an implement held in, and worked by the hand, as distinguished from one moved by machinery: *carpenter's, gardener's, blacksmith's tools* &c.; **b** that part of a machine or mechanical contrivance which actually does the cutting, shaping &c.; usually *machine tool*; **c** specif., a tool used by a bookbinder in decorating the cover of a book. **2.** The means whereby an occupation is pursued; aid in, equipment for, intellectual work: *books are the tools of a scholar*; *the tools of one's trade.* **3.** (usually derogatory) A person used by another to perform actions, esp. of a discreditable character, on his behalf, without the real mover appearing; a cat's-paw, a servile confederate who acts as the instrument of another's will; person who acts entirely at the instigation of another; a puppet.

tool (II.), vb. trans. & intrans., fr. prec. **A.** trans. **1.** To use a tool upon; specif., to decorate back or edges of a book-cover with a tool. **2.** (colloq.) To drive a person in a leisurely manner in a vehicle: *let me tool you down to the station.* **B.** intrans. (colloq.) To ride or drive oneself in an easy, leisurely way; also *tool along*, to bowl along: *tooling along the road in fine style.*

tool-box, -chest, n. Box specially designed, and used, for keeping tools.

tooler, n. [1. to͞oler; 2. tūlə]. **tool (II.)** & **-er.** Broad chisel for dressing stone.

tooling, n. [1. to͞oling; 2. tūliŋ]. See prec. & **-ing. 1.** Mode of dressing stone, so that the marks of the chisel are left. **2.** Ornamentation, often gilt, made by pressing with a tool, on book bindings.

toon, n. [1. to͞on; 2. tūn]. Hind. *tun, tuna.* An East Indian tree with fine-grained reddish wood, used for furniture-making; sometimes known as Indian mahogany.

toot, vb. intrans. & n. [1. to͞ot; 2. tūt]. Prob. imitative; the same word in very similar form exists in Du. & Scand. languages. **1.** vb. To blow a horn; to sound like the note of a horn, to hoot. **2.** n. The sound of tooting or hooting.

tooth (I.), n. [1. to͞oth; 2. tūþ]. O.E. *tōþ*, M.E. *tōth* &c., fr. earlier **tanþ-*; cogn. w. O.S. *tand*; O.H.G. *zand*, Germ. *zahn*; Goth. *tunþus*; fr. participial base *(*e*)*dent-*, *(*o*)*dont-* &c., fr. **ed-*, whence also **eat**; cogn. w. Scrt. *danta*; Gk. *odóntos*, see **odont-**; Lat. *dent-*, see **dental**; cp. also **tusk. 1.** One of the hard, ivory-like objects in the gums of human beings and the lower animals, which serve to masticate food, and, for the latter, as weapons of attack and defence. Phrs. *to cast something in a person's teeth*, to reproach him with it; *in the teeth of*, in opposition to; in spite of; *to draw a person's teeth*, (i.) to deprive him of his chief ground of complaint; (ii.) to render him harmless, mollify him; *to fight, oppose, tooth and nail*, with the utmost fierceness or energy; *armed to the teeth*, very completely armed; (*to escape*) *by* (properly *with*) *the skin of one's teeth*, by very slight margin, very narrowly; *to have a sweet tooth*, to be fond of sweet things; *to set one's teeth on edge*, disgust, cause to shudder; *to show one's teeth*, to exhibit anger, resentment &c. **2.** Any of various objects resembling, or supposed to resemble, a tooth; e.g. one of the separate divisions of a comb or saw; one of the projecting points or cogs on a wheel &c.

tooth (II.), vb. trans. & intrans., fr. prec. **1.** trans. To furnish (a wheel &c.) with teeth. **2.** intrans. To interlock, as the teeth or cogs on two engaged wheels.

toothache, n. [1. to͞othāk; 2. tūþeik]. Pain in the nerves of the teeth.

tooth-billed, adj. [1. to͞oth bild; 2. tūþ bild]. Having a bill the edges of which have projections or notches.

tooth-brush, n. Small brush for washing the teeth.

toothful, n. [1. to͞othfool; 2. tūþful]. (of brandy &c.) A small draught.

tooth-paste, n. Cleansing, antiseptic paste used in brushing the teeth.

toothpick, n. [1. to͞othpik; 2. tūþpik]. Small instrument with pliable point and end, of quill, gold &c., for dislodging portions of food from between the teeth.

tooth-powder, n. Medicated, gritty powder, used on tooth-brush, for cleaning the teeth.

toothsome, adj. [1. to͞othsum; 2. tūþsəm]. **tooth (I.)** & **-some.** Dainty, choice, agreeable to the taste.

tootle, vb. intrans. & n. [1. to͞otl; 2. tūtl]. Freq. of **toot. 1.** vb. To toot, or hoot, repeatedly but not loudly, on a flute, horn &c. **2.** n. The sound made by one who tootles.

top (I.), n. [1. top; 2. tɔp]. O.E. *topp*, 'summit'; O.H.G. *zopf*, 'tuft of hair; top of a tree'; O.N. *toppr*, 'tuft of hair; crest, summit'. **1. a** The highest part of anything; summit: *the top of the head, of a hill, house, tree*; Phrs. *the top of the tree, ladder*, highest point of success, excellence; highest rank; *from top to toe*, from head to foot; *to come out on top*, to beat others in a contest, be successful in life; *on top of everything else* &c., in addition to, as a last straw; **b** the upper portion of a flat surface: *the top of the page.* **2.** Specif., kind of platform near the head of a ship's mast, to which part of rigging is fastened, and upon which men stand in taking in sail &c.; also (pl.) *the tops.* **3.** A tuft springing from the top of anything. **4.** Upper surface, outer side of anything: *on the top of the ground.* **5.** That part of a plant above the ground; contrasted with the root. **6.** The greatest degree of intensity, fullest extent: *at the top of one's voice*, very loud; *the top of one's speed.* Phr. *to the top of one's bent*, as much as one could desire. **7.** The highest, most honourable, position, rank; the highest place attainable: *the top of one's profession*; *the top of a class.* **8.** Specif., a long fibre of wool after combing, fashioned into a continuous sliver for spinning, contrasted with *noil*, the short fibre.

top (II.), adj., fr. prec. **1.** Nearest to, or at the top; highest: *the top shelf, layer, step*; *top right-hand corner* (of a page &c.); *top rung of a ladder* &c. Phr. (fig.) *top rung*, highest point of success, chief position. **2.** Having the greatest degree of intensity: *top speed*; *top price(s)*, highest price reached. **3.** Chief, foremost, highest in rank &c.: *the top place in a class.*

top (III.), vb. trans., fr. **top (I.). 1.** To furnish with a top, cover top of. **2.** To cut off top of: *to top a tree.* **3.** To touch, strike, on upper part, above the centre: *to top a golf-ball.* **4.** To reach to the top of, come level with: *the wood just tops the rising ground.* **5.** To surpass in height, reach beyond top of: *he tops his father by half a head*; (also fig.) be superior to: *his performance tops all previous records.*

top (IV.), n. O.E. *top*; fr. M.H.G. *topf*; etymol. doubtful. Child's toy of wood or metal, usually pear-shaped and tapering to a point, or round, having a central metal point upon which it is made to spin either by whipping, or by means of a string wound round it and unwound by a sudden jerk.

topaz, n. [1. tṓpaz; 2. tóupæz]. Lat., fr. Gk. *tópazos*; etymol. uncertain. Semi-precious stone, usually yellow, but sometimes white, or bluish.

top-boot, n. Riding boot reaching to just below the knee, having a band of light-coloured leather round the top.

topcoat, n. [1. tópkōt; 2. tɔ́pkóut]. Coat worn above another coat; overcoat.

top-dress, vb. trans. To apply top-dressing to.

top-dressing, n. Manure applied on the surface of the ground.

tope (I.), vb. intrans. & trans. [1. tōp; 2. toup]. Fr. *toper*; etymol. doubtful. **1.** intrans. To drink alcoholic liquor frequently and to excess. **2.** trans. To drink (strong liquor) frequently and excessively.

tope (II.), n. Etymol. unknown. A small kind of shark; dogfish.

tope (III.), n. Hind. *tōp.* Cylindrical tower surmounted by a cupola, containing a Buddhist shrine.

topee. See **topi.**

topek, n. [1. tṓpek; 2. tóupɛk]. Eskimo *tupek.* Eskimo hut of wood or some substance other than snow.

toper, n. [1. tṓper; 2. tóupə]. **tope (I.)** & **-er.** One who topes; a drunkard.

topgallant, adj. [1. tópgálant; 2. tɔ́pgǽlənt]. (naut.) Designating a position above top-mast and below royal-mast.

top-hamper, n. **1.** The upper rigging of a ship **2.** The upper, smaller boughs or the thinner upper part of the stem of a large tree.

top-hat, n. Tall hat, silk hat.

top-heavy, adj. Ill-balanced through having the upper part too heavy for the base; inclined to topple over.

Tophet, n. [1. tṓfet; 2. tóufet]. Heb. *topheth*, 'place to be spat upon'. Place in valley of Hinnom, near Jerusalem, where rubbish was perpetually being burnt, and where sacrifices to Moloch were performed.

top-hole, adj. (slang) Excellent, first-rate, tip-top.

tophus, n. [1. tṓfus; 2. tóufəs], fr. Fr., in Engl. sense; cp. **tufa.** Calcareous deposit round the teeth; gouty concretion in, or on, a joint.

topi, topee, n. [1. tṓpē; 2. tóupi]. Hind. *tōpi.* A pith hat or helmet, usually *sola topi.*

topiary, n. [1. tṓpiari; 2. tóupiəri]. Lat. *topiārius*, 'landscape gardener', fr. *topia*, 'mural decoration depicting landscapes of fanciful character', fr. Gk. *tópos*, 'place', see next word. The art of cutting living trees, esp. yews and boxes, into shapes of animals, birds, and other objects.

topic, n. [1. tópik; 2. tɔ́pik]. Gk. *topikós*, 'belonging to a place; concerning *tópoi*, i.e. commonplaces', fr. *tópos*, 'a place'; prob. cogn. w. Lith. *tàpti*, 'to become'; possibly also w. O.E. *þafian*, 'to consent', assuming that the orig. meaning was 'to yield place to', cp. **allow** for similar development. **1.** Theme, subject, of thought; also, subject of discourse, conversation, discussion &c. **2.** One of the forms of argument employed in probable, as distinct from demonstrative, reasoning; source from which arguments may be drawn.

topical, adj. [1. tópikl; 2. tɔ́pikl]. Prec. & **-al. 1.** Connected with a subject of current or local interest. **2.** Of the nature of a topic or general principle. **3.** (med.) Affecting a particular area of the body only.

topically, adv. Prec. & **-ly.** In a topical manner.

topknot, n. [1. tópnot; 2. tɔ́pnɔt]. **1.** A tuft or bunch, projecting from the top of anything; specif. **a** tuft of hair or curl on the top of the head; **b** (colloq.) the head itself. **2.** Species of flounder.

topless, adj. [1. tóples; 2. tɔ́plis]. **top (I.)** & **-less.** Having the top so high as to be invisible; hence very lofty, of a height so great that it cannot be estimated: '*the topless towers of Ilium*' (Marlowe's 'Faustus').

top-light, n. Lantern in a ship's tops.

topmast, n. [1. tópmahst; 2. tɔ́pmāst]. Mast between the lower and the topgallant mast.

topmost, adj. [1. tópmōst; 2. tɔ́pmoust]. Highest; chief, highest in importance or position.

topo-, pref., fr. Gk. *tópos*, 'place', see **topic.**

topographer, n. [1. topógrafer; 2. təpɔ́grəfə]. **topo-** & **-grapher.** One who describes a place or area; student of, one skilled in, topography.

topographic(al), adj. [1. tòpográfik(l); 2. tòpəgrǽfik(l)]. **topo-** & **graphic(al)**. Connected with topography; descriptive of an area or locality.

topographist, n. [1. topógrafist; 2. təpɔ́grəfist]. **topography** & **-ist**. Topographer.

topography, n. [1. topógrafi; 2. təpɔ́grəfi]. **topo-** & **-graphy**. **1.** Systematic, detailed, description of a place, city &c., or of an area of country. **2.** General characteristics and relative disposition of geographical and other features of a region.

topology, n. [1. topóloji; 2. təpɔ́lədži]. **topo-** & **-logy**. Study of topography.

toponomy, n. [1. topónomi; 2. təpɔ́nəmi], fr. **topo-** & Gk. *ónoma*, 'name', see **onomatopoeia**. Nomenclature, **a** of places; **b** of regions of the body.

topper, n. [1. tóper; 2. tɔ́pə]. **top (II.)** & **-er**. **1.** Something which lies or is placed on the top; **a** large stone used as top course of a wall, often set edgewise; **b** (slang) a top-hat. **2.** (colloq.) Person who, thing which, tops or surpasses others; specif., term of praise of persons, a good fellow, good sort; a thoroughly admirable and likable person.

topping (I.), vbl. n. [1. tóping; 2. tɔ́piŋ]. **top (II.)** & **-ing**. **1.** Act of one who tops or removes top. **2.** Part removed from, cut off, the top of anything. **3.** That which forms the top of anything.

topping (II.), adj., fr. Pres. Part. of **top (II.)**. Higher than, superior to; hence (colloq.) term of indiscriminate praise; excellent, very good, first-rate; agreeable, delightful: *a topping fellow*; *a topping dinner* &c.

toppingly, adv. Prec. & **-ly**. (colloq.) In a topping manner, excellently: *the car ran simply toppingly*.

topple, vb. intrans. & trans. [1. tópl; 2. tɔ́pl]. Freq. formed fr. **top (II.)**, lit. 'to fall because top-heavy'. **1.** intrans. **a** To totter, rock; to overbalance, to be on the point of falling; **b** *topple over*, to lose balance and fall over; **c** *topple down*, (of an edifice, pile, single object) to tumble down; tip over. **2.** trans. **a** To cause to totter or to be unsteady; **b** *topple over*, push over; **c** *topple down*, to send tumbling down.

topsail, n. [1. tópsl; 2. tɔ́psl]. Square sail next above lowest.

top-sawyer, n. **1.** Man who occupies upper place in sawing in a pit. **2.** (archaic) Person occupying prominent, important position in life.

top-shaped, adj. **top (III.)**. Shaped like a top; pear-shaped.

topsides, n. pl. [1. tópsīdz; 2. tɔ́psáidz]. Upper part of ship's sides, above water.

topsyturvy, adv., adj., n. [1. tópsitérvi; 2. tɔ́psitə́vi]. *topsy-=top so*; for *-turvy* cp. O.E. *tearflian*, 'to roll'. **1.** adv. & adj. Upside-down, in confusion; upset, confused, the wrong way about. **2.** n. State of confusion, a muddle.

topsyturvydom, n. [1. tòpsitérvidum; 2. tòpsitə́vidəm]. Prec. & **-dom**. Condition of upset and confusion, whether in material objects or in ideas, affairs &c.; an inversion of natural order and conditions.

toque, n. [1. tōk; 2. touk]. Fr., fr. Celt. **1.** Small, close-fitting, round hat, esp. as worn by women. **2.** Monkey found in Ceylon, *Macaca pileata*, the hair on the head of which gives it the appearance of wearing a cap.

tor, n. [1. tōr; 2. tō]. O.E. *torr*; a Celt. loan-word; cp. O.W. *torr*; W. *tor*, 'a boss'. A high rocky pointed hill; now chiefly of such hills on Dartmoor.

torah, n. [1. tóra; 2. tṓrə]. Heb. **a** A law, precept; **b** divine revelation of law; specif., the Pentateuch.

toran, n. [1. tóran; 2. tṓrən]. Scrt. *tōrana*, 'archway, gate'. The ceremonial gateway to a Buddhist temple.

torch, n. [1. torch; 2. tōtʃ]. M.E., fr. O. Fr. *torche*, 'rag, wisp', fr. L. Lat. *torca*, fr. Lat. **torqua*, variant of *torquis, torques*, 'twisted neck-chain, collar' &c., see **torque**, fr. base *torquēre*, 'to turn, twist, wind' &c.; see also **tort**. **1. a** Piece of inflammable wood or wood soaked in inflammable substance, such as resin, pitch &c., which flares when kindled and is used to give light; a flambeau, a link; **b** (fig.) something which produces spiritual enlightenment or enthusiasm for worthy things: *the torch of learning* &c. Phr. *to hand on the torch*, to transmit a tradition of culture and spiritual enlightenment. **2.** One of various devices for giving light, esp. *electric torch*, small electric lamp carried in the hand.

torchlight, n. [1. tórchlīt; 2. tṓtʃlait]. Light shed by torches; (attrib.) *torchlight procession*, one in which those taking part carry torches.

torchon, n. used attrib. [1. tórshon; 2. tṓʃɔ̃, -ɔn]. Fr., 'a crumpled rag, wisp of cloth' &c.; see **torch**. *Torchon lace*, strong, coarse lace, made on a pillow; *torchon paper*, strong, hard paper with a rough surface, used for water-colour painting.

torcular, n. [1. tórkūlar; 2. tṓkjulə]. Lat., 'that which twists; a wine-press'; see **torque**. Tourniquet used by surgeons.

toreador, n. [1. tóreadōr; 2. tóriədō]. Span. Cp. Lat. *taurus*, 'bull'. See **taurus**. Mounted bull-fighter, cp. *torero*.

tore, vb. [1. tōr; 2. tō]. Pret. of **tear (I.)**; fr. M.E. P.P. type *tore(n)*, see **torn**. Cp. O.E. Pret. *tær*; M.E. *tar*.

torero, n. [1. torárō; 2. tɔréərou]. Span. See **toreador**. A bull-fighter on foot.

toreutic, adj. & n. [1. torūtik; 2. tərjū́tik]. Gk., fr. *toreutós*, 'worked in relief', fr. *toreúein*, 'to bore through; to work in relief'; cp. also *toreús*, 'graving tool of a sculptor'; connected w. Gk. *teírō*, fr. **ter-jō*, 'rub away, wear away'; cp. further Lat. *terere*, 'to rub to pieces, bruise, grind', *terebra*, 'instrument for boring', cp. **terebra, teredo, & triturate**; cogn. w. O.E. *þrāwan*, 'to twist, turn round', see **throw (I.)**, & O.E. *þrǣd*, see **thread (I.)**. **1.** adj. Pertaining to chased, embossed, wrought work, esp. in metal. **2.** n. (pl.) *Toreutics*, carved, embossed work.

torfaceous, adj. [1. torfáshus; 2. tōféiʃəs]. O.N. *torf*, see **turf**, & **-aceous**. Pertaining to, growing in, bogs or mosses.

torii, n. sing. & pl. [1. tóriē; 2. tṓrii]. Jap. A structure of wood of two posts with lintel, forming an entrance-way to a Shinto temple.

torment (I.), n. [1. tórment; 2. tṓmənt]. Fr., fr. Lat. *tormentum*, 'instrument with which anything is turned, a windlass; an instrument of torture; torture, pain, anguish'; for **torquementum*, fr. *torquēre*, 'to twist' &c.; see **torque**. **1. a** Severe suffering, anguish, pain, of mind or body; **b** pain deliberately inflicted on another; torture. **2.** That which gives rise to mental irritation, worry, annoyance, anxiety: *his undutiful sons are the torment of his life*.

torment (II.), vb. trans. [1. tormént; 2. tōmént], fr. prec. **1.** To inflict extreme pain and suffering upon; to torture. **2.** To cause severe suffering to: *to be tormented by toothache*. **3.** To annoy, tease, worry, harass: *to torment a person with perpetual questions, with one's complaints, with constant demands for money* &c.

tormentil, n. [1. tórmentil; 2. tṓməntil]. Fr. *tormentille*, a woodland plant, supposed to relieve toothache &c., see **torment (I.)**. Rosaceous plant, genus *Potentilla*, with four-petalled yellow flowers, and an astringent root, used in medicine and in tanning.

tormenting, adj. [1. torménting; 2. tōméntiŋ], fr. Pres. Part. of **torment (II.)**. Causing torment, bodily pain, anxiety, annoyance &c.

tormentingly, adv. Prec. & **-ly**. So as to cause torment.

tormentingness, n. See prec. & **-ness**. Quality of being tormenting; annoyance.

tormentor, n. [1. torménter; 2. tōméntə]. **torment (II.)** & **-or**. **1.** Person who inflicts bodily or mental suffering upon another. **2.** Kind of harrow. **3.** Long meat-fork used on board ship by the cooks.

tormentress, n. [1. torméntres; 2. tōméntris]. See prec. & **-ess**. Woman who torments.

tormina, n. pl. [1. tórmina; 2. tṓminə]. Lat., 'pains in the bowels, gripes'; fr. base *torq-*, 'to twist' &c., see **torque**. (med.) Griping pains in the bowels.

torn, vb. [1. torn; 2. tōn]. O.E. (*ġe*)*toren*; M.E. *tōren*; P.P. of **tear (I.)**.

tornado, n. [1. tornádō; 2. tōnéidou]. Span. *tronada*, 'thunderstorm', fr. *tronar*, 'to thunder', fr. Lat. *tonāre*; influenced by Lat. *tornāre*, 'to turn'. Violent, narrowly localized storm; hurricane; specif., rotary storm of extreme violence accompanied by a whirlwind and a cloud resembling a water-spout in appearance, occurring in West Africa, at beginning and end of rainy season, and in America during the summer months.

tornadic, adj. [1. tornádik; 2. tōnǽdik]. Prec. & **-ic**. Pertaining to, having the character of, a tornado.

torose, torous, adj. [1. tōrṓs, tórus; 2. tōróus, tṓrəs]. Lat. *torōsus*, 'brawny'; see **torus** & **-ous**. (zool. and bot.) Knobbed as with muscle; having surface covered with rounded projections.

torosity, n. [1. tōrósiti; 2. tōrɔ́siti]. Prec. & **-ity**. Quality of being torose.

torpedo (I.), n. [1. torpḗdō; 2. tōpídou]. Lat. *torpēdo*, 'numbness', fr. *torpēre*, 'to be numb, inactive; to be stupefied'; prob. fr. base *(*s*)*terep-* &c., 'numb, stiff', whence, w. *s-*, O.E. *steorfan*, 'to die', see **starve**, & fr. **terp-*, O.E. (*ġe*)*deorf*, 'hardship', cp. also O.E. *þearfian*, 'to be indigent', & *þearf*, Pret. Pres., 'require; be compelled'. See also **torpid**. **1.** Also *torpedo fish*, the electric ray, which kills its prey with an electric shock. **2. a** A cigar-shaped apparatus filled with explosive discharged on impact, propelled and steered by mechanism, used for destroying or injuring enemy ships at sea; **b** similarly shaped heavy bomb discharged from an aeroplane or airship. **3.** Any of various kinds of explosive or detonating cartridge.

torpedo (II.), vb. trans., fr. prec. **a** To attack with a torpedo; **b** to strike or destroy with a torpedo.

torpedo-boat, n. Small, fast vessel, used for firing torpedoes.

torpedo-boat destroyer, n. Vessel of larger size, and still faster than a torpedo-boat, the purpose of which is to overtake and destroy one of these belonging to the enemy and to attack other vessels by launching torpedoes.

torpedo-netting, n. Heavy steel netting hung from booms used as a protection against attack by torpedoes.

torpedo station, n. Naval base for torpedo-boats and their supplies.

torpedo-tube, n. Steel tube through which torpedoes are discharged by compressed air.

torpid (I.), adj. [1. tórpid; 2. tṓpid]. Lat. *torpidus*, 'benumbed, stupefied'; fr. *torpēre*, 'to be numb' &c.; see **torpedo (I.)**. **1.** (in physical sense) Inactive, sluggish. **2.** (of the mind) Dull, lethargic, apathetic.

torpid (II.), n., fr. prec., facetiously in reference to their supposed inactivity. **1.** Usually *torpids*, boat-races rowed at Oxford in Lent term between the second crews of colleges. **2.** Boat with eight oars in which these races are rowed.

torpidity, n. [1. torpíditi; 2. tōpíditi]. **torpid (I.)** & **-ity**. State or quality of being torpid.

torpidness, n. [1. tórpidnes; 2. tṓpidnis]. See prec. & **-ness**. Torpidity.

torpor, n. [1. tórper; 2. tṓpə]. Lat., 'numbness, stupefaction'; fr. same base as **torpid (I.)**. **1.** Loss of power of motion; state of inactivity accompanied by partial insensibility. **2.** Dullness, inactivity, of the mind.

torporific, adj. [1. tòrporífik; 2. tòpərífik]. *torpori-*, stem of prec., & **-fic**. Tending to produce torpor.

torquate, torquated, adjs. [1. tórkwāt, torkwā́ted; 2. tṓkweit, tōkwéitid]. Lat. *torquātus*, 'wearing a collar or neck-chain', fr.

torquis &c., ' collar ', see **torque**, & **-ate**. (zool.) Having a ring round the neck distinct in colour from the rest of the feathers or fur.

torque, n. [1. tork; 2. tōk]. Lat. *torques*, ' necklace ' &c.; fr. *torquēre*, ' to twist, bend ' &c.; fr. same base also Scrt. *tarkúš*, ' spindle '; cp. also Goth. *þwairhs*, ' angry ', O.E. *þweorh*, ' crosswise; perverse ', O.N. *þwerr*, ' across ', see **thwart (I.)**; cp. also **torment**. **1.** A twisted ring, or chain, worn round the neck by the ancient Teutons, Gauls &c. **2.** (mechan.) A twisting force or movement.

torrefaction, n. [1. tòrefákshun; 2. tòrifǽkʃən]. Lat. *torrefact-*, P.P. type of *torrefacere*, see next word, & **-ion**. Act, process, of torrefying; state of being torrefied.

torrefy, vb. trans. [1. tórefī; 2. tórifai]. Fr. *torréfier*, Lat. *torrefacere*, fr. *torrēre*, ' to parch, roast, scorch ', see **torrid**, & **-fy**. To dry by exposure to heat; to scorch, roast.

torrent, n. [1. tórent; 2. tórənt]. Lat. *torrent-(em)*, Pres. Part. of *torrēre*, ' to parch, scorch, burn, boil, rage ', see **torrid**. **a** A violent rush; a pouring, rapidly flowing stream, of water, or other liquid, or of lava; a stream of water flowing down a steep incline; **b** (fig.) also applied to (i.) a rush of rapidly uttered words; (ii.) violent outburst of abuse, grief &c.

torrential, adj. [1. torénshal; 2. tərénʃəl]. Prec. & **-ial**. Like a torrent, flowing, falling, with great violence.

torrentially, adv. Prec. & **-ly**. After the manner of a torrent; flowing violently.

Torricellian, adj. [1. tòriséliаn; 2. tòriséliən], fr. Torricelli, Italian physicist, 1608–47, & **-an**. Relating to, discovered by, Torricelli, esp. *Torricellian tube, vacuum* &c., in which mercury was first employed in measuring the pressure of the atmosphere, thus originating the mercury barometer.

torrid, adj. [1. tórid; 2. tórid]. Lat. *torridus*, ' parched, dried up '; fr. base **tors-*, **ters-*, whence also Scrt. *taršáyati*, ' makes thirsty, starves '; *taršaš*, ' thirst '; *tŗšyati*, ' thirsts '; Gk. *térsomai*, ' become dry '; *tarsiá*, ' drying frame '; Goth. *(ga)þairsan*, ' to dry ' (fr. **ters-*), *þaursus*, ' dry ', *þaurstei*, ' thirst '; O.E. *þyrst*, see **thirst (I.)**. **a** Parched, dried up, by the sun; **b** very hot: *torrid zone*, that between the tropics of Cancer and Capricorn.

torsel, n. [1. tórsl; 2. tōsl]. O. Fr., ' bundle ', dimin. of *torce*, ' something twisted, bunch ', fr. Lat. *torqu-*, ' to twist ' &c., see **torque**. Piece of wood, or iron, let into a stone or brick wall, to support the end of a beam.

torsion, n. [1. tórshun; 2. tóʃən]. L. Lat., fr. *tort-*, P.P. type of *torquēre*, ' to twist ', see **torque** & **tort** & **-ion**. **1.** Act of twisting, e.g. young shoots in early summer, to check growth; or the end of an artery which has been severed, to prevent haemorrhage. **2.** State of being twisted. **3.** (mechan.) Force with which a twisted wire, spring &c. tends to return to its untwisted state or form; *torsion balance*, apparatus used for measuring minute differences of electric and other forces, by the twisting and untwisting of a wire, spring &c.

torsional, adj. [1. tórshunal; 2. tóʃənəl]. Prec. & **-al**. Pertaining to, causing, due to, torsion.

torsive, adj. [1. tórsiv; 2. tósiv]. Stem *tors-*, as in prec., & **-ive**. (bot.) Twisted spirally.

torsk, n. [1. torsk; 2. tōsk]. Scand.; O.N. *thorskr*, cp. Germ. *dorsch*. A valuable food fish, of the cod family, found in N. Atlantic.

torso, n. [1. tórsō; 2. tósou]. Ital., fr. Lat. *thyrsos*, ' stalk, stem ', fr. Gk. *thúrsos*, see **thyrsus**. **1.** The upper part of the human body; trunk. **2.** Piece of sculpture which has been mutilated by removal of head and limbs. **3.** Any piece of work which is unfinished, incomplete.

tort, n. [1. tort; 2. tōt]. Fr., ' injury ', fr. Lat. *tortum*, P.P. of *torquēre*, ' to twist ' &c., see **torque**. (law) An injurious, harmful action, not involving a breach of contract, for which a civil action can be brought.

torticollis, n. [1. tòrtikólis; 2. tòtikólis]. Prec. & Lat. *collum*, ' neck ', see **collar (I.)**. Twisted or stiff neck due to rheumatism.

tortile, adj. [1. tórtīl, -il; 2. tótail, -il]. Lat. *tortilis*, ' twisted ', fr. *tort-*, P.P. type of *torquēre*, see **tort**, & **-ile**. Twisted, coiled, wreathed.

tortility, n. [1. tortíliti; 2. tōtíliti]. Prec. & **-ity**. State of being twisted.

tortilla, n. [1. tortíla; 2. tōtílə]. Span. dimin. of *torta*, ' cake ', fr. Lat. *torta*, ' twisted roll ', fr. *tort-*, P.P. type of *torquēre*, see **tort**. Thin flat cake of maize flour, baked on iron plates, the typical bread of Mexicans &c.

tortious, adj. [1. tórshus; 2. tóʃəs]. **tort** & **-ious**. Of the nature of, implying, a tort.

tortiously, adv. Prec. & **-ly**. In a tortious manner.

tortoise, n. [1. tórtus; 2. tótəs]; affected & artificial [1. tórtoiz; 2. tótɔiz]. M.E. *tortuce*, Fr. *tortues*, pl. of *tortue*, fr. Lat. *tortus*, ' crooked, twisted ', P.P. of *torquēre*, ' to twist ', see **torque** & **tort**. Kind of reptile with complete scaly covering for the upper and under surfaces of the body, the head and legs being capable of protrusion beyond, or retraction within, the shell; a land turtle.

tortoise-shell, n. [1. tórtushèl; 2. tótəʃèl]. **1.** The material forming the hard external covering of the tortoise, esp. when polished and used for manufacture of various ornamental and useful objects. **2.** Tortoise-shell butterfly.

tortoise-shell butterfly, n. Common black and brownish-yellow butterfly with markings resembling those on polished tortoise-shell.

tortoise-shell cat, n. Female cat with dark brown, yellow, and black markings.

tortuosity, n. [1. tòrtūósiti; 2. tòtjuósiti]. Next word & **-ity**. State of being tortuous; a winding, a twist, turn &c. (in physical and moral sense).

tortuous, adj. [1. tórchoous, tórtūus; 2. tótʃuəs, tótjuəs]. Lat. *tortuōsus*, ' twisting ', fr. *tortus*, ' a twist ', fr. P.P. of *torquēre*, ' to twist ', see **tort**, **torque**. **1.** Full of twists, turns, and windings. **2.** (in non-material sense, of the mind, methods, aims &c.) Not straightforward; devious, disingenuous.

tortuously, adv. Prec. & **-ly**. In a tortuous manner; with turns and twists.

tortuousness, n. See prec. & **-ness**. Condition of being tortuous; a tortuosity.

torturable, adj. [1. tórchurabl; 2. tótʃərəbl]. **torture** & **-able**. Capable of being tortured.

torturableness, n. Prec. & **-ness**. Quality of being torturable.

torture (I.), n. [1. tórchur; 2. tótʃə]. Fr., fr. Lat. *tortūra*, ' a twisting; torment ', fr. base *torq-* as in *torquēre*, ' to twist ' &c., see **torque**, **tort**, & **-ure**. **1.** Act of deliberately inflicting severe bodily pain upon, of causing extreme physical suffering to, another, as a punishment, from revenge, or from love of cruelty &c.: *to put to the torture*. **2.** Extreme, intolerable, pain; anguish, agony, of body or mind: *to suffer the tortures of the damned*.

torture (II.), vb. trans., fr. prec. **1.** To inflict physical torture upon as a punishment, or in order to extract a confession. **2.** To cause extreme agony to, of body or mind: *tortured by gout, by doubt and anxiety; don't torture me by keeping me in suspense*.

torturer, n. [1. tórchurer; 2. tótʃərə]. Prec. & **-er**. One who inflicts torture.

torturing, adj. [1. tórchuring; 2. tótʃəriŋ], fr. Pres. Part. of **torture (II.)**. Causing torture of mind or body; tormenting, agonizing.

torturous, adj. [1. tórchurus; 2. tótʃərəs]. **torture (I.)** & **-ous**. (rare) Connected with, of the nature of, causing, torture.

torula, n. [1. tórūla; 2. tórjulə]. Mod. Lat., Lat. *torulus*, ' little mound; a tuft ' &c.; dimin. of *torus*, ' a prominence '; a knot, bulge ' &c.; see **torus**. **1.** A genus of fungus. **2.** Chain of bacteria. **3.** (bot.) Small torus.

toruliform, adj. [1. tórūliform; 2. tórjulifōm]. Prec. & **-form**. Shaped like a torula.

torus, n. [1. tórus; 2. tórəs]. Lat., ' a prominence; a boss, knot, or bulge; a knoll, mound '; etymol. obscure. **1.** A round convex moulding used in the bases of columns. **2.** (bot.) Modified end of flower-stalk forming receptacle for the floral leaves. **3.** (anat.) A rounded muscular protuberance.

Tory, n. [1. tóri; 2. tóri]. Perh. fr. Ir. *toiridhe*, ' pursuer ', orig. applied to one of a class of outlaws in 16th & 17th cents., who professed to be royalists. **1.** Originally applied to a member of the party who were loyal to King James II. in 1688, opposed the Revolution, and who later favoured the Stuarts and opposed the accession of George I. on the death of Anne; a Jacobite; contrasted with *Whig*. **2.** Term at present time denoting a strong Conservative, esp. of the old-fashioned kind, who upholds the constitution, the Church, and the landed interest; contrasted with so-called Liberal Unionists, or Unionists; also attributively: *Tory party, principles* &c.

Toryism, n. [1. tóriizm; 2. tóriizəm]. Prec. & **-ism**. Political principles and practice of Tories.

tosh, n. [1. tosh; 2. tɔʃ]. Origin unknown. (slang) Rubbish, rot, nonsense.

tosher, n. [1. tósher; 2. tóʃə]. Corrupt. of **unattached**. (colloq., slang) Unattached student at a university.

toss (I.), vb. trans. & intrans. [1. taws, tos; 2. tōs, tɔs]. Etymol. doubtful. **A.** trans. **1. a** To fling, throw, with the hand: *to toss a ball*; also **b** (of a horse) to fling his rider from his back; also *toss off*. **2.** To fling, jerk, with a sudden swift upward movement: *to toss the head*, esp. as expressive of spirited protest, contempt &c., or (of horses) of vigour and fire. **3.** Specif. **a** (of a bull) to lift with the horns and fling into the air; **b** (of the sea in agitation) to fling (ships &c.) violently up and down, to cause to rise and fall with violence. **4.** (fig.) To cause agitation of mind to; to cast from one set of circumstances to another: *tossed about in the storms of life*. **5.** To give a fillip to and cause to spin into the air; in Phr. *to toss a coin*, specif., to decide for or against something according as head or tail comes uppermost. **B.** intrans. **1.** To fling oneself about from restlessness &c.: *to toss on a bed of pain*; also *toss about*: *to toss about on one's bed all night*. **2. a** (of the waves &c.) To be agitated, to leap up; **b** (of plumes or other floating, wavering objects) to sway in the air, float, tremble, rise and fall, be alternately raised and lowered with the movements of the wearer: *tossing plumes, crests, banners* &c. **3.** To be tossed in a ship &c.: *tossing for days on the ocean*. **4.** To spin a coin and allow the result to determine action; to bet upon result of a spun coin: *to toss for*. Phr. *I'll toss you for it*; also *toss up*: *let's toss up who has first choice*, or *for first choice*.

toss (II.), n., fr. prec. Act of tossing (in various senses); **a** *a toss from a bull*; **b** fact of being thrown by a horse; Phr. *to take a toss*, to be thrown, have a fall; **c** act of tossing, jerking, flinging up, the head: *a knowing, pert, proud, toss of the head*; **d** act of tossing, of spinning, a coin; result of this: *to win the toss*.

toss-up, n. [1. táws up; 2. tɔ́s áp]. **a** Act of tossing, spinning, a coin; hence, **b** an even chance: *it's a toss-up whether he succeeds or not*.

tot (I.), n. [1. tot; 2. tɔt]. Origin doubtful. A small, young child: *a tiny tot*.

tot (II.), n. & vb. trans. Lat., ' so many '; prob. also influenced by, or associated w., **total**. **1.** n. **a** Aggregate, amount resulting from the addition of a row of figures; **b** an allotted portion, small glass, of drink. [By many included under **tot (I.)**.] **2.** vb. Usually *tot up*, to add up.

total (I.), adj. [1. tṓtl; 2. tóutl]. Lat. *tōtālis*, fr. *tōtus*, ' all, the whole of, entire '; for **towetos*, connected w. Lat. *tumēre*, ' to swell ', see **tumid, tumour, tumulus**. **1.** Entire; including, constituting, the whole; omitting nothing: *the total amount owed was* . . . **2.** Complete, utter, absolute; unqualified: *total absurdity; total eclipse; total loss; total* *abstinence*, complete abstention from alcoholic drink.

total (II.), n., fr. prec. Whole, complete amount or number: *the total of his gains amounted to millions.*

total (III.), vb. trans. & intrans., fr. **total** (I.). **1.** trans. To add up the whole of and ascertain total amount or number. **2.** intrans. To amount to as a whole, when every item is added.

totality, n. [1. tōtáliti; 2. toutǽliti]. **total** (I.) & **-ity**. The whole sum, quantity, number; entirety.

totalization, n. [1. tòtalīzā́shun; 2. tòutəlaizéiʃən]. **totalize** & **-ation**. Act of totalizing; state of being totalized.

totalizator, totalizer, n. [1. tṓtalīzâter, tṓtalīzer; 2. tóutəlaizèitə, tóutəlaizə]. Machine for registering and indicating bets on the pari-mutuel system, in which the odds are calculated on the basis that the total amount of money staked is divided among those who have backed the winning horse, with a percentage deducted for expenses &c.

totalize, vb. trans. & intrans. [1. tṓtalīz; 2. tóutəlaiz]. **a** trans. To ascertain total of; **b** intrans., to make use of a totalizator.

totally, adv. [1. tṓtali; 2. tóutəli]. **total** (II.) & **-ly**. Entirely, completely, wholly.

tote (I.), n. [1. tōt; 2. tout]. Abbr. of **totalizator**.

tote (II.), vb. trans. Origin obscure. (chiefly U.S.A.) To carry, convey, lift.

totem, n. [1. tṓtem; 2. tóutem]. Prob. fr. Am. Ind. (anthrop.) **1.** Class of natural phenomena, or objects, esp. a species of animal or plant, between which and himself, or his family or tribe, the savage believes that an intimate and mysterious tie exists. **2.** A representation of the totem.

totemic, adj. [1. tōtémik; 2. toutémik]. Prec. & **-ic**. Connected with a totem, or with totemism.

totemism, n. [1. tṓtemizm; 2. tóutemizəm]. See prec. & **-ism**. Belief in totems; system of social custom based on this.

totemist, n. [1. tṓtemist; 2. tóutemist]. **totem** & **-ist**. Member of a community or tribe possessing a totem.

totemistic, adj. [1. tòtemístik; 2. tòutemístik]. Prec. & **-ic**. Connected with totems, or totemism; totemic.

tother, t'other, adj. & pron. [1. túdher; 2. táðə], fr. M.E. *þet ōþer*, pronounced & written *þe toþer*; now interpreted as equiv. to 'the other'. (obs., provinc., or colloq. slang) The other; **1.** adj., as in: *tother day*; **2.** pron., as in: *not to know one from tother.*

totidem verbis, adv. [1. tótidem vẽrbis; 2. tótidem vʌ́bis]. Lat., 'in as many words'.

toties quoties, adv. [1. tótiēz kwótiēz; 2. tótiīz kwɔ́tiīz]. Lat., 'as often . . ., so often'. Every time.

toto caelo, adv. [1. tṓtō sḗlō; 2. tóutou sílou]. Lat., 'by the whole heaven'. By an enormous amount; entirely: *to disagree toto caelo.*

totter, vb. intrans. [1. tóter; 2. tɔ́tə]. M.E. *toteren*; cp. Du. *touteren*, 'to swing'; Norw. dial. *totra*, 'to quiver'. **1.** To walk with shaky, uncertain, faltering steps. **2. a** (of a building &c.) To be shaky, insecure; to be, or appear to be, about to tumble down; **b** (fig.) to be ruined, to come to an end, be overtaken by destruction: *the great empire was tottering to its fall.*

tottery, adj. [1. tóteri; 2. tɔ́təri]. Prec. & **-y**. Shaky, insecure, faltering.

toucan, n. [1. tōōkán; 2. túkǽn], fr. Braz. Port. *tucana*, fr. native name. One of several species of bird from tropical S. America, having an enormous, coloured beak and bright-coloured plumage.

touch (I.), vb. trans. & intrans. [1. tuch; 2. tatʃ], fr. O. Fr. *touchier* &c.; cp. Ital. *toccare*; Span. *tocar*; borrowed by Romance fr. Gmc., cp. O.E. *tucian*, 'to ill-treat, afflict'; orig. meaning 'to twitch, tug, pluck'; cogn. w. O.H.G. *zucchen*, 'to twitch, pluck'; an intensive formed fr. Gmc. base **tug-*, **teuχ-* &c., as in O.E. *tēon*, fr. **teuhan*, 'to draw', see **tow** (I.), & **tug** (I.); cogn. w. Lat. *dūcere*, 'to draw, lead' &c., see **duct**, & words ending in *-duce*. **A.** trans. **1.** To be, stand, lie, up against, in contact with: *the creeper is touching the window*; *the overhanging bough touches the water.* **2. a** To feel with the hand or fingers; to lay the hand upon; to handle, finger, lightly; to bring some part of the body into contact with: *to touch every lamp-post in passing*; *visitors are requested not to touch the exhibits*; *to touch a dog with one's foot*; Phrs. *to touch one's hat*, make a sign of greeting; *touch one's hat to*, to greet, express respect for, in this way; *to touch a person on the arm, shoulder*, call his attention in this way; **b** specif., to lay the hand on with a view to healing: *Dr. Johnson, as a child, was touched by Queen Anne for scrofula.* **3.** In various special senses implying physical contact; (usually in neg. sentences) **a** to taste, partake of (food or drink): *I haven't touched food all day*; *he couldn't touch his dinner*; *I couldn't touch anything*, I am not hungry; *I daren't touch lobster*; **b** to play (musical instrument): *I haven't touched the piano for months*; **c** to misappropriate, take to one's own use unlawfully: *to touch money that doesn't belong to one*; **d** to mishandle; ill-treat, molest: *what is the child crying for? I never touched him*; **e** to molest, affect injuriously: *the law can't touch him*; **f** to disturb, interfere with, move out of place: *nothing must be touched until the police have been*; **g** to concern, occupy, oneself with; to set about: *I haven't been able to touch my work all day.* **4.** To reach (to), come up to, go as far as, attain: *his head nearly touches the ceiling*; *the glass just touched 90 yesterday*; Phr. *to touch bottom*, (fig.) to reach lowest point of demerit, depravity &c. **5.** To deal with, affect, involve, include, be related to: *what you say does not touch the point at issue*; *the new law doesn't touch my case at all.* **6. a** To affect emotionally, stir feelings and emotions of; to move: *to touch the heart*; *his generosity touched me profoundly*; *he was greatly touched by the universal sympathy*; **b** to arouse, excite, irritate (passions &c.): *his vanity and self-esteem were touched no less than his sense of duty.* **7.** To equal, rival in merit, be as good as, come up to: *there is nothing to touch a hot bath when you are tired*; *there are few things to touch sea air for bracing you up.* **8.** (colloq. slang) To extract money from, esp. as a loan; attempt to borrow from: *to touch a man for a fiver.* **9.** To treat of, deal with, lightly and casually: *we touched many topics in our talk*; see also *touch on*, below. **10.** To receive, esp. as a stipend or salary: *to touch 1000 rupees a month.* **B.** intrans. **1.** To be in contact: *his nose and chin appear almost to touch.* **2.** To practise touching, or laying the hand upon, as formerly the kings of England and France, for king's evil: *James II. used to touch regularly and is said to have wrought many cures.* **C.** Followed by adverb or preposition. *Touch at*, intrans., (of a ship) *to touch at a port*, to visit for a brief time in the course of a voyage. *Touch on*, intrans., to refer to: *there are many other points which I have no time to touch on now.* *Touch up*, trans., **1.** to excite, stimulate; **2.** to put touches to in order to repair, improve appearance of. *Touch upon*, intrans., same as *touch on.*

touch (II.), n. See prec. **1.** Sense or sensation of feeling communicated by the nerves in the skin: *the sense of touch*; *soft to the touch.* **2.** Act, fact, of touching, or bringing the hand &c. into contact with, something; contact thus formed: '*O for the touch of a vanished hand*' (Tennyson). Phr. *in touch with*, in social or intellectual relation. **3. a** A light, slight, passing contact; faint stroke or impulse: *so fragile that the slightest touch will break it*; **b** (fig.) a slight degree of persuasion, moral pressure, suggestion: '*Ask me no more . . . for at a touch I yield*' (Tennyson). **4.** Something resembling a slight stroke; a mild attack of disease &c.: *a touch of gout, fever, lumbago*; *a touch of the sun*, slight sunstroke. **5.** Characteristic movement of keys of a piano, mode in which these respond to the fingers of the player. **6.** Characteristic, individual, mode of touching **a** a musical instrument, such as piano: *a light, firm, good, heavy, touch*; **b** particular mode of applying a brush in painting, or a chisel in sculpture &c.: *easy to recognize the touches of the master*; **c** particular mode of verbal expression: *a happy touch, a characteristic touch* (in a speech &c.). **7.** Characteristic mode of behaviour, individual manner of doing something, or of dealing with a situation: *the Nelson touch.* **8.** A stroke given, action performed, in the execution of a piece of work: *to put the finishing touches*; *a few deft, last touches.* **9.** Test, trial, proof; only in Phrs. *to put, bring, something to the touch*; *a near touch*, (colloq.) a close shave. **10.** A slight but perceptible amount; slight appearance, trace; a tinge, suggestion, dash, smack: *a touch of colour*; *a touch of bitterness in the voice*; *a touch of acidity to the taste*; *a touch of genius, of vulgarity*; *one touch of Nature.* **11.** (slang) A thing for which a certain price is asked: *a shilling touch.* **12.** (football) Part of the field beyond the flags. **13.** A child's game in which one player pursues and attempts to catch, or touch, any of the others, putting person so touched temporarily out of action.

touchable, adj. [1. túchabl; 2. tátʃəbl]. **touch** (I.) & **-able**. That can or may be touched; capable of being touched; tangible.

touchableness, n. Prec. & **-ness**. Capacity of being touched.

touch-and-go, adj. & n. [1. túch an(d) gṓ; 2. tátʃ ən(d) góu]. **1.** adj. Uncertain, risky, chancy: *a touch-and-go business.* **2.** n. A risky, dangerous, situation or affair.

touch body, corpuscle, n. One concerned in sense of touch; tactile body.

touch down, n. Placing of hand by player on ball when in touch-in-goal, behind his own goal-line, in Rugby football, which renders the ball dead.

touched, adj. [1. tucht; 2. tatʃt]. P.P. of **touch** (I.). Various specific uses: **1.** Emotionally moved, stirred, affected. **2.** Slightly mad, crazy; also *touched in the upper storey.* **3.** Phr. *touched in the wind*, broken-winded, short-winded, short of breath.

toucher, n. [1. túcher; 2. tátʃə]. **touch** (I.) & **-er**. That which touches; specif. **1.** (slang) a close shave; in Phr. *as near as a toucher*, very nearly. **2.** (bowls) Bowl that touches the jack before coming to rest.

touch-hole, n. Vent in old-fashioned guns through which the gunpowder was fired.

touchily, adv. [1. túchili; 2. tátʃili]. **touchy** & **-ly**. In a touchy manner.

touchiness, n. [1. túchines; 2. tátʃinis]. See prec. & **-ness**. Quality of being touchy.

touching (I.), adj. [1. túching; 2. tátʃiŋ], fr. Pres. Part. of **touch** (I.). Pathetic, moving.

touching (II.), prep. Regarding, concerning, with regard to, in reference to: *touching the subject of our conversation . . .*

touchingly, adv. **touching** (I.) & **-ly**. In a touching manner; pathetically.

touch-in-goal, n. (Rugby football) Each of the four corners between the touch-lines and goal-lines, if respectively produced.

touch-line, n. Side line bounding the field of play in Association and Rugby football.

touch-me-not, n. [1. túch mi nòt; 2. tátʃ mi nɔ̀t]. Garden balsam, or noli-me-tangere whose ripe seed-pods explode at a touch.

touch-paper, n. Paper impregnated with nitre, used formerly for firing gunpowder.

touch-piece, n. Gold coin formerly presented by English sovereigns to the persons whom they touched for king's evil.

touchstone, n. [1. túchstōn; 2. tátʃstoun]. **1.** Black siliceous stone formerly used to test purity of gold and silver, which left a streak on the stone when rubbed upon it. **2.** Anything taken as a test, standard, or criterion.

touchwood, n. [1. túchwood; 2. tátʃwud]. Decayed wood, dried and used as tinder; also dried fungus used for same purpose.

touchy, adj. [1. túchi; 2. tátʃi]. Cp. provinc. **tetchy**. Easily offended, irritable; morbidly sensitive.

tough, adj. [1. tuf; 2. taf]. O.E. *tōh*, M.E. *tough*; fr. earlier **tanχ*, cp. O.H.G. *zāhi*, Mod. Germ. *zäh*, 'tough'; the nasal, lost before *-h*, still remains in the O.E. cogn. *(ġe-)tenġe*, 'near by, close to; occupying the mind; pressing', fr. **(ga)tangi*; O.S. *(bi)tengi*, 'oppressive'; cp. also O.E. *(ġe)tang*, 'in contact with'. The primitive sense of the base is 'closely pressed together, dense, tenacious'; cognates outside Gmc. have not been identified. **1.** (of material things) a Firm, resistant, of close, dense, consistency, resembling gristle or rubber; capable of being bent, but not liable to break or tear; difficult to cut or bite: *tough meat, leather, fibre* &c.; **b** (of human beings and animals) very strong and vigorous; resistant; having a powerful constitution and well-knit frame; robust, hardy; Phr. *a tough customer*, strong, robust person, one difficult to overcome and subdue; one likely to become violent if attacked; **c** also as noun (slang, U.S.A.) *a tough*, a criminal, ruffianly person, cp. *rough*. **2.** (in non-material sense) **a** (of mind, character &c.) Firm, possessing or evincing fortitude; tenacious, stubborn; **b** (of a task &c.) difficult, laborious, to carry out; uphill work: *a tough job, proposition* &c.; cp. such Phrs. as *a tough nut to crack*; *tough row to hoe* &c.

toughen, vb. trans. & intrans. [1. túfn; 2. táfən]. Prec. & **-en**. **1.** trans. **a** To make tough; **b** to render hardy and vigorous. **2.** intrans. To become tough.

toughish, adj. [1. túfish; 2. táfiʃ]. **tough** & **-ish**. Rather tough.

toughly, adv. [1. túfli; 2. táfli]. **tough** & **-ly**. In a tough manner; strenuously, with vigour.

toughness, n. [1. túfnes; 2. táfnis]. See prec. & **-ness**. Quality of being tough (in all senses).

toupee, n. [1. tōōpā; 2. tūpei]. Fr. *toupet*, dimin., fr. Gmc.; connected w. **top (I.)**. A tuft, esp. a tuft of hair on the front of the head; usually, a false front of hair.

tour (I.), n. [1. toor; 2. tuə]. Fr., see **turn**. **1.** A prolonged journey consisting of successive visits to different places; a series of short journeys from place to place; a round of visits: *a foreign tour*; *a tour of inspection*; *the grand tour*, journey through France and other European countries, formerly considered as necessary to put final touches on the education of a young man of the world. **2.** (mil.) A turn of duty.

tour (II.), vb. intrans. & trans., fr. prec. **1.** intrans. To undertake, make, a tour; to travel; also *tour about*; *tour through*. **2.** trans. To journey through, visit, as part of a tour: *to tour France and Italy*.

tourbillion, n. [1. toorbílyun; 2. tuəbíljən]. Fr. *tourbillon*, 'whirlwind'. Kind of firework which spins in the air, producing the effect of a spiral column of fire.

tour de force, n. [1. tóor de fórs; 2. túə də fɔ̃s]. Fr. Action requiring special skill or effort.

touring, adj. [1. tōōring; 2. túəriŋ, tɔ̃riŋ]. Pres. Part. of **tour (II.)**. *Touring car*, large motor-car designed for touring.

tourist, n. [1. tōōrist; 2. túərist]. **tour (I.)** & **-ist**. Person who goes on a tour; one who travels about from place to place as a visitor, without having a fixed abode in any of the places he visits.

tourmalin(e), n. [1. tōōrmalēn, -in; 2. túəməlīn, -in]. Fr., fr. Singhalese *tōramalli*, 'the carnelian'. A composite mineral of various colours, often transparent, used as a gem; the mineral has special optical properties and is used for making certain optical instruments, e.g. the *tourmaline tongs*.

tournament, n. [1. tōōr-, tórnament; 2. túə-, tɔ̃nəmənt]. M.E. *turnement*, fr. O. Fr. *tornoiement*, 'a turning, wheeling', fr. *tornoier*, 'to wheel, turn repeatedly'. See **turn (I.)**. **1. a** Mediaeval assembly to witness the knightly sport of jousting; **b** series of contests between mounted men in armour, armed with the lance, with which weapon each combatant tried to unhorse his opponent; also series of tilting matches and similar sports. **2.** (modern usage) A series of sports, or a series of matches between groups of players, in the same game, lawn-tennis, croquet &c.; usually a competition for a championship; also applied to a series of contests in chess.

tourney, n. & vb. intrans. [1. tórni, tōōrni; 2. tɔ̃ni, túəni]. O. Fr. *tornei, tornoi*, 'a turning'; see **tournament**. **1.** n. A tournament in mediaeval sense. **2.** vb. To take part in a tournament, to joust.

tourniquet, n. [1. tóor-, tórniket, -kā; 2. túə-, tɔ̃niket, -kei]. Fr., 'turnstile', also in Engl. sense. See prec. Device used by surgeons for applying pressure by means of a screw to arteries to stop bleeding during operations or from accident.

tousle, vb. trans. [1. tóuzl; 2. táuzl]. Connected w. **tussle**. To make untidy and dishevelled; to tumble, ruffle: *tousled hair*.

tous-les-mois, n. [1. tōō lā mwah; 2. tū lei mwā]. Fr., 'every month'; origin uncertain. Kind of starch made from the tubers of canna, used for adulterating arrowroot and cocoa.

tout, vb. intrans. & n. [1. tout; 2. taut]. Origin doubtful; O.E. *tōtian*, 'to peep, pry', sometimes cited in connexion w. this word, wd. have become **toot* [tūt]. **1.** vb. **a** To endeavour to obtain customers or clients by persistent and importunate offers of goods or services to persons who want neither; to pester persons to give their custom; to cadge; **b** *tout round*, to go about furtively in the hope of picking up scraps of private information, esp. concerning condition and chances of horses entered for a race. **2.** n. **a** Person who importunes and pesters those whom he hopes to have as customers; **b** one who professes to have, and endeavours to sell, information concerning likely winners of horse-races; a tipster.

tout court, adv. [1. tōō kōōr; 2. tū kúə]. Fr., 'quite briefly'. Without further formality, addition, explanation: *they addressed him as 'Bishop' tout court*; *I told him tout court that his services were not required*.

tout ensemble, n. [1. tōōt onsómbl; 2. tūt ɑ̃sɑ̃bl]. Fr., 'all together, the whole'. General effect, taken as a whole, without reference to single parts or details.

touter, n. [1. tóuter; 2. táutə]. **tout** & **-er**. More usually *tout*. One who touts.

tow (I.), vb. trans. & n. [1. tō; 2. tou]. O.E. *togian*, 'to pull, draw', M.E. *towen*; formed fr. Gmc. type **tug-*, of base **teug-*, **teuh-* &c., 'to draw, drag, pull'; cp. O.E. *tēon*, 'to draw' &c.; cogn. w. Lat. *dūcere*, 'to lead, draw' &c., see **duct, duke**, & cp. **tug (I.)**. **1.** vb. **a** To draw (a barge &c.) along in the water by a rope, by power exerted by a horse or person moving along on the land, esp. in a canal or narrow river, the horse &c. walking along a path by the side of the water; **b** (of a ship) to draw along in the water another vessel which has broken down, or one wishing to enter or leave a port or an estuary where navigation is difficult; **c** to pull a motor-car or other vehicle along a road by means of a cable attached to a horse or to another motor-car &c. **2.** n. **a** Act of towing; chiefly in Phrs. *to take in tow*; *to have (person) in tow*, (fig.) (i.) have him under one's care, guidance; (ii.) to have a person in attendance upon one, at one's disposal: *the cinema star had a number of admirers in tow*. **b** vessel &c. which is being towed.

tow (II.), n. O.E. *tow-*, only in compounds, 'a spinning, weaving'; cogn. w. **taw (I.)** & **tool (I.)**. Coarse fibre of hemp, from which ropes are made.

towage, n. [1. tōij; 2. tóuidž]. **tow (I.)** & **-age**. **a** Act of towing; **b** fee charged for towing a vessel &c.

toward (I.), adj. [1. tōard; 2. tóuəd]. O.E. *tōweard*, 'facing; imminent; future'; see **to (I.)**; the second element is a form of the O.E. base *weorþ-*, as in *weorþan*, 'to become, happen' &c.; cogn. w. Lat. *vertere*, 'to turn', see **vertigo** & **verse (I.)**, **version** &c. (obs. or archaic) **1.** Imminent, about to happen, at hand. **2.** Reverse of *froward*; docile, tractable, compliant.

toward (II.), prep., also **towards** [1. tuwórd(z); 2. təwɔ̃d(z)], more rarely [1. tord(z); 2. tɔ̃d(z)]. Same as **toward (I.)**. O.E. *tōweard, tōweardes*. *Towards* gen. used in prose writing & in speaking. **1. a** (of relation in space) In the direction of: *towards the sun, the south, the sky* &c.; Phr. (now facet.) *I look(s) towards you*, formula used in drinking a person's health; **b** expressing direction of a tendency, result of an action: *moving towards better things*; *drifting towards war*; *striving towards a better understanding*. **2.** (of time) Approaching, round about, just before, specified hour or period: *he died towards six o'clock, towards dawn*; *the present tense plural in -en died out of common use towards the end of the 15th century*. **3.** With regard to, in respect of: *to feel kindly, well-disposed, towards a person*.

towardly, adj. [1. tōardli; 2. tóuədli]. **toward (I.)** & **-ly**. (archaic) Kindly, well-disposed, gentle.

towardness, n. [1. tōardnes; 2. tóuədnis]. See prec. & **-ness**. (archaic) Quality of being toward.

towel, n. & vb. trans. [1. tóuel, -il; 2. táuel, -il], vulg. [tauəl]. M.E. *towaille* &c., fr. O. Fr. *touaille*, fr. Low Lat. *toacula*; fr. Gmc. source, fr. some such form as **þwahila-*, cp. O.H.G. *dwahila*, M.H.G. *twähele, dwähele*, Mod. Germ. *zwehle*, 'towel'; fr. Gmc. base **þwah-*, 'to wash', cp. O.S. *thwahan*, Goth. *þwahan*, O.E. *þwēan*, 'to wash'; cp. also Goth. *þwahl*, 'bath', O.H.G. *dwahal*, O.E. *þwēal*, 'a washing, an ointment'. **1.** n. Cloth used for drying the person after washing; *oaken towel*, (archaic slang) a cudgel for administering a beating. **2.** vb. **a** To dry or rub with a towel; **b** (slang) to thrash.

towel-horse, n. A wooden frame on which towels may be hung.

towelling, n. [1. tóueling; 2. táueliŋ]. **a** Strips of cloth, specially woven, from which towels are cut; **b** (slang) a thrashing.

tower (I.), n. [1. tour; 2. táuə]. M.E., fr. O. Fr. *tour*; fr. Lat. *turris*, 'a tower for defence; a castle, high building'; prob. fr. Gk. *túrrhis, túrsis*, 'a tower'; origin & connexions doubtful. A lofty building, high in proportion to its diameter; a tower may be either round or square, and either isolated from other buildings, or forming a lofty part of a building, though distinct from the rest structurally and to the eye. Phr. *a tower of strength*, person who can be relied upon fo[r] help and support.

tower (II.), vb. intrans., fr. prec. **a** (of an[y] tall object) To rise, rear itself: *the mountains seemed to tower to the clouds*; also *tower up*; **b** *tower above*, to be much taller, higher, than, rise far above: *he towered above the crowd*; (also fig.) to exceed in power of mind, genius, character &c.: *to tower above one's fellow-workers*.

towering, adj. [1. tóuering; 2. táuəriŋ]. Pres. Part. of prec. **1.** Lofty, rising to a great height. **2.** (fig.) In Phr. *towering rage, passion*, excessive, violent.

town, n. [1. toun; 2. taun]. O.E. *tūn*, 'enclosure, yard; estate, farm; village, town'; cogn. w. Mod. Germ. *zaun*, 'hedge, fence', O.H.G. *zūn*; cogn. w. O. Celt. *-dūnum*, 'fortress, city'; O. Ir. *dūn*, 'fortress'. Orig. meaning 'hedge, fence, that which encloses; then, that which is enclosed or fenced in'. **1.** (gen. sense) **a** Large group of houses and other buildings with fixed, distinguishing name; larger than a *village*, but not entitled by charter or usage to the name of 'city', q.v.; Phr. *man about town,* fashionable, gay man of leisure, esp. in London; **b** the inhabitants of such a unit of population collectively: *the talk of the town*; **c** specif., a place where a market is regularly held; also *market town.* **2.** Specif. **a** *London,* in such Phrs. as *to live in, go up to, town* (often with cap.); *out of town,* away from London; in the country; **b** *the town,* the nearest market town, or important centre, in a rural neighbourhood. **3.** (Scots & Nthn. Engl.) A farm-house with its outbuildings.

town-clerk, n. Official, usually a lawyer, under a municipality, who keeps records of its proceedings and advises on legal questions.

town council, n. Governing body of a town or city.

town councillor, n. Member of a town council.

town crier, n. [1. tóun kríer; 2. táun kráiə]. Person employed by a municipality to make public announcements.

townee, n. [1. tòuné; 2. tàuní]. **town & -ee.** (univ. slang; disparaging and derogatory term) Person, esp. a tradesman, living in Oxford or Cambridge, who is not a member of the university.

town hall, n. Building in which a town council holds its meetings, and where the business of a municipality is transacted.

town house, n. Private residence in a town; esp. as contrasted with the *country house* of the same person.

townified, adj. [1. tóunifīd; 2. táunifaid]. See **town & -fy & -ed.** Pertaining to a town, or to a person living in and accustomed to a town; contrasted with *countrified.*

townsfolk, n. pl. [1. tóunzfōk; 2. táunzfouk]. **a** Inhabitants of towns; contrasted with those who live in the country; **b** the inhabitants of a particular town.

township, n. [1. tóunship; 2. táunʃip]. **1.** Ancient administrative unit, co-extensive with a parish. **2.** (U.S.A.) A unit of local administration in a county.

townsman, n. [1. tóunzman; 2. táunzmən]. **a** Man who lives in a town, as distinct from a country dweller; **b** inhabitant of a particular town; *fellow-townsman,* person belonging to the same town as another.

townspeople, n. pl. [1. tóunzpēpl; 2. táunzpīpl]. Townsfolk.

tow-path, n. Path running along the bank of a river or canal, used by horses towing barges.

tow-rope, n. Rope used in towing vessels.

toxaemia, n. [1. toksḗmia; 2. təksímiə]. See **toxic & haema-.** Blood-poisoning.

toxic, adj. [1. tóksik; 2. tɔ́ksik]. Lat. *toxicum,* 'poison in which arrows were dipped; a poison generally'; fr. Gk. *toxikón,* neut. of *toxikós,* 'connected with a bow', fr. *tóxon,* 'a bow'. The common view of a relationship between this word & Lat. *taxus,* 'yew', is not absolutely well authenticated since the latter never means 'bow' in Lat. nor the former 'yew' in Gk. Pertaining to, of the nature of, caused by, poison.

toxicant, adj. & n. [1. tóksikant; 2. tɔ́ksikənt]. Prec. & **-ant. 1.** adj. Producing toxic results. **2.** n. Toxic drug or agent.

toxico-, pref. Form fr. Gk. *toxikós,* see **toxic,** used in compounds. Poison.

toxicological, adj. [1. tòksikolójikl; 2. tɔ̀ksikəlɔ́džikl]. Prec. & **-logy & -ic & -al.** Connected with poisons or with toxicology.

toxicologist, n. [1. tòksikólojist; 2. tɔ̀ksikɔ́lədžist]. Next word & **-ist.** Student of poisons, their nature, and their effects on the living organism.

toxicology, n. [1. tòksikóloji; 2. tɔ̀ksikɔ́lədži]. **toxico- & -logy.** Systematic study of the nature and effects of poisons.

toxin, n. [1. tóksin; 2. tɔ́ksin]. Gk. *tóxon,* 'bow'; for mod. sense see **toxic, & -in.** A poisonous organic substance.

toxophilite, n. [1. toksófilīt; 2. təksɔ́filait]. Gk. *tóxon,* see **toxic,** & *phílos,* 'loving', see **philo-, & -ite.** A lover, a practitioner, of archery; one skilled in shooting with the bow.

toxophilitic, adj. [1. tòksofilítik; 2. tɔ̀ksɔfilítik]. Prec. & **-ic.** Pertaining to archers or to archery.

toy, n. & vb. intrans. [1. toi; 2. tɔi]. Cp. Du. *tuig,* 'tool, implement; stuff'; cogn. w. Germ. *zeug*; cp. Du. *speeltuig,* Germ. *spielzeug,* 'plaything'; ultimately fr. same base as O.E. *tēon,* 'to draw, lead'; see **tow (I.). 1.** n. **a** A child's plaything; **b** any object which serves to amuse and distract; hence, **c** a trifle, bauble, thing of no value or importance. **2.** vb. **a** To indulge in dalliance; *toy with,* to caress amorously, sport with; **b** to trifle with, linger over carelessly: *to toy with the wing of a pheasant*; **c** to let the mind dwell on lightly, to consider casually and superficially: *to toy with an idea.*

toy dog, n. Very small lap-dog; *toy terrier,* very small breed of terrier.

toyshop, n. [1. tóishop; 2. tɔ́iʃɔp]. Shop where children's playthings &c. are sold.

tra-, pref. for **trans-,** in certain words derived fr. Lat. as *tradition* &c.

trabeated, adj. [1. trábeàted; 2. trǽbièitid]. Lat. *trabs,* 'beam'; prob. cogn. w. Gk. *téremnon,* fr. **terebnon,* 'anything closed; room, chamber'; O.W. *treb,* 'dwelling'; Lith. *trobà,* 'building', & perh. O.E. *þorp,* 'village', q.v. under **thorp, & -ate & -ed.** (archit.) Built with horizontal beams or lintels; not arcuate.

trabeation, n. [1. tràbeáshun; 2. træbiéiʃən]. See prec. & **-ion.** (archit.) Straight, distinguished from arched, construction; an entablature.

trabecula, n. [1. trabékūla; 2. træbékjulə]. Lat., 'little beam', dimin. of *trabs,* see **trabeated.** (anat.) Small rod, or bundle, esp. bundle of fibres or connective tissue in framework of an organ.

trabecular, adj. [1. trabékūlar; 2. træbékjulə]. Prec. & **-ar.** Pertaining to, consisting of, trabeculae.

trabeculate, adj. [1. trabékūlāt; 2. træbékjuleit]. **trabecula & -ate.** Trabecular.

trace (I.), n. [1. trās; 2. treis]. M.E. *trays,* pl., fr. O. Fr., *trais, traits*; see **trait.** Part of harness, consisting of two straps or chains, one end of which is fastened on either side, to the hames on the collar, of a draft animal, and connected at the other end with the vehicle or other object to be drawn. Phr. (fig.) *to kick over the traces,* to break loose from discipline, be guilty of unruly conduct.

trace (II.), vb. trans. M.E. *trācen,* fr. O. Fr. *tracier,* L. Lat. *tractiāre,* formed fr. *tract-(um),* P.P. of *trahere,* 'to draw'; see **tract (I.). 1.** To draw, delineate, mark out with lines &c.; often *trace out*: **a** (on paper &c.) *to trace (out) a map, plan* &c.; **b** to lay out, mark out (plans of buildings &c.), on the ground. **2.** To follow exactly, with a pen or pencil, on thin, transparent paper &c., the lines of writing, or of a drawing placed below, and appearing through, the paper &c., on which one is working. **3.** To write, esp. deliberately, carefully, laboriously: *as I trace these words to you I am deeply moved* &c. **4. a** To perceive and follow a visible track: *to trace a person's footsteps in the snow* &c.; **b** to make out, discern: *I scarce could trace her features in the gloom*; **c** to find, reach, by following a series of clues: *to trace one's long-lost relations*; *to trace a criminal*; **d** to find, come upon, put one's hand on: *I am unable to trace the document to which you refer*; **e** to reason out, discover the various stages of, follow from point to point; work out the links of a chain of facts: *to trace the etymology of a word*; *the history, origin, of a family* &c. **5.** To follow, proceed along (a particular path or route); to walk, traverse; tread: *we traced the winding mazes of the wood.*

trace (III.), n. See prec. **1.** Mark made by something which has passed; track, trail, footstep, furrow &c.: *we could plainly see the traces of big game along the river-bank.* Phrs. *on the traces of, hot on the traces of* &c., on the trail, following keenly, about to come up with. **2. a** Visible marks, signs, evidence, left by some earlier event; vestige: *war had left its traces on the countryside*; *every trace of the crime had been removed*; **b** (in non-material sense) recognizable evidence, result, of earlier experience, circumstances &c.: *sorrow and disappointment had left their trace(s) upon his character.* **3.** A very small amount; a slight but perceptible smack, tinge, touch; **a** (of material things) *just a trace of onion in the salad*; *no trace of scent on the handkerchief*; **b** (of non-material things) *he betrayed not a trace of fear, emotion* &c.

traceability, n. [1. tràsabíliti; 2. trèisəbíliti]. **traceable & -ity.** Quality of being traceable.

traceable, adj. [1. trásabl; 2. tréisəbl]. **trace (II.) & -able.** Capable of being traced.

traceableness, n. Prec. & **-ness.** Quality, fact, of being traceable; traceability.

tracer, n. [1. tráser; 2. tréisə]. **trace (II.) & -er.** Person who, thing which, traces (in various senses); specif. **a** a device for tracing patterns on cloth &c.; **b** a person employed to trace out and find missing articles &c.; cp. also *tracer shell,* shell fired from a gun leaving a trail of smoke through the air, so that error in aim or trajectory &c. may be corrected.

tracery, n. [1. tráseri; 2. tréisəri]. **trace (III.) & -ery. 1.** A series, system, group, of lines forming a kind of pattern, as though deliberately traced: *the delicate tracery of light and shade.* **2.** Specif. (archit.) system of decorative ramifications of open stonework in the upper part of windows.

trachea, n. [1. trakḗa; 2. trəkíə]. Mod. Lat., fr. Lat. *trachia,* fr. Gk. *trākheia (artēría),* lit. 'rough artery', fr. *trākhús,* 'harsh, rough, rugged'; cogn. w. Gk. *thrássein,* 'to disturb'; O.N. *dreggjar,* 'dregs' (see **dreg**); O. Prussian *dragios,* 'lees'. The wind-pipe; that part of the air-passage in vertebrates between the lungs and the back of the mouth.

tracheal, adj. [1. trakḗal; 2. trəkíəl]. Prec. & **-al.** Pertaining to, connected with, the trachea.

trachelo-, pref., fr. Gk. *trákhēlos,* 'neck, throat'; etymol. doubtful.

trachelotomy, n. [1. tràkēlótumi; 2. trækilɔ́təmi]. Prec. & **-tomy.** (surg.) Incision in the neck of the uterus.

tracheo-, pref. See **trachea.** Concerned with, involving, the trachea.

tracheocele, n. [1. trákeosēl; 2. tréikiousīl]. Prec. & **-cele.** Goitre.

tracheotomy, n. [1. tràkeótumi; 2. trèikiɔ́təmi]. **tracheo- & -tomy.** Operation consisting in making an incision in the trachea.

trachoma, n. [1. trakóma; 2. trəkóumə]. Gk. *trákhōma,* 'roughness'; see **trachea & -oma.** (med.) Disease characterized by roughness on inner surface of eyelids.

trachyte, n. [1. trákīt; 2. trǽkait]. Gk. *trākhús,* 'rough', see **trachea, & -ite.** Light-coloured volcanic rock with very rough surface when fractured.

tracing, n. [1. trásing; 2. tréisiŋ]. **trace (II.) & -ing.** Writing or drawing traced; reproduction of pattern, writing &c., made by following lines of the original which are visible through superimposed paper &c.

tracing-paper, n. Tough semi-transparent paper upon which tracings are made.

track (I.), n. [1. trak; 2. træk]. O. Fr. *trac,* 'track of horses &c.; trace'; origin doubtful; perh. fr. Gmc. source; cp. Du. *trek,* 'act of drawing'. **1. a** Mark left on the ground, or on surface of water, by something which has passed over it: *the track of a wagon, wheel* &c.; *the track of a vessel*; by extension also: *the track of a meteor*; **b** specif., a footprint, trace, vestige, made on the ground by man or beast. Phrs. *on the track of,* in pursuit; *to make tracks* (slang), to depart hurriedly; *to make tracks for,* go, run, towards; *to cover up one's tracks,* conceal one's plans, actions, designs &c.; *off the track* (fig.), on wrong path, following wrong line; *to lose track of* (fig.), lose sight of, be no longer in touch with (a person or thing). **2.** (in non-material sense) Signs, evidence, of a person's work, actions, designs &c.: *he has left his tracks everywhere in the affairs and organization of the office*; (often in bad sense) signs of intrigue &c. **3. a** A path, rough road, worn by use rather than properly made; Phrs. (fig.) *the beaten track*, the ordinary routine of action; the commonplace and conventional; *he never leaves the beaten track*, never launches out, never shows initiative, never does anything original; **b** a line of railway, including both rails; **c** a course, path, on which races are run.

track (II.), vb. trans., fr. prec. **1.** To follow the track of; trail, pursue by following tracks; *track down*, to run down, pursue to lair or hiding-place and capture. **2.** To make out, trace, by means of visible remains &c. **3.** To tow a vessel by a rope from the bank.

trackage, n. [1. trákij; 2. trǽkidž]. **track** (I.) & **-age**. **a** Railway tracks collectively; **b** extent of these.

tracker, n. [1. tráker; 2. trǽkə]. **track** (II.) & **-er**. **1.** One who traces or tracks out a person or thing. **2.** One who tows a vessel from the bank.

trackless, adj. [1. trákles; 2. trǽklis]. **track** (I.) & **-less**. **1. a** Not crossed by a path or track; untrodden: *a trackless waste*; **b** not having tracks or rails: *trackless trams*. **2.** Leaving no track, footprint, or other mark of passage.

tracklessly, adv. Prec. & **-ly**. Without leaving a track.

tracklessness, n. See prec. & **-ness**. Fact, quality, of being trackless.

tract (I.), n. [1. trakt; 2. trækt]. Lat. *tractus*, 'a drawing, draught; extent, distance; district, region; a space of time'; fr. *tract-(um)*, P.P. type of *trahere*, 'to draw'; the group of words to wh. this is related is disputed; Walde gives two possibilities: (1) fr. **dhragho-* & cogn. w. O.E. *dragan*, see **draw** (I.); (2) fr. **trăgh-* & cogn. w. O. Ir. *traig*, 'fast'. **1. a** A continuous stretch, or expanse, of country; a region, area, district: *a tract of land*; also *tract of forest, woodland* &c., unbroken stretch; **b** expanse of water; **c** expanse of sky. **2.** (of time) Continuous period, unbroken duration; lapse, extent. **3.** (anat.) System of organs or parts of the body which fulfil a specific function or set of functions: *digestive tract*.

tract (II.), n. For **tractate**. A brief written dissertation or treatise; a pamphlet; esp. one designed to enforce some specific religious or political doctrine or theory.

tractability, n. [1. tràktabíliti; 2. træktəbíliti]. **tractable** & **-ity**. Quality, condition, of being tractable; docile.

tractable, adj. [1. tráktabl; 2. trǽktəbl]. Lat. *tractābilis*, 'manageable; yielding'; fr. base of *tractāre*, 'to drag about; to touch; to manage'; formed fr. *tract-(um)*, P.P. type of *trahere*, 'to draw' &c. See **tract** (I.) & cp. **trace** (II.). **1.** Capable of being easily wrought. **2.** Capable of being easily managed; open to persuasion and influence; controllable.

Tractarian, n. [1. traktárian; 2. træktéəriən]. **tract** (II.) & **-arian**. **a** One of the founders of Tractarianism; **b** a believer in the principles of Tractarianism.

Tractarianism, n. [1. traktárianizm; 2. træktéəriənizəm]. Prec. & **-ism**. Movement, in the Church of England, called also the *Oxford Movement*, started by the writers of the 'Tracts for the Times', Keble, Newman, Pusey, Hurrell Froude, and others, published in Oxford in the thirties and forties of the 19th cent. The main points of these teachings were a revolt against the extreme Protestantism which had become characteristic of the Church of England as a whole, an appeal in matters of faith and practice to the early fathers, and to the Anglican High Church divines of the 17th cent., such as Andrewes, Laud &c., and the insistence upon sacramental doctrine.

tractate, n. [1. tráktāt; 2. trǽkteit]. Lat. *tractātus*, 'a touching, handling; a treatment'; see **treat** & **treatise** & cp. **tract** (II.). A treatise, an excursus, essay.

traction, n. [1. trákshun; 2. trǽkʃən], fr. Lat. *tract-(um)*, P.P. type of *trahere*, 'to draw', see **trace** (II.), & **tract** (I.) & **-ion**. **1.** Act, process, of drawing; process of causing to move along by drawing. **2.** Method by which locomotive power is obtained; transport, esp. along roads: *motor, steam, traction*.

tractional, adj. [1. trákshunal; 2. trǽkʃənəl]. Prec. & **-al**. Pertaining to traction.

traction-engine, n. Locomotive engine generally driven by steam, used for drawing heavy trucks along roads.

tractive, adj. [1. tráktiv; 2. trǽktiv]. See **tract** (I.) & **-ive**. Having the function or property of drawing; tractional.

tractor, n. [1. trákter; 2. trǽktə]. **tract** (I.) & **-or**. That which draws; specif. **a** a traction-engine; **b** motor vehicle used for drawing agricultural machines, other vehicles &c.

trade (I.), n. [1. trād; 2. treid]. M.E., 'a path'; connected w. **tread**. **1.** A handicraft, a skilled employment: *the trade of a saddler, of a blacksmith, a wheelwright* &c. **2. a** Business, commercial transactions, esp. those of buying and selling commodities; traffic, barter: *engaged in trade*, contrasted with one of the liberal professions; *Board of Trade*, (i.) one of the great Government departments, dealing with commerce and industry &c., strictly a committee of the Privy Council, its ministerial chief, *President of the Board of Trade* is usually a Cabinet Minister; (ii.) in U.S.A., a Chamber of Commerce; **b** often specif., retail business, shopkeeping, contrasted with *commerce*: *his father was in trade*, i.e. kept a shop. **3.** Occupation, employment of any kind; a calling: *the trade of war*. **4.** Group of persons engaged in some particular trade; specif., *the trade*, the brewers and distillers; sellers of liquor. **5.** (in pl.) *The trades*, trade-winds.

trade (II.), vb. intrans. & trans., fr. prec. **1.** intrans. To engage in, carry on trade, or a trade: *to trade with Russia*; *to trade in furs* &c. Phr. *to trade (up)on*, to presume upon, attempt to derive advantage from, esp. to exploit in an unscrupulous manner: *to trade (up)on one's father's reputation*; *to trade upon a person's tender heart*. **2.** trans. To barter, exchange: *to trade knives and beads with natives for skins*.

trade board, n. A board composed of equal numbers of representatives of employers and employed with a few nominated neutral members, appointed in certain industries by the Board of Trade, to fix minimum rates of wages &c.

trade-mark, n. Registered name, symbol, device, used by a manufacturer to distinguish the goods made by him from others.

trade-name, n. **1.** Name by which an article or commodity is known among those who trade in it. **2.** Name by which an individual or a firm of traders is known in the commercial world.

trade price, n. Price charged by manufacturers for their goods to those who deal in them.

trader, n. [1. tráder; 2. tréidə]. **trade** (II.) & **-er**. **1.** One engaged in trade or commerce; a merchant: *an African trader*. **2.** A trading vessel.

tradesfolk, n. pl. [1. trádzfōk; 2. tréidzfouk]. Tradespeople.

tradesman, n. [1. trádzman; 2. tréidzmən]. **1.** Person engaged in trade, esp. in retail trade; a shopkeeper. **2.** A handicraftsman, a skilled worker.

tradespeople, n. pl. [1. trádzpēpl; 2. tréidzpīpl]. Persons engaged in retail trade, shopkeepers; the families of tradesmen; tradesmen as a class.

tradeswoman, n. [1. trádzwooman; 2. tréidzwumən]. Woman engaged in retail trade.

trade union, n. Legalized association of workers, clerks, or other employees in a particular trade, formed to protect the rights of the members by means of collective bargaining with the employers.

trade-unionism, n. Principles and methods followed by trade unions; system of having trade unions.

trade-unionist, n. Member of a trade union; supporter of the principles of trade-unionism.

trade-wind, n. Wind which blows continuously from N.E. on north side of equator, and from S.E. on south side.

trading, adj. [1. tráding; 2. tréidiŋ]. Engaged in, carrying on, trade or commerce: *a trading concern*.

tradition, n. [1. tradíshun; 2. trədíʃən]. Lat. *trāditiōn-(em)*, fr. *trādit-(um)*, P.P. of *trādere*, 'to give over, deliver, surrender; to betray', & **-ion**; *trādere* is for *trans*, 'over, beyond' &c., see **trans-**, & *dare*, 'to give', see **dower** (I.) & **donation**, & cp. **traitor** & **treason**. **1.** (legal) Act of handing over to, of delivering into the hands of, another; delivery. **2.** Belief, habit, practice, principle, handed down verbally from one generation to another, or acquired by each successive generation from the example of that preceding it: *the great traditions of the British Army*; *to keep up the family traditions*; *it is a misfortune to inherit no traditions*. **3. a** Doctrine, based on divine revelation, statement of alleged occurrence &c., transmitted orally though not recorded in documents, concerning matters of religious belief, or great religious teachers; **b** belief in occurrence of events in the remote past of the history of a race, tribe, family, based upon oral transmission from generation to generation. **4.** Group of principles in art or letters based on the accumulated practice and experience of a series of generations: *the Dryden tradition*.

traditional, adj. [1. tradíshunal; 2. trədíʃənəl]. Prec. & **-al**. **a** Based on, arising from, tradition; hence, **b** in accordance with, adhering to tradition; old-fashioned.

traditionalism, n. [1. tradíshunalizm; 2. trədíʃənəlizəm]. Prec. & **-ism**. **a** Adherence, exaggerated tendency to adhere, to tradition; **b** doctrine that religious belief must be based upon tradition of divinely revealed truth, and traditional interpretation of the Scriptures.

traditionalist, n. [1. tradíshunalist; 2. trədíʃənəlist]. See prec. & **-ist**. One firmly attached to tradition; believer in traditionalism.

traditionalistic, adj. [1. tradìshunalístik; 2. trədìʃənəlístik]. Prec. & **-ic**. Pertaining to, characterized by, traditionalism.

traditionally, adv. [1. tradíshunali; 2. trədíʃənəli]. **traditional** & **-ly**. By, in accordance with, tradition.

traditionary, adj. [1. tradíshunari; 2. trədíʃənəri]. **tradition** & **-ary**. Traditional.

traditor, n. [1. tráditer; 2. trǽditə]. Lat., see **tradition** & **-or**, & see **traitor**. Early Christian who betrayed his fellow-Christians under persecution, or who handed over the Scriptures or sacred vessels to the Roman authorities.

traduce, vb. trans. [1. tradús; 2. trədjús]. Lat. *trādūcere*, 'to lead, bring, across'; see **trans-** & **duke** & **duct**. To hold up to contempt; to disparage, run down, defame, blacken the character of; to calumniate.

traducer, n. [1. tradúser; 2. trədjúsə]. Prec. & **-er**. One who traduces; a calumniator.

traducian, adj. [1. tradúsian; 2. trədjúsiən]. **traduce** (see Lat. sense) & **-ian**. Connected with, pertaining to, traducianism or traducianists.

traducianism, n. [1. tradúsianizm; 2. trədjúsiənizəm]. Prec. & **-ism**. Doctrine that the human soul is procreated along with the body in the act of generation.

traducianist, n. [1. tradúsianist; 2. trədjúsiənist]. See prec. & **-ist**. Adherent of traducianism.

traduction, n. [1. tradúkshun; 2. trədákʃən]. Fr., 'translation from one language to another', fr. Lat. *trāductiōn-(em)*, 'a transferring', fr. *traduct-(um)*, P.P. type of *trādūcere*, see **traduce** & **-ion.** (rare) **1.** Act of transferring from one to another. Specif. **2.** process of procreating the soul along with the body. **3.** Translation.

traffic (I.), n. [1. tráfik ; 2. trǽfik]. Fr. *trafic*, Ital. *traffico*, L. Lat. *trafficum*; origin unknown. **1.** Act, or process, of buying and selling goods; barter, trade, commerce. **2.** Passage to and fro; coming and going of pedestrians, vehicles, goods, over roads, or railways; also, movement of vessels, passengers, and cargoes between ports.

traffic (II.), vb. intrans. Fr. *trafiquer*; see prec. To trade, carry on the business of bartering, buying and selling goods; to deal in merchandise.

tragacanth, n. [1. trágakanth ; 2. trǽgəkænþ]. Lat. *tragacanthum*, fr. Gk. *tragákantha*, lit. 'goat thorn', fr. *trágos*, 'he-goat', wh. is perh. fr. same orig. base as Lat. *turgere*, 'to swell', see **turgid**, & *ákantha*, 'thorn, thorn tree'; see **acanthus.** Kind of gum obtained from an Asiatic plant, *Astragalus*, used in pharmacy.

tragedian, n. [1. trajḗdian ; 2. trədžídiən]. M.E. & O. Fr. *tragedien*, 'writer of tragedies'; see **tragedy. 1.** Writer of tragedies. **2.** Actor of tragedy.

tragedienne, n. [1. trazhèdién ; 2. trǽžèdién]. Fr., fem.; see prec. Tragic actress.

tragedy, n. [1. trájedi ; 2. trǽdžidi]. M.E. & O. Fr. *tragedie*, fr. Lat. *tragoedia*, fr. Gk. *tragōidía*, cp. *tragōidós*, 'tragic poet and singer', orig. prob. 'goat singer', so called because the singers were clothed in goat-skins, or because a he-goat was the prize; cp. *trágos*, 'he-goat', under **tragacanth**, & *ōidós*, 'singer', cp. *ōidḗ*, 'song' &c., q.v. under **ode. 1.** A form of dramatic composition; **a** in ancient tragedy the principal personages were conceived of, and represented, as being by force of circumstances, the natural trend of events, or by some peculiarity of character, inevitably driven, as by fate, to the final catastrophe; **b** in modern usage, a tragedy is simply a solemn play in which the principal personages pass through a series of misfortunes, and end unhappily. **2.** The act of composing or representing tragedies. **3.** (popular usage) A sad, lamentable, event; one causing or involving death and unhappiness.

tragic, more rarely **tragical**, adj. [1. trájik(l); 2. trǽdžik(l)]. Fr. *tragique*, fr. *tragicus*, fr. Gk. *tragikós*, 'pertaining to a tragedy; stately, majestic'; fr. *trágos*, see prec. **1.** Pertaining to, connected with, dramatic tragedy: *the tragic art*; *a tragic actor*. **2. a** (of events and actions) Involving calamity, death, destruction; calamitous; **b** (of persons, expression &c.) evincing, exhibiting, great unhappiness; mournful.

tragically, adv. Prec. & **-ly.** In a tragic manner; calamitously.

tragicalness, n. See prec. & **-ness.** Quality, fact, of being tragic.

tragi-comedy, n. [1. tráji kómedi ; 2. trǽdži kómidi]. See **tragedy** & **comedy.** Play, series of events, in which tragic and comic elements intermingle.

tragi-comic, adj. [1. tráji kómik ; 2. trǽdži kómik]. Exhibiting both tragic and comic scenes or elements.

tragopan, n. [1. trágōpan ; 2. trǽgoupæn]. Gk., name of a fabulous bird, fr. *trágos*, 'he-goat', see **tragacanth**, & **Pan** (III.) (name of the god). Asiatic pheasant with fleshy erectile horns and bright-coloured wattles.

trail (I.), vb. trans. & intrans. [1. trāl ; 2. treil]. O. Fr. *traillier*, 'to tow a boat; to follow a deer by trailing'; prob. fr. Lat. *trāgula*, 'a drag-net; a small sledge'; fr. *trahere*, 'to draw', see **tract** (I.) & **trace** (II.). **A.** trans. **1. a** To drag along the ground: *to trail one's skirt through the dust* &c.; Phr. (fig.) *to trail one's coat* (as though daring people to tread on it), to give provocation, invite attack; (mil.) *to trail arms*, to carry a rifle or pike with the butt-end near the ground, and the muzzle or point sloping forward; **b** to drag through the water: *to trail an oar*, allow the blade to drag over the surface of the water; *to trail a fishing line*, draw it along in the water after a boat. **2.** To follow the track of, to track: *to trail a deer*. **B.** intrans. **1.** To hang down loosely, so as to sweep the ground: *her long train trailed in the mud*. **2.** To straggle, grow, or be placed, in an extended line from some fixed point; to stream out: *creepers trailing over the roofs and walls*; *seaweed trailing over the rocks*.

trail (II.), n. See prec. **1.** Visible mark, track, wake, left by anything that has passed; also any other evidence of its passage left by an animal or thing, such as scent: *on the trail of*. **2.** Path, track, esp. through bush or wild country, worn by those who have passed; course, line of route followed through wild country. **3.** That extended part of a gun-carriage which rests upon the ground.

trailer, n. [1. trāler ; 2. tréilə]. **trail** (I.) & **-er. 1.** One following the trail of another person or of an animal. **2.** Straggling growth of a plant, a long runner of a creeping plant. **3.** A vehicle of any kind drawn or trailed by another.

train (I.), vb. trans. & intrans. [1. trān ; 2. trein]. O. Fr. *trahiner*, cp. Mod. Fr. *traîner*, 'to drag, draw along'; L. Lat. *trahinare*, formed fr. *trahere*, 'to draw', see **tract** (I.) & **trace** (II.). **A.** trans. **1. a** To submit (a person) to discipline and instruction, to educate; to bring up, rear, in habits of good behaviour and conduct: *to train a child, a horse* &c.; **b** to exercise in some specific mental, moral, or bodily discipline; to accustom to specific bodily exercises, or particular mode of reasoning; to cause to acquire skill, deftness, facility; to bring to a certain standard, by systematic practice: *to train a child to obey, to read music at sight, to be a good gymnast* &c.; **c** to produce, form, by training: *to train a cricketer*; *to train hospital nurses, airmen, botanists* &c.; *to train racehorses* &c. **2.** To cause (plants) to grow in a desired direction by bending, tying &c.: *to train roses against a wall*. **3.** To direct upon, towards, a given point: *to train guns on a fort* &c. **B.** intrans. **1.** To carry out the process of training, educating, instructing, either generally, or for some specific purpose and along special lines. **2.** To bring oneself to required pitch of physical condition by dieting &c., and of skill and precision in movement, by steady practice, for a specific contest or form of sport: *to train for a boat race, for a boxing match, for mountain-climbing*.

train (II.), n. See prec. **1.** A body of attendants, a retinue: *the prince and his train*. **2.** A procession, cortège; a number of persons, vehicles &c. forming a continuous line, series, file: *a funeral train*. **3.** Part of a dress, robe, cloak, cope &c., made long so as to extend along the ground behind the wearer. **4.** Series of railway coaches or trucks, coupled together, and drawn as a unit by one or more locomotives: *when does the train start for London?* Phr. *by train*, by the railway, as contrasted with *by road, sea, air* &c.; also *railway train*. **5.** A series, sequence, of connected ideas &c.: *a train of thought, of reasoning*; (more rarely) *a train of words*. **6.** Course of action; process of movement, preparation, development; esp. in such Phr. as *to put things in train*, to start, prepare for, action &c.; *everything is now in train for the attack*. **7.** A continuous line, esp. of gunpowder, extending from a given point up to some explosive object or substance which it is desired to blow up.

train (III.), vb. intrans., fr. prec. **4.** To travel by railway train.

train-band, n., for *trained band*. A company of trained citizens capable of being used for defence, started in London in 14th cent., which in the 18th cent. developed into the more highly organized militia.

train-bearer, n. Page or other attendant who holds up the train of the robe of a high personage on a ceremonial occasion, of bride at wedding &c.

trainer, n. [1. trāner ; 2. tréinə]. **train** (I.) & **-er.** One who trains; specif., person who trains men for athletic competitions or horses for racing.

train-ferry, n. **a** A vessel specially built to carry a railway train and transport it and its passengers and freight across water; **b** service of such vessels.

training, n. [1. trāning ; 2. tréiniŋ]. **train** (I.) & **-ing. 1. a** Act or process of forming, educating, instructing, disciplining: *training of mind and body*; *the training of teachers*, instruction given them in methods and practice of their profession; **b** state of being trained, practised, disciplined, in some branch of mental or physical proficiency: *in first-rate training for a race* &c.

training-college, n. Institution for instructing young teachers in the theory and art of their profession; a normal school.

training-ship, n. Vessel, usually moored in an estuary, in which the art and practice of seamanship is taught to boys.

training-stable, n. Stables, exercising ground &c. where racehorses are trained.

train-oil, n., fr. Du. *traen*, 'tear from the eye; train-oil'; cp. Germ. *träne*, 'tear'. Thick kind of lubricating oil made from whale blubber.

traipse, see **trapse.**

trait, n. [1. trā ; 2. trei]. Fr., 'a stroke; a feature', orig. P.P. of *traire*, 'to draw', fr. Lat. *tract-(um)*, P.P. of *trahere*, see **tract** (I.) & **trace** (II.). **1.** (rare) A stroke, touch: *a trait of humour*. **2.** A characteristic feature, distinguishing mark: *the chief traits of a person's character*.

traitor, n. [1. trāter ; 2. tréitə]. M.E. *traitour* &c., fr. O. Fr. *traïteur*, fr. Lat. *trāditor*, 'betrayer'; fr. *trādit-(um)*, P.P. type of *trādere*, 'to deliver, surrender'; see **traditor.** One who betrays a person or a cause to whom he owes allegiance; specif., one who is disloyal to his king and country, and who consorts with, and betrays secrets to, his country's enemies to the detriment of his native land.

traitorous, adj. [1. trāturus ; 2. tréitərəs]. Prec. & **-ous. a** Pertaining to, of the nature of, a traitor or of treachery; **b** guilty of treachery, disloyal.

traitorously, adv. Prec. & **-ly.** In a traitorous manner.

traitorousness, n. See prec. & **-ness. a** Quality of being traitorous; **b** traitorous conduct.

traitress, n. [1. trātres ; 2. tréitris]. **traitor** & **-ess.** A female traitor.

trajectory, n. [1. trajékturi ; 2. trədžéktəri]. Lat. *trāject-(um)*, P.P. type of *trājicere*, 'to throw across', & **-ory**; see **trans-** & **jet** (III.). Path followed by a projectile fired at a given incline, and passing through the air at a given speed.

tram (I.), n. [1. tram ; 2. træm]. Fr. *trame*, Lat. *trāma*, 'woof, weft', perh. for **tragh-sma*, cp. *trahere*, 'to draw' &c., see **tract** (I.) & **trace** (II.); another suggestion is that first element is *trans*, 'across', see **trans-.** Double twisted thread, esp. such forming weft of velvet or other silk fabrics.

tram (II.), n. & vb. intrans. Perh. Scand.; etymologists compare Swed. dial. *tromm*, 'a log'; Norw. *tram*, 'wooden doorstep'; but connexion in sense w. Engl. word is very vague. **1.** n. **a** Large, heavy, public vehicle plying for hire, carrying passengers, and running on rails laid on a road; **b** truck used in coal-mines for conveying coal to entrance of mine. **2.** vb. To travel by tram.

tram-car, n. Vehicle running on a rail laid upon a road; a tram.

tram-line, n. **a** One of the rails, these taken together, upon which a tram runs; **b** the whole route upon which rails for trams are laid.

trammel (I.), n. [1. tráml ; 2. trǽml]. Fr. *tramail*, earlier *trémail*, 'net', fr. L. Lat.

tremaculum fr. *trēs*, 'three, triple', see **tri-**, & *macula*, 'a spot; mesh of a net', see **macula**, & **mail** (I.). **1.** (archaic) A net for catching birds. **2.** A shackle for controlling motions of a horse. **3.** Something which acts as a check or means of restraint; something which hampers and impedes movement and action; (esp. in fig. or non-material sense) *the trammels of the flesh*; *the trammels imposed by poverty* &c. **4.** Hook for hanging a pot over a fire; a pot-hook; a figure (ʅ) in form of this. **5.** Instrument for drawing ellipses. **6.** One of various devices for adjusting and aligning parts of a machine. **7.** (pl.) A beam-compass: *pair of trammels*.

trammel (II.), vb. trans., fr. prec. To impose trammels upon; (chiefly fig.) to hamper, impede, restrain.

tramontana, n. [1. tràmontáhna; 2. træ̀mɔntána]. Ital.; see next word. Dry, strong, cold wind from the Adriatic.

tramontane, adj. & n. [1. tramóntān, trámontān; 2. træmɔ́ntein, trǽmɔntein]. Fr., fr. Ital. *tramontano*, fr. Lat. *trans*, 'across', see **trans-**, & *montānus*, 'of the mountains', see **mountain**. **1.** adj. Coming from, lying, beyond the mountains; (from Ital. standpoint) foreign, barbarous. **2.** n. A stranger, a foreigner.

tramp (I.), vb. intrans. & trans. [1. tramp; 2. træmp]. M.E. *trampen*; L.G. *trampen*, 'to trample'; cp. Goth. *(ana)trimpan*, 'to press down'; cp. **trample** (I.) & **trapse**. **1.** intrans. **a** To walk, tread, heavily: *heavy footsteps tramping overhead*; **b** to plod along; to go on foot, in distinction to riding or going in a vehicle: *we shall have to tramp as there is no means of conveyance*; **c** (from n.) to travel on foot for long distances, after the manner of a tramp. **2.** trans. To traverse by tramping: *to tramp the streets all night*. Phr. *to tramp it*, to walk, go on foot.

tramp (II.), n., fr. prec. **1.** A homeless vagrant who wanders along the roads from place to place, sleeping out, and living by mendicancy, and by doing occasional short jobs of work. Phr. *to look like a tramp*, present a dirty, disreputable, shabby appearance. **2.** A long, esp. a tedious and laborious, journey on foot. **3.** Sound of a heavy tread, as of a regiment &c. marching past. **4.** Cargo steamer making short journeys to any port as occasion arises, not always between the same ports, and not going on regular voyages. **5.** Flat plate of iron on upper edge of blade of a spade to protect boot when pressing the spade into the ground.

trample (I.), vb. trans. & intrans. [1. trámpl; 2. trǽmpl]. M.E. *trampelen*; freq. of **tramp** (I.). **1.** trans. To tread heavily and repeatedly upon so as to crush: *to trample grapes*; *to trample grass down*; also *trample down (growing corn &c.)*; (also fig.) to suppress: *to trample down one's feelings*; *to trample upon a person*, to oppress, domineer over. **2.** intrans. To perform the act of trampling: *to hear a person trampling about overhead*.

trample (II.), n., fr. prec. **a** The act of trampling; **b** sound of trampling.

tram-rail, n. **a** Rail upon which trams run; **b** (pl.) whole system of such rails at given place.

tramway, n. [1. trámwā; 2. trǽmwei]. Road laid with rails for trams; (also loosely) a tram.

tran-, pref. Form of **trans-** used before words beginning w. *s-*.

trance, n. [1. trahns; 2. trāns]. M.E., 'fright, access of fear', fr. O. Fr. *transe*, 'a swoon', fr. *transir*, 'to chill, penetrate deeply with cold, to benumb', fr. Lat. *transīre*, 'to pass over'; see **transire**. **1.** (med.) Bodily condition attended with unconsciousness, in which complete insensibility occurs, and the vital functions are reduced to a very low ebb, the general appearance being that of profound and prolonged slumber. **2.** Condition in which mystics believe that the soul leaves the body and passes into other spheres of being, seeing visions, and receiving enlightenment concerning spiritual mysteries.

tranquil, adj. [1. trángkwil; 2. trǽŋkwil]. Cp. Fr. *tranquille*, fr. Lat. *tranquillus*, 'quiet, calm, still'; prob. fr. *trans*, 'over' &c., w. intens. sense, see **trans-**, & **-quil-nos*, fr. same base as *quiēs*, 'rest, repose', see **quiet**. **a** (of material things) Calm, serene; not disturbed or agitated: *the tranquil air*; *tranquil waters of a lake* &c.; **b** (of non-material things) not excited; unruffled; not disturbed by violent emotions; peaceful: *a tranquil life*; *a tranquil heart*; **c** expressing no agitation or excitement; exhibiting serenity and calm: *a tranquil gaze, face, voice*.

tranquillity, n. [1. trangkwíliti; 2. træŋkwíliti]. **tranquil** & **-ity**. State of being tranquil; **a** material calm, peacefulness, quietness; **b** calmness, serenity, of mind; composure.

tranquillization, n. [1. tràngkwilīzáshun; 2. træ̀ŋkwilaizéiʃən]. See **tranquillize** & **-ation**. Act of tranquillizing; state of being tranquillized.

tranquillize, vb. trans. & intrans. [1. trángkwilīz; 2. trǽŋkwilaiz]. **tranquil** & **-ize**. **1.** trans. To cause to become tranquil; to quieten, appease, calm down. **2.** intrans. To become tranquil; to die down, abate, become quiet.

trans-, pref. Lat. *trans*, 'across, over, beyond, on farther side of'. In most Engl. words this pref. is pronounced indifferently w. either [ah, ā] or [a, æ], even by the same speaker. In compounds, *trans-* has the senses: **a** 'over, across': *transīre*, 'to go over, across'; **b** 'through, through and through': *transfīgere*, 'to pierce through'; **c** 'beyond': *transalpīnus*, 'lying beyond the Alps'. In Lat. compounds, *trans* remains unchanged before vowels, & often before cons. other than *s-*. Before the latter, *tran-* is the form used; before cons. it sometimes appears as *trā-*, as in *trādo*, 'to give over, deliver' &c., see **tradition**, also *transdo*. In most Engl. words where *trans-* occurs the compound comes direct fr. Lat. As a living suff. it usually has sense of 'beyond, on farther side of', as in *trans-Caucasian*.

transact, vb. trans. & intrans. [1. trahnzákt; 2. trānzǽkt]. Lat. *transact-(um)*, P.P. type of *transigere* for *-agere*, 'to carry through, settle, dispatch'; see **trans-** & **act** (I.). **1.** trans. To carry through, perform, conduct (business, negotiations &c.). **2.** intrans. To settle, put through, a piece of business.

transaction, n. [1. trahnzákshun; 2. trānzǽkʃən]. Prec. & **-ion**. **1.** Act or process of conducting, settling (a piece of business): *the transaction of affairs* &c. **2.** Something transacted, carried out, negotiated; a piece of business: *engaged in various transactions*. **3.** (in pl.) Account, record, of business transacted; specif., record of papers read before a learned society; Proceedings: *Transactions of the Philological Society*. **4.** (law) Compromise of a dispute by mutual concession and agreement.

transalpine, adj. & n. [1. tràhnzálpīn; 2. trànzǽlpain], fr. Lat. *transalpīnus*, see **trans-** & **Alpine**. **1.** adj. Situated, living, from Italian point of view, beyond the Alps. **2.** n. Person living beyond the Alps.

transatlantic, adj. [1. tràhnzatlántik; 2. trànzətlǽntik]. **a** Situated, living, across the Atlantic; **b** going, making a voyage, across the Atlantic: *transatlantic liner*.

transcend, vb. trans. & intrans. [1. trahnsénd; 2. trānsénd]. Lat. *transcendere*, 'to step over, surmount; to surpass'; **trans-** & *scandere*, 'to climb, ascend'; see **scan** & **scandal** & second element in **ascend** & **descend**. **1.** To go beyond, overstep: *to transcend the limits of decency*. **2.** To be superior to, to surpass, excel: *the genius of Shakespeare transcends that of all other human beings*.

transcendence, **-ency**, n. [1. trahnséndens(i); 2. trānséndəns(i)]. Lat. *transcendentia*, see next word & **-ce**, **-cy**. **1.** Quality of being transcendent. **2.** Specif. (theol.) essential attribute of God in being superior to, apart from, and not subject to, the conditions and limitations of the material universe.

transcendent (I.), adj. [1. trahnséndent; 2. trānséndənt]. Lat. *transcendent-(em)*, Pres. Part. of *transcendere*, see **transcend**. **1.** Surpassing, excelling, superior to, others in quality or extent: *transcendent merit, beauty*; also *transcendent folly* &c. **2.** Transcendental. **3.** (theol., of God) Possessing transcendency; see **transcendence, 2.**

transcendent (II.), n., fr. prec. Person or thing which is transcendent.

transcendental, adj. [1. tràhnsendéntl; 2. trànsendéntl]. **transcendent** (I.) & **-al**. **1.** (philos., of human experience and knowledge) Of a character which is a priori; intuitive, gained by intuition; contrasted with *empirical*. **2.** (popular) Vague, fanciful, visionary; abstruse: *transcendental style (of writing)*.

transcendentalism, n. [1. tràhnsendéntalizm; 2. trànsendéntəlizəm]. Prec. & **-ism**. System of philosophy which emphasizes the intuitive rather than the empirical elements in thought and knowledge.

transcendentalist, n. [1. tràhnsendéntalist; 2. trànsendéntəlist]. See prec. & **-ist**. Believer in transcendentalism.

transcendentalize, vb. trans. [1. tràhnsendéntalīz; 2. trànsendéntəlaiz]. **transcendental** & **-ize**. To make, regard as, transcendental.

transcendentally, adv. [1. tràhnsendéntali; 2. trànsendéntəli]. See prec. & **-ly**. In a transcendental manner.

transcontinental, adj. [1. tráhnzkontinéntal; 2. trànzkɔntinéntəl]. Passing across, traversing, the Continent, or a continent.

transcribe, vb. trans. [1. trahnskríb; 2. trānskráib]. Lat. *transcrībere*, 'to write, copy, from one document to another; to copy off'; see **trans-** & **scribe** (I.). To copy; to write out, write down.

transcript, n. [1. tráhnskript; 2. tránskript]. Lat. *transcript-(um)*, P.P. type of *transcrībere*, see prec., & **trans-** & **script**. Something transcribed; a copy written from another document.

transcription, n. [1. trahnskrípshun; 2. trānskrípʃən]. Prec. & **-ion**. **1.** Act, process, of transcribing. **2.** A transcript, copy.

transcurrent, adj. [1. trahnzkúrent; 2. trānzkárənt]. Lat. See **trans-** & **current** (I.), adj. Extending, running, across.

transect, vb. trans. [1. trahnsékt; 2. trānsékt], fr. Lat. *transect-(um)*, P.P. of *transecāre*, 'to put across'; see **trans-** & **sect**. To cut across.

transection, n. [1. trahnsékshun; 2. trānsékʃən]. Prec. & **-ion**. **a** Act, process, of cutting across; **b** a transverse section.

transenna, n. [1. trahnséna; 2. trānsénə]. Lat., 'a grating, lattice; fowler's net'. Etymol. entirely obscure. Screen of stone or metal lattice-work enclosing a shrine.

transept, n. [1. trán-, tráhnsept; 2. trǽn-, tránsept], fr. **trans-** & Lat. *septum*, 'a hedge; an enclosure'; see **septum**. That extension on either side of the nave of a church which crosses at right angles before the apse or choir.

transfer (I.), vb. trans. & intrans. [1. trahnzfér; 2. trānzfə̃]. Lat. *transferre*, 'to carry over, transport' &c.; see **trans-** & **-ferous**. **A.** trans. **1.** **a** To move, shift (person or thing) from one place to another, remove from one place or position and place in another: *to transfer a book from a table to a shelf*; *to transfer a boy to another school*; also *to transfer a name to a different list*; **b** (of non-material action) *to transfer one's affections, allegiance &c. to a new object*. **2.** Specif., to convey, deliver over (property, shares &c.), into possession of, vest in, another. **3.** (lithography &c.) To print, take an impression, from one surface to another. **B.** intrans. Specif., to change one's place from one tram, train, boat, to another.

transfer (II.), n. [1. tráhnzfĕr; 2. trǽnzfā]. See prec. **1.** Act of transferring, state of being transferred; specif. **a** conveyance, transference, of any kind of property or the right in it, by any means, to another person; **b** legal instrument by which such conveyance is effected. **2.** Picture, device, design, made so that it can be transferred from one surface to another, esp. a highly coloured picture on very thin paper, fixed to a thicker paper, which on being immersed in water becomes detached from this, and can be transferred, and made to adhere to, another sheet or object.

transferability, n. [1. tràhnzferabíliti; 2. trànzfərəbíliti]. See next word & **-ity.** Condition, property, of being transferable.

transferable, adj. [1. trahnzférabl, tráhnzferabl; 2. trānzfə́rəbl, trǽnzfərəbl]. **transfer (I.)** & **-able.** Capable of being transferred; (specif. of rights, or documents attesting these) capable of being legally conveyed to, or vested in, another person: *transferable vote*, method of electing parliamentary and other candidates, in which the voter signifies on the ballot-paper the name of the candidate to whom his vote should be transferred if no candidate obtains an absolute majority.

transferee, n. [1. tràhnzferḗ; 2. trànzfərī́]. **transfer (I.)** & **-ee.** Person to whom anything, esp. a legal right or interest, is transferred.

transference, n. [1. tráhnzferens; 2. trǽnzfərəns]. **transfer (I.)** & **-ence.** Act of transferring; **a** conveyance; **b** passage from one place &c. to another.

transferential, adj. [1. tràhnzferénshal; 2. trànzfərénʃəl]. Prec. & **-ial.** Pertaining to, of the nature of, a transfer or transference.

transferor, n. [1. tràhnzferṓr; 2. trànzfərɔ́]. **transfer (II.)** & **-or.** One who transfers, esp. a legal right or interest.

transferrer, n. [1. trahnzférer; 2. trānzfə́rə]. See prec, & **-er.** Transferor (in gen. sense).

transfiguration, n. [1. tràhnzfigūrā́shun; 2. trànzfigjəréiʃən, trànsfigəréiʃən]. See **transfigure** & **-ation.** A marked change of form or of appearance; specif. (cap.) **a** the miraculous change in the form and face of the Saviour, described in Matt. xvii.; **b** feast held by the Church in commemoration of this, on Aug. 6th.

transfigure, vb. trans. [1. trahnzfíger; 2. trānzfígə]. Fr. *transfigurer*, fr. Lat. *transfigūrāre*, 'to change in shape, to transform'; see **trans-** & **figure (I.).** To alter the shape and appearance of; to transform; esp. to make more beautiful and glorious.

transfix, vb. trans. [1. trahnzfíks; 2. trānzfíks], fr. Lat. *transfix-(um)*, P.P. type of *transfīgere*, 'to pierce through'; fr. **trans-** & *fīgere*, 'to fasten, fix, attach', see **fix (I.).** To pierce through, penetrate; to impale: *to transfix a bird with an arrow*; (also fig.) to affect profoundly: *to be transfixed with terror.*

transfixion, n. [1. trahnzfíkshun; 2. trānzfíkʃən]. Prec. & **-ion. a** Act of transfixing; **b** state of being transfixed.

transform, vb. trans. [1. trahnzfórm; 2. trānzfɔ́m]. Fr. *transformer*, fr. Lat. *transformāre*, 'to change shape of'; see **trans-** & **form (I.).** **1.** To alter the outward shape and appearance of to such an extent as to cause to appear something different: *he was quite transformed by the removal of his beard.* **2. a** To change into a different substance, alter the nature of, transmute: *attempts to transform one metal into another are no longer considered practicable*; **b** to alter the essential character, functions, uses, of: *to transform a cottage into a mansion, a conventicle into a church.* **3.** To change the spiritual nature and character of: *to transform a criminal into a decent member of society.*

transformable, adj. [1. trahnzfórmabl; 2. trānzfɔ́məbl]. Prec. & **-able.** Capable of being transformed.

transformation, n. [1. tràhnzformā́shun; 2. trànzfəméiʃən]. Lat.; see prec. & **-ation. a** Act of transforming; **b** condition of being transformed (in various senses both material and non-material).

transformation scene, n. Theatrical scene which gradually changes before the eyes of the audience; specif., one at the end of a pantomime, in which the characters in this change into those of the harlequinade.

transformative, adj. [1. trahnzfórmativ; 2. trānzfɔ́mətiv]. Fr. *transformatif*; **trans-** & **formative (I.).** Tending, serving, to transform.

transformator, n. [1. tráhnzformàter; 2. trǽnzfəmèitə]. See prec. & **-or.** Mechanical device for altering strength of an electric current; transformer.

transformer, n. [1. trahnzfórmer; 2. trānzfɔ́mə]. **transform** & **-er.** Person who, thing which, transforms; esp. one of various mechanical devices in electricity or wireless for altering continuous into alternating current or the voltage of a continuous current.

transformism, n. [1. trahnzfórmizm; 2. trānzfɔ́mizəm]. **transform** & **-ism.** Biological doctrine, now obsolete, also called *mutability of species*, that entirely new species may arise from others already existing, chiefly through the modifying influence of environment.

transfuse, vb. trans. [1. trahnzfū́z; 2. trānzfjū́z], fr. Lat. *transfūs-(um)*, P.P. of *transfundere*, 'to pour from one (vessel) into another, to pour off'; see **trans-** & **fuse (I.).** **1.** To pour (liquid) from one receptacle into another. **2.** To transfer (blood) from veins of one person or animal into those of another. **3.** (in non-material sense) To instil into, penetrate deeply with, imbue: *to transfuse one's own enthusiasm into one's audience.*

transfusion, n. [1. trahnzfū́zhun; 2. trānzfjū́žən]. Lat. *transfūsiōn-(em)*, 'a pouring from one vessel into another'; **trans-** & **fusion.** **1.** Act, process, of transfusing in all senses; esp. *transfusion of blood.* **2.** An intermingling, interpenetration, of different elements, properties, qualities.

transfusive, adj. [1. trahnzfū́siv; 2. trānzfjū́siv]. **transfuse** & **-ive.** Tending to transfuse, serving to bring about transfusion.

transgress, vb. trans. & intrans. [1. trahnzgrés; 2. trānzgrés]. Fr. *transgresser*, fr. Lat. *transgress-(um)*, P.P. of *transgredi*, 'to step across'; fr. **trans-** & *gradi*, 'to step, walk', fr. *gradus*, 'a step', see **grade (I.)** & **gradus. A.** trans. **1.** To overstep, go beyond, exceed: *to transgress the bounds of decency, the limitations of an agreement* &c. **2.** To violate, infringe, break: *to transgress the law, the Divine commands* &c. **B.** intrans. To commit a breach of the law; to violate a moral principle; to sin.

transgression, n. [1. trahnzgréshun; 2. trānzgréʃən]. Lat. *transgressiōn-(em)*, 'a going across, a passage', fr. *transgress-(um)*, see prec. & **-ion.** Act of transgressing; the overstepping of a moral bound or limit, a violation of a moral principle or rule of conduct; a misdeed, a sin.

transgressional, adj. [1. trahnzgréshunal; 2. trānzgréʃənəl]. Prec. & **-al.** Pertaining to transgression.

transgressive, adj. [1. trahnzgrésiv; 2. trānzgrésiv]. Fr. *transgressif*, fr. Lat. *transgressīvus*; **transgress** & **-ive.** Prone, tending, to transgress.

transgressor, n. [1. trahnzgrésur; 2. trānzgrésə]. Lat.; **transgress** & **-or.** One who transgresses; **a a** breaker of laws or rules; **b** a violator of moral principles; a sinner.

tranship, vb. See **trans-ship.**

transience, transiency, n. [1. tráhnsiens(i); 2. trǽnsiəns(i)]. **transient** & **-ce, -cy.** Quality, fact, of being transient.

transient, adj. [1. tráhnsient; 2. trǽnsiənt]. As though fr. Lat. *transient-(em), Pres. Part. of *transīre*, 'to pass through, to pass'; on anal. of **ambient**; see **transire.** Passing, tending to pass away; lasting but a short time; fleeting, brief, momentary; contrasted with *lasting, permanent*; **a** (of material things) *a transient smile*; *a transient flush in the sky*; **b** (of non-material things) *transient pleasures, joys, success* &c.

transiently, adv. Prec. & **-ly.** For a moment; in a brief space of time; not permanently.

transilient, adj. [1. trahnsílient; 2. trānsíliənt]. Lat. *transilient-(em)*, Pres. Part. of *transilīre*, 'to spring over, or across'; fr. **trans-** & *salīre*, 'to leap'; see **salient (I.).** (anat., of nerve-fibres) Passing from one convolution of the brain to another; not adjacent.

transilluminate, vb. trans. [1. tràhnzilū́minā̆t; 2. trànziljū́mineit]. **trans-** & **illuminate.** To cause light to pass through; esp. to pass light through some part of the body for purposes of examination, as by X-rays.

transillumination, n. [1. tràhnzilūminā́shun; 2. trànziljūminéiʃən]. Prec. & **-ion.** Act, process, of transilluminating.

transire, n. [1. tràhnzíre; 2. trǽnzáiəri]. Lat. infin., 'to go through'; see **trans-** & base *i-, 'to go', discussed under **itinerate.** Document issued by Custom-house officials describing cargo of a ship, enabling it to be cleared, and setting forth names of consignors and consignees.

trans-isthmian, adj. [1. tràhnz ísmian; 2. trǽnz ísmiən]. **trans-** & **isthmus** & **-an.** Across an isthmus or through a ship-canal through an isthmus, as through the Panama or Suez Canal: *a trans-isthmian canal*; *trans-isthmian traffic.*

transit (I.), n. [1. tráhnzit; 2. trǽnzit]. Lat. *transitus*, 'a going over, a passage', fr. *transit-(um)*, P.P. type of *transire*, 'to pass over', see **transire.** **1.** Passage through. **2.** Act, process, of conveying, sending, transmitting, causing to pass: *the transit of goods*; Phr. *in transit*, said of goods during time which elapses between the moment of their being sent off and that of the receipt by the person to whom they are consigned. **3.** Passage of a heavenly body, esp. of Venus or Mercury, across sun's disk, or across field of vision of a telescope, or apparent passage of a star across meridian.

transit (II.), vb. trans., fr. prec. (of a heavenly body) To pass across the sun's disk.

transit-circle, instrument, n. Instrument for observing the transit of heavenly bodies.

transition, n. [1. trahnzíshun; 2. trānzíʃən]. Lat. *transitiōn-(em)*, 'a passing over, passage'; see **transit (I.)** & **-ion.** **1.** Change, passage, **a** from one place, or kind of place, to another: *a sudden transition from the plain to hilly country*; **b** passage, alteration, from one set of conditions, mode of existence, state &c. to another: *a gradual transition from a tropical to a cold climate*; *a rapid transition from poverty to wealth*; *a natural transition from grave to gay*; *a period of transition* &c. **2.** (used attrib.) Indicating a process of gradual change and modification: *transition period*, one occurring between two well-marked, characteristic periods; *Transition English*; *Early Transition*, phase of English between Old and Middle English; *Late Transition*, that between Middle and Modern English.

transitional, adj. [1. trahnzíshunal; 2. trānzíʃənəl]. Prec. & **-al.** Pertaining to, occurring, existing, under conditions of transition; marked by, characterized by, change from one state of things to another.

transitionally, adv. See prec. & **-ly.** In a transitional manner.

transitionary, adj. [1. trahnzíshunari; 2. trānzíʃənəri]. **transition** & **-ary.** Transitional.

transitive, adj. [1. tráhnzitiv; 2. trǽnzitiv], fr. L. Lat. *transitīvus*; see **transit (I.)** & **-ive.** **1.** (gram., of vbs.) Governing a direct object; *transitive verb*, one expressing an action which passes directly on to, and affects, the object, as *to strike the iron while it is hot*, contrasted with *intransitive*, as *to strike while the iron is hot.* **2.** Having the property of passing or making a transit from one person or thing to another: *transitive heat*

transitively, adv. Prec. & **-ly**. In a transitive manner; by use of a transitive verb.

transitiveness, n. See prec. & **-ness**. Quality of being transitive.

transitivity, n. [1. tràhnzitíviti; 2. trǎnzitíviti]. **transitive** & **-ity**. Property of being transitive; capacity of passing from one person or thing to another.

transitorily, adv. [1. tráhnziturili; 2. trǎnzitərili]. **transitory** & **-ly**. In a transitory manner; for a time only.

transitoriness, n. [1. tráhnziturines; 2. trǎnzitərinis]. Next word & **-ness**. Quality, state, of being transitory.

transitory, adj. [1. tráhnzituri; 2. trǎnzitəri]. Lat. *transitōrius*, 'adapted for passing through'; see **transit** (**I.**) & **-ory**. Not lasting, tending to pass away, enduring but for a time; fleeting, evanescent: *this transitory life.*

translatable, adj. [1. trahnzlátabl; 2. trānzléitəbl]. See next word & **-able**. Capable of being translated.

translate, vb. trans. & intrans. [1. trahnzlāt; 2. trānzléit], fr. L. Lat. *translatāre*, formed fr. *translāt-(um)*, P.P. type of *transferre*, 'to carry over', see **transfer** (**I.**); **trans-**, & *lāt-*, wh. stands for **tlāt-*; see base **tl-* under **tolerate** & **thole**. **A.** trans. **1. a** (archaic) To remove, transfer, from one place to another; specif. **b** to remove, transfer, (a bishop) from one see to another; **c** to remove the body or relics of a saint, confessor, or martyr from one place to another. **2.** Specif., to remove, carry away, bodily, direct to heaven without death of the body: *Enoch is said to have been translated to heaven.* **3.** To turn from one language into another; to render in one language what has been written or spoken in another. **4.** To render what is expressed or conceived in one medium into another: *to translate promises, schemes &c. into actions; to translate phonetic symbols into sounds.* **B.** intrans. **1.** To translate what is uttered or written in one language into another: *I can read Danish but can't translate into it.* **2.** To be capable of translation: *poetry does not translate easily.*

translation, n. [1. trahnzláshun; 2. trānzléiʃən]. Lat. *translātiōn-(em)*, 'a removing, transferring, from one place to another'; also of language, 'a version, translation', see **translate** & **-ion**. **1.** Act, process, of translating, **a** the transference of a bishop from one see to another; **b** removal to heaven without bodily death; **c** removal of body or relics of a saint &c. from one place to another. Specif. **2. a** act of translating from one language into another; **b** something which is translated; esp. a version in a particular language of something originally written or uttered in a different language.

translational, adj. [1. trahnzláshunal; 2. trānzléiʃənəl]. Prec. & **-al**. Pertaining to, connected with, translation.

translative, adj. [1. tráhnzlativ; 2. trǎnzlətiv]. Lat. *translātīvus*, 'belonging to transference; capable of being transferred'; see **translate** & **-ive**. **a** Connected with, denoting, a transfer of property; **b** indicating, expressing, a transference of meaning, state &c.

translator, n. [1. trahnzláter; 2. trānzléitə]. Lat. See **translate** & **-or**. One who translates; esp. one who translates from one language into another.

transliterate, vb. trans. [1. trahnzlíterāt; 2. trānzlítəreit], fr. **trans-** & Lat. *lit(t)era*, 'letter', see **letter** (**I.**) & **literal** & **-ate**. To write what is actually or commonly written with the symbols of a given alphabet in the corresponding symbols of another: *in this Dictionary, Greek is always transliterated with Roman letters.*

transliteration, n. [1. tràhnzliteráshun; 2. trǎnzlitəréiʃən]. Prec. & **-ion**. **a** Act of transliterating; **b** written word &c. which has been transliterated.

translucence, **translucency**, n. [1. trahnzlûsens(i); 2. trānzljûsəns(i)]. Next word & **-ce**, **-cy**. Property, condition, of being translucent.

translucent, adj. [1. trahnzlûsent; 2. trānzljûsənt]. Lat., 'shining through'; see **trans-** & **lucent**. Allowing rays of light to pass through; transparent or semi-transparent.

transmarine, adj. [1. tràhnzmarḗn; 2. trǎnzmərîn]. **trans-** & **marine** (**I.**). adj. Situated, living, coming from, beyond, on the other side of, the sea.

transmigrant, adj. [1. trahnzmígrant; 2. trānzmáigrənt]. **trans-** & **migrant**. Migrating from one place or condition to another.

transmigrate, vb. intrans. [1. trahnzmígrāt; 2. trānzmáigreit]. **trans-** & **migrate**. **1.** To migrate, go, from one place or country to another. **2.** (of the soul) To pass at death into another body.

transmigration, n. [1. tràhnzmīgráshun; 2. trǎnzmaigréiʃən]. **trans-** & **migration**. **1.** Act of migrating from one place or country to another. **2.** (specif. Hinduism &c.) The passage of the soul at death into another body, human or animal; metempsychosis; usually, *the transmigration of souls.*

transmigrator, n. [1. tràhnzmīgráter; 2. trǎnzmaigréitə]. **transmigrate** & **-or**. One who transmigrates.

transmigratory, adj. [1. trahnzmígraturi; 2. trānzmáigrətəri]. **transmigrate** & **-ory**. Given to, liable to, transmigration.

transmissibility, n. [1. tràhnzmisibíliti; 2. trǎnzmisibíliti]. Next word & **-ity**. Condition, quality, of being transmissible; capacity of being transmitted.

transmissible, adj. [1. trahnzmísibl; 2. trānzmísibl]. *transmiss-* as in **transmission** & **-ible**. Capable of being transmitted.

transmission, n. [1. trahnzmíshun; 2. trānzmíʃən]. **trans-** & **mission**. **a** Act of transmitting; **b** condition of being transmitted.

transmit, vb. trans. & intrans. [1. trahnzmít; 2. trānzmít]. Lat. *transmittere*, 'to send, convey, across; to allow to pass through; to hand over'; **trans-**, & see **missile** & **mission** for base of second element. **A.** trans. **1.** To hand over, cause to be received, pass on (by a physical action): *to transmit a package by rail, a letter by hand.* **2.** To pass on, convey, hand on, or down, **a** by heredity: *parents transmit their characters and features to their offspring*; **b** by inheritance and descent: *to transmit property, a title, to one's heirs.* **3.** To permit passage of, allow to pass along, serve as medium for: *wires transmit an electric current.* **4.** To communicate, pass on, tell: *to transmit news; to transmit a tradition to the younger generation.* **B.** intrans. (law) To descend by transmission.

transmitter, n. [1. trahnzmíter; 2. trānzmítə]. Prec. & **-er**. **a** One who transmits: '*No tenth transmitter of a foolish face*' (Savage, 'The Bastard'); **b** that which transmits; part of a telephone or telegraphic apparatus which sends on the message; specif., apparatus by means of which wireless waves are sent out.

transmogrification, n. [1. tràhnzmogrifikáshun; 2. trǎnzmɔgrifikéiʃən]. See next word & **-fication**. Act of transmogrifying; a complete change or transformation.

transmogrify, vb. trans. [1. trahnzmógrifī; 2. trānzmɔ́grifai]. Mod. coinage. To cause to change completely in appearance or character; to transform, transmute.

transmutability, n. [1. tràhnzmūtabíliti; 2. trǎnzmjūtəbíliti]. Next word & **-ity**. Quality, fact, of being transmutable.

transmutable, adj. [1. trahnzmûtabl; 2. trānzmjûtəbl]. **transmute** & **-able**. Capable of being transmuted.

transmutably, adv. Prec. & **-ly**. So as to be transmutable.

transmutation, n. [1. tràhnzmūtáshun; 2. trǎnzmjūtéiʃən]. Lat. *transmūtātiōn-(em)*. **transmute** & **-ation**. **1. a** Act or process of transmuting; complete change in nature, form, or conditions; transformation; *transmutations of fortune*, ups and downs, fluctuations; **b** state of being transmuted. **2.** Specif. **a** (biol.) change of one species into another (a process now called *mutation*); **b** (alchem.) *transmutation of metals*, supposed conversion of base metals into gold.

transmutationist, n. [1. tràhnzmūtáshunist; 2. trǎnzmjūtéiʃənist]. Prec. & **-ist**. Believer in the transmutation of species or of metals.

transmutative, adj. [1. trahnzmûtativ; 2. trānzmjûtətiv]. Lat. *transmūtāt-(um)*, P.P. type of *transmūtāre*, 'to change over', see **transmute**, & **-ive**. Connected with, resulting from, transmutation.

transmute, vb. trans. [1. trahnzmût; 2. trānzmjût]. Lat. *transmūtāre*, 'to change, shift'; see **trans-** & **mutable**. To change from one form, character, set of conditions, into another; to transform.

transoceanic, adj. [1. tráhnzōsheánik; 2. trǎnzouʃiǽnik]. Across the ocean; **a** situated on the other side of, beyond, an ocean; **b** crossing an ocean.

transom, n. [1. tránsum; 2. trǽnsəm]. Lat. *transtrum*, 'a cross-timber, beam running from side to side in a vessel'; formed fr. **trans-**, w. formative *-tr-*, expressing an agent or instrument. **a** Horizontal stone or wooden beam or bar across the top of a doorway or of a window, or across the middle of a window; **b** beam or timber fixed across the stern-post of a vessel; **c** any cross-timber or strut used in building and engineering.

transom-window, n. Window over the transom of a door.

transpadane, adj. [1. trahnzpádān; 2. trānzpéidein], fr. Lat. *transpadānus*, fr. *trans*, 'across', see **trans-**, & *Padus*, the river Po, & **-an(e)**. Situated, lying beyond, i.e. north of, the river Po.

transparence, n. [1. trahnspárens; 2. trānspéərəns]. **transparent** & **-ce**. Transparency **1**.

transparency, n. [1. trahnspárensi; 2. trānspéərənsi]. **transparent** & **-cy**. **1.** Quality of being transparent. **2.** Something which is transparent; specif., a picture or device, concealed externally between thin sheets of paper, cloth &c., but becoming visible if looked at against a light.

transparent, adj. [1. trahnspárent; 2. trānspéərənt]. Lat. *transpārent-(em)*, Pres. Part. of *transpārēre*, fr. **trans-** & *pārēre*, 'to appear'; see **appear** & **pare**. **1.** (of matter) **a** Permeable to light; having the property of letting rays of light pass through, and therefore of allowing objects and images behind or beneath, to be clearly seen; reverse of *opaque*; **b** (of fabric) open, having an open texture or mesh, so that what lies beneath is scarcely concealed: *transparent muslin* &c. **2.** (of style) Clear, limpid, lucid, easy to be understood. **3.** (of the character and spiritual qualities) Candid, frank, not attempting to hide or dissemble: *transparent honesty, sincerity* &c.

transparently, adv. Prec. & **-ly**. In a transparent manner (lit. and fig.).

transparentness, n. See prec. & **-ness**. Quality of being transparent.

transpierce, vb. trans. [1. trahnspḗrs; 2. trānspíəs]. **trans-** & **pierce**. To pierce through; to transfix.

transpirable, adj. [1. trahnspírabl; 2. trānspáiərəbl]. **transpire** & **-able**. Capable of being given off in vapour.

transpiration, n. [1. tràhnspiráshun; 2. trǎnspiréiʃən]. **transpire** & **-ation**. **a** Process of transpiring, of exhaling vapour; **b** moisture given off in form of vapour.

transpiratory, adj. [1. trahnspíraturi; 2. trānspáiərətəri]. Lat. *transpīrāt-(um)*, P.P. type of *transpīrāre*, see **transpire**, & **-ory**. Pertaining to, connected with, transpiration.

transpire, vb. intrans. & trans. [1. trahnspír; 2. trānspáiə]. Fr. *transpirer*, 'perspire' &c., fr. Lat. *transpīrāre*, **tran-** & *spīrāre*, 'to breathe, blow; to exhale'; see **spirant**. **A.** intrans. **1.** To exhale, give off, watery vapour. **2.** To pass off, be exhaled, in form of watery vapour. 3. (of events, or news concerning them) To become known, leak out: *nothing transpired of all that happened*; *what occurred did not transpire*; *it transpired that the Emperor was dead.* 4. (incorrect and vulg. usage) To take place, happen, occur: *grave events transpired which did not become known for many hours.* B. trans. To excrete, exhale through the pores, give off in form of vapour.

transplant, vb. trans. & intrans. [1. trahnspláhnt; 2. trānsplánt]. See **trans-** & **plant** (I.). 1. trans. **a** To dig up, remove (plant &c.) from where it is growing, and re-plant in another place; **b** to remove (persons) from one place of abode, and re-settle them elsewhere. 2. intrans. **a** (of persons) To perform the act of transplanting; **b** (of plants) to be capable of being transplanted, to bear transplantation.

transplantation, n. [1. tràhnsplahntáshun; 2. trànsplāntéiʃən]. Prec. & **-ation**. **a** Act of transplanting (growing trees &c.); **b** removal of skin &c. by a surgeon, from one part of the body or from body of a given person, and the setting of it in another part, or in the body of another person &c.; **c** removal of persons settled in one place, and resettling of them elsewhere.

transplanter, n. [1. trahnspláhnter; 2. trānsplántə]. **transplant** & **-er**. **a** Person who transplants; **b** mechanical device for transplanting trees &c.

transpontine, adj. [1. trahnzpóntīn; 2. trānzpóntain]. **trans-** & Lat. *pont-*, 'a bridge', see **pons**, & **-ine**. Lying on the other side of a bridge; (specif. usage) referring to a type of melodrama formerly popular in theatres on the south side of London Bridge: *a transpontine drama, hero* &c.

transport (I.), vb. trans. [1. trahnzpórt; 2. trānzpɔ́t]. Lat. *transportāre*, 'to carry across', see **trans-** & **port** (IV.). 1. To carry, transfer, from one place to another: *to transport passengers and luggage* &c. 2. Specif., to convey criminals to a penal settlement, to banish as punishment for crime: *transported for sheep-stealing.* 3. (fig.) To take out of oneself, to ravish, charm, by powerful emotion: *transported with delight, grief* &c.

transport (II.), n. [1. tráhnzport; 2. tránzpɔ̄t], fr. prec. 1. Act or process of transporting; carriage, conveyance: *the transport of goods* &c. 2. **a** Vessel engaged in transporting goods and passengers: specif. **b** ship carrying troops. 3. Violent, overwhelming emotion; gust of feeling, ecstasy: *a transport of joy, horror, rage* &c.

transportability, n. [1. tràhnzportabíliti; 2. trànzpɔ̄təbíliti]. Next word & **-ity**. Quality, state, of being transportable.

transportable, adj. [1. trahnzpórtabl; 2. trānzpɔ́təbl]. **transport** (I.) & **-able**. Capable of being transported, carried, conveyed.

transportation, n. [1. tràhnzportáshun; 2. trànzpɔ̄téiʃən]. **transport** (I.) & **-ation**. 1. Act of transporting; conveyance, transport. 2. Fact of being sent to penal settlement; punitive banishment: *transportation for life.*

transporter, n. [1. trahnzpórter; 2. trānzpɔ́tə]. **transport** (I.) & **-er**. **a** One who transports; (in various senses) *transporter of goods* &c.; **b** machine, apparatus, for carrying goods from one place to another, a conveyor.

transposal, n. [1. trahnzpózl; 2. trānzpóuzl]. See next word & **-al**. **a** Act of transposing; **b** something transposed.

transpose, vb. trans. & intrans. [1. trahnzpóz; 2. trānzpóuz]. Fr. *transposer*; see **trans-** & **pose** (I.). A. trans. 1. **a** To change the respective places or order of things; to put one thing in the place or order formerly occupied by another, and the latter in that place where, or order in which, the former stood; **b** to alter relative position and order (of words) in a sentence. 2. (mus.) To put into a different key. B. intrans. 1. Specif., to put piece of music into a different key. 2. To be capable of, lend itself to, transposition: *the sentence is ambiguous as it stands—won't it transpose?*

transposition, n. [1. tràhnzpozíshun; 2. trànzpəzíʃən]. **trans-** & **position** (I.). Act of transposing; result of this.

transpositive, adj. [1. trahnzpózitiv; 2. trānzpɔ́zitiv]. See prec. & **-ive**. Consisting in transposition.

trans-ship, vb. trans. [1. trahnz shíp; 2. trānz ʃíp]. **trans-** & **ship**. To remove, transfer (goods or passengers) from one ship to another, the voyage being continued in the latter.

trans-shipment, n. [1. trahnz shípment; 2. trānz ʃípmənt]. Prec. & **-ment**. Act of trans-shipping.

transubstantiate, vb. trans. [1. tràhnsubstánshiāt; 2. trànsəbstǽnʃieit]. Med. Lat. *transubstantiāt-(um)*, P.P. of *transubstantiāre*; see **trans-** & **substantiate**. To change into another substance, to transmute.

transubstantiation, n. [1. tráhnsubstànshiáshun; 2. tránsəbstǽnʃiéiʃən]. Med. Lat. *transubstantiātiōn-(em)*. See prec. & **-ion**. Doctrine that in the Eucharist a change is wrought in the elements at consecration, whereby the whole substance of these is transmuted into the very Body and Blood of Christ, nothing of the bread and wine remaining except the appearance.

transudation, n. [1. tràhnsūdáshun; 2. trànsjūdéiʃən]. See **transude** & **-ation**. **a** Process of transuding; **b** moisture which transudes.

transudatory, adj. [1. trahnsúdaturi; 2. trānsjúdətəri]. See next word & **-ory**. Pertaining to, of the nature of, transudation.

transude, vb. intrans. [1. trahnsúd; 2. trānsjúd]. **tran-** & Lat. *sūdāre*, 'to sweat, perspire'; see **sudation** & **sweat** (I.). To pass out through, or as through, the pores, in form of perspiration.

transversal, adj. & n. [1. trahnzvérsl; 2. trānzvə́səl]. **transverse** & **-al**. 1. adj. Transverse. 2. n. Line that intersects other lines.

transversality, n. [1. tràhnzvērsáliti; 2. trànzvəsǽliti]. Prec. & **-ity**. Quality of being transversal.

transversally, adv. [1. trahnzvérsali; 2. trānzvə́səli]. See **transversal** & **-ly**. Transversely.

transverse, adj. & n. [1. trahnzvérs, tráhnzvērs; 2. trānzvə́s, tránzvəs]. Lat. *transversus*, also *trāversus*, 'going, lying, across, or athwart', fr. **trans-** & *vers-(um)*, P.P. type of *vertere*, 'to turn', see **version**; cp. also **traverse** (I.). 1. adj. Passing, lying, placed, so as to cross; cross-wise. 2. n. Something which lies in a transverse direction.

transversely, adv. [1. trahnzvérsli; 2. trānzvə́sli]. Prec. & **-ly**. In a transverse direction.

tranter, n. [1. tránter; 2. trǽntə]. Etymol. doubtful; Med. Lat. has *travetārius*. (provinc.) Hawker, carrier.

trap (I.), n. [1. trap; 2. træp]. Swed. *trappa*, 'stair'. Any of various kinds of dark-coloured, igneous rocks; also *trap-rock*; so called because they occur in masses rising one above another somewhat in the form of flights of stairs.

trap (II.), n. M.E. has *trappen*, 'to clothe, furnish with trappings &c.'; origin doubtful, cp. Span. *trapo*, 'cloth'. Connexion w. Fr. *drap*, 'cloth', see **drape**, is doubtful. (colloq., usually pl. *traps*) Personal possessions, clothes &c.; luggage.

trap (III.), n. O.E. *træppe*, M.E. *trappe*, origin unknown. 1. A mechanical or other material device for catching or snaring animals, birds &c.; a pitfall; a snare, a gin. 2. (fig.) **a** A stratagem, an artful scheme, device, or plan to ensnare and deceive, or to lead (persons) into an awkward dilemma; **b** anything having a deceptive, misleading appearance; a take-in, a pitfall. 3. Instrument used in trap-ball, consisting of a wooden arm with a pivot in the middle, raised from the ground below the pivot; one end retains a ball and the other is struck downwards, causing the ball to fly up; the ball is then struck and driven in desired direction. 4. Apparatus from which live or clay pigeons are released for shooting at. 5. Bend in the upper end of a drain-pipe, just below the opening, which holds a certain amount of water, and thus prevents noxious gases from escaping from the sewer. 6. A horse carriage, esp. one with only two wheels. 7. A trap-door.

trap (IV.), vb. trans. & intrans., fr. prec. A. trans. 1. **a** To catch in, or as in, a trap; to snare; also **b** (fig.) to catch by artifice and stratagems; to cozen, deceive. 2. To supply (drain &c.) with a trap or traps. B. intrans. To set traps; practise occupation of a trapper.

trapan, vb. trans. See **trepan** (II.).

trap-ball, n. Old game played with trap and ball.

trap-door, n. Hinged flap, opening upwards from a ceiling or roof, giving entrance to a loft &c.; one giving access from below the stage of a theatre, for sudden appearance of demons, ghosts &c.; *trap-door spider*, a kind of spider which nests in a cylindrical hole in the ground which it closes by a hinged door.

trapes, vb. See **trapse**.

trapeze, n. [1. trapéz; 2. trəpíz]. Fr. *trapèze*, fr. Gk. *trapézion*, see **trapezium**. Short, swinging horizontal bar, suspended from two ropes, used by gymnasts and acrobats.

trapeziform, adj. [1. trapéziform; 2. trəpízifɔ̄m]. Prec. & **-form**. Having the form of a trapezium.

trapezium, n. [1. trapézium; 2. trəpíziəm]. Lat., fr. Gk. *trapézion*, 'a little table'; dimin. fr. *trápeza*, 'a table', fr. *tétra-*, 'four', see **tetra-**, & *péza*, 'a foot', q.v. under **pedal** (I.). (geom.) Four-sided plane figure, no two lines of which, or according to another definition, only two, are parallel.

trapezoid, adj. & n. [1. trápezoid; 2. trǽpezɔid]. Prec. & **-oid**. 1. adj. Having the form of a trapezium; also *trapezoidal*. 2. n. Trapezium.

trapper, n. [1. tráper; 2. trǽpə]. **trap** (IV.) & **-er**. Person who traps animals; specif., one who traps animals for their skins.

trappings, n. pl. [1. trápingz; 2. trǽpiŋz]. See **trap** (II.). 1. Harness, accoutrements, caparison, of a horse; esp. elaborately ornamented harness and adjuncts used on ceremonial occasions. 2. Ceremonial or official dress; elaborate uniform with decorations.

Trappist, n. [1. trápist; 2. trǽpist], fr. monastery of La Trappe in Normandy. Member of a branch of Cistercian order of monks who observe strict silence among themselves.

trappy, adj. [1. trápi; 2. trǽpi]. **trap** (III.) & **-y**. Full of snares or traps; tricky.

trapse, trapes, traipse, vb. intrans. [1. trāps; 2. treips]. Perhaps related to, or the same as, obs. or dial. *trape, trappe*, & cogn. w. M. Du. *trappen*, Norw. dial. *trappa*, 'to tread, stamp'; cp. w. infixed nasal, **trample**. To ramble or gad about aimlessly.

trap-shooting, n. Shooting at live or clay pigeons released from a trap.

trash, n. [1. trash; 2. træʃ]. Cp. O.N. *tros*, 'rubbish, twigs &c. collected for fuel'. Origin doubtful. **a** Worthless stuff, rubbish; shoddy, cheap material; **b** literary or artistic work of very poor quality.

trashily, adv. [1. tráshili; 2. trǽʃili]. **trashy** & **-ly**. In a trashy manner or style.

trashiness, n. [1. tráshines; 2. trǽʃinis]. See next word & **-ness**. Quality of being trashy; esp. in non-material sense: *the trashiness of much modern writing.*

trashy, adj. [1. tráshi; 2. trǽʃi]. **trash** & **-y**. Worthless, rubbishy (of material and non-material things).

trass, n. [1. tras; 2. træs]. Du. *tras*, perh. fr. Ital. *terrazza*, see **terrace**. A volcanic earth, used as a hydraulic cement.

trattoria, n. [1. tràtoréa; 2. trætɔría]. Ital. An Italian eating-house.

trauma, n. [1. tráwma; 2. trṓmə]. Gk. *traûma*, 'a wound; damage'; perh. fr. same base as Gk. *trúein*, 'to wear down, or out'; cp. Lat. *terere*, 'to rub, wear away', see **teredo, termite** & words there referred to. (med.) A bodily injury, a wound.

traumatic, adj. [1. trawmátik; 2. trōmǽtik]. fr. Gk. *traumat-*, stem of *traûma*, see prec., & **-ic.** Pertaining to, caused by, following after or in consequence of, a wound or other bodily injury: *traumatic neurasthenia* &c.

traumatism, n. [1. tráwmatizm; 2. trṓmətizəm]. See prec. & **-ism.** General pathological condition produced by severe wounds or injuries.

travail, n. & vb. intrans. [1. trávāl; 2. trǽveil]. O. Fr. *traváil*, 'toil'; *travailler*, 'to labour, work'; perh. fr. L. Lat. *trepalium*, 'an instrument of torture'; fr. *trēs*, 'three', see **tri-**, & *pālus*, 'a stake', see **pale (I.)**. **1.** n. Pains of childbirth; labour. **2.** vb. **a** To feel the pains of childbirth, be in labour; **b** to toil painfully and laboriously.

travel (I.), vb. intrans. & trans. [1. trávl; 2. trǽvl]. Same word as prec.; derived fr. type accentuated on first syll. fr. early period. **A.** intrans. **1.** To move along, go, proceed: *a tram travels along a rail.* **2.** To make a journey; to go from place to place, esp. to journey for long distances, in remote places: *to travel on the Continent.* **3.** Specif., to journey from place to place with a view to selling goods or to obtaining orders for goods from customers; to ply the business of a commercial traveller. **B.** trans. To pass through or over (tract of country) in travelling; to traverse, journey through: *to travel the whole world in search of novelty.*

travel (II.), n., fr. prec. **1.** (rare) Process of travelling; movement; mode, rate, of movement or progress (of parts of machine &c.). **2.** (chiefly pl.) **a** Journeys, journeyings, wanderings; esp. long journeys, in foreign and remote parts: *travels abroad*; *back from one's travels*; **b** narrative, book containing this, of travels, and adventures occurring during these: *a book of travels.*

travelled, adj. [1. trávld; 2. trǽvld], fr. P.P. of **travel (I.)**. Having experience of travelling; having travelled widely.

traveller, n. [1. tráv(e)ler; 2. trǽv(ə)lə]. **travel (I.)** & **-er.** **a** One who travels; specif. **b** one who travels to obtain orders for a trading firm: *a commercial traveller.*

traveller's cheque, n. Cheque, usually for relatively small amount, issued by a banker to a client travelling abroad, payable by any agent of the bank which issues it.

traveller's-joy, n. Species of clematis, *Clematis vitalba.*

traveller's tale, n. A fantastic, exaggerated, highly coloured narrative; a tall story, story of fictitious adventures and exploits.

traversable, adj. [1. tráversabl; 2. trǽvəsəbl]. **traverse (I.)** & **-able.** Capable of being traversed; passable.

traverse (I.), vb. trans. & intrans. [1. trávers; 2. trǽvəs]. Fr. *traverser*, fr. O. Fr. *travers*, 'across'; see **transverse.** **A.** trans. **1.** To pass, run, lie, be placed, across: *the railway line traverses the road at this point.* **2.** **a** To cross, pass over, travel across: *to traverse the desert, the ocean* &c.; **b** (fig.) to go over, treat of, deal with, in discussion, argument, exposition: *I need not traverse that ground in my present lecture.* **3.** **a** To oppose, call in question, take exception to: *I must traverse several points in your statement*; **b** (law) to deny (allegation of other party). **4.** **a** (artillery) To move, turn sideways or laterally, in aiming: *to traverse a gun*; **b** (carpentry) to plane (wood) across the grain; **c** (mach.) to swivel, turn (lathe &c.) laterally. **B.** intrans. To execute a traverse, **a** in fencing; **b** in riding.

traverse (II.), adj. & adv.; see prec. **1.** adj. Lying across; formed, cut, crosswise: *traverse trench.* **2.** adv. Crosswise.

traverse (III.), n., fr. prec. **1.** Something which traverses, which lies across; **a** a dividing bar or partition; **b** a structural part, a beam, transom &c., crossing a ceiling, lying across top of a door &c.; **c** a path made across face of a cliff, glacier &c. in mountaineering; **d** earthwork placed at right angles to the front of a trench or covered way, dividing it into bays, thus giving protection against enfilade fire and localizing effect of shell-bursts. **2.** (fig.) Circumstance, event, which thwarts, hinders, a purpose or action; specif. (law) a formal denial of fact alleged by opposite party in a suit. **3.** A cross movement; **a** (fencing) movement made in opposing or counteracting an attack; **b** oblique, crosswise, forward movement of a horse.

traverser, n. [1. tráverser; 2. trǽvəsə]. **traverse (I.)** & **-er.** One who, that which, traverses; specif., device in form of platform on wheels moving laterally, used in shifting railway carriages from one line of rails to another; also *traverse-table.*

travertin(e), n. [1. trávertin; 2. trǽvətin]. Ital. *travertino*, Lat. *Tiburtīnus* (*lapis*), 'Tibur (stone)', now Tivoli. Hard, calcareous deposit of limy springs, used in Italy for building.

travesty, vb. trans. & n. [1. trávesti; 2. trǽvəsti], fr. Fr. *travesti*, P.P. of *travestir*, 'to disguise; make ridiculous', fr. **trans-** & Lat. *vestīre*, 'to clothe', see **vest (I.)**. **1.** vb. **a** To cause to appear ridiculous; to caricature, to burlesque, mimic; to imitate (deliberately) in such a manner as to bring ridicule upon: *to travesty a person's manner, mode of speech, style* &c.; **b** to render absurd, represent, perform badly, misinterpret, through incompetence or lack of skill: *to travesty the part of Hamlet, the position of chairman.* **2.** n. **a** A deliberate burlesque, parody, comical imitation or mimicry; **b** an incompetent performance; a distortion, perversion, misconception: *a travesty of justice, of discipline* &c.

trawl, vb. trans. & intrans. & n. [1. trawl; 2. trōl]. O. Fr. *troller*, 'to move about, go to and fro, in a desultory fashion'; see **troll (I.)**. **1.** vb. **a** trans. To drag along after a vessel: *to trawl a net, a fishing-line*; **b** intrans., to practise trawling: *first we tried throwing a fly, and then we trawled.* **2.** n. **a** A fishing-net with a wide mouth, held open by a frame, and dragged along the bottom of the sea; also *trawl-net*; **b** a long line having short lines coming at intervals from it, with baited hooks attached, stretched out, and buoyed, and anchored at both ends; also *trawl-line.*

trawler, n. [1. tráwler; 2. trṓlə]. Prec. & **-er.** **a** Person who trawls; **b** vessel used in trawling.

trawling, n. [1. tráwling; 2. trṓliŋ]. See prec. & **-ing.** Act or process of using a trawl-net or trawl-line for catching fish.

tray, n. [1. trā; 2. trei]. M.E. *treie* &c.; origin doubtful; possibly fr. an O.E. *træǵ, or *treǵ, & connected by gradation w. O.E. *trōg*, see **trough.** A flat, round, oval, or oblong board, plate, slab, of wood, metal, papier mâché &c., with edges slightly raised, used for holding, or carrying, light articles such as glass, china, crockery, silver &c., or for handing such articles or letters &c.

treacherous, adj. [1. trécherus; 2. trétʃərəs]. See **treachery** & **-ous.** **1.** **a** (of persons) Disloyal, false, apt to betray; unreliable; liable to break a pledge or a promise; perfidious; **b** (of actions, and bodily movements) expressing, involving, treachery and deceit, betrayal, disloyalty &c.: *a treacherous glance, smile, move* &c.; **c** (of mental functions) unreliable, uncertain, apt to fail: *a treacherous memory.* **2.** **a** (of animals) Not to be depended upon, liable to turn on their masters; **b** (of inanimate things) not as good as they appear, liable to disappoint expectation, not justifying hopes which they arouse: *treacherous ice, branch*, liable to break, though seeming sound; *treacherous weather*, bright but cold, or likely to turn to rain &c.

treacherously, adv. Prec. & **-ly.** In a treacherous manner.

treacherousness, n. See prec. & **-ness.** **a** Treacherous action, treachery; **b** disloyalty, falseness of heart and character.

treachery, n. [1. trécheri; 2. trétʃəri]. M.E., fr. O. Fr. *trech-*, *tricherie*, cp. *trechier*, 'to deceive'; cp. **trickery** & see **trick (I.)**. Disloyal action, betrayal; breach of trust, allegiance, or of plighted word; perfidy.

treacle, n. [1. trḗkl; 2. tríkl]. O. Fr. *triacle*; cp. Provenç. *triacla*, *tiriaca*; fr. Lat. *thēriaca*, 'antidote against poisonous beasts'; fr. Gk. *thēriakḗ*; see **theriac.** **1.** (obs.) **a** A sovran remedy, cure against poison, esp. of venomous reptiles &c. or disease; **b** remedy, balm, for spiritual ills. **2.** Thick, syrupy substance which drains out of sugar in the process of refining; molasses.

treacly, adj. [1. trḗkli; 2. tríkli]. Prec. & **-ly.** **a** Having a thick, sticky consistency, like that of treacle; **b** covered with treacle; **c** (fig.) unctuous: *a treacly smile.*

tread (I.), vb. intrans. & trans. [1. tred; 2. tred]. O.E. & O.S. *tredan*; M.E. *trēden*; O.H.G. *tretan*; Goth. *trudan* (*u* is difficult to equate w. the other forms); O.N. *troða*; not found outside Gmc., unless the base may be connected remotely w. that in Gk. *drómos*, a 'running', q.v. under **dromedary.** **A.** intrans. To walk, step, go; specif. (poet.) to go on foot, contrasted with *creep*; *tread on, upon*, to put one's foot upon; **a** to crush with the foot: *to tread (up)on a black beetle*; **b** to step, walk, upon (by mistake): *to tread upon a slide and fall down*; *tread down*, **a** to crush down, by treading: *to tread down flowers*; **b** to suppress, oppress, overpower: '*No hungry generations tread thee down*' (Keats, 'Nightingale'); also *to tread down one's feelings*; *tread under*, crush down; oppress; *tread out*, crush, cause to flow or come out, by treading: *to tread out the juice of the grape*; *to tread out the corn*; *tread in*, press into the earth by treading. **B.** trans. **1.** To beat, press down, by treading: *to tread a path through the grass.* **2.** To traverse, walk, pass, over; (often fig.) *to tread the paths of exile.* Phr. *to tread the boards*, be an actor. **3.** To execute on foot, by walking, dancing: '"*Now tread we a measure," said young Lochinvar*' (Scott). **4.** (of male birds) To have connexion with (the female).

tread (II.), n., fr. prec. **1.** **a** Act of treading, footstep: *the tread of armed men*; **b** mode of treading, or walking, stepping: *a sprightly, airy tread.* **2.** Thing, or part of something, designed for treading on; specif. **a** the flat, upper surface of a stair or step; **b** part of a boot or shoe which presses on the ground; **c** part of tire of a wheel which rests, presses, upon the ground. **3.** Copulation of male bird.

treadle, n. [1. trédl; 2. trédl]. O.E. *tredel*, fr. **tread (I.)**. Part of a machine on which the foot rests in working a crank which turns a wheel; e.g. in a bicycle, sewing-machine &c.

treadmill, n. [1. trédmil; 2. trédmil]. Mill worked by persons who tread upon steps made on the periphery; formerly used as a punishment, and also as a means of exercise, for convicts.

treason, n. [1. trḗzn; 2. trízn]. M.E. *tresun*, *traisoun* &c., fr. O. Fr. *traïson*, fr. Lat. *trāditiōn-(em)*, 'delivering up'; see **tradition.** **1.** Betrayal of trust, treachery, perfidy. **2.** Specif., disloyalty, treachery, to one's king and country; any attempt to overthrow government or well-being of a state to which one owes allegiance; the crime of giving comfort to the king's enemies; *high treason*, outrage offered to the king's person, to that of his consort, or that of his heir; attempt to depose the king or to levy war against him.

treasonable, adj. [1. trḗzunabl; 2. tríznəbl]. Prec. & **-able.** Pertaining to, involving, of the nature of, treason; treacherous, disloyal, perfidious.

treasonableness, n. See prec. & **-ness.** Quality of being treasonable.

treasonably, adv. Prec. & **-ly.** In a treasonable manner.

treason-felony, n. An act of high treason.

treasure (I.), n. [1. trézhur; 2. tréžə]. M.E. *tresor, tresour*; fr. O. Fr., fr. Lat. *thēsaurus*, fr. Gk. *thēsaurós*, 'a store laid up, treasure; a treasure-house; receptacle for treasure, a casket'; prob. an old, obscured compound; origin unexplained. **1.** Valuables stored up and carefully kept; esp. money, plate, jewels. **2.** Money: *the War cost the country great sacrifices in blood and treasure.* **3.** Something of great value, beauty, or rarity; object to which great importance is attached: *treasures of art in museums and picture galleries; the unique MS. of Beowulf is among the priceless treasures of the British Museum Library.* **4. a** A person (child or young woman) to whom one is devotedly attached; esp. as affectionate mode of address: *my treasure!*; **b** a person who is invaluable by reason of competence in his business, reliability of character, serviceableness &c.: *my new butler is a perfect treasure.*

treasure (II.), vb. trans., fr. prec. **1. a** To store, hoard up, keep as, treasure; also *treasure up*: *to treasure up money and jewels*; **b** to retain in the mind and memory, dwell on with affection, cherish fondly: *to treasure a person's memory; to treasure up in one's heart the recollection of former days* &c. **2. a** (of objects &c.) To set store by, regard as valuable, attach value and importance to: *that is not a book that I treasure very highly*; **b** (of persons) to feel warm affection for: *we cannot treasure our friends too much.*

treasure-house, n. Place, building, where treasure is kept; a treasury.

treasurer, n. [1. trézhurer; 2. tréžərə]. O. Fr. *tresorier*; **treasure** (II.) & **-er**. **a** An officer in charge of the funds, and who manages the finances, of a society, institution &c.; **b** title of various officers of state, or of Royal household; *Lord High Treasurer*, now obsolete; *Treasurer of the Household.*

treasure trove, n. [1. trézhur tróv; 2. tréžə tróuv]. See **treasure** (I.) & **trover**. Gold or silver articles, bullion or coin, found hidden in the earth, for which no owner can be traced, the right to which lies in the Crown.

treasury, n. [1. trézhuri; 2. tréžəri], fr. O. Fr. *tresorie*; **treasure** (I.) & **-y**. **1. a** Place for storing of treasure; treasure-house; **b** (cap.) place where public revenues are stored; **c** department of state which collects public revenue, and controls taxation and the expenditure of public moneys; this department is controlled by the *Lords of the Treasury*, the nominal head of which is the First Lord of the Treasury, usually the Prime Minister or Leader of the House; the Chancellor of the Exchequer, and Junior Lords, the chief of which are the *Patronage Secretary*, who acts as chief whip, and the *Financial Secretary*, acting as assistant to the Chancellor of Exchequer. **2.** A literary collection or anthology: *the 'Golden Treasury'.*

Treasury bench, n. The front bench on the right-hand side of the Speaker in the House of Commons, on which sit the principal members of His Majesty's Government.

Treasury bill, n. A form of bill of exchange for raising short-term loans, offered for tender and issued to the highest bidder.

Treasury note, n. A form of currency note for £1 and 10s. respectively, issued by the Treasury from 1914 to 1928.

Treasury solicitor, n. A legal official, who acts in all cases taken to secure payments due to the Treasury, as King's Proctor and formerly as Public Prosecutor.

treat (I.), vb. trans. & intrans. [1. trēt; 2. trīt]. O. Fr. *traitier*, fr. Lat. *tractāre*, 'to drag, draw; to handle, manage; to perform, transact; to use, conduct oneself towards; to discuss, reflect upon'. See **tract** (I.) & **trace** (II.). **A.** trans. **1. a** To conduct, demean, oneself, behave, towards, to use: *to treat one's servants with consideration; to treat a dog kindly*; **b** to have a certain mental attitude towards; to consider, regard; to hold a certain view concerning, and express it in words and behaviour: *to treat the whole thing as a joke; to treat one's position as a means of securing one's own ends.* **2.** To cause to undergo, submit (objects) to, some special process, for a particular purpose; specif. **a** to deal with chemically: *to treat (a substance) with sulphuric acid*; **b** to apply to, cover with &c.: *to treat dry leather with grease; to treat fruit trees with chemical mixtures*; **c** to give medical or surgical care to, prescribe for: *to treat a man for gout.* **3.** To deal with, take as a theme for consideration, discussion, exposition &c.: *many aspects of the subject are not treated at all by the author.* **4.** To pay expenses of, or for, to bear the cost of entertaining (another), esp. to pay for some exceptional pleasure: *to treat a person to a new suit, to a good dinner, to a box at the opera.* Phr. *to treat oneself to (a bottle of champagne)*, to have as an exceptional indulgence. **B.** intrans. **1.** *Treat of*, to deal with, take as subject of discourse, discussion &c.: *the sermon treated of sin and death.* **2.** *Treat with*, to negotiate, discuss terms with, transact business with: *it is humiliating to have to treat with a rogue.* **3.** To stand expenses, bear the costs of entertainment: *whose turn is it to treat next?*

treat (II.), n., fr. prec. **1.** Event, circumstance, condition, which affords satisfaction and pleasure; esp. something unusual and therefore the more enjoyed: *it was a treat to hear a good sermon again; a great treat to me to be in the country; a fine day is a rare treat; if you are a good boy you shall come down to dessert as a treat.* **2.** Entertainment planned to give pleasure: *a Sunday School treat.* **3.** (colloq. and rare) **a** Act of treating, or bearing cost of entertainment &c.; chiefly in Phr. *to stand treat*, bear expenses of amusement &c. for another; **b** turn (of person) to treat.

treating, n. [1. trḗting; 2. trītiŋ]. Act of bearing another's expenses of eating and drinking; ordering and paying for food and drink for another: *treating in restaurants was forbidden during the war.*

treatise, n. [1. trḗtiz; 2. trītiz]. A.-Fr. *tretiz*, prob. connected w. **treat** (I.), Lat. *tract-*, in sense of something drawn up, or something treated of; cp. **tractate**. Systematic written account of something; an excursus, a monograph.

treatment, n. [1. trḗtment; 2. trītmənt]. **treat** (I.) & **-ment**. **1.** Way of behaving to, of using, treating; usage: *hard, rough, unkind, favourable, treatment.* **2.** Act, mode, of treating, managing, caring for, attempting to cure; act of subjecting to particular process: *a new treatment for black spot in roses, for consumption; medical, surgical, treatment.*

treaty, n. [1. trḗti; 2. trīti]. O. Fr. *traitie*, fr. Lat. *tractāt-(um)*, P.P. of *tractāre*, 'to handle' &c.; see **treat** (I.). **1.** Negotiation, act of bargaining, discussion of terms and conditions; in Phr. *in treaty for (a house &c.)*, in process of making arrangements, of coming to terms. **2.** Specif., an agreement, engagement, covenant, contract, agreed upon, and entered into, between different states or rulers.

treble (I.), adj. [1. trébl; 2. trébl]. M.E., fr. O. Fr.; fr. Lat. *triplus*, 'threefold'; see **triple**. **1.** Threefold, triple. **2.** (mus.) Pertaining to what was formerly the third part, that is, the higher notes, sung by boys' voices; hence high, shrill.

treble (II.), n., fr. prec. **a** The treble part or notes; **b** a treble voice.

treble (III.), vb. trans. & intrans. **a** trans. To make threefold: *to treble one's income*; **b** intrans., to become, increase, threefold: *expenses have trebled.*

trebuchet, n. [1. trébūshā; 2. trébjuʃei]. O. Fr., 'a trap, gin'; cp. Fr. *trébucher*, 'to stumble'; fr. Fr. *tré*, fr. **trans-**, & Gmc. word for *belly*, cp. O.H.G. *būh*, Mod. Germ. *bauch*, 'belly'. Obsolete military apparatus for hurling stones.

trecentist, n. [1. trāchéntist; 2. treitʃéntist]. Next word & **-ist**. Writer or painter of the trecento; imitator of these.

trecento, n. & adj. [1. trāchénō; 2. treitʃéntou]. Ital., 'three hundred', for 'thirteen hundred'. The fourteenth century as expressed in the great poets and painters of this period in Italy.

trechometer, n. [1. trekómeter; 2. trekɔ́mitə], fr. base of Gk. *trékhein*, 'to run', see **troche**, & **-meter**. Device for range-finding; a hodometer.

tree (I.), n. [1. trē; 2. trī]. O.E. *trēo*, M.E. *trē*; O.S. *treo*; Goth. *triu*; cogn. w. Gk. *drûs*, 'tree, oak', see **dryad**, & *dóru*, 'beam, shaft, spear'; see also **trim** (I.). **1.** A perennial plant with a woody stem, or trunk, and boughs; often employed in distinction to *bush*, or *shrub*, of a plant which has considerable height of trunk in proportion to the reach of its boughs, and one whose stem is devoid of boughs for some considerable distance from the ground; roses are called indifferently *bushes* or *trees*. Phr. *up a tree*, in a fix. **2. a** Any of several objects made of timber (for which the word *tree* was formerly used), esp. in compounds: *axle-tree, boot-tree, saddle-tree, whipple-tree* (see these words); also **b** (archaic or obs., except Bib.) the Cross of Christ. **3.** Usually, *family tree*, **a** a diagram showing descent or development from a common ancestor or source, formerly drawn in form of a tree with stem and branches: *tree of Jesse*; hence, **b** a pedigree; lineage, descent.

tree (II.), vb. trans. & intrans., fr. prec. **1.** trans. **a** To drive up or into a tree; **b** (fig. and colloq.) to place in a dilemma, put in a difficult or awkward position. **2.** intrans. To form, grow into, a tree.

tree calf, n. Leather of fine calfskin, highly polished and grained to resemble polished wood; used for binding books.

tree-creeper, n. Small bird, *Certhia familiaris*, which creeps about the trunks and branches of trees in search of insects.

tree-fern, n. Large, tree-like fern of warm countries, with woody stem and branching leaves.

tree-frog, n. Small frog, genus *Hyla*, that climbs trees by means of small suckers on its toes.

tree-kangaroo, n. Small arboreal marsupial of Australia.

treeless, adj. [1. trḗles; 2. trīlis]. **tree** (I.) & **-less**. Bare of trees.

tree-nail, trenail, n. [1. trḗnāl, trénl; 2. trīneil, trénl]. A long pin or nail of hard wood for fastening planks to a ship's timbers.

tree-peony, n. Chinese peony, *Paeonia Moutan*, growing in form of a shrub, with woody stem and branches.

trefoil, n. [1. tréfoil; 2. trífɔil]. O. Fr. *trefueil*, fr. Lat. **trifolium**. **1.** Clover. **2.** (archit.) Conventionalized, carved, representation of clover leaf.

trek, vb. intrans. & n. [1. trek; 2. trɛk], fr. Cape Du.; cogn. w. **track** (I.). **1.** vb. **a** To travel, make a journey, in an ox-waggon; **b** to wander far afield in search of a fresh place of abode; to migrate. **2.** n. **a** Journey performed in an ox-waggon; **b** migration.

trellis, n. & vb. trans. [1. trélis; 2. trélis]. M.E. *trelis*, O. Fr. *treliz*; cp. Mod. Fr. *treillis*, formerly 'sackcloth', then 'trellis', fr. resemblance of lattice-work to the coarse mesh; fr. Low Lat. *trilīcius*, fr. Lat. *trilīx*, 'woven with three sets of leashes; triple-twilled'; **tri-** & *līcium*, 'thrum, or ends of a weaver's thread', see second element of **oblique** (I.). **1.** n. Light wooden structure formed of laths crossing each other and nailed together; similar structure of wire &c.; used as a screen and for training climbing plants. **2.** vb. To supply with a trellis; to screen off with a trellis.

trellis-work, n. Structure in form of a trellis; lattice-work.

tremble (I.), vb. intrans. [1. trémbl; 2. trémbl]. Fr. *trembler*, fr. L. Lat. *tremulāre*, formed fr. Lat. *tremulus*, 'quivering'; see **tremulous**. **1. a** To be shaken, agitated, with rapid, brief, intermittent, involuntary movements of the muscles, esp. such as are caused by fear, cold, excessive weakness; to shiver, to quake; **b** (fig.) to quail, be dismayed, terrified, seized with fear: *the stoutest hearts trembled at the sound.* **2.** (fig.) To experience great anxiety, perturbation of mind; to have grave misgivings or apprehensions: *I tremble for your safety; I tremble to think what might have happened.* **3.** (of the earth) To be shaken, as with earthquake; to quiver, as from the shock of a heavy body falling. **4.** (of light, fluttering or swaying objects) To be agitated with a rapid vibratory movement, to oscillate, be stirred, as by the wind, to flutter: *leaves of the poplars tremble; flags tremble in the gale;* Phr. (*his fate &c.*) *is trembling in the balance,* has reached the critical moment in which it will be decided one way or the other. **5.** To be tremulous, shaky, to give the impression of trembling or vibrating: *his voice trembled.*

tremble (II.), n., fr. prec. Involuntary act of trembling, shivering, shaking; a tremor, quiver &c. Phr. (colloq.) *all of a tremble,* shaking, trembling; greatly agitated and perturbed.

trembler, n. [1. trémbler; 2. trémblə]. See prec. & **-er.** One who, thing which, trembles.

trembling, n. [1. trémbling; 2. trémbliŋ]. **tremble (I.)** & **-ing.** State of one who trembles; **a** bodily shivering; **b** mental agitation. Phr. *in fear and trembling,* with great misgiving, diffidently.

tremblingly, adv., fr. Pres. Part. of **tremble (I.)** & **-ly. a** With physical, material trembling; **b** with fear and mental agitation; fearfully.

tremendous, adj. [1. treméndus; 2. triméndəs]. Lat. *tremendus,* 'causing quaking and shivering; dreadful, terrible', & **-ous**; fr. *tremere,* 'to quake, shiver'; see **tremble (I.)** & **tremulous. 1. a** Awe-inspiring, overpowering, possessing great importance; momentous: *the tremendous events of the war;* hence, **b** (popularly) (i.) considerable in size, very large, huge, immense, enormous: *a tremendous house; tremendous applause;* (ii.) as adverb *a tremendous long way;* (also colloq.) *tremendous great* (*horse, book, jump, shout* &c.). **2.** (colloq.) In various rather vague senses, implying importance, magnitude &c.: *to get a tremendous fright; it is a tremendous thing for me,* a great advantage; *it means a tremendous lot to him,* is of vital importance.

tremendously, adv. Prec. & **-ly.** In a tremendous manner, to a tremendous extent; (colloq., as emphatic) very much, very: *tremendously improved; tremendously pleased to see you; I'm tremendously obliged to you.*

tremendousness, n. See prec. & **-ness.** (rare) State, quality, of being tremendous.

tremolo, n. [1. trémolō; 2. tréməlou]. Ital., fr. Lat. *tremulus,* see **tremulous.** Tremulous, vibratory, quivering, effect deliberately produced in the tones of the singing voice, or in those of a wind or string instrument, e.g. in the organ or the violin &c.

tremor, n. [1. trémur; 2. trémə]. Lat., 'a shaking, quivering', fr. *tremere,* 'to quiver' &c., see **tremulous.** A shaking, quivering, trembling, palsy; **a** of the limbs, voice, of leaves &c.; **b** (of the mind) (i.) a quailing of the spirit or courage, a qualm &c.: *he faced death without a tremor;* also, (ii.) a thrill: *a tremor of excitement.*

tremulous, adj. [1. trémūlus; 2. trémjuləs]. Lat. *tremulus,* 'shaking, quivering', & **-ous**; fr. base of *tremere,* 'to shiver, tremble' &c., cp. Gk. *trémein,* 'to shiver', & *trómos,* 'a trembling, quaking'; cogn. w. O.S. *thrimman,* 'to leap'; & Goth. *þramstei,* 'grasshopper'; ultimately prob. an extension of base seen in *terrēre,* 'to frighten'; see **terror, terrible. 1.** Shaky; quivering, trembling; fluttering: *a tremulous hand; tremulous eyelids; tremulous plumes* &c. **2.** Timid, fearful: *tremulous maidens;* nervous, hesitating, vacillating.

tremulously, adv. Prec. & **-ly.** In a tremulous manner.

tremulousness, n. See prec. & **-ness.** State, quality, of being tremulous.

trench (I.), vb. trans. & intrans. [1. trench; 2. trentʃ]. O. Fr. *trenchier,* 'to cut', cp. Ital. *trinciare;* prob. connected w. **truncate,** cp. **trunk. A.** trans. **1. a** To cut furrows or trenches in; **b** to cultivate, dig (land) thoroughly, by making series of parallel trenches, each one of which is filled with the soil taken from the one dug immediately after it. **2.** (mil.) To cut entrenchments in; to protect with trenches. **B.** intrans. *Trench upon,* to encroach, infringe, upon: *to trench upon the sphere, rights, time &c., of another.*

trench (II.), n. M.E. & O. Fr. *trenche,* fr. prec. Long, narrow opening, ditch, furrow, cut or dug in the earth; specif., one made for soldiers to stand in, with the excavated earth thrown up in front, as protection from enemy's fire.

trenchancy, n. [1. trénshansi; 2. trénʃənsi]. Next word & **-cy.** Quality of being trenchant.

trenchant, adj. [1. trénshant; 2. trénʃənt]. In M.E., fr. O. Fr.; Pres. Part. of *trenchier,* 'to cut'; see **trench (I.). a** (chiefly poet.) Having a cutting edge, cutting, sharp: *a trenchant blade;* **b** (in non-material sense) keen, incisive, biting, penetrating: *a trenchant humour, wit, style.*

trench-coat, n. Short waterproof coat worn by a soldier in the trenches in war.

trencher (I.), n. [1. trénchor; 2. tréntʃə]. **trench (I.)** & **-er.** One who cuts or digs trenches.

trencher (II.), n. O. Fr. *trencheor,* 'platter (for cutting on)'. **trench (I.). 1.** Wooden platter formerly used for cutting food, and as a plate from which food was eaten, now chiefly for cutting bread. **2.** (fig.) What is on a trencher; food.

trencher-man, n. One who eats from a trencher; esp. *a good, a poor, trencher-man,* a hearty, a small, eater.

trench-fever, n. A form of low, intermittent, infectious fever, transmitted by lice, suffered by troops after serving in the trenches during the War.

trench-foot, n. An affection of the feet and legs suffered by troops during the War after service in the trenches, due to long soddening in cold and muddy water; in severe cases ending in moist gangrene, as distinct from the dry gangrene of frost-bite.

trench mortar, n. A small, easily portable kind of mortar used for throwing bombs &c. short distances, from trench to trench.

trend, vb. intrans. & n. [1. trend; 2. trend]. Origin doubtful, but connected w. O.E. *trendel* & *tryndel,* 'a wheel'; *trendlian,* 'to make round', & *trinde,* 'round lump'; cp. **trundle 1.** vb. (rarish) **a** To bend, be bent, inclined, slope, go, in a particular direction; **b** (fig.) to have a particular tendency. **2.** n. **a** Inclination, course, direction: *trend of a coastline;* **b** (fig.) general tendency, line, course, drift: *the trend of public feeling; the trend of events.*

trental, n. [1. tréntl; 2. tréntl]. Low Lat. *trentale,* fr. Lat. *trīginta,* 'thirty', cp. Fr. *trente,* & see **tri-.** Series of thirty Masses for the dead.

trente-et-quarante, n. [1. trónt ā karónt; 2. trɑ̃t ei kærɑ̃t]. Fr., 'thirty and forty'. Gambling card-game played on a specially marked table.

trepan (I.), also **trephine**, vb. trans. & n. [1. trepán, trefín; 2. tripǽn, trifáin]. Fr. *trépan,* fr. L. Lat. *trepanum,* fr. Gk. *trúpanon,* 'a borer'; cp. *trūpân,* 'to bore', fr. *trûpa,* 'a hole'; ultimately connected w. base **ter-,* 'to bore, rub away'; see **toreutic** & words there referred to. **1.** vb. (surg.) To remove, by cutting, (a portion of bone from the skull) to relieve pressure on the brain. **2.** n. Saw for performing this operation.

trepan (II.), vb. trans., fr. O. Fr. *trappan,* n., perh. a loan-word connected w. **trap (III.).** (archaic) To ensnare, lure, delude.

trepang, n. [1. trepáng; 2. tripǽŋ]. Malay. Sea-slug, bêche-de-mer, used by Chinese for making soup.

trephine, vb. trans. & n. [1. trefín; 2. trifáin]. Fr. *tréfine;* see **trepan (I.). 1.** vb. To trepan. **2.** n. A trepan.

trepidation, n. [1. trèpidáshun; 2. trèpidéiʃən]. Lat. *trepidātiōn-(em),* formed fr. P.P. of *trepidāre,* 'to bustle about anxiously, be in a state of alarm'; fr. *trepidus,* 'agitated, disturbed, alarmed'; cogn. w. Gk. *trépein,* 'to burn'; cp. also **trope. 1.** State of alarm; quaking, nervous fluster. **2.** Involuntary trembling or twitching of the limbs, as in paralysis &c.

trespass (I.), vb. intrans. [1. tréspas; 2. tréspəs]. O. Fr. *trespasser,* 'to go beyond; to die'; see **trans-** & **pass (I.). 1.** (obs.) To die. **2.** To go unlawfully upon another's land: *to trespass in search of game.* **3.** To encroach, infringe, upon: *to trespass upon a person's leisure, time* &c. **4.** To go beyond, exceed, what is morally right and lawful; to offend, sin, commit an offence: *to trespass against the moral law; 'as we forgive them that trespass against us'.*

trespass (II.), n. O. Fr. *trespas,* see prec. **1.** Act of trespassing upon another's land. **2. a** Act of sin, an offence against God; **b** an injury inflicted upon another person.

trespasser, n. [1. tréspaser; 2. tréspəsə]. **trespass (I.)** & **-er.** One who trespasses upon the land of another.

tress, n. & vb. trans. [1. tres; 2. tres]. M.E. *tresse,* 'lock of hair', fr. Fr. *tresse;* vb. fr. Fr. *tresser,* 'to plait, twist'; fr. Low Lat. *tricia,* fr. Lat. *trīcae,* pl., 'trifles, toys; subterfuges, tricks'; connected w. *torquēre,* 'to twist', see **torque. 1.** n. **a** Lock of hair, ringlet, plait; esp. of long hair on a woman's head; (poet. or facet.) hair of the head generally: *golden, scanty, tresses;* **b** (rare) spray, cluster, of flowers. **2.** vb. To fasten, bind up, arrange (the hair).

tressed, adj. [1. trest; 2. trest]. Prec. & **-ed. a** Having tresses; **b** bound, twisted up.

tressure, n. [1. tréshur; 2. tréʃə]. **tress** & **-ure. 1.** Fillet, band for the hair; head-dress. **2.** (her.) A double fillet round the shield, some distance from edge, ornamented with fleurs-de-lis.

tressy, adj. [1. trési; 2. trési]. **tress** & **-y.** Adorned with tresses.

trestle, n. [1. trésl; 2. trésl]. M.E., fr. O. Fr. *trestel,* Low Lat. **transtellum,* dimin. of *transtrum,* 'cross-beam' &c., see **transom. 1.** Wooden structure consisting of a piece of timber lying horizontally, and supported by braced legs; used to support planks forming a table, platform &c. **2.** A large framework of braced open timber or steel work, used as the support of a *trestle-bridge.*

trestle-table, n. Table of movable planks resting upon trestles.

tret, n. [1. tret; 2. tret]. Fr. *traite,* 'transport', see **trait, tract (I.).** Allowance made to buyers of certain goods for wastage during transit.

trews, n. pl. [1. trōōz; 2. trūz]. See **trousers** Trousers made of tartan cloth worn by Highlanders, esp. in Scottish non-kilted regiments.

trey, n. [1. trā; 2. trei], fr. O. Fr. *treis,* 'three', fr. Lat. *trēs,* see **three.** The three at dice or cards.

tri-, pref. Lat., or Gk. *tri-,* 'three, threefold, thrice'; form of Lat. *trēs, tria,* Gk. *treîs, tria;* Scrt. *tráyaš,* 'three'; see **three, thrice.** Three, threefold.

triable, adj. [1. tríabl; 2. tráiəbl]. **try (I.)** & **-able.** Capable of being, worthy to be, tried.

triad, n. [1. tríad; 2. tráiæd]. Lat. *triad-(is),* genit., fr. Gk. *triád-(os);* see **tri-.** Group of three persons or things; specif. **a** (chem.) trivalent element or radical, one with valency or combining power of three; **b** (mus.) chord of three tones; **c** form of Celtic poetical composition, in which the subjects are grouped in threes: *'Three things that ruin wisdom: ignorance, inaccurate knowledge, forgetfulness'.*

trial, n. [1. trial; 2. tráiəl]. **try** (I.) & **-al**. **1.** Act of trying, testing, proving (in various senses); **a** a test of strength, speed, skill &c. in comparison with that of another; a match to decide relative proficiency; **b** act of testing the qualities, merits &c. of anything by using it: *to give a thing a trial*; Phr. *to have something on trial*, in order to test it; **c** test of a person's character, temper, courage, patience, fortitude, honour, &c. **2. a** Something which afflicts or grieves; a trying experience; adversity, ill-fortune, trouble: *the loss of friends is among the most frequent trials of life*; **b** an annoyance, source of irritation; a nuisance: *a dog that barks all night is rather a trial.* **3.** A judicial inquiry in a court of law; **a** examination of evidence to establish the guilt or innocence of a prisoner charged with a crime: *a criminal trial*; *a trial for theft*; *the trial of a man for murder*; **b** legal proceedings to determine the rights and wrongs of a civil case, to substantiate or negative a claim &c.

triangle, n. [1. triánggl; 2. tráiæŋgl]. **tri-** & **angle** (I.). **1. a** Geometrical figure bounded by three lines forming three angles; **b** piece of ground, object, having approximately this form; Phr. *the eternal triangle*, three persons, consisting of a married pair and the lover of either. **2.** Musical instrument consisting of a thin steel rod bent into the form of a triangle with one open end, suspended from a cord and sounded by being struck with another steel rod. **3. a** Framework of three poles fixed in the ground at suitable distances, the tops being fastened together, to which military offenders were formerly bound, to receive corporal punishment; **b** structure of similar form, with pulley hanging from the top, used for hoisting weights.

triangular, adj. [1. triánggūlar; 2. traiǽŋgjulə]. **tri-** & **angular**. **1.** Having the form of a triangle; three-cornered. **2.** Involving three persons or parties: *triangular fight, pact* &c.

triangularity, n. [1. trianggūláriti; 2. tràiæŋgjulǽriti]. Prec. & **-ity**. Property of being triangular.

triangularly, adv. [1. triánggūlarli; 2. traiǽŋgjuləli]. See prec. & **-ly**. In triangular shape or form.

triangulate, vb. trans. & adj. [1. triánggūlāt; 2. traiǽŋgjuleit]. **triangle** & **-ate**. **1.** vb. To divide into triangles for purpose of surveying, measuring heights, distances &c. **2.** adj. Consisting of triangles, having form of a triangle.

triangulation, n. [1. trianggūláshun; 2. tràiæŋgjuléiʃən]. Prec. & **-ion**. Process of surveying by triangulating the area.

Trias, n. [1. trías; 2. tráiəs]. See **triad**. (geol.) **a** Period preceding the Jurassic; **b** system of rocks formed during this period; so called by the Germans from their threefold division of the period.

Triassic, adj. [1. triásik; 2. traiǽsik]. Prec. & **-ic**. Pertaining to the Trias.

tribal, adj. [1. tríbl; 2. tráibl]. **tribe** & **-al**. Connected with, belonging to, a tribe: *tribal legends, feeling* &c.

tribalism, n. [1. tríbalizm; 2. tráibəlizəm]. Prec. & **-ism**. System of tribal organization, tribal sentiment, customs &c.; characteristic features of a tribe or of its organization &c.

tribasic, adj. [1. tribásik; 2. tràibéisik]. **tri-** & **basic**. (chem.) Having three hydrogen atoms in the molecule.

tribe, n. [1. trīb; 2. traib]. In M.E., fr. Lat. *tribus*, 'one of the three divisions of the Roman people'; orig. 'village'; cogn. w. O. Ir. *treb*; perh. fr. *tri-*, 'third', used in gen. sense of 'division', & base **bhu-*, 'to become, grow' &c.; see this further under **future** (I.), **folio** (I.); cp. also **physic** (I.) & **be**. **1.** Social unit, a community, consisting of groups of families, or clans, descended, or originally supposed to be descended, from a common ancestor, together with their slaves and others living with the community; later, the bond between the families of a tribe consists more in common customs and institutions than in actual consanguinity. **2.** Class, group, of persons having, or assumed to have, the same characteristics, occupation, habits, ideals &c.: *lawyers and all their tribe*; *the whole tribe of politicians.* **3.** (biol., often loosely) Group: *the dog tribe.*

tribesman, n. [1. tríbzman; 2. tráibzmən]. **tribe** & **man**. Member of a tribe.

tribesmanship, n. [1. tríbzmanship; 2. tráibzmənʃip]. Prec. & **-ship**. Membership of a tribe.

triblet, tribolet, n. [1. tríblet, tríbolet; 2. tríblit, tríbəlɛt]. Fr. *triboulet*; Lat. *tribulus*, fr. Gk. *tribolos*, 'instrument with three prongs, a caltrop'; **tri-** & *bólos*, 'a throw', connected w. *bállein*, 'to throw', see **ballistics**, & dimin. **-et**. Instrument for making rings, nuts &c.

tribrach, n. [1. trí-, tríbrak; 2. trái-, tríbræk]. Gk. *tribrakhus*, 'consisting of three shorts'; **tri-** & *brakhús*, 'short', see **brachi-**. (prosody) Foot of three short syllables.

tribrachic, adj. [1. tribrákik; 2. traibrǽkik]. Prec. & **-ic**. Pertaining to, formed of, a tribrach.

tribulation, n. [1. tribūláshun; 2. tribjuléiʃən]. L. Lat. *tribulātiōn-(em)*, fr. P.P. of *trībulāre*, 'to afflict', fr. *trībulum*, 'instrument for thrashing', fr. *trī-*, cp. perf. *trī-vi*, of *terere*, 'to rub' &c., see **teredo** & **triturate**, & **-ion**. **1.** State of mental suffering; grief, distress: *in great tribulation.* **2.** Anything which causes suffering; an affliction, a trial: *beset by tribulations of all kinds.*

tribunal, n. [1. tribúnl; 2. traibjúnl]. Lat., 'raised platform where magistrates sat; judgement seat'; see **tribune** (I.). **1.** Seat, bench, upon which judges and magistrates sit when hearing cases. **2.** Court of justice; any court empowered to inquire into and decide an issue.

tribunary, adj. [1. tríbūnari; 2. tríbjūnəri]. **tribune** & **-ary**. Connected with, pertaining to, a tribune or tribunes.

tribunate, n. [1. tríbūnāt; 2. tríbjūneit]. **tribune** & **-ate**. **a** Office, status, of tribune; **b** tenure of this office.

tribune (I.), n. [1. tríbūn; 2. tríbjūn]. Lat. *tribūnus*, 'chieftain, headman of a tribe; a military officer with consular power; a civil magistrate'; cp. Fr. *tribun*; see **tribe**. **1.** (Rom. hist.) Military or civil officer elected by the people to safeguard their liberties. **2. a** A popular champion; **b** title of a newspaper.

tribune (II.), n. Fr., fr. Ital. or Med. Lat. *tribūna*, prob. fr. Lat. *tribūnal*, see **tribunal**. **1. a** Raised dais for magistrate's chair in Roman basilica; **b** bishop's throne, and part of church containing this, in basilican church. **2.** Raised dais for speakers addressing an assembly; specif., such a platform in the French Chamber of Deputies.

tribunicial, -itial, adj. [1. tribūníshl; 2. tribjuniʃl]. See **tribune** (I.). Pertaining to, befitting, a tribune.

tributary (I.), adj. [1. tríbūtari; 2. tríbjutəri]. Lat. *tribūtārius*, see **tribute** & **-ary**. **1.** Paying tribute to a higher authority, as acknowledgement of the other's superiority or overlordship: *tributary kings.* **2.** Bringing, contributing, supplies, additions, to; esp. *a tributary stream*, one flowing into a larger one.

tributary (II.), n., fr. prec. **1.** State or head of state paying tribute to another. **2.** A river or stream which discharges its waters into a larger river or stream.

tribute, n. [1. tríbūt; 2. tríbjūt]. Lat. *tribūtum*, 'stated payment, contribution, tax levied on citizens'; fr. P.P. of *tribuere*, 'to divide, distribute; to assign, allot'; see **tribe**. **1.** Enforced payment of an annual sum imposed by a conqueror, or made in order to secure some benefit, such as immunity from attack &c. **2.** Payment made by an individual to a sovereign or other overlord; a tax. **3.** Act performed, words uttered, testifying approbation of, esteem, respect, affection for, a person, quality, action: *a tribute of admiration*; *a tribute to the bravery of the dead*; *to pay a tribute to*, express approbation of, admiration &c. for, utter words of praise &c.

tricar, n. [1. tríkar; 2. tráikā]. **tri-** & **car**. A small kind of motor-car with two front wheels and driving wheel behind.

trice (I.), vb. trans. [1. trīs; 2. trais]. M.E. *trīsen*; cp. Swed. *trissa*, 'a pulley'. To haul up (a sail) and make fast.

trice (II.), n. Origin obscure. A brief space of time, an instant; chiefly in Phr. *in a trice*, in an instant, in the twinkling of an eye.

triceps, n. [1. tríseps; 2. tráiseps]. Lat. adj., 'having three heads', fr. **tri-** & *-ceps*, fr. *caput*, 'head', as in **biceps**. Extensor muscle at the back of the upper arm.

tricerium, tricerion, n. [1. trisérium, -ion; 2. traisíəriəm, -iən]. Lat., fr. Gk. *trikḗrion*, **tri-** & *kērós*, 'wax', see **cere-**. (Gk. Ch.) Three-branched candlestick used by the bishop in blessing.

trichiasis, n. [1. trikíasis; 2. trikáiəsis]. Gk. *trikhiāsis*, fr. *thríx*, genit. *trikhós*, 'hair', see **trich(o)-**. **a** Affection of the eyelashes in which these turn inwards and cause irritation; **b** occurrence of hairlike filaments in the urine.

trichina, n. [1. trikína; 2. trikáinə]. Mod. Lat. coinage, fr. Gk. *trikhinos*, 'hairy'; see prec. Minute, very fine, parasitic worm occurring in the flesh of diseased pigs, and sometimes introduced into the human body by means of imperfectly cooked pork.

trichinosis, n. [1. trikinósis; 2. trikinóusis]. Prec. & **-osis**. Disease produced by the presence of trichinae in the system.

trich(o)-, pref. fr. Gk. *trikho-*, stem of *thríx*, 'a hair'; origin obscure.

trichoma, trichome, n. [1. trikóma, tríkōm; 2. traikóumə, tráikoum]. Gk. *trikhōma*, 'growth of hair', see prec. Any outgrowth, such as hair, nail &c., from the epidermis.

trichord, n. & adj. [1. tríkord; 2. tráikōd]. **tri-** & **chord** (I.). **a** n. A three-stringed musical instrument, as lyre or lute; **b** adj., having three strings.

trichosis, n. [1. trikósis; traikóusis]. **tricho-** & **-osis**. Disease of the hair.

trichotomous, adj. [1. trikótumus; 2. traikótəməs]. Next word & **-ous**. Connected with, of the nature of, trichotomy.

trichotomy, n. [1. trikótumi; 2. traikótəmi]. Gk. *trikha*, 'threefold', see **tri-** & **-tomy**. Threefold division; esp. division of human nature into body, soul, and spirit.

trichromatic, adj. [1. trikrōmátik; 2. tràikroumǽtik]. **tri-** & **chromatic**. Three coloured.

trick (I.), n. [1. trik; 2. trik]. In M.E., 'an artifice; a trifle'; in pl. 'odds and ends, knick-knacks'. Origin doubtful; perh. connected w. **treachery**; cp. Du. *trek*, 'trick', wh. may or may not be same word as *trek*, 'a pull, drawing' (cp. *trekken*, 'to draw'); & O. Fr. *triche*, n., & *trikier*, variant of *trichier*, 'to cheat' &c. The relations & origins of all these words are obscure. **1. a** An artifice, dodge, deception, deliberate contrivance to deceive and hoodwink; a swindle, a piece of imposture: *to obtain money by a trick*; *none of your tricks with me*; Phr. *the tricks of the trade*, devices practised by the dishonest in any given trade or business to deceive and outwit customers; **b** an illusion: *a trick of the senses, of the imagination*; *tricks of the memory*, unreliability, temporary failure. **2. a** A mischievous action; a playful, roguish prank, a whimsical practical joke; a harmless deception perpetrated without evil intent: *to play a trick upon*; *full of merry tricks*; also **b** (in bad sense) a mean, underhand prank: *that was a dirty trick*; *a nasty trick to play.* **3. a** A personal habit, an unconscious idiosyncracy, or oddity, of manner, behaviour, speech &c.; a mannerism: *queer little tricks of gesture and pronunciation*; *a* *trick of scratching his head*; **b** an affectation, a foppish mannerism, deliberate eccentricity; esp. *tricks of style*. **4.** A conjurer's artifice in imitation of magic, an act of sleight-of-hand, a piece of jugglery; Phr. *that just does, will just do, the trick*, just accomplishes its purpose. **5.** (card games) A unit of scoring; the cards played in one round. **6.** (see second M.E. sense of pl. cited in etymol.) In Phr. *the whole bag of tricks*, the whole matter and everything connected with it.

trick (II.), vb. trans. & intrans. See prec. **A.** trans. **1.** To swindle, cheat, impose upon: *he found the coin was false and that he had been tricked*; *to trick a person out of his money*, to obtain money by fraud; *to trick a person into doing something*, to induce him to do it by false representations, to lure, inveigle, him into doing it. **2.** *Trick out*, more rarely *trick up*, (fr. earlier sense of n., 'trifle, bauble, trinket' &c.) to deck, adorn, bedizen: *tricked out in jewels and finery*. **B.** intrans. To practise trickery.

trickery, n. [1. tríkeri; 2. tríkəri]. O. Fr. *triquerie*, dial. variant of *tricherie*, see **trick (I.)** & **-ery**. Act of tricking; fraud, knavery.

trickish, adj. [1. tríkish; 2. tríkiʃ]. **trick (I.)** & **-ish**. Inclined to trickery; undependable, rascally.

trickishly, adv. Prec. & **-ly**. In a trickish manner.

trickishness, n. See prec. & **-ness**. Quality of being trickish.

trickle, vb. intrans. & trans. & n. [1. tríkl; 2. tríkl]. Origin dubious. **1.** vb. **a** intrans. To flow slowly or in a thin stream: *the pipe was so small that the water could only trickle*; *tears trickled down her face*; *blood was trickling from the wound*; **b** trans., to cause to trickle. **2.** n. A thin flow: *the stream had shrunk to a mere trickle*.

trickster, n. [1. tríkster; 2. tríkstə]. **trick (II.)** & **-ster**. A cheat, a dishonest rogue, a swindler.

tricksy, adj. [1. tríksi; 2. tríksi]. **trick (I.)** & *-s-* (cp. *tipsy*) & **-y**. Artful, crafty; deceptive.

tricky, adj. [1. tríki; 2. tríki]. See prec. & **-y**. **1.** (of persons) Inclined to play tricks; unreliable, shifty. **2.** (of things) **a** Intricate, complicated, catchy; ingenious: *a tricky lock*; *a tricky brake, lamp* &c.; **b** difficult to follow, involved: *a tricky argument, problem* &c.

triclinic, adj. [1. trīklínik; 2. traiklínik]. **tri-** & **clinic**. (of crystals) Having three axes inclined at oblique angles to each other.

triclinium, n. [1. trīklínium; 2. traikláiniəm]. Lat., fr. Gk. *tríklīnion*; fr. **tri-** & *klínē*, 'couch', see **clinic**. (class. antiq.) **a** A set of three couches set on three sides of a table for dining; **b** dining-room arranged with such tables.

tricolo(u)r, n. [1. tríkolòr, tríkulur; 2. tráikəlɔ̀, tráikalə]. Fr. (*drapeau*) *tricolore*, 'flag of three colours', as n. See **tri-** & **colour (I.)**. A national flag composed of three colours, arranged in equal stripes, esp. the French national flag consisting of red, white, and blue stripes of equal width.

tricot, n. [1. tríkō; 2. tríkou]. Fr., 'knitting'. **a** A coarse, large-stitched knitting; fabric of this; **b** garment, jersey, made of this.

tric-trac, n. [1. trík trak; 2. trík træk]. Fr. An early, difficult, and complicated form of backgammon.

tricuspid, adj. [1. trìkúspid; 2. tràikáspid]. **tri-** & **cusp** (*-id-* is part of stem of latter). Having three cusps or points.

tricycle, n. [1. trísikl; 2. tráisikl]. **tri-** & **cycle (I.)**. Cycle with three wheels; practically obsolete, except as tradesman's carrier.

tricyclist, n. [1. trísiklist; 2. tráisiklist]. Prec. & **-ist**. Rider of a tricycle.

trident, n. [1. trídent; 2. tráidənt]. Lat. *trident-(em)*, 'three-pronged spear', fr. **tri-** & **dent-**, 'tooth; prong', see **dental**. A three-pronged spear; esp. one represented as the characteristic symbol of Neptune and of naval power.

tridentate, adj. [1. trìdéntāt; 2. tràidénteit]. Prec. & **-ate**. Having three prongs or divisions.

Tridentine, adj. & n. [1. trìdéntīn; 2. tràidéntain]. Med. Lat. *Tridentum*, 'Trent'. **1.** adj. Belonging to, connected with, Trent, or the Council of Trent (1545-63). **2.** n. One who accepts the doctrines defined as *de fide* by the Council of Trent.

tried, adj. [1. trīd; 2. traid], fr. P.P. of **try (I.)**. Proved, tested, reliable, well established: *a tried friend, friendship*; *a book of tried excellence*. Phr. *old and tried*.

triennial, adj. & n. [1. triénial; 2. traiéniəl], fr. Lat. *triennium*, 'space of three years', fr. **tri-** & *annus*, 'year', see **annual (I.)**, & **-al**. **1.** adj. **a** Lasting for three years; **b** occurring, appearing, once in every three years. **2.** n. **a** Something that lasts for, or occurs once in, three years; **b** specif., a Mass said every day for three years for the repose of the soul of a deceased person.

trier, n. [1. trīer; 2. tráiə]. **try (I.)** & **-er**. **a** One who tries, attempts; **b** one who tests, esp. one who tests judicially.

trierarch, n. [1. tríerark; 2. tráiərāk]. Lat. *triērarchus*, fr. Gk. *triḗrarkhos*, 'commander of a trireme'; see **trireme** & **arch-**. **1.** Commander of a trireme. **2.** (in anct. Athens) Person who built and fitted out a trireme for the service of the state.

trierarchy, n. [1. tríeràrki; 2. tráiəràki]. Prec. & **-y**. Office, functions, of a trierarch.

trifid, adj. [1. trífid; 2. tráifid]. Lat. *trifidus*, 'cleft in three parts; three-forked'; **tri-** & *fid-*, form of base occurring in perf. of *findere*, 'to split'; see this under **fissile**, & cp. **bite**. (zool. and bot.) Divided into three lobes or sinuses; tridentate.

trifle (I.), n. [1. trífl; 2. tráifl]. M.E. *trīfle*, *trūfle*, O. Fr. *trufle*, *trufe*, 'mockery, trickery'. Origin unknown; prob. same word as **truffle**. **1.** **a** Thing of no value; small, insignificant object: *a few trifles for your birthday*; **b** unimportant subject, a paltry matter; **a** worthless, trivial idea: *a mind occupied with, interested in, trifles*. Phrs. *he doesn't stick at trifles, not the man to stick at trifles*, he is entirely without scruples. **2.** A sweet dish made of cake soaked in wine, filled with jam, stuck over with almonds, and covered thickly with whipped cream. **3.** **a** (colloq.) A very small amount: *just the merest, a mere, trifle of sugar in my tea*; **b** (adverbially) slightly, somewhat: *a trifle sad, dull, annoyed* &c.

trifle (II.), vb. intrans. & trans. M.E. *trīfelen*; see prec. **A.** intrans. **1.** **a** To speak jestingly, lightly, idly; **b** to speak and act without seriousness, speak insincerely; to play fast and loose, to promise without intending to fulfil: *I beg you not to trifle with me*; *in no mood for trifling*; *not a man to trifle with*; *I did but trifle*, didn't mean what I said. **2.** **a** To spend one's time idly; to lounge, dawdle, potter about, engage in frivolous pursuits: *he trifled through the best years of his life*; **b** to linger over, toy with, play with: *to trifle with, over, a light meal*. **B.** trans. To waste in trifling; chiefly *trifle away*: *to trifle away one's time, one's time away*.

trifler, n. [1. trífler; 2. tráiflə]. Prec. & **-er**. One who trifles; a frivolous, superficial person.

trifling, adj. [1. trífling; 2. tráifliŋ], fr. Pres. Part. of **trifle (II.)**. Slight, unimportant, trivial; of small account, inconsiderable: *a trifling error, remark, jest* &c.; *a trifling ailment*.

triflingly, adv. Prec. & **-ly**. In a trifling manner; to a slight, trifling, extent.

trifoliate, adj. [1. trìfóliāt; 2. tràifóulieit]. See next word & **-ate**. Having three leaves or leaflets.

trifolium, n. [1. trīfólium; 2. traifóuliəm]. Lat., 'trefoil', lit. 'three-leaved plant'; see **tri-** & **folio (I.)**. Large genus of plants; the clovers.

triforium, n. [1. trīfórium; 2. traifɔ́riəm]. L. Lat., formed fr. **tri-**, & *foris*, 'door', q.v. under **forum**. Gallery with arched openings running along the nave and transepts of a church, above the main arches.

triform, adj. [1. tríform; 2. tráifɔ̄m]. Lat. *triformis*, see **tri-** & **-form**. **a** Having three parts; **b** having a triple character or nature.

triformity, n. [1. trìfórmiti; 2. tràifɔ́miti]. Prec. & **-ity**. Quality, state, of being triform.

trifurcate, adj. & vb. intrans. and trans. [1. trífĕrkāt; 2. tràifʌ́keit]. **tri-** & Lat. *furca*, see **fork (I.)**, & **-ate**. **1.** adj., also *trifurcated*. Having three branches; forking in three. **2.** vb. To branch out, divide, into three.

trifurcation, n. [1. trìfĕrkáshun; 2. traifʌ̄kéiʃən]. Prec. & **-ion**. **a** Process of branching into three; **b** place where a road, stream, bough &c. trifurcates.

trig, adj. [1. trig; 2. trig]. O.N. *tryggr*, cogn. w. **true**. Smart, trim, in good order and condition.

trigamist, n. [1. trígamist; 2. trígəmist]. **trigamy** & **-ist**. One who has three wives or husbands at the same time.

trigamous, adj. [1. trígamus; 2. trígəməs]. See next word & **-ous**. **1.** Thrice married; having three wives or three husbands at same time. **2.** (bot.) Having male, female, and hermaphrodite flowers on same stem.

trigamy, n. [1. trígami; 2. trígəmi]. Gk. *trigamia*, see **tri-** & **-gamy**. Triple marriage; state of having three wives or husbands at the same time.

trigeminous, adj. [1. trījéminus; 2. traidžéminəs]. Lat. *trigeminus*, 'three at a birth'; **tri-** & *geminus*, 'a twin', see **Gemini**, & **-ous**. Being one of three born at one birth.

trigger, n. [1. tríger; 2. trígə]. Earlier *tricker*; cp. Du. *trekker*, fr. *trekken*, 'to pull'; cp. **trek**. Lever which releases a spring; specif., one releasing the hammer of a firearm.

triglot, adj. [1. tríglot; 2. tráiglət]. **tri-** & Gk. *glôtta*, 'tongue, language', variant of *glôssa*, see **gloss (III.)**, **glossary**. Written in, speaking, three languages.

triglyph, n. [1. tríglif; 2. tráiglif]. Gk. *trígluphos*, 'thrice-carved ornament', see **tri-** & **glyph**. Three-grooved tablet repeated at equal distances along the frieze in Doric architecture.

triglyphic, adj. [1. trīglífik; 2. traiglífik]. Prec. & **-ic**. Connected with, consisting of, triglyphs.

trigon, n. [1. trígon; 2. tráigən]. Gk. *trígōnon*, 'triangle; musical instrument in this form'; see **tri-** & under **-gon**. **1.** **a** A triangle; **b** (anct. Gk.) triangular lyre. **2.** (astrol.) Division, group, of three signs of the zodiac.

trigonal, adj. [1. trí-, trígonal; 2. trái-, trígənəl]. Prec. & **-al**. (of a cross-section) Triangular.

trigonometric(al), adj. [1. trìgonométrik(l); 2. trìgənəmétrik(l)]. **trigonometry** & **-ic** (& **-al**). Pertaining to, based on, trigonometry.

trigonometry, n. [1. trìgonómetri; 2. trìgənɔ́mitri]. **trigon** & *-o-* of stem & **-metry**. Branch of mathematics dealing with the relations of the sides and angles of triangles.

trigonous, adj. [1. trí-, trígunus; 2. trái-, trígənəs]. **trigon** & **-ous**. Three-cornered, having three angles.

trigraph, n. [1. trígrahf; 2. tráigrāf]. **tri-** & **graph**. Group of three graphic symbols used to express a single sound; e.g. *sch*=[s], in *schism*.

trilateral, adj. & n. [1. trīláteral; 2. trailǽtərəl]. **tri-** & **lateral (I.)**. **a** adj. Having three sides; **b** n., three-sided figure or enclosed space.

trilby, n. [1. trílbi; 2. trílbi], fr. name of novel by George du Maurier. A soft felt hat.

trilemma, n. [1. trīléma; 2. trailémə]. Gk., see **tri-** & **lemma**, & cp. **dilemma**. Choice between three things or three courses of action.

trilinear, adj. [1. trilínear; 2. trailíniə]. **tri-** & **linear.** Pertaining to, enclosed by, three lines.

trilingual, adj. [1. trilínggwal; 2. trailíŋgwəl]. **tri-** & **lingual.** Speaking, written in, three languages.

triliteral, adj. & n. [1. trilíteral; 2. trailítərəl]. **tri-** & **literal.** **a** adj. Spelt with three letters; **b** n., word so spelt.

triliteralism, n. [1. trilíteralizm; 2. trailítərəlizəm]. See prec. & **-ism.** Property, condition, of being triliteral; specif. of Semitic languages, fact of having words consisting of 'roots' which have three fixed consonant sounds, the vowels varying in cognate words according to the sense.

trilith, trilithon, n. [1. trílith, trílithon; 2. tráiliþ, tráiliþon]. **tri-** & Gk. *líthos*, 'stone', see **litho-.** A prehistoric stone monument, consisting of two upright stones supporting a third stone as lintel.

trill (I.), vb. intrans. & trans. [1. tril; 2. tril]. Cp. Fr. *triller*; Ital. *trillare*; prob. imitative of sound. **a** intrans. To make a vibrating sound with the tongue, utter such a note with the voice, or produce such a note on an instrument; **b** trans., to pronounce (a sound), sing, or play (a note) with vibratory effect.

trill (II.), n. Fr. *trille*; Ital. *trilla*; see prec. **1.** (singing &c.) **a** A rapid alternation of the voice between two notes, producing a vibratory effect; a shake; **b** a similar effect in a bird's song; a warble; **c** similar alternation of tone, and same effect, produced on a musical instrument. **2.** (phon.) Consonantal sound produced by a rapid vibratory movement, **a** of the point of the tongue—[r] in Scots; **b** of the uvula—[r] in French.

trilling, n. [1. tríling; 2. tríliŋ]. **tri-** & **-ling**; cp. Germ. *drilling*, fr. form of *drei*, 'three'. One of three children born at one birth.

trillion, n. [1. tríliun; 2. tríliən], fr. Fr.; **tri-** w. ending on anal. of **million.** **a** A million million million; expressed by a unit and 18 zeros; **b** (Fr. & Am. usage) a million million; expressed by a unit and 12 zeros.

trilobate, adj. [1. trilóbāt; 2. trailóubeit]. **tri-** & **lobate.** (bot. &c.) Having three lobes.

trilobite, n. [1. trílobīt; 2. tráiləbait]. See prec. & **-ite.** An extinct marine arachnid with trilobate body, found as fossils in Cambrian and Silurian strata.

trilogy, n. [1. tríloji; 2. tríləd͡ʒi]. Gk. *trilogía*; see **tri-** & **-logy.** **a** Series of three Greek dramas performed consecutively on the same day; **b** any connected series of three literary or musical compositions.

trim (I.), vb. trans. & intrans. [1. trim; 2. trim]. O.E. *trymman*, 'to make strong, fortify; to arrange, array', fr. O.E. *trum*, 'firm, strong, healthy'; cogn. w. Lat. *dūrus*, 'hard, strong', wh. is for **drūros*, see **durable**; cp. further Gk. *drūmós*, 'oak-coppice', & *drūs*, 'oak', q.v. under **dryad.** The base **derewomeant* orig. 'tree-trunk', & the adj. derived fr. this had the sense 'hard, firm, as a tree' &c. See also **tree** (I.). General sense, to set in order, bring to a desired shape, condition &c.; various specialized uses. **A.** trans. **1.** To clean up, smooth (wick of a lamp), so that it will burn; to arrange (a fire), make compact, put in condition favourable to combustion. **2.** To make tidy, shapely; cut into desired shape and size: *to trim a hedge*; *to trim one's moustache, one's nails* &c.; *trim oneself up*, make oneself clean and neat. **3.** (naut.) **a** To adjust balance of, distribute weight in (a boat), so that she floats level in the water; **b** to arrange (sails) in position suitable for sailing. **4.** To ornament, attach edging, fringe, lace &c. to: *to trim a jacket with fur*; to adorn with ribbons, flowers &c.: *to trim a* (*woman's*) *hat.* **B.** intrans. To perform act of trimming (in various senses); specif. (fig.) to waver in one's principles, adjust one's sentiments, or the expression of them, to modify one's policy &c. to suit circumstances, public opinion &c.

trim (II.), n. See prec. **a** Condition, mode of adjustment or arrangement; order: *to put a home, garden &c. in good, proper, trim*; **b** bodily condition; **c** frame of mind, state of intellectual balance, mental disposition.

trim (III.), adj., fr. **trim** (I.). Neat, trig, spruce; in good order; in condition suited for a particular purpose or function.

trimester, n. [1. triméster; 2. triméstə]. Fr. *trimestre*, fr. *trimestris*, 'of three months'; **tri-** & *mensis*, 'month', see **meno-.** Period of three months; school or university term of this length.

trimeter, n. [1. trímeter; 2. trímitə]. See **tri-** & **metre** (I.). (prosody) A verse of three measures.

trimetric(al), adj. [1. trimétrik(l); 2. trimétrik(l)]. Prec. & **-ic** (& **-al**). Pertaining to, of the nature of, a trimeter.

trimly, adv. [1. trímli; 2. trímli], fr. **trim** (III.) & **-ly.** In trim, neat, condition or manner.

trimmer, n. [1. trímer; 2. trímə]. **trim** (I.) & **-er.** **1.** **a** Person who trims (in various senses); **b** instrument for trimming or clipping &c. **2.** Specif., person who sacrifices principle to expediency; a time-server.

trimming, n. [1. tríming; 2. trímiŋ]. See prec. & **-ing.** **1.** Action of one who trims. **2.** **a** Material, ornamental edging, border, frill &c. used to trim a garment; ornamental edging to a table dish; **b** (fig.) flowers of speech, ornamental redundancies of speech. **3.** Adjuncts, accessories: *boiled beef and trimmings.*

trimness, n. [1. trímnes; 2. trímnis], fr. **trim** (III.) & **-ness.** Condition of being trim; tidiness, order, neatness.

trine, adj. & n. [1. trīn; 2. train]. Lat. *trīnus*, 'threefold'; see **tri-.** **1.** adj. Threefold, triple. **2.** n. **a** A group of three; **b** (astrol.) aspect of planets 120° apart; Phr. *in trine.*

tringle, n. [1. tríngl; 2. tríŋgl]. Fr.; origin doubtful. **1.** Rod for curtain, or for bed canopy. **2.** **a** (archit.) Narrow, square moulding; **b** (artillery) bar on gun platform which takes up the recoil of the gun on discharge.

Trinitarian, adj. & n. [1. trinitárian; 2. triniténriən]. **trinity** & **-arian.** **1.** adj. Pertaining to the Trinity, or to the doctrine of the Trinity. **2.** n. Believer in the doctrine of the Trinity.

Trinitarianism, n. [1. trinitárianizm; 2. triniténriənizəm]. Prec. & **-ism.** The doctrine of the Trinity; faith in this.

trinitrotoluene, n. [1. trīnítrōtólūēn; 2. trainàitroutóljuìn]. **tri-**, **nitro-**, & **toluene.** Abbr. T.N.T., a high explosive obtained by action of nitric and sulphuric acid on toluene.

trinity, n. [1. tríniti; 2. tríniti]. M.E. *trinitee*, L. Lat. *trīnitāt-*(*em*), see **trine** & **-ity.** **1.** Combination of three (objects or persons) considered as forming a unity. **2.** Specif. (theol., cap.) the union of the three divine persons, Father, Son, Holy Ghost, in the Godhead.

Trinity House, n. A corporate body which licenses pilots, erects and maintains lighthouses, buoys &c.

Trinity Sunday, n. The Sunday next after Whitsunday; the day on which the feast of the Blessed Trinity is kept.

trinket, n. [1. tríngket; 2. tríŋkit]. M.E. *trenket*, 'small ornamental knife'; O. Fr. *trenquet*, cp. *tranchier*, 'to cut'; see **trench** (I.). **a** Small ornament, a jewel, a bauble; **b** small, insignificant, trivial object; a worthless trifle.

trinomial, adj. & n. [1. trinómial; 2. trainóumiəl], cp. Lat. *trinōminis*, adj., 'having three names'. See **tri-** & **nominal.** The above word is formed as though fr. **trinōmius* & *-ālis*; see **-al.** **1.** adj. **a** (alg.) Having, consisting of, three terms; **b** (bot. and zool.) composed of three names or words; more usually *trinominal*, q.v. **2.** n. (alg.) Expression, equation, consisting of three terms.

trinominal, adj. [1. trinóminal; 2. trainóminəl]. Lat., see prec. Having three names; esp. (bot. and zool.) *trinominal system*, of describing animals or plants by genus, species, and subspecies.

trio, n. [1. tréō; 2. tríou]. Ital., fr. Lat. *tri-*, 'three'; see **tri-.** **1.** Musical composition **a** for three voices, **b** for three instruments. **2.** Group of three persons or things.

triolet, n. [1. tréōlā, tréōlet; 2. tríoulei, tríoulet]. Fr. Prec. & **-let.** Poem of eight lines with rhymes in the order *abaaabab.*

trior, n. See **trier.**

trip (I.), vb. intrans. & trans. [1. trip; 2. trip]. M.E. *trippen*; cp. Swed. *trippa*; prob. connected w. Germ. *treppe*, 'flight of steps', & w. **trap** (III.), a snare. **A.** intrans. **1.** To move nimbly along with light, rapid, graceful steps. **2.** **a** To stumble, catch one's foot in an obstacle in walking or running and lose one's balance so as to fall, or nearly to fall; also *trip up*; **b** to perform the act of tripping another: *it is not legitimate to trip in football.* **3.** (fig.) **a** To commit an error, be guilty of an offence, or indiscretion in behaviour: *he was caught tripping several times and at last was dismissed*; **b** to make an error in statement of fact, be inaccurate; **c** to halt, hesitate, stumble, over a word &c. in speaking; to make a slip of the tongue. **B.** trans. **1.** (rare) To dance lightly and nimbly: '*Come and trip it as ye go, On the light fantastic toe*' (Milton, 'L'Allegro', 33-34); *to trip a measure.* **2.** **a** To cause to stumble or fall, *e.g.* by putting an obstacle in the way of the feet and suddenly checking forward progress, or (in wrestling) by catching and pulling away a leg; also *trip up*; **b** *trip up*, to detect in an error of statement, or in conduct in another; to catch (person) in a lapse from truth or honesty. **3.** To upset plans of, to outwit, cause to fail in enterprise. **4.** To loose (an anchor) from bottom of sea by means of cable.

trip (II.), n., fr. prec. **1.** A journey, tour; an excursion; esp. one of short duration for purposes of pleasure; a jaunt, an outing: *a trip to the Continent, to the seaside.* **2.** A light, nimble, rapid motion forward on the feet. **3.** **a** Act of tripping or stumbling; a false step, a slip, lurch forward; **b** act of causing another to stumble or fall; wrestler's device for causing opponent to lose his footing. **4.** (fig.) A slip, a faux pas, an offence, in conduct; a slip of the tongue, an error in statement &c.

tripartite, adj. [1. trīpártīt; 2. traipátait]. **tri-** & **part** (I.) & **-ite.** **1.** Divided into, consisting of, three parts. **2.** Existing, arranged between, three parties.

tripartition, n. [1. trīpartíshun; 2. traipātíʃən]. **tri-** & **partition.** Division into three parts.

tripe, n. [1. trīp; 2. traip]. Fr., origin unknown. **1.** (obs. or vulg.) The entrails, the guts. **2.** Part of the stomach of an animal of the ox kind, used as food. **3.** (slang) Worthless stuff, rubbish; applied to inferior literary work.

tripedal, adj. [1. trīpédl; 2. traipídl]. **tri-** & **pedal** (I.). Having three feet.

trip-hammer, n. A tilt-hammer.

triphthong, n. [1. trífthong; 2. trífþoŋ]. **tri-** & second element as in **diphthong.** A combination, or series, of three vowel sounds, of which only one is stressed; e.g. [áiə] as in *fire.*

triplane, n. [1. trīplān; 2. tráiplein]. **tri-** & **plane** (V.). Aeroplane with three supporting planes.

triple, adj. & vb. trans. & intrans. [1. trípl; 2. trípl]. Fr., fr. Lat. *triplus*; see **tri-** & cp. formation of *duplus* under **double** (I.). **1.** adj. Threefold. **2.** vb. **a** trans. To multiply, increase, threefold; **b** intrans., to become three times as great, to treble.

triplet, n. [1. tríplet; 2. tríplit]. Prec. & **-et.** Group, series, of three; **a** three lines rhyming together; **b** three notes played or sung in time of two; **c** any one of three children born at one birth.

triplex, adj. & n. [1. trípleks; 2. trípleks]. Lat., 'triple'; fr. **tri-** & base *plic-*, 'fold', see **plicate.** **1.** adj. **a** Threefold; **b** producing threefold effect. **2.** n. (mus.) Triple time.

triplicate, adj., n., & vb. trans. [1. tríplikāt; 2. tríplikeit]. Lat.; see **tri-** & **plicate**. **1.** adj. Threefold; esp. reproduced in three identical copies. **2.** n. One of three identical things or copies. **3.** vb. To make three copies of; to treble.

triplication, n. [1. trìplikáshun; 2. trìplikéiʃən]. Prec. & **-ion**. **a** Act of triplicating; **b** that which is triplicated.

triplicity, n. [1. trī-, triplísiti; 2. trai-, triplísiti]. Lat. *triplic-*, stem of **triplex**, & **-ity**. State of being threefold.

tripod, n. [1. trípod; 2. tráipɔd]. Gk. *tripod-*, 'three-legged'; see **tri-** & **pedal (I.)**. **1.** A stand, table, stool &c. standing on three legs. **2.** Specif., three-legged stool, or altar, of bronze, on which the priestess sat in the temple of Apollo at Delphi when giving the answers of the oracle.

tripoli, n. [1. trípoli; 2. trípəli], fr. name of place in Africa. Friable, siliceous deposit; also called *rotten-stone*.

tripos, n. [1. trípos; 2. tráipɔs]. Gk. *trípous*, nom., of wh. the stem is seen in **tripod**. Honours examination at University of Cambridge; formerly the list of successful candidates in the examination; from the three-legged stool upon which the M.A. sat who delivered the satirical Latin speech at the degree-giving on Ash Wednesday.

tripper, n. [1. tríper; 2. trípə]. **trip (I.)** & **-er**. One who takes trips; a tourist, an excursionist.

tripping, adj. [1. tríping; 2. trípiŋ], fr. Pres. Part. of **trip (I.)**. Walking with light, rapid, nimble steps.

trippingly, adv. Prec. & **-ly**. **a** As though tripping; nimbly; **b** (of speech, utterance) flowingly, fluently, readily.

triptych, n. [1. tríptik; 2. tríptik]. Gk. *triptukhos*, 'consisting of three layers, or plates', fr. **tri-** & *ptúx*, genit. *ptukhós*, 'layer, fold'; the origin of latter is doubtful. Cp. **diptych**. Picture or carving upon three panels placed side by side; esp. one as altar-piece with large central panel and a smaller one on either side.

triquetra, n. [1. trīkwétra; 2. traikwétrə]. Lat., fem. of *triquetrus*, 'having three corners'; fr. **tri-** & second element orig. **quadros*, 'sharp, pointed', cogn. w. O.E. *hwæt*, 'sharp; bold' &c., q.v. under **whet (I.)**. Ornament consisting of three arcs interlaced.

triquetrous, adj. [1. trīkwétrus; 2. traikwétrəs]. Prec. & **-ous**. Having three acute angles or edges.

trireme, n. [1. trírēm; 2. tráiərīm]. Lat. *trirēmis*, 'having three banks of oars'; fr. **tri-** & *rēmus*, 'oar', fr. **retsmos*, cogn. w. O.E. *rōðor*, 'oar', see **rudder**, & **row (II.)**. Ancient galley, esp. a Greek galley, with three benches for rowers.

Trisagion, n. [1. triságion; 2. trisǽgiɔn]. Gk. *trís*, 'three times', see under **tri-**, & *hágion*, neut., 'holy', q.v. under **hagiology**. Greek hymn which invokes God three times as holy.

trisect, vb. trans. [1. trīsékt; 2. traisékt], fr. Lat. **tri-** & *sect-(um)*, P.P. of *secāre*, 'to cut'; see **sect**. To divide, cut, into three, esp. three equal parts (specif. geom.).

triskelion, n. [1. triskélion; 2. triskéliɔn], fr. Gk. *triskelés*, 'three-legged', fr. **tri-** & *skélos*, 'leg', see **isosceles**. Name given to a device of three curves or branches joined at a centre, developing into the three legs of the coins of ancient Sicily, and of the arms of the Isle of Man.

trismus, n. [1. trízmus; 2. trízməs]. Latinized fr. Gk. *trismós*, 'a squeaking, creaking', cp. *trízein*, 'to squeak, creak', fr. base **streid-*, **strid-*, cp. Lat. *strīdēre*, 'to creak, rattle' &c., see **strident**. (med.) Lockjaw.

trisyllabic, adj. [1. trìsilábik; 2. trìsilǽbik]. **tri-** & **syllabic**. Having three syllables.

trisyllable, n. [1. trisílabl; 2. trisíləbl]. **tri-** & **syllable (I.)**. Word of three syllables.

tritagonist, n. [1. trītágunist; 2. traitǽgənist]. Gk. *tritagōnistḗs*, fr. *trítos*, 'third', cp. **third (I.)**. & *agōnistḗs*, 'actor'; see **agonistic**. Cp. **protagonist**. Character third in importance in a Greek play.

trite, adj. [1. trīt; 2. trait]. Lat. *trīt-(um)*, P.P. of *terere*, 'to rub, wear away'; see also **teredo** & **toreutic**; prob. cogn. w. **throw (I.)**. Lacking novelty and freshness; commonplace, hackneyed, banal: *a trite remark, expression*.

tritely, adv. Prec. &- **ly**. In a trite manner.

triteness, n. See prec. & **-ness**. Condition, quality, of being trite.

tritheism, n. [1. trīthēizm; 2. tráiþiizəm]. **tri-** & **theism (II.)**. Heretical opinion that as each of the Persons of the Trinity is God, there are therefore three Gods.

tritheist, n. [1. trīthēist; 2. tráiþiist]. **tri-** & **theist**. Believer in tritheism.

Triton, n. [1. trītun; 2. tráit(ə)n]. Gk. *Trītōn*. **a** (Gk. mythol.) A minor sea-god, son of Poseidon and Amphitrite, depicted with a fish's tail, and holding a conch shell as a trumpet; also, one of a number of demi-gods resembling Triton. Phr. *a Triton among minnows*, of important personage among people of little or no consequence; **b** a genus of marine gastropod molluscs with large spiral shells.

triturable, adj. [1. trítūrabl; 2. trítjurəbl]. L. Lat. *tritur-*, as in next word, & **-able**. Capable of being triturated.

triturate, vb. trans. [1. trítūrāt; 2. trítjəreit]. L. Lat. *trītūrāt-(um)*, P.P. of *trītūrāre*, 'to grind, pulverize', formed fr. Lat. *trīt-(um)*, P.P. of Lat. *terere*, see **trite**. To rub, grind down, pulverize, reduce to a fine powder.

trituration, n. [1. trìtūráshun; 2. trìtjəréiʃən]. Prec. & **-ion**. Act or process of triturating.

triumph (I.), n. [1. tríumf; 2. tráiəmf]. Lat. *triumphus*, earlier *triumpus*, 'solemn procession attending entrance of a general into Rome after an important victory'; fr. Gk. *thriambos*, 'procession in honour of Bacchus'; the etymol. is doubtful; some authorities interpret as 'a dance in three-time', & derive fr. Gk. *trís*, 'thrice', & a hypothetical **ambos*, 'a dance', supposed to be cogn. w. Scrt. *ángam*, 'a limb', O.H.G. *ancha*, 'leg'; others believe that *thriambos* & *dīthúrambos*, see **dithyramb**, are borrowed fr. Asia Minor, the source being unidentifiable. **1.** Victory, ascendancy: *the triumph of good over evil*; achievement, success: *the triumphs of modern science*. Phr. *in triumph*, with victory, having achieved success. **2.** **a** Sense of, feeling of, exultation over, success achieved, victory gained &c.: *he could hardly conceal his triumph at the result of the election*; *a note of triumph in his voice*; **b** outward expression of sense of success &c.: *there was triumph in the eye of the conqueror*. **3.** Something which constitutes a victory, which is the expression of achievement and success: *Pope's life was a triumph over weakness and ill-health.*

triumph (II.), vb. intrans. Fr. *triompher*, Lat. *triumphāre*; see prec. **1.** To win the victory, achieve success: *we hope that in the end righteousness will triumph*; *triumph over*, to defeat, obtain ascendancy over: *good sense has triumphed over unreasoning impetuosity*. **2.** To feel and express joy and satisfaction at success; to exult; commonly *triumph over*: *it is ungenerous to triumph over a defeated enemy*.

triumphal, adj. [1. trīúmfl; 2. traiámfl]. Lat. *triumphālis*, 'belonging to a triumph'; see **triumph (I.)** & **-al**. Pertaining to a triumph; expressing triumph: *a triumphal procession, arch* &c.

triumphant, adj. [1. trīúmfant; 2. traiámfənt]. Lat. *triumphant-(em)*, Pres. Part. of *triumphāre*, see **triumph (II.)**. **1.** Victorious, successful: *triumphant generals*; *the triumphant progress of knowledge*. **2.** a Feeling exultation; **b** expressing exultation, manifesting a sense of successful achievement or of victory: *a triumphant shout*; *triumphant bearing*.

triumphantly, adv. Prec. & **-ly**. **1.** Successfully, victoriously: *to return triumphantly from the wars*. **2.** Exultingly, so as to express joy in, assurance of, success: *to smile triumphantly*.

triumvir, n. [1. trīúmvēr; 2. traiámviə]. Lat., fr. *trium*, genit. pl. of *trēs*, 'three', see **tri-**, & *vir*, 'a man', see **virile**. The *triumviri* were three men holding a public office conjointly, a board of three joint commissioners. A *triumvir* was one of these.

triumvirate, n. [1. trīúmvirāt, -it; 2. traiámvireit, -it]. Lat. *triumvirātus*, 'office, dignity, of a triumvir; a group of triumvirs'; see prec. & **-ate**. **a** A group of three having conjoint authority; specif. **b** (Rom. hist.) one of two such associations formed in Rome in 60 B.C. and 43 B.C.

triune, adj. [1. trīūn; 2. tráijūn]. **tri-** & Lat. *ūnus*, 'one', see **union**. Three in one.

triunity, n. [1. trīūniti; 2. traijūniti]. Prec. & **-ity**. **a** Fact, condition, of being triune; **b** a trinity.

trivet, n. [1. trívet; 2. trívit]. O.E. *trefet*, fr. Low Lat. form of Lat. *triped-*, 'three-footed'; see **tri-** & **pedal (I.)**. Iron stand with three legs for holding a pot or kettle; iron utensil with three projections on lower surface, made to hook over bars of a grate and support a kettle &c. Phr. *right as a trivet*, all right.

trivial, adj. [1. trívial; 2. tríviəl]. Lat. *triviālis*, 'belonging to the cross-roads or public streets'; hence 'commonplace, vulgar, ordinary'; fr. **tri-** & *via*, 'a way', see **trivium**. **1.** (archaic) Commonplace, ordinary: '*The trivial round*'. **2.** **a** Unimportant, of small value, not weighty; insignificant, trifling, negligible: *a trivial remark*; *a trivial mind*; **b** inconsiderable, slight, not severe: *a trivial injury*; *trivial expenses*.

triviality, n. [1. trìviáliti; 2. trìviǽliti]. Prec. & **-ity**. **1.** Quality, condition, of being trivial. **2.** A trivial thing; a trifling, trite, unimportant idea, piece of work &c.

trivially, adv. [1. tríviali; 2. tríviəli]. **trivial** & **-ly**. In a trivial, trifling, manner.

trivialness, n. [1. trívialnes; 2. tríviəlnis]. See prec. & **-ness**. Quality of being trivial; triviality.

trivium, n. [1. trívium; 2. tríviəm]. Lat., 'place where three roads meet; public square; highway', fr. **tri-** & *via*, 'a way, road', see **via**. The initial course of study in mediaeval schools, consisting of the three liberal arts, grammar, rhetoric, and logic; corresponding to the B.A. course of later universities; cp. *quadrivium*.

-trix. Lat. suff. expressing a female agent; corresponding to masc. *-tor*.

trocar, trochar, n. [1. trṓkar; 2. tróukā]. Fr. *trocart*, fr. *trois*, 'three', & *carre*, 'side of a square', fr. Lat. *quadra*, see **quadrate (I.)**. Surgical piercing instrument with triangular point used for drawing off fluid from the body.

trochaic, adj. & n. [1. trōkáik; 2. troukéiik]. See **trochee** & **-ic**. **1.** adj. Pertaining to, composed in, trochees. **2.** n. A trochaic verse or line.

troche, n. [1. trṓkē; 2. tróukī]. Gk. *trokhós*, 'something which runs round; a round wheel; a round ball or cake'; connected w. *trékhein*, 'to run'; this base is seen in O.E. *þrǣgan*, 'to run', see **thrall**. Small, round, flat lozenge of medicinal drugs.

trochee, n. [1. trṓkē; 2. tróukī]. Lat. *trochaeus*, fr. Gk. *trokhaîos*, 'tripping, running', see prec. A metrical foot consisting (in Greek and Latin) of a long syllable followed by a short; or (in English and other languages where stress metre prevails) of a stressed syllable followed by an unstressed.

trochilus, n. [1. trókilus; 2. trɔ́kiləs]. Lat., fr. Gk. *trokhílos*, lit. 'a runner'; applied to several small birds; connected w. base **trekh-*, 'to run'; see **troche**. **1.** A small bird, a variety of sandpiper, said to accompany the crocodile and clear it of leeches and other parasites. **2.** (ornith., cap.) A genus of humming-birds.

trochlea, n. [1. tróklea; 2. trɔ́kliə]. Lat., 'a block containing a pulley', fr. Gk. *trokhilia*, 'a pulley'; for Gk. *trokh-*, *trekh-*, see prec. (anat.) Cartilage in a joint resembling a pulley in function.

trochlear, adj. [1. tróklear; 2. trɔ́kliə]. Prec. & **-ar.** (anat.) Pertaining to a trochlea: *trochlear muscle.*

trocho-, pref. Gk. *trokhós*, 'wheel'; see **troche.**

trochoid, adj. [1. trŏkoid; 2. tróukɔid]. Prec. & **-oid.** **a** Working like a wheel, i.e. rotating on own axis; **b** wheel-shaped.

trochometer, n. [1. trōkómeter; 2. troukɔ́mitə]. **trocho-** & **-meter.** Hodometer or trechometer.

troco, n. [1. trŏkō; 2. tróukou]. Span. *truco*; origin doubtful. Obsolete game played on a lawn with wooden balls and spoon-shaped cues.

trod, vb. [1. trod; 2. trɔd]. Pret. of **tread (I.)**, fr. M.E., P.P. type *trode(n)*, see **trodden.** Cp. O.E. Pret. *træd*; M.E. *trad.*

trodden, vb. [1. tródn; 2. trɔ́dn]. P.P. of **tread**; O.E. *(ġe)troden*; M.E. *troden.*

troglodyte, n. [1. tróglodīt; 2. trɔ́glədait]. Gk. *trōglodútēs*, 'one who creeps into holes'; fr. *trṓglē*, 'a hole', cp. *trṓgein*, 'to gnaw', fr. base **trōg-*, **terg-* &c., cogn. w. Goth. *þairkō*, 'hole', & O.E. *þȳrel*, 'hole', see **nostril** & **through (I.).** The second element is formed fr. *dúein*, 'to enter', the origin of wh. is uncertain. **1.** Primitive cave-dweller, caveman; (fig.) recluse. **2.** *Troglodytes parvulus*, the common wren.

troglodytic, adj. [1. tròglodítik; 2. trɔ̀glədítik]. Prec. & **-ic.** Pertaining to a troglodyte.

trogon, n. [1. trŏgon; 2. tróugɔn]. Invented word, fr. Gk. *trṓgōn*, Pres. Part. of *trṓgein*, 'to gnaw', see prec. Typical genus of a family of brilliantly coloured birds, chiefly of S. America.

troika, n. [1. tróika; 2. trɔ́ikə]. Russ., cp. *tri*, 'three'; cogn. w. **tri-.** Carriage sledge, drawn by three horses harnessed abreast.

trois-temps, n. [1. trwáh tom; 2. trwá tã]. Fr., 'three time'. The musical time or rhythm of a waltz.

Trojan, adj. & n. [1. trŏjan; 2. tróudžən]. Lat. *Trojānus*, fr. *Troia*, 'Troy'. **1.** adj. Belonging to, connected with, Troy. **2.** n. Inhabitant of Troy. Phr. *to work like a Trojan*, work industriously and laboriously.

troll (I.), vb. intrans. & trans. [1. trōl; 2. troul], fr. O. Fr. *troller*, prob. of Gmc. origin; cp. Germ. *trollen*, 'to roll, troll'; M.H.G. sense, 'to run with short steps'; etymol. doubtful. **A.** intrans. **1.** To fish by trailing or spinning a revolving bait or lure, esp. behind a boat. **2.** (archaic or obs.) To pass the bottle round. **B.** trans. **1.** (rare) To fish (area of water) by trolling. **2.** To sing in a careless, light-hearted manner: *to troll a stave.*

troll (II.), n. O.N. & Swed. Fabulous creature, either a giant or a mischievous dwarf.

trolley, n. [1. tróli; 2. trɔ́li]. Perh. fr. **troll (I.)**, see **trawl.** **1.** Any of various vehicles; **a** a light cart usually on two wheels, pushed by hand; **b** a strong low truck on four wheels, running on rails, for moving stones and other heavy objects. **2.** Steel arm with pulley projecting from electric tram-car, running along overhead wire and conveying current to the car; (also attrib.) *trolley-car*, *-pole* &c.

trolley-lace, n. Origin doubtful. Coarse lace the pattern on which is outlined in thick threads.

trollius, n. [1. trólius; 2. trɔ́liəs]. Mod. Lat., fr. Hung. *torolya*, the name of the plant. Genus of ranunculaceous plants, with globe-shaped yellow or orange flowers.

trollop, n. [1. trólop; 2. trɔ́ləp], fr. **troll (I.)** in old sense 'roll'; cp. Fr. *rouleuse* for meaning. A slatternly, disreputable woman.

trombone, n. [1. trómbōn; 2. trɔ́mboun]. Ital., fr. *tromba*, 'trumpet', see **trump (I.)**, & **-oon.** Powerful brass wind instrument consisting of a tube bent and rebent on itself, with a bell-shaped end, and a sliding section, by moving which the various notes are made.

trommel, n. [1. trómel; 2. trɔ́məl]. Germ., 'a drum', q.v. Revolving sieve used in cleansing ores.

tromometer, n. [1. tromómeter; 2. trɔmɔ́mitə], fr. Gk. *trómos*, 'a trembling', cogn. w. **tremor**, & **-meter.** Instrument for measuring earth tremors.

trompe, n. [1. tromp; 2. trɔmp]. Fr., see **trump (I.).** Apparatus for making powerful draught in a blast furnace, by means of falling water; water-bellows.

troop (I.), n. [1. trōōp; 2. trūp]. Fr., see **troupe.** **1.** A number of people. **2.** (specif. mil.) A division of a cavalry squadron, commanded by a captain, and corresponding to a company in an infantry regiment. **3.** Specif. (pl.) military forces.

troop (II.), vb. intrans. & trans., fr. prec. **1.** intrans. To move forward in large numbers; to flock: *people came trooping out of the theatre.* **2.** trans. In Phr. (mil.) *to troop the colour*, to perform ceremony of escorting the colour through the regiment on parade.

trooper, n. [1. trōōper; 2. trūpə]. **troop** & **-er.** Private soldier in a cavalry regiment. Phr. *to swear like a trooper*, to swear fluently and forcibly.

troop-ship, n. Vessel carrying soldiers; a transport.

Tropaeolum, n. [1. tropēolum; 2. trɔpíələm]. Latinized dimin. of Gk. *trópaion*, 'trophy', see **trophy**; so called fr. the shield-shaped leaves & scarlet flowers of the plant. Genus of slender S. American climbing plants with masses of scarlet or orange flowers, including the nasturtium and canary creeper.

trope, n. [1. trōp; 2. troup]. Gk. *trópos*, 'turn, direction, way', fr. same base as *trépein*, 'to turn'; cogn. w. O. Lat. *trepit*, 'turns'; see under **trepidation.** Figure of speech; figurative, metaphorical, use of a word.

-trope, suff. Gk. *tropḗ*, 'a turning'; cogn. w. prec. Used in compounds, e.g. *heliotrope*, *zoetrope* &c., in sense of 'that which turns'.

trophic, adj. [1. trófik; 2. trɔ́fik]. Gk. *trophikós*, fr. *trophḗ*, 'food, nourishment'; fr. same base **dh(e)rebh-*, &c., as *tréphein*, 'to make firm; to feed, nourish, to cherish'; cp. further Gk. *trophālis*, 'curdled milk'; *thrómbos*, 'clot, lump', fr. **dhro(m)bh-*, see **thrombosis.** Cp. also Lith. *drabnùs*, 'thick, fat'; & see **draff.** Connected with nutrition.

trophy, n. [1. trŏfi; 2. tróufi]. Fr. *trophée*, Ital. *trofeo*, Lat. *trophaeum*, *tropaeum*, fr. Gk. *trópaion*, fr. neut. of *tropaios*, 'connected with turning, or with a change; connected with defeat'; hence token of an enemy's defeat, consisting of shields, helmets &c., hung on trees or posts. See **trope.** **1.** Memorial, token, of victory; something taken from a defeated enemy; spoils of victory. **2.** **a** Something preserved in memory of victory, success, achievement; **b** specif., group of such objects, such as weapons, heads or antlers of stags &c., arranged in picturesque design, and fixed on wall as an ornament: *trophies of the chase* &c.

-trophy, suff. Gk. *-trophia*, fr. *trophḗ*, 'nourishment'; see **trophic.** Form used in compounds, *atrophy*, *hypertrophy*, with sense of 'nutrition'.

tropic, n. & adj. [1. trópik; 2. trɔ́pik]. In M.E., fr. Lat. *tropicus*, fr. Gk. *tropikós* (*kúklos*) 'pertaining to a turn'; see **trope.** **1.** n. **a** Each of the parallels of latitude about 23½ degrees N. (*tropic of Cancer*) and S. (*tropic of Capricorn*) of the Equator, bounding zone where sun reaches zenith; **b** region of the earth lying between the two parallels of latitude; usually *the tropics.* **2.** adj. Belonging to the tropics.

tropical, adj. [1. trópikl; 2. trɔ́pikl]. **tropic** & **-al.** **1.** Occurring in, characteristic of, the tropics: *tropical vegetation, diseases* &c. **2.** (of weather, temperature &c.) Resembling that of the tropics; very hot, sultry. **3.** Pertaining to, of the nature of, a trope; figurative.

tropically, adv. Prec. & **-ly.** **a** In a tropical state &c.; **b** figuratively.

tropic bird, n. One of several kinds of bird resembling a tern, found in the tropics.

tropist, n. [1. trŏpist; 2. tróupist]. **trope** & **-ist.** One who indulges in figures of speech or tropes.

tropological, adj. [1. tròpolójikl; 2. trɔ̀pəlɔ́džikl]. See next word & **-ic** & **-al.** Characterized by tropes.

tropology, n. [1. tropóloji; 2. trɔpɔ́lədži]. **trope** & **-logy.** **1.** Figurative, metaphorical, mode of speech; use of tropes. **2.** Specif., method of interpreting Scripture so as to make words bear a figurative meaning.

troppo, adv. [1. trópō; 2. trɔ́ppou]. Ital. Cp. Fr. *trop*, 'too much'. (mus.) Too much; esp. *non troppo*, not to excess.

trot (I.), vb. intrans. & trans. [1. trot; 2. trɔt]. M.E. *trotten*, fr. O. Fr. *trotter*; prob. of Gmc. origin; cp. O.H.G. *trottōn*, wh. is cogn. w. **tread (I.).** **A.** intrans. **1.** Specif. **a** (of horse, mule &c.) to move along at a trot; **b** (of persons) to ride at a trot. **2.** (of human beings) To move along with short, rapid steps; used **a** to express the motion of a jerky, irregular run; and **b** that of a hurried walking pace in which short steps are taken; contrasted with *stride.* **3.** *Trot along*, (colloq.) **a** to move off rapidly to perform some specific task: *you had better trot along and feed the dogs*; **b** to take one's departure: *good-bye, I must trot along now.* **B.** trans. **1.** To cause to move at a trot: *to trot a horse.* **2.** *Trot round*, (colloq.) to conduct (a person) from one place to another in succession: *I'll trot you round Oxford and show you the colleges.* **3.** *Trot out*, **a** to put (a horse) through its paces so as to show it off, produce, exhibit, show off for another's inspection; (colloq.) **b** to bring out, and submit (a thing) for another's approval or acceptance: *to trot out one's best wines*; **c** to submit, bring forward (a proposal, suggestion &c.) for consideration; to bring to another's notice: *he trotted out all the old arguments.*

trot (II.), n., fr. prec. **1.** **a** The rapid pace of a horse &c., between pacing and galloping, in which the fore and hind legs on the same side move forward at once, in regular succession; **b** a ride on a horse &c., at this pace. **2.** (colloq.) **a** The movement of a rapid walk or run of human beings; **b** a spell of rapid exercise on foot; a quick walk, a jog. Phrs. *(always) on the trot*, *to be kept on the trot*, continuously moving, constantly busy. **3.** (colloq.) A small child, a toddler.

troth, n. [1. trōth; 2. trouþ]. Variant of **truth**; M.E. *trowthe.* (archaic) Faith, fidelity, word of honour; chiefly in Phr. *to plight one's troth*, to pledge one's word; specif. in marriage.

trotter, n. [1. tróter; 2. trɔ́tə]. **trot (I.)** & **-er.** One who, that which, trots (in various specif. senses): **1.** A horse specially bred and used for trotting. **2.** **a** The foot of a sheep or pig, esp. thought of as food; **b** (colloq. and facet.) the foot of a person, esp. of a child or young girl.

trottoir, n. [1. trótwar; 2. trɔ́twā]. Fr., fr. **trot (I.).** Pavement, side-walk, for pedestrians, at the side of a road.

troubadour, n. [1. trōōbadōr; 2. trūbədɔ̄]. Fr., fr. Provenç. *trobador*; either formed fr. *trobar*, 'to find, invent, compose poetry', cp. Fr. *trouver*, q.v. under **trove**, **trover**, & **trouvère**; or fr. a Low Lat. **tropāre*, 'to make tropes, to sing', cp. Lat. *tropus*, 'a trope; a song', fr. Gk., see **trope.** A mediaeval lyric and amatory poet of a school that flourished in Provence and the south of France, during late 11th and down to end of 13th centuries.

trouble (I.), vb. trans. & intrans. [1. trúbl; 2. trábl]. O. Fr. *trobler*, *troubler*, fr. L. Lat. *turbulāre*, 'to disturb, agitate', fr. *turbula*, dimin. of *turba*, 'a crowd'; see **turbulent.** **A.** trans. **1.** (of physical action) To agitate, cause to become ruffled, put into violent motion: *to trouble the waters.* Phr. *troubled waters*, disturbed, confused state of affairs. **2.** To cause agitation of mind to, to vex, render anxious, to perturb, to harass: *he was greatly troubled about his son's misconduct*; *what troubles me is the thought of her sufferings.* **3. a** To cause annoyance to, to pester, inconvenience, importune, worry, esp. with demands to do something, complaints &c.; to disturb: *he is always troubling me about his private affairs*; *I'm sorry to trouble you about such trivial matters*; also **b** in polite requests: *I fear I must trouble you to come upstairs*; *may I trouble you to pass the salt*; (also ironical) *I'll trouble you to hold your tongue.* **4.** To cause physical pain or discomfort to: *his wound troubles him a good deal*; *much troubled by gout.* **5.** To be a source of difficulty to, to compel to make an effort: *the learning of languages never troubled him much.* **B.** intrans. **1.** To take pains, give oneself trouble; to make an effort: *he never even troubled to answer*; *don't trouble to write*; *if it is inconvenient to come, don't trouble.* **2.** To feel anxious, to be in a state of mental agitation; to worry: *I shall not trouble if I never see him again.*

trouble (II.), n., fr. prec. **1.** Mental agitation, grief, care, affliction: *one could read trouble on his face*; *a heart full of trouble*; Phr. *in trouble,* (i.) sad, afflicted; (ii.) in danger of being punished for an offence; *to get into trouble,* render oneself liable to punishment; *to ask for trouble,* to behave in such a way as to court danger, disaster; to lay oneself open to opposition and attack; to create difficulties for oneself. **2. a** Difficulty, necessity for special effort or exertion: *I had some trouble in reading his handwriting*; *he opened the safe without any trouble*; **b** effort, labour, pains: *to take trouble*; *thank you for all your trouble on my behalf.* **3.** Cause, source, of trouble; something which afflicts, which causes grief or annoyance: *life is full of petty troubles*; *tell me all your troubles.* **4.** State of political or social unrest, disturbance, confusion. **5. a** An ailment; physical or mental ill-health: *heart trouble, mental trouble*; **b** specif. (popular) childbirth, confinement: *Mrs. Jones is over her trouble.*

troublesome, adj. [1. trúblsum; 2. tráblsəm]. Prec. & **-some.** Causing trouble (in various senses); **a** difficult, wearisome, laborious: *a troublesome job*; **b** persistently harassing; *a troublesome cough*; **c** unruly, undisciplined, obstreperous: *a troublesome child.*

troublesomely, adv., fr. prec. Prec. & **-ly.** In a troublesome manner.

troublous, adj. [1. trúblus; 2. trábləs]. **trouble (II.)** & **-ous.** (archaic) Characterized by troubles; disturbed, unsettled; esp. *troublous times.*

trough, n. [1. trawf, trof, truf; 2. trōf, trɔf, traf]. O.E. *trōg, trōh,* 'a hollowed wooden vessel'; O.N. *trōg*; possibly connected w. **tree (I.). 1. a** A wooden vessel, or receptacle; esp. a long, narrow, open one used for holding water or food for animals; **b** a similar vessel of iron or stone; **c** wooden vessel in which dough is kneaded. **2.** A hollow, narrow channel between two waves: *the trough of the sea.* **3.** (meteor.) Line in a cyclonic area in which barometric pressure reaches the lowest point.

trounce, vb. trans. [1. trouns; 2. trauns]. Fr. *tronce,* 'a stump, thick piece of wood', variant of *tronche*; see **truncheon. a** To beat severely, castigate thoroughly; **b** (fig.) to castigate verbally; to criticize, censure, severely.

troupe, n. [1. trōōp; 2. trūp]. Fr., 'band, troop'; see also **troop**; origin uncertain. Derivation has been suggested fr. L.G. *dorp,* 'a village', cogn. w. Engl. **thorp.** A band of actors or of other performers on the stage.

trousered, adj. [1. tróuzerd; 2. tráuzəd]. See **trousers** & **-ed.** Wearing, clothed in, trousers.

trousering, n. [1. tróuzering; 2. tráuzəriŋ]. **trousers** & **-ing.** (tailor's word) Material from which trousers are made.

trousers, n. pl. [1. tróuzerz; 2. tráuzəz]. Formerly *trouses,* fr. Fr. *trousse,* 'bundle'; see **trousse** & **truss (I.)** & cp. **trews. a** Male outer garment extending from the waist to the ankle, covering the lower part of the body and having a separate tubular covering for each leg; also *pair of trousers*; **b** long frilled drawers reaching to the foot worn by women in early 19th cent. Rarely used in sing., & chiefly in such Phrs. as *the leg of my trouser*; also in compounds *trouser-button, trouser-leg, trouser-stretcher.*

trousse, n. [1. trōōs; 2. trūs]. Fr., 'a bundle'; see **truss (I.).** Case for holding a surgeon's smaller instruments.

trousseau, n. [1. trōōsō; 2. trūsou]. Fr., 'bundle; clothes given to a bride', fr. O. Fr. *trossel,* dimin. of **trousse.** Outfit of clothes, jewellery, and other personal belongings provided for a woman on her marriage.

trout, n. [1. trout; 2. traut]. O.E. *truht,* fr. Lat. *tructa,* fr. Gk. *trṓktēs,* 'a nibbler, gnawer', fr. *trṓgein,* 'to gnaw'; see **troglodyte.** Any of various species of small or moderate-sized edible fish of genus *Salmo,* found in rivers and lakes, whose flesh resembles somewhat that of the salmon, but is more delicate in taste and texture, and of a lighter pink in colour; the colour of the skin varies from silvery white to brown, and is in many species sprinkled with pink spots.

trouvère, n. [1. trōōvār; 2. trūvɛə]. O. Fr. & Mod. Fr.; see **troubadour.** One of a school of poets belonging to Northern France, who flourished from 11th to 14th cent., and composed chiefly narrative poems—the so-called 'Chansons de geste'.

trove, adj. [1. trōv; 2. trouv]. O. Fr. *trové,* 'found'. See next word. Only in Phr. *treasure trove,* q.v.

trover, n. [1. trōver; 2. tróuvə]. O. Fr., 'to find', cp. Mod. Fr. *trouver,* Ital. *trovare,* 'to find'; according to Meyer-Lübke, orig. 'to disturb, frighten, start, stir up (fish), fr. Lat. *turbāre,* 'to disturb', fr. *turba,* 'uproar, disorder, confusion', see **turbid, turbulent.** (law) **1.** Acquisition of personal property by finding or otherwise than by purchase. **2.** Action at law to recover goods, or the value of goods (assumed by a legal fiction to have been found), wrongfully detained.

trow, vb. intrans. [1. trou; 2. trau]. O.E. *trūwian,* 'to trust, believe'; connected w. **true.** (obs. or deliberately archaic) To suppose, believe; generally, *I trow.*

trowel, n. [1. tróuel; 2. tráuil]. Fr. *truelle,* 'mason's trowel', fr. L. Lat. *truella,* dimin. of Lat. *trua,* 'ladle', cp. also Lat. *trulla*; cogn. w. Gk. *torúnē,* 'implement for stirring'; prob. fr. base **twer-,* 'to stir', whence also O.E. *þweran,* 'to stir'; cp. also O.E. *þwirel,* 'a whisk for whipping cream' &c. Connexion w. words in *st-,* e.g. **stir (I.), storm (I.),** is purely speculative. One of various small hand implements, of which the chief are **a** one with a flat blade, usually pointed, for spreading mortar (*mason's trowel*); Phr. *to lay it on with a trowel,* to flatter grossly; **b** one with a hollowed-out blade and sharpened edge for lifting small plants, stirring and scooping out the earth in planting &c. (*gardener's trowel*).

troy, adj. & n. [1. troi; 2. trɔi], fr. Troyes in France. Only in *troy weight*; *so many ounces troy* &c.; indicating method of weighing, standard of weight used for gold and silver, in pounds, ounces, pennyweights, grains; one pound troy consists of 12 oz.

truancy, n. [1. trōōansi; 2. trūənsi]. Next word & **-cy. a** Act of playing truant; **b** state of being a truant.

truant, n. & adj. [1. trōōant; 2. trúənt]. O. Fr., 'a vagrant'; prob. fr. Celt., cp. W. *truan,* 'wretched'. **1.** n. **a** Person who absents himself from his duties for his own pleasure and without just cause; **b** specif., boy or girl who stays away from school. Phr. *to play truant,* remain away from one's duties, esp. to shirk school. **2.** adj. Shirking duty; staying away from school.

truce, n. [1. trōōs; 2. trūs]. Apparently fr. M.E. *trēwes,* pl. of *trēwe,* 'fidelity, pledge; truce', fr. *trēwe,* 'true, faithful', see **true (I.). 1.** Cessation of hostilities, generally for a considerable period, by arrangement between the commanders of opposing forces, upon terms agreed upon by both parties; *flag of truce,* a white flag borne by party sent to ask for a truce; *truce of God,* suspension of all warfare, enforced by the Mediaeval Church at stated holy seasons. **2.** Cessation, intermittence; esp. in such Phr. as *a truce to jesting* &c.

truck (I.), n. & vb. trans. [1. truk; 2. trak]. M.E. *truken,* 'to exchange'; cp. O. Fr. *troque,* 'exchange, sale, bargain', fr. Flem. *trok,* 'pay; sale'; cp. also A.-Fr. *troquier,* 'to barter'; perh. connected w. Du. *trekken,* 'to draw'; see **trek. 1.** n. **a** Barter, exchange; hence, commerce, intercourse: *to have no truck with a person,* have nothing to do with him; **b** small wares; hence, objects of small value; rubbish, nonsense; *truck system* (of wages), payment in kind instead of in cash; *Truck Acts,* various statutes abolishing the truck system. **2.** vb. (rare) To exchange, barter.

truck (II.), n. & vb. trans., fr. Lat. *trochus,* 'an iron hoop', fr. Gk. *trokhós,* 'a wheel', q.v. under **trochee. 1.** n. **a** Any of various strongly built, low vehicles, running on small, strong wheels, used for conveying heavy weights; e.g. (i.) two-wheeled barrow used by railway porters for moving luggage; (ii.) an open waggon on a railway for transporting heavy goods, coal, iron &c.; **b** the framework and wheels upon which a railway carriage is built. **2.** vb. To place (goods) in or on a truck.

truckage, n. [1. trúkij; 2. trákidž]. Prec. & **-age. a** Conveyance of goods by truck; **b** charge made for this.

truckle (I.), n. [1. trúkl; 2. trákl]. Dimin. of **truck (II.). 1.** (obs.) A small wheel. **2.** A small cylindrical cheese; also *truckle cheese.* **3.** A truckle-bed.

truckle (II.), vb. intrans., fr. prec. Orig., to sleep on a truckle-bed, hence to behave as befits one who sleeps on a truckle-bed, i.e. as one in a servile relation to another. To cringe, behave in a servile, obsequious manner; also *truckle to,* cringe to, submit to (a person) as a servant to his master.

truckle-bed, n. See **truckle (I.).** A small, low bed, esp. one on wheels; formerly one occupied by a servant, which could be pushed under that of his master in the daytime.

truckler, n. [1. trúkler; 2. tráklə]. **truckle (II.)** & **-er.** One who truckles; a servile, obsequious person.

truculence, -cy, n. [1. trúkūlens(i), trōōk-; 2. trákjələns(i), trūk-]. Lat. *truculentia,* 'savageness, harshness'; next word & **-ce, -cy.** Quality of being truculent.

truculent, adj. [1. trúkūlent, trōōkūlent; 2. trákjulənt, trūkjulənt], fr. Lat. *truculentus,* 'savage, cruel, harsh, grim, stern', fr. *truc-,* base of *trux,* w. same meaning; the etymol. is uncertain. Fierce, harsh, overbearing, arrogant, haughtily defiant.

truculently, adv. Prec. & **-ly.** In a truculent manner.

trudge, vb. intrans. & n. [1. truj; 2. tradž]. Origin uncertain; the various forms commonly adduced fr. O.N. or Mod. Scand. dial. appear to agree neither in form nor meaning w. the Engl. word. **1.** vb. To walk along laboriously and wearily; to pursue a tedious and tiring course on foot. **2.** n. **a** A long, tedious, laborious walk; **b** a long walk undertaken for the sake of exercise rather than for pleasure: *let's go for a good trudge.*

trudgen, n. [1. trújen; 2. trádžən], fr. J. Trudgen, swimmer who popularized the stroke. Also *trudgen stroke* (erroneously *trudgeon*), swimming stroke in which the arms are brought over the head alternately and the head kept well down.

true (I.), adj. [1. trōō; 2. trū]. O.E. (*ge*)*trēowe, -trīewe,* 'faithful, trusty, honest', M.E. *trēwe*;

O.S. *triuwi*; Germ. *trau*; Goth. *triggws*; O.N. *tryggr*. **1.** Faithful, loyal, constant, staunch; reverse of *perfidious*: *good men and true*; *true to one's king, principles*; *a man should remain true to his wife*. Phr. *true as steel*. **2. a** In accordance with fact, veracious; contrasted with *false*: *a true story*; *what you say is not true*; Phrs. *to come true*, to happen as was foretold, be realized in fact; *true as gospel*; **b** (more rarely of persons) adhering to, telling, the truth, truthful; **c** *the true*, something which is true, truth: '*Who battled for the True, the Just*' (Tennyson, 'In Mem.' lv. 5). **3.** Genuine, actual, authentic; not a sham, not counterfeited: '*I am the true vine*'; *a true son of his race*; in accordance with a standard, pattern, ideal; exact, accurate: *a true copy, version, reproduction*; *a true Christian*; *true to type*; *weights and measures ought to be strictly true*; *the true time*.

true (II.), adv., fr. prec. **1.** Truly: *tell me true*. **2.** In accordance with ancestral type; of animals, *to breed true*; of plants from seed, *to come true*.

true (III.), vb. trans., fr. **true** (I.). To make true, accurate; to adjust accurately, make straight &c.: *to true (up) a machine* &c.

true bill, n. A bill of indictment found to be based on prima-facie evidence and endorsed as such by a grand jury.

true-blue, adj. & n. **1.** adj. **a** Of a fast and lasting blue colour; **b** (fig., of persons) adhering rigidly and uncompromisingly to a principle, party &c. **2.** n. **a** True-blue colour; **b** (fig.) true-blue person.

true-bred, adj. **1.** Of pure and genuine breed: *a true-bred West Highland terrier*. **2.** (of persons) Well bred; possessing real breeding in manner, character &c.

true-hearted, adj. Faithful, loyal.

true-love, n. O.E. *trēowlufu*, 'faithful love', M.E. *truelove* &c. Beloved being, sweetheart.

true-love, or **true-lover's, knot**, n. Intricate knot of two interlaced bows, hard to untie, symbolical of the lasting nature of love.

trueness, n. [1. trōōnes; 2. trūnis]. **true** (I.) & **-ness**. Quality of being true; **a** truth, veracity; **b** fidelity; **c** accuracy, exactness.

truffle, n. [1. trúfl, trōōfl; 2. tráfl, trūfl]. O. Fr. *truffle, truffe*; origin doubtful; perh. connected w. **tuber**. Round, edible fungus, with pungent flavour, growing below the ground, used for flavouring, esp. in pâté de foie gras.

truism, n. [1. trōōizm; 2. trūizəm]. **true** (I.) & **-ism**. A statement the truth of which is self-evident; a trite saying the truth of which no one disputes, and which it is unnecessary to utter.

trull, n. [1. trul; 2. tral]. Cp. Mod. Germ. *trolle*; variant of **troll** (II.). A slatternly, disreputable woman; a low strumpet.

truly, adv. [1. trōōli; 2. trūli]. **true** (I.) & **-ly**. In a true manner (in various senses); **a** faithfully, loyally: *to serve a person truly*; formula concluding letters: *yours (very) truly*; **b** veraciously: *tell me truly what you think*; **c** genuinely, actually, essentially: *a truly good man*; *to be truly happy*; in Phr. *truly I am puzzled* &c., really, speaking honestly.

trumeau, n. [1. trōōmō; 2. trūmou]. Fr.; etymol. doubtful; possibly of Gmc. origin. (archit.) Piece of wall or pillar between two windows or other openings in a wall.

trump (I.), n. [1. trump; 2. tramp]. M.E. *trumpe, trompe*, Fr. *trompe*; perh. fr. Lat. *triumphus*, see **triumph**. The sound made by a trumpet or a sound resembling this: *the last trump*, that of the day of judgement.

trump (II.), n. & vb. trans. & intrans. Ultimately same word as prec. **1.** n. **a** The last card dealt by the dealer, dealt to himself and left face upwards on the table; this and any card of same suit takes any card of other suits; also any card of a suit declared by bidding &c. to be trumps, as at bridge; **b** a card belonging to the trump suit; **c** (fig.) a good-natured, obliging person: *he behaved like a regular trump*. **2.** vb. To take (a trick) with a trump-card.

trump (III.), vb. trans. Fr. *tromper*, 'to deceive'; orig. 'to blow a trumpet'. (gen.) *Trump up*, to fabricate, concoct, deliberately and with intent to deceive: *to trump up an accusation, a charge, against*.

trump-card, n. **a** Last card in a pack, dealt to himself by the dealer and turned up; see **trump** (II.); **b** (fig.) the chief and most effective means in one's possession of obtaining one's purpose, gaining one's point &c. Phr. *to play one's trump-card*, to make use of one's best weapon for gaining one's end.

trumpery, n. & adj. [1. trúmperi; 2. trámpəri]. Fr. *tromperie*, 'deceit', fr. *tromper*, 'to deceive', same word as that meaning 'to blow a trumpet'. **1.** n. Showy, meretricious object or material, of small value; rubbish; nonsense. **2.** adj. Showy but worthless; rubbishy; weak and ineffective: *trumpery ornaments*; *trumpery arguments*.

trumpet (I.), n. [1. trúmpet; 2. trámpit]. M.E. *trompete*, Fr. *trompette*, dimin. of *trompe*, see **trump** (I.). **1.** Musical wind instrument consisting of a long metal tube, usually bent several times upon itself, having a mouthpiece, a wide end where the air passes out, and stops worked by the fingers which form the different notes. Phr. *to blow one's own trumpet*, praise oneself. **2.** Instrument shaped like a trumpet, esp. an instrument for intensifying sounds, e.g. an *ear-trumpet*, used for speaking to deaf persons; kind of horn for intensifying sounds produced by a phonograph, gramophone &c., or transmitted by wireless. **3.** Sound produced by a trumpet.

trumpet (II.), vb. trans. & intrans., fr. prec. **1.** trans. **a** To proclaim by, or as by, a trumpet; **b** (fig.) to announce widely and loudly: *to trumpet a person's fame abroad*. **2.** intrans. (of elephant) To utter characteristic cry through the trunk.

trumpet-call, n. **a** Call made by sounding a trumpet; **b** (fig.) imperative call or summons to action.

trumpeter, n. [1. trúmpeter; 2. trámpitə]. **trumpet** (II.) & **-er**. **1.** One who plays on a trumpet. **2.** One of several kinds of birds with long neck and legs, found in S. America.

trumpet-flower, n. Name applied to various plants with trumpet-shaped flowers, e.g. honeysuckle, datura &c.

trumpeting, n. [1. trúmpeting; 2. trámpitiŋ]. **trumpet** (II.) & **-ing**. **a** Sound made by blowing a trumpet; **b** cry made by elephants.

trumpet-shaped, adj. Shaped like a trumpet, i.e. hollow, and broadening gradually from a narrow end towards a broad bell, or cup-shaped mouth.

truncal, adj. [1. trúngkl; 2. tráŋkl]. **trunk** & **-al**. Belonging to the trunk or to the body.

truncate, vb. trans. & adj. [1. trungkāt; 2. traŋkéit]. Lat. *truncātum*, P.P. of *truncāre*, 'to cut off'. See **trunk**. **1.** vb. To cut off, shorten, lop. **2.** adj. Shortened as by lopping; e.g. of spiral shells the point of which is broken or worn off.

truncated, adj. [1. trungkāted; 2. traŋkéitid]. Prec. & **-ed**. **a** Shortened by, or as though by, lopping; maimed; **b** (of writings, speeches &c.) abbreviated, drastically reduced in length, esp. in such a way as to produce effect of incompleteness; mutilated.

truncation, n. [1. trungkāshun; 2. traŋkéiʃən]. **truncate** & **-ion**. Act of truncating.

truncheon, n. [1. trúnshun; 2. tránʃən]. M.E. *tronchoun*, 'broken shaft', O. Fr. *tronchon*, variant of Fr. *tronçon*, fr. L. Lat. formation fr. Lat. *truncus*, 'stem, stock, trunk of a tree' &c.; see **trunk**. A short thick staff or cudgel, esp. one used by policeman; the baton of office of the Earl Marshal.

trundle, n. & vb. trans. & intrans. [1. trúndl; 2. trándl]. O.E. *tryndel, trendel*, 'a ring, a circle, a wheel', cp. *trind(e)*, 'a round lump', & *trendlian*, 'to make round'; cp. **trend** (I.). **1.** n. A small broad, strong wheel. **2.** vb. **a** trans. To cause to roll along, to bowl: *to trundle a hoop, a cask* &c.; **b** intrans., to roll, be capable of being rolled.

trundle-bed, n. A low bed on wheels, capable of being easily wheeled about; a truckle-bed.

trunk, n. [1. trungk; 2. traŋk]. Fr. *tronc*, Lat. *truncus*, (1) adj., 'maimed, mutilated'; hence, (2) 'stem or bole of a tree', orig. 'the stem with the boughs lopped off'; etymol. doubtful; possibly fr. same base as O.E. *þringan*, 'to press, crowd', see **throng**. **1.** The main stem of a tree. **2.** The body of a man or an animal, not including the head or limbs. **3.** The main body or line (of railways, telephones; also of an artery) as distinct from side-lines and branches; cp. *trunk call* (on telephone). **4.** Receptacle, with lid on hinges, made of hide, leather, or other materials; esp. as used by travellers for transporting their clothes &c. **5.** (for **trump** (I.), cp. Fr. *trompe*) The proboscis, or long tube-like prehensile organ, formed by extension of the nose of an elephant. **6.** (pl.) *Trunks*, trunk-hose.

trunk-hose, n. Short full breeches covering the lower part of the trunk and part of the thighs, as worn in 16th and 17th cents.

trunk-line, n. Main line of a railway, telegraph, or telephone system.

trunnel, n. [1. trúnl; 2. tránəl]. Corrupt variant of tree-nail.

trunnion, n. [1. trúniun; 2. tránian], fr. Fr. *trognon*, 'core of a fruit'; according to Meyer-Lübke, formed fr. Lat. *truncus*, see **trunk**. One of two parts, or gudgeons, projecting horizontally from either side of a cannon, or other heavy cylindrical apparatus, serving as pivots upon which it rests and by means of which its angle can be altered.

truss (I.), n. [1. trus; 2. tras]. Fr. *trousse*, 'bundle', O. Fr. *tros, tourse*, fr. Lat. *thyrsus*, 'stalk, stem', fr. Gk. *thúrsos*, see **thyrsus**. **1.** A bundle, package; esp. *a truss of hay, straw*, oblong package of compressed hay or straw tightly tied with bands of coarse string which pass round it a short distance from either end; *a truss of hay* or *straw* is a specific measure, the former being 60 lb. (new), the latter 36 lb. **2.** A cluster of blossom growing on a single stem. **3.** Combination of timbers or of iron rods forming a rigid framework, used in building and engineering. **4.** Apparatus used to give support by applying continuous pressure in cases of rupture.

truss (II.), vb. trans.; see prec. **1.** To bind up into a truss or bundle. **2. a** To tie tightly and secure wings of (a fowl) close to the body before cooking; **b** *truss up*, to tie up limbs close to the body and hang up. **3.** To support (part of building) by a truss, framework, girder &c.

trust (I.), n. [1. trust; 2. trast]. M.E. *trust, trist*; prob. Scand., cp. O.N. *traust*, 'confidence'; Swed. *tröst*, 'consolation'; cogn. w. Goth. *trausti*, 'a covenant', & **true** (I.). **1.** Firm conviction in another's reliability, integrity, honour; implicit confidence, faith, reliance: '*Put not your trust in princes*'. Phr. *to take something on trust*, to believe that it is what it appears or is asserted to be, without looking closely into the evidence for oneself. **2.** Duty or task, responsibility, committed to, imposed upon, one, which one is morally bound to undertake: *I regard it as a sacred trust to fulfil my father's last wishes*. **3.** Something committed to one's charge and care, to be used for the benefit of another; specif. (law) **a** the vesting of the legal ownership of property in a person or persons, *trustees*, for the benefit of another or others, the *cestui que trust*; **b** property so vested. **4.** A combination of several commercial firms or businesses, effected for the purpose of regulating conditions of business and the price of commodities; or, less justifiably, for the purpose of obtaining control of a particular branch of business activity, and a monopoly of certain articles of commerce.

trust (II.), vb. trans. & intrans. M.E. *trusten* &c.; see prec. **A.** trans. **1.** To place reliance, confidence, in; to rely upon; have faith in integrity of: *I trust him as I would myself*; *not a man to be trusted.* **2.** To allow to do something, or go somewhere, with full assurance that one's confidence will not be abused: *he may be trusted to do the work well*; *I wouldn't trust that man round the corner.* **3. a** To entrust (a person) with something: *I should not like to trust him with large sums of money*; **b** to entrust (a thing) to the care of: *I wouldn't trust my watch to him.* **4.** To have a confident expectation that something will happen, or does exist, or is in the condition that one desires; to hope: *I trust (that) nothing will prevent our meeting*; *I do trust you will be successful*; *I trust this is the book you wanted*; also absol., *you are feeling better, I trust.* **5.** To have a firm conviction that, to believe: '*The knight's bones are dust, And his good sword rust, His soul is with the saints, I trust*' (Coleridge, 'Knight's Tomb'). **B.** intrans. To perform the mental act of trusting: *it is hard to trust where respect is lacking.*

trustee, n. [1. trustḗ; 2. trastī]. **trust (I.)** & **-ee.** **1.** One to whom a trust is committed: *we are trustees of our country's honour.* **2.** One holding property in trust for another.

trustful, adj. [1. trústfool; 2. trástful]. **trust (I.)** & **-ful.** Disposed to trust, confiding.

trustfully, adv. Prec. & **-ly.** In a trustful manner.

trustiness, n. [1. trústines; 2. trástinis]. **trusty** & **-ness.** Quality of being trusty.

trustless, adj. [1. trústles; 2. trástlis]. **trust (I.)** & **-less.** Not to be trusted; unreliable, disloyal.

trustworthiness, n. [1. trústwẽrdhines; 2. trástwɅ̄ðinis]. See next word & **-ness.** Reliability, dependability.

trustworthy, adj. [1. trústwẽrdhi; 2. trástwɅ̄ði]. **trust (I.)** & **worthy (I.).** **a** (of persons) Worthy of trust; reliable, dependable, honourable; **b** (of statements) worthy of credence, consonant with fact, accurate.

trusty, adj. [1. trústi; 2. trásti]. **trust (I.)** & **-y.** **a** (of persons) Deserving to be trusted; faithful, loyal, staunch: *a trusty servant*; **b** (archaic, of things) reliable, to be counted on to serve their purpose: *my trusty sword, steed.*

truth, n. [1. trōōth; 2. trūþ]. O.E. *trēoþ*, *trīewþ*, 'good faith, fidelity', M.E. *treuþe*; see **true (I.)** & **-th.** **1.** Moral quality of being true and honest; sincerity, loyalty, trustiness: *to doubt a person's truth.* **2.** Conformity to fact and reality to the utmost extent that these are discoverable by the human mind; verity. **3.** Conformity to fact in statement; veracity; the reverse of *a lie*: *to tell, speak, the truth*; *the truth is, you ought never to have come.* **4. a** Ascertained fact in science; sound, reliable doctrine in religion, esp. as known by revelation: *biological truth*; *Gospel, Christian, truth*; **b** an established principle or law: *the great truths of morals, science, philosophy* &c. **5.** Accuracy, exactness, in formation and adjustment in mechanism; esp. in Phr. *out of truth.*

truthful, adj. [1. trōōthfool; 2. trūþful]. Prec. & **-ful.** **a** (of persons) Habitually speaking the truth, veracious; **b** (of statements) in accordance with the truth, true.

truthfully, adv. Prec. & **-ly.** In a truthful manner; in accordance with truth; with truth, veraciously.

truthfulness, n. See prec. & **-ness.** Quality of being true; veracity.

try (I.), vb. trans. & intrans. [1. trī; 2. trai]. M.E. *trien*, 'to select'; cp. Fr. *trier*, 'to set apart, select', fr. L. Lat. *tritāre*, 'to rub down, separate the grain from the husk'; formed fr. *trīt-*, P.P. type of *terere*, 'to rub, grind, thresh', q.v. under **trite.** **A.** trans. **1.** (obs.) To pick out (the best) from the rest; to separate one sort from another. **2.** Also *try out*, to separate the dross from the ore, impure matter from the pure substance; to refine; to assay, test purity of (metals); also of whale blubber, so as to extract the oil. **3. a** To test (qualities), put to the test or proof: *to try one's skill, strength*; **b** to put a strain upon; make demands upon: *his patience, courage, was severely tried*; *it tries the eyes to read in a bad light*; **c** to afflict, cause suffering to: *he has been very sorely tried*; *rheumatism tries me a good deal.* **4. a** To make use of in order to test properties of, to find out by using how far something will serve one's purpose, prove a remedy, be to one's taste &c.: *I have tried all the makes of safety razor blades*; *try our pills for dyspepsia*; *have you tried tea with a slice of lemon in it?*; **b** *try on*, (i.) to test fit of (clothes) by putting them on: *to try a coat on*; *to try on a new coat*; (ii.) *to try it on*, to do something audacious, to test how far one will be allowed to go. **5.** To make an effort to do, to attempt: *he tried an impossible feat*; *don't try more than you can do.* **6.** To test by means of experiment, to carry out an experiment in order to discover: *try which is the highest note you can sing*; *try how far you can jump.* **7. a** To conduct judicial inquiry into, hear arguments concerning, in a court of law: *to try a case*; **b** to conduct trial of, inquire into innocence or guilt of: *to try a criminal.* **B.** intrans. To endeavour, exert oneself, make an attempt or effort (to do something): *I doubt if I can do it, but I'll try*; *I have never tried to ski*; *he makes very little progress though he tries hard*; *try to please your employers, to do your duty*; frequently *try and* (in colloq. speech): *try and be punctual*; *now try and repeat it correctly*; *do try and behave better*; Phr. *to try one's best, one's hardest*, do as well as one can; use one's utmost efforts.

try (II.), n. See prec. **1.** (colloq.) An attempt: *have a try at.* **2.** (Rugby football) Touch down behind opponent's goal and within the touch-in-goal, on which the ball is brought out and a place kick is taken aimed between the goal-posts, above the cross-bar; a try, if not thus converted, counts 3 points, as opposed to 5 for a goal.

trying, adj. [1. trīing; 2. tráiiŋ], fr. Pres. Part. of **try (I.).** **1.** Tending to try, test, put a strain upon; (i.) provoking, exasperating: *trying to the temper*; *a trying person to deal with*; (ii.) exacting: *a trying bit of work.* **2. a** Fatiguing, irksome, wearisome: *a trying journey*; **b** afflicting, grievous, painful: *a trying time, situation, experience.*

trypanosome, n. [1. trípanosōm; 2. trípanəsoum], fr. Gk. *trúpanon*, 'borer, piercer', see **trepan (I.)**, & *sôma*, 'body', see **somatic.** A minute whip-like parasite, belonging to the genus *Trypanosoma*, transmitted to the blood of man and animals by the bite of the tsetse-fly, q.v., and causing disease (see below).

trypanosomiasis, n. [1. trìpanōsōmíasis; 2. trìpənousoumáiəsis]. Prec. & **-iasis.** Disease caused by presence of a trypanosome in the blood, specif., sleeping sickness in man, nagana in cattle.

trypsin, n. [1. trípsin; 2. trípsin]. Invented Germ. word fr. Gk. *trúein*, 'to rub, consume', cogn. w. Lat. *terere*, see **trite**, & **pepsin.** (physiol.) A digestive ferment or enzyme formed in the pancreatic juice.

trysail, n. [1. trísl; 2. tráisl]. **try (I.)** & **sail (I.).** A small fore-and-aft sail attached to a gaff.

tryst, n. & vb. trans. & intrans. [1. trīst, trist; 2. traist, trist]. M.E., fr. O. Fr. *triste, tristre*, 'waiting or watching place'; prob. of Scand. origin, see **trust (I.).** **1.** n. **a** Engagement to meet; **b** agreed upon, appointed, meeting-place. **2.** vb. To promise to meet at agreed time and place.

tsar. See **czar.**

tsetse-fly, n. [1. tsétsi flī; 2. tsétsi flai]. Cape Du. fr. Native Afr. An African fly, *Glossina*, which acts as intermediate host of the parasitic trypanosome, q.v., and thus infects the blood of man and animals, one species being the carrier of sleeping sickness, to man, another of nagana, q.v., or tsetse-fly disease, to cattle.

tuatara, n. [1. tooatáhra; 2. tuətárə]. Maori. A large lizard-like reptile, genus *Sphenodon*, once common in New Zealand.

tub, n. & vb. intrans. [1. tub; 2. tab]. M.E. *tubbe*, cp. Du. *tobbe*; perh. fr. Lat. *tubus*, see **tube.** **1.** n. **a** Wooden vessel made in various shapes, often in form of a cask; used for various purposes, e.g. *wash-tub, butter-tub, rain-water tub* &c.; **b** (colloq.) a bath: *to take one's tub, a cold tub, every morning*; **c** boat used in practising rowing; **d** a kind of bucket or box used for conveying coal or ore in mines from the workings to the shaft. **2.** vb. (colloq.) To take a bath.

tuba, n. [1. tûba; 2. tjúbə]. Lat., 'trumpet'; see **tube.** **a** A type of brass wind musical instrument with deep tone, including the bombardon and euphonium; **b** a reed stop in an organ.

tubal, adj. [1. tûbl; 2. tjúbl]. **tube** & **-al.** Pertaining to, connected with, a tube.

tubby, adj. [1. túbi; 2. tábi]. **tub** & **-y.** **1.** Shaped like a tub; fat, squat, and round. **2.** (of musical instruments) Lacking resonance, giving out a dull sound.

tube, n. [1. tūb; 2. tjūb]. Lat. *tubus*, 'a pipe, tube'; cogn. w. *tuba*, 'trumpet'; etymol. uncertain. **1. a** Long hollow cylinder, or pipe, of any size, of various materials, and used for many purposes: *glass tube, metal tube*; *a tube of paint*; *vacuum tube* &c.; **b** an organ of the body in form of a tube; esp. *bronchial tubes.* **2.** Underground electric railway system in London, the lines of which are laid in enormous steel tubes.

tuber, n. [1. tûber; 2. tjúbə]. Lat., 'a bump, swelling, protuberance'; contains the same base **tu-* as **tumid, tumour**, w. different formative elements. Modified part of stem of certain plants, such as the potato and Jerusalem artichoke, containing buds whence new plants are formed.

tubercle, n. [1. tûberkl; 2. tjúbəkl]. Lat. *tuberculum*, dimin. of **tuber.** **1.** Small rounded protuberance on part of an animal or plant. **2.** (pathol.) Small granular morbid growth in the substance of an organ of the body, such as the lungs, causing the disease known as *tuberculosis.*

tubercular, adj. [1. tūbẽrkūlar; 2. tjubɅ́kjulə]. Prec. & **-ar.** **a** Connected with, of the nature of, a tubercle; **b** affected by tuberculosis; tuberculous.

tubercularize, vb. trans. [1. tūbẽrkūlarīz; 2. tjubɅ́kjuləraiz]. Prec. & **-ize.** To infect with tubercle or tuberculosis.

tuberculosis, n. [1. tūbẽrkūlṓsis; 2. tjubɅ́kjulóusis]. Formed fr. Lat. *tubercul-*, see **tubercle**, & **-osis.** Infectious disease of the tissues of an organ of the body caused by the tubercle bacillus, which produces disintegration of the organ or part affected, as *pulmonary tuberculosis*, phthisis &c.

tuberculous, adj. [1. tūbẽrkūlus; 2. tjubɅ́kjuləs]. See prec. & **-ous.** **a** Having tubercles; **b** affected by tuberculosis.

tuberose, n. [1. tûberōz; 2. tjúbərouz]. Orig., an adj., fr. **tuber** & **-ose.** See also **tuberous.** Bulbous plant, *Polianthes tuberosa*, resembling a lily, cultivated in gardens for its spikes of blossom.

tuberosity, n. [1. tûberósiti; 2. tjúbərɔ́siti]. See prec., **tuberous**, & **-ity.** Quality of being tuberous.

tuberous, adj. [1. tûberus; 2. tjúbərəs]. **tuber** & **-ous.** **a** Producing, growing from, tubers; **b** covered with rounded excrescences; knobby.

tubing, n. [1. tûbing; 2. tjúbiŋ]. **tube** & **-ing.** **1.** A series, collection, system, of tubes. **2.** A length, portion, piece, of tube: *india-rubber tubing.*

tubular, adj. [1. tûbūlar; 2. tjúbjulə]. Lat. *tubulus*, dimin. of *tubus*, 'tube', & **-ar.** **a** Having the form of a tube or pipe; **b** provided with tubes.

tubule, n. [1. tûbūl; 2. tjúbjūl]. Lat. *tubulus*, see prec. A small tube.

tuck (I.), vb. trans. & intrans. [1. tuk; 2. tak]. M.E. *tucken*, 'to pull, draw'; usually derived by dictionary makers fr. Continental Gmc.; but it is possibly fr. O.E. *tūcian*, 'to afflict', the primary meaning of wh. may well have been 'to pluck, tug, pull'; cp. provinc. Engl. 'to tuck peas, beans, fruit &c.', i.e. to pluck, gather. The word is prob. an anct. doublet fr. base **tug*-, 'pull, draw' &c. See **tow** (**I.**) & **tug** (**I.**). **A.** trans. **1.** To gather (loose folds of cloth or garments, loose ends of cord, line &c.) together tightly, and push away out of sight behind other folds, or under something firmly fixed; also *tuck in*: *tuck one's handkerchief into one's pocket*; *tuck up*, to fold back and fasten firmly, as to *tuck up one's shirt-sleeves*; *to tuck a child up in bed*, pull the sheets and blankets well over him and push the ends under mattress; *tuck away*, to place securely and neatly; also to hide away where discovery is difficult: *a great deal of learning is tucked away in the notes* (*of the book*). **2.** (new formation from n.) To put a tuck or tucks in (a sleeve &c.). **B.** intrans. **1.** To make tucks. **2.** (colloq.) **a** *Tuck in*, to eat hungrily and copiously; **b** *tuck into*, trans.

tuck (**II.**), n., fr. prec. **1.** Permanent fold or hem, made and sewed, in a skirt, in the sleeve of a shirt &c. **2.** (schoolboy slang) Food, esp. food of an attractive character, eaten rather from greed than hunger; sweetmeats, cakes; tasty meats, delicacies.

tuck (**III.**), n. Fr. *toquer*, Nthn. form of *toucher*, see **touch** (**I.**), & cp. **tocsin.** The sound, roll, of a drum.

tucker, n. [1. túker; 2. tákə]. **tuck** (**I.**) & **-er.** **1.** Piece of linen formerly worn by women, folded across the breast; now only in Phr. *one's best bib and tucker*, best, smartest, clothes. **2.** Device for making tucks in clothes.

tucket, n. [1. túket; 2. tákit]. Cp. Ital. *toccata*, 'a prelude', P.P. fem. of *toccare*; see **touch.** A flourish of trumpets, a fanfare.

tuck-shop, n. Shop at a school where 'tuck' is sold; a confectioner's, a sweet shop.

-tude, suff. Lat. *-tūdō*, genit. *-tūdinis*; suff. used to form abstract ns. fr. Lat. adjs. or P.P.'s: *plenitude*, fr. Lat. *plēnum*, 'full', &c.

Tudor, adj. [1. tūdor; 2. tjūdə], fr. name of a family descended fr. Owen Tudor, members of wh. occupied the throne of England & included all monarchs fr. Henry VII. to Elizabeth inclusive. Pertaining to, made in, characteristic. of, the age of the Tudors: *Tudor architecture, style* &c.; *Tudor rose*, one combining the red rose of Lancaster and the white rose of York, used as royal badge of England after marriage of Henry VII. (of Lancaster) with Elizabeth, heiress of York.

Tuesday, n. [1. tūzdi; 2. tjūzdi]. O.E. *Tīwesdæg*, M.E. *Tēwesday*, fr. *Tīw*, the name of an anct. Gmc. war god; the name is cogn. w. Gk. *Zeús*, Lat. *Jū-piter*; see **jovial** & **Jupiter** & **deity.** Third day of the week, between Monday and Wednesday.

tufa, n. [1. tūfa; 2. tjūfə]. Cp. Ital. *tufo*, 'soft', fr. Lat. *tōfus, tōphus*, 'volcanic rock'; Oscan-Umbrian loan-word; origin unknown. Porous rock of volcanic origin, also called 'tuff'.

tufaceous, adj. [1. tūfáshus; 2. tjūféiʃəs]. Prec. & **-aceous.** Connected with, resembling, tufa.

tuff. See **tufa.**

tuft (**I.**), n. [1. tuft; 2. taft]. M.E. *tuft*; origin doubtful; perh. connected w. **top** (**I.**). **1.** A bunch, bundle, cluster, of anything resembling threads, fastened together at the base or growing thickly from a common point: *a tuft of feathers, grass, hair.* **2.** (obs. slang) A person of importance, a swell; from the *tuft* or gold tassel formerly worn in their college caps by noblemen at English universities.

tuft (**II.**), vb. trans. & intrans., fr. prec. **a** trans. To furnish with tufts; **b** intrans., to form, grow, into tufts.

tufted, adj. [1. túfted; 2. táftid], fr. P.P. of prec. **a** Having, provided with, a tuft or tufts; **b** growing thickly in tufts.

tuft-hunter, n. See **tuft** (**I.**), **2.** (archaic) One who seeks the acquaintance of, and behaves obsequiously to, persons of importance, wealth, or distinguished birth, formerly called 'tufts'; a toady, a sycophant.

tufty, adj. [1. túfti; 2. táfti]. **tuft** (**I.**) & **-y.** Growing in, forming, tufts.

tug (**I.**), vb. trans. & intrans. [1. tug; 2. tag]. M.E. *tuggen*; Scand., cp. O.N. *toga*, 'to pull'; cogn. w. **tow** (**I.**). **1.** trans. **a** To pull violently; to exert effort, to strain, in pulling; to haul; **b** to pull suddenly and jerkily. **2.** intrans. To exert effort in pulling; often *tug at.*

tug (**II.**), n., fr. prec. **1.** The act of tugging; a sudden, violent pull. **2.** Small steamer with powerful engines, used to tow large vessels into, or out of, a harbour &c.

tug of war, n. [1. tùg uv wŏr; 2. tàg əv wɔ́]. Contest of strength in which each of two parties, pulling in different directions on the same rope, attempts to pull the other across a line marked on the ground.

tuition, n. [1. tūíshun; 2. tjuíʃən]. Lat. *tuitiōn-(em)*, 'a looking after, guardianship, defence'; fr. *tuit-(um)*, P.P. of *tuēri*, 'to look after, guard, protect'; see **tutor** (**I.**). **1.** (archaic or obs.) Guardianship, care of a pupil or ward. **2.** **a** Act of teaching; **b** instruction given by a tutor or teacher.

tulip, n. [1. tūlip; 2. tjūlip]. Fr. *tulipe*, O. Fr. *tulipan*, cp. Ital. *tulipano*, fr. Turk. *tulbend*, 'turban', fr. supposed resemblance of flower to this; see **turban.** Liliaceous plant with many species, genus *Tulipa*, growing from bulbs, and having bright-coloured bell-shaped flowers, supported on stiff stalks.

tulip root, n. Disease in oats characterized by a swelling in the stem resembling the bulb of a tulip.

tulip tree, n. N. American tree, *Liriodendron tulipiferum*, allied to the magnolia, with red or yellow flowers resembling those of the tulip.

tulip wood, n. Wood of tulip tree, used in cabinet-making.

tulle, n. [1. tool; 2. tul], fr. name of a town in France. Soft, silky material, used for making women's garments.

tulwar, n. [1. túlwar; 2. tálwə]. Hindi. Kind of curved sabre used among N. Indian tribes.

tumble (**I.**), vb. intrans. & trans. [1. túmbl; 2. támbl]. Apparently a freq. form fr. O.E. *tumbian*, 'to dance, tumble'; cp. also Du. *tuimelen*, 'to fall', & Swed. *tumla.* **A.** intrans. **1.** **a** To fall heavily and clumsily; also *tumble down*; *tumble over*, (i.) to fall down, be upset; (ii.) to stumble, trip up over (an obstacle): *to tumble over a hassock*; **b** to move forward in a disorderly, violent manner, to rush helter-skelter: *to tumble into a room anyhow.* **2.** To toss about, roll over, as with restlessness and discomfort: often *to tumble and toss.* **3.** To turn somersaults, as an acrobat. **4.** (slang) *Tumble to* (a suggestion &c.), to take in, grasp, understand. **B.** trans. **1.** To cause to tumble; to overturn, upset, throw down; frequently, *tumble over* (*something*): *his horse tumbled him over a bank*; also *tumble out*: *to tumble passengers out of a carriage.* **2.** To put into confusion, disturb, rumple, ruffle: *to tumble a bed, one's clothes, hair* &c.

tumble (**II.**), n., fr. prec. Act of tumbling; **a** a fall, a toss; **b** an acrobat's somersault &c.

tumble-down, adj. [1. túmbl doun; 2. támbl daun]. Dilapidated, ruinous, shabby: *a tumble-down house.*

tumbler, n. [1. túmbler; 2. támblə]. **tumble** (**I.**) & **-er.** **1.** An acrobat who throws somersaults. **2.** Kind of domestic pigeon which makes movements resembling somersaults while in flight. **3.** One of several movable portions of the internal mechanism of a lock, which has to be made to occupy a certain position by the working of the key before the bolt can be shot. **4.** Drinking-glass without a foot, standing flat on its own bottom.

tumbrel, -il, n. [1. túmbril; 2. támbril]. Connected w. Fr. *tomber*, 'to fall', of Gmc. origin; cp. O.E. *tumbian*, 'to dance, tumble', & see **tumble** (**I.**). **a** A heavy cart, made to tip backwards from the shafts, for carting and shooting dung and refuse &c.; **b** name given by historians to the carts in which the victims of the French Revolution were taken to the guillotine; **c** light two-wheeled military cart for carrying ammunition, tools &c.

tumefacient, adj. [1. tūmefásient; 2. tjūmiféiʃiənt]. Lat., Pres. Part. of *tumefacere*, 'to cause to swell, to inflate'; see **tumid** & **fact.** Causing swelling.

tumefaction, n. [1. tūmefákshun; 2. tjūmifǽkʃən]. Lat., fr. *tumefact-(um)*, P.P. type of *tumefacere*, see prec., & **-ion.** **1.** The process of swelling. **2.** A swelling, a tumour.

tumefy, vb. trans. & intrans. [1. tūmefī; 2. tjūmifai]. Fr. *tuméfier*; see under **tumid** & **-fy.** **a** trans. To cause to swell; **b** intrans., to swell up.

tumescent, adj. [1. tūmésent; 2. tjumésənt]. Lat., Pres. Part. of *tumescere*, 'to begin to swell, swell up', inchoat. of *tumēre*, 'to swell'; see **tumid.** Inclined to swell up; slightly swollen.

tumid, adj. [1. tūmid; 2. tjūmid]. Lat. *tumidus*, 'swollen, protuberant'; cp. Lat. *tumēre*, 'to swell'; *tumor*, 'swelling, protuberance', see **tumour**; *tumulus*, 'raised heap of earth'; w. this base etymologists connect a large number of words; O.E. *þūma*, see **thumb**; O.E. *þēoh*, see **thigh**; see further **thousand** & **taurus.** Puffed up, swollen, inflated (in material and non-material senses).

tumidity, n. [1. tūmíditi; 2. tjūmíditi]. Prec. & **-ity.** State of being tumid.

tumour, n. [1. tūmor; 2. tjūmə]. Lat. *tumor*, 'a swelling; protuberance'; see under **tumid.** A swelling in some part of the body; an abnormal growth and increase of size in some of the tissues, whether benign or malignant.

tumult, n. [1. tūmult; 2. tjūmalt]. Lat. *tumultus*, 'an uproar, violent commotion, disturbance'; fr. base **tum*-, 'to swell', see **tumid.** **1.** **a** Uproar, confused noise, as that made by the voices and movements of large crowds; hence, **b** the noise of a disturbance; a disturbance, commotion, turbulence. **2.** Profound and violent disturbance, agitation, commotion, **a** of the forces of nature; **b** of the mind; great mental excitement and confusion.

tumultuary, adj. [1. tūmúltūari; 2. tjumáltjuəri]. Lat. *tumultuārius*, see prec. & **-ary.** Of the nature of a tumult; confused; agitated.

tumultuous, adj. [1. tūmúltūus; 2. tjumáltjuəs]. Lat. *tumultuōsus*, 'full of bustle and confusion; turbulent, restless'; see **tumult** & **-ous.** **1.** Characterized by tumult and disturbance; uproarious, noisy: *a tumultuous meeting, assembly.* **2.** Greatly agitated, deeply stirred: *tumultuous passions.*

tumultuously, adv. Prec. & **-ly.** In a tumultuous manner.

tumultuousness, n. See prec. & **-ness.** State, quality, of being tumultuous.

tumulus, n., pl. **tumuli** [1. tūmūlus, -ī; 2. tjūmjuləs, -ai]. Lat., 'heap of earth, a mound'; fr. base 'to swell', as in **tumid** &c. An artificially raised mound, esp. an ancient burial mound or barrow.

tun, n. & vb. trans. [1. tun; 2. tan]. O.E. *tunne*, 'a cask'; also in O.H.G. &c.; origin doubtful. **1.** n. A large cask or vat for storing, also for fermenting, beer and wine; formerly a specific measure of 252 gallons. **2.** vb. To enclose and store in a tun.

tuna, n. [1. tūna; 2. tjūnə]. Span. form of **tunny.** The great tunny, esp. of the Pacific, Californian, coast of N. America.

tunable, adj. [1. tūnabl; 2. tjūnəbl]. **tune** (**II.**) & **-able.** **a** Capable of being tuned; **b** capable of yielding a tune; hence, melodious: *a tunable voice.*

tunableness, n. Prec. & **-ness.** Quality of being tunable.

tunably, adv. See prec. & **-ly.** Harmoniously, melodiously.

tundra, n. [1. túndra; 2. tándrə]. Russ. Barren plain in N. Russia or other arctic region, constituting a frozen, or partially frozen, desert, which produces only mosses and lichens in the way of vegetation.

tundun, n. [1. túndun; 2. tándan]. Native. The bull-roarer, q.v., of Australian aborigines.

tune (I.), n. [1. tūn; 2. tjūn]. M.E., fr. A.-Fr. *tune*, fr. O. Fr. *ton*; variant of **tone (I.).** **1. a** Air, melody, with or without harmony: *a good, a poor, a catchy, popular, tune*; *a difficult tune to remember*; **b** quality of having a well-marked air: *the piece has very little tune about it.* **2.** Harmony, agreement in tone, pitch &c., with a definite standard: *to sing in, out of, tune*; *your fiddle isn't in tune.* Phrs. (fig.) *in tune, out of tune, with* (one's surroundings &c.), congenial, uncongenial; *to be charged to the tune of* (such an amount), implying extortionate charge; *to sing another tune, change one's tune*, change one's way of talking; as from respectful to insolent or vice versa &c.

tune (II.), vb. trans. & intrans., fr. prec. **A.** trans. **1. a** To bring (musical instrument) into tune, adjust the pitch of the strings &c. to the required degree; **b** *tune up*, to bring to a desired degree, or standard, of efficiency, excellence, health &c. **2.** To bring (wireless apparatus) into relation with waves of a certain length. **B.** intrans. **1.** *Tune in*, to tune wireless apparatus (see **resonance**). **2.** *Tune up*, **a** (of instruments in orchestra) to start tuning; **b** to begin to play or to sing.

tuneful, adj. [1. tū́nfool; 2. tjū́nful]. **tune (I.)** & **-ful. a** Exhibiting a well-marked air; **b** melodious, harmonious; producing song and melody: *the tuneful choir of birds* &c.

tunefully, adv., fr. prec. Prec. & **-ly.** In a tuneful manner.

tunefulness, n. See prec. & **-ness.** Quality of being tuneful.

tuneless, adj. [1. tū́nles; 2. tjū́nlis]. **tune (I.)** & **-less. a** Lacking an air; harsh, unmelodious; **b** not producing melody, unmusical.

tuner, n. [1. tū́ner; 2. tjū́nə]. **tune (II.)** & **-er. 1.** One who tunes musical instruments: *piano tuner* &c. **2. a** Device attached to pipe for tuning an organ; **b** device for tuning electrical current &c.

tungsten, n. [1. túngsten; 2. táŋstən]. Swed., fr. *tung*, 'heavy', & *sten*, 'stone'. A rare metallic element, found in combination with other minerals, grey in colour and very hard, and only fusible at very high temperatures, used in an alloy of steel and for making the filaments of incandescent electric lamps.

tungstic, tungstous, adj. [1. túngstik, túngstus; 2. táŋstik, táŋstəs], fr. prec. & **-ic, -ous.** (chem.) Of, pertaining to, tungsten.

tunic, n. [1. tū́nik; 2. tjū́nik]. Lat. *tunica*, 'thin undergarment with sleeves' (worn by both sexes); also 'coating, membrane, husk'; fr. early form **ktun-ica*, Heb. loan-word; cp. also Gk. *khitṓn*, fr. Heb. *kithonet*, 'garment worn next skin', cp. **chiton. 1.** Any of various loose garments, esp. as worn by the ancients or modern Orientals. **2.** Regimental coat worn by British officers and private soldiers; the name is properly restricted to one particular kind of coat, namely, that worn for full dress, made of scarlet cloth. **3.** Natural covering, integument, husk.

Tunicata, n. pl. [1. tūnikā́tā; 2. tjūnikéitə]. Lat., 'covered by a tunic, coated'; see prec. Group of marine animals with thick outer covering, membrane, or tunic.

tunicate, adj. & n. [1. tū́nikāt; 2. tjū́nikeit]. See prec. **1.** adj. (bot. and zool.) Having several coats or layers of covering. **2.** n. Member of the group of Tunicata.

tunicle, n. [1. tū́nikl; 2. tjū́nikl]. Lat. *tunicula*, dimin. of *tunica*, see **tunic. 1.** Close-fitting vestment, smaller than the dalmatic, worn by deacons at Eucharist, and by bishops under the dalmatic when pontificating. **2.** Thin, natural, outer covering.

tuning-fork, n. [1. tū́ning fork; 2. tjū́niŋ fōk]. Instrument of steel with two prongs, which, on being struck, gives out a particular note; used as a standard in tuning musical instruments.

tunnel, n. & vb. trans. & intrans. [1. túnl; 2. tánl]. O. Fr. *tonnel*, dimin. of *tonne*, see **tun. 1.** n. A passage, usually cylindrical in form, cut underground; e.g. one cut through a hill or mountain for the laying of a railway line &c. **2.** vb. **a** trans. To cut a tunnel through: *to tunnel a hill* &c.; **b** intrans., to cut a tunnel.

tunny, n., also **tunny fish** [1. túni (fish); 2. táni (fiʃ)]. Ital. *tonno*, Lat. *thunnus*, fr. Gk. *thúnnos*, also *thū́nos*; origin obscure; prob., according to Boisacq, a pre-Hellenic loan-word. Large, edible fish of the mackerel family, with somewhat oily flesh, found in Mediterranean, also, as the great tunny, *Thunnus thynnus*, in the Atlantic, where it is known as 'horse-mackerel', and in the N. Pacific, the tuna.

tup, n. [1. tup; 2. tap]. M.E. *tuppe*; origin doubtful. A ram.

tu quoque, n. [1. tū kwṓkwe; 2. tjū kwóukwi]. Lat., 'thou also'. A retort of 'you are, or did, the same as I', so you can't blame me.

Turanian, adj. [1. tūrā́nian; 2. tjuréiniən]. Of race and language, Ural-Altaic, q.v.

turban, n. [1. tėrban; 2. tə́bən]. Earlier *turbant, turband*; cp. Ital. *turbante*, fr. Turk. *tulbend.* See also **tulip. 1.** Head-dress worn by men in the East consisting of a long strip of silk, or cotton cloth, wound round and round the head. **2.** Woman's head-dress, resembling the Oriental turban, worn at end of 18th and beginning of 19th cent.

turbary, n. [1. tėrbəri; 2. tə́bəri]. Low Lat. *turbāria*, 'place where peat is dug', fr. *turba*, 'turf, peat'; see **turf. a** Right to dig turf or peat on the land of another; **b** place where peat is dug.

turbid, adj. [1. tėrbid; 2. tə́bid]. Lat. *turbidus*, 'confused, disordered; thick, muddy'; cp. *turbāre*, 'to confuse, bewilder', also *turba*, 'uproar, confusion, tumult; a crowd'. See **turbinal, turbulent**, & cp. **thorp. a** (of liquids) Having the sediment disturbed; hence thick, muddy; **b** (fig.) confused, disturbed; lacking clarity.

turbidity, n. [1. tėrbíditi; 2. təbíditi]. Prec. & **-ity.** Condition, quality, of being turbid.

turbidly, adv. [1. tėrbidli; 2. tə́bidli]. **turbid** & **-ly.** In a turbid manner.

turbidness, n. [1. tėrbidnes; 2. tə́bidnis]. See prec. & **-ness.** Turbidity.

turbinal, adj. [1. tėrbinal; 2. tə́binəl]. Lat. *turbin-*, stem of *turbō*, 'violent, circular motion; something that spins, a top; something spiral and twisted, a whorl', & **-al**; perh. fr. same base as *turba*, 'uproar' &c. See **turbid.** (anat. and zool.) Having the form of a spiral or scroll.

turbinate, adj. [1. tėrbināt; 2. tə́bineit]. *turbin-*, as in prec., & **-ate. 1.** Whirling like a top. **2.** Shaped like a top or like an inverted cone. **3.** (anat.) Of some bones, scroll-shaped.

turbination, n. [1. tėrbinā́shun; 2. təbinéiʃən]. Prec. & **-ion. 1.** Act or movement of spinning like a top. **2.** Something turbinate in shape.

turbine, n. [1. tėrbīn; 2. tə́bain]. Lat. *turbin-*, see **turbinal.** Wheel, serving as a motor, which is rotated by means of a stream of water or steam, under pressure over rotating vanes on the shaft, and thus used to generate electric power or to drive a steamship &c.

turbit, n. [1. tėrbit; 2. tə́bit]. Origin doubtful. Kind of fancy pigeon with short head and beak and a frill.

turbot, n. [1. tėrbut; 2. tə́bət]. Fr., O. Fr. *torbout*; perh. fr. Lat. *turbō*, 'top', see **turbinal**, fr. shape of the fish, & obscure suff.; cp. **halibut.** Large flat sea-fish, with firm, white flesh much sought after as food.

turbulence, n. [1. tėrbūlens; 2. tə́bjuləns]. Lat. *turbulentia*, see next word & **-ce. a** Turbulent conduct; unruliness, commotion; **b** unsettled social or civic condition; lack of order, discipline, and quiet; disturbance, lawlessness.

turbulent, adj. [1. tėrbūlent; 2. tə́bjulənt]. Fr., fr. Lat. *turbulentus*, fr. *turba*, 'disorder, confusion' &c., see **turbinal** & cp. **turbid. a** In commotion, in violent movement, fiercely agitated: *turbulent waves*; **b** unruly, vehement, boisterous, ill-controlled: *a turbulent character*; *turbulent passions* &c.; **c** uproarious, insubordinate, disorderly: *a turbulent mob.*

Turcophil(e), adj. & n. [1. tėrkōfil; 2. tə́koufil]. **Turk** & **-phil(e). 1.** adj. Admiring the Turks and their political and social qualities. **2.** n. A Turcophil person.

Turcophobe, adj. & n. [1. tėrkōfōb; 2. tə́koufoub]. See prec. & **-phobe. 1.** adj. Hating and fearing the Turks, their civilization, political influence &c. **2.** n. A Turcophobe person.

turdine, adj. [1. tėrdīn; 2. tə́dain]. Lat. *turdus*, 'a thrush', for **trzdos*; cp. Lith. *strūsdas*; O.N. *þrǫstr*; O.E. *þrostle*, see **throstle** & **thrush**, & cp. **struthious.** Connected with the thrush genus, *Turdus*, or family, *Turdidae*, of birds including the thrush, ousel, blackbird &c.

tureen, n. [1. tūrḗn; 2. tjurín]. Fr. *terrine*, 'earthen vessel', fr. Lat. *terra*, 'earth', see **terra.** Boat-shaped dish for holding soup.

turf, n. [1. tėrf; 2. təf]. O.E. & M.E. *turf*; cp. O.N. *torf*; cogn. w. Scrt. *darbha*, 'tuft of grass'. **1. a** Thin upper stratum of the earth covered with grass; lawn, sward; **b** a sod. **2.** Mass of compressed ancient vegetable fibre, dead grass &c., peat; esp. as used for fuel. **3.** Horse-racing: *on the turf*, engaged in racing.

turfy, adj. [1. tėrfi; 2. tə́fi]. Prec. & **-y. a** Abounding in, covered with, turf; **b** having character or appearance of turf.

turgescence, n. [1. tėrjésens; 2. tədžésəns]. Next word & **-ce. a** Process of swelling; **b** condition of being turgescent; **c** bombast.

turgescent, adj. [1. tėrjésent; 2. tədžésənt]. Lat. *turgescent-(em)*, Pres. Part. of *turgescere*, inchoative of *turgēre*, 'to swell'; see **turgid. a** Swelling, inflated; **b** (fig., of style &c.) pompous, bombastic.

turgid, adj. [1. tėrjid; 2. tə́džid]. Lat. *turgidus*, 'inflated, distended'; cp. *turgēre*, 'to swell'; contains the base **tu-*, 'to swell', see **tumid. 1.** Swollen, puffed up. **2.** (of style &c.) Inflated, bombastic, pompous.

turgidity, n. [1. terjíditi; 2. tədžíditi]. Prec. & **-ity.** State, quality, of being turgid.

turgidly, adv. [1. tėrjidli; 2. tə́džidli]. See prec. & **-ly.** In a turgid manner.

turion, n. [1. tū́rion; 2. tjúəriən]. Lat. *turiōn-(em)*, 'shoot, sprout'; connected w. base **tu-*, 'to swell' &c.; see **turgid** & **tumid.** (bot.) Scaly shoot developed from a subterranean bud.

Turk, n. [1. tėrk; 2. tək]. Fr. *Turc*, Ital. *Turco*; prob. of Tatar origin. **1.** Member of the Turkish race; specif. of Osmanli or Ottoman branch. **2.** (facet.) An unruly, unmanageable, mischievous boy; esp. *a regular young Turk.*

turkey (I.), n. [1. tėrki; 2. tə́ki]. So called fr. belief that the birds came orig. fr. Turkey. Large domestic gallinaceous bird introduced from America, whose flesh is prized as food, and largely eaten in England at Christmas time.

Turkey (II.), country of Ottoman Turks. Used attributively in various combinations. *Turkey carpet*, one made of wool, with a thick pile, usually with pattern of bold design in red, blue, and green; *Turkey red*, a scarlet pigment obtained from madder or synthetically from coal-tar; *Turkey towel*, rough kind of bath towel.

turkey buzzard, n. A kind of vulture, *Cathartes aura*, common in South and Central America.

turkey-cock, n. **a** A male turkey; **b** (fig.) a strutting, pompous person.

Turki, adj. & n. [1. tóorkē; 2. túəkī]. Pers., 'Turk'. **1.** adj. Of, belonging to, a group of Ural-Altaic languages and races, which includes Turkish. **2.** n. This language, group, or race.

Turkish, adj. & n. [1. têrkish; 2. tə́kiʃ]. **Turk** & **-ish. 1.** adj. Belonging to, connected with, Turkey, the Turks, or their language, which is Turki much mixed with Arabic and Persian. **2.** n. The language of the Turks.

Turkish bath, n. A hot-air or steam bath, inducing extreme perspiration, followed by shampooing and massage &c.

Turkish delight, n. A sweetmeat made of gelatine flavoured and coated with powdered sugar.

Turkish pound, n. 100 piastres, value about 18s. 2d., usually written £T.

Turk's head, n. A long-handled broom or brush with head of feathers, used for dusting ceilings &c.

turmalin(e), n. See **tourmalin.**

turmeric, n. [1. têrmerik; 2. tə́mərik]. Supposed to be fr. Fr. *terre-mérite*, itself perh. a corrupt. of Arab. *kurkum*, 'curcuma', q.v. An aromatic plant of the ginger family, the root of which is ground to a powder, and used as a condiment, a medicine, and a dye.

turmeric paper, n. Paper impregnated with turmeric, used as a test for alkali, in contact with which it turns brown, and for boric acid, which turns it reddish brown.

turmoil, n. [1. têrmoil; 2. tə́moil]. Origin doubtful. Perh. fr. intens. *tur-* for **tra-** & **moil.** Agitation, uproar, unrest, confusion, tumult.

turn (I.), vb. trans. & intrans. [1. têrn; 2. tən]. M.E. *turnen, tournen* &c., fr. O.E. *tyrnan*, & *turnian*, 'to revolve', intrans., also combined w. O. Fr. *torner, tourner*; O.E. & Fr. both fr. Lat. *tornāre*, 'to polish, round off, fashion', fr. *tornus*, 'a lathe; a graver's tool'; borrowed fr. Gk. *tórnos*, 'turner's wheel; graver's chisel'; prob. cogn. w. Lat. *teres*, 'rubbed, rounded off, well turned, smooth', cp. *terere*, 'to rub, wear down' &c., & Gk. *teírein*, 'to rub', fr. **ter-ĵ-*; see **teredo, toreutic, trite, triturate. A.** trans. **1. a** To shape, cut out, on a lathe: *to turn brass*; *to turn a candlestick out of brass*; **b** (fig.) to polish, shape, execute, in an elegant manner; give a graceful form to: *to turn a compliment, an epigram*; *to turn a couplet* &c. **2.** To give a circular motion to, cause to revolve, spin round; to wind: *to turn a handle, a wheel*; also *to turn the leaves of a book.* Phr. *to turn (a person) round one's little finger*, to influence him as one chooses. **3. a** (of physical act or process) To cause to assume a particular, often a different, position; to move, cause to face, or be inclined in particular direction; to direct: *to turn one's head*; *turn your eyes this way*; *turn the camera more to the right*; Phrs. *to turn one's back on* (various fig. senses), to refuse to recognize or to associate with; to have nothing more to do with; to express disapproval of, or contempt for &c.; *to turn a deaf ear to*, refuse to listen or to attend to; *to turn one's steps*, to go; *turn tail*, to run away; *not to turn a hair*, to be quite unaffected, unperturbed; *to turn the edge of (a knife* &c.), to blunt; **b** (of intellectual action) in Phr. *turn one's thoughts, attention, efforts* &c. to direct, concentrate (thoughts &c.). **4. a** To guide, cause to go in particular direction, alter course of: *to turn one's horse to the hills*; *to turn a beast into a field*; **b** to deflect, persuade to pursue different course of action: *when once he has made up his mind, nothing will turn him.* **5. a** To reverse position of, so that the upper surface lies underneath, and the lower surface upwards: *to turn things upside-down*; *to turn a chop on a gridiron*; Phr. *to turn an honest penny*, to earn a profit; **b** to cause outer surface of anything to be on the inside, and vice versa: *to turn something inside out*; *to have a suit turned.* Phr. *to turn one's coat*, change one's opinions and principles; to give up one's old allegiance and accept a new one. **6. a** To bring, cause to pass, into a specified condition: *his behaviour turns me sick*; *the success of others turns him green with envy*; *thundery weather turns milk sour*; **b** specif., to render (food) curdled, sour, tainted, corrupt &c.: *the heat has turned the milk.* **7. a** To change, transmute (things, feelings &c.) into something different: *to turn water into wine*; *to turn love to hate*; **b** to translate: *to turn a passage into Latin.* **8.** To disturb, upset, derange: *the mere sight of food turns my stomach.* Phrs. *to turn a person's head*, upset mental balance; render conceited: *flattery has turned his head*; *to turn (person's) brain*, make him mad. **9. a** To reach, and pass, a certain point in time, period of life &c.: *it has just turned four*; *he has not yet turned sixty*; **b** *to turn a* (or *the*) *corner*; (i.) to go up a street branching off that in which one is; (ii.) (fig.) *turn the corner*, to reach and pass successfully, a crisis in illness, or in one's affairs. **10.** (mil.) *To turn an enemy's flank*, pass round, take up position behind or across; to outflank. **11.** To use, employ, for particular purpose: *to turn one's hand to useful work*; *turn to account*, make use of. **B.** intrans. **1. a** To use a lathe; **b** (of material) to be capable of being shaped or turned on a lathe. **2. a** To perform revolutions, to rotate, as on a pivot or axis; **b** (fig.) to depend, hinge, upon, be involved in: *the whole dispute turns on a single point.* **3. a** To direct one's course towards, pursue, a particular direction: *to turn to the right*; *to turn west*; Phr. *not to know where, which way, to turn*, to be at end of one's resources, be hard pressed, desperate &c.; **b** to direct one's thought, attention, glance &c., towards: *to turn to the last page.* **4. a** To reverse one's course or direction, and pursue an opposite one; to retrace one's steps: *he turned and went away in a rage*; *it is time to turn now if we wish to get home in time for dinner*; **b** (fig.) to reverse one's course of action. **5.** To alter one's position, move from the side on which one is lying, on to the other: *to turn in bed, in one's sleep.* Phrs. *enough to make* (someone who is dead) *turn in his grave*, would shock and distress him, very much; *the worm turns*, even the patient and humble show resentment after a certain point; *to turn turtle*, to capsize. **6.** (of tide) To change from ebb to flow, or vice versa; (also fig.) *the tide has turned*, the course of affairs has altered, events are beginning to develop favourably or unfavourably. **7. a** To alter in specified way, in physical character, appearance, composition, general condition &c.; to pass into a specified state, to become: *the weather is turning colder*; *the milk has turned sour*; *water turns to ice*; *he turned very red*; *to turn sick*; **b** to change one's opinions, principles, profession &c.: *to turn Tory*; *to turn soldier, cook, schoolmaster* &c.; *to turn traitor*; *to turn Christian.* **8.** Specif. (of food &c.) to pass into first stage of decay, sourness, acidity &c.: *the milk has turned.* **C.** Followed by adverbs or prepositions. *Turn aside*, **1.** trans., to divert, put on a different course; **2.** intrans., to pursue a new course, deviate. *Turn away*, **1.** trans., to reject, refuse entrance to, dismiss: *to turn crowds away from the door* &c.; **2.** intrans., to turn in different direction; direct one's attention, refuse to look; show contempt or disapproval. *Turn back*, **1.** trans., to refuse to allow to proceed, cause to return; **2.** intrans., to return, retrace one's steps; (fig.) to discontinue course of action. *Turn against*, **1.** trans., to make (person) hostile to; **2.** intrans., to become hostile to, oppose. *Turn down*, **1.** trans., **a** to fold down: *to turn down one's collar*; **b** to diminish intensity of by lowering: *to turn down the light*; **c** (fig.) to reject, refuse to consider: *to turn down a proposal* &c.; **2.** intrans., **a** to be folded down; **b** to be capable of being lowered. *Turn in*, **1.** trans., to cause to point or incline inwards: *to turn in one's toes*; **2.** intrans., **a** to be inclined inwards: *his toes turned in*; **b** (colloq.) to go to bed. *Turn off*, **1.** trans., **a** to check, shut off, supply or flow of, by turning a tap &c.: *to turn off water, gas*; **b** to dismiss from service: *to turn off workmen (from one's employ)*; **2.** intrans., **a** (of persons &c.) to leave road on which one is walking &c., and go up another leading from it; **b** (of roads &c.) to branch off, bifurcate. *Turn out*, **1.** trans., **a** to dismiss, eject, expel: *to turn a person out of the room, of his office, situation, a club* &c.; **b** to put horses, cattle &c. out to grass, as contrasted with keeping them in a stable; **c** to produce as result of labour and skill: *to turn out beautiful fabrics from the looms*; **d** to furnish with equipment, clothing &c., to fit out, dress: *an exquisitely turned out young woman*; **e** to turn off, to extinguish: *to turn out the light, the gas*; **2.** intrans., **a** to point, be inclined, outwards: *his toes turn out too much*; **b** to go out, esp. as result of expulsion: *to turn out of one's house*; **c** to get up from bed; **d** to come out in order to perform some duty: *the fire brigade turned out as soon as the alarm was given*; **e** to prove, be shown to be: *he turned out an excellent administrator*; *the day is turning out fine*; Phr. *to turn out well*, to be satisfactory, a success &c.; *as it turned out*, as it chanced, happened. *Turn over*, **1.** trans., **a** to reverse position of, cause to roll over: *to turn over the pages of a book*, to look through while turning; Phr. *to turn over a new leaf*, make amends for past, behave better; **b** to hand over, transfer, to: *to turn one's business over to one's son*; **c** to ponder, consider, dwell upon: *to turn (the matter) over in one's mind*; **d** to handle, take in, in the course of business: *the business turns over several thousands a year*; **2.** intrans., to alter one's position by rolling over: *to turn over in bed.* *Turn to*, intrans., **a** to rely upon, trust to, apply to: *to turn to a friend for help*; **b** (absol.) to set to, set to work, act with vigour. *Turn up*, **1.** trans., to bend up, cause to incline upwards, bring lower side, or end, uppermost: *to turn up the ends of one's trousers*; *to turn up the soil*, plough or dig it. Various special uses: *a to turn a child up*, put face downwards over one's knee to whip him; *to turn up a decanter*, empty the last drops it contains into one's glass; *to turn up one's nose at*, to feel and show contempt for, to despise; *to turn up one's toes*, (colloq.) to die; *his conduct, the sight, turned me up*, disgusted, nauseated me. **2.** intrans. **a** To incline, be inclined, bend, slope, upwards: *the bough turns up at the end*; *her nose turns up*; **b** (i.) (of persons) to appear, come on the scene, visit one, esp. casually and unexpectedly: *my brother has just turned up from India*; *he turned up in London the other day*; *I shouldn't think he'll turn up tonight*; (ii.) (of objects) to come to light, be found, esp. by accident: *the book I lost hasn't turned up yet*; *I wouldn't waste time looking for your knife, it will turn up some day*; Phr. *to wait for something to turn up*, await the course of events passively, in the hope that some favourable opportunity, or some piece of good fortune, will come to one. *Turn upon*, trans., **a** to attack; **b** to depend upon.

turn (II.), n., fr. O. Fr. *torn*, later *tour*; see prec. **1.** Act or process of turning; rotation, revolution: *the turn of a wheel*; a turning movement: *a turn of the wrist*; movement made in a particular direction: *a turn to the right.* **2.** Something which turns or winds; a bend, curve: *a turn in a road, in a river.* **3. a** Change in direction, reverse movement: *the turn of the tide*; Phr. *the turn of the tide*, (fig.) reversal of fortune; **b** change, new departure, vicissitude, in affairs, fortune, health &c.: *matters, affairs, have taken a bad turn*; *the patient has taken a turn for the better, for the worse.* **4. a** A spell of action, bout of activity: *to take a turn at the oars*; **b** a form of activity, an action, regarded as affecting another in some particular way: *to do one a good turn*, render him a service; *a bad turn*, a disservice. Phr. *one good turn deserves another*. **5.** A short spell of exercise, a walk, ride &c.: *let us take a turn along the sea-front*. **6.** Opportunity which recurs at regular intervals; right, or obligation to do, or enjoy something at certain recurring periods, which alternate with periods during which others are liable to the obligation or enjoy the right: *everyone must take his turn to keep watch*; *it is your turn to have dinner next*; *my turn will come*. Phrs. *by turns, turn and turn about*, alternately. **7.** Special need, requirement, exigency: *this stick will serve my turn to beat him with*. **8.** Special aptitude, bent, predisposition: *a distinct turn for music*. **9.** A short performance on the stage, display of agility, skill &c. lasting for a brief period, forming a definite part of an entertainment: *a variety entertainment with several good and some poor turns*. **10.** Special form, shape, cast; characteristic style: *a peculiar turn of mind*. **11.** (colloq.) Physical or moral shock, a qualm, a jar; esp. *it gave me quite a turn*. **12.** Phr. (food) *done to a turn*, cooked with absolute perfection, neither underdone, nor over-cooked.

turncoat, n. [1. tẽrnkōt; 2. tʌ́nkout]. (contemptuous) Person who changes his political or religious opinions and principles, esp. one who does so from interested motives.

turncock, n. [1. tẽrnkok; 2. tʌ́nkɔk]. Man employed by water company to regulate the water from the mains &c.

turned, adj. [1. tẽrnd; 2. tʌ̄nd]. P.P. of **turn** (I.). (print.) *A turned letter*, one inverted or reversed.

turner, n. [1. tẽrner; 2. tʌ́nə], fr. **turn** (I.) & **-er**. One who practises turning with a lathe as a skilled trade.

turnery, n. [1. tẽrneri; 2. tʌ́nəri]. Fr. *tournerie*. **1.** Art of turning with a lathe. **2. a** (coll.) Objects turned with a lathe; **b** ornamentation wrought with a lathe.

turning, n. [1. tẽrning; 2. tʌ́niŋ]. **turn** (I.) & **-ing**. **1.** A winding, twisting, bend: *turnings and twistings of a road, river* &c. **2.** Place where one road branches off from another: *first turning to the right*. **3.** Act, art, of turning with a lathe; turnery.

turning-point, n. Point or place of turning; (usually in non-material sense) point at which a new departure is made; crisis: *the turning-point of an illness, of a career*.

turnip, n. [1. tẽrnip; 2. tʌ́nip]. First element of doubtful origin; the second is O.E. *nǣp*, M.E. *nēpe*, 'turnip', early loan-word fr. Lat. *nāpus*, 'turnip'; cp. Gk. *nāpu*, later form of *sinā́pi*, 'mustard'; prob. of Egyptian origin. See **sinapism** & cp. second element in **parsnip**. **1. a** Plant, *Brassica campestris*, var. *rapa*, with globular or long root, with a sweetish or, when old, hot taste; used as a vegetable and for feeding sheep and cattle; **b** specif., the edible root of this plant. **2.** (slang) A large, clumsy, common silver watch.

turnip fly, n. **a** A hymenopterous insect, *Athalia spinarum*, whose larva feeds on turnip-leaves; **b** small beetle (also *turnip-flea*), *Phyllotreta nemorum*, which feeds on young turnip-leaves.

turnip-tops, n. pl. Leaves and stems of the turnip, esp. the young sprouts from previous season's root, considered as a vegetable.

turnkey, n. [1. tẽrnkē; 2. tʌ́nkī]. Person who keeps the keys of the cells in a prison.

turn-out, n. [1. tẽrn óut; 2. tʌn áut]. **1.** Gathering, assembly, of persons who have come together for a particular purpose: *quite a good turn-out at the lecture*. **2.** (colloq.) A carriage, horses, and servants, considered as a whole or ensemble: *a smart turn-out*.

turnover, n. [1. tẽrnōver; 2. tʌ́nouvə]. **1.** Something bent or folded over; specif., a kind of pie made by doubling or folding over a piece of dough. **2.** Amount of money handled, taken in, and paid out in a business within a given time. **3.** Article in a newspaper extending from one page on to another.

turnpike, n. [1. tẽrnpīk; 2. tʌ́npaik]. Gate kept closed across a road and not opened to passengers until they have paid toll; a toll-gate, originally a pointed bar turning on a pivot, worked by the keeper.

turnpike road, n. One which has a turnpike across it.

turnsole, n. [1. tẽrnsōl; 2. tʌ́nsoul]. Fr. *tournesol*; **turn** (I.) & Lat. *sol*, 'sun', see **sol** (I.). Plant whose flowers are supposed always to face the sun; sunflower.

turnspit, n. [1. tẽrnspit; 2. tʌ́nspit]. One of a small breed of dog used formerly for turning a spit upon which meat was cooked.

turnstile, n. [1. tẽrnstīl; 2. tʌ́nstail]. Mechanical device consisting of a heavy revolving gate so constructed that only one person can pass at a time; used at the entrance of theatres, on piers &c., to regulate speed of entrance while tickets are collected.

turnstone, n. [1. tẽrnstōn; 2. tʌ́nstoun]. Popular name for a shore bird, allied to the plover, which turns over the pebbles on a beach in search of food.

turn-table, n. Circular revolving platform upon which rails are laid corresponding with those of a railway line, used for reversing locomotives.

turn-up, n. [1. tẽrn úp; 2. tʌn ʌ́p]. **1.** Something turned up, as *the turn-up of one's trousers*. **2.** (colloq.) A commotion, a row; a fight or noisy wrangle.

turpentine, n. [1. tẽrpentīn; 2. tʌ́pəntain]. O. Fr. *terbentine*, Lat. *terebinthinus*, 'turpentine tree', fr. Gk. *terébinthos*, see **terebinth**. **1.** Oily, fluid or semi-fluid, sticky substance secreted by pine trees. **2.** Popular name for *spirits of turpentine*, distilled from turpentine; used for mixing with paints and varnishes.

turpentine tree, n. Terebinth tree.

turpeth, n. [1. tẽrpeth; 2. tʌ́pɛþ]. O. Fr. *turbith*, fr. Pers. *turbid*, 'a purge'. The root of an Asiatic plant, used as a purgative.

turpitude, n. [1. tẽrpitūd; 2. tʌ́pitjūd]. Fr., fr. Lat. *turpitūdo*, 'ugliness, foulness', fr. *turpis*, 'ugly, foul, filthy; shameful, base'; cogn. w. O. Lat. *trepit*, 'turns away', see **trepidation**; fundamental sense of adj. is 'revolting, causing one to turn away'. Wickedness, depravity, infamy.

turps, n. [1. tẽrps; 2. tʌ̄ps]. Popular abbreviation of spirits of turpentine.

turquoise, n. [1. tẽrkwoiz, tẽrkwahz; 2. tʌ́kwɔiz, tʌ́kwāz], formerly [1. tẽrkis; 2. tʌ́kis]. Fr. fem. adj., 'Turkish'. **a** Semi-precious stone, opaque, and bright blue or greenish blue in colour; **b** bright blue or greenish colour, like that of the turquoise, (also attrib.) *turquoise blue, green*.

turret, n. [1. túret; 2. tárit]. Fr. *tourette*, 'little tower'; see **tower** (I.) & **-et**. **1.** A small tower, esp. one built out and projecting from a larger building. **2.** (nav.) Revolving, tower-like, armoured structure upon which a ship's guns are mounted.

turreted, adj. [1. túreted; 2. táritid]. Provided with a turret or turrets.

turret-gun, n. Ship's gun mounted upon a turret.

turriculate(d), adj. [1. turíkūlāt(ed); 2. taríkjuleit(id)]. Lat. *turricula*, 'little tower', dimin. of *turris*, 'tower', see **tower** (I.), & **-ate**. **a** Provided with small turrets; **b** (of shells) resembling a turret in shape.

turtle (I.), n. [1. tẽrtl; 2. tʌ̄tl]. Lat. *turtur*, 'dove', imitative of bird's note; usually *turtle-dove*. Any of various kinds of wild dove with soft cooing note; supposed to show great affection for, and fidelity to, its mate; hence (fig.) *a pair of turtle-doves*, lovers.

turtle (II.), n. Form perh. suggested by prec., fr. Span. *tortuga*, 'tortoise'; see **tortoise**. A marine tortoise; reptile of various species, having the body enclosed in a hard bony shell; several kinds have edible flesh, especially used for soup. Phr. *to turn turtle*, (chiefly of a ship) to capsize.

Tuscan, adj. & n. [1. túskan; 2. táskən]. Lat. *Tuscānus*. **1.** adj. **a** Pertaining to Tuscany; **b** (archit.) of, pertaining to, the Tuscan order, of late Roman origin, plain in style, with unfluted columns. **2.** n. **a** Inhabitant of Tuscany; **b** language of Tuscany.

tush (I.), interj. & vb. intrans. [1. tush; 2. taʃ]. Imitative. (archaic) **a** interj. Exclamation expressive of contempt or impatience; **b** vb., to utter this exclamation.

tush (II.), n. O.E. *tūsć*, for earlier **tunsk-*, cp. Goth. *tunþ-us*, 'tooth', gradational variant of Gmc. **tanþ-*, whence O.E. *tōþ*, see **tooth**; the form presupposes an orig. **dn̥t-ko-*, the suff. being adjectival. Cp. **tusk**. One of the long prominent side teeth of a horse.

tushery, n. [1. túsheri; 2. táʃəri]. **tush** (I.) & **-ery**. Term applied by R. L. Stevenson to affected literary archaisms.

tusk, n. & vb. trans. [1. tusk; 2. task]. In M.E., fr. O.E. *tūx*, metathesized form of O.E. *tūsć*, see **tush** (II.); *tūx* undergoes a later metathesis to *tŭsk*. **1.** n. **a** An enormously long prominent tooth which always projects outside the mouth, found esp. in the elephant, in the walrus, and similar marine animals, and on a smaller scale in the wild boar; **b** (facet.) a human tooth, esp. when exceptionally long and prominent. **2.** vb. To strike at, wound, gore, with the tusks.

tusked, adj. [1. tuskt; 2. taskt]. Prec. & **-ed**. Having tusks.

tusker, n. [1. túsker; 2. táskə]. An elephant or boar with large tusks.

tussal, adj. [1. túsal; 2. tásəl], fr. Lat. *tussis*, 'cough', origin doubtful, & **-al**. (med.) Pertaining to, connected with, a cough.

tussicular, adj. [1. tusíkūlar; 2. tasíkjulə]. Lat. *tussicula*, 'slight cough', dimin. of *tussis*, see prec., & **-ar**. Having the character of a slight cough.

tussive, adj. [1. túsiv; 2. tásiv]. Lat. *tussis*, 'cough', see **tussal**, & **-ive**. Connected with, due to, a cough.

tussle, n. & vb. intrans. [1. túsl; 2. tásl]. Etymol. doubtful; possibly connected w. **tousle**. **1.** n. A fight; a rough struggle; a strenuous effort. **2.** vb. To engage in a rough, violent struggle.

tussock, n. [1. túsuk; 2. tásək]. Etymol. obscure. A tuft, thick bunch, of grass &c.

tussock grass, n. Grass which grows in tufts on damp, marshy soil; specif., species of tall tufted grass of the Falkland Islands and Patagonia.

tussock moth, n. Kind of moth whose caterpillar has tufts of hair on its back.

tussocky, adj. [1. túsuki; 2. tásəki]. Prec. & **-y**. Full of tussocks; tufty.

tussore, n. [1. túsōr; 2. tásɔ̄], **tussah, tussar, tusseh, tusser, tussur**, fr. Hind. *tassar*, 'shuttle'. **1.** Indian undomesticated silkworm that feeds on oak leaves. **2. a** Coarse, fawn-coloured fibre produced by these silkworms; **b** fabric woven from this.

tut, interj. & vb. [1. tut; 2. tat]. Conventionalized spelling attempting to express sound. **a** interj. Exclamation of impatience, annoyance &c.; **b** vb., to give utterance to such an exclamation.

tutelage, n. [1. tū́telij; 2. tjū́tilidž]. Lat. *tūtēla*, 'charge, guardianship', fr. *tūtus*, 'safe, secure', see **tuition** & **tutor**, & **-age**. **1.** Act of protecting, of acting as guardian. **2.** State of being under guardianship, in the protection of a tutor.

tutelar, tutelary, adj. [1. tū́telar(i); 2. tjū́tilə(ri)]. Lat. *tūtēla*, see prec., & **-ar** (& **-y**). Having guardianship; acting as a guardian or protector; protective: *tutelar(y) power, deities*.

tutor (I.), n. [1. tū́tur; 2. tjū́tə]. Lat., 'protector, defender, legal guardian', fr. base *tūt-*, P.P. type of *tuēri*, 'to guard, protect'; cogn. w. Goth. *þiuþ*, 'good', n.; perh. ultimately connected w. base of *tumēre*, 'to swell', see **tumid**; see further **tuition, tute-**

lage, tutelar. Less probable is Brugmann's derivation of this group fr. the base *tugʷhō- &c., seen in Gk. *sophós*, 'wise', see **sophism.** **1.** (Rom. law) One having charge of a person below the age of puberty, and of his property; a guardian. **2.** A teacher, instructor; **a** college official, usually a specialist in some branch of learning, who directs the studies of undergraduates at Oxford and Cambridge; contrasted with a university professor; **b** a private instructor; often a person living with the family of his pupil; **c** a coach, a teacher who prepares young men for some particular examination.

tutor (**II.**), vb. trans. & intrans., fr. prec. **a** trans. To act as tutor to; **b** intrans., to engage in tutorial work, perform the duties of a tutor.

tutoress, n. [1. tútores; 2. tjûtərɛs]. **tutor** (**I.**) & **-ess.** Woman tutor.

tutorial, adj. & n. [1. tūtórial; 2. tjūtɔ́riəl]. **tutor** (**I.**) & **-ial.** **1.** adj. **a** Pertaining to a tutor or to his duties; **b** pertaining to, of the nature of, tuition. **2.** n. (Oxford slang) A spell of instruction given by a college tutor.

tutorially, adv. Prec. & **-ly.** After the manner of a tutor.

tutorship, n. [1. tûtership; 2. tjûtəʃip]. **tutor** (**I.**) & **-ship.** **a** Office, functions, of a tutor; **b** an engagement, appointment, as tutor.

tutsan, n. [1. tútsan; 2. tátsən]. Fr. *toute-saine*, lit. 'entirely wholesome or healthy'. Cp. **total** (**I.**) & **sane.** The plant St.-John's-wort, *Hypericum Androsaemum*, from which a healing ointment was formerly made.

tutti, adj. [1. tóoti; 2. tútti]. Ital., 'all'. (mus. direction) All players, instruments, or voices.

tutti-frutti, n. [1. tóoti fróoti; 2. tútti frútti]. Ital., 'all fruits'. Sweetmeat made of a mixture of various kinds of preserved fruits.

tutty, n. [1. túti; 2. táti]. Fr. *tutie*, fr. Arab. *tūtiyā*, 'vitriol'. Brown substance obtained from flues of furnaces in which zinc is smelted; a crude oxide of zinc.

tuum, pron. [1. tûum; 2. tjûəm]. Lat. neut. sing. of possessive pron. of 2nd pers., cogn. w. **thou.** Thine; in Phr. *meum and tuum*, see **meum.**

tu-whitt, tu-whitt tu-whoo, n. [1. tōō wít tōō wōō; 2. tū wít tū wû]. Imitative of the cry of the owl.

tuxedo, n. [1. tuksédō; 2. taksídou], fr. name of a country club, Tuxedo Park, New York. (U.S.A.) Dinner jacket.

tuyère, n. [1. twéyār; 2. twíjɛə]. Fr., 'pipe', connected w. *tuyau*, q.v. under **tewel.** Pipe through which air is pumped into a furnace.

twaddell, n. [1. twódl; 2. twɔ́dl]. After name of inventor. Kind of hydrometer.

twaddle, n. & vb. intrans. [1. twódl; 2. twɔ́dl]. Prob. variant of **tattle.** **1.** n. Empty, foolish, trite talk; nonsense: *to talk mere twaddle.* **2.** vb. To talk twaddle.

twain, adj. & n. [1. twān; 2. twein]. O.E. *twēgen*, masc., 'two', M.E. *twēine, twēyen* &c. See **two.** (archaic or poet.) Two: *(to cut) in twain*, asunder, in two parts; '*and never the twain shall meet*'.

twang, n. & vb. trans. & intrans. [1. twang; 2. twæŋ]. Imitative. **1.** n. **a** A sharp sound, as of the string of a fiddle &c. suddenly and sharply plucked; **b** nasalized speech utterance; effect produced by speaking through the nose: *an American twang.* **2.** vb. **a** To pluck the string of a musical instrument sharply so that it gives forth a twang; **b** (rarely) to speak with a nasal twang.

twayblade, n. [1. twấblād; 2. twéibleid], fr. O.E. *twēge(n)*, 'two', see **twain, & blade.** A plant of the orchidaceous family, genus *Listera*, with two broad leaves, opposite each other, on the stem; also N. American species of the genus *Liparis.*

tweak, vb. trans. & n. [1. twēk; 2. twīk]. Variant of **twitch** (**I.**); the formal relation to M.E. *twikken* is not clear. **1.** vb. To pluck, nip, or pinch with a sharp, sudden, jerky action. **2.** n. A sharp, sudden nip, pinch, or plucking.

tweed, n. [1. twēd; 2. twīd]. Hardly fr. **twill**, as sometimes suggested, as the two kinds of cloth have no resemblance; prob. fr. name of Scottish river. A soft woollen cloth, usually woven from yarns of several colours or shades, but without a regular pattern; primarily used of cloth woven in Scotland.

tweedle-dum and tweedle-dee, ns. [1. twḗdl dúm an(d) twēdl dḗ; 2. twídl dám ən twídl dí]. Imit. of high-pitched note; first quoted in O.E.D. in Phr. *tweedle-dum and tweedle-dee* of two musicians (1725). Designation of two persons who are considered very alike in appearance, character, opinion, or behaviour &c.; more rarely of things, modes of conduct &c. which are very much alike and differ chiefly in name.

'tween, prep. [1. twēn; 2. twīn]. Abbr. for **between.**

tweeny, n. [1. twḗni; 2. twíni]. Prec. & **-y.** (colloq.) A young servant girl who helps two other maids with their work; also *tweeny-maid.*

tweezers, n. pl. [1. twḗzerz; 2. twízəz], fr. obs. *tweeze*, 'a small pocket-case', Fr. Fr. *étui*, 'case'; fr. such a phr. as *a pair of twees*, 'a folding case'; hence *tweezers*, primarily instrument carried in a case. Small pair of pincers used for grasping a small blood-vessel, plucking out thorns from the flesh &c.

twelfth, adj. & n. [1. twelfth; 2. twelfþ]. O.E. *twelfta*, M.E. *twelfte*; see **twelve.** **1.** adj. Next in order after eleventh; ordinal adj. of *twelve.* **2.** n. **a** The twelfth thing; **b** a twelfth part.

Twelfth-night, n. Evening of twelfth day after Christmas, that is, of the Feast of the Epiphany.

twelve, adj. & n. [1. twelv; 2. twɛlv]. O.E. *twelf*, M.E. *twelf, twelve*; cp. O.S. *twelif*; O.H.G. *zwelif*; Goth. *twalif.* The word is compounded of the elements in **two & leave** (**II.**); cp. also **eleven**; & the primitive sense is 'two over' or 'two in addition' (to ten). **1.** adj. One more than eleven, two more than ten; a dozen. **2.** n. **a** The number one more than eleven; Phr. *the twelve*, the twelve Apostles; **b** symbol for this: *put down a twelve*; **c** colloquial abbreviation for 12 o'clock.

twelvemo, n. [1. twélvmō; 2. twélvmou]. A duodecimo, written 12mo.

twelvemonth, n. [1. twélvmunth; 2. twélvmanþ]. A year: *this day twelvemonth*; *it will take a twelvemonth to finish.*

twentieth, adj. & n. [1. twéntieth; 2. twéntiiþ]. O.E. *twentigoða*; see **twenty & -th.** **1.** adj. Ordinal of twenty. **2.** n. **a** Thing next in order after the nineteenth; **b** one of twenty equal parts.

twenty, adj. & n. [1. twénti; 2. twénti]. O.E. *twēntig*, M.E. *twenti*; O.S. *twēntig*; O.H.G. *zweinzug*; cp. Goth. *twai tigjus*, 'two tens'; see **twain & -ty & ten.** **1.** adj. One more than nineteen. **2.** n. **a** The number following nineteen; **b** symbol for this; **c** collection of twenty things; a score.

twi-, pref. O.E. *twi*, 'two, double'; see **twice, twain, & two.**

twibill, n. [1. twíbil; 2. twáibil], Prec. & **bill** (**I.**). **1.** (obs.) Sword, battle-axe, with two blades. **2.** Mattock with two cutting edges.

twice, adv. [1. twīs; 2. twais]. M.E. *twies*, formed fr. O.E. *twiwa, twiga*, 'twice', w. the addition of genit. suff. *-es*, used adverbially; cp. O.H.G. *zwi-*; O.N. *tvi-*; cogn. w. Scrt. *dvi-*; Gk. *di-*; Lat. *bi-* for **dwi-*, see **bi- & two.** Two times: *to do something twice.* Phrs. *to think twice* (before doing &c.), to ponder well, hesitate; *not to think twice about*, (i.) not to think of again, to forget, disregard; (ii.) to do (something) without hesitation, reluctance, or misgiving; *I shouldn't think twice about refusing his offer*; *twice as good as*; *twice as much*, in double quantity, to a double degree.

twicer, n. [1. twíser; 2. twáisə]. See prec. & **-er.** One who does something twice; specif. **a** Presbyterian who goes to church twice a year; **b** printer who is both compositor and pressman.

twice-told, adj. Told, narrated, constantly; hence, hackneyed, commonplace.

twiddle, vb. trans. & intrans. & n. [1. twídl; 2. twídl]. O.N. *tvidla*, 'to stir'. **1.** vb. **a** trans. To twist, twirl; Phr. *to twiddle one's thumbs*, spend one's time idly, to have no serious occupation; **b** intrans., to shake, tremble, vibrate. **2.** n. **a** The action or motion of twiddling; **b** a vibration, shake, flourish, of the voice or of a musical instrument; **c** a twisting, wavy line.

twig (**I.**), vb. intrans. & trans. [1. twig; 2. twig]. Cp. Ir. *tuigaim*, 'I understand'. (slang) **a** intrans. To have understanding of, follow, catch on to (a proposal, explanation &c.): *I don't quite twig, will you tell me again?*; **b** trans., to understand, apprehend shrewdly: *to twig a person's meaning.*

twig (**II.**), n. O.E. *twig*, 'branch, stalk' cp. O.H.G. *zwig*; prob. connected w. **twi- & two.** Thin slender branch, or end of branch, of a tree. Phr. (slang) *to hop the twig*, to die.

twiggy, adj. [1. twígi; 2. twígi]. Prec. & **-y.** Covered with, abounding in, twigs.

twilight, n. [1. twílīt; 2. twáilait]. 15th cent.; see **twi- & light** (**I.**). **1.** **a** Half-light, subdued light just before and after sundown; **b** the time when such light prevails; period between late afternoon or evening and night. Phr. *twilight of the gods* (anct. Gmc. mythol.), the great struggle in which the gods and giants will destroy each other; also (attrib.) *twilight sleep*, condition of semi-unconsciousness induced by narcotics for relieving the pains of childbirth. **2.** (fig.) Obscurity of meaning; imperfect comprehension.

twill, n. & vb. trans. [1. twil; 2. twil]. Cp. O.E. *twilic*, 'woven double', see **twi-**; cp. M.H.G. *zwilich*, 'of two threads'; perh. formed on anal. of Lat. *bilix*, 'two-threaded', fr. **bi-**, 'double', & the base of *licium*, 'thread, something worn'. The Mod. Engl. word is prob. borrowed fr. a L.G. dial., *twillen*, 'to make double'. **1.** n. **a** Fine diagonal rib in fabric, formed by the mode of weaving; **b** cloth so woven. **2.** vb. To weave (cloth) with a twill.

twin, adj., n., & vb. [1. twin; 2. twin]. O.N. *tvinnr*, 'double', O.E. *getwinnas*, 'twins'; see **twi-.** **1.** adj. Specif. **a** being one of two children born at one birth: *twin brothers, sisters*; **b** double, twofold: *twin blades in a knife*; **c** closely connected or related, nearly resembling each other: *twin houses, projects* &c.; **d** closely connected in affection, mode of thought; having spiritual affinity: *twin souls.* **2.** n. **a** Either of two persons or animals born at one birth; **b** (pl.) two persons, animals, things, which closely resemble each other in appearance, character, activities, function &c.; specif., compound crystal, with pair of crystals in exactly reversed position on opposite side of axis; **c** (cap.) *the Twins*, constellation and sign of the zodiac, also called *Gemini*, i.e. Castor and Pollux. **3.** vb. To form (into) twin crystals.

twin-born, adj. Born at one birth.

twine, n. & vb. trans. & intrans. [1. twīn; 2. twain]. O.E. *twīn*, 'linen', implying fabric made of double or twisted thread; later in present sense of n. From base in **twi- & two.** **1.** n. **a** Twisted threads of jute, hemp &c., formed into a strong line, used for tying parcels &c.; string; **b** act or process of twining; **c** a twist, convolution. **2.** vb. **a** trans. To twist, wind, form into (wreaths): *to twine garlands for the feast*; *to twine one's arms round*, to embrace; **b** intrans., to twist, wreathe, encircle, form into winding folds: *in the woodland the ivy twines*; *ivy twines round the trunks of trees.*

twiner, n. [1. twíner; 2. twáinə]. Prec. & **-er.** That which twines; esp. a rambling, twisting plant.

twinge, n. & vb. intrans. [1. twinj; 2. twin(d)ž]. The n. is fr. the vb., but is now far more frequently used than the latter; O.E. *twengan*, 'to press, pinch', M.E. *twingen*, 'to afflict'; origin doubtful. **1.** n. **a** A sudden, sharp, shooting pain, a pang, a qualm: *a twinge of toothache, of lumbago* &c.; **b** a sudden mental qualm, sharp stab of remorse: *a twinge of conscience, compunction.* **2.** vb. To throb, shoot, with sudden pain.

twinkle, vb. intrans. & n. [1. twíngkl; 2. twíŋkl]. O.E. *twinclian*, 'to twinkle', M.E. *twinclien*, cp. M.H.G. *zwinken, zwingen*, 'to blink, wink'. **1.** vb. **a** (of lights, stars &c.) To produce effect of winking, to flash, sparkle, intermittently; to scintillate; **b** (of the eyes) to wink, blink (rare); to light up with sudden gleam of mirth &c.; **c** to move rapidly in different directions, to flash into sight and disappear by turns: *feet twinkling in the dance* &c. **2.** n. **a** (i.) An intermittent gleam, flash, sparkle; a scintillation; (ii.) a fleeting expression of mirth or humour in the eye; **b** a rapid, flashing movement, a twinkling.

twinkling, n. [1. twíngkling; 2. twíŋkliŋ]. Prec. & **-ing. 1.** A rapid, flickering movement; a momentary glimpse caught of this: *the twinkling of a rabbit's tail.* Phr. *the twinkling of an eye*, a brief instant of time. **2.** Intermittent flashing or sparkling of light: *the twinkling of the stars.*

twinning, n. [1. twíning; 2. twíniŋ]. **twin**, vb., & **-ing.** Formation of twin crystals.

twirl, vb. trans. & intrans. & n. [1. twërl; 2. twʌl]. Freq. of O.E. *þweran*, 'to stir, churn', cogn. w. *þwǣre*, 'a churn'; cogn. w. Lat. *trua*, 'a ladle', & *trulla*, 'a dipper, scoop', q.v. under **trowel. 1.** vb. **a** trans. To cause to revolve, whirl, or spin round: *to twirl one's moustache*; to twist so as to impart a rotatory movement to, to flourish: *to twirl a cane*; **b** intrans., to whirl, spin round. **2.** n. **a** Act of twirling; a whirling, a rotatory movement; **b** something twirled; a twist, coil; **c** a flourish, a twisting line, a twiddle.

twist (I.), n. [1. twist; 2. twist]. O.E. *twist* in the compound *mæst-twist*, 'mast-rope, stay'; formed fr. base in **twi-** & **two. 1.** Mass, bundle, formed by winding, twining, plaiting, flexible strands or some soft substance; **a** a hank of thread or yarn; **b** particular kind of yarn; **c** kind of coarse tobacco twisted into a tight roll; **d** loaf made of dough twisted into spiral form. **2.** A spinning, twisting, motion imparted to an object in throwing or striking it, which causes it to deviate suddenly from the original direction it follows: *to give a twist to a ball.* **3.** Act of twisting, bending; torsion, flexure: *to give a twist to a rope, to a person's arm.* **4.** A bend, coil, kink, turn, convolution: *a twist in a rope.* **5. a** Deviation, departure, from a straight line; curve, tortuosity: *a twist in a road, stream*; **b** (fig., in moral sense) (i.) departure from probity and uprightness in character or conduct; disingenuousness, lack of straightforwardness, candour, honesty: *a twist in one's nature*; also (ii.) abnormality, peculiar warped tendency of mind.

twist (II.), vb. trans. & intrans. M.E. *twisten*, see prec. **A.** trans. **1.** To plait, twine, interweave: *to twist threads into yarn, strands of jute &c. into a rope*; *to twist flowers into a wreath.* **2.** To wreathe, encircle with, wind round: *to twist wreaths round a column.* **3.** To impart spiral form to by torsion, that is by holding ends of and turning hands in opposite directions; to wring: *to twist a stick, a cloth* &c. **4.** (fig.) To distort, wrest, interpret in a sense at variance with true meaning: *to twist what is said so as to give a wrong impression.* **B.** intrans. **1. a** To assume spiral form; to wind, coil; to be distorted, to curve; **b** to writhe. **2.** To deviate suddenly from a straight line and move in different direction: *a cricket ball twists on the wicket.* **3. a** To move forward in a curving, winding path; to pursue a tortuous course: *the road, stream, turns and twists a good deal*; **b** (fig.) to be guilty of duplicity, to pursue a disingenuous line of conduct with a view to deceive.

twister, n. [1. twíster; 2. twístə]. Prec. & **-er. 1.** Person who twists (in various senses); specif. (fig.) one who speaks or acts insincerely, an unreliable, dishonest person, a dodger. **2.** Thing that twists; **a** a ball which turns suddenly in different direction, which breaks or screws; **b** machine for twisting threads; **c** (i.) a difficult task or problem; (ii.) word or combination of sounds difficult to pronounce; also *tongue-twister.*

twisty, adj. [1. twísti; 2. twísti]. **twist** (I.) & **-y. a** Abounding in twists and turns, curving, winding; **b** (fig., of persons) fond of and practising deception and intrigues; disingenuous, tortuous, dishonest, unreliable.

twit, vb. trans. [1. twit; 2. twit]. O.E. *ætwītan*, 'to reproach, blame', w. loss of the unstressed initial vowel; the first element is **at**; the second is the base *wīt, wit-* &c., 'to see, to know', wh. also expresses blame, hostility &c., cp. O.E. *witan*, 'to reproach with', *wīte*, 'torture, misery', Goth. *fraweitan*, 'to avenge', *fraweit*, 'punishment, vengeance'; see under **wit** (I.) & cp. **vision** (I.), & **idea, idol.** To reproach (a person) with (a fault, weakness, defect &c.); to bring such up against him; to remind (person) of (fault &c.) and taunt him with it: *to twit a person with*, or (more rarely) *about, his timidity, conceit, humble origin* &c.

twitch (I.), vb. trans. & intrans. [1. twich; 2. twitʃ]. M.E. *twicchen*; cp. O.E. *twiccian*, 'to pluck (fruit)', see **tweak**; connected w. O.E. *tucian*, 'pluck; oppress', see **tuck** (I.). **1.** trans. **a** To pluck, pull, with a sudden, jerking movement: *to twitch a cloth off a table*; *his cup was suddenly twitched from his hand*; **b** to move (something) with sudden jerky or tremulous motion: *a horse twitches his ears, tail* &c.; *to twitch one's eyelids.* **2.** intrans. To be seized, agitated, by a spasmodic, convulsive (usually involuntary), muscular movement: *his face twitched with pain, emotion* &c.; *a horse's ears twitch.*

twitch (II.), n. See prec. **1.** Act of twitching; process of being twitched; **a** a sharp, sudden pull, tweak or jerk; **b** a convulsive movement of part of the body. **2.** Something used for twitching; specif., a device consisting of a short handle with a cord attached which is twisted tightly round the upper lip of a horse, and held, to make him stand still while being clipped, shod, or subjected to some operation.

twitter, vb. intrans. & n. [1. twíter; 2. twítə]. M.E. *twiteren*; prob. imitative. **1.** vb. **a** (of birds) To utter a running series of shrill, intermittent notes, as at dawn or nightfall: '*And gathering swallows twitter in the skies*' (Keats, 'To Autumn'); **b** (of persons) to talk with a rapid, unresonant utterance, expressive of feebleness, timidity, and futility. **2.** n. **a** Sound made by birds that twitter; **b** rapidly uttered, feeble, futile speech or chatter. Phr. *in a twitter*, in an excited, nervous condition which tends to evoke shrill, rapid chatter.

twittering, n. [1. twítering; 2. twítəriŋ]. Prec. & **-ing.** Sounds, collectively, as uttered by birds or persons that twitter.

'twixt, prep. [1. twikst; 2. twikst]. Abbr. for **betwixt.**

two, adj. & n. [1. tōō; 2. tū]. O.E. *twā* (fem. & neut.), see also **twain**; M.E. *twō*; O.S. *twā* (fem.); O.H.G. *zwei*; Goth. *twai*; O.N. *tveir*; cogn. w. Lat. *duo*; Gk. *dúo*, see **dual**; Scrt. *dvā(u)*; O. Slav. *duva, dva*; see also **bi-, dis-. 1.** adj. One more than one; twice one. Phrs. *to cut in two*, divide into two parts; *to put two and two together*, to draw the obvious conclusion; *one or two*, a few. **2.** n. **a** A pair, group of two persons or things; *in two's and three's*, in small groups or batches; **b** symbol representing the number two—2, II., ii.

two-edged, adj. Having two cutting edges: *a two-edged sword*; also fig., *a two-edged compliment*, one that is ambiguous, and may be interpreted as an insult.

two-faced, adj. **a** Having two faces; **b** (fig.) double-faced, false.

twofold, adj. & adv. [1. tōōfōld; 2. tūfould]. **a** adj. Double; **b** adv., doubly.

two-handed, adj. **1.** Having two hands. **2.** Requiring two hands to lift, move, use &c.: *a two-handed sword.* **3.** (of games) Played by two persons.

two-headed, adj. Having two heads.

two-legged, adj. Having two legs; contrasted with *four-legged.*

two-line, adj. (typog., of a letter on page) Occupying the space, having the height, of two lines of specified type: *two-line brevier.*

twopence, n. [1. túpens; 2. tápəns]. The sum, value, of two pennies considered as a unity; formerly a coin of this value.

twopenny, adj. & n. [1. túpeni; 2. tápəni]. **1.** adj. Of the value or price of twopence: *a twopenny bun.* **2.** n. (slang) Head, in Phr. *tuck in your twopenny.*

twopenny-halfpenny, adj. [1. túpeni hápeni; 2. tápəni héipəni]. Insignificant, contemptible, trivial: *twopenny-halfpenny squabbles.*

two-ply, adj. **a** Having double thickness; **b** woven double; **c** having two strands.

two-power standard, n. Principle of naval construction based on having a navy equal to a combination of the navies of the two next strongest powers.

two-seater, n. Motor-car designed to seat two people.

two-sided, adj. Having two sides; having two aspects; having a double bearing.

twosome, n., orig. adj. [1. tōōsum; 2. tūsəm]. Game played by two players only.

two-speed, adj. Adaptable to two different speeds: *two-speed gear.*

two-step, n. **a** A dance in polka time; **b** music composed for such a dance.

-ty (I.), suff. forming abstract ns. fr. adj.; fr. Fr. *-té*, fr. Lat. *-tāt-*; *piety*, Fr. *piété*, Lat. *pietāt-(em)*, fr. *pius* &c.

-ty (II.), suff. O.E. *-tiġ*, 'ten', cp. O.E. *tīen*, '10', Goth. *tigus*, 'group of ten', *taihun*, '10'; see **ten.** Suffix used to denote so many times ten: *twenty, thirty* &c.

Tyburn, n. [1. tíburn; 2. táibən]. Former place of execution in London, close to present Marble Arch. *Tyburn tippet*, halter for hanging a criminal; *Tyburn tree*, the gallows.

tycoon, n. [1. tíkōōn; 2. taikūn]. Jap. *taikun*, 'great ruler'. Title applied formerly to the hereditary commander-in-chief, the shogun, in Japan; office and title now abolished.

tyke. See **tike.**

tyler. See **tiler.**

Tylopod, n. [1. tílopod; 2. táiləpɔd], fr. Gk. *túlos*, 'lump, knot', fr. base **tu-*, 'to swell', see **tumid, tumour** &c., & *pod-*, stem of *poús*, 'foot', see **pedal** (I.). Member of a division of ruminant mammals, including the camels, llamas &c.

tylosis, n. [1. tilósis; 2. tailóusis]. Gk. *túlos*, 'lump, knot', see prec. & **-osis. 1.** (med.) A thickening, hardening, of tissue. **2.** (bot.) Irregular mass of cells formed by growth of one plant cell into another.

tymp, n. [1. timp; 2. timp]. See next word. Covering of opening in a blast-furnace, through which molten metal and slag pass.

tympan, n. [1. tímpan; 2. tímpən]. Shortened form of **tympanum.** Thin sheet of paper, parchment &c., in a printing press, placed between the platen and the upper surface of the paper which is being printed.

tympanic, adj. [1. timpánik; 2. timpǽnik]. **tympanum** & **-ic. 1.** Pertaining to, resembling, a tympanum or drum. **2.** Specif., pertaining to the tympanum of the ear.

tympanites, n. [1. timpanítēz; 2. timpənáitīz]. Gk., see **tympanum** & **-ite.** Tightening, distension, of the abdomen, due to accumulation of gas in the intestines.

tympanitis, n. [1. timpanítis; 2. timpənáitis]. **tympanum** & **-itis.** Inflammation of the membrane of the middle ear.

tympano-, pref. Form of **tympanum** used in compounds.

tympanum, n. [1. tímpanum; 2. tímpənəm]. Lat., fr. Gk. *túmpanon*, 'a kettle-drum', also *túpanon*, fr. base *tup-*, as in Gk. *túptein*, 'to strike'; cogn. w. Scrt. *túmpati*, *tupáti*, 'he strikes'; O. Slav. *tŭpati*, 'to palpitate'; see also **type** (I.). **1.** (anat.) The drum or membrane of the ear. **2.** (archit.) Flat triangular space enclosed by the sides of a pediment or gable at the end of buildings; similar space over a door, between the lintel and the arch.

Tynewald, n. [1. tínwold; 2. táinwəld]. O.N. *þing-vǫllr*, lit. 'assembly field', the first element is cogn. w. Engl. **thing**, the second perh. w. Engl. **weald**. The legislative assembly or parliament of the Isle of Man.

type (I.), n. [1. tīp; 2. taip]. Fr., fr. Lat. *typus*, 'figure, image', fr. Gk. *túpos*, 'a blow; mark of a blow; impress of a seal; stamp on a coin; original pattern, model, mould'; fr. base *tup-*, 'to strike'; see **tympanum**. **1.** (rare) Characteristic mark; sign, stamp, impress. **2.** Person, thing, action, event, which is a symbol, or prefiguration, of some other person, thing, action &c.: *the king's sceptre is a type of royal authority*; *the slaying of the lamb at the Passover is a type of Christ's death*. **3. a** Mode of form or structure, combination of physical features, characteristic of all the members of a group: *each of the great races of mankind exhibits a definite type*; **b** class or group, which is recognizable as such by the possession of certain characteristic features and peculiarities of structure &c.: *Australia has many types of animal and plant life not found in other continents*; *it is now disputed whether there is such a thing as a criminal type*; *true to type*, exhibiting the distinguishing features of a class. **4.** Class or group, also a member or example of such, distinguished by having certain material or moral qualities common to the whole class: *this is just the type of house I require*; *men of his type are not to be trusted*. **5.** A member of a class or group regarded as exhibiting the characteristics and qualities of the class in a very complete manner, and as constituting a standard; pattern, model: *a perfect type of English country gentleman*. **6. a** Block of metal, more rarely of wood, upon the upper surface of which a letter or other symbol is cast or cut, from which an impression is taken in printing; **b** (collectively) a set, collection, of types: *books are stereotyped to avoid keeping large quantities of type lying idle*; Phr. *in type*, set up in the press all ready for printing; **c** style, shape, kind, of type: *the type of the book is admirable*.

type (II.), vb. trans. & intrans., fr. prec. **1.** trans. (rarely) To typify, be a type of. **2. a** trans. To print (words) with a typewriter, to typewrite; **b** intrans., to use a typewriter.

-type, suff., fr. **type** (I.). **1.** Representative, exemplar: *prototype*. **2.** Print, mode of printing, of reproduction: *autotype*, *stereotype*.

type-founder, n. One who casts type for printing.

type-foundry, n. Place where metal is cast into type.

type-setter, n. Compositor in printing works.

typewrite, vb. trans. & intrans. [1. típrīt; 2. táiprait]. **a** trans. To print, copy, with a typewriter; **b** intrans., to make use of a typewriter.

typewriter, n. [1. típrìter; 2. táipràitə]. Machine worked by the fingers, which transmits printed characters to paper, used instead of handwriting.

typewritten, adj. [1. típritn; 2. táipritn], fr. P.P. of **typewrite**. Copied, written, on a typewriter.

typhlitis, n. [1. tiflítis; 2. tifláitis]. Coined fr. Gk. *tuphlós*, 'blind, closed' (for cognates see **deaf**), on anal. of med. Lat. *caecum*, & **-itis**. Inflammation of the caecum.

typhoid, adj. & n. [1. tífoid; 2. táifɔid]. See **typhus** & **-oid**. **a** adj. Resembling, of the nature of, typhus; *typhoid fever*, an infectious fever, originally thought to be a form of typhus, but now known to be due to a bacillus, *typhoid bacillus*, conveyed by infected drinking water, milk, or food; the disease is now usually styled *enteric fever*; **b** n., typhoid fever.

typhoidal, adj. [1. tīfóidl; 2. taifɔ́idl]. Prec. & **-al**. Pertaining to, resembling, typhoid fever.

typhomania, n. [1. tīfōmánia; 2. tàifouméiniə]. **typhus** & **mania**. Delirium characteristic of typhus fever.

typhonic, adj. [1. tīfónik; 2. taifónik]. See next word & **-ic**. Pertaining to, of the nature of, a typhoon.

typhoon, n. [1. tīfóon; 2. taifún]. Earlier *tuffoon*, Port. *tufão*; prob. fr. Gk. *tūphôn*, 'furious storm, hurricane'; fr. base **dhū-* &c.; see **typhus** & words there referred to. The Chinese *tai fêng*, 'great wind', may possibly have been the starting-point, but the above quite unrelated Gk. word is responsible for the form of the word we use. Violent whirlwind, a hurricane; specif., one occurring in China seas.

typhous, adj. [1. tífus; 2. táifəs]. **typhus** & **-ous**. Connected with, of the nature of, typhus.

typhus, n. [1. tífus; 2. táifəs], fr. Gk. *tûphos*, 'smoke, mist, cloud'; cp. *tūphein*, 'to smoke', for **thūph-*, cogn. w. Scrt. *dhūpa*, 'smoke'; fr. base **dhū-* &c., q.v. under **dust** (I.) & **fume** (I.). Contagious fever due to a bacillus conveyed by lice, fleas, and other parasites, causing great weakness, and accompanied by red spots on the body; formerly called *jail fever* and *putrid fever*.

typic, adj. [1. típik; 2. típik]. Fr. *typique*, Lat. *typicus*, fr. Gk. *tupikós*; **type** (I.) & **-ic**. Typical.

typical, adj. [1. típikl; 2. típikl]. Prec. & **-al**. **1.** Possessing, exhibiting, so fully the characteristics of a type as to serve as an example, specimen, or representative of this: *a typical Oxford don*; *a typical British officer* &c. **2.** Symbolical, emblematic: *the Passover was typical of Christ's death*.

typically, adv. [1. típik(a)li; 2. típik(ə)li]. Prec. & **-ly**. In a typical manner.

typify, vb. trans. [1. típifī; 2. típifai]. See **type** (I.) & **-fy**. **1.** To be a type, symbol, of, to prefigure. **2.** To exhibit essential characteristic features of; to exemplify.

typist, n. [1. típist; 2. táipist]. **type** (II.) & **-ist**. Person who works a typewriting machine.

typo-, form of Gk. *túpos* used in compounds; see **type** (I.).

typographer, n. [1. tīpógrafer; 2. taipɔ́grəfə]. **typo-** & **-graph** & **-er**. One who has to do with type and printing; a printer.

typographic(al), adj. [1. tīpográfik(l); 2. tàipəgrǽfik(l)]. See prec. & **-ic** & (**-al**). Connected with, pertaining to, the art of printing.

typographically, adv. Prec. & **-ly**. As regards printing.

typography, n. [1. tīpógrafi; 2. taipɔ́grəfi]. **typo-** & **-graphy**. **a** The art of printing from type; **b** style of printing, mode of arrangement of type.

typology, n. [1. tīpóloji; 2. taipɔ́lədži]. **typo-** & **-logy**. **a** Doctrine that events &c. recorded in the New Testament are prefigured in the Old; **b** treatise on the types of Scripture.

tyrannical, adj. [1. ti-, tīránikl; 2. ti-, tairǽnikl]. Lat. *tyrannicus*, fr. Gk. *turannikós*; see **tyrant** & **-ic** & **-al**. Characteristic of, natural to, befitting, resembling, a tyrant; hence, oppressive, arbitrarily harsh, despotic.

tyrannically, adv. Prec. & **-ly**. In a tyrannical, oppressive manner; harshly and unjustly.

tyrannicidal, adj. [1. tirànisídl; 2. tirǽnisáidl]. Next word & **-al**. Pertaining to the killing of a tyrant, or of tyrants.

tyrannicide, n. [1. ti-, tīránisīd; 2. ti-, tairǽnisaid]. Lat. (i.) *tyrannicīdium*, 'killing of a tyrant'; (ii.) *tyrannicīda*, 'killer of a tyrant'; see **tyrant** & **-cide**. **1.** Act of killing a tyrant. **2.** One who kills a tyrant.

tyrannize, vb. intrans. [1. tíranīz; 2. tírənaiz]. Fr. *tyranniser*, fr. Gk. *turannízein*, 'to play the part of a tyrant'; see **tyrant** & **-ize**. To play the tyrant; to rule, exert authority harshly, arbitrarily, and unjustly; *tyrannize over*.

tyrannous, adj. [1. tíranus; 2. tírənəs]. O. Fr. *tiran-*, see **tyrant**, & **-ous**. Like a tyrant, tyrannical.

tyrannously, adv. Prec. & **-ly**. In a tyrannous manner.

tyrannousness, n. See prec. & **-ness**. **a** Quality of being tyrannous; **b** tyrannous conduct.

tyranny, n. [1. tírani; 2. tírəni]. M.E., fr. O. Fr. *tirannie*, fr. Gk. *turannía*, 'rule of a tyrant'; see **tyrant** & **-y**. **1.** (Gk. hist.) Government, jurisdiction, of a tyrant in old sense (see **tyrant**, **1**). **2.** Harsh, arbitrary, unjust exercise of authority; despotism, oppressive rule. **3.** A tyrannical action; an example of the exercise of despotic power, or of an unduly rigorous discipline.

tyrant, n. [1. tírant; 2. táiərənt]. M.E. *tirant*, fr. O. Fr. *tirant*, earlier *tiran*; fr. Lat. *tyrannus*, fr. Gk. *túrannos*, 'an absolute prince or ruler; a cruel, unjust ruler'. According to some authorities the word is of Phrygian origin; others connect w. the base in Lith. *tverti*, 'to seize'; others again w. Scrt. *tūrvati*, 'to subjugate'. **1.** (anct. Gk. hist.) An absolute ruler; applied to one who had seized the supreme power, as contrasted with a hereditary king. **2. a** A despotic, harsh, unjust, arbitrary, ruler; one who oppresses his people; **b** any masterful person who exerts his authority in a cruel, oppressive manner.

tyre. See **tire** (II.), **3**.

tyro. See **tiro**.

tyro-, pref., fr. Gk. *tūrós*, 'cheese'; prob. fr. same base as Lat. *turgēre*, 'to swell'; see **turgid**, & second element of **butter** (I.). Occurs as prefix in a few scientific words, e.g. *tyrotoxicon*, poisonous substance occurring in putrid cheese, milk, or butter.

tzar, **tzarina** &c. See **czar** &c.

tzetze-fly. See **tsetse-fly**.

Tzigany, adj. & n. [1. tsigáhni; 2. tsigáni]. Fr. *tzigane*, fr. Magyar *c(z)igány*. **a** adj. Pertaining to a (Hungarian) gipsy; **b** n., a Hungarian gipsy.

U

U, u, [1. ū; 2. jū]. The twenty-first letter of the English alphabet; for use in abbreviations &c. see list at end of Dictionary.

uberous, adj. [1. úberus; 2. júbərəs]. Lat. *ūber*, 'a teat, breast, udder'; also as adj., 'rich, full, fertile'; for suff. see **-ous**. *Uber* is cogn. w. Gk. *oûthar*; Scrt. *úhar*, 'udder', also w. O.E. *ūder*, see **udder**. (rare) Plentiful, copious; fertile.

uberrima fides, n. [1. ūbérima fídēz; 2. jūbérimə fáidīz]. Lat. superl. of *ūber*, 'fruitful' &c., see prec.; for *fidēs*, 'faith', see **fidelity**. (law) The most complete good faith, esp. applied to contracts entered into by parties standing in a particular relation of mutual trust, as guardian and ward, solicitor and client &c.

ubiety, n. [1. ubíeti; 2. jūbáiiti]. Neo-Lat. *ubietāt-*, stem of *ubietas*, 'wheresoever', formed fr. Lat. *ubi*, 'where', for **cubi*, as in *alicubi*, 'elsewhere'; Aryan **kʷu-* &c. (orig. a pronominal stem) appears also in Scrt. *kvá*, 'where, whither'; Gk. *póteron*, 'whether' &c.; see also under **how & where (I.)**. (philos.) Whereness; quality or state of being in a place in relation to another thing; abstract, relative position.

Ubiquitarian, n. [1. ûbikwitárian; 2. jùbikwitéərian]. Formed fr. **ubiquity & -arian.** (theol.) One who believes in the ubiquity or omnipresence of the body of Christ in all things, not only in heaven and the Eucharist, a doctrine held by certain Lutheran theologians.

Ubiquitarianism, n. [1. ūbikwitárianizm; 2. jūbìkwitéərianizm]. Prec. & **-ism.** (theol.) Doctrine of the Ubiquitarians.

ubiquitous, adj. [1. ūbíkwitus; 2. jūbíkwitəs]. **ubiquity & -ous.** Being, existing, found, present, everywhere, omnipresent.

ubiquitously, adv. Prec. & **-ly.** In a ubiquitous manner; as if present everywhere.

ubiquitousness, n. See prec. & **-ness.** State of being ubiquitous or present everywhere.

ubiquity, n. [1. ūbíkwiti; 2. jūbíkwiti], fr. O. Fr. *ubiquite*, as if fr. Lat. **ubīquitas*, fr. *ubīque*, 'everywhere', see **ubiety, & -ity.** State, quality, of being ubiquitous; presence, existence, in every place or an indefinite number of places at the same time; omnipresence. Phr. *the ubiquity of the king*, (law) the assumed presence of the sovereign in all his courts of justice in the person of his judges.

ubi supra, adv. [1. úbi súpra; 2. júbi sjúprə]. Lat., 'where above'. In the place above mentioned; as reference in book to a work, passage &c. cited previously.

U-boat, n. [1. ú bôt; 2. jú bòut]. A German submarine; these in the German navy were lettered U followed by a numeral, as abbreviation of *Unter-see boot*, lit. 'under-sea boat, submarine'.

udal, n. [1. údal; 2. júdəl], also *odal*, fr. O.N. *ōðal*, Dan. *odel*, cogn. w. O.H.G. *uodil*, 'farm'. (legal hist.) A form of land tenure, *udal tenure*, existing in Scotland prior to the establishment of the feudal system, and still existing in Orkney and Shetland, in which land is held by right of uninterrupted possession and descends to all the children equally; *udal man, woman*, male, female, owner by udal; udaller.

udaller, n. [1. údaler; 2. júdələ]. Prec. & **-er.** Owner of land by udal tenure.

udder, n. [1. úder; 2. ádə]. O.E. *ūder*, M.E. *uddir* &c.; O.H.G. *ūtār*, Mod. Germ. *euter*; cogn. w. Lat. *über*, see **uberous.** The large, pendulous external milk gland with more than one teat or nipple, esp. of cows, sheep, goats &c.

-uddered, adj. [1. úderd; 2. ádəd]. Prec. & **-ed.** Having so many or such udders: *double-, two-uddered* &c.; *large-, small-uddered.*

udderless, adj. [1. úderles; 2. ádəlis]. **udder & -less.** Deprived of udders or nourishment from the mother; hence, motherless: *udderless lambs.*

-ude, suff. [1. ūd; 2. jūd], fr. Lat. *-ūdo*, forming abstract ns. fr. adjs. & P.P.'s w. stems ending in *-t*; see **-tude.**

udograph, n. [1. údōgrahf; 2. júdougrāf]. See first element of **udometer & -graph.** An automatic, self-registering rain-gauge.

udometer, n. [1. ūdómeter; 2. jūdɔ́mitə], fr. Lat. *ūdus*, 'wet', contracted fr. **uoidus*, 'wet, damp, moist', cogn. w. Gk. *hugrós*, 'wet, moist'; further related to Scrt. *ukšati*, 'he sprinkles'; prob. also to Scrt. *ukšan-*, 'ox'; see also **ox**; for suff. see **-meter.** A rain-gauge.

udometric, adj. [1. ûdōmétrik; 2. jùdoumétrik]. Prec. & **-ic.** Pertaining to a rain-gauge or measurement of rainfall by such instrument.

udometry, n. [1. ûdómetri; 2. jùdɔ́mitri]. Measurement of rainfall by a udometer or rain-gauge.

ugh, interj. [1. ugh; 2. aχ]. Imitative. An expression of disgust, contempt, disapproval, and dislike.

uglify, vb. trans. [1. úglifī; 2. áglifai]. **ugly (I.) & -fy.** To make ugly; to spoil the beauty or attractiveness of.

uglily, adv. [1. úglili; 2. áglili]. **ugly (I.) & -ly.** In an ugly manner.

ugliness, n. [1. úglines; 2. áglinis]. **ugly (I.) & -ness.** Condition, quality, of being ugly.

ugly (I.), adj. [1. úgli; 2. ágli]. Scand., fr. O.N. *uggligr*, 'fearful, horrible, awful', fr. *uggr*, 'fear', cogn. w. **awe (I.)**; the suff. is O.N. *-ligr*, see **-ly.** 1. Repulsive, unpleasing to the sight; hideous, unbecoming, the opposite of *beautiful, handsome*, or *pleasing* or *becoming*: *an ugly face*; *ugly building*; *ugly clothes*; *ugly way of doing the hair.* 2. Offensive to the moral sense, repulsive, vile, unpleasantly suggestive, disreputable: *ugly customs and habits*; *an ugly crime*; *there are ugly rumours about his past.* 3. Threatening, menacing; foreboding danger or unpleasantness: *ugly weather*; *the sky has an ugly look*; *the crowd made an ugly rush*; *the situation becomes more ugly every day*; *an ugly wound.* Phr. *an ugly customer* (colloq.), a dangerous, rough, violent, person.

ugly (II.), n., fr. prec. 1. (colloq.) An ugly person or thing. 2. A shade attached to the front part of a bonnet, worn during the middle part of the 19th cent.

Ugrian, adj. & n. [1. úgrian; 2. júgriən], fr. Ugra, name of the country on both sides of the Ural Mountains & **-ian.** 1. adj. Of, belonging to, the Eastern division of the races and their languages, known as the Finno-Ugrian or Finnic peoples, including the Ostyaks and Voguls of Asiatic Russia, and specif., the Hungarians and Magyars. 2. n. a A member of these races; b one of the languages spoken by them.

Ugric, adj. [1. úgrik; 2. júgrik]. See prec. & **-ic.** Ugrian.

uhlan, n. [1. o͞oláhn; 2. ūlán]. Germ., fr. Pol. *ulan*, 'lancer', fr. Turk. and Tatar *oglān*, 'son, child'; also as title of a chief. A light cavalry soldier, armed with a lance, of the pre-War German or Austrian armies.

ukase, n. [1. ūkáz; 2. jukéiz]. Fr., fr. Russ. *ukaz*, 'edict; order, decree', fr. *ukazat*, 'to order'. An edict or decree having the force of law on proclamation, as in Tsarist Russia.

ukulele, n. [1. úkuláli; 2. jùkəléili]. Hawaiian, lit. 'jumping insect, flea'. A Hawaiian musical stringed instrument, shaped like a guitar or banjo and twanged with the fingers or plectrum.

ulcer, n. [1. úlser; 2. álsə], fr. Fr. *ulcère*, fr. Lat. *ulcer-(em)*, stem of *ulcus*, 'a sore'; cogn. w. Gk. *hélkos*, 'wound, abscess', cp. Scrt. *arçaš*, 'haemorrhoids'. See **helcosis.** 1. An open sore, discharging pus, whether on the external surface of the skin or on an internal mucous membrane: *a varicose ulcer*; *gastric ulcer* &c. 2. (fig.) A source of moral contagion, corruption; corrupting, festering influence, a moral sore: *the ulcer of discontent, envy* &c.

ulcerate, vb. trans. & intrans. [1. úlserāt; 2. álsərèit], fr. Lat. *ulcerāt-(um)*, P.P. type of *ulcerāre*, 'to make sore'; see prec. & **-ate.** 1. trans. a To cause the formation of an ulcer in; to infect with an ulcer or ulceration; rare except in P.P. as adj.: *ulcerated sore throat, gums, leg* &c.; b to corrupt morally. 2. intrans. To become ulcerated; to form ulcers.

ulceration, n. [1. ùlseráshun; 2. àlsəréiʃən]. Prec. & **-ion.** a Ulcerated condition; b process of becoming ulcerated.

ulcerative, adj. [1. úlserativ; 2. álsərətiv]. **ulcerate & -ive.** 1. Tending to cause or produce ulcers; ulcerating. 2. Infected with ulcers; ulcerous.

ulcered, adj. [1. úlserd; 2. álsəd]. **ulcer & -ed.** Affected by an ulcer; ulcerated; festered.

ulcerous, adj. [1. úlserus; 2. álsərəs], fr. Lat. *ulcerōsus*; **ulcer & -ous.** 1. a Of the nature of an ulcer; sore and discharging pus: *an ulcerous wound*; b (fig.) corrupting, festering: *an ulcerous hatred.* 2. Affected by an ulcer or ulcers; ulcerated: *an ulcerous leg, gums* &c.

ulcerously, adv. Prec. & **-ly.** In an ulcerous manner.

ulcerousness, n. See prec. & **-ness.** State of being ulcerous or ulcerated.

-ule, dimin. suff., fr. Lat. words ending in *-ulus, -a, -um*; as *globule*, or in mod. formations on anal. of Lat., as *pillule.*

ulema, n. [1. óolema; 2. úlimə], fr. Arab. *'ulamā*, 'learned men', pl. of *'alim*, 'wise, learned', fr. *'alama*, 'to know, be wise'. Men learned in Moslem theology and law, specif., the college of doctors of sacred law, presided over by the Sheikh-ul Islam of Turkey.

uliginose, uliginous, adj. [1. ūlíjinōs, -us; 2. jūlídžinous, -əs], fr. Lat. *ūlīginōsus*, 'damp, wet, marshy', fr. *ūlīgin-(em)*, stem of *ūlīgo*, 'moisture, dampness, marshiness'; for **ūviligo*, w. dial. *l* for earlier *d*; cp. *ūvidus, ūdus*, 'moist, damp'; see first element of **udometer.** 1. Oozy, muddy, slimy. 2. (bot.) Growing in swampy, muddy places.

ullage, n. [1. úlij; 2. álidž], fr. Provenç. *ulhage*, in O. Fr. *eullage, ouillage*, fr. Provenç. *ulha*, 'to fill up (cask) to the bung or eye'; ultimately fr. Lat. *oculus*, 'eye', see **ocular, & -age.** The amount by which a cask or bottle of liquor is short of being full.

ulmaceous, adj. [1. ulmáseus; 2. alméiʃəs]. Mod. formation fr. Lat. *ulmus*, 'the elm', see **elm, & -aceous.** (bot.) Of, belonging to, the family of trees, *Ulmaceae*, which includes the elms.

ulmic, adj. [1. úlmik; 2. álmik]. **ulmin & -ic.** (chem.) Of, pertaining to, obtained from, ulmin: *ulmic acid*, an acid found in humus.

ulmin, n. [1. úlmin; 2. álmin]. New formation, fr. Lat. *ulmus*, 'elm', see **elm, & -in.** (chem.) A brown, sticky substance found on elms and other trees, and also in decaying vegetable mould or humus; one of the chemical constituents of humus.

ulna, n., pl. **ulnae**, [1. úlna, -nē; 2. álnə, -nī]. Lat., 'elbow'; fr. **olenā*, fr. Gk. *ōlénē*, 'elbow'; cogn. w. Goth. *aleina*; O.E. *eln*; see **ell & elbow.** (anat.) The inner of the two bones of the forearm, or of the two similar bones of the fore-limb of vertebrate animals.

ulnar, adj. [1. úlnar; 2. álnə]. Prec. & **-ar.** (anat.) Pertaining to, situated on, the same side as the ulna: *ulnar artery, nerve, vein.*

ulno-, pref. Form of **ulna** used in compounds; *ulnocarpal*, pertaining to the ulna and carpus.

ulotrichous, adj. [1. ūlótrikus; 2. jūlɔ́trikəs], fr. Gk. *oulóthrix*, genit. *oulótrikhos*, 'woolly haired', fr. *oûlos*, 'curly, woolly', & *thrix, trikhós*, 'hair'. The first element is for **wolnos*, & is cogn. w. Lat. *lāna*, 'wool', fr. **wlāna*, see **lanate**; & O.E. *wull*, see **wool**; for second element see **tricho-.** (ethnol.) Having woolly hair; esp. of the woolly-haired or negroid races.

ulster, n. [1. úlster; 2. álstə], fr. Ulster, the N.E. province of Ireland. A long heavy loose overcoat, usually furnished with a belt, and sometimes with a small hood which hangs down the back when not used for protecting the head.

ulterior, adj. [1. ultérior; 2. altíəriə]. Lat., 'farther, beyond', compar. of an old adj. **ulter*, the base of wh. is seen in *ultrā & ultro*, & in O. Lat. *uls, ols*, 'beyond', cp. also O. Lat. *ollus*, 'that one', later *ille.* 1. (of position) Lying on the farther side of or beyond a specified boundary line: *on the ulterior side of the river.* 2. (of time) Following, succeeding in the future; later in time; prospective: *ulterior steps will be taken to secure this object*; *the ulterior consequences of his act.* 3. (of motives, aims, intentions &c.) More remote; not plainly avowed; undisclosed: *ulterior* *motives*; *ulterior objects, plans* &c.; *for the sake of ulterior ends.*

ulteriorly, adv. Prec. & **-ly**. In an ulterior manner; more remotely.

ultima, adj. & n. [1. última; 2. áltimə]. Lat., fem. sing. of *ultimus*, 'last, latest', superl. of **ulter*, see **ulterior**. **1.** adj. Last, final; in Phrs. *ultima ratio*, the last, final reason or argument or sanction, force or violence; *ultima ratio regum*, 'the final argument of kings', war and its instruments; *ultima Thule*, furthest Thule, an island placed by ancient geographers north of the British Isles; hence, any far-distant, unknown land. **2.** n. The final syllable of a word.

ultimate, adj. [1. últimat; 2. áltimit], fr. Lat. *ultimāt-(um)*, P.P. type of *ultimāre*, 'to be at the last, to come to an end', fr. *ultimus*, 'last', see prec. word. **1.** (of place) Farthest, most distant, beyond which one cannot go: *to the ultimate ends of the earth*; *the ultimate regions of space.* **2.** (of time) Last, latest, final: *man's ultimate end, destiny*; *to look forward to an ultimate peace.* **3.** Last in a series, chain of succession, or consequences: *the ultimate results of one's action.* **4.** Final, fundamental; beyond further analysis, primary: *ultimate causes, principles*; *the ultimate sources of belief.*

ultimately, adv. Prec. & **-ly**. In an ultimate manner; finally, in the end, at last.

ultimateness, n. See prec. & **-ness**. State, quality, of being ultimate; finality.

ultimatum, n. [1. ùltimā́tum; 2. àltiméitəm], pl. *ultimata*, or *ultimatums*. Lat., neut. sing. of P.P. of *ultimāre*, 'to come to an end'. Formed fr. *ultimus*, 'last', see **ultimate**. The last word, final expression of intentions &c.; specif., the final terms, admitting of no further discussion, proposed by a government or other administrative or executive body, or by an individual, in negotiating with another; the rejection of an ultimatum by the party to whom it is presented implies the end of friendly negotiations and a resort to methods designed to compel compliance with the will of the party presenting it.

ultimo, adv., abbr. *ult.* [1. últimō; 2. áltimou], fr. Lat. *ultimō*, sc. *mense*, 'in the last month'; see **ultima**. In the month preceding the present or current month: *in answer to your letter of the 16th ultimo*; cp. *instant* and *proximo.*

ultimogeniture, n. [1. últimōjénichur; 2. áltimoudžénitʃə]. Prec. & **-geniture**. (law) A system of inheritance by which landed property descends to the youngest son, as in Borough-English, contrasted with *primogeniture.*

ultra, adj. & n. [1. últra; 2. áltrə]. Lat. adv. & prep., 'beyond, on the other, far side of', see **ulterior**. **1.** adj. Extreme in views, opinions &c.; favouring extreme principles: *an ultra Conservative, Protestant* &c. **2.** n. One who holds extreme opinions &c.; an extremist: *a thorough-paced ultra.*

ultra-, pref., fr. prec., quite freely used w. adjs. & derivative ns., indicating, to an excessive degree or extent, beyond what is customary, ordinary, natural, proper, or reasonable; *ultra-conservative*; *ultra-fashionable*; *an ultra-Protestant* &c.; only words with a special meaning are given separate entries.

ultraism, n. [1. últraìzm; 2. áltrəizəm]. **ultra-** & **-ism**. The holding of extreme, esp. political, opinions.

ultraist, n. [1. últraist; 2. áltrəist]. As prec. & **-ist**. One who holds extreme opinions.

ultramarine (I.), adj. [1. últramarḗn; 2. áltrəmərín]. **ultra-** & **marine (I.)**. Situated beyond the sea or seas; overseas: *ultramarine dominions*; *ultramarine trade.*

ultramarine (II.), n. & adj., fr. Ital. *oltramarino*, 'beyond the seas', w. first syll. Latinized; applied to lapis lazuli, wh. had to be imported. **1.** n. A brilliant pure blue pigment, originally obtained from powdered lapis lazuli, now artificially produced from kaolin, silica, sulphate and carbonate of soda &c. **2.** adj. Of blue colour, as in this pigment.

ultra-microscopic, adj. **ultra-** & **microscopic**. Beyond the range of the microscope; too small to be visible under the microscope.

ultramontane, adj. & n. [1. últramóntān; 2. áltrəmóntein]. See **ultra-** & **montane**; cp. Fr. *ultramontain*, Ital. *oltramontano*, fr. L. Lat. *ultramontānus*, in Class. Lat. *trāmontānus*, see **tramontane**. **1.** adj. **a** Beyond, on the other side of, the mountains, i.e. the Alps; applied to Italians by northern peoples as living on the south side, and vice versa; **b** specif., pertaining to, supporting, the extreme claims of the Papacy to absolute authority in all matters of faith and discipline, over-riding general Councils, together with refusal to allow any independence to national Roman Catholic Churches outside Italy; a term used by opponents of the full enforcement of the decrees of the Vatican Council of 1870. **2.** n. **a** One who lives beyond the Alps; **b** (cap.) a supporter of the ultramontane policy in the Roman Catholic Church.

ultramontanism, n. [1. últramóntinizm; 2. áltrəmóntinizəm]. Prec. & **-ism**. Principles, policy, of the ultramontanes.

ultramontanist, n. [1. últramóntinist; 2. áltrəmóntinist]. **ultramontane** & **-ist**. An ultramontane.

ultramundane, adj. [1. últramúndān; 2. áltrəmándein]. **ultra-** & **mundane**. (rare) Beyond, outside, the world, or the limits of the solar system.

ultra-red, adj. **ultra-** & **red**. (phys.) Of those rays of the spectrum which are below the red, the lowest visible rays; infra-red.

ultra-violet, adj. **ultra-** & **violet**. (phys.) Of those electro-magnetic waves which in the spectrum fall between the visible violet and the X-rays.

ultra vires, adv. or adj. [1. últra vírēz; 2. áltrə váiəriz]. Lat., 'beyond powers or strength'; **ultra** & *vīrēs*, pl. of *vīs*, 'force, strength', see **virile**. (law) Beyond, transcending, power or authority; exceeding the powers granted by law; used esp. of actions taken by the directors of a company or by municipal or local authorities in excess of their powers.

ululant, adj. [1. úlūlant; 2. júljulənt], fr. Lat. *ululant-(em)*, Pres. Part. of *ululāre*, see next word. Howling, hooting.

ululate, vb. intrans. [1. úlūlāt; 2. júljuleit], fr. Lat. *ululāt-(um)*, P.P. type of *ululāre*, 'to howl'; imitative. To howl, hoot, as wolves, owls &c.

ululation, n. [1. ùlūlā́shun; 2. jùljuléiʃən]. Prec. & **-ion**. **a** The sound of lamentation; howling, wailing; **b** the act of howling &c.; used of the cries of owls, wolves &c., also of human wailing.

umbel, n. [1. úmbl; 2. ámbl], fr. Lat. *umbella*, 'a little shade, a sunshade, parasol', dimin. of *umbra*, 'shade, shadow', q.v. under **umbra**. (bot.) A type of flower cluster or inflorescence in which the stalks radiate from a single point forming a flat or convex head of flowers.

umbellal, adj. [1. úmbelal; 2. ámbeləl]. **umbel** & **-al**. (bot.) Umbellate.

umbellar, adj. [1. úmbelar; 2. ámbelə]. As prec. & **-ar**. (bot.) Umbellate.

umbellate, adj. [1. úmbelāt; 2. ámbeleit]. **umbel** & **-ate**. (bot.) Having umbels; arranged in umbels.

umbellet, n. [1. úmbelet; 2. ámbelet]. **umbel** & **-et**. (bot.) An umbellule.

umbelliferous, adj. [1. ùmbelíferus; 2. àmbelífərəs]. **umbel** & **-ferous**. (bot.) **a** Bearing, having, umbels; **b** belonging to the Umbelliferae, a large order of plants chiefly characterized by the umbels of their inflorescence.

umbelliform, adj. [1. umbéliform; 2. ambélifɔm]. **umbel** & **-form**. (bot.) Having the form or shape of an umbel.

umbellule, n. [1. úmbelūl; 2. ámbeljūl]. **umbel** & **-ule**. (bot.) One of the secondary umbels in a compound umbelliferous plant; umbellet.

umber (I.), n. [1. úmber; 2. ámbə], fr. O. Fr. *ombre*, in this sense short for *terre d'ombre*, 'earth for giving shadow' to pictures, fr. Lat. *umbra*, 'shade, shadow'; see **umbra**. **1.** An earthy, mineral pigment of a yellowish-brown colour, in raw or natural state, and with a reddish tint when burnt or calcined. **2.** **a** The grayling (fish); **b** umber-bird or umbrette.

umber (II.), adj., fr. prec. Of dark-brown colour.

umber (III.), vb. trans. To colour, paint, with umber.

umber-bird, n. An African wading-bird, *Scopus umbretta*, allied to the herons, of dark-brown plumage, large bill and crested head; the umbrette.

umbilical, adj. [1. umbílikl; 2. ambílikl]. See **umbilicus** & **-al**. **1.** Of, pertaining to, situated in the region of, the umbilicus or navel: *umbilical cord*, the navel cord, the rope-like structure joining the foetus of a mammal to the placenta and containing the *umbilical veins and arteries*, through which blood passes to and from the placenta; *umbilical hernia*, hernia of the bowels at or near the umbilicus. **2.** In the position of, shaped like, an umbilicus or navel: *an umbilical pillar* of a dome or vault; *umbilical opening*, in a dome. **3.** (rare) Descended from the mother's side.

umbilicate, adj. [1. umbílikāt; 2. ambílikeit]. **umbilicus** & **-ate**. **1.** **a** Having an umbilicus or navel; **b** having a depression in the centre like an umbilicus. **2.** Shaped like an umbilicus.

umbilication, n. [1. ùmbilikā́shun; 2. àmbilikéiʃən]. Prec. & **-ion**. A navel-like depression.

umbilicular, adj. [1. ùmbilíkūlar; 2. àmbilíkjulə]. **umbilicus** & **-ule** & **-ar**. Of, pertaining to, the umbilicus; umbilical.

umbilicus, n. [1. ùmbilíkus; 2. àmbiláikəs]. Lat. *umbilīcus*, cogn. w. Gk. *omphalós*, & **navel**; cp. **umbo**. **1.** The anatomical name for the navel, q.v. **2.** **a** A circular navel-like central depression, as in certain shells; **b** the hilum or 'eye' of beans and other seeds. **3.** (Rom. antiq.) The boss at each end of the wooden staff on which manuscripts were rolled. **4.** (geom.) **a** (obs.) Focus; **b** point on a surface through which all lines of curvature pass.

umbiliform, adj. [1. umbíliform; 2. ambílifɔm]. Prec. & **-form**. Shaped like an umbilicus.

umble pie, n. [1. úmbl pí; 2. ámbl pái]. See **humble pie**, & for etymol. see next word.

umbles, n. [1. úmblz; 2. ámblz]. Also *numbles*, M.E. *noumbles*, fr. O. Fr. *nombles*, properly *lombles*, fr. L. Lat. *lumbulus*, dimin. of *lumbus*, 'loin', see **lumbar**. (obs.) The entrails of a deer.

umbo, n. [1. úmbō; 2. ámbou]. Lat., 'a convex elevation; the boss of a shield', cogn. w. **umbilicus**. **1.** The boss of a shield, usually in the centre and having a corresponding depression on the other or internal side. **2.** Any round, elevated protuberance, usually with corresponding depression; **a** (anat.) part of the drum of the ear where it joins the malleus; **b** (bot.) protuberance on the top surface of various fungi; **c** (zool.) similar protuberance forming the first stage in the development of a valve in the shells of various molluscs.

umbonal, adj. [1. úmbonal; 2. ámbənəl], fr. Lat. *umbōn-(em)* & **-al**. Pertaining to, situated near, the umbo.

umbonate, adj. [1. úmbonāt; 2. ámbəneit]. As prec. & **-ate**. Shaped like an umbo or boss.

umbra, n., learned pl. **umbrae** [1. úmbra, úmbrē; 2. ámbrə, ámbrī]. Lat., 'shade, shadow'; said by Walde to be fr. **unkʷs-ra*, 'shadow, shade', & cogn. w. Lith. *ùnks-na*, 'shade', & *úkanas*, 'cloudy'. **1.** (astron.) **a** The complete or perfect shadow thrown in an eclipse by the moon, earth &c., leaving

none of the sun's light visible, opposed to *penumbra*; **b** the central, darkest part of a sun-spot. **2.** (Rom. antiq.) An uninvited guest who comes as the shadow of an invited guest.

umbraculiferous, adj. [1. úmbrakūlíferus; 2. ámbrəkjulífərəs]. **umbraculum** & **-ferous**. (bot.) Bearing umbracula.

umbraculiform, adj. [1. umbrákūliform; 2. ambrǽkjulífōm]. As prec. & **-form**. (bot.) Shaped like an umbraculum.

umbraculum, n., pl. **umbracula** [1. umbrákūlum, -la; 2. ambrǽkjuləm, -lə]. Lat., 'umbrella', dimin. of **umbra**. (bot.) An umbrella-shaped appendage, as in such plants as the liverwort.

umbrage, n. [1. úmbrij; 2. ámbridž], fr. Fr. *ombrage*, 'shadow, suspicion', fr. Lat. *umbra*, 'shade, shadow', see **umbra** & **-age**. **1.** (poet.) **a** Shadow, shade: '*In the deep umbrage of a green hill's shade*' (Byron, 'Childe Harold'); **b** a shadow, reflection: '*His semblable is his mirror; . . . his umbrage, nothing more*' (Shakespeare, 'Hamlet'). **2.** Suspicion of slight or injury; feeling of offence or resentment: *to give, take, umbrage.*

umbrageous, adj. [1. umbrājus; 2. ambréidžəs]. Prec. & **-ous**. **1.** Shady; giving, affording, shade; shaded, enjoying shade. **2.** (rare) Disposed to take umbrage; suspicious, resentful.

umbrageously, adv. Prec. & **-ly**. In an umbrageous manner.

umbrageousness, n. See prec. & **-ness**. Condition, quality, of being umbrageous.

umbral, adj. [1. úmbral; 2. ámbrəl]. **umbra** & **-al**. (astron.) Connected with, pertaining to, an umbra or complete shadow; contrasted with *penumbral.*

umbrella, n. [1. umbréla; 2. ambrélə]. Ital., also more commonly *ombrella*, dimin. of *ombra*, 'shade', fr. Lat. **umbra**. **1. a** A light, folding framework of flexible ribs of steel &c., radiating from, and sliding up and down on, a stick, covered with silk, gingham, or other material; carried above the head as a protection against rain or against the sun, though in the latter case usually termed 'parasol' or 'sunshade'; **b** a similar device of elaborate and decorative character borne by attendants above the head of Eastern and African potentates as a symbol of dignity. **2.** (zool.) The umbrella-shaped disk forming the upper part of the body of a jelly-fish, by the expansion and contraction of which it swims.

umbrella ant, n. A South American ant which devours leaves, which it carries to its nest over its back; also called the *parasol ant.*

umbrella bird, n. A Central and S. American bird, of black plumage, with a large umbrella-shaped, erectile crest.

umbrella pine, n. A Japanese pine tree with an umbrella-shaped crown, and pine-needles clustered like umbrellas to the twigs.

umbrella shell, n. A marine gastropod mollusc, forming a genus, *Umbrella*, with thick foot and small shell partially covering the body.

umbrella tree, n. A North American dwarf magnolia, *Magnolia tripetala*, with leaves arranged in an umbrella-like cluster at the end of the branches.

umbrette, n. [1. umbrét; 2. ambrét], fr. Fr. *ombrette*, dimin. of *ombre*, 'umber'. The umber-bird.

Umbrian, adj. & n. [1. úmbrian; 2. ámbriən]. Lat. & Ital. *Umbria* & **-an**. **1.** adj. Pertaining to the ancient or modern Umbria, Central Italy, its people, language &c.; *Umbrian school* of painting, of Perugino and his pupil Raphael. **2.** n. **a** A native of Umbria; **b** the language of ancient Umbria.

umbriferous, adj. [1. ùmbríferus; 2. àmbrífərəs]. Lat. *umbrifer*, see **umbra** & **-ferous**. Casting, giving, a shade; shady.

umiak, n. [1. óomiak; 2. úmiæk]. Eskimo. An Eskimo boat of skins stretched over a wooden framework, used by women; cp. *kayak.*

umlaut, n. & vb. trans. [1. óomlout; 2. úmlaut]. Germ. *um*, 'round, about', & *laut*, 'sound'. **1.** n. (philol.) Term invented by Grimm, and adopted by all German, and formerly by most English grammarians, to denote the change of a vowel in Germanic languages through the influence of another vowel, chiefly *i* (or *j*) or *u*, in the following syllable; the process is now often called *i-*, *j-*, or *u-* mutation in English; example O.E. *mȳs* from **mūsi-*, 'mice'. **2.** vb. (rare) To change or mutate a vowel by this process.

umpirage, n. [1. úmpīrij; 2. ámpaiəridž]. **umpire** & **-age**. (rare, archaic) **a** Position, authority, of an umpire; **b** decision, ruling, of an umpire.

umpire (I.), n. [1. úmpīr; 2. ámpaiə]. M.E. *numpere*; the mod. form is due to *a numpire* being taken for *an umpire*; cp. **apron, adder** &c.; fr. O. Fr. *nomper*, 'not equal, peerless; odd'; hence, 'the odd man, third man with a casting vote', (cp. O.N. *oddemaðr*, 'odd man', in sense of arbitrator), fr. *non*, 'not', & *par*, 'equal', see **par** (I.) & **peer** (I.). A person chosen to judge, decide, arbitrate upon a question in dispute; specif. **a** person chosen to enforce the rules of, and see fair play in, a game, and to decide doubtful points in favour of one side or other; **b** (law) a third person called in to decide when arbitrators have failed to agree.

umpire (II.), vb. intrans. & trans., fr. prec. **1.** intrans. To act as umpire: *will you umpire for our side, for us?; he umpired in the last test match.* **2.** trans. To act as umpire in: *to umpire a championship game at Wimbledon.*

umpteen, adj. [1. úmptēn; 2. ámptīn]. Invented on analogy of *thirteen* &c. See **-teen**. (slang) Many, a large number of.

un- (I.), pref. O.E. *un-*, O.H.G. & Goth. *un-*; O.N. *ū-*; M.E. *un-*; cogn. w. Scrt. *an-*, *a-*, Gk. *an-*, *a-*, see **a-** & **an-**; Lat. *in-*, see **in-** (II.); Ir. & W. *an*; this pref. is cogn. w. the negatives Lat. *nē*, Scrt. *nā*, Gk. *nē-*; O.E. *ne*, Goth. *ni*, 'not'; see also **no** (I.), **not, nor** (I.). The force of the pref. *un-* is purely neg., & usually expresses simply 'not' when used before adj. or adv., & 'lack of, reverse of', before ns. It is used: **a** before adjs., whether primary, as *unhappy*, or derived fr. Pres. Part., *unwilling, unbecoming*, or fr. P.P., *unwanted, unsought, undone* = 'not done', *unforgotten* &c.; **b** before advs., as *unhappily, unchastely* &c.; **c** before abstract ns. derived fr. adjs., such as *unhappiness, unsuitability, unimportance* &c.; **d** before a certain number of primary ns., as in *unrest, unfaith, untruth* &c. The pref. even when unstressed retains the character of the vowel sound, being always [an] & never [ən]. As regards mode of stressing, the following principles cover most cases. **1.** Words compounded w. *un-* usually retain the same conditions of stress as when uncompounded, e.g. *háppy, unháppy; abáshed, unabáshed; reliability, unreliability.* In the two last the pref. itself may receive slight secondary stress, *ùnabáshed* &c. **2. a** The pref. itself is completely unstressed when the chief stress falls on the syll. immediately following it, e.g. *unháppy, uncháste*; **b** the pref. is strongly stressed in sentences where positive & neg. forms are contrasted, as in *some men are háppy, some are únhàppy*; **c** (i.) when the pref. is strongly stressed in this way, the following syll., if normally bearing the chief stress, receives only secondary stress. (ii.) In words where the chief stress does not normally fall immediately after the pref. as in *ùnreliable*, this strong syll. receives only the secondary stress when the pref. bears the chief (contrasting) stress, e.g. *reliable and únreliable.* **3. a** When used before long words wh. when uncompounded have both a strong & a secondary stress, such as *reliability*, the pref. itself also receives a secondary stress, as *ùnreliability*; **b** when in such words the pref. is emphasized (in contrast), & receives the principal stress, that syll. wh. has normally the principal stress now has secondary stress, & that wh. normally has the secondary stress receives a still weaker degree of stress, sufficient, however, to distinguish it fr. the completely unstressed sylls., e.g. *únreliability* (1 3 2). The numbers above the sylls. refer to the relative degree of stress wh. each receives.

un- (II.), pref. O.E. *on-* & *un-*, M.E. *un-*; the fuller form is preserved in O.E. *ondswarian*, see **answer**; cp. Du. *ont-*, O.H.G. *ant-* & *int-*, Mod. Germ. *ant-*, *ent-*; cogn. w. Gk. *anti-*; see **anti-**. A pref. used before vbs., expressing **a** the reversal of the action of the vb. to wh. it is attached, as *undo, unlace, unlock* &c.; **b** deprivation, separation; removal, as *unfrock, undress, unsex, unearth, unhorse.* The remarks on stressing & pronunciation under **un-** (I.) apply also to **un-** (II.).

unabashed, adj. [1. ùnabásht; 2. anəbǽʃt, ànəbǽʃt]. **un-** (I.) & **abash(ed)**. Not abashed; **a** unashamed, shameless; **b** not intimidated, preserving composure of mind and bearing.

unabated, adj. [1. ùnabāted; 2. ànəbéitid]. **un-** (I.) & **abate(d)**. Not abated, undiminished; preserving full intensity.

unabating, adj. [1. ùnabāting; 2. ànəbéitiŋ]. Not abating; continuing with full intensity.

unabbreviated, adj. [1. ùnabréviàted; 2. ànəbríviéitid]. **un-** (I.) & **abbreviate(d)**. Not abbreviated, preserving full length; unshortened.

unabetted, adj. [1. ùnabéted; 2. ànəbétid]. **un-** (I.) & **abet(ted)**. Not abetted.

unabiding, adj. [1. ùnabíding; 2. ànəbáidiŋ]. **un-** (I.) & **abiding**. Not abiding; not lasting; transient, transitory.

unable, adj. [1. unābl; 2. anéibl]. **un-** (I.) & **able**. **1.** Not able; incapable: *unable to do anything.* **2.** (rare, poet.) Feeble, weak, impotent.

unabolished, adj. [1. ùnabólisht; 2. ànəbɔ́liʃt]. **un-** (I.) & **abolish(ed)**. Not abolished; still in force or current; not repealed.

unabridged, adj. [1. ùnabríjd; 2. ànəbrídžd]. **un-** (I.) & **abridge(d)**. Not abridged, unshortened; given in full.

unabsorbable, adj. [1. ùnabsórbabl; 2. ànəbsɔ́bəbl]. **un-** (I.) & **absorb** & **-able**. Not absorbable; incapable of being absorbed.

unabsorbed, adj. [1. ùnabsórbd; 2. ànəbsɔ́bd]. **un-** (I.) & **absorb(ed)**. Not absorbed.

unabsorbent, adj. [1. ùnabsórbent; 2. ànəbsɔ́bənt]. **un-** (I.) & **absorbent**. Not absorbent.

unaccented, adj. [1. ùnaksénted; 2. ànəkséntid]. **un-** (I.) & **accent(ed)**. Not accented, having no accent; specif., of syllables, unstressed.

unaccentuated, adj. [1. ùnaksénťūàted; 2. ànæksénťjuèitid]. **un-** (I.) & **accentuate(d)**. Not accentuated; not emphasized or brought into prominence.

unacceptability, n. [1. ùnaksèptabíliti; 2. ànəksèptəbíliti]. **un-** (I.) & **acceptability**. **a** Condition of being unacceptable or unwelcome; **b** lack of welcome or pleasing qualities.

unacceptable, adj. [1. ùnakséptabl; 2. ànəkséptəbl]. **un-** (I.) & **acceptable**. Not acceptable; unwelcome; not giving satisfaction.

unacceptably, adv. Prec. & **-ly**. In an unacceptable manner.

unaccommodating, adj. [1. ùnakómadàting; 2. ànəkɔ́mədèitiŋ]. **un-** (I.) & **accommodating**. Not accommodating, not disposed to be compliant or obliging.

unaccompanied, adj. [1. ùnakúmpanid; 2. ànəkámpənid]. **un-** (I.) & **accompany** & **-ed**. Not accompanied; **a** without a companion: **b** (mus.) without an accompaniment.

unaccomplished, adj. [1. ùnakómplisht; 2. ànəkɔ́mpliʃt]. **un-** (I.) & **accomplish(ed)**. Not accomplished. **1.** Not completed or brought to a conclusion; not achieved. **2.** Having no accomplishments, not clever or skilful.

unaccountability, n. [1. ùnakòuntabíliti; 2. ànəkàuntəbíliti]. See next word & **-ity.** State, quality, of being unaccountable.

unaccountable, adj. [1. ùnakóuntabl; 2. ànəkáuntəbl]. **un-** (I.) & **accountable. 1.** Not to be accounted for; inexplicable. **2.** Not responsible.

unaccountably, adv. Prec. & **-ly.** In an unaccountable manner; inexplicably, strangely.

unaccredited, adj. [1. ùnakrédited; 2. ànəkréditid]. **un-** (I.) & **accredit(ed).** Not accredited.

unaccustomed, adj. [1. ùnakústumd; 2. ànəkástəmd]. **un-** (I.) & **accustomed. 1.** (with *to*) Not accustomed; unused, not habituated, unfamiliar with: *unaccustomed to hot climates, public speaking.* **2.** Not customary; unusual, strange: *with unaccustomed rudeness; his unaccustomed absence.*

unachievable, adj. [1. ùnachévabl; 2. ànətʃívəbl]. **un-** (I.) & **achieve** & **-able.** Not to be achieved; incapable of achievement.

unachieved, adj. [1. ùnachévd; 2. ànətʃívd]. **un-** (I.) & **achieve(d).** Not achieved.

unacknowledged, adj. [1. ùnaknólejd; 2. ànəknɔ́lidʒd]. **un-** (I.) & **acknowledge(d).** Not acknowledged; **a** (i.) not recognized, or admitted: *an unacknowledged branch of the family;* (ii.) not returned: *an unacknowledged greeting;* (iii.) (of letters &c.) not answered; **b** not confessed, owned: *unacknowledged crimes, faults* &c.

unacquainted, adj. [1. ùnakwánted; 2. ànəkwéintid]. **un-** (I.) & **acquaint(ed).** Not acquainted; having no acquaintance with, or knowledge of.

unacquirable, adj. [1. ùnakwírabl; 2. ànəkwáiərəbl]. **un-** (I.) & **acquire** & **-able.** Not acquirable, not to be acquired; unprocurable.

unacquired, adj. [1. ùnakwírd; 2. ànəkwáiəd]. **un-** (I.) & **acquire(d).** Not acquired.

unactable, adj. [1. unáktabl; 2. anǽktəbl]. **un-** (I.) & **act** & **-able.** Not actable; not fit or suitable for acting.

unacted, adj. [1. unákted; 2. anǽktid]. **un-** (I.) & **act(ed). 1.** Not acted, not done, accomplished, or performed. **2.** Not produced, performed, on the stage.

unadaptable, adj. [1. ùnadáptabl; 2. ànədǽptəbl]. **un-** (I.) & **adaptable.** Not adaptable.

unadapted, adj. [1. ùnadápted; 2. ànədǽptid]. **un-** (I.) & **adapt(ed).** Not adapted; unsuitable for specified purpose.

unaddicted, adj. [1. ùnadíkted; 2. ànədíktid]. **un-** (I.) & **addicted.** Not addicted (*to*).

unaddressed, adj. [1. ùnadrést; 2. ànədrést]. **un-** (I.) & **address(ed).** Not addressed; (of letter &c.) having no address written upon it.

unadjusted, adj. [1. ùnajústed; 2. ànədʒástid]. **un-** (I.) & **adjust(ed).** Not adjusted, not settled; unregulated.

unadministered, adj. [1. ùnadmínisterd; 2. ànədmínistəd]. **un-** (I.) & **administer(ed).** Not administered.

unadmired, adj. [1. ùnadmírd; 2. ànədmáiəd]. **un-** (I.) & **admire(d).** Not admired.

unadmitted, adj. [1. ùnadmíted; 2. ànədmítid]. **un-** (I.) & **admit(ted).** Not admitted.

unadmonished, adj. [1. ùnadmónisht; 2. ànədmɔ́niʃt]. **un-** (I.) & **admonish(ed).** Not admonished; uncorrected; not warned or cautioned.

unadorned, adj. [1. ùnadórnd; 2. ànədɔ́nd]. **un-** (I.) & **adorn(ed).** Not adorned, without adornment; simple, plain.

unadulterated, adj. [1. ùnadúlterāted; 2. ànədáltərèitid]. **un-** (I.) & **adulterate(d). 1.** Not adulterated; free from adulteration. **2.** Free from sophistication; genuine, pure, unmixed: *unadulterated praise, nonsense.*

unadventurous, adj. [1. ùnadvénchurus; 2. ànədvéntʃərəs]. **un-** (I.) & **adventurous. 1.** Lacking a spirit of adventure; not venturesome or enterprising. **2.** Not attended by adventures; safe, uneventful: *an unadventurous journey.*

unadvisability, n. [1. ùnadvìzabíliti; 2. ànədvàizəbíliti]. **un-** (I.) & **advisability.** State, quality, of being unadvisable.

unadvisable, adj. [1. ùnadvízabl; 2. ànədváizəbl]. **un-** (I.) & **advisable.** Not advisable; not to be recommended; inexpedient.

unadvised, adj. [1. ùnadvízd; 2. ànədváizd]. **un-** (I.) & **advise(d).** Not advised; **a** not having received advice; **b** imprudent, rash.

unadvisedly, adv. [1. ùnadvízedli; 2. ànədváizidli]. Prec. & **-ly.** Without proper advice; without due consideration; imprudently, rashly.

unaffected, adj. [1. ùnafékted; 2. ànəféktid]. **un-** (I.) & **affected.** Not affected. **1.** *Unaffected by,* **a** not moved, changed, or altered: *the ground was unaffected by the recent wet weather;* **b** unmoved, uninfluenced: *he was quite unaffected by the appeal.* **2.** Free from affectation; **a** not marked by affectation or mannerisms; plain, simple: *unaffected manners; an unaffected, direct style;* **b** not assumed out of affectation; genuine, sincere, not pretended; not put on or hypocritical: *unaffected grief; he expressed unaffected delight; unaffected kindness of heart.*

unaffectedly, adv. Prec. & **-ly.** In an unaffected manner.

unaffiliated, adj. [1. ùnafíliāted; 2. ànəfílièitid]. **un-** (I.) & **affiliate(d).** Not affiliated (*to*).

unafflicted, adj. [1. ùnaflíkted; 2. ànəflíktid]. **un-** (I.) & **afflict(ed).** Not afflicted.

unafraid, adj. [1. ùnafrád; 2. ànəfréid]. **un-** (I.) & **afraid.** Not afraid; undismayed.

unaggressive, adj. [1. ùnagrésiv; 2. ànəgrésiv]. **un-** (I.) & **aggressive.** Not aggressive; pacific.

unaided, adj. [1. unáded; 2. anéidid]. **un-** (I.) & **aid(ed).** Not aided; unassisted; without aid, help, or assistance: *he did it unaided; by his unaided efforts.*

unaired, adj. [1. unárd; 2. anéəd]. **un-** (I.) & **air(ed).** Not aired; **a** not ventilated, deprived of air: *an unaired room;* **b** not dried by airing; damp: *unaired bed, sheets.*

unalarmed, adj. [1. ùnalármd; 2. ànəlámd]. **un-** (I.) & **alarm(ed).** Not alarmed, undismayed; not startled.

unalarming, adj. [1. ùnalárming; 2. ànəlámiŋ]. **un-** (I.) & **alarming.** Not alarming; not causing or tending to cause alarm.

unalleviated, adj. [1. ùnalévīāted; 2. ànəlívièitid]. **un-** (I.) & **alleviate(d).** Not alleviated, not lessened, mitigated, or relieved.

unallied, adj. [1. ùnalíd; 2. ànəláid]. **un-** (I.) & **allied.** Not allied, having no relation or connexion: *unallied species, genera* &c.

unallotted, adj. [1. ùnalóted; 2. ànəlɔ́tid]. **un-** (I.) & **allot(ted).** Not allotted.

unallowable, adj. [1. ùnalóuabl; 2. ànəláuəbl]. **un-** (I.) & **allowable.** Not allowable, not permissible.

unallowed, adj. [1. ùnalóud; 2. ànəláud]. **un-** (I.) & **allow(ed).** Not allowed; not permitted; forbidden.

unalloyed, adj. [1. ùnalóid; 2. ànəlɔ́id]. **un-** (I.) & **alloy(ed).** Not alloyed. **1.** (of metals) Free from alloy; pure. **2.** (of feelings &c.) Unmixed, unqualified: *unalloyed happiness.*

unalluring, adj. [1. ùnalúring; 2. ànəljɔ́riŋ]. **un-** (I.) & **alluring.** Not alluring.

unalterability, n. [1. unàwlterabíliti; 2. anɔ̀ltərəbíliti]. **un-** (I.) & **alterability.** Condition, quality, of being unalterable; unalterableness.

unalterable, adj. [1. unáwlterabl; 2. anɔ́ltərəbl]. **un-** (I.) & **alterable.** Not alterable; incapable of being altered; fixed, unchangeable.

unalterableness, n. Prec. & **-ness.** Unalterability.

unalterably, adv. See prec. & **-ly.** In an unalterable manner.

unaltered, adj. [1. unáwlterd; 2. anɔ́ltəd]. **un-** (I.) & **alter(ed).** Not altered, unchanged.

unaltering, adj. [1. unáwltering; 2. anɔ́ltəriŋ]. **un-** (I.) & **alter** & **-ing.** Not altering; constant, unchanging.

unamazed, adj. [1. ùnamázd; 2. ànəméizd]. **un-** (I.) & **amaze(d).** Not amazed.

unambiguous, adj. [1. ùnambígūus; 2. ànæmbígjuəs]. **un-** (I.) & **ambiguous.** Not ambiguous; clear, plain; not having a doubtful meaning; leaving no room for doubt.

unambiguously, adv. Prec. & **-ly.** Not ambiguously; plainly, clearly.

unambiguousness, n. See prec. & **-ness.** Condition, quality, of being unambiguous.

unambitious, adj. [1. ùnambíshus; 2. ànæmbíʃəs]. **un-** (I.) & **ambitious.** Not ambitious; modest, unpretentious.

unambitiously, adv. Prec. & **-ly.** In an unambitious manner; modestly, unpretendingly.

unambitiousness, n. See prec. & **-ness.** Condition, quality, of being unambitious.

unamenable, adj. [1. ùnaménabl; 2. ànəmínəbl]. **un-** (I.) & **amenable.** Not amenable: *unamenable to treatment, discipline* &c.

unamendable, adj. [1. ùnaméndabl; 2. ànəméndəbl]. **un-** (I.) & **amend** & **-able.** Not amendable, incapable of being amended.

unamended, adj. [1. ùnaménded; 2. ànəméndid]. **un-** (I.) & **amend(ed).** Not amended.

un-American, adj. [1. ùn amérikan; 2. àn əmérikən]. **un-** (I.) & **American.** Not American; not in accordance with American (United States) customs, principles &c.

unamiability, n. [1. unàmiabíliti; 2. anèimiəbíliti]. **un-** (I.) & **amiability.** Condition, quality, of being unamiable; moroseness, surliness; disobligingness.

unamiable, adj. [1. unámiabl; 2. anéimiəbl]. **un-** (I.) & **amiable.** Not amiable; disagreeable, disobliging.

unamiably, adv. Prec. & **-ly.** In an unamiable manner.

unamusing, adj. [1. ùnamúzing; 2. ànəmjúziŋ]. **un-** (I.) & **amusing.** Not amusing.

unanalysable, adj. [1. unànalízabl; 2. anænəláizəbl]. **un-** (I.) & **analyse** & **-able.** Not analysable; not capable of analysis or being analysed.

unanalysed, adj. [1. unánalīzed; 2. anǽnəlàizd]. **un-** (I.) & **analyse(d).** Not analysed.

unanchor, vb. trans. & intrans. [1. unángkur; 2. anǽŋkə]. **un-** (II.) & **anchor. 1.** trans. To loosen, set free (ship), from an anchor or anchorage. **2.** intrans. To be set free from an anchor &c.; to weigh anchor.

unaneled, adj. [1. ùnanéld; 2. ànəníəld]. **un-** (I.) & **anele(d).** (archaic) Not aneled, unanointed; without having the sacrament of extreme unction administered: '*unhousel'd, disappointed, unaneled*' (Shakespeare, 'Hamlet').

unanimated, adj. [1. unánimāted; 2. anǽnimèitid]. **un-** (I.) & **animate(d).** Not animated.

unanimiter, adv. [1. ùnanímiter; 2. jùnənímitə]. Lat., see next word. (law) Unanimously.

unanimity, n. [1. ùnanímiti; 2. jùnənímiti], fr. Fr. *unanimité,* fr. Lat. *ūnanimitāt-(em);* see **unanimous** & **-ity.** State, quality, of being unanimous: *the unanimity of the Cabinet; the unanimity of the applause.*

unanimous, adj. [1. ūnánimus; 2. junǽniməs], fr. Lat. *ūnanimus,* 'of one mind', fr. *ūnus,* 'one', & *animus,* 'mind', see **unity, one,** & **animus. 1.** (of persons) Being of one mind; agreeing in opinion and decision: *the Cabinet was unanimous; the meeting was unanimous in refusing to listen to the speaker.* **2.** Held, formed, passed, given with the agreement of all: *a unanimous vote of thanks; greeted with unanimous applause.*

unanimously, adv. Prec. & **-ly.** In a unanimous manner; with unanimity.

unannealed, adj. [1. ùnanéld; 2. ànəníəld]. **un-** (I.) & **anneal(ed).** (of glass, metals) Not annealed; not heated first and then cooled slowly.

unannounced, adj. [1. ùnanóunst; 2. ànənáunst]. **un-** (I.) & **announce(d).** Not announced; without previous announcement.

Phr. *to enter unannounced*, without one's name being first called out.

unanointed, adj. [1. ùnanóinted; 2. ànənóintid]. **un-** (I.) & **anoint(ed)**. Not anointed.

unanswerability, n. [1. unàhnserabíliti; 2. anànsərəbíliti]. **un-** (I.) & **answerable** & **-ity**. Condition, state, of being unanswerable.

unanswerable, adj. [1. unáhnserabl; 2. anánsərəbl]. **un-** (I.) & **answerable**. Not answerable; incapable of being answered or refuted; conclusive.

unanswerableness, n. Prec. & **-ness**. Unanswerability.

unanswerably, adv. See prec. & **-ly**. In an unanswerable manner; conclusively.

unanswered, adj. [1. unáhnserd; 2. anánsəd]. **un-** (I.) & **answer(ed)**. Not answered; **a** left without an answer, unreplied to: *an unanswered letter, question, appeal*; **b** not refuted: *the criticism remains unanswered*; *unanswered accusations*; **c** not returned or requited: *unanswered affection*.

unanticipated, adj. [1. ùnantísipàted; 2. ànæntísipèitid]. **un-** (I.) & **anticipate(d)**. Not anticipated or expected; unexpected.

unapocryphal, adj. [1. ùnapókrifl; 2. ànəpɔ́krifl]. **un-** (I.) & **apocryphal**. Not apocryphal, genuine; canonical.

unapostolic, adj. [1. unàpostólik; 2. anæ̀pəstɔ́lik]. **un-** (I.) & **apostolic**. Not apostolic; having no apostolic authority; contrary to apostolic usage.

unappalled, adj. [1. ùnapáwld; 2. ànəpɔ́ld]. **un-** (I.) & **appal(led)**. Not appalled; undaunted, unafraid.

unapparel, vb. trans. [1. ùnapárel; 2. ànəpǽr(ə)l]. **un-** (II.) & **apparel**. (archaic) To remove the apparel of; to undress, unclothe.

unapparelled, adj. [1. ùnapáreld; 2. ànəpǽr(ə)ld]. **un-** (I.) & **apparel(led)**. Not apparelled; unclothed, without apparel.

unapparent, adj. [1. ùnapárent; 2. ànəpéərənt]. **un-** (I.) & **apparent**. Not apparent, not visible, not manifest.

unappealable, adj. [1. ùnapélabl; 2. ànəpíləbl]. **un-** (I.) & **appealable**. Not appealable; **a** incapable of being taken to a higher court: *an unappealable case*; **b** incapable of being appealed from: *an unappealable decision, judge*.

unappeasable, adj. [1. ùnapḗzabl; 2. ànəpízəbl]. **un-** (I.) & **appeasable**. Not appeasable; incapable of being appeased, satisfied, placated, or satiated: *unappeasable hunger, anger*.

unappeased, adj. [1. ùnapḗzd; 2. ànəpízd]. **un-** (I.) & **appease(d)**. Not appeased; unsatisfied.

unappetizing, adj. [1. unápetìzing; 2. anǽpitàiziŋ]. **un-** (I.) & **appetizing**. Not appetizing; not appealing favourably to the taste; repellent, causing disgust.

unappetizingly, adv. Prec. & **-ly**. In an unappetizing manner.

unapplied, adj. [1. ùnaplíd; 2. ànəpláid]. **un-** (I.) & **apply** & **-ed**. Not applied; not used for a specific purpose or object.

unappreciated, adj. [1. ùnapréshiàted; 2. ànəpríʃièitid]. **un-** (I.) & **appreciate(d)**. Not appreciated; not valued.

unappreciative, adj. [1. ùnapréshiativ; 2. ànəpríʃiətiv]. **un-** (I.) & **appreciative**. Not appreciative.

unapprehended, adj. [1. ùnaprehénded; 2. ànæprihéndid]. **un-** (I.) & **apprehend(ed)**. Not apprehended; **a** not taken into custody; still at large: *the criminal remains unapprehended*; **b** not understood, not clearly perceived: *such theories are unapprehended by ordinary people*.

unapprehensive, adj. [1. ùnaprehénsiv; 2. ànæprihénsiv]. **un-** (I.) & **apprehensive**. Not apprehensive; **a** not feeling apprehension, not suspicious or suspecting; not fearful; **b** not quick or ready at apprehension or understanding.

unapprehensiveness, n. Prec. & **-ness**. Condition, quality, of being unapprehensive.

unapprised, adj. [1. ùnapríz d; 2. ànəpráizd]. **un-** (I.) & **apprise(d)**. Not apprised, not informed or told of beforehand.

unapproachability, n. [1. ùnapròchabíliti; 2. ànəpròutʃəbíliti]. **un-** (I.) & **approachability**. Condition, quality, of being unapproachable; inaccessibility, unapproachableness.

unapproachable, adj. [1. ùnapróchabl; 2. ànəpróutʃəbl]. **un-** (I.) & **approachable**. Not approachable; inaccessible; exhibiting a frigid aloofness of manner or character.

unapproachableness, n. Prec. & **-ness**. Unapproachability.

unapproachably, adv. See prec. & **-ly**. In an unapproachable manner; inaccessibly.

unappropriated, adj. [1. ùnaprópriàted; 2. ànəpróuprieitid]. **un-** (I.) & **appropriate(d)**. Not appropriated; specif. **a** (of funds, money &c.) not granted for, not applied to, or used for, a specific purpose; **b** (of land &c.) not granted to, or taken by, a person, company &c., to the exclusion of others.

unapproved, adj. [1. ùnapróōvd; 2. ànəprúvd]. **un-** (I.) & **approve(d)**. Not approved; not having received approval.

unapproving, adj. [1. ùnapróōving; 2. ànəprúviŋ]. **un-** (I.) & **approve** & **-ing**. Not approving; disapproving.

unapprovingly, adv. Prec. & **-ly**. In an unapproving manner.

unapt, adj. [1. unápt; 2. anǽpt]. **un-** (I.) & **apt**; cp. **inept**. Not apt; **a** not ready, quick; slow, unskilful: *unapt to learn*; *unapt at games*; **b** not accustomed to, not inclined to: '*unapt to weep*' (Shakespeare, '1 Henry VI.'); **c** not fit, not suitable, not appropriate: *an unapt quotation*.

unaptly, adv. Prec. & **-ly**. In an unapt manner; not aptly; inappropriately.

unaptness, n. See prec. & **-ness**. State, quality, of being unapt.

unargued, adj. [1. unárgūd; 2. anágjūd]. **un-** (I.) & **argue(d)**. Not argued; not disputed; not debated.

unarm, vb. trans. & intrans. [1. unárm; 2. anám]. **un-** (II.) & **arm** (III.). **1.** trans. **a** To deprive of arms, armour, or other means of offence or defence; to disarm; **b** (by transf., poet.) to deprive of means of inflicting injury. **2.** intrans. To lay down one's arms; to render oneself incapable of offence or defence.

unarmed, adj. [1. unármd; 2. anámd]. Prec. & **-ed**. **1.** **a** Lacking arms, armour &c.; **b** not wearing, unprovided with, weapons or other means of attack or defence. **2.** (zool. and bot.) Not having points, prickles, spines, or other defensive protection.

unarmoured, adj. [1. unármurd; 2. anámad]. **un-** (I.) & **armour(ed)**. Not armoured; not protected by armour, esp. of cruisers and other war-vessels.

unarraigned, adj. [1. ùnarānd; 2. ànəréind]. **un-** (I.) & **arraign(ed)**. Not arraigned, not brought to trial.

unarranged, adj. [1. ùnarānjd; 2. ànəréin(d)žd]. **un-** (I.) & **arrange(d)**. **1.** Not arranged, not placed in order; not classified. **2.** Not planned, prepared beforehand: *our meeting was fortuitous and quite unarranged*.

unarrayed, adj. [1. ùnarād; 2. ànəréid]. **un-** (I.) & **array(ed)**. Not arrayed; **a** not drawn up in array or line of battle; not arranged in order; **b** not dressed in array, not decked out for display; unadorned.

unarrested, adj. [1. ùnarésted; 2. ànəréstid]. **un-** (I.) & **arrest(ed)**. Not arrested.

unartful, adj. [1. unártfl; 2. anátfl]. **un-** (I.) & **artful**. Not artful; **a** not cunning; **b** artless, frank, genuine; **c** without art or skill; unskilful.

unartificial, adj. [1. ùnartifíshl; 2. ànātifíʃl]. **un-** (I.) & **artificial**. Not artificial; free from artifice, natural, simple.

unartistic, adj. [1. ùnartístik; 2. ànātístik]. **un-** (I.) & **artistic**. Not artistic; specif., not concerned with art or artists; contrasted with *inartistic*, contrary to the rules of art.

unascertainable, adj. [1. ùnasertānabl; 2. ànæsətéinəbl]. **un-** (I.) & **ascertainable**. Not ascertainable; not capable of being ascertained or known with certainty.

unascertained, adj. [1. ùnasertānd; 2. ànæsətéind]. **un-** (I.) & **ascertain(ed)**. Not ascertained.

unashamed, adj. [1. ùnashāmd; 2. ànəʃéimd]. **un-** (I.) & **ashamed**. Not ashamed; unabashed; shameless, exhibiting effrontery.

unasked, adj. [1. unáhskt; 2. anáskt]. **un-** (I.) & **ask(ed)**. Not asked; unsolicited; unsought.

unaspirated, adj. [1. unáspiràted; 2. anǽspirèitid]. **un-** (I.) & **aspirate(d)**. Not aspirated; not pronounced or written with an aspirate.

unaspiring, adj. [1. ùnaspíring; 2. ànəspáiəriŋ]. **un-** (I.) & **aspire** & **-ing**. Not aspiring; unambitious, modest.

unassailable, adj. [1. ùnasālabl; 2. ànəséiləbl]. **un-** (I.) & **assailable**. Not assailable; **a** proof against attack: *an unassailable fortress, position*; **b** irrefutable, incontestable: *unassailable arguments*.

unassayed, adj. [1. ùnasād; 2. ànəséid]. **un-** (I.) & **assay(ed)**. Not assayed; **a** not tried or attempted; **b** not subjected to a metallurgical or other assay or test; untested.

unassignable, adj. [1. ùnasínabl; 2. ànəsáinəbl]. **un-** (I.) & **assignable**. **a** Not assignable; not capable of transference by assignment; **b** not attributable: *results unassignable to any known cause*.

unassimilated, adj. [1. ùnasímilàted; 2. ànəsímilèitid]. **un-** (I.) & **assimilate(d)**. Not assimilated.

unassisted, adj. [1. ùnasísted; 2. ànəsístid]. **un-** (I.) & **assist(ed)**. Not assisted.

unassuming, adj. [1. ùnasúming; 2. ànəsjúmiŋ]. **un-** (I.) & **assuming**. Not assuming; unpresuming, modest.

unassured, adj. [1. ùnashórd; 2. ànəʃɔ́d]. **un-** (I.) & **assure(d)**. Not assured; **a** having no assurance, not confident or bold; **b** not insured against loss; not holding a policy of assurance or insurance.

unatoned, adj. [1. ùnatónd; 2. ànətóund]. **un-** (I.) & **atone(d)**. Not atoned; unexpiated.

unattached, adj. [1. ùnatácht; 2. ànətǽtʃt]. **un-** (I.) & **attached**. Not attached. Specif. **1.** (law) not seized or attached for debt. **2.** (mil., of officers) Not assigned to a particular regiment or other unit. **3.** (univ.) Not attached to a particular college, though a member of the university; non-collegiate. **4.** Not fastened.

unattainable, adj. [1. ùnatānabl; 2. ànətéinəbl]. **un-** (I.) & **attainable**. Not attainable; impossible of attainment; out of reach.

unattainableness, n. Prec. & **-ness**. Condition, quality, of being unattainable.

unattempted, adj. [1. ùnatémpted; 2. ànətémptid]. **un-** (I.) & **attempt(ed)**. Not attempted.

unattended, adj. [1. ùnaténded; 2. ànəténdid]. **un-** (I.) & **attend(ed)**. Not attended. **1.** Having no attendants; not escorted or waited on. **2.** Receiving no attention, not attended to; undressed: *unattended wounds*.

unattested, adj. [1. ùnatésted; 2. ànətéstid]. **un-** (I.) & **attest(ed)**. Not attested; lacking attestation; not supported by evidence of a witness &c.

unattractive, adj. [1. ùnatráktiv; 2. ànətrǽktiv]. **un-** (I.) & **attractive**. Not attractive; unprepossessing, plain; repellent.

unattractively, adv. Prec. & **-ly**. In an unattractive manner; so as to fail to attract.

unattractiveness, n. See prec. & **-ness**. Condition, quality, of being unattractive.

unaugmented, adj. [1. ùnawgménted; 2. ànɔ̄gméntid]. **un-** (I.) & **augment(ed)**. Not augmented; specif. (Gk. gram.) having no augment prefixed.

unauthentic, adj. [1. ùnawthéntik; 2. ànɔ̄þéntik]. **un-** (I.) & **authentic**. Not authentic; apocryphal; not genuine.

unauthenticated, adj. [1. ùnawthéntikàted; 2. ànɔþéntikèitid]. **un- (I.)** & **authenticate(d)**. Not authenticated; not shown or proved to be true.

unauthorized, adj. [1. unáwthorìzd; 2. anɔ́þəràizd]. **un- (I.)** & **authorize(d)**. Not authorized; having no proper authority or sanction.

unavailable, adj. [1. ùnavâlabl; 2. ànəvéiləbl]. **un- (I.)** & **available**. Not available; not within one's reach, not at one's disposal.

unavailing, adj. [1. ùnavâling; 2. ànəvéiliŋ]. **un- (I.)** & **avail** & **-ing**. Not availing; not effectual or effective; fruitless, vain.

unavailingly, adv. Prec. & **-ly**. In an unavailing manner; without avail; fruitlessly.

unavenged, adj. [1. ùnavénjd; 2. ànəvéndžd]. **un- (II.)** & **avenge(d)**. Not avenged.

unavoidable, adj. [1. ùnavóidabl; 2. ànəvóidəbl]. **un- (I.)** & **avoidable**. **1.** Not avoidable; incapable of being avoided; not to be prevented or escaped; inevitable. **2.** Not voidable; incapable of being rendered null and void.

unavoidably, adv. Prec. & **-ly**. In an unavoidable manner; in a way that cannot be avoided.

unavowed, adj. [1. ùnavóud; 2. ànəváud]. **un- (I.)** & **avow(ed)**. Not avowed, not acknowledged; unconfessed.

unawakened, adj. [1. ùnawâkend; 2. ànəwéikənd]. **un- (I.)** & **awaken(ed)**. **1.** Not awakened; not roused from sleep. **2.** Not yet aroused; dormant, quiescent: *unawakened passions, ambition* &c.

unaware, adj. [1. ùnawâr; 2. ànəwéə]. **un- (I.)** & **aware**. (only used pred.) Not aware, not knowing or noticing; ignorant; not awake to or conscious of: *unaware of their danger; they remained unaware that war was near.*

unawares, adv. [1. ùnawârz; 2. ànəwéəz]. Prec. & advbl. suff. *-s*. **1.** Without knowing or noticing; unintentionally, undesignedly: *to do something unawares; he slew his father unawares.* **2.** Without warning, unexpectedly, by surprise: *to be taken unawares, to take a person unawares*, to be surprised, to surprise. Phr. *at unawares*, by surprise.

unbacked, adj. [1. unbákt; 2. anbǽkt]. **un- (I.)** & **back(ed)**. Not backed. **1.** (of horse) Not ridden before, not broken in. **2. a** Without supporters or backers, unsupported, unaided; **b** (of horse in a race &c.) having no bets made upon it.

unbag, vb. trans. [1. unbág; 2. anbǽg]. **un- (II.)** & **bag (II.)**. To take out, let go, from a bag: *to unbag a ferret.*

unbagged, adj. [1. unbágd; 2. anbǽgd], fr. P.P. of prec. **1.** Let loose, taken out of a bag. **2.** Not placed or kept in a bag.

unbaked, adj. [1. unbâkt; 2. anbéikt]. **un- (I.)** & **bake(d)**. **a** Not baked; **b** (fig.) immature, crude.

unbalance, vb. trans. [1. unbálans; 2. anbǽləns]. **un- (II.)** & **balance (II.)**. To upset, destroy, the balance of; to throw off or out of balance or equipoise, physical or mental: *the water jump will unbalance several of the riders; his financial anxieties went far to unbalance him (his mind).*

unbalanced (I.), adj. [1. unbálanst; 2. anbǽlənst], fr. P.P. of prec. Thrown out of balance or equipoise; thrown, put, off one's balance; upset, unsteady (of physical or mental states): *an unbalanced rider, seat on a horse; an unbalanced mind.*

unbalanced (II.), adj. **un- (I.)** & **balance(d)**. Not balanced. **1. a** Not fitted with a balance or counterweight, not counterpoised rightly: *a pair of unbalanced scales*; **b** (i.) lacking balance or equipoise; unsteady: *an unbalanced type of character*; (ii.) lacking restraint or poise: *an unbalanced style of writing.* **2.** (commerc.) Not brought to a balance, not equal on debit and credit sides: *unbalanced books, accounts* &c.

unballast, vb. trans. [1. unbálast; 2. anbǽləst]. **un- (II.)** & **ballast (II.)**. To discharge, remove, the ballast from: *to unballast a ship, balloon* &c.

unballasted (I.), adj. [1. unbálasted; 2. anbǽləstid]. P.P. of prec. Freed from, discharged of, ballast; having discharged its ballast: *the ship, balloon, was by this time unballasted.*

unballasted (II.), adj. **un- (I.)** & **ballast(ed)**. Not ballasted; **a** not provided with ballast: *an unballasted ship* &c.; *an unballasted railway track*; **b** unsteady, lacking ballast or a steadying influence: *an unballasted character, type of mind* &c.

unbank, vb. trans. [1. unbángk; 2. anbǽŋk]. **un- (II.)** & **bank (II.)**. **1.** (of fires, furnaces &c.) To loosen, take away, the ashes banked on the top of a fire, so as to cause it to burn brightly again: *unbanked fire, furnace.* **2.** (of rivers &c.) To remove or damage the banks so as to cause an overflow.

unbanked, adj. [1. unbángkt; 2. anbǽŋkt]. **un- (I.)** & **bank(ed)**. Not banked: **a** having no banks or sides; **b** not placed in a bank: *unbanked cheques, money* &c.

unbaptized, adj. [1. ùnbaptìzd; 2. ànbæptáizd]. **un- (I.)** & **baptize(d)**. Not baptized; not having received the sacrament of baptism.

unbar, vb. trans. [1. unbár; 2. anbá]. **un- (II.)** & **bar (II.)**. To remove, take away, a bar or bars from; to unfasten, unbolt, to throw open: *to unbar a gate, door; unbar the prison*; (also fig.) *get rid of tariffs and unbar the channels of trade; the path to knowledge is now unbarred.*

unbarbed, adj. [1. unbárbd; 2. anbábd]. **un- (I.)** & **barb(ed)**. Not barbed, not furnished with barbs or reversed points.

unbarbered, adj. [1. unbárberd; 2. anbábəd]. **un- (I.)** & **barber(ed)**. Not barbered; unshaven, unkempt.

unbark, vb. trans. [1. unbárk; 2. anbák]. **un- (II.)** & **bark (I.)**. To strip the bark from, to deprive of bark.

unbated, adj. [1. unbâted; 2. anbéitid]. **un- (I.)** & **bate(d)**. (rare or poet.) Unabated; **a** not bated or abated, not diminished: '*unbated fire*' (Shakespeare, 'Merchant of Venice'); **b** (of weapon) not blunted, without a button on the point: '*You may choose A sword unbated*' (Shakespeare, 'Hamlet').

unbathed, adj. [1. unbâdhd; 2. anbéiðd]. **un- (I.)** & **bathe(d)**. **a** Not bathed; unwashed; **b** not wetted, dry.

unbear, vb. trans. [1. unbâr; 2. anbéə]. **un- (II.)** & **bear (I.)**. To remove or unloose the bearing-rein of a horse.

unbearable, adj. [1. unbârabl; 2. anbéərəbl]. **un- (I.)** & **bearable**. Not bearable, not to be borne; intolerable, insupportable.

unbearably, adv. Prec. & **-ly**. In an unbearable manner; to an unbearable extent.

unbearded, adj. [1. unbērded; 2. anbíədid]. **un- (I.)** & **beard(ed)**. Not bearded; **a** having no beard; beardless: *an unbearded face, youth*; **b** not having beards or awns: *unbearded wheat, barley* &c.

unbeaten, adj. [1. unbētn; 2. anbítn]. **un- (I.)** & **beaten**. **1.** Not flogged. **2.** Not beaten by the feet; untrodden. Phr. *unbeaten track*: (i.) an unexplored region of the earth; (ii.) (fig.) unexplored region of thought, scientific investigation &c. **3. a** Unconquered: *an unbeaten army*; **b** not surpassed or excelled in competition of any kind: *unbeaten as a tennis-player; an unbeaten steeple-chaser; an unbeaten record.*

unbeautiful, adj. [1. unbûtifl; 2. anbjūtifl]. **un- (I.)** & **beautiful**. Not beautiful; ugly, plain.

unbecoming, adj. [1. ùnbekúming; 2. ànbikámiŋ]. **un- (I.)** & **becoming**. Not becoming, not suitable; unsuitable. **1.** Not befitting; unbefitting, not appropriate to, not suited for: *conduct unbecoming to a gentleman; expenditure, house &c. unbecoming in a person of his class.* **2.** Improper, unseemly, indecent: *unbecoming conduct, language.* **3.** Not suiting, not suited to, detracting from the attractiveness of: *unbecoming style of dress, fashions* &c.; *a pretty face spoiled by an unbecoming hat.*

unbecomingly, adv. Prec. & **-ly**. In an unbecoming manner; unsuitably, improperly.

unbecomingness, n. See prec. & **-ness**. Condition, quality, of being unbecoming.

unbed, vb. trans. [1. unbéd; 2. anbéd]. **un- (II.)** & **bed (II.)**. To lift (plant), move from a bed.

unbedded, adj. [1. unbéded; 2. anbédid]. **un- (I.)** & **bed(ded)**. Not bedded; **a** not placed or planted in a bed; **b** (archaic) not brought to bed; unwedded, virgin; **c** (of stone) not firmly fixed on its bed; loosened from, not laid upon, its bed.

unbefitting, adj. [1. ùnbefíting; 2. ànbifítiŋ]. **un- (I.)** & **befitting**. Not befitting; unbecoming.

unbefriended, adj. [1. ùnbefrénded; 2. ànbifréndid]. **un- (I.)** & **befriend(ed)**. Not befriended; not aided or helped by friends; friendless.

unbegotten, adj. [1. ùnbegótn; 2. ànbigɔ́tn]. **un- (I.)** & **begotten**. Not begotten; not generated; specif. (of God) self-existent, eternal.

unbeguiled, adj. [1. ùnbegīld; 2. ànbigáild]. **un- (I.)** & **beguile(d)**. Not beguiled; not deceived.

unbeknown, **unbeknownst**, adj. & adv. [1. ùnbenōn(st); 2. ànbinóun(st)]. **un- (I.)**, **be-**, & **know** & **-n**. (illit. or colloq., with *to*). **1.** adj. Unknown, not known. **2.** adv. Without the knowledge of: *he did it unbeknownst to me.*

unbelief, n. [1. ùnbelēf; 2. ànbilíf]. **un- (I.)** & **belief**, cp. O.E. *ungelēafa*. Withholding of belief or faith; refusal to believe; want of faith; disbelief, scepticism, esp. in matters of religion or divine revelation: '*He upbraided them with their unbelief*' (Mark xvi. 14).

unbelievability, n. [1. ùnbelèvabíliti; 2. ànbilìvəbíliti]. **un- (I.)** & **believable** & **-ity**. Condition of being unbelievable.

unbelievable, adj. [1. ùnbelēvabl; 2. ànbilívəbl]. **un- (I.)** & **believable**. Not believable, not to be believed, incredible.

unbelievably, adv. Prec. & **-ly**. In an unbelievable manner; to an unbelievable degree or extent; incredibly.

unbeliever, n. [1. ùnbelēver; 2. ànbilívə]. **un- (I.)** & **believer**. One who does not or who refuses to believe, esp. in religion or in a divine revelation; an infidel, pagan; a sceptic.

unbelieving, adj. [1. ùnbelēving; 2. ànbilíviŋ]. **un- (I.)** & **believing**. Refusing to believe; not believing; incredulous, sceptical.

unbelievingly, adv. Prec. & **-ly**. In an unbelieving manner.

unbeloved, adj. [1. ùnbelúvd; 2. ànbilávd]. **un- (I.)** & **beloved**. Not beloved.

unbelt, vb. trans. [1. unbélt; 2. anbélt]. **un- (II.)** & **belt (II.)**. **1.** To remove, loosen, the belt of; to ungird. **2.** To take off by loosening or removing a belt: *to unbelt a sword.*

unbend, vb. trans. & intrans. [1. unbénd; 2. anbénd]. **un- (II.)** & **bend (I.)**. **A.** trans. **1. a** (in physical senses) To free, change, release, from a bent position; to straighten, flatten out: *to unbend a bow*, by unstringing it; *to unbend a link, staple* &c., by hammering it flat; **b** (in non-physical senses) to relax, relieve from effort, strain, or constraint: *to unbend the mind; to unbend oneself in congenial company.* **2.** (naut.) **a** To unfasten from yards and stays: *to unbend the sails*; **b** to cast off or loose: *to unbend a cable*, from the anchor; **c** to untie: *to unbend a rope.* **B.** intrans. **1.** To become unbent, to cease to be bent; to become straght or flat: *the bow unbends when the string is loosened.* **2.** To relax one's rigidity of bearing, to abandon coldness and constraint; to get rid of, behave without, stiffness of manner; to be affable: *he only unbends in the family circle.*

unbending, adj. [1. unbénding; 2. anbéndiŋ]. Pres. Part. of prec. **1. a** Not pliant or easily bent; stiff, rigid; **b** (fig., of character &c.) not easily moved from one's intentions, principles, line of conduct &c.; inflexible, resolute, determined; unyielding, obstinate: '*the stern unbending Tories*'. **2.** Becoming relaxed from effort or constraint, becoming free from constraint or stiffness in manner; given, yielding, to relaxation or amusement: *a few unbending hours of ease; found him in a gay, unbending mood.*

unbendingly, adv. Prec. & **-ly.** In an unbending manner.

unbeneficed, adj. [1. unbénefist; 2. anbénifist]. **un- (I.)** & **benefice(d).** Not beneficed; not holding an ecclesiastical benefice or incumbency: *the unbeneficed clergy.*

unberufen, adj. [1. óonberóofen; 2. únbirūfən]. Mod. Germ., 'not called, summoned'. Phrase used to deprecate the intervention of fate, after boasting, making a too-confident statement as to the future &c.; a form of verbal warding off the unlucky, corresponding to touching wood in the same circumstances.

unbeseem, vb. trans. [1. ùnbesém; 2. ànbisím]. **un- (II.)** & **beseem.** (rare) To do anything unbecoming or unworthy of; to be unbecoming or unworthy of.

unbeseeming, adj. [1. ùnbeséming; 2. ànbisímiŋ]. **un- (I.)** & **beseem** & **-ing.** Not beseeming; unbefitting, unbecoming.

unbeseemingly, adv. Prec. & **-ly.** In an unbeseeming manner.

unbesought, adj. [1. ùnbesáwt; 2. ànbisɔ́t]. **un- (I.)** & **besought**, see **beseech.** Not besought; not entreated; not asked for.

unbespoken, adj. [1. ùnbespóken; 2. ànbispóukən]. **un- (I.)** & **bespoken.** See **bespeak.** Not bespoken, not ordered or reserved in advance.

unbestowed, adj. [1. ùnbestód; 2. ànbistóud]. **un- (I.)** & **bestow(ed).** Not bestowed, not given.

unbias, vb. trans. [1. unbías; 2. anbáiəs]. **un- (II.)** & **bias.** (rare) To free from, get rid of, bias or prejudice.

unbiased, unbiassed, adj. [1. unbíast; 2. anbáiəst]. **un- (I.)** & **bias** & **-ed.** Not biased; without preconceived notions; unprejudiced.

unbiblical, adj. [1. unbíblikl; 2. anbíblikl]. **un- (I.)** & **biblical.** Not biblical, not contained in the Bible, not authorized by the Bible.

unbidden, adj. [1. unbídn; 2. anbídn]. **un- (I.)** & **bid(den).** Not bidden; **a** not commanded, not ordered; freely given; spontaneous; **b** not invited; uninvited.

unbigoted, adj. [1. unbíguted; 2. anbígətid]. **un- (I.)** & **bigoted.** Not bigoted.

unbind, vb. trans. [1. unbínd; 2. anbáind]. **un- (II.)** & **bind. 1. a** To unfasten, untie what was bound or fastened; to loose: *to unbind the ropes*; **b** to release, free from bonds: *to unbind a prisoner*; to unfasten: *she unbound her hair.* **2.** To remove the binding from: *to unbind a book.*

unbishop, vb. trans. [1. unbíshop; 2. anbíʃəp]. **un- (II.)** & **bishop. 1.** To deprive of, degrade from, the rank and dignity of a bishop; to take away a bishopric: *the Queen threatened to unbishop him.* **2.** To deprive of the rank of an episcopal see or bishopric: *to unbishop a diocese, cathedral town.*

unbitt, vb. trans. [1. unbít; 2. anbít]. See **un- (II.)** & **bitts.** To uncoil, unfasten, as the turns of rope or cable, from a bitt.

unbitted, adj. [1. unbíted; 2. ənbítid]. **un- (I.)** & **bit(ted).** Not bitted, not restrained by a bit or bridle.

unbitten, adj. [1. unbítn; 2. anbítn]. **un- (I.)** & **bitten.** Not bitten.

unblamable, adj. [1. unblámabl; 2. ambléiməbl]. **un- (I.)** & **blame** & **-able.** Not blamable; blameless, innocent.

unbleached, adj. [1. unblécht; 2. anblítʃt]. **un- (I.)** & **bleach(ed).** Not bleached; left in its natural colour: *unbleached calico.*

unblemished, adj. [1. unblémisht; 2. anblémiʃt]. **un- (I.)** & **blemish(ed).** Not blemished; **a** not marked with physical blemishes or stains; **b** morally pure, without fault; spotless: *an unblemished reputation, character* &c.

unblended, adj. [1. unblénded; 2. anbléndid]. **un- (I.)** & **blend(ed).** Not blended, not mixed with other kinds; pure, unmixed.

unblessed, unblest, adj. [1. unblést; 2. anblést]. **un- (I.)** & **blessed, blest.** Not blessed or blest; accursed; unhappy.

unblock, vb. trans. [1. unblók; 2. anblɔ́k]. **un- (II.)** & **block (II.).** To remove a block from; to clear away an obstacle or that which blocks.

unblooded, adj. [1. unblúded; 2. anbládid]. **un- (I.)** & **blood(ed).** Not blooded, not having pure blood or descent; not thoroughbred: *an unblooded horse.*

unbloody, adj. [1. unblúdi; 2. anbládi]. **un- (I.)** & **bloody.** Not bloody; **a** not stained or marked with blood; **b** not accompanied by bloodshed; specif., *the unbloody sacrifice of the Eucharist*; **c** not bloodthirsty.

unblotted, adj. [1. unblóted; 2. anblɔ́tid]. **un- (I.)** & **blot(ted).** Not blotted; **a** not marked with blots or stains; **b** not blotted out, not erased or deleted.

unblown, adj. [1. unblṓn; 2. anblóun]. **un- (I.)** & **blow(n).** Not blown; **a** not sounded, as of trumpet, signal by trumpet &c.; **b** not in full bloom, not in flower, still in bud; **c** not exhausted by running, still having wind.

unblushing, adj. [1. unblúshing; 2. anbláʃiŋ]. **un- (I.)** & **blushing.** Not blushing; without a blush of shame; unashamed, shameless, barefaced.

unblushingly, adv. Prec. & **-ly.** In an unblushing manner; shamelessly.

unblushingness, n. See prec. & **-ness.** State, quality, of being unblushing; shamelessness.

unbodied, adj. [1. unbódid; 2. anbɔ́did]. **un- (I.)** & **(II.)** & **-bodied.** Freed from the body, disembodied; incorporeal, spiritual.

unboiled, adj. [1. unbóild; 2. anbɔ́ild]. **un- (I.)** & **boil(ed).** Not boiled; not brought to the boiling-point.

unbolt, vb. trans. [1. unbṓlt; 2. anbóult]. **un- (II.)** & **bolt (II.).** To draw back the bolt or bolts of; to unfasten, open (a door &c.), by drawing back the bolt.

unbolted (I.), adj. [1. unbṓlted; 2. anbóultid]. **un- (I.)** & **bolted (I.).** Not bolted, not fastened by bolting.

unbolted (II.), adj. **un- (I.)** & **bolted (II.).** (of flour &c.) Not bolted, not sifted or strained; not having the bran removed.

unbone, vb. trans. [1. unbṓn; 2. anbóun]. **un- (II.)** & **bone (I.).** To rid of bone, to remove the bones from (meat).

unbonnet, vb. intrans. & trans. [1. unbónet; 2. anbɔ́nit]. **un- (II.)** & **bonnet (II.). 1.** intrans. To remove one's bonnet or cap; to take off the hat as a salutation: *to unbonnet to a person.* **2.** trans. To remove the bonnet or hat from; esp. by knocking it off.

unbonneted, adj. [1. unbóneted; 2. anbɔ́nitid], fr. P.P. of prec. Not bonneted, without a bonnet or cap on; bareheaded, uncovered.

unbookish, adj. [1. unbóokish; 2. anbúkiʃ]. **un- (I.)** & **bookish.** Not bookish; **a** not devoted to books or reading; **b** not gaining knowledge from books alone, not depending merely on books.

unboot, vb. trans. & intrans. [1. unbóot; 2. anbút]. **un- (II.)** & **boot (II.). 1.** trans. To remove, take off the boots of, esp. riding boots. **2.** intrans. To take off one's boots.

unborn, adj. [1. unbórn; 2. anbɔ́n]. **un- (I.)** & **born.** Not yet born; still to be born; future: *unborn generations.*

unborrowed, adj. [1. unbórōd; 2. anbɔ́roud]. **un- (I.)** & **borrow(ed).** Not borrowed; not copied or plagiarized; original.

unbosom, vb. trans. [1. unbóozum; 2. anbúzəm]. **un- (II.)** & **bosom. 1.** To disclose, display, confess: *to unbosom one's feelings, thoughts, secrets* &c. **2.** (reflex.) *To unbosom oneself*, to open one's heart, to reveal one's intimate feelings, hopes, plans; to confess.

unbought, adj. [1. unbáwt; 2. anbɔ́t]. **un- (I.)** & **bought.** Not bought; **a** not acquired by payment; given freely and without price; **b** not sold, left unsold; **c** not bought over or gained by money or bribes.

unbound (I.), adj. [1. unbóund; 2. anbáund]. P.P. of **unbind.** Freed from bonds or shackles: *the prisoner was left unbound.*

unbound (II.), adj. **un- (I.)** & **bound (VI.).** Not bound, not in binding, loose (of books, papers &c.).

unbounded, adj. [1. unbóunded; 2. anbáundid]. **un- (I.)** & **bound (II.)** & **-ed.** Not bounded; **a** not bounded by material confines or limits; limitless: *unbounded space*; **b** unrestricted, unlimited; boundless: *unbounded pride, ambition, joy* &c.

unboundedly, adv. Prec. & **-ly.** In an unbounded manner.

unboundedness, n. See prec. & **-ness.** State, quality, of being unbounded.

unbowed, adj. [1. unbóud; 2. anbáud]. **un- (I.)** & **bow(ed). 1.** Not bowed, not bent or curved. **2.** Not conquered, undefeated, unsubdued.

unbox, vb. trans. [1. unbóks; 2. anbɔ́ks]. **un- (II.)** & **box (III.).** To take out of, remove from, a box.

unbrace, vb. trans. [1. unbrás; 2. anbréis]. **un- (II.)** & **brace (II.). 1.** To free from a brace or braces; to loosen: *to unbrace the yards of a ship, a drum* &c. **2.** To relax, to free from tension: *to unbrace the muscles, nerves* &c.; *to unbrace the mind.*

unbraced (I.), adj. [1. unbrást; 2. anbréist]. P.P. of prec. Freed from a brace or braces.

unbraced (II.), adj. **un- (I.)** & **brace(d). a** Not braced, without braces; **b** relaxed.

unbraid, vb. trans. [1. unbrád; 2. anbréid]. **un- (II.)** & **braid (I.).** To separate the braids or strands of; to unfasten, unweave, the braids of, as of hair &c.

unbred, adj. [1. unbréd; 2. anbréd]. **un- (I.)** & **bred.** Not bred; **a** not begotten, not reared; unborn; **b** without breeding; ill-bred; **c** not bred up to, not trained or taught.

unbreech, vb. trans. [1. unbréch, -brích; 2. anbrítʃ, -brítʃ]. **un- (II.)** & **breech. a** To remove the breeches of: **b** to free the breech of a cannon from fastenings.

unbreeched, adj. [1. unbrícht; 2. anbrítʃt]. **un- (I.)** & **breech(ed).** Not breeched; (of boy) not yet put into breeches or trousers, still in short clothes.

unbribable, adj. [1. unbríbabl; 2. anbráibəbl]. **un- (I.)** & **bribable.** Not bribable; not open to bribes, incorruptible.

unbridle, vb. trans. [1. unbrídl; 2. anbráidl]. **un- (II.)** & **bridle (II.). 1.** To take off, loosen, the bridle of: *to unbridle a horse.* **2.** (fig.) To free from constraint or restraint: *to unbridle the tongue* &c.

unbridled, adj. [1. unbrídld; 2. anbráidld]. **un- (I.)** & **bridle(d).** Not bridled; not controlled, free from all restraint, esp. (fig.) violent: *unbridled passions, language* &c.

unbroken, adj. [1. unbróken; 2. anbróukən]. **un- (I.)** & **broken.** Not broken. **1.** Not broken in two or up; not shattered, whole, intact: *an unbroken window, mast* &c. **2.** Not subdued, not crushed or weakened: *unbroken spirit, morale.* **3.** Not interrupted; continuous: *unbroken fine weather, sleep, peace.* **4.** Not broken in, not trained to saddle or bridle: *an unbroken colt.* **5.** (also *unbroke*) Not opened up by the plough, untilled, virgin: *unbroken soil, land.* **6.** Not violated; kept: *unbroken promises, word, faith* &c. **7.** Not surpassed, not beaten: *an unbroken record.*

unbrotherliness, n. [1. unbrúdherlines; 2. anbráðəlinis]. See next word & **-ness.** State, quality, of being unbrotherly.

unbrotherly, adj. [1. unbrúdherli; 2. anbráðəli]. **un- (I.)** & **brotherly.** Not brotherly; not showing normal feelings of, or acting as, one brother to another; unfriendly.

unbuckle, vb. trans. [1. unbúkl; 2. anbákl]. **un- (II.)** & **buckle.** To unfasten the buckle of; to release from a buckle: *to unbuckle a strap, belt, shoe &c.*; *to unbuckle a sword from its belt.*

unburden, vb. trans. [1. unbĕrdn; 2. anbə́dn]. **un-** (II.) & **burden** (II.). **1.** To take away, remove, relieve of, a burden or load. **2.** (fig.) To throw off, as a load, from the mind, by confession, disclosure: *to unburden one's heart, mind, conscience*; *to unburden one's heart to another.*

unburdened, adj. [1. unbĕrdnd; 2. anbə́dnd]. **un-** (I.) & **burden(ed)**. Not burdened; not weighed down, loaded, with cares, sins, secrets &c.

unburied (I.), adj. [1. unbérid; 2. anbérid]. P.P. of **unbury**. Disinterred, exhumed, dug up from the grave.

unburied (II.), adj. **un-** (I.) & **buried**. Not buried, not interred.

unburned, unburnt, adj. [1. unbĕrnd, -t; 2. anbə́nd, -t]. **un-** (I.) & **burn(ed)**, **burn(t)**. Not burned; not burned up.

unbury, vb. trans. [1. unbéri; 2. anbéri]. **un-** (II.) & **bury**. To disinter, exhume.

unbusinesslike, adj. [1. unbíznislīk; 2. anbíznislaik]. **un-** (I.) & **business-like**. Not businesslike; lacking, not evincing, business capacity.

unbutton, vb. trans. [1. unbútn; 2. anbátn]. **un-** (II.) & **button**. **a** To undo, unfasten, the buttons of, to open by disengaging the buttons from the buttonholes; **b** (fig.) to unbend.

uncage, vb. trans. [1. unkáj; 2. ankéidž]. **un-** (II.) & **cage** (II.). To release, set free, from a cage.

uncalled, adj. [1. unkáwld; 2. ankɔ́ld]. **un-** (I.) & **call(ed)**. Not called, not summoned, not invited.

uncalled-for, adj. [1. unkáwld for; 2. ankɔ́ld fɔ]. Not demanded or required by the situation and circumstances; gratuitous, impertinent; brought forward without excuse or reason; obtruded: *an uncalled-for rebuke, insult, remark &c.*; *his exhibition of temper was quite uncalled for.*

uncandid, adj. [1. unkándid; 2. ankǽndid]. **un-** (I.) & **candid**. Not candid, not frank, open, or sincere; disingenuous.

uncandidly, adv. Prec. & **-ly**. In an uncandid manner; not candidly.

uncannily, adv. [1. unkánili; 2. ankǽnili]. **uncanny** & **-ly**. In an uncanny manner; weirdly, mysteriously.

uncanniness, n. [1. unkánines; 2. ankǽninis]. Next word & **-ness**. State, quality, of being uncanny.

uncanny, adj. [1. unkáni; 2. ankǽni]. **un-** (I.) & **canny**. Producing a sense of awe, mystery, dread; weird.

uncanonical, adj. [1. ùnkanónikl; 2. ànkənɔ́nikl]. **un-** (I.) & **canonical**. Not canonical; **a** not according to the canon law; *uncanonical hours*, hours during which it is not allowed to hold a marriage service; **b** not contained in the canon of the Bible: *uncanonical books*, the Apocrypha.

uncanonically, adv. Prec. & **-ly**. In an uncanonical manner.

uncanonized (I.), adj. [1. unkánonīzd; 2. ankǽnənaizd]. **un-** (I.) & as next word. Not canonized as a saint.

uncanonized (II.), adj. **un-** (II.) & **canonize(d)**. Deprived of the status of a canonized saint.

uncap, vb. trans. & intrans. [1. unkáp; 2. ankǽp]. **un-** (II.) & **cap**. **1.** trans. To take off the cap or cover from. **2.** intrans. To take one's cap or hat off in salutation.

uncared-for, adj. [1. unkárd for; 2. ankéəd fɔ]. **un-** (I.) & **care(d)** (II.). Not cared for; neglected.

uncart, vb. trans. [1. unkárt; 2. ankát]. **un-** (II.) & **cart**. **1.** To discharge, unload, from a cart. **2.** (stag hunting) To set (deer) loose or free from the cart in which it is carried to the meet.

uncase, vb. trans. [1. unkás; 2. ankéis]. **un-** (II.) & **case**. To remove from a case or covering; specif., to remove from the case and display (the colours of a regiment).

uncatalogued, adj. [1. unkátalògd; 2. ankǽtəlɔ̀gd]. **un-** (I.) & **catalogue(d)**. Not catalogued; not appearing or found in any catalogue.

uncate, adj. [1. únkāt; 2. ánkeit], fr. Lat. *uncus*, 'hook', & **-ate**, see **uncinate**. Hooked, uncinate.

uncaught, adj. [1. unkáwt; 2. ankɔ́t]. **un-** (I.) & **caught**. Not caught, not captured or taken prisoner.

uncaused, adj. [1. unkáwzd; 2. ankɔ́zd]. **un-** (I.) & **cause(d)**. Not caused; existing without an antecedent cause, self-existent, uncreated, eternal.

unceasing, adj. [1. unsésing; 2. ansísiŋ]. **un-** (I.) & **cease** & **-ing**. Not ceasing, without ceasing or stopping; incessant, continual.

unceasingly, adv. Prec. & **-ly**. In an unceasing manner; without ceasing, continually.

uncelebrated, adj. [1. unsélebrāted; 2. ansélibrèitid]. **un-** (I.) & **celebrate(d)**. **a** Not celebrated, not famous; **b** not observed or kept by celebrations.

uncensored, adj. [1. unsénsurd; 2. ansénsəd]. **un-** (I.) & **censor(ed)**. Not censored; published, printed &c. without a censor's examination or permission.

uncensured, adj. [1. unsénshurd; 2. ansénʃəd]. **un-** (I.) & **censure(d)**. Not censured, not blamed; exempt from censure or blame.

unceremonious, adj. [1. unsèremṓnius; 2. ansèrimóuniəs]. **un-** (I.) & **ceremonious**. Not ceremonious; **a** without ceremony or formality; informal, easy, familiar: *an unceremonious gathering, entertainment*; *an unceremonious farewell*; *talked to me in a quite unceremonious way*; **b** not expressing, observing, or practising ceremony; hence also abrupt, discourteous, in manner: *he is rather too unceremonious for my taste*; *unceremonious treatment*; *a sharp, unceremonious dismissal.*

unceremoniously, adv. Prec. & **-ly**. In an unceremonious manner; without ceremony; familiarly; abruptly, rudely.

unceremoniousness, n. See prec. & **-ness**. Quality of being unceremonious.

uncertain, adj. [1. unsĕrtin; 2. ansə́tin]. **un-** (I.) & **certain**. Not certain. **1. a** Not certainly known; doubtful, problematical: *the date of their arrival is uncertain*; *the danger is plain, success is uncertain*; Phr. *a lady of uncertain age*, no longer young, yet not old; middle-aged; **b** not having certain knowledge, not assured or sure of: *I am quite uncertain as to my movements, as to when I shall leave &c.*; *he is uncertain of success.* **2. a** Not certain or sure in action or purpose; undecided, vacillating; unsteady: *a person of uncertain character*; *his aim was somewhat uncertain*; **b** liable to change; variable; not to be depended or relied on; capricious, unreliable: *an uncertain temper*; *uncertain weather*; *he is a good golfer, but very uncertain.*

uncertainly, adv. Prec. & **-ly**. In an uncertain manner; not certainly, without certainty.

uncertainty, n. [1. unsĕrtinti; 2. ansə́tinti]. **un-** (I.) & **certainty**. Condition, quality, of being uncertain; absence, lack, of certainty; **a** want of certain knowledge, state of not being sure or assured of: *to be in a state of uncertainty*; *uncertainty as to one's fate, as to results &c.*; legal Phr. *void for uncertainty*, of bequests, documents &c., in which the intention is stated in terms too vague to be carried out with certainty; **b** state of not being certainly known or predictable; doubtful: *the uncertainty of life*; **c** undependableness, tendency to vary; esp. *uncertainty of temper.*

uncertificated, adj. [1. ùnsertífikāted; 2. ànsətífikèitid]. **un-** (I.) & **certificate(d)**. Not certificated, not having obtained a certificate.

uncertified, adj. [1. unsĕrtifīd; 2. ansə́tifaid]. **un-** (I.) & **certify** & **-ed**. Not certified; not guaranteed.

unchain, vb. trans. [1. unchā́n; 2. antʃéin]. **un-** (II.) & **chain**. To free, loose, from a chain; to unfasten the chain of.

unchallengeable, adj. [1. unchálenjabl; 2. antʃǽlindžəbl]. **un-** (I.) & **challengeable**. Not challengeable; not to be challenged, called to account or question.

unchallenged, adj. [1. unchálenjd; 2. antʃǽlindžd]. **un-** (I.) & **challenge(d)**. Not challenged; unquestioned, not disputed.

unchangeability, n. [1. unchā̀njabíliti; 2. antʃèin(d)žəbíliti]. **un-** (I.) & **changeability**. State, quality, of being unchangeable, unchangeableness.

unchangeable, adj. [1. unchā́njabl; 2. antʃéin(d)žəbl]. **un-** (I.) & **changeable**. Not changeable; not liable to change; immutable.

unchangeableness, n. Prec. & **-ness**. Unchangeability.

unchangeably, adv. See prec. & **-ly**. In an unchangeable manner.

unchanged, adj. [1. unchā́njd; 2. antʃéin(d)žd]. **un-** (I.) & **change(d)**. Not changed; unaltered, remaining the same.

unchanging, adj. [1. unchā́njing; 2. antʃéin(d)žiŋ]. **un-** (I.) & **change** & **-ing**. Not changing, not varying; not liable to undergo change; invariable.

unchangingly, adv. Prec. & **-ly**. In an unchanging manner; without changing.

uncharged, adj. [1. unchárjd; 2. antʃádžd]. **un-** (I.) & **charge(d)**. Not charged. **1.** Not loaded; not fitted with a charge. **2.** Not charged with a crime, not accused.

uncharitable, adj. [1. uncháritabl; 2. antʃǽritəbl]. **un-** (I.) & **charitable**. Not charitable. **1.** (rare) Not disposed to almsgiving, not giving generously to charitable objects. **2.** Not ruled by, or acting in accordance with, the virtue of charity; censorious, unforgiving, judging harshly of others.

uncharitableness, n. Prec. & **-ness**. Quality of being uncharitable.

uncharitably, adv. See prec. & **-ly**. In an uncharitable manner.

uncharted, adj. [1. unchárted; 2. antʃátid]. **un-** (I.) & **chart(ed)**. **a** Not marked on a chart or map; **b** not mapped, not described or delineated on a chart or map.

unchartered, adj. [1. unchárterd; 2. antʃátəd]. **un-** (I.) & **chartered**. Not chartered, not having a charter of incorporation; unlicensed.

unchary, adj. [1. unchā́ri; 2. antʃéəri]. **un-** (I.) & **chary**. Not chary; **a** not frugal or sparing; **b** not cautious, rash.

unchaste, adj. [1. unchā́st; 2. antʃéist]. **un-** (I.) & **chaste**. Not chaste; incontinent.

unchastely, adv. Prec. & **-ly**. In an unchaste manner.

unchastened, adj. [1. unchā́send; 2. antʃéisnd]. **un-** (I.) & **chasten(ed)**. Not chastened.

unchastised, adj. [1. ùnchastīzd; 2. àntʃæstáizd]. **un-** (I.) & **chastise(d)**. Not chastised; unpunished.

unchastity, n. [1. unchástiti; 2. antʃǽstiti]. **unchaste** & **-ity**. Want of chastity; incontinence; state, quality, of being unchaste.

unchecked, adj. [1. unchékt; 2. antʃékt]. **un-** (I.) & **check(ed)**. Not checked. **1. a** Not stopped or reduced (in motion); **b** not disciplined, restrained, or controlled. **2.** Not examined or tested.

unchivalrous, adj. [1. unshívlrus; 2. anʃívlrəs]. **un-** (I.) & **chivalrous**. Not chivalrous, wanting in chivalry.

unchristian, adj. [1. únkríschan; 2. ankrístʃən]. **un-** (I.) & **Christian**. Not Christian; **a** (rare) not belonging to the Christian religion; heathen; **b** not in accordance with the spirit of Christianity, uncharitable; unbecoming a Christian.

unchristianize, vb. trans. [1. unkríschanīz; 2. ankrístʃənaiz]. **un-** (II.) & **christianize**. To cause to abandon Christianity.

unchristianly, adj. & adv. [1. unkríschanli; 2. ankrístʃənli]. **unchristian** & **-ly**. **a** adj. Unchristian; **b** adv., in an unchristian way.

unchurch, vb. trans. [1. unchĕrch; 2. antʃʌ́tʃ]. **un- (II.)** & **church**. To deprive of the rights and privileges of the Church; to expel from the Church, to excommunicate.

uncia, n., pl. **unciae** [1. únsia, -ē; 2. ánsiə, -ī]. Lat., for **oincia*, 'unity', fr. *ūnus*, O. Lat. *oinos*, 'one', see **uni-**, & cp. **inch (I.)** & **ounce (I.)**. (Rom. antiq.) One twelfth part, **a** of the *libra* or pound, an ounce, esp. as coin, one-twelfth of the **as**; **b** of the *pes*, or foot, an inch.

uncial, adj. & n. [1. únshal, únsial; 2. ánʃəl, ánsiəl], fr. Lat. *unciālis*, 'pertaining to an ounce or inch'; prec. & **-al**. The term *litterae unciāles*, 'letters an inch high', was used by St. Jerome of very large letters, not necessarily an inch in height. **1.** adj. Designating, pertaining to, consisting of, written in, a type of large MS. letter, used from the 4th to the 9th centuries A.D., differing from the capital 'majuscules' and the later cursive 'minuscules'. **2.** n. **a** An uncial letter; **b** a MS. written in uncial letters.

unciferous, adj. [1. unsíferus; 2. ansífərəs], fr. Lat. *unc-(us)*, 'hook', see **uncus**, & **-ferous**. (zool.) Bearing a hook or hook-like structure.

unciform, adj. [1. únsiform; 2. ánsifōm]. See prec. & **-form**. (anat. and zool.) Shaped like a hook; hook-shaped.

uncinal, adj. [1. unsínl; 2. ansáinl], fr. L. Lat. *uncīn-(us)*, variant of Lat. *uncus*, 'hook', see **uncus**, & **-al**. Hook-like, uncinate.

uncinate, adj. [1. únsināt; 2. ánsineit], fr. Lat. *uncīnāt-(us)*, fr. *uncīnus*, see prec. (anat., bot., and zool.) Hooked, bent like a hook; uncate; bearing hooked spines or prickles.

uncircumcised, adj. [1. unsĕrkumsīzd; 2. ansʌ́kəmsaizd]. **un- (I.)** & **circumcise(d)**. **a** Not having undergone the rite of circumcision; hence, non-Jewish or Hebraic; Gentile; **b** (fig.) unregenerate, heathen, pagan.

uncircumcision, n. [1. ùnsĕrkumsízhun; 2. ànsʌ̄kəmsížən]. **un- (I.)** & **circumcision**. **a** Non-circumcision; state of being uncircumcised; **b** (Bib.) *the uncircumcision*, the Gentiles.

uncircumstantial, adj. [1. ùnsĕrkumstánshl; 2. ànsʌ̄kəmstǽnʃəl]. **un- (I.)** & **circumstantial**. Not circumstantial, not given in detail, not examined in detail or going into details.

uncivil, adj. [1. unsívl; 2. ansívl]. **un- (I.)** & **civil**. **1.** Not civil or courteous; rude, impolite, ill-mannered: *uncivil language, manners, treatment* &c. **2.** (rare) Not civilized; barbarian: *an uncivil state of society*.

uncivilized, adj. [1. unsívilīzd; 2. ansívilaizd]. **un- (I.)** & **civilize(d)**. Not civilized; barbarous, savage.

uncivilly, adv. [1. unsívili; 2. ansívili]. **uncivil** & **-ly**. In an uncivil manner; rudely.

unclad, adj. [1. unklád; 2. anklǽd]. **un- (I.)** & **clad**, P.P. of **clothe**. Not clad; unclothed.

unclaimed, adj. [1. unklāmd; 2. ankléimd]. **un- (I.)** & **claim(ed)**. Not claimed.

unclasp, vb. trans. [1. unkláhsp; 2. anklásp]. **un- (II.)** & **clasp (I.)**. To loose, unfasten, the clasp of; to open something fastened by a clasp; to open something clasped: *to unclasp a brooch*; *to unclasp a box, case* &c.; *to unclasp one's hands*.

unclassed, adj. [1. unkláhst; 2. anklást]. **un- (I.)** & **class(ed)**. **1.** Not classed, not placed in a class. **2.** Not placed first, second, or third in a competition.

unclassified, adj. [1. unklásifīd; 2. anklǽsifaid]. **un- (I.)** & **classify** & **-ed**. Not classified; not arranged according to a classification.

uncle, n. [1. úngkl; 2. áŋkl]. A.-Fr., Mod. Fr. *oncle*, fr. Lat. *avunculus*, 'one's mother's brother', lit. 'a little grandfather', fr. *avus*, 'grandfather', & suff. *-unculus*; see **atavism** & cp. **avuncular**. **1.** **a** The brother of one's father or mother; **b** the husband of one's aunt. Phr. *Uncle Sam*, the United States of America, as personified in its government or a typical citizen. **2.** (Southern U.S.A.) A term of friendly or familiar address to an old negro: *Uncle Tom's Cabin*: *Uncle Remus* &c. **3.** (slang) The pawnbroker: *he has left his watch with his uncle*; cp. French slang, *ma tante*.

-uncle, suff., fr. Lat. *-unculus*, a variant of suff. *-culus*, cp. *carbuncle, furuncle* &c.; also *-uncule*, as in *homuncule*, or as Lat., *ranunculus*.

unclean, adj. [1. unklḗn; 2. anklín]. **un- (I.)** & **clean**. Not clean; **a** dirty, filthy, unwashed; **b** not ceremonially or ritually clean; **c** impure, unchaste, obscene.

uncleanliness, n. [1. unklénlines; 2. anklénlinis]. See next word & **-ness**. State, quality, of being uncleanly.

uncleanly, adj. [1. unklénli, -klḗnli; 2. anklénli, -klínli]. **un- (I.)** & **cleanly**. Not cleanly; having dirty habits, not attentive to cleanliness.

uncleanness, n. [1. unklḗnnes; 2. anklínnis]. **unclean** & **-ness**. State, quality, of being unclean, esp. in a moral sense; impurity, unchastity.

uncleared, adj. [1. unklḗrd; 2. anklíəd]. **un- (I.)** & **clear(ed)**. Not cleared. **1.** Not removed, not taken away; not freed from what should be cleared or removed: *the table is still uncleared*; *land uncleared of weeds, timber* &c. **2.** Not acquitted, not freed from a charge or accusation: *his character remains uncleared of a terrible suspicion*.

unclench, unclinch, vb. trans. [1. unklénch, -klínch; 2. anklén(t)ʃ, -klín(t)ʃ)]. **un- (II.)** & **clench, clinch**. To open, force open, what is clenched: *to unclench one's fist, teeth*.

unclerical, adj. [1. unklérikl; 2. anklérikl]. **un- (I.)** & **clerical**. Not clerical; **a** not characteristic of the clergy; lay: *unclerical dress*; **b** not befitting, unbecoming in, clerics: *very unclerical language*.

uncleship, n. [1. úngklship; 2. áŋklʃip]. **uncle** & **-ship**. (rare) Condition, relationship, of an uncle.

unclinch. See **unclench**.

uncloak, vb. trans. & intrans. [1. unklṓk; 2. anklóuk]. **un- (II.)** & **cloak**. **1.** trans. To remove the cloak from; to uncover. **2.** intrans. To take off one's cloak.

unclog, vb. trans. [1. unklóg; 2. anklɔ́g]. **un- (II.)** & **clog**. To free from a clog or obstruction; to remove that which clogs.

unclose, vb. trans. & intrans. [1. unklṓz; 2. anklóuz]. **un- (II.)** & **close**. To open, unfasten.

unclosed, adj. [1. unklṓzd; 2. anklóuzd]. **un- (I.)** & **close** & **-ed**. Not closed or shut, **a** open: *an unclosed door*; **b** not enclosed or shut in: *an unclosed view*; **c** not finished or concluded: *an unclosed controversy, argument*.

unclosured, adj. [1. unklṓzhurd; 2. anklóužəd]. **un- (I.)** & **closure(d)**. Not closured; not ended by the use of the parliamentary closure.

unclothe, vb. trans. [1. unklṓdh; 2. anklóuð]. **un- (II.)** & **clothe**. To remove, strip off, the clothes of; to divest of clothing.

unclothed, adj. [1. unklṓdhd; 2. anklóuðd]. **un- (I.)** & **clothe(d)**. Not clothed, naked.

unclouded, adj. [1. unklóuded; 2. ankláudid]. **un- (I.)** & **cloud(ed)**. Not clouded, not obscured by mist or cloud; clear, bright: *unclouded skies*; (also fig.) bright, serene: *a life of unclouded happiness*.

unclutch, vb. trans. [1. unklúch; 2. anklátʃ]. **un- (II.)** & **clutch**. To disengage a clutch; to free from a clutch.

unco', adj., adv., & n. [1. únkō; 2. ánkou]. Scots. variant of **uncouth**. **1.** adj. Strange, wonderful, weird: *an unco' sicht*. **2.** adv. Very, exceedingly, remarkably, excessively: *unco' guid*, exceedingly good; *the unco' guid*, excessively good people, usually with suggestion of hypocrisy. **3.** n. An extraordinary, strange, remarkable person or thing.

uncock, vb. trans. [1. unkók; 2. ankɔ́k]. **un- (II.)** & **cock (II.)**. To lower the hammer of a cocked gun without discharging it.

uncoffined, adj. [1. unkófind; 2. ankɔ́find]. **un- (I.)** & **coffin(ed)**. Not enclosed in a coffin.

uncoil, vb. trans. & intrans. [1. unkóil; 2. ankɔ́il]. **un- (II.)** & **coil**. **1.** trans. To unwind, to unfasten the coils of: *to uncoil a rope*. **2.** intrans. To unwind, to come out of coils: *the snake slowly uncoiled*.

uncoined, adj. [1. unkóind; 2. ankɔ́ind]. **un- (I.)** & **coin(ed)**. Not coined; **a** not minted into coins: *uncoined silver*; **b** (fig.) not counterfeit; genuine, unfeigned: '*A fellow of plain, uncoined constancy*' (Shakespeare, 'Henry V.').

uncollected, adj. [1. ùnkolékted; 2. ànkəléktid]. **un- (I.)** & **collect(ed)**. Not collected; **a** not collected or gathered together, not brought to one place or point; scattered: *uncollected rays of light*; **b** not gathered in, not demanded and received: *uncollected taxes*; **c** not brought under control; disordered: *uncollected wits*.

uncoloured, adj. [1. unkúlurd; 2. ankáləd]. **un- (I.)** & **colour(ed)**. Not coloured; **a** not painted in colours; left in natural colours; drawn in black and white; **b** (fig.) not exaggerated, not heightened by imagination; related with simplicity and truth; plain, unvarnished: *a plain uncoloured tale*.

uncombed, adj. [1. unkṓmd; 2. ankóumd]. **un- (I.)** & **comb(ed)**. Not combed; tangled, unkempt.

uncombined, adj. [1. ùnkombínd; 2. ànkəmbáind]. **un- (I.)** & **combine(d)**. Not combined; not formed into a combination or compound.

un-come-at-able, adj. [1. ùn kum át abl; 2. àn kam ǽt əbl]. (colloq.) Not to be come at; not attainable, inaccessible.

uncomeliness, n. [1. unkúmlines; 2. ankámlinis]. **uncomely** & **-ness**. State, quality, of being uncomely; **a** want of beauty, plainness, ugliness; **b** lack of decency or seemliness; unseemliness.

uncomely, adj. [1. unkúmli; 2. ankámli]. **un- (I.)** & **comely**. Not comely; **a** not beautiful or graceful; plain, ugly; **b** not seemly or becoming; indecent.

uncomfortable, adj. [1. unkúmfortabl; 2. ankámfətəbl]. **un- (I.)** & **comfortable**. Not comfortable, physically or mentally; **a** feeling, experiencing, discomfort, disagreeably placed or situated; uneasy: *to be uncomfortable in tight boots*; *to feel uncomfortable with strangers, about the political situation* &c.; **b** causing discomfort or uneasiness; awkward: *an uncomfortable hat, seat*; *the country is in an uncomfortable predicament*; *an uncomfortable prospect of increased taxation*.

uncomfortableness, n. Prec. & **-ness**. State, quality, of being uncomfortable; discomfort.

uncomfortably, adv. See prec. & **-ly**. In an uncomfortable manner.

uncomforted, adj. [1. unkúmforted; 2. ankámfətid]. **un- (I.)** & **comfort(ed)**. Not comforted; unconsoled.

uncommendable, adj. [1. ùnkoméndabl; 2. ànkəméndəbl]. **un- (I.)** & **commendable**. Not commendable; not to be commended, not worthy of commendation.

uncommercial, adj. [1. ùnkomĕrshl; 2. ànkəmʌ́ʃəl]. **un- (I.)** & **commercial**. Not commercial, **a** not engaged in, not pertaining to, commerce or trade: *an uncommercial nation*; *uncommercial interests, undertaking* &c.; **b** not in accordance with commercial principles or usage: *an uncommercial system of taxation*; **c** not actuated by desire of financial profit: *very uncommercial in his aims*.

uncommissioned, adj. [1. ùnkomíshund; 2. ànkəmíʃənd]. **un- (I.)** & **commission(ed)**. Not commissioned, not entrusted with a commission or duty; not authorized.

uncommitted, adj. [1. ùnkomíted; 2. ànkəmítid]. **un- (I.)** & **commit(ted)**. Not committed. **1.** Not done, not effected: *scarcely a crime left uncommitted*. **2.** Not pledged or bound (to): *he is still uncommitted to any definite course of action*. **3.** Not referred to a parliamentary committee, not yet in the committee stage: *the bill remains uncommitted.*

uncommon, adj. & adv. [1. unkómun; 2. ankɔ́mən]. **un-** (I.) & **common** (I.). **1.** adj. Not common; **a** not commonly found, or occurring; infrequent, rare: *an uncommon bird;* **b** not usual; strange, extraordinary, remarkable: *an uncommon act of courage, charity* &c. **2.** adv. (colloq., illit.) Uncommonly, remarkably: *I feel uncommon queer; uncommon good beer in this pub.*

uncommonly, adv. Prec. & **-ly**. **1.** In an uncommon manner; not commonly; infrequently, rarely: *a bird uncommonly found in England.* **2.** To an uncommon degree, remarkable; very: *it is uncommonly cold for the time of year; an uncommonly tall man.*

uncommonness, n. State, quality, of being uncommon; infrequency, rarity; strangeness.

uncommunicable, adj. [1. ùnkomûnikabl; 2. ànkəmjûnikəbl]. **un-** (I.) & **communicable.** Not communicable, not to be communicated; incapable of being imparted or shared.

uncommunicated, adj. [1. ùnkomûnikâted; 2. ànkəmjûnikèitid]. **un-** (I.) & **communicate**(d). Not communicated; **a** not disclosed or made known to others; **b** not imparted to, not shared with, others.

uncommunicative, adj. [1. ùnkomûnikativ; 2. ànkəmjûnikətiv]. **un-** (I.) & **communicative.** Not communicative; not disposed to communicate information; reserved, taciturn.

uncommunicativeness, n. Prec. & **-ness.** State, quality, of being uncommunicative.

uncompanionable, adj. [1. ùnkumpániunabl; 2. ànkəmpǽnjənəbl]. **un-** (I.) & **companionable.** Not companionable; unsociable.

uncomplaining, adj. [1. ùnkompláning; 2. ànkəmpléiniŋ]. **un-** (I.) & **complain** & **-ing.** Not complaining, making no complaints; patient, long-suffering.

uncomplainingly, adv. Prec. & **-ly.** In an uncomplaining manner, without complaint; resignedly.

uncomplaisant, adj. [1. ùnkumplásant; 2. ànkəmpléisənt]. **un-** (I.) & **complaisant.** Not complaisant; not obliging or courteous.

uncomplaisantly, adv. Prec. & **-ly.** In an uncomplaisant manner.

uncompleted, adj. [1. ùnkumplḗted; 2. ànkəmplítid]. **un-** (I.) & **complete**(d). Not completed; not finished, incomplete.

uncomplicated, adj. [1. unkómplikâted; 2. ankómplikèitid]. **un-** (I.) & **complicated.** Not complicated; not involved or intricate; simple.

uncomplimentary, adj. [1. ùnkompliméntari; 2. ànkəmpliméntəri]. **un-** (I.) & **complimentary.** Not complimentary; rude, discourteous.

uncompounded, adj. [1. ùnkompóunded; 2. ànkəmpáundid]. **un-** (I.) & **compound**(ed). Not compounded; not formed into a compound; unmixed; simple.

uncomprehensive, adj. [1. ùnkomprehénsiv; 2. ànkəmprihénsiv]. **un-** (I.) & **comprehensive.** Not comprehensive. **1.** Not inclusive of a large number or quantity. **2.** (rare) Not able to comprehend or understand.

uncompromising, adj. [1. unkómpromîzing; 2. ankómprəmàiziŋ]. **un-** (I.) & **compromise** & **-ing.** Not compromising; **a** not given to making compromises; admitting of no compromise; **b** inflexible, determined, decided, unyielding; strict.

uncompromisingly, adv. Prec. & **-ly.** In an uncompromising manner; without compromise.

unconcealed, adj. [1. ùnkonsḗld; 2. ànkənsíəld]. **un-** (I.) & **conceal**(ed). Not concealed; shown, displayed, openly.

unconcern, n. [1. ùnkonsẽrn; 2. ànkənsɜ́n]. **un-** (I.) & **concern.** Absence of, freedom from, concern, anxiety, care; indifference, apathy: *he regards such matters with complete unconcern.*

unconcerned, adj. [1. ùnkonsẽrnd; 2. ànkənsɜ́nd]. **un-** (I.) & **concern**(ed). Not concerned. **1.** **a** *Unconcerned in,* not implicated, uninvolved, not taking part in: *he was unconcerned in the conspiracy;* **b** *unconcerned with,* not interested in, not affected by: *to be unconcerned with politics.* **2.** *Unconcerned about,* free from concern or anxiety; easy in mind: *to be unconcerned about the future.* **3.** (absol.) Unperturbed; unmoved, apathetic.

unconcernedly, adv. [1. ùnkunsẽrnedli; 2. ànkənsɜ́nidli]. Prec. & **-ly.** In an unconcerned manner; indifferently, without concern.

uncondemned, adj. [1. ùnkondémd; 2. ànkəndémd]. **un-** (I.) & **condemn**(ed). Not condemned; **a** not found guilty or sentenced to punishment; **b** not blamed or disapproved of.

uncondensed, adj. [1. ùnkondénst; 2. ànkəndénst]. **un-** (I.) & **condense**(d). Not condensed.

unconditional, adj. [1. ùnkondíshunal; 2. ànkəndíʃənəl]. **un-** (I.) & **conditional.** Not conditional, not subject to or limited by conditions or reservations; absolute, not dependent on terms: *demanded an unconditional surrender; gave an unconditional refusal; made an unconditional offer to purchase.*

unconditionality, n. [1. ùnkondìshunáliti; 2. ànkəndìʃənǽliti]. Prec. & **-ity.** State, quality, of being unconditional.

unconditionally, adv. [1. ùnkondíshunali; 2. ànkəndíʃənəli]. See prec. & **-ly.** Without conditions or terms; absolutely: *to surrender, accept, unconditionally.*

unconditioned, adj. [1. ùnkondíshund; 2. ànkəndíʃənd]. **un-** (I.) & **condition**(ed). Not conditioned, not subject to conditions; unconditional; specif. (philos.) not subject to limitations or relations; absolute, infinite.

unconfessed, adj. [1. ùnkonfést; 2. ànkənfést]. **un-** (I.) & **confess**(ed). Not confessed; **a** not acknowledged or admitted: *an unconfessed crime;* **b** not having confessed one's sins and received absolution: *to die unconfessed.*

unconfined, adj. [1. ùnkonfínd; 2. ànkənfáind]. **un-** (I.) & **confine**(d). Not confined; **a** not fastened up; loose, free: *with tresses unconfined;* **b** unrestricted, not subject to restrictions and limitations; free, unchecked: *thoughts and speculations unconfined by prejudice or fear.*

unconfirmed, adj. [1. ùnkonfẽrmd; 2. ànkənfɜ́md]. **un-** (I.) & **confirm**(ed). Not confirmed. **1.** Not corroborated, not established by authoritative statement: *unconfirmed rumours.* **2.** Not having received the rite of confirmation.

unconformability, n. [1. ùnkonfòrmabíliti; 2. ànkənfɔ̀məbíliti]. See next word & **-ity.** State, quality, of being unconformable.

unconformable, adj. [1. ùnkonfórmabl; 2. ànkənfɔ́məbl]. **un-** (I.) & **conformable.** Not conformable, not conforming, not consistent; specif. (geol.) exhibiting unconformity: *unconformable strata.*

unconformably, adv. Prec. & **-ly.** In an unconformable manner; without conformity.

unconformity, n. [1. ùnkonfórmiti; 2. ànkənfɔ́miti]. **un-** (I.) & **conformity.** Want, absence, of conformity; specif. (geol.) break in continuity in series of strata, due to interruption of the process of formation.

unconfused, adj. [1. ùnkonfûzd; 2. ànkənfjúzd]. **un-** (I.) & **confuse**(d). Not confused; **a** free from confusion or disorder; **b** not embarrassed.

unconfusedly, adv. [1. ùnkonfûzedli; 2. ànkənfjúzidli]. Prec. & **-ly.** Not in a confused manner; without confusion or embarrassment.

uncongenial, adj. [1. ùnkonjḗnial; 2. ànkəndʒíniəl]. **un-** (I.) & **congenial.** Not congenial; **a** not sympathetic, not agreeing with one's character, temperament &c.: *in uncongenial company;* **b** distasteful, repugnant: *an uncongenial task.*

uncongeniality, n. [1. ùnkonjènialiti; 2. ànkəndʒìniǽliti]. Prec. & **-ity.** State, quality, of being uncongenial.

uncongenially, adv. [1. ùnkonjḗniali; 2. ànkəndʒíniəli]. See prec. & **-ly.** In an uncongenial manner.

unconnected, adj. [1. ùnkonékted; 2. ànkənéktid]. **un-** (I.) & **connect**(ed). Not connected; **a** not joined or linked physically together; separated: *unconnected lines of railway;* **b** not joined by a chain of causation: *events seemingly unconnected;* **c** not allied by ties of relationship: *families bearing the same name but unconnected;* **d** not logically connected; incoherent; disconnected; disjointed, rambling: *an unconnected narrative; loose, unconnected arguments.*

unconnectedly, adv. Prec. & **-ly.** In an unconnected manner; without connexion.

unconquerable, adj. [1. unkóngkerabl; 2. ankɔ́ŋkərəbl]. **un-** (I.) & **conquerable.** Not conquerable; incapable of being conquered or subdued; indomitable, invincible.

unconquerably, adv. Prec. & **-ly.** So as to be unconquerable; invincibly.

unconquered, adj. [1. unkóngkerd; 2. ankɔ́ŋkəd]. **un-** (I.) & **conquer**(ed). Not conquered; unsubdued, undefeated.

unconscientious, adj. [1. únkònshiénshus; 2. ánkɔ̀nʃiénʃəs]. **un-** (I.) & **conscientious.** Not conscientious, unscrupulous.

unconscientiously, adv. Prec. & **-ly.** In an unconscientious manner; unscrupulously.

unconscientiousness, n. See prec. & **-ness.** State, quality, of being unconscientious.

unconscionable, adj. [1. unkónshunabl; 2. ankɔ́nʃənəbl]. **un-** (I.) & *conscionable,* 'governed by conscience, scrupulous; reasonable', formed irregularly fr. **conscience.** **1.** **a** Not governed or restrained by conscience; unscrupulous: *unconscionable usurers; unconscionable subterfuges;* **b** (law) unfair, exceeding the limits of conscientious dealing: *an unconscionable bargain.* **2.** Not reasonable; excessive, inordinate: '*an unconscionable time a-dying*' (Charles II.).

unconscionably, adv. Prec. & **-ly.** In an unconscionable manner; to an unconscionable degree.

unconscious, adj. [1. unkónshus; 2. ankɔ́nʃəs]. **un-** (I.) & **conscious.** Not conscious. **1.** (with *of*) Not knowing; not alive to, unaware: *they were unconscious of any danger; unconscious of one's mistake, of one's absurd appearance* &c. **2.** Deprived of consciousness; in a state when all power of perception is lost: *after the accident he was unconscious for several days; he still remains in an unconscious condition.* **3.** Not apprehended or realized by the consciousness; not the result of will, not deliberately intended: *unconscious humour.* **4.** Taking place, carried out, without the participation of conscious will; involuntary: *unconscious movements; unconscious cerebration,* working of the mind without conscious effort; *the unconscious,* as n., in psychology and psycho-analysis, the unconscious elements and working of the mind, as distinct from and in contrast with the conscious. **5.** Non-conscious, not possessed of self-consciousness or of perception: *unconscious nature.*

unconsciously, adv. Prec. & **-ly.** Not consciously; in an unconscious manner; without consciousness.

unconsciousness, n. See prec. & **-ness.** Condition of being unconscious; absence, lack, of consciousness.

unconsecrated, adj. [1. ùnkónsekrâted; 2. ànkɔ́nsikrèitid]. **un-** (I.) & **consecrate**(d). Not consecrated.

unconsenting, adj. [1. ùnkonsénting; 2. ànkənséntiŋ]. **un-** (I.) & **consent** & **-ing.** Not consenting, withholding consent; nonacquiescent.

unconsidered, adj. [1. ùnkonsíderd; 2. ànkənsídəd]. **un-** (I.) & **consider**(ed). Not considered, disregarded, not taken into consideration; negligible.

unconstitutional, adj. [1. unkònstitúshunal; 2. ankɔ̀nstitjúʃənəl]. **un- (I.)** & **constitutional.** Not constitutional; not in accordance with, opposed to, the principles of the constitution of a state.

unconstitutionality, n. [1. unkònstitùshunáliti; 2. ankɔ̀nstitjùʃənǽliti]. Prec. & **-ity.** Quality of being unconstitutional.

unconstitutionally, adv. [1. unkònstitúshunali; 2. ankɔ̀nstitjúʃənəli]. See prec. & **-ly.** In an unconstitutional manner; in breach of the constitution.

unconstrained, adj. [1. ùnkonstránd; 2. ànkənstréind]. **un- (I.)** & **constrain(ed).** Not constrained. **1.** Free from restraint or compulsion; free to act or not. **2.** Not done under compulsion; done voluntarily. **3.** Free from constraint of manner, unembarrassed, not self-conscious; easy.

unconstrainedly, adv. [1. ùnkonstránedli; 2. ànkənstréinidli]. Prec. & **-ly.** In an unconstrained manner.

unconsumed, adj. [1. ùnkonsúmd; 2. ànkənsjúmd]. **un- (I.)** & **consume(d).** Not consumed.

unconsummated, adj. [1. unkónsumàted; 2. ankɔ́nsəmèitid]. **un- (I.)** & **consummate(d).** Specif. (of marriage) not consummated.

uncontainable, adj. [1. ùnkontánabl; 2. ànkəntéinəbl]. **un- (I.)** & **contain** & **-able.** Not containable; not to be contained or held in; irrepressible.

uncontaminated, adj. [1. ùnkontáminàted; 2. ànkəntǽminèitid]. **un- (I.)** & **contaminate(d).** Not contaminated; pure, unsullied (in material and spiritual sense).

uncontemplated, adj. [1. unkóntemplàted; 2. ankɔ́ntɛmplèitid]. **un- (I.)** & **contemplate(d).** Not contemplated; not expected.

uncontested, adj. [1. ùnkontésted; 2. ànkəntéstid]. **un- (I.)** & **contest(ed).** Not contested; specif., *an uncontested election*, one without a rival candidate.

uncontracted, adj. [1. ùnkontrákted; 2. ànkəntrǽktid]. **un- (I.)** & **contract(ed).** Not contracted; not shrunk or made smaller.

uncontradicted, adj. [1. unkòntradíkted; 2. ankɔ̀ntrədíktid]. **un- (I.)** & **contradict(ed).** Not contradicted; not denied, undisputed.

uncontrollability, n. [1. ùnkontròlabíliti; 2. ànkəntròuləbíliti]. See next word & **-ity.** State of being uncontrollable.

uncontrollable, adj. [1. ùnkontrólabl; 2. ànkəntróuləbl]. **un- (I.)** & **controllable.** Not controllable, incapable of being controlled or restrained; ungovernable, unmanageable: *an uncontrollable temper*; *uncontrollable children* &c.

uncontrollably, adv. Prec. & **-ly.** In an uncontrollable manner; beyond control.

uncontrolled, adj. [1. ùnkontróld; 2. ànkəntróuld]. **un- (I.)** & **control(led).** Not controlled; free from control, unrestrained.

uncontrolledly, adv. [1. ùnkontróledli; 2. ànkəntróulidli]. Prec. & **-ly.** In an uncontrolled manner; without control or restraint; freely.

uncontroversial, adj. [1. unkòntrovérshl; 2. ankɔ̀ntrəvə́ʃl]. **un- (I.)** & **controversial.** Not controversial; not a subject of, or giving rise to, controversy.

uncontroverted, adj. [1. unkòntrovérted; 2. ankɔ̀ntrəvə́tid]. **un- (I.)** & **controvert(ed).** Not controverted; undisputed, indisputable.

unconventional, adj. [1. ùnkonvénshunal; 2. ànkənvénʃənəl]. **un- (I.)** & **conventional.** Not conventional; **a** not in strict accordance with established custom and usage; **b** free and easy in manner; not strictly observant of the accepted rules and customs in manners, dress &c.

unconventionality, n. [1. únkonvènshunáliti; 2. ánkənvènʃənǽliti]. Prec. & **-ity.** Condition of being unconventional; freedom from established custom or usage.

unconventionally, adv. [1. ùnkonvénshunali; 2. ànkənvénʃənəli]. See prec. & **-ly.** In an unconventional manner.

unconversable, adj. [1. ùnkonvérsabl; 2. ànkənvə́səbl]. **un- (I.)** & **conversable.** Not conversable; not free or easy in conversation; not easy to get on with; unsociable.

unconversant, adj. [1. unkónversant; 2. ankɔ́nvəsənt]. **un- (I.)** & **conversant.** Not conversant; not familiarly acquainted with.

unconverted, adj. [1. ùnkonvérted; 2. ànkənvə́tid]. **un- (I.)** & **convert(ed).** Not converted. **1.** Not changed into or exchanged for another substance or body; not changed in substance or form. **2.** Not changed or converted in mind or heart; **a** not brought into acquaintance with Christianity or other specified religion; still in a state of heathendom; specif. **b** not having undergone conversion in special sense; not having felt the workings of faith and religion in the heart, or realized the inward truth of these. **3.** Not persuaded of, brought round to, some specified body of opinion.

unconvertible, adj. [1. ùnkonvértibl; 2. ànkənvə́tibl]. **un- (I.)** & **convertible.** Not capable of being converted or changed into something else; specific usages: **a** (of any form of money) not convertible into another form; **b** *unconvertible terms*, not capable of being used one for the other, not synonymous.

unconvinced, adj. [1. ùnkonvínst; 2. ànkənvínst]. **un- (I.)** & **convince(d).** Not convinced, unpersuaded.

unconvincing, adj. [1. ùnkonvínsing; 2. ànkənvínsiŋ]. **un- (I.)** & **convincing.** Not convincing; not bringing conviction.

unconvincingly, adv. Prec. & **-ly.** In an unconvincing manner.

uncooked, adj. [1. unkóokt; 2. ankúkt]. **un- (I.)** & **cook(ed).** Not cooked; raw.

uncord, vb. trans. [1. unkórd; 2. ankɔ́d]. **un- (II.)** & **cord.** To unfasten, undo knots, and remove cords from (a box, trunk &c.).

uncork, vb. trans. [1. unkórk; 2. ankɔ́k]. **un- (II.)** & **cork.** **a** To draw the cork from, take the cork out of: *to uncork a bottle of wine*; **b** (colloq.) to set loose what is bottled up, to give vent to: *to uncork one's feelings.*

uncorrected, adj. [1. ùnkorékted; 2. ànkəréktid]. **un- (I.)** & **correct(ed).** Not corrected; not revised; not rebuked.

uncorroborated, adj. [1. ùnkoróboràted; 2. ànkərɔ́bəreitid]. **un- (I.)** & **corroborate(d).** Not corroborated; unconfirmed.

uncorroded, adj. [1. ùnkoróded; 2. ànkəróudid]. **un- (I.)** & **corrode(d).** Not corroded, not impaired by rust; not acted on by acid.

uncorrupted, adj. [1. ùnkorúpted; 2. ànkəráptid]. **un- (I.)** & **corrupted.** Not corrupted; **a** not putrefied; **b** not morally corrupted; not bought with bribes.

uncorruptible, adj. [1. ùnkorúptibl; 2. ànkəráptibl]. **un- (I.)** & **corruptible.** Not corruptible, not liable to moral corruption; incorruptible.

uncountable, adj. [1. unkóuntabl; 2. ankáuntəbl]. **un- (I.)** & **count** & **-able.** Not countable, not to be counted; innumerable, countless.

uncounted, adj. [1. unkóunted; 2. ankáuntid]. **un- (I.)** & **count(ed).** Not counted, unnumbered.

uncountenanced, adj. [1. unkóuntenanst; 2. ankáuntinənst]. **un- (I.)** & **countenance(d).** Not countenanced; unsupported by others; not sanctioned.

uncouple, vb. trans. [1. unkúpl; 2. ankápl]. **un- (II.)** & **couple (II.)** **a** To loose from a couple or leash: *to uncouple greyhounds*; **b** to disconnect from couplings, to separate: *to uncouple railway trucks.*

uncoupled, adj. [1. unkúpld; 2. ankápld]. **un- (I.)** & **couple(d).** Not coupled, not joined together; disconnected.

uncourteous, adj. [1. unkórteus, -kérteus; 2. ankɔ́tiəs, -kə́tiəs]. **un- (I.)** & **courteous.** Not courteous; discourteous, rude.

uncourteously, adv. Prec. & **-ly.** In an uncourteous manner; discourteously, rudely.

uncourteousness, n. See prec. & **-ness.** Want of courtesy; discourtesy.

uncourtliness, n. [1. unkórtlines; 2. ankɔ́tlinis]. See next word & **-ness.** State of being uncourtly; want, absence, of courtliness.

uncourtly, adj. [1. unkórtli; 2. ankɔ́tli]. **un- (I.)** & **courtly.** Not courtly, not trained in, or used to, the manners of a court; unpolished, unrefined.

uncouth, adj. [1. unkóoth; 2. ankúþ]. O.E. *uncūð*, 'unknown, strange', **un- (I.)** & *cūþ*, 'known', cp. O.S. *cūð*, O.H.G. *chund*, Goth. *kunþs*; fr. base seen in **cunning, can (I.)**; cp. also **know.** **1.** (archaic and obs.) Unknown, strange, unfamiliar, mysterious: '*Find out His uncouth way*' (Milton, 'P. L.' II. 407). **2.** Awkward, unrefined, clumsy, boorish: *an uncouth rustic*; *of uncouth manners, appearance* &c.

uncouthly, adv. Prec. & **-ly.** In an uncouth manner.

uncouthness, n. See prec. & **-ness.** State, quality, of being uncouth.

uncovenanted, adj. [1. unkúvenanted; 2. ankávənəntid]. **un- (I.)** & **covenant(ed).** Not covenanted. **1.** Not founded on, not promised by, a covenant; specif. (theol.) *uncovenanted mercies of God*, mercies of salvation extended by God to those outside the Covenant of Grace and Redemption through Christ. **2.** Not bound by a covenant or agreement; specif., *Uncovenanted Civil Service*, a branch of the Indian Civil Service, members of which are appointed without examination, have no right to a pension, and may retire at will.

uncover, vb. trans. & intrans. [1. unkúver; 2. ankávə]. **un- (II.)** & **cover (I.).** **A.** trans. **1. a** To remove a cover or covering from: *to uncover a dish of food*; *to uncover a protected cricket pitch* &c.; **b** to remove the covering from (any part of the body): *to uncover the face, feet* &c., esp. *to uncover the head, uncover oneself*, to take off the hat or other head-covering as a sign of salutation or respect. **2. a** (by transf. or fig.) To lay open to view, to disclose, lay bare: *to uncover one's position*; *to uncover one's heart to*; specif. **b** (mil.) to disclose position of troops by deploying to right and left the leading lines which cover them. **3.** To remove cover or protection from; to leave unguarded, unprotected. **B.** intrans. To take off the hat or other head-covering as a salutation or in token of respect: *everyone uncovered when the signal sounded.*

uncovered, adj. [1. unkúverd; 2. ankávəd]. **un- (I.)** & **cover(ed).** Not covered; **a** devoid of cover; bare, unprotected: *the position lies quite uncovered and open to attack*; **b** with the hat off: *to stand uncovered.*

uncoveted, adj. [1. unkúveted; 2. ankávitid]. **un- (I.)** & **covet(ed).** Not coveted.

uncowl, vb. trans. [1. unkóul; 2. ankául]. **un- (II.)** & **cowl.** **a** To remove the cowl from: *to uncowl one's face, head*; **b** to take the cowl away from, to deprive of right to wear the cowl: *to uncowl a monk.*

uncreate (I.), vb. trans. [1. ùnkreát; 2. ànkriéit]. **un- (II.)** & **create.** (rare) To reverse the process of creation in respect of; wipe out of existence, annihilate: '*Who can uncreate thee thou shalt know*' (Milton, 'P. L.' v. 895).

uncreate (II.), adj. **un- (I.)** & (archaic) **create(d).** Not created; uncreated: '*The Father uncreate, the Son uncreate*' &c. (Athanasian Creed).

uncreated, adj. [1. ùnkreáted; 2. ànkriéitid]. **un- (I.)** & **create(d).** **1.** Not yet created, not existing, non-existent. **2.** Self-existing, existing eternally; existing, having its origin, independently of creation; uncreate.

uncredited, adj. [1. unkrédited; 2. ankréditid]. **un- (I.)** & **credit(ed).** Not credited, not believed.

uncrippled, adj. [1. unkrípld; 2. ankrípld]. **un-** (I.) & **cripple**(d). Not crippled; **a** not lamed; not injured in the limbs: *hands, feet, uncrippled by gout*; **b** not damaged or injured, not prevented by injury or loss from movement or activity: *the ships remained uncrippled by the heavy fire; the business is uncrippled in spite of the heavy loss incurred.*

uncritical, adj. [1. unkrítikl; 2. ankrítikl]. **un-** (I.) & **critical**. Not critical; **a** not disposed, unwilling, to criticize: *an enthusiastic and uncritical audience*; **b** not capable of criticism, wanting in powers of critical judgement, unable to criticize: *the uncritical applause of the uneducated*; **c** not according to the rules or principles of criticism: *an uncritical appreciation, estimate, review* &c.

uncritically, adv. Prec. & **-ly**. In an uncritical manner.

uncriticized, adj. [1. unkrítisīzd; 2. ankrítisaizd]. **un-** (I.) & **criticize**(d). Not criticized; not subjected to criticism.

uncropped, adj. [1. unkrópt; 2. ankrɔ́pt]. **un-** (I.) & **crop**(**ped**). Not cropped. **1.** (of land) Not sown, planted, with crops. **2.** (of crops) Not reaped, gathered in, or harvested. **3.** (of hair, ears) Not trimmed, not lopped or cut short.

uncross, vb. trans. [1. unkráws; 2. ankrɔ́s]. **un-** (II.) & **cross**. To change from a crossed position; to put straight what is crossed: *to uncross one's legs.*

uncrossed, adj. [1. unkráwst; 2. ankrɔ́st]. **un-** (I.) & **cross**(**ed**). Not crossed. **1.** Not placed across one another: *knives must lie uncrossed on the table.* **2.** (of cheque) Not crossed so as to indicate that it must be paid through an account at a bank. **3.** Not thwarted, not opposed: *a rapid rise to power uncrossed by any rivals.*

uncrown, vb. trans. [1. unkróun; 2. ankráun]. **un-** (II.) & **crown**. To deprive of a crown, to dethrone, depose from position as king (lit. and fig.).

uncrowned, adj. [1. unkróund; 2. ankráund]. **un-** (I.) & **crown**(**ed**). Not crowned; **a** not yet crowned; not having gone through the ceremony of coronation; **b** having the power but not the title of king: *some called Parnell the uncrowned king of Ireland.*

unction, n. [1. úngkshun; 2. áŋkʃən]. O. Fr., Mod. Fr. *onction*, fr. Lat. *unctiōn-(em)*, 'anointing'; fr. *unct-(um)*, P.P. type of *unguere*, 'to anoint', see **unguent**, & **-ion**. **1.** Act of anointing with oil as a ceremony or rite or symbol of consecration; **a** in the sacrament given to the dying in the Roman Catholic and Orthodox Churches, the blessed oil being applied to the head, hands, feet, and chest: *Extreme Unction*; **b** in the coronation of the king. **2.** Act of applying, by rubbing or smearing, oil, ointment, or unguent for medical purposes. **3. a** That which is used in anointing; an oil, ointment, or unguent; **b** (fig.) anything which soothes or assuages: '*Lay not that flattering unction to your soul*' (Shakespeare, 'Hamlet'). **4. a** A quality in language, voice, manner, or style which expresses or excites deep feeling or fervour, esp. religious fervour: *unction is no longer admired in a preacher; the sermons of to-day lack unction*; **b** exaggerated, affected, fervour; insincere emotion, sympathy, or suavity, gush, unctuousness: *the unction of a Pecksniff*; **c** relish, gusto, enjoyment: *an amusing story told with unction.*

unctuous, adj. [1. úngktūus; 2. áŋktjuəs], fr. O. Fr. *unctueus*, Mod. Fr. *onctueux*, fr. L. Lat. *unctuōsus*, fr. Lat. *unctus*, 'an anointing, unguent'; see prec. & **-ous**. **1.** Of the nature of an unguent or ointment; **a** greasy, oily; **b** having a soapy, greasy feeling or touch, as some minerals, e.g. fuller's earth, soapstone &c. **2.** Full of unction, esp. of simulated, exaggerated fervour or emotion; insincerely suave or gushing: *an unctuous person; an unctuous voice, manner* &c.

unctuously, adv. Prec. & **-ly**. In an unctuous manner; with affected, exaggerated, unction.

unctuousness, n. See prec. & **-ness**. Condition, quality, of being unctuous (lit. and fig.).

unculled, adj. [1. unkúld; 2. ankáld]. **un-** (I.) & **cull**(**ed**). Not culled, ungathered; not separated.

uncultivable, adj. [1. unkúltivabl; 2. ankáltivəbl]. **un-** (I.) & **cultivable**. Not cultivable; not capable of cultivation or tillage.

uncultivated, adj. [1. unkúltivàted; 2. ankáltivèitid]. **un-** (I.) & **cultivate**(d). Not cultivated. **1.** Not tilled, not employed for agricultural purposes, production of food &c.: *uncultivated land.* **2.** (fig.) **a** Not practised, not promoted, neglected: *uncultivated art, talents* &c.; **b** not improved or fostered by study, care &c.: *an uncultivated genius.* **3.** Not civilized; barbarous, rude, uncultured: *uncultivated races*, not refined by instruction and education.

uncultured, adj. [1. unkúlchurd; 2. ankáltʃəd]. **un-** (I.) & **culture**(d). Not cultured; uneducated, uncultivated.

uncurb, vb. trans. [1. unkẽrb; 2. ankə́b]. **un-** (II.) & **curb**. To free from a curb, to loosen the curb of, to ride on the snaffle only: *to uncurb a horse*; (also fig.) to unloose, let loose from control: *to uncurb one's passions.*

uncurbed, adj. [1. unkẽrbd; 2. ankə́bd]. **un-** (I.) & **curb**(**ed**). Not curbed; **a** not provided with a curb: *an uncurbed bridle*; **b** (fig.) not checked or controlled; unrestrained: *uncurbed passions, ambitions* &c.

uncurl, vb. trans. & intrans. [1. unkẽrl; 2. ankə́l]. **un-** (II.) & **curl**. **1.** trans. To put, take, out of curl, to straighten out from curl. **2.** intrans. **a** To come out of curl, come uncurled, to become straight; **b** to unroll, come out of a curled-up posture.

uncursed, adj. [1. unkẽrst; 2. ankə́st]. **un-** (I.) & **curse**(d). Not cursed; free from a curse.

uncurtailed, adj. [1. ùnkẽrtā́ld; 2. ànkə̀téild]. **un-** (I.) & **curtail**(**ed**). Not curtailed; not cut short, unabbreviated; existing, given, in full.

uncurtain, vb. trans. [1. unkẽrtin; 2. ankə́tin]. **un-** (II.) & **curtain**. To remove a curtain from; to draw aside the curtains of; to disclose, reveal.

uncurtained, adj. [1. unkẽrtind; 2. ankə́tind]. **un-** (I.) & **curtain**(**ed**). Not curtained; **a** having no curtains; **b** having the curtains drawn aside or back.

uncus, n., pl. **unci** [1. úngkus, únsī; 2. áŋkəs, ánsai]. Lat., 'hook', fr. Gk. *ógkos*; see also under **angle** (I.). (anat., zool.) A hook, barb; a hook-like appendage or process.

uncushioned, adj. [1. unkóoshund; 2. ankúʃənd]. **un-** (I.) & **cushion**(**ed**). Not cushioned; not provided with, not resting on, cushions; not padded.

uncustomary, adj. [1. unkústumari; 2. ankástəməri]. **un-** (I.) & **customary**. Not customary; not according to the usual custom.

uncustomed, adj. [1. unkústumd; 2. ankástəmd]. **un-** (I.) & **custom**(**ed**). **1.** Not liable to, or charged with, customs duty. **2.** Not having paid customs duty.

uncut, adj. [1. unkút; 2. ankát]. **un-** (I.) & **cut** (I.). Not cut; specif., of books, with margins of the pages not trimmed or cut down from the original width, as for binding.

undam, vb. trans. [1. undám; 2. andǽm]. **un-** (II.) & **dam** (II.). To remove a dam from, clear obstruction from: *to undam a river, reservoir* &c.

undamaged, adj. [1. undámijd; 2. andǽmidžd]. **un-** (I.) & **damage**(d). Not damaged, having suffered no damage; uninjured, unspoilt; sound, whole.

undammed, adj. [1. undámd; 2. andǽmd]. **un-** (I.) & **dam**(**med**) (III.). Not dammed; not blocked, obstructed, or held back by a dam.

undamned, adj. [1. undámd; 2. andǽmd]. **un-** (I.) & **damned**. Not damned; uncondemned.

undamped, adj. [1. undámpt; 2. andǽmpt]. **un-** (I.) & **damp**(**ed**). Not damped; **a** not disheartened; **b** specif. (elect.) of oscillations, maintained with increasing amplitude.

undate, adj. [1. úndāt; 2. ándeit], fr. Lat. *unda*, 'a wave', & **-ate**; cogn. w. Scrt. *undati*, 'it springs; it moistens'; & *udán*, 'water'; Gk. *hudōr*, 'water', see **hydro-**; O.E. *wæter*, see **water** (I.). Wavy, undated.

undated (I.), adj. [1. úndāted; 2. ándeitid]. Prec. & **-ed**. (bot.) Wavy, undulate.

undated (II.), adj. [1. undā́ted; 2. andéitid]. **un-** (I.) & **date**(d). **a** Not dated; bearing no date, as a document, cheque &c.; **b** not having the time fixed or agreed upon.

undaunted, adj. [1. undáwnted; 2. andɔ́ntid]. **un-** (I.) & **daunt**(**ed**). Not daunted, not dismayed or cowed by fear; fearless, courageous.

undauntedly, adv. Prec. & **-ly**. In an undaunted manner; fearlessly.

undauntedness, n. See prec. & **-ness**. Condition, quality, of being undaunted.

undazzled, adj. [1. undázld; 2. andǽzld]. **un-** (I.) & **dazzle**(d). Not dazzled; not blinded, as by too much brightness.

undé, adj. [1. úndi; 2. ándi], fr. Fr. *ondé*, see **undate**. (her.) Wavy.

undebated, adj. [1. ùndebā́ted; 2. àndibéitid]. **un-** (I.) & **debate**(d). Not debated; undiscussed.

undebauched, adj. [1. ùndebáwcht; 2. àndibɔ́tʃt]. **un-** (I.) & **debauch**(**ed**). Not debauched; **a** not corrupted in morals; **b** not dissolute in behaviour.

undecagon, n. [1. undékagon; 2. andékəgən], fr. Lat. *undec-(im)*, 'eleven', *ūnus*, 'one', & *decem*, 'ten', & **-gon**. (geom). A plane figure, having eleven angles and eleven sides.

undeceive, vb. trans. [1. ùndesḗv; 2. àndisív]. **un-** (II.) & **deceive**. To cause to be no longer deceived, to disillusion; to open the eyes of, to cause to see things as they really are: *he believes that he is certain to win, and I have not the heart to undeceive him.*

undeceived, adj. [1. ùndesḗvd; 2. àndisívd]. **un-** (I.) & **deceive**(d). Not deceived; not under the influence of illusion or self-deception: *undeceived by false hopes and promises, he prepared for the worst.*

undecennial, adj. [1. ùndesénial; 2. àndiséniəl]. Lat. *undecim*, 'eleven', see first element of **undecagon**, & for suff. see that of **decennial**. Occurring, observed, every eleventh year.

undecided, adj. [1. ùndesīded; 2. àndisáidid]. **un-** (I.) & **decided**. Not decided. **1. a** Not yet settled or determined: *an undecided question*; **b** (of weather) unsettled; **c** not having made up one's mind: *I'm undecided whether to go or stay.* **2.** Lacking decision of character; irresolute, incapable of coming to a decision: *an undecided character.* **3.** Not clearly marked, not definite in form or outline; vague, unpronounced: *a person of undecided features.*

undecidedly, adv. Prec. & **-ly**. In an undecided manner; irresolutely, waveringly.

undecidedness, n. See prec. & **-ness**. State, quality, of being undecided.

undecipherable, adj. [1. ùndesī́ferabl; 2. àndisáifərəbl]. **un-** (I.) & **decipherable**. Not decipherable; incapable of being deciphered; illegible.

undeck, vb. trans. [1. undék; 2. andék]. **un-** (II.) & **deck** (I.). (poet.) To deprive, divest, of adornments: '*Undeck the pompous body of a king*' (Shakespeare, 'Richard II.').

undecked (I.), adj. [1. undékt; 2. andékt]. **un-** (I.) & **deck**(**ed**). Not decked out or adorned.

undecked (II.), adj. **un-** (I.) & **deck** (II.), & **-ed**. (of boats) Not furnished with a deck.

undeclared, adj. [1. ùndeklā́rd; 2. àndikléəd]. **un-** (I.) & **declare**(d). **1.** Not declared, not made known, not disclosed. Specif. **2.** (of goods subject to customs duty) Not exhibited to officials of the customs for assessment of duty.

undedicated, adj. [1. undédikàted; 2. andédikèitid]. **un-** (I.) & **dedicate**(d). Not dedicated. **1.** **a** (of church) Not consecrated, not dedicated to a patron saint; **b** (of book) not dedicated to a patron; without a dedication. **2.** (of a road) Not handed over to a public authority but maintained at private expense by the makers or the owners of property along it.

undeeded, adj. [1. undéded; 2. andídid]. **un-** (I.) & **deed**(ed). (law) Not transferred by deed.

undefended, adj. [1. ùndeféndcd; 2. àndiféndid]. **un-** (I.) & **defend**(ed). Not defended. **1.** **a** Not defended; unprotected, without defence or protection, defenceless: *an undefended town*; **b** not supported or maintained by argument, excuse &c.: *an undefended act, measure* &c. **2.** **a** Not defended by counsel: *an undefended prisoner*; **b** without a defence being entered or put forward: *an undefended charge, action at law* &c.

undefiled, adj. [1. ùndefíld; 2. àndifáild]. **un-** (I.) & **defile**(d) (I.). Not defiled, unpolluted; pure; unmixed with baser elements.

undefined, adj. [1. ùndefínd; 2. àndifáind]. **un-** (I.) & **define**(d). Not defined. **1.** Not clearly marked; indefinite, vague. **2.** Not explained or described by a definition.

undeify, vb. trans. [1. undéifī; 2. andíifai]. **un-** (II.) & **deify**. To degrade from the position of a deity or god; to deprive of the sanctity of, rites and worship due to, a god.

undelayed, adj. [1. ùndelád; 2. àndiléid]. **un-** (I.) & **delay**(ed). Not delayed, not held back by delays.

undelegated, adj. [1. undélegàted; 2. andéligèitid]. **un-** (I.) & **delegate**(d). Not delegated, not transferred or committed to another: *undelegated powers or authority*.

undelivered, adj. [1. ùndelíverd; 2. àndilívəd]. **un-** (I.) & **deliver**(ed). Not delivered; **a** not set free, released, liberated: *an undelivered prisoner*; **b** not handed over, not distributed: *undelivered message, letters, parcels* &c.; **c** not pronounced, uttered, recited: *an undelivered speech, address*.

undemanded, adj. [1. ùndemáhnded; 2. àndimándid]. **un-** (I.) & **demand**(ed). Not demanded, not claimed or asked for.

undemonstrable, adj. [1. ùndemónstrabl; 2. àndimónstrəbl]. **un-** (I.) & **demonstrable**. Not demonstrable, incapable of being demonstrated.

undemonstrated, adj. [1. undémonstràted; 2. andémənstrèitid]. **un-** (I.) & **demonstrate**(d). Not demonstrated; not proved by demonstration.

undemonstrative, adj. [1. ùndemónstrativ; 2. àndimónstrətiv]. **un-** (I.) & **demonstrative**. Not demonstrative, not effusive, not addicted to strong expression of feeling, opinion &c.; reserved.

undemonstratively, adv. Prec. & **-ly**. In an undemonstrative manner.

undeniable, adj. [1. ùndeníabl; 2. àndináiəbl]. **un-** (I.) & **deniable**. Not deniable; **a** not capable of being denied or refuted; indisputable: *undeniable truth, evidence* &c.; **b** decidedly excellent: *of undeniable antecedents*; **c** unmistakable: *an undeniable Jew*.

undeniably, adv. Prec. & **-ly**. In an undeniable manner; indisputably, unmistakably.

undenominational, adj. [1. ùndenòmináshunal; 2. àndinòminéiʃənəl]. **un-** (I.) & **denominational**. Not denominational; specif., not restricted to, not in accordance with the characteristic tenets of any particular religious denomination: *undenominational education*.

undenounced, adj. [1. ùndenóunst; 2. àndináunst]. **un-** (I.) & **denounce**(d). Not denounced. **1.** **a** Not openly charged with, not informed against: *the conspirators remain undenounced*; **b** not inveighed against, not repudiated. **2.** Not formally terminated: *the treaty is still undenounced though obsolete*.

undependable, adj. [1. ùndepéndabl; 2. àndipéndəbl]. **un-** (I.) & **dependable**. Not dependable, not to be depended on; untrustworthy.

undeplored, adj. [1. ùndeplórd; 2. àndiplɔ́d]. **un-** (I.) & **deplore**(d). Not deplored, unlamented.

undeposed, adj. [1. ùndepózd; 2. àndipóuzd]. **un-** (I.) & **depose**(d). Not deposed.

undepraved, adj. [1. ùndeprávd; 2. àndipréivd]. **un-** (I.) & **deprave**(d). Not depraved, not corrupted in morals.

undepreciated, adj. [1. ùndepréshiàted; 2. àndipríʃièitid]. **un-** (I.) & **depreciate**(d). Not depreciated; **a** not disparaged, not belittled: *an undepreciated reputation*; **b** not lowered or reduced in value: *undepreciated currency*.

undepressed, adj. [1. ùndeprést; 2. àndiprést]. **un-** (I.) & **depress**(ed). Not depressed; esp. in mind, spirits; not dejected, not cast down: *undepressed by their losses*.

undeprived, adj. [1. ùndeprívd; 2. àndipráivd]. **un-** (I.) & **deprive**(d). Not deprived; not dispossessed of.

under (I.), prep. [1. únder; 2. ándə]. O.E. & M.E. *under*; O.S. *undar*; O.H.G. *untar*, Du. *onder*, Germ. *unter*, O.N. *undir* &c.; cogn. w. Lat. *infrā*, 'below'. See **infra**, & cp. Scrt. *adhaš*, 'below'. **1.** In, at, to a lower place or position than; below, the opposite of *over*; cp. *beneath* and *above*: *to lie down under a tree*; *you will find it under the seat*; *river flowing under a bridge*; **a** with sense of submersed in, covered by: *under the water*; *under the ground*; *hid his face under the bedclothes*; **b** inside, within: *under the skin*; *under the lee of*, to leeward of, sheltered from the wind by; **c** at the foot of: *village nestling under a hill*; *stand under the wall*; in various Phrs.: *under foot*, beneath one's feet, trodden; *under one's nose*, right in front of one, close to, so that one cannot help seeing it or noticing it; *under one's eye*, in sight; *under hatches*, with hatches closed down; safely secured; *under cover*, sheltered. **2.** With sense of sustaining, being loaded with or oppressed by (lit. and fig.): *cannot march under such a load*; *broke down under the burden of sorrow, care, debts* &c. Phr. *under arms*, armed. **3.** In sense of being in certain conditions or states (lit. and fig.) analogous to that of position under or beneath: **a** as subjected to, undergoing: *died under an operation, under the surgeon's knife*; *to be brave under trials and adversities*; *confessed under torture, the rack*; Phrs. *to be under a cloud*, be in disgrace, suspected, out of favour; *under fire*, fired upon; *under sail*, driven by wind; *under sentence of death, ten years' penal servitude* &c., sentenced to; **b** as in course of: *road under repair*; *bill now under discussion*; **c** as controlled or governed by: *England under the Stuarts*; *under the authority of the law*; **d** implying obligation, liability: *the terms under a contract*; *under a vow of secrecy*; *to give evidence under oath*; **e** as included in, in the same division or class as: *spiders, mites, ticks &c. are dealt with under (the head of) Arachnida*; **f** as indicating shelter, cover, or disguise &c.: *went under a false name*; *under the pretence of collecting for charity*; **g** as indicating a general state: *under such conditions, under the circumstances*; **h** during, in the time of: *under the later Roman Empire, under the Third French Republic*. **4.** Less than, inferior to: **a** (of position) *no one under (rank of) a colonel*; **b** (of age) *all children under 10 years old*; Phr. *under age*, not 21 years old; **c** in less time than: *cannot reach the place under two hours*; *run a hundred yards under ten seconds*; **d** (of price, value &c.) *won't sell under £1000*; **e** (of number, quantity &c.): *under 50 people were there*; *under 100 acres in area*.

under (II.), adj., fr. prec. Lower, subordinate, inferior; usually compounded, with or without hyphen, as *under-tenant, an underlease* &c.; see **under-**.

under (III.), adv.; see prec. In a lower, inferior, position, usually in various verbal Phrs.: *to bring, go, keep, under*, bring to, descend to, keep in, a lower condition; *to knuckle under*, to submit to slavishly.

under-, pref., fr. prec., w. force of prep., adv., or adj. **1.** Below, beneath: *underclothes, underfoot* &c.; *to underbid, to underline*. **2.** From beneath: *undermine, underprop*. **3.** Not completely, insufficient: *understaff, understatement*. **4.** Inferior, subordinate: *underling* &c.

underact, vb. trans. & intrans. [1. ùnderákt; 2. àndərǽkt]. **under-** & **act**. **1.** trans. To act (stage play) without sufficient passion, vigour, spirit; to act in such a manner that a character or part is insufficiently emphasized: *to underact the character of Macbeth*; *the play was underacted throughout*. **2.** intrans. To act in the above way.

underaction, n. [1. únderàkshun; 2. ándərǽkʃən]. **under-** & **action**. Subordinate action; action not essential to the main action; an episode.

under-agent, n. [1. únder ájent; 2. ándər éidʒənt]. **under-** & **agent**. A subordinate agent.

underarm, adj. & adv. [1. únderàrm; 2. ándərɑ̀m]. **under-** & **arm** (I.). (cricket, tennis) Bowled, served, with the fore-arm and hand, the elbow held downwards; underhand: *an underarm delivery, service*; *he bowls underarm*.

underbid, vb. trans. [1. ùnderbíd; 2. àndəbíd]. **under-** & **bid**. To bid or offer less than; to offer a less price for a service or contract; to offer to sell goods, contract to perform some service, at a lower price than: *our commercial rivals can underbid us in foreign markets*.

underbidder, n. [1. ùnderbíder; 2. àndəbídə]. Prec. & **-er**. One who underbids; **a** one who has successfully offered a lower price for supply of goods, for contract of service &c.: *our underbidders for coal in Europe*; **b** one who has failed to buy an object &c. at an auction, usually the person who has bid next highest price to the successful bidder: *the picture fell at £10,000 to Messrs. A; the underbidders were Messrs. B.*

underbitten, adj. [1. ùnderbítn; 2. àndəbítn]. **under-** & **bitten**. (etching) Not bitten in on the copper sufficiently deep for printing.

underbrace, vb. trans. [1. ùnderbrás; 2. àndəbréis]. **under-** & **brace** (II.). To brace, tie, fasten, together below or underneath: *to underbrace rafters, girders* &c.

underbraced, adj. [1. ùnderbrást; 2. àndəbréist]. **under-** & **brace**(d). Insufficiently braced or supported.

underbred, adj. [1. ùnderbréd; 2. àndəbréd]. **under-** & **bred**. Not well-bred, not thoroughbred; showing ignorance of the standards of manners, and the customs of polite society; not animated by the ideals and traditions of manners and conduct current among well-bred persons; ill-bred.

underbrush, n. [1. únderbrùsh; 2. ándəbrʌ̀ʃ]. **under-** & **brush** (I.). Undergrowth, underwood.

underbuy, vb. trans. [1. ùnderbí; 2. àndəbái]. **under-** & **buy**. To buy at a lower price than its real value or than the price at which it is offered; to buy cheaper than another.

undercharge (I.), vb. trans. [1. ùnderchárj; 2. àndətʃádž]. **under-** & **charge** (I.). **1.** To charge less than the true or fair price for; to charge too little for: *this account is undercharged*; *you have undercharged me for, on, this bill, for the books sent* &c. **2.** To load with an insufficient charge: *to undercharge a gun*.

undercharge (II.), n. [1. úndercharj; 2. ándətʃàdž]. An insufficient charge.

under-clay, n. [1. únder klá; 2. ándə kléi]. **under-** & **clay**. A bed, stratum, of clay beneath a coal seam.

under-clerk, n. [1. ùnder klárk; 2. àndə klák]. **under-** & **clerk**. A subordinate clerk.

under-clerkship, n. [1. ùnder klárkship; 2. àndə klákʃip]. Prec. & **-ship**. Position, office, of an under-clerk.

undercliff, n. [1. úndercliff; 2. ándəklif]. **under-** & **cliff**. A raised terrace or secondary cliff beneath a main or upper cliff, formed by fallen rock &c. from above.

underclothed, adj. [1. ùnderklṓdhd; 2. àndəklóuðd]. **under- & clothe(d).** Insufficiently clothed.

underclothes, n. pl. [1. únderklṓ(dh)z; 2. ándəklòu(ð)z]. **under- & clothes.** Clothes worn under the outer clothes, esp. those worn next the skin; undergarments, underclothing.

underclothing, n. [1. únderklṑdhing; 2. ándəklòuðiŋ]. **under- & clothing.** Underclothes.

undercoat, n. [1. únderkṑt; 2. ándəkòut]. **under- & coat. a** A coat worn under another; **b** the growth of short hair beneath the longer, outer hair of an animal's coat.

undercroft, n. [1. únderkràwft; 2. ándəkrɔ̀ft]. **under-** & obs. *croft*, 'vault'; cp. Dut. *krocht*, O.H.G. *chruft*, ad. fr. Lat. *crupta*, *crypta*, see **crypt.** A vaulted chamber beneath a church or other building; a crypt.

undercurrent, n. [1. únderkùrent; 2. ándəkàrənt]. **under- & current (II.). 1.** A current of water, as in a river, sea &c., flowing beneath the surface and in a contrary direction to that of the main or upper current. **2.** (fig.) A tendency, influence, as of opinion, feeling &c., not definitely expressed or apparent on the surface, sometimes running contrary to, or different from, the general or more obvious tendency: *amid the general acclamation an undercurrent of doubt and suspicion may be traced.* **3.** Specif. (gold min.) a large shallow box at the side of a main sluice with a steeper fall.

undercut (I.), vb. trans. [1. ùnderkút; 2. àndəkát]. **under- & cut. 1.** To cut away a lower part of anything so as to leave a projecting edge; to cut away from underneath (a raised, curved, or sculptured design), so that it should stand out in high relief: *moulding deeply undercut.* **2.** To cut, reduce, prices of goods, so as to sell cheaper than another: *to undercut prices; to undercut a commercial rival.* **3.** (golf) To hit a ball so that it rises sharply and falls dead without much run.

undercut (II.), n. [1. únderkùt; 2. ándəkàt]. **a** The tender meat on the lower or under side of the bone of a sirloin of beef; **b** (boxing) a blow delivered with an upward swing or punch of the arm.

under-develop, vb. trans. [1. ùnder devélop; 2. àndə divéləp]. **under- & develop.** (photog., of plate or film) To develop insufficiently.

under-developed, adj. [1. ùnder devélopt; 2. àndə divéləpt]. Not sufficiently developed; **a** not developed physically or mentally: *an under-developed child, mind*; **b** (photog., of plate or film) insufficiently developed.

underditch, vb. trans. [1. ùnderdích; 2. àndədítʃ]. **under- & ditch.** To dig an underground or deep ditch to drain heavy soil: *to underditch a field.*

underdo, vb. trans. [1. ùnderdóó; 2. àndədú]. **under- & do.** To cook, as meat, insufficiently; usually in P.P. pass., *underdone.*

underdog, n. [1. ùnderdóg, únderdòg; 2. àndədɔ́g, ándədɔ̀g]. **under- & dog (I.).** Also *the under dog*; **a** the dog which gets the worst of it in a fight with another dog; **b** (fig.) one who comes off badly in the struggle of life: *we naturally tend to sympathize with the underdogs.*

underdone, adj. [1. ùnderdún; 2. àndədán]. P.P. of **underdo. a** Insufficiently cooked, too raw: *the mutton's underdone again*; **b** not cooked too thoroughly; left slightly red or raw: *I like beef rather underdone.*

underdose (I.), vb. trans. [1. ùnderdṓs; 2. àndədóus]. **under- & dose (II.). a** To administer an insufficient dose to: *to underdose a patient*; **b** (reflex.) to take an insufficient dose: *to underdose oneself.*

underdose (II.), n. [1. únderdṑs; 2. ándədòus]. An insufficient dose.

underdrain (I.), vb. trans. [1. ùnderdrā́n; 2. àndədréin]. **under- & drain.** To drain, as land, by cutting drains or trenches below the surface.

underdrain (II.), n. [1. únderdrā̀n; 2. ándədrèin]. A drain or trench cut below the surface of the ground.

underdraw, vb. trans. [1. ùnderdráw; 2. àndədrɔ́]. **under- & draw.** To draw without enough definiteness or spirit.

underdress, vb. trans. & intrans. [1. ùnderdrés; 2. àndədrés]. **under- & dress. a** To dress inadequately or too scantily; to wear insufficient clothes; **b** to dress more simply and plainly than the occasion demands.

underestimate (I.), vb. trans. [1. ùnderéstimāt; 2. àndəréstimeit]. **under- & estimate.** To estimate at below the true figure; to undervalue, underrate, miscalculate: *to underestimate the cost of a holiday*; *to underestimate a person's abilities* &c.; *to underestimate a distance.*

underestimate (II.), n. [1. ùnderéstimat; 2. àndəréstimit]. An estimate below the true value or cost; an inadequate estimate.

underestimation, n. [1. úndèrestimā́shun; 2. ándərèstiméiʃən]. **underestimate (I.) & -ion.** An underestimate.

under-expose, vb. trans. [1. ùnder ekspṓz; 2. àndər ɛkspóuz]. **under- & expose.** (photog.) To expose a plate or film for too short a time.

under-exposure, n. [1. ùnder ekspṓzhur; 2. àndər ɛkspóužə]. (photog.) Exposure of plate &c. for too short a time.

underfeed, vb. trans. & intrans. [1. ùnderfḗd; 2. àndəfíd]. **under- & feed. a** trans. To feed with too little or inadequate food; to supply with too little food: *never underfeed children*; **b** intrans., to eat less than normal amount of food: *the doctor advises me to underfeed for a bit.*

under-fired, adj. [1. ùnder fīrd; 2. àndə fáiəd]. **under- & fire(d).** (of pottery &c.) Not sufficiently fired or baked.

underflow, n. [1. únderflṑ; 2. ándəflòu]. **under- & flow (II.).** An undercurrent.

underfoot, adv. [1. ùnderfóot; 2. àndəfút]. **under- & foot (I.).** Under, beneath, one's feet; underneath; **a** *it is very damp underfoot*; **b** (fig.) in subordinate position, in subjection: *he kept his subjects underfoot.*

underframe, n. [1. únderfrā̀m; 2. ándəfrèim]. **under- & frame (II.).** A frame below another frame; a supporting frame for an upper part or body, as of the chassis of a motor-car &c.

underfur, n. [1. únderfêr; 2. ándəfə̀]. **under- & fur (I.).** The short, thick, soft fur beneath the coarser and long hair of certain furbearing animals, as seals, beavers &c.

undergarment, n. [1. úndergàrment; 2. ándəgàmənt]. **under- & garment.** A garment worn under outer garments, usually one worn next the skin; (pl.) underclothes.

undergird, vb. trans. [1. ùndergérd; 2. àndəgə́d]. **under- & gird (I.). a** To gird below or round the bottom of: '*to undergird the ship*' (Acts xxvii. 17); **b** to place girders beneath or below: *to undergird a roof.*

undergo, vb. trans. [1. ùndergṓ; 2. àndəgóu]. O.E. *undergān*; **under- & go.** To experience, endure, suffer; to be subjected to: *to undergo fatigue, a long journey* &c.; *he has undergone an operation.*

undergraduate, n. [1. ùndergrádūit; 2. àndəgrǽdjuit]. **under- & graduate (I.). 1.** A member of a university who has not taken his or her first or bachelor's degree. **2.** (attrib.) Of, pertaining to, an undergraduate or undergraduates.

undergraduateship, n. [1. ùndergrádūitship; 2. àndəgrǽdjuitʃip]. Prec. & **-ship.** Status, position, of an undergraduate.

underground (I.), adv. [1. ùndergróund; 2. àndəgráund]. **under- & ground (I.). a** (in physical sense) Under, beneath, the ground, below the surface of the earth: *miners who work underground*; **b** (fig.) secretly, surreptitiously, in an obscure, hidden manner: *schemes are being concocted underground.*

underground (II.), adj. & n. [1. úndergròund; 2. ándəgràund]. **1.** adj. **a** (in physical sense) Situated, moving, beneath the surface of the ground: *an underground cellar, basement*; *an underground railway* &c.; **b** (fig.) secret, surreptitious, obscure: *underground intrigues, influence* &c. **2.** n. An underground railway: *to travel by the Underground.*

undergrown, adj. [1. ùndergrṓn; 2. àndəgróun]. **under- & grown.** Not sufficiently or fully grown or developed; underdeveloped.

undergrowth, n. [1. úndergrṑth; 2. ándəgròuþ]. **under- & growth.** That which grows below something else; small trees, bushes, shrubs, growing beneath the larger trees in a wood; underbrush.

underhand (I.), adv. [1. ùnderhánd; 2. àndəhǽnd]. **under- & hand. 1.** (cricket, tennis &c.) With the hand and arm below the elbow or shoulder; contrasted with *overarm* or *overhand*: *to bowl, serve, underhand.* **2.** (fig.) Secretly, clandestinely, not openly; contrasted with *above-board*: *he worked underhand to discredit his political rivals.*

underhand (II.), adj. [1. únderhànd; 2. ándəhǽnd]. **1.** (cricket &c.) Delivered, served, with the hand and arm below the elbow or shoulder: *underhand bowling, service.* **2.** (fig.) Secret, clandestine, not open and above-board: *underhand intrigues.*

underhanded, adj. [1. ùnderhánded; 2. àndəhǽndid]. Prec. & **-ed. a** Underhand, clandestine, secret; **b** insufficiently supplied with hands or assistants; short-handed.

underhandedly, adv. Prec. & **-ly.** In an underhanded manner; underhand.

underhew, vb. trans. [1. ùnderhū́; 2. àndəhjú]. **under- & hew.** To hew a log of timber by cutting away a portion below the surface so that it appears of larger cubic content than it really is.

underhung, adj. [1. ùnderhúng; 2. àndəháŋ]. **under- & P.P. of hang. a** (of lower jaw) Projecting beyond the upper jaw; **b** having the lower jaw so projecting: *an underhung face*; *she is slightly underhung.*

underived, adj. [1. ùndirī́vd; 2. àndiráivd]. **un- (I.) & derive(d).** Not derived. **1.** Original, not dependent on anything else: *absolute, underived power or authority.* **2.** Not traced to its original source; without derivation.

under-king, n. [1. únder king; 2. ándə kiŋ]. **under- & king.** A subordinate, inferior, vassal king.

underlaid, adj. [1. únderlā̀d; 2. ándəlèid]. P.P. of **underlay.** Laid, placed, underneath; specif. (print.) having something laid underneath to raise the type or impression: *an underlaid plate.*

underlap, vb. trans. & intrans. [1. ùnderláp; 2. àndəlǽp]. **under- & lap (II.).** To extend, project, to be folded under, the edge of something above; contrasted with *overlap*: *one plank slightly underlaps the other*; *an underlapping plank.*

underlay (I.), vb. trans. & intrans. [1. ùnderlā́; 2. àndəléi]. O.E. *underleċġan*, **under- & lay (III.). 1.** trans. To lay, place, something under or beneath something; specif. (print.) to support, raise, type &c. by laying something, as a sheet of paper or cardboard, beneath it, so as to throw the impression up: *to underlay a plate, block* &c. **2.** intrans. (min., of veins, lodes &c.) To incline from a perpendicular direction, to hade.

underlay (II.), n. [1. únderlā; 2. ándəlei]. **a** Paper, cardboard, placed beneath type, block &c., to raise the impression; **b** (min.) dip, inclination, of a vein or lode, from the perpendicular; hade.

underlay (III.), Pret. of **underlie.**

underlease, n. [1. únderlēs; 2. ándəlīs]. **under- & lease.** The lease by a tenant or lessee of part of the term of his lease to another; a sublease.

underlet, vb. trans. [1. ùnderlét; 2. àndəlét]. **under- & let (II.). a** To let at a lower rent than its real or full value; **b** to sublet.

underletting, n. [1. ùnderléting; 2. àndəlétiŋ]. **under- & let(ting).** The letting of a house, land &c., **a** below its full value; **b** to a subtenant; subletting.

underlie, vb. trans. [1. ùnderlí; 2. àndəlái]. Pret. *underlay*, P.P. *underlain*; O.E. *underlicgan*, **under-** & **lie** (III.). **1.** To lie, be placed, under or beneath; (also absol., esp. in Pres. Part.) *the coal measures which underlie the English Channel*; *gravel underlain by clay*; *the underlying strata.* **2.** (in non-physical sense) To form the basis or foundation of: *the principles which underlie our foreign policy.*

underline (I.), vb. trans. [1. ùnderlín; 2. àndəláin]. **under-** & **line** (III.). **1.** To mark with a line underneath, as a sign of emphasis or to indicate to the printer that the words are to be printed in italics. **2.** To emphasise, lay stress upon: *the sudden summoning of the Cabinet underlines the seriousness of the situation.*

underline (II.), n. [1. únderlīn; 2. ándəlain]. **under-** & **line** (II.). **a** A line drawn under a word, phrase &c., as a sign of emphasis; **b** (theatr.) an announcement of a forthcoming play, printed at the foot of the announcement, bill &c., of a current play.

underlinen, n. [1. únderlinen; 2. ándəlinin]. **under-** & **linen.** Underclothing of linen or other material; body-linen.

underling, n. [1. únderling; 2. ándəliŋ]. M.E., **under-** & **-ling.** (contemptuous) Person in a subordinate position, one occupying a humble office without authority or responsibility.

underlooker, n. [1. únderlòoker; 2. ándəlùkə]. **under-** & **look** & **-er.** (coal min.) An official who inspects the condition of a mine below the surface; an underviewer.

underman, vb. trans. [1. ùndermán; 2. àndəmǽn]. **under-** & **man** (II.). To supply, furnish, with too few men, esp. too small a crew for a ship: *to underman a ship*; *they set sail much undermanned*, i.e. short-handed.

undermasted, adj. [1. ùndermáhsted; 2. àndəmástid]. **under-** & **mast** & **-ed.** (of ship) Having too few or too small masts for the necessary or full spread of sail.

under-master, n. [1. ùnder máhster; 2. àndə mástə]. **under-** & **master.** A subordinate master at a school; any master other than the headmaster.

undermentioned, adj. [1. ùnderménshund; 2. àndəménʃənd]. **under-** & **mention(ed).** Mentioned, alluded to, below or later.

undermine, vb. trans. [1. ùndermín; 2. àndəmáin]. **under-** & **mine** (III.). **1. a** To dig a mine, excavate ground under something in order to cause its fall or destruction by an explosion or collapse: *to undermine a fortress, line of trenches, wall* &c.; **b** to wear away the base or foundations of, by erosion: *the sea is undermining the cliffs of the south coast.* **2.** (fig.) **a** To weaken, to sap, by secret, underhand means; to injure by insidious attacks: *to undermine a person's influence, reputation* &c.; **b** to wear away, impair: *dissipation has undermined his health.*

underminer, n. [1. ùnderminer; 2. àndəmáinə]. Prec. & **-er.** One who undermines.

undermost, adj. [1. úndermōst; 2. ándəmoust]. **under** (I.) & **-most.** Lowest in position, rank &c.

underneath, adv. & prep. [1. ùndernéth; 2. àndəníþ]. M.E. *undirnethe*; see **under-** & **(be)neath. 1.** adv. In, at, to a lower place; beneath, below: *the river flowing underneath.* **2.** prep. Under, below: *the river flowing underneath the bridge.*

underogatory, adj. [1. ùndirógaturi; 2. àndirógətəri]. **un-** (I.) & **derogatory.** Not derogatory; not disparaging or detracting.

underpay, vb. trans. [1. ùnderpā́; 2. àndəpéi]. **under-** & **pay** (I.). To pay inadequately or insufficiently: *underpaid workmen.*

underpayment, n. [1. ùnderpā́ment; 2. àndəpéimənt]. Prec. & **-ment.** Inadequate, insufficient, pay.

underpin, vb. trans. [1. ùnderpín; 2. àndəpín]. **under-** & **pin** (II.). To support (wall, bank &c.) by additional props of stone, brick, timber &c. introduced below, or so as to take the place of, existing foundations.

underpinning, n. [1. ùnderpíning; 2. àndəpíniŋ]. Prec. & **-ing. a** Act of supporting by props of stone &c. below foundations; **b** the props or other material used for this purpose.

underplay (I.), vb. intrans. & trans. [1. ùnderplā́; 2. àndəpléi]. **under-** & **play** (I.) **1.** intrans. (cards) To lose a trick intentionally by playing a low card instead of a higher one in the hand, in view of later advantages; to finesse. **2.** trans. To play a part inadequately, to underact.

underplay (II.), n. [1. únderplā; 2. ándəplei]. Act of underplaying.

underplot, n. [1. únderplot; 2. ándəplɔt]. **under-** & **plot** (III.). A subordinate, secondary, plot in a novel or play.

under-populated, adj. [1. ùnder pópūlāted; 2. àndə pɔ́pjuleitid]. **under-** & **populate(d).** Insufficiently populated in relation to the extent and fruitfulness &c. (of an area).

underpraise, vb. trans. [1. ùnderprā́z; 2. àndəpréiz]. **under-** & **praise.** To praise less than is deserved.

under-produce, vb. intrans. [1. ùnder prodús; 2. àndə prədjús]. **under-** & **produce.** To produce commodities below the general demand for such commodities, with the object of forcing up prices.

under-production, n. [1. ùnder prodúkshun; 2. àndə prədákʃən]. **under-** & **production.** Production of commodities below the demand, or below normal rate of production.

under-proof, adj. [1. ùnder pro͞of; 2. àndə prúf]. **under-** & **proof** (II.). Containing less alcohol than proof spirit.

underprop, vb. trans. [1. ùnder próp; 2. àndəprɔ́p]. **under-** & **prop** (II.). To place a prop under; to support from below by props.

underquote, vb. trans. [1. ùnderkwṓt; 2. àndəkwóut]. **under-** & **quote.** To quote, or offer goods for sale, at a lower price than others; to offer a lower price than.

underrate, vb. trans. [1. ùnderā́t; 2. àndəréit]. **under-** & **rate** (II.). To rate, value, too low, to place too low an estimate on; to underestimate: *one should not underrate the abilities of one's enemies.*

under-reckon, vb. trans. [1. ùnder rékun; 2. àndə rékən]. **under-** & **reckon.** To reckon too low; to underestimate.

under-ripe, adj. [1. ùnder ríp; 2. àndə ráip]. **under-** & **ripe.** Not fully ripe.

underrun, vb. trans. [1. ùnderún; 2. àndərán]. **under-** & **run. 1.** (rare) To run, pass, under: *the boat underran the bridge.* **2.** (specif. naut.) To examine a cable, hose &c., by lifting it and passing it through the hands.

underscore, vb. trans. [1. ùnderskṓr; 2. àndəskɔ́]. **under-** & **score** (II.). To underline.

under-secretary, n. [1. ùnder sékretari; 2. àndə sékrit(ə)ri]. **under-** & **secretary.** An assistant, subordinate secretary, esp. of Government departments; *Parliamentary Under-Secretary*, a member of the Ministry, vacating office at change of Government; *Permanent Under-Secretary*, member of the Civil Service, the official head of a department.

under-secretaryship, n. [1. ùnder sékretariship; 2. àndə sékrit(ə)riʃip]. Prec. & **-ship.** Position, status, of an under-secretary.

undersell, vb. trans. [1. ùndersél; 2. àndəsél]. **under-** & **sell.** To sell commodities at a lower price than: *to undersell one's rivals in trade.*

underseller, n. [1. ùnderséler; 2. àndəsélə]. Prec. & **-er.** One who undersells.

under-servant, n. [1. ùnderse̊rvant; 2. àndəsʌ́vənt]. **under-** & **servant.** A subordinate, inferior, servant.

underset (I.), vb. trans. [1. ùnderset; 2. àndəsét]. **under-** & **set** (I.). To support, prop (a wall, roof &c.), by masonry, brickwork &c.

underset (II.), n. [1. únderset; 2. ándəset]. **under-** & **set** (II.). (naut.) A set, current, beneath the surface of water, contrary to the general set of the water or to the wind.

under-sheriff, n. [1. únder shérif; 2. ándə ʃérif]. **under-** & **sheriff.** A deputy sheriff.

under-shirt, n. [1. únder shėrt; 2. ándə ʃʌ̀t]. **under-** & **shirt.** A shirt worn next the skin; a vest.

undershot, adj. **under-** & **shot** (II.). **1.** [1. úndershòt; 2. ándəʃɔ̀t] (of water-wheel) Moved, driven, by water flowing under it, contrasted with *overshot.* **2.** [1. ùndershót; 2. àndəʃɔ́t] (of jaw) Underhung.

undershrub, n. [1. úndershrùb; 2. ándəʃràb]. **under-** & **shrub** (I.). A small shrubby plant.

undersign, vb. trans. [1. ùndersín; 2. àndəsáin]. **under-** & **sign** (II.). To sign a document &c. at the foot; to write one's name at the end of a letter or document.

undersigned, adj. [1. úndersīnd, ùndersínd; 2. ándəsàind, àndəsáind]. In *the undersigned members*, those members whose names are signed below (at end of a document); *we the undersigned*, we who have signed our names below.

undersized, adj. [1. ùndersízd; 2. àndəsáizd]. **under-** & **-sized.** Of less than the normal or average size; dwarfish, stunted.

underskirt, n. [1. únderskėrt; 2. ándəskʌ̀t]. **under-** & **skirt.** A skirt worn under another or outer skirt; petticoat.

undersleeve, n. [1. únderslēv; 2. ándəslīv]. **under-** & **sleeve.** A sleeve worn under an outer sleeve.

undersoil, n. [1. úndersòil; 2. ándəsòil]. **under-** & **soil.** Subsoil.

undersong, n. [1. úndersòng; 2. ándəsɔ̀ŋ]. **under-** & **song.** The burden, refrain, of a song.

understand, vb. trans. & intrans. [1. ùnderstánd; 2. àndəstǽnd]. O.E. *understandan*, lit. 'to stand under, beneath'; the sense-development is not clear; Skeat, giving *under* here the sense of 'among', compares Lat. *intelligere*, fr. *inter*, 'between', cp. **intelligence**; O.E. has *undergietan*, lit. 'to under get', in same sense, cp. also O.N. *undirstanda*. **A.** trans. **1.** To comprehend, perceive, the meaning of; to grasp the meaning, purport, of; to hear, read, and interpret to oneself: *I can hear your voice but cannot understand you*; *can you understand German? please understand me, I absolutely refuse.* Phr. *to make oneself understood*, to make one's language, meaning, clear. **2.** To apprehend by the mind, to grasp, take in the idea of; to perceive the full significance or force of: *we do not yet understand the nature of electricity*; *does the child understand the meaning of an oath?*; *try and understand my difficulties.* Phr. *to understand one another*, (i.) to come to an understanding or agreement with another; (ii.) to be clearly aware of, though not necessarily sharing, each other's opinions, intentions &c.; (iii.) to be on good terms through comprehending and sympathizing each with the other's aims &c. **3.** To learn, be informed of: *we understand from an unofficial source that the measure is to be dropped.* Phr. *to give to understand*, to tell, inform. **4. a** To assume, infer; to take as meant or implied, often indicating surprise, warning &c.: *I understood him to say that*; *what are we to understand from such contradictory statements?*; **b** to supply mentally though not expressed: *when we say X is a millionaire, are we to understand pounds or dollars?* **B.** intrans. **1.** To have understanding; to have the powers, faculties, of mental comprehension; to be an intelligent being: *do animals understand?*; *the people listen but will not understand.* **2.** To be informed, to learn, hear, be told: *the news is better, so I understand.*

understandable, adj. [1. ùnderstándabl; 2. àndəstǽndəbl]. Prec. & **-able.** Able to be understood; intelligible.

understanded, adj. [1. ùnderstánded; 2. àndəstǽndid]. P.P. of **understand**: used in 16th cent. (archaic) Understood: '*language understanded of the people*', plain, ordinary language or words (Art. of Relig. xxiv.).

understanding (I.), n. [1. ùnderstánding; 2. àndəstǽndiŋ]. **understand** & abstract suff. **-ing.** **1.** Act of one who understands; mental grasp, comprehension, knowledge; discernment: *he tried to get some understanding of the question.* **2.** Intelligence; power, faculty, of comprehension or thought; sense: *a person of understanding*; *God give us understanding.* **3.** Agreement, unity of thought, feeling &c.; that which is mutually agreed upon or understood: *to have an understanding with another*; *to come to a definite understanding about.* Phr. *on the understanding that,* on such terms or conditions as are stated. **4.** (pl., colloq., facet.) Legs: *he has a sound pair of understandings.*

understanding (II.), adj., fr. Pres. Part. of **understand.** Intelligent, discerning, sensible: *an understanding man.*

understandingly, adv. [1. ùnderstándingli; 2. àndəstǽndiŋli]. Prec. & **-ly.** (rare or archaic) In an understanding manner; with understanding, intelligence, discernment.

understate, vb. trans. [1. ùnderstát; 2. àndəstéit]. **under-** & **state** (III.). Not to state fully or adequately, not to bring out all the points of; to minimize in statement, put forward with studied moderation; reverse of *exaggerate*: *to understate one's abilities, claims, case* &c.

understatement, n. [1. ùnderstátment; 2. àndəstéitmənt]. Prec. & **-ment.** **1.** Act of understating. **2.** A statement which errs on the side of moderation, which does not represent with completeness all the aspects of a case; reverse of *exaggeration.*

understock, vb. trans. [1. ùnderstók; 2. àndəstɔ́k]. **under-** & **stock.** **1.** To put less stock on (land) than it will properly carry. **2.** To furnish (shop, store &c.) with smaller supply of commodities or stock than the demand and requirements warrant.

understood, vb. [1. ùnderstóod; 2. àndəstúd]. Pret. & P.P. of **understand.**

understrapper, n. [1. úndersträper; 2. ándəstræ̀pə]. **under-** & **strap** & **-er.** (colloq.) An underling, a subordinate; an inferior agent, official or employee.

under-stratum, n. [1. úndersträtum; 2. ándə strèitəm]. **under-** & **stratum.** A substratum; a layer or stratum of earth on which the soil rests.

understudy, n. & vb. trans. [1. úndersträdi; 2. ándəstàdi]. **under-** & **study.** **1.** n. One who studies or learns the part of the regular actor in order to be able to play it in his absence. **2.** vb. **a** To study a theatrical part for this purpose: *to understudy Hamlet*; **b** to act as understudy to: *to understudy Irving in 'Hamlet'.*

undertake, vb. trans. & intrans. [1. ùnderták; 2. àndətéik]. M.E. *undertaken.* **under-** & **take.** **A.** trans. **1.** To take upon oneself, to lay oneself under an obligation to do: *to undertake a responsible post*; *to undertake a task, responsibility* &c.; *he has undertaken too much*; *to undertake to do anything*; *to undertake that it is so.* **2.** To engage in, take steps to perform, embark upon: *to undertake a journey.* **3.** (archaic) To challenge, engage with another in a contest, an argument. **B.** intrans. **1.** (archaic) To be guarantee for; to take on oneself a duty for another: *to undertake for another.* **2.** (colloq.) To carry on the business of, to be, an undertaker.

undertaker, n. [1. úndertàker; 2. ándətèikə]. Prec. & **-er.** One who undertakes or engages to perform some task &c.; a contractor. **1.** Specif., one whose business and trade it is to undertake all duties connected with the burial of the dead; one who manages funerals. **2.** (hist., usually cap. and in pl., *the Undertakers*) **a** The settlers on the forfeited lands of the Earl of Desmond in Ireland, at the end of the 16th century; **b** a party of members of the Parliament of 1614 who undertook to manage elections, secure supplies and passage of bills &c. in the interest of James I.

undertaking, n. [1. ùndertáking; 2. àndətéikiŋ]. **undertake** & **-ing.** **1.** That which is undertaken; an enterprise, task: *a difficult, dangerous, undertaking.* **2.** Promise, guarantee, obligation: *an undertaking to pay the debt within six months.* **3.** The professional activities, the trade, of an undertaker.

under-tenancy, n. [1. únder tènansi; 2. ándə tènənsi]. **under-** & **tenancy.** A tenancy, lease, held from or under another tenant or lessee, and not directly from the landlord; a subtenancy.

under-tenant, n. [1. únder tènant; 2. ándə tènənt]. **under-** & **tenant.** A tenant under another tenant; a subtenant.

under-timed, adj. [1. ùnder tímd; 2. àndə táimd]. **under-** & **time**(d). (photog.) Underexposed.

undertint, n. [1. úndertìnt; 2. ándətìnt]. **under-** & **tint** (I.). A subdued, faint, tint or colour; undertone.

undertone, n. [1. úndertòn; 2. ándətòun]. **under-** & **tone** (I.). **1.** A subdued tone or note; low, subdued voice: *to speak in undertones.* **2.** A subdued, faint, colour; an undertint.

undertook, vb. [1. ùndertóok; 2. àndətúk]. Pret. of **undertake.**

undertow, n. [1. úndertò; 2. ándətòu]. **under-** & **tow** (I.). The backward flow, drag, or pull of a wave or the sea after it breaks on the shore; underset.

undervaluation, n. [1. ùndervàlūáshun; 2. àndəvæ̀ljuéiʃən]. **under-** & **valuation.** Act of undervaluing; a valuation, estimate, of anything which is below its real value or worth.

undervalue, vb. trans. [1. ùndervál̄u; 2. àndəvǽlju]. **under-** & **value.** To value at less than the real worth; to set too low a value upon.

underwear, n. [1. únderwàr; 2. ándəwèə]. **under-** & **wear** (II.). (shop term) Clothes worn below others; underclothing, undergarments.

underwent, vb. [1. ùnderwént; 2. àndəwént]. Pret. of **undergo.**

underwing, n. [1. únderwìng; 2. ándəwìŋ]. **under-** & **wing.** Any kind of various nocturnal moths with conspicuous, banded markings on the under or posterior wings.

underwood, n. [1. únderwood; 2. ándəwud]. **under-** & **wood.** Undergrowth, underbrush.

underwork (I.), vb. trans. & intrans. [1. ùnderwérk; 2. àndəwə́k]. **under-** & **work.** **1.** trans. **a** To exact too little work from; to put to work for too short a time: *to underwork a machine, horse* &c.; **b** to work for a lower price than: *one trader tries to underwork another.* **2.** intrans. To work inadequately, to do less work than one should or is capable of: *a modern tendency to underwork.*

underwork (II.), n. [1. únderwèrk; 2. ándəwə̀k]. Inferior, subordinate, work; slack, inadequate, work.

underworld, n. [1. únderwèrld; 2. ándəwə̀ld]. **under-** & **world.** **1.** The lower, nether, world; the infernal regions; place of departed spirits; hell: *spirits from the underworld.* **2.** (poet. and rare) The world on the other side of the globe; the antipodes: '*the first light glimmering on a sail That brings our friends up from the underworld*' (Tennyson, 'Princess', iv. 45). **3.** That part of a community who live entirely by vice and crime: *gangster leaders or the kings of the underworld.*

underwrite, vb. trans. & intrans. [1. ùnderrít; 2. àndəráit]. **under-** & **write.** **A.** trans. **1.** To write below or underneath, to subscribe (rare, except in P.P.): *the underwritten signatures, names,* the undersigned. **2.** Specif. **a** to execute, by the signature of one's name to the document, and deliver a policy of insurance, esp. of marine insurance, guaranteeing, on payment of a premium, to make good loss or damage to the property insured; to take a risk on a policy of (marine) insurance: *to underwrite a ship, cargo* &c.; *to underwrite any kind of risk*; **b** to undertake, guarantee, to buy such of the stock or shares to be issued by a company as are not subscribed for by the public, for a named consideration or commission of so much per cent. **B.** intrans. To be in business as an underwriter.

underwriter, n. [1. únderìter; 2. ándəràitə]. Prec. & **-or.** **a** One whose business it is to underwrite policies, esp. of marine insurance: *an underwriter at Lloyd's*; **b** one who underwrites the shares newly issued by a company.

underwriting, n. [1. únderìting; 2. ándəràitiŋ]. **underwrite** & **-ing.** The business of an underwriter.

undescribed, adj. [1. ùndeskríbd; 2. àndiskráibd]. **un-** (I.) & **describe**(d). Not described.

undescried, adj. [1. ùndeskríd; 2. àndiskráid]. **un-** (I.) & *descried,* P.P. of **descry.** Not descried; undiscovered, unseen.

undeserved, adj. [1. ùndezérvd; 2. àndizə́vd]. **un-** (I.) & **deserve**(d). Not deserved; unmerited.

undeservedly, adv. [1. ùndezérvedli; 2. àndizə́vidli]. Prec. & **-ly.** In an undeserved manner; without deserving praise or blame.

undeserving, adj. [1. ùndezérving; 2. àndizə́viŋ]. **un-** (I.) & **deserving.** Not deserving; a not meritorious, having earned no claim (to help &c.) by personal virtue: *the undeserving poor*; **b** *undeserving of,* not meriting, unworthy of: *undeserving of pity.*

undesignated, adj. [1. undézignàted; 2. andézignèitid]. **un-** (I.) & **designate**(d). Not designated; unspecified; undescribed; unappointed.

undesigned, adj. [1. ùndezínd; 2. àndizáind]. **un-** (I.) & **design**(ed). Not designed; not intended, unintentional.

undesignedly, adv. [1. ùndezínedli; 2. àndizáinidli]. Prec. & **-ly.** In an undesigned manner; unintentionally.

undesigning, adj. [1. ùndezíning; 2. àndizáiniŋ]. **un-** (I.) & **designing.** Not designing; not engaged in crafty schemes; not having ulterior motives; ingenuous.

undesirability, n. [1. ùndezírabíliti; 2. àndizàiərəbíliti]. See next word & **-ity.** Condition, quality, of being undesirable; undesirableness.

undesirable, adj. & n. [1. ùndezírabl; 2. àndizáiərəbl]. **un-** (I.) & **desirable.** **1.** adj. Not desirable, not to be desired; having no qualities to recommend (him, it): **a** *an undesirable alien*; **b** *undesirable manners, language* &c.; **c** *he called at a most undesirable moment.* **2.** n. An undesirable person.

undesirableness, n. Prec. & **-ness.** Undesirability.

undesirably, adv. See prec. & **-ly.** In an undesirable manner.

undesired, adj. [1. ùndezírd; 2. àndizáiəd]. **un-** (I.) & **desire**(d). Not desired; **a** unwished for, unwanted; **b** not asked for, unsolicited.

undesirous, adj. [1. ùndezírus; 2. àndizáiərəs]. **un-** (I.) & **desirous.** Not desirous of, not desiring: *undesirous of distinctions, rank* &c.

undestroyable, adj. [1. ùndestróiabl; 2. àndistrɔ́iəbl]. **un-** (I.) & **destroyable.** Not destroyable; indestructible.

undetected, adj. [1. ùndetékted; 2. ànditéktid]. **un-** (I.) & **detect**(ed). Not detected, undiscovered.

undetermined, adj. [1. ùndetérmind; 2. ànditə́mind]. **un-** (I.) & **determine**(d). **1.** Not determined; not settled, fixed, or decided: *one question still remained undetermined.* **2.** Irresolute, vacillating, vague: *an undetermined character.*

undeterred, adj. [1. ùndetérd; 2. àndità́d]. **un-** (I.) & **deter**(red). Not deterred.

undeveloped, adj. [1. ùndevélopt; 2. àndivéləpt]. **un-** (I.) & **develop**(ed). Not developed. **1.** (of persons &c.) **a** (in physical sense) Not fully grown; not grown to normal size for its age: *an undeveloped child, muscles, body* &c.; **b** *an undeveloped mind, character.* **2.** (of land) Not put to its fullest use, whether for cultivation or building.

undeviating, adj. [1. undéviàting; 2. andívièitiŋ]. **un-** (I.) & Pres. Part. of **deviate.** Not deviating; **a** not departing from a straight course, not wandering into by-paths; **b** not turning aside from a fixed line in conduct, purpose, principle.

undeviatingly, adv. Prec. & **-ly.** In an undeviating manner.

undevout, adj. [1. ùndevóut; 2. àndiváut]. **un-** (I.) & **devout.** Not devout.

undevoutly, adv. Prec. & **-ly.** In an undevout manner.

undies, n. [1. úndiz; 2. ándiz]. Abbr. of **underclothes**, w. dimin. ending. (colloq.) Women's underclothes.

undifferentiated, adj. [1. ùndiferénshiàted; 2. àndiferénʃieitid]. **un-** (I.) & **differentiate(d).** Not differentiated; homogeneous.

undiffused, adj. [1. ùndifúzd; 2. àndifjúzd]. **un-** (I.) & **diffuse(d).** Not diffused.

undigested, adj. [1. ùndijésted; 2. àndidžéstid]. **un-** (I.) & **digest(ed).** Not digested; **a** not yet assimilated by the organs of digestion; not absorbed into the system; **b** not fully assimilated by the mind; not analysed, arranged, correlated: *undigested facts, theories* &c.

undignified, adj. [1. undígnifìd; 2. andígnifaid]. **un-** (I.) & **dignified.** Not dignified; inconsistent with, wanting in, dignity.

undiluted, adj. [1. ùndilúted; 2. àndailjútid]. **un-** (I.) & **dilute(d).** Not diluted; not mixed with extraneous matter; at full strength, unweakened by admixture of other elements.

undiminished, adj. [1. ùndimínisht; 2. àndimíniʃt]. **un-** (I.) & **diminish(ed).** Not diminished, not lessened; retaining full force, quality &c.

undimmed, adj. [1. undímd; 2. andímd]. **un-** (I.) & **dim(med).** Not dimmed.

undine, n. [1. oondén; 2. undín], fr. Mod. Germ., taken fr. Fr. *ondine*, fr. Lat. *unda*, 'wave', see **undulate** (I.). A female water-sprite, or elemental spirit, who, according to the system of Paracelsus, obtained a human soul by marrying, and bearing a child to, a mortal; cp. *salamander, gnome*, and *sylph*; whence (cap.) the name of the principal character in La Motte Fouqué's romance 'Undine'.

undiplomatic, adj. [1. ùndiplōmátik; 2. àndiploumǽtik]. **un-** (I.) & **diplomatic.** Not diplomatic; blunt, tactless.

undiplomatically, adv. [1. ùndiplōmátikali; 2. àndiploumǽtikəli]. Prec. & **-al** & **-ly.** Not diplomatically.

undirected, adj. [1. ùndirékted; 2. àndiréktid]. **un-** (I.) & **direct(ed).** Not directed. **1.** Left without direction or guidance: *undirected zeal.* **2.** Not addressed; having no address affixed: *undirected letters.*

undiscerned, adj. [1. ùndizérnd; 2. àndizʌ́nd]. **un-** (I.) & **discern(ed).** Not discerned; unperceived; not perceived clearly in the mind.

undiscernible, adj. [1. ùndizérnibl; 2. àndizʌ́nibl]. **un-** (I.) & **discernible.** (rare) Not discernible.

undiscerning, adj. [1. ùndizérning; 2. àndizʌ́niŋ]. **un-** (I.) & **discerning.** Not discerning; deficient in mental or moral discernment; dull of perception; obtuse.

undiscerningly, adv. Prec. & **-ly.** In an undiscerning manner; without discernment.

undischarged, adj. [1. ùndischárjd; 2. àndistʃádžd]. **un-** (I.) & **discharge(d).** Not discharged. **1.** Not fulfilled or carried out: *an undischarged duty.* **2.** Not freed from obligation; not having received a discharge: *undischarged bankrupt.* **3.** Not fired: *an undischarged gun.*

undisciplined, adj. [1. undísiplind; 2. andísiplind]. **un-** (I.) & **discipline(d).** Not disciplined; **a** not subject, or having been subjected, to mental or moral training and control: *an undisciplined mind, character* &c.; **b** specif., not properly exercised in military discipline; not trained to obey orders; not observing due order and discipline: *not an army but an undisciplined mob.*

undisclosed, adj. [1. ùndisklṓzd; 2. àndisklóuzd]. **un-** (I.) & **disclose(d).** Not disclosed; kept secret, undivulged.

undiscomfited, adj. [1. ùndiskúmfited; 2. àndiskámfitid]. **un-** (I.) & **discomfit(ed).** Not discomfited; undefeated.

undisconcerted, adj. [1. ùndìskunsérted; 2. andìskənsʌ́tid]. **un-** (I.) & **disconcert(ed).** Not disconcerted.

undiscouraged, adj. [1. ùndiskúrijd; 2. àndiskáridžd]. **un-** (I.) & **discourage(d).** Not discouraged.

undiscoverable, adj. [1. ùndiskúverabl; 2. àndiskávərəbl]. **un-** (I.) & **discoverable.** Not discoverable; not to be discovered.

undiscoverably, adv. Prec. & **-ly.** So as not to be discovered.

undiscovered, adj. [1. ùndiskúverd; 2. àndiskávəd]. **un-** (I.) & **discover(ed).** Not discovered, not found out; unknown.

undiscriminated, adj. [1. ùndiskrímìnàted; 2. àndiskrímìnèitid]. **un-** (I.) & **discriminate(d).** Not discriminated; not separated or distinguished; indiscriminate.

undiscriminating, adj. [1. ùndiskrímìnàting; 2. àndiskrímìnèitiŋ]. **un-** (I.) & **discriminating.** Not discriminating; not exhibiting discrimination; uncritical.

undiscriminatingly, adv. Prec. & **-ly.** In an undiscriminating manner; without discrimination.

undiscussed, adj. [1. ùndiskúst; 2. àndiskást]. **un-** (I.) & **discuss(ed).** Not discussed; undebated; not argued.

undisfigured, adj. [1. ùndisfígurd; 2. àndisfígəd]. **un-** (I.) & **disfigure(d).** Not disfigured.

undisguised, adj. [1. ùndisgízd; 2. àndisgáizd]. **un-** (I.) & **disguise(d).** Not disguised. **1.** Not covered or veiled under a disguise, mask &c. **2.** Open, plain, avowed, unconcealed: *with undisguised pleasure, hatred; he made an undisguised attack.*

undisguisedly, adv. [1. ùndisgízedli; 2. àndisgáizidli]. Prec. & **-ly.** In an undisguised manner; without disguise; frankly.

undismayed, adj. [1. ùndismád; 2. àndisméid]. **un-** (I.) & **dismay(ed).** Not dismayed; not terrified; not disheartened.

undisparaged, adj. [1. ùndispárijd; 2. àndispǽridžd]. **un-** (I.) & **disparage(d).** Not disparaged.

undispatched, adj. [1. ùndispácht; 2. àndispǽtʃt]. **un-** (I.) & **dispatch(ed).** Not dispatched, not sent.

undispelled, adj. [1. ùndispéld; 2. àndispéld]. **un-** (I.) & **dispel(led).** Not dispelled.

undispersed, adj. [1. ùndispérst; 2. àndispʌ́st]. **un-** (I.) & **disperse(d).** Not dispersed; kept together.

undisplayed, adj. [1. ùndisplád; 2. àndispléid]. **un-** (I.) & **display(ed).** Not displayed.

undisposed, adj. [1. ùndispṓzd; 2. àndispóuzd]. **un-** (I.) & **dispose(d).** Not disposed; **a** not inclined; unwilling, indisposed: *undisposed to do* &c.; **b** not disposed of, not set apart, not allocated to a specific use, not distributed: *undisposed property*; **c** (rare, archaic) unwell, indisposed.

undisputed, adj. [1. ùndispúted; 2. àndispjútid]. **un-** (I.) & **dispute(d).** Not disputed; unquestioned.

undissected, adj. [1. ùndisékted; 2. àndiséktid]. **un-** (I.) & **dissect(ed).** Not dissected.

undissembled, adj. [1. ùndisémbld; 2. àndisémbld]. **un-** (I.) & **dissemble(d).** Not dissembled; undisguised, open, unfeigned.

undissembling, adj. [1. ùndisémbling; 2. àndisémbliŋ]. **un-** (I.) & Pres. Part. of **dissemble.** Not dissembling, free from dissimulation; frank, honest.

undissolved, adj. [1. ùndizólvd; 2. àndizɔ́lvd]. **un-** (I.) & **dissolve(d).** Not dissolved.

undistinguishable, adj. [1. ùndistínggwishabl; 2. àndistíŋgwiʃəbl]. **un-** (I.) & **distinguishable.** Not distinguishable; not to be known apart; not clearly separable.

undistinguishably, adv. Prec. & **-ly.** In an undistinguishable manner.

undistinguished, adj. [1. ùndistínggwisht; 2. àndistíŋgwiʃt]. **un-** (I.) & **distinguished.** Not distinguished. **1.** Not regarded as distinct or separate. **2.** Having no distinction; commonplace, ordinary, mediocre.

undistressed, adj. [1. ùndistrést; 2. àndistrést]. **un-** (I.) & **distress(ed).** Not distressed; not troubled, physically or mentally.

undistributed, adj. [1. ùndistríbuted; 2. àndistríbjutid]. **un-** (I.) & **distribute(d).** Not distributed; specif. (log.) of a middle term used with different quantity in the major and minor premise, thus concealing a fallacy in the conclusion.

undisturbed, adj. [1. ùndistérbd; 2. àndistʌ́bd]. **un-** (I.) & **disturb(ed).** Not disturbed; **a** not moved or placed in another position; **b** not worried or distressed in mind.

undiversified, adj. [1. ùndivérsifìd; 2. àndaivʌ́sifaid]. **un-** (I.) & **diversify** & **-ed.** Not diversified; uniform.

undivided, adj. [1. ùndivíded; 2. àndiváidid]. **un-** (I.) & **divide(d).** Not divided; **a** not separated or broken into two or more parts; whole, continuous: *an undivided line, property* &c.; **b** not distracted; not directed or concentrated upon more than one object: *undivided attention.*

undivulged, adj. [1. ùndivúljd; 2. àndaivál(d)žd]. **un-** (I.) & **divulge(d).** Not divulged.

undo, vb. trans. [1. undóó; 2. andú]. **un-** (II.) & **do.** **1.** To reverse what has been done; to annul: *what's done cannot be undone; attempt to undo the past, the mischief, an injury to others* &c. **2. a** To unfasten, unloose, untie: *to undo a button, one's clothes, collar* &c.; **b** to free from what encloses, fastens; to unbutton, unfasten, (person's clothes &c.) and free him &c.: *he is choking, undo him; undo a parcel.* **3.** (archaic) To bring to ruin, poverty &c.; to ruin, damage, the character, fortunes, of: *his extravagance will undo him some day.*

undock, vb. trans. [1. undók; 2. andɔ́k]. **un-** (II.) & **dock** (II.). To take (vessel) out of a dock.

undoer, n. [1. undóóer; 2. andúə]. **undo-** & **-er.** One who undoes; specif., one who brings another to ruin &c.: *this faithless friend was his undoer.*

undoing, n. [1. undóóing; 2. andúiŋ]. **undo** & **-ing.** **1.** Act of reversing what has been done; reversal, annulment of the past: *there can be no undoing of the injury done to him.* **2.** Act of untying, unfastening: *the undoing of a parcel* &c. **3. a** Act or process of bringing to ruin: *it is melancholy to see the gradual undoing of a great man*; **b** cause, source, of ruin, destruction, misfortune &c.: *his overweening self-confidence proved his undoing in the end.*

undomesticated, adj. [1. ùndōméstikàted; 2. àndouméstikèitid]. **un-** (I.) & **domesticate(d).** **1.** (of animals) Not tamed, unaccustomed to live in contact with, or under care of man; wild. **2.** (of human beings) Not fond of home, unsuited for family life in the domestic circle.

undone (I.), adj. [1. undún; 2. andán], fr. P.P. of **undo.** **1.** Unfastened, unloosed, untied. **2.** Ruined; brought to misery.

undone (II.), adj. **un-** (I.) & P.P. of **do.** Not done; not carried out; uncompleted: *'left undone those things which we ought to have done'; half his work is undone.*

undoubted, adj. [1. undóuted; 2. andáutid]. **un-** (I.) & **doubt(ed).** Not doubted or called in question; indisputable; genuine, indubitable: *undoubted evidence; an undoubted masterpiece; an undoubted Rembrandt.*

undoubtedly, adv. Prec. & **-ly.** Without doubt or question; indubitably.

undoubting, adj. [1. undóuting; 2. andáutiŋ]. **un-** (I.) & **doubting.** Not doubting; not suspectir·.

undoubtingly, adv. Prec. & **-ly.** In an undoubting manner; unsuspectingly.

undrape, vb. trans. [1. undráp; 2. andréip]. **un-** (II.) & **drape**. To remove drapery, covering, or clothing from; to uncover, unclothe.

undraped, adj. [1. undrápt; 2. andréipt]. **un-** (I. & II.) & **drape(d)**. Not draped; unclothed; with drapery removed.

undreamed, -dreamt, adj. [1. undrémd, -drém(p)t; 2. andrímd, -drém(p)t]. **un-** (I.) & **dream(ed)**. (chiefly *undreamed-, undreamt-of*) Not dreamed or dreamt of; not conceived or thought of; unimagined, unexpected, unsuspected: *an undreamt-of success; wonders still undreamt of.*

undress (I.), vb. trans. & intrans. [1. undrés; 2. andrés]. **un-** (II.) & **dress**. **1.** trans. To take clothes off, strip, divest of clothing. **2.** intrans. To take one's clothes off.

undress (II.), n. [1. úndrès; 2. ándrès]. **a** Ordinary dress, as distinguished from 'full or parade dress', as of military and naval or other uniform; **b** loose, informal dress, déshabille.

undressed (I.), adj. [1. undrést; 2. andrést]. P.P. of **undress** (I.). Having the clothing removed, without clothing; nude; specif., having one's day clothing removed, and in night attire.

undressed (II.), adj. **un-** (I.) & **dress(ed)**. (of wounds, leather &c.) Not dressed.

undrilled, adj. [1. undríld; 2. andríld]. **un-** (I.) & **drill(ed)**. Not drilled.

undrinkable, adj. [1. undríngkabl; 2. andríŋkəbl]. **un-** (I.) & **drinkable**. Not drinkable.

undue, adj. **un-** (I.) & **due** (I.). **1.** [1. úndū; 2. ándjū] Not according to what is right or proper; **a** excessive, immoderate: *treated the matter with undue haste; had an undue fondness for whisky;* **b** improper: *undue influence*, influence improperly exercised over another, so as to induce him to do what he otherwise would not have done, as in making a will &c.; undue influence is sufficient to invalidate a will if established; **c** unbecoming, unsuitable, to the occasion: *undue levity.* **2.** [1. undú; 2. andjú] Not yet due or owing (rare, except of a bill of exchange or other negotiable instrument).

undulate (I.), adj. [1. úndūlāt; 2. ándjulèit], fr. Lat. *undulātus*, 'wavy, undulated', rare & post-class., fr. *undula, dimin. of Lat. *unda*, 'wave, water'; cp. Lat. *ūdus*, 'wet'; cogn. w. Gk. *húdōr*, 'water', see **hydro-**, & Engl. **water** & **wet**; the Lat. *und-* is seen also in *abound, redundant, surround* &c. (rare, except bot., of leaves &c.) Wavy, having a wavy or undulating margin.

undulate (II.), vb. intrans. See prec. **1.** (of a moving surface) To rise and fall in a regular series of alternate ridges and furrows (of the surface of the sea, or other large sheet of water; of standing corn swept by the wind &c.). **2.** (of a firm surface) To be diversified by a series of gently rising and falling curved slopes: *the land undulates as far as the eye can see.* **3.** (of an edge) To be cut or shaped into a series of alternately concave and convex curves.

undulating, adj. [1. úndūlàting; 2. ándjulèitiŋ]. Pres. Part. of prec. Undulated, wavy; having undulation; esp. of surface of ground.

undulatingly, adv. Prec. & **-ly**. In an undulating manner.

undulation, n. [1. ùndūláshun; 2. àndjuléiʃən]. **undulate** (II.) & **-ion**. **1. a** Undulating motion, like that of waves on surface of water, standing corn &c.; **b** a wavy, undulating contour; **a** gentle sloping rise or hollow on the surface of the ground. **2.** (phys.) Vibratory movement in the ether or other liquid or elastic substance, esp. of a wave of light or sound.

undulatory, adj. [1. úndūlaturi; 2. ándjulətəri]. **undulate** (II.) & **-ory**. Pertaining to, caused by, of the nature of, undulations, on water, the surface of the ground, or in the ether; *undulatory theory* (of light &c.), wave theory.

unduly, adv. [1. undúli; 2. andjúli]. **undue** & **-ly**. In an undue manner; **a** to an undue extent; immoderately, excessively: *unduly heated by the arguments;* **b** improperly: *unduly influenced by another.*

undutiful, adj. [1. undútifl; 2. andjútifl]. **un-** (I.) & **dutiful**. Not dutiful; rebellious.

undutifully, adv. Prec. & **-ly**. In an undutiful manner.

undutifulness, n. See prec. & **-ness**. State of being undutiful.

undying, adj. [1. undíing; 2. andái-iŋ]. **un-** (I.) & Pres. Part. of **die**. **a** Immortal, everlasting: *undying glory, fame;* **b** unceasing, never-ending: *with undying hatred.*

unearned, adj. [1. unérnd; 2. anə́nd]. **un-** (I.) & **earn(ed)**. Not earned, not gained by personal services or work; specif., *unearned income*, income derived from investments, as distinguished from salary, wages, fees for work done, and subject to a higher rate of income tax; *unearned increment*, increase in value of landed property due to causes other than expenditure of the owner in developing it, such as increased demand from growth of population, expenditure of public money &c.

unearth, vb. trans. [1. unérth; 2. anə́þ]. **un-** (II.) & **earth**. **1. a** To dig out of, up from, the earth: *to unearth a buried treasure;* **b** to drive (fox &c.) from its earth or burrow, with a terrier &c. **2.** (fig.) To discover, bring to light, by diligent search: *to unearth hitherto unknown documents, a secret, a mystery* &c.

unearthliness, n. [1. unérthlines; 2. anə́þlinis]. See next word & **-ness**. State, quality, of being unearthly.

unearthly, adj. [1. unérthli; 2. anə́þli]. **un-** (I.) & **earthly**. **a** Not earthly, not of this world; supernatural: *unearthly light, appearance, beauty;* **b** mysterious, weird, ghastly: *an unearthly scream.*

uneasily, adv. [1. unézili; 2. anízili]. **uneasy** & **-ly**. In an uneasy manner.

uneasiness, n. [1. unézines; 2. anízinis]. See next word & **-ness**. State of being uneasy.

uneasy, adj. [1. unézi; 2. anízi]. **un-** (I.) & **easy**. **1. a** Not enjoying bodily ease; uncomfortable, restless: *uneasy in tight clothes;* **b** not firmly settled: *uneasy in the saddle;* (fig.) *uneasy on the throne.* **2. a** Disturbed in mind, anxious; perturbed: *to feel uneasy about the future, the weather* &c.; **b** arising from, causing, anxiety or uneasiness of mind; disturbing: *uneasy dreams, fears* &c. **3.** (of manner &c.) Evincing lack of ease; constrained, awkward, embarrassed, self-conscious.

uneatable, adj. [1. unétabl; 2. anítəbl]. **un-** (I.) & **eatable**. Not eatable.

uneaten, adj. [1. unétn; 2. anítn]. **un-** (I.) & **eat(en)**. Not eaten.

uneconomic(al), adj. [1. ùnēkonómik(l); 2. ànīkənɔ́mik(l)]. **un-** (I.) & **economic(al)**. Not economic; **a** not in accordance with the principles of economics: *uneconomic expenditure, prices, wages* &c.; **b** not economical; extravagant, wasteful: *an uneconomic manager.*

unedifying, adj. [1. unédifling; 2. anédifài-iŋ]. **un-** (I.) & **edifying**. Not edifying; not tending to moral edification; degrading: *an unedifying spectacle.*

unedited, adj. [1. unédited; 2. anéditid]. **un-** (I.) & **edit(ed)**. Not edited; specif., not published before, of literary and other works.

uneducated, adj. [1. unédūkàted; 2. anédjukèitid]. **un-** (I.) & **educate(d)**. Not educated; illiterate.

unembarrassed, adj. [1. unembárast; 2. animbǽrəst]. **un-** (I.) & **embarrass(ed)**. Not embarrassed; **a** free from mental or money troubles; **b** free from awkwardness of manner; easy.

unemotional, adj. [1. ùnemóshunl; 2. ànimóuʃənəl]. **un-** (I.) & **emotional**. Not emotional; not readily feeling or showing strong emotion; not liable to having the emotions strongly roused.

unemployable, adj. [1. ùnemplóiabl; 2. ànimplɔ́iəbl]. **un-** (I.) & **employable**. Not employable; **a** not usable; **b** not capable of being employed for labour.

unemployed, adj. & n. [1. ùnemplóid; 2. ànimplɔ́id]. **un-** (I.) & **employ(ed)**. **1.** adj. Not employed; **a** not used or put to use or profit: *unemployed talents, energies, capital* &c.; **b** not occupied: *to have a few hours a day unemployed;* **c** not employed or engaged in regular labour; out of work: *an unemployed labourer, craftsman.* **2.** n. (coll.) *The unemployed*, body of workmen out of work at a specified time or in a specified district.

unemployment, n. [1. ùnemplóiment; 2. ànimplɔ́imənt]. **un-** (I.) & **employment**. **a** State of being unemployed or out of work; **b** the fluctuating number of workers out of work at any specific moment or in any specific district: *statistics of unemployment; what is the unemployment of this area?;* also (attrib.) as *unemployment benefit*, payment made to unemployed workers under various insurance acts; *unemployment insurance*, insurance against unemployment by means of contributions from workers, employers, and the State, in a specific industry.

unencumbered, adj. [1. ùnenkúmberd; 2. àninkámbəd]. **un-** (I.) & **encumber(ed)**. Not encumbered, without encumbrances; specif., of landed estates, not burdened with mortgages or other charges, such as life interests, annuities &c.

unending, adj. [1. unénding; 2. anéndiŋ]. **un-** (I.) & **end(ing)**. Not ending; **a** eternal, everlasting: *in unending bliss;* **b** never ceasing; ceaseless, continuous: *unending toil; unending chatter.*

unendingly, adv. Prec. & **-ly**. In an unending manner; **a** eternally; **b** ceaselessly.

unendowed, adj. [1. ùnendóud; 2.ànindáud]. **un-** (I.) & **endow(ed)**. Not endowed; without endowments.

unendurable, adj. [1. ùnendúrabl; 2.ànindjɔ́rəbl]. **un-** (I.) & **endurable**. Not endurable; not to be endured, intolerable.

un-English, adj. [1. unínglish; 2. aníŋgliʃ]. **un-** (I.) & **English**. Not English; not like, not characteristic of, Englishmen or their ways &c.

unenlightened, adj. [1. ùnenlítnd; 2. ànin-láitnd]. **un-** (I.) & **enlightened**. Not enlightened; in state of intellectual darkness; benighted.

unenterprising, adj. [1. unénterprìzing; 2. anéntəpràiziŋ]. **un-** (I.) & **enterprising**. Not enterprising; unwilling to embark on new enterprises; unadventurous.

unenviable, adj. [1. unénviabl; 2. anénviəbl]. **un-** (I.) & **enviable**. Not enviable, not to be envied.

unequable, adj. [1. unékwabl; 2. aníkwəbl]. **un-** (I.) & **equable**. Not equable; **a** not even or uniform; **b** easily put out or troubled; uncertain in temper.

unequal, adj. [1. unékwal; 2. aníkwəl]. **un-** (I.) & **equal**. Not equal; **a** not of the same size, weight, length &c.; **b** not equally matched; uneven, ill-matched; **c** not of the same merit or quality throughout; **d** followed by *to*, not sufficient for, not up to: *unequal to the task.*

unequalled, adj. [1. unékwald; 2. aníkwəld]. **un-** (I.) & **equal(led)**. Not equalled or to be equalled; unrivalled, unmatched, unparalleled.

unequally, adv. [1. unékwali; 2. aníkwəli]. **unequal** & **-ly**. In an unequal manner.

unequivocal, adj. [1. ùnekwívokl; 2. ànikwívəkl]. **un-** (I.) & **equivocal**. Not equivocal; without equivocation; not ambiguous; clear, plain, straightforward.

unequivocally, adv. Prec. & **-ly**. In an unequivocal manner.

unerring, adj. [1. unéring; 2. anə́riŋ]. **un-** (I.) & **err(ing)**. Not erring; not making, incapable of making, any mistake; not missing; not failing; sure, certain: *unerring aim; unerring judgement, insight* &c.

unerringly, adv. Prec. & **-ly**. In an unerring manner.

unessential, adj. [1. ùnesénshl; 2. ànisénʃəl]. **un-** (I.) & **essential**. Not essential; not belonging to the essence; not indispensable; not necessary; unimportant.

uneven, adj. [1. unḗven; 2. anívən]. **un-** (I.) & **even** (II.). Not even; **a** not level or smooth, rough: *uneven surfaces, road*; **b** not uniform, unequal, not equable: *of uneven temper*; **c** not of uniform or equal quality throughout: *an uneven performance*; **d** not divisible by two without remainder; odd: *uneven numbers*.

unevenly, adv. Prec. & **-ly**. In an uneven manner.

uneventful, adj. [1. ùnevéntfl; 2. ànivéntfl]. **un-** (I.) & **eventful**. Not eventful; not characterized by numerous noteworthy or important events: *an uneventful life, year* &c.

uneventfully, adv. Prec. & **-ly**. In an uneventful manner.

unexampled, adj. [1. ùnegzáhmpld; 2.ànigzámpld]. **un-** (I.) & **example(d)**. Without example; unprecedented, unparalleled; exceptional.

unexceptionable, adj. [1. ùneksépshunabl; 2. àniksépʃənəbl]. **un-** (I.) & **exceptionable**. Not exceptionable; not subject or liable to exceptions; unobjectionable; irreproachable; perfect, excellent.

unexceptionably, adv. Prec. & **-ly**. In an unexceptionable manner.

unexecuted, adj. [1. unéksekûted; 2. anéksikjûtid]. **un-** (I.) & **execute(d)**. Not executed; esp. of legal document, not finally signed and witnessed.

unexhausted, adj. [1. ùnegzáwsted; 2. ànigzɔ́stid]. **un-** (I.) & **exhaust(ed)**. Not exhausted; esp. not consumed, not entirely used up, still producing something; *unexhausted improvements*, such as manure put on agricultural land of which the benefit has not ceased.

unexpected, adj. [1. ùnekspékted; 2. àníkspéktid]. **un-** (I.) & **expect(ed)**. Not expected; not provided for; coming without warning; unforeseen, sudden.

unexpectedly, adv. Prec. & **-ly**. In an unexpected manner.

unexpired, adj. [1. ùnekspírd; 2. ànikspáiəd]. **un-** (I.) & **expire(d)**. Not expired, esp. of lease or tenancy, of which a portion of the term has still to run.

unexpressive, adj. [1. ùneksprésiv; 2. àníksprésiv]. **un-** (I.) & **expressive**. **1.** Inexpressive. **2.** (obs.) Inexpressible, ineffable: '*he . . . hears the unexpressive nuptial song, In the blest kingdoms meek of joy and love*' (Milton, 'Lycidas', 176–7).

unexpurgated, adj. [1. unékspurgâted; 2. anékspəgèitid]. **un-** (I.) & **expurgate(d)**. Not expurgated, of book &c., with no passages suppressed; published in full with no omissions.

unfading, adj. [1. unfâding; 2. anféidiŋ]. **un-** (I.) & Pres. Part. of **fade**. Not fading; not liable to fade or pass away; imperishable: esp. *unfading glory*; (in material sense chiefly poet.) *unfading flowers*.

unfailing, adj. [1. unfâling; 2. anféiliŋ]. **un-** (I.) & **fail(ing)**. Not failing, not liable to fail; **a** not running or falling short; inexhaustible: *an unfailing supply of water, source of amusement*; *unfailing courage*; **b** not likely to mislead or disappoint; staunch: *an unfailing champion, friend, defender* &c.

unfailingly, adv. Prec. & **-ly**. In an unfailing manner; without failing.

unfair, adj. [1. unfâr; 2. anféə]. **un-** (I.) & **fair** (II.). Not fair; **a** unjust, inequitable; showing, resulting from, a lack of impartiality: *an unfair judge, judgement* &c.; **b** having recourse to tricks and shifts and mean devices; dishonest: *an unfair player, opponent*; **c** based on, derived from, tricky, mean, dishonest methods: *an unfair advantage*; *unfair means* &c.

unfairly, adv. Prec. & **-ly**. In an unfair manner.

unfairness, n. See prec. & **-ness**. Quality of being unfair.

unfaith, n. [1. únfâth; 2. ánfeiþ]. **un-** (I.) & **faith**. (rare and poet.) Want of faith; lack of honour, untrustworthiness; distrust: '*Faith and unfaith can ne'er be equal powers*' (Tennyson, 'Merlin and Vivien', 388).

unfaithful, adj. [1. unfâthfl; 2. anféiþfl]. **un-** (I.) & **faithful**. Not faithful. **1. a** not observing vows, obligations, duty &c.: *an unfaithful servant*; **b** disloyal: *an unfaithful friend, subject*. **2.** Specif., not true to marriage vows; guilty of adultery: *an unfaithful wife, husband*. **3.** Not true to fact, inaccurate: *an unfaithful version, transcript*.

unfaithfully, adv. Prec. & **-ly**. In an unfaithful manner.

unfaithfulness, n. See prec. & **-ness**. State of being unfaithful.

unfaltering, adj. [1. unfáwltering; 2. anfɔ́lt(ə)riŋ]. **un-** (I.) & **falter(ing)**. Not faltering. **1. a** Steady, not stumbling: *with unfaltering steps*; **b** not trembling: *unfaltering voice, tone*; **c** not shifting; intent: *unfaltering gaze*. **2.** (fig.) Unhesitating, resolute, undeviating; inflexible: *unfaltering courage, determination*.

unfamiliar, adj. [1. ùnfamíliar; 2. ànfəmíliə]. **un-** (I.) & **familiar**. Not familiar. **1. a** Not well known, not recognized as being known before; strange: *unfamiliar faces*; *an unfamiliar landscape*; **b** unaccustomed, unknown: *an unfamiliar language*. **2.** *Unfamiliar with*, unacquainted with, not accustomed to, inexperienced in: *quite unfamiliar with the habits of refined society*.

unfamiliarity, n. [1. ùnfamìliáriti; 2. ànfəmìliǽriti]. Prec. & **-ity**. Want of familiarity.

unfamiliarly, adv. [1. ùnfamíliarli; 2. ànfəmíliəli]. See prec. & **-ly**. In an unfamiliar manner.

unfashionable, adj. [1. unfáshunabl; 2. anfǽʃənəbl]. **un-** (I.) & **fashionable**. Not fashionable; behind, not in accordance with, the fashion.

unfashionably, adv. Prec. & **-ly**. In an unfashionable manner.

unfashionableness, n. See prec. & **-ness**. State, quality, of being unfashionable.

unfashioned, adj. [1. unfáshund; 2. anfǽʃənd]. **un-** (I.) & **fashion(ed)**. Not fashioned, unshaped; shapeless.

unfasten, vb. trans. [1. unfáhsn; 2. anfásn]. **un-** (II.) & **fasten**. To loose, free from, a fastening; to unbind, untie, unfix, undo.

unfastened (I.), adj. [1. anfáhsnd; 2. anfásnd]. P.P. of prec. Loosed, freed, from a fastening.

unfastened (II.), adj. **un-** (I.) & **fasten(ed)**. Not fastened.

unfathered, adj. [1. unfáhdherd; 2. anfáðəd]. **un-** (I.) & **father(ed)**. **a** Having no father; fatherless; **b** not acknowledged by his, its, father, begetter, or author.

unfatherly, adj. [1. unfáhdherli; 2. anfáðəli]. **un-** (I.) & **fatherly**. Not fatherly; unbecoming a father; harsh, cruel.

unfathomable, adj. [1. unfádhumabl; 2. anfǽðəməbl]. **un-** (I.) & **fathom** & **-able**. Not fathomable; **a** not to be fathomed or plumbed; bottomless: *unfathomable sea, lake*; **b** not to be fully grasped by the mind; inexplicable, insoluble: *an unfathomable mystery*.

unfathomed, adj. [1. unfádhumd; 2. anfǽðəmd]. **un-** (I.) & **fathom(ed)**. Not fathomed; unplumbed (lit. and fig.).

unfavourable, adj. [1. unfâvurabl; 2. anféivərəbl]. **un-** (I.) & **favourable**. Not favourable; unpropitious, adverse.

unfavourableness, n. Prec. & **-ness**. State of being unfavourable.

unfavourably, adv. See prec. & **-ly**. In an unfavourable manner.

unfeasible, adj. [1. unfḗzibl; 2. anfízibl]. **un-** (I.) & **feasible**. Not feasible; not to be done; impracticable.

unfeathered, adj. [1. unfédherd; 2. anféðəd]. **un-** (I.) & **feather(ed)**. Not feathered; having no feathers, unfledged.

unfed, adj. [1. unféd; 2. anféd]. **un-** (I.) & **fed**. Not fed.

unfeeling, adj. [1. unfḗling; 2. anfíliŋ]. **un-** (I.) & **feel(ing)**. Not feeling; lacking feeling(s); callous, hard-hearted.

unfeelingly, adv. Prec. & **-ly**. In an unfeeling manner.

unfeigned, adj. [1. unfând; 2. anféind]. **un-** (I.) & **feign(ed)**. Not feigned; real, sincere, genuine.

unfeignedly, adv. [1. unfânedli; 2. anféinidli]. Prec. & **-ly**. In an unfeigned manner; sincerely.

unfelt, adj. [1. unfélt; 2. anfélt]. **un-** (I.) & **felt** (II.). Not felt.

unfeminine, adj. [1. unféminin; 2. anféminin]. **un-** (I.) & **feminine**. Not feminine; unwomanly.

unfermented, adj. [1. ùnferménted; 2. ànfəméntid]. **un-** (I.) & **ferment(ed)**. Not fermented.

unfertile, adj. [1. unfĕrtīl; 2. anfə́tail]. **un-** (I.) & **fertile**. Not fertile; infertile (perhaps the more usual form).

unfertilized, adj. [1. unfĕrtilīzd; 2. anfə́tilaizd]. **un-** (I.) & **fertilize(d)**. Not fertilized.

unfetter, vb. trans. [1. unféter; 2. anfétə]. **un-** (II.) & **fetter** (II.). To free, loose, from fetters or chains, to set at liberty (lit. and fig.).

unfettered (I.), adj. [1. unféterd; 2. anfétəd], fr. P.P. of prec. Freed from fetters.

unfettered (II.), adj. **un-** (I.) & **fetter(ed)**. Not hampered or restricted in thought or action; independent, free.

unfigured, adj. [1. unfígurd; 2. anfígəd]. **un-** (I.) & **figure(d)**. Not figured; not decorated or marked with figures.

unfilial, adj. [1. unfílial; 2. anfíliəl]. **un-** (I.) & **filial**. Not filial; not becoming a son or child; undutiful.

unfilially, adv. Prec. & **-ly**. In an unfilial manner.

unfilterable, adj. [1. unfílterabl; 2. anfíltərəbl]. **un-** (I.) & **filterable**. Not filterable; specif. (biol.) of certain micro-organisms that pass through all filtering media.

unfinished, adj. [1. unfínisht; 2. anfíniʃt]. **un-** (I.) & **finish(ed)**. Not finished; **a** not completed, not brought to completion: *an unfinished house, story*; **b** not highly wrought; rough, unpolished: *an unfinished style*.

unfirm, adj. [1. unfĕrm; 2. anfə́m]. **un-** (I.) & **firm**. Not firm; shaky, likely to fall down or apart, of structures &c.; cp. different use of *infirm*.

unfit (I.), adj. [1. unfít; 2. anfít]. **un-** (I.) & **fit** (IV.). Not fit. **1.** Not sound; diseased, defective, in body or mind: *unfit to plead* &c.; *the unfit* (coll. pl.), those who are unfit in any sense. **2.** Unsuited, unsuitable for, not adapted to, some specified purpose: *unfit for such a profession*; *mind unfit for a philosopher*; *unfit to conduct such delicate inquiries*; *unfit for work*; *houses unfit for human habitation*.

unfit (II.), vb. trans. **un-** (II.) & **fit** (III.). To deprive of fitness, physical or mental; to make unsuitable; disqualify: *drink unfits a man for work*; *his age unfits him for such a position*.

unfitly, adv. [1. unfítli; 2. anfítli]. **unfit** (I.) & **-ly**. In an unfit manner or condition.

unfitness, n. [1. unfítnes; 2. anfítnis]. See prec. & **-ness**. Condition of being unfit.

unfitted (I.), adj. [1. unfíted; 2. anfítid]. P.P. of **unfit** (II.). Rendered unfit or unsuitable; deprived of fitness, disqualified: *unfitted for such a position* &c.

unfitted (II.), adj. **un-** (I.) & **fit(ted)**. Not fitted, furnished, or supplied with: *houses unfitted with baths*.

unfitting, adj. [1. unfíting; 2. anfítiŋ]. **un-** (I.) & **fitting** (I.). Not fitting; unbecoming, unsuitable.

unfittingly, adv. Prec. & **-ly**. In an unfitting manner.

unfix, vb. trans. [1. unfíks; 2. anfíks]. **un-** (II.) & **fix**. To make not fixed; to remove from a fixed position: *unfix bayonets!*

unfixed (I.), adj. [1. unfíkst; 2. anfíkst]. P.P. of prec. Removed from a fixed position.

unfixed (II.), adj. **un-** (I.) & **fix(ed)**. Not fixed.

unflagging, adj. [1. unflágging; 2. anflǽgiŋ]. **un-** (I.) & **flag(ging)**. Not flagging, not drooping; unremitting: *unflagging spirits, zeal, energy* &c.

unflaggingly, adv. Prec. & **-ly**. In an unflagging manner.

unflattering, adj. [1. unflátering; 2. anflǽtəriŋ]. **un-** (I.) & **flattering**. Not flattering.

unflatteringly, adv. Prec. & **-ly**. In an unflattering manner.

unfledged, adj. [1. unfléjd; 2. anflédžd]. **un-** (I.) & **fledge(d)**. Not yet fully fledged or feathered; (fig.) not fully developed, immature.

unfleshed, adj. [1. unflésht; 2. anfléʃt]. **un-** (I.) & **flesh(ed)**. Not fleshed; not yet dipped in blood; not yet used in fighting: *an unfleshed sword.*

unfleshly, adj. [1. unfléshli; 2. anfléʃli]. **un-** (I.) & **fleshly**. Not fleshly, not worldly; spiritual.

unflinching, adj. [1. unflínshing; 2. anflínʃiŋ]. **un-** (I.) & **flinch(ing)**. Not flinching, not shrinking; steadfast, unyielding, resolute.

unflinchingly, adv. Prec. & **-ly**. In an unflinching manner.

unfold, vb. trans. & intrans. [1. unfṓld; 2. anfóuld]. **un-** (II.) & **fold**. **A.** trans. **1. a** To open the folds of; to unwrap and spread out what is folded: *to unfold a newspaper, a tablecloth* &c.; **b** to expand, spread open: *plant unfolds its leaves, flower its buds.* **2.** (by transf. and fig.) To open, reveal, disclose, display: *to unfold one's plans*; '*I could a tale unfold*'. **B.** intrans. (of leaves, buds &c.) To become open or expanded: *buds unfold in the sunshine.*

unforeseen, adj. [1. ùnforsḗn; 2. ànfɔ̄sín]. **un-** (I.) & **foresee(n)**. Not foreseen; unexpected.

unforgettable, adj. [1. ùnforgétabl; 2. ànfəgétəbl]. **un-** (I.) & **forgettable**. Not forgettable; not to be forgotten, ever memorable.

unforgivable, adj. [1. ùnforgívabl; 2. ànfəgívəbl]. **un-** (I.) & **forgivable**. Not forgivable; not to be forgiven; unpardonable.

unforgiven, adj. [1. ùnforgívn; 2. ànfəgívən]. **un-** (I.) & **forgive(n)**. Not forgiven, not pardoned.

unforgiving, adj. [1. ùnforgíving; 2. ànfəgíviŋ]. **un-** (I.) & **forgiving**. Not forgiving.

unforgotten, adj. [1. ùnforgótn; 2. ànfəgɔ́tn]. **un-** (I.) & **forgot(ten)**. Not forgotten; remembered.

unformed, adj. [1. unfórmd; 2. anfɔ̄́md]. **un-** (I.) & **form(ed)**. Not yet formed; not fully developed; untrained.

unfortunate, adj. & n. [1. unfórchunit; 2. anfɔ̄́tʃənit]. **un-** (I.) & **fortunate**. **1.** adj. **a** Not fortunate; unlucky, unhappy; unsuccessful; **b** not accompanied by good fortune: *an unfortunate day.* **2.** n. An unfortunate person; specif., a prostitute.

unfortunately, adv. Prec. & **-ly**. In an unfortunate manner.

unfounded, adj. [1. unfóunded; 2. anfáundid]. **un-** (I.) & **found(ed)**. Not founded on fact; without foundation, baseless: *unfounded accusations, reports, hopes* &c.

unframed, adj. [1. unfrāmd; 2. anfréimd]. **un-** (I.) & **frame(d)**. Not framed; not furnished with a frame, as a picture, drawing &c.

unfree, adj. [1. unfrḗ; 2. anfrí]. **un-** (I.) & **free**. (rare) Not free; not enjoying liberty; in a state of slavery or subjection; specif. (legal hist.) of tenure of land in which the service to be performed was uncertain and fixed more or less at the will of the feudal lord.

unfrequented, adj. [1. ùnfrekwénted; 2. ànfrikwéntid]. **un-** (I.) & **frequent(ed)**. Not frequented; seldom or rarely visited or used by people: *an unfrequented valley, road* &c.

unfriended, adj. [1. unfrénded; 2. anfréndid]. **un-** (I.) & **friend** & **-ed**. Having no friends; not befriended.

unfriendliness, n. [1. unfréndlines; 2. anfréndlinis]. See next word & **-ness**. Unfriendly feeling, conduct, manner; hostility.

unfriendly, adj. & adv. [1. unfréndli; 2. anfréndli]. **un-** (I.) & **friendly**. **1.** adj. Not friendly; unkind; hostile: *an unfriendly act.* **2.** adv. (rare and archaic) In an unfriendly manner: *I do not mean it unfriendly.*

unfrock, vb. trans. [1. unfrók; 2. anfrɔ́k]. **un-** (II.) & **frock**. To remove the frock from; specif., to deprive of the status of a priest, degrade from the priesthood; (in P.P. as adj.) *an unfrocked priest.*

unfruitful, adj. [1. unfrōōtfl; 2. anfrū́tfl]. **un-** (I.) & **fruitful**. Not fruitful; **a** (rare or archaic) not yielding fruit; barren, unprolific, unproductive: *an unfruitful vine, tree, land*; **b** not yielding results; vain, fruitless: *our efforts at reform were at first unfruitful.*

unfruitfully, adv. Prec. & **-ly**. In an unfruitful manner; without result.

unfruitfulness, n. See prec. & **-ness**. Condition of being unfruitful.

unfulfilled, adj. [1. ùnfoolfíld; 2. ànfulfíld]. **un-** (I.) & **fulfil(led)**. Not fulfilled; not achieved; unrealized, unaccomplished: '*Inheritors of unfulfilled renown*' (Shelley, 'Adonais'); *our hopes remain unfulfilled.*

unfunded, adj. [1. unfúnded; 2. anfándid]. **un-** (I.) & **fund** & **-ed**. (of debt) Not funded; floating.

unfurl, vb. trans. & intrans. [1. unfḗrl; 2. anfǝ́l]. **un-** (II.) & **furl**. **1.** trans. To unroll, spread out: *to unfurl sails, a flag* &c. **2.** intrans. To become unfurled.

unfurnished, adj. [1. unfḗrnisht; 2. anfǝ́niʃt]. **un-** (I.) & **furnish(ed)**. Not furnished; esp. of rooms &c. without furniture.

ungainliness, n. [1. ungā́nlines; 2. angéinlinis]. See next word & **-ness**. Condition of being ungainly.

ungainly, adj. [1. ungā́nli; 2. angéinli]. M.E. *ungeinliche*, as adv., w. suff. *-liche*, see **-ly**, added to *ungein*, 'awkward, inconvenient', fr. **un-** (I.) & O.N. *gegn*, 'ready, convenient, serviceable', cogn. w. *gegna*, 'to meet', *gegn*, 'against'; see further **again** & **against**. Awkward, clumsy.

ungallant, adj. **un-** (I.) & **gallant**. **1.** [1. ungálant; 2. angǽlənt] Not gallant, not evincing gallantry. **2.** [1. ùngalánt; 2. àngəlǽnt] Not polite, esp. not showing due deference and courtesy to women.

ungallantly, adv. Prec. & **-ly**. In an ungallant manner.

ungarbled, adj. [1. ungárbld; 2. angā́bld]. **un-** (I.) & **garble(d)**. Not garbled; not mutilated or falsified for the purpose of misleading; accurate; plain, straightforward: *ungarbled report, statement, version* &c.

ungenerous, adj. [1. unjénerus; 2. andžénərəs]. **un-** (I.) & **generous**. Not generous; **a** not lavish or liberal; **b** mean; unfair.

ungenerously, adv. Prec. & **-ly**. In an ungenerous manner.

ungenial, adj. [1. unjḗnial; 2. andžíniəl]. **un-** (I.) & **genial** (I.). Not genial; not kindly; unsociable.

ungentle, adj. [1. unjéntl; 2. andžéntl]. **un-** (I.) & **gentle**. Not gentle; **a** not of gentle birth; **b** rude, rough.

ungentlemanlike, adj. [1. unjéntlmanlīk; 2. andžéntlmənlàik]. **un-** (I.) & **gentlemanlike**. Unbefitting, unlike, a gentleman; unlike the manners or conduct of a gentleman; ill-bred, vulgar, caddish.

ungentlemanliness, n. [1. unjéntlmanlines; 2. andžéntlmənlinis]. See next word & **-ness**. State of being ungentlemanly.

ungentlemanly, adj. [1. unjéntlmanli; 2. andžéntlmənli]. **un-** (I.) & **gentlemanly**. Often used now for *ungentlemanlike.*

un-get-at-able, adj. [1. ùn get át abl; 2. àn get ǽt əbl]. **un-** (I.) & **get-at-able**. Not get-at-able; not easily reached, inaccessible: *he lives in a remote, un-get-at-able village.*

ungird, vb. trans. [1. ungḗrd; 2. angǝ́d]. **un-** (II.) & **gird**. To remove the girdle from; to unloose one's girdle.

ungirt (I.), adj. [1. ungḗrt; 2. angǝ́t]. **P.P.** of prec. With girdle loosed or removed.

ungirt (II.), adj. **un-** (I.) & P.P. of **gird**. Having no girdle on.

unglazed, adj. [1. unglā́zd; 2. angléizd]. **un-** (I.) & **glaze(d)**. **a** Not glazed; **b** not covered by or fitted with glass.

ungodliness, n. [1. ungódlines; 2. angɔ́dlinis]. See next word & **-ness**. State of being ungodly.

ungodly, adj. [1. ungódli; 2. angɔ́dli]. **un-** (I.) & **godly**. Not godly; neglectful of God; not fearing or worshipping God; impious, wicked; *the ungodly*, wicked people.

ungovernable, adj. [1. ungúvernabl; 2. angávənəbl]. **un-** (I.) & **governable**. Not governable; incapable of restraint; wild, unruly: *ungovernable rage, passions* &c.

ungraceful, adj. [1. ungrā́sfl; 2. angréisfl]. **un-** (I.) & **graceful**. Not graceful; awkward, clumsy.

ungracefully, adv. Prec. & **-ly**. In an ungraceful manner.

ungracious, adj. [1. ungrā́shus; 2. angréiʃəs]. **un-** (I.) & **gracious**. Not gracious; not courteous, generous-minded, or kindly; churlish.

ungraciously, adv. Prec. & **-ly**. In an ungracious manner.

ungrammatical, adj. [1. ùngramátikl; 2. àngrəmǽtikl]. **un-** (I.) & **grammatical**. Not grammatical; not according to the rules of grammar.

ungrammatically, adv. Prec. & **-ly**. In an ungrammatical manner.

ungrateful, adj. [1. ungrā́tfl; 2. angréitfl]. **un-** (I.) & **grateful**. Not grateful. **1.** Not feeling or expressing gratitude. **2.** Not repaying one's labour; irksome, disagreeable; unpleasing: *an ungrateful task.*

ungratefully, adv. Prec. & **-ly**. In an ungrateful manner.

ungratefulness, n. See prec. & **-ness**. State of being ungrateful; ingratitude.

ungratified, adj. [1. ungrátifīd; 2. angrǽtifaid]. **un-** (I.) & P.P. of **gratify**. Not gratified; unsatisfied.

ungrounded, adj. [1. ungróunded; 2. angráundid]. **un-** (I.) & **ground(ed)**. Not well grounded; lacking grounds or reasons; unfounded.

ungrudging, adj. [1. ungrújing; 2. angrádžiŋ]. **un-** (I.) & **grudging**. Not grudging; unstinted, unsparing: *ungrudging attention, praise* &c.

ungrudgingly, adv. Prec. & **-ly**. In an ungrudging manner; freely, generously.

ungual, adj. [1. úngwal; 2. áŋgwəl], fr. Lat. *unguis*, 'nail, hoof, claw', cogn. w. Gk. *ónux*, 'nail', see **onyx**; O.E. *nægel*, 'nail', see **nail** (I.), & **-al**. Pertaining to, having, a nail, claw, talon, hoof &c.

unguarded, adj. [1. ungárded; 2. angā́did]. **un-** (I.) & **guard(ed)**. Not guarded; showing a lack of circumspection or caution; careless, thoughtless, incautious: *an unguarded remark, expression* &c.; *in an unguarded moment*, when off one's guard.

unguardedly, adv. Prec. & **-ly**. In an unguarded manner.

unguent, n. [1. úngwent; 2. áŋgwənt], fr. Lat. *unguent-(um)*, 'ointment', fr. *unguere, ungere*, 'to anoint', see **unctuous** & **unction**, & cp. **ointment** & **anoint**. An ointment.

unguided, adj. [1. ungī́ded; 2. angáidid]. **un-** (I.) & **guide(d)**. Not guided; lacking a guide or guidance.

unguiform, adj. [1. únggwiform; 2. áŋgwifɔ̄m], fr. Lat. *unguis*, see **ungual**, & **-form**. Shaped like, in the form of, a nail, claw, or hoof.

ungulate, adj. & n. [1. úngg̃ūlāt; 2. áŋgjuleit], fr. Lat. *ungula*, 'hoof', also 'claw, talon'; dimin. form, without force, of *unguis*, 'nail, claw', see **ungual**, & **-ate**. **1.** adj. (zool.) **a** Having hoofs; **b** belonging to the order or group, *Ungulata*, hoofed mammals, including the ruminants, swine, horses &c. **2.** n. A hoofed mammal.

unhackneyed, adj. [1. unháknid; 2. anhǽknid]. **un-** (I.) & **hackneyed**. Not hackneyed; not trite or stale; fresh, original.

unhallowed, adj. [1. unhálōd; 2. anhǽloud]. **un-** (I.) & **hallow(ed)**. Not hallowed or consecrated; unholy, profane, wicked.

unhampered, adj. [1. unhámperd; 2. anhǽmpəd]. **un-** (I.) & **hamper(ed)**. Not hampered; free, untrammelled.

unhand, vb. trans. [1. unhánd; 2. anhǽnd]. **un-** (II.) & **hand**. To take the hands off or from; to release, let go, from one's grasp.

unhandsome, adj. [1. unhánsum; 2. anhǽnsəm]. **un-** (I.) & **handsome**. **1.** Not handsome in appearance; ugly, plain. **2.** Ungenerous, mean; ungracious.

unhandy, adj. [1. unhándi; 2. anhǽndi]. **un-** (I.) & **handy**. **1.** Not near at, or ready to, hand; not convenient. **2.** Not handy; awkward, clumsy.

unhang, vb. trans. [1. unháng; 2. anhǽŋ]. **un-** (II.) & **hang**. **a** To remove from a hanging position; **b** to clear (wall &c.) of hangings.

unhappily, adv. [1. unhápili; 2. anhǽpili]. **unhappy** & **-ly**. In an unhappy manner. **1.** Unfortunately: *unhappily we unintentionally offended him.* **2.** Without happiness, miserably: *they lived unhappily together.*

unhappiness, n. [1. unhápines; 2. anhǽpinis]. See prec. & **-ness**. State of being unhappy; misery.

unhappy, adj. [1. unhápi; 2. anhǽpi]. **un-** (I.) & **happy**. Not happy; unfortunate. **1.** Miserable, wretched: *an unhappy life.* **2.** Unlucky: *an unhappy meeting, ship.* **3.** Unsuitable, out of place, not felicitous: *an unhappy remark.*

unharmed, adj. [1. unhármd; 2. anhámd]. **un-** (I.) & **harm(ed)**. Not harmed, uninjured, undamaged; safe and sound.

unharness, vb. trans. [1. unhárnes; 2. anhánis]. **un-** (II.) & **harness**. **a** To take (horse &c.) out of the shafts and remove harness from; **b** to strip armour or harness from.

unhasp, vb. trans. [1. unháhsp; 2. anhásp]. **un-** (II.) & **hasp**. To loose, free, unfasten, from a hasp; as a chain, bracelet &c.

unhealthily, adv. [1. unhélthili; 2. anhélþili]. **unhealthy** & **-ly**. In an unhealthy manner.

unhealthiness, n. [1. unhélthines; 2. anhélþinis]. See prec. & **-ness**. State of being unhealthy.

unhealthy, adj. [1. unhélthi; 2. anhélþi]. **un-** (I.) & **healthy**. Not healthy; **a** wanting in health, not in sound health; diseased in body or mind; **b** not conducive to bodily or mental health; unwholesome: *an unhealthy occupation, district* &c.; **c** indicating want of health: *an unhealthy complexion.*

unheard, adj. [1. unhẽrd; 2. anhə́d]. **un-** (I.) & **hear(d)**. Not heard; **a** not perceived by the ear; **b** not given a hearing; not listened to: *to be condemned unheard.*

unheard-of, adj. [1. unhẽrd ov; 2. anhə́d ɔv]. Not heard of before; unprecedented: *an unheard-of calamity.*

unheeded, adj. [1. unhḗded; 2. anhídid]. **un-** (I.) & **heed(ed)**. Not heeded; disregarded; unnoticed.

unheedful, adj. [1. unhḗdfl; 2. anhídfl]. **un-** (I.) & **heedful**. Not heedful; unheeding, not paying regard, careless.

unheeding, adj. [1. unhḗding; 2. anhídiŋ]. **un-** (I.) & **heed(ing)**. Not heeding; inattentive, unheedful, careless.

unhelm, vb. trans. & intrans. [1. unhélm; 2. anhélm]. **un-** (II.) & **helm**. **a** trans. To take off the helm or helmet of; **b** intrans., to take off one's helmet.

unhelpful, adj. [1. unhélpfl; 2. anhélpfl]. **un-** (I.) & **helpful**. Not helpful; affording no help.

unhelpfully, adv. Prec. & **-ly**. In an unhelpful manner.

unheralded, adj. [1. unhéralded; 2. anhérəldid]. **un-** (I.) & **herald(ed)**. Not heralded; unannounced, unproclaimed; unforetold.

unheroic, adj. [1. ùnheróik; 2. ànhiróuik]. **un-** (I.) & **heroic**. Not heroic; lacking heroism.

unhesitating, adj. [1. unhézitàting; 2. anhézitèitiŋ]. **un-** (I.) & Pres. Part. of **hesitate**. Not hesitating; **a** acting without hesitation; prompt, ready: *unhesitating in his obedience*; **b** performed, given, without hesitation: *unhesitating reply, obedience* &c.

unhesitatingly, adv. Prec. & **-ly**. Without hesitation.

unhinge, vb. trans. [1. unhínj; 2. anhín(d)ž]. **un-** (II.) & **hinge** (II.). **1.** To take off, remove from, the hinges: *to unhinge a door* &c. **2.** (fig.) To throw (the mind) out of its normal course, to cause madness: *to unhinge the mind*; *a mind unhinged by troubles.*

unhistorical, adj. [1. ùnhistórikl; 2. ànhistórikl]. **un-** (I.) & **historical**. Not historical; not in accordance with the facts of history.

unhistorically, adv. Prec. & **-ly**. In an unhistorical manner.

unhitch, vb. trans. [1. unhích; 2. anhítʃ]. **un-** (II.) & **hitch**. To free from a hitch or from being hitched; to unfasten.

unholily, adv. [1. unhṓlili; 2. anhóulili]. **unholy** & **-ly**. In an unholy manner.

unholiness, n. [1. unhṓlines; 2. anhóulinis]. See next word & **-ness**. State of being unholy.

unholy, adj. [1. unhṓli; 2. anhóuli]. **un-** (I.) & **holy**. Not holy; **a** not sacred or consecrated, profane; **b** wicked, impious; **c** (colloq.) as mere intensive epithet: *an unholy row* &c.

unhonoured, adj. [1. unónord; 2. anɔ́nəd]. **un-** (I.) & **honour(ed)**. Not honoured.

unhook, vb. trans. [1. unhóok; 2. anhúk]. **un-** (II.) & **hook**. **a** To remove from a hook; **b** to detach hooks, so as to unfasten: *to unhook a dress.*

unhoped, adj. [1. unhṓpt; 2. anhóupt]. **un-** (I.) & **hope(d)**. Not hoped; unexpected; also, more usual, *unhoped for*, as *unhoped-for success* &c.

unhopeful, adj. [1. unhṓpfl; 2. anhóupfl]. **un-** (I.) & **hopeful**. Not hopeful.

unhorse, vb. trans. [1. unhórs; 2. anhɔ́s]. **un-** (II.) & **horse**. To throw, cause to fall, from a horse.

unhouse, vb. trans. [1. unhóuz; 2. anháuz]. **un-** (II.) & **house**. To deprive of, drive from, a house or shelter; to deprive of means of living in a house.

unhoused (I.), adj. [1. unhóuzd; 2. anháuzd]. P.P. of prec. Deprived of, expelled from, a house or houses.

unhoused (II.), adj. **un-** (I.) & **house(d)**. Not provided with a house or houses.

unhouseled, adj. [1. unhóuzld; 2. anháuzld]. **un-** (I.) & **housel(ed)**. (archaic) Not having received the Eucharist.

unhuman, adj. [1. unhū́man; 2. anhjúmən]. **un-** (I.) & **human**. Not human, cp. *inhuman.*

unhurt, adj. [1. unhẽrt; 2. anhə́t]. **un-** (I.) & **hurt**. Not hurt; undamaged, uninjured.

uni-, pref. Form of Lat. *ūnus*, 'one', used to form compounds. Lat. *ūnus*, O. Lat. *oinos*, is cogn. w. Gk. *oînos*, *oinē*, 'the one on a die'; Goth. *ains*, O.E. *ān*, see **one** (I.). Formed, consisting of, having, only one element; single-; freely used in scientific terminology, as *uni-articulate*, single-jointed, *unisexual* &c.

Uniat(e), n. [1. úniat; 2. júniət], fr. Russ. *uniyata*, 'united', fr. *uniya*, 'union', fr. Lat. *ūnus*, see **one** (I.). A member of various Eastern Christian Churches which, while retaining the Greek liturgy, rites, customs &c., acknowledge the supremacy of the Pope and are thus members of the Roman Church; (also attrib.) *the Uniate churches.*

uniaxial, adj. [1. ùniáksial; 2. jùniǽksiəl]. **uni-** & **axial**. Having one axis or single line of growth.

unibranchiate, adj. [1. ùnibrángkiāt; 2. jùnibrǽŋkieit]. **uni-** & **branchiate**. Having a single branchia or gill.

unicameral, adj. [1. ùnikámeral; 2. jùnikǽmərəl]. **uni-** & Lat. *camera*, 'chamber', see **camera**, & **-al**. (of legislative bodies) Having a single chamber.

unicapsular, adj. [1. ùnikápsūlar; 2. jùnikǽpsjulə]. **uni-** & **capsule** & **-ar**. (bot.) Having a single capsule.

unicellular, adj. [1. ùnisélūlar; 2. jùniséljulə]. **uni-** & **cellular**. (biol.) Composed of a single cell.

unicoloured, adj. [1. ūnikùlurd; 2. júnikàləd]. **uni-** & **colour(ed)**. Having only one colour, uniform in colour.

unicorn, n. [1. ūnikòrn; 2. júnikɔ̀n], fr. Lat. *ūnicornis*, 'one-horned'; also in Vulgate 'the unicorn'; fr. **uni-** & *cornu*, 'horn'. See **corn** (III.) & **horn** (I.). **1.** **a** A fabulous animal, usually described and depicted with the body and head of a horse, a lion's or horse's tail, the hind quarters of an antelope, and a single twisted horn; **b** as word used in A.V. (*unicornis* in Vulgate) to translate Heb. *r'ēm*, in R.V. 'wild ox'. **2.** (her.) A figure of a unicorn as a supporter, formerly used for the Scottish royal arms, and since the Union the left-hand supporter facing the lion in the British royal arms. **3.** A team of three horses driven two abreast and a third as leader in front between them. **4.** Applied attributively **a** to the narwhal, *unicorn fish*; **b** to a moth, *unicorn moth*, the caterpillar of which has a single horny growth; **c** to a mollusc, *unicorn shell*, with a horny spike projecting from the forepart of the shell.

unicostate, adj. [1. ùnikóstāt; 2. jùnikɔ́steit]. **uni-** & **costate**. (bot., of leaves) Having a single, primary rib.

unicuspid, adj. [1. ùnikúspid; 2. jùnikáspid]. **uni-** & **cusp**. (of teeth) Having a single cusp.

unidea'd, unideaed, adj. [1. ùnīdḗad; 2. ànaidíəd]. **un-** (I.) & **idea'd**. Having no ideas; without imagination, stupid, dull.

unideal, adj. [1. ùnīdḗal; 2. ànaidíəl]. **un-** (I.) & **ideal**. Not ideal; **a** materialistic, realistic; **b** dull, prosaic, ordinary.

unidentified, adj. [1. ùnīdéntifīd; 2. ànaidéntifaid]. **un-** (I.) & P.P. of **identify**. Not identified.

unidimensional, adj. [1. ùnidīménshunal; 2. jùnidaiménʃənəl]. **uni-** & **dimensional**. Having only one dimension, as a geometrical line.

unidiomatic, adj. [1. ùnidiōmátik; 2. ànidioumǽtik]. **un-** (I.) & **idiomatic**. Not idiomatic.

unidirectional, adj. [1. ùnidirékshunal; 2. jùnidirékʃənəl]. **uni-** & **direction** & **-al**. Having only one direction; esp. of electric currents, flowing in one direction only, continuous.

unifiable, adj. [1. ūnifīabl; 2. júnifàiəbl]. **unify** & **-able**. Capable of being unified.

unification, n. [1. ùnifikā́shun; 2. jùnifikéiʃən]. **uni-** & **-fication**; see **unify**. **a** Act of unifying; **b** state of being unified.

unifier, n. [1. ūnifīer; 2. júnifaiə]. **unify** & **-er**. One who, that which, unifies.

uniflagellate, adj. [1. ùniflájelāt; 2. jùniflǽdžileit]. **uni-** & **flagellate** (II.). (of bacteria &c.) Having only one flagellum or whip-like process.

unifoliate, adj. [1. ùnifṓliāt; 2. jùnifóulieit]. **uni-** & **foliate**. (bot.) Having one leaf.

uniform (I.), adj. [1. ūniform; 2. júnifɔ̃m], fr. Fr. *uniforme*, fr. Lat. *ūniformis*, 'having one form', see **uni-** & **form** (I.). **1.** (of various things) Having the same form, shape, or pattern; agreeing with each other in some particular; conforming to some common standard: *all must wear a dress of uniform pattern*; *articles of uniform weight* &c. **2.** (of single object &c.) Not varying or changing from time to time or place to place: *keep the room at a uniform temperature.* **3.** Homogeneous.

uniform (II.), n., fr. prec. A prescribed form of dress worn as an official costume to distinguish members of an organized body; esp. the official dress worn by soldiers, sailors, police, members of the Diplomatic body &c., when on duty, and on ceremonial occasions.

uniformed, adj. [1. únifòrmd; 2. júnifɔ̄md]. Prec. & **-ed**. **a** Furnished with, habitually wearing, a uniform: *uniformed constabulary*; **b** actually wearing a uniform: *a uniformed constable guarded the door.*

uniformity, n. [1. ùnifórmiti; 2. jùnifɔ̄miti], fr. L. Lat. *ūniformitāt-(em)*, see **uniform** (I.) & **-ity**. Quality, state, of being uniform; sameness, consistency, homogeneity; conformity to one pattern, standard, or rule.

uniformly, adv. [1. únifòrmli; 2. júnifɔ̄mli]. **uniform** (I.) & **-ly**. In a uniform manner; without change or variation.

unify, vb. trans. [1. únifī; 2. júnifai], fr. L. or Med. Lat. *ūnificāre*, cp. Fr. *unifier*, see **uni-** & **-fy**. To cause to be one; to reduce to unity or uniformity.

Unigenitus, n. [1. ùnijénitus; 2. jùnidžénitəs]. Med. Lat., 'only begotten'. The name of a Papal Bull, issued in 1713, by Clement XI. against Jansenism, from the word with which it begins.

unilateral, adj. [1. ùniláteral; 2. jùnilǽtərəl]. **uni-** & **lateral**. **a** Having, arranged on, affecting, one side only; one-sided; specif. **b** (law) binding, obligatory, for one party only, as by a deed poll: *unilateral contract.*

unilaterally, adv. Prec. & **-ly**. In a unilateral manner.

uniliteral, adj. [1. ùnilíteral; 2. jùnilítərəl]. **uni-** & **literal**. Having, consisting of, one letter only.

unilluminated, adj. [1. ùnilúminàted; 2. ànilјúminèitid]. **un-** (I.) & **illuminate(d)**. Not illuminated (lit. and fig.).

unillustrated, adj. [1. unílustràted; 2. anìləstrèitid]. **un-** (I.) & **illustrate(d)**. Not illustrated; without illustrations.

unilocular, adj. [1. ùnilókūlar; 2. jùnilɔ́kjulə]. **uni-** & **locular**. (bot. and zool.) Having one cell or cavity.

unimaginable, adj. [1. ùnimájinabl; 2. ànimǽdžinəbl]. **un-** (I.) & **imaginable**. That cannot be imagined; inconceivable.

unimaginative, adj. [1. ùnimájinativ; 2. ànimǽdžinətiv]. **un-** (I.) & **imaginative**. Not imaginative; without imagination.

unimpaired, adj. [1. ùnimpárd; 2. ànimpέəd]. **un-** (I.) & **impair(ed)**. Not impaired; not weakened, diminished, or damaged.

unimpeachability, n. [1. ùnimpèchabíliti; 2. ànimpìtʃəbíliti]. See next word & **-ity**. State of being unimpeachable; exemption from being called in question or doubted; freedom from fault or blame.

unimpeachable, adj. [1. ùnimpéchabl; 2. ànimpítʃəbl]. **un-** (I.) & **impeachable**. Not impeachable; not liable to be called in question or doubted; irreproachable; blameless.

unimpeachably, adv. Prec. & **-ly**. In an unimpeachable manner.

unimpeded, adj. [1. ùnimpéded; 2. ànimpídid]. **un-** (I.) & **impede(d)**. Not impeded; unhindered.

unimportance, n. [1. ùnimpórtans; 2. ànimpɔ̄təns]. **un-** (I.) & **importance**. State of being unimportant; want, lack, of importance; insignificance, triviality.

unimportant, adj. [1. ùnimpórtant; 2. ànimpɔ̄tənt]. **un-** (I.) & **important**. Not important; of no weight or value; insignificant; trivial.

unimposing, adj. [1. ùnimpózing; 2. ànimpóuziŋ]. **un-** (I.) & **imposing**. Not imposing, unimpressive, in appearance.

unimpressionable, adj. [1. ùnimpréshunabl; 2. ànimpréʃənəbl]. **un-** (I.) & **impressionable**. Not impressionable.

unimpressive, adj. [1. ùnimprésiv; 2. ànimprésiv]. **un-** (I.) & **impressive**. Not impressive.

unimproved, adj. [1. ùnimproõvd; 2. ànimprúvd]. **un-** (I.) & **improve(d)**. Not improved, esp. of land, not cultivated; not developed for building &c.: *unimproved site value*, land value as divested of all improvements.

unincumbered. See **unencumbered**.

uninflammable, adj. [1. ùninflámabl; 2. àninflǽməbl]. **un-** (I.) & **inflammable**. Not inflammable.

uninflated, adj. [1. ùninflàted; 2. àninfléitid]. **un-** (I.) & **inflate(d)**. Not inflated.

uninflected, adj. [1. ùninflékted; 2. àninfléktid]. **un-** (I.) & **inflect(ed)**. Not inflected; esp. of a language or a word, having no inflexions.

uninfluenced, adj. [1. unínflooenst; 2. anínfluənst]. **un-** (I.) & **influence(d)**. Not influenced.

uninfluential, adj. [1. ùninflooénshl; 2. àninfluénʃ(ə)l]. **un-** (I.) & **influential**. Not influential; having no influence.

uninformed, adj. [1. ùninfórmd; 2. àninfɔ̄md]. **un-** (I.) & **informed**. Not informed; **a** having no information concerning, not told of; **b** lacking information or knowledge; untaught, ignorant.

uninhabitable, adj. [1. ùninhábitabl; 2. àninhǽbitəbl]. **un-** (I.) & **inhabitable**. Not inhabitable; not fit to be lived in.

uninhabited, adj. [1. ùninhábited; 2. àninhǽbitid]. **un-** (I.) & **inhabit(ed)**. Not inhabited; deserted, empty.

uninitiated, adj. [1. ùniníshiàted; 2. àniníʃieitid]. **un-** (I.) & **initiate(d)**. Not initiated.

uninjured, adj. [1. unínjurd; 2. aníndžəd]. **un-** (I.) & **injure(d)**. Not injured.

uninspired, adj. [1. ùninspírd; 2. àninspáiəd]. **un-** (I.) & **inspire(d)**. Not inspired; without, lacking, inspiration.

uninstructed, adj. [1. ùninstrúkted; 2. àninstráktid]. **un-** (I.) & **instruct(ed)**. Not instructed; untaught.

uninstructive, adj. [1. ùninstrúktiv; 2. àninstráktiv]. **un-** (I.) & **instructive**. Not instructive.

unintelligent, adj. [1. ùnintélijent; 2. àntélidžənt]. **un-** (I.) & **intelligent**. Not intelligent; stupid.

unintelligently, adv. Prec. & **-ly**. In an unintelligent manner; stupidly.

unintelligibility, n. [1. ùnintèlijibíliti; 2. àntèlidžibíliti]. **un-** (I.) & **intelligibility**. State of being unintelligible; lack of intelligibility.

unintelligible, adj. [1. ùnintélijibl; 2. àntélidžəbl]. **un-** (I.) & **intelligible**. Not intelligible.

unintelligibly, adv. Prec. & **-ly**. In an unintelligible manner.

unintentional, adj. [1. ùninténshunal; 2. àninténʃənəl]. **un-** (I.) & **intentional**. Not intentional; not deliberate; involuntary.

unintentionally, adv. Prec. & **-ly**. In an unintentional manner; involuntarily.

uninterested, adj. [1. unínterested; 2. anínt(ə)ristid]. **un-** (I.) & **interest(ed)**. Not interested.

uninteresting, adj. [1. unínteresting; 2. anínt(ə)ristiŋ]. **un-** (I.) & **interesting**. Not interesting; dull.

uninterestingly, adv. Prec. & **-ly**. In an uninteresting manner.

unintermitted, adj. [1. ùnintermíted; 2. àntəmítid]. **un-** (I.) & **intermit(ted)**. Not intermitted; uninterrupted.

unintermitting, adj. [1. ùnintermíting; 2. àntəmítiŋ]. **un-** (I.) & **intermit(ting)**. Not intermitting; ceaseless, continuous.

unintermittingly, adv. Prec. & **-ly**. Without intermission; ceaselessly, continuously.

uninterrupted, adj. [1. ùninterúpted; 2. àntəráptid]. **un-** (I.) & **interrupt(ed)**. Not interrupted.

uninterruptedly, adv. Prec. & **-ly**. Without interruption.

uninventive, adj. [1. ùninvéntiv; 2. àninvéntiv]. **un-** (I.) & **inventive**. Not inventive; without the faculty of invention.

uninvited, adj. [1. ùninvíted; 2. àninváitid]. **un-** (I.) & **invite(d)**. Not invited; having received no invitation.

uninviting, adj. [1. ùninvíting; 2. àninváitiŋ]. **un-** (I.) & **inviting**. Not inviting; unattractive; repellent.

uninvolved, adj. [1. ùninvólvd; 2. àninvɔ́lvd]. **un-** (I.) & **involve(d)**. Not involved; simple, direct.

Unio, n. [1. ūniō; 2. júniou]. Lat., 'union, unity; a single large pearl', see next word & cp. **onion**. (zool.) A genus of freshwater mussels, having a pearly shell, and producing pearls.

union, n. [1. únium; 2. júniən]. Fr., fr. Lat. *ūniōn-(em)*, 'unity, union'; fr. *ūnus*, 'one', see **uni-**. **1. a** Act of uniting or joining two or more things into one: *to promote, accomplish, the union between two families, states* &c.; **b** state of being united in marriage; a marriage. **2.** State of being united: *a lasting union*; specif., a political combination or fusion of two countries under a single sovereign or government, as *the Union of England and Scotland, 1707*; *of Great Britain and Ireland, 1801* &c. **3.** A combination of various political or administrative bodies for a specific common purpose: *the Latin monetary union*; *the postal union.* **4.** Specif. **a** a combination of parishes for administration of the Poor Law under a Public Assistance Authority; **b** the workhouse administered by such body: *to go into the union*; *tramping from one union to another.* **5.** That part of a national flag which symbolizes the political union of two or more states, occupying usually the upper canton next the staff: *to fly a flag union down*, as signal of distress; hence a union flag or jack (see below). **6.** A trade union.

Union flag, n. [1. úniun flág; 2. júniən flǽg]. The national flag of Great Britain, signifying the union of England, Scotland, and Ireland, being a combination of the crosses of St. George, St. Andrew, and St. Patrick; commonly known as the *Union Jack*, whether flown as a jack or not.

unionism, n. [1. úniunìzm; 2. júniənizəm]. **union** & **-ism**. Specif. **1. a** the political principle of uniting under a central government the various kingdoms, states, provinces, dominions, forming the British Empire; the principle of maintaining the unity of the Empire, as distinct from establishing 'Home Rule' or independent governments in each portion or province; **b** specif., these principles as applied to Ireland. **2.** Principles of trade-unionism.

unionist, n. [1. úniunist; 2. júniənist]. **union** & **-ist**. **1. a** One who advocates the political principles of unionism within the Empire; specif. **b** a member of the party which, basing itself on these principles, opposed Home Rule for Ireland; **c** name often applied latterly, until the establishment of the Irish Free State, to the Conservative party in Great Britain. **2.** A member of a trade union; supporter of trade-union principles.

Union Jack, n. [1. úniun ják; 2. júniən džǽk]. The Union flag of Great Britain when flown as a jack, q.v.; (in common usage) the Union flag.

uniparous, adj. [1. ūníparus; 2. jūnípərəs]. **uni-** & *-parous*, fr. Lat. *parere*, 'to bring forth, beget', & **-ous**; cp. **parent**. **a** (of animals) Producing, normally, only one at a birth; **b** (of plants) having a single axis or stem.

unipartite, adj. [1. únipártīt; 2. júnipátait]. **uni-** & **part** & **-ite**. **1.** Not divided into parts. **2. a** (math.) Characterizing a single set of objects of the same kind; **b** (of curves) having all its real points comprised in one series through infinity or finity.

unipersonal, adj. [1. ùnipérsunal; 2. jùnipɔ́sənəl]. **uni-** & **personal**. (theol., of the Godhead) Consisting of, existing as, a single person.

unipolar, adj. [1. ùnipólar; 2. jùnipóulə]. **uni-** & **polar**. Having only one pole or kind of polarity.

unique, adj. [1. ūnék; 2. júník]. Fr., fr. Lat. *ūnicus*, 'one and no more, only, single', fr. *ūnus*, 'one'. Single in kind or excellence; having no like or equal; unmatched, unequalled, unparalleled: *a unique event; perhaps a unique survival; this picture is thought to be unique*; (in illit. usage) remarkable, wonderful, singular, and hence used wrongly with comparatives: *we had rather a unique experience; she dresses in a most unique fashion.*

uniquely, adv. Prec. & **-ly**. In a unique manner.

uniqueness, n. See prec. & **-ness**. State, quality, of being unique.

uniradial, uniradiate, adj. [1. ûnirâdial, -iat; 2. jûniréidiəl, -iət]. **uni-** & **radial, -ate.** Having one radius, ray, or arm.

unirrigated, adj. [1. unírigâted; 2. aníri-gèitid]. **un-** (I.) & **irrigate(d).** Not irrigated; not under irrigation.

unisexual, adj. [1. ûnisékshooal; 2. jûnisék-ʃuəl]. **uni-** & **sexual.** (bot.) Having one sex only, male or female, with stamen or pistil; not hermaphroditic.

unisolated, adj. [1. unísolâted; 2. anáisəlèitid]. **un-** (I.) & **isolate(d).** Not isolated.

unison, n. [1. ûnizun; 2. jûnizən], fr. M.E. *unis(s)on*, Lat. *ūnisonus*, adj., 'having one sound', fr. **uni-** & *sonus*, 'sound', see **sound** (I.). **a** Harmony, concord, agreement, in sound; specif. **b** (mus.) identity of pitch: *to sing in unison*, to sing so that all the voices sing the same note, without producing harmony.

unisonance, n. [1. ûnisónans; 2. jûnisóunəns]. Next word & **-ce.** Accordance, agreement, of sounds.

unisonant, adj. [1. ûnisónant; 2. jûnisóunənt]. See prec. & **-ant.** Sounding together, agreeing in sound.

unissued, adj. [1. uníshūd; 2. aníʃjūd]. **un-** (I.) & **issue(d).** Not issued, esp. of shares of a company authorized but held in reserve and not issued to the public for subscription.

unit, n. [1. ûnit; 2. jûnit]. A shortened form of **unity. 1.** A single individual object or person; a group of objects or persons regarded **a** as forming a unity or whole complete in itself; or **b** as forming that into which a whole may be divided most conveniently for a specific purpose: *a division is now regarded as the unit of an army; the parish, we may say, has almost ceased to be the unit of local government.* **2.** (math.) The least whole number, one. **3.** (phys.) Any determinate single quantity used as a standard by which other quantities are measured or expressed: *international electrical units, as the volt, ohm* &c.; *units of mass, energy* &c.

Unitarian, n. & adj. [1. ûnitârian; 2. jûni-téəriən], fr. **unity** & **-arian**, on anal. of **Trinitarian. 1.** n. Member of a religious body which rejects the doctrine of the Trinity and the Divinity of Christ, and asserts that God is unipersonal. **2.** adj. Pertaining to this body and their beliefs; pertaining to any set of religious doctrines which deny the Divinity of Christ and the existence of the Trinity.

Unitarianism, n. [1. ûnitârianizm; 2. jûni-téəriənizəm]. Prec. & **-ism.** Religious doctrines and philosophy of Unitarians.

unitary, adj. [1. ûnitari; 2. jûnitəri]. **unit** & **-ary. 1.** Pertaining to a unit or units: *unitary system, method* &c. **2.** Single; not double or divided: *unitary government; a unitary state.*

unite, vb. trans. & intrans. [1. ûnít; 2. jūnáit], fr. Lat. (rare or post-class.) *ūnīt-(um)*, P.P. type of *ūnīre*, 'to make one, join', fr. *ūnus*, 'one', see **uni-. A.** trans. **1.** To join several things, objects, together, into one, bring into close contiguity, and form into a single whole; to combine, amalgamate: *to unite pieces of metal with solder; to unite two neighbouring portions of land.* **2.** To join, bring, together into close social or family relationship: *to unite two families by marriage; to unite one's son to a suitable wife.* **3.** To possess, exhibit, equally, as elements of character, mind, habit &c., several qualities, traits, accomplishments &c.: *he unites the best qualities of the gentleman and the Christian.* **B.** intrans. **1.** (of physical process) To become joined together; become one or a whole; to combine, coalesce: *oil and water will not unite.* **2.** To become associated, to join, become one, in opinions, principles &c.: *all parties can unite in patriotic sentiment in a national crisis.* **3.** To become associated, join together, in action; to act as one: *let us unite in singing 'God save the King', in resisting foreign aggression* &c.

united, adj. [1. ûnîted; 2. jūnáitid], fr. P.P. of prec. **1.** Joined together; **a** joined politically, as *United Kingdom of Great Britain and (Northern) Ireland; the United States of America* &c.; **b** joined in spirit, sympathy, affection; not divided by disagreements and quarrels: *a united family.* **2. a** Associated together for purposes of common action: *the united forces of Christendom resisted Mohammedan aggression*; **b** arising from, based on, association for a common purpose: *united action.*

unitedly, adv. Prec. & **-ly.** In a united manner; harmoniously.

unitive, adj. [1. ûnitiv; 2. jûnitiv], fr. L. Lat. *ūnītīvus*, see **unity** & **-ive.** Having the power of uniting; tending to unite.

unity, n. [1. ûniti; 2. jûniti], fr. O. Fr. *unité*, fr. Lat. *ūnitāt-(em)*; fr. *ūnus*, 'one', see **uni-. 1.** State of being one, single, individual; grouping, arrangement, of component elements or parts so as to form or produce the sense of a single coherent whole: *to find unity in diversity; the plan and underlying idea which give unity to a work of art; the dramatic unities*, those of time, place, and action which the perfect classical drama was supposed to observe. **2.** Oneness of spirit; harmony, agreement, of aims, interests, feeling, thought &c.; amity, concord: *national unity; family unity; to live in unity with all men; 'Give to all nations unity, peace, and concord'* (The Litany). **3.** Specif. **a** (math.) any definite quantity taken as one; the number one; **b** (law) joint tenancy of a property by two or more persons.

univalence, -cy, n. [1. ûnivâlens(i); 2. jûni-véiləns(i)]. **uni-** & **valence, -cy.** (chem.) State, quality, of being univalent.

univalent, adj. [1. ûnivâlent; 2. jûnivéilənt]. **uni-** & **-valent.** (chem.) Having a valency or combining power of one.

univalve, adj. & n. [1. ûnivalv; 2. jûnivælv]. **uni-** & **valve. a** adj. (of molluscs) Having only one valve or shell, not bivalve; **b** n., mollusc with only one valve or shell.

universal (I.), adj. [1. ûnivérsl; 2. jûnivə́sl]. **universe** & **-al. 1. a** Pertaining to the universe; referring to, embracing, the whole world or the whole of created things: *the universal Church*; **b** involving the whole world or universe; complete, absolute: *'Universal ruin'* (Milton, 'P. L.' vi. 797); **c** affecting, held, done, used, by everybody; widespread: *the almost universal belief is that vaccination has nearly stamped out smallpox; superstition is universal among savages; a universal practice; a universal language*, one artificially and deliberately compiled with a view to its being learnt and spoken by people of all races; a real language that actually is spoken in all parts of the world: *English is fast becoming a universal language.* **2. a** Applicable to every member of a genus; general; contrasted with *particular*; (esp. log.) affirmed or denied of a whole class: *a universal proposition; a universal negative*; e.g. *no man is infallible*; **b** true of, applying to, all cases: *universal rules.* **3.** (mechan.) Capable of being used for objects of all shapes and sizes; adaptable for all purposes; moving in all directions: *a universal spanner, bevel, joint* &c. **4.** (law) Pertaining to, applying to, including, the whole of a person's rights, advantages, duties, arising from a specified position, capacity, relation: *a universal successor, legacy, partnership, trustee* &c.

universal (II.), n. Med. Lat. *universale*; see prec. **1.** (log.) **a** A universal proposition; **b** that which may be predicated of anything; any one of the five predicables. **2.** (philos.) A general concept; an abstract, general term.

universalism, n. [1. ûnivérsalizm; 2. jûnivə́-səlizəm]. **universal** (I.) & **-ism.** The theological belief that ultimately all mankind will be saved.

universalist, n. [1. ûnivérsalist; 2. jûnivə́-səlist]. See prec. & **-ist.** Believer in universalism.

universalistic, adj. [1. ûnivërsalístik; 2. jûni-vəsəlístik]. Prec. & **-ic.** Pertaining to universalism.

universalize, vb. trans. [1. ûnivérsalīz; 2. jûni-və́səlaiz]. **universal** (I.) & **-ize.** To make, treat as, universal.

universe, n. [1. ûnivers; 2. jûnivəs], fr. Fr. *univers*, fr. Lat. *ūniversum*, 'the whole world, the universe', neut. sing. as n., of *universus*, adj., 'turned, combined into one, all collectively; whole, general, universal', fr. **uni-**, 'one', & *vers-(um)*, P.P. of *vertere*, 'to turn', see **version. 1.** The whole system of suns, planets &c. existing in space; the cosmos. **2.** The whole system of created things viewed as a whole. Phr. *to behave as though one owned the universe*, to give oneself airs of inordinate importance and authority. **3.** The world.

university, n. [1. ûnivérsiti; 2. jûnivə́siti]. M.E. *universite*, fr. Fr. *université*, fr. Lat. *ūniversitāt-(em)*, *ūniversitas*, 'the whole; whole number of things; the universe, the world; (as a term of law) number of persons associated together as one body; community; a corporation'. The use of the term in Med. Lat. for a university in the present sense is prob. due to such a body being a *universitas facultatum*, or combination of all the Faculties, but there was also possibly an idea of the whole of learning being taught. See **universe** & **-ity. 1.** An institution for the purpose of educating students in the arts and sciences and all the higher branches of learning, with a body of professors and other teachers conducting examinations and conferring degrees. In the cases of Oxford, Cambridge, and London, the university consists of and includes a number of different individual colleges, separate foundations, having a very large degree of independence, and each providing courses of instruction in addition to those provided by the university in the narrower sense. **2.** The members of a university collectively; the governing body or bodies of a university: *the opinion of the university is* &c.; *the university has elected X their Chancellor.* **3.** Team, crew, athletes &c. representing a university: *the university was beaten by an innings.*

universology, n. [1. ûnivërsóloji; 2. jûnivə-sɔ́lədži]. See **universal** & **-logy.** Science which deals with everything pertaining to the universe or to the whole range of human activities.

univocal, adj. & n. [1. ûnivókl; 2. jûnivóukl]. **uni-** & **vocal. 1.** adj. **a** Speaking with a single voice; having only one meaning, not equivocal; **b** (mus.) having unison; played, sung, in unison. **2.** n. **a** A word having only one meaning; **b** (log.) a generic term applied in one sense only to all the species it includes.

univocally, adv. Prec. & **-ly.** In a univocal manner.

unjaundiced, adj. [1. unjáhndist, -jáwndist; 2. andžɑ́ndist, -džɔ́ndist]. **un-** (I.) & **jaundice(d).** Not jaundiced; not affected by feelings of envy or jealousy; unprejudiced.

unjoin, vb. trans. [1. unjóin; 2. andžɔ́in]. **un-** (II.) & **join.** To separate that which is joined; to disjoin.

unjoint, vb. trans. [1. unjóint; 2. andžɔ́int]. **un-** (II.) & **joint** (III.). To separate the joints; to unfasten what is jointed; to disjoint.

unjust, adj. [1. unjúst; 2. andžást]. **un-** (I.) & **just.** Not just; **a** not animated by justice; acting contrary to just principles: *an unjust judge; the unjust*, unjust persons; in Phr. *on the just and the unjust*, everybody; **b** contrary to justice, not conformable with just principles: *an unjust sentence.*

unjustifiable, adj. [1. ùnjustifíabl; 2. àndžastifáiəbl]. **un-** (**I.**) & **justifiable.** Not justifiable, without justification.

unjustifiably, adv. Prec. & **-ly.** In an unjustifiable manner; to an unjustifiable extent.

unjustly, adv. [1. unjústli; 2. andžástli]. **unjust** & **-ly.** In an unjust manner.

unkempt, adj. [1. unkém(p)t; 2. ankém(p)t]. fr. **un-** (**I.**) & M.E. *kempt, kembed*, P.P. of obs. O.E. *cemban*, 'to comb', see **comb.** **a** (obs.) Not combed; **b** untidy, shaggy; badly dressed, neglected: *unkempt appearance.*

unkennel, vb. trans. [1. unkénl; 2. ankénl]. **un-** (**II.**) & **kennel** (**II.**). To loose, drive (dogs &c.) from a kennel.

unkind, adj. [1. unkínd; 2. ankáind]. **un-** (**I.**) & **kind** (**II.**). Not kind; harsh, cruel, inconsiderate.

unkindliness, n. [1. unkíndlines; 2. ankáindlinis]. **unkindly** (**I.**) & **-ness.** State of being unkindly; an unkindly action.

unkindly (**I.**), adj. [1. unkíndli; 2. ankáindli]. **un-** (**I.**) & **kindly** (**I.**). Not kindly; ungracious, unfriendly, harsh.

unkindly (**II.**), adv. **un-** (**I.**) & **kindly** (**II.**). In an unkind manner.

unkindness, n. [1. unkíndnes; 2. ankáindnis]. **unkind** & **-ness.** State of being unkind; an unkind action.

unking, vb. trans. [1. unkíng; 2. ankíŋ]. **un-** (**II.**) & **king.** (rare) To deprive of rank and status of king; to depose.

unkingly, -like, adj. [1. unkíngli, -līk; 2. ankíŋli, -laik]. **un-** (**I.**) & **kingly, -like.** Not kingly or kinglike; not royal; unworthy of a king.

unknightly, adj. [1. unnítli; 2. annáitli]. **un-** (**I.**) & **knightly.** Not knightly or chivalrous; unworthy of a knight.

unknit, vb. trans. [1. unnít; 2. annít]. **un-** (**II.**) & **knit.** (esp. fig.) To undo what has been knitted or fastened together.

unknot, vb. trans. [1. unnót; 2. annɔ́t]. **un-** (**II.**) & **knot** (**II.**). To untie that which is knotted; to unloose the knots from.

unknowable, adj. [1. unnóabl; 2. annóuəbl]. **un-** (**I.**) & **knowable.** Not knowable; not capable of being known; (esp. philos.) beyond the powers or limits of man's intelligence; also as noun: *the unknowable*, that which cannot be known, the absolute, the first cause, the ultimate reality of things.

unknowing, adj. [1. unnóing; 2. annóuiŋ]. **un-** (**I.**) & Pres. Part. of **know.** Not knowing; ignorant, unwittir .

unknowingly, adv. Prec. & **-.y.** Not knowingly; ignorantly.

unknown, adj. & n. [1. unnón; 2. annóun]. **un-** (**I.**) & **know(n).** **1.** adj. Not known; **a** not within one's knowledge; unascertained: *address unknown; an unknown country*; **b** not within one's experience; not to be described or told; incalculable: *to experience unknown delights*; **c** (math.) to be ascertained or found out, as of quantities in equations, usually denoted by the later letters of alphabet: *x, y, z are the unknown quantities*; Phr. *an unknown quantity*, person, thing, whose influence, power &c. is not yet known or calculable. **2.** n. *The unknown*, that which is unknown; an unknown quantity: *to venture into the unknown*, into an unexplored, unknown region, country, or domain of thought or experience: *the unknown is always mysterious and attractive; the Great Unknown*, name given to the author of the Waverley Novels (Sir Walter Scott) before his identity had been revealed.

unlabelled, adj. [1. unlábld; 2. anléibld]. **un-** (**I.**) & **label(led).** Not labelled.

unlaboured, adj. [1. unlábur̥d; 2. anléibəd]. **un-** (**I.**) & **laboured.** Not laboured; done without great effort; (esp. of style) easy, spontaneous.

unlace, vb. trans. [1. unlás; 2. anléis]. **un-** (**II.**) & **lace** (**II.**). **1.** To undo the laces of, to unfasten that which is laced; to free from laces or being laced: *to unlace one's boots, stays* &c.; *unlace a woman*, unlace her stays. **2.** Old phr. of the chase, *to unlace a boar*, to cut it up when killed.

unlade, vb. trans. [1. unlád; 2. anléid]. **un-** (**II.**) & **lade.** To unload, **a** to take out the cargo or load from: *to unlade a ship*; **b** to take out, remove from: *to unlade the cargo from a ship; to unlade hay from cart* &c.; **c** to discharge: *ship will unlade cargo today.*

unladen, adj. [1. unládn; 2. anléidn]. **un-** (**I.**) & **lade(n).** Not laden, not burdened (esp. fig.): *unladen with sorrow, anxieties* &c.

unladylike, adj. [1. unládilīk; 2. anléidilaik]. **un-** (**I.**) & **ladylike.** Not ladylike; not worthy of a lady; vulgar, common.

unlaid, adj. [1. unlád; 2. anléid]. **un-** (**I.**) & P.P. of **lay.** Not laid; **a** not placed, fixed, or arranged: *the table is still unlaid*; **b** not put at rest, not allayed: *an unlaid, restless spirit*; specif. **c** (of paper) without parallel watermark lines.

unlamented, adj. [1. ùnlaménted; 2. ànləméntid]. **un-** (**I.**) & **lament(ed).** Not lamented; not mourned; unregretted.

unlash, vb. trans. [1. unlásh; 2. anlǽʃ]. **un-** (**II.**) & **lash.** To unfasten that which is lashed; to loose the lashings of.

unlatch, vb. trans. [1. unlách; 2. anlǽtʃ]. **un-** (**II.**) & **latch.** To undo, release, the latch of (as of a door).

unlawful, adj. [1. unláwfl; 2. anlɔ́fl]. **un-** (**I.**) & **lawful.** Not lawful; forbidden or not permitted by the law; illegal: *unlawful assembly*, a meeting of three or more persons for purposes forbidden by law or in such a manner as to endanger or be likely to endanger the public peace.

unlawfully, adv. Prec. & **-ly.** In an unlawful manner.

unlawfulness, n. See prec. & **-ness.** State of being unlawful.

unlay, vb. trans. [1. unlá; 2. anléi]. **un-** (**II.**) & **lay** (**III.**). (naut.) To untwist the strands of (a rope &c.).

unlearn, vb. trans. [1. unlérn; 2. anlǽn]. **un-** (**II.**) & **learn.** To forget what one has learnt; to lose the memory of; to learn the opposite of what one has been taught, esp. of erroneous teaching or methods.

unlearned (**I.**), adj. [1. unlérned, -lérnd; 2. anlǽnid, -lǽnd]. **un-** (**I.**) & **learned.** Not learned; ignorant, illiterate; also with definite article, as collective plural noun: *the unlearned*, the ignorant mob.

unlearned (**II.**), **unlearnt**, adj. [1. unlérnd, unlérnt; 2. anlǽnd, anlǽnt]. **un-** (**I.**) & **learn(ed).** Not learnt: *unlearned lessons.*

unlearnedly, adv. [1. unlérnedli; 2. anlǽnidli]. **unlearned** (**I.**) & **-ly.** In an unlearned manner; illiterately, ignorantly.

unleash, vb. trans. [1. unlḗsh; 2. anlíʃ]. **un-** (**II.**) & **leash.** To free from, let go from, a leash.

unleavened, adj. [1. unlévnd; 2. anlévnd]. **un-** (**I.**) & **leaven(ed).** Not leavened; made without leaven (of bread; also fig.).

unled, adj. [1. unléd; 2. anléd]. **un-** (**I.**) & P.P. of **lead** (**IV.**). Not led, not guided; without guidance or leaders.

unleisured, adj. [1. unlézhur̥d; 2. anlέžəd]. **un-** (**I.**) & **leisured.** Not leisured; having little or no leisure; hard-worked, busy.

unleisurely, adj. [1. unlézhurli; 2. anlέžəli]. **un-** (**I.**) & **leisurely.** Not leisurely; hurried.

unless, conj. [1. unlés; 2. anlés]. Earlier *onless(e)*, followed by a *that* clause, *on less(e) that ye wait* &c.; the orig. sense being, 'on the less supposition than, in a less case than'; fr. **on**, in earlier sense of 'in', & **less.** If not, supposing that not, except that: *I shall not go unless the weather is fine; unless you work harder you will never pass your examination; unless you are a perfect fool you will behave properly to your uncle.*

unlettered, adj. [1. unléterd; 2. anlétəd]. **un-** (**I.**) & **letter(ed).** Illiterate, uneducated; without knowledge or love of literature.

unlicensed, adj. [1. unlísenst; 2. anláisənst]. **un-** (**I.**) & **license(d).** Not licensed.

unlicked, adj. [1. únlikt; 2. ánlikt]. **un-** (**I.**) & **lick(ed).** Cp. Phr. *lick into shape*, q.v. under **lick.** (chiefly attrib.) Not licked into shape; in Phr. *an unlicked cub*, a crude, conceited, impudent, underbred young fool.

unlighted, adj. [1. unlíted; 2. anláitid]. **un-** (**I.**) & **light(ed).** Not lighted; unlit.

unlike, adj. & prep. [1. unlík; 2. anláik]. **un-** (**I.**) & **like.** **1.** adj. Not like; dissimilar, different, having little or no resemblance: *the two cases are quite unlike; no two people could be more unlike in appearance or character.* **2.** prep. Not like, having no resemblance to, different from, in appearance, character &c.: *the picture is quite unlike him; how unlike you to forget your dinner; unlike his predecessor, he was more concerned with his own future than his duty.*

unlikelihood, n. [1. unlíklihood; 2. anláiklihud]. **unlikely** & **-hood.** State, fact, of being unlikely; improbability, unlikeliness: *the unlikelihood of the fine weather continuing; unlikelihood of success.*

unlikeliness, n. [1. unlíklines; 2. anláiklinis]. See next word & **-ness.** State of being unlikely; unlikelihood.

unlikely, adj. [1. unlíkli; 2. anláikli]. **un-** (**I.**) & **likely.** Not likely; **a** improbable: *in the unlikely event of* &c.; *a victory is unlikely but not impossible*; **b** not likely to succeed; unpromising: *engaged on an unlikely adventure.*

unlimber, vb. trans. [1. unlímber; 2. anlímbə]. **un-** (**II.**) & **limber** (**I.**). To detach and take away the limber from (gun) so as to prepare for action.

unlimited, adj. [1. unlímited; 2. anlímitid]. **un-** (**I.**) & **limited.** Not limited; **a** having no limits; boundless: *the unlimited expanse of the sky, of ocean*; **b** unrestricted, not confined and narrow: *an unlimited field for talents, enterprise* &c.; **c** not restricted in amount or extent; unconditional: *unlimited liability; unlimited discretion, authority*; **d** unbounded; very great, excessive: *he has unlimited assurance, impudence.*

unlimitedly, adv. Prec. & **-ly.** In an unlimited manner.

unlimitedness, n. See prec. & **-ness.** State of being unlimited.

unline, vb. trans. [1. unlín; 2. anláin]. **un-** (**II.**) & **line** (**IV.**). To remove the lining from, take lining out of.

unlink, vb. trans. [1. unlíngk; 2. anlíŋk]. **un-** (**II.**) & **link** (**II.**). To undo, separate, unfasten the links of; separate that which is linked together.

unliquidated, adj. [1. unlíkwidàted; 2. anlíkwidèitid]. **un-** (**I.**) & **liquidate(d).** Not liquidated, (esp. law) of damages, not fixed or determined.

unlit, adj. [1. unlít; 2. anlít]. **un-** (**I.**) & *lit*, P.P. of **light.** Not lit; unlighted, dark.

unload, vb. trans. & intrans. [1. unlṓd; 2. anlóud]. **un-** (**II.**) & **load.** **A. 1.** trans. **a** To remove the load, cargo &c. from: *to unload a ship, truck, cart* &c.; **b** also, *to unload cargo from a ship, goods from a truck* &c. **2.** To remove the charge from: *unload a gun.* **3.** (of stocks and shares) To get rid of one's holding, sell out. **B.** intrans. To discharge cargo, load: *the ships will unload tomorrow.*

unlocated, adj. [1. ùnlōkáted; 2. ànloukéitid]. **un-** (**I.**) & **locate(d).** Not located; unplaced; (U.S.A.) not surveyed.

unlock, vb. trans. [1. unlók; 2. anlɔ́k]. **un-** (**II.**) & **lock.** To undo, open, lock of (a locked door, box &c.); (fig.) *to unlock one's heart*, reveal one's feelings.

unlooked-for, adj. [1. unlóokt fôr; 2. anlúkt fɔ]. **un-** (**I.**) & **look(ed)** & **for.** Not looked-for; unexpected.

unloose, unloosen, vb. trans. [1. unlōōs(n); 2. anlús(n)]. **un-** (**II.**) & **loose(n).** To make loose; to loose; to set free.

unlovable, adj. [1. unlúvabl; 2. anlávəbl]. **un-** (**I.**) & **lovable.** Not lovable; not likely or worthy to be loved; not exciting love; disagreeable, repellent.

unloved, adj. [1. unlúvd; 2. anlávd]. **un- (I.)** & **love(d)**. Not loved.

unloveliness, n. [1. unlúvlines; 2. anlávlinis]. **unlovely** & **-ness**. Ugliness.

unlovely, adj. [1. unlúvli; 2. anlávli]. **un- (I.)** & **lovely**. Not lovely; ugly, unpleasing, unattractive, in physical and moral senses.

unloverlike, adj. [1. unlúverlīk; 2. anlávəlaik]. **un- (I.)** & **loverlike**. Not loverlike; not characteristic of, or like, (that of) a lover.

unloving, adj. [1. unlúving; 2. anláviŋ]. **un- (I.)** & **loving**. Not loving; not affectionate; cold, harsh.

unlovingly, adv. Prec. & **-ly**. In an unloving manner.

unluckily, adv. [1. unlúkili; 2. anlákili]. **unlucky** & **-ly**. In an unlucky manner; unfortunately.

unluckiness, n. [1. unlúkines; 2. anlákinis]. Next word & **-ness**. State of being unlucky.

unlucky, adj. [1. unlúki; 2. anláki]. **un- (I.)** & **lucky**. Not lucky; **a** unfortunate, unsuccessful; always meeting with bad luck: *an unlucky gambler; lucky at cards, unlucky in love*; **b** ill-omened, inauspicious, not bringing good luck; *Friday is an unlucky day; green is thought an unlucky colour*; **c** not happily chosen, ill-timed, inopportune: *an unlucky moment for their meeting; a most unlucky speech.*

unmade, adj. [1. unmā́d; 2. anméid]. **un- (I.)** & *made*, P.P. of **make**. Not made.

unmaidenly, adj. [1. unmā́dnli; 2. anméidnli]. **un- (I.)** & **maidenly**. Not maidenly, unbecoming a maiden; immodest.

unmaintainable, adj. [1. ùnmāntā́nabl; 2. ànmeintéinəbl]. **un- (I.)** & **maintainable**. Not maintainable.

unmake, vb. trans. [1. unmā́k; 2. anméik]. **un- (II.)** & **make**. To destroy what has been made; to change the form or qualities of; to annul.

unman, vb. trans. [1. unmán; 2. anmǽn]. **un- (II.)** & **man**. **1.** To deprive of manly spirit, courage, fortitude &c.: *quite unmanned by the terrible news, by the sight* &c. **2.** (rare) To deprive (a ship) of its crew.

unmanageable, adj. [1. unmánijabl; 2. anmǽnidžəbl]. **un- (I.)** & **manageable**. Not manageable; not easily controlled or regulated.

unmanlike, adj. [1. unmánlīk; 2. anmǽnlaik]. **un- (I.)** & **manlike**. Not manlike; unlike mankind; not human.

unmanliness, n. [1. unmánlines; 2. anmǽnlinis]. **unmanly** & **-ness**. State of being unmanly.

unmanly, adj. [1. unmánli; 2. anmǽnli]. **un- (I.)** & **manly**. Not manly; cowardly; effeminate; womanly.

unmannerliness, n. [1. unmánerlines; 2. anmǽnəlinis]. See next word & **-ness**. State of being unmannerly.

unmannerly, adj. [1. unmánerli; 2. anmǽnəli]. **un- (I.)** & **mannerly**. Not mannerly; rude, ill-mannered, ill-bred.

unmarked, adj. [1. unmárkt; 2. anmā́kt]. **un- (I.)** & **mark(ed)**. Not marked; **a** having no marks; **b** not noticed: *the mistake passed unmarked.*

unmarketable, adj. [1. unmárketabl; 2. anmā́kitəbl]. **un- (I.)** & **marketable**. Not marketable; not fit or suitable for market; unsalable.

unmarriageable, adj. [1. unmárijabl; 2. anmǽridžəbl]. **un- (I.)** & **marriageable**. Not marriageable; not fit or old enough for marriage.

unmarried, adj. [1. unmárid; 2. anmǽrid]. **un- (I.)** & *married*, P.P. of **marry**. Not married; single.

unmask, vb. trans. & intrans. [1. unmáhsk; 2. anmā́sk]. **un- (II.)** & **mask**. **1.** trans. **a** To remove the mask from; to take a mask off; **b** to reveal true character of; to expose: *to unmask a traitor, his treachery.* **2.** intrans. **a** To take off one's mask; **b** to reveal one's true character.

unmasked, adj. [1. unmáhskt; 2. anmā́skt]. P.P. of prec. **a** With mask removed; **b** revealed, exposed.

unmatchable, adj. [1. unmáchabl; 2. anmǽtʃəbl]. **un- (I.)** & **match (II.)** & **-able**. Not matchable; not to be matched.

unmatched, adj. [1. unmácht; 2. anmǽtʃt]. **un- (I.)** & **match(ed)**. Not matched; matchless, without an equal.

unmated, adj. [1. unmā́ted; 2. anméitid]. **un- (I.)** & **mate(d)**. Not mated; having no mate.

unmaterial, adj. [1. ùnmatḗrial; 2. ànmətíəriəl]. **un- (I.)** & **material**. Not material; not composed of material, cp. *immaterial.*

unmaterialized, adj. [1. ùnmatḗrialīzd; 2. ànmətíəriəlaizd]. **un- (I.)** & **materialize(d)**. Not materialized; not in bodily shape or form; not fully developed.

unmatured, adj. [1. ùnmatū́rd; 2. ànmətjúəd]. **un- (I.)** & **mature(d)**. (esp. of wine) Not matured; cp. *immature.*

unmeaning, adj. [1. unmḗning; 2. anmíniŋ]. **un- (I.)** & **mean(ing)**. Empty of meaning or significance; senseless, meaningless.

unmeaningly, adv. Prec. & **-ly**. In an unmeaning manner.

unmeant, adj. [1. unmént; 2. anmént]. **un- (I.)** & **mean(t)**. Not meant; unintended, unintentional.

unmeasured, adj. [1. unmézhurd; 2. anméžəd]. **un- (I.)** & **measure(d)**. **1.** Not measured. **2. a** Boundless, limitless: *unmeasured tracts of desert*; **b** abundant, unstinted: *unmeasured liberality.* **3.** Without due limits; immoderate, excessive: *unmeasured abuse; in unmeasured terms.*

unmechanical, adj. [1. ùnmekánikl; 2. ànmikǽnikl]. **un- (I.)** & **mechanical**. Not mechanical.

unmeet, adj. [1. unmḗt; 2. anmít]. **un- (I.)** & **meet (III.)**. Not meet or fit; unsuitable.

unmelodious, adj. [1. ùnmelṓdius; 2. ànmilóudiəs]. **un- (I.)** & **melodious**. Not melodious; discordant, unmusical.

unmelodiously, adv. Prec. & **-ly**. In an unmelodious manner.

unmelodiousness, n. See prec. & **-ness**. Quality of being unmelodious.

unmentionable, adj. [1. unménshunabl; 2. anménʃənəbl]. **un- (I.)** & **mentionable**. Not mentionable; not fit to be mentioned; as n., (obs. or rare) *unmentionables*, facetious euphemism for 'trousers'.

unmerchantable, adj. [1. unmérchantabl; 2. anmā́tʃəntəbl]. **un- (I.)** & **merchantable**. Not merchantable; not fit for sale, through defect of quality, quantity &c.; unsalable, unmarketable.

unmerciful, adj. [1. unmérsifl; 2. anmā́sifl]. **un- (I.)** & **merciful**. Not merciful; showing no mercy; pitiless, cruel.

unmercifully, adv. Prec. & **-ly**. In an unmerciful manner; mercilessly.

unmerited, adj. [1. unmérited; 2. anméritid]. **un- (I.)** & **merit(ed)**. Not merited; undeserved.

unmethodical, adj. [1. ùnmethódikl; 2. ànmiþɔ́dikl]. **un- (I.)** & **methodical**. Not methodical; lacking method; confused, muddled.

unmetrical, adj. [1. unmétrikl; 2. anmétrikl]. **un- (I.)** & **metrical**. Not metrical; not according to the rules of metre; not metrically arranged.

unmetrically, adv. Prec. & **-ly**. In an unmetrical manner.

unmilitary, adj. [1. unmílitari; 2. anmílitəri]. **un- (I.)** & **military**. Not military; not like or worthy of a soldier; unsoldierly.

unmindful, adj. [1. unmī́ndfl; 2. anmáindfl]. **un- (I.)** & **mindful**. Not mindful; forgetful; regardless.

unmindfully, adv. Prec. & **-ly**. In an unmindful manner.

unmistakable, adj. [1. ùnmistā́kabl; 2. ànmistéikəbl]. **un- (I.)** & **mistakable**. Not mistakable; not to be mistaken; leaving no room for error or misunderstanding; clearly recognizable.

unmistakably, adv. Prec. & **-ly**. In an unmistakable manner.

unmitigated, adj. [1. unmítigā̀ted; 2. anmítigèitid]. **un- (I.)** & **mitigate(d)**. Not mitigated: unqualified, absolute: *an unmitigated nuisance; an unmitigated liar, blackguard* &c.

unmixed, adj. [1. unmíkst; 2. anmíkst]. **un- (I.)** & **mix(ed)**. Not mixed; uniform in character throughout; pure, unqualified: *not an unmixed blessing*, a condition, situation, not entirely satisfactory.

unmodernized, adj. [1. unmódernīzd; 2. anmɔ́dənaizd]. **un- (I.)** & **modernize(d)**. Not modernized; not brought up to date, old-fashioned.

unmodified, adj. [1. unmódifīd; 2. anmɔ́difaid]. **un- (I.)** & *modified*, P.P. of **modify**. Not modified; without modification.

unmolested, adj. [1. ùnmōlésted; 2. ànmouléstid]. **un- (I.)** & **molest(ed)**. Not molested; left in peace.

unmoor, vb. trans. [1. unmṓr, móor; 2. anmɔ́, -múə]. **un- (I.)** & **moor (III.)**. To free (ship &c.) from moorings; to loose the moorings of; to weigh one of several anchors by which ship is moored.

unmoral, adj. [1. unmóral; 2. anmɔ́rəl]. **un- (I.)** & **moral**. Not moral; not concerned with, or related to, morals or morality; nonmoral; contrasted with *immoral.*

unmounted, adj. [1. unmóunted; 2. anmáuntid]. **un- (I.)** & **mount** & **-ed**. Not mounted. **1.** Not on horseback; standing, going, on foot. **2.** Not having a mount or setting, as a picture, jewellery &c.

unmourned, adj. [1. unmórnd; 2. anmɔ́nd]. **un- (I.)** & **mourn(ed)**. Not mourned; unregretted.

unmoved, adj. [1. unmṓovd; 2. anmúvd]. **un- (I.)** & **move(d)**. Not moved (chiefly in moral sense); **a** not having feelings and emotions stirred; **b** not to be deflected or dissuaded from a purpose or determination.

unmoving, adj. [1. unmṓoving; 2. anmúviŋ]. **un- (I.)** & **moving**. Not moving; **a** fixed, stationary, motionless; **b** not affecting, not arousing, feeling or emotion.

unmuffle, vb. trans. [1. unmúfl; 2. anmáfl]. **un- (II.)** & **muffle**. **a** To remove muffler, scarf, or other covering from the face, throat &c.; **b** to remove the muffling from a drum, bell, oars &c.

unmurmuring, adj. [1. unmérmering; 2. anmā́məriŋ]. **un- (I.)** & Pres. Part. of **murmur**. Not murmuring; uncomplaining.

unmurmuringly, adv. Prec. & **-ly**. Without a murmur or complaint.

unmusical, adj. [1. unmū́zikl; 2. anmjúzikl]. **un- (I.)** & **musical**. Not musical; **a** not pleasing, as music, to the ear; discordant (of sound, voice &c.); **b** not skilled or versed in, not caring for, indifferent to, music.

unmusically, adv. Prec. & **-ly**. In an unmusical manner.

unmutilated, adj. [1. unmū́tilā̀ted; 2. anmjútilèitid]. **un- (I.)** & **mutilate(d)**. Not mutilated.

unmuzzle, vb. trans. [1. unmúzl; 2. anmázl]. **un- (II.)** & **muzzle**. **a** To remove the muzzle from, to free (dog &c.) from a muzzle; **b** (fig.) to allow to speak freely, to remove restrictions on utterance or expression of opinions &c.: *the Press is unmuzzled at last.*

unnail, vb. trans. [1. unnā́l; 2. annéil]. **un- (II.)** & **nail**. To remove the nails from; to unfasten that which is nailed.

unnamable, adj. [1. unnā́mabl; 2. annéiməbl]. **un- (I.)** & **namable**. Not namable; not to be named or described.

unnamed, adj. [1. unnā́md; 2. annéimd]. **un- (I.)** & **name(d)**. Not named; having no name; not mentioned.

unnatural, adj. [1. unnáchural; 2. annǽtʃərəl]. **un- (I.)** & **natural**. **1.** Not natural; **a** contrary to, violating, the laws or common order of nature; monstrous: *unnatural crimes* &c.; **b** not in accordance with what usually happens; not to be expected, out of the ordinary course: *it is unnatural not to love one's children*. 2. Not exhibiting normal, natural feelings: *an unnatural parent, child* &c.

unnaturalized, adj. [1. unnáchuralīzd; 2. annǽtʃərəlàizd]. **un-** (I.) & **naturalize**(d). Not naturalized.

unnaturally, adv. [1. unnáchurali; 2. annǽtʃərəli]. **unnatural** & **-ly**. In an unnatural manner.

unnaturalness, n. [1. unnáchuralnes; 2. annǽtʃərəlnis]. See prec. & **-ness**. State of being unnatural.

unnavigable, adj. [1. unnávigabl; 2. annǽvigəbl]. **un-** (I.) & **navigable**. Not navigable.

unnecessarily, adv. [1. unnésesarili; 2. annésisərili]. **unnecessary** & **-ly**. In an unnecessary manner.

unnecessariness, n. [1. unnésesarines; 2. annésisərinis]. See prec. & **-ness**. State of being unnecessary.

unnecessary, adj. & n. [1. unnésesari; 2. annésis(ə)ri]. **un-** (I.) & **necessary**. **1.** adj. Not necessary; superfluous; not required by the circumstances of the case; needless, useless. **2.** n. (rare, usually pl.) Things which are unnecessary.

unneeded, adj. [1. unnḗded; 2. annídid]. **un-** (I.) & **need**(ed). Not needed; needless; unwanted.

unneedful, adj. [1. unnḗdfl; 2. annídfl]. **un-** (I.) & **needful**. Not needful; not requisite; not indispensable.

unneedfully, adv. Prec. & **-ly**. In an unneedful manner.

unnegotiable, adj. [1. ùnnegṓshiabl; 2. ànnigóuʃiəbl]. **un-** (I.) & **negotiable**. Not negotiable; not to be negotiated, esp. of bills of exchange &c.

unneighbourliness, n. [1. unnā́burlines; 2. annéibəlinis]. See next word & **-ness**. Quality of being unneighbourly.

unneighbourly, adj. [1. unnā́burli; 2. annéibəli]. **un-** (I.) & **neighbourly**. Not neighbourly; unfriendly, unsociable.

unnerve, vb. trans. [1. unnḗrv; 2. annʌ́v]. **un-** (II.) & **nerve**. To deprive of, cause to lose, nerve; to unman.

unnerved, adj. [1. unnḗrvd; 2. annʌ́vd]. P.P. of prec. Deprived of nerve; having lost one's courage.

unnoted, adj. [1. unnṓted; 2. annóutid]. **un-** (I.) & **note**(d). Not noted; unheeded; unmarked.

unnoticed, adj. [1. unnṓtist; 2. annóutist]. **un-** (I.) & **notice**(d). Not noticed; unobserved.

unnourished, adj. [1. unnúrisht; 2. annáriʃt]. **un-** (I.) & **nourish**(ed). Not nourished, insufficiently nourished.

unnumbered, adj. [1. unnúmberd; 2. annámbəd]. **un-** (I.) & **number**(ed). Not numbered, uncounted; innumerable, countless.

unobjectionable, adj. [1. ùnobjékshunabl; 2. ànəbdžékʃənəbl]. **un-** (I.) & **objectionable**. Not objectionable; not open to objection; inoffensive.

unobliging, adj. [1. ùnoblī́jing; 2. ànəbláidžiŋ]. **un-** (I.) & **obliging**. Not obliging; disobliging.

unobliterated, adj. [1. ùnōblíterāted; 2. ànoublítərèitid]. **un-** (I.) & **obliterate**(d). Not obliterated.

unobscured, adj. [1. ùnobskū́rd; 2. ànəbskjṓd]. **un-** (I.) & **obscure**(d). Not obscured.

unobservant, adj. [1. ùnobzḗrvant; 2. ànəbzʌ́vənt]. **un-** (I.) & **observant**. Not observant; lacking powers of observation.

unobtainable, adj. [1. ùnobtā́nabl; 2. ànəbtéinəbl]. **un-** (I.) & **obtainable**. Not obtainable; out of one's reach.

unobtrusive, adj. [1. ùnobtrṓōsiv; 2. ànəbtrū́siv]. **un-** (I.) & **obtrusive**. Not obtrusive; modest, retiring.

unobtrusively, adv. Prec. & -ly. In an unobtrusive manner.

unobtrusiveness, n. See prec. & **-ness**. State, quality, of being unobtrusive.

unoccupied, adj. [1. unókūpīd; 2. anɔ́kjupaid]. **un-** (I.) & *occupied*, P.P. of **occupy**. Not occupied; a (of house, seat &c.) untenanted; b (of persons) disengaged.

unoffending, adj. [1. ùnofénding; 2. ànəféndiŋ]. **un-** (I.) & **offending**. Not offending; harmless, inoffensive.

unofficial, adj. [1. ùnofíshl; 2. ànəfíʃl]. **un-** (I.) & **official**. Not official; not announced through official channels.

unofficially, adv. Prec. & **-ly**. In an unofficial manner; not officially.

unopened, adj. [1. unṓpend; 2. anóupənd]. **un-** (I.) & **open**(ed). Not opened; closed, shut.

unoperated, adj. [1. unóperāted; 2. anɔ́pəreitid]. **un-** (I.) & **operate**(d). Not operated, not worked; not in operation or at work.

unopposed, adj. [1. unopṓzd; 2. anəpóuzd]. **un-** (I.) & **oppose**(d). Not opposed.

unorganized, adj. [1. unórganīzd; 2. anɔ́gənàizd]. **un-** (I.) & **organize**(d). Not organized; specif. (biol.) lacking organic structure.

unoriginal, adj. [1. ùnoríjinal; 2. ànərídžinəl]. **un-** (I.) & **original**. Not original; having no originality; derived from other sources; derivative, imitative.

unornamental, adj. [1. ùnornaméntl; 2. ànɔ̄nəméntl]. **un-** (I.) & **ornamental**. Not ornamental; plain; ugly, unsightly.

unorthodox, adj. [1. unórthodoks; 2. anɔ́þədɔks]. **un-** (I.) & **orthodox**. Not orthodox.

unostentatious, adj. [1. ùnostentā́shus; 2. ànɔstəntéiʃəs]. **un-** (I.) & **ostentatious**. Not ostentatious; unassuming; not boastful; not showy or glaring.

unostentatiously, adv. Prec. & **-ly**. In an unostentatious manner.

unostentatiousness, n. See prec. & **-ness**. Quality of being unostentatious.

unowed, adj. [1. unṓd; 2. anóud]. **un-** (I.) & **owe**(d). Not owed, not due.

unowned, adj. [1. unṓnd; 2. anóund]. **un-** (I.) & **own**(ed). Not owned; without a master; unacknowledged.

unpacified, adj. [1. unpásifīd; 2. anpǽsifaid]. **un-** (I.) & *pacified*, P.P. of **pacify**. Not pacified; not subdued or at peace.

unpack, vb. trans. & intrans. [1. unpák; 2. anpǽk]. **un-** (II.) & **pack**. **1.** trans. **a** To open and take out the contents of: *to unpack a trunk, box, package* &c.; **b** to take out from trunk or package: *to unpack one's clothes, the wedding presents* &c. **2.** intrans. To carry out the process of unpacking trunks &c.: *I shan't unpack until tomorrow morning.*

unpacked, adj. [1. unpákt; 2. anpǽkt]. P.P. of prec. Removed from trunk &c.; emptied of contents.

unpaged, adj. [1. unpā́jd; 2. anpéidžd]. **un-** (I.) & **page**(d). Not paged; not having the pages numbered.

unpaid, adj. [1. unpā́d; 2. anpéid]. **un-** (I.) & P.P. of **pay**. Not paid. **1.** (of bills, debt &c.) Not discharged, not cancelled by payment. **2.** (of persons, office &c.) **a** Not receiving payment; without salary or wages; honorary: *an unpaid secretary*; **b** not paid for, performed gratuitously: *unpaid work* &c.

unpaired, adj. [1. unpā́rd; 2. anpéəd]. **un-** (I.) & **pair**(ed). Not paired; specif., not having arranged for a parliamentary 'pair', or member voting in the opposite sense to oneself, in an approaching division.

unpalatable, adj. [1. unpálatabl; 2. anpǽlətəbl]. **un-** (I.) & **palatable**. Not palatable; **a** disagreeable, unpleasing, to the taste; nasty: *unpalatable medicine* &c.; **b** displeasing to the mind, offensive to the susceptibilities: *they must be told the truth, however unpalatable it may be.*

unpalatably, adv. Prec. & **-ly**. In an unpalatable manner.

unparalleled, adj. [1. unpáralèld; 2. anpǽrəlèld]. **un-** (I.) & **parallel**(ed). Not to be paralleled; incomparable; unprecedented.

unpardonable, adj. [1. unpárdunabl; 2. anpā́d(ə)nəbl]. **un-** (I.) & **pardonable**. (of conduct, actions) Not pardonable; not deserving pardon; inexcusable.

unpardonably, adv. Prec. & **-ly**. In an unpardonable manner.

unparental, adj. [1. ùnparéntl; 2. ànpəréntl]. **un-** (I.) & **parental**. Not parental; unlike, unworthy of, a father or mother.

unparented, adj. [1. unpā́rented; 2. anpéərəntid]. **un-** (I.) & (II.) & **parent**(ed). Without a parent; orphaned; deserted by the parents.

unparliamentary, adj. [1. ùnparlaméntari; 2. ànpāləméntəri]. **un-** (I.) & **parliamentary**. Not parliamentary; not permissible in parliament; contrary to the usage, rules &c. of parliament; esp. *unparliamentary language*, abuse, strong language in general.

unpatriotic, adj. [1. ùnpatriótik; 2. ànpætriɔ́tik]. **un-** (I.) & **patriotic**. Not patriotic.

unpatriotically, adv. [1. ùnpatriótikali; 2. ànpætriɔ́tikəli]. Prec. & **-al** & **-ly**. In an unpatriotic manner.

unpatronized, adj. [1. unpátrunīzd; 2. anpǽtrənàizd]. **un-** (I.) & **patronize**(d). Not patronized.

unpaved, adj. [1. unpā́vd; 2. anpéivd]. **un-** (I.) & **pave**(d). Not paved; without paving or pavement.

unpeaceful, adj. [1. unpḗsfl; 2. anpísfl]. **un-** (I.) & **peaceful**. Not peaceful, not at peace or at rest; restless, unquiet.

unpedantic, adj. [1. ùnpedántik; 2. ànpidǽntik]. **un-** (I.) & **pedantic**. Not pedantic.

unpedigreed, adj. [1. unpédigrēd; 2. anpédigrìd]. **un-** (I.) & **pedigree**(d). Having no pedigree.

unpeg, vb. trans. [1. unpég; 2. anpég]. **un-** (II.) & **peg** (II.). To remove the pegs from, to unfasten what is pegged down or pegged together; specif. (of prices, currency &c.) to remove regulations fixing or pegging prices &c.

unpen, vb. trans. [1. unpén; 2. anpén]. **un-** (II.) & **pen** (I.). To release, as sheep &c., from a pen.

unpensioned, adj. [1. unpénshund; 2. anpénʃənd]. **un-** (I.) & **pension**(ed). Not pensioned; not eligible for a pension; not receiving a pension.

unpeople, vb. trans. [1. unpḗpl; 2. anpípl]. **un-** (II.) & **people** (II.). To remove the population from; to depopulate.

unpeopled, adj. [1. unpḗpld; 2. anpípld]. **un-** (I.) & **people**(d). Not populated.

unperceived, adj. [1. ùnpersḗvd; 2. ànpəsívd]. **un-** (I.) & **perceive**(d). Not perceived; unnoticed.

unperforated, adj. [1. unpḗrforāted; 2. anpʌ́fəreitid]. **un-** (I.) & **perforate**(d). Not perforated; specif., of older issues of postage-stamps, having no perforations to enable one stamp to be torn from those next it in the sheet.

unperformed, adj. [1. ùnperfórmd; 2. ànpəfɔ́md]. **un-** (I.) & **perform**(ed). Not performed; not done or carried out.

unperjured, adj. [1. unpḗrjurd; 2. anpʌ́džəd]. **un-** (I.) & **perjure**(d). Not perjured.

unpersuadable, adj. [1. ùnpērswā́dabl; 2. ànpʌswéidəbl]. **un-** (I.) & **persuadable**. Not persuadable; not to be persuaded; not open to persuasion.

unpersuaded, adj. [1. ùnpērswā́ded; 2. ànpʌswéidid]. **un-** (I.) & **persuade**(d). Not persuaded.

unpersuasive, adj. [1. ùnpērswā́siv; 2. ànpʌswéisiv]. **un-** (I.) & **persuasive**. Not persuasive.

unperturbed, adj. [1. ùnpertḗrbd; 2. ànpətʌ́bd]. **un-** (I.) & **perturb**(ed). Not perturbed; unruffled, calm, undisturbed; not alarmed.

unperused, adj. [1. ùnperṓōzd; 2. ànpirū́zd]. **un-** (I.) & **peruse**(d). Not perused; unread; not read through.

unphilosophical, adj. [1. ùnfilosófikl; 2. ànfìləsɔ́fikl]. **un-** (I.) & **philosophical**. Not philosophical; wanting in philosophy; contrary to philosophical principles.

unphilosophically, adv. Prec. & **-ly**. In an unphilosophical manner.

unphilosophicalness, n. See prec. & **-ness**. State of being unphilosophical.

unpick, vb. trans. [1. unpík; 2. anpík]. **un-** (**II.**) & **pick** (**II.**). To undo, loosen, unfasten, remove (stitches &c.) by picking.

unpicked (**I.**), adj. [1. unpíkt; 2. anpíkt]. P.P. of prec. Picked loose; unfastened by picking.

unpicked (**II.**), adj. **un-** (**I.**) & **pick**(**ed**). **a** Not picked out, not selected or chosen; **b** (of flowers) not picked, plucked, or gathered.

unpiloted, adj. [1. unpíloted; 2. anpáilətid]. **un-** (**I.**) & **pilot**(**ed**). Not piloted; not guided by a pilot; (also fig.) undirected, unguided.

unpin, vb. trans. [1. unpín; 2. anpín]. **un-** (**II.**) & **pin** (**II.**). To unfasten what is pinned together; to remove pins from.

unpitied, adj. [1. unpítid; 2. anpítid]. **un-** (**I.**) & P.P. of **pity**. Not pitied; having received no pity: '*Thy fate unpitied, and thy rites unpaid*' (Pope, 'Unfortunate Lady', 48).

unpitying, adj. [1. unpíti-ing; 2. anpíti-iŋ]. **un-** (**I.**) & Pres. Part. of **pity**. Feeling no pity; callous, remorseless.

unpityingly, adv. Prec. & **-ly**. In an unpitying manner.

unplaced, adj. [1. unplást; 2. anpléist]. **un-** (**I.**) & **place**(**d**). Not placed; (esp. of horses) not placed among the first three in a race.

unplait, vb. trans. [1. unplát; 2. anplǽt]. **un-** (**II.**) & **plait** (**II.**). To unfasten the plaits of, as hair &c.

unplanned, adj. [1. unplánd; 2. anplǽnd]. **un-** (**I.**) & **plan**(**ned**). Not planned; not provided for in plans; not properly thought out.

unplanted, adj. [1. unpláhnted; 2. anplántid]. **un-** (**I.**) & **plant**(**ed**). Not planted.

unplausible, adj. [1. unpláwzibl; 2. anplɔ́zibl]. **un-** (**I.**) & **plausible**. Not plausible.

unplausibly, adv. Prec. & **-ly**. In an unplausible manner.

unplayable, adj. [1. unpláabl; 2. anpléiəbl]. **un-** (**I.**) & **playable**. Not playable; **a** of a ball at cricket or tennis, that cannot be played or effectively taken and dealt with by the player receiving it; **b** (of ground) not fit to play on.

unpleasant, adj. [1. unplézant; 2. anplézənt]. **un-** (**I.**) & **pleasant**. Not pleasant; **a** disagreeable, offensive, causing disgust, discomfort, or repulsion to any of the senses: *an unpleasant sight, smell, voice* &c.; **b** provoking moral disapproval or dislike; shocking the taste, the sense of propriety: *an unpleasant person*; *unpleasant manners*; *an unpleasant subject*.

unpleasantly, adv. Prec. & **-ly**. In an unpleasant manner.

unpleasantness, n. See prec. & **-ness**. State or quality of being unpleasant. **1. a** Lack of positive or good qualities; sense of want of external beauty, comfort, charm &c.: *the unpleasantness of a neighbourhood, landscape*; **b** presence of repellent and disgusting physical qualities or properties: *the unpleasantness of a smell, sight* &c. **2.** Qualities or conditions which shock, repel, disgust the mind, something which offends the taste, sense of propriety &c.: *the unpleasantness of a person's manners*. **3.** Lack of agreement between persons; disagreement, misunderstanding, friction, quarrel: *we have had a slight unpleasantness with our landlady*.

unpleasing, adj. [1. unplézing; 2. anplíziŋ]. **un-** (**I.**) & **pleasing**. Not pleasing; not giving pleasure, disagreeable, unattractive.

unpledged, adj. [1. unpléjd; 2. anplédžd]. **un-** (**I.**) & **pledge**(**d**). **a** Not pledged; not promised; **b** not pawned.

unpliable, adj. [1. unplíabl; 2. anpláiəbl]. **un-** (**I.**) & **pliable**. Not pliable (in lit. and fig. senses).

unpliant, adj. [1. unplíant; 2. anpláiənt]. **un-** (**I.**) & **pliant**. Not pliant; stiff, stubborn.

unploughed, adj. [1. unplóud; 2. anpláud]. **un-** (**I.**) & **plough**(**ed**). Not ploughed; not tilled or cultivated.

unplug, vb. trans. [1. unplúg; 2. anplág]. **un-** (**II.**) & **plug** (**II.**). To remove the plug from.

unplugged, adj. [1. unplúgd; 2. anplágd]. **un-** (**I.**) & **plug**(**ged**). Not plugged.

unplumbed, adj. [1. unplúmd; 2. anplámd]. **un-** (**I.**) & **plumb**(**ed**). Not plumbed, unfathomed (lit. and fig.): *unplumbed depths of ignorance*.

unpoetical, adj. [1. ùnpōétikl; 2. ànpouétikl]. **un-** (**I.**) & **poetical**. Not poetical; prosaic.

unpoetically, adv. Prec. & **-ly**. In an unpoetical manner.

unpointed, adj. [1. unpóinted; 2. anpóintid]. **un-** (**I.**) & **pointed**. Not pointed. **1.** Without a point; blunt. **2.** Without vowel points or diacritical marks. **3.** (of joints between the stones or bricks in masonry) Not pointed by an external streak of mortar or cement.

unpolished, adj. [1. unpólisht; 2. anpɔ́lišt]. **un-** (**I.**) & **polish**(**ed**). Not polished; (in lit. and fig. senses): *unpolished stone, style, manners* &c.

unpolitical, adj. [1. ùnpōlítikl; 2. ànpoulítikl]. **un-** (**I.**) & **political**. Not political; not interested in or concerned with politics; cp. *impolitic*.

unpolled, adj. [1. unpṓld; 2. anpóuld]. **un-** (**I.**) & **poll**(**ed**). Not polled; specif. (of voters) not having cast a vote; (of votes) not cast or registered at the polling station.

unpolluted, adj. [1. ùnpolū́ted; 2. ànpəljū́tid]. **un-** (**I.**) & **pollute**(**d**). Free from pollution; pure.

unpopular, adj. [1. unpópūlar; 2. anpɔ́pjulə]. **un-** (**I.**) & **popular**. Not popular; not a general favourite; out of popular favour or fashion.

unpopularity, n. [1. ùnpopūláriti; 2. ànpɔpjulǽriti]. Prec. & **-ity**. State of being unpopular; popular disfavour.

unpopularly, adv. [1. unpópūlarli; 2. anpɔ́pjuləli]. See prec. & **-ly**. In an unpopular manner.

unpossessed, adj. [1. unpozést; 2. anpəzést]. **un-** (**I.**) & **possess**(**ed**). **a** Not possessed; not owned, not held in possession; **b** *unpossessed of*, not in possession (of).

unposted, adj. [1. unpṓsted; 2. anpóustid]. **un-** (**I.**) & **post**(**ed**). Not posted. **1.** Not placed in or delivered to the post. **2.** Not posted up, not in possession of information; uninformed.

unpractical, adj. [1. unpráktikl; 2. anprǽktikl]. **un-** (**I.**) & **practical**. Not practical; cp. *impracticable*.

unpracticality, n. [1. ùnpraktikáliti; 2. ànpræktikǽliti]. Prec. & **-ity**. State of being unpractical.

unpractically, adv. [1. unpráktikali; 2. anprǽktikəli]. See prec. & **-ly**. In an unpractical manner.

unpractised, adj. [1. unpráktist; 2. anprǽktist]. **un-** (**I.**) & **practise**(**d**). Not practised; **a** not put into practice; **b** unskilled, inexperienced.

unprecedented, adj. [1. unprésedènted; 2. anprésidèntid]. **un-** (**I.**) & **precedented**. Without a precedent; for which there is no prior example; unparalleled; novel.

unprecedentedly, adv. Prec. & **-ly**. In an unprecedented manner.

unpredicted, adj. [1. ùnprēdíkted; 2. ànprīdíktid]. **un-** (**I.**) & **predict** & **-ed**. Not predicted.

unprefaced, adj. [1. unpréfast; 2. anpréfist]. **un-** (**I.**) & **preface**(**d**). Not prefaced; **a** without a preface; **b** without warning or introduction.

unprejudiced, adj. [1. unpréjūdist; 2. anprédžjudist]. **un-** (**I.**) & **prejudice** & **-ed**. Not prejudiced; free from, without, prejudice, or bias; impartial, fair.

unpremeditated, adj. [1. ùnprēméditàted; 2. ànprīméditèitid]. **un-** (**I.**) & **premeditate**(**d**). Not premeditated; done &c. without premeditation; not deliberately planned or thought out previously; unprepared.

unprepared, adj. [1. ùnprepā́rd; 2. ànpripɛ́əd]. **un-** (**I.**) & **prepare**(**d**). Not prepared; **a** done without preparation; impromptu: *an unprepared retort, reception*; **b** not ready: *you caught me unprepared*.

unpreparedness, n. [1. ùnprepā́r(e)dnes; 2. ànpripɛ́ə(ri)dnis]. Prec. & **-ness**. State of being unprepared.

unprepossessing, adj. [1. unprèpozésing; 2. anprìpəzésiŋ]. **un-** (**I.**) & **prepossessing**. Not prepossessing; unattractive, unpleasing.

unpresentable, adj. [1. ùnprezéntabl; 2. ànprizéntəbl]. **un-** (**I.**) & **presentable**. Not presentable; specif. **a** not suitable to present in refined and highly civilized society; ill-mannered, ill-bred, ungentlemanlike; **b** unattractive in appearance; plain, ill-favoured.

unpresuming, adj. [1. ùnprezū́ming; 2. ànprizjū́miŋ]. **un-** (**I.**) & **presuming**. Not presuming; without presumption; unassuming; modest.

unpresumptuous, adj. [1. ùnprezúmptūus; 2. ànprizámptjuəs]. **un-** (**I.**) & **presumptuous**. Not presumptuous.

unpretending, adj. [1. ùnpreténding; 2. ànpriténdiŋ]. **un-** (**I.**) & **pretend** & **-ing**. Not making pretences; not pretending to be what one is not; unassuming; modest, humble.

unpretendingly, adv. Prec. & **-ly**. In an unpretending manner.

unpretentious, adj. [1. ùnpreténshus; 2. ànpriténʃəs]. **un-** (**I.**) & **pretentious**. Not pretentious.

unpretentiously, adv. Prec. & **-ly**. In an unpretentious manner.

unpreventable, adj. [1. ùnprevéntabl; 2. ànprivéntəbl]. **un-** (**I.**) & **preventable**. Not preventable; not to be prevented, inevitable.

unpriced, adj. [1. unpríst; 2. anpráist]. **un-** (**I.**) & **price**(**d**). Having no fixed price; without prices stated or marked.

unpriestly, adj. [1. unprḗstli; 2. anpríistli]. **un-** (**I.**) & **priestly**. Not priestly; **a** not like a priest; **b** not characteristic of, not befitting, a priest.

unprincely, adj. [1. unprínsli; 2. anprínsli]. **un-** (**I.**) & **princely**. Not princely; not worthy of, not befitting, a prince.

unprincipled, adj. [1. unprínsipld; 2. anprínsipld]. **un-** (**I.**) & **principle**(**d**). **a** Having no fixed moral principles; unscrupulous, dishonest: *an unprincipled rogue*; **b** not based on, governed, or dictated by, not in accordance with, moral principles: *unprincipled conduct*.

unprintable, adj. [1. unpríntabl; 2. anpríntəbl]. **un-** (**I.**) & **printable**. Not printable; too indecent or profane to be printed.

unprinted, adj. [1. unprínted; 2. anpríntid]. **un-** (**I.**) & **print** & **-ed**. Not printed; existing only in MS. form.

unprivileged, adj. [1. unprívilejd; 2. anprívilidžd]. **un-** (**I.**) & **privilege**(**d**). Not privileged; without special privileges.

unprized, adj. [1. unprízd; 2. anpráizd]. **un-** (**I.**) & **prize**(**d**). Not prized; not valued highly.

unprobed, adj. [1. unprṓbd; 2. anpróubd]. **un-** (**I.**) & **probe**(**d**). Not probed; (chiefly fig.) not looked into, not examined, thoroughly.

unproclaimed, adj. [1. ùnproklā́md; 2. ànprəkléimd]. **un-** (**I.**) & **proclaim**(**ed**). Not proclaimed; unannounced.

unprocurable, adj. [1. ùnprokū́rabl; 2. ànprəkjɔ́rəbl]. **un-** (**I.**) & **procurable**. Not procurable; not to be procured.

unproductive, adj. [1. ùnprodúktiv; 2. ànprədáktiv]. **un-** (**I.**) & **productive**. Not productive; barren; unprofitable; ineffective.

unproductively, adv. Prec. & **-ly**. In an unproductive manner.

unproductiveness, n. See prec. & **-ness**. State of being unproductive.

unprofaned, adj. [1. ùnprofā́nd; 2. ànprəféind]. **un-** (**I.**) & **profane**(**d**). Not profaned: '*thy cheek unprofaned by a tear*' (T. Moore).

unprofessional, adj. [1. ùnprofésbunal; 2. ànprəféʃənəl]. **un- (I.)** & **professional.** Not professional. **1.** Not having a profession; not belonging to a specified, or to any, profession: *unprofessional people; the unprofessional mind.* **2.** Contrary to the rules, etiquette &c. of a profession: *unprofessional conduct.*

unprofessionally, adv. Prec. & **-ly.** From an unprofessional point of view; in an unprofessional manner.

unprofitable, adj. [1. unprófitabl; 2. anprɔ́fitəbl]. **un- (I.)** & **profitable.** Not profitable; **a** yielding no profit; entailing loss; **b** yielding no advantage or favourable results.

unprofitably, adv. Prec. & **-ly.** In an unprofitable manner.

unprogressive, adj. [1. ùnprogrésiv; 2. ànprəgrésiv]. **un- (I.)** & **progressive.** Not progressive; not in favour of social or political progress; reactionary.

unprolific, adj. [1. ùnprolífik; 2. ànprəlífik]. **un- (I.)** & **prolific.** Not prolific; infertile.

unpromising, adj. [1. unprómising; 2. anprɔ́misiŋ]. **un- (I.)** & **promising.** Not promising; not likely to be successful; not holding out good prospects.

unprompted, adj. [1. unprómpted; 2. anprɔ́mptid]. **un- (I.)** & **prompt(ed).** Not prompted; without prompting, spontaneous, on one's own initiative.

unpronounceable, adj. [1. ùnpronóunsabl; 2. ànprənáunsəbl]. **un- (I.)** & **pronounceable.** Not pronounceable; difficult, or impossible, to pronounce.

unprop, vb. trans. [1. unpróp; 2. anprɔ́p]. **un- (II.)** & **prop.** To remove the props, or support, from; to deprive of support.

unprophetic, adj. [1. ùnprofétik; 2. ànprəfétik]. **un- (I.)** & **prophetic.** Not prophetic.

unpropitious, adj. [1. ùnpropíshus; 2. ànprəpíʃəs]. **un- (I.)** & **propitious.** Not propitious; inauspicious; ill-omened; unlucky.

unpropitiously, adv. Prec. & **-ly.** In an unpropitious manner.

unpropitiousness, n. See prec. & **-ness.** State of being unpropitious.

unproportional, adj. [1. ùnpropórshunal; 2. ànprəpɔ́ʃənəl]. **un- (I.)** & **proportional.** Not proportional.

unprosperous, adj. [1. unprósperus; 2. anprɔ́spərəs]. **un- (I.)** & **prosperous.** Not prosperous.

unprotected, adj. [1. ùnprotékted; 2. ànprətéktid]. **un- (I.)** & **protect(ed).** **1.** Lacking protection or a protector; liable to attack or molestation: *an unprotected female.* **2.** Not fortified, or armoured: *an unprotected town, cruiser.* **3.** Specif., not protected by a tariff: *unprotected industries.*

unprotested, adj. [1. ùnprotésted; 2. ànprətéstid]. **un- (I.)** & **protest(ed).** Not protested, esp. of bills of exchange.

unprovable, adj. [1. unpróovabl; 2. anprúvəbl]. **un- (I.)** & **provable.** Not provable; incapable of proof.

unproved, adj. [1. unpróovd; 2. anprúvd]. **un- (I.)** & **prove(d).** Not proved.

unprovided, adj. [1. ùnprovíded; 2. ànprəváidid]. **un- (I.)** & **provide(d).** Not provided; **a** not supplied, or furnished with; **b** not ready, not prepared for.

unprovoked, adj. [1. ùnprovókt; 2. ànprəvóukt]. **un- (I.)** & **provoke(d).** Not provoked; done without provocation: *an unprovoked assault* &c.

unpublished, adj. [1. unpúblisht; 2. anpábliʃt]. **un- (I.)** & **publish(ed).** Not published; **a** not made public or generally known; **b** not printed and published.

unpucker, vb. trans. [1. unpúker; 2. anpákə]. **un- (II.)** & **pucker.** To remove, get rid of, puckers or wrinkles from.

unpunctual, adj. [1. unpúngkchooal; 2. anpáŋktʃuəl]. **un- (I.)** & **punctual.** Not punctual; not up to time for appointments &c.; arriving, doing something, happening, after the hour fixed.

unpunctuality, n. [1. ùnpungkchooáliti; 2. ànpaŋktʃuǽliti]. Prec. & **-ity.** State, quality, of being unpunctual.

unpunctually, adv. [1. unpúngkchooali; 2. anpáŋktʃuəli]. See prec. & **-ly.** So as to be unpunctual.

unpunctuated, adj. [1. unpúngkchooàted; 2. anpáŋktʃuèitid]. **un- (I.)** & **punctuate** & **-ed.** Not punctuated; without stops or marks of punctuation.

unpunishable, adj. [1. unpúnishabl; 2. anpániʃəbl]. **un- (I.)** & **punishable.** Not punishable; not entailing punishment.

unpunished, adj. [1. unpúnisht; 2. anpániʃt]. **un- (I.)** & **punish(ed).** Not punished; having escaped punishment.

unpurchasable, adj. [1. unpérchasabl; 2. anpátʃəsəbl]. **un- (I.)** & **purchasable.** Not purchasable, not to be bought at any price.

unpurged, adj. [1. unpérjd; 2. anpádžd]. **un- (I.)** & **purge(d).** Not purged; esp., of crimes or offences &c., not cleared or atoned for by confession, and submission to a sentence by a court of law.

unpurified, adj. [1. unpúrifid; 2. anpjɔ́rifaid]. **un- (I.)** & P.P. **of purify.** Not purified.

unpuzzle, vb. trans. [1. unpúzl; 2. anpázl]. **un- (II.)** & **puzzle (I.).** To puzzle out, decipher, solve (a puzzle, problem &c.).

unquailing, adj. [1. unkwáling; 2. ankwéiliŋ]. **un- (I.)** & **quail(ing).** Not quailing, not shrinking from or before.

unqualified, adj. [1. unkwólifid; 2. ankwɔ́lifaid]. **un- (I.)** & P.P. of **qualify.** Not qualified. **1.** Without the necessary legal, or natural, qualifications for: *an unqualified medical practitioner; to be unqualified to teach, preach, advise others.* **2.** Not modified, not restricted by qualifications, exceptions &c., absolute: *an unqualified assertion, denial, statement*; (also colloq.) downright: *he is an unqualified liar.*

unquelled, adj. [1. unkwéld; 2. ankwéld]. **un- (I.)** & **quell(ed).** Not quelled; not put down.

unquenchable, adj. [1. unkwénchabl; 2. ankwéntʃəbl]. **un- (I.)** & **quenchable.** Not quenchable; not to be quenched: *unquenchable thirst, enthusiasm* &c.

unquenchably, adv. Prec. & **-ly.** In an unquenchable manner.

unquestionable, adj. [1. unkwéschunabl; 2. ankwéstʃənəbl]. **un- (I.)** & **questionable.** Not questionable, not to be questioned or doubted; indisputable, certain.

unquestionably, adv. Prec. & **-ly.** In an unquestionable manner; undoubtedly; to a degree, in a manner, beyond all question.

unquestioned, adj. [1. unkwéschund; 2. ankwéstʃənd]. **un- (I.)** & **question(ed).** Not questioned; not called in question; undoubted; not examined or disputed.

unquestioning, adj. [1. unkwéschuning; 2. ankwéstʃəniŋ]. **un- (I.)** & **question(ing).** Not questioning; asking no questions, unhesitating; without questions asked: *his unquestioning supporters; their unquestioning loyalty.*

unquestioningly, adv. Prec. & **-ly.** In an unquestioning manner; without question or hesitation.

unquiet, adj. [1. unkwíet; 2. ankwáiət]. **un- (II.)** & **quiet.** Not quiet; restless, disturbed, uneasy: *unquiet minds; an unquiet age.*

unquietly, adv. Prec. & **-ly.** In an unquiet manner.

unquietness, n. See prec. & **-ness.** State, quality, of being unquiet.

unquotable, adj. [1. unkwótabl; 2. ankwóutəbl]. **un- (I.)** & **quotable.** Not quotable; not suitable for quotation; unfit to be quoted or repeated.

unquoted, adj. [1. unkwóted; 2. ankwóutid]. **un- (I.)** & **quote(d).** Not quoted.

unransomed, adj. [1. unránsumd; 2. anrǽnsəmd]. **un- (I.)** & **ransom(ed).** Not ransomed.

unrated, adj. [1. unráted; 2. anréitid]. **un- (I.)** & **rate(d).** Not rated. **1.** Not subject to a local or other rate. **2.** Not included in a rate or class.

unravaged, adj. [1. unrávijd; 2. anrǽvidžd]. **un- (I.)** & **ravage(d).** Not ravaged; not plundered or devastated.

unravel, vb. trans. [1. unrávl; 2. anrǽvl]. **un- (II.)** & **ravel.** **1.** To disentangle, separate (what is ravelled or tangled together): *to unravel a skein of wool, the threads of a tangled skein* &c. **2.** (fig.) To clear up, to solve (a mystery &c.): *to unravel a plot (of story* &c.).

unreachable, adj. [1. unréchabl; 2. anrítʃəbl]. **un- (I.)** & **reachable.** Not reachable; not to be reached; unattainable.

unread, adj. [1. unréd; 2. anréd]. **un- (I.)** & P.P. of **read.** Not read; **a** (of books) not perused; **b** (of persons) not well read; not scholarly; unlearned; illiterate.

unreadable, adj. [1. unrédabl; 2. anrídəbl]. **un- (I.)** & **readable.** Not readable. **1.** Illegible: *unreadable handwriting.* **2.** (of book, style &c.) Not attractive to read; impossible, difficult, to read without boredom; dull, uninteresting. **3.** Not fit to be read.

unreadily, adv. [1. unrédili; 2. anrédili]. **unready** & **-ly.** In an unready manner; without readiness or promptitude.

unreadiness, n. [1. unrédines; 2. anrédinis]. See next word & **-ness.** State, quality, of being unready.

unready, adj. [1. unrédi; 2. anrédi]. **un- (I.)** & **ready.** Not ready. **1.** Not prepared. **2.** Not quick in mental reactions; not prompt, slow, lacking alertness of mind.

unreal, adj. [1. unréal; 2. anríəl]. **un- (I.)** & **real.** Not real; not based on reality; imagined, visionary, unsubstantial.

unreality, n. [1. ùnreáliti; 2. ànriǽliti]. Prec. & **-ity.** State of being unreal; want of reality.

unrealizable, adj. [1. ùnrealízabl, unréalizabl; 2. ànriəláizəbl, anríəlaizəbl]. **un- (I.)** & **realizable.** Incapable of being realized; illusory.

unrealized, adj. [1. unréalizd; 2. anríəlaizd]. **un- (I.)** & **realize(d).** Not realized; unfulfilled.

unreally, adv. [1. unréali; 2. anríəli]. **unreal** & **-ly.** In an unreal manner.

unreason, n. [1. unrézn; 2. anrízn]. **un- (I.)** & **reason.** Lack of reason; stupidity, folly, absurdity.

unreasonable, adj. [1. unrézunabl; 2. anríznəbl]. **un- (I.)** & **reasonable.** Not reasonable. **1.** Not animated by, amenable to, reason; acting on impulse, without taking full account of circumstances and conditions; making extravagant claims; capricious; expecting more than can reasonably be looked for: *an unreasonable person.* **2.** Not governed by reason: *unreasonable conduct.* **3.** Beyond, overstepping the bounds of, what is reasonable; immoderate: *an unreasonable claim, demand*; specif. (of price, charge &c.) too high, exorbitant.

unreasonableness, n. Prec. & **-ness.** Quality of being unreasonable.

unreasonably, adv. See prec. & **-ly.** In an unreasonable manner; to an unreasonable extent.

unreasoning, adj. [1. unrézuning; 2. anrízəniŋ]. **un- (I.)** & **reasoning.** Not reasoning, not using reason, not guided by reason; irrational; unreasonable; *the unreasoning multitude; an unreasoning hatred.*

unreasoningly, adv. Prec. & **-ly.** In an unreasoning manner.

unrebuked, adj. [1. ùnrebúkt; 2. ànribjúkt]. **un- (I.)** & **rebuke(d).** Not rebuked; without incurring, or receiving, rebuke; unchecked by rebuke.

unrecallable, adj. [1. ùnrekáwlabl; 2. ànrikɔ́ləbl]. **un- (I.)** & **recallable.** Not recallable.

unrecalled, adj. [1. ùnrekáwld; 2. ànrikɔ́ld]. **un- (I.)** & **recall(ed).** Not recalled.

unreceipted, adj. [1. ùnresḗted ; 2. ànrisítid]. **un- (I.)** & **receipt(ed)**. Not receipted.

unreceivable, adj. [1. ùnresḗvabl ; 2. ànrisívəbl]. **un- (I.)** & **receivable**. Not receivable.

unreceived, adj. [1. ùnresḗvd ; 2. ànrisívd]. **un- (I.)** & **receive(d)**. Not received.

unreciprocated, adj. [1. ùnresíprokā̀ted ; 2. ànrisíprəkèitid]. **un- (I.)** & **reciprocate(d)**. Not reciprocated.

unreckoned, adj. [1. unrékund ; 2. anrékənd]. **un- (I.)** & **reckon(ed)**. Not reckoned ; not included in a reckoning or estimate.

unreclaimed, adj. [1. ùnreklā́md ; 2. ànrikléimd]. **un- (I.)** & **reclaim(ed)**. Not reclaimed (in material and moral senses), cp. *irreclaimable.*

unrecognizable, adj. [1. unrékognīzabl ; 2. anrékəgnáizəbl]. **un- (I.)** & **recognizable**. Not recognizable.

unrecognized, adj. [1. unrékognīzd ; 2. anrékəgnáizd]. **un- (I.)** & **recognize(d)**. Not recognized ; not having received due recognition or reward : *humble, unrecognized merit.*

unrecompensed, adj. [1. unrékumpènst ; 2. anrékəmpènst]. **un- (I.)** & **recompense(d)**. Not recompensed ; without reward or recompense.

unreconciled, adj. [1. unrékunsīld ; 2. anrékənsáild]. **un- (I.)** & **reconcile(d)**. Not reconciled ; not reunited to friendship ; not made to agree.

unrecorded, adj. [1. ùnrekórded ; 2. ànrikɔ́did]. **un- (I.)** & **record(ed)**. Not recorded ; not placed on record ; not found in records.

unrectified, adj. [1. unréktifīd ; 2. anréktifaid]. **un- (I.)** & P.P. of **rectify**. Not rectified. **1.** Not put right or corrected. **2.** (chem.) Not purified or refined.

unredeemable, adj. [1. ùnredḗmabl ; 2. ànridíməbl]. **un- (I.)** & **redeemable**. Not redeemable, cp. *irredeemable.*

unredeemed, adj. [1. ùnredḗmd ; 2. ànridímd]. **un- (I.)** & **redeem(ed)**. Not redeemed. **1.** Not fulfilled or carried out : *unredeemed promises.* **2.** Not taken out of pawn, by payment of sum advanced, with interest : *sale of unredeemed pledges.* **3.** Having no redeeming quality ; unmitigated : *a stupid, pretentious play unredeemed by the saving quality of humour.* **4.** Not recovered, of areas of country lost to a foreign State : *unredeemed Italy*, cp. *irredentist.* **5.** Not recalled by payment of value : *an unredeemed bill of exchange.*

unredressed, adj. [1. ùnredrést ; 2. ànridrést]. **un- (I.)** & **redress(ed)**. Not redressed.

unreel, vb. trans. & intrans. [1. unrḗl ; 2. anríəl]. **un- (II.)** & **reel (II.)**. To unwind, become unwound, from a reel.

unrefined, adj. [1. ùnrefīnd ; 2. ànrifáind]. **un- (I.)** & **refine(d)**. Not refined. **1.** Not purified or clarified : *unrefined sugar* &c. **2.** Having no refinement ; unpolished, coarse, vulgar : *unrefined manners, society.*

unreflecting, adj. [1. ùnreflékting ; 2. ànrifléktiŋ]. **un- (I.)** & **reflect(ing)**. **1.** Not reflecting light. **2.** Not using the mind in reflection ; unthinking, thoughtless.

unreflectingly, adv. Prec. & **-ly**. In an unreflecting manner ; without reflection.

unreformable, adj. [1. ùnrefórmabl ; 2. ànrifɔ́məbl]. **un- (I.)** & **reform** & **-able**. Not reformable.

unreformed, adj. [1. ùnrefórmd ; 2. ànrifɔ́md]. **un- (I.)** & **reform(ed)**. Not reformed.

unrefuted, adj. [1. ùnrefū́ted ; 2. ànrifjū́tid]. **un- (I.)** & **refute(d)**. Not refuted ; not disproved.

unregarded, adj. [1. ùnregárded ; 2. ànrigā́did]. **un- (I.)** & **regard(ed)**. Not regarded ; disregarded ; neglected.

unregeneracy, n. [1. ùnrejénerasi ; 2. ànridžénərəsi]. **un- (I.)** & **regeneracy**. State of being unregenerate.

unregenerate, adj. [1. ùnrejénerat ; 2. ànridžénərit]. **un- (I.)** & **regenerate**. Not regenerate ; esp. (theol.) not reconciled to God through regeneration.

unregistered, adj. [1. unréjisterd ; 2. anrédžistəd]. **un- (I.)** & **register(ed)**. Not registered.

unregretted, adj. [1. ùnregréted ; 2. ànrigrétid]. **un- (I.)** & **regret(ted)**. Not regretted ; unlamented.

unregulate(d), adj. [1. unrégulāt(ed) ; 2. anrégjuleit(id)]. **un- (I.)** & **regulate(d)**. Not regulated ; undisciplined.

unrehearsed, adj. [1. ùnrehérst ; 2. ànrihə́st]. **un- (I.)** & **rehearse(d)**. Not rehearsed ; occurring spontaneously, and without design ; unpremeditated : *an unrehearsed effect.*

unrein, vb. trans. [1. unrā́n ; 2. anréin]. **un- (II.)** & **rein**. To unloose the reins of ; to give the rein to, release (esp. fig.).

unreined, adj. [1. unrā́nd ; 2. anréind]. **un- (I.)** & **rein(ed)**. Not reined in ; unrestrained, unbridled : *unreined passions.*

unrelated, adj. [1. ùnrelā́ted ; 2. ànriléitid]. **un- (I.)** & **relate(d)**. Not related.

unrelenting, adj. [1. ùnrelénting ; 2. ànriléntiŋ]. **un- (I.)** & **relent** & **-ing**. Not relenting ; relentless ; inflexible ; merciless.

unrelentingly, adv. Prec. & **-ly**. In an unrelenting manner.

unreliability, n. [1. ùnrelīabíliti ; 2. ànrilàiəbíliti]. **un- (I.)** & **reliability**. State of being unreliable.

unreliable, adj. [1. ùnrelíabl ; 2. ànriláiəbl]. **un- (I.)** & **reliable**. Not reliable, not to be relied on ; untrustworthy.

unreliably, adv. Prec. & **-ly**. In an unreliable manner.

unrelieved, adj. [1. ùnrelḗvd ; 2. ànrilívd]. **un- (I.)** & **relieve(d)**. Not relieved.

unreligious, adj. [1. ùnrelíjus ; 2. ànrilídžəs]. **un- (I.)** & **religious**. Not concerned or connected with religion ; not involving, or involved in, religious ideas or questions ; nonreligious ; cp. *irreligious.*

unremembered, adj. [1. ùnremémberd ; 2. ànrimémbəd]. **un- (I.)** & **remember(ed)**. Not remembered ; forgotten.

unremitting, adj. [1. ùnremíting ; 2. ànrimítiŋ]. **un- (I.)** & **remit(ting)**. Without remission ; unceasing, incessant ; not relaxing effort ; persistent, persevering : *unremitting toil, energy.*

unremittingly, adv. Prec. & **-ly**. In an unremitting manner ; unceasingly.

unremunerative, adj. [1. ùnremū́nerativ ; 2. ànrimjū́nərətiv]. **un- (I.)** & **remunerative**. Not remunerative ; unprofitable.

unrenewed, adj. [1. ùnrenū́d ; 2. ànrinjū́d]. **un- (I.)** & **renew(ed)**. Not renewed.

unrenounced, adj. [1. ùnrenóunst ; 2. ànrináunst]. **un- (I.)** & **renounce(d)**. Not renounced.

unrenovated, adj. [1. unrénovāted ; 2. anrénəveitid]. **un- (I.)** & **renovate(d)**. Not renovated.

unrepair, n. [1. ùnrepā́r ; 2. ànripéə]. **un- (I.)** & **repair**. State of disrepair, dilapidation.

unrepealed, adj. [1. ùnrepḗld ; 2. ànripíəld]. **un- (I.)** & **repeal(ed)**. Not repealed.

unrepentance, n. [1. ùnrepéntans ; 2. ànripéntəns]. **un- (I.)** & **repentance**. Lack of repentance ; state of being unrepentant ; impenitence.

unrepentant, adj. [1. ùnrepéntant ; 2. ànripéntənt]. **un- (I.)** & **repentant**. Not repentant ; showing no repentance ; impenitent.

unrepentantly, adv. Prec. & **-ly**. Without repentance ; impenitently.

unrepining, adj. [1. ùnrepīning ; 2. ànripáiniŋ]. **un- (I.)** & **repine** & **-ing**. Not repining ; uncomplaining.

unrepiningly, adv. Prec. & **-ly**. In an unrepining manner, without complaint.

unreported, adj. [1. ùnrepórted ; 2. ànripɔ́tid]. **un- (I.)** & **report(ed)**. Not reported ; specif., not to be found in the legal or parliamentary reports.

unrepresentative, adj. [1. unrèprezéntativ ; 2. anrèprizéntətiv]. **un- (I.)** & **representative**. Not representative.

unrepresented, adj. [1. unrèprezénted ; 2. anrèprizéntid]. **un- (I.)** & **represent(ed)**. Not represented.

unreprieved, adj. [1. ùnreprḗvd ; 2. ànriprívd]. **un- (I.)** & **reprieve(d)**. Not reprieved.

unreproachful, adj. [1. ùnreprṓchfl ; 2. ànripróutʃfl]. **un- (I.)** & **reproachful**. Not reproachful.

unreproved, adj. [1. ùnreprōōvd ; 2. ànriprū́vd]. **un- (I.)** & **reprove(d)**. Not reproved ; without incurring, unchecked by, reproof.

unrequisite, adj. [1. unrékwizit ; 2. anrékwizit]. **un- (I.)** & **requisite**. Not requisite ; unnecessary.

unrequited, adj. [1. ùnrekwīted ; 2. ànrikwáitid]. **un- (I.)** & **requite(d)**. Not requited ; **a** not returned or reciprocated : *unrequited affections* ; **b** not recompensed : *unrequited labours* ; **c** unavenged : *wickedness does not go altogether unrequited.*

unrescinded, adj. [1. ùnresínded ; 2. ànrisíndid]. **un- (I.)** & **rescind(ed)**. Not rescinded ; not revoked or cancelled.

unresented, adj. [1. ùnrezénted ; 2. ànrizéntid]. **un- (I.)** & **resent(ed)**. Not resented.

unresenting, adj. [1. ùnrezénting ; 2. ànrizéntiŋ]. **un- (I.)** & **resenting**. Not resenting ; not feeling or showing resentment.

unresentingly, adv. Prec. & **-ly**. In an unresenting manner ; without resentment.

unreserve, n. [1. ùnrezérv ; 2. ànrizə́v]. **un- (I.)** & **reserve (II.)**. Want of reserve in speech or behaviour.

unreserved, adj. [1. ùnrezérvd ; 2. ànrizə́vd]. **un- (I.)** & **reserve(d)**. Not reserved. **1.** Free from reserve in speech, manner, character ; **a** frank, open ; **b** not possessing or showing proper restraint and decorum. **2.** Free from reservations, restrictions, or qualifications ; unrestricted, unqualified : *in unreserved agreement.* **3.** Not allotted or booked in advance, not kept for specific persons or purposes : *unreserved seats*, at theatre &c.

unreservedly, adv. [1. ùnrezérvedli ; 2. ànrizə́vidli]. Prec. & **-ly**. In an unreserved manner ; without reserve or reservations.

unreservedness, n. [1. ùnrezérv(e)dnes ; 2. ànrizə́v(i)dnis]. See prec. & **-ness**. State, quality, of being unreserved in speech, manner &c.

unresisted, adj. [1. ùnrezísted ; 2. ànrizístid]. **un- (I.)** & **resist(ed)**. Not resisted ; unopposed.

unresisting, adj. [1. ùnrezísting ; 2. ànrizístiŋ]. **un- (I.)** & **resist(ing)**. Not resisting, not offering resistance ; yielding.

unresistingly, adv. Prec. & **-ly**. Without resistance.

unresolved, adj. [1. ùnrezólvd ; 2. ànrizɔ́lvd]. **un- (I.)** & **resolve(d)**. Not resolved. **1. a** Lacking resolution ; irresolute, undecided ; **b** not having made a decision ; uncertain. **2. a** Not separated or analysed into its component (material) parts or elements ; **b** not analysed, disentangled, or made clear in, or to, the mind ; unsolved, not cleared up : *an unresolved mystery* ; *my doubts are still unresolved.*

unrespected, adj. [1. ùnrespékted ; 2. ànrispéktid]. **un- (I.)** & **respect(ed)**. Not respected ; despised : *an unrespected old age.*

unresponsive, adj. [1. ùnrespónsiv ; 2. ànrispɔ́nsiv]. **un- (I.)** & **responsive**. Not responsive, not reacting easily or readily to a physical, intellectual, or emotional stimulus ; not impressionable ; not readily accessible to an emotional or intellectual appeal.

unresponsively, adv. Prec. & **-ly**. In an unresponsive manner.

unresponsiveness, n. See prec. & **-ness**. State of being unresponsive.

unrest, n. [1. unrést ; 2. anrést]. **un- (I.)** & **rest (I.)**. Restlessness, disquiet ; **a** state of disturbance or agitation ; esp. *political, industrial, unrest* ; **b** anxious, disturbed state of mind.

unrestful, adj. [1. unréstfl ; 2. anréstfl]. **un- (I.)** & **restful**. Not restful ; **a** not conducive to peace of mind ; **b** restless, fidgety.

unrestfully, adv. Prec. & **-ly**. In an unrestful manner.

unrestfulness, n. See prec. & **-ness**. State of being unrestful.

unresting, adj. [1. unrésting; 2. anréstiŋ]. **un- (I.)** & **rest(ing)**. Not resting, taking no rest; untiring: *unresting activity, energy*.

unrestingly, adv. Prec. & **-ly**. In an unresting manner.

unrestrained, adj. [1. ùnrestrā́nd; 2. ànristréind]. **un- (I.)** & **restrain(ed)**. Not restrained; without restraint or control; uncontrolled; unreserved.

unrestrainedly, adv. [1. ùnrestrā́nedli; 2. ànristréinidli]. Prec. & **-ly**. In an unrestrained manner.

unrestraint, n. [1. ùnrestrā́nt; 2. ànristréint]. **un- (I.)** & **restraint**. Lack of restraint, lack of self-control.

unrestricted, adj. [1. ùnrestríkted; 2. ànristríktid]. **un- (I.)** & **restrict(ed)**. Not restricted; free from restrictions, limitations &c.

unretarded, adj. [1. ùnretárded; 2. ànritádid]. **un- (I.)** & **retard(ed)**. Not retarded; unhampered, undelayed.

unrevealed, adj. [1. ùnrevḗld; 2. ànrivíəld]. **un- (I.)** & **reveal(ed)**. Not revealed; hidden, secret; not divulged.

unrevenged, adj. [1. ùnrevénjd; 2. ànrivéndʒd]. **un- (I.)** & **revenge(d)**. Not revenged; unavenged.

unrevised, adj. [1. ùnrevī́zd; 2. ànriváizd]. **un- (I.)** & **revise(d)**. Not revised.

unrevoked, adj. [1. ùnrevṓkt; 2. ànrivóukt]. **un- (I.)** & **revoke(d)**. Not revoked.

unrewarded, adj. [1. ùnrewórded; 2. ànriwɔ́did]. **un- (I.)** & **reward(ed)**. Not rewarded.

unrhetorical, adj. [1. ùnretórikl; 2. ànritɔ́rikl]. **un- (I.)** & **rhetorical**. Not rhetorical; free from false rhetoric; simple, straightforward, in style and expression.

unrhymed, adj., pred. [1. unrī́md; 2. anráimd]; attrib. [1. únrīmd; 2. ánraimd]. **un- (I.)** & **rhyme(d)**. Not rhymed; written without rhymes.

unrhythmical, adj. [1. unríthmikl; 2. anríþmikl]. **un- (I.)** & **rhythmical**. Not rhythmical.

unrhythmically, adv. Prec. & **-ly**. Without rhythm.

unridable, adj. [1. unrī́dabl; 2. anráidəbl]. **un- (I.)** & **ridable**. Not ridable; incapable of being ridden.

unridden, adj. [1. unrídn; 2. anrídn]. **un- (I.)** & **ridden**. Not ridden.

unriddle, vb. trans. [1. unrídl; 2. anrídl]. **un- (II.)** & **riddle (II.)**. To solve the riddle of; to explain, interpret: *unriddle this mystery*.

unrifled, adj. [1. unrī́fld; 2. anráifld]. **un- (I.)** & **rifle(d)**. Not rifled; not plundered or robbed.

unrig, vb. trans. [1. unríg; 2. anríg]. **un- (II.)** & **rig (I.)**. To strip (ship &c.) of rig or rigging.

unrigged, adj. [1. unrígd; 2. anrígd]. **un- (I.)** & **rig(ged)**. (of ship) Not rigged; without rigging.

unrighteous, adj. [1. unrī́chus; 2. anráitʃəs]. **un- (I.)** & **righteous**. Reverse of *righteous*. **1.** Not pious; wicked, ungodly; Phr. *the unrighteous*, wicked people. **2.** Unjust, not in accordance with justice and equity: *an unrighteous judgement*.

unrighteously, adv. Prec. & **-ly**. In an unrighteous manner.

unrighteousness, n. See prec. & **-ness**. Wickedness, ungodliness.

unrip, vb. trans. [1. unríp; 2. anríp]. **un- (II.)** & **rip (I.)**. To rip open; to rip out stitches from.

unripe, adj. [1. unrī́p; 2. anráip]. **un- (I.)** & **ripe**. Not yet ripe; immature (lit. and fig.): *unripe fruit; an unripe mind; land unripe for development*.

unripeness, n. Prec. & **-ness**. State of being unripe; immaturity.

unrisen, adj. [1. unrízn; 2. anrizn]. **un- (I.)** & **rise(n)**. Not yet risen.

unrivalled, adj. [1. unrī́vld; 2. anráivld]. **un- (I.)** & **rival(led)**. Having no rival; unsurpassed, unequalled.

unrivet, vb. trans. [1. unrívet; 2. anrívit]. **un- (II.)** & **rivet**. To remove rivets from; to unfasten what is riveted.

unrobe, vb. trans. & intrans. [1. unrṓb; 2. anróub]. **un- (II.)** & **robe**. **a** trans. To take off (the), esp. official, robe(s) of; to disrobe, undress; **b** intrans., to take off one's own robes.

unroll, vb. trans. & intrans. [1. unrṓl; 2. anróul]. **un- (II.)** & **roll**. **a** trans. To roll back, open, what is rolled up; **b** intrans., to become unrolled; to unfold.

unromantic, adj. [1. ùnrōmántik; 2. ànroumǽntik]. **un- (I.)** & **romantic**. Not romantic; lacking in romance; commonplace, matter-of-fact.

unromantically, adv. [1. ùnrōmántikali; 2. ànroumǽntikəli]. Prec. & **-al** & **-ly**. In an unromantic manner.

unroof, vb. trans. [1. unro͞of; 2. anrū́f]. **un- (II.)** & **roof (II.)**. To take off, carry away, the roof of (house); to destroy the roof of.

unroofed, adj. [1. unro͞oft; 2. anrū́ft]. **un- (I.)** & **roof(ed)**. Not roofed; having lost its roof.

unroot, vb. trans. [1. unro͞ot; 2. anrū́t]. **un- (II.)** & **root (II.)**. To pull, tear, up by the root; to uproot; to eradicate.

unround, vb. trans. [1. unróund; 2. anráund]. **un- (II.)** & **round**, vb. (phon.) To pronounce (vowel) with lips drawn back to natural position, instead of being protruded: *the sound* [ȳ] *when unrounded becomes* [ī].

unroyal, adj. [1. unróial; 2. anrɔ́iəl]. **un- (I.)** & **royal**. Not royal; not like or not worthy of, not befitting, a king.

unroyally, adv. Prec. & **-ly**. In an unroyal manner.

unruffled, adj. [1. unrúfld; 2. anráfld]. **un- (I.)** & **ruffle(d)**. Not ruffled; not agitated or disturbed; calm, serene (lit. and fig.).

unruled, adj. [1. unro͞old; 2. anrū́ld]. **un- (I.)** & **rule(d)**. Not ruled. **1.** Not marked with lines or rulings. **2.** Not governed; uncontrolled.

unruliness, n. [1. unro͞olines; 2. anrū́linis]. See next word & **-ness**. State of being unruly.

unruly, adj. [1. unro͞oli; 2. anrū́li], fr. 15th cent.; fr. **un- (I.)**, **rule (I.)**, & **-ly**. Not obedient, or subservient, to rule or restraint; disorderly, ungovernable, disobedient, refractory.

unsaddle, vb. trans. & intrans. [1. unsádl; 2. ansǽdl]. **un- (II.)** & **saddle (II.)**. **a** trans. To take the saddle off (horse &c.); **b** intrans., to unsaddle one's horse.

unsafe, adj. [1. unsā́f; 2. anséif]. **un- (I.)** & **safe (I.)**. Not safe; dangerous.

unsafely, adv. Prec. & **-ly**. In an unsafe manner.

unsafeness, n. See prec. & **-ness**. State of being unsafe.

unsaid, adj. [1. unséd; 2. anséd]. **un- (I.)** & **said**. Not said; unspoken: *things better left unsaid*.

unsaintly, adj. [1. unsā́ntli; 2. anséintli]. **un- (I.)** & **saintly**. Not saintly.

unsalability, n. [1. ùnsālabíliti; 2. ànseiləbíliti]. See next word & **-ity**. State of being unsalable.

unsalable, adj. [1. unsā́labl; 2. anséiləbl]. **un- (I.)** & **salable**. Not salable; that cannot be sold; unmarketable.

unsalaried, adj. [1. unsálarid; 2. ansǽlərid]. **un- (I.)** & **salaried**. Not salaried, not receiving a salary; unpaid, honorary.

unsanctified, adj. [1. unsángktifīd; 2. ansǽŋktifaid]. **un- (I.)** & **sanctified**. Not sanctified; unholy.

unsanctioned, adj. [1. unsángkshund; 2. ansǽŋkʃənd]. **un- (I.)** & **sanction(ed)**. Not sanctioned; unauthorized.

unsanitary, adj. [1. unsánitari; 2. ansǽnit(ə)ri]. **un- (I.)** & **sanitary**. Not sanitary; unhealthy; insanitary.

unsated, adj. [1. unsā́ted; 2. anséitid]. **un- (I.)** & **sate(d)**. Not sated; unsatisfied.

unsatisfactorily, adv. [1. unsàtisfáktorili; 2. ansæ̀tisfǽktərili]. **unsatisfactory** & **-ly**. In an unsatisfactory manner.

unsatisfactoriness, n. [1. unsàtisfáktorines; 2. ansæ̀tisfǽktərinis]. See prec. & **-ness**. State of being unsatisfactory.

unsatisfactory, adj. [1. unsàtisfáktori; 2. ansæ̀tisfǽktəri]. **un- (I.)** & **satisfactory**. Not satisfactory; giving no satisfaction.

unsatisfied, adj. [1. unsátisfīd; 2. ansǽtisfaid]. **un- (I.)** & **satisfy** & **-ed**. Not satisfied; unappeased.

unsatisfying, adj. [1. unsátisfīing; 2. ansǽtisfaiiŋ]. **un- (I.)** & **satisfying**. Not satisfying.

unsatisfyingly, adv. Prec. & **-ly**. In an unsatisfying manner.

unsaturated, adj. [1. unsáchurāted; 2. ansǽtʃəreitid]. **un- (I.)** & **saturate(d)**. Not saturated.

unsavourily, adv. [1. unsā́vurili; 2. anséivərili]. **unsavoury** & **-ly**. In an unsavoury manner.

unsavouriness, n. [1. unsā́vurines; 2. anséivərinis]. See next word & **-ness**. State of being unsavoury.

unsavoury, adj. [1. unsā́vuri; 2. anséivəri]. **un- (I.)** & **savoury**. Not savoury; uninviting, unattractive; unpleasant, disgusting.

unsay, vb. trans. [1. unsā́, únsā; 2. anséi, ánsei]. **un- (II.)** & **say**. To recall, retract (what has been said).

unscalable, adj. [1. unskā́labl; 2. anskéiləbl]. **un- (I.)** & **scalable**. Not scalable; not to be scaled; unclimbable.

unscale, vb. trans. [1. unskā́l; 2. anskéil]. **un- (II.)** & **scale**. To remove scales from (boilers &c.).

unscannable, adj. [1. unskánabl; 2. anskǽnəbl]. **un- (I.)** & **scannable**. (of verse) Not scannable; impossible to scan.

unscared, adj. [1. unskā́rd; 2. anskέəd]. **un- (I.)** & **scare(d)**. Not scared; not frightened.

unscarred, adj. [1. unskárd; 2. anskā́d]. **un- (I.)** & **scar(red)**. Not scarred; without a scar or wound.

unscathed, adj. [1. unskā́dhd; 2. anskéiðd]. **un- (I.)** & **scathe(d)**. Not scathed; physically or morally uninjured.

unscented, adj. [1. unsénted; 2. anséntid]. **un- (I.)** & **scent(ed)**. Not scented; having, yielding, no perfume: *an unscented rose*.

unscholarly, adj. [1. unskólarli; 2. anskɔ́ləli]. **un- (I.)** & **scholarly**. Not scholarly; **a** devoid of scholarship; **b** not done after the manner of a scholar.

unschooled, adj. [1. unsko͞old; 2. anskū́ld]. **un- (I.)** & **school(ed)**. Not schooled; not taught, not trained or disciplined; not experienced: *unschooled in deceit, in vice*.

unscientific, adj. [1. unsīentífik; 2. ansàiəntífik]. **un- (I.)** & **scientific**. Not scientific; not in accordance with scientific principles or methods.

unscientifically, adv. [1. unsīentífikali; 2. ansàiəntífikəli]. Prec. & **-al** & **-ly**. In an unscientific manner.

unscreened, adj. [1. unskrḗnd; 2. anskrínd]. **un- (I.)** & **screen(ed)**. Not screened. **1.** Not sheltered by a screen. **2.** Not passed through a screen or riddle; unsifted.

unscrew, vb. trans. & intrans. [1. unskro͞o; 2. anskrū́]. **un- (II.)** & **screw**. **1.** trans. **a** To remove, draw out screw(s) from: *to unscrew the lid of a coffin*; **b** to loosen and withdraw (screw) by turning it reverse way. **2.** intrans. **a** To become unscrewed; **b** to permit of being unscrewed: *the nut won't unscrew*.

unscriptural, adj. [1. unskrípchural; 2. anskríptʃərəl]. **un- (I.)** & **scriptural**. Not scriptural; not in conformity with or according to the Bible.

unscripturally, adv. Prec. & **-ly**. In an unscriptural manner.

unscrupulous, adj. [1. unskrōōpūlus; 2. anskrūpjuləs]. **un- (I.)** & **scrupulous.** Not scrupulous; without scruples or moral principles; unprincipled.

unscrupulously, adv. Prec. & **-ly.** In an unscrupulous manner.

unscrupulousness, n. See prec. & **-ness.** State of being unscrupulous.

unseal, vb. trans. [1. unsēl; 2. ansíəl]. **un- (II.)** & **seal (IV.).** To break or remove the seal of, to open that which is sealed, as a letter &c.

unsealed, adj. [1. unsēld; 2. ansíəld]. **a un- (I.), b un- (II.),** & see prec. **a** Not sealed up; not under seal; **b** having the seal broken or removed.

unseam, vb. trans. [1. unsēm; 2. ansím]. **un- (II.)** & **seam.** To cut, rip open, the seams of.

unsearchable, adj. [1. unsěrchabl; 2. ansə́tʃəbl]. **un- (I.)** & **searchable.** Not to be discovered or found out by searching; mysterious; inscrutable.

unseasonable, adj. [1. unsēzonabl; 2. ansízənəbl]. **un- (I.)** & **seasonable.** Not seasonable; **a** occurring out of its proper or normal season of the year, unusual for the season: *unseasonable weather, heat* &c.; **b** done, said, at the wrong time, ill-timed, untimely; inopportune: *unseasonable humour.*

unseasonableness, n. See prec. & **-ness.** State of being unseasonable.

unseasonably, adv. Prec. & **-ly.** In an unseasonable manner.

unseasoned, adj. [1. unsēznd; 2. ansízn̩d]. **un- (I.)** & **season(ed).** Not seasoned. **1.** Without seasoning or flavouring. **2.** Not matured or ripened.

unseat, vb. trans. [1. unsēt; 2. ansít]. **un- (II.)** & **seat. 1.** To displace (rider) from his seat on horseback; to throw. **2.** To remove from, dispossess of, a seat in Parliament, either by votes at an election, or by a decision in court that election was invalid.

unseated, adj. [1. unsēted; 2. ansítid]. **un- (I.)** & **seat(ed).** Not provided or furnished with a seat or seats.

unseaworthiness, n. [1. unsēwěrdhines; 2. ansíwāðinis]. See next word & **-ness.** State of being unseaworthy.

unseaworthy, adj. [1. unsēwěrdhi; 2. ansíwāði]. **un- (I.)** & **seaworthy.** Not seaworthy; not in fit condition to undertake a sea voyage.

unseconded, adj. [1. unsékonded; 2. ansékəndid]. **un- (I.)** & **second(ed). 1.** Not seconded, helped, assisted. **2.** (of a motion) Not seconded when proposed. **3.** Not provided with, supported by, a second at a duel.

unsectarian, adj. [1. ùnsektárian; 2. ànsektéəriən]. **un- (I.)** & **sectarian.** Not sectarian; **a** free from the prejudices and narrowness of religious sects; **b** not in accordance with the tenets of any specific sect.

unsectarianism, n. [1. ùnsektárianizm; 2. ànsektéəriənizəm]. Prec. & **-ism.** Freedom from sectarian prejudices.

unsecured, adj. [1. ùnsekūrd; 2. ànsikjɔ́d]. **un- (I.)** & **secure(d).** Not secured; (esp. of debts and creditors) not covered by assets &c.

unseductive, adj. [1. ùnsedúktiv; 2. ànsidáktiv]. **un- (I.)** & **seductive.** Not seductive.

unseeing, adj. [1. unsēing; 2. ansí-iŋ]. **un- (I.)** & **seeing.** Not seeing; unobservant; blind; unsuspecting.

unseemliness, n. [1. unsēmlines; 2. ansímlinis]. See next word & **-ness.** State of being unseemly.

unseemly, adj. [1. unsēmli; 2. ansímli]. **un- (I.)** & **seemly.** Not seemly; not becoming or befitting; improper, indecent.

unseen, adj. & n. [1. unsēn; 2. ansín]. **un- (I.)** & **seen,** see **see (I.). 1.** Not seen; not visible: *unseen dangers*; *the unseen,* what is unseen, the invisible, spiritual world. **2. a** Only in *unseen translation, passage,* translation of unprepared passages in a foreign tongue, ancient or modern; **b** *an unseen,* a passage set for translation in an examination, without previous preparation; an unseen passage.

unseizable, adj. [1. unsēzabl; 2. ansízəbl]. **un- (I.)** & **seizable.** Not to be seized.

unseldom, adv. [1. unséldum; 2. anséldəm]. **un- (I.)** & **seldom.** (rare) Not seldom; often.

unselected, adj. [1. ùnselékted; 2. ànsiléktid]. **un- (I.)** & **select(ed).** Not selected.

unselfish, adj. [1. unsélfish; 2. ansélfiʃ]. **un- (I.)** & **selfish.** Not selfish; thinking of others rather than of oneself; altruistic.

unselfishly, adv. Prec. & **-ly.** In an unselfish manner.

unselfishness, n. See prec. & **-ness. a** State, quality, of being unselfish; **b** unselfish actions.

unsensational, adj. [1. ùnsensáshunal; 2. ànsenséiʃənəl]. **un- (I.)** & **sensational.** Not sensational; not causing or likely to cause a sensation.

unsensationally, adv. Prec. & **-ly.** In an unsensational manner.

unsent, adj. [1. unsént; 2. ansént]. **un- (I.)** & **sent.** Not sent.

unsentimental, adj. [1. ùnsentiméntl; 2. ànsentiméntl]. **un- (I.)** & **sentimental.** Not sentimental.

unseparated, adj. [1. unséparàted; 2. ansépərèitid]. **un- (I.)** & **separate(d).** Not separated; undivided.

unserviceable, adj. [1. unsěrvisabl; 2. ansə́visəbl]. **un- (I.)** & **serviceable.** Not serviceable; unfit for use.

unserviceably, adv. Prec. & **-ly.** In an unserviceable manner.

unset (I.), vb. trans. [1. unsét; 2. ansét]. **un- (II.)** & **set (I.).** To undo the setting of; to remove (jewel &c.) from its setting.

unset (II.), adj., attrib. [1. únset; 2. ánset]; pred. [1. unsét; 2. ansét]. **un- (I.)** & P.P. of **set (I.).** Not set (in various senses of the verb): *unset limb, jewel* &c.

unsettle, vb. trans. [1. unsétl; 2. ansétl]. **un- (II.)** & **settle (II.). 1.** To change from a fixed or settled position or state. **2.** To disturb in mind, feelings &c.; to disarrange; to throw into a state of unrest, agitation &c.; to render unsettled: *to unsettle a person's opinions, affections* &c.; *to unsettle a boy at school.*

unsettled, adj. [1. unsétld; 2. ansétld]. **un- (I.)** & **settle(d).** Not settled (in various senses); **a** changeable, unstable: *unsettled weather*; **b** unpaid: *unsettled claims, debts*; **c** unallocated, not allotted; not subject to a deed of settlement: *an unsettled estate*; *unsettled lands* &c.

unsettling, adj. [1. unsétling; 2. ansétliŋ]. **unsettle** & **-ing.** Disturbing: *unsettling news.*

unsevered, adj. [1. unséverd; 2. ansévəd]. **un- (I.)** & **sever(ed).** Not severed.

unsex, vb. trans. [1. unséks; 2. anséks]. **un- (II.)** & **sex.** To deprive of sex; esp. to deprive (woman) of her feminine qualities; commonly in P.P. as adj. *unsexed.*

unshackle, vb. trans. [1. unshákl; 2. anʃǽkl]. **un- (II.)** & **shackle.** To loose, unfasten, the shackles of; to free from shackles.

unshackled, adj. [1. unshákld; 2. anʃǽkld]. **un- (I.)** & **shackle(d).** Not shackled (esp. in fig. sense); unrestrained: *unshackled by conventions, conscientious scruples* &c.

unshaded, adj. [1. unshāded; 2. anʃéidid]. **un- (I.)** & **shade(d).** Not shaded; free from shade; not showing differences of light and shade, esp. of a drawing &c.

unshadowed, adj. [1. unshádōd; 2. anʃǽdoud]. **un- (I.)** & **shadow(ed).** Not shadowed, not overcast by shadow; (esp. fig.) not darkened, not rendered sad and gloomy: *a life unshadowed by any calamity.*

unshakable, adj. [1. unshākabl; 2. anʃéikəbl]. **un- (I.)** & **shakable.** (esp. fig.) Not shakable; not to be shaken or upset; firmly established: *unshakable loyalty.*

unshaken, adj. [1. unshāken; 2. anʃéik(ə)n]. **un- (I.)** & **shake(n).** Not shaken; (esp. fig.) firm, steady, unwavering: *unshaken courage, resolution* &c.

unshapeliness, n. [1. unshāplines; 2. anʃéiplinis]. See next word & **-ness.** State of being unshapely.

unshapely, adj. [1. unshāpli; 2. anʃéipli]. **un- (I.)** & **shapely.** Not shapely; ill-formed, ill-proportioned; misshapen.

unshaven, adj. [1. unshāven; 2. anʃéivən]. **un- (I.)** & **shave(n).** Not shaven; **a** not newly shaven; **b** wearing a beard.

unsheathe, vb. trans. [1. unshēdh; 2. anʃíð]. **un- (II.)** & **sheathe.** To take out, draw (sword &c.); (fig.) *to unsheathe the sword,* to declare or begin war.

unshed, adj. [1. unshéd, únshed; 2. anʃéd, ánʃed]. **un- (I.)** & **shed (I.).** Not shed; esp. *unshed tears.*

unsheltered, adj. [1. unshélterd; 2. anʃéltəd]. **un- (I.)** & **shelter(ed).** Not sheltered; exposed, unprotected; specif., *unsheltered industries,* those which are subject to competition by imports of the same kind from foreign countries.

unship, vb. trans. [1. unshíp; 2. anʃíp]. **un- (II.)** & **ship (II.). a** To discharge, unload (cargo &c.), from a ship; **b** to disembark (passengers) from a ship; **c** to remove (oar) from rowlock, or (tiller) from place in a boat &c. where it is fixed or fitted.

unshod, adj. [1. unshód; 2. anʃɔ́d]. **un- (I.)** & **shod.** Not shod; barefoot.

unshoe, vb. trans. [1. unshōō; 2. anʃū]. **un- (II.)** & **shoe (I.).** To remove shoes from (horse &c.).

unshorn, adj. [1. unshórn; 2. anʃɔ́n]. **un- (I.)** & **shorn.** Not shorn; having the hair long and needing to be cut.

unshrinkable, adj. [1. unshríngkabl; 2. anʃríŋkəbl]. **un- (I.)** & **shrink** & **-able.** Not shrinkable; made so as not to shrink from wet (of flannel, cloth).

unshrinking, adj. [1. unshríngking; 2. anʃríŋkiŋ]. **un- (I.)** & **shrinking.** Not shrinking; undaunted; unhesitating, unflinching.

unshriven, adj. [1. unshrívn; 2. anʃrívn]. **un- (I.)** & **shrive(n).** Not shriven; not having confessed, done penance, and received absolution from a priest.

unshut, adj. [1. unshút, únshut; 2. anʃát, ánʃat]. **un- (I.)** & P.P. of **shut.** Not shut; wide open; not capable of shutting: '*great whales . . . with unshut eye*' (M. Arnold).

unshutter, vb. trans. [1. unshúter; 2. anʃátə]. **un- (II.)** & **shutter.** To remove, open, the shutters from windows of.

unsifted, adj. [1. unsífted; 2. ansíftid]. **un- (I.)** & **sift(ed).** Not sifted (lit. and fig.).

unsighted, adj. [1. unsíted; 2. ansáitid]. **un- (I.)** & **sight(ed).** Not sighted. **1.** Not seen, not brought within view. **2. a** (of gun &c.) Not provided with sights; **b** (of shot) aimed without use of sights.

unsightliness, n. See next word & **-ness.** State, quality, of being unsightly.

unsightly, adj. [1. unsítli; 2. ansáitli]. **un- (I.)** & **sightly.** Not sightly; displeasing to the sight; ugly.

unsigned, adj. [1. unsínd; 2. ansáind]. **un- (I.)** & **sign(ed).** Not signed; not identified by the signature of author &c.

unsinged, adj. [1. unsínjd; 2. ansíndžd]. **un- (I.)** & **singe(d).** Not singed.

unsisterly, adj. [1. unsísterli; 2. ansístəli]. **un- (I.)** & **sisterly.** Not sisterly, not behaving like a sister; unbecoming in, unworthy of, a sister.

unskilful, adj. [1. unskílfl; 2. anskílfl]. **un- (I.)** & **skilful.** Not skilful; wanting skill or dexterity; clumsy, awkward.

unskilfully, adv. Prec. & **-ly.** In an unskilful manner.

unskilfulness, n. See prec. & **-ness.** State of being unskilful.

unskilled, adj. [1. unskíld; 2. anskíld]. **un- (I.)** & **skill(ed).** Not skilled; not possessing or requiring special skill or training; specif. *unskilled labour,* manual labour which it requires little or no special skill or training to perform.

unslaked, adj. [1. unslākt; 2. ansléikt]. **un-** (I.) & **slake(d)**. Not slaked. **1.** (of thirst) Not satisfied; unassuaged. **2.** (of lime) Not mixed with water.

unsleeping, adj. [1. unslēping; 2. anslīpiŋ]. **un-** (I.) & **sleep(ing)**. Not sleeping, (usually fig.) tireless, alert, constantly watchful: *unsleeping vigilance.*

unsling, vb. trans. [1. unslíng; 2. anslíŋ]. **un-** (II.) & **sling** (I.). **a** To remove (an object, a rifle &c.) from the place where it has been slung; **b** (naut.) to release from slings, remove the slings from (cargo, yards &c.).

unsociability, n. [1. ùnsōshabíliti; 2. ànsouʃəbíliti]. See next word & **-ity**. State, quality, of being unsociable.

unsociable, adj. [1. unsóshabl; 2. ansóuʃəbl]. **un-** (I.) & **sociable**. Not sociable; disinclined, unsuited, to mix in society; reserved.

unsociably, adv. Prec. & **-ly**. In an unsociable manner.

unsocial, adj. [1. unsóshl; 2. ansóuʃl]. **un-** (I.) & **social**. Not social; not promoting, antagonistic to, the social relations of individuals or nations.

unsoiled, adj. [1. unsóild; 2. ansóild]. **un-** (I.) & **soil(ed)**. Not soiled;, clean.

unsolaced, adj. [1. unsólast; 2. ansólist]. **un-** (I.) & **solace(d)**. Not solaced; not comforted or relieved.

unsold, adj. [1. unsōld; 2. ansóuld]. **un-** (I.) & **sold**. Not sold; still on the market and open for sale.

unsolder, vb. trans. [1. unsóder, -sólder; 2. ansódə, -sóldə]. **un-** (II.) & **solder**. To remove solder from; to divide, separate (what has been soldered).

unsoldierly, adj. [1. unsōljerli; 2. ansóuldžəli]. **un-** (I.) & **soldierly**. Not soldierly; not like, not worthy of, unbecoming in, a soldier.

unsolicited, adj. [1. únsolísited; 2. ànsəlísitid]. **un-** (I.) & **solicit(ed)**. Not solicited; not asked or requested; gratuitous.

unsolvable, adj. [1. unsólvabl; 2. ansólvəbl]. **un-** (I.) & **solvable**. Not solvable; not to be solved; cp. *insoluble.*

unsolved, adj. [1. unsólvd; 2. ansólvd]. **un-** (I.) & **solve(d)**. Not solved.

unsophisticated, adj. [1. ùnsofístikàted; 2. ànsəfístikèitid]. **un-** (I.) & **sophisticate(d)**. Not sophisticated; **a** simple-minded, ingenuous, inexperienced, innocent; **b** not adulterated; pure, genuine.

unsophisticatedly, adv. Prec. & **-ly**. In an unsophisticated manner.

unsophisticatedness, n. See prec. & **-ness**. State of being unsophisticated.

unsought, adj. [1. unsáwt; 2. ansɔ́t]. **un-** (I.) & P.P. of **seek**. Not sought; not looked for; unasked, unsolicited.

unsound, adj. [1. únsóund; 2. ánsáund]. **un-** (I.) & **sound** (III.). Not sound (in various senses of the word), as **a** not in sound or healthy condition: *an unsound horse*; *to have an unsound heart*; Phr. *of unsound mind*, insane; **b** decayed, rotten: *unsound fruit, fish, timber*; **c** not based on sound reasoning; ill-founded, fallacious: *unsound arguments*; *a thoroughly unsound scheme* &c.

unsounded, adj. [1. unsóunded; 2. ansáundid]. **un-** (I.) & **sound(ed)**. Not sounded; unfathomed, unplumbed.

unsoundly, adv. [1. unsóundli; 2. ansáundli]. **unsound** & **-ly**. In an unsound manner.

unsoundness, n. [1. unsóundnes; 2. ansáundnis]. See prec. & **-ness**. State of being unsound.

unsown, adj. [1. unsṓn; 2. ansóun]. **un-** (I.) & **sow(n)**. Not sown.

unsparing, adj. [1. unspáring; 2. anspéəriŋ]. **un-** (I.) & **sparing**. Not sparing. **1.** Not showing mercy or forgiveness; hard, severe: *an unsparing taskmaster.* **2.** Not parsimonious; liberal, profuse, lavish: *unsparing kindness, generosity*; *unsparing in his offers of help* &c.

unsparingly, adv. Prec. & **-ly**. In an unsparing manner.

unsparingness, n. See prec. & **-ness**. State of being unsparing.

unspeakable, adj. [1. unspékabl; 2. anspíkəbl]. **un-** (I.) & **speak** & **-able**. Not capable of being uttered, expressed in words; indescribable, ineffable; **a** (in good sense) *unspeakable blessing, delight* &c.; **b** (in bad sense) too bad, horrible &c., to mention or describe: *unspeakable torments, misery*; (colloq.) *his manners are unspeakable.*

unspeakableness, n. Prec. & **-ness**. State of being unspeakable (chiefly in bad sense).

unspeakably, adv. See prec. & **-ly**. In an unspeakable manner; to an unspeakable degree.

unspecialized, adj. [1. unspéshalīzd; 2. anspéʃəlaizd]. **un-** (I.) & **specialize(d)**. Not specialized; specif. (biol., of organism, organ &c.) not specially modified or adapted for particular functions.

unspecified, adj. [1. unspésifīd; 2. anspésifaid]. **un-** (I.) & P.P. of **specify**. Not specified; not particularly indicated or stated.

unspeculative, adj. [1. unspékūlativ; 2. anspékjulətiv]. **un-** (I.) & **speculative**. Not speculative; not given to (mental) speculation.

unspent, adj. [1. unspént; 2. anspént]. **un-** (I.) & **spent**. Not spent; not tired, unexhausted.

unspilt, adj. [1. unspílt; 2. anspílt]. **un-** (I.) & P.P. of **spill** (I.). Not spilt.

unspiritual, adj. [1. unspírichooal; 2. anspíritʃuəl]. **un-** (I.) & **spiritual**. Not spiritual; wanting in spirituality; worldly, material.

unspirituality, n. [1. ùnspìrichooáliti; 2. ànspìritʃuǽliti]. Prec. & **-ity**. State, quality, of being unspiritual.

unspiritually, adv. [1. unspírichooali; 2. anspíritʃuəli]. See prec. & **-ly**. In an unspiritual manner.

unspoiled, unspoilt, adj. [1. unspóild, -spóilt; 2. anspóild, -spóilt]. **un-** (I.) & P.P. of **spoil**. Not spoiled; undamaged.

unspoken, adj. [1. unspṓken; 2. anspóukən]. **un-** (I.) & P.P. of **speak**. Not spoken; unuttered.

unspontaneous, adj. [1. ùnspontáneus; 2. ànspəntéiniəs]. **un-** (I.) & **spontaneous**. Not spontaneous; produced, or appearing to be produced, by deliberate effort; laboured, forced.

unspontaneously, adv. Prec. & **-ly**. In an unspontaneous manner.

unsporting, adj. [1. unspórting; 2. anspɔ́tiŋ]. **un-** (I.) & **sporting**. (colloq.) Not sporting; unsportsmanlike.

unsportsmanlike, adj. [1. unspórtsmanlīk; 2. anspɔ́tsmənlaik]. **un-** (I.) & **sportsmanlike**. Not sportsmanlike; not behaving according to, done in defiance of, the rules and principles of sportsmanship; unchivalrous.

unspotted, adj. [1. unspóted; 2. anspótid]. **un-** (I.) & **spot(ted)**. Not spotted; (esp. fig.) untainted with guilt, uncontaminated: *unspotted from the world*; immaculate: *unspotted honour.*

unstable, adj. [1. unstábl; 2. anstéibl]. **un-** (I.) & **stable** (I.). Not stable; **a** unsteady, easily upset; liable to shift, or be shifted, in position or direction; changeable; not firmly fixed; **b** (in moral sense) wavering, unreliable; inconstant; unbalanced.

unstained, adj. [1. unstánd; 2. anstéind]. **un-** (I.) & **stain(ed)**. Not stained; (esp. fig.) unblemished, untarnished, in character, reputation &c.

unstamped, adj. [1. unstámpt; 2. anstǽmpt]. **un-** (I.) & **stamp(ed)**. Not stamped; (of letters, documents &c.) without a stamp affixed.

unstarched, adj. [1. unstárcht; 2. anstátʃt]. **un-** (I.) & **starch(ed)**. Not starched; **a** not stiffened with starch; limp; **b** not stiff in manner and bearing &c.; easy, natural.

unstated, adj. [1. unstáted; 2. anstéitid]. **un-** (I.) & **state(d)**. Not stated; not expressed in definite terms.

unstatesmanlike, adj. [1. unstátsmanlīk; 2. anstéitsmənlaik]. **un-** (I.) & **statesmanlike**. Not statesmanlike.

unstatutable, adj. [1. unstátūtabl; 2. anstǽtjutəbl]. **un-** (I.) & **statutable**. Not statutable; not warranted by statute.

unsteadfast, adj. [1. unstédfast; 2. anstédfəst]. **un-** (I.) & **steadfast**. Not steadfast; wavering in courage &c., irresolute.

unsteadfastly, adv. Prec. & **-ly**. In an unsteadfast manner.

unsteadfastness, n. See prec. & **-ness**. Quality of being unsteadfast.

unsteadily, adv. [1. unstédili; 2. anstédili]. **unsteady** & **-ly**. In an unsteady manner.

unsteadiness, n. [1. unstédines; 2. anstédinis]. See prec. & **-ness**. State of being unsteady.

unsteady, adj. [1. unstédi; 2. anstédi]. **un-** (I.) & **steady**. Not steady. **1.** Shaky, unstable, not firm; easily upset or thrown down: *unsteady on one's feet*; *an unsteady post.* **2.** (in moral sense) **a** Variable, changeable, wavering, unreliable, not constant in character: *unsteady of purpose*; **b** not irreproachable in conduct; dissipated, profligate.

unstep, vb. trans. [1. unstép; 2. anstép]. **un-** (II.) & **step**. (naut.) To remove (mast) from step or socket.

unstick, vb. trans. [1. unstík; 2. anstík]. **un-** (II.) & **stick** (I.). To separate what is stuck together.

unstimulated, adj. [1. unstímūlàted; 2. anstímjulèitid]. **un-** (I.) & **stimulate(d)**. Not stimulated.

unstinted, adj. [1. unstínted; 2. anstíntid]. **un-** (I.) & **stint(ed)**. Not stinted; lavish.

unstipulated, adj. [1. unstípūlàted; 2. anstípjulèitid]. **un-** (I.) & **stipulate(d)**. Not stipulated.

unstitch, vb. trans. [1. unstích; 2. anstítʃ]. **un-** (II.) & **stitch** (II.). To undo what is stitched together; to remove stitches from.

unstocked, adj. [1. unstókt; 2. anstókt]. **un-** (I.) & **stock(ed)**. Not stocked, not provided with supplies: *an unstocked larder.*

unstop, vb. trans. [1. unstóp; 2. anstóp]. **un-** (II.) & **stop**. **a** To remove, take out, a stopper from; **b** to clear away a stoppage.

unstopped, adj. [1. unstópt; 2. anstópt]. **un-** (I.) & **stop(ped)**. Not stopped; specif. (phon.) **a** (of air-passage) not closed, partially open; **b** (of consonants) formed with the air-passage partially open.

unstrained, adj. [1. unstránd; 2. anstréind]. **un-** (I.) & **strain(ed)**. Not strained. **1.** Not passed through a strainer or filter. **2.** Not subjected to strain; unforced, easy, natural.

unstrap, vb. trans. [1. unstráp; 2. anstrǽp]. **un-** (II.) & **strap** (II.). To loosen, undo, the straps of; to remove straps from.

unstratified, adj. [1. unstrátifīd; 2. anstrǽtifaid]. **un-** (I.) & P.P. of **stratify**. (geol.) Not stratified.

unstressed, adj. [1. unstrést; 2. anstrést]. **un-** (I.) & **stress(ed)**. Not stressed; **a** not emphasized; **b** (of syllables or words in a sentence) not uttered with force or stress; not bearing the chief or any stress or accent.

unstring, vb. trans. [1. unstríng; 2. anstríŋ]. **un-** (II.) & **string** (II.). **1.** To loosen or remove the string or strings from (any stringed instrument). **2.** To remove from a string, to unthread: *to unstring a necklace of pearls.*

unstrung, adj. [1. unstrúng; 2. anstráŋ]. P.P. of prec. Relaxed, out of control, no longer subject to the will: *his nerves are all unstrung.*

unstudied, adj. [1. unstúdid; 2. anstádid]. **un-** (I.) & P.P. of **study** (II.). Not studied; attained without conscious art or effort; unpremeditated, spontaneous, easy, natural: *unstudied graces*; *an unstudied pose.*

unsubdued, adj. [1. ùnsubdúd; 2. ànsəbdjúd]. **un-** (I.) & **subdue(d)**. Not subdued; unconquered; unrepressed.

unsubmissive, adj. [1. ùnsubmísiv; 2. ànsəbmísiv]. **un-** (I.) & **submissive**. Not submissive, not readily yielding obedience; not subservient.

unsubmissively, adv. Prec. & **-ly**. In an unsubmissive manner.

unsubmissiveness, n. See prec. & **-ness**. State of being unsubmissive.

unsubstantial, adj. [1. ùnsubstánshl; 2. ànsəbstǽnʃl]. **un-** (**I.**) & **substantial**. Not substantial. **1.** (in physical sense) Lacking substance or solidity, not solid or heavy; light, flimsy: *an unsubstantial protection against the weather*; *an unsubstantial meal* &c. **2.** (in non-physical sense) Lacking reality or substance; unreal, visionary: *unsubstantial hopes, dreams, arguments* &c.

unsubstantiality, n. [1. ùnsubstànshiáliti; 2. ànsəbstænʃiǽliti]. Prec. & **-ity**. State of being unsubstantial.

unsubstantially, adv. [1. ùnsubstánshali; 2. ànsəbstǽnʃəli]. See prec. & **-ly**. In an unsubstantial manner.

unsubstantiated, adj. [1. ùnsubstánshiàted; 2. ànsəbstǽnʃièitid]. **un-** (**I.**) & **substantiate(d)**. Not substantiated, confirmed, or proved: *unsubstantiated evidence, report* &c.

unsuccess, n. [1. ùnsuksés; 2. ànsəksés]. **un-** (**I.**) & **success**. Want of success; failure.

unsuccessful, adj. [1. ùnsuksésfl; 2. ànsəksésfl]. **un-** (**I.**) & **successful**. Not successful; **a** meeting with failure, disappointment, or misfortune; missing success: *an unsuccessful man, business* &c.; **b** not producing the desired results: *unsuccessful efforts* &c.

unsuccessfully, adv. Prec. & **-ly**. In an unsuccessful manner; without success.

unsuitability, n. [1. ùnsūtabíliti; 2. ànsjūtəbíliti]. See next word & **-ity**. State of being unsuitable; unsuitableness.

unsuitable, adj. [1. unsū́tabl; 2. ansjū́təbl]. **un-** (**I.**) & **suitable**. Not suitable, not fitting or adapted for; not fulfilling requirements; unbecoming.

unsuitableness, n. Prec. & **-ness**. Unsuitability.

unsuitably, adv. See prec. & **-ly**. In an unsuitable manner.

unsuited, adj. [1. unsū́ted; 2. ansjū́tid]. **un-** (**I.**) & **suit(ed)**. Not suited, not fit or adapted, for; ill-matched, incompatible.

unsullied, adj. [1. unsúlid; 2. ansálid]. **un-** (**I.**) & P.P. of **sully**. Not sullied; unblemished, untarnished: *unsullied glory, reputation* &c.

unsummed, adj. [1. unsúmd; 2. ansámd]. **un-** (**I.**) & **sum(med)**. Not summed or counted.

unsummoned, adj. [1. unsúmund; 2. ansámənd]. **un-** (**I.**) & **summon(ed)**. Not summoned, not called upon to appear; uninvited.

unsung, adj. [1. unsúng; 2. ansáŋ]. **un-** (**I.**) & **sung**. Not sung; not celebrated in poetry: '*Unwept, unhonoured, and unsung*' (Scott, 'Last Minstrel', vi. 1).

unsunned, adj. [1. unsúnd; 2. ansánd]. **un-** (**I.**) & **sun(ned)**. Not warmed or lighted by the sun.

unsunny, adj. [1. unsúni; 2. ansáni]. **un-** (**I.**) & **sunny**. Not sunny; dark, gloomy.

unsupplied, adj. [1. ùnsuplíd; 2. ànsəpláid]. **un-** (**I.**) & P.P. of **supply**. Not supplied; not furnished (with).

unsupported, adj. [1. ùnsupórted; 2. ànsəpɔ̄tid]. **un-** (**I.**) & **support(ed)**. Not supported.

unsuppressed, adj. [1. ùnsuprést; 2. ànsəprést]. **un-** (**I.**) & **suppress(ed)**. Not suppressed.

unsure, adj. [1. unshṓr; 2. anʃɔ̄]. **un-** (**I.**) & **sure**. Not sure; **a** unsafe; insecure; **b** uncertain.

unsurmountable, adj. [1. ùnsurmóuntabl; 2. ànsəmáuntəbl]. **un-** (**I.**) & **surmountable**. Not surmountable; not to be surmounted or overcome; insuperable.

unsurmounted, adj. [1. ùnsurmóunted; 2. ànsəmáuntid]. **un-** (**I.**) & **surmount(ed)**. Not surmounted.

unsurpassable, adj. [1. ùnsurpáhsabl; 2. ànsəpā́səbl]. **un-** (**I.**) & **surpassable**. Not surpassable, not to be surpassed.

unsurpassably, adv. Prec. & **-ly**. In an unsurpassable manner.

unsurpassed, adj. [1. ùnsurpáhst; 2. ànsəpā́st]. **un-** (**I.**) & **surpass(ed)**. Not surpassed.

unsusceptible, adj. [1. ùnsuséptibl; 2. ànsəséptibl]. **un-** (**I.**) & **susceptible**. Not susceptible; insusceptible.

unsuspected, adj. [1. ùnsuspékted; 2. ànsəspéktid]. **un-** (**I.**) & **suspect(ed)**. Not suspected; not supposed or known to exist.

unsuspectedly, adv. Prec. & **-ly**. In an unsuspected manner.

unsuspecting, adj. [1. ùnsuspékting; 2. ànsəspéktiŋ]. **un-** (**I.**) & **suspect** & **-ing**. Not suspecting; having no suspicion.

unsuspectingly, adv. Prec. & **-ly**. In an unsuspecting manner.

unsuspicious, adj. [1. ùnsuspíshus; 2. ànsəspíʃəs]. **un-** (**I.**) & **suspicious**. Not suspicious; **a** without suspicion; **b** not arousing suspicion.

unsuspiciously, adv. Prec. & **-ly**. In an unsuspicious manner.

unsuspiciousness, n. See prec. & **-ness**. State of being unsuspicious.

unsustainable, adj. [1. ùnsustā́nabl; 2. ànsəstéinəbl]. **un-** (**I.**) & **sustainable**. Not sustainable, not to be sustained; not to be encouraged or upheld: *an unsustainable position, opinion* &c.

unsustained, adj. [1. ùnsustā́nd; 2. ànsəstéind]. **un-** (**I.**) & **sustain(ed)**. Not sustained; not upheld; unsupported.

unswathe, vb. trans. [1. unswā́dh; 2. answéið]. **un-** (**II.**) & **swathe**. To remove the swathings or bandages of.

unswayed, adj. [1. unswā́d; 2. answéid]. **un-** (**I.**) & **sway(ed)**. Not swayed or influenced (by); unbiassed, unprejudiced.

unswear, vb. trans. [1. unswā́r; 2. answéə]. **un-** (**II.**) & **swear**. To recant, recall, on oath (that which has been sworn); to abjure.

unsweetened, adj. [1. unswḗtnd; 2. answítnd]. **un-** (**I.**) & **sweeten(ed)**. Not sweetened.

unswerving, adj. [1. unswérving; 2. answə́viŋ]. **un-** (**I.**) & **swerve** & **-ing**. Not swerving, (esp. fig.) firm, constant, undeviating: *unswerving loyalty*.

unswervingly, adv. Prec. & **-ly**. In an unswerving manner; undeviatingly.

unsworn, adj. [1. unswórn; 2. answɔ́n]. **un-** (**I.**) & **sworn**. Not sworn; not put on oath.

unsymbolical, adj. [1. ùnsimbólikl; 2. ànsimbɔ́likl]. **un-** (**I.**) & **symbolical**. Not symbolical.

unsymmetrical, adj. [1. ùnsimétrikl; 2. ànsimétrikl]. **un-** (**I.**) & **symmetrical**. Not symmetrical.

unsymmetrically, adv. Prec. & **-ly**. Without symmetry.

unsympathetic, adj. [1. ùnsimpathétik; 2. ànsimpəþétik]. **un-** (**I.**) & **sympathetic**. Not sympathetic; **a** not showing sympathy with or to; hard, callous; **b** antipathetic.

unsympathetically, adv. [1. ùnsimpathétikali; 2. ànsimpəþétikəli]. Prec. & **-al** & **-ly**. In an unsympathetic manner.

unsystematic, adj. [1. ùnsistemátik; 2. ànsistimǽtik]. **un-** (**I.**) & **systematic**. Not systematic.

unsystematically, adv. [1. ùnsistemátikali; 2. ànsistimǽtikəli]. Prec. & **-al** & **-ly**. In an unsystematic manner; without system.

untack, vb. trans. [1. unták; 2. antǽk]. **un-** (**II.**) & **tack** (**II.**). To undo, unfasten (what is tacked together); to remove tacks from.

untactful, adj. [1. untáktfl; 2. antǽktfl]. **un-** (**I.**) & **tactful**. Not tactful; lacking tact; tactless.

untactfully, adv. Prec. & **-ly**. In an untactful manner.

untactfulness, n. See prec. & **-ness**. State of being untactful; want of tact.

untainted, adj. [1. untā́nted; 2. antéintid]. **un-** (**I.**) & **taint(ed)**. Not tainted; (esp. in fig. sense) without blemish or taint of guilt, shame &c.

untalented, adj. [1. untálented; 2. antǽləntid]. **un-** (**I.**) & **talent(ed)**. Not talented; without talents or talent.

untamable, adj. [1. untā́mabl; 2. antéiməbl]. **un-** (**I.**) & **tamable**. Not tamable.

untamableness, n. Prec. & **-ness**. State of being untamable.

untamably, adv. See prec. & **-ly**. In an untamable manner.

untamed, adj. [1. untā́md; 2. antéimd]. **un-** (**I.**) & **tame(d)**. Not tamed; **a** wild, undomesticated; **b** not subdued, controlled, disciplined: *untamed passions*.

untangle, vb. trans. [1. untánggl; 2. antǽŋgl]. **un-** (**II.**) & **tangle** (**II.**). To loose, free from a tangle; to unravel, disentangle.

untanned, adj. [1. untánd; 2. antǽnd]. **un-** (**I.**) & **tan(ned)**. Not tanned; **a** (of hides) not dressed; **b** (of human skin) not sunburnt.

untarnished, adj. [1. untárnisht; 2. antā́niʃt]. **un-** (**I.**) & **tarnish(ed)**. Not tarnished (lit. and fig.).

untasted, adj. [1. untā́sted; 2. antéistid]. **un-** (**I.**) & **taste(d)**. Not tasted; not yet enjoyed.

untaught, adj. [1. untáwt; 2. antɔ̄́t]. **un-** (**I.**) & **taught**. **1.** Not taught; uninstructed; illiterate, ignorant. **2.** Acquired without teaching: *those untaught graces of style*.

untaxed, adj. [1. untákst; 2. antǽkst]. **un-** (**I.**) & **tax(ed)**. Not taxed; free from, not liable to, taxation.

unteach, vb. trans. [1. untḗch; 2. antítʃ]. **un-** (**II.**) & **teach**. To cause to forget what has been taught; to teach the contrary of what has been learnt or a different method of learning.

unteachable, adj. [1. untḗchabl; 2. antítʃəbl]. **un-** (**I.**) & **teachable**. Not teachable; incapable of being taught.

unteachableness, n. Prec. & **-ness**. State of being unteachable.

untearable, adj. [1. untā́rabl; 2. antéərəbl]. **un-** (**I.**) & **tear** & **-able**. Not tearable; incapable of being torn.

untechnical, adj. [1. untéknikl; 2. antéknikl]. **un-** (**I.**) & **technical**. Not technical.

untemper, vb. trans. [1. untémper; 2. antémpə]. **un-** (**II.**) & **temper** (**I.**). To take away, remove, the temper of (metal).

untempered, adj. [1. untémperd; 2. antémpəd]. **un-** (**I.**) & **temper(ed)**. Not tempered; (esp. fig.) not modified or qualified: *untempered abuse, harshness*; *justice untempered with mercy*.

untenability, n. [1. ùntēnabíliti; 2. àntīnəbíliti]. See next word & **-ity**. State, quality, of being untenable.

untenable, adj. [1. untḗnabl; 2. antínəbl]. **un-** (**I.**) & **tenable**. Not tenable; not to be defended or maintained: *an untenable position* (lit. and fig.).

untenably, adv. Prec. & **-ly**. In an untenable state.

untenantable, adj. [1. unténantabl; 2. anténəntəbl]. **un-** (**I.**) & **tenantable**. Not tenantable; not fit to be let to or be occupied by a tenant.

untenanted, adj. [1. unténanted; 2. anténəntid]. **un-** (**I.**) & **tenant(ed)**. Not tenanted; unoccupied by a tenant; vacant.

untended, adj. [1. unténded; 2. anténdid]. **un-** (**I.**) & **tend(ed)**. Not tended; neglected, uncared for.

unterrified, adj. [1. untérifīd; 2. antérifaid]. **un-** (**I.**) & P.P. of **terrify**. Not terrified.

untested, adj. [1. untésted; 2. antéstid]. **un-** (**I.**) & **test(ed)**. Not tested; untried.

untether, vb. trans. [1. untédher; 2. antéðə]. **un-** (**II.**) & **tether**. To loose from a tether; to set free (what has been tethered).

unthanked, adj. [1. unthángkt; 2. anþǽŋkt]. **un-** (**I.**) & **thank(ed)**. Not thanked.

unthankful, adj. [1. unthángkfl; 2. anþǽŋkfl]. **un-** (**I.**) & **thankful**. Not thankful; ungrateful.

unthankfully, adv. Prec. & **-ly**. Without thanks or gratitude.

unthankfulness, n. See prec. & **-ness**. State of being unthankful; ingratitude.

unthink, vb. trans. [1. unthíngk; 2. anþíŋk]. **un-** (**II.**) & **think.** (rare) To dismiss from the thoughts; to change one's thoughts or mind about.

unthinkable, adj. [1. unthíngkabl; 2. anþíŋkəbl]. **un-** (**I.**) & **thinkable.** Not thinkable; not to be thought of; (colloq.) extremely improbable or unlikely.

unthinking, adj. [1. unthíngking; 2. anþíŋkiŋ]. **un-** (**I.**) & Pres. Part. of **think.** Not thinking; thoughtless, heedless, inconsiderate.

unthinkingly, adv. Prec. & **-ly.** In an unthinking manner; thoughtlessly.

unthought (**of**), adj. [1. untháwt (ov); 2. anþɔ̄t (ɔv)]. **un-** (**I.**) & **thought** (**II.**). Not thought of, having never entered one's thoughts; unimagined; highly improbable, quite unexpected.

unthoughtful, adj. [1. unthāwtfl; 2. anþɔ̄tfl]. **un-** (**I.**) & **thoughtful.** Not thoughtful; inconsiderate, heedless.

unthoughtfully, adv. Prec. & **-ly.** In an unthoughtful manner.

unthoughtfulness, n. See prec. & **-ness.** Lack of thoughtfulness; thoughtlessness, inconsiderateness.

unthread, vb. trans. [1. unthréd; 2. anþréd]. **un-** (**II.**) & **thread** (**II.**). To remove, take out, the thread or threads from; (also fig.) to find one's way through, or out of, to disentangle (a mystery &c.).

unthrift, n. [1. únthrift; 2. ánþrift]. **un-** (**I.**) & **thrift.** (archaic) Want, lack, of thrift; thriftlessness.

unthriftily, adv. [1. unthríftili; 2. anþríftili]. **unthrifty** & **-ly.** In an unthrifty manner.

unthriftiness, n. [1. unthríftines; 2. anþríftinis]. See prec. & **-ness.** State of being unthrifty, lack of thrift; extravagance, wastefulness.

unthrifty, adj. [1. unthríftì; 2. anþríftì]. **un-** (**I.**) & **thrifty.** Not thrifty; thriftless, extravagant, wasteful.

unthrone, vb. trans. [1. unthrṓn; 2. anþróun]. **un-** (**II.**) & **throne.** To remove from a throne; to dethrone, to depose (a king).

unthwarted, adj. [1. unthwórted; 2. anþwɔ̄tid]. **un-** (**I.**) & **thwart**(**ed**). Not thwarted, not frustrated or crossed in purpose.

untidily, adv. [1. untídili; 2. antáidili]. **untidy** & **-ly.** In an untidy manner.

untidiness, n. [1. untídines; 2. antáidinis]. See prec. & **-ness.** State of being untidy.

untidy, adj. [1. untídi; 2. antáidi]. **un-** (**I.**) & **tidy.** Not tidy; lacking neatness and order; disarranged, in confusion.

untie, vb. trans. [1. untí; 2. antái]. **un-** (**II.**) & **tie** (**II.**). To undo, unfasten, what is tied, as a package &c.; to undo knot in.

untied, adj. [1. untíd; 2. antáid]. **a** fr. **un-** (**I.**); **b** fr. **un-** (**II.**) & **tie**(**d**). **a** Not tied; **b** unfastened, loosed from tie.

until, prep. & conj. [1. untíl; 2. antíl]. In M.E.; variant of **unto**; see **un-** (**II.**) & **till** (**I.**). (of time) **1.** prep. Till, so far as, as late as, up to: *until his death*; *wait until four o'clock.* **2.** conj. Up to the time when: *wait here until I come*; *until he returns, nothing can be done.*

untiled, adj. [1. untíld; 2. antáild]. **un-** (**I.**) & **tile**(**d**). Not tiled. **1.** (of roofs &c.) Not covered with tiles. **2.** (freemasonry, of lodge) Not closed or guarded by the tiler.

untilled, adj. [1. untíld; 2. antíld]. **un-** (**I.**) & **till**(**ed**). Not tilled; uncultivated.

untimeliness, n. [1. untímlines; 2. antáimlinis]. Next word & **-ness.** State of being untimely.

untimely (**I.**), adj. [1. untímli; 2. antáimli]. **un-** (**I.**) & **timely.** **1.** Not occurring at the normal time; unseasonable; specif., occurring, done, before its time; too early; premature: *an untimely death.* **2.** Done, said, occurring, at an unsuitable time; inopportune: *an untimely remark.*

untimely (**II.**), adv. **a** Prematurely; **b** inopportunely.

untinctured, adj. [1. untíngkchurd; 2. antíŋktʃəd]. **un-** (**I.**) & **tincture**(**d**). Not tinctured; (usually fig.) unmixed with, unaffected by (some quality), without a flavour or taste of: *cruelty untinctured by remorse.*

untinged, adj. [1. untínjd; 2. antíndžd]. **un-** (**I.**) & **tinge**(**d**). Not tinged; not coloured or modified with (some quality).

untiring, adj. [1. untíring; 2. antáiəriŋ]. **un-** (**I.**) & **tiring.** Not tiring; unwearying, unflagging: *with untiring energy.*

untiringly, adv. Prec. & **-ly.** In an untiring manner.

untithed, adj. [1. untídhd; 2. antáiðd]. **un-** (**I.**) & **tithe**(**d**). Not tithed, not subject to tithe.

untitled, adj. [1. untítld; 2. antáitld]. **un-** (**I.**) & **title**(**d**). Not titled; having no title.

unto, prep. [1. úntoo; 2. ántu]. In M.E., fr. **und to*; *und-*, *un-*, 'as far as', as in **until**, cp. O. Fris. & O.S. *und*, 'until', & **to.** (archaic, Bib., and formal) To.

untold, adj. [1. úntṓld; 2. ántóuld]. **un-** (**I.**) & P.P. of **tell.** Not told. **1.** Not recounted or related; not revealed or communicated: *left the story, secret, untold.* **2.** Not counted, beyond counting: *untold wealth.*

untormented, adj. [1. ùntorménted; 2. àntɔ̄méntid]. **un-** (**I.**) & **torment**(**ed**). Not tormented.

untouchable, adj. [1. untúchabl; 2. antátʃəbl]. **un-** (**I.**) & **touchable.** Not touchable; not to be touched; specif., of the pariah or non-caste peoples of India; also as noun: *an untouchable*, a non-caste person.

untouched, adj. [1. untúcht; 2. antátʃt]. **un-** (**I.**) & **touch**(**ed**). Not touched.

untoward, adj. [1. untṓward; 2. antóuəd]. **un-** (**I.**) & **toward** (**I.**). (archaic) **a** Perverse, froward: '*this untoward generation*' (Acts ii. 40); **b** unlucky, inconvenient, awkward: *a most untoward event.*

untowardly, adv. Prec. & **-ly.** In an untoward manner.

untraceable, adj. [1. untrásabl; 2. antréisəbl]. **un-** (**I.**) & **traceable.** Not traceable, not to be traced; not to be found.

untrained, adj. [1. untránd; 2. antréind]. **un-** (**I.**) & **train**(**ed**). Not trained. **1.** Not disciplined in mind; not having received a training in the methods of some particular kind of intellectual work. **2.** Not trained or exercised in some form of physical activity; specif. **a** not trained for some form of athletic exercise; **b** not trained as a soldier in military exercises.

untrammelled, adj. [1. untrámld; 2. antrǽmld]. **un-** (**I.**) & **trammel**(**led**). Not trammelled; free from impediments or restrictions; unhampered.

untransferable, adj. [1. ùntrahnsférabl; 2. àntrānsfə́rəbl]. **un-** (**I.**) & **transferable.** Not transferable; not to be transferred.

untranslatability, n. [1. ùntrahnzlātabíliti; 2. àntrānzlèitəbíliti]. See next word & **-ity.** State, quality, of being untranslatable.

untranslatable, n. [1. ùntrahnzlátabl; 2. àntrānzléitəbl]. **un-** (**I.**) & **translatable.** Not translatable; unadapted to, incapable of, translation.

untranslated, adj. [1. ùntrahnzláted; 2. àntrānzléitid]. **un-** (**I.**) & **translate**(**d**). Not translated.

untravelled, adj. [1. untrávld; 2. antrǽvld]. **un-** (**I.**) & **travel**(**led**). Not travelled; **a** not having travelled; without experience of travel in foreign countries; **b** not traversed, untrodden, by travellers.

untraversed, adj. [1. untráverst; 2. antrǽvəst]. **un-** (**I.**) & **traverse**(**d**). Not traversed. **1.** Not passed over or crossed. **2.** Not denied or controverted.

untried, adj. [1. untríd; 2. antráid]. **un-** (**I.**) & P.P. of **try.** Not tried; not yet experienced; not having passed a preliminary trial.

untrodden, adj. [1. untródn; 2. antrɔ́dn]. **un-** (**I.**) & P.P. of **tread.** Not trodden on; unfrequented.

untroubled, adj. [1. untrúbld; 2. antrábld]. **un-** (**I.**) & **trouble** & **-ed.** Not troubled; **a** undisturbed in mind, unperturbed, unperplexed; **b** (in material sense) calm, unruffled, not stirred into movement: *the untroubled surface of a lake.*

untrue, adj. [1. untrōō; 2. antrū]. **un-** (**I.**) & **true.** Not true. **1. a** False, not in accordance with the truth or with facts; **b** unfaithful, disloyal. **2.** Not exactly conforming or corresponding to, not in agreement with, a particular standard, pattern, or measure: *untrue to type*; *the angles are untrue and out of the square.*

untruly, adv. [1. untrōōli; 2. antrūli]. Prec. & **-ly.** In an untrue manner.

untrustworthiness, n. [1. untrústwĕrdhines; 2. antrástwāðinis]. Next word & **-ness.** State, quality, of being untrustworthy.

untrustworthy, adj. [1. untrústwĕrdhi; 2. antrástwāði]. **un-** (**I.**) & **trustworthy.** Not trustworthy; not to be relied and depended on; shifty, undependable.

untruth, n. [1. untrōōth; 2. antrūþ]. **un-** (**I.**) & **truth.** **a** Quality of being untrue; falsity; lack of veracity: *marked by dissimulation and untruth*; *quick to discern the untruth in such rumours*; **b** an untrue statement, a falsehood, a lie: *never told an untruth in his life.*

untruthful, adj. [1. untrōōthfl; 2. antrūþfl]. **un-** (**I.**) & **truthful.** Not truthful; **a** given to saying what is untrue; not adhering to the truth in one's statements; apt to tell lies; **b** not in accordance with the truth; untrue, unveracious, lying: *an untruthful account, description.*

untruthfully, adv. Prec. & **-ly.** In an untruthful manner.

untruthfulness, n. See prec. & **-ness.** Quality of being untruthful; **a** habit, practice, of lying; **b** falsehood, absence of veracity (in a statement &c.).

untuck, vb. trans. [1. untúk; 2. anták]. **un-** (**II.**) & **tuck.** To undo, unfold, what is tucked up; to free, unfasten, tucks in.

untune, vb. trans. [1. untū́n; 2. antjū́n]. **un-** (**II.**) & **tune** (**II.**). To put out of tune, to make untuneful or discordant.

untuned, adj. [1. untū́nd; 2. antjū́nd]. **un-** (**I.**) & **tune**(**d**). Not tuned, not in tune.

untuneful, adj. [1. untū́nfl; 2. antjū́nfl]. **un-** (**I.**) & **tuneful.** Not tuneful; discordant.

untunefully, adv. Prec. & **-ly.** In an untuneful manner.

unturf, vb. trans. [1. untérf; 2. antə́f]. **un-** (**II.**) & **turf.** To remove the turf from.

unturned, adj. [1. untérnd; 2. antə́nd]. **un-** (**I.**) & **turn**(**ed**). Not turned (over); esp. in Phr. *leave no stone unturned*, use every effort, leave nothing undone or untried.

untutored, adj. [1. untū́tord; 2. antjū́təd]. **un-** (**I.**) & **tutor**(**ed**). Not tutored; not taught; uninstructed; hence, rude, barbarous, uncultivated.

untwine, vb. trans. & intrans. [1. untwín; 2. antwáin]. **un-** (**II.**) & **twine**, vb. **1.** trans. To unwind, loosen, undo, what is twined; to untwist. **2.** intrans. To become untwined.

untwist, vb. trans. & intrans. [1. untwíst; 2. antwíst]. **un-** (**II.**) & **twist** (**II.**). **1.** trans. To undo, loosen, what is twisted; to unravel, disentangle. **2.** intrans. To become untwisted.

unurged, adj. [1. unérjd; 2. anə́dzd]. **un-** (**I.**) & **urge**(**d**). Not urged.

unused, adj. **un-** (**I.**) & **use**(**d**). **1.** [1. unū́zd; 2. anjū́zd] Not used; not made use of, not in use: *an unused room.* **2.** [1. unū́st; 2. anjū́st] Unaccustomed to; unfamiliar with, inexperienced in, not habituated to: *unused to society, to foreign travel*; *quite unused to public speaking.*

unusual, adj. [1. unū́zhooal; 2. anjū́žuəl]. **un-** (**I.**) & **usual.** Not usual; uncommon, rare; unfamiliar, strange; exceptional, odd.

unusually, adv. Prec. & **-ly.** In an unusual manner; (colloq.) to a high degree, extremely: *an unusually nice person.*

unutilized, adj. [1. unū́tilīzd; 2. anjū́tilaizd]. **un-** (**I.**) & **utilize**(**d**). Not utilized; not made use of, not turned to account.

unutterable, adj. [1. unúterabl; 2. anátərəbl]. **un-** (**I.**) & **utterable.** Not to be uttered; **a** unspeakable, inexpressible, indescribable: *unutterable despair*; *in unutterable confusion*; **b** so bad as to be beyond description; indescribable; hence out-and-out, thoroughgoing: *an unutterable scoundrel.*

unutterably, adv. Prec. & **-ly.** In an unutterable manner.

unuttered, adj. [1. unúterd; 2. anátəd]. **un-** (**I.**) & **utter(ed).** Not uttered; existing in the mind but unspoken: *unuttered prayers.*

unvaccinated, adj. [1. unváksinàted; 2. anvǽksinèitid]. **un-** (**I.**) & **vaccinate(d).** Not vaccinated.

unvalued, adj. [1. unválūd; 2. anvǽljūd]. **un-** (**I.**) & **value(d).** Not valued; **a** not prized or esteemed; **b** not held in esteem; not considered valuable.

unvanquished, adj. [1. unvángkwisht; 2. anvǽŋkwiʃt]. **un-** (**I.**) & **vanquish(ed).** Not vanquished; unconquered.

unvaried, adj. [1. unvārid; 2. anvéərid]. **un-** (**I.**) & P.P. of **vary.** Not varied; **a** not varying, always the same; constant, enduring: *unvaried kindness*; *unvaried hostility*; **b** showing no variety; monotonous, tedious: *the unvaried routine of daily duties.*

unvarnished, adj. [1. unvárnisht; 2. anvániʃt]. **un-** (**I.**) & **varnish(ed).** Not varnished; **a** not covered with a coat of varnish; **b** (fig.) not embellished or tricked out; plain, simple: *an unvarnished tale.*

unvarying, adj. [1. unvāriiŋ; 2. anvéəri-iŋ]. **un-** (**I.**) & **vary(ing).** Not varying; not altering or changeable; constant; invariable.

unvaryingly, adv. Prec. & **-ly.** In an unvarying manner.

unveil, vb. trans. & intrans. [1. unvál; 2. anvéil]. **un-** (**II.**) & **veil** (**II.**). **1.** trans. **a** To remove the veil or covering from: *to unveil one's face, oneself*; *to unveil a statue*, to perform the public ceremony of disclosing to view a newly erected statue; **b** (fig.) to disclose, reveal, make plain (what is secret): *to unveil a secret plan, one's purpose.* **2.** intrans. **a** To take the veil off one's face or person; **b** to reveal oneself; to show one's true character.

unventilated, adj. [1. unvéntilàted; 2. anvéntilèitid]. **un-** (**I.**) & **ventilate(d).** Not ventilated; **a** (of rooms &c.) not adequately supplied with fresh air; hence stuffy, airless; **b** not submitted to discussion: *unventilated grievances.*

unveracious, adj. [1. ùnverāshus; 2. ànvəréiʃəs]. **un-** (**I.**) & **veracious.** Not veracious; (chiefly applied to statements &c.) lacking veracity, untruthful.

unverifiable, adj. [1. unvérifīabl; 2. anvérifaiəbl]. **un-** (**I.**) & **verifiable.** Not verifiable; not capable of being verified.

unverified, adj. [1. unvérifīd; 2. anvérifaid]. **un-** (**I.**) & P.P. of **verify.** Not verified, not proved or established as true.

unversed, adj. [1. unvérst; 2. anvə́st]. **un-** (**I.**) & **versed.** Not versed or skilled in.

unvexed, adj. [1. unvékst; 2. anvékst]. **un-** (**I.**) & **vex(ed).** Not vexed.

unvindicated, adj. [1. unvíndikàted; 2. anvíndikeitid]. **un-** (**I.**) & **vindicate(d).** Not vindicated.

unviolated, adj. [1. unvíolàted; 2. anváiəleitid]. **un-** (**I.**) & **violate(d).** Not violated; (lit. and fig.) kept inviolate.

unvisited, adj. [1. unvízited; 2. anvízitid]. **un-** (**I.**) & **visit(ed).** Not visited; unfrequented.

unvitiated, adj. [1. unvíshiàted; 2. anvíʃieitid]. **un-** (**I.**) & **vitiate(d).** Not vitiated; unspoiled; pure, not corrupted.

unvoiced, adj. [1. unvóist; 2. anvóist]. **un-** (**I.**) & **voice(d).** **a** Not expressed or uttered; **b** (phon.) not voiced; uttered without vibration of the vocal chords.

unvouched, adj. [1. unvóucht; 2. anváutʃt]. **un-** (**I.**) & **vouch(ed).** Not vouched (for); not attested.

unwaked, -wakened, adj. [1. unwākt, -wākend; 2. anwéikt, -wéikənd]. **un-** (**I.**) & **wake(ne)d.** Not waked or awakened.

unwalled, adj. [1. unwáwld; 2. anwɔ́ld]. **un-** (**I.**) & **wall(ed).** Not walled; without walls or fortifications.

unwanted, adj. [1. unwónted; 2. anwɔ́ntid]. **un-** (**I.**) & **want(ed).** Not wanted.

unwarily, adv. [1. unwārili; 2. anwéərili]. **unwary** & **-ly.** In an unwary manner; incautiously.

unwariness, n. [1. unwārines; 2. anwéərinis]. See prec. & **-ness.** State of being unwary.

unwarlike, adj. [1. unwórlīk; 2. anwɔ́laik]. **un-** (**I.**) & **warlike.** Not warlike; unmilitary; pacific.

unwarned, adj. [1. unwórnd; 2. anwɔ́nd]. **un-** (**I.**) & **warn(ed).** Not warned.

unwarped, adj. [1. unwórpt; 2. anwɔ́pt]. **un-** (**I.**) & **warp(ed).** Not warped; not biassed; unprejudiced.

unwarrantable, adj. [1. unwórantabl; 2. anwɔ́rəntəbl]. **un-** (**I.**) & **warrantable.** Not warrantable; unjustifiable, indefensible; improper.

unwarrantably, adv. Prec. & **-ly.** In an unwarrantable manner.

unwarranted, adj. [1. unwóranted; 2. anwɔ́rəntid]. **un-** (**I.**) & **warrant(ed).** Not warranted; **a** without a warrant or guarantee; **b** unauthorized.

unwary, adj. [1. unwāri; 2. anwéəri]. **un-** (**I.**) & **wary.** Not wary; incautious; unguarded; rash.

unwashed, adj. [1. unwósht; 2. anwɔ́ʃt]. **un-** (**I.**) & **wash(ed).** Not washed; **a** dirty: Phr. *the great unwashed*, the mob; **b** not touched or reached by the sea, river &c.

unwasted, adj. [1. unwāsted; 2. anwéistid]. **un-** (**I.**) & **waste(d).** Not wasted.

unwatched, adj. [1. unwócht; 2. anwɔ́tʃt]. **un-** (**I.**) & **watch(ed).** Not watched; unguarded.

unwatchful, adj. [1. unwóchfl; 2. anwɔ́tʃfl]. **un-** (**I.**) & **watchful.** Not watchful; careless.

unwatchfully, adv. Prec. & **-ly.** In an unwatchful manner.

unwatchfulness, n. See prec. & **-ness.** Quality, state, of being unwatchful; lack of vigilance.

unwatered, adj. [1. unwáwterd; 2. anwɔ́təd]. **un-** (**I.**) & **water(ed).** Not watered; **a** not diluted; **b** not supplied with water; **c** not sprinkled, moistened, irrigated, with water.

unwavering, adj. [1. unwāvering; 2. anwéivəriŋ]. **un-** (**I.**) & **wavering.** Not wavering; steadfast, firm.

unwaveringly, adv. Prec. & **-ly.** In an unwavering manner.

unweaned, adj. [1. unwēnd; 2. anwínd]. **un-** (**I.**) & **wean(ed).** Not yet weaned; still at the breast.

unwearable, adj. [1. unwārabl; 2. anwéərəbl]. **un-** (**I.**) & **wearable.** Not wearable; **a** not fit to be put on and worn; **b** not to be worn out.

unwearied, adj. [1. unwērid; 2. anwíərid]. **un-** (**I.**) & **wearied.** Not wearied; not tired; unfatigued; indefatigable.

unweary, adj. [1. unwēri; 2. anwíəri]. **un-** (**I.**) & **weary.** Not weary.

unwearying, adj. [1. unwēriing; 2. anwíəri-iŋ]. Prec. & **-ing.** Not wearying; showing no weariness; untiring, indefatigable; persistent.

unwearyingly, adv. Prec. & **-ly.** In an unwearying manner.

unweave, vb. trans. [1. unwēv; 2. anwív]. **un-** (**II.**) & **weave.** To undo what is woven; to separate the threads of.

unwed, -wedded, adj. [1. unwéd(ed); 2. anwéd(id)]. **un-** (**I.**) & **wed(ded).** Not wedded; unmarried, single.

unweighed, adj. [1. unwād; 2. anwéid]. **un-** (**I.**) & **weigh(ed).** Not weighed; not duly pondered or considered.

unwelcome, adj. [1. unwélkum; 2. anwélkəm]. **un-** (**I.**) & **welcome.** Not welcome.

unwell, adj. [1. unwél; 2. anwél]. **un-** (**I.**) & **well** (**IV.**). Not well in health; ailing, indisposed; specif., sick, suffering from nausea.

unwept, adj. [1. unwépt; 2. anwépt]. **un-** (**I.**) & P.P. of **weep.** Not wept for; unmourned, unlamented.

unwhipped, adj. [1. unwípt; 2. anwípt]. **un-** (**I.**) & P.P. of **whip.** Not whipped, esp. of one needing a whipping: *an unwhipped cub.*

unwholesome, adj. [1. unhṓlsum; 2. anhóulsəm]. **un-** (**I.**) & **wholesome.** Not wholesome. **1. a** Bad for the health; likely to cause disease; **b** suffering from bad health; unhealthy. **2.** Morally unhealthy; tending to promote immorality: *an unwholesome book.*

unwholesomeness, n. Prec. & **-ness.** State, quality, of being unwholesome.

unwieldiness, n. [1. unwēldines; 2. anwíəldinis]. See next word & **-ness.** State of being unwieldy.

unwieldy, adj. [1. unwēldi; 2. anwíəldi]. **un-** (**I.**) & obs. *wieldy*, 'easy to wield or handle', see **wield** & **-y.** Not easy to handle or move; bulky, unmanageable; ponderous, clumsy.

unwifely, adj. [1. unwífli; 2. anwáifli]. **un-** (**I.**) & **wifely.** Not wifely; unlike a wife; not befitting or worthy of a wife.

unwill, vb. trans. [1. unwíl; 2. anwíl]. **un-** (**II.**) & **will.** To will the exact reverse of what one has willed, or has been willed to do.

unwilling, adj. [1. unwíling; 2. anwíliŋ]. **un-** (**I.**) & **willing.** Not willing; reluctant, disinclined.

unwillingly, adv. Prec. & **-ly.** In an unwilling manner, against one's will.

unwillingness, n. See prec. & **-ness.** State of being unwilling.

unwind, vb. trans. & intrans. [1. unwínd; 2. anwáind]. **un-** (**II.**) & **wind** (**IV.**). **1.** trans. To wind off what has been wound; to loose, separate, what has been wound. **2.** intrans. To become unwound.

unwinking, adj. [1. unwíngking; 2. anwíŋkiŋ]. **un-** (**I.**) & **wink(ing).** Preserving a steady gaze without a tremor of an eyelid; open-eyed, wide awake; (fig., rare) vigilant.

unwisdom, n. [1. unwízdum; 2. anwízdəm]. **un-** (**I.**) & **wisdom.** Reverse of wisdom; folly, unwise conduct.

unwise, adj. [1. unwíz; 2. anwáiz]. **un-** (**I.**) & **wise.** Not wise; foolish, imprudent.

unwisely, adv. [1. unwízli; 2. anwáizli]. Prec. & **-ly.** In an unwise manner; foolishly.

unwished, adj. [1. unwísht; 2. anwíʃt]. **un-** (**I.**) & **wish(ed).** Not wished (for), not desired.

unwitnessed, adj. [1. unwítnest; 2. anwítnist]. **un-** (**I.**) & **witness(ed).** Not witnessed; **a** not seen; **b** uncorroborated by a witness; **c** not signed by a witness.

unwitting, adj. [1. unwíting; 2. anwítiŋ]. **un-** (**I.**) & Pres. Part. of **wit** (**II.**). Not witting; unknowing, unconscious, unintentional.

unwittingly, adv. Prec. & **-ly.** In an unwitting manner; unconsciously, inadvertently.

unwomanly, adj. [1. unwóomanli; 2. anwúmənli]. **un-** (**I.**) & **womanly.** Not womanly; not characteristic of, unbefitting, a (good) woman.

unwon, adj. [1. unwún; 2. anwán]. **un-** (**I.**) & **won.** Not won; not gained.

unwonted, adj. [1. unwṓnted; 2. anwóuntid]. **un-** (**I.**) & **wonted.** Not wonted; unaccustomed; unusual; infrequent, rare.

unwontedly, adv. Prec. & **-ly.** In an unwonted manner.

unwontedness, n. See prec. & **-ness.** State, quality, of being unwonted.

unwooded, adj. [1. unwóoded; 2. anwúdid]. **un-** (**I.**) & **wood(ed).** Not wooded, not covered with woods or forests.

unwooed, adj. [1. unwōōd; 2. anwúd]. **un-** (**I.**) & **woo(ed).** Not wooed; uncourted.

unwork, vb. trans. [1. unwérk; 2. anwə́k]. **un-** (**II.**) & **work** (**II.**). To undo, destroy, what has been worked or done.

unworkable, adj. [1. unwĕrkabl; 2. anwákəbl]. **un-** (I.) & **workable.** Not workable; difficult or impossible to work, manage, or carry out: *an unworkable machine, plan* &c.

unworked, adj. [1. unwĕrkt; 2. anwákt]. **un-** (I.) & **work(ed).** Not worked.

unworkmanlike, adj. [1. unwĕrkmanlīk; 2. anwákmənlaik]. **un-** (I.) & **workmanlike.** Not workmanlike; not like the work of a good and skilled craftsman; badly, unskilfully, done.

unworldliness, n. [1. unwĕrldlines; 2. anwáldlinis]. See next word & **-ness.** An unworldly habit of mind; unworldly conduct.

unworldly, adj. [1. unwĕrldli; 2. anwáldli]. **un-** (I.) & **worldly.** Not worldly; **a** not of this world; spiritual; **b** spiritually minded; not concerned with material or worldly things; specif., not seeking worldly advantage and gain.

unworn, adj. [1. unwórn; 2. anwɔ́n]. **un-** (I.) & **worn.** Not worn; **a** not showing signs of wear; **b** (of clothes) having never been worn; **c** not usually worn.

unworthily, adv. [1. unwĕrdhili; 2. anwáðili]. **unworthy** & **-ly.** In an unworthy manner.

unworthiness, n. [1. unwĕrdhines; 2. anwáðinis]. See next word & **-ness.** State, quality, of being unworthy.

unworthy, adj. [1. unwĕrdhi; 2. anwáði]. **un-** (I.) & **worthy.** **1.** Not worthy; lacking moral worth, not having or deserving respect, worthless: *an unworthy person.* **2.** Not deserving some specified position, reward &c.; not possessing the moral or intellectual requirements for a specified position, rank, status: *an unworthy member of the Church; a humble, but, I fear, an unworthy pupil of a great teacher.* **3.** *Unworthy of,* **a** not deserving: *unworthy of respect, of promotion; reports unworthy of credence;* **b** below the dignity of, unbecoming in: *conduct unworthy of a gentleman.*

unwound, adj. [1. unwóund; 2. anwáund]. **a un-** (II.); **b un-** (I.) & **wound** (III.). **a** Wound off, freed from windings; unwrapped, untwisted, disentangled; **b** not wound.

unwounded, adj. [1. unwōōnded; 2. anwúndid]. **un-** (I.) & **wound(ed).** Not wounded; without, not having received, a wound.

unwoven, adj. [1. unwóven; 2. anwóuvən]. **un-** (I.) & **woven.** Not woven.

unwrap, vb. trans. [1. unráp; 2. anrǽp]. **un-** (II.) & **wrap** (I.). To undo, unfold, or open what is wrapped; to take off the wrappings from (parcel &c.).

unwrapped, adj. [1. unrápt; 2. anrǽpt]. **a un-** (II.); **b un-** (I.) & P.P. of **wrap** (II.). **a** Unfolded; freed from wrappings; **b** not wrapped (up).

unwritten, adj. [1. unrítn; 2. anrítn]. **un-** (I.) & P.P. of **write.** Not written. Not embodied in or reduced to writing: *unwritten law,* **a** customary or common law, as opposed to *statute;* **b** an assumed rule or custom by which a verdict of acquittal is given in cases of crime committed in defence of, or in revenge for seduction or attempt on the virtue of, a wife, daughter &c.

unwrought, adj. [1. unráwt; 2. anrɔ́t]. **un-** (I.) & **wrought.** Not wrought; not worked or manufactured; not elaborated or worked up.

unwrung, adj. [1. unrúng; 2. anráŋ]. **un-** (I.) & **wrung.** Not wrung, esp. in Phr. *my, his, withers are unwrung,* not touched by charge, accusation &c.

unyielding, adj. [1. unyḗlding; 2. anjíldiŋ]. **un-** (I.) & **yield(ing).** Not yielding; **a** incapable of being bent or moved; rigid; **b** refusing to alter a decision, opinion &c., inflexible, obstinate, determined.

unyieldingly, adv. Prec. & **-ly.** In an unyielding manner.

unyoke, vb. trans. [1. unyṓk; 2. anjóuk]. **un-** (II.) & **yoke** (II.). To loose, free from, the yoke; to disconnect, separate.

unyoked, adj. [1. unyṓkt; 2. anjóukt]. **a un-** (II.); **b un-** (I.) & **yoke**(d). **a** Freed, loosed, from the yoke; **b** not yoked.

unzealous, adj. [1. unzélus; 2. anzéləs]. **un-** (I.) & **zealous.** Not zealous.

up (I.), adv. [1. up; 2. ap]. O.E. *ūpp,* 'up', *uppe,* 'on high, up'; M.E. *up;* cp. O.S. *uppa, uppe;* O.H.G. *ūf, ūfe;* Goth. *iup,* 'up, upwards'; the orig. Gmc. form was **upp,* fr. Aryan **upná;* the Gmc. type fr. Aryan **up-* has *f* as in Goth. *ufar,* O.E. *ofer,* see **over.** The following are a few cognates: Scrt. *úpa,* 'towards; on, upon'; & *upa-más,* 'uppermost'; Gk. *hupér,* 'over', see **hyper-,** &, in spite of the difference of meaning, also *hupó,* 'under', see **hypo-;** further Lat. *sub,* 'under', orig. 'from below towards, from below upwards'; see also etymol. of **sub-** & discussion there of changes in meaning. Above, aloft, on high; reverse of *down.* **1. a** Expressing (i.) movement from a lower to a higher position: *to go up to the top of a hill; come up here and look at the view;* Phr. *to get up,* rise from bed; *to go up to the University, up to Oxford, Cambridge;* (ii.) movement from South to North: *to run up North, up to Scotland;* **b** expressing (i.) rest at, or in, a higher place or position: *to stay up in the hills; to sleep up at the top of the house; to live several storeys up;* Phrs. *to be up, stay up (all night),* not to be in bed, not to go to bed; *to be up and doing,* alert and active; *up at Oxford, up at the University,* in residence at Oxford &c.; *shall you be up during the Vac.?,* residing in Oxford; (ii.) rest at or in, being at or in, a northerly part of the country: *to live up in Scotland;* (iii.) motion to, rest at, the metropolis or nearest important centre; *up to, up in, London, in town, up in Glasgow* (from country); *up from the country.* **2.** After various verbs expressing movement, *fly up, pull up, throw up, jump up, stand up* &c.; and others expressing continuance in same position or state: *lie up, sit up* &c. See under the verbs severally. **3.** Expressing change, development, from an inferior or simpler, to a superior or more complex state: *to bring, train, up a child; a plant grows up from a seed; many large cities have sprung up from very humble beginnings.* **4.** Expressing the passage from an inferior to a superior social grade, official or other worldly position &c.: *to come up from poverty to affluence; up from the ranks;* Phr. *to come, move, up in the world,* rise in social scale. **5.** Expressing the coming into importance, under notice, consideration &c.: *the question came up for discussion, came up in conversation* &c.; *the case is up before the High Court; up before the local Bench* &c. Phrs. *is anything up?,* anything happening; *what's up (with you)?,* what's the matter?, what do you complain of?, &c.; *it's up to me, you &c., to do* &c., it is my business, is incumbent on me &c. **6.** *Up to, up with,* **a** abreast of, alongside of, at the same distance from the starting-point, or from the objective: *I could not get, catch, up to him; slow down a bit and let me come up with you;* **b** (fig.) expressing equality, or approximation to, in merit, success, attainments &c.: *he is not up to his father as a scholar;* Phr. *not up to his job* &c., incompetent to carry it out. **7.** Expressing completeness, finality &c.; after various verbs: *to eat up everything on the table; to finish up work up; to tear up a letter; to dry up; burnt up to a cinder; shrivelled up; to boil up, heat up* &c. Phrs. *it's all up,* there is no more hope; *it's all up with him,* he is dying, is ruined, is done for &c.; *the game is up,* the thing is at an end, there's nothing more to be done, it's all over. **8.** Expressing **a** (physical) an increase in intensity, loudness, activity &c.: *to speak up, sing up, keep the voice up; to play up, buck up; to light up; blow the fire up; to flare up; the hunt is up; the temperature has gone up; the cider is very much up,* highly charged with gas, effervescing; **b** increased intensity in mental activity, feeling, passion &c.: *his temper is up; to fire up* (fig.), become suddenly angry; *his spirits went up;* **c** expressing various conceptions of increase, enhancement &c.; (i.) (of price, value &c.): *consols are up this morning; prices have gone up;* (ii.) (of moral estimate): *he has gone up considerably in my opinion;* **d** (rise in musical pitch) *I can't get up to that note; the piano is up a tone.* **9.** Expressing condition of inactivity, being out of use, put by, or aside: *laid up with gout; put up your swords into their sheaths; to lay up treasure.* **10.** *Up to,* (colloq.) occupied with, engaged in: *what have you been up to?; he's up to no good,* engaged in some wickedness, mischief &c. **11.** *Up against,* (colloq.) faced, confronted with (difficulty &c.). **12.** *Up and down,* (i.) rising and falling: *to bob up and down;* (ii.) backwards and forwards, to and fro: *to walk up and down.* (*N.B.*—For various idiomatic uses of *up* after vbs., other than those mentioned, see under the various vbs. themselves.)

up (II.), prep. See prec. **1. a** From a lower to, or at, a higher position, place, spot: *to walk, live, up a mountain; to go up a ladder; to climb up a tree;* **b** to a position of greater importance, superiority &c.: *to work one's way up a form, a school* &c.; *he went steadily up the social scale.* **2.** From the direction of a river's mouth towards its source; in the contrary direction to the current: *to row up the stream; to walk up the river bank;* also *to live, camp, further up the stream,* nearer the source than a spot specified or understood. **3.** Along a road, away from speaker, or farther in a given direction from a specified spot: *to walk up the road, street, lane.* **4.** Away from the sea towards the interior of a country: *to travel up (the) country.*

up (III.), adj., fr. **up** (I.). Tending towards, in direction of, a higher position; only in a few expressions: *on the up grade,* tending to rise; *the up train,* that which goes towards a big city, esp. to London; *up line,* railway line on which the up trains run; *the up side,* that side of a railway station on which is the up line; *up platform,* that on the up line.

up (IV.), n., fr. prec. Only in Phr. *ups and downs,* rise and fall, fluctuation (in various senses): *ups and downs of fortune, of health;* also *a house full of ups and downs,* numerous small staircases, landings &c.

up (V.), vb. intrans. O.E. has *uppian,* 'to rise', fr. *ūp(p),* see **up** (I.), but M.E. *uppen,* 'to bring up, disclose', is fr. O.E. *yppen,* fr. **ūppjan.* The present word is almost certainly a new formation. (colloq. and vulg. or facet.) To rise, get up; to start into activity; only in such Phrs. as *he ups and says* &c.; *he up* (Past.) *and struck me, sauced me* &c.

up-, pref., fr. **up** (I.), (II.), or (III.), used in compounds in the varying senses of these. See the following words.

up-and-down, adj. [1. úp an(d) dóun; 2. áp ən dáun]. Fluctuating, varying, alternately rising and falling (in material and non-material senses): *an up-and-down motion; an up-and-down road, country* &c.; *an up-and-down life,* one distinguished by variations of fortune &c.

Upanishad, n. [1. ōōpáhnishahd; 2. upániʃad]. Scrt. Lit. 'a sitting-down' (at another's feet to be taught by him). A class of metaphysical treatises, one of the divisions of the Vedas.

upas (**tree**), n. [1. ū́pas (trē); 2. júpəs (trī)]. Malay. (Jav.), 'poison', esp. *pūku ūpas,* 'the poison tree'. **a** The antiar, a large tree, *Antiaris toxicaria,* of Java and the adjacent islands, allied to the fig, which yields a very poisonous milky sap; from an unfounded traveller's tale, it was believed to destroy every living thing within a radius of many miles, whence *upas tree* is used of anything of poisonous or corrupting influence; **b** the poisonous juice, *antiar,* derived from this tree.

upbear, vb. trans. [1. upbā́r; 2. apbɛ́ə]. **up-** & **bear** (I.). To hold up, to sustain, support; usually poet. & in P.P.: '*Upborne with indefatigable wings*' (Milton, 'P. L.', II. 408).

upbraid, vb. trans. [1. upbrād; 2. apbréid]. M.E. *upbreiden*, 'to reproach'; fr. **up-** & O.E. *bregdan*, 'to throw, brandish; to pluck'; cp. also the O.E. n. *brægd, bregd, gebregd* &c., 'skill, cunning; trick, deceit'. For etymol. see **braid**. To censure, reproach, scold, chide: *he upbraided her fiercely*; also *upbraid with*, to charge, reproach with.

upbraiding, adj. & n. [1. upbrāding; 2. apbréidiŋ]. Prec. & **-ing**. **a** adj. (fr. Pres. Part.) Reproachful: *upbraiding looks* &c.; **b** n., reproach, reproof.

upbraidingly, adv. Prec. & **-ly**. In an upbraiding manner; reproachfully.

upbringing, n. [1. úpbringing, upbrínging; 2. ápbriŋiŋ, apbríŋiŋ]. **up-** & *bringing*, as vbl. n. of 'to bring up' children &c. A bringing up, education, mode of training, nurture: *the result of his good, bad, upbringing.*

upcast, adj. & n. [1. úpkahst; 2. ápkāst]. **up-** & **cast** (I.). **1.** adj. Cast, directed, upwards: *with upcast looks*; cp. *downcast*. **2.** n. **a** That which is cast or thrown up; **b** a casting or throwing upwards, specif., a shaft in a mine through which air passes up after ventilation.

upcountry, n. & adj. [1. úpkùntri; 2. ápkàntri]; adv. [1. upkúntri; 2. apkántri]. **up-** & **country**. (a colonial usage) **a** n. The interior, part of country, area, away from the coast, or up a river: *the upcountry is barren*; **b** adj., pertaining to the interior, away from the coast: *an upcountry farm*; **c** adv., (colloq.) in a direction towards the interior, away from the coast: *travelled upcountry for a hundred miles.*

upgrowth, n. [1. úpgrōth; 2. ápgrouþ]. **up-** & **growth**. **a** Process of growing up; **b** that which grows up.

upheaval, n. [1. uphḗvl; 2. aphívl]. **upheave** & **-al**. **a** Act, process, of heaving or lifting up, as by a natural cataclysm; **b** sudden change, disturbance, upset, in ideas, habits, social conditions, circumstances of life &c.

upheave, vb. trans. [1. uphḗv; 2. aphív]. **up-** & **heave**. To heave, or lift, up, to raise: said especially of a great cataclysm of nature such as volcanic action, earthquake &c.

uphill, attrib. adj. [1. úphil; 2. áphil]; pred. adj. & adv. [1. uphíl; 2. aphíl]. **up-** & **hill**. **1.** adj. **a** Going, sloping, up; ascending; passing towards higher ground: *an uphill climb, road* &c.; *the road is uphill all the way*; **b** difficult, laborious: *an uphill task*. **2.** adv. Towards the top, or higher areas, of a hill, slope, or incline: *to go, run, uphill.*

uphold, vb. trans. [1. uphṓld; 2. aphóuld]. **up-** & **hold**. **1.** To hold up, support, keep from falling: *slender columns uphold the great dome*; *strong arms upheld him while he hung in mid-air*. **2.** **a** To give moral support and encouragement to: *your praise and sympathy have upheld me greatly*; **b** to approve, give countenance to: *I cannot uphold such unscrupulous conduct*; **c** to confirm, maintain: *the Court of Appeal upheld Mr. Justice X's ruling.*

upholder, n. [1. uphṓlder; 2. aphóuldə]. Prec. & **-er**. One who upholds; supporter, defender.

upholster, vb. trans. [1. uphṓlster; 2. aphóulstə]. Back-formation fr. next word. **1.** To provide, furnish, with carpets, curtains, furniture &c.: *to upholster a house, room* &c. **2.** **a** To provide with stuffing, springs, coverings: *to upholster a sofa or chair*; **b** to cover (chair &c.) with some material.

upholsterer, n. [1. uphṓlsterer; 2. aphóulstərə]. Earlier *upholdster*, also *upholder*, orig. an auctioneer or broker, one who 'holds up' goods for inspection and sale. The suff. *-ster* is substituted on the anal. of *maltster*, & perh. influenced by association w. *holster*; the final (redundant) *-er* may be compared w. that in *fruiterer, poulterer* &c. **a** One who supplies upholstered furniture, carpets, curtains &c. for a house or room; **b** one who repairs and covers chairs, sofas &c. with upholstery.

upholstery, n. [1. uphṓlsteri; 2. aphóulstəri]. Prec. & **-y**. **1.** The work and trade of an upholsterer: *to learn upholstery*. **2.** **a** Such goods, articles of household furniture, as are supplied by an upholsterer, including chairs, sofas, carpets, hangings; specif. **b** stuffing and coverings of chairs and sofas; **c** the way in which this work is carried out: *highly skilled upholstery.*

uphroe, n. [1. ū́frō; 2. jū́frou]. Corrupt. of Du. *juffrouw*, 'young woman; pulley', fr. *jung*, 'young', & *frouw*, 'woman'. (naut.) A block of wood pierced with holes through which cords for an awning are passed.

upkeep, n. [1. úpkēp; 2. ápkīp]. **up-** & **keep** (II.). **a** Act of keeping up or maintaining; specif., maintenance of land, houses &c. in good condition and repair; **b** money spent on, the cost of, such maintenance.

upland, n. & adj. [1. úpland; 2. áplənd]. **up-** & **land**. **1.** n. High land or ground; upper level of ground by a river, in a valley, or on foothills of a mountain; also in pl., *uplands*, upland country. **2.** adj. Pertaining to, situated in, the uplands, high in situation: *an upland road, farm*; *upland country* &c.

uplift (I.), vb. trans. [1. uplíft; 2. aplíft]. **up-** & **lift** (II.). (archaic) To lift up, raise, elevate: *with uplifted hands, eyes*; also in moral sense: *spirits uplifted by the news.*

uplift (II.), n. [1. úplift; 2. áplift], fr. prec. **a** Uplifting; upheaval: *an uplift of strata*; **b** (an Americanism) moral, spiritual elevation, emotional fervour: *preacher celebrated for his uplift.*

upmost, adj. & adv. [1. úpmōst; 2. ápmoust]. Archaic, for **uppermost**.

upon, prep. [1. upón; 2. əpón]. O.E. *úppon*, M.E. & Early Mod. *úppen*; **up** (I.) & **on** (I.). The distinction in usage between *on* and *upon* is very slight. It may be said that the two are almost always interchangeable, but that generally speaking, *upon* is less colloquial than *on*. *Upon* is often preferred when it follows a verb, esp. at end of a sentence: *nothing to go upon*; *not a chair to sit upon*; *very little to live upon*. On the other hand, while we could say either *her picture still hangs on*, or *upon, the wall*, we should probably not say *which wall did you hang it upon?*, but rather *on*. *Upon* is preferred in some Phr. such as *upon my word*. See idiomatic uses of *upon* after verbs under these.

upper (I.), adj. [1. úper; 2. ápə]. Compar. of **up**. **1.** Higher in physical position; placed, situated above: *upper seats, the upper circle*, in theatre &c.; *shave the upper lip*; Phrs. *to have the upper hand of*, to be superior to, have authority or power over; *to get the upper hand of*, obtain advantage or power over; *upper storey*, (colloq.) the head, brains; specif., *upper case*, that holding capital letters &c. in printing; hence capital letters. **2.** Higher in rank, dignity &c.: *the Upper House*, House of Lords, Senate &c.; *upper servants*, butler, housekeeper &c. Phr. *the upper ten (thousand)*, the highest ranks in society, the aristocracy.

upper (II.), n. (usually pl. *uppers*) Part of a shoe or boot above the sole: esp. in Phr. *down on one's uppers*, out at heel, with boots worn out, hence, desperately poor, in low water financially.

upper-cut, n. **upper** (I.) & **cut**. (boxing) A short-arm blow, delivered upwards at opponent's chin or jaw.

uppermost, adj. & adv. [1. úpermōst; 2. ápəmoust]. **upper** & **-most**. **1.** adj. Highest in position, rank, influence; predominant. **2.** adv. In the highest position, at the top.

uppish, adj. [1. úpish; 2. ápiʃ]. **up** (III.) & **-ish**. Inclined to be presuming; impudent, cheeky.

uppishly, adv. Prec. & **-ly**. In an uppish manner.

uppishness, n. See prec. & **-ness**. State, quality, of being uppish; presumption, impudence.

upraise, vb. trans. [1. upráz; 2. apréiz]. **up-** & **raise**. (archaic) To raise, to lift up: (usually in P.P.) *with hands upraised to heaven*; *with voice upraised in anger.*

upright (I.), adj. & n. [1. úprit; 2. áprait]. O.E. *ūp(p)riht*, **up-** & **right**. **A.** adj. **1.** Erect, pointing directly upwards; vertical, perpendicular: *an upright tree, pillar*; *pattern with upright lines*; *take an upright position*; *has an upright, athletic figure*; specif., *upright piano*, one in which the strings are laid vertically, distinct from *a grand piano*. **2.** Possessing, showing, moral rectitude and integrity; honourable. **B.** n. Upright post, beam &c., esp. one used to support a structure.

upright (II.), adv. [1. uprít; 2. apráit]. In an upright position: *to stand, walk, upright.*

uprightly, adv. [1. uprítli; 2. apráitli]. **upright** (I.) & **-ly**. In an upright manner; chiefly in moral sense.

uprightness, n. [1. uprítnes; 2. apráitnis]. See prec. & **-ness**. State of being morally upright; integrity.

uprise, vb. intrans. [1. upríz; 2. apráiz]. **up-** & **rise**. (poet.) To rise, stand, get up.

uprising, n. [1. uprízing; 2. apráiziŋ]. Prec. & **-ing**. **a** Act of rising, esp. from bed: '*New every morning is the love Our wakening and uprising prove*' (Ken's Morning Hymn); **b** an insurrection, revolt; a rising: *the uprising was suppressed with great difficulty.*

uproar, n. [1. úprōr; 2. áprɔ̄]. Earlier *uprore*; borrowed fr. Du. *oproer*, 'commotion, tumult; sedition', fr. *op*, 'up' & *roeren*, 'to stir, move'; cogn. w. O.E. *hrēran*, 'to stir, agitate', O.S. *hrōrian*; O.H.G. *ruoren*, 'to move', cp. Mod. Germ. *aufruhr*, 'tumult'. Present spelling is due to association w. *roar*. Violent, excited, noisy tumult; clamour, rowdy disturbance: *the town, meeting, was in an uproar.*

uproarious, adj. [1. uprṓrius; 2. aprɔ́riəs]. Prec. & *-i-* & **-ous**. **a** Making an uproar; distinguished by disturbance and noise; violently rowdy: *an uproarious meeting*; *uproarious revellers*; **b** boisterous, noisy, tumultuous: *uproarious applause, laughter.*

uproariously, adv. Prec. & **-ly**. In an uproarious manner.

uproariousness, n. See prec. & **-ness**. State of uproar; noisy disturbance; noisy hilarity.

uproot, vb. trans. [1. uprŏŏt; 2. aprū́t]. **up-** & **root** (II.). **1.** **a** To root up, tear up by the roots: *to uproot a tree* &c.; **b** (fig.) to remove from established or natural abode or residence: *pathetic exiles uprooted from their homelands.* **2.** (in fig. sense) To destroy as from the root, to eradicate, extirpate: *long-established customs and habits are hard to uproot.*

uprouse, vb. trans. [1. upróuz; 2. apráuz]. **up-** & **rouse**. To rouse, stir up.

upset (I.), vb. trans. & intrans. [1. upsét; 2. apsét]. **up-** & **set**. **1.** trans. **a** To turn upside-down, throw down; to overset, overturn, to capsize: *to upset a boat, motor-car* &c.; **b** to defeat, overthrow: *to upset a government* &c.; **c** to disturb, to put out of gear, frustrate: *you have upset all my plans*; also **d** (i.) to disturb mind of, distress: *the bad news completely upset him*; *much upset by his friend's coldness*; (ii.) to injure the health of, render ill: *I think it must have been the lobster last night that upset me.* **2.** intrans. To be overturned: *the car upset after a violent skid*; *if you don't sit still, the boat will upset.*

upset (II.), n. [1. upsét; 2. ápsét], fr. prec. **a** A fall, overturning, tumble: *a bad upset from a dog-cart*; **b** disturbance of normal, quiet, orderly conditions; state of disorder and confusion: *the sudden departure of all our servants caused rather an upset*; **c** a disagreement, quarrel: *a bit of an upset with his father.*

upset (III.), adj. [1. upset; 2. ápsɛt]. Set up, fixed; only in Phr. *upset price*, the lowest price at which property or an article will be sold, as at an auction; reserve price.

upshot, n. [1. úpshot; 2. ápʃɔt]. **up-** & **shot** (IV.), in sense of 'share, reckoning'. The final issue of anything; conclusion, end, general result or effect: *the upshot of the whole trouble.*

upside, also **up side**, n. [1. úpsīd; 2. ápsaid]. **up-** & **side**. **a** The top or upper side; **b** the side, as of a railway line or platform, on which an up train travels, as to London or nearest principal town or terminus.

upside-down, adv. [1. úpsīd dóun; 2. ápsaid dáun]. Changed for M.E. *up so down*, 'up and so down'; associated w. *up side*. **a** With the top or upper part or side underneath or inverted: *turn the box upside-down*; **b** in confusion or disorder; higgledy-piggledy, topsy-turvy: *turned the room upside-down to hunt for a lost collar-stud.*

upsides, adv. [1. upsídz; 2. apsáidz]. **up-** & **side(s)**. (provinc. in Phr.) *To be upsides with*, to be equal to, get the better of person, thing.

upstair(s), adj. [1. úpstār(z); 2. ápstɛə(z)]. **up-** & **stair**. Belonging to, situated on, an upper storey; above stairs: *an upstair(s) room.*

upstairs, adv. [1. upstárz; 2. apstéəz]. **up-** & **stair(s)**. Towards, in, an upper storey; at the top of a staircase, above stairs; to, in, a higher storey than that in which speaker is, or to which reference is made: *go upstairs and look at the view*; *upstairs in bed*; *my room is upstairs again after the third flight.*

upstanding, adj. [1. upstánding; 2. apstǽndiŋ]. **up-** & **stand(ing)**. Standing upright, well set-up in figure: *a fine, upstanding young fellow.*

upstart, n. [1. úpstart; 2. ápstāt]. **up-** & **start**. **a** Person who has started or sprung up suddenly from a low position to wealth or importance; a parvenu: *the crowd of upstarts who pushed themselves into prominence after the war*; **b** an insolent and arrogant nobody: *he could snub an upstart with a look*; (also attrib.) *these upstart pushers into society.*

upstream, adv. & adj. [1. upstrḗm; 2. apstrīm]. **up-** & **stream**. **a** adv. Against the stream or current; **b** adj., moving against the stream or current.

upstroke, n. [1. úpstrōk; 2. ápstrouk]. **up-** & **stroke**. An upward line or stroke, as in writing &c.

uptake, n. [1. úptāk; 2. ápteik]. **up-** & **take**. **a** (rare) Act of taking or lifting up; **b** (a Scots Phr.) understanding, power of apprehension, intellectual grasp: *quick, slow, in the uptake.*

upthrow, n. [1. úpthrō; 2. ápþrou]. **up-** & **throw**. A throwing up, upheaval; specif. (geol.) displacement upwards on one side of a fault.

upthrust, n. [1. úpthrust; 2. ápþrast]. **up-** & **thrust**. A thrusting upwards; specif. (geol.) elevation of part of the crust of the earth; upheaval.

upturn, vb. trans. [1. uptérn; 2. aptə́n]. **up-** & **turn**. To turn up, to throw up.

upward, adj. [1. úpward; 2. ápwəd]. **up-** & **-ward**. Directed, turned, moving, to a higher place or in a higher direction, ascending (lit. and fig.): *an upward course, glance*; *the constant upward move of prices, taxation &c.*; *an upward trend in social customs and manners.*

upwardly, adv. Prec. & **-ly**. In an upward direction; upwards.

upwards, (also poet. or liter.) **upward**, adv. [1. úpward(z); 2. ápwəd(z)]. In an upward direction, towards a higher position: *to move, look, upwards.* Phrs. *and upwards*, and more: *soldiers of ten years' service and upwards*; *upwards of*, more than: *upwards of a million unemployed.*

uraemia, n. [1. ūrḗmia; 2. jūrīmiə]. Neo-Lat., fr. Gk. *oûron*, see **urine**, & *haîma*, 'blood', see **haemo-**. A morbid condition of the blood, due to the failure of the kidneys and bladder to carry away by natural secretion various toxic substances.

uraemic, adj. [1. ūrḗmik; 2. jūrīmik]. Prec. & **-ic**. Affected by, characteristic of, uraemia.

uraeus, n. [1. ūrḗus; 2. jūríəs]. Neo-Lat.; fr. Gk. *ouraîos*, 'pertaining to a tail, tailed', fr. *ourá*, 'tail', see **uro- (II.)**. A figure of the sacred or king cobra with head erect and hood expanded, worn, as a symbol of kingship, by the kings of Ancient Egypt.

Ural-Altaic, adj. & n. [1. ū́ral altā́ik; 2. júərəl æltéi-ik], fr. the Ural & Altaic Mountains of Asia. **1.** adj. Pertaining to, **a** a racial group of people lying between these ranges; **b** a group of agglutinative languages spoken in Eastern Europe and Central Asia, including Finnish, Turki, Mongol &c. **2.** n. Ural-Altaic language.

uralite, n. [1. ū́ralīt; 2. júərəlait]. As found first in the Ural Mountains. A kind of hornblende.

Urania, n. [1. ūrā́nia; 2. ju(ə)réiniə]. Lat., fr. Gk. *ouranía*, fem. of *ouránios*, 'heavenly', fr. *ouranós*, 'heaven', fr. **oworanos*; cogn. w. Scrt. *varunaś*, 'the god of the evening sky'. (class. mythol.) **a** The Muse of Astronomy; **b** epithet of Aphrodite (Venus); spiritual love, as opposed to *pándēmos*, sexual love.

uranic, adj. [1. ūránik; 2. juréinik]. **uranium** & **-ic**. (chem.) Pertaining to, containing, uranium, as *uranic acid.*

uranium, n. [1. ūrā́nium; 2. ju(ə)réiniəm], fr. name of the planet *Uranus*, discovered by Herschel a few years before. (chem.) A white, malleable, metallic, radioactive element, found in pitchblende; used as an alloy in steel manufacture.

urano-, pref. Form used in compounds, fr. Gk. *ouranós*, 'heaven', see **Urania**; as *uranography*, description of the heavens and heavenly bodies; *uranometry*, measurement of stellar distances.

uranous, adj. [1. ūrā́nus; 2. ju(ə)réinəs]. **uranium** & **-ous**. (chem.) Pertaining to, containing, uranium, esp. of compounds of lower valency than uranic compounds.

Uranus, n. [1. ū́ranus; 2. jú(ə)rənəs]. Lat., fr. Gk. *ouranós*, 'heaven', see **Urania**. **a** (Gk. mythol.) The husband of Gaia, the Earth, and father of Cronos (Saturn) and the Titans; **b** (astron.) the seventh of the major planets, farthest from the sun, except Neptune and Pluto, discovered 1781 by Sir W. Herschel.

urban, adj. [1. érban; 2. ə́bən], fr. Lat. *urbānus*, 'of the city', fr. *urbs*, 'a city'; prob. fr. **wr̥bhis*, 'place surrounded by a hedge'; cp. Lith. *vir̃bas*, 'a twig, a rod'; fr. the same base w. a different gradational form comes the first syll. of **verbena**. Pertaining to, situated, living in, a city or town, as distinguished fr. *rural*: *urban population &c.*; *urban district council*, an administrative district and its council, for local government purposes.

urbane, adj. [1. ērbā́n; 2. əbéin], fr. Lat. *urbānus*, see prec., in sense of 'polished, refined, well-bred'. Polished, refined, affable, courteous.

urbanely, adv. Prec. & **-ly**. In an urbane manner; courteously.

urbanity, n. [1. ērbániti; 2. əbǽniti], fr. Lat. *urbānitāt-(em)*, see **urbane** & **-ity**. Grace and affability of manner, bearing, character; gracious and polished courtesy.

urbanization, n. [1. ērbanizā́shun; 2. əbənaizéiʃən]. See next word & **-ation**. **a** Act, process, of urbanizing; **b** state of being urbanized.

urbanize, vb. trans. [1. ḗrbanīz; 2. ə́bənaiz]. **urban** & **-ize**. To make urban; to change from a rural to an urban condition or character.

urceolate, adj. [1. érseolāt; 2. ə́siəleit], fr. Lat. *urceolus*, dimin. of *urceus*, 'an urn, pitcher', cogn. w. Gk. *úrkhā*, 'an earthen vessel for salted fish'; further Lith. *waršas*, 'basket used for catching fish'. The original *urceus* was perhaps a rude wicker-work frame plastered w. clay. See also **urn**. (bot.) Shaped like a pitcher or urn, as the flowers of various plants.

urchin, n. [1. érchin; 2. ə́tʃin]. M.E. *urchon*, also *irchon*, fr. O. Fr. *herichon*, variant of *ireçon*, whence Mod. Fr. *hérisson*, formed w. dimin. *-on* fr. Lat. *ēricius*, expanded form of *ēr* for **hēr*, 'hedgehog', cogn. w. Gk. *khḗr*, lit. 'the bristly, prickly creature'; fr. base **gʹher-*, **gʹhers-*, 'to become stiff, to bristle'; cp. Scrt. *hŕšatē*, 'becomes stiff, bristles, rises; shudders'; see further cogn. under **horror, hirsute, gorse**. **1.** (provinc.) A hedgehog. **2.** Sea-urchin, the echinus. **3. a** (archaic) Goblin, an imp, who was supposed to take the form of a hedgehog; **b** a mischievous, roguish boy.

Urdu, n. [1. óordōō; 2. úədū]. Hind., 'camp,' esp. in *urdū-zabān*, 'camp language'; cp. **horde**. A form of Hindustani, spoken chiefly by the Moslem races in India; it has a large admixture of Persian and Arabic words.

-ure, suff. Fr., fr. Lat. *-ūra*, suff. used to form ns. for P.P. type of vbs. Many words thus formed in Fr. are derived direct fr. Lat., e.g. *nature, literature &c.*; others are formed in Fr. itself, as *tournure, bordure*, &c. The force of the suff. is, **a** an act, process, existence, as *culture &c.*; **b** result of an act, *picture &c.*; **c** collective body of official persons, *legislature, judicature.*

urea, n. [1. ūrḗa; 2. juəríə]. Neo-Lat., formed fr. **urine**. A crystalline, soluble compound found in the urine of mammals, birds and some reptiles; also obtained synthetically from ammonium cyanate.

ureal, adj. [1. ūrḗal; 2. juəriəl]. Prec. & **-al**. Pertaining to, containing, urea.

uredo, n. [1. ūrḗdō; 2. juərídou]. Lat., 'a burning; a blight'; fr. *ūrere*, P.P. *us-tum*, 'to burn, scorch'; see second element of **combustion**. **a** A kind of rust-fungus, affecting plants; **b** a burning, itching sensation, as in nettle-rash &c.

ureter, n. [1. ūrḗter; 2. juərítə], fr. Gk. *ourētḗr*, fr. *ouréin*, 'to pass urine', see **urine**. An excretory duct of the kidney conveying urine to the bladder.

ureteritis, n. [1. ūrēterítis; 2. juərītəráitis]. Prec. & **-itis**. Inflammation of the ureter.

urethra, n. [1. ūrḗthra; 2. juəríþrə]. Lat., fr. Gk. *ourḗthra*, see **ureter**. The canal or passage through which urine is discharged from the bladder.

urethral, adj. [1. ūrḗthral; 2. juəríþrəl]. Prec. & **-al**. Pertaining to the urethra.

urethritis, n. [1. ūrēthrítis; 2. juərīþráitis]. **urethra** & **-itis**. Inflammation of the urethra.

urethroscope, n. [1. ūrḗthroskōp; 2. juəríþrəskoup]. See prec. & **-scope**. Instrument for the examination of the interior of the urethra.

uretic, adj. [1. ūrḗtik; 2. ju(ə)rétik], fr. Gk. *ourētikós*, see **ureter** & **-ic**. Pertaining to the urine; diuretic.

urge (I.), vb. trans. [1. ērj; 2. ədž]. A late word, fr. 16th cent., fr. Lat. *urgēre*, fr. **wr̥g-*, 'to drive, urge', cogn. w. Gk. *eírgein*, fr. **wergj-*, 'to repress, constrain'; further Goth. *wrikan*, 'to persecute', O.E. *wrecan*, 'to drive, expel; to avenge', see **wreak**. **1.** To drive, press, impel, push forward, whether by blows, threats, or by persuasive words &c.: *to urge a horse on*; *he urged (on) the crew to greater efforts.* **2.** To press, persuade, encourage, exhort, insistently and vigorously: *to urge a person to do something*; *we are urged to economize in every way.* **3.** To bring forward, bring to notice, or to the attention, pressingly and insistently; to press, insist upon: *to urge the necessity for immediate action*; *let me urge upon you the importance of this measure.*

urge (II.), n., fr. prec. (mod. Americanism, to be avoided) Powerful, spiritual impulse; sense of being compelled to do something; strong impelling motive, incentive: *an urge to go and convert the heathen*; *to feel the urge of ambition.*

urgency, n. [1. érjensi; 2. ə́džənsi], fr. Fr. *urgence*. Next word & **-cy**. Quality of being urgent. **1.** Stress, exigency, pinch: *the urgency of poverty.* **2.** The need for haste, necessity for immediate action; pressing character: *a matter of great urgency.* **3.** Insistence, importunity: *the urgency of a claimant.*

urgent, adj. [1. ĕrjent; 2. ʌ́dʒənt]. Fr., fr. Lat. *urgent-(em)*, Pres. Part. of *urgēre*, 'to press, force, impel'. See **urge (I.)**. **1.** (of circumstances) Extremely pressing, demanding immediate attention or action; gravely important: *urgent necessity*; *in urgent need of help*. **2. a** (of persons) Using great insistence in demanding; pressing, plying, with persistence and importunity: *an urgent suitor*; **b** (of pleas, demands &c.) made, pressed, with insistence and importunity.

urgently, adv. Prec. & **-ly**. In an urgent manner; insistently; to an urgent degree.

-uria, form used as suff. in compounds, fr. Gk. suff.- *ouría*, fr. *oûron*, see **urine**; as *dysuria*, difficulty in passing urine; *pyuria*, urine containing pus &c.

uric, adj. [1. úrik; 2. júərik, jɔ́rik], fr. **urine** & **-ic**. Pertaining to, found in, urine; esp. *uric acid*, a white, almost insoluble acid, forming the chief constituent of the urine of birds and reptiles, and existing also, in small quantities, in normal mammalian urine, but in morbid conditions deposited as calculi or stone in the kidney and bladder, or as concretions in the joints of gouty subjects &c.

urim and thummim, ns. [1. úrim ən(d) thúmim; 2. júərim ən(d) þámim]. Heb. pls., lit. 'light' & 'perfection'. Two objects, mentioned in the Bible, first in connection with the casting of lots, secondly as kept in the breastplate of the High Priest.

urinal, n. [1. úrinal; 2. jɔ́rinəl]. O. Fr., fr. L. Med. Lat. *ūrīnāle*, 'a urinal', neut. sing. of Lat. *ūrīnālis*, adj., 'pertaining to urine', see **urine** & **-al**. **1.** Vessel into which urine may be discharged, esp. one of a special shape, easy of use by sick persons in bed. **2.** A fixed receptacle, or series of receptacles for urine, in a covered place, esp. one for the use of the public; a lavatory.

urinary, adj. [1. úrinari; 2. júərinəri]. See **urine** & **-ary**, cp. Med. Lat. *ūrīnārium*. Pertaining to urine: *urinary diseases, organs* &c.

urinate, vb. intrans. [1. úrināt; 2. júərineit], fr. Med. Lat. *ūrīnāt-(um)*, P.P. type of *ūrīnāre*; see **urine** & **-ate**. To pass urine, micturate.

urine, n. [1. úrin; 2. júərin, jɔ́rin]. O. Fr., fr. Lat. *ūrīna*, cogn. w. Gk. *oûron*, 'urine', & Scrt. *vāri*. A yellow-coloured fluid secreted by the kidneys, passed by the ureter into the bladder and thence discharged from the body through the urethra.

urino-, pref. Form used in compounds, fr. prec., as *urinogenital*, pertaining to the urinary and reproductive organs; *urinometer*, instrument for measuring the specific gravity of urine.

urn (I.), n. [1. ĕrn; 2. ʌn], fr. Fr. *urne*, fr. Lat. *urna* for **urcna*, cogn. w. *urceus*, 'pitcher', see **urceolate**. **1.** A vase-shaped vessel, of pottery or metal, usually with a foot or pedestal and rounded in the centre with narrow neck, used to contain the ashes of the dead: *a cinerary, funeral, urn*; also, a sculptured representation of such on a tomb: '*storied urn or animated bust*' (Gray's 'Elegy'). **2.** A large metal vessel with tap, heated by a spirit lamp or other method, in which tea, coffee &c. can be kept hot and served to a large number of people.

urn (II.), vb. trans., fr. prec. (very rare) To place, preserve (as ashes of the dead), in an urn.

urnful, n. [1. ĕrnfool; 2. ʌ́nful]. **urn (I.)** & **-ful**. As much as an urn will hold.

uro- (I.), pref. Form used in compounds, fr. Gk. *oûron*, see **urine**, w. same force as *urino-*, as *urology*, science dealing with the urinary organs, their diseases &c.; *urosepsis*, septic condition due to disease of these organs.

uro- (II.), pref. Form used esp. in anatomical terminology, fr. Gk. *ourá*, 'tail', allied to *órros*, 'rump, base of the spine', fr. **órsos*, cogn. w. O.H.G. *ars*, O.E. *ærs*; as *urodaeum* (Neo-Lat. w. second element fr. Gk. *hodós*, 'way, passage'), the cloacal cavity of birds and reptiles.

Ursa, n. [1. ĕrsa; 2. ʌ́sə]. Lat., 'she-bear', fem. of *ursus*, 'bear', fr. **urcsos*, cogn. w. Gk. *árktos*, see **arctic**. Name of two northern constellations, *U. Major*, the Great Bear, Charles's Wain, the Plough; *U. Minor*, the Little Bear, which contains the Pole Star.

ursine, adj. [1. ĕrsīn; 2. ʌ́sain], fr. Lat. *ursīnus*, fr. *ursus*, 'bear', see prec., & **-ine**. Pertaining to, like, a bear.

urticaceous, adj. [1. ĕrtikáshus; 2. ʌtikéiʃəs], fr. Lat. *urtīca*, 'nettle', origin very doubtful, & **-aceous**. (bot.) Pertaining to the nettle family, *Urticaceae*, of plants and shrubs.

urticaria, n. [1. ĕrtikária; 2. ʌtikéəriə]. Neo-Lat., see prec. (med.) Nettle-rash.

urticate, vb. trans. [1. ĕrtikāt; 2. ʌ́tikeit], fr. Med. Lat. *urticāt-(um)*, *urticāre*, fr. Lat. *urtīca*, 'nettle', see **urticaceous**. To sting, as a nettle; to whip with nettles, in order to restore circulation &c.

urtication, n. [1. ĕrtikáshun; 2. ʌtikéiʃən]. See next word & **-ion**. Itching, tingling, burning, sensation on the skin, as from nettle stings, or in nettle-rash.

urubu, n. [1. ŏŏrooboŏ; 2. úrubū]. Native name. The black vulture of the Amazon districts &c. of S. America.

urus, n. [1. úrus; 2. júərəs]. Lat., fr. Gmc., cp. O.H.G., O.E. *ūr*; cogn. w. Scrt. *usrá-*, 'ox'. See also **aurochs**. The wild ox of Europe, the aurochs.

us, pron. pl. [1. us; 2. as]. Objective case of **we**; O.E. *ūs*, dat., fr. **uns-*; M.E. *ous, ūs*; O.H.G. *uns*; Goth. *uns*; Aryan type **ns*, cogn. w. Lat. *nōs*; Gk. dual. *nṓ*, pl. *nemâs*; Scrt. *nās*; O. Slav. *nasŭ*.

usable, adj. [1. úzabl; 2. júzəbl]. **use (I.)** & **-able**. Capable of being, fit to be, used.

usage, n. [1. úzij; 2. júzidʒ]. M.E., fr. O. Fr.; fr. L. Med. Lat. *ūsagium*, *ūsaticum*, see **use (I.)** & **-age**. **1. a** Way, manner, of using, treating, handling; treatment: *such delicate instruments will not stand rough usage*; *good usage has preserved them*; **b** way of using a word to express a particular sense, shade of meaning &c. **2.** Habitual practice, long established use or custom, esp. as establishing a legal right, an acknowledged standard &c.: *to keep an old usage alive*; *some modern usages could be dispensed with*; *common usage has accustomed us to this*.

usance, n. [1. úzans; 2. júzəns]. O. Fr.; see **use** & **-ance**. (commerc.) Time allowed by custom for the payment of foreign bills of exchange.

use (I.), n. [1. ūs; 2. jūs]. M.E. *ūs*, O. Fr. *ūs*, fr. Lat. *ūs-us*, n., 'usage, custom, use'; also P.P. of *ūti*, 'to use'; the older Lat. form is *oisus, oiti*. Further connexions highly uncertain. In the legal sense (see **6** below), the word is strictly fr. O. Fr. *oes, ues*, 'profit, benefit', fr. Lat. *opus*, 'work, need, employment', see **opus**, but was levelled in pronunciation w. O. Fr. *us*, 'use'. **1.** Act of employing, or using anything; employment in, application to, some purpose or service: *to teach, learn, the use of tools, implements* &c.; *the proper use of one's faculties, limbs*; *the use of the telephone is growing very rapidly*; *the use of coal for domestic fires ought to be diminished*. Phrs. *to be in use*, be used, employed; *to be, fall, out of use*, cease to be used; *with use*, by using constantly; *to make use of, put to use*. **2. a** Capacity, power, of using: *to lose the use of one's legs, eyes* &c.; **b** liberty, right to use: *he put the use of his house, purse &c., at my disposal*; **c** need, opportunity, occasion, for using: *will there be any further use for big battleships in war?* **3. a** Usefulness, utility; advantage, purpose served: *to be of use, of no use*; *what's the use of so many officials?*; *is there any use in discussing the matter further?*; **b** purpose, end, object, for which something is used: *to find a use for old scrap iron*; *to have no further use for anything*; (colloq.) *to have no use for*, to dislike, see no merits in. **4.** Custom, usage, habit, continued practice, wont (slightly archaic): *it was his use to walk ten miles every day*; *according to an ancient use*. Specif. **5.** (eccles.) a special ritual or liturgy as observed by a church or diocese: *the Roman, Orthodox, Anglican use*; *the use of Sarum, Bangor* &c. **6.** (law) The profit or benefit from lands or tenements held in trust for another; the beneficial or equitable as contrasted with the legal ownership; profit or benefit from a trust.

use (II.), vb. trans. [1. ūz; 2. jūz], fr. O. Fr. *user*, fr. L. Lat. *ūsāre*, 'to use', formed fr. Lat. *ūs-(um)*, P.P. type of *ūti*, 'to use'; see prec. word. **A.** trans. **1.** To employ, to apply to a purpose, to put to a useful service; to handle usefully or properly; **a** in physical sense, of implements &c.: *to learn to use a saw*; **b** of mental action: *to use information to serve one's ends*; *to know how to use books*. **2.** (of one's faculties, body &c.) To exercise, employ actively, to put to use (in physical and mental sense): *to use one's legs*, to walk; *one's eyes*, to look; *one's ears*, to hear; *to use one's brains, wits*, to think. **3.** To consume, exhaust, expend: *to use a ton of coal in a month*; *how many eggs has the cook used for this omelette?*; *too little paint has been used on the gate*; *use up*, to consume completely, exhaust altogether: *the coal is all used up*; *to use up one's energy in fruitless efforts*; *to feel used up*, feel quite exhausted. **4.** To bring to bear, put into operation: *to use care, diligence*; *to use all one's skill*. **5.** To behave toward, treat, in some specified way: *to use a person well or ill*; *to ill-use*; (archaic, ending of letters) *yours as you shall use me*. **6.** To have the use of, avail oneself of: *use my house as if it were your own*; *may I use your telephone?* **B.** intrans. **a** (i.) (archaic except in pret.) To be accustomed, make a practice, have the habit, be wont: '*Were it not better done, as others use, To sport with Amaryllis in the shade?*' (Milton, 'Lycidas', 67-8); (ii.) pret. [jūst]: *I used to see him often*; *I used to smoke pipes when I was young*; (iii.) in neg. sentences, *use(d)n't* (to), (illit. or vulg.) *didn't use (to)*, [júsnt, dídnt jūs(tu)]; **b** impersonal constructions: *it used to be said*; *there used to be a house here*.

used, adj. [1. ūst; 2. jūst], fr. P.P. of **use (II.)**. Accustomed, habituated, inured to; experienced in: *you'll soon get used to our ways*; *quite used to one's new surroundings*; *I'm not used to being spoken to like that*; *used to hardship, to hard work*; *used to every comfort and luxury*; *he is not used to good society yet*.

useful, adj. [1. úsfl; 2. júsfl]. **use (I.)** & **-ful**. Of use; serviceable, advantageous, productive of good results, helpful (in material and non-material senses): *a stout stick is useful in emergencies as a weapon*; *a useful remedy to have by one*; *to give useful advice*; *a useful book for young students*.

usefully, adv. Prec. & **-ly**. In a useful manner; so as to serve a useful purpose: *I can't usefully intervene at this point*.

usefulness, n. See prec. & **-ness**. State, quality, of being useful.

useless, adj. [1. úsles; 2. júslis]. **use (I.)** & **-less**. Of no use, unserviceable; not producing or productive of good results; serving no useful purpose, ineffectual: *a well-advertised but quite useless remedy*; *material aid is now useless*; *good advice is useless for some people*.

uselessly, adv. Prec. & **-ly**. In a useless manner.

uselessness, n. See prec. & **-ness**. State, quality, of being useless.

user (I.), n. [1. úzer; 2. júzə]. **use (I.)** & **-er**. One who uses or employs anything: *users of this remedy will probably be disappointed*.

user (II.), n., fr. O. Fr., infin. as n., see **use (I.)**. (law) Use or enjoyment of property; presumptive right to such by prescription.

ushabti, n. [1. ŏŏshábti; 2. uʃǽbti]. Egyptian, lit. 'answerer'. A small figure, in the form of a mummy, made of stone or wood, and later, of glazed faience, representing a servant &c., and deposited in an ancient Egyptian tomb with the body in order to accompany and serve the dead person in the other world.

usher (I.), n. [1. úsher; 2. áʃə]. M.E. *uschere, huissher*, fr. A.-Fr. *usser*, O. Fr. *ussier, (h)uissier*, fr. Lat. *ōstiārius*, 'door-keeper, porter', fr. *ōstium*, 'door, entrance', fr. *ōs, ōris*, 'mouth', see **oral. 1. a** Official in charge of the door or entrance to a court, hall &c., who admits or keeps out the public, shows people to their seats, keeps order and silence &c.: *an usher of the High Court of Justice* &c.; **b** one of several officials, *gentlemen ushers*, of the Royal Household, who precede ceremonial processions &c., specif., a high official of the principal orders of knighthood, as *Gentleman Usher of the Black Rod*, i.e. of the Garter &c. **2.** (obsolesc., except as term of contempt) An under-master at a school for boys.

usher (II.), vb. trans., fr. prec. **1.** To act as usher or introducer; to walk before and conduct; to show in, introduce, announce: *a footman ushered me to the drawing-room; I was ushered in with great ceremony.* **2.** (fig. or poet.) *Usher in*, to precede, to herald, to be the harbinger of: *the song of birds that ushers in the dawn; the passing of the first Reform Bill ushered in a new era in English politics.*

ushership, n. [1. úshership; 2. áʃəʃip]. **usher** (I.) & **-ship.** Post, situation, of an usher, esp. in a school; an under-mastership.

usquebaugh, n. [1. ùskwibáw; 2. àskwibɔ́], fr. Ir. *uisge beatha*, lit. 'water of life; whisky', The first element is fr. O. Ir. *usce, uisce*, 'water', fr. **wud-ko-*; cogn. w. Scrt. *udán-*, 'water'; Gk. *húdōr*, see **hydro-**; Lat. *unda*, 'wave', see **undulate**; O. Slav. *voda*, 'water', see **vodka**; O.E. *wæter*, 'water', & *wǣt*, see **water** & **wet.** The second element is fr. O. Ir. *bethu*, 'life', cogn. w. Gk. *bíos*, see **bio-**; Lat. *vīta*, 'life', see **vital**; O.E. *cwicu*, 'living', see **quick.** (archaic) Whisky.

ustulation, n. [1. ùstūláshun; 2. àstjuléiʃən], fr. obs. *ustulate*, 'to burn, scorch', & **-ion**, fr. Lat. *ustulāt-(um), ustulāre*, in same sense, fr. *ūrere, ust-(um)*, 'to burn', see second element in **combustion.** (rare and obs.) Scorching, burning, (esp. chem.) the drying by heat of moist substances as a preparatory stage of reducing them to powder.

usual, adj. [1. úzhooal; 2. júʒuəl], fr. Fr. *usuel*, fr. Lat. *ūsuālis*, fr. *ūsu-*, stem of *ūsus*, 'use', see **use** (I.), & **-al.** In accordance with ordinary use, practice, custom, habit; such as is commonly met with in ordinary experience; such as is to be expected under given circumstances; habitual; commonplace, ordinary, familiar; the reverse of *strange, exceptional, extraordinary*: *the wedding was celebrated with the usual rites; the usual tale which such people tell; he said all the usual things; the usual people were there; it is usual for the king to open Parliament in person; it is not usual for shops to open on Sundays.* Phrs. *as usual*, in accordance with what is usual, in the ordinary way; *the usual (thing)*, that which is usually done, said, received &c.

usually, adv. Prec. & **-ly.** As a matter of habit, custom &c.; generally, in the ordinary way: *one usually takes one's hat off in the house; he usually spent the morning at work, in bed.*

usualness, n. See prec. & **-ness.** (rare) State, quality, of being usual; commonplaceness.

usucaption, also **usucapion**, n. [1. ūzūkápshun, -kápiun; 2. jūzjukǽpʃən, -kéipiən], fr. Lat. *ūsucaptiōn-(em)*, 'prescription', fr. *ūsucapt-*, P.P. type of *ūsucapere*, 'to obtain, possess, by long use or prescription'; fr. *ūsus*, 'use', see **use, user,** & **captive.** (Rom. and civil law) Acquisition of right or title to property by uninterrupted use or possession for specified period of time; prescription.

usufruct, n. [1. úzūfrukt; 2. júzjufrakt], fr. Lat. *ūsusfructus*, in same sense, fr. *ūsus*, 'use', see prec., & *fructus*, 'fruit', see **fruit.** (Rom. and civil law) Right to the use and profits of property belonging to another without damage to it or waste.

usufructuary, n. [1. ūzūfrúktūari; 2. jūzjufráktjuəri], fr. L. Lat. *ūsusfructuārius*, see prec. & **-ary.** One having the usufruct of property.

usurer, n. [1. úzhurer; 2. júʒərə]. In M.E., fr. O. Fr. *usurier*, fr. L. Lat. *ūsuārius*, see **usury** & **-er. a** (archaic and Bib.) One who lends money at interest; **b** one who lends money at exorbitant or illegal rates of interest; an extortionate money-lender.

usurious, adj. [1. ūzhóōrius; 2. juʒɔ́riəs]. **usury** & **-ous. a** Of the nature of usury, involving usury: *a usurious rate of interest, loan, bond* &c.; **b** practising usury, extortionate.

usuriously, adv. Prec. & **-ly.** In a usurious manner; with usury.

usuriousness, n. See prec. & **-ness.** State, quality, of being usurious.

usurp, vb. trans. & intrans. [1. ūzérp; 2. jūzə́p]. M.E., fr. Fr. *usurper*, fr. Lat. *ūsurpāre*, 'to gain, acquire', in bad sense, 'to seize, usurp'; for *ūsu-rapere*, fr. *ūsu-*, see **use** (I.), & *rapere*, 'to seize'. See **rapid** & **rapt. 1.** trans. To seize, take, assume, possession of, without right or by force: *to usurp the throne, office, power, the functions of a dictator* &c. **2.** intrans. (rare or archaic) *Usurp (up)on*, to encroach upon.

usurpation, n. [1. ūzerpáshun; 2. jūzəpéiʃən], fr. Lat. *ūsurpātiōn-(em)*, fr. *ūsurpāt-(um)*, P.P. type of *ūsurpāre*, see prec., & **-ion.** Act of usurping; wrongful or violent seizure of power, authority &c.: *the usurpation of a throne; a flagrant usurpation on the prerogatives of others.*

usurper, n. [1. ūzérper; 2. jūzə́pə]. **usurp** & **-er.** One who usurps; esp. one who wrongfully takes, accepts, holds, kingly status and authority in place of the rightful heir.

usurpingly, adv. [1. ūzérpingli; 2. jūzə́piŋli]. Pres. Part. of **usurp** & **-ly.** By usurpation.

Usury, n. [1. úzhuri; 2. júʒəri]. M.E. *usure, usurie, userie*, fr. Fr. *usure*, fr. Lat. *ūsūra*, 'use, enjoyment'; also 'interest, usury', fr. *ūsus*, see **use** (I.), & **-ure** & **-y. 1 a** (archaic an . Bib.) Practice of lending money at interest; **b** the lending of money at illegal or exorbitant rates of interest: *various statutes have been passed to check or limit usury.* **2.** Interest charged or received (often fig.): *she returned his love and devotion with usury.*

ut (I.), conj. [1. ut; 2. at]. Lat., 'as', fr. same base (w. different formative suff.) as *u-bi*, 'where', see **ubiety.** Chiefly in phr. *ut supra, infra*, as shown above, below.

ut (II.), n. [1. oot; 2. ut]. See **gamut.** The first or key note in the musical scale of Guido d' Arezzo, now, in solmization, replaced by *Do.*

utas, n. [1. útas; 2. jútæs]. M.E., fr. A.-Fr. *utaves*, fr. O. Fr. *oitauve*, fr. Lat. *octāva (diēs)*, 'eighth day', see **octave.** (eccles., rare or archaic) The octave or eight days of a feast.

utensil, n. [1. ūténsl; 2. jūténsl], fr. M. Fr. *utensile*, Mod. Fr. *ustensile*, fr. Lat. *ūtensilis*, 'fit for use', esp. in neut. pl. *ūtensilia*, 'things for use', for **ūtentilis*, fr. *ūtent-*, Pres. Part. stem of *ūti*, 'to use', see **use** (II.). **a** Any object or implement, a tool, usually one of moderate size, used for a specified purpose: *writing utensils; farming utensils*; **b** specif., a vessel of any kind used in the household or the dairy.

uterine, adj. [1. úterīn; 2. jútərain]. Fr., fr. L. Lat. *uterīnus*, see next word & **-ine. 1.** (med.) Pertaining to the uterus or womb: *uterine artery, disease* &c. **2.** Born of the same mother but by a different father: *uterine brother(s)*; so also *uterine descent* &c.

uterus, n., pl. **uteri** [1. úterus, -ī; 2. jútərəs, -ai]. Lat., 'womb', cogn. w. Scrt. *udára-*, 'belly'. The womb.

utilitarian (I.), adj. [1. ūtilitárian; 2. jùtilitéəriən]. A mod. word coined fr. **utility** & **-arian** by Bentham. **1.** Conducing to, aiming at, utility; materially or practically useful; serving material or practical ends (often in derogatory sense): *from the merely utilitarian point of view; true education cannot be purely utilitarian or professional.* **2.** Pertaining to the Utilitarians, or to their school of thought.

Utilitarian (II.), n., fr. prec. A follower of the political philosophy of Jeremy Bentham and John Stuart Mill, which makes utility, in the widest sense, the test of the rightness of political and moral action, and virtue to consist in promoting the happiness of the greatest number.

Utilitarianism, n. [1. ūtilitárianizm; 2. jutilitéəriənizəm]. Prec. & **-ism.** (philos.) The political and ethical theory of the Utilitarians, namely, that the end and criterion of all individual and political action should be the greatest happiness of the greatest number.

utility, n. [1. ūtíliti; 2. jūtíliti], fr. Fr. *utilité*, fr. Lat. *ūtilitāt-(em)*, fr. *ūtilis*, 'useful', fr. *ūt-*, a form of the base seen in *ūsus*, see **use** (I.); cp. also infin. *ūti*, Pres. *ūtor* &c. **1.** State, property, quality, of being useful; usefulness, advantageousness, the being profitable. Phr. *of no utility*, useless. **2.** Usually *utilities*, useful things; (theatr. slang) *utility man*, man capable of playing various kinds of minor parts; general handy-man.

utilizable, adj. [1. útilīzabl; 2. jútilaizəbl]. **utilize** & **-able.** Capable of being utilized or used.

utilization, n. [1. ūtilīzáshun; 2. jūtilaizéiʃən]. **utilize** & **-ation. a** Act of utilizing; **b** state of being utilized.

utilize, vb. trans. [1. útilīz; 2. jútilaiz]. Fr., fr. *utiliser*, a mod. word fr. Lat. *ūtilis*, 'useful', see **utility**, & **-ize.** To put to use, make use of; to turn to profitable use or account.

utmost (I.), adj. [1. útmost; 2. átmoust]. O.E. *ūtemest*, M.E. *ūtemest* &c., superl. of *ūt(e)*, 'out', see **out**; the O.E. ending is an old double superl. suff.; this was later influenced in form by *most*, see **-most. 1.** Outermost, situated at farthest extreme or limit; farthest, most extreme: *to the utmost ends of the earth; utmost limits; filled to its utmost capacity.* **2.** To, of, the greatest, highest, degree: *in the utmost danger and misery; ready to help with the utmost pleasure.*

utmost (II.), n., fr. prec. The most that can be done; the most possible; the greatest possible effort: *that is the utmost that I can do; try your utmost to succeed; to the utmost of one's power* &c.

Utopia, n. [1. ūtópia; 2. jūtóupiə], lit. 'nowhere', coined by Sir Thomas More, fr. Gk. *ou*, 'not' (etymol. unknown), & *tópos*, 'place,' see **topic. 1.** (cap.) The name of the imaginary island governed on a perfect political and social system, giving the title to More's book, 'Utopia', published 1516. **2.** Any ideal community or state; an ideally perfect social and political system, usually with the implication that such is impossible of realization: *the foundation of Utopias in imagination will never cease; the new Utopia has failed.* **3.** Any literary work describing such an ideal state or system: *Samuel Butler's Utopia is styled 'Erewhon'.*

Utopian, adj. & n. [1. ūtópian; 2. jūtóupiən]. Prec. & **-an. 1.** adj. **a** Pertaining to, characteristic of, a Utopia, ideally perfect but impracticable; chimerical, visionary: *Utopian schemes*; **b** apt to form or imagine Utopias: *a Utopian dreamer.* **2.** n. Inhabitant of a Utopia.

utricle, n. [1. útrikl; 2. jútrikl]. Fr., fr. Lat. *ūtriculus*, 'a little bag', dimin. of *ūter*, 'leather sack or bag', a collateral form of **uterus.** (physiol.) **a** A cell or sac in an animal or plant, esp. an air sac or vesicle in certain aquatic plants, as the bladderworts (*Utricularia*) &c.; **b** a cavity in the labyrinth of the inner ear.

utricular, adj. [1. ūtríkūlar; 2. jūtríkjulə], fr. Lat. *utriculus*, see prec. & **-ar.** Pertaining to, resembling, a utricle.

utter (I.), adj. [1. úter; 2. átə]. O.E. *ūtera*,

ūtra, 'outer', M.E. *ūt(t)ere*, an old compar. adj. formed fr. O.E. *ūt*, see **out**; shortening of the old long vowel takes place in M.E. in the first syll. of a three-syllabled word. **1.** Outer, situated on the outside; now obs. except in the rarely used *utter bar, barrister*, for those members of the bar who have not been called within the bar; the junior bar, those who are not King's Counsel or, formerly, serjeants-at-law. **2. a** Complete, total: *utter darkness, misery, ruin* &c.; **b** unconditional, final, peremptory: *an utter refusal, denial* &c.; **c** unqualified, absolute: *an utter scoundrel*; *the utter folly of such a policy.*

utter (II.), vb. trans. M.E. fr. *uttren*, formed fr. *uttere*, see prec., or formed again later fr. the adv. or adj. **1.** (orig. meaning) To put out, or forth, now only **a** *to utter a libel*, publish it; **b** *to utter false coin, notes* &c., to produce and put these into circulation; *charged with forging and uttering cheques* &c. **2. a** (i.) To produce audibly by means of the vocal organs; to pronounce: *to utter a vowel sound*; *not a sound was uttered*; *the last words to be uttered*; also (ii.) to breathe out, to emit through the mouth: *to utter a groan, a sigh*; **b** to express, make known, by word of mouth or in writing: *to utter one's thoughts, feelings* &c.

utterable, adj. [1. úterabl; 2. átərəbl]. Prec. & **-able.** (rare) Capable of being uttered.

utterance (I.), n. [1. úterans; 2. át(ə)rəns]. **utter (II.)** & **-ance.** **1.** Act of uttering or expressing in words &c.: *to give utterance to one's feelings.* **2.** Mode, style, manner, of speaking; pronunciation, delivery: *a thick, clear, slovenly, utterance* &c. **3.** That which is uttered; spoken or written expression of thoughts, opinions &c.; pronouncement: *the pompous utterances of the platform, the press* &c. **4.** (rare) Act of uttering or circulating; putting, passing, into circulation: *utterance of false coin.*

utterance (II.), n. M.E., fr. Fr. *oultrance*, see **outrance**, & **ultra**; influenced in form by association w. *utter*, adj. (archaic, poet.) Extremity; the uttermost: *to the utterance*, (Shakespeare, 'Macbeth').

utterer, n. [1. úterer; 2. átərə]. **utter (II.)** & **-er.** One who utters (in various senses): *an utterer of slander, of false coins* &c.

uttering, n. [1. útering; 2. átəriŋ]. **utter (II.)** & **-ing.** **a** Act of expressing in words &c.; **b** act of circulating: *the forging and uttering of a cheque.*

utterly, adv. [1. úterli; 2. átəli]. **utter (I.)** & **-ly.** To the fullest extent; completely, totally: *utterly exhausted, ruined* &c.

uttermost, adj. & n. [1. útermōst; 2. átəmoust]. **utter (I.)** & **-most.** **1.** adj. **a** Farthest away, farthest out: *to the uttermost ends of the earth*; **b** extreme, utmost; being of the highest, greatest, degree: *the uttermost limit of forbearance.* **2.** n. The utmost; highest degree or extremity: *to the uttermost of one's power, capacity* &c.

utterness, n. [1. útemes; 2. átənis]. **utter (I.)** & **-ness.** Quality of being extreme; completeness: *the utterness of his folly and wickedness.*

uvula, n., pl. **uvulae** [1. ū́vūla, -lē; 2. jū́vjulə, -lī], fr. Fr. *uvula*, fr. L. or Med. Lat. *ūvula*, dimin. of Lat. *ūva*, 'a grape, bunch of grapes, uvula'; fr. **oiwā*; cogn. w. Gk. *óā*, Ionic *óē, oiē* for **oiwā-*, 'service-tree; a berry'. (anat.) **a** A fleshy, hanging protuberance in the centre of the posterior part of the soft palate; **b** similar protuberance in the cerebellum and the bladder.

uvular, adj. [1. ū́vūlar; 2. jū́vjulə]. Prec. & **-ar.** Pertaining to the uvula; specif. (phon.) velar.

uvulitis, n. [1. ūvūlítis; 2. jūvjuláitis]. See prec. & **-itis.** Inflammation of the uvula.

uxorious, adj. [1. ukzṓrius; 2. akzṓriəs], fr. Lat. *uxōrius*, 'pertaining to, excessively fond of, a wife', fr. *uxor*, 'wife'; perh. orig. 'she who is led home', fr. base seen in Lat. *vehere*, 'to draw' &c., see **vehicle**; cp. Lith. *vedú*, 'I lead, conduct', & Scrt. *vadhū́-*, 'bride'. Excessively fond of or devoted to one's wife; too submissive to the will of one's wife.

uxoriously, adv. Prec. & **-ly.** In an uxorious manner.

uxoriousness, n. See prec. & **-ness.** State, quality, of being uxorious.

V

V, v [1. vē; 2. vī]. **a** The twenty-second letter of the alphabet; for use in abbreviations &c. see end of Dictionary; **b** the Roman symbol for the numeral 5; **c** a V-shaped object.

vac, n. [1. vak; 2. væk]. Colloq. abbr. of **vacation.**

vacancy, n. [1. vā́kansi; 2. véikənsi]. Through Fr. *vacance*, or directly fr. L. or Med. Lat. *vacantia*, fr. Lat. *vacant-(em)*, see **vacant**, & **-ancy.** **1.** (in physical senses) **a** Condition, state, of being vacant, unoccupied, or empty; emptiness: *to gaze on the vacancy of the polar ice-fields*; *look down from the precipice into vacancy*; **b** an empty, unoccupied, unfilled, space; a vacant space: *there is still a vacancy for another villa in the new road.* **2. a** State of being mentally vacant; absent-mindedness, lack of interest, listlessness; inanity, vacuity: *an expression of vacancy on his face*; *sudden periods of vacancy preceded his breakdown*; **b** state of being unoccupied or freed from work or business; inactivity, want of occupation: *an active, busy man dreads the vacancy of retirement*; **c** a gap, blank, deficiency: *it will fill a vacancy in our knowledge.* **3.** A vacant, unfilled, unoccupied, post, situation, or office; form of employment waiting to be filled: *there are still a few vacancies on the staff to be filled*; *his death has caused a vacancy in the Cabinet.*

vacant, adj. [1. vā́kant; 2. véikənt]. Through O. Fr. or directly fr. Lat. *vacant-(em)*, Pres. Part. type of *vacāre*, 'to be empty; to be unoccupied or without an owner; to lack or be without; to be free from toil, be at leisure'. The base is seen also in Lat. *vānus*, 'void, vacant; fruitless', see **vain**; cp. also **vacuous.** **1.** Empty, void, not filled by anything; having no material contents: *look down into vacant space*; *the vast and vacant regions of infinite space.* **2. a** Not occupied by man; uninhabited; not populated or developed: *the vacant regions of the North-West*; *vacant prairies clamouring for colonists*; **b** not held or occupied by owner or tenant; untenanted: *many vacant farms*; *increase of vacant houses in a town*; Phr. *vacant possession*, legal or auctioneer's term implying that immediate occupation and possession of house, farm &c. is offered; **c** not engaged or let; not already booked: *not a room vacant in the hotel*; *many vacant seats in the theatre*; **d** no longer occupied: *the vacant chair.* **3.** (of office, benefice &c.) Not held, filled, or occupied by anyone; left unoccupied by death, resignation &c.; waiting to be filled: *situations vacant*; *the resignation of Lord X leaves an important Cabinet post vacant.* **4.** (of periods of time) Not occupied by work or business; not engaged; leisured: *some occupation to fill the vacant hours*; *keep a day next week vacant if you can.* **5.** (of mental state, character &c.) **a** Not active or occupied with serious work or thought; empty, idle, vacuous: '*the loud laugh that spoke the vacant mind*' (Goldsmith, 'Deserted Village', 122); *to lead a silly, vacant life*; **b** characteristic of, expressing, such an unoccupied, empty mind: *a vacant stare, look* &c.

vacantly, adv. Prec. & **-ly.** In a vacant manner: *to stare, laugh, vacantly.*

vacate, vb. trans. [1. vakā́t, vākā́t; 2. vəkéit, veikéit], fr. Lat. *vacāt-(um)*, P.P. type of *vacāre*, 'to be empty; to be free from' &c., see **vacant.** **1.** To make, leave, vacant; to go away, depart from and leave unoccupied: *to vacate a house, rooms* &c.; *the enemy vacated the town as we advanced.* **2.** To give up, to resign from; to leave unfilled or unoccupied: *to vacate the throne*; *one bishopric vacated by death and two by translation*; *to vacate a seat in parliament.* **3.** (mil.) To remove, order to leave position, camp &c.: *all troops must be vacated from the town before noon.* **4.** (law) To render void; to annul, cancel, invalidate: *to vacate a contract, deed, registration* &c.

vacation, n. [1. vakā́shun; 2. vəkéiʃən]. Lat. *vacātiōn-(em)*, fr. *vacāt-*, see prec., & **-ion.** **1.** Act of vacating or leaving vacant, unfilled or unoccupied: *his sudden vacation of office is unexplained.* **2.** Period during which an office, benefice &c. is left vacant: *the vacation of the benefice was prolonged.* **3.** A fixed, stated, interval in a year during which the ordinary business, work, study &c. is suspended; used esp. of courts of law and of a university; period when the courts are 'up' or not sitting, or when the university is 'down' or not in residence: *the Christmas, Easter, vacation*; *the long vacation*, that which occupies the summer months.

vaccinal, adj. [1. váksinal; 2. væksinəl]. Fr., see **vaccine** & **-al.** Pertaining to vaccine or vaccination.

vaccinate, vb. trans. [1. váksinā̀t; 2. væksinèit], fr. **vaccine** & **-ate**; it was ad. fr. Fr. *vacciner*, c. 1803, in place of the earlier *inoculate.* **1.** To inoculate (child, person) with the vaccine, i.e. the virus, of cowpox, in the form of calf-lymph, as a protection against smallpox. **2.** To inoculate with other kinds of vaccine.

vaccination, n. [1. vàksinā́shun; 2. væksinéiʃən]. Prec. & **-ion.** Inoculation with a vaccine, esp. that of cowpox or vaccinia, as a protection against smallpox.

vaccinationist, n. [1. vàksinā́shunist; 2. væksinéiʃənist]. Prec. & **-ist.** One who advocates vaccination, esp. compulsory vaccination as protection against smallpox.

vaccinator, n. [1. váksinā̀ter; 2. væksineitə]. **vaccinate** & **-or.** **1.** Person, esp. public (medical) official, who performs compulsory vaccination on children and others. **2.** Instrument, scarifier, used in vaccination.

vaccine, n. [1. váksēn; 2. væksīn], fr. Fr. *vaccin*, fr. Lat. *vaccīnus*, 'pertaining to cows', fr. *vacca*, 'cow', cogn. w. Scrt. *vaçā́*, 'cow', prob. connected w. Scrt. *vā́çati*, 'cries, lows', & cogn. w. Lat. *vōx*, see **vocal.** **1.** n. **a** The virus of cowpox, 'vaccinia', obtained now from calves specially inoculated with the disease, in the form of lymph and used in vaccination for protection against smallpox; **b** the virus of other diseases, culture of the bacteria of such diseases as plague &c., used as inoculation against such diseases; cp. **serum.** **2.** (attrib.) Pertaining to a vaccine: *vaccine therapy*, treatment, prevention, of diseases by means of inoculation with a vaccine.

vaccinia, n. [1. vaksínia; 2. væksíniə]. Neo-Lat., fr. prec. Cowpox, a disease cognate with smallpox, now especially inoculated into calves for the purpose of obtaining a vaccine in form of lymph, used in vaccination against smallpox.

vaccinic, adj. [1. vaksínik; 2. væksínik]. **vaccine** & **-ic.** Pertaining to a vaccine or vaccines; **vaccinal.**

vacillate, vb. intrans. [1. vásilāt; 2. vǽsilẹit], fr. Lat. *vacillāt-(um)*, P.P. type of *vacillāre*, 'to sway, waver, vacillate', formed as if fr. an adj., **vacillus*, fr. base **wak*ʷ-, q.v. under **vehicle**. **1.** (somewhat rare) To sway, oscillate; to stagger. **2.** To waver in mind, intentions &c.; to hesitate, to change from one opinion to another; to alternate between two opinions or courses of action.

vacillating, adj. [1. vásilàting; 2. vǽsilèitiŋ], fr. Pres. Part. of prec. Hesitating, wavering, in opinion or action.

vacillatingly, adv. Prec. & **-ly**. In a vacillating manner.

vacillation, n. [1. vàsilā́shun; 2. vǽsiléiʃən], fr. Lat. *vacillātiōn-(em)*; see **vacillate** & **-ion**. Act of vacillating, wavering, or hesitating in opinions, intentions, action; hesitation, unsteadiness of opinion or character.

vacuity, n. [1. vakū́iti; 2. vəkjúiti], fr. Lat. *vacuitāt-(em), vacuitas*, fr. *vacuus*, 'empty', see **vacuous** & **-ity**. **1.** (rare or obs.) Emptiness, empty space. **2.** Emptiness of mind; lack of ideas, interest &c.: *vacuity of mind*; *vacuity of expression*.

vacuolar, vacuolate, adjs. [1. vákūolar, -āt; 2. vǽkju(ə)lə, -eit]. See next word & **-ar** & **-ate**. (biol.) Pertaining to, containing, a vacuole or vacuoles.

vacuole, n. [1. vákūōl; 2. vǽkjuoul]. Fr., a dimin. formed fr. Lat. **vacuum**. (biol.) A small vesicle or cavity, as in plant tissue, protoplasm &c., containing fluid or air.

vacuous, adj. [1. vákūus; 2. vǽkjuəs], fr. Lat. *vacuus*, 'empty, void; free from toil, care &c.', cogn. w. *vacāre*, see **vacant**, & **-ous**. **1.** Empty (archaic or obs. in physical sense). **2.** a Vacant in mind, empty-headed; stupid, unintelligent, meaningless: *an idle and vacuous young fellow*; *a vacuous stare*; b unoccupied, purposeless, idle; not profitably or usefully employed: *a selfish, vacuous life*.

vacuously, adv. Prec. & **-ly**. In a vacuous manner; vacantly, idly.

vacuousness, n. See prec. & **-ness**. State, quality, of being vacuous.

vacuum, n. [1. vákūum; 2. vǽkjuəm], pl. *vacuums*, learned pl. *vacua*. Lat.; neut. sing. of *vacuus*, 'empty', see **vacuous**. **1.** Space empty or devoid of all matter or content: *nature abhors a vacuum*. **2.** Specif., space or vessel from which the air has by various means been wholly or partially exhausted: *the vacuum of a barometer, in the atmosphere* &c. **3.** (lit. or fig.) Any space unoccupied or unfilled; a void, blank: *to leave a vacuum difficult to fill*; (also facetiously) *feel a vacuum in the lower regions*, be hungry.

vacuum brake, n. A continuous brake, used on railway trains, worked by the action of compressed air on a vacuum.

vacuum cleaner, n. An apparatus used for removing dust and dirt from carpets, curtains, upholstery &c. by means of suction.

vacuum flask, n. A double-walled vessel, with the air exhausted in the space between the walls, thus forming a vacuum; flask in which liquids may be kept either hot or cold for a considerable period; cp. *thermos flask*.

vacuum gauge, n. Gauge for measuring pressure in a vacuum.

vacuum pump, n. a Pump for exhausting air from an enclosed space and creating a vacuum; air-pump; b pump by which water is raised by pressure of air and steam on a vacuum.

vacuum tube, n. A sealed glass tube or vessel containing exhausted or highly rarefied air or gas with electrodes at each end through which a current of electricity is passed exhibiting various electrical, radio-active, and other phenomena; a special type called 'thermionic valve' is used in wireless telephony.

vade-mecum, n. [1. vā́de mḗkum; 2. véidi míkəm]. Lat., 'go with me'; Lat. *vādere*, 'to go', is related by gradation to *vadum*, 'ford', & cogn. w. O.E. *wadan*, 'to go, wade', see **wade**; O.H.G. *watan*, O.N. *vaða* &c. A handbook or manual that one carries about with one for quick reference; often used as title for such a book.

vagabond (I.), adj. [1. vágabond; 2. vǽgəbənd, -bɔnd]. O. Fr., fr. Lat. *vagābundus*, 'wandering', formed w. gerundive suff. *-bundus*, fr. *vagāri*, 'to wander, roam, about', see **vagary**. **1.** a Wandering, roaming, from place to place without a fixed abode or settled mode of life: *vagabond family of beggars*; *the vagabond classes*; *a vagabond singer* &c.; b inclined to live a wandering life; not steady or settled in character; worthless: *a vagabond kind of fellow*. **2.** Characteristic of wanderers; wandering, roving, irregular: *lead a vagabond life*; *vagabond habits*.

vagabond (II.) n., fr. prec. a One who wanders about without a fixed abode or regular means of livelihood; a tramp, vagrant: *actors were once classed with rogues and vagabonds*; (legal) an idle, disorderly person, as included under various *Vagrancy Acts* &c.; b (as term of abuse or reproach) an idle, worthless fellow: *she called her husband a lazy old vagabond*.

vagabond (III.), vb. intrans., fr. prec. (rare) To wander, roam, about, like a vagabond: *to go vagabonding all the world over*.

vagabondage, n. [1. vágabòndij; 2. vǽgəbɔ̀ndidž]. Fr.; see prec. words & **-age**. a State, character, of a vagabond; vagabond life or habits: *the charm of vagabondage which some people feel*; *to take to vagabondage*; b people living a vagabond life; the vagabond class; vagabonds collectively: *all the vagabondage of the countryside were there*.

vagabondism, n. [1. vágabondizm; 2. vǽgəbəndizəm, -bɔnd-]. **vagabond** & **-ism**. Habit of living a vagabond life; vagabondage.

vagabondize, vb. intrans. [1. vágabondiz; 2. vǽgəbəndaiz]. See prec. & **-ize**. To live as a vagabond; to wander about.

vagal, adj. [1. vā́gal; 2. véig(ə)l]. See **vagus** & **-al**. (anat.) Pertaining to, affecting, the vagus or pneumogastric nerve.

vagarious, adj. [1. vagā́rius; 2. vəgéəriəs]. See **vagary** & **-ous**. Full of, characterized by, vagaries; erratic, capricious.

vagary, n. [1. vagā́ri; 2. vəgéəri], fr. 17th cent., usually in verbal phrs., 'to make, lead &c. a vagary'; also in form *fegary, figary*; apparently borrowed as a n., fr. Lat. *vagāri*, 'to wander, roam, about', fr. *vagus*, 'wandering'; the base is prob. a variant form of that seen in **vacillate**; cp. **vague** & distinguish **vagrant**. **1.** (orig. meaning, now obs.) A wandering, ramble, an aimless excursion: *they led us a pretty vagary*; (also fig.) *the vagaries of the mind*. **2.** A prank, freak; whimsical, erratic, eccentric, fancy, act, conduct; caprice, whim: *the vagaries of a pampered film-star*; *the usual vagaries of fashion*; '*straight they changed their minds, . . . and into strange vagaries fell*' (Milton, 'P. L.', vi. 613-14).

vagina, n. [1. vajína; 2. vədžáinə]. Lat. *vāgina*, 'sheath, scabbard', fr. **vāsgina*; cogn. w. *vās*, 'vessel', see **vase** & cp. **vest** (I.). A sheath or sheath-like covering; specif. a (anat.) the canal leading from the female external organ of generation to the uterus; b (bot.) the sheath formed by a leaf round a stem, as in grasses.

vaginal, adj. [1. vajínal; 2. vədžáinl]. Prec. & **-al**. **1.** Pertaining to, connected with, the vagina. **2.** Sheath-like, serving as a sheath: *vaginal process*, of the temporal bone.

vaginate(d), adj. [1. vájināt(ed); 2. vǽdžinèit(id)]. See **vagina** & **-ate**. (bot.) Sheathed, closed in a vagina, as the leaf-stalk of grasses &c.

vaginitis, n. [1. vàjinítis; 2. vǽdžináitis]. **vagina** & **-itis**. (med.) Inflammation of the vagina.

vago-, pref. Form, fr. **vagus**, used in anatomy & physiology, in compounds denoting connexion w. that nerve: *vago-accessory, -sympathetic* &c.

vagrancy, n. [1. vā́gransi; 2. véigrənsi]. See **vagrant** & **-ancy**. State of being vagrant; habit, act, of wandering from place to place without settled abode or means of livelihood; vagrants or tramps collectively: *vagrancy has increased since the war*; *statistics, suppression, of vagrancy*; *Vagrancy Acts*, various statutes, of wide application, dealing with rogues, vagabonds, idle and disorderly persons &c.

vagrant (I.), adj. [1. vā́grant; 2. véigrənt]. M.E. *vagaraunt, vagraunt*, fr. A.-Fr. *wakerant*, O. Fr. *wan(l)erant*, Pres. Part. of *walerer*, 'to walk, wander about', also *wal-, waucrant*; of Gmc. origin, see **walk**, but confused w. & assimilated to Lat. *vagāri*, 'to wander', cp. **vagabond** & **vagary**. **1.** Wandering, roaming, from place to place; nomadic, itinerant, living the life of a vagabond or tramp: *a band of vagrant minstrels, beggars* &c.; *the vagrant tribes of the desert*. **2.** Characteristic of a wanderer or vagabond devoted to wandering or vagrancy: *a vagrant life*; *vagrant habits*. **3.** (fig.) Flitting hither and thither, wayward, roving: *vagrant thoughts, fancies* &c.

vagrant (II.), n., see prec. One who wanders from place to place; a vagabond, a tramp; person with no settled abode or livelihood; an idle and disorderly person.

vagrantly, adv. [1. vā́grantli; 2. véigrəntli]. **vagrant** (I.) & **-ly**. In a vagrant, wandering manner; as a vagrant or tramp.

vagrom, adj. [1. vā́grom; 2. véigrəm]. Dogberry's corruption of **vagrant** in 'Much Ado about Nothing'.

vague, adj. [1. vāg; 2. veig]. Fr., 'wandering', fr. *vaguer*, 'to wander', fr. Lat. *vagāri*, see **vagary**, or fr. *vagus*, 'wandering'. **1.** Perceived indistinctly by the senses; not clearly defined; blurred; indeterminate, shadowy, indefinable; difficult to recognize with certainty: *a vague and shadowy outline*; *a vague, subtle odour*; *a vague taste of bitter almonds*; *the rather vague quality of unstressed vowels in English*. **2.** Not clearly perceived, grasped, conceived by the mind; indefinite, lacking precision: *vague hopes, ideas*; *his knowledge is rather vague*; *I haven't the vaguest notion what to do, where I left my umbrella*. **3.** Not expressed or defined with clearness and precision; ambiguous, equivocal, conveying an uncertain meaning; loosely phrased: *vague answers, statements, promises*; *the powers of the Board are purposely left vague*. **4.** (of persons) a Absent-minded, distrait, appearing not to be fully alive to what is taking place or being said; not having clear ideas &c.: *she is so vague that I never feel sure whether she realizes who one is*; b expressing oneself without precision, not given to clear-cut statements; not making wishes, opinions, intentions &c. absolutely clear and unambiguous: *he is very vague as to what he really wants*.

vaguely, adv. Prec. & **-ly**. In a vague way.

vagueness, n. See prec. & **-ness**. State, quality, of being vague.

vagus, n. [1. vā́gus; 2. véigəs], fr. Lat., 'wandering', see **vagary**. (anat.) The pneumogastric nerve.

vail (I.), n. [1. vāl; 2. veil]. Shortened form of **avail**, in sense of 'profit, aid'. (archaic) A gratuity, tip; servant's perquisites.

vail (II.), vb. trans. & intrans.; shortened form fr. *avale*, fr. Fr. *avaler*, 'to cast down, let fall', fr. *à val*, 'to the valley, downwards', cp. **avalanche**. (obs., except as liter. or poet. archaism) a trans. (i.) To take off, doff (hat &c.): '*vailed was her lofty crest*' (Spenser, 'F.Q.', III. 9, 20); '*The bonnets . . . were now at once vailed in honour of the royal warrant*' (Scott); (ii.) to lower, allow to fall; '*He looked but once, and vail'd his eyes again*' (Tennyson) &c.; b intrans. or absol., to take off hat &c.; lower one's head &c. as sign of greeting or respect.

vain, adj. [1. vān; 2. vein]. M.E. *vayn, veyn, vain* &c., fr. O. Fr. *vein, vain*, fr. Lat. *vānus*, 'empty, vain'; cogn. w. Goth. *wans*, 'lacking'; O.H.G., O.S., O.E. *wan*, 'lacking, deficient'; O.N. *vanr*, see **want**; further Gk. *eûnis*, 'deficient' Scrt. *ūnáš*, 'incomplete'. **1. a** Without result; useless, idle, fruitless, futile, unavailing: *all our efforts were vain*; *in the vain hope of success*; *it is vain to try to escape*; Phr. *in vain* (adv.), (i.) to no end or purpose, uselessly, fruitlessly: *to try in vain to succeed*; *all our efforts were in vain*; *in vain did I point out how time was getting on*; *these men have laboured and died in vain*; (ii.) (fr. Low Lat.) *in vanum nomen Dei assumere*, 'take the name of God in vain', to use it lightly, heedlessly, or profanely; also *take a person's name in vain*, speak of him slightingly, without due respect; **b** trivial; concerned with trifles; slight, petty, unsubstantial: *the vain day-dreams of youth*; *to waste one's life in vain pleasures*; *vain delights* &c. **2.** Having no real significance or foundation; unreal, baseless, empty: *vain threats, boasting, protestations of affection* &c. **3.** Ostentatious, concerned with outward show only; lacking real worth; hollow: *the vain pomps of a court*; *how vain are earthly splendours*. **4.** Having an exaggerated sense or opinion of one's own importance, personal appearance, one's possessions, talents, abilities &c.; conceited, self-satisfied, self-complacent: *a very vain man*; *adulation is apt to make men vain*; *vain of*, proud of, feeling self-satisfaction at: *little boys are naturally vain of their first long trousers*.

vainglorious, adj. [1. vànglṓrius; 2. vèinglṓriəs], fr. **vainglory** & **-ous**. Med. Lat. has *vānaglōriōsus*. **a** Given to, filled with, vainglory; inordinately, ostentatiously, vain or proud of one's actions, abilities &c.; boastful: *the defeat of these vainglorious athletes was popular*; **b** characteristic of, arising out of, exhibiting, vainglory: *vainglorious confidence*.

vaingloriously, adv. Prec. & **-ly**. In a vainglorious manner.

vaingloriousness, n. See prec. & **-ness**. Quality, condition, character, of being vainglorious.

vainglory, n. [1. vànglṓri; 2. vèinglṓri]. M.E. *vainglorie*; fr. O. Fr. *vaine gloire*, Med. Lat. *vāna glōria*, see **vain** & **glory**. Inordinate, ostentatious pride or vanity; boastfulness.

vainly, adv. [1. vā́nli; 2. véinli]. **vain** & **-ly**. **1.** Uselessly, in vain, futilely: *vainly tried to speak*. **2.** Conceitedly: *vainly proud of his appearance*.

vainness, n. [1. vā́nnes; 2. véinnis]. **vain** & **-ness**. Quality, state, of being vain, useless, or futile.

vair, n. [1. vār; 2. vɛə]. In M.E. & O. Fr., fr. Lat. *varius*, 'varied, parti-coloured', see **various** & cp. **minever**. **1.** (hist. and archaic) A parti-coloured fur, bluish grey and white, esp. that of a kind of squirrel, used as a trimming or lining for robes of knights. **2.** (her.) One of the heraldic furs, represented by rows of small shields or bells, alternately azure and argent unless otherwise mentioned.

Vaisya, n. [1. vī́shia; 2. váiʃiə]. Scrt. *vaiśya*, 'settler, peasant', fr. base *viś-*, 'to dwell', cogn. w. Lat. *vīcus*, 'village'; see **vicinity**. The third of the great Hindu castes, including agriculturists and merchants.

vaivode. See **voivode**.

vakeel, vakil, vakul, n. [1. vakḗl; 2. vækíəl]. Hind., fr. Arab. *wakīl*. **a** A deputy, representative; minister, ambassador; **b** a native attorney or pleader in the law courts.

valance, n. [1. válans; 2. vǽləns]. Of uncertain origin; fr. 15th cent.; usually supposed to be the name of a material made at Valence, in France, used for curtains; possibly fr. a hypothetical A.-Fr. *valance, fr. *valer, Fr. *avaler*, 'to let down, fall', see **avalanche** & **vail (II.)**. A hanging border of drapery for a window, shelf &c., esp. one that hangs from the framework of a bed to the floor.

vale (I.), n. [1. vāl; 2. veil], fr. O. Fr. *val*, fr. Lat. *vallis*, 'valley', cogn. w. Gk. *hélos*, 'low, marshy ground by a river'. Valley, esp. a low-lying wide tract of land between hills; a dale; now chiefly poet., but surviving in such Place-Names as *Vale of Evesham*, *of Aylesbury*, *of the White Horse*. Phr. *this vale of tears, woe, misery*; *earthly vale* &c., the world, this mortal life.

vale (II.), interj. & n. [1. vā́li; 2. véili]. Lat., 2nd pers. sing. imperat. of *valēre*, 'to be well, strong', see **valiant**. **a** interj. Farewell, good-bye; **b** n., a farewell; a farewell greeting, letter &c.: *to say, take, write, one's vale*.

valediction, n. [1. vàledíkshun; 2. vǽlidíkʃən]. Formed fr. Lat. *valedict-(um)*, P.P. type of *valedīcere*, 'to say farewell', & **-ion**, see **vale (II.)** & **diction**. **a** Act of saying farewell; bidding good-bye to; a farewell; **b** word(s) of farewell.

valedictory, adj. & n. [1. vàledíkturi; 2. vǽlidíktəri]. Lat. *valedict-*, see prec., & **-ory**. **1.** adj. Spoken, uttered, in saying farewell; of the nature of a valediction: *valedictory speech, letter* &c. **2.** n. (chiefly U.S.A.) A valedictory speech, address &c.

valence. See **valency**.

Valencia, n. [1. valénshia; 2. vəlénʃiə]. Name of town and province in Spain. (usually in pl.) A kind of cloth, of wool, with silk or cotton warp, usually with a fine stripe.

Valenciennes, n. [1. vàlensḗnz; 2. vælənsínz], or as Fr. [1. válonsién; 2. valɑ̃sjɛn]. Name of town in France, celebrated for its lace. A variety of bobbin lace made here or in Belgium.

valency, valence, n. [1. vā́lens(i); 2. véiləns(i)], fr. L. Lat. *valentia*, 'power, strength', fr. *valent-(em)*, Pres. Part. type of *valēre*, 'to be well, strong', see **valiant**. (chem.) Term used in defining the combining powers of atoms in molecular compounds, hydrogen, as univalent and unvarying in its valency, being the standard of comparison.

-valent, suff., fr. Lat. *valent-(em)*, see prec. Having a specified valency or combining power; e.g. *univalent*.

valentine, n. [1. válentīn; 2. vǽləntain], fr. O. Fr. *Valentin*, fr. Lat. *Valentīnus*, name of two early saints, whose feast day was Feb. 14th, *Valentine's day*, when birds were supposed to begin mating; hence the day when sweethearts were chosen. **1.** A sweetheart, lover: *will you be my valentine?* **2.** A card decorated with emblems and messages of love, and formerly sent to persons of the opposite sex on Valentine's day; also *mock-valentine*, a scurrilous, satirical picture sent to make fun of person of opposite sex on this day.

valerian, n. [1. valḗrian; 2. vəlíəriən], fr. O. Fr. *valeriane*, Med. Lat. *valeriāna*, fr. *valeriānus*, adj., formed fr. Lat. proper name *Valerius*, or fr. *Valeria*, a province in Pannonia. **a** A genus of perennial herbs, wild or cultivated, with small red or white flowers in clusters; **b** the root of *Valeriana officinalis*, which has a nauseous smell and is used medicinally in nervous diseases or hysteria.

valerianic, adj. [1. valèriánik; 2. vəlìəriǽnik]. Prec. & **-ic**. (chem.) Obtained, derived, from the root of valerian.

valeric, adj. [1. válerik; 2. vǽlərik]. See **valerian** & **-ic**. (chem.) Valerianic.

valet, n. & vb. trans. [1. válet; 2. vǽlit]; vulg. [1. válā; 2. vǽlei], fr. O. Fr. *valet*, earlier *vaslet*. See **varlet** & cp. **vassal**. **1.** n. A gentleman's personal servant, who looks after his clothes, helps him in dressing &c. **2.** vb. To act as valet to; to attend, wait, on as personal servant: *the butler valets me very well*.

valet de pied, n. [1. válā de pyā́; 2. vǽlei də pjéi]. Fr. A footman.

valetudinarian, adj. & n. [1. vàletùdinā́rian; 2. vǽlitjùdinɛ́əriən]. See **valetudinary** & **-an**. **1.** adj. **a** Having constant poor health; perpetually ailing **b** engrossed in the state of one's health, and apprehensive of illness, often without cause; valetudinary. **2.** n. One who is in constant poor health; a chronic invalid; person unduly preoccupied with the state of his health.

valetudinarianism, n. [1. vàletùdinā́rianizm; 2. vǽlitjùdinɛ́əriənizəm]. See prec. & **-ism**. The state of mind or body of a valetudinarian.

valetudinary, adj. & n. [1. vàletū́dinari; 2. vǽlitjúdinəri], fr. Fr. *valetudinaire*, fr. Lat. *valētūdinārius*, 'sickly, infirm', also as n. 'an invalid'; formed w. adj. suff. & *-ārius*, see **-ary**, fr. *valētūdin-(em)*, *valētūdo*, 'state of health, whether good or bad', fr. *valēre*, 'to be well, strong'; see **valiant**. Valetudinarian, now the more usual word.

Valhalla, n. [1. valhála; 2. vælhǽlə]. Cp. Mod. Germ. & Fr. *walhalla*. Ad. fr. O.N. *Valhöl*, 'the hall of the slain in battle', fr. *valr*, 'the slain' (cogn. w. O.E. *wæl*, 'slaughter, the slain; a dead body', & prob. O.E. *wōl*, 'pestilence'), & *höll*, 'a royal hall', cogn. w. **hall**. **1.** (Scand. mythol.) The hall of Odin in Asgard, where the souls of heroes slain in battle feast, attended by the Valkyries. **2.** A hall or other building in which a nation's illustrious dead are buried or commemorated, and where their statues or monuments are placed; a Pantheon.

vali, n. [1. valḗ; 2. vælí]. Turk. & Arab. *valī*. The civil governor of a Turkish *vilayet* or province.

valiance, n. [1. válians; 2. vǽliəns], fr. O. Fr. *vaillance*. See **valiant** & **-ance**. (obs. or archaistic) Bravery, courage; a brave, valiant deed.

valiant, adj. [1. váliant; 2. vǽliənt]. In M.E. in various forms, 'strong, brave, courageous', fr. O. Fr. *valant, vailant, vaillant*, Pres. Part. of *valoir*, 'to be worth, to be good for, to serve', fr. Lat. *valēre*, 'to be strong and vigorous, to be healthy; to be strong enough to do some specific thing, to be able; to be powerful, have influence; to have a specific value, to be worth'. The base is cogn. w. that in O.E. (*ġe*)*weald*, 'power, strength', & *wealdan*, 'to have control over, to rule; to wield (weapon)'. See **wield**. **1.** (provinc.) Strong, sturdy, of body; stalwart. **2.** Courageous, brave, heroic (of persons and acts): *our valiant soldiers, their valiant deeds* &c.

valiantly, adv. Prec. & **-ly**. In a valiant manner; with valour; bravely.

valid, adj. [1. válid; 2. vǽlid], fr. Fr. *valide*, fr. Lat. *validus*, 'strong', fr. *valēre*, 'to be strong &c.', see under **valiant**. **1.** (rare or archaistic) Sound, strong, in body or health; cp. *invalid*, n. **2.** Having legal force and authority, properly and formally executed; sound in law: *a valid contract, marriage* &c. **3.** Well founded, soundly based; capable of being supported and defended; not open to objection: *valid arguments*; *have you any valid reason against the proposal?*; *there is no valid objection to* &c.

validate, vb. trans. [1. válidāt; 2. vǽlideit], fr. Med. Lat. *validāt-(um)*, P.P. type of *validāre*, 'to make valid', see prec., & **-ate**. To render, declare to be, valid: *to validate a treaty, election* &c.; but cp. the negative *invalidate*.

validity, n. [1. valíditi; 2. vəlíditi], fr. L. or Med. Lat. *validitāt-(em)*, *validitas*, see **valid** & **-ity**. State, quality, of being valid; **a** legal force or authority; quality of being legally binding and enforceable: *the validity of a marriage, of a contract* &c.; **b** soundness, strength, force, cogency (of an argument, objection &c.).

validly, adv. [1. válidli; 2. vǽlidli]. **valid** & **-ly**. In a valid manner; with validity.

valise, n. [1. valḗz; 2. vəlíz]. Fr., fr. Ital. *valigia*, cp. Med. Lat. *valesia, valisia, valixia*; Span. *balija*; etymol. unknown, possibly of Arab. origin. A small portmanteau or travelling bag, formerly one carried strapped to a horse's saddle; now obsolescent, except as official term for a soldier's kitbag.

Valkyr, Valkyria, n. [1. válkḗr, valkíria; 2. vǽlkiə, vælkíriə]. Valkyrie.

Valkyrie, n. [1. valkíri; 2. vælkáiəri], more rarely [1. válkiri; 2. vǽlkiri]. O.N. *Valkyrja*, lit. 'chooser of the slain'; the exact equivalent *wælcyrige* is found in O.E.; for the first element see **Valhalla**; the second is formed fr. **kur-*, a form of the O.N. *kjósa*, O.E. *ċēosan*, 'to choose', see **choose**, & cp. **kur-* in Germ. *kurfürst*. (Scand. mythol.) One of the twelve war-goddesses, handmaids of Odin, who ride through the air over a battlefield, choose those who are to be slain, and guide them to, and serve them in, Valhalla.

vallation, n. [1. valâshun; 2. vælèiʃən], fr. L. Lat. *vallātiōn-(em)*, fr. *vallāt-(um)*, P.P. type of *vallāre*, 'to build a vallum or wall'. See **vallum**. A rampart, earthwork; more commonly *circumvallation*.

vallecula, n., pl. **valleculae** [1. valékūla, -lē; 2. vælékjulə-, -li]. L. Lat. dimin. of *vallis*, see **valley**. (anat. and bot.) A groove, channel, fossa, furrow, cleft.

valley, n., pl. **valleys** [1. váli; 2. væli], fr. O. Fr. *valee* (Mod. Fr. *vallée*), earlier form *vallede*, cp. Ital. *vallata*, fr. Lat. *vallis*, 'valley', see **vale (I.)**. **1.** A tract of land lying between mountains or hills, generally traversed by a stream or river, or containing a lake; usually narrower than a vale and lying between steeper slopes. Phr. *the valley of the shadow of death*, the dread hour of impending death, from Psalm xxiii. **2.** (geog.) A large river basin or flat country drained by a river system: *the Thames valley; valley of the Euphrates and Tigris*. **3.** (building and archit.) The internal angle formed by two sloping roofs or by a roof and a wall.

vallonia. See **valonia**.

vallum, n. [1. válum; 2. væləm]. Lat., 'a wall'; orig. 'a stockade, defence of stakes'; a coll. neut., fr. *vallus*, 'stake'; prob. cogn. w. Gk. *hêlos*, 'nail or stud'. See also **wall (I.)**. (Roman antiq.) A defensive rampart set with stakes, a palisaded earthwork, formed of earth cast up from the ditch, also built of and strengthened with stone, sods of turf &c.

valonia, vallonia, n. [1. valónia; 2. vælóuniə]. Ital. *vallonia*, fr. Mod. Gk. *balania*, 'evergreen oak, ilex', fr. *baláni*, anct. Gk. *bálanos*, 'acorn', see **balaniferous**. The dried acorn cup of a species of ilex, or evergreen oak, *Quercus Aegilops*, or valonia oak, used in tanning, dyeing, and ink-making.

valorous, adj. [1. válorus; 2. vælərəs]. O. Fr. *valeureux*, Med. Lat. *valorōsus*, see **valour & -ous**. **a** (of persons) Possessing, exhibiting, valour; brave, intrepid, courageous; **b** (of actions) requiring valour from those who perform them; displaying, performed with, valour.

valorously, adv. Prec. & **-ly**. In a valorous manner; with valour.

valour, n. [1.válur; 2. vælə], fr. O. Fr. *valour*, Mod. Fr. *valeur*, 'value; bravery'; fr. L. Lat. *valōr-(em)*, stem of *valor*, 'worth, value; courage', fr. *valēre*, 'to be strong, worth' &c., see **valiant**. Courage of a noble and lofty quality; continuous, active, bravery exhibited in actions performed in the face of personal danger.

valse, n. & vb. [1. vahls; 2. vāls]. Fr. form of **waltz**.

valuable (I.), adj. [1. válūabl; 2. væljuəbl], fr. **value (II.)** & **-able**. **1.** (rare) Capable of being valued or estimated: *rarities once in a public museum or library cease to be valuable in terms of money* (cp. the more common negative form, *invaluable*). **2. a** Having monetary or exchange value; worth something which can be expressed in terms of money, exchange, or benefit; in legal Phr. *valuable consideration*; **b** having considerable or great value, worth a good deal of money or exchange value; precious, costly: *collection of valuable pictures; a valuable property for sale; catalogue of the valuable kinds of wood of the Empire*. **3.** Having a use or value; capable of serving a useful and important purpose; possessing and exhibiting qualities which are prized and esteemed as necessary for the performance of specific duties and functions: *a valuable public servant; gave me valuable service, information; a book which will be very valuable for teachers*.

valuable (II.), n. See prec. (usually in pl.) Objects of value; valuable goods or possessions: *plate, jewels, and other valuables; lost all their valuables in the fire*.

valuableness, n. [1. válūablnes; 2. væljuəblnis]. **valuable (I.)** & **-ness**. Condition, quality, of being valuable.

valuably, adv. [1. válūabli; 2. væljuəbli]. See **valuable (I.)** & **-ly**. In a valuable manner; usefully: *his support has helped the cause most valuably*.

valuation, n. [1. vàlūâshun; 2. væljuéiʃən], fr. **value (II.)** & **-ation**. **1. a** Act of valuing, of settling, or estimating, the value, or proper price, of anything: *engaged in the valuation of property for probate; the quinquennial valuation of ratable buildings*; **b** value or price so estimated and arrived at: *I was offered the fixtures at a moderate valuation*. **2.** Estimation, degree of appreciation, in which a person, or his moral or intellectual qualities, are held: *to take a man at (on) his own valuation; they put his services at the highest valuation*.

value (I.), n. [1. válū; 2. væljū]. O. Fr., fem. sing. of *valu*, P.P. of *valoir*, 'to be worth', fr. Lat. *valēre*; see **valiant**. **1. a** Worth, that quality or property of anything which renders it desirable or useful: *the value of sunlight, fresh air, exercise, for health; the value of good books, education*; **b** (i.) worth of anything as compared with that of other things; degree of such worth: *to be of great, little, no value; your help was of value to me*; (ii.) estimation, valuation: *to set a high value on one's abilities*. **2.** Worth of anything as estimated in terms of something else for which it can be exchanged, either in other goods, labour, services, or, esp., in money or other standard medium of exchange; purchasing power, monetary price: *economic, exchange, value; to pay, give, get, full value for something; the value of this kind of picture has fallen greatly*. Phr. *for value received*, form used in promissory notes for stating valuable consideration. **3.** (in various specific uses) **a** Precise import, meaning, bearing, force; *the value of a word in a given phrase* &c.; **b** relative proportion of light and shade in a picture or drawing, as distinct from that of colour; **c** length or duration of a note of music; **d** quantity denoted by an algebraic symbol or expression; **e** (pl.) relative ethical standards.

value (II.), vb. trans., fr. prec. **1.** To estimate the value or worth of, to assign a price or value to; to put a price on, fix a price for, to appraise: *I value the house and contents at £10,000; to value an estate for probate*. **2.** (in moral sense) **a** To rate at a specified degree of worth, to hold in specified degree of esteem: *to value one's life highly, not at all*; **b** (absol.) to attach a high degree of value to, rate highly: *I shall always value your friendship; we do not always value advice from others*.

valued, adj. [1. válūd; 2. væljūd]. P.P. of prec. Highly esteemed, greatly regarded; considered as being of great value to some specified person; precious: *one's most valued possession; a valued friend of the late king*.

valueless, adj. [1. válūles; 2. væljulis]. **value (I.)** & **-less**. Of no value or use; worthless, destitute of value (in material or non-material sense): *valueless pictures, stocks and shares; a book valueless for its purpose; valueless advice*.

valuelessness, n. [1. válūlesnes; 2. væljulisnis]. Prec. & **-ness**. State, quality, of being valueless.

valuer, n. [1. válūer; 2. væljuə]. **value (II.)** & **-er**. One who fixes or assesses the monetary or material value of anything; specif., person who estimates values and prices professionally as a matter of business: *a surveyor and valuer; valuer for probate* &c.

valuta, n. [1. valūta; 2. vəljūtə]. Ital., 'value', q.v. The value of a national currency as fixed in terms of a foreign currency, exchange value of a currency in relation to a specified foreign currency in distinction from its internal value; also attributively.

valval, valvar, adj. [1. válval, -ar; 2. vælvəl, -ə]. **valve** & **-al, -ar**. Valvular, chiefly in botanical terminology.

valvate, adj. [1. válvāt; 2. vælveit]. **valve** & **-ate**. (bot.) Meeting at the edges without overlapping (of leaves and sepals).

valve, n. [1. valv; 2. vælv]. Fr., fr. Lat. *valva*, 'leaf of a folding-door', usually in pl. *valvae*, 'a folding-door'; cogn. w. *volvere*, 'to roll', see **volute**. **1.** One of the leaves of a folding door, now rare except as applied to lock-gates, sluices &c. **2.** Any of various devices which open and shut, like the leaves of a folding door, thus regulating the passage of air, liquid, gas &c. through an opening, tube, pipe &c., often acting automatically, as *the safety-valve* of a steam-engine, *the slide* or *key valves* of musical wind instruments &c. **3.** (in various specific uses) **a** (anat.) A membrane in a vein, artery or lymphatic which allows the passage one way only of the blood or lymph; **b** (bot.) one of the separable parts of a pod, pericarp, or capsule; **c** (zool.) one of the two shells of molluscs such as the oyster, or of the several parts of the shell of compound molluscs. **4.** (wireless) A special form of vacuum tube used for the reception of messages, as *thermionic valve* &c.; (also attrib.) *valve set*, one fitted with such valves, distinct from *crystal set*.

valved, adj. [1. valvd; 2. vælvd]. **valve** & **-ed**. Furnished, fitted, with valves; also in compounds, having so many valves: *three-valved* &c.

valveless, adj. [1. válvles; 2. vælvlis]. **valve** & **-less**. Having no valves; not provided with a valve or valves.

valvular, adj. [1. válvūlar; 2. vælvjulə], fr. Lat. *valvulae*, dimin. of *valvae*, see **valve**, & **-ar**. **1.** Pertaining to, affecting, a valve or valves, esp. those of the heart: *valvular disease*. **2.** Consisting, made up, of valves or segments, esp. of plant formations.

valvulitis, n. [1. vàlvūlítis; 2. vælvjuláitis]. See prec. & **-itis**. (med.) Inflammation of the valves of the heart.

vambrace, n. [1. vámbrās; 2. væmbreis]. Earlier *vantbrace* (cp. Milton, 'Samson', 1151), fr. A.-Fr. *vantbras* for *avant-bras*, fr. *avant*, 'before, in front', see **advance**, & *bras*, 'arm', see **brace (I.)**. A piece of armour for the forearm.

vamoose, vamose, vb. intrans. [1. vamóoz, vamṓz; 2. væmúz, væmóuz], fr. Span. *vamos*, 'let us go'. (slang, U.S.A., often as imperat.) To go away, decamp, get off.

vamp (I.), n. [1. vamp; 2. væmp]. M.E. *vaumpé*, fr. O. Fr. *avampié*, later *avant-pied*, 'forepart of the foot', fr. *avant*, 'before', see **advance (I.)**, & *pied*, 'foot', see **pedal (I.)**. **1. a** That part of a boot or shoe which covers the front part of the foot; **b** a piece of leather used in repairing the front part of a boot or shoe; a patch to a boot or shoe. **2.** (a back-formation from vb.) Something vamped or patched up; a patchwork, esp. a simple, improvised musical accompaniment to a song &c.

vamp (II.), vb. trans. & intrans., fr. prec. **1.** trans. **a** To repair (boot &c.) by putting a new vamp on it; to repair, mend (worn boots and shoes); **b** *vamp up*, to patch up, renew, furbish up, (anything) so as to look like new: *to vamp up some old furniture* &c.; **c** (by transf.) to patch together, make something out of old or used material; to make a patchwork of: *to vamp up a farce, new business for a play* &c.; **d** specif. (mus.) to improvise (an accompaniment) in a simple, crude way, to a song, dance &c. **2.** intrans. To improvise a simple accompaniment to a song &c., on the piano &c.

vamp (III.), n. & vb. trans. & intrans.; abbr. of **vampire**. (slang) **1.** n. An adventuress, a woman who uses her physical charms to extort or extract money from her victims; a female blood-sucker. **2.** vb. To fascinate (men) and extract money from them.

vampire, n. [1. vámpīr; 2. væmpaiə]. Fr., fr. Magyar or Serbian *vampir*, also found in

Russ., Bulgarian, Pol. & other Slav. languages in various forms as *vepir, upyr* &c.; prob. fr. a Turk. *uber*, 'witch'; the word has been borrowed fr. Slav. sources in other European languages, as Germ. *vampyr*. **1.** An evil, malignant spirit with the power of entering and reviving a corpse; person whose dead body is thus revived, and renews its life at night by visiting and sucking the blood of sleepers. **2.** (by transf.) An unscrupulous, malignant extortioner, male or female; a blood-sucker, a ruthless blackmailer or money-lender. **3.** A vampire bat. **4.** (in a theatre) A kind of trap in the floor of the stage working by springs, allowing a demon &c. to appear or disappear suddenly.

vampire bat, n. Either of two small blood-sucking bats, *Desmodus* and *Diphylla*, of tropical S. America, which suck the blood of animals, esp. horses, and are said to attack human beings in their sleep.

vampirism, n. [1. vámpīrizm; 2. vǽmpaiərizəm]. **vampire** & **-ism.** **a** Habits, practices, of a vampire; **b** superstitious belief in vampires.

vamplate, n. [1. vámplāt; 2. vǽmpleit], fr. Fr. *avant-plat*, cp. **vambrace** & **plate (I.)**. (hist.) An iron guard-plate for the hand, fixed on a lance.

van (I.), n. & vb. trans. [1. van; 2. væn]. Shortened form of **caravan. 1.** n. **a** A large covered vehicle for the conveyance of goods by road: *furniture van* &c.; **b** a covered truck or closed carriage on a railway: *guard's van; luggage, goods, van;* **c** closed vehicle for conveying prisoners by road: 'Black Maria'; **d** a caravan, in sense **2**; (also attrib.) *van boy, van dwellers* &c. **2.** vb. To place (goods) in, convey (goods) by, a van.

van (II.), n. Shortened form of **vanguard. 1.** The front of an army or fleet, when in battle formation or moving to battle; the leading division of an army or fleet. **2.** The leading part of any troop or concourse of people moving forward: *the van of a procession* &c. **3.** (fig.) Those who lead and are in the front of any forward intellectual, social, or political movement: Phrs. *in the van of*, leading; *to lead the van of* &c.

van (III.), n., fr. Lat. *vannus*, see **fan (I.)**. (archaic or dial.) **a** A winnowing fan or machine; **b** (poet.) the wing of a bird; **c** a shovel used for washing ore.

vanadate, n. [1. vánadāt; 2. vǽnədeit]. **vanadium** & **-ate.** (chem.) A salt of vanadic acid.

vanadic, adj. [1. vanádik, -ādik; 2. vænǽdik, -éidik]. See prec. & **-ic.** (chem.) Pertaining to, containing, vanadium: *vanadic acid;* esp. of compounds in which vanadium has a higher valence than in *vanadious* compounds.

vanadious, adj. [1. vanádius; 2. vænéidiəs]. See prec. & **-ous.** (chem.) Of compounds of vanadium with lower valence than vanadic compounds.

vanadium, n. [1. vanádium; 2. vænéidiəm]. Invented word, fr. *vanadis*, an Old Norse title for the Scand. goddess *Freyja*. (chem.) A rare metallic element, found in certain iron, lead, and uranium ores, used esp. in making alloys of steel.

Vandal (I.), n. [1. vándl; 2. vǽndl]. L. Lat. *Vandalus*, usually in pl. *Vandali*, also *Vandilii;* in O.E. *Wendlas*, pl. of *Wendil*, O.N. *Vendill*. **1.** One of the Germanic races, closely related to the Goths, which invaded Western Europe in 5th century A.D., sacking Rome under their leader Genseric in 455, settling in Gaul and Spain and finally in N. Africa; traditionally regarded as the great destroyers of Roman civilization, art, and literature. **2.** (by transf., with or without cap.) One who through ignorance and lack of taste and sensibility sweeps away or spoils beautiful things in art or nature: *the vandals who cover the countryside with cigarette tins and chocolate boxes; 19th century vandals often pulled down mediaeval buildings to make room for new ones of churchwarden's Gothic.*

vandal (II.), adj., fr. prec. **1.** (hist., cap.) Pertaining to the Vandals: *the Vandal invasions, invaders* &c. **2. a** Barbarous; ruthlessly, ignorantly, destructive of beauty and culture: *the vandal despoilers of our churches;* **b** characterized by such destruction: *the vandal defacement of the countryside.*

Vandalic, adj. & n. [1. vandálik; 2. vændǽlik]. Prec. & **-ic. a** adj. Of, characteristic of, the Vandals or a vandal; **b** n., the language of the Vandals.

vandalism, n. [1. vándalizm; 2. vǽndəlizəm]. **Vandal (I.)** & **-ism. a** (cap.) The characteristic spirit or conduct of the Vandals; **b** (usually without cap.) hostility to things of art, beauty &c.; vandalization.

vandalization, n. [1. vàndalīzā́shun; 2. vændəlaizéiʃən]. **vandalize** & **-ation. a** Act of vandalizing; ignorant, tasteless, ruthless destruction of beautiful things; **b** state of being vandalized; barbarous destruction.

vandalize, vb. trans. [1. vándalīz; 2. vǽndəlaiz]. **Vandal (I.)** & **-ize.** To treat (objects of art, or the face of the countryside) like a vandal; to destroy, or make hideous, things of beauty in art or nature wilfully and ignorantly.

Vandyke (I.), n. [1. vandī́k; 2. vændáik], fr. Engl. spelling of A. Van Dyck, Flemish painter, 1599–1641, the Court painter of Charles I. **1.** (cap.) A portrait or painting by Vandyke. **2.** Specif. (with or without cap.) **a** a deep lace falling collar with deeply indented edge, as frequently seen in portraits of and by Vandyke; **b** any deeply indented or zigzag edge or border; one of the points or indentations of such an edge or border.

Vandyke (II.), adj., fr. prec. **1.** (cap.) **a** Of, by, Vandyke, the painter: *a Vandyke portrait;* **b** resembling a picture by, or in the style of, *Vandyke*: *a Vandyke beard*, a close-cut, pointed one; *Vandyke brown*, a deep brown. **2.** (usually cap.) Deeply indented, bordered with vandykes, zigzagged: *Vandyke collar* &c.

vandyke (III.), vb. trans., fr. **Vandyke (I.)**. To indent edge, border with vandykes.

vane, n. [1. vān; 2. vein]. O.E. *fana*, 'flag', cogn. w. Lat. *pannus*, see **pane (I.)**. The *v-* in present-day form is a survival of M.E. Southern dialect. See **gonfalon. 1.** A weathercock. **2. a** The sail of a windmill; **b** the blade of a ship's or aeroplane's propeller; **c** movable sight of a surveyor's levelling staff, quadrant &c.; **d** the web of a feather.

Vanessa, n. [1. vanésa; 2. vənésə]. Origin of name uncertain. (entom.) A genus of butterflies, including the peacock and red admiral &c.

vang, n. [1. vang; 2. væŋ]. Du., 'a catch', fr. *vangen*, 'to seize, catch', see **fang (I.)**. (naut.) One of two guys from the peak of a gaff to deck used to keep it steady.

vanguard, n. [1. vángàrd; 2. vǽŋgād], fr. Fr. *avant-garde*, fr. *avant*, 'before', see **advance**, & *garde*, **guard. 1.** Advanced troops of an army or military force; the van; also the leading squadron of a fleet in battle formation. **2.** (fig.) The leaders of an intellectual, social, or political movement.

vanilla, n. [1. vaníla; 2. vəníla]. Ad. fr. Span. *vainilla*, dimin. of *vaina*, 'sheath, pod', see **vagina**, fr. the shape of the fruit of the plant. **a** A climbing orchidaceous plant, of genus *Vanilla*, esp. *Vanilla planifolia* of tropical America, with scented flowers and pods or beans which yield an aromatic substance used for flavouring ices, confectionery &c.; **b** the extract obtained from vanilla pods.

vanish, vb. intrans. [1. vánish; 2. vǽniʃ]. M.E. *vanissen*, fr. O. Fr. *e(s)vanniss-*, Pres. Part. stem of *e(s)vanir*, fr. Lat. *ēvānescere*, 'to fade, vanish away', fr. *e-* for **ex-** & *vānescere*, 'to fade, vanish, become empty', fr. *vānus*, 'empty', see **vain** & cp. **evanescent. 1.** To disappear, pass out of sight; to become invisible: *shadows vanish with the dawn; as we entered the figure vanished.* **2.** To fade away, to decay and disappear: *all the colour has vanished from the picture.* **3.** To cease to exist, to come to an end: *all our hopes of a speedy success vanished at the news; the fears of overnight vanish with the morning.* **4.** (math.) To become zero.

vanishing point, n. [1. vánishing pòint; 2. vǽniʃiŋ pòint]. **a** The converging point in a perspective drawing &c. at which receding parallel lines appear to meet; **b** (colloq.) point at which anything comes to an end, or tends to disappear: *our money, strength, has reached the vanishing point.*

vanity, n. [1. vániti; 2. vǽniti]. M.E. *vanite*, fr. Fr. *vanité*, fr. Lat. *vānitāt-(em)*, 'emptiness, worthlessness', fr. *vānus*, 'empty' &c., see **vain**, & **-ity. 1.** Quality of being vain, empty or worthless; futility, unsubstantiality; worthlessness, emptiness: *the vanity of human wishes, of earthly greatness.* **2.** That which is vain, worthless; an unprofitable, futile thing, act &c.: '*to renounce the pomps and vanity of this wicked world*' (Catechism); '*all is vanity, saith the Preacher*'. **3.** Quality of being personally vain; exaggeratedly high opinion of, and pride in, one's own appearance, physical or mental capacities &c.; conceit: *a man's vanity is his tenderest spot; an injury to vanity will never be forgiven.*

vanity bag, n. A small ornamental hand-bag which women carry to hold a mirror, powder-puff, and cosmetics with which to make up their complexion.

Vanity Fair, n. The world of idle amusements and luxury; the fashionable world of society; fr. Bunyan's 'Pilgrim's Progress'.

vanquish, vb. trans. & intrans. [1. vángkwish; 2. vǽŋkwiʃ]. M.E. *venkisen, venkusen, venquisshen* &c., fr. A.-Fr. *venquiss-*, O. Fr. *veinquiss-*, Pres. Part. stem of *venquir, veinquir*, Mod. Fr. *vaincre*, 'to conquer', fr. Lat. *vincere, vict-(um)*, 'to conquer', see **vincible. 1.** trans. To conquer, defeat, overcome, reduce to subjection; to subdue, in physical and non-physical senses: *to vanquish the enemy in battle, one's opponents in argument, the temptations of the flesh* &c. **2.** intrans. To be victorious.

vanquishable, adj. [1. vángkwishabl; 2. vǽŋkwiʃəbl]. Prec. & **-able.** Capable of being vanquished, overcome, or subdued; cp. *invincible.*

vanquished, adj. & n. [1. vángkwisht; 2. vǽŋkwiʃt], fr. P.P. of **vanquish. a** adj. Conquered, defeated; subdued: *our vanquished enemy; vanquished temptations;* **b** n., *the vanquished*, defeated person or persons.

vanquisher, n. [1. vángkwisher; 2. vǽŋkwiʃə]. See prec. & **-er.** Conqueror, victor.

vantage, n. [1. váhntij; 2. vántidž]. Variant of **advantage.** Advantage, gain, profit, now archaic or obs. except as, **a** commonly used in calling score in lawn-tennis, and **b** Phrs. *vantage-ground, point of vantage*, superior, commanding position; favourable position (lit. and fig.) from which to attack an opponent or ward off his attack.

vanward, adj. & adv. [1. vánward; 2. vǽnwəd]. **van (II.)** & **-ward. a** adj. Placed, coming, in the van or front: '*The vanward clouds of evil days*' (Keats); **b** adv., towards the van; forward.

vapid, adj. [1. vápid; 2. vǽpid], fr. Lat. *vapidus*, 'that has lost its vapour or life; flavourless, insipid'; cp. *vappa*, 'flat, stale wine', see **vapour (I.)**. **1.** (in material sense, rare) Tasteless, flavourless; insipid, flat. **2.** (in non-material sense) Lifeless, uninteresting; lacking point, pungency, salt; insipid, dull: *vapid platitudes; the dialogue was vapid and commonplace; vapid compliments.*

vapidity, n. [1. vapíditi; 2. væpíditi]. Prec. & **-ity.** Quality, state, fact, of being vapid; insipidity, vapidness.

vapidly, adv. [1. vápidli; 2. vǽpidli]. See prec. & **-ly.** In a vapid manner.

vapidness, n. [1. vápidnes; 2. væ̍pidnis]. See prec. & **-ness**. Vapidity.

vaporability, n. [1. vâporabíliti; 2. vèipərəbíliti]. **vaporable** & **-ity**. State, quality, of being vaporable.

vaporable, adj. [1. vâporabl; 2. véipərəbl]. See **vapour** & **-able**. Capable of being vaporized or converted into vapour.

vaporific, adj. [1. vâporífik; 2. vèipərífik]. See **vapour** & **-fic**. Producing vaporization.

vaporimeter, n. [1. vâporímeter; 2. veipərímitə]. See prec. & **-meter**. Instrument for measuring the volume or pressure of vapour.

vaporization, n. [1. vâporīzâshun; 2. vèipəraizéiʃən]. **vaporize** & **-ation**. Act, or process of vaporizing, of converting into vapour; process of becoming vapour.

vaporize, vb. trans. & intrans. [1. vâporīz; 2. véipəraiz]. **vapour** & **-ize**. **1.** trans. To convert into vapour. **2.** intrans. To be converted into, to pass off as, vapour.

vaporizer, n. [1. vâporīzer; 2. véipəraizə]. Prec. & **-er**. Apparatus for converting substances, such as oils, into vapour.

vaporous, adj. [1. vâporus; 2. véipərəs], fr. Lat. *vapōrus* or *vapōrōsus*, see **vapour** & **-ous**. **a** Resembling, having the character or consistency of, vapour; **b** filled with vapour; foggy, steamy; **c** (archaic) having the vapours, fanciful.

vapour (I.), n. [1. vâper; 2. véipə]. Through A.-Fr. *vapour*, O. Fr. *vapeur*, or direct fr. Lat. *vapōr*, 'steam, vapour', cogn. w. Gk. *kapnós*, 'smoke', *kapúein*, 'to breathe forth'; Scrt. *kapis*, 'incense', Lith. *kvâpas*, 'breath, fragrance'; all fr. base *k^wap-; related also to Goth. *(af-)hwapjan*, 'to choke', fr. Aryan variant *k^wab-. Cp. **cupid**. **1. a** A visible diffusion, exhalation, of moisture floating in the air, as fog, mist, steam &c., arising from the action of heat on water, damp ground &c.; **b** specif. (phys.) the gaseous state or form to which a solid or liquid may be reduced by the action of heat; a liquid or solid substance reduced by heat to a gaseous, elastic condition. **2.** (fig.) **a** Something unsubstantial, transitory, or fleeting; an idle fancy, freak of imagination: *his brain clouded by vapours and dreams*; *all his schemes were but the vapour of an excited imagination*; **b** (archaic) futile, empty boasting; vapouring. **3.** (in pl.) **a** (anct. med.) Morbid condition of body and mind due to supposed exhalations from the stomach; such exhalations; **b** *the vapours*, hysteria, mental depression, hypochondria: *a fit of the vapours once fashionable among young ladies.*

vapour (II.), vb. intrans., fr. prec. **1.** (rare) To pass off as vapour, to evaporate, be exhaled. **2.** To boast, brag; indulge in empty high-flown chatter.

vapour-bath, n. **a** A bath in hot vapour or steam; **b** closed place, apparatus, for such a bath. Phr. (of a place, part of the country) *like a vapour-bath*, very hot, steamy, relaxing.

vapourer, n. [1. vâperer; 2. véipərə]. **vapour** (II.) & **-er**. **1.** One who vapours or boasts; a flatulent, pretentious chatterer. **2.** (entom.) Moth of genus *Orgyia*, with wingless female, very destructive to vegetation.

vapouring (I.), n. [1. vâpering; 2. véipəriŋ]. **vapour** (II.) & **-ing**. Often *vapourings*. Empty high-flown talk.

vapouring (II.), adj., fr. Pres. Part. of **vapour** (II.). **a** Empty and pretentious; **b** full of vapours; hysterical, hypochondriacal.

vapoury, adj. [1. vâperi; 2. véipəri]. **vapour** (I.) & **-y**. Full of vapour; misty, clouded with mist or vapour.

vapulation, n. [1. vàpūlâshun; 2. væ̀pjuléiʃən], fr. Lat. *vāpulāt-(um)*, *vāpulāre*, 'to be flogged, whipped'; etymol. uncertain. (rare or facetiously archaistic) A beating, flogging.

vapulatory, adj. [1. vápūlaturi; 2. væ̍pjulətəri]. See prec. & **-ory**. Pertaining to flogging or beating.

vaquero, n. [1. vakârō; 2. vækéərou]. Span., 'cowherd', fr. *vaca*, 'cow', fr. Lat. *vacca*, see **vaccine**. (in Spanish America, Mexico &c.) A drover; a man in charge of cattle, horses, or mules; a herdsman; cowboy.

Varangian, n. & adj. [1. varánjian; 2. værǽndžiən], fr. Med. Lat. *Varangus*, fr. Med. Gk. *Bára(n)ggos*, through Slav., fr. O.N. *Væringi*, pl. *Væringjar*, 'confederate, ally', fr. *vārar*, 'pledges, oaths'. **1.** n. **a** One of the Northman rovers who harried the Baltic and founded a dynasty in Russia in 9th and 10th centuries; **b** one of the 'Varangian Guard'. **2.** adj. **a** Pertaining to the Varangians; **b** composed of Varangians, esp. *Varangian Guard*, a bodyguard of the Byzantine emperors, recruited from Varangians and other Northern peoples of Europe.

varec, n. [1. várek; 2. væ̍rɛk]. Fr., also *varech*, of Gmc. origin; see **wreck** (I.). Calcined ash of seaweed used in manufacture of iodine &c.; kelp.

variability, n. [1. vâriabíliti; 2. vèəriəbíliti]. See **variable** & **-ity**. Quality, condition, of being variable; liability, tendency, to variation.

variable (I.), adj. [1. vâriabl; 2. véəriəbl]. Fr., fr. L. Lat. *variābilis*, see **vary** & **-able**. **1.** Liable to vary; tending to vary; changeable, fluctuating, not constant or steady: *variable weather, temperature, wind* &c.; *a man of variable character, temper* &c. **2.** Capable of being varied or changed; admitting of variation in degree &c.: *prices are variable according to the exchanges.* **3.** Specific uses: **a** (astron.) periodically changing in apparent magnitude or brightness: *variable stars*; **b** (biol.) liable to variation; tending to deviate from type, aberrant: *variable species*; **c** (math.) increasing or decreasing, indeterminate: *variable quantities.*

variable (II.), n., fr. prec. **a** A variable quantity, an indeterminate quantity, one subject to increase or decrease; **b** a variable star.

variableness, n. [1. vâriablnes; 2. véəriəblnis]. **variable** (I.) & **-ness**. State, quality, of being variable; liability to change or vary.

variably, adv. [1. vâriabli; 2. véəriəbli]. See prec. & **-ly**. In a variable manner.

variance, n. [1. vârians; 2. véəriəns]. O. Fr., fr. Lat. *variantia*; **variant** & **-ce**. **1.** Act or fact of varying; variation; a change, alteration: *some variance of temperature is to be expected*; *such sudden variance of public taste is remarkable.* **2.** Active disagreement between persons in opinions, tastes, ideals &c.; strife, dissension, antagonism; esp. in Phr. *at variance (with)*, differing, in a state of estrangement (from); holding dissentient views (from), opposed to &c.: *old friends now at variance*; *he was at variance with his colleagues on one subject only*; *such opinions are quite at variance with those he formerly held.* **3.** (law) Discrepancy between two portions in legal proceedings, as between a statement in pleadings and evidence in proof of it.

variant, adj. & n. [1. vâriant; 2. véəriənt]. O. Fr., fr. Lat. *variant-(em)*, Pres. Part. of *variāre*, see **vary** & **-ant**. **1.** adj. **a** Differing, varying, from one another or from some standard which is accepted as normal; esp. *variant reading* (Lat. *varia lectio*), a reading, as in a MS. &c., different from the accepted reading, or from that in another text; **b** varying, showing variation, varied: *to obtain variant results from what is apparently the same process.* **2.** n. A variant form, reading, version &c.; something which is appreciably different from something else with which it has a common origin or close connexion: *hame and home are dialectal variants of the same word*; *different MSS. of the same work often contain variants introduced by copyists.*

variation, n. [1. vâriâshun; 2. vèəriéiʃən]. O. Fr., fr. Lat. *variātiōn-(em)*, fr. *variāt-(um)*, P.P. type of *variāre*, see **vary** & **-ation**. **1. a** Act, process, or fact of varying in form, state, degree, quality &c., from type, standard, the normal &c.; alteration, modification: *variation of temperature, colour, tone* &c.; *a principle without variation*; *subject, liable, to, capable of, variation*; **b** amount, extent, rate, of change: *slight, marked, great, variations in temperature, price* &c. **2.** Specif. **a** (astron.) deviation or change in the mean motion or orbit of a heavenly body; **b** (biol.) deviation or divergence of an organism in structure, or of a function in mode of operation, from that which is typical or usual in the group or species to which it belongs; **c** (magnetism) deviation of the magnetic needle from true North and South; declination; **d** (math.) relation between changes of quantities which vary as each other; permutation; **e** (mus.) repetition of a theme or melody with various, usually progressive, developments; any elaboration of a simple theme.

variational, adj. [1. vâriâshunal; 2. vèəriéiʃənəl]. Prec. & **-al**. Pertaining to, marked by, characteristic of, arising from, variation.

varicated, adj. [1. várikâted; 2. væ̍rikèitid]. See **varix** & **-ate** & **-ed**. (of shells) Having varices or ridges.

varicella, n. [1. vàriséla; 2. væ̀riséla]. An irregular, mod. dimin. of **variola**. (med.) Chicken-pox.

varicocele, n. [1. várikōsēl; 2. væ̍rikousīl]. See **varicose** & **-cele**. A varicose condition or enlargement of the veins of the spermatic cord or of the scrotum.

varicoloured, adj. [1. vârikùlurd; 2. véərikàləd]. See **various** & **colour(ed)**. Of various colours; variegated, parti-coloured.

varicose, adj. [1. várikōs; 2. væ̍rikous], fr. Lat. *varicōsus*, fr. *varic-(em)*, *varix*, see **varix**, & **-ose**. **a** Suffering from, affected by, a varix or varices, or abnormally dilated veins: *a varicose leg, patient, symptom* &c.; **b** abnormally dilated; of veins, esp. those of the leg; hence *varicose ulcer*, such a vein when ulcerated; **c** designed for varicose veins: *varicose bandage* &c.

varicosis, n. [1. vàrikṓsis; 2. væ̀rikóusis]. See prec. & **-osis**. (med.) State of having varicose veins or of being varicose; varicosity.

varicosity, n. [1. vàrikósiti; 2. væ̀rikɔ́siti]. See prec. & **-ity**. Varicosis.

varied, adj. [1. vârid; 2. véərid], fr. P.P. of **vary**. **1.** Exhibiting variety; various: *varied scenes*; *birds of the most varied kinds*; *indulge in varied pleasures, ideas.* **2.** Changing, differing, from time to time; characterized by variety: *live a varied life*; *delightfully varied scenery.*

variedly, adv. Prec. & **-ly**. In a varied manner; with many or constant changes.

variegate, vb. trans. [1. vârigāt; 2. véərigeit], fr. L. Lat. *variegāt-(um)*, P.P. type of *variegāre*, 'to make of various colours', fr. *varius*, see **various**, & *ag-*, stem of *agere*, 'to drive, do' &c., see **agent**. To diversify the colour of, to mark with different colours.

variegated, adj. [1. vârigâted; 2. véərigèitid], fr. P.P. of prec. **1.** Diversified in colour; parti-coloured; streaked with various colours. **2.** (fig.) **a** Diversified by change, variety of experience &c.: *a variegated career*; **b** exhibiting different qualities intermingled: *a character strangely variegated with good and evil.*

variegation, n. [1. vârigâshun; 2. vèərigéiʃən]. See prec. & **-ion**. Diversified colouration; intermingled streaks or patches of colour.

variety, n. [1. varíeti; 2. vəráiəti], fr. O. Fr. *variete*, fr. Lat. *varietāt-(em)*, fr. *varius*, see **various**, & **-ty**. **1.** Quality of being various; reverse of *monotony*; absence of sameness; diversity in external objects or conditions, or of qualities &c.: *the variety of town life*; *the extraordinary variety of his character*; *variety is what the public wants.* **2.** A number or collection, group, of various or different things: *to have a great variety to choose from*; *a variety of excellent dishes*; *owing to a variety of causes.* **3. a** Something varying from others of the same kind; a different kind or form of something; a kind, sort: *a rare variety of old English glass*; *a collection of stamps with many* *varieties*; *distinguish the varieties of strata, of Gothic architecture* &c.; specif. **b** (biol.) a group or member of a group of animals or plants, differing from related groups, but not so far as to allow them to be classified as a separate species or subspecies, esp. the various kinds or breeds of domesticated animals or cultivated plants; **c** any one of the types of speech, or dialects, into which one original dialect or language has been differentiated. **4.** That form of entertainment which is given at a *variety theatre* or music-hall, a mixed entertainment of individual singers, acrobats, comedians, dancers &c., each giving a separate, distinct turn; known in U.S.A. as *vaudeville*: *variety seemed to have been killed by the films and by revues*; also attrib.: *variety show, artist* &c.

variform, adj. [1. vàriform; 2. vέərifɔ̄m], fr. **various** & **-form**. Varied in form, having various forms.

variola, n. [1. varíola, vàrióla; 2. vəráiələ, vὲərióulə]. Med. Lat., fr. Lat. *varius*, see **various**. (med.) Smallpox.

variolar, adj. [1. varíolar, vàriólar; 2. vəráiələ, vὲərióulə]. Prec. & **-ar**. (med.) Pertaining to variola or smallpox; pitted like those attacked by smallpox.

variolite, n. [1. váriōlīt; 2. vέərioulait]. See prec. & **-ite**. A kind of diorite in which whitish spherules of other rock are embedded, giving a pitted appearance like that of smallpox.

varioloid, adj. & n. [1. váriōlòid; 2. vέərioulɔid], fr. **variola** & **-oid**. **a** adj. Resembling smallpox; **b** n., a mild form of smallpox, as modified by previous vaccination.

variolous, adj. [1. varíolus, vàriólus; 2. vəráiələs, vὲərióuləs]. **variola** & **-ous**. Variolar.

variometer, n. [1. vàriómeter; 2. vὲəriɔ́mitə]. fr. **various** & **-meter**. (elect.) **a** An instrument for the comparison of magnetic forces; **b** device for varying the magnetic inductance in a circuit, used in wireless receiving sets for adjustment of wave-lengths &c.

variorum, adj. [1. vàriórum; 2. vὲəriɔ́rəm]. Lat., genit. pl. of *varius*, **various**, lit. 'of various persons'. *Variorum edition*, Lat. *editio cum notis variorum*, with notes of various commentators &c.

various, adj. [1. várius; 2. vέəriəs]. fr. Lat. *varius*, 'changing, varying; varied'; etymol. dubious. **1.** Different, diverse; having, showing, many different characteristics; varied: *the effects of this disease are various in different cases*; '*Party leaders . . . maintaining . . . their various opinions*' ('The Gondoliers', Gilbert). **2. a** Possessing and exhibiting a variety of qualities, talents &c.; many-sided, versatile; rare or archaic, but familiar from Dryden's '*A man so various, that he seemed to be Not one, but all mankind's epitome*' ('Absalom and Achitophel', i. 545-6); **b** diversified by many and different experiences, adventures, occupations; reverse of monotonous: (The Muse) '*Eyes the calm sunset of thy various day*' (Pope, 'To Earl of Oxford', 38). **3. a** Several, many; also, of several different sorts or kinds: *various people declared they had seen the man*; *there are various reasons for believing*; **b** (colloq. and vulg. as pron. or elliptically as **n.**) *various of the speakers were inaudible*; *we were assured by various that . . .*

variously, adv. Prec. & **-ly**. In a various manner; in various ways.

variousness, n. See prec. & **-ness**. State, quality, of being various or diversified; variety.

varix, n., pl. **varices** [1. váriks, várisēz; 2. vέəriks, vǽrisīz]. Lat., 'dilated vein'; etymol. doubtful; connected w. *varus*, 'a blotch, pimple'; Walde connects this word w. the base of Lat. *vermis*, 'worm', see **vermi-**. **1.** (med.) A varicose vein. **2.** (zool.) A projecting ridge or rib on surface of certain shells.

varlet, n. [1. várlet; 2. vάlit]. O. Fr., 'groom; a youth'; earlier *vaslet*, whence **valet**; *vaslet* is for ***vasalet*, dimin. of *vas(s)al*, see **vassal**. **1.** (hist.) A groom, attendant; personal servant of a knight or squire; a manservant. **2.** (archaic) A low fellow, rogue, rascal.

varmint, n. [1. vármint; 2. vάmint]. Variant of **vermin**; a pronunciation current in 17th and 18th cents., even among speakers of the higher class. (colloq., slang, or dial.) Rascal, mischievous boy, scamp; esp. *a young varmint*.

varnish (I.), n. [1. várnish; 2. vάniʃ]. M.E. *vernisshe* &c., fr. O. Fr. *vernis*, cp. Ital. *vernice*, Span. *barniz*; Med. Lat. has *vernicium* & Med. Gk. *bernikē*; etymol. unknown. **1.** A gum or resin dissolved in oil or spirit and forming a solution which after application to the surface of wood, leather, metal &c., dries and hardens into a glossy, translucent coating. **2.** (by transf.) A natural glossy surface, as on the leaves of holly, ivy &c.; artificial glaze on pottery. **3.** (fig.) Outward superficial brilliance or polish; gloss; specious appearance or show, serving as a covering for some deficiency &c.: *his occasional association with good society had imparted a certain varnish to his manners*; *even the apologists of the Borgias find it difficult to put a varnish on their characters*.

varnish (II.), vb. trans.; fr. O. Fr. *vernisser*, fr. *vernis*, see prec.; later form *vernir*. **1.** To cover, paint over, with varnish; give a coat of varnish to (a picture, piece of furniture &c.). **2.** (fig.) To cover over with a superficial attractiveness; to gloze over; to hide with a fair, outward appearance: *a hard, merciless character varnished with an attractive air of geniality*; *they hope to varnish their unpopular policy with some vague promises of social reform*.

varnishing day, n. [1. várnishing dā; 2. vάniʃiŋ dei]. Day before the public opening of an exhibition of pictures, on which the artists are able to put the finishing touches to their exhibits.

'Varsity, adj. & n. [1. vársiti; 2. vάsiti]. Colloq. form of *university*: *at the 'Varsity*; *'Varsity match, team* &c.

varsovienne, n. [1. vàrsōvién; 2. vàsouvién]. Fr., fr. *Varsovie*, 'Warsaw'. A kind of dance, based, in rhythm &c., on Polish national dances.

varus, n. [1. várus; 2. vέərəs], fr. Lat. *vārus*, adj., 'bent, crooked', prob. for ***vākros*, fr. same base as in *vacillāre*, see **vacillate**. (med.) A form of clubfoot; in full, *talipes varus*.

vary, vb. intrans. & trans. [1. vári; 2. vέəri], fr. Fr. *varier*, fr. Lat. *variāre*, 'to change, vary', fr. *varius*, see **various**. **1.** intrans. To change, become different; to undergo a change from one condition to a different one: *colours varying with every change of light*; *the weather varies from hour to hour*; *his principles have never varied*. **2.** trans. To cause to change in form, substance, character &c.; to alter; to make different, to modify: *to vary one's plans*; *to vary a patient's treatment*; *to vary the rules, procedure of a court* &c.; *to vary one's meals, method of work* &c.

vas, n., pl. **vasa** [1. vas, vása; 2. væs, véisə]. Lat. *vās*, 'vessel, vase', etymol. uncertain. (anat.) A vessel or duct, as *vas deferens*, excretory, spermatic duct.

vasal, adj. [1. vásl; 2. véisl]. Prec. & **-al**. Pertaining to a vas.

vascular, adj. [1. váskūlar; 2. vǽskjulə], fr. Lat. *vāsculum*, dimin. of *vās*, see **vas**, & **-ar**. (physiol.) Of plants and animals, pertaining to, containing, consisting of, the vessels, ducts &c.: *vascular system*, the circulatory system of blood-vessels, lymphatics, ducts &c.: *vascular tissue*, containing, full of, blood and other vessels &c.

vascularity, n. [1. vàskūláriti; 2. væskjulǽriti]. Prec. & **-ity**. State of being vascular; vascular form.

vascularization, n. [1. vàskularizáshun; 2. væskjuləraizéiʃən]. See next word & **-ation**. **a** Act, process, of vascularizing; **b** state of being vascularized.

vascularize, vb. trans. [1. váskūlarīz; 2. vǽskjuləraiz]. **vascular** & **-ize**. To render, cause to become, vascular.

vasculum, n., pl. **vascula** [1. váskūlum, -a; 2. vǽskjulə(m)]. Lat. dimin. of *vās*, cp. **vascular**. **1.** A small vessel or vase-shaped organism; an ascidian. **2.** A small cylindrical metal case with opening on one side, used by collectors for carrying botanical specimens.

vase, n. [1. vahz; 2. vāz]; archaic [1. vawz; 2. vɔ̄z]; spelling pronunciation [1. vāz; 2. veiz]. Fr., fr. Lat. *vās*, 'vessel', see **vas**. **1. a** A general term for a vessel, usually of a decorative kind, of many shapes and sizes, made of glass, pottery, porcelain, or metal, used chiefly as an ornament; **b** a vessel usually more or less tall and slender, but variously shaped, used to contain cut flowers. **2.** Specif., *Greek*, formerly *Etruscan, vase*, type of vessel of baked earthenware, made in many varying sizes and forms, and diversely decorated, used as cinerary urns, and for many other purposes, ceremonial and domestic, e.g. for holding wine, water &c. as drinking vessels: *black, red-figured vases* &c.; so *vase painting*. **3.** A sculptured representation of such a vessel in marble or other stone, used as an architectural feature or as a decorative object.

vaseline, n. [1. váselēn; 2. vǽsəlīn]. Modern concoction fr. Germ. *wasser*, 'water', & Gk. *élaion*, 'oil', & **-ine**. A trade and proprietary name of a soft petroleum jelly, without smell or taste, and usually of a yellow colour, used as the basis of ointments, as a lubricant &c.

vasi-, pref. Form fr. Lat. *vās*, 'vessel', see **vas** & **vascular**; used in compounds: *vasiform*, adj., **a** of the shape of a vas or blood-vessel; tubular; **b** shaped like a vase.

vaso-, pref. Form fr. same source as above, used in physiol. & anatomy, in sense of pertaining to, affecting, vascular system, esp. of nerves, drugs &c.; *vaso-constrictor*, constricting, *-dilator*, dilating, or *-motor*, controlling, the blood and other vessels.

vassal, n. [1. vásl; 2. vǽsl]. O. Fr.; represented in Low & Med. Lat. by *vassallus*, or in the more orig. form *vassus*, 'servant, retainer'; a Celt. word, cp. Bret. *goaz*, fr. W. *gwas*, 'youth, servant'; cp. **valet** & **varlet**. **1.** (Med. hist., feudalism) One who has vowed fealty and done homage to a superior lord, and holds land from him by so doing; a feudal tenant, feudatory. **2.** (by transf. or fig.) One who is in a subordinate position to another; a dependant, devoted subject; bondman. **3.** (attrib.) Pertaining to, like, a vassal; subject; servile: *vassal homage, fealty*; *a vassal kingdom* &c.

vassalage, n. [1. vásalij; 2. vǽsəlidʒ]. O. Fr., Mod. Fr. *vasselage*, Med. Lat. *vassalāgium*; see **vassal** & **-age**. **a** State of being a vassal; allegiance, fealty due from a vassal to his superior; **b** dependence, subordinate position, servitude.

vast, adj. [1. vahst; 2. vāst], fr. Fr. *vaste*. Walde distinguishes two Lat. words, *vāstus*, 'huge, immense; shapeless', & *vāstus*, 'barren, void, waste, empty'; Lewis & Short, who give only one word, include under it all the above meanings. The type *vāst-* is cogn. w. O.H.G. *wuosti*, 'barren, empty', O.S. *wōsti*, & O.E. *wēste*, w. same meaning; O. Ir. *fās*, 'empty'. See also **waste** (I.). The form *vāst-* is fr. ***wazdhos*, & cogn. w. O. Ir. *fot*, 'length'. **1.** Of great size, breadth &c.; very extensive, huge, enormous, immense: **a** (in physical sense) *vast expanse of desert, ocean* &c.; *the vast mountains of the Andes*; *buildings become ever vaster in London*; **b** (in non-physical sense) *vast plans of development*; *a scheme of vast scope*. **2.** Very great in number, amount, or quantity: *spent vast sums of money*; *drank vast quantities of beer*; *a vast crowd of people*. **3. a** Very great: *there is a vast difference between* &c.; *of vast importance*; *a vast improvement*; **b** (archaistic, as a colourless intens.): *it gives me vast pleasure*. **4.** (as n., with art.) *A vast, the vast, of ocean, water* &c., immense tract.

vastly, adv. Prec. & **-ly**. **1.** To a vast, enormous, extent: *the Empire that was so vastly enlarged in the 19th century; this book adds vastly to our knowledge.* **2.** Greatly, as mere intensive; very, to a very large extent: *vastly superior to*; (also archaic) *am vastly pleased, obliged* &c.: *vastly pleasant*, extremely amusing.

vastness, n. See prec. & **-ness**. Quality of being vast; immensity, hugeness; vast size.

vasty, adj. [1. váhsti; 2. vásti]. **vast** & **-y**. Vast, immense: Shakespeare, '1 Henry IV.' III. i. 52, '*I can call spirits from the vasty deep*'; '*The vasty hall of death*' (M. Arnold, 'Requiescat').

vat, n. & vb. trans. [1. vat; 2. væt]. Southern dial. variant of O.E. *fæt*, M.E. *vat, fat*, 'a vessel' (cp. **vane, vixen**), O.N. *fat*, Du. *vat*, Germ. *fass*, 'cask, tub', cogn. w. O.H.G. *fazzōn*, 'to hold; to catch, seize; contain', the orig. meaning of word being 'container'. Cp. *wine fat* in N.T., wh. shows the usual Midl. form of O.E. *f-*. **1.** n. A large vessel for containing liquids, esp. in process of fermentation, maturing, manufacture &c., as in brewing, tanning, dyeing &c. **2.** vb. To place, store, mature, in a vat: *old vatted whiskies* &c.

Vatican, n. [1. vátikan; 2. vǽtikən]. Fr., fr. Lat. *Vāticānus*, sc. *mons*, one of the hills of ancient Rome. **1. a** The palace, with its library, museum, chapels &c. of the Pope in Rome, built on the Vatican hill, the official residence of the Pope and centre of Papal government; hence **b** the Papacy, Papal authority and government; Phr. *thunders of the Vatican*, excommunication, anathemas, of the Roman Church. **2.** (attrib.) *Vatican library, gallery* &c.; *Vatican Council*, that of 1869-70, which established the doctrine of Papal Infallibility &c.

Vaticanism, n. [1. vátikanizm; 2. vǽtikənizəm]. Prec. & **-ism**. The principle, system, of Papal supremacy and infallibility; ultramontanism.

vaticinal, adj. [1. vatísinl; 2. vætísinl], fr. Lat. *vāticinus*, see **vaticinate** & **-al**. (rare) Pertaining to, of the nature of, vaticination or prophecy; prophetic.

vaticinate, vb. trans. & intrans. [1. vatísināt; 2. vætísineit], fr. Lat. *vāticināt-(um)*, P.P. type of *vāticinārī*, 'to prophesy, foretell', fr. *vātes*, 'prophet, seer'; cogn. w. Goth. *wōþs*, 'possessed, mad'; O.E. *wōd*, 'frenzied, mad'; O.H.G. *wuot*, 'mad; madness'; also O.E. *wōþ*, 'voice; melody, song'; O.N. *ōdr*, 'song, poetry', fr. **wod*. See also **Edda** & cp. **Wednesday**. **a** trans. To prophesy, foretell; **b** intrans., to utter prophecies.

vaticination, n. [1. vàtisināshun; 2. vætisinéiʃən], fr. Lat. *vāticinātiōn-(em)*; see prec. & **-ion**. **a** Act of prophesying or foretelling; **b** a prophecy.

vaticinator, n. [1. vatísināter; 2. vætísineitə]. Lat., see prec. & **-or**. Prophet, seer.

vaudeville, n. [1. vṓdvil; 2. vóudvil]. Fr., corrupt. of earlier (*chanson de*) *Vau de Vire*, i.e. of the valley, or gorge, of the Vire, in Normandy, where Basselin, the best-known composer of such songs, lived. **1.** (Fr. liter. hist.) **a** A light, convivial song such as those of Basselin, c. 1400-50; **b** a form of light, satirical, topical verse, often accompanied by songs, dances, and pantomime, popular in the 17th cent., written in couplets. **2. a** (Engl. usage) A form of light, musical comedy; **b** (U.S.A.) a variety or music-hall entertainment.

vault (I.), n. [1. vawlt; 2. vōlt]. M.E. *voute, vowte*, fr. O. Fr. *voute, voulte, vaute* &c., Mod. Fr. *voûte*, fr. Low Lat. *vol(u)ta*, fr. P.P. of Lat. *volvere*, 'to roll', cp. **volute** & see **volume**. **1.** An arched roof or ceiling; the covering of an open space by stone or brick supported on a continuous series of arches, as in the 'barrel' vault, or on connected arched ribs meeting in a central point and depending on thrust and counter-thrust for stability, the intersecting or 'groined' vault. **2.** A vaulted chamber or space, specif. **a** an underground cellar or chamber with arched roof: *wine vaults*; **b** a strong room in which safes are kept: *safety vault*; **c** an underground brick or stone chamber in which coffins are laid in a cemetery and, formerly, beneath the flooring of a church, in a crypt &c.: *family vault*. **3. a** Any naturally formed subterranean cavern with arching roof; **b** an arched cavity in the body of an animal &c. **4.** (fig.) The arched canopy of the sky: *the blue vault of heaven*.

vault (II.), vb. trans., fr. prec. **a** To cover, roof over with a vault; to build a vault over; **b** (fig.) to cover as with a vault.

vault (III.), vb. intrans. & trans., fr. M. Fr. *volter*, 'to leap, gambol', cp. Ital. *volta*, 'the turn, swerve, bound, of a horse'; cp. **vault** (I.), wh. is the same word w. differentiation of meaning. **1.** intrans. To leap, spring, with a single movement, esp. with the support of the hand or hands or of a leaping-pole: *to vault over a gate, ditch; to vault on to a horse, into the saddle*. **2.** trans. To leap over, with support of the hand: *to vault a gate*.

vault (IV.), n., fr. prec. Leap, jump, with single movement with support of hand &c.

vaulted, adj. [1. váwlted; 2. vṓltid]. P.P. of **vault** (II.). **a** Built with vaults, or as a vault; arched: *a vaulted roof*; **b** covered by a vault: *vaulted aisle, chamber* &c.

vaulter, n. [1. váwlter; 2. vṓltə]. **vault** (III.) & **-er**. One who vaults or leaps.

vaulting (I.), n. [1. váwlting; 2. vṓltiŋ], fr. **vault** (II.) & **-ing**. **a** The construction, building, of a vault or vaults; **b** a vaulted building; **c** the vaults, collectively, of a roof &c.

vaulting (II.), n. & adj., fr. **vault** (III.) & **-ing**; **2** is fr. Pres. Part. of same. **1.** n. Act of leaping with support of the hand &c. **2.** adj. Leaping with a vault; (also fig.) fr. *vaulting ambition* (Shakespeare, 'Macbeth'), that vaults over, surmounts, all obstacles.

vaunt (I.), vb. intrans. & trans. [1. vawnt; 2. vōnt]. M.E. *avaunten* (cp. **avaunt**), also later without the intens. *a-*; fr. O. Fr. (*se*) *vanter*, 'to boast', fr. Low Lat. *vānitāre*, 'to flatter', fr. Lat. *vānitas*, see **vanity** & **vain**. **1.** intrans. **a** *Vaunt of*, to boast about, proclaim in boastful terms: *to vaunt of one's skill*; **b** *vaunt over*, to triumph over malevolently and boastfully: *to vaunt over another's failure*. **2.** trans. **a** To boast, brag about: *to vaunt one's skill*; (also as adj. fr. P.P.): *his vaunted courage*; **b** to proclaim the merits of, to praise highly, celebrate: *to vaunt the beauties of the Scottish lochs*.

vaunt (II.), n., fr. prec. Boasting; boastful language; a boast.

vaunter, n. [1. váwnter; 2. vṓntə]. **vaunt** (I.) & **-er**. One who vaunts; a boaster, braggart.

vavasour, n. [1. vávasōr; 2. vǽvəsɔ̄]. O. Fr.; in Med. Lat. *vavassor, valvassor, vasvassor*, apparently a corrupt. of *vassus vassorum*, 'vassal of vassals', see **vassal**. (Med. hist.) A term, of varying applications, for a subordinate or mediate vassal; a person holding a fief from one who was himself the vassal to another; also a vassal who had subordinate vassals himself.

veal, n. [1. vēl; 2. vīəl]. M.E. *veel*, 'calf; veal', fr. O. Fr. *veël*, later, as in Mod. Fr., *veau*, fr. Lat. *vitellus*, dimin. of *vitulus*, 'calf'; cogn. w. Gk. *italós*, fr. **witalos*; Scrt. *vatsa*, 'calf'; the orig. meaning is 'yearling', cp. Gk. *étos* for **wetos*, 'year'; wh. base is seen also in Lat. *vetus*, 'old', see **veteran**; further in O.E. *weþer*, see **wether**. The flesh of a calf, as used for food; the word was used occasionally for the living animal as late as 18th cent.

vector, n. [1. vékter; 2. véktə]. Lat., 'carrier, bearer, conveyer', fr. *vect-(um)*, P.P. type of *vehere*, 'to convey', see **vehicle**, & **-or**; see also **weight** (I.). (math.) A quantity involving direction as well as magnitude.

vectorial, adj. [1. vektṓrial; 2. vɛktṓriəl]. Prec. & **-i-** & **-al**. (math.) Pertaining to vectors.

Veda, n. [1. vā́da; 2. véidə]. Scrt. *vēda*, 'knowledge; sacred book of wisdom', fr. base **weid-, *woid-, *wid-*, q.v. also under **idol, idea, -oid, vision** (I.), **wit** (I.). One of the four ancient sacred books of the Hindus.

Vedanta, n. [1. vādánta; 2. veidǽntə]. Scrt., fr. **Veda** & *anta*, 'end'. The system of Hindu pantheistic philosophy.

Veddah, n. [1. véda; 2. védə]. Cingalese, 'hunter'. Member of the primitive, aboriginal race inhabiting the jungles of Ceylon.

vedette, n. [1. vedét; 2. vɛdét]. Fr., fr. Ital. *vedetta*, fr. *vedere*, 'to see', fr. Lat. *vidēre*, see **vision**. A mounted sentry, placed in advance of an outpost.

Vedic, adj. [1. vā́dik; 2. véidik]. **Veda** & **-ic**. Pertaining to the Vedas: *Vedic literature* &c.

veer, vb. intrans. & trans. [1. vēr; 2. viə], fr. Fr. *virer*, 'to turn round, change direction', cp. Span. *virar, birar*, Ital. *virare*; of doubtful etymol.; L. Lat. has *virāre*, wh. has been referred to stem seen in Lat. *viriae*, pl., 'bracelets', dimin. form *viriola*, & second element in **environ**, the orig. meaning being 'to twist, wind round'; this base is also seen in **wire** (I.) & **withy**. **1.** intrans. **a** To shift, change, turn, in position or direction: *the wind, the vane, has veered round to the south*; specif. (of a ship) to change course as preparation for tacking; Phrs. *veer and haul*, to pay out and haul in (rope) alternately; *veer out*, pay out; **b** (fig.) to change about, shift, from one opinion, belief, set of feelings, intentions &c., to another; *to veer round to the opposite party* &c. **2.** trans. To alter, change, the course of, as a ship &c.

veeringly, adv. [1. vḗringli; 2. víəriŋli], fr. Pres. Part. of prec. & **-ly**. In a veering, shifting manner; with change of direction, esp. of mind or opinion.

Vega (I.), n. [1. vḗga; 2. vígə]. Med. Lat., fr. Arab. *wāqis*, adj., 'falling'. The brightest star in the constellation Lyra.

vega (II.), n. [1. vā́ga; 2. véigə]. Span. A low-lying damp or grassy tract of ground, esp. in South America; also tobacco field, in Cuba.

vegetable (I.), adj. [1. véjetabl; 2. védžitəbl]. Fr., fr. L. Lat. *vegetābilis*, 'enlivening, animating', w. suff. *-bilis*, fr. Lat. *vegetāre*, 'to arouse, animate, invigorate', fr. *vegetus*, 'vigorous, active, lively', fr. *vegēre*, 'to be active, lively; to quicken, arouse'; the base is seen in the Lat. derivatives **vigil** & **vigour**; also in O.E. *wacor*, 'watchful, vigilant', cp. *wacan*, 'to awake, be born', see **wake** (I.). A fuller form of this base, **aweg-*, is seen in Lat. *augēre* for **awegēre*, 'to cause to grow, to increase', see **augment** (I.) & **eke** (II.), & cp. **hygiene**. Pertaining to, belonging to, composed of, comprising, including, affecting, of the nature of, plants, or plant life: *the vegetable kingdom; vegetable life* &c.; *vegetable tissue; vegetable as distinct from mineral drugs; vegetable diseases* &c.

vegetable (II.), n., fr. prec. **1.** Anything that grows in the ground; any form of plant life. Phr. *to become a mere vegetable*, said of a person who is thoroughly inactive in mind and body. **2.** Specif., the edible leaves, stalks, flowers, seeds, pods, or roots of certain plants specially cultivated for human food; greens, greenstuff; in common colloquial usage a distinction is made between *potatoes* and *vegetables*, the latter including peas, beans, cabbage of all kinds, asparagus, turnips, carrots &c.; *green vegetables*, (i.) those whose leaves &c. are eaten, as distinct from the roots; (ii.) vegetables cooked green and fresh, as distinct from dried peas &c.; *vegetable dish*, one in which vegetables are brought to table.

vegetable ivory, n. A hard white seed or nut of a South American palm, which is used as a substitute for ivory in manufacture of buttons &c.

vegetable marrow, n. A kind of edible gourd, *Cucurbita Pepo ovifera*.

vegetal, adj. [1. véjetal; 2. védžit(ə)l]. Fr., fr. Lat. *vegetus*, see **vegetable**, & **-al**. **1.** Pertaining to, of the nature of, a plant or vegetable; vegetable: *vegetal life, structure* &c. **2.** (physiol.) Pertaining to growth or the functions; especially concerned with growth or maintenance of life in living organisms, both animals and plants; vegetative.

vegetarian, n. & adj. [1. vèjetárian; 2. vèdžitéərian]. A modern, coined word, fr. *veget-*, see **vegetable (II.)**, & **-arian**. **1.** n. One whose food consists solely or mainly of vegetables, fruit, nuts &c.; one who, on principle, abstains from all forms of animal food, esp. from such as involves the taking of animal life. **2.** adj. **a** Pertaining to vegetarians, their principles &c.: *vegetarian society, system, principles* &c.; **b** consisting solely of vegetables, providing vegetables only as food: *vegetarian diet, dishes, restaurant* &c.

vegetarianism, n. [1. vèjetárianizm; 2. vèdžitéəriənizəm]. See prec. & **-ism**. Principles, practice, of vegetarians; abstention from all animal foods.

vegetate, vb. intrans. [1. véjetāt; 2. védžiteit], fr. Lat. *vegetāt-(um)*, P.P. type of *vegetāre*, 'to give life and vigour to, to animate', fr. *vegetus*, see **vegetable (I.)**. **a** To grow, pass one's life, like a plant; live a purely physical life, devoid of all intellectual and spiritual activities; **b** to live a dull, monotonous, unvaried life with few social or other distractions.

vegetation, n. [1. vèjetáshun; 2. vèdžitéiʃən], fr. L. Lat. *vegetātiōn-(em)*, see prec. & **-ion**. **1.** Act, process, of growing or vegetating; plant growth and development: *vegetation is at its height in spring*. **2.** Plants collectively: *a tropical, luxuriant, vegetation*; *the vegetation is sparse*.

vegetative, adj. [1. véjetativ; 2. védžitətiv], fr. Med. Lat. *vegetātīvus*, see **vegetate** & **-ive**. **1.** Having the capacity of growth; growing: *the vegetative as opposed to the reproductive system of plants*. **2.** Pertaining to, connected with, growth: *vegetative functions*; *during the vegetative stage*. **3.** Productive of growth or vegetation: *vegetative soils*. **4.** (fig.) Living an inactive life; vegetating, passive; passed in mere sloth or idleness: *a placid, vegetative sort of character, existence*.

vegetatively, adv. Prec. & **-ly**. In a vegetative manner.

vegetativeness, n. See prec. & **-ness**. State, quality, of being vegetative.

vehemence, rarely **vehemency**, n. [1. vḗemens(i); 2. víəməns(i)], fr. L. Lat. *vehementia*, see **vehement** & **-ency**. State, quality, of being vehement; violence, intensity, impetuosity, force, eagerness; in material and non-material sense: *the vehemence of the storm, attack* &c.; *carried away by the vehemence of his own eloquence, passions* &c.

vehement, adj. [1. vḗement; 2. víəmənt]. O. Fr., fr. Lat. *vehement-(em), vehemens*, 'eager, violent, furious, vehement; forcible, vigorous', the first element is fr. the base *vehere*, 'to carry, convey', see under **vehicle**. Orig. sense, 'transported (as with strong emotion), carried out of oneself'. The form *vehemens* was probably orig. participial: **vehemenos*. **1.** Acting with great material force, strength or violence; furious: *vehement heat, wind*; *a vehement current* &c. **2.** (in non-material sense) Passionate, **a** (of actions, emotions &c.) impetuous, eager, ardent: *vehement opposition, strife*; *vehement desire, hatred* &c.; **b** (of persons) exhibiting vehemence of character, passion &c.: *a vehement partisan, opponent* &c.

vehemently, adv. Prec. & **-ly**. In a vehement manner; with vehemence; ardently, passionately.

vehicle, n. [1. vḗikl; 2. víikl, víəkl], fr. Lat. *vehiculum*, 'carriage, conveyance', formed w. dimin., see **-cule**, fr. base of *vehere*, 'to bear, carry, convey', this base **wegh-*, **wogh-*, is seen in Scrt. *vahati*, 'he carries, conveys'; Gk. (Pamphylian) *ékhos* for **wekhos*, 'wagon', *(w)ekhétō*, 'let him bring'; *ókhos* for **wokhos*, 'wagon'; Goth. *(ga)wigan*, 'to shake, to move'; O.E. *wegan*, 'to carry', see **weigh (I.)**, also **way**. **1.** That in which anything can be carried; esp. a wheeled carriage, cart, car, or other conveyance by which persons or goods may be transported by land. **2.** A means of transmission; a medium, in various senses: *the ether is the vehicle of light and electric waves*; *a sweet syrup is a good vehicle for the administration of nauseous drugs*; *milk is often a vehicle of infection*. **3.** A means of communicating ideas: *English is a noble vehicle of human thought*.

vehicular, adj. [1. vehíkūlar; 2. vīhíkjulə], fr. L. Lat. *vehiculāris*, see prec. & **-ar**. Pertaining to, concerned with, consisting of, carried by, vehicles: *vehicular transport*; *vehicular traffic*.

vehmgericht, n. [1. vám-, fámgeright; 2. véim-, féimgərijt]. Germ., also *fehmgericht*, fr. *vehme*, *fehme*, 'judgement, punishment', origin doubtful, & *gericht*, 'jurisdiction, court, tribunal', cp. **right (I.)**. **a** A special form of criminal jurisdiction, prevalent in Germany, esp. in Westphalia, during the Middle Ages until the 16th cent., exercised by judges chosen from those pledged by oaths to secrecy, trying serious crimes with power of life and death, and usually though not necessarily sitting in secret; **b** a court of this kind.

vehmic, also **fehmic**, adj. [1. vámik, fámik; 2. véimik, féimik]. See prec. & **-ic**. Pertaining to the vehmgericht: *vehmic courts*.

veil (I.), n. [1. vāl; 2. veil], fr. O. Fr. *veile*, Mod. Fr. *voile*, fr. Lat. *vēlum*, 'sail; piece of cloth; curtain, veil'; see **velum**. **1.** A covering for the face or head, esp. as worn by women, either (i.) as by Moslem women, nuns &c., to conceal their features, or (ii.) as a protection against sun, wind &c., or (iii.) at the dictates of fashion; Phr. *to take the veil*, to become a nun.. **2.** (eccles.) **a** A curtain or cloth hanging, esp. that dividing the Sanctuary from the main body of the Jewish Temple; **b** a piece of drapery of silk &c., used to cover a chalice, crucifix &c., esp. during Lent. **3.** **a** Something which covers and hides (an object) from the sight: *a veil of mist over the landscape*; **b** something which obscures the mental vision; something which renders complete and clear mental perception difficult: *the facts are hidden in a veil of mystery*. **4.** (bot. and zool.) Velum.

veil (II.), vb. trans., fr. O. Fr. *veiler*, fr. Lat. *vēlare*, 'to veil, conceal', see prec. **1.** To cover with, or as with, a veil; to throw a veil over: *to veil one's face, head* &c. **2.** **a** To conceal, hide from sight: *clouds veiled the sun*; **b** to conceal from another's mental perception; to render imperceptible to mental observation; to disguise, dissimulate: *to veil one's dislike, suspicion*; *his malevolence was veiled by an urbane manner*.

veiled, adj. [1. vāld; 2. veild], fr. P.P. of prec. **1.** Wearing a veil, with head and face &c. covered by a veil: *the veiled Tuaregs*; *veiled nun*; *with veiled eyes*. **2.** Concealed, disguised, masked: *veiled hatred* &c.

veiling, n. [1. váling; 2. véiliŋ]. **veil (II.)** & **-ing**. Soft, thin material suitable for veils &c.

veilless, adj. [1. válles; 2. véillis]. **veil (I.)** & **-less**. Without a veil; unveiled.

vein (I.), n. [1. vān; 2. vein]. M.E. & Fr. *veine*, fr. Lat. *vēna*; possibly for **vexna*, & connected w. base seen in *vehere*, 'to carry, convey', see **vehicle**. **1.** One of the tubular vessels which convey the blood returned from the capillaries to the heart, cp. *artery*; (loosely) any blood-vessel. **2.** Something resembling a vein in appearance; as **a** one of the fine ribs or branches of the framework of a leaf, insect's wing &c.; **b** a coloured streak or mark, natural or artificial, in stone, wood &c. **3.** A fissure, cleft, in rock, earth &c., filled with a different rock, or mineral ore; a seam, lode. **4.** **a** Distinctive strain or tendency or characteristic quality which runs through a man's nature as a vein of ore &c. through rock &c.; a streak: *he had a strong vein of humour, of cruelty*; *his characteristic vein of sarcasm*; **b** mood, disposition: *to be in the vein for composing, writing* &c.

vein (II.), vb. trans., fr. prec. To mark, cover, with veins; usually in P.P. *veined*.

veininess, n. [1. vánines; 2. véininis]. **veiny** & **-ness**. State, quality, of being veiny.

veinless, adj. [1. vánles; 2. véinlis]. **vein (I.)** & **-less**. Lacking veins; unveined.

veiny, adj. [1. váni; 2. véini]. **vein (I.)** & **-y**. Covered with, full of, veins; showing the veins prominently, on face, hand &c.

velamen, n., pl. **velamina** [1. velámen, -ina; 2. veléimen, -inə]. Lat., 'covering', fr. *vēlāre*, see **velum**. (anat.) A membrane, velum.

velar, adj. & n. [1. vḗlar; 2. vílə], fr. Lat. *vēlāris*, see **velum** & **-ar**. **1.** adj. Connected with, related to, arising from, the velum or soft palate; *velar consonants*, those formed by the back of the tongue in proximity to the velum. **2.** n. A velar consonant, i.e. a back consonant.

velarium, n. [1. vēlárium; 2. viléəriəm]. Lat. See prec. **a** (Rom. antiq.) The large awning which could be stretched over the auditorium of an amphitheatre or theatre as protection against the sun; **b** (zool.) a membranous rim, in certain jelly-fish.

veld(t), n. [1. velt, felt; 2. velt, felt]. S.-Afr. Du., fr. Du. *veld*, cogn. w. **field (I.)**. The open grass-country, mostly treeless, of S. Africa.

veld(t)-schoen, n. [1. vélt, félt, shōōn; 2. vélt, félt, ʃūn]. S.-Afr. Du. See prec. & **shoe (I.)**. Shoe made of untanned hide, as used in S. Africa by natives and Boer farmers &c.

velite, n. [1. vḗlit; 2. vílait], fr. Lat. *vēlīt-*, stem of *vēles*, cogn. w. *vēlox*, 'swift', see **velocity**. (Rom. antiq.) Light-armed soldier, skirmisher.

velleity, n. [1. velḗiti; 2. velíiti], fr. Med. Lat. *velleitāt-(em), velleitas*, fr. Lat. *velle*, 'to will, wish', see **voluntary (I.)**; cp. also **will (I.)**. (philos.) Imperfect volition, the weakest form of desire.

vellicate, vb. trans. & intrans. [1. vélikāt; 2. vélikeit], fr. Lat. *vellicāt-(um)*, P.P. type of *vellicāre*, freq. of *vellere*, 'to pluck, twitch; to tear, pull off', earlier **vels-*; fr. base **vel-*, **vol-* &c., 'to tear, break', seen also in **vulture, vulnerable**; & in Lat. *vellus*, 'sheepskin with wool left on', see **villus**. From another grade of the same base is Lat. *lāna* for **wlana*, 'wool', see **laniferous**; & further, O.E. *wull*, see **wool (I.)**. (rare) To twitch; to contract, move, convulsively or spasmodically.

vellication, n. [1. vèlikáshun; 2. vèlikéiʃən]. Prec. & **-ion**. (med.) A spasmodic, convulsive local twitching of muscular tissue, esp. of the face.

vellum, n. [1. vélum; 2. véləm]. Earlier *velym, velim*, fr. O. Fr. *velin*, w. change of final *n* to *m*, as in **venom**; Mod. Fr. *vélin*; fr. *vel*, 'veal', or fr. Lat. *vitulīnus*, 'belonging to a calf', *vitulus*, see **veal**; the L. Lat. name for 'vellum' was *pellis vitulīna*. A fine calfskin parchment, used for MSS. or for binding.

velocipede, n. [1. velósipēd; 2. velósipīd]. Fr.; modern concoction fr. Lat. *vēlōci-*, *vēlox*, 'swift', see **velocity**, & *ped-(em)*, *pēs*, 'foot', see **pedal (I.)**. Name formerly given to, **a** a kind of hobby-horse on wheels propelled by the rider's feet touching, and pushing off from, the ground; **b** the earliest form of bicycle; a bone-shaker.

velocity, n. [1. velósiti; 2. vilósiti], fr. Fr. *vélocité*, fr. Lat. *vēlōcitāt-(em)*, *vēlōcitas*, 'swiftness', fr. *vēlōci-*, *vēlox*, 'swift', for **wegslo-*, fr. the base of *vehere*, 'to carry' &c., see **vehicle**. **1.** **a** Swiftness, speed, rapidity of motion: *darted off with the velocity of a bird*; *what limit is there to an aeroplane's velocity?*; **b** quickness, rapidity of action or of events: *the world was rushed into war with startling velocity*. **2.** Rate of motion, rapidity relative to time: *at a velocity of 100 miles per hour*; *muzzle velocity*, that of projectile on leaving the gun or rifle.

velours, n. [1. velóor; 2. velúə]. Fr.; O. Fr. *velour, velous*, fr. Lat. *villōsus*, 'shaggy', see **velvet**. **a** A material with a soft pile like that of velvet; **b** hat of this material.

velum, n., pl. **vela** [1. vēlum, -a; 2. vílə(m)]. Lat., 'sail; piece of cloth, curtain, veil'; etymol. disputed; prob. for *vecslom; fr. base *weg-, 'to weave'; cp. Ir. *figim*, 'I weave'; O.H.G. *wickilin*, 'woollen yarn for spinning'; see further under **wick** (of candle). **1.** (anat.) The soft palate. **2. a** (bot.) A membranous covering seen in certain fungi; **b** (zool.) a membranous organ in jelly-fish, molluscs &c.

velure, n. [1. velūr; 2. vɛljúə], fr. O. Fr. See **velours**. A variant of velours, q.v.

velvet (I.), n. [1. vélvet; 2. vélvit]. A.-Fr., fr. L. or Med. Lat. *ve(e)lvētum*, apparently for **velluētum*, a variant form of *vellūtum*, whence Ital. *velluto*; fr. Lat. *villus*, 'shaggy, rough hair', cogn. w. *vellus*, 'fleece of wool'; cp. Lat. *vellere*, 'to pluck'; see **vellicate**. The Lat. adj. *villōsus*, 'shaggy', gave O. Fr. *velous*, later *velours*, 'velvet', see **velours**. **1.** A textile, properly of silk or of silk on a cotton or linen backing, with a thick, close, soft pile or nap on one side. **2.** The soft, velvety covering of newly grown antlers of deer. **3.** Any soft surface resembling velvet in touch or appearance, as on a peach, cheek &c.; or of mossy stone, tree trunk &c.; Phr. *to be on velvet*, to be in a safe or advantageous position, esp. in money matters, specif. in betting or speculation, so that whatever happens one may win but cannot lose.

velvet (II.), adj., fr. prec. **1.** Made of velvet; Phr. *iron hand in the velvet glove*, sternness, force, ruthlessness, concealed by a suave, courteous manner. **2.** Like, resembling, velvet, to the touch or in appearance; soft, velvety, often in names of plants, animals &c.: *velvet ant, moss, sponge* &c.

velveteen, n. [1. vèlvetēn; 2. vèlvitín], fr. Fr. *velvetine*. **velvet** & **-een**, variant of **-ine**, indicating an imitation or derivative. An imitation velvet made of cotton; *velveteens*, breeches made of this, often worn by gamekeepers; hence, a gamekeeper.

velvety, adj. [1. vélveti; 2. vélviti]. **velvet** (I.) & **-y**. Like velvet; having the texture of velvet to the touch; smooth and non-astringent to the taste: *a velvety wine*.

venal, adj. [1. vēnl; 2. vínl]. Through O. Fr. or directly fr. Lat. *vēnālis*, 'for sale, purchasable; that can be bought or bribed'; fr. *vēnum*, also *vēnus*, for *vesn-, 'sale'; cp. Scrt. cogn. *vasnál*, 'purchase price', *vasnam*, 'reward'; further Gk. *ônos* for **wōsnos*, 'price'. **1.** (of persons) Capable of being bought or bribed; influenced by hope of reward; mercenary, corrupt: *a venal judge, politician; a venal police force; the venal races of the Levant* &c. **2.** (of actions and motives) Controlled, influenced, by hope of gain or reward; springing from, instigated by, corrupt, mercenary, motives.

venality, n. [1. vēnáliti; 2. vinǽliti], fr. Fr. *vénalité*, fr. L. Lat. *vēnālitāt-(em)*, see **venal** & **-ity**. Quality of being venal; mercenary behaviour.

venally, adv. [1. vēnali; 2. vínəli]. **venal** & **-ly**. In a venal manner; corruptly.

venatic, adj. [1. vēnátik; 2. vinǽtik], fr. Lat. *vēnāticus*, fr. *vēnāri*, 'to hunt', see **venery** (I.) & **venison**. (rare, archaistic) Pertaining to the chase or hunting.

venation, n. [1. vēnāshun; 2. vinéiʃən], fr. Lat. *vēna*, see **vein** & **-ation**. The arrangement or system of veins in a leaf or insect's wing.

vend, vb. trans. [1. vend; 2. vɛnd], fr. O. Fr. *vendre*, fr. Lat. *vendere*, 'to sell', fr. *vēnum dāre*, 'to offer for sale', fr. *vēnum*, 'price, sale', see **venal**, & *dāre*, 'to give, offer', see **date** (I.), **donation**. To sell or offer for sale; chiefly a legal term, or used in sense of to peddle (small wares).

vendace, n. [1. véndās; 2. véndeis]. Apparently fr. O. Fr. *vendese*, Mod. Fr. *vandoise*, 'dace'; etymol. doubtful. A small freshwater fish, genus *Coregonus*, of some Scottish and English lakes.

Vendean, adj. & n. [1. vendēan; 2. vɛndíən], fr. Fr. *Vendéen*, fr. Vendée, department in N.W. France. **1.** adj. Of La Vendée, esp. in connexion with the struggle there against the Revolution in 1793. **2.** n. An inhabitant of La Vendée; participator in the struggle against the Revolution.

vendee, n. [1. vendē; 2. vɛndí]. **vend** & **-ee**. (legal) Person to whom anything is sold; purchaser.

Vendémiaire, n. [1. vàhndāmiár; 2. vɑ̃demiɛ̄r]. Fr., fr. Lat. *vindēmia*, 'vintage', see **vintage**. The first month, Sept. 22nd to Oct. 21st, of the French Revolutionary calendar.

vender, n. [1. vénder; 2. véndə]. **vend** & **-er**. One who vends, sells, or offers to sell; cp. *vendor*.

vendetta, n. [1. vendéta; 2. vɛndétə]. Ital., 'revenge', fr. Lat. *vindicta*, see **vindictive**. A blood feud; family vengeance, esp. as practised through generations, as in Corsica.

vendibility, n. [1. vèndibíliti; 2. vɛ̀ndibíliti]. See next word & **-ity**. Quality of being vendible or salable.

vendible, adj. [1. véndibl; 2. véndibl], fr. Lat. *vendibilis*, see **vend** & **-ible**. Salable.

vendor, n. [1. vendór; 2. vɛndɔ́]. **vend** & **-or**. One who sells or offers for sale; vender; esp. (legal) the seller of real property: *the law of vendor and purchaser*; contrasted with *vendee*.

veneer (I.), vb. trans. [1. venḗr; 2. vənίə]. Earlier *faneer, fineer*, fr. Germ. *furniren*, 'to inlay, veneer', lit. 'to furnish with pieces of inlay', fr. Fr. *fournir*, 'to furnish', itself fr. O.H.G., see **furnish**. **1.** To cover, overlay, (object of common wood) with a thin sheet of fine wood, or (a piece of fine wood) with a thin sheet of wood of same kind, but of better grain and texture; also, similarly, to overlay (wood, stone &c.) with a thin plate of ivory, marble, mother-of-pearl &c. **2.** (fig.) To attempt to conceal beneath a specious appearance of refinement and polish something which is essentially unrefined and coarse: *his innate vulgarity was veneered with an affectation of ease and geniality*.

veneer (II.), n., fr. prec. **1.** (cabinet-making) A thin plate or layer of wood of fine grain and texture, laid and glued over wood of inferior quality and appearance, so as to produce the impression that the wood so treated is of fine quality throughout. **2.** (fig.) A superficial appearance of some quality, mode of behaviour &c., assumed as being superior to that which it is designed to hide; a specious gloss: *a thin veneer of education, good breeding, respectability* &c.; *a Scotch accent with a veneer of cockney*.

veneering, n. [1. venḗring; 2. vənίəriŋ]. **veneer** (I.) & **-ing**. **1.** Process of applying veneer to wood. **2.** Material used as veneer.

venenate, vb. trans. [1. vénenāt; 2. vénɛneit], fr. Lat. *venēnāt-(um)*, P.P. type of *venēnāre*, 'to infect with poison', fr. *venēnum*, 'poison', see **venom**. (rare, med.) To poison, infect with poisonous substance.

venenation, n. [1. vènenāshun; 2. vènenéiʃən]. Prec. & **-ion**. Poisoning.

venerability, n. [1. vènerabíliti; 2. vènərəbíliti], fr. L. Med. Lat. *venerābilitāt-(em)*, see next word & **-ity**. Quality of being venerable.

venerable, adj. [1. vénerabl; 2. vénərəbl], fr. O. Fr., fr. Lat. *venerābilis*, fr. *venerāri*, see **venerate**, & **-able**. **1. a** (of persons) Worthy of being venerated; deserving honour and respect; esp. **b** (of persons and things) deserving respect and veneration as having lived long and honourably, or having lasted for a very long time: *the venerable commander, prelate* &c.; also *a venerable building, a venerable oak* &c. Thus venerable comes to mean 'old', but nearly always with the implication of 'deserving respect': *venerable age, antiquity*. **2.** Specif., an ecclesiastical title, **a** in the Anglican Church, for an archdeacon: *the Venble. Archdeacon Brown* &c.; **b** in Roman Catholic Church, for one who has passed the first stage of canonization, prior to beatification; *the Venerable Bede* (traditional title). **3.** (of things) Held in great honour and esteem for historical, religious associations &c.: *venerable ruins* &c.

venerableness, n. Prec. & **-ness**. Venerability.

venerably, adv. See prec. & **-ly**. In a venerable manner.

venerate, vb. trans. [1. vénerāt; 2. vénəreit], fr. Lat. *venerāt-(um)*, P.P. type of *venerāri*, 'to reverence, worship, venerate'; fr. *vener-*, stem of *venus*, 'love, desire', see **Venus**. **1.** To reverence, revere; to regard with feelings of profound respect. **2.** To worship, adore.

veneration, n. [1. vènerāshun; 2. vènəréiʃən], fr. Lat. *venerātiōn-(em)*, see prec. & **-ion**. Act of venerating; deep respect and reverence accorded to persons, objects, qualities, or actions.

venerator, n. [1. vénerāter; 2. vénəreitə]. Lat., see **venerate** & **-or**. One who venerates or reverences.

venereal, adj. [1. venḗreal; 2. venίəriəl], fr. Lat. *venereus*, fr. *vener-*, stem of *venus*, 'sexual love, desire', see **Venus**, & **-al**. Pertaining, due, to sexual intercourse; esp. *venereal diseases*, as syphilis, gonorrhoea &c.

venery (I.), n. [1. véneri; 2. vénəri], fr. O. Fr. *venerie*, fr. *vener*, 'to hunt', fr. Lat. *vēnāri*, 'to hunt; to seek after, pursue'; cogn. w. Scrt. *vēti*, 'follows after'; more remotely w. O.H.G. *weida*, 'fodder, pasture, pasture-ground; the chase', fr. base **wēi-*, **wai-*, & **-ery**. (archaic) Hunting, the chase: *learned in all the arts of venery*; '*a boke of venerie*'.

venery (II.), n., fr. Lat. *vener-*, stem of *venus*, 'sexual love, desire', see **Venus**. (archaic) Sexual love; indulgence in sexual gratification.

venesection, n. [1. vènesékshun; 2. vìnisékʃən], fr. Med. Lat. *vēnae sectio*, 'cutting of a vein', see **vein** (I.) & **section** (I.). (med.) The opening of a vein to let blood; blood-letting, as formerly practised as a remedy; phlebotomy.

Venetian, adj. & n. [1. venēshan; 2. viníʃən], fr. Med. Lat. *Venetiānus*, fr. *Venetia*, Venice. **1.** adj. Pertaining to, made in, used in, Venice: *Venetian glass*, from Murano; *Venetian blind*, one made of movable slats of wood; *Venetian mast*, spirally painted pole used in street decorations. **2.** n. Inhabitant, native, of Venice.

vengeance, n. [1. vénjans; 2. véndžəns]. M.E., fr. O. Fr., fr. *venger*, 'to avenge', & **-ance**, fr. Lat. *vindicāre*, see **vindicate**. **1.** The infliction of punishment or exaction of retribution for wrong done or received; often with sense of vindictive punishment: '*Vengeance is mine, I will repay*' (Rom. xii. 19). Phr. *to take vengeance upon*, exact retribution from. **2.** An instance of this: *a fearful vengeance*. Phr. (colloq.) *with a vengeance*, to a high degree, to an extreme extent, very thoroughly: *he laid about him with a vengeance*.

vengeful, adj. [1. vénjfl; 2. véndžfl], fr. obs. *venge*, 'to avenge', see prec., & **-ful**. Vindictive, revengeful.

vengefully, adv. Prec. & **-ly**. Revengefully, vindictively.

vengefulness, n. See prec. & **-ness**. Revengefulness, vindictiveness.

venial, adj. [1. vēnial; 2. víniəl]. O. Fr., fr. L. Lat. *veniālis*, 'gracious; pardonable, venial'; fr. Lat. *venia*, 'grace, kindness, pardon, mercy', fr. base seen in **venerate** & **Venus**. **a** Pardonable, excusable; trivial, unimportant: *a venial error*; *such childish, venial faults*; **b** (theol.) entitled to remission of punishment and to forgiveness: *venial sin*; contrasted with *mortal sin*.

veniality, n. [1. vèniáliti; 2. vìniǽliti]. See prec. & **-ity**. Quality of being venial, pardonable, or excusable.

venially, adv. [1. vēniali; 2. víniəli]. **venial** & **-ly**. In a venial manner.

venire facias, n. [1. veníre fásias; 2. vináiəri fǽsiæs]. Lat., 'cause, make, to come'. (legal hist.) Name of a judicial writ, now obsolete, issued to a sheriff ordering him to summon certain persons as jurors.

venison, n. [1. vénzun; 2. vénz(ə)n], vulgarly [vénizən], fr. O. Fr. *veneson, veneison*, Mod. Fr. *venaison*, fr. Lat. *vēnātiōn-(em)*, 'hunting, the chase', fr. *vēnāri*, 'to hunt', see **venery (I.)**. The flesh of deer, as food; formerly applied to the flesh of various other animals, such as the boar &c., killed in the chase.

Venite, n. [1. veníti; 2. vináiti]. Lat., 'come ye', 2nd pers. pl. imperat. of *venīre*, 'to come', see **venue**, & cp. **event** & **come**. **a** Name of the ninety-fifth psalm, 'O come, let us sing unto the Lord', in Lat. '*Venite, exultemus Domino*', esp. as the Canticle sung at Morning Prayer before the Psalms for the day; **b** a musical setting for this.

venom, n. [1. vénum; 2. vénəm]. M.E. *venym, venim*, fr. O. Fr. *venim, venin*, fr. Lat. *venēnum*, 'a drug, potion; a poisonous drug &c.; poison'; the suggestion that this is for *venesnom, & orig. meant 'a love potion', fr. **Venus**, is now considered improbable. No convincing etymol. is offered. **1. a** The poisonous fluid secreted from glands in certain reptiles, such as snakes, scorpions, and some insects, such as wasps, bees &c., injected by bite or sting; **b** (now rare) any poison or poisonous thing. **2.** (fig.) Malignity, spite, malice; venomous conduct, language &c.: *the venom of malignant tongues*; *she cast a look of venom at him* &c.

venomed, adj. [1. vénumd; 2. vénəmd]. Prec. & **-ed**. Poisoned; charged with, full of, venom; often in fig. sense: *a venomed tongue* &c.; more usually *envenomed*.

venomous, adj. [1. vénumus; 2. vénəməs]. M.E. *venimous*, fr. O. Fr. *venimeux*, fr. Lat. *venēnōsus*, see **venom** & **-ous**. **1.** Secreting poison, infecting with poison: *venomous snakes* &c. **2.** (fig.) Full of venom or malice; malignant, spiteful, maleficent: *a venomous opponent*; *she had a venomous tongue*; *these venomous attacks on his character*.

venomously, adv. Prec. & **-ly**. In a venomous manner; malignantly.

venomousness, n. See prec. & **-ness**. State, quality, of being venomous.

venose, adj. [1. vēnōs; 2. vīnous], fr. Lat. *vēnōsus*, 'full of veins', fr. *vēna*, see **vein**, & **-ose**, **-ous**. (bot.) Full of veins, veined, veiny; cp. *venous*.

venosity, n. [1. vēnósiti; 2. vīnɔ́siti]. Prec. & **-ity**. **1.** Quality, state, of being venose or veined. **2.** Quality of being venous; **a** (of organs &c.) presence, excess, of venous, as opposed to arterial, blood; **b** (of arterial blood) admixture of venous blood.

venous, adj. [1. vēnus; 2. vīnəs], fr. Lat. *vēnōsus*, see **venose**. **1.** (physiol.) Pertaining to, contained in, the veins, distinguished from *arterial*: *venous blood*. **2.** (bot.) Venose, full of veins; veiny.

vent (I.), n. [1. vent; 2. vent]. M.E. *fent*, fr. O. Fr. *fente*, 'cleft, slit, cranny', fr. *fendre*, 'to cleave, split', fr. Lat. *findere, fiss-(um)*, see **fissile**; to this word many of the meanings of **vent (II.)** are often referred; the O.E.D. keeps them entirely separate. **1.** A slit or opening in a garment, common in the slashed garments of the 15th and 16th cents.; now only as a tailor's term for the slit at the back of a coat. **2.** (obs. or hist.) Opening or crenel in a battlemented wall.

vent (II.), n., fr. O. Fr. *vent*, fr. Lat. *ventus*, 'wind', see **ventilate** & **wind (I.)**; or fr. or influenced by O. Fr. *esvent*, Fr. *évent*, 'a breaking, bursting forth', fr. *e(s)venter*, 'to break forth', fr. *es-, e-*, see **ex-**, & *vent*, 'wind', as above. **1.** Aperture, hole, outlet, passage, in anything, which allows air, liquid &c. to escape, or admits air, as *the vent of a cask, of a fire-arm* &c.; *a vent in the crater of volcano* &c.; specif., the anal or cloacal opening of birds, reptiles, and fishes. **2.** Means of exit; outlet; power, opportunity to escape, esp. in Phr. **a** *to find (a) vent for* (in material or non-material senses): *the enclosed steam must find a vent or burst the boiler*; *he found some vent for his emotion in violent exercise, bad language* &c.; **b** *to give vent to*, to give means of escape to, provide outlet for (usually in non-material sense), to express, give utterance to: *to give vent to one's anger* &c. **3.** Act of an otter in coming to the surface to breathe.

vent (III.), vb. trans. & intrans. In sense **1**, fr. O. Fr. *venter*; other senses fr. n., see **vent (II.)**. **A.** trans. **1.** To provide a vent for; to make a vent in; specif., *to vent a cask*, to bore through the wooden bung in the top so as to allow gas to escape. **2.** To give vent to, to discharge, allow to escape: *the chimneys vented their smoke in great clouds*; *to vent one's wrath, indignation, high spirits*. **B.** intrans. Specif. (of a hunted otter), to come to surface of water in order to breathe.

vent (IV.), n., fr. Fr. *vente*, 'sale', fr. *vendre*, 'to sell', see **vend**. (archaic or obs.) Market, opening, for sale of goods; in such Phr. as *to find a vent for* &c., it is difficult to distinguish from same phrase in **vent (II)**.

ventage, n. [1. véntij; 2. véntidž]. **vent (II.)** & **-age**. **1. a** Means of escape for air, gas, liquid &c.; **b** means of relief to the emotions. Phr. *to give ventage to anger, indignation, rage* &c. **2.** A finger-hole in a musical wind instrument.

ventail, n. [1. véntāl; 2. vénteil]. O. Fr. *ventaile*, fr. *vent*, 'wind', see **ventilate.** (hist.) The lower movable part of the visor of a helmet.

venter, n. [1. vénter; 2. véntə]. Lat., 'belly, womb'; for **vend-tro*, fr. base **wened-*, wh. is explained by some as a nasalized form of that seen in Scrt. *utáram*, 'belly', & Lat. *uterus*; see **uterus**. **1.** (anat.) The abdominal cavity in insects and other invertebrate animals. **2.** (law, O. Fr. in origin) Womb; hence (by transf.) mother, as in such Phr. as *born of a second venter* &c.

vent-hole, n. **vent (II.)** & **hole**. Hole, aperture, for passage of air, light, smoke, gas &c.

ventiduct, n. [1. véntidùkt; 2. véntidàkt], fr. Lat. *venti-, ventus*, 'wind', see **ventilate** & **duct**. (archit.) A pipe or other passage used for passage of air in ventilating a building, room &c.

ventilate, vb. trans. [1. véntilāt; 2. véntileit], fr. Lat. *ventilāt-(um)*, P.P. type of *ventilāre*, 'to brandish in the air; to fan, winnow; to set in motion; to agitate', fr. *ventus*, 'wind'; cp. W. *gwynt*, Bret. *gwent*; Aryan type **awe-*, 'to blow', cp. Gk. *áēmi* for **áwēmi*, 'I blow', & see **air** & **wind (I.)**. **1.** To cause fresh air to circulate in (a room, building, mine &c.); to render (the air of a room &c.) fresh and cool by adopting various means for the withdrawal or escape of vitiated, and the continual supply of fresh, air. **2.** To expose (blood) to, and purify by, the free action of oxygen; to aerate. **3.** (fig.) To allow, cause, to become known, and to be freely and widely discussed; to submit for investigation: *to ventilate a grievance*; *the new policy has now been freely ventilated*.

ventilation, n. [1. vèntiláshun; 2. vèntiléiʃən], fr. Lat. *ventilātiōn-(em)*, see prec. & **-ion**. **1. a** Admission, free circulation, of fresh air into an enclosed space or chamber; **b** state of room &c. in relation to the free circulation of fresh air: *the ventilation of the crowded room was appalling*; **c** means of ventilating; apparatus adopted for ventilating: *the ventilation of the mine broke down*. **2.** Free discussion of a subject; public examination and debate: *a full ventilation of grievances*.

ventilative, adj. [1. véntilativ; 2. véntilətiv]. **ventilate** & **-ive**. Pertaining to, tending to produce or facilitate, ventilation.

ventilator, n. [1. véntilāter; 2. véntileitə]. **ventilate** & **-or**; Lat. *ventilātor* only in sense of 'one who winnows grain'. **1.** Apparatus used in drawing out exhausted or stagnant, and admitting fresh, cool, air to room, building, mine &c. **2.** One who ventilates or submits a subject &c. for examination and discussion: *he was a great ventilator of grievances by letters to the daily press*.

ventless, adj. [1. véntles; 2. véntlis]. **vent (II.)** & **-less**. Having no vent or outlet.

Ventôse, n. [1. vahntṓz; 2. vãtóuz], fr. Lat. *ventōsus*, 'windy', fr. *ventus*, 'wind', see **ventilate**. Sixth month of the French Revolutionary calendar, from Feb. 19th to Mar. 20th.

vent-peg, n. **vent (II.)** & **peg**. A small peg of wood driven into the vent-hole of a cask or barrel, used to allow escape of excess of gas from the liquor, and to permit enough air to enter for the liquor to be drawn off through the tap.

ventral, adj. [1. véntral; 2. véntrəl], Fr., fr. Lat. *ventrālis*, fr. *venter*, 'belly', see **venter**, & **-al**. Pertaining to the belly or abdominal region; esp. situated on the under side or that opposite the back; cp. *dorsal*; *ventral fin*, of fish, one situated on the under side of the body behind the pectoral fins.

ventrally, adv. Prec. & **-ly**. In a ventral position or direction.

ventri-, pref. Form of Lat. *venter*, 'belly', used in compounds; see **venter**.

ventricle, n. [1. véntrikl; 2. véntrikl], fr. Fr. *ventricule*, or directly fr. Lat. *ventriculus*, dimin. of **venter**. A cavity in an organ of the body, as in the brain or larynx; specif., one of the two chambers of the heart, receiving the blood from the auricles and discharging it into the arteries.

ventricular, adj. [1. ventríkūlar; 2. ventríkjulə]. Prec. & **-ar**. Pertaining to, affecting, a ventricle, as of the brain or heart.

ventriloquial, adj. [1. vèntrilṓkwial; 2. vèntrilóukwiəl], fr. Lat. *ventriloquus*, lit. 'one who speaks from his belly; ventriloquist'; **ventriloquy** & **-al**. Pertaining to, produced by, ventriloquism: *the ventriloquial art*; *ventriloquial effects*.

ventriloquially, adv. Prec. & **-ly**. By means of ventriloquism.

ventriloquism, n. [1. ventrílokwizm; 2. ventríləkwizəm]. **ventriloquy** & **-ism**. Art of, skill in, so modifying the voice in speaking, or producing sounds with the vocal organs, that the voice, or the sound made, appears to come from a place remote from, or a person other than, the actual speaker.

ventriloquist, n. [1. ventrílokwist; 2. ventríləkwist]. **ventriloquy** & **-ist**. One who is skilled in ventriloquism; esp. a professional entertainer in this art.

ventriloquize, vb. intrans. & trans. [1. ventrílokwīz; 2. ventríləkwaiz]. **ventriloquy** & **-ize**. **a** intrans. To practise ventriloquy; **b** trans., to utter, speak, ventriloquially.

ventriloquy, n. [1. ventrílokwi; 2. ventríləkwi], fr. Fr. *ventriloquie*, fr. Med. Lat. *ventriloquium*, see **ventri-**, & base *loqui*, 'to speak', see **loquacious**, & **-y**. Ventriloquism.

ventripotent, adj. [1. ventrípotent; 2. ventrípətənt]. Fr. See **ventri-** & **potent**. **a** Big-bellied; **b** having a large capacity or appetite for food.

ventro-, pref. Form of **venter**, 'belly', in compounds, as *ventro-dorsal*, pertaining to, extending from, the ventral and dorsal parts of the body; *ventro-lateral*, pertaining to the ventral and lateral parts of the body.

venture (I.), n. [1. vénchur; 2. véntʃə]. Aphetic form of earlier M.E. *aventure*, fr. O. Fr., fr. L. Lat. *adventūra*, 'adventure', q.v., formed as if fem. of *adventūrus*, Fut. Part. of Lat. *advenīre*, 'to come to, happen', fr. **ad-** & *venīre*, 'to come', see **venue**. **1.** Chance, fortune, luck, event, not to be calculated; contingency; rare or archaic, except in Phr. *at a venture*, at random, without foreseeing or calculating the results. **2. a** Enterprise, undertaking, of a hazardous nature; some course of action attended by risk or danger of loss; **b** specif., a financial or commercial speculation: *a bold venture is often successful*; *a lucky, profitable, disastrous, venture*.

venture (II.), vb. trans. & intrans. See prec. **A.** trans. **1.** To expose to risk or danger, to run the chance of losing; to risk, hazard: *to venture one's life, happiness, on a doubtful* *enterprise*; (also reflex.) *venture oneself*. **2.** To stake, risk, for monetary or other gain: *to venture £1000, all one's wealth* &c.; *to venture a fortune on a single chance.* Proverbial Phr. *nothing venture, nothing have*, no gain without some risk. **3.** To undertake the risk of, dare to go &c.: *will you venture a flight in an aeroplane, a climb down these rocks?*; *I won't venture a step farther.* **4.** To put forward, advance, express, in a tentative, diffident, undogmatic manner: *to venture an opinion, criticism* &c. **B.** intrans. **1.** Also *venture on, upon*, **a** to dare, be bold enough, to go; to risk oneself by going: *I should not venture too near the edge if I were you*; *to venture on a stormy sea*; **b** to take the risk of (doing something): *will you venture on another glass of wine?* **2.** To presume, to make so bold as, go so far as: *I venture to assert that* &c.; *I should not venture to offer an opinion*; in polite formulae expressing diffidence: *if I might venture to make a remark*; *may I venture to ask your opinion?*

venturer, n. [1. vénchurer; 2. véntʃərə]. Prec. & **-er**. One who ventures; an adventurer; used esp. of the old 16th and 17th trading companies: *the Merchant Venturers of Bristol.*

venturesome, adj. [1. vénchursum; 2. véntʃəsəm]. **venture (I.)** & **-some**. **a** (of persons) Daring, foolhardy, rash; **b** (of actions &c.) involving risk or danger; rash, hazardous, dangerous.

venturesomely, adv. Prec. & **-ly**. In a venturesome manner.

venturesomeness, n. See prec. & **-ness**. State, quality, of being venturesome.

venue, n. [1. vénū; 2. vénjū]. Fr., 'arrival, coming', fem. of *venu*, P.P. of *venir*, 'to come', fr. Lat. *venīre*, 'to come', fr. **gwenīre*, earlier **gwemīre*; Aryan base **gʷem-*, cp. Scrt. *gam-*, 'to come, go', Gk. *bainein*, see **basis**; Goth. *qiman*, O.E. *cuman*, earlier **cwiman*; see **come**. **a** (law) The locality or place to which a jury is summoned for the trial of a case, originally in the neighbourhood where the cause of action has arisen or a crime been committed. Phr. *to change the venue*, to alter the place of trial, remove it to another county, to Central Criminal Court &c.; **b** (popular) meeting-place.

Venus, n. [1. vḗnus; 2. vínəs]. Lat. *venus, veneris*, 'desire, sexual love; beauty'; (cap.) 'the goddess of beauty and love'; the same base is seen in **venerate**; also in O.E. *wynn*, 'joy, delight', see **winsome**; in O.E. *wȳscan*, 'to desire, wish', see **wish (I.)**. **1.** (mythol.) The Roman, Latin, goddess of beauty and growth, later identified with the Greek Aphrodite, goddess of sexual love; *Mount of Venus* (palmistry), protuberance on the palm, at base of the thumb. **2.** (astron.) The second of the major planets in order from the sun, appearing as the evening and morning star, Hesperus and Lucifer. **3. a** A statue, picture of the goddess: *the Venus di Milo*; **b** a beautiful woman. Phr. *pocket Venus*, a beautiful, petite woman, of exquisite form and features.

Venus's comb, n. **a** A kind of marine shell-fish with spiny edges; **b** a plant, akin to the parsley, with fruit toothed like a comb.

Venus's flower-basket, n. A kind of sponge, shaped like a tube of delicate network, found in East Indian waters.

Venus's fly-trap, n. An insectivorous plant, *Dionaea muscipula*, of the Carolina coast, N. America, cultivated as a curiosity.

Venus's slipper, n. Lady's slipper; the wild orchid, *Cypripedium*; also the garden calceolaria.

veracious, adj. [1. veráshus; 2. veréiʃəs], fr. Lat. *vērāci-*, stem of *vērax*, 'truthful, speaking the truth', fr. *vērus*, 'true'; fr. **vesros*, 'that which is', fr. the Aryan base **wes-*, 'to be', see **was**; cogn. w. O.H.G. *wār*, 'true', for **wǣz*; see also **verify** & **very (I.)**. For similar development of meaning cp. **sooth**. **1.** (of person &c.) Truthful, observant of the truth, habitually speaking the truth; trustworthy: *a veracious witness* &c. **2.** (of statement &c.) Founded on the truth or on fact; true; to be believed: *a veracious narrative*; *veracious evidence.*

veraciously, adv. Prec. & **-ly**. In a veracious manner.

veraciousness, n. See prec. & **-ness**. Veracity.

veracity, n. [1. verásiti; 2. virǽsiti], fr. Fr. *véracité*. See **veracious** & **-ity**. **a** Quality of habitually speaking the truth; truthfulness: *his veracity is unquestioned*; **b** agreement with the facts or the truth; truth: *one doubts the veracity of such statements.*

veranda(h), n. [1. veránda; 2. vərǽndə]. Introduced in 18th cent. fr. India & taken to be a native word; it represents Port. & Span. *varanda*, 'railing, balustrade, balcony', prob. fr. *vara*, 'rod, pole', fr. Lat. *vāra*, 'forked pole on which fishing nets are spread'. Covered space with a roof and pavement, in immediate proximity to the wall of a house, some windows of which open on to it; the front and sides are open or partially glazed, and the roof is supported at the back by the house wall and in front by pillars.

veratria, veratrine, n. [1. verā́tria, -trin; 2. veréitriə, -trin], fr. Lat. *vērātrum*, 'hellebore'. A bitter, poisonous alkaloid obtained from the root of various kinds of hellebore, used externally in medicine, in an ointment for the relief of neuralgia and rheumatism.

verb, n. [1. vĕrb; 2. vʌ̄b], fr. Fr. *verbe*, fr. Lat. *verbum*, 'word', cogn. w. O.E. *word*, see **word**; fr. base **werē-*, 'to speak'; whence also Gk. *eírō*, 'I say', fr. **werjō*, & *rhḗtōr*, 'orator', for **wrḗtōr*, see **rhetoric** & **word**; Scrt. *vratám*, 'order, command, law'. (gram.) The part of speech which expresses existence or action and affirms or predicates that a person or thing *is, does*, or *suffers* something.

verbal, adj. [1. vĕrbl; 2. vʌ́bl]. Fr., fr. L. Lat. *verbālis*, see prec. & **-al**. **1.** Pertaining to, concerned with, words; expressed in, or composed of, words: *verbal felicities, mistakes*; *verbal wit*; *a good verbal memory*, one retentive of the exact words, or wording of something heard or read; *verbal inspiration*, the direct influence of God assumed to have inspired every actual word of the Holy Scriptures. **2.** Dealing, concerned, with the words only, not with the substance: *a purely verbal criticism*; *a verbal pedantry*; *the difference between the two accounts is merely verbal.* **3.** Literal, word for word: *a verbal translation.* **4.** Oral, by word of mouth, spoken, not embodied in a written document: *a verbal contract*; *a verbal message will suffice.* **5.** (gram.) Pertaining to, derived from, a verb: *verbal inflexions*; *verbal nouns and adjectives.*

verbalism, n. [1. vĕrbalizm; 2. vʌ́bəlizəm]. Prec. & **-ism**. **1.** Expression in words; that which is expressed in words; use, choice, of words. **2.** Undue attention to the mere words; verbal criticism and pedantry.

verbalist, n. [1. vĕrbalist; 2. vʌ́bəlist]. **verbal** & **-ist**. One given too much to verbalism; a verbal critic.

verbalization, n. [1. vĕrbalīzáshun; 2. vʌbəlaizéiʃən]. See next word & **-ation**. **a** Act of verbalizing; **b** state of being verbalized.

verbalize, vb. trans. [1. vĕrbalīz; 2. vʌ́bəlaiz]. **verbal** & **-ize**. **a** To convert into a verb; **b** to put into words.

verbally, adv. [1. vĕrbali; 2. vʌ́bəli]. **verbal** & **-ly**. By word of mouth, by means of, in, uttered words; contrasted with *in writing.*

verbascum, n. [1. vĕrbáskum; 2. vʌbǽskəm]. Lat., 'mullein'. (bot.) A genus of herbaceous plants, the mulleins, with tall spikes of clustered yellow, white, or purple flowers.

verbatim, adv., adj., & n. [1. verbā́tim; 2. vʌbéitim]. Lat., fr. *verbum*, 'word', see **verb**. **1.** adv. Word for word, in exactly the same words; literally: *to report a speech, translate a book, verbatim.* **2.** adj. Following words exactly; reporting word for word: *a verbatim report, translation.* **3.** n. A verbatim report.

verbena, n. [1. verbḗna; 2. vəbínə]. **Lat.**, usually in pl. *verbēnae*, 'leaves and branches of laurel, myrtle, olive' &c., used in sacred ceremonies'; allied to *verber*, usually in pl. *verbera*, 'rods', cp. **reverberate**, cogn. w. Gk. *rhábdos*, 'rod', for **wrábdos*, & *hráptein*, 'to sew, stitch'; cp. also **warp (I.)**, & see **vervain**. (bot.) A genus of herbaceous plants, the vervains, esp. several cultivated species with blue, white, crimson, purple, or striped flowers; *lemon-scented verbena* with fragrant leaves is not a true verbena but belongs to the genus *Lippia.*

verbiage, n. [1. vĕrbiij; 2. vʌ́biidž]. Fr., fr. *verbe*, see **verb**, & **-age**. **a** The use of too many, of unnecessary, words; verbosity, prolixity, circumlocution; **b** (depreciatory) actual words used, choice of words.

verbose, adj. [1. vĕrbṓs; 2. vʌbóus], fr. Lat. *verbōsus*, fr. *verbum*, 'word'; see **verb** & **-ose**. **a** (of speakers, writers) Using a large, unnecessary, number of words; prolix, long-winded; **b** (of style, verbal expression) characterized by too many words, overloaded with words; wordy.

verbosely, adv. Prec. & **-ly**. In a verbose manner.

verboseness, n. See prec. & **-ness**. Verbosity.

verbosity, n. [1. vĕrbósiti; 2. vʌbɔ́siti], fr. Fr. *verbosité*, see **verbose** & **-ity**. Quality of being verbose; prolixity, wordiness, verboseness.

verb. sap., Phr. [1. vĕrb sáp; 2. vʌ́b sǽp], abbr. fr. Lat. phr. *verbum sat est sapienti.* A word is enough for the wise.

verdancy, n. [1. vĕrdansi; 2. vʌ́dənsi]. See **verdant** & **-ancy**. Quality, state, of being verdant; greenness; **a** (lit.) *the verdancy of the fields and woods*; **b** (fig.) greenness, rawness, crudity, immaturity of knowledge, character, judgement; innocence, simplicity, arising from inexperience: *with the rashness typical of his youthful verdancy.*

verdant, adj. [1. vĕrdant; 2. vʌ́dənt]. Not till 16th cent.; formed w. adjectival suff. **-ant**, fr. O. Fr. *verd*, Mod. Fr. *vert*, 'green', cp. **verdure**, used much earlier; O. Fr. had *verdissant, verdeant, verdoyant*, Pres. Part., fr. *verdir*, 'to become green'; ultimately fr. Lat. *viridis*, 'green; fresh, young', see **vert (I.)**. **1.** Green, of the colour of fresh, young grass or foliage; covered with green, growing herbage: *the verdant grass, trees, leaves*; *verdant lawns*; *a smiling, verdant landscape.* **2.** Youthful, inexperienced, unsophisticated, simply innocent: *in his verdant youth.*

verd-antique, n. [1. vārd antḗk; 2. vέəd ātík]. Fr., fr. earlier *verd*, now *vert*, 'green', see prec., & **antique**. **a** A kind of serpentine marble mottled or veined with green; also a green variety of porphyry; **b** the green incrustation or patina, the result of long exposure to the air, seen on ancient bronzes &c.

verdantly, adv. [1. vĕrdantli; 2. vʌ́dəntli]. **verdant** & **-ly**. In a verdant green; freshly, youthfully.

verderer, n. [1. vĕrderer; 2. vʌ́dərə]. A.-Fr., also *verder*, fr. Fr. *verd, vert*, 'green', see **vert (I.)**; the Med. Lat. word was *viridārius*, fr. Lat. *viridis*, 'green'. (legal hist.) An official of the king's forests who sees to the maintenance of the *vert*, i.e. the green wood, the protection of the venison or deer therein and punishment of all trespassers &c.

verdict, n. [1. vĕrdikt; 2. vʌ́dikt]. M.E. *verdit*, fr. A.-Fr. *verdit*, O. Fr. *voirdit*, fr. Lat. *vērē dictum*, 'truly said', in Med. Lat. *vērēdictum*, 'verdict', fr. *vērē*, 'truly', fr. *vērus*, 'true', see **veracious**, **very (I.)**, & *dictum*, P.P. of *dīcere*, 'to say', see **diction**. **1.** The finding or decision of a jury given to a judge on an issue of fact in any cause, civil or criminal, submitted to them: *a verdict for the plaintiff, defendant, of guilty or not guilty*; *open verdict* &c. **2.** A decision, judgement, opinion, pronounced on anything: *a popular verdict in* *favour of the government; my verdict differs from yours in this matter.*

verdigris, n. [1. vĕrdigrēs; 2. vā́digris]. M.E. *verdegrece*, fr. O. Fr. *vert de Grece*, later *vert de gris*, lit. 'green of Greece', in Med. Lat. *viride grecum*, 'Greek green', fr. *vert* 'green', see **vert** (I.). The second element is popularly associated w. the word **grease**. **a** The green or greenish-blue deposit or incrustation, forming on copper or brass vessels &c. as a rust; **b** (chem.) a poisonous blue or green acetate of copper, obtained by the action of acetic acid on copper, employed as a pigment and mordant in dyeing &c.

verdigrised, adj. [1. vĕrdigrēst; 2. vā́digrist]. Prec. & **-ed**. Coated, covered, with verdigris.

verditer, n. [1. vĕrditer; 2. vā́ditə], fr. O. Fr. *verd de terre*, lit. 'green of earth', fr. *verd*, *vert*, 'green', see **vert** (I.), & *terre*, fr. Lat. *terra*, 'earth', see **terra**. A blue or green pigment obtained from azurite or malachite, both being chemically copper carbonates.

verdure, n. [1. vĕrjur, vĕrdūr; 2. vā́džə, vā́djə]. Fr., fr. O. Fr. *verd*, later *vert*, 'green', see **vert** (I.), fr. Lat. *viridis*, see **viridity**, & **-ure**. **1. a** Green vegetation; grass, herbage; **b** the fresh, green colour of growing herbage &c. **2.** (fig.) Freshness, vigour, as of youth.

verdured, adj. [1. vĕrjurd; 2. vā́džəd]. Prec. & **-ed**. Covered with verdure.

verdureless, adj. [1. vĕrjurles; 2. vā́džəlis]. See prec. & **-less**. Destitute, deprived, of verdure; barren, bare of grass &c.

verdurous, adj. [1. vĕrjurus; 2. vā́džərəs]. **verdure** & **-ous**. Abounding in, covered with, verdure; green and fresh.

verge (I.), n. [1. vĕrj; 2. vādž]. O. Fr., 'wand, rod', fr. Lat. *virga*, 'twig, rod, wand'; see **virgate** (I.). **1.** A wand or staff of office, now only used of such as are borne before ecclesiastical dignitaries in processions &c. **2.** (hist.) **a** A rod or stick placed by the lord of the manor in the hand of a tenant on admission to his land, esp. in copyholds, whence Phr. *tenant by the verge*; **b** the jurisdiction of the Lord Steward of the Household and the area of this jurisdiction, within a certain distance of the royal palace: as *within the verge*; *coroner of the verge*, the King's Coroner, whose jurisdiction lies within the palace precincts. **3.** A small rod or spindle as in a watch or linotype machine. **4.** (now the chief usage) Border, edge, brink, margin; the horizon; **a** (in phys. sense) (i.) grass edge of road, garden bed or border; (ii.) (poet.) '*a sail That sinks with all we love below the verge*' (Tennyson, 'Princess', iv. 47); **b** (fig.) a state bordering on one which is specified: *on the verge of tears, of a collapse; on the verge of war.* **5.** The projecting edge or border of tiles or slates on a roof; hence, *verge-board*, now *barge-board*, q.v.

verge (II.), vb. intrans.; fr. Lat. *vergere*, 'to bend, turn, incline'; the meaning has prob. been influenced by prec. word. The base is *wereĝ- &c., 'to bend, turn, twist', & appears also in Scrt. *varjati*, 'turns', *vṛjinás*, 'crooked'; Lith. *veržiù*, 'to snare'; & further in many Gmc. words; cp. **wrench**, **wring**, **wrinkle**, **wrong**. Another form of the base *wer-, 'to twist', appears in **vermi-**, & **worm**. **1.** To bend, incline, descend, towards or in a certain direction: *the sun now verging toward the horizon; we were gradually verging nearer the cliff.* **2.** (fig.) To be on the verge of; to tend towards, approach, border on, some specified state or condition; chiefly *verge on*: *such a remark verges on impertinence; he appears to be verging on insanity, delirium*; also *verge towards*: *we seem to be verging towards a quarrel.*

verge-board. See **barge-board**.

verger, n. [1. vĕrjer; 2. vā́džə]. O. Fr., fr. *verge*, 'rod, wand'; see **verge** (I.), & **-er**; the Med. Lat. word was *virgārius*. **a** One who bears a verge, or wand or staff of office, as before ecclesiastical dignitaries; **b** specif., an official attached to a church, who shows worshippers to their seats &c.

veridical, adj. [1. verídikl; 2. verídikl], fr. Lat. *vēridicus*, fr. *vērus*, 'true', see **veracious** & **very** (I.), & *dīc-*, stem of *dīcere*, 'to speak, say', see **diction**. Veracious, truthful; corresponding with the facts or real things; esp. of various psychical phenomena, as dreams, hallucinations, mediumistic messages &c.

veridically, adv. Prec. & **-ly**. In a veridical manner; veraciously.

verifiability, n. [1. vèrifīabíliti; 2. vèrifàiəbíliti]. See next word & **-ity**. State, fact, of being verifiable.

verifiable, adj. [1. vérifīabl; 2. vérifàiəbl]. See **verify** & **-able**. Capable of being verified, or proved to be true.

verification, n. [1. vèrifikā́shun; 2. vèrifikéiʃən], fr. O. Fr. *verificacion*, fr. Med. Lat. *vērificāt-(um)*, *vērificāre*, see **verify**, & **-fication**. **a** Act of verifying; **b** state of being verified; confirmation of the truth of anything by examination of and comparison with the real facts.

verify, vb. trans. [1. vérifī; 2. vérifai], fr. O. Fr. *verifier*, fr. Med. Lat. *vērificāre*, fr. Lat. *vērus*, 'true', see **veracious**, & **-fy**. **1.** To prove, confirm the truth of; to check, ascertain, make sure of, by examination of and comparison with facts: *to verify one's references, statements, details* &c. **2.** To confirm, fulfil; to bear out; to prove to be true by result: *events have verified the prophecy*; *his suspicion was speedily verified.* **3.** (law) To authenticate, prove the authenticity of, by proofs, affidavit &c.: *to verify documents, claims, pleadings* &c.

verily, adv. [1. vérili; 2. vérili], fr. **very** (I.), in orig. sense of 'true', & **-ly**. In very truth; truly, really, without doubt, certainly (now archaic or liter.): *Verily I say unto you*; principally used as a mere emphatic: *verily this is a strange saying.*

verisimilar, adj. [1. vèrisímilar; 2. vèrisímilə], fr. Lat. *vērisimilis* & **-ar**. See next word. (rare) Having the appearance of truth; likely, probable.

verisimilitude, n. [1. vèrisimílitūd; 2. vèrisimílitjūd]. fr. Lat. *vēri-similitūdin-(em)*, fr. *vērus*, 'true', see **veracious**, & *similitūdo*, 'likeness, similitude', see **similitude**. The appearance of truth; apparent probability, likelihood.

veritable, adj. [1. véritabl; 2. véritəbl]. O. Fr. See **verity** & **-able**. True, real, genuine, actual.

veritably, adv. Prec. & **-ly**. In a veritable manner.

verity, n. [1. vériti; 2. vériti], fr. O. Fr. *verite*, Mod. Fr. *vérité*, fr. Lat. *vēritāt-(em)*, fr. *vērus*, 'true', see **veracious**, & **-ity**. **1.** Quality of being true; truth; truthfulness: *a man of unquestioned verity*; *to doubt the verity of a statement.* **2.** Something which is stated, and is to be accepted as true; a fundamental and essential truth: *the verities of the Christian religion.* Phr. *of a verity*, in truth, as a truth.

verjuice, n. [1. vĕrjōōs; 2. vā́džūs], fr. O. Fr. *vertjus*, *verjus*, fr. *vert*, 'green', see **vert** (I.), & *jus*, see **juice**. The acid, sour juice of green, unripe grapes or apples; often fig., of sour looks, temper &c.

vermeil, n. & adj. [1. vĕrmāl; 2. vā́meil]. O. Fr., see **vermilion**. **1.** n. **a** (poet. and liter.) Vermilion colour, bright red, of lips &c. '*What need a vermeil-tinctured lip for that?*' (Milton, 'Comus', 751); **b** silver gilt, gilded bronze. **2.** adj. Bright, vermilion red in colour.

vermi-, pref. Form used in compounds, fr. Lat. *vermis*, 'worm'; orig. 'that which twists, writhes, turns', fr. base *wer-, 'twist, turn', whence a number of words w. this sense; cp. the nearest cogn. **worm**, also **wrench** & **wring**, & perh. also **work**.

vermicelli, n. [1. vĕrmiséli; 2. vāmiséli]. Ital., pl. of *vermicello*, 'little worm', fr. Lat. *vermiculus*, dimin. of *vermis*, 'worm', see prec. A paste of wheat-flour &c., of the same kind as macaroni, made into very slender, worm-like threads.

vermicide, n. [1. vĕrmisīd; 2. vā́misaid]. See **vermi-** & **-cide**. **a** A drug, used medicinally, for killing intestinal, parasitic worms; an anthelmintic; **b** a chemical substance used for killing earth-worms.

vermicular, adj. [1. vĕrmíkūlar; 2. vāmíkjulə], fr. L. Lat. *verminulāris*, fr. Lat. *vermiculus*, dimin. of *vermis*, see **vermi-**. **1.** Shaped like a worm; vermiform; having convolutions or wavy markings, as of a collection of worms. **2.** Moving like a worm, with sinuous, wavy motion; peristaltic.

vermiculated, adj. [1. vĕrmíkūlāted; 2. vāmíkjuleitid], fr. Lat. *vermiculāt-(um)*, P.P. of *vermiculāri*, 'to be full of worms, worm-eaten'; See prec. **a** Worm-eaten; **b** (archit.) decorated with deeply cut convolutions, of stonework &c.; **c** decorated with, having a wavy pattern of, sinuous lines.

vermiculation, n. [1. vĕrmikulā́shun; 2. vàmikjuléiʃən]. See prec. & **-ion**. **1.** A wavy, sinuous, peristaltic movement in the intestines. **2.** (archit.) Vermiculated work.

vermiform, adj. [1. vĕrmifòrm; 2. vā́mifɔ̀m]. **vermi-** & **-form**. Having the shape of a worm; specif. (anat.) *vermiform appendix*, a small blind tube issuing from the large intestine, the seat of appendicitis; *vermiform process*, a part of the median lobe of the cerebellum.

vermifuge, n. [1. vĕrmifūj; 2. vā́mifjūdž]. **vermi-** & **-fuge**. A medicinal drug which expels intestinal parasitic worms; an anthelmintic.

vermilion, n., adj., & vb. trans. [1. vermílion; 2. vəmíliən], fr. O. Fr. *vermeillon*, *vermillon*, fr. *vermeil*, 'vermilion', fr. Lat. *vermiculus*, dimin. of *vermis*, 'worm', i.e. 'the cochineal insect', see **vermi-** & cp. **crimson**. **1.** n. **a** A brilliant scarlet pigment, obtained from sulphide of mercury in its natural form (cinnabar) or artificially; (also loosely) lead oxide, minium or red lead; **b** the colour of this pigment, a brilliant scarlet. **2.** adj. Having the colour of vermilion. **3.** vb. To colour, dye, vermilion (chiefly poet.).

vermin, n. [1. vĕrmin; 2. vā́min], fr. O. Fr. *vermine*, fr. Low Lat. **vermina*, fr. Lat. *vermis*, 'worm', see **vermi-**. A collective name for, **1.** Animals, including some birds, usually small, which are noxious or harmful, esp. (i.) those which prey upon game, poultry &c., as weasels, hawks, owls &c.; also (ii.) applied to those which are generally destructive, as rats and mice &c. **2.** Insects, usually wingless or creeping, of disgusting look or habit, esp. those which infest dirty houses, clothes &c., or are parasites upon the person, as lice, bugs, fleas &c. **3.** Pestilent human beings; the criminal and predatory classes of society; low riff-raff, the scum or dregs of the population.

verminate, vb. intrans. [1. vĕrmināt; 2. vā́mineit], fr. Lat. *vermināt-(um)*, P.P. type of *vermināre*; fr. *vermis*, see **vermi-**. **1.** To be infested with parasitic worms. **2.** To breed parasitic vermin, such as lice.

verminous, adj. [1. vĕrminus; 2. vā́minəs], fr. **vermin** & **-ous**, cp. Fr. *vermineux*; Lat. *verminōsus*, means 'full of worms, wormy.' **1.** Infested with insect vermin, e.g. bugs, fleas, lice &c.: *verminous persons.* **2.** Caused by such parasitic vermin: *verminous diseases* &c. **3.** (as term of contempt &c.) Resembling vermin in character; base, degraded; noxious.

verminously, adv. Prec. & **-ly**. In a verminous state or manner.

vermouth, n. [1. vĕrmōōt; 2. vā́mūt], fr. Fr. *vermout*, fr. Germ. *wermuth*, O.H.G. *wermot*, 'wormwood' of wh. the exact equiv. *wermōd* occurs in O.E. The etymol. is quite obscure. See also **wormwood**. An alcoholic beverage made of white wine fortified with spirit and flavoured with various bitter tonic substances such as wormwood; used, often with gin added, as an *apéritif*, also as a basis for cocktails; it may be sweet, 'Italian', or dry, 'French vermouth'.

vernacular, adj. & n. [1. vernákūlar; 2. vənǽkjulə]. Formed w. suff. **-ar**, fr. Lat. *vernā-*

culus, 'born in one's house, of slaves; native'; fr. *verna*, 'slave born in his master's house'; the etymol. of this word is much disputed. Walde says the connexion w. the idea of a 'slave' is secondary, the essential idea being 'common life, community', thus *verna* was 'one born within the community, or the house; within doors'; it derives fr. base **wer-*, 'to shut'; see **vestibule**, Lat. *vestibulum*, for **versostibulum*; see also **aperient**. **1.** adj. Pertaining to the country in which one was born; native, indigenous; now only used of language, in following senses, **a** commonly spoken or used by the people of a country, district &c.: *the vernacular languages of India*; *a vernacular idiom*; **b** written in such language: *the vernacular poems of Burns*; *newspapers in vernacular Greek*; **c** using such language: *Barnes, the vernacular poet of Dorset* &c. **2.** n. A vernacular language, or dialect; specif. (i.) a regional, provincial dialect, as distinguished from the standard, literary language; (ii.) (facet.) type of language supposed to be popularly current, i.e. strong language, profanity: *he addressed me forcibly in the vernacular*, i.e. swore at me.

vernacularism, n. [1. vernákūlarizm; 2. vənǽkjuləriz̧əm]. See prec. & **-ism.** A vernacular usage or idiom.

vernacularization, n. [1. vernákūlarīzā́shun; 2. vənǽkjulərdizéiʃən]. See next word & **-ation.** Act of vernacularizing or making vernacular.

vernacularize, vb. trans. [1. vernákūlarīz; 2. vənǽkjuləraiz]. **vernacular** & **-ize.** To make vernacular, adapt to the usage of a vernacular language.

vernacularly, adv. [1. vernákūlarli; 2. vənǽkjuləli]. **vernacular** & **-ly.** In a vernacular manner, according to vernacular usage &c.; in popular language, profanely.

vernal, adj. [1. vérnl; 2. vʌ́nl], fr. Lat. *vernālis*, fr. *vernus*, 'pertaining to spring', for **vērinos*, formed fr. *vēr*, 'spring', fr. **vēsr, vesr*, cogn. w. Gk. *éar* for **wesar*, 'spring', *earinós*, 'springlike', for **wesarinos*; cp. Scrt. *vasantaś*; O. Slav. *vesna*, 'early part of the year, spring'; Lith. *vasarà*, 'summer'; O.N. *var*. Further attempted identifications of this base are very doubtful. **1.** Belonging to, occurring, coming, in the spring: '*Or sight of vernal bloom, or summer's rose*' (Milton, 'P. L.' iii. 43); *the vernal equinox*; *the vernal migration of birds*. **2.** Like, appropriate to, suggestive of, the spring: *vernal weather*; *the vernal aspect of the woods and fields*. **3.** (fig.) Having the freshness and strength natural and suited to the spring time of life: *the vernal spirits of youth*.

vernant, adj. [1. vérnant; 2. vʌ́nənt], fr. Lat. *vernant-*, Pres. Part. of *vernāre*, 'to appear like spring', to flourish, see prec. Springlike, coming in spring: '*else had the spring Perpetual smiled on earth with vernant flowers*' (Milton, 'P. L.').

vernation, n. [1. vernā́shun; 2. vʌnéiʃən], fr. Lat. *vernātiōn-(em)*, 'a snake's sloughing of skin in spring', fr. *vernāt-(um)*, P.P. type of *vernāre*, 'to be like the spring, to be verdant, to bloom, to grow young', fr. *vēr*, 'spring', see prec. (bot.) The arrangement of the growing leaves within the bud.

Verner's Law, n. [1. vérnerz láw; 2. vʌ́nəz lɔ́]. Statement by Karl Verner in 1877 of the precise conditions under which the Aryan consonants *p, t, k*, appear in Gmc. as the voiced sounds *b, d, g*, instead of as the voiceless *f*, þ, χ, as is more common. The law may be briefly stated thus: When, in Aryan, the accent fell on any other syllable of the word than that immediately preceding the *p, t, k*, these sounds appear in Gmc. as voiced open consonants, usually written *b, d, g*, in the old languages. The law explains a large number of forms previously regarded as 'exceptions' to Grimm's Law, and may be considered as supplemental to this.

vernicle, n. [1. vérnikl; 2. vʌ́nikl]. O. Fr., for *veronicle, veronique*, fr. Med. Lat. *veronica*, fr. St. Veronica; & **-le**; in Gk. *Berenīkē*; a popular derivation of the name was fr. the hybrid form *vera ikonica*, fr. Gk. *eikon*, 'true image'. **a** The handkerchief or napkin, Lat. *sudarium*, of St. Veronica with which Christ wiped His face as He carried the Cross, and which was miraculously imprinted with His portrait; **b** a reproduction of the face of Christ, in various forms, esp. such as were carried as badges or signs by pilgrims in the Middle Ages.

vernier, n. [1. vérnier; 2. vʌ́niə], fr. the inventor, P. Vernier, a French mathematician (1580–1637). A small, movable, graduated slip of wood, ivory &c., fixed to scale of surveying instrument &c., and used to subdivide divisions of this.

vernis martin, n. [1. várnē mártan; 2. vɛrnī martæ̃]. Fr. *vernis*, see **varnish.** A fine green varnish with powdered gold, used in the reign of Louis XV. by the Martin family of cabinet-makers.

veronal, n. [1. véronal; 2. vérənəl]. Germ., invented as a trade-name. A powerful soporific drug, in the form of a white, slightly bitter powder.

Veronica, n. [1. verónika; 2. vərɔ́nikə]. Named after St. Veronica, in Gk. *Berenīkē*, cp. **vernicle.** (bot.) Genus of herbs or plants with spikes of blue, pink, or white flowers.

verricule, n. [1. vérikūl; 2. vérikjūl], fr. Lat. *verriculum*, 'net', fr. *verrere*, 'to sweep', & **-cule**; cogn. w. Gk. *érrhein*, 'to move with difficulty'; O.S. *werran*, 'to confuse'; & perh. w. Goth. *wairsiza*; O.E. *wyrsa*, 'worse', see **worse.** (entom.) Tuft of hairs.

verruca, n. [1. veróōka; 2. verūkə]. Lat. *verrūca*, 'excrescence, swelling; wart'; for **versūca*; cogn. w. Scrt. *várṣman-*, 'height, point'; O. Slav. *vrŭhŭ*, 'point, peak'; O.E. *wearh, weart*, 'wart' (fr. **wars(u)h?*). **a** (med.) A wart on the hand or face; **b** (zool.) wart-like excrescence on the skin of animals.

verrucose, adj. [1. veróōkōs; 2. verūkous], fr. Lat. *verrūcōsus*, see prec. & **-ose.** Warty; covered with warts or wart-like excrescences.

versatile, adj. [1. vérsatīl; 2. vʌ́sətail], fr. Lat. *versātilis*, 'turning round, revolving; versatile'; fr. *vers-(um)*, P.P. type of *vertere*, 'to turn', see **version.** **1.** (in physical sense, rare, except in bot. and zool.) Capable of revolving, swinging, or turning freely in different directions, as an anther, joint, muscle &c. **2.** (of character, mental characteristics) **a** Changeable, inconstant, fickle, capricious: *versatile affection, disposition* &c.; **b** readily and easily applied, adaptable, to different subjects in turn; many-sided: *a versatile genius*; *a versatile but erratic mind*; (also of persons) having a versatile mind, talented in various ways: *a versatile writer, actor* &c.

versatilely, adv. Prec. & **-ly.** In a versatile manner.

versatility, n. [1. vērsatíliti; 2. vʌ̀sətíliti]. Fr. *versatilité*, see **versatile** & **-ity.** Quality, character, of being versatile; capacity for doing many different things, varied ability; many-sidedness of character, interests, or abilities.

vers de société, n. [1. vār de sosiātā; 2. vɛr də sosiete]. Fr. Society verse; poetry of a light, easy, witty kind, dealing with familiar social events, habits &c.

verse (I.), n. [1. vērs; 2. vʌs]. M.E., fr. O. Fr. *vers*, 'division of a poem, stanza', fr. Lat. *versus*, 'a furrow; a line, row; a line of poetry, verse'; fr. *vers-(um)*, P.P. type of *vertere*, 'to turn'; see **version.** **1. a** A metrical line containing a certain number of feet or accented syllables, arranged according to a definite metrical rule; a line of poetry as metrically arranged: *a hexameter, iambic, Alexandrine &c. verse*; **b** (pl.) a set of such, as translated into Greek or Latin: *to set Latin, Greek, verses*. **2.** Metrical composition or structure: *Latin verse*; *his prose lapses into verse at moments of emotion*; *free verse*, such composition of an irregular nature, untrammelled by rules of prosody &c. **3.** A division of a poem consisting of several lines, forming in itself a unity, and having a definite structure as regards number of lines and rhymes and the arrangement of the latter. **4.** Poetry: *English lyrical verse*. **5.** One of the sections or short divisions into which a chapter of the Bible is divided. Phr. *to give chapter and verse for*, give the exact reference, authority &c., for any statement.

verse (II.), vb. trans. & intrans., fr. prec. **1.** trans. To express in verse, to make verses about: *to verse one's emotions*; *he versed the praises of the conqueror*. **2.** intrans. To compose, make, verses: *taught to verse*.

versed, adj. [1. vërst; 2. vʌst], fr. Lat. *versātus*, P.P. of *versāri*, 'to turn, move about in a place; to be circumstanced, situated, in; to be engaged, occupied, in', freq. form of *vertere*, 'to turn', formed fr. *vers-(um)*, P.P. type. See **version.** Skilled, practised, experienced, *in* some subject, art &c.

versed sine, n., fr. Mod. Lat. *versus sinus*, P.P. of *vertere*, 'to turn', see **version**, & **sine.** (math.) Reversed sine.

verset, n. [1. vérset; 2. vʌ́sɛt]. **verse** & **-et.** Short musical prelude, played on an organ before a church service.

versicle, n. [1. vérsikl; 2. vʌ́sikl], fr. Lat. *versiculus*, 'a little verse', dimin. of *versus*, see **verse.** A short verse; specif., one of the short, liturgical verses, often taken from the Psalms, intoned or read by the officiating minister and answered by the responses of the choir and congregation.

versicoloured, adj. [1. vérsikulurd; 2. vʌ́sikàləd], fr. Lat. *versicolor*, fr. *vers-(um)*, *vertere*, 'to turn, change', see **version**, & *color*, **colour**, & **-ed.** Changing, varying, in colour; iridescent.

versification, n. [1. vērsifikā́shun; 2. vʌ̀sifikéiʃən], fr. Lat. *versificātiōn-(em)*, see **versify** & **-ation.** **a** Art, practice, of versifying or of making verse; **b** mode, style, of metrical composition; metre, prosody.

versifier, n. [1. vérsifier; 2. vʌ́sifaiə]. Next word & **-er.** One who versifies; usually in deprecatory sense, verse-monger, poetaster.

versify, vb. trans. & intrans. [1. vérsifī; 2. vʌ́sifai], fr. Fr. *versifier*, fr. Lat. *versificāre*, see **verse** & **-fy.** **1.** trans. **a** To turn into verse from a prose form, to translate into verse; **b** to tell, recount, in verse. **2.** intrans. To compose verses.

versifying, n. [1. vérsifiing; 2. vʌ́sifaiiŋ]. See prec. & **-ing.** The making, composing, of verses; versification.

version, n. [1. vérshun; 2. vʌ́ʃən]. Fr., fr. Lat. *versiōn-(em)*, fr. *vers-(um)*, fr. **vert-tom*, P.P. of *vertere*, 'to turn', & **-ion.** The base **wert-* is found in Scrt. *vártatē*, 'he turns, rolls'; Gk. *rhatánē* for **wrat-*, fr. **wr̥t-*, 'a stirrer, ladle'; O. Slav. *vrŭtěti*, 'to turn, twist'; the base exists in all Gmc. languages, e.g. O.H.G. *werdan*, O.E. *weorþan*, 'to become, turn out, happen', see **worth (III.)** & **weird** (I.); cp. also *-vert* in **convert** &c.; also **vertex** & **vortex.** **1.** A translation or rendering of a book, passage &c., from one language into another: *the Authorized, Revised, Versions of the Bible*; *a neat version of some of Horace's Odes*; *a comparison of the French and English versions of the document shows some divergencies*. **2.** An account, statement, of something from a personal or particular point of view: *the police gave a different version of the incident from that of the prisoner*.

vers libre, n. [1. vār lébr; 2. vɛr líbr]. Fr. Free verse; verse with no regular metrical system but arranged in lines of irregular length and with certain rhythms or rhythmical structure.

vers librist(e), n. [1. vār lébrist; 2. vɛr líbrist]. Fr. Prec. & **-ist(e).** Writer of free verse.

verso, n. [1. vérsō; 2. vʌ́sou]. Lat., sc. *folio*, 'leaf', abl. sing. of *versus*, 'turned', see **version.** **a** The left hand or reverse of a page of a book; used esp. of a folded sheet of vellum or paper, cp. *recto*; **b** the reverse of a coin, medal &c., cp. *obverse*.

verst, n. [1. vërst; 2. vʌ̄st], fr. Russ. *versta* for **vert-ta*, fr. *vertyet*, 'to turn', fr. base discussed under **version**. A Russian measure of length, 3500 Engl. ft., about ⅔ of a mile.

versus, prep. [1. vérsus; 2. vʌ̄səs]. Lat., see **version**. Against (abbr. *v.* or *vs.*); esp. in describing a case at law: *Rex* v. *Jones, Smith* v. *Robinson* &c.; also in matches, *Lancashire* v. *Yorkshire*.

vert (I.), n. [1. vërt; 2. vʌ̄t]. O. Fr., Fr., earlier form *verd*, fr. Lat. *viridis*, 'green', see **viridity**. **1.** (forest law) **a** The green growth of a forest, esp. as cover for deer: *vert and venison*; **b** right to cut the greenwood in a forest; cp. *verderer*. **2.** (her.) The colour or tincture green.

vert (II.), vb. intrans. & n.; abbr. of *convert* or *pervert*. (colloq.) **1.** vb. To change one's religious faith; esp. to abandon Protestantism for Roman Catholicism, or vice versa. **2.** n. A convert or pervert to or from Roman Catholicism.

vertebra, n., pl. **vertebrae** [1. vértebra, -ē; 2. vʌ̄tibrə, -ī]. Lat., fr. base of *vertere*, 'to turn', see **version**. (anat.) One of the joints of the backbone or spinal column in vertebrate animals; (pl.) *the vertebrae*, the backbone or spinal column in vertebrate animals.

vertebral, adj. [1. vértebral; 2. vʌ̄tibrəl]. Prec. & **-al**. **a** Pertaining to, situated near, the vertebrae or joints of the spine; **b** composed of vertebrae: *vertebral column*, the spine.

vertebrally, adv. Prec. & **-ly**. By means of vertebrae.

vertebrate, adj. & n. [1. vértibrat, -āt; 2. vʌ̄tibrit, -eit], fr. Lat. *vertebrātus*, 'jointed, articulated', fr. *vertebra*, see **vertebra**, & **-ate**. **1.** adj. Having a spinal column or vertebrae; belonging to the Vertebrata or group of animals which have a spinal column, including mammals, birds, reptiles, fish, and batrachians. **2.** n. A vertebrate animal; member of the Vertebrata.

vertebration, n. [1. vêrtebráshun; 2. vʌ̄tibréiʃən]. See prec. & **-ion**. Arrangement, division, into vertebrae.

vertex, n., pl. **vertices** [1. vérteks, -isēz; 2. vʌ̄teks, -isīz]. Lat., variant of *vortex*, q.v. for differentiation of meaning; 'the top, crown, of the head; highest point, top, summit; the pole, zenith'; fr. base of *vertere*, 'to turn', the orig. sense being that wh. turns about itself; see **version** &c. The highest or principal point; top, summit; specif. **a** (anat.) crown of the head; **b** (astron.) the zenith; **c** (geom.) the point or angle of a figure opposite to the base.

vertical, adj. [1. vértikl; 2. vʌ̄tikl]. Fr., fr. Lat. *vertic-(em)*, *vertex*, see prec., & **-al**. **1.** Situated at the vertex or highest point; directly overhead, at the zenith: *the vertical point of the heavens*. **2.** Perpendicular, at right angles to the plane of the horizon; upright; opposed to *horizontal*: *a vertical line* &c. **3.** Directed downwards or upwards at right angles to the plane of the ground: *a vertical wall, fall* &c. **4.** (elliptically as n.) *The vertical*, vertical line, position; the perpendicular.

verticality, n. [1. vêrtikáliti; 2. vʌ̄tikǽliti]. Prec. & **-ity**. Quality, condition, of being vertical.

vertically, adv. [1. vértikali; 2. vʌ̄tikəli]. See prec. & **-ly**. In a vertical manner, position, direction; directly overhead or below.

verticil, verticel, n. [1. vértisil; 2. vʌ̄tisil], fr. Lat. *verticillus*, dimin. of *vertex*, 'whorl of a spindle', see **vertex**. (bot.) A circle of leaves, florets &c., round a central axis; a whorl.

verticillate, adj. [1. vërtísilāt; 2. vʌ̄tísileit]. Prec. & **-ate**. (bot., of leaves &c.) Arranged in verticils or whorls.

vertiginous, adj. [1. vërtíjinus; 2. vʌ̄tídžinəs], fr. Lat. *vertīginōsus*, fr. *vertīgin-(em)*, *vertīgo*, see **vertigo**, & **-ous**. **1.** Turning, whirling, round and round: *vertiginous current, wind* &c. **2.** Dizzy, giddy, suffering from vertigo: *to feel, grow, vertiginous at great heights*. **3.** Causing, inducing, vertigo or giddiness: *a vertiginous height, precipice* &c.

vertiginously, adv. Prec. & **-ly**. In a vertiginous manner; dizzily, giddily.

vertigo, n. [1. vértigō; 2. vʌ̄tigou]. Lat. *vertīgo*, 'giddiness', fr. base in *vertere*, 'to turn', see **version**. The medical term for the sensation of giddiness, dizziness, or swimming in the head, often accompanied by faintness, experienced after turning rapidly round and round, or during an attack of sea-sickness, or when at a great height.

vertu. See **virtu**.

vervain, n. [1. vérvān; 2. vʌ̄vein], fr. O. Fr. *verveine*, fr. Lat. *verbēna*. Popular name of various species of *Verbena*, esp. the common wild verbena, *V. officinalis*.

verve, n. [1. vërv; 2. vʌ̄v]. Fr., etymol. obscure; in O. Fr. it meant 'an odd humour, fancy'; perh. fr. a Low Lat. **verva*, fr. Lat. *verba*, 'words, talk', see **verb**. Display of vigour and liveliness of spirit and imagination; gusto, in the work of a poet, painter, or other artist.

vervet, n. [1. vérvet; 2. vʌ̄vet]. Fr.; etymol. doubtful; usually supposed to be fr. a combination of *vert*, 'green', & *grivet*, a name of a small grey monkey, fr. *gris*, 'grey'. A small Central and S. African monkey, *Cercopithecus pygerythrus*, with greyish-green fur and black extremities and red patch at base of tail.

very (I.), adj. [1. véri; 2. véri]. M.E. *verai, verray* &c., fr. O. Fr. *verai*, later & Mod. Fr. *vrai*; fr. Low Lat. **vēracus*, fr. Lat. *vērāc-* 'true', stem of *vērax*, see **veracious**. **1.** **a** Having the true, proper character of a person or thing; truly and really that which the word implies; genuine, actual, real: '*Very God of very God*' (Nicene Creed); *this is my very son*; also in such Phrs. as: *in very truth, deed* &c.; **b** exactly that which is implied by the noun qualified, just the same as, neither more nor less than: *for very shame they must confess*; *for very pity's sake have mercy*. **2.** Used intensively or emphatically: **a** *the very*, actual, same, identical; *caught in the very act*; *the very fact of your hesitating proves* &c.; *the very question I wanted to ask*; *the very thing I was looking for*; **b** (with *this, that* &c.) *this very day, at that very moment*; **c** (with possessive) *did it under your very eyes*; *his very look betrayed him*. **3.** With *a* and comparative, or *the* and superlative: *a verier humbug would be hard to meet*; *the veriest scoundrel unhung*.

very (II.), adv., fr. prec. **1.** In a high degree, to a great extent, exceedingly, extremely; **a** (with adjs.) *very large, small*; *very hot, cold*; *very dangerous* &c.; Phrs. *very good*, as form of assent or agreement; also *very well*, often with sense of reluctance or compulsion: *oh, very well! if you insist*; **b** (with vbl. adjs.) *a very dazzling light*; *a very puzzling question*; *a very interesting book*; *substance very resistant to cold*; **c** (with P.Ps.) (i.) when used as adjs.: *a very valued friend*; *a very over-weighted car*; *a very harassed mind*; *wore a very worried look*; (ii.) otherwise, *very much*: *was very much pleased, annoyed*; *this road is very much used by travellers*; **d** (with neg.) usually in sense of moderately, rather: *not a very good bit of work*, rather bad; *I don't sing very well*, i.e. I sing pretty badly; *I am not very keen on going there*, I don't want to go. **2.** Before superlative, used intensively or emphatically: *the very last thing I should have expected*; *he came the very next day*; *the very best thing you can do*. **3.** Emphasising complete identity or difference: *he used the very same words as I had*; *said the very opposite of what I expected.* Phrs. *my, your, his &c. very own*, mine &c. absolutely, beyond dispute; with possession not shared by another: *the property is my very own*; *if you make good use of the book you shall have it for your very own*.

Very light, n. [1. véri līt; 2. véri láit], fr. S. W. Very, of U.S.A. navy, inventor, 1877. A form of signal in which coloured lights or flares are fired from a large-bore pistol, used with a code for signalling at night.

vesica, n. [1. vésika; 2. vésikə]. Lat. *vēsīca*, 'bladder; blister', cogn. w. Scrt. *vasti*, 'bladder'. **a** (anat.) Bladder, esp. the urinary bladder in animals or the swim-bladder of fish, whence *vesica piscis*, term used in Gothic architecture and painting, as design for seals &c., for a pointed oval, often forming an aureole or glory for a sacred figure; **b** (bot.) a small sac or cyst, vesicle.

vesical, adj. [1. vésikl; 2. vésikl]. Prec. & **-al**. Pertaining to a vesica or bladder.

vesicant, adj. & n. [1. vésikant; 2. vésikənt]. See next word & **-ant**. **a** adj. Causing, raising, blisters; blistering; **b** n., a blistering substance.

vesicate, vb. trans. & intrans. [1. vésikāt; 2. vésikeit], fr. Lat. *vēsīca*, in sense of 'blister', & **-ate**. (med.) **a** trans. To raise a blister on, to blister; **b** intrans., to become blistered.

vesicle, n. [1. vésikl; 2. vésikl], fr. Lat. *vēsīcula*, 'a small blister, sac' &c., dimin. of **vesica**. A small membranous cavity or sac; esp. one filled with air or fluid, as in the animal body, on a leaf &c.

vesico-, pref. Form fr. **vesica**, used to form compounds denoting connexion or relationship with the bladder.

vesicular, adj. [1. vesíkūlar; 2. vesíkjulə], fr. Lat. *vēsīcula*, see **vesicle**, & **-ar**. **a** Shaped like a vesicle or small cyst or sac; **b** having, composed of, vesicles.

vesiculate, adj. [1. vesíkūlāt; 2. vesíkjuleit]. See prec. & **-ate**. Vesicular.

vesper, n. [1. vésper; 2. véspə]. Lat., also *vespera*, 'evening, the even-tide; the evening star', cogn. w. Gk. *hésperos*, fr. **wesperos*, adj. & n., 'evening, evening star', *hesperā*, 'evening'; O. Slav. *večerŭ*, 'evening'. The specif. eccles. use is derived fr. O. Fr. *vespres*, Mod. Fr. *vêpres*, fr. Lat. *vesperae*, pl., cp. **matins**. **1.** (cap.) The evening star, Hesperus, the planet Venus appearing as the evening star in the west. **2.** (pl.) Evensong, the evening service, the sixth of the canonical hours of the Roman Catholic and Orthodox Greek Churches. *Sicilian Vespers*, (hist.) the massacre of the French in Sicily, which began at Palermo, at the hour of Vespers on Easter Monday, 1282.

vespertilionid, adj. & n. [1. vèspertílionid; 2. vèspətílianid]. Mod. Lat. *Vespertilionidae*, fr. Lat. *vespertilio*, 'a bat', fr. *vesper*, 'evening', see prec. (zool.) **a** adj. Belonging to the large group, *Vespertilionidae*, of insectivorous bats, which includes the common European bats; **b** n., one of this group of bats.

vespertine, adj. [1. véspertīn; 2. véspətain], fr. Lat. *vespertīnus*, 'belonging to the evening; western', see **vesper**. **a** Pertaining to, done, occurring, in the evening; **b** (of animals &c.) appearing in the evening; **c** (astron.) setting at evening or just after sunset.

vespiary, n. [1. véspiari; 2. véspiəri]. On anal. of **apiary**, fr. Lat. *vespa*, 'wasp'; fr. **vopsa*, fr. Aryan base **webh-*, 'to weave, spin'; cp. O. Prussian *wobse*, 'gadfly'; see **wasp** & **weave**. A wasp's nest.

Vespidae, n. pl. [1. véspidē; 2. véspidī]. Med. Lat., fr. Lat. *vespa*, 'wasp', see prec. & **-idae**. (zool.) One of the families of wasps, including the social wasps and hornets.

vespiform, adj. [1. véspifòrm; 2. véspifɔ̄m], fr. Lat. *vesp-(a)*, 'wasp', see prec., & **-form**. Formed like, resembling, a wasp; wasp-like.

vespine, adj. [1. véspīn; 2. véspain]. See prec. & **-ine**. Pertaining to wasps.

vessel, n. [1. vésl; 2. vésl]. O. Fr., also *vaissel*, Mod. Fr. *vaisseau*, esp. in sense of 'ship', fr. Lat. *vascellum*, rare variant of *vasculum*, dimin. of *vās*, see **vase**, & cp. **vascular**. **1.** **a** A general term for any hollow article or utensil serving as a receptacle for liquids, food, or other substance, usually round in shape, as a jug, pot, pan, dish &c., esp. as designed for domestic use; **b** (fig., from Bib. usage) person regarded as that which contains or receives some mental or spiritual quality: *a vessel of wrath*; *a chosen vessel*; *woman the weaker vessel* &c. 2. A ship, usually of a larger kind than one styled 'boat'. 3. a (anat.) Any one of the tubes, canals, or ducts which contain and circulate the blood or other fluid contents or secretions of the animal body: *blood-vessel*; *the lymphatic vessels* &c.; b (bot.) a cellular tube or duct containing and circulating the sap in plants.

vest (I.), n. [1. vest; 2. vest], fr. Lat. *vestis*, 'garment; covering for the body, clothes'; fr. Aryan base **wes-*, 'to put on, clothe'; cogn. w. Scrt. *vas-*, 'to put on', *vastra*, 'garment', Gk. *esthḗs*, 'clothing', *hénnūmi*, fut. *hésō*, for **wésnumi*, 'I clothe, put on', Goth. (*ga*)*wasjan*, 'to clothe', O.E. *werian*, 'to wear (clothes)', see **wear** (I.). 1. (archaic or obs.) Robe, vestment, clothing. 2. Undergarment of wool, silk &c. worn on the upper part of the body next the skin. 3. (shop term) A waistcoat: *gent's black coat and vest with striped trousers*.

vest (II.), vb. trans. & intrans., fr. O. Fr. *vestir*, Mod. Fr. *vêtir*, fr. Lat. *vestīre*, 'to clothe', fr. *vestis*, see prec. A. trans. 1. To clothe with, put on, a robe or garment, (chiefly in eccles. usage of liturgical vestments) *a priest vested with chasuble, alb, and stole*; *the celebrant vests himself in the sanctuary*. 2. a To invest, endow with, to put in possession of, secure possession to: *to vest a person with rights in an estate, property* &c.; b to confer an immediate fixed right of present or future possession of: *to vest property, rights, authority, in a person*. B. intrans. 1. (of rights, property &c.) To become fixed or vested in a person. 2. To array oneself, esp. put on vestments of ceremony: *a chaplain assists the bishop to vest*.

Vesta, n. [1. vésta; 2. véstə]. Lat.; cogn. w. Gk. *hestia* for **westia*, 'hearth, home', also (cap.) 'the goddess of the home'; etymol. doubtful, but cp. **combustion**. 1. (Roman mythol.) The goddess of flocks and herds and of the household, homestead; also goddess of fire and the household hearth, for whom a sacred communal fire was kept always burning in her temple. 2. (astron.) The name of one of the earlier discovered minor planets or asteroids. 3. (without cap.) A wax match.

vestal, adj. & n. [1. véstl; 2. véstl], fr. Lat. *Vestālis*, see prec. & **-al**. 1. adj. a (Roman mythol.) Belonging to, dedicated to, the goddess Vesta, esp. *vestal virgin*, one of the virgins, vowed to perpetual chastity, whose duties included keeping the sacred *vestal fire* safe and perpetually burning in the temple at Rome; b (by transf.) chaste, pure, virgin. 2. n. A vestal virgin; a virgin, a pure, chaste woman; a nun.

vested, adj. [1. vésted; 2. véstid], fr. P.P. of **vest** (II.). Fixed, settled, secured in the possession of a person; specif. (law) not contingent or in state of suspension: *vested rights, interests* &c.

vestibular, adj. [1. vestíbūlar; 2. vestíbjulə]. See next word & **-ar**. Pertaining to, serving as, a vestibule.

vestibule, n. [1. véstibūl; 2. véstibjūl], fr. Lat. *vestibulum*, 'entrance or fore-court to a house'; various explanations have been proposed, of wh. Walde favours the derivation fr. **ver(o)stabulum*, 'place before the door', fr. **vero*, 'door', lit. 'means of closure', q.v. under **vernacular** & **aperient**, & *stabulum*, 'standing-place; habitation; stable', see **stable** (II.). 1. a A covered entrance to a house; ante-chamber, entrance hall, lobby; b (U.S.A.) enclosed platform at end of a railway train. 2. (anat.) A communicating channel or chamber, esp. the central cavity in the ear.

vestige, n. [1. véstij; 2. véstidž]. Fr., fr. Lat. *vestīgium*, 'footprint, step, track'; prob. for **verstīgium*, derived fr. *verrere*, 'to sweep, brush along', w. suff. on anal. of *fastīgium*, 'gable', for **farstigium*, cp. Scrt. *bhṛṣtiś*, 'point, prong', & see **bristle** (I.). 1. (rare or poet.) The mark of a foot left on the ground; footprint, track, spoor, of man or animal. 2. a A visible trace, material sign, or mark left behind by something destroyed or vanished; any material evidence of something no longer existing: *only a few vestiges of the great building remain*; *the last vestiges of prehistoric life and culture*; b (biol.) a rudimentary, degenerate survival of a former organ or structure: *the vestige of a tail in the human body*; *the pineal gland may be the vestige of a third eye*. 3. (in non-material sense) A perceptible trace, slight survival, or indication: *not a vestige left of former hatred or jealousy*; *soon there will hardly be left a vestige of our former rights and liberty*.

vestigial, adj. [1. vestíjial; 2. vestídžiəl]. See prec. & **-al**. Surviving as a vestige or indication of something which has passed away, disappeared; (esp. biol.) rudimentary, atrophied, degenerate: *vestigial organs, structure* &c.

vesting, n. [1. vésting; 2. véstiŋ]. **vest** (II.) & **-ing**. 1. The act of putting on robes or vestments: *the vesting of a priest* &c. 2. Act of confirming, settling, the legal possession: *vesting of property in trustees* &c.

vestment, n. [1. véstment; 2. véstmənt], fr. O. Fr. *vestement*, Mod. Fr. *vêtement*, fr. Lat. *vestīmentum*, 'clothing', fr. *vestis*, 'a garment', see **vest** (I.), & **-ment**. a A robe, dress; esp. one of the liturgical articles of dress worn by the officiating clergy during divine service, as *Mass vestments*, those ordered to be worn by priests and deacons at the celebration of the Eucharist, the essential or principal Mass vestment being the chasuble, q.v.; in general, the dress worn by the clergy and choir during divine service, as cassock, stole, and surplice; b specif., *the vestment*, the chasuble; used already in the 15th cent. in this special sense.

vestry, n. [1. véstri; 2. véstri], fr. O. Fr. *vestiarie, vestiaire*, fr. Lat. *vestiārium*, 'chest, cupboard for clothes, wardrobe', fr. *vestis*, 'garment', see **vest** (I.), & **-ry**. 1. Building or chamber attached to a church in which the vestments, surplice, cassocks &c. of the clergy and choir, or the liturgical vestments, if any, are kept and put on before a service, and where the Communion vessels are stored when not in use; also used for such church business as signing of registers and other parochial matters; when attached to a cathedral or other large church it is usually styled *sacristy*. 2. A similar building or chamber in a nonconformist chapel where chapel business is carried on, prayer-meetings are held &c. 3. Body of ratepayers of parish which elects churchwarden and manages the business of the church, presided over by the rector or vicar, and meeting usually in the vestry; formerly having general administrative secular powers in the parish, but now superseded by the parish council when not embodied in a large local administrative unit such as a rural or urban district council &c.

vestry clerk, n. The clerk to a vestry; parish clerk.

vestrydom, n. [1. véstridum; 2. véstridəm]. See **vestry** & **-dom**. Government by a parish vestry; esp. referring to the formerly often inefficient and corrupt administration by the old vestries; cp. *bumbledom*.

vestryman, n. [1. véstriman; 2. véstrimən]. Member of a parish vestry.

vesture, n. [1. véschur; 2. véstʃə]. O. Fr., Mod. Fr. *vêture*, fr. Lat. *vestis*, see **vest** (I.), & **-ure**. a Garments, clothing, raiment; a garment, robe &c.; now chiefly poetical or reminiscent of Biblical usage in '*They cast lots upon my vesture*'; '*the Queen in a vesture of gold*' (Ps. 45); b (poet.) covering in nature: *a vesture of mist, of verdure* &c.

vestured, adj. [1. véschurd; 2. véstʃəd]. Prec. & **-ed**. a Dressed, robed; b covered as with a vesture.

vesturer, n. [1. véschurer; 2. véstʃərə]. **vesture** & **-er**. An official of a cathedral or collegiate church in charge of ecclesiastical vestments.

Vesuvian, adj. & n. [1. vesúvian; 2. vəsjúviən], fr. Vesuvius & **-an**. 1. adj. Of, pertaining to, resembling, the volcano Vesuvius, near Naples. 2. n. (obsolesc., without cap.) A kind of fusee.

vet (I.), n. [1. vet; 2. vet]. Colloq. abbr. of **veterinary** (surgeon).

vet (II.), vb. trans., fr. prec. a (colloq.) To examine, treat (animal, human being) medically or surgically; b (colloq.) to examine (manuscripts &c.) critically; *he got a publisher's reader to vet his first novel*.

vetch, n. [1. vech; 2. vetʃ], fr. O. Fr. *veche*, fr. Lat. *vicia*, 'vetch', cp. Germ. *wicke*; prob. fr. the base **wei-*, 'to bind', seen in Lat. *vītis*, 'the vine', *viēre*, 'to twine' &c., see **vine**. A climbing or trailing leguminous plant of many varieties, esp. *Vicia sativa* or tare, used as green fodder.

vetchy, adj. [1. véchi; 2. vétʃi]. Prec. & **-y**. Made of, full of, vetches.

veteran, n. & adj. [1. véteran; 2. vétərən], fr. Lat. *veterānus*, 'old, veteran', adj. & n.; fr. *veter-(is), vetus*, 'old'; cp. also Lat. *vitulus*, 'yearling, calf', see **veal**, cogn. w. Scrt. *vatsáś*, 'year'; Gk. *étos* for **wétos*, 'a year'; O. Slav. *vetŭχŭ*, 'old'; cp. also O.E. *weþer*, 'sheep' &c., see **wether**. 1. n. One old and experienced in service, esp. an old tried soldier or sailor. 2. adj. Old and experienced, tried in service: *a veteran soldier, member of Parliament* &c.

veterinarian, adj. & n. [1. vèterinárian; 2. vètərinéəriən]. See next word & **-an**. a adj. Veterinary; b n., a veterinary surgeon.

veterinary, adj. & n. [1. véterinari; 2. vétərinəri], fr. Lat. *veterīnārius*, fr. *veterīnus*, 'belonging to beasts of burden, draught animals', esp. *veterīna*, sc. *bestia*, 'a draught animal'; fr. *vetus, veteris*, 'old', draught animals being those too old for other purposes; see **veteran**. 1. adj. Pertaining to, concerned with, affecting, the diseases of animals, esp. cattle and other domestic animals: *veterinary science, surgeon* &c. 2. n. A veterinary surgeon.

veto (I.), n. [1. vḗtō; 2. vītou]. Lat. *veto*, 'I forbid'; *vetāre*, 'to oppose, forbid', appears first in the form *votāre*, the etymol. of wh. is very doubtful; the Roman tribunes of the people used the word in the exercise of their power of blocking measures of the Senate or acts of other magistrates. 1. a The constitutional right or power residing in various persons or bodies, as a sovereign, a legislative assembly &c., of forbidding or preventing the carrying out of an enactment or act of administration: *the veto of the Crown has not been exercised since the reign of Queen Anne*; b an exercise of this power or right: *the veto of the Lords has fortunately hung the bill up for the present*; specif., *local veto*, right of a locality by vote to prohibit the sale of alcoholic liquor within the area as a measure of temperance reform. 2. (in gen. sense) Prohibition, refusal to allow anything to be done, said &c.: *to put, set, a veto on a proposal*; *a public veto on such performances was only to be expected*.

veto (II.), vb. trans., fr. prec. a Specif., disallow, prevent enaction of (a measure, proposal, bill), by exercising the veto: *the Crown may, but never does, veto a bill that has passed both Houses*; b to refuse to allow, prohibit absolutely (an action, conduct &c.): *in public schools smoking by the boys is vetoed*.

vetturino, n. [1. vètoorḗnō; 2. vèturíno]. Ital., fr. *vettura*, 'carriage', fr. L. Lat. *vectūra*, fr. *vect-(um)*, P.P. type of *vehere*, 'to draw, carry', see **vehicle**. Driver of a hackney or hired carriage in Italy.

vex, vb. trans. [1. veks; 2. veks], M.E. *vexen*, fr. O. Fr. *vexer*, fr. Lat. *vexāre*, 'to agitate, shake, toss; to harass, trouble, vex'; prob. fr. *vex-*, variant form of P.P. of *vehere*, 'to draw, carry', cp. *convex* & see **vehicle**. a To irritate, disturb, distress, cause worry to, by petty annoyances, esp. in mind; to cause grief to; b to render mildly angry, excite mild wrath of; esp. in P.P. as adjective: *I shall be seriously vexed if you speak to me like that*; also *vexed with* (*a person*), angry with.

vexation, n. [1. veksā́shun; 2. vɛkséiʃən], fr. Lat. *vexātiōn-(em)*, fr. *vexāt-(um)*, P.P. type of *vexāre*, see **vex**, & **-ation**. **1.** State of being vexed; esp. mental distress, irritation, feeling of annoyance or worry: '*vanity and vexation of spirit*'; *much to my vexation I just missed a chance of a good profit*. **2.** Cause of distress or annoyance; worry: *all the trifling vexations one has to put up with*.

vexatious, adj. [1. veksā́shus; 2. vɛkséiʃəs]. See prec. & **-ous**. **1.** Causing vexation; troublesome, irritating, annoying: *moving house is a vexatious business*; *how vexatious to miss one's train!* **2.** (law) Undertaken for trivial reasons, done for purpose of annoyance or irritation: *a vexatious suit or action*.

vexatiously, adv. Prec. & **-ly**. In a vexatious manner.

vexatiousness, n. See prec. & **-ness**. State of being vexatious.

vexillum, n., pl. **vexilla** [1. veksílum, -a; 2. vɛksíləm, -ə]. Lat., 'military ensign; standard'; for **vĕcslom*; variant of *vēlum*, 'veil' &c., see **velum** & **veil**. **1. a** The military standard of a company of the Roman legion, being a small square cloth hung from a cross-bar borne on a pole; **b** a company of soldiers under such a standard. **2.** (eccles.) A scarf wrapped round a bishop's pastoral staff. **3. a** (zool.) The web of the feather of a bird; **b** (bot.) the larger upper petal in flowers such as the sweet-pea.

vexing, adj. [1. véksing; 2. véksiŋ], fr. Pres. Part. of **vex**. Causing vexation; annoying, irritating; troublesome.

vexingly, adv. Prec. & **-ly**. In a vexing manner, so as to cause vexation.

via (I.), n. [1. vía; 2. váiə]. Lat. *via*, 'path, street, highway; passage, channel; pipe'; fr. **wĕja-*, whence also Lat. *venor*, 'to hunt, follow after', see **venery (I.)**; Scrt. *vēti*, 'he follows, pursues, strives after'; *vī-thī-*, 'row, street, way'; perh. also Gk. *oi-mos*, 'way, road', for **woi-*. Only in *via media* [1. vía mēdia; 2. váiə mídiə]. Lat., 'middle path'; (fig.) a moderate course between two extremes; esp. of Church of England as lying between the extremes of Roman Catholicism and Protestantism; *Via Lactea*, n. [1. vía láktea; 2. váiə lǽktiə]. Lat., 'Milky Way'.

via (II.), prep. Abl. of Lat. *via*, see prec. By way of, passing through, calling at: *to travel via London*; as indication on luggage: *Tunbridge Wells via Reading and Redhill* &c.

viability, n. [1. viabíliti; 2. vàiəbíliti]. Next word & **-ity**. Condition of being viable; capacity for living.

viable, adj. [1. víabl; 2. váiəbl]. Fr., fr. *vie*, 'life', Lat. *vīta*, see **vital**, & **-able**. Capable of living; a having all the organs &c. at such a state of development as to enable life to be carried on; said esp. of a newly born infant; **b** able to live in a particular climate and environment.

viableness, n. [1. víablnes; 2. váiəblnis]. Prec. & **-ness**. Viability.

viaduct, n. [1. víadukt; 2. váiədakt]. Lat. *via*, see **via (I.)**, *ducta*, 'conducted', see **duct**. A long bridge, supported upon a series of arches and pillars, which carries a road or railway line across a valley or gorge.

vial, n. [1. víal; 2. váiəl]. M.E. *viole*, fr. variant of Fr. *fiole*, fr. Lat. *phiala*, fr. Gk. *phiálē*, 'cup, bowl, drinking-bowl'; etymol. doubtful. A small glass bottle for medicine &c. Phr. (Bib.) (*to pour out*) *the vials of one's wrath*.

viameter, n. [1. viámeter; 2. vaiǽmitə]. **via** (I.) & **-meter**. Instrument for measuring distances on roads; a hodometer.

viand, n. [1. víand; 2. váiənd]. Fr. *viande*, 'food, meat', fr. L. Lat. *vivanda*, Lat. *vivenda*, neut. pl. gerundive, fr. *vivere*, 'to live'; see **vivid** & **vital**; cp. **vivandière**. Article of food; more often collectively *viands*.

viatic, adj. [1. viátik; 2. vaiǽtik]. Lat. *viāticus*, 'pertaining to a road or to a journey', see **via (I.)** & **-atic**. Connected with a journey, with travels.

viaticum, n. [1. viátikum; 2. vaiǽtikəm]. Lat., neut. sing. of *viāticus* as n., see prec., 'provision for a journey; allowance of soldiers on service'. **1.** (rare) Provisions for a journey. **2.** The consecrated wafer, the Host, as administered to the dying.

vibracular, adj. [1. vībrákūlar; 2. vaibrǽkjulə]. See next word & **-ar**. Pertaining to, caused by, of the nature of, vibracula.

vibraculum, n., pl. **vibracula** [1. vībrákūlum, -a; 2. vaibrǽkjuləm, -ə]. Lat., formed fr. *vibra-*, see **vibrate**, w. dimin. suff., see **-cule**. Filamentous spine-like organ of certain polyzoans, by means of the vibratory movements of which food is brought within reach.

vibrancy, n. [1. víbransi; 2. váibrənsi]. **vibrant** & **-cy**. State or property of being vibrant; resonance.

vibrant, adj. [1. víbrant; 2. váibrənt]. Fr., fr. Lat. *vibrant-(em)*, Pres. Part. of *vibrāre*, see **vibrate**. **a** Vibrating, tremulous; **b** (of sound, the voice) setting up vibrations, resonant.

vibrate, vb. intrans. & trans. [1. vībrā́t, víbrāt; 2. vaibréit, váibreit], fr. Lat. *vibrāt-(um)*, P.P. type of *vibrāre*, 'to set in tremulous motion, cause to move rapidly to and fro; to shake, to agitate'; expanded fr. base **wei-*, 'to tremble' &c.; also fr. this base are O.H.G. *wipf*, 'swing, impetus', *wipfil*, 'top of a tree', *wimpal*, 'veil, headgear', see **wimple**. The base in its simpler form is seen in Lat. *viēre*, 'to twist, bend', *vītis*, 'grape vine'; see further under **viti-**, **vine**, & **withy**. **A.** intrans. **1. a** To move rapidly to and fro, to oscillate; esp. to quiver, thrill, with incessant, tremulous, rapid movement, as of a thin, or tightly stretched, flexible or elastic body: *a fiddle string vibrates when touched with the bow*; *the atmosphere vibrates in response to the oscillations of a fiddle string*; **b** (fig.) to be deeply stirred emotionally, have the feelings profoundly moved; to thrill: *to vibrate with passion, at a person's touch* &c. **2. a** To move, swing, steadily backwards and forwards between two points; e.g. of a pendulum; **b** (rare, fig.) to hesitate between two opinions, courses of action &c. **B.** trans. To cause to vibrate.

vibratile, adj. [1. víbratīl; 2. váibrətail]. **vibrate** & **-ile**. Capable of vibrating, tending to vibrate.

vibratility, n. [1. vībratíliti; 2. vàibrətíliti]. Prec. & **-ity**. Property of being vibratile.

vibration, n. [1. vībrā́shun; 2. vaibréiʃən]. **vibrate** & **-ion**. **1. a** Rapid, tremulous, oscillating movement to and fro, as of a tense elastic, or fluid body; **b** (fig.) tremulous stirring, or thrilling, of the emotions. **2.** (more rarely) Steady swinging movement to and fro. **3.** Act or process of causing (a body) to vibrate.

vibrational, adj. [1. vībrā́shunal; 2. vaibréiʃənəl]. Prec. & **-al**. Pertaining to, connected with, of the nature of, vibration.

vibrative, adj. [1. víbrativ; 2. váibrətiv]. **vibrate** & **-ive**. Of the nature of, causing, vibration.

vibrato, n. [1. vibráhtō; 2. vibrátou]. Ital., P.P. of *vibrare*, see **vibrate**. Tremulous effect produced by variation of emphasis or loudness in the same note.

vibrator, n. [1. vibrā́tor; 2. vaibréitə]. **vibrate** & **-or**. That which vibrates.

vibratory, adj. [1. víbraturi; 2. váibrət(ə)ri]. **vibrate** & **-ory**. Vibrative.

vibrio, n. [1. víbriō; 2. víbriou]. Neo-Lat., formed fr. *vibrāre*, see **vibrate**. Kind of bacteria which are endowed with the power of vibratory or undulatory movement.

vibrioid, adj. & n. [1. víbrioid; 2. víbriɔid]. Prec. & **-oid**. **1.** adj. Like a vibrio. **2.** n. A vibrioid body, or vibrio.

vibrissa, n., pl. **vibrissae** [1. vībrísa, -ē; 2. vaibrísə, -i]. Lat., fr. base of **vibrate**. Stiff hair in the human nostril; hair round the muzzle of mammals, the whiskers of the cat &c.

vibrograph, n. [1. víbrograhf; 2. váibrəgrāf]. Base of **vibrate** & **-graph**. Device for recording vibrations.

vibroscope, n. [1. víbroskōp; 2. váibrəskòup]. Base of **vibrate** & **-scope**. Instrument for observing and recording vibrations.

vibroscopic, adj. [1. vībroskópik; 2. vàibrəskɔ́pik]. Prec. & **-ic**. Pertaining to, observed by, the vibroscope.

viburnum, n. [1. vībérnum; 2. vaibʌ́nəm]. Lat., translated as 'the wayfaring tree'. The element *vi-* is fr. base in Lat. *viēre*, 'to twine' &c., see under **viti-** & **vibrate**, & refers to the habit of the tree; the second element is like that in **laburnum** & is unexplained. A genus of shrubs and trees, the guelder roses, wild and cultivated in gardens for their flowers and foliage.

vicar, n. [1. víkar; 2. víkə]. M.E. *vicair*, *vicar* &c., fr. O. Fr. *vicaire*, in eccles. sense, fr. Lat. *vicārius*, 'a deputy, substitute, proxy', see **vicarious**. **1.** Deputy; rare except in Phr. *the Vicar of Christ*, title claimed by, and accorded to, the Pope; *Vicar-general*, deputy of the Pope or of an Archbishop. **2.** The incumbent of an English parish who is not a rector, i.e. one who does not receive the great tithes, but is paid a stipend from other sources; formerly called a *perpetual curate*. The parish of a vicar is either a new one carved out of a larger, older parish, the rector retaining the old parish church and the great tithes, or one in which these tithes belong to a layman or a corporation.

vicarage, n. [1. víkarij; 2. víkəridž]. **vicar** & **-age**. **1.** The residence of a vicar. **2.** (more rarely) The office of a vicar.

vicar-apostolic, n. (R.C. Ch.) **1.** Archbishop or bishop to whom the Pope delegated his authority. **2.** An ecclesiastic exercising episcopal jurisdiction in a diocese during a vacancy, or on account of the illness of the bishop. **3.** A titular bishop exercising his functions in a country where there are no episcopal sees.

vicar-capitular, n. (R.C. Ch.) Person elected by the Chapter (in England) to rule the diocese, after the death of a bishop, until the new bishop is appointed.

vicar-choral, n. Clergyman or layman whose duty it is to sing part of the service in a cathedral.

vicar-forane, n. [1. víkar fórin; 2. víkə fɔ́rin]. Lat. *forāneus*, see **foreign**. (R.C. Ch.) Priest appointed by the bishop to exercise certain limited jurisdiction in a particular town &c. within the diocese.

vicarial, adj. [1. vikā́rial; 2. vikɛ́əriəl]. **vicar** & **-ial**. **1.** Pertaining to, acting as, a vicar. **2.** (rare) Vicarious.

vicariate, n. [1. vikā́riat; 2. vikɛ́əriət]. **vicar** & **-i-** & **-ate**. Office of a vicar; period of tenure of this.

vicarious, adj. [1. vīkā́rius; 2. vaikɛ́əriəs]. Lat. *vicārius*, 'substituted, delegated', fr. *vicis*, 'change, interchange, alternation', see **vice (IV.)**, & **-ary**, & **-ous**. **1.** Connected with, pertaining to, a vicar or deputy; deputed: *vicarious authority*. **2.** Performing duties as the substitute or deputy of another: *a vicarious ruler, agent*. **3.** Performed, undergone, by one person &c., on behalf of, in the place of, another: *the vicarious sufferings, sacrifice, of Christ*. **4.** (med.) *Vicarious haemorrhage*, one taking place from an organ other than the normal one, the usual flow from the latter being suppressed.

vicariously, adv. Prec. & **-ly**. In a vicarious manner; as a deputy; by deputy.

vicariousness, n. See prec. & **-ness**. State, quality, of being vicarious.

vice (I.), n. [1. vīs; 2. vais]. In M.E., fr. O. Fr. fr. Lat. *vitium*, 'fault, defect, blemish; moral fault; crime'; perh. cogn. w. O.E. *wīdl*, 'defilement, impurity'; the etymol. is disputed; perh. fr. the base in Lat. *viēre*, 'to bend, twine' &c., see **viti-**, in the sense of 'bending aside, departure, from the normal or healthy condition'. **1.** A grave moral fault;

ingrained defect in the character: *avarice and cruelty are among the most detestable vices.* **2. a** Immoral, degrading, conduct or habit; gross wickedness, depravity, lewdness: *vice of all kinds exists, unfortunately, in all big cities*; **b** *the Vice*, a character in English Morality plays, usually a buffoon, who represented some particular vice. **3.** Specif., *vice in a horse*, bad, incorrigible tricks and habits, such as bolting, shying, rearing &c., which make the animal difficult to ride or drive with comfort. **4. a** Physical defect or disability; diseased taint: *he has certain vices of constitution which render his life precarious*; **b** defect, blemish, imperfection in organization, social structure &c.: *the vices of our social system*; **c** a fault in, a bad form of, expression; esp. *a vice of literary style, oratory, drawing* &c.

vice (II.), n. & vb. trans. M.E., fr. O. Fr. *vis*, 'a screw; a winding stair', fr. Lat. *vītis*, 'a vine', fr. base **vī-* in *viēre*, 'to twist together, to weave', see **viti-**. **1.** n. A device, usually of iron, and screwed to a bench, consisting of two parts worked by a screw so as to be brought together and held immovable at the desired distance apart, used by smiths, and workers in wood or metal, for gripping, holding, an object in a given position while being carved, chiselled, hammered or otherwise worked on; Phrs. *as firm as a vice*; *a grip like a vice* &c. **2.** vb. (rare) To grip, hold firm, in a vice.

vice (III.), n. Colloq. abbr. for *vice-chancellor*, *vice-president* &c.

vice (IV.), prep. [1. vísi; 2. váisi]. Lat., abl. of *vicis*, 'change, interchange, alternation, reciprocal succession'; cogn. w. Gk. *eikō* for **weikō*, 'I yield, draw back, give way' &c.; Scrt. *višti*, 'changeable'; further (Gmc. *k* fr. Aryan *kn-*), O.S. *wīkan*, O.E. *wīcan*, 'to give way, collapse', O.H.G. *wīhhan*; O.E. *wāc*, 'weak', O.N. *veikr*, fr. **waik-*, see **weak**; & prob. O.E. *wīcu*, see **week.** Instead of, in the place of: *an examiner in Greek will be appointed vice Mr. Jones, who retires*; *to be Brigade Major vice Captain X.*

vice-, pref. [1. vīs; 2. vais]. Fr., for etymol. see prec. Prefix placed before the names of offices and ranks to express: **a** persons entitled, qualified, appointed, to hold such offices as deputies for others and to perform certain delegated functions: *vice-agent, vice-sheriff, vice-warden* &c.; **b** expressing a rank next in order below that to which the prefix is attached: *vice-admiral.*

vice-admiral, n. Officer in the navy next in rank below an admiral.

vice-admiralty, n. Rank, office, of a vice-admiral; term of this office.

vice-chairman, n. Permanent officer of a company, corporation, deliberative body &c., who presides at the meetings in the absence of the chairman.

vice-chairmanship, n. Office of a vice-chairman; term of this.

vice-chamberlain, n. Deputy of a chamberlain or lord chamberlain.

vice-chancellor, n. **1.** Formerly (down to 1873) a judge appointed to the Chancery Court of England. **2.** The chief executive officer of a University acting also as deputy of the Chancellor.

vice-consul, n. The deputy of a consul; official appointed by a government to watch commercial interests of its subjects in a foreign country, in a town, when these subjects are not sufficiently numerous or the business sufficiently important for a consul.

vice-consulate, n. Residence, office, term of office, of a vice-consul.

vice-consulship, n. Status, office, of a vice-consul; term of this office.

vicegerent, n. [1. vīsjérent; 2. vaisdžíərənt]. **vice** & **gerent.** One who rules as the deputy of another; *God's vicegerent*, the Pope.

vice-governor, n. Deputy governor.

vice-governorship, n. Office, term of office, of vice-governor.

vicennial, adj. [1. vīsénial; 2. vaiséniəl]. Lat. *vīcennium*, 'period of 20 years', *vīcēni*, '20', & *annus*, 'year', see **annual**, & **-al.** The first element is cogn. w. Lat. *vīginti*, fr. **vīkntói*; Scrt. *viçati*; Gk. *eikosi*; O.W. *uceint*, 'twenty'. The meaning is 'two tens', fr. base **wī-*, **wei-*, &c., 'two', see **divide**; & **k mt*, earlier **dk m-t-*, 'ten, a decade', see **hundred, deca-.** Lasting for, recurring every, twenty years.

vice-presidency, n. Office, term of office, of vice-president.

vice-president, n. Deputy of a president.

viceregal, adj. [1. vīsrégl; 2. vaisrígl]. **vice-** & **regal** (I.). Pertaining to, connected with, a viceroy or vicereine: *the viceregal palace, ball* &c.

vicereine, n. [1. vísrān; 2. váisrein]. **vice-** & Fr. *reine*, 'queen', fr. Lat., see **regina.** Wife of a viceroy.

viceroy, n. [1. vísroi; 2. váisrɔi]. **vice-** & Fr. *roi*, 'king', fr. Lat., see **rex.** One who rules a country, province, colony, in the name and with the authority of, and as representing, the sovereign.

viceroyal, adj. [1. vīsróial; 2. vaisrɔ́iəl]. Prec. & **-al.** (rare) Viceregal.

viceroyalty, n. [1. vīsróialti; 2. vaisrɔ́iəlti]. Prec. & **-ty.** The dignity and office of a viceroy; term of this office.

viceroyship, n. [1. vísroiship; 2. váisrɔiʃip]. Viceroyalty.

vice versa, adv. [1. vísi vérsa; 2. váisi vʌ́sə]. Lat., **vice** (IV.) & abl. fem. of P.P. of *vertere*, 'to turn', see **version.** Conversely, the relations being reversed: *I dislike him, and vice versa*, i.e. and he dislikes me; *he's afraid of horses, and vice versa*, i.e. horses are nervous with him.

Vichy water, n. [1. véshi wawter; 2. víʃi wɔ̄tə]. Mineral medicinal water obtained from the springs of Vichy, France.

vicia, n. [1. vísia; 2. vísiə]. Lat., 'a vetch'; fr. base **vei-* &c. as in Lat. *viēre*, 'to twist, bend', see under **viti-.** The vetch family of plants.

vicilin, n. [1. vísilin; 2. vísilin], fr. prec. Chemical substance found in the broad bean, pea, and other fabaceous plants.

vicinage, n. [1. vísinij; 2. vísinidž], fr. Lat. *vīcīnus*, 'near, neighbouring', fr. *vīcus*, 'district, quarter, of a city; village, hamlet'; fr. **woikos*; cogn. w. Gk. *oîkos*, fr. **woikos*, 'house', see first element of **economy**: Scrt. *vēćáš*, 'house', & *vić*, 'dwelling-place'; Goth. *weihs*, 'village'; cp. further, O.E. *wīc*, 'dwelling, village', either borrowed direct fr. Lat. *vīcus*, or fr. **wīkná*, cp. Pl.-Ns. in *-wich*, & **wick** (II.); for suff. see **-age. 1.** Area, tract of country, place, lying near by; neighbourhood, neighbouring country or place; vicinity. **2.** Common rights arising to neighbouring tenants of the same barony.

vicinal, adj. [1. vísinal; 2. vísinəl]. Lat. *vīcīnālis*, 'neighbouring', fr. *vīcīn-*, see prec. & **-al.** Neighbouring.

vicinism, n. [1. vísinizm; 2. vísinizəm]. Lat. *vīcīn-*, see **vicinage**, & **-ism.** (biol.) Tendency of forms to vary owing to the influence of related forms living in the same vicinity.

vicinity, n. [1. visíniti; 2. visíniti]. Fr. *vicinité*, fr. Lat. *vīcīnitāt-(em)*, 'neighbourhood', fr. *vīcīn-*, as in **vicinage**, & **-ity. 1.** State of being near; nearness, propinquity. **2.** Neighbouring area, adjacent regions, neighbourhood.

vicious, adj. [1. víshus; 2. víʃəs]. O. Fr. *vicious*, fr. Lat. *vitiōsus*, fr. *vitium*, see **vice** (I.) & **-ous. 1.** Affected by, characterized by, practising, vice; grossly immoral, lewd: *a vicious book*; *a vicious life*; *a vicious person.* **2.** Malignant, spiteful, malevolent: *a vicious look, speech, blow.* **3.** Faulty, imperfect, defective (in various senses): *a vicious text* (of an author), corrupt: *a vicious style, pronunciation*, full of faults and blemishes; vulgar; *a vicious argument*, one logically defective. Phr. *a vicious circle*, (i.) a set of undesirable circumstances which act and react detrimentally upon each other, so that one condition or circumstance leads to another, which in turn intensifies and aggravates the former, and so on; (ii.) (in reasoning) a conclusion based upon an unsound premise, and serving as the basis for establishing the former. **4.** (of a horse) Showing vice; having certain bad tricks and habits; badly trained, hard to manage.

viciously, adv. Prec. & **-ly.** In a vicious manner.

viciousness, n. See prec. & **-ness. 1.** Quality of being vicious; **a** gross wickedness, immorality; vice; **b** malignity, ill nature, spite. **2.** Faultiness, defectiveness.

vicissitude, n. [1. vīsísitud; 2. vaisísitjūd]. Fr., fr. Lat. *vicissitūdo*, 'change, interchange, alternation'; formed fr. Lat. *vicis*, 'change', see **vice** (IV.) & **-tude. 1.** Irregular alternation, change, mutation, esp. of circumstances, experience, worldly condition; ups-and-downs of life: *the vicissitudes of fate.* **2.** (obs. or poet.) Regular change and succession, orderly alternation: '*Where light and darkness . . . Lodge and dislodge by turns, which makes . . . Grateful vicissitude, like day and night*' (Milton, 'P. L.' vi. 6-8).

vicissitudinary, adj. [1. vīsisitū́dinari; 2. vàisisitjū́dinəri]. Lat. *vicissitūdin-*, stem of *vicissitūdo*, see prec., & **-ary.** Characterized by, liable to, vicissitude.

vicissitudinous, adj. [1. vīsisitū́dinus; 2. vàisisitjū́dinəs]. Same stem as prec. & **-ous.** Vicissitudinary.

victim, n. [1. víktim; 2. víktim]. Fr. *victime*, fr. Lat. *victima*, 'beast of sacrifice, victim'; formed fr. **vict-*, 'something consecrated', fr. base **wīk-*, 'sacred'; cogn. w. Goth. *weihs* (=*wīhs*), 'holy', *weihan*, 'to make holy, consecrate', *weiha*, 'priest'; O.H.G. *wīhan*, Mod. Germ. *weihen*, 'to consecrate, devote' &c. The orig. meaning seems to be 'to set apart', cp. Scrt. *viktár*, 'separated off, set apart'. **1.** Human being or animal devoted, consecrated, to a god, or to God, slain, and offered as a sacrifice. **2. a** Person or living creature that is the object of, and that suffers from, another's anger, ill-will, persecution, evil passions &c.: *the victim of malice, dislike, hatred* &c., *the victim of another's greed* &c.; **b** one who suffers through, is a prey to, some bad qualities, or defects, in his own character or behaviour: *the victim of his own folly, cowardice, extravagance* &c.; **c** one who suffers through the operation of external circumstances and conditions which he cannot control: *a victim of poverty, of the war, of disease* &c.; Phr. *the victim of circumstances*, a wrongdoer who sins owing to the stress of forces and conditions which overmaster him, so that he is not wholly responsible. **3.** A person who is brought under the sinister influence of another, and is deceived and injured by him: *the victim of a swindler*; (facet.) *fell a victim to the lady's charms*, was captivated by these.

victimizable, adj. [1. víktimīzabl; 2. víktimàizəbl]. **victimize** & **-able.** Capable of being, liable to be, victimized.

victimization, n. [1. viktimīzáshun; 2. vìktimaizéiʃən]. See prec. & **-ation.** Condition of being victimized; act, process, of victimizing.

victimize, vb. trans. [1. víktimīz; 2. víktimaiz]. **victim** & **-ize.** To make a, or the, victim of; to cause to suffer; **a** to deceive, cheat: *victimized by rogues*; **b** to cause to suffer, or endure: *I was victimized the whole evening by the worst bore in the room.*

victor, n. [1. víktor; 2. víktə]. Lat., 'conqueror', formed fr. *vict-(um)*, P.P. type of *vincere*, 'to vanquish', see **vincible**, & **-or.** One who is successful in battle or in a contest; a conqueror, vanquisher, winner; (also attrib.) '*See where the victor victim bleeds*' (Shirley).

victoria, n. [1. viktória; 2. viktɔ́riə]. Lat., 'victory'; fr. *vict-* as in **victor**, & see **-ory**; used as proper name. Name of a light, low, four-wheeled carriage, drawn by one or two horses, having two seats looking towards the driver's back, a movable hood, and a box for the coachman; named after Queen Victoria.

Victoria Cross, n. Abbr. V.C., commonly called [1. vḗ sḗ; 2. vī sī]. Decoration, founded by Queen Victoria in 1856, awarded to soldiers and sailors for an act of remarkable bravery in the presence of the enemy; it consists of a bronze Maltese cross, suspended from a crimson ribbon, for the Army, or from a dark blue one for the Navy. V.C. is also applied to a holder of the decoration: *he is a V.C. and a D.S.O.*

victoria lily, n. Gigantic S. American water-lily, *Victoria regia.*

Victorian, adj. & n. [1. viktórian; 2. viktɔ́riən]. **victoria & -an.** **1.** adj. Pertaining to, characteristic of, living, made, in the reign of Queen Victoria: *Victorian habits, dress, furniture; Victorian statesmen, writers* &c. **2.** n. A person, esp. a writer or other public character, living during the reign of Queen Victoria.

Victorian Order, n. Order founded in 1896 by Queen Victoria, and awarded for personal service to the sovereign.

victorine, n. [1. viktorḗn; 2. víktərīn], fr. woman's name. **1.** Fur tippet with long narrow ends, formerly worn by women. **2.** A kind of peach.

victorious, adj. [1. viktórius; 2. viktɔ́riəs]. Lat. *victōriōsus*; see **victory & -ous.** Having the victory in a battle, in war, or in a contest of any kind: *victorious troops; the victorious football team.*

victoriously, adv. Prec. & **-ly.** In a victorious manner; with victory; so as to win.

victoriousness, n. See prec. & **-ness.** (rare) Condition, quality, of being victorious.

victory, n. [1. víktori; 2. víktəri]. M.E., fr. O. Fr. *victorie*, fr. Lat. *victōria*, see **victoria.** **1. a** Success in battle or in a contest of any kind; act or fact of defeating an enemy in the field, or an opponent in a dispute, competition, game &c.; conquest, act of winning; **b** success in any kind of effort or struggle: *a victory over every difficulty, over one's lower self* &c. **2.** (cap.) Roman goddess of victory.

victress, n. [1. viktres; 2. viktris], fr. **victor & -ess.** Female victor.

victual, n. & vb. trans. & intrans. [1. vítl; 2. vitl]. M.E., fr. O. Fr. *vitaille*, fr. Lat. *victuālia*, neut. pl., 'provisions', formed fr. *victus*, 'nourishment, fr. *vict-(um)*, P.P. type of *vīvere*, 'to live', see **vital.** **1.** n. Generally *victuals*, food, provisions. **2.** vb. **a** trans. To supply, provide with, food or stores; **b** intrans., (i.) to procure, take in, stores (of a ship &c.); (ii.) to consume food.

victualler, n. [1. vítaler; 2. vítələ]. Prec. & **-er.** **1.** One who provides victuals; (now chiefly) *licensed victualler*, one licensed to sell alcoholic liquor; an innkeeper, a publican. **2.** A ship carrying provisions and stores for other ships, or supplying military forces; also *victualling ship.*

victualling, n. [1. vítaling; 2. vítəliŋ]. See **victual & -ing.** *Victualling bill*, list of stores to be used on a voyage, and held in bond, furnished to Customs authorities; *victualling house*, eating-house; *victualling note*, one issued by Naval Paymaster, authorizing a ship's steward to supply food to a seaman; *victualling office*, one supplying naval stores &c.; *victualling ship*, victualler; *victualling yard*, one in which naval supplies are stored.

vicuna, vicuña, n. [1. vīkū́na, vikṓōnya; 2. vaikjū́nə, vaikū́njə]. Span. *vicuña*, fr. Peruv. **1.** Ruminant animal of Peru, Bolivia, and Ecuador, closely related to the llama; hunted for its fine wool. **2.** Fine, woolly cloth made from the wool of the vicuna, or from some wool resembling this; also *vicuna cloth.*

vide, vb. [1. vídi; 2. váidi]. Imperat. sing. of Lat. *vidēre*, 'to see'; cogn. w. a series of Gk. words, meaning 'see' and 'know', q.v. under **-oid; idea; idol;** for Gmc. cognates see **wit (I.)**; cp. also **vision.** See; used in referring to a passage &c., quoted in a book &c.: *vide* (or *v.*) *p.* 30 &c.; q.v., *quod vide*, which see.

videlicet, adv. [1. vi-, vīdḗliset; 2. vi-, vaidī́liset]. Lat., for *vidēre licet*, 'it is permitted to see'; abbr. *viz.*, wh. is commonly rendered *namely.* Generally used to introduce a fuller explanation, or expansion, of what has been stated so briefly as to demand a further elaboration: *the animal kingdom may be divided into three great groups, viz. the vertebrates, invertebrates, and protozoa.*

vidette. See **vedette.**

vidimus, n. [1. vidimus; 2. váidiməs]. Lat. *vidimus*, 'we have seen', perf. pl. of *vidēre*, see **vide.** A formal inspection of documents.

vidual, adj. [1. vidūal; 2. vidjuəl]. Lat. *vidua*, 'widow' & **-al**; see **divide & widow.** Pertaining to, connected with, a widow, or widows.

viduate, n. [1. vídūāt; 2. vidjueit]. Lat. *vidua*, see prec., & **-ate.** Position or status of a widow; condition of being a widow.

vie, vb. intrans. [1. vī; 2. vai]. M.E. *vīen*, fr. *envīen*, see **envy.** *Vie with*, to strive with for superiority in any form; to contest place of superiority with; to rival: *to vie with another for power* &c.; *various kinds of vegetation vying with each other for supremacy; in my opinion few fruits can vie with the apple.*

Viennese, adj. & n. [1. vienḗz; 2. vieníz]. Vienna & **-ese. a** adj. Belonging to, coming from, Vienna; **b** n., (sing. & pl.) inhabitant of Vienna.

vi et armis, adv. [1. vī et ármis; 2. vái et ámis]. Lat., 'by force and arms', see **vis.** (law) By force and with arms, as showing how damage to person or property was caused.

view (I.), n. [1. vū; 2. vjū]. M.E. *veue*, 'the sense of sight', fr. O. Fr., P.P. Fem. of *veoir*, 'to see', fr. Lat. *vidēre*, see **vide & vision.** **1.** Act of seeing; inspection, examination, by eye; sight: *this ruin is well worth our view; the jury had a view of the body; a private view* (of pictures on exhibition). Phr. *to keep, have, something in view*, under observation, within range of vision, under one's eye; also (fig.) in one's mind or memory; *on view*, on exhibition; *in full view of*, so as to be visible to, or from. **2. a** Something that is seen; impression presented to the eye; a prospect, a sight, a scene: *a fine view of the surrounding country, of the proceedings, of the Lord Mayor's show*; specif. **b** a prospect of nature, of a tract of country or natural scenery: *I want a house with a view.* **3.** A representation in art, photography &c., of a scene, esp. of a landscape, a building &c.: *to do, take, some views of the Lakes, of a cathedral* &c. **4. a** Mental impression; a critical survey based on a mental examination of anything; an estimate, sizing-up: *I have not yet formed a clear view of the situation; he presented quite a new view of the affair; I take a grave view of his conduct*; **b** an intellectual judgement, an opinion: *to hold extreme views; what are your views on Protection?; in my view it would be unwise to proceed further with the matter*; Phr. *in view of*, considering, seeing, having regard to. **5.** Design, plan, intention; expectation: *I will try to meet your views in every way; I have quite other views for my son's future; I have views on a meal at the next town.* Phrs. *with a view to, with the view of*, with the intention of.

view (II.), vb. trans., fr. prec. **1.** To inspect, look at: *to view the pictures, a house and grounds* &c.; specif., *to view the body* (of jury at an inquest). Phr. *an order to view*, authoritative permission to inspect (house, estate &c.) **2.** (poet., obsolesc.) To see, look upon: '*that dear home she ne'er might view again*' (T. Haynes Bayly). **3.** To contemplate, look forward to: *I can only view the future with misgiving.* **4.** To take a specified view of, hold specified opinion concerning; to estimate: *I view his conduct in the gravest light.*

viewable, adj. [1. vūabl; 2. vjūəbl]. Prec. & **-able.** Capable of being viewed; visible.

view-finder, n. **view (I.) & finder.** The small aperture in a camera with a mirror in which is shown the view of that which is to be photographed.

view-hallo(o), n. [1. vū haló; 2. vjū həlū́]. The hallo(o) or call of huntsman when the fox is viewed on breaking cover.

viewless, adj. [1. vū́les; 2. vjū́lis]. **view (I.) & -less.** (poet.) **a** Invisible: '*Each stair . . . drawn up to heaven sometimes Viewless*' (Milton, 'P. L.' iii. 516-18); **b** unseeing, blind.

viewy, adj. [1. vū́i; 2. vjū́i]. **view (I.) & -y.** Full of views and opinions, esp. of fantastic views; visionary; cranky.

vigil, n. [1. vijil; 2. vidžil]. Lat. *vigilia*, 'wakefulness, sleeplessness', fr. *vigil*, 'awake, wakeful, alert', fr. the base in *vigēre*, 'to be lively, to flourish'; this base is cogn. w. that in Lat. *vegēre*, 'to move, to excite' &c., see **vegetable**; cp. also **wake (I.)**. **1.** The act of being awake; the act of watching, e.g. in a sick-room, or over the dead. **2. a** Devotional waking and watching; *vigils*, nocturnal devotions; **b** specif., the night spent in prayer before a feast of the Church; the eve of a feast-day.

vigilance, n. [1. víjilans; 2. vidžiləns]. Lat. *vigilantia*; see **vigilant & -ce.** **1.** Watchfulness, alertness. **2.** (med.) Insomnia, sleeplessness.

vigilance committee, n. **1.** (chiefly U.S.A.) Voluntary, self-chosen body of citizens who assume responsibility for the preservation of order, and the summary punishment of crime in a community which has no regular government, or in one in which the government is temporarily inadequate. **2.** More usually *watch committee*, a similar voluntary local body in a town looking for breaches of morals, infringement of licensing laws &c. and reporting to the police, instigating prosecutions &c.

vigilant, adj. [1. víjilant; 2. vidžilənt], fr. Lat. *vigilant-(em)*, Pres. Part. of *vigilāre*, 'to watch, be wakeful', formed fr. *vigil*, 'wakeful' &c., see **vigil.** Watchful, alert; keenly alive to possible danger, and to the necessity of securing safety; attentive, wary.

vigilantly, adv. Prec. & **-ly.** In a vigilant manner; with vigilance.

vigilantness, n. See prec. & **-ness.** State, quality, of being vigilant; vigilance.

vignette (I.), n. [1. vinyét; 2. vinjét]. Fr., dimin. fr. *vigne*, 'vine', see **vine, & -ette.** **1.** (obs.) Originally, a decoration consisting of conventionalized representation of vine leaves, tendrils, and bunches of grapes. **2. a** A small ornamental design placed at the beginning or end of chapters or of books; **b** a picture or photograph which merges gradually in the surrounding background, without a definite boundary line. **3. a** A small delicate illustration on the page of a book; **b** a short highly-wrought picture in words.

vignette (II.), vb. trans., fr. prec. To depict in the form of a vignette.

vignettist, n. [1. vinyétist; 2. vinjétist]. **vignette (I.) & -ist.** A maker of vignettes.

vigoroso, adv. [1. vigorṓsō; 2. vigərṓusou]. Ital., fr. L. Lat. *vigōrōsus*, see **vigorous.** (musical direction) With vigour.

vigorous, adj. [1. vigorus; 2. vigərəs]. L. Lat. *vigōrōsus*, see **vigour & -ous.** **1.** Abounding in bodily or mental vigour, vitality; strong, potent; virile. **2. a** Exhibiting vigour in bodily growth, activity, action; active, lively: *a vigorous plant; a vigorous player; a vigorous attack*; **b** showing, acting with, intellectual vigour and strength of character; forcible, forceful; animated: *a vigorous thinker; a vigorous writer, style* &c.; *a vigorous commander.*

vigorously, adv. Prec. & **-ly.** In a vigorous manner.

vigorousness, n. See prec. & **-ness.** Condition, quality, of being vigorous; vigour.

vigour, n. [1. vigor; 2. vigə]. M.E., fr. O. Fr. *vigour*, Lat. *vigor*, 'liveliness, activity, force'; fr. base in *vigēre*, 'to be lively', q.v. under **vigil, & cp. vegetable.** **1. a** Animal strength, force, potency, vitality; **b** powers of intellect, mental strength. **2. a** Strength, force, as exhibited in power of growth or of movement or action; activity; strength of bodily constitution; **b** force of character; **c** forceful, powerful action.

viking, n. [1. víking; 2. váikiŋ]. Affectedly & erroneously [víkiŋ]. O.N. *víkingr*; prob. fr. *víg*, 'a fight, battle'; cp. O.E. *wíg*, 'war'; cogn. w. Lat. *vic-*, form of *vincere*, 'to conquer', see **victor** & **vincible**; popularly confused w. *sea-king*, as though the second element in both words were the same, although there is in reality no connexion. An ancient Scandinavian pirate; one of the northern adventurers who from the 8th to the 10th century ravaged and plundered nearly every coast in Europe.

vilayet, n. [1. vìlayét, viláhyet; 2. vìlájét, vilájɛt]. Turk. *vilâyet*; see **Blighty**. One of the chief provinces of the old Ottoman Empire.

vile, adj. [1. vīl; 2. vail]. M.E., fr. O. Fr. *vil*, fr. Lat. *vīlis*, 'of small price or value; trifling, paltry, common'; etymol. unexplained; objections have been taken to each of the attempted solutions. **1.** (rare, archaic) Of no account, common, mean: *silver was held a vile thing in the days of Solomon*; '*our vile body*' (Phil. iii. 21). **2.** Morally degraded and debased; depraved; sinful. **3.** (colloq., as term of disapprobation) Highly objectionable; of bad, inferior, quality; atrocious, shocking: *a perfectly vile hat*; *a very vile phrase.*

vilely, adv. Prec. & **-ly.** In a vile manner; (colloq.) very badly: *the dinner is vilely cooked*; *a vilely written letter.*

vileness, n. See prec. & **-ness.** State, quality, of being vile.

vilify, vb. trans. [1. vílifī; 2. vílifai]. Lat. *vilificāre*, 'to esteem of small value', see **vile** & **-fy.** **1.** To speak ill of, to defame, traduce. **2.** (rare and archaic) To render vile; to degrade.

vilipend, vb. trans. [1. vílipend; 2. vílipend]. Lat. *vilipendere*, 'to hold in light esteem, to despise', fr. *vīlis*, see **vile**, & *pendere*, 'to weigh, estimate', see **pendant.** To speak slightingly of, to disparage.

villa, n. [1. víla; 2. vílə]. Lat. *villa*, 'a country house, seat, farm, villa', for **vicsla*, fr. *vicus*, 'hamlet, village', see **vicinage.** **a** A house of some pretensions, or pretentiousness, detached, and with some ground round it, usually in a suburban area; also used **b** of a house, sometimes of considerable size in fairly large grounds, with a few acres of vineyard, olive-trees &c., used as a residence for part of the year, in Italy or the south of France: *a villa on the Riviera.*

villadom, n. [1. víladum; 2. víladəm]. Prec. & **-dom.** Suburban society.

village, n. [1. vílij; 2. vílidž]. M.E., fr. O. Fr., fr. Lat. *villāticus*, 'connected with a villa, or country house', see **villa.** A collection of houses, larger than a hamlet, in a country district, usually an ancient settlement, containing a church and forming the residential nucleus of a parish.

village community, n. Term used by 19th century writers on early society, to designate a primitive organized agricultural community, concerning the precise structure of which some difference of opinion exists.

villager, n. [1. vílijer; 2. vílidžə]. **village & -er.** One who lives in a village; a countryman; specif., one of the poorer, labouring inhabitants of a village.

villain, n. [1. vílan; 2. vílin, -ən]. M.E. *villain*, *villein*, fr. O. Fr., fr. L. Lat. *villānus*, 'pertaining to a villa, or farm', see **villa.** **1.** (hist.) Now usually spelt *villein*; **a** originally, a free-born peasant, one of an inferior class of landholders; **b** later (13th cent.) the term was applied to a class of serfs, adscript to the soil, and with no rights except to some degree of protection from their lord, by whom they could, however, be removed at will from such lands as they enjoyed. Later still the position of this class improved, so that they became free, and gradually, as regards tenure, developed into the class of copyholders. **2.** (obs. or archaic) A low-born person, a churl; a rustic boor. **3. a** A scoundrel; one likely to commit, or who has committed, grave crimes; an infamous knave; **b** used playfully and affectionately, as: *the young villain has finished the jam*; cp. similar use of *rascal* and *rogue.*

villa(i)nage, n. See **villeinage.**

villainous, adj. [1. vílanus; 2. vílənəs]. **villain & -ous.** **1.** Characteristic of a villain, **3 a**; infamous, exhibiting wickedness and rascality: *a villainous countenance*; *villainous conduct.* **2.** (colloq.) As general expression of disapproval; thoroughly bad in quality; badly done or made; ugly, nasty &c.: *a villainous piece of mutton, suit of clothes, dinner* &c.

villainously, adv. Prec. & **-ly.** **a** In a villainous manner; after the manner of a villain; **b** very badly: *a villainously delivered sermon* &c.

villainousness, n. See prec. & **-ness.** **a** State or quality of being villainous; **b** villainous conduct.

villainy, n. [1. vílani; 2. víləni]. M.E., fr. O. Fr. *vile(i)nie*; see **villain & -y.** **1.** (obs.) Boorishness, rudeness, discourtesy. **2.** Villainous conduct; great wickedness, rascality, blackguardism.

villanella, n. [1. vìlanéla; 2. vìlənélə]. Ital., see **villa, -an, & -elle.** Old Italian rustic dance accompanied by singing.

villanelle, n. [1. vìlanél; 2. vìlənél]. Fr. form of prec. A poem, esp. in French, usually of 19 lines, and with only two rhymes.

villatic, adj. [1. vilátik; 2. vilǽtik]. Lat. *villāticus*, 'pertaining to a farm', see **village.** **a** Pertaining to a country-house; **b** pertaining to a farm; rustic; **c** domestic: '*the perched roosts and nests in order rang'd Of tame villatic fowl*' (Milton, 'Samson', 1695; contrasted with *the eagle*).

villegiatura, n. [1. vilèjatóora; 2. vilèdžatúra]. Ital. *villagio*, see **village & -ture.** **a** Stay in the country; rustication; **b** a villa, house, in the country.

villein, n. [1. vílin; 2. vílin]. Spelling variant of **villain, 1**, with differentiation of meaning fr. **villain, 2, 3.**

villeinage, n. [1. vílinij; 2. vílinidž]. Prec. & **-age.** (feud. law) **a** Status of a villein, see **villain, 1**; **b** tenure by which a villein or villain held his land; copyhold.

villiform, adj. [1. víliform; 2. vílifɔ̄m]. See **villus & -form.** Resembling villi in form and appearance; resembling pile of velvet.

villosity, n. [1. vilósiti; 2. vilɔ́siti]. **villous & -ity.** Condition or quality of being villous.

villous, adj. [1. vílus; 2. víləs]. Lat. *villōsus*, 'hairy, shaggy', see **villus & -ous.** Covered with fine, woolly hairs; having a nap like velvet.

villus, n., pl. **villi** [1. vílus, -ī; 2. víləs, -ai]. Lat., 'shaggy hair, tuft of hair'; a dialectal variant of Lat. *vellus*, 'fleece; pelt with wool left on it'; see **vellicate.** **1.** One of the minute processes resembling hairs which cover the mucous membrane of the intestines, giving a velvety appearance. **2.** One of the soft, woolly hairs found on some fruits and flowers.

vim, n. [1. vim; 2. vim]. Lat., acc. of *vīs*, 'force', see **vis.** (colloq.) Energy, vigour; spirit, abandon, go.

vimen, n. [1. vímen; 2. váimɛn]. Lat., 'a pliant twig, a switch; an osier', fr. the base of *viēre*, 'to bend, twist, twine', see **vine & viti-.** A long, slender, pliant shoot or branch.

viminal, adj. [1. víminl; 2. váiminl]. Stem of prec. & **-al.** **a** Pertaining to, of the nature of, resembling, a shoot or osier; **b** tending to produce long, slender shoots.

vimineous, adj. [1. vimíneus; 2. vaimíniəs]. Stem of **vimen & -eous.** Viminal; consisting, made, of pliant stems.

vinaceous, adj. [1. vināshus; 2. vainéiʃəs]. See **vine & -aceous.** **a** Pertaining to, resembling, the vine, or grapes; **b** having the colour of red wine.

vinaigrette, n. [1. vìnāgrét; 2. vìneigrét]. Fr., fr. *vinaigre*, see **vinegar & -ette.** **a** A small gold or silver box with a perforated inner lid, for carrying on the person, containing a small portion of sponge soaked in aromatic vinegar; **b** a smelling-bottle.

vincibility, n. [1. vìnsibíliti; 2. vìnsibíliti]. Next word & **-ity.** Quality of being vincible.

vincible, adj. [1. vínsibl; 2. vínsibl]. Lat. *vincibilis*, 'that can be easily gained', fr. *vincere*, 'to conquer, defeat; to gain'; nasalized form of base **wīc-*, as in perf. *vīci*, 'I have conquered'; cogn. w. Goth. *weihan*; O.E. & O.H.G. *wīgan*, 'to fight'; see further **victor.** (rare) Conquerable; not invincible.

vincibleness, n. [1. vínsiblnes; 2. vínsiblnis]. See prec. & **-ness.** Vincibility.

vinculum, n. [1. víngkūlum; 2. víŋkjuləm]. Lat., 'that with which anything is bound, a bond, a fetter', fr. base of *vincīre*, 'to bind, fetter'; an expansion of base **vi-*, 'to bend, twist', as in *viēre*, cp. **viburnum & vimen** & see **vine & viti-.** **1.** A bond, a tie. **2.** (math.) A straight, horizontal line placed over two or more numbers of a compound quantity.

vindicability, n. [1. vìndikabíliti; 2. vìndikəbíliti]. Next word & **-ity.** Quality of being vindicable.

vindicable, adj. [1. víndikabl; 2. víndikəbl]. See next word & **-able.** Capable of being vindicated or justified.

vindicate, vb. trans. [1. víndikāt; 2. víndikeit], fr. Lat. *vindicāt-(um)*, P.P. of *vindicāre*, 'to lay legal claim to anything; to revenge, avenge, take vengeance on'; formed fr. *vindic-*, stem of *vindex*, 'one who lays legal claim to anything, a claimant; a protector, deliverer; an avenger'; the origin of *vin-* is disputed; the second element is the base **deik'-*, **dik'-*, 'to show, point out' &c., q.v. under **diction.** **1.** To establish the justice and validity of, to make good, to prove, obtain recognition of: *to vindicate one's claim, rights.* **2.** To disprove, dispose of, aspersions, accusations, imputations against; to establish integrity or soundness of: *to vindicate one's honour, character, honesty* &c.; *to vindicate one's judgement*; also, to defend (person) from imputations &c.

vindication, n. [1. vìndikáshun; 2. vìndikéiʃən]. Prec. & **-ion.** Act of vindicating; state of being vindicated; **a** establishment of claims &c.; **b** justification, defence, exculpation, from or against accusations, imputations &c.

vindicative, adj. [1. vindíkativ; 2. vindíkətiv]. **vindicate & -ive.** Tending to vindicate; of the nature of vindication.

vindicatively, adv. Prec. & **-ly.** So as to vindicate.

vindicativeness, n. See prec. & **-ness.** Quality of being vindicative.

vindicatory, adj. [1. víndikaturi; 2. víndikətəri]. **vindicate & -ory.** Vindicative.

vindictive, adj. [1. vindíktiv; 2. vindíktiv]. Lat. *vindict-*, 'punishment, vengeance, revenge', see **vindicate, & -ive.** **a** Animated by, arising from, characterized by, a desire for revenge; bearing a grudge, revengeful: *a vindictive character, spirit, action*; **b** punitive: *vindictive damages*, heavy damages awarded against a defendant with the intention of punishing him.

vindictively, adv. Prec. & **-ly.** In a vindictive manner.

vindictiveness, n. See prec. & **-ness.** **a** Quality of being vindictive; **b** a vindictive action or spirit.

vine, n. [1. vīn; 2. vain]. M.E., fr. O. Fr. *vigne*, fr. Lat. *vinea*, 'a plantation of grapes, a vineyard', fr. *vīnum*, 'wine', for **woinom*; cogn. w. Gk. *oínē*, 'the vine', *oînos*, 'wine', for **woin-*; cp. further Lat. *vītis*, 'grape vine; vine-branch', wh. together w. *vīnum*, goes back to the base **vī-* &c., 'to bend, to twist, to twine, ramble', as in Lat. *viēre*, 'to bend, twist' &c.; see further under **viti-**, & cp. **vimen.** O.E. *wīn*, see **wine**, is borrowed direct fr. Lat. *vīnum.* **1.** The plant, *Vitis*, esp. species *V. vinifera*, which bears grapes. **2.** Any plant with long, slender, pliant stems and tendrils, which twists and climbs or rambles; esp. the trailing shoots and stems of such a plant: *a hop-vine*; *the vines of a melon, of a pea* &c.

vine-beetle, n. Kind of beetle that destroys the shoots and leaves of the vine.

vine-borer, n. Reddish-brown weevil which bores into the stems of the vine.

vine-dresser, n. One who tends and prunes grape-vines.

vinegar, n. [1. vínegar; 2. vínigə]. M.E. *vinegre*, Fr. *vinaigre*, lit. 'sour wine', see **vine** & **eager.** A liquid of extreme acidity, used as a preservative and a condiment, made by the fermentation of diluted wine, beer, or cider.

vinegar eel, n. Minute worm found in vinegar and in sour or fermenting vegetable substances.

vinegar plant, n. Microscopic fungus which produces vinegar by causing fermentation of wine &c.

vinegar tree, n. Kind of sumach the acid berries of which are sometimes used to flavour vinegar.

vinegary, adj. [1. vínegari; 2. vínigəri]. **vinegar** & **-y.** **1. a** Saturated with, tasting of, vinegar; **b** very sour, or acid. **2.** (fig.) Expressing ill-temper, bitterness, malignity &c.: *a vinegary smile.*

vine maple, n. Kind of American maple with recumbent stems which strike root and form a dense thicket.

vinery, n. [1. víneri; 2. váinəri]. **vine** & **-ry.** Heated glass-house in which grapes are grown.

vineyard, n. [1. vínyerd; 2. vínjəd]. **vine** & **yard.** An enclosed piece of ground in which grape-vines are grown.

vingt-et-un, n. [1. vánt ā ē; 2. vǣteǒ]. Fr., 'twenty-one'. Card game in which each player attempts to obtain from the dealer cards showing a total of 21 pips and no more.

vinic, adj. [1. vínik; 2. váinik]. Lat. *vīnum*, 'wine', see **vine,** & **-ic.** Pertaining to, occurring in, wine.

vinicultural, adj. [1. vìnikúlchural; 2. vìnikáltʃərəl]. **viniculture** & **-al.** Pertaining to viniculture.

viniculturalist, n. [1. vìnikúlchuralist; 2. vìnikáltʃərəlist]. Prec. & **-ist.** Person who engages in viniculture.

viniculture, n. [1. vínikulchur; 2. vínikaltʃə]. **vine-**, fr. Lat. *vīnum*, see **vine,** & **culture.** The cultivation of the vine; viticulture.

viniferous, adj. [1. viníferus; 2. vainífərəs]. Lat. *vīnum*, 'wine', see **vine,** & **-ferous.** Producing wine.

vinification, n. [1. vìnifikā́shun; 2. vìnifikéiʃən]. **vini-** as in prec. words, & **-fication.** Process whereby grape or other fruit juice becomes alcoholic by fermentation.

vinificator, n. [1. vínifikàtor; 2. vínifikèitə]. See prec. & **-or.** Apparatus for collecting alcoholic vapours in wine making.

vin ordinaire, n. [1. ván ordinā́r; 2. vǣn ɔ̄dinɛ́ə]. Fr., 'common wine'. The cheap wine most abundantly produced in a given district in France; commonly mixed with water.

vinosity, n. [1. vīnósiti; 2. vainɔ́siti]. Lat. *vīnōsitāt-(em)*, see **vinous** & **-ity.** Quality of being vinous.

vinous, adj. [1. vínus; 2. váinəs]. Lat. *vīnōsus*, 'full of, drunk with, wine; tasting of wine', fr. *vinum*, 'wine', see **vine,** & **-ous.** **1.** Connected with wine; **a** having the properties, taste, smell, of wine; **b** wine-coloured. **2. a** Inspired by wine: *vinous mirth*; **b** affected by wine: *in a somewhat vinous condition.*

vintage, n. [1. víntij; 2. víntidž]. M.E. *vindage, vendage*, fr. O. Fr. *vendenge*, cp. Mod. Fr. *vendange*, 'the gathering of grapes', fr. Lat. *vīndēmia*, 'grape-gathering', fr. *vinum*, 'wine', see **vine,** & an abstract suff. formed fr. *dēmere*, 'to take away', formed fr. *dē*, 'away, from', see **de-**, & *emere*, 'to take, receive'; later, 'to purchase', see second element in **exempt, redeem,** & **pre-emption**; the Mod. Engl. word has been influenced in form by association w. **vintner.** **1. a** Act of gathering and collecting grapes from the vines for wine-making; **b** the period in a season during which this takes place. **2.** The yield of wine grapes in a given year: *a poor, an abundant, vintage this year*; *the great vintages of the seventies.* **3.** Vintage wine: *he brought out his rare old vintages.*

vintager, n. [1. víntijer; 2. víntidžə]. Prec. & **-er.** Grape-gatherer.

vintage wine, n. That made from the vintage of a specially good year, carefully set apart as the wine of that particular year.

vintner, n. [1. víntner; 2. víntnə]. M.E. *viniter, vintener*, fr. O. Fr. *vinetier*, fr. *vinet*, dimin. of *vin*, 'wine', fr. Lat. *vīnum*, see **vine,** & **-er.** **1.** A wholesale seller of wine; a wine merchant. **2.** *The Vintners, Vintners' Company*, one of the great, ancient City livery companies of London.

vinum, n. [1. vínum; 2. váinəm]. Lat., 'wine', see **vine.** (pharm.) Medicated wine; medicinal substance dissolved in wine.

viny, adj. [1. víni; 2. váini]. **vine** & **-y.** Pertaining to, resembling, abounding in, vines.

viol, n. [1. víol; 2. váiəl]. M.E., fr. Fr. *viole*, fr. Ital. or Span. *viola*, or Provenç. *viula.* Origin uncertain; the Provenç. may be fr. an earlier **viudla*, w. metathesis, fr. **vidula*, fr. L. Lat. *vitula*, 'a viol', see **fiddle,** but this is very doubtful. Musical instrument of the fiddle family; the size and the number of strings vary; varieties are *bass-viol*, or double bass; *viol da braccio*; see also next word.

viola (I.), n. [1. víola, vióla; 2. váiələ, vióulə]. Ital. See prec. Specif., the *viol(a) da braccio*, or tenor violin, larger than the ordinary violin, and smaller than the 'cello; played held in the left hand; its strings are tuned c g d a; the strings are thicker than those of a violin, and the tone deeper; *viola da gamba*, a larger type, held between the legs, resembling the 'cello.

viola (II.), n. [1. víola; 2. váiələ]. Lat., according to Walde, a dimin. of **via-*, borrowed fr. Gk. *ion*, earlier **wion-*; perh. related to the base in Gk. *itus*, 'edge or rim', wh. is prob. cogn. w. Lat. *viēre*, to bend, twist', see **viti-** & **vine,** the viola or violet being used in weaving wreaths and crowns. Genus of flowering plants, of the family *Violaceae*, including the pansy; the flowers are predominatingly blue, purple, white, and yellow, in various shades.

violable, adj. [1. víolabl; 2. váiələbl]. See **violate** & **-able.** Capable of being violated.

Violaceae, n. pl. [1. vīolā́siē; 2. vàiouléisi-ī]. See **viola (II.)** & **-aceae.** (bot.) Large family of flowering plants including violet and viola.

violaceous, adj. [1. vīolā́shus; 2. vàiouléiʃəs]. See prec. & **-aceous.** **a** (bot.) Belonging to the family Violaceae; **b** having the colour of violets, of a blue purple.

violate, vb. trans. [1. víolāt; 2. váiəleit], fr. Lat. *violāt-(um)*, P.P. type of *violāre*, 'to treat with violence; to injure, dishonour', formed fr. *viol-*, as in Lat. *violent-(em)*, see **violent,** wh. is an expansion of *vīs*, 'strength, force', see **vis.** **1.** (obs. or archaic) To treat with violence, mishandle, abuse. **2.** To desecrate, profane, treat with indignity (that which is sacred): *to violate a tomb, a shrine, a church* &c. **3. a** To infringe, break, disregard, act in contradiction to (*a promise, oath, treaty* &c.); **b** to touch, seize, possess, wrongfully: '*to violate The sacred fruit forbidden*' (Milton, 'P. L.', ix. 903-4). **4.** To have carnal knowledge of, possess, (a woman) by force; to rape, to ravish.

violation, n. [1. vìolā́shun; 2. vàiəléiʃən]. Lat. *violātiōn-(em)*, see prec. & **-ion.** Act of violating; state of being violated (in various senses); **a** desecration; **b** infringement, breaking (of an oath &c.); **c** interruption of, breaking into (a sleep, privacy &c.); **d** rape.

violence, n. [1. víolens; 2. váiələns]. Fr., fr. Lat. *violentia*, see **violent** & **-ce.** **1. a** Energetic, forcible action; effort vigorously exerted; impetuosity, vehemence: *to attack an enemy with violence*; **b** powerful, impetuous, tumultuous movement: *the violence of the wind and waves*; also **c** of non-material effort or vigour: *violence of invective, of a person's passions, emotions* &c. **2.** Force, strength, effort, exerted with undue, unnecessary, or unlawful vehemence and rigour; roughness; turbulence; (in material and non-material sense) *to handle a prisoner, a patient, with violence*; *the mob behaved with great violence*; *crimes of violence*; *the speech was uncompromising, but free from violence.* **3.** Injury, insult, profanation offered to what is sacred: *you have done violence to my deepest convictions*; *to do violence to the holy things of God.* **4.** Specif., rape.

violent, adj. [1. víolent; 2. váiələnt]. Fr., fr. Lat. *violent-(em)*, see **violate.** **1.** Characterized by very forcible, vehement, rapid, often sudden, movement; boisterous, tumultuous, impetuous: *a violent storm, wind, earthquake.* **2. a** Requiring, exhibiting, a powerful voluntary exertion of muscular strength: *violent efforts, exertion, struggle to escape*; *a violent blow*; **b** showing results of, caused by, some powerful stimulus independent of the will; severe, intense: *a violent cough, spasm* &c. **3.** Due to a powerful external physical cause; caused by violence; unnatural: *a violent death.* **4.** Characterized by, arising from, violence of the emotions and passions: *a violent rage, a violent speech* &c. **5.** (as intens.) **a** Very great, of intense severity: *a violent toothache*; *a violent attack of the gout*; **b** exaggerated, extreme: *a violent contrast of colour.* Phr. (law) *a violent presumption*, one based on evidence that is practically conclusive.

violescent, adj. [1. vìolésent; 2. vàiəlésənt]. **viola** & **-escent.** Tending towards the colour of violets.

violet (I.), n. [1. víolet; 2. váiəlit]. Fr. *violette*, see **viola (I.)** & **-et(te).** **1.** Flower or plant of the viola species; specif., a common sort, wild or cultivated, with strongly scented flowers, purple, mauve, or white, also a rather similar flower found in woods &c. without a scent. **2.** The colour resembling that of violets, a bluish-purple, found at the higher end of the spectrum.

violet (II.), adj., fr. prec. Having the colour of violets; bluish-purple.

violet-powder, n. Toilet-powder scented with the perfume of violets.

violet-root, n. Trade name for orris-root.

violin, n. [1. violín; 2. vàiəlín]. Ital. *violino*, dimin. of **viola** (I.). A fiddle; smaller instrument of the viola family, having a treble tone and four strings, g, d, a, e, held in left hand and supported under the chin, the notes being formed by the fingers of left hand upon the strings, which are set in vibration with a bow.

violinist, n. [1. violínist; 2. vàiəlínist]. Prec. & **-ist.** A player of the violin.

violist, n. [1. víolist; 2. váiəlist]. **viol** or **viola (I.)** & **-ist.** Player of the viol or viola.

violoncellist, n. [1. vēolonchélist; 2. vìələntʃélist]. Next word & **-ist.** Player of the violoncello.

violoncello, n. [1. vēolonchélō; 2. vìələntʃélou]. Ital., dimin. of *violone*, 'a large viola'; see **viola (I.).** A bass viol; stringed instrument similar in shape to a viola and a violin, but much larger than the former; played by being held between the knees and fingered like a violin. The strings are very thick and have a bass tone.

violone, n. [1. vēōlṓnā; 2. vìoulóunei]. Ital., see **violoncello.** **1.** The largest instrument of the viola family; the contra-bass, or double bass. **2.** An organ stop with similar quality of tone.

viper, n. [1. vīper; 2. váipə]. Fr. *vipère*, fr. Lat. *vīpera*; fr. base **wei-p-*, **wei-b-*, 'to move rapidly, twist, coil', see discussion under **vibrate** & **vine**; the type **woip-* occurs in Goth. *(bi)-waibjan*, 'to weave round, wind about'. **1.** Any of several venomous snakes, of which the adder is the only one found in Britain. Phr. *to cherish a viper in one's bosom*, to show kindness to one who proves an unworthy and ungrateful traitor. **2.** A malignant, ungrateful, treacherous person.

viperiform, adj. [1. vīperiform; 2. váipərifōm]. Prec. & **-form**. Shaped like, resembling, a viper.

viperine, adj. [1. vīperin; 2. váipərin]. **viper** & **-ine**. Pertaining to, resembling, of the nature of, a viper.

viperish, adj. [1. vīperish; 2. váipəriʃ]. **viper** & **-ish**. Like a viper in character; malignant, treacherous.

viperous, adj. [1. vīperus; 2. váipərəs]. **viper** & **-ous**. Viperish.

viperously, adv. Prec. & **-ly**. In a viperous way.

viperousness, n. See prec. & **-ness**. Quality of being viperous; malignity, spite, treachery.

virago, n. [1. virágō; 2. viréigou]. Lat., 'a man-like, vigorous maiden; a female warrior', fr. *vir*, 'a man', see **virile**. A violent, brawling female; a loud-voiced, ill-tempered, scolding woman; a vixen, termagant, shrew.

virelai, n. [1. vírelā; 2. vírəlei]. O. Fr. *vireli*, perh. orig. a meaningless refrain, later *-lai*, through association w. **lay (I.)**. One of several kinds of Old French poems, having two rhymes and a refrain, or in stanza form, the stanzas being interlocked by recurrent rhymes.

virescence, n. [1. virésens; 2. virésəns]. **virescent** & **-ce**. **a** Process of becoming, state of being, green; greenness; **b** specif. (bot.) abnormal greenness in petals of flowers usually white or coloured.

virescent, adj. [1. virésent; 2. virésənt]. Lat. *virescent-(em)*, Pres. Part. of *virescere*, 'to grow green', freq. of *virēre*, 'to be green, to be fresh and vigorous; to flourish', cp. *viridis*, 'green'; prob. related to *vīvere*, 'to live'; see **viridity** & words there referred to. Becoming, turning, green; greenish.

virgate (I.), adj. [1. vĕrgāt; 2. vágeit]. Lat. *virgātus*, 'made of twigs or osiers', fr. *virga*, 'twig, sprout, switch, rod'; this is for earlier **vizgā-*, the basal meaning of wh. seems to be 'a pliant shoot or twig'; cogn. w. Scrt. *vēškáś*, 'a noose'; O.H.G. *wisk*, 'a whisk, switch', see **whist (II.)**, w. wh. cp. O.E. *wioxian*, fr. **wiscian*, 'to clean (a house &c.)', lit. 'to sweep it with a whisk or besom of twigs', for suff. see **-ate**. (bot.) Rod- or wand-shaped.

virgate (II.), n. L. Lat. *virgāta, virgāta terrae*, a land measure; cp. **rod** in sense of a measure. Same word as prec. Old English measure of land equal to a quarter of an acre.

Virgilian, adj. [1. vĕrjilian; 2. vǽdžiliən], fr. name of Virgil, Latin poet, & **-an**. Connected with, in the style of, Virgil.

virgin (I.), n. [1. vĕrjin; 2. vǽdžin]. M.E., fr. O. Fr. *virgine*, fr. Lat. *virgin-(em)*, 'a virgin'; stem of **Virgo**. **1. a** A woman who has had no carnal knowledge of a man; **b** a member of a female religious or other order bound by vows of chastity. **2. a** *The Virgin*, the Mother of Christ, the Virgin Mary; **b** *a Virgin*, picture or statue of the Virgin Mary. **3.** (more rarely) A man who has had no carnal knowledge of women. **4.** Female insect that produces eggs without impregnation. **5.** The sign of the zodiac, *Virgo*.

virgin (II.), adj., fr. prec. **1.** Being a virgin, chaste: '*For I was ever virgin save for thee*' (Tennyson). Phr. *the Virgin Queen*, Queen Elizabeth. **2.** Characteristic of, befitting, a virgin; chaste, modest: *virgin blushes*; *virgin fancies*. **3.** Untouched, untrampled, undefiled, unsullied: *virgin snow*. **4.** Undisturbed, unapproached; unmixed; never yet used; never before cultivated; in various Phrs.: *virgin forest*, from which no timber has been cut; *virgin gold*, pure, unalloyed; *virgin honey*, that which flows from an unopened comb, without pressure; *virgin oil*, that produced from the first, light pressure of olives; *virgin parchment*, that made from the skins of new-born lambs; *a virgin peak*, one which has never yet been scaled; *virgin soil*, (i.) land which has never before been cultivated; (ii.) (fig.) said of a mind which is unsophisticated and untouched by prejudice, or which is new to a particular range of ideas.

virginal (I.), adj. [1. vĕrjinal; 2. vǽdžinəl]. Fr. *virginal*, fr. Lat. *virginālis*, see **virgin (I.)** & **-al**. Belonging to, befitting, becoming in, a virgin; unsullied, pure, innocent: *virginal bloom, modesty* &c.; *virginal generation*, parthenogenesis; *virginal membrane*, the hymen.

virginal (II.), n., fr. prec.; prob. so called fr. being commonly played by young men & girls. A kind of spinet, with one string to a note, square and without legs, popular in the 16th and 17th centuries; (also in pl.) *the virginals*.

virginhood, n. [1. vĕrjinhood; 2. vǽdžinhud]. **virgin** & **-hood**. State of being a virgin.

Virginia, n. [1. vĕrjínia; 2. vǽdžíniə]. One of the States of N. America; named after the *Virgin Queen* (Elizabeth). *Virginia creeper*, Ampelopsis, ornamental rambling and climbing plant with large leaves, which turn red in autumn, grown on the walls of buildings; *Virginia tobacco*, also called simply *Virginia*, tobacco grown in Virginia and other Southern States of U.S.A.

Virginian, adj. & n. [1. vĕrjínian; 2. vǽdžíniən]. Prec. & **-an**. **a** adj. Belonging to, coming from, the State of Virginia; **b** n., a native of Virginia.

virginity, n. [1. vĕrjíniti; 2. vǽdžíniti]. M.E., fr. Fr. *virginité*, fr. Lat. *virginitāt-(em)*, see **virgin** & **-ity**. State, quality, of being a virgin.

virgo, n. [1. vĕrgō; 2. vágou]. Lat., 'virgin'; etymol. doubtful, but most prob. connected w. Lat. *virga*, 'young, pliant shoot, twig', see **virgate (I.)**; cp. *young sprig*, for a youth. **1.** (cap.) The constellation, known also as *the Virgin*, the sixth sign of the zodiac. **2.** *Virgo intacta*, Lat., 'intact virgin', a woman or girl who is a complete virgin, never approached by a man.

virgulate, adj. [1. vĕrgūlāt; 2. vágjuleit]. Lat. *virgula*, dimin. of *virga*, 'a rod' &c., see **virgate**, & **-ate**. Rod-shaped.

virgule, n. [1. vĕrgūl; 2. vágjūl]. Fr., fr. Lat. *virgula*, see prec. A comma in punctuation.

viridescence, n. [1. viridésens; 2. viridésəns]. Next word & **-ce**. **1.** Greenness, verdancy, verdure; colour of grass or of young foliage. **2.** Freshness, vigour, youthful vitality.

viridescent, adj. [1. viridésent; 2. viridésənt]. Lat. *viridescent-(em)*, Pres. Part. of *viridescere*, 'to grow green', formed fr. *viridis*, 'green', see **viridity**, & freq. suff. See **-esce**. Greenish, verging on green in colour.

viridity, n. [1. viríditi; 2. viríditi]. Lat. *viriditāt-(em)*, fr. *viridis*, 'green', & **-ity**; *viridis* for **gʷir-* is connected w. Lat. *virēre*, 'to be green, to bloom, to flourish', see **virescent**; cp. the cognates, Gk. *dierós*, fr. **gʷieros*, 'moist, fresh, juicy; fresh, active'; Scrt. *jirāś*, 'lively, active, stirring', also for **gʷīr-*, & O. Slav. *žirŭ*, fr. *gʷiru-*, 'pasture'. The underlying base is **gʷī-*, 'to live, be lively' &c., whence Lat. *vivere*, 'to live', see **vivacious**, & *vīta*, 'life', see **vital**; cp. also **verdant, verdure, vert (I.)**. **a** Greenness, esp. of grass or young foliage; **b** mental or bodily freshness, liveliness, springiness: *to show a healthy viridity in old age*.

virile, adj. [1. víril; 2. virail], more rarely [1. vīrīl; 2. váiərail]. Lat. *virīlis*, 'belonging to a man, male, masculine; manly, firm, vigorous, spirited', fr. *vir*, 'a male person, a man'; cogn. w. Goth. *wair*, 'man'; O.H.G., O.S., & O.E. *wer*, see first element in **werewolf**; Scrt. *vīraś*, 'man, hero'; Lith. *výras*, 'man'. The word is ultimately fr. the base in Lat. *vīs*, 'strength, vigour', for *vīr-*, see **vis**; cp. also **virtue**. **1.** Having the physical attributes and qualities of fully grown, mature man; specif., capable of procreation, not impotent. **2.** Having the characteristics of a man in habits, mind, character; male, masculine, manly; contrasted with *womanly, feminine*: *virile strength, courage, voice, glance*; *a virile intelligence*. **3.** Hence, strong, vigorous, forceful, forcible, spirited, sturdy, robust: *a virile government*; *a virile mind*; *a virile literary style*.

virilescence, n. [1. virilésens; 2. virilésəns]. Next word & **-ce**. The acquiring of male characters by a female animal when old or sterile.

virilescent, adj. [1. virilésent; 2. virilésənt]. Lat. *viril-*, see **virile**, & inchoative suff., see **-esce**. Tending to acquire male characters; of female animals in old age and sterility.

virility, n. [1. viríliti; 2. viríliti]. Lat. *virīlitāt-(em)*. See **virile** & **-ity**. Quality of being virile; **a** potency, power of procreation; **b** masculinity of character &c., manliness; **c** vigour, force, robustness: *virility of style*.

virose, adj. [1. vīrōs; 2. váiərous]. Lat. *vīrōsus*, 'poisonous', fr. *vīrus*, 'poison', see **virus**, & **-ose**. Poisonous; having a bad smell, fetid.

virous, adj. [1. vīrus; 2. váiərəs]. Prec. w. suff. **-ous**. Virose.

virtu, n. [1. vertōō; 2. vǽtū]. Ital. *virtù*, 'excellence', see **virtue**. **1.** Esp. in Phr. *object, article, of virtu*, object &c. possessing qualities of artistic merit, and value, of rarity and exquisite workmanship. **2.** Love for, knowledge of, fine art and craftsmanship; fondness for antiquities and curios.

virtual, adj. [1. vĕrchooal, vĕrtūal; 2. vǽtʃuəl, vǽtjuəl]. Fr. *virtuel*; see **virtue** & **-al**. Being in effect and essence, though not in name, that specified; being for all practical purposes though not defined as such: *the Prime Minister is the virtual ruler of the country*.

virtuality, n. [1. vĕrchooáliti, vĕrtūáliti; 2. vǽtʃuǽliti, vǽtjuǽliti]. Prec. & **-ity**. State, quality, of being virtual.

virtually, adv. [1. vĕrchooali; 2. vǽtʃuəli]. **virtual** & **-ly**. In point of fact, to all intents and purposes: *the dialect of the City of London in the 12th and 13th centuries was virtually the same as that of Essex*.

virtue, n. [1. vĕrchōō; 2. vǽtʃu, -ū]. M.E., fr. O. Fr. *vertú*, Lat. *virtūt-(em)*, stem of *virtus*, 'manliness, manhood; excellence, virtue, merit; moral perfection, virtue; courage, valour; value', fr. *vir*, 'a man', see **virile**. **1.** Positive, active, quality or property; capacity to affect a definite, specific result; potency: '*When that Aprille with his shoures sote . . . had . . . bathéd every veyne in swich licóur, Of which vertú engendred is the flour*' (Chaucer, Prol. of 'C. T.', 1-4); *Jesus perceived that virtue had gone out of Him when a woman touched Him in the crowd*; *every quack extols the virtue of the nostrums which he sells*. Phrs. *by virtue of*, by means of, through the instrumentality of; *in virtue of*, on the strength of, on the ground of: *promoted in virtue of his high descent, rather than of his abilities*. **2.** Good quality, merit, value: *a place which lacks the virtue of beauty, but has at least that of being bracing*. **3. a** Moral excellence; the practice of goodness; integrity, uprightness of character, honourable conduct, rectitude: *we have all been taught to love virtue, but we too often forget it in our conduct*; **b** some specific moral excellence: *humility is a virtue difficult to attain to*. Phrs. *the cardinal virtues*, prudence, fortitude, temperance, justice; *theological, Christian, virtues*, faith, hope, charity; *to make a virtue of necessity*, affect to do from a sense of duty that which one is compelled to do. **4.** Chastity, esp. in a woman: *it is hard for a poor, unprotected girl to preserve her virtue in a dissolute city*. Phr. *a lady of easy virtue*, one who is unchaste. **5.** One of the orders of celestial beings: '*Thrones, dominations, princedoms, virtues, powers*' (Milton, 'P. L.', v. 601).

virtuosity, n. [1. vĕrtūósiti; 2. vʌtjuɔ́siti]. **virtuoso** & **-ity**. **1.** Quality, state, of being a virtuoso. **2.** High degree of technical skill and dexterity in one of the fine arts, esp. in music. **3.** Fondness for, knowledge of, articles of virtu.

virtuoso, n. [1. vĕrtūósō, vĕrtōō-; 2. vʌtju-óusou, virtū-], pl. **virtuosos**, **virtuosi** [1. vĕrtōōósē; 2. virtūóusī]. Ital., fr. Lat. *virtuōsus*, see **virtuous**. **1.** A person with a high degree of technical skill as a performer in one of the fine arts, esp. in music. **2.** Person with an intimate knowledge of curios, antiques &c.

virtuous, adj. [1. vĕrchoous; 2. vʌtʃuəs]. Lat. *virtuōsus*, see **virtue** & **-ous**. **1.** Having, practising, moral virtue; morally good; honourable. **2.** Specif. (of women) chaste.

virtuously, adv. Prec. & **-ly**. In a virtuous manner.

virtuousness, n. See prec. & **-ness**. Quality of being virtuous; the practice of virtue.

virulence, -cy, n. [1. vírūlens(i); 2. vírju-ləns(i)]. Next word & **-ce** or **-cy**. Quality, state, of being virulent (in material and non-material senses).

virulent, adj. [1. vírūlent; 2. vírjulənt]. Fr., fr. Lat. *virulentus*, 'poisonous', see **virus**. **1.** Poisonous, venomous; deadly, noxious, extremely severe: *a virulent disease*; *measles of the most virulent kind*. **2.** Malignant, bitter, spiteful: *virulent animosity, abuse* &c.

virulently, adv. Prec. & **-ly**. In a virulent manner, to a virulent degree; with virulence.

virus, n. [1. vírus; 2. váiərəs]. Lat., 'a slimy liquid, slime; a poisonous liquid, poison; pungency'; for *vīzus, cogn. w. Gk. *iós*, 'poison', fr. *wisos; Scrt. *viśím*, 'poison'; connected w. Scrt. *veśati*, 'melts, liquefies'; also w. Lat. *viscum*, 'mistletoe', lit. 'the sticky berry', see **viscum**. **1.** (med.) The active organic element or poison which infects with and produces contagious disease: *the virus of scarlet fever, of rabies, anthrax* &c. **2.** Any influence which causes moral corruption, which affects adversely the mind or the spirit: *the virus of revolution, of sedition, heresy* &c.

vis, n. [1. vis; 2. vis]. Lat. *vīs*, pl. *vīres*, 'physical or mental strength; force, vigour, power, energy; hostile force, strength, violence'; cogn. w. Gk. *ís* for *wís, 'strength, force, nerve, thew, sinew'; Scrt. *váyaś*, 'vital force'; connected w. Lat. *vir*, 'man', see **virile**. Used in various Phrs.: *vis animi*, 'force of soul', courage; *vis inertiae*, 'force of inertia', tendency of bodies to remain at rest if resting, or to move uniformly in a straight line if moving; *vis medicātrix nātūrae*, 'healing power of nature', natural power of recovery, tendency to throw off disease; *vis mortua*, 'dead force', tendency towards motion; *vis mōtīva*, power of producing mechanical effect; *vis vīva*, 'living force', measure of a body's mass multiplied by the measure of its velocity. In plural, see **ultra vires**.

visa, n. & vb. [1. vēza; 2. vízə]. See **visé**.

visage, n. [1. vízij; 2. vízidž]. Fr., fr. O. Fr. *vis*, 'face', cp. **vis-à-vis**, fr. Lat. *vīsus*, 'sight, faculty of seeing; a look, a glance', see **vision (I.)**, & **-age**. The face, countenance, of a human being; rarely applied to the face of an animal.

visaged, adj. [1. vízijd; 2. vízidžd]. Prec. & **-ed**. Having a specified kind of visage; esp. in compounds: *dark-visaged, long-visaged* &c.

visard. See **visor**.

vis-à-vis, adv. & n. [1. víz a vē; 2. víz ə ví]. Fr., 'face to face', fr. *vis*, 'face', see **visage**. **1.** adv. Opposite: *he and I sat vis-à-vis at meals during the voyage.* **2.** n. **a** Person placed, sitting, opposite to another: *I haven't yet spoken to my vis-à-vis*; **b** a conveyance in which passengers sit facing one another; **c** S-shaped couch or seat in which persons sitting at the ends face each other.

viscacha, n. [1. viskácha; 2. viskǽtʃə]. Span., fr. S. American. S. American burrowing rodent, resembling, but larger than, a chinchilla, with valuable soft grey fur.

viscaria, n. [1. viskária; 2. viskéəriə], fr. Lat. *viscum*, 'mistletoe; birdlime', see **viscum** & **viscous**. Alpine plant with upright viscous stems.

viscera, n. pl. [1. vísera; 2. vísərə]. Lat., pl. of *viscus*, 'internal organs of an animal'; according to Walde, most prob. fr. base *wei- &c., 'to twist, wind round', as in Lat. *viēre*, 'to twist, twine' &c., see **vine** & **viti-**. The internal organs of the animal body, esp. the heart, lungs, bowels, liver &c.

visceral, adj. [1. víseral; 2. vísərəl]. Prec. & **-al**. Pertaining to, connected with, of the nature of, viscera.

viscerate, vb. trans. [1. víserāt; 2. vísəreit]. **viscera** & **-ate**. (rare) To eviscerate, remove the viscera from.

visceri-, viscero-, pref. Forms of **viscera** used in compounds: *visceri-pericardial*, of the body cavity of molluscs, which is divided into two parts, the upper containing the heart, the lower the other viscera; *viscero-motor*, conducting motor impulses to the viscera.

viscid, adj. [1. vísid; 2. vísid]. Lat. *viscidus*, 'sticky', fr. *viscum*, 'mistletoe, birdlime', see **viscum**. Glutinous, sticky; having a syrupy consistency.

viscidity, n. [1. visíditi; 2. visíditi]. Prec. & **-ity**. Stickiness, adhesiveness.

viscin, n. [1. vísin; 2. vísin]. See **viscum** & **-in**. Sticky substance occurring in the berries of the mistletoe.

viscose, n. [1. vískōs; 2. vískous]. See prec. & **-ose**. Form of cellulose used in artificial silk manufacture.

viscosity, n. [1. viskósiti; 2. viskɔ́siti]. **viscous** & **-ity**. Stickiness; property in viscous fluids whereby resistance is offered to rearrangement of the molecules.

viscount, n. [1. víkount; 2. váikaunt]. O. Fr. *viscomte*, see **vice (IV.)** & **count (III.)**. Male person holding the rank of nobility immediately below that of earl; often as second title of an earl, and used as courtesy title by his eldest son before he succeeds.

viscountess, n. [1. víkountes; 2. váikauntis]. Prec. & **-ess**. Wife of a viscount; courtesy title often borne by wife of an earl's eldest son; lady holding this rank in her own right.

viscountship, n. [1. víkountship; 2. váikaunt-ʃip]. See prec. & **-ship**. Viscounty.

viscount(c)y, n. [1. víkount(s)i; 2. váikaunt(s)i]. **viscount** & **-y**. Rank, status, of a viscount.

viscous, adj. [1. vískus; 2. vískəs]. Lat. *viscōsus*, 'sticky', fr. *viscum*, 'birdlime', see **viscum**, & **-ous**. Sticky, glutinous, adhesive; possessing viscosity.

viscum, n. [1. vískum; 2. vískəm]. Lat., 'mistletoe; birdlime'; cogn. w. Gk. *ixós* for *wiskos, 'mistletoe, birdlime'; O.H.G. w. dimin. suff. *wīhsela*, Mod. Germ. *weichsel*, 'wild cherry'; fr. the Gmc. word, w. different suff., comes O. Fr. *guisne* for *wisn-, Mod. Fr. *guigne*, 'wild cherry'; the *-n-* suff. occurs also in the O. Slav. cogn. *višnja*; cp. also O. Fr. *guis*, Mod. Fr. *gui*, 'mistletoe', fr. a Gmc. *wisk-. Walde suggests that the base is ultimately connected w. **virus**. **1.** The mistletoe, a parasitic plant bearing greenish-white berries filled with a sticky glutinous substance. **2.** Birdlime, often made from the berries of the mistletoe.

visé, n. & vb. trans. [1. vēzā; 2. vízei]. Fr., P.P. of *viser*, 'to inspect', formed fr. *vis*, 'a look, glance', see **vis-à-vis**. **1.** n. Also *visa*, official endorsement on a passport showing that it has been examined and authenticated. **2.** vb. To put a visé upon (a passport).

visibility, n. [1. vizibíliti; 2. vizibíliti]. **visible** & **-ity**. State, quality, of being visible; specif., state of the atmosphere and light in reference to the distance at which objects can be clearly seen.

visible, adj. [1. vízibl; 2. vízibl]. Fr., fr. Lat. *visibilis*, fr. *vīs-*, a form of base *vid- &c., 'to see', see **vision (I.)**, & **-ible**. **1.** To be seen; perceptible, apparent, to the eye; discoverable by the eye: *lights no longer visible*; *many stars are visible by the help of a telescope, but not to the naked eye*; *without visible means of support*; *the visible church*, the whole body of the faithful throughout the world; *visible horizon*, farthest distance that can be seen from a given spot; *visible speech*, a system of phonetic notation invented by Melville Bell (1819–1905), later known as the Organic Alphabet, by means of which each speech-sound is represented by a symbol indicating the actual positions of the vocal organs. **2.** (as n.) *The visible*, the material, visible world, contrasted with the invisible or spiritual world.

visibleness, n. Prec. & **-ness**. Visibility.

visibly, adv. See prec. & **-ly**. In a visible manner, to a visible extent; so as to be visible; perceptibly, appreciably: *visibly excited, moved*; *not visibly larger than it was an hour ago.*

vision (I.), n. [1. vízhun; 2. vížən]. Lat. *vīsiōn-(em)*, 'act or sense of seeing, sight; apparition, appearance; a notion'; fr. *vīs-*, type seen in P.P. of *vidēre*, 'to see', see also **vide**; *vīs- arises fr. *vīd-to, whence *vīsso-, whence *vīs-, w. simplification of *-ss-* after a long vowel. The Aryan base is *weid-, *woid-, *wid-, 'to know, to see'; for other cognates see **-oid, idea, idol** (Gk.), & **wit (I.), wise (I.)** (Gmc.). **1. a** The sense by which light, colour, form, are perceived by the eye; power, faculty, of seeing; sight; **b** the act of sight, actual seeing. **2. a** Faculty of forming mental images, pictures of objects and conditions, esp. the power of seeing things in the mind as they really are; imagination, insight, intuition: *vision is as indispensable to a statesman as to a poet*; **b** specific mental picture evoked by the power of the prophetic imagination; a poet's dream: '*Saw the vision of the world, and all the wonder that would be*' (Tennyson, 'Locksley Hall'); '*The poet's vision of eternal fame*' (Pope, 'Dunciad', iii. 12). **3. a** Something seen; a sight, a spectacle, a view: *the bride was a lovely vision*; *I had only a momentary vision of the sea*; **b** something seen or believed to be seen under conditions which are abnormal; a sight prophetically revealed to the bodily eyes by supernatural means; an appearance, supposed to be more substantial than a dream, of objects, scenes, or events which, though real, are not actually present in a material state to the eye of the beholder; an apparition, a phantasm.

vision (II.), vb. trans., fr. prec. (very rare) To perceive in the form of a vision.

visional, adj. [1. vízhunal; 2. vížənəl]. **vision (I.)** & **-al**. Pertaining to, of the nature of, a vision.

visionary (I.), adj. [1. vízhunari; 2. vížənəri]. **vision (I.)** & **-ary**. **1.** Pertaining to, of the nature of, a vision; seen in a vision: *a visionary form beckoned me to follow.* **2.** Existing only in visions; having no reality or substance; unsubstantial, imaginary, unreal, chimerical; impossible of realization; impracticable: *madmen often live amid visionary splendours*; *visionary schemes, projects* &c. **3.** (of persons) Given to seeing visions; **a** dreamy, imaginative, idealistic; **b** given to forming impracticable, unworkable schemes; unpractical; flighty, viewy.

visionary (II.), n., fr. prec. **1.** One who sees visions; a dreamer, an idealist; one having prophetic vision; a mystic. **2.** One who dreams of, hopes for, impossible things; one who lives in an unreal world of his own and forms impracticable, unsubstantial projects, and plans that are impossible to carry out.

visit (I.), vb. trans. & intrans. [1. vízit; 2. vízit]. Fr. *visiter*, fr. Lat. *vīsitāre*, 'to see frequently; to go to see'; freq. of *vīsāre*, 'to look at often or attentively; to behold, survey; to go to see, visit'; formed fr. *vīs-*, as in *vīsum*, P.P. of *vidēre*, 'to see', see **vide**, & **vision (I.)**. **A.** trans. **1.** To go to see, call upon, (a person) as a social duty, out of friendliness, friendship, or as an act of kindness: *to visit a new neighbour, an old friend, a sick person.* **2.** To go to see, examine, inspect, as a matter of professional duty, or as an official: *a doctor visits his patients; a bishop cannot visit every parish in his diocese every year.* **3.** a To go to (a place): *to visit foreign countries, a picture gallery* &c.; b to be habitually or constantly at; to frequent: *to visit public-houses and low haunts.* **4.** To come to or upon with some definite object, or with some definite result; a (archaic) to come upon with blessing: '*He hath visited and redeemed his people*'; b to attack: *plague and famine often visit India.* **B.** intrans. To make, pay, visits: *to visit in the country; to visit at strange houses.*

visit (II.), n. Fr. *visite*, fr. prec. **1.** Act of visiting; a a journey to the house of another in order to see and converse with him; a friendly call; b a call made for professional, business, or official reasons: *my doctor charges half a guinea for each visit; a visit from a tax-collector, an inspector of drains, a policeman*; c journey to a specific object or place for the purpose of inspecting or becoming acquainted with it: *a visit to the Tower, to London* &c. **2.** A temporary sojourn or stay in a house, at a place, other than one's habitual place of residence: *I don't live here, I'm only on a visit; a brief visit to Ireland; to pay a round of visits in country houses.*

visitable, adj. [1. vízitabl; 2. vízitəbl]. **visit** (I.) & **-able.** **1.** To which a visit may be made; worth visiting: *hardly anything visitable in the place.* **2.** Desirable to visit; of such social standing as to warrant a visit: *a few visitable neighbours.*

visitant, adj. & n. [1. vízitant; 2. vízitənt]. Lat. *visitant-(em)*, Pres. Part. of *vīsitāre*, see **visit** (I.). **1.** adj. (rare) Visiting. **2.** n. a (poet. or rhet.) A passing visitor, a temporary guest; esp. an important, august, visitor: *a glorious visitant from some brighter sphere*; b specif., a migratory bird; c (cap.) a nun of the Order of Visitation in R.C. Church.

visitation, n. [1. vìzitáshun; 2. vìzitéiʃən]. Lat. *vīsitātiōn-(em)*, see **visit** (II.) & **-ation.** **1.** Act of visiting; state of being visited; a visit. **2.** Specif., an official, ceremonial, visit of a high official or dignitary for purposes of inspection, conference, giving of admonition and instruction &c.: *archdeacons hold periodical visitations in their archdeaconries; visitation of the sick*, (i.) visit of a clergyman to sick parishioners; (ii.) office for such occasions in Prayer Book. **3.** a Visit of a herald to inquire into the right to bear arms, or to hear claims for grants of arms, to persons within his province; b official document recording results of a herald's visitation. **4.** (colloq.) A protracted visit: *I fear we have paid you a regular visitation.* **5.** Special act (i.) of divine favour, or, (ii.) more commonly, of wrath; a calamity, an awe-inspiring event, thought of as directly retributive: *plague was formerly regarded as a visitation of God for the people's sins; the late gale was a disastrous visitation.* **6.** (zool.) An unusually large migration of birds or animals, or one taking place at an unusual season. **7.** (cap.) Festival commemorating the visit of St. Elizabeth to the B.V.M.

visitatorial, adj. [1. vìzitatórial; 2. vìzitətóriəl]. L.L. *visitātor*, 'visitor', & **-ial.** Pertaining to, connected with, an official visitor, superintendent &c., or his visitations: *visitatorial powers, functions* &c.; *Visitatorial Board*, (Oxford University) a permanent body having powers of supervision and control over the teachers and other officers of the University in the performance of their duties.

visiting, adj. [1. víziting; 2. vízitiŋ]. Pres. Part. of **visit** (I.). *Visiting card*, small strip of cardboard with name and address of caller engraved upon it, left at houses on the occasion of a visit. Phr. *on visiting terms*, having social relations sufficiently intimate for the exchange of visits.

visitor, n. [1. vízitor; 2. vízitə]. **visit** (I.) & **-or**, cp. Fr. *visiteur.* **1.** One who visits; a caller: *we had quite a number of visitors this afternoon.* **2.** Person making a temporary stay at a place, in a house, other than his own place of abode: *we had a succession of visitors all the summer; visitors' book*, one kept, according to law, in an hotel, in which the names and addresses of visitors are written; book kept in private house, in which guests inscribe their names and the dates of their arrival and departure. **3.** (usually cap.) Official specially appointed to make visits of inspection to a corporate body, institution &c. to hear statements of grievances, to give a ruling on the interpretation of statutes, and generally to act as superintendent and adviser.

visor, vizor, visard, vizard, n. [1. vízor(d); 2. váizə(d)]. M.E., fr. A.-Fr. *visere*, O. Fr. *visiere*, fr. O. Fr. *vis*, 'face', see **vis-à-vis.** **1.** Part of a helmet which could be raised or lowered to cover and protect the face. **2.** The peak of a cap.

vista, n. [1. vísta; 2. vístə]. Ital., 'sight, view', fem. of *visto*, P.P. of *vedere*, Lat. *vidēre*, see **view, vision** (I.), **vide.** **1.** A view, prospect, esp. one seen through a long narrow space enclosed on either side, as by rows of trees, sides of a mountain &c.; also the narrow space itself before it opens out. **2.** Mental view or prospect; long series of memories of past events and experiences &c. called up before the mind's eye; also a series of such mental pictures representing hopes and anticipations for the future: *to look back through the vistas of the past; I seem to see long vistas of future happiness.*

visual, adj. [1. vízhūal, vízūal; 2. vížjuəl, vizjuəl]. O. Fr., fr. Lat. *visuālis*, fr. *visus*, 'sight', see **vision** (I.), & **-al.** **1.** Connected, concerned, with the sense of sight: *visual images, sensations*; used in sight: *the visual nerve.* **2.** Perceived by the eye, visible: *the apparition was visual, not a product of the imagination.*

visuality, n. [1. vìzhūáliti, vìzūáliti; 2. vìžjuǽliti, vìzjuǽliti]. Prec. & **-ity.** Condition, quality, of being visual; visibility.

visualization, n. [1. vìzhū-, vìzūalīzáshun; 2. vìžju-, vìzjuəlaizéiʃən]. **visualize** & **-ation.** **1.** Act, process, power, of visualizing. **2.** Mental image created by visualizing; that which is visualized. **3.** Faculty of producing vivid mental images in others by artistic description.

visualize, vb. trans. & intrans. [1. vízhū-, vízūalīz; 2. vížju-, vízjuəlaiz]. **visual** & **-ize.** **1.** trans. To render visual; specif., to call up a clear image of in the mind, to see with the eye of the mind: *I find it difficult to visualize the garden as it will be after the alterations; if I shut my eyes I can visualize the scene and the actors, as I actually saw them.* **2.** intrans. To carry out the process, perform the act, of visualizing: *some people can recall a sound or a tune mentally, but are quite unable to visualize.*

visualizer, n. [1. vízhū- vízūalīzer; 2. vížju-, vízjuəlàizə]. Prec. & **-er.** Person who visualizes, one who is able to visualize; specif., one whose mental images are mainly visual.

visually, adv. [1. vízhūali, vízūali; 2. vížjuəli, vízjuəli]. **visual** & **-ly.** In a visual manner; so as to become visual.

vita glass, n. [1. víta glahs; 2. váitə glās]. Trade and proprietary name, fr. Lat. *vita*, 'life'; see next word. A special kind of glass, for windows &c., which does not exclude the health-giving ultra-violet rays of the sunlight.

vital, adj. [1. vítl; 2. váitl]. Lat. *vītālis*, 'belonging to life', fr. *vīta*, 'life', & **-al**; *vīta*, 'life, livelihood, way of life', is for **vīvita*, fr. Lat. base in *vivere*, 'to live, be alive; to lead a specified kind of life; to remain, endure'; the Aryan base is **gʷīw-*, **gʷei(w)-* &c., wh. has many derivatives in most Aryan languages; close cognates w. Lat. *vita*, fr. **gʷīwita*, are Gk. *biotēs*, 'life, means of life', *bioteia*, 'way of life, livelihood', for **gʷiwot-*, cp. *bios*, 'course of life', see **bio-**; O. Ir. *biad*, 'means of life'; *bethu*, 'life', fr. **gʷiwot-*; Goth. *qius*, 'living', see **quick** (I.); further cognates under this word & **bio-**; see also **zoo-.** **1.** Connected with, pertaining to, having to do with, essential to, arising from, animal life: *vital functions, power*; *vital part* (of the body); *vital movements; vital warmth; vital wound*, one in a vital part; mortal; *vital statistics*, those dealing with the duration of life, and conditions affecting this, in a given area. **2.** a Having life, living (rare or archaic in physical sense); b full of life, vitality, and spirit; lively, animated: *his style was always vital and interesting.* **3.** Essential to the existence of something, necessary, essential to some object or purpose; important, momentous: *vital to one's purpose, to a scheme; this paragraph is vital; of vital importance.*

vitalism, n. [1. vítalizm; 2. váitəlìzəm]. Prec. & **-ism.** Doctrine that organic life is the result of a principle outside of, and distinct from, the operation of physical forces; contrasted with *mechanism.*

vitalist, n. [1. vítalist; 2. váitəlist]. **vital** & **-ist.** Adherent of vitalism.

vitalistic, adj. [1. vìtalístik; 2. vàitəlístik]. Prec. & **-ic.** Pertaining to vitalism or to vitalists; of the nature of vitalism.

vitality, n. [1. vitáliti; 2. vaitǽliti]. Lat. *vītālitāt-(em).* See **vital** & **-ity.** **1.** Vital force, animal life; strength, bodily vigour; capacity to live: *vitality is greatly reduced in old age.* **2.** Vigour, liveliness, elasticity, of mind; spirit, animation; expression of this in literature and art. **3.** Capacity to last, quality of permanence, durability: *much of the poetry of every age is of merely transitory value and lacks vitality.*

vitalization, n. [1. vìtalīzáshun; 2. vàitəlaizéiʃən]. See next word & **-ation.** Act, process, of vitalizing; state of being vitalized.

vitalize, vb. trans. [1. vítalīz; 2. váitəlaiz]. **vital** & **-ize.** a To give, impart, vitality to, to make alive, endow with life: *good food vitalizes the blood*; b (more frequent in non-material sense) (i.) to give spirit, animation, to, make living: *to vitalize a dull subject of study*; (ii.) to revive, render active and vital: *to vitalize one's religion, the patriotic spirit* &c.

vitalizer, n. [1. vítalīzer; 2. váitəlàizə]. Prec. & **-er.** He who, that which, vitalizes.

vitals, n. pl. [1. vítlz; 2. váitlz]. **vital**, as n. a The vital organs; the parts of the body necessary to life and health, esp. the heart, lungs, liver, bowels &c.; b (fig.) that which is of the essence of anything; the inner kernel: *to tear the vitals out of a subject*, get at the real gist.

vitamin, n. [1. vítamin; 2. váitəmin]. Word coined fr. Lat. *vita*, 'life'. See **vital** & **amine.** Any one of various substances, the chemical nature of which is imperfectly known, present in the food, in its natural state, of man and animals, derived originally from plants, and essential to health and life, deficiency or lack of which causes such diseases as beri-beri, rickets, scurvy &c.; vitamins are classified as being soluble in fat or in water, and are divided into classes A, B, C &c.; they are found in butter-fat, cod-liver oil, green leaves, yeast, some fresh fruits &c.

vitel-. See **vitello-.**

vitellarian, adj. [1. vìtelárian; 2. vìteléəriən]. **vitellarium** & **-an.** Connected with the vitellarium.

vitellarium, n. [1. vìtelárium; 2. vìteléəriəm]. See **vitellus** & **-ary.** Part of the ovary in certain lowly organisms producing yolk-filled cells, distinct from the true eggs.

vitelligenous, adj. [1. vitelíjenus; 2. vìtelídžinəs]. See **vitellus** & **-genous.** Yolk-producing, of certain cells in the ovaries of insects.

vitellin, n. [1. vitélin; 2. vitélin]. **vitellus** & **-in.** A protein found in the yolk of an egg.

vitelline, adj. [1. vitélin; 2. vitélain]. **vitellus** & **-ine.** (embryology) Pertaining to the yolk of an egg.

vitello-, **vitel-**, pref. Forms of **vitellus** used in compounds.

vitellus, n. [1. vitélus; 2. vitéləs]. Lat., 'a little calf; the yolk of an egg', dimin. of *vitulus*, 'a calf'; see **vitular**. Yolk of an egg; (archaic) entire contents of an egg-shell.

viti-, pref. denoting connexion w. the vine, or w. vines; fr. Lat. *vītis*, 'grape-vine, vine branch'; cogn. w. O. Slav. *vitī*, 'something twisted'; O.H.G. *wīda*, 'willow', & O.E. *wiðig*, 'a willow; a band', see **withy**; fr. base seen in Lat. *viēre*, 'to twist, twine'. See **vine**.

vitiate, vb. trans. [1. víshiāt; 2. víʃieit], fr. Lat. *vitiāt-(um)*, P.P. of *vitiāre*, 'to make faulty, to mar; to taint, corrupt' &c., fr. *vitium*, 'defect, blemish, vice'. See **vice** (I.). **1.** To render faulty, to detract from, destroy force or merit of: *to vitiate an argument by exaggeration of statement.* **2.** To sully, make impure; to taint, contaminate, pollute: *gas may vitiate the air of a room.* **3.** To destroy validity of, render ineffective, to deprive of force as a legal instrument: *to vitiate a will, a contract* &c.

vitiated, adj. [1. víshiāted; 2. víʃieitid], fr. P.P. of prec. Made defective; contaminated, impure.

vitiation, n. [1. vìshiāshun; 2. viʃiéiʃən]. **vitiate** & **-ion**. Act or process of vitiating; state of being vitiated; **a** contamination, pollution; **b** invalidation.

viticultural, adj. [1. vìti-, vìtikúlchural; 2. vàiti-, vìtikáltʃərəl]. Next word & **-al**. Pertaining to the culture of the vine or to grape-growing.

viticulture, n. [1. víti-, vítikùlchur; 2. váiti-, vítikàltʃə]. **viti-** & **culture**. Cultivation of the vine; grape-growing.

viticulturist, n. [1. vìti-, vìtikúlchurist; 2. vàiti-, vìtikáltʃərist]. Prec. & **-ist**. A grape-grower.

vitiosity, n. [1. vìshiósiti; 2. viʃiɔ́siti]. Lat. *vitiōsitāt-(em)*, 'faultiness, corruption', fr. *vitiōsus*, see **vicious**, & **-ity**. Corruption, viciousness.

vitreo-, pref. Form of Lat. *vitreus*, 'glass, glassy', fr. *vitrum*, 'glass', used in compounds. The origin of this rather late word is doubtful; Walde suggests that it may be either a loan fr. Gmc. representing some such type as **hwītra*, comparative meaning 'whitish', see **white**, or may be orig. identical w. *vitium*, 'woad', on account of the blue colour of much early glass. See **woad**.

vitreous, adj. [1. vítreus; 2. vítriəs]. Lat. *vitreus*. See prec. & **-ous**. **1.** Resembling glass; transparent, glassy: *vitreous rocks*; *vitreous humour*, transparent, jelly-like substance which fills the hinder portion of the eye-ball. **2.** Pertaining to, made of, glass.

vitrescence, n. [1. vitrésens; 2. vitrésəns]. Next word & **-ce**. Tendency to become glass.

vitrescent, adj. [1. vitrésent; 2. vitrésənt]. Lat. *vitrum*, 'glass'. See **vitreo-** & **-escent**. Tending to become glass.

vitrescible, adj. [1. vitrésibl; 2. vitrésibl]. Fr., *vitresc-*, as in prec., & **-ible**. Capable of becoming glass or glassy.

vitri-, pref. Form of Lat. *vitrum*, 'glass', used in compounds. See **vitreo-**.

vitric, adj. [1. vítrik; 2. vítrik]. Lat. *vitrum*, 'glass'. See **vitreo-** & **-ic**. Having the character of glass; glass-like.

vitrics, n. pl. [1. vítriks; 2. vítriks]. See prec. Art of glass working and manufacture; study of this.

vitrifaction, n. [1. vìtrifákshun; 2. vìtrifǽkʃən]. **vitri-** & **-faction**. Vitrification.

vitrifacture, n. [1. vítrifàkchur; 2. vìtrifǽktʃə]. **vitri-** & **-facture**. Glassmaking; manufacture of glassware.

vitrifiability, n. [1. vìtrifìabíliti; 2. vìtrifàiəbíliti]. Next word & **-ity**. Capacity of being, liability to be, vitrified.

vitrifiable, adj. [1. vítrifìabl; 2. vítrifàiəbl]. **vitrify** & **-able**. Capable of being vitrified.

vitrification, n. [1. vitrifikáshun; 2. vìtrifikéiʃən]. **vitri-** & **-fication**. Act, process, of vitrifying; state of being vitrified.

vitriform, adj. [1. vítriform; 2. vítrifɔ̄m]. **vitri-** & **-form**. Having the appearance and consistency of glass; glass-like.

vitrify, vb. trans. & intrans. [1. vítrifī; 2. vítrifai]. **vitri-** & **-fy**. **1.** trans. To convert into glass; to cause to become vitriform, esp. by heat. **2.** intrans. To become converted into glass; to become vitriform.

vitriol, n. [1. vítriol; 2. vítriəl]. In M.E., fr. Fr.; fr. Lat. *vitreolus*, 'made of, resembling, glass', dimin. form of *vitreus*. See **vitreo-**. The name is due to the glassy lustre exhibited by some of the sulphuric acid salts. **1.** (chem.) A sulphate of any of various metals —copper, iron, zinc, known respectively as blue, green, and white vitriol; *oil of vitriol*, also merely *vitriol*, an oily, highly corrosive liquid distilled from blue vitriol; this substance is sometimes used by criminals, esp. women, to blind and disfigure the faces of those against whom they have a grudge: *to throw vitriol over, at.* **2.** Corrosive, biting, caustic mode of expression: *to put plenty of vitriol in a speech, a review.*

vitriolate, vb. trans. [1. vítriōlāt; 2. vítrioulеit]. Prec. & **-ate**. **a** To convert into vitriol; to subject to the effects of vitriol; **b** to throw vitriol at or over.

vitriolation, n. [1. vìtriōláshun; 2. vìtrioulèiʃən]. Prec. & **-ion**. Act, process, of vitriolating.

vitriolic, adj. [1. vìtriólik; 2. vìtriɔ́lik]. **vitriol** & **-ic**. **1.** Connected with, consisting of, resembling, vitriol. **2.** (fig.) Biting, corrosive; heated, fiery, vehement: *vitriolic temper*; *vitriolic invective, eloquence* &c.

vitriolizable, adj. [1. vítriolìzabl; 2. vítriəlàizəbl]. **vitriolize** & **-able**. Capable of being converted into vitriol.

vitriolization, n. [1. vìtriolīzáshun; 2. vìtriəlaizéiʃən]. **vitriolize** & **-ation**. Act, process, of vitriolizing; state of being vitriolized.

vitriolize, vb. trans. [1. vítriolīz; 2. vítriəlaiz]. **vitriol** & **-ize**. **a** To attack, injure (a person), by throwing vitriol at or over; also **b** to convert into vitriol.

Vitruvian, adj. [1. vitrōōvian; 2. vitrúviən], fr. name of Vitruvius Pollio, a Roman architect in the age of Augustus. Pertaining to, connected with, Vitruvius or his work. *Vitruvian scroll*, undulating decoration used in friezes.

vitta, n., pl. **vittae** [1. víta, -ē; 2. vítə, -ī]. Lat., 'a band, fillet, chaplet; a sacerdotal fillet'; perh. fr. **vītwa*, fr. base of *vīta*, 'life', see **vital**, w. *-wa* suff., doubling of *-t-* before *-w-*, & shortening of preceding vowel. (bot.) Oil-bearing tube in the fruit of certain umbelliferous plants.

vittate, adj. [1. vítāt; 2. víteit]. Prec. & **-ate**. Having vittae.

vitular, adj. [1. víchoolar; 2. vítʃulə], fr. Lat. *vitulus*, 'calf', & **-ar**. Orig. meaning of *vitulus* is 'a yearling animal'; cp. Lat. *vetus*, 'old, having lived, or lasted, many years', see **veteran**; cogn. w. Gk. *étos*, 'year', for **wetos*, whence Gk. *éteion*, 'yearling animal'; cp. w. different derivative suff. Scrt. *vatšáš*, 'yearling calf, lamb'; Goth. *wiþrus*, 'a lamb'; O.E. *weþer*, see **wether**; cp. further **veal**, **veterinary**. Pertaining to, connected with, a calf or calves; *vitular apoplexy*, that to which cows are liable when calving.

vitulary, adj. [1. víchoolari; 2. vítʃuləri]. Prec. & **-y**. Vitular.

vituline, adj. [1. víchoolīn; 2. vítʃulain]. Lat. *vitulīnus*, fr. *vitulus*, 'calf', see **vitular**, & **-ine**. Pertaining to a calf, or to veal.

vituperable, adj. [1. vitū́perabl; 2. vaitjū́pərəbl]. Lat. *vituperābilis*, 'blameworthy'. See next word & **able**. Deserving vituperation.

vituperate, vb. trans. [1. vitū́perāt; 2. vaitjū́pəreit]. Lat. *vituperāt-(um)*, P.P. of *vituperāre*, 'to censure, blame, disparage'; fr. Lat. *vitium*, 'fault, defect', see **vice** (I.), & *parāre*, 'to prepare, provide'. See **parade**, **pare**. To rate, scold, soundly; to abuse loudly and forcibly; to dress down, trounce.

vituperation, n. [1. vìtūperáshun; 2. vàitjūpəréiʃən]. Prec. & **-ion**. Act of vituperating; loud, vehement, abuse; verbal castigation.

vituperative, adj. [1. vitū́perativ; 2. vaitjū́pərətiv]. See prec. & **-ive**. **a** Uttering abuse; given to rating and scolding; **b** abusive, denunciatory: *a vituperative speech.*

viva (I.), interj. & n. [1. vēva; 2. vívə]. Ital., 'let him live, long live...' **1.** interj. Long (may he) live, uttered as a greeting, welcome &c. **2.** n. The cry *viva*; hence (*vivas*), shouts of greeting, applause &c.: *the hall resounded with the vivas of the crowd.*

viva (II.), n. & vb. trans. & intrans. [1. víva; 2. váivə]. Lat., for **viva voce**. **1.** n. Examination conducted viva voce. **2.** vb. **a** trans. To submit (person) to a viva; to examine (person) orally; **b** intrans., to conduct a viva voce examination.

vivace, adv. [1. viváhchā; 2. vivátʃe]. Ital., 'vivaciously'. See **vivacious**. (musical direction) Vivaciously, with spirit and liveliness.

vivacious, adj. [1. vīváshus; 2. vaivéiʃəs]. Lat. *vīvāci-*, stem of *vīvax*, 'tenacious of life; lively, vigorous', fr. *vīvere*, 'to live'. See **vital** & **vivid** & **-ous**. Full of life and spirit; lively, sprightly, animated, gay.

vivaciously, adv. Prec. & **-ly**. In a vivacious manner.

vivaciousness, n. See prec. & **-ness**. Quality of being vivacious.

vivacity, n. [1. vīvásiti; 2. vaivǽsiti]. Lat. *vīvācitāt-(em)*, 'tenacity of life'. See **vivacious** & **-ity**. Liveliness, sprightliness, gaiety, playfulness.

vivandière, n. [1. vēvandiár; 2. vīvãdiẽr]. L. Lat. *vivanda*, 'provisions', see **viand**, & *-ière*, Fr. fem. of **-ier**. Female who formerly accompanied a French army and sold provisions and liquor to the troops.

vivarium, n. [1. vīvárium; 2. vaivéəriəm]. Lat., 'enclosure in which game and fish are kept alive; a preserve'; fr. base *vīv-*, as in *vīvere*, 'to live', see **vital**; for suff. see **-ary**. An enclosure or preserve in which (terrestrial) animals live, as far as possible, under natural conditions.

viva voce, adv., adj., & n. [1. víva vósi; 2. váivə vóusi]. Lat., 'with the living voice', abl. fem. of *vivus*, 'living', see **vivacious** & **vital**, & abl. of *vox*, 'voice', see **vox**, **vocal**, & **voice**. **1.** adv. **a** Out loud: *to speak viva voce*; **b** by means of the voice, by word of mouth, orally; contrasted with *in writing*. **2.** adj. Uttered with the voice, oral; *viva-voce examination*, one conducted by word of mouth, instead of by written questions and answers. **3.** n. A viva-voce examination.

vive, interj. [1. vēv; 2. vīv]. Fr., 'let him live, long live...', 3rd pers. pres. subj. of *vivre*, 'to live', fr. Lat. *vīvere*, see **vivacious** & **vital**. *Vive le roi, la reine, le Président, la France* &c., long live the King, Queen, President, France &c. See also **qui vive**.

vives, n. [1. vīvz; 2. vaivz]. O. Fr. *avives*, fr. Span. *adwivas*, fr. Arab. *al-dhiba*. Disease of the ear in young horses.

vivi-, pref. Form of Lat. *vīvus*, 'living', used in compounds; the etymological relations of this base are discussed under **vital**.

vivid, adj. [1. vívid; 2. vívid]. Lat. *vīvidus*, 'full of life, living, animated; full of vigour', fr. base *vīv-*, 'life, live', see prec. & **vital**. Full of life, vigour, liveliness &c. (in various senses). **1.** Vigorous, abounding in force, animated, lively: *a vivid imagination*; *a vivid personality.* **2.** **a** (of colour and visual images) Clear, bright, intense, brilliant; reverse of *dull, subdued, indistinct*: *vivid colouring*; *the vivid green of leaves in spring*; *a vivid reflection in water*; *a vivid flash of lightning*; **b** bringing a clear and life-like image before the mind: *a vivid description*; *a vivid picture of life in the fields.*

vividly, adv. Prec. & **-ly**. In a vivid manner; with vividness.
vividness, n. See prec. & **-ness**. Quality of being vivid.
vivificate, vb. trans. [1. vī-, vivífikāt; 2. *vai-*, *vivífikeit*]. **vivi-** & **-fic** & **-ate**. (rare) To put life into, to vivify; to revive.
vivification, n. [1. vìvifikáshun; 2. vìvifikéiʃən]. Prec. & **-ion**. Act, process, of vivifying; condition of being vivified.
vivify, vb. trans. [1. vívifī; 2. *vívifai*]. **vivi-** & **-fy**. To give life or liveliness to; to animate, quicken, revive.
viviparity, n. [1. vìvipáriti; 2. vàivipǽriti]. See **viviparous** & **-ity**. State, quality, of being viviparous.
viviparous, adj. [1. vīvíparus; 2. *vaivípərəs*]. **vivi-** & *par-*, fr. base in Lat. *parere*, 'to bear, bring forth (young)', see **parent**, & **-ous**. Bringing forth young alive and fully formed and immediately capable of independent life; contrasted with *oviparous*.
viviparously, adv. Prec. & **-ly**. In a viviparous manner.
viviparousness, n. See prec. & **-ness**. Quality of being viviparous.
vivisect, vb. trans. & intrans. [1. vìvisékt; 2. vìvisékt]. **vivi-** & base **sec-*, 'to cut', see **secant** & **sect**. **1.** trans. To dissect (animal) while alive, to practise vivisection upon. **2.** intrans. To practise vivisection.
vivisection, n. [1. vìvisékshun; 2. vìvisékʃən]. Prec. & **-ion**. The practice of performing operations upon living animals, of inoculating them with the germs of disease &c., in order to observe their behaviour and symptoms, to test remedies and, generally, to enlarge medical, pathological, or biological knowledge.
vivisectional, adj. [1. vìvisékshunal: 2. vìvisékʃənəl]. Prec. & **-al**. Connected with, arising from, of the nature of, vivisection.
vivisectionist, n. [1. vìvisékshunist; 2. vìvisékʃənist]. **vivisection** & **-ist**. **1.** One who practises vivisection. **2.** One who approves of and advocates the practice of vivisection.
vivisector, n. [1. vívisektor; 2. vívisɛktə]. **vivisect** & **-or**. One who practises vivisection.
vixen, n. [1. víksn; 2. víksn]. O.E. *fyxen*, 'female fox', fr. **fuhs-in-*, see **fox**. **1.** A female fox. **2.** An ill-tempered, vinegary, shrewish, spiteful woman.
vixenish, adj. [1. víksenish; 2. víksəniʃ]. Prec. & **-ish**. Like a vixen in character; spiteful, malicious.
viz. See **videlicet**.
vizier, n. [1. vizḗr; 2. vizíə]. Turk. *vezīr*, 'counsellor', fr. Arab. *wezīr*, *wazīr*, lit. 'one who bears burdens'. High State official in Mohammedan countries, esp. in the old Ottoman Empire. *Grand Vizier*, chief minister of state.
vizierate, vizirate, n. [1. vizḗrāt; 2. vizíəreit]. Prec. & **-ate**. The office, status, of a vizier; term of this.
Vlach. See **Wallach**.
vocable, n. [1. vṓkabl; 2. vóukəbl]. Fr., fr. Lat. *vocābulum*, 'that by which anything is called, designation, name'; fr. base **vōc-*, as in *vōc-em*, fr. *vox*, 'voice', & *vocāre*, 'to call', see **vocation**, & **vox**. A word, esp. one regarded as composed of certain sounds without reference to meaning.
vocabulary, n. [1. vōkábūlari; 2. voukǽbjuləri]. Lat. *vocābulum*, see prec. & **-ary**. **1.** The stock of words employed by an individual speaker, author, class of persons &c.; range, scope, of language: *an ordinary labourer is said to have a vocabulary of only a few hundred words*; *Shakespeare's rich vocabulary*. **2.** Alphabetical list of the principal words as found in a particular work or language, or used in some special branch of study, together with a translation of each into another language, or explanations in elucidation of the meaning.
vocal, adj. [1. vṓkl; 2. vóukl], fr. Lat. *vōcālis*, 'uttering a voice or sound; sounding, sonorous, vocal', fr. *vōc-(em)*, *vox*, 'voice', & **-al**; for an account of the base *vōc-* &c. see **vox**. **1.** Pertaining to the voice or to voice production: *the vocal organs*; *vocal chords*, vibrating membranes in the glottis which produce voice. **2.** Uttered, produced, by the voice; spoken or sung: *vocal music*, that intended for singing; contrasted with *instrumental*. **3.** Filled with the sound of voices; endowed with a voice: '*hill or valley, fountain, or fresh shade, Made vocal by my song*' (Milton, 'P. L.', v. 203-4). **4.** Expressing oneself or itself in words; giving vent in speech or language: *public opinion has at last become vocal*; *this class may be very vocal and noisy, but carries little weight*.
vocalic, adj. [1. vōkálik; 2. voukǽlik]. Prec. & **-ic**. Pertaining to, consisting of, of the nature of, a vowel sound or sounds.
vocalism, n. [1. vṓkalizm; 2. vóukəlizəm]. **vocal** & **-ism**. **a** Use of the voice and vocal organs in speech, song &c.; **b** (rare) system of vowel sounds used in a given language.
vocalist, n. [1. vṓkalist; 2. vóukəlist]. **vocal** & **-ist**. A singer.
vocality, n. [1. vōkáliti; 2. voukǽliti]. **vocal** & **-ity**. Quality of being vocal; resonance.
vocalization, n. [1. vòkalīzáshun; 2. vòukəlaizéiʃən]. **vocalize** & **-ation**. **a** Act of vocalizing; method of utterance, esp. of the singing voice; **b** the use of vowel signs in writing certain languages, where they are usually omitted, as in Hebrew, Arabic &c.
vocalize, vb. trans. & intrans. [1. vṓkalīz; 2. vóukəlaiz]. See **vocal** & **-ize**. **A.** trans. **1.** (phon.) **a** To make vocal; to utter with voice; **b** to make vocalic or syllabic. **2.** To point or supply vowel signs to (written form of a language such as Hebrew which commonly omits these). **B.** intrans. To use the voice, to sing.
vocally, adv. [1. vṓkali; 2. vóukəli]. **vocal** & **-ly**. In a vocal manner; by voice or speech, in words.
vocation, n. [1. vōkáshun; 2. voukéiʃən]. Fr., fr. Lat. *vocātiōn-(em)*, 'a summons; invitation', fr. *vocāt-(um)*, P.P. type of *vocāre*, 'to call'. See **vocal** & **vox** & **-ion**. **1.** (theol.) **a** God's calling or invitation to an individual or nation to a life of salvation by grace; specif., a call to a religious life, as to the ministry; the divine guidance towards a spiritual or religious life; **b** that form of spiritual life to which one has been called by God. **2.** A special fitness, aptitude, talent, for a particular occupation or profession; a calling: *to have little or no vocation for business life*; *to find one's vocation in life*. **3.** Habitual occupation, followed as a means of livelihood; profession, business, walk in life, calling.
vocational, adj. [1. vōkáshunal; 2. voukéiʃənəl]. Prec. & **-al**. Relating, adapted, preparatory, to a vocation, profession, or occupation: *vocational education, school* &c.
vocationally, adv. Prec. & **-ly**. In a vocational manner; from the point of view of a vocation.
vocative, adj. & n. [1. vókativ; 2. vɔ́kətiv], fr. O. Fr. *vocatif, -ive*, fr. Lat. *vocātīvus*, sc. *casus*, fr. *vocāt-(um)*, P.P. type of *vocāre*, 'to call', see **vocation** & **vox** & **-ive**. **1.** adj. Used in addressing or calling a person or object: *vocative case*. **2.** n. The vocative case.
vociferance, n. [1. vōsíferans; 2. vousífərəns]. See next word & **-ce**. Shouting, noise, clamour.
vociferant, adj. [1. vōsíferant; 2. vousífərənt], fr. Lat. *vōciferant-(em)*, Pres. Part. of *vōciferārī*, see next word. Vociferating, shouting, clamorous.
vociferate, vb. trans. & intrans. [1. vōsíferāt; 2. vousífəreit], fr. Lat. *vōciferāt-(um)*, P.P. type of *vōciferārī*, 'to cry, call out, to shout'; fr. *vōci-*, stem of **vox**, & *-fer*, see under **-ferous**, & **-ate**. **1.** trans. To shout, utter with a loud voice; to bawl out: *to vociferate oaths*; *the crowd vociferated 'Sit down!'* **2.** intrans. To bawl, shout, utter loud cries.
vociferation, n. [1. vōsìferáshun; 2. vousìfəréiʃən], fr. Lat. *vōciferātiōn-(em)*; see prec. & **-ion**. Shouting, bawling; clamour.
vociferator, n. [1. vōsíferātor; 2. vousífəreitə]. Lat., see **vociferate** & **-or**. One who vociferates; shouter, bawler.
vociferous, adj. [1. vōsíferus; 2. vousífərəs]. Lat. *vōci-*, stem of *vox*, 'voice', see **vox**, & **-ferous**. **1.** Having plenty of voice; using the voice with energy, making a loud outcry, clamorous: *a vociferous mob*; *birds were so vociferous that I woke up*. **2.** Uttered with a loud voice; noisy, loud: *vociferous cheers*.
vociferously, adv. Prec. & **-ly**. In a vociferous manner; noisily.
vociferousness, n. See prec. & **-ness**. Quality of being vociferous.
vodka, n. [1. vódka; 2. vɔ́dkə]. Russ., dimin. of O. Slav. & Russ. *vodá*, 'water'; cogn. w. Gk. *húdōr*, 'water'; Goth. *watō*; O.E. *wæter*, see **water, wash,** & **wet**; Lat. *unda*, 'wave', see **undulate**. A Russian spirituous drink, distilled formerly from rye, maize, or potatoes.
voe, n. [1. vō; 2. vou], fr. O.N. *vāgr*, Mod. Icel. *vōgr*. A creek, inlet, or small bay in the Orkney and Shetland Islands.
vogue, n. [1. vōg; 2. voug]. Fr., 'swaying motion, as of boat, sway, drift, course', fr. *voguer*, 'to sway, set sail', as in Phr. *vogue la galère*, lit. 'let the galley set sail', hence 'let things take their course whatever happens'; the word is found in Ital. as *vogare*, & in Span. as *bogare*, 'to row', & is of Gmc. origin; cp. O.H.G. *wāg*, later *wōg*, 'wave', O.E. *wǣg*, 'wave', a form of the Gmc. base **weȝ-*, 'to carry, bear', see **weigh**. **1.** The prevailing fashion; popular mode, custom, practice at the time: *the vogue of very short skirts* &c.; *a mere passing vogue*; *what will the next vogue be?* **2.** Popularity, popular acceptance or favour: *to have a short vogue*. Phr. *in vogue*, in fashion, fashionable; *all the vogue*, the latest thing, the dernier cri.
voice (I.), n. [1. vois; 2. vɔis]. M.E. & O. Fr. *vois* &c., fr. Lat. *vōci-*, stem of *vōx*, 'voice', see **vox**. **1.** Sound produced, uttered, through the mouth by the human organs of speech, in speaking, singing, laughing; also used of the vocal sounds produced by birds, and, more rarely, of those made by other animals. **2.** Specif. (phon.) that kind of sound produced by the organs of speech when the air-stream sets up vibrations in the vocal chords; contrasted with *breath*. **3.** The sound or sounds produced by the human organs of speech considered in relation to their quality, individual character, peculiar characteristic timbre and so on: *his master's voice*; *a good, poor, strong, loud, sweet, harsh, voice*. Phr. *to lift up one's voice*, to speak. **4.** Faculty, power, of using the voice; desire and capacity to speak: *indignation gave me voice*. **5. a** Any sound regarded as resembling, or as comparable to, that of the human voice: '*Earth with her thousand voices praises God*' (Coleridge, 'Vale of Chamouni'); *the voice of the stream, of the waves* &c.; **b** anything regarded as resembling the human voice as a means of expression, as delivering a message &c.: '*E'en from the tomb the voice of Nature cries*' (Gray's 'Elegy'); *the voice of the law*; *the voice of conscience*. **6.** Wish, desire, opinion, choice, esp. as expressed in a vote or less formally indicated: *to give one's voice for war*. Phr. *to have a voice in*, have a choice, have the right to express an opinion or wish, to have some influence in a decision. **7.** (gram.) Form of a verb which shows the relation of the subject to the action. See **active, passive**.
voice (II.), vb. trans., fr. prec. **1.** To give utterance to, to express: *to voice the feelings of a meeting*. **2.** (phon.) To utter (a speech, sound) with voice, that is, pronounce it with vibration of the vocal chords.
voiced, adj. [1. voist; 2. vɔist]. P.P. of prec. (phon.) Uttered with voice, i.e. with vibration of the vocal chords: *voiced sounds, consonants* &c.; contrasted with *voiceless*.

-voiced, adj. Having a specified kind of voice: *sweet-voiced, loud-voiced* &c.

voiceful, adj. [1. vóisfl; 2. vɔ́isfl]. **voice (I.)** & **-ful.** Having a voice; sonorous, sounding.

voiceless, adj. [1. vóisles; 2. vɔ́islis]. **voice** & **-less.** **1. a** Having no voice; **b** having lost (temporarily) the power of speech. **2.** (phon.) Uttered without voice, uttered with breath alone; unvoiced.

voicelessly, adv. Prec. & **-ly.** In a voiceless manner; without voice.

voicelessness, n. See prec. & **-ness.** The quality of being voiceless.

voicing, n. [1. vóising; 2. vɔ́isiŋ]. **voice (II.)** & **-ing.** (phon.) Act or process of producing voice; act of uttering speech sounds with vibration of the vocal chords.

void (I.), adj. [1. void; 2. vɔid]. In M.E., fr. O. Fr. *vuit, vuide, voide*, fr. L. Lat. *vocitum*, 'empty', dialectal for Lat. *vacāt-(um)*, P.P. of *vacāre*, 'to be empty, to be void of, free from', see **vacate** & **vacant.** **1.** Empty, vacant: '*without form, and void*' (Gen. i. 2). **2.** Having no occupant, holder, or tenant: *a void benefice, farm, dwelling-house* &c. **3.** Lacking, wanting, deficient in, devoid of: *a landscape void of all beauty*; *a person quite void of common honesty.* **4.** Legally invalid, of no effect: *the contract was declared void on account of the insanity of one of the parties*; also *null and void.*

void (II.), n., fr. prec. **1. a** An empty space, a vacuum; *the void*, space, infinity; **b** an unoccupied house, esp. rated as such. **2.** (fig.) A sense of emptiness, vacancy, loss: *his death has left a void in our lives which can never be filled*; (commonly) *an aching void (in one's heart)*, deep sense of irreparable loss.

void (III.), vb. trans., fr. **void (I.).** **1.** To discharge, evacuate: *to void excrement, a stone from the bladder.* **2.** To make null and void; to make invalid, of no effect; to nullify.

voidable, adj. [1. vóidabl; 2. vɔ́idəbl]. **void (III.)** & **-able.** Capable of being made, or judged, as of no effect; capable of being nullified.

voidance, n. [1. vóidans; 2. vɔ́idəns]. **void (III.)** & **-ance.** **1.** Act of voiding; evacuation; casting away, removal. **2.** (eccles.) **a** Act of ejecting from a benefice; **b** state of being void; vacancy (of a benefice).

voided, adj. [1. vóided; 2. vɔ́idid], fr. P.P. of **void (III.).** (her., of an ordinary) Having central part removed or cut away, and showing the tincture of the field in the vacant space.

voider, n. [1. vóider; 2. vɔ́idə]. **void (III.)** & **-er.** (her.) An ordinary, consisting of a figure with two concave sides, occupying the greater part of the field.

voile, n. [1. vwahl; 2. vwāl]. Fr., 'a veil', fr. Lat. *vēlum*, see **velum** & cp. **veil.** A thin cotton, woollen, or silken material used for women's dresses.

voivode, n. [1. vóivōd; 2. vɔ́ivoud]. Russ. *voevoda*, 'leader in war'. Title formerly borne by the reigning princes of Moldavia and Wallachia.

volant, adj. [1. vṓlant; 2. vóulənt]. Fr., fr. Lat. *volant-(em)*, Pres. Part. of *volāre*, for **gʷol-*, 'to fly'; cogn. w. Scrt. *garút*, 'wing', fr. **gʷol-*; further relations doubtful, but perh. fr. same base as Lat. *volvere*, 'to roll, turn, tumble', see **volute** & second element in **devolve, revolve.** **1. a** (zool.) Flying, capable of flying; **b** (her.) represented as flying. **2.** Passing rapidly through the air as though flying on wings.

Volapük, n. [1. vólapōōk, -pook; 2. vɔ́ləpūk, -puk]. 'World's speech'. Artificial language invented by J. M. Schleyer in 1879 with the object of providing a means of intercourse between all nations of the world; superseded long since in public estimation by Esperanto, Ido, and similar inventions.

volar, adj. [1. vṓlar; 2. vóulə]. Lat. *vola*, 'palm of hand; sole of foot'; for **gwela* or **gwola*, conn. w. base **geu(l)-*; cogn. w. Gk. *gúalon*, 'a hollow, cave'; Scrt. *gōlaś*, 'ball'; O.N. *kjōlr*, O.E. *ċēol*, 'keel, ship', see **keel (I.).** Pertaining to the palm or the sole.

volatile, adj. [1. vólatil; 2. vɔ́lətail]. Fr., fr. Lat. *volātilis*, 'flying, winged; rapid; fleeting, transitory', fr. *volāt-(um)*, P.P. type of *volāre*, 'to fly', see **volant.** **1.** Tending to waste, to be carried off by evaporation, vaporization &c.; easily vaporizable (of spirituous liquids). **2.** (fig.) Tossed hither and thither by the caprice of the moment, lacking concentration of purpose; changeable, wayward, fickle.

volatileness, n. Prec. & **-ness.** Volatility.

volatility, n. [1. vòlatíliti; 2. vɔ̀lətíliti]. See prec. & **-ity.** Quality, mental characteristic, of being volatile.

volatilizable, adj. [1. vòlatilízabl; 2. vɔ̀lətilάizəbl]. **volatilize** & **-able.** Capable of being volatilized.

volatilization, n. [1. volátilīzā́shun; 2. vɔlǽtilaizéiʃən]. **volatilize** & **-ation.** Process of volatilizing; state of being volatilized.

volatilize, vb. trans. & intrans. [1. vólatilīz; 2. vɔ̀lətilaiz]. **volatile** & **-ize.** **1.** trans. To render volatile, cause to evaporate. **2.** intrans. To evaporate, pass off in vapour.

vol-au-vent, n. [1. vól ō vòn; 2. vɔ́l ou vã]. Fr. Kind of raised pie made of puff paste, filled with chicken, game, fish &c.

volcanic, adj. [1. volkánik; 2. vɔlkǽnik]. **volcano** & **-ic.** **1.** Pertaining to, of the nature of, produced by, due to action of, a volcano or of volcanoes: *volcanic activity*; *volcanic eruption* &c.; *volcanic bomb*, a round, hollow mass of lava; *volcanic glass*, glass-like substance formed by the rapid cooling of lava; obsidian. **2.** (fig.) Resembling a volcano in violence; ebullient, violent, intense: *a volcanic character*; *volcanic energy.*

volcanicity, n. [1. vòlkanísiti; 2. vɔ̀lkənísiti]. Prec. & **-ity.** State, quality, of being volcanic.

volcanism, n. [1. vólkanizm; 2. vɔ́lkənizəm]. **volcano** & **-ism.** **a** Volcanic action; **b** combination of natural forces which produces volcanic action.

volcanist, n. [1. vólkanist; 2. vɔ́lkənist]. **volcano** & **-ist.** Student of volcanoes and volcanic action.

volcanization, n. [1. vòlkanīzā́shun; 2. vɔ̀lkənaizéiʃən]. Next word & **-ation.** Process of subjecting or of being subjected to volcanic heat.

volcanize, vb. trans. [1. vólkanīz; 2. vɔ́lkənaiz]. **volcano** & **-ize.** To subject to the action of volcanic heat.

volcano, n. [1. volkā́nō; 2. vɔlkéinou]. Ital., fr. Lat. *Vulcānus*, see **Vulcan.** Hill or mountain having a deep vent in the summit from which lava, ashes, gases &c., coming from the interior of the earth, are ejected continuously or periodically. Phr. *extinct volcano*, (i.) one which has ceased to be active; (ii.) a person who is no longer productive, one who has lost his vigour, spirit, enthusiasm, creative energy, and capacity for thought and action.

volcanological, adj. [1. vòlkanōlójikl; 2. vɔ̀lkənoulɔ́dʒikl]. **volcano** & **-logy** & **-ic** & **-al.** Pertaining to volcanology or volcanologists.

volcanologist, n. [1. vòlkanólojist; 2. vɔ̀lkənɔ́lədʒist]. **volcanology** & **-ist.** Student of volcanology.

volcanology, n. [1. vòlkanóloji; 2. vɔ̀lkənɔ́lədʒi]. **volcano** & **-logy.** The science which deals with volcanoes, their causes, and attendant phenomena.

vole (I.), n. & vb. intrans. [1. vōl; 2. voul], fr. Fr. *voler*, 'to fly', fr. Lat. *volāre*, see **volant.** **a** n. The winning of all the tricks in a deal in certain card games; **b** vb., to make a vole.

vole (II.), n. For *vole mouse*, fr. O.N. *vollr*, 'field', cogn. w. O.E. *wēald, wāld*, see **wold.** One of various kinds of rat-like rodent mammals, genus *Microtus*, with blunt noses, short tails, and thickish bodies: *field vole*, field-mouse; *water-vole*, water-rat.

volet, n. [1. vólā; 2. vɔ́lei]. Fr., 'shutter'. **vole (I.)** & **-et.** One of the panels of a triptych.

volitant, adj. [1. vólitant; 2. vɔ́litənt]. Lat. *volitāre*, 'to fly', freq. of *volāre*, see **volant.** (zool.) Flying.

volitation, n. [1. vòlitā́shun; 2. vɔ̀litéiʃən]. Lat. *volitāt-(um)*, P.P. type of *volitāre*, 'to fly', see prec., & **-ion.** Act of flying; capacity to fly.

volition, n. [1. vōlíshun; 2. vouliʃən]. Med. Lat. *volitiōn-(em)*, formed fr. base **vol-*, 'to wish, will', cp. Lat. *volo*, 'I wish' &c., infin. *velle*; cogn. w. Scrt. *vṛnāti* &c., 'he chooses, desires, prefers', for **vḷ-*; *váranam* for **val-*, 'act of choosing, wishing'; Goth. *wiljan*, 'to will', O.E. *willan*, see **will (II.)**; O. Slav. *voliti*, 'to will, desire', *volja*, 'the will, desire' &c.; Gk. *elpis*, 'hope', for **wel-*. **1.** Act of willing or choosing; exercise of the will. **2.** Power of exercising a choice, of forming an intention or a determination; will.

volitional, adj. [1. vōlíshunal; 2. vouliʃənəl]. Prec. & **-al.** Connected, having to do, with volition or the will; of the nature of volition; arising from, due to, volition.

volitionally, adv. Prec. & **-ly.** By volition.

volitionary, adj. [1. vōlíshunari; 2. vouliʃənəri]. **volition** & **-ary.** Volitional.

volitionless, adj. [1. vōlíshunles; 2. vouliʃənlis]. **volition** & **-less.** Lacking volition; having no power of will.

volitive, adj. [1. vólitiv; 2. vɔ́litiv]. See **volition** & **-ive.** Pertaining to, arising from, the will.

Volkslied, n. [1. fólkslēd; 2. fɔ́lkslīd]. Mod. Germ. Folk-song, national song or air.

Volksraad, n. [1. fólksrahd; 2. fɔ́lksrād]. Du., see **folk**, & *raad*, 'counsel' &c., cogn. w. O.E. *rǣd*, 'advice, counsel', see under **read.** National legislative body in the old Orange Free State.

volley (I.), n. [1. vóli; 2. vɔ́li], fr. Fr. *volée*, 'a flight; discharge of a number of guns', fr. Lat. *volātum*, P.P. of *volāre*, 'to fly', see **volant.** **1.** A number of missiles discharged at the same time against a common objective: *a volley of arrows, of stones*; if not specified, *a volley* implies at the present time, a number of shots fired simultaneously from fire-arms or from cannon. **2.** (fig.) A rapid, continuous, noisy utterance, a torrent (of oaths, imprecations, abuse &c.), esp. when directed against a particular person, party, set of circumstances &c. **3.** In various ball games, **a** as tennis &c., the striking and return of the ball before it touches the ground; **b** as cricket &c., the delivery of ball full pitch at batsman or wicket; *half-volley*, ball pitched and struck just after it touches the ground.

volley (II.), vb. trans. & intrans., fr. prec. **1.** trans. **a** (i.) (rare) To direct, fire, (missiles) in a volley; (ii.) in ball games, to deliver or strike by a volley; **b** to utter (abuse &c.) in a volley. **2.** intrans. **a** To fire a volley; **b** to deliver or hit a volley.

volplane, vb. intrans. & n. [1. vólplān; 2. vɔ́lplein], fr. Fr. *vol planer*, see **volant** & **plane (V.).** **a** vb. (of aeroplane or pilot) To descend by a long and somewhat steep glide after shutting off the engine; **b** n., such a descent.

volt (I.), n. [1. volt; 2. vɔlt]. Fr., see **vault (I.).** **1.** (fencing) Rapid step to escape a thrust. **2.** Pace of a horse in which it steps with high springy movements of the legs.

volt (II.), n., fr. name of the Italian, A. Volta, d. 1827. Unit of electromotive force or potential difference; defined as the electromotive force which, steadily applied to a resistance of 1 ohm, will produce a current of 1 ampère.

volta, n., pl. **volte** [1. vólta, -ā; 2. vɔ́lta, -e]. Ital., 'time'. (mus.) *Una volta*, 'once'; *due volte*, 'twice'.

voltage, n. [1. vóltij; 2. vɔ́ltidž]. **volt (II.)** & **-age.** Amount of electromotive current measured in volts.

voltaic, adj. [1. voltā́ik; 2. vɔltéi-ik]. *Volta*, see **volt (II.)**, & **-ic.** Designating electricity produced by, apparatus producing electricity by, chemical action.

Voltairian, adj. & n. [1. voltárian; 2. voltéər-iən], fr. name of French philosopher Voltaire & **-ian**. **1.** adj. Pertaining to Voltaire and his mode of thought. **2.** n. Adherent of the doctrines and principles of Voltaire.

Voltair(ian)ism, n. [1. voltár(ian)izm; 2. voltéər(iən)izəm]. See prec. & **-ism**. Philosophical doctrines of Voltaire; specif., religious scepticism.

voltameter, n. [1. voltámeter; 2. voltǽmitə], fr. *Volta*, see **volt (II.)**, & **-meter**. (obs.) Instrument for measuring electrical force.

volte-face, n. [1. vòlt fáhs; 2. vɔ̀lt fás]. Fr. A complete turn round, so as to face the opposite way; **a** reversal of physical, bodily, position; **b** a change of front, complete reversal of opinions, mental attitude &c.

voltite, n. [1. vóltīt; 2. vɔ́ltait], fr. **volt (II.)** & **-ite**. A kind of insulating material for covering electric wires.

voltmeter, n. [1. vóltmēter; 2. vɔ́ltmītə]. **volt (II.)** & **-meter**. (elect.) Instrument for measuring potential difference in volts.

volubility, n. [1. vòlūbíliti; 2. vɔ̀ljubíliti]. See next word & **-ity**. Habit, quality, of being voluble; extreme fullness, fluency, of utterance and expression; talkativeness.

voluble, adj. [1. vólūbl; 2. vɔ́ljubl]. Lat. *volūbilis*, fr. base of *volvere*, 'to roll', see **volute**. Having, speaking with, a great flow of words; fluent in speech; talkative.

volume, n. [1. vólūm; 2. vɔ́ljəm, -jum]. Fr., fr. Lat. *volūmen*, 'a roll; book written on parchment and rolled up'; fr. base of *volvere*, 'to turn, roll', see **volute**. **1.** A book, a tome; collection of printed or written sheets bound up together and forming a unity, whether forming a complete literary work or a portion of one: *a library of many thousand volumes; a work in six volumes; Volume I. has just appeared* (abbr. as *vol.*). Phr. *to speak volumes for*, to afford strong, favourable, or confirmatory testimony. **2.** A considerable mass, body, amount: *a great volume of water; volume of smoke, vapour*, large, dense cloud; (fig.) *a great volume of sound*, a powerful gust, blast. **3.** **a** Solid content, bulk, mass, amount: *the total volume of masonry, débris, earth, covering the ruins is enormous*; **b** space occupied by a liquid, gas &c. measured in cubic units, as feet, inches &c.; **c** (special use) *a voice of great, little, volume*, resonant quality, capacity for filling a large space.

-volumed, adj. [1. vólūmd; 2. vɔ́ljəmd, -jūmd]. Consisting of so many volumes: *many-volumed, three-volumed.*

volumenometer, n. [1. volūmenómeter; 2. voljūminɔ́mitə]. Lat., see **volume** & **-meter**. Instrument for measuring the volume of a solid body.

volumetric(al), adj. [1. vòlūmétrik(l); 2. vɔ̀ljumétrik(əl)]. **volume** & **-metric** (& **-al**). Pertaining to the measurement of volume.

voluminal, adj. [1. volúminal; 2. vəljúminəl]. Lat. *volūmin-*, stem of *volūmen*, see **volume**, & **-al**. Pertaining to volume.

voluminosity, n. [1. volùminósiti; 2. vəljùminɔ́siti]. Lat. *volūminōsus*, see **voluminous**, & **-ity**. Quality, condition, of being voluminous.

voluminous, adj. [1. volúminus; 2. vəljúminəs], fr. Lat. *volūmin-*, stem of *volūmen*, see **volume**, & **-ous**. Having considerable volume; occupying much space; bulky, abundant; extensive: *voluminous robes; voluminous correspondence.*

voluminously, adv. Prec. & **-ly**. To a voluminous extent or degree.

voluminousness, n. See prec. & **-ness**. Quality, condition, of being voluminous.

voluntarily, adv. [1. vóluntarili; 2. vɔ́ləntərili]. See voluntary & **-ly**. In a voluntary manner; freely, of one's own accord, without compulsion.

voluntariness, n. [1. vóluntarines; 2. vɔ́ləntərinis]. See prec. & **-ness**. Quality of being voluntary.

voluntarism, n. [1. vóluntarizm; 2. vɔ́ləntərizəm]. **voluntary** & **-ism**. System, as of religious education, military enlistment &c., which depends entirely on voluntary action.

voluntary (I.), adj. [1. vóluntari; 2. vɔ́ləntəri]. Lat. *voluntārius*, cp. *voluntāt-(em)*, 'free will', fr. base in *volo*, 'I wish, desire' &c., see **volition**, & **-ary**. **1.** Acting of one's own free will, by one's own desire, without compulsion, constraint, or necessity: *a voluntary worker, helper.* **2.** Done, performed, rendered, freely and at one's own choice; not compulsory; unconstrained: *voluntary services, work, tasks; a voluntary confession; voluntary contributions.* **3.** Brought about, carried on, supported, by voluntary effort, expenditure &c.: *a voluntary hospital; voluntary school*, one supported by a religious body; as distinguished from a state or Council school. **4.** Deliberate: *voluntary waste* (of owner's property by tenant's act or order). **5.** Specif. (physiol.) affected by, depending on, the action of the will: *voluntary muscles*, those under the control of the will; *voluntary movements*; contrasted with *involuntary.*

voluntary (II.), n., fr. prec. An organ solo played in a church, esp. before or after a service.

volunteer (I.), n. [1. vòluntḗr; 2. vɔ̀ləntíə]. Formed fr. *volunt-*, as in **voluntary** &c., & **-eer**. **1.** Person who voluntarily offers to perform specific services, esp. such as involve danger or arduous effort; one not compulsorily enrolled for such service, but coming forward of his own free will, and primarily from a sense of duty rather than from hope of reward: *volunteers were called for to act as special constables, as engine-drivers* &c. Phr. *one volunteer is worth two pressed men* (orig. of service in the Navy), service given freely and willingly is more effective than that exacted under compulsion. **2.** Specif., a member of a voluntary military organization for defensive purposes, with branches all over England, officially recognized in 1859 as the *National Rifle Association.* This force was later reorganized and known as the *Territorial Army.*

volunteer (II.), vb. trans. & intrans., fr. prec. **1.** trans. To offer freely and voluntarily: *to volunteer one's services, help, a subscription* &c. Phr. *to volunteer a remark, an opinion*, to speak, intervene in a discussion, offer an opinion, without being directly invited or consulted. **2.** intrans. **a** To offer voluntarily to perform certain services: *I asked if anyone present would undertake to collect money for the hospital, but no one volunteered*; specif. **b** to offer oneself for military service: *during the first few days of the Great War many thousands volunteered.*

voluptuary, n. [1. volúptūari; 2. vouláptjuəri]. Lat. *voluptu-*, as in next word, & **-ary**. A voluptuous person; one fond of, addicted to, sensual pleasure.

voluptuous, adj. [1. volúptūus; 2. vouláptjuəs]. Formed fr. Lat. type *volupt-*, as in *voluptas*, 'pleasure', w. addition of *-u-*, on the model of *sensu-ous, virtu-ous*, & **-ous**. The base of *voluptas* is that of *volo*, 'I desire, wish' &c., see **volition**. **a** Fond of, addicted to, sensual pleasure; sensual: *a voluptuous person*; **b** tending to promote sensual or sensuous delight; tending to excite sensual desire: *a voluptuous atmosphere, book, picture*; **c** expressing desire: *a voluptuous glance.*

voluptuously, adv. Prec. & **-ly**. In a voluptuous manner.

voluptuousness, n. See prec. & **-ness**. State, quality, of being voluptuous; voluptuous cast of mind; voluptuous habits.

volute, n. [1. volút; 2. vəljút]. Fr., 'snail shell', fr. Lat. *volūta*, P.P. fem. of *volvere*, 'to roll, turn', fr. the Aryan base **wolw-*, **welw-*, whence also Gk. *elúein*, 'to roll', for **welw-*, see **helix**; Scrt. *valaya*, 'circle'; Lith. *welti*, 'to roll'; Goth. *walwjan*, 'to roll', O.E. *wealwian*, 'to roll round', see **wallow**, & cp. **walk, wallop**, & **gallop**; also *-volve* in **devolve, evolve** &c. **1.** (archit.) The spiral scroll forming the principal feature in Ionic and Corinthian capitals. **2.** (zool.) Any of various kinds of tropical snail (gasteropod) with beautiful shells.

voluted, adj. [1. volúted; 2. vəljútid]. Prec. & **-ed**. (archit.) Decorated with volutes.

volution, n. [1. volúshun; 2. vəljúʃən]. **volute** & **-ion**. **a** Spiral, whorls, of a shell; **b** (anat.) a convolution.

volutoid, adj. & n. [1. volūtòid; 2. vɔ́ljutɔid]. **volute** & **-oid**. **a** adj. Shaped like a volute; **b** n., volutoid shell &c.

vomit (I.), vb. intrans. & trans. [1. vómit; 2. vɔ́mit], fr. Lat. *vomit-(um)*, P.P. type of *vomere*, 'to vomit'; cogn. w. Gk. *emein*, 'to vomit', *emetikós*, 'provoking sickness', for **wem-*, see **emetic**. **A.** intrans. **1.** To discharge the contents of the stomach through the mouth, to be sick. **2.** (of volcano) To discharge lava, ashes &c. through the crater. **B.** trans. **1.** **a** To discharge from the stomach through the mouth: *to vomit one's dinner*; **b** (fr. n., archaic) to cause to vomit by administering an emetic: *in the 17th and 18th centuries people were periodically vomited, purged, and bled.* **2.** (fig.) To pour forth vehemently in speech, to utter with violence and volubility: *to vomit insults, abuse, curses* &c.; also to give forth in printed or written form: *the reptile Press vomited its libels; every scribbler vomited filthy lampoons.* **3.** To emit, pour out, belch forth suddenly or impetuously, copiously, and more or less continuously: *a chimney vomits forth smoke; the guns vomited fire, shells; dragons were said to vomit fire and smoke; excursion trains hourly vomited crowds of trippers into quiet country districts.*

vomit (II.), n. M.E. *vomite*, fr. Lat. *vomitus*, 'a vomiting', see prec. **1.** **a** Matter vomited from the stomach; **b** (fig.) something of an abusive or disreputable character, uttered by word of mouth or written &c.: *the foul vomit of lampoonists.* **2.** Act of vomiting. **3.** Drug which causes vomiting; an emetic.

vomiting, n. [1. vómiting; 2. vɔ́mitiŋ]. **vomit** & **-ing (II.)**. Act of one who vomits; retching, sickness.

vomitive, adj. & n. [1. vómitiv; 2. vɔ́mitiv]. **vomit (I.)** & **-ive**. **a** adj. Tending to cause vomiting; **b** n., drug which causes vomiting; an emetic.

vomitory, adj. & n. [1. vómituri; 2. vɔ́mitəri]. **vomit (I.)** & **-ory**. **a** adj. Causing vomiting, vomitive; **b** n., drug which does this; an emetic.

vomiturition, n. [1. vòmitūríshun; 2. vɔ̀mitjuríʃən], fr. Lat. *vomitus*, 'act of vomiting'; see **vomit (II.)**. **a** Strong but abortive desire to vomit, violent retching; **b** frequent vomiting.

voodoo, n. & vb. trans. [1. vóodōō; 2. vúdu]. Creole Fr., not fr. Fr. *Vaudois*, Waldensian, but fr. a native Dahomey word, *vodu*. **1.** n. Witchcraft, kind of black magic, practised among negroes in W. Indies and United States. **2.** vb. To bewitch, affect, with voodoo.

voodooism, n. [1. vóodōōizm; 2. vúdúizəm]. Prec. & **-ism**. Practice of, belief in, voodoo.

voodooist, n. [1. vóodōōist; 2. vúdúist]. **voodoo** & **-ist**. Believer in, practitioner of, voodoo.

-vora, suff. fr. neut. pl. of Lat. *-vorus*, 'eating', used to form ns. designating animals classified according to the kind of food they eat: *carnivora*, 'flesh-eating animals'; see **-vorous**, & etymol. under **voracious**.

voracious, adj. [1. voráshus; 2. vəréiʃəs]. Lat. *vorāci-*, stem of *vorax*, 'hungry, greedy', fr. base **gʷer-*, **gʷor-*, seen in *vorāre*, 'to devour'; & also in Gk. *borá*, 'food'; *brôma*, 'food'; Scrt. *garāś*, 'drink'; *gargaraš*, 'gulf'. Eager to consume food; at once greedy and hungry; ravenous; urgently requiring food; (fig.) *a voracious reader.*

voraciously, adv. Prec. & **-ly**. In a voracious manner.

voraciousness, n. See prec. & **-ness**. State, quality, of being voracious; voracity.

voracity, n. [1. vorásiti; 2. vərǽsiti]. Fr. *voracité*, 'greed' &c., fr. Lat. *vorāci-*, see **voracious**, & **-ity**. State, quality, of being voracious; eagerness, capacity, to devour; greed springing from hunger; also figurative.

-vore, suff. Fr., fr. Lat. *-vorus*, see **-vorous** & **voracious.** Suffix forming name of an animal designated from the character of its food: *carnivore*, a flesh-eating animal.

-vorous, suff. fr. Lat. *-vorus*, see prec. & **voracious** & **-ous**, forming adjectives meaning 'eating such and such food': *carnivorous*, flesh-eating &c.

vortex, n. [1. vórteks; 2. vɔ̃teks], pl. **vortexes, vortices** [1. vórtisēz; 2. vɔ̃tisīz]. Lat., 'whirlpool, eddy'; gradational variant fr. base **vert-*, 'to turn', see **version. 1. a** Fluid in rotational motion; a whirlpool, powerful eddy; **b** whirling motion or mass. **2.** (fig.) Any social or intellectual movement, system &c., a set of social or other conditions possessing such liveliness and intensity that they are considered as absorbing and engulfing completely those who approach them: *the vortex of war, revolution, religious controversy* &c.

vortical, adj. [1. vórtikl; 2. vɔ̃tikl], fr. Lat. *vortic-*, stem of **vortex**, & **-al**. Resembling, of the nature of, a vortex.

vortically, adv. Prec. & **-ly**. So as to form a vortex.

vorticism, n. [1. vórtisizm; 2. vɔ̃tisizəm], fr. **vortex** & **-ism**. An artistic movement on futurist lines, in which nature is imaginatively reconstructed in formal designs, its practitioners using vortices much as the cubists use cubes.

vorticist, n. [1. vórtisist; 2. vɔ̃tisist]. See prec. & **-ist**. One who practises or advocates vorticism.

vorticose, adj. [1. vórtikōs; 2. vɔ̃tikous]. *vortic-*, as in **vortical**, & **-ose**. Having a vortex; abounding in vortices.

vortiginous, adj. [1. vortíjinus; 2. vɔ̃tídžinəs]. Cp. **vortex** & **vertiginous**. Whirling, eddying, resembling a vortex; vortical.

votable, adj. [1. vṓtabl; 2. vóutəbl]. **vote** (**II.**) & **-able**. **a** Entitled, competent, to vote; **b** able to be voted for.

votaress, n. [1. vṓtarès; 2. vóutərès]. See **votary** & **-ess**. A female votary.

votary, n. [1. vṓtari; 2. vóutəri], fr. Lat. *vōtum*, 'a vow, a wish', see next word, & **-ary**. **1.** Person vowed, devoted, to the service of **a** god: *the ancient gods sometimes destroyed their votaries.* **2. a** Ardent adherent, supporter, advocate of a cause, ideal, system &c.: *a votary of celibacy, of total abstinence, of vegetarianism* &c.; **b** one who is much addicted to a certain pursuit: *a votary of pleasure*; *a votary of athletic sports, of hunting* &c.

vote (**I.**), n. [1. vōt; 2. vout]. Fr., fr. Lat. *vōtum*, 'wish; vow', for **vovetum*, fr. P.P. of *vovēre*, 'to vow; to wish for'; cogn. w. Scrt. *vāghát-*, 'one who offers a sacrifice'; Aryan base **(e)wĕgʷh-, *(e)wōgʷh-*, 'to offer sacrifice, pray, vow', whence also Gk. *eúkhomai* 'to pray'; *eukhḗ*, 'vow; wish'. **1.** Formal expression, by ballot or show of hands &c., of one's wish, choice, opinion, esp. in regard (i.) to the election of a candidate for a post, or as a member of Parliament or other legislative or administrative body; or (ii.) to the passing of a resolution, law, measure, sanctioning or prohibiting some specific form of action. Phr. *to cast a vote*, express one's opinion by voting. **2.** The choice, will, opinion of an individual, or of a party, thus formally expressed: *I gave my vote to X*, voted for him; *the Conservative vote was unanimously given against the measure*; *one man one vote.* **3.** The right to vote, at parliamentary elections, or on other occasions when matters are decided by votes: *at what age should women have a vote?*; *he was present at the committee, but without a vote.*

vote (**II.**), vb. intrans. & trans., fr. prec. **A.** intrans. To exercise the right to express one's wishes, opinion &c. by casting a vote; to give a vote: *you may attend the meeting but you may not vote*; *shall you vote for or against the resolution?*; *vote for Brown and cheap bread*; *my mind is not made up, so I would rather not vote.* **B.** trans. **1.** In such Phrs. as: *to vote a measure through*, get it passed by voting; *to vote a person into Parliament*, elect him by votes; *to vote down a measure*, defeat it by voting. **2.** To assign, allot, bestow, by vote: *Parliament often votes considerable sums of money to successful generals.* **3.** To regard as, feel to be and designate as: *he was generally voted a public nuisance*; *the public voted the new play a distinct success.* **4.** (colloq.) *I vote (that) we go to the theatre to-night* &c., I suggest, propose that &c.; let us (go &c.).

voteless, adj. [1. vṓtles; 2. vóutlis]. **vote** (**I.**) & **-less**. Lacking a vote or the right to vote.

voter, n. [1. vṓter; 2. vóutə]. **vote** (**II.**) & **-er.** One who votes; specif. **a** one entitled to vote at parliamentary elections; **b** person actually casting a vote on a specific occasion.

voting, n. [1. vṓting; 2. vóutiŋ]. **vote** (**II.**) & **-ing**. Act of one who votes; the exercise of the right to vote: *voting paper*, official form on which votes are recorded at a ballot.

votive, adj. [1. vṓtiv; 2. vóutiv]. Lat. *vōtīvus*, 'belonging to a vow; given in consequence of a vow'; see **vote** (**I.**) & **-ive.** Dedicated, devoted, consecrated, to a particular purpose, in fulfilment of **a** vow: *a votive offering, sacrifice.*

vouch, vb. intrans. & trans. [1. vouch; 2. vautʃ], fr. O. Fr. *voucher*, 'to cite, or call in aid, in a suit', fr. Lat. *vocāre*, 'to call', see **vocal** & **vox. 1.** intrans. Chiefly *vouch for*, to guarantee, answer for (a person's honesty &c.); assert, confirm (statement or assertion), undertake: *he is a perfectly honest man for whom I can vouch*; *I can't vouch for it that the house is not already sold*; (also more rarely) *vouch that* &c. **2.** trans. (very rare) To declare, guarantee to be: *will you vouch him honest?*

voucher, n. [1. vóucher; 2. váutʃə]. Prec. & **-er.** He who, that which, vouches for something; specif., a document which establishes some fact or the authenticity of something, esp. that money has been paid.

vouchsafe, vb. trans. [1. vouchsā́f; 2. vautʃséif]. M.E. *vouchen sāfe*, 'to undertake that it is safe'; see **vouch** & **safe.** To condescend to grant; to give as an act of grace: *can you vouchsafe me a few minutes' conversation*; *I think he might at least have vouchsafed an answer.*

voussoir, n. [1. vṓōswar; 2. vúswā]. Fr., cogn. w. *voute*, **vault.** Any of the wedge-shaped stones forming an arch, as of a bridge or vault.

vow (**I.**), n. [1. vou; 2. vau]. O. Fr. *vou, veu*, fr. Lat. *vōtum*, see **vote** (**I.**). **1.** A solemn and, under ordinary circumstances, an inviolable promise, pledge, or undertaking, made under an oath, to God, or taking God to witness, to do, or to abstain from doing, something: *a vow of celibacy*; *marriage vows*; *to be under a vow, to be bound by a vow*; *to take, make a vow*, to bind oneself by vow. **2.** Content, implication, of a vow; action &c. to which one is pledged by a vow.

vow (**II.**), vb. trans., fr. prec. **1.** To make a solemn promise or vow; to promise faithfully: *to vow that one will be loyal to the king.* **2.** To make vow, promise under oath, to do or make: *to vow a pilgrimage to the Holy Land.* **3.** To promise solemnly to give: *the king vowed an abbey to God for his victory.* **4.** To devote, dedicate, consecrate, esp. under a vow: *to vow oneself to a life of self-sacrifice*; *vowed to poverty and obedience.* **5.** Archaic, in colloquial Phr. *to vow and declare*, often merely emphatic for to assert; archaic and colloquial as in *I vow you are in a pretty mess*, I must say . . . **6.** To state emphatically, to assert as an intention, resolution &c.: *he vowed he would never return to such an unpleasant place.*

vowel, n. [1. vóuil, -el; 2. váuil, -ɛl, -əl], fr. O. Fr. *vouel*, cp. Mod. Fr. *voyelle*, fr. Lat. *vocālis (littera)*, 'vocal letter'; see **vocal. 1.** (phon.) A speech sound, usually voiced, formed by the tongue, and sometimes with the participation of the lips, in the utterance of which the air-passage in the mouth is never sufficiently constricted to produce audible friction; contrasted with *consonant. Vowel gradation*, see **gradation**; *vowel mutation*, see **mutation. 2.** Graphic symbol representing a vowel sound.

vowel harmony, n. Phonological principle observable in the Finno-Ugric languages, whereby the vowel sounds in the second and subsequent syllables of words are assimilated in phonetic character to that in the first syllable—a front vowel being followed by front vowels, back by back.

vowelize, vb. trans. [1. vóuilīz; 2. váuilaiz]. **vowel** & **-ize.** (rare) **1.** To change a consonantal sound into a vowel sound: *final -j in Gothic is vowelized to -i.* **2.** To add the vowel symbols or points in a Hebrew or Arabic text.

vowelless, adj. [1. vóuilles; 2. váuillis]. **vowel** & **-less.** Lacking vowels; pronounced without a vowel or vowels.

vowel-like, adj. **vowel** & **-like.** Resembling a vowel in phonetic or acoustic properties; esp. having the power of forming a syllable; syllabic; e.g. the *l* in *bottle* [bótl].

vox, n. [1. voks; 2. vɔks]. Lat., 'voice, sound, tone, cry, call'; genit. *vōc-is*; fr. same base as Lat *vocāre*, 'to call' &c., see **vocal** & **vocation**, & vbs. ending in *-voke.* This base, wh. appears in Lat. as *vŏc-, vōc-*, represents Aryan **wokʷ-, wōkʷ-, wekʷ-*, & occurs in Scrt. *vačiti*, 'he speaks', *vakaš*, 'sound', & in Gk. *épos*, 'word, song, narrative', see **epic.** Cp. also **voice.** *Vox barbara*, a linguistic barbarism, i.e. a hybrid formation or concoction; *vox humāna*, one of the stops in an organ, the quality and tone of which resemble those of the human voice; *vox populi*, the voice of the people; public opinion.

voyage (**I.**), n. [1. vói-ij; 2. vɔ́i-idž, vɔidž], fr. O. Fr. *veiage, voiage*, 'journey', fr. Lat. **viaticum.** A journey by sea or on another large sheet of water; used especially of a long sea journey: *a voyage to Australia, round the world*; but also, occasionally, of short journeys by sea: *one has a brief but often a rough voyage from Dover to Calais*; *crossing* would be the more usual word here.

voyage (**II.**), vb. intrans. & trans., fr. prec. **1.** intrans. To make a voyage, to travel by sea, to undertake a long sea journey. **2.** trans. (very rare and poet.) To journey upon, or through, to traverse: '*Long were to tell What I have done, what suffered, with what pain Voyaged the unreal, vast, unbounded deep*' (Milton, 'P. L.', x. 469–71).

voyager, n. [1. vóiajer; 2. vɔ́iədžə]. Prec. & **-er.** A traveller by water; specif., an adventurous explorer of the ocean.

vraisemblable, adj. [1. vresombláhbl; 2. vresɑ̃blábl]. Fr., 'having the appearance of truth'. Seeming true; having plausibility, within the bounds of probability.

vraisemblance, n. [1. vresombláhns; 2. vresɑ̃blɑ̃s]. Fr., 'verisimilitude'. The quality of being vraisemblable; verisimilitude.

Vulcan, n. [1. vúlkan; 2. válkən]. Lat. *Vol-, Vulcānus*, name of the Roman god of fire & metal-working; cogn. w. Scrt. *ulká*, 'a fire-brand', for **wḷká-. Vulcan powder*, a high explosive.

Vulcanist, n. [1. vúlkanist; 2. válkənist]. Prec. & **-ist.** (geol.) One who held the Plutonic theory, namely, that most geological phenomena have been caused by the action of fire in the interior of the earth.

vulcanite, n. [1. vúlkanīt; 2. válkənait]. **vulcan** & **-ite.** Form of india-rubber produced by an admixture of sulphur; ebonite.

vulcanization, n. [1. vùlkanizā́shun; 2. vàlkənaizéiʃən]. Next word & **-ation.** Process of vulcanizing rubber.

vulcanize, vb. trans. [1. vúlkanīz; 2. válkənaiz]. **Vulcan** & **-ize.** To treat (rubber) by mixing with sulphur to increase its elasticity.

vulgar, adj. [1. vúlgar; 2. válgə]. Lat. *vulgāris*, 'belonging to the multitude; general, usual, common, commonplace, vulgar'; fr. *vulgus*, 'the multitude', see **vulgus**, & **-ar**

1. Pertaining to the multitude, hence common, in common or ordinary use, having currency among the mass of the people, usual; obs. except in Phr. *the vulgar tongue*, the vernacular. 2. Pertaining to the common people as contrasted with the upper and more civilized classes: *vulgar life, circles* &c. 3. a Characteristic of the people, as contrasted with the upper and more refined or polite classes of society; not current in refined circles; low, base, unrefined; indelicate; ill-bred: *vulgar manners, language*; *a vulgar accent, way of speaking*; b not conforming to, unfamiliar with, the manners and customs of good society; lacking delicacy of feeling; bad, coarse, indecorous: *a vulgar fellow*; as n., *the vulgar*, vulgar people.

vulgarian, n. [1. vulgárian; 2. valgéəriən]. Lat. *vulgāri-*, stem of *vulgāris*, see prec., & **-an**. A vulgar, flamboyant, person; esp. a pretentious person, often one newly enriched, without good breeding, decent manners, or delicacy of feeling; a bounder.

vulgarism, n. [1. vúlgarizm; 2. válgərizəm]. **vulgar** & **-ism**. 1. Vulgar behaviour; vulgarity. 2. A vulgar, unrefined mode of speech; a mode of pronunciation, choice of words, grammatical form, not current among the well-bred and refined classes of society; a solecism.

vulgarity, n. [1. vulgáriti; 2. valgǽriti]. See **vulgar** & **-ity**. Quality of being vulgar; vulgar behaviour; coarseness, commonness of moral fibre, lack of refinement and delicacy in feeling; rudeness, ill-breeding; pretentious, offensive arrogance and display, coupled with bad taste and bad manners; indecorum.

vulgarization, n. [1. vùlgarīzáshun; 2. vàlgəraizéiʃən]. **vulgarize** & **-ation**. 1. Act, process, of rendering vulgar; state of having become vulgar. 2. (rare) Act of rendering more widely known and current; popularization.

vulgarize, vb. trans. [1. vúlgarīz; 2. válgəraiz]. **vulgar** & **-ize**. 1. To make vulgar, common, unrefined, commonplace: *the tripper has vulgarized many of the loveliest spots in England*. 2. (rare) To render better known; to popularize.

vulgarly, adv. [1. vúlgarli; 2. válgəli]. **vulgar** & **-ly**. 1. Commonly, generally, popularly: *vulgarly supposed to be a cure* &c. 2. In a vulgar manner; with vulgarity: *to behave, speak, vulgarly*.

Vulgate, n. [1. vúlgat; 2. válgit]. Lat. *vulgāta ēditio*, lit. 'popular edition', fr. fem. of *vulgātus*, P.P. of *vulgāre*, 'to make general, common, or universal', formed fr. *vulgus*, 'the multitude' &c., see **vulgus** & **vulgar**. Latin translation of the Scriptures made towards the end of the 4th cent., recognized by the Roman Church as authentic and authoritative.

vulgus, n. [1. vúlgus; 2. válgəs]. Lat., 'the great mass of the people; the masses, the multitude, the people, the common run'; cogn. w. Scrt. *várgaś*, 'division, section, group'; not connected with **folk**. 1. The common people, the multitude. 2. (archaic or obs.) A collection of exercises in Latin or Greek verse used in schools.

vulnerability, n. [1. vùlnerabíliti; 2. vàlnərəbíliti]. Next word & **-ity**. Quality, condition, of being vulnerable.

vulnerable, adj. [1. vúlnerabl; 2. válnərəbl]. Lat. *vulnerābilis*, fr. *vulner-*, stem of *vulnus*, earlier *volnus*, 'wound'; cogn. w. Gk. *oulē*, fr. **wolnā*, 'a scar'; prob. fr. same base as that in Lat. *vellere*, 'to pluck, pull, tear', see **villus**, **vellicate**. Capable of being, liable to be, wounded; open to, susceptible of, not protected against, attack, injury, criticism.

vulnerably, adv. Prec. & **-ly**. So as to be vulnerable.

vulnerary, adj. & n. [1. vúlnerari; 2. válnərəri]. Lat. *vulner-*, see **vulnerable**, & **-ary**. 1. adj. Used, useful, for healing wounds. 2. n. A remedy for wounds.

vulpicide, n. [1. vúlpisīd; 2. válpisaid]. Lat. *vulpi-*, stem of *vulpes*, 'fox', see **vulpine**, & **-cide**. 1. Person who shoots or traps foxes. 2. The killing of foxes otherwise than by the normal method of hunting them.

vulpine, adj. [1. vúlpīn; 2. válpain], fr. Lat. *vulpīnus*, 'pertaining to, like, a fox; crafty', fr. *vulpēs*, 'a fox', earlier *volp-*, & **-ine**. The Lat. name for fox may either be fr. Aryan base **kʷelpi-*, **kʷolpi-*, whence also, fr. variant **kʷelb-*, O.E. *hwelp*, 'young dog', see **whelp** (I.), or, as seems more probable, fr. Aryan **wulkʷi-*, **wulpi-*, fr. a different grade of wh. comes Lith. *wilpiszis*, 'wild cat'; fr. another variant, **wl̥kʷos*, comes Lat. *lūpus*, 'wolf', see **lupine** & cp. **wolf** (I.). Pertaining to, resembling, a fox; a having the appearance of a fox: *vulpine countenance*; b like a fox in character; sly, crafty.

vulpinism, n. [1. vúlpinizm; 2. válpinizəm]. Prec. & **-ism**. (rare) Guile, craftiness, slyness.

vulture, n. [1. vúlchur; 2. váltʃə]. M.E. *vultur*, fr. O. Fr. *voltur*, fr. Lat. *vultur*, *voltur*, name of the bird, connected w. *vellere*, 'to pluck', see **vellicate** & words there referred to. 1. Large bird of prey, allied to the hawks and eagles, which lives chiefly on carrion. 2. (fig.) An unscrupulous, rapacious rogue and extortioner who preys upon his fellow-creatures.

vulturine, adj. [1. vúlchurīn; 2. váltʃərain]. Prec. & **-ine**. Pertaining to, resembling, a vulture in appearance or habits: *vulturine eagle*.

vulturous, adj. [1. vúlchurus; 2. váltʃərəs]. **vulture** & **-ous**. Having the characteristics of the vulture; rapacious.

vulva, n. [1. vúlva, 2. válvə]. Lat., also *volva*, 'wrapper, covering; the womb', connected w. *volvere*, 'to turn, roll, fold' &c., see **volute**. External orifice of female genital organs.

vulvar, adj. [1. vúlvar; 2. válvə]. Prec. & **-ar**. Pertaining to the vulva.

vulvitis, n. [1. vulvítis; 2. valváitis]. **vulva** & **-itis**. Inflammation of the vulva.

vulvo-, pref. Form of **vulva** used in compounds: *vulvo-uterine*, pertaining to, affecting, the vulva and the uterus.

W

W, w [1. dúbl-ū; 2. dábl-ju]. The twenty-third letter of the alphabet. For abbreviations &c. see list at end of Dictionary.

wabble. See **wobble**.

wacke, n. [1. wáke; 2. wǽkə], fr. Mod. Germ. *wacke*; M.H.G. *wacke*, O.H.G. *wacko*, 'gravel'. Soft, greyish or brownish rock developed from decomposed trap-rock.

wad (I.), n. [1. wod; 2. wɔd]. Prob. fr. Swed. *vadd*, 'wadding'; cp. Mod. Germ. *watte*, fr. Du. *watje*. According to Kluge, the word first appears in 1380, as Med. Lat. *wadda*. 1. a Small mass or lump of soft, fibrous material packed round or between objects to prevent shifting and rattling, concussion &c.; or used to stop up an opening; specif. b disk of leather, felt &c. to hold charge in position in gun &c. 2. Collection of sheets, esp. of bank-notes, pressed or folded together so as to form a compact bundle.

wad (II.), vb. trans., fr. prec. 1. To pack, press (soft material), into a wad. 2. a To pack, pad, stuff, with a wad; b to stop up (opening) with a wad. 3. To line (garment &c.) with wadding, to give warmth, softness &c.

wadable, adj. [1. wádabl; 2. wéidəbl]. **wade** (I.) & **-able**. Capable of being waded.

wadding, n. [1. wóding; 2. wɔ́diŋ]. **wad** & **-ing**. 1. Soft, fluffy material used for stuffing, packing, lining garments &c.; esp. cotton-wool in sheets. 2. Felt or other material used for gun-wads.

waddle, vb. intrans. & n. [1. wódl; 2. wɔ́dl]. **wade** & **-le**. 1. vb. To walk with short steps and a rolling gait, as of a stout, short-legged person, or a heavy short-legged bird, esp. a duck &c. 2. n. Act of waddling; a heavy, ungraceful gait accompanied by a roll from side to side as each foot is placed on the ground.

waddling, adj. [1. wódling; 2. wɔ́dliŋ], fr. Pres. Part. of prec. Inclined to waddle; characterized by a waddle.

waddlingly, adv. Prec. & **-ly**. In a waddling manner.

waddy, n. [1. wódi; 2. wɔ́di]. Australian. Wooden war-club of Australian aborigines.

wade (I.), vb. intrans. & trans. [1. wād; 2. weid]. O.E. *wadan*; M.E. *wāden*, 'to go'; cp. O. Fris. *wada*; O.H.G. *watan*; O.N. *vaða*, 'to go, walk'; cogn. w. Lat. *vādere*, 'to go', seen in **vade-mecum**, *vadum*, 'ford'; *vadāre*, 'to wade'. A. intrans. 1. a To walk through water, liquid mud, wet snow &c., or other penetrable substance: *to wade across a stream*; *to wade through the mud*; also b (fig.) '*to wade through slaughter to a throne*' (Gray's 'Elegy'). 2. Specif., to walk in the water of a river while fly-fishing. 3. (fig.) To peruse, go through laboriously, with effort: *to wade through a book*. 4. *Wade in*, a to enter, advance into shallow water, on foot, not swimming: *he waded in and rescued the drowning child*; b (fig.) to enter, take part in, intervene, in a fight, piece of business, discussion &c.: *he must needs wade in and delay the business with petty objections*. B. trans. To cross, traverse (piece of water) by wading, ford: *to wade a stream*.

wade (II.), n., fr. prec. Act, spell, of wading.

wader, n. [1. wáder; 2. wéidə]. Prec. & **-er**. 1. One who, that which, wades; specif., a wading bird. 2. (pl.) *Waders*, long waterproof garments covering feet and legs and coming up above the waist, worn by fly-fishermen &c.

wadi, wady, n. [1. wódi; 2. wɔ́di]. Arab. *wādī*. (in Arabia &c.) a Watercourse, river-bed, which is dry except in rainy season; b an oasis.

wading, adj. [1. wáding; 2. wéidiŋ]. Pres. Part. of **wade** (I.). *Wading bird*, one which has long legs enabling it to walk in shallow water to obtain food, such as a crane, a heron &c.

Wafd, n. [1. wahft, waft; 2. waft, wæft]. Arab. Name of the extreme Nationalist party in Egypt.

wafer (I.), n. [1. wáfer; 2. wéifə]. M.E. *wāfre*, 'thin cake', fr. O. Fr. *waufre*, of Gmc. origin; cp. O.H.G. *waba*, 'honeycomb'; cogn. w. **weave** (I.), **web**. 1. A very thin sheet or disk of flour, used for various purposes: a small disk formerly used for sealing letters &c.; b small disk used in Holy Communion. 2. A small disk of red paper affixed to a document in place of a seal. 3. A thin sweet, cake, or biscuit, esp. one eaten with ices. Phr. *as thin as a wafer*, very thin.

wafer (II.), vb. trans., fr. prec. To fasten with a wafer.

wafery, adj. [1. wáferi; 2. wéifəri]. **wafer** & **-y**. Resembling a wafer in thinness and consistency.

waffle, n. [1. wófl; 2. wɔ́fl], fr. Du. *wafel*, cogn. w. **wafer**. Thin, crisp cake of batter cooked over the fire in a waffle-iron.

waffle-iron, n. Iron cooking utensil, consisting of two shallow pans hinged together and reversible.

waft (I.), vb. trans. [1. wahft: 2. wāft]. Prob. a variant of **wave**; or possibly a back-formation fr. obs. *wafter*, 'convoying ship', the latter perh. fr. Du. *wachter*, 'guard', cogn. w. **watch** (I.) & **wake** (I.). To carry lightly and buoyantly through the air or water; to bear smoothly along: *the leaves were wafted along by the breeze; a distant song was wafted to our ears.*

waft (II.), n., fr. prec. **1.** Smooth movement, sweep, of flying or floating body. **2.** Hint of fragrance; faint odour, whiff.

wag (I.), vb. trans. & intrans. [1. wag; 2. wæg]. M.E. *waggen*, prob. fr. M. Swed. *wagga*, 'to oscillate, fluctuate'; cogn. w. O.E. *wagian*, M.E. *wāwien*, 'to move'; O.H.G. *wagōn*; Goth. *wagjan*, 'to move'; cogn. w. O.E. *weġan*, 'to carry'; see **weigh** (I.), & cp. also **wag(g)on, wain. A.** trans. **1.** To cause to oscillate, shake (object fastened at one end) lightly up and down or from side to side: *to wag one's forefinger.* **2.** Specif. (of a dog) *to wag the tail*, to move it rapidly to and fro as expression of pleasure &c. **B.** intrans. (of object fastened at one end) To move quickly and lightly up and down or from side to side: *the dog's tail wags when his master appears; their heads wagged in time to the music.* Phrs. *to set tongues, chins, wagging*, cause people to talk, esp. to provoke mild scandal; *so the world wags*, thus human affairs go on.

wag (II.), n., fr. prec. Motion of wagging; single movement forming part of oscillation: *the dog replied with a wag of its tail.*

wag (III.), n. Earlier *wag-halter*, a person likely to swing at the end of a rope, i.e. to be hanged; hence a rascal; commonly used playfully. A jester; a merry, roguish person; one fond of quips and jokes; a humorous person, one full of comical, laughable sayings.

wage (I.), n. [1. wāj; 2. weidž]. M.E. *wāge*, fr. O. Fr. *wage*; fr. Low Lat. *wadium*, 'a pledge'; of Gmc. origin; cp. Goth. *wadi*, 'a pledge', & *(ga)wadjōn*, 'to pledge'; cp. O.E. *wedd*, 'pledge, agreement', see **wed. gage** (I.) is fr. a Fr. variant. **1.** (archaic) Recompense, reward; often in plural treated as singular: '*the wages of sin is death*'; '*Thou thy worldly task hast done, Home art gone, and ta'en thy wages*' (Shakespeare, 'Cymbeline', iv., song). **2. a** Payment made at regular intervals in return for services; now chiefly used of payment made for manual labour, the contract between the parties being terminable at short notice; contrasted with *stipend* and *salary*: *I pay my man a good weekly wage*; Phr. *a living wage*, one adequate for the support of recipient; **b** more usually in plural, *wages*, the periodical payment earned by, and made to, domestic servants and manual labourers generally: *a reliable workman can earn good wages; take your month's wages and go at once; when wages are high, prices are high.*

wage (II.), vb. trans. M.E. *wāgen*, O. Fr. *wagier*, 'to pledge, promise, engage', fr. *wage*, 'a pledge', see prec. To carry on, conduct, prosecute (war, a campaign).

wage-earner, n. [1. wāj ẽrner; 2. wéidž ʌ̄nə]. Person working for wages.

wageless, adj. [1. wājles; 2. wéidžlis]. **wage** (I.) & **-less.** Receiving no wages.

wager (I.), n. [1. wājer; 2. wéidžə]. M.E. *wāgeoure*, fr. O. Fr. *wageure*, fr. L. Lat. *wadiatūra*, fr. *wadiāre*, 'to pledge', fr. *wadium*, 'a pledge', see **wage** (I.). **1.** Engagement between two persons to risk money on the outcome of an event; bet. **2.** (hist.) *Wager of battle*, mode of trial by personal combat; *wager of law*, mode of defence in which defendant, together with a number of witnesses, swears to his innocence, absence of liability &c.

wager (II.), vb. trans., fr. prec. **1. a** To bet, risk, offer as stake: *to wager half a crown on a race*; **b** to pledge: *to wager one's reputation on.* **2.** To bet (that): *I would not wager that I shall succeed.*

wage(s)-fund, n. [1. wāj(ez) fŭnd; 2. wéidž(iz) fʌnd]. (polit. econ.) That part of the capital of a community which is to be expended on wages and salaries.

waggery, n. [1. wágeri; 2. wǽgəri]. **wag** (III.) & **-ery.** Waggish behaviour or sayings; drollery, comicality.

waggish, adj. [1. wágish; 2. wǽgiʃ]. **wag** (III.) & **-ish.** Inclined to, of the nature of, waggery; comical, droll: *a waggish fellow; a waggish look, speech* &c.

waggishly, adv. Prec. & **-ly.** In a waggish manner.

waggishness, n. See prec. & **-ness.** Quality of being waggish; waggery.

waggle (I.), vb. intrans. & trans. [1. wágl; 2. wǽgl]. Freq. of **wag** (I.); see **-le.** (colloq.) To move slightly backwards and forwards, to oscillate.

waggle (II.), n., fr. prec. (colloq.) A slight backward and forward movement.

wag(g)on, n. [1. wágun; 2. wǽgən], fr. Du. *wagen*; cogn. w. **wain. 1.** Strong, four-wheeled vehicle used for carrying heavy loads, often drawn by two or more horses, and sometimes with removable top or cover. **2.** Railway truck.

wag(g)on-boiler, n. Steam-boiler of semi-cylindrical shape, like that of cover of waggon.

wag(g)oner, n. [1. wáguner; 2. wǽgənə]. **wag(g)on** & **-er.** Driver of waggon; man in charge of waggon(s) and horses &c.

wag(g)on-roof, n. Roof of semi-cylindrical shape.

wag(g)on-vault, n. Semicircular vault.

wagonette, n. [1. wàgunét; 2. wæ̀gənét]. **wag(g)on** & **-ette.** Four-wheeled open carriage, with two seats facing each other behind the coachman's box.

wagon-lit, n. [1. vàgon lḗ; 2. væ̀gō lí]. Fr. Railway carriage fitted with beds.

wagtail, n. [1. wágtāl; 2. wǽgteil]. **wag** (I.) & **tail.** One of a genus, *Motacilla*, of small birds with long wings, and tail feathers which move constantly up and down as the bird runs along the ground.

Wahabi, -ee, n. [1. wahháhbi; 2. wahā́bi]. Member of Puritanical Mohammedan sect founded in the 18th cent. in Central Arabia by Abd-el-Wahhab, who died about 1792.

waif, n. [1. wāf; 2. weif]. In M.E., fr. O.N. *veif*, 'something flapping or waving'; meaning influenced by O. Fr. *waif*, fr. L. Lat. *waivium*, 'goods thrown away by a thief in flight', also fr. O.N. See **waive. 1. a** A homeless, straying, wandering person or animal; Phr. *waifs and strays*, homeless, abandoned children; **b** a person or animal of miserable, poverty-stricken, neglected appearance. **2.** Object without an owner, esp. something which drifts in water or is blown by the wind, or brought by unknown agency.

wail (I.), vb. intrans. & trans. [1. wāl; 2. weil]. M.E. *wailen*, fr. O.N. *væla*, 'to lament', fr. *væ*, 'woe'; cogn. w. **woe. A.** intrans. **1.** (of living creatures and of the wind) To utter or produce a long, shrill, lugubrious or plaintive cry or sound; to shriek, howl. **2.** To express sorrow or regret; to lament: *to wail over one's misfortunes.* **B.** trans. To bewail; to lament, grieve over: *to wail one's sorrows.*

wail (II.), n. See prec. **a** Wailing sound; prolonged, plaintive sound produced by a living creature or by the wind &c.; **b** a complaint, expression of regret, grief, annoyance &c.

wailful, adj. [1. wā́lfool; 2. wéilful]. Prec. & **-ful.** In the nature of a wail; plaintive: *a wailful cry.*

wailing (I.), adj. [1. wā́ling; 2. wéiliŋ]. Pres. Part. of **wail** (I.). Of the nature of, resembling, a wail.

wailing (II.), vbl. n. **wail** & **-ing.** The sound of a wail.

wailingly, adv. **wailing** (I.) & **-ly.** In a wailing manner.

wain, n. [1. wān; 2. wein]. O.E. *wæġn*, M.E. *wain*, 'waggon'; cp. O. Fris. *wain*; O.N. *vagn*; O.H.G. *wagan*; in gradational relation to O.E. *weġan*, 'to carry', see **weigh** (I.); cp. also **vehicle.** (chiefly poet.) A waggon; *Charles's Wain*, the constellation also called the Plough, the Great Bear, and Ursa Major.

wainscot, n. & vb. trans. [1. wénskut, wā́nskōt; 2. wénskət, wéinskout, -kət], fr. Du. *wagenschot*; the first element is doubtful; perh. cogn. w. O.E. *wāg*, 'wall', but by some referred to Du. *wage*, 'a wave', in reference to the grain of wood; the second element means 'board'; etymol. doubtful; cp. **camp-shot. 1.** n. **a** Originally applied to a fine oak used for panelling imported from Holland; now, any wooden panelling on a wall, but esp. the wooden panel at the base of, and running round, the wall of a room just above the floor; **b** name of various moths of the sub-family Orthosiidae, with streaked wing markings. **2.** vb. To affix wainscot to (wall).

wainscoting, n. [1. wénskuting; 2. wénskətiŋ]. Prec. & **-ing. a** Material for wainscot; **b** wooden panelling on a wall.

waist, n. [1. wāst; 2. weist]. M.E. *wāst*, 'stature; waist'; cp. O.H.G. *wahst*; Goth. *wahstus*, 'growth'; cogn. w. O.E. *wæstm*, 'growth', fr. base of *weahsan, weaxan*, 'to grow', see **wax** (III.). **1. a** Narrowest part of human trunk, between ribs and hip-bones: *to have a sash round one's waist; a large, small, waist*, one of large, small, circumference; **b** well-marked narrowing and slimness of the figure at the waist: *waists have gone out of fashion.* **2.** Part of woman's garment corresponding to the waist. Specif. U.S.A., a woman's blouse or bodice; also *shirt-waist.* **3.** Part of an object resembling the human waist in shape and position; central, narrowed portion, e.g. of a violin. **4.** (naut.) Middle part of ship, between quarter-deck and forecastle.

waist-band, n. Band, part of garment, fitting round the waist.

waist-belt, n. Belt worn round the waist.

waist-cloth, n. Loin-cloth.

waistcoat, n. [1. wéskut, wā́s(t)kōt; 2. wéskət, wéis(t)kout]. Close-fitting, usually sleeveless garment worn under a coat and reaching to the waist.

waist-deep, adj. & adv. **1.** adj. **a** Reaching up to the waist: *the water was waist-deep*; **b** covered up to the waist: *to be waist-deep in bracken.* **2.** adv. So as to reach the waist.

waisted, adj. [1. wā́sted; 2. wéistid]. **waist** & **-ed.** Having a waist; shaped to form a waist; also in compounds: *long-, short-, small-waisted* &c.

waist-high, adj. & adv. High enough to reach to the waist.

wait (I.), vb. intrans. & trans. [1. wāt; 2. weit]. M.E. *waiten*, fr. O. Fr. *waitier* (also *gaitier*), 'to watch, wait', fr. *waite*, 'watcher', fr. O.H.G. *wahta*, 'watcher', fr. *wahhēn*, 'to be awake'; see further under **wake** (I.). **A.** intrans. **1.** To remain in expectation of something happening; to delay action &c., until a particular time, until an event has taken place: *the train is due, so we shall not have long to wait; don't wait if I am late; let us wait in the shade; you mustn't keep him waiting; wait until you are asked; please wait a minute; we have waited for hours.* **2.** To act as waiter, serve and hand round dishes at table &c.: *to wait at table; she will never learn to wait.* **B.** trans. To await, wait for, remain in expectation of, on the watch for: *to wait one's chance; to wait a person's return; to wait one's convenience, pleasure* &c. Phr. *to wait dinner, tea, luncheon* &c. *for* (a person), to put off having (dinner &c.) until he arrives. **C.** Followed by adverbs and prepositions with special meanings. *Wait for*, intrans., to remain in expectation of, await; delay action, resumption of action, departure &c., until specified time, person's arrival &c.: *I will wait for you at the gate; we have been waiting for the clock to strike; to wait for a person's reply; to wait for* *a signal.* *Wait (up)on*, **1.** (archaic) to call upon, pay one's respects to; **2.** (archaic) **a** to escort; **b** (fig.) to accompany, attend: *may good luck wait upon you*; **3.** to serve, attend upon, act as attendant on, fetch and carry for: *to be waited on hand and foot*; **4.** to follow as result, be a consequence of: '*Now good digestion wait on appetite*' (Shakespeare, 'Macbeth', iii. 4).

wait (II.), n., fr. prec. **a** Act of waiting; Phrs. *to lie in wait (for)*, remain hidden and waiting to waylay or attack; *to lay wait for*, prepare an ambush for; **b** time during which one waits: *a long, tedious wait.*

wait (III.), n., fr. O. Fr. *waite*, 'watcher'; see **wait** (I.). (chiefly in pl.) *The waits*, a band of persons who go from house to house and sing Christmas carols.

waiter, n. [1. wâter; 2. wéitə]. **wait** (I.) & **-er.** **1.** A male servant who serves guests at meals in public restaurants and hotels. **2.** Tray, salver, for handing dishes &c.

waiting, n. [1. wâting; 2. wéitiŋ]. **wait** & **-ing.** Act or occupation of one who waits. Phr. *in waiting*, in attendance, esp. on royalty: *lady-in-waiting*; *lords, grooms, in waiting.*

waiting-maid, n. Female personal attendant.

waiting-room, n. Room at railway station for the use of persons waiting for trains; sitting-room in a house for person awaiting an interview with a medical man &c.

waitress, n. [1. wâtres; 2. wéitris]. **waiter** & **-ess.** Female waiter at a hotel or restaurant.

waive, vb. trans. [1. wāv; 2. weiv]. M.E. *waiven*, fr. A.-Fr. *wayver*; of Gmc. origin; cp. O.N. *veifa*, 'to fluctuate, vibrate'; cogn. w. O.E. *wǣfian*, 'to be astonished at, to hesitate'; O.H.G. *weibōn*, 'to be unsteady'; cogn. w. Lat. *vibrāre.* See **vibrate** & cp. **waif.** To relinquish, esp. temporarily, refrain from insisting on or pressing: *to waive one's rights, a claim* &c.

waiver, n. [1. wâver; 2. wéivə]. A.-Fr. *wayver*, infin. as n.; see prec. Legal renunciation, relinquishing of claim &c.

wake (I.), vb. intrans. & trans. [1. wāk; 2. weik]. There are two closely related vbs. in O.E., *wacian*, 'to be awake, watch', & *wacan*, 'to originate, rise, be born'; M.E. *wāken*, 'to be awake, watch, keep vigil'; O.H.G. *wahhēn*; O.N. *vaka*, 'to be awake'; Goth. *wakan*; cp. further O.E. *wacor*, 'watchful'; O.H.G. *wahhar*, 'lively'; O.N. *vakr*, 'vigilant'; cogn. w. Lat. *vegēre*, 'to be active; to arouse', see **vegetable**; cp. **watch** (I.). **A.** intrans. **1.** To be, remain, awake: '*He wakes or sleeps with the enduring dead*' (Shelley, 'Adonais', xxxviii., 3). Phr. *in our waking hours*, those during which we are awake. **2. a** Also *wake up*, to return to consciousness from sleep: *I wake (up) early*; *to wake up with a start*; **b** to return to consciousness from a state resembling sleep: *to wake from a stupor, hypnotic trance* &c.; **c** to become mentally alert following condition of dullness and torpor: *it is time for you to wake up and attend to your business.* Phr. *to wake to (a realization of danger* &c.), become conscious of, realize. **3.** To come to life, become active; to emerge from a state of inactivity and quiescence: *his conscience woke and smote him*; *many fierce and angry passions wake during controversy.* **B.** trans. Also *wake up*, **1.** To cause to wake, rouse: *the noise woke me (up)*; *wake me at seven.* Phr. *to wake the echoes*, make a loud noise. **2.** To rouse, provoke mental alertness in, to stimulate into activity of mind: *the shock seemed to wake him up and make him less lethargic.* **3.** To excite, rouse, recall to activity, render lively; to stir: *to wake memories of the past*; *to wake passions.*

wake (II.), n., fr. prec. **1.** (hist.) **a** Festival of dedication of church, preceded by all-night vigil; **b** festivity, merrymaking, in celebration of this. **2. a** Vigil beside a corpse, kept up throughout the night preceding the funeral; **b** festivities accompanying a wake; (frequent among the poorer classes in Ireland). **3.** Annual holiday taken by workers in the industrial towns of Lancashire, Yorkshire &c.

wake (III.), vb. trans., fr. prec. To hold a wake over (dead person).

wake (IV.), n., fr. O.N. *vök*, 'hole in ice'; cp. O.N. *vökr*, 'damp'; cogn. w. Gk. *hugrós*, 'moist'; Scrt. *ukšati*, 'sprinkles'; Lat. *ūvidus*, 'wet'; *(h)ūmor*, 'moisture', see **humour** (I.). Long streak of smooth water behind moving vessel. Phr. *in the wake of*, (i.) (of vessel) following in the track of; (ii.) (fig.) following as consequence of; *wars bring misery in their wake.*

wakeful, adj. [1. wākfool; 2. wéikful]. **wake** (I.) & **-ful.** **1.** Watchful, vigilant, alert. **2. a** Remaining awake, unable to sleep; **b** *a wakeful night*, one passed with little or no sleep.

wakefully, adv. Prec. & **-ly.** In a wakeful manner.

wakefulness, n. See prec. & **-ness.** State of being wakeful.

waken, vb. intrans. & trans. [1. wâken; 2. wéikən]. O.E. *wæcnan*, 'to be born, have origin'; M.E. *waknen*, 'to be awakened', fr. *wacan*, 'to have origin, arise', see **wake** (I.). **1.** intrans. **a** To wake up, be awakened; **b** to recover consciousness, be roused. **2.** trans. **a** To cause to wake, rouse up; **b** to rouse to activity, stir up.

wake-robin, n. Wild arum.

Walach(ian). See **Wallach, Wallachian.**

Waldenses, n. pl. [1. wòldénsēz; 2. wɔldénsīz], fr. Peter Waldo, of Lyons, founder of the sect. Sect of Puritan reformers in Western Church, still persisting in the region of the Cottian Alps, founded about 1170, and much persecuted in 16th and 17th cents.

Waldensian, adj. [1. wòldénsian; 2. wɔldénsiən]. Prec. & **-ian.** Pertaining to the Waldenses.

wald-horn, n. [1. váhlt horn; 2. vált hɔ̄n], fr. Germ. *wald*, 'forest', see under **wold**, & **horn.** Hunting-horn.

wale, n. & vb. trans. [1. wāl; 2. weil]. O.E. *walu*, 'weal, stripe; bar, gunwale'; M.E. *wāle*; cp. O.N. *vǫlr*; O. Fris. *walu*; Goth. *walus*, 'rod'; cogn. w. Lith. *(ap)valùs*, 'round'; Lat. *vallus*, 'pillar'; *vallēs*, 'valley'; see **vallum, valley, wall. weal** (II.) is a variant. **1.** n. Raised streak formed on the flesh by a blow from a whip, stick &c. **2.** vb. To raise wales on, mark with wales.

wale-knot, n. Also *wall-knot*, mode of interweaving strands at end of rope to prevent unravelling.

Waler, n. [1. wâler; 2. wéilə], fr. New South Wales. One of a breed of horses imported into India from Australia.

Walhalla. See **Valhalla.**

walk (I.), vb. intrans. & trans. [1. wawk; 2. wɔ̄k]. O.E. *walcan*, 'to roll, fluctuate, whirl, twist'; M.E. *walken*, 'to move, go, roll, walk'; O.H.G. *walkan*, 'to strike, beat'; cp. O.N. *valka*, 'to roll'; Du. *walken*, 'to press'; Mod. Germ. *walken*, 'to full (cloth)'; cogn. w. Scrt. *valgati*, '(he) hops'. **A.** intrans. **1. a** To move along by putting alternately each foot in front of the other, and advancing at a moderate pace; contrasted with *sit*, or *stand still*; to pace along: *to walk slowly, steadily, up and down*; *children learn to walk at 13 months or so*; *it is too cold to stand about, you had better walk a bit*; Phr. *walking lady, gentleman*, actor who appears on the stage, but has no spoken part; **b** specif. (of a ghost) to be seen moving, stirring, in a specific place, to be visible, to haunt a place: *the ghost walks at midnight.* **2.** a (of persons) To move along at a comparatively slow or walking pace; contrasted with *to run*: *I'm quite out of breath with running, I must walk for a bit*; **b** (of a horse &c.) to move along at the slowest pace; contrasted with *to trot, canter, gallop.* **3.** To go on foot, as opposed to riding, or being conveyed in a vehicle: *let us stop the carriage and get down and walk*; *shall we go by car or walk?* **4.** (archaic) To conduct oneself, to behave, order one's conduct, mode of life &c.: '*to walk humbly with one's God*'. **B.** trans. **1. a** To cause to go at a walk: *to walk one's horse down hill*; **b** to lead, accompany, at a walk: *to walk a horse up and down*; *to walk a man all over the town*; Phr. *to walk a person off his legs*, tire him out by making him walk too far; **c** specif., *to walk a puppy*, to train and exercise him. **2.** To traverse on foot: *I have walked this country for miles round.* Phrs. (archaic) *to walk the hospitals*, attend cases, watch operations, in hospital, as part of practical training for medical profession; *to walk the boards*, to act on the stage; *to walk the plank*, be murdered by pirates by being compelled to walk up a plank which tips up and precipitates one into the sea; *to walk the chalk*, to demonstrate that one is sober by walking along a narrow chalk line. **3.** To traverse a specified distance on foot: *to walk a mile.* **4.** To contend with, pit oneself against, in walking: *I'll walk you ten miles any day you like.* **C.** Followed by adverbs and prepositions with special meanings. *Walk about*, intrans., to walk here and there, stroll up and down &c. *Walk away*, **1.** intrans., to depart at a walk; **2.** trans., to lead away at a walk. *Walk away from*, intrans., (lit. and fig.) to outstrip with ease in a contest. *Walk away with*, intrans., to carry off. *Walk in*, intrans., to enter, come, go in. *Walk into*, intrans., (slang) **a** to eat heartily of, devour; **b** to abuse, rail at, pitch into. *Walk off*, **1.** intrans., to depart at a walk; **2.** trans., to cause to walk off. *Walk off with*, intrans., to carry off; to steal: *the page-boy has walked off with the spoons.* *Walk out with*, intrans., (of lower classes) to be in initial stages of courtship with, prior to formal engagement. *Walk over*, trans., (in contest, race &c.) **a** to pass over (course) at walking pace in absence of other competitors; **b** to have an easy victory over.

walk (II.), n., fr. prec. **1.** Action of walking, **a** (of person) pace in which the feet are moved forward successively, without taking both off the ground simultaneously; **b** (of quadruped) slowest pace, two feet at least being always on the ground: *to go at a walk*; *to drop into a walk.* **2.** Manner of walking, characteristic gait, carriage: *one can often recognize a person by his walk*; *a dignified, a shambling, walk.* **3.** Spell of walking; journey, excursion, on foot, esp. for exercise or recreation: *to go for a walk*; *to take a walk*; *we had a long, tiring walk.* **4. a** Route traversed on foot: *this is my favourite walk*; **b** specif., regular route, beat, of hawker &c. Phr. *walk of*, or *in, life*, (i.) station, position, rank in society: *persons in the humbler walks of life*; (ii.) habitual occupation, profession: *he chose the Bar as his walk in life.* **5.** (archaic) Mode of ordering one's life and behaviour; general conduct. **6.** Place, strip of ground, set apart for walking; path, promenade: *a grass, gravel, walk*; *a walk bordered with a yew-hedge.* **7.** District, enclosure, piece of ground, for exercising animals, pasturing sheep &c.; also in compounds, *sheep-walk* &c.

walkable, adj. [1. wáwkabl; 2. wɔ̄kəbl]. **walk** (I.) & **-able.** Capable of being walked: *a walkable distance.*

walker, n. [1. wáwker; 2. wɔ̄kə]. **walk** (I.) & **-er.** **1. a** One who walks, a pedestrian; **b** person who habitually practises and enjoys walking as an exercise: *not much of a walker.* **2.** Bird which moves along the ground by successive steps instead of hopping.

walking, vbl. n. [1. wáwking; 2. wɔ̄kiŋ]. **walk** (I.) & **-ing.** The act or motion of one who walks: *to be fond of, to dislike, walking.*

walking-dress, n. Dress suitable for wearing out of doors.

walking-fern, n. North American evergreen fern whose fronds bend backwards and take root at the tip.

walking-gentleman, -lady, n. Actor, actress, who takes a part needing little skill but a good appearance.

walking-leaf, n. Leaf-insect.

walking-papers, n. (slang) Dismissal from employment.

walking-stick, n. **1.** Stick carried in the hand while walking. **2.** Insect with long, slender body and legs; stick-insect.

walking-ticket, n. Walking-papers.

walking-tour, n. Extended excursion, journey for pleasure, on foot.

walk-over, n. [1. wàwk ôver; 2. wɔ̄k óuvə]. (sporting) Easy or unopposed victory.

Walkyrie. See **Valkyrie.**

wall (I.), n. [1. wawl; 2. wɔ̄l]. O.E., M.E. *wall*; cp. O. Fris., O.S. *wal*; M.H.G. *wall*; early loan-word fr. Lat. *vallum*, 'wall, rampart', fr. *vallus*, 'stake, palisade; pillar'; see **vallum.** **1. a** Solid structure of stones, bricks, timbers, sods &c., usually relatively thin in proportion to its height and length, and erected as barrier, partition, means of defence, enclosure &c.: *to build the walls of a house*; *the garden is surrounded by a wall*; Phrs. *wall of partition, party wall*, wall dividing rooms, gardens &c.; *retaining wall*, one supporting bank of earth &c.; *blank wall*, unbroken by doors, windows &c.; *walls have ears*, one is liable to be overheard; *to be able to see through a brick wall*, have remarkable perceptive power; *to run one's head against a wall*, attempt obvious impossibilities; *with one's back to the wall*, at bay; *wooden walls*, the old wooden men-of-war, considered as the true protection of England against her enemies; **b** specif., defensive wall of town &c. **2.** Extended, densely packed group of objects resembling a wall in appearance or function: *a wall of bayonets.* **3.** Side of, partition in, a cavity, organ, vessel &c. of animals or plants: *the walls of the heart* &c. **4.** (min.) One of the rock-surfaces enclosing the lode. **5.** That side of the pavement in a street nearest to the walls of the houses &c., and therefore farthest from the gutter or kennel; hence various Phrs.: *to give a person the wall*, allow him to pass on the inside; *to take the wall of*, refuse to yield the inner side of the pavement and cause another pedestrian to pass on the outside near the edge of the pavement; *to push, drive, thrust (a person) to the wall*, thrust him aside, treat with contempt; *to go to the wall*, to be thrust aside as useless and ineffective.

wall (II.), vb. trans., fr. prec. **1.** To surround, protect, defend, with a wall; often P.P., *walled towns.* **2.** Usually *wall up*, to block up (space, opening &c.) with a wall.

walla(h), n. [1. wóla; 2. wɔ́lə], fr. Hind., agent-suff. *-wālā.* (Anglo-Indian) Person engaged in specified occupation or employed in specific business; equivalent to man, fellow: *punkah walla(h)*, the servant whose job it is to keep the punkah going. Phr. *competition walla(h)*, term applied in contempt by the now extinct generation of British military officers, or civilian officials, in India, who owed their entry into the East India Company's service to interest and nomination, to those who passed in by examination.

wallaby, n. [1. wólabi; 2. wɔ́ləbi]. Native Australian. Species of small kangaroo.

Wallach, n. [1. wólak; 2. wɔ́læk]. Slav., ultimately fr. O.H.G. *walh*, 'foreigner', q.v. under **Welsh.** Member of one of the Romance-speaking peoples of Roumania.

Wallachian, adj. & n. [1. wolákian; 2. wɔléi-kiən]. Prec. & **-ian.** **1.** adj. Pertaining to the Wallachs or their language. **2.** n. **a** A Wallach; **b** language of the Wallachs.

wallaroo, n. [1. wòlaroo͞; 2. wɔ̀lərū́]. Native Australian. One of the larger varieties of kangaroo.

wall-creeper, n. Small insectivorous bird.

wall-cress, n. Kind of arabis.

wallet, n. [1. wólet; 2. wɔ́lit]. Etymol. doubtful; possibly a variant of M.E. *watel*, 'hurdle; basket, bag'; see **wattle.** **1.** (archaic) Bag or scrip carried by traveller, pilgrim &c. and containing food and other necessaries. **2.** Flat leather case or pocket-book for carrying bank-notes, papers &c. **3.** Small leather bag or case for tools &c.

wall-eye, n. Back-formation fr. next word. **1. a** Opacity of the cornea of the eye; **b** white appearance of eye affected in this way. **2.** Eye showing large proportion of cornea on account of squint &c.

wall-eyed, adj. M.E. *wawl-ēʒed*, fr. O.N. *vagl eygðr*, fr. *vagl*, 'beam in the eye', *eygðr*, 'eyed, having eyes', fr. *auga*, 'eye', q.v. under **eye.** The etymol. of the first element is unknown. Affected with wall-eye.

wall-fern, n. Small evergreen fern; polypody.

wallflower, n. [1. wáwlflòur; 2. wɔ́lflàuə]. **1.** Garden perennial of the mustard family, genus *Cheiranthus*, with clusters of fragrant, yellow, red, or brown flowers. **2.** Woman at a ball who, from lack of partners, cannot dance and occupies a seat against the wall of the ball-room.

wall-fruit, n. Fruit produced by trees trained on a garden wall.

wall-game, n. A variety of football played at Eton.

wall-knot, n. Variant of **wale-knot.**

wall-less, adj. [1. wáwlles; 2. wɔ́llis]. **wall (I.)** & **-less.** Having no wall.

wall-moss, n. Stonecrop.

Walloon, n. & adj. [1. wolóo͝n; 2. wɔlū́n], fr. O. Fr. *Wallon*, fr. Gmc. **walh*, O.H.G. *walh*, 'foreigner', see **Welsh.** **1.** n. **a** One of a people of mixed descent living in Belgium and the adjoining part of France; **b** French dialect spoken by Walloons. **2.** adj. Of, pertaining to, the Walloons or their dialect.

wallop, vb. intrans. & trans. [1. wólup; 2. wɔ́ləp]. Origin somewhat obscure; certainly of Gmc. origin, but perh. derived through O. Fr.; a variant of **gallop**, & formerly used in English in that sense; possibly connected w. O.E. *weallan*, 'to boil, to be agitated'. See **well (I.)** & cp. **potwalloper.** **1.** intrans. (archaic or provinc.) To move along rapidly but heavily; esp. *to wallop along.* **2.** trans. To beat severely, to thrash.

walloping, adj. [1. wóluping; 2. wɔ́ləpiŋ]. Pres. Part. of prec. (slang) Of large size; big, strapping, whacking: *a walloping great hare.*

wallow (I.), vb. intrans. [1. wólō; 2. wɔ́lou]. O.E. *wealwian*; M.E. *walwen*, 'to turn, roll'; cp. Goth. *walwjan*, 'to roll'; *waltan*, 'to turn round'; cogn. w. Lat. *volvere*, 'to turn, roll', see **volute**; Gk. *elúein*, 'to wind'; *élutron*, 'sheath', see **elytron**; Scrt. *varútram*, 'outer garment'; *ulūtaš*, 'python'; O. Slav. *valiti*, 'to revolve'; cp. also **waltz** & **welter (I.).** **1.** To roll about, flounder, in liquid or semi-liquid substance: *to wallow in the mire, mud, water* &c. Phr. *wallowing in money*, very rich. **2.** (fig.) To indulge in to excess, plunge into, revel in: *to wallow in sensuality* &c.

wallow (II.), n., fr. prec. Hollow, pool, mud-hole, in which an animal habitually wallows.

wallowing, n. [1. wólōing; 2. wɔ́louiŋ]. **wallow** & **-ing.** The floundering, rolling, movement of an animal that wallows.

wall-painting, n. Decorative painting, picture, on the wall of room &c.

wall-paper, n. Paper, often highly decorated in colours, used for covering interior walls and ceilings of rooms.

wall-pepper, n. Stonecrop.

wall-plate, n. Timber in or on top of a wall to take the pressure of beam, girder &c.

wall-rue, n. Small evergreen fern, *Asplenium Ruta-muraria*, growing on cliffs &c.

Wallsend, n. [1. wáwlzend; 2. wɔ́lzɛnd], fr. Wallsend in Northumberland. Fine grade of household coal.

Wall Street, n. Street in New York City. American money-market.

walnut, n. [1. wáwlnut; 2. wɔ́lnat]. O.E. *w(e)alhhnutu*, fr. *w(e)alh*, 'foreign', see **Welsh**, & **nut.** **1.** Edible nut of oily consistency, and rough irregular surface, contained between two very hard, easily separable shells, outside which is a thick pulpy husk. **2. a** The tree (*Juglans*) producing these nuts; **b** hard, finely grained timber of this tree, used in cabinet-making and for gunstocks.

walnut-tree, n. Same as **walnut, 2, a.**

Walpurgis-night, n., semi-Germ. [1. vàhl-pĕrgis nīt; 2. vàlpágis nàit], fr. Germ. *Walpurgis (nacht)*, fr. St. Walpurga, abbess of Heidenheim, died c. 779. Witches' festival on the Brocken, on the eve of May 1st.

walrus, n. [1. wól-, wáwlrus; 2. wɔ́l-, wɔ́lrəs], fr. Du., fr. Swed. *vallross*, transposed fr. Icel. *hrosshvalr*, fr. *hross*, 'horse', & *hvalr*, 'whale'; cp. O.E. *horshwæl*, 'walrus'; see **whale** & **horse.** Large, amphibious, seal-like mammal with long, drooping tusks, found in Arctic seas.

waltz (I.), n. [1. wawls; 2. wɔ̄ls]. Mod. Germ. fr. *walzen*, 'to revolve'; cp. O.E. *waltan*, 'to turn round'. See **welter (I.).** **1.** Dance for couples, with smooth, even step, to music in 3 or 2 time. **2.** Musical composition to which this is danced.

waltz (II.), vb. intrans. & trans., fr. prec. **1.** intrans. **a** To dance a waltz; **b** to dance, twirl, skip about rapidly, with joy, excitement &c. **2.** trans. To cause to waltz; to lay hold of (person) and dance about with (him or her): *waltz me round again.*

wampee, n. [1. wompḗ; 2. wɔmpī́], fr. Chinese, fr. *hwang*, 'yellow', & *pī*, 'skin'. **1.** Berry with tough, yellow rind and edible pulp. **2.** Tropical tree, growing in China, East Indies &c., producing this fruit.

wampum, n. [1. wómpum; 2. wɔ́mpam], fr. N. American Ind. *wampum(peag)*, fr. *wompi*, 'white', & *ompumpeag*, 'string of beads or money'. Beads made of shells, worn in strings by N. American Indians as money or ornament.

wan, adj. [1. won; 2. wɔn]. O.E. *wann*, 'livid, dark'; M.E. *wan*, 'faint, pale'; perh. connected w. **wane.** Pallid, pale, colourless (esp. through illness, anxiety &c.), sickly; (also poet. of sky, atmosphere &c.) neither dark nor light; livid; palish, colourless.

wand, n. [1. wond; 2. wɔnd]. M.E. *wand*, fr. O.N. *vǫndr*, 'rod'; cp. Goth. *wandus*, 'rod'; Goth. *wandjan*, 'to turn round' O.E. *windan*, 'to wind', see **wind (IV.).** The primitive meaning seems to be 'something pliable'. Long, slender rod, esp. **a** one carried in the hand as symbol of office &c.; **b** conductor's baton; **c** conjuror's light rod: *the wand of the magician.*

wander, vb. intrans. & trans. [1. wónder; 2. wɔ́ndə]. O.E. *wandrian*; M.E. *wandrien*, 'to wander'; cp. M. Du. *wanderen*; M.H.G. *wandern*, 'to wander'; fr. same base, w. *i*-mutation, O.E. *wenden*, 'to turn', see **wend (I.)**; *windan*, 'to wind', see **wind (IV.).** **A.** intrans. **1. a** To move from place to place, or from one object to another, without a specific route or purpose; to roam, ramble, rove: *to wander through the woods*; *to wander from flower to flower*; *to wander about the world*; **b** (of the eyes, glance &c.) to shift from point to point, stray. **2. a** To deviate from the proper course, go out of one's way, to stray, go astray: *to wander out of one's way*; *to wander off the track*; **b** to depart from a clear and logical line of thought; to go aside from a subject of thought or discussion, become diffuse or confused: *to wander from the point.* **3. a** To become incoherent in thought and expression; to ramble in one's mind, be delirious, and unconscious of what one is saying: *he is wandering, is wandering in his mind, as the result of high fever*; **b** (of the mind, thoughts, attention) to lack concentration, go wool-gathering, to be preoccupied, distrait, absent-minded. **B.** trans. To traverse, roam over, journey through at random, without settled course.

wanderer, n. [1. wónderer; 2. wɔ́ndərə]. Prec. & **-er.** One who wanders; person given to wandering.

wandering (**I.**), n. [1. wóndering; 2. wɔ́ndəriŋ]. **wander** & **-ing. 1.** (gen. in pl.) **a** An aimless ramble; **b** widely extended journeyings; travels from place to place: *to return from one's wanderings.* **2.** (gen. in pl.) Incoherent or delirious speech: *the vapid wanderings of insanity.*

wandering (**II.**), adj. fr. Pres. Part. of **wander. 1.** Moving about in a rambling, purposeless manner; roving, strolling. Phr. *wandering Jew,* (i.) legendary character condemned to perpetual wandering on account of an insult offered to Christ on the road to the Crucifixion; (ii.) person addicted to wandering from country to country; (iii.) kind of trailing plant. **2.** Moving about within the body, not attached, floating: *wandering cell* &c.

wanderingly, adv. Prec. & **-ly.** In a wandering manner.

wanderoo, n. [1. wònderōō; 2. wɔ̀ndərú], fr. Cingalese *wanderu.* **a** Large, black, langur monkey of Ceylon and Malabar, with light-coloured or grey mane and ruffs; **b** the lion-tailed Indian macaque.

wane (**I.**), vb. intrans. [1. wān; 2. wein]. O.E. *wanian,* 'to diminish, decline, fade, wane'; M.E. *wanien* & *wānen,* 'to lessen, wane, grow pale'; cp. O.H.G. *wanōn*; O.N. *vana*; O. Fris. *wania,* 'to decline'; cp. further O.E., O.H.G. *wan,* Goth. *wans,* O.N. *vanr,* 'wanting'; cogn. w. Lat. *vānus,* 'empty; useless', see **vain**; Gk. *eûnis,* 'bereaved of', for **ewənis*; see also **want. 1.** To grow less, to diminish; to become less in amount, intensity, power &c.: **a** *our supply of ammunition steadily wanes*; **b** chiefly used of non-material things and of qualities: *waning influence, popularity*; *his strength is slowly waning.* **2.** Specif. (of the moon and certain other heavenly bodies) to expose an ever smaller part of the illuminated surface to the earth; contrasted with *wax.*

wane (**II.**), n., fr. prec. Act or process of waning; decline; esp. in Phr. *on the wane.*

wanghee. See **whanghee.**

wangle, vb. trans. [1. wánggl; 2. wǽŋgl]. Weekley derives tentatively fr. provinc. *wangle,* 'to shake, totter', & compares M.E. *wankel,* 'unstable', O.E. *wancol*; this is cogn. w. O.H.G. *wankōn,* 'to totter', Mod. Germ. *wanken.* **wink** is perh. in gradational relation to these. On the other hand, the word is quite recent, though since the War in widespread use, so that an obscure provinc. origin seems improbable. Further, the present usage is very remote fr. the idea of 'tottering'. May the word not rather be a humorous concoction fr. a combination of 'wily' & 'to angle' in fig. sense, or something of the kind? (recent slang) To obtain by diplomacy or artifice: *to wangle a few days' extra leave*; *to wangle five pounds out of a person.*

wanion, n. [1. wónyun; 2. wɔ́njən], fr. *waniand,* M.E. Nthn. Pres. Part. of **wane,** w. reference to waning moon as unpropitious. Archaic Phr. *with a wanion on, to,* ill-luck to (as imprecation).

wanly, adv. [1. wónli; 2. wɔ́nli]. **wan** & **-ly.** With a wan appearance; (also fig.) dismally, bleakly: *to smile wanly.*

wanness, n. [1. wónnes; 2. wɔ́nnis]. See prec. & **-ness.** State or quality of being wan.

want (**I.**), n. [1. wont; 2. wɔnt]. M.E. *want,* fr. O.N. *vant,* 'deficiency', fr. neut. form of *vanr,* 'lacking', see **wane**; for another example of this neut. suff. *-t* see **scant. 1.** State of being absent; lack, deficiency: *to suffer from want of food, air*; *want of common sense, tact* &c. **2.** State of being without; **a** need; absence of something felt to be necessary: *to be in want of food*; *the building seems to be in want of repair*; *I feel the want of a real friend*; **b** specif., destitution, indigence, penury; insufficiency, lack, of means of livelihood: *to live in want*; *to know the bitterness of want.* **3.** (chiefly pl.) Thing or things desired and felt to be necessary; requirements: *my wants are few*; *you should try to reduce your wants*; *I will supply all your essential wants.* Phr. *a long-felt want,* something for which the necessity has long been felt, but which is not available.

want (**II.**), vb. trans. & intrans. M.E. *wanten,* fr. O.N. *vanta,* 'to be lacking', fr. *want,* 'deficiency'; see prec. **A.** trans. **1.** To lack, be deficient in; to fall, or be, short of; to require addition of in order to reach specified or desired standard or quality: *the house only wants a few more rooms to be perfect*; *the book wants a page at the end*; *he certainly does not want intelligence,* or *is not wanting in* &c.; *your coat wants an inch or so of the proper length,* is an inch or so short of . . . **2. a** To need, have need of, to require; feel the necessity for: *children want plenty of sleep*; *we shan't want a fire today*; *I shall want dinner for four*; *you badly want a new hat* = you ought to have; *what do you want?*; *shall you want anything more tonight, sir?*; (colloq.) *what you want is a good thrashing,* i.e. what would do you good is &c.; **b** to desire to obtain, procure, get hold of, buy &c.: *I want some evening ties, please*; *I want some hot water at once.* **3.** To desire to have, wish for, have a longing for: **a** *I want many things that I can't have*; *he wants everything he sees*; **b** (followed by infin.) (i.) *I want to see what is going on*; *I want you to be happy*; (ii.) (with neg.) *I don't want you to be hurt* = want you to avoid being; *he doesn't want to go* = wants not to go. **4.** (i.) To be so circumstanced that it is desirable to do (something specified); to be obliged to do; ought, must: *you want to have your teeth seen to*; *one wants to be very careful in handling poisons*; (ii.) (with neg.) *you don't want to be rude* = you needn't, oughtn't, to be; *you don't want to overdo it for a bit* = mustn't overdo it; *he doesn't want to be treated too severely* = does not require &c. **5.** Specif. **a** to desire to see or to speak to, to require presence of: *tell the boy I want him*; *you won't be wanted this afternoon*; *I want you for a minute or two*; **b** P.P. in special Phr. *wanted by the police, wanted for* (*murder* &c.), being sought for as a suspicious person, as being suspected to be guilty of (murder). **B.** intrans. **1. a** To lack, be lacking or absent; (impers.) *it wanted only this last outrage,* that alone was lacking; *it wants but one word more and I shall turn you out,* if you utter one more word &c.; *it wants half an hour to the appointed time*; *it wants just a minute to the hour*; **b** (in Pres. Part.) *nothing is wanting to make the party a success*; *style and dignity are quite wanting from the play*; **c** specif. (colloq.) lacking normal intelligence, defective in mind: *such a strange boy, he seemed to me to be slightly wanting* (see also **wanting** (**I.**)). **2. a** To be destitute, to lack the necessities of life: *he must not be allowed to want in his old age*; **b** *want for,* to be without, be unable to obtain: *he shall want for nothing that care and affection can bestow.*

wanting (**I.**), adj. [1. wónting; 2. wɔ́ntiŋ], fr. Pres. Part. of **want** (**II.**). (pred.) **1. a** Deficient, defective; lacking some essential and necessary quality: *wanting in some respects, in initiative* &c.; *weighed and found wanting*; **b** specif., (absol.) deficient in intelligence, partly imbecile (see prec., **B. 1, c**). **2.** Lacking, absent, missing: *there is a volume wanting to complete the set.*

wanting (**II.**), Pres. Part. as prep. Without, less, in the absence of: *wanting a leader, nothing could be done.*

wantless, adj. [1. wóntles; 2. wɔ́ntlis]. **want** (**I.**) & **-less.** Without a want.

wanton (**I.**), adj. [1. wóntun; 2. wɔ́ntən]. M.E. *wantowen, wantoun,* fr. pref. *wan-,* 'without, lacking', cogn. w. **want,** & M.E. *towen,* O.E. *togen,* P.P. of *tēon,* 'to draw, pull; to bring up, educate', q.v. under **tow** (**I.**). **1.** Unrestrained, not under control; specif. **a** frolicsome, capricious, irresponsible: *a wanton kid, child*; *wanton play, tricks* &c.; **b** wild, wayward in growth or arrangement; luxuriant, unchecked or uncontrolled: '*golden tresses . . . Dishevelled, but in wanton ringlets waved*' (Milton, 'P. L.', iv. 305–6); **c** without motive, purposeless; irresponsible, arbitrary: *wanton destruction.* **2.** Unchaste, loose, licentious.

wanton (**II.**), n., fr. prec. Wanton person, esp. an unchaste woman.

wanton (**III.**), vb. intrans. **a** To frolic, sport, without restraint: '*The birds that wanton in the air*' (Lovelace, 'To Althea'); **b** to luxuriate, flourish, run riot, produce, in limitless abundance and prodigality: '*Nature here Wantoned as in her prime*' (Milton, 'P .L.', v. 394–5).

wantonly, adv. [1. wóntunli; 2. wɔ́ntənli]. **wanton** (**I.**) & **-ly.** In a wanton manner; esp. without motive; unnecessarily, gratuitously: *wantonly cruel.*

wantonness, n. [1. wóntunnes; 2. wɔ́ntənnis]. See prec. & **-ness.** State or quality of being wanton; **a** light-heartedness, irresponsibility; **b** dissolute conduct, unchastity.

wapentake, n. [1. wápentāk; 2. wǽpənteik]. L.O.E. *wǣpentæc,* 'expression of consent or loyalty by touching weapon; district governed by leader thus appointed', fr. O.N. *vāpntak,* fr. *vāpn,* 'weapon', q.v. under **weapon,** & *taka,* 'to touch', see **take.** An old division of one of the counties of Yorks., Lincs., Derby, Leics., Rutland, Notts., corresponding to a hundred elsewhere.

wapiti, n. [1. wópiti; 2. wɔ́piti], fr. N. Am. Ind. *wapitik.* Large N. American antlered deer, *Cervus canadensis,* related to red deer; called 'elk' in popular usage.

war (**I.**), n. [1. wōr; 2. wɔ̄]. M.E., fr. O. Fr. *werre,* of Gmc. origin; cp. O.H.G. & O.S. *werran,* 'to confuse, hinder, injure'; cp. O.N. *vǫrr,* 'stroke of oar'; cogn. w. Lat. *verrere,* 'to sweep; to draggle, trail', see **verricule**; Gk. *érrein* for **wer-* 'to move painfully'; O. Slav. *vrěšti,* 'to thresh'. **1. a** Open conflict between nations, active international hostility carried on by force of arms; *civil war,* between two parties in the same nation; *holy war,* in support or defence of religious cause; *private war,* between individuals or families. Phrs. *to make, wage, war* (*on*); *to declare war* (*on*), make formal announcement (to government of another nation) of intention to make war; hence (fig.) proclaim one's hostility to; *to go to the wars,* see active service in army; *to have been in the wars,* show signs of physical injuries &c.; *at war,* engaged in war; *on a war footing,* (of army &c.) at full strength, prepared for war; *war to the knife,* irreconcilable hostility; *war of elements,* storm, tempest; *art of war,* strategy; *council of war*; *declaration of war,* formal announcement of intention to make war; *seat of war,* district in which war is being carried on, scene of campaign; *sinews of war,* (fig.) money necessary for carrying on war; *to carry the war into the enemy's camp,* (fig.) to attack, or make complaint against, a hostile person or body alleging the same grounds as those alleged against oneself; **b** armaments, instruments, engines, of war: '*bring forth all my war, My bow and thunder*' (Milton, 'P. L.', vi. 712-13). **2.** Hostility, bitterness of spirit: *to have war in one's heart.*

war (**II.**), vb. intrans., fr. prec. To contend, strive, compete: *war with, against.* Phr. *warring elements,* opposed, irreconcilable.

waratah, n. [1. wáhratah; 2. wárətā]. Native. Australian shrub bearing clusters of crimson or scarlet flowers.

warble (**I.**), vb. intrans. & trans. [1. wórbl; 2. wɔ̄bl]. M.E. *werblen,* 'to blow' (of the wind), 'to sound', fr. O. Fr. *werbler,* of Gmc. origin; cp. O.H.G. *wirbel,* 'whirl'; Mod. Germ. *wirbeln,* 'to whirl', cogn. w. **whirl. 1.** intrans. **a** (of bird) To sing with trills and vibrations; **b** (of person) (i.) to sing with trills and tremolo effect, suggestive of birds' song; (ii.) to sing generally. **2.** trans. **a** (of bird or person) To utter, produce (a song, notes) with a series of roulades and trills; cp. Milton's '*the warbled string*' ('Arcades', 87), one made vibrant, trilled; **b** to sing (a song). (N.B. The earlier usage seems always to imply 'trilling' and the like, and not merely 'singing' in a general sense; Milton has '*Warble his native wood-notes wild*' (of Shakespeare, 'L'Allegro', 134); of the notes of Orpheus which were '*warbled to the string*' ('Il Penseroso', 106); and '*Fountains, and ye that warble as ye flow, Melodious murmurs*' ('P. L.', v. 195).)

warble (**II.**) n., fr. prec. Act, sound, of warbling.

warble (**III.**), n. Etymol. doubtful; cp. M. Swed. *varbulde*, 'boil'. **a** Larva of the bot-fly; **b** small hard tumour on horses or cattle caused by this.

warbler, n. [1. wórbler; 2. wɔ̄blə]. **warble** (**I.**) & **-er**. Person who, bird which, warbles; specif., the popular name of a genus *Sylvia* and sub-family *Sylviinae* of singing birds, usually small, including the sedge- and reed-warbler, the white-throat, willow-wrens &c.

warbling, n. [1. wórbling; 2. wɔ̄bliŋ]. **warble** (**I.**) & **-ing**. **a** A trill, a roulade; **b** (poet.) a song: *plaintive warblings of the birds*.

war-bonnet, n. Feather-trimmed, ceremonial head-dress of N. American Indian.

war-cloud, n. Signs, circumstances, indicating imminence of war.

war-cry, n. Word, name &c. shouted as a signal or rallying-cry in battle.

ward (**I.**), n. [1. word; 2. wɔ̄d]. (1) O.E. *weard*, masc., 'watchman, guardian'; (2) O.E. *weard*, fem., 'guard, protection'; M.E. *ward*; cp. O.H.G. *wart*; O.N. *vǫrðr*, 'warden, keeper'; O.H.G. *warta*, 'guardianship'; Goth. *wardja*, 'guard'; see **ware** (**II.**), & cp. **guard**. **1.** Now only in Phr. *watch and ward*, act of guarding, protection. **2.** State of being under control, esp. **a** (of minor) control of guardian, esp. in Phr. *in ward*; **b** (archaic) custody, confinement: *to put a person in ward*; **c** (archaic) warder, guard, now esp. in compounds: *hayward* &c. **3.** A minor under control of guardian; *ward in Chancery*, under guardianship of Court of Chancery. **4.** Division of a city, or (archaic) of a forest, for administrative purposes. **5.** Section, specific room, of building; specif. **a** (of hospital) *fever, isolation, ward*; **b** (of prison) *condemned ward* &c.; **c** (of workhouse) *casual ward* &c. **6.** Projection, ridge, notch, in a lock, or in a key, intended to prevent insertion and turning of any but a particular key in a given lock. **7.** (fencing) a Guard; **b** parry.

ward (**II.**), vb. trans. O.E. *weardian*, 'to guard', fr. *weard*, 'guard', see prec. **1.** (archaic) To defend, protect, act as guardian to. **2.** *Ward off*, to avert, turn aside, repel; to take measures to guard oneself against: *to ward off a blow, an attack*; *to ward off sleep, a cold* &c.

-ward, -wards, suff. O.E. *-weard*, M.E. *-ward-(es)*; cp. O.H.G. *-wert*; Goth. *-wairþs*, 'having specified direction'; cogn. w. O.E. *weorðan*, 'to become', see **worth** (**III.**); Lat. *vertere*, 'to turn', see **version, vertex**. With meaning, 'in specified direction', & forming **a** *-ward*, adj., e.g. *forward, inward* &c.; **b** *-ward(s)*, adv., e.g. *backwards, afterwards, westwards, homeward(s)*; **c** *-ward(s)*, prep., e.g. *toward(s)*. Also as living suff., esp. in facetious compounds, *bedward* &c.: '*When the young Augustus Edward Most reluctantly goes bedward*' (Calverley).

war-dance, n. Savages' ceremonial dance before battle, or to celebrate a victory.

warden (**I.**), n. [1. wórdn; 2. wɔ̄dn]. M.E., fr. O. Fr. *wardein*, fr. Gmc. **ward-*, 'guard', see **ward** (**I.**), & **-ian**, & cp. **guardian**. **1.** (archaic) Watchman, guard. **2.** (in official titles) a Person having control, jurisdiction, authority, over specific district &c.; governor: *Warden of the Marches, of the Cinque Ports* &c.; **b** the title of the head of five colleges in Oxford University, and of some schools; one of two principal officers in Freemasons' lodge, *Senior and Junior Warden*. **3.** Church-warden: *Vicar's warden, people's warden*.

warden (**II.**) also **wardon**, n. Weekley suggests connexion w. **ward** (**I.**) & interprets as 'keeping pear': he cites Cotgrave, who gives *poire de garde*, 'a warden, or winter peare, a peare which may be kept verie long'. Variety of cooking pear.

wardenship, n. [1. wórdnship; 2. wɔ̄dnʃip]. **warden** (**I.**) & **-ship**. Office or jurisdiction of warden.

warder, n. [1. wórder; 2. wɔ̄də]. **ward** (**II.**) & **-er**. **1.** (archaic) Watchman, guard, still surviving in the name *Tower Warders*, of the guards of the Tower of London, wrongly called Yeomen of the Guard. **2.** Prison guard, gaoler. **3.** Staff symbolic of authority carried by sovereign, commander &c.

ward-mote, n. **ward** (**I.**) & **moot** (**I.**) Meeting of inhabitants of city ward.

Wardour Street, n. [1. wórder strēt; 2. wɔ̄də strīt]. London street formerly containing many antique furniture shops &c. *Wardour-street English*, a style pervaded with bogus archaism.

wardress, n. [1. wórdres; 2. wɔ̄dris]. **warder** & **-ess**. Female gaoler.

wardrobe, n. [1. wórdrōb; 2. wɔ̄droub]. M.E.; cp. O. Fr. *garderobe*; see **ward** (**I.**) & **robe**. **1.** A large piece of furniture including divisions for hanging clothes, and often also with drawers. **2.** Person's stock of clothes: *to renew one's wardrobe*.

ward-room, n. Common room on warship for commissioned naval officers below the rank of commanding officer and above that of sub-lieutenant.

wardship, n. [1. wórdship; 2. wɔ̄dʃip]. **ward** (**I.**) & **-ship**. State of being a guardian; office of guardian, tutelage: *to be under the wardship of*.

ware (**I.**), n. [1. wār; 2. wɛə]. O.E. *waru*; M.E. *wāre*, 'goods, wares'; cp. Mod. Germ. *ware*; M. Du. *ware*, 'goods'; O.N. *vara*, 'skin, fleece; merchandise'; cogn. w. Scrt. *ūrā*; Gk. *arnós*, 'lamb' (genit.), fr. **arén* for **war-*; Lat. *vervex*, 'wether'. **1.** **a** (in compounds) Manufactured articles of commerce: *ironware, hardware* &c.; **b** specif., pottery; often preceded by qualifying word: *stoneware*; *Staffordshire wares*. **2.** (pl.) *Wares*, things offered for sale, goods, merchandise.

ware (**II.**), adj. O.E. *wær*, 'cautious, aware'; M.E. *war*, 'wary'; cp. O.S. *war*; O.H.G. *(gi)war*; O.N. *var*; Goth. *wars*, 'watchful'; O.E. *bewarian*; O.H.G. *biwarōn*, 'to guard, defend'; cogn. w. Lat. *verēri*, 'to observe anxiously, revere, fear', see **revere**; Gk. *oûros* for **wor-wos*, 'watchman'; *horáein* for **wor-*, 'to see'; cp. w. extensional suff., Goth. *wardja*; O.H.G. *warto*; O.E. *weard*, 'watchman', cp. **ward.** (poet.) Alert, vigilant: '*You'll find me ware and waking, As you found me long ago*' (Newbolt, 'Drake's Drum').

ware (**III.**), vb. trans. [1. wār, wōr; 2. wɛə, wɔ̄]. O.E. *warian*, 'to guard, guard against', fr. *war*, 'heedful', see prec. **1.** (esp. hunting, imperat.) Beware, look out for: *ware hounds!*; *ware wire!* **2.** (colloq.) To guard against, avoid.

warehouse (**I.**), n. [1. wārhous; 2. wɛ́əhaus]. **ware** (**I.**) & **house** (**I.**). **1.** Storehouse for goods before distribution to retailers &c.; store for furniture &c. temporarily unwanted; repository. **2.** Large retail shop, store.

warehouse (**II.**), vb. trans. [1. wārhouz; 2. wɛ́əhauz]. **ware** (**I.**) & **house** (**II.**). To store (esp. furniture) temporarily in a warehouse.

warehouseman, n. [1. wārhousman; 2. wɛ́əhausmən]. **1.** Man employed in warehouse. **2.** Keeper, owner, of a warehouse; specif., one who keeps or owns a wholesale establishment, for Manchester or cotton goods or for woollen and other textiles &c.

warfare, n. [1. wórfār; 2. wɔ̄fɛə]. **war** (**I.**) & **fare** (**III.**). **a** Act or process of waging war: *the science of warfare*; **b** state of being at war; active hostility, strife.

war-game, n. Kriegspiel.

war-god, n. Deity presiding over, and invoked in, war.

war-head, n. Explosive cap on torpedo as used in time of war.

war-horse, n. **a** (archaic) A horse used in battle, a charger; **b** *a seasoned old war-horse*, a person with long experience in political struggle, and affairs generally; a veteran.

warily, adv. [1. wārili; 2. wɛ́ərili]. **wary** & **-ly**. In a wary manner.

wariness, n. [1. wārines; 2. wɛ́ərinis]. See prec. & **-ness**. State or quality of being wary.

warlike, adj. [1. wórlīk; 2. wɔ̄laik]. **war** (**I.**) & **-like**. **1.** Of, pertaining to, characteristic of, war; martial. **2.** Inclined for, tending to, war; bellicose.

warlock, n. [1. wórlok; 2. wɔ̄lɔk]. O.E. *wǣrloga*, 'traitor'; M.E. *warloghe*, 'traitor, sorcerer', fr. O.E. *wǣr*, 'truth'; cogn. w. Lat. *vērax*, 'truthful', q.v. under **veracious**, & O.E. *loga*, 'liar', fr. base seen in O.E. *(ge)logen*, P.P. of *lēogan*, 'to lie', see **lie** (**I.**). (archaic) A sorcerer, wizard, magician.

war-lord, n. Military leader, general, chiefly as translating German *Kriegsherr*, in reference to the Kaiser, as such.

warm (**I.**), adj. [1. worm; 2. wɔ̄m]. O.E. *wearm*, M.E. *warm*, 'warm'; O.S., O.H.G. *warm*; O.N. *varmr*, 'warm'; fr. base **gʷhor-m-*, **gʷher-m-* &c., 'warm'; whence also Lat. *formus*, 'warm'; Gk. *thermós*, 'warm', see **thermo-**; Scrt. *gharmáś*, 'glow'; O. Prussian *gorme*, 'heat'. **1.** **a** Giving sensation of mild, pleasant heat; implying lower temperature than *hot*: *warm water*; *this water is barely warm*; *a warm iron*; **b** often used as equivalent of *hot*, and to imply a considerable degree of temperature: *I find the day, the room, rather warm*. The context must determine whether **a** or **b** is intended; then *to get warm* may mean either (i.) an agreeable, comfortable, temperature, as: *come and get warm by the fire*, or (ii.) to put oneself in a state of excessive heat: *I got warm playing in the sun*; *warm weather, climate*; *a warm room*; specif., *warm blood*, that of mammals and birds, having a normal temperature ranging between 98° and 112°; imparting or promoting heat: *a warm fire*; *warm clothes*. Phrs. *warm work*, (i.) work which makes one hot; (ii.) a strenuous, arduous, dangerous occupation; *a warm corner, to make things warm for a person*, harass him by attacks or annoyances. **2.** Ardent, enthusiastic, devoted: *warm support(er)*; *a warm welcome*. **3.** Affectionate, sympathetic, responsive: *a warm heart*. **4.** (fig.) Heated, excited, vehement: *the disputants grew warm*. Phr. *in warm blood*, in passion. **5.** (of colour) Deep, intense, in shade, giving suggestion of warmth, esp. having red or yellow as basis. **6.** **a** (hunting, of scent) Fresh, recently made, strongly marked; **b** (of seeker in children's hiding games) close to the object sought. Phr. *you are getting warm*, you are on the right track of what you are seeking; you are getting near the truth. **7.** (colloq.) Well-to-do, comfortably off.

warm (**II.**), vb. trans. & intrans., fr. prec. **A.** trans. **1.** To make warm, raise temperature of: *to warm one's hands, oneself, at the fire*; *the sun has warmed the air*; also *warm up*: *kindly warm up the mutton*, make it hot again. **2.** To animate, excite, cause to glow with feeling or enthusiasm: *to warm one's heart*. **B.** intrans. To become warm or warmer: *the pudding is warming in the oven*; also *warm up*: *the room will soon warm up*. Phr. *to warm to one's work*, become keenly interested in it, intent upon it.

warm (**III.**), n., fr. prec. Act or process of warming, process of being warmed: *to have a warm by the fire*.

warm-blooded, adj. [1. wórm blùded; 2. wɔ̄m blàdid]. **1.** Having warm blood; specif. (of mammals and birds) having a normal temperature above that of the surrounding medium; contrasted with *cold-blooded*. **2.** Having an ardent temperament; having the passions and emotions easily roused.

warmer, n. [1. wórmer; 2. wɔ̄mə]. **warm (I.)** & **-er.** That which warms, device for warming; esp. in compounds: *foot-warmer* &c.

warm-hearted, adj. Having a warm heart; kind, sympathetic.

warm-heartedly, adv. Prec. & **-ly.** In a warm-hearted manner.

warm-heartedness, n. See prec. & **-ness.** State of being warm-hearted.

warming, n. [1. wórming; 2. wɔ̄miŋ]. **warm (II.)** & **-ing.** **a** Act of warming; process of being warmed; **b** (slang) a thrashing: *to give a boy's jacket a good warming.*

warming-pan, n. Round, flat, covered metal vessel with long handle, formerly filled with live coals and used for airing or heating a bed.

warmish, adj. [1. wórmish; 2. wɔ̄miʃ]. **warm (I.)** & **-ish.** Fairly warm.

warmly, adv. [1. wórmli; 2. wɔ̄mli]. **warm (I.)** & **-ly.** In a warm manner.

warmth, n. [1. wormth; 2. wɔ̄mþ]. **warm (I.)** & **-th.** **1.** A moderately high temperature; contrasted with *cold.* **2.** Enthusiasm, ardour, cordiality: *the warmth of one's welcome.* **3.** Emotional excitement, vigour, vehemence; anger: *to reply with some warmth.*

warn, vb. trans. [1. worn; 2. wɔ̄n]. O.E. *wearnian, war(e)nian,* 'to beware of'; M.E. *warnen,* 'to warn, admonish'; influenced by O.N. *varna,* 'to warn'; cp. O.H.G. *warnōn*; fr. stem **war-*, 'heedful', see **ware (II.).** **1.** To advise (a person) to be careful, put on his guard against possible risk, danger &c.; to admonish: *to warn a person of danger, of the consequences of an action* &c.; *to warn a person against another*; *I warn you that you will be punished.* **2.** To intimate, be a signal to: *the gong warned us that it was time to dress for dinner.*

warning (I.), n. [1. wórning; 2. wɔ̄niŋ]. Prec. & **-ing.** **1.** Act of one who, that which, warns; notice, hint, of, caution against, possible danger, consequences of action &c.; admonition: *the General received a warning of the coming attack*; *to take warning by another's example.* **2.** Something which warns; indication of something about to happen; premonition: *the branch fell without the slightest warning.* **3.** Specif., notice given by employer to servant, or by servant to employer, of intention to terminate engagement: *I have given the cook warning*; *a month's warning,* notice to quit situation, or of intention to leave, at the end of a month.

warning (II.), adj., fr. Pres. Part. of **warn.** Serving, intended, to warn; admonitory, cautionary: *a warning signal, look* &c. Phr. *warning colours,* (zool., entom. &c.) conspicuous marks or colourings on poisonous insects &c. supposed to give warning to other creatures.

warningly, adv. Prec. & **-ly.** In a warning manner; so as to convey a warning.

War Office, n. Government department controlling the army and all matters connected with war, under the Secretary of State for War.

warp (I.), vb. trans. & intrans. [1. worp; 2. wɔ̄p]. M.E. *warpen,* fr. O.N. *varpa,* 'to throw, bend'; cp. O.E. *weorpan,* 'to throw'; *wearp,* 'warp'; O.H.G. *werfen*; Goth. *wairpan,* 'to throw'. **A.** trans. **1.** **a** To alter shape of, bend, twist, distort: *the heat has warped the timber*; **b** (in moral sense) to bias, distort, pervert: *to warp the mind, judgement*; *his whole character was warped.* **2.** (naut.) To bring (vessel) into specific place or position by hauling on ropes attached to fixed object: *to warp a boat out into the channel.* **3.** To fertilize (land) by spreading it with alluvial deposit. **B.** intrans. **1.** To become distorted, bent, twisted, by shrinkage, contraction &c.: *the table-top has warped.* **2.** (naut., of ship) To be moved, change position, by means of warps.

warp (II.), n., fr. O.E. *wearp*; M.E. *warp,* see prec. **1.** Threads running lengthwise in a fabric and crossed by woof. **2.** Rope, fastened to a fixed point, as buoy, anchor &c., used in warping vessel. **3.** Distortion in timber, wooden object &c., caused by contraction &c. **4.** Alluvial deposit, silt.

war-paint, n. **a** Paint applied to the face and other exposed parts of the body by savages before battle; **b** (fig.) full dress, complete ceremonial uniform &c.

war-path, n. Route of Red Indians on military expedition. Phr. *on the war-path,* (also fig.) planning an attack, preparing to launch an attack, to embark on hostile action of any kind; in fighting mood.

warplane, n. Military aeroplane.

warrant (I.), n. [1. wórant; 2. wɔ́rənt]. M.E. *warant,* fr. O. Fr. *warant, guarant,* 'safeguard, guarantee'; of Gmc. origin; cp. O.H.G. *werēnto,* 'guarantor', fr. *werēn,* 'to guarantee, vouch'; cp. O. Fris. *wera,* 'to vouch for'. Cp. variant **guarantee.** **1.** Justification, authority, reasonable grounds: *you have no warrant for such a statement.* **2.** That which authorizes, gives sanction for, an action; esp. a document authorizing a specified course of action; (in various special senses); **a** a writ issued by a competent legal authority, authorizing an arrest, a search &c.; **b** document authorizing payment of money: *a dividend warrant*; **c** certificate of appointment of a naval or military officer below commissioned rank (see **warrant officer**); **d** similar certificate issued to certain tradesmen supplying the Royal household, styled *royal warrant-holders.*

warrant (II.), vb. trans., fr. prec. **1.** To justify, constitute sufficient ground for: *nothing can warrant this intrusion.* **2.** To vouch for, guarantee, certify as: *I'll warrant him a perfectly honest man*; trade Phr. *warranted real silk.* To declare, assert confidently: *he never was so handsomely treated before, I'll warrant,* i.e. I would wager that my statement is true.

warrantable, adj. [1. wórantabl; 2. wɔ́rəntəbl]. Prec. & **-able.** **1.** Capable of being justified. **2.** (of deer) In sixth year, old enough to be hunted.

warrantee, n. [1. wòranté; 2. wɔ̀rəntí]. **warrant** & **-ee.** Person to whom warrant is given.

warranter, n. [1. wóranter; 2. wɔ́rəntə]. **warrant** & **-er.** Warrantor.

warrant officer, n. Highest rank of non-commissioned officer.

warrantor, n. [1. wóranter; 2. wɔ́rəntə]. **warrant** & **-or.** One who gives a warranty to another.

warranty, n. [1. wóranti; 2. wɔ́rənti]. M.E., O. Fr. *warantie,* fr. fem. P.P. of *warantir,* 'to warrant', fr. *warant,* n., see **warrant (I.).** **1.** Sufficient reason, justification, or authority: *you have no warranty for that statement.* **2.** (law) Assurance, undertaking, expressed or implied on part of vendor that property sold is his, that it fulfils the requirements specified, and is in accordance with his description of it.

warren, n. [1. wóren; 2. wɔ́rən]. M.E., fr. O. Fr. *warene,* fr. *warir,* 'to preserve', of Gmc. origin; cp. O.S. & O.H.G. *warōn,* 'to take care of', cogn. w. **ware (III.).** **1.** (law) **a** A tract of ground the right to enclose which, for the purpose of keeping or preserving hares, rabbits, partridges, pheasants, has been granted by the king: *beasts of warren*; **b** also *free warren,* the right or privilege to keep a warren: *rights of warren*; a warren ranks next in dignity to a *park.* **2.** Tract of land, usually honeycombed with burrows, in which rabbits breed and abound. Phr. *packed like, as thick as, rabbits in a warren,* of a densely crowded population.

warrigal, n. [1. wórigal; 2. wɔ́rigəl]. Native. Australian dingo.

warrior, n. [1. wórier; 2. wɔ́riə]. M.E. *werreour,* fr. O. Fr.; see **war** & **-iour, -ior.** (now chiefly poetical) Soldier, fighter; esp. an experienced fighting-man, veteran.

war-ship, n. Man-of-war, battleship.

war-song, n. Song sung before, or in celebration of, a battle.

wart, n. [1. wort; 2. wɔ̄t]. O.E. *wearte*; M.E. *wart*; cp. O.H.G. *warza*; M. Du. *warte*; O.N. *varta,* 'wart'; cp. further O.E. *weorr,* 'wart'; cogn. w. Lat. *verrūca,* 'wart', see **verruca**; Scrt. *váršman-*, 'height, point'; Lith. *viršùs,* 'the upper'. **1.** Small, hard growth on surface of skin. **2.** Small, hard excrescence on bark of tree &c.

wart disease, n. Fungoid growth to which potatoes are liable.

warted, adj. [1. wórted; 2. wɔ̄tid]. **wart** & **-ed.** Having warts on the surface, skin &c.

wart-grass, -weed, n. Kind of spurge the juice of which is used to remove warts.

wart-hog, n. African wild hog, *Phacochoerus,* with hard excrescence on either side of face, and tusks curving upwards.

warty, adj. [1. wórti; 2. wɔ̄ti]. **wart** & **-y.** Resembling, of the nature of, covered with, warts.

war-wearied, adj. [1. wốr wērid; 2. wɔ̄ wiərid]. War-worn.

war-whoop, n. Red Indians' war-cry.

war-worn, adj. Injured in, wearied by, war.

wary, adj. [1. wāri; 2. wɛ́əri]. **ware (II.)** & **-y.** Cautious; on the look-out for danger &c.; circumspect.

was, vb. [1. woz; 2. wɔz]. O.E. *wæs,* 1st & 3rd pers. sing. Pret. of *wesan,* 'to be'; cp. O.S. & Goth. *was*; cp. O.S. & O.H.G. infin. *wesan,* Goth. *wisan*; cp. further Goth. *wizōn,* 'to live'; Scrt. *vásati,* '(he) dwells, remains, stays', & *vastu-*, 'seat, place'; Gk. *ástu* for **wastu,* 'a city'; cp. also **were.** Past tense sing. 1st and 2nd person of **be.**

wash (I.), vb. trans. & intrans. [1. wosh; 2. wɔʃ]. O.E. *wasċan,* M.E. *wasshen,* 'to wash'; cp. O.S., O.H.G. *wascan*; prob. fr. earlier **wat-ska-*, fr. base **wat-*, 'water', see **water,** & cp. **wet.** **A.** trans. **1.** **a** To cleanse by application of, immersion in, water or other liquid: *to wash one's hands, oneself, one's clothes, the dishes* &c.; Phr. *to wash one's hands of,* disclaim further responsibility for; **b** (in moral sense) to purify, render guiltless. **2.** Usually *wash away, off, out* &c.; **a** (in physical sense) to remove by application of water &c.: *to wash the dust off*; *to wash a stain out*; also **b** (in moral sense) to purge, do away: *to wash away one's guilt, sin.* **3.** To serve as a cleansing agent for: *the soap that won't wash clothes.* **4.** (of water of the sea, a lake, river) To come into contact with; to flow past, lap, bathe, lave: *the sea washes the cliffs*; *the castle walls are washed by the waters of the river.* **5.** To hollow out, produce, by flowing over and removing substance: *the rain washes channels in the ground.* **6.** To carry along, transport, by the movement or drift of water: *washed ashore by the tide, waves.* **7.** To separate, sift, heavier parts of (ore &c.) by shaking in water. **8.** To cover with a thin coat of metal or of paint &c. **B.** intrans. **1.** To wash oneself, one's hands &c., perform one's ablutions: *unpleasant to wash in cold water.* **2.** To wash clothes, household linen &c.: *to wash once a week.* **3.** (of fabric, colour, paint &c.) To be able to stand washing without deterioration: *will this material wash?* Phr. *that theory &c. won't wash,* will not bear investigation, won't go down, is unconvincing, cannot be accepted. **4.** To reach and plash or lap against or over: *the waters of the lake wash upon the shore.* **C.** Followed by adverbs or prepositions with special meanings. *Wash against,* intrans., to come up to and splash or lap against: *the waves wash against the houses at high tide.* *Wash down,* trans., **1.** to cleanse by washing, apply a stream of water to: *to wash down the walls*; **2.** **a** to drive down by flow or rush of water: '*It may be that the gulfs will wash us down*' (Tennyson, 'Ulysses', 62); **b** in such Phr. as *a meal washed down by a draught of ale,* accompanied by, taken immediately before. *Wash out,* **1.** trans., to remove by washing: *to wash out a blood-stain*; also fig. colloq., to give up, abandon as futile, as a plan, suggestion, &c., cp. **wash-**

out, below; 2. intrans., to be removed by washing: *the stain won't wash out*; Phr. (colloq.) *to be, look, feel, washed out,* be, look, pale and worn; to feel exhausted. *Wash up,* trans., & intrans. (absol.), to wash (dishes, cutlery &c.) after use at meals &c.

wash (II.), n., fr. prec. **1. a** Act of washing: *to have a wash*; *to give a thing a wash*; **b** process of being washed. Phrs. *to send clothes to the wash,* send them to the laundry to be washed; *at the wash,* at the laundry, in process of being washed. **2.** (familiar) Clothes, household linen &c., ready to be sent to the laundry, in the process of being washed, or just returned from the laundry: *the wash goes on Monday and comes back on Saturday*; *to hang out the wash to dry.* **3. a** Movement to and fro, outward flow, of water: *the wash of the waves*; **b** sound produced by this; **c** backward movement or current in water caused by steamer's screw or by oars. **4. a** Liquid or semi-liquid refuse from kitchen &c., esp. as food for pigs; **b** weak, thin liquid intended for consumption: *I don't like tea, soup &c. that is only wash*; **c** the fermented wort in the distillation of spirits. **5.** Medicinal lotion: *a wash for the eyes, hair &c.*; also in compounds: *mouth-wash, hair-wash* &c. **6. a** Thin, flat application of water-colour, distemper &c. put on in liquid state; **b** thin coating of metal. **7.** Alluvial deposit, sediment, silt.

washable, adj. [1. wóshabl; 2. wɔ́ʃəbl]. **wash** (I.) & **-able.** Capable of being washed without deterioration.

wash-basin, n. Basin for washing in.

wash-board, n. Corrugated board on which clothes &c. may be scrubbed.

wash-boiler, n. Vessel for boiling clothes &c. after washing.

wash-bottle, n. Apparatus for purifying gases &c.

wash-bowl, n. [1. wósh bōl; 2. wɔ́ʃ boul]. Large basin for washing dishes &c.

wash-cloth, n. Piece of material used in washing dishes &c.

wash-day, n. Washing-day.

washer, n. [1. wósher; 2. wɔ́ʃə]. **wash** (I.) & **-er. 1. a** Person who, that which, washes; specif. **b** washing-machine. **2.** Small perforated disk of metal, rubber &c. used to tighten joint, nut &c.

washerwoman, n. [1. wósherwòoman; 2. wɔ́ʃəwùmən]. Woman employed to do household washing &c.

wash-hand-basin, n. [1. wósh (h)and bâsn; 2. wɔ́ʃ (h)ænd béisn]. Wash-basin.

wash-hand-stand, n. [1. wósh (h)and stând; 2. wɔ́ʃ (h)ænd stǽnd]. Wash-stand.

wash-house, n. Room or building in which clothes &c. are washed.

washily, adv. [1. wóshili; 2. wɔ́ʃili]. **washy** & **-ly.** In a washy manner.

washiness, n. [1. wóshines; 2. wɔ́ʃinis]. See prec. & **-ness.** State or quality of being washy.

washing, n. [1. wóshing; 2. wɔ́ʃiŋ]. **wash** (I.) & **-ing. 1. a** Act of one who washes, process of cleansing: *engaged in washing*; **b** process of being washed: *children sometimes dislike, though they frequently need, washing.* **2. a** Collection of articles ready to be sent to, or just returned from, the laundry; **b** clothes and other articles in process of being washed: *to hang out the washing to dry.* **3.** Liquid, substance, washed off in process of cleaning anything: *the washings of plates and dishes.*

washing-day, n. Day on which household washing is done, or clothes &c. are sent to the laundry.

washing-machine, n. Mechanical apparatus for washing clothes &c.

washing-stand, n. Wash-stand.

Washington, n. [1. wóshingtun; 2. wɔ́ʃiŋtən]. Town in N. America, seat of government of U.S.A. Government of U.S.A.

washingtonia, n. [1. wòshingtṓnia; 2. wɔ̀ʃiŋtóuniə]. Named after George Washington. Genus of palms of Southern California, with white flowers and fan-shaped leaves.

washing-up, n. Process of washing dishes &c. used at meals.

wash-leather, n. Chamois leather, or substitute for this.

wash-out, n. [1. wósh out; 2. wɔ́ʃ aut]. **1.** Erosion of earth by flood &c. **2.** (slang) Ineffective, disappointing, unsuccessful, person or enterprise &c.; a failure: *he was a wash-out as a lecturer*; *the attempt was a complete wash-out.*

wash-pot, n. **a** Vessel containing liquid tin for coating tin-plate; **b** (archaic, Bib.) any vessel in which something is washed: '*Moab is my wash-pot*'.

wash-stand, n. Flat-topped piece of furniture for holding basin and other requisites for personal ablutions.

wash-tub, n. Large wooden tub in which clothes &c. are washed.

washy, adj. [1. wóshi; 2. wɔ́ʃi]. **wash** (II.) & **-y. 1.** (of drink or liquid food) Thin, weak, highly diluted. **2.** (of colour) Pale, without intensity or depth. **3.** (fig., of style &c.) Feeble, insipid, lacking in force or character.

wasp, n. [1. wosp; 2. wɔsp]. O.E. *wæfs, wæps, wæsp*; M.E. *waspe*; cp. O.H.G. *wafsa, wefsa*; cogn. w. Lat. *vespa*; O. Prussian *wobse*; O. Slav. *vosa,* 'wasp', Lith. *vapsà,* 'horsefly'; fr. stem **webh-, *wobh-* &c., 'to weave', w. reference to appearance of nest. See **weave. a** Family of hymenopterous insects with slender waist and powerful sting; specif. **b** the common variety, *Vespa vulgaris,* with alternate yellow and black stripes.

wasp-bee, n. Bee with colouring like that of wasp.

wasp-fly, n. Fly with black and yellow stripes.

waspish, adj. [1. wóspish; 2. wɔ́spiʃ]. **wasp** & **-ish.** Ill-tempered, spiteful; sour, shrewish: *a waspish person*; expressing ill-temper and malignity; biting: *a waspish nature, speech* &c.

waspishly, adv. Prec. & **-ly.** In a waspish manner.

waspishness, n. See prec. & **-ness.** State or quality of being waspish.

wasp-waisted, adj. Having a very slender or much-compressed waist.

wassail (I.), n. [1. wósl, wásl, wásāl; 2. wɔ́sl, wǽsl, wǽseil &c.]. M.E. *wesseil,* for *wes,* 'be', & O.N. *heil,* 'whole'; the O.E. formula of greeting, *wes þū hāl,* 'be thou whole, or sound'; see **was** & **whole.** (obs. or lit.) **1.** Carousal, merry drinking-bout; feasting. **2.** Ale &c. drunk at such festivity.

wassail (II.), vb. intrans. M.E. *wesseilen*; fr. prec. To take part in a wassail, drink healths; to carouse.

wassail-bowl, -cup, -horn, n. Drinking vessel used at a wassail; festive potations, junketing.

wast, vb. [1. wost; 2. wɔst]. 2nd person Pret. sing. of **be.** See **was.**

wastage, n. [1. wâstij; 2. wéistidž]. **waste** (II.) & **-age. a** Process of wasting; **b** a wasteful loss; **c** amount wasted.

waste (I.), adj. [1. wāst; 2. weist]. M.E. *wāst,* fr. O. Fr. *wast,* fr. M.H.G. *wast,* fr. Lat. *vastus,* 'empty; waste, desert'. See **vast. 1.** Not cultivated or occupied by man; desolate, unproductive, either from natural causes or through destructive effect of war &c.: *waste land, a waste space.* Phrs. *to lie waste,* remain uncultivated; *to lay waste,* destroy, ravage. **2.** Not wanted; useless, superfluous; thrown aside as worthless; left over after an action or process: *waste matter, scraps*; *waste effort*; *waste products.*

waste (II.), vb. trans. & intrans., fr. O. Fr. *waster,* fr. Lat. *vastāre,* 'to lay waste, devastate', fr. *vastus,* 'empty, waste'. See **vast. A.** trans. **1.** To expend or use extravagantly or uselessly; squander, be prodigal of: *to waste one's time, money, energy &c.* **2.** To lay waste, devastate. **3.** To cause to shrink and diminish; cause to lose vigour, strength, substance &c.; to sap, blight: *a frame wasted by disease.* Phr. *a wasting disease,* causing emaciation and lack of strength. **4.** (law) To allow (property &c.) to be impaired through neglect &c. **B.** intrans. **1. a** Also *waste away,* to lose substance or strength, become emaciated; **b** (of time) to pass gradually, be consumed. **2.** To be wasted, run to waste.

waste (III.), n., fr. **waste** (I.). **1.** Desolate expanse of land or water; desert, uncultivated region; barren or devastated tract. **2.** Gradual diminution, reduction, in amount, substance, vigour &c. **3.** Act of wasting; state of being wasted; extravagant, unprofitable, or ineffective use or expenditure. **4.** Something wasted; waste material; useless, superfluous, or rejected matter; refuse. **5.** (law) Damage, impairment, of property &c. through neglect &c.

waste-basket, n. Waste-paper-basket.

waste-book, n. Book in which commercial transactions are entered temporarily.

wasteful, adj. [1. wâstfool; 2. wéistful]. **waste** (III.) & **-ful. 1. a** Extravagant; given to unprofitable, reckless, expenditure: *a wasteful man*; **b** tending to cause, involving, waste and extravagance: *a wasteful process, wasteful habits* &c.; **c** liable to waste or to be wasted: *a wasteful substance.* **2.** (poet.) Resembling, having the character of, a desolate waste (cp. **waste** (III.), **1**): '*the vast immeasurable abyss, Outrageous as a sea, dark, wasteful, wild*' (Milton, 'P. L.' vii. 211-12).

wastefully, adv. Prec. & **-ly.** In a wasteful manner.

wastefulness, n. See prec. & **-ness.** Quality of being wasteful.

wasteless, adj. [1. wâstles; 2. wéistlis]. **waste** (III.) & **-less.** Not liable to waste.

waste-paper-basket, n. Basket kept in a room, for holding waste scraps of paper, old letters and envelopes.

waste-pipe, n. Pipe for carrying off waste or surplus water.

waster, n. [1. wâster; 2. wéistə]. **waste** (II.) & **-er. 1.** A wasteful, extravagant, useless person. **2.** Thing spoilt in manufacture.

wastrel, n. [1. wâstrel; 2. wéistrəl]. **waste** (II.) & dimin. suff. *-rel.* Idle, extravagant, good-for-nothing fellow; a waster.

watch (I.), n. [1. woch; 2. wɔtʃ]. O.E. *wæċċe*; M.E. *wacche,* 'vigil; watch'; cp. O.H.G. *wacha*; fr. stem seen in O.E. *wacian,* 'to be awake', see **wake** (I.). **1.** (archaic) Vigil, wakefulness; forbearance, abstention, from sleep: *in the night watches*; *passed like a watch in the night.* **2.** Act of watching; alertness, vigilance; constant observation, look-out: *to keep watch*; *to be on the watch for a person or expected event &c.*; *to keep watch and ward.* **3.** (archaic) **a** Person employed to watch or guard; a watchman; **b** party of persons employed for this purpose. **4.** One of the periods of three or four hours into which the night was formerly divided: *the evening, morning, watch &c.* **5.** (naut.) **a** Spell of duty on board ship, four hours except in the case of the *dog-watch,* q.v.; **b** one of the two divisions of a ship's crew taking alternate watches: *starboard, port, watch.* **6.** Small timepiece worked by a coiled spring, usually enclosed in a flat, round case suitable for carrying on the person; cp. *clock.*

watch (II.), vb. intrans. & trans. O.E. *wæċċan,* formed fr. base of *wacian,* 'to be awake, to keep watch'; see prec. **A.** intrans. **1. a** To remain awake and alert; to be vigilant: '*watch and pray*'; **b** to keep vigil: *to watch beside a sick-bed.* **2. a** To play the part of a spectator; to observe, look on at events: *he remained silent during the whole scene and merely watched*; **b** *watch for,* to be on the look-out for; await with vigilance the arrival or occurrence of something: *to watch for the procession to go by*; *to watch for an opportunity to speak, for a chance to pounce.* **3. a** To be on guard, act as sentinel or look-out; **b** *watch over,* to guard, protect, have in one's care; keep an observant eye on: *to watch* *over flocks*; *to watch over the destinies of a nation.* B. trans. 1. a To look at, observe, as a spectator; to direct the attention upon; esp. to consider attentively a series of actions or of moving objects: *to watch a procession pass*; *to watch the crowd from a window*; *to watch a person's face*; b to direct the mind upon, keep oneself acquainted with (a series of events): *to watch the development of affairs.* 2. To keep under observation: *spies and suspicious persons are carefully watched*; *a good nurse watches her patient continuously.* 3. a To guard; to observe for the purpose of protecting: *David as a boy watched his father's sheep*; b (specif. of a barrister) *to watch a case for an interested party*, to be present in court during the hearing, and ensure as far as possible that nothing is said or done to the prejudice of his client. 4. To be on the look-out for: *to watch a favourable opportunity.*

watch-box, n. Sentry-box.

watch-case, n. Metal outer case containing mechanism of watch.

watch-chain, n. Chain for securing watch to clothing &c.

watch-dog, n. a Dog guarding property &c., giving warning of approach of strangers &c.; b person who keeps a vigilant look-out against possible infringement of, or injury attempted to, some particular group of interests, rights &c.

watcher, n. [1. wócher; 2. wɔ́tʃə]. **watch (II.)** & **-er.** One who watches.

watch-fire, n. Fire kept burning at night by camp-guards, or as signal &c.

watchful, adj. [1. wóchfool; 2. wɔ́tʃful]. **watch (I.)** & **-ful.** Vigilant, on the watch, alert, observant.

watchfully, adv. Prec. & **-ly.** In a watchful manner.

watchfulness, n. See prec. & **-ness.** State or quality of being watchful.

watch-glass, n. Thin, round piece of glass fixed over the face of a watch.

watch-guard, n. Chain, strap, cord &c. for fastening watch to clothing &c.

watch-gun, n. Gun fired at changing of watch.

watch-house, n. Building occupied by guard.

watch-key, n. Key for winding up a watch.

watchmaker, n. [1. wóchmàker; 2. wɔ́tʃmèikə]. Person whose trade is to make and repair watches.

watchman, n. [1. wóchman; 2. wɔ́tʃmən]. 1. (hist.) Member of guard formerly patrolling streets at night. 2. Man employed to guard buildings &c. at night.

watch-night, n. New Year's Eve, esp. as celebrated by religious services.

watch-oil, n. Fine oil for lubricating mechanism of watch.

watch-pocket, n. Small pocket, usually in a waistcoat, for holding a watch.

watch-spring, n. Spring which actuates the movement in mechanism of a watch.

watch-stand, n. Small stand which supports a watch in such a way that its face can be seen.

watch-tower, n. Lofty tower from which a wide view can be obtained of the surrounding country, upon which sentinels were placed formerly to give warning of approach of an enemy.

watchword, n. [1. wóchwërd; 2. wɔ́tʃwʌd]. 1. Password, countersign. 2. Word or phrase intended to embody the principles of a party, cause &c.

water (I.), n. [1. wáwter; 2. wɔ́tə]. O.E. *wæter*; M.E. *wāter*; cp. O.H.G. *wassar*; O.S. *watar*; O.N. *vatu*, 'water'; cogn. w. Gk. *húdōr*, 'water', see **hydro-**; Scrt. *udán-*, 'wave'; O. Slav. *voda*, see **vodka**; Lith. *vandũ*; O. Prussian *unds*, 'water'; the base is **wed-*, **wod-*, **ud-*, 'water'; cp. also **wash, wet.** 1. A widely distributed, nearly colourless, transparent, liquid, composed of hydrogen and oxygen, either pure or containing mineral or other matter in solution: *fresh, salt, hot, cold water* &c.; *hard, soft, water* (see **hard, soft**); sometimes in compounds, indicating source &c.; *rain-, spring-, river-, sea-, ground-water* &c.; *mineral waters*, characterized by specific mineral ingredient; *strong waters*, (archaic) spirits; *table waters*, bottled for use at meals; *holy water*, water which has been blessed and is used for various religious purposes; Phrs. *water bewitched*, (colloq.) very weak tea &c.; *water of life* (Bib.), spiritual refreshment; *waters of forgetfulness*, oblivion, death; *in deep water(s)*, in difficulties, tribulation; struggling; *in smooth water(s)*, prosperous, having an easy progress; (*like*) *a fish out of water*, out of one's element, in unaccustomed and uncongenial surroundings; *written in water* (of name, fame &c.), soon forgotten, transient; *to back water*, to go backwards in rowing-boat by reversing motion of oars; *to fish in troubled waters*, endeavour to profit by discords &c.; *to get into hot water*, get into trouble; *to drink the waters*, take prescribed quantity of medicine-water treatment at a spa; *to go through fire and water*, undergo great hardships; *to hold water*, (of theory, statement &c.) admit of proof, investigation &c.; *to keep one's head above water*, contrive to avoid succumbing to financial embarrassments; manage to hold one's own, in various senses; *to pour oil on the waters*, to induce calm, serenity; (*to spend money &c.*) *like water*, extravagantly, lavishly; *to throw cold water on* (*a plan* &c.), discourage. 2. (often pl.) Body of water: *the waters of the lake*; *the head-waters of the Amazon.* 3. Tide, state of tide, at specific moment: *high, low, water*; Phr. *in low water*, in want of money &c. 4. (in compounds) Solution of vegetable or mineral substance in water: *rose-water, soda-water* &c. 5. Liquid secretion of animal body, e.g. tears, perspiration, urine &c.: *water on the brain, knee*, accumulation of serous fluid. Phr. *to make, pass, water*, discharge urine. 6. Quality, lustre, brilliance, of precious stone, esp. diamond; Phrs. *of the first water*, of the finest quality; (also fig.) embodying in a high degree the characteristic qualities of a type or class.

water (II.), vb. trans. & intrans., fr. prec. A. trans. 1. To sprinkle with water, moisten, irrigate: *to water the garden, plants* &c. Phr. *to water one's pillow with tears.* 2. To provide (animals &c.) with water for drinking. 3. To supply with moisture, streams &c.: *the country is watered by large rivers.* 4. To dilute with water: *to water the whisky, milk* &c.; also *water down*, (i.) to dilute (milk &c.) with water; (ii.) to weaken force, pungency, cogency, expressiveness, of (a statement &c.) by alterations and omissions, in order to make it more generally acceptable to the timid or half-hearted. 5. (chiefly in P.P.) To give a wavy pattern to surface of (textile fabric): *watered silk.* 6. (finance) To increase number of shares in (stock &c.) without increasing actual capital. B. intrans. 1. a (of animal &c.) To drink water, go to watering-place; b (of engine, ship &c.) to take in a supply of water. 2. To have increased secretion, become filled with water: *the light makes one's eyes water*; *one's mouth waters*, through anticipation of food &c. Phr. *to make one's mouth water*, to fill one with longing to possess or enjoy.

water-anchor, n. Floating, wooden framework used to check leeway of ship.

water-bailiff, n. Custom-house official inspecting ships entering port.

water-bed, n. Rubber mattress filled with water.

water-beetle, n. General name for various aquatic beetles (*Dytiscus*) which live habitually under the surface of water.

water-bellows, n. Apparatus by means of which air for a forge is forced into, and expelled from, a wooden tube through sloping holes by the pressure of falling water; also called a *trompe.*

water-bird, n. Bird frequenting water; aquatic bird.

water-biscuit, n. Thin, hard biscuit made of flour and water.

water-blink, n. In arctic regions, cloud-like appearance on the horizon indicating the presence of open water.

water-blister, n. Blister on the skin, containing serous fluid.

water-boatman, n. Aquatic insect, *Notonecta*, with boat-shaped body and long legs.

water-borne, adj. (of mail, goods &c.) Transported by water.

water-bottle, n. 1. Glass bottle holding drinking-water for table or bedroom use. 2. Metal flask for water, as part of military equipment &c.

water-brash, n. Form of indigestion with vomiting of bitter, watery liquid.

water-buck, n. Large S. African antelope, with white stripe on buttocks, genus *Cobus.*

water-buffalo, n. Indian buffalo.

water-butt, n. Large cask for collecting rain-water.

water-carriage, n. Transportation of goods by water.

water-carrier, n. a Person employed to carry water; b (cap.) the constellation of Aquarius.

water-cart, n. Cart for carrying water, esp. one with device for watering roads.

water-chute, n. Boarded slope down which toboggans rush into a pool of water, as a form of amusement.

water-clock, n. Clock regulated by flow of water.

water-closet, n. Privy with pan flushed out by water.

water-colour, n. 1. Pigment diluted with water instead of oil. 2. Picture painted with such pigments. 3. (also pl.) Art of painting with such pigments.

water-colourist, n. [1. wáwter kùlurist; 2. wɔ́tə kàlərist]. Painter in water-colour.

water-cooled, adj. [1. wáwter kōōld; 2. wɔ́tə kûld]. *Water-cooled engine*, one in which the cylinders are kept from overheating by the circulation of water round them; contrasted with *air-cooled.*

watercourse, n. [1. wáwterkòrs; 2. wɔ́təkɔ̀s]. 1. Body of running water, stream. 2. Channel for stream &c.

watercress, n. [1. wáwterkrès; 2. wɔ́təkrès]. Creeping herb *Nasturtium officinale*, growing in water and used in salads.

water-cure, n. Medical treatment by application of water; hydropathy.

water-drinker, n. One who drinks water; specif., one who abstains from alcohol.

water-dropwort, n. [1. wáwter drópwërt; 2. wɔ́tə drɔ́pwʌt]. Poisonous plant, genus *Oenanthe*, resembling celery.

watered, adj. [1. wáwterd; 2. wɔ́təd], fr. P.P. of **water (II.)**. 1. Supplied with streams &c.; irriguous: '*a quiet water'd land, a land of roses*' (Rolleston, 'Clonmacnois'). 2. (of silk &c.) Having a pattern of wavy lines.

waterfall, n. [1. wáwterfàwl; 2. wɔ́təfɔ̀l]. Body of water descending perpendicularly or nearly so; cascade.

water-finder, n. Person who is able to find a spring of water in the ground by means of divining-rod; a dowser.

water-flag, n. Yellow iris.

water-flea, n. Small fresh-water crustacean.

waterfowl, n. [1. wáwterfòul; 2. wɔ́təfàul]. (usually coll.) Aquatic birds.

water-gas, n. Illuminating or power-gas derived, produced, by passing steam through red-hot coke or anthracite and decomposing it.

water-gate, n. 1. Gate for checking or releasing flow of water. 2. Gate opening from building on to river, lake &c.

water-gauge, n. Gauge indicating level of water in tank, boiler &c.

water-glass, n. 1. Tube with glass bottom for observing objects under water. 2. Transparent solution of silica &c. sprayed over fresco painting to preserve it; also used for preserving eggs.

water-hammer, n. Concussion of water when its flow through pipe &c. is suddenly checked.

water-hen, n. Moorhen.

water-hyacinth, n. Tropical plant with spikes of blue flowers and thick, tangled leaf-stalks.
water-ice, n. Confection of frozen water, fruit-juice, and sugar &c.
water-inch, n. Amount of water flowing in twenty-four hours through a hole one inch in diameter.
wateriness, n. [1. wáwterines; 2. wɔ̄tərinis]. watery & **-ness**. Quality of being watery.
watering-can, n. [1. wáwtering kàn; 2. wɔ̄təriŋ kæn]. Vessel with long spout, often fitted with perforated nozzle, for watering plants.
watering-cart, n. Cart carrying a supply of water and fitted with a device for watering roads.
watering-place, n. **1.** Pool to which animals resort to drink. **2. a** Health resort with medicinal springs; **b** seaside resort.
watering-pot, n. Watering-can.
water-jacket, n. Casing containing water and surrounding cylinder &c. for cooling purposes.
water-joint, n. Water-tight joint.
water-junket, n. Sandpiper.
water-lens, n. Magnifying lens consisting of water enclosed in a brass cell with a glass bottom.
waterless, adj. [1. wáwterles; 2. wɔ̄təlis]. **water** & **-less**. Without water.
water-level, n. **1.** Surface of body of water, esp. as datum for measurement. **2.** (geol.) Irregular upper surface of ground-water; upward limit of saturation. **3.** Levelling instrument in which the position of a drop of water indicates horizontality.
water-lily, n. Plant, *Nymphaea*, with flat, heart-shaped leaves, and large, white, yellow, pink, or blue flowers, which float on the surface of water.
water-line, n. **1.** Line along ship's side corresponding to water-level; *load-*, *light-water-line*, level reached by water when ship is loaded, empty. **2.** Line forming part of watermark.
water-logged, adj. **a** (of wood or wooden objects) Saturated or filled with water and having lost buoyancy; **b** (of the ground) soaked with water beyond saturation-point, so that it remains swampy; **c** (of a ship) rendered almost unmanageable, through water leaking excessively into hold.
water-main, n. Chief pipe in system of water-supply.
waterman, n. [1. wáwterman; 2. wɔ̄təmən]. **1.** Boatman, ferryman &c. plying for hire. **2.** Oarsman: *a good, bad, waterman* &c.
watermanship, n. [1. wáwtermanship; 2. wɔ̄təmənʃip]. Prec. & **-ship**. Skill in management of oars.
watermark, n. & vb. trans. [1. wáwtermàrk; 2. wɔ̄təmàk]. **1.** n. **a** Design imprinted on surface of paper, showing quality, date or place of manufacture &c., and faintly visible when the paper is held against the light; **b** (i.) mark or line showing the height to which water has risen, as *high-watermark*, on a beach &c.; (ii.) fig. *high-watermark*, the highest attainable point or degree of excellence; *low-watermark*, lowest attainable degree of demerit. **2.** vb. To imprint a watermark on (paper) in process of manufacture.
water-meadow, n. Low-lying meadow periodically inundated by river &c.
water-melon, n. Large, edible, sweet, pulpy fruit of a trailing plant of the gourd family.
water-mill, n. Mill worked by water-power.
water-mocassin, n. Poisonous N. American snake.
water-monkey, n. Long-necked, earthenware water-jar of eastern countries.
water-motor, n. Motor driven by water pressure.
water-nymph, n. Spirit haunting river, lake &c.; naiad.
water-pillar, n. Pillar with swinging spout for supplying steam-engines with water.
water-pipe, n. Pipe for conveying water.
water-plane, n. **1.** Plane in which water-line lies, level with surface of water. **2.** Sea-plane.
water-plate, n. Plate with double bottom enclosing space for hot water.
water-platter, n. Variety of water-lily.
water-polo, n. Ball-game played by swimmers, the object being to throw the ball into the goal of the opposing side.
water-power, n. Power generated by pressure, fall &c. of water.
waterproof, adj., n., & vb. trans. [1. wáwterproof; 2. wɔ̄təprûf]. **1.** adj. Proof against water, capable of excluding or resisting water, not permitting water to pass through. **2.** n. Waterproof coat &c. **3.** vb. To make waterproof by coating with rubber &c.
water-rail, n. Long-legged, short-winged wading bird; the common rail.
water-ram, n. Hydraulic ram.
water-rat, n. Popular name for the water-vole.
water-rate, n. Official charge made for public water-supply.
water-sail, n. (naut.) Sail below lower studding-sail.
water-seal, n. Body of water held in a trap &c. to prevent passage of gas &c.
watershed, n. [1. wáwtershèd; 2. wɔ̄təʃèd], fr. **water** (I.) & **shed** (I.), in earlier sense to divide, separate. **a** Elevation dividing two river valleys or basins; line of division between two river-systems; **b** (a loose incorrect usage) river-basin; catchment area.
water-shoot, n. Pipe, trough, gutter, for discharging water from roof &c.
water-side, n. Edge, margin, of body of water.
water-skin, n. Bag of skin for carrying water.
water-soldier, n. Water plant, *Stratiotes*, rooted at bottom of water and having sword-like leaves and flowers above the surface.
water-spider, n. Kind of spider which lives in a bell-shaped nest under water.
waterspout, n. [1. wáwterspout; 2. wɔ̄təspaut]. Pillar of water drawn upward by a funnel-shaped mass of whirling cloud which descends vertically to meet it.
water-sprite, n. Supernatural being haunting river, lake &c.
water-supply, n. **1.** System of procuring and storing water to supply house, town &c. **2.** Water used or supplied by such a system.
water-table, n. **1.** Water-level. **2.** (archit.) Moulding, projecting ledge &c. designed to throw off water from building.
water-tiger, n. Destructive larva of a kind of water-beetle.
watertight, adj. [1. wáwtertīt; 2. wɔ̄tətait]. **a** Capable of resisting passage of water; fixed or fitted tightly enough to prevent water passing through; **b** (fig., of argument &c.) perfectly sound, unassailable.
water-tower, n. Structure containing raised tank designed to furnish pressure necessary to system of water-supply.
water-vole, n. Kind of aquatic rodent, *Microtus amphibius*, often called the water-rat.
water-wagtail, n. Wagtail.
water-way, n. **1.** Navigable channel. **2.** Channel round edge of ship's deck to carry off water.
water-wheel, n. Wheel turned by flow of water.
water-witch, n. **1.** Water-finder. **2.** Any one of several kinds of diving bird.
water-withe, n. West Indian vine with branches full of watery juice.
waterworks, n. [1. wáwterwèrks; 2. wɔ̄təwàks]. **a** System of buildings, machinery, reservoirs, pipes &c. for supplying water to town &c. Slang Phr. *to turn on the waterworks*, shed tears; **b** (colloq.) the bladder and urinary organs generally.
water-worn, adj. (of rock, pebble &c.) Rounded, smoothed, polished, by action of water.
watery, adj. [1. wáwteri; 2. wɔ̄təri]. **water** (I.) & **-y**. **1.** Consisting of water; cp. such poet. Phr. as *watery waste*, *wilderness*, the sea; '*He must not float upon his watery bier Unwept*', the sea, in which Lycidas had perished (Milton). **2.** Containing, full of, saturated with, water; specif. a (of eyes) having a weak, moist appearance, as though they were watering; **b** (of boiled food) containing too much water, sodden. **3. a** (of liquid) Over-diluted with water; thin, weak, insipid: *watery tea, soup* &c.; **b** hence, (fig.) insipid, without force or character. **4.** (of moon or sky) Indicating approach of rain.
watt, n. [1. wot; 2. wɔt], fr. James Watt, inventor, d. 1819. Unit of electrical power, the equivalent to work at the rate of one joule per second, 746 watts = 1 h.p.
Watteau, n. [1. wótō; 2. wɔ́tou], fr. name of Antoine Watteau, French painter (1684–1721); with reference to costumes &c. shown in his paintings. *Watteau back*, back of woman's dress, arranged to form a long pleat from neck to hem; *Watteau bodice*, with square neck-opening.
wattle (I.), n. [1. wótl; 2. wɔ́tl]. O.E. *watol*, 'hurdle'; M.E. *watel*, 'hurdle; basket, bag'. Origin uncertain; cp. O.E. *wætla*, 'bandage'. **1.** Structure of wickerwork on a framework of stiffer rods, used in form of hurdles. **2.** Fleshy excrescence hanging from neck of bird, esp. turkey. **3.** Barbel of fish. **4.** Kind of acacia of Australia and S. Africa.
wattle (II.), vb. trans. To make of, construct with, wattle-work.
wattle-and-daub, n. [1. wótl an(d) dáwb; 2. wɔ́tl ən(d) dɔ̄b]. Wattle-work daubed with clay, mud &c.; used for the walls of rough huts.
wattle-bird, n. Australian bird with wattle below each ear.
wattled, adj. [1. wótld; 2. wɔ́tld]. **wattle** (I.) & **-ed**. **1.** Made of, covered with, wattle-work. **2.** (of birds and fish) Having wattles.
wattle-work, n. Hurdle &c. made of wattles.
wattling, n. [1. wótling; 2. wɔ́tliŋ]. **wattle** (II.) & **-ing**. Wattle-work.
watt-meter, n. **watt** & **-meter**. Instrument measuring electrical power in terms of watts.
waul, vb. intrans. [1. wawl; 2. wɔ̄l]. Imitative. To cry, howl, squall, like a cat.
wave (I.), vb. intrans. & trans. [1. wāv; 2. weiv]. O.E. *wafian*, 'to wave, brandish', M.E. *wāven*; cp. O.N. *vafa*; M.H.G. *waben*, 'to wave, fluctuate'; cp. **waver**. **A.** intrans. **1.** (of flexible object) To move to and fro in air or water with curving, sinuous, motion; to sway, sweep to and fro; to stream, fluctuate: *flags, branches, wave in the breeze*; *waving corn*; *seaweed waves below the surface of the water.* **2.** (of line or surface) To be arranged, lie, in a series of curves; to have alternate curving elevations and depressions, undulate: *one's hair waves.* **3.** To signal by waving hand &c.: *to wave in farewell* &c. **B.** trans. **1.** To cause to move to and fro with a sweeping motion; to brandish, flourish: *to wave one's hand*; *to wave a wand*; also (of flags) to allow to stream in the wind, to flaunt: '*Wave, Munich, all thy banners wave!*' (Campbell, 'Hohenlinden'). **2.** To signal to by waving: *the leader waved his men on with his sword*; *to wave a person away*; *to wave away a proposal* &c., signify disapproval of by a waving gesture, to brush it aside. **3.** To express by a wave of the hand &c.: *to wave a farewell.* **4.** To give an undulating surface, edge, appearance, to: *to wave one's hair.*
wave (II.), n., prob. fr. or due to association w. prec. The O.E. word was *wǣg*, M.E. *wawe*, wh. was ousted by *wave* in 16th cent. **1. a** A swelling, curving ridge on the surface of the sea or other large sheet of water in motion; a billow; **b** specif. (poet.) *the waves*, the sea. **2.** An undulation, or undulating movement, in any surface, resembling in appearance that caused by wind on the surface of water: '*Waves of shadow went over the wheat*' (Tennyson, 'Poet's Song'). **3.** (phys.) Any disturbance which is periodic in both space and time. The interval between its repetition in space is its *wave-length*· the interval of time is its *period*, and the reciprocal of its period is its *frequency*. **4.** An

undulating mark or streak on a surface, e.g. in a silk fabric, reflecting light differently from the rest of the surface. 5. One of a series of wide curves or curls in a substance such as the hair. 6. A waving movement, a shaking to and fro: *a wave of the hand.* 7. An emotional or intellectual impulse, movement, tendency, a gust of feeling &c.: *a wave of religious passion, of enthusiasm, of indignation,* &c.

wave-length, n. a The distance between the crests of two adjacent waves in water; b (phys.) regular interval of space between each recurrence of a periodic disturbance.

waveless, adj. [1. wâvles; 2. wéivlis]. **wave (II.) & -less.** Without waves.

wavelet, n. [1. wâvlet; 2. wéivlit]. **wave (II.) & -let.** A small wave, a ripple.

waver, vb. intrans. [1. wâver; 2. wéivə]. M.E. *wäveren*, 'to waver'; cp. M.H.G. *waberen*, O.N. *vafra*, 'to waver'; **wave (I.) & -er.** 1. To move unsteadily, to shift with irregular movements from place to place, or to and fro; to fluctuate; to tremble, to flicker, to come and go: *a wavering shadow, mist, light, cloud of smoke.* 2. To totter, recede and show signs of breaking or giving way: *the line wavered and finally broke before the shock of the cavalry.* 3. a To halt between two opinions, to vacillate, to shilly-shally; b to remain undecided between two courses of action; to be irresolute, to lack fixity of purpose; to yield, give way: *inflexible in his resolve, he never wavered in spite of abuse and denunciation.*

waverer, n. [1. wâverer; 2. wéivərə]. Prec. & **-er.** One who wavers; an irresolute, vacillating person.

wavering, adj. [1. wâvering; 2. wéivəriŋ], fr. Pres. Part. of **waver.** a Flickering, quivering; b hesitating, vacillating.

waveringly, adv. Prec. & **-ly.** In a wavering manner.

wavily, adv. [1. wâvili; 2. wéivili]. **wavy & -ly.** In a wavy manner; with undulations.

waviness, n. [1. wâvines; 2. wéivinis]. Next word & **-ness.** State or quality of being wavy.

wavy (I.), adj. [1. wâvi; 2. wéivi]. **wave (II.) & -y.** 1. Inclined to wave, waving, e.g. as grass, plumes &c. in the wind. 2. (of surface or line) Having, showing, undulating curves, alternately convex and concave: *a wavy line; wavy hair.*

wavy (II.), wavey, n., fr. Am. Ind. *wawa.* North American Arctic goose; snow-goose.

wawl. Variant of **waul.**

wax (I.), n. [1. waks; 2. wæks]. O.E. *weax*; M.E. *wax*; cp. O. Fris. *wax*; O.H.G. *wahs*; O.N. *vax*, 'wax'; prob. cogn. w. O.H.G. *waba*, 'honeycomb', & w. **weave, web, wick (I.).** 1. a Plastic, yellow, fatty substance secreted by bees and used by them in construction of cells; b prepared wax, bleached and purified, used for manufacture of candles, for modelling &c. Phr. *like wax (in one's hands* &c.), easily influenced. 2. Substance resembling wax in appearance, consistency &c.; specif. a also *vegetable wax*, waxy substance exuded by some plants; b also *ear-wax*, substance secreted by ear; cerumen; c also *mineral wax*, ozocerite; d *cobbler's wax*, kind of resin used by shoemakers to coat thread.

wax (II.), vb. trans., fr. prec. To cover, coat, impregnate, treat, with wax.

wax (III.), vb. intrans. O.E. *weaxan*; M.E. *waxan*, 'to grow'; cp. O.H.G. *wahsan*; O. Fris. *waxa*; O.N. *vaxa*, 'to grow'; Goth. *wahsjan*, 'to grow'; cogn. w. Scrt. *vakšanam*, 'growth, increase'; *úkšati*, 'he strengthens'; Gk. *aéxein*, 'to increase', earlier **awex-*; cp. also Lat. *augēre*, 'to cause to grow', see **augment, auction.** 1. To increase, grow larger; now used chiefly of the moon, to present the appearance of growing in size in passing towards the phase of full moon; contrasted with *wane.* 2. To pass into a specified state; to become: *to wax merry; their mirth waxed loud;* (archaic) *to wax old and feeble.*

wax (IV.), n. Etymol. unknown. (school slang) Fit of anger, rage, esp. in Phr. *to be in, get into, a wax.*

wax-berry, n. The candle-berry.

waxbill, n. [1. wáksbil; 2. wǽksbil]. Small kind of weaver-bird with beak having appearance of sealing-wax.

wax candle, n. Candle made of wax.

wax-chandler, n. Maker of, dealer in, wax candles.

wax-cloth, n. Cloth coated or treated with wax for polishing floor, furniture &c.

wax doll, n. Doll with head and extremities made of prepared beeswax &c.

waxen, adj. [1. wáksen; wǽksən]. **wax (I.) & -en.** 1. a (archaic) Made of wax; b resembling wax in appearance; esp. (i.) smooth, unwrinkled; also (ii.) colourless: *a waxen complexion.* 2. (archaic) Impressionable, easily melted or influenced; yielding: '*the waxen hearts of men*' (Tennyson, 'In Mem.' xxi. 8).

wax-end, n. Shoemaker's waxed thread.

wax-flower, n. Tropical Asiatic plant with thick, glossy leaves and waxy flowers, *Hoya carnosa.*

waxiness, n. [1. wáksines; 2. wǽksinis]. **waxy & -ness.** State or quality of being waxy.

wax-insect, n. Insect secreting wax.

wax-light, n. Wax candle, taper &c.

wax-moth, n. Moth liable to infest bee hives and lay its eggs on the combs.

wax-myrtle, n. American shrub producing nuts coated with white wax from which candles are made; the candle-berry.

wax-painting, n. Encaustic painting.

wax-palm, n. South American palm producing vegetable wax.

wax-paper, n. Paper made waterproof by coating with wax.

wax-plant, n. Plant producing waxy flowers; the wax-flower.

wax-pocket, n. One of the cavities of the under side of bee's abdomen in which wax is secreted.

wax tree, n. Tree yielding vegetable wax.

waxwing, n. [1. wákswing; 2. wǽkswiŋ]. Small bird, *Ampelis*, with feathers tipped with red, horny appendages.

waxwork, n. [1. wákswẽrk; 2. wǽkswāk]. Figure modelled in wax; esp. wax effigy of the human figure dressed for exhibition &c.; *waxworks*, an exhibition of such figures.

waxy (I.), adj. [1. wáksi; 2. wǽksi]. **wax (I.) & -y.** 1. Pertaining to, resembling, treated with, having the consistency of, wax. 2. (specif. of complexion, skin &c.) Having a pallid, translucent appearance. 3. (of organ of body, tissue &c.) Affected by a morbid change towards a structure of waxy appearance.

waxy (II.), adj. **wax (IV.) & -y.** (school slang) Angry, annoyed.

way, n. [1. wā; 2. wei]. O.E. *weg*; M.E. *wei*, 'way'; cp. O.S., O.H.G. *weg*; O. Fris. *wei*; O.N. *vegr*; Goth. *wigs*, 'way'; cp. also O.E. *wegan*, 'to carry, move', see **weigh**; *wægn*, 'cart', see **wain**; cogn. w. Lat. *vehere*, 'to drive, carry', see **vehicle**; Gk. *ókhos* for **wokhos*, 'waggon'; Lith. *vežimas*, 'cart'. 1. a Road, track, path, trail, leading from one place to another: *a rough, winding way*; Phrs. *covered way*, roofed-in passage, path &c.; *Appian, Icknield, Fosse, Way* &c., names of Roman roads; *permanent way*, railway track; *six-foot way*, space between two sets of rails on railway track; *Milky Way*, see **milky**; *the Way of the Cross*, (i.) series of representations of the stages on the road to Calvary; (ii.) set of devotions referring to these stages; Phr. *to pave the way for*, prepare for, facilitate approach or introduction of: *to pave the way for reform* &c.; b also in compounds, *highway, byway* &c. 2. Route followed, or to be followed, in going from place to place: *do you know the way?; this is the way home; to find, lose, one's way; to ask, point out, the way; which is the way out?* Phrs. *the longest way round is the shortest way home*, short cuts are often not reliable (lit. and fig.); *to take one's way*, go; *to go one's way*, depart; *to lead the way*, (lit. and fig.) go in front, act as leader; *to see one's way to*, feel that one is able to (do something); *to go out of one's way to*, make special effort to; *to put oneself out of the way*, take trouble; *to go the way of all flesh, of all the earth*, die; *the parting of the ways*, (fig.) moment for decisive action along one of two opposed lines; *by way of*, by a route passing through; *by the way*, (i.) during journey; (ii.) (fig., introducing an irrelevancy) in passing, incidentally; *on the way*, travelling, passing from one place to another; going or approaching; *out of the way*, unusual, unfamiliar: *he has done nothing out of the way*; *out-of-the-way* (attrib. adj.), remote, inaccessible: *an out-of-the-way place.* 3. Direction, point towards which motion takes place: *he went that way; which way were you looking?* 4. Distance traversed, or to be traversed; distance between two points: *it is only a little way to the town; we have still some way to go; England is a long way from Australia; the roots go a long way down.* 5. a Passage from point to point; progress, advance: *to make one's way; to make the best of one's way*, go as fast as possible; b (lit. and fig.) forward movement, tendency or power to advance; momentum: *to make, gather, lose, way.* Phrs. *to be under way, to have way on*, (esp. of ship) be moving forward; (also fig.) *preparations are now under way* &c. 6. (lit. and fig.) Freedom to advance, opportunity for progress; space for unimpeded forward movement: *to make way (for); to be in one's way; to get out of one's way; to clear the way.* Phrs. *to put (person) out of the way*, kill him &c.; *to put one in the way of*, give an opportunity to; *to give way*, yield, cease to resist. 7. Method, mode of procedure, manner of achieving an object or performing an action; course of action: *the right or wrong way of doing something; to try new ways of working; to speak in a careless way; do it your own way.* Phrs. *to have one's own way*, get what one wants; *to my &c. way of thinking*, in my opinion; *by way of*, (i.) with intention of, with a view to; (ii.) as substitute for: *to say a few words by way of introduction; in the way of (business* &c.), in the ordinary course of. 8. a Characteristic method, customary procedure, habit: *it's not his way to be generous; the way of the world*; b specific manner of life, habits: *to like old-fashioned ways; to live &c. in a small way*, unpretentiously, on a small scale. 9. Scope, sphere of attention, occupation, action &c.: *such things have never come (in) my way.* Phr. *to be in the drapery &c. way*, trade as draper &c. 10. a State, condition; (colloq.) *to be in a bad way*; Phr. *in the family way*, pregnant; b specif. (slang) state of agitation: *she is in a terrible way.* 11. Respect, regard, particular: *they are in no way similar; it is good in some ways; bad in every way.* 12. (pl.) Lines of framework of timber down which ship slides when launched.

way-bill, n. List of passengers or goods carried by public conveyance.

way-board, n. Thin seam of rock lying between two thicker strata.

wayfarer, n. [1. wâfârer; 2. wéifɛ̀ərə]. **way & fare (III.) & -er.** Person passing from one place to another, traveller.

wayfaring, adj. [1. wâfâring; 2. wéifɛ̀əriŋ]. **way & fare (III.) & -ing.** Passing from place to place; travelling, itinerant.

wayfaring tree, n. European shrub with white flowers and black berries, common in hedgerows; viburnum.

waylay, vb. trans. [1. wālâ; 2. weiléi]. **way & lay (III.).** To lie in wait for in order to attack &c.; to ambush.

way-leave, n. Right of way; specif., right to carry minerals, goods &c. over another's property.

way-mark, n. Milestone or other indication on public way.
way-post, n. Sign-post.
-ways, adv. suff. representing O.E. *weġes*, genit. of *weġ*, 'way'; **way** & **-es**. Used to form advs. indicating position, direction &c.: *sideways, always, lengthways* &c.
way-shaft, n. For *weigh-*. Rocking shaft in steam-engine.
wayside, n. & adj. **1**. n. Side, margin, of path or road. **2**. adj. Found, situated, at the side of the road: *wayside flowers*.
wayward, adj. [1. wāward; 2. wéiwəd]. Earlier *awayward*; **away** & **-ward**. Not yielding to control; perverse, capricious, wilful.
waywardly, adv. Prec. & **-ly**. In a wayward manner.
waywardness, n. See prec. & **-ness**. State or quality of being wayward.
way-worn, adj. Wearied by travel, esp. on foot.
wayzgoose, n. [1. wāzgōōs; 2. wéizgūs]. 17th cent. *waygoose*; etymol. unknown. Annual entertainment held by printing-house employees.
we, pron., 1st pers. pl. [1. wē; 2. wī]. O.E., M.E. *wē*; O.S. *wī*; Du. *wij*; O.H.G. *wir*; Goth. *weis*; cogn. w. Scrt. *vayám*, 'we'.
weak, adj. [1. wēk; 2. wīk]. M.E. *wēke*, fr. O.N. *veikr*, wh. is cogn. w. O.E. *wāc*, 'weak; slender', M.E. *wōk*, now obs.; cp. O.S. *wēc*; O.H.G. *weich*, 'weak'; cp. w. Gk. *eikein*, 'to yield, draw back'; Lat. *vicis*, 'change'; *vicissim*, 'in turn', see **vice (IV.)** & **vicissitude**. **1**. **a** Not strong; lacking in vigour, strength, firmness, solidity, durability &c.; easily disturbed, shaken, broken down &c.; not able to resist force, pressure &c.: *weak supports, foundations*; *weak wrists*; *weak defences*; **b** (of person or group of persons &c.) easily overcome, unable to attack or resist: *a weak side, team* &c.; Phr. *the weaker sex*, women; **c** liable to attack, offering little resistance: *the weak points, spots, of a fortification* &c. Phr. *the weak point* (of a person, scheme, argument &c.), quality &c. most open to attack. **2**. **a** Enfeebled by illness, injury, age &c.; frail, lacking in strength and vigour: *to be too weak to walk*; **b** of delicate constitution, not robust; **c** (of organ of body) not functioning with normal force or efficiency: *a weak heart*. **3**. (of senses or organs of sense) Lacking in perceptive power, not normal in action: *weak hearing*; *weak eyes, sight* &c.; *a weak voice*, one that is feeble and lacking in resonance. **4**. (of mind &c.) Not reaching normal standard of intelligence; lacking in mental power; feeble, deficient. **5**. (of person or character) Lacking in moral force, tending to irresolution, wanting in decision, stability &c.; vacillating. **6**. (of action) Not forcible, decisive, firm; showing lack of firmness, resolution, courage &c.: *weak refusal, argument, resistance, defence* &c. **7**. Inadequately supplied with something necessary for particular purpose: *a weak hand at cards*. **8**. (of statement, argument &c.) Insufficiently supported by facts &c.; lacking cogency; unconvincing, illogical. **9**. Not efficient in, not good at; below required standard: *weak in spelling, in Latin*. **10**. Much diluted, watery, insipid: *weak tea*. **11**. (of style) Lacking in force, vigour, conciseness &c. **12**. (commerc., of trade &c.) Not active, lacking in briskness. **13**. (gram.) **a** *Weak verb*, in English and other Germanic languages, one forming past tense & past participle by addition of *-d* or *-t*; **b** *weak declension* (of nouns and adjectives), belonging originally to the so-called *-n-* stems, that is, having stems ending in *-n-* to which the case-endings are added; in Old English, except in genitive plural, the case suffixes are lost, leaving only *-n*, which takes the place of these; the dative plural of weak declensions is identical with that of the strong.
weaken, vb. trans. & intrans. [1. wēkn; 2. wīkən]. Prec. & **-en**. **1**. trans. **a** (of material action) (i.) To render bodily weak or weaker; to reduce power of resistance, cause to lose strength and vigour, intensity: *his illness has permanently weakened him*; (ii.) to reduce stability of, diminish capacity of bearing strains, weights, pressure &c.: *you will weaken the bridge if you reduce the number of arches*; *the sea-wall has been weakened by the force of the storm*; **b** (of non-material action) to reduce, detract from, intellectual force, cogency, convincingness of: *to weaken an argument by exaggerated statement, one's case by claiming too much* &c. **2**. intrans. **a** (rare, in material sense) To become bodily weaker, lose force and vigour: *he seems to be weakening daily*; **b** (in non-material sense) to become less assured and determined; to be shaken in one's opinion; to offer less resistance, be inclined to give way: *I was afraid he would weaken when he heard the plausible arguments on the other side*; *he still makes a show of opposition, but he is obviously weakening*.
weak-eyed, adj. Having weak eyes.
weak-headed, adj. Weak-minded.
weakish, adj. [1. wēkish; 2. wīkiʃ]. **weak** & **-ish**. Somewhat weak.
weak-kneed, adj. [1. wēk nēd; 2. wīk nīd]. (chiefly fig.) Weak in resolution, lacking determination and firmness of character.
weakling, n. [1. wēkling; 2. wīkliŋ]. **weak** & **-ling**. Person &c. lacking in physical or moral strength.
weakly (I.), adj. [1. wēkli; 2. wīkli]. **weak** & **-ly**. Not robust; feeble, sickly.
weakly (II.), adv. **weak** & **-ly**. In a weak manner.
weak-minded, adj. Lacking in intelligence, feeble-minded.
weakness, n. [1. wēknes; 2. wīknis]. **weak** & **-ness**. **1**. State or quality of being weak; specif. a bodily infirmity, debility, feebleness: *the weakness and helplessness of old age*; **b** intellectual feebleness, imbecility: *weakness of mind, brain-power*; **c** feebleness of character, irresolution, instability of will; **d** (rare) lack of strength in material objects; insecurity, liability to be upset, broken down &c.: *the weakness of a lock, of a hedge, a wall* &c. **2**. Characteristic defect, failing, weak point in character &c.: *his chief weakness is being too easily amenable to flattery, a fondness for the bottle*. **3**. (colloq.) **a** Predilection, particular taste, fondness: *a weakness for apple-dumplings*; **b** thing for which one has a weakness: *detective novels are a weakness of many hard-working students*. **4**. Lack of cogency, unconvincingness, illogicality, absence of ground: *the weakness of an argument, of a case* &c. **5**. Imperfection, defectiveness, inadequacy: *the weakness of a man's classical knowledge*; *weakness in scholarship*. **6**. Feebleness in action, effort &c.: *the weakness in resistance shown by the enemy*.
weak-sighted, adj. Lacking in strength of vision.
weal (I.), n. [1. wēl; 2. wīəl]. O.E. *wela*, 'prosperity'; M.E. *wēle*; cp. O.E. *wel*, 'well', see **well (III.)**. Prosperity, welfare, state of well-being; now only in Phr. *in weal and woe*; *the public weal* &c.
weal (II.), n. See **wale**. A mark or ridge on living flesh, raised by a blow from a rod or lash.
weald, n. [1. wēld; 2. wīəld]. O.E. (Saxon) *wēald*, M.E. *weeld*, 'forest, wold'; cp. O.E. *wāld*, see **wold**, wh. is an Anglian variant. *The Weald*, district of southern England comprising parts of Kent, Sussex, Surrey, Hampshire.
weald-clay, n. (geol.) Clay, limestone, and sandstone beds forming part of the Wealden series.
Wealden, adj. & n. [1. wēldn; 2. wīəldn]. **weald** & **-en**. **1**. adj. Pertaining to, resembling, the Weald, esp. in its characteristic geological formation. **2**. n. (geol.) Series of sandstone and clay strata forming the lower part of the Lower Cretaceous system.
wealth, n. [1. welth; 2. welþ]. M.E. *welþe*, pleasure, happiness, wealth'; **weal (I.)** & **-th**. **1**. Plentiful supply, abundance, profusion: *a wealth of flowers, words, affection* &c. **2**. Abundance of material resources, riches, accumulation of property: *a man of considerable wealth*; *to possess wealth is not always to be happy*. **3**. (archaic) Well-being, prosperity: '*Grant him in health and wealth long to live*' (Prayer for King's Majesty).
wealthily, adv. [1. wélthili; 2. wélþili]. **wealthy** & **-ly**. In a wealthy manner.
wealthiness, n. [1. wélthines; 2. wélþinis]. Next word & **-ness**. State of being wealthy.
wealthy, adj. [1. wélthi; 2. wélþi]. **wealth** & **-y**. Possessing, characterized by, wealth.
wean (I.), vb. trans. [1. wēn; 2. wīn]. O.E. *wenian*, 'to accustom, train, make familiar; to wean'; M.E. *wēnen*, 'to wean'; cp. O.H.G. *wennan*; M. Du. *wennen*; O.N. *venja*, 'to accustom'; cp. O.N. *vanr*; cp. further, with different vowel grade, O.H.G. *(gi)won*; O.E. *wuna*, 'accustomed', see **wont (I.)**; O.E. *wunian*, 'to dwell'; ultimately all fr. base **wen-* &c., 'to love'; see also **wish, Venus**. **1**. To accustom (child or other young mammal) to food other than its mother's milk. **2**. (also *wean away*) To withdraw (person &c.) gradually from former habit, occupation, object of affection &c.; to estrange, distract, draw away, alienate, esp. by substitution of fresh interests, associations &c.
wean (II.), n. Apparently fr. Scots *wee ane*, 'little one'. (Scots) Child.
weanling, n. [1. wēnling; 2. wīnliŋ]. **wean (I.)** & **-ling**. Newly weaned child or other mammal.
weapon, n. [1. wépun; 2. wépən]. O.E. *wǣpen*; M.E. *wēpen*, 'weapon'; cp. O.H.G. *wāfen*; O. Fris. *wēpen*; O.N. *vāpn*, 'weapon'; Goth. *wēpna*, pl. The short vowel in present form is due to M.E. shortening before two consonants in inflected forms: *wĕpnes* &c. **1**. **a** Material object, instrument, tool, designed, or used, as means of attack or defence; **b** organ of animal or plant used for similar purpose. **2**. Intellectual or moral means of attack or defence: *the strike as a political weapon*; *tariffs as a weapon for bargaining*.
weaponless, adj. [1. wépunles; 2. wépənlis]. Prec. & **-less**. Without a weapon.
wear (I.), vb. trans. & intrans. [1. wār; 2. wɛə]. O.E. *werian*, 'to wear (clothes); to clothe', M.E. *wēr(i)en*, 'to wear (clothes)'; apparently a specialized use of *werian*, 'to protect, defend'; cp. O.E. *waru*, 'defence'; cp., however, in special sense Goth. *wasjan*, 'to clothe', & *wasti*, 'garment', cogn. w. Lat. *vestis*, 'garment'; see **vest (I.)** & cognates there given. It looks as if some of the present meanings, such as 'to fatigue, exhaust, wear out' &c., were due to association w. an entirely different word—O.E. *wōrian*, 'to crumble, wear away', wh. is connected w. O.E. *wēriġ*, 'weary', & *wēriġean*, 'to weary, exhaust', see **weary**. **A**. trans. **1**. **a** To be covered, clothed, with, have upon the person as a garment, or as an ornament: *to wear a frock-coat, a white waistcoat, wool next the skin, a pair of top-boots, a clean collar* &c.; *to wear mourning*; *to wear a wreath of flowers*; *to wear diamonds*; Phr. *to wear one's heart on one's sleeve*, to show one's feelings readily; to have emotions which are easily roused; **b** to have as a characteristic of one's personal appearance, to have as an appendage to one's person: *to wear one's hair waved, parted in the middle*; *to wear side-whiskers*. **2**. **a** To bear, exhibit, as a characteristic expression of face, cast of features &c.: *to wear a troubled look, a harassed expression*; *her features wore a pleasant smile*; **b** (of external nature or other objects) to give an impression of, to exhibit, to be clad in: '*This city now doth like a garment wear The beauty of the morning*' (Wordsworth, 'On Westminster Bridge'). **3**. To sustain, carry, bear, as closely associated with one: *to wear one's honours*

with modesty and grace. **4.** To remove part of, cause wastage of substance from, as by attrition; to produce a furrow, depression, in surface of by frequent passage, friction &c.: *the constant flow of water has worn the stone*; *steps worn by the feet of thousands*; *to wear one's shoes into holes.* **5.** To produce injury to, diminution of substance, attrition in; to beat, smooth, down, as by constant use, frequent passage over, rough handling and usage, friction &c.: *to wear ruts on a road*; *to wear a track across a field*; *a rope at last wears a groove in a stout stanchion.* **6.** To cause bodily or mental fatigue to; to exhaust, waste: *sorrow and anxiety wear one more than hard work*; *a constitution worn by years of hardship*; also *wear out.* **B.** intrans. **1.** To last, remain unimpaired, withstand the stress of hard usage: *this material will wear for ever*; *you will find that this colour won't wear.* **2.** To offer specified kind or amount of resistance to usage, severe treatment &c.: *shoddy clothes never wear well*; *these clothes have worn splendidly.* Phr. (of persons) *to wear well*, bear one's years lightly, show few signs of age. **3.** To pass, traverse a period of time, advance: *the day, one's life, wears towards its close*; '*never morning wore To evening, but some heart did break*' (Tennyson, 'In Mem.' vi.). **C.** Followed by adverbs with special meanings. *Wear away*, **1.** trans., to remove, efface, as by friction, to rub out: *time has worn away the inscription*; *the feet of many generations have worn away the steps.* **2.** intrans., (of time) to pass, esp. tediously, to drag out: *the long day wore away.* *Wear down*, trans., **a** to reduce, lessen height of, by friction: *to wear one's heels down*; *the steps have been worn down*; **b** (fig.) to break down, reduce, as by constant attack or importunity: *to wear down opposition.* *Wear off*, **1.** trans., to rub off, remove, reduce, by constant friction; **2.** intrans., **a** to be removed, lessened, by friction: *the nap will wear off*; **b** (fig.) to pass away, become less: *the strangeness, his roughness &c., will wear off in time.* *Wear out*, **1.** trans., **a** to render shabby, threadbare, dilapidated; to reduce value or usefulness of by usage: *to wear out one's clothes, a machine* &c.; **b** to exhaust: *his temper, patience &c., is worn out*; **c** to exhaust in body or mind, to tire out by excessive bodily or mental strain: *hardship and penury wore him out before his time*; **2.** intrans., to become worn out: *the clothes will soon wear out.*

wear (**II.**), n., fr. prec. **1. a** Wearing of, act of wearing (clothes &c.): *a suit for Sunday wear*; **b** act of using; usage: *a carpet which has been many years in wear*; *it shows signs of wear*, i.e. of having been used. **2.** Amount of diminution in usefulness, effectiveness, value, which an article undergoes in the process of normal use: *in fixing the rent of a furnished house one must allow for wear.* Phrs. *wear and tear*, natural dilapidation caused by time and usage; specif., *fair wear and tear*, such as is considered permissible for a person hiring an article to cause by normal usage, without being called upon to compensate owner.

wear (**III.**), vb. trans. & intrans. Variant of **veer.** (naut.) **1.** trans. To bring (ship) about by putting the helm up. **2.** intrans. (of ship) To go about before the wind.

wear (**IV.**), n. [1. wēr; 2. wīə]. See **weir.**

wearable, adj. [1. wárabl; 2. wέərəbl]. **wear** (**I.**) & **-able.** Capable of being worn; fit to be worn.

weariless, adj. [1. wḗriles; 2. wíərilis]. **weary** (**I.**) & **-less.** (rare) Incapable of being wearied.

wearily, adv. [1. wḗrili; 2. wíərili]. **weary** (**I.**) & **-ly.** In a weary manner.

weariness, n. [1. wḗrines; 2. wíərinis]. See prec. & **-ness.** State or quality of being weary; fatigue, tiredness.

wearing, adj. [1. wáring; 2. wέəriŋ], fr. Pres. Part. of **wear** (**I.**). Exhausting; tending to fatigue body or mind: *a wearing task*; *children are often very wearing.*

wearing-apparel, n. Clothes, garments.

wearing-iron, n. Wearing-plate.

wearing-plate, n. Plate designed to guard part of a machine &c. from friction.

wearisome, adj. [1. wḗrisum; 2. wíərisəm]. **weary** (**I.**) & **-some.** Tending to cause weariness; tiresome, tiring, tedious.

wearisomely, adv. Prec. & **-ly.** In a wearisome manner.

wearisomeness, n. See prec. & **-ness.** State or quality of being wearisome.

weary (**I.**), adj. [1. wḗri; 2. wíəri]. O.E. *wēriġ*; M.E. *wēri*, 'weary'; fr. **wōr-iġ*, cp. O.E. *wōrian*, 'to crumble', & O.S. *wōrig*, *-ag*, 'weary'; O.H.G. *wuorag*, 'drunk'; cogn. w. Gk. *hōrākiân*, 'to be giddy, faint'; cp. further O.N. *órar*, 'fits of madness'; Gk. *ôros* for **wōr-*, 'sleep'. **1.** Tired, fatigued, exhausted, by effort. **2.** *Weary of*, tired of, bored by, impatient of: *to be weary of life*; *to be weary of a person's chatter, nonsense* &c. **3.** Causing weariness; tedious, irksome: *a weary world, life.*

weary (**II.**), vb. trans. & intrans., fr. prec. **A.** trans. **1.** To make weary; to tire, fatigue, exhaust. **2.** To bore, wear out patience of, harass: *to weary a person with idle talk.* **B.** intrans. **1.** To grow weary; become fatigued. **2.** *Weary of*, to become bored by, lose patience with: *to weary of too much gaiety.* **3.** *Weary for*, to long for, yearn after; to miss greatly, long for presence of: *she wearies for her absent children.*

weasand, n. [1. wḗzand, wizand; 2. wízənd, wizənd]. O.E. *wǣsend*, *wāsend*; M.E. *wēsand*; cp. O.H.G. *weisunt*; O. Fris. *wāsende.* (archaic) Trachea, windpipe; esp. in Phr. *to cut, slit, his weasand.*

weasel, n. [1. wḗzl; 2. wízl]. O.E. *wesle*; M.E. *wēsele*; cp. O.H.G. *wisela*, 'weasel'; Du. *wezel*; Dan. *väsel.* Small, carnivorous, reddish-brown quadruped, *Putorius nivalis*, of the polecat family, with long body and short legs; related to stoat, ferret &c. Phr. *to catch a weasel asleep*, catch an habitually alert person off his guard.

weasel-faced, adj. [1. wḗzl fâst; 2. wízl fèist]. Having a thin, sharp-featured, mean face.

weather (**I.**), n. [1. wédher; 2. wéðə]. O.E., M.E. *weder*, 'storm'; cp. O.S. *wedar*; O.H.G. *wetar*; O.N. *veðr*, 'storm'; cogn. w. O. Slav. *vedro*, 'good weather'; cp. also O. Slav. *vĕtrŭ*, 'storm'; *vĕjati*, 'to blow'; Lith. *vĕtra*, 'storm'; O. Prussian *wetro*, 'wind'; connected w. Lat. *ventus*; Scrt. *vātaš*; O.E. *wind*, 'wind', see **wind** (**I.**). General atmospheric conditions prevailing at a specific time and place, as regards temperature, amount of moisture in the air, direction &c. of wind, clouds &c.: *bad, good, fine, wet, hot, windy, weather* &c. Phrs. (naut.) *to make good, bad, weather*, experience such weather; *April weather*, sunshine and showers alternately; *under the weather*, depressed, indisposed, not up to the mark; *under stress of weather*, affected by, under compulsion of, bad weather.

weather (**II.**), vb. trans. & intrans., fr. prec. **A.** trans. **1.** (esp. geol.) To affect surface of, to disintegrate (rock &c.), by action of rain, wind &c. **2.** To expose to action of weather; to season. **3.** To slope (roof-slates, boards &c.) downwards, in order that rain may drain off. **4.** (naut.) To pass, sail, to windward of: *to weather a point.* **5.** To come through successfully, survive: *to weather a storm*; also fig.: *to weather a financial crisis* &c. **B.** intrans. To be affected, disintegrated, by atmospheric action, as stones &c.

weather (**III.**), adj., fr. **weather** (**I.**). (naut.) Windward; facing, turned towards, direction of wind: *the weather bow, beam* &c. Phrs. *to have the weather ga(u)ge of*, to be to windward of; (fig.) to gain an advantage over; *to keep one's weather eye open*, be on the alert.

weather-beaten, adj. Showing effects of exposure to sun, wind, rain; hence, having a rough, hearty, sunburnt, reddened complexion.

weather-board, vb. trans. To supply with weather-boarding.

weather-boarding, -boards, n. Series of overlapping boards designed to throw off rain from house &c.

weather-bound, adj. Detained by bad weather.

weather-bureau, n. Meteorological office.

weather-chart, n. Map showing distribution of atmospheric characteristics.

weather-cloth, n. Canvas screen fixed to ship's bridge to give protection from rain, wind &c.

weathercock, n. [1. wédherkòk; 2. wéðəkɔ̀k]. **1.** Revolving plate or bar, often in shape of a cock, fixed on vertical rod and indicating direction of wind. **2.** (fig.) Fickle, capricious person; a flibbertigibbet.

weather-contact, n. Leakage of electricity from one telegraph-wire to another caused by damp.

weather-cross, n. Weather-contact.

weather-forecast, n. Forecast of weather to be expected during an ensuing period of 12, 24, hours &c.

weather ga(u)ge. See **weather** (**III.**).

weather-glass, n. Barometer.

weathering, n. [1. wédhering; 2. wéðəriŋ]. **weather** (**II.**) & **-ing.** **1.** (archit.) Slight slope given to surface in order that rain &c. may drain off. **2.** Atmospheric action on rock &c.

weatherliness, n. [1. wédherlines; 2. wéðəlinis]. Next word & **-ness.** State or quality of being weatherly.

weatherly, adj. [1. wédherli; 2. wéðəli]. **weather** & **-ly.** (naut.) Capable of sailing close to the wind without making much leeway.

weather-map, n. Weather-chart.

weathermost, adj. [1. wédhermòst; 2. wéðəmòust]. Farthest to windward.

weather-moulding, n. Projecting moulding on wall &c. designed to throw off rain.

weather-proof, adj. Capable of resisting rough weather.

weather-prophet, n. Person making forecast of weather.

weather-service, n. Institution for collecting and distributing meteorological information.

weather-stain, n. Discolouration through exposure.

weather-station, n. Meteorological observation-post.

weather-strip, n. Strip of leather, wood &c. for keeping out draughts, rain &c.

weather-tiles, n. pl. Overlapping tiles as substitute for weather-boarding.

weather-vane, n. Weathercock.

weather-wise, adj. Able to foretell the weather.

weather-worn, adj. Affected by exposure to rough weather.

weave (**I.**), vb. trans. & intrans. [1. wēv; 2. wīv]. O.E. *wefan*, M.E. *wēven*; cp. O.H.G. *weban*; O.N. *vefa*, 'to weave'; M. Du. *weven*, 'to move to and fro; to weave'; M.H.G. *webelen*, 'to fluctuate'; O.N. *vafra*, 'to move to and fro'; *(kongur)vāfa*, 'spider'; cogn. w. Scrt. *(ūrṇa)vābhiš*, 'spider', lit. 'wool-weaver'; fr. base **wĕbh-* &c., 'to weave'; see also **web.** **A.** trans. **1. a** To form (threads) into a web, tissue, fabric, by intertwining on a loom; **b** to make (fabric &c.) out of threads, on a loom. **2. a** To form (a wreath, garland) by twisting and intertwining stalks of leaves and flowers &c.; **b** to twist (leaves, flowers &c.) into a wreath. **3.** To pass, twist, in and out among: *to weave ribbons through one's hair.* **4.** (fig.) **a** To construct by an act of the mind and imagination: *to weave a romance, story, round a person or incident*; **b** *to weave facts, incidents &c. into a continuous narrative*, to arrange, treat, display (facts &c.) so as to form (them) into a narrative &c. **B.** intrans. To practise weaving.

weave (**II.**), n., fr. prec. Style of weaving, manner in which threads &c. are interlaced to form a fabric.

weaver, n. [1. wḗver; 2. wívə]. **weave (I.)** & **-er**. **1.** Person habitually engaged in weaving on a loom. **2.** Member of an ancient Company of the City of London—*the Weavers*—founded 1130. **3.** Weaver-bird.

weaver-bird, n. Small finch-like bird constructing a pouch-shaped woven nest.

weazand. See **weasand**.

weazen(ed). See **wizen(ed)**.

web, n. [1. web; 2. wεb]. O.E., M.E. *webb*; fr. **wōbja*; gradational variant of base of **weave**; cp. O.H.G. *weppi*; Du. *web*; O.N. *vefr*, 'web'. **1. a** Woven fabric; textile formed by interlacing threads on a loom; Phr. (fig.) *a web of intrigue* &c., an intricate system; **b** piece of fabric woven in a single length. **2.** Network of threads spun by spider &c.; cobweb. **3.** Membrane between the digits of aquatic bird, flying animal &c. **4.** Set of barbs on either side of the shaft of a feather; vane. **5.** Roll of printing-paper. **6.** Thin plate of metal, sometimes perforated, connecting heavier parts of machinery &c.

webbed, adj. [1. webd; 2. wεbd]. Prec. & **-ed**. United, having the digits united, by a web: *water-birds have webbed feet.*

webbing, n. [1. wébing; 2. wébiŋ]. **web** & **-ing**. **1. a** Narrow strip of strong, woven material used in upholstery, saddlery &c.; **b** edging of a fine fabric made in stronger material. **2.** Tapes used to guide web in printing-machine.

web-eye, n. Ophthalmic disease in which the eye becomes covered with a film.

web-eyed, adj. Prec. & **-ed**. Affected with web-eye.

web-fingered, adj. Having the fingers connected by membranes.

web-foot, n. Foot the toes of which are joined together by membranes, as those of aquatic birds.

web-footed, adj. Prec. & **-ed**. Having web-feet.

web-toed, adj. Having the toes joined by membranes.

web-wheel, n. Wheel with disk or plate instead of spokes.

web-worm, n. Larva which spins itself a web as shelter.

wed, vb. trans. & intrans. [1. wed; 2. wεd]. O.E. *weddian*, 'to promise, pledge', M.E. *wedden*, 'to pledge; to wed'; fr. O.E. *wedd*, 'pledge, agreement'; cp. M.H.G. *wetten*; O.N. *veðja*; Goth. *-wadjōn*, 'to pledge'; O. Fris. *wed*; O.H.G. *wetti*; Goth. *wadi*, 'pledge, compact'; cogn. w. Lat. *vas*, stem *vad-*, 'pledge'; Lith. *vadũti*, 'to redeem a pledge'; cp. **gage (I.)** & **wager (I.)**. **A.** trans. **1.** To take as husband or wife; to marry. **2.** To join in marriage; perform marriage ceremony over, or for. **3.** To give in marriage, cause to marry: *to wed one's daughter to a soldier.* In senses **1, 2, 3** the word is archaic or rhetorical, though the P.P. as adjective is in common use; see **wedded**. **4.** (fig.) To unite, join, combine: *to wed simplicity with art.* **B.** intrans. To take a husband or wife; to be married.

wedded, adj. [1. wéded; 2. wédid], fr. P.P. of prec. **1. a** Married, in the state of matrimony: *the wedded pair*; **b** pertaining to, derived from, matrimony: *wedded bliss.* **2.** (fig.) Devoted, firmly attached (to): *wedded to one's profession*; *I am not wedded to that particular plan* &c., am not committed to it, do not insist on it.

wedding, n. [1. wéding; 2. wédiŋ]. **wed** & **-ing**. **a** Marriage ceremony; **b** this together with the festivities connected with it; *silver wedding*, 25th, *golden wedding*, 50th, *diamond wedding*, 60th, anniversary of a marriage.

wedding-breakfast, n. Festivity accompanied by a banquet, attended by the principal parties and the guests after a wedding.

wedding-cake, n. Rich cake covered with almond paste and highly ornamented with white sugar and silvered decorations, usually cut by the bride at a wedding-breakfast, and afterwards distributed in small pieces to friends.

wedding-day, n. **a** Day upon which a particular wedding is celebrated; **b** anniversary of this.

wedding-favour, n. White rosette worn in honour of wedding.

wedding-ring, n. Ring placed by the bridegroom upon the bride's finger at the time of marriage, and ever afterwards worn by her.

wedge (I.), n. [1. wej; 2. wedž]. O.E. *wecǵ*, M.E. *wegge*; cp. O.H.G. *weggi*; M. Du. *wegghe*; O.N. *veggr*, 'wedge'; cp. further O.H.G. *waganso*; O.N. *vangnsi*, 'ploughshare'; cogn. w. Lat. *vōmer*; O. Prussian *wagnis*, 'ploughshare'; Lith. *vágis*, 'wedge'. **1.** A piece of wood or metal relatively thick at one end, and gradually tapering to a thin edge at the other, used for splitting wood, or for rendering immovable separate parts or objects between which there is too much space, &c.; one of the elementary mechanical powers. Phr. *the thin end of the wedge*, a slight, unimportant action or event which may have considerable results later; esp. an incipient attempt to achieve important results by means which at first are hardly noticeable. **2.** A wedge-shaped object, e.g. **a** a hunch of cheese, bread &c. in this form; **b** *a wedge of troops, population* &c., body of troops &c. disposed in such a form.

wedge (II.), vb. trans., fr. prec. **1.** To fix, make firm, compress, with a wedge: *to wedge a door to keep it open (or shut), a window to prevent it from rattling.* **2.** To split, cleave, by means of a wedge. **3.** Usually *wedge oneself in*, to squeeze oneself in forcibly through or into narrow space.

wedge-shaped, adj. Having the shape of a wedge.

wedge-tailed, adj. (of bird &c.) Having the tail in the shape of a wedge.

wedgewise, adv. [1. wéjwīz; 2. wédžwaiz]. **wedge (I.)** & **-wise**. In the manner of a wedge.

Wedgwood, n. [1. wéjwood; 2. wédžwud], fr. name of inventor, Josiah Wedgwood (1730–1795). Fine earthenware made at the Wedgwood works in Staffordshire.

Wedgwood-blue, n. Shade of blue typical of some varieties of Wedgwood ware.

wedlock, n. [1. wédlok; 2. wédlɔk]. O.E. *wedlāc*, 'wedlock', M.E. *wedlōc*; fr. O.E. *wedd*, 'pledge', see **wed**, & *lāc*, 'sport, game; movement; gift (to bride &c.)'; cp. O.N. *leikr*; O.H.G. *leich*; Goth. *laiks*, 'sport'; Goth. *laikan*, 'to spring, hop, fly'; cogn. w. Gk. *elelizein*, 'to shake'; Lith. *láigyti*, 'to run about wildly'; the form of second element may be due to association w. O.E. *loc*, 'enclosure; settlement' &c. The married state, matrimony. Phr. *born in wedlock*, of legally married parents.

Wednesday, n. [1. wénzdi; 2. wénzdi]. O.E. *Wōdnesdæǵ*; M.E. *Wodenes-*, *Wednesdai*; fr. O.E. *Wōden*, Gmc. god, & **day**; cp. O.H.G. *Wuotan*; O.S. *Wōden*; O.N. *Oðinn*; the name is connected w. Goth. *wōds*, O.E. *wōd*, 'raging, possessed'; cp. O.E. *wōþ*, 'voice, song'; O.N. *ōðr*, 'poetry, song'; cogn. w. Lat. *vātēs*, 'prophet, seer', see **vaticinate**. Fourth day of the week. Phr. *Ash Wednesday*, first day of Lent.

wee, adj. [1. wē; 2. wī], fr. M.E. *wei*, M. Scots *wē*, 'bit', fr. O.E. *wǣǵe*, 'weight, balance', see **wey**. (Scots and provinc.) Very small, tiny; in England chiefly in *a wee bit* (as adv.): *a wee bit tedious*, i.e. rather, slightly.

weed (I.), n. [1. wēd; 2. wīd]. O.E. *wēod*, M.E. *wēd*, 'weed'; cp. O.S. *wiod*. Etymol. unknown. **1. a** Any plant which grows where it is not wanted, in a garden among cultivated plants, or in a field among crops; esp. applied to hardy, rank-growing plants which tend to choke those which it is desired to cultivate; Phrs. *to grow like a weed*, to grow rampantly; *the soothing weed*, tobacco; **b** (slang) a cigar. **2.** A thin, lanky, badly grown person or animal, one in poor condition.

weed (II.), vb. trans. & intrans. O.E. *wēodian*, 'to weed'; see prec. **A.** trans. **1.** To clear (ground) of weeds; to remove weeds from (ground). **2.** *Weed out*, to remove, eliminate (esp. weak, undesirable, elements &c.) by selective process: *to weed out useless books from one's library, undesirable persons from a community* &c. **B.** intrans. To perform the act of weeding.

weeder, n. [1. wḗder; 2. wídə]. Prec. & **-er**. **a** Person employed to pull up weeds; **b** mechanical device for removing weeds.

weed-grown, adj. Overgrown with weeds.

weediness, n. [1. wḗdines; 2. wídinis]. **weedy** & **-ness**. State of being weedy.

weeding-fork, n. [1. wḗding fòrk; 2. wídiŋ fɔ̀k]. Fork used in removing weeds.

weedless, adj. [1. wḗdles; 2. wídlis]. **weed (I.)** & **-less**. Without, free from, weeds.

weeds, n. [1. wēdz; 2. wīdz]. Pl. form, fr. O.E. *(ǵe)wǣde*, M.E. *wēde*, 'garment'; cp. O.S. *wādi*; O.H.G. *wāt*; O.N. *vāð*, 'garment'; cogn. w. Gk. *othónē* (fr. **wothónē*), 'linen, fine cloth'; Lith *áudmi*, 'to weave'. Only in Phr. *widow's weeds*, widow's mourning dress.

weedy, adj. [1. wḗdi; 2. wídi]. **weed (I.)** & **-y**. **1.** Containing, overgrown with, weeds. **2.** (of persons and animals) Thin, lanky, and weak; badly grown, in poor condition, weakly.

week, n. [1. wēk; 2. wīk]. O.E. *wice*, M.E. *wēke*, 'week'; O.H.G. *wehha*; O.N. *vika*; Goth. *wikō*, 'week'; connected w. the base in O.H.G. *wehsal*, 'exchange; change'; O.N. *vixla*, 'to exchange'; O.E. *wīce*, 'exchange'; cogn. w. Lat. *vicis*, 'change, alternation, turn'; *vicissim*, 'in turn', see **vicissitude**; & cp. further **weak**. **1. a** A period of any seven successive days: *he came for a week and stayed a month*; Phr. *today week*, a week counting backwards or forwards from today; *Saturday &c. week*, a week backwards or forwards from Saturday; **b** specif., a period extending from any Sunday to the following Saturday inclusive: *this week, next week*; *Easter Week*, that beginning on Easter Sunday; *Holy Week*, the one immediately preceding Easter. **2.** (colloq.) Period embracing all the working days of the week, that is, the whole week with the exception of Sunday: *he spends the week in town, but is at home on Sundays.*

week-day, n. **1.** Any day of the week with the exception of Sunday. **2.** (attrib.) Occurring on, pertaining to, a week-day: *week-day services.*

week-end, n. & vb. intrans. **1.** n. Period usually from part of Friday, or from Saturday, to Monday morning: *to have one's week-ends free.* **2.** vb. To spend a week-end (usually in specified place).

weekly (I.), adj. & n. [1. wḗkli; 2. wíkli]. **week** & **-ly**. **1.** adj. **a** Performed, due, occurring, appearing, regularly every week: *weekly wages*; *weekly publication*; **b** performed during the week: *weekly work.* **2.** n. Weekly newspaper or other periodical.

weekly (II.), adv. **week** & **-ly**. Once a week, every week: *wages paid, a room cleaned, weekly.*

ween, vb. trans. [1. wēn; 2. wīn]. O.E. *wēnan*, 'to hope, expect; to think, have an opinion'; M.E. *wēnen*, 'to hope, suppose'; cp. O. Fris. *wēna*; cp. O.H.G. *wānan*; O.S. *wānian*; O.N. *vǣna*; Goth. *wēnjan*, 'to expect, suppose'; cp. also the ns. O.E. *wēn*, 'hope, expectation, belief'; Goth. *wēns*; O.H.G. *wān*; cogn. w. Lat. *venus*, 'charm, love', see **Venus**; Scrt. *vaniś*, 'desire, wish'; cp. also **winsome, wish**. (archaic) **a** To think, believe, be of opinion; to trow: '*they ween'd she was escaped away*' (Spenser, 'F. Q.' v. 2. 25); **b** to hope, expect: '*by force or fraud Weening to prosper*' (Milton, 'P. L.' vi. 794-5).

weep, vb. intrans. & trans. [1. wēp; 2. wīp]. O.E. *wēpan*; M.E. *wēpen*, 'to weep, bewail'; O.H.G. *wuofan*; O. Fris. *wēpa*; O.N. *ǣpa*; Goth. *wōpjan*, 'to weep, cry out'; fr. **wōp-*

jan, cp. O.E., O.S. *wōp*; O.N. *ōp*, 'lamentation'; cogn. w. O. Slav. *vabiti*, 'to summon, call up'; cp., w. different formative suff., Lat. *vāgīre*, 'to cry, squeal'; Gk. *iakhḗ*, 'a cry', for **wi-wagh-*; *ēkhéein*, 'sound, echo', for **wēgh-*; see **echo**. **A.** intrans. **1. a** To shed tears, cry; **b** *weep for*, to lament, bewail: *to weep for one's sins.* **2.** To exude moisture &c.; to be covered with condensed moisture. **3.** (of trees) To droop gracefully, to have pendent boughs. **B.** trans. **1.** To shed: *to weep bitter tears.* **2.** To show, exude, drip (moisture), give out (moisture) in drops. **3.** To shed tears for, to lament, bewail: *to weep one's sad fate.*

weeper, n. [1. wḗper; 2. wīpə]. **weep** & **-er.** **1.** One who weeps or mourns; esp. a hired mourner, or undertaker's assistant, at a funeral. **2.** Garment &c. as symbol of mourning; specif. **a** hat-band or scarf of black crape; **b** widow's crape veil; **c** (pl.) widow's white cuffs.

weeping (I.), adj. [1. wḗping; 2. wīpiŋ], fr. Pres. Part. of **weep**. **1.** Dripping, exuding, or giving off moisture; *weeping eczema*, characterized by moist exudation; *weeping pipe*, designed to drip slowly. **2.** (of trees) Having the branches bent downwards, curving, drooping towards the ground: *weeping ash, willow* &c.

weeping (II.), vbl. n., fr. **weep** & **-ing.** Act of one who weeps; lamentation, wailing.

weeping-gas, n. Tear-gas.

weepingly, adv. [1. wḗpingli; 2. wīpiŋli]. **weeping** (I.) & **-ly.** Tearfully.

weet, vb. trans. & intrans. [1. wēt: 2. wīt]. M.E. *wēten*, 'to know'; variant of **wit** (I.). (archaic) To know, perceive, recognize: '*he kist her wearie feet, And lickt her lilly hands with fawning tong, As he her wronged innocence did weet*' (Spenser, 'F. Q.' i. 3. 6).

weever, n. [1. wḗver; 2. wīvə]. O. Fr. *wivre*, 'wyvern, weever'; see **wivern.** Genus of fishes with very sharp, poisonous dorsal spines.

weevil, n. [1. wḗv(i)l; 2. wīv(*i*)l]. O.E. *wifol*, *-il*; M.E. *wēvel*, 'weevil'; cp. O.S. *-wivil*; O.H.G. *wibil*, 'weevil'; fr. base of **weave.** One of various small beetles with elongated snouts which feed upon plants, grain, fruit, cork &c.; often in compounds, *boll-, corn-, rice-weevil* &c.

weevilled, adj. [1. wḗv(i)ld; 2. wīv(*i*)ld]. Prec. & **-ed.** Damaged, infested, by weevils.

weevil(l)y, adj. [1. wḗvili; 2. wīvili]. **weevil** & **-y.** Infested by weevils.

weft, n. [1. weft; 2. weft]. O.E. *weft*, fr. base of *wefan*, 'to weave', see **weave**, & n. suff. *-t.* **a** Threads interwoven with warp, q.v.; **b** (loosely) thing woven, web.

weigh (I.), vb. trans. & intrans. [1. wā; 2. wei]. O.E. *wegan*, 'to carry, move'; M.E. *weien*, 'to bear; to weigh'; cp. O.H.G. *wegan*; O.N. *vega*; Goth. *(ga)wigan*, 'to move, carry'; cogn. w. Lat. *vehere*, 'to carry, bring, drive', see **vehicle**; Gk. *ókhos*, 'cart'; Scrt. *váhati*, 'drives, carries'; cp. also **wain, way.** **A.** trans. **1.** To test, ascertain, weight of by means of scales or balances. **2.** To turn over in the mind, to ponder, consider critically; to form an estimate of; to compare and contrast so as to ascertain relative value of: *to weigh a proposal*; *to weigh the advantages and disadvantages.* Phr. *to weigh one's words*, choose them carefully. **3.** *Weigh anchor*, (i.) raise it from water; hence, (ii.) to start on a voyage. **B.** intrans. **1.** To have a specified weight: *it weighs little, heavily* &c.; *how much do you weigh?*; *it weighs a ton.* **2.** To have moral or logical weight and importance; to count for something; to exert moral or intellectual influence: *personal considerations ought not to weigh at all in the matter.* **C.** Followed by adverb or preposition with special meanings. *Weigh down*, trans., **a** to press down, bend down: *the fruit is so thick that it weighs down the branches*; **b** to cause depression of mind, to oppress: *weighed down by grief.* *Weigh in*, intrans., (specif. of jockey) to be weighed, in order to prove that weight is up to stipulated amount; Phr. *to weigh in with*, to bring (fact, argument &c.) to bear on discussion. *Weigh out*, **1.** trans., to measure out, divide, take portions of, by weight: *to weigh out rations, materials for a cake* &c.; **2.** intrans., (of jockey) to be weighed after a race. *Weigh upon*, trans., to be burdensome to, to afflict, be oppressive: *the matter weighed upon his conscience.* *Weigh with*, trans., to affect the judgement of, have moral or intellectual influence upon: *what weighs with me most in deciding to oppose the measure is the impossibility of carrying out its provisions*; *selfish interests don't weigh with him at all.*

weigh (II.), n., fr. prec. Act or process of weighing. Phr. *under weigh*, variant of *under way*, see **way.**

weighable, adj. [1. wā́abl; 2. wéiəbl]. **weigh** (I.) & **-able.** Capable of being weighed.

weighage, n. [1. wā́ij; 2. wéiidž]. **weigh** (I.) & **-age.** Fee paid for weighing of goods.

weigh-beam, n. Steelyard hung in a frame.

weigh-bridge, n. Instrument for weighing carts &c. and their loads.

weigh-house, n. Building for official weighing of goods.

weighing-machine, n. [1. wā́ing mashḗn; 2. wéiiŋ məʃīn]. Instrument for determining weight of person, heavy objects &c.

weigh-lock, n. Canal lock with apparatus for weighing vessels.

weight (I.), n. [1. wāt; 2. weit]. M.E. *weiht*, new formation fr. **weigh.** The O.E. form was *(ge)wiht*, M.E. *wiht.* **1.** The property which makes bodies tend to move towards the centre of the earth by virtue of gravity, the degree of this tendency being in proportion to the mass of the body; the property of being heavy: *vapours and gases appear to have hardly any weight.* **2. a** Specific amount of heaviness, actual relative amount which body weighs as shown by a balance: *a full-grown man has a weight of ten stone upwards*; **b** weight considered as a burden; an oppressive degree of heaviness: *in ancient times horses often sank beneath the weight of a rider in full armour.* **3.** Event, circumstances, material or non-material conditions which are burdensome and oppressive; something which weighs upon and oppresses the mind, or cripples action &c.; a burden: *the weight of public responsibility*; *a weight of care, sorrow* &c. Phr. *that is a great weight off my mind*, a relief from anxiety, responsibility, and the like. **4. a** Intellectual or moral influence and importance; value, significance: *a man of weight in council*; *an argument of great weight*; **b** preponderating fact, circumstance, argument, which exerts influence, supplies a motive for action, determines a decision, and so forth: *considerations of self-interest had no weight with him.* **5.** Mode of weighing, particular system or standard by which weight is ascertained: *avoirdupois, apothecary's, weight.* **6.** A heavy mass; name of various objects; **a** one of a series of lumps or disks of metal used as standards in ascertaining the weight of a body on a balance; **b** (i.) mass of metal, or other heavy substance, used to press down, and keep in place, light objects, esp. *paper-weight*; (ii.) heavy mass of metal suspended from a wheel in a large clock, which serves gradually to unwind a spring and keep the machinery in motion.

weight (II.), vb. trans., fr. prec. **1. a** To add weight to, make heavy; to load: *a stick weighted with lead*; *weight down*, to fasten down with a weight; **b** to burden, overload, oppress: *weighted with a rifle and heavy uniform.* **2.** To adulterate, load (fabric &c.), with a foreign, esp. a mineral, substance.

weightily, adv. [1. wā́tili; 2. wéitili]. **weighty** & **-ly.** In a weighty manner; (esp. fig.) with moral weight and importance.

weightiness, n. [1. wā́tines; 2. wéitinis]. See prec. & **-ness.** Quality of being weighty (in material and non-material senses).

weightless, adj. [1. wā́tles; 2. wéitlis]. **weight** (I.) & **-less.** With little or no weight; light.

weighty, adj. [1. wā́ti; 2. wéiti]. **weight** (I.) & **-y.** **1.** Heavy, of considerable weight: *a package too weighty for the post.* **2. a** (of persons) Exhibiting moral or intellectual power; wielding influence: *a weighty speaker*; **b** cogent, convincing: *a weighty argument, utterance, reason.* **3.** Important, full of significance, momentous: *weighty matters of state.*

weir, wear, n. [1. wēr; 2. wiə]. O.E. *wer*; M.E. *wēre*, 'weir, dam, pond'; cp. O.E. *werian*, 'to defend; to dam up (a pool)'; cp. Mod. Germ. *wehr*, 'defence'; Goth. *warjan*, 'to defend'; cogn. w. Scrt. *varūtár*, 'protector'; Gk. *érusthai* for **wer-*, 'to save, preserve'. **1.** Dam constructed to raise level of part of stream or to hinder or divert flow of water. **2.** Structure of stakes or wattles erected in a stream as fish-trap.

weird (I.), n. [1. wērd; 2. wiəd]. O.E. *wierd*, M.E. *werd, wird*, 'fate'; cp. O.H.G. *w(u)rt*; O.S. *wurd*, 'fate', fr. stem seen in O.E. *weorðan*, 'to become', see **worth** (III.). (archaic or provinc.) Fate, destiny; cp. Scots Phr. *to dree one's weird*, work out, undergo, one's destiny.

weird (II.), adj., fr. prec. **1.** Connected with, pertaining to, fate; esp. *the weird sisters*, the Fates. **2.** Supernatural, uncanny, eerie. **3.** (slang) Strange, odd, queer: *ultra-fashionable dress sometimes gives people rather a weird appearance.*

weirdly, adv. Prec. & **-ly.** In a weird manner.

weirdness, n. See prec. & **-ness.** State or quality of being weird.

Weismannism, n. [1. vísmanizm; 2. váismanizəm], fr. its propounder, August Weismann (1834-1914). A theory of heredity in which the germ-plasm is regarded as the basis, the possibility of the transmission of acquired characters being denied.

Welch (I.), adj. & n. [1. welsh; 2. welʃ]. Variant of **Welsh** (I.), used in name of the *Welch Regiment*, and the *Royal Welch Fusiliers.*

welch (II.), vb. Variant of **welsh** (II.).

welcome (I.), adj. [1. wélkum; 2. wélkəm], fr. O.N. *velkominn*, 'welcome', see **well** (III.). The O.E. is *wilcuma*, 'welcome guest', lit. 'one who comes in accordance with one's will or desire', see **will** (I.); M.E. has both the Engl. *wilcume* & the Scand. *welcume.* **1.** (of person) Received with pleasure into one's presence, society &c.; giving pleasure by one's presence, visit, companionship &c.: *a welcome guest* &c. Phr. *to make (a person) welcome*, exhibit, express, satisfaction at his arrival, presence &c. **2.** *Welcome to*, **a** free, having full permission, to the use or enjoyment of: *you are welcome to any book in my library*; also **b** (followed by infin.) free, having permission to do something, go somewhere &c.: *you are quite welcome to come and go as you please*; **c** (iron.) *you are welcome to your own opinion, to any opinion you like, to go to the devil your own way* = it is a matter of indifference to me. **3.** (of events, circumstances &c.) Affording pleasure by occurrence, greeted with satisfaction; opportune: *a welcome relief from pain*; *a holiday is very welcome after a long spell of work*; *financial help would be very welcome.* **4.** In elliptical construction: *welcome, little stranger!*; *welcome home again!*; i.e. you are welcome.

welcome (II.), n., fr. prec. Act of welcoming; expression, by word or deed, of satisfaction and pleasure at a person's arrival, presence, companionship &c.: *to receive a hearty, a cold, welcome.*

welcome (III.), vb. trans., fr. **welcome** (I.). **1.** To give a welcome to; to express gratification at arrival or presence of: *I welcome you to my house*; *the king was enthusiastically welcomed by the large crowds.* **2. a** To feel and express satisfaction at an action, utterance, event &c.: *I shall welcome the coming of warm weather*; *we welcome the Prime Minister's assurances*; **b** to accept, receive, with satisfaction: *I welcome your help, your criticism, the suggestion* &c.

welcomeness, n. [1. wélkumnes; 2. wélkəmnis]. **welcome (I.)** & **-ness.** (rare) Quality of being welcome.

weld (I.), n. [1. weld; 2. weld]. M.E. *welde*; perh. connected w. O.E. *wald*, 'forest', see **wold**, & cp. **luteous.** Annual herb yielding a yellow dye; dyer's weed.

weld (II.), vb. trans. & intrans., fr. M.E. *wellen*, 'to boil, bubble up; to melt, weld'; see **well (II.)**. **A.** trans. **1.** To unite (pieces or masses of metal heated to a plastic condition) by hammering or pressure. **2.** (of non-material action) To unite; to join into a compact whole: *the incidents are welded into an interesting narrative*; *to weld the different elements of a party together.* **B.** intrans. (of metal) To undergo, be in a suitable condition for, welding: *different metals weld at different temperatures.*

weld (III.), n., fr. prec. Joint formed by welding.

weldability, n. [1. wèldabíliti; 2. wèldəbíliti]. See next word & **-ity.** State or quality of being weldable.

weldable, adj. [1. wéldabl; 2. wéldəbl]. **weld (I.)** & **-able.** Capable of being welded.

welfare, n. [1. wélfār; 2. wélfɛə]. **well (III.)** & **fare (III.)**. Well-being, prosperity; state of bodily or spiritual health, of satisfactory progress &c. Phr. *welfare work*, organized effort to improve or preserve the physical and general well-being of shop employees, factory workers &c.

welk, vb. trans. & intrans. [1. welk; 2. welk]. M.E. *welken*, cp. M. Du. *welken*; O.H.G. *welchen*, 'to fade, decay, rot'; O.H.G. *welc(h)*, 'moist'; cogn. w. O. Slav. *vlaga*, 'moisture'; *vlŭgŭku*, 'moist'; Lett. *wélgans*, 'damp'; cp. **gauche.** (archaic) To wither, fade, shrivel, shrink. Used by Spenser both trans.: '*But now sad Winter welked hath the day*' ('Shep. Cal.', Nov.); and intrans.: '*By that, the welked Phœbus gan availe, His weary waine*' ('Shep. Cal.', Jan.).

welkin, n. [1. wélkin; 2. wélkin]. O.E. *wolcen*, M.E. *wolken, welken*, 'cloud'; cp. O.S., O.H.G. *wolcan*, 'cloud'; perh. fr. the same base as **welk.** (poet.) Sky, vault of heaven; otherwise now current chiefly in Phr. *to make the welkin ring* (with shouting &c.).

well (I.), n. [1. wel; 2. wel]. O.E., M.E. *welle*, 'spring, fountain', cp. O.H.G. *wella*, 'wave'; O.N. *vella*, 'torrent'; cp. further O.E. *wellen*, 'to boil, bubble up, well up, flow'; *weallan*, 'to boil'; O. Fris. *walla*, O.H.G. *wallan*, 'to boil'; cogn. w. Goth. *walwjan*, *waltjan*; O.H.G. *walzan*, 'to revolve'; Lat. *volvere*, 'to turn, roll, revolve', see **volute** & words there referred to. **1.** a Shaft, usually cylindrical and lined with brick, stone &c., sunk in the ground to collect water from a subterranean source; **b** a boring from which oil gushes. **2.** Natural spring; (in Place-Names &c.) e.g. *Chadwell* (Essex), i.e. O.E. *ċealde well.* **3.** (fig.) Source of supply; fount: '*that renowned Poet . . . Dan Chaucer, well of English undefyled, On Fames eternall beadroll worthie to be fyled*' (Spenser, 'F. Q.' iv. 2. 32). **4.** Any of various enclosed spaces, more or less deep, and supposed to resemble a well; **a** relatively narrow shaft in a building formed by enclosing an area or court by the walls of surrounding buildings; **b** open space from ground-floor to the top of a house in which a staircase is placed; **c** enclosed chamber in the hold of a ship or fishing-boat; **d** hollowed-out depression in a desk made to contain an ink-pot. **5.** Specif., *the well of the court*, space in front of the judge's seat in law court, usually occupied by solicitors.

well (II.), vb. intrans. O.E. *wellan*, 'to boil, bubble up', see prec. To spring, gush, start, from, or as from, a spring or well: *streams well from the ground*; *blood wells from a wound*; *tears well from the eyes* &c.; also *well up, forth.*

well (III.), adv. O.E. & M.E. *wel*, 'well; in a great degree; very; fully'; O.S. *wel*; O.H.G. *wela*; Goth. *waila*; O.N. *vel*; fr. same base as **will (II.)**, orig. sense being 'according to one's desire'. **1.** In a pleasing, desirable, satisfactory manner: *to dine well*; *to sleep well.* Phr. *to live well, do oneself well*, to fare sumptuously; *to stand well with*, be in good graces of. **2.** Skilfully, in a proper manner: *to play and sing well*; *to speak well*; *to do a thing well.* **3.** a In a becoming, seemly manner; suitably, with propriety: *to behave well*; *to treat a person well*; *his modesty became him well*; **b** in a manner suitable to the occasion; in a way suitable under the circumstances: *you may quite well plead illness as an excuse*; *you can't very well pretend you didn't hear.* **4.** **a** (i.) To the full extent; fully, thoroughly: *a stone well and truly laid*; *he had to abandon his journey before it was well begun*; *he ought to be well beaten*; *shake the bottle well*; (ii.) (archaic, before numbers) fully, quite: '*At night was come into that hostelrye Wel nyne and twenty in a companye*' (Chaucer, Prol. of 'C. T.' 24); **b** to a considerable degree, extent: *well on in years*; *lean well back*; *I am well forward with my work*; *I should like very well to come.* **5.** *As well*, in addition, besides: *I'll have some meat and some pudding as well.* **6.** In various idiomatic Phrs., sometimes with force of an interjection: **a** *it's all very well*, expressing ironic disagreement with, protest against, doubt concerning, something which has been said or done: *it's all very well to say that you are sorry, but . . .*; **b** expressing expectation: *well, what next? tell me all about it*; **c** expressing acquiescence, submission to the inevitable: *well, well, I suppose there's nothing more to be said!*; **d** (*just*) *as well*, with equal advantage, reason, justification &c.; without prejudice or injury, harm &c.: *you might just as well make a clean breast of it*; *one might as well throw money away as spend it in betting*; *as well be hung for a sheep as a lamb*; **e** in beginning or resuming a narrative: *well, it was like this*; *well, as I was saying* &c.; **f** expressing comprehension of, or agreement with, what has been, and indicating that a stage or phase has been disposed of, and that it is time for the next: *very well* (*then*), *now go on*; *very well, in that case I shall refuse absolutely.*

well (IV.), adj., fr. prec. (only in pred. use). **1.** In good health, physically strong; contrasted with *ill*: *to be, to look, to feel, well*; *I hope you are pretty well*; *I'm not very well today*; *you can't work when you are not well.* **2.** Suitable, advisable, satisfactory: *it were, would have been, well for him if* &c.; *it would be as well to ask permission.* **3.** In a satisfactory state; favourable, propitious; comfortable: *all is not well with him*; *we are very well where we are*; *past midnight and all well!* Phr. *well enough*, tolerable, fairly good or satisfactory: *the rooms are well enough, but we don't like the landlady.*

well (V.), n., fr. prec. That which is good, satisfactory, or to be desired: *let well alone*, don't interfere with a satisfactory state of affairs.

welladay, interj. [1. wèladá; 2. wèlədéi]. Variant of **wellaway.**

well-advised, adj. Prudent, judicious, considered: *a well-advised step, action* &c.

well-appointed, adj. [1. wèl apóinted; 2. wèl əpóintid]. Having good, adequate, well-chosen appointments, equipment &c.: *a well-appointed house, expedition* &c.

wellaway, interj. [1. wèlawá; 2. wèləwéi]. O.E. *wālā wā*, see **woe, lo.** (archaic) Exclamation of grief, lamentation; equivalent to *alack-a-day.*

well-balanced, adj. [1. wél bálanst; 2. wél bǽlənst]. (chiefly used of the mind) Sane, steady, judicious.

well-behaved, adj. [1. wèl behávd; 2. wèl bihéivd]. Having good manners; behaving well.

well-being, n. **a** Bodily comfort: *a sense of physical well-being*; **b** prosperity, progress; sound moral or social conditions: *the well-being of the community at large.*

well-born, adj. Of good, noble, or distinguished family.

well-bred, adj. Having, exhibiting, good breeding; of good family and polite manners.

well-chosen, adj. Chosen with judgement; apt, suitable to the occasion, appropriate: *well-chosen words* &c.

well-conditioned, adj. **a** In sound bodily condition; **b** having good manners and behaviour.

well-conducted, adj. [1. wèl kundúkted; 2. wèl kəndáktid]. Of good, orderly, behaviour; behaving in a moral manner.

well-connected, adj. [1. wél kunékted; 2. wél kənéktid]. Having high family connexions; related to people of distinction and good standing.

well-cooked, adj. [1. wèl kóokt; 2. wèl kúkt]. **a** Skilfully cooked and served; **b** thoroughly cooked, well-done.

well-deck, n. Space on deck surrounded by upper decks.

well-directed, adj. [1. wél dirékted; 2. wél diréktid]. Accurately or skilfully placed or aimed: *a well-directed blow*; carefully prepared, and applied in a suitable direction: *well-directed effort.*

well-dish, n. Meat dish with depression at one end to catch gravy.

well-disposed, adj. [1. wèl dispṓzd; 2. wèl dispóuzd]. **a** Having friendly and kindly disposition and feelings towards one's fellow-men; **b** favourably inclined towards specific persons, ideas, schemes &c.

well-doer, n. Person who performs moral obligations.

well-doing, n. Virtuous conduct; good actions.

well-done, adj. Thoroughly cooked; contrasted with *underdone.*

well-favoured, adj. Having a good, prepossessing appearance; comely, handsome.

well-found, adj. Adequately and suitably equipped.

well-founded, adj. [1. wèl fóunded; 2. wèl fáundid]. Based on facts: *well-founded suspicions* &c.

well-graced, adj. [1. wèl grāst; 2. wèl gréist]. Attractive, having many good qualities.

well-grounded, adj. **1.** Adequately trained in the elements of a subject. **2.** Well-founded.

well-head, n. **a** Source of a spring or fountain; **b** a coping of stone, lead &c., sometimes of ornamental form, surrounding the head of a well.

well-hole, n. Central, well-like shaft in building, surrounded by walls, stairs &c.

well-informed, adj. Having extensive knowledge.

Wellingtonia, n. [1. wèlingtṓnia; 2. wèliŋtóuniə]. Named after 1st Duke of Wellington & **-ia.** Genus of large Californian pines; sequoia.

Wellingtons, n. pl. [1. wélingtunz; 2. wéliŋtənz], fr. 1st Duke of Wellington. Also *Wellington boots*, boots reaching up to the knee.

well-intentioned, adj. Well-meaning; desiring to do the right thing; well-meant; springing from good motives.

well-judged, adj. [1. wél jujd; 2. wél džadžd]. Judicious; appropriate, timely: *a well-judged reply, action, blow* &c.

well-knit, adj. Firmly jointed, compact, powerful, sinewy: *a well-knit frame, figure* &c.

well-liking, adj. In good condition, having prosperous appearance.

well-looking, adj. Handsome, comely.

well-made, adj. **a** Specif. (of body &c.) well-proportioned, strongly knit; **b** (of handiwork) skilfully shaped, fitted, put together.

well-mannered, adj. Possessing good manners; polite, well-bred.

well-marked, adj. Possessing characteristic features; distinct, definite, unmistakable: *well-marked differences.*

well-meaning, adj. Having good intentions.

well-meant, adj. [1. wèl mént; 2. wèl mént]. Done, said &c. with good intention.
well-nigh, adv. Very nearly.
well-off, adj. [1. wél áwf; 2. wél ɔ́f]. (chiefly pred.) **a** Possessing ample financial resources; wealthy, well-to-do; **b** fortunate, advantageously situated; **c** *well-off for*, well supplied with, possessing abundance of.
well-oiled, adj. [1. wél oild; 2. wél ɔild]. (fig.) **a** Flattering, intended to cajole; **b** (slang) having drunk quite as much as is good for one; mellow, slightly tipsy.
well-ordered, adj. [1. wèl órderd; 2. wèl ɔ́dəd]. Well arranged or organized.
well-padded, adj. **a** (of furniture &c.) Thoroughly provided with padding, cushions &c.; **b** (of persons, facet.) plump, stoutish, cushiony.
well-pleasing, adj. (archaic) Highly agreeable.
well-proportioned, adj. Exhibiting due, symmetrical, proportions.
well-read, adj. **a** Possessing extensive reading and information; well acquainted with literature: *a well-read person*; **b** *well-read in*, possessing deep knowledge of, well trained and instructed in (some specific branch of learning).
well-reputed, adj. Of good repute.
well-room, n. Building where water from mineral spring is served out.
well-rounded, adj. [1. wèl róunded; 2. wèl ráundid]. **a** (of the person) Plump; portly, chubby; **b** (of style, sentence &c.) well and elegantly proportioned, gracefully balanced and finished off.
well-seeming, adj. Apparently satisfactory.
well-seen, adj. (slightly archaic) Versed, accomplished, in some specified branch of learning: *well-seen in Latin.*
well-set, adj. (esp. of body) Firmly knit, strong, and sinewy.
well-sinker, n. Person employed in making wells.
well-spoken, adj. Having a pleasing address and manner of speech; specif. **a** having a cultivated pronunciation; speaking like an educated person; **b** speaking with courtesy and urbanity.
well-spring, n. Source of a spring; well-head.
well-timed, adj. [1. wèl tímd; 2. wèl táimd]. Performed, executed, said &c. at an appropriate or opportune moment.
well-to-do, adj. [1. wèl to dóō; 2. wèl tə dú]. In prosperous financial circumstances; wealthy, well-off; also as collective n., *the well-to-do*, the richer classes; contrasted with *the poor, the needy.*
well-trodden, adj. **a** Often traversed, beaten down by the feet of many passers-by; **b** (fig.) often explored, worked at, elaborated, before; therefore hackneyed, lacking freshness.
well-turned, adj. (of compliment, phrase &c.) Turned, expressed, with grace.
well-wisher, n. [1. wél wisher; 2. wél wiʃə]. Person who is kindly disposed to another or to a cause &c.
well-worn, adj. (fig.) Hackneyed, commonplace, stale.
Welsh (I.), adj. & n. [1. welsh; 2. welʃ]. O.E. *welisċ*, 'foreign', M.E. *wel(i)sh*, fr. *w(e)alh*, 'foreigner', esp. applied to a Celt. inhabitant of Britain, & **-ish**; cp. O.N. *Valskr*; O.H.G. *Walhisc.* **1.** adj. Of, pertaining to, Wales, its people or its language; *Welsh mutton*, meat of small, Welsh breed of sheep. **2.** n. **a** *The Welsh*, the people of Wales; **b** *Welsh*, language of Wales.
welsh, welch (II.), vb. intrans. & trans. Etymol. unknown. **1.** intrans. (of bookmaker &c.) To abscond with stake-money without paying winners of bets. **2.** trans. To cheat (winner of bet) by absconding with money staked.
Welshman, Welshwoman, ns. [1. wélshman, -wooman; 2. wélʃmən, -wumən]. **Welsh** (I.) & **man, woman.** Male, female, native of Wales.
welsh rabbit, incorrectly **rarebit**, n. Toasted cheese.
welt (I.), n. [1. welt; 2. welt]. M.E. *welte*; cp. O.E. *w(i)eltan, wæltan*, 'to roll', see **welter** (I.). **1.** Leather strip stitched into shoe to strengthen join between sole and upper. **2.** Piece of ribbed knitting finishing top of sock &c. **3.** Inflamed stripe raised on skin by blow; wale, weal.
welt (II.), vb. trans., fr. prec. **1.** To furnish (shoe &c.) with a welt. **2.** **a** To raise welts on (skin); **b** (colloq.) to strike, thrash.
welter (I.), vb. intrans. & n. [1. wélter; 2. wéltə], fr. O.E. *w(i)eltan*, 'to roll, turn, overturn', M.E. *welten*, 'to overturn', & **-er.** Cp. O.N. *velta*; M.H.G. *welzen*, 'to turn, revolve', see **waltz**; Goth. *waltjan*, 'to roll'; cogn. w. Lat. *volvere*, 'to turn, roll', see **volute**; cp. also **well** (I.), **wallow** (I.). **1.** vb. To wallow, roll, tumble, about, be rolled in: *weltering in gore.* **2.** n. Surging, tumult, confusion; disorderly mass: (in material and non-material senses) *the welter of the waves, of a crowd*; *a welter of confused ideas.*
welter (II.), n. Etymol. doubtful; perh. fr. **welt** (II.), 2, & **-er.** (boxing, racing &c.) Heavy weight; chiefly in compounds: *welter-race, welter-weight* &c.
wen (I.), n. [1. wen; 2. wen]. O.E., M.E. *wenn*; cp. Du. *wen*; M.L.G. *wene*, 'wen'; etymol. doubtful. Indolent tumour on surface of body; esp. one on the scalp or neck. Phr. *The Great Wen*, London, so called by Cobbett.
wen (II.), n. O.E. *wenn*, S.E. variant of *wynn*, 'joy', see **winsome**, used on account of its initial letter; this letter was also called *wēn*, 'hope, expectation'; cp. **thorn.** The old English letter ƿ = *w*.
wench, n. [1. wench; 2. wentʃ]. M.E. *wenche(l)*, 'child'; fr. O.E. *wenċel*, n. 'child', adj. 'weak'; cp. O.E. *wancol*, 'feeble'; O.H.G. *wanchal*, 'tottering'; *wankōn*, 'to totter'; O.N. *vakka*, 'to be unsteady'; cogn. w. Scrt. *vaŋgati*, 'limps'; Lat. *vagāri*, 'to wander', see **vagary.** Prob. cogn. w. **wince.** **1.** (archaic or facetious) A girl, young woman, esp. servant, country girl. **2.** (archaic) Prostitute.
wend (I.), vb. trans. & intrans. [1. wend; 2. wend]. O.E. *wendan*, M.E. *wenden*, 'to turn, go'; fr. gradational type **wand-*, as seen in Pret. of O.E. *windan*, see **wind** (IV.), & **went.** **1.** trans. To turn, direct, proceed on; only in Phr. *to wend one's way.* **2.** intrans. (archaic) To go, betake oneself.
Wend (II.), n., fr. Germ. *Wende.* Member of a Slavonic race living in parts of Northern and Eastern Germany.
Wendic, adj. [1. wéndik; 2. wéndik]. Prec. & **-ic.** Of, pertaining to, the Wends or their language.
Wendish, adj. & n. [1. wéndish; 2. wéndiʃ]. See prec. & **-ish.** **1.** adj. Of, pertaining to, the Wends. **2.** n. The language of the Wends.
Wenlock, adj. [1. wénlok; 2. wénlɔk]. Shropshire Place-Name. (geol.) Pertaining to the middle division of the Silurian system of rock.
Wensleydale, n. [1. wénzlidāl; 2. wénzlideil]. Yorkshire Place-Name. Kind of cheese.
went, vb. [1. went; 2. went]. Pret. of **wend** (I.), now used as Pret. of **go.**
wentletrap, n. [1. wéntltràp; 2. wéntltræp], fr. Du. *wenteltrap*, earlier 'spiral staircase', fr. *wentel*, 'turning', fr. stem of *winden*, 'to turn', q.v. under **wind** (III.), & *trap*, 'stair, step'. Univalve shellfish with spiral shell.
wept, vb. [1. wept; 2. wept]. Pret. & P.P. of **weep.**
were, vb. [1. wār, wer; 2. weə, wə]. Pret. pl. of **be.** O.E. *wǣron*; M.E. *wēren*; cp. O.H.G. *wārun*; fr. earlier **wǣz-*, fr. a gradational variant of the base **wes-*, seen in **was.**
werewolf, werwolf, n. [1. wérwoolf; 2. wíəwulf]. O.E. *werewulf*, fr. *wer*, 'man'; cp. Goth. *wair*; O.H.G. *wer*; O.N. *verr*, 'man'; cogn. w. Lat. *vir*, 'man', see **virile,** & *wulf*, see **wolf.** (folklore) Person who assumed voluntarily or involuntarily the shape of a wolf, either permanently or periodically.
wert, vb. [1. wĕrt; 2. wʌt]. (archaic) 2nd pers. sing. Pret. of **be**; cp. **were** & **wast.**
Wertherism, n. [1. wérterizm; 2. wʌ́tərizəm], fr. *Werther*, hero of Goethe's novel, 'Die Leiden des jungen Werthers', 1774. Extravagant, morbid, and sickly sentimentality.
Wesleyan, adj. & n. [1. wézlian, wèzlḗan; 2. wézliən, wèzlíən] (pronounced [1. wés-; 2. wés-] by members of the body), fr. name of founder, John Wesley, d. 1791. **1.** adj. Of, pertaining to, John Wesley, or the body of Methodist dissenters named after him. **2.** n. Member of this body.
Wesleyanism, n. [1. wezléanizm; 2. wezlíənizəm]. Prec. & **-ism.** Method, doctrine, of the Wesleyans, or of their founder, John Wesley.
west (I.), adv. [1. west; 2. west]. O.E., M.E. *west*; cp. Du., Germ. *west*, 'west'; prob. orig., 'of the setting sun', & fr. stem **we-*, 'down'; cp. Scrt. *avā́š*, 'down'; *avástād*, 'below'; cp. also Lat. *vesper*, 'evening', see **vesper**; Gk. *hésperos*, 'evening', see **Hesperian.** Towards, in the direction of, the setting sun; in or towards the region faced by person observing the setting sun at the equinox from the line of the equator: *to look, face, go, sail, west*; Phr. *to go west*, to die; *to sail due west*, exactly towards W. point of compass. Phr. *west of*, farther west than.
west (II.), adj., fr. prec. **1.** Of, pertaining to, situated in, facing, the west: *a west window, room,* &c.; *west end* (of church), end, part, opposite to the altar; *west-country*, south-western and south-west midland part of England. **2.** (of wind) Blowing from the west.
west (III.), n., fr. prec. **1.** **a** One of the cardinal points of the compass, opposite to east; **b** region of earth, sky &c. lying in this direction. **2.** Western part of continent, country, county &c.; specif. **a** Western Europe, Occident; Phr. *the Empire of the West*, Western Empire (see **western**); **b** West of England; **c** Western United States, west of Alleghany mountains, or including prairie and Pacific states.
west-country, n. & adj. **1.** n. South-western and south-west midland England. **2.** adj. Of, pertaining to, the west-country.
west-countryman, -woman, n. Native of west-country.
West End, n. A somewhat loose term applied to the district of London in which are the residences of fashionable society, higher-class shops, hotels, theatres &c., roughly including the area from Trafalgar Square to Hyde Park; also, by transf., the society living in this district.
West-end, adj. Of, pertaining to, the West End of London.
westering, adj. [1. wéstering; 2. wéstəriŋ], fr. obs. *wester*, fr. M.E. *westren*, 'to go west', fr. **west** (I.). Turning, tending, towards the west.
westerly, adj. & adv. [1. wésterli; 2. wéstəli], fr. **west** on anal. of **easterly.** **1.** adj. **a** Of, pertaining to, the west; western; **b** directed, proceeding, towards the west: *a westerly course*; **c** (of wind) coming from the west. **2.** adv. Towards the west.
western (I.), adj. [1. wéstern; 2. wéstən]. **west** & **-ern.** **1.** Of, pertaining to, situated in, coming from, characteristic of, the west. Phrs. *Western Church*, Papal branch of the Catholic Church; *Western Empire*, western part, including Rome, of the Roman Empire as divided by Theodosius in 395. **2.** (of wind) Blowing from the west; westerly.
western (II.), n., fr. prec. Native of the west; westerner.
westerner, n. [1. wésterner; 2. wéstənə]. **western** (I.) & **-er.** Native of the west, esp. of the Western United States.
westernize, vb. trans. [1. wésterniz; 2. wéstənaiz]. **western** (I.) & **-ize.** To introduce western civilization into (esp. Oriental countries, races &c.).

westernmost, adj. [1. wésternmòst; 2. wéstənmòust]. **western (I.)** & **-most.** Farthest towards the west.

West Indian, adj. West Indies & **-ian.** Of, pertaining to, coming from, the West Indies.

westing, n. [1. wésting; 2. wéstiŋ]. **west (I.)** & **-ing.** Distance traversed by, movement of, ship in westerly direction.

Westminster, n. [1. wéstmìnster; 2. wéstmìnstə]. **1.** District of London. **2.** Westminster Abbey. **3.** The Houses of Parliament; (also fig.) parliamentary politics &c. **4. a** Westminster School; **b** member of this school; *old Westminster*, former pupil of the school.

west-north-west, adj., adv., & n. [1. wést nòr(th) wést; 2. wést nɔ̄(þ) wést]. (In or towards) direction or point midway between W. & N.W.

west-south-west, adj., adv., & n. [1. wést sòu(th) wést; 2. wést sàu(þ) wést]. (In or towards) direction or point midway between W. &. S.W.

westward, adj., adv., & n. [1. wéstward; 2. wéstwəd]. **west (I.)** & **-ward.** **1.** adj. Tending towards, lying towards, the west. **2.** adv. Towards the west. **3.** n. Westward region or direction.

westwards, adv. [1. wéstwardz; 2. wéstwədz]. **west (I.)** & **-wards.** Towards the west.

wet (I.), adj. [1. wet; 2. wet]. O.E. *wǣte*; M.E. *wēte*, 'wet'; cp. O. Fris. *wēt*; O.N. *vātr*, 'wet'; cogn. w. **water.** **1.** Covered, saturated, dripping, or moistened with liquid: *wet clothes, cheeks, umbrellas, wood, leaves* &c.; *the grass is wet with dew.* Phrs. *a wet bargain*, one clinched and celebrated by drinks; *wet blanket*, see **blanket**; *wet bob* (Eton slang), see **bob (VI.)**; *wet pack*, medical treatment of patient by wrapping him in wet sheets covered with dry blankets; *wet through, wet to the skin*, with one's clothes soaked. **2.** Characterized by constant or abundant rain: *a wet day, season, month*; *wet weather.* **3.** (Am. slang) Not prohibiting the sale of alcoholic liquor: *a wet state*, one in which such liquor is obtainable; contrasted with *dry*.

wet (II.), n., fr. prec. **1.** Liquid, wet substance, moisture. **2.** (vulg. slang) A drink. **3.** (U.S.A.) An anti-Prohibitionist.

wet (III.), vb. trans. O.E. *wǣtan*; M.E. *wēten*, 'to wet, moisten'; fr. **wet (I.)**. To apply liquid to, sprinkle, cover, saturate, with liquid. Phr. *to wet one's whistle*, drink.

wet-bulb thermometer, n. Thermometer with bulb kept moist and used in conjunction with a dry-bulb thermometer in a hygrometer.

wet dock, n. Dock filled with water.

wether, n. [1. wédher; 2. wéðə]. O.E., M.E. *weðer*, 'sheep, lamb'; cp. Germ. *widder*; O.N. *veðr*; Goth. *wiþrus*, 'lamb'; cogn. w. Scrt. *vatsá-* 'calf, yearling'; *vatsará*, 'year'; Lith. *vetuszas*, 'old'; Lat. *vitulus*, 'calf', orig., 'yearling'; *vetus*, 'old'; see **veteran, vitular.** Castrated ram.

wetness, n. [1. wétnes; 2. wétnis]. **wet (I.)** & **-ness.** State or condition of being wet.

wet-nurse, n. & vb. trans. **1.** n. Woman who suckles another's child. **2.** vb. To act as wet-nurse to.

wet-plate, n. Photographic plate treated with collodion and exposed while still wet from sensitizing bath.

wetting, n. [1. wéting; 2. wétiŋ]. **wet (III.)** & **-ing.** State of being, process of becoming or being made, wet.

wettish, adj. [1. wétish; 2. wétiʃ]. **wet (I.)** & **-ish.** Fairly wet.

wey, n. [1. wā; 2. wei]. O.E. *wǣge*; M.E. *wēȝe*, 'weight, weighing-machine, wey'; cp. O.N. *vāg*; O.H.G. *wāga*, 'scales'; cp. further O.E. *wegan*, 'to carry, move', & see **weigh.** Unit of weight varying in amount with different substances, usually 182 lb. (of wool).

whack (I.), vb. trans. & intrans. [1. wak; 2. wæk]. Imitative. **1.** trans. To strike, slap, sharply and with audible sound. **2.** intrans. To give sharp, resounding blows.

whack (II.), n., fr. prec. **1.** Sharp, audible blow with stick &c. **2.** (slang) Allotted, suitable, or adequate portion; due share.

whacker, n. [1. wáker; 2. wǽkə]. **whack (I.)** & **-er.** (slang) **a** Unusually large person or thing; **b** a lie.

whacking (I.), n. [1. wáking; 2. wǽkiŋ]. **whack (I.)** & **-ing.** Act of striking with stick &c.; a beating.

whacking (II.), adj., fr. Pres. Part. of **whack (I.)**. (slang) Tremendous, thundering: *a whacking lie*; as adv., *a whacking big horse.*

whale (I.), n. [1. wāl; 2. weil]. O.E. *hwæl*; M.E. *whal, whāle*; cp. O.N. *hvalr*; O.H.G. *wal*, 'whale'; cogn. w. Lat. *squalus*, 'large fish'; perh. cogn. w. Gk. *áspalos*, 'fish'; Gk. *skúlion*, 'dog-fish'. Large, fish-like, warm-blooded aquatic mammal, order *Cetacea*, with short, broad, flattened fore-limbs; hunted for its oil, whalebone, spermaceti &c. Phrs. (colloq.) *very like a whale*, expressing ironical agreement with an incredible statement or promise; *he's a regular whale for work* &c., a very diligent, laborious worker; *a whale at tennis*, very good at it.

whale (II.), vb. intrans. To engage in whaling.

whale-back, n. Type of boat with rounded covering on deck, for use in rough seas.

whale-boat, n. **a** Boat employed in whaling; **b** ship's boat resembling this.

whalebone, n. [1. wálbōn; 2. wéilboun]. Thin, horny, flexible substance found in a series of plates in the upper jaw of some varieties of whale; used for light framework, for stiffening fabric &c.

whale-calf, n. Young whale.

whale-fin, n. (commerc.) Whalebone.

whale-fishery, n. **1.** Business of catching whales; whaling. **2.** Part of sea or coast where whaling is carried on.

whale-head, n. Central African bird of heron family with broad, hooked beak.

whale-line, n. Stout rope used for harpoons in whaling.

whaleman, n. [1. wálman; 2. wéilmən]. Man employed in whaling.

whale-oil, n. Oil obtained from whale's blubber.

whaler, n. [1. wáler; 2. wéilə]. **whale (II.)** & **-er.** **1.** Ship engaged in whale-fishery. **2.** Man employed in whaling.

whaling, n. [1. wáling; 2. wéiliŋ]. **whale (II.)** & **-ing.** The pursuit and killing of whales.

whaling-gun, n. Apparatus for discharging harpoon &c. at whale.

whaling-master, n. Captain of whaler.

whang (I.), vb. trans. & intrans. [1. wang; 2. wæŋ]. Imitative. **1.** trans. To strike with a clanging, resounding blow. **2.** intrans. To clang, resound as result of a blow.

whang (II.), n. See prec. Clanging, resounding blow, bang.

whanghee, wangee, n. [1. wanggḗ; 2. wæŋgí]. fr. Chinese *hwang.* A Chinese variety of bamboo, used for walking-sticks.

wharf (I.), n. [1. worf; 2. wɔ̄f]. O.E. *hwerf*, 'dam'; M.E. *wherfe*, 'wharf'; cp. M.L.G., M. Du. *werf*, 'wharf'; cp. further O.N. *hvarf*, 'act of turning'; fr. the base in O.E. *hweorfan*, 'to turn'; O.N. *hverfa*; O.H.G. *hwerfan*, 'to turn round'; Goth. *hwairban*, 'to go round'; cogn. w. Gk. *karpós*, 'wrist', see **carpus.** Structure of timber or stone, alongside which ships may be moored for receiving and discharging goods &c.

wharf (II.), vb. trans., fr. prec. **1.** To moor (vessel) to a wharf. **2.** To unload, store (goods), on a wharf.

wharfage, n. [1. wórfij; 2. wɔ̄fidž]. Prec. & **-age.** Dues paid for use of a wharf for mooring, loading, or unloading a ship.

wharfinger, n. [1. wórfinjer; 2. wɔ̄findžə]. Earlier *wharfager*; see **wharfage** & **-er.** Owner of wharf where vessels are unloaded, cargoes shipped and unshipped &c.

what (I.), adj. [1. wot; 2. wɔt]. O.E. *hwæt*; M.E. *w(h)at*; neut. form of interrog. pron. *hwā*, 'who'; O.H.G. *hwaz*; cogn. w. Lat. *quod*, 'that, in that'; see **who.** **1.** (interrog.) Asking for specification of quality, kind, amount, identity &c. of person or thing referred to: *what kind of food do they eat?*; *what supplies have they?*; *what places did you go to?*; *what weather did you have?*; *what man are you speaking of?*; *what ship is that?*; (also in indirect questions) *do you know what ship that is?* **2.** (rel.) That, those, which; as much, as many as, of the kind that &c.: *bring what parcels you can carry*; *wear what clothes you please.* Phr. *what time*, see **time (I.)**. **3.** (exclamatory) How great &c., implying surprise, disapproval &c. of the quality, amount &c. of something: *what fools they are!*; *what waste!*; *what a miserable day!*; *what strange people!*

what (II.), pron., fr. prec. **1.** (interrog.) Asking for specification of identity, quality, quantity, amount, &c.; what thing: *what did he do, say* &c.*?*; *what do you know about it?*; *what has happened?*; *what is his name?* Phrs. (often elliptical) *what about it?* = *what do you know, shall we do &c. about . . . ?*; *what next?* = *what will happen &c. next?*, expressing surprise at event, conduct &c.; *what though the skies may fall* &c. = *what does it matter?*; *what if we should fail* &c.*?* = *what will be the result?*; *what?* = *what did you say* &c.*?*; *what for?*, for what reason?; *what is he?*, what is his occupation?; *what of it?*, what does it matter?; *what-d'you-call-him, it* &c., used as substitute for forgotten name &c. **2.** (rel.) The thing(s) which, that which: *what I say is true*; *he told me what to say*; *I will do what I can*; *what happened was quite an accident*; *that is what I heard*; *what I always say is . . .* Phrs. *I know what!* = *I know what we will, or ought to, do* &c., introducing new plan &c.; *to know what's what*, know the real, proper, or genuine thing &c. **3.** (exclamatory) What a large amount, how much &c.; what things &c.: *what these ancient walls could tell us!*

whate'er, adj. & pron. [1. wòtár; 2. wɔ̀téə]. Contracted fr. **next word.** (poet.) Whatever.

whatever (I.), adj. [1. wòtéver; 2. wɔ̀tévə]. **what (I.)** & **ever.** **1.** What (with additional emphasis); of any kind, degree &c.: *whatever orders he gives are obeyed*; *whatever excuses he may make, we will not believe him.* **2.** (in negative clause, emphasizing negation) Of any kind, at all: *I can see nothing whatever*; *no motive whatever can excuse his conduct.*

whatever (II.), pron. **what (II.)** & **ever.** (rel., emphatic form of **what (II.)**) Anything, everything that, all that; no matter what: *whatever happens, he is safe*; *I am right, whatever you may think*; *take whatever you like*; *whatever I do I'm always wrong*; *whatever you do, don't drink too much* = *on no account are you to . . .*

what-not, n. [1. wót not; 2. wɔ́t nɔt]. Piece of furniture usually consisting of slender uprights supporting a set of shelves for holding odds & ends, ornaments, books &c.

what's-his-name, pron. [1. wótsiznām; 2. wɔ́tsizneim]. Discourteous, contemptuous mode of referring to a person whose name one cannot, or which one affects not to, remember: *not a soul there except old what's-his-name.*

whatso, adj. & pron. [1. wótsō; 2. wɔ́tsou]. **what** & **so.** (archaic) Same as **whatsoever.**

whatsoe'er, adj. & pron. [1. wòtsōár; 2. wɔ̀tsouéə]. Contracted from next word. (poet.) Whatsoever.

whatsoever, adj. & pron. [1. wòtsōéver; 2. wɔ̀tsouévə]. **what** & **so** & **ever.** Emphatic and rhetorical form of **whatever.**

whaup, n. [1. wawp; 2. wɔ̄p]. Imitative. (chiefly Scots) Curlew.

wheal (I.), n. [1. wēl; 2. wīəl]. M.E. *whēle*, 'pustule'; cp. O.E. *hwelian*, 'to suppurate'; *hwyle*, 'boil, tumour'; perh. cogn. w. Lett. *kwēle*, 'inflammation of a wound'. Small, inflamed tumour, a pustule.

wheal (II.), n., fr. Corn. *hwel.* Mine; specif., tin-mine.

wheat, n. [1. wēt; 2. wīt]. O.E. *hwǣte*; M.E. *whēte*; cp. O.S. *hwēti*; O.H.G. *hweiti*; O.N. *hveiti*; Goth. *hwaiteis*, 'wheat'; cogn. w. **white (I.)**. **1.** Annual, or biennial, cereal plant, *Triticum*, esp. *T. sativum*, bearing a spike of edible seeds. **2.** Edible grain produced by this plant, usually ground and made into bread &c., and forming a staple food.

wheatear, n. [1. wḗtèr; 2. wítiə]. Earlier *white-ears* (cp. Fr. *cul-blanc*); **white (I.)** & **arse**. Small, grey and white, thrush-like migratory bird, *Saxicola oenanthe*.

wheaten, adj. [1. wḗtn; 2. wítn]. **wheat** & **-en**. Of, composed of, containing, of the colour of, wheat.

wheat-fly, n. Insect whose larvae are injurious to wheat.

wheat-grass, n. Couch-grass.

Wheatstone bridge, n. [1. wḗtstun bríj; 2. wítstən brídž]. An electrical device for measuring an unknown by a known resistance. It was invented by S. H. Christie (d. 1865), but was named after Sir C. Wheatstone (d. 1875).

wheedle, vb. trans. [1. wḗdl; 2. wídl]. Prob. fr. O.E. *wǣdlian*, M.E. *wēdlien*, 'to beg'; fr. O.E. *wǣdl*, 'poverty'; the latter is perh. connected w. O.H.G. *weisso*, Mod. Germ. *waise*, 'an orphan'; cp. also O.E. (*wudu*)-*wāsa*, 'faun, satyr', lit. 'waif of the woods'. **1. a** To influence by crafty flattery, bring artful persuasion to bear upon; to coax, cajole: *to wheedle a person into doing something*; **b** to beguile, deceive (person) by flattery and cajolery. **2.** To obtain (thing from person &c.) by coaxing or flattery: *to wheedle something out of a person.*

wheedling, adj. [1. wḗdling; 2. wídliŋ], fr. Pres. Part. of prec. Insinuatingly persuasive; using, characterized by, seductive flattery and blandishments.

wheedlingly, adv. Prec. & **-ly**. In a wheedling manner.

wheel (I.), n. [1. wēl; 2. wīəl]. O.E. *hwēol*, *hweogol*; M.E. *whēle*; cp. M. Du. *weel*, *wiel*; Dan. *hiul*; O.N. *hjōl*, 'wheel'; all fr. reduplicated type **hwehwlo*- &c.; cogn. w. Gk. *kúklos*, 'circle, wheel', fr. **kʷekʷlo*-, see **cycle**; Scrt. *čakráś*, 'wheel'; Lith. *kāklas*, 'neck'; cp. further, without reduplication, O.N. *hvel*, 'wheel'; O. Prussian *kelan*; O. Slav. *kolo*, 'wheel'; Gk. *pélein*, 'to turn'; *pólos*, 'pivot, axis', see **pole (III.)**; Lat. *colere*, 'to engage in, occupy oneself with, cultivate, inhabit'; see **colony**. **1.** Disk, or circular rim and concentric disk connected by radiating bars (spokes), having, or capable of, rotatory motion, and used to facilitate movement of body, esp. vehicle, or to transmit or modify motion in machine &c.; (often in compounds) *Catherine-wheel, cog-wheel, spinning-wheel, steering-wheel* &c., q.v. Phrs. *Fortune's wheel*, symbolic representation of vicissitudes of life; *to break (person) on the wheel*, kill or injure by binding on revolving wheel and striking with iron bar, as mediaeval form of torture: *to put a spoke in one's wheel*, hinder, prevent progress; *to put one's shoulder to the wheel*, make an effort to assist progress of undertaking, cause &c.; *wheels within wheels*, referring to a complicated and involved combination of motives or influences, acting and reacting on each other. **2.** Specif. **a** a bicycle; **b** steering-wheel; **c** spinning-wheel; **d** round, horizontal disk revolving on a spindle, on which a potter shapes his clay: *potter's wheel*. **3. a** Wheeling, sweeping or revolving motion: *the wheel of birds* &c.; **b** specif., movement of line of troops &c. as on a pivot.

wheel (II.), vb. trans. & intrans., fr. prec. **A.** trans. **1. a** To cause (wheeled vehicle &c.) to move; to propel, pull, on wheels: *to wheel a truck, barrow* &c.; **b** to propel (person, load &c.) in a wheeled vehicle or barrow. **2.** To cause (line of men &c.) to turn as on a pivot. **B.** intrans. **1. a** Often *wheel round*, to move, swing, round so as to face another direction; **b** (of line of troops &c.) to swing round as on a pivot. Phr. *right, left, wheel*, words of command to carry out this movement. **2.** (of bird &c.) To move in a sweeping, circular course. **3.** To ride a bicycle &c.

wheel-and-axle, n. A wheel fixed to and revolving on an axle, one of the elementary mechanical powers.

wheelbarrow, n. [1. wḗlbarō; 2. wíəlbærou]. Strong, usually oblong, receptacle of wood or thin iron sheets, having a single low wheel in front, and short stout legs, with shafts or handles for pushing, set at right angles to the legs behind; used for transporting small loads by hand.

wheel-chair, n. Chair mounted, and moving, on wheels.

wheeled, adj. [1. wēld; 2. wiəld]. **wheel (I.)** & **-ed**. Provided with a wheel or wheels; often in compounds, *two-, four-wheeled* &c.

wheeler, n. [1. wḗler; 2. wílə]. **wheel (II.)** & **-er**. **1.** One who, that which, wheels. **2.** Wheel-horse. **3.** In compounds, *four-wheeler* &c., vehicle with specified number of wheels. **4.** Wheelwright.

wheel-horse, n. Horse, or one of two horses, harnessed to the pole or shafts of a vehicle and preceded by leader(s).

wheel-house, n. Shelter erected round ship's helm; pilot-house.

wheelless, adj. [1. wḗlles; 2. wíəllis]. **wheel (I.)** & **-less**. Without wheels.

wheel-lock, n. **1.** Ancient form of gun-lock, with steel wheel whirling round and striking flint when released by trigger. **2.** Obsolete type of pistol &c., with wheel-lock.

wheelman, n. [1. wḗlman; 2. wíəlmən]. Cyclist.

wheel-seat, n. End of axle, fitting on to hub.

wheel-tread, n. Part of tire or rim that touches road &c.

wheel-window, n. Circular window with tracery radiating from centre.

wheelwright, n. [1. wḗlrīt; 2. wíəlrait]. **wheel (I.)** & **wright**. Person engaged in making or repairing wheels or wheeled vehicles.

wheeze (I.), vb. intrans. & trans. [1. wēz; 2. wīz]. O.E. *hwēsan*; M.E. *whēsen*, fr. **hwōsjan*; cp. O.E. *hwōsta*, 'a cough'; O.H.G. *huosto*; cogn. w. Lith. *koseti*, 'to cough'. **1.** intrans. To breathe with a rattling, grating, rasping, whistling sound due to phlegm in the throat or bronchial tubes. **2.** trans. To utter with a wheezing sound.

wheeze (II.), n., fr. prec. **1.** Wheezing sound, noisy breathing. **2.** (slang) Actor's interpolated remark, joke &c.; gag; a joke in general: *a good wheeze*, an amusing anecdote.

wheezily, adv. [1. wḗzili; 2. wízili]. See **wheezy** & **-ly**. In a wheezy manner.

wheeziness, n. [1. wḗzines; 2. wízinis]. See next word & **-ness**. State or quality of being wheezy.

wheezy, adj. [1. wḗzi; 2. wízi]. **wheeze (I.)** & **-y**. **a** Speaking, breathing, with a wheeze; **b** performed, uttered, with wheezing: *wheezy breathing*; *a wheezy laugh*.

whelk (I.), n. [1. welk; 2. wεlk]. O.E. *wiluc*, M.E. *wilk, welk*; prob. cogn. w. Gk. *hélix*, 'spiral'; *helikē*, 'spiral shell' &c., see **helix**; fr. stem **wel*-, **wol*- &c., 'to turn, revolve', seen in **volute**, **wallow**, **well (I.)** &c. Marine, edible, gastropod mollusc with univalve spiral shell having few whorls.

whelk (II.), n. M.E. *whelke*; cp. **wheal (I.)** & dimin. suff. **-ock**. Pimple, small inflamed swelling.

whelked, adj. [1. welkt; 2. wεlkt]. Prec. & **-ed**. Marked or covered with pustules, pimply.

whelm, vb. trans. [1. welm; 2. wεlm]. M.E. *whelmen*, 'to turn over'; the word seems, in form & later meaning, to be the result of association between O.E. *helmian*, 'to cover over', see **helm(et)**, & (*ā*)*hwelfan*, 'to cover; to overwhelm'; the latter is cogn. w. O.S. *bihwelbian*, 'to cover over, to arch over', O.H.G. *welben*, Mod. Germ. *wölbe*; further cognates are Gk. *kólpos*, 'bosom, gulf'; Lat. *culcita*, 'pillow'. It is possible that the O.E. poetical word *welman*, *wielman*, 'to boil, surge, rage' &c., used of the sea, wh. survives in its old sense in M.E. *welmen*, may also have influenced the form. (poet.) To flow over, overwhelm, engulf, submerge &c. (in material and non-material senses): '*Where thou perhaps, under the whelming tide, Visit'st the bottom of the monstrous world*' (Milton, 'Lycidas', 157-8); *whelmed in ruin, in sorrow* &c.

whelp (I.), n. [1. welp; 2. wεlp]. O.E. *hwelp*, M.E. *whelp*, 'puppy'; cp. O.S. *hwelp*; O.H.G. *welf*; O.N. *hvelpr*; connexion w. Lat. *vulpes*, 'fox', see **vulpine**, is doubtful. **1. a** Puppy; **b** cub of lion, tiger, seal &c. **2.** Ill-bred, mannerless boy or youth.

whelp (II.), vb. intrans. & trans., fr. prec. **1.** intrans. (of animal) To bring forth young: '*sea-monsters whèlped And stabled*' (Milton, 'P. L.' xi. 751-2); (also contemptuously of woman). **2.** trans. To bring forth (whelps).

when (I.), adv. [1. wen; 2. wεn]. O.E. *hwænne*, M.E. *whan(ne)*, 'when', cp. O.S., Goth. *hwan*, 'when'; O.H.G. *wanne*; fr. pronominal base seen in **who**. **1.** (interrog.) At what time or period, on what occasion: *when will you come?*; *when did it begin to rain?*; *when did you see him last?* **2. a** At the moment, during the time that: *it was raining when we started*, *when we were out*; *I will see you when I return*; in elliptical Phr. *a dog wags his tail when pleased*; *say when* = tell me when you have enough, used when pouring drink into another's glass; **b** on any occasion that, whenever: *it is cold when it snows*; **c** after the time that: *he will go when he has had his dinner*; **d** just then, at that moment: *we were about to start when it began to rain*; **e** in spite of the fact that, although: *he keeps on talking when he knows it annoys us*; **f** considering the fact that: *how can I explain when you won't listen?* **3.** (as n., rare) The time at which: *the when and the where*.

when (II.), pron., fr. prec. **1.** (rel.) At or during which: *during the time when you were away*; *at a moment when we were busy*. **2.** (interrog. or rel. after prep.) What or which time or moment: *till when shall you be here?*; *since when have you been here?*; *we came a week ago, since when the weather has been bad*.

whence, adv. & rel. pron. [1. wens; 2. wεns], fr. M.E. *whennes*, formed fr. **when** & advbl. suff. *-es*. (archaic) **1.** (interrog.) From what place, from what source: *whence did you come?*; *whence comes this great river, all this uproar?* The usual construction would be, *where did you come from?* &c. Phr. *whence comes it that . . .?*, how is it that? **2. a** The place or source from which: *tell me whence you come*; also *from whence*; **b** to the place from which: *go back whence you came.*

whencesoever, adv. [1. wènssōéver; 2. wènssouévə]. Prec. & **so** & **ever**. From whatever place, source &c.

whene'er, adv. [1. wenár; 2. wenέə]. Contracted fr. next word. (poet.) Whenever.

whenever, adv. [1. wenéver; 2. wenévə]. **1.** At whatever time; as soon as; at the moment that, no matter when: *I'll see him whenever he likes to come*. **2.** On whatever occasion, as often as: *I hope you'll come and play whenever you feel inclined*.

whensoever, adv. [1. wènsōéver; 2. wènsouévə]. **when** & **so** & **ever**. Whenever (emphatic).

where (I.), adv. [1. wār; 2. wεə]. O.E. *hwǣr*; M.E. *whēre*; cp. O.S. *hwār*; O.H.G. *wār*; O.N. *hvār*; Goth. *hwar*; orig. locative of pronominal base seen in **who**, **when** &c.; cp. Lat. *cūr*, 'why'; fr. **kʷō-r*, old locative of pron. **kʷoi*, Lat. *quī*, 'who'; Scrt. *kar-hi*, 'when'; Lith. *kùr*, 'where'. **1.** (interrog.) **a** (implying motion) To or towards what place, in what direction, whither: *where are you going?*; **b** (implying rest) at or in what place, situation, position, or part: *where are you going to stay?*; *where is my hat?*; *where does the river rise?*; *where did you hear that tale?*; **c** in what respect or condition: *where does it* *concern us?*; *where will you be if you offend him?*; *where is the use of being obstinate?* **2.** (introducing dependent clause) **a** (implying motion) To what place, in what direction: *let him go where he likes*; **b** (implying rest) in or at what place or part: *we must camp where we can get water*; *he knows where they are*; *things are never where one wants them*; **c** in what respect, at what point, in which circumstances: *one never knows where to have him*, at what point he is vulnerable.

where (II.), pron., fr. prec. **1.** (interrog.) **a** (followed by *from*) From what place &c.: *where have you come from?*; (followed by *to*) to what place: *where are you going to?* **2.** (rel.) **a** At, to, or in which: *that is the place where he lives*; *this is the point where we stuck*; also **b** *this is where I live*, the place in or at which; *this is where we get out*; **c** *from where*, from the place which; *to where*, to the place which; **d** the respect, the circumstances, conditions in which: *that's just where you're wrong*.

where-, pref., compounded with preps., **a** denoting in what place, part, respect &c.; e.g. *whereas, wherever* &c.; **b** see **whereby, wherein, wherewith.**

whereabouts, adv. & n. [1. wârabòuts; 2. wέərəbàuts]. **1.** adv. **a** (interrog.) In what place, where approximately: *whereabouts did you put it?*; **b** (rel.) the place where &c.: *I like to know whereabouts you are.* **2.** n. Approximate place or position, locality, situation: *his present whereabouts is unknown.*

whereas, conj. [1. wâráz; 2. weərǽz]. **1.** Formula in opening legal documents, in consideration of the fact that, since, in view of specified circumstances: *whereas it hath seemed good to the King's Majesty.* **2.** When on the other hand, while; used in contrasting two statements: *whereas in her youth she was slim and beautiful, in later years she became fat and hideously ugly.*

whereat, adv. [1. wârát; 2. weərǽt]. **1.** (interrog., archaic and rare) At, about, what: *whereat was he annoyed?* **2.** (rel.) **a** At, about, which: *the things whereat you are displeased*; **b** upon which: '. . . *They vote: whereat his speech he thus renews*' (Milton, 'P. L.' ii. 389).

whereby, adv. [1. wârbī; 2. weəbái]. **1.** (interrog.) By what, by what means, how: *whereby may we be saved?* **2.** (rel.) By means of which: *a plan whereby we may escape.*

where'er, adv. [1. wârár; 2. weəréə]. Contracted fr. **wherever.** (poet.) Wherever.

wherefore, adv. & n. [1. wárfōr; 2. wέəfɔ̄]. **1.** adv. **a** (interrog.) For what reason, why: *wherefore do you weep?*; **b** (rel.) for which reason: *he was angry, wherefore I was afraid.* **2.** n. Reason, cause; in Phr. *the why and the wherefore.*

wherefrom, adv. [1. wârfróm; 2. weəfrɔ́m]. (rare) From which, whence.

wherein, adv. [1. wârín; 2. weərín]. **1.** (interrog.) In what point, respect, particular: *wherein do they differ?* **2.** (rel.) In which; in which place, respect, circumstance: *points wherein we differ.*

whereinsoever, adv. [1. wârìnsōéver; 2. weərìnsouévə]. Prec. & **so** & **ever.** In whatever respect, part &c.

whereinto, adv. [1. wàrintóō; 2. wèərintú]. **1.** (interrog.) Into what. **2.** (rel.) Into which: *the shelter whereinto he crept.*

whereof, adv. [1. wâróf; 2. weərɔ́f]. Of which, of what: *the matter whereof we spoke.*

whereon, adv. [1. wârón; 2. weərɔ́n]. **1.** (interrog.) Upon what: *whereon is your trust?* **2.** (rel.) On, upon, which: *the rock whereon the house is built.*

whereout, adv. [1. wâróut; 2. weəráut]. (rare) Out of which.

wheresoever, adv. [1. wàrsōéver; 2. wèərsouévə]. **where** & **so** & **ever.** Emphatic for **wherever.**

wherethrough, adv. [1. wârthróō; 2. weəþrú]. Through which.

whereto, adv. [1. wârtóō; 2. weətú]. **1.** (interrog.) For what, for what purpose? **2.** (rel.) **a** To which (place &c.): *the point whereto they hasten*; **b** to which (question, remark &c.): *he asked them their business, whereto they replied* &c.

whereunder, adv. [1. wârúnder; 2. weərándə]. (rare) Under which: *the trees whereunder they rested.*

whereunto, adv. [1. wàruntóō; 2. wèərantú]. Whereto.

whereupon, adv. [1. wàrupón; 2. wèərəpɔ́n]. **1.** (interrog.) Whereon, on what. **2.** (rel.) Upon which, after, in consequence of, following upon which: *they showed signs of yielding, whereupon we renewed the attack.*

wherever, adv. [1. wârévėr; 2. weərévə]. In, to, at, whatever place, in any place: *sit wherever you like*; *he will get lost wherever he goes.*

wherewith, adv. [1. wârwídh; 2. weəwíð]. **1.** (interrog., archaic) With what: *wherewith shall they be fed?* **2.** (rel., archaic) With which: *we have nothing wherewith to feed them.*

wherewithal, adv. & n. [1. wârwidhàwl; 2. wέəwiðɔ̀l]. **1.** adv. (archaic) Wherewith. **2.** n. Resources, esp. necessary money: *he lacked the wherewithal to bring up and educate his family.*

wherry, n. [1. wéri; 2. wéri]. Etymol. unknown. **1.** Light row-boat used for passengers on river, lake &c. **2.** Broad, heavy barge used on Norfolk Broads.

wherryman, n. [1. wériman; 2. wérimən]. Man in charge of a wherry.

whet (I.), vb. trans. [1. wet; 2. wet]. O.E. *hwettan*, 'to sharpen, make keen'; M.E. *whetten*; cp. O.H.G. *wezzan*; Goth. *(ga-)hwatjan*, 'to sharpen'; O.N. *hvetja*; fr. **hwatjan*, cp. O.E. *hwæt*, 'sharp, keen, active, brave'; O.S. *hwat*; O.H.G. *hwaz*; cogn. w. Lat. *(tri)quetrus*, 'three-cornered'. **1.** To sharpen, put an edge on (a knife, scythe &c.), esp. with a hone. **2.** To stimulate, excite (appetite, curiosity).

whet (II.), n., fr. prec. Act of whetting, **a** a knife &c.; **b** appetite &c.

whether (I.), pron. [1. wédher; 2. wéðə]. O.E. *hwæðer*; M.E. *w(h)eþer*, 'which of two'; cp. O.S. *hwethar*; O.H.G. *hwedar*; O.N. *hvárr*; Goth. *hwaþar*; fr. pronominal base seen in **who**, & **-ther.** Cp. Gk. *kóteros, póteros*, 'which of two'; Scrt. *kataráś*; Lith. *katràs*; O. Slav. *kotorŭ*, 'which'. (archaic or obs.) Which of the two.

whether (II.), conj., fr. prec. Expresses doubt, alternative possibility; correlative *or*, or *or whether*; in various constructions: *I don't know whether to go away or stay where I am*; *I wonder whether he will go himself or whether he will send you*; *I don't know whether it is raining or not*; *he asked whether he could help*; *whether we help or not, the enterprise will fail.* Phr. *whether or no*, in either case.

whetstone, n. [1. wétstōn; 2. wétstoun]. O.E. *hwetstān*; **whet** & **stone.** **a** Stone used for whetting, and putting sharp edge to knives, scythes &c.; **b** person who, problem, subject &c. which, provokes and stimulates mental action.

whey, n. [1. wā; 2. wei]. O.E. *hwæg*; M.E. *whei.* Clear watery liquid left when the curd is separated from milk, as by the action of rennet.

whey-faced, adj. [1. wā fàst; 2. wéi fèist]. Of sallow or pallid complexion through ill-health, fear &c.

which (I.), adj. [1. wich; 2. witʃ]. O.E. *hwelč* &c., 'which? of what sort? what kind of?' fr. *hwa-līc*, 'what like'; cp. O.S. *hwilīc*; O.H.G. *hwelīh*; Goth. *hwileiks*; see **who** & **like** (I.). **1.** (interrog.) What individual person or thing?, what group of persons or things?; used to demand selection, specification, identification, of one or more things from a number, class &c.: *which books did you choose?*; *which piece of cake will you have?*; *which teacher of all those you were under did you like best?* **2.** (rel., rare) The specific thing referred to: *he told me all he had suffered, which things were well-nigh incredible.*

which (II.), pron., fr. prec. **1.** (interrog.) In demanding selection, identification, specification, choice between two or more alternative persons, things &c.: *which of the members were present?*; *which is the right road?*; *which would you like?* Phr. *which is which?*, asking for more explicit distinction between two persons or things. **2.** (rel.) **a** (not used now in reference to persons) The thing, circumstance &c. referred to in an antecedent sentence or clause; that individual thing or group of things: *all the documents which I have examined are forgeries*; *this is the book which I chose*; *this fact, which I think you have forgotten, proves the contrary*; *I lost my way, which delayed me considerably*; Phr. (archaic) *the which*, which; **b** (archaic) referring to person(s), (chiefly Bib. and liturgical) *our Father, which art in heaven.*

whichever, adj. & pron. [1. wichéver; 2. witʃévə]. **which** & **ever.** (indef. rel.) Any individual from several persons or things specified: *I will take whichever piece you reject*; *pray take whichever suits you best.*

whichsoever, adj. & pron. [1. wìchsōéver; 2. wìtʃsouévə]. **which** & **so** & **ever.** (rare) Whichever (emphatic).

whidah-bird, n. [1. wída bẽrd; 2. wídə bȧd]. Apparently orig. *widow-bird*, later influenced by Place-Name *Whidah*, on W. African coast. West African weaver-bird, with black plumage, the male of which has tail-feathers twice its own length.

whiff (I.), n. [1. wif; 2. wif]. Imitative of sound of sniffing, inhaling, or the like. **1. a** A puff, a breath, slight gust: *a whiff of air, of sea-air*; **b** a light puff or breath of air having a characteristic odour; a slight odour: *I got a whiff of a good cigar as he passed*; *I thought I noticed a slight whiff of the stable about him.* Phr. *to take a whiff or two* (of a pipe &c.), to have a brief smoke. **2.** (colloq.) A small cigar.

whiff (II.), vb. intrans., fr. prec. To emit a slight, light, odour.

whiff (III.), n. Etymol. unknown. Light, outrigged sculling boat.

whiff (IV.), n. Etymol. unknown. A flat-fish, esp. a dab.

whiff (V.), vb. intrans. Etymol. unknown. To fish with hand-line from a moving boat, drawing the bait along near surface of water.

whiffle, vb. intrans. & trans. [1. wifl; 2. wifl]. **whiff** (I.) & **-le.** **a** intrans. (of wind &c.) To veer, blow lightly; **b** trans., to disperse, scatter, as with a puff of wind.

whiffy, adj. [1. wífi; 2. wífi]. **whiff** (I.) & **-y.** Emitting a slight, fitful, but unpleasant odour; smelly.

Whig, n. [1. wig; 2. wig], fr. obs. *Whiggamore*, nickname of Presbyterians in Scotland in 17th cent.; etymol. doubtful, possibly fr. Scot. *whig*, 'drive', & **mare** (II.). **1.** Member of the party, earlier called Roundheads, which during the 17th and early 18th cents. opposed the Royal prerogative and Episcopacy, upheld the supremacy of Parliament, and favoured toleration for Dissenters; later in the 18th cent. the Whigs were the party who opposed the Stuarts and supported the Hanoverian and Protestant succession. The Whigs developed in the 19th cent. into the Liberal party. The word expresses the antithesis of everything expressed by *Tory.* **2.** (chiefly derisive) A straight-laced, narrow-minded person who is, or is believed to be, a prey to trifling moral scruples, to be opposed to mirth and conviviality.

Whiggery, n. [1. wígeri; 2. wígəri]. Prec. & **-ery.** (contemptuous) The political principles, moral attitude, of Whigs.

Whiggish, adj. [1. wígish; 2. wígiʃ]. **Whig** & **-ish.** Pertaining to, characteristic of, a Whig; savouring of Whiggery.

Whiggishly, adv. Prec. & **-ly.** After the manner of a Whig.

Whiggishness, n. See prec. &-**ness**. Whiggish state of mind, principles, practice.

Whiggism, n. [1. wígizm; 2. wígizəm]. **Whig** & **-ism.** Doctrine, principles, of the Whigs.

while (**I.**), n. [1. wīl; 2. wail]. O.E. *hwīl*, 'space of time', M.E. *whīl*; O.H.G. *hwīla*; Goth. *hweila*; O.N. *hvīla*, 'space of time'; cogn. w. Lat. *quiēs*, 'rest', see **quiet**; (*tran*)*quillus*, 'quiet', see **tranquil.** Space of time, period: *to stay for a while*; *to rest a while*; *it took a long while to do*; *a while ago*; *in a little while*, soon; *once in a while*, occasionally. Phrs. *the while*, during that time, at the same time: *he went about his work and sang the while*: *worth one's while*, repaying one for time and trouble bestowed; *to make it worth one's while*, to reward, pay one adequately; (also in pejorative sense) to bribe.

while (**II.**), vb. trans., fr. prec., but prob. confused or associated w. **wile.** *While away* (*time*), to spend, cause to pass in such a way as to reduce the tedium.

while (**III.**), conj., fr. **while** (**I.**). **1.** During the time that; as long as: *sit down while you are waiting*; *it was raining while we were out*; *the lark sings while on the wing*; at a moment in the space of time that: *he had an accident while on the way here.* **2.** Though, at the same time (implying a contrast): *he became an earl, while his brother was only made a knight.*

whiles, conj. [1. wīlz; 2. wailz]. O.E. *hwīles*, genit. of *hwīl*; see **while.** (archaic) While.

whilom, adv. & adj. [1. wílum; 2. wáiləm]. O.E. *hwīlum*, 'in the times, at times', dat. pl. of *hwīl*, 'time'; used as adv.; see **while** (**I.**). (archaic) **1.** adv. At one time, formerly. **2.** attrib. adj. Former, quondam.

whilst, conj. [1. wīlst; 2. wailst]. Earlier *whiles*, advbl. genit. of **while** (**I.**), & *-t*, for addition of wh. cp. **amongst.** While.

whim, n. [1. wim; 2. wim], fr. O.N. *hvīma*, 'to let the eyes wander'; connected w. Norw. *kvima*, 'to flutter', cp. **whimsy. 1.** A passing fancy; a trifling desire, an irresponsible caprice; a fad, a crotchet. **2.** Winch for use in a vertical mine-shaft.

whimbrel, n. [1. wímbrel; 2. wímbrəl]. Earlier *whimrel*, fr. imitation of bird's cry, & dimin. suff. *-rel.* Species of small curlew, the jack curlew.

whimper (**I.**), vb. intrans. & trans. [1. wímper; 2. wímpə]. Prob. imitative; cp. Mod. Germ. *wimmern*, 'to whimper'. **1.** intrans. To cry weakly, fretfully, plaintively; to utter feeble cries, as of a frightened child or young animal. **2.** trans. (rare) To utter in a whimpering voice.

whimper (**II.**), n., fr. prec. Feeble, fretful cry, wail, whine.

whimpering, adj. [1. wímpering; 2. wímpəriŋ]. **whimper** (**I.**) & **-ing.** Inclined to whimper; resembling, of the nature of, a whimper.

whimperingly, adv. Prec. & **-ly.** With, in, a whimper.

whimsical, adj. [1. wímzikl; 2. wímzikl]. **whimsy** & **-ic** & **-al. 1.** Given to whimsies, capricious, fanciful. **2.** Quaint, fantastic.

whimsicality, n. [1. wìmzikáliti; 2. wìmzikǽliti]. Prec. & **-ity. 1.** Quality of being whimsical (in both senses of adj.). **2. a** Caprice, fad, crotchet; **b** a quaint, original fancy.

whimsically, adv. [1. wímzikali; 2. wímzikəli]. **whimsical** & **-ly.** In a whimsical manner.

whimsy, n. [1. wímzi; 2. wímzi]. Connected w. Norw. *kvimsa*, 'to skip', fr. *kvima*, 'to flutter', cp. also **whim.** Capricious idea, freak, whim.

whimwham, n. [1. wímwam; 2. wímwæm]. Redupl. form of **whim.** (archaic) **1.** Whimsical idea; a whimsy, a fad, a crotchet. **2.** Toy, trifle, plaything.

whin (**I.**), n. [1. win; 2. win]. Cp. Norw. *hvin*, a kind of grass. Gorse; gorse bushes.

whin (**II.**), n. Etymol. unknown. One of several varieties of hard basaltic rock, also called greenstone, trap, &c.; diabase; used for roadmaking.

whinberry, n. [1. wínberi; 2. wínbəri], fr. O.E. *winberig*, 'grape'. **wine** & **berry**, influenced by **whin** (**I.**). Whortleberry.

whin-chat, whinchat, n. [1. wínchat; 2. wíntʃæt]. Small brown and reddish bird, allied to the wheatear.

whine (**I.**), vb. intrans. & trans. [1. wīn; 2. wain]. O.E. *hwīnan*, 'to shriek', esp. of an arrow &c. flying through the air; M.E. *whīnen*; cp. O.N. *hvīna*, 'to whirr'; Dan. *hvine*, 'to shriek'. **1.** intrans. **a** (of animal, esp. dog, or of child) To utter prolonged wailing cry; **b** (of person) to complain, esp. about trifles; to utter constant, fretful, childish complaints. **2.** trans. To utter in whining tone.

whine (**II.**), n., fr. prec. **1.** Prolonged, wailing, plaintive cry of dog, child &c. **2.** Fretful, childish complaint.

whinger, n. [1. wínger; 2. wíŋə]. Origin doubtful; perh. connected w. **whine**, & imitative of sound of stroke. Dagger or short sword.

whining, adj. [1. wīning; 2. wáiniŋ], fr. Pres. Part. of **whine.** Habitually complaining; snivelling: *a whining rascal*; uttered with or in a whine.

whiningly, adv. Prec. & **-ly.** In a whining manner.

whinny, vb. intrans. & n. [1. wíni; 2. wíni], fr. **whine** (**I.**). **1.** vb. (of horse) To neigh gently and playfully. **2.** n. A gentle neigh of a horse, expressive of pleasure, friendly greeting &c.

whinsill, n. [1. wínsil; 2. wínsil]. **whin** (**II.**) & **sill.** (geol.) Sheet of intrusive basalt.

whinstone, n. [1. wínstōn; 2. wínstoun]. Same as **whin** (**II.**).

whinyard, n. [1. wínyard; 2. wínjəd]. (obs.) Variant of **whinger**, with ending suggested by *poniard.*

whip (**I.**), vb. trans. & intrans. [1. wip; 2. wip]. M.E. *whippen*; cp. M. Du. *wippe*, 'to skip'; Mod. Germ. *wippen*, fr. L.G. source, 'to move up & down'; O.H.G. *wipf*, 'swing'; M.H.G. *wīfen*, 'to swing'; cogn. w. Lith. *wýbur-iu*, 'to oscillate'; Lat. *vibrāre*, 'to swing, shake', see **vibrate**; see also **wimple. A.** trans. **1. a** To apply a whip to, to strike with a lash: *to whip a horse*; Phr. *to whip up one's horse*, cause to start or to increase pace by whipping; **b** to strike with a pliable stick; to flog in any way, as incitement or punishment &c.: *to whip a naughty child* &c.; Phrs. *to whip eggs*, whisk them into a froth; *to whip a stream*, to fish with a fly, continually throwing the line over a piece of water; **c** to effect, remove &c. by whipping; *to whip sense into, the nonsense out of, a child* &c.; **d** (hunting) to control (hounds) by means of whip &c., esp. in Phr. *to whip in, off* &c.; hence transferred to control of members of political party in House of Commons &c. **2.** (colloq.) To defeat, overcome, beat. **3.** To bind, lash (rope, rope-end &c.), by wrapping in repeated coils of twine &c. **4.** To join, fasten (seam, frill &c.) by oversewing rolled edges. **B.** intrans. **1.** To use a whip &c. for beating, flogging &c. **2.** To move with great rapidity and suddenness: *he whipped upstairs in a flash.* **C.** Followed by preposition or adverb. *Whip out*, **1.** trans., **a** to draw, pull, snatch, out with a sudden swift action: *to whip out a knife*; **b** to utter suddenly and violently, rap out: *to whip out an oath, a reply* &c.; **2.** intrans., to make a hasty exit: *to whip out of a door. Whip off*, **1.** trans., **a** to snatch suddenly away: *to whip a cloth off the table*; **b** to carry away, cause to accompany one in a sudden swift departure: *he whipped me off to play bridge*; **c** to drive away by whipping; **2.** intrans., to depart hastily, or with sudden, rapid motion: *to whip off to the continent. Whip round*, intrans., to turn round suddenly and swiftly: *he had his back to me but whipped round in a second when I shouted. Whip up*, trans., **a** to make (horse) start, or increase speed, by whipping; **b** to seize with a sudden grab, to snatch up: *to whip up a pistol and shoot an intruder*; **c** to gather, collect: *to whip up an audience, subscriptions.*

whip (**II.**), n., fr. prec. **1.** Object consisting of lash attached either to a long, pliant, or to a short, stiff, handle, for delivering blows as punishment or to incite (animal &c.) to increased effort. **2.** Driver (of horses), esp. in Phr. *a good, an accomplished, whip.* **3.** Hunt servant controlling hounds in hunting-field. **4.** (Parliament) **a** Person appointed by a party to enforce discipline among, ensure attendance of, members at voting time, meetings of committees &c.; the chief whip of the Government is the Patronage Secretary of the Treasury; **b** message, appeal, issued by a party whip to members to attend sessions, divisions &c. of Parliament: *a three-line whip*, underlined three times, as sign of urgency; also any urgent appeal to action to supporters of a cause &c. **5.** Whip-and-derry.

whip-and-derry, n. [1. wíp an(d) déri; 2. wíp ən(d) déri]. See **derrick.** Hoisting apparatus consisting of rope and pulley.

whip-cord, n. **1.** Hard, tightly twisted cord made of hemp and used for whip-lashes. **2.** A strong, tough woven fabric with ribs resembling whip-cord.

whip-fish, n. Fish having a dorsal spine elongated into a long filament.

whip-gin, n. Block for use in whip-and-derry apparatus.

whip-hand, n. Hand used to hold whip. Phr. *to have the whip-hand of*, have control of, mastery over, the upper hand of.

whipper-in, n. [1. wíper ín; 2. wípər ín]. Hunt official managing hounds; whip.

whipper-snapper, n. [1. wíper snáper; 2. wípə snǽpə]. Small, insignificant but uppish person; one who is negligible in mind, person, and standing, but yet is inclined to be impudent and presuming.

whippet, n. [1. wípet; 2. wípit]. Etymol. doubtful. **1.** Small, cross-bred, greyhound-like dog used for racing. **2.** Light, small, armoured army tank capable of rapid movement.

whipping, n. [1. wíping; 2. wípiŋ]. **whip** (**I.**) & **-ing. 1. a** Punishment inflicted with a whip or stick; a thrashing; **b** a defeat inflicted in a contest or match of any kind; a beating. **2.** Lashing of twine securing end of rope &c.

whipping-boy, n. (hist.) Boy formerly educated with, and taking chastisement in place of, a prince or child of exalted birth.

whipping-post, n. Stake &c. to which a malefactor is bound to receive a flogging.

whipping-top, n. Child's top kept spinning by lashing with whip.

whipple-tree, n. [1. wípl trē; 2. wípl trī], fr. **whip** (**I.**), 'to move up and down, to and fro'. The movable bar of a cart, plough &c. to which the traces of a horse are hitched; swingle-tree.

whip-poor-will, n. [1. wìporwíl; 2. wìpəwíl]. Imitative of bird's cry. Small, American nocturnal bird allied to goatsucker or night-jar.

whippy, adj. [1. wípi; 2. wípi]. **whip** (**II.**) & **-y.** Resembling a long-handled whip in slenderness and pliancy; hence, slender, inclined to bend along the whole length; reverse of *stiff* or *stocky.*

whipster, n. [1. wípster; 2. wípstə]. **whip** & **-ster.** Insignificant person.

whir(**r**), vb. intrans. & n. [1. wěr; 2. wʌ̄]. Prob. imitative; but cp. Dan. *hvirre*, 'to whirl', cogn. w. **whirl. 1.** vb. **a** To revolve, vibrate, move, with great rapidity; **b** to produce a buzzing sound by such movement. **2.** n. **a** Rapid rotating or vibratory motion; **b** sound produced by this.

whirl (**I.**), vb. intrans. & trans. [1. wěrl; 2. wʌ̄l]. M.E. *whirlen*, fr. O.N. *hvirfla*, 'to whirl'; cp. M. Du. *werveleln*; M.H.G. *wirbelen*, 'to whirl, rotate'; O.N. *hvirfill*, 'circle'; O.H.G. *wirbel*, 'whirlwind'; cp. further O.E. *hweorfan*, 'to turn', see **wharf**; cp. also, w. different formative element, Lat.

vertere, 'to turn'; see **version** & words there referred to. **A.** intrans. **1.** To rotate, spin, gyrate, rapidly, on an axis: *a whirling top; the sails of the windmill whirl round and round.* **2.** To pass quickly along a circular course, move swiftly in an orbit: *the horses whirled round the circus-ring; dancers whirl round a ballroom.* **3.** (of vehicle or person in vehicle) To move swiftly, spin, dash: *the carriage whirled out of sight.* **4. a** (of brain) To be giddy, confused, bewildered; to reel; **b** (of thoughts &c.) to be in confusion, throng swiftly and disconnectedly. **B.** trans. **1.** To cause to revolve, rotate, move swiftly about a centre or point, or in a more or less circular course: *he whirled his stick about his head; he whirled his partner off round the room; the wind whirled the snowflakes in eddies.* **2.** To convey rapidly (implying revolving or eddying motion, of wheeled vehicle &c.): *the cart whirled him down the hill.*

whirl (II.), n., fr. prec. **a** Whirling motion, rapid revolution; **b** (fig.) confusion of mind, bewilderment: *my thoughts are, brain is, in a whirl.*

whirl-bone, n. Ball-and-socket joint.

whirligig, n. [1. wĕrligìg; 2. wálĭgìg]. **whirl** (I.) & **gig**. **1. a** Mechanical device, toy &c. designed to rotate rapidly on an axis; specif. **b** a merry-go-round. **2.** (fig.) That which passes with rapid changes or revolutions: *the whirligig of time* &c. **3.** Water-beetle, of bright, metallic appearance, moving in swift circles to catch its prey.

whirling-table, n. [1. wĕrling tàbl; 2. wálĭŋ tèibl]. Apparatus for demonstrating effects of centrifugal force.

whirlpool, n. [1. wĕrlpōōl; 2. wálpūl]. Violent, rapid, movement of water in a circular sweep; rapid, circular eddy.

whirlwind, n. [1. wĕrlwind; 2. wálwind]. Swift, circular movement of cylindrical or funnel-shaped column of air.

whirr. See **whir(r)**.

whisk (I.), n. [1. wisk; 2. wisk]. Cp. Dan. *viske*; cp. Mod. Germ. *wischen*, 'to wipe'; O.H.G. *wisk*, 'wisp'; & further, O.E. *weoxian*, 'to wipe down a horse'; cogn. w. Lat. *virga*, 'rod', see **virgate**. **1.** Small bunch of light twigs, bristles, straw, feathers &c. for use as brush; sometimes in compounds: *fly-whisk* &c. **2.** Light, metal instrument for beating eggs, cream &c. to a froth.

whisk (II.), vb. trans. & intrans., fr. prec. **A.** trans. **1.** Usually *whisk off, away*, **a** to remove, flick off, with light, brushing movement, sweep lightly and briskly: *to whisk flies away; whisk crumbs off one's coat;* **b** to carry off, cause to accompany one, with impetuous, rapid action: *they whisked him off to see the sights.* **2.** To wave, sweep, twitch lightly and quickly through the air: *the cow whisked her tail.* **3.** To beat, agitate, lightly, whip: *to whisk eggs, cream* &c. **B.** intrans. To move, esp. depart, disappear, with rapid, abrupt, motion: *to whisk round, out of sight, out of the room* &c.

whisk (III.), n., fr. prec. Sudden, light, sweeping movement: *with a whisk of the tail.*

whisker, n. [1. wísker; 2. wískə]. **whisk** (I.) & **-er**. **1.** Usually pl., *whiskers*, hair growing on the sides of a man's face. **2.** (usually pl.) The long bristles growing at side of mouth of cat, tiger &c.

whiskered, adj. [1. wískerd; 2. wískəd]. Prec. & **-ed**. Having, wearing, whiskers.

whiskey, n. See **whisky**.

whiskified, adj. [1. wískifìd; 2. wískifaid]. Next word & **-fy** & **-ed**. (colloq.) Under the influence of, affected by, whisky.

whisky (I.), also **whiskey**, n. [1. wíski; 2. wiski], fr. Gael. *uisge-(beatha)*, see **usquebaugh**. Alcoholic liquor obtained by the distillation of malted grain, esp. barley.

whisky (II.), n., fr. **whisk** (I.). Light, two-wheeled vehicle; gig.

whisky-jack, n. Canadian jay.

whisky-liver, n. Alcoholic disease of liver; cirrhosis.

whisky-toddy, n. Hot whisky and water; usually flavoured with lemon and sugar.

whisper (I.), vb. intrans. & trans. [1. wísper; 2. wíspə]. O.E. *hwisprian*; M.E. *whispren*; cp. M. Du. *wisperen*; cp. Mod. Germ. *wispern*; O.H.G. *wispalōn*, 'to whisper'; also w. different formative element, O.N. *hvīsta*, 'to whisper'; *hvissa*, 'to buzz'; cogn. w. O. Slav. *svistati*, 'to whisper'. **A.** intrans. **1. a** To speak in a low voice, without the resonance produced by vibration of the vocal chords; **b** (specif. phon.) to utter speech-sounds with a definite contraction of the glottis, differing from the condition in *voice* on the one hand, and in *breath* on the other. **2.** (poet., of breeze, leaves &c.) To make a faint sound, suggestive of whispering, by gentle motion; to murmur, rustle. **B.** trans. **1. a** To utter (words, sounds) in a whisper; **b** (fig.) to tell as a secret, or as something not to be revealed. **2.** To put about furtively, circulate as a rumour: *the strangest things were whispered concerning him.*

whisper (II.), n., fr. prec. **1. a** Act of whispering; subdued speech, uttered without vibration of vocal chords: *to speak in a whisper;* **b** (specif. phon.) articulation produced with a slight but definite contraction of the glottis. **2. a** That which is whispered; remark &c. made in a whisper; **b** rumour, secret communication. **3.** Gentle rustling, murmuring sound, of leaves, wind &c.

whisperer, n. [1. wísperer; 2. wíspərə]. **whisper** (I.) & **-er**. **a** One who whispers; **b** a tale-bearer, a privy gossip.

whispering (I.), n. [1. wíspering; 2. wíspəriŋ]. **whisper** (I.) & **-ing**. Whispered speech.

whispering (II.), adj., fr. Pres. Part. of **whisper** (I.). Speaking in, producing, a whisper.

whispering-gallery, n. Gallery, usually in a dome, where, owing to the construction, a sound uttered without any great resonance travels a considerable distance; there is a well-known example of this in the dome of St. Paul's Cathedral.

whisperingly, adv. [1. wísperingli; 2. wíspəriŋli]. **whispering** (II.) & **-ly**. In a whisper; in a manner resembling a whisper.

whist, whisht (I.), interj. & vb. intrans. [1. wist, wisht; 2. wist, wiʃt]. Conventionalized imitation of natural sound. **1.** interj. Exclamation of warning, to demand silence. **2.** vb. To be silent; to cease speaking.

whist (II.), n. [1. wist; 2. wist]. Earlier **whisk**, fr. quick movements of players in taking cards fr. table. Game of cards played by two pairs of players with pack of 52 cards, in which ten, five, points are required for game; *progressive whist*, a number of games of whist played simultaneously at different tables, one or more players from each passing at intervals to the next.

whist-drive, n. Social function at which progressive whist is played.

whistle (I.), vb. intrans. & trans. [1. wísl; 2. wísl]. O.E. *hwistlian*; M.E. *whistlen*, 'to whistle'; imitative; cp. O.N. *hvīsla, hvīsta*, 'to whisper'; perh. connected w. **whisper**. **A.** intrans. **1.** To produce a shrill, clear, piping note, or sound, or a series of such notes; **a** (of human beings) by pursing up the lips and forcing the air through them, altering the note by changing position of the tongue; **b** (of birds) by forcing air through the beak; **c** (of mechanical device) by forcing air or steam through a narrow aperture. **2.** Specif. (of human beings) to produce a series of characteristic musical notes, or a tune, by whistling. **3.** (of moving body) To produce a clear, shrill sound by rapid passage through the air: *the bullets whistled round our ears.* **4.** (of wind) To produce a shrill, clear, continuous sound by blowing through a narrow chink or aperture. **B.** trans. **1.** To utter, produce (an air), by whistling: *to whistle a tune.* **2.** To summon by whistling: *to whistle a dog back.*

whistle (II.), n., fr. prec. **1.** Shrill, clear, piping sound produced by whistling. **2.** Device, instrument, for producing such a sound: *penny whistle*, small *tin whistle; steam whistle*, with sound produced by jet of steam. Phr. *to pay for one's whistle*, pay dearly for insignificant action or object. **3.** Throat, esp. in slang Phr. *to wet one's whistle*, to drink.

whistler, n. [1. wísler; 2. wíslə]. **whistle** (I.) & **-er**. One who, that which, whistles; specif. **a** broken-winded horse, producing a whistling sound in breathing; **b** one of several species of birds.

whistling, adj. & vbl. n. [1. wísling; 2. wísliŋ], fr. Pres. Part. of **whistle** (I.). **1.** adj. Producing a sound resembling a whistle; esp. as descriptive epithet for bird or animal, e.g. *whistling duck, eagle, marmot, thrush* &c. **2.** n., fr. **whistle** (I.) & **-ing**. The sound produced by person who, or thing which, whistles: *the whistling of the wind.*

whit (I.), n. [1. wit; 2. wit]. O.E. *wiht*, 'thing, creature'; M.E. *wight*; cp. O.S., O.H.G. *wiht*; Goth. *waihts*, O.N. *vætt*, 'thing'; cogn. w. O. Slav. *vešti*, 'thing'; cp. **wight**. Smallest amount, minute particle, jot; chiefly in Phrs. *not a whit, no whit.*

Whit (II.), **Whitsun**, adj. [1. wít(sun); 2. wít(sən)], fr. M.E. *hwīte (sunnedei)*, lit. 'white Sunday', fr. the white robes worn by persons to be baptized, christenings being most numerous on this day. Of, pertaining to, following, Whitsunday; only in Phrs. *Whit Monday, Tuesday; Whit week; Whitsun week.*

white (I.), adj. [1. wīt; 2. wait]. O.E. *hwīt*; M.E. *whīt*; cp. O.S. *hwīt*; O.H.G. *hwīz*; O.N. *hvītr*; Goth. *hweits*, 'white'; cogn. w. Scrt. *çvitrá*, *çvētáś*, 'white, light'; O. Slav. *světŭ*, 'light'; Lith. *szvaitýti*, 'to brighten'. **1.** Having the colour of unstained snow; or the luminous appearance of sunlight reflected from a surface without the absorption of any of the visible rays of the spectrum; colourless; opposed to *black*; largely, partly, or nearly white: *as white as snow; white clouds; white hair*, having lost its colour and become silvery, esp. through age; *white meat*, poultry, rabbit, veal. **2.** (of animal, bird, plant &c.) Entirely or partly white, or with characteristic white markings: *white crab, goat, poplar, owl, wagtail* &c. Phr. *a white crow*, a rarity. **3. a** Of fair complexion, of the colouring of the Caucasian race as distinct from the yellow, brown, red, and black races: *the white races; a white man*, (also fig., colloq.) honourable, sincere, man; **b** pale, pallid, through illness, fatigue, fear &c. **4.** (of wine) Of clear, amber or golden colour, contrasted with *red*. **5.** Beneficent, working or used for good purpose: *white magic; a white witch*; contrasted with *black*.

white (II.), n., fr. prec. **1.** White or whitish colour. **2.** White pigment, often with qualifying epithet, *flake-, zinc-white; Chinese, Dutch, white* &c. **3.** White object, substance, matter; specif. **a** white fabric: *to dress in white;* **b** also *white of egg*, colourless, albuminous liquid surrounding yolk of egg; **c** white part of cornea surrounding iris of eye; **d** white butterfly, esp. the cabbage butterfly. **4.** Member of fair-skinned, Caucasian race; white man. **5.** (pl.) *Whites*, leucorrhoea.

white (III.), vb. trans., fr. **white** (I.). (archaic) To whiten, make white.

white-, pref. representing **white** (I.), forming adjectival compounds descriptive of bird, animal, insect &c.; e.g. *white-crested, -necked, -tailed* &c., having a white crest, neck, tail &c.

white alloy, n. White metal.

white ant, n. Termite.

whitebait, n. [1. wītbāt; 2. wáitbeit]. Fry of several varieties of edible fish, sprat, herring &c., eaten as a delicacy.

whitebeam, n. [1. wītbēm; 2. wáitbīm]. Flowering shrub or small tree, *Sorbus aria*, with whitish down on lower surface of leaves.

white bear, n. Polar bear.

whiteboy, n. [1. wītboi; 2. wáitbɔi]. Member of white-robed gang of Irish agricultural agitators of 18th cent.

white-cap, n. The redstart.
white-caps, n. pl. Foam-crested waves.
Whitechapel cart, n. [1. wítchapl kárt; 2. wáittʃæpl kắt], fr. Whitechapel in East End of London. Tradesman's light, two-wheeled cart.
white corpuscle, n. Leucocyte.
white currant, n. Variety of *Ribes*, with glistening, whitish berries.
white elephant, n. a Light grey variety of elephant venerated in Burma and Siam; b unwanted, burdensome possession.
white ensign, n. St. George's red cross on a white ground, the flag of Royal Navy; cp. *red ensign.*
white feather, n. Symbol of cowardice.
white fish, n. Fish which have white flesh and are not oily; i.e. excluding salmon, mackerel &c.
white flag, n. Symbol of surrender or truce.
White Friar, n. Carmelite.
white-gum, n. Infant's white rash.
Whitehall, n. [1. wít-hawl; 2. wáithōl]. Street in London where many Government offices are situated. a British Government; b (fig.) departmental government.
white-handed, adj. Having white hands; (fig.) innocent, unspotted, blameless.
white-heart (-cherry), n. Large yellowish-white variety of cherry.
white heat, n. Temperature at which metals become white; also fig. of passion, enthusiasm &c.
white-horses, n. pl. Foam-crested waves, white-caps.
white-hot, adj. (of metal &c.) Raised to white heat; also fig. of enthusiasm &c.
White House, n. Official residence of President of U.S.A. at Washington.
white-iron, n. **1.** Thin sheets of iron coated with tin. **2.** A brittle variety of cast-iron.
white-land, n. Soil consisting of whitish clay.
white lead, n. Pigment made of lead carbonate and hydrated lead oxide.
white light, n. Natural, colourless sunlight.
white-lipped, adj. Having pallid lips, through fear, illness &c.
white-livered, adj. [1. wít liverd; 2. wáit livəd]. Cowardly.
whitely, adv. [1. wítli; 2. wáitli]. **white (I.) & -ly.** With a white appearance.
white metal, n. Pewter, or any other alloy of silvery appearance.
whiten, vb. trans. & intrans. [1. wítn; 2. wáitn]. **white (I.) & -en. 1.** trans. To make, cause to grow, white, give white colour to. **2.** intrans. To become, grow, turn, white, assume white appearance.
whiteness, n. [1. wítnes; 2. wáitnis]. **white (I.) & -ness.** State or quality of being white.
whitening, n. [1. wítning; 2. wáitniŋ]. **whiten & -ing.** Dried and prepared chalk for use in whitewash, for polishing &c.; also *whiting.*
white paper, n. Government report giving information on specific subject.
white rent, n. Annual tax on tinners in Devon and Cornwall, payable to the Prince of Wales as lord of the Duchy of Cornwall.
white sheet, n. Garb of penitent, esp. in Phr. *to stand in a white sheet,* make confession.
white slave, n. Girl entrapped, and usually exported, as prostitute; also attrib., *white-slave traffic.*
whitesmith, n. [1. wítsmith; 2. wáitsmiþ]. Tradesman working in tin, silver &c.
white squall, n. Sudden squall at sea, arising in fine weather, without clouds.
white-thorn, n. Hawthorn.
white-throat, n. Small European warbler.
whitewash (I.), n. [1. wítwosh; 2. wáitwɔʃ]. **1.** Solution of lime, white when dry, used to coat walls &c. of rooms, outhouses &c. **2.** (fig.) Mode of description, report &c. designed to clear, justify, person's name, actions &c.
whitewash (II.), vb. trans., fr. prec. **1.** To coat, daub, with whitewash. **2.** (fig.) To attempt to rehabilitate (person or his character) by explaining away, or putting favourable interpretation upon, bad actions, concealing defects, setting good qualities in high relief &c. **3.** To free from debt by passing through bankruptcy court.
whither (I.), adv. [1. wídher; 2. wíðə]. O.E. *hwider,* M.E. *whider*; fr. pronominal base seen in **who, & -ther**; cp. **whether. 1.** (interrog.) To or towards what place, in what direction: *whither did they go?* **2.** (introducing dependent clause) To the place which, to any place that: *let him go whither he will.*
whither (II.), pron., fr. prec. (rel.) To or towards which: *the place whither they went.*
whither (III.), n., fr. prec. Place to which one goes, is going; destination: *we know not the whence nor the whither of our destinies.*
whithersoever, adv. [1. wídhersōèver; 2. wíðəsouèvə]. **whither & so & ever.** (archaic) To whatever place, in any direction whatever.
whitherward, adv. [1. wídherward; 2. wíðəwəd]. **whither & -ward.** (archaic) In which or what direction, towards what point.
whiting (I.), n. [1. wíting; 2. wáitiŋ]. **white (III.) & -ing.** Dried, purified, and powdered chalk for polishing, making colour-wash &c.
whiting (II.), n. **white (I.) & -ing.** Small, edible, European sea-fish, *Gadus merlangus,* of the cod family.
whiting-pout, n. Fish with inflatable membrane over the eyes.
whitish, adj. [1. wítish; 2. wáitiʃ]. **white (I.) & -ish.** Fairly white.
whitleather, n. [1. wítledher; 2. wítlɛðə]. **white (I.) & leather.** Leather whitened by dressing with alum.
whitlow, n. [1. wítlō; 2. wítlou]. M.E. *whit(f)lawe,* influenced by **white,** O.N. *kwika,* 'quick below the nail', see **quick (III.), & flaw (I.).** Earlier *quick-(f)lawe.* Small, inflamed tumour, usually below the skin, on the end-joint of a finger.
whitlow-grass, n. Small, white-flowered cruciferous plant.
Whit Monday, n. Day after Whitsunday, an English Bank Holiday.
Whitsun. See **Whit (II.).**
Whitsunday, n. [1. witsúndi; 2. witsándi]. O.E. *on hwītan Sunnan dæg,* M.E. *hwīte sunnedei,* see **Whit (II.) & Sunday.** Seventh Sunday after Easter, commemorating the descent of the Holy Spirit on the Day of Pentecost.
Whitsuntide, n. [1. wítsuntīd; 2. wítsəntàid]. **Whitsun & tide.** Week-end or week including Whitsunday.
Whitsun week, n. Week beginning with Whitsunday.
whittle (I.), n. [1. witl; 2. witl]. M.E. *þwitel,* 'whittle, jack-knife', fr. O.E. *þwītan,* 'to cut up', & **-le.** Cp. O.N. *þveitr,* 'enclosed piece of land', see **thwaite.** Large sheath-knife or butcher's knife.
whittle (II.), vb. trans. & intrans., fr. prec. **A.** trans. **1.** To pare, slice thin shavings off (piece of wood), with a knife. **2.** To construct (object) by carving and trimming piece of wood &c. **3.** (fig.) To reduce gradually in amount: *to whittle down a person's salary; to whittle down a statement,* to weaken, destroy force of; also *whittle away* (a doctrine), to minimize its significance, explain it away. **B.** intrans. To shape, trim, carve, a piece of wood into desired shape by slicing shavings with a knife.
whity, whitey, adj. [1. wíti; 2. wáiti]. **white (I.) & -y.** Fairly white; whitish; sometimes in compounds: *whity-brown* &c., white tinged with brown.
whiz(z), n. & vb. intrans. [1. wiz; 2. wiz]. Imitative. **1.** n. Humming and hissing sound produced by body flying rapidly through the air. **2.** vb. To rush through the air at great speed, producing a hissing or buzzing sound in the passing.
whizzbang, n. [1. wízbang; 2. wízbæŋ]. Prec. & **bang (I.)**; imitative. (mil. slang) A light, high velocity shell, the sound of approach and explosion being almost simultaneous.
who, pron. [1. hōō; 2. hū]. O.E. *hwā,* M.E. *hwō, hō*; cp. Goth. *hwa*; O. Swed. *hvar*; O.H.G. *hwer,* 'who'; fr. Aryan **kʷo-* &c.' & cogn. w. Gk. *pê, pôs,* 'how'; *póthi,* 'where', fr. **kʷo-*; Scrt. *kaś,* 'who'; O. Slav. *kŭto*; Lith. *kàs,* 'who'; Lat. *quod,* 'that'; cp. also Lat. *quis,* 'who'; Scrt. *kím*; O. Slav. *čĭto,* 'what'; Gk. *tís,* 'who?'; all fr. stem **kʷo-, *kʷi-, *kʷoi-* &c., 'who? what', in many pronominal & advbl. forms, see **what, when, whether, where, why. 1.** (interrog.) What or which person: *who is there?; who(m) did you see?; who do you think you are?; who was he speaking to?; whose ugly face is that?; whose is it?* **2.** (rel.) a That person, the one mentioned in preceding clause or sentence: *the man who was here is an artist; I don't know the people who live next door; is there anyone who can be trusted?; I know the man whom you mean; that is the boy whose head was punched; he struck his opponent, who promptly returned the blow*; b (in elliptical constructions) the person(s) that, any person(s) that, he that: *who delays, pays; whom the gods would destroy, they first make mad.*
whoa. See **wo.**
whoe'er, pron. [1. hōōār; 2. hūέə]. Contracted form of next word. (poet.) Whoever.
whoever, pron. [1. hōōéver; 2. hūévə]. **who & ever.** (rel., indef., without antecedent expressed) Who, the person, any person, anybody, be he who he may, that: *whoever comes first may have it; give it to who(m)ever you like; whose-ever it is, you must return it.*
whole (I.), adj. [1. hōl; 2. houl]. O.E. *hāl,* M.E. *hōl*; cp. O.S., O. Fris. *hēl*; O.H.G. *heil*; O.N. *heili*; Goth. *hails,* 'complete, whole, sound'; cogn. w. O. Prussian *kailūstikan,* 'health'; O. Slav. *cĕlŭ,* 'complete'. The spelling *w-, wh-,* wh. is fairly common in scattered examples in the 16th cent., seems to express a variant dialectal pronunciation long since extinct except in certain provinc. forms. See also **hale (I.), heal, health, holy. 1.** In a sound condition of health; intact; not injured or diseased: '*the multitude wondered, when they saw . . . the maimed to be whole*' (Matt. xv. 31); *lucky to get off with a whole skin.* **2.** Complete in all its parts, unbroken, unimpaired; intact, entire: *not a single whole cup or saucer in the house.* **3.** All of anything, including every part, complete, undivided, without subtraction of any element or aspect: *whole cities were destroyed; the whole country was swept by a violent storm; I can't deal now with the whole question, but must select one or two points; one's whole mind, energies &c.; to eat a whole sheep at a sitting; to roast an ox whole,* without cutting it up. Phr. *to go the whole hog,* to do a thing thoroughly, hold an opinion with complete conviction; to be whole-hearted, go all lengths.
whole (II.), n., fr. prec. **1.** All there is; every part, member, aspect; the complete sum, amount, quantity, of anything; the entirety: *the whole is greater than its parts; the whole of one's property, family &c.; the whole of the affairs of state devolve upon him; the whole of the Christian religion.* **2.** A unity, an undivided, unbroken individual entity with all parts duly proportioned, adjusted, and interrelated; a complete system: *the Catholic faith is a whole, and cannot be divided into a number of separate and distinct tenets.* Phr. *on the whole,* all things considered.
whole-bound, adj. (of book) Bound entirely in leather.
whole-coloured, adj. Entirely of one colour.
whole-hearted, adj. Acting, done, felt, with the whole heart; devoted, sincere, single-minded: *whole-hearted enthusiasm, support* &c.
whole-heartedly, adv. Prec. & **-ly.** In a whole-hearted manner.
whole-heartedness, n. See prec. & **-ness.** Quality of being whole-hearted.
whole-hogger, n. [1. hōl hóger; 2. hóul hɔ́gə]. One who does a thing, supports a cause &c. to the utmost limit, and without reservations or misgivings; see Phr. *to go the whole hog,* under **whole (I.), 3.**

whole-hoofed, adj. Not having cloven hoofs.

whole-length, adj. & n. **1.** adj. *Whole-length portrait* &c., one representing person's whole figure. **2.** n. A whole-length portrait &c.

wholemeal, n. & adj. [1. hṓlmēl; 2. hóulmīəl]. **1.** n. Flour containing all the constituents of the grain. **2.** adj. Made of wholemeal: *wholemeal bread* &c.

wholeness, n. [1. hṓlnes; 2. hóulnis]. **whole (I.)** & **-ness.** State of being whole; completeness.

whole number, n. Number involving no fractions; integer.

wholesale, n., adj., & adv. [1. hṓlsāl; 2. hóulseil]. **1.** n. Sale of goods in bulk or quantity; contrasted with *retail*; chiefly in Phr. *by wholesale.* **2.** adj. **a** Pertaining to, carried on by, sale of goods in bulk: *wholesale prices*; *wholesale trade*; **b** selling by wholesale: *wholesale trader*; **c** (fig.) involving large amounts, on a large scale: *wholesale destruction*; *a wholesale liar.* **3.** adv. **a** By wholesale, in bulk or quantity: *to buy goods wholesale*; **b** hence (fig.) on a large scale, indiscriminately: *to incur debts, waste one's money, wholesale.*

wholesaler, n. [1. hṓlsāler; 2. hóulseilə]. A wholesale trader.

wholesome, adj. [1. hṓlsum; 2. hóulsəm]. **whole (I.)** & **-some.** **1.** Favourable to, promoting, health; salubrious, good for one, healthful: *wholesome food, surroundings* &c. **2.** Conducive to moral well-being; salutary: *a little wholesome punishment*; *a clean, wholesome story.*

wholesomely, adv. Prec. & **-ly.** In a wholesome manner.

wholesomeness, n. See prec. & **-ness.** State or quality of being wholesome.

whole-souled, adj. Acting, feeling, experienced, with one's whole soul; whole-hearted; *a whole-souled supporter*; *whole-souled devotion.*

wholly, adv. [1. hṓlli, hṓli; 2. hóulli, hóuli]. **whole (I.)** & **-ly.** **1.** Completely, in all parts or respects, entirely: *few men are wholly bad.* **2.** Altogether, without qualification: *I don't wholly agree.*

whom, pron. [1. ho͞om; 2. hūm]. Objective case of **who**; O.E. *hwām* (dat.), M.E. *whōm*; now often replaced colloquially by *who*: *I don't know who(m) you mean.*

whoop, vb. intrans. & n. [1. ho͞op; 2. hūp], fr. Fr. *houper*, imitative. **1.** vb. To utter a whoop, esp. that heard in whooping-cough. **2.** n. Loud cry or shout: *whoops of joy.*

whooper swan, n. [1. ho͞oper swón; 2. hūpə swɔ́n]. Whooping swan.

whooping-cough, n. [1. ho͞oping kàwf; 2. hūpiŋ, húpiŋ, kɔ̄f, kɔ́f]. Also *hooping-cough*, infectious disease of children, characterized by paroxysms of coughing which end in loud whoops, *Pertussis.*

whooping swan, n. The wild swan, *Cygnus musicus.*

whop, vb. trans. [1. wop; 2. wɔp]. Etymol. doubtful. **1.** To beat, thrash. **2.** (fig.) To overcome, vanquish, defeat.

whopper, n. [1. wóper; 2. wɔ́pə]. Prec. & **-er.** (slang) Anything especially large or fine; specif., a lie of remarkable magnitude and shamelessness.

whopping (I.), n. [1. wóping; 2. wɔ́piŋ]. **whop** & **-ing.** **1.** Thrashing, beating. **2.** Defeat.

whopping (II.), adj. & adv., fr. Pres. Part. of **whop.** (slang) **a** adj. Especially large or fine of its kind; **b** adv., very, extremely; chiefly *whopping great* (*fish* &c.).

whore, n. & vb. intrans. [1. hōr; 2. hɔ̄]. O.E., M.E. *hōre*; cp. O.H.G. *huora*; O.N. *hōrr*; M. Du. *hoere*, 'fornicator'; Goth. *hōrs*, 'adulterous'; cogn. w. Lat. *cārus*, 'dear', see **caress**; Lett. *kārs*, 'covetous'; Scrt. *cārus*, 'beloved'. **1.** n. **a** A woman who is guilty of sexual immorality; **b** a prostitute. **2.** vb. To indulge in fornication.

whoredom, n. [1. hórdum; 2. hɔ́dəm]. Prec. & **-dom** (obs.) Fornication.

whoremonger, n. [1. hórmùngger; 2. hɔ́màŋgə]. (archaic) A fornicator.

whorl, n. [1. wërl; 2. wʌ̄l]. M.E. *whorvil*, fr. stem of O.E. *hweorfan*, 'to turn', see **wharf**, & **-le**; cp. M. Du. *worvel*, 'spindle-whorl'. **1.** Disk used to balance or steady a spindle. **2.** (bot.) Group of petals, leaves, stamens &c. arranged in a circle about a point. **3.** (esp. zool.) Single turn of spiral (in shell &c.).

whorled, adj. [1. wërld; 2. wʌ̄ld]. Prec. & **-ed.** Having, arranged in, whorls.

whortleberry, n. [1. wërtlberi; 2. wʌ́tlbəri]. Earlier *hurtleberry*, possibly connected w. O.E. *horta*, 'bilberry'. Bilberry, whinberry.

whose, pron. [1. ho͞oz; 2. hūz]. Possessive case of **who.**

whoso, pron. [1. ho͞osō; 2. húsou]. **who** & **so.** (archaic) The person(s) that; whoever.

whosoever, pron. [1. ho͞osōéver; 2. hūsouévə]. **who** & **so** & **ever.** (archaic) Whoso.

why (I.), adv. [1. wī; 2. wai]. O.E. *hwī*, *hwȳ*, instrumental case of *hwā*, *hwæt*, 'who, what'; see **who.** **1.** (interrog.) For what reason?, with what intent?, on what grounds?, wherefore?: *why are you here?*; *why do you think so?*; *do you know why he was late?*; *you say you are unhappy; why?* Phr. *why so?*, for what reason, on what grounds? **2.** (introducing dependent clause, with or without antecedent expressed) Because of which, by reason of which; the reason for which: *tell us the reason why you came*; *this is why I came.*

why (II.), n., fr. prec. The reason, cause, purpose, ground; esp. in Phr. *the why and wherefore* (*of an action, situation* &c.).

why (III.), interj., fr. **why** (I.). Expressing surprise, protestation &c., or merely introducing a new idea: *what, going out? why, it's quite dark*; *why, he told me he was only fifty*; *why, it's nearly five o'clock.*

whydah. See **whidah-bird.**

wick (I.), n. [1. wik; 2. wik]. O.E. *wice*, 'wick of lamp' &c., M.E. *wicke*, &c.; cp. O.H.G. *wieche*, M. Du. *wieke*, 'wick'; cogn. w. O.E. *wōcig*, 'net, snare', & w. **wax** (I.). **a** Twisted strands of thread forming the centre of a wax candle or taper, and projecting beyond one end, which when lighted burn with a small flame until the wax is consumed; **b** piece of woven material, flat, or in form of a tube, having one end immersed in the oil of a lamp, and the other end left in suitable position for lighting; the incandescent and illuminating properties of such a wick are derived from the oil which it sucks up.

wick (II.), n. Prob. fr. O.N. *vīk*, 'creek, bay', w. sense fr. O.E. *wīc*, 'dwelling, village'. The word is prob. an early loan fr. Lat. *vīcus*, 'village, hamlet', wh. is cogn. w. Gk. *oikos*, 'house', see under **economy.** Village, place &c. Now obsolete except in compounds such as **bailiwick**, and in Place-Names; *-wich*, in *Greenwich* &c., is from the O.E. word.

wicked, adj. [1. wíkid; 2. wíkid]. M.E. *wikked*, fr. *wikke*, 'evil', & **-ed.** Cp. O.E. *wicce*, 'witch', see **witch**; cogn. w. O.E. *wīcan*, 'to fall, grow feeble'; *wāc*, 'weak, pliant', see **weak.** **1.** Evil, morally reprehensible; sinful; reverse of *good, virtuous, pious*; **a** (of persons) deliberately thinking or practising what is evil; habitually opposed to virtue, piety, justice; vicious, depraved; **b** (of thoughts and actions) springing from, inspired by, of the nature of, sin, depravity, vice. **2.** Mischievous; playfully naughty, roguish.

wickedly, adv. Prec. & **-ly.** In a wicked manner.

wickedness, n. See prec. & **-ness.** **1.** State of being wicked: *the wickedness of our hearts.* **2.** **a** Wicked thought or action: *to practise wickedness*; **b** specific wicked act.

wicker, n. & adj. [1. wíker; 2. wíkə]. Orig. sense, 'pliant rod, osier', fr. Scand.; cp. Swed. dial. *vikker*, 'willow', M. Swed. *wika*, 'to bend', cogn. w. O.E. *wīcan*, 'to grow feeble, fall'; *wāc*, 'weak, pliant', see **wicked, weak.** **1.** n. Fabric made of interwoven osiers, or other pliant stems; used for baskets, light furniture &c. **2.** adj. Made of wicker: *wicker tables* &c.

wickered, adj. [1. wíkerd; 2. wíkəd]. Prec. & **-ed.** Made of or covered with wicker-work.

wicker-work, n. & adj. **1.** n. **a** Wickers wrought into a fabric; **b** things made of this; **c** act, art, of making such objects. **2.** adj. Made of wicker.

wicket, n. [1. wíkit; 2. wíkit]. M.E. *wiket*, fr. A.-Fr. *wiket*; of Gmc. origin, & prob. connected w. O.N. *vīkja*, 'to move, turn'. **1.** Small door or gate, esp. one at side, or forming part of, larger one. **2.** Small opening, hatch, in wall, door &c. closed by sliding panel, grating &c. **3.** Half-door, barring lower half of doorway, as in stable &c. **4.** (cricket) **a** Group of three upright stumps with two bails, defended by batsman; Phrs. *to take a wicket*, (of bowler) get batsman out; *to keep wicket*, act as wicket-keeper, q.v.; *two &c. wickets down*, two &c. batsmen out; *to win by two &c. wickets*, with three batsmen still to be got out; **b** state of pitch, chiefly in Phr. *a good, hard, dry, wicket* &c.

wicket-door, -gate, n. Same as **wicket, 1.**

wicket-keeper, n. Fieldsman standing immediately behind wicket for catching, stumping, and saving byes.

widdershins. Variant of **withershins.**

wide (I.), adj. [1. wīd; 2. waid]. O.E. *wīd*; M.E. *wide*; O.S. *wīd*; O.H.G. *wīt*; O.N. *vīðr*; prob. cogn. w. Lat. (*dī*)*videre*, 'to separate', see **divide.** **1.** Of great or comparatively great extent from side to side; broad: *a wide road, river, ribbon, ditch, skirt* &c.; *wide margins*; *a wide forehead*; *the gate is not wide enough.* Phr. *to give a wide berth to*, avoid, keep out of the way of. **2.** Having specified measurement from side to side: *how wide is it?*; *a foot wide.* **3.** **a** Of great extent; spacious, vast: *a wide expanse of desert*; *the wide sea*; *wide dominions*; *the wide world*, whole world; *wide intervals*; **b** (i.) covering, occurring over, a wide area: *a wide distribution*; (ii.) affecting a large circle of persons: *a wide appeal.* **4.** Striking, falling, being, at some distance from a specific point or object: *the bullet was wide of the mark, target* &c.; *a wide ball*, at cricket; (also fig.) *a remark, reply* &c. *wide of the mark*, irrelevant, not to the point; *wide of the truth*, deviating from it. **5.** (in non-material sense) **a** Of extensive scope, range, and grasp: *wide knowledge*; *scholarship*; **b** (i.) not narrow or restricted; catholic, liberal, comprehending many and different objects: *a man of wide interests, sympathies* &c.; (ii.) far-seeing, taking large views: *wide vision*; (iii.) broad, general; reverse of *minute* and *specialized*: *education at the school stage should be wide and humane.*

wide (II.), adv., fr. prec. **1.** Widely, to a considerable extent, to a distance; esp. in Phr. (*to search &c.*) *far and wide.* **2.** Extensively; to full extent: *with eyes wide open*; *open your mouth wide.* Phr. *to have one's eyes wide open*, (i.) to be alert, shrewd; (ii.) to be fully alive to what is happening; *to open one's mouth too wide*, (i.) to be greedy and grasping; (ii.) to be too ambitious, undertake more than one can perform. **3.** Remotely, to a considerable distance from specific point: *to fall, shoot, wide of the mark*; also, to *speak wide of the mark*, not to the point.

wide (III.), n., fr. **wide** (I.). (cricket) Also *wide ball*, one bowled so as to pass wicket out of reach of batsman, adding one run to score of latter's side.

wide-awake (I.), adj. [1. wīd awā́k; 2. wáid əwéik]. **a** Thoroughly awake; **b** alert, vigilant, wary.

wide-awake (II.), n. [1. wīd awāk; 2. wáid əweik]. A soft felt hat with a broad, floppy brim and a low crown; the name is now as obsolete as the hat to which it was applied.

widely, adv. [1. wīdli; 2. wáidli]. **wide** (I.) & **-ly.** **1.** (referring to spatial conditions) **a** At wide intervals, so as to occur over a wide area: *widely scattered, distributed, over Europe*; *widely separated*; **b** so as to affect persons in different parts of a wide area: *to appeal widely for support; widely known.* **2.** (referring to degree, extent, of diversity &c.): *widely unlike, different; to differ widely,* (i.) to have little or no resemblance; (ii.) to disagree considerably, hold quite different opinions.

widen, vb. trans. & intrans. [1. wīdn; 2. wáidn]. **wide** (I.) & **-en.** **1.** trans. To make wider, increase width, extent, scope, of; to broaden: **a** (in material sense) *to widen a ditch;* **b** (in non-material sense) *to widen one's outlook, one's intellectual horizon.* **2.** intrans. (in material and non-material senses) To become, grow, wider; to extend, expand.

widespread, adj. [1. wīdspred; 2. wáidsprɛd]. Having a wide distribution, extending over large area: *a widespread tendency, superstition &c.; to become less widespread.*

widgeon, n. [1. wíjun; 2. wídžən], fr. O. Fr. *vigeon*, fr. Lat. *vipiōnem*, nom. *vipio*, 'kind of small crane', according to Pliny a Balearic word. A short-billed, short-legged migratory wild duck, *Mareca penelope*, the drake having a chestnut head and neck and light patch on forehead.

widish, adj. [1. wīdish; 2. wáidiʃ]. **wide (I.)** & **-ish.** Somewhat wide.

widow (I.), n. [1. wídō; 2. wídou]. O.E. *widwe*; M.E. *widewe*; cp. Mod. Germ. *witwe*; O.S. *widowa*; Goth. *widuwō*; cogn. w. Lat. *vidua*; Scrt. *vidhávā*; O. Slav. *vĭdova*; O. Prussian *widdewū*, 'widow'; cp. further Gk. *(ē)itheos*, 'unmarried'; Lat. *(dī)videre*; see **divide** & words there referred to. Woman whose husband has died, and who remains unmarried. Phrs. *grass widow,* woman temporarily separated from her husband; *widow's peak,* hair growing downwards in a point, at centre of forehead; *widow's weeds,* see **weeds**; *widow's cruse, mite,* see **cruse, mite (I.)**; *widow's cap,* one made of lawn and with long streamers behind.

widow (II.), vb. trans., fr. prec. **1.** To make a widow or widower, bereave of husband or wife; esp. in P.P.: *widowed by war; thrice-widowed.* **2.** (fig., chiefly poet.) To deprive, bereave, esp. by death or disaster: '*a dying king, Laid widow'd of the power in his eye*' (Tennyson, 'Passing of Arthur').

widow-bird. See **whidah-bird.**

widower, n. [1. wídōer; 2. wídouə]. **widow (I.)** & **-er.** Man whose wife has died, and who has remained unmarried.

widowhood, n. [1. wídōhòod; 2. wídouhùd]. **widow (I.)** & **-hood.** Condition of being a widow.

widow woman, n. (Bib., colloq. and facet.) A widow.

width, n. [1. width; 2. widþ]. **wide (I.)** & **-th**; not in O.E.; new formation on anal. of **length.** **1.** (material and non-material senses) State or quality of being wide: *a river of considerable width; width of mind.* **2.** Measurement from side to side: *to have a width of four feet.* **3.** Piece of material of full width as manufactured: *to join two widths.*

wield, vb. trans. [1. wēld; 2. wiəld]. Formally, most prob. fr. O.E. *(ġe-)wěldan*, 'to subdue, dominate', but the meaning is derived fr. the cogn. O.E. *wealdan*, 'to have control over; to wield (a weapon); to rule, govern'; (the Mod. form can be explained, however, as derived either fr. a Sthn. variant of this, or on the anal. of the mutated 3rd pers. sing. pres.). Both vbs. are formed fr. O.E. *weald*, 'power'; cp. O.S. *waldan*; O.H.G. *waltan*, 'to govern'; Goth. *waldan*; cogn. w. Lat. *valēre*, 'to be strong' &c., q.v. under **valiant.** **1. a** To have control or power over; chiefly in Phr. *to wield the sceptre,* to rule as king; **b** to have at one's command: *to wield influence.* **2.** To handle, make use of (some implement or weapon grasped by the hands): *to wield a sword, an axe, a flail &c.;* Phr. *to wield the pen,* to write.

wife, n. [1. wīf; 2. waif]. O.E., M.E. *wīf*, 'woman, wife'; cp. O.S. *wīf*; O.H.G. *wīb*; O.N. *vīf*. Etymol. unknown. **1.** Married woman, spouse: *husband and wife; a man and his wife; his lawful, wedded, wife; she has been a good wife to him.* Phrs. *to have a wife,* be married; *to take (a woman) to wife,* to marry her. **2.** (archaic) A woman; esp. *an old wife,* a feeble old woman of humble rank. Phr. *old wives' tale,* a foolish, fantastic story, told and believed by the credulous.

wifehood, n. [1. wífhood; 2. wáifhud]. Prec. & **-hood.** Condition of being a wife.

wifeless, adj. [1. wífles; 2. wáiflis]. **wife** & **-less.** Without a wife.

wifelike, adj. [1. wíflīk; 2. wáiflaik]. **wife** & **-like.** **a** Like a wife; **b** suitable, appropriate, for a wife; **c** appertaining to a wife.

wifely, adj. [1. wífli; 2. wáifli]. **wife** & **-ly.** Wifelike.

wig (I.), n. [1. wig; 2. wig]. Abbr. fr. **periwig.** **1.** A covering for the head, made of hair; **a** head-dress of human hair, worn by the bald, or by actors &c., made to imitate naturally-growing hair; **b** head-dress of horse hair, made in various forms, worn in 17th and 18th cents. as a fashionable ornament; similar head-dress still worn in court &c. by judges and counsel. Phr. *wigs on the green,* (i.) a rough, hand-to-hand fight; (ii.) a heated public altercation or dispute. **2.** (facet. and colloq.) A natural head of hair: *you had better brush your untidy wig.*

wig (II.), vb. trans. Perh. orig. in physical sense, fr. idea of striking person on the head, knocking his wig off &c.; cp. somewhat similar transference of meaning in such vbs. as *to jacket, dress down,* & Phrs. *comb his hair, dust his jacket for him* &c. (slang) To blame severely, take to task; to rate, scold.

wigan, n. [1. wígan; 2. wígən], fr. name of town in S. Lancashire. Kind of stiff canvas used for stiffening hems of garments, collars &c.

wig-block, n. Round block, shaped more or less like a human head, used to hold wigs while being combed &c.

wigged, adj. [1. wigd; 2. wigd]. **wig (I.)** & **-ed.** Having, wearing, a wig.

wigging, n. [1. wíging; 2. wígiŋ]. **wig (II.)** & **-ing.** (slang) **a** Severe scolding, a rating; a dressing-down.

wiggle, vb. trans. & intrans. [1. wígl; 2. wígl]. Variant of **waggle**, or blend of this & **wriggle.** (colloq.) **1.** trans. To cause to move with a slight but rapid movement: *to wiggle one's little finger.* **2.** intrans. To make slight, jerky, nervous movements; to wriggle.

wight, n. [1. wīt; 2. wait]. O.E. *wiht*, 'creature, thing'; see **whit (I.)**. (archaic or facet.) Creature, person, human being: *a luckless wight.*

wigless, adj. [1. wígles; 2. wíglis]. **wig (I.)** & **-less.** Without a wig.

wig-maker, n. Tradesman who makes and sells wigs and deals in human hair.

wigwam, n. [1. wígwam, -wom; 2. wígwæm, -wɔm] fr. N. Am. Indian *weekuwom*. N. American Indian's roughly made, conical tent of poles hung with bark, hides &c.

wild (I.), adj. [1. wīld; 2. waild]. O.E. *wilde*; M.E. *wilde*, 'wild, savage, uncultivated'; cp. O.S. *wilde* O.H.G. *wildi*; O.N. *villr*; Goth. *wilþeis*, 'wild'. Further etymol. doubtful. **1. a** (of birds, beasts &c.) Living in original, natural state; not domesticated, not in subjection to man; contrasted with *tame*: *wild animals;* Phr. *to be drawn by wild horses,* form of torture; **b** easily startled, shy: *the deer are very wild.* **2.** (of plants &c.) Uncultivated, not planted or tended by man; growing naturally: *wild roses, cherries* &c. Phrs. *to run wild,* (i.) grow without training or cultivation; (ii.) (fig. of persons) to grow up without due control; *to sow one's wild oats,* to indulge in those follies and dissipations supposed to be natural to youth. **3.** (of man) Uncivilized, savage, in a primitive state of culture. **4.** (of land) Left in, or having reverted to, natural, uncultivated, and uninhabited state: *wild mountain regions; a wild and desolate country.* **5.** Disarranged, disturbed, disordered: *wild hair, attire &c.; in a state of wild confusion.* **6.** Dissipated; fond of riotous, extravagant, wanton pleasure and excitement; reverse of *steady, sedate*: *rather wild as a young man.* **7.** Disturbed, violently agitated, tumultuous, turbulent, stormy, boisterous: *a wild sea; a wild night; wild cheers.* **8.** In a condition of mental excitement or disturbance, roused to a state of enthusiasm or frenzy, distracted; **a** excited by joy, desire &c.: *they are wild to go; wild with delight; wild excitement;* Phr. *to be wild about* (person, cause &c.), intensely devoted to; **b** mentally deranged, crazy, frantic: *he has a wild look; wild laughter;* Phr. *to drive wild,* to render, distracted; **c** (colloq.) very angry: *it made me wild to listen to such nonsense.* **9.** Rash, ill-advised; reckless; ill-aimed; done or said at random: *wild talk, accusation, shooting; wild schemes.*

wild (II.), adv., fr. prec. Wildly, esp. without care, consideration, or proper aim: *to shoot wild.*

wild (III.), n., fr. **wild (I.)**. **a** Land in natural, uncultivated state; wilderness: '*Till from the garden and the wild A fresh association blow*' (Tennyson, 'In Mem.' ci. 5); **b** remote, savage, uncivilized country: *the wilds of Africa; the call of the wild.*

wild-boar, n. Kind of pig, *Sus scrofa*, still found wild in parts of Europe, from which domesticated swine have descended.

wild-cat, n. **1.** Large, very fierce, undomesticated cat found in N. Scotland and other parts of Europe &c. **2.** (attrib.) In Phr. *wild-cat schemes,* fantastic, visionary, impracticable schemes.

wild-duck, n. One of various kinds of wild, freshwater ducks.

wildebeest, n. [1. wĕldebàst; 2. wíldəbèist]. S. Afr. Du.; see **wild (I.)** & **beast.** Variety of large antelope; gnu.

wilder, vb. trans. [1. wílder; 2. wíldə]. Prob. abbr. fr. **bewilder.** (poet.) To mislead, bewilder, perplex.

wilderness, n. [1. wíldernes; 2. wíldənis], fr. M.E. *wildern*, 'desert', fr. O.E. *wildēor, wilder*, 'wild beast', fr. *wilde*, 'wild', see **wild (I.)**, & *dēor*, 'animal', see **deer**, & **-ness.** **1.** Uncultivated, sometimes barren, region, wholly or for the most part uninhabited; desert; specif., that region in which the children of Israel wandered forty years before reaching the Promised Land. **2.** Vast, desolate expanse of land or water: *a wilderness of waters.* Phr. *a wilderness of streets, houses,* long, monotonous series of dull, squalid streets or houses. **3.** Part of garden allowed to grow naturally, without cultivation.

wildfire, n. [1. wíldfīr; 2. wáildfàiə]. **1.** Combustible, highly inflammable compound, formerly used to set fire to hostile ships &c.; Greek fire. Chiefly in Phr. *to spread like wildfire,* very rapidly. **2.** Phosphorescent light, e.g. St. Elmo's fire.

wild-fowl, n. Wild birds hunted as game.

wild-goose, n. Undomesticated goose. Phr. *a wild-goose chase,* a futile enterprise; search for something which can never be found, or which has no existence.

wilding, n. [1. wílding; 2. wáildiŋ]. **wild (I.)** & **-ing.** **1.** Uncultivated plant, esp. among cultivated plants, or one that has sprung naturally from originally cultivated stock. **2.** Fruit of such a plant.

wildish, adj. [1. wíldish; 2. wáildiʃ]. **wild (I.)** & **-ish.** Somewhat, inclined to be, wild.

wildly, adv. [1. wíldli; 2. wáildli]. **wild (I.)** & **-ly.** In a wild manner.

wildness, n. [1. wíldnes; 2. wáildnis]. **wild (I.)** & **-ness.** **a** State or quality of being wild (in various senses of adj.); **b** wild, dissipated conduct or habits: *wildnesses of youth.*

wild-wood, n. Natural forest-land.

wile, n. & vb. trans. [1. wīl; 2. wail]. O.E. *wīl*; M.E. *wile*, 'trick'; etymol. doubtful. **1.** n. (usually pl.) Means of enticing, persuading, or cajoling; cunning stratagem, ruse, craft: *to* *defeat the wiles of the devil.* 2. vb. a To entice, lure, mislead; b in Phr. *to wile away the time,* to spend it pleasantly; confused with **while (II.)**.

wilful, adj. [1. wilfool; 2. wílful]. **will (I.)** & **-ful.** 1. (of person or character) Obstinately and perversely determined to have one's own way; headstrong, stubborn, wayward; capricious. 2. (of action) Springing from deliberate intention; premeditated; not the result of sudden passion or of accident: *wilful waste, destruction*; specif., *wilful murder.*

wilfully, adv. Prec. & **-ly.** In a wilful manner.

wilfulness, n. See prec. & **-ness.** a Quality of being wilful; b wilful conduct.

wilily, adv. [1. wílili; 2. wáilili]. **wily** & **-ly.** In a wily manner.

wiliness, n. [1. wílines; 2. wáilinis]. **wily** & **-ness.** State or quality of being wily; craft, cunning.

will (I.), n. [1. wil; 2. wil]. O.E. *willa,* 'will', see **will (II.)**. 1. Faculty of controlling one's thoughts and actions, of determining and directing the activities of mind or body; cp. *volition*: *freedom of the will.* 2. Power of imposing one's influence and controlling force on oneself or others; strength of will: *a strong will; he has no will of his own.* 3. Energy directed to a particular end; enthusiasm in action: *to work with a will.* 4. Definite intention, determined course of action: *where there's a will there's a way; against one's will; to take the will for the deed.* 5. Disposition, feelings towards others; now chiefly in compounds: *good-, ill-will.* 6. That which one wills; purpose, intention: *God's will be done; to work one's will, have one's will.* 7. Personal right of action; discretion; esp. in Phr. *at will,* when and how one pleases; *tenant at will,* liable to be dispossessed without notice. 8. Legal document by which a person makes disposition of his property, taking effect after his death: *one's last will and testament; to make, draw up, a will.*

will (II.), vb. trans. & intrans. O.E. *willan*; M.E. *willen,* 'to desire, wish'; cp. O.S. *willian*; O.H.G. *wellan*; O.N. *vilja*; Goth. *wiljan,* 'will'; cogn. w. Goth. *waljan*; O.H.G. *wellan,* 'to choose'; Goth. *wilja,* O.E. *willa,* 'will', n.; O.H.G. *wala,* 'choice'; cogn. w. Lat. *velle,* 'to wish'; *voluptas,* 'pleasure', see **voluptuous** & **volition**; Gk. *elpís,* 'hope'; Scrt. *varanam,* 'choice'; *vṛṇītē,* 'chooses, prefers'; Lith. *vēlyju,* 'to wish'; *viltis,* 'hope'; O. Slav. *volją,* 'will', vb. **A.** trans. 1. To be desirous of, wish, be anxious or eager for: (archaic) *what would you?; let him do what he will; would that he were come; I would to heaven I had stayed.* 2. To resolve, decide, upon (action &c.) by exercise of the will; make choice of: *whatever he wills he may accomplish.* 3. To control (person &c.) by means of the will, exercise power over: *to will oneself to fall asleep; to will a person to look at one.* **B.** intrans. To be desirous, anxious, or eager; to exercise the will: *it must be as God wills; they had to obey, whether they would or not.*

will (III.), auxil. vb., fr. prec. The auxil. is usually unstressed & is then, in ordinary speech, reduced to [l], written *'ll.* When it follows a personal pron. *will* ceases to be syllabic, & is attached as a final consonant to the preceding syll., *i.e.* the pron.: *I'll, he'll, she'll, we'll, you'll, they'll* = [ail, hīl, jūl, ðeil] &c. After words ending in voiceless consonants *'ll,* [l] has force of a syll.: *this'll, what'll* &c. After words ending in voiced consonants *'ll* is sounded [əl]: *Jones'll come* = [džóunzəl kàm], *the king'll be pleased* = [ðə kiŋəl bi plīzd]. *Will* only retains its full form in natural, rapid speech (1) when strongly stressed, & this only happens when the idea, or function, expressed by the *will* is emphasized: *if he says that he'll come, he will* = [*if* (h)i séz ðət hìl kám, hi wíl], *boys will be boys* = [bóiz wíl bi bóiz], & so on; (2) initially, in interrog. sentences, even when the stress is weak: *will he come, do you think?* 1. (expressing future pure and simple) *You never know what he'll do next; we'll be there in good time; you'll hurt yourself if you're not careful; what'll be the end of it all?* 2. (i.) (expressing a certain degree of purpose and intention alongside of futurity) *I'll certainly go and see him if you like; I'll be a good boy for the future*; (ii.) (expressing firm resolution; strongly stressed) *I will be obeyed; he will have his joke.* 3. (expressing habitual or repeated action) *There he'll sit hour after hour without saying a word.* 4. (expressing natural process or action, inevitability) *Boys will be boys; accidents will happen.* 5. (expressing inference, expectation that the facts will turn out to be as stated) *This'll be our train, I fancy; I suppose she would be about 40 when she died.* (For negative constructions with **will,** see **won't.**)

will (IV.), vb. trans., fr. **will (I.), 8.** a To devise, bequeath, by means of a will, leave as legacy: *to will one's property away from one's natural heirs*; b to bequeath property &c. to.

-willed, adj. [1. wild; 2. wild]. **will (I.)** & **-ed.** Having a will of specific quality: *strong-, weak-willed* &c.

willet, n. [1. wílet; 2. wílit]. Imitative. Large N. American sandpiper.

willing, adj. [1. wíling; 2. wíliŋ]. **will (II.)** & **-ing.** 1. Favourably disposed, inclined (for action); desirous, eager (to do something): '*Willing to wound, and yet afraid to strike*' (Pope, 'Epist. to Arbuthnot', 203); *if you would like me to intervene, I'm quite willing.* 2. a (of living beings) Ready and eager to help, or to perform tasks proposed or allotted; serviceable: *a willing guide, heart; a willing horse; he doesn't know his job very well, but he's willing and obliging*; b (of services, actions) rendered, performed, offered, willingly.

willingly, adv. Prec. & **-ly.** In a willing manner; gladly, readily.

willingness, n. See prec. & **-ness.** Quality of being willing.

will-less, adj. [1. willes; 2. wíllis]. **will (I.)** & **-less.** Without will-power, wanting in volition.

will-o'-the-wisp, n. [1. wíl o dhe wísp; 2. wíl ə ðə wísp], fr. personal name *Will,* & **wisp** in sense of 'bundle of tow, straw &c., used as torch'. Ignis fatuus.

willow (I.), n. [1. wílō; 2. wílou]. O.E. *wiliġ, weliġ*; M.E. *wilghe, wilwe*; cp. M. Du. *wilghe*; cogn. w. Gk. *helíkē,* 'willow', for **welik-*; Scrt. *válśaś,* 'shoot, pliant twig'; fr. base **wel-,* **wol-,* 'to turn'; see **well (I.), wallow, volute** &c. 1. Any tree or shrub of the genus *Salix,* many species of which are found in the Northern hemisphere, esp. in watery ground; most species have slender, pliant branches, and some yield strong timber, used for cricket-bats &c.; *weeping willow,* kind with long, drooping branches. Phr. *to wear the willow,* as symbol of mourning. 2. A cricket-bat, as made of willow wood: *to wield the willow,* to bat.

willow (II.), vb. trans. & n., fr. prec., fr. use of willow branches for beating fibre. 1. vb. To clean (fibres) by beating in a machine. 2. n. Also *willowing-machine,* machine with revolving spikes for cleaning fibre.

willow-herb, n. Any of many species of herb, *Epilobium,* some tall, with pale, pinkish-purple flowers and long leaves like those of willow.

willow-pattern, n. a Chinese design for china, with pagodas, a river, willow trees, a bridge upon which are three persons, and two birds flying overhead, usually printed or painted in blue on white ground; b china bearing this design.

willow-warbler, n. Bird resembling chiff-chaff.

willow-wren, n. Small bird belonging to the warblers.

willowy, adj. [1. wílōi; 2. wíloui]. **willow (I.)** & **-y.** 1. Abounding in willows. 2. Slender, supple, and graceful: *a willowy figure.*

will-power, n. Strength of will, ability to control, endure, determine course of events &c.

will-worship, n. (archaic) Self-invented, arbitrary, form of religion.

willy nilly, adv. [1. wíli níli; 2. wíli níli]. Variant of *will I* or *he, nill I* or *he*; see **will (II.)** & **nill.** Whether one will or not; inevitably, of necessity.

wilt (I.), vb. [1. wilt; 2. wilt]. 2nd pers. sing. pres. of **will (II.)**.

wilt (II.), vb. intrans. & trans. Etymol. doubtful; possibly connected w. **welk.** 1. intrans. (of plant &c.) To lose freshness and strength; to fade, droop. 2. trans. To cause to fade, droop; to wither.

Wilton, n. [1. wíltun; 2. wíltən], fr. town in Wiltshire. Also *Wilton carpet,* kind of Brussels carpet with cut pile, made at, or similar to those made at, Wilton, formerly made at Axminster.

wily, adj. [1. wíli; 2. wáili]. **wile** & **-y.** Full of, characterized by, wiles; artful, crafty, cunning.

wimple, n. [1. wímpl; 2. wímpl]. O.E., M.E. *wimpel,* 'neck-covering, cloak'; cp. M. Du. *wimpel,* 'streamer'; O.N. *vimpill*; O.H.G. *wimpal,* 'veil'; cp. further M.H.G. *wifen,* 'to swing'; O.H.G. *wipf,* 'swing'; cogn. w. Lat. *vibrāre,* 'to swing, vibrate'; Lith. *wÿburiu,* 'to wave'; see **vibrate**; cp. **whip (II.)**. Cloth of linen, silk &c. folded about head so as to expose the face; now worn in W. Europe only by nuns.

wimpled, adj. [1. wímpld; 2. wímpld]. Prec. & **-ed.** Wearing a wimple.

win (I.), vb. trans. & intrans. [1. win; 2. win]. O.E. *winnan,* 'to toil, suffer, fight'; *ġewinnan,* 'to gain, conquer'; M.E. *winnen,* 'to strive; to win'; cp. O.S., O.H.G. *winnan*; O.N. *vinna*; O.H.G. *giwinnan,* 'to strive after'; cogn. w. Scrt. *vánati,* 'wishes, desires; fights for, wins'; *vánaś,* 'desire'; Lat. *venus,* 'love', see **Venus**; fr. base **wen-,* 'to wish'; see also **wont, winsome, wish.** **A.** trans. 1. a To gain, obtain, acquire, by effort, esp. in competition, against opposition &c.: *to win a prize, the victory, a laurel wreath, honour, a lady's hand, golden opinions* &c.; Phrs. *to win one's spurs,* (i.) (hist.) achieve knighthood by valiant service; hence (ii.) to do something which proves one's real value; *to win ore,* extract it from mine; b to reach, arrive at, with effort: *to win the shore, the mountain-top* &c. Phr. *to win one's way,* (chiefly fig.) to succeed in life, a career &c. by dint of effort. 2. To achieve victory in: *to win a race, battle, game* &c. Phr. *to win the day, field,* be victorious. 3. To gain: *to win all hearts; he won the jury over to his side.* **B.** intrans. 1. To win a contest, fight, game, race &c.; be victorious, prevail: *he is sure to win; may the best man win; to win by a length, a head, a neck.* Phrs. *to win hands down,* (colloq.) to be easily successful. 2. *Win clear, win out, win through,* to come, get, through or out, to escape, with difficulty.

win (II.), n., fr. prec. Act of winning; victory, success in a contest: *to celebrate a win; another win for Lancashire.*

wince, vb. intrans. & n. [1. wins; 2. wins]. M.E. *winc(h)en,* 'to kick out; to start; to draw back'; cp. O. Fr. *guenchir, guincir,* fr. O.S. *wenkien*; cogn. w. O.H.G. *wanchōn,* 'to draw back'; O.H.G. *wanchal*; O.E. *wancol,* 'unstable', see **wench**; O.H.G. *winkan,* 'to move sideways, start; wink'; O.E. *wincian,* 'to wink, nod', see **wink**; cogn. w. Lat. *vagāri,* 'to wander', see **vagary.** 1. vb. To start or draw back suddenly, to shrink away; to show sensitiveness to sudden bodily or moral pain or shock; to flinch: *to wince under the blows; to bear pain without wincing; brutal, vulgar jests make her wince.* Phr. *let the galled jade wince,* let him who considers that an insult &c. is levelled at him resent it. 2. n. Involuntary movement, recoil, shrinking, caused by mental or physical pain.

wincey, n. [1. wínsi; 2. wínsi]. Perh. coined fr. *woolsey and linsey.* Strong cotton and wool fabric.

winch, n. [1. winch; 2. wintʃ]. O.E. *wince*, 'pulley'; M.E. *winche*, 'winch, windlass'; cogn. w. Lith. *vingis*, 'bow, curve'; Scrt. *váŋgati*, 'limps'; Lat. *vagāri*, 'to wander', see **vagary**; cp. further O.E. *wincian*, 'to nod, wink', see **wink**; *wancol*, 'unstable', see **wench**. **1.** Windlass, esp. with revolving drum worked by a crank. **2.** Crank for use as a handle.

Winchester, n. [1. wínchester; 2. wíntʃistə], fr. place-name in U.S.A. Kind of repeating rifle.

wind (I.), n. [1. wind; 2. wind]. Pronounced [wīnd; waind] to end of 18th cent., & still often so rhymed by poets. Cp. **wind (III.)**. O.E., M.E. *wind*; cp. Goth. *winds*; O.S. *wind*; O.H.G. *wint*; O.N. *vindr*, 'wind'; cogn. w. Lat. *ventus*, see **ventilate**; W. *gwynt*; cp. further O.E. *wedar*, see **weather**; O. Prussian *wetro*, 'wind'; O. Slav. *vedro*, 'good weather'; Scrt. *vāti*, 'blows'; *vāyúš*, 'wind, air'; O. Slav. *vějati*; O.H.G. *wājan*; O.E. *wāwan*, 'to blow'; Gk. *áēmi*, 'I blow'; *aḗtēs*, 'wind'; *āḗr*, 'air', fr. **awē-*, see **air**. **1.** Air set in motion by natural causes, esp. when moving rapidly enough to be perceptible: *a gentle, strong, hot, cold, wind*; *favourable, variable, winds*; *a wet wind*, one bringing rain; *contrary, fair, winds*, unfavourable, favourable, to navigation &c.; *constant winds*, blowing always in same direction over specific area; *periodical winds*, those changing their direction at specific periods; *north, west, S.E., wind* &c., blowing from specified direction; *the wind rises, falls*, becomes stronger, weaker; *(to) the four winds*, to all points of the compass, broadcast; *a capful of wind*, small gust; *against the wind, in the wind's eye, in the teeth of the wind*, towards the direction from which the wind is blowing; *between wind and water*, (i.) line where surface of water meets vessel's hull; (ii.) (fig.) part of human body between the thorax and the abdomen: *hit between wind and water*; *by the wind*, (naut.) close-hauled; *down wind, before the wind*, in the direction of, carried along by, the wind; *(to know, find out, see) how the wind blows, lies*, what direction affairs are taking, tendency of public opinion &c.; *in the wind*, in process of development, discussion &c., esp. secretly: *what's in the wind?, there's something in the wind*; *to cast (prudence, one's reputation* &c.) *to the winds*, act without consideration for it; *to get, have, the wind of*, have advantage over, be in more favourable position; *to go, run &c. like the wind*, very fast; *to raise the wind* (slang), raise funds; *to sail close to the wind*, (fig.) to verge on dishonesty, illegality, impropriety &c.; *to take the wind out of one's sails*, render action of abortive by anticipating and counteracting it. Phrs. *To put the wind up* (person), to frighten; *get the wind up*, be frightened (army slang). **2.** Air set in motion by artificial, mechanical, means &c.: *the wind from the bellows*; *the wind of the passing train*. **3. a** Scent borne by the wind; (hence fig.) **b** rumour, hint: *to get wind of*, hear as rumour &c. **4.** Gas produced in stomach or bowels by acidity, indigestion &c.; flatulence. **5. a** Breath; regularity or force of breathing, lung power: *to lose, get, one's wind*; *sound in wind and limb*; *broken wind*, impaired breathing (esp. of horse); *second wind*, regularity of breathing regained during violent exercise after first breathlessness; **b** part of body below diaphragm, blow on which temporarily checks breathing: *to hit one in the wind*. **6.** Empty talk, purposeless or extravagant use of words. **7.** (mus.) Wind-instruments in an orchestra; contrasted with strings; *brass wind*, trumpets &c.; *wood-wind*, flutes &c.

wind (II.), vb. trans., fr. prec. **1.** To scent, detect by scent: *the hounds winded the quarry*. **2.** To exhaust the breath of, cause to breathe with an effort: *to be winded by running*. **3.** To recover the wind of, give opportunity of getting breath to: *to stop in order to wind the horses*.

wind (III.), vb. trans. [1. wīnd; 2. waind], fr. **wind (I.)**. **1.** To sound a call or signal on (horn, bugle &c.). **2.** To sound, produce, on wind-instrument: *to wind a call* &c.

wind (IV.), vb. intrans. & trans. [1. wīnd; 2. waind]. O.E. *windan*; M.E. *winden*, 'to wind; to go, circle round'; cp. O.S. *windan*; O.H.G. *wintan*; O.N. *vinda*; Goth. *windan*, 'to wind, turn, twist'; cp. further Goth. *wandjan*; O.E. *wenden*, 'to turn', see **wend (I.)**; Goth. *wandus*; O.N. *vǫndr*, 'supple rod', see **wand**. **A.** intrans. **1. a** (of series or line of moving beings) To go, pass along: '*The lowing herd winds slowly o'er the lea*' (Gray's 'Elegy'); **b** to pass by a curving, tortuous course: '*And as the boat-head wound along The willowy hills and fields among*' (Tennyson, 'Lady of Shalott'). **2. a** (of road, stream, course) To run, flow, lead, in bends and twistings; **b** (of stairway) to pass upwards or downwards in spirals round a central structure. **3.** *Wind round*, (of a serpent, climbing plant &c.) to coil, twine, round. **B.** trans. **1. a** (i.) To turn, cause to revolve: *to wind a handle*; (ii.) to raise, draw up, by winding: *to wind a bucket, water, from a well*; **b** to start mechanism of by winding; (i.) to tighten spring of (watch or clock) by turning a key; (ii.) to raise weights of (certain kinds of clock) by turning a handle. **2.** To form into a ball by a series of circular movements, by coiling up evenly on itself, or round something as a basis: *to wind wool*; *to wind thread on to a reel, a line on to a stick* &c. Phr. *to (be able to) wind a person round one's little finger*, bend him to one's will, make him do what one pleases. **3.** To enfold with, wrap round, twine round: *to wind one's arms round a person's neck*; *wind a shawl round a baby, a baby in a shawl* &c. **4.** *To wind one's way*, to pursue one's course, esp. deliberately, cautiously. **C.** Followed by adverbs & preps. *Wind off*, trans., to remove by unwinding, uncoiling: *to wind cotton off a reel*. *Wind up*, **1.** trans., **a** to coil round and round, form into a ball: *to wind up wool, string* &c.; **b** to recoil, or increase tightness of spring to fullest extent, in order to set, or keep, going: *to wind up a watch*; **c** to increase intensity of feeling of: *wound up to a high pitch of excitement*; **d** to bring to an end, terminate, conclude: *to wind up a speech by a quotation*; *the Chancellor wound up the debate*; *to wind up a company*, dissolve it; **2.** intrans., (of person) to stop, conclude: *I hope this tedious speaker will soon wind up*; (of trading company) to go into liquidation.

wind (V.), n., fr. prec. **1.** Act of winding; turn of handle, crank &c.; single turn in winding wool &c. **2.** Bend, curve, turn, twist; winding: *the winds of a path, stream* &c.

windage, n. [1. windij; 2. windidž]. **wind (I.)** & **-age**. **1. a** Amount of deviation of projectile from its normal course owing to wind; **b** allowance for such deflection made in aiming. **2.** Difference between diameter of projectile and that of bore of gun from which it is discharged.

windbag, n. [1. wíndbag; 2. windbæg]. (slang) A person who talks much but says little; one who utters platitudes in a high-flown, verbose style.

wind-bound, adj. Delayed by contrary winds.

wind-break, n. Fence, hedge &c. breaking force of wind.

wind-chest, n. Box in organ from which compressed air is supplied to the pipes.

wind-colic, n. Pain due to flatulence.

wind-cutter, n. Upper lip of mouth of organ pipe.

wind-egg, n. **a** Imperfect egg with very thin shell; **b** unfertilized egg.

winder, n. [1. wínder; 2. wáində]. **wind (II.)** & **-er**. One who, that which, winds; esp. a mechanical apparatus for winding thread &c.

windfall, n. [1. wíndfawl; 2. windfōl]. **1.** Fruit blown down by wind. **2.** Unexpected piece of good luck; specif., unanticipated legacy or sum of money received.

wind-fanner, n. Windhover.

windflower, n. [1. wíndflòuer; 2. windflduə]. Wood anemone.

wind-gall, n. Soft swelling on horse's fetlock.

wind-gauge, n. **1.** Instrument for measuring force of wind. **2.** Indicator showing amount of air in wind-chest of organ. **3.** Device fixed on gun indicating force of wind and allowance to be made for windage.

windhover, n. [1. wínd-hòver; 2. windhɔ̀və]. Kestrel.

windily, adv. [1. wíndili; 2. windili]. **windy** & **-ly**. In a windy manner.

windiness, n. [1. wíndines; 2. windinis]. **windy** & **-ness**. State or quality of being windy.

winding (I.), adj. [1. wīnding; 2. wáindiŋ], fr. Pres. Part. of **wind (IV.)**. Tending to wind; having numerous turns and twists, constantly curving in a different direction: *a winding stream, path, passage* &c.; *a winding staircase*, one built in a spiral.

winding (II.), n. **wind (IV.)** & **-ing**. **a** Twist, turn, curve, bend, of winding course; coil, spiral, of coiled object; esp. **b** (pl.) *windings*, series of bends or curves of stream, road &c.

windingly, adv. [1. wīndingli; 2. wáindiŋli]. **winding (I.)** & **-ly**. With many windings.

winding-sheet, n. Sheet used to wrap a corpse; a shroud.

winding-up, n. **a** Act or process of concluding; state of being concluded; termination; specif. **b** liquidation of a company.

wind-instrument, n. Musical instrument, the notes of which are produced by air, esp. by breath.

wind-jammer, n. [1. wínd jàmer; 2. wínd džæ̀mə]. Large, swift sailing ship.

windlass, n. & vb. trans. [1. wíndlas; 2. wíndləs]. M.E. *windelas*, prob. fr. A.-Fr. *windas*, fr. O.N. *vindáss*, fr. *vinda*, 'to wind', fr. base in **wind (IV.)**, & *āss*, 'beam, pillar'; cp. Goth. *ans*, 'beam'; cogn. w. Gk. *ánios*, 'burdensome'; *anía*, 'trouble'; & prob. w. Lat. *onus*, 'burden', see **onus**. **1.** n. Apparatus for hoisting or hauling by means of a rope or wire wound on to a horizontal drum &c. **2.** vb. To hoist by means of a windlass.

windless, adj. [1. wíndles; 2. windlis]. **wind (I.)** & **-less**. Without wind; still, calm: *a windless day*.

windlestraw, n. [1. wíndlstràw; 2. wíndlstrɔ̀]. O.E. *windelstrēaw*, fr. *windel*, 'twisting', fr. **wind (IV.)** & **straw (I.)**. Dry, withered grass-stalk.

windmill, n. [1. win(d)mil; 2. win(d)mil]. **1.** Mill for grinding corn turned by the pressure of the wind upon the sails. **2.** Any apparatus resembling the sails of a windmill which, when made to revolve by wind pressure, performs certain work, esp. that of pumping water.

window, n. [1. wíndō; 2. windou]. M.E. *windohe, windowe*, fr. O.N. *vindauga*; see **wind (I.)** & **eye**. Opening in the wall or roof of a building to admit light, usually filled with panes of glass fixed in a movable frame; similar glazed opening in a closed vehicle; *to break a window*, break one or more panes of glass in a window.

window-box, n. **1.** Hollow recess in a window-frame in which the sash-weight moves. **2.** Box on window-sill for growing plants.

window-dressing, n. Art of arranging goods in shop-window.

windowed, adj. [1. wíndōd; 2. windoud]. **window** & **-ed**. Having, furnished with, windows.

windowless, adj. [1. wíndōles; 2. windoulis]. **window** & **-less**. Without windows.

window-pane, n. Pane of glass in a window.

window-seat, n. Broad seat fitted below a window, so adapted that a person using it can see out.

windpipe, n. [1. wíndpīp; 2. windpaip]. Air-passage between mouth and lungs; trachea.

windrow, n. [1. wíndrō; 2. windrou]. Line of hay raked into a low ridge after cutting, and left to dry before putting into cocks.

wind-sail, n. Canvas funnel or tube for ventilating ship's hold &c.

wind-screen, n. Transparent plate of glass &c. to shelter driver of motor &c. from wind.

Windsor, n. [1. wíndzer; 2. wíndzə], fr. Windsor in Berkshire, where is the royal palace of Windsor Castle. *The House and Family of Windsor*, the style, adopted 1917, of the reigning dynasty of Great Britain and Ireland; *Windsor chair*, wooden chair with curving back and sides; *Windsor soap*, also *brown Windsor*, kind of cheap brown, scented toilet soap; *Windsor uniform*, uniform worn, at Windsor Castle only, by members of the royal family and certain officers of the Household, consisting of a dark blue evening-dress coat with scarlet collar, facings, and cuffs, white waistcoat, and black breeches or trousers.

wind-spout, n. Revolving column of air; tornado, whirlwind.

wind-stick, n. (slang) Propeller of aeroplane.

wind-swept, adj. Exposed to winds.

wind-tight, adj. Not permitting the passage of, impervious to, wind.

windward, adj. & n. [1. wíndward; 2. wíndwəd]. **wind** (I.) & **-ward. 1.** adj. Facing, exposed to, the direction from which the wind is blowing: *the windward side.* **2.** n. Windward side or region: *the boat passed to windward.* Phr *to get to windward of*, to get an advantage over.

windy, adj. [1. wíndi; 2. wíndi]. **wind** (I.) & **-y. 1.** Abounding in, exposed to, wind: *a windy day; windy weather; a windy spot; the windy side of the house.* **2.** Addicted to, characterized by, empty verbosity: *a windy speaker; windy rhetoric.* **3.** (slang) Having the wind up; nervous, frightened.

wine (I.), n. [1. win; 2. wain]. O.E.; M.E. *win*; O.H.G. *wīn*; O.N. *vīn*; Goth. *wein*; very ancient loan-word fr. Lat. *vīnum*, 'wine', see **vine. 1.** Fermented grape-juice. Phr. *Adam's wine*, water; *in wine*, intoxicated; *to take wine with (a person)*, to raise one's glass ceremoniously, bow to the person, and drink to his health. **2.** Fermented juice of other fruit or flowers, the kind being usually specified: *currant, cowslip, elderberry, dandelion, wine* &c. **3.** (univ.) A friendly evening party, usually of limited size, at which wine is drunk: *to have a wine in one's rooms.* **4.** (med.) Medicinal solution of drug in wine. **5.** Also *wine-colour*, colour of red wine.

wine (II.), vb. intrans., fr. prec. To drink wine, esp. to indulge to excess in wine-drinking.

winebag, n. [1. wínbag; 2. wáinbæg]. **1.** Wineskin. **2.** (slang) Winebibber.

winebibber, n. [1. wínbìber; 2. wáinbìbə]. Person given to excessive drinking of wine.

winebibbing, n. [1. wínbìbing; 2. wáinbìbiŋ]. Excessive indulgence in wine.

winebottle, n. [1. wínbòtl; 2. wáinbɔ̀tl]. **1.** Glass bottle for wine. **2.** Wineskin.

winebowl, n. [1. wínbōl; 2. wáinboul]. Bowl used for drinking wine.

wine-carriage, n. Wheeled vessel for passing a decanter or bottle of wine round table.

wine-cellar, n. Cellar in which wine is stored.

wine-cooler, n. Vessel for holding ice in which bottle of wine is placed to cool.

winecup, n. [1. wínkup; 2. wáinkap]. Cup from which wine is drunk.

winefat, n. [1. wínfat; 2. wáinfæt]. The second element is an old, Nthn. or Midland, form of **vat.** (Bib. and archaic) Wine-press; cp. Is. lxiii. 2.

wineglass, n. [1. wínglahs; 2. wáinglās]. **1.** Drinking-glass, varying in size and shape, used for wine. **2.** (as measure) Usually, sherry glass.

wineglassful, n. [1. wínglahsfòol; 2. wáinglāsfùl]. Prec. & **-ful.** Amount contained in a wineglass, about two fluid ounces.

wineless, adj. [1. wínles; 2. wáinlis]. **wine** & **-less.** Without wine.

wine-marc, n. Refuse left after juice has been crushed from grapes.

wine-palm, n. Variety from which palm wine is made.

wine-press, n. Apparatus for pressing juice from grapes for making wine.

winery, n. [1. wíneri; 2. wáinəri]. **wine** & **-ry.** Establishment where wine is made.

wineskin, n. [1. wínskin; 2. wáinskin]. Animal's skin made into a bag for holding wine.

wine-stone, n. Tartar deposited by wine.

wine-vault, n. **1.** Cellar for storing wine. **2.** Cellar, shop, bar, where wine is sold and consumed.

wine-whey, n. Drink made of wine, whey, and sugar.

wing (I.), n. [1. wing; 2. wiŋ]. M.E. *weng, wing*, fr. O.N. *vengja*, 'wing'; cp. change (in pronunciation) of *e* to *i* before *-ng* in *England* &c.; cogn. w. Swed. *vinge* 'wing'; further etymol. doubtful. **1.** One of the fore-limbs, including bones, feathers &c., by means of which a bird flies. Phrs. *grey-goose wing*, arrow; *on the wings of the wind*, very swiftly; *fear &c. lent him wings*, made him go extra fast; *to clip the wings of*, limit activities of; *to take to itself wings*, depart, vanish, quickly; *under the wing of*, under the protection of; *on the wing*, (i.) in flight; (ii.) (fig.) in the act or process of departing; *to take wing*, to fly away; to depart. **2.** Organ, usually membranous, by means of which an insect, bat, flying-fish &c. propels itself through the air. **3.** One of the broad, flat surfaces by means of which an aeroplane is supported in the air. **4. a** Structure resembling a wing in position, appearance &c.; specif. **b** projection at side or end of building, at right angles to main part; **c** (pl.) sides of stage; scenery placed in this position. **5.** Appendage resembling a wing in shape or position; specif. **a** thin, flat membrane attached to some kinds of seed, by means of which it is carried through the air; **b** one of the two side petals of a flower of the bean family. **6. a** Division of army, member of team &c. working on one side of main body: *right, left, wing*; **b** a division, consisting of three squadrons, of the Royal Air Force.

wing (II.), vb. trans. & intrans., fr. prec. **A.** trans. **1.** To give wings to, furnish (arrow &c.) with wings. **2.** (lit. and fig.) To set in motion, start in flight; impel rapidly, increase speed of: *to wing an arrow at its mark; horror winged his steps; jealousy winged his shafts.* **3.** (of birds) To fly over, traverse on the wing: '*Part loosely wing the region*' (Milton, 'P. L.' vii. 425); also *to wing the air; wing its way through the air; wings its flight*, flies. **4.** To wound (bird) in the wing, or (person) in the arm. **B.** intrans. To fly through the air on wings: *the angel wings heavenwards.*

wing-beat, n. Single complete movement of bird's wing in flying.

wing-case, n. Thickened horny development of fore-wing of some insects, forming a protective cover for posterior wing.

wing-commander, n. Officer in Royal Air Force corresponding in rank to a commander in navy, or a lieutenant-colonel in the army.

wing-covert, n. One of the small feathers at joint of wing, covering base of flying feathers.

winged, adj. [1. wingd; 2. wiŋd]. **wing** (I.) & **-ed.** Having, furnished with, wings; *the winged god*, Mercury; *the winged horse*, Pegasus.

wing-footed, adj. (poet.) Flying as on wings; swift.

wingless, adj. [1. wíngles; 2. wíŋlis]. **wing** (I.) & **-less.** Without wings.

winglet, n. [1. wínglet; 2. wíŋlit]. **wing** (I.) & **-let.** Small wing.

wing-sheath, n. Wing-case.

wing-spread, n. Width across extended wings from tip to tip.

wing-stroke, n. Wing-beat.

wink (I.), vb. intrans. & trans. [1. wingk; 2. wiŋk]. O.E. *wincian*, 'to nod, wink'; M.E. *winken*; cp. M.H.G. *winken*; see **wince. A.** intrans. **1.** (of person) **a** To open and close eyelids quickly, blink; **b** to lower and raise one eyelid, esp. as signal or hint to another person; see *wink at.* **2.** (of eye) To close and open rapidly. Phr. (slang) *like winking*, very swiftly. **3.** (of light, star &c.) To shine, flash, intermittently or fitfully; twinkle. **B.** trans. To close and open (eye) rapidly. **C.** Followed by preposition. *Wink at*, **1.** to give a hint or signal to a person by lowering and raising one eyelid quickly; **2.** to connive at, ignore deliberately (misconduct, an abuse &c.).

wink (II.), n., fr. prec. Act of winking: **a** momentary closing of eyes: *I have not slept a wink, did not get a wink of sleep*; Phr. *forty winks*, short nap; **b** rapid closing and opening of one eye to convey a signal, hint &c. Phr. (slang) *to tip (a person) the wink*, give him a hint.

winkle, n. [1. wíngkl; 2. wíŋkl]. O.E. *-wincla*, 'shell-fish' (with spiral shell); cogn. w. O.E. *wincian*, 'to nod, wink'; see **wink**; O.H.G. *wanchōn*, 'to draw back, start, move sideways'; Lat. *vagāri*, 'to wander'; see **vagary** & words there referred to. Edible shell-fish, sea-snail, periwinkle.

winner, n. [1. wíner; 2. wínə]. **win** (I.) & **-er. 1.** One who, that which, wins; specif., a horse that wins a race: *the evening papers will give all the winners.* **2.** *-winner*, earner, see **bread-winner.**

winning, adj. [1. wíning; 2. wíniŋ], fr. Pres. Part. of **win** (I.). **1.** Victorious in contest &c.: *the winning horse, team, side* &c. **2.** Giving, leading to, victory in contest, game &c.: *the winning hit, stroke, shot, move* &c. **3.** Charming, attractive, engaging: *winning manners, smile, personality* &c.

winningly, adv. Prec. & **-ly.** In a winning manner; engagingly.

winning-post, n. Post marking end of racecourse.

winnings, n. [1. winingz; 2. wíniŋz]. **win** (I.) & **-ing.** Amount won, esp. money won in betting.

winnow, vb. trans. [1. wínō; 2. wínou]. O.E. *windwian*; M.E. *wind(e)wen, winewen*, 'to winnow'; cp. Goth. *(dis)winþjan*, 'to throw apart'; O.H.G. *wintōn*, 'to winnow'; cogn. w. Lat. *vannus*, 'winnowing fan', see **van** (III.) & **fan** (I.); *ventilāre*, 'to blow, winnow', see **ventilate**; Gk. *ainein* (fr. *wanj-), 'to separate grain from chaff'; Lith. *vėtau*, 'to winnow'; cogn. also w. **wind** (I.). **1. a** To separate (grain &c.) from husks, chaff &c. by allowing a current of air to play upon it; **b** to separate, remove, clear off (chaff &c.) from grain by means of a current of air. **2.** (fig.) **a** To separate, sort out, discern, sift, what is good, true, reliable &c., from what is bad, worthless, doubtful &c.: *to winnow the facts from a mass of words*; **b** to separate (what is false, inferior &c.) from what is good or reliable. **3.** (poet.) **a** To beat with or as with wings; to agitate, stir, (of Satan) '*with quick fan Winnows the buxom air*' (Milton, 'P. L.' v. 269-70); **b** (of air) to pass through and stir.

winsome, adj. [1. wínsum; 2. wínsəm]. O.E. *wynsum*, 'pleasant', M.E. *winsome*; fr. *wynn*, 'joy, pleasure', q.v. under **wish,** & **-some.** Engaging, attractive; sweet and charming: *a winsome maiden, smile, face* &c.; *winsome manners.*

winsomely, adv. Prec. & **-ly.** In a winsome manner.

winsomeness, n. See prec. & **-ness.** Quality of being winsome.

winter (I.), n. [1. wínter; 2. wíntə]. O.E., M.E. *winter*; cp. O.S., O.H.G. *winter*; Goth. *wintrus*, 'winter'; prob. orig., 'the white or snowy season', cp. O. Gaul. *vindo-*, 'white'; W. *gwynn.* **1.** Coldest season of the year, between autumn and spring, usually considered to include, in Northern hemisphere, the months of December, January, February; (astron.) from autumn solstice (Dec. 22nd) to vernal equinox (Mar. 20th). Phr. *hard winter*, a very cold one. **2.** (poet.) Year, esp. in reckoning age of old person: *a man of eighty winters.*

winter (II.), vb. intrans. & trans., fr. prec. **1.** intrans. To spend, live during, the winter: *to winter in Italy, on the Riviera* &c. **2.** trans. To keep, graze (cattle &c.) during the winter.

winter (III.), adj., fr. **winter** (I.). Occurring in, characteristic of, used or occupied in, carried on during, the winter: *winter frosts, clothes, quarters, sports, apples* &c.; *winter sleep*, hibernation.

winter-apple, n. One which ripens during the winter.

winterberry, n. [1. wínterbèri; 2. wíntəbèri]. Red-berried N. American shrub; black alder.

winter garden, n. Large conservatory, warmed, stocked with semi-tropical trees and shrubs, and used as a smoking and sitting room.

winter-green, n. Genus of low-growing, evergreen plants, *Gaultheria*, the leaves of which yield an aromatic oil, used for flavouring and scenting.

winterless, adj. [1. wínterles; 2. wíntəlis]. **winter** (I.) & **-less**. Without cold season.

winter-lodge, n. (bot.) Bulb &c. enclosing embryo during winter.

winterly, adj. [1. wínterli; 2. wíntəli]. **winter** & **-ly**. Wintry.

winter sports, n. Open-air sports, skiing, skating &c. indulged in, esp. in Switzerland, Norway &c., in winter.

wintertide, n. [1. wíntertìd; 2. wíntətàid]. Season of winter.

wintriness, n. [1. wíntrines; 2. wíntrinis]. Next word & **-ness**. Quality of being wintry.

wintry, adj. [1. wíntri; 2. wíntri]. **winter** & **-y**. **1.** Characteristic of winter; cold, stormy, snowy &c. **2.** (fig.) Cold, unfriendly, frigid, in manner, expression &c.: *a wintry smile, greeting* &c.

winy, adj. [1. wíni; 2. wáini]. **wine** & **-y**. Resembling, having colour or taste of, wine.

winze, n. [1. winz; 2. winz]. Perh. connected w. **wind** (I.). Small mine-shaft for ventilation or communication between two levels.

wipe (I.), vb. trans. [1. wīp; 2. waip]. O.E. *wīpian*; M.E. *wīpen*, 'to wipe'; cp. O.H.G. *wipf*, 'impulse, movement'; *wipfil*, 'the top of a tree', lit. 'the swaying part'; also O.H.G. *weif*, 'a band'; Goth. *waips*, 'a crown'; *weipan*, 'to crown'; O.N. *veipr*, 'cloth for binding the head'; cogn. w. Lat. *vibrāre*, 'to move rapidly, brandish, shake' &c., see **vibrate**. **A.** trans. **1.** To pass a cloth or other material over surface of, in order to clean or dry, rub gently, esp. with absorbent material: *to wipe the dishes after they have been washed*; *wipe the floor with a damp cloth*; Phr. *to wipe the floor with* (person), (slang) to defeat utterly in debate or controversy; *to wipe one's eyes*, dry tears; Phr. *to wipe a person's eye* (*for him*), (slang) to rebuff, humiliate, check, by harsh action or speech. **2.** To remove, clean off, by rubbing with cloth or other absorbent material: *to wipe the mud off with a handful of grass*; *to wipe one's tears away*. **B.** Followed by adverb. *Wipe off*, trans., **a** to remove by wiping, rub off, erase. *Wipe out*, trans., **1.** to clean (vessel &c.) by rubbing round interior; **2. a** to remove, erase, by wiping: *to wipe out a mark, stain* &c.; **b** (fig.) to erase, obliterate, cancel effects of: *to wipe out an insult, debt* &c.; **c** to destroy utterly, exterminate (a military force, a race, family &c.). *Wipe up*, trans., to take up by mopping or rubbing with a cloth &c.: *to wipe up spilt milk*.

wipe (II.), n., fr. prec. **1.** Act of wiping, state of being wiped: *to give the floor a wipe*. **2.** (slang) A blow, a clip, a biff. Phr. *a wipe in the eye*, (also fig.) a rebuff, snub. **3.** (vulg. slang) Handkerchief.

wiper, n. [1. wíper; 2. wáipə]. **wipe** (I.) & **-er**. One who, that which, wipes; device, material for wiping; esp. in compounds, e.g. *pen-wiper*, q.v.

wire (I.), n. [1. wīr; 2. waiə]. O.E., M.E. *wīr*; cp. O.H.G. *wiara*, 'wire'; O.N. *virr*, 'spiral'; Swed. *vira*, 'to twist'; cogn. w. Lat. *viriae*, 'armlet'; of Celt. origin, cp. O. Ir. *fiar*, 'bent'; fr. base **wei-*, **wi-*, 'to bend', seen also in Lat. *viēre*, 'to twist, weave'; Scrt. *vyájati*, 'winds'; Gk. *ítus*, 'rim of shield'; O.E. *wiðig*, 'band; willow', see **withy**. **1.** Fine-drawn, slender, flexible thread, rod &c. of metal: *copper, iron, steel, wire* &c.; *telegraph, telephone, wires*; *barbed wire*, see **barb** (I.). Phr. *to pull the wires*, (i.) to move puppets by means of wires &c., hence, (ii.) to control affairs through secret influence; *a live wire*, (i.) one charged with electricity, hence (ii.) a vigorous, pushing, vital person. **2. a** Telegraphy as means of communication: *to send a message by wire*; **b** (colloq.) a telegram: *to send, receive, a wire*.

wire (II.), vb. trans. & intrans., fr. prec. **A.** trans. **1. a** To secure, fasten, stiffen, connect &c. with wire: *to wire the stems of flowers*; *to wire beads together*; **b** to snare, catch (birds, rabbits &c.), with wires. **2.** To provide with wire; to lay wire or wires in, for any purpose: *to wire a house for electric light*. **3.** To communicate by telegraph: *to wire the news to a person*. **B.** intrans. To send a telegram: *please wire as soon as you hear*. **C.** Followed by adverb. *Wire in*, intrans., (slang) to engage energetically in some enterprise; to set to work vigorously: *you had better wire in and finish the job*.

wire-cloth, n. Fabric woven of wire.

wire-cutter(s), n. Instrument for cutting wire.

wire-dancer, n. Acrobat who performs on a taut wire.

wiredraw, vb. trans. [1. wírdràw; 2. wáiədrɔ̄]. **1.** To draw out (metal) into wire by passing it through holes of required diameter. **2.** To treat (argument &c.) with excessive subtlety or over-refinement.

wire-edge, n. Very thin edge formed on a cutting instrument by over-grinding or honing, which turns over or peels off when the instrument is used.

wire-entanglement, n. Form of military defence consisting of barbed wire stretched and twisted in and out between and round stout stakes firmly planted in the ground.

wire-gauge, n. Gauge for measuring size of round wire.

wire-gauze, n. Thin fabric woven of wire.

wire-gun, n. Cannon made of an iron tube with wire wound round it.

wire-haired, adj. Having short, rough, stiff hair; esp. describing a breed of fox-terrier.

wire-heel, n. Disease affecting horse's foot.

wireless, adj. & n. [1. wírles; 2. wáiəlis]. **wire** & **-less**. **1.** adj. Without wire(s); specif. **a** connected with, pertaining to, a system of telegraphy or telephony in which sounds or signals are conveyed from a transmitting station to various receiving stations, through the ether direct, by means of radiating electric waves; **b** (of message &c.) transmitted by wireless. **2.** n. **a** Wireless telegraphy or telephony; **b** a message sent by this means.

wireless-cabin, n. Wireless-room.

wireless operator, n. Ship's wireless telegrapher.

wireless-room, n. Room on a ship containing wireless installation.

wireless station, n. Place equipped for transmitting and receiving wireless messages &c.

wire-netting, n. Network of thin wire, made with various sizes of mesh, used for fencing &c.

wire-puller, n. Person who pulls the wires; specif., one who brings secret influence to bear to effect a purpose.

wire-rope, n. Rope of twisted wire.

wire-worm, n. Stiff, worm-like larva which attacks the roots of plants.

wire-wove, adj. (of paper) Smooth and unlined, made in a frame of wire-gauze.

wirily, adv. [1. wírili; 2. wáiərili]. **wiry** & **-ly**. In a wiry manner.

wiriness, n. [1. wírines; 2. waiərinis]. **wiry** & **-ness**. Quality of being wiry.

wiring, n. [1. wíring; 2. wáiəriŋ]. **wire** & **-ing**. System of wires for conveying electric current &c.

wiry, adj. [1. wíri; 2. wáiəri]. **wire** (I.) & **-y**. **1.** Resembling wire in being thin, stiffish, but flexible. **2.** (of persons &c.) Strong and tough, capable of physical endurance; sinewy without being especially large or muscular.

wis, vb. [1. wis; 2. wis]. Bogus vb. used in sham archaism (used by Spenser) in *I wis*, supposed to mean 'I know, ween'; due to misinterpretation of M.E. *y-wis, i-wis*, 'certainly', fr. O.E. *ġewis*. This sham Pres. was no doubt partly a back-formation fr. the genuine Pret. *wiste*, 'knew'; see **wist**. Browning actually has *you wis!*

wisdom, n. [1. wízdum; 2. wízdəm]. O.E. *wīsdōm*; M.E. *wīsdom*; **wise** & **-dom**. **1.** The quality of being wise; sound judgement, sagacity. **2.** (archaic) Learning, knowledge, science: *the wisdom of the ancients*. **3.** (cap.) Name of two books of the Apocrypha, *Wisdom* (*of Solomon*), and *Wisdom of Jesus, the son of Sirach*, usually known as *Ecclesiasticus*.

wisdom-tooth, n. Third molar of human being, usually cut about the twentieth year. Phr. *to cut one's wisdom-teeth*, acquire a mature judgement by age and experience.

wise (I.), adj. [1. wīz; 2. waiz]. O.E., M.E. *wīs*; cp. O.S., O.H.G. *wīs*; O.N. *viss*; Goth. *weis*, 'wise'; fr. earlier **wīss-*, fr. Aryan **wid-tō*, fr. base **wid-*, **weid-*, 'to see; to know'; see further under **wit** (I.), **vide, idea**. **1. a** (of persons) Having sound judgement; sagacious, prudent, shrewd; **b** (of thought or action) informed with, springing from, based on, wisdom, sagacity, prudence; **c** (of utterance, sayings, writings) embodying, expressing, wisdom. **2.** Having knowledge of, information upon, some subject: *I was none the wiser for his explanation*. Phr. (Am.) *to put a person wise to, on* (a matter, a situation &c.), give him full information, explanation &c. concerning it; *wise woman*, (archaic) one supposed to be versed in some branch of occult science, having mysterious powers, (i.) a witch; (ii.) a midwife.

wise (II.), n. O.E., M.E. *wīse*, 'way, manner'; cp. O.S., O.H.G. *wīsa*, 'manner'; O.E. *wīsian*, 'to show, guide', lit. 'to put wise'; cogn. w. **wise** (I.), & cp. **guise**. (archaic) Way, manner, fashion: *in any wise*; *in no wise*; *on this wise*; *in stately wise*.

-wise, suff. representing prec., used w. ns. & advs. to form advs. of manner, e.g. *lengthwise, likewise, crosswise* &c.

wiseacre, n. [1. wízàker; 2. wáizèikə], fr. M. Du. *wijs-segger*, fr. Germ. *weissager*, wh. was formed by popular etymol., as though *weis*, 'wise', see **wise**, & *sager*, 'sayer', see **say**, really fr. M.H.G. *wīzago*; 'sage, prophet'; cp. O.E. *wītiga*; *wīz(z)ago*, 'sage, prophet'; cp. O.E. *wītiga*; O.N. *vitki*, 'sage'; fr. base of **wise** & **wit**. Person who assumes an air of wisdom.

wish (I.), vb. trans. & intrans. [1. wish; 2. wiʃ]. O.E. *wȳscan*; M.E. *wischen*, 'to wish'; cp. O.H.G. *wunskan*; M. Du. *wunschen*, 'to wish'; O.H.G. *wunsc*; cogn. w. O.E. *wynn*, 'joy', see **winsome**; *wunian*, 'to remain, live', see **wont**; O.E. (*gi*)*winnan*, 'to obtain', see **win**; cogn. w. Lat. *venus*, 'love, charm'; see **Venus**; Scrt. *vánaš*, 'desire'. **A.** trans. **1.** To desire, crave, want, feel a longing for: *I will do what you wish*; *you may have whichever you wish*. **2. a** To feel and express a desire that oneself or another should have something, obtain a benefit, be in a specified condition &c.; to invoke (good or evil) upon: *to wish oneself at home, anywhere but where one is*; *won't you wish me good luck?*; *I wish you a happy life, a good journey, good health* &c.; *I don't wish you any harm*; Phr. (colloq.) *to wish a person further*, to feel annoyance or boredom at his presence and wish he were gone; **b** (in weakened sense) to bid: *I wish you good-bye, good morning, farewell* &c. Phr. *I'll wish you good morning*, formula for abrupt dismissal, or of sudden, happy departure. **3.** (followed by *that* and dependent clause, often with *that* suppressed) To desire, be anxious and desirous that: *I wish* (*that*) *you wouldn't make such a noise*; *don't you* *wish (that) we were at home?; I wish I could see him now.* **B.** intrans. *Wish for,* to desire; to desire to possess, long for; to desire coming of &c.: *We are apt to wish for what we can't have; it is no good wishing for rain with the glass so high.*

wish (**II.**), n., fr. prec. **1.** Desire, longing, craving: *a wish for better times; he has no wish to live.* **2.** Expression of desire, specif. **a** request, order: *to obey one's slightest wish;* **b** expressed hope for another's success &c.: *you have our good wishes; with every good wish.* **3.** That which one wishes, object of desire: *you shall have your wish; you must carry out your father's last wish(es); my dearest wish is to see you prosperous and happy.*

-wisher, n. [1. wísher; 2. wíʃə]. **wish** (**I.**) & **-er.** One who wishes, as in *well-wisher.*

wishful, adj. [1. wíshfool; 2. wíʃful]. **wish** (**II.**) & **-ful.** (followed by infin.) Having a specified wish, desirous; anxious, willing: *wishful to depart; wishful to please.*

wishing-bone, n. [1. wíshing bōn; 2. wíʃiŋ bòun]. Forked bone in front of breast of bird; when this is pulled apart by two persons, the one subsequently holding the longer part is supposed to be entitled to the fulfilment of a wish; also *wish-bone.*

wishing-cap, n. Fabulous magic cap, supposed to accomplish the wishes of the wearer.

wish-wash, n. [1. wísh wosh; 2. wíʃ wɔʃ]. Redupl. form of **wash.** (colloq.) Insipid, watery drink; wash.

wishy-washy, adj. [1. wíshi wòshi; 2. wíʃi wɔ̀ʃi]. Redupl. form of **washy.** (colloq.) **a** Thin, tasteless, weak, sloppy: *wishy-washy tea* &c.; **b** (fig.) insipid, without force, sloppy: *wishy-washy talk, sentiment* &c.

wisp, n. [1. wisp; 2. wisp]. M.E. *wisp, wips;* cp. L.G. *wiep;* Swed. dial. *vipp;* O.N. *vippa,* 'wisp'; perh. cogn. w. **wipe.** Small bunch, tuft, handful of straw, hay &c.; thin, straggly lock of hair.

wispy, adj. [1. wíspi; 2. wíspi]. Prec. & **-y.** Like, forming, a wisp: *wispy hair,* thin and straggly.

wist, vb. [1. wist; 2. wist]. O.E. & M.E. *wiste,* Pret. of *witan,* 'to know', a Pret. Pres. vb., see **wit** (**I.**). O.E. *wiste* was itself a new formation, the orig. form, also preserved in O.E., being *wisse.* This being an isolated type of Pret. in O.E., a form w. the normal suff. *-te* was made on the anal. of *cyste,* 'kissed' &c. (archaic, Bib.) Knew: *wist ye not* &c.

wistaria, n. [1. wistâria; 2. wistéəriə], fr. name of Caspar Wistar, American professor of anatomy, d. 1818. Genus of climbing plants of the bean family, with long clusters of pale purplish flowers.

wistful, adj. [1. wístfool; 2. wístful]. Prob. fr. *wishful,* w. differentiation of meaning, influenced by obs. *wistly,* fr. *wisly,* 'prudently', fr. O.E. *wīsliċe,* 'wisely' &c., w. M.E. shortening of long vowel before *-sl-.* **1.** Indicating, expressing, unfulfilled longing; pathetically eager, esp. for something unobtained or unobtainable; yearning: *wistful eyes, look, voice* &c. **2.** Pensive, musing: *he grew silent and wistful.*

wistfully, adv. Prec. & **-ly.** In a wistful manner.

wistfulness, n. See prec. & **-ness.** State or quality of being wistful.

wit (**I.**), vb. trans. & intrans. [1. wit; 2. wit]. O.E. *witan,* 'to know' (Pret. Pres. vb.); M.E. *witen,* also *wēten,* cp. **weet**; cp. O.S., Goth. *witan;* O.H.G. *wizzan;* O.N. *vita,* 'to know'; cogn. w. Lat. *vidēre,* 'to see', see **vide**; Gk. *oida,* 'know'; *eidon,* 'saw'; *idéa,* 'appearance', see **idea**; Scrt. *vḗda,* 'I know', see **Veda**; O. Slav. *vidĕti,* 'to see'; *vĕdĕ,* 'I know'; cp. further O.E. *wīs,* 'wise', see **wise** (**I.**); also other forms of the vb. under **wot** & **wist.** (archaic and defective) This type only survives now in Phr. *to wit,* namely, that is to say.

wit (**II.**), n. O.E., M.E. *witt,* 'mind, intelligence'; cp. O. Fris. *wit;* O.S. *(gi)wit;* M. Du. *wite;* O.H.G. *wizzi;* O.N. *vit;* Goth. *-witi,* 'wit'; cogn. w. prec. **1.** (sing. or pl.) Mind, understanding, mental power or perception; activity, alertness, of mind: *to exercise one's wit; a man of quick, little, wit* &c.; *to depend on one's mother wit,* natural intelligence. Phrs. *the five wits,* (archaic) (i.) the senses; (ii.) the mind; mental faculties; *out of one's wits,* insane, demented; *to have, keep, one's wits about one,* be alert and resourceful; *to be at one's wits' end,* (i.) not know what to do or say; (ii.) be without financial resources: *to live by one's wits,* earn one's living by haphazard, unscrupulous methods, without settled occupation or work. **2. a** Defined by Dryden in relation to poetry as being in the wider sense 'propriety of language', and in narrower sense 'sharpness of conceit'; **b** in present-day usage the word means, (i.) a faculty or quality of mind which perceives unexpected relations between ideas not usually associated, and the power of clothing such perceptions in a happy, neat, epigrammatic form; (ii.) the expression of such perception of relations between ideas in a felicitous, striking way.

wit (**III.**), n., fr. prec. Person possessing wit in sense **2.**

witch (**I.**), n. [1. wich; 2. witʃ]. O.E. *wiċċe,* '(female) witch'; cp. O.E. *wicca,* 'wizard'; fr. O.E. *wiccian,* 'to bewitch'; cp. M.L.G. *wicken;* connected w. **wicked. 1.** Woman in league with, or under the influence of, evil spirits and in possession of occult powers; female follower of the black art, female sorcerer. Phrs. *white witch,* one using her powers for beneficent purposes; *witches' Sabbath,* see **Sabbath. 2.** Ugly, malevolent old woman; a hag, a crone. **3.** Fascinating, bewitching woman, who uses her beauty and charm to influence people.

witch (**II.**), vb. trans., fr. prec. To bewitch, enchant, cast a magic spell over.

witch-, pref. See **wych-.**

witchcraft, n. [1. wíchkrahft; 2. wítʃkrāft]. Power and practices of a witch; sorcery.

witch-doctor, n. Magician, medicine man among savage tribes.

witchery, n. [1. wícheri; 2. wítʃəri]. **witch** & **-ery. 1.** Powers of a witch; witchcraft. **2.** (fig.) Bewitching effect, fascination, magic.

witch-hazel, wych-hazel, n. [1. wích hāzl; 2. wítʃ heizl]. See **wych-**; the twigs were, & are, used as divining rods, to wh. cause the more usual spelling is due. **a** A N. American shrub, *Hamamelis virginica,* with yellow late-flowering blossoms; also formerly in England name of the hornbeam and the wych-elm; **b** astringent medicinal substance extracted from *Hamamelis.*

witching, adj. [1. wíching; 2. wítʃiŋ]. **witch** (**II.**) & **-ing.** Capable of bewitching; captivating, fascinating.

witchingly, adv. Prec. & **-ly.** In a witching manner.

witch-knots, n. Small tangled clumps of twigs on branch of oak &c., caused by fungi.

witch-meal, n. The pollen of the club-moss.

witenagemot, n., formerly ignorantly pronounced [1. witenágemōt; 2. witinǽgimout], now more correctly [1. wítena yemót; 2. wítәna jemóut], O.E. *witena ġemōt,* fr. *witena,* genit. pl. of *wita,* 'wise man, counsellor', see **wit**, & *(ġe)mōt,* 'meeting', see **moot.** (hist.) Public national assembly of the Anglo-Saxons.

with, prep. [1. widh; 2. wið]. O.E. *wiþ* expresses opposition, hostility to; protection against; rest near, or opposite to; separation from; association with; in later M.E. the word has the senses of 'together with; among; by means of', replacing O.E. *mid* in these senses; cp. O.S., O. Fris. *wið;* O.N. *við;* cogn. w. O.E. *wiðer;* O.H.G. *widar;* Goth. *wiþra,* 'against'; fr. base **wi-,* 'two', cp. second element of **divide,** & **widow. 1.** Against, in opposition to; only after verbs and nouns expressing struggle, hostility &c.: *to fight, struggle, contend, with;* also *a fight, battle &c. with savages.* **2.** Expressing association; **a** in action: in the company of: *to ride, walk, dine, shoot, drink &c. with one's friends;* **b** association by physical propinquity: alongside of: *to live, sleep, sit, stay &c. with;* **c** expressing community and reciprocity of action: *to play cricket with; to discuss politics with.* **3.** Expressing association in aims and interests; assistance, alliance; on the side of, side by side with: *in the Great War we fought with the French against the Germans.* **4.** Expressing agreement in, harmony of, opinions, ideals &c.: *'Burns, Shelley, were with us'* (Browning, 'Lost Leader'); *I am entirely with you in this; 'he that is not with me is against me'* (Matt. xii. 30). **5. a** Indicating the object of thought, attention, preoccupation: *the lecture was concerned with early English poetry;* **b** denoting the object of an action: *to deal with each piece of business as it arises.* **6.** Indicating contrast and comparison: *compare Pope's treatment of Nature with that of Wordsworth.* **7. a** Expressing an attribute or possession: *a lady with golden hair; a man with ten thousand a year;* **b** expressing temporary association or possession: *'Methinks I see her now, With the wreath of orange blossoms, Upon her snowy brow'* (T. Haynes Bayly); *the man with the frock-coat and bowler hat;* **c** expressing manner in adverbial phrases: *standing with his hands in his pockets; with an ugly smile on his face; he came home with a black eye.* **8. a** Expressing a cause; on account of: *I am dying with hunger; roses wet with dew; eyes dim with tears;* **b** indicating the instrument; by means of: *he struck me with a stick; to light a house with electricity; to amuse oneself with a book;* **c** indicating material or content: *stuffed with straw; a hole filled with rubbish.* **9.** Expressing coincidence in time, simultaneity of two actions or occurrences; at the same time as: *to rise with the lark; to come home with the milk; with the death of Queen Victoria a great epoch ended.* **10.** Expressing correspondence; **a** in proportion to, in the same degree as: *to move with the age; it grew colder with the approach of sunset;* **b** in the same direction as: *the shadow moves with the sun.* **11.** After certain verbs expressing **a** physical separation: *I parted with him at the door;* **b** separation, division, in opinion; disagreement: *to quarrel with, differ with* (a person) &c. **12.** Notwithstanding, in spite of: *with all his wealth he is unhappy.* **13.** To the accompaniment of; indicating manner: *he greeted me with smiles; 'come before his presence with a song'* (Ps. c. 1).

with-, pref. Same as prec. **1.** Expresses departure, removal, see **withdraw. 2.** Expresses refusal, see **withhold.**

withal, adv. & prep. [1. widháwl; 2. wiðɔ́l]. Prec. & **all.** (archaic) **1.** adv. In addition, besides, moreover: *a man of breeding and a very honest fellow withal.* **2.** prep. = with, esp. when expressing the instrument, at the end of a sentence: *the sword he used to defend himself withal.*

withdraw, vb. trans. & intrans. [1. widhdráw; 2. wiðdrɔ́]. **with-** & **draw. A.** trans. **1.** To draw back, pull aside, move backwards from position: *she put out her hand and then withdrew it; to withdraw one's head from the window.* **2.** To take away, recall, remove: *to withdraw troops from a country; to withdraw a book, coins &c. from circulation.* **3.** To recall, retract, contradict (one's statement, remark, promise &c.). **B.** intrans. **a** To move, draw, back; to retire, recede: *the troops withdrew; to withdraw from one's presence;* **b** to go back on one's word, back out of an undertaking: *after all your promises you can't withdraw now.*

withdrawal, n. [1. widhdráwal; 2. wiðdrɔ́əl]. Act or process of withdrawing.

withdrawing-room, n. [1. widhdráwing room; 2. wiðdrɔ́iŋ rum]. (archaic) Drawing-room.

withe, n. [1. widh, with; 2. wið, wiþ]. O.E. *wiððe;* M.E. *wiþþe,* 'withy; fetter; chaplet'; cp. O. Fris. *withthe;* O.H.G. *wida;* O.N. *við(ja);* M. Du. *wiede,* 'willow, withy'; O.H.G. *wid,* 'cord of twisted branches';

cogn. w. Gk. *itéa*, 'willow'; Scrt. *vītáš*, 'twisted'; *vītikā*, 'band'; Lith. *výtis*, 'willow branch'; Lett. *vitols*; Lat. *viēre*, 'to bind, twist', *vīnum*, 'vine'; see **viti-** & **vine**, & cp. **withy**. Flexible band of twisted osier or other tough pliant shoots, used for tying up faggots &c.

wither, vb. intrans. & trans. [1. wídher; 2. wíðə]. Prob. fr. O.N. *viðra*, 'to wither'; cp. M.E. *wideren, wederen*, 'to expose to the weather', fr. O.E. *weder*, see **weather**. **A.** intrans. **1.** (of plants and flowers) To dry up, shrivel, shrink, wilt, fade, whether as a natural process or as result of exposure to excessive heat or drought. **2.** (of affections, hopes &c.) To grow weaker, die away, be blighted. **B.** trans. **1.** To cause (flowers &c.) to wither. **2.** To blight (affections, hopes &c.), cause to die down and diminish in intensity. **3.** To disconcert, rebuff, snub, reduce to confusion and silence: *she withered him with a scornful glance.*

withered, adj. [1. wídherd; 2. wíðəd], fr. P.P. of prec. **1.** (of plants &c.) **a** Faded, shrivelled, parched from lack of water; **b** having attained maturity and died down. **2.** (of persons) Having a dried-up, faded, wrinkled appearance. **3.** (of hopes &c.) Diminished, blighted.

withering, adj. [1. wídhering; 2. wíðəriŋ], fr. Pres. Part. of prec. Tending to, having power to, wither; **a** (lit.) *a withering drought, sun*; **b** (fig.) *a withering glance, sarcasm* &c.

witheringly, adv. Prec. & **-ly**. In a withering manner.

withers, n. [1. wídherz; 2. wíðəz], fr. O.E., M.E. *wiðer*, 'against', see **with**, as part on wh. collar presses. Part of a horse's shoulder at the base of the neck. Phr. *my, his &c. withers are unwrung*, that does not affect me, him &c.

withershins, adv. [1. wídhershinz; 2. wíðəʃinz]. Scots, fr. M.L.G. *weddersins*, fr. *wider*, 'against', cp. prec., & *sin*, 'way, direction'. In a direction contrary to the apparent course of the sun; counter-clockwise.

withhold, vb. trans. [1. with-, widhhṓld; 2. wiþ-, wiðhóuld]. O.E. *wiðhāldan*; **with-** & **hold**. **1.** To hold, keep back, refrain from using or allowing to act, restrain from action: *to withhold one's hand*; *the sun withheld his light.* **2.** To refrain from granting, refuse to bestow: *to withhold one's consent, help, favour* &c.

within (I.), adv. [1. widhín; 2. wiðín]. O.E. *wiðinnan*; M.E. *wiþinnen*, 'on the inside'; **with-** & **in.** (archaic) On the inside, in the interior, internally: *the banana is yellow outside and cream-coloured within*; specif. **a** in the house, indoors: *to stay within*; *is Mrs. Smith within?*; '*the king's daughter is all glorious within*' (Ps. xlv. 14); **b** in the heart or mind, inwardly: *to be pure within.*

within (II.), n., fr. prec. The interior, inner part, inside: *seen from within, the cave looks larger.*

within (III.), prep. See **within** (I.). **1. a** Inside, in the interior of, in the inner part of: *within the building*; *to call from within the house*; *within doors*, indoors; Phr. *wheels within wheels*, secret agencies at work; **b** in the inward, mental part of: *hope sprang up within him.* **2. a** Inside the limit, scope, range, compass, power, of: *within hearing, earshot*; *within call*; *within sight of home*; *within one's powers*; *within the meaning of the Act*; *within the law*, not transgressing it; Phr. (of athlete &c.) *to be running, fighting &c. well within himself*, keeping a reserve of effort; **b** so as to be limited by, and not to exceed, amount of: *to live within one's income.* **3.** Inside of, not exceeding the limits of a specified time or distance: *to return within two hours (of one's departure* &c.); *within a few miles of London*; *within an easy walk of*, at a distance easily covered in a walk; *within an ace of death*, barely escaping.

without (I.), adv. [1. widhóut; 2. wiðáut]. O.E. *wiþūtan*; M.E. *wiþūten*, 'without, beyond'; **with-** & **out. a** On the exterior, outside, externally: *fair without and foul within*; specif. **b** outside the house, building &c.: *the messenger stands without.*

without (II.), n., fr. prec. The exterior, outside: *to look at a thing from without.*

without (III.), prep. See **without** (I.). **1.** (archaic) On the outside of, external to: *without the gate, house* &c.; '*a green hill . . . Without a city wall*' (Mrs. Alexander); *without doors*, out of doors. **2.** Not having, using; unaccompanied by; destitute, in want, of; free from, lacking: *without money, home, or friends*; *he cannot walk without a stick*; *to be without servants*; *the child came without its nurse*; *without hope of reward*; *without stint*; *without ceremony*; *all without exception*; *without rhyme or reason*; *without fear and without reproach*; *without doubt*, doubtless, certainly; *without fail*, for certain; *without end*, interminable, everlasting; *without number*, innumerable; *without prejudice* (see **prejudice**); *without regard for*, having no consideration for. Phr. *that goes without saying*, is too obvious to be mentioned. **3.** (before Pres. Part. or vbl. n. in *-ing*) Having neglected to; in such a way as to avoid: *to travel without taking a ticket*; *go in without waking him*; *without shedding of blood.*

without (IV.), conj., fr. prec. (archaic or vulg.) Unless, except, but: *you will never succeed without you work hard*; *he never goes out without he loses his umbrella.*

withstand, vb. trans. & intrans. [1. widhstánd; 2. wiðstǽnd]. O.E. *wiðstandan*, 'to resist'; **with-** & **stand. 1.** trans. To oppose, resist, endure force or attack of, esp. resist successfully: *to withstand the enemy, temptation* &c. **2.** intrans. (chiefly poet.) To offer resistance, endure.

withy, n. [1. wídhi; 2. wíði]. O.E. *wiðig*, variant of *wiððe*, 'withe', see **withe.** A young willow or osier plant.

withy-bed, n. Plantation of osiers or willows.

witless, adj. [1. wítles; 2. wítlis]. **wit** (II.) & **-less.** Lacking in, destitute of, wit; dull, foolish.

witlessly, adv. Prec. & **-ly.** In a witless way.

witlessness, n. See prec. & **-ness.** State or quality of being witless.

witling, n. [1. wítling; 2. wítliŋ]. **wit** (II.) & **-ling.** Person of little intelligence.

witness (I.), n. [1. wítnes; 2. wítnis]. O.E., M.E. *witnes(s)*; cp. O.H.G. *(gi)wiznessi*; **wit** (I.) & **-ness. 1.** Evidence in support of theory, statement &c.; testimony, corroboration: *to give witness on behalf of*; *bear witness to, of*; *to support another's witness.* **2.** Person who is able to give a first-hand account of an incident, state of affairs &c.; one who has personal knowledge of an event; eye-witness. **3.** Person or thing furnishing proof: *the empty cupboard was a witness of his poverty*; *he is a living witness to the success of the scheme.* **4.** (law) **a** Person giving evidence under oath in a court of law; **b** person who appends his signature by the side of that of the person who executes a document &c., in testimony of having seen the latter sign.

witness (II.), vb. trans. & intrans., fr. prec. **A.** trans. **1. a** (archaic) To give or furnish evidence of, testify to: *none could witness that he was present*; **b** to show, give, evidence of: *his expression witnessed his discomfiture.* **2.** To be present as an eye-witness of, to see personally: *many people witnessed the incident.* **3.** Specif., *to witness a person's signature*, to write one's own signature by the side of his, in testimony of having seen him sign; also *to witness a document*, act as witness to the signing of it. **B.** intrans. To give evidence, bear witness, testify: *to witness against one*; *to witness to a person's conduct*; *witness Heaven!*

witness-box, n. Enclosure in law-court in which a witness stands to give evidence.

-witted, adj. [1. wíted; 2. wítid]. **wit** (II.) & **-ed.** Having wits of specified quality: *quick-, slow-witted* &c.; *half-witted*, imbecile.

witticism, n. [1. wítisizm; 2. wítisizəm], fr. **witty**, on anal. of **solecism** &c. Witty remark, phrase &c.

wittily, adv. [1. wítili; 2. wítili]. **witty** & **-ly.** In a witty manner.

wittiness, n. [1. wítines; 2. wítinis]. **witty** & **-ness.** Quality of being witty.

wittingly, adv. [1. wítingli; 2. wítiŋli]. Pres. Part. of **wit** (I.) & **-ly.** Consciously, intentionally, by design.

wittol, n. [1. wítol; 2. wítəl], fr. M.E. *wodewale*, 'green woodpecker'; cp. M.H.G. *witewal*; M. Du. *wedewal.* (archaic) Husband who condones his wife's unfaithfulness; a compliant, accommodating cuckold.

witty, adj. [1. wíti; 2. wíti]. O.E. *witiġ*; M.E. *witi*, 'witty, skilful'; **wit** (II.) & **-y.** Possessed of, displaying, wit: *a witty speaker, speech* &c.

wive, vb. trans. & intrans. [1. wīv; 2. waiv]. O.E. *wīfian*; M.E. *wiven*, 'to marry', fr. *wīf*, 'woman, wife', see **wife.** (archaic) **1.** trans. To take as wife, marry. **2.** intrans. To take a wife, get married.

wivern, wyvern, n. [1. wívern; 2. wáivən]. M.E. *wivere*, 'serpent', fr. O. Fr. *wivre*, fr. Lat. *vīpera*, 'viper'; see **viper.** (her.) Fabulous monster, depicted with the head and tail of a dragon, wings, and two legs.

wizard, n. [1. wízard; 2. wízəd]. M.E. *wisard*; prob. fr. *wīs*, 'wise', & **-ard. 1.** Magician, sorcerer. **2.** Person possessing apparently magical powers, one who works wonders; a fascinating, charming person, able to influence others.

wizardry, n. [1. wízardri; 2. wízədri]. Prec. & **-ry. a** Powers or practices of a wizard; sorcery; **b** charm, fascination.

wizen(ed), weazen(ed), adj. [1. wízen(d), wḗzen(d); 2. wízən(d), wízən(d)]. O.E. *wisnian*; M.E. *wisenen*, 'to dry up'; cp. O.H.G. *wesenēn*; O.N. *visna*, 'to shrivel'; cogn. w. Lat. *viēscere*, 'to fade, shrivel'; Lith. *výstu*, 'wither'; perh. cogn. w. Lat. *vīrus*, 'moisture, slime, sap, poison', see **virus.** Dried up, shrivelled, shrunken: *a wizen(ed) old man*; *a wizen(ed) complexion*; *wizened apples.*

wizier. See **vizier.**

wo, whoa, interj. [1. wō; 2. wou]. Cry uttered to a horse; stop!

woad, n. [1. wōd; 2. woud]. O.E. *wād*; M.E. *wōd*; cp. O.H.G. *weit*; O. Fris., M. Du. *weed*; Goth. *wizdila*, 'woad'; cogn. w. Lat. *vitrum*, 'woad', perh. also w. Gk. *isátis*, 'woad' (fr. **wis-*). **1.** Herbaceous plant, *Isatis tinctoria*, of the mustard family, with clusters of yellow flowers and leaves yielding a blue dye. **2.** Blue dye obtained from this plant.

wobble, wabble (I.), vb. intrans. [1. wóbl; 2. wɔ́bl], fr. M.E. *wappen*, 'to beat', & **-le. 1. a** To sway unsteadily from side to side; to oscillate, be shaky and unsteady: *the bridge does not feel safe, it wobbles*; *the jelly wobbles*; **b** specif. (of wheels) to rock while rotating, revolve unsteadily. **2.** (fig.) To waver in purpose; to vacillate, hesitate, be inconstant in principles and opinions.

wobble (II.), n., fr. prec. **1.** Unsteady, rocking, swaying, motion; oscillation. **2.** (fig.) Vacillation in principles; instability in opinions; weakness of purpose.

woe, n. [1. wō; 2. wou]. O.E. *wā*; M.E. *wō*, 'calamity, sorrow'; cp. O.S., O.H.G. *wē*; O.N. *vǣ, vei*; Goth. *wai*, 'sorrow'; cogn. w. Lat. *vae*, 'cry of pain'; Lett. *wai*, 'alas'; *waidi*, 'lament, need'. **1.** (archaic and poet.) Sorrow, grief, trouble, misery. Phrs. *weal and woe* (see **weal** (I.)); *woe is me!*, alas!; *woe be to . . .*, *woe betide . . .*, a curse be upon; *a face of woe*, a lugubrious countenance; *a tale of woe*, recitation of sorrows and grievances. **2.** Cause of sorrow; affliction, calamity: *to tell all one's woes.*

woebegone, adj. [1. wṓbegàwn, -gòn; 2. wóubigɔ̀n, -gɔn]. **woe** & O.E. *begān*, M.E. *begoon*, P.P. of O.E. *begān*, 'to possess, occupy, surround'; **by** & **go.** Of sorrowful appearance, doleful, mournful.

woeful, adj. [1. wṓfool; 2. wóuful]. **woe** & **-ful.** Causing, characterized by, expressive of, woe; mournful: *a woeful day, spectacle, cry* &c.

woefully, adv. Prec. & **-ly.** In a woeful manner.

woke, vb. [1. wōk; 2. wouk]. O.E. *wōc*; M.E. *wook*; Pret. of **wake (I.).** The Mod. Engl. pronunciation, where one wd. have expected [1. wook; 2. wuk], cp. **took**, has been explained by Zachrisson as due to the influence of *spoke, spoken*; the infins. **wake (I.)** & **speak** were pronounced w. the same vowel [1. ā; 2. ē] by many speakers in the 17th & 18th cents.

woken, vb. [1. wṓken; 2. wóukən]. P.P. of **wake (I.).** The vowel is perh. due to the influence of that of **spoken**, see prec. Cp. O.E. (*ġe*)*wacen*, M.E. *wāken*.

wold, n. [1. wōld; 2. would]. O.E. *wāld*, 'forest, woodland'; M.E. *wōld*; cp. O.S., O.H.G. *wald*, Du. *woud*, 'forest'; O.N. *vollr*, 'uncultivated land'; prob. cogn. w. Gk. *lásios*, 'tufted, wooded', earlier **wlát-jo-*; Russ. *vóloti*, 'fibre'; Lith. *váltis*, 'ear of corn'. Cp. variant **weald.** Tract of elevated, uncultivated, open country.

wolf (I.), n. [1. woolf; 2. wulf]. O.E. *wulf*; M.E. *wulf, wolf*; cp. O.H.G. *wolf*; Goth. *wulfs*; O.N. (fem.) *ylgr*; cogn. w. Scrt. *vṛ́kaš*; Gk. *lúkos*, see **lycanthropy**; Lat. *lūpus*, see **lupine**; O. Prussian *vilkis*; Lett. *wilks*; O. Slav. *vlŭkŭ*, 'wolf'; fr. base **wl̥kʷ-os*, 'wolf'. Cp. **vulpine.** **1.** One of several species of savage, carnivorous, gregarious quadrupeds of the dog family, esp. *Canis lupus* of northern latitudes, often preying on sheep and cattle. Phrs. *a wolf in sheep's clothing*, person of mild appearance and manners, but of a sinister and malevolent nature; *to cry wolf*, raise a false alarm; *to keep the wolf from the door*, stave off want or destitution; *to have a wolf by the ears*, be in a dangerous dilemma. **2.** Rapacious, greedy, person. **3.** (mus.) Discords heard from keyboard instrument when tuned according to a system of unequal temperament.

wolf (II.), vb. trans., fr. prec. To devour ravenously and rapidly, as from hunger or greed: *to wolf one's dinner*, also *wolf down*, gulp down, swallow hungrily.

wolf-cub, n. **1.** Young wolf. **2.** Member of the junior branch of the Boy Scouts.

wolf-dog, n. **1.** Dog for hunting or guarding sheep &c. against wolves. **2.** Hybrid between dog and wolf.

wolf-fish, n. Large voracious fish of Atlantic coasts.

wolf-hound, n. *Irish, Russian, wolf-hound*, breeds of large dogs originally kept for hunting wolves.

wolfish, adj. [1. wóolfish; 2. wúlfiʃ]. **wolf (I.)** & **-ish.** Resembling a wolf, esp. in nature; cruel, fierce, rapacious.

wolfishly, adv. Prec. & **-ly.** In a wolfish manner.

wolfishness, n. See prec. & **-ness.** Quality of being wolfish.

wolfram, n. [1. wóolfram; 2. wúlfrəm]. Mod. Germ., fr. *wolf*, see **wolf**, *rahm*, 'cream'; for the second element, cp. O.E. *rēam*; Du. *room*; O.N. *rjómi*, 'cream'. **1.** Mineral ore yielding tungsten. **2.** (now rare) Tungsten.

wolframite, n. [1. wóolframīt; 2. wúlfrəmait]. Prec. & **-ite.** Wolfram.

wolf's-bane, n. Aconite, esp. species found in the Alps &c., with yellowish flowers.

wolf's-claws, n. Also *wolf's-foot*, club-moss.

wolf's-fist, n. Puff-ball.

wolf's-foot, n. Wolf's-claws.

wolfskin, n. [1. wóolfskin; 2. wúlfskin]. **a** Skin of wolf; **b** rug, cloak &c. made of this.

wolf's-milk, n. Kind of spurge, with sticky, milky sap.

wolf-spider, n. **a** Tarantula; **b** spider that chases its prey instead of entrapping it in a web.

wolf-tooth, n. Small extra tooth sometimes developing in horse in front of molar.

wolverene, -ine, n. [1. wóolverēn; 2. wúlvərīn]. Formed as dimin. of **wolf (I.).** **1.** Carnivorous mammal, *Gulo luscus*, of N. American forests, with strong limbs and bushy tail; skunk-bear or glutton. **2.** The skin of this animal as fur.

woman (I.), n. [1. wóoman; 2. wúmən]. O.E. *wīfman*; M.E. *wimman, wumman*; **wife** & **man.** **1.** Human being of female sex; **a** as contrasted with *man*; Phrs. *woman of the world*, one who is sophisticated, accustomed to society &c.; *single woman*, spinster; *to play the woman*, give way to unmanly weakness, weep &c.; *women's rights*, legal equality with men; *my good woman*, patronizing mode of address; **b** adult human female, as contrasted with *child, girl*: *my daughter will soon be a woman.* **2.** Women in general, female part of human race, womankind: *woman is weaker than man.* Phr. *born of woman*, mortal. **3.** Lady-in-waiting: *one of the queen's women.* **4.** Feminine character, emotions, qualities &c.: *there is little of the woman in her.* **5.** Man with feminine or effeminate qualities: *the governors are a set of old women.* **6.** (attrib.) Female: *woman-doctor* &c.

woman (II.), vb. trans., fr. prec. (rare) **1.** To cause to act like a woman, make effeminate or weak. **2.** To address as, refer to as a 'woman', instead of using the supposedly more dignified term 'lady'.

-woman, as suff., denoting woman connected with, occupied with, some specified object or profession &c.; or of specified nationality &c., e.g. *churchwoman, dairywoman, Englishwoman, horsewoman, needlewoman* &c.

woman-hater, n. [1. wóoman hâter; 2. wúmən hèitə]. Man with habitual aversion to women; a misogynist.

womanhood, n. [1. wóomanhòod; 2. wúmənhùd]. **woman (I.)** & **-hood.** Condition of being a woman; character or qualities of women in general.

womanish, adj. [1. wóomanish; 2. wúməniʃ]. **woman (I.)** & **-ish.** (usually in disparaging sense) Characteristic of or resembling a woman; weak, effeminate: *womanish sentiment.*

womanishly, adv. Prec. & **-ly.** In a womanish manner.

womanishness, n. See prec. & **-ness.** State or quality of being womanish.

womanize, vb. trans. & intrans. [1. wóomanīz; 2. wúmənaiz]. **woman (I.)** & **-ize.** **1.** trans. To make womanish, effeminate. **2.** intrans. (colloq.) To practise sexual intercourse with women outside wedlock.

womankind, n. [1. wóomankìnd; 2. wúmənkàind]. **woman (I.)** & **-kind.** Women collectively. Phr. *one's womankind*, women of one's family or household.

womanless, adj. [1. wóomanles; 2. wúmənlis]. **woman (I.)** & **-less.** Without women.

womanlike, adj. [1. wóomanlìk; 2. wúmənlàik]. **woman (I.)** & **-like.** Resembling or characteristic of a woman.

womanliness, n. [1. wóomanlines; 2. wúmənlinis]. Next word & **-ness.** Quality of being womanly.

womanly, adj. [1. wóomanli; 2. wúmənli]. **woman (I.)** & **-ly.** **a** Having the good qualities of a woman; tender, sympathetic, kind &c.; **b** suited, natural to, a woman: *womanly feelings, intuition, modesty* &c.

womb, n. [1. wōōm; 2. wūm]. O.E. *wāmb*, M.E. *wōmb*, 'belly, womb'; cp. O.H.G., Goth. *wamba*; O.N. *vōmb*; Dan. *vom.* Organ in female mammal in which the offspring are developed until the time of birth; uterus. Phrs. *falling of the womb*, downward displacement, prolapsus uteri; *fruit of the womb*, children (Isaiah xiii. 18); *in the womb of time*, in the unknown future.

wombat, n. [1. wómbat; 2. wɔ́mbæt], fr. Australian native *womback, wombar.* Marsupial, nocturnal, herbivorous mammal of Australia and Tasmania, genus *Phascolomys*, of several species.

womenfolk, n. [1. wíminfòk; 2. wíminfòuk]. **a** Women in general, womankind; **b** *the, one's, womenfolk*, women of a family or household &c.

won(n) (I.), vb. trans. [1. wun; 2. wan]. O.E. *wunian*, 'be accustomed; to dwell, inhabit', M.E. *wun(i)en, wonen*; cp. O.H.G. *wonēn*, 'to inhabit'; *giwonēn*, 'to be accustomed'; cogn. w. Goth. *wunan*, 'to take pleasure'; cp. further O.E. *wynn*, 'joy', see **wish, winsome**; Lat. *venus*, 'love', see **Venus**; Scrt. *vánaš*, 'desire'. See also **win.** See **wont (I.)** & **(II.).** Obs. vb. still used by Spenser: '*the noblest knight alive Prince Arthur is, that wonnes in Faerie lond*' ('F. Q.' ii. 3. 18).

won (II.), vb. [1. wun; 2. wan]. O.E. (*ġe*)*wunnen*; M.E. *wunne(n), wonne(n)*; P.P. of **win**, now used also as Pret.; cp. O.E., M.E. Pret. sing. *wann.*

wonder (I.), n. [1. wúnder; 2. wándə]. O.E. *wundor*, M.E. *wonder*; cp. O.H.G. *wuntar*; M. Du. *wonder*; O.N. *undr*, 'miracle, wonder'; perh. cogn. w. O.E. *wandian*, 'to flee from, to fear; to revere'; O.E. *wenden*, 'to turn, go', see **wend**; *windan*, 'to turn, twist', see **wind (IV.).** **1.** Object, person, incident &c. that excites a feeling of surprised admiration; a prodigy, miracle, marvel: *the seven wonders of the world*; *it is a wonder that he is still alive.* Phrs. *to do, work, wonders*, work with marvellous results; *signs and wonders*, miracles, portents; *a nine days' wonder*, event creating temporary sensation; (*it is*) *no wonder* (*that*), it is not surprising that: *no wonder you are late after such a night*; *for a wonder*, it is a surprising thing: *he is punctual today for a wonder*; *he's a perfect wonder*, a remarkable person. **2.** Feeling, emotion, of awe, astonishment, surprise, and admiration, excited by marvellous object, person, incident &c., feeling of awe aroused by something unexpected, apparently impossible &c.: *to be filled with wonder*; *to stare in wonder*; *their wonder increased.*

wonder (II.), vb. intrans. & trans. O.E. *wundrian*, M.E. *wundrien*, 'to wonder'; fr. O.E. *wundor*, 'miracle', see prec. **A.** intrans. To experience wonder, feel amazement, to marvel: *I wondered to see you there*; *I don't wonder at his anxiety*; *I wonder at you*, expressing disapproval. **B.** trans. **1.** *Wonder that*, to be amazed, marvel, feel astonishment at: *I wonder* (*that*) *you were able to escape*; *can you wonder that he refused?* **2.** To be desirous of knowing, feel curiosity about, be anxious to learn: *I wonder who he is*; *I can't help wondering if we were wise to do it.* Also as polite formula introducing a request: *I wonder whether I might ask you* &c., *whether I might trouble you to . . .*

wonderberry, n. [1. wúnderberi; 2. wándəbɛri]. A cross between the raspberry and the dewberry.

wonderful, adj. [1. wúnderfool; 2. wándəful]. **wonder (I.)** & **-ful.** **1.** Surpassing what was known or expected, arousing wonder, amazing, marvellous: *wonderful courage*; *a wonderful wealth of flowers*; *a wonderful sight*; *wonderful scenery*; *a wonderful escape.* **2.** (slang, often used as more or less meaningless intens.) Very good, splendid: *a wonderful dinner, sermon, frock* &c.

wonderfully, adv. Prec. & **-ly.** In a wonderful manner.

wondering, adj. [1. wúndering; 2. wándəriŋ]. Pres. Part. of **wonder (II.).** Feeling or expressing wonder; marvelling, amazed.

wonderingly, adv. Prec. & **-ly.** In a wondering manner.

wonderland, n. [1. wúnderlànd; 2. wándəlæ̀nd]. Real or imaginary country of marvels, surprising beauty or fertility &c.; fairyland.

wonderment, n. [1. wúnderment; 2. wándəmənt]. **wonder** & **-ment.** Wonder, astonishment, amazement.

wonder-struck, adj. Deeply affected by some marvellous sight or event &c.; overcome with wonder.

wonder-worker, n. Person who works miracles.

wondrous, adj. & adv. [1. wúndrus; 2. wándrəs], fr. obs. *wonders*, genit. of **wonder (I.)** used as adv. & adj., see **-es**; now altered on the anal. of adjs. in **-ous.** (chiefly poet.) **1.** adj. Exciting wonder; wonderful. **2.** adv. Extraordinarily, wonderfully: *wondrous kind, beautiful* &c.

wondrously, adv. Prec. & **-ly**. In a wondrous manner, to a wondrous degree.

wondrousness, n. See prec. & **-ness**. State or quality of being wondrous.

wonky, adj. [1. wóngki; 2. wɔ́ŋki]. Apparently a new word, but formed fr. an old base; cp. O.E. *wancol*, 'wavering', & Mod. Germ. *wanken*, 'to totter' &c. From another gradational form of the base comes **wink.** (slang) **a** Shaky, tottery, unsteady; groggy, dicky: *wonky on one's legs*; *the wall, this tooth, is a bit wonky*; *the Company seems rather wonky*; **b** frail, in uncertain health; **c** wavering, unreliable, shilly-shallying.

wont (I.), adj. [1. wōnt; 2. wount]; archaic [1. wunt; 2. want]. M.E. *wuned*, P.P. of *wunien, wunen*, O.E. *wunian*, 'to be accustomed', see next word; cp. O.H.G. *giwon*; O.N. *vanr*, 'accustomed'. (pred.) Accustomed, habituated: *as he was wont to do.*

wont (II.), vb., new formation fr. prec.; M.E. *wuned*, infin. *wunien*; O.E. *wunian*, 'to dwell; to be accustomed'; see **won (I.)**. (poet. or archaic) Only in Pres. 2nd and 3rd pers. (pl. rare); chiefly in the construction *as he wonts, as thou wontest*, (to do), as he is, as thou art, accustomed, used, (to do). The past tense is also *wont.*

wont (III.), n., fr. P.P. of prec. Usual practice, habit, custom. Prob. fr. impers. construction *her &c. was wont*, wh. became *her wont was, it was his, her, wont*: *it was her wont to rise at six.* Phr. *use and wont*, custom.

won't, vb. [1. wōnt; 2. wount], fr. M.E. *wol not*, 'will not'. (colloq.) Will not.

wonted, adj. [1. wṓnted, wúnted; 2. wóuntid, wántid], fr. **wont (I.)** & **-ed.** (attrib.) Accustomed, customary, usual: *to return at one's wonted hour.*

wonyer, n. [1. wúnyer; 2. wánjə], fr. **won**, 'dwell, inhabit', & **-yer.** This word appears in Shakespeare, '1 Henry IV.' II. i. 73 (Cambr. Shakesp.), in the form *oneyers*, '*burgomasters and great oneyers*'. Various conjectures have been made by the Editors, but by far the most convincing is that of Mr. J. M. Robertson, who takes it to be for *wonyer*, the origin of wh. is as above. The meaning wd. thus be 'inhabitants, dwellers', & in this passage, prob. 'citizens'. The spelling is easily accounted for. The word *one* was pronounced by a large number of speakers in the 16th cent. pretty much as at present, & is often spelt *wone, won* (e.g. by Henry VIII. & Queen Elizabeth among others). Thus *won*, 'dwell', & *one* were pronounced alike, & just as *wone* was written for the latter, so, in the Shakespeare passage, *one* is written, or printed, for the former. This is known as an 'inverted spelling'.

woo, vb. trans. [1. wōō; 2. wū]. O.E. *wōgian*; M.E. *wōwen*, 'to woo'; lit. 'to bend, incline, in a certain direction'; fr. stem seen in O.E. *wōh, wōg*, 'bent'; hence 'crooked, perverse'; cp. O.S. *wāh*, 'perverse'; Goth. *unwāhs*, 'blameless'; cogn. w. Scrt. *vakrás*, 'bent'. **a** To seek in marriage, try to gain the affections of; to court, make love to; **b** (hence fig.) to try to win, attempt to obtain: *to woo fame, fortune, slumber*; *to woo the muses*, cultivate, practise, the arts.

woobut, oubit, n. [1. ōōbit; 2. úbit]. M.E. *wolbude*, fr. **wool**, & O.E. *budda*, M.E. *bude*, 'weevil, beetle'. Hairy caterpillar, esp. woolly-bear.

wood, n. [1. wood; 2. wud]. O.E. *wudu*, 'forest; timber', earlier **widu*; M.E. *wōde*; cp. O.H.G. *vitu*; M. Du. *wede*; O.N. *viðr*, 'wood'; cogn. w. W. *gwydd*; Gael. *fiodh*, 'wood'. **1.** Tract of tree-covered land; number of trees growing in a group and covering a comparatively large space; forest: *a wood of larches*; *to ride through the wood(s)*; *a house in the middle of the wood.* Phrs. *to be out of the wood*, out of danger or difficulty; *don't halloo till you are out of the wood*, don't congratulate yourself on success too soon; *to be unable to see the wood for the trees*, have one's mental vision obscured by details. **2.** Solid fibrous substance of which the hard part of a tree or shrub is composed, esp. as cut for manufacturing or other use; timber. Phrs. *in the wood*, (of wine) in cask; *from the wood*, straight from the cask, not bottled. **3.** (mus.) *The wood*, part of orchestra including wind-instruments made of wood.

wood-agate, n. Petrified wood.

wood-anemone, n. Wild anemone, having white flowers tinged with purple.

woodbine, -bind, n. [1. wóodbīn(d); 2. wúdbain(d)]. Honeysuckle.

wood-block, n. Block of fine-grained wood engraved with design for printing.

Woodbury-type, n. [1. wóodburi tīp; 2. wúdbəri taip], fr. name of inventor. **1.** Method of engraving in which a print is transferred from gelatine to a metal plate, from which further prints are made. **2.** Print produced by this method.

wood-carving, n. **1.** Act or method of carving designs or figures in wood. **2.** Piece of carving, sculpture, in wood.

woodchuck, n. [1. wóodchuk; 2. wúdtʃak]. Formed by popular etymol. fr. N. Am. Indian *wejack.* Small, brown, burrowing rodent of N.E. America, variety of marmot.

woodcock, n. [1. wóodkok; 2. wúdkɔk]. A migratory game-bird, *Scolopax rusticula*, of the same family as the snipe and sandpiper.

wood-craft, n. Knowledge of, skill in, adapting oneself to conditions of life, hunting &c. in the forest.

wood-cut, n. **1.** Engraving on block of wood used for printing. **2.** Picture, design &c. produced by printing from wood-block.

wood-cutter, n. **1.** Person engaged in cutting wood, felling trees &c. **2.** Wood-engraver.

wooded, adj. [1. wóoded; 2. wúdid]. **wood** & **-ed.** Covered with, abounding in, woods: *wooded hills, a well-wooded country.*

wooden, adj. [1. wóod(e)n; 2. wúd(ə)n]. **wood** & **-en.** **1.** Made of wood: *wooden steps, spoons.* Phrs. *wooden walls*, ships; *wooden-head*, stupid person, blockhead. **2. a** Stiff, motionless, inexpressive &c. as though carved from wood: *a wooden smile, stare, expression* &c.; **b** (of action) stiff, clumsy, ungraceful. **3.** (of character, type of intelligence &c.) Rigid, unyielding, unadaptable.

wood-engraver, n. **1.** Person who makes wood-cuts. **2.** Beetle boring beneath bark of tree.

wooden-headed, adj. Dull, stupid, unintelligent.

wooden-headedness, n. Dullness, stupidity.

woodenly, adv. [1. wóodenli; 2. wúdənli]. **wooden** & **-ly.** In a wooden manner.

woodenness, n. [1. wóodennes; 2. wúdənnis]. See prec. & **-ness.** State or quality of being wooden.

wood-fibre, n. Fibre obtained from wood and used for making paper &c.

wood-gas, n. Kind of illuminating-gas, obtained from wood.

wood-house, n. Building for storing wood.

wood-ibis, n. N. American stork, white, with black wings and tail.

woodiness, n. [1. wóodines; 2. wúdinis]. **woody** & **-ness.** State or quality of being woody.

woodland, n. [1. wóodland; 2. wúdlənd]. **1.** Land covered with forest; woods. **2.** (attrib.) Characteristic of, belonging to, growing, living, in, the woods: *woodland scenery*; *woodland flowers.*

woodlark, n. [1. wóodlark; 2. wúdlāk]. Small lark with spotted breast.

wood-leopard, n. Leopard moth.

woodless, adj. [1. wóodles; 2. wúdlis]. **wood** & **-less.** Destitute of woods.

wood-louse, n. Small land crustacean found in or under logs &c.

woodman, n. [1. wóodman; 2. wúdmən]. Person engaged in the care of woods, and in felling of trees.

wood-note, n. (usually pl.) **a** Song of bird; **b** (fig.) natural, artless verse.

wood-nymph, n. **1.** Nymph inhabiting woodland; dryad. **2.** Kind of moth. **3.** Kind of humming-bird.

wood-opal, n. Silicified fossil wood.

wood-paper, n. Paper made from wood-pulp.

wood-pavement, n. Pavement composed of wooden blocks.

woodpecker, n. [1. wóodpèker; 2. wúdpèkə]. Any one of a large number of species of birds, family *Picidae*, with parti-coloured plumage and strong, sharp beak, with which they extract insects from the bark of trees.

wood-pie, n. Spotted woodpecker.

wood-pigeon, n. Kind of wild pigeon, ring-dove.

wood-pulp, n. Wood-fibre reduced to pulp and treated chemically for making paper.

wood-reeve, n. Official superintending woods and forests.

woodruff, n. [1. wóodruf; 2. wúdraf]. O.E. *wudurōfe*, M.E. *woderōve.* Woodland herb, *Asperula odorata*, with clusters of white scented flowers.

woodshed, n. [1. wóodshed; 2. wúdʃed]. Shed where firewood is cut and stacked.

woodsman, n. [1. wóodzman; 2. wúdzmən]. Person living in or employed in the woods; one skilled in wood-craft.

wood-sorrel, n. Genus of herbs, esp. *common wood-sorrel*, small, white-flowered herb with creeping rhizome, the wild oxalis.

wood-tar, n. Tar obtained from wood by distillation.

wood-warbler, n. Variety of American warbler.

wood-wasp, n. **a** Wasp making its nest in rotten wood; **b** wasp that hangs its nest from a branch.

wood-wind, n. Wooden wind-instruments as a section of an orchestra.

wood-wool, n. Fine shavings of pine &c. used for dressing wounds &c.

woodwork, n. [1. wóodwĕrk; 2. wúdwāk]. Wooden structure, esp. wooden parts of building, doors, wainscots, window-frames &c.; contrasted with *plaster work, stone-work* &c.

woody, adj. [1. wóodi; 2. wúdi]. **wood** & **-y.** **1.** Resembling, of the nature of, consisting of, wood: *woody stems.* **2.** Covered with, abounding in, woods; wooded.

woody nightshade, n. Bitter sweet.

wooer, n. [1. wōōer; 2. wūə]. **woo** & **-er.** One who woos; suitor.

woof, n. [1. wōōf; 2. wūf]. O.E. *āwef, ōwef*; M.E. *oof*, 'woof'; fr. **a-**, & *wef*, 'web', fr. *wefan*, 'to weave', see **weave.** Cross-threads in woven fabric; weft; contrasted with *warp.*

wooing, n. [1. wōōing; 2. wūiŋ]. **woo** & **-ing.** Act of one who woos; courtship.

wool (I.), n. [1. wool; 2. wul]. O.E. *wull*; M.E. *wulle, wolle*; cp. O.H.G. *wolla*; Goth. *wulla*, 'wool'; cogn. w. Lett. *wilna*; Lith. *vìlna*, 'wool'; O. Prussian *wilna*, 'coat'; Lat. *lāna*; Scrt. *ū́rṇā*; Gk. *lēnos*, 'wool'; fr. base **wl̥nā-* &c., 'wool'. Cp. **avulsion** & **vellicate.** **1.** Soft, elastic hair, with scaly fibres, forming the fleece of the sheep; applied also to the coat of some varieties of goat, llama, alpaca &c.; used in the manufacture of many textile fabrics. Phrs. *dyed in the wool*, dyed before spinning; *much cry and little wool*, a fuss about nothing. **2.** Thread spun from wool; woollen yarn. **3.** Fabric woven or knitted of wool. **4.** Short, soft downy fur forming under-coat of fur-bearing animal. **5. a** Negro's crisp, curly hair; **b** (slang) person's hair; Phr. *to lose one's wool*, get excited and angry. **6.** Fibrous substance resembling wool in appearance, texture &c.; often in compounds, *cotton-, wood-wool* &c.; Phr. *to pull the wool over a person's eyes,* deceive, hoodwink, him; *mineral wool*, mass of fine thread-like substance obtained by exposing molten slag to a strong blast. **7.** As adj.: *wool merchant*; *wool sales* &c.

wool (II.), vb. trans., fr. prec. To pull tufts or wisps of wool out of a sheep's fleece; said of a dog which chases and snaps at sheep.

wool-ball, n. Ball of matted wool sometimes found in sheep's stomach.

wool-carding, n. [1. wóol kàhrding; 2. wúl kȧdiŋ]. Preparation of wool-fibres by carding.

wool-combing, n. Method of preparing wool for spinning by combing and straightening fibres.

wool-dyed, adj. [1. wóol dīd; 2. wúl daid]. Dyed in the wool before spinning.

-wooled, adj. [1. woold; 2. wuld]. **wool** (I.) & **-ed.** Having wool of specified kind: *long-wooled* &c.

wool-fat, n. Natural oil found in sheep's wool; lanolin.

wool-fell, n. Sheep's skin and fleece.

wool-gathering, n. & adj. **1.** n. Absent-mindedness, preoccupation of mind, state of inattention to what goes on around one. **2.** adj. In a condition of absent-mindedness. Phr. *one's wits have gone wool-gathering.*

wool-grower, n. Person raising sheep for the wool.

wool-hall, n. Wool merchant's place of business.

woollen, adj. & n. [1. wóolen; 2. wúlən]. **wool** (I.) & **-en.** **1.** adj. Made of wool: *woollen cloth, stockings* &c. **2.** n. Woollen fabric or garment: *dressed in woollen*; (also in pl.) *woollens must be washed carefully.*

woollen-draper, n. Retail dealer in woollen garments and fabrics.

woollenette, n. [1. wòolenét; 2. wùlənét]. **woollen** & **-ette.** Light woollen fabric.

woolliness, n. [1. wóolines; 2. wúlinis]. Next word & **-ness.** State or quality of being woolly.

woolly, adj. & n. [1. wóoli; 2. wúli]. **wool** (I.) & **-y.** **1.** adj. **a** Pertaining to, resembling, of the nature of, made of, covered with, wool or wool-like down: *woolly sheep*; *a woolly fibre*; *woolly hair*; *woolly clothes*; **b** (fig.) indistinct, vague, blurred; lacking clearness, definiteness, precision; reverse of clear-cut, precise &c.; with various applications: *woolly painting, thinking*; *a woolly mind*; *a woolly voice* &c. **2.** n. Sweater or other woollen garment.

woolly-bear, n. Caterpillar of the tiger-moth.

wool-oil, n. Wool-fat.

wool-pack, n. Bale of wool containing 240 lb.

woolsack, n. [1. wóolsak; 2. wúlsæk]. **1.** Wool-stuffed cushion on which the Lord Chancellor sits as presiding officer of House of Lords. **2.** (fig.) Office of Lord Chancellor: *many a young lawyer has dreams of the woolsack.*

woolsey, n. [1. wóolzi; 2. wúlzi], fr. **linsey-woolsey.** Linsey-woolsey.

wool-staple, n. Quality of wool, considered specially as regards the length of the fibre.

wool-stapler, n. (archaic) Wool merchant.

wool-work, n. Embroidery in wool.

woorali, woorara, n. [1. wōōráhli, wōōráhra; 2. wūrάli, wūrάrə], fr. S. Am. Indian *wurali.* South American poisonous herb, curare, q.v.

wootz, n. [1. wōōts; 2. wūts], fr. native word. A variety of steel made in India.

wop (I.). See **whop.**

Wop (II.), n. Origin doubtful. (Am. slang) Name given to any immigrant into the United States from the south of Europe, esp. from Italy.

word (I.), n. [1. wërd; 2. wʌ̄d]. O.E. *word*, 'word; what is said; speech; sentence', M.E. *wōrd*; O.H.G. *wort*; O.S. *word*; Goth. *waurd*; cogn. w. Lat. *verbum*; O. Prussian *wirds*, 'word'; Lith. *vardas*, 'name'; fr. base **wer-dh-*, 'word', expanded fr. **werē-* &c., 'to speak', seen in Gk. *eirein*, 'to say' (fr. **werjō-*); *rhēsis*, 'speech'; *rhētōr*, 'orator', see **verb** & cp. **rhetor**; Scrt. *vratám*, 'order'; O. Slav. *rota*, 'oath'; possibly also, w. *-k-* extension, Goth. *wrōhs*, 'accusation'; O.E. *wrēgan*, 'to accuse'. **1.** The simplest element of speech; a group of speech-sounds, or even a single sound, serving as the name of an object, representing an idea, or indicating the relation between ideas: *words are classified as parts of speech*; *a word of two syllables*; *an English word*; *to use long words*; *I can't hear a word (of what) you say*; *to say a few words*, make a few remarks, a short speech; *words without actions are of little use*; *to put one's thoughts into words.* Phrs. *(a man) of few words*, habitually taciturn; *in a word*, in short, to sum up; *to have no words for*, be unable to describe; *play upon words*, pun; *a word and a blow*, impetuous action; *the last word*, (i.) latest authoritative pronouncement; (ii.) *last word in*, of something embodying the most recent discoveries and improvements: *the last word in wireless, in comfort* &c.; *to have the last word*, make a crushing, unanswerable, final remark in a dispute; *the last word has not yet been said on (a subject)*, there are further arguments to be considered, fresh facts still to be discovered; *word for word*, literally; verbatim; *word of command*, direction indicating specific movement to soldiers drilling &c. **2.** Written or printed word, group of graphic symbols representing a word: *to write a few words*; *to cross out a word.* **3.** (often pl.) Thing said, speech, remark: *to listen to one's concluding words.* Phrs. *warm, hot, words*, angry speech; *fair words*, flattering, conciliatory, speech; *big words*, boasting; *by word of mouth*, orally; *on, with, the word*, immediately after specific word has been uttered; *a word in, out of, season*, advice offered seasonably, inopportunely; *a word in one's ear*, confidential remark, hint &c.; *to have words (with)*, quarrel (with); *can I have a word with you?*, a private conversation with; *to suit the action to the word*, carry out an action mentioned; *to eat one's words*, to retract what one has said, apologize for insult &c.; *to bandy words with*, argue, dispute, with; *to put in a word for*, speak in defence or recommendation of; *to waste one's words*, speak in vain; *no good wasting words on*, (i.) useless to argue with (a person); (ii.) useless to discuss (a subject); *to hang on one's words*, listen eagerly to. **4.** Command, order, direction, spoken signal: *his word is law*; *to give the word to fire.* Phrs. *mum's the word*, the matter is not to be mentioned; *sharp's the word*, hurry up. **5.** Password: *to give the word.* **6.** Message, communication; tidings: *to send word to a person*; *to receive word of one's coming*; *I have had no word from him since he left.* **7.** Promise, assurance: *to give, pledge, keep, break, one's word*; *a man of his word*; *to be as good as one's word*, live up to one's promises; *word of honour*, statement made, promise given, upon one's honour; *upon*, or *'pon, my word!*, exclamation of surprise; *upon my word (I don't know what to make of it* &c.), I assure you that I really don't &c. **8.** (theol.) **a** *The Word*, translating Gk. *Lógos*; the second person of the Trinity before the Incarnation; **b** (i.) the Holy Scriptures; (ii.) specif., the Gospel message: *to preach the Word to the heathen*; also *God's Word, Word of God*; *ministers of the Word*, the clergy.

word (II.), vb. trans., fr. prec. To put into, express in, words; to phrase, turn: *I should word it rather differently*; *a beautifully worded address* &c.

word-blind, adj. Unable, through mental defect, to understand written or printed words.

word-book, n. A recent Germanizing affectation based on Mod. Germ. *wörterbuch*; cp. also Du. *woordenbock* & Swed. *ordbok.* Lexicon, dictionary.

word-deaf, adj. Unable, through mental defect, to understand spoken words.

word-formation, n. Mode of forming words by inflexion, or by other suffixes, or by composition.

wordily, adv. [1. wërdili; 2. wʌ́dili]. **wordy** & **-ly.** In a wordy manner; verbosely.

wordiness, n. [1. wërdines; 2. wʌ́dinis]. **wordy** & **-ness.** Quality of being wordy.

wording, n. [1. wërding; 2. wʌ́diŋ]. **word** (II.) & **-ing.** The way in which anything is said; choice and arrangement of words in expressing specific ideas, esp. in writing; phrasing.

wordless, adj. [1. wërdles; 2. wʌ́dlis]. **word** (I.) & **-less.** Without words; incapable of speech.

word-painter, n. Person skilled in word-painting.

word-painting, n. The act of calling up an image, a scene, an action, or an event before the mind by verbal description; vivid description of actions, events &c.

word-perfect, adj. Knowing, and able to repeat, a passage, a part in play &c., word for word, by heart.

word-picture, n. A description of an object, scene, event &c. which is so vivid as to call up before the mind that which is described.

word-play, n. **1.** Subtle discussion or exchange of repartee, verbal fencing. **2.** Play on words.

word-splitting, n. [1. wërd spliting; 2. wʌ́d splìtiŋ]. Over-subtle argument, sophistry.

word-square, n. Arrangement, one below another, of a set of selected words of equal length so that each may be read from top to bottom or from side to side.

wordy, adj. [1. wërdi; 2. wʌ́di]. **word** (I.) & **-y.** **1.** Consisting of, expressed in, words: *wordy warfare.* **2. a** Given to using too many words; prolix, verbose: *a wordy speaker*; **b** expressed in an unnecessary number of words; verbose, diffuse: *his style is too wordy.*

wore, vb. [1. wōr; 2. wɔ̄]. Pret. of **wear.**

work (I.), n. [1. wërk; 2. wʌ̄k]. O.E. *weorc*, 'work (act and result); action; a building; a fortification'; M.E. *werk, worc*; O.S. *werk*; O.H.G. *werach*; cogn. w. Gk. *érgon*, 'action, work', for **wergon*, see **erg**; also Gk. *órganon*, 'instrument', for **worg-* see **organ.** Generally, any form of physical or intellectual activity engaged in for the purpose of accomplishing a desired end. **1.** Bodily or intellectual labour deliberately performed and directed to some specific object; purposeful activity: *he does the work of two men*; *the work of building a house, of writing a dictionary, is exacting*; *many men, rich and poor, appear to do no work.* Phrs. *to set to work*, start doing something; *at work upon*, engaged in, occupied with. **2.** Labour of specific kind performed as a person's regular occupation and employment, esp. **a** as a means of livelihood; handicraft, trade, profession &c.: *the work of a stone-mason, of a miner, an agricultural labourer* &c.; *a clerk does his work at a desk, a surgeon does his at an operating table*; *the man had been out of work for many weeks*; *father has gone to (his) work*; Phr. *at work*, specif., engaged in one's regular business; **b** special study, scientific investigation, research &c. **3.** Particular task, duty, undertaking, which one is morally or legally bound to perform, or which one has set oneself to accomplish: *I have a lot of work I must do tonight.* Phr. *to have one's work cut out (for one)*, to have a difficult task before one. **4.** Object, stuff, materials, instruments, of any kind at, or with which, one is working: *bring your work out into the garden*; specif., embroidery, needlework. **5.** Something produced by manual or intellectual work; **a** artistic creations of the craftsman: *the work of silversmiths, sculptors, and other artificers*; **b** creations of imagination; writings, paintings, musical compositions &c.: *a work, the works, of Scott, Keats, Beethoven, Velazquez*; specif., *the works of* ——, usually the complete set of works, musical compositions, pictures, of a writer, composer, painter &c. **c** (sing.) the product of the intellectual imaginative activity of the artist, craftsm:

author &c., considered from the point of view of form, structure, style: *one can hardly fail to recognize the work of Milton, of Velazquez, of Grinling Gibbons, when one sees it.* **6.** (in pl.) Various kinds of engineering structures, such as bridges, docks, embankments &c. **7.** Any of various structures wrought by hand or by machinery; usually preceded by a qualifying word, or as the second element of a compound: *iron-work, basket-work, earthwork* &c. (See each word.) **8.** (in pl., often with sing. construction) Establishment where industry or manufacturing is carried on: *brick works, iron works* &c.; *many owners of factories spend most of their lives at the works.* **9. a** Those essential parts of a machine which move, and either themselves perform the functions for which the machine was designed, or set up the necessary movements in other parts: *the works of a watch, a piano*; **b** (colloq., facet.) the internal organs of the body, esp. of the thorax and abdomen. **10. a** Activity, or action generally: *the devil and all his works*; *it was the work of a moment to cut off the light*; **b** the result of some specific process, operation, action: *this is the work of an enemy.* **11.** (theol.) Good deeds performed by religious persons, which if springing from a true and lively faith are pleasing to God and an element, through the merits of Christ, in effecting the salvation of the soul; contrasted from the latter point of view with *Faith*; *works of supererogation*, such works performed over and above what is necessary for the individual's salvation. **12.** (phys.) The result of a transference of one kind of energy into another.

work (II.), vb. intrans. & trans. O.E. *wyrċan*, M.E. *wirchen* wd. have become Mod. Eng. [wʌ̄tʃ]; the present vb. is a new formation fr. the n., q.v. See also **wrought.** **A.** intrans. **1. a** To expend effort, engage in mental or physical activity, to some specific end; to toil, labour, exert oneself: *to work hard*; *to work with a will*; *to work for a good master*; *to work for the public good*; *you have worked too long*; Phrs. *to work against*, to oppose, use one's influence &c. against; *to work against time*, strive to finish a task within limited time; **b** specif., to do needlework &c., sew, embroider. **2. a** (of mechanism, an organ of the body &c.) To perform its normal function, operate, have some form of activity, be in action: *his heart is working badly*; *the saw-mill is not working*; *the electric bell won't work*; *the door works on a spring*; *to work smoothly, freely, stiffly*; **b** (fig.) to be successful, effective; achieve desired result: *the charm worked, failed to work*; *the plan worked well.* **3. a** (usually followed by adv.) To make, wear, a way, a passage; to pass in a specific direction, esp. gradually, encountering opposition: *his elbow has worked through the sleeve*; *the root worked down between the stones*; *we worked south through the forest*; also *to work through a list*; *to work round to the point from which the discussion started*; **b** (followed by adj.) to come gradually, as result of repeated movement, into a specified condition: *to work loose, free* &c. **4.** To be employed, have regular occupation: *he is not working just now*; *he works in a jam factory, for a farmer.* **5.** (lit. and fig.) To be in a state of agitated activity; to twitch: *his features worked with excitement.* **6. a** To ferment; **b** (fig.) to permeate by slow degrees and produce results: *just drop a judicious hint and leave it to work in his mind.* **7.** (hort., of dormant bud) To become active, to shoot. **B.** trans. **1. a** To control or supply motion of, operate, cause to function: *to work a machine*; *to work a treadle with one's foot*; *the mill-wheel is worked by the stream*; **b** to compel to work: *to work one's servants unmercifully*; **c** to move, bring into action: *to work one's jaws.* **2. a** To expend effort upon, labour in, do or direct work of, operate in: *to work a farm*; *the silver-mines are no longer worked*; *to work a house with one servant*; *the fisherman works the stream*; **b** to solve (a sum, problem &c.). **3. a** To prepare, treat, by applying intermittent pressure, kneading, hammering &c.: *to work dough to the right consistency*; *to work iron* (see **wrought**); **b** to prepare, cultivate (soil &c.) by digging, ploughing &c. **4.** To bring about, effect, accomplish: *to work a miracle*; *time works many changes*; *to work one's will*; *to work wonders.* **5. a** To achieve a passage, penetrate, by exertion: *to work one's way upwards, through the jungle* &c.; **b** to obtain by labour: *to work one's passage* (on a ship), pay for it in work. **6. a** (reflex.) To pass into specified condition, as result of repeated movements: *the rope has worked itself loose*; **b** to bring oneself into specified frame of mind, or bodily condition: *to work oneself into a temper, a fever* &c. **7. a** To embroider, produce (design &c.), in needlework: *to work a design on a banner*; **b** to make a design on, in needlework &c.: *to work a robe with lilies in silver thread.* **C.** Followed by adverb or preposition. *Work at*, intrans., to elaborate, apply oneself to: *he is working at a new invention*; to study, apply one's energies to learning: *to work at history and literature.* *Work for*, intrans., to strive, work, with specified object in view: *to work for peace, for a prize* &c. *Work in*, **1.** trans., to introduce, put in, mingle: *the lecture would be improved if you could work in a few jokes*; **2.** intrans., to combine well, fit in: *his plans will not work in with ours.* *Work off*, trans., **1.** to dispose of, get rid of, palm off: *he worked off all his oldest goods*; *to work off a stale joke on a victim*; **2.** to get rid of by expending: *to work off superfluous energy.* *Work on, upon*, intrans., to influence, have an effect on, act upon. *Work out*, **1.** trans., **a** to discover by study and application; to reckon, calculate, compute (amount, solution &c.): **b** to exhaust: *the mine was worked out long ago*; *the subject was soon worked out as a topic of conversation*; **c** to develop, elaborate, amplify, plan out (a scheme &c.); **2.** intrans., **a** (of problem &c.) to admit of solution; **b** (of amount) to be calculated, appear as result of reckoning: *it works out at £5 each.* *Work up*, trans., **1.** to build up gradually, by effort, industry &c.: *to work up one's custom, reputation* &c.; **2. a** to promote, instigate, foment: *to work up a rebellion, a friendly feeling* &c.; **b** to arouse, excite, strong emotion in: *to work up an audience to a state of frenzy*; also *to work up the feelings &c. of an audience*; **3. a** to combine and manipulate (raw materials) into a finished work: *to work up a lump of clay into a bust*; **b** to elaborate and develop (a piece of work) into something more highly wrought: *to work up a sketch into a picture* &c.

workability, n. [1. wẽrkabíliti; 2. wʌ̀kəbíliti]. See next word & **-ity.** State of being workable.

workable, adj. [1. wẽrkabl; 2. wʌ́kəbl]. **work** (II.) & **-able.** **a** Capable of being worked, cultivated, worked upon: *the ground is too wet to be workable*; **b** capable of being executed, carried out; practicable: *a workable plan.*

workableness, n. Prec. & **-ness.** State or quality of being workable; practicability.

workably, adv. See prec. & **-ly.** In a workable manner.

workaday, adj. [1. wẽrkadā; 2. wʌ́kədei]. Characteristic of, suitable for, ordinary working days; hence ordinary, dull, commonplace: *this workaday world, life* &c.

work-bag, n. Bag for holding materials for needlework &c.

work-basket, n. Basket for holding materials necessary for needlework &c.

work-box, n. Box for holding materials for sewing &c.

workday, n. [1. wẽrkdā; 2. wʌ́kdei]. Day on which ordinary work is carried on; contrasted with *Sunday*, or *holiday.*

worker, n. [1. wẽrker; 2. wʌ́kə]. **work** (II.) & **-er.** **a** One who, that which, works; specif. **b** worker-ant, -bee &c.

worker-ant, n. One of the main body of ants (undeveloped females) which carry on the work of the community.

worker-bee, n. One of the main body of bees in a hive (contrasted with *drones*, or *queens*) which collect honey.

workhouse, n. [1. wẽrkhous; 2. wʌ́khaus]. Institution, supported by public funds, in which the paupers of a parish or larger area are maintained.

working (I.), adj. [1. wẽrking; 2. wʌ́kiŋ], fr. Pres. Part. of **work** (II.). **1.** Occupied by, spent in, work: *working hours.* **2.** Required for actual financial needs of commercial enterprise, firm &c.: *working capital, expenses.* **3.** Adapted to requirements of constructor or person elaborating a scheme, theory &c.: *a working drawing, plan* &c.; *a working hypothesis.* **4.** Engaged actively in work, not merely supervising: *a working builder.*

working (II.), n. **work** (II.) & **-ing.** **1.** Act, operation, activity, process: *the working of conscience*; *the workings of nature.* **2.** Mode, manner, according to which an action or process takes place: *the exact working of wireless telephony cannot be understood without a training in physics.* **3.** (usually pl.) That part of a mine or quarry which is being worked.

working-class, n. Manual workers collectively.

working-day, n. **1.** [1. wẽrking dā; 2. wʌ́kiŋ dei]. One on which ordinary work is carried on, workday; contrasted with a holiday. **2.** [1. wẽrking dā́; 2. wʌ́kiŋ déi]. Number of hours recognized as normal day's work.

working-man, n. Member of working-class; man employed in manual work.

working-out, n. Development of detail, elaboration of drafted scheme &c.

workless, adj. [1. wẽrkles; 2. wʌ́klis]. **work** (I.) & **-less.** Having no work, without employment.

workman, n. [1. wẽrkman; 2. wʌ́kmən]. **1.** Man employed in manual work; labourer, artisan, mechanic &c. **2.** One who does, or makes, something, considered from the point of view of the quality of his work; a craftsman: *a very decent fellow but a poor workman.* Phr. *a bad workman finds fault with his tools*, inefficient people always find excuses for their failures.

workmanlike, adj. [1. wẽrkmanlīk; 2. wʌ́kmənlaik]. Prec. & **-like.** Like, suitable for, characteristic of, a skilled workman.

workmanship, n. [1. wẽrkmanship; 2. wʌ́kmənʃip]. **workman** & **-ship.** **1. a** The special skill of a craftsman; **b** this thought of in relation to its quality: *the exquisite workmanship of Cellini.* **2.** Something produced as the result of work, skill &c.: *this box is my workmanship.*

work-people, n. Manual workers collectively; persons employed by a master to do manual labour.

work-room, n. Room in which work is done.

workshop, n. [1. wẽrkshop; 2. wʌ́kʃɔp]. Room or building in which work, esp. a handicraft, is carried on.

work-shy, adj. Unwilling to work.

work-table, n. Table with furnished fittings and accessories for needlework.

workwoman, n. [1. wẽrkwooman; 2. wʌ́kwumən]. Woman employed in manual work; specif., one employed in needlework.

world, n. [1. wẽrld; 2. wʌ̄ld]. O.E. *weorold*; M.E. *wer(e)ld, wor(e)ld*; cp. O.S. *werold*; O.H.G. *weralt*, 'world'; a very old compound fr. stem **wer-*, 'man', see first element of **werewolf**, & **ald-*, 'age, generation of men'; see **old, eld.** **1.** The earth and the heavens; the universe. Phrs. *not for the world*, not on any account; *for all the world like*, exactly like; *to be all the world to*, be everything to. **2.** The earth and its inhabitants; the human race; mankind as a whole: *great reformers* *generally have the world against them at first; Athanasius against the world; the whole world suffered in the Great War.* **3.** Mode, form, of life or existence: *this world and the next; too good for this world; the world to come,* the future state; '*He ... Allur'd to brighter worlds, and led the way*' (Goldsmith, 'Deserted Village', 170); *the other world,* existence after this present life, heaven. **4.** Human life on earth; specif. **a** individual life and experience in the world: *how is the world using you?, the world goes very well with me;* **b** individual outlook on life; range of thought, and emotional experience &c.: *his world was a very narrow one;* **c** habits, customs, way of life, mode of thought &c., of mankind in general: *to see much of the world in every part of the globe.* **5. a** The purely material concerns of human life as contrasted with the spiritual: *the world, the flesh, and the devil; he forsook the world and turned his thoughts to heaven;* **b** the part of mankind chiefly occupied with material concerns, worldly persons. **6. a** Humanity considered in its social aspect; organized society: *he retired to the country and shut out the world;* '*The world forgetting, by the world forgot*' (Pope, 'Eloisa to Abelard', 208); **b** some particular phase or section of society: *the ancient world; the fashionable world; I do not move in his world.* Phr. *man of the world,* one versed and experienced in life and society. **7.** A particular sphere, or range, of organized activities, occupations, interests; persons identified with any of these: *the world of commerce; the dog world; the sporting, racing, world; the scientific world.* **8.** One of the great primary divisions of natural objects; kingdom: *the animal, vegetable, mineral, world.* **9.** One of the hemispheres of the globe and its inhabitants; *the New World,* America; *the Old World,* Europe, Asia, Africa, as known before the discovery of America. **10.** One of the heavenly bodies thought of as having inhabitants and as constituted like our earth: *we are surrounded in space by innumerable worlds which may resemble our own.* **11.** As a symbol of vast size, amount, number; a host, a sea: *a world of troubles, of sin* &c.

world-language, n. **a** Language used throughout the world; **b** an artificial language intended for universal use.

worldliness, n. [1. wērldlines; 2. wʌ́ldlinis]. **worldly & -ness.** State or quality of being worldly.

worldling, n. [1. wērldling; 2. wʌ́ldliŋ]. **world & -ling.** Worldly person.

worldly, adj. [1. wērldli; 2. wʌ́ldli]. **world & -ly.** **1.** Pertaining to the present world; earthly, mundane: *worldly interests, pleasures, ambitions, affairs; worldly goods, property, possessions; worldly wisdom,* experience in the ways of men, shrewdness in dealing with human affairs, esp. in advancing one's own interests. **2.** Devoted to, concerned chiefly with, the material affairs of life; having the mind mainly bent on success in life, material riches, glory, prosperity &c.

worldly-minded, adj. Concerned mainly with, interested in, mundane matters.

worldly-mindedness, n. State of being worldly-minded.

worldly-wise, adj. Possessed of worldly wisdom.

world-old, adj. As old as the world, hence, of extreme antiquity.

world-power, n. Political state whose policy affects the world.

world-weary, adj. Generally discontented with life and earthly conditions.

world-wide, adj. Extending over the whole world: *world-wide fame.*

worm (I.), n. [1. wērm; 2. wʌm]. O.E. *wyrm;* M.E. *wurm,* 'serpent, worm, dragon'; cp. O.H.G. *wurm;* M. Du. *worm;* O.N. *ormr;* Goth. *waurms,* 'worm, serpent'; cogn. w. Lat. *vermis,* earlier **vormis,* 'worm'; see **vermi-.** **1. a** One of several varieties of legless, invertebrate animals, including earthworms, tapeworms &c. Phrs. *food for worms,* of dead person; *even a worm will turn,* the most oppressed, humblest or meekest person will retaliate under sufficient pressure; *the worm of conscience,* remorse; **b** a mean-spirited, abject, contemptible person. **2.** Spiral grooving on a screw. **3.** Spiral arrangement of pipes in a still. **4.** Worm-like organ in human or animal body, specif., membrane under tongue of dog.

worm (II.), vb. trans. & intrans., fr. prec. **A.** trans. **1. a** *Worm one's way,* to make one's way along cautiously and gradually, in spite of obstacles and difficulties; also (fig.) *to worm one's way into society, into a person's confidence* &c., to wriggle in, insinuate oneself by stealth, cunning, and persistence; **b** also *worm oneself in,* same as **a.** **2.** To remove worms from, esp. *to worm a dog,* purge him of intestinal worms. **3.** To extract (information &c.) by cajolery, insistent questioning &c.: *to worm secrets out of a person.* **B.** intrans. (rare) To crawl, wriggle, along like a worm.

worm-cast, n. Cylindrical mass of earth excreted by earth-worm, left on surface of the ground.

worm-eaten, adj. [1. wērm ētn; 2. wʌ́m ītn]. **1.** Gnawed, bored into, perforated, by weevils &c.: *worm-eaten wood* &c. **2.** (fig.) Old, worn, out-of-date: *worm-eaten regulations, customs* &c.

worm-fishing, n. Angling with worm as bait.

worm-gear, n. Gear-wheel with teeth arranged to engage with a worm of a screw.

worm-hole, n. Hole bored by worm in earth, or by a weevil in wood &c.

worm-holed, adj. [1. wērm hōld; 2. wʌ́m hould]. Riddled with worm-holes.

worminess, n. [1. wērmines; 2. wʌ́minis]. **wormy & -ness.** State of being wormy.

worm-seed, n. **a** Seed of certain plants used as a vermifuge; **b** plant yielding this seed, esp. a herb of the Levant.

worm-wheel, n. Wheel in worm-gear.

wormwood, n. [1. wērmwood; 2. wʌ́mwud]. Not connected w. **worm** (I.). O.E., M.E. *wermōd;* cp. O.H.G. *werimuote;* etymol. doubtful; cp. **vermouth;** Du. *wermoet.* Aromatic, bitter perennial herb, *Artemisia absinthium,* wild and cultivated, with downy, segmented leaves and yellow flowers, used in the manufacture of absinth, vermouth &c. Phr. (fig.) *gall and wormwood,* bitter humiliation and mortification; circumstance causing these.

wormy, adj. [1. wērmi; 2. wʌ́mi]. **worm** (I.) **& -y.** Infested with, abounding in, bored through by, worms.

worn, adj. [1. worn; 2. wōn]. P.P. of **wear.** O.E. *(ge)woren.* M.E. *wōr(e)n.* **1.** Injured, impaired, made thin &c. by use, wear &c.: *worn garments.* **2.** Pinched, showing signs of exhausting toil, care &c.: *a worn and haggard face.*

worriless, adj. [1. wúriles; 2. wárilis]. **worry** (II.) **& -less.** Without worries.

worriment, n. [1. wúriment; 2. wárimənt]. **worry** (I.) **& -ment.** **1.** Vexation, anxiety, worry. **2.** Cause of uneasiness, anxiety, or vexation.

worry (I.), vb. trans. & intrans. [1. wúri; 2. wári]. O.E. *wyrgan;* M.E. *wurȝen,* 'to choke, strangle, tear, worry'; cp. O.H.G. *wurgan;* O. Fris. *werga;* M. Du. *worghen,* 'to choke'; cp. further O.S. *wurgil,* 'band, cord'; cogn. w. Lith. *veržiu,* 'to bind, compress'; Lett. *werst,* 'to turn, twist'; O. Slav. *vrěsti,* 'to bind'; Gk. *erkhatáein,* 'to hedge in'; Lat. *vergere,* 'to bend, bow', see **verge** (II.); fr. base **wer(e)g-, *wr̥g-* &c., 'to bend, curve, turn'; cp. further forms w. nasal under **wring, wrong.** **A.** trans. **1.** (of dog &c.) To seize (quarry), shake and lacerate with the teeth: *the dog worried the rat.* Phr. *to worry the sword,* to make a quick succession of feints in fencing, in an attempt to distract opponent. **2. a** To cause annoyance to, to pester, harass, by constant importunity &c.: *to worry a person with perpetual questions, demands;* **b** to annoy with persistent, importunate demands: *he was always worrying her to marry him.* **3. a** To cause uneasiness and anxiety to: *his prolonged absence worries me; don't let that worry you;* **b** to cause wearing bodily pain or discomfort to: *his old wound, toothache &c. worries him a good deal.* **B.** intrans. To be anxious, troubled, uneasy: *don't worry if you are late.* Phr. *to worry along,* manage to get on in spite of difficulties.

worry (II.), n., fr. prec. **1.** (of dog &c.) Act of worrying. **2.** Feeling of wearing anxiety and uneasiness: *to show signs of worry.* **3.** That which worries, cause of anxiety or annoyance: *to have many worries.*

worrying, adj. [1. wúriing; 2. wáriiŋ], fr. Pres. Part. of **worry** (I.). Causing worry, anxiety, irritation; annoying, vexatious: *to have a worrying time.*

worryingly, adv. Prec. & **-ly.** So as to cause worry.

worse (I.), compar. adj. [1. wērs; 2. wʌs]. O.E. *wyrsa,* M.E. *wurs;* cp. O.S. *wirs(a);* O.H.G. *wirs;* Goth. *wairs,* 'worse'; cogn. w. O.S., O.H.G. *werran,* 'to confuse, mix up'; further w. Lat. *verrere,* 'to sweep, brush'; see **verricule.** **1.** Bad in a higher degree: *there could be no worse misfortune; this road is even worse than the other; the worse for wear.* **2.** (pred.) **a** In a less satisfactory physical condition, more ill: *the patient is worse this morning; he grew rapidly worse; he is none the worse for the accident;* **b** more badly situated, in less satisfactory condition or circumstances: *he will not be the worse for the change.*

worse (II.), compar. adv. O.E. *wyrs,* see prec. **1. a** In a worse manner, to a worse extent: *he sings worse than ever;* **b** *none the worse,* no less; all the better: *to like (a person) none the worse for being outspoken* &c.; *to think none the worse of,* to esteem more highly. **2.** To a greater degree, with more severity: *it is blowing worse than before.*

worse (III.), n., fr. **worse** (I.). Worse thing, something more unsatisfactory or evil: *worse remains to tell.* Phr. *to go from bad to worse,* deteriorate steadily.

worsen, vb. trans. & intrans. [1. wērsen; 2. wʌ́sən]. **worse** (I.) **& -en.** **1.** trans. To make worse. **2.** intrans. To become worse.

worship (I.), n. [1. wērship; 2. wʌ́ʃip]. O.E. *weorðscipe;* M.E. *wur(ð)shipe,* 'dignity, honour, worship'; **worth** (I.) **& -ship.** **1.** (archaic and obs.) Honour, dignity; status, character, which commands the highest respect: *a man of great worship.* **2.** *Your, his, Worship,* conventional formula of respect used in addressing, or referring to, a magistrate on the bench; also as title of a mayor: *his Worship the Mayor of B.* **3. a** The highest form of veneration and adoration, accorded only to a deity; **b** religious observances: *divine worship, public worship.* **4.** Intense love and admiration; respect, veneration, felt for anything: *the worship of beauty, money, intellect, success* &c.

worship (II.), vb. trans. & intrans., fr. prec. **A.** trans. **1.** To accord worship to, to revere and adore as God. **2. a** To regard with great or excessive admiration or reverence; idolize, adore: *to worship one's wife, money;* **b** to honour, show respect for: '*with my body I thee worship*' (Marriage Service). Phr. *to worship the ground a person treads on,* entertain the intensest affection for him (her). **B.** intrans. **1.** To take part in religious observances: *many people have worshipped in this church.* **2.** To feel deep reverence, adoration: *to worship at the shrine of beauty.*

worshipful, adj. [1. wērshipfōol; 2. wʌ́ʃipfùl]. **worship** (I.) **& -ful.** (archaic, except in titles of respect) Worthy of honour, respected: *the Worshipful Company of Fishmongers; the Worshipful the Master* (masonic).

worshipfully, adv. Prec. & **-ly.** In a worshipful manner.

worshipfulness, n. See prec. & **-ness.** Quality of being worshipful.

worshipper, n. [1. wērshiper; 2. wʌ́ʃipə]. **worship** (II.) **& -er.** One who worships.

worst (**I.**), adj. [1. wërst; 2. wʌst]. O.E. *wyrsta*; M.E. *wurst*; **worse** (**I.**) & **-est.** **a** Bad, severe, harmful, to the highest possible degree; exhibiting bad qualities to a more intense degree than any other or others of the same kind: *the worst dinner I ever ate*; **b** most intense: *the worst frost for a hundred years.*

worst (**II.**), adv. O.E. *wyrst*; see prec. In the worst manner, most badly: *there were many who played badly, but he played worst.*

worst (**III.**), n., fr. **worst** (**I.**). That which is worst; worst person or thing; worst part, circumstance, event, result &c.: *of all bad kings, John was probably the worst*; *to prepare for the worst*; *to keep the worst for the last*; *tell me the worst*; *the worst of the winter must be past*; *the storms are at their worst in February*; *he always makes the worst of his troubles.* Phrs. *at worst*, under the most unfavourable circumstances; *to see somebody, something, at his, its, worst*, under the worst aspects; *do your worst, let him do his worst*, formula of defiance; *to get the worst of it*, be defeated; *if the worst comes to the worst*, if the most disastrous thing should happen, should it turn out as badly as possible; *the worst of it is that . . .*, the most unfortunate, unfavourable, circumstance is, it happens most unfortunately that.

worst (**IV.**), vb. trans., fr. prec. To defeat, gain a victory over, vanquish in a contest, overthrow.

worsted, n. & adj. [1. wóosted; 2. wústid], fr. Worste(a)d, in Norfolk, orig. place of manufacture. **1.** n. Twisted woollen yarn of long staple. **2.** adj. Made of worsted: *worsted socks* &c.

wort (**I.**), n. [1. wërt; 2. wʌt]. O.E. *wyrt*; M.E. *wurt*, 'root, herb'; cp. O.S. *wurt*; O.H.G. *wurz*; O.N. *urt*; Goth. *waurts*, 'root, plant, herb'; cogn. w. Lat. *rādix*, 'root', see **radix**; Gk. *rhādix*, 'branch, rod'; *rhiza*, 'root', see **rhizo-**; cp. further O.N. *rōt*, 'root', see **root.** (chiefly in compounds) Herb, plant, e.g. *milkwort, ragwort.*

wort (**II.**), n. M.E. *wurte*; O.E. *-wyrte*; cp. M.H.G. *würze*; M. Du. *worte*, 'wort in brewing'; prob. fr. same stem as prec. Infusion of malt before fermentation.

worth (**I.**), adj. [1. wërth; 2. wʌþ]. O.E. *wyrðe*; M.E. *wurþe*, 'worthy'; cp. O.S. *werth*; O.H.G. *wert*; O.N. *verðr*; Goth. *wairþs*, 'worthy'. (pred.) **1.** Having a specified value: *you can have it for sixpence, but it is worth more*; *it is worth little, much*; *it is not worth a penny*; (poet.) *it is little, nothing, worth.* **2.** Deserving of, meriting, giving adequate return for: *it is worth seeing*; *worth the trouble.* Phrs. *the game isn't worth the candle*, see **candle**; *to be worth one's salt*, see **salt**; *worth while*, (colloq.) *worth it*, worth the time, trouble, spent on it, worth the difficulty, danger &c. incurred; *not worth a damn*, quite worthless. **3.** Having property to the value of, possessions amounting to: *what is he worth? he is worth several millions.* Phr. *run &c. for all you are, one is, worth*, exerting the utmost strength, making every effort.

worth (**II.**), n. O.E. *weorð, wurð, wyrð*, 'worth, price; ransom; honour, dignity', see prec. **1. a** Material value or price of anything: *a jewel of great worth*; **b** spiritual qualities of mind and character, moral excellence: *few knew his true worth.* **2.** Amount of anything purchasable for a given sum; number of specified coins equivalent to one of higher value: *half a crown's worth of oranges*; *a shilling's worth of bird-seed*; *two shillings' worth of coppers*; also in the compounds, *pennyworth, ha'p'orth* &c.

worth (**III.**), vb. intrans. O.E. *weorðan*, M.E. *worthen*, 'to become'; cp. O.S. *werthan*; O.H.G. *werdan*; O.N. *verða*; Goth. *wairþan*, 'to become'; cp. Goth. *-wairþs*; O.E. *-weard*, 'in specified direction', see **-ward**; cogn. w. Lat. *vertere*, 'to turn', see **version**; Scrt. *vártatē*, 'turns, rolls, goes'. To betide, befall; poet., in Phr. *woe worth*, ill betide; cp. M.E. *wo mote worþen*: '*Woe worth the chase, woe worth the day!*' (Scott, 'Lady of the Lake', I. ix.).

worthily, adv. [1. wërdhili; 2. wʌ́ðili]. **worthy** & **-ly.** In a worthy manner.

worthiness, n. [1. wërdhines; 2. wʌ́ðinis]. See prec. & **-ness.** Quality of being worthy.

worthless, adj. [1. wërthles; 2. wʌ́þlis]. **worth** (**II.**) & **-less. a** Of no worth; valueless; useless; **b** (specif. of persons) unprincipled, unreliable, of no character.

worthlessly, adv. Prec. & **-ly.** In a worthless manner.

worthlessness, n. See prec. & **-ness.** Quality of being worthless.

worthy (**I.**), adj. [1. wërdhi; 2. wʌ́ði]. **worth** (**II.**) & **-y. 1. a** Meriting honour or respect; virtuous, estimable, of good character: *a worthy man*; **b** deserving approval and support: *a worthy cause.* **2.** Fitted by character or quality for, suited to; deserving: *courage worthy of a better cause*; *a worthy adversary*; *worthy to be considered*; *worthy of death, reward* &c.

worthy (**II.**), n., fr. prec. **a** Person of importance and of estimable character; eminent person; a notable; *the Worthies of England*; *the Nine Worthies*; **b** (ironic) equivalent to *person, merchant*: *who is the worthy with the bald head and a beard?*

wot, vb. [1. wot; 2. wɔt], fr. O.E. *wāt*, 'I know', M.E. *wōt*; a Pret. Pres. fr. O.E. *witan*, 'to know', see **wit** (**I.**). (archaic) I know; the 3rd sing. now usually *wots*, on anal. of other vbs.; but note archaic form in Phr. *God wot*, in M.E. *Godot*, 'God knows'.

would, vb. [1. wood; 2. wud]. O.E., M.E. *wolde*, Pret. of **will** (**III.**).

would-be, adj. & adv. [1. wóod bē; 2. wúd bī]. (attrib.) Expressing a quality or state desired or intended: *a would-be poet*; *would-be poetical phrases.*

wound (**I.**), n. [1. wōōnd; 2. wūnd]. O.E., M.E. *wund*, 'wound'; cp. O.E. *wund*, 'wounded'; O.S. *wunda*; O.H.G. *wunda*; Du. *wond*, 'wound'; prob. cogn. w. O.E. *winnan*, 'to fight' &c.; see **win. 1. a** Injury to any part of the body in which the skin, and often the muscular tissue, is penetrated, cut, torn &c.: *wounds received in battle*; *a fatal, mortal, wound*; *an open, contused, wound*; **b** in obs. Phr. *God's wounds*; as oath; see **zounds. c** injury to plant &c., involving cutting or tearing of bark &c. **2.** Injury to the feelings, self-respect, honour, affections &c.; an insult, affront.

wound (**II.**), vb. trans., fr. prec. To inflict a wound upon; to hurt, injure, the body or the feelings: *the shell wounded him in the head*; *he was profoundly wounded in his deepest affections.*

wound (**III.**), vb. [1. wound; 2. waund]. O.E. (*ġe*)*wunden*, M.E. *wunde*(*n*), P.P. of **wind** (**IV.**); now used also as Pret.; cp. O.E. Pret. *wand.*

woundily, adv. Obs., fr. **woundy**, q.v.

woundless, adj. [1. wōōndles; 2. wūndlis]. **wound** (**I.**) & **-less.** Free from wounds, uninjured.

wound-wort, n. Plant formerly used as remedy for wounds.

woundy, adj. [1. wōōndi; 2. wūndi]. **wound** (**I.**), **1 b**, & **-y.** Profane but rather mild and meaningless epithet, used colloquially as intensive in 17th or first half of 18th cent.; apparently more or less equivalent to *confounded*; cp. '*There was a neighbour's daughter I had a woundy kindness for*' (Farquhar, 'Twin Rivals', 1702).

wourali. See **woorali.**

wove(**n**), adj. [1. wōv(en); 2. wóuv(ən)], fr. P.P. of **weave**; M.E. (*i*)*wōve*(*n*), on the anal. of **stolen** &c.; cp. O.E. P.P. (*ġe*)*wefen.* Made by weaving: *woven fabrics*; *wove paper*, smooth paper made on wire-gauze frame.

wow, n. [1. wou; 2. wau]. (slang, U.S.A.) A great success; something wonderful, extraordinary.

wrack, n. [1. rak; 2. ræk]. M.E. *wrac*, 'wreck', prob. fr. O.N. *wrak*, 'a wreck; refuse, trash'; cp. the O.E. cogn. *wræcu*, 'vengeance; misery'; also the cognates *wræċċa, wreċċa*, 'an exile'; lit. 'one driven out', see **wretch**, & cp. *wrecan*, 'to drive, expel', see **wreak** & **wreck** (**I.**). The fundamental meaning is 'what is driven about, or away'. **1.** (archaic or poet.) Ruin, destruction: *everything is gone to wrack*; cp. Phr. *wrack*, now usually *rack, and ruin*, see **rack** (**III.**). **2.** Marine vegetation cast up on the shore.

wraith, n. [1. rāth; 2. reiþ]. Etymol. doubtful; perh. a variant of **wreath. a** Apparition of a living person, or of one who has recently died, foretelling or announcing his death; **b** a spectre, ghost, disembodied spirit generally.

wrangle, vb. intrans. & n. [1. ránggl; 2. rǽŋgl]. M.E. *wranglen*, 'to wrangle'; prob. a gradational variant of **wring** (**I.**) & **-le. 1.** vb. To take part in a heated or noisy discussion or quarrel, dispute angrily, brawl. **2.** n. Noisy altercation, quarrel.

wrangler, n. [1. ránggler; 2. rǽŋglə]. Prec. & **-er. 1.** Person who wrangles, brawler. **2.** (Cambridge University) Person placed in first class of mathematical tripos; (the name has reference to the public disputation in which candidates formerly took part); *senior wrangler*, person heading the list of wranglers in any year when the order of merit was published, now obsolete.

wranglership, n. [1. rángglership; 2. rǽŋgləʃip]. Prec. & **-ship.** Position of wrangler.

wrap (**I.**), vb. trans. & intrans. [1. rap; 2. ræp]. M.E. *wrappen*; etymol. doubtful. Cp. obs. *wlappen*, 'to wrap', & see **lap** (**II.**). **A.** trans. **1.** To fold round, enfold, cover, roll up, envelop, (a person or thing) in (a folding material or garment): *to wrap a parcel in paper*; *to wrap a child in a shawl*; also *wrap up* (*a parcel in paper*) or *wrap a parcel up in paper*; *to wrap oneself, or another, up in a cloak*; specif., *to wrap oneself up* (*well*), put on warm clothes. **2.** (in non-material sense) **a** To enshroud in, surround with, envelop (oneself): *he wraps himself in an impenetrable reserve*; Phr. *wrapped up in*, devoted to, entirely absorbed by, preoccupied with: *wrapped up in his children, in his work*; **b** to disguise, conceal: *he wraps up a sensitive diffidence of nature in a rather boisterous manner*; *to wrap up a censure in a polite formula.* **3.** To place, arrange, fold (of flexible material) so as to cover: *wrap paper round it*; *to wrap one's cloak round one.* **B.** intrans. **1.** Usually *wrap up*, to cover, enfold oneself, in wraps; specif., to put on a number of warm clothes: *mind you wrap up well.* **2.** *Wrap over*, to overlap.

wrap (**II.**), n., fr. prec. **1.** Material used for wrapping: *to take a mummy out of its wraps.* **2.** Specif., a garment, cloak &c., or a rug or other piece of fabric used for wrapping up and protecting the person from cold: *take plenty of wraps with you in the car.*

wrappage, n. [1. rápij; 2. rǽpidž]. **wrap** (**I.**) & **-age.** Material used for wrapping.

wrapper, n. [1. ráper; 2. rǽpə]. **wrap** (**I.**) & **-er.** One who, that which, wraps; material used for wrapping; specif. **a** slip of paper used to wrap up newspaper &c. for posting; **b** loose paper cover for book; **c** light dressing-gown; **d** tobacco-leaf of good quality used for outer layer of cigar.

wrapping, n. [1. ráping; 2. rǽpiŋ]. **wrap** (**I.**) & **-ing.** Material, piece(s) of fabric &c., in which a thing is wrapped: *put plenty of wrapping round it*; *a mummy is enclosed in many wrappings.*

wrapt. See **rapt.**

wrasse, n. [1. ras; 2. ræs], fr. W. *gwrachen.* Family of brightly coloured, European sea-fish, often with very thick lips, found inshore near rocky coasts.

wrath, n. [1. rawth; 2. rɔþ]. The O.E. n. is *wrǣþþo, wrǣþu*, 'anger', w. mutation; **the unmutated form** *wrāþ* **occurs in the adj.**

meaning 'angry' &c.; cp. O.S. *wrēð*, O.H.G. (*w*)*reidi*, O.N. *reiðr*, 'angry'. Perh. cogn. w. Lat. *irrītāre*, 'to provoke, enrage', if this is fr. **in-wrīt-āre*; see **irritate**; cp. **writhe** & **wroth**. Deep, intense, anger and indignation.

wrathful, adj. [1. ráwthfool; 2. rɔ́þful]. Prec. & **-ful**. **a** Feeling or expressing wrath; angry, deeply indignant, incensed; **b** animated by wrath: *wrathful indignation.*

wrathfully, adv. Prec. & **-ly**. In a wrathful manner.

wreak, vb. trans. [1. rēk; 2. rīk]. O.E. *wrecan*, 'to drive, push; to avenge'; M.E. *wrēken*, 'to avenge'; cp. O.S. *wrekan*; O.H.G. *rehhan*, 'to punish, avenge'; O.N. *reca*; O. Fris. *wreka*, 'to drive, oppress, revenge'; Goth. *wrikan*, 'to pursue'; cogn. w. Lat. *urgēre*, 'to push, force, drive', see **urge**; O. Slav. *vragŭ*, 'enemy'; Lith. *vargas*, 'oppression'. See **wrack** & **wreck**. **1.** (archaic) To avenge. **2.** To carry out, inflict, put into operation: *to wreak vengeance, one's wrath, malice &c., upon a person.*

wreath, n. [1. rēth; 2. rīþ]. O.E. *wrǣþ*, 'band, wreath', fr. **wrāþi-*; cp. O.E. *wrīðan*, 'to twist', Pret. sing. *wrāþ*; see **writhe** & **wraith**. **1. a** A circle made of twisted branches, sprays &c., often adorned with leaves and flowers, used as decoration for tombs and other monuments, in commemorations and celebrations, as a crown for a poet; a garland; **b** (fig.) as symbol of the honour and veneration paid to a poet or conqueror; **c** carved or other representation of a wreath. **2.** A curling, eddying, drifting spiral, streak, wisp &c., esp. of smoke, vapour, mist &c.; also a light, drifting mass of sand, snow &c.

wreathe, vb. trans. & intrans. [1. rēdh; 2. rīð]. Formed fr. prec. The final consonant of the vb. is voiced because orig. followed by a suff.; cp. *breathe*, contrasted w. *breath*. **A.** trans. **1.** To twist, wind, weave, into a wreath: '*From his slack hand the garland wreathed for Eve Down dropt*' (Milton, 'P. L.' ix. 892-3). **2.** To adorn, hang, encircle, with, or as with, a wreath: *the bays that wreathe the poet's brow.* Phr. *wreathed in smiles*, smiling. **3.** To wind round, clasp, entwine: *to wreathe one's arms about a person.* **B.** intrans. (of smoke, mist, plants, &c.). To move, coil, in, or as in, wreaths.

wreck (I.), n. [1. rek; 2. rɛk]. Variant of **wrack**; O.E. *wræc*, 'exile, misery', M.E. *wrac, wrec*; cp. O.E. *wrecan*, 'to drive, expel', see **wreak**. **1.** Destruction, esp. **a** such disablement of a ship by winds and waves that she has to be abandoned; **b** destruction of other objects, esp. the demolition of houses and buildings generally, by fire, storm &c. **2.** Ruin, the bringing to nought, upsetting, annihilation (of one's fortunes, plans, hopes &c.). **3. a** A ship that has been wrecked and abandoned at sea; a ship cast on a reef, or the shore, and broken up by the force of the waves &c.; **b** a ruined building demolished by fire, storm &c.; Phr. *a* (*mere*) *wreck of his former self*, said of a person who is emaciated and weakened by ill-health or the ravages of some disease; **c** ruined hopes, plans &c.

wreck (II.), vb. trans. & intrans., fr. prec. **A.** trans. **1.** To cause wreck, **a** to a ship; **b** to a train, building &c. **2.** To ruin, destroy, bring to nought (plans, hopes &c.). **B.** intrans. **1.** (rare, chiefly fig.) To be destroyed, come to grief: *our plans will wreck, if at all, on our own lack of conviction.* **2.** To be concerned with a wreck, either as a rescuer or as a plunderer.

wreckage, n. [1. rékij; 2. rékidž]. **wreck** & **-age**. **1.** Material from a ship, building &c. that has been wrecked; remnants, dilapidated fragments left from a wreck. **2.** (fig.) Act or process of wrecking: *to witness the wreckage of one's hopes.*

wrecked, adj. [1. rekt; 2. rɛkt], fr. P.P. of **wreck**. Involved in a wreck; having suffered from, having been damaged by, wreck: *wrecked ship, sailors.*

wrecker, n. [1. réker; 2. rékə]. **wreck** & **-er**. **1. a** One who, that which, wrecks; specif. **b** person who attempts to lead ship to destruction on a coast in order that he may plunder the wreckage. **2.** Person employed in recovering cargo &c. from wrecked ship.

wrecking, adj., fr. Pres. Part. of **wreck** (II.). Causing ruin, tending to destroy; esp. *a wrecking amendment, motion*, one designed to frustrate a previous motion, or a bill.

wreck-master, n. Official appointed to take charge of cargo &c. from wrecked vessel.

wren, n. [1. ren; 2. rɛn]. O.E. *wrǣnna*, name of the bird; M.E. *wrenne*; prob. fr. O.E. *wrǣne*, 'lecherous'; etymol. unknown. Name of a genus, *Troglodytes*, of small passerine song-birds with rounded wings and short, erect tail; also name of certain warblers, esp. the *willow-wren*, and of the kinglet or *golden-crested wren.*

wrench (I.), n. [1. rench; 2. rentʃ]. O.E. *wrenċ*, 'trick, artifice'; M.E. *wrench*, 'guile'; cp. M.H.G. *ranc*, 'deceit'; cp. further O.E. *wrincle*, see **wrinkle**; *wringan*, 'to twist', also **wring**, **wrong** & words there referred to. **1. a** Sudden violent twist, jerk, pull, strain: *to pull out a tooth with one wrench*; **b** injury inflicted on a joint, tendon, muscle by a wrench: *to give one's knee a wrench.* **2.** (fig.) Painful emotion comparable to a physical wrench in its intensity, esp. such an emotion felt at separation, abrupt discontinuance of old habits and occupations &c.: *it was a terrible wrench to leave the old home; the wrench of parting with one's children.* **3.** Tool for grasping and turning nuts &c.

wrench (II.), vb. trans. O.E. *wrenċan*, 'to twist, turn'; fr. prec. **1.** To pull with a sudden, sharp, violent, jerk: *to wrench a plant out of the ground; to wrench a box open; cows wrench the grass.* **2. a** To twist, jerk, and tear from normal position (a tendon, ligament &c. of the body); **b** (fig.) to distort, pervert, give a twist to (meaning of what is said, facts, words).

wrest (I.), vb. trans. [1. rest; 2. rɛst]. O.E. *wrǣstan*; M.E. *wrasten, wresten*, 'to twist, wrest'; cp. Du. *vriste*; O.N. *reista*, 'to twist'; fr. stem **wrei-*, **wri-* &c., 'to turn, twist'; see **writhe**. **1. a** To pull away forcibly, tear, wrench away: *to wrest a weapon from one's grasp*; **b** (also fig.) to extract by toil and pains; to extort: *to wrest a living from the barren ground; to wrest her secrets from Nature.* **2.** To distort, pervert, turn away from its true meaning, intent &c.: *you must not wrest my words from their obvious meaning in that way.*

wrest (II.), n., fr. prec. Key for tuning a stringed instrument, esp. a harp.

wrest-block, n. Part of piano-frame to which wrest-pins are fastened.

wrestle (I.), vb. intrans. & trans. [1. résl; 2. résl]. O.E. *wrǣstlian*; M.E. *wrestlen*; cp. M. Du. *wrastelen*. **wrest** (I.) & **-le**. **1.** To struggle with opponent by grappling with and endeavouring to throw him, by lifting and levering, esp. in a contest of strength and skill; constructions: (i.) (absol.) *I saw the champions wrestle*; (ii.) *to wrestle with*; (iii.) (trans. use) *to wrestle a man for a prize, I'll wrestle you for it.* **2.** (fig.) *Wrestle with*, to strive, contend with, struggle against, make an effort to deal with or overcome: *to wrestle with a task, difficulty, temptation* &c. Phr. *to wrestle with God*, pray with great earnestness.

wrestle (II.), n., fr. prec. **1.** Act of wrestling, specif., wrestling-bout. **2.** (fig.) A struggle, tussle, strenuous effort to deal with a difficult task.

wrestler, n. [1. résler; 2. réslə]. **wrestle** (I.) & **-er**. One who wrestles; specif., a trained person who regularly engages in wrestling matches.

wrestling, n. [1. résling; 2. résliŋ]. **wrestle** (I.) & **-ing**. Act of person who wrestles; specif., the art of overpowering and throwing, pulling down an opponent by various grapples, locks, modes of lifting and tripping &c.

wrest-pin, n. Steel pin in a piano to which one end of each string is fixed, by turning which the instrument is tuned.

wretch, n. [1. rech; 2. rɛtʃ]. O.E. *wræċċa*, 'exile; wretch'; M.E. *wrecche*; fr. stem seen in O.E. *wrecan*, 'to drive; to expel', see **wreak**; cp. O.H.G. *reccho*; O.S. *wrekkio*, 'exile, wretch'. **1.** Person involved in utter distress; miserable, thoroughly unhappy or unfortunate person; *poor wretch*, often pityingly contemptuous. **2. a** Base, contemptible scoundrel; an abandoned ruffian: *the servants of a revolution are often wretches devoid of mercy or conscience*; **b** (i) (playful and affectionate) as in *the little wretch did all she could to tease him*=little rogue; (ii) (archaic) *the pretty wretch.*

wretched, adj. [1. réched; 2. rétʃid]. Prec. & **-ed**. **1. a** (i.) Miserable, unhappy, deeply depressed in mind: *boys are often wretched when they first go to school*; (ii.) (implying some degree of censure) unfortunate: *the wretched man had lost all his money*; **b** suffering extreme bodily discomfort: *to feel thoroughly wretched with influenza*; **c** causing wretchedness and discomfort of mind or body: *a wretched business, state of things* &c.; *a wretched cold, toothache, pain in the side.* **2.** (of external surroundings) squalid, mean, poverty-stricken; full of discomfort; dismal, depressing: *a wretched hovel; what a wretched place to live in.* **3.** Of poor quality, inferior; thoroughly bad: *the play was wretched stuff; the food at this hotel is wretched; wretched accommodation; his voice and delivery are wretched.*

wretchedly, adv. Prec. & **-ly**. In a wretched manner.

wretchedness, n. See prec. & **-ness**. State or quality of being wretched.

wretchlessness, n., variant of **recklessness**. The *w-* is due to association with *wretch*: '*the Devil doth thrust them*' (i.e. '*curious and carnal persons*') '*either into desperation, or into wretchlessness of most unclean living*' (No. xvii., Articles of Religion, Prayer Book).

wrick, **rick**, vb. trans. & n. [1. rik; 2. rik]. M.E. *wricken*, 'to move, jerk, twist'; cp. Dan. *vrikke*; Swed. *vricka*; Du. *wrikken*, 'to move to and fro'; cogn. w. **wring** (I.). **1.** vb. To twist, sprain slightly: *to wrick one's neck, back* &c. **2.** n. Slight sprain, twist, of a joint.

wriggle (I.), vb. intrans. & trans. [1. rígl; 2. rígl]. Freq. of **wrig-*, fr. same base as **wry**; cp. L.G. *wriggeln*. **A.** intrans. **1. a** To twist and turn (the body) this way and that, with rapid, jerky motions; to squirm, to fidget about: *keep still, and don't wriggle; to wriggle about*; **b** *wriggle along*, move along, proceed, with wriggling motions; **c** *wriggle out* (of a hole, tight place &c.), (i.) manage to escape by wriggling; also (ii.) (fig.) to escape from an awkward situation by cunning; *to wriggle out of a bargain, undertaking*, find a pretext for not sticking to it. **2.** (fig.) To give evasive answers to questions, to dodge, to equivocate. **3.** To betray uneasiness of mind, to show embarrassment: *the implied criticism made him wriggle.* **B.** trans. **a** (reflex.) *To wriggle oneself along, into, free* &c., move along, penetrate, extricate oneself by means of wriggling; (also fig.); **b** *wriggle one's way*, to make one's way by wriggling.

wriggle (II.), n., fr. prec. Wriggling motion; twist, squirm.

wriggler, n. [1. rígler; 2. ríglə]. **wriggle** (I.) & **-er**. **1.** Person or animal that wriggles; specif., a worm or wriggling insect; *red wriggler*, worm used for fishing. **2.** One who equivocates; one who evades his promises.

wright, n. [1. rīt; 2. rait]. O.E. *wyrhta*; M.E. *wirhte, wrihte*, 'carpenter, workman, wright', fr. base **wurk-*, gradational variant of **werk-* &c., 'work', seen in O.E. *weorc*, 'work', see **work**; O.E. *wyrċan*, 'to work'. **a** (archaic) A worker, a constructive workman, artificer; **b** now chiefly in compounds, *ship-, wheelwright* &c.; also *playwright.*

wring (I.), vb. trans. [1. ring; 2. riŋ]. O.E. *wringan*; M.E. *wringen*, 'to wring, twist';

cp. M. Du. *wringhen*; O.H.G. *ringan*, 'to twist'; Goth. *wruggō*, 'noose, snare'; O.N. *rangr*; Swed. *vrång*, 'twisted; wrong', see **wrong**, & **wrangle**. **1.** To twist and press, twist strongly; to strain, squeeze, compress by twisting: *to wring clothes (out)*, squeeze and twist them to remove moisture. Phrs. *to wring the neck of* (chicken &c.), kill by twisting neck of; *wringing wet*, wet enough to wring water out of; *to wring one's hands*, (fig.) to feel and express sorrow and despair; *to wring the hand of* (another person), to clasp it warmly, expressing cordiality; *it wrings my heart*, causes anguish, pity, sorrow &c. **2. a** To extract, press out by wringing: *to wring moisture out of clothes*; **b** (fig.) to extort by persistent persuasion, by compulsion &c.: *to wring money out of a stingy person*; *to wring a reluctant promise, answer &c., from a person.*

wring (II.), n., fr. prec. Action of wringing; squeeze.

wringer, n. [1. rínger; 2. ríŋə]. **wring** (I.) & **-er**. One who, that which, wrings; specif., machine with rollers for pressing water out of clothes.

wrinkle (I.), n. [1. ríngkl; 2. ríŋkl]. O.E. *wrincle*; M.E. *wrinkel*; cp. M. Du. *wrinkel*; cogn. w. O.E. *wrenċan*, 'to twist', see **wrench**. **a** Small depression, furrow, or ridge caused by crumpling or puckering a flexible surface; specif. **b** crease or pucker produced by contraction of skin through old age &c.: '*Time writes no wrinkle on thine azure brow*' (Byron, 'Childe Harold', iv. 182).

wrinkle (II.), vb. trans. & intrans., fr. prec. **1.** trans. To form wrinkles in, to pucker, crease: *to wrinkle (up) one's forehead*, as in perplexity. **2.** intrans. To become wrinkled, to pucker.

wrinkle (III.), n. O.E. *wrenċ*, 'an artifice, a trick', w. dimin. suff.; cp. O.E. *wrenċan*, 'to twist'; & see **wrench**. Ingenious hint, suggestion or device; dodge; useful piece of advice.

wrinkly, adj. [1. ríngkli; 2. ríŋkli]. **wrinkle** (I.) & **-y**. Full of wrinkles.

wrist, n. [1. rist; 2. rist]. O.E., M.E. *wrist*; cp. O.N., M.H.G. *rist*, 'instep'; O. Fris. *(hond)-wirst*, 'wrist'; fr. base seen in O.E. *wrīðan*, 'to turn', see **writhe**; ultimate meaning, 'the turning joint'. **1.** Joint between fore-arm and hand; the carpus. **2.** Method of using, skill in using, wrist in art, craft, sport &c. **3.** Wrist-pin.

wristband, n. [1. rízband; 2. rízbənd]. (archaic) The band at the lower part of a shirt sleeve.

wrist-drop, n. Paralysis of the muscles controlling the hand, which prevents the straightening of the hand and interferes with its active use.

wristlet, n. [1. rístlet; 2. rístlit]. **wrist** & **-let**. Band worn round the wrist for support, warmth, ornament, for holding a watch &c.; also attrib.: *a wristlet watch.*

wrist-pin, n. (mechan.) Pin, peg, shaft, on which a connecting-rod turns.

writ, n. [1. rit; 2. rit]. O.E. *(ġe)writ*, 'something written'; M.E. *writ*; see **write**. **1.** (archaic) That which is written; document, writing; now only in *holy, sacred, writ*, the Bible. **2.** (law) An instrument or document issued in the king's name to a particular person, enjoining specific action or instructing him to abstain from action.

write, vb. intrans. & trans. [1. rīt; 2. rait]. O.E. *wrītan*, 'to engrave, draw, write'; M.E. *wrīten*, 'to write'; cp. O.S. *wrītan*, 'to tear, scratch; to write'; O.H.G. *rīzan*, Mod. Germ. *reissen*, 'to tear'; O.N. *rīta*, to write'; O.E. *ġewrit*, 'writing'; Goth. *writs*, 'stroke, line, point'. No cognates known outside Gmc. **A.** intrans. **1.** To trace on a surface symbols representing letter(s) or word(s), esp. on paper, parchment &c.: *to learn to write*; *to write well, illegibly* &c. **2.** To communicate in writing, send letter or written message: *he promised to write*; *I write every week to my family when absent.* **3.** To engage in literary composition, compose book(s), article(s) &c.; to practise the trade of author: *to write for a living*; *to write amusingly, well* &c. Phr. *to write oneself out*, write so much that one's vein is exhausted. **B.** trans. **1.** To put down, trace (symbols representing letters, words), on paper, parchment, or other surface: *to write one's name*; *to write notes in the margin*; *to write shorthand*; *to write Chinese characters.* Phrs. *to write a good, legible, hand*, produce good, legible writing; *writ(ten) in water*, leaving no permanent mark or record; *writ large*, widely proclaimed, clearly visible and recognizable: *the character and spiritual outlook of Milton are writ large in every page of 'Paradise Lost'.* **2. a** To express, state, put down, in writing (as an opinion or fact): *it is written that . . .*; *a great scholar has written that . . .*; **b** to communicate in writing, tell by means of a letter: *be sure to write me all your news.* **3. a** Specif., to produce, create, as a literary or artistic composition: *to write a book, article, poem, review* &c.; **b** to draw up, put down, in writing: *to write a letter.* **4. a** To fill up, cover, with writing: *to write several pages*; **b** to fill in, insert necessary writing in: *to write a cheque, certificate* &c. **5.** To designate, describe as, in writing: *he writes himself 'Colonel'.* **6.** (fig.) To show clearly, give clear signs of, imprint indelibly: *his selfishness, fear &c. is written on, all over, his face*; *the tendencies of the times are written in current events.* **C.** Followed by adverb. *Write down*, trans., **1.** To put down, record, in writing: *to write down an address*; *write it down before you forget it*; **2.** to depreciate in writing; **3.** to describe as, put down for: *I should write him down a fool.* *Write off*, trans., **1.** to compose quickly and easily; **2. a** to cancel, write a statement annulling (debt &c.); **b** to regard as cancelled. *Write out*, trans., to write in full, put whole of into writing; Phr. *to write out fair*, make fair copy of. *Write up*, trans., **1.** to praise in writing, compose a eulogy of; **2.** to elaborate, exaggerate, details of (event), in writing; **3.** to fill up, complete, bring up to date &c., in writing: *to write up a report, one's diary.*

writer, n. [1. rīter; 2. ráitə]. **write** & **-er**. **1.** One who writes; specif. **a** person who practises literary composition; an author; **b** a clerk, esp. in a government office; **c** *writer to the signet*, Scottish solicitor. **2.** Book giving instructions for writing, esp. foreign language.

writer's cramp, n. Muscular affection of the hand and fingers, due to excessive and prolonged use of the pen.

writership, n. [1. rītership; 2. ráitəʃip]. **writer** & **-ship**. Position, rank, of writer in an office &c.

writhe (I.), vb. intrans. & trans. [1. rīdh; 2. raið]. O.E. *wrīðan*, M.E. *wrīðen*, 'to twist, turn, writhe'; cp. O.H.G. *rīdan*; O.N. *rīða*, 'to turn'; O.H.G. *(w)reid*, 'crinkled'; cogn. w. O.E. *wrāð*, 'angry'; see **wrath** & **wreath**, & cp. **wrist**. **A.** intrans. **1.** To twist, contort, the body about; to squirm: *to writhe in agony.* **2.** (fig.) To undergo acute mental discomfort, to wince in spirit: *to writhe under a person's taunts.* **B.** trans. (rare) To cause to writhe, to twist; (chiefly reflex.) *to writhe oneself.*

writhe (II.), n., fr. prec. Act, motion, of writhing.

writhen, adj. [1. rídhen; 2. ríðən]. O.E. *wriðen*, P.P. of *wrīðan*, see **writhe** (I.). (archaic or poet.) Twisted, distorted.

writing, n. [1. rīting; 2. ráitiŋ]. **write** & **-ing**. **1.** Act of one who writes. Phr. *to put a thing in writing*, record it in written form. **2.** Lettering, an inscription, written by hand; written document; contrasted with something printed or engraved. **3. a** Act of literary composition: *fond of, busy with one's, writing*; **b** (pl.) the literary works of an author: *the writings of Pope*; *hitherto unpublished writings of X.* **4.** Method, style, of writing, handwriting; penmanship.

writing-case, n. Case for holding writing-materials.

writing-desk, n. **1.** Folding case or box containing writing materials, with hinged cover, part of which when opened forms a sloping slab on which paper can be placed for writing. **2.** Piece of furniture in various forms, having a receptacle for papers &c., and a table convenient for writing.

writing-ink, n. Ink prepared for writing; contrasted with *printer's ink.*

writing-paper, n. Paper prepared for writing, esp. for letters &c.

writing-table, n. Table used, or specially made, for writing at.

written, adj. [1. rítn; 2. rítn], fr. P.P. of **write**; O.E. *(ġe)writen*; M.E. *writen*. **a** Expressed, set down, in writing; specif., *written language*, that type used in writing and literature, distinguished from the colloquial by certain features of dialect, construction, and vocabulary; contrasted with *spoken language*; **b** in writing, inscribed; contrasted with *verbal*: *written orders* &c.

wrong (I.), adj. [1. rong; 2. rɔŋ], fr. O.E. *wrang*, n., fr. Scand.; cp. O.N. *rangr*; Swed. *vrång*, 'crooked, wrong'; cogn. w. Goth. *wruggō*, 'snare, noose'; O.H.G. *ringan*, 'to twist'; O.E. *wringan*, 'to turn, twist', Pret. *wrang*, see **wring**; also w. different final consonant, O.E. *wrenċ*, 'trick, guile', see **wrench**; O.H.G. *renken*, 'to twist'; cogn. w. Lat. *vergere*, 'to bend, be inclined, turn, lean', see **verge** (II.); Scrt. *vrjinás*, 'crooked; false'; Lith. *veržiù*, 'to snare'; Lett. *werst*, 'to turn'; Gk. *erkhatáein*, 'to hedge in'. Orig. sense 'twisted; morally distorted'. **1.** Not in accordance with what is morally right or just; reprehensible, wicked, sinful: *it is wrong to tell lies*; *how very wrong of him to mislead you in this way.* **2. a** (of statements, opinions, calculations, beliefs) Not in accordance with ascertained fact, with the truth, or with reason; erroneous, based on ignorance; misleading, inaccurate, incorrect: *we know now that many of the old scientific teachings were wrong*; *certain doctrines have been ruled out by the Church as definitely wrong and heretical*; *you have got all your sums wrong*; **b** (i.) not in accordance with what has been fixed or decided: *the wrong day, the wrong station*; (ii.) not what is asked for or desired: *you've brought the wrong book.* **3.** (of persons) Mistaken in opinions, having been misled; having misunderstood, been ignorant of, or misstated facts: *you were quite wrong in what you said*; *the ancients thought the sun went round the earth, but they were wrong.* **4.** Unsuited for particular purpose, not adapted to produce desired result: *the wrong way to do it, to set about it.* **5.** Unsuited to a particular time; unseasonable, inopportune; unsuitable for particular circumstances, or for a given company: *quite the wrong clothes for the evening, for the hot weather*; *he always says and does the wrong thing in society*; *just the wrong story to tell a bishop.* Phrs. *to go wrong*, (of persons) (i.) to lapse from the strict path of rectitude; (ii.) to come to grief, go to the bad; (iii.) (of actions, plans, affairs) to fail, end disastrously: *in the wrong box*, in an awkward or disconcerting position; *to get hold of the wrong end of the stick*, to misconceive, have mistaken impression of, a fact, statement, intention &c.; *wrong fount* (usually abbr., *w.f.*), direction to printer that type is from a different fount from that required; *wrong side out*, inside out; *on the wrong side of* (30 &c.), older than.

wrong (II.), adv., fr. prec. In a wrong manner; **a** incorrectly, erroneously, inaccurately, mistakenly: *you have done it wrong*; *to guess, answer, wrong*; Phr. *to get it wrong*, (i.) to miscalculate, reckon (a sum) incorrectly; (ii.) to misunderstand, misconceive; **b** unsuitably, in a manner not adapted to secure desired result: *you are treating him all wrong.*

wrong (III.), n. O.E. *wrang*, 'wrong', see **wrong** (I.). **1. a** Wrongful act; action at variance with what is right, with justice, duty &c.; sin, wickedness, evil-doing: *to distinguish between right and wrong*; *to do wrong*; **b** injustice, injury: *to suffer wrong*; *you do him wrong*, have an unjust, or too low an, opinion of him. **2.** (law, pl.) **a** Infringement of the rights of persons; **a** *private wrongs*, privation of the private or civil rights of an individual as such; also termed *civil injuries*; **b** *public wrongs*, a breach or violation of public rights and duties, which affect the whole community considered as such; these are distinguished as *crimes* and *misdemeanours*. **3.** State in which responsibility attaches for wrongful action, mistake &c.: *to be in the wrong*. Phr. *to put one in the wrong*, make him appear responsible for mistake &c.

wrong (IV.), vb. trans., fr. prec. **1.** To do wrong to, injure, treat wrongfully, unjustly: *an honest man will not knowingly wrong another*. **2.** To have an unjust opinion of, impute evil to undeservedly: *I wronged you in believing you unfaithful*.

wrongdoer, n. [1. róngdòoer; 2. rɔ́ŋdùə]. Person who does wrong; sinner, evildoer.

wrongdoing, n. [1. róngdòoing; 2. rɔ́ŋdùiŋ]. Commission of a wrongful act; evil-doing, offence, crime; sin.

wrongful, adj. [1. róngfool; 2. rɔ́ŋful]. **wrong** (III.) & **-ful**. Wrong; unjust; criminal.

wrongfully, adv. Prec. & **-ly**. In a wrongful manner; unjustly; illegally.

wrongfulness, n. See prec. & **-ness**. Quality of being wrongful.

wrong-headed, adj. Persevering in a wrong course; perverse, stubbornly mistaken.

wrongly, adv. [1. róngli; 2. rɔ́ŋli]. **wrong** (I.) & **-ly**. In a wrong manner; erroneously; wickedly.

wrongous, adj. [1. rónggus; 2. rɔ́ŋgəs]. **wrong** (I.) & **-ous**. (Scots law) Illegal, unjust, inequitable.

wrote, vb. [1. rōt; 2. rout]. O.E. *wrāt*, M.E. *wroot*, Pret. of **write**.

wroth, adj. [1. rōth, roth; 2. rouþ, rɔþ]. O.E. *wrāþ*, M.E. *wrōþ*, 'angry'; cp. O.S. *wrēþ*; O.N. *reiðr*, 'angry, hostile'; O.H.G. (*w*)*reid*, 'crooked, crumpled'; see **wrath** & **writhe**. (archaic, Bib., and poet.) Angry, incensed.

wrought (I.), vb. intrans. & trans. Pret. & P.P. [1. rawt; 2. rōt]. O.E. *worhte*, 'worked', Pret. of *wyrċan*, 'to work', M.E. *wrohte*; P.P. O.E. (*ge*)*worht*, M.E. *worht*, *wroht*. Now replaced by new Pret. *worked* in ordinary English. **A.** intrans. (archaic, poet., or provinc.) Worked, laboured, toiled: *he wrought very hard at his task*. Phr. *he wrought upon me to . . .*, persuaded me. **B.** trans. **1. a** Effected, produced, brought about; (i.) Pret.: *he wrought a great change in the spirit of his age*; (ii.) P.P.: *what evil he has wrought!*; **b** (Pret. & P.P.) made, constructed. **2.** Used as Pret. of *work* in sense of to treat metal by hammering &c.

wrought (II.), adj. O.E. (*ġe*)*worht*; M.E. *wroht*, *wrouht*; P.P. of O.E. *wyrċan*, 'to work', q.v. under **work**. Specif., *wrought iron*, worked by hammering; contrasted with *cast iron*.

wrung, vb. [1. rung; 2. raŋ]. Pret. & P.P. of **wring**; O.E. (*ġe*)*wrungen*, P.P.; M.E. *wrung*(*en*); now used also as Pret. Cp. O.E. Pret. *wrang*.

wry, adj. [1. rī; 2. rai]. M.E. *wrīe*, 'twisted', fr. *wrīen*, 'to turn, twist', cp. O.E. *wrigian*, 'to turn; go forward'. Cp. **wriggle**. Crooked, distorted, pulled or bent aside, twisted; rare except in *to make a wry face*, to pull a grimace expressing disgust.

wrybill, n. [1. rībil; 2. ráibil]. Species of plover.

wryly, adv. [1. rīli; 2. ráili]. **wry** & **-ly**. In a wry manner.

wrymouth, n. [1. rīmouth; 2. ráimauþ]. Sea-fish with vertical mouth-opening.

wry-mouthed, adj. Having a crooked mouth.

wryneck, n. [1. rīnek; 2. ráinɛk]. Bird related to woodpecker, able to twist its neck to a considerable angle.

wryness, n. [1. rīnes; 2. ráinis]. **wry** & **-ness**. State of being wry; distortion, crookedness.

Wyandotte, n. [1. wīandot; 2. wáiəndɔt], fr. name of tribe of N. American Indians. Breed of domestic fowls.

wych-, **wich-**, **witch-**, pref. [1. wich; 2. witʃ]. O.E. *wiċe*, M.E. *wiche*, 'wych-elm'; cogn. w. **wicker**. (in names of trees) *Wych-elm*, *Ulmus montana*, with drooping branches and pointed leaves; *wych-hazel*, see **witch-hazel**.

wye, n. [1. wī; 2. wai]. **a** Letter Y; **b** Y-shaped object.

Wykehamist, n. [1. wíkamist; 2. wíkəmist], fr. William of Wykeham, d. 1404, founder of school, & **-ist**. Member of Winchester College; *Old Wykehamist*, former member.

wynd, n. [1. wind; 2. waind]. Spelling variant of **wind** (IV.). (Scots) Alley, narrow lane between walls &c.

wyvern. See **wivern**.

X

X, x [1. eks; 2. ɛks]. **a** Twenty-fourth letter of alphabet; for use in abbreviations &c. see end of Dictionary; **b** the Roman symbol for the numeral 10; **c** (alg.) principal unknown quantity; hence **d** an unknown or mysterious factor or influence; **e** *double-*, *triple-x*, ale of specific strength, marked xx or xxx on cask.

xanth(o)-, pref., fr. Gk. *xanthós*, 'fair, yellow', for **k̑*(*ə*)*san-*; cogn. w. Lat. *cascus*, 'hoary, old'; *cānus*, 'grey, ashen'; fr. earlier **kasno-*; cogn. w. O.E. *hasu*; O.N. *hǫss*, 'greyish brown'; O.E. *hara*, 'hare', see **hare**; O. Prussian *sasins*, 'hare'. Yellow.

xanthein(e), n. [1. zánthiin; 2. zǽnþiin]. Prec. & **-in**. Soluble yellow colouring-matter in flowers.

Xanthian, adj. [1. zánthian; 2. zǽnþiən], fr. Xanthus, in Lycia, Asia Minor, & **-ian**. Pertaining to Xanthus; *Xanthian marbles*, sculptures discovered on this site and now in the British Museum.

xanthic, adj. [1. zánthik; 2. zǽnþik]. **xanth(o)-** & **-ic**. Yellow, yellowish; *xanthic flowers*, having yellow as typical colour and varying to white or red.

xanthin, n. [1. zánthin; 2. zǽnþin]. **xanth(o)-** & **-in**. **1.** Insoluble yellow colouring-matter in flowers. **2.** Crystalline compound contained in animal secretions.

Xanthippe, n. [1. zantípi, -thípi; 2. zæntípi, -þípi]. Gk., name of the wife of Socrates. An ill-tempered, shrewish woman or wife.

xanthite, n. [1. zánthīt; 2. zǽnþait]. **xanth(o)-** & **-ite**. Kind of yellowish-brown rock.

xantho-, pref. See **xanth(o)-**.

xanthochroi, n. pl. [1. zànthókrōī; 2. zæ̀nþókrouai]. **xanth(o)-** & Gk. *khróa*, 'skin, complexion', cp. Gk. *khrôma*, 'skin, colour', see **chromo-**. Blond, blue-eyed races.

xanthomelanous, adj. [1. zánthomélanus; 2. zǽnþəmélənəs]. **xanth(o)-** & Gk. *melān-*, stem of *mélās*, 'black', see **melanism**, & **-ous**. Black-haired and dark- or olive-skinned.

xanthophyll, n. [1. zánthofil; 2. zǽnþəfil]. **xanth(o)-** & Gk. *phúllon*, 'leaf', see **phyllo-**. Yellow pigment colouring autumn leaves.

xanthous, adj. [1. zánthus; 2. zǽnþəs]. **xanth(o)-** & **-ous**. Of yellow or Mongolian type.

xebec, **zebec(k)**, n. [1. zḗbek; 2. zíbɛk]. Cp. Ital. *sciabecco*, Fr. *chebec*, prob. of Eastern origin. Small three-masted vessel used on the Mediterranean.

xenelasia, n. [1. (g)zènēlásia; 2. (g)zɛ̀niléisiə]. Gk. *xenēlasia*, 'expulsion of foreigners', fr. *xénos*, 'stranger, guest', fr. **ghsenwo-*; cogn. w. Lat. *hostis*, 'stranger, enemy', see **host** (I.); & *élasis*, 'a driving away', fr. *elaúnein*, 'to drive, drive out'; cogn. w. Lat. *alacer*, 'quick, active', see **alacrity**; Goth. *aljan*, 'zeal'; O.E. *ellen*, 'courage'. Constitutional custom in ancient Sparta of preventing aliens from settling in the country.

xen(o)-, pref., fr. Gk. *xénos*, 'stranger, guest', see prec. **a** Relating to hospitality; **b** external.

xenial, adj. [1. (g)zénial; 2. (g)zéniəl]. Prec. & **-ial**. Of, pertaining to, denoting, relations between guest and host.

xenogamy, n. [1. zenógami; 2. zɛnɔ́gəmi]. **xen(o)-** & **-gamy**. Cross-fertilization.

xenogenous, adj. [1. zenójenus; 2. zɛnɔ́dʒinəs]. **xen(o)-** & **-genous**. Produced by external agency.

xenon, n. [1. zénon; 2. zénɔn]. Gk., neut. form of *xénos*, 'strange', see **xen(o)-**. Heavy, inert gas present in the air, first isolated in 1898.

xer(o)-, pref. Representing Gk. *xērós*, 'dry'; cogn. w. Scrt. *kṣārás*, 'burning'; Lat. *serēnus*, 'dry, clear, calm', see **serene**. Dry; dryness.

xeransis, n. [1. zērànsis; 2. ziərǽnsis]. Gk. *xḗransis*, 'drying up', fr. *xērainein*, 'to dry', fr. *xērós*, 'dry', see prec. Drying up, desiccation.

xeranthemum, n. [1. zērànthemum; 2. ziərǽnþiməm], fr. **xer(o)-** & Gk. *ánthemon*, 'flower', q.v. under **anther**, **anthology**. The everlasting flower.

xerasia, n. [1. zērázia; 2. ziəréiziə]. Gk. *xērasia*, 'dryness', fr. *xērainein*, 'to dry', fr. *xērós*, 'dry', see **xer(o)-**. Morbid dryness of the hair.

xerophilous, adj. [1. zērófilus; 2. ziərɔ́filəs]. **xer(o)-** & **-philous**. (of plant) Drought-loving, living in dry climate.

xerophthalmia, n. [1. zērofthálmia; 2. ziərɔfþǽlmiə]. **xer(o)-** & **ophthalmia**. Variety of conjunctivitis.

xerophyte, n. [1. zḗrofīt; 2. zíərɔfait]. **xer(o)-** & **-phyte**. Xerophilous plant.

xiph(i)-, **xipho-**, pref. Representing Gk. *xíphos*, 'sword'; etymol. doubtful. Sword-shaped; e.g. *Xiphidae*, swordfishes; *xiphisternum*, xiphoid appendage.

xiphoid, adj. [1. zífoid; 2. zífɔid]. Prec. & **-oid**. Sword-shaped; *xiphoid appendage*, *process*, sword-shaped, cartilaginous process at the lower extremity of the sternum.

xoanon, n. [1. (g)zṓanòn; 2. (g)zóuənɔ̀n]. Gk. *xóanon*, 'piece of sculpture in wood; statue of a deity'; cp. Gk. *xúein*, 'to scrape, scratch, polish'; *xustón*, 'polished spear-shaft'; *xustḗr*, 'graving-tool'; *xuréein*, 'to shave'; cogn. w. Scrt. *kṣurás*, 'razor'; cp. also, w. infixed nasal, Scrt. *kṣṇā́uti*, 'he rubs, whets'; O.N. *snǫggr*, 'shorn'. Primitive wooden statue of a deity.

x-rays, n. pl. [1. éks ráz; 2. éks réiz]. Pref. implies that their precise nature was unknown. Röntgen rays.

xyl(o)-, pref. Representing Gk. *xúlon*, 'wood, timber', fr. **kʷsulom*; cogn. w. O.N. *súla*; Goth. *sauls*; O.H.G. *sūl*, 'column'; see also **sill**. Wood.

xylem, n. [1. zīlem; 2. záilɛm]. See prec. & **-m**. Woody tissue forming part of a vegetable body.

xylobalsamum, n. [1. zīlobáwlsamum; 2. zailɔbɔ́lsəməm]. **xyl(o)-** & see **balsam**. Dried twigs of the balm-of-Gilead tree.

xylocarp, n. [1. zílokàrp; 2. záilǝkàp]. **xyl(o)-** & Gk. *karpós*, 'fruit', see **carpel**. **a** Hard woody fruit; **b** tree bearing such fruit.

xylograph, n. [1. zílogràhf; 2. záilǝgràf]. **xyl(o)-** & **-graph**. **a** Wood-engraving, esp. of early type; **b** representation of, or impression from, grain of wood as decoration.

xylographer, n. [1. zīlógrafer; 2. zailógrǝfǝ]. Prec. & **-er**. Wood-engraver.

xylographic, adj. [1. zìlográfik; 2. zàilǝgrǽfik]. **xyl(o)-** & **-graphic**. Pertaining to, produced by means of, xylography.

xylography, n. [1. zilógrafi; 2. zailógrǝfi]. **xyl(o)-** & **-graphy**. The art of wood-engraving.

xylonite, n. [1. zílonīt; 2. záilǝnait], fr. Gk. *xúlon*, 'wood', see **xyl(o)-**, & **-ite**. Celluloid.

xylophagous, adj. [1. zīlófagus; 2. zailófǝgǝs]. **xyl(o)-** & **-phagous**. (of insect) Feeding on, boring into, wood.

xylophone, n. [1. zílofōn; 2. záilǝfoun]. **xyl(o)-** & **-phone**. Musical instrument of percussion, consisting of a series of wooden bars, graduated in length.

xyster, n. [1. zíster; 2. zístǝ]. Gk. *xustḗr*, 'graving-tool'; fr. base of *xúein*, 'to scratch, scrape'; for **ksū-*, cp. Scrt. *kṣurá́ś*, 'razor'. See also **xoanon**. Instrument for scraping membrane from bones.

xystus, n. [1. (g)zístus; 2. (g)zístǝs]. Lat. *xystus*, fr. Gk. *xustós*, 'covered colonnade, with polished floor, in gymnasium', fr. *xustós*, 'polished', as prec. **1.** (class. antiq.) Covered portico used for athletic exercises. **2.** Garden walk.

Y

Y, y [1. wī; 2. wai]. **a** Twenty-fifth letter of alphabet; for use in abbreviations see end of Dictionary; **b** (alg.) second unknown quantity; **c** Y-shaped object, arrangement &c.

Y- (I.), pref. [1. wī; 2. wai]. Representing prec. Y-shaped; e.g. *Y-cartilage, Y-ligament* &c.; *Y-branch*, forked pipe &c.; *Y-level*, spirit-level with Y-shaped supports; *Y-moth*, with Y-shaped mark on upper wings; *Y-track*, short, Y-shaped railway track at right angles from a main line, used to enable engine to reverse direction.

y- (II.), pref. [1. i; 2. i]. O.E. *ġe-*, M.E. *i-*, *y-*; pref. used in O.E. to form trans. fr. intrans. vbs., also, gen., before P.P.'s of vbs.; to form coll. ns. &c.; cp. O.H.G. *gi-*, Goth. *ga-*. Now used only in archaic P.P. **yclept**. Mistaken for pers. pron. in *iwis*, written *I wis*, see **wis**.

-y (I.), suff. representing **a** Fr. *-ie*, Lat. *-ius*, *-ia*, *-ium*, in abstract ns. & adjs., e.g. *augury, century, family, fury*; *necessary, contrary*; or **b** Fr. *-ie*, Lat. *-ia*, fr. Gk. *-iā*, e.g. *history, -logy, homily*.

-y (II.), suff. representing O. Fr. n. suff. *-e, -ee*, fr. Lat. P.P.'s in *-ātus, -a, -um*, e.g. *army, city, entry, treaty*. The suff. is also used to form ns. fr. vbs. on anal. of these, e.g. *expiry*.

-y (III.), suff. forming ns., w. dimin. sense, **a** fr. other ns., e.g. *baby, dolly, pussy*; **b** fr. adjs., e.g. *darky*. Sometimes appears as *-ie*, e.g. *laddie, lassie*.

-y (IV.), suff. forming adjs., **a** fr. O.E. *-iġ*, M.E. *-y* (cogn. Lat. *-ic-*), e.g. *many, holy*; & by anal., fr. mod. ns., *lumpy, horsy, stony, shiny* &c.; **b** fr. adjs. of colour, e.g. *yellowy*, esp. in compounds, *bluey-grey* &c.; **c** chiefly poet., fr. other adjs., e.g. *stilly*.

-y (V.), n. suff. representing O.E. *-iġ*, M.E. *-i(e)*, e.g. *body, lady*.

yacht (I.), n. [1. yot; 2. jɔt], fr. Du. *jacht*, fr. stem of *jagen*, 'to hunt', w. reference to speed of vessel; cp. O.H.G. *jagōn*, 'to hunt'; etymol. doubtful. **a** Vessel, whether propelled by sails or by mechanical power, designed for pleasure-cruising; specif. **b** small, light sailing-vessel used for racing &c.

yacht (II.), vb. intrans., fr. prec. To sail, race &c. in a yacht.

yacht-club, n. Club for yachtsmen, esp. for yacht-racing.

yachting, n. [1. yóting; 2. jɔ́tiŋ]. **yacht** (II.) & **-ing**. Art or practice of sailing in, or managing, a yacht.

yachtsman, n. [1. yótsman; 2. jɔ́tsmǝn]. One who habitually sails a yacht.

yaffle, yaffil, n. [1. yáfl; 2. jǽfl]. Imitative of cry. (provinc.) The green woodpecker.

yager, n. [1. yáger; 2. jéigǝ], fr. Germ. *jäger*, 'hunter', fr. *jagen*, O.H.G. *jagōn*, 'to hunt', q.v. under **yacht**. Member of one of various German infantry or cavalry corps, usually riflemen.

yahoo, n. [1. yàhhóō; 2. jàhú]. Coined by Swift in *Gulliver's Travels* (Voyage to the Houyhnhnms). **1.** One of a fictitious race of loathsome and vicious creatures, described by Swift, having the forms of men but the habits of lower animals; intended as a satire on the human race. **2.** An ungainly, coarse, rude, mannerless person.

Yahveh, n. [1. yahvá; 2. jāvéi], fr. Heb. *yahaveh*, see **Jehovah**. Jehovah.

Yahvist, n. [1. yáhvist; 2. jávist], fr. prec. & **-ist**. Jehovist.

Yahvistic, adj. [1. yàhvístik; 2. jàvístik]. Prec. & **-ic**. Jehovistic.

yak, n. [1. yak; 2. jæk]. Tibetan *gyak*. Wild and domesticated, long-haired, bovine quadruped of Central Asiatic mountains, used as a beast of burden.

yam, n. [1. yam; 2. jæm], fr. Port. *inhame*, fr. African. **1.** Fleshy, edible root of a tropical, climbing plant, *Dioscorea Batatas*. **2.** Any plant of the *Dioscorea* family, producing edible tubers.

Yama, n. [1. yáhma; 2. jámǝ]. Scrt. *Yama*. Hindu god and judge of the dead.

yamen, -un, n. [1. yáhmen; 2. jámǝn]. Chinese. Mandarin's official residence; office of public department.

yank (I.), vb. trans. & n. [1. yangk; 2. jæŋk]. Etymol. unknown. **a** vb. (slang) To pull sharply, with a jerk; **b** n., a sudden hard pull.

Yank (II.), n. Abbr. fr. next word. (slang) Yankee.

Yankee, n. [1. yángki, -ē; 2. jǽŋki, -ī]. Possibly fr. *Jankin*, dimin. of *Jan*=John, applied by Dutch settlers of New York to the English colonists of Connecticut. **1.** Specif., an inhabitant of New England, U.S.A., esp. a descendant of the original settlers. **2.** (colloq. in England) Any inhabitant of the United States, esp. one of British descent; an American.

Yankeedom, n. [1. yángkidom; 2. jǽŋkidǝm]. Prec. & **-dom**. Yankees collectively.

yankeefied, adj. [1. yángkifīd; 2. jǽŋkifaid]. **Yankee** & **-fy**. Imbued with, exhibiting, Yankee characteristics or ideas; Americanized.

Yankeeism, n. [1. yángkiizm; 2. jǽŋkiizǝm]. **Yankee** & **-ism**. Yankee characteristic(s).

yap, vb. intrans. & n. [1. yap; 2. jæp]. Imitative. **1.** vb. (of a dog) To utter a sharp, shrill bark or series of barks; to yelp. **2.** n. Sharp, excited yelp or bark.

yapon, n. [1. yápon; 2. jǽpɔn]. Prob. Am. Indian. An evergreen shrub of the southern United States of America.

yapp, n. [1. yap; 2. jæp]. Name of inventor. Style of bookbinding, with limp cover projecting beyond the edges.

Yarborough, n. [1. yárburo; 2. jábǝrǝ], fr. an Earl of Yarborough who betted against the possibility of such a hand. A hand at bridge or whist containing no card higher than a nine.

yard (I.), n. [1. yard; 2. jād]. O.E. *ġerd*, M.E. *ʒerde, yerde*, 'rod, staff; yard'; O.S. *gerda*; O.H.G. *gerta*; Du. *garde*; O.N. *gaddr*, 'rod'; Goth. *gazds*, 'point, sting'; cogn. w. Lat. *hasta*, 'staff, shaft, spear'; see **hastate**. **1. a** Unit of length, 36 inches, 3 feet; **b** piece of material a yard in length. **2.** (naut.) Long, nearly cylindrical spar, tapering towards the ends, fastened to mast and used to support sails; *square, lateen, yard*, forming a right, oblique, angle with the mast; (in compounds, indicating mast or sail to which the yard is attached) *lower-, topsail-yard* &c. Phr. *to man the yards*, to station sailors, be stationed, on the yards, esp. as form of salute. **3.** (archaic) Male organ of generation.

yard (II.), n. & vb. trans. O.E. *ġeard*; M.E. *ʒard*, 'piece of land, garden, yard'; cp. O.S. *gard*, 'enclosure, dwelling'; O.H.G. *gart*, 'circle'; O.N. *garðr*, 'hedge, enclosure'; Goth. *gards*, 'house'; cogn. w. Lat. *hortus*, 'garden'; *(co)-hors*, 'yard, enclosure; company, cohort; crowd', see **cohort, court** (I.), **garden**, & **garth**; cp. further Goth. *gairdan*, O.S. *gyrdan*, 'to gird', see **gird** (I.). **1.** n. **a** Enclosed, or partially enclosed, space, often paved, used for various purposes, near or adjoining a house, stable, or other building; often particularized in compounds: *farm-yard, rick-yard, stable-yard* &c.; **b** piece of open ground fenced off, in which some particular occupation is carried on: *a builder's, stone-mason's yard*; *railway yard*, open space near a station where trucks &c. are kept; specif., *the Yard*, Scotland Yard, as headquarters of the Criminal Investigation Department. **2.** vb. To put (cattle) into stock-yard.

yardage, n. [1. yárdij; 2. jádidž]. Prec. & **-age**. **1.** Right of enclosing cattle &c. in stock-yard. **2.** Sum payable for this right.

yard-arm, n. (naut.) Either half of yard.

yard-man, n. Man employed in railway yard.

yard-master, n. Manager of railway yard.

yard-measure, n. Tape, wooden or steel rod, measuring one yard and marked in feet, inches &c.

yard-stick, n. Wooden or metal yard-measure.

yard-wand, n. Yard-stick.

yare, adj. [1. yār; 2. jɛǝ]. O.E. *ġearu*, 'ready, prepared'; M.E. *ʒare, yāre*. Cogn. w. O.S. *garu*, O.H.G. *garo*; cp. also **gear** (I.). (archaic) **a** Ready, prepared; **b** moving quickly, active.

yarn (I.), n. [1. yarn; 2. jān]. O.E. *ġearn*; M.E. *ʒarn*, 'yarn'; O.N. *garnar*, 'entrails'; Gk. *khordḗ*, 'intestines; catgut; cord', see **cord**; Scrt. *hirá*, 'vein'; Lat. *haru-(spex)*, 'diviner inspecting entrails'; cp. **hernia**. **1. a** Fibrous material spun for weaving, knitting &c.; **b** specif., thread composed of two or more twisted strands of yarn; **c** twisted fibres prepared for rope-making. **2.** (colloq., orig. naut.) **a** A tale, narrative; Phr. *spin a yarn*, tell a story; also to exaggerate, tell a traveller's tale; **b** a false, exaggerated report or statement; an ill-founded rumour; **c** a friendly conversation, a chat.

yarn (II.), vb. intrans., fr. prec. (colloq., orig. naut.) **a** To tell a yarn; **b** to talk at length, to chatter; to hold a long conversation.

yarn-beam, n. Roller on which warp-threads are wound in a loom.

yarrow, n. [1. yárō; 2. jǽrou]. O.E. *ġearwe*; M.E. *ʒar(o)we*, 'yarrow'; cp. O.H.G. *gar-(a)wa*; Du. *gerw*, 'yarrow'. Highly astringent perennial herb, *Achillea millefolium*, with clusters of small white flowers, milfoil.

yashmak, n. [1. yáshmak; 2. jǽʃmæk], fr. Arab. Veil worn by Mohammedan women.

yataghan, n. [1. yátagàn; 2. jǽtəgæ̀n], Turkish. Turkish sword with double-curved blade and no cross-piece.

yaw, vb. intrans. & n. [1. yaw; 2. jɔ̄], fr. O.N. *jaga*, 'to curve back', orig. 'to hunt', cp. O.H.G. *jagōn*, 'to hunt'; see **yager, yacht.** (naut.) **1.** vb. (of ship or aircraft) To fall away from the course, move or steer unsteadily. **2.** n. Act of yawing; unsteady motion in, falling away from, ship's or aircraft's course.

yawl (I.), vb. intrans. & n. [1. yawl; 2. jɔ̄l]. Variant of **yowl**. Perh. influenced by **bawl**.

yawl (II.), n., fr. Du. *jol*; cp. Dan. *jolle.* **1.** Small, cutter-rigged sailing-vessel. **2.** Small ship's boat, jolly-boat.

yawn (I.), vb. intrans. & trans. [1. yawn; 2. jɔ̄n]. O.E. forms are *gānian* & *gīnan*, 'to yawn'; also *ginian, ġeonian*; M.E. *gōnen, yōnen, ȝeonien* &c. Cogn. w. Lat. *hiāre*, see **hiatus**. The Mod. form owes its initial to O.E. *ġeonian* &c., & the vowel is perh. imitative. **A.** intrans. **1.** To open the mouth owing to an involuntary muscular contraction, the tendency to which often arises from drowsiness. Phr. *to make a person yawn*, cause him to become sleepy; hence, to bore him. **2.** To open wide, be wide open, to gape: *a gulf, abyss, chasm &c., yawned in front of us.* **B.** trans. To utter with a yawn.

yawn (II.), n., fr. prec. The act of yawning, involuntary opening of the mouth.

yawning, adj. [1. yáwning; 2. jɔ̄niŋ], fr. Pres. Part. of **yawn** (I.). Wide open, gaping: *a yawning pit, cavern* &c.

yawningly, adv. Prec. & **-ly**. With a yawn.

yaws, n. [1. yawz; 2. jɔ̄z]. Prob. fr. African. Skin disease prevalent among negroes in the tropics, characterized by blains on various parts of the body; called also framboesia.

yclept, adj. [1. iklépt; 2. iklépt]. O.E. *ġecleopod*; M.E. *icleped*; P.P. of *clipian, cleopian*, 'to call'. Used by Spenser, & cp. Milton: '*Come thou Goddess fair and free, In heaven yclept Euphrosyne*' ('L'Allegro', 11-12). (archaic or facet.) Called, having the name of, known as.

ye (I.), pron. [1. yē; 2. jī], unstressed [1. (y)i; 2. (j)i]. O.E. *ġē*; M.E. *ȝē*; cp. Du. *gij*; Mod. Germ. *ihr*; Goth. *jus*. Cogn. w. Lith. *jūs*; Scrt. *yūyám*, 'you'. (archaic and poet.) Old nom. pl. of pron. of 2nd pers. *Ye* began to be superseded by *you* in nom. by the middle of 16th cent., but many writers keep the forms distinct much later. The Authorized Version always does so. As nom. the form survives in *how d'ye do?*=[haudidú], in the now obs. or provinc. *hark ye, look ye* [háki, lúki]. On the other hand, *ye* is used not infrequently instead of *you*, in the acc. & dat., in colloq. style in 16th & 17th cents., & still survives in the old-fashioned *thank ye* [þǽŋki]. This usage is prob. due orig. to the anal. of *thee*. See also **you**.

ye (II.), def. art. [1. dhē; 2. ðī], archaic method of printing *the*, due to 15th-cent. confusion of þ (see **thorn**) & *y*; sometimes ignorantly pronounced [1. yē; 2. jī], as a pseudo-archaism: *ye olde shoppe* &c.

yea, interj. & n. [1. yā; 2. jei]. O.E. *ġēa, ġǣ*; M.E. *ȝē, ȝā*, 'yes'; cp. O.S., O.H.G., O.N. *jā*; O. Fris. *jē*; Goth. *jā*, 'yes'; *jai*, 'certainly'; fr. the pronominal stem **i-*, **ei-*, wh. occurs also in it. (archaic) **1.** interj. **a** Yes, expressing affirmation; **b** moreover, not only that but: '*Nature's whole wealth, yea, more, A Heav'n on Earth,* (Milton, 'P. L.', iv. 407-8). **2.** n. Affirmative statement, expression of affirmation or agreement; Phr. '*Let your yea be yea*'.

yean, vb. trans. & intrans. [1. yēn; 2. jīn]. O.E. *ēanian*; M.E. *ēnen*, 'to yean'; cp. Du. *oonen*, 'to yean'; prob. formed fr. Gmc. base **agʷna-*, 'lamb'; cogn. w. Lat. *agnus*, 'lamb'; Gk. *amnós*, earlier *abnos*; O. Slav. *(j)agne*, 'lamb'. **1.** trans. To bring forth (lamb or kid). **2.** intrans. (of sheep or goat) To bring forth a lamb or kid.

yeanling, n. [1. yḗnling; 2. jínliŋ]. Prec. & **-ling**. Young lamb or kid.

year, n. [1. yēr, yër; 2. jiə, jɜ̄]. O.E. *ġēr*; M.E. *ȝēr*; cp. O.S. & O.H.G. *jār*; O.N. *ār*; Goth. *jēr*, 'year'; cogn. w. Gk. *hōrā*, 'period, season'; *hôros*, 'year', see **hour**; O. Slav. *jara*, 'spring'; prob. also Lat. *hornus*, 'of this year', earlier **hōjōrīnos*, fr. Instrumental **hō jōro-*, 'in this year'. **1. a** Period of time taken by the earth to revolve once round the sun; called specifically *astronomical, natural, equinoctial, solar, tropical year*; *common year*, this period reckoned as 365 days; *leap year, bissextile year*, of 366 days; **b** time taken by the sun to return to the same apparent position among the fixed stars; also called *astral, sidereal year*; **c** *lunar year*, period of twelve lunar months. **2.** Unit of time, period of 365 days (in leap-year, 366 days) reckoned from Jan. 1st to Dec. 31st next following, also *calendar, civil, legal year*: *this year*; *next year* &c.; *new, old, year*, year just beginning, ending; *this year of grace, year of our Lord*, of the Christian era. Phrs. *year in, year out*, continuously through the years; *from year to year*, every year; *in the year one*, very long ago. **3.** Period of 365 days reckoned from any or from a specific date: *it is just a year since I saw him*; *just a year ago*; *in a year's time*; *academic, school, year*, one reckoned from beginning of session in the autumn; *Christian, Church, year*, from Advent; *a year and a day*, period designated to ensure lapse of full year. **4.** (pl.) Age: *young, old, for one's years*; *a man of his years*; *to reach years of discretion.*

year-book, n. **1.** Annual publication giving statistics, reports &c., up to date. **2.** (hist.) One of a series of annual reports of courts of justice from Edward III. to Henry VIII.

yearling, n. & adj. [1. yḗr-, yḗrling; 2. jíə-, jɜ́liŋ]. **year** & **-ling**. **1.** n. **a** Animal in its second year; **b** (racing) colt one year old from January 1st of year of foaling. **2.** adj. A year old.

year-long, adj. Lasting, persisting, throughout the year, for a whole year.

yearly, adj. & adv. [1. yḗr-, yḗrli; 2. jíə-, jɜ́li]. **year** & **-ly**. **1.** adj. Occurring **a** once a year; **b** every year. **2.** adv. Every year, annually.

yearn, vb. intrans. [1. yërn; 2. jɜ̄n]. O.E. *ġernan*; M.E. *ȝernen*; cp. O.S. *gernean*; O.H.G. *gernen*; O.N. *girna*; Goth. *gairnjan*, 'desire, long'; O.H.G. *gern*, 'eager, desirous'; cogn. w. Lat. *hori, hortāri*, 'to incite, exhort', see **hortation**; Scrt. *háryati*, 'desires'; Gk. *khaírein*, 'to rejoice'; *kháris*, 'grace; joy; favour', cp. **eucharist**. **a** (followed by *for* or *after*) To desire earnestly and tenderly; to feel a tender longing towards: *to yearn for home*; *to yearn after one's absent friends*; **b** to desire, long: *I am yearning to make myself useful.*

yearning (I.), adj. [1. yḗrning; 2. jɜ́niŋ], fr. Pres. Part. of prec. Animated by, expressing, desire; longing: *a yearning look.*

yearning (II.), n. **yearn** & **-ing**. Strong desire for something; wistful longing.

yearningly, adv. [1. yḗrningli; 2. jɜ́niŋli]. **yearning** (I.) & **-ly**. In a yearning manner.

yeast, n. [1. yēst; 2. jist]. O.E. *ġest*; M.E. *ȝēste*, 'yeast'; cp. M.H.G., *jest*, 'foam'; O.H.G. *iesan*, 'to ferment'; cogn. w. Gk. *zéein*, 'to boil'; *zóē*, 'foam', see second element of **eczema**; Scrt. *yásati*, 'to boil'; cp. also **enzyme** & **zymosis**. **1.** Fungoid growth consisting of a yellowish, frothy substance, with cells germinating in contact with saccharine liquid and producing alcoholic fermentation; used in brewing, distilling, bread-making &c. **2.** Mass of dried yeast compressed into a cake for keeping &c.

yeastiness, n. [1. yḗstines; 2. jístinis]. **yeasty** & **-ness**. State or quality of being yeasty.

yeast-powder, n. Baking-powder used as substitute for yeast.

yeasty, adj. [1. yḗsti; 2. jísti]. **yeast** & **-y**. **1.** Consisting of, or covered with, froth. **2.** (fig.) **a** In a state of ferment; restless, unsettled: *yeasty thoughts* &c.; **b** unsubstantial, trifling, frivolous: *yeasty words* &c.

yelk, n. [1. yelk; 2. jɛlk]. See **yolk.**

yell (I.), vb. intrans. & trans. [1. yel; 2. jɛl]. O.E. *ġellan*; M.E. *ȝellen*, 'to yell, shout'; cp. O.H.G. *gellan*, 'to yell, shriek'; *galm*, 'sound'; prob. cogn. w. Gk. *khelidṓn*, 'swallow'. Cp. also O.E. *galan*, 'to sing, scream', see last syll. of **nightingale**. **1.** intrans. **a** To utter a yell, cry loudly and sharply: *to yell with pain* &c.; **b** specif., to laugh loudly and suddenly, indulge in a prolonged burst of laughter. **2.** trans. To utter, express, with a yell: *to yell an order.*

yell (II.), n., fr. prec. **1.** Loud, sharp outcry, scream; vocal expression, often involuntary, of sudden strong emotion, pain &c.: *a yell of pain, fear, defiance* &c. **2.** (U.S.A.) Specific cry, phrase, series of vocal sounds, used by college students as an organized cheer of encouragement, salute &c.

yellow (I.), adj. [1. yélō; 2. jélou]. O.E. *ġeolo*; M.E. *ȝelowe*; cp. O.H.G. *gelo*, 'yellow'; cogn. w. Lat. *helvus*, 'tawny'; Lith. *želvas*, 'greenish'; cp. further Scrt. *háriš*, 'yellow, greenish'; O. Slav. *zelenu*, 'green'; Gk. *khlōrós*, 'green', see also **chloral**, & **gold**. **1.** Of the colour found between green and orange in the spectrum, similar to the colour of gold, daffodils, buttercups &c.; Phrs. *yellow boy*, (slang) gold coin; *yellow looks*, sour, suspicious glances. **2.** (of race or person) Yellow-skinned, Mongolian; Phr. *yellow peril*, supposed danger of the yellow races obtaining world-power. **3.** (low slang) Cowardly, lacking spirit and pluck.

yellow (II.), n., fr. prec. **1. a** Yellow colour; **b** yellow pigment. **2.** (archaic) *Yellows*, jaundice.

yellow (III.), vb. trans. & intrans., fr. **yellow** (I.). **1.** trans. To give a yellow colour to, turn yellow. **2.** intrans. To grow yellow.

yellow-, pref. representing **yellow** (I.). **1.** (in names of animals, insects, plants &c.) Of a yellow colour. **2.** (with name of part of body, forming names of plants, animals &c.) Of a yellow colour in specified part, e.g., *yellow-bill*; *yellow-tail*; *yellow-jacket* &c. **3.** (in names of animals, plants &c., compounded w. adjs. formed fr. parts of body) e.g. *yellow-backed, yellow-legged* &c.

yellowback, n. [1. yélōbàk; 2. jéloubæ̀k]. (archaic) A cheap novel, esp. of an exciting, sensational character, formerly issued bound in boards covered with shiny yellow paper, with a picture on the front.

yellow-bird, n. N. American goldfinch.

yellow-book, n. Official report of French or Chinese government, issued with a yellow paper cover.

yellow box, n. Australian box-tree.

yellow cartilage, n. Elastic wall of artery.

yellow earth, n. Yellow ochre.

yellow fever, n. Acute, infectious, malignant, tropical fever, marked by jaundice, black vomit, and bleeding &c., caused by a micro-organism conveyed by the bite of a mosquito.

yellow-gum, n. Infants' black jaundice.

yellow-hammer, n. Earlier *yellow ammer*, fr. **yellow** (I.) & O.E. *amore*, a kind of bird; cp. O.H.G. *amer*, 'yellow-hammer'. Small, European bunting, *Emberiza citrinella*, with yellow head, neck, and breast.

yellowish, adj. [1. yélōish; 2. jélouiʃ]. **yellow** (I.) & **-ish**. Somewhat yellow.

yellow jack, n. Yellow fever.

yellowly, adv. [1. yélōli; 2. jélouli]. **yellow** (I.) & **-ly**. In a yellow manner; so as to give an impression of yellowness.

yellow metal, n. Alloy of 60 parts copper and 40 parts zinc.

yellowness, n. [1. yélōnes; 2. jélounis]. **yellow** (I.) & **-ness**. Quality of being yellow.

yellow ochre, n. Kind of clay coloured with oxide of iron, used as pigment.

yellow press, n. Sensational newspapers.

yellow-rattle, n. Yellow-flowered herb.

yellow spot, n. Point of most acute vision in the retina.

yellow wood, n. Tree yielding yellow timber.

yellow wort, n. A plant of the gentian family, the flowers of which are used medicinally.

yellowy, adj. [1. yélōi; 2. jéloui]. **yellow (I.)** & **-y**. Yellow, yellowish.

yelp, vb. intrans. & n. [1. yelp; 2. jɛlp]. O.E. *ġelpan*, 'to boast'; M.E. *ȝelpen*, cp. M.H.G. *gelfen*; O.N. *gjalpa*, 'to yelp'. **1.** vb. To utter a yelp, to yap. **2.** n. Short, sharp cry or bark, a yap, of rage or pain, esp. of a dog.

yen, n. [1. yen; 2. jɛn]. Jap., fr. Chinese *yüan*, 'round; a dollar'. Unit of Japanese coinage, worth about 2s. 1d.

yeoman, n. [1. yṓman; 2. jóumən]. M.E. *ȝēman*, *ȝōman*, 'manservant, steward'; cp. O. Fris. *gāman*, 'villager'. The origin of the first element is rather doubtful, & it is uncertain fr. what source the word got into M.E. O.E. **ġeā* is not found, but it has been suspected to lurk in the Pl.-N. *Ely*, O.E. *Eli-ge*, *-ga*. The meaning was presumably 'village, district', & its cognates must be sought in O. Fris. *gā*, *gō*, 'village', O.H.G. *kawi*, *goui* &c., Mod. Germ. *gau*, 'village, township' &c.; Goth. *gawi*. On the other hand, O.E.D. suggests not entirely without some plausibility that the word stands for *yongman*, w. the sense of 'page, retainer' &c., & adduces early forms *yemman*, *yomman*. **1.** (hist.) Owner of free land to the value of forty shillings yearly, thereby entitled to certain rights. Phr. *yeoman('s) service*, effective assistance. **2.** Farmer cultivating his own land, a small landowner. **3.** Member of yeomanry force of cavalry. **4.** *Yeoman of the Guard*, in full, *His Majesty's Body Guard of the Yeomen of the Guard*, member of a royal bodyguard founded in 1485, and now employed solely in ceremonial duties.

yeomanly, adj. [1. yṓmanli; 2. jóumənli]. Prec. & **-ly**. Of, resembling, characteristic of, a yeoman.

yeomanry, n. [1. yṓmanri; 2. jóumənri]. **yeoman** & **-ry**. **1.** Yeomen collectively. **2.** Territorial, formerly volunteer, cavalry force recruited chiefly from country districts.

-yer, suff. expressing an agent. Now used only in a few words—*lawyer*, *bowyer*, *sawyer*. From earlier **-ier**; cp. **-eer**; or formed as fr. *-ien* vbs., & **-er**; cp. M.E. *luvien*, 'to love', whence earlier *luvier*, *loveyer* instead of *lover*; cp. **wonyer**.

yerba, n. [1. yérba; 2. jɜ́bə]. Span. *yerba (maté)*, 'the herb maté'. Paraguay tea, maté.

yercum, n. [1. yérkum; 2. jɜ́kəm], fr. Tamil *erukku*. Fibre of an E. Indian plant called mudar, which resembles flax.

yes, interj. or advbl. particle [1. yes; 2. jɛs]. O.E. *ġiese*, *ġese*, fr. *ġeā swā*, **yea** & **so**. **1.** Expressing affirmation, consent, **a** esp. in answer to a question: *are you ready? yes*; **b** expressing acquiescence in what has been said: *this is an excellent book; yes, it is*. **2.** (uttered with rising tone) **a** Expressing interrogation; is it so? &c. in reply to another's statement: *he is a very unscrupulous fellow. Yes?*; **b** also following a statement of one's own, with sense do you understand?, do you agree?, is that clear? &c.: *we first go two miles west, then bear to the north and continue in a straight line for several miles—yes?* **3.** As emphasising or amplifying a statement; moreover, in addition: *he will insult you, yes, and cheat you as well.*

yester-, pref. representing O.E. *ġeostran-*, M.E. *ȝestren-*, 'yester-'; cp. O.H.G. *gestaron*, 'yesterday'; Goth. *gistra(dagis)*, 'tomorrow'; cogn. w. Lat. *here*, earlier **hezi*, 'yesterday', fr. **ghes-*; *hesternus*, 'of yesterday'; Scrt. *hyáš*; Gk. *khthés*, 'yesterday'. (chiefly poet.) Forming nouns and adverbs, **a** with the sense 'of yesterday', e.g. *yester-night*, *-eve* &c.; **b** with the sense 'last, preceding', e.g. *yesteryear*, (poet.) past times.

yesterday, n. & adv. [1. yésterdi; 2. jéstədi]. O.E. *ġeostran dæġ*, 'yesterday'; see prec. & **day**. **1.** n. **a** The day before today, the day just past. Phr. *(a thing) of yesterday*, something of but recent growth, appearance &c.; **b** (pl.) past times, former days: '*A man of cheerful yesterdays*' (Wordsworth, 'Excursion', vii. 536); **c** (attrib.) *yesterday morning, evening, night*. **2.** adv. On the day before today: *he went away yesterday.*

yestreen, n. & adv. [1. yestrḗn; 2. jɛstrín]. Contracted fr. *yester-even*; see **yester-**. (Scots) **a** n. Yester-even, the evening of yesterday; **b** adv., on the evening of yesterday.

yet (I.), adv. [1. yet; 2. jɛt]. O.E. *ġet*; M.E. *ȝet*; cp. O. Fris. *(j)eta*; M.H.G. *ieze*, 'yet, now'. **1.** (usually with neg.) **a** Up to this time, until now, heretofore: *he has not come yet*; *I know nothing yet*; **b** up to a specified point of time in the past: *when dawn broke the reinforcements had not yet arrived.* **2.** At this present time, now: *need you go yet?*; *I can't come just yet.* **3.** Still, up to and including the present time, even now: *he is yet alive*; *while there is yet time*; *he loves her yet*; *the work is yet unfinished.* Phr. *as yet*, up to now, so far. **4.** In addition, besides: *he has yet much to say*; *there is work yet to be done*; *we have yet more to ask.* **5.** Before a future time, some day: *he will yet be victorious*; *he may surprise you yet.* **6.** Even, as much as: *he will not accept help nor yet advice.* **7.** (with compar.) Still, even, additionally, even more: *travelling is yet more rapid today than it was ten years ago.* **8.** Nevertheless, in spite of that: *the house was humble, yet clean*; *poor, yet honest.*

yet (II.), conj., fr. prec. Nevertheless, but still: *appearances are against him, yet I cannot think him guilty.*

yew, n. [1. ū; 2. jū]. O.E. *ēow*, *īw*; M.E. *eu*, 'yew'; cp. O.H.G. *īwa*, Mod. Germ. *eibe*; Du. *ijf*; O.N. *ȳr*; cp. also O.E. *eoh*; O.H.G. *īche*, 'yew'. **1.** Evergreen coniferous tree, *Taxus baccata*, with small, slender, densely growing, dark-green leaves and rough bark. **2.** Close-grained, durable wood obtained from the yew, used formerly for making bows.

yew tree, n. Same as **yew**, **1**.

Yg(g)drasil, n. [1. ígdrasil; 2. ígdrəsil]. O.N. *(askr) Yggdrasils*, perh. 'ash of the horse of Yggr' or Odin. (Norse mythol.) Great tree of the universe, whose roots and branches bind together heaven, earth, and hell.

Yiddish, n. & adj. [1. yídish; 2. jídiʃ], fr. Jewish pronunciation of Germ. *jüdisch*, 'Jewish', fr. *Jude*, 'Jew', O.H.G. *judeo*, fr. Lat. *judaeus*, 'Jew'; see **Judaic**. **1.** n. Mixed dialect with German, Hebrew, and Slavonic elements, used by German Jews, largely spoken in the East End of London. **2.** adj. Spoken, written &c., in Yiddish.

yield (I.), vb. trans. & intrans. [1. yēld; 2. jiəld]. O.E. *ġelden*; M.E. *ȝeelden*, 'to pay'; cp. O.H.G. *geltan*, 'to pay; to be worth'; O.N. *gjalda*, 'to pay'; Goth. *-gildan*, 'to requite'; Du. *gelden*, 'to cost'. **A.** trans. **1. a** To produce, give, as result of a natural process: *the land yields heavy crops*; *cows yield milk*; **b** to produce in return for effort, trouble &c.: *my labours, researches, yielded but a poor result*; **c** to produce as financial return: *investments yield a profit.* **2.** To give up, relinquish under pressure, compulsion &c., surrender: *to yield a fortress to the enemy.* **3.** To concede, grant: *to yield precedence to another*; *to yield a point in argument.* **B.** intrans. **1.** To produce, give a return for effort &c.: *the land yields abundantly.* **2.** (often with *to*) **a** To give way, submit, cease resistance: *he will never yield*; *to yield to pressure, to force.* Phr. *I yield to none (in my admiration for him* &c.), I do not admit that anyone (admires him &c.) more than I do; **b** (of material object) to give way to, or before, physical pressure: *the door yielded to a strong push*; '*Oft did the harvest to their sickle yield*' (Gray's 'Elegy'); **c** (of diseases) *to yield to treatment*, be amenable to, become less acute, be cured, as result of.

yield (II.), n., fr. prec. Amount produced; result, profit, return.

yielding, adj. [1. yélding; 2. jíəldiŋ], fr. Pres. Part. of **yield (I.)**. **a** Tending to bend; capable of being bent or altered in shape; flexible, not rigid; **b** easily influenced, liable to yield to persuasion; compliant; reverse of *stubborn.*

yieldingly, adv. Prec. & **-ly**. In a yielding manner.

-yl, suff. representing Gk. *hū́lē*, 'wood, forest, timber; material; matter'; etymol. doubtful. Used to form chemical terms denoting a radical, q.v., e.g. *methyl.*

ylang-ylang, n. [1. iláng ilàng; 2. ilǽŋ ilæ̀ŋ]. Philippine. Malayan tree with fragrant flowers.

yodel, vb. intrans. & trans., & n. [1. yṓdl; 2. jóudl], fr. Germ. *jodeln*, prob. imitative. **1.** vb. **a** intrans. To produce a yodel; **b** trans., to sing (a song) by yodelling. **2.** n. Series of musical notes uttered by the voice, in form of a kind of warble or run, passing alternatively from chest voice to falsetto, and vice versa.

yoga, n. [1. yṓga; 2. jóugə]. Hind. System of philosophy and practice of esoteric meditation, having as object the union of the individual human spirit with that of the universe.

yogh, n. [1. yogh; 2. jɔχ]. Prob. fr. M.E. *ȝoc*, 'yoke', see **yoke**, wh. begins w. this letter. The Middle English letter ȝ.

yogi, n. [1. yṓgi; 2. jóugi]. Hind. Devotee of yogism.

yogism, n. [1. yṓgizm; 2. jóugizəm]. Prec. & **-ism**. Doctrines of the yoga.

yo-heave-ho, interj. [1. yō hēv hō; 2. jou hīv hou]. (naut.) Cry used in heaving the anchor &c.

yoho, interj. [1. yōhṓ; 2. jòuhóu]. Yo-heave-ho.

yoick, vb. intrans. & trans. [1. yoik; 2. jɔik], fr. next word. **1.** intrans. To cry yoicks. **2.** trans. To encourage, urge on (hounds), with the cry of 'Yoicks'.

yoicks, interj. [1. yoiks; 2. jɔiks]. Etymol. unknown. Huntsman's cry to hounds.

yoke (I.), n. [1. yōk; 2. jouk]. O.E. *ġeoc*; M.E. *ȝoc*, *ȝōke*; cp. O.H.G. *joh*; Goth. *juk*; cogn. w. Lat. *jugum*, 'yoke', see **jugate**; Gk. *zugón*, 'yoke', see **zyg(o)-**; Scrt. *yugám*, 'yoke, pair'; conn. w. Lat. *jungere*, 'to join', see **join**. **1.** Cross-piece forming part of harness of, and shaped to fit necks of, draught-animals, oxen &c. Phr. *to pass, come, under the yoke*, to submit to defeat; from ancient Roman custom of causing conquered enemy to pass beneath an uplifted yoke, or an arch of spears, as a symbol of servitude. **2.** Object resembling a yoke in shape; specif. **a** wooden bar or frame shaped to fit person's shoulders and used for carrying milkpails &c.; **b** cross-bar from which a bell is hung; **c** cross-bar on rudder, to which steering-lines are fastened; **d** coupling for pipes; **e** part of garment cut or designed to fit shoulders. **3. a** Pair of oxen, for ploughing &c.; **b** *yoke of land*, amount of land ploughed by a pair of oxen in a day. **4.** (fig.) Sway, domination, authority: *the yoke of an oppressor.* **5.** (rare) Moral or legal bond.

yoke (II.), vb. trans. & intrans.; see prec. **A.** trans. **1.** To put a yoke upon, harness with a yoke. **2.** To join together, to unite: (chiefly fig.) *yoked in marriage.* **B.** intrans. (rare) *Yoke together*, to be joined.

yoke-bone, n. Cheek-bone, malar, joining bones of head and face.

yoke-fellow, n. Person joined or associated with one in work &c. or in marriage.

yokel, n. [1. yṓkl; 2. jóukl]. Prob. **yoke** & **-el**. Countryman, rustic.

yoke-lines, n. Pair of lines attached to yoke of rudder for steering small boat.

yokemate, n. [1. yṓkmāt; 2. jóukmeit]. Yoke-fellow.

yolk, n. [1. yōk; 2. jouk]. O.E. *ġeolca*, 'yolk'; M.E. *ȝolke*; connected w. O.E. *ġeolu*, 'yellow', see **yellow**. **1.** Yellow central mass of egg. **2.** Fatty secretion in sheep's wool.

yolk-bag, n. Yolk-sac.

yolked, adj. [1. yōkt; 2. joukt]. **yolk** & **-ed**. Having a yolk; sometimes in compounds, e.g. *double-yolked*, with two yolks.

yolk-sac, n. Membranous sac attached to an embryo from which nutrition is derived.

yolky, adj. [1. yṓki; 2. jóuki]. **yolk** & **-y.** Containing or resembling yolk.

yon, adj., adv., & pron. [1. yon; 2. jɔn]. O.E. *ġeon*; M.E. *ȝon*, 'yon'; cp. O. Fris. *jene*; O.H.G. *jener*; O.N. *enn*; Goth. *jains*, 'that'; cogn. w. Scrt. *yáś*, 'which, who'; Gk. *hós*, 'that'; fr. pronominal stem ***i-** &c., seen in **it** &c. (archaic or provinc.) **1.** adj. That one yonder. **2.** adv. Yonder, over there. **3.** pron. Yonder person or thing: *did you ever see the like of yon?*

yonder, adj. & adv. [1. yónder; 2. jɔ́ndə]. M.E. *ȝonder*; **yon** & **-ther.** **1.** adj. In that (more or less remote) place, over there. **2.** adv. Over there: *yonder stands an oak.*

yore, n. [1. yōr; 2. jɔ̄]. O.E. *ġēara*, *ġ(e)āra*, M.E. *ȝōre*, 'formerly', adv. fr. n. *ġēar*, 'year', see **year.** Only in *of yore*, formerly, long ago; *days of yore*, in ancient times.

York (I.), n. [1. york; 2. jɔ̄k], fr. Place-Name York; O.E. *Eoforwic*, adaptation of Brito-Lat. *Eboracum*. *York-and-Lancaster rose*, red-and-white variety, named from respective badges of Lancastrians and Yorkists in Wars of the Roses.

york (II.), vb. trans., fr. next word. To bowl (person) out with a yorker.

yorker, n. [1. yórker; 2. jɔ̄kə]. Prob. fr. York, Pl.-N. (cricket) Ball which pitches immediately in front of batsman's block.

Yorkist, adj. & n. [1. yórkist; 2. jɔ̄kist]. **York** & **-ist.** **1.** adj. Of, pertaining to, the house of York, family descended from Edmund, son of Edward III. **2.** n. Adherent of House of York in Wars of the Roses.

Yorkshire, adj. [1. yórksher; 2. jɔ̄kʃə], fr. name of county. Of, pertaining to, originating in Yorkshire; *Yorkshire flannel*, made of undyed wool; *Yorkshire grit*, grit used for polishing; *Yorkshire pudding*, baked batter eaten with meat; *Yorkshire terrier*, small, long-haired variety.

you, pron. [1. ū; 2. jū]; unstressed [ju]. O.E. *ēow*, dat. of *ȝē*, pl. pron. of 2nd pers., see **ye**; M.E. *ȝou*, which was already used in respectful address to a single person. **1.** Used as nominative and objective case of pronoun of 2nd person, singular and plural. By the middle of 16th cent., while *you* is still often kept distinct from nominative *ye*, the two forms are used indifferently by many, and some writers (e.g. Queen Elizabeth) appear to use *you* only, as at present. **2.** indef. pron. One, anyone: *you never can tell*; *you often find that just when you want something you haven't got it by you.* **3.** (reflex., archaic) Yourself: *stay and rest you on this bank.*

young (I.), adj. [1. yung; 2. jaŋ]. O.E. *ġeong*; M.E. *ȝung*; cp. O.S., O. Fris., O.H.G. *jung*; Goth. *juggs*, 'young'; cogn. w. Lat. *juvenis*, 'young', see **juvenile**; *juvencus*, 'bullock'; Scrt. *yuvaśáś*, 'youthful'; *yúvā*, 'young'; Lith. *jáunas*; O. Slav. *junŭ*, 'young'. **1.** **a** (of men and other living creatures) In the early stages of life, in a period of life not long after birth; contrasted with *old* or *middle-aged*: *a young man, animal, plant* &c.; *a young tree*, one planted only a short time, not fully grown; Phrs. *a young family*, one consisting of small children; *the young person*, inexperienced, unsophisticated youth collectively; *(look here), young man*, familiar, slightly condescending form of address; **b** applied to the younger of two persons of same name or family, to distinguish a son from his father, or a man from his elder brother &c.: *young Jones, the young Mrs. Brown* &c.; *younger branch of family*, descended from a younger son. **2.** Characteristic of youth; **a** having the appearance, habits &c. of youth; fresh, vigorous, not decrepit: *a man is as young as his arteries*; *young for his age, years*; **b** enjoyed, possessed, by young persons: *young love*; *young ambitions*; Phr. *young blood*, fresh, vigorous, triumphant youth; **c** embodying new ideas, tendencies &c., esp. in names of progressive political parties, movements &c.: *Young England*; *Young Turks.* **3.** Having had a comparatively short historical existence. **4.** (of periods of time, seasons &c.) Not far advanced, having begun but a short time before: *the night, the century, is still young.* **5.** Inexperienced; not inured: *young in crime.*

young (II.), n., fr. prec. (coll.) The offspring of animals: *every animal will defend its young to the utmost of its powers.* Phr. (of female animals) *with young*, pregnant.

youngish, adj. [1. yúngish; 2. jáŋiʃ]. **young** & **-ish.** Fairly young; barely middle-aged.

youngling, n. [1. yúngling; 2. jáŋliŋ]. **young** & **-ling.** (poet.) Young child, animal &c.

youngster, n. [1. yúngster; 2. jáŋstə]. **young** & **-ster.** A young man; a child, esp. a boy.

younker, n. [1. yúngker; 2. jáŋkə], fr. Du. *jonker*, fr. *jong*, 'young', cogn. w. **young**, & *heer*, 'sir'; cp. Germ. *Herr*, O.H.G. *hērro*, *hēriro*, 'lord, master', fr. compar. of *hēr*, 'distinguished, respected', orig. 'old' (Mod. Germ. *hehr*); cp. O.E. *hār*, 'grey, hoary', see **hoar.** (archaic) Young man, youngster.

your, adj. [1. yōr, ūr; 2. jɔ̄, juə]. O.E. *ēower*; genit. pl. of *ġē*, 'you', see **ye**; M.E. *eour, ower*, & *ȝour, your*, w. *y-* on anal. of nom.; cp. O.S. *iuwar*; O.H.G. *iuwer*; Goth. *izwara*, 'of you'. **1.** Pertaining or belonging to you. **2.** (archaic and colloq.) Used to give indefinite, general sense to following noun: *your true savage can never be thoroughly civilized.*

yours, pron. & predic. adj. [1. yorz, ūrz; 2. jɔ̄z, juəz]. M.E. *youres.* **your** & **-es.** **1.** pron. Possessive of *you*, **a** the thing or things belonging to you; used absolutely: *this seat is yours*; **b** also preceded by *of*: *a little whim of yours*; *I saw a friend of yours.* **2.** adj. **a** Belonging to you: *the credit is much more yours than mine*; **b** at your service, devoted to you: in formulae at close of letters: *yours truly, faithfully, affectionately*; *yours to command.* **3.** As n. Those (persons) belonging to you, your nearest and dearest: *all good wishes to you and yours.*

yourself, pron. [1. yor-, ūrsélf; 2. jɔ̄-, juəsélf]. **your** & **-self.** **1.** Emphatic form of *you*: *you told me so yourself*; *do it yourself*, implying *you* rather than someone else; *(all) by yourself*, (i.) alone, without company; (ii.) by your own efforts, without help from others. **2.** (reflex.) *Don't hurt yourself*; *you will wear yourself out.*

youth, n. [1. yōōth; 2. jūþ]. O.E. *ġeóguþ*, fr. **jugunþ*; M.E. *ȝuweþe, youhþe* &c.; O.S. *juguth*; O.H.G. *jugund*, 'youth'; cogn. w. Lat. *juventa, -tus*, 'youth'; see **young, -th.** **1.** Early life; **a** specif., period of life between childhood and physical maturity; adolescence; contrasted with *childhood* on one hand and *manhood* on the other; **b** young manhood or young womanhood; period of life before middle age; contrasted with *middle age* or *old age*: *the wife of his youth*; *after thirty we feel that youth is slipping away*; (fig.) *the youth of nations*, early period in their history or development. **2.** Physical and mental characteristics of youth; buoyancy, vigour: *the way to keep one's youth is to exercise both mind and body regularly.* **3.** A young man: *a most agreeable youth*; *a bevy of youths and maidens.* **4.** Young persons of both sexes collectively: *the youth of the place.*

youthful, adj. [1. yōōthfool; 2. jūþfəl]. Prec. & **-ful.** **1.** Possessing youth; young, not old: *a youthful bride, mother.* **2.** Pertaining to, characteristic of, suitable for, youth: *youthful ambitions* &c.; *a youthful appearance, smile*; *her clothes were too youthful for her face and figure.*

youthfully, adv. Prec. & **-ly.** In a youthful manner.

youthfulness, n. See prec. & **-ness.** State or quality of being youthful.

yowl, vb. intrans. & n. [1. youl; 2. jaul]. Cp. Du. *jolen*; O.N. *gaula*, 'to yell'. Imitative. **a** vb. To howl dismally; **b** n., a dismal howl.

ytterbic, adj. [1. itérbik; 2. itʌ́bik]. See next word & **-ic.** Connected with, pertaining to, ytterbium.

ytterbium, n. [1. itérbium; 2. itʌ́biəm], fr. Place-Name Ytterby, in Sweden, place of discovery. Rare element, forming colourless salts.

yttric, adj. [1. ítrik; 2. ítrik]. See **yttrium** & **-ic.** Pertaining to yttrium.

yttriferous, adj. [1. itríferus; 2. itrífərəs]. **yttro-** & **-ferous.** Containing yttrium.

yttrious, adj. [1. ítrius; 2. ítriəs]. See **yttrium** & **-ous.** Derived from yttrium.

yttrium, n. [1. ítrium; 2. ítriəm], fr. Place-Name Ytterby, in Sweden, place of discovery. Rare metal, found as a greyish powder.

yttro-, pref. representing prec. Forming names of minerals containing yttrium, e.g. *yttrocerite*, a violet-coloured mineral sometimes found in quartz.

yucca, n. [1. yúka, yooka; 2. jákə, júkə]. Span., fr. Am. Indian. Genus of plants of the lily family, indigenous to Central America, Mexico &c., having a dense crown of stiff, thick, sword-shaped leaves and large white flowers.

yuga, n. [1. yōōga; 2. júgə]. Hind., fr. Scrt. *yugá-*, 'era, age'. Any one of the four cycles into which the duration of the world is divided in the Hindu religious writings.

yule, n. [1. yōōl; 2. jūl]. O.E. *ġeōl*, M.E. *ȝōl*; cp. O.N. *jōl.* Etymol. unknown. Christmas season or festival.

yule-log, n. Log burnt as part of Christmas celebrations.

yule-tide, n. Christmas.

Z

Z, z [1. zed; 2. zɛd]. **a** The twenty-sixth letter of the alphabet; for use in abbreviations &c. see list at end of Dictionary; **b** (alg.) third unknown quantity.

zaffre, zaffer, n. [1. záfer; 2. zǽfə], fr. Fr. *zafre*, perh. fr. Arab. Blue pigment made from cobalt ore and silica, used in enamelling, glass-painting &c.

zamindar, n. [1. zámindar; 2. zǽmindā]. See **zemindar.**

zany, n. [1. zāni; 2. zéini], fr. Fr. *zani*, fr. Ital. *zanni*, abbr. fr. *Giovanni*, John. **1.** (hist.) Buffoon who mimics the chief clown and other actors in a theatrical performance. **2.** A fantastic, foolish person; a buffoon, a merry-andrew.

Zanzibari, n. & adj. [1. zànzibáhri; 2. zæ̀nzibári], fr. Place-Name Zanzibar. **1.** n. Native of Zanzibar. **2.** adj. Of, coming from, Zanzibar.

zaptieh, n. [1. záptiā; 2. zǽptiei]. Turkish. Turkish policeman.

Zarathustrian. See **Zoroastrian.**

zareba, zariba, n. [1. zarēba; 2. zərībə], fr. Arab. *zariba*, 'pen, enclosure'. (in the Soudan &c.) Camp or village enclosed for protection by hedge or stockade.

zeal, n. [1. zēl; 2. zīəl], fr. O. Fr. *zele*, fr. L. Lat. *zēlus*, 'zeal', fr. Gk. *zēlos*, 'emulation; zeal', possibly cogn. w. Slovene *jal*, 'envy' O. Slav. *jaru*, 'furious'; Scrt. *yávan*, 'persecutor'. Intense enthusiasm for person, cause, enterprise &c.; ardour, fervour.

zealot, n. [1. zélot; 2. zélət], fr. O. Fr. *zelote*, fr. Lat. *zēlōtes*, fr. Gk. *zēlōtḗs*, 'zealous follower', fr. *zēlos*, 'emulation', see prec., & **-ot.** Person with excessive enthusiasm for an object, cause &c.; a fanatic.

zealotry, n. [1. zélotri; 2. zélətri]. Prec. & **-ry.** Practice or feeling of a zealot.

zealous, adj. [1. zélus; 2. zéləs]. **zeal & -ous.** Acting with, characterized by, expressing, zeal.

zealously, adv. Prec. & **-ly.** In a zealous manner; with zeal.

zebec(k), n. See **xebec.**

zebra, n. [1. zébra; 2. zíbrə]. Port., fr. Afr. Genus of African quadrupeds related to the horse and ass, with light-coloured body, marked with dark brown or black stripes.

zebra-, pref. implying stripiness: *zebra-antelope, -fish* &c.

zebra-wood, n. Striped wood obtained from a tree found in Guiana.

zebrine, adj. [1. zébrīn; 2. zíbrain]. **zebra & -ine.** Resembling, allied to, the zebra.

zebu, n. [1. zébū; 2. zíbjū], fr. Fr. *zébu*, fr. Tibetan *mdzopo.* Large animal of the bovine family, with a hump; domesticated in India and China.

zed, n. [1. zed; 2. zɛd], fr. Fr. *zède*, fr. Lat., fr. Gk. *zēta*, sixth letter of alphabet; according to Boisacq, prob. formed fr. Heb. *zajin*, on anal. of *ēta, thēta.* Name of the letter *z.*

zedoary, n. [1. zédōari; 2. zédouəri], fr. O. Fr. *zedoaire*, fr. Med. Lat., fr. Pers. *zadwar.* Cp. **setwall.** An aromatic drug used in India as a medicine and stimulant.

zeitgeist, n. [1. tsítgīst; 2. tsáitgaist]. Germ., fr. *zeit*, 'time', q.v. under **tide**, & *geist*, 'spirit', q.v. under **ghost.** Spirit of the times; general body of opinions and intellectual tendencies prevalent at a particular period.

Zelanian, adj. [1. zilánian; 2. ziléiniən], fr. Latinized form (*Nova*) *Zelania*, 'New Zealand', & **-an.** Connected with, belonging to, New Zealand.

zeloso, adv. [1. zelṓsō; 2. zɛlóusou]. Ital., fr. Lat. *zēlōsus*, 'emulous', see **jealous.** (direction in mus.) Fervently, energetically.

zemindar, n. [1. zémindàr; 2. zémindā], fr. Pers. *zemīndār*, 'landholder', *zamīn*, 'land', & *-dar*, suff. indicating the agent. (in India, esp. Bengal) **a** A person holding land for which he pays revenue to the Government; **b** a landholder generally.

zemstvo, n. [1. zémstvō; 2. zémstvou]. Russ., fr. *zemlya*, 'land', cogn. w. Lith. *žẽme*; Scrt. *kšā́š*; Lat. *humus*, 'earth'; see **humus.** Provincial, elective, economic assembly in the old Russian Empire.

zenana, n. [1. zenáhna; 2. zinā́nə]. Pers. *zenāna*, 'of women', fr. *zan*, 'woman'; cp. Scrt. *jániš*, 'woman'; cogn. w. Gk. *gunḗ*, 'woman', see **gyno-**; O.E. *cwene*, 'woman', see **quean**; *cwēn*, 'wife, queen', see **queen.** Apartments in an Indian native house in which the women are secluded; *zenana mission*, one for religious, medical, and educational reform among Indian women.

Zend, n. [1. zend; 2. zɛnd], fr. O. Pers. *zend*, 'commentary'; named fr. that upon the Parsee scriptures. Ancient form of Old Persian, called also Old Bactrian, in which the Avesta is written; a language belonging, together with Sanscrit and the modern Indian languages, to the Aryan branch of Aryan speech.

Zend-Avesta, n. [1. zénd avésta; 2. zénd avéstə], fr. Pers. *Avistāk va Zand*, 'text and commentary'. The sacred writings of the Zoroastrians; also applied to the interpretation of these in Pehlevi.

zenith, n. [1. zénith; 2. zéniþ], fr. O. Fr. *zenith*, fr. O. Span. *zenit*, fr. Arab. *semt*, 'way, path', abbr. fr. *semt-er-ras*, 'way of the head'. **1.** Point of the heavens directly above the observer. **2.** (fig.) Culminating point, highest degree of intensity, strength, success &c.: *at the zenith of one's fame, powers* &c.

zenithal, adj. [1. zénithal; 2. zéniþəl]. Prec. & **-al.** Of, pertaining to, the zenith.

zenith-distance, n. Angular distance of a heavenly body from the zenith.

zeolite, n. [1. zéolīt; 2. zíəlait], fr. Gk. *zé-(ein)*, 'to boil', see second element of **eczema**, & **-lite.** Hydrous silicate found in the cavities of lava.

zephyr, n. [1. zéfer; 2. zéfə], fr. Fr. *zéphire*, fr. Lat. *zephyrus*, fr. Gk. *zéphuros*, 'west wind'; perh. cogn. w. *zóphos*, 'darkness'. **1. a** (cap.) West wind; **b** (poet.) soft wind, gentle breeze. **2. a** Fine, very thin, woollen material; **b** under-garment made from such material.

Zeppelin, n. [1. zépelin; 2. zépəlin], fr. name of inventor, Count von Zeppelin, d. 1917. Large dirigible airship.

zero, n. [1. zḗrō; 2. zíərou], fr. Fr., fr. Ital., contracted fr. *zefiro*, fr. Arab. *çifr*, see **cipher. 1.** Arabic numeral 0, a cipher, a nought; symbol of nothingness. **2. a** Central point in a scale from which positive and negative quantities are reckoned; specif. **b** central point of scale of temperature; in centigrade thermometer, freezing-point of water; **c** *zero hour*, (mil.) precise time from which the times of the various operations in an offensive are calculated. **3.** (fig.) Lowest point in scale of comparison or reckoning; nothingness: *our hopes were reduced to zero.*

zest, n. [1. zest; 2. zɛst], fr. O. Fr. *zeste*, 'lemon-peel used for flavouring; skin of walnut kernel', fr. Lat. *schistos*, 'split', fr. Gk. *skhistós*, 'divided', fr. *skhízein*, 'to cleave', see **schism. 1.** Piquant addition, flavouring, relish; (chiefly fig.) piquancy, stimulating quality, esp. in Phr. *to give a zest to* (*pleasure* &c.). **2.** Keenness, enjoyment, gusto, ardour: *to enter into a game, a piece of work &c. with zest.*

zeta, n. [1. zḗta; 2. zítə]. Gk. name of symbol ζ, the sixth letter in Greek alphabet, which expressed either [dz] or [zd]. See **zed.**

zetetic, adj. [1. zētétik; 2. zītétik], fr. Gk. *zētētikós*, 'searching, inquiring', fr. *zētētḗs*, 'seeker', fr. *zētéein*, 'to search after, inquire into', fr. earlier **djātej-*, fr. stem **djā-*, **djə-*, 'to hasten towards, strive after'; cp. Gk. *(di)zēmai*, 'strive to reach'; *zálē*, 'storm at sea'. (rare) Proceeding by inquiry: *zetetic method.*

zeugma, n. [1. zū́gma; 2. zjū́gmə]. Gk. *zeûgma*, 'band, bond, yoke', fr. *zeúgnūmi*, 'I yoke, bind'; cp. Gk. *zeûgos*, 'harness'; *zugón*, 'yoke', see **zyg(o)- & yoke.** Figure of grammar in which a verb or adjective is applied to two nouns, to only one of which it is strictly applicable either grammatically or logically; see also **syllepsis.**

zeugmatic, adj. [1. zūgmátik; 2. zjūgmǽtik], fr. Gk. *zeúgmatos*, genit. of *zeûgma*, 'yoke', see prec., & **-ic.** Characterized by zeugma.

Zeus, n. [1. zūs; 2. zjūs]. Gk. *Zeús*; cp. Scrt. *dyāúš*, 'heaven'; Lat. *deus*, 'god', see **deity**, & words there referred to. Supreme Olympian deity of ancient Greeks.

zeuxite, n. [1. zū́ksīt; 2. zjū́ksait], fr. Gk. *zeûxis*, 'joining', fr. *zeúgnūmi*, 'I join, yoke, bind', see **zeugma**, & **-ite.** Kind of pale brown tourmaline.

zibet, n. [1. zíbet; 2. zíbet], fr. Ital. *zibetto*, fr. Arab. *zabad.* Asiatic or Indian civet-cat.

zigzag, n., adj., adv., & vb. intrans. [1. zígzag; 2. zígzæg], fr. Fr., fr. Germ. *zickzack*, redupl. fr. *zacke*, 'tooth', cogn. w. **tack. 1.** n. A line having a series of short angular deviations from the straight, turning or winding now in one direction, now in another; anything having such a form or course. **2.** adj. Having, forming, describing, a zigzag. **3.** adv. So as to follow or describe a zigzag line: *the road ran zigzag across the hills.* **4.** vb. **a** To move in, follow, a zigzag course: *he zigzagged slowly homewards after dinner*; **b** (of road, river) to run, be shaped, in zigzags.

zillah, n. [1. zíla; 2. zílə], fr. Hind. *dilah.* District in British India under the control of a deputy-commissioner or collector.

zinc, n. & vb. trans. [1. zingk; 2. ziŋk]. Germ. *zink*; etymol. doubtful. **1.** n. Bluish-white metallic element, used in the industrial arts; *zinc oxide*, white pigment used as substitute for oxide of lead. **2.** vb. To treat, coat, with zinc.

zincic, adj. [1. zíngkik; 2. zíŋkik]. Prec. & **-ic.** Of, pertaining to, derived from, zinc.

zinciferous, adj. [1. zingkíferus; 2. ziŋkífərəs]. **zinc** & *-i-* & **-ferous.** Yielding, producing, zinc.

zincification, n. [1. zìngkifikáshun; 2. zìŋkifikéiʃən]. See **zincify & -fication.** Act of zincifying; state of being zincified.

zincify, vb. trans. [1. zíngkifī; 2. zíŋkıfai]. **zinc** & *-i-* & **-fy.** To coat or impregnate with zinc.

zinco, n. [1. zíngkō; 2. zíŋkou]. Abbr. fr. **zincograph.** Zincograph.

zinco-, pref. representing **zinc & -o-.** Zinc, e.g. *zincograph, zincotype* &c.

zincograph (I.), n. [1. zíngkogràhf; 2. zíŋkəgrāf]. **zinco- & -graph. a** Design in relief on zinc plate; **b** picture produced by printing from such a plate.

zincograph (II.), vb. intrans. & trans., fr. prec. **1.** intrans. To produce pictures by zincographic process. **2.** trans. To print, produce (design, picture), from a zincograph.

zincographer, n. [1. zingkógrafer; 2. ziŋkógrəfə]. Prec. & **-er.** Person employed or skilled in zincographing.

zincographic, adj. [1. zìngkográfik; 2. zìŋkəgrǽfik]. **zincograph (I.) & -ic.** Of, pertaining to, of the nature of, a zincograph.

zincography, n. [1. zìngkógrafi; 2. zìŋkógrəfi]. **zinco- & -graphy.** Process of producing design in relief on zinc plates for printing.

zincoid, adj. [1. zíngkoid; 2. zíŋkɔid]. **zinco- & -oid.** Resembling zinc.

zincotype, n. [1. zíngkotīp; 2. zíŋkətàip]. **zinco- & type.** Zincograph.

zincous, adj. [1. zíngkus; 2. zíŋkəs]. **zinc & -ous.** Of, pertaining to, derived from, zinc.

zingaro, n., pl. **zingari** [1. zíngarō, -i; 2. zíŋgərou, -i]. Ital. Ultimately fr. Pers. or Indian word meaning 'blacksmith'; cp. Pehlevi *asinkār*, 'blacksmith'. Gipsy.

zinke, n. [1. tsíngke; 2. tsíŋkə]. Mod. Germ. Old form of musical wind-instrument with leather-covered, slightly tapering tube.

zinky, adj. [1. zíngki; 2. zíŋki]. **zinc & -y.** Made of, containing, or resembling, zinc.

zinnia, n. [1. zínia; 2. zíniə], fr. J. G. Zinn, German botanist, d. 1759. Genus of annual herbs of the aster family, with bright-coloured, composite flowers.

Zion, n. [1. zíon; 2. záiən]. Eccles. Lat. *Sīon*, fr. Heb. *Tsiyōn*, 'hill'. **1. a** Hill in Jerusalem; **b** the city of Jerusalem. **2.** (fig.) **a** Ancient Hebrew theocracy; **b** the Christian Church; **c** heaven, the Heavenly Jerusalem.

Zionism, n. [1. zíonìzm; 2. záiənìzəm]. Prec. & **-ism.** Movement with the object of re-settlement of the Jews in Palestine and the establishment of a national home there.

Zionist, n. [1. zíonìst; 2. záiənìst]. **Zion & -ist.** Adherent of Zionism.

Zionwards, adv. [1. zíonwardz; 2. záiənwədz]. **Zion & -wards.** Heavenwards.

zip, n. [1. zip; 2. zip]. Imitative. Light, whizzing sound, as of bullet passing through the air.

zircon, n. [1. zérkon; 2. zə́kən], fr. Arab. *zarkun*, 'cinnabar', fr. Pers. *zargūn*, 'gold-coloured'. Silicate of zirconium, variously coloured; varieties are the hyacinth and the jargoon.

zirconate, n. [1. zérkonāt; 2. zə́kəneit]. Prec. & **-ate.** Salt of zirconic acid.

zirconic, adj. [1. zerkónik; 2. zəkónik]. **zircon & -ic.** Of, derived from, zirconium.

zirconium, n. [1. zerkṓnium; 2. zəkóuniəm]. **zircon & -ium.** Blackish or greyish metallic element found in combination with silica.

zither, n. [1. zíther; 2. zíþə]. Germ., fr. Lat. *cithara*, see **cither(n).** Musical instrument with flat sounding-board and strings plucked with a plectrum.

zitherist, n. [1. zítherist; 2. zíþərist]. Prec. & **-ist**. Player on the zither.
zloty, n. [1. zlóti; 2. zlóti]. Pol. Polish coin = 10d.
-zoa suff. [1. zóa; 2. zóuə], representing pl. of Gk. *zōon*, 'animal', see **zoo-**.
Zoar, n. [1. zóar; 2. zóuə]. With reference to story of Lot, Genesis xix. 22. Place of refuge.
zodiac, n. [1. zódiàk; 2. zóudiæk], fr. Fr. *zodiaque*, fr. Lat. *zōdiacus*, fr. Gk. *zōdiakós*, 'containing animals', fr. *zṓdion*, 'small figure'; pl., 'signs of zodiac', dimin. of *zōon*, 'animal, living creature'; fr. *zōós*, 'living', see **zoo-**. **1. a** An imaginary belt in the heavens, having the ecliptic in the centre, within which the moon and all the principal planets have their paths; divided into twelve sections or signs; **b** the region in the heavens enclosed by the zodiac. **2.** A figure representing the zodiac and its divisions, each with its appropriate symbol.
zodiacal, adj. [1. zòdíakl; 2. zòudáiəkl]. Prec. & **-al**. Of, pertaining to, situated within, the zodiac: *zodiacal light*, faintly luminous, apparently triangular tract of sky sometimes seen in the west after dusk or in the east before dawn, chiefly in the tropics.
zoetrope, n. [1. zóetròp; 2. zóuitròup], fr. Gk. *zōḗ*, 'life', fr. *zōós*, 'living', see **zoo-**, & *trópos*, 'a turn', see **-trope**, & **trepidation**. Toy with revolving cylinder showing series of pictures in apparent motion; wheel of life.
zoic, adj. [1. zóik; 2. zóuik], fr. Gk. *zōikós*, fr. *zōon*, 'animal', see **zoo-**, & **-ic**. **a** Of, pertaining to, characterized by, animal life; specif. **b** (geol., of rock) containing fossils of plants or animals.
Zolaesque, adj. [1. zòlaésk; 2. zòuləésk], fr. *Zola*, see next word, & **-esque**. Resembling, characteristic of, the style and manner of Zola.
Zolaism, n. [1. zólaìzm; 2. zóuləizəm], fr. Emile Zola, French novelist, d. 1902, & **-ism**. Literary style and method characteristic of Zola; vigorous but coarse naturalism.
Zolaist, n. [1. zólaist; 2. zóuləist], fr. *Zola*, see prec. Writer in the style of Zola.
Zolaistic, adj. [1. zòlaístik; 2. zòuləístik]. Prec. & **-ic**. Of, resembling, the style of Zola.
zollverein, n. [1. tsól-, zólferìn; 2. tsɔ́l-, zɔ́lfərain]. Germ., fr. *zoll*, 'tax', see **toll (III.)**, & *verein*, 'union', fr. pref. *ver-*, cogn. w. **for-**, & *ein*, 'one', see **one**. Union of states having a common tariff of duties on imports from other countries, and free trade among themselves.
zonal, adj. [1. zónal; 2. zóunəl]. **zone** & **-al**. Of, pertaining to, arranged or marked out in, zones.
zonally, adv. Prec. & **-ly**. In a zonal manner.
zonary, adj. [1. zónari; 2. zóunəri]. **zone** & **-ary**. Resembling a belt in form or appearance.
zonate, adj. [1. zónāt; 2. zóuneit]. **zone** & **-ate**. (bot., zool.) Marked with bands.
zone (I.), n. [1. zōn; 2. zoun], fr. Fr., fr. Lat. *zōna*, fr. Gk. *zṓnē*, 'belt, girdle'; cp. Gk. *zṓnnūmi*, 'I gird'; *zōstós*, 'girdled'; cogn. w. Zend *yāsta-*, 'girded'; Lith. *jūsta*, 'belt'; O. Slav. *(po)-jasŭ*, 'girdle'. **1.** (archaic or poet.) Girdle, belt: '*that milky way, Which nightly, as a circling zone, thou seest Powdered with stars*' (Milton, 'P.L.', vii. 579-81). **2.** Belt, band, stripe, area, distinguished from surface &c. on either side by appearance, colour, characteristics, formation &c. **3.** (geog.) One of the five regions into which the surface of the earth is divided by imaginary lines parallel to the equator; *frigid zones*, within Arctic and Antarctic circles; *torrid zone*, between tropics of Cancer and Capricorn; *temperate zones*, between torrid and frigid zones. **4.** (math.) Portion of surface of sphere, cone, cylinder, &c. enclosed between two parallel planes at right angles to its axis.
zone (II.), vb. trans., fr. prec. To mark, encircle, with a zone.
zonular, adj. [1. zónūlar; 2. zóunjulə]. **zone** & **-ule** & **-ar**. Of, pertaining to, in the shape of, a small belt or band.
Zoo, n. [1. zōō; 2. zū]. Abbr. fr. **zoological**. Zoological garden, esp. the Zoological Gardens in London.
zoo-, pref. representing Gk. *zōós*, 'living'; *zōon*, 'animal'; cp. Gk. *zā́ō*, *zên*, 'to live'; earlier **gʷjōjō-* &c.; cp. Gk. *bíos*, 'life', fr. stem **gʷej-* &c., 'to live', see **bio-** & words there referred to. Of animals or animal life.
zooblast, n. [1. zóoblahst; 2. zóuəblāst]. **zoo-** & Gk. *blastós*, 'sprout', see **blastoderm**. Animal cell.
zoochemistry, n. [1. zòokémistri; 2. zòuəkémistri]. Chemistry of solid and fluid constituents of animal body.
zoodynamics, n. [1. zòodīnámiks; 2. zòuədainǽmiks]. Animal physiology.
zoogamy, n. [1. zōógami; 2. zouɔ́gəmi]. **zoo-** & **-gamy**. Sexual reproduction.
zoogeny, n. [1. zōójeni; 2. zouɔ́džini]. **zoo-** & **-geny**. Doctrine of the origin of living beings.
zoogeography, n. [1. zóojiógrafi; 2. zóuədžiɔ́grəfi]. Science of geographical distribution of animals.
zoography, n. [1. zōógrafi; 2. zouɔ́grəfi]. **zoo-** & **-graphy**. Descriptive zoology.
zooid (I.), adj. [1. zóoid; 2. zóuɔid]. **zoo-** & **-oid**. Resembling, but not completely being, an animal organism.
zooid (II.), n., fr. prec. **1.** An organic body or cell possessing independent locomotion. **2.** An animal organism produced by fission, or some similar process, and not by direct sexual reproduction, and having an imperfect individuality.
zoolatrous, adj. [1. zōólatrus; 2. zouɔ́lətrəs]. See next word & **-ous**. Pertaining to, characterized by, zoolatry.
zoolatry, n. [1. zōólatri; 2. zouɔ́lətri]. **zoo-** & **-latry**. Worship of animals.
zoolite, n. [1. zóolīt; 2. zóuəlait]. **zoo-** & **-lite**. Fossil animal.
zoological, adj. [1. zòolójikl; 2. zòuəlɔ́džikl]. **zoo-** & **-logy** & **-ic** & **-al**. **a** Connected with, pertaining to, zoology; **b** connected with animal life and structure.
zoological garden(s), n. Large garden or park in which wild animals of all kinds are kept for exhibition.
zoology, n. [1. zòóloji; 2. zòuɔ́lədži]. **zoo-** & **-logy**. Branch of biology dealing with the structure, physiology, classification of animals.
zoom, vb. intrans. [1. zōōm; 2. zūm]. Etymol. doubtful. (aeron.) To compel an aeroplane to ascend rapidly and at a steep angle.
zoomagnetism, n. [1. zòomágnetizm; 2. zòuəmǽgnitizəm]. Animal magnetism.
zoomancy, n. [1. zóomànsi; 2. zóuəmæ̀nsi]. **zoo-** & **-mancy**. Divination by observing the behaviour of animals.
zoomorphic, adj. [1. zòomórfik; 2. zòuəmɔ́fik]. **zoo-** & Gk. *morphḗ*, 'form, shape', see **morphology**, & **-ic**. Pertaining to, represented by, animal forms; having the forms of animals.
zoomorphism, n. [1. zòomórfizm; 2. zòuəmɔ́fizəm]. See prec. & **-ism**. The conception and representation of gods in the form of animals.
zoophysics, n. [1. zòofíziks; 2. zòuəfíziks]. Science of the physical structure of animal bodies.
zoophyte, n. [1. zóofīt; 2. zóuəfait]. **zoo-** & **-phyte**. Invertebrate animal of plant-like form, including sea-anemones, sponges &c.
zoophytic, adj. [1. zòofítik; 2. zòuəfítik]. Prec. & **-ic**. Pertaining to, of the nature of, zoophytes.
zoophytology, n. [1. zòofītóloji; 2. zòuəfaitɔ́lədži]. See prec. & **-logy**. The study of zoophytes.
zooplastic, adj. [1. zòoplástik; 2. zòuəplǽstik]. Pertaining to that form of surgery in which living tissue from an animal is grafted on to a human body.
zoopsychology, n. [1. zòosīkóloji; 2. zòuəsaikɔ́lədži]. Psychology of animals other than man.
zoosperm, n. [1. zóospĕrm; 2. zóuəspə̀m]. **1.** Spermatozoon. **2.** Zoospore.
zoospore, n. [1. zóospòr; 2. zóuəspɔ̀]. Spore capable of independent motion.
zootaxy, n. [1. zóotàksi; 2. zóuətæ̀ksi], fr. **zoo-** & Gk. *táxis*, 'arrangement', see **taxis**, & **-y**. The classification of animals.
zootheism, n. [1. zóothèizm; 2. zóuəþìizəm]. Religious system based on the worship of animals.
zootomy, n. [1. zòótomi; 2. zòuɔ́təmi]. **zoo-** & **-tomy**. **1.** Dissection of animals. **2.** Animal anatomy.
zoril, n. [1. zóril; 2. zɔ́ril], fr. Fr. *zorille*, fr. Span. *zorrilla*, dimin. of *zorra*, 'fox'. Small African carnivorous quadruped resembling skunk.
Zoroastrian, Zarathustrian, adj. & n. [1. zòroástrian, zàrathōōstrian; 2. zɔ̀rɔǽstriən, zæ̀rəþústriən], fr. Lat. *Zōroastres*, 'Zarathustra', fr. O. Pers. *Zarathustra*, founder of Pers. religion. **1.** adj. Pertaining to Zoroaster and his religion. **2.** n. An adherent, worshipper, of Zoroaster.
Zoroastrianism, n. [1. zòroástrianism; 2. zɔ̀rɔǽstriənizəm]. Prec. & **-ism**. Religious system of ancient Persia and of the Parsees, based on the recognition of the dual principle of good and evil or light and darkness.
zouave, n. [1. zōōahv; 2. zūáv]. Fr., fr. name of Kabyle tribe. Member of French, light-armed corps of infantry, originally recruited from Algerians and wearing Eastern uniform.
zounds, interj. [1. zoundz; 2. zaundz]. Contracted fr. *God's wounds*. Archaic exclamatory expression.
zucchetta, zucchetto, n. [1. tsukéta, -étō; 2. tsukétə, -étou]. Ital., dimin. of *zucca*, 'gourd'. Skull-cap worn by ecclesiastics.
zuffolo, n. [1. tsúfolō; 2. tsúfəlou]. Ital. *zufolo*, 'whistle'. A small flageolet.
Zulu, n. [1. zōōlōō; 2. zúlū]. Native. **1.** Member of a people of the Bantu or Kaffir family of S. Africa. **2.** Language of this people.
zwieback, n., Anglicized to [1. zwḗbahk; 2. zwíbāk]. Germ. *zwie*, 'twice', & *backen*, 'bake'. Cp. etymol. of **biscuit**. Kind of thin rusk; consisting of a slice cut from a lightly baked loaf, baked again till crisp.
Zwinglian, adj. & n. [1. zwíngglian; 2. zwíŋgliən], fr. name of Zwingli, Swiss Protestant reformer, d. 1531, & **-an**. **1.** adj. Pertaining to the doctrines of Zwingli. **2.** n. Follower of Zwingli, one of whose characteristic doctrines was that in the Eucharist the presence of Christ in the elements is not an objective fact, but depends upon the faith of the recipient, and that the service is merely commemorative and has no sacrificial character.
zyg(o)-, pref. representing Gk. *zugón*, 'yoke', cogn. w. Scrt. *yugám*; Lat. *jugum*, see **jugate**; Goth. *juk*; O.E. *ġeoc*, 'yoke', see **yoke**; cp. also Gk. *zeûgos*, 'harness'; *zeûgma*, 'bond, yoke', see **zeugma**. Existing in pairs; shaped like a yoke.
zygal, adj. [1. zígal; 2. záigəl]. **zyg(o)-** & **-al**. Having the shape of a yoke; H-shaped; esp. of brain fissures.
zygapophysis, n. [1. zìgapófizis; 2. zàigəpɔ́fizis]. **zyg(o)-** & Gk. *apóphusis*, 'offshoot; process of a bone', see **apo-** & **physic**. Articulating portion of vertebra.
zygodactyl, n. [1. zìgodáktil; 2. zàigɔdǽktil]. See **zyg(o)-** & **dactyl**. Bird with toes arranged in pairs, two pointing forward and two backward.
zygodactylous, adj. [1. zìgodáktilus; 2. zàigɔdǽktiləs]. Prec. & **-ous**. Of the nature of a zygodactyl.
zygoma, n. [1. zī-, zìgóma; 2. zai-, zìgóumə], fr. Gk. *zúgōma*, 'yoke', fr. *zugóein*, 'to yoke together', fr. *zugón*, 'yoke', see **zyg(o)-**, & **-m**. The cheek-bone.
zygomatic, adj. [1. zī-, zìgomátik; 2. zai-, zìgəmǽtik], fr. Gk. *zugṓmatos*, genit. of *zúgōma*, see prec., & **-ic**. Pertaining to, situated near, the zygoma; *zygomatic arch*, bony ridge

forming part of the framework of the face, and consisting of the union of the upper jaw-bone and the cheek-bone.

zygophyte, n. [1. zígofīt; 2. záigəfàit]. **zyg(o)-** & **-phyte.** Plant in which reproduction is effected by means of zygospores.

zygosis, n. [1. zī-, zìgṓsis; 2. zài-, zìgóusis], fr. Gk. *zugôsis*, 'joining', see **zyg(o)-** & **-osis.** (biol.) Coalescence of two cells; conjugation.

zygospore, n. [1. zígospōr; 2. záigəspɔ̄]. **zyg(o)-** & **spore.** Zygote.

zygote, n. [1. zígōt; 2. záigout], fr. Gk. *zugōtos*, 'yoked', fr. *zugóein*, 'to yoke together', see **zygoma.** Product of coalescence of two sexual cells or gametes; a zygospore.

zymosis, n. [1. zī-, zìmṓsis; 2. zài-, zimóusis], fr. Gk. *zūmōsis*, 'fermentation', fr. *zūmoûn*, 'to ferment', fr. *zū́mē*, 'leaven', fr. *zéein*, 'to boil', cp. Gk. *zóē*, 'foam'; cogn. w. Scrt. *yásati*, 'to boil'; O.H.G. *iesan*, 'to ferment'; O.E. *ġest*, 'yeast', see **yeast,** & **eczema,** & cp. **enzyme. 1.** Fermentation. **2.** Zymotic disease.

zymotic, adj. [1. zī-, zìmótik; 2. zài-, zìmɔ́tik], fr. Gk. *zūmōsis*, 'fermentation', see prec., & **-otic.** Pertaining to, produced by, fermentation; *zymotic diseases*, epidemic, endemic or sporadic diseases produced by propagation of living germs introduced from without.

zymurgy, n. [1. zímërji; 2. záimə̄dži], fr. Gk. *zū́mē*, 'leaven', see **zymosis,** & *-ourg-(os)*, fr. *érg-(on)*, 'work', see **ergon.** Branch of applied chemistry dealing with the science of wine making, brewing, and distilling.

Addenda and Corrigenda

HERE are printed corrections of a few errors in the text which came to the Editor's notice while the Dictionary was passing through the press, together with definitions of certain words inadvertently omitted from their alphabetical positions in the body of the work.

P. 5. **abstention,** n. [**1.** absténshun; **2.** əbsténʃən]. Fr., fr. Lat. *abstention-(em)*, fr. *abstent-(um)*, P.P. type of *abstinere*, see **abstain.** The act of abstaining from any action; specif. **a** act of abstaining from any form of enjoyment, e.g. from food &c.; abstinence; **b** refusal to record one's vote.

P. 5. **abstraction,** n. (1. abstrákshun; 2. əbstrǽkʃən]. Fr., fr. Lat.; see **abstract (I.)** & **-ion. 1. a** (i.) Act of abstracting; (ii.) condition of being abstracted; withdrawal, removal; **b** (euphemistic) unlawful removal; theft, stealing. **2. a** Mental act of regarding things from an abstract point of view; **b** something so considered. **3.** Preoccupied state of mind; absent-mindedness, abstractedness.

P. 11. **actuate.** Pronunciation **No. 1** [áktūāt, ákchooāt].

P. 15. **adscititious,** adj. [1. àdsitíshus; 2. ædsitíʃəs], fr. Lat. *adscit-(um)*, P.P. type of *adsciscere*, 'to approve, adopt; to receive, admit (person)'; inceptive fr. *adscire*, 'to take, associate with oneself', fr. **ad-** & *scire*, 'to know', see **science,** & **-itious.** Additional, supplemental; adventitious.

P. 17. **advertisement.** Pronunciation No. 1 [advértisement].

P. 34. **anaglyph.** After 'cameo', add 'Picture obtained by printing a pair of prints one above the other in red and green inks, producing a stereoscopic effect when viewed through spectacles having one green and one red lens'.

P. 38. **anna.** Delete 'no coin of one anna exists'.

P. 76. **ban (II.), e.** For 'med. hist', read 'Med. hist'.

P. 130. Transfer words 'used in medicine, as a sedative &c.', from **bromine** to **bromide.**

P. 133. **bugle.** For 'small brass trumpet', read 'small trumpet'.

P. 134. **bullace.** After 'dark purple', add 'or yellow'.

P. 143. **calabar bean.** For 'by oculists for dilating', read 'for contracting the pupil of'.

P. 154. **carline (III.),** n., also *carling* (1. kárlin; 2. kálin). Etymol. doubtful; cp. Fr. *carlingue*. A wooden beam, generally fitted at right angles to and below the main deck timbers of a wooden ship, to strengthen the deck in way of openings.

P. 161. **cathode.** For 'Negative electrode . . . current leaves', read 'Negative pole of a cell, Crookes tube, or other current-passing apparatus'.

P. 171. **change (II.).** For **cambion** read **cambium.**

P. 297. **derrick.** For 'early 18th', read '17th or even (?) late 16th'.

P. 348. **east-north-east,** n., adj., & adv. (In or towards) direction or point midway between east and north-east.

P. 348. **east-south-east,** n., adj., & adv. (In or towards) direction or point midway between east and south-east.

P. 350. **economist,** n. [1. ēkónomist; 2. ĭkɔ́nəmist]. See **economy** & **-ist. 1.** (rare) One who manages domestic or other affairs. **2.** One given to economizing; a thrifty person. **3.** A student of, authority on, the science of political economy.

P. 362. **emulsion.** For 'An oily liquid . . . consistency', read 'A mixture of two liquids, one in the form of minute globules produced by a third substance, often in the form of a white liquid'. For 'curative purposes', read 'for preventive and curative purposes'.

P. 417. **fifth, 2. c.** For 'five semitones', read 'three tones and a semitone'.

P. 418. **figwort,** n. Any one of a large and widely spread genus of herbs, natural order Scrophulariaceae, with greenish-purple or yellow flowers, and usually an unpleasant smell.

P. 455. **Free Church.** For 'part of the Presbyterian Church . . . 1929)', read 'Part of the Presbyterian Church, the minority of the former Free Church which failed to enter the Union with the United Presbyterian Church in 1900'.

P. 464. **funny-bone.** Delete 'sensitive'. Add 'The sensitiveness of this part of the arm is due to the ulnar nerve which passes between the end of the bone of the upper arm (humerus) and that of the larger bone (ulna) of the forearm. The name *funny-bone* is a popular joke based on the anatomical term *humerus* (q.v.).'

P. 467. **gaga,** adj. [*gága*]. Imitative of stammering. (slang) **a** Reduced to state of gibbering bewilderment and incapacity, as by fright, nervous shock &c.; **b** affected by permanent weakening of the mind; cracked, dotty; Phr. to *go gaga*.

P. 474. Under **gay.** After **1. a** insert '(i.)'. After words '*laugh* &c.' in this section insert '(*in spite of ill health he is always gay*; Phr. *the gayest of the gay*; (ii.) (of persons and their social life) enjoying, filled with, frequent social gatherings, engagements and amusements: *we were very gay in town this season*'.

P. 483. Under **girl** indication of pronunciation should read—(1. garl, gə̄l) (this is now rather old-fashioned; the more usual pronunciation, even among good speakers, is now—[1. gërl; 2. gə̄l]. After **3. a** add 'Phr. *one's best girl*, she who for the moment is the object of special admiration and devotion'.

P. 494. **goof,** n. (gūf) origin unknown. A silly fellow; a clumsy, awkward, oafish person.

P. 494. **gorblimy,** interjec. & n. [gɔ̄blaimi], fr. *Gaud* (=God) *blind me*. **a** interjec. Low expletive of surprise or annoyance; **b** n. military hat with the round flat crown unstiffened by a wire frame, so that it flops rather like that of a tam-o'-shanter.

P. 528. **hare,** vb. intrans. (slang) To run like a hare, run very fast, hurry: *you had better hare down to the post*; also *hare away*, to run away, esp. to fly in order to escape pursuit.

P. 531. **hat (I.).** Last line but one, just before '*my hat!*' insert '*to keep something under one's hat*, keep it to oneself, not divulge it; *a good deal under his hat*, a powerful mind, learning &c.; *lame under the hat*, of weak mind; foolish, lacking intelligence'.

P. 536. **hearing,** n. Add '**3.** Something heard, news; esp. in Phr. *that's a good hearing*, something that is pleasing to hear'.

P. 564. **hot (III.)** vb. trans. & n., fr. **hot (I.).** (colloq.) **1.** vb. **a** Also *hot up*, to warm up food already cooked which has become cold; **b** (fig.) to revive, put new life into, stimulate (a cause, business, enterprise &c.) which is declining. **2.** n. A stimulus, re-animation, revivification.

P. 573. After **hydro,** n., insert—[1. hídrō; 2. háidrou].

P. 631. **jim-jams,** n. pl. [džímdžæmz] (slang) *The jim-jams*, **a** delirium tremens; **b** a highly nervous, over-wrought state of mind; jumpiness, fussy excitability; the willies.

P. 660. **lewdsby,** n. [ljū́dzbi], facet, formation fr. **lewd** w. *by*, Pl. N. ending. A lewd, loose, immoral person.

P. 686. **loony bin,** n. (slang) Lunatic asylum, madhouse.

P. 686. **loopy,** adj. (lūpi]. (slang) Weak in the intellect, slightly mad; dippy, batty.

P. 687. **Lord-Lieutenant.** For 'Governor-General of the Free State of N. Ireland' read 'Governor of Northern Ireland'.

P. 799. Under **omnibus. 2.**—after words 'number of persons', add '; *omnibus volume*, one containing several complete novels, or short stories by the same author, or by several authors'.

P. 800. After **oneyer**—add **(I.).**

P. 800. **oneyer (II.).** n. See **wonyer.**

P. 844. **pen (III.).** add '**3.** A female swan'.

P. 861. **pi (II.).** For '(school slang)' read

'(school and Univ. slang).' Definition should read—**a** Pious; religious; **b** connected w., expressing, setting forth, religious or moral ideas and principles.

P. 864. **pi-jaw,** n. (1. píjaw; 2. páidʒɔ]. See **pi (II.)** & **jaw (I.) 5. b.** (school slang) Religious or moral address; a sermon.

P. 1017. **ride (II.).** After **1. b** . . . *carriage.* add '; Phr. (Amer. gangster slang) *to take* (person) *for a ride,* take him out into the country in a motor car and murder him'.

P. 1126. Under **sixpence,** in **b** Phrs. after words 'of no consequence' add '; *the same old sixpence,* of person, implying that he is unchanged either for better or for worse'.

P. 1185. Under **step (II.)** in **A. 2.** after word 'intervene', insert '; *step on the gas, step on it,* to accelerate in a motor car; hence to drive at high speed; to hurry'.

P. 1232. For '**tab**' read '**tab (I.)**'.

P. 1232. **tab (II.),** n. abbrev. of **Cantab** q.v. Same sense as Cantab, but not a polite mode of reference.

P. 1244. **telautograph.** For 'Electrical . . . distance' read 'Trademark for facsimile telegraph for reproducing writing, &c'.

P. 1387. **wench,** at end, after 'Prostitute', add '**3.** vb. To frequent company of prostitutes'.

P. 1387. **wenching,** vbl. n., fr. prec. (archaic) Practice of sexual intercourse outside wedlock.

P. 1396. **willies,** n. pl. (wíliz] adapted fr. *bewilder* ? (slang) *the willies.* State of nervous excitement caused by fear or shock; temporary mental incapacity, jumpiness, and so on: *a fit of the willies, it gave me the willies*'.

P. 1399. **w(e)isenheim,** n. Facet. use of Germ.-Jewish name. (American slang) A knowing, sharp-witted person; applied ironically to one who prides himself on possessing the latest information, and an infallible judgement, and on being cleverer than other people.

P. 1401. **wobbler,** n., fr. **wobble (I.)** & **-er.** One who wobbles; specif. one who is unstable and vacillating in opinions, principles &c.

Familiar Abbreviations

In these pages we give a reasonably full list of the abbreviations commonly used in speech and in writing. We have included also a number which, though no longer current, are still to be met with in standard works of reference.

A, argon (chem.).
a., aged (of racehorse over six years old).
A1, at Lloyd's, first-class ship on the register; also first-class in physique, health &c.
A.A., Automobile Association; Associate in Arts.
A.A.A., Amateur Athletic Association.
A.A.C., Lat. *anno ante Christum*, in the year before Christ.
A.A.G., Assistant Adjutant-General.
A.A.I., Associate of the Auctioneers' Institute.
A. and M., Ancient and Modern (hymn-book).
A.A. of A., Automobile Association of America.
A.A.Q.M.G., Acting Assistant Quarter-master-General.
A.A.U., Amateur Athletic Union (of U.S.A.).
A.B., able-bodied seaman; Lat. *Artium Baccalaureus*, Bachelor of Arts, usually B.A.
A.B.A., Amateur Boxing Association.
abbr., **abbrev.**, abbreviation, abbreviated.
ABC, the alphabet; alphabetical railway guide.
A.B.C., Aerated Bread Co.
abd., abdicated.
ab init., Lat. *ab initio*, from the beginning.
abl., ablative.
abp., archbishop.
A.B.S., American Bible Society.
abs., absolute; abstract.
absol., absolute(ly).
abt., about.
A.C., Appeal Court; Appeal Cases in this court (in law reports); Alpine Club; Aero Club; Athletic Club; Lat. *anno Christi*, in the year of Christ, A.D.; Lat. *ante Christum*, before Christ, B.C.
a/c, account.
A.C.A., Associate of the Institute of Chartered Accountants.
acc., account; accusative.
accel., accelerando (mus.).
acct., account; accountant.
accus., accusative.
A.C.G.I., Associate of the City & Guilds of London Institute.
A.C.I.S., Associate of the Chartered Institute of Secretaries.
A.C.P., Associate of the College of Preceptors.
A.C.S., Additional Curates Society.
A.C.U., Auto-cycle Union.
A.D., Lat. *anno Domini*, in the year of our Lord.
a.d., after date.
ad., adapted; advertisement.
adag., adagio (mus.).
A.D.C., Aide-de-camp; Amateur Dramatic Club (esp. of Cambridge University).
ad eund., Lat. *ad eundem (gradum)*, admitted to the same degree (at another university).
ad fin., Lat. *ad finem*, at, to, the end.
ad inf., Lat. *ad infinitum*, to infinity.
ad int., Lat. *ad interim*, meanwhile.
Adj., Adjutant.
adj., adjective.
Adjt., Adjutant.
ad lib., Lat. *ad libitum*, at pleasure.
ad loc., Lat. *ad locum*, at the place.
Adm., Admiral, Admiralty; Administrator.
Adml., Admiral.
admor., administrator.
A.D.O.S., Assistant Director of Ordnance Stores.
Adv., Advent; Advocate.
adv., adverb.
adv., Lat. *adversus*, against.
ad val., Lat. *ad valorem*, according to the value.
advbl., adverbial.
advt., advertisement.
Æ, third-class ship at Lloyd's.
aeg., Lat. *aeger*, ill.
aegrot., Lat. *aegrotat*, he is ill, in Engl. univs., certificate that student is too ill to take examination.
A.E.L.T.C., All England Lawn Tennis Club.
aeron., aeronautics.
aet., ***aetat.***, Lat. *aetatis*, aged (so many years).
A.E.U., Amalgamated Engineering Union.
A.F., Admiral of the Fleet.
A.F.A., Amateur Football Association.
A.F.B.S., American & Foreign Bible Society.
A.F.C., Air Force Cross.
A.F.M., Air Force Medal.
A.-Fr., Anglo-French (Anglo-Norman).
Afr., African.
A.F.R.Ae.S., Associate Fellow of the Royal Aeronautical Society.
A.G., Adjutant-General; Attorney-General; Accountant-General; Agent-General; German, *Aktiengesellschaft*, joint-stock company.
Ag, Lat. *argentum*, silver (chem.).
agric., agriculture.
A.G.S.M., Associate of the Guildhall School of Music.
Agt., Agent.
Agt.-Gen., Agent-General.
A.H., Lat. *anno Hegirae*, in the year of the Hegira.
A.H.S., Lat. *anno humanae salutis*, in the year of human salvation.
A.I., American Institute.
A.I.A., Associate of the Institute of Actuaries.
A.I.C., Associate of the Institute of Chemistry.
A.I.C.E., Associate of the Institution of Civil Engineers.
A.I.D., Army Intelligence Department.
A.I.F., Australian Imperial Force.
A.I.Mech.E., Associate of the Institution of Mechanical Engineers.
A.I.S.A., Associate of the Incorporated Secretaries' Association.
A.K.C., Associate of King's College, London.
Al, aluminium (chem.).
Ala., Alabama (U.S.A.).
Alas., Alaska.
Alban., St. Albans, in signature of Bishop.
A.L.C.M., Associate of the London College of Music.
Ald., Alderman; Aldine.
Alex., Alexander.
alg., algebra.
A.L.S., Associate of the Linnean Society.
alt., alternate; altitude.
Alta., Alberta, Canada.
A.M., Lat. *Artium Magister*, Master of Arts, usually M.A.; Albert Medal; Lat. *anno mundi*, in the year of the world.
a.m., Lat. *ante meridiem*, before noon.
Am., American.
A.M.C., Army Medical Corps (since 1898, R.A.M.C.).
A.M.D.G., Lat. *ad majorem Dei gloriam*, to the greater glory of God.
A.M.I.C.E., Associate Member of the Institution of Civil Engineers.
A.M.I.E.E., Associate Member of the Institution of Electrical Engineers.
A.M.I.Mech.E., Associate Member of the Institution of Mechanical Engineers.
amp., ampère.
A.M.S., Army Medical Staff.
amt., amount.
anal., analogy; analysis.
anat., anatomy.
anct., ancient.
Angl., Lat. *Anglice*, in English.
Angl., Anglican.
anon., anonymous.
anr., another.
anthropol., anthropology.
antiq., antiquity.
A.N.Z.A.C. (**Anzac**), Australian and New Zealand Army Corps, in Great War.
A.O., Army Order.
a/o, account of.
A.O.C., Army Ordnance Corps (since 1918, R.A.O.C.).
A.O.D., Ancient Order of Druids; Army Ordnance Department.
A.O.F., Ancient Order of Foresters.
A.O.H., Ancient Order of Hibernians.
aor., aorist.
ap., Lat. *apud*, according to, in the works of, in literary references.
A.P.D., Army Pay Department.
Apl., April.
A.P.M., Assistant Provost-Marshal.
Apoc., Apocalypse; Apocrypha.
app., appendix; appointed; apprentice.
appro., approval, approbation.
approx., approximate(ly).
Apr., April.
A.P.S., Aborigines Protection Society.
A.Q.M.G., Assistant Quartermaster-General.
A.R., Lat. *anno regni*, in the year of the reign; annual return.
A.R.A., Associate of the Royal Academy.
Arab., Arabic.
A.R.A.M., Associate of the Royal Academy of Music.
A.R.B.A., Associate of the Royal Society of British Artists.
arbor., arboriculture.
A.R.C., Automobile Racing Club.
A.R.C.A., Associate of the Royal College of Art; Associate of the Royal Cambrian Academy.
archaeol., archaeology.
archit., architecture.
A.R.C.I., Associate of the Royal Colonial Institute.
A.R.C.M., Associate of the Royal College of Music.
A.R.C.O., Associate of the Royal College of Organists.
A.R.C.S., Associate of the Royal College of Science.
A.R.E., Associate of the Royal Society of Painter-Etchers and Engravers.
Argyl., Argyllshire.
A.R.I.B.A., Associate of the Royal Institute of British Architects.
A.R.I.C.S., Professional Associate of the Royal Institution of Chartered Surveyors.
arith., arithmetic.
Ariz., Arizona (U.S.A.).
Ark., Arkansas (U.S.A.).
A.R.M.S., Associate of the Royal Society of Miniature Painters.
A.R.P.S., Associate of the Royal Photographic Society.
A.R.R., Lat. *anno regni regis (reginae)*, in the year of the king's (queen's) reign.
arr., arrives (of train &c.).
A.R.S.A., Associate of the Royal Scottish Academy; Associate of the Royal Society of Arts.
A.R.S.L., Associate of the Royal Society of Literature.
A.R.S.M., Associate of the Royal School of Mines (now Royal College of Science).

A.R.S.W., Associate of the Royal Scottish Society of Painters in Water Colours.
art., article.
A.R.W.A., Associate of the Royal West of England Academy.
A.R.W.S., Associate of the Royal Society of Painters in Water Colours.
A.-S., Anglo-Saxon.
As, arsenic (chem.).
A.S.A., Amateur Swimming Association.
A.S.A.A., Associate of the Society of Incorporated Accountants and Auditors.
Asaph., St. Asaph, in signature of Bishop.
A.S.C., Army Service Corps (since 1918, R.A.S.C.
A.Sc., Associate in Science.
A.S.E., Amalgamated Society of Engineers.
A.S.L.E. & F., Associated Society of Locomotive Engineers and Firemen.
A.S.R.S., Amalgamated Society of Railway Servants.
Assn., association.
Assoc., associate, association.
Asst., assistant.
astrol., astrology.
astron., astronomy.
A.T.C.L., Associate of Trinity College (of Music), London.
At(t).-Gen., Attorney-General.
attrib., attributive(ly).
at. wt., atomic weight.
A.U., Ångström unit (physics).
Au, Lat. *aurum*, gold (chem.).
A.U.C., Lat. *anno urbis conditae* or *ab urbe condita*, in the year of, or from the foundation of the city (Rome).
Aug., August.
Aus., Austria; Austrian.
auxil., auxiliary.
A.V., Authorized Version.
av., average.
avdp., avoirdupois.

B, boron (chem.); black (of pencil-lead).
B., Bay.
b., born; (cricket) bowled, bye.
B.A., Lat. *Baccalaureus Artium*, Bachelor of Arts; British Academy; British Association.
Ba, barium (chem.).
bacter., bacteriology.
B. Agr(ic)., Bachelor of Agriculture.
Balto-Slav., Balto-Slavic.
B. & S., brandy and soda.
B. & W., Bath and Wells, in signature of Bishop.
Bart., Baronet.
Bart's, St. Bartholomew's Hospital.
Bath. & Well., Bath and Wells, in signature of Bishop.
Batt., Battery; Battalion.
Battn., Battalion.
BB, double black (of pencil-lead).
B.B., Blue Book.
BBB, treble black (of pencil-lead).
B.B.C., British Broadcasting Corporation.
B.C., Before Christ; British Columbia.
B.Ch., Lat. *Baccalaureus Chirurgiae*, Bachelor of Surgery.
B.Ch.D., Bachelor of Dental Surgery.
B.C.L., Bachelor of Civil Law.
B.Com., Bachelor of Commerce.
B.C.S., Bengal Civil Service.
B.D., Bachelor of Divinity.
Bde., Brigade.
Bde. Maj., Brigade Major.
B.D.S., Bachelor of Dental Surgery.
B.E., Bachelor of Engineering; (Order of the) British Empire; Board of Education.
b.e., bill of exchange.
Be, beryllium (chem.).
B.E.A., British East Africa.
Beds, Bedfordshire.
B.E.F., British Expeditionary Force, in Great War.
Belg., Belgium; Belgian.
B.Eng., Bachelor of Engineering.
Berks, Berkshire.
B.E.S.A., British Engineering Standards Association.
B. ès L., Fr. *Bachelier ès Lettres*, Bachelor of Letters.
B. ès S., Fr. *Bachelier ès Sciences*, Bachelor of Science.
B.F.B.S., British and Foreign Bible Society.
B.G.G.S., Brigadier-General, General Staff.
B'ham, Birmingham.
B'head, Birkenhead.
b.h.p., brake horse-power.
B.I., British India.
Bi, bismuth (chem.).
Bib., Biblical.
bibliog., bibliography; bibliographical.
biog., biography; biographical.
biol., biology; biological.
bk., book, bank.
bkg., banking.
bkrpt., bankrupt.
bkt., basket.
B.L., Bachelor of Law; black letter; breech-loading.
b.l., bill of lading.
bl., barrel; bale.
B.Litt., Bachelor of Letters (Literature).
B.LL., Bachelor of Laws, more commonly LL.B.
B.M., Bachelor of Medicine, more commonly M.B.; Lat. *Beata Maria*, Blessed Mary, the Virgin, more commonly B.V.M.; Lat. *beatae memoriae*, of blessed memory; Brigade Major; British Museum.
B.M.A., British Medical Association.
B.M.E., Bachelor of Mining Engineering.
B.M.J., British Medical Journal.
B.Mus., Bachelor of Music, more commonly Mus. Bac.; British Museum.
B.N.C., Brasenose College, Oxford.
B.N.O.C., British National Opera Company.
b.o., branch office; buyer's option.
B.O.A., British Olympic Association; British Optical Association.
B.O.A.F.G., British Order of Ancient Free Gardeners.
B. of E., Bank of England; Board of Education.
B. of H., Band of Hope; Board of Health.
B. of T., Board of Trade.
bomb., bombardier.
Bom. C.S., Bombay Civil Service.
Bom. S.C., Bombay Staff Corps.
B.O.P., Boys' Own Paper.
bor., borough.
bos'n, boatswain.
bot., botany; botanical.
B.P., British Pharmacopoeia; the British public (humorous).
b.p., below proof (of spirits); bills payable; birthplace; boiling-point.
B.-P., Baden-Powell.
bp., bishop.
B.P.B., bank post bills.
Bp. Suff., Bishop Suffragan.
B.Q., Lat. *bene quiescat*, may he (she) rest well.
Br, bromine (chem.).
Br., Brother; Brigade; Brig; Bombardier; Bugler.
b.r., bills receivable.
Brazil., Brazilian.
B.R.C.S., British Red Cross Society.
b. rec., bills receivable.
Brecon, Brecknockshire.
Bret., Breton.
brev., brevet; brevier.
Brig., Brigade; Brigadier.
Brig.-Gen., Brigadier-General.
Brit., Britain; British; Britannia.
Brit. Mus., British Museum.
Brit. Pharm., British Pharmacopoeia.
Britt., Lat. *Brit(t)an(n)iarum*, of (all) the Britains, on coins.
bro., brother.
Bros., Brothers (commercial).
bryol., bryology.
B.S., Bachelor of Surgery; Bachelor of Science (U.S.A.).
b.s., balance sheet; bill of sale.
B.S.A., British South Africa; Birmingham Small Arms Co.; British School at Athens.
B.S.C., Bengal Staff Corps.
B.Sc., Bachelor of Science.
B.S.L., Botanical Society of London.
B.S.R., British School at Rome.
Bt., Baronet.
bt., bought.
B.Th., Bachelor of Theology.
B.Th.U., British thermal unit.
B.T.U., (elect.) Board of Trade unit.
Bty., Battery.
bu., bushel.
Bucks, Buckinghamshire.
Bulg., Bulgaria; Bulgarian.
B.V., Bible Version (of the Psalms).
B.V.M., Lat. *Beata Virgo Maria*, the Blessed Virgin Mary.
B.W., Board of Works; bonded warehouse; Black Watch.
B.W.G., Birmingham wire gauge.
B.W.I., British West Indies.
B.W.T.A., British Women's Temperance Association.

C, Roman numeral, *centum*, 100; carbon (chem.).
C., Cape; Catholic; Centigrade; Conservative.
c., Lat. *circa*, *circum*, *circiter*, about; cent; centime; chapter; child; (cricket) caught.
C3, lowest in physique, state of health, efficiency, &c.
C.A., Chartered Accountant; Chief Accountant; Commercial Agent; County Alderman; Court of Appeal; Church Association; Church Army.
Ca, calcium (chem.).
ca., cathode (elect.).
ca., Lat. *circa*, about.
cad., cadenza (mus.).
caet. par., see **cet. par.**
C.A.F., Curates' Augmentation Fund.
Cal., California (U.S.A.).
C. Am., Central America(n).
Cambs., Cambridgeshire.
Can., Canada; Canon; Canto; *Cantoris* (of choir).
c. & b., caught and bowled (cricket).
Cant., Canticles (O.T.); Canterbury.
Cantab., Cambridge University; member of Cambridge University.
cantab., cantabile (music).
Cantuar., Lat. *Cantuariensis*, of Canterbury, in signature of Archbishop.
cap., Lat. *capitulum*, chapter; capital letter; number of statute in year of reign of sovereign; captain.
caps., capital letters.
Capt., Captain.
Car., Lat. *Carolus*, Charles.
Card., Cardinal.
Cardig., Cardiganshire.
Carib., Caribbean.
Carliol., Carlisle, in signature of Bishop.
Carmarths., Carmarthenshire.
cat., catalogue; catechism.
Cath., Catholic; Cathedral.
cath., cathode (elect.).
Cathol., Catholic; Catholikos.
cav., cavalry; caveat (law).
C.B., Companion of the Bath (civil or military); confined to barracks, as punishment in army; Cape Breton (Canada); County Borough.
Cb, columbium (chem.).
C.B.E., Commander of the British Empire.
C.B.S., Confraternity of the Blessed Sacrament; Church Building Society.
C.C., Caius College (Cambridge); Cape Colony; Chamber of Commerce; Circuit Court; Common Council(man), City of London; County Council(lor); County Court; Cricket Club; Cycling Club.
c.c., cubic centimetre.
C.C.C., Corpus Christi College, Oxford and Cambridge; Central Criminal Court.
C.C.P., Court of Common Pleas; Code of Civil Procedure.
C.C.S., Ceylon Civil Service; Casualty Clearing Station.
C.D., Chancery Division.
Cd, cadmium (chem.).
Cd., Command Paper, up to 1918 (see **Cmd.**).

cd., could.
C.D. (Acts), Contagious Diseases (Acts).
c.d.v., carte-de-visite (photograph).
C.E., Civil Engineer; Chief Engineer; Church of England.
Ce, cerium (chem.).
Cels., Celsius (thermometer).
Celt., Celtic.
C.E.M.S., Church of England Men's Society.
Cent., Centigrade.
cent., Lat. *centum*, 100; central; century.
Cent. Am., Central America(n).
cert., **certif.**, certificate; certified.
C.E.S.S.I., Church of England Sunday School Institution.
Cestr., Chester, in signature of Bishop.
cet. par., Lat. *ceteris paribus*, other things being equal.
C.E.T.S., Church of England Temperance Society.
C.E.U., Christian Endeavour Union.
C.E.W.M.S., Church of England Working Men's Society.
C.F., Chaplain to the Forces.
cf., Lat. *confer*, compare.
C.F.G., Fr. *Confédération Générale de Travail*, General Confederation of Labour.
c.f.i., cost, freight, and insurance.
C.G., Captain-General; Captain of the Guard; Coast Guard; Coldstream Guards; Commissary-General; Consul-General.
cg., centigramme.
C.G.H., Cape of Good Hope.
C.G.M., Conspicuous Gallantry Medal.
C.G.S., Chief of the General Staff; centimetre-gramme-second system of scientific measurement.
C.H., Companion of Honour; Custom House; Court House.
Ch., Church; Chancery.
Chap., Chaplain; Chapter.
Chap.-Gen., Chaplain-General.
Chas., Charles.
Ch.B., Lat. *Chirurgiae Baccalaureus*, Bachelor of Surgery.
Ch.Ch., Christ Church, Oxford University.
chem., chemistry; chemical.
Ches., Cheshire.
Chev., Fr. *Chevalier*, knight.
Chin., China; Chinese.
Ch.J., Chief Justice.
Ch.M., Lat. *Chirurgiae Magister*, Master of Surgery.
Chmn., Chairman.
chq., cheque.
Chron., Chronicles (O.T.).
chron., chronology; chronological.
chrs., chambers.
C.I., (Imperial Order of the) Crown of India (for ladies); Channel Islands.
Cicestr., Chichester, in signature of Bishop.
C.I.D., Criminal Investigation Department, Scotland Yard.
C.I.E., Companion of the Indian Empire.
c.i.f.c., cost, insurance, freight, and commission.
C.I.G.S., Chief of the Imperial General Staff.
C.I.Mech.E., Companion of the Institution of Mechanical Engineers.
C.-in-C., Commander-in-Chief.
circ., Lat. *circa, circiter, circum*, about.
cit., citation; cited.
C.I.V., City Imperial Volunteers.
C.J., Chief Justice.
C.L., Commander of the Order of Leopold (Belgium).
Cl, chlorine (chem.).
cl., centilitre.
Clar., Clarendon (printing type).
class., classics; classical; classification.
C.L.B., Church Lads' Brigade.
cld., cleared (goods, shipping); coloured.
C.M., Lat. *Chirurgiae Magister*, Master of Surgery; Church Missionary; Certificated Master; Corresponding Member; common metre (of hymns).
c.m., Lat. *causa mortis*, by reason of death.
cm., centimetre.
C.M.A.S., Clergy Mutual Assurance Society.
Cmd., Command Paper, from 1919 (see **Cd.**).
cmdg., commanding.
C.M.G., Companion of St. Michael and St. George.
C.M.R., Cape Mounted Rifles.
C.M.S., Church Missionary Society.
C.O., Commanding Officer; Colonial Office; Crown Office; Criminal Office.
Co, cobalt (chem.).
Co., Company; County.
c/o, care of.
C.O.D., cash on delivery.
C. of E., Church of England.
C. of G.H., Cape of Good Hope.
C. of S., Chief of Staff.
cogn., cognate.
Col., Colossians (N.T.); Colonel.
col., colony; colonial; colour(ed); college; column.
Coll., College.
coll., collective(ly).
collat., collateral.
colloq., colloquial.
Colo., Colorado (U.S.A.).
Coloss., Colossians (N.T.).
Col.-Sergt., Colour-Sergeant.
Com., Commander; Commissioner; Committee; Commodore; Commonwealth; Communist.
com., common; commune; commerce; communications; comedy; commentary; commission.
Comdg., Commanding.
Comdr., Commander.
Comdt., Commandant.
Com.-in-C., Commander-in-Chief.
commerc., commercial.
Commn., Commission.
Commr., Commissioner.
comp., company; comparative; compare; compositor; compound.
compar., comparative.
Com. Serj., Common Serjeant (City of London).
Comy.-Gen., Commissary-General.
Con., Consul.
con., Lat. *contra*, against; conics.
conch., conchology.
conf., Lat. *confer*, compare.
Cong., Congress; Congregation.
conj., conjunction; conjunctive; conjugation.
Conn., Connecticut (U.S.A.).
conn., connected.
Cons., Consul; Conservative.
cons., consonant.
Conserv., Conservative.
Consols, Consolidated Stock.
constr., construction.
contr., contracted; contraction; contrary.
Co-op., Co-operative (Stores).
Cop., Copernican.
C.O.P.E.C. (Copec), Conference on Politics, Economics, and Citizenship (Ch. of Eng.).
Copt., Coptic.
Cor., Corinthians (N.T.); Coroner.
Corn., Cornwall; Cornish.
corol., corollary.
Corp., Corporal; Corporation.
correl., correlative.
Corr. Mem. or **Fell.**, Corresponding Member or Fellow (of a foreign learned society or academy).
corrupt., corruption.
C.O.S., Charity Organisation Society.
cos, cosine.
cosec, cosecant.
cosmog., cosmogony; cosmography.
coss., Lat. *consules*, consuls.
cot, cotangent.
cox, coxswain.
Coy., Company.
C.P., Carriage Paid; Carter Paterson; Clerk of the Peace; Common Pleas; Central Provinces (India); Court of Probate.
c.p., candle-power.
cp., compare.
C.P.C., Clerk of the Privy Council.
Cpl., Corporal.
C.P.R., Canadian Pacific Railway.
C.P.R.E., Council for the Preservation of Rural England.
C.P.S., Lat. *Custos Privati Sigilli*, Keeper of the Privy Seal.
C.R., Lat. *Carolus Rex*, Charles, King; Caledonian Railway.
Cr, chromium (chem.).
Cr., Crown; credit(or).
cr., created.
cresc., crescendo (mus.).
crim. con., criminal conversation, i.e. adultery in old divorce law.
crystal., crystallography.
C.S., Chemical Society; Civil Service; Clerk to the Signet; Common Serjeant; Court of Session; *Custos Sigilli*, Keeper of the Seal.
Cs, caesium (chem.).
C.S.A., Confederate States of America, Confederate States Army.
C.S.C., Conspicuous Service Cross.
C.S.I., Companion of the Star of India.
C.S.M., Company Sergeant-Major.
C.S.S.A., Civil Service Supply Association.
C.T., Certificated Teacher; Commercial Traveller.
Ct., Count; Court.
ct., caught (cricket); cent.
C.T.C., Cyclists' Touring Club.
Cte., Fr. *Comte*, Count.
Ctesse., Fr. *Comtesse*, Countess.
Cu, Lat. *cuprum*, copper (chem.).
C.U.A.C., Cambridge University Athletic Club.
C.U.A.F.C., Cambridge University Association Football Club.
cub., cubic.
C.U.B.C., Cambridge University Boat Club.
C.U.C.C., Cambridge University Cricket Club.
C.U.G.C., Cambridge University Golf Club.
C.U.H.C., Cambridge University Hockey Club.
cum., cumulative.
Cumb., Cumberland.
cum div., with dividend.
Cum. Pref., Cumulative Preference (shares).
C.U.M.S., Cambridge University Musical Society.
cur., current; currency.
C.U.R.F.C., Cambridge University Rugby Football Club.
C.V.O., Commander of the Royal Victorian Order.
c.w.o., cash with order.
C.W.S., Co-operative Wholesale Society.
cwt., hundredweight.
cyl., cylinder.
Cym., Cymric.

D, Roman numeral, 500.
D., Don; Dom; Lat. *Deus*, God.
d., date; daughter; delete; Lat. *denarius*, penny, pence; died; dollar.
d——, damn.
D.(A.)A.G., Deputy (Assistant) Adjutant-General.
dag., decagramme.
D.A.H., disordered action of the heart.
Dak., Dakota (U.S.A.).
dal., decalitre.
dam., decametre.
Dan., Daniel (O.T.); Danish.
D.A.Q.M.G., Deputy Assistant Quartermaster-General.
dat., dative.
dau., daughter.
d.b., day-book.
D.B.E., Dame Commander of the British Empire.
dbk., drawback.
D.C., District of Columbia (U.S.A.); direct current (elect.).
D.C., Ital. *da capo* (mus.), repeat from the beginning.
D.C.L., Doctor of Civil Law.
D.C.L.I., Duke of Cornwall's Light Infantry.
D.C.M. Distinguished Conduct Medal.
D.C.S., Deputy Clerk of Session.

D.D., Doctor of Divinity.
D.D.; **d.d.**, Lat. *dono dedit*, gave as a gift.
d——d, damned.
D.D.D., Lat. *dat, dicat, dedicat*, gives, devotes, and dedicates.
D.D.S., Doctor of Dental Surgery.
deb., debenture.
Dec., December; Decorated (archit.); *Decani* (of choir).
dec., deceased.
dec(l.), declension.
Def., Deferred (stocks or shares); Defendant.
def., definite; definition.
deg., degree.
Del., Delaware (U.S.A.).
del(e)., delete.
del(t)., Lat. *delineavit*, he (she) drew (it).
Dem., Democrat.
demon(s)., demonstrative.
D.Eng., Doctor of Engineering.
Dent., dental; dentistry; dentist.
dep., departs (of train &c.); deputy; department.
dep(t)., department.
deriv., derivation.
Deut., Deuteronomy.
D.F., Lat. *defensor fidei*, Defender of the Faith, usually F.D.; Dean of the Faculty; direction finding.
D.F.C., Distinguished Flying Cross.
D.F.M., Distinguished Flying Medal.
dft., defendant; draft.
D.G., Lat. *Dei gratia*, by the grace of God; Lat. *Deo gratias*, thanks to God; Director-General; Dragoon Guards.
dg., decigramme.
dial., dialect.
diam., diameter.
D.I.C., Diploma of the Imperial College.
dict., dictionary.
diff., differ; difference; different.
dim., diminuendo (mus.).
dimin., diminutive.
Dioc., Diocese; Diocesan.
Dir., Director.
dis., **disc(t).**, discount.
Dist., District.
dist., distinguish(ed).
Div., Division (army).
div., dividend; division.
D.L., Deputy-Lieutenant.
dl., decilitre.
D.L.I., Durham Light Infantry.
D.Lit., Doctor of Literature.
D.Litt., (at Aberdeen) Doctor of Letters.
D.L.O., Dead Letter Office (now R.L.O., Returned Letter Office).
D.M., Doctor of Medicine, now usually M.D.; Deputy Master.
dm., decimetre.
D.M.R.E., Diploma in Medical Radiology and Electrology.
D.Mus., Doctor of Music, now Mus.D(oc.).
D.N.B., Dictionary of National Biography.
do., ditto, the same.
doc., document.
D.O.M., Lat. *Deo optimo maximo*, to God the best and greatest.
Dom., Lat. *Dominus*, Lord, Master; Dominion.
D.O.M.S., Diploma in Ophthalmic Medicine and Surgery.
Dor., Doric.
D.O.R.A., Defence of the Realm Act(s).
doz., dozen(s).
D.P., double pole.
D.P.H., Diploma in, Department of, Public Health.
D.Ph., Doctor of Philosophy, usually Ph.D.
D.Phil., Doctor of Philosophy.
D.P.I., Director of Public Instruction.
D.P.O., Distributing Post Office.
dpt., department.
D.Q.M.G., Deputy Quartermaster-General.
D.R., dead reckoning.
Dr., Doctor; debtor.
dr., drachm; drawer (banking).
dram. pers., Lat. *dramatis personae*, characters of the play.
D.S., Ital. *dal segno* (mus.), from the sign.
d.s., days after sight (on bills of exchange).
D.S.C., Distinguished Service Cross.
D.Sc., Doctor of Science.
D.S.M., Distinguished Service Medal.
D.S.O., Distinguished Service Order.
d.s.p., Lat. *decessit sine prole*, died without issue.
D.T., (colloq.) delirium tremens.
D.Theol., Doctor of Theology.
D.T.M., Diploma in Tropical Medicine.
Du., Dutch.
Dunelm., Durham, in signature of Bishop.
D.V., Lat. *Deo volente*, God willing.
D.V.M., Doctor of Veterinary Medicine.
d.v.p., Lat. *decessit vita patris*, died during lifetime of father.
D.V.S., Doctor of Veterinary Science or Surgery.
dwt., pennyweight.
dyn., dynamics.
D.Z., Doctor of Zoology.

E, erbium (chem.).
E., earth; east; eastern (London postal district); second-class ship at Lloyd's; Egyptian, in £E.
ea., each.
E. & O.E., errors and omissions excepted (mercantile).
E.B., Encyclopædia Britannica.
Ebor., fr. Lat. *Eboracensis*, of *Eboracum*, York, in signature of Archbishop.
E.C., east central (London postal district).
Eccl(es)., Ecclesiastes (O.T.).
eccl(es)., ecclesiastical.
Ecclus., Ecclesiasticus (O.T., Apoc.).
econ., economics.
E.C.U., English Church Union.
ed., edited; edition; editor.
Edin., Edinburgh.
edit., edited; edition; editor.
E.D.S., English Dialect Society.
eds., editors.
educ., education.
Edw., Edward.
E.E., Envoy Extraordinary; errors excepted (mercantile).
E.E.T.S., Early English Text Society.
e.g., Lat. *exempli gratia*, for example.
Egyptol., Egyptology.
E.I., East Indian; East Indies; East India.
E.I.C., East India Company.
ejusd., Lat. *ejusdem*, of the same.
el., elected,
eld., eldest.
elect., electricity.
Eliz., Elizabeth; Elizabethan.
Elz., Elzevir.
E.M.D.P., electromotive difference of potential.
E.M.F., electromotive force.
Emp., Emperor, Empress.
E.M.U., electromagnetic units.
Ency., Encyclop(a)edia.
E.N.E., east-north-east.
Eng., England; English.
eng., engineer, engineering; engraver, engraving.
engin., engineering.
Engl., English.
ent(om)., entomology; entomological.
Ent. Sta. Hall, Entered at Stationers' Hall.
Env. Extr., Envoy Extraordinary.
Ep., Epistle.
E.P.D., Excess Profits Duty.
Eph., Ephesians (N.T.).
Epiph., Epiphany.
episc., episcopal.
eq., equal, equivalent.
equiv., equivalent.
E.R., East Riding, Yorkshire.
E.R. (et I.), Lat. *Edwardus Rex (et Imperator)*, Edward King (and Emperor).
eschat., eschatology.
E.S.E., east-south-east.
esp(ec)., especially.
Esq(re)., Esquire.
est(ab)., established.
Esth., Esther (O.T.).
E.S.U., electrostatic units.
et al., Lat. *et alibi*, and elsewhere; *et alia*, and other things; *et alii*, and other people.
E.T.C., Eastern Telegraph Co.
etc., Lat. *et cetera*, and (the) other things.
eth., ethics, ethical.
ethnol., ethnology, ethnological.
et seq., et sqq., Lat. *et sequens, et sequentia*, and the following.
E.T.U., Electrical Trades Union.
etymol., etymology, etymological.
euphem., euphemism, euphemistically.
Ex., Exodus (O.T.).
ex., examined; example; except.
exam., examination.
Exc., Excellency.
exc., except.
exc., Lat. *excudit*, he (she) engraved (it).
ex div., ex dividend.
Exod., Exodus (O.T.).
ex off., Lat. *ex officio*, by virtue of office.
Exon., Exeter, in signature of Bishop.
exor., executor.
exp., export, exporter.
Ez., Ezra (O.T.).
Ezek., Ezekiel (O.T.).

F, firm (of pencils).
F., Fahrenheit; French.
f., farthing; fathom; foot; filly; folio; franc.
f, Ital. *forte*, loud (mus.).
F.A., Football Association.
f.a.a., free of all average.
facet., facetious.
F.A.C.S., Fellow of the American College of Surgeons.
fac(s)., facsimile.
F.A.G.S., Fellow of the American Geographical Society.
Fahr., Fahrenheit.
F.A.I., Fellow of the Auctioneers' Institute.
F.A.L.P.A., Fellow of the Incorporated Society of Auctioneers and Landed Property Agents.
F.A.S., Fellow of the Society of Arts; do. of the Antiquarian Society (Edinburgh); do. of the Anthropological Society.
f.a.s., free alongside ship.
F.B., Fire Brigade; Fenian Brotherhood; Free Baptist.
F.B.A., Fellow of the British Academy.
F.B.H., fire brigade hydrant.
F.B.I., Federation of British Industries.
F.B.S., Fellow of the Botanical Society; **F.B.S.E.**, do. of the Botanical Society of Edinburgh.
F.C., Football Club; Free Church (Scotland).
F.C.A., Fellow of the Institute of Chartered Accountants.
fcap., foolscap.
F.C.G.I., Fellow of the City and Guilds of London Institute.
F.C.I.I., Fellow of the Chartered Insurance Institute.
F.C.I.S., Fellow of the Chartered Institute of Secretaries.
F.C.O., Fellow of the College of Organists, now F.R.C.O.
F.C.P., Fellow of the College of Preceptors.
fcp., foolscap.
F.C.S., Fellow of the Chemical Society.
F.D., Lat. *fidei defensor*, Defender of the Faith; also D.F.
Fe, Lat. *ferrum*, iron (chem.).
Feb(y)., February.
fec., Lat. *fecit*, he (she) did, made (it).
fed., federal; federated.
F.E.I.S., Fellow of the Educational Institute of Scotland.
fem., feminine.
F.E.S., Fellow of the Entomological Society; Fellow of the Ethnological Society.
feud., feudal(ism).
ff., folios; following pages.
ff, Ital. *fortissimo*, very loud (mus.).
F.F.A., Fellow of the Faculty of Actuaries.

ffy., faithfully.
F.G., Foot Guards.
f.g.a., free of general average.
F.G.S., Fellow of the Geological Society.
F.H., fire hydrant.
F.I.A., Fellow of the Institute of Actuaries.
F.I.A.A., Fellow Architect Member of the Incorporated Association of Architects and Surveyors.
F.I.A.S., Fellow Surveyor Member of the Incorporated Association of Architects and Surveyors.
F.I.A.T., Ital. *Fabrica Italiana Automobile Torino*, make of motor-car.
F.I.C., Fellow of the Institute of Chemistry.
F.I.C.A., Fellow of the Institute of Chartered Accountants.
F.I.C.S., Fellow of the Institute of Chartered Shipbrokers.
F.I.D., Fellow of the Institute of Directors.
Fid. Def., Lat. *fidei defensor*, Defender of the Faith.
fi. fa., Lat. *fieri facias* (law).
fig., figure (illustration); figurative(ly).
F.I.Inst., Fellow of the Imperial Institute.
F.I.J., Fellow of the Institute of Journalists.
fin., financial; finis; finished.
Finn., Finnish.
F.Inst.P., Fellow of the Institute of Physics.
F.I.O., Fellow of the Institute of Ophthalmic Opticians.
F.I.P.I., Fellow of the Institute of Patentees (Inc.).
F.I.S.A., Fellow of the Incorporated Secretaries Association.
F.I.S.E., Fellow of the Institution of Structural Engineers.
F.J.I., Fellow of the Institute of Journalists.
F.K.C.(L.), Fellow of King's College (London).
Fl, fluorine (chem.).
fl., florin.
fl., Lat. *floruit*, he (she) flourished, lived.
f.l., Lat. *falsa lectio*, false reading (of MS. &c.).
F.L.A., Fellow of the Library Association.
Fla., Florida (U.S.A.).
F.L.A.A., Fellow of the London Association of Accountants.
F.L.A.S., Fellow of the Land Agents' Society.
Flem., Flemish.
flor., Lat. *floruit*, he (she) flourished, lived.
F.L.S., Fellow of the Linnean Society.
F.M., Field-Marshal.
fm., fathom.
F.M.S., Federated Malay States.
F.O., Foreign Office; Field Officer; full organ (mus.).
fo., folio.
f.o.b., free on board.
fol., folio; following.
foll., following.
f.o.r., free on rail.
fort., fortification.
F.P., fire-plug; field punishment.
fp., foot-pound; foolscap.
fp, Ital. *forte piano*, loud and soft (mus.).
f.p.a., free of particular average.
F.Phys.S., Fellow of the Physical Society.
F.P.S., Fellow of the Philosophical Society; Fellow of the Philharmonic Society; Fellow of the Philological Society.
Fr., Father; France, French; Friar.
fr., franc; from.
F.R.A.I., Fellow of the Royal Anthropological Institute.
F.R.A.M., Fellow of the Royal Academy of Music.
F.R.Ae.S., Fellow of the Royal Aeronautical Society.
F.R.A.S., Fellow of the Royal Astronomical Society; Fellow of the Royal Asiatic Society.
F.R.B.S., Fellow of the Royal Botanic Society.
F.R.C.I., Fellow of the Royal Colonial Institute.
F.R.C.M., Fellow of the Royal College of Music.
F.R.C.O., Fellow of the Royal College of Organists.
F.R.C.P., Fellow of the Royal College of Physicians; **F.R.C.P.E.**, do. of Edinburgh; **F.R.C.P.I.**, do. of Ireland.
F.R.C.S., Fellow of the Royal College of Surgeons; **F.R.C.S.E.**, do. of Edinburgh; **F.R.C.S.I.**, do. of Ireland.
F.R.C.V.S., Fellow of the Royal College of Veterinary Surgeons.
F.R.Econ.Soc., Fellow of the Royal Economic Society.
freq., frequentative; frequently.
F.R.F.P.S., Fellow of the Royal Faculty of Physicians and Surgeons.
F.R.G.S., Fellow of the Royal Geographical Society.
F.R.Hist.S., Fellow of the Royal Historical Society.
F.R.Hort.S., Fellow of the Royal Horticultural Society.
Fri., Friday.
F.R.I.B.A., Fellow of the Royal Institute of British Architects.
F.R.I.C.S., Fellow of the Royal Institution of Chartered Surveyors.
Frl., Fräulein.
F.R.Met.S., Fellow of the Royal Meteorological Society.
F.R.M.S., Fellow of the Royal Microscopical Society.
F.R.N.S.A., Fellow of the Royal Naval School of Architects.
F.R.P.S., Fellow of the Royal Photographic Society.
F.R.P.S.L., Fellow of the Royal Philatelic Society, London.
F.R.S., Fellow of the Royal Society.
F.R.S.A., Fellow of the Royal Society of Arts.
F.R.S.A.I., Fellow of the Royal Society of Antiquaries of Ireland.
F.R.San.I., Fellow of the Royal Sanitary Institute.
F.R.S.E., Fellow of the Royal Society of Edinburgh.
F.R.S.G.S., Fellow of the Royal Scottish Geographical Society.
F.R.S.L., Fellow of the Royal Society of Literature.
F.R.S.S., Fellow of the Royal Statistical Society.
F.R.S.S.A., Fellow of the Royal Scottish Society of Arts.
F.R.U.I., Fellow of the Royal University of Ireland.
F.S., Fleet Surgeon.
fs., foot-second.
F.S.A., Fellow of the Society of Antiquaries; Fellow of the Society of Arts.
F.S.A.A., Fellow of the Society of Incorporated Accountants and Auditors.
F.S.I., Fellow of the Sanitary Institution.
F.S.R., Field Service Regulations.
F.S.S., Fellow of the Statistical Society, now F.R.S.S.
ft., foot, feet.
F.T.C.D., Fellow of Trinity College, Dublin.
F.T.C.L., Fellow of Trinity College (of Music), London.
fur., furlong.
fut., future.
F.W.B., four wheel brake; Free Will Baptist.
F.W.D., four wheel drive.
F.Z.S., Fellow of the Zoological Society of London; **F.Z.S.Scot.**, do. of Scotland.

g., guinea; gramme.
G.A., General Assembly.
Ga., Georgia (U.S.A.).
Ga, gallium (chem.).
Gael., Gaelic.
Gal., Galatians (N.T.).
gal., gallon.
Gaul., Gaulish.
gaz., gazette; gazetteer.
G.B., Great Britain.
G.B. & I., Great Britain and Ireland.
G.B.E., Knight (or Dame) Grand Cross of the British Empire.
G.C., Grand Chaplain, Grand Chapter (freemasonry).
G.C.B., Knight Grand Cross of the Bath.
G.C.C., Gonville and Caius College, Cambridge.
G.C.F., greatest common factor.
G.C.H., Knight Grand Cross of Hanover.
G.C.I.E., Knight Grand Commander of the Indian Empire.
G.C.L.H., Knight Grand Cross of the Legion of Honour.
G.C.M., greatest common measure.
G.C.M.G., Knight Grand Cross of St. Michael and St. George.
G.C.R., Great Central Railway, now part of L.N.E.(R.).
G.C.S.I., Knight Grand Commander of the Star of India.
G.C.V.O., Knight Grand Cross of the Royal Victorian Order.
Gdns., Gardens.
Gds., Guards.
Ge, germanium (chem.).
Gen., General; Genesis (O.T.).
gen., gender; genus; general(ly); generic.
geneal., genealogy.
genit., genitive.
Genl., General.
Geo., George.
geod., geodesy.
geog., geography.
geol., geology.
geom., geometry.
G.E.R., Great Eastern Railway, now part of L.N.E.(R.).
ger., gerund.
Germ., German; Germany.
G.F.S., Girls' Friendly Society.
G.F.T.U., General Federation of Trade Unions.
G.G., Grenadier Guards.
g.gr., great gross, 144 dozens.
G.H.Q., General Headquarters.
Gib., (colloq.), Gibraltar.
G.J.C., Grand Junction Canal.
Gk., Greek.
G.L., Grand Lodge (freemasonry).
Gl, glucinum (chem.).
Glam., Glamorganshire.
Glos., Gloucestershire.
gloss., glossary.
Glo'ster, Gloucester.
Gloucs., Gloucestershire.
G.M., Grand Master (orders of knighthood and freemasonry); Gold Medallist (Bisley).
gm., gramme.
G.M.B., Great Master of the Bath; good merchantable brand (of metals).
Gmc., Germanic.
G.M.I.E., Grand Master of the Indian Empire.
G.M.M.G., Grand Master of St. Michael and St. George.
G.M.S.I., Grand Master of the Star of India.
G.M.T., Greenwich Mean Time.
G.N.R., Great Northern Railway.
G.O., General Order.
G.O.C., General Officer Commanding; **G.O.C. in C.**, do. in Chief.
G.O.M., Grand Old Man (originally of W. E. Gladstone).
G.O.P., Girls' Own Paper.
Goth., Gothic.
Gov., Governor.
Gov.-Gen., Governor-General.
Govt., Government.
G.P., general practitioner (doctor); general paralysis of the insane (also G.P.I.); Lat. *Gloria Patri*, Glory to the Father.
G.P.D.S.T., Girls' Public Day School Trust.
G.P.I., general paralysis of the insane.
G.P.M., Grand Past Master (freemasonry).
G.P.O., General Post Office.
G.R., General Reserve.
G.R. (et I.), Lat. *Georgius Rex (et Imperator)*, George, King (and Emperor).
Gr., Greek.
gr., gramme; grain.
gram., grammar.
Gr. Gds., Grenadier Guards.
grm., gramme.
G.S., General Staff; General Service.
g.s., grandson.

G.S.N.C., General Steam Navigation Co.
G.S.O., General Staff Officer.
G.T., Good Templar.
Gt. Br., Great Britain.
guar., guarantee(d).
G.W.R., Great Western Railway.
gym., gymnasium ; gymnastics.

H, hydrogen (chem.) ; hard (of pencil-lead).
H., hydrant.
h., hour.
H.A., heavy artillery.
H.A. & M., Hymns Ancient and Modern.
Hab., Habakkuk (O.T.).
hab., Lat. *habitat*, he lives.
Hab. Corp., Habeas Corpus (writ).
H.A.C., Honourable Artillery Company.
Hag., Haggai (O.T.).
H.A.L., *Hamburg-Amerika Linie* (German steamship company).
h. and c., hot and cold (water supply).
Hants, Hampshire.
HB, hard black (of pencil-lead).
H.B.C., Hudson's Bay Company.
H.B.M., His (Her) Britannic Majesty.
H.C., House of Commons ; Heralds' College.
hcap., handicap.
H.C.F., highest common factor.
H.C.M., His (Her) Catholic Majesty.
H.C.S., Home Civil Service.
hd., hogshead.
hdbk., handbook.
hdqrs., headquarters.
H.E., His Excellency ; His Eminence ; high explosive.
He, helium (chem.).
Heb., Hebrew ; Hebrews (N.T.).
hectog., hectogramme.
hectol., hectolitre.
hectom., hectometre.
H.E.I.C., Honourable East India Company.
Hellen., Hellenic ; Hellenistic.
her., heraldry.
Herts, Hertfordshire.
HF, hard firm (of pencil-lead).
H.F., high frequency.
hf., half.
hf.-bd., half-bound.
H.F.R.A., Honorary Fellow of the Royal Academy.
H.G., High German ; Horse Guards ; His (Her) Grace.
Hg, Lat. *hydrargyrum*, mercury (chem.).
hg., hectogramme ; heliogram.
H.G.D.H., His (Her) Grand Ducal Highness.
H.H., His (Her) Highness ; His Holiness (the Pope).
HH, double hard (of pencil-lead).
hhd., hogshead.
HHH, trebly hard (of pencil-lead).
H.I.H., His (Her) Imperial Highness.
H.I.M., His (Her) Imperial Majesty.
Hind., Hindustani ; Hindi.
hist., history ; historical.
H.J.(S.), Lat. *hic jacet* (*sepultus*), here lies (buried).
H.K., House of Keys (Isle of Man).
H.L., House of Lords.
hl., hectolitre.
H.L.I., Highland Light Infantry.
H.M., His (Her) Majesty.
hm., hectometre.
H.M.A., His Majesty's Airship ; Head Masters' Association.
H.M.C., His Majesty's Customs.
H.M.I.(S.), His Majesty's Inspector (of Schools).
H.M.P., Lat. *hoc monumentum posuit*, erected this monument.
H.M.S., His Majesty's Ship ; His Majesty's Service.
H.M.S.O., His Majesty's Stationery Office.
H.O., Home Office.
Hon., Honourable ; Honorary.
Honble., Honourable.
Hon. Sec., Honorary Secretary.
hor., horizon.
horol., horology.
hort., horticulture ; horticultural.
Hos., Hosea (O.T.).
H.P., House Physician.
h.p., horse-power ; half-pay ; high pressure.
h.p.n., horse-power nominal.
H.Q., Headquarters.
H.R., House of Representatives ; Highland Railway.
hr., hour.
H.R.C.A., Honorary Member of the Royal Cambrian Academy.
H.R.E., Holy Roman Empire, Emperor.
H.R.H., His (Her) Royal Highness.
H.R.H.A., Honorary Member of the Royal Hibernian Academy.
H.R.I.P., Lat. *hic requiescit in pace*, here rests in peace.
Hrs., Hussars.
H.R.S.A., Honorary Member of the Royal Scottish Academy.
H.S., House Surgeon.
H.S.E., Lat. *hic situs* (*sepultus*) *est*, here is laid (buried).
H.S.H., His (Her) Serene Highness.
h.t., high tension (elect.).
Hung., Hungary ; Hungarian.
Hunts, Huntingdonshire.
H.W., high water.
h.w., hit wicket (cricket).
Hy., Henry.
hydr., hydraulics.
hydro, hydropathic establishment.
hydrostat., hydrostatics.

I, Roman numeral ; iodine (chem).
I., Idaho (U.S.A.) ; Island.
I.A., Indian Army ; Incorporated Accountant.
Ia., Iowa (U.S.A.).
I.A.A.M., Incorporated Association of Assistant Masters.
I.A.O.S., Irish Agricultural Organization Society.
I.A.R.O., Indian Army Reserve of Officers.
ib., ***ibid.***, Lat. *ibidem*, in the same place.
i/c, in charge of.
I.C.E., Institution of Civil Engineers.
Icel., Icelandic ; Iceland.
ichth., ichthyology.
icon., iconography.
I.C.S., Indian Civil Service.
I.D., Intelligence Department.
id., Lat. *idem*, the same.
Ida., Idaho (U.S.A.).
I.D.B., illicit diamond buyer, buying (South Africa).
I.D.N., Lat. *in Dei nomine*, in the name of God.
i.e., Lat. *id est*, that is.
I.E.E., Institution of Electrical Engineers.
I.F.S., Irish Free State.
I.F.T.U., International Federation of Trade Unions.
I.G., Inspector-General.
ign., Lat. *ignotus*, unknown, of painter &c.
i.h.p., indicated horse-power.
IHS, Lat. *Jesus Hominum Salvator*, Jesus, Saviour of Mankind ; properly ΙΗΣ, in Greek, the first three letters of ΙΗΣΟΥΣ, Jesus.
Ill., Illinois (U.S.A.).
ill., illustration ; illustrated.
illit., illiterate.
I.L.O., International Labour Office, Geneva (League of Nations).
I.L.P., Independent Labour Party.
imit., imitative.
Imp., Imperial ; Lat. *Imperator*, Emperor, *Imperatrix*, Empress.
imp., Lat. *imprimatur*, let it be printed ; imported.
imperat., imperative.
imperf., imperfect ; imperforated (stamps).
impers., impersonal.
I.M.S., Indian Medical Service.
In, indium (chem.).
in., inch.
I.N.A., Institution of Naval Architects.
I.N.C., Lat. *in nomine Christi*, in the name of Christ.
inc., incorporated.
incl., including ; inclusive.
incog., Ital. *incognito*, unknown.
incorp., incorporated.
I.N.D., Lat. *in nomine Dei*, in the name of God.
Ind., Indian, India ; Indiana (U.S.A.).
ind., independent ; indicated ; index.
indecl., indeclinable.
indef., indefinite.
indic., indicative.
Ind.T., **Ind. Terr.**, Indian Territory (U.S.A.).
inf., infantry.
inf., Lat. *infra*, below.
infin., infinitive.
infra dig., Lat. *infra dignitatem*, beneath one's dignity.
init., Lat. *initio*, at, from, the beginning.
I.N.J., Lat. *in nomine Jesu*, in the name of Jesus.
in lim., Lat. *in limine*, on the threshold, at the outset.
in pr., Lat. *in principio*, in the beginning.
I.N.R.I., Lat. *Jesus Nazarenus Rex Judaeorum*, Jesus of Nazareth, King of the Jews.
insc., inscribed (stock).
insep., inseparable.
Insp., Inspector.
Insp.-Gen., Inspector-General.
I.N.S.T., Lat. *in nomine Sanctae Trinitatis*, in the name of the Holy Trinity.
inst., instant (the present month) ; institute ; institution, instrument(al).
Inst. Act., Institute of Actuaries.
Inst. C.E., Institution of Civil Engineers.
Inst. E.E., Institution of Electrical Engineers.
Inst. M.E., Institution of Mechanical Engineers.
Inst. N.A., Institution of Naval Architects.
instr., instrument(al).
int., interest ; internal ; interior ; interpreter ; international.
int. al., Lat. *inter alia*, among other things.
intens., intensive.
inter., interrogation, interrogative ; intermediate.
interj., interjection.
internat., international.
interrog., interrogative.
intrans., intransitive.
intro(d)., introduction.
inv., invented, inventor ; invoice.
inv(en)., Lat. *invenit*, he (she) invented, discovered (it).
I.O.F., Independent Order of Foresters.
I. of M., Isle of Man.
I. of W., Inspector of Works.
I.O.G.T., International Order of Good Templars.
I.O.O.F., Independent Order of Oddfellows.
I.O.P., Institute of Painters in Oil Colours.
IOU., I owe you (loose form of promissory note).
I.P.D., Lat. *in praesentia Dominorum*, in the presence of the Lords of Session.
ipecac., ipecacuanha.
I.P.L., Lat. *In partibus infidelium*, in the regions of unbelievers.
i.q., Lat. *idem quod*, the same as.
I.R., Inland Revenue.
Ir, iridium (chem.).
Ir., Irish ; Ireland.
I.R.A., Irish Republican Army.
I.R.B., Irish Republican Brotherhood.
I.R.O., Inland Revenue Office.
iron., ironical(ly).
irreg., irregular.
I.S., Irish Society.
Is., Isaiah (O.T.) ; Island.
I.S.C., Indian Staff Corps.
Isl., Island.
I.S.M., Incorporated Society of Musicians.
I.S.O., Imperial Service Order.
isth., isthmus.
I.T., Indian Territory (U.S.A.) ; Inner Temple (Inn of Court).
Ital., Italian ; Italy.
ital., italics.
I.W., Isle of Wight.
I.W.T.D., Inland Water Transport Department.

I.W.W., Industrial Workers of the World.
I.Y., Imperial Yeomanry.
I.Z., I Zingari (Cricket Club).

J, broad-pointed pen marked J.
J., Judge, Justice; joule (elect.).
J.A., Judge-Advocate.
J.A.G., Judge Advocate-General.
Jam., James (N.T.); Jamaica.
Jan., January.
Jap., Japanese.
Jas., James.
Jav., Javanese.
J.C., Lat. *jurisconsultus*, jurisconsult; Justice Clerk.
J.C.D., Lat. *Juris Civilis Doctor*, Doctor of Civil Law.
J.C.R., Junior Common Room (Oxford University).
J.D., Lat. *Jurum Doctor*, Doctor of Laws.
Jer., Jeremiah (O.T.).
JHS, see **IHS**.
J.I.C., Joint Industrial Council.
jn., junction.
Jno., John.
jnr., junior.
Jo., Joel (O.T.).
Jos., Joseph; Josiah.
Josh., Joshua (O.T.).
J.P., Justice of the Peace.
jr., junior.
J.U.D., Lat. *Juris utriusque Doctor*, Doctor of both (Civil and Canon) Laws.
Jud., Judith (O.T., Apoc.).
Jud(g)., Judges (O.T.).
Jul., July.
Jun., June.
jun., junior.
junc., junction.
Jun. Opt., Junior Optime (Camb. Univ. Math. Tripos).
junr., junior.

K, Lat. *kalium*, potassium (chem.).
Kal., Lat. *kalendae*, Calends.
Kan., Kansas (U.S.A.).
K.B., Knight Bachelor; King's Bench.
K.B.E., Knight Commander of the British Empire.
K.C., King's Counsel; King's College.
kc., kilocycle.
K.C.B., Knight Commander of the Bath.
K.C.H., Knight Commander of Hanover.
K.C.I.E., Knight Commander of the Indian Empire.
K.C.M.G., Knight Commander of St. Michael and St. George.
K.C.S.I., Knight Commander of the Star of India.
K.C.V.O., Knight Commander of the Royal Victorian Order.
K.G., Knight of the Garter.
kg., kilogramme.
K.G.C.B., Knight Grand Cross of the Bath, more usually G.C.B.
K.G.F., Knight of the Golden Fleece.
K.H., Knight of Hanover.
K.H.C., Honorary Chaplain to the King.
K.H.P., Honorary Physician to the King.
K.H.S., Honorary Surgeon to the King.
K.-i-H., Kaisar-i-Hind.
kilo(g)., kilogramme.
kilo(l)., kilolitre.
kilo(m)., kilometre.
K.K., Germ. *Kaiserlich, Königlich*, Imperial, Royal, i.e. of German Empire and Kingdom of Prussia.
K.K.K., Ku Klux Klan (U.S.A.).
kl., kilolitre(s).
K.L.H., Knight of the Legion of Honour.
K.L.I., King's Light Infantry.
K.M., Knight of Malta.
km., kilometre(s).
Knt., Knight.
Knt. Bach., Knight Bachelor.
K.O.S.B., King's Own Scottish Borderers.
K.O.Y.L.I., King's Own Yorkshire Light Infantry.
K.P., Knight of St. Patrick.
K.R., King's Regulations.
Kr, krypton (chem.).
K.R.R., King's Royal Rifles.
K.S., King's Scholar.
K.S.I., Knight of the Star of India.
K.T., Knight of the Thistle; Knight Templar.
Kt., Knight.
Kt. Bach., Knight Bachelor.
kv., kilovolt.
kw., kilowatt.
Ky., Kentucky (U.S.A.).

L, Roman numeral, 50.
L., Lake; Liberal; Late; left.
£, Lat. *libra*, pound sterling.
l., left; lira; litre.
L.A., Literate in Arts; Law Agent; Legislative Assembly.
La, lanthanum (chem.).
La., Louisiana (U.S.A.).
Lab., Labrador.
L.A.C., London Athletic Club; Licentiate of the Apothecaries' Company.
L.A.H., Licentiate of Apothecaries' Hall, Dublin.
L.A.M., London Academy of Music.
Lam., Lamentations (O.T.).
Lancs., Lancashire.
L. & N.E.R., see **L.N.E.(R.)**.
L. & S.W.R., London and South-Western Railway, now part of S.R.
L. & Y.R., Lancashire and Yorkshire Railway, now part of L.M.S.(R.).
lang., language.
L.A.S., Lord Advocate of Scotland.
Lat., Latin.
lat., latitude.
lb., Lat. *libra*, pound(s).
l.b., (cricket) leg-bye.
L.B. & S.C.R., London, Brighton and South Coast Railway, now part of S.R.
l.b.w., (cricket) leg before wicket.
L.C., Lord Chancellor; Lord Chamberlain; left centre (of stage).
l.c., (print.) lower case; Lat. *loco citato*, in place cited; letter of credit.
L.C. & D.R., London, Chatham and Dover Railway, now part of S.R.
L.C.B., Lord Chief Baron (obs.).
L.C.C., London County Council(lor).
L.Ch., **L.Chir.**, Licentiate in Surgery.
L.C.J., Lord Chief Justice.
L.C.M., least common multiple.
L.-Corp., Lance-Corporal.
L.C.P., Licentiate of the College of Preceptors.
L.-Cpl., Lance-Corporal.
L.D., Doctor of Letters (U.S.A.); Lady Day; Lat. *laus Deo*, praise be to God.
Ld., Lord; Limited.
L.Div., Licentiate in Divinity.
L.D.S., Licentiate in Dental Surgery; Lat. *laus Deo semper*, praise be to God for ever.
£E., Egyptian pound.
Leics., Leicestershire.
L. ès L., Fr. *Licencié ès Lettres*, Licentiate of Letters.
Lett., Lettish.
Lev., Leviticus (O.T.).
L.F., low frequency.
L.F.P.S., Licentiate of the Faculty of Physicians and Surgeons (Glasgow).
L.G., Low German; Life Guards.
L.G.B., Local Government Board.
L.G.O.C., London General Omnibus Co.
l.h., left hand.
L.I., Light Infantry; Long Island (U.S.A.).
Li, lithium (chem.).
Lib., Library, Librarian; Liberal.
Lic. Med., Licentiate in Medicine.
Lieut., Lieutenant.
Lieut.-Col., **-Gen.**, **-Gov.**, Lieutenant-Colonel, -General, -Governor.
Lincs., Lincolnshire.
Linn., Linn(a)ean; Linnaeus.
lit., literal(ly); litre.
Lit.D. See **Litt.D.**
liter., literature; literary.
Lith., Lithuania; Lithuanian.
litho(g)., lithograph; lithography.
Lit. Hum., Lat. *Literae Humaniores*, Final Classical Honour School, Oxford University, usually known as 'greats'.
Litt.D., Lat. *Literarum Doctor*, Doctor of Letters (Literature).
liturg., liturgy; liturgical.
L.J., Lord Justice (of Appeal).
L.L., Lord-Lieutenant.
ll., lines.
L.L.A., Lady Literate in Arts.
LL.B., *Legum Baccalaureus*, Bachelor of Laws.
LL.D., *Legum Doctor*, Doctor of Laws.
LL.JJ., Lords Justices of Appeal.
LL.M., *Legum Magister*, Master of Laws.
L.M., Licentiate in Midwifery; Lord Mayor.
L.M.B.C., Lady Margaret Boat Club (St. John's College, Cambridge).
L.M.S., London Missionary Society.
L.M.S.(R)., London, Midland and Scottish (Railway).
L.M.S.S.A., Licentiate in Medicine and Surgery of the Society of Apothecaries.
L.M.T., length, mass, time (physics).
L.N.E.(R.), London and North-Eastern (Rly.).
L.N.W.R., London and North-Western Railway, now part of L.M.S.(R.).
loc. cit., Lat. *loco citato*, in the place cited.
log., logarithm; logic.
Lond., London.
Londin., also **London.**, London, in signature of Bishop.
long., longitude.
loq., Lat. *loquitur*, (he) speaks.
L.P., Lord Provost; Labour Party.
l.p., large paper (edition); long primer (type); low pressure.
L'pool, Liverpool.
L.P.S., Lord Privy Seal.
L.R.A.M., Licentiate of the Royal Academy of Music.
L.R.C., Leander Rowing Club; London Rowing Club.
L.R.C.P., Licentiate of the Royal College of Physicians; **L.R.C.P.E.**, do. Edinburgh; **L.R.C.P.I.**, do. Ireland.
L.R.C.S., Licentiate of the Royal College of Surgeons; **L.R.C.S.E.**, do. Edinburgh; **L.R.C.S.I.**, do. Ireland.
L.R.C.V.S., Licentiate of the Royal College of Vetinary Surgeons.
L.R.F.P.S.G., Licentiate of the Royal Faculty of Physicians and Surgeons, Glasgow.
Lrs., Lancers.
L.S., Linnean Society; Lat. *loco sigilli*, in the place of the seal (legal documents).
L.S.A., Licentiate of the Society of Apothecaries.
L.S.B., London School Board (obs.).
L.S.D., Lightermen, Stevedores and Dockers.
£.s.d., Lat. *librae, solidi, denarii*, pounds, shillings, pence.
Lt., Lieutenant.
l.t., (electricity) low tension.
£T., pound Turkish.
L.T.A., Lawn Tennis Association; London Teachers' Association.
L.T.C., Lawn Tennis Club.
L.T.C.L., Licentiate of Trinity College of Music (London).
Lt.-Col., Lieutenant-Colonel.
Lt.-Comm., Lieutenant-Commander (R.N.).
Ltd., Limited.
Lt.-Gen., **-Gov.**, Lieutenant-General, -Governor.
Lt. Inf., Light Infantry.
L.T.M., Licentiate of Tropical Medicine.
L.U., Liberal Unionist.
L.V., Licensed Victuallers.
L.W.L., load water line.
LXX, Roman numeral, 70; the Septuagint.

M, Lat. *mille*, 1000, Roman numeral.
M., maiden (over, cricket); Fr. *Monsieur*.
m., mark (coin); married; metre; mile; minute.
M.A., Master of Arts; Military Academy.
M.A.B., Metropolitan Asylums Board.
Macc., Maccabees (O.T., Apoc.).
mach., machinery.

mag., magazine.
mag(n)., magnetism; magneto.
M.Agr(ic)., Master of Agriculture (U.S.A.).
Maj., Major.
Maj.-Gen., Major-General.
Mal., Malachi (O.T.).
Malay., Malayan.
Mancun., Lat. *Mancunium*, Manchester, in signature of Bishop.
Man(it)., Manitoba (Canada).
manuf., manufactured; manufacturer; manufacturing; manufactory.
Mar., March.
mar., married.
March., Marchioness.
Marq., Marquess.
masc., masculine.
Mass., Massachusetts (U.S.A.).
math(s)., mathematics.
matric., matriculation.
Matt., Matthew (N.T.).
M.B., Lat. *Medicinae Baccalaureus*, Bachelor of Medicine.
M.B.E., Member of the British Empire.
M.B.W., Metropolitan Board of Works (obs., now L.C.C.).
M.C., Master of Ceremonies; Member of Congress; Member of Council; Military Cross.
M.C.C., Marylebone Cricket Club.
M.Ch., Lat. *Magister Chirurgiae*, Master of Surgery.
Mch., March.
M.Ch.D., Master of Dental Surgery.
M.Ch.Orth., Master of Orthopaedic Surgery.
M.Com., Master of Commerce (Birmingham).
M.Comm., Master of Commerce and Administration (Manchester).
M.C.P., Member of the College of Preceptors.
M.C.S., Madras Civil Service; Malay Civil Service.
M.D., Lat. *Medicinae Doctor*, Doctor of Medicine.
Md., Maryland (U.S.A.).
Mddx., Middlesex.
Mdlle. See **Mlle.**
Mdme. See **Mme.**
M.D.S., Master in Dental Surgery.
M.Du., Middle Dutch.
Mdx., Middlesex.
M.E., Methodist Episcopal; Middle English; Mining (Mechanical) Engineer.
Me., Maine (U.S.A.).
M^{e}., Fr. *maître*, title applied to barristers, etc.
meas., measure.
M.E.C., Member of Executive Council.
mech(an)., mechanical; mechanics.
Med., Mediaeval.
med., medical; medicine.
Medit., Mediterranean (Sea).
M.E.F., Mediterranean Expeditionary Force (Great War).
mem., Lat. *memento*, remember; memorandum.
memo., Lat. *memorandum*, to be remembered.
M.Eng., Master of Engineering.
M. ès A., Fr. *Maître ès Arts*, Master of Arts.
Messrs., Fr. *Messieurs*, Gentlemen; also as pl. of Mr.
Met., Metropolitan.
metal(l)., metallurgy.
metaph., metaphorical; metaphysical, metaphysics.
meteor., meteorology.
Meth(od)., Methodist.
meton., metonymy.
Met. R., Metropolitan Railway.
mf, Ital. *mezzo forte* (mus.), moderately loud.
M.F.B., Metropolitan Fire Brigade (obs., now L.C.C.).
mfd., manufactured.
mfg., manufacturing.
M.F.H., Master of Fox Hounds.
M.F.N., Most Favoured Nation.
M.Fr., Middle French.
m.g., machine-gun.
mg., milligramme.
M.G.C., Machine-Gun Corps.
M.G.G.S., Major-General, General Staff.
Mgr., Ital. *Monsignor*, of Papal dignitaries.
M.H.A., Member of House of Assembly.
M.H.G., Middle High German.
M.H.K., Member of the House of Keys (Isle of Man).
mho, unit of conductivity, reciprocal of the ohm (elect.).
M.H.R., Member of the House of Representatives.
M.Hy., Master of Hygiene.
M.I., Mounted Infantry.
Mic., Micah (O.T.).
M.I.C.E., Member of the Institution of Civil Engineers.
Mich., Michaelmas; Michigan (U.S.A.).
M.I.E.E., Member of the Institution of Electrical Engineers.
M.I.J., Member of the Institute of Journalists.
mil., military; militia.
Mil. Att., Military Attaché.
M.I.Mar.E., Member of the Institute of Marine Engineers.
M.I.M.E., Member of the Institution of Mechanical Engineers; Member of the Institution of Mining Engineers.
M.I.Mech.E., Member of the Institution of Mechanical Engineers.
M.I.Min.E., Member of the Institution of Mining Engineers.
M.I.M.M., Member of the Institution of Mining and Metallurgy.
Min., Minister; Ministry.
min., mineralogy; mining; minute.
M.I.N.A., Member of the Institution of Naval Architects.
mineral., mineralogy.
Minn., Minnesota (U.S.A.).
Min. Plen., Minister Plenipotentiary.
M.Inst.C.E., Member of the Institution of Civil Engineers.
M.Inst.E.E., Member of the Institution of Electrical Engineers.
M.Inst.Mar.E., Member of the Institute of Marine Engineers.
M.Inst.Mech.E., Member of the Institution of Mechanical Engineers.
M.Inst.Met., Member of the Institute of Metals.
M.Inst.Min.E., Member of the Institution of Mining Engineers.
M.Inst.M.M., Member of the Institution of Mining and Metallurgy.
misc., miscellaneous; miscellany.
Miss., Mississippi (U.S.A.).
M.J.I., Member of the Institute of Journalists; now commonly M.I.J.
M.J.S., Member of the Japan Society.
mk., mark (coin).
mkt., market.
ml., millilitre.
M.L.A., Member of the Legislative Assembly; Modern Language Association.
M.L.C., Member of the Legislative Council.
M.L.G., Middle Low German.
Mlle., Fr. *Mademoiselle.*
M.L.S.B., Member of the London School Board (obs.).
M.M., Master Mason; Military Medal.
MM., Majesties; Fr. *Messieurs.*
mm., millimetre.
Mme., Fr. *Madame.*
Mn, manganese (chem.).
M.O., Medical Officer; Money Order.
Mo, molybdenum (chem.).
Mo., Missouri (U.S.A.).
mo., month.
Mod., Modern.
Mods., Moderations (Oxford University).
M.O.H., Master of Otter Hounds; Medical Officer of Health; Ministry of Health.
mol. wt., molecular weight.
Mon., Monday; Monmouthshire.
Mons., Fr. *Monsieur.*
Mont., Montana (U.S.A.).
M.O.O., Money Order Office.
morph(ol)., morphology.
M.P., Member of Parliament; Metropolitan Police; Military Police.
m.p., melting-point.
mp, Ital. *mezzo piano* (mus.), moderately soft.
M.Ph., Master of Philosophy (U.S.A.).
m.p.h., miles per hour.
M.P.S., Member of the Pharmaceutical Society; do. of the Philological Society; do. of the Physical Society.
M.R., Master of the Rolls; Midland Railway, now part of L.M.S.(R.); Municipal Reform Party, L.C.C.
Mr., Mister.
M.R.A.S., Member of the Royal Academy of Science; Member of the Royal Asiatic Society.
M.R.C.C., Member of the Royal College of Chemistry.
M.R.C.P., Member of the Royal College of Physicians; **M.R.C.P.E.**, do. of Edinburgh; **M.R.C.P.I.**, do. of Ireland.
M.R.C.S., Member of the Royal College of Surgeons; **M.R.C.S.E.**, do. of Edinburgh; **M.R.C.S.I.**, do. of Ireland.
M.R.C.V.S., Member of the Royal College of Veterinary Surgeons.
M.R.G.S., Member of the Royal Geographical Society.
M.R.I., Member of the Royal Institution.
M.R.I.A., Member of the Royal Irish Academy.
Mrs., Mistress.
M.R.S.L., Member of the Royal Society of Literature.
M.R.U.S.I., Member of the Royal United Service Institution.
M.S., Master in Surgery; Military Secretary.
m.s., month's sight.
MS., manuscript.
M.S.A., Master of Science and Art (U.S.A.); Member of the Society of Arts.
M.S.C., Madras Staff Corps; Medical Staff Corps.
M.Sc., Master of Science.
M.S.H., Master of Stag Hounds.
M.S.I., Member of the Sanitary Institute; Member of the Surveyors' Institution.
M.S.L., mean sea-level.
MSS., manuscripts.
M.T., mechanical transport.
Mt., mount(ain).
M'ter, Manchester.
mth., month.
Mt. Rev., Most Reverend.
mus., music; museum.
Mus.B(ac)., Bachelor of Music.
Mus.D(oc)., Doctor of Music.
Mus.M., Master of Music.
M.V., motor vessel.
M.V.O., Member of the Royal Victorian Order.
M.W., Most Worshipful; Most Worthy.
M.W.B., Metropolitan Water Board.
M.W.G.M., Most Worshipful (Worthy) Grand Master (freemasonry).
Mx., Middlesex.
myth(ol)., mythological; mythology.

N, nitrogen (chem.).
N., Nationalist; New; north.
n., neuter; nominative; noon; noun.
N.A., Nautical Almanac; North America(n).
Na, Lat. *natrium*, sodium (chem.).
n/a, no account (on cheques).
Nah., Nahum (O.T.).
N.A.S., National Academy of Science, U.S.A.
Nat., National; Nationalist; Natal.
nat. hist., natural history.
Nat. Ord., Natural Order.
nat. phil., natural philosophy.
nat. sc., natural science.
naut., nautical.
nav., naval; navigating; navigation; navy.
N.B., New Brunswick; North Britain; North British; Lat. *nota bene*, note well.
n.b., no ball (cricket).
Nb, niobium (chem.).
N.B.A., North British Academy.
N.B.R., North British Railway, now part of L.N.E.(R.).
N.C., North Carolina (U.S.A.).
n.c., nitro-cellulose.

N.C.C.V.D., National Council for Combating Venereal Diseases.
N.C.O., non-commissioned officer.
N.C.U., National Cyclists' Union.
n.d., no date, not dated (on cheques &c.).
N. Dak., North Dakota (U.S.A.).
N.D.L., *Norddeutscher Lloyd* (German steamship company).
N.E. New England; no effects (banking, on cheque); north-east; north-eastern (London postal district).
Ne, neon (chem.).
Neb(r)., Nebraska (U.S.A.).
N.E.D., New English Dictionary; see **O.E.D.**
neg., negative.
Neh., Nehemiah (O.T.).
nem. con., Lat. *nemine contradicente*, no one contradicting.
nem. dis., Lat. *nemine dissentiente*, nobody dissenting.
N.E.R., North-Eastern Railway, now part of L.N.E.(R.).
Neth., Netherlands.
neut., neuter; neutral.
Nev., Nevada (U.S.A.).
N.F., Newfoundland; Norman French.
Nfd., **Nfld.**, Newfoundland.
N.H., New Hampshire (U.S.A.).
N. Heb., New Hebrides.
n.h.p., nominal horse-power.
N.H.R.U., National Home Reading Union.
N.H.R(ules), National Hunt Rules.
N.I., Native Infantry; Northern Ireland.
Ni, nickel (chem.).
N.I.D., Naval Intelligence Department.
ni. pr., Lat. *nisi prius* (law).
N.J., New Jersey (U.S.A.).
N.L., National Liberal; Navy League.
N.L.C., National Liberal Club.
N.L.F., National Liberal Federation.
N.L.I., National Lifeboat Institution.
n.m., nautical mile(s).
N. Mex., New Mexico (U.S.A.).
N.N.E., north-north-east.
N.N.W., north-north-west.
N.O., Natural Order (bot. and zool.); New Orleans (U.S.A.).
n.o., not out (cricket).
No., *numero*, number.
N.O.D., Naval Ordnance Department.
nol. pros., Lat. *nolle prosequi* (law).
nom(in)., nominative; nominal.
Non-Coll., Non-Collegiate.
non. com., non-commissioned (officer).
Noncon., Nonconformist.
non obst., Lat. *non obstante*, notwithstanding.
non pros., Lat. *non prosequitur*, he does not prosecute.
non seq., Lat. *non sequitur*, it does not follow.
n.o.p., not otherwise provided.
Norm., Norman.
Northants, Northamptonshire.
Northumb., Northumberland.
Norvic., Norwich, in signature of Bishop.
Norw., Norway; Norwegian.
Nos., numbers.
Notts, Nottinghamshire.
Nov., November.
N.P., Notary Public.
n.p., new paragraph.
N.P.D., North Polar distance.
N.P.L., National Physical Laboratory.
N.R., North Riding (Yorkshire).
nr., near.
N.R.A., National Rifle Association.
N.S., New Style, of Gregorian Calendar; Nova Scotia; Lat. *non satis*, not sufficient (funds) on cheques, do. (in excellence) on examination papers &c.
N.S.A., National Skating Association.
N.S.I.C., *Noster Salvator Jesus Christus* (Our Saviour Jesus Christ).
N.S.L., National Service League; National Sunday League.
N.S.P.C.C., National Society for Prevention of Cruelty to Children.
N.S.Trip., Natural Science Tripos (Cambridge University).
N.S.W., New South Wales (Australia).
N.T., New Testament; Northern Territory (Australia).
Nthn., northern.
N.U., Northern Union (Rugby football).
n.u., name unknown.
N.U.J., National Union of Journalists.
Num., Numbers (O.T.).
num., numerals; number.
numis., numismatics.
N.U.R., National Union of Railwaymen.
N.U.S.E.C., National Union of Societies for Equal Citizenship.
N.U.T., National Union of Teachers.
N.U.W.S.S., National Union of Women's Suffrage Societies.
N.U.W.T., National Union of Women Teachers.
N.V., New Version.
N.V.M., Nativity of the Virgin Mary.
N.W., north-west; north-western (London postal district).
N.W.M.P., North-West Mounted Police (Canada), now R.C.M.P.
N.W.P(rov)., North-West Provinces (India).
N.W.T., North-Western Territories (Canada).
N.Y., New York (state, U.S.A.).
N.Y.C., New York City (U.S.A.).
N.Y.K., Jap. *Nippon Yusen Kaisha*, Japan Mail Steamship Company.
N.Z., New Zealand.

O, oxygen (chem.).
O., Ohio (U.S.A.); Old.
o., over(s) (cricket).
o/a, on account of.
O.B., outside broadcast.
ob., Lat. *obiit*, (he) died.
Obad., Obadiah (O.T.).
obb., obbligato (mus.).
obdt., obedient.
O.B.E., Officer of the British Empire.
obj., object; objection; objective.
obs., observation; obsolete.
obsol(esc)., obsolescent.
ob.s.p., Lat. *obiit sine prole*, died without issue.
obstet., obstetrics.
O.C., Officer Commanding; Old Catholic.
o'c., o'clock.
Oct., October.
oct., octavo.
O.D., Old Dutch; Ordnance Data.
O. Dan., Old Danish.
O.E., Old English; Old Etonian.
O.E.D., Oxford English Dictionary.
O.F., Odd Fellows; Old French.
off., offered; office; official; officinal.
offg., officiating.
offic., official.
O.F.M., Order of Friars Minor.
O. Fr., Old French.
O. Fris., Old Frisian.
O.F.S., Orange Free State.
O.H.B.M.S., On His (Her) Britannic Majesty's Service.
O.H.G., Old High German.
O.H.L., Oxford Higher Local (examinations).
O.H.M.S., On His (Her) Majesty's Service.
O. Ir., Old Irish.
O.K., All Correct (orl k'rect).
Okla., Oklahoma (U.S.A.).
O.L., Officer of the Order of Leopold, Belgium.
Ol., Olympiad.
O.L.G., Old Low German.
Olym., Olympiad.
O.M., Order of Merit.
O.M.I., Oblate of Mary Immaculate.
O.N., Old Norse.
onomat., onomatopoeia.
Ont., Ontario.
O.P., Old Playgoers (club); Old Prices (theatr. hist.); opposite prompt (side, in theatre); Order of Preachers; out of print (of books).
o.p., over proof (spirits).
op., Lat., *opus*, a work.
op. cit., Lat. *opere citato*, in the work cited.
o. pip., (signallers' slang) observation post.
o.p.n., Lat. *ora pro nobis*, pray for us.
opp., opposes; opposite.
opt., Lat. *optimus*, best, *optime* (adv.); optative; optics; optical; optional.
O.R., Official Receiver; Official Referee.
Or., Orient(al).
orat., oratorical; oratory.
O.R.C., Orange River Colony (now O.F.S.); Order of the Red Cross.
ord., ordained; order; ordinary; ordnance
Ore(g)., Oregon (U.S.A.).
orig., original(ly).
ornith., ornithology.
ors., others.
Os, osmium (chem.).
O.S., Old Saxon; Old Style (Julian Calendar); Order of Servites; ordinary seaman; Ordnance Survey.
o.s., only son.
O.S.A., Order of St. Augustine.
O.S.B., Order of St. Benedict.
O.S.D., Order of St. Dominic.
O.S.F., Order of St. Francis.
O. Slav., Old Slavonic.
O.S.N.C., Orient Steam Navigation Company.
o.s.p., Lat. *obiit sine prole*, died without issue.
O. Swed., Old Swedish.
O.T., Old Testament.
O.T.C., Officers' Training Corps.
O.U.A.C., Oxford University Athletic Club.
O.U.A.F.C., Oxford University Association Football Club.
O.U.B.C., Oxford University Boat Club.
O.U.C.C., Oxford University Cricket Club.
O.U.D.S., Oxford University Dramatic Society.
O.U.G.C., Oxford University Golf Club.
O.U.H.C., Oxford University Hockey Club.
O.U.R.F.C., Oxford University Rugby Football Club.
Oxon., Oxfordshire; Oxford University; Oxford, in signature of Bishop.
oz., ounce(s).

P, phosphorus (chem.).
P., Pawn (chess); Progressive (party, L.C.C.); President.
p., page; participle; past; perch; pint; population.
p, Ital. *piano*, soft (mus.).
Pa., Pennsylvania (U.S.A.).
P.A., Press Association.
p.a., per annum.
paint., painting.
Pal., Palestine.
pal., palaeography; palaeontology.
palaeog., palaeography.
palaeont., palaeontology.
P. & O., Peninsular and Oriental (steamship line).
par., paragraph; parallel; parenthesis; parish.
parl., parliament; parliamentary.
pars., paragraphs.
part. participle; particular.
P.A.S., Principal Assistant Secretary.
pass., passive.
P.A.T.A., Proprietary Articles Trade Association.
path(ol)., pathology.
Pat. Off., Patent Office.
Paym., Paymaster.
Paym.-Gen., Paymaster-General.
payt., payment.
P.B., Lat. *Pharmacopoeia Britannica*, British Pharmacopoeia; Plymouth Brother, Brethren; Prayer Book; Primitive Baptist(s).
Pb, Lat. *plumbum*, lead (chem.).
P.C., Privy Council(lor); Police Constable; Perpetual Curate.
p.c., Lat. *per centum*, by the hundred; post card.
P.C.R.C., Poor Clergy Relief Corporation.
P.C.S., Principal Clerk of Session.
P.D., potential difference.
Pd, palladium (chem.).
pd., paid.
P.D.A.D., Probate, Divorce, and Admiralty Division.

pdr., pounder (of gun, fish &c.).
P.E., Protestant Episcopal; Presiding Elder.
ped., pedal (mus.): pedestrian.
P.E.F., Palestine Exploration Fund.
P.E.I., Prince Edward Island.
pen(in)., peninsula.
Penn., Pennsylvania (U.S.A.).
Pent., Pentateuch.
per an., Lat. *per annum*, per year, yearly.
per cent, Lat. *per centum*, per hundred.
perf., perfect; perforated (stamps).
perh., perhaps.
per pro(c)., Lat. *per procurationem*, by proxy, as agent &c.
Pers., Persia; Persian.
pers., person.
Peruv., Peruvian.
Pet., Peter (N.T.).
Petriburg., Peterborough, in signature of Bishop.
petrol., petrology.
P.F., Procurator Fiscal.
pf, Ital. *piano-forte*, soft, then loud (mus.).
pfd., preferred.
P.G., paying guest.
P.G.A., Professional Golfers' Association.
P.G.D., Past Grand Deacon (freemasonry).
P.G.M., Past Grand Master (freemasonry).
phar(m)., pharmaceutical; pharmacist; pharmacology; pharmacy.
Ph.B., Bachelor of Philosophy.
Ph.D., Doctor of Philosophy.
Phil., Philippians (N.T.).
phil., philosophy; philology.
Philem., Philemon (N.T.).
philol., philology.
phil(os)., philosophy; philosophical.
phon(et)., phonetics.
phonog., phonography.
phot(og)., photography.
Phr., phrase.
phren., phrenology.
phys., physics; physical; physician; physicist; physiology.
physiol., physiology.
pinx., Lat. *pinxit*, he (she) painted (it).
pk., peck.
P.L., Primrose League; Poet Laureate; Lat. *Pharmacopoeia Londinensis*, London Pharmacopoeia.
pl., place; plural; plate.
P.L.A., Port of London Authority.
P.L.C., Poor Law Commissioners.
Plen., Plenipotentiary.
P.-L.-M., Paris-Lyon-Mediterranée (railway).
Pl.-N., Place-Name.
plup(f)., pluperfect.
P.M., Past Master (freemasonry); Prime Minister; Police Magistrate; Postmaster; Provost Marshal.
p.m., Lat. *post meridiem*, after noon; Lat. *post mortem*, autopsy (colloq.).
pm., premium.
P.M.G., Postmaster-General; Paymaster-General.
P.M.O., Principal Medical Officer.
p.n., promissory note.
pnxt., Lat. *pinxit*, he (she) painted (it).
P.O., Petty Officer (nav.); Postal Order; Post Office.
p.o.d., pay on delivery.
poet., poetry; poetical.
Pol., Poland; Polish.
pol., political.
pol. econ., political economy.
polit., political; politics.
P.O.O., Post Office Order.
P.O.P., (photog.) printing out paper.
pop., popular; population.
Port., Portugal; Portuguese.
pos., position; positive.
P.O S.B., Post Office Savings Bank.
posit., position; positive.
poss(ess)., possessive.
P.P., Parish Priest (R.C.); past participle; Lat. *Pastor Pastorum*, Shepherd of the Shepherds, as title of the Pope; Past President; Lat. *Pater patriae*, father of his country.
p.p., per pro(c).
pp., pages.
pp, Ital. *pianissimo*, very soft (mus.).
P.P.C., Fr., *pour prendre congé*, to take leave.
p.p.i., policy proof of interest (insurance).
ppp, Ital. *pianississimo*, as softly as possible (mus.).
P.P.S., additional postscript.
P.R., Prize Ring (obs.); Lat. *Populus Romanus*, the Roman people; Proportional Representation.
Pr., Priest; Primitive; Prince; Provençal.
pr., pair; per; present; price; printer; pronoun.
P.R.A., President of the Royal Academy.
P.R.B., Pre-Raphaelite Brotherhood.
P.R.C., Lat. *post Romam conditam*, after the foundation of Rome.
P.R.C.A., President of the Royal Cambrian Academy.
Preb., Prebendary; prebend.
prec., preceding.
pred., predicate, predicatively.
Pref., Preface; Preference; preferred (stock and shares).
pref., prefix.
prelim., preliminary (examination).
prem., premium.
prep., preparation; preparatory (school &c.); preposition.
Pres., President.
pres., present; presumptive.
Presb., Presbyter; Presbyterian.
Pres. Part., present participle.
pret., preterite.
prev., previously.
Pri., Private (mil.).
Prim., Primary; Primate; Primitive.
Prin., Principal.
print., printer; printing.
priv., private; privative.
prem., premium.
P.R.H.A., President of the Royal Hibernian Academy.
pro., professional (cricketer, footballer &c.).
Prob., Probate (Division and Law Reports).
prob., probably.
Proc., Proceedings; Proctor.
Prof., Professor.
Prom., promenade (concert); promontory.
pron., pronominal; pronoun; pronounced; pronunciation.
prop., properly; property; proprietary; proposition.
propr., proprietary; proprietor.
pros., prosody.
Prot., Protestant.
pro tem., Lat. *pro tempore*, for the time being.
Prov., Provençal; Proverbs (O.T.); Province; Provost.
Provenç., Provençal.
Prov. G.M., Provincial Grand Master (freemasonry).
provinc., provincial.
prox., Lat. *proximo*, next month.
prox. acc., Lat. *proxime accessit*, he came next, as in examination for prize &c.
P.R.S., President of the Royal Society.
prs., pairs.
P.R.S.A., President of the Royal Scottish Academy.
P.R.S.E., President of the Royal Society of Edinburgh.
Prus(s)., Prussia; Prussian.
P.S., Permanent Secretary; Police Sergeant; Lat. *post scriptum*, postscript; Privy Seal; prompt side (in theatre).
p.s., (mil.) passed School (of Instruction).
Ps., Psalms (O.T.).
P.S.A., Pleasant Sunday Afternoons (movement).
p.s.a., Graduate of the Royal Air Force Staff College.
p.s.c., Graduate of the Military (or Naval) Staff College.
pseud., pseudonym, pseudonymous.
P.S.N.C., Pacific Steam Navigation Co.
psych., psychic, psychical.
psychol., psychological, psychology.
P.T., Physical Training; Pupil Teacher; post town.
Pt, platinum (chem.).
pt., part; payment; pint(s).
Pte., Private.
P.T.O., please turn over.
pub., publisher; published; publication; public; public house.
P.U.C., Lat. *post urbem conditam*, after the foundation of the city (Rome).
punct., punctuation.
P.V., Priest Vicar.
P.W.D., Public Works Department.
pwt., (usually dwt.) pennyweight.
pxt., Lat. *pinxit*, he (she) painted (it).

Q., queen; question; coulomb (elect.).
q., quasi; query; quintal.
Q.A.B., Queen Anne's Bounty.
Q.B., Queen's Bench; Queen's Bays (2nd Dragoon Guards).
Q.B.D., Queen's Bench Division (law reports).
Q.C., Queen's Counsel.
q.d., Lat. *quasi dicat*, as if one should say; Lat. *quasi dictum*, as if said.
q.e., Lat. *quod est*, which is.
Q.E.D., Lat. *quod erat demonstrandum*, which was to be proved (applied to a geometrical or other theorem).
Q.E.F., Lat. *quod erat faciendum*, which was to be done (applied to a geometrical or other problem).
Q.E.I., Lat. *quod erat inveniendum*, which was to be found.
Q.F., quick-firing (gun).
Q.M., Quartermaster.
qm., Lat. *quomodo*, by what means.
Q.M.A.A.C., Queen Mary's Army Auxiliary Corps (**W.A.A.C.**).
Q.M.G., Quartermaster-General.
Qmr., Quartermaster.
Q.M.S., Quartermaster-Sergeant.
qn., question.
qq.v., Lat. *quae vide*, which (things) see.
qr(s)., quarter(s); quire(s).
Q.S., Quarter Sessions.
Q.T., (slang) on the quiet, in Phr. *on the strict Q.T.*, privately, in secret.
qt., quantity; quart(s).
qto., quarto.
qu., Lat. *quasi*, as if; *quaere*, query.
quad., quadrangle; quadrant; quadrat; quadruple.
quart., quarterly.
Q.U.B., Queen's University, Belfast.
Que., Quebec.
Queensl., Queensland.
quor., quorum.
quot., quotation; quoted.
q.v., Lat. *quod vide*, which see (in references); Lat. *quantum vis*, as much as you wish.
qy., query.

R., Railway; Réaumur (therm.); Republican; Lat. *rex*, king, *regina*, queen, in criminal action at law; right; river; rook or castle (chess); ohm, unit of electrical resistance.
r., right; rod; rood; run(s) (cricket); rupee.
℞, Lat. *recipe* (in medical prescriptions).
R, rupee(s).
R.A., Royal Academician; Royal Academy; Rear-Admiral; Road Association; Royal Arch (freemasonry); Royal Artillery.
Ra, radium (chem.).
R.A.A., Royal Academy of Arts.
R.A.C., Royal Agricultural College; Royal Automobile Club; Royal Arch Chapter (freemasonry).
rad., Lat. *radix*, root (math.); radical.
R.-Adm., Rear-Admiral.
R.A.E., Royal Air Force Establishment.
R.Ae.S., Royal Aeronautical Society.
R.A.F., Royal Air Force; Royal Aircraft Factory.
R.A.G.C., Royal and Ancient Golf Club, St. Andrews.

rall., Ital. *rallentando*, gradually slower (mus.).
R.A.M., Royal Academy of Music.
R.A.M.C., Royal Army Medical Corps.
R.A.N., Royal Australian Navy.
R.A.O.B., Royal Antediluvian Order of Buffaloes.
R.A.O.C., Royal Army Ordnance Corps.
R.A.P.C., Royal Army Pay Corps.
R.A.S., Royal Agricultural Society; Royal Asiatic Society; Royal Astronomical Society.
R.A.S.C., Royal Army Service Corps.
R.A.V.C., Royal Army Veterinary Corps.
R.B., Rifle Brigade.
Rb, rubidium (chem.).
R.B.A., Royal Society of British Artists.
R.B.S., Royal Society of British Sculptors.
R.C., Red Cross; Roman Catholic; right centre (of stage).
R.C.A., Royal Cambrian Academy, Academician; Royal Canadian Academy; Royal College of Art; Railway Clerks' Association.
R.C.I., Royal Colonial Institute (now R.E.S.).
R.C.M., Royal College of Music (London).
R.C.M.P., Royal Canadian Mounted Police, formerly N.W.M.P.
R.C.N., Royal Canadian Navy.
R.C.O., Royal College of Organists.
R.C.P., Royal College of Physicians.
R.C.S., Royal College of Surgeons; Royal Corps of Signals.
R.C.V.S., Royal College of Veterinary Surgeons.
R.D., Refer to drawer (on cheques); Royal Dragoons; Royal Naval Reserve (and Volunteer Reserve) Decoration; Rural Dean.
Rd., Road.
R.D.C., Royal Defence Corps; Rural District Council.
R.D.S., Royal Drawing Society; Royal Dublin Society.
R.D.Y., Royal Dockyard.
R.E., Royal Engineers; Royal Society of Painter-Etchers and Engravers; Royal Exchange.
Rear-Adm., Rear-Admiral.
Rec., Recorder.
rec., recipe.
recd., received.
recit., recitative (mus.).
recogns., recognizances (law).
rect., rectified.
red., reduced.
redupl., reduplicated.
Ref., Referee; Reformation.
ref., referred; reference; reformed.
Ref. Ch., Reformed Church.
refd., referred.
refl(ex)., reflexive.
Reg., Lat. *regina*, queen; Registrar; Register.
reg., registered; regular(ly).
regd., registered.
Reg.-Gen., Registrar-General.
Reg. Prof., Regius Professor.
Regt., Regent; regiment.
rel., religion; religious; relative.
relig., religion.
Reliq., Lat. *reliquiae*, remains.
Rep., Representative; Republic; Report; Reporter.
repr., reprinted.
Repub., Republic; Republican.
R.E.S., Royal Empire Society (formerly R.C.I.).
res., reserve; resigned; resident; residence.
ret(d)., retired; returned; retained.
R. et I., Lat. *Rex* (*Regina*) *et Imperator* (*Imperatrix*), King (Queen) and Emperor (Empress), in British Royal signature.
retnr., retainer (law).
Rev., Reverend; Revelation (N.T.); Review.
rev., revolution (mechan.); reverse(d); revised; revision; revenue.
Rev. Ver., Revised Version (Bible).
R.F., Fr. *République française*, French Republic; Royal Fusiliers.
R.F.A., Royal Field Artillery.
R.F.C., Royal Flying Corps (now R.A.F.).
R.Fus., Royal Fusiliers.
R.G.A., Royal Garrison Artillery.
R.G.G., Royal Grenadier Guards.
R.G.S., Royal Geographical Society.
Rgt., regiment.
R.H., Royal Highlanders; Royal Highness.
Rh, rhodium (chem.).
r.h., right hand.
R.H.A., Royal Horse Artillery; Royal Hibernian Academy, Academician.
rhet., rhetoric; rhetorical.
R.H.G., Royal Horse Guards.
R.Hist.S., Royal Historical Society.
R.H.S., Royal Humane Society; Royal Horticultural Society; Royal Historical Society.
R.I., Rhode Island (U.S.A.); Royal Institute (of Painters in Water Colours); Royal Institution.
R.I.A., Royal Irish Academy.
R.I.B.A., Royal Institute of British Architects.
R.I.C., Royal Irish Constabulary.
R.I.M., Royal Indian Marine.
R.I.P., Lat. *requiescat in pace*, may he (she) rest in peace.
rit(ard)., Ital. *ritardando*, gradually slower (mus.).
R.L.O., Returned Letter Office.
R.L.S., Robert Louis Stevenson.
Rly., Railway.
R.M., Royal Marines; Resident Magistrate (Ireland); Royal Mail.
rm., ream.
R.M.A., Royal Military Academy (Woolwich); Royal Marine Artillery; Royal Military Asylum.
R.M.C., Royal Military College (Sandhurst).
R.Met.S., Royal Meteorological Society.
R.M.L.I., Royal Marine Light Infantry.
R.M.S., Royal Mail Service; Royal Mail Steamer; Royal Microscopical Society; Royal Society of Miniature Painters.
R.M.S.P., Royal Mail Steam Packet (Co.).
R.N., Royal Navy.
R.N.A.F., Royal Naval Air Force (now R.A.F.).
R.N.A.S., Royal Naval Air Service (now R.A.F.).
R.N.A.V., Royal Naval Artillery Volunteers.
R.N.D., Royal Naval Division.
R.N.L.I., Royal National Lifeboat Institution.
R.N.R., Royal Naval Reserve.
R.N.V.R., Royal Naval Volunteer Reserve.
R.O., Receiving Office, Order; Receiving Officer; Relieving Officer; Recruiting Officer; Returning Officer.
Ro., Lat. *recto*, on the right-hand page.
Robt., Robert.
Roffen., Rochester, in signature of Bishop.
R. of O., Reserve of Officers.
R.O.I., Royal Institute of Oil Painters.
Rom., Romans (N.T.); Rome; Roman; Romance (lang.).
rom., roman type.
Rom. Cath., Roman Catholic.
Roy., Royal.
R.P., Royal Society of Portrait Painters.
R.P.D., Regius Professor of Divinity; Lat. *Rerum Politicarum Doctor*, Doctor of Political Science.
r.p.m., revolutions per minute.
R.P.S., Royal Photographic Society.
rpt., report.
R.R., Right Reverend.
Rr., Rear.
R.R.C., (Lady of) the Royal Red Cross.
R.S., Royal Society.
Rs., rupees.
R.S.A., Royal Scottish Academy, Academician; Royal Society of Antiquaries.
R.S.D., Royal Society of Dublin.
R.S.E., Royal Society of Edinburgh.
R.S.F.S.R., Russian Socialist Federal Soviet Republic (Russia proper).
R.S.Fus., Royal Scots Fusiliers.
R.S.L., Royal Society of Literature; Royal Society of London.
R.S.M., Regimental Sergeant-Major; Royal School of Mines; Royal Society of Medicine.
R.S.O., Railway Sub-Office; Railway Sorting Office.
R.S.P.C.A., Royal Society for the Prevention of Cruelty to Animals.
R.S.S., Lat. *Regiae Societatis Socius*, Fellow of the Royal Society
R.S.V.P., Fr. *répondez s'il vous plaît*, please reply.
R.S.W., Royal Scottish Society of Painters in Water Colours.
R/T, radio-telegraphy.
R.T.C., Royal Tank Corps.
Rt. Hon., Right Honourable.
R.T.O., Railway Transport Officer.
Rt. Rev., Right Reverend.
R.T.S., Religious Tract Society; Royal Toxophilite Society.
R.U., Rugby Union (football).
Ru, ruthenium (chem.).
R.U.I., Royal University of Ireland.
R.U.Rif., Royal Ulster Rifles.
R.U.S.I., Royal United Service Institution.
R.U.S.Mus., Royal United Service Museum.
Russ., Russia; Russian.
R.V., Revised Version; Rifle Volunteers.
R.V.C., Rifle Volunteer Corps.
R.V.O., Royal Victorian Order.
R.W., Right Worshipful, Worthy.
R.W.A., Royal West of England Academy.
R.W.D.G.M., Right Worshipful Deputy Grand Master (freemasonry).
R.W.G.M., Right Worshipful Grand Master.
R.W.G.S., Right Worthy Grand Secretary.
R.W.G.T., Right Worthy Grand Templar; Right Worthy Grand Treasurer.
R.W.G.W., Right Worthy Grand Warden.
R.W.S., Royal Society of Painters in Water Colours.
R.W.S.G.W., Right Worshipful Senior Grand Warden.
Rx, tens of rupees.
Ry., Railway.
R.Y.S., Royal Yacht Squadron.

S, sulphur (chem.).
S., Saint; Signor; Señor; Socialist; soprano; south.
s., second; shilling; singular; son; substantive.
S.A., Salvation Army; South Africa; South America; South Australia.
s.a., Lat. *sine anno*, without date.
S.A.C., Scottish Automobile Club.
S.A.E., Society of Automobile Engineers.
Salop, Shropshire.
Sam., Samuel (O.T.).
S. and M., Sodor and Man, in signature of Bishop.
Sarum., Salisbury, in signature of Bishop.
S.A.S., Lat. *Societatis Antiquariorum Socius*, Fellow of the Society of Antiquaries.
Sask., Saskatchewan.
Sat., Saturday.
S.A.T.B., soprano, alto, tenor, bass.
S.B., simultaneous broadcast.
Sb, Lat. *stibium*, antimony (chem.).
S.C., Lat. *senatus consultum*, decree of the senate; South Carolina (U.S.A.).
s.c., small capital letters.
Sc, scandium (chem.).
sc., scene (play); scruple (weight).
sc., Lat. *scilicet*, namely, being understood; Lat. *sculpsit*, he (she) engraved (it).
Scand., Scandinavian.
S.C.A.P.A. (Scapa), Society for Checking the Abuses of Public Advertising.
s.caps., small capital letters.
Sc.B., Lat. *Scientiae Baccalaureus*, Bachelor of Science.
Sc.D., Lat. *Scientiae Doctor*, Doctor of Science.
sch., scholar; school; schooner.
sched., schedule.
sci., science; scientific.
sci. fa., Lat. *scire facias*, do you cause to know (law).
scil., Lat. *scilicet*, namely, being understood.
S.C.L., Student of Civil Law.
S.C.M., Student Christian Movement.
Scot., Scotland; Scottish.

scr., scruple (weight).
Script., Scripture.
Scrt., Sanscrit.
sculp., sculptor ; sculpture.
sculps., Lat. *sculpsit*, he (she) engraved (it).
sculpt., sculptor ; sculpture.
S.D., Senior Deacon (freemasonry).
s.d., several dates.
s.d., Lat. *sine die*, without day (appointed), indefinitely.
sd., said.
S. Dak., South Dakota (U.S.A.).
S.D.F., Social Democratic Federation.
S.D.P., Social Democratic Party.
S.E., south-east ; south-eastern (London postal district).
Se, selenium (chem.).
S.E. & C.R., South-Eastern and Chatham Railway, now part of S.R.
Sec., Secretary.
sec., second.
Sec. Leg., Secretary of Legation.
S.E.C.R., South-Eastern and Chatham Railway, now part of S.R.
sect., section.
secy., secretary.
sel., selected ; selection.
Sem., Seminary ; Semitic.
Sen., Senator ; Senate ; Senior.
Sen. Opt., Senior Optime.
senr., senior.
Sep(t)., September ; Septuagint, usually LXX.
seq., seqq., Lat. *sequens, sequentia*, the following.
S.E.R., South-Eastern Railway, now part of S.R.
ser., series.
Serb., Serbia ; Serbian.
Serg(t)., Sergeant.
Serj(t)., Serjeant.
servt., servant.
S.F., Sinn Fein.
s.f., Lat. *sub finem*, towards the end.
sf, Ital. *sforzando*, with sudden emphasis (mus.).
S.F.A., Scottish Football Association.
sfz, Ital. *sforzando*, with sudden emphasis (music).
S.G., Solicitor-General ; specific gravity.
S.G.W., Senior Grand Warden (freemasonry).
S.H., School House.
sh., shilling.
shd., should.
s.h.p., shaft horse-power.
s.h.v., Lat. *sub hac voce*, or *hoc verbo*, under this word.
Si, silicon (chem.).
S.I.C., specific inductive capacity.
sig., signature.
S.I.M., Sergeant Instructor of Musketry.
sim., similar(ly) ; simile.
sin, sine (trigonometry).
sing., singular ; single.
S.J., Society of Jesus (Jesuits).
S.J.C., Supreme Judicial Court (U.S.A.).
Skr(t)., Sanskrit.
S.L., Serjeant-at-Law.
Slav., Slavonic ; Slavic.
s.l.p., Lat. *sine legitima prole*, without legitimate offspring.
S.M., Sergeant-Major ; short metre ; silver medallist (Bisley).
S.M.Lond.Soc., Lat. *Societatis Medicae Londoniensis Socius*, Member of the London Medical Society.
S.M.M., Lat. *Sancta Mater Maria*, Holy Mother Mary.
S.M.O., Senior Medical Officer.
s.m.p., Lat. *sine mascula prole*, without male issue.
S.M.T.O., Senior Mechanical Transport Officer.
Sn, Lat. *stannum*, tin (chem.).
S.O., Staff Officer ; Sub-Office ; Stationery Office.
s.o., seller's option.
Soc., Society ; Socialist.
sociol., sociology ; sociological.
sol., solicitor ; solution.
Sol.-Gen., Solicitor-General.
Som., Somerset.
Song of Sol., Song of Solomon (O.T.).
sop., soprano.
SOS, wireless code signal for ships &c. in extreme distress.
sost(en)., Ital. *sostenuto*, sustained (mus.).
sov., sovereign.
S.P., small paper (edition) ; small pica (typography) ; starting price (betting).
s.p., Lat. *sine prole*, without issue.
Sp., Spain ; Spanish.
Span., Spanish.
S.P.C.A., Society for the Prevention of Cruelty to Animals, now R.S.P.C.A.
S.P.C.C., Society for the Prevention of Cruelty to Children, now N.S.P.C.C.
S.P.C.K., Society for the Promotion of Christian Knowledge.
S.P.E., Society for Pure English.
spec., special ; specification.
specif., specific(ally).
S.P.G., Society for the Propagation of the Gospel.
sp. gr., specific gravity.
spirit., spiritualism.
S.P.Q.R., Lat. *Senatus Populusque Romanus*, the Senate and People of Rome ; small profits and quick returns.
S.P.R., Society for Psychical Research.
s.p.s., Lat. *sine prole superstite*, without surviving issue.
S.P.S.P., St. Peter and St. Paul (papal seal).
spt., seaport.
S.P.V.D., Society for the Prevention of Venereal Diseases.
sq., square.
sq., Lat. *sequens*, the following.
Sqd. Ldr., Squadron Leader (R.A.F.).
sqn., squadron.
sqq., Lat. *sequentia*, the following.
S.R., Southern Railway.
Sr, strontium (chem.).
Sr., Senior ; Señor.
S.R.I., Lat. *Sacrum Romanum Imperium*, Holy Roman Empire.
S.R.S., Lat. *Societatis Regiae Socius*, Fellow of the Royal Society.
S.S., screw steamer ; Secretary of State ; steamship ; Straits Settlements ; Sunday School.
SS., Saints ; (Collar of) Esses ; Lat. *Sanctissimus*, Most Holy.
S.S.C., Solicitor of the Supreme Court, Scotland ; Lat. *Societas Sanctae Crucis*. Society of the Holy Cross.
SS.D., Lat. *Sanctissimus Dominus*, Most Holy Lord (the Pope).
S.S.E., south-south-east.
S.S.F.A., Soldiers' and Sailors' Families Association.
S.S.J.E., Society of St. John the Evangelist.
S.S.U., Sunday School Union.
S.S.W., south-south-west.
St., Saint ; Street ; Strait.
st., stone (weight) ; stumped (cricket) ; stanza stet.
stacc., staccato (mus.).
Staffs., Staffordshire.
stat., statics ; stationary ; statistics ; statute.
S.T.B., Lat. *Sacrae Theologiae Baccalaureus*, Bachelor of Sacred Theology.
S.T.D., Lat. *Sacrae Theologiae Doctor*, Doctor of Theology.
Ste., Fr. *Sainte*, feminine of Saint.
stereo, stereotype.
ster(l)., sterling.
St. Ex., Stock Exchange.
stg., sterling.
Sthn., southern.
Stip., Stipendiary (magistrate).
S.T.L., Lat. *Sacrae Theologiae Lector*, Reader in Sacred Theology.
S.T.M., Lat. *Sacrae Theologiae Magister*, Master of Sacred Theology.
stn., station.
S'ton, Southampton.
S.T.P., Lat. *Sacrae Theologiae Professor*, Professor of Sacred Theology.
str., steamer ; stroke oar.
S.T.S., Scottish Text Society.
sub., subaltern ; subject ; submarine boat ; subscription ; substitute ; suburb.
subj., subject ; subjective ; subjectively ; subjunctive.
subst., substantive ; substitute.
suc(c)., succeeded ; successor.
suff., sufficient ; suffix.
Suff(r)., Suffragan.
sug(g)., suggested ; suggestion.
Sun., Sunday.
sup., superior ; supreme ; supplement.
sup., Lat. *supra*, above.
super., superintendent ; supernumerary.
superl., superlative.
supp(l)., supplement ; supplementary.
supr., supreme.
supt., superintendent.
surg., surgeon ; surgery ; surgical.
Surg.-Gen., Surgeon-General.
Surr., Surrogate.
surv., surveying ; surveyor ; surviving.
Surv.-Gen., Surveyor-General.
sus. per. col(l)., Lat. *suspensio per collum*, hanging by the neck (as capital punishment).
S.V., Lat. *Sancta Virgo*, Holy Virgin ; Lat. *Sanctitas Vestra*, Your Holiness.
s.v., Lat. *sub voce*, under the word, heading &c.
S.W., Senior Warden (freemasonry) ; south-west ; south-western (London postal district).
Sw., Swed., Sweden ; Swedish.
S.W.G., standard wire gauge.
Swit., Switzerland.
S.Y., steam yacht.
syll., syllable.
sym., symbol ; symphony.
syn., synonym ; synonymous.
syst., system.

T., tenor ; Turkish, in £T.
t., taken (betting) ; tempo (mus.) ; ton.
t., Lat. *tempore*, in the time of.
T.A., telegraphic address ; Territorial Army.
Ta, tantalum (chem.).
tal. qual., Lat. *talis qualis*, just as they come.
tan., tangent (math.).
t. and o., taken and offered (betting).
tar-mac., tar-macadam.
Tasm., Tasmania.
Tb, terbium (chem.).
T.B., torpedo boat ; tuberculosis.
T.B.D., torpedo boat destroyer.
T.C., Tank Corps ; temporary constable ; Town Councillor.
T.C.D., Trinity College, Dublin.
T.C.F., Touring Club de France.
T.D., Telegraph, Telephone, Department ; Territorial Officers' Decoration.
Te, tellurium (chem.).
tech(n)., technical(ly) ; technology.
technol., technology.
t.e.g., top edges gilt.
tel., telegram ; telegraph ; telephone.
teleg., telegram ; telegraph ; telegraphy.
teleph., telephone ; telephony.
telg., telegram.
temp., temperature ; temporary.
temp., Lat. *tempore*, in the time of.
ten., tenor.
ten., Ital. *tenuto* (mus.), held, sustained.
Tenn., Tennessee (U.S.A.).
term., termination ; terminology.
Ter(r)., Terrace ; Territory.
Test., Testament ; testamentary ; testator.
Teut., Teutonic.
Tex., Texas (U.S.A.).
text. rec., Lat. *textus receptus*, the received, accepted text.
T.F., Territorial Force.
Th, thorium (chem.).
Th., Thomas.
theat(r)., theatre ; theatrical.
theol., theological ; theology.
theor., theorem.
theos., theosophy.
therap., therapeutics.
therm., thermometer.
Thess., Thessalonians (N.T.).

Tho(s)., Thomas.
Thurs., Thursday.
T.H.W.M., Trinity high-water mark.
Ti, titanium (chem.).
T.I.H., Their Imperial Highnesses.
Tim., Timothy (N.T.).
tinct., tincture.
Tit., Titus (N.T.).
tit., title.
Tl, thallium (chem.).
T.M., trench mortar.
T.M.O., telegraph money order.
tn., ton.
T.N.T., trinitrotoluene (high explosive).
T.O., Telegraph, Telephone, Office; Transport Officer; turn over.
Tob., Tobit (O.T., Apoc.)
Toc H., Talbot House.
tonn., tonnage.
topog., topographical; topography.
tp., township; troop.
tpr., trooper.
Tr., Treasurer; Trustee.
tr., transactions; translate; translator; transport; transpose.
trans., transactions; transitive; translation; transport.
transf., transference; transferred.
transl., translated; translation.
T.R.C., Thames Rowing Club; tithe rent charge.
Treas., Treasurer; Treasury.
T.R.H., Their Royal Highnesses.
trig., trigonometry.
trop., tropic(s); tropical.
Trs., trustees.
trs., transpose.
Truron., Truro, in signature of Bishop.
T.S.H., Their Serene Highnesses.
T.S.O., Town Sub-Office.
T.T., torpedo tubes.
T.U., Trades Union.
T.U.C., Trades Union Congress; Trades Union Council.
Tues., Tuesday.
Turk., Turkey; Turkish.
2LO, London (broadcasting).
T.W.U., Transport Workers' Union.
T.Y.C., Thames Yacht Club.
typ(og)., typographical; typography.

U, uranium (chem.).
U., Unionist.
u., uncle.
U.C., Upper Canada.
u.c., upper case (printing).
U.C.L., University College, London.
U.D.C., Union of Democratic Control; Urban District Council.
U.F.(C.), United Free (Church of Scotland).
U.G.S.S.S., Union of Girls' Schools for Social Service.
u i., Lat. *ut infra*, as below.
U.J.D., Lat. *Utriusque Juris Doctor*, Doctor of both (Civil and Canon) Laws.
U.K., United Kingdom.
U.K.A., United Kingdom Alliance.
ult., Lat. *ultimo*, in the last preceding month.
U.M.F.C., United Methodist Free Churches.
unabr., unabridged.
Unit., Unitarian.
univ., university; universal(ly).
unm., unmarried.
U.P., United Presbyterian (Church).
u.p., under proof.
up., upper.
U.P.C., United Presbyterian Church.
U.S., United Services; United States.
u.s., Lat. *ut supra*, as above.
U.S.A., United States of America; United States Army.
U.S.M., United States Mail; United States Marine.
U.S.M.A., United States Military Academy.
U.S.N., United States Navy.
U.S.N.A., United States Naval Academy.
U.S.P., United States Pharmacopoeia.
U.S.S., United States Senate; United States ship or steamer.
U.S.S.C., United States Supreme Court.
U.S.S.R., Union of Socialist Soviet Republics (Russia).
usu., usually.
U.S.V., United States Volunteers.
Ut., Utah (U.S.A.).
ut dict., Lat. *ut dictum*, as said.
ut inf., Lat. *ut infra*, as below.
ut sup., Lat. *ut supra*, as above.

V, Roman numeral, 5; vanadium (chem.).
V., volt (elect.).
v., verb; verse; versus.
v., Lat. *vice*, in the place of; Lat. *vide*, see; Ital. *voce*, voice.
V.A., Victoria and Albert (Order); Vicar Apostolic; Vice-Admiral; Volunteer Artillery.
Va., Virginia (U.S.A.).
v.a., Lat. *vixit annos*, lived (so many) years.
V.A.D., Voluntary Aid Detachment (nursing service, Territorial Force).
V.-Adm., Vice-Admiral.
val., value.
V. and M., Virgin and Martyr.
var., variant; variation; variety.
var. lect., Lat. *varia lectio*, variant reading (of MS. &c.).
Vat., Vatican.
vb., verb.
vbl., verbal.
V.C., Vice-Chancellor; Vice-Chairman; Vice-Consul; Victoria Cross.
V.D., Volunteer (Officers') Decoration; venereal disease.
v.d., various dates.
V.D.H., valvular disease of the heart.
Ven., Venerable.
verb. (sat) sap., Lat. *verbum sat sapienti*, a word is enough to the wise.
Vert., Vertebrata.
vet, veterinary surgeon.
veter., veterinary.
v.f., very fair.
V.G., Vicar-General.
v.g., very good.
v.i., verb intransitive.
Vic., Victoria (queen).
Vice-Adm., Vice-Admiral.
Vice-Pres., Vice-President.
Vict., Victoria (Australia).
vid., Lat. *vide*, see.
Vigorn., see **Wigorn.**
vil., village.
Vis(ct)., Viscount.
viz., Lat. *videlicet*, namely.
v.l., Lat. *varia lectio*, variant reading (of MS. &c.).
v/m, volts per metre.
V.O., (Royal) Victorian Order.
Vo., Lat. *verso*, on the left-hand page.
voc., vocative.
vocab., vocabulary.
Vol., Volunteer; Volume.
V.P., Vice-President.
V.R.C., Volunteer Rifle Corps.
V.R. (et I.), *Victoria Regina (et Imperatrix)*, Victoria, Queen (and Empress).
V.Rev., Very Reverend.
V.S., veterinary surgeon.
v.s., Lat. *vide supra*, see above; Ital. *volti subito* (mus.), turn over quickly.
vs., Lat. *versus*, against.
V.S.C., Volunteer Staff Corps.
v.t., verb transitive.
Vt., Vermont (U.S.A.).
V.T.C., Volunteer Training Corps.
Vulg., Vulgate.
vulg., vulgar(ly).
vv., verses.
vv.ll., Lat. *variae lectiones*, variant readings (of MS. &c.).
vy., very.

W, (chem.) tungsten (wolfram).
W., west; Welsh; western (London postal district).
w., wicket, wide (cricket); with; wife.
W.A., Western Australia; West Africa.
W.A.A.C., Women's Army Auxiliary Corps (Q.M.A.A.C.).
w.a.f., with all faults.
W.A.F.F., West African Frontier Force.
W.Afr.R., West African Regiment.
War., Warwickshire.
Wash., Washington (U.S.A.).
W. Aust., Western Australia.
W.B., Water Board; way bill.
W.C., west central (London postal district); Wesleyan Chapel.
w.c., water closet; without charge.
W.D., War Department; Works Department.
wd., would.
W.E.A., Workers' Educational Association.
Wed., Wednesday.
w.f., wrong fount (printing).
W.F.L., Women's Freedom League.
W. Gmc., West Germanic.
wh., which.
W'hampton, Wolverhampton.
whf., wharf.
W.I., West Indies; West India; West Indian.
Wigorn., Worcester, in signature of Bishop.
Wilts., Wiltshire.
Winton., Winchester, in signature of Bishop.
W.I.R., West India Regiment.
Wis(c)., Wisconsin (U.S.A.).
Wisd., Wisdom (of Solomon) (O.T., Apoc.).
wk., week; weak.
W/L, wave length.
Wm., William.
W.M.S., Wesleyan Missionary Society.
W.N.L.F., Women's National Liberal Federation.
W.N.W., west-north-west.
W.O., War Office; warrant officer.
Wor., Worshipful.
Worcs., Worcestershire.
W.P., weather permitting.
W.P.B., waste-paper basket.
W.R., West Riding, Yorkshire.
W.R.A.F., Women's Royal Air Force.
W.R.N.S., Women's Royal Naval Service.
W.S., West Saxon; Writer to the Signet.
W.S.P.U., Women's Social and Political Union.
W.S.W., west-south-west.
W.T., wireless telegraphy, telephony.
wt., weight.
W.U.S.L., Women's United Service League.
W. Va., West Virginia (U.S.A.).
Wyo., Wyoming (U.S.A.).

X, Roman numeral, 10.
x-cp., ex coupon.
xd, x-d., x-div., ex dividend.
Xe, xenon (chem.).
x-i., ex interest.
Xmas, Christmas.
x-n., ex new shares.
Xt(ian)., Christ(ian).
XX, XXX, double-X, triple-X, indicating strength of ales.

Yb, ytterbium (chem.).
yd., yard.
yday., yesterday.
Yeo(m)., Yeomanry.
Y.L.I., Yorkshire Light Infantry.
Y.M.C.A., Young Men's Christian Association.
Yorks., Yorkshire.
Y.P.S.C.E., Young People's Society for Christian Endeavour.
yr., year; your; younger.
Y.R.A., Yacht Racing Association.
yrs., years; yours.
Yt, yttrium (chem.).
Y.W.C.A., Young Women's Christian Association.

Zech., Zechariah (O.T.).
Zeph., Zephaniah (O.T.).
Zn, zinc (chem.).
zool., zoology; zoological.
Zr, zirconium (chem.).
Z.S., Zoological Society.

Appendix

By HUGH BUSS, M.A. (1936)

Revised and Enlarged

By ERIC PARTRIDGE (1952)

The following entries have, whenever possible, been made to read as continuations of entries that will be found in the body of the Dictionary. The word 'Add :' means 'Add, at the end of the entry in the Dictionary, or of the division of it just mentioned'. The absence of any word 'Add :' in an entry shows that it is not such a continuation but has been newly added.

Two additional abbreviations have been used : Dict. = (in) the body of the Dictionary. Suppl. = (in) this Supplement.

Unless otherwise stated, references are to the body of the Dictionary.

abstract, adj. Add : **2.** In art : characterized by designs representing nothing recognizable.

abstraction. Add : **4.** In art : an abstract composition.

ace, adj. Superlative, as in *an ace pilot.*

acidize [ásidiz]. To acidify.

acoustic mine. A naval mine touched off by the sound-vibrations of a vessel's propellers or engines. Cp. **magnetic mine,** Suppl.

acrophobia [ákrofôbia]. See **acro-** & **phobia.** A morbid fear of heights.

actinomycin [aktinomísin]. See **actino-** & **myco-** & **-in.** An anti-microbic substance abstracted from actinomyces.

activate [aktivāt]. To render active or capable of reacting.

ad-lib. To speak or play *ad libitum,* to improvise.

adsorb [ad'sorb], fr. **ad-** & *sorb-* (as in *absorb*). To condense and then hold by *adsorption*—the adhesion of molecules to the surfaces of solids. *Adsorbate,* an adsorbed substance.

aerobatic, adj. [1. årobátik; 2. éərəbǽtik]. See **aero-** & **acrobat** & **-ic.** Of, pertaining to, performing, aerobatics.

aerobatics, n., fr. prec. (The performance of) feats of skill or of daring, in piloting aircraft through spectacular motions in the air; stunt flying.

age (I.), n. **2.** Add : Phr. *to be* (or *act*) *one's age,* (slang, orig. U.S.) to behave in a reasonable manner, as befits one's years.

aide-mémoire, n. [1. åd māmwàhr ; 2. éd memwår]. Fr., 'memorandum'. A note sent by a government through its Foreign Office to another Power, stating clearly its attitude on a point at issue.

air (I.), n. **1. c** Add : *to be on the air,* (i.) be broadcasted, (ii.) to be broadcasted from time to time.

air brake. Any device that reduces the speed of an aircraft.

air-condition. To equip with air-freshening apparatus.

aircraftman, n. [1. årkrahftman ; 2. éə-krāftmən]. **aircraft** & **man.** Man in the ranks of the Royal Air Force.

airfield. An aerodrome.

airlift. Transportation of supplies (esp. food) by air.

airlock. A chamber with doors that prevent entry of gas to an air-raid shelter.

airstrip or **landing strip.** An improvised runway—or landing-place for aircraft.

airworthiness, n. [1. årwĕrdhines; 2. éəwǝ̄ðinis]. See next word & **-ness.** State, quality, of being airworthy.

airworthy, adj. [1. årwĕrdhi ; 2. éəwǝ̄ði]. **air** & **-worthy.** (of aircraft) Fit to undertake a flight ; sound in all parts, construction, &c.

alert, n. An air-raid warning ; the period for which the warning holds good.

all-clear, n. A signal indicating that enemy aircraft have gone.

allelomorph, n. [1. alélomorf ; 2. əlīloumōf]. Gk. *allēlōn,* 'of each other', & Gk. *morphḗ,* 'shape', see **morphology.** (biol.) One of any pair of organisms related, in respect of a particular feature, as dominant to recessive.

allergic, adj. Corresponding to **allergy.** Hence, loosely, *allergic to,* irritated by or inimical towards. *He is allergic to the cinema.*

all-in, adj. **1.** attrib. (of cost, insurance, arbitration, &c.) All-inclusive, including every possible item, contingency or dispute. **2.** (colloq.) *All-in wrestling, an all-in contest,* a type of wrestling match in which only very few kinds of foul are recognized. **3.** pred. (slang, orig. U.S.) (of persons) Tired out, exhausted.

all-out, adv., fig., prob. from motoring 'with all throttles out'. (slang) Using all one's strength and resources unreservedly : *to go all-out,* strive with all one's might.

altitude, n. **1. b** Phr. *grabbing for altitude,* (slang) (i.) trying to climb above an enemy in aerial combat; (ii.) (fig.) becoming furiously angry.

amenity. Add : **c** anything that renders, e.g. a house, more convenient or attractive.

amino [amino]. Combining-form of **amine.**

analysis, n. Add : **3.** Psycho-analysis (of a person) : *under analysis.*

Anderson shelter. A small air-raid shelter consisting of corrugated iron roof, usually covered with earth, and a light frame sunk into the ground.

and how ! An intensive tag, as in *He's sick—and how !*

angle (I.), n. Add : **3.** (slang, orig. U.S.) *To get, use a new angle on something,* find a new way of thinking about it.

anoxia [anoksia], fr. *an-,* 'not', & *oxygen* & *-ia* (as in *hysteria*). Deficiency of oxygen.

antibiotic, adj. [antibīótik], corresponding to *antibiosis* [antibīósis], such an association between organisms as is detrimental to the life (cp. **bio-**) of one of them.

anti-social. Add : **2.** Unfriendly; morose.

apartheid [apart'hīd]. Policy of social *apartness* or segregation in South Africa.

A + B theorem, n. Major C. H. Douglas's contention that, if A denotes every firm's payments to individuals (wages, salaries, dividends) and B denotes its payments to other firms (for raw materials, plant, bank charges, &c.), consumers, while their total incomes = A, must be charged in prices at the rate of A + B, if not more. See **Social Credit,** Suppl.

apneusis, n. [1. apnúsis ; 2. æpnjúsis], fr. a- (priv.) & Gk. *pneûsis,* 'a breathing', fr. *pneûsai,* 'to breathe' ; see **pneuma.** (med.) Suspension of breathing ; apnoea.

Arcos, n. [1. árkos ; 2. ákɔs]. Abbr. fr. *All-Russian Co-operative Society* (U.S.S.R.). Anglo-Russian Trade Delegation.

armour or (U.S.A.) **armor.** Add : **3.** Armoured forces and their vehicles collectively —e.g. tanks, mechanized field artillery, etc.

arrive, vb. intrans. Add : **4.** (fr. mod. Fr. *arriver*) To achieve success and recognition.

asdic [ásdik]. Apparatus for detection of submarines. (Initial-word from *A*nti-*S*ubmarine *D*etection *I*nvestigation *C*ommittee.)

astronomic(al), adj. Add : **2.** (colloq., of figures, &c.) Not unlike the inconceivably large figures used in measuring astronomical distances ; astoundingly big, immense.

Atlantic Charter. An Anglo-American formulation of national policy, made by Prime Minister Churchill and President Roosevelt on 14 August 1941.

atom bomb. Journalistic for *atomic bomb,* first used in 1945. Hence *the Atomic Age,* that era of world history which commenced in August 1945.

aureomycin [aw'reōmísin], fr. *aureo-,* 'golden', & *myco,* 'fungoid', & **-in.** A golden-yellow antibiotic sometimes effectual where penicillin and streptomycin have failed.

autarchy [awtarki], fr. Gk. *autarkhia,* 'absolute power'. Absolute rule. Contrast :

autarky [awtarki], fr. Gk. *autarkeia,* 'self-sufficiency'. A nation's economic self-sufficiency.

authoritarian, b adj. Add : specif., of, pertaining to, a dictatorship ; anti-democratic, non-parliamentary and oppressive towards civil liberties.

auto - radio - gram, n. Radio - gramophone fitted with a device for changing records automatically several times.

auxin [oukśin], fr. Gk. *auxein,* 'to increase', & **-in.** A member of a group of organic acids that, by cellular elongation, assist the growth of plants.

axe, vb. trans., fr. Phr. *the axe.* (See **axe,** Dict.) (Colloq. & chiefly in P.P.) To dismiss, dispense with, as a measure of drastic economy.

axis. Add : **4.** An alliance made by two or more great powers to show their solidarity and to render mutual support, as *the Berlin-Rome-Tokyo axis.*

Babbitt, n. [1. bábit ; 2. bǽbit], fr. George F. Babbitt, central figure of a novel by Sinclair Lewis. A business man, or the like, typical of the low cultural and ethical standards associated with 20th-century commercialism.

baby, n. **1.** Add : Phr. *to be left holding the baby,* (colloq., fig.) to be left with all the trouble, responsibility, &c., on one's hands ; Add : **4.** (slang, orig. U.S.) Man's girl friend.

baby sitter. One who tends babies while the parents are out.

bakelite, n. [1. båkelīt ; 2. béikəlait], fr. Baekeland, inventor. A synthetic resin of the phenol-aldehyde type very widely used instead of wood, pottery, &c.

balletomania, n. [1. báletománia ; 2. bælitəméiniə]. **ballet** & **-mania.** Extravagant enthusiasm for witnessing performances of ballet.

ballyhoo, fr. *Ballyhooly,* a jovial village of County Cork. Sensational advertisement or propaganda. Hence *hooey,* untrustworthy advertisement ; nonsense.

band-pass, adj. (wireless) Constructed on a special principle so that the receiving set will pass a predetermined width of frequencies : *band-pass tuning.*

bang-up, adj. [1. báng úp; 2. bæŋ áp]. (U.S. slang) Very high class, excellent. Cp. **slap-up.**

bankocracy, n. [1. bangkókrasi; 2. bæŋkɔ́krəsi]. **bank & -cracy,** 'government'. **1.** Dictation or control of state policy by a bank or banks. **2.** Bank directors, as dictators or controllers of state policy.

bankster, n. [1. bángkster; 2. bæŋkstə]. **bank & -ster.** (colloq.) Derogatory term for a partisan of bankocracy.

banzai. Add: **2.** Often apprehended as 'hurrah!'

barbecue, n. Add: **c** hence an open-air social entertainment at which a pig or an ox is roasted whole.

barbiturate [barbitúrāt], ultimately the *barb-* of **barbate & -ate.** A sedative drug of *barbituric* acid.

barometer, n. Add: **2.** (fig. & gen.) Any readily ascertainable factor that can be consulted as a safe indicator of more elusive fluctuations: *by-elections as a barometer of public opinion.*

barysphere, n. [1. bárisfēr; 2. bǽrisfiər]. See **baro- & sphere.** (geol.) Internal substance of the earth, enclosed by the lithosphere.

Basic, Basic English, n. & attrib. n. **1. n.** The English Language systematically restricted to a vocabulary of 850 words (together with compounds and combinations of these), not counting words that may be considered as technical or of international currency: *Lamb's Stories from Shakespeare in Basic.* **2.** attrib. n. Of, or belonging to, rendered in, Basic English: *the Basic Rules of Reason,* principles of logic expounded in Basic English.

bathysphere, n. [1. báthisfēr; 2. bǽþisfiə]. See **bathos & sphere.** Hollow sphere constructed so that it can be let down to a considerable depth in the sea (and, e.g., bring up sample of water).

bawl (I.), vb. trans. **3.** Add: **c** *to bawl* (a person) *out,* (U.S. slang) to reprove, reprimand him.

bay (II.), n. Add to **4.**: **a** compartment in the fuselage of an aircraft.

bazooka [bazóōka]. Perhaps from a resemblance to Bob Burns, the radio comedian's sound-contraption. An American small anti-tank gun.

beach-head, or as one word. Such small area on a beach as is taken and held by a force covering the landing of troops or, later, of supplies, as *the Normandy beach-head.*

beacon (I.), n. **2.** Add: **b** (*Belisha*) *beacon,* a sign, consisting of a yellow globe on a metal post, indicating where pedestrians may safely cross the street.

beam, off the beam. Astray, mistaken, originally with reference to *radio beam,* a wireless directional signal. (Slangy.)

bean, n. Add: **2.** (slang, orig. U.S.) Head: *to bat someone on the bean,* hit him on the head.

beat (I.), vb. trans. Add: **6.** *Beat up,* (slang, orig. U.S.) to maltreat cruelly, treat with brutal violence.

beauty parlour, n. (colloq.) Shop fitted out for women's hairdressing, massage, &c.

beetle (IV.), vb. intrans., facet. fr. **beetle (I.).** (slang) **a** To hurry, esp. *to beetle off, beetle along*; **b** to go, depart.

bell, n. **1.** Phrs. Add: *to ring the bell,* (slang, orig. U.S.) to be successful, get good results (fig., from a strength-testing mechanism which rings when heavily punched).

bellyache, vb. intrans. [1. béliāk; 2. bélieik]. See **belly, 2.** (Am. slang) to complain, whine.

besbozhnik, n., pl. *-niki* [1. besbózhnik; 2. besbɔ́žnik]. Russ., *bes,* 'without', *bog,* 'god', *-nik* (suff.). (U.S.S.R.) Member of the League of the Godless, for anti-religious propaganda.

bibful, n. [1. bíbfool; 2. bíbfùl], fr. **bib (I.) & -ful, 2.** Enough to cover a bib. *To slobber a bibful* (of words), (U.S. slang) to talk freely, have much to say; sometimes iron.; cp. **spit (III.) B. 1. b.**

bid (II.), n. Add: **2.** An attempt. (Journalistic.)

big end, n. Abbr. of *big end bearing.* (motor-cars) The bearing or joint where the piston rod joins the crank shaft.

biotin [bíotin]. A crystalline vitamin that assists growth. Formerly *vitamin H.*

bird, n. **3.** Phr. Add: *to give someone the bird,* (slang) orig. theatr., give him a rough house, now gen., get rid of, snub him curtly, rudely; *to get the bird,* be given it.

biro [bḗro]. From the proprietary name *Biro.* Loosely used for any ball-bearing pen of the fountain type.

bit (I.), n. Add: **4.** Slang for *piece of flesh,* a girl or woman. See **piece (I.), 6.**

black out, black-out, vb. intrans. & n. **1.** vb. (theatr.) To switch off all lights during a performance, purposely leaving the stage in complete darkness. **2.** n. **a** (theatr.) Instance, period, of blacking out; **b** (transf.) a temporary failure of the electric light anywhere; **c** (fig.) a temporary loss of memory. **3.** To prevent artificial light from shining outside (a building). Hence, *the black-out* as an air-raid precaution. As *a black-out,* it bears the sense 'a brief faint', a sense deriving probably from the failure of a supply of electricity.

Blackshirt, n. [1. blákshērt; 2. blǽkʃʌ̄t], fr. the black shirt worn as uniform. A member of the Fascist party. See **Fascist.**

Blimp, n. [blimp]. Imitative word. *Colonel Blimp,* figure in cartoons by Low caricaturing an extreme diehard type of outlook.

blitz, n. (hence the verb), short for **blitzkrieg** [blitskrēg], literally, 'lightning war'. A war conducted at tremendous speed and with great violence. *The London Blitz,* the air warfare waged by the Nazis upon London in September 1940—May 1941.

bloc, n. Fr., 'block'; see next entry.

block (I.), n. Add: **8.** Group of countries, political parties, &c., with some common policy.

block (II.), vb. Add: **5.** To prevent the exchange of (*funds, moneys, credits*) for a foreign currency; to prevent (a foreigner) from using his legal moneys in any country other than that where the moneys are banked.

blood (-) bath. An exterminatory form of **purge,** Suppl.

blood group, n. (med.) All persons having the same type of blood, as recognized for purposes of transfusion; there are four such types and only certain combinations of them are safe.

bloody-minded. Add: **2.** Hence, colloquially, unhelpful, obstructive.

blue print, n. & (hyphened or as one word) vb. A photographic print, blue-grounded and white-lined, used for copying drawings of machinery used for architects' plans; to make a blue print of. Hence, loosely, any diagram or, even more loosely, any detailed plan.

body-line, adj. (cricket) *body-line bowling,* fast bowling aimed at the body of the batsman with the object of defeating him by intimidation, if he does not previously retire hurt.

Bofors [bṓfors] **gun.** Originally manufactured at the Bofors works in Sweden, this is a double-barrelled anti-aircraft gun firing up to 120 rounds a minute.

boko, n. [1. bṓkō; 2. bóukou]. (slang) The human head.

boloney, baloney, n. [1. bolṓni; 2. bəlóuni]. **a** Insincere talk; **b** nonsensical talk.

bomb (-) sight, or as one word. A device for aiming bombs from the air.

bone (I.), n. **1.** Add: *to cut* (costs, &c.) *to the bone,* reduce them to the minimum.

bonehead, n. [1. bṓnhed; 2. bóunhed]. (Am. slang.) **a** blockhead; **b** fool's mistake.

boob, n. [1. bōōb; 2. būb]. Slang, abbr. of booby.

booby trap. A grenade or a small mine attached to or concealed in some otherwise harmless object. Invented by the Germans in 1914–1918 and perfected by them in 1939–1945.

boot (I.), n. **2.** Extant in motor-cars.

bottled, adj. Add: **2.** (slang) Intoxicated.

bottle-neck, n. Short strip of narrow road through which considerable traffic has to pass. **2.** Any activity, or source of supply, causing delay in availability or production of related goods.

bounce (I.), B. vb. trans. Add: **3.** (slang. orig. U.S.) To dismiss from a post.

bounce (II.), n. Add: **3.** (slang, orig. U.S.) *The* (*grand*) *bounce,* dismissal from a post.

bowler hat, get a or **one's** or **the.** From the exchange of military for civilian clothes. To be dismissed from the Army.

box up, vb. trans. (slang) To bungle and mess up, make chaotic.

box-up, n. (Slang.) **a** Instance of causing utter confusion by bungling; **b** confusion so caused.

bracket, as in *upper-income-brackets,* (those who earn) large incomes. (Jargon.)

brain trust, n. **a** A group of advisers called in by President Franklin D. Roosevelt; **b** (by extension) any group of 'experts'. As used by the B.B.C. and, metaphorically by Britons, the form is (*the*) *Brains Trust.*

brave new world. A cliché, drawn from Aldous Huxley's satirical novel thus titled and published in 1932. Latterly, the world after the 1939–1945 war; esp. the **Welfare State,** Suppl.

break (II.), n. Add: **6.** (Am. slang) A run of luck (usu. qualified by an adj.): *a bad break*; *a lucky break.* **7.** (Am. slang) A breach of good manners or of social discretion.

bridgehead. Add: **2.** An advanced position, defended as a base for invading or penetrating.

brief (II.), vb. Add to **b**: To instruct (esp. **a** bomber crew) in route, target, timing, weather, etc.

bromide, n. Add: **2.** (Am. slang) **a** A dull, utterly conventional and uninventive person; **b** a remark characteristic of such **a** person; a cliché.

browned off. War-weary, tired of life, thoroughly disgruntled. (Military become general slang.) Perhaps from food done brown.

Brownian movement, n. (phys.) Erratic movement imposed on suspended particles by bombardment from molecules of the suspending medium.

Brownshirt, n. [1. bróunshērt; 2. bráunʃʌ̄t], fr. the brown shirt worn as uniform. A member of the Nazi party. See **Nazi.**

Buchmanism, n. [1. bóokmunizm; 2. búkmənizm], fr. Rev. Frank Buchman, its originator. The so-called 'Oxford Groups', an undenominational Protestant movement of the 1930's, emphasizing individual divine guidance and the method of evangelistic 'team-work'.

Buchmanite, n. & adj. [1. bóokmunīte; 2. búkmənait]. prec. & **-ite. a** n. An adherent of Buchmanism; **b** adj., of, pertaining to, Buchmanism.

bulldozer, fr. **bull-doze.** A tractor-driven vehicle, with blunt ram, for clearing ground.

bum, n., adj. & vb. intrans. **1.** n. **a** Buttocks; **b** (Am. slang) vagabond, tramp. **2.** adj. (slang, orig. U.S.) Worthless, rotten. **3.** vb. intrans. (slang) To tramp about, hike.

bumper, n. Add: **2.** Metal projection on the front or back of a motor vehicle to take the first shock of a collision. **3.** (attrib., cp. **1.**) *Bumper book,* book containing little matter, but deceptively large in appearance.

burg, n. [1. bērg; 2. bʌ̄g], fr. Germ. *burg,* 'stronghold, &c.', formerly 'walled town'. (colloq. & facet., orig. U.S.) A town.

burp, vb. intrans. [1. bĕrp; 2. bɅp]. Imitative. (U.S. slang) To belch, eructate.

business, n. **2. b** Phr. Add: *out of business,* bankrupt.

butt (IV.), vb. Add: **B.** intrans. *Butt in,* (colloq.) to intrude, to break in upon proceedings, conversation, &c.

by-pass, bypass, vb. trans. To make a detour round; hence, to ignore (something) in achieving one's purpose.

calypso [kalipsō]. An improvised ballad that, chanted to an African rhythm, is composed and sung by West Indian natives at carnivals and public events.

camera man, n. (films) Man responsible for the lighting and, in conjunction with the director, for the angles from which shots are taken.

can (III.), vb. trans. Add: **2.** (fig., Am. slang) To cease, stop, put a stop to (anything).

canasta [kanasta]. A card-game that originated in Argentina, went to the U.S.A. and finally (1950) reached Britain. It resembles—but is more difficult than—**gin rummy** (Suppl.).

canned, adj. Add: **b** (slang) intoxicated.

cannibalize [kanibalīz]. To salvage parts of damaged or superseded machines (esp. aircraft) and use them to assemble a usable one; to dismantle a machine to obtain parts usable as replacements.

carry (I.), vb. At **C.** *carry on,* **b** Add: (iii.) to do one's job or one's duty.

cash, vb. Add: **B.** intrans. Phr. *to cash in,* (colloq.; lit. & fig.) realize one's assets, 'make hay while the sun shines'.

cat (I.), n. **1. a** Phr. Add: *the cat's whiskers,* (slang, orig. U.S., with many variants) something quite out of the ordinary, remarkable, excellent, esp. iron., i.e. in person's own estimation.

cat burglar, n. (colloq.) Burglar who enters a building by climbing in, e.g., through a skylight.

category. Add: **c** hence, any class or classification, as in *his medical category.* Hence, *to categorize, recategorize,* to classify, reclassify, medically.

ceiling. Add: **d** the upper limit, esp. the maximum price or the maximum production.

cell. Add: **4.** The smallest practicable unit devoted to the study and promotion of a religious or political movement, as esp. for the propagation of Communism.

cert, n. Slang abbr. of *certainty,* sense **2,** Dict.

chamber (I.), n. 4. Add: **c** the coiled horn enclosed in a gramophone.

change (I.), vb. **B.** intrans. Add: **5.** (in motor driving) *To change up, change down,* change to a higher, lower, gear.

Check! (Elliptical for 'I check that and find it correct'.) Right! Correct! Agreed! (Originally and mostly American.)

chemurgy [kemurji], fr. *chemistry* & *-urgy,* (technical) working. That branch of chemistry which deals with the industrial utilization of raw materials.

chipper, adj. [1. chíper; 2. tʃípə]. (U.S. slang) Lively, in good form, in good spirits.

chisel (II.), vb. Add: **B.** intrans. *Chisel in,* (colloq.) to intrude, interfere.

choke (II.), n. Add: **2.** Device for closing the air inlet in a petrol engine. **3.** (wireless) Coil for reducing the strength of an electric current by self-induction.

Christiania (turn), often shortened to **Christy.** From *Christiania,* former name of Oslo. In skiing, a swinging turn.

cine [sinā] **camera.** A camera for taking motion pictures.

clam, n. Add: **2.** (fig., Am. slang) A silent, uncommunicative person. **3.** vb. intrans. (Am. slang) To be, or become, silent, uncommunicative.

clean (I.), adj. **1.** Phr. Add: *come clean,* (gangster slang) make a clean breast of it. Add: **7. a** Free from dishonesty; **b** free from obscenity; cp. **dirty (I. 3.,** Dict.).

clean-up, n. Add: **c** (slang, orig. U.S.) organized action to eradicate crime or corruption in a certain sphere or locality.

climate. Add: **2.** General trend of attitudes, opinions, beliefs, in a community, a people, a nation; e.g. *the climate of opinion.*

cloak-and-dagger boys or **work.** 'Secret Service' men or work, esp. during a war; (men engaged actively in) Intelligence.

cobber, n. [1. kóber; 2. kɔ́bə]. (Australian slang) A chum, pal.

cold-storage, n. **a** Add: also fig.

cold war. Employment of propaganda, intimidation, obstruction and other subversive activities to obtain advantages otherwise obtainable only by aggression.

collaborationist. One who, in occupied territory, collaborates—works helpfully—with the enemy.

collage [kollahzhé], fr. Fr. *coller,* 'to glue or paste'. That abstract form of Surrealist art which consists in the apparently fortuitous collocation of such objects as pieces of string, match-boxes, cards, tickets, pasted to a ground of cardboard or canvas.

collective, adj. **2.** *collective (farm),* see **kolkhos,** Suppl.; *collective security,* (League of Nations) security for nations, obtained not by arming independently but by trusting in the united strength of the League as sufficient to restrain or resist an aggressor.

collectivize, vb. trans. [1. kuléktivīz; 2. kəléktivaiz), fr. prec. & **-ize.** To reorganize on collective lines.

comfort station. (American.) A lavatory.

Comintern, n. [1. kómintĕrn; 2. kɔ́mintɅn]. Abbr. for 'Communist International'. Committee elected by the Communist parties of all countries to co-ordinate and direct the activities of those parties.

commando. Add: **2.** A band of specially-trained shock-troops; hence, the member of such a band or unit.

commentator. Add: **2.** One who broadcasts summaries of news.

commercialese or **officese.** The cumbrous and ludicrous jargon affected by commerce and trade.

compensation, n. Add: **3.** (psycho-analysis) Cultivation of some trait or accomplishment as an offset to a feeling of inferiority that may be due to some physical or other disability.

concentration camp, n. Place converted into, improvised as, a prison, e.g. for political prisoners or prisoners of war.

condition (II.), vb. trans. **2.** Add: **b** to adopt measures for keeping (e.g. merchandise, air) in a state of freshness; **c** (psychol.) to induce by association of stimuli to behave in a predetermined way in given circumstances; *conditioned reflex,* capacity to act in a familiar way to a new stimulus.

conditioning, n. prec. & **-ing.** Process, effect, of being conditioned (as in prec.).

conga [kongga], fr. *Congo.* A Cuban dance with an African origin and rhythm.

conk (II.), vb. intrans. Imitative word. (slang) To cease functioning; to become suddenly exhausted and inert; also *conk out.*

-conscious, suff. used to form adjs. expressing persons' full awareness of their connexion with (something): *class-conscious.*

-consciousness, suff. forming ns. from prec.

consolidate. Add: **3.** To summarize, to render an abstract of, to incorporate the gist of (reports, memoranda, &c.). *To consolidate the various reports from battalions.*

consumer credit, n. A proposed kind of money credit, non-repayable, to be issued to the public in part claim for their share of the potential output of commodities. See **Social Credit.**

contact [kontakt], vb. trans. To establish contact with. *To contact one's immediate superior.*

continuation (-) school. A special class of school for the education of those young persons aged 15 (16)-18 who have left school in the ordinary sense.

continuity, n. Add: **e** special captions inserted between sections of a film to bridge over and explain, e.g. an imaginary interval of time; also attrib.: *continuity writer, clerk.*

conurbation. The bringing of outlying towns and villages within the local-government jurisdiction of a great city.

co-op, n. Slang abbr. of (consumers') **co-operative society.**

co-operator, n. [1. kōóperāter; 2. kouɔ́pəreitə]. **co-operate** & **-or.** One who co-operates; specif., member of a consumers' co-operative society.

core (I.), n. **4.** Add: **b** *the hard core* (esp. of unemployment), irreducible residuum.

corny. (American slang; origin much disputed.) Old-fashioned or painfully obvious—or both. Of music: banal, unsophisticated; sentimental and facile.

corporation, n. **1.** Add: **d** (Fascist Italy) body representing employers and employees of an industry and responsible, under the State, for its direction, &c.

corporative, adj. Add: **b** of, pertaining to, having under it, corporations, as in prec.; *the corporative State.*

counter intelligence. A body of men and women employed by Intelligence to prevent information from reaching, and to supply false information to, the enemy.

crack (II.), n. Add: **4.** (slang, orig. U.S.) A witticism, a sententious, often a sarcastic, remark: *a wise crack*; cp. **crack (I.), A 2.**

crackers, adj. [1. krákerz; 2. krǽkəz]. (slang) Mentally unbalanced; insane, dotty.

cramp (III.), vb. trans. **3.** (fig.) Add: Phr. (of persons or things, colloq.) *to cramp one's style,* put one ill at ease.

crash (I.), vb. **A.** intrans. Add: **4.** *Crash in (on),* (slang) to intrude (on). **B.** trans. (slang) To intrude into (a party, &c.) as a gate-crasher, q.v. Suppl.

crush (II.), n. Add: **3.** Drink made of the juice of crushed fruit; squash; chiefly in compounds: *orange crush,* &c. **4.** (slang) *To have (got) a crush on* (a person or thing), be very fond of.

crypto-. Add: Esp. in *crypto-Fascist, crypto-Nazi, crypto-Communist,* &c., whether noun or adjective; a quite unsuspected yet firm adherent of, e.g., Communism.

cut (I.), vb. **C.** *Cut in* (intrans.); Add: specif.; **a** While driving a motor vehicle, to overtake and get in front of another motor vehicle, in circumstances which make it dangerous or inconsiderate to do so; **b** (in ballroom dancing, of a man) to claim another man's partner from him while he is dancing with her.

cut (III.), n. Insert as **7.** (films) An abrupt, instantaneous change from one shot to the next. (Re-number **7** as **8, 8** as **9.**)

cutey, cutie, n. [1. kūti; 2. kjūti], fr. **cute** & **-y (III.).** (U.S. slang) A bright, rather smart, young girl.

cyclotron [sīklōtron], fr. **cyclo-** & *-tron* as in *electron.* In physics, a machine used for bombarding the nuclei of atoms.

day, n. **3.** Add: **c** Phr. (slang) *call it a day,* reckon the day's work or main occupation finished, i.e. leave off anything.

D Day. '*Deliverance Day*'—the day (June 6, 1944) on which the allies invaded France. Hence, *D day,* any day appointed for initiating a tactical operation.

dead (I.), adj. **5. a.** Add: Phr. *dead from the neck up,* (slang, orig. U.S.) brainless, devoid of intelligence.

dead pan. (American slang.) A 'poker face'—a countenance showing neither emotion nor even interest.

deal (III.), n. **1.** Add: *a raw deal,* (grossly) unfair treatment; cp. **raw (II.),** Dict. Add: **3. a** *The New Deal,* President Franklin D. Roosevelt's attempted liberal reconstruction of the administrative and economic system in the U.S.A.; **b** (by extension) any similar or comparable attempt at reconstruction.

debunk, vb. trans. [1. dḕbúnk; 2. dībánk], fr. **de-** & **bunk (III.).** (slang) To unmask, to divest of humbug.

deck. Add: **3.** (Naval and Air Force slang) *The deck,* land, as opposed to *the drink,* sea.

decontaminate, vb. trans. [1. dḕkuntáminàt; 2. dīkəntǽmineit], fr. **de-** & **contaminate.** To rid of, purify from, contamination; specif., to rid of poison gas used in warfare.

décor. French word; cp. **decoration.** Artistic arrangement of accessories, esp. in dramatic settings.

decorative. Add: **2.** (Of persons) unusually agreeable to regard; showily handsome, glamorously beautiful—and quite useless.

deep (I.), adj. **1. a** Phr. Add: *to go (in) off the deep end,* (colloq. & fig.) (i.) to make the plunge; (ii.) to give vent to anger, vituperation.

defence in depth. A defensive system wherein points of resistance and obstruction are disposed in successive layers or clusters.

definitely, adv. Add: **b** (colloq.) yes indeed.

degauss [degouś]. To provide (steel ship) with device against magnetic mines; invented by Karl F. Gauss, German mathematician and scientist.

de-ice. To free from, to protect against, an accumulation of ice upon, e.g., the wings of an aircraft.

denationalize. Add: **3.** To restore to private ownership an industry or other activity that has been State-owned *(nationalized).*

dendrite, n. Add: **2.** (anat.) Branching twig of a nerve cell.

deposit (II.), n. Add: **2.** An overdraft.

depress, vb. trans. **2.** Add: **b** (chiefly P.P. pass.) to deprive of trade and prosperity; *depressed areas,* regions so affected.

dicoumarin. See **di-** & **coumarin.** A crystalline chemical compound, derived from sweet clover.

dilantin [dīlańtin]. A blend of *di*phenyl & hyd*antoin.* A synthetic drug employed against epilepsy.

dilution, n. **1. b**; Add: specif., the introduction of some semi-skilled workers into a body of skilled workers.

dim (I.), adj. Add: **4.** Slang abbr. of *dim-witted,* stupid.

dipper, n. Add: **e** contrivance for dipping and raising the headlights of a motor-car while driving it.

director, n. Add: **c** (films) person having supreme control of the actual production of a film; cp. **producer,** Suppl.; *assistant director,* person responsible for assembling actors at the right time and for all details connected with the floor.

dispersion, n. Add: **3.** (chem.) A system in which one component consists of discrete particles (usually of colloidal dimensions) dispersed in the other component, which is a continuous medium called the vehicle.

dissociated, adj. P.P. of *dissociate.* (psycho-analysis) Suffering from loss of, failure to develop, some normal type(s) of association: *dissociated personality*; cp. **integrated,** Suppl.

dissociation, n. Add: specif., (psycho-analysis) Fact, instance, of being dissociated, as in prec.

dissolve (II.), n. (films) (The device, effect, of) making one shot dissolve into the next, growing less and less, while the new shot grows more and more, distinct.

distributism, n. [1. distríbūtizm; 2. distríbjūtizm]. **distribute** & **-ism.** Doctrine that the solution of economic problems lies, not in transferring ownership of land and capital to the state, but in distributing it from the few to all adult citizens.

distributist, n. & adj. [1. distríbūtist; 2. distríbjūtist]. prec. & **-ist. a** n. Advocate, adherent of distributism; **b** adj., of, pertaining to, distributism.

distributive, adj. Add: **3.** Distributist.

distributor, n. [1. distríbūter; 2. distríbjūtə]. **distribute** & **-or.** Person or thing that distributes; specif., (motor-cars) device which determines the order in which the plugs shall spark.

dive bomber. A bomber (plane) that can dive close to its target. Verb: *dive-bomb.*

documentary, n. A *documentary film,* one presenting artistically, yet authoritatively, a phase of history past or in the making.

dog (I.), n. **1. a**; Add: *the dogs,* (slang) greyhound races or racing: *he's lost money at the dogs*; Add: **d** (Am. colloq., facet. for sausage-meat) *hot dog,* hot sausage sandwiched in bread. **2.**; Add: **c** (Canadian slang) side, swagger: *black sheep putting on dog,* swaggering Englishman who has had to leave England in disgrace.

doggone, attrib. adj. [1. dógon; 2. dɔ́gən], fr. the phr. *to go to the dogs.* (Am. slang) Accursed, miserable, confounded.

doing, n., in pl. Add: **2.** (slang) Casual and facet. substitute word for a thing the name of which one cannot, or affects not to, remember; what-d'you-call-it: *pass the doings to me.*

doll (II.), vb. trans. & intrans., fr. **doll (I.).** *Doll up,* (slang) dress up in best clothes.

dollar gap. That deficiency in dollar-exchange which happens when a country's imports from a *dollar area* (a country whose exchange is based upon the American dollar) exceed, in value, its exports to that area (esp. the U.S.A.).

dome (I.), n. **2.** Add: **c** (slang, orig. U.S.) the human head.

dominant, adj. & n. Add: **3.** adj. & n. (biol.) (A Mendelian character) that prevails over a recessive and wholly or partially determines some feature of the organism.

doodle, vb. intrans. (A fanciful word.) To draw aimlessly, absent-mindedly. The practice is *doodling.*

doodlebug. From preceding term & *bug,* 'a cockroach'. An ugly but efficient utility van. (Army slang.) Hence, the German flying bomb of the latter half of 1944.

dope (I.), n. See p. 1417. To **c** Add: *inside dope,* a tip from racing-stables or the like; Phr. *to spill the dope,* give inside information; *to upset the dope,* turn out widely, disconcertingly otherwise than as forecasted. Add: **3.** (U.S. slang) A senseless, idiotic person. Now applied to any dull-witted person. **4.** (slang) Motor spirit.

double (III.), n. Add: **6.** A linked bet on two separate events, receiving heavier odds because of the greater risk to the backer.

Douglasism, n. [1. dúglasizm; 2. dágləsizm]. See **Social Credit.**

Douglasite, n. & adj. [1. dúglasīt; 2. dágləsait]. **1.** n. Social Crediter, q.v. Suppl. **2.** adj. Of, or connected with, the doctrine of Social Credit or with the Social Credit movement.

drain (II.), n. **1.** Add: Phr. *to go down the drain,* (slang) go from bad to worse.

draught (I.), n. **2. d** Add: Phr. *to feel the draught,* (colloq. & fig.) be in financial straits.

dream up. To imagine idly, to devise fancifully. (colloq.)

drink (II.), n. Add: **2.** See **deck,** Suppl.

drophead coupé, n. (motor-cars) Coupé such that the roof folds down.

dub (II.), vb. trans. Add: **2.** (From *double*). To add sound-effects, esp. speech, to a film—or to a televised production.

duck (I.), n. Add: **4.** A combination of barge and large truck, capable of movement on either water or land. Although a vehicle, it takes like a duck to water.

dust-up, n. [1. dúst úp; 2. dást áp]. See **dust (I.). 2.** (colloq.) A commotion, disturbance, row, free fight.

Dutch treat, n. (U.S. colloq.) An occasion to which each of the party brings his own refreshments; *to go Dutch,* to adopt this arrangement.

easy (I.), adj. **2. a** Add: Phr. (slang) *easy on the eye,* pleasant to look at. **4.** Add: *on Easy Street* (slang, orig. U.S.).

eat (I.). C. b *eat up*; Add: also fig., to cover (distance or ground) rapidly: *to eat up the road.*

eats, n. [1. ēts; 2. īts]. (slang) Eatables.

E-boat. (From enemy *boat.*) A German motor torpedo-boat of 1939–1945.

economic. To **2.** add *economic factor—man* (there's no such animal)—*necessity.*

ectogenesis, n. [1. ѐktojénesis; 2. ѐktoudžénəsis]. **ecto-** & **genesis.** (biol.) A predicted method of generating and developing human embryos, not in the uterus, but in the laboratory.

ectogenetic, adj. [1. ѐktojenétik; 2. ѐktoudžənétik]. prec. & **genetic.** Of, pertaining to, produced by, ectogenesis.

edit, vb. trans. **2.** Add: **b** *to edit a film,* piece it together, cutting out superfluous strips and revising montage.

efficiency-sense. Consciousness of one's own, or a perception of others', degree of efficiency.

eidetic, adj. [1. īdétik; 2. aidétik], fr. Gk. *eidētikós,* adj. fr. *eîdos* 'form, appearance', cogn. w. Gk. *ideîn* 'to see'. (psychol.) (of images) Reviving an optical impression with hallucinatory clearness.

eight-ball, behind the. At a grave disadvantage. American slang, from the fact that when the cue ball has the 8 ball between it and its object, the cue ball is badly placed.

elder statesman. (A term borrowed from Japan.) A statesman retired from the House of Commons, yet, because of great reputation, still influential.

Electra [ēlektra] **complex.** That which, in adolescent girls or young women, corresponds to the **Oedipus complex** in males. In Greek myth, Electra deeply loved her father.

electronics [ēlektrońiks]. The science of electrons—a branch of physics.

elevenses, n. [1. elévnziz; 2. ilévnziz], facet. double pl. of **eleven.** (slang) Mid-morning refreshment, e.g. coffee and biscuits.

emmetropia, n. [1. èmetrṓpia; 2. èmətróupiə]. Gk. *émmetros,* adj. '(being) in due measure', & Gk. *ṓps,* 'eye'. Normal sight.

emulsion, n. Add: **3.** (chem.) Colloidal dispersion of a liquid in a liquid.

encirclement. The isolation of one country by another or by several others.

endocrinology, n. [1. èndōkrinóloji; 2. èndoukrinɔ́lədži]. See **endocrine** & **-ology.** (physiol.) The theory and experimental study of the internal secretions of the ductless glands.

engram, n. [1. éngram; 2. éngræm], fr. Gk. *en,* 'in', & **-gram,** fr. Gk. *eggráphein,* 'to inscribe, incise, engrave'. (psychol.) Presumed pattern of nerve-paths, due partly to heredity and partly to previous experience of the individual, and tending to cause specific behaviour; the physiological basis of a habit.

epicritic, adj. [1. èpikrítik; 2. èpikrítik]. See **epi-** & **critic.** (physiol.) (of sensations) Accurately localized and estimated; opposed to **protopathic,** Suppl.

epidiascope, n. [1. èpidíaskōp; 2. èpidáiəkoup]. See **epi-** & **dia-** & **-scope.** Instrument for projecting a magnified image of a small picture on to a white screen.

equity. Add **3.** As *Equity*: a British co-operative society of actors and actresses.

erg, n. Add: **2.** (technocracy) A proposed unit for measuring the value of commodities according to the amount of mechanical energy consumed in the production of them.

ergolatry, n. [1. ĕgólatri; 2. ɜ̄gólətri]. See **ergon** & **-latry.** Idolization of work as a thing good in itself, whether directed towards a good purpose or not.

ergosophy, n. [1. ĕrgósofi; 2. ɜ̄gósəfi], fr. **ergon** & Gk. *sophía*, 'wisdom'. Wisdom in the systematic utilization of physical sources of energy.

erk. An aircraftman, esp. an A.C.2. Air Force slang: *air*craftman.

ersatz, adj. (German *Ersatz*, a replacement, a substitute) Substitute, as in *ersatz coffee*; temporary, as in *ersatz girl*; hence, inferior.

escapism, n. [1. eskápizm; 2. ɛskéipizm]. **escape** & **-ism.** Escaping, tendency to escape, from unpleasant or intractable realities into fantasy.

escapist, n. & adj. [1. eskápist; 2. ɛskéipist]. **escape** & **-ist. a** n. One who has a tendency to escapism; **b** adj., having this characteristic or tendency.

ethanolamine [ethanolomēn], fr. *ethanol*, 'an ethyl alcohol', & **-amine.** Any of the three amino alcohols. A colourless alkaline liquid, used in soap-making.

evacuee [ēvakūē]. One who is *evacuated*—withdrawn from a place of danger (esp. London)—in wartime.

evasive action. The action of aircraft so manœuvring as to escape enemy aircraft or flak.

exchange (II.), n. **2. b**; Add: *Exchange Equalization Fund* or *Account*, a reserve fund set aside and used by the Bank of England on behalf of the Treasury for stabilizing the foreign exchange value of the pound sterling, since the abandonment of the gold standard.

exhibitionism, n. [1. èksibíshunizm; 2. èksibíʃənizm]. **exhibition** & **-ism. 1.** (psycho-analysis) Morbid eagerness to display one's naked body. **2.** Excessive propensity for focussing the attention of others on oneself.

exhibitionist, n. & adj. [1. èksibíshunist; 2. èksibíʃənist]. prec. & **-ist. a** n. One who is given to exhibitionism; **b** of, pertaining to, manifesting, exhibitionism.

existentialism. (Cp. **existential.**) The somewhat negative, almost despairing philosophy of Jean-Paul Sartre, French man of letters.

expendable, -ible. Supplies or personnel involved in a calculated risk.

extrasensory perception; abbr.: **E.S.P.** Perceptive powers (as in telepathy) not yet scientifically explained.

eye (I.), n. **1. c** Phr. Add: *easy on the eye*, (slang) good-looking, of pleasing appearance.

face-lifting, n. See **lift** (I.), Suppl.

fade, vb. intrans. **A. 1. b** Add: specif. (wireless) to become weaker through fading.

fade-in, n. (films) The gradual appearance of a new shot on the screen out of darkness into full intensity.

fade-out, n. **a** (films) The gradual disappearance of a shot on the screen from full intensity into darkness; **b** (colloq. & fig.) gradual withdrawal from publicity.

fading, n., fr. **fade,** Suppl. (wireless) The periodical weakening of tone experienced in reception, esp. on medium wave-lengths.

fall (I.), vb. intrans. **B.** Add: *Fall for*, (slang, orig. U.S.) to fall a victim to, be captivated by, the charm, &c., of (a person or thing).

fantastic. Add: **c** ludicrous, grossly absurd.

Fascism, n. Add: **2.** Any similar or comparable movement or tendency elsewhere than in Italy: **boiled-shirt Fascism.**

Fascist, n. & adj. Add: **3.** (Person) having convictions, sympathies or tendencies similar or comparable to those of the Italian Fascists.

favouring, vbl. n. (films) Regulating the volume of sound recorded, by movement of the sound-boom, e.g. towards the actor who is speaking.

feather (II.), vb. trans. Add: **4.** To reduce the air-resistance of an aircraft by feathering the propeller: cp. sense **3. a.**

Federal prose, familiarly known as *gobbledygook*. That which, in the U.S.A., answers to the **officialese,** Suppl., or **Whitehallese** of Great Britain. Cumbrous official language. The second term, *gobbledygook*, imitates a pompous utterance.

fellow traveller. (Translation of Russian *popuchiki*.) One who, without being a member of the Communist party, sympathizes with the cause of Communism.

ferricillin [ferrisil'in]. *Ferric* salt of peni*cillin*, Suppl.

ferry (I.), vb. Add: **2.** To deliver, e.g. aircraft under their own power. **3.** To convey troops or supplies by regular air service.

Fifth Column, Sixth Column. (An adherent is a *Fifth Columnist*.) '"Franco," said Freeth, rather pontifically for him, "coined the term 'Fifth Column' when his forces were threatening Madrid" during the Spanish Civil War of 1936–1939. "If my memory serves me right, they were converging on the city in what war correspondents call a four-pronged drive, and Franco said in a broadcast that he had a fifth column inside Madrid. . . . The point is that he invented a new and very useful label. Less belligerent than *francs tireurs*, less political than Quislings, less operational than the underground, the Fifth Column is a convenient and accepted designation for the enemy in your midst. Or anyhow for the enemy's sympathizers."' On the next page (160) Freeth says, 'But in this country, and in America too, it's the Sixth Column that's the menace', and, asked what he means, he continues, 'Meaning the rare but very dangerous individuals who have turned traitor for no apparent reason at all. . . . The Sixth Column' is 'composed of cool, level-headed individuals who don't work for any particular cause, who don't care whether or not they are rewarded . . . who haven't really any special grievance against their own country, or any special liking for her enemies. They just take to treachery.' (From Peter Fleming, *The Sixth Column*, 1951, with the author's generous permission.) *Webster's Dictionary* defines the Sixth Column as 'the aggregate of persons in a country at war who assist the subversive activities of the fifth column, esp. by defeatist talk, spreading rumours, and the like'.

fighter. Add: **2.** A fighter aircraft. (Cp. **pursuit plane** below).

finger-tip control, n. Arrangement of controls in a motor-car, such that they can be operated without removing the hand from the steering-wheel.

fit (I.), n. **1.** Add: *to throw a fit*, to be, to behave as one, shocked, infuriated, outraged.

Five Year Plan, n. (U.S.S.R.) Comprehensive scheme for industrial and general development of resources, to cover a period of five years; the first such scheme was begun in 1928.

fixation. Add: **2.** As in *mother fixation*, this denotes a desire, esp. a sexual desire, that has ceased and become fixed at an immature stage of development; in short, it constitutes one of the more important manifestations of *arrested development*.

flak. Anti-aircraft fire; strictly, German a.-a. fire. An initial word from German *Flieger-abwehrkanone*, anti-aircraft gun.

flame (I.), n. **1.** Add: as interj., (slang) euphemism for 'hell'.

flap (II.), n. Add: **4.** Fussed excitement, (almost) panic. Also vb. intrans., to get flustered, to panic. (Slang; from birds flapping wings as they fly off.)

flash-back, n. (films) Episode beginning with a sudden change to an earlier point of time.

flat (II.), adv. **2.** Add: Phr. *to go flat out*, cp. **all-out,** Suppl.; *flat spin*, see **spin,** Suppl.

flat spin. Motion of an aircraft almost horizontal and rotating about its vertical axis. Hence, the slangy *go into a flat spin*, to become extremely flustered.

flick (II.), n., fr. *flicker*. (slang) A motion picture, film, cinema show; also pl.

flood-light, vb. trans. To illuminate (a building) with powerful electric lamps directed upwards and away from the spectator's eye.

flood lighting, n. The kind of illumination described in prec.

floor (I.), n. **2.** Add: **b** the part of a film studio where the actors perform.

floor show. An informal-seeming entertainment presented among the 'guests' at a night-club.

flop (I.), vb. intrans. **1.** Add: **c** (fig. & slang) to be a failure, a fiasco.

flop (III.), n. Add: *to go flop*, (fig. & slang) to be a failure, a fiasco.

fluorescent lighting. The light emitted by cathode-ray from tubular electric lamps.

fly (I.), n. **1.** Phr. Add: (slang) *there are no flies on* (a person), he is very active (and efficient).

flying bomb. A pilotless 'aircraft' steered gyroscopically and laden with high explosives.

for (I.), prep. **2.** Add: Phr. (colloq.) *to be in for trouble, &c., to be in for it*, (slang) *to be for it* [fór it], have trouble, punishment, a reprimand, in store for one; *to be out for trouble, for a row, &c.*, (colloq.) be intending to cause it; *to be out for* (anything), (colloq.) have it as one's aim.

fox-hole or as one word (American); **slit trench** (British). The former is smaller, but both are very short, narrow trenches, just deep enough to protect the one or two occupants (*foxhole*) or the two or several occupants (*slit trench*). Mere slits in the ground, they have names only rarely used before 1940.

fraternize. Add: **2.** Hence, of soldiers that, from opposing armies, meet briefly on friendly terms; in 1939–1945, also of soldiers making friends with civilians.

free-for-all, n. Cp. Phr. *a free fight*, under **free** (I.), **9. a.** (Am. colloq.) A rough and tumble, a row.

Free Money, n. Money which, as advocated by Silvio Gesell, automatically depreciates in value at a rate approximately equal to the average rate of depreciation in the value of commodities.

freeze (I.), vb. Add: **3.** To immobilize (foreign-owned credits) by legislative measures.

frig, n. [1. frij; 2. fridž]. Slang abbr. for **refrigerator.**

front (I.), n. **2.** Add: **e** (fig.) any sphere of conflict; **f** a coalition of political forces, united front: *popular front* (fr. Fr. *front populaire*). Add: **7.** (Perhaps from sense **2. d**) As in *the Communist front*; **b** the nominal head of an enterprise, a committee, a delegation; **c** in the American underworld, a gang's (or mob's) liaison with the outer world.

Führer, the; Führerprinzip. (Adoptions from German; English usually omits the diæresis.) Hitler; the principle of personal leadership (literally, leader-principle) in Hitler's Germany.

fundamentalism, n. Add: **c** (colloq.) naïve adherence to traditional beliefs of any kind, e.g. to Free Trade.

futilitarian, n. & adj. [1. fūtilitárian; 2. fjūtilitéəriən]. Formed facet. fr. **futile** & **utilitarian.** (facet.) **a** (one who is) made arid by narrowly utilitarian aims; **b** (one who is) pessimistic in outlook.

future in it, (there's) no. It's dangerous (Air Force slang applied to an aerial sortie); hence, It's fruitless or useless.

gain control, n. (wireless) Volume control increasing and decreasing the amplification of a wireless receiver.

gangsterism, n. [1. gángsterizm; 2. gǽŋstərizm]. **gangster & -ism.** Gangster-like behaviour.

gat, n. [1. gat; 2. gæt]. Am. slang abbr. of **Gatling-gun.**

gate-crash, vb. intrans. (slang) To effect entrance to a dance, party or entertainment without invitation or ticket of admission.

gate-crasher, n., fr. prec. (slang) One who gate-crashes.

gauleiter. (German; literally, district-leader.) A provincial political governor in Nazi Germany.

gee, interj. [1. jē; 2. dži]. Abbr. for **God** or for **Jesus.** (Slang, orig. U.S.)

gel, n. [1. jel; 2. džel]. Abbr. fr. **gelatine.** (chem.) A colloid which, under suitable conditions, has set or formed a jelly.

gen [jen]. Information—indeed, this slang word derives fr. '*gen*eral information'.

genotype, n. [1. jénotīp; 2. dženoutaip]. Gk. *génos*, 'birth, breed, &c.', see **genus & type.** (biol.) Hereditary genetic constitution of an organism.

genteelism. A would-be polite or superior term. Coined by the Fowler brothers from **genteel & -ism.**

gentleman, n. **4.** Add: Phr. *gentleman's agreement*, **a** mutual understanding (i.) with no guarantee but the honour of those entering into it; (ii.) (euphemistically) with a more or less dishonest aim.

geopolitics [jéōpolitiks]. The anglicized form of the German *Geopolitik*, that branch of learning which deals with the influence of geography upon politics and sociology.

Gesellite, n. & adj. **1.** n. Follower of Silvio Gesell. **2.** adj. Of, pertaining **to,** the doctrine of Free Money, q.v. Suppl.

gestalt, n. [1. geshtált; 2. gəʃtǽlt], Germ. 'form'. (psychol.) An organized whole in experience; chiefly used attrib.: *gestalt psychology*, a theory which explains psychological phenomena by their relations to organized wholes, at least some of which are immediately given in experience.

Gestapo, n. [1. geshtáhpo; 2. gəʃtápou]. Abbr. fr. Germ. *geheime Staatspolizei*, 'secret state police'. The secret police organization of the Nazi régime in Germany. **2.** Humorously, the police.

get (I.), vb. trans. & intrans. **A. 1.** Phr. Add: *to get religion, socialism, films*, &c., (colloq.) become preoccupied with. **B.** intrans. Add: **5.** *Get!* (imperat., slang), abbr. for 'get along!' **C.** Add: *Get* (an idea, &c.) *across*, trans. (colloq., orig. U.S.), get the public to accept it. *Get away with*; **b** Add: *to get away with it*, (colloq.) perpetrate something impudent, forbidden or risky without being punished, prevented, reprimanded, hurt, &c. *Get off*; Add: **d** (slang, orig. U.S.) to go wrong, make a mistake; esp. *to tell someone where he gets off. Get off with*, (slang) to establish amorous relations with (someone); *get off* (of two persons), to get off with each other. *Get over*, Add: **f** *to get* (a thing) *over*; (i.) finish and have done with it; (ii.) get it across (as above, Suppl.).

getaway, n. [1. gétawā; 2. gétəwei]. **get (I.), C.** (slang) Escape: *to make a get-away.*

Get cracking! Get busy! This Armed Forces' slang phrase (1939–1945) has outlived such others as *Get mobile!* and *Get weaving!*—this last injunction was Air Force only.

G.I., fr. '*g*eneral *i*ssue'; often elaborated to **G.I. Joe,** where *Joe* merely connotes 'guy, fellow'. (American slang) A private soldier.

gigolo, n. [1. jígolō; 2. džígəlou]. Fr., formed fr. *gigole*, 'loose woman'. Male dancing partner, &c.

ginger (I.), n. **2. a** Add: also attrib.: *ginger group*, a minority acting as a spur to a more passive majority.

gin rummy. An American variation (mostly for two persons) of **rummy (II.).**

give (I.), vb. **A.** trans. **1.** Phr. Add: *not to give a damn (for)*, (slang) not to care at all; cp. **care (II.), 1. b.**

give-away, n., fr. **give (I.) C. & away.** (slang) **a** A betrayal (usu. unintentional) of something intended to be kept hidden from observation or knowledge; **b** an act of giving, or throwing, away an opportunity or something which should have been retained.

glacine, n. [1. glásēn; 2. glǽsīn]. See **glacial & -ine (VI.). a** A substance similar in nature and use to cellophane, but semi-opaque and less glossy.

glamorous; glamour. Add, respectively: **2.** and **c.** The adj. corresponding to *glamour*, (usually) **a** person's **glossy** or artificial attractiveness, esp. for the opposite sex.

glossy, n. A glossy magazine, i.e. a magazine with glossy paper and usually with romanticized illustrations.

G-man, n. [1. jémàn; 2. dzímæn.] Abbr. of **government man.** (U.S.) One of the American secret police.

gobbledygook [gobeldigook]. See **Federal prose,** Suppl.

godbooster, n. [1. gódbōōster; 2. gódbūstə], fr. **god & boost & -er.** (U.S. slang) A minister of religion, a preacher.

godbox, n., fr. **god & box, 5.** (U.S. slang) A church or chapel.

gold bloc(k), n. Since 1931, the group of countries still on the gold standard, after Great Britain and many other countries went off it.

gold bullion standard, n. A modified gold standard whereby a central bank is obliged to exchange its notes only for bar gold (value about £1,560 each bar).

gold currency standard, n. The gold standard, in the strict sense.

gold-digger, n. Add: **2.** (slang, orig. U.S.) (fig.) An adventuress who deliberately cultivates admirers for the sake of what money she can extract from them.

gold exchange standard, n. A modified gold standard whereby a central bank is permitted to base part of its note issue, not on its own gold reserves, but on foreign exchange of a country that is on the gold standard.

gold standard, n. **a** The monetary system by which a unit of currency is based strictly on gold, and a central bank is obliged to exchange its notes for gold on demand, and there is no restriction on the flow of gold into and out of a country; **b** loosely, for *gold bullion standard* or *gold exchange standard*, q.v.

gone for a Burton. Of persons: dead. Of things: destroyed; lost. Air Force slang, perhaps euphemistically, for 'He's gone for a glass of Burton' (ale).

gong (II.), vb. trans. (slang, orig. U.S., of motor police) To notify (the driver of a motor vehicle) by signal that he must stop.

gongster, n. [1. góngster; 2. góŋstə]. prec. & **-ster.** (slang, orig. U.S.) Motor police officer who gongs people.

goo, n. [1. gōō; 2. gū]. (Am. slang) **a** Any sticky substance; **b** (fig.) sickly sentiment.

good (I.), adj. **1.** Add **d** *to be feeling good*, (slang, orig. U.S.) to be in good health and spirits. **2. b** Phr. Add: *not so good!* (colloq. iron) what a bad mistake, what a failure, &c.!

good (II.), n. **4.** (pl.) **b** Add: *the goods* (fig., slang) **a** The requisite qualities: *he has the goods*, is thoroughly well qualified and competent; **b** exactly what is wanted: *I tell you, it's the goods, he's the goods.*

good looker, n. (slang) A handsome person.

gooey, adj. [1. gōōi; 2. gúi]. **goo & -y (IV.).** (Am. slang) **a** Sticky, gummy; **b** sentimental.

goofer, n. [1. gōōfer; 2. gúfə]. **goof,** p. 1418, & **-er.** (Am. slang) Dupe; victim.

goofy, adj. [1. gōōfi; 2. gúfi]. **goof,** p. 1418, & **-y (IV.).** (Am. slang) Daft, stupid.

goo-goo eyes, n. (slang, orig. U.S.) Ogling.

goon. A slang term, probably the blend of '*go*rilla' and 'bab*oon*', deriving immediately from the sub-human creatures presented in a comic strip by E. C. Segar († 1938). In American slang: a thug. Among British prisoners of war, a German guard or sentry.

goosey (II.), goosy, adj. [1. gōōsi; 2. gúsi]. **goose & -y (IV.), a.** (colloq.) **a** (of persons) Scared, &c.; see **goose-flesh,** Dict.; **b** (of things) such as to make one scared, &c.

Gosplan, n. [1. gósplan; 2. gósplæn]. Russ., *gosudarstvo*, 'state'. (U.S.S.R.) State planning committee of the Soviet Union.

Gostorg, n. [1. góstorg; 2. góstōg]. Russ., *gos*, abbr. of *gosudarstvo*, 'state', & *torg*, 'trade'. State trading department of the U.S.S.R.

gracing, n. Abbr. of **greyhound-racing.** (vulg. slang) Participating in, witnessing, greyhound races.

gramicidin [gramiśidin], fr. *Gram*, a Danish physician, & **-cide & -in.** An antibacterial that is efficacious against certain dangerous bacteria but, if introduced into the blood stream, destroys the red cells.

Greenshirt, n. One belonging to that section of the Douglasite movement which parades in green for the purpose of advertising the doctrine of Social Credit. Also attrib.

gremlin. A puckishly interfering little goblin that haunts aircraft (esp. when **operational**); although always mischievous and indeed tiresome, gremlins seldom cause a fatal accident. Now a part of British folklore. Hence, the word is perhaps a blend of '*grin*ning gob*lin*'; *grinlin* would pass easily into *grimlin*, thence into *gremlin.*

grid, n. Add: **c** specif., *the grid*, the system of overhead wires supported by iron pylons that distributes electric current from main generating stations to towns and intervening villages.

grill (II.), vb. **A.** trans. **1.** Add: **d** (slang) to subject to intimidation and harshness, e.g. in examination of suspects.

grilling, n., fr. prec. & **-ing.** Process of being 'grilled', as in prec.

grim, adj. Add: **c** (slang, usu. pred.) Rather trying, mildly distressing.

gripe (I.), vb. Add: **2.** intrans. (fig., Am. slang) To complain, whine. Cp. **bellyache,** Suppl.

gripe (II.), n. **2.** Add: **b** (fig., sing., Am. slang) a cause of annoyance.

guinea-pig. Add: **3.** Any human subject of medical or other scientific experimentation.

gump, n. [1. gump; 2. gamp], fr. Mr. Gump, name of a butt in the comic papers. (U.S. slang) A fool, blockhead, noodle.

gut (I.), n. **2.** Add: **c** pl. (Am. slang) Impudence, insolence. Cp. **nerve (1. 3. a).**

gyropilot. See **gyro- & pilot.** A gyroscopic control keeping an aircraft level and on its course.

had it, I've—he's—&c. I—he—won't get it. that's the end for me, him, &c. A Royal Air Force catch-phrase that has gained a very wide currency; probably from such an issue of, e.g., clothing as cannot, without payment, be repeated.

hair-do. (colloq.) A hair style; coiffure.

half-track. A caterpillar tread of the endless-band type; hence, in U.S.A., a carrier (of personnel) equipped with half-tracks.

hammer and sickle. A crossed hammer and sickle, an emblem—indicative of industrial worker and farm labourer—adopted (1923) for the national flag by the U.S.S.R.

hang-over, n. (slang) Unpleasant after-effects of alcoholic indulgence.

hard-boiled, adj. Add: **2. a** (of persons) Shrewd, hard-headed, exacting; **b** (of schemes, &c.) practical, esp. in a financial sense.

hari-kari. Incorrect for **hara-kiri.**

have, vb. trans. **A.** (end of). Various Phrs. & idioms. Add: *to have a person on,* (slang) to deceive him.

have-on, n. [1. hǽvon; 2. hævǿn], fr. prec. (slang) An instance of having a person, or people, on.

hay (I.), n. **a** Phr. Add: *to hit the hay,* (slang) retire to bed.

hay-wire, adj. (U.S. slang) Crazy, mad.

headliner, n. [hédlainə]. **headline & -er.** (slang, orig. U.S.) A principal performer, e.g. in a variety entertainment.

heat (I.), n. Add: **10.** Esp. *to turn on the heat* (American slang). Of, e.g., the police: to carry out an intense investigation. The criminal says, *the heat is on.* Hence, loosely, to play one's best against an (inferior) opponent. Perhaps from the action of an acetylene torch.

Heaviside layer, n. [1. hévisīd; 2. hévisaid], fr. name of discoverer. See **ionosphere,** Suppl.

heavy water. Any water heavier than ordinary water, esp. that containing heavy oxygen.

heeby-jeebies, n. pl. [1. hḗbijḗbiz; 2. hībidžībiz]. (slang, orig. U.S.) State of alarm and trepidation.

heel (I.), n. Add: **4.** (American slang) A mean-spirited, thoroughly untrustworthy fellow. From the heel of the foot—the lowest part of an upright body.

Heil! [hīl]. Hail! The Nazis' traditional salute to Hitler.

he-man, n. [1. hḗ mán; 2. hī mǽn]. **he & man** (pleonastic emphasis). (slang, orig. U.S.) A sturdy and virile man, attractive to most women.

herd, n. **2.** Add: *herd instinct,* gregariousness and mass-imitation.

Herrenvolk. German for 'master people' (literally, *Herren* is the plural of *Herr,* lord, master): a name with which the Germans graced themselves from the late 1920's until ca. 1944.

het up, adj. [hɛt áp], P.P. of **heat (II.) & up.** (slang, orig. U.S.) Emotionally disturbed, agitated; esp., annoyed: *all het up,* thoroughly so.

high-hat, n. & vb. trans. (slang, orig. U.S.) **1.** n. Supercilious person. **2.** vb. trans. To talk (patronizingly) down to.

high-pressure, adj. **b** Add: intensive: *high-pressure salesmanship, methods* (of business).

high-stepper, n. Add: **c** supercilious, presumptuous person; social climber.

hiker, n. [1. hī́ker; 2. háikə]. **hike & -er.** (colloq.) One who hikes, or is hiking.

hitch-hike, vb. intrans. To travel about with the help of lifts from motor vehicles.

Hitlerism, n. [1. hítlerizm; 2. hítlərizm], fr. *Hitler* & **-ism.** See **Nazism.**

hock, vb. trans. [1. hok; 2. hɔ́k]. (U.S. slang) **2.** Add: **b** To pawn, put in pledge.

hock shop. (U.S. slang) Pawn-shop.

-hog, element of abuse in slang compounds: *road-hog, speed-hog.* **a** n. One who selfishly and regardlessly drives a car at high speed; **b** vb. intrans., to *road-hog,* &c., to behave in such a way.

hokum, hocum, n. [1. hókum; 2. hóukəm], ? fr. **hocus-pocus & bunkum.** (U.S. slang) Stale, outworn conventional situations and recipes for a plot, &c., in plays, novels and the like; esp. Phr.: *the same old hokum.*

homo, adj. & n. [1. hṓmō; 2. hóumou]. Abbr. of **homosexual.** (slang) **a** adj. Homosexual; **b** n., a homosexual person.

hooey, n. [1. hṓōi; 2. húi]. (slang, orig. U.S.) **a hokum,** Suppl.; **b boloney,** Suppl.; **c** See **ballyhoo,** Suppl.

hooky (II.), n. (slang, orig. U.S.) *To play hooky,* play truant.

hoot (I.), vb. intrans. **1. a** Add: Phr. *to hoot with laughter,* (slang) to laugh uproariously.

hoot (II.), n. Add: Phr. (slang) *not to care a hoot* (or *two hoots*), not at all; Add: **b** (slang) a reason for uproarious laughter, a great joke: *What a hoot!*

horn (II.), vb. Add: **B.** intrans. *Horn in,* (colloq. orig. U.S.) to intrude, interfere, butt in.

hot (I.), adj. Add: **7.** (mus.) Having an elaborate and stimulating jazz rhythm. **8.** (financ.) (of Treasury Bonds) Just issued. **9.** *Hot money,* (slang, orig. U.S.) dangerous, because connected with some crime or illegality.

hot-gospeler, n. [1. hótgóspeler; 2. hɔ́tgɔ́spələ], fr. **hot (5.) & gospel & -er.** (U.S. slang) A revivalist preacher.

hound (I.). 3. Add: **b** In compounds, (U.S. slang) an uncomplimentary term for one who habitually hunts after a certain thing: *news-hound,* hunter after newspaper 'copy'; *publicity hound,* one who is always trying to get himself into the news; *smut-hound,* self-appointed investigator and censor of public morals; *sin-hound,* prison chaplain.

how. 4. b Add: also absol., (U.S. slang) *and how,* (yes) in the extreme, to a remarkable extent, on a big scale: *it was a swell party, and how.*

human, adj. Add: **3.** n. (colloq. & usu. in pl.) A human being.

(a) hundred-per-cent, adj. & adv. (U.S. colloq.) Complete(ly): *a hundred-per-cent he-man.*

hundred-per-center, n. prec. & **-er.** (U.S. slang) **a** Fervent American patriot; **b** whole-hogger.

hunky-dory, pred. adj. [1. húngki dṓri; 2. háŋki dṓri]. (slang, orig. U.S.) Quite all right, fine, excellent.

hush-hush, adj., fr. **hush (IV.).** (colloq.) Kept secret and so (sometimes intentionally) rather mysterious.

hydrogen bomb. An atomic bomb designed to be many times more powerful than the plutonium bomb and having heavy hydrogen as the principal ingredient.

hydroponics [hīdrōpóniks], fr. **hydro-** & Gk. *ponos,* 'labour', & **-ics.** The growing of esp. vegetables with their roots not in soil but in an aqueous solution containing the essential salts.

hypertension; adj. **hypertensive.** See **hyper- & tension.** (With) an unhealthily high blood pressure.

hypoplasia, n. [1. hīpōplázia; 2. hàipoupléiziə]. See **hypo- & plasma & -ia.** (anat.) Under-developed condition of any part of an organism.

id. Add: **2.** In psycho-analysis: the basic complex or mass of life tendencies whence come the ego and the **libido,** Suppl.

ignitron [ignítron], a blend of '*ignite*' & '*electron* tube'. A rectifier containing mercury and, at the commencement of each cycle, re-struck by an electrode energized by an auxiliary circuit.

immunology, n. [1. imūnóloji; 2. imjūnɔ́lədži]. See **immune & -logy.** The study of immunity from disease, infection, &c., and the conditions governing it.

implant [implant], n. In the treatment of cancer, a radium-containing tube inserted into diseased tissue.

indicator, n. Add: **b** (chem.) A compound which by means of a change in colour indicates a chemical change.

inflationary gap-spiral. A *gap* between purchasing power and purchasable goods; as the gap widens, it tends to initiate an inflationary spiral or vicious circle.

insufflator. Add: **2.** In fingerprinting, a mechanical device for blowing powder onto the surfaces likely to hold impressions.

integrate (hence **integration**). Add: **3.** Merely to co-ordinate. (Whitehallese and, derivatively, journalese.) Cp.:

integrated, adj., P.P. of **integrate.** (psychol.) Successfully combined, co-ordinated, into a whole; cp. **dissociated,** Suppl.

intelligence, n. **1. a** Add: *intelligence test,* (psychol.) supposedly scientific method of classifying persons according to their mental powers.

interventor. A professional—or, at the least, an official—intervener. (Jargon.)

ionosphere, n. [1. iónosfēr; 2. aiɔ́nəsfiə]. **ion & sphere.** The ionized region high up in the stratosphere from which wireless waves are reflected.

iron (III.), vb. trans. **1.** Add: *to iron out,* (fig.) keep (e.g. prices) from fluctuating.

iron curtain, behind the. In Russia itself, its satellites, and the Russian zone of Germany. (Impossible to see through and difficult to pass.)

iron lung. A device for maintaining artificial respiration; esp. when, through infantile paralysis, the chest muscles fail to work.

iron ration. An emergency ration contained in a tin or can.

-ish (I.). Add: **d** adv. (of time, colloq.) round about: *4.30-ish.*

isolationism, n. [1. īsolāshunizm; 2. aisəléiʃənizm]. **isolation & -ism.** A policy aiming at the greatest possible freedom for a nation from dependence on other nations, whether politically or economically.

isolationist, n. & adj. [1. īsolāshunist; 2. aisəleiʃənist]. **isolation & -ist. a** n. One who advocates or adopts a policy of isolationism; **b** adj., of, pertaining to, isolationism.

isostasy, n. [1. īsóstasi; 2. aisɔ́stəsi]. See **iso- & stasis.** (geol.) The hypothesis that between the land or water surface and the centre of the earth there is the same amount of matter under every unit of surface area.

isostatic, adj. [1. īsostátik; 2. aisoustǽtik]. See prec. & **static.** Of, pertaining to, isostasy.

jalopy, jaloppy [jalopi]. (American slang, 'of unknown origin'. Perhaps, however, in view of the facts that the word was first used, in 1925, in gangster-ridden Chicago and that the first recorded printed version has the spelling *jaloppi,* the original word was an Italian gangster's mis-hearing, and consequent elliptical use, of some such phrase as *a jallopy car* (or automobile), where *jallopy* signifies 'messy'—cp. the American slangy, virtually synonymous *heap,* a cheap or ordinary car—and is the adjective of *jallop,* a variant of *jalap,* a purgative; cp. also the Scottish and North Country *jallup,* a lively purgative, and the English dialectal *jollop,* a semi-fluid mess, and even the Australian *jollop,* a purgative.) An old, an outmoded or a dilapidated motor-car, a sense now (1952) creeping into British English; in U.S.A., occasionally of an old or outmoded aircraft (cf. the slang senses of *bus*: car; aircraft).

jeep. A utility cross-country vehicle, half car and half van (or truck). Probably elliptical for *G.P. vehicle, G.P.* being '(for) *g*eneral *p*urposes'; the form *jeep* seems to have been suggested by the sound emitted by a rat-like wonder-worker in E. C. Segar's comic strip *Popeye*—cf. **goon,** Suppl.

jerk (I.), n. **1.** Add: **b** (slang) *to get a jerk on* (*with* something), to hurry up, be quick (doing it).

jet liner or **jetliner.** An airliner that is jet-propelled.

jigger (I.), n. Add: **3.** (slang, orig. U.S.) Any appliance or mechanical device; a contraption. **4.** A glass that, holding 1½ fluid ounces, is used in mixing drinks, esp. cocktails.

jitters, n. pl. [1. jíterz; 2. džítəz]. *The jitters,* (Am. slang) 'the creeps', nervous fluster, trepidation.

job (I.), n. **1.** Phr. Add: *on the job,* busily at work.

ju-jitsu. See **ju-jutsu.**

juke box, juke joint. The *juke box,* an automatic player—set in motion by the insertion of a nickel—of phonograph records, so called because it characterizes a *juke joint,* a low roadhouse or dance-hall, but originally a shack frequented by Negro workers as a resort for drinking and dancing. For *box* cp. *musical box*; for *joint* see **joint (I.), 7. a**; *juke* appears to be a Negro word—as, very probably, is **jazz.**

key word. A word that either solves a problem or forms the most important or pertinent, or the illustrative, word in a phrase or a sentence.

kibitz [kib′its], **kibitzer** [kib′ítser]. The former ('to be, act as, a kibitzer') derives from the latter ('a meddlesome onlooker, at a game of cards; hence, any giver of unwanted advice'); and the latter, a Yiddish word, comes from colloquial Ger. *kiebitzen,* to look on at a card-game, itself from *Kiebitz,* or *Kibitz,* a meddlesome spectator, figurative employment of *Kiebitz,* a lapwing, the name (cp. **pewit**) being echoic.

kick (II.), n. **d** Add: Phr. *to get a kick out of something,* to find it stimulating, amusing, enjoyable.

killer. Add: **2.** As life becomes more deadly, the word increasingly tends to mean 'one who hunts in order to kill'; we even speak of a *killer ship.*

klystron [klistron], fr. Gk. *klustēr,* 'a syringe', & *-tron* as in *electron.* An electron tube that multiplies the oscillation-frequency of individual electrons and then converts their energy into such waves of very high frequency as flows in a radio beam that is used either in directing artillery fire or in television.

knee-action spring, n. A type of independent motor-car spring.

knock-out, n. & adj. Add: **3.** adj. (in competitions) Such that a competitor or team defeated in any round does not compete again: *knock-out competition, knock-out system.*

kolkhos, n. [1. kólkos; 2. kɔ́lkɔs]. Russ., abbr. of *kollektivii,* 'collective', & *khos,* base of *khozyaistvo,* 'household', &c. (U.S.S.R.) Collective farm organized, esp. under Five Year Plan, by pooling of peasant holdings. Cp. **sovkhos,** Suppl.

Komintern, n. See **Comintern.**

Komsomol, n. [1. kómsomol; 2. kɔ́msəməl]. Russ., abbr. of *kommunisticheskii soyus,* 'union', & *molodyozhi,* 'youth'. (U.S.S.R.) Communist League of Youth.

kulak, n. [1. kōōlak; 2. kūlæk], Russ., 'fist, grasper'. (U.S.S.R.) Independent well-to-do peasant: a class 'liquidated' under the system of 'collectives'.

lam, be on the, to be a fugitive from justice; **lam, take it on the,** to evade the police, or to avoid danger or serious trouble, by recourse to flight. (American slang—originally cant—of obscure origin.)

landing strip. See **airstrip.**

land mine. A mine that is buried in the ground; loosely (1940–1944), an aerial mine.

lattice, n. Add: **4.** The regular and more or less reticulate arrangement of atoms in a crystal.

Laurentian, n. & adj. [1. lōrénshian; 2. lōrénʃiən]. **1.** n. A follower or ardent admirer of D. H. Lawrence. **2.** adj. Of, pertaining to, a Laurentian; tending to make a religion of primitiveness and sex.

lay (III.), vb. **C.** *Lay off,* trans., to dismiss (an employee) temporarily through slackness of trade, &c.

Lebensraum [lābensroum]. Living room, i.e. living space, 'a place in the sun'. A German word, connoting an (alleged) need for national expansion.

leftist [left′ist]. A member of the political Left; a Socialist.

left-wing, adj. Of, pertaining to, the political Left; progressive.

lemon, n. **1.** Add: Phr. (slang) *the answer's a lemon,* the question is problematic; *to hand someone a lemon,* swindle him in a transaction.

lenticulated (or **lenticular**) film. In cinematography, a film that has lenticular embossings and is used for the production of motion pictures in natural colours.

leucotome [lōōkōtōm], **leucotomy** [lōōkotōmi], fr. Gk. *leukos,* 'white' (as is the cerebral cortex), & **-tome** or **-tomy,** 'a cutting, an incision'. The former is a rotating blade used in the latter, an operation for cutting into a lobe of the brain.

libido, n. [1. libído, libēdo; 2. libáidou, libídou], Lat. See **libidinous.** (psycho-analysis) Psychic urge, vital impetus, total life energy. Used by Freud for 'energy, a compulsive desire, deriving from the sexual instinct', and by Jung for 'energy deriving from the urge to live'.

lift (I.), vb. trans. **A. 5.** Add: **c** *to lift a person's face,* when the muscles of it have sagged, to restore it by surgical treatment to a more normal shape.

line (II.), n. Add: **17.** (slang, orig. U.S.) Information, special or inside information: *to get a line on,* obtain information about.

line-up, n. See **line (III.), B.** (colloq.) Alignment.

Link trainer. A mechanical device (named after its American initiator, Edward Link) enabling student pilots to learn to fly by using the normal instruments yet without going into the air.

liquidate, vb. trans. **1.** Add: **c** (colloq., orig. U.S.S.R.) to put an end to, suppress, stamp out (anything regarded as a public nuisance). Add: **3.** To kill, to murder, esp. if it be done systematically. Noun: *liquidation.*

literarism [literariʒm], fr. *literary* on *literalism.* Employment of very literary terms; such a word or phrase.

living room. See **Lebensraum,** Suppl.

load-shedding. Reduction of electricity supply in order to forestall an excessive strain upon a generating plant.

Locarno (agreement, pact), n. [1. lōkáhnō; 2. loukánou], fr. the Locarno treaty of 1925. Any international treaty binding each of three or more nations to give full military assistance against the aggressor, in the event of one nation signatory to the treaty being attacked by any of the others; a regional pact: *an Eastern Locarno,* a treaty of this kind between nations in Eastern Europe.

location scene, n. (films) Scene produced not in the studio but at some chosen spot elsewhere.

logorrhoea, n. [1. lògorēa; 2. lɔ̀gourīə]. **logo-** & Gk. *rhoia,* 'a flow, flowing'. (facet. allusion to *diarrhoea*) Excessive flow of words; wordiness, verbosity, prolixity.

lorry-hop, vb. intrans. To travel by getting lifts on lorries and other motor vehicles.

lousy, adj. Add: **c** (slang) *lousy with,* very well provided with; esp., *lousy with money.*

lowdown, n., fr. criminals' slang usage. (slang. orig. U.S.) True facts, correct information: *I'm giving you the lowdown.*

Luftwaffe [lōōftwahffĕ]. A German word, literally 'air weapon', to denote the air force of the Third Reich.

lush. Fr. **luscious,** this is the Royal Navy's answer to *smashing* (see **smasher** in Suppl.).

Machine Age, the. A phrase coined in the 1920's to describe that stage of civilization which, since ca. 1914, has been dominated by machines.

Mae West. A life-saving jacket worn by pilots flying over a sea. Coined by the R.A.F. in honour of the famous American film actress, the term was originally slang; by 1943 it had become official.

magnetic mine. A naval mine exploded immediately a magnetic needle is deflected by the nearness of a ship's metal hull.

magneto-, pref. Add: *magnetometer,* instrument for measuring the strength of the earth's magnetic field.

make-up, n. Add: **d** components: *elements in one's make-up,* fundamental qualities of one's nature.

-making, adjectival suffix in compound with other adjectives. (colloq.) Such as to make one this or that: *sick-making, shy-making.*

malarkey (or **-ky**) [malarki], occasionally **malak(k)y** [malaki]. American slang, fr. the modern form of Gk. *malakia,* softness, fr. *malakos,* soft: cp. esp. the Modern Gk. *maláka,* softening of the brain, and the fig. use of *soft soap.* The *arky* pronunciation may have been influenced by *larky,* mischievous. A deliberately misleading statement or story; blarney. *Don't give me the old malarkey!*

mammogen [mamōgen], fr. *mammo-,* combining-form (cf. **mammary**), & **-gen.** A hormone that promotes the growth of the mammary gland.

man. Add: **11.** At many English Public Schools for boys, *man* denotes a fellow-pupil.

manage (I.). **A.** vb. trans. **2.** Add: **c** (financ.) *a managed currency,* one that is off the gold standard and for whose stability the central bank is responsible.

manganin [manganin]. An alloy that, containing **manganese,** is used for making the wire of resistance standards.

man-sized, adj. (Am. slang) Large, difficult enough to occupy or tax a man's energies: *a man-sized job.*

maquis. Add: **2.** Hence, *les* (or English *the*) *Maquis,* those French guerilla fighters who opposed the Nazis in rural France, esp. in the scrublands of the central and southern regions of eastern France.

margin. Add: **4.** In psychology, that part—the marginal portion—of the field of consciousness which, at any given moment, is apprehended only vaguely.

Marxian, n. & adj. [1. máhksian; 2. máksiən]. Next word & **-ian. 1.** n. Follower of Karl Marx; adherent of Marxism. **2.** adj. Of, pertaining to, Marxism or Karl Marx.

Marxism, n. [1. máhksizm; 2. máksizm], fr. Karl Marx (1818–1883) & **-ism.** The doctrine of Karl Marx concerning the materialistic (i.e. economic) interpretation of history, the class struggle caused by capitalistic appropriation of 'surplus-value', and the ultimate triumph of the proletariat, leading to a system of Communism.

Marxist, n. & adj. [1. máhksist; 2. máksist], fr. prec. & **-ist.** Marxian.

matey, adj. [1. māti; 2. méiti]. **mate** (II.), **1.** & **-y** (IV.) **a** (colloq.) Sociable, companionable, friendly.

mean (I.), n. **4. a** Add: Phr. *means test,* official inquiry as to what means of subsistence an applicant for unemployment benefit can already obtain from members of the family and household where he lives: *family means test, household means test.*

means test. A test made of a retired, or of a temporarily unemployed, person's financial means, to determine respectively his pension or his unemployment pay.

mechanization, n. [1. mèkanīzā́shun; 2. mèkənaizéiʃən]. **mechanize** & **-ation.** **a** Technical transformation, for the sake of increased efficiency, by substituting machinery for direct human effort; **b** (specif.) the transformation of military units, redesigning them for mobility and resistance to gun-fire.

mechanized units. Those units of an army which are mechanically operated and transported.

mental (I.), adj. **1.** Add: **c** (slang, pred. & often by hyperbole) mentally deficient, feeble-minded; stupid.

meson [meśon], short for alternative **mesotron** [meśōtron], fr. **meso-** and the *-tron* of *electron.* A particle that has a mass roughly 200 times that of the electron and that transmits the forces that cause the atom to cohere.

mezzo-brow, n. & adj. [1. métsōbrou; 2. métsoubrau]. (Person) intermediate between highbrow and low-brow (colloq.).

micro-climate, -climatology. The latter is a science that deals with the former: and the former signifies the climate of a (usually small) area wherein the weather conditions are essentially the same and observable as a climatic entity.

micro-film. A (strip of) film for photographing, on a reduced scale, such things as manuscripts and periodicals.

micronize [mī́kronīz]. To pulverize into very fine particles. The corresponding noun is *micronization.*

micro-waves, n. Radio-waves of wavelength less than 1 metre.

mike, n. [1. mīk; 2. maik]. Slang abbr. of *microphone.*

militarist, adj. Directly from and answering to the noun **militarist.**

mill (I.), n. **1. a** Add: Phr. (colloq.) *to go through the mill,* to be severely disciplined, to get a gruelling.

milling, vbl. n. **1. b** (colloq.) (The act of) being 'put through the mill', severely disciplined; a gruelling experience.

mind, vb. **B.** intrans. **1.** Add: *mind out,* (slang) look out, (and) keep (or get) out of the way.

-minded, adjectival suffix. **1.** (preceded by an adj. or adv.) Having such-and-such a turn of mind: *politically-minded.* **2. a** (colloq.) Alive to the importance of such-and-such: *air-minded,* keenly interested in civil aviation, &c.; **b** (commerc. slang) willing to pay money for such-and-such: *telephone-minded, refrigerator-minded.*

minicam [mińikam]. A *mini*ature *cam*era.

mitt, n. Abbr. of **mitten.** (slang, orig. U.S.) Hand: *he gave me the frozen mitt,* shook my hand very coldly, showed marked unfriendliness to me; *I tipped his mitt,* (i.) shook him by the hand; (ii.) (fig.) disclosed what was in it, i.e. exposed his plans or intentions.

mixing, vbl. n. (films) Re-recording such as to mix in, e.g., music with the actors' voices.

mock-up. A structural model, natural-size, complete, accurate, esp. of an aircraft; used instructionally and, for manufacturers, constructively.

Mogul. Add: **2.** In American slang, a *mogul* is a magnate, esp. at Hollywood.

money, n. **5.** Phrs. Add: *it's money for jam,* (slang) good remuneration or profit for little or no trouble; *to be in the money,* hobnobbing with the rich.

Mongolian. 1. adj. Add: **b** *Mongolian idiocy,* Mongolism.

Mongolism, n. [1. móngg olizm; 2. mɔ́ŋgəlizm]. **mongol** & **-ism.** A form of mental deficiency accompanied by physical resemblance to the Mongolian race.

monitor, vb. trans., fr. the noun. To act as a monitor, or checker, in respect of (matter coming over the air, esp. in wartime).

monomark, n. [1. mónōmark; 2. mɔ́noumāk], (trade name) fr. **mono-** & **mark.** Mark, consisting chiefly of letters of the alphabet, which an individual person can use in the place of a permanent address and for the identification of his belongings.

monoscope [mońōskōp]. In television: a cathode-ray tube designed to produce a **video** (Suppl.) signal of a still picture.

montage, n. Add: **b** (more strictly) cut, cuts, designed to elicit an emotional response not registered in the shots themselves.

motorize, vb. trans. [1. mṓtorīz; 2. móutəraiz], fr. **motor (I.), 2.** & **-ize.** (esp., military units) To transform by substituting motor for horse transport.

mouthful. 3. (fig. & sometimes iron., colloq.) *To say a mouthful,* say something striking, important.

mud, n. Phr. Add: (person's) *name is mud,* (colloq.) he has lost any prestige, good name, credit, he once had.

museum-piece, n. **a** Valuable object in, suitable for, a museum; **b** (fig.) person or thing of special interest or value, esp. if not up-to-date.

nance, n. [1. nans; 2. næns]. Abbr. of next word. An effeminate male person.

nancy, adj. & n. [1. nánsi; 2. nǽnsi], fr. the girl's name, Nancy. **a** n. An effeminate male person; **b** adj., of this nature; Phr. *a nancy boy.*

natter. To chatter, often with a suggestion of querulousness. A dialectal word ('to work clatteringly, to potter noisily': obviously echoic) adopted by the Armed Forces in 1939–1945.

navicert [nā́visert], a blend of '*navi*gation *cert*ificate'. A consular exemption from stoppage by Naval patrol; the Royal Navy's permission to a ship to continue its voyage.

Nazi, n. & adj. [1. náhtsē; 2. nátsi]. Germ., abbr. of *Nazionalsozialist(ische).* **1.** n. **a** A member of the National Socialist party, formed by Adolf Hitler at Munich in 1925 with the aim of making Germany united and powerful after ridding it of Communism, Social Democracy, &c. Success in the election of Jan. and March 1933 enabled this party to establish itself, ruthlessly sweeping away all opposition. Cp. **Fascist. b** A member of the actively pro-German party since formed in one of several other states, such as Austria. **2.** adj. Of, or pertaining to, the Nazis or their system, aims or methods.

Nazism, Naziism, n. [1. náhtsizm, náhtsēizm; 2. nātsizm, nátsiizm]. The political system, the aims or the methods of the Nazis.

necking, vbl. n. (slang) Hugging, petting (demonstratively).

needle (II.), vb. trans. Add: **3.** (colloq.) To prick repeatedly with gibes or doubts, often in order to irritate someone into intended action.

neon, n. Add: *neon sign,* lettering, &c., usually forming an advertisement, lit up by means of neon light.

neoprene [nḗōprēn], fr. **neo-** & chloro*prene* (*chloro-,* as in *chloroform* & *prene,* itself short for *isoprene,* an arbitrary word containing **iso-** & **-ene**). A synthetic plastic, more impermeable than rubber.

Nep, n. [1. nep; 2. nɛp]. Russ., abbr. of *novaya ekonomicheskaya politika.* (U.S.S.R.) The New Economic Policy, permitting a controlled capitalism in certain trades, from 1921 till the first Five Year Plan; *Nep man,* private entrepreneur or trader under Nep.

neper [nā́per], fr. John Napier or Naper, the inventor of logarithms. The ratio-unit of two amounts of power (e.g. output and intake).

nerts, interj. & n. [1. nërts; 2. nʌts]. Imitative (vulg. slang). See **pshaw. a** interj. **b** n., *nerts to you!* I (deliberately) say to you 'Nerts!'

network. Add: **3.** A system of related yet not necessarily inter-related units; as of airfields.

neutrino, n. [1. nūtrḗnō; 2. njūtrínou]. **neutron** & **-ine (VI.). b** (phys.) Electrically neutral particle having the same mass as an electron.

neutron, n. [1. nū́tron; 2. njū́trɔn]. **neuter** & ending on the anal. of **electron.** (phys.) Particle having about the same mass as a proton, but without electrical charge. It is thought to consist of a proton combined with an electron.

new look, the. The longer and fuller dresses introduced in mid-1947 and thus named early in 1948. A reversion to an earlier, more gracious, less skimpy mode.

New Order, the. The political order enforced in Nazi Germany and, by Hitler, intended for the outer world.

news, n. pl. Add: **c** anything that the public can be induced to read about in newspapers: *cats are news now; news value,* (degree of) salability as news.

news reel, n. A talking-film giving items of current or recent news.

Nissen [nisen] **hut.** A barrel-shaped sleeping-hut, much used by the British Army in 1914–1918 and later. It had been invented by Lt.-Col. P. Nissen, who died in 1930.

nitwit, n. [1. nítwit; 2. nítwit], fr. **nit** (negative) & **wit.** (U.S. slang) A dolt, blockhead.

no man, n. (Am. slang) An unobliging and contrary man who refuses to join in. Cp. **yes man,** Suppl.

Non-co-operation, n. The Indian movement, led by Mahatma Gandhi, of non-violent civil disobedience to British rule.

non-skid, adj. Designed so as not to skid.

non-starter, n. [1. nòn stárter; 2. nɔ̀n stātə]. (colloq.) A person, or horse, that fails to start as a competitor in a race. Also fig.

nose-dive, nosedive, n. & vb. intrans. Add: **2. a** n. A débâcle, precipitate downward trend in fortune, &c.; **b** vb., to take such a downward trend.

nucleus, n. Add: **4.** (phys.) The positively charged central core of an atom.

nut, n. Add: **6.** (Am. slang) An idiot, dolt.

nuts, adj. See prec. & **nut, 2.,** Dict. (slang) Cracked, crazy, dotty.

nylon. (An arbitrary word, concocted by the inventors and marketers.) A synthetic material that is derived from coal, water and air, and is used esp. in making stockings; hence, elliptically for a *nylon stocking.*

Oerlikon [eŕlēkōn: American; eŕlikon: British] or **oerlikon,** fr. *Oerlikon* in Switzerland. A rapid-firing automatic anti-aircraft gun, used esp. against dive bombers.

officese. See **commercialese,** Suppl.

officialese. Official jargon; cp. **Federal prose,** Suppl.

okay, adv. & adj. [1. ò kā́; 2. òu kéi], = O.K.

oke, adv. & adj. [1. ōk; 2. ouk]. Abbr. fr. prec. (slang) Quite all right.

okey doke, adv. & adj. [1. ṓki dṓk; 2. óuki dóuk], fr. prec. & *doke,* meaningless rhyming syllable. (slang) Quite all right.

on (I.), prep. Add: **9.** At the expense of, **a** (financially): *have this one on me;* **b** (generally): *the joke's on him;* **c** *that's a new one on me,* is news to me (i.e. shows up my ignorance).

once-over, n. (slang, orig. U.S.) Cursory survey, hasty examination: *to give* (person or thing) *the once-over.*

one (II.), n. **2.** Add: **b** *a one,* (colloq. & vulg.) an odd, strange, eccentric, person: *you are a one!*

one-track, adj. **a** (of railways, &c.) Having only a single line of rails; **b** (fig.) one-idea'd: *a one-track mind.*

one way, one-way, adj. Restricted to one direction: *one-way traffic*, lit. & fig.

operational [operáshunal]. Engaged in, pertaining to, battle; esp. of aircraft and duties.

operative word, the. (colloq.) The most important word, the pertinent word, 'the key word', in a phrase or a sentence.

organized [organīzd or organīzd], fr. **organize, 2.** Mostly in *be*, or *to get, organized*, the latter esp. in the imperative. To have arranged, to arrange, things advantageously for oneself; *to organize*, to obtain cleverly or surreptitiously, fr. the German *organisieren*, to 'scrounge' or 'wangle' something.

out for, to be. See **for**, Suppl.

outsize(d), adj. [dutsdiz(d)]. (of ready-made clothes; & gen., colloq.) Exceptionally large.

overcall, vb. trans. & intrans. [ōuvə kɔ̄l]. (in bridge) **A.** trans. **a** To outbid; **d** *to overcall one's hand*, bid higher than it justifies; also fig. **B.** intrans. **a** To outbid one's partner or opponent; **b** to overcall one's hand.

over-compensation, n. (psycho-analysis) Excess of compensation, often taking the form of an overbearing manner; see **compensation**, Suppl.

overtone. Add: **2.** An implication; some aim, purpose, motive over and above the apparent. Cp. **undertone**, Suppl.

Oxford Group, n. See **Buchmanism.**

Oxford-Grouper, n. (colloq.) An adherent of the 'Oxford Groups'.

panatrope, n. [1. pánatrōp; 2. pǽnətroup]. See **pan-** & **trope.** Electrical contrivance, consisting of pick-up, amplifier and loud-speaker, for making audible the sounds recorded on a gramophone record.

panic, vb. intrans. & vb. trans., fr. the noun. To get into a panic, to become panicky; to cause (others) to do so.

panning, vbl. n. Abbr. fr. **panorama.** (films) **a** Sweeping horizontally with the camera to get a panoramic effect; **b** the visual effect so produced.

pansy, n. Add: adj. & vb. trans. & intrans. Also add: (slang) **2.** n. (fig.) An effeminate male person given to self-adornment. **3.** adj. **a** (of persons) Effeminate and given to self-adornment; **b** (of things) of, pertaining to, or in any way reminiscent of, such persons; chic. **4.** vb. **a** trans., also *pansy up*, to render (oneself or one's intimate belongings) pansy or chic: **b** intrans., with reflexive meaning.

pants, n. Add: **c** (slang, orig. U.S.) Phr. *a kick in the pants*, i.e. on the buttocks; but chiefly fig., (the administering of) a sharp check or rebuff.

Panzer [pantser], German for 'armour'. In combination, e.g. *Panzer division*, it signifies 'armoured'.

parachutist. Add: **2.** A soldier trained to make a parachute landing and, immediately he lands, to begin fighting.

parity. Add: **3.** The difference between what esp. a farmer gets for his produce and what he has to pay out.

park, vb. trans. Add: **3.** (slang) **a** To place a thing on one side or in some spot chosen for safety or convenience; **b** (facet., pretending that a person is an inanimate object) (i.) to leave (e.g. a child) in someone's charge; (ii.) to place in position, plant: *park yourself here.*

parlary [pahrlahri] or **parlyaree** [pahrliarē]. The Italianate vocabulary of circus-hands, sideshow-men, organ-grinders, troupers (itinerant actors and actresses: see **troupe**). For instance, It. *letto*, a bed, yields *letty*, bed, (hence) lodgings.

partisan (I.). **2. b** revived during the war of 1939–1945.

part-time, adj. Employed for, taking up, only part of the working day: *a part-time worker, a part-time job.*

part-timer, n. (colloq.) Part-time worker.

party (I.), n. **2. a** Add: *hen party, stag party*, party consisting entirely of females, of males; *petting party*, see below.

party line. The *line*, of course, of policy adopted by any political party, esp. the Socialist party of Britain. The term originated among the Communists: the line they have to toe.

pass (I.), vb. **B.** trans. **5. a** Add: Phr. *to pass the buck*, hand on something embarrassing. **C.** Add: *Pass out*, (colloq.) (i.) to faint, become unconscious; (ii.) to become dead drunk; (iii.) to die.

peak year, n. A year for which statistics recording some selected data reach a maximum point as compared with surrounding years.

pedocal [ped'okal], fr. Gk. *pedon*, 'ground', & L. *calx* (genitive *calcis*), 'lime'. In agriculture: a soil that belongs to that major kind which is characterized by a zone of calcium. Adj. *pedocalcic.*

peel off. (of aircraft, esp. bombers) To veer away to the outside of a formation, esp. from the base of an echelon, in order to dive steeply.

penatin [pen'atin], a blend of '*peni*cillium *notatum*' (a particular mould) and the 'chemical' suffix **-in.** An anti-bacterial substance. Cp.:

penicillin [pen'-i-sil-in or pe-nis'-il-in], fr. *penicill*ium (a genus of fungi) & **-in**; *penicillium* is a Scientific Latin derivative fr. L. *penicillum* (variant of *penicillus*, a pencil), so named from the tufts at the ends of the conidiophores (bearers of asexual spores). A potently anti-bacterial, non-poisonous, acid substance extracted from a green mould (*penicillium notatum*) and used against such diseases as pneumonia and meningitis. Discovered in 1928 by Dr., later Sir, Alexander Fleming, Scottish bacteriologist, and mass-produced in U.S.A. from 1942 onwards.

perishing, adj. Add: **2.** (colloq., in place of an expletive) Confounded, infernal.

perm, n. Slang abbr. of **permanent wave** (colloq., hairdressing).

Peter Pan, fr. the eponymous boy hero of Sir James Barrie's play (1904). A man retaining the zest, freshness, fancy and imagination of a boy; sometimes derogatively for a childish man.

petting, vbl. n., fr. **pet (II.).** Caressing; *a petting party*, bout of caressing.

phase, n. Add: **4.** (physical chem.) One component of a heterogeneous mixture.

phenomenology, n. [1. fenòmenóloji; 2. finɔ̀minɔ́lədži]. **phenomenon** & **-logy.** A recent school of philosophical thought originating from Husserl, which claims to reject rational concepts and judgements and to start from reality as it appears in pure intuition.

phenotype, n. [1. fénotīp; 2. fínoutaip]. See (first element in) **phenomenon** & **type.** (biol.) The part of its hereditary constitution that an organism actually displays.

phon [fon]. (Cp. **-phone.**) A unit in the measurement of loudness. Cp.:

phoneme [fōnēm], fr. Gk. *phōnēma*, 'a sound'. A group of those variants of one speech-sound which result from varying phonetic conditions.

phoney [fōni], preferable to **phony.** (American slang, adopted in Britain, late in 1939, as a result of the American phrase, *the phoney war.* The American underworld used *fawney* (later *phoney*) *man* for a vendor of imitation jewellery, from the English underworld's *fawney man*, an operator of *fawney-dropping*, whereby the gullible were tricked into buying a finger-ring (*fawney*) dropped on the pavement; English *fawney* derives from Irish *fainne*, a finger-ring.) False, faked, pretended; thoroughly dishonest; based upon—leading up to—reminiscent or indicative of—foul play or a criminal racket. In the R.A.F. of 1934–1945 and after, *phoney gen* has meant 'false information', esp. if deliberately false.

photo(-)finish. Such a finish to a race as demands an examination of the photograph in order to determine the winner.

photogenic [fōtōgēnik], adj. applied to one whose photographs flatter him or her—or to anyone who constitutes a subject agreeable to photograph.

phut, adv. [1. fut; 2. fat], fr. Hind. *phatna*, 'to split, burst'. *To go phut*, become suddenly broken; collapse, end in nothing.

phylogeny, n. [1. filójeni; 2. failɔ́dženi]. See **phylogenesis** & **-y.** Phylogenesis.

physical chemistry, n. Chemistry interpreted in terms of physics.

piat [píat], fr. the official description, '*pro*jector, *i*nfantry, *a*nti-*t*ank'. A light, anti-tank gun used by the British Army during the latter part of the war of 1939–1945.

pick (II.), vb. trans. **c** *Pick up.* **3.** Add: **d** (slang) to take into custody, arrest. Add: *Pick on*, to single (someone) out and pester, badger (him).

pick-up, n. Device by which the sound-track on a gramophone record causes corresponding variation in an electric current in a loud speaker.

piece of cake, it's a. That's easy! (R.A.F. slang (1939–1945) that has gained a wide currency. A piece of cake is supposedly easy to eat.)

piezo-electric effect, n. [1. piézō; 2. paiízou], fr. Gk. *piézein*, 'to press'. The production of an electro-motive force in certain crystals by means of pressure.

pigeon pair, fr. the affection existing between a pair of pigeons. A boy and a girl as the complete offspring in a family.

pink (VI.), vb. intrans. Imitative word. (of petrol engines) To make a metallic sound, caused by premature explosion; to knock (**B. b**).

pin-up, n. Such a photograph, or picture from a magazine, of a girl as a man in the Services might wish to pin up on the wall (&c.) by his bed or his bunk.

pipe (II.), vb. **A.** intrans. **2.** Add: **d** Phr. (colloq.) *to pipe down*, become less cock-sure, less exorbitant.

place (I.), n. **2.** and **8.** Add: *place in the sun*, *a* or *one's.* See **Lebensraum,** Suppl.; probably a translation of the French *une place au soleil.* The definition at **sun (I.),** n., **1.,** needs to be modified: prominence—for an individual at least—is no longer required.

plane table, n. **plane (IV.)** & **table.** Drawing board mounted on a tripod and used, e.g., by surveyors.

plate (I.), n. **7.** a Add: (iii.) Phr. *to hand someone something on a plate*, (fig.) surrender something gratuitously.

plutonium [plōōtōnium]. Cp. **Plutonic.** The principal ingredient of—the fundamental element in—the atomic bomb; it is an artificial element prepared from uranium.

pocket battleship. A comparatively small battleship carrying a very heavy armament.

point (I.), n. Add: **A. 6.** A unit in any rationing system, esp. for food.

pointer, n. Add: **3.** *pointer* (*ad.*), (commerc. slang) Small advertisement indicating where a larger one is to be found.

polio [pōliō]. A shortening of *acute anterior poliomyelitis* (cp. **poliomyelitis**), the full medical name for infantile paralysis.

polystyrene [polistírēn], a combination of **poly-** and *styrene* (a hydrocarbon distilled from **storax**: cp. **-ene**). A transparent and colourless plastic.

pop-shop, n. (slang) Pawn-shop.

positron, n. [1. pózitron; 2. pɔ́zitrɔn], *positive* & ending on the anal. of *electron.*

(phys.) Positively charged particle having mass equal to that of the electron.

pot-bound, adj. **a** (of a plant) Suffering from insufficiency of space for its roots in a pot; **b** (fig.) suffering from lack of room to expand.

powder room. A woman's lavatory in, e.g., a hotel or a club. (Where women go to powder their noses.)

power politics. A translation of Germ. *Machtpolitik,* international politics conducted upon a basis of ' Might is right '.

prang. Echoic—cp. **bang.** (Air Force slang.) To bomb (a target) heavily; to crash one's own, or an enemy, aircraft.

precision bombing ; precision instruments. The former is effected by an expert use of a certain combination (and kind) of the latter; the latter are adapted to delicate work and accurate results.

predictor. Add: **2.** An instrument whereby one controls anti-aircraft fire.

prefab [prĕfab]. Short for *prefabricated dwelling* (or *house*).

preselector gear, n. (motor-cars) Gearing device such that the gear about to be engaged is previously selected.

prick (I.), n. To **1.** add: **b** the penis. (Now vulgar.)

priority. Add: **2.** Preference by government-granted permission and according to a government-determined scale of importance.

producer, n. **1.** Add: **c** person who takes the initiative and financial responsibility in producing a film; cp. **director,** Suppl.

prom, n. Abbr. of **Promenade Concert.**

prosthetic. Add: **2.** In biochemistry: denoting, or belonging to, such a group, or such a radical, of a different kind as has been substituted in, or added to, a compound.

protagonist. To **2.** add: now occasionally used of an instrument or any other non-human factor.

protocol (I.), n. Add: **4.** In diplomacy: the rigid code setting forth the degree of obedience, the order of precedence, the rules of official and social behaviour.

protopathic, adj. [1. prōtōpáthik; 2. prō*u*to*u*pǽpik]. See **proto- & pathos & -ic.** (physiol.) (of sensations) Not accurately localized nor accurately estimated; opposed to **epicritic,** Suppl.

pseudo, adj., fr. **pseudo-.** (colloq., of things material and immaterial) Not genuine, not real; sham, counterfeit: *all this panelling is pseudo.* Sometimes of persons; see **bogus,** Suppl.

psychotic [psīkótik]. The adjective answering to **psychosis.**

public relations. The relations of, e.g., the Army with civilians, or those of a Ministry, or a large firm, with the outside public.

punch-drunk, adj. Stupefied, whether temporarily or permanently, by having been severely or frequently punched on the head. (A boxing colloquialism.)

punk (I.), n. Add: **c** adj. (slang, orig. U.S.) Rotten, worthless, no good at all.

purge (II.), n. Add: **3.** Hence, a political liquidating: cp. **liquidate,** Suppl.

pursuit plane. The American equivalent of **fighter,** Suppl.

put (I.), vb. **A.** trans. **1.** Add: *to stay put,* (colloq. of a thing) to stay where, or as, it is put. **C.** *Put over,* Add: **b** trans., (colloq. orig. U.S.) to get the public to accept (an idea, &c.).

quisling [kwiz'ling]. A traitor that, his country having been conquered, becomes an influential puppet of the conquerors, as did Major Vidkun *Quisling,* when, in April 1940, the Germans overran Norway and he accepted the head-ship of a Nazi-sponsored government. (In 1945 he died a traitor's death.) Cp. **Fifth Column.**

racism [rāsizm]. A nation's assumption of racial superiority (cp. **Herrenvolk,** Suppl.); a policy based upon this assumption.

radar [rādar], fr. '*ra*dio *d*etecting *a*nd *r*anging (or, *r*ange-finding) '. A radio device for the detection of enemy aircraft.

radio, n. Add: **c** a wireless receiving set.

radio-, pref. Add: **b** to wireless: *radio-gramophone.*

radio-gram, n. Colloq. abbr. for next word.

radio-gramophone, n. Combined wireless receiving set and gramophone with pick-up. (See **pick-up,** Suppl.)

radiolocation [rādiōlōkáshun]. The detection of the position and the course of enemy aircraft by the use of radiolocators; collectively, radiolocators constitute radar.

rake-off, n. (colloq.) Pecuniary profit made illegitimately by one or more persons concerned in a transaction; also, middle-man's profit.

ranger. Add: **3.** A *Ranger* is the American form of the British Commando (the individual).

raspberry, n. Add: Phr. (slang, orig. U.S.) *to give, hand* (a person), *a raspberry,* insult by a gesture of contempt.

ray (II.), n. **2.** Add: *cosmic rays,* a penetrating radiation producing ionization and coming from an extra-terrestrial source.

reaction. Add to **5. c** (loosely) an emotional or intellectual response; an opinion.

reaction control, n. Device for increasing the receptivity of a wireless receiving set.

real Mackay (British) or **McCoy** (American), **the.** (Slang.) The best of its kind; very good; esp., genuine and good. The very old *Mackay* form originated among the clan Mackay; the American alteration (*McCoy*) commemorates the famous boxer, 'Kid' McCoy.

recordist, n. [1. rekórdist; 2. rikáudist]. **record (I.) & -ist.** Person responsible for everything connected with the audible part of a film during its production.

rectification, n. Add: **4.** (elect.) The process of converting an alternating into a direct current.

red. Add: **3.** A *Red* is a Communist.

reducing, n. See **slimming,** Suppl.

reflate, vb. trans. & intrans. [1. rēflát; 2. rīfléit]. See **re- & inflate. 1.** trans. To increase (the amount of money in circulation) towards what it was before a period of deflation began. See **inflate. 2.** intrans. To increase the amount of money in circulation, as in **1.**

reflation, n. [1. rēfláshun; 2. rīfléiʃən]. **reflate & -ion.** Act or process of reflating; state of being reflated.

register (II.), vb. **A.** trans. **1.** Add: **c** (i.) (of a film) To depict, express (usu. some emotion); (ii.) (by extension, gen.; colloq.) To express, represent.

relativistic, adj. [1. rèlativístik; 2. rèlətivístik], fr. **relativist & -ic.** In accordance with the principles of, accepting the postulates of, relativity: *relativistic, as opposed to Newtonian, mechanics.*

re-recording, vbl. n. (film-producing) Changing the sound-track by mixing or by adding a voice or voices to it.

reticulate. To **2. a** add: To distribute—esp. over a large area—by means of a *network* of roads, channels, conductors, &c.

retread, n. & vb. trans. [1. rētréd; 2. rītréd], fr. **re- & tread (II.), 2. c. a** n. Motor-tyre the original tread of which has been removed and replaced by new rubber; **b** vb. trans., to furnish with new treads.

revisionism, n. [1. revízhunizm; 2. rivížənizm]. **revision & -ism.** Policy, advocacy, of revising something; specif., of revising (i.) the Versailles and associated treaties; (ii.) Marxism.

revisionist, n. & adj. prec. & **-ist.** (One who works, or is) in favour of revisionism.

rewarding, adj. Profitable; very agreeable. A modern vogue-word.

rexine, n. [1. réksēn; 2. réksīn]. A type of imitation cloth used for bookbinding, &c.

rheology, n. [1. rēóloji; 2. rīɔ́lədži]. **rheo- & -logy.** The scientific study of the flow of liquids, gases and plastic substances.

ribbon development, n. The uncontrolled building of houses and shops along main roads, esp. those leading out of towns.

road(-)block. A defensive block—against enemy tanks, mechanized artillery, motor cyclists—built across a road at a tactical point.

road-hog, n. & vb. intrans. See **-hog,** Suppl.

rocket (I.). Add: **2.** (Slang.) A reprimand: it blows the recipient sky-high.

rod, n. **1.** Add: **e** (Am. slang) revolver, gun.

roll (II.), vb. intrans. **C.** *Roll in;* Add: (slang) to pay a casual or unexpected visit, to arrive. *Roll up;* Add: **3.** To keep a rendezvous, put in an appearance; to arrive (in large numbers).

Ronin [rō'nin], fr. Japanese, literally, 'wave man'. A hired bravo; earlier, a rather disreputable knight-errant, who, separated from his feudal lord, wandered—like a wave—restlessly about the country.

rough-house, vb. intrans., fr. Phr. *a rough house,* see under **rough (I.), 4. a.** To behave rowdily; to brawl.

roundabout, adj. & n. Add: **3.** n. Arrangement of the roadways at a junction, such that traffic circulates in one direction round a central object or space.

routineer, n. [1. rōōtinḗr; 2. rūtiníə]. **routine & -eer.** One who is efficient in routine work, but, through lack of imagination and originality, is unable to deal with wide issues and great changes, and expects others to be like himself.

rubber (III.), vb. Abbr. of next word.

rubber-neck, n. & vb. intrans. [1. rúbernek; 2. rábənɛk]. (slang, U.S. origin) **a** n. One who peers and pries about inquisitively; **b** vb., to pry, peer about inquisitively.

rubber stamp, rubber-stamp, n. & vb. trans. **1.** n. **a** Ill-considered and quasi-mechanical approval or authorization; **b** a person who gives such authorization or approval. **2.** vb. trans. To authorize, as if mechanically, without consideration.

rube, n. [1. rōōb; 2. rūb]. (U.S. slang) A rustic, country bumpkin.

sabotage, vb. trans fr. the noun. To wreck or ruin a plan, a policy, a political programme. (Jargon.)

sadist, n. [1. sáhdist; 2. sádist], fr. **sadism & -ist.** Person who displays sadism.

sadistic, adj. [1. sadístik; 2. sādístik, sədístik], fr. prec. & **-ic.** (Characteristic) of, pertaining to, a sadist.

saga. Add: **3.** Short for *saga novel,* whether the very long family novel during several generations or the usually long novel about a community; sometimes called the *roman fleuve,* Fr. for ' river(-like) novel '.

salariat(e), n. [1. salắriat; 2. səlɛ́əriət], fr. **salary (I.) & -ate.** Salaried workers as a class.

sales-resistance, n. (commerc. slang, orig. U.S.) Resistance to salesmanship, refusal to buy or order goods, &c.

samba. From African (Negro) through Portuguese. A Brazilian dance of the 1920's and 1930's, not unknown in U.S.A.

sanction (I.), n. **2.** Insert: **b** (League of Nations) chiefly pl., measures concerted by League members against an aggressor nation, in order to coerce it into acceptance of arbitration: *financial sanctions,* restriction or cessation of loan credits; *economic sanctions,* restriction or cessation of trade with it; *military sanctions,* force, e.g. a naval blockade.

sanctionist, adj. & n. [1. sángkshunist; 2. sǽŋkʃənist]. prec. & **-ist.** Person advocating, supporting, sanctions as in prec.

sap, n. Abbr. of **saphead.**

scene, n. **4. a** Add: in films, a shot: see **shot,** Suppl.

schadenfreude, n. [1. sháhdenfroider; 2. ʃádənfròidə]. Germ. fr. *schaden,* 'injury', & *freude,* 'joy'. Malicious joy at the misfortunes of others.

schizoid, adj. & n. [1. skízoid; 2. skáizoid]. See next word & **-oid.** Mildly schizophrenic (person).

schizophrenia, n. [1. skīzōfrénia; 2. skàizoufríniə]. See **schizo- & phrenic.** Dementia praecox.

schizophrenic, adj. [1. skīzōfrénik; 2. skàizoufrénik]. prec. & **-ic.** Suffering from, liable to, dementia praecox.

scientific attitude. That cool, sceptical, judicial attitude which characterizes, or is supposed to characterize, scientists, esp. in their researches.

scorched earth (policy). A concerted plan, carried out thoroughly by the Russians in 1941, to deprive the enemy of supplies by burning or otherwise destroying everything before abandoning an area.

scram, n. & vb. intrans. [1. skram; 2. skræm], fr. **scramble.** (U.S. slang) **1.** n. A hasty departure. **2.** vb. intrans. To depart hastily, esp. imperat.: *Scram!* off with you!

screen (IV.), vb. trans. Add: **2.** Hence, to investigate the antecedents and the political views of candidates for (esp. governmental) employment.

screwball. From such a ball as, in baseball, screws or wobbles in its flight from pitcher to striker. (American slang.) A crazy or, at the best, an eccentric person.

screwy, adj. Add: **3.** (U.S. slang) Not quite right in the head, slightly mad. See Phr. *to have a screw loose,* under **screw (I.) 1.**

scrip (II.), n. Add: **c** Paper or token money issued not by a bank or by a state treasury, but by a municipality or by some organization for production and exchange, and backed not by gold but by goods. Also attrib.: *scrip money; scrip group,* group of persons using this medium of exchange.

sedimented, adj. [1. sédimèntid; 2. sédimèntid], fr. **sediment.** (chem.) Having formed a sediment.

seersucker, n. [1. sérsuker; 2. síəsakə]. (orig. U.S.) A light linen or cotton fabric. (A Hindi word, from Persian.)

self-expression. The chief means of self-realization. A term much used by a slightly outmoded school of psychiatrists and educators—but do they know they're outmoded?

semantics. Add: **2.** A so-called science that deals with the relation between signs (symbols) and that to which they refer; a science dealing with the relation between signs and the human beings using them or having them imposed; esp. the employment of symbols as a means towards the systematization of the language of science.

send (I.), vb. **C.** Add: *Send over,* to broadcast, trans.

sense (I.), n. Add: **B.** In combination with another noun, intuitive understanding and good judgement in a particular sphere: *road sense;* but, for **horse-sense,** see Dict.

sensum, n., pl. *sensa* [1. sénsum, -a; 2. sénsəm, -ə], Lat. (P.P. neut. of *sentire,* 'to feel'), 'a thing felt'; see **sense.** (philos.) (Term used for) the immediate content of sensation (to avoid pre-judging whether this content is mental or physical).

seppuku, fr. Japanese. The ceremonial form of suicide practised by Japanese officers—a superior form of **hara-kiri.**

sequence, n. **3.** Add: **d** (films) succession of shots together forming a main division of a film.

servo (-assisted) break, n. (motor-cars) Some form of break such that the motion of the car reinforces the breaking which the driver applies to the shoes.

set (III.), adj. **3.** Add: **b** (slang, orig. U.S.) ready to begin; ready to start away: esp., *all set,* quite ready.

sez you, adverbial phr. [1. sèz yōō; 2. sèz yû], for *says* (i.e. say) *you.* (slang, orig. U.S.) (iron.) As you say, (but I doubt it, or I don't believe it); sometimes interrog.

shadow factory. Either a framework easily completed if the occasion demand completion or a mock-factory designed to mislead enemy air pilots.

Shangri-La, fr. *Shangri,* an arbitrary name, and Tibetan *la,* a mountain pass. Coined by James Hilton in his novel *The Lost Horizon,* 1933, to denote an idyllic land, an agreeable Utopia.

shape of things to come, the. A slightly pompous synonym for 'the future', taken immediately from H. G. Wells's *The Shape of Things to Come. The Ultimate Revolution,* 1933. Cp. **brave new world,** Suppl.

shemozzle, n. [1. shemózl; 2. ʃimózl]. (U.S.; orig., slang) A rough and tumble, a row, an uproar.

Sherlock Holmes and **Dr. Watson,** from the detective and his medical friend in Arthur Conan Doyle's collections of short detective stories, beginning with *The Adventures of Sherlock Holmes,* 1891, and ending a quarter-century later. Any scientific detective; hence, any person showing detective ability; Dr. Watson—cp. the catch-phrase, *Elementary, my dear Watson*—represents a slightly pompous, rather dull commentator-friend.

shock-absorber, n. (motor-cars) A device for damping out excessive road vibration and counteracting the effects of axle movement.

shoot (I.), vb. **A.** trans. **4.** Phr. Add: *to shoot down* (person or crowd), suppress, dispose of by shooting and killing or wounding; *to shoot down* (aircraft), bring down by gunfire; *shot down,* (slang, fig.) decisively defeated in an argument.

short time, n. Employment cut down to some fraction of full time, with a corresponding curtailment of wages.

shot (III.), n. **7.** Add: **c** An example, short continuous piece, of cinema photography: *an unusually interesting shot. Long shot,* shot taken from long distance; *mid-shot,* shot taken from medium distance; *crane shot, zoom shot,* shot taken while the camera is moved by a crane; *model shot,* shot taken, not of the subject represented, but of a (small-scale) model of it. Add: **8.** Phr. (colloq., U.S.) *big shot,* an important person.

show (II.), n. **2. a** Add: (ii.) (colloq.) stage performance: *leg show,* revue, &c., in which the legs of the chorus are a prominent feature.

show-down, n., fr. the 'showing down' (i.e. showing face-upwards on the table) of the cards after bidding, &c., in certain card games. (slang) **a** Any test of real strength and backing in a struggle, e.g. between political parties. Phr. *if it comes to a show-down;* **b** a frank avowal of, or exchange of confidences about, personal motives.

siblings, n. pl. [1. síblingz; 2. síbliŋz], fr. **sib & -ling (I.).** (biol). Offspring of the same parents.

sign, vb. **B.** intrans. **3.** Add: **b** *sign in, out, off,* &c., sign one's name as being, going to be, in, out, away from, &c.

signature tune, often shortened to **signature.** A tune that has come—or is intended—to be recognized as the identifier of an orchestra or a programme, esp. in radio or television; hence, any musical number, or any group of sounds, constituting such an identifier.

significant. Add to **2. c** esp. in the art term, *significant form,* form with values and implications additional to the representational.

Silent Service, the. The Royal Navy—from its tradition of reticence.

simp, n. (U.S. slang.) Abbr. of **simpleton.**

siren, 3. Add: During the war of 1939–1945, the siren that announced the advent and then the departure of enemy raider aircraft.

sissy, n. & adj. [1. sísi; 2. sísi]. **a** n. An effeminate (male) person; **b** adj., of this nature.

sit-down strike, often merely **sit-down.** A downing of tools and a refusal to be ejected from the scene of work until a claim has been met or a complaint satisfied.

Sitzkrieg. Literally, 'sitting war'; in humorous opposition to *Blitzkrieg* (see **blitz,** Suppl.). 'The Phoney War' of September 1939–March 1940.

Sixth Column, the. See **Fifth Column, the.**

sixty-four dollar question, the. The crucial question—from the literal sense: that final question which, successfully answered, brings to the answerer, at a quiz, the sum of 64 dollars, but which, failed, loses him the 32 dollars he has already won, after having won an initial 16 dollars (a sum risked when he elects to answer the second question).

skin game, n. Cp. **skin (II.) 1. 2.** (slang) Fraud, deception, swindling.

slack, n. Add: **5.** See **sprung rhythm,** Suppl.

slam (I.), vb. trans. **1.** Add: **d** (fig.) (Am. slang) To criticize, censure.

slant (II.), n. Add: **2.** (slang, orig. U.S.) A view, opinion; cp. **angle,** Suppl.

slick, adj. **1.** Add: **c** (of persons or things, slang) smart but unsound, specious.

slim (II.), vb. intrans. (colloq.) To practise slimming.

slimming, n. & adj. [1. slíming; 2. slímiŋ], fr. prec. (colloq.) **1.** n. Measures, treatment adopted by a person, esp. through diet or drugs, with the object of making her, or his, figure slimmer. **2.** adj. Of, pertaining to, slimming: *slimming diet,* &c.

slip (I.), vb. **A.** intrans. **2.** *slip up;* Add: also fig., (colloq.) to make a mistake.

slit trench. See **fox-hole.**

slosh, n. Add: **2.** (slang) A heavy resounding blow.

slosh (II.), vb. trans. Cp. **slop (II.) & slap (I.). 1.** *To slosh* (paint, &c.) *on,* (colloq.) spread it thickly, audibly (and clumsily). **2.** (slang) To hit with a resounding blow.

smasher. Add: **3.** (slang) Any superlative or very attractive person or thing. *What a smasher!* or *That car is a smasher.*

smashing, adj. Add: **2.** A slangy superlative (cf. the preceding entry), as in *We had a smashing time.*

smear (II.), vb. Add: **4.** (Orig. American slang, mostly political. Now a world-wide and general colloquialism, verging upon Standard English.) To blacken the character of (someone), esp. in a public, widespread manner. Cf. *Your name will be smeared all over the front pages of the popular press.*

smoke-screen, n. Add: **2.** (fig.) Anything done or put forward as a blind, to conceal one's real aims and activities.

smorgasbord or, as in Swedish, **smörgåsbord** [smurgōsboord']. A luncheon or a supper that, imitatively of Sweden, is served buffet-style and consists of a bewildering variety of hors-d'œuvre, meats, desserts, savouries, and what-have-you.

snack-bar, n. (Shop with a) bar or counter at which light refreshments are sold.

snap (I.), vb. **B.** intrans. Add: **6.** Phr. *snap into it,* (slang, orig. U.S.) to make a vigorous start, act with decision, enthusiasm.

snatch, vb. trans. Add to **A. 5.** (American underworld term.) To kidnap; hence *the snatch racket,* kidnapping as a business.

snip (II.), n. Add: **4.** (slang) A cert; see **certainty, 2.,** Dict.

Social Credit, n. The mainly financial

doctrine of Major C. H. Douglas. It claims that the potential abundance which industrial technique can now produce (with less and less labour) is 'the unearned increment of association', belongs to the whole community and ought to be made available to all as consumers, by certain changes in monetary policy, including the issue of National Dividends of Consumer Credit. See also **A + B theorem**, Suppl.

Social Crediter, n. Advocate, adherent of Social Credit; see prec.

socialite. A person moving in, belonging actively to, Society. (Originally American colloq., now general journalese.)

soften. Add: **3.** (Also *soften up.*) With aerial bombing and other bellicose preliminaries to weaken both the physical and the moral resistance in an area or a region about to be attacked or invaded.

sol (III.), n. Abbr. fr. **solution.** (chem.) A colloidal solution.

solute, n. [1. sólūt; 2. sɔ́ljūt]. See **solution.** (chem.) The dissolved substance in a solution.

sound (VI.), vb. **A.** trans. **1.** Add: **b** transf., To explore (the upper air, esp. the stratosphere and tropopause), e.g. by means of a balloon fitted with automatic recording instruments, and ascertain its temperature, density, movement, &c., at different heights, latitudes, &c.

sound-boom, n., fr. **sound (I).** & **boom (I.)**, **1.** (films) Apparatus for moving a microphone about as required during a shot.

sound-box, n. The part of a gramophone which contains the diaphragm.

sound camera, n. Camera which records the sounds on the sound-track of a film.

sound-head, n. That part of a film-projector which emits audible sound picked up from the sound-track.

sound-track, n. That part of a sound-film on which accompanying sounds are recorded.

sour (I.), adj. **2.** Add: Phr. *to be sour on*, (U.S. slang) to hate, detest.

sour (III.), vb. **2.** intrans. Add: **b** (fig.) *to sour on*, (U.S. slang) to change from liking to disliking (a person or thing).

sourtop, n. [1. sóuertop; 2. sáuətop], fr. **sour (I.)**, **2.** & **top**, 'head'. (U.S. slang) Morose, disagreeable person.

sovkhos, n. [1. sóvkos; 2. sɔ́vkɔ́s]. Russ., abbr. of **soviet** & *khos*, see **kolkhos** '**farm**'. (U.S.S.R.) State farm instituted on rationalized methods, esp. under Five Year Plan. Cp. **kolkhos**, Suppl.

Sovnarkom, n. [1. sóvnarkom; 2. sɔ́vnākɔ́m]. Russ., abbr. of *soviet, narod*, 'people', & *komissar.* (U.S.S.R.) Soviet of people's commissaries.

so what? Phr. (slang, orig. U.S.) What of that? What has it to do with the matter in hand? What is the bearing of your remark? Has it any?

sozzled, adj. [1. sozld; 2. sɔ́zld]. Probably imitative word; cp. **soak (I.)**, **B. 2.** & **muzzy** & **fuddle.** (slang) Intoxicated.

special, adj. **3.** Add: *special areas*, industrial regions in a condition of chronic depression.

speed-cop, n. (slang, orig. U.S.) Policeman on the watch for offences against the speed-limit.

spigotty, adj. [1. spígoti; 2. spígəti], ? origin. (U.S. slang) Strangely interesting, romantic.

spin (II.), n. Add: **3.** Phr. *to get into a flat spin*, (i.) (aeron.) to spin round horizontally without hope of recovery; (ii.) (fig. & colloq.) to get into inextricable difficulties.

spiv, spivvery [spiv′eri], perhaps fr. '*spiff*ing'. One who earns a living without legitimate employment; (*spivvery*) such 'activities', spivs collectively. From the underworld, it had, by 1947, risen to slang; by 1949 it was official.

split personality. The personality of one who seems to combine two sharply opposed characters—a *Dr. Jekyll and Mr. Hyde.*

sponson [spońson]. In a seaplane: that air-filled protrusion from the hull which, while the plane rests upon the water, steadies it.

sprog. (R.A.F. slang, probably from a fusion of *sprocket* and *cog.*) A recruit; an aircraftman during his first year of service. Hence, by extension, any tyro or newcomer—e.g. a baby.

sprung rhythm. That type of poetic rhythm which Gerard Manley Hopkins (1844–1889) revived from Middle English, refurbished and, through Dr. Robert Bridges's edition (1918), popularized among the English poets of the 1930's and ever since. The stress falls always on the first syllable of the foot; the feet vary in length from one to four or even five syllables; not all the verse-lines of a poem need be in sprung rhythm.

squeeze (II.), n. Add: **4.** The *squeezing*-out, i.e. elimination, of a competitor by making it difficult for him to obtain replacements at an economic price. In the underworld, *put the squeeze on* connotes severe pressure, sometimes blackmail.

stab (II.), n. Add: **c an attempt**: *to have a stab at* (something).

stag (II.), vb. intrans. (Stock Exchange) To act in the manner of a stag; see **stag (4.)**, Dict.

stag party, n. See **party**, Suppl.

stakhanovite, n. & adj. [1. stakáhnofīt; 2. stækānəfait], fr. Stakhanov, a Russian miner who, in 1935, succeeded in increasing his individual output prodigiously. **a** n. One of those Russian workers belonging to a rank-and-file movement for the increase of industrial output through rationalization and individual initiative; **b** adj., of, pertaining to, that movement.

Stalag [stal′ag], fr. Germ. *Stammlager*, a base camp. A German camp for prisoners of war; strictly, for non-commissioned officers and men.

stamped scrip, n. Scrip money that has to be stamped at stated intervals (e.g. monthly) at a cost to the holder equalling its automatic depreciation in value; see **Free Money & scrip (II.)**, Suppl.

stand (I.), vb. **C.** *Stand off*; Add: trans., to discharge (an employee) temporarily, owing to slackness of trade, &c.

stay-in, attrib. adj. *Stay-in strike*, a strike in which the employees remain on the premises of the employers; *stay-in tactics.*

stem (II.), vb. Add: **2.** vb. intrans. (Of a word) to originate, as in *Most English words stem from Indo-European radicals.*

Sten gun, a blend of *S*heppard and *T*urpin of *En*gland, the designers, or of *S*heppard, *T*urpin, and *En*field, where, originally, this automatic carbine was manufactured. Less accurate than the *tommy gun*, it is far cheaper to make and, being much simpler, is less likely to go wrong.

stick (I.), vb. **A.** trans. **2.** Add: **d** (slang) to put; (gangster slang) *stick 'em up!* put up your hands!

stick, n. Add: **7.** A number (usually 3, 4, 5 or 6) of bombs released, at regular intervals, in a line before, on, after the target.

stiff (II.), n. **2.** Add: **b** a stupid or clumsy person; esp. *big stiff*, an utter fool or bungler.

still (II.), n. Add: **2.** A single snapshot abstracted from a motion film and, in many cases, displayed as a photograph.

sting (I.), vb. **A.** intrans. **3.** (fig.); Add: **c** (slang) to make (a person) pay an exorbitant price, to fleece.

stirrup pump. A light, portable hand pump, held firmly—with its intake in a bucket—on the ground, and having a stirrup (or a brace) in which the operator sets one foot.

stockpile, n. and vb. A somewhat redundant Americanism for 'a stock' and 'to stock', with esp. reference to raw materials.

stooge, n. [1. stōōj; 2. stūdž]. (slang, orig. U.S.) **a** (theatr.) Butt in slapstick comedy; **b** scapegoat. **2.** Hence, an assistant, a learner. Hence:

stooge, vb. To be an assistant or a learner; *to stooge around*, to loiter either expectantly or time-killingly.

storm trooper, n. Member of the semi-military nucleus of the Nazi party.

storm troops, n. **1.** Military units reserved for arduous offensive engagements. **2.** Body of storm troopers.

stratosphere, n. [1. strátōsfēr; 2. strǽtousfiə]. See **stratum & sphere.** The upper and more rarefied part of the atmosphere above the tropopause; see **tropo-sphere & tropopause**, Suppl.

stream-lined, now usually one word. (Cp. **stream line.**) Of an aircraft: so smoothly constructed, externally, as to offer the least resistance to the air; hence, of any other machine or manufactured object, exhibiting the fewest possible angles and protuberances; hence, slangily, of attractively slim—*not* skinny—girls.

streptomycin [streptōmísin]. A powerful anti-bacterial substance produced from fungus: cp. **aureomycin & penicillin** (both in Suppl.).

stress (I.), n. **5.** Add: Since ca. 1930, the word has acquired an additional meaning, which combines the ideas of 'distress' and 'storm and stress'.

strip-tease. A music-hall or other turn in which, usually towards or at the end, an actress strips herself, piece by piece, to the barest minimum permissible by law.

stroboscope, n. [1. stróboskōp; 2. strɔ́bəskoup]. See **strophe & -scope.** A device for studying periodic motion by means of intermittent glimpses.

stuff (I.), n. Add: **4.** (slang) In the phr. *to do one's stuff*, special accomplishment or subject; prearranged performance or harangue: *Now then, do your stuff!*

stylus bar, n. [1. stílus bàr; 2. stáiləs bå]. See **style & bar.** Rod conveying vibrations from the point of a gramophone needle to the centre of the diaphragm.

stymied [stī′mēd], fr. golf. (colloq.) Baffled, circumvented.

sublimate, vb., and **sublimation**, as used in psycho-analysis. To divert an impulse or a desire into a higher cultural or intellectual level; (*sublimation*) such a diversion.

submachine-gun. See **tommy gun**, Suppl.

subotnik, n. [1. soobótnik; 2. subɔ́tnik]. Russ., fr. *subota*, 'Saturday', & **-nik** (suff.). (U.S.S.R.) Labour freely given to the State on off days.

sub-stratosphere. That region of the atmosphere which, lying below the stratosphere yet above 3½ miles from the earth, requires, for aviation, certain protective devices, such as oxygen masks.

sucker, n. Add: **6.** (Am. slang) **a** Ill-informed and gullible stock market speculator; *sucker list*, list of such people for the use of dishonest company promoters; **b** any gullible and easily exploitable person.

sugar daddy, n. (slang, orig. U.S.) An elderly man who takes about, or keeps as his mistress, a young woman and, consciously or unconsciously, allows himself to be exploited by her as a liberal source of revenue and luxuries.

sulfa, occasionally **sulpha.** A group of organic drugs related to sulfanilamide (the amide of sulfanilic acid). They destroy certain disease-bearing or -producing bacteria.

sunk, adj. Add: **2.** pred. (slang) Utterly frustrated, in a desperate situation or fix; *now we're sunk*, that finishes our chances.

super (II.), adj., fr. the prefix **super-**, **(g & h).** (slang) Excellent; unusually good, useful, clever, &c.

supercharge. To maintain an atmospheric pressure as near normal as possible within the cabin of an aircraft flying at great altitudes —by means of a supercharger (or pressurizer).

superhet, adj. [1. sū́perhet; 2. sjū́pəhɛt]. Abbr. of *superheterodyne*. **super–,** (**h**), & **heterodyne.** (colloq.) *type of radio reception.*

supernova. A **nova** hundreds of times as bright as a normal one.

supersonic, adj. [soópersoník]. In physics: relating to vibrations with frequencies greater than those affecting the human ear—i.e. more than 20,000 per second.

suppression. Add: **2.** The conscious exclusion of an idea or a desire, from conscious continuance.

supraconductivity, n. Increased electrical conductivity at exceptionally low temperatures.

Sûreté Générale, la [lah soortā́ zhānārahl], or **the.** That branch of the French police which safeguards the State against subversive acts and practices.

surrealism, n. [1. sūrḗalizm; 2. sùríəlizm], fr. Fr. *surréalisme*; see **sur– (II.)** & **realism.** A recent movement in literature and art which originated in France. Its subject-matter is derived chiefly from 'the unconscious', even from dreams, and its emphasis on immediacy and spontaneity, with a minimum of conscious elaboration, makes it an exaggerated antithesis of academic art.

surrealist, n. & adj. [1. sūrḗalist; 2. sùríəlist]. See prec. & **–ist. 1.** n. An exponent or adherent of surrealism. **2.** adj. Of, pertaining to, or exemplifying, surrealism.

suspension, n. Add: specif. (phys. chem.) a liquid containing finely divided and stably suspended solid particles.

suspensoid, n. [1. suspénsoid; 2. səspénsoid], fr. **suspension** & **–oid.** (chem.) The disperse phase in a suspension.

swastika. Add: **2.** A rectilinear swastika adopted by the Third Reich as its official emblem.

swill (II.), n. Add: **4.** (U.S. slang) *Swell swill*: (i.) Garbage the inspection of which suggests a luxurious standard of living; (ii.) excellent food and drink.

swing music, now usually **swing.** That manner of playing jazz which submerges the melody in individual variations or interpretations of the main theme.

swish (III.), adj. (slang) Strikingly smart or stylish.

swop, swap (II.), n. Add: Phr. *to take a swop*, (commerc. slang) meet with a rebuff in salesmanship.

synchro-mesh, n. Abbr. of *synchronized mesh*. (motor-cars) A device in the gearbox for making the gears engage automatically at their correct speed.

synthetic. Add: **3.** Hence, artificial, disingenuous.

tab, n. Add: **2.** On an aircraft: a small airfoil hinged to, or inset into, a control surface (e.g. an aileron or the rudder).

tabloid press, n. Contemptuous collective term for illustrated newspapers that give only scanty and compressed news.

tactical. Add: **2.** Esp. of an airforce: designed to assist an army during a battle or potential battle.

task force, or as one word. An expeditionary or other 'special mission' force composed, if necessary, of men from all three Services and controlled by one commander; or a compact naval force.

Tass (II.), n. Russ., abbr. fr. *Telegraphnoye Agentstvo Sovyetskovo Soyuza.* (U.S.S.R.) Telegraphic Agency of the Soviet Union.

taxi dancer. A dancer employed to dance with customers in a dance hall, a night club, a café; she dances, as it were, to a meter, the customer paying for each dance.

teaser, n. Add: **3.** *Teaser (ad.)*, (commerc. slang) advertisement designed to stimulate curiosity by holding out hopes of a startling future announcement.

technocracy, n. [1. tèknókrasi; 2. tèknókrəsi]. See **technic** & **–cracy.** A type of social organization, imagined and advocated by a group of Americans, in which engineers and technicians would exercise a decisive control of industry, maintaining output at the maximum in the interests of the public as consumers. See also **erg,** Suppl.

technocrat, n. [1. téknokràt; 2. téknəkræ̀t]. See **technic** & **–crat. 1.** An advocate of technocracy. **2.** An engineer or technician, as controller of production in such a régime.

technocratic, adj. [1. tèknokrátik; 2. tèknəkrǽtik]. prec. & **–ic.** Having the characteristics of a technocrat, or of a technocracy.

teen-ager. A young person aged anything from 13 to 19.

telegenic, adj. [telejēnik], fr. **tele–,** from afar, & *-genic*, as in **photogenic,** Suppl. Coming out well, photographically, on television.

teleprinter. A teletypewriter.

teleview, vb. trans. and intrans. [télevū']. To watch on a television screen.

televise, vb. trans. [televīz]. To transmit by television.

televisor, n. [1. televīsor; 2. télivaisə]. See **television** & **–or (2).** Instrument for receiving audio-signals and converting them into visual signals.

tell, vb. **A.** trans. **3. b**; Add: Phr. *you're telling me!* (slang) don't, or there's no need to tell me that!

test pilot. A pilot engaged to test thoroughly, in flight, the first example of a newly designed, or of a remodelled, aircraft.

That Man. Hitler. Misappropriated and given a clever twist by the late Tommy Handley in his serial radio programme, Itma: It's That Man Again.

thermoduric, adj. [thermōdūrik], fr. **thermo–** & (en)*dur*(e) & **–ic.** Capable of withstanding great heat.

thermoplastic [thermōplastik]. Free from *thermosetting* reaction—a reaction consisting in a permanent rigidity induced by the application of heat

Third Reich [rīk], **the,** a translation of *das dritte Reich*, literally, the third kingdom. Germany as a totalitarian State, 1933–1945.

thixotropy, n. [1. thiksótropi; 2. þiksótrəpi], fr. Gk. *thixis*, 'a touching', fr. base *thig-* in *thiggánein*, 'to touch', cogn. w. *touch*, &c., & **–trope.** (chem.) Property of a substance, apparently a liquid, whereby it can pass from gel to sol on agitation, and back to gel on standing.

Thompson submachine-gun. See **tommy gun,** Suppl.

three-point landing. The skilful landing of an aircraft on all three wheels.

thrombin, n. [1. thrómbin; 2. þrɔ́mbin], fr. Gk. *thrómbos*, 'a clot', & **–in.** (physiol.) The substance in the blood which causes clotting.

thrombopenia, n. [1. thròmbōpḗnia; 2. þrɔmboupíniə], fr. prec. & Gk. *penía*, 'poverty'. (physiol.) Deficiency of thrombine in the blood.

thromboplastin [thrombōplastin], fr. *thrombo-* (as in **thrombosis**) & *plast* (as in **plastic**) & **–in.** An extract from the brain-tissue of cattle in a solution of sodium chloride; used as a haemostatic.

throw (I.), vb. **A.** trans. Add: **9.** (slang) To give (as a social gesture, e.g. a dinner, a cocktail party). Phr. *to throw a fit*, (slang) see **fit (I.), 1.,** Suppl.

throwaway, n. (slang) An advertising circular, leaflet.

throw-out, n. Article thrown aside, esp. in the factory where it is made, as defective or useless.

thumb a lift. Either to ask for or to obtain a ride in a passing vehicle (jeep, car, &c.) by pointing a demonstrative thumb in the direction one wishes to travel. *I managed to thumb a lift for most of the way.*

tiddly, adj. [1. tídli; 2. tídli]. (slang) Intoxicated. **2.** In first-class order; (of clothes) best, smart. (Naval slang from **tidy.**)

tie (I.), n. **2.** Add: Phr. *the old school tie*, (fig. & colloq.) (i.) snobbishness of, (ii.) solidarity, freemasonry among, members of certain Public Schools, &c.

tie (II.), vb. **C.** *Tie up*, **3.** Add: Phr. *to tie* (person) *up (in knots)*, (colloq.) put into (great) difficulties.

tie-up, n. (commerc. slang) Arrangement for the display of advertised goods simultaneously with advertisement of them in the press.

tightwad, n. [1. tī́twod; 2. táitwɔd]. **tight (6. b)** & **wad (I.), 2.** (Am. slang) A miser.

time-lag, n. Interval of time between one phenomenon and another which is associated with it or caused by it.

Titoism [tē̆tōizm]. The Yugoslavian—i.e. Marshal Tito's special—sort of Communism.

T-man. (American slang, on the analogy of *G-man.*) A Treasury man, esp. an investigator into tax-evasion.

Tocharian or **Tokharian** [tokā́rian]. The language—it is one of the Indo-European languages—spoken by the Tocharians, an Asiatic people known to the ancient Greeks as *Tokharoi.*

token, adj., fr. the noun. Paid or done in partial fulfilment of a debt or other obligation.

Tokharian. See **Tocharian,** Suppl.

tommy gun, n.; **tommy-gun,** vb. trans. A Thompson submachine-gun, a light, portable, one-man quick-firing gun, which one can fire either in bursts or in single shots. From one of the inventors, General J. I. Thompson (1860–1940) of the United States Army. The form *tommy gun* and the corresponding verb were originally terms employed by the American underworld.

tomogram, tomographic, tomography. The third is that diagnostical technique (the *tomographic* method) which employs such *tomograms* or X-ray photographs as do not, for the section being examined, exhibit the shadows of structures whether in front of or behind that section. (*Tomo-*, fr. Gk. *tomos*, a cut(ting); cp. **–gram** and **–graphy.**)

tone-arm, n. The part of a gramophone connecting the sound-box to the horn.

topectomy [to'pektōmi], fr. Gk. *topos*, 'a place', & *ek*, 'out of', & **–tome.** A surgical operation that, designed to relieve mental disease, is achieved by removal of parts of the brain tissue.

topliner, n. See **headliner,** Suppl.

tops, the. The best there is, whether among persons or among things. Predicatively, however, also *tops*. *He's the tops*, the best in his group or kind; *He's tops*, he's a fine fellow. An American colloquialism adopted in Britain, partly by 1944, fully by 1951.

totalitarian, adj. [1. tòtalitā́rian; 2. tòutælitéəriən]. **totality** & **–arian. a** (concerned with) Arrogating (to the State and the ruling party) all rights and every liberty of choice, including those normally belonging to individuals and various corporate bodies: *the totalitarian State*; **b** conscripting a country's entire resources in population and material.

totalitarianism [totalitā́rianizm]. The abstraction—the Abstract Noun—answering to the preceding.

total war is short for **total warfare**: war in which no regard is paid to the safety of civilians.

tourist class. The sole class of passenger on some ocean-going ships; on others, the class next below the first. Also adj., as in *She's a tourist-class ship.*

track (I.), n. Add: **4.** The band of a tractor of the caterpillar type; also, the tread of a motor-car tyre.

tracking, vbl. n., fr. **track (I.).** (films) **a** Moving the camera nearer and nearer to, or further away from, the subject; **b** the visual effect so produced.

trafficator, n. Abbr. of **traffic-indicator.** (motor-cars) Automatic red pointer for warning traffic whenever the driver intends to change direction.

trailer, n. Add: **4.** Parts of a forthcoming film shown on the screen at a public performance, to advertise the film.

trainee [trānē]. A person under training.

transcribe. Add: **2.** To broadcast by transcription—i.e. by electrical transcription.

trauma. Add: **2.** Hence, a mental injury.

traumatic acid. A crystalline acid that helps to repair the damaged parts of plants.

tricot. Add: **2.** A very tight-fitting garment worn by ballet dancers.

Trojan horse. A Nazi device—the placing of such agents inside a country marked out for invasion as will direct the activities of the Fifth Column and do sabotage work. (During the Trojan War, the Greeks insinuated into Troy a wooden horse containing soldiers who, the opportunity occurring, opened the gates and initiated the sack of the town.)

tropopause, n. [1. trópōpawz; 2. trɔ́poupɔ̄z], fr. **troposphere & pause.** A belt of atmosphere, about two miles thick, between the troposphere and the stratosphere, i.e. from seven to twelve miles above sea-level.

troposphere, n. [1. trópōsfēr; 2. trɔ́pousfiə]. See **trope & sphere.** That part of the atmosphere which immediately surrounds the earth, reaching up as far as the tropopause, and in which increase of height is associated with decrease of temperature; cp. **stratosphere,** Suppl.

trouper [trōōper]. See **parlary,** Suppl.

trust (I.), n. **3.** Add: **c** *investment trust,* a joint-stock company whose profits are drawn from investments distributed among a number of other companies and from the judicious buying and selling of investments; *fixed trust,* investment trust whose capital is permanently invested in a few securities.

try (I.), vb. **A.** trans. **6.** Add: **b** *to try* (a thing) *out,* (colloq.) (i.) test it thoroughly, (ii.) give it a trial.

try-on, n. [tráiən]. See **try, A. 4. b** (ii.). (slang) An instance of 'trying it on', seeing how far one will be allowed to go in some piece of audacity.

try-out, n. [tráiaut]. See **try,** Suppl. (slang) **a** An instance of trying something out; **b** something that is being tried out.

turbo-supercharger. A turbine compressor that supplies rarefied air to the engine of an aircraft, in order to increase the climbing rate and the engine's efficiency.

turn (I.), vb. **A.** trans. Add: **11.** *To turn a film,* be responsible for the action of the camera in the production of a film.

turn-out, n. Add: **3.** (colloq.) Way in which, degree of smartness with which, a person is dressed and groomed.

twin. 2. n. **a** Add: *identical twins,* twins developed from the same fertilized ovum and therefore of identically the same genotype; *fraternal twins,* twins developed from different ova and spermatozoa and therefore of different genotypes, though from the same pregnancy.

tycoon. Add: **2.** Hence, a magnate; a very important person in industry or commerce.

type, n., fr. sense **5.** A person of a specific character, esp. *a good* (or *a bad*) *type.* Originally, R.A.F. slang; by 1951, colloq. Perhaps influenced by the Fr. slang *type,* a humorous fellow.

type, v. Add: **3.** vb. trans. To assign to a type (or classification), to determine the type of; hence, to identify. Hence, *typable* and its negative, *untypable.*

udarnik, n., pl. *-niki* [1. ōōdárnik; 2. ūdánik]. Russ. *udar,* 'a blow', & *-nik* (suff.). (U.S.S.R.) Shock-brigader, usu. in an industrial sense.

ultra-short, adj. & n. See **wave-length,** Suppl.

umbrella. Add: **3.** A protective force of aircraft, esp. fighters, to cover the operations of sea and land forces.

unc, n. [1. ungk; 2. aŋk]. Slang abbr. of **unconscious** (q.v., **4.,** Dict.).

underground movement, the; often simply **the underground.** (A translation of Fr. *le* (*mouvement*) *souterrain.*) The secret organized forces of resistance within an occupied country, as esp. in France during the years 1940–1944.

undertone. Add: **3.** A significance underlying the avowed or the manifest meaning of an action or a course of action or a prevailing tendency. Cp. **overtone,** Suppl.

underworld, n. **3.** Add: **b** social circles in which obscure and possibly sinister moves, bargains, &c., are made: *political underworld.*

unitage [ūnitij]. A specification of what, precisely, constitutes a unit in any system of measurement.

unstick, vb. trans. Add: Phr. *to come unstuck,* (slang) to get into difficulties.

untypable. See **type,** vb., Suppl.

up-and-up, n. Phr. (slang) *to be on the up-and-up,* to be succeeding, making progress, having a run of prosperity.

upgrade, vb. trans. [upgrād]. To raise (someone) to a higher grade, to promote; to put a higher price on (a product).

up-stage, adj. [1. úp stāj; 2. áp stèidž]. **up & stage.** (colloq.) Supercilious, stand-offish, apt to give oneself airs.

urge (II.), n. Also—probably from *body urge* —applied to physical desire.

Vansittartism [Vansitartizm]. The belief (strongly held and ably publicized by Baron Vansittart of Denham) that Germany should be permanently demilitarized, protractedly occupied, thoroughly re-educated, as a vital means of preserving world peace.

V.E. Day; V.J. Day; V sign. The Day on which *v*ictory in *E*urope—in *J*apan—was achieved by the surrender of Germany (and her European allies) and of Japan at the end of the war of 1939–1945 in the two main theatres; the *V* (Victory) *sign* was made by the index and middle fingers upraised and spread to form a V.

vehicle, n. **2.** Add: specif. (chem.) medium in which a substance is dispersed to form a suspension or an emulsion.

vernacular, n. Add: **3.** A vernacular as opposed to the Scientific name of an animal or a plant.

Vichyite [Vḗshē-īt]. An adherent of the *Vichy* government (July 1940–November 1942) of France—a government bound to collaborate economically with the Nazis.

video, adj. [vēdāō], fr. Lat. *video,* 'I see'. Of, for, in, by the transmission—or the reception —of the image in television.

vinyl resin. A thermoplastic resin formed from a vinyl compound. *Vinyl* (from Lat. *vinum,* wine—cp. **vine & -yl**): a radical of which ethylene is the hydride.

virtual wealth, n. The aggregate of goods and services that a community theoretically could at any time exchange for the aggregate of its money.

vitamer [vītamer], a blend of *vita*min & iso*mer.* A compound that makes good a vitamin deficiency.

V.J. Day. See **V.E. Day,** Suppl.

Voks, n. [1. voks; 2. vɔks]. Russ., fr. *Vsesoyuznoye Obschestvo Kulturnoy Svyazi,* 'All-Union Society for Cultural Relations'. (U.S.S.R.) Soviet-Union Society for Cultural Relations with foreign countries.

Volkswagen. A German word, literally '(the) people's waggon or vehicle'. A small, cheap, mass-produced motor-car.

V sign. See **V.E. Day,** Suppl.

wacky or **whacky,** perhaps fr. '*whacked* on the head'. (American slang.) Crazy; extremely eccentric.

wad, (I.), n. **2.** Add: **b** (gen. slang.) money.

waffle (II.), vb. intrans. Imitative word. (slang) To talk nonsense, blether.

walk (I.), vb. **C.** Add: *Walk out* (of an assembly), walk out ostentatiously to show strong disapproval or contempt. *Walk out on,* (slang, orig. U.S.) decamp, clear off, leaving (person) in the lurch. Cp. **on (9.),** Suppl.

walkie-talkie. A two-ways radio-telephonic set that can be carried like a knapsack.

war guilt. The degree to which a nation is responsible for causing a war; or that to which an individual maltreats prisoners of war, civilians in occupied territory, and others.

war of nerves. Psychological warfare.

water-waggon, n. Wheeled vehicle for carrying water; Phr. *gone on the water-waggon,* (slang, orig. U.S.) having forsworn all alcoholic drinks; for *on,* see **diet,** Dict.

Watson, Dr. See **Sherlock Holmes,** Suppl.

wave, suff. Abbr. for **wave-length,** in the adjs. *short-wave, medium-wave* and *long-wave*; see next word.

wave-length, n. **b** Add: *long,* 600-30,000 metres; *medium,* 100-600 metres; *short,* 10-100 metres; *ultra-short,* 1-10 metres.

wave mechanics, n. A development of quantum mechanics in which matter is treated as a wave motion.

Wehrmacht [vār'markt]. Germany's armed forces, as a whole; literally, the German word means 'defence force'.

Welfare State. A state, or a country, in which the government pretends to provide security and even happiness for all.

Weltanschauung [velt'anshoúoong]; **Weltpolitik** [velt'politik]; **Weltschmerz** [velt'-schmerts]. Respectively, 'world view', a philosophical conception of the world as a whole; 'world politics, world policy', the imperialism implicit in German international policy, esp. in the 1930's; 'world pain, world bitterness', a rather sentimental pessimism concerning the character and fate of the human race.

wet (I.), adj. Add: **4.** (slang) (of persons or things) Unacceptable, distasteful; foolish; sloppy, sentimental; *you're all wet,* quite off the track. **5.** n. (slang) One who is wet, as in **4.**

whacky. See **wacky,** Suppl.

whale (I.), n. Add: *a whale of a,* (slang, orig. U.S.) a very big: *a whale of a lot.*

Whitehallese. The British equivalent of **Federal Prose,** Suppl., Whitehall being the residential area of the British governmental ministries. More widely known as **officialese,** Suppl., or official jargon.

whodunit, fr. 'Who done it?'—the illiterate form of 'Who did it?'—who committed the crime? A murder-mystery story, esp. a detective novel.

whoopee, interj. & n. [1. wóopē; 2. wúpī]. (slang) **a** interj. Expressing gaiety and exhilaration; **b** n., riotous gaiety; Phrs. *to make whoopee; whoopee period,* (U.S.) period of prosperity.

wide (I.), adj. **3. a** Add: (slang) *to the wide* (sc. world), utterly: *done to the wide,* utterly exhausted, done-for.

win (I.), vb. **B.** intrans. *Win back,* (colloq.) to recover lost ground by strenuous efforts.

window-shopping, vbl. n. & adj. (colloq.) Gazing at what is displayed in shop windows.

wings. The insignia—an outspread pair of bird's wings—gained by a pilot when he officially attains to that rank in the Air Force.

wipe, n. **1.** Add: **b** (films) (the device, effect, of) making one shot appear to be peeled off revealing another as if it had been underneath it.

wipe-out, n. & attrib. n. (wireless) **1. n. a** The effect which a wireless transmitting station has of rendering all messages on its own wave-length inaudible within a certain radius; **b** the zone thus affected. **2.** n. attrib.: *wipe-out zone* or *area*.

wise (I.). **2.** Add: (U.S. slang) *wise guy*, a disconcertingly, irritatingly well-informed or conceited person, one who 'knows it all'; a would-be-smart exposer of frauds; an iconoclast.

wise crack, wise-crack, n. & vb. intrans. **1.** n. **a** A witticism, a sententious, esp. a sarcastic, remark; **b** one who makes such remarks. **2.** vb. To make such remarks.

wish, n. Add: **4.** (psycho-analysis) An unconscious desire which is tending to translate itself into action through some bodily mechanism, but which may be diverted or inhibited.

wish-fulfilment, n. (psycho-analysis) Fulfilment of a desire, either in a dream or in phantasy as expressed, e.g. in some inadvertent gesture or verbal error.

wishful thinking. A taking for real, or for accomplished, what one wishes were so; esp. self-delusion, not necessarily of an objectionable kind.

witch hunt. An ostensibly virtuous, really self-advertising, search for persons to victimize or to make morally responsible for the shortcomings of others.

wiz, whiz, n., prob. punning on **whiz(z)** & **wizard.** (U.S. slang) An expert.

wizard, adj., fr. **wizard, 1.** (slang) **a** (of persons or things) Clever, ingenious; **b** (chiefly of things) fascinating, attractive.

wog, n. [1. wog; 2. wɔg], fr. **golliwog.** (slang) A negro. **2.** Any dark-skinned, or coffee-skinned, native.

wolf (I.), n. **1.** Add: Phr. (colloq. & facet.) *Who's afraid of the big bad wolf?* such-and-such villain or bug-bear is not so formidable as may appear. Add: **4.** (slang, orig. American) A conscienceless philanderer—the human male as a sexual hunter. Often humorously of any man very fond—or even quite normally fond—of women.

wolfpack. A flotilla of submarines (esp. German) surfacing more or less simultaneously at night in the midst of a convoy and loosing their torpedoes.

wood. Add: **4.** A bowl (heavy wooden ball) used in the game of bowls.

work (I.), n. **5.** Add: **c** *a nasty piece of work*, (slang) an objectionable person. **9.** Add: **c** (gangster slang) *give him the works*, fire every cartridge in the revolver or gun at him.

worry (I.), vb. **B.** intrans. Phr. Add: *I should worry*, (colloq., iron.) should not mind, should be glad.

wuzzy, n. [1. wúzi; 2. wázi]. Muzzy.

X disease. A yellowish-red virosis (disease caused by a **virus**) of the peach; characteristics: watery green spots on leaves; often, shedding of leaves; shrivelling of fruit.

xeric [zērik], fr. Gk. *xeros*, 'dry': cp. **xer(o)-.** In botany: (of plants) lacking moisture, (of soil) that is arid.

X-unit, n. The unit, $10^{-11} \times 1$ cm., used for wave-lengths of X- and gamma-rays.

Yak. The most famous Russian fighter plane (designed by Alexander *Yak*ovlev) of the years 1941–1945.

yen (II.), n. (Am. slang) A yearning, ambition: *a yen for knowledge, a yen to write.*

yes man, n. (slang, orig. U.S.) A man who lacks initiative and obsequiously assents to the opinions of others.

yob. Originally the back-slang for *boy*; by 1950, almost Standard English (familiar S.E., that is). An ill-mannered, uncouth lad; a lout, with the connotation 'clumsy and downright ignorant'

Zero. A Japanese fighter plane, light and very easily manœuvrable—so named from the '00' of the Japanese year 2600 (A.D. 1940), when this make of plane was introduced, a date appearing in the markings.

zip, n. Add: *zip fastener*, ingenious metallic attachment to clothing, &c., enabling it to be undone or done up with a single pull; Add: **b** (fig., slang) brisk energy or vigour.

zip (II.), vb. trans. & intrans. (slang) **A.** intrans. To dart, shoot; also fig.; Phr. *to zip across the horizon*, (Am. slang) come suddenly into fame, prominence, notoriety. **B.** trans. *Zip up*, to put (more) briskness and vigour into (something).

zoom, vb. intrans. & trans. [1. zōōm; 2. zūm]. Imitative. (Slang.) **A.** vb. intrans. **1.** To climb vertically in an aeroplane. **2.** (fig.) To boom, make a great hit. **B.** trans. To boost, advertise by high-pressure methods.

zoom, n., fr. prec. Vertical climb in flying.

zoot suit. A flashily cut and loudly coloured suit, originally in U.S.A., hence (?) also in South Africa. This slang term is not, as usually stated, of obscure origin: *suit* (of clothes) has merely been qualified by a distortion of Dutch *zoet*, sweet, good: for flashy fellows, such a suit is their best suit.

zymase [zīmās], fr. *zyme*, 'a ferment' (Gk. *zumē*, 'a leaven'). Any of a group of enzymes originally found in yeasts and in bacteria. Cp. **zymosis.**